Broadway Musicals, 1943–2004

Broadway Musicals, 1943–2004

John Stewart

foreword by HAL PRINCE

McFarland & Company, Inc., Publishers
Jefferson, North Carolina, and London

LIBRARY OF CONGRESS CATALOGUING-IN-PUBLICATION DATA

Stewart, John, 1952–
Broadway musicals, 1943–2004 / John Stewart ; foreword by Hal Prince.
p.   cm.
Includes bibliographical references and index.

ISBN 0-7864-2244-0 (library binding : 50# alkaline paper)

1. Musicals — New York (State) — New York — Encyclopedias.   I. Title.
ML102.M88S74   2006   782.1'4'09747103 — dc22   2005024680

British Library cataloguing data are available

Manufactured in the United States of America

*McFarland & Company, Inc., Publishers
Box 611, Jefferson, North Carolina 28640
www.mcfarlandpub.com*

For
Gayle Winston

Contents

Foreword

Who is this John Stewart? Who is the man who, in one short lifetime, has produced exhaustive encyclopedias, covering Australian film, Africa's states and their rulers, two volumes on Antarctica — the *Library Journal*'s candidate for the best reference book of the year (1990), the moons of the solar system, Italian film personnel, the holdings of the British Empire, and now Broadway Musicals?

I suspect there must be other books similarly titled, but Mr. Stewart's is nothing less than a guide to every Broadway musical ever produced since 1943 (and most of the important ones before that), its presenters, directors, designers, its casts. It includes not only original productions, but reworked productions and revivals.

I covet INFORMATION and I suppose, predictably, I resent criticism, especially the professional kind. This amazing and invaluable resource contains NO OPINIONS.

Surely this is the most complete (and fascinating!) reference book of its kind in print, and no theater professional or enthusiastic observer should be without it.

— Hal Prince

Preface

The subject always comes around to Broadway musicals. The reminiscences, the "favorite shows" game, and of course, the questions — who? what? when? why? Someone's going to try to look up the answers, especially if there's a debate going, or better still, a wager. Where do you go to find these answers? A library would need on hand all back annual issues of *Theatre World* and *Best Plays* and copies of old *Playbills*, and that's asking a lot. Even the Lincoln Center Library isn't able to go that far.

There are some good sites on the Internet, but (as of this writing) all of them are evolving, and none of them have anywhere near the depth necessary to answer many of the questions you're likely to come up against.

Hence this book, with its twin objectives of deep coverage and wide appeal. Its coverage begins with March 31, 1943, the momentous night that the "first modern musical" — *Oklahoma!* — made its debut on Broadway. However all is not lost from those pre–*Oklahoma!* days, by any means. Many older shows have been revived since 1943 — *Show Boat, Pal Joey, Porgy and Bess,* to name but three very famous ones, are therefore in this book. One might say, simplistically but with some truth, that the only pre–*Oklahoma!* shows the reader won't find are those that producers have considered unrevivable.

Given the universal acceptance of *Oklahoma!* as the first modern musical, we must ask, What is a Broadway musical? I'd never considered that this might be an issue, but it is. This question really breaks down into two parts — What is Broadway? and What is a musical?

Taking the last part first: What is a musical? We also see the terms musical play or musical comedy or musical drama, and indeed, several other nonce terms as well. Well, a musical is a show with music and lyrics and a libretto, acted and sung and danced by players on the stage (the libretto is less formally called the book, hence the term "book musical"). It is a story told with music, like an opera, but with the libretto being spoken rather than sung.

My own road to a suitable definition of the term "musical" began by excluding certain types of stage productions. The most obvious are straight plays (either comedies or dra-

mas) without music. Straight plays are not covered in this book, even if they had a song or two as incidental music.

Then there's that animal called a play with music. There is a distinction between a musical play and a play with music, but sometimes that distinction is blurred. Usually a "play with music" is a straight play with some musical numbers in it — more than just incidental music, but not enough to warrant calling it a musical. Importantly, the music does not advance the story. Occasionally a musical will advertise itself as a "play with music" when it is really a musical. *Park* is an example. But most of the time I could not justify including a "play with music."

Revues? What about them? What about *New Faces of 1952*, for example? I could not really leave that out — too many readers would be too disappointed. And if I put that one in, I could not leave out the subsequent *New Faces* shows, or any other musical revues. However, non-musical revues (of which there are many) or revues with very little music are not included.

What about Broadway presentations such as ice shows, magic shows, special concerts, one-night specials, one-night tributes, roasts, one-person shows, poetry shows, mime, monologues, specialty performances, "albums," parades of stars, foreign exotica, Yiddish musicals aimed mainly at the Jewish market, ballet and dance companies (both domestic and overseas), circuses, acrobatic shows? I could not justify these except *The Magic Show* itself, which is a genuine musical. However, commercially running shows that took the form of a musical tribute — for instance, *Eubie!, Sophisticated Ladies,* and *Dream* — really do qualify as musicals, as do certain purely dance shows such as *Fosse, Contact, Kat and the Kings* (who says a musical has to have a libretto?). So, they are in.

Operas. This is a gray area, and again a subjective call. *Porgy and Bess* — an opera, yes, but also one of the great musicals — is in, as are several (but not all) by Gian-Carlo Menotti. It depends whether they are generally thought of as musicals or as operas, despite whatever advertising they may have had at the time of production.

Operettas, such as *The Vagabond King* and *The Merry*

1

Widow, are mostly in if they were presented as and are generally viewed as musicals. Gilbert and Sullivan's comic operas are out, with the exception of the 1981 production of *The Pirates of Penzance,* which was a genuine Broadway musical.

That gives a pretty comprehensive picture of what I came to consider a "musical" for the purposes of this book — with the reader, I hope, always in mind.

The problem of what to do with shows that did not meet my criteria, but which the reader might expect to find herein, would be resolved later. The next question to be addressed was "What is Broadway"— or, what is a Broadway theatre?

The definition of "Broadway theatre" has changed over the years. Perhaps the best definition is a theatre within the confines of the "Broadway Box," i.e., a geographical area of Midtown Manhattan centering around the street called Broadway, within which lie a number of theatres with a seating capacity of 499 or more that have traditionally been called Broadway theatres. However, the Broadway Box itself has changed shape and size with time, as old theatres disappeared and new ones came in. But there are certain rigid rules. For example, a theatre with only 100 seats even if it falls within the Broadway Box, could never be called a Broadway theatre. A theatre in Brooklyn, even if it has 2,000 seats, could never be called a Broadway theatre. There must be some reasonable proximity to the Great White Way, and there must be a certain minimum number of seats. If a theatre doesn't qualify, and is still in Manhattan, it is called Off Broadway (I use the spelling Off Broadway throughout this book, as adjective and adverb, and have sometimes abbreviated it to OB, especially in the appendix). If it is not a traditional Off Broadway house, then it is called Off Off Broadway (OOB). If it is farther out than Manhattan, it is called "regional theatre."

Apart from these standards, a certain amount of the "Broadway" classification has been determined by tradition, which sometimes leads to confusion. Even in well-informed circles, the following are from time to time listed in reputable publications as Broadway: the Public, the Circle in the Square (now called the Circle in the Square Downtown to distinguish it from the Circle in the Square Uptown on Fiftieth Street, which is a Broadway theatre), City Center, New York State Theatre at Lincoln Center (Lincoln Center operates two other theatres: one upstairs, The Vivian Beaumont [Broadway], and one downstairs, The Mitzi E. Newhouse [Off Broadway]), Town Hall, Madison Square Garden Theatre, and Radio City Music Hall. Nevertheless, these are not traditionally regarded as Broadway theatres, and they are not included in this book. Some theatres, such as the Edison, are (now) called Limited Broadway or Middle Broadway. I have chosen to exclude these.

If a bona fide Broadway musical ever had another production at one of these theatres, then that performance is covered in the main part of the book, not as its own entry, but under the heading of the genuine Broadway production.

Sometimes a show would open under Broadway contracts, but in an Off Broadway theatre. This might be because a show was waiting for a Broadway house, but had to play the first part of its run in an Off Broadway house. This happened to *Man of La Mancha* and *Grease,* to name but two. In that case, although the house may still be Off Broadway, the production is considered Broadway, and therefore eligible for the Tony Awards.

So, an important definition of a Broadway show (rather than a Broadway theatre) is one that qualifies for the Tony Awards. However, that depends to some extent on the persuasion and pressure brought to bear by interested parties on the Tony Awards Committee at any given time. More of this below.

What about shows that closed out of town on their way to Broadway, or those few that actually got to their designated Broadway theatre but closed during previews? Although they were Broadway-bound, I do not consider them Broadway because they did not have a recognized Broadway run.

But still there was the thought that a reader might not find a particular show — a musical revue, a Broadway-bound show that did not make it, a play with music, a musical that played a non–Broadway house, a musical that was playing Broadway at the very moment *Oklahoma!* opened, ones that opened in 2005 (i.e. after the cut-off of this book), a famous foreign show that did not make Broadway, and other shows that for one reason or another I feel do not qualify for the main part of this book. The best example may be *The Fantasticks.* So, rather reluctantly, I had to face what I always knew: that I was obliged to create an appendix for such shows.

So, if you are looking for a show and it is not in the main part of the book, then it probably will be in the appendix, which also lists most of the main London productions that never had a showing on Broadway, and also some from other countries. But this appendix is only a help-list, not a complete list. Although perhaps larger than a normal appendix, and containing, I think, most shows a reader might reasonably expect to find, it is not comprehensive. It is certainly secondary to the main part of the book. In order to list all musicals and revues, etc., that never played Broadway during our time frame, one would have to write a separate book (much bigger than this one). However, I hope there will not be many disappointments at not finding a show in one part of the book or another.

The main text treats every Broadway musical ever to open from March 31, 1943, through Dec. 31, 2004, even for one performance, in considerable depth (there are 772 individual entries). The shows are arranged alphabetically, and are numbered for index purposes. Essentially the entry for each show is composed of three main sections: Before Broadway, the Broadway Run, and After Broadway. More specifically, the format breaks down as follows:

First comes the title of the Broadway musical, in large bold italics. The title is followed by a description of the plot. Next comes the Before Broadway section, which discusses the period before that particular production's official opening night in its Broadway theatre. Out-of-town tryouts are covered, as well as pre–1943 or earlier non–Broadway) productions of the musical.

The second section of each entry covers the Broadway run. Under this heading come all the data one would expect: theatre or theatres; dates that the show ran at each theatre (often a show would move to another theatre during its run); the number of Broadway previews (if any), and when they began; the number of performances during the official run (whenever the show played at more than one Broadway theatre during its run, it will say "Total of x performances"); and "Presented by" (this is the producer, unless otherwise stated), followed by the crew credits, arranged roughly thus: Music; Lyrics; Book; Based on [source]; Director; Choreographer; Sets; Costumes; Lighting; Sound; Musical Supervisor: Musical Director; Orchestrations; Dance Music Arrangements; Cast recording details; Press; Casting; General Manager; Company Manager; Production Stage Manager; Stage Manager; Assistant Stage Manager.

Sometimes the credits in a program (or playbill), especially more recent ones, are very extensive. For the sake of space, I regretfully chose to omit certain credits, unless they listed someone of real note or general interest. Those I didn't have space for include attorneys, insurance, advertising, poster designers, interns, assistants and associates in most departments, electricians, carpenters, props, fly men, spot light operators, wardrobe, hair, wigs, production managers, production supervisors, and executive producers.

An explanation of the term "production stage manager" is necessary here. Actors' Equity Association (known as Equity) does not recognize this term, at least not in its rules or contract form, not even today. Equity demands that in a musical there must be a stage manager (or general stage manager), first assistant stage manager and second assistant stage manager. In older productions one will see these terms. However, in real life, over the years the general stage manager (or stage manager) has become the production stage manager, the first assistant manager has become the stage manager, and the second assistant manager has become the assistant stage manager.

Following the crew credits is the cast listing, in order of appearance (unless otherwise stated, or unless otherwise obvious). An example of a cast entry is: JOE BLOW: Fred Graham (2) ☆, *Jim Dendy* (from 2/4/63). At left is the character in CAPS AND SMALL CAPS; then a colon; then the actor who played that character, usually with dates of his or her run; then replacements (in italics) and dates. In parentheses by certain actors' names appear numbers, for example "(2)." These refer to the actors' billing positions on opening night. There is a star (☆) after some billing position indicators — this means that the actor starred (i.e., had his or her name above the title). Any name in italics signifies a replacement.

Standbys and understudies are listed. These terms need some explanation because for years they have been the subject of much confusion. What's the difference between a standby and an understudy? Ask that question of any ten

actors who have been either understudies or standbys (or both) and you'll get ten different answers. The facts are: a standby is an understudy, but an understudy is not necessarily (and probably is not) a standby. Standbys are understudies who have negotiated "standby" terms for themselves in the contract (i.e., in the program they will be distinguished as "standbys"). Equity does not recognize the term "standby," at least not in its production contract rules. It does, however, demand that all parts for which contracts are issued, except for stars and bit players, shall be covered by understudies (which means a star does not have to have an understudy, but, in fact, will often have a standby and an understudy). "Standby" has been a term used for decades, but it was not used in playbills or yearbooks until the 1960s, so for those earlier productions it is sometimes difficult to determine exactly who was a standby. The safest guide, and the one that has been used in this book, is that an actor who is listed as understudy for one of the leading players, and who does not have a regular role in the production, is a standby (however, sometimes, rarely, and just to confuse the matter, the standby will have a regular role). In the old days standbys would have to call in half an hour before the beginning of each performance to see if they were needed. If not, depending on the terms of the standby contract, they could either go about their business and forget about that night's performance (some actors have had roles in other shows to go to, sometimes out of town, but never a conflicting Broadway show), or they would have to stay within 15 minutes of the theatre and leave a number with the stage manager where they might be reached. Nowadays, standbys have beepers (an understudy does not need a beeper), and if they're needed they are beeped.

A regular understudy almost always has a regular role in the production, often as an ensemble member. He or she is ready to go on in the understudied role at all times if needed. A "general understudy" covers a number of roles and is not usually a regular member of the cast. Chorus or ensemble members are covered by "swings" or "partial swings" (a "partial swing" covers an absent ensemble member only in a specific production number or numbers).

Orchestra (or band) members are listed after the cast.

Then comes the act and scene breakdown which runs along these lines. *Act I*: *Scene 1* The footpath: "Musical Number" (Joe, Fred, Company) [the hit]; *Scene 2* The store; midnight: Sketch (by Jim Walton). Spoof of doctors. Sung by Betty Warren. Danced by Nikos Kourtoil. *Act II*: *Scene 1* The store; the following day: "Sketch and Song" (m/l: Howard Jones; sketch by Joe Fine); *Scene 2* The Howard house: "Musical Number" (reprise) (Company) [this reprise was dropped during the run].

The characters who performed each musical number will be in parentheses next to the title of the number. If it is a sketch, then the characters and actors will generally be listed, in a style similar to a main cast list.

Sometimes I simply could not break the musical numbers down into their scenes — the best I could do was act by act, and so that it is how I have presented those shows (they are relatively few).

Most of the musical numbers are songs, but some are dance numbers, and these will generally be noted as such (i.e., "dance"). The musical numbers do not always have quotation marks around them if they are dances.

Next comes information on various aspects of the show and its reception: the preview period, opening night and post-opening night; reviews and awards (winners and nominations); and other items of interest. Only a very basic summary of the reviews is given.

The third principal section in an entry is "After Broadway," which includes tours, London productions, Off Broadway revivals, movie versions, television versions, and some others, all arranged chronologically.

In this third section I have listed only those productions that I consider to be of some significance or interest. To list all productions of a show such as *Oklahoma!* would be next to impossible, of course. The amount of information on these later productions also varies, but perforce it had to be limited. The cast in these listings are not necessarily given in order of appearance, as they are in the Broadway run.

There had to be two indexes, one for song titles, and one for personnel (and the occasional dog, or pig).

Throughout the book I have endeavored to standardize (and correct) spellings of personal names. This needs explanation. A person's name will often be seen spelled in different ways, meaning somewhere there is an error. I have chosen to use the *New York Times* as my guide, but sometimes they are in error too.

With all the personal names indexed I tried to parse them as well as I could. So Robert Jones, Robert H. Jones, Bob Jones, Rob Jones, Robbie Jones, and Bobby Jones — are they all the same person? I have done my best here, but if the attempt falls short occasionally, then so be it. I have in no way attempted to correct the song titles.

Looking at the song index the reader may well spot a certain cavalier approach to punctuation. This is a very deliberate approach, born out of the fact that in many instances there seems to be no correct way to punctuate a song. It is not important whether it is a comma, or a dash; or if three dots come at the end, or if there is an ending exclamation point, etc. If it is not important to the composer, then it is not important to this index. The object of the song index is for the reader to find the song title. However, when it comes to the book itself, the song is punctuated according to the sources I found it in.

This book is about people, of course, but its thrust is the shows, the Broadway shows. So, as for biographical information, as much as I would have liked to have tinkered in this area in the index (for example, for Gayle Stine I would have loved to have put something like "Producer of a string of Broadway and Off Broadway comedies and dramas in the '50s and '60s, married movie director Ron Winston, went into the hotel and restaurant business, and has for many years owned the famous River House in the mountains of North Carolina," or, for, say, George Elmer, "Producer and manager of numerous productions, On and Off Broadway," or, for Gracie Luck, "American actress/writer of three continents, also known as Susan Kramer; most recently well-known for the book *Max and Friends,*" or, for Hal Prince, "Almost universally acknowledged as the greatest single contributor to the Broadway musical stage") I did not have the nerve, and it would, again, have made the book an impossible size.

Thanks to Cindy Jones, of Winston-Salem Library, Renee Landau, Pete Masterson, Carlin Glynn, Norman Twain, and more than special thanks to Bert L. Klein and Honoree Van De Nelsen.

Chronology of Openings

The chronology below is arranged by "Broadway year," i.e. June 1 to May 31, rather than by regular calendar year (Jan. 1 to Dec. 31).

Mar 31, 1943 — *Oklahoma!*
Apr 1, 1943 — *Ziegfeld Follies of 1943*

June 1, 1943 — May 31, 1944 (23)

Jun 8, 1943 — *The Student Prince*
Jun 17, 1943 — *Early to Bed*
Jun 29, 1943 — *The Vagabond King*
Aug 4, 1943 — *The Merry Widow*
Aug 12, 1943 — *Chauve-Souris 1943*
Sep 4, 1943 — *Blossom Time*
Sep 8, 1943 — *Laugh Time*
Sep 9, 1943 — *My Dear Public*
Sep 13, 1943 — *Porgy and Bess*
Sep 16, 1943 — *Bright Lights of 1944*
Sep 19, 1943 — *A Tropical Revue*
Oct 1, 1943 — *Hairpin Harmony*
Oct 7, 1943 — *One Touch of Venus*
Nov 5, 1943 — *Artists and Models*
Nov 11, 1943 — *What's Up?*
Nov 17, 1943 — *A Connecticut Yankee*
Dec 2, 1943 — *Carmen Jones*
Jan 13, 1944 — *Jackpot*
Jan 28, 1944 — *Mexican Hayride*
Apr 8, 1944 — *Follow the Girls*
Apr 19, 1944 — *Allah Be Praised!*
Apr 24, 1944 — *Helen Goes to Troy*
May 18, 1944 — *Dream with Music*

June 1, 1944 — May 31, 1945 (18)

Jun 15, 1944 — *Take a Bow*
Aug 21, 1944 — *Song of Norway*
Sep 12, 1944 — *Star Time*
Oct 5, 1944 — *Bloomer Girl*
Nov 16, 1944 — *Sadie Thompson*
Nov 22, 1944 — *Rhapsody*
Dec 7, 1944 — *The Seven Lively Arts*
Dec 23, 1944 — *Laffing Room Only*

Dec 26, 1944 — *A Tropical Revue*
Dec 27, 1944 — *Sing Out, Sweet Land!*
Dec 28, 1944 — *On the Town*
Jan 10, 1945 — *A Lady Says Yes*
Jan 27, 1945 — *Up in Central Park*
Mar 22, 1945 — *The Firebrand of Florence*
Apr 19, 1945 — *Carousel*
May 21, 1945 — *Blue Holiday*
May 24, 1945 — *Memphis Bound*
May 31, 1945 — *Hollywood Pinafore*

June 1, 1945 — May 31, 1946 (19)

Jun 1, 1945 — *Concert Varieties*
Jul 18, 1945 — *Marinka*
Sep 6, 1945 — *Mr Strauss Goes to Boston*
Sep 27, 1945 — *Carib Song*
Oct 6, 1945 — *Polonaise*
Oct 16, 1945 — *The Red Mill*
Nov 8, 1945 — *The Girl from Nantucket*
Nov 10, 1945 — *Are You with It?*
Nov 22, 1945 — *The Day Before Spring*
Dec 21, 1945 — *Billion Dollar Baby*
Jan 5, 1946 — *Show Boat*
Jan 21, 1946 — *Nellie Bly*
Feb 6, 1946 — *Lute Song*
Feb 13, 1946 — *The Duchess Misbehaves*
Mar 7, 1946 — *Three to Make Ready*
Mar 30, 1946 — *St Louis Woman*
Apr 18, 1946 — *Call Me Mister*
May 16, 1946 — *Annie Get Your Gun*
May 31, 1946 — *Around the World (in Eighty Days)*

June 1, 1946 — May 31, 1947 (14)

Jul 8, 1946 — *Tidbits of 1946*
Sep 5, 1946 — *Yours Is My Heart*
Sep 17, 1946 — *Gypsy Lady*

Nov 4, 1946 — *Park Avenue*
Nov 7, 1946 — *Bal Negre*
Dec 5, 1946 — *If the Shoe Fits*
Dec 26, 1946 — *Beggar's Holiday*
Dec 26, 1946 — *Toplitzky of Notre Dame*
Jan 9, 1947 — *Street Scene*
Jan 10, 1947 — *Finian's Rainbow*
Jan 21, 1947 — *Sweethearts*
Mar 12, 1947 — *The Chocolate Soldier*
Mar 13, 1947 — *Brigadoon*
Apr 3, 1947 — *Barefoot Boy with Cheek*

June 1, 1947 — May 31, 1948 (12)

Jun 2, 1947 — *Louisiana Lady*
Oct 2, 1947 — *Music in My Heart*
Oct 9, 1947 — *High Button Shoes*
Oct 10, 1947 — *Allegro*
Dec 5, 1947 — *Caribbean Carnival*
Dec 11, 1947 — *Angel in the Wings*
Dec 26, 1947 — *The Cradle Will Rock*
Jan 15, 1948 — *Make Mine Manhattan*
Jan 29, 1948 — *Look Ma, I'm Dancin'!*
Apr 30, 1948 — *Inside U.S.A.*
May 5, 1948 — *Hold It!*
May 6, 1948 — *Sally*

June 1, 1948 — May 31, 1949 (16)

Jun 3, 1948 — *Sleepy Hollow*
Sep 9, 1948 — *Hilarities*
Sep 15, 1948 — *Small Wonder*
Sep 16, 1948 — *Heaven on Earth*
Sep 20, 1948 — *Magdalena*
Oct 7, 1948 — *Love Life*
Oct 11, 1948 — *Where's Charley?*
Oct 19, 1948 — *My Romance*
Nov 13, 1948 — *As the Girls Go*
Dec 16, 1948 — *Lend an Ear*
Dec 29, 1948 — *The Rape of Lucretia*

Dec 30, 1948—*Kiss Me, Kate*
Jan 13, 1949—*Along Fifth Avenue*
Jan 22, 1949—*All for Love*
Feb 22, 1949—*Carousel*
Apr 7, 1949—*South Pacific*

June 1, 1949— May 31, 1950 (15)

Jul 15, 1949—*Miss Liberty*
Sep 6, 1949—*Ken Murray's Blackouts of 1949*
Oct 13, 1949—*Touch and Go*
Oct 30, 1949—*Lost in the Stars*
Oct 31, 1949—*Regina*
Nov 25, 1949—*Texas, Li'l Darlin'*
Dec 8, 1949—*Gentlemen Prefer Blondes*
Jan 6, 1950—*Happy as Larry*
Jan 17, 1950—*Alive and Kicking*
Jan 20, 1950—*Dance Me a Song*
Feb 2, 1950—*Arms and the Girl*
Mar 15, 1950—*The Consul*
Mar 23, 1950—*Great to Be Alive!*
Apr 27, 1950—*Tickets Please*
May 18, 1950—*The Liar*

June 1, 1950— May 31, 1951 (16)

Jun 28, 1950—*Michael Todd's Peep Show*
Oct 5, 1950—*Pardon Our French*
Oct 12, 1950—*Call Me Madam*
Nov 2, 1950—*The Barrier*
Nov 24, 1950—*Guys and Dolls*
Dec 13, 1950—*Let's Make an Opera*
Dec 14, 1950—*Bless You All*
Dec 21, 1950—*Out of this World*
Jan 29, 1951—*Where's Charley?*
Feb 6, 1951—*Jotham Valley*
Feb 19, 1951—*Razzle Dazzle*
Mar 29, 1951—*The King and I*
Apr 18, 1951—*Make a Wish*
Apr 19, 1951—*A Tree Grows in Brooklyn*
May 14, 1951—*Flahooley*
May 29, 1951—*Oklahoma!*

June 1, 1951— May 31, 1952 (13)

Jun 13, 1951—*Courtin' Time*
Jun 21, 1951—*Seventeen*
Jul 19, 1951—*Two on the Aisle*
Oct 8, 1951—*Music in the Air*
Nov 1, 1951—*Top Banana*
Nov 12, 1951—*Paint Your Wagon*
Jan 2, 1952—*Pal Joey*
Jan 8, 1952—*Kiss Me, Kate*
Mar 21, 1952—*Three Wishes for Jamie*
Apr 16, 1952—*Four Saints in Three Acts*
May 5, 1952—*Of Thee I Sing*
May 8, 1952—*Shuffle Along*
May 16, 1952—*New Faces of 1952*

June 1, 1952— May 31, 1953 (10)

Jun 25, 1952—*Wish You Were Here*
Oct 14, 1952—*Buttrio Square*
Oct 27, 1952—*My Darlin' Aida*
Dec 15, 1952—*Two's Company*
Feb 11, 1953—*Hazel Flagg*
Feb 18, 1953—*Maggie*
Feb 25, 1953—*Wonderful Town*
Mar 10, 1953—*Porgy and Bess*
May 7, 1953—*Can-Can*
May 28, 1953—*Me and Juliet*

June 1, 1953— May 31, 1954 (7)

Sep 8, 1953—*Carnival in Flanders*
Dec 3, 1953—*Kismet*
Dec 10, 1953—*John Murray Anderson's Almanac*
Mar 5, 1954—*The Girl in Pink Tights*
Apr 8, 1954—*By the Beautiful Sea*
Apr 20, 1954—*The Golden Apple*
May 13, 1954—*The Pajama Game*

June 1, 1954— May 31, 1955 (14)

Sep 13, 1954—*Hayride*
Sep 30, 1954—*The Boy Friend*
Oct 11, 1954—*On Your Toes*
Oct 20, 1954—*Peter Pan*
Nov 4, 1954—*Fanny*
Dec 1, 1954—*Hit the Trail*
Dec 27, 1954—*The Saint of Bleecker Street*
Dec 30, 1954—*House of Flowers*
Jan 27, 1955—*Plain and Fancy*
Feb 24, 1955—*Silk Stockings*
Apr 6, 1955—*Three for Tonight*
Apr 18, 1955—*Ankles Aweigh*
May 5, 1955—*Damn Yankees*
May 26, 1955—*Seventh Heaven*

June 1, 1955— May 31, 1956 (8)

Jun 20, 1955—*Almost Crazy*
Sep 6, 1955—*Catch a Star!*
Sep 27, 1955—*Hear! Hear!*
Nov 10, 1955—*The Vamp*
Nov 30, 1955—*Pipe Dream*
Mar 15, 1956—*My Fair Lady*
Mar 22, 1956—*Mr. Wonderful*
May 3, 1956—*The Most Happy Fella*

June 1, 1956— May 31, 1957 (11)

Jun 13, 1956—*Shangri-La*

Jun 14, 1956—*New Faces of 1956*
Nov 15, 1956—*Li'l Abner*
Nov 26, 1956—*Cranks*
Nov 29, 1956—*Bells Are Ringing*
Dec 1, 1956—*Candide*
Dec 6, 1956—*Happy Hunting*
Mar 1, 1957—*Ziegfeld Follies of 1957*
Apr 13, 1957—*Shinbone Alley*
Apr 15, 1957—*Brigadoon*
May 14, 1957—*New Girl in Town*

June 1, 1957— May 31, 1958 (11)

Aug 20, 1957—*Simply Heavenly*
Sep 10, 1957—*Mask and Gown*
Sep 26, 1957—*West Side Story*
Oct 17, 1957—*Copper and Brass*
Oct 31, 1957—*Jamaica*
Nov 6, 1957—*Rumple*
Dec 19, 1957—*The Music Man*
Jan 23, 1958—*The Body Beautiful*
Feb 4, 1958—*Oh Captain!*
Feb 21, 1958—*Portofino*
Apr 3, 1958—*Say, Darling*

June 1, 1958— May 31, 1959 (11)

Oct 11, 1958—*Goldilocks*
Nov 5, 1958—*Maria Golovin*
Nov 11, 1958—*La Plume de Ma Tante*
Dec 1, 1958—*Flower Drum Song*
Dec 22, 1958—*Whoop-Up*
Feb 5, 1959—*Redhead*
Mar 9, 1959—*Juno*
Mar 19, 1959—*First Impressions*
Apr 23, 1959—*Destry Rides Again*
May 12, 1959—*The Nervous Set*
May 21, 1959—*Gypsy*

June 1, 1959— May 31, 1960 (15)

Aug 4, 1959—*Billy Barnes Revue*
Oct 7, 1959—*Happy Town*
Oct 22, 1959—*Take Me Along*
Nov 2, 1959—*The Girls Against the Boys*
Nov 16, 1959—*The Sound of Music*
Nov 23, 1959—*Fiorello!*
Nov 25, 1959—*Once Upon a Mattress*
Dec 7, 1959—*Saratoga*
Feb 10, 1960—*Beg, Borrow or Steal*
Mar 8, 1960—*Greenwillow*
Apr 14, 1960—*Bye, Bye, Birdie*
Apr 20, 1960—*From A to Z*
Apr 27, 1960—*West Side Story*
Apr 28, 1960—*Christine*
May 23, 1960—*Finian's Rainbow*

June 1, 1960— May 31, 1961 (12)

Sep 29, 1960—*Irma La Douce*

Oct 17, 1960—*Tenderloin*
Nov 3, 1960—*The Unsinkable Molly Brown*
Dec 3, 1960—*Camelot*
Dec 16, 1960—*Wildcat*
Dec 26, 1960—*Do, Re, Mi*
Jan 12, 1961—*Show Girl*
Jan 16, 1961—*The Conquering Hero*
Mar 1, 1961—*13 Daughters*
Apr 3, 1961—*The Happiest Girl in the World*
Apr 13, 1961—*Carnival!*
May 18, 1961—*Donnybrook!*

June 1, 1961— May 31, 1962 (16)

Jun 13, 1961—*The Billy Barnes People*
Oct 3, 1961—*Sail Away*
Oct 10, 1961—*Milk and Honey*
Oct 12, 1961—*Let It Ride!*
Oct 14, 1961—*How to Succeed in Business Without Really Trying*
Oct 23, 1961—*Kwamina*
Nov 2, 1961—*Kean*
Nov 18, 1961—*The Gay Life*
Dec 27, 1961—*Subways Are for Sleeping*
Jan 27, 1962—*A Family Affair*
Feb 1, 1962—*New Faces of 1962*
Mar 15, 1962—*No Strings*
Mar 19, 1962—*All American*
Mar 22, 1962—*I Can Get It for You Wholesale*
May 8, 1962—*A Funny Thing Happened on the Way to the Forum*
May 19, 1962—*Bravo Giovanni*

June 1, 1962— May 31, 1963 (10)

Oct 3, 1962—*Stop the World—I Want to Get Off*
Oct 20, 1962—*Mr. President*
Nov 10, 1962—*Nowhere to Go but Up*
Nov 17, 1962—*Little Me*
Jan 6, 1963—*Oliver!*
Mar 18, 1963—*Tovarich*
Apr 15, 1963—*Sophie*
Apr 19, 1963—*Hot Spot*
Apr 23, 1963—*She Loves Me*
May 16, 1963—*The Beast in Me*

June 1, 1963— May 31, 1964 (14)

Sep 30, 1963—*The Student Gypsy, or the Prince of Liederkranz*
Oct 3, 1963—*Here's Love*
Oct 17, 1963—*Jennie*
Oct 24, 1963—*110 in the Shade*
Dec 8, 1963—*The Girl Who Came to Supper*
Jan 16, 1964—*Hello, Dolly!*
Feb 6, 1964—*Rugantino*
Feb 16, 1964—*Foxy*

Feb 27, 1964—*What Makes Sammy Run?*
Mar 26, 1964—*Funny Girl*
Apr 4, 1964—*Anyone Can Whistle*
Apr 7, 1964—*High Spirits*
Apr 17, 1964—*Cafe Crown*
May 26, 1964—*Fade Out—Fade In*

June 1, 1964— May 31, 1965 (15)

Jun 2, 1964—*Folies Bergere*
Sep 11, 1964—*Wiener Blut (Vienna Life)*
Sep 22, 1964—*Fiddler on the Roof*
Sep 30, 1964—*Oh, What a Lovely War*
Oct 20, 1964—*Golden Boy*
Oct 27, 1964—*Ben Franklin in Paris*
Nov 10, 1964—*Something More!*
Nov 23, 1964—*Bajour*
Dec 15, 1964—*I Had a Ball*
Feb 6, 1965—*Kelly*
Feb 16, 1965—*Baker Street*
Mar 18, 1965—*Do I Hear a Waltz?*
Apr 25, 1965—*Half a Sixpence*
May 11, 1965—*Flora, the Red Menace*
May 16, 1965—*The Roar of the Greasepaint—The Smell of the Crowd*

June 1, 1965— May 31, 1966 (15)

Aug 2, 1965—*Oliver!*
Oct 4, 1965—*Pickwick*
Oct 10, 1965—*Drat! The Cat!*
Oct 17, 1965—*On a Clear Day You Can See Forever*
Nov 13, 1965—*Skyscraper*
Nov 22, 1965—*Man of La Mancha*
Nov 29, 1965—*Anya*
Dec 10, 1965—*The Yearling*
Dec 14, 1965—*La Grosse Valise*
Jan 29, 1966—*Sweet Charity*
Mar 7, 1966—*Wait a Minim!*
Mar 18, 1966—*Pousse Café*
Mar 29, 1966—*"It's a Bird ... It's a Plane ... It's Superman"*
May 21, 1966—*A Time for Singing*
May 24, 1966—*Mame*

June 1, 1966— May 31, 1967 (9)

Sep 21, 1966—*Annie Get Your Gun*
Oct 18, 1966—*The Apple Tree*
Nov 20, 1966—*Cabaret*
Nov 26, 1966—*Walking Happy*
Dec 5, 1966—*I Do! I Do!*
Dec 15, 1966—*A Joyful Noise*
Mar 28, 1967—*Sherry!*
Apr 11, 1967—*Illya Darling*
Apr 26, 1967—*Hallelujah, Baby!*

June 1, 1967— May 31, 1968 (11)

Oct 23, 1967—*Henry, Sweet Henry*
Dec 7, 1967—*How Now, Dow Jones*
Jan 18, 1968—*The Happy Time*
Jan 27, 1968—*Darling of the Day*
Feb 4, 1968—*Golden Rainbow*
Mar 3, 1968—*Here's Where I Belong*
Apr 4, 1968—*The Education of H*Y*M*A*N K*A*P*L*A*N*
Apr 10, 1968—*George M!*
Apr 23, 1968—*I'm Solomon*
Apr 29, 1968—*Hair*
May 2, 1968—*New Faces of 1968*

June 1, 1968— May 31, 1969 (12)

Oct 20, 1968—*Her First Roman*
Oct 23, 1968—*Maggie Flynn*
Nov 17, 1968—*Zorba*
Dec 1, 1968—*Promises, Promises*
Jan 2, 1969—*The Fig Leaves Are Falling*
Jan 22, 1969—*Celebration*
Jan 26, 1969—*Red, White and Maddox*
Feb 3, 1969—*Canterbury Tales*
Feb 6, 1969—*Dear World*
Mar 16, 1969—*1776*
Mar 18, 1969—*Come Summer*
Mar 22, 1969—*Billy*

June 1, 1969— May 31, 1970 (14)

Oct 23, 1969—*Jimmy*
Dec 2, 1969—*Buck White*
Dec 4, 1969—*La Strada*
Dec 18, 1969—*Coco*
Feb 14, 1970—*Gantry*
Feb 26, 1970—*Georgy*
Mar 15, 1970—*Purlie*
Mar 26, 1970—*Minnie's Boys*
Mar 29, 1970—*Look to the Lilies*
Mar 30, 1970—*Applause*
Apr 8, 1970—*Cry for Us All*
Apr 14, 1970—*The Boy Friend*
Apr 22, 1970—*Park*
Apr 26, 1970—*Company*

June 1, 1970— May 31, 1971 (11)

Oct 19, 1970—*The Rothschilds*
Nov 10, 1970—*Two by Two*
Dec 18, 1970—*The Me Nobody Knows*
Dec 28, 1970—*Lovely Ladies, Kind Gentlemen*
Jan 15, 1971—*Ari*
Jan 19, 1971—*No, No, Nanette*

Feb 25, 1971—*Oh! Calcutta!*
Apr 4, 1971—*Follies*
Apr 15, 1971—*70, Girls, 70*
Apr 24, 1971—*Frank Merriwell (or Honor Challenged)*
May 5, 1971—*Earl of Ruston*

June 1, 1971—
May 31, 1972 (15)

Jun 1, 1971—*You're a Good Man, Charlie Brown*
Oct 12, 1971—*Jesus Christ Superstar*
Oct 20, 1971—*Ain't Supposed to Die a Natural Death*
Oct 31, 1971—*On the Town*
Nov 2, 1971—*The Grass Harp*
Dec 1, 1971—*Two Gentlemen of Verona*
Dec 7, 1971—*Wild and Wonderful*
Dec 19, 1971—*Inner City*
Mar 22, 1972—*The Selling of the President*
Mar 30, 1972—*A Funny Thing Happened on the Way to the Forum*
Apr 9, 1972—*Sugar*
Apr 18, 1972—*Lost in the Stars*
May 1, 1972—*Different Times*
May 16, 1972—*Don't Play Us Cheap*
May 21, 1972—*Heathen!*

June 1, 1972—
May 31, 1973 (16)

Jun 7, 1972—*Grease*
Jun 22, 1972—*Man of La Mancha*
Sep 15, 1972—*Jacques Brel Is Alive and Well and Living in Paris*
Oct 9, 1972—*Dude*
Oct 12, 1972—*Hurry, Harry*
Oct 19, 1972—*Mother Earth*
Oct 23, 1972—*Pippin*
Nov 19, 1972—*Ambassador*
Nov 28, 1972—*Via Galactica*
Dec 27, 1972—*Purlie*
Jan 8, 1973—*Tricks*
Feb 6, 1973—*Shelter*
Feb 25, 1973—*A Little Night Music*
Mar 13, 1973—*Irene*
Mar 18, 1973—*Seesaw*
May 13, 1973—*Cyrano*

June 1, 1973—
May 31, 1974 (10)

Sep 5, 1973—*The Desert Song*
Oct 18, 1973—*Raisin*
Nov 1, 1973—*Molly*
Nov 13, 1973—*Gigi*
Dec 9, 1973—*The Pajama Game*
Jan 27, 1974—*Lorelei*
Feb 13, 1974—*Rainbow Jones*
Mar 6, 1974—*Over Here!*
Mar 10, 1974—*Candide*
May 28, 1974—*The Magic Show*

June 1, 1974—
May 31, 1975 (11)

Sep 23, 1974—*Gypsy*
Oct 6, 1974—*Mack and Mabel*
Dec 19, 1974—*Where's Charley?*
Dec 23, 1974—*Good News!*
Jan 5, 1975—*The Wiz*
Jan 7, 1975—*Shenandoah*
Feb 26, 1975—*The Night that Made America Famous*
Mar 3, 1975—*Goodtime Charley*
Mar 9, 1975—*The Lieutenant*
Mar 10, 1975—*The Rocky Horror Show*
Mar 19, 1975—*Doctor Jazz*

June 1, 1975—
May 31, 1976 (16)

Jun 3, 1975—*Chicago*
Oct 19, 1975—*A Chorus Line*
Oct 21, 1975—*Treemonisha*
Oct 22, 1975—*Me and Bessie*
Nov 6, 1975—*Hello, Dolly!*
Nov 13, 1975—*A Musical Jubilee*
Dec 21, 1975—*Very Good Eddie*
Jan 4, 1976—*Home Sweet Homer*
Jan 11, 1976—*Pacific Overtures*
Feb 17, 1976—*Rockabye Hamlet*
Mar 2, 1976—*Bubbling Brown Sugar*
Mar 25, 1976—*My Fair Lady*
Apr 25, 1976—*Rex*
May 1, 1976—*The Threepenny Opera*
May 4, 1976—*1600 Pennsylvania Avenue*
May 27, 1976—*Something's Afoot*

June 1, 1976—
May 31, 1977 (15)

Jun 22, 1976—*Godspell*
Jun 27, 1976—*Pal Joey*
Jul 21, 1976—*Guys and Dolls*
Jul 22, 1976—*Let My People Come*
Sep 19, 1976—*Going Up*
Sep 25, 1976—*Porgy and Bess*
Oct 9, 1976—*The Robber Bridegroom*
Dec 20, 1976—*Music Is*
Dec 22, 1976—*Your Arms Too Short to Box with God*
Dec 28, 1976—*Fiddler on the Roof*
Apr 17, 1977—*I Love My Wife*
Apr 18, 1977—*Side by Side by Sondheim*
Apr 21, 1977—*Annie*
May 2, 1977—*The King and I*
May 7, 1977—*Happy End*

June 1, 1977—
May 31, 1978 (12)

Sep 15, 1977—*Man of La Mancha*
Oct 5, 1977—*Hair*
Oct 29, 1977—*The Act*

Nov 23, 1977—*Jesus Christ Superstar*
Feb 19, 1978—*On the Twentieth Century*
Mar 1, 1978—*Timbuktu!*
Mar 5, 1978—*Hello, Dolly!*
Mar 27, 1978—*Dancin'*
May 9, 1978—*Ain't Misbehavin'*
May 10, 1978—*Angel*
May 13, 1978—*Runaways*
May 14, 1978—*Working*

June 1, 1978—
May 31, 1979 (14)

Jun 19, 1978—*The Best Little Whorehouse in Texas*
Sep 20, 1978—*Eubie!*
Oct 22, 1978—*King of Hearts*
Nov 12, 1978—*Platinum*
Dec 14, 1978—*Ballroom*
Dec 21, 1978—*A Broadway Musical*
Jan 11, 1979—*The Grand Tour*
Jan 11, 1979—*Sarava*
Feb 11, 1979—*They're Playing Our Song*
Feb 14, 1979—*Whoopee!*
Mar 1, 1979—*Sweeney Todd*
Apr 8, 1979—*Carmelina*
May 13, 1979—*The Utter Glory of Morrissey Hall*
May 31, 1979—*I Remember Mama*

June 1, 1979—
May 31, 1980 (16)

Jun 25, 1979—*Got Tu Go Disco*
Jul 31, 1979—*But Never Jam Today*
Sep 6, 1979—*Peter Pan*
Sep 25, 1979—*Evita*
Oct 7, 1979—*The 1940s Radio Hour*
Oct 8, 1979—*Sugar Babies*
Oct 11, 1979—*The Most Happy Fella*
Dec 13, 1979—*Oklahoma!*
Dec 20, 1979—*Comin' Uptown*
Feb 12, 1980—*Canterbury Tales*
Feb 14, 1980—*West Side Story*
Mar 27, 1980—*Reggae*
Apr 27, 1980—*Happy New Year*
Apr 30, 1980—*Barnum*
May 1, 1980—*A Day in Hollywood/ A Night in the Ukraine*
May 14, 1980—*Musical Chairs*

June 1, 1980—
May 31, 1981 (19)

Jun 2, 1980—*Your Arms Too Short to Box with God*
Jun 3, 1980—*It's So Nice to Be Civilized*
Jun 15, 1980—*Fearless Frank*
Aug 25, 1980—*Forty-Second Street*
Sep 14, 1980—*Charlie and Algernon*
Oct 16, 1980—*Brigadoon*

Oct 23, 1980—*Tintypes*
Nov 30, 1980—*Perfectly Frank*
Dec 14, 1980—*Onward Victoria*
Jan 8, 1981—*The Pirates of Penzance*
Jan 21, 1981—*Shakespeare's Cabaret*
Jan 28, 1981—*The Five O'clock Girl*
Mar 1, 1981—*Sophisticated Ladies*
Mar 5, 1981—*Bring Back Birdie*
Mar 15, 1981—*Broadway Follies*
Mar 29, 1981—*Woman of the Year*
Apr 16, 1981—*Copperfield*
Apr 30, 1981—*Can-Can*
May 3, 1981—*The Moony Shapiro Songbook*

June 1, 1981— May 31, 1982 (14)

Aug 18, 1981—*My Fair Lady*
Oct 12, 1981—*Marlowe*
Nov 10, 1981—*Oh, Brother!*
Nov 15, 1981—*Camelot*
Nov 16, 1981—*Merrily We Roll Along*
Nov 17, 1981—*The First*
Dec 20, 1981—*Dreamgirls*
Jan 21, 1982—*Little Me*
Jan 24, 1982—*Joseph and the Amazing
    Technicolor Dreamcoat*
Feb 4, 1982—*Pump Boys and Dinettes*
Mar 21, 1982—*Little Johnny Jones*
May 7, 1982—*Is There Life After High School?*
May 9, 1982—*Nine*
May 27, 1982—*Do Black Patent
    Leather Shoes Really Reflect Up?*

June 1, 1982— May 31, 1983 (13)

Jun 2, 1982—*Blues in the Night*
Jun 23, 1982—*Cleavage*
Jun 27, 1982—*Play Me a Country Song*
Jul 8, 1982—*Seven Brides for Seven Brothers*
Sep 8, 1982—*Your Arms Too Short to
    Box with God*
Sep 23, 1982—*A Doll's Life*
Oct 7, 1982—*Cats*
Oct 24, 1982—*Rock 'n' Roll! The First
    5,000 Years*
Feb 13, 1983—*Merlin*
Mar 6, 1983—*On Your Toes*
Apr 24, 1983—*Show Boat*
May 1, 1983—*My One and Only*
May 11, 1983—*Dance a Little Closer*

June 1, 1983— May 31, 1984 (13)

Jul 24, 1983—*Mame*
Aug 21, 1983—*La Cage aux Folles*
Oct 16, 1983—*Zorba*
Nov 10, 1983—*Amen Corner*
Nov 20, 1983—*Marilyn: An American Fable*
Nov 21, 1983—*Doonesbury*
Dec 4, 1983—*Baby*
Dec 21, 1983—*The Tap Dance Kid*

Feb 9, 1984—*The Rink*
Apr 5, 1984—*The Human Comedy*
Apr 29, 1984—*Oliver!*
May 2, 1984—*Sunday in the Park with George*
May 24, 1984—*The Wiz*

June 1, 1984— May 31, 1985 (7)

Nov 11, 1984—*The Three Musketeers*
Jan 7, 1985—*The King and I*
Jan 31, 1985—*Harrigan 'n' Hart*
Apr 8, 1985—*Leader of the Pack*
Apr 14, 1985—*Take Me Along*
Apr 16, 1985—*Grind*
Apr 25, 1985—*Big River*

June 1, 1985— May 31, 1986 (11)

Jul 2, 1985—*Singin' in the Rain*
Sep 18, 1985—*Song and Dance*
Oct 9, 1985—*Tango Argentino*
Nov 7, 1985—*The News*
Dec 2, 1985—*The Mystery of Edwin Drood*
Dec 18, 1985—*Jerry' Girls*
Dec 19, 1985—*Wind in the Willows*
Jan 23, 1986—*Jerome Kern Goes to Hollywood*
Jan 28, 1986—*Uptown...It's Hot!*
Apr 10, 1986—*Big Deal*
Apr 27, 1986—*Sweet Charity*

June 1, 1986— May 31, 1987 (10)

Aug 7, 1986—*Honky Tonk Nights*
Aug 10, 1986—*Me and My Girl*
Aug 21, 1986—*Rags*
Oct 16, 1986—*Raggedy Ann*
Oct 22, 1986—*Into the Light*
Nov 17, 1986—*Oh Coward!*
Nov 24, 1986—*Smile*
Feb 19, 1987—*Stardust*
Mar 12, 1987—*Les Miserables*
Mar 15, 1987—*Starlight Express*

June 1, 1987— May 31, 1988 (15)

Jun 28, 1987—*Dreamgirls*
Oct 1, 1987—*Roza*
Oct 15, 1987—*Late Nite Comic*
Oct 19, 1987—*Anything Goes*
Oct 29, 1987—*Cabaret*
Oct 29, 1987—*Don't Get God Started*
Nov 5, 1987—*Into the Woods*
Nov 12, 1987—*Teddy and Alice*
Jan 26, 1988—*The Phantom of the Opera*
Jan 28, 1988—*Sarafina!*
Mar 24, 1988—*The Gospel at Colonus*
Apr 14, 1988—*Mail*
Apr 28, 1988—*Chess*
May 1, 1988—*Romance/Romance*
May 12, 1988—*Carrie*

June 1, 1988— May 31, 1989 (7)

Aug 15, 1988—*Ain't Misbehavin'*
Dec 26, 1988—*Legs Diamond*
Jan 26, 1989—*Black and Blue*
Feb 26, 1989—*Jerome Robbins' Broadway*
Apr 7, 1989—*Chu Chem*
Apr 13, 1989—*Welcome to the Club*
Apr 27, 1989—*Starmites*

June 1, 1989— May 31, 1990 (11)

Aug 8, 1989—*Shenandoah*
Sep 14, 1989—*Sweeney Todd*
Oct 19, 1989—*Dangerous Games*
Nov 2, 1989—*Meet Me in St. Louis*
Nov 5, 1989—*3 Penny Opera*
Nov 9, 1989—*Prince of Central Park*
Nov 12, 1989—*Grand Hotel*
Nov 16, 1989—*Gypsy*
Dec 11, 1989—*City of Angels*
Apr 8, 1990—*Aspects of Love*
Apr 22, 1990—*Truly Blessed: A Musical
    Celebration of Mahalia Jackson*

June 1, 1990— May 31, 1991 (10)

Oct 18, 1990—*Once on This Island*
Nov 1, 1990—*Oh, Kay!*
Nov 4, 1990—*Buddy*
Nov 18, 1990—*Fiddler on the Roof*
Nov 29, 1990—*Shogun*
Dec 13, 1990—*Peter Pan*
Apr 11, 1991—*Miss Saigon*
Apr 25, 1991—*The Secret Garden*
Apr 28, 1991—*Gypsy*
May 1, 1991—*The Will Rogers Follies*

June 1, 1991— May 31, 1992 (11)

Nov 27, 1991—*Peter Pan*
Dec 8, 1991—*Nick and Nora*
Feb 13, 1992—*The Most Happy Fella*
Feb 19, 1992—*Crazy for You*
Apr 8, 1992—*Five Guys Named Moe*
Apr 14, 1992—*Guys and Dolls*
Apr 16, 1992—*Metro*
Apr 21, 1992—*The High Rollers Social and
    Pleasure Club*
Apr 24, 1992—*Man of La Mancha*
Apr 26, 1992—*Jelly's Last Jam*
Apr 29, 1992—*Falsettos*

June 1, 1992— May 31, 1993 (8)

Aug 26, 1992—*Anna Karenina*
Dec 10, 1992—*My Favorite Year*

Mar 4, 1993 — *The Goodbye Girl*
Apr 18, 1993 — *Ain't Broadway Grand*
Apr 22, 1993 — *The Who's Tommy*
Apr 25, 1993 — *Blood Brothers*
Apr 28, 1993 — *Tango Pasion*
May 3, 1993 — *Kiss of the Spider Woman*

June 1, 1993 — May 31, 1994 (12)

Jun 10, 1993 — *She Loves Me*
Jun 21, 1993 — *Camelot*
Nov 10, 1993 — *Joseph and the Amazing Technicolor Dreamcoat*
Nov 21, 1993 — *Cyrano — The Musical*
Dec 9, 1993 — *My Fair Lady*
Dec 16, 1993 — *The Red Shoes*
Mar 3, 1994 — *Damn Yankees*
Mar 24, 1994 — *Carousel*
Apr 18, 1994 — *Beauty and the Beast*
May 9, 1994 — *Passion*
May 10, 1994 — *The Best Little Whorehouse Goes Public*
May 11, 1994 — *Grease!*

June 1, 1994 — May 31, 1995 (5)

Oct 2, 1994 — *Show Boat*
Nov 17, 1994 — *Sunset Boulevard*
Mar 2, 1995 — *Smokey Joe's Café*
Mar 23, 1995 — *How to Succeed in Business Without Really Trying*
Apr 10, 1995 — *Gentlemen Prefer Blondes*
Jun 15, 1995 — *Chronicle of a Death Foretold*
Oct 5, 1995 — *Company*
Oct 19, 1995 — *Hello, Dolly!*
Oct 22, 1995 — *Swingin' on a Star*
Oct 25, 1995 — *Victor/Victoria*
Mar 27, 1996 — *State Fair*
Apr 11, 1996 — *The King and I*
Apr 18, 1996 — *A Funny Thing Happened on the Way to the Forum*
Apr 25, 1996 — *Bring in 'da Noise, Bring in 'da Funk*
Apr 28, 1996 — *Big*
Apr 29, 1996 — *Rent*

June 1, 1996 — May 31, 1997 (11)

Nov 14, 1996 — *Chicago*
Nov 24, 1996 — *Juan Darien: A Carnival Mass*
Dec 19, 1996 — *Once Upon a Mattress*
Mar 20, 1997 — *Play On!*
Mar 26, 1997 — *Annie*
Apr 3, 1997 — *Dream: The Johnny Mercer Musical*
Apr 23, 1997 — *Titanic*
Apr 24, 1997 — *Steel Pier*
Apr 26, 1997 — *The Life*
Apr 28, 1997 — *Jekyll and Hyde*
Apr 29, 1997 — *Candide*

June 1, 1997 — May 31, 1998 (12)

Jun 19, 1997 — *Forever Tango*
Aug 14, 1997 — *1776*
Oct 16, 1997 — *Side Show*
Oct 23, 1997 — *Triumph of Love*
Nov 11, 1997 — *The Scarlet Pimpernel*
Nov 13, 1997 — *The Lion King*
Nov 24, 1997 — *Street Corner Symphony*
Jan 18, 1998 — *Ragtime*
Jan 29, 1998 — *The Capeman*
Mar 12, 1998 — *The Sound of Music*
Mar 19, 1998 — *Cabaret*
Apr 27, 1998 — *High Society*

June 1, 1998 — May 31, 1999 (12)

Oct 22, 1998 — *Footloose*
Nov 12, 1998 — *Little Me*
Nov 22, 1998 — *On the Town*
Nov 23, 1998 — *Peter Pan*
Dec 17, 1998 — *Parade*
Jan 14, 1999 — *Fosse*
Feb 4, 1999 — *You're a Good Man, Charlie Brown*
Mar 4, 1999 — *Annie Get Your Gun*
Mar 24, 1999 — *Rollin' on the T.O.B.A.*
Apr 22, 1999 — *The Civil War*
Apr 25, 1999 — *The Gershwins' Fascinating Rhythm*
Apr 26, 1999 — *It Ain't Nothin' but the Blues*

June 1, 1999 — May 31, 2000 (13)

Aug 19, 1999 — *Kat and the Kings*
Oct 21, 1999 — *Saturday Night Fever*
Nov 17, 1999 — *Tango Argentino*
Nov 18, 1999 — *Kiss Me, Kate*
Nov 21, 1999 — *Putting It Together*
Dec 2, 1999 — *Marie Christine*
Dec 9, 1999 — *Swing!*
Jan 11, 2000 — *James Joyce's The Dead*
Mar 23, 2000 — *Aida*
Mar 30, 2000 — *Contact*
Apr 13, 2000 — *The Wild Party*
Apr 16, 2000 — *Jesus Christ Superstar*
Apr 27, 2000 — *The Music Man*

June 1, 2000 — May 31, 2001 (10)

Oct 26, 2000 — *The Full Monty*
Nov 15, 2000 — *The Rocky Horror Show*
Nov 30, 2000 — *Seussical*
Dec 10, 2000 — *Jane Eyre*
Mar 11, 2001 — *A Class Act*
Apr 5, 2001 — *Follies*
Apr 12, 2001 — *Bells Are Ringing*
Apr 19, 2001 — *The Producers*

Apr 26, 2001 — *The Adventures of Tom Sawyer*
May 2, 2001 — *Forty-Second Street*

June 1, 2001 — May 31, 2002 (8)

Sep 20, 2001 — *Urinetown*
Oct 18, 2001 — *Mamma Mia*
Oct 25, 2001 — *Thou Shalt Not*
Oct 28, 2001 — *By Jeeves*
Mar 14, 2002 — *Sweet Smell of Success*
Mar 21, 2002 — *Oklahoma!*
Apr 30, 2002 — *Into the Woods*
May 18, 2002 — *Thoroughly Modern Millie*

June 1, 2002 — May 31, 2003 (12)

Aug 15, 2002 — *Hairspray*
Aug 18, 2002 — *The Boys from Syracuse*
Oct 17, 2002 — *Flower Drum Song*
Oct 20, 2002 — *Amour*
Oct 24, 2002 — *Movin' Out*
Dec 5, 2002 — *Man of La Mancha*
Dec 9, 2002 — *Dance of the Vampires*
Mar 27, 2003 — *Urban Cowboy*
Apr 10, 2003 — *Nine*
Apr 10, 2003 — *A Year with Frog and Toad*
May 1, 2003 — *Gypsy*
May 4, 2003 — *The Look of Love*

June 1, 2003 — May 31, 2004 (12)

Jul 24, 2003 — *Big River*
Jul 31, 2003 — *Avenue Q*
Oct 10, 2003 — *Little Shop of Horrors*
Oct 16, 2003 — *The Boy from Oz*
Oct 31, 2003 — *Wicked*
Nov 13, 2003 — *Taboo*
Nov 23, 2003 — *Wonderful Town*
Dec 4, 2003 — *Never Gonna Dance*
Feb 26, 2004 — *Fiddler on the Roof*
Apr 22, 2004 — *Assassins*
Apr 29, 2004 — *Bombay Dreams*
May 2, 2004 — *Caroline, or Change*

June 1, 2004 — Dec 31, 2004 (6)

Jul 22, 2004 — *The Frogs*
Jul 24, 2004 — *Forever Tango*
Aug 19, 2004 — *Dracula: The Musical*
Oct 21, 2004 — *Brooklyn: The Musical*
Dec 2, 2004 — *Pacific Overtures*
Dec 9, 2004 — *La Cage aux Folles*

Broadway Musicals

1. *The Act*

A fading Hollywood actress tries a comeback as a nightclub act at the Hotel Las Vegas. Her memories and tribulations as she climbed to stardom.

Before Broadway. Martin Scorsese, Liza Minnelli, John Kander & Fred Ebb, and Larry Gaines were all from the 1977 film *New York, New York*. In Chicago they put together an adult-oriented musical, *In Person* (known by some there as *Liza with a Zero*) at a cost of about $900,000. It moved to the Orpheum Theatre, San Francisco, where it was produced by the San Francisco Civic Light Opera, 7/19/77–8/27/77. Although they had already settled on the new title *The Act*, they decided temporarily to call it *Shine it On* because, aside from the fact that it was the name of one of the songs, San Francisco was the home of the American Conservatory Theatre (ACT), and they didn't want to risk a conflict of names. Then it moved to Los Angeles. Not long after the L.A. opening, Mr. Scorsese was fired and replaced by Gower Champion (even though Scorsese received final director credit). In the cast Larry Gaines was replaced by Lorry Goldman, who was replaced by Arnold Soboloff before Broadway; and actors Roger Minami and Christopher Barrett were added to the script. The number "Love Songs" was cut. Before the show hit Broadway, it had spent another $320,000, yet amassed $450,000 in operating profits during its 15-week, record-breaking tryout tour. But it was not in good shape when it got to Broadway; in fact it never had been. The *Los Angeles Times* said its opening there "looked more like the rehearsal," and everyone blamed this on Mr. Scorsese spending more time in Miss Minnelli's dressing room than on the set. Gower Champion had only three weeks to repair the damage.

The Broadway Run. MAJESTIC THEATRE, 10/29/77–7/1/78. 6 previews from 10/22/77. 233 PERFORMANCES. The Cy Feuer & Ernest H. Martin production presented by The Shubert Organization; MUSIC: John Kander; LYRICS: Fred Ebb; BOOK: George Furth (based on his original book); DIRECTOR: Martin Scorsese; CHOREOGRAPHER: Ron Lewis (with Gower Champion); SETS: Tony Walton; COSTUMES: Halston; LIGHTING: Tharon Musser; SOUND: Abe Jacob; MUSICAL DIRECTOR: Stanley Lebowsky; ORCHESTRATIONS: Ralph Burns; DANCE MUSIC ARRANGEMENTS: Ronald Melrose; VOCAL & CHORAL ARRANGEMENTS: Earl Brown; CAST RECORDING on DR; PRESS: Merle Debuskey; CASTING: Gordon Hunt; GENERAL MANAGER: Joseph Harris & Ira Bernstein; PRODUCTION STAGE MANAGER: Phil Friedman; STAGE MANAGER: Robert Corpora; ASSISTANT STAGE MANAGER: Richard Lombard. *Cast:* LENNY KANTER: Christopher Barrett (6); MICHELLE CRAIG: Liza Minnelli (1) ☆; NAT SCHREIBER: Arnold Soboloff (3); DAN CONNORS: Barry Nelson (2) ☆, *Gower Champion* (during Mr. Nelson's vacation, from 5/25/78); ARTHUR: Roger Minami (5); CHARLEY PRICE: Mark Goddard (7); MOLLY CONNORS: Gayle Crofoot (4), *Laurie Dawn Skinner*; THE BOYS: Wayne Cilento (*Danny Buraczeski*), Michael Leeds, Roger Minami, Albert Stephenson; THE GIRLS: Carol Estey & Laurie Dawn Skinner (*Claudia Asbury*). **Standbys:** Dan: Mace Barrett & Christopher Barrett; Michelle: Claudia Asbury (dance standby); Nat/Charley: Christopher Barrett; Molly: Laurie Dawn Skinner; **Dance Alternates:** Claudia Asbury (*Karen Di Bianco*), Brad Witsger (*Steve Anthony*). **Act I: Scene 1** "Shine it On" (Michelle & Chorus); **Scene 2** "It's the Strangest Thing" (Michelle); **Scene 3**; **Scene 4** "Bobo's" (Michelle & Dancers); **Scene 5** "Turning" (Shaker Hymn); **Scene 6** "Little Do They Know" (Boys & Girls); **Scene 7** "Arthur (in the Afternoon)" (Michelle & Arthur] [re-written version of "Mamie in the Afternoon," which had been cut from *A Family Affair*]; **Scene 8**; **Scene 9** "Hollywood, California" (Michelle & Dancers) [dropped during the run]; **Scene 10**; **Scene 11** "The Money Tree" (Michelle). **Act II: Scene 1** "City Lights" (Michelle & Chorus); **Scene 2** "There When I Need Him" (Michelle); **Scene 3**; **Scene 4** "Hot Enough for You?" (Michelle & Dancers), "Little Do They Know" (reprise) (Boys & Girls); **Scene 5** Finale: "My Own Space" (Michelle) [replaced after opening with "Walking Papers" (Michelle)].

This was the first Broadway musical to charge $25 for a top seat. Ernie Martin, the producer, correctly foresaw the panning critics would give it — a couple did give it favorable reviews — but he wrongly foresaw a long run. John Simon, the *New York* magazine critic, gave Liza Minnelli a notoriously devastating review, more a personal attack. Miss Minnelli won a Tony Award, and there were also nominations for score, choreography, costumes, lighting, and for Barry Nelson. On 12/8/77 a fire in Miss Minnelli's apartment, while she was sleeping, was put out quickly by firemen, but she had inhaled too much smoke to be able to go on, and the show was canceled for that night. Miss Minnelli missed 26 of the 233 performances and, as she had no understudy, the show was repeatedly canceled; the producers received $230,000 in insurance payouts. Later George Furth sued the producers for a million dollars for reducing his royalties to help pay for Gower Champion's. Stanley Donen also sued, claiming he had brought them all together and was then frozen out.

2. *The Adventures of Tom Sawyer*

Tom lives with his Aunt Polly on the Mississippi, in St. Petersburg, Missouri, in 1844, and falls in love with Becky, the Judge's daughter, and witnesses Injun Joe, the half-breed, killing Doctor Robinson.

Before Broadway. It was Mike Ockrent's idea, and was almost five years in the making. On 11/26/96 there was a staged reading, with songs. DIRECTOR: Don Scardino. *Cast:* TOM: Sean Kennedy; AUNT POLLY: Cass Morgan; HUCK: Hunter Foster; JOE: Christopher Innvar; JUDGE: Dennis Parlato; BECKY: Jolie Jenkins; WIDOW DOUGLAS: Polly Holliday. The Broadway opening date of spring 1997 was put back to spring 1998, but that didn't work either. Don Scardino backed out as director. Allan Carr and Elizabeth Williams were involved, but Mr. Carr died and other producers came in. The show was due to open on Broadway in the 1999–2000 season, but that was postponed until 4/4/01, then 4/3/01. It was planned to miss New Haven and go straight to Broadway due to the size of the sets. On 10/28/00 a sampler CD was made, with the same main cast as would play on Broadway, except Beth Fowler (Widow Douglas). In the end it did try out, at the Shubert Theatre, New Haven, 3/4/01–3/11/01. Previews from 2/27/01. The cast was the same as for the subsequent Broadway run, except Alex Boyd as one of the Boys (he was replaced by Erik J. McCormack), and Michael McCormick and Gregg Rainwater in the chorus (replaced for Broadway by Patrick Boll and John Herrera).

The Broadway Run. MINSKOFF THEATRE, 4/26/01–5/13/01. 34 previews from 3/27/01. 21 PERFORMANCES. PRESENTED by James M. & James L. Nederlander & Watt/Dobie Productions; MUSIC/LYRICS: Don Schlitz; BOOK: Ken Ludwig; BASED ON the novel by Mark Twain; DIRECTOR: Scott Ellis; CHOREOGRAPHER: David Marques; ADDITIONAL CHOREOGRAPHY: Jodi Moccia; SETS: Heidi Ettinger; COSTUMES: Anthony Powell; LIGHTING: Kenneth Posner; SOUND: Lew Mead; MUSICAL DIRECTOR: Paul Gemignani; ORCHESTRATIONS: Michael Starobin; DANCE & INCIDENTAL MUSIC: David Krane; PRESS: Boneau/Bryan-Brown; CASTING: Jim Carnahan; GENERAL MANAGER: Devin Keudell; COMPANY MANAGER: Sean Free; STAGE MANAGER: David Hyslop; ASSISTANT STAGE MANAGER: Scott Taylor Rollison. *Cast:* TOM SAWYER: Joshua Park (1) ✧; BEN ROGERS: Tommar Wilson; GEORGE BELLAMY: Joe Gallagher: LYLE BELLAMY: Blake Hackler; JOE HARPER: Erik J. McCormack; ALFRED TEMPLE: Pierce Cravens; AMY LAWRENCE: Ann Whitlow Brown; LUCY HARPER: Mekenzie Rosen-Stone; SUSIE ROGERS: Elan; SABINA TEMPLE: Nikki M. James; SALLY BELLAMY: Stacia Fernandez; SERENY HARPER: Donna Lee Marshall; LUCINDA ROGERS: Amy Jo Phillips; NAOMI TEMPLE: Sally Wilfert; AUNT POLLY: Linda Purl (4) ✧; SID SAWYER: Marshall Pailet (12) ✧; DOC ROBINSON: Stephen Lee Anderson; REV. SPRAGUE: Tommy Hollis (10) ✧; LANYARD BELLAMY: Richard Poe (11) ✧; GIDEON TEMPLE: Ric Stoneback; LEMUEL DOBBINS: John Christopher Jones (9) ✧; HUCKLEBERRY FINN: Jim Poulos (2) ✧; MUFF POTTER: Tom Aldredge (7) ✧; INJUN JOE: Kevin Serge Durand (8) ✧; JUDGE THATCHER: John Dossett (5) ✧; BECKY THATCHER: Kristen Bell (3) ✧; WIDOW DOUGLAS: Jane Connell (6) ✧; PAP: Stephen Lee Anderson; ENSEMBLE: Stephen Lee Anderson, Ann Whitlow Brown, Elan, Stacia Fernandez, Joe Gallagher, Blake Hackler, Donna Lee Marshall, Erik J. McCormack, Amy Jo Phillips, Richard Poe, Mekenzie Rosen-Stone, Ric Stoneback, Sally Wilfert. *Understudies:* Tom: Blake Hackler & Erik J. McCormack; Huck: Joe Gallagher & Tommar Wilson; Becky: Nikki M. James & Kate Reinders; Aunt Polly: Stacia Fernandez & Sally Wilfert; Widow Douglas: Stacia Fernandez & Amy Jo Phillips; Amy: Kate Reinders; Sid: Pierce Cravens; Judge/Injun Joe: Patrick Boll & Richard Poe; Lanyard/Gideon/Doc: Patrick Boll, Richard Poe, John Herrera; Muff: John Herrera; Lemuel/Sprague: Stephen Lee Anderson & John Herrera; Ben/Joe: Michael Burton. *Swings:* Patrick Boll, Michael Burton, John Herrera, Kate Reinders, Elise Santora. *Orchestra:* SYNTHESIZER: Nicholas Archer; CONCERTMASTER: Marilyn Reynolds; VIOLINS: Andrea Andros & Jonathan Kass; VIOLA: Shelley Holland-Moritz; CELLO: Deborah Assael; FIDDLE: Blake Hackler; WOODWINDS: Scott Shachter, Martha Hyde, Kelly Peral, Thomas Sefcovic; FRENCH HORN: Lawrence Di Bello; TRUMPETS: Hiro Noguchi & Phil Granger; TROMBONE: Dean Plank; PIANO: Paul Ford; GUITARS: Andrew Schwartz, Gregory Utzig, Gordon Titcomb; DULCIMER: Erik J. McCormack; BASS: Kermit Driscoll; DRUMS: Larry Lelli; PERCUSSION: Charles Descarfino. *Act I: Scene 1* A meadow, and the town of St. Petersburg: "Hey, Tom Sawyer" (Boys, Tom, Aunt Polly, Dobbins, Sprague, People of St. Petersburg); *Scene 2* The fence in front of Tom's house: "Smart Like That" (Tom, Huck, The Boys) [during tryouts this number was performed by Tom, Ben, Boys]; *Scene 3* The graveyard: "Hands All Clean" (Injun Joe) [this replaced "Spirits" (Injun Joe) during the first week of tryouts], "The Vow" (Tom & Huck); *Scene 4* On the way to the church: "Ain't Life Fine" (People of St. Petersburg); *Scene 5* Outside the schoolhouse: "It Just Ain't Me" (Huck); *Scene 6* Inside the schoolhouse: "To Hear You Say My Name" (Tom & Becky); *Scene 7* The alley behind the jail: "Murrel's Gold" (Injun Joe, Muff, Tom, Huck); *Scene 8* Inside the courthouse: "The Testimony" (Tom & People of St. Petersburg). *Act II: Scene 1* The school, and the town: "Here's My Plan" (Tom) [during tryouts this was the first song in Act I Scene 1], "Ain't Life Fine" (reprise) (Boys & Girls); *Scene 2* Tom's bedroom: "This Time Tomorrow" (Aunt Polly); *Scene 3*

Widow Douglas's front porch: "I Can Read" (Huck & Widow Douglas); *Scene 4* The picnic grounds, Cardiff Hill: "You Can't Can't Dance" (Judge, Aunt Polly, People of St. Petersburg), "Murrel's Gold" (reprise) (Injun Joe); *Scene 5* McDougal's Cave: "Angels Lost" (Aunt Polly, Judge, People of St. Petersburg), "Light" (Tom), "Angels Lost" (reprise) (Becky); *Scene 6* Inside and outside the church: "Light" (reprise) (People of St. Petersburg), "Ain't Life Fine" (reprise) (Sprague & The People of St. Petersburg) [this reprise was cut during tryouts], Finale (Tom, Huck, Becky, Boys, Girls).

Broadway reviews were not good, and the show was a disappointing failure. Closing notices were posted on 5/7/01, and the show closed after the 5/13/01 matinee. It received a Tony nomination for sets. The show cost $8 million.

3. *Aida*

Aida is a Nubian princess captured by Radames, an Egyptian soldier who is also the fiancé of Pharaoh's daughter, Amneris. Aida becomes a royal slave, and finally leads a revolt. Zoser was a high priest and Amneris's religious adviser.

Before Broadway. Elton John and Tim Rice began work on the project in 1995. In 1996 Disney became involved, and they held auditions that year and in 1997; by 1998 it was called *Elaborate Lives; The Legend of Aida*. In 6/98 Heather Headley and Sherie Rene Scott were cast. The show's first incarnation was at the ALLIANCE THEATRE, ATLANTA. First dress rehearsal was 9/12/98, when a technical problem with the opening and closing pyramid brought an end to the performance. It was finished in concert fashion. Two further dress rehearsals, on 9/13/98, went fine. After a benefit performance on 9/16/98, previews began on 9/17/98. It opened officially on 10/7/98, to mixed reviews. During the run the pyramid malfunctioned a couple of times, bringing the performance to an end each time (again, finished in concert fashion). The run ended on 11/8/98. In 12/98 director Robert Jess Roth was replaced by Robert Falls; set designer Stanley A. Meyer by Bob Crowley; and a new choreographer, Wayne Cilento, was brought on board. The character of Nehebka, Amneris's handmaiden, had her name changed to Hefnut before the show opened (although it changed back again in time for Broadway). There were 28 in the cast, including: AIDA: Heather Headley; RADAMES: Hank Stratton; AMNERIS: Sherie Rene Scott; HEFNUT: Jenny Hill (Mary Bentley-Lamar was originally going to play the role); ZOSER: Rich Hebert; SHU, A HANDMAIDEN: Pamela Gold. The album, released on 3/23/99 by Rocket/Island Records, was called "Elton John and Tim Rice's *Aida*" (*Aida* was now the name the show was tending to go by). These were the tracks on that album (with the recording artists in parentheses): "Another Pyramid" (Sting), "How I Know You" (James Taylor), "Written in the Stars" (Elton John & LeAnn Rimes), "Enchantment Passing Through" (Dru Hill), "My Strongest Suit" (Spice Girls), "Easy as Life" (Tina Turner), "I Know the Truth" (Elton John & Janet Jackson), "Amneris's Letter" (Shania Twain), "Like Father, Like Son" (Lenny Kravitz), "Not Me" (BoysIIMen), "Elaborate Lives" (Elton John), "A Step Too Far" (Elton John, Heather Headley, Sherie Rene Scott), "The Gods Love Nubia" (Kelly Price), "The Messenger" (Elton John & Lulu). The three stars, Heather Headley, Sherie Rene Scott, and Adam Pascal, were confirmed in their Broadway roles on 4/21/99. Linda Woolverton remained with the show, but David Henry Hwang had been brought in after Atlanta to help on the book (he was first known as "creative consultant," but would eventually achieve co-librettist credit). Broadway rehearsals began on 9/20/99, and a much-revised and very different *Aida* (the official name now) opened for previews on 11/12/99, at the Palace Theatre, Chicago. During a preview on 11/13/99 Heather Headley and Adam Pascal were in a box-like "coffin" being transported across the front of the stage about eight feet above the floor, and it fell, crashing to the stage. Injuries were minor, but performances were canceled until 11/18/99. The show opened officially on 12/9/99, to divided reviews (Heather Headley got good ones; Adam Pascal got bad ones, so his role was built up for Broadway). The Palace Theatre, on Broadway, was renovated at great expense for this show. At the Broadway matinee preview of 2/27/00 Elton John stormed out when he felt that a couple of pieces of incidental music were out-of-date. This upset several members of the production.

The Broadway Run. PALACE THEATRE, 3/23/00–9/5/04. 31 previews from 2/25/00. 1,852 PERFORMANCES. The Alliance Theatrical Company production, PRESENTED BY Hyperion Theatricals (under the direction of Peter Schneider & Thomas Schumacher); MUSIC: Elton John; LYRICS: Tim Rice; BOOK: Linda Woolverton, with Robert Falls & David Henry Hwang; BASED ON the book by Linda Woolverton & Robert Falls, which was based on Linda Woolverton's book, which was based on Leontyne Price's children's book version of Verdi's 1871 opera; DIRECTOR: Robert Falls; CHOREOGRAPHER: Wayne Cilento; SETS/COSTUMES: Bob Crowley; LIGHTING: Natasha Katz; SOUND: Steve Canyon Kennedy; MUSICAL DIRECTOR: Paul Bogaev, *Yolanda Segovia*; ORCHESTRATIONS/VOCAL ARRANGEMENTS: Steve Margoshes, Guy Babylon, Paul Bogaev; DANCE MUSIC ARRANGEMENTS: Bob Gustafson, Jim Abbott, Gary Seligson; CAST RECORDING on Buena Vista, released on 6/13/00; PRESS: Boneau/Bryan-Brown; CASTING: Bernard Telsey; GENERAL MANAGER: Alan Levey; COMPANY MANAGER: Michael Sanfilippo, *Lizbeth Cone* (from 4/8/00), *Dave Ehle* (6/15/00–5/5/02), *Lisa Rao* (from 5/5/02); PRODUCTION STAGE MANAGER: Clifford Schwartz, *Paul J. Smith*; STAGE MANAGER: Paul J. Smith, *Lois Griffing*; ASSISTANT STAGE MANAGERS: Caroline Ranald Curvan & Valerie Lau-Kee Lai. **Cast:** AMNERIS: Sherie Rene Scott (3) (until 2/25/01), *Taylor Dayne* (2/27/01–9/8/01), *Idina Menzel* (9/9/01–1/27/02), *Felicia Finley* (1/29/02–6/29/03), *Mandy Gonzalez* (6/30/03–1/4/04), *Jessica Hendy, Lisa Brescia*; RADAMES: Adam Pascal (2) (until mid-June 2003), *Patrick Cassidy* (during Mr. Pascal's absence due to an injured back 6/25/02– 6/30/02; *William Robert Gaynor* 7/1/02. Mr. Pascal returned 7/2/02), *Matt Bogart* (during Mr. Pascal's vacation from 7/30/02. Mr. Pascal returned 8/13/02), *Matt Bogart* (on 10/1/02), *Adam Pascal* (until 6/15/03), *Richard H. Blake* (6/17/03–6/29/03), *Will Chase* (6/30/03–6/27/04); *Adam Pascal* (from 6/28/04); AIDA: Heather Headley (1) (until 9/9/01), *Maya Days* (due to take over 9/11/01, but the attack on NYC postponed that until 9/13/01. She played it until 1/27/02), *Simone* (from 1/29/02), *Merle Dandridge* (for 4 performances over the 3/8/02 weekend), *Maya Days* (during Simone's vacation 8/20/02–8/31/02. Simone returned 9/1/02, but left 6/15/03 when her mother died), *Saycon Sengbloh* (6/17/03–6/29/03), *Toni Braxton* (6/30/03–11/16/03), *Michelle Williams* (11/18/03–2/15/04), Deborah Cox (from 2/17/04); MEREB: Damian Perkins (5), *Delisco* (i.e. James D. Beeks); ZOSER: John Hickok (4), *Donnie Kehr* (until 1/4/04), *Mickey Dolenz* (from 1/6/04); PHARAOH: Daniel Oreskes (7), *Graeme Malcolm, Tom Nelis*; NEHEBKA: Schele Williams (8), *Nikki Renee Daniels, Melodye Perry*; AMONASRO: Tyrees Allen (6), *Robert Jason Jackson*; ENSEMBLE: Robert M. Armitage, Troy Allen Burgess, Franne Calma, Bob Gaynor, Kisha Howard, Tim Hunter, Youn Kim, Kyra Little, Kenya Unique Massey, Corinne McFadden, Phineas Newborn III, Jody Ripplinger, Eric Sciotto, Samuel N. Thiam, Jerald Vincent, Schele Williams, Natalia Zisa, *Raymond Rodriguez* (added by 00–01), *Ben Cameron, Tim Crasky, Nikki Renee Daniels (Lori Ann Strunk), Rhett George, Mandy Gonzalez, Karine Newborn, Alice Rietveld, Solange Sandy, Michael Serapiglia, Steve Geary, Terra Lynn Arrington, Afi Bryant, John Jacquet Jr., Mahi Kekumu, Grasan Kingsberry, Nina Lafarga, Allison Thomas Lee, Noa Neve, Chuck Saculla, Brooke Wendle*. **Standbys:** Aida: Thursday Farrar, *Maya Days, Schele Williams, Saycon Sengbloh, Ta'rea Campbell*; Radames: *Matt Bogart, Will Chase, Richard H. Blake, Cheyenne Jackson*; Pharaoh/Zoser: Neal Ben Ari, *Todd Alan Johnson, Jeb Brown*; Amneris: *Darcie Roberts & Mandy Gonzalez, Jessica Hendy*. **Understudies:** Aida: Schele Williams, *Nikkie Renee Daniels, Lori Ann Strunk*; Pharaoh: Robert M. Armitage, *Bob Gaynor, Chuck Saculla*; Zoser: Troy Allen Burgess, *Raymond Rodriguez*; Amneris: Franne Calma & Kelli Fournier; Radames: Bob Gaynor, Raymond Rodriguez, Eric Sciotto, *Chuck Saculla*; Mereb: Tim Hunter & Phineas Newborn III, *Rhett George, Koh Mochizuki, Mahi Kekumu*; Nehebka: Kyra Little & Endalyn Taylor-Shellman, *Solange Sandy, Afi Bryant*; Amonasro: Samuel N. Thiam & Jerald Vincent, *James Harkness, Raymond Rodriguez, Grasan Kingsberry*. **Swings:** Chris Payne Dupre, Kelli Fournier, Timothy Edward Smith, Endalyn Taylor-Shellman. *Silvia Aruj, Koh Mochizuki, Martin Samuel, Darrell Grand Moultrie, Derrick Williams, Reginald Holden Jennings, Josy Ripplinger, Solange Sandy.* **Orchestra:** CONCERTMASTER: Ron Oakland; KEYBOARDS: Jim Abbott, Bob Gustafson, Rob Mikulski; DRUMS: Gary Seligson; PERCUSSION: Gary Seligson & Dean Thomas; BASS: Gary Bristol; ACOUSTIC & ELECTRIC GUITAR: Bruce Uchitel & Jon Herington; CELLO: Amy Ralske;

VIOLA: Carol Landon; VIOLIN: Robin Zeh; FRENCH HORN: Russ Rizner; OBOE/ENGLISH HORN: Jim Roe; FLUTE/ALTO FLUTE/PICCOLO: Melanie Bradford. *Act I:* "Every Story is a Love Story" (Amneris), "Fortune Favors the Brave" (Radames & Soldiers) [a new song since the Chicago tryout], "The Past is Another Land" (Aida), "Another Pyramid" (Zoser & Ministers), "How I Know You" (Mereb & Aida), "My Strongest Suit" (Amneris & Women of the Palace), "Enchantment Passing Through" (Radames & Aida), "My Strongest Suit" (reprise) (Amneris & Aida), "The Dance of the Robe" (Aida, Nehebka, Nubians), "Not Me" (Radames, Mereb, Aida, Amneris), "Elaborate Lives" (Radames & Aida) [formerly Aida alone] "The Gods Love Nubia" (Aida, Nehebka, Nubians). *Act II:* "A Step Too Far" (Amneris, Radames, Aida), "Easy as Life" (Aida), "Like Father, Like Son" (Zoser, Radames, Ministers), "Radames's Letter" (Radames), "How I Know You" (reprise) (Mereb), "Written in the Stars" (Aida & Radames), "I Know the Truth" (Amneris), "Elaborate Lives" (reprise) (Aida & Amneris), "Every Story is a Love Story" (reprise) (Amneris).

Broadway reviews were very divided. The show won Tonys for score, sets, lighting, and for Heather Headley, and was nominated for costumes. On the weekend of 3/8/02 Simone, then playing Aida, was injured, and couldn't go on. Neither could her two understudies, Maya Days and Schele Williams. So Merle Dandridge, understudy on the tour, had to be drafted. After the weekend she returned to the tour. Michelle Williams was rumored to be replacing Simone as Aida, but Toni Braxton took the role. The show missed a performance due to the 8/14/03 power blackout. On 5/4/04 it was announced that the show would be closing on 9/5/04. The show made back its investment in 99 weeks, and went on to make a profit of $12 million. Deborah Cox extended her stay from 6/13/04 to the end of the run.

After Broadway. TOUR. Opened on 4/6/01, at the Orpheum Theatre, Minneapolis. Previews from 3/27/01. It had the same basic crew as for Broadway. The tour included stints at the Ahmanson Theatre, Los Angeles, 11/7/01–1/5/02; the Kennedy Center, Washington, DC, 7/9/02–8/19/02; and the Canon Theatre, Toronto, 5/7/03–5/31/03 (its first Canadian run). **Cast:** AIDA: Simone (Nina Simone's daughter), *Paulette Ivory* (from 3/27/02); RADAMES: Patrick Cassidy, *Jeremy Kushnier* (from 3/27/02), *Ryan Link* (4/15/03– 4/20/03 during Mr. Kushnier's vacation); AMNERIS: Kelli Fournier, *Lisa Brescia*; MEREB: Eric L. Christian, *Jacen R. Wilkerson*; ZOSER: Robert Neary, *Neal Ben Ari, Mickey Dolenz* (2/25/03–1/04); PHARAOH: Peter Kapetan. **Understudies:** Amneris: Julie P. Danao; Radames: Ryan Link from 9/02.

NORTH SHORE MUSIC THEATRE, Beverly, Mass., 10/26/04–11/21/04. This was the first regional production of *Aida*. DIRECTOR: Stafford Arima; CHOREOGRAPHER: Patricia Wilcox; MUSICAL DIRECTOR: Andrew Graham; LIGHTING: Kirk Bookman. **Cast:** AIDA: Montego Glover; RADAMES: Brad Anderson; AMNERIS: Jeanine LaManna; ZOSER: John Schiappa.

4. *Ain't Broadway Grand*

A musical biography of showman Mike Todd. Set in New York and Boston, in the summer and fall 1948, as he produces the fictional musical *Of the People*.

Before Broadway. It tried out in Philadelphia, as *Mike*. Marianne Tatum played Gypsy Rose. It was revised many times before Broadway.

The Broadway Run. LUNT–FONTANNE THEATRE, 4/18/93–5/9/93. 27 previews from 3/26/93. 25 PERFORMANCES. A Tra-La-La (Moira McFadden, John Whitley, Charles J. Siedenburg) production, PRESENTED BY Arthur Rubin; MUSIC: Mitch Leigh; LYRICS: Lee Adams; BOOK: Thomas Meehan & Lee Adams; DIRECTOR: Scott Harris; CHOREOGRAPHER: Randy Skinner; SETS: David Mitchell; COSTUMES: Suzy Benzinger; LIGHTING: Ken Billington; SOUND: Otts Munderloh; MUSICAL SUPERVISOR/ VOCAL ARRANGEMENTS: Neil Warner; MUSICAL DIRECTOR: Nicholas Archer; ORCHESTRATIONS: Chris Bankey; DANCE MUSIC ARRANGEMENTS: Scot Woolley; CAST RECORDING on Music Makers; PRESS: Fred Nathan Company; CASTING: Gayle Kenerson; GENERAL MANAGER: Peter H. Russell; PRODUCTION STAGE MANAGER: Frank Marino; STAGE MANAGER: John Actman; ASSISTANT STAGE MANAGER: Donna A. Drake. **Cast:** BOBBY CLARK: Gerry Vichi (4) ✫; GYPSY ROSE LEE: Debbie Shapiro Gravitte (2) ✫;

MIKE TODD: Mike Burstyn (1) ✩; HARRIET POPKIN: Alix Korey; LOU, THE STAGE MANAGER: Bill Nabel; MURRAY PEARL: Mitchell Greenberg; REUBEN PELISH: David Lipman; JOAN BLONDELL: Maureen McNamara (3) ✩; MARVIN FISCHBEIN: Gabriel Barre; WALDO KLEIN: Bill Kux; WALLY FARFLE: Scott Elliott; DEXTER LESLIE: Richard B. Shull; JAEGER: Merwin Goldsmith; LINDY'S WAITERS: Bill Corcoran, Jerold Goldstein, Bill Nabel; THELMA: Caitlin Carter; FLOYD: Patrick Wetzel; ROCCO: Luis Perez, *Peter Gregus* from 4/30/93; FRANKIE THE BARTENDER: Scott Fowler; HERBIE THE OFFICE BOY: Jerold Golstein. *Of the People* Cast I: PRESIDENT & HIS CABINET: Timothy Albrecht, Bill Corcoran, Scott Elliott, Scott Fowler, Jerold Goldstein, Rod McCune, Bill Nabel, Luis Perez, Mimi Cichanowicz Quillin, Patrick Wetzel; RIVERSIDE DRIVE STREETWALKER: Beverly Britton; LILI: Ginger Prince; SHERYL: Jennifer Frankel; LINDA: Mimi Cichanowicz Quillin. *Of the People* Cast II: PRESIDENT & HIS CABINET: Leslie Bell, Beverly Britton, Caitlin Carter, Colleen Dunn, Jennifer Frankel, Lauren Goler-Kosarin, Elizabeth Mills, Ginger Prince, Mimi Cichanowicz Quillin, Carol Denise Smith; ENSEMBLE: Timothy Albrecht, Leslie Bell, Beverly Britton, Caitlin Carter, Bill Corcoran, Colleen Dunn, Scott Elliott, Scott Fowler, Jennifer Frankel, Jerold Goldstein, Lauren Goler-Kosarin, Joe Istre, Rod McCune, Elizabeth Mills, Bill Nabel, Luis Perez, Ginger Prince, Mimi Cichanowicz Quillin, Carol Denise Smith, Patrick Wetzel. *Standby*: Mike: P.J. Benjamin. *Understudies*: Gypsy Rose: Mimi Cichanowicz Quillin; Joan: Beverly Britton; Bobby/Jaeger: Jerold Goldstein; Marvin/Waldo: Scott Elliott; Murray/Reuben: Bill Nabel; Harriet: Ginger Prince; Dexter: Merwin Goldsmith. *Swings*: Kelli Barclay, James Horvath, Lynn Sullivan. *Orchestra*: REEDS: Lawrence Feldman, Bill Meade, Roger Rosenberg, Lauren Goldstein; TRUMPETS: David Stahl & Don Downs; TROMBONE: David Bargeron; BASS TROMBONE: Alan Raph; FRENCH HORNS: Paul Riggio & Chris Costanzi; CONCERTMASTER: Barry Finclair; VIOLINS: Robert Zubrycki, Carlos Villa, Rebekah Johnson, Valerie Levy, Susan Gellert; CELLI: Anne Callahan & Curtis Woodside; BASS: Raymond Kilday; DRUMS: Ronald Zito; PERCUSSION: Ian Finkel; KEYBOARDS: Michael Dansicker, Wayne Abravanel, Mark Lipman. *Act I*: *Scene 1* The stage of the Alvin Theatre: "Girls Ahoy" (Bobby, Gypsy Rose, Ensemble); *Scene 2* Backstage at the Alvin Theatre: "Ain't Broadway Grand" (Mike, Harriet, Murray, Reuben, Ensemble), "Class" (Mike & Chorus Girls); *Scene 3* Backstage at a production meeting: "The Theater, the Theatre" (Marvin & Waldo), "Ain't Broadway Grand" (reprise) (Mike, Harriet, Murray, Dexter, Marvin, Waldo, Wally, Ensemble); *Scene 4* Lindy's Restaurant: "Lindy's" (Jaeger, Waiters, Company), "It's Time to Go" (Gypsy Rose & Ensemble); *Scene 5* The Bar at "21": "Waiting in the Wings" (Joan), "You're My Star" (Mike & Ensemble); *Scene 6* Todd's office; *Scene 7* *Of the People* show curtain; *Scene 8* The Oval Office: "A Big Job" (President & Ensemble); *Scene 9* The stage of the Colonial Theatre, Boston: "Ain't Broadway Grand" (reprise) (Company). *Act II*: *Scene 1* The street in front of Lindy's: "Ain't Broadway Grand" (reprise) (Jaeger & Waiters); *Scene 2* Todd's suite, Ritz Carlton Hotel, Boston: "They'll Never Take Us Alive" (Mike, Harriet, Murray); *Scene 3* Riverside Drive, near Grant's Tomb: "On the Street" (Mike), "The Man I Married" (Joan & Female Ensemble); *Scene 4* A costume shop: "The Theater, The Theatre" (reprise) (Harriet & Murray), "Maybe, Maybe Not" (Gypsy Rose); *Scene 5* Rehearsal backstage at the Alvin Theatre: "Tall Dames and Low Comedy" (Bobby & Ensemble); *Scene 6* The Beverly Hills Hotel, Beverly Hills, California: "He's My Guy" (Joan); *Scene 7* Behind the curtain at the Alvin Theatre; *Scene 8* The Oval Office: "A Big Job" (reprise) (President & Ensemble); *Scene 9* Backstage at the Alvin Theatre: "You're My Star" (reprise) (Mike), "Ain't Broadway Grand" (reprise) (Company).

Broadway reviews were not grand at all. The show received a Tony nomination for choreography.

5. *Ain't Misbehavin'*

Subtitled *The New Fats Waller Musical Show*. The atmosphere was as a Harlem nightclub of those times. A re-creation of the world and style of Mr. Waller, not an impersonation.

Before Broadway. The idea began when Richard Maltby Jr. and Murray Horwitz were listening to Fats Waller recordings in Mr. Horwitz's apartment. It opened originally as an Off Broadway limited-run cabaret entertainment at the 65-seat MANHATTAN THEATRE CLUB, 2/8/78– 3/5/78. 28 PERFORMANCES. *Cast*: Nell Carter, Andre De Shields, Armelia McQueen, Ken Page, Irene Cara (*Charlaine Woodard*), Luther Henderson (piano).

The Broadway Run. LONGACRE THEATRE, 5/9/78–1/28/79; PLYMOUTH THEATRE, 1/29/79–1/24/81; BELASCO THEATRE, 1/26/81– 2/21/82). 14 previews from 4/28/78. Total of 1,604 PERFORMANCES. PRESENTED BY Emanuel Azenberg, Dasha Epstein, the Shubert Organization, Jane Gaynor, Ron Dante; MUSIC: 18 songs written by the late Thomas "Fats" Waller (1904–1943), including instrumentals with new lyrics by Richard Maltby Jr. or Murray Horwitz, as well as 12 others recorded by Fats Waller but not written by him; LYRICS: by miscellaneous writers; BASED ON an idea by Murray Horwitz & Richard Maltby Jr.; CONCEIVED BY/DIRECTOR: Richard Maltby Jr.; ASSOCIATE DIRECTOR: Murray Horwitz; CHOREOGRAPHER: Arthur Faria; SETS: John Lee Beatty; COSTUMES: Randy Barcelo; LIGHTING: Pat Collins; SOUND: Otts Munderloh; MUSICAL SUPERVISOR/ORCHESTRATIONS/ARRANGEMENTS: Luther Henderson; CONDUCTOR: Hank Jones; VOCAL ARRANGEMENTS: William Elliott & Jeffrey Gutcheon; CAST RECORDING on RCA Victor; PRESS: Bill Evans; CASTING: Johnson — Liff; COMPANY MANAGER: Maurice Schaded, *John M. Kirby* by 78–79; PRODUCTION STAGE MANAGER: Richard Evans, *Lani Ball* by 78–79; STAGE MANAGER: D.W. Koehler, *Bruce Birkenhead & Linda Cohen* by 79–80, *D.W. Koehler* by 80–81. *Cast*: Nell Carter (*Avery Sommers* from 5/15/79, *Zoe Walker, Yvette Freeman* from 9/24/79, *Roz Ryan* from 79–80), Andre De Shields (*Alan Weeks* from 3/5/79, *Lonnie McNeil* from 3/81), Armelia McQueen (*Yvette Freeman* by 78–79, *Teresa Bowers* from 9/24/79, *Loretta Bowers* by 79–80), Ken Page (*Ken Prymus* from 9/24/79, *Jason Booker* by 79–80), Charlaine Woodard (*Debbie Allen* by 3/5/79, *Adriane Lenox* from 9/24/79). *Pianist*: Luther Henderson (*Frank Owens* by 78–79, *Hank Jones* by 79–80). *Standbys*: Judy Gibson (for Miss Carter), Judy Gibson (for Miss McQueen — 78; *Vivian Jett* 78–79), Yolanda Graves (for Miss Woodard & Miss Allen), Irving Lee (for Mr. De Shields 1978; and for Mr. Page), Eric Riley (for Mr. Weeks 78–80), Zoe Walker (for Miss Sommers). *Other Standbys*: Ellia English (78–80), Annie Joe Edwards (78), Ms. Heaven (78), George Merritt (78–80), Shezwae Powell (79–80), Gail Boggs (79–80). *Onstage Musicians*: SAX: Seldon Powell; DRUMS: Joe Marshall; BASS: Lisle Atkinson; CLARINET: Alex Foster; TRUMPET: Virgil Jones; TROMBONE: Janice Robinson. *Act I*: "Ain't Misbehavin'" (m: Harry Brooks & FW; l: Andy Razaf; 1929) [from *Hot Chocolates*] (voc arr: Jeffrey Gutcheon) (Company), "Lookin' Good but Feelin' Bad" (m: FW; l: Lester A. Santly; 1929) (voc arr: Jeffrey Gutcheon) (Company), "Tain't Nobody's Biz-ness if I Do" (m/l: Porter Grainger & Everett Robbins; 1922; add l: Maltby & Horwitz) (Andre & Company) [this was the first song recorded by FW], "Honeysuckle Rose" (m: FW; l: Andy Razaf; 1929) [from *Load of Coal*] (Ken & Nell), "Squeeze Me" (m: FW; l: Clarence Williams; 1925) (Armelia), "Handful of Keys" (m: FW; 1933; l: Maltby & Horwitz) (based on an idea by Marty Grosz) (voc arr: William Elliott) (Company), "I've Got a Feelin' I'm Fallin'" (m: FW & Harry Link; l: Billy Rose; 1929) [from the movie *Applause*] (Nell & Company), "How Ya Baby" (m: FW; l: J.C. Johnson; 1938) (Charlaine, Andre, Company), "The Jitterbug Waltz" (m: FW; 1942; l: Maltby) (voc arr: William Elliott) (Company), "The Ladies Who Sing with the Band" (m: FW; l: George Marion Jr.; 1943) [from *Early to Bed*] (Andre & Ken) [this number comprised: "Yacht Club Swing" (m: FW & Herman Autry; l: J.C. Johnson; 1938) (Charlaine); "When the Nylons Bloom Again" (m: FW; l: George Marion Jr.; 1943) (from *Early to Bed*) (voc arr: Jeffrey Gutcheon) (Armelia, Charlaine, Nell); "Cash for Your Trash" (m: FW; l: Ed Kirkeby; 1942) (Nell); "Off-Time" (m: FW & Harry Brooks; l: Andy Razaf; 1929) (voc arr: Jeffrey Gutcheon) (Company)], "The Joint is Jumpin'" (m: FW; l: Andy Razaf & J.C. Johnson; 1938) (Company). *Act II*: Entr'acte (Ensemble), "Spreadin' Rhythm Around (Us)" (m: Jimmy McHugh; l: Ted Koehler; 1935) [from the movie *King of Burlesque*] (add l: Maltby) (Company), "Lounging at the Waldorf" (m: FW; 1936; l: Maltby) (voc arr: William Elliott) (Armelia, Charlaine, Ken, Nell), "The Viper's Drag" ("The Reefer Song") (traditional) (m: FW. Instrumental; 1943) (Andre & Company), "Mean to Me" (m/l: Roy Turk & Fred E. Ahlert; 1929) (Nell), "Your Feet's Too Big" (m/l: Ada Benson & Fred Fisher; 1936) (Ken), "That Ain't Right" (m/l: Nat "King" Cole;

1943; add l: Maltby & Horwitz) (Andre, Armelia, Company), "Keepin' Out of Mischief Now" (m: FW; l: Andy Razaf; 1932) (Charlaine), "Find Out What They Like (and How They Like It)" (m: FW; l: Andy Razaf; 1929) (Armelia & Nell), "This is So Nice" (m: FW; l: George Marion Jr.; 1943) (Nell) [only in the 1988 revival], "Fat and Greazy" (m/l: Porter Grainger & Charlie Johnson; 1936) (Andre & Ken), "(What Did I Do to Get So) Black and Blue" (m: FW & Harry Brooks; l: Andy Razaf; 1929) [from *Hot Chocolates*] (voc arr: William Elliott) (Company), Finale [songs by others which FW made hits, comprising: "I'm Gonna Sit Right Down and Write Myself a Letter" (m: Fred E. Ahlert; l: Joe Young; 1933) (Ken), "Two Sleepy People" (m: Hoagy Carmichael; l: Frank Loesser; 1938) (from the movie *Thanks For the Memory*) (Armelia & Ken), "I've Got My Fingers Crossed" (m: Jimmy McHugh; l: Ted Koehler; 1935) (Armelia, Charlaine, Ken), "I Can't Give You Anything but Love" (m: Jimmy McHugh; l: Dorothy Fields; 1928) (from *Blackbirds of 1928*) (Andre & Charlaine), "It's a Sin to Tell a Lie" (m/l: Billy Mayhew; 1933) (Nell & Company), "Honeysuckle Rose" (reprise) (Company)].

Note: the songs not written by Fats Waller were, like his own songs, recorded by him (FW = Fats Waller).

It opened on Broadway to rave reviews. The show won Tony Awards for musical, direction of a musical, and for Nell Carter (this is what made her a star), and was also nominated for choreography, and for Charlaine Woodard.

After Broadway. TOUR. Opened on 2/28/79, in Boston. *Cast*: Teresa Bowers (*Debra Byrd* from 9/79; *Loretta Bowers* from 5/80), Yvette Freeman (*Yvonne Talton Kersey* from 9/79; *Roz Ryan* from 5/80), Ben Harney (*Lonnie McNeil* from 9/79), Adriane Lenox (*Jackie Lowe* from 9/79), Ken Prymus (*Evan Bell* from 9/79).

TOUR. Opened on 4/17/79, in Fort Lauderdale. *Cast*: Terri White, David Cameron, Adrienne West, Clent Bowers, Gail Boggs.

TOUR. Opened on 9/24/79, in San Francisco. It featured the original Broadway cast.

TOUR. Opened on 12/11/79, at the Aquarius Theatre, Hollywood. *Cast*: Nell Carter, Andre De Shields, Armelia McQueen (*Debra Byrd*), Jackie Lowe, Ken Page (*Ken Prymus*).

LONDON, 3/22/79. *Cast*: Annie Jo Edwards, Andre De Shields, Jozella Reed, Evan Bell, Charlaine Woodard.

NBC TV. 6/21/82. A two-hour version, with the original Broadway cast.

6. *Ain't Misbehavin' (Broadway revival)*

This was the 10th-anniversary revival, with the original cast. The number "This Is So Nice" was added (see the original 1978 entry for song list).

The Broadway Run. AMBASSADOR THEATRE, 8/15/88–1/15/89. 8 previews. 176 PERFORMANCES. PRESENTED BY The Shubert Organization, Emanuel Azenberg, Dasha Epstein, Roger Berlind; MUSIC/ LYRICS: see the original 1978 production for details; CONCEIVED BY: Richard Maltby Jr.; BASED ON an idea by Murray Horwitz & Richard Maltby Jr.; DIRECTOR: Richard Maltby Jr.; ASSOCIATE DIRECTOR: Murray Horwitz; CHOREOGRAPHER: Arthur Faria; SETS: John Lee Beatty; COSTUMES: Randy Barcelo; LIGHTING: Pat Collins; SOUND: Tom Morse; MUSICAL SUPERVISOR/ ARRANGEMENTS/CONDUCTOR: Luther Henderson; VOCAL AND MUSICAL CONCEPTS: Jeffrey Gutcheon; VOCAL ARRANGEMENTS: William Elliott & Jeffrey Gutcheon; PRESS: Bill Evans & Associates; CASTING: Johnson — Liff & Zerman; GENERAL MANAGEMENT: Berg/Birkenhead; PRODUCTION STAGE MANAGER: Scott Glenn; STAGE MANAGER: Linnea Sundsten, *Tracy Crum*; ASSISTANT STAGE MANAGER: Peter Lawrence. *Cast*: Nell Carter (1) (*Terri White* from 12/20/88), Andre De Shields (*Eric Riley*), Armelia McQueen (*Patti Austin* from 12/20/88), Ken Page (*Ken Prymus* from 12/20/88), Charlaine Woodard (*Jackie Lowe* from 12/20/88). **Pianist**: Luther Henderson. **Standbys**: Kecia Lewis-Evans (for Nell/Armelia), Jackie Lowe (for Charlaine), Eric Riley (for Andre), Ken Prymus (for Ken). **Onstage Musicians**: ALTO SAX/CLARINET: Ken Adams; TENOR SAX/CLARINET: George Barrow; DRUMS: Ken Crutchfield; BASS: Arvell Shaw; TRUMPET: Stanton Davis; TROMBONE: Porter Poindexter.

Reviews were generally very good, and this production won a Tony nomination for revival.

After Broadway. TOUR. Opened during the 95–96 season, and closed on 7/21/96, in San Francisco. It got great reviews. There was talk of it going to Broadway, but it never happened. DIRECTOR/CHOREOGRAPHER: Arthur Faria; SETS: John Lee Beatty; COSTUMES: Bob Mackie; LIGHTING: Pat Collins; SOUND: Peter Fitzgerald; MUSICAL DIRECTOR: William Foster McDaniel. *Cast*: The Pointer Sisters (Ruth, Anita, June), Eugene Barry-Hill, Michael-Leon Wooley.

CENTER STAGE, Baltimore. Closed on 2/23/03 (after an extension due to record-breaking box-office returns), then it went to the ARENA STAGE, Washington, DC. This production was a joint venture of both theatres. DIRECTOR: Ken Roberson. *Cast*: Raun Ruffin, Amy Jo Phillips, Janeece Aisha Freeman, Doug Eskew, E. Faye Butler.

PAPER MILL PLAYHOUSE, New Jersey, 9/12/03–10/19/03. Previews from 9/10/03. DIRECTOR: Ken Roberson; SETS: Neil Patel; COSTUMES: Paul Tazewell; SOUND: David F. Shapiro; MUSICAL DIRECTOR: William Foster McDaniel. *Cast*: E. Faye Butler, Darius de Haas, Doug Eskew, Angela Robinson, NaTasha Yvette Williams.

7. *Ain't Supposed to Die a Natural Death*

Subtitled *Tunes from Blackness*. For obvious reasons this musical is generally referred to as *Natural Death*. A series of vignettes, presented in poetic recitatives with musical accompaniment (rather than songs) adding up to a sombre portrait of a black ghetto today. Set in the present.

Before Broadway. First staged at Sacramento State College, by Paul Carter Harrison.

The Broadway Run. ETHEL BARRYMORE THEATRE, 10/20/71– 11/10/71; AMBASSADOR THEATRE, 11/17/71–7/30/72. 10 previews from 10/8/71. Total of 325 PERFORMANCES. PRESENTED BY Eugene V. Wolsk, Charles Blackwell, Emanuel Azenberg, Robert Malina; MUSIC/ LYRICS/BOOK: Melvin Van Peebles; DIRECTOR: Gilbert Moses; SETS: Kert Lundell; COSTUMES: Bernard Johnson; LIGHTING: Martin Aronstein; SOUND: Jack Shearing; MUSICAL SUPERVISOR/MUSICAL DIRECTOR: Harold Wheeler; CONDUCTOR: Arthur Jenkins; CAST RECORDING on A & M Records; PRESS: Merle Debuskey & Faith Geer; PRODUCTION STAGE MANAGER: Nate Barnett, Helaine Head; STAGE MANAGER: Helaine Head, James S. Lucas Jr.; ASSISTANT STAGE MANAGER: Ted Lange. *Cast*: Gloria Edwards (*Lauren Jones* from 5/9/72), Dick Anthony Williams (*Charles Adu* from 5/9/72), Ralph Wilcox, Barbara Alston, Joe Fields, Marilyn B. Coleman, Arthur French, Carl Gordon, Madge Wells, Lauren Jones (*Cecelia Norfleet* from 1/4/72), Clebert Ford, Sati Jamal, Jimmy Hayeson, Tony Brealond, Beatrice Winde, Albert Hall, Garrett Morris, Bill Duke, Minnie Gentry. *Standbys*: Ted Lange, Joan Pryor, Phylicia Ayers-Allen, Roger Robinson. *Musicians*: Harold Wheeler, Arthur Jenkins, Richard Pratt, Bill Salter, Lloyd Davis, Charles Sullivan, Robert Carten. *Act I*: "Just Don't Make No Sense" (Arthur), "Coolest Place in Town" (Gloria, Lauren), "You Can Get Up Before Noon without Being a Square" (Ralph), "Mirror, Mirror on the Wall" (Joe), "Come Raising Your Leg on Me" (Marilyn), "You Gotta Be Holdin' Out Five Dollars on Me" (Carl & Madge), "Sera Sera Jim" (Lauren, *Cecelia*), "Catch That on the Corner" (Clebert), "The Dozens" (Jimmy), "Funky Girl on Motherless Broadway" (Toney). *Act II*: "Tenth and Greenwich" (Beatrice), "Heh Heh (Chuckle) Good Mornin' Sunshine" (Arthur), "You Ain't No Astronaut" (Jimmy), "Three Boxes of Longs, Please" (Albert), "Lily Done the Zampoughi Every Time I Pulled Her Coattail" (Garrett & Barbara), "I Got the Blood" (Bill), "Salamaggi's Birthday" (Dick Anthony, Charles), "Come on Feet, Do Your Thing" (Sati), "Put a Curse on You" (Minnie), Finale: "Just Don't Make No Sense" (reprise) (Company).

Broadway reviews were divided, and there were a few raves. During the run Arthur French was placed first in order of appearance. The show received Tony nominations for musical, score, book, direction of a musical, sets, lighting, and for Beatrice Winde.

After Broadway. CLASSICAL THEATRE OF HARLEM, 10/1/04– 11/21/04 (closing date extended from 10/31/04). Previews from 9/29/04. This was the first revival of note. *Cast*: Ty Jones, Ron Simons, Tracy Jack,

Glenn Turner, Neil Dawson, Shamika Cotton, Carmen Baruka, Ralph Carter, Rashad Ernesto Greene, J. Kyle Manzay, Yusef Miller, Lizan Mitchell, Simone Moore, Nyambi Nyambi, Althea Vyfhius, Kendra Ware, Robyn Landiss Walker.

8. *Alive and Kicking*

A musical revue.

Before Broadway. On 1/10/50 it opened at the Hershey Community Theatre, Pennsylvania, for tryouts that ran for five days. The number "If You Don't Love Me" (m: Hoagy Carmichael; l: Paul F. Webster & Ray Golden), in Act II, was cut.

The Broadway Run. WINTER GARDEN THEATRE, 1/17/50–2/25/50. 46 PERFORMANCES. PRESENTED BY William R. Katzell & Ray Golden; MUSIC/LYRICS/ SKETCHES: various authors; SKETCH EDITOR: William R. Katzell; DIRECTOR: Robert H. Gordon; CHOREOGRAPHER: Jack Cole; SETS/COSTUMES: Raoul Pene du Bois; LIGHTING: Mason Arvold; MUSICAL DIRECTOR/VOCAL ARRANGEMENTS: Lehman Engel; ORCHESTRATIONS: George Bassman; PRESS: George & Dorothy Ross, Madelin Blitzstein; GENERAL MANAGER: Michael Goldreyer; STAGE MANAGERS: Michael Ellis & Perry Bruskin. *Act I: Scene 1* "Alive and Kicking" (m: Hal Borne; l: Ray Golden & Sid Kuller) (voc arr: George Bassman). Sung by June Brady, Patricia Bybell, Margery Oldroyd, Laurel Shelby, Louise Kirtland, Jack Cassidy, Arthur Maxwell, Sam Kirkham, Ray Stephens, Earl William, Singers. MILKMAN: Bobby Van; THE GIRL: Dolores Starr; Dancers; *Scene 2* "Pals of the Pentagon" (sketch by Ray Golden & I.A.L. Diamond; m/l: Harold Rome). Rival military branches agree to agree on women. UNDERSECRETARY: Jack Russell; ARMY: David Burns (2); NAVY: Carl Reiner (5); AIRFORCE: Mickey Deems; SECRETARY: Eve Lynn; *Scene 3* "I Didn't Want Him" (m: Irma Jurist; l: Leonard Gershe). A blues number. Sung by June Brady. Danced by Jack Cole (1) & Gwen Verdon. *Scene 4* "What a Delightful Day" (m: Sammy Fain; l: Paul Francis Webster & Ray Golden). An English song by a Madrigal trio. Introduction by Carl Reiner (5). MADRIGAL TRIO: Jack Gilford (4), Margery Oldroyd, Madelaine Chambers. *Scene 5* Meet the Authors (sketch by Jerome Chodorov). A spoof on a literary luncheon. CHAIRWOMAN: Louise Kirtland; DR. HIRMA FLICK: Carl Reiner (5); VIOLA TREMAINE: Louise Lonergan (3); DR. ALLEN DRAWBRIDGE: David Burns (2); WAITER: Sam Kirkham; *Scene 6* "A World of Strangers" (m: Sammy Fain; l: Paul Francis Webster & Ray Golden). Sung by Arthur Maxwell & Patricia Bybell; *Scene 7* "Abou Ben Adhem" (m/l: Ray Golden; adapted from the poem by Leigh Hunt). Original dance music by Billy Kyle. SERGEANT: Jack Russell; BOY: Rex Thompson; TRIO: Sam Kirkham, Jack Cassidy, Ray Stephens; ABOU: Jack Cole (1); ABOU'S WIFE: Gwen Verdon; ANGEL: Marie Groscup. Danced by Velerie Camille, Jean Harris, Dolores Starr, George Bockman, Marc Hertsens, Paul Olson, Jack Miller; *Scene 8* "Cry, Baby (Cry)" (m/l: Harold Rome). Sung by Louise Lonergan (3), Rae Abruzzo, Laurel Shelby; *Scene 9* I Never Felt Better (sketch by Joseph Stein & Will Glickman). Barney tries to give up cigarette smoking. WIFE: Louise Kirtland; BARNEY: Jack Gilford (4); CHARLIE: Carl Reiner (5); *Scene 10* "One Word Led to Another" (m: Hal Borne; l: Ray Golden). Sung & danced by Bobby Van; *Scene 11* Calypso Celebration, including the song "Love, It Hurts So Good" (m/l: Harold Rome). Dance music: Billy Kyle. Sung by Louise Lonergan (3). Danced by Jack Cole & His Dancers (Marie Groscup & Gwen Verdon) (1). Singers: Jack Cassidy, Sam Kirkham, Graham Lee, Jack Russell, Ray Stephens, Earl William, Jay Harnick, Rae Abruzzo, Margaret Baxter, Patricia Bybell, Madelaine Chambers, Fay De Witt, Eve Lynn, Margery Oldroyd, Laurel Shelby, Louise Kirtland, Sylvia Chaney, Jeanne Bal, Bryn Corey. Dancers: George Bockman, Kenneth Davis, Marc Hertsens, Paul Olson, Jack Miller, Velerie Camille, Ruth Davis, Jean Harris, Dolores Starr. *Act II: Scene 1* "(There's a) Building Going Up" (m: Sammy Fain; l: Paul Francis Webster & Ray Golden). Lead Singer: Arthur Maxwell. Singers: June Brady, Patricia Bybell, Eve Lynn, Margery Oldroyd, Laurel Shelby, Louise Kirtland, Jack Cassidy, Sam Kirkham, Jack Russell, Ray Stephens, Earl William, Rex Thompson, Singers; *Scene 2* "My Day of Rest" (m/l: Lucille Kallen, Max Liebman, Mickey Deems). Sung by Mickey Deems; *Scene 3* Hippocrates Hits the Jackpot (sketch by Henry Morgan & Joseph Stein). A burlesque of doctors; Dr. Frisbee

performs an operation for a radio give-away show called *Stop the Operation.* FIRST MAN: Jack Cassidy; DR. WALSH: Carl Reiner (5); FIRST NURSE: Laurel Shelby; WOMAN: Louise Kirtland; PATIENT: Mickey Deems; DR. FRISBEE: David Burns (2); ANNOUNCER: June Brady; SECOND NURSE: Fay De Witt; ANESTHETIST: Ray Stephens; *Scene 4* "Propinquity" (m: Sonny Burke; l: Paul Francis Webster & Ray Golden). Sung by Jack Russell. Danced by Jack Cole (1) & Gwen Verdon. Singers: Jack Cassidy, Graham Lee, Sam Kirkham, Margery Oldroyd, Madelaine Chambers, Rae Abruzzo. Dancers: Marie Groscup & Dancers; *Scene 5* "I'm All Yours" (m: Leo Schumer; l: Mike Stuart & Ray Golden). Sung by: AGNES: Jessie Elliott; GEORGE: Bobby Van; *Scene 6* Once Upon a Time (sketch by Joseph Stein & Will Glickman). An Elizabethan actor auditions for a role in a Shakespeare play. DIRECTOR: Carl Reiner (5); FLOOGELMAN: Jack Gilford (4); MISS HONEYSUCKLE: Louise Lonergan (3); MIKE: Mickey Deems; *Scene 7* "One! Two! Three!" (m: Sonny Burke; l: Paul Francis Webster & Ray Golden). Sung by Earl William, Patricia Bybell, Graham Lee, Rae Abruzzo. Danced by Gwen Verdon, Marie Groscup, Dancers; *Scene 8* "French with Tears" (m/l: Harold Rome). A spoof of Edith Piaf. Sung by Louise Lonergan (3); *Scene 9* "Cole Scuttle Blues" (dance) (m: Billy Kyle). Danced by Jack Cole and His Dancers (Marie Groscup & Gwen Verdon) (1); *Scene 10* Finale (Entire Company). *Singers:* Rae Abruzzo, Margaret Baxter, Madelaine Chambers, Fay De Witt, Sylvia Chaney, Jeanne Bal, Bryn Corey, Graham Lee, Jay Harnick. *Dancers:* Velerie Camille, Ruth Davis, Jean Harris, George Bockman, Kenneth Davis, Marc Hertsens, Paul Olson, Jack Miller, Dolores Starr.

Broadway reviews were divided — mostly bad. The show won a Donaldson Award for choreography.

9. *All American*

A musical satire. Eastern European immigrant Fodorski arrives in the USA to teach engineering at the Southern Baptist Institute of Technology, but winds up applying his skills to football strategy. Madison Avenue makes him famous.

Before Broadway. Ron Moody was the first choice as star, then Charles Boyer, then Ray Bolger. Mel Brooks wrote Act I of the book, but never got around to finishing the whole thing (so it is said). Act II was written by the rest of the creative staff. The numbers "I'm Not in Philadelphia" and "Pripoz Diva Se" were not used. The show tried out in Philadelphia, where the number "Back to School Again" was cut. "Born Too Late" (m: Charles Strouse; l: Fred Tobias) was also cut.

The Broadway Run. WINTER GARDEN THEATRE, 3/19/62–5/26/62. 80 PERFORMANCES. PRESENTED BY Edward Padula in association with L. Slade Brown; MUSIC: Charles Strouse; LYRICS: Lee Adams; BOOK: Mel Brooks; Based on the 1950 novel *Professor Fodorski*, by Robert Lewis Taylor; DIRECTOR: Joshua Logan; CHOREOGRAPHER: Danny Daniels; SETS/LIGHTING: Jo Mielziner; COSTUMES: Patton Campbell; MUSICAL DIRECTOR/DANCE MUSIC ARRANGEMENTS: John Morris; ORCHESTRATIONS: Robert Ginzler; MUSICAL CONTINUITY: Trude Rittman; CAST RECORDING on CBS, recorded 3/25/62 at CBS Studios, New York; PRESS: Bill Doll, Dick Williams, Robert Ganshaw, Midori Tsuji; GENERAL MANAGER: Michael Goldreyer; COMPANY MANAGER: David Lawlor; STAGE MANAGER: George Wagner; ASSISTANT STAGE MANAGERS: Fred Kimbrough & Bob Bakanic. *Cast:* AIRLINE STEWARDESS: Lori Rogers; FLIGHT ATTENDANT: Robert Lone; HEAD IMMIGRATION OFFICER: Barney Martin; IMMIGRATION OFFICER: Michael Gentry; FLEISSER: Mort Marshall; SHINDLER: David Thomas; FEINSCHVEIGER: Bernie West; KATRINKA: Betty Oakes; IMMIGRANTS: Will B. Able, Jed Allan, Don Atkinson, Vicki Belmonte, Bonnie Brody, Bill Burns, Trudy Carole, John Drew, Anthony Falco, Mary Jane Ferguson, Catherine Gale, Joseph Gentry, Linda Rae Hager, Warren Hays, Jerry Howard, Bill Landrum, George Lindsey, Selma Malinou, Joe McWherter, Norman Riggins, Bill Starr, Sharon Vaughn; PROFESSOR FODORSKI: Ray Bolger (1); TAXIS: Michael Gentry, Barney Martin, Fred Randall, Norman Riggins, Will B. Able; POLICEMAN: Jed Allan; GORILLA: Bob Bakanic; BRIDE: Bonnie Brody; MANNIKIN: Mary Jane Ferguson; PEDDLER: Will B. Able; CHEWING GUM GIRL: Bonnie Brody; DRUNK: Mort Marshall; CON ED WORKER: Joseph Gentry; COWBOYS:

Bill Burns & Robert Lone; PARK AVENUE COUPLE: Betty Oakes & David Thomas; SIGHTSEEING TOUR GUIDE: Bernie West; 2ND SIGHTSEEING TOUR GUIDE: George Lindsey; ELIZABETH HAWKES-BULLOCK: Eileen Herlie (2); SUSAN: Anita Gillette (4); EDWIN BRICKER: Ron Husmann (3); DR. SNOPES: Bernie West; COACH HULKINGTON (HULK) STOCKWORTH: Mort Marshall; ASSISTANT COACH: Barney Martin; MOOSE: George Lindsey; FOOTBALL PLAYERS: Jed Allan, Bill Burns, John Drew, Joseph Gentry, Michael Gentry, Jerry Howard, Bill Landrum, Joseph McWherter, Fred Randall, Bill Starr; PRESIDENT PIEDMONT: Will B. Able; PROFESSOR DAWSON: David Thomas; PROFESSOR WHITE: Warren Hays; 1ST BOY: Robert Lone; 1ST GIRL: Trudy Carole; 2ND GIRL: Karen Sargent; 2ND BOY: Ed Kresley; HOUSE MOTHER: Betty Oakes; BATON TWIRLER: Karen Sargent; RED STERN: Barney Martin; HENDERSON: Fritz Weaver (5); WHISTLER'S MOTHER: Betty Oakes; CRAVEN: Jed Allan; PHILLIPS: Anthony Falco; WYLER: Bill Burns; HOMECOMING QUEEN: Sharon Vaughn; SECRETARY: Betty Oakes; FARQUAR: Bill Starr; FOUNTAINHEAD: Bob Bakanic; SINGERS: Jed Allan, Vicki Belmonte, Bonnie Brody, Bill Burns, John Drew, Anthony Falco, Catherine Gale, Warren Hays, Selma Malinou, Norman Riggins, Lori Rogers, Sharon Vaughn. DANCERS: Don Atkinson, Bob Bakanic, Trudy Carole, Cathy Conklin, Mary Jane Ferguson, Linda Rae Hager, Ed Kresley, Bill Landrum, Robert Lone, Charlene Mehl, Karen Sargent, Kip Watson. *Understudies*: Fodorski/Henderson: Will B. Able; Elizabeth: Betty Oakes; *Swing Boy*: Frank Virgulto. *Act I: Scene 1* Idlewild Airport (New York); today: "Melt Us" (Fodorski & Immigrants); *Scene 2* New York and panorama of America: "What a Country!" (Fodorski & Company); *Scene 3* Dean's office, S.B.I.T. (Southern Baptist Institute of Technology): "Our Children" (Fodorski & Elizabeth), "Animal Attraction" (Susan & Bricker), "Our Children" (reprise) (Fodorski & Elizabeth); *Scene 4* Football field; *Scene 5* Classroom, S.B.I.T.: "Back to School" (Students) [added during the run], "We Speak the Same Language" (Fodorski & Bricker); *Scene 6* On the campus: "I Can Teach Them!" (Fodorski, Elizabeth, Bricker, Dawson); *Scene 7* Classroom, S.B.I.T.: "It's Fun to Think" (Fodorski, Professors, Students); *Scene 8* Front porch of Elizabeth's house: "Once Upon a Time" (Fodorski & Elizabeth); *Scene 9* Front porch of girls' dormitory; *Scene 10* Susan's room in girls' dormitory: "Nightlife" (Susan & Girls); *Scene 11* On the window of Susan's room: "I've Just Seen Her" (Bricker), "Once Upon a Time" (reprise) (Elizabeth) [dropped during the run]; *Scene 12* Locker room: "Physical Fitness" (Football Team), "The Fight Song" (Fodorski & Football Team); *Scene 13* Football field & stadium: "What a Country!" (reprise) (Fodorski & Company). *Act II: Scene 1* Office of Exploiters Unlimited; *Scene 2* Exterior & interior of Union Building, S.B.I.T.: "I Couldn't Have Done it Alone" (Bricker & Susan), "If I Were You" (Fodorski & Elizabeth); *Scene 3* Fodorski's seduction: "Have a Dream" (Fodorski, Henderson, Company); *Scene 4* On the campus: "I've Just Seen Him" (reprise) (Susan); *Scene 5* Office of Fodorski Foundation: "I'm Fascinating" (Fodorski), "Once Upon a Time" (reprise) (Elizabeth); *Scene 6* Bricker's room in boys' dormitory: "The Real Me" (Elizabeth); *Scene 7* On the campus: "It's Up to Me" (Fodorski); *Scene 8* The Cotton Bowl: "The Fight Song" (reprise) (Fodorski & Company); *Scene 9* Classroom, S.B.I.T.: "It's Fun to Think" (reprise) (Company).

Broadway reviews were extremely divided, and the show flopped. Ray Bolger couldn't pull it off. The number "Which Way?" was added after the opening. The show received Tony nominations for direction of a musical, and for Ray Bolger.

10. *All for Love*

A musical revue.

The Broadway Run. MARK HELLINGER THEATRE, 1/22/49– 5/7/49. 121 PERFORMANCES. PRESENTED BY Sammy Lambert & Anthony Brady Farrell; MUSIC/LYRICS: Allan Roberts & Lester Lee; SKETCH EDITOR: Max Shulman; DIRECTOR: Edward Reveaux; CHOREOGRAPHER: Eric Victor; SETS: Edward Gilbert; COSTUMES: Billy Livingston; MUSICAL DIRECTOR: Clay Warnick; ORCHESTRATIONS: Ted Royal, Don Walker, Russell Bennett, Hans Spialek; PRESS: Willard Keefe & David Tebet; COMPANY MANAGER: Edward O'Keefe; STAGE MANAGERS: Paul E. Porter, Ralph Simone, Phil Dakin. *Act I: Scene 1* "All for Love"

(Singing & Dancing Ensembles); *Scene 2* Fashion Expert (sketch by Jane Bishir). MANAGER OF BLATZ DEPARTMENT STORE: Milton Frome; RENEE MULFINGER: Grace Hartman (1) ☆; SIGNOR PIGNATELLI: Paul Hartman (1) ☆; *Scene 3* "My Baby's Bored" (Patricia Wymore & Budd Rogerson); *Scene 4* Morris, My Son (sketch by Billy K. Wells). A take-off of the movie *Edward, My Son*. FOREWORD: Bert Wheeler (2) ☆; WITHERS: Milton Frome; IVY: Janie Janvier; LORD MALCOLM TWONKEY: Bert Wheeler (2) ☆; OLIVE: Patricia Wymore; *Scene 5* "The Big Four" (music paraphrased by Peter Howard Weiss). PRODUCER: Milton Frome; FIRST SECRETARY: Carol Lee; SECOND SECRETARY: Prue Ward; OFFICE BOY: Jack Warner; AGENTS: Frank Stevens, Cary Conway, Sid Lawson, Thomas Bowman; JERRY REDBREAST: Eric Kristen; AGGIE DEE: Tiny Shimp; MR. X JACKSON: Peter Gladke; ELLEN LA MOURIS: Onna White; Dancing Girls & Boys; *Scene 6* Isolde (sketch by Ted Luce, Grace & Paul Hartman). TREADWELL: Paul Hartman (1) ☆; BARTON: Bert Wheeler (2) ☆; ISOLDE: Grace Hartman (1) ☆; WAGERNICK: Dick Smart, *Larry Douglas*. "Why Can't it Happen Again?" (m: Michel Emer; l: Sammy Gallop) (Kathryne Mylroie), "My Heart's in the Middle of July" [Featured singers: Dick Smart (*Larry Douglas*) & Leni Lynn (*Gloria Benson*). Specialty Dance: Patricia Wymore, Budd Rogerson, Dancing & Singing Ensembles; *Scene 7* Lament [Bert Wheeler (2) ☆]; *Scene 8* "It's a Living" [Grace & Paul Hartman (1) ☆]; *Scene 9* "(On the) *Benjamin B. Odell*." Production number set in 1899 aboard a Hudson River day steamer. BOY: Dick Smart, *Larry Douglas*; GIRL: Leni Lynn, *Gloria Benson*; POLICEMAN: Milton Frome; CAPTAIN: Bert Wheeler (2) ☆; CHAMBERMAID: Grace Hartman (1) ☆; PURSER: Paul Hartman (1) ☆; SAILORS: Robert Thompson & Peter Gladke; BALLOON MAN: Robert Shawley; LITTLE GIRL: June Graham; LITTLE BOY: Richard D'Arcy; ALSO WITH: Patricia Wymore, Milada Mladova, Katie Mylroie, Budd Rogerson, Dancing & Singing Ensembles. *Act II: Scene 1* "Prodigal Daughter" (ballet music by Peter Howard Weiss). DOROTHY (CRYSTAL): June Graham; FIRST MAN IN HER LIFE: Richard D'Arcy; HONKY-TONK GIRLS: Yvonne Tibor, Helen Wenzel, Tiny Shimp, Janet Bethel, Norma Doggett; JEWEL: Milada Mladova; SHADOW: Onna White; And Singing & Dancing Ensembles; *Scene 2* Message to Our Sponsor [Bert Wheeler (2) ☆]. A spoof on TV; *Scene 3* Sea Diver (sketch by Jane Bishir). Beebe is a deep-sea diver who fishes out a mermaid. PROFESSOR PISCES BEEBE: Paul Hartman (1) ☆; MRS. BEEBE: Grace Hartman (1) ☆; SAILOR: Dick Smart, *Larry Douglas*; *Scene 4* "Run to Me, My Love" [Leni Lynn (*Gloria Benson*) & Dick Smart (*Larry Douglas*)]; *Scene 5* Mary Maggie McNeil (sketch by Ted Luce, Grace & Paul Hartman). MAKE-UP GIRL: Janie Janvier; CHIEF PETERSON: Bert Wheeler (2) ☆; SONYA: Jean Handzlik; LEROY: Milton Frome; MARY MAGGIE MCNEIL: Grace Hartman (1) ☆; CAMERAMEN: Cary Conway & Sid Lawson; HOBART HAVERMILL: Paul Hartman (1) ☆; MAKE-UP GIRL: Marilyn Frechette; WARDROBE MAN: John Henson; BOY: Bob Shawley; *Scene 6* "No Time for Love" ("No Time for Nothin' but You") (Patricia Wymore & Be-Bop Boys); *Scene 7* Flying Mare (sketch by Max Shulman). Bert Wheeler as a female wrestler. GUS, FIRST WRESTLER: Paul Reed; AL, SECOND WRESTLER: Arthur Carroll; MCNULTY: Milton Frome; HAROLD MINAFEE: Bert Wheeler (2) ☆; GEORGEIUS GEORGIA: Verne Rogers; REFEREE: Richard D'Arcy; SECONDS: John Henson & Bob Shawley; *Scene 8* "(A) Dreamer with a Penny" [Dick Smart (*Larry Douglas*)]; *Scene 9* "The Farrell Girl" (Budd Rogerson & Boys); *Scene 10* "Oh, How Fortunate You Mortals Be" (Kathryne Mylroie); *Scene 11* Finale (Entire Company). *Singing Ensemble*: Gloria Benson, Ann Blackburn, Ruth Edberg, Arlyne Frank, Marilyn Frechette, Janie Janvier, Helena Schurgot, Tom Bowman, Arthur Carroll, Cary Conway, John Henson, Sid Lawson, Frank Stevens. *Dancing Ensemble*: Janet Bethel, Norma Doggett, Jean Handzlik, Carol Lee, Tiny Shimp, Yvonne Tibor, Prue Ward, Helen Wenzel, Onna White, Eric Kristen, Verne Rogers, Bob Thompson, Jack Warner.

This was the first show to play at the Mark Hellinger, which was owned by Anthony Brady Farrell (at that point the husband of Katie Mylroie). June Graham and Milada Mladova were the principal dancers. The show was roundly panned by the critics. It was the first Broadway show to lose more than half a million dollars.

11. *Allah Be Praised!*

Set in New York, Persia and Hollywood, between Feb. 20

and 29, 1948 (i.e., in the future). An emir, also a Dartmouth graduate, returns to Persia, where he has a harem stocked with 365 American girls, one for every day of the year. Two senators — Tex, from Texas, and Marcia, from Maryland — go to investigate a lend-lease possibility. Tex's sister, Carol, is there too, as the 366th wife (once every 4 years). Tex and Marcia fall in love. Suddenly the emirate finds oil.

Before Broadway. During Boston tryouts Alfred Bloomingdale, the producer (and department store magnate) disregarded play doctor Edward Howard's advice to discontinue this revue before going to Broadway. This was a mistake. John Hoysradt was a nightclub comedian. Evelyne & Beatrice were known as the Kraft Sisters.

The Broadway Run. ADELPHI THEATRE, 4/20/44–5/6/44. 20 PERFORMANCES. PRESENTED BY Alfred Bloomingdale; MUSIC: Don Walker & Baldwin "Beau" Bergersen; LYRICS/BOOK: George Marion Jr.; DIRECTORS: Robert H. Gordon & Jack Small; CHOREOGRAPHER: Jack Cole; SETS/LIGHTING: George Jenkins; COSTUMES: Miles White; MUSICAL DIRECTOR: Ving Merlin; VOCAL ARRANGEMENTS: Don Walker. **Cast:** CASWELL· Jack Albertson; RECEPTIONIST: Helen Bennett; TEX O'CARROLL: Edward Roecker; CLERK: Sheila Bond; CITIZEN: Joey Faye; ABDUL: Sid Stone; BULBUL: Jack Albertson; CAROL O'CARROLL: Mary Jane Walsh (3); ROBERTA: Marge Ellis; PAULA: Lee Joyce; DORIS: Mary McDonnell; TUBAGA: Anita Alvarez; EMIR: John Hoysradt (2); ZARAH: Milada Mladova (5); YOUSSOUF: Joey Faye (4); NIJ O'CARROLL: Pittman Corry; DULCY ROBOT: Margie Jackson; BEATRICE: Beatrice Kraft; EVELYNE: Evelyne Kraft; MARCIA MASON MOORE: Patricia Morison (1); MIMI McSLUMP: Jayne Manners; MATRON: Helen Bennett; MERCHANT: Tom Powers; McGRAB, A TRAINEE: Natalie Wynn; GIRLS ABOUT TEHERAN: Eleanor Hall & Louise Jarvis; OTHER TRAINEES: Lee Joyce, Susan Scott, Marge Ellis, Mari Lynn, Barbara Neal, Alice Anthony, Olga Suarez, Margie Jackson, Mary McDonnell, Dorothy Bird, Ila Marie Wilson, Grace Crystal, Gloria Crystal, Hazel Roy, Muriel Bruenig, Pat Welles; PHOTOGRAPHERS: Mischa Pompianov, Ray Arnett Jr., Remi Martel, Jack Baker, Jacy McCord [also known as J.C. McCord], Johnny Oberon, Tom Powers, Jack L. Nagle, William Lundy, Forrest Boncher [later known as Forrest Bonshire]. **Act I: Scene 1** Bureau of Missing Persons, New York, Feb. 20, 1948; **Scene 2** The minarets of Sultanbad, Feb. 29, 1948; **Scene 3** The emir's palace; siesta time; **Scene 4** The palace gardens; twilight, a few hours later; **Scene 5** The emir's palace; the same evening. **Act II: Scene 1** The minarets of Sultanbad; later that night; **Scene 2** The harem sleeping porch; **Scene 3** Hollywood, California; **Scene 4** The harem sleeping porch. **Act I:** "The Persian Way of Life" (m: Don Walker) (Carol); Dance (Tubaga & Doris), "Allah Be Praised" (m: Don Walker) (Tex), Dance (staged by Dan Eckley) (Clerk & Nij), "What's New in New York?" (m: Beau Bergersen) (Carol), "Leaf in the Wind" (m: Beau Bergersen) (Marcia), Dance (Evelyne & Beatrice), "Katinka to Eva to Frances" (m: Don Walker) (Emir), Dance (Tubaga), "Let's Go Too Far" (m: Don Walker) (Tex & Marcia), Dance (Zarah & Nij), Finaletto & Ballet (Entire Company). **Act II:** "Getting Oriental Over You" (m: Don Walker) (Carol), Dance (Clerk, Zarah, Beatrice, Evelyne), "Let's Go Too Far" (reprise) (Youssouf & Mimi), "Secret Song" (m: Beau Bergersen) (Marcia & Tex), "Sunrise on Sunset" (m: Beau Bergersen) (Tex), Finale (Entire Company).

The show was panned, it flopped, and Al Bloomingdale lost $160,000.

12. *Allegro*

This was the first Rodgers and Hammerstein musical not based on an original source. The saga of doctor Joe Taylor, Jr., from his birth in a small midwestern town in 1905, son of country doctor Joseph Taylor and his wife Marjorie, to age 35 (the original concept had been to take him through to death). Joe is not seen until he is 16 (his story before that is narrated by his parents and grandmother). We see his education, his courting of local bad belle Jennie, her rejection of him for another boy, Joe's brief involvement with Beulah, Joe going to college while Jennie waits for him, and his marriage to Jennie. Act II has him, after the 1929 stock market crash, joining the staff of a large Chicago hospital pandering to hypochondriacs. Charlie is his old schoolfriend also on the staff. Joe discovers that his wife is unfaithful, divorces her and returns to his home town with his secretary Emily, who really loves him, to practice medicine there the way it should be practiced. The show had abstract sets, multi-level performing areas and a Greek chorus. Scenes merged into each other, i.e. before one scene ended another had begun. In effect, the writers designed it as the first truly integrated show, i.e. not only did the book, music, lyrics, and choreography advance the story, so did the sets, lighting, costumes, etc., thus taking it beyond *Oklahoma!* in that respect.

Before Broadway. It was Oscar Hammerstein II's idea to do a show about a doctor. He had been good friends with his doctor, and Richard Rodgers' father and brother were both doctors. The number "Driving at Night" was not used (it was used later, however, in the 1996 production of *State Fair*). There were a lot of trying changes in rehearsals. The show tried out from 9/1/47, at the Shubert Theatre, New Haven. Mabel and the Shakespeare Student were played by Annabelle Lyon; Dot by Charlotte Howard; and Mrs. Mulhouse by Virginia Poe. The numbers "I Have Let the Time Run On" and "Sitting on the Porch in the Moonlight" were cut, as was "My Wife" (which was re-shaped into "Younger than Springtime" and used in *South Pacific*). In New Haven, when Lisa Kirk was singing "The Gentleman is a Dope," she fell into the orchestra pit, was caught by a couple of cellists, yanked back on stage, and continued the song as if nothing had happened. Apparently Agnes de Mille was not up to the task of directing, and she was helped out by Richard Rodgers (on songs) and Oscar Hammerstein (on book).

The Broadway Run. MAJESTIC THEATRE, 10/10/47–7/10/48. 315 PERFORMANCES. PRESENTED BY The Theatre Guild; MUSIC: Richard Rodgers; LYRICS/BOOK: Oscar Hammerstein II; DIRECTORS: Agnes de Mille and (uncredited) Oscar Hammerstein II & Richard Rodgers; CHOREOGRAPHER: Agnes de Mille; ASSISTANT TO THE CHOREOGRAPHER: Dania Krupska; SETS/LIGHTING: Jo Mielziner; COSTUMES: Lucinda Ballard; MUSICAL DIRECTOR: Salvatore Dell'Isola; ORCHESTRATIONS: Robert Russell Bennett; CHORAL DIRECTOR: Crane Calder; CHORAL SPEECH DIRECTOR: Josephine Callan; MUSIC FOR DANCES ARRANGED BY: Trude Rittman; PRESS: Joseph Heidt & Peggy Phillips; CASTING: John Fearnley; PRODUCTION SUPERVISORS: Lawrence Langner & Theresa Helburn; PRODUCTION ASSISTANT: Stephen Sondheim, *Paul Crabtree*; COMPANY MANAGER: Peter Davis; STAGE MANAGERS: Robert Calley & Herman Kantor; ASSISTANT STAGE MANAGER: Glenn Scandur. **Cast:** MARJORIE TAYLOR: Annamary Dickey (3); DR. JOSEPH TAYLOR: William Ching; MAYOR: Edward Platt; GRANDMA TAYLOR: Muriel O'Malley; FRIENDS OF JOEY: Ray Harrison (*Edward Weston, Robert Herget, Sam Steen, Stanley Simmons*) & Frank Westbrook; JENNIE BRINKER: Roberta Jonay (2); PRINCIPAL: Robert Byrn; MABEL: Evelyn Taylor; BICYCLE BOY: Stanley Simmons; GEORGIE: Harrison Muller, William Bradley (alternate); HAZEL SKINNER: Kathryn Lee; CHARLIE TOWNSEND: John Conte (4); DR. JOSEPH "JOE" TAYLOR JR.: John Battles (1); MISS LIPSCOMB: Susan Svetlik, *Ruth Ostrander*; CHEERLEADERS: Charles Tate (*Frank Westbrook, John Laverty*) & Sam Steen; COACH: Wilson Smith; NED BRINKER: Paul Parks; ENGLISH PROFESSOR: David Collyer; CHEMISTRY PROFESSOR: William McCully; GREEK PROFESSOR: Raymond Keast; BIOLOGY PROFESSOR: Robert Byrn; PHILOSOPHY PROFESSOR: Blake Ritter; SHAKESPEARE STUDENT: Susan Svetlik, Ruth Ostrander (alternate — she later took over role); BERTRAM WOOLHAVEN: Ray Harrison, *Robert Herget, Sam Steen, Stanley Simmons*; MOLLY: Katrina Van Oss, *Susan Svetlik*; BEULAH: Gloria Wills, *Katrina Van Oss*; MINISTER: Edward Platt; MILLIE: Julie Humphries; DOT: Sylvia Karlton, Irene Maxine (alternate); ADDIE: Patricia Bybell; DR. BIGBY DENBY: Lawrence Fletcher; MRS. MULHOUSE: Frances Rainer, *Clara Knox*; MRS. LANSDALE: Lily Paget; JARMAN, A BUTLER: Bill Bradley; MAID: Jean Houloose; EMILY WEST: Lisa Kirk (5); DOORMAN: Tom Perkins, *Bernard Green*; BROOK LANSDALE: Stephen Chase; BUCKLEY: Wilson Smith; SINGING GIRLS: Patricia Bybell, Priscilla Hathaway (*Christina Lind*), Charlotte Howard, Julie Humphries, Helen Hunter, Sylvia Karlton, Josephine Lambert, Gay Laurence, Mary

O'Fallon, Lily Paget, Yolanda Renay, Mia Stenn, Devida Stewart, Lucille Udovick, Nanette Vezina, *Ruth Vrana*; SINGING BOYS: Robert Arnold, Tommy Barragan, Robert Byrn, Joseph Caruso, Victor Clarke, David Collyer, Bernard Green, Clarence Hall, James Jewell, Raymond Keast, Walter Kelvin, William McCully, Robert Neukum, Ralph Patterson, Tom Perkins (left during the run), Edward Platt, David Poleri, Robert Reeves, Blake Ritter, Glenn Scandur, Wilson Smith, Wesley Swails, Gene Tobin; DANCING GIRLS: Patricia Barker, Andrea Downing, Patricia Gianinoto, Jean Houloose, Therese Miele, Mariane Oliphant, Ruth Ostrander, Frances Rainer (*Clara Knox*), Susan Svetlik, Jean Tachau, Evelyn Taylor, *Melissa Hayden*; DANCING BOYS: William Bradley, Daniel Buberniak, Bob Herget, John Laverty, Ralph Linn, Harrison Muller, Stanley Simmons, Sam Steen, Charles Tate, Frank Westbrook, Edward Weston, Ralph Williams, *James Barron, Edmund Howland*. **Understudies**: Joe Jr.: James Jewell; Marjorie/Grandma: Lily Paget & Julie Humphries, *Charlotte Howard*; Emily: Julie Humphries; Dr. Taylor: Wilson Smith; Jennie: Katrina Van Oss & Sylvia Karlton; Beulah: Sylvia Karlton & Mary O'Fallon, *Katrina Van Oss*; Molly: Sylvia Karlton & Mary O'Fallon; Charlie: Robert Reeves; Milly: Mary O'Fallon; Denby: Blake Ritter, *David Collyer*; Minister: Blake Ritter; Addie: Helen Hunter; Dot: Christina Lind, *Devida Stewart*; Hazel: Patricia Barker & Ruth Ostrander, *Susan Svetlik*; Coach/Buckley: Robert Byrn; Brook: William McCully; Ned: David Collyer; Philosophy Professor: Ralph Patterson; Georgie: Bill Bradley. **Act I**: His home town and his college town: "Joseph Taylor Jr" (Entire Ensemble), "I Know it Can Happen Again" (Grandma); "One Foot, Other Foot" (Singing Ensemble & Ballet). Specialists: Kathryn Lee, Patricia Barker, Bob Herget (Ray Harrison); "Winters Go By" [only in the 1994 revival], "A Fellow Needs a Girl" (Dr. Taylor & Marjorie) [a hit]; "Freshman Dance" [(Ensemble). As They Imagine They Are: Evelyn Taylor & Harrison Muller]; "A Darn Nice Campus" [(Joe Jr). Cheerleaders: Sam Steen & Charles Tate]; "The Purple and Brown" (Freshmen) [1994 City Center revival had "Wildcats" here], "So Far" (Beulah) [a hit], "You are Never Away" [(sung by Dr. Taylor & Vocal Chorus). Danced by Jennie] [a hit]; "(What) a Lovely Day for the Wedding" (Singing Ensemble & Ned) [cut from the cast album], "It May Be a Good Idea for Joe" (Charlie), "Wedding" ("To Have and to Hold" & "Wish Them Well") (Singing Ensemble) [1994 City Center revival had here: "Winters Go By" (reprise)/"To Have and to Hold"/"Wish Them Well"]. **Act II**: A large city: "Money isn't Ev'rything" (Jennie, Hazel, Addie, Millie, Dot), "Hazel Dances" (dance) (Kathryn Lee), "Yatata, Yatata, Yatata" (Charlie & Ensemble) [cut from the cast album], "The Gentleman is a Dope" (Emily) [a hit], "Allegro" (Emily, Charlie, Joe Jr., Singing Ensemble, Kathryn Lee, Ballet), "Come Home" (Marjorie); Finale (Entire Company).

This was R & H's eagerly-awaited musical immediately after *Carousel*, and it disappointed. It was their first failure. Reviews were very divided. When it opened on Broadway the show had already sold 250,000 tickets, and had $750,000 in the box office. It won Donaldson Awards for music, lyrics, and book.

After Broadway. TOUR: 11/48–6/49. It took in 16 cities. **Cast**: Roberta Jonay.

Oscar Hammerstein II was working on a revised version for TV when he died.

CITY CENTER, 3/2/94–3/5/94. 4 PERFORMANCES. Part of the *Encores!* concert series. DIRECTOR: Susan H. Schulman; CHOREOGRAPHER: Lar Lubovitch; SETS: John Lee Beatty; COSTUMES: Catherine Zuber; SOUND: Tony Meola; MUSICAL DIRECTOR: Rob Fisher. HOSTS: Stephen Sondheim & Christopher Reeve. **Cast**: MARJORIE: Carolann Page; DR. JOSEPH TAYLOR: John Cunningham; GRANDMA: Celeste Holm; YOUNG JENNIE: Gretchen Kingsley; JENNIE: Donna Bullock; HAZEL: Nancy Johnston; CHARLIE: Jonathan Hadary; JOE: Stephen Bogardus; BEULAH: Karen Ziemba; MINISTER: Robert Ousley; MILLIE: Sherry D. Boone; ADDIE: Elizabeth Acosta; DENBY: Erick Devine; MRS. LANSDALE: Susan Cella; EMILY: Christine Ebersole; BROOK: Martin Van Treuren.

Richard Nelson re-wrote *Allegro* in the late 1990s, but nothing came of this project.

THE REVISED **Allegro**: This version had a revised book (and only the book was revised), adapted with the blessing of the Rodgers & Hammerstein Organization. There was a staged reading, 8/6/02. **Cast**: Patrick

Wilson, Marc Kudisch, Lauren Kennedy. Then it had a run at the SIGNATURE THEATRE, Arlington, Virginia, 1/6/04–2/29/04 (run extended from 2/22/04). BOOK ADAPTED BY: Joe DiPietro; DIRECTOR: Eric Schaeffer; SETS: Eric Grims; COSTUMES: Gregg Barnes & Eric Grims; SOUND: Elsie Jones; LIGHTING: Ken Billington; MUSICAL DIRECTOR: Jon Kalbfleisch; NEW ORCHESTRATIONS: Jonathan Tunick. **Cast**: MARJORIE: April Harr Blandin; JOSEPH TAYLOR SR.: Harry A. Winter; JENNIE: Laurie Saylor; HAZEL: Jenna Sokolowski; CHARLIE: Stephen Gregory Smith; JOSEPH TAYLOR JR.: Will Gartshore; NED/DR. DENBY: Dan Manning; DR. LANSDALE: Carl Randolph; ETHEL/MISS LANSDALE: Donna Migliaccio; SALLY ANN: Tracy Lynn Olivera; MURIEL: Dana Krueger; VINCENT: Nan Casey; ETHAN: Eric Thompson; MITZI: Lauren Williams.

FAIRVIEW LIBRARY THEATRE, North York, Ontario, 2/19/04–2/28/04. This was the original version, PRESENTED BY the Civic Light Opera Company. DIRECTOR/SETS/COSTUMES/MUSICAL DIRECTOR: Joe Cascone. **Cast**: JOE: Bryan Chamberlain.

13. *Almost Crazy*

A musical revue.

Before Broadway. Certain sketches were dropped en route to Broadway: The Time, the Place and the Boy (replaced with Mother's Day), Coffee Break, Chemical Reactions, and Lament of the Dying Lady. The order of songs and sketches was considerably re-arranged.

The Broadway Run. LONGACRE THEATRE, 6/20/55–7/2/55. 16 PERFORMANCES. PRESENTED BY John S. Cobb; MUSIC/LYRICS/SKETCHES: various writers; SKETCH DIRECTOR: Christopher Hewett; DIRECTOR: Lew Kesler; CHOREOGRAPHER: William Skipper; SETS/LIGHTING: John Robert Lloyd; COSTUMES: Stanley Simmons; MUSICAL DIRECTOR: Al Rickey; ORCHESTRAL ARRANGEMENTS: Ted Royal; PRESS: Richard Falk; GENERAL MANAGER: Leon Spachner; PRODUCTION STAGE MANAGER: Walter Rinner; STAGE MANAGERS: Frederick Nay & Richard Towers. **Act I**: **Scene 1** "Everything's Gonna Be Much Worse Next Year" (m: Lew Kesler; l: James Shelton). LADIES OF THE ENSEMBLE: Rita Tanno, Betty Colby (4), Karen Anders (5), Mildred Hughes, Joan Morton, Lorna Del Maestro, Ann York, Kay Medford (1); QUARTETTE: William Skipper, Alvin Beam, Kevin Scott (6), Nick Dana; **Scene 2** "Mother's Day" (m: Portia Nelson; l: Joyce Geary). Sung by Mildred Hughes, Karen Anders (5), Ann York; **Scene 3** "Why Not Me?" (m: Ed Scott; l: Sam Rosen). Sung & danced by Phyllis "The Leg" Dorne & Ron Cecill; **Scene 4** Fort Knox, New York (sketch by Lester Judson); **Scene 5** "But it's Love" (m: Ray Taylor; l: Hal Hackady). Sung & danced by Gloria Smith, Ann York, Lorna Del Maestro, Rita Tanno, Joan Morton, William Skipper, Alvin Beam, Nick Dana, Ron Cecill; **Scene 6** "Don't Bait for Fish You Can't Fry" (m/l: Portia Nelson). Sung by Babe Hines (3); **Scene 7** This is a Living (sketch by Hal Hackady). RALPH DEADWOOD: Kevin Scott (6); MARY SMILES WINTER: Kay Medford (1); A MODEL: Mildred Hughes; THE HUSBAND: James Shelton (2); MAXINE MADISON: Karen Anders (5); **Scene 8** "Where is the Girl?" (m/l: James Shelton). Sung by Betty Colby (4) & Kevin Scott (6); **Scene 9** "Mother's Day" (reprise). Sung by Mildred Hughes, Karen Anders (5), Ann York; **Scene 10** "Goin' to the Moon" (m: Ed Scott; l: Lenny Adelson). Sung by Rita Tanno, James Shelton (2), Vincent Beck, Kay Medford (1), Richard Towers; **Scene 11** "Down to Eartha" (m/l: Ray Taylor). Sung by Betty Colby (4); **Scene 12** "Chat Noire" (m: Ray Taylor; l: Jim Kaye). Sung by Kevin Scott (6). CHAT NOIRE: Joan Morton; BARTENDER: Fred Nay; COP: Nick Dana; SAILOR: Ron Cecill; STREET CLEANER: Fred Nay; THE MOUSE: Alvin Beam; **Scene 13** "I Can Live without It" (m/l: Ray Taylor). Sung by Karen Anders (5); **Scene 14** If I Knew You Were Coming (sketch by Robert A. Bernstein). ANNOUNCER: Karen Anders (5); WIFE: Kay Medford (1); HUSBAND: James Shelton (2); **Scene 15** "Come and Get Cozy with Me" (m: Lew Kesler; l: Carley Mills). LIFEGUARD: Kevin Scott (6); HIS GIRL: Karen Anders (5); KITTY'S ROOMMATE: Kay Medford (1); KITTY'S BEAU: James Shelton (2); LOVERS: Betty Colby (4), Vincent Beck, Company. **Act II**: **Scene 1** "As We Told You" (m: Lew Kesler; l: James Shelton). LADIES OF THE ENSEMBLE: Rita Tanno, Betty Colby (4), Karen Anders (5), Mildred Hughes, Joan Morton, Ann York, Lorna Del Maestro, Gloria Smith; Quartette: William Skipper, Alvin Beam, Nick

Dana, Ron Cecill; *Scene 2* "Burlesque" (m: Bill Russell; l: Stan Hagler). QUEENIE: Gloria Smith; BIG QUEENIE: Kay Medford (1); BARKER: Fred Nay; THE BARITONE: Kevin Scott (6); *Scene 3* "Vertigo" (m: Ray Taylor; l: Helen Bragdon). MISTRESS OF THE VILLA: Betty Colby (4); TENDER OF THE GRAPES: Vincent Beck; *Scene 4* I Thought So Too (sketch by James Shelton). DOCTOR: Richard Towers; 1ST WOMAN: Lorna Del Maestro; 1ST MAN: Kevin Scott (6); 2ND MAN: James Shelton (2); 2ND WOMAN: Rita Tanno; 3RD WOMAN: Kay Medford (1); *Scene 5* "Easy" (m/l: James Shelton). Sung by Babe Hines (3); *Scene 6* "Always Tell the Truth" (m/l: Portia Nelson; dial: Hal Hackady). TRUTH: Joan Morton; VERACITY: Kay Medford (1); *Scene 7* "Mother's Day" (reprise). Sung by Mildred Hughes, Ann York, Karen Anders (5); *Scene 8* "Here Come the Blues" (m: Gene de Paul; l: Don Raye). Sung by William Skipper. Danced by William Skipper, Joan Morton, Lorna Del Maestro, Mildred Hughes, Phyllis "The Leg" Dorne; *Scene 9* "More Fish." Sung by Karen Anders (5); *Scene 10* "Love in the Barnyard" (m/l: Ray Taylor). Sung by Babe Hines (3). Danced by Gloria Smith, Lorna Del Maestro, Rita Tanno, Phyllis "The Leg" Dorne, Ron Cecill, Alvin Beam, Nick Dana, William Skipper; *Scene 11* Love Me or Leave Me (sketch by Kay Medford & James Shelton). The Grump: James Shelton (2); Ruth: Kay Medford (1); *Scene 12* Finale (Entire Company).

Broadway reviews were bad.

14. *Along Fifth Avenue*

Musical revue set on Fifth Avenue.

Before Broadway. During tryouts Bob Gordon (unbilled) replaced Charles Friedman as director. In the cast Jackie Gleason, who had slimmed down drastically, replaced the fatally ill Willie Howard (who died the day before opening night). The numbers "If" (m: Gordon Jenkins; l: Tom Adair), "With You So Far Away" (m: Gordon Jenkins; l: Tom Adair) and "Maybe it's Because" (m: Johnnie Scott; l: Harry Ruby) were cut.

The Broadway Run. BROADHURST THEATRE, 1/13/49–2/19/49; IMPERIAL THEATRE, 2/21/49–6/18/49. Total of 180 PERFORMANCES. PRESENTED BY Arthur Lesser; MUSIC: Gordon Jenkins; ADDITIONAL MUSIC: Richard Stutz, Johnnie Scott, Philip Kadison; LYRICS: Tom Adair; ADDITIONAL LYRICS: Milton Pascal, Harry Ruby, Thomas Howell, Nat Hiken; SKETCHES: Charles Sherman & Nat Hiken; DIRECTOR: Robert H. Gordon; CHOREOGRAPHER: Robert Sidney; SETS: Oliver Smith; COSTUMES: David ffolkes; LIGHTING: Peggy Clark; MUSICAL DIRECTOR: Irving Actman; MUSICAL & VOCAL ARRANGEMENTS: Gordon Jenkins; PRESS: Richard Maney & Frank Goodman; GENERAL MANAGER: Eddie Lewis; STAGE MANAGERS: B.D. Kranz, Samuel Liff, Ted Cappy. *Act I: Scene 1* "Fifth Avenue" (m: Gordon Jenkins; l: Tom Adair). Virginia Gorski (*Evelyn Ward*) & Company; *Scene 2* Sweet Surrender (sketch by Nat Hiken). Set in Lord & Taylor's; Miss Herkimer is a girl at the perfume counter who sprays a man with an aphrodisiac, and an effeminate customer standing nearby is affected. MISS HERKIMER: Nancy Walker (1), *Betty Kean*; MR. FARQUHAR: George S. Irving; MR. HIGGINS: Dick Bernie; *Scene 3* "The Best Time of Day" (m: Gordon Jenkins; l: Tom Adair). Carol Bruce (4) (*Jane Kean*), with Dante Di Paolo, Bob Neukum, Ken Renner, Bert Sheldon; *Scene 4* "A Window on the Avenue" (m: Gordon Jenkins). WINDOW DRESSER: Zachary Solov; GIRLS: Shellie Farrell, Marian Horosko, Gretchen Houser; BOYS: Harry Asmus, Howard Malone, Wallace Seibert; *Scene 5* "If This is Glamour!" (m: Richard Stutz; l: Rick French). Nancy Walker (1) (*Betty Kean*); *Scene 6* The Fifth Avenue Label (sketch by Charles Sherman). NURSE: Joyce Mathews; DOCTOR: Dick Bernie; AMBULANCE DRIVER: Lee Krieger; PATIENT: Jackie Gleason (2); INSURANCE ADJUSTER: George S. Irving; MODELS: Ted Allison, Ken Renner, Walter Stane; *Scene 7* "Skyscraper Blues" (m: Gordon Jenkins; l: Tom Adair). Sung by Donald Richards (*Hayes Gordon*). Danced by: GIRL: Viola Essen; BOY: Zachary Solov (ballet dancer); LOVERS: Marian Horosko & Wallace Seibert; YOUNG GIRLS: Franca Baldwin & Shellie Farrell; STREET WALKERS: Tessie Carrano, Gretchen Houser, Janet Sayers; MEN: Harry Asmus, Dante Di Paolo, Walter Stane; *Scene 8* Hank Ladd (3) (monologist); *Scene 9* "I Love Love in New York" (m: Gordon Jenkins; l: Tom Adair). Scene: Washington Square. HURDY-GURDY MAN: Lee Krieger; FIRST COUPLE: Carol Bruce (4) (*Jane Kean*) & Don Richards (*Hayes Gordon*); SECOND COUPLE: Virginia Gorski (*Evelyn Ward*) & Johnny Coy; GIRLS: Franca Baldwin, Shellie Farrell, Marian Horosko, Gretchen Houser, Carol Nelson, Janet Sayers; BOYS: Harry Asmus, Dante Di Paolo, Howard Malone, Wallace Seibert, Zachary Solov, Walter Stane; *Scene 10* "The Fugitive from Fifth Avenue" (m: Richard Stutz; l: Nat Hiken). Three Foreign Legionnaires enter, dying of thirst. The Fugitive appears, in immaculate Legion uniform, with ascantily-dressed great-looking blonde carrying his golf bags, and brushing the other legionnaires aside, says "Do you mind if we play through?" CAPTAIN: Lee Krieger; LEGIONNAIRES: Ted Allison, Dick Bernie, George S. Irving; THE FUGITIVE: Jackie Gleason (2); *Scene 11* Hank Ladd (3) (monologist); *Scene 12* "Santo Dinero" (m: Richard Stutz; l: Milton Pascal). Nancy Walker (1) (*Betty Kean*), Viola Essen, Zachary Solov, Wallace Seibert, Lee Krieger, Singing & Dancing Ensembles. *Act II*: *Scene 1* "In the Lobby" (m: Gordon Jenkins; l: Tom Adair). Singing & Dancing Ensembles; *Scene 2* What's in the Middle? (sketch by Charles Sherman). COUNTER GIRL: Nancy Walker (1), *Betty Kean*; CUSTOMER: Jackie Gleason (2); OTHER CUSTOMERS: Dick Bernie, Leonard Claret, Lee Krieger; MANAGER: George S. Irving; ASSISTANT COUNTER GIRL: Joyce Mathews; ASSISTANT MANAGER: Bert Sheldon; *Scene 3* "Weep No More" (m: Gordon Jenkins; l: Tom Adair). Sung by Carol Bruce (4) (*Jane Kean*); *Scene 4* Mr. Rockefeller Builds His Dream House (sketch by Mel Tolkin & Max Liebman). A gentleman (really John D. Rockefeller) talking to a group of sightseers. GUIDE: Lee Krieger; VISITORS: Singing Ensemble; GENTLEMAN: Hank Ladd (3); *Scene 5* "Challenge" (m: Mel Pahl & Richard Stutz). A competition between ballet dancer Viola Essen & tap dancer Johnny Coy; *Scene 6* "Chant d'Amour" (m: Gordon Jenkins; l: Nat Hiken). Sung by Nancy Walker (1) (*Betty Kean*) to her beau "Irving"; *Scene 7* "Vacation in the Store" (m: Gordon Jenkins; l: Tom Adair) (courtesy of Lord & Taylor). TRIO: Gloria Hayden, Candace Montgomery, Tina Prescott; ALSO WITH: Nancy Walker (1) (*Betty Kean*), Jackie Gleason (2), Don Richards (*Hayes Gordon*), Johnny Coy, Virginia Gorski (*Evelyn Ward*), Zachary Solov, Lee Krieger, Wallace Seibert, & Company; *Scene 8* Hank Ladd (3) (monologist); *Scene 9* "Call it Applefritters" (m: Richard Stutz; l: Milton Pascal). Set in a cafeteria. A boy gets a custard pie in the face. Sung by: BOY: Hank Ladd (3); GIRL: Carol Bruce (4), *Jane Kean*; *Scene 10* Murder on Fifth Avenue (sketch by Charles Sherman). Daisy accidentally swallows poison, thinking it's whiskey; the police interrogate her, and tell her to keep moving to ward off the effects of the poison. DETECTIVE: Dick Bernie; PHILIP ASHTON: Donald Richards, *Hayes Gordon*; MRS. SCHUYLER: Joyce Mathews; BUTLER: Ted Allison; INSPECTOR MALONEY: Jackie Gleason (2); DAISY: Nancy Walker (1), *Betty Kean*; MRS. ASHTON: Louise Kirtland; DR. BROWN: George S. Irving; *Scene 11* "A Trip Doesn't Care at All" (m: Philip Kadison; l: Thomas Howell). PAM: Judythe Burroughs (an eight-year-old black actress); CHRIS: Don Richards, *Hayes Gordon*; *Scene 12* Finale: "Fifth Avenue" (reprise) (Entire Company). SINGING ENSEMBLE: Joan Coburn, Gloria Hayden, Candace Montgomery, Tina Prescott, Dorothy Pyren, Lucille Udovick, Ted Allison, Lenny Claret, Bob Neukum, Ken Renner, Bert Sheldon. DANCING ENSEMBLE: Franca Baldwin, Tessie Carrano, Shellie Farrell, Marian Horosko, Gretchen Houser, Carol Nelson, Janet Sayers, Harry Asmus, Ted Cappy, Dante Di Paolo, Howard Malone, Walter Stane. *Standbys*: Viola: Franca Baldwin; Carol: Tina Prescott; Nancy: Dorothy Pyren; George: Ted Allison; Johnny: Leonard Claret; Don: Bert Sheldon.

Broadway reviews were evenly divided. Viola Essen won a Donaldson Award for best female dancer.

15. *Ambassador*

Lambert, a Massachusetts man "you can set your watch by," is sent to Paris in 1906 by his employer and fiancée Amelia, to rescue her son Chad from the grip of a middle-aged French woman, Marie. Lambert falls for Marie, and for the first time in his life acts spontaneously, and stays in France with Marie while Chad goes home.

Before Broadway. An American production that had failed to find Broadway financing, it opened at HER MAJESTY'S THEATRE, London, on 10/19/71, at a cost of $265,000, which came from more than 100 American backers who all flew over for the premiere. Reviews were divided, but mostly bad; the show failed after three months. There was a London cast recording on RCA. **Cast**: Danielle Darrieux, Howard Keel, Neville Jason, Judith Paris, Margaret Courtenay, Nevil Whiting. "A Man You Can Set Your Watch By," "It's a Woman," "Lambert's Quandary," "Lilas," "The Right Time, The Right Place," "Surprise," "Charming," "All of My Life," "What Can You Do with a Nude?," "Love Finds the Lonely," "Tell Her," "La Femme," "Young with Him," "I Thought I Knew You," "What Happened to Paris?," "La Nuit d'Amour," "Am I Wrong?," "Mama," "That's What I Need Tonight," "You Can Tell a Lady by Her Hat," "This Utterly Ridiculous Affair," "Not Tomorrow," "Thank You, No." In 1972 the show was re-written for the USA. It had an inconsequential summer run in Philadelphia. Robert Upton was replaced as co-librettist by Anna Marie Barlow, and Gillian Lynne as choreographer by Joyce Trisler.

    The Broadway Run. Lunt–Fontanne Theatre, 11/19/72–11/25/72. 20 previews, 11/2/72–11/17/72. 9 performances. Presented by Gene Dingenary, Miranda D'Ancona, Nancy Levering; Music: Don Gohman; Lyrics: Hal Hackady; Book: Don Ettlinger & Anna Marie Barlow; Based on the 1903 novel *The Ambassadors*, by Henry James; Director: Stone Widney; Choreographer: Joyce Trisler; Sets/Costumes: Peter Rice; Costume Supervisor: Sara Brook; Lighting: Martin Aronstein; Musical Director/Vocal Arrangements: Herbert Grossman; Orchestrations: Philip J. Lang; Dance Music Arrangements: Trude Rittman; Press: Reginald Denenholz & Timothy A. Burke; General Manager: Norman Maibaum; Company Manager: Malcolm Allen; Production Stage Manager: Alan Hall; Stage Manager: Mary Porter Hall; Assistant Stage Manager: Robert L. Hultman. **Cast**: Flower Girl: Patricia Arnell; Lewis Lambert Strether: Howard Keel (1) ☆; Waymarsh: David Sabin (3); Marie de Vionnet: Danielle Darrieux (2) ☆; Gloriani: Carmen Mathews (4); Waiter: Dwight Arno; Bilham: Michael Goodwin; Chad: Michael Shannon; Jeanne de Vionnet: Andrea Marcovicci (6); Dancing Master: Larry Giroux; Artist: Larry Giroux; Guide: Jack Trussel; Waiter: Robert L. Hultman; Innkeeper's Wife: Marsha Tamaroff; Bellboy: Nikolas Dante; Lady in Park: Dixie Stewart; Amelia Newsome: M'el Dowd (5); Germaine: Patricia Arnell; Cabaret Dancers: Alexis Hoff, Phillip Filiato, Suzanne Sponsler, Larry Giroux; Headwaiter: Robert L. Hultman; Hotel Manager: Jack Trussel; People of Paris: Janis Ansley, Patricia Arnell, Dwight Arno, Marcia Brooks, Nikolas Dante, Richard Dodd, Vito Durante, Phillip Filiato, Lynn Fitzpatrick, Larry Giroux, Charlie Goeddertz, Gerald Haston, Alexis Hoff, Robert L. Hultman, Douglas E. Hunnikin, Genette Lane, Betsy Ann Leadbetter, Nancy Lynch, Linda-Lee MacArthur, Adam Petroski, Dean Russell, Salicia Saree, Ellie Smith, Suzanne Sponsler, Dixie Stewart, Marsha Tamaroff, Jack Trussel, Chester Walker. **Standbys**: Strether: Steve Arlen; Marie: Margot Moser. **Understudies**: Gloriani: Linda-Lee MacArthur; Amelia: Marsha Tamaroff; Waymarsh: Jack Trussel; Chad: Michael Goodwin; Jeanne: Patricia Arnell; Bilham: Dean Russell; Germaine: Lynn Fitzpatrick. **Act I: Scene 1** Gare St. Lazare [this scene was deleted before Broadway opening night, and its song, "Lambert's Quandary" (Lambert), was placed in the new Scene 1 (see below)]; **Scene 1** The Tuileries [before Broadway opening night this had been Scene 2, minus "Lambert's Quandary" (see above)]: "Lilas" (Flower Girl), "Lambert's Quandary" (Lambert), "I Know the Man" (Marie); **Scene 2** Chad's apartment [before Broadway opening night this had been Scene 3; Scene 3 had been Scene 4, etc. There had been 10 scenes in Act I]; **Scene 3** Gloriani's garden: "The Right Time, The Right Place" (Gloriani's Guests), "She Passed My Way" (Marie & Guests), Valse (dance) (Gloriani's Guests); **Scene 4** Terrace of Lambert's apartment: "Something More" (Lambert); **Scene 5** A park: "Love Finds the Lonely" (Jeanne); **Scene 6** Notre Dame Cathedral: "Kyrie Eleison" (Choir); **Scene 7** The Left Bank: "Surprise" (Marie, Lambert, People of the Left Bank); **Scene 8** Terrace of Lambert's apartment: "Happy Man" (Lambert); **Scene 9** An inn at St. Cloud. **Act II: Scene 1** The Tuileries: "Lilas, What Happened to Paris" (Lambert & Flower Girl); **Scene 2** Lambert's apartment: "Young with Him" (Marie), "Too Much to Forgive" (Lambert); **Scene 3** A secluded part of the Bois de Boulogne: "Why Do Women Have to Call it Love" (Gloriani & Waymarsh); **Scene 4** Chad's apartment; **Scene 5** Marie's garden: "Mama" (Jeanne), "That's What I Need Tonight" (Marie & Lambert); **Scene 6** Le Petit Moulin Cabaret: "Maxixe—Habanera" (dance) (Cabaret Dancers & People of

Paris), "That's What I Need Tonight" (reprise) (Lambert, Marie, People of Paris), "Gossip" (Ladies of Paris); **Scene 7** Marie's garden: "Not Tomorrow" (Marie); **Scene 8** A bridge: "All of My Life" (Lambert); **Scene 9** The hotel lobby: "Thank You, No" (Lambert); **Scene 10** A bridge.

    It opened on Broadway in a big way, was panned big-time, and flopped, at a cost of $360,000. Don Gohman committed suicide shortly thereafter.

16. *Amen Corner*

    Set in a sanctified storefront church in Harlem and in an adjoining apartment, in the early 1960s.

    The Broadway Run. Nederlander Theatre, 11/10/83–12/4/83. 12 previews from 11/1/83. 28 performances. Presented by Prudhomme Productions (Edward Mann, Judith Henry, Joel Goldstein, Gil Gerard); Music/Vocal Arrangements: Garry Sherman; Lyrics: Peter Udell; Book: Philip Rose & Peter Udell; Based on the 1953 play *The Amen Corner*, by James Baldwin; Director: Philip Rose; Choreographer: Al Perryman; Sets: Karl Eigsti; Costumes: Felix E. Cochren; Lighting: Shirley Prendergast; Sound: Peter J. Fitzgerald; Musical Director: Margaret Harris; Orchestrations: Garry Sherman & Dunn Pearson; Dance Music Arrangements: Dunn Pearson & George Butcher; Cast recording on CBS; Press: Fred Nathan & Associates; General Management: Theatre Now; Company Manager: Helen V. Meier; Production Stage Manager: Mortimer Halpern; Stage Managers: Dwight R.B. Cook & Sherry Lambert. **Cast**: Margaret Alexander, pastor of the church: Rhetta Hughes (1) ☆, Sister Moore, elder of the church: Jean Cheek (7); Odessa, Margaret's older sister: Ruth Brown (2); David, Margaret's son: Keith Lorenzo Amos (4); Sister Boxer, elder of the church: Helena-Joyce Wright (5); Brother Boxer, elder of the church: Chuck Cooper (6); Luke, Margaret's husband: Roger Robinson (3); Members of the Congregation: Loretta Abbott, Leslie Dockery, Cheryl Freeman, Gene Lewis, Denise Morgan, Lewis Robinson, Renee Rose, Vanessa Shaw, Jeffrey V. Thompson; Dancers: Loretta Abbott, Leslie Dockery, Renee Rose. **Understudies**: Margaret: Denise Morgan; Odessa: Venida Evans; Sister Moore: Vanessa Shaw; Sister Boxer: Cheryl Freeman; Brother Boxer: Jeffrey V. Thompson; David: Lewis Robinson; Luke: Gene Lewis. **Swing Dancers**: Venida Evans & Leonard Piggee. **Act I**: **Scene 1** Church; Sunday morning: "Amen Corner" (Margaret); **Scene 2** Apartment; later that morning: "That Woman Can't Play No Piano" (David & Friends), "In the Real World" (Brother Boxer), "You Ain't Gonna Pick up Where You Left Off" (Margaret & Luke); **Scene 3** Apartment; late afternoon, the following Saturday: "In the Real World" (reprise) (Sister Boxer), "We Got a Good Thing Goin'" (Luke & David); **Scene 4** Church; same afternoon: "In His Own Good Time" (Sister Boxer, Brother Boxer, Sister Moore, Odessa, Congregation); **Scene 5** Apartment; same afternoon: "Heat Sensation" (Luke), "Every Time We Call it Quits" (Luke). **Act II**: Entr'acte (Orchestra); **Scene 1** Apartment; early Sunday morning: "Somewhere Close By" (Odessa), "Leanin' on the Lord" (Sister Moore, Brother Boxer, Sister Boxer, Odessa, Congregation), "I'm Already Gone" (David), "Love Dies Hard" (Margaret), "Every Time We Call it Quits" (reprise) (Luke & Margaret), "Rise up and Stand Again" (Margaret).

    Reviews were very bad. Rhetta Hughes was nominated for a Tony.

17. *Amour*

    An intimate musical, with no intermission, and sung through. Set in Paris about 1950. Dusoleil (Dutilleul in the French original), a mild mannered office clerk, discovers that he can walk through walls. He revenges himself on his mean boss, courts Isabelle, the girl he has adored from afar and who has a sadistic Prosecutor husband who locks her up at night, and becomes a Robin Hood figure known as Passepartout, a crime hero to the masses.

    Before Broadway. Lewis Cleale and Sarah Litzsinger were announced in their roles on 7/19/02. Broadway previews began on 9/21/02 (put back from 9/20/02). Set problems interrupted the flow of previews, and the evening performance of 9/24/02, and the matinee of 9/25/02 were canceled.

The Broadway Run. MUSIC BOX THEATRE, 10/20/02–11/3/02. 31 previews from 9/21/02. 17 PERFORMANCES. PRESENTED BY the Shubert Organization, Jean Doumanian Productions, USA Ostar Theatricals; MUSIC/ORCHESTRATIONS: Michel Legrand; TRANSLATED BY: Jeremy Sams from the 1997 French musical *Le Passe-Muraille* (*The Man Who Could Pass Through Walls*), which had a (French) book by Didier Van Cauwelaert, and which was in turn adapted from the French short story by Marcel Ayme; DIRECTOR: James Lapine; CHOREOGRAPHER: Jane Comfort; SETS: Scott Pask; COSTUMES: Dona Granata; LIGHTING: Jules Fisher & Peggy Eisenhauer; SOUND: Dan Moses Schreier; ILLUSION DESIGNER: Jim Steinmeyer; MUSICAL DIRECTOR/VOCAL ARRANGEMENTS: Todd Ellison; CAST RECORDING on Sh-K-Boom, made on 4/7/03 and released on 7/8/03; PRESS: Bill Evans & Associates; CASTING: Bernard Telsey; GENERAL MANAGEMENT: Niko Associates; COMPANY MANAGER: Tom Senter; PRODUCTION STAGE MANAGER: Leila Knox; STAGE MANAGER: David Sugarman; ASSISTANT STAGE MANAGER: Jonathan Donahue. *Cast*: DUSOLEIL: Malcolm Gets (1) ✿; ISABELLE: Melissa Errico (2) ✿; CLAIRE: Nora Mae Lyng; BERTRAND: Christopher Fitzgerald; CHARLES: Lewis Cleale; MADELEINE: Sarah Litzsinger; PAINTER: Norm Lewis; NEWSVENDOR: Christopher Fitzgerald; WHORE: Nora Mae Lyng; POLICEMEN: John Cunningham & Bill Nolte; PROSECUTOR: Lewis Cleale; DOCTOR: John Cunningham; BOSS: Bill Nolte; PRESIDENT OF THE TRIBUNAL: John Cunningham; ADVOCATE: Christopher Fitzgerald. *Standbys*: Claire/Isabelle: Jessica Hendy; Madeleine/ Whore: Jessica Hendy; Boss/Charles: Matthew Bennett; Doctor/Policeman: Matthew Bennett; President/Prosecutor: Matthew Bennett; Advocate/Bertrand: Christian Borle; Dusoleil/Newsvendor/Painter: Christian Borle. *Understudy*: Sarah Litzsinger (Isabelle). *Orchestra*: PIANOS: Todd Ellison & Antony Geralis; PERCUSSION: Bill Hayes; WOODWINDS: Ben Kono; BASS: Mark Vanderpoel. Overture (Dusoleil, Isabelle, Charles), "Office Life" (Dusoleil, Charles, Claire), "Going Home Alone" (Dusoleil), "Other People's Stories" (Dusoleil & Isabelle), "The Street Vendor's Waltz" (Dusoleil, Isabelle, Charles), "Dusoleil Walks Through the Wall" (Dusoleil), "The Doctor" (Dusoleil & Doctor), "An Ordinary Guy" (Dusoleil), "Dusoleil's Revenge" (Dusoleil, Prosecutor, President), "Somebody" (Isabelle), "Prosecutor's Song" (Prosecutor), "Whore's Lament" (Dusoleil & Whore), "Monsieur Passepartout" (Dusoleil, Cleale, Cunningham), "Special Time of Day" (Dusoleil & Isabelle), "Waiting" (Dusoleil), "The Latest News" (Newsvendor & Painter), "Dusoleil in Jail" (Dusoleil, Isabelle, Claire), "Painter's Song" (Painter), "Isabelle on Her Balcony" (Dusoleil, Isabelle, Charles), "Transformation" (Dusoleil, Isabelle, Charles), "The Advocate's Plea" (President & Advocate), "The Trial" (Dusoleil, Isabelle, Prosecutor), "Duet for Dusoleil and Isabelle" (Dusoleil, Isabelle, Charles), "Whistling Ballet" (Dusoleil, Cunningham, Painter), "Amour" (Dusoleil & Isabelle), "Dusoleil Meets the Press" (Dusoleil, Isabelle, Cleale), "Serenade" (Dusoleil, Isabelle, Cleale).

Broadway reviews were divided. The show closed after the 11/3/02 matinee because people stayed away. The show, which cost over $3 million, lost $4.5 million. The cast recording was made with the original Broadway cast. It had a bonus track, "An Ordinary Guy" (sung by Michel Legrand; Malcolm Gets also recorded that version of the song). The show received Tony nominations for musical, score, book, and for Malcolm Gets and Melissa Errico. Especially after the release of the cast album, the show gained a certain cult following.

After Broadway. The show was reconceived, and had a run at the Goodspeed Opera House's Norma Terris Theatre, in Connecticut, 8/11/05–9/4/05, as part of the Goodspeed's developmental season. There were still nine actors, but the size of the production was scaled down. DIRECTOR: Darko Tresnjak (replaced Gary Griffin).

18. *Angel*

Set in the autumn of 1916. Eliza turns her Altamount, North Carolina, home into a boarding house, and puts her quest for money ahead of her sons Ben and Eugene.

Before Broadway. Originally called *All the Comforts of Home*, it was going to be produced at Circle in the Square, with the same main crew

as for the musical *Shenandoah*, but it didn't work out. It finally tried out as *Look Homeward, Angel*, at the Northstage Theatre Restaurant, Glen Cove, Long Island, but didn't work there. Presented by Norman Main. The number "It's Gotta Be Dixie" was cut. Then it moved to Broadway.

The Broadway Run. MINSKOFF THEATRE, 5/10/78–5/13/78. 6 previews. 5 PERFORMANCES. PRESENTED BY Philip Rose & Ellen Madison; MUSIC: Gary Geld; LYRICS: Peter Udell; BOOK: Ketti Frings & Peter Udell; BASED ON the 1957 Pulitzer Prize-winning play *Look Homeward Angel*, by Ketti Frings, which was based on Thomas Wolfe's 1929 autobiographical novel of that name; DIRECTOR: Philip Rose; CHOREOGRAPHER: Robert Tucker; SETS: Ming Cho Lee; COSTUMES: Pearl Somner; LIGHTING: John Gleason; SOUND OPERATOR: Bill Weingart; MUSICAL DIRECTOR/DANCE MUSIC ARRANGEMENTS: William Cox; ORCHESTRATIONS: Don Walker; PRESS: Merle Debuskey & Leo Stern; CASTING: Lynda Watson; GENERAL MANAGER: Helen Richards; COMPANY MANAGER: Charles Willard; PRODUCTION STAGE MANAGER: Steve Zweigbaum; STAGE MANAGER: Arturo E. Porazzi; ASSISTANT STAGE MANAGER: Paul Myrvold. *Cast*: HELEN GANT: Donna Davis; BEN GANT: Joel Higgins (4); MRS. FATTY PERT: Patti Allison (7); MRS. SNOWDEN: Grace Carney; EUGENE GANT: Don Scardino (3); ELIZA GANT: Frances Sternhagen (1) ✿; WILL PENTLAND: Elek Hartman; FLORRY MANGLE: Rebecca Seay; MRS. CLATT: Justine Johnston; JAKE CLATT: Gene Masoner; MR. FARRELL: Billy Beckham; MISS BROWN: Jayne Barnett; LAURA JAMES: Leslie Ann Ray (5); W.O. GANT: Fred Gwynne (2) ✿; DR. MAGUIRE: Daniel Keyes; JOE TARKINGTON: Rex David Hays; REED McKINNEY: Carl Nicholas; TIM LAUGHRAN: Norman Stotz; MADAME VICTORIA: Patricia Englund (6). *Standbys*: W.O. Gant: Peter Walker; Eliza: Ann Gardner. *Understudies*: Mme Victoria: Ann Gardner; Eugene/Farrell: Dennis Cooley; Ben/Jake: Paul Myrvold; Laura/Helen/Florry: Leoni Norton; Fatty/Miss Brown: Laura Waterbury. *Act I*: The Dixieland Boarding House: "Angel Theme" (Orchestra), "All the Comforts of Home" (Boarders), "Like the Eagles Fly" (Ben), "Make a Little Sunshine" (Eliza, Eugene, Ben), "Fingers and Toes" (W.O., Tim, Reed, Joe), "Fatty" (Ben), "Astoria Gloria" (Fatty & Boarders), "Railbird" (Eugene), "If I Ever Loved Him" (Laura), "A Dime Ain't Worth a Nickel" (Ben & Fatty), "I Got a Dream to Sleep On" (Eugene), "Drifting" (Eliza). *Act II*: *Scene 1* Gant's marble yard and shop; one week later: "I Can't Believe it's You" (W.O., Victoria), "Feelin' Loved" (Eugene & Laura); *Scene 2* Dixieland Boarding House; that evening: A Medley (Ben, Fatty, Eliza, Laura); *Scene 3* Dixieland; two weeks later, just before dawn: "Tomorrow I'm Gonna Be Old" (W.O.), "Feelin' Loved" (reprise) (Eugene & Laura), "How Do You Say Goodbye" (Laura), "Gant's Waltz" (W.O. & Eliza), "Like the Eagles Fly" (reprise) (Eugene).

On Broadway it received terrible reviews and flopped. Frances Sternhagen was nominated for a Tony.

19. *Angel in the Wings*

An intimate musical revue.

Before Broadway. This show came from the summer circuit, where it was originally called *Heaven Help the Angels*. It opened on 6/23/47, at Bucks County Playhouse, New Hope, Pa., starring the Hartmans and Viola Roache. Eileen Barton replaced Connie Baxter during the pre-Broadway tour.

The Broadway Run. CORONET THEATRE, 12/11/47–9/4/48. 308 PERFORMANCES. PRESENTED BY Marjorie & Sherman Ewing; MUSIC/LYRICS: Bob Hilliard & Carl Sigman; SKETCHES: Hank Ladd, Ted Luce, Grace & Paul Hartman; DIRECTOR: John Kennedy; CHOREOGRAPHER: Edward Noll; SETS/LIGHTING: Donald Oenslager; COSTUMES: Julia Sze; MUSICAL DIRECTOR: Phil Ingalls; MUSICAL ARRANGEMENTS: David Mann & Fred Barovick; PRESS: Bill Doll & Dick Williams; GENERAL MANAGER: William Herz Jr.; COMPANY MANAGER: James Troup, *Warren P. Munsell Jr.*; STAGE MANAGER: Herman Glazer; ASSISTANT STAGE MANAGER: Alan Green, *Dave Brennan*. *Act I*: *Scene 1* The Hartmans (Grace & Paul Hartman) (1) ✿; *Scene 2* Hank Ladd (2) (he was a monologist and introduced the acts); *Scene 3* "Long Green Blues" [Hank Ladd (2)]. The dancers: Nadine Gae & Peter Hamilton (3) (*Marie-Jeanne & Robert Pagent*); *Scene 4* "Up Early with the Upjohns." NETTIE: Grace Hartman (1) ✿; HORACE: Paul Hartman (1) ✿; WILFORD: Robert Stanton (4), *Larry Semon*; CHARLIE: Johnny Barnes (6); LULA BELLE: Elaine

Stritch (7); *Scene 5* "Holler Blue Murder." Sung by Eileen Barton (8) (*Eugenie Baird*); *Scene 6* Reminiscences [Hank Ladd (2)]; *Scene 7* Professor De Marco and Company [The Hartmans (1) ✮]; *Scene 8* "Breezy." Sung by Patricia Jones (*Mildred Fenton*) & Bill McGraw (*Tommy Morton*). Danced by Nadine Gae & Peter Hamilton (3) (*Marie-Jeanne & Robert Pagent*)]; *Scene 9* "Swingeasy." THE KILLER: Hank Ladd; LEFTY: Robert Stanton (4), *Larry Semon*; THE KID: Johnny Barnes (6); THE STRANGER: Paul Hartman (1) ✮; 3 "GONE CATS": Viola Roache, Janet Gaylord, Alan Green; *Scene 10* "Civilization" (Bongo, Bongo, Bongo). Sung by Elaine Stritch (7)] [this song was already a big hit]; *Scene 11* "Apoliagia" [Hank Ladd (2)]; *Scene 12* "The Glamorous Ingabord." A parody of singer Hildegarde. HEADWAITER: Bill McGraw (9), *Tommy Morton*; MRS. TIDWORTH: Viola Roache (5), *Dulcie Cooper*; MR. TIDWORTH III: Robert Stanton (4), *Larry Semon*; MRS. BLODGETT: Grace Hartman (1) ✮; MR. BLODGETT: Paul Hartman (1) ✮; WAITER: Johnny Barnes (6); Ingabord: Elaine Stritch (7). *Act II: Scene 1* "Tambourine." Sung by Eileen Barton (8) (*Eugenie Baird*). Dance: Johnny Barnes (6)]. Assisted by Hank Ladd (2); *Scene 2* "Trailer Trouble." GEORGE: Paul Hartman (1) ✮; CHARLIE: Johnny Barnes (6); RUTH: Grace Hartman (1) ✮; MILLY: Elaine Stritch (7); LT JACKSON: Robert Stanton (4), *Larry Semon*, JOE: Bill McGraw (9), *Tommy Morton*; *Scene 3* "If it Were Easy to Do." Sung by Eileen Barton (8) (*Eugenie Baird*). Danced by Nadine Gae & Peter Hamilton (3) (*Marie-Jeanne & Robert Pagent*)]; *Scene 4* "The Serious Note" [Hank Ladd (2)]; *Scene 5* "The Thousand Islands Song" ("I Left My Love on One of the Thousand Islands"). Sung by Hank Ladd (2) and: FLORENCE: Nadine Gae (3), *Marie-Jeanne*; *Scene 6* "The Salina Select Garden Club." Dauntless explorers interpret a native dance to a group of ladies at a garden club. MRS. SCHULTZ: Viola Roache (5), *Dulcie Cooper*; MRS. HUTCHINSON: Grace Hartman (1) ✮; DR. HUTCHINSON, W.T.: Paul Hartman (1) ✮; SCENE 7 "The Big Brass Band from Brazil" (Entire Company).

It got great Broadway reviews. The Hartmans won the first ever Tonys for best actor and actress in a musical. Paul also won a Donaldson Award.

20. *Ankles Aweigh*

Wynne, a starlet, is making a movie on location in Sicily. Her boyfriend is a navy lieutenant, who she marries, thus violating part of her movie contract. Helped by her sister Elsey and two of her husband's navy pals, Wynne is smuggled aboard her husband's ship, which then sails for French Morocco, where the lieutenant is accused of being a spy. A throwback to the old burlesque material of 1920s and 30s. The Kean Sisters impersonated the Gabor Sisters, Mary Martin in *Peter Pan* and Marlene Dietrich.

Before Broadway. Oscar Hammerstein II (nicknamed Oc) and his partner Richard Rodgers (nicknamed Dick) invested money in this show. During rehearsals Lew Parker (who married Betty Kean) replaced Myron McCormick in the cast. The show tried out in New Haven, where Mark Dawson replaced Sonny Tufts. Fred F. Finklehoffe was replaced as coproducer by Anthony B. Farrell. Jerome Robbins tried to doctor it for two weeks during the Boston tryout, but it was a flop as it hit Broadway at the same time that producers Reginald Hammerstein (Oc's brother) and Howard Hoyt quit.

The Broadway Run. MARK HELLINGER THEATRE, 4/18/55–9/17/55. 176 PERFORMANCES. PRESENTED BY Howard Hoyt, Reginald Hammerstein, Anthony Brady Farrell; MUSIC: Sammy Fain; LYRICS: Dan Shapiro; BOOK: Guy Bolton & Eddie Davis; DIRECTOR: Fred F. Finklehoffe; CHOREOGRAPHER: Tony Charmoli; SETS/LIGHTING: George Jenkins; COSTUMES: Miles White; MUSICAL DIRECTOR/ CHORAL DIRECTOR: Salvatore Dell'Isola; VOCAL & ORCHESTRAL ARRANGEMENTS: Don Walker; DANCE MUSIC DEVISER: Roger Adams; ADDITIONAL DANCE MUSIC DEVISER: Donald Pippin; PRESS: George Ross & Madi Blitzstein; CASTING: Jack Lenny; GENERAL MANAGER: Jesse Long; STAGE MANAGERS: Neil Hartley & Herman Shapiro. *Cast:* RUSS: Ed Hanley; CAMERA MAN: Ray Mason; TOMMY: Bill Costin; PIZZA CART MAN: Frank Conville; ELSEY: Betty Kean (1); WYNNE: Jane Kean (1); DINKY: Lew Parker (2); SPUD: Gabriel Dell (4); LT BILL KELLEY: Mark Dawson (3);

NATIVE GIRL: Nancy Walters; CAPTAIN ZIMMERMAN: Mark Allen; ADMIRAL POTTLES: Will Hussung; CHIPOLATA: Thelma Carpenter (6); JOE MANCINNI: Mike Kellin (5); TONY: Herb Fields; LUCIA: Betty George; THE DUCHESS: Karen Shepard; SHORE PATROL: Skeet Guenther; DANCERS: Dick Alderson, Sandi Bonner, Hank Brunjes, Gene Carrons, Don Emmons, Patty Fitzsimmons, Skeet Guenther, Marilyn Marsh, Meri Miller, Marianne Olsen, Jack Purcell, Marsha Rivers, John Smolko, Nina Starkey, Gloria Stevens, Jack Timmers, Patricia White, Ethel Winter; SINGERS: Marilynn Bradley (7), Thelma Dare, Herb Fields, Henry Hamilton, Warren Kemmerling, Michael King, Ellen McCown, Virginia Martin, Ray Mason, Janet Pavek, Jack Rains, Karen Shepard, Hobe Streiford, Nancy Walters. ***Understudies***: Wynne: Virginia Martin; Bill: Ray Mason; Dinky: Frank Conville; Spud: Ed Hanley; Chipolata: Karen Shepard. *Act I: Scene 1* Montefino, the piazza; afternoon: "Italy" (Boys & Girls), "Old-Fashioned Mothers" (Elsey & Wynne), "Skip the Build-Up" (Elsey & Dinky), "Nothing at All" (Wynne & Bill), "Walk Like a Sailor" (Wynne, Dinky, Spud, Girls, Elsey, Hank Brunjes, Skeet Guenther); *Scene 2* USS *Alamo*, below decks; that night; *Scene 3* El Dahli night spot, Morocco; early the next morning: "Headin' for the Bottom (Blues)" (Chipolata, Girls, Night Spot Patrons), "Nothing Can Replace a Man" (Wynne & Boys), "Here's to Dear Old Us" (Elsey, Dinky, Spud); *Scene 4* A bedroom in El Dahli: "His and Hers" (Wynne & Bill); *Scene 5* Montefino, the piazza: "La Festa" (Natives, Boys, Girls). Soloist: Ray Mason. *Act II: Scene 1* Hotel Argento, Montefino; next day: "Ready Cash" (Croupiers & Gamblers), "Kiss Me and Kill Me with Love" (Wynne & Bill), "Honeymoon" (Elsey & Girls), "The Villain Always Gets It" (Boys & Girls); *Scene 2* A street in Montefino: "The Code" (Joe's Henchmen); *Scene 3* Joe's room; *Scene 4* Aboard the USS *Alamo*; the following night: "Walk Like a Sailor" (reprise) (Dancing Boys & Girls), "Eleven O'clock Song" (Elsey & Wynne), Finale (Entire Company).

It got very bad Broadway reviews. The show was simply outdated before it began, even though Walter Winchell and Ed Sullivan both defended it. It continued only at the expense of Anthony Brady Farrell (owner of the Mark Hellinger Theatre; he had kicked *Plain and Fancy* out to accommodate this musical), but it finally closed when the cast started to leave. Equity agreed to let Mr. Farrell institute salary cuts, so Jane Kean, Mark Dawson and Thelma Carpenter (featured singer) quit, leaving Betty Kean to play sister to an understudy. The show continued to pile up expenses as it ran, and closed to a deficit of $340,000 on an investment of $275,000.

After Broadway. GOODSPEED OPERA HOUSE, Conn, 1989. NEW BOOK: Charles Busch; DIRECTOR/CHOREOGRAPHER: Dan Siretta; SETS: Eduardo Sicangco; NEW MUSICAL ARRANGEMENTS: Tom Fay. *Cast:* RUSSELL: Peter Bartlett; LORRAINE: D'Jamin Bartlett; GLORIA: Monica Carr; DINKY: Ken Lundie; SPUD: Bobby Clark; BILL: Mark McGrath; ADMIRAL: Kevin Cooney; JOE: Bob Cuccioli; LUCIA: Debbie Petrino; ALSO WITH: Maria Calabrese, Aimee Turner. Critics hated it; audiences liked it.

21. *Anna Karenina*

Anna's obsessive love for Vronsky leads to her doom.

The Broadway Run. CIRCLE IN THE SQUARE UPTOWN, 8/26/92–10/4/92. 18 previews from 8/11/92. 46 PERFORMANCES. PRESENTED BY Circle in the Square; MUSIC: Daniel Levine; LYRICS/BOOK: Peter Kellogg; ADAPTED FROM the novel by Leo Tolstoy; DIRECTOR: Theodore Mann; CHOREOGRAPHER: Patricia Birch; SETS: James Morgan; COSTUMES: Carrie Robbins; LIGHTING: Mary Jo Dondlinger; SOUND: Fox & Perla; MUSICAL DIRECTOR/DANCE MUSIC ARRANGEMENTS: Nicholas Archer; ORCHESTRATIONS: Peter Matz; PRESS: Maria Somma & Patty Onagan; CASTING: Judy Henderson & Alycia Aumuller; COMPANY MANAGER: Susan Elrod; PRODUCTION STAGE MANAGER: Wm Hare; STAGE MANAGER: Jack Gianino. *Cast:* COUNT ALEXIS VRONSKY: Scott Wentworth (3) ✮; ANNA KARENINA: Ann Crumb (1) ✮; CONSTANTINE LEVIN: Gregg Edelman (7); TRAIN CONDUCTOR: David Pursley; PRINCE STEPHEN OBLONSKY (STIVA): Jerry Lanning (4); PRINCESS KITTY SCHERBATSKY: Melissa Errico (5); DUNYASHA, KITTY'S MAID: Naz Edwards; KORSUNSKY, MASTER OF CEREMONIES: Gabriel Barre; MEN AT

THE BALL: Larry Hansen & Ray Wills; GUARD AT THE STATION: Larry Hansen; MASHA, WOMAN AT THE STATION: Amelia Prentice; SERYOZHA KARENIN, ANNA'S SON: Erik Houston Saari (6); ANNUSHKA, KARENIN'S MAID: Darcy Pulliam; NICOLAI KARENIN, ANNA'S HUSBAND: John Cunningham (2) ✩; FYODOR, A SERVANT: David Pursley; BASSO: David Pursley; PRINCESS ELIZABETH TVERSKY (BETSEY): Jo Ann Cunningham; WOMAN AT PARTY: Naz Edwards; FINANCE MINISTER: Ray Wills; MAN AT PARTY: Gabriel Barre; PRINCE YASHVIN, A CAPTAIN: Ray Wills; VASILIY, VRONSKY'S SERVANT: Larry Hansen; LEVIN'S FOREMAN: David Pursley; PEASANT: Gabriel Barre; GINA, ITALIAN NURSE: Amelia Prentice. *Understudies*: Anna: Melissa Errico; Vronsky: Ray Wills; Kitty: Amelia Prentice; Karenin: Larry Hansen; Levin: Gabriel Barre; Stiva: David Pursley. *Swings*: Jonathan Cerullo & Audrey Lavine. *Extras*: Jeremy Black & Billy Hipkins. *Orchestra*: PIANOS: Nicholas Archer & David Geist; WOODWINDS: Walter Kane & Edward Zuhlke; TRUMPET: Lorraine Cohen-Moses; CELLO: Beverly Lauridsen; PERCUSSION: David Carey. *Act I*: Russia; 1870s: *Prologue* St. Petersburg Train Station: "On a Train" (Anna, Vronsky, Levin, Chorus); *Scene 1* Moscow Train Station; next morning: "There's More to Life Than Love" (Stiva & Anna); *Scene 2* Kitty Scherbatsky's house; later the same day: "How Awful" (Kitty), "Would You?" (Levin), "In a Room" (Levin, Kitty, Anna, Vronsky); *Scene 3* A ball; a few days later: Waltz and Mazurka (Anna, Kitty, Vronsky, Stiva, Chorus); *Scene 4* A small station between Moscow & St. Petersburg; the next night; *Scene 5* Anna's house in St. Petersburg: "Nothing Has Changed" (Anna); *Scene 6* Prince Tversky's home; that night: "Lowlands" (Basso); *Scene 7* Croquet lawn; several weeks later: "Rumors" (Chorus); *Scene 8* Kitty's house: "How Many Men" (Kitty); *Scene 9* A small dance in St. Petersburg: "We Were Dancing" (Vronsky); *Scene 10* On the way home: "I'm Lost" (Anna); *Scene 11* Anna's house: "Karenin's List" (Karenin); *Scene 12* Vronksy's apartment: "Waiting for You" (Anna & Vronsky). *Act II*: Russia & Italy; 1870s: *Scene 1* Anna's house; three months later: "This Can't Go On" (Anna, Vronsky, Karenin); *Scene 2* Levin's estate and Italy: "Peasant's Idyll" (Chorus) [cut during previews], "That Will Serve Her Right" (Levin); *Scene 3* A villa in Rome: "Everything's Fine" (Anna & Vronksy); *Scene 4* Kitty's house: "Would You?" (reprise)(Levin & Kitty); *Scene 5* A hotel in Moscow: "Everything's Fine" (reprise) (Anna); *Scene 6* Karenin's house: "Only at Night" (Karenin); *Scene 7* St. Petersburg Train Station: Finale (Anna & Chorus).

Several actors were singled out by Broadway reviewers for their great voices, but the show was given generally bad reviews. It received Tony nominations for score, book, and for Gregg Edelman and Ann Crumb.

22. *Annie*

Set in New York City during the Depression. Annie, an 11-year-old red-headed girl escapes, with her dog Sandy, from the orphanage and the awful matron Miss Hannigan; through the services of secretary Grace, she is invited to spend Christmas with Grace's boss, Warbucks, the richest man in America. Warbucks becomes very fond of Annie and adopts her, after failed efforts by Miss Hannigan to reclaim her.

Before Broadway. Several movies about the comic strip *Little Orphan Annie* had been made: in 1919; 1932 (with Mitzi Green as Annie and Edgar Kennedy as Warbucks); 1938 (Anne Gillis as Annie; Budd Schulberg one of the screenwriters). In 1971, after buying *Arf: The Life and Hard Times of Little Orphan Annie*, an anthology of strips of the character, Martin Charnin conceived the idea of a musical of *Little Orphan Annie*. He obtained the rights from the *Chicago Tribune*, and brought in Thomas Meehan and Charles Strouse; by mid-1973 they had written a new story involving only the three recurring comic characters in the strip. i.e. Annie, Daddy Warbucks and Sandy the dog. But they couldn't raise the money. It first ran at the Goodspeed Opera House, Connecticut, from 8/10/76 (previews from 8/8/76). It was panned. Mike Nichols, who saw the show and loved it, came in as the guiding genius and helped transform it. On 1/22/77 rehearsals began for pre-Broadway tryouts. Dorothy Loudon also came aboard. The original Annie (Kristen Vigard) was fired (Martin Charnin could see "no sadness in her"), and replaced by Andrea McArdle, who had been cast as Pepper. Miss McArdle learned

the role in three days, and got a standing ovation. It tried out at the Kennedy Center, Washington, DC, 3/5/77–4/2/77 (previews from 3/1/77). During this run it played at the White House and became the favorite of Jimmy Carter. After Washington it went to Broadway.

The Broadway Run. ALVIN THEATRE, 4/21/77–9/13/81; ANTA THEATRE, 9/16/81–10/24/81; EUGENE O'NEILL THEATRE, 10/29/81–12/6/81; URIS THEATRE, 12/10/81–1/2/83. Total of 2,377 PERFORMANCES. A production of Irwin Meyer, Stephen R. Friedman, Lewis Allen, Alvin Nederlander Associates (James M. Nederlander), in association with Peter Crane, the John F. Kennedy Center for the Performing Arts (Roger L. Stevens), Icarus Productions (Mike Nichols), PRESENTED BY Mike Nichols; MUSIC: Charles Strouse; LYRICS: Martin Charnin; BOOK: Thomas Meehan; BASED ON Harold Gray's *New York Daily News* comic strip (since 8/5/24) *Little Orphan Annie*; DIRECTOR: Martin Charnin; CHOREOGRAPHER: Peter Gennaro; SETS: David Mitchell; COSTUMES: Theoni V. Aldredge; LIGHTING: Judy Rasmuson; SOUND: Herb Syers; MUSICAL DIRECTOR: Peter Howard, *Arnold Gross* (80–82); ORCHESTRATIONS: Philip J. Lang; DANCE MUSIC ARRANGEMENTS: Peter Howard; CAST RECORDING on Columbia; PRESS: David Powers & Barbara Carroll; CASTING: *Peter Cereghetti*; Sandy & Arf owned & trained by William Berloni; GENERAL MANAGERS: Gatchell & Neufeld; COMPANY MANAGER: Drew Murphy (gone by 80–81), *Dennis Durcell* (by 77–78), *Douglas C. Baker* (78–81), *Steven H. David* (80–81), *Sandy Carlson*; PRODUCTION STAGE MANAGER: Janet Beroza (77–79), *Brooks Fountain* (from 79); STAGE MANAGER: Jack Timmers, *Barrie Moss* (from 79); ASSISTANT STAGE MANAGER: Patrick O'Leary (77–81), *Roy Meachum* (gone by 80–81), *Steven David* (79–80), *Larry Mengden* (from 80). *Cast:* THE (SIX) ORPHANS: MOLLY: Danielle Brisebois, *Jennine Babo* (from 78–79), *Roxanne Dundish* (from 80); PEPPER: Robyn Finn, *Penny Marie Chaney* (from 78–79), *Jenn Thompson* (from 79–80), *Caroline Daly* (80–82), *Stephanie Vine* (82–83); DUFFY: Donna Graham, *Randall Ann Brooks* (from 79–80), *Stacey Lynn Brass* (80–81), *Sherry Dundish* (81–83); JULY: Janine Ruane, *Kathy-Jo Kelly* (77–78), *Sarah Jessica Parker* (from 78–79), *Jodi Ford* (from 78–79), *Martha Byrne* (80–82), *Becky Snyder* (82–83); TESSIE: Diana Barrows, *Kim Fedena* (from 78–79), *Tiffany Blake* (from 78–79), *Jennine Babo* (81–83); KATE: Shelley Bruce, *Kim Fedena* (78), *Karen Schleifer* (78–80), *Tara Kennedy* (80–82), *Nicole Nowicki* (82–83); ANNIE: Andrea McArdle (1) ✩, *Shelley Bruce* (from 3/7/78), *Sarah Jessica Parker* (from 3/6/79), *Allison Smith* (from 1/29/80), *Alyson Kirk* (from 9/8/82); MISS AGATHA HANNIGAN: Dorothy Loudon (3) ✩, *Alice Ghostley* (from 8/15/78), *Dolores Wilson* (from 8/21/79), *Alice Ghostley* (from 1/29/80), *Betty Hutton* (9/17/80–10/8/80), *Alice Ghostley*, *Marcia Lewis* (from 4/29/81), *Ruth Kobart* (during Miss Lewis's vacation 2/24–3/10/82), *June Havoc* (from 10/6/82); BUNDLES MCCLOSKEY: James Hosbein, *R. Martin Klein* (by 79–80); APPLE SELLER: David Brummel (by 79–80), *Timothy Jecko* (from 80–81) [a new role by 79–80]; 1ST DOG CATCHER: Steven Boockvor, *Gary Gendell* (by 77–78), *Larry Ross* (by 79–80); 2ND DOG CATCHER: Donald Craig, *Richard Walker* (by 79–80); SANDY: Sandy; LT WARD: Richard Ensslen; HARRY: Raymond Thorne, *Alfred Toigo* (from 78–79), *Raymond Thorne* (by 79–80); SOPHIE THE KETTLE: Laurie Beechman, *Chris Jamison* (from 78–79), *Shelly Burch* (from 79–80), *Beth McVey* (from 81–82); GRACE FARRELL: Sandy Faison (4) ✩, *Lynn Kearney* (from 1/22/79), *Mary Bracken Phillips* (from 8/79), *Kathryn Boule* (from 7/29/80), *Anne Kerry* (from 4/29/81), *Lauren Mitchell* (from 1/13/82); DRAKE: Edwin Bordo; MRS. PUGH: Edie Cowan, *Henrietta Valor* (by 80–81), *Lola Powers* (from 81–82); MRS. GREER: *Ann Ungar* (by 80–81), *Donna Thomason* (by 80–81) [a new role by 79–80]; CECILLE: Laurie Beechman (7), *Chris Jamison* (from 78–79), *Edie Cowan* (by 79–80), *Marianne Sanazaro* (by 80–81); ANNETTE: Penny Worth, *Ann Ungar* (77–78), *Chris Jamison* (by 79–80), *Shelly Burch* (from 79–80), *Beth McVey* (from 81–82); OLIVER "DADDY" WARBUCKS: Reid Shelton (2) ✩, *Keene Curtis* (during Mr. Shelton's vacation, 2/6/78–2/27/78), *John Schuck* (during Mr. Shelton's vacation, 7/3/79–7/24/79), *Keene Curtis* (from 79), *John Schuck* (from 12/25/79), *Harve Presnell* (12/17/80–1/7/81), *John Schuck*, *Rhodes Reason* (from 6/23/81), *Harve Presnell* (from 9/1/81); A STAR TO BE: Laurie Beechman (7); ROOSTER HANNIGAN: Robert Fitch (5) ✩, *Gary Beach* (from 1/29/80), *Richard Sabellico* (from 4/29/81), *Guy Stroman* (during Mr. Sabellico's vacation, 81–82), *Bob Morrissey* (from 8/4/82), *Michael Calkins* (from 9/19/82); LILY: Barbara Erwin (8), *Annie McGreevey* (from 9/78), *Barbara Erwin* (from 5/29/79), *Rita Rudner* (from 1/29/80), *Dorothy*

Stanley (from 2/11/81); BERT HEALY: Donald Craig, *Richard Ensslen* (by 80–81); FRED MCCRACKEN: Bob Freschi, *John Deyle* (from 78–79), *Larry Ross* (by 80–81); JIMMY JOHNSON: Steven Boockvor, *Gary Gendell* (by 77–78), *David Brummel* (by 79–80), *Timothy Jecko* (from 80–81); SOUND EFFECTS MAN: James Hosbein, *R. Martin Klein* (from 79–80); BONNIE BOYLAN: Laurie Beechman (7), *Chris Jamison* (from 78–79), *Ann Ungar* (by 79–80), *Donna Thomason* (by 80–81); CONNIE BOYLAN: Edie Cowan, *Marianne Sanazaro* (by 80–81); RONNIE BOYLAN: Penny Worth, *Ann Ungar* (by 77–78), *Chris Jamison* (by 79–80), *Shelly Burch* (from 79–80), *Beth McVey* (from 81–82); NBC PAGE: Mari McMinn, *Edie Cowan* (by 79–80), *Henrietta Valor* (by 80–81), *Lola Powers* (from 81–82); KALTENBORN'S VOICE: Donald Craig; FDR: Raymond Thorne (6), *Alfred Toigo* (during Mr. Thorne's absence, 78–79), *Tom Hatten* (during Mr. Thorne's vacation, 8/18/82–8/31/82); HAROLD ICKES: James Hosbein, *R. Martin Klein* (by 79–80); LOUIS HOWE: Bob Freschi, *John Deyle* (from 78–79), *David Brummel* (by 79–80), *Timothy Jecko* (from 80–81); HENRY MORGENTHAU: Richard Ensslen; CORDELL HULL: Donald Craig, *Richard Walker* (by 79–80); FRANCES PERKINS: Laurie Beechman, *Chris Jamison* (from 78–79), *Edie Cowan* (by 79–80), *Henrietta Valor* (by 80–81), *Lola Powers* (from 81–82); HONOR GUARD: Steven Boockvor, *Gary Gendell* (by 77–78), *Larry Ross* (by 79–80); JUSTICE BRANDEIS: Richard Ensslen; HOOVERVILLE-ITES/POLICEMEN/WARBUCKS' SERVANTS/NEW YORKERS: Laurie Beechman, Steven Boockvor, Edwin Bordo, Edie Cowan, Donald Craig, Richard Ensslen, Barbara Erwin, Bob Freschi, James Hosbein, Mari McMinn, Penny Worth. ***Standby***: Annie: Kristen Vigard (77–78). **Understudies**: Annie: Shelley Bruce (77–78), *Diana Barrows* (by 77–78), *Tiffany Blake* (by 79–80), *Becky Snyder* (from 81); Warbucks: Raymond Thorne; Miss Hannigan: Penny Worth (77–78), *Henrietta Valor* (79–81), *Lola Powers* (from 81); Grace: Mari McMinn (77–78), *Donna Thomason* (from 79); Rooster: Steven Boockvor (77–78), *Gary Gendell* (78), *Larry Ross* (from 79); Duffy/Pepper/Kate/Tessie: Janine Ruane (77–78), *Kim Fedena* (77–78), *Laura Kerr* (79–80), *Sonia Bailey* (80–81), *Stephanie Vine* (from 81); Molly: Shelley Bruce (77–78), *Tara Kennedy* (79–80), *Sherry Dundish* from 80); July: Donna Graham (77–78), *Laura Kerr* (79–80), *Stephanie Vine* (from 81); FDR: Donald Craig (77–78), *Roy Meachum* (from 79); Harry: Donald Craig (77–78); Lily: Edie Cowan (77–78), *Jane Robertson* (79–81), *Beth McVey* from 81; Drake: Bob Freschi (77–78), *Timothy Jecko* (from 80); Bert: Bob Freschi (77–78), *Richard Walker* (from 79); Sandy: Arf (77–78), *O'Malley* (80–81), *Honey* (from 81); Ensemble Alternates: Don Bonnell (77–82), *Barrie Moss* (79–80), *Roy Meachum* (79–82), *Jane Robertson* (79–81), *Mimi Wallace* (81–82). **Act I**: Dec. 11–19, 1933: *Scene 1* The New York Municipal Orphanage (Girls' Annex): "Maybe" (Annie), "It's the Hard Knock Life" (Annie & Orphans), "It's the Hard-Knock Life" (reprise) (Orphans); *Scene 2* St. Marks Place: "Tomorrow" (Annie) [the big hit]; *Scene 3* A Hooverville under the 59th Street Bridge: "We'd Like to Thank You (Herbert Hoover)" (Hooverville-ites); *Scene 4* The Orphanage: "Little Girls" (Miss Hannigan); *Scene 5* The Warbucks Mansion at 5th Avenue and 82nd Street: "I Think I'm Gonna Like It Here" (Grace, Annie, Drake, Cecille, Annette, Mrs. Pugh, Servants); *Scene 6* New York City: "N.Y.C." (Warbucks, Grace, Annie, Star-to-Be, New Yorkers); *Scene 7* The Orphanage: "Easy Street" (Miss Hannigan, Rooster, Lily); *Scene 8* Warbucks's study: "You Won't Be an Orphan for Long" (Grace, Drake, Mrs. Pugh, Cecille, Annette, Servants, Warbucks). **Act II**: Dec. 21–25, 1933: *Scene 1* NBC Radio Studio at 30 Rockefeller Center; the Orphanage: "You're Never Fully Dressed without a Smile" (Bert Healy, Boylan Sisters, "The Hour of Smiles" Family); *Scene 2* The Orphanage: "You're Never Fully Dressed without a Smile" (reprise) (Orphans), "Easy Street" (reprise) (Miss Hannigan, Rooster, Lily); *Scene 3* Washington: The White House: "Tomorrow" (reprise) (Annie, FDR, Warbucks, Cabinet); *Scene 4* The Great Hall at the Warbucks Mansion: "Something Was Missing" (Warbucks), "I Don't Need Anything but You" (Warbucks & Annie); *Scene 5* The East Ballroom at the Warbucks Mansion: "Annie" (Grace, Drake, Staff), "Maybe" (reprise) (Annie), "A New Deal for Christmas" (Annie, Warbucks, Grace, FDR, Staff).

Annie was rapturously received by critics and public. It won Tonys for musical, score, book, choreography, sets, costumes, and for Dorothy Loudon, and was nominated for direction of a musical, and for Reid Shelton and Andrea McArdle. The show paid back its initial investment of $800,000 in just eight months. On 3/24/79 14-year-old Sarah Jessica Parker, playing Annie, broke a tooth mid-song, and had to be replaced by

her understudy. In 12/79 Sarah Jessica Parker, then playing Annie, was fired, the producers claiming she had outgrown the role. That wasn't all. 14 other cast members were replaced. The producers said they wanted to refresh the show. Equity was disturbed by this, and brought in a new rule to stop this sort of thing. In 9/81 the show was kicked out of the Alvin to make way for the incoming *Merrily We Roll Along*. In 1/82 Irwin Meyer and Stephen Friedman, two of the producers of *Annie*, and also co-owners of the 46th Street Theatre, got six-month prison terms for a tax shelter scam. On the last night of *Annie*, when the curtain went down, Martin Charnin announced that a sequel would be made. *Annie* became the third-longest running Broadway musical of the 1970s, and made a $20 million profit.

After Broadway. TOUR. Opened on 3/23/78 at the O'Keefe, Toronto, and closed on 9/6/81, at the Kennedy Center, Washington, DC. MUSICAL DIRECTOR: Glen Clugston. *Cast*: ANNIE: Kathy-Jo Kelly, *Dara Brown* (1/79–2/8/79), *Kathy-Jo Kelly, Mary K. Lombardi* (from 4/79), *Theda Stemler* (from 9/30/80), *Louanne* (from 5/20/81), *Becky Snyder*; HANNIGAN: Jane Connell, *Ruth Kobart*; SANDY: Sandy; GRACE: Kathryn Boule, *Jan Pessano, Ellen Martin, Kathleen Marsh, Martha Whitehead* (from 11/25/80); WARBUCKS: Norwood Smith, *John Schuck* (for a week); ROOSTER: Gary Beach, *Bob Morrisey, Michael Calkins* (from 8/26/80); LILY: Lisa Raggio, *Dorothy Holland, Jacalyn Switzer, Pamela Matteson* (from 7/15/80); FDR: Sam Stoneburner, *Stephen Everett, Randall Robbins* (from 8/26/80).

TOUR. Opened on 6/22/78, at the Curran Theatre, San Francisco. MUSICAL DIRECTOR: Milton Greene. *Cast*: ANNIE: Patricia Ann Patts, *Louanne, Marisa Morell, Kristi Coombs* (from 12/29/80), *Regina Meredith*; HANNIGAN: Jane Connell; SANDY: Sandy, *Buttercup*; GRACE: Kathryn Boule, *Lisa Robinson, Krista Neumann* (from 1/7/81), *Ann Peck* (from 10/13/81); WARBUCKS: Keene Curtis, *Reid Shelton* (from 12/28/79); ROOSTER: Swen Swenson, *Tom Offt, Michael Calkins* (from 9/30/81), *Gary Beach* (from 4/30/82); LILY: Connie Danese, *Jacalyn Switzer, Edie Cowan, Dorothy Holland, Linda Lauter, Maggy Gorrill* (from 11/4/80), *Linda Manning* (from 11/3/81); FDR: Tom Hatten, *Alan Wikman* (from 12/17/80), *Randall Robbins* (from 12/22/81).

TOUR. Opened on 10/3/79, at the State Fair Music Hall, Dallas. MUSICAL DIRECTOR: Arthur Greene. *Cast*: KATE: Mollie Hall, *Alyson Kirk, Sharon Jordan*; ANNIE: Rosanne Sorrentino, *Bridget Walsh* (from 3/27/81); HANNIGAN: Patricia Drylie, *Kathleen Freeman* (from 3/27/81); SANDY: Sandy, *Moose*; GRACE: Deborah Jean Templin, *Lauren Mitchell* (from 3/27/81), *Kathryn Boule* (from 1/13/82); WARBUCKS: Harve Presnell, *Jack Collins* (12/17/80–1/7/81), *Harve Presnell, Rhodes Reason* (from 8/31/81); ROOSTER: Michael Leeds, *Dennis Parlato* (from 10/4/80), *J.B. Adams* (from 8/25/81), *Jon Rider* (from 2/22/82); LILY: Katharine Buffaloe, *Wendy Kimball* (from 10/4/80); FDR: Jack Denton, *David Green* (from 3/29/82).

TOUR. Opened on 7/31/81, at the Kennedy Center, Washington, DC, and closed there on 9/5/81. It re-opened on 9/11/81, at Eisenhower Hall, West Point, NY. *Cast*: ANNIE: Mollie Hall, *Kathleen Sisk* (from 8/31/82); HANNIGAN: Ruth Williamson; SANDY: Roxanne; GRACE: Lynne Wintersteller, *Donna Thomason* (from 9/12/82); WARBUCKS: Ron Holgate, *Gary Holcombe* (from 9/12/82); ROOSTER: Guy Stroman, *William McClary* (from 4/6/82), *Dick Decareau* (from 9/26/82); LILY: Ann Casey; FDR: William Metzo.

LONDON. Opened on 5/3/78. 1,485 PERFORMANCES. *Cast*: ANNIE: Andrea McArdle, *Anne-Marie Gwatkin* (from 6/78); HANNIGAN: Sheila Hancock, *Maria Charles* (from 7/79); GRACE: Judith Paris; WARBUCKS: Stratford Johns; ROOSTER: Kenneth Nelson; LILY: Clovissa Newcombe; FDR: Damon Sanders.

THE MOVIE. 1982. Ray Stark purchased the rights for Columbia for $9.5 million, a record at that time. The movie, directed by John Huston, flopped, and its failure hurt the long-running Broadway show. It cost $40 million. There were four new songs: "Sign," "We Got Annie," "Dumb Dog" (a re-hash of the Strouse—Adams number "Together," which had been used in their 1978 Broadway failure *A Broadway Musical*) and "Let's Go to the Movies" (a new Strouse—Charnin number that replaced "N.Y.C."). The movie did not use "Annie," "A New Deal for Christmas," "Something Was Missing," "We'd Like to Thank You (Herbert Hoover)," "You Won't Be an Orphan for Long." *Cast*: ANNIE: Aileen Quinn; WARBUCKS: Albert Finney; HANNIGAN: Carol Burnett; LILY: Bernadette Peters; GRACE: Ann Reinking; ALSO WITH: Tim Curry.

TOUR. Opened on 1/3/86, at the Auditorium, Rochester, NY. DIRECTOR: Sam A. Jerriss; CHOREOGRAPHER: Carla Roetzer Vitale; MUSICAL DIRECTOR: Corinne Jerriss Aquilina. *Cast:* ANNIE: Sarah Bethany Reynolds; HANNIGAN: Teri Gibson; WARBUCKS: Robert Tiffany; MOLLY: Erin Daly; GRACE: Leslie Castay; SANDY: Moose. *Understudies*: Annie: Stephanie Kae Seeley; Warbucks: Michael Mulheren.

Annie 2: Miss Hannigan's Revenge. This was the first *Annie* sequel. Set in 1934, six weeks after the ending of the original *Annie*. Miss Hannigan escapes detention after being jailed for trying to defraud Warbucks. She plots revenge on Annie and Warbucks. Warbucks has been ordered by Congresswoman Christmas, head of United Mothers of America, to find a mother for Annie within 90 days, or lose her. He figures Grace (played by Lauren Mitchell) is too young for him, so he instigates a national competition. Hannigan teams with ex-con Lionel McCoy, who falls in love with her. He becomes one of Warbucks' chauffeurs. Hannigan plans to marry Warbucks, and get rid of him and Annie. A big make-up job by Lionel's friend Maurice makes Hannigan look like a winner. She turns up at Yankee Stadium, where the results are going to be determined, posing as Charlotte O'Hara, and is chosen as a finalist. Hannigan finds tough street kid Kate, who is Annie's double; she is substituted for the real Annie, who is kidnapped at Coney Island. Hannigan wins the contest & is about to be married to Warbucks, but at the last moment Grace uncovers the plot & rescues Annie from drowning. Warbucks then marries Grace. "1934," "You Ain't Seen the Last of Me," "A Younger Man," "How Could I Ever Say No?," "The Lady of the House," "Beautiful," "He Doesn't Know I'm Alive," "You! You! You!," "When You Smile," "Just Let Me Get Away with This One," "Coney Island," "All I've Got is Me," "Cortez," "Tenement Lullaby," "I Could Get Used to This." On 9/11/89 open auditions were held in New York to find an actress to play Annie in this sequel. 11-year-old Danielle Findley was chosen. It first ran at the KENNEDY CENTER, Washington, DC, 1/4/90–1/20/90. Previews from 12/22/89. Kennedy Center previews were greeted by stunned silence (it was that bad). DIRECTOR: Martin Charnin; CHOREOGRAPHER: Danny Daniels; SETS: David Mitchell; COSTUMES: Theoni V. Aldredge; LIGHTING: Ken Billington; SOUND: Abe Jacob; MUSICAL DIRECTOR: Peter Howard; ORCHESTRATIONS: Michael Starobin; ADDITIONAL ORCHESTRATIONS: Larry Wilcox. *Cast:* ANNIE: Danielle Findley; HANNIGAN: Dorothy Loudon; WARBUCKS: Harve Presnell; FDR: Raymond Thorne; SANDY: Beau; MRS. MARIETTA CHRISTMAS: Marian Seldes; LIONEL McCOY: Ronny Graham; GRACE: Lauren Mitchell; DRAKE: Terrence P. Currier; FELIX FRANKFURTER: Laurent Giroux; LUPE: Corinne Melancon; NUSSBAUM/ED/BARNEY SULLIVAN/FORD BOND: Bill Nolte; SLAM/MISS MELISSA DABNEY: Karen Murphy; EUBANKS/HOT DOG VENDOR: Don Percassi; DETENTION GUARD: Dorothy Stanley; PEABODY/PIANIST/JENKINS: Bobby Clark; MYRNA: Karen L. Byers; PATSY: Mary-Pat Green; DEUTCH/SGT CLANCY/KALTENBORN: J.K. Simmons; TICKTIN/ARNOLD: Michael Duran; ROCHELLE: Sarah Knapp; MARIE: Michelle O'Steen; PUNJAB: Gerry McIntyre; THE ASP: Fiely Matias; BABE RUTH: T.J. Meyers; MAURICE: Scott Robertson; WALTER S. DOBBINS/FATHER PULLAM/FLETCHER/SEAMAN: Brian Everat Chandler; MONICA: Juliana Marx; FUNGO: Courtney Earl; FISHMONGERS: Mary-Pat Green & Ellyn Arons; LEE DeFOREST: Oliver Woodall; FIORELLO LaGUARDIA: Michael Cone; AIDE: Jane Bodle. It got terrible reviews. Mike Nichols, Tommy Tune and Peter Stone all offered suggestions. There were many changes during the run at Kennedy Center, and after a month had altered considerably. It never reached Broadway, where it was not only scheduled (at the Marquis Theatre, for 3/1/90) but had racked up $4 million in advance sales (it had already cost $7 million to make).

Annie 2. The disaster *Annie 2: Miss Hannigan's Revenge* was revised at a workshop, as *Annie 2,* then produced at the GOODSPEED OPERA HOUSE, Conn., 5/17/90–7/8/90, during which enormous changes in book, score and cast were made. Commissioner Stark was now the villain, and Miss Hannigan was eliminated as a character. Fran Riley was Stark's sister who insinuates her way into Warbucks' bed. "He'll Be Here," "When You Smile," "Changes," "Perfect Kid," "That's the Kind of Woman," "A Younger Man," "But You Go On," "Rich Girls," "Annie Two," "He Doesn't Know," "If I Wasn't Around," "I Can Do No Wrong," "Live a Long, Long Time," "All Dolled Up," "Cortez," "Tenement Lullaby," "Isn't This the Way to Go," "My Daddy," Finale. DIRECTOR: Mar-

tin Charnin; CHOREOGRAPHER: Peter Gennaro; COSTUMES: Theoni V. Aldredge; LIGHTING: Ken Billington; MUSICAL DIRECTOR: Steven M. Alper. *Cast:* ANNIE: Lauren Gaffney; SANDY: Chelsea; WARBUCKS: Harve Presnell; COMMISSIONER MARGARET G. STARK: Marian Seldes; FDR: Raymond Thorne; FRANCES RILEY: Helen Gallagher; DRAKE: Scott Robertson; HENRY DRUMMOND: Laurent Giroux; MISS SHERMAN/ABIGAIL DABNEY: Karen Murphy; CECILLE/GLENDA: Paula Leggett. It was planned to bring the new show to Broadway for the 1990–91 season, but they couldn't find the money.

Annie Warbucks. This was the second *Annie* sequel, variously and unofficially known as *Annie 3.* First it was workshopped at the Goodspeed Opera House, Conn. Warbucks must find a wife within 60 days in order to make his adoption of Annie stick. "When You Smile," "Above the Law," "Changes," "The Other Woman," "That's the Kind of Woman," "A Younger Man," "'Cause of You," "But You Go On," "Everything is Nothing without You," "Love," "Somebody's Gotta Do Somethin'," "You Owe Me, Tootsie," "All Dolled Up," "Tenement Lullaby," "It Would Have Been Wonderful," "I Guess Things Happen for the Best," "The Day They Say I Do," Finale (these songs were re-arranged on tour). As a production it had its world premiere at MARRIOTT'S LINCOLNSHIRE THEATRE, 1/29/92. Then it played Chicago, then went off on a nationwide tour, but it never made Broadway. DIRECTOR: Martin Charnin; CHOREOGRAPHER: Pete Gennaro; SETS: Thomas M. Ryan; COSTUMES: Nancy Missimi; LIGHTING: Diane Ferry Williams; SOUND: Randy Allen Johns; MUSICAL DIRECTOR: Michael Duff. *Cast:* ANNIE WARBUCKS: Lauren Gaffney; SANDY: Chelsea; OLIVER WARBUCKS: Harve Presnell; GRACE FARRELL: Jennifer Nees, *Marguerite MacIntyre*; ALVIN T. PATTERSON: Kingsley Leggs, *M.W. Reid*; FDR: Raymond Thorne. There were also several other new characters. It then ran Off Broadway, at VARIETY ARTS THEATRE, 8/9/93–1/30/94. 38 previews from 7/6/93. 200 PERFORMANCES. DIRECTOR: Martin Charnin; CHOREOGRAPHER: Pete Gennaro; SETS: Ming Cho Lee; COSTUMES: Theoni V. Aldredge; LIGHTING: Ken Billington; SOUND: Tom Sorce; ORCHESTRATIONS: Keith Levenson; CAST RECORDING on: Angel. *Cast:* ANNIE: Kathryn Zaremba; SANDY: Cindy Lou; WARBUCKS: Harve Presnell; GRACE: Marguerite MacIntyre; DRAKE: Kip Niven; MRS. PUGH/DR. MARGARET WHITTLEBY: Brooks Almy; SIMON WHITEHEAD: Joel Hatch; MOLLY: Ashley Pettet; PEPPER: Missy Goldberg; TESSIE: Elisabeth Zaremba; KATE: Rosie Harper; PEACHES: Natalia Harris; MRS. SHEILA KELLY: Donna McKechnie; WARBUCKS' ACCOUNTANTS: Michael E. Gold & Steve Steiner; FLETCHER/DAVID LILIENTHAL/MR. STANLEY: Michael E. Gold; HARRY/SENATOR ARTHUR I. VANDENBERG: Steve Steiner; COMMISSIONER HARRIET DOYLE: Alene Robertson; MISS CLARK/GLADYS: Colleen Fitzpatrick; TRAINMAN/MAN IN STETSON HAT: J.B. Adams; HOBOES: Steve Steiner & Jennifer Neuland; ALVIN: Harvey Evans; C.G. PATTERSON: Jackie Angelescu; ELLA PATTERSON: Molly Scott; FDR: Raymond Thorne. "A New Deal for Christmas," "Annie isn't Just Annie Anymore," "Above the Law," "Changes," "The Other Woman," "That's the Kind of Woman," "A Younger Man," "But You Go On," "When You Smile," "I Got Me," "Love," "Somebody's Gotta Do Somethin'," "Leave it to the Girls," "All Dolled Up," "Tenement Lullaby," "It Would Have Been Wonderful," "Wedding, Wedding," "I Always Knew." *Annie Warbucks* got a big revival at the WALNUT STREET THEATRE, Philadelphia, 9/14/04–10/24/04. Previews from 9/7/04. DIRECTOR: Charles Abbott; CHOREOGRAPHER: Mary Jane Houdina; SETS: Charles S. Kading; COSTUMES: Colleen McMillan; MUSICAL DIRECTOR/VOCAL DIRECTOR: Sherman Frank. *Cast*: WARBUCKS: Patrick Quinn; GRACE: Amy Bodnar; FDR: John-Charles Kelly; ANNIE: Andie Belkoff & Christiana Anbri; SHEILA KELLY: Mary Martello; COMMISSIONER DOYLE: Alene Robertson.

23. *Annie (Broadway revival)*

Before Broadway. This 20th anniversary Broadway production was part of a national tour. The tour and Broadway stint were announced on 4/24/96. Although Martin Charnin directed, this was a separate production from another 1996 Goodspeed production that he also directed. A new number had been added: "You Make Me Happy" (Hannigan & Grace), the first song in Act I, Scene 7 (this song didn't work, and never made it into the *Annie* canon). Act I Scene 2 was now Lower Broadway;

the Hooverville in Act I Scene 3 was now near the East 10th Street Gas Works; the setting of Act I Scene 6 was now From Fifth Avenue to Times Square. The 2nd song in Act II Scene 2 was a reprise of "Easy Street" (Hannigan, Rooster, Lily). The tour opened on 11/29/96, at Theatre Under the Stars, Houston (TUTS) (previews from 11/26/96), and closed on 3/9/97, in Montreal. The tour had same basic crew and cast as for the subsequent Broadway run, with the notorious exception of Joanna Pacitti, who played Annie 106 times from the beginning of the tour until 2/23/97, when the producers fired her for not acting well enough. 12-year-old Miss Pacitti had won the role in a national competition held at Macy's, in New York City (Andrea McArdle, the original Annie, was one of the judges who helped pick her), and sued Macy's in a long, drawn-out case which she finally lost. Miss McArdle and Dorothy Loudon both sided with Miss Pacitti. Miss Pacitti's understudy, 8-year-old Brittny Kissinger, replaced her on 2/25/97. If later rumors were true that Miss Pacitti had been offered an alternating role with Brittny Kissinger, then she didn't take it up (later that year she did play Annie in a regional production in Raleigh, NC). Zappa, who had been playing Sandy on tour, was demoted to understudy in favor of Cindy Lou when it came to Broadway. Roz Ryan played Hannigan on tour, and was replaced by Nell Carter on 1/3/97. For part of the tour Sally Struthers stood in for Miss Carter, Lisa Gunn stood in for Colleen Dunn as Grace, and Laurent Giroux stood in for Jim Ryan as Rooster. After the tour closed in Montreal, it went to Broadway, where previews began on 3/14/97 (the date was put back from 3/13/97). The show had been due to open on Broadway on 3/27/97, but that date was brought forward a day.

The Broadway Run. MARTIN BECK THEATRE, 3/26/97–10/19/97. 14 previews from 3/14/97. 238 PERFORMANCES. PRESENTED BY Timothy Childs & Rodger Hess, Jujamcyn Theatres, in association with Terri B. Childs & Al Nocciolino; MUSIC: Charles Strouse; LYRICS: Martin Charnin; BOOK: Thomas Meehan; BASED ON the comic strip *Little Orphan Annie*; DIRECTOR: Martin Charnin; CHOREOGRAPHER: Peter Gennaro; SETS: Kenneth Foy; COSTUMES: Theoni V. Aldredge; LIGHTING: Ken Billington; SOUND: T. Richard Fitzgerald; MUSICAL SUPERVISOR/MUSICAL DIRECTOR: Keith Levenson; ORIGINAL ORCHESTRATIONS: Philip J. Lang; PRESS: Peter Cromarty & Company; CASTING: Stuart Howard & Amy Schecter; ANIMALS: William Berloni; GENERAL MANAGER: Marvin A. Krauss; COMPANY MANAGERS: Kim Sellon & Kathleen Turner; PRODUCTION STAGE MANAGER: Bryan Young; STAGE MANAGER: Jeffrey M. Markowitz; ASSISTANT STAGE MANAGER: Becky Garrett. **Cast**: ANNIE: Brittny Kissinger (3); MOLLY: Christiana Anbri (until 7/26/97), *Kristen Alderson* (from 8/97); PEPPER: Cassidy Ladden; DUFFY: Mekenzie Rosen-Stone (until 7/26/97), *Bianca Collins* (from 8/97); JULY: Casey Tuma; TESSIE: Lyndsey Watkins (until 7/26/97), *Courtney Leigh* (from 8/97); KATE: Melissa O'Malley (until 7/26/97), *Jemini Quintos* (from 8/97); MISS HANNIGAN: Nell Carter (1) ☆, *Barbara Tirrell* (8/21/97– 8/26/97 during Miss Carter's hernia operation); BUNDLES MCCLOSKEY: Michael E. Gold; APPLE SELLER: Brad Wills; DOG CATCHERS: Tom Treadwell & Sutton Foster; SANDY: Cindy Lou; SGT THAYER: Michael E. Gold; LT WARD: Drew Taylor; SOPHIE THE KETTLE: Barbara Tirrell; FRED: Tom Treadwell; GRACE FARRELL: Colleen Dunn (5); DRAKE: MichaelJohn McCann; MRS. PUGH: Barbara Tirrell; CECILLE: Sutton Foster; MRS. GREER: Elizabeth Richmond; ANNETTE: Kelley Swaim; OLIVER "DADDY" WARBUCKS: Conrad John Schuck (2) ☆ [this was John Schuck; he added his father's name to his own in 1997]; A STAR TO BE: Sutton Foster; ROOSTER HANNIGAN: Jim Ryan (6); LILY: Karen Byers-Blackwell (7); BERT HEALY: MichaelJohn McCann; FRED MCCRACKEN: Brad Wills; JIMMY JOHNSON: Tom Treadwell; SOUND EFFECTS MAN: Michael E. Gold; BONNIE BOYLAN: Elizabeth Richmond; CONNIE BOYLAN: Kelley Swaim; RONNIE BOYLAN: Sutton Foster; OXYDENT *Hour of Smiles* PRODUCER: Jennifer L. Neuland; H.V. KALTENBORN'S VOICE: Bryan Young; FDR: Raymond Thorne (4); ICKES: Brad Wills; HOWE: Tom Treadwell; HULL: Drew Taylor; PERKINS: Barbara Tirrell; MORGENTHAU: MichaelJohn McCann; HONOR GUARD: Michael E. Gold; JUSTICE BRANDEIS: Drew Taylor; HOOVERVILLE-ITES/WARBUCKS' STAFF/NEW YORKERS: Sutton Foster, Michael E. Gold, MichaelJohn McCann, Jennifer L. Neuland, Elizabeth Richmond, Kelley Swaim, Drew Taylor, Barbara Tirrell, Tom Treadwell, Brad Wills. **Understudies**: Annie/Tessie/Pepper/Duffy/July: Alexandra Kiesman; Warbucks: Drew Taylor; Grace: Kelly Swaim & Christy Tarr; Lily: Jennifer L. Neuland & Christy Tarr; Hannigan: Barbara Tirrell; FDR: Tom Treadwell; Rooster: Michael E. Gold;

Molly: Mekenzie Rosen-Stone; Kate: Casey Tuma; Sandy: Zappa (until 7/26/77), Sparky. **Swings**: J.B. Adams & Christy Tarr. **Orchestra**: VIOLIN: Blair Lawhead; CELLO: Marisol Espada; TRUMPETS: Donald Downs & Craig Johnson; TROMBONE: Joseph Petrizzo; TUBA: Alan Raph; SAXOPHONES: Vincent Della Rocca, Timothy Ries, Donald Haviland; BASS: Ray Kilday; FLUTE: Marco Granados; GUITAR: Ed Hamilton; DRUMS: Mark Mule; KEYBOARDS: Christine Cadarette & Anne Shuttlesworth.

Broadway reviews were divided, mostly negative. This revival of *Annie* was nominated for a Tony as best revival of a *musical*. On 7/26/97 Christiana Anbri and Melissa O'Malley were fired; Mekenzie Rosen-Stone and Lyndsey Watkins left voluntarily; Zappa was zapped. During the run the producers shortened the show by 15 minutes (to 2½ hours), which included cutting a few scenes and "We'd Like to Thank You (Herbert Hoover)." On 7/21/97 it was announced that the show would close at the Sunday matinee, 10/26/97, in order to continue with the tour. Actually it closed early, at the evening performance of 10/19/97.

After Broadway. CONTINUATION OF THE TOUR. The tour resumed the day after the show closed on Broadway, at the Performing Arts Center, Providence, Rhode Island, with the Broadway cast intact. After three months of touring Sally Struthers replaced Nell Carter on 1/5/98. Lisa Gunn replaced Colleen Dunn as Grace, and Kay Story replaced her on 7/30/98; Laurent Giroux replaced Jim Ryan as Rooster. The tour ended in 3/99.

VICTORIA PALACE THEATRE, London, 9/30/98–2/28/99. Previews from 9/22/98. DIRECTOR: Martin Charnin. **Cast**: ANNIE: Charlene Barton; HANNIGAN: Lesley Joseph; WARBUCKS: Kevin Colson.

TV. *Wonderful World of Disney*, 11/7/99. This was a new $10 million TV production. All of the Broadway score was used except: "We'd Like to Thank You," "You Won't Be an Orphan for Long," "Annie," "A New Deal for Christmas." WRITER: Irene Mecchi; DIRECTOR/CHOREOGRAPHER: Rob Marshall. **Cast**: ANNIE: Alicia Morton; HANNIGAN: Kathy Bates; PEPPER: Marissa Rago; ROOSTER: Alan Cumming; GRACE: Audra McDonald; STAR TO BE: Andrea McArdle; MR. BUNDLES: Ernie Sabella; LILY: Kristin Chenoweth; WARBUCKS: Victor Garber.

PAPER MILL PLAYHOUSE, New Jersey, 11/1/02–12/8/02. This was the 25th Anniversary production. Previews from 10/30/02. DIRECTOR: Greg Ganakas; CHOREOGRAPHER: Linda Goodrich; MUSICAL DIRECTOR: Tom Helm. **Cast**: ANNIE: Sarah Hyland; WARBUCKS: Rich Hebert; HANNIGAN: Catherine Cox; ROOSTER: Jim Walton; LILY ST. REGIS, ROOSTER'S GIRLFRIEND: Tia Speros; GRACE: Crista Moore; FDR: Eric Michael Gillett; SANDY: Buster; ENSEMBLE: Kenneth Kantor, Anna McNeely.

FOX THEATRE, Atlanta, 1/14/04–1/18/04. PRESENTED BY Theatre Under the Stars, Atlanta; DIRECTOR: Martin Charnin. **Cast**: ANNIE: Christiana Anbri; HANNIGAN: Marcia Lewis-Bryan; WARBUCKS: Conrad John Schuck. The orphan chorus was boosted in size from the regular 6 to 20. The number "We'd Like to Thank You, Herbert Hoover" was in it (some regional productions omit this one). This production featured (for the first time in the U.S.A.) the new song "Why Should I Change a Thing?" (Warbucks), which Martin Charnin had written the lyrics for at the suggestion of Anthony Warlow, who had starred in the 1999 Australian production which Mr. Charnin directed in Sydney and Melbourne (the 15th time Mr. Charnin had directed a production of *Annie*). Charles Strouse wrote the music for this new song, and the song will go into the *Annie* canon. After Atlanta the show went on a small tour: Columbus, Hartford, Detroit.

TOUR. This planned Equity tour was to open in 8/05 in San Francisco. DIRECTOR: Martin Charnin. It used the new song "Why Should I Change a Thing?" It was aiming for Broadway.

24. *Annie Get Your Gun*

Annie Oakley (1860–1926), an illiterate hillbilly sharpshooter from near Cincinnati, is persuaded to join Buffalo Bill's traveling Wild West show. She falls for star marksman, Frank, whom she eclipses as the ace shot. She shoots out candles while riding on a motorcycle at Minneapolis Fair Grounds. Frank quits, and joins Pawnee Bill's Far East Show. Chief Sitting Bull, delighted with Annie, adopts her into his Sioux tribe, and even invests in Buffalo

Bill's show. Annie and the show tour Europe with spectacular success. Annie is decorated by most of the leading monarchs. But the show is broke. Annie realizes Buffalo Bill and Pawnee Bill must merge to survive. She sells her medals to raise funds. While performing at Governors Island, New York, she realizes, thanks to Sitting Bull, that the only way to win her man is to let him win.

Before Broadway. Dorothy Fields came up with the idea of a musical about Annie Oakley, for her and her brother Herbert to do the lyrics, and for Jerome Kern to do the music. She visited Ethel Merman, who was in the hospital after the birth of her daughter, and Miss Merman agreed to play the role. After Mike Todd rejected the idea, the lyricists took it to Rodgers and Hammerstein, who agreed to produce. Jerry Kern died of a stroke on 11/11/45, the day after he arrived in New York City from California, so they went for Irving Berlin. At first they hesitated because Mr. Berlin always wrote his own lyrics, and the Fieldses were already set as lyricists (Mr. Berlin finally wrote the music and lyrics). Moreover, Mr. Berlin, used to writing old-fashioned musicals which revolved around the songs, rather than the new fashioned way of integrating all the elements of a musical into the story, wasn't sure he could learn these new tricks in time. However, the producers gave him the script and urged him to try. He came up with 10 songs in 8 days, including (according to Josh Logan) "Anything You Can Do, I Can Do Better" during a taxi ride. He almost discarded "(There's No Business Like) Show Business" when he felt Rodgers and Hammerstein weren't excited enough about it. It turned out to be Mr. Berlin's most successful show. The tryouts in New Haven and Boston were well-received. The original Broadway debut date of 4/25/46 was postponed for three weeks due to a structural fault at the Imperial. During a run-through several large pieces of overhanging scenery had crashed to the stage, nearly killing Richard Rodgers. The Shuberts, who owned the Imperial, quickly booked the show into their Philadelphia theatre while repairs were made. Rumors began that the crash was faked, that the show was in trouble. The numbers "With Music" and "Take it in Your Stride (Whatever the Fates Decide)" were both cut before Broadway. "Let's Go West" was cut too, but published separately in 1949. *Annie Get Your Gun* was the only hit musical Rodgers & Hammerstein produced that they themselves did not write.

The Broadway Run. IMPERIAL THEATRE, 5/16/46–2/12/49. 1,147 PERFORMANCES. PRESENTED BY Richard Rodgers & Oscar Hammerstein II; MUSIC/LYRICS: Irving Berlin; BOOK: Herbert & Dorothy Fields; DIRECTOR: Joshua Logan; ASSISTANT DIRECTOR: Ruth Mitchell; CHOREOGRAPHER: Helen Tamiris; ASSISTANT CHOREOGRAPHER: Daniel Nagrin; SETS/LIGHTING: Jo Mielziner; COSTUMES: Lucinda Ballard; MUSICAL DIRECTOR: Jay S. Blackton; ORCHESTRA DIRECTOR: John Passaretti; ORCHESTRATIONS: Philip J. Lang, Russell Bennett, Ted Royal; VOCAL ARRANGEMENTS: Joe Moon; PIANO ARRANGEMENTS: Helmy Kresa; CAST RECORDING on Decca. It featured Ethel Merman and Ray Middleton, but virtually no one else from the actual musical; PRESS: Michel Mok; CASTING: John Fearnley; GENERAL MANAGER: Morris Jacobs; COMPANY MANAGER: Maurice Winters; GENERAL STAGE MANAGER: Charles Atkin; STAGE MANAGER: John Sola; ASSISTANT STAGE MANAGER: Beau Tilden. *Cast:* LITTLE BOY: Warren Berlinger, *Clifford Sales*; LITTLE GIRL: Mary Ellen Glass, *Jane Earle* (from 47–48); CHARLIE DAVENPORT: Marty May (4); IRON TAIL: Daniel Nagrin, *Jack Beaber* (alternate from 46–47), *William Weslow* (from 47–48); YELLOW FOOT: Walter John, *Earl Sauvain* (by 6/1/46), *Fred Rivetti* (from 46–47); MAC (PROPERTY MAN): Cliff Dunstan, *Pete Civello* (alternate in 47–48), *Harold Gordon* (from 47–48); 1ST COWBOY: Rob Taylor, *Wes Bowman* (from 47–48), *Robert Nash* (from 47–48); 2ND COWBOY: Bernard Griffin, *Arthur Ulisse* (from 47–48); 3RD COWBOY: Jack Pierce, *Marc West* (by 47–48), *Gordon West* (from 47–48); 1ST COWGIRL: Mary Grey, *Andrea Downing* (from 46–47), *Janice Bodenhoff* (by 47–48), *Ruth Mitchell* (from 47–48); 2ND COWGIRL: Franca Baldwin, *Evelyn Giles* (by 6/1/46), *Margaret Banks* (by 6/1/47), *Gloria Gordon* (from 47–48); FOSTER WILSON: Art Barnett; COOLIE: Beau Tilden, *Phil McEneny* (from 46–47); DOLLY TATE: Lea Penman, *Betty Lou Holland*; WINNIE TATE: Betty Ann Nyman, *Betty Lou Holland* (from 47–48); TOMMY KEELER: Kenny Bowers, *William Skipper* (from 47–48); FRANK BUTLER: Ray Middleton (2); GIRL WITH BOUQUET: Katrina Van Oss, *Barbara Gaye* (from 47–48); ANNIE OAKLEY: Ethel Merman (1) ✩, *Mary Jane Walsh* (alternate in 47–48); MINNIE (ANNIE'S SIS-

TER): Nancy Jean Raab, *Camilla de Witt* (from 46–47), *Marlene Cameron* (from 47–48); JESSIE (ANOTHER SISTER): Camilla de Witt, *Beverly Sales* (from 46–47), *Mary Ellen Glass* (from 47–48); NELLIE (ANOTHER SISTER): Marlene Cameron, *Kam Moran* (from 47–48); LITTLE JAKE (HER BROTHER): Clifford Sales, *Bobby Hookey*, *Clifford Tatum Jr.*(from 46–47); HARRY: Don Liberto, *Robert Dixon* (from 47–48); MARY: Ellen Hanley, *Helene Whitney* (from 46–47), *Barbara Barlow* (by 6/1/47); COL. WILLIAM F. CODY (BUFFALO BILL): William O'Neal; MRS. LITTLE HORSE: Alma Ross; MRS. BLACK TOOTH: Elizabeth Malone; MRS. YELLOW FOOT: Nellie Ranson; TRAINMAN: John Garth III; WAITER: Leon Bibb; PORTER: Clyde Turner; RIDING MISTRESS: Lubov Roudenko; MAJ. GORDON LILLIE (PAWNEE BILL): George Lipton; CHIEF SITTING BULL: Harry Bellaver (3); MABEL: Mary Woodley; LOUISE: Ostrid Lind; NANCY: Dorothy Richards; TIMOTHY GARDNER: Jack Byron, *Pete Civello* (from 46–47); ANDY TURNER: Earl Sauvain, *Joseph Cunneff* (from 46–47); CLYDE SMITH: Victor Clarke, *Noel Gordon* (by 6/1/46); JOHN: Rob Taylor, *Wes Bowman* (from 47–48), *Robert Nash* (from 47–48); FREDDIE: Robert Dixon; WILD HORSE (CEREMONIAL DANCER): Daniel Nagrin, *Jack Beaber* (alternate in 46–47 and 47–48), *William Weslow* (from 47–48); PAWNEE'S MESSENGER: Walter John, *Milton Watson* (by 6/1/46); MAJOR DOMO: John Garth III; 1ST WAITER: Clyde Turner; 2ND WAITER: Leon Bibb; MR. SCHUYLER ADAMS: Don Liberto, *Joseph Cunneff* (from 47–48); MRS. SCHUYLER ADAMS: Dorothy Richards; DR. PERCY FERGUSON: Bernard Griffin, *Arthur Ulisse* (from 47–48); MRS. PERCY FERGUSON: Marietta Vore; DEBUTANTE: Ruth Vrana [role cut 47–48]; MR. ERNEST HENDERSON: Art Barnett; MRS. ERNEST HENDERSON: Truly Barbara, *Rose Marie Elliott* (from 46–47); SYLVIA POTTER-PORTER: Marjorie Crossland; MR. CLAY: Rob Taylor, *Wes Bowman* (from 47–48), *Robert Nash* (from 47–48); MR. LOCKWOOD: Fred Rivetti; GIRL IN PINK: Christina Lind, *Jet MacDonald* (by 6/1/46), *Claire Saunders* (from 46–47), *Christina Lind* (from 46–47), *Pat Dexter* (from 47–48); GIRL IN WHITE: Mary Grey, *Andrea Downing* (from 46–47), *Madeleine Detry* (by 6/1/47); SINGING GIRLS: Truly Barbara (*Rose Marie Elliott*), Ellen Hanley (*Barbara Barlow*), Christina Lind (*Jet MacDonald* by 6/1/46, *Claire Sanders* from 46–47, *Christina Lind* from 46–47, *Pat Dexter* from 47–48), Ostrid Lind, Dorothy Richards, Ruth Strickland, Katrina Van Oss, Marietta Vore, Ruth Vrana, Mary Woodley, *Bernice Saunders*, *Roslynd Lowe*; SINGING BOYS: Jack Byron (*Pete Civello*), Victor Clarke (*Noel Gordon*), Robert Dixon, Bernard Griffin (*Arthur Ulisse*), Marvin Goodis, Vincent Henry, Don Liberto (*Joseph Cunneff*), Fred Rivetti, Earl Sauvain, Rob Taylor (*Wes Bowman*), Ray Hyson, *Edward Pfeiffer*; DANCING GIRLS: Franca Baldwin (*Gloria Gordon*), Tessie Carrano, Madeleine Detry, Cyprienne Gabelman, Barbara Gaye, Evelyn Giles, Mary Grey (*Janice Bodenhoff, Ruth Mitchell*), Harriett Roeder, *Bernice Brady*; DANCING BOYS: Jack Beaber (*William Weslow*), John Begg, Michael Maule, Duncan Noble, Jack Pierce (*Gordon West*), Paddy Stone, Ken Whelan, Parker Wilson. *Dusty McCaffrey.* **Understudies**: Foster/Mac: Wes Bowman; Ernest/Messenger: Wes Bowman; Tommy: Gordon West; Winnie/Riding Mistress: Barbara Gaye; Sylvia: Marietta Vore; Iron Tail/Wild Horse: William Weslow; Trainman/ Major Domo: Leon Bibb. ***Act I*: *Scene 1*** The Wilson House, a summer hotel on the outskirts of Cincinnati, Ohio; July: "(Colonel) Buffalo Bill" (Charlie & Ensemble), "I'm a Bad, Bad Man" (Frank & Girls) (danced by Duncan Noble, Paddy Stone, Parker Wilson, Ensemble), "Doin' What Comes Natur'lly" (Annie, Sisters, Brothers, Wilson) [a hit], "The Girl That I Marry" (Frank) [a big hit], "You Can't Get a Man with a Gun" (Annie) [a hit], "(There's No Business Like) Show Business" (Buffalo Bill, Charlie, Frank, Annie) [the big hit]; *Scene 2* A Pullman parlor in an overland steam train; six weeks later: "They Say it's Wonderful" (Frank & Annie), "Moonshine Lullaby" (Annie & Trio); *Scene 3* The Fair Grounds at Minneapolis, Minnesota; a few days later: "I'll Share it All with You" (tap dance devised by Harry King) (Winnie & Tommy); *Scene 3a* The arena of the Big Tent [sometimes this scene is listed as Scene 4, which altered the numbering of the next two scenes in Act I]: Ballyhoo (danced by Riding Mistress & Show People), "(There's no Business Like) Show Business" (reprise) (Annie), "My Defenses Are Down" (Frank & Boys); *Scene 4* A dressing-room tent; the same day [sometimes this scene is listed as Scene 5]; *Scene 5* The arena of the Big Tent; later that night [sometimes this scene is listed as Scene 6]: Wild Horse Ceremonial Dance (Wild Horse, Braves & Maidens), "I'm an Indian Too" (Annie), Adoption Dance (Annie, Wild

Horse, Braves), "You Can't Get a Man with a Gun" (reprise) (Annie). *Act II*: *Scene 1* The deck of a cattle boat; eight months later: "(I Got) Lost in His Arms" (Annie & Ensemble); *Scene 2* Ballroom of the Hotel Brevoort, New York; next night: "Who Do You Love, I Hope?" (Winnie & Tommy) (danced by Winnie, Tommy, Ensemble), "I'll Share it All with You" (dance) (reprise), "(I Got the) Sun in the Morning" (Annie & Ensemble) (danced by Lubov Roudenko, Daniel Nagrin, Show People), "They Say it's Wonderful" (reprise) (Annie & Frank), "The Girl that I Marry" (reprise) (Frank); *Scene 3* Aboard a ferry, en route to Governor's Island; next morning; *Scene 4* Governor's Island. Near the Fort; immediately following: "Anything You Can Do (I Can Do Better)" (Annie & Frank) [a big hit], "(There's No Business Like) Show Business" (reprise) (Entire Company).

On Broadway opening night the audience, expecting a troubled show, were polite but not effusive during Act I, but during Act II they loosened up and began to enjoy it. Brooks Atkinson, the *New York Times* theatre critic, called the book, dances and songs "undistinguished," but all the critics loved Merman. The show won Donaldson Awards for music, lyrics, director, and for Ethel Merman. Miss Merman made $3,000 a week, plus 10 per cent of the gross. Irving Berlin got $2,500 a week from the box office, $100,000 from the original cast album, $500,000 from the sheet music and $650,000 from the movie rights. It was the most expensive musical to that time. Annie Get Your Gun was the third-longest running Broadway musical of the 1940s.

After Broadway. COLISEUM, London, 6/7/47–4/29/50. 1,304 PERFORMANCES. PRESENTED BY Helen Tamiris; DIRECTOR: Charles Hickman; CHOREOGRAPHER: Helen Tamiris; ASSISTANT CHOREOGRAPHER: Daniel Nagrin. Aside from the two stars, it was an all-British cast. *Cast:* IRON TAIL: Paddy Stone, *Tony Repetski*; DOLLY: Barbara Babington; WINNIE: Wendy Toye, *Nancy Willard*; TOMMY: Irving Davies; FRANK: Bill Johnson; ANNIE: Dolores Gray; BUFFALO BILL: Ellis Irving, *Robert Moore*; SITTING BULL: John Garside; SCHUYLER: Bernard Quinn; SYLVIA: Betty Hare.

FIRST AUSTRALASIAN TOUR. Took in: His Majesty's Theatre, Melbourne, 7/19/47–5/12/48; Theatre Royal, Adelaide, 5/15/48–7/10/48; His Majesty's Theatre, Brisbane, 7/13/48–8/21/48; Theatre Royal, Sydney, 8/27/48–8/31/49. Then to NZ, where it played 12 cities, then back to Australia: His Majesty's Theatre, Brisbane, 3/3/50–4/1/50; Empire Theatre, Perth, 4/10/50–5/20/50; Theatre Royal, Adelaide, 5/25/50–6/8/50; His Majesty's Theatre, Melbourne, 6/10/50–7/11/50; Empire Theatre, Sydney, 7/13/50–8/23/50. PRESENTED BY J.C. Williamson's. DIRECTOR: Carl Randall. *Cast:* CHARLIE: Carl Randall, *Peter French, Robert Healey*; DOLLY: Marie La Verre, *Shirley Mae Donald*; WINNIE: Elizabeth Gaye, *Ann Donald, Maggie Fitzgibbon*; TOMMY: Billy Kershaw, *Donald Kirk*; FRANK: Webb Tilton, *Earl Covert, Hayes Gordon*; ANNIE: Evie Hayes; BUFFALO BILL: Claude Fleming; PAWNEE BILL: Charles Crawford, *Frank Martin, Graeme Bent*; SITTING BULL: Sydney Wheeler, *Alec Kellaway*.

FIRST U.S. TOUR. Opened in 10/47, and closed in 1949, after 19 months. *Cast:* FRANK: John Raitt; ANNIE: Mary Martin, *Billie Worth*. Mary Martin won a special 1948 Tony Award for bringing the show to so many people.

THE MOVIE. 1950. The numbers "Who Do You Love, I Hope" and "Moonshine Lullaby" were cut. *Cast:* CHARLIE: Keenan Wynn; DOLLY: Benay Venuta; FRANK: Howard Keel; ANNIE: Betty Hutton [Judy Garland had been first choice]; BUFFALO BILL: Louis Calhern; PAWNEE BILL: Edward Arnold; SITTING BULL: J. Carroll Naish.

Annie du Far-West. The French production ran for a year at the THEATRE DU CHATELET, Paris, 1950. *Cast:* Lili Fayol, Marcel Merkes.

NEW AUSTRALASIAN TOUR. Took in: His Majesty's Theatre, Melbourne, 7/5/52–7/31/52; Theatre Royal, Sydney, 12/5/52–1/28/53; Theatre Royal, Adelaide, 4/28/53–5/5/53. *Cast:* WINNIE: Maggie Fitzgibbon; FRANK: Hayes Gordon; ANNIE: Evie Hayes; SITTING BULL: Alec Kellaway.

1957 U.S. TOUR. DIRECTOR: Vincent J. Donehue. *Cast:* DOLLY: Reta Shaw; FRANK: John Raitt; ANNIE: Mary Martin; BUFFALO BILL: William O'Neal. On 11/27/57 it aired on NBC TV. Richard Halliday (Mary Martin's husband) produced.

CITY CENTER, NYC, 2/19/58–3/2/58. 16 PERFORMANCES. PRESENTED BY the New York City Center Light Opera Company; DIREC-TOR: Donald Burr; CHOREOGRAPHER: Helen Tamiris; SETS: George Jenkins; COSTUMES: Florence Klotz; LIGHTING: Peggy Clark; MUSICAL DIRECTOR: Frederick Dvonch. *Cast:* CHARLIE: Jack Whiting; IRON TAIL/WILD HORSE: Stuart Hodes; YELLOW FOOT: Edward Villella; WILSON: Leo Lucker; DOLLY: Margaret Hamilton; WINNIE: Rain Winslow; TOMMY: Richard France; FRANK: David Atkinson; ANNIE: Betty Jane Watson; LITTLE JAKE: Flip Mark; BUFFALO BILL: James Rennie; PORTER/MAJOR DOMO: John Buie; 2ND PORTER: Walter P. Brown; RIDING MISTRESS: Ruthanna Boris; PAWNEE BILL: William Le Massena; SITTING BULL: Harry Bellaver; THE SCHUYLERS: Jack Rains & Basha Regis; SYLVIA: Claire Waring; SINGERS INCLUDED: Patricia Finch, Kenneth Ayers, Ralph W. Farnworth, Sam Kirkham, Casper Roos, Ralph Vucci; DANCERS INCLUDED: Iva March.

25. *Annie Get Your Gun (1966 Broadway revival)*

Before Broadway. Irving Berlin wrote a new number for this 20th-Anniversary production: "An Old Fashioned Wedding." He cut "Who Do You Love, I Hope" and "I'll Share it All with You." Also, the songs and dances performed by the young lovers were cut, as the young lovers were no longer in the show. "Who Needs the Birds and Bees," composed by Mr. Berlin for this revival, was cut. The book was slightly revised, and the secondary love interest was cut. Certain characters, notably Winnie, were cut, and there was some re-arranging of the order of characters. This revival first ran at the NEW YORK STATE THEATRE, 5/31/66–7/9/66. 47 PERFORMANCES. It had the same basic crew as for the subsequent Broadway run, except that associate conductor Jonathan Anderson took over from Franz Allers for the Broadway run; same cast too, except Jaclynn Villamil (Mrs. Black Tooth) and Jaime Rogers (Wild Horse). Also Vicki Belmonte and Ronn Carroll were dropped from the singing chorus when it came time to move to Broadway; and three members of the dancing chorus: Jaclynn Villamil, Anne Wallace, and Jeremy Ives (there was only one replacement in this section: Carolyn Dyer). There was some criticism that Ethel Merman was too old to play love scenes with the much younger Bruce Yarnell (some wags dubbed the show *Granny Get Your Gun*), but the show received glowing reviews. Many felt it was better than the original. After its New York State Theatre run it went on a brief tour, and re opened on Broadway.

The Broadway Run. BROADWAY THEATRE, 9/21/66–11/26/66. 78 PERFORMANCES. PRESENTED BY Music Theatre of Lincoln Center (Richard Rodgers, president and producing director); MUSIC/LYRICS: Irving Berlin; ORIGINAL BOOK: Herbert & Dorothy Fields; BOOK REVISED BY: Dorothy Fields; DIRECTOR: Jack Sydow; CHOREOGRAPHER: Danny Daniels; SETS: Paul C. McGuire; COSTUMES: Frank Thompson; LIGHTING: Peter Hunt; MUSICAL DIRECTOR: Jonathan Anderson; ORCHESTRATIONS: Robert Russell Bennett; DANCE MUSIC ARRANGEMENTS: Richard De Benedictis; PRESS: Richard Maney, Frank Goodman, Martin Shwartz; GENERAL MANAGER: Henry Guettel; COMPANY MANAGER: Ronald Bruguiere; PRODUCTION STAGE MANAGER: William Ross; STAGE MANAGERS: J.P. Regan, Charles Blackwell, Iris O'Connor. *Cast:* LITTLE BOY: Jeffrey Scott; LITTLE GIRL: Deanna Melody; CHARLIE DAVENPORT: Jerry Orbach, *Jim Lynn*; DOLLY TATE: Benay Venuta; IRON TAIL: Brynar Mehl; YELLOW FOOT: Gary Jendell; MAC: John Dorrin; FOSTER WILSON: Ronn Carroll; FRANK BUTLER: Bruce Yarnell (2); THE SHY GIRL: Diana Banks; ANNIE OAKLEY: Ethel Merman (1); LITTLE JAKE (HER BROTHER): David Manning; HER (THREE) SISTERS: NELLIE: Donna Conforti; JESSIE: Jeanne Tanzy; MINNIE: Holly Sherwood; COL. WM F. CODY (BUFFALO BILL): Rufus Smith; MRS. LITTLE HORSE: Mary Falconer; MRS. BLACK TOOTH: Eva Marie Sage; MRS. YELLOW FOOT: Kuniko Narai; INDIAN BOY: Jeffrey Scott; CONDUCTOR: Jim Lynn, *Ben Laney*; PORTER: Beno Foster; WAITER: David Forssen; MAJ. GORDON LILLIE (PAWNEE BILL): Jack Dabdoub; CHIEF SITTING BULL: Harry Bellaver; THE WILD HORSE: Tony Catanzaro; PAWNEE'S MESSENGER: Walt Hunter; MAJOR DOMO: Ben Laney; MR. SCHUYLER ADAMS: Ronn Carroll; MRS. SCHUYLER ADAMS: Patricia Hall; DR. PERCY FERGUSON: Marc Rowan; MRS. FERGUSON: Bobbi Baird; MAJ. T.L.C. "TOMMY" KEELER: Walt Hunter; MR. ERNEST HENDERSON: Grant Spradling; MRS. ERNEST HENDERSON: Lynn Carroll; MRS. SYLVIA POTTER-PORTER: Mary

Falconer; MR. CLAY: John Dorrin; SINGERS: Kenny Adams, Bobbi Baird, Chrysten Carroll, Lynn Carroll, Audrey Dearden, John Dorrin, Lynn Dovel, Mary Falconer, David Forssen, Beno Foster, Patricia Hall, Walt Hunter, Ben Laney, Jim Lynn, Florence Mercer, Marc Rowan, Grant Spradling, Susan Terry; DANCERS: Diana Banks, Bjarne Buchtrup, Tony Catanzaro, Frank Derbas, Joanne Di Vito, Carolyn Dyer, Rozann Ford, Ronn Forella, Marcelo Gamboa, Barbara Hancock, Gary Jendell, Daniel Joel, Ruth Lawrence, Brynar Mehl, Gene Myers, Kuniko Narai, Eva Marie Sage, Evelyn Taylor. ***Standbys***: Annie: Eileen Rodgers; Frank: Jack Dabdoub; Dolly: Iris O'Connor. ***Understudies***: Sitting Bull: Ronn Carroll; Charlie: Jim Lynn; Pawnee Bill: Walt Hunter; Buffalo Bill: John Dorrin; Wild Horse: Ronn Forella; Little Jake: Jeffrey Scott; Minnie: Joanne Di Vito; Nellie/Jessie: Deanna Melody; Wilson/Adams/ Tommy: David Forssen; Mac/Clay: Ben Laney; Porter: Grant Spradling; Waiter/ Major Domo: Marc Rowan; Conductor: Kenny Adams; Mrs. Little Horse/Sylvia/Mrs. Adams: Susan Terry. ***Act I***: ***Scene 1*** The Wilson House, a summer hotel on the outskirts of Cincinnati, Ohio; July: "Colonel Buffalo Bill" (Charlie, Dolly, Ensemble), "I'm a Bad, Bad Man" (Frank & Girls), "Doin' What Comes Naturally" (Annie, Children, Wilson), "The Girl that I Marry" (Frank), "You Can't Get a Man with a Gun" (Annie), "There's No Business Like Show Business" (Annie, Frank, Buffalo Bill, Charlie); ***Scene 2*** A Pullman parlor in an overland steam train; six weeks later: "They Say it's Wonderful" (Annie & Frank), "Moonshine Lullaby" (Annie, Trio, Children); ***Scene 3*** The fair Grounds at Minneapolis, Minnesota; a few days later: Wild West Pitch Dance (Wild Horse & Dancers), "There's No Business Like Show Business" (reprise) (Annie), "My Defenses Are Down" (Frank & Boys); ***Scene 4*** The arena of the Big Tent; later that night: Wild Horse Ceremonial Dance (Wild Horse & Indian Braves), "I'm an Indian Too" (Annie), Adoption Dance (Annie, Wild Horse, Braves), "You Can't Get a Man with a Gun" (reprise). ***Act II***: ***Scene 1*** The deck of a cattle boat; eight months later: "I Got Lost in His Arms" (Annie & Singers); ***Scene 2*** The ballroom of the Hotel Brevoort (New York City), "I Got the Sun in the Morning" (Annie & Company), "Old Fashioned Wedding" (Annie & Frank), "The Girl that I Marry" (reprise) (Frank); ***Scene 3*** Aboard a ferry, en route to Governor's Island; the next morning; ***Scene 4*** Governor's Island, near the fort; immediately following: "Anything You Can Do" (Annie & Frank), "There's No Business Like Show Business" (reprise) (Ensemble), Finale: "They Say it's Wonderful" (reprise) (Entire Company).

This revival was nominated for two Tonys: direction of a musical, and choreography. The Broadway production was televised by NBC on 3/19/67.

After Broadway. ***Annie es un Tiro***. The Mexican production opened in Mexico City in 1976. DIRECTOR: Jose Luis Ibanez. **Cast:** ANNIE: Silvia Pinal.

DOROTHY CHANDLER PAVILION, Los Angeles. Opened 6/21/77. 56 PERFORMANCES. PRESENTED BY Cy Feuer & Ernest Martin, for the San Francisco and Los Angeles Civic Light Opera; DIRECTOR: Gower Champion (he also re-structured the musical); CHOREOGRAPHERS: Gower Champion & Tony Stevens; SETS/LIGHTING: Robert Randolph; COSTUMES: Alvin Colt; MUSICAL DIRECTOR: Jack Lee. **Cast:** CHARLIE: Gavin MacLeod; FRANK: Harve Presnell; ANNIE: Debbie Reynolds; ALSO WITH: Art Lund, Bibi Osterwald, Tony Stevens.

JONES BEACH THEATRE, New York, 6/29/78–9/4/78. DIRECTOR: Richard Barstow; CHOREOGRAPHER: Bert Michaels; SETS: Karl Eigsti; LIGHTING: Richard Nelson; MUSICAL DIRECTOR: Jay Blackton. **Cast:** CHARLIE: Don Potter; DOLLY: Travis Hudson; WILSON: Ralph Vucci; FRANK: Harve Presnell; ANNIE: Lucie Arnaz; BUFFALO BILL: Jack Dabdoub; SITTING BULL: Alan North; SYLVIA: Dixie Stewart.

TOUR. The first night of the tour was 3/2/93, in Baltimore, but it opened officially on 3/3/93, at the Houston Grand Opera. PRESENTED BY Tom McCoy, Tom Mallow, ATP/Dodger/PACE Theatrical Group, and the Kennedy Center; DIRECTOR: Susan H. Schulman; CHOREOGRAPHER: Michael Lichtefeld; SETS: Heidi Landesman & Joel Reynolds; COSTUMES: Catherine Zuber; LIGHTING: Ken Billington; MUSICAL DIRECTOR: Brian W. Tidwell. **Cast:** CHARLIE: Paul V. Ames; DOLLY: KT Sullivan, *Robin Lusby*; FRANK: Brent Barrett; ANNIE: Cathy Rigby; SITTING BULL: Mauricio Bustamante; BUFFALO BILL: Erick Devine; SYLVIA: Robin Lusby; THE ADAMSES: Bill Bateman & Lynn Shuck.

VIVIAN BEAUMONT THEATRE, Broadway, 3/8/98. One-concert per-

formance. Guests wore western or casual gear, and there was dinner afterwards at the Tavern on the Green. Cast: FRANK: Peter Gallagher; ANNIE: Patti LuPone; SITTING BULL: Eli Wallach.

26. *Annie Get Your Gun* (1999 Broadway revival)

Before Broadway. In 1997, when plans were being made to bring the show to Broadway again, the two choices to play Annie were Geena Davis and Bernadette Peters. By early 1998 James Naughton was being rumored for the role of Frank. After Patti LuPone played Annie in the 1998 concert at Lincoln Center, her name came up too. But Miss Peters emerged as the only real contender. On 8/6/98 Tom Wopat got the news that he was to be Frank. The book had been slightly revised. A new prologue, with Frank & Company singing "(There's No Business Like) Show Business," and Buffalo Bill's intro to the show's concept was also new. Rehearsals began on 11/2/98. It tried out at the Kennedy Center, in Washington, DC (its only pre-Broadway stop, despite a national tour having been announced earlier), 1/7/99–2/4/99 (previews from 12/29/98). The Broadway opening date of 2/20/99 was pushed back to 3/4/99.

The Broadway Run. MARQUIS THEATRE, 3/4/99–9/1/01. 35 previews from 2/2/99. 1,046 PERFORMANCES. PRESENTED BY Barry & Fran Weissler, in association with Kardana Productions, Michael Watt, Irving Welzer, Hal Luftig; MUSIC/LYRICS: Irving Berlin; ORIGINAL BOOK: Herbert & Dorothy Fields; NEW BOOK/ADDITIONAL MATERIAL: Peter Stone (with Graciela Daniele); DIRECTOR: Graciela Daniele; CHOREOGRAPHERS: Graciela Daniele & Jeff Calhoun; SETS: Tony Walton; COSTUMES: William Ivey Long; LIGHTING: Beverly Emmons; SOUND: G. Thomas Clark; SUPERVISING MUSICAL DIRECTOR/VOCAL & INCIDENTAL MUSIC ARRANGEMENTS: John McDaniel; MUSICAL DIRECTOR/DANCE MUSIC ARRANGEMENTS: Marvin Laird; NEW ORCHESTRATIONS: Bruce Coughlin; NEW CAST RECORDING on Angel, released on 4/20/99; PRESS: Pete Sanders Group; CASTING: Betsy D. Bernstein & Howie Cherpakov, Red Sky Productions, Stuart Howard, Howard Meltzer, Amy Schecter; GENERAL MANAGEMENT: Nina Lannan Associates; COMPANY MANAGER: Michael Gill; STAGE MANAGER: Richard Hester, *Jim Woolley & Rick Steiger*. **Cast:** BUFFALO BILL: Ron Holgate (3), *Christopher Coucill* (from 9/99), *Dennis Kelly* (from 1/00), *Conrad John Schuck*; FRANK BUTLER: Tom Wopat (2) ☆ (until 9/2/00), *Patrick Cassidy* (from 9/6/00), *Brent Barrett* (1/26/01–6/22/01), *Tom Wopat* (from 6/23/01); DOLLY TATE: Valerie Wright (4), *Michelle Blakely, Valerie Wright, Kerry O'Malley*; TOMMY KEELER: Andrew Palermo (6), *Randy Donaldson, Eric Sciotto*; WINNIE TATE: Nicole Ruth Snelson (9), *Emily Rozek, Claci Miller*; MAC, THE PROPMAN: Kevin Bailey, *Tom Schmid*; CHARLIE DAVENPORT: Peter Marx (7) (he was formerly known as Peter Slutsker); FOSTER WILSON: Ronn Carroll (5), *Gerry Vichi*; CHIEF SITTING BULL: Gregory Zaragoza (8), *Kevin Bailey, Larry Storch*; ANNIE OAKLEY: Bernadette Peters (1) ☆, *Susan Lucci* (during Miss Peters' vacation, 12/27/99– 1/16/00; this was Miss Lucci's Broadway debut; Miss Peters returned 1/18/00, and left the show 9/2/00), *Cheryl Ladd* (from 9/6/00), *Reba McEntire* (1/26/01–6/22/01), *Crystal Bernard* (from 6/23/01); (THREE) KIDS: JESSIE OAKLEY: Cassidy Ladden (11), *Jenny Rose Baker, Jewel Restaneo*; NELLIE OAKLEY: Mia Walker (12), *Ashley Rose Orr, Laura M. Gilberson, Blair Restaneo*; LITTLE JAKE: Trevor McQueen Eaton (10), Eddie Brandt, *Nicholas Jonas*; RUNNING DEER: Kevin Bailey, *Tom Schmid*; BALLERINA: Keri Lee; HOOP DANCE SPECIALTY: Adrienne Hurd, Kent Zimmerman; EAGLE FEATHER: Carlos Lopez; DINING CAR WAITER: Brad Bradley; SLEEPING-CAR PORTER: Patrick Wetzel; MOONSHINE LULLABY TRIO: Cleve Asbury, Brian O'Brien, David Villella; PAWNEE BILL (MAJOR GORDON LILLIE): Ronn Carroll (5), *Gerry Vichi*; MESSENGER: Kevin Bailey, *Tom Schmid*; BAND LEADER: Marvin Laird; MRS. SCHUYLER ADAMS: Julia Fowler, *Deanna Dys*; SYLVIA POTTER-PORTER: Jenny-Lynn Suckling, *Kimberly Dawn Neumann*; ENSEMBLE: Shaun Amyot, Kevin Bailey (*Tom Schmid*), Brad Bradley, Randy Donaldson, Madeleine Ehlert, Julia Fowler, Kisha Howard (*Hollie Howard*), Adrienne Hurd (*Kent Zimmerman*), Keri Lee, Carlos Lopez, Desiree Parkman, Eric Sciotto, Kelli Bond Severson, Timothy Edward Smith, Jenny-Lynn Suckling, David Villella, Patrick Wetzel, *Jason Gillman, Elisa Heinsohn, Rommy Sandhu, David*

Eggers, Emily Hsu, Brian O'Brien, Carolyn Ockert. **Standbys**: Annie/ Dolly: Michelle Blakely & Karyn Quackenbush. **Understudies**: Annie: Valerie Wright; Frank: Christopher Coucill (*David Hess*) & Kevin Bailey (*Tom Schmid*); Dolly: Valerie Wright (*Deanna Dys*) & Jenny-Lynn Suckling (*Karyn Quackenbush*); Tommy: Carlos Lopez & Shaun Amyot; Buffalo Bill: Christopher Coucill; Nellie/Jessie: Blair Goldberg, *Ashley Rose Orr, Jewel Restaneo*; Winnie: Keri Lee & Kisha Howard (*Hollie Howard*), Kimberly Dawn Neumann, Kate Levering & *Alice Rietveld*; Sitting Bull/Pawnee Bill/Foster: Kevin Bailey & Patrick Wetzel, *Brad Bradley*; Little Jake: Mia Walker, *Ashley Rose Orr, Jenny Rose Baker, Blair Restaneo*; Charlie: Brad Bradley & Patrick Wetzel; Hoop Dance Specialty: David Villella; "The Girl that I Marry" Dancer: Leasen Beth Almquist. **Swings**: Leasen Beth Almquist (*Jenny-Lynn Suckling*), Patti D'Beck (*Kent Zimmerman*), Rick Spaans. **Orchestra**: TRUMPET I: Chris Jaudes; TRUMPET II: Joe Mosello; TRUMPET III: Larry Lunetta; TENOR TROMBONE: Dale Kirkland; BASS TROMBONE/TUBA: Morris Kianuma; FRENCH HORN: Roger Wendt; BASS: William Ellison; GUITAR/BANJO: Ed Hamilton; PERCUSSION: Beth Ravin; DRUMS: Cubby O'Brien; WOODWINDS I: Les Scott; WOODWINDS II: Morty Silver; WOODWINDS III: Ken Dybisz; WOODWINDS IV: Terrence Cook; WOODWINDS V: John Campo; CONCERTMASTER/STAGE SOLO: Todd Reynolds; VIOLIN II: Victor Schultz; VIOLIN III: Heidi Stubner; VIOLIN IV: Nina Simon; VIOLIN/VIOLA: Richard Clark; CELLO I: Clay Ruede; CELLO II: Marisol Espada; SYNTHESIZER: Nicholas Archer. **Act I**: "There's No Business Like Show Business" (Frank & Company), "Doin' What Comes Natur'lly" (Annie, Kids, Wilson), "The Girl that I Marry" (Frank & Annie), "You Can't Get a Man with a Gun" (Annie), "There's No Business Like Show Business" (reprise) (Frank, Buffalo Bill, Charlie, Annie), "I'll Share it All with You" (Tommy, Winnie, Company), "Moonshine Lullaby" (Annie, Kids, Ensemble Trio), "There's No Business Like Show Business" (reprise) (Annie), "They Say it's Wonderful" (Annie & Frank), "My Defenses Are Down" (Frank & Young Men), The Trick (Annie & Company), Finale Act I: "You Can't Get a Man with a Gun" (reprise) (Annie). **Act II**: Entr'acte (Orchestra); "The European Tour" (Annie & Company), "(I Got) Lost in His Arms" (Annie), "Who Do You Love, I Hope" (Tommy, Winnie, Company), "I Got the Sun in the Morning" (Annie & Company), "An Old Fashioned Wedding" (Annie & Frank), "The Girl that I Marry" (reprise) (Frank), "Anything You Can Do" (Annie & Frank), "They Say it's Wonderful" (reprise) (Annie, Frank, Company), Finale Ultimo (Company).

Broadway reviews were somewhat divided, but generally good. The show won Tonys for revival of a musical and for Bernadette Peters, and Tom Wopat was nominated. Susan Lucci was scheduled to stand in for the vacationing Bernadette Peters from 12/23/99, but was sidelined with flu until 12/27/99. Cheryl Ladd was announced as Annie on 8/10/00. During her tenure box-office receipts dropped off sharply. Reba McEntire was originally due to take over on 1/28/01, but this date was put forward to 1/26/01. Her leaving date was scheduled for 5/27/01, but she was so hot in the role, and box-office receipts were almost back at 100 per cent, that this was extended until 6/22/01. Closing notices were posted on 8/27/01, and the show closed on 9/1/01 (ahead of the scheduled closing date of 10/01).

After Broadway. TOUR. Opened on 7/25/00, at Dallas Music Hall, and closed there on 8/6/00, then continued with the tour. This version was revised yet again. The entr'acte and the number "I'll Share it All with You" were cut. DIRECTOR/CHOREOGRAPHER: Jeff Calhoun. **Cast**: ANNIE: Marilu Henner, *Karyn Quackenbush* (4/3/01–4/15/01), *Crystal Bernard* (from 4/17/01); FRANK: Rex Smith, *Tom Wopat* (from 10/31/00), *Rex Smith* (4/17/01–6/5/01); SITTING BULL: Larry Storch; DOLLY: Susann Fletcher, *Julia Fowler* (from 5/8/01); WILSON/PAWNEE BILL: Charles Goff; CHARLIE: Joe Hart; BUFFALO BILL: George McDaniel; WINNIE: Claci Miller, *Carolyn Ockert* (from 12/27/00); TOMMY: Eric Sciotto, *Randy Donaldson* (from 1/9/01), *Sean Michael McKnight* (from 4/3/01); BUFFALO BILL: George McDaniel.

About 450 stage productions of *Annie Get Your Gun* are done each year in the USA alone.

27. *Anya*

Bounine, former general of Cossacks in the Czarist army, is now a taxi-driver in Berlin. In 1925 he finds a girl in a psychiatric hospital (she'd tried to jump into the river, but had been rescued), and she claims to be Anastasia, youngest daughter of the murdered Czar. They try to pass her off as Anastasia. She and Bounine have a relationship, despite his mistress Genia. Katrina ran the local cafe.

Before Broadway. Michael Kermoyan replaced George London during rehearsals.

The Broadway Run. ZIEGFELD THEATRE, 11/29/65–12/11/65. 16 previews 11/15/65–11/27/65. 16 PERFORMANCES. PRESENTED BY Fred R. Fehlhaber; MUSIC/LYRICS: Robert Wright & George Forrest; BOOK: George Abbott & Guy Bolton; BASED ON the drama *Anastasia*, Guy Bolton's adaptation of the 1948 French play *La Tsarina*, by Marcelle Maurette. It opened at the Lyceum, on Broadway, on 12/29/54, with Viveca Lindfors as Anna, Joe Anthony as Bounine, and also with Vivian Nathan, Eugenie Leontovich, Hurd Hatfield; MUSIC BASED ON themes by Russian composer Sergei Rachmaninoff; DIRECTOR: George Abbott; CHOREOGRAPHER: Hanya Holm; SETS: Robert Randolph; COSTUMES: Patricia Zipprodt; LIGHTING: Richard Casler; MUSICAL DIRECTOR: Harold Hastings; ORCHESTRATIONS: Don Walker; CAST RECORDING on United Artists; PRESS: Mary Bryant & Robert Pasolli; GENERAL MANAGER: Carl Fisher; PRODUCTION STAGE MANAGER: John Allen; STAGE MANAGER: Frank Gero; ASSISTANT STAGE MANAGER: Bob Bernard. **Cast**: ANYA: Constance Towers (1) ✫; NURSE: Patricia Hoffman; BOUNINE: Michael Kermoyan (2) ✫; JOSEF: Boris Aplon (6); COUNT DRIVINITZ: Lawrence Brooks; COUNT DORN: Adair McGowan; SERGEI: Jack Dabdoub; YEGOR: Walter Hook; KATRINA: Irra Petina (4) ✫; PETROVIN: Ed Steffe (7); BALALAIKA PLAYER: Konstantin Pio-Ulsky; GENIA, COUNTESS HOHENSTADT: Karen Shepard (9); CHERNOV: George S. Irving (5); OLGA: Laurie Franks; MASHA: Rita Metzger; SLEIGH DRIVER: Lawrence Boyll; ANOUCHKA: Elizabeth Howell; TINKA: Barbara Alexander; MOTHER: Maggie Task; FATHER: Michael Quinn; DOWAGER EMPRESS: Lillian Gish (3) ✫; PRINCE PAUL: John Michael King (8); COUNTESS DRIVINITZ: Elizabeth Howell; 1ST POLICEMAN: Lawrence Boyll; 2ND POLICEMAN: Bernard Frank; POLICE SERGEANT: Howard Kahl; BARONESS LIVENBAUM: Margaret Mullen (10); DANCERS: Barbara Alexander, Kip Andrews, Steven Boockvor, Ciya Challis, Randy Doney, Patricia Drylie, Juliette Durand, Joseph Nelson. SINGERS: Darrell Askey, Lawrence Boyll, Bernard Frank, Laurie Franks, Les Freed, Horace Guittard, Patricia Hoffman, Walter Hook, Howard Kahl, Adair McGowan, Rita Metzger, Richard Nieves, J. Vernon Oaks, Mia Powers, Lourette Raymon, Robert Sharp, John Taliaferro, Diane Tarleton, Maggie Task. **Understudies**: Anya: Karen Shepard; Bounine: Lawrence Brooks; Empress: Margaret Mullen; Katrina: Maggie Task; Chernov/Petronin: Jack Dabdoub; Paul: Horace Guittard; Genia: Lourette Raymon; Baroness: Elizabeth Howell; Tinka: Ciya Challis; Josef: Bernard Frank. **Act I**: **Choral Prelude**: "Anya" (from Piano Concerto No. 1, Opus I; *Etudes Tableaux*, Opus 33, No. 2) (Chorus); **Scene 1** The sanatorium, Berlin; 1925: "A Song from Somewhere" (from Trio Elegiaque, Opus 9; Symphony No. 2, Opus 27; Melodie, Opus 3, No. 5) (Anya); **Scene 2** The Cafe Czarina: "Vodka, Vodka!" (from *Polka Italienne*) (Katrina, Josef, Émigrés), "So Proud" (from Symphony No. 1, Opus 13; Piano Concerto No. 3, Opus 30) (Bounine, Chernov, Petrovin, Josef), "Homeward" (from Prelude, Opus 23, No. 5) (Katrina & Émigrés); **Scene 3** The chateau: "Snowflakes and Sweethearts" ("The Snowbird Song") (from *Polka on a Theme de W.R.*; Valse, Suite for Two Pianos, Opus 17, No. 2; "Thou, My Beloved Harvest Field," Opus 4, No. 5) (Yinka, Anya, Father, Mother, Peasants), "On That Day" (from String Quartet in G Minor; "A Dream," Opus 38, No. 5) (Chernov, Petrovin, Josef, Katrina); **Scene 4** The library: "Anya" (reprise) (Bounine), "Six Palaces" (from *Etudes Tableaux*, Opus 33, No. 7; Barcarolle, Suite for Two Pianos, Opus 5, No. 1; Polichinelle, Opus 3, No. 4; Mazurka, Opus 10, No. 7) (Anya, Bounine, Chernov, Petrovin). Livadia, on the Black Sea: YOUNG PRINCE PAUL: Randy Doney; YOUNG ANYA: Barbara Alexander. The Palace of Peterhof: The Winter Palace: DOWAGER EMPRESS: Lillian Gish; **Scene 5** The courtyard: "Hand in Hand" (from *Romance*, Suite for Two Pianos, Opus 17, No. 3) (Anya & Paul), "This is My Kind of Love" (from Piano Concerto No. 2, Opus 18) (Anya & Bounine); **Scene 6** The library; **Scene 7** The chateau: "On That Day" (reprise) (Paul & Investors). **Act II**: **Scene 1** The chateau: "That Prelude!" (from Prelude in C Sharp Minor, Opus 3, No. 2) (Bounine, Katrina, Petrovin, Josef, Chernov, Sergei, Yegor, Masha, Olga,

Policemen); *Scene 2* The Empress's drawing-room in Copenhagen: "A Quiet Land" (from Symphony No. 2, Opus 27) (Anya); *Scene 3* The courtyard: "Here Tonight, Tomorrow Where?" (from *Danse Hongroise*, Opus 5, No. 2; "So Many Hours," Opus 4, No. 6) (Chernov, Petrovin, Josef), "Leben Sie Wohl" (from Prelude, Opus 23, No. 5; Polichinelle, Opus 3, No. 4) (Katrina & Policemen), "If This is Goodbye" (from Piano Concerto No. 2, Opus 18) (Anya & Bounine); *Scene 4* The library: "Little Hands" (from Vocalise, Opus 34, No. 14) (Empress & Anya); *Scene 5* The chateau: "All Hail the Empress" (from Symphony No. 1, Opus 13) (Émigrés), Choral Finale (Chorus).

Broadway critics destroyed the show. Set designer Robert Randolph was nominated for a Tony, for his entire year's output (including *Anya*). The show lost $415,000. It was the last show to play the Ziegfeld, which was demolished after *Anya* closed.

After Broadway. The show was later re-named *The Anastasia Affair*. In 1967 it was revived in stock, as *I, Anastasia*, with a new book by Jerry Chodorov, and a new score. Willi Burke played Anna. In 1981 *I, Anastasia*, with Judy Kaye and Len Cariou, closed before Broadway. It had some new songs — "Drawn to You," "Now is My Moment," "That Song," "Think Upon Something Beautiful," "Two Waltzes." In 1986 Edwin Lester was planning to produce it for his Los Angeles & San Francisco Civic Light Opera Companies, but it didn't happen.

Revived often, but not on Broadway, the show has been renamed (and re-worked) at least once more — as *The Anastasia Game*.

28. *Anyone Can Whistle*

"A musical fable," "a wild new musical," an unconventional allegorical musical satire about a "not too distant town" which has been manufacturing a product that never wears out, and thus is now in a depression. Cora, the corrupt mayoress, and her henchmen cook up a fake miracle — water from a rock — to bring in more business. Fay, a nurse who can't whistle, and whose frigidity is only relaxed when she disguises herself in a red wig and calls herself "Ze Lady from Lourdes," meets Hapgood, ostensibly a doctor, but actually the latest addition to her "Cookie Jar" (local asylum for the "socially pressured"). Fay, egged on by Hapgood, destroys the asylum's records, and sets her cookies free as the townfolk realize the miracle is a fake. Fay is finally able to whistle, and a genuine fountain springs from the rock.

Before Broadway. Originally called *The Natives are Restless*, then *Side Show*, it was an unusual show, to say the least. Kermit Bloomgarden had problems raising the money. However, investors included Jule Styne, Frank Loesser, Irving Berlin, Richard Rodgers. This was a first musical for Angela Lansbury, Harry Guardino and Lee Remick. During rehearsals Gabriel Dell replaced Henry Lascoe (who died of a heart attack). It tried out at the Forrest, Philadelphia, 3/2/64–3/21/64, and two weeks into tryouts dancer Tucker Smith fell into the pit, injuring a musician. Philly reviews were negative and it went straight to Broadway.

The Broadway Run. MAJESTIC THEATRE, 4/4/64–4/11/64. 12 previews from 3/24/64. 9 PERFORMANCES. PRESENTED BY Kermit Bloomgarden & Diana Krasny; MUSIC/LYRICS: Stephen Sondheim; BOOK/DIRECTOR: Arthur Laurents; CHOREOGRAPHER: Herbert Ross; SETS: William & Jean Eckart; COSTUMES: Theoni V. Aldredge; LIGHTING: Jules Fisher; MUSICAL DIRECTOR/VOCAL ARRANGEMENTS: Herbert Greene; ORCHESTRATIONS: Don Walker; DANCE MUSIC ARRANGEMENTS: Betty Walberg; CAST RECORDING on CBS, recorded on 4/12/64. Largely thanks to the album the show gained a cult following; PRESS: James D. Proctor & Louise Weiner; GENERAL MANAGER: Joseph Harris; PRODUCTION STAGE MANAGER: James S. Gelb; STAGE MANAGER: Don Doherty & Louis Kosman. *Cast:* SANDWICH MAN: Jeff Killion; BABY JOAN: Jeanne Tanzy; MRS. SCHROEDER: Peg Murray; TREASURER COOLEY: Arnold Soboloff (5); CHIEF MAGRUDER: James Frawley (6); COMPTROLLER SCHUB: Gabriel Dell (4); CORA HOOVER HOOPER: Angela Lansbury (2); THE BOYS: Sterling Clark, Harvey Evans, Larry Roquemore, Tucker Smith; FAY APPLE: Lee Remick (1); J. BOWDEN HAPGOOD: Harry Guardino (3); DR. DETMOLD: Don Doherty; GEORGE: Larry Roquemore; JANE: Janet Hayes; JOHN: Harvey Evans; MARTIN: Lester Wilson;

OLD LADY: Eleanore Treiber; TELEGRAPH BOY: Alan Johnson; OSGOOD: Georgia Creighton; ENSEMBLE (COOKIES, NURSES, DEPUTIES, TOWNSPEOPLE, PILGRIMS, TOURISTS): Susan Borree, Sterling Clark, Georgia Creighton, Eugene Edwards, Dick Ensslen, Harvey Evans, Janet Hayes, Loren Hightower, Bettye Jenkins, Alan Johnson, Patricia Kelly, Jeff Killion, Barbara Lang, Paula Lloyd, Barbara Monte, Jack Murray, Odette Phillips, William Reilly, Hanne Marie Reiner, Larry Roquemore, Tucker Smith, Don Stewart, Eleanore Treiber, Lester Wilson. **Understudies:** Fay: Barbara Lang; Cora: Peg Murray; Detmold: Harvey Evans; Hapgood: Don Stewart; Cooley: Tucker Smith; Magruder: Dick Ensslen; Baby Joan: Bettye Jenkins; Mrs. Schroeder: Georgia Creighton. *Act I: Scene 1* The town: "I'm Like the Bluebird" (Company) [not on the cast album], "Me and My Town" (Cora & Boys); *Scene 2* The miracle: "Miracle Song" (Cora, Cooley, Townspeople, Tourists, Pilgrims), "There Won't Be Trumpets" [cut for Broadway]; *Scene 3* The interrogation: "Simple" (The Interrogation) (Hapgood & Company). *Act II: Scene 1* The celebration: "A-1 March" (The Cookies) [not on the cast album]; *Scene 2* The romance: "Come Play Wiz Me" (Fay, Hapgood, Boys), "Anyone Can Whistle" (Fay); *Scene 3* The parade: "A Parade in Town" (Cora); *Scene 4* The release: "Everybody Says Don't" (Hapgood), Don't Ballet (Fay, Hapgood, Cookies). VARIATION 1: Loren Hightower, Odette Phillips, Eleanore Treiber; VARIATION 2: Barbara Monte; VARIATION 3: Alan Johnson & Paula Lloyd; VARIATION 4: Tucker Smith; VARIATION 5: Lester Wilson & Hanne Marie Reiner; VARIATION 6: William Reilly, Sterling Clark, Eleanore Treiber, Larry Roquemore, Harvey Evans, Bettye Jenkins. *Act III: Scene 1* The conspiracy: "I've Got You to Lean On" (Cora, Schub, Cooley, Magruder, Boys); *Scene 2* The confrontation: "See What it Gets You" (Fay); *Scene 3* The Cookie Chase: The Cookie Chase (Waltzes) (Cora, Fay, Schub, Company). DANCING DEPUTIES: Larry Roquemore, Tucker Smith, Harvey Evans; OLD LADY: Eleanore Treiber; WALTZ 1: Odette Phillips; WALTZ 2: Barbara Monte; WALTZ 3: Bettye Jenkins & Alan Johnson; WALTZ 4: Schub, Paula Lloyd, Hanne Marie Reiner, Susan Borree, Patricia Kelly; WALTZ 5: Sterling Clark; WALTZ 6: Bettye Jenkins; PAS DE DEUX: Hanne Marie Reiner & William Reilly; GALLOP: Loren Hightower; FINALE: Company; *Scene 4* The Farewell: "There's Always a Woman" [cut for Broadway], "With So Little to Be Sure Of" (Fay & Hapgood), Finale (Company) [not on the cast album].

Some references say that there were only two acts, "Don't" being the end of Act I. Actually that was only the intermission. There were really three acts, as above.

Broadway reviews were divided (a couple of raves, but the *New York Times* said it lacked imagination and wit). It received a Tony nomination for choreography.

After Broadway. CHURCH OF THE HEAVENLY REST, NYC, 3/14/80–4/4/80. 19 PERFORMANCES. PRESENTED BY The York Players; DIRECTOR: Fran Soeder; CHOREOGRAPHER: Cal Del Pozo; SETS: James Morgan. *Cast:* COOLEY: Ralph David Westfall; SCHUB: Sam Stoneburner; CORA: Gaylea Byrne; FAY: Rosemary McNamara; HAPGOOD: Gary Krawford; JANE: Kathy Morath; ENSEMBLE INCLUDED: Gail Lohla.

47TH STREET THEATRE, NYC, 11/4/92–11/22/92. PRESENTED BY Opening Doors Productions; DIRECTOR: Tom Klebba; CHOREOGRAPHER: Barry McNabb; COSTUMES: Wade Laboissonniere; MUSICAL DIRECTOR: Darren R. Cohen. *Cast:* NARRATOR: Tim Connell; FAY: Wendy Oliver; HAPGOOD: Chris Innvar.

CARNEGIE HALL, NYC, 4/5/95. One-night AIDS benefit concert for Gay Men's Health Crisis. PRESENTED BY Peter Bogyo; CHOREOGRAPHIC ASSOCIATE: Robert La Fosse; SETS: Heidi Landesman; COSTUMES: Theoni V. Aldredge; LIGHTING: Jules Fisher; SOUND: Otts Munderloh; MUSICAL DIRECTOR: Paul Gemignani; NEW CAST RECORDING on Columbia. *Cast:* HOSTESS: Angela Lansbury; MRS. SCHROEDER: Maureen Moore; MAGRUDER: Ken Page; COOLEY: Chip Zien; SCHUB: Walter Bobbie; CORA: Madeline Kahn; THE BOYS: Sterling Clark, Harvey Evans, Evan Pappas, Eric Riley, Tony Stevens; FAY: Bernadette Peters; HAPGOOD: Scott Bakula; DETMOLD: Nick Wyman; SOPRANO: Harolyn Blackwell; WESTERN UNION BOY: Sterling Clark; CHORUS: Joan Barber, Gerry Burkhardt, Susan Cella, Madeleine Doherty, Colleen Fitzpatrick, Joy Franz, Betsy Joslyn, Joseph Kolinski, David Lowenstein, Seth Malkin, Michael X. Martin, Marin Mazzie, Karen Murphy, Bill Nolte, Robert Ousley, Darcy Pulliam, Nancy Ringham, Francis Ruivivar, Martin Van Treuren, Walter Willison.

BRIDEWELL THEATRE, London, 1/8/03–2/15/03. Previews from 1/2/03. The book was re-written by Arthur Laurents and approved by Steve Sondheim. This London production was a test run for the revised version in 2 acts. PRESENTED BY Gryphon; DIRECTOR: Michael Gieleta; SETS: Frances Rodriguez-Weil; LIGHTING: Mike Robertson; MUSICAL DIRECTOR: Mark Etherington. *Cast:* COOLEY: Mark Heenehan; MAGRUDER: Aaron Shirley; SCHUB: James Smillie; CORA: Paula Wilcox; FAY: Janie Dee; HAPGOOD: Edward Baker Duly.

MATRIX THEATRE, Los Angeles. Opened 2/18/03. This was the revised version. PRESENTED BY Carole Black; ADAPTED BY: Michael Michetti (into two acts); DIRECTOR: Michael Michetti; CHOREOGRAPHER: Larry Sousa; SETS: Evan Bartoletti (inspired by Andy Warhol); MUSICAL DIRECTOR: Darryl Archibald. *Cast:* FAY: Misty Cotton; CORA: Ruth Williamson; HAPGOOD: John Bisom.

CHICAGO, 5/25/04–7/3/04. Previews from 5/21/04. PRESENTED BY the Pegasus Players. This was the revised version; the non-Equity Pegasus Players had presented the original version in 1988 to much acclaim.

THE PAVILION, Ravinia Festival, Chicago, 8/26/05–8/27/05. Part of the Sondheim 75 series, to celebrate Steve Sondheim's 75th birthday in 2005. This was the version used at Carnegie Hall in 1995. DIRECTOR: Lonny Price; MUSICAL DIRECTOR: Paul Gemignani. *Cast:* Patti LuPone, Audra McDonald, Michael Cerveris.

29. *Anything Goes*

Set in the 1930s. A cruise on the ocean liner S.S. *American* to Europe, and the characters on it: Reno, a celebrity evangelist turned nightclub singer; her friend Billy, who stowed away to be near debutante Hope, whom he loves; Moon-Face Martin, Public Enemy No. 13, posing as a priest. It opened with Cole Porter singing "Anything Goes" as the lights dim, then the orchestra played a jazzy arrangement of the overture. It ended with a huge picture of Mr. Porter descending from the ceiling.

Before Broadway. The original production, first called *Bon Voyage*, and then *Hard to Get*, was the brainwave of producer Vinton Freedley; it ran at the ALVIN THEATRE, from 11/21/34. 420 PERFORMANCES. It was the 4th-longest running Broadway musical of the 1930s. DIRECTOR: Howard Lindsay; CHOREOGRAPHER: Robert Alton; SETS: Donald Oenslager; MUSICAL DIRECTOR: Earl Busby; ORCHESTRATIONS: Russell Bennett & Hans Spialek. *Cast:* RENO: Ethel Merman; BILLY: William Gaxton; MOON: Victor Moore; OAKLEIGH: Leslie Barrie; HOPE: Bettina Hall; SNOOKS: Drucilla Strain; BABE: Vivian Vance. *Act I: Scene 1* The Weylin Caprice Bar: "I Get a Kick Out of You"; *Scene 2* The afterdeck; midnight sailing: "Bon Voyage"; *Scene 3* Mr. Whitney's and Dr. Moon's cabins: "All Through the Night"; *Scene 4* The afterdeck; same morning: "Sailors' Chantey," "Where Are the Men?," "You're the Top"; *Scene 5* Sir Evelyn's cabin; *Scene 6* The deck: "Anything Goes." *Act II: Scene 1* The lounge; that evening: "Public Enemy Number One," "Blow, Gabriel, Blow"; *Scene 2* The brig; five days later: "Be Like the Bluebird," "All Through the Night" (reprise); *Scene 3* Conservatory of Sir Evelyn's home in England: "Buddie Beware" [replaced soon after opening by a reprise of "I Get a Kick Out of You"], "The Gypsy in Me," Finale.

It was filmed in 1936. DIRECTOR: Lewis Milestone. *Cast:* Ethel Merman, Charlie Ruggles, Bing Crosby, Ida Lupino, Arthur Treacher, Margaret Dumont. There were two NBC TV versions in the 1950s. The first, on 10/2/50, with Martha Raye and John Conte. The second, on 2/28/54, with Ethel Merman, Frank Sinatra, Bert Lahr, Sheree North. In 1956 there was another movie, with the same title but little else, except five songs from the show. *Cast:* Bing Crosby, Donald O'Connor, Jeanmaire, Mitzi Gaynor, Buzz Miller, Ernie Flatt.

The famous Off Broadway revival ran at the ORPHEUM THEATRE, 5/15/62–12/9/62. 239 PERFORMANCES. PRESENTED BY Jane Friedlander, Michael Parver, Gene Andrewski; DIRECTOR: Lawrence Kasha; CHOREOGRAPHER: Ron Field; MUSICAL DIRECTOR: Julian Stein. *Cast:* RENO: Eileen Rodgers, *Sheila Smith*; BILLY: Hal Linden; MOON: Mickey Deems; HOPE: Barbara Lang; SIR EVELYN: Kenneth Mars; ALSO WITH: Robert Fitch, Diane McAfee.

PAPER MILL PLAYHOUSE, New Jersey, 3/27/74–5/12/74. DIRECTOR: Lawrence Kasha; MUSICAL DIRECTOR: Glen Clugston. Then it toured. *Cast:* Ann Miller, Coley Worth, Isabelle Farrell, Louise Kirtland, Roland Young.

TOUR. Opened on 7/80, and closed on 11/80, in Los Angeles. PRESENTED BY Steven Bohm. *Cast:* Ginger Rogers, Sid Caesar.

MEXICO CITY, 1986. *Cast:* RENO: Rocio Banquells; BILLY: Julio Aleman.

The Broadway Run. VIVIAN BEAUMONT THEATRE, 10/19/87–9/3/89. 44 previews from 9/11/87. 804 PERFORMANCES. PRESENTED BY Lincoln Center Theatre; MUSIC/LYRICS: Cole Porter; ORIGINAL BOOK: Guy Bolton & P.G. Wodehouse, Howard Lindsay & Russel Crouse; NEW BOOK: Timothy Crouse & John Weidman; DIRECTOR: Jerry Zaks; CHOREOGRAPHER: Michael Smuin; SETS/COSTUMES: Tony Walton; LIGHTING: Paul Gallo; SOUND: Tony Meola; MUSICAL DIRECTOR: Edward Strauss, *Jim Coleman* (added by 88–89); ORCHESTRATIONS: Michael Gibson; DANCE MUSIC ARRANGEMENTS: Tom Fay; CAST RECORDING on RCA, made on 12/7/87; PRESS: Merle Debuskey; CASTING: Risa Bramon & Billy Hopkins; GENERAL MANAGER: Steven C. Callahan; COMPANY MANAGER: Lynn Landis; PRODUCTION STAGE MANAGER: George Darveris; STAGE MANAGER: Chet Leaming; ASSISTANT STAGE MANAGER: Leslie Loeb. *Cast:* LOUIE: Eric Y.L. Chan, *Marc Oka*; ELISHA WHITNEY: Rex Everhart; FRED: Steve Steiner; BILLY CROCKER: Howard McGillin, *Gregg Edelman* (from 5/25/89); RENO SWEENEY: Patti LuPone (1), *Linda Hart* (during Miss LuPone's vacation, from 6/28/88; Miss LuPone was back 7/5/88; *Leslie Uggams* (from 3/21/89); YOUNG GIRL: Michele Pigliavento, *Jane LaBanz*; SAILOR: Alec Timmerman, *Dale Hensley*; CAPTAIN: David Pursley; PURSER: Gerry Vichi; CHANTEY QUARTET [also known as the Lady Fair Quartet]: Steve Steiner, Larry Cahn, Dale Hensley, Leslie Feagen; REPORTER #1: Robert Kellett; PHOTOGRAPHER: Gerry McIntyre, *Dan Fletcher*; REPORTER #2: Larry Cahn, *Ken Shepski, Larry Cahn*; PURITY: Daryl Richardson, *Karen E. Fraction*; CHASTITY: Barbara Yeager, *Michaela Hughes*; CHARITY: Maryellen Scilla; VIRTUE: Jane Lanier, *Kim Darwin*; MINISTER: Richard Korthaze; LUKE: Stanford Egi, *Ronald Yamamoto*; JOHN: Toshi Toda; HOPE HARCOURT: Kathleen Mahony-Bennett, *Nancy Opel* (from 10/4/88); MRS. EVANGELINE HARCOURT: Anne Francine, *Ellen Hanley*; LORD EVELYN OAKLEY: Anthony Heald, *Walter Bobbie* (from 4/14/89); G-MAN #1: Dale Hensley; G-MAN #2: Leslie Feagan; ERMA: Linda Hart, *Jane Seaman, Maryellen Scilla* (from 4/89), *Linda Hart* (from 7/89); MOONFACE MARTIN: Bill McCutcheon, *Gerry Vichi* (from 8/8/89); WOMAN IN BATHCHAIR: Jane Seaman; HER NIECE: Alice Ann Oakes; COUNTESS: Pat Gorman; THUGGISH SAILORS: Mark Chmiel, Dan Fletcher (*Joe Deer*), Lacy Darryl Phillips (*Garry Q. Lewis*), Lloyd Culbreath; SHIP'S CREW/PASSENGERS: Eric Y.L. Chan, Mark Chmiel, Dan Fletcher, Robert Kellett, Jane Lanier, Gerry McIntyre, Alice Ann Oakes, Lacy Darryl Phillips, Michele Pigliavento, Daryl Richardson, Maryellen Scilla, Alec Timmerman, Barbara Yeager, *Robert Ashford*. **Understudies:** Whitney: David Pursley & Leslie Feagan; Evangeline: Jane Seaman & Pat Gorman; Erma: Barbara Yeager & Jane Seaman; Oakley/Crocker: Larry Cahn & Dale Hensley; Reno: Pat Gorman & Jane Seaman; Hope: Michele Pigliavento & Jane Lanier; Martin: Gerry Vichi & Leslie Feagan; Luke/John: Eric Y.L. Chan; Minister: Leslie Feagan; Captain: Steve Steiner & Robert Kellett; Purser: Gerry McIntyre & Alec Timmerman; 1st Reporter: Gerry McIntyre; Sailor: Mark Chmiel & Dan Fletcher; Photographer: Mark Chmiel; 2nd Reporter: Robert Kellett; Young Girl: Jane Seaman & Barbara Yeager; Fred: Gerry McIntyre & Lacy Darryl Phillips; Purity: Alice Ann Oakes & Michele Pigliavento; Chastity: Daryl Richardson & Maryellen Scilla; Charity: Alice Ann Oakes & Daryl Richardson; Virtue: Maryellen Scilla & Alice Ann Oakes; Woman in Bath Chair: Pat Gorman & Daryl Richardson; Niece: Michele Pigliavento. **Swings:** Rob Ashford, Amy O'Brien, Michelle O'Steen, Paul Geraci (*Gib Jones*). **Musicians:** Kamau Adilifu, Dennis Anderson, Raymound Beckenstein, Bruce Bonvissuto, William Butler, Burt Collins, Garfield Fobbs, Laurie A. Frink, Eric Kivnick, Ronald Raffio, Seymour Red Press, John W. Redsecker, Roger Rosenberg, Santo Russo, Andrew Stein. *Act I: Prelude* (Orchestra); *Scene 1* A smoky Manhattan bar: "I Get a Kick Out of You" (Reno), "(There's) No Cure Like Travel" [newly added in 1987] (Sailor, Girl, Crew); *Scene 2* The afterdeck of an ocean liner shortly before sailing: "Bon Voyage" (Company); *Scene 3* On deck; that evening: "You're the Top" (Reno & Billy), "Easy to Love" (Billy) [from the movie *Born to Dance*, and newly added in 1987]; *Scene 4* Mr. Whitney's stateroom: "I Want to Row on the Crew" (Whitney) [from *Paranoia*, and newly added in 1987]; *Scene 5* The ship's deck; mid-morning: "Sailors' Chantey" (Chantey Quartet), "Friendship" (Reno & Moonface) [from *Du Barry Was a Lady*, and newly added in 1962]; *Scene 6* Lord Evelyn's stateroom; *Scene 7* The ship's deck: "It's De-Lovely" (Billy & Hope) [from *Red, Hot and Blue*, and newly added in 1962]; *Scene 8* The ship's deck; early the following morning: "Anything Goes" (Reno & Company). *Act II*: Entr'acte (Orchestra); *Scene 1* The ship's nightclub: "Public Enemy # 1" (Company), "Blow, Gabriel, Blow" (Reno & Company), "Goodbye, Little Dream, Goodbye" (Hope) [from the London production of *O Mistress Mine*, and newly added in 1987]; *Scene 2* The brig: "Be Like the Bluebird" (Moonface), "All Through the Night" (Billy, Hope, Men); *Scene 3* The ship's deck: "The Gypsy in Me" (Lord Evelyn); *Scene 4* The brig; *Scene 5* The ship's deck: "Buddie Beware" (Erma & Sailors), Finale: "I Get a Kick Out of You"/"Anything Goes" (reprise) (Company).

Note: "newly added in 1962" means for the 1962 Off Broadway production; "newly added in 1987" means for this production.

This production was the most successful. It had a new, up-to-date book by the sons of the original librettists, and several new Cole Porter songs (as the 1962 Off Broadway production had had). "Heaven Hop," "Let's Step Out," "Let's Misbehave," and "Take Me Back to Manhattan," all new in 1962, were not used here. The critics raved. It won Tonys for revival, choreography, and for Bill McCutcheon, and was also nominated for direction of a musical, lighting, sets, costumes, and for Howard McGillin, Patti LuPone, and Anthony Heald.

After Broadway. Tour. Opened on 10/19/88, at the Shubert Theatre, New Haven, and closed on 1/15/89, at the Benedum Theatre, Pittsburgh. Musical Director: Jim Coleman. *Cast*: Reno: Leslie Uggams; Billy: Rex Smith; Moonface: Rip Taylor; Erma: Susan Terry; Whitney: Gordon Connell; Captain: Kenneth Kantor; Evangeline: Julie Kurnitz; Oakleigh: Paul V. Ames; Hope: Rebecca Baxter; Chorus included: Lynn Sterling & Garry Q. Lewis.

Prince Edward Theatre, London. Opened on 7/4/89. *Cast*: Reno: Elaine Paige; Billy: Howard McGillin, *John Barrowman* (from 10/89); Moonface: Bernard Cribbins; Whitney: Harry Towb; Evangeline: Ursula Smith; Erma: Kathryn Evans; Lord Evelyn: Martin Turner; Hope: Ashleigh Sendin.

Tour. Opened on 9/12/89, in Costa Mesa, Calif. *Cast*: Reno: Mitzi Gaynor; Billy: Scott Stevenson; Moonface: Robert Nichols; Whitney: Gordon Connell; Evangeline: Evelyn Page; Erma: Dorothy Kiara; Lord Evelyn: Richard Sabellico; Hope: Donna English.

Lincoln Center, 4/1/00. One-performance benefit concert to honor a great contributor to the Lincoln Center, Joe Cullman on his 90th birthday. *Cast*: Reno: Patti LuPone; Also with: Howard McGillin, Linda Hart, Boyd Gaines, John Jellison, John Cunningham, Kaitlin Hopkins, Elizabeth Hubbard, Mike McGrath.

Paper Mill Playhouse, New Jersey, 9/6/00–10/15/00. Director: Lee Roy Reams; Choreographer: Michael Lichtefeld; Lighting: F. Mitchell Dana; Musical Director: Tom Helm. *Cast*: Reno: Chita Rivera; Moonface: Bruce Adler; Billy: George Dvorsky; Hope: Stacey Logan; Lord Evelyn: Patrick Quinn.

Freud Playhouse, Los Angeles, 9/17/02–9/29/02. Part of the *Reprise!* series. This production used the updated text of the 1987 Broadway production. Director: Glenn Casale. *Cast*: Billy: Brent Barrett; Reno: Rachel York; Evangeline: Sally Struthers; Hope: Anastasia Barzee; Lord Evelyn: Larry Cedar; Moonface: Jason Graae; Erma: DeLee Lively.

Olivier Theatre, London 12/18/02–2/8/03. Previews from 12/11/02. This revival was a huge success, then it went into repertory until 3/22/03. It was Trevor Nunn's last musical as director of the Royal National Theatre (which the Olivier is part of). Choreographer: Stephen Mear; Sets: John Gunter; Costumes: Anthony Powell; Lighting: David Hersey; London cast recording released on 9/22/03. *Cast*: Reno: Sally Ann Triplett; Eli: Denis Quilley; Billy: John Barrowman; Hope: Mary Stockley; Moonface: Martin Marquez. It re-ran at the Theatre Royal, Drury Lane, London, 10/7/03–5/1/04 (previews from 9/23/03), and was replaced *My Fair Lady*.

Hobby Center, Houston, 1/27/05–2/13/05. Presented by The-

atre Under the Stars; Director: Roy Hamlin; Choreographer: Gregory Daniels; Lighting: Richard Winkler; Costumes: Christopher "Kit" Bond; Musical Director: John Visser. *Cast*: Reno: Dee Hoty; Billy: Matt Cavenaugh; Hope: Kaytha Coker; Sir Evelyn: George Dvorsky; Moonface: Robert Creighton; Bonnie: Jennifer Cody; Whitney: Kevin Cooney; Mrs. Harcourt: Susan Shofner; Captain: Ron Solomon; Bishop Dodson: Jim Shaffer.

30. *Applause*

Set in and around New York City. Margo, a famous actress, befriends Eve, a young fan who tries to steal not only Margo's roles but also her boyfriend, Bill. Finally Margo gets her man and Eve becomes a star.

Before Broadway. In 1966 Charles Strouse and Lee Adams were contracted to write the score, and in 1968 Lauren Bacall agreed to star. In 1969 Comden & Green replaced the original librettist, Sidney Michaels, updating the story to 1970s Broadway and eliminating the acidic drama critic played by George Sanders in the movie *All About Eve*, upon which the musical was based. The wise-cracking maid, played by Thelma Ritter in the movie, was replaced by homosexual hairdresser Duane. Penny Fuller replaced Diane McAfee as Eve during the Baltimore tryouts. Ron Field was almost fired, but Miss Bacall insisted he remain. The numbers "It Was Always You" and "Love Comes First" were cut.

The Broadway Run. Palace Theatre, 3/30/70–5/27/72. 4 previews. 896 performances. Presented by Joseph Kipness & Lawrence Kasha, in association with Nederlander Productions & George M. Steinbrenner III; Music: Charles Strouse; Lyrics: Lee Adams; Book: Betty Comden & Adolph Green; Based on the 1950 movie *All About Eve*, written by Joseph Mankiewicz, which was based on Mary Orr's 1946 short story *The Wisdom of Eve* (Margola Cranston was the character's name in that story), which in turn was based on a real-life incident that Austrian actress Elisabeth Bergner and her husband, producer Paul Czinner, had with an unscrupulous young actress they befriended during the war. It was made into a radio play in 1949; Director/Choreographer: Ron Field; Sets: Robert Randolph; Costumes: Ray Aghayan; Lighting: Tharon Musser; Assistant Lighting: Ken Billington; Sound: Jack Shearing; Musical Director/Vocal Arrangements: Donald Pippin; Orchestrations: Philip J. Lang; Dance & Incidental Music Arrangements: Mel Marvin; Cast recording on ABC; Press: Bill Doll & Company; General Manager: Philip Adler; Company Manager: S.M. Handelsman, *Milton Pollack* (added by 71–72); Production Stage Manager: Terence Little, *Robert L. Borod, Donald Christy*; Stage Manager: Donald Christy, *Lanier Davis*; Assistant Stage Managers: Lanier Davis, *John Herbert* (by 70–71) & Howard Kahl. *Cast*: Tony Announcer: John Anania; Tony Host: Alan King; Margo Channing: Lauren Bacall (1) ☆, *Anne Baxter* (from 7/19/71), *Arlene Dahl* (from 5/1/72); Eve Harrington: Penny Fuller (2), *Patti Davis* (during Miss Fuller's vacation, 4/16/71–5/3/71), *Janice Lynde* (from 11/22/71), *Diane McAfee*; Howard Benedict: Robert Mandan (4), *Lawrence Weber* (from 4/19/71), *Franklin Cover* (from 1/17/72); Bert: Tom Urich (10); Buzz Richards: Brandon Maggart (6); Bill Sampson: Len Cariou (3), *Keith Charles* (from 5/3/71), *John Gabriel* (from 5/1/72); Duane Fox: Lee Roy Reams (7), *Gene Foote* (during Mr. Reams's vacation in 70–71), *Tom Rolla* (from 11/22/71), *Larry Merritt* (from 4/24/72), *Christopher Chadman*; Karen Richards: Ann Williams (5), *Gwyda DonHowe* (from 8/24/70), *Penny Hagan* (from 12/13/71) [Miss Hagan's name changed to Phebe Hagan on 5/1/72]; Bartender: Jerry Wyatt; Peter: John Anania (9); Dancer in Bar: Sammy Williams [a new role added by 71–72], *Gene Aguirre*; Bob: Howard Kahl, *John Herbert*; Piano Player: Orrin Reiley, *Joseph Neal*; Stan Harding: Ray Becker (11); Danny: Bill Allsbrook, *Larry Merritt, Gene Aguirre*; Bonnie: Bonnie Franklin (8), *Carol Petri* (4/29/71–6/21/71), *Bonnie Franklin, Leland Palmer* (9/6/71–11/22/71), *Bonnie Franklin* [the character's name was changed to Nancy while Miss Petri was playing it, but from then the name matched with the first name of actress]; Carol: Carol Petri, *Renee Baughman* (for Miss Petri while she was standing in for Bonnie Franklin, 4/29/71–6/21/71), *Kathleen Robey*; Joey: Mike Misita, *Christopher Chadman, John Medeiros*;

MUSICIANS: Gene Kelton, Nat Horne, David Anderson; TV DIRECTOR: Orrin Reiley, *Joseph Neal*; AUTOGRAPH SEEKER: Carol Petri, *Renee Baughman* (for Miss Petri while she was playing Bonnie), *Kathleen Robey*; SINGERS: Laurie Franks (*Peggy Hagen*), Ernestine Jackson (gone by 70–71), Howard Kahl (*John Herbert*), Sheilah Rae (*Patti Davis*), Orrin Reiley (*Joseph Neal*), Jeannette Seibert, Henrietta Valor (gone by 70–71), Jerry Wyatt, *Gail Nelson, Merrill Leighton, Judy McCauley, Jozella Reed, Peggy LeRoy*; DANCERS: Bill Allsbrook (*Larry Merritt*), David Anderson, Renee Baughman, Joan Bell, Debi Carpenter, John Cashman, Jon Daenen (*Wayne Boyd*), Nikolas Dante, Patti D'Beck, Marilyn D'Honau (*Bonnie Walker, Marilyn D'Honau*), Gene Foote, Nat Horne, Gene Kelton, Marybeth Kurdock, Mike Misita (*Christopher Chadman, John Medeiros*), Ed Nolfi, Carol Petri (*Kathleen Robey*), Sammy Williams (*Gene Aguirre*), *Paul Charles, Jay Fox, Richard Dodd*. **Understudies**: Eve: Sheilah Rae, *Patti Davis*; Bill: Tom Urich; Howard: John Anania; Buzz: Ray Becker; Karen: Laurie Franks, *Peggy Hagen*; Duane: Gene Foote; Bonnie: Carol Petri, *Patti D'Beck*; Bert/Stan: Jerry Wyatt; Peter: Lanier Davis, *John Herbert*. **Act I**: **Scene 1** The Tony Awards; **Scene 2** Margo's dressing-room: "Backstage Babble" (First Nighters), "Think How it's Gonna Be" (Bill), "But Alive" (Margo & Boys); **Scene 3** The Village Bar: "But Alive" (continued) (Margo & Boys); **Scene 4** Margo's living-room: "The Best Night of My Life" (Eve), "Who's That Girl?" (Margo); **Scene 5** Margo's dressing-room; **Scene 6** Joe Allen's: "Applause" (Bonnie & Gypsies); **Scene 7** Margo's bedroom: "Hurry Back" (Margo); **Scene 8** Margo's living-room: "Fasten Your Seat Belts" (Buzz, Karen, Howard, Duane, Bill, Guests); **Scene 9** Backstage: "Welcome to the Theatre" (Margo). **Act II**: **Scene 1** Buzz & Karen's Connecticut home: "Inner Thoughts" (Karen, Buzz, Margo), "Good Friends" (Margo, Karen, Buzz); **Scene 2** Margo's dressing-room: "The Best Night of My Life" (reprise) (Eve); **Scene 3** Joe Allen's: "She's No Longer a Gypsy" (Bonnie, Duane, Gypsies); **Scene 4** Margo's living-room: "One of a Kind" (Bill & Margo); **Scene 5** Backstage: "One Halloween" (Eve); **Scene 6** Margo's dressing-room: "Something Greater" (Margo); **Scene 7** Backstage: Finale (Margo & Company).

It got rave reviews on Broadway, and was a major triumph for Lauren Bacall. The show won Tony Awards for musical, direction of a musical, choreography, lighting, and for Lauren Bacall, and was nominated for sets, costumes, and for Len Cariou, Brandon Maggart, Bonnie Franklin, and Penny Fuller.

After Broadway. TOUR. Opened on 11/29/71, at the Royal Alexandra Theatre, Toronto. *Cast:* MARGO: Lauren Bacall, *Eleanor Parker* (from 6/27/72); EVE: Virginia Sandifur, *Penny Fuller* (from 4/25/72), *Janice Lynd* (from 6/27/72); HOWARD: Norwood Smith; BUZZ: Ted Pritchard; BILL: Don Chastain, *George McDaniel* (from 6/27/72); DUANE: Lee Roy Reams, *Orrin Reiley* (from 6/27/72); KAREN: Beverly Dixon; PETER: Burt Bier; LELAND: Leland Palmer, *Candy Brown* (from 6/27/72) [this was the old Bonnie role]; JOEY: Christopher Chadman.

TOUR. Opened on 9/22/72, at the Masonic Auditorium, Scranton, Pa., and closed on 5/5/73, at the Veterans Memorial Auditorium, Providence, Rhode Island, after 114 cities. PRESENTED BY William Court Cohen, Edward H. Davis & Columbia Artists Theatrical Corporation, in association with Robert C. Schuler; CHOREOGRAPHER: Ed Nolfi; MUSICAL DIRECTOR: Michael Rose. *Cast:* MARGO: Patrice Munsel; EVE: Diane McAfee; HOWARD: Ed Fuller; BERT: Alan Jordan, *Brad Tyrrell*; BILL: Virgil Curry; KAREN: Lisa Carroll, *Ann Gardner*; PIA: Pia Zadora.

LONDON. Opened on 11/16/72. *Cast:* MARGO: Lauren Bacall; EVE: Angela Richards; HOWARD: Basil Hoskins; BUZZ: Rod McLennan; BILL: Ken Walsh; DUANE: Eric Flynn; KAREN: Sarah Marshall.

CBS-TV, 3/15/73. *Cast:* MARGO: Lauren Bacall; EVE: Penny Fuller; HOWARD: Robert Mandan; BILL: Larry Hagman; KAREN: Sarah Marshall.

TOURING REVIVAL. Conceived in 7/95. Rehearsals began in 8/96. Comden & Green and Strouse & Adams were all involved with this tour, and the slight revisions that took place. It was updated from the late 60s to the 1971–1972 period. New songs: "Margo," "I Don't Want to Grow Old" (the new finale), and "She Killed Them" (Duane). The title song was now the opening number. The tour kicked off with a stint at the Paper Mill Playhouse, Millburn, New Jersey, 9/11/96–10/19/96. PRESENTED BY Barry & Fran Weissler; DIRECTOR: Gene Saks; SETS: Michael Anania; MUSICAL DIRECTOR: John McDaniel; PRODUCTION SUPERVISOR: Tommy

Tune. *Cast:* MARGO: Stefanie Powers; EVE: Kate Jennings Grant; HOWARD: Nick Wyman; BUZZ: Stuart Zagnit; BILL: John Dossett; DUANE: Darrell Carey; KAREN: Janet Aldrich; ALSO WITH: Belle Calaway, Marc Calamia, Deidre Goodwin. The creators showed up opening night, along with Mary Orr (who wrote the original 1946 story). Stefanie Powers starred instead of the proposed Raquel Welch (who quit to do a TV series), and was criticized by some during previews as being too lightweight to carry the show, but she certainly could dance, and Ann Reinking, the choreographer, tailored the show to her strengths. After it closed at the Paper Mill it continued with the 22-week tour, first at Tampa Bay Performing Arts Center, from 10/22/96. There were Broadway hopes as early as 7/96; on 10/18/96 it was announced that it would arrive on Broadway in 4/97; but it never happened. The tour closed on 11/24/96, in Columbus, Ohio, for "re-tooling."

FREUD PLAYHOUSE, UCLA, Calif., 5/10/05–5/10/05. Part of the *Reprise!* series.

31. *The Apple Tree*

Before Broadway. It was originally called *Come Back! Go Away! I Love You!* Jerry Bock, Sheldon Harnick and Jerome Coopersmith wanted to do three separate one-act musical plays strung together (a first on Broadway). They picked *Boule de Suif*, by Guy de Maupassant; *Angel Levine*, by Bernard Malamud; and *Martin, the Novelist*, by Marcel Ayme. But they dropped those components in favor of *Show Biz*, by Bruce Jay Friedman; *Young Goodman Brown*, by Nathaniel Hawthorne, and *Extracts from Adam's Diary*, by Mark Twain. The plan was to trace the progress of man's relationship with woman. Hawthorne's work was replaced with *The Lady or the Tiger?* and *Show Biz* with *Passionella*. As for *Passionella*, this had been a one-act play, part of a summer stock tryout in 1962 called *The World of Jules Feiffer*, directed by Mike Nichols, with music by Stephen Sondheim, and Dorothy Loudon as the sniveling chimney sweep (Gower Champion was to have directed it on Broadway, but it never happened). Bock & Harnick wrote their own version of *Passionella*. Mike Nichols suggested Al Freeman Jr. as Adam, but the producer thought that a black Adam would be a gimmick. Three months before rehearsals began Jerome Robbins was replaced as choreographer by Lee Becker Theodore. Jerome Coopersmith departed before Broadway, as did the number "I'm Lost."

The Broadway Run. SHUBERT THEATRE, 10/18/66–11/25/67. 13 previews from 10/5/66. 463 PERFORMANCES. PRESENTED BY Stuart Ostrow; MUSIC: Jerry Bock; LYRICS: Sheldon Harnick; BOOK: Jerry Bock & Sheldon Harnick; ADDITIONAL BOOK MATERIAL: Jerome Coopersmith; BASED ON: 1/ the 1904 journal *Extracts from Adam's Diary (translated from the original Ms.)*, by Mark Twain; 2/ the 1882 short story *The Lady or the Tiger?*, by Frank R. Stockton; 3/ the 1953 cartoon story *Passionella*, by Jules Feiffer; DIRECTOR: Mike Nichols [his first musical]; CHOREOGRAPHER: Lee Becker Theodore; ADDITIONAL MUSICAL STAGING: Herbert Ross [he actually replaced Lee Becker, despite the credits]; SETS/COSTUMES: Tony Walton; LIGHTING: Jean Rosenthal; SOUND: Robert Liftin; MUSICAL DIRECTOR/VOCAL ARRANGEMENTS/ADDITIONAL SCORING: Elliot Lawrence; ORCHESTRATIONS: Eddie Sauter; CAST RECORDING on Columbia; PRESS: Harvey B. Sabinson, Lee Solters, Harry Nigro, Jay Russell; CASTING: Michael Shurtleff; ANIMATION FILM SEQUENCE of Barbara Harris: Richard Williams; GENERAL MANAGERS: Joseph Harris & Ira Bernstein; PRODUCTION STAGE MANAGER: Jerry Adler, *George Thorn*; STAGE MANAGER: George Thorn, *Joe Dooley*; ASSISTANT STAGE MANAGER: Tom Porter. Star billing was rotated among the three stars. **Cast Standbys**: For Alan Alda: Ken Kercheval & Hal Linden; For Larry Blyden: Ken Kercheval; For Barbara Harris: Phyllis Newman. **Understudy**: For Barbara Harris: Carmen Alvarez. **General Understudies**: Bill Reilly, Ceil Delli, Scott Pearson.

THE DIARY OF ADAM AND EVE. Time: Saturday, June 1; Place: Eden; Deals with the dawn of humanity & innocence. *Cast:* ADAM: Alan Alda (3), *Ken Kercheval* (from 3/27/67), *Hal Holbrook* (from 4/6/67), *Alan Alda* (from 7/3/67); EVE: Barbara Harris (1), *Phyllis Newman* (all matinees from 11/23/66, and also stood in for Miss Harris during vacation, 7/10/67–7/31/67), *Carmen Alvarez* (matinees from 8/9/67), *Sue Ann Langdon* (evenings only, from 11/1/67); SNAKE: Larry Blyden (2). "Here in Eden" (Eve); "Feelings" (Eve); "(This) Eve" (Adam); "Friends" (Eve); "The Apple Tree" ("Forbidden Fruit") (Snake); "Beautiful, Beautiful World" (Adam); "It's a Fish" (Adam); "Go to Sleep, Whatever You Are" (Eve); "What Makes Me Love Him?" (Eve).

THE LADY OR THE TIGER? Time: A Long time ago; Place: A semi-barbaric kingdom; A warrior who dares to love his princess is put to the test of opening one of two doors behind which he will find either a beautiful girl who he must marry, or a tiger. The princess tips her warrior which door to open — but to which fate will she consign him, female rival or tiger? Incidentally, Princess Barbara has an accent mark over the second "a." **Cast:** BALLADEER: Larry Blyden (2); KING ARIK: Marc Jordan (8); PRINCESS BARBARA: Barbara Harris (1), *Phyllis Newman* (all matinees from 11/23/66, and also stood in for Miss Harris during vacation, 7/10/67–7/31/67), *Carmen Alvarez* (matinees from 8/9/67), *Sue Ann Langdon* (evenings only, from 11/1/67); PRISONER: Jay Norman; PRISONER'S BRIDE: Jaclynn Villamil; NADJIRA: Carmen Alvarez (4); CAPTAIN SANJAR: Alan Alda (3), *Ken Kercheval* (from 3/27/67), *Hal Holbrook* (from 4/6/67), *Alan Alda* (from 7/3/67); GUARD: Robert Klein (9), *David McCorkle*; KING ARIK'S COURT: Jackie Cronin (5), Michael Davis (6), Neil F. Jones (7), Barbara Lang (10), Mary Louise (11), *Ceil Delli, Sal Pernice*. "I'll Tell You a Truth" (Balladeer), "Make Way" (King's Court & Arik), "Forbidden Love (in Gaul)" (Barbara & Sanjar), "The Apple Tree" ("Forbidden Fruit)" (reprise) (Balladeer), "I've Got What You Want" (Barbara), "Tiger, Tiger" (Barbara), "Make Way" (reprise) (King's Court), "Which Door?" (Sanjar, Barbara, Arik & Court), "I'll Tell You a Truth" (reprise) (Balladeer).

PASSIONELLA. Time: Now; Place: Here. By using a fairy godmother, a girl chimney sweep realizes her dream of becoming a movie star, only to discover that her idolized Prince Charming in his black leather jacket is also a phoney. **Cast:** NARRATOR: Larry Blyden (2); ELLA/PASSIONELLA: Barbara Harris (1), *Phyllis Newman* (all matinees from 11/23/66, and also stood in for Miss Harris during vacation, 7/10/67–7/31/67), *Carmen Alvarez* (matinees from 8/9/67), *Sue Ann Langdon* (evenings only from 11/1/67); MR. FALLIBLE: Robert Klein (9), *David McCorkle*; PRODUCER: Marc Jordan (8); FLIP/THE PRINCE CHARMING: Alan Alda (3), *Ken Kercheval* (from 3/27/67), *Hal Holbrook* (from 4/6/67), *Alan Alda* (from 7/3/67); SUBWAY RIDERS/EL MOROCCO PATRONS/FANS/FLIP'S FOLLOWING/ MOVIE SET CREW: Carmen Alvarez, Jackie Cronin, Michael Davis, Neil F. Jones, Marc Jordan, Robert Klein (*David McCorkle*), Barbara Lang, Mary Louise, Jay Norman, Jaclynn Villamil (12), *Ceil Delli, Sal Pernice*. "Oh, To Be a Movie Star" (Ella), "Gorgeous" (Passionella), "(Who, Who, Who, Who) Who is She?" (Company), "I Know" (Ella) [this number was added shortly after opening], "Wealth" (Passionella). "You Are Not Real" (Flip & Company), "George L." (Ella & George).

The show got generally excellent Broadway reviews. Barbara Harris won a Tony, and the show was also nominated for musical, composer & lyricist, direction of a musical, choreography, costumes, and for Alan Alda.

After Broadway. TOUR. Opened on 10/24/68, at the Rajah Theatre, Reading, Pa., and closed on 3/20/69, after 63 cities. DIRECTOR/CHOREOGRAPHER: James Moore; SETS: Leo B. Meyer; MUSICAL DIRECTOR: Philip Fradkin. **Cast:** Will MacKenzie, Rosemary Prinz, Tom Ewell.

OFF BROADWAY REVIVAL. 3/24/87–4/11/87. 20 PERFORMANCES. PRESENTED BY the York Theatre Company; DIRECTOR/CHOREOGRAPHER: Robert Nigro; MUSICAL DIRECTOR: David Krane. **Cast:** Kathy Morath, John Sloman, Rufus Bonds Jr., Ron La Rosa, Lyle Garrett, Kevin Wallace.

GOODSPEED OPERA HOUSE, Conn., 10/28/99–12/19/99. Previews from 10/8/99. Ted Pappas heard a 1966 demo recording of the original show, which had "Talkin' Truth" (Flip) on it before it was cut. He asked Sheldon Harnick if he could insert it into the Goodspeed production, so Mr. Harnick wrote a new scene for Passionella's acting teacher (who now got the song). Mr. Harnick changed a line in the song, to bring it more up to date. Jerry Bock and Sheldon Harnick appeared on opening night. DIRECTOR: Ted Pappas; SETS: James Noone; COSTUMES: David

C. Woolard; LIGHTING: David F. Segal; MUSICAL DIRECTOR: Michael O'Flaherty. **Cast:** Kevin Ligon, Joanna Glushak, John Scherer, Sloan Just.

The Diary of Adam and Eve segment was produced Off Off Broadway at the 45TH STREET THEATRE, 8/4/04–8/15/04, in repertory with Stephen Sondheim's *Marry Me a Little*. Admission to each show was separate. DIRECTOR: Michael Klimzak; MUSICAL DIRECTOR: John Clayton. **Cast:** J. Brandon Savage & Laura Gruet (in her New York debut).

CITY CENTER, NYC, 5/12/05–5/16/05. *The Apple Tree* was presented as part of the *Encores!* series of staged readings. **Cast:** Kristin Chenoweth.

32. *Are You with It?*

A humble insurance company actuary misplaces a decimal point, is fired, and is persuaded by "Goldie," an Acres of Fun Carnival barker, to join the show, where he concentrates on a new type of figure, i.e. Vivian's. He uncovers a scam by the carnival's owner to rob the Nutmeg Insurance Company, and gets his old job back. Cleo was the carnival's fat black lady. Bunny was a sexy tent-dancer, with risqué songs. There was a trio of singing and dancing midgets.

The Broadway Run. NEW CENTURY THEATRE, 11/10/45– 4/27/46; SHUBERT THEATRE, 4/30/46–6/29/46. Total of 264 PERFORMANCES. PRESENTED BY Richard Kollmar & James W. Gardiner; MUSIC: Harry Revel; LYRICS: Arnold B. Horwitt; BOOK: Sam Perrin & George Balzer; ADAPTED FROM the novel *Slightly Perfect*, by George Malcolm-Smith; DIRECTOR: Edward Reveaux; CHOREOGRAPHER: Jack Donohue; SETS/LIGHTING: George Jenkins; COSTUMES: Willa Kim (from sketches by Raoul Pene du Bois); MUSICAL DIRECTOR: Will Irwin; ORCHESTRATIONS: Joe Glover, Hans Spialek, Ted Royal, Don Walker, Walter Paul; VOCAL ARRANGEMENTS/VOCALIZATIONS SUPERVISOR: H. Clay Warnick; NO CAST RECORDING; PRESS: Bernard Simon & Dorothy Ross; GENERAL MANAGER: Leo Rose; GENERAL STAGE MANAGER: Frank Coletti; STAGE MANAGER: George Hunter; ASSISTANT STAGE MANAGER: Jimmy Allen. **Cast:** MARGE KELLER: Jane Dulo (6); MR. BIXBY: Sydney Boyd; MR. MAPLETON: Johnny Stearns; WILBUR HASKINS: Johnny Downs (2); VIVIAN REILLY: Joan Roberts (1); POLICEMAN: Duke McHale (8); "GOLDIE": Lew Parker (3); BARTENDER: Lou Wills Jr.(9); CARTER: Lew Eckels; SNAKE CHARMER'S DAUGHTER: Jane Deering (5), *Kathryn Lee, Jeanne Coyne*; CICERO: Bunny Briggs (10); CLEO: June Richmond (7); A BARKER: Johnny Stearns; BALLOON SELLER: Mildred Jocelyn; BUNNY LA FLEUR: Dolores Gray (4); SALLY SWIVELHIPS: Diane Adrian, *Gretchen Houser*; GEORGETTA: Buster Shaver (11); OLIVE: Olive; GEORGE: George; RICHARD: Richard; STRONG MAN: William Lundy, *Ray Arnett*; AERIALIST: Jane Deering, *Kathryn Lee*; OFFICE BOY: Hal Hunter; QUARTET: 1ST MUSICIAN: Lou Hurst; 2ND MUSICIAN: David Lambert; 3RD MUSICIAN: Jerry Duane; 4TH MUSICIAN: Jerry Packer; LOREN: Loren Welch [character cut during the run]; GIRLS: Dorothy Bennett, Vivian Cook, Jeanne Coyne, Pompey Cross (*Cece Eames*), Dorothy Drew, Suzanne Graves, Beth Green, Betty Heather, Penny Holt, Gretchen Houser, Joan Kavanagh, Charlotte Lorraine, Pat Marlowe, June Morrison, Renee Russell, Bette Valentine, Doris York, *Kay Popp*; BOYS: Jimmy Allen, Jerry Ames, Eddie Feder, Bill Julian, John Laverty, Don Miraglia, Tommy Morton, George Thornton. *Ray Arnett, John Martin, Matt Mattox, Eddie Vale.* **Act I: Scene 1** A boarding house in Hartford, Conn.; at 7.45 on a summer morning; **Scene 2** Bushnell Park, Hartford; a moment later; **Scene 3** Office of the Nutmeg Insurance Company; **Scene 4** Bushnell Park; a few minutes later; **Scene 5** Joe's Barroom; **Scene 6** Behind the tent of the "Plantation Minstrels"; **Scene 7** The midway; "Acres of Fun"; **Scene 8** Behind the Minstrel tent; **Scene 9** Two train compartments; **Scene 10** Behind the tent; **Scene 11** The midway. **Act II: Scene 1** Office of the Nutmeg Insurance Company; **Scene 2** Behind the tent; **Scene 3** "Acres of Fun" in Worcester; **Scene 4** The tent; **Scene 5** The train; **Scene 6** Carter's office on the train; **Scene 7** Inside the Midway Frolics tent; **Scene 8** The midway. **Act I:** "Five More Minutes in Bed" (Marge & Ensemble). Dancers: Jane Deering, Kathryn Lee, Jeanne Coyne; "Nutmeg Insurance" (Wilbur, Marge, Bixby, Mapleton, Ensemble), "Slightly

Perfect" (Vivian & Wilbur), "When a Good Man Takes to Drink" (Vivian & Policeman), "When a Good Man Takes to Drink" (reprise) (Vivian, Policeman, Bartender), "Poor Little Me" (Cleo), "Are You with It?" (Bunny, Quartette, Ensemble), "This is My Beloved" (Vivian & Wilbur), "Slightly Slightly" (Olive, George, Richard). Dance: Buster & Olive; "Vivian's Reverie" (ballet) (music adapted by Will Irwin from scenes by Harry Revel) (Aerialist, Strong Man, Circus Performers). *Act II*: "Send Us Back to the Kitchen" (Marge & Girls). Dance by Office Boy; "Here I Go Again" (Vivian & Quartette), "You Gotta Keep Saying 'No'" (Bunny), "Just Beyond the Rainbow" (Cleo & Ensemble). Dance by Cicero; "In Our Cozy Little Cottage of Tomorrow" (Bunny & Goldie), Finale (Entire Company).

The show received divided reviews, and some raves.

After Broadway. THE MOVIE. 1948. DIRECTOR: Jack Hively. It had a totally new score by Sidney Miller and Inez James. *Cast:* Donald O'Connor, Olga San Juan, Lew Parker.

33. *Ari*

Also called: *Leon Uris' Ari*. Set in Cyprus in 1947. Ari tries to get children from Nazi concentration camp past British blockade into Palestine.

Before Broadway. The show tried out at the National Theatre, Washington, DC, 12/22/70–1/2/71, then went to Broadway.

The Broadway Run. MARK HELLINGER THEATRE, 1/15/71–1/30/71. 12 previews from 1/6/71. 19 PERFORMANCES. PRESENTED BY Ken Gaston & Leonard J. Goldberg, in association with Henry Stern; MUSIC: Walt Smith; ADDITIONAL MUSIC: William Fisher; LYRICS/BOOK: Leon Uris (based on the first half of his 1957 novel *Exodus*); DIRECTOR: Lucia Victor; CHOREOGRAPHER: Talley Beatty; SETS: Robert Randolph; COSTUMES: Sara Brook; LIGHTING: Nananne Porcher; MUSICAL DIRECTOR/VOCAL ARRANGEMENTS: Stanley Lebowsky; ORCHESTRATIONS: Philip J. Lang; DANCE & INCIDENTAL MUSIC ARRANGEMENTS: Peter Howard; PRESS: David Lipsky; GENERAL MANAGER: Victor Samrock; COMPANY MANAGER: James Awe; PRODUCTION STAGE MANAGER: Wade Miller; STAGE MANAGER: Jack Timmers; ASSISTANT STAGE MANAGERS: Dorothy Hanning & Didi Francis. CAST: JOAB: Joseph Della Sorte (11); ZEV: Mark Zeller (8); DAVID: Martin Ross (5); MANDRIA, THE GREEK: C.K. Alexander (6); GENERAL SUTHERLAND: Jack Gwillim (9); MAJOR CALDWELL: Jamie Ross (10); ARI BEN CANAAN: David Cryer (1) ☆; MARK PARKER: Norwood Smith (7); KITTY FREMONT: Constance Towers (2) ☆; DOV: John Savage (3); KAREN: Jacqueline Mayro (4); BENJY: Roger Morgan; ARMETEAU: Alexander Orfaly; HIS FRIEND: Edward Becker; CAPTAIN HENLEY: Casper Roos; REFUGEE CHILDREN: Tracey Eman, Kelley Boa, Mona Daleo, Toni Lund, Lynn Reynolds, Timmy Ousey, Todd Jones, Johnny Welch, Tony Dean; DANCERS: Bryant Baker, Bjarne Buchtrup, Ron Crofoot, Richard Dodd, Pi Douglass, Richard Maxon, Ronn Steinman, Carol Estey, Reggie Israel, Karen L. Jablons, Joanna Mendl, Gayle Pines, Deborah Strauss; SINGERS: Edward Becker, Ted Bloecher, Bennett Hill, Henry Lawrence, Art Matthews, Casper Roos, D. Brian Wallach, Bonnie Marcus, Patricia Noal, Susan Schevers, Suzanne Horn. **Standby:** Kitty: Rita Gardner. **Understudies:** Ari: Norwood Smith; Karen: Patricia Noal & Bonnie Marcus; Benjy: Timmy Ousey; Dov: Ronn Steinman; Armeteau: Henry Lawrence; Sutherland: Casper Roos; Caldwell/Henley: Art Matthews; Timmy/Tony: Todd Jones. *Act I:* "Children's Lament" (Children); *Scene 1* Beach near Famagusta, Cyprus; at night: "Yerushaliam" (Ari), "The Saga of The Haganah" (David, Zev, Joab, Mandria); *Scene 2* Mandria's house; immediately thereafter: "The Saga of the Haganah" (reprise) (Mandria); *Scene 3* A waterfront cafe; the next night: "Give Me One Good Reason" (Kitty); *Scene 4* Detention camp, children's compound; the following afternoon: "Dov's Nightmare" (Dov & Victims of Holocaust), "Karen's Lullaby" (Karen); *Scene 5* A waterfront cafe, quayside, Larnaca; a few days later: "Aphrodite" (Mandria & Armeteau); *Scene 6* Detention camp, children's compound; the following week: "My Galilee" (Ari & Palestinians); *Scene 7* A military camp; a week later: "The Lord Helps Those Who Help Themselves" (David & Palestinians); *Scene 8* Detention camp; a few days later: "Alphabet Song" (Karen & Children), Tactics;

Scene 9 The dispensary: "Give Me One Good Reason" (reprise) (Kitty); *Scene 10* Mandria's house; a few days after. British HQ; the same day. Mandria's house; the following afternoon: "My Brother's Keeper" (Ari). *Act II: Scene 1* A hidden cove; the next morning: "The Exodus" (David & Ensemble); *Scene 2* Gen. Sutherland's quarters; noon: "He'll Never Be Mine" (Kitty); *Scene 3* Detention camp; 2 pm: "One Flag" (Karen & Children); *Scene 4* Military camp; 5 pm: "The Lord Helps Those Who Help Themselves" (reprise) (Mandria); *Scene 5* Dockside, Kyrenia; 6 pm; *Scene 6* Parker's hotel room; immediately thereafter; *Scene 7* Aboard the *Exodus*, Kyrenia Harbor; the 80th hour of the hunger strike through the 120th hour: "I See What I Choose to See" (Karen & Dov), "Hora-Galilee" (dance) (Karen, Dov, Children, Palestinians), "Ari's Promise" (Ari); *Scene 8* Dockside, Kyrenia; immediately thereafter: Finale (reprises of "Ari's Promise" and "The Exodus") (Company).

One major mistake was to try musicalizing the first half of Leon Uris' great book, and another was letting Mr. Uris write the lyrics and libretto. The question asked about why this musical was produced in the first place was "why?" If it was to get to the Jewish theatre-party market it didn't work. It was panned on Broadway (Martin Gottfried in *Women's Wear Daily* devastated it). A concentration camp ballet didn't help. First-time producers Gaston & Goldberg were both in their 20s.

34. *Arms and the Girl*

Set in Ridgefield, Fairfield Co., Conn., during the Revolutionary War. Jo is committed in the fight for independence. She carries sword and rifle, and dresses in men's clothing. But she's a bungler, and causes confusion instead. She becomes involved with a runaway slave who takes the name of whatever state she's in at the time (originally Virginia, then Pennsylvania, and now Connecticut). Franz is a Hessian deserter, with whom Jo has an affair. At the end, when George Washington arrives, Jo expects to be decorated for her services, but the general tells her to stay the hell out of the revolution. Bundling (an unmarried couple sleeping together, with a board between them) was an old New England custom much featured in both the play and the publicity. Aaron was a local officer, married to Prudence.

Before Broadway. Morton Gould replaced Burton Lane during rehearsals. The show got mixed reviews in Philadelphia, but very good ones in Boston. The numbers "I'm Scared," "Johnny Cake," and "Little Old Cabin Door" were cut before Broadway.

The Broadway Run. FORTY-SIXTH STREET THEATRE, 2/2/50–5/27/50. 134 PERFORMANCES. PRESENTED BY the Theatre Guild, in association with Anthony Brady Farrell; MUSIC: Morton Gould; LYRICS: Dorothy Fields; BOOK: Herbert & Dorothy Fields, Rouben Mamoulian; BASED ON the 1933 comedy *The Pursuit of Happiness*, by Alan Child & Isabelle Louden (i.e. Theatre Guild principals Lawrence Langner & his wife Armina Marshall); DIRECTOR: Rouben Mamoulian; CHOREOGRAPHER: Michael Kidd; SETS: Horace Armistead; COSTUMES: Audre; MUSICAL DIRECTOR: Frederick Dvonch; ORCHESTRATIONS: Morton Gould & Philip J. Lang; PUBLICITY DIRECTOR: Joseph Heidt; PRODUCTION SUPERVISORS: Lawrence Langner & Theresa Helburn; COMPANY MANAGER: George Oshrin; STAGE MANAGERS: John Cornell & Herman Magidson. CAST: CONNECTICUT: Pearl Bailey (4), *Delores Martin*; FRANZ: Georges Guetary (2), *John Tyers*; JO KIRKLAND: Nanette Fabray (1), *Mary O'Fallon*; THAD JENNINGS: Seth Arnold; TWO SONS OF LIBERTY: Andrew Aprea & Victor Young; TOWN CRIER: William J. McCarthy; CAPT. AARON KIRKLAND: Florenz Ames; DRUMMER: Jerry Miller; SERGEANT: Norman Weise; PRUDENCE KIRKLAND: Eda Heinemann; COMFORT KIRKLAND: Lulu Belle Clarke; BEN: Sterling Hall; MATTHEW: Joseph Caruso; A MILITIAMAN: Peter Miceli; ABIGAIL: Mimi Cabanne; BETSY: Joan Keenan; COL. MORTIMER SHERWOOD: John Conte (3); AIDE TO GENERAL CURTIS: Daniel O'Brien; GEN. LUCIUS CURTIS: Cliff Dunstan; JOHN: Paul Fitzpatrick; DAVID: Philip Rodd; AIDE TO GEN. WASHINGTON: Robert Rippy; GEN. GEORGE WASHINGTON: Arthur Vinton; DANCERS: Edmund Balin, Barbara Ferguson, Peter Gennaro, Annabelle Gold, Maria Harriton, William Inglis, Robert Josias, Barbara McCutcheon, Patricia Muller, Arthur Partington, Marc West, Onna White, Fern Whitney, Lou Yetter; SINGERS: Howard Andreola, Andrew Aprea, Mimi Cabanne, Joseph Caruso, Sterling Hall, Katherine Hennig, Joan Keenan, Peter Miceli, Daniel O'Brien, Mary O'Fallon, Frederick Olsson, Robert Rippy, Shirley Robbins, Patricia Rogers, Helen Stanton, Bettina Thayer, Donald Thrall, William Thunhurst, Norman Weise, Victor Young. **Standbys**: Franz: Stephen Douglass; Connecticut: Delores Martin. **Understudies**: Jo: Mary O'Fallon; Sherwood: Andy Aprea. **Act I**: **Scene 1** Hayloft of Thad Jennings' barn, Ridgefield, Conn.; 1776; **Scene 2** Village Green; a few hours later; **Scene 3** Behind the Kirkland barn; immediately following; **Scene 4** Meeting House; same evening; **Scene 5** Outside the Meeting House; **Scene 6** Parlor of the Kirkland home. **Act II**: **Scene 1** The Kirkland parlor; **Scene 2** The Boston Post Road; early next morning; **Scene 3** Behind the Kirkland barn; **Scene 4** Village Green. **Act I**: "A Girl with a Flame" (Jo), "That's What I Told Him Last Night" (Aaron & Girls), "I Like it Here" (Franz); "That's My Fella" (Jo) (danced by Arthur Partington & Barbara McCutcheon, and: FIRST TWO COUPLES: Fern Whitney, Maria Harriton, William Inglis, Edmund Balin; WHITTLER AND GIRL: Marc West & Annabelle Gold; DEACON: Lou Yetter; SIREN: Onna White; BUTTERFLY CATCHER & GIRL: Peter Gennaro & Patricia Muller; THE PURSUED: Robert Josias; PATIENT ONE: Shirley Robbins; "A Cow and a Plough and a Frau" (Franz), "Nothin' for Nothin'" (Connecticut), "He Will Tonight" (Jo & Girls), "Don't Talk" (Sherwood), "Plantation in Philadelphia" (Jo, Franz, Connecticut, Sherwood, Company) (danced by Boys & Girls) [the show-stopper], "You Kissed Me" (Jo). **Act II**: "Don't Talk" (reprise) (Sherwood), "I'll Never Learn" (Jo & Franz), "There Must Be Something Better than Love" (Connecticut), "She's Exciting" (Franz), "Mister Washington! Uncle George" (Boys & Girls), "A Cow and a Plough and a Frau" (reprise) (Joe & Franz).

Broadway reviews were divided, but basically favorable. Pearl Bailey stole the show, and three weeks after the opening she was raised to star billing. The cast was plagued by illnesses; all three principal players quit before three months into the run. One evening the big white horse ridden by George Washington dumped on stage.

35. *Around the World (in Eighty Days)*

A musical extravaganza, including motion pictures, a circus, a train plunging over a collapsing bridge, the landing of the U.S. Marines up the aisles of the theatre. Set in 1872. On a wager, Fogg attempts to travel the world in 80 days, attended by his manservant Passepartout, and pursued by Fix.

Before Broadway. Mike Todd, the original producer, withdrew early. Robert Davison constructed 34 sets. The numbers "Slave Auction" and "Snagtooth Gertie" were not used. The show opened at the Boston Opera House, on 4/28/46. Orson Welles played Fix for one performance, to show the designated actor how to play it, but he was so good that the actor quit, and Welles continued to play it; it then played at the Shubert Theatre, New Haven, 5/7/46; and at the Shubert Theatre, Philadelphia, 5/14/46. The number "Missus Aouda" was cut before Broadway.

The Broadway Run. ADELPHI THEATRE, 5/31/46–8/3/46. 74 PERFORMANCES. A Mercury Theatre production, PRESENTED BY Orson Welles; MUSIC/LYRICS: Cole Porter; BOOK: Orson Welles (he adapted it from the 1873 Jules Verne novel); DIRECTOR: Orson Welles; EXECUTIVE DIRECTOR: Richard Wilson; CHOREOGRAPHER: Nelson Barclift; SETS: Robert Davison; COSTUMES: Alvin Colt; LIGHTING: Peggy Clark; MUSICAL DIRECTOR: Harry Levant; ORCHESTRATIONS: Russell Bennett & Ted Royal; VOCAL ARRANGEMENTS: Mitchell Ayres; FILM EDITOR: Irving Lerner; CIRCUS ARRANGER: Barbette; PRESS: Frank Goodman; GENERAL MANAGER: Hugo Schaaf; GENERAL STAGE MANAGER: Henri Caubisens; ASSISTANT STAGE MANAGERS: James Wicker, Spencer James, Phil King. **Cast**: A BANK ROBBER: Brainerd Duffield; A POLICE INSPECTOR: Guy Spaull; DICK FIX, A COPPER'S NARK: Orson Welles; LONDON BOBBIES: Nathan Baker, Jack Pitchon, Myron Speth, Gordon West; A LADY: Genevieve Sauris; MR. PHILEAS FOGG: Arthur Margetson (1); AVERY JEVITY, 1ST EARL OF CRAVENAW: Stefan Schnabel; MOLLY MUGGINS, AN IRISH NURSEMAID: Julie Warren (3); "PAT" PASSEPARTOUT, A YANKEE MANSERVANT TO FOGG: Larry Laurence (4) [Mr. Laurence was really

Enzo Stuarti]; MR. BENJAMIN CRUETT-SPEW: Brainerd Duffield; MR. RALPH RUNCIBLE: Guy Spaull; SIR CHARLES MANDIBOY: Bernard Savage; LORD UPDITCH: Billy Howell; A SERVINGMAN: Bruce Cartwright; ANOTHER SERVINGMAN: Gregory McDougall; A STATION ATTENDANT: Billy Howell; MEERAHLAH, A DANCER: Dorothy Bird; TWO DANCING FELLAS: Lucas Aco & Myron Speth; BRITISH CONSUL IN SUEZ: Bernard Savage; AN ARAB SPY: Stefan Schnabel; A 2ND ARAB SPY: Brainerd Duffield; SNAKE CHARMERS: Eddy Di Genova, Victor Savidge, Stanley Turner; A FAKIR: Lucas Aco; MAURICE GOODPILE, CONDUCTOR ON THE GREAT INDIAN PENINSULA R.R.: Guy Spaull; A SIKH: Spencer James; MRS. AOUDA, AN INDIAN PRINCESS: Mary Healy (2); A HIGH PRIEST: Arthur Cohen; VARIOUS SINISTER CHINESE: Phil King, Billy Howell, Lucas Aco, Nathan Baker; LEE TOY: Jackie Cezanne; TWO DAUGHTERS OF JOY: Lee Morrison & Nancy Newton; MR. OKA SAKA, PROPRIETOR OF THE OKA SAKA CIRCUS: Brainerd Duffield; CIRCUS ARTISTS: THE FOOT JUGGLERS: The Three Kanasawa; THE ROLLING GLOBE LADY: Adelaide Corsi; THE CONTORTIONIST: Miss Lu; THE HAND BALANCER: Ishikawa; THE AERIALISTS: Mary Broussard, Lee Vincent, Patricia Leith, Virginia Morris; ASSISTANTS: Billy Howell, Lucas Aco, Gregory McDougall, Myron Speth; THE SLIDE FOR LIFE: Ray Goody; ROUSTABOUTS: Jack Pitchon & Tony Montell [end of Circus Artist section]; CLOWNS: MOTHER: Stefan Schnabel; FATHER: Nathan Barker; CHILD: Bernie Pisarski; BRIDE: Cliff Chapman; GROOM: Larry Laurence; MINISTER: Arthur Cohen; POLICEMAN: Jack Cassidy; MONKEY MAN: Eddy Di Genova; KIMONA MAN: Allan Lowell; FIREMEN: Bruce Cartwright & Gordon West; DRAGON: Daniel De Paolo; AN ATTENDANT: Stanley Turner [end of Clown section]; A BARTENDER: Eddy Di Genova; MEXICAN DANCERS: Dorothy Bird & Bruce Cartwright; LOLA, THE PROPRIETRESS OF A CAFE: Victoria Cordova (5); SOL, A STATION MASTER IN SAN FRANCISCO: Brainerd Duffield; SAM, A STAGECOACH DRIVER: Billy Howell; JIM, A RAILROAD CONDUCTOR OF THE CENTRAL PACIFIC R.R.: James Aco; JAKE, A RAILROAD ENGINEER: Spencer James; A MEDICINE MAN OF THE OJIBWAY: Stefan Schnabel; OTHER MEDICINE MEN: George Spelvin & Billy Howell; JAIL GUARD: Allan Lowell; SINGING GENTLEMEN: Kenneth Bonjukian, Jack Cassidy, Arthur Cohen, Daniel De Paolo, Eddy Di Genova, Allan Lowell, Tony Montell, Jack Pitchon, Victor Savidge, Stanley Turner; DANCING GENTLEMEN: Lucas Aco, Nathan Baker, Bruce Cartwright, Billy Howell, Phil King, Gregory McDougall, Myron Speth, Gordon West; SINGING LADIES: Florence Gault, Natalye Greene, Arline Hanna, Marion Kohler, Rose Marie Patane, Genevieve Sauris, Gina Siena, Drucilla Strain; DANCING LADIES: Mary Broussard, Jackie Cezanne, Eleanore Gregory, Patricia Leith, Virginia Morris, Lee Morrison, Nancy Newton, Miriam Pandor, Virginia Sands, Lee Vincent.

Note: George Spelvin is a name traditionally used on Broadway to denote an actor in a double role. So, we don't know who Mr. Spelvin is. **Act I**: Overture (Orchestra); **Scene 1** Movies; **Scene 2** Interior of Jevity's Bank, London, England; **Scene 3** Movies; **Scene 4** Hyde Park: "Look What I Found" (Molly, Pat, Singers); **Scene 5** A London street; **Scene 6** Mr. Fogg's flat in London: "There He Goes, Mr. Phileas Fogg" (Fogg & Pat); **Scene 7** A street before the Whist Club, London: "There He Goes, Mr. Phileas Fogg" (reprise) (Fogg, Pat, Dancers, Singers); **Scene 8** The Card Room of the Whist Club; **Scene 9** Fogg's flat; **Scene 10** The Charing Cross Railroad Station; **Scene 11** Suez, Egypt: "Meerahlah" (Singing Boys). Dance (Meerahlah & Dancers); **Scene 12** The end of railway tracks in British India; **Scene 13** The Great Indian Forest; **Scene 14** The Pagoda of Pilagi: "Suttee Procession" (Mrs. Aouda, Dancers, Singers); **Scene 15** A jungle encampment in the Himalayas: Dance (Dancers); **Scene 16** Aboard the S.S. *Tankadere*, on the China Sea: "Sea Chantey" (Singing Boys), "Should I Tell You I Love You?" (music from "If I Hadn't a Husband," an unused song from *The Seven Lively Arts*) (Aouda); **Scene 17** Movies; **Scene 18** A street of evil repute in Hong Kong; **Scene 19** Interior of an Opium Hell in the same city: "Pipe Dreaming" (Pat & Singing Chorus); **Scene 20** The Oka Saka Circus, Yokohama, Japan: "Oka Saka Circus" (dance) (Circus Performers). **Act II**: Entr'acte (Orchestra); **Scene 1** Movies; **Scene 2** Lola's, a low place in Lower California: Dance (Dorothy Bird, Bruce Cartwright, Jackie Cezanne, Dancers), "If You Smile at Me" (Lola), "Pipe Dreaming" (reprise) (Pat), "If You Smile at Me" (reprise) (Molly); **Scene 3** The railroad station in San Francisco; **Scene 4** Movies; **Scene 5** A passenger car on the Central Pacific Railway:

Somewhere in the Rocky Mountains; *Scene 6* The Perilous Pass at Medicine Bow; *Scene 7* A water stop on the banks of the Republican River; *Scene 8* The peak of Bald Mountain: "Wherever They Fly the Flag of Old England" (Fogg & Singing Girls), "The Marines' Hymn" (Aouda & Singing Boys); *Scene 9* The harbor, Liverpool, England; *Scene 10* The gaol in Liverpool; *Scene 11* A cell in Liverpool Gaol: "Should I Tell You I Love You?" (reprise) (Aouda); *Scene 12* A street in London; *Scene 13* Outside the London Whist Club; *Scene 14* Grand Tableau: Finale (Entire Company).

On Broadway the show got a couple of very good reviews but mostly unfavorable ones, partly due to the comparatively poor quality of Cole Porter's hurriedly-written score, and partly because it opened so soon after *Annie Get Your Gun*. On 6/2/46 Orson Welles on his radio program, threatened to put a voodoo curse on the critics who were knocking his show. It lost $300,000 (it cost an initial $200,000). It was overproduced by far (55 stagehands ran the production). This venture wrecked Mr. Welles financially, and was the cause of his European exile.

After Broadway. THE MOVIE. Mike Todd acquired the film rights from the financially struggling Orson Welles and subsequently made the movie *Around the World in 80 Days* out of it in 1956, with none of the stage material, but with many guest stars. *Cast*: FOGG: David Niven; PASSEPARTOUT: Cantinflas; FIX: Robert Newton; AOUDA: Shirley MacLaine.

36. *Artists and Models*

Also known as *Artists and Models* (1943). An expensive musical revue (it cost $125,000 and lost $225,000), the sixth and last in a series of the same name. Producer Lou Walters ran the Broadway nightclub The Latin Quarter.

The Broadway Run. BROADWAY THEATRE, 11/5/43–11/27/43. 28 PERFORMANCES. PRESENTED BY Lou Walters & Don Ross, in association with E.M. Loew & Michael Redstone; MUSIC/LYRICS: Dan Shapiro, Milton Pascal, Phil Charig, Ervin Drake; BOOK: Lou Walters, Don Ross, Frank Luther; CONCEIVED BY/DIRECTOR: Lou Walters; DIALOGUE DIRECTOR: John Kennedy; CHOREOGRAPHER: Natalie Kamarova (assisted by Lauretta Jefferson); SETS: Watson Barratt; COSTUMES: Katherine Kuhn; MUSICAL DIRECTOR: Max Meth; ORCHESTRATIONS: Hans Spialek, Ted Royal, Don Walker, Emil Gerstenberger, Charlie Cooke; VOCAL ARRANGEMENTS: Buck (i.e. Clay) Warnick. *Act I*: *Scene 1* "Parade of Models" (models with perfume names walk elegantly down a flight of steps and stand at footlights). VELVET NIGHT: Mira Stephans; GOLDEN DAY: Nancy Callahan; MY SIN: Jackie Jordan; MIDNIGHT MADNESS: Joan Myles; MELODY MOOD: Ruth Dexter; STAR SAPPHIRE: Gail Banner; TEMPEST TOPAZ: Lana Holmes; AMBER GLOW: Iris Amber; BRIDAL BLUSH: Helen Heller; CORAL CROWN: Edna Ryan; BLITHE HARBOR: Lillian Moore; ROSE BLOOM: Grace de Witt; BLUE HEAVEN: Maureen Cunningham; DUSKY DAWN: Patti Robins; RADIANT RUBY: Carmelita Lanza; *Scene 2* Three comedians, Jackie Gleason (2), Marty May (4), Billy Newell (6), rush out to explain the proceedings in a prologue; *Scene 3* Minstrelsy (minstrel songs): "Way up North in Dixie Land" [Marty May (4), Jackie Gleason (2), Billy Newell (6), the Radio Aces (Joe & Lou Stoner, Marty Drake) (7), the Three Businessmen of Rhythm and Pearl, the Peters Sisters (Mattye, Ann, Virginia), Minstrel Men, Minstrel Girls, Ensemble], "Swing Low, Sweet Harriet" (blues shouter) [sung by Jane Froman (1)]; *Scene 4* Burlesque. Comedy routine: Candy Butcher: Jackie Gleason (2); Song: "How'ja Like to Take Me Home?" [Collette Lyons (5) as a blonde in a short skirt]; Striptease [fake striptease; the Worth Sisters (Toni & Mimi)]; Sketch: Taken for a Ride: BOZE-O-SNIDER: Jackie Gleason (2); SLIDING WILLIE WESTON: Marty May (4); MIKE SPECKS: Billy Newell (6); GYSPY ROSE CORIO: Collette Lyons (5); MARGIE SMART: Billie Boze; GEORGIA SUDDEN: Barbara Bannister; *Scene 5* Hollywood: *The Road to Manasooris*. A Super-Duper epic in Technicolor. Is the tropical island's virgin really a virgin? VIRGIN PRINCESS: Mayla; CHIEF DANASOORIS: Jackie Gleason (2); BEACHCOMBER: Don Saxon; KAY TOWNSEND: Mildred Law; MARGIE "BOO-BOO" LE MAY: Collette Lyons (5); BOB STEVENS: Nick Long; GIRLS OF MANASOORIS: Billie Boze, Barbara Bannister, Grace de Witt; SCHWARTZESOORIS: The Peters Sisters (Mattye, Ann, Virginia); CAPTAIN OF MARINES: Ben Yost.

"Isle of Manasooris" (sung by Mayla & Island Beauties). S~~___~~ Roebuck" (what are the pages of the famous catalogue use~~___~~ areas?) [Jackie Gleason (2) & Collette Lyons (5)]. Lover's ~~___~~ tive (Mayla). Dance of the Cobra (Harold & Lola); *Scene 6* R~~___~~ Latecomers [Marty May (4)]; *Scene 7* Concert [Frances Faye (2~~___~~ & Harps in Swing (Harp Ensemble: Helen Thomas, Margaret~~___~~ Catherine Johnk, Ann Roberts)]; *Scene 8* Vaudeville. Song: "~~___~~ Dakota, South Dakota Moon" [Jackie Gleason (2), Marty May (4), B~~___~~ Newell (6); *Scene 9* Blues song: "My Heart is on a Binge Again" [su~~___~~ by Jane Froman (1)]; *Scene 10* "New York Heartbeat" (ballet) (m: Monsieur Georges F. Kamaroff; staging/ch: Mme Natalie Kamarova). BALLERINA: Carol King; DANCER: Slava Toumine; ALSO WITH: Nick Long, the Worth Sisters (Toni & Mimi), Mayla, the Three Businessmen of Rhythm and Pearl, the Ben Yost Singers, Corps de Ballet, Dancing Girls, Specialty Girls, American Beauties. *Act II*: *Scene 1* Circus. EQUESTRIENNES: Sheila Bond, Jeanne Blanche, Gertrude Erdey, Lee Loprete; JUNGLE DENIZENS: Mira Stephans, Ruth Dexter, Lana Holmes, Iris Amber, Joan Myles, Jackie Jordan, Gail Banner, Nancy Callahan; PONIES: Ballet & Dancing Girls; BIRDS OF PARADISE: The Worth Sisters (Toni & Mimi); CARNIVORI: Betty Jane Hunt, Mullen Sisters, Patsy Lu Rains; CLOWNS: The Ben Yost Singers (octet: Albert Cazentre, William Hogue, Alfred Jimenez, Arthur Laurent, Jack Leslie, Fred Peters, Jack Paddock, Torine Rella); AERIAL BALLET: Chat Chilvers, Betty Hackett, Corinne Rose, Florence Walsh; TRAINER: Joseph Hahn; LION TAMER: Mildred Law; *Scene 2* Questionnaire (special material by Bud Burston). Song: "What Does the Public Want?" [the Radio Aces (Joe & Lou Stoner, Marty Drake) (7)]; *Scene 3* Specialty (Gloria LeRoy); *Scene 4* Revue. Song: "You Are Romance" (blues) [Jane Froman (1), Don Saxon, the Ben Yost Singers, Dancers, Specialty Girls, Ballet Boys, Raye & Naldi (i.e. Mary Raye & Mario Naldi)].Song: "Blowin' My Top" (Nick Long, Don Saxon, Mildred Law, Specialty Girls); *Scene 5* Sketch: Afternoon Tea [Collette Lyons (5)]; *Scene 6* Drama. Submarine U-Boat X37 (blonde stowaway found by the captain and lieutenant). CAPTAIN ANSCHLUSS: Jackie Gleason (2); LT. EINGEMACHT: Billy Newell (6); BYSTANDER: Marty May (4); SEAMEN: Lou Stoner & Marty Drake; BOATSWAIN: Joe Stoner; STOWAWAY: Billie Boze; *Scene 7* Blues song: "Let's Keep it That Way" (m: Abner Silver; l: Milton Berle & Ervin Drake) [sung by Jane Froman (1)]; *Scene 8* Finale (Every Show Has One). Song: "You'll Know that it's Me" (Entire Company). *Specialty Dancers*: Sheila Bond, Gloria LeRoy, Jeanne Blanche, Lee Loprete, The Mullen Sisters (twins), Gertrude Erdey, Betty Jane Hunt, Patsy Lu Rains, Mary-Jo Ball; *Dancing Girls*: Ellen Taylor, Maureen Cunningham, Wynn Stanley, Lillian Moore, Edna Ryan, Helen Heller, Grace de Witt, Frances Gardner; *Ballet Girls*: Carmelita Lanza, Virginia Harriot, Jane Sproule, Patti Robins, Irene Vernon, Nancy Newton, Didi Foret, Margaret Neil, Leandra Hines, Anita Divine; *Ballet Boys*: Charles Beckman, Joseph Hahn, Harold Haskin, Slava Toumine (i.e. Sviatoslav Toumine); *Models*: Iris Amber, Gail Banner, Nancy Callahan, Ruth Dexter, Lana Holmes, Jackie Jordan, Joan Myles, Mira Stephans.

This was singer Jane Froman's first show after her plane crash, and she performed sitting down. Reviews were divided, mostly bad. The show made way for the incoming *Carmen Jones*.

37. *As the Girls Go*

Lucille is the first woman president of the USA. Husband Waldo is the First Gentleman, and takes advantage of his position to chase girls. Son Kenny is having a romance with Kathy.

Before Broadway. It began as a satire, but in the light of the terrible pre-Broadway tryout in Boston, where it was criticized very badly by the local press, it was re-worked substantially into what was essentially an old-style "legs" revue, starring Bobby Clark in his last Broadway show. Then it went to New Haven for more tryouts with the re-worked material.

The Broadway Run. WINTER GARDEN THEATRE, 11/13/48–7/9/49; BROADWAY THEATRE, 9/14/49–1/14/50. Total of 414 PERFORMANCES. PRESENTED BY Michael Todd; MUSIC: Jimmy McHugh; LYRICS: Harold Adamson; BOOK: William Roos; DIRECTOR/SETS: Howard Bay; CHORE-

As the Girls Go

etch: "Sears —
...d for in rural
...ryst Narra-
...sume for
(piano)
Ross,
orth
ly

ASSISTANT TO HOWARD BAY: Horace
...i; MUSICAL DIRECTOR: Max Meth;
...AL DIRECTOR/VOCAL ARRANGE-
...ll; GENERAL MANAGER: Ben F.
...Jones; ASSOCIATE STAGE MAN-
...MANAGER: Freddie Nay. *Cast:*
...UCILLE THOMPSON WELLING-
...ON: Bill Callahan (3); MICKEY
...TOMMY WELLINGTON: Donny Har-
...THY ROBINSON: Betty Jane Watson (5),
...obart Cavanaugh (6); GUARD: Jack Russell;
...SITOR: John Brophy; MISS SWENSON: Cavada
...TLER: Curt Stafford; DAUGHTERS OF THE BOSTON TEA
...aire Grenville, Claire Louise Evans, Lois Bolton, Marjorie
...n; FLOYD ROBINSON: Douglas Luther; DIANE: Mildred Hughes;
PHOTOGRAPHER: Kenneth Spaulding; ROSS MILLER: Jack Russell;
DAPHNE: Dorothea Pinto; PHOTOGRAPHER: William Reedy; BLINKY JOE:
Dick Dana (8); DARLENE: Rosemary Williamson; SECRET SERVICE MEN:
George Morris & John Sheehan; SECRET SERVICE WOMEN: Gregg Sher-
wood (*June Kirby*) & Truly Barbara; CHILDREN: Marlene Cameron,
Pauline Hahn, Norma Marlowe, Jonathan Marlowe, Clifford Sales,
Eugene Steiner; SECRETARY: Ruth Thomas; PRESIDENT OF POTOMAC
COLLEGE: Douglas Luther; PREMIERE DANSEUSE: Kathryn Lee (4); SHOW-
GIRLS: Truly Barbara, Pat Gaston, Mildred Hughes, Mickey Miller,
Dorothea Pinto, Gregg Sherwood (*June Kirby*), Ruth Thomas, Rosemary
Williamson; DANCING ENSEMBLE: Jeanett Aquilina, James Brock,
Carmina Cansino, Arline Castle, Charles Chartier, Babs Claire, Peter
Conlow, Jessie Elliott, James Elsegood, Yvette Fairhill, Christina Frerichs,
Patty Ann Jackson, Margaret Jeanne Klein, Frances Krell, Ila McAvoy, Pat
Marlowe, Toni Parker, Joyce Reedy, William Reedy, Bobby Roberts,
Joseph Schenck, Eugene "Buddy" Schwab, Diane Sinclair, Kenneth
Spaulding, Norma Thornton, Larry Villani; SINGING ENSEMBLE: Bob
Burkhardt, Dean Campbell, Barbara Davis, Lydia Fredericks, Betty
George, John Gray, Pearl Hacker, Douglas Luther, Abbe Marshall, Ellen
McCown, George Morris, Jack Russell, Jack Sheehan, Judy Sinclair, Curt
Stafford, Jo Sullivan. *Understudies*: Lucille: Claire Louise Evans; Kenny:
Kenneth Spaulding; Kathy: Ellen McCown; Mickey: Marlene Cameron;
Tommy: Clifford Sales; Barber: Dick Dana; Miss Swenson: Diane Sin-
clair; Blinky Joe: Jack Russell; Premiere Danseuse: Carmina Cansino.
Act I: Scene 1 Roxy Theatre; Jan. 20, 1953; *Scene 2* The Truman White
House balcony; early in the morning; *Scene 3* The White House barber
shop; the following morning; *Scene 4* The White House grounds; immediately following; *Scene 5* The Chartreuse Room in the White House;
that spring; *Scene 6* A corridor in the White House; the following afternoon; *Scene 7* The rumpus room; immediately following; *Scene 8* A
hotel room; *Scene 9* The White House grounds; the next afternoon;
Scene 9a A newspaper office; *Scene 9b* A boudoir; *Scene 10* The American Cannes Beach Club; *Scene 11* A corridor in the White House; *Scene
12* The White House barber shop; that evening; *Scene 13* Kathy's bedroom; that night; *Scene 13a* A telephone company switchboard; *Scene
13b* Kenny's bedroom; *Scene 14* The lobby of the Mayflower Hotel; later;
Scene 15 The Union Depot, Washington, D.C.; the next afternoon. *Act
II: Scene 1* The Union Depot, Washington, D.C.; that night; *Scene 2*
The Campus Inn; later; *Scene 3* A street in Washington; later, at night;
Scene 4 The Chartreuse Room in the White House; Sunday breakfast,
June 3; *Scene 5* The college campus; the next morning; *Scene 6* The Gold
Room in the White House; later, in the evening. *Act I*: "As the Girls Go"
(Waldo & Girls), "Nobody's Heart but Mine" (Kathy & Kenny),
"Brighten up and Be a Little Sunbeam" (Waldo & Children), "Rock,
Rock, Rock" (Kenny & Kathy), "It's More Fun than a Picnic" (Mickey
& Children), "American Cannes" (Waldo & Girls), "You Say the Nicest
Things, Baby" (Kathy, Kenny, Singing Girls), "I've Got the President's
Ear" (Waldo & Girls), "Holiday in the Country" (Entire Company). *Act
II*: "There's No Getting Away from You" (voc arr: Bus Davis) (Kenny,
Singing & Dancing Ensemble). Dance (ch for Miss Lee by Hermes Pan)
(Skip, Kathryn Lee, Dancing Ensemble); "(I Got) Lucky in the Rain"
(Kenny, Kathy, Ensemble). Dance (ch: Hermes Pan) (Kathryn Lee & Bill
Callahan); "Fathers Day" (The Family), "It Takes a Woman to Get a
Man" (Waldo & Ensemble), "You Say the Nicest Things, Baby" (reprise)
(Waldo & Madame President), Finale (Entire Company).

It was the first Broadway show to charge $7.20 for orchestra seats.
Broadway reviews were generally excellent; although it ran for a year, it
still lost money (it cost a record $340,000). Bobby Clark painted spec-
tacles on his face as part of his act, and this led to eye trouble, so much
so that performances had to be suspended, 7/9/49–9/14/49. The show
won a Tony for musical direction.

38. *Aspects of Love*

Often called a "soap opera set to music," it is an extremely
complex through-composed story about incestuous relationships.
The story begins in 1964 with Alex recounting the story of his life.
Then a flashback to 1947 when, at 17, he falls for 25-year-old
Rose, star of a touring acting company. They spend two weeks
together at his Uncle George's unoccupied country estate. George
is in Rome with his mistress Giulietta, but returns unexpectedly.
Alex returns to the Army, George and Giulietta continue their
affair but George eventually marries Rose (who has also had an
affair with Giulietta). George and Rose have a daughter Jenny (at
least Jenny may be George's; she may also be Alex's). About 12
years later Alex returns to visit George & Rose and Jenny falls
madly in love with him. George dies & Alex falls in love with
Giulietta.

Before Broadway. It was first done in 1983 as a "cabaret" production at the annual music festival at Andrew Lloyd Webber's Sydmonton
estate. Then it opened at the PRINCE OF WALES THEATRE, London, on
4/17/89. 1,325 PERFORMANCES. *Cast*: ROSE: Ann Crumb; ALSO WITH:
Michael Ball, Kevin Colson, Kathleen Rowe McAllen, Diana Morrison,
Sally Smith, David Greer. Roger Moore, set to co-star as George, bowed
out on 3/13/89, feeling he wasn't up to the singing.

The Broadway Run. BROADHURST THEATRE, 4/8/90–3/2/91. 22
previews. 377 PERFORMANCES. PRESENTED BY The Really Useful Theatre
Company; MUSIC: Andrew Lloyd Webber; LYRICS: Don Black & Charles
Hart; BOOK: Andrew Lloyd Webber; BASED ON the novelized autobi-
ography by David Garnett (Virginia Woolf's nephew); DIRECTOR: Trevor
Nunn; CHOREOGRAPHER: Gillian Lynne; SETS/COSTUMES: Maria Bjorn-
son; LIGHTING: Andrew Bridge; SOUND: Martin Levan; MUSICAL DIREC-
TOR: Paul Bogaev; ORCHESTRATIONS: David Cullen & Andrew Lloyd
Webber; LONDON CAST RECORDING on Polydor; PRESS: Fred Nathan
Company; CASTING: Johnson—Liff & Zerman; GENERAL MANAGE-
MENT: Gatchell & Neufeld; COMPANY MANAGER: Mary Miller; PRO-
DUCTION STAGE MANAGER: Perry Cline; STAGE MANAGER: Elisabeth
Farwell; ASSISTANT STAGE MANAGER: Michael J. Passaro. *Cast*: ROSE
VIBERT, A FRENCH ACTRESS: Ann Crumb, *Elinore O'Connell (from 9/90),
Sarah Brightman (from 12/14/90)*; ALEX DILLINGHAM, A YOUNG ENG-
LISHMAN: Michael Ball; GEORGE DILLINGHAM, ALEX'S UNCLE, AN
ENGLISH PAINTER: Kevin Colson, *Walter Charles, John Cullum (from
10/22/90), Barrie Ingham (from 1/7/91)*; GIULIETTA TRAPANI, AN ITAL-
IAN SCULPTRESS: Kathleen Rowe McAllen; MARCEL RICHARD, AN ACTOR-
MANAGER: Walter Charles; JENNY DILLINGHAM (AGED 12), DAUGHTEROF
ROSE & GEORGE: Deanna DuClos; JENNY, AGED 14: Danielle DuClos;
ELIZABETH, GEORGE'S HOUSEKEEPER: Suzanne Briar; HUGO LE MEUNIER,
ROSE'S FRIEND: Don Goodspeed; JEROME, GEORGE'S GARDENER: Philip
Clayton; AT THE CAFE: ACTORS: Philip Clayton, John Dewar, Marcus
Lovett, Kurt Johns; ACTRESSES: Elinore O'Connell, Lisa Vroman,
Wysandria Woolsey; STAGE MANAGER: Don Goodspeed; ASSISTANT
STAGE MANAGER: Jane Todd Baird; WAITER: Gregory Mitchell; MAN ON
DATE: Eric Johnson; HIS DATE: Suzanne Briar; AT THE FAIRGROUND:
1ST BARKER: Eric Johnson, *R.F. Daley (from 12/19/90)*; 2ND BARKER:
Kurt Johns; ALEX'S FRIENDS: Don Goodspeed & Philip Clayton; THEIR
GIRLFRIENDS: Elinore O'Connell & Lisa Vroman; ALEX'S DATE: Jane
Todd Baird; WAR VETERAN: John Dewar; HIS WIFE: Suzanne Briar;
LOCAL MEN: Marcus Lovett & Gregory Mitchell; LOCAL WOMAN:
Wysandria Woolsey; IN VENICE: GONDOLIER: Kurt Johns; HOTEL
CASHIER: Lisa Vroman; NUN: Elinore O'Connell; DOCTOR: John Dewar;
HOTELIER: Eric Johnson, *R.F. Daley (from 12/19/90)*; PHARMACIST:
Wysandria Woolsey; REGISTRAR: Eric Johnson, *R.F. Daley (from

12/19/90); ASSISTANT REGISTRAR: John Dewar; IN ROSE'S DRESSING ROOM: ROSE'S FRIENDS: Jane Todd Baird, Suzanne Briar, Philip Clayton, John Dewar, Kurt Johns, Eric Johnson (*R.F.Daley* from 12/19/90), Marcus Lovett, Gregory Mitchell, Elinore O'Connell, Lisa Vroman, Wysandria Woolsey; AT THE CIRCUS: CLOWNS: Gregory Mitchell, Marcus Lovett, Philip Clayton, John Dewar; KNIFE THROWER: Kurt Johns; HIS ASSISTANT: Wysandria Woolsey; AT THE WAKE: YOUNG PEASANT: Gregory Mitchell; OTHER ROLES: Ensemble. *Understudies*: Rose: Elinore O'Connell & Wysandria Woolsey; Giulietta: Lisa Vroman & Wysandria Woolsey; Alex: Don Goodspeed; George: Walter Charles; Marcel: Eric Johnson, *R.F. Daley* (from 12/19/90); Jenny at 14: Jane Todd Baird; Jenny at 12: Brooke Sunny Moriber; Hugo: Marcus Lovett. *Swings*: Wiley Kidd, Brad Oscar, Anne Marie Runolfsson. *Orchestra*: CONCERTMASTER: Sanford Allen; VIOLIN: Dale Stuckenbruck; VIOLA: Jenny Hansen; CELLO: Mark Shuman; BASS: Deb Spohnheimer; HARP: Grace Paradise; FLUTES: Diva Goodfriend-Koven & Lawrence Feldman; PICCOLO/ALTO FLUTE: Diva Goodfriend-Koven; OBOE/ENGLISH HORN: Blair Tindall; CLARINETS: Jon Manasse & Lawrence Feldman; BASS CLARINET: Jon Manasse; SAXOPHONE: Lawrence Feldman; FRENCH HORN: Russell Rizner; PIANO/CELESTE: Paul Sportelli; SYNTHESIZERS: Nicholas Archer; PERCUSSION: Louis Oddo. *Act I. Prologue*: On the terrace at Pau; 1964: "Love Changes Everything" (Alex); FRANCE; 1947: A small theatre in Montpellier (Rose, Marcel, Ensemble); A cafe in Montpellier: "Parlez-vous Francais"/"The Cafe" (Rose, Alex, Ensemble); The railway station (Alex & Rose); In a train compartment: "Seeing is Believing" (Alex & Rose); The house at Pau (Alex & Rose); A sculpture exhibition in Paris: "A Memory of a Happy Moment" (George & Giulietta); In many rooms in the house at Pau (Rose & Alex); On the terrace (Rose, Alex, George); Outside the bedroom (Rose & Alex); Up in the Pyrenees: "Chanson d'enfance" (Rose); The house at Pau (Rose & Alex); The railway station (Rose & Marcel); TWO YEARS PASS…: A fairground in Paris: "Everybody Loves a Hero" (Barkers & Ensemble); George's flat in Paris: "She'd Be Far Better off with You" (Alex, George, Rose, Elizabeth); Giulietta's studio in Venice: "Stop. Wait. Please" (Giulietta, George, Ensemble); A registry office (Rose, George, Registrars, Giulietta, Guests); A military camp in Malaya (Alex). *Act II*: THIRTEEN YEARS LATER…: A grand theatre in Paris: "Leading Lady" (Marcel & Ensemble); At the stage door (Rose & Alex); George's house at Pau: "Other Pleasures" (George, Jenny, Alex, Rose); A cafe in Venice/The house at Pau: "There is More to Love" (Giulietta & Rose); The garden at Pau (George, Rose, Alex): "Mermaid Song" (Jenny & Alex); The countryside around the house (Jenny & Alex); TWO YEARS PASS…: The garden at Pau (Jenny, Alex, Rose); On the terrace: "The First Man You Remember" (George & Jenny); Up in the Pyrenees (Jenny & Alex); In the vineyard at Pau (Company); A circus in Paris: "The Journey of a Lifetime" (Company); Outside the circus: "Falling" (George, Rose, Alex, Jenny); Jenny's bedroom in Paris (Alex & Jenny); The vineyards at Pau: "Hand Me the Wine and the Dice" (Giulietta, Ensemble, Rose, Jenny, Alex, Marcel, Hugo); A hayloft (Giulietta & Alex); On the terrace (Alex, Jenny, Rose, Giulietta): "Anything but Lonely" (Rose).

On Broadway reviews were divided, mostly bad, and it ran as long as it did only because it had advance sales of over $11 million, and because of the Lloyd Webber name. It received Tony nominations for musical, score, book, direction of a musical, and for Kevin Colson and Kathleen Rowe McAllen.

After Broadway. TOUR. Opened on 4/13/92, in Toronto. PRESENTED BY Broadway in Concert, LIVENT, The Really Useful Theatre Company of Canada; DIRECTOR: Robin Phillips; SETS: Philip Silver; MUSICAL SUPERVISOR: Michael Reed. *Cast*: ROSE: Linda Balgord; ALEX: Ron Bohmer; GEORGE: Barrie Ingham; MARCEL: David Masenheimer; ENSEMBLE INCLUDED: Bonnie Schon.

PALO ALTO PLAYERS, Calif., 4/26/02–5/12/02. This was a revised revival. The hayloft scene was cut. DIRECTOR/CHOREOGRAPHER: Mike Ward.

39. *Assassins*

A long-awaited Stephen Sondheim revue-like piece, with no intermission, about presidential assassins and would-be assassins.

John Wilkes Booth (1838–1865), actor, shot and k[...] Lincoln at Ford's Theatre, Washington, DC; Cha[...] (1841–1882), disappointed office seeker, shot and ki[...] Garfield at the Baltimore & Potomac railroad station, [...]ton, DC; Leon Czolgosz (1873–1901), Polish anarchist, s[...] killed William McKinley at the Pan American Expositio[...] Buffalo; Giuseppe Zangara (1900–1933), Italian bricklayer, s[...] and killed Mayor Anton Cermak of Chicago, in Miami. Cerma[...] was sitting next to Franklin D. Roosevelt; Lee Harvey Oswal[...] (1931–1963), shot and killed John F. Kennedy in Dallas; Samuel Byck (1930–1974), unemployed tire salesman, attempted to fly a commercial airplane into Richard Nixon's White House in 1974; Lynette "Squeaky" Fromme (b. 1948), Manson-groupie, attempted to shoot Gerald Ford in Sacramento; Sara Jane Moore (b. 1930), fanatic, attempted to shoot Gerald Ford in San Francisco; John W. Hinckley Jr. (b. 1955), failure and Jodie Foster freak, shot but did not kill Ronald Reagan in Washington, DC.

Before Broadway. Steve Sondheim was on a panel at Stuart Ostrow's Musical Theatre Lab when he read a play by Charles Gilbert about a fictional assassination. Mr. Gilbert had made notes about actual assassins, including letters and anecdotes from and about them, and this gave Sondheim the idea for a new musical. Several years later, with permission from Mr. Gilbert, Sondheim and John Weidman began working on the musical, which was originally going to cover all of history, but which was narrowed down to U.S. presidential assassins and wannabes, a sort of portrayal of the frustration of the American dream. It is not historically accurate.

It first played Off Broadway, at PLAYWRIGHTS HORIZONS, 1/27/91–2/16/91. 48 previews from 12/18/90. Limited run of 25 PERFORMANCES. MUSIC/LYRICS: Stephen Sondheim; BOOK: John Weidman; BASED ON an idea by Charles S. Gilbert Jr.; DIRECTOR: Jerry Zaks; CHOREOGRAPHER: D.J. Giagni; SETS: Loren Sherman; COSTUMES: William Ivey Long; LIGHTING: Paul Gallo; SOUND: Scott Lehrer; MUSICAL DIRECTOR: Paul Gemignani; ORCHESTRATIONS: Michael Starobin; CAST RECORDING on RCA, made 3/6/91–3/7/91. *Cast:* PROPRIETOR: William Parry; LEON CZOLGOSZ: Terrence Mann; JOHN HINCKLEY: Greg Germann; CHARLES GUITEAU: Jonathan Hadary; GIUSEPPE "JOE" ZANGARA: Eddie Korbich; SAMUEL BYCK: Lee Wilkof; LYNETTE "SQUEAKY" FROMME: Annie Golden; SARAH JANE MOORE: Debra Monk; JOHN WILKES BOOTH: Victor Garber; BALLADEER: Patrick Cassidy; DAVID HEROLD: Marcus Olson; BARTENDER: John Jellison; EMMA GOLDMAN: Lyn Greene; JAMES GARFIELD: William Parry; JAMES BLAINE: John Jellison; HANGMAN: Marcus Olson; WARDEN: John Jellison; BILLY: Michael Shulman; GERALD FORD: William Parry; LEE HARVEY OSWALD: Jason Alexander; BYSTANDERS: Joy Franz, Lyn Greene, John Jellison, Marcus Olson, William Parry, Michael Shulman; FAIRGOERS: Joy Franz, Lyn Greene, John Jellison, Marcus Olson, William Parry, Michael Shulman. *Understudies*: Ted Brunetti, Joy Franz, Davis Gaines, John Jellison, Julia Kiley, J.R. Nutt, Marcus Olson, William Parry. *Musicians*: PIANO: Paul Ford; DRUMS/PERCUSSION: Paul Gemignani; SYNTHESIZERS: Michael Starobin. Opening: "Everybody's Got the Right" (Proprietor, Czolgosz, Hinckley, Guiteau, Zangara, Byck, Fromme, Moore), "The Ballad of Booth" (Balladeer, Booth, Herold), "How I Saved Roosevelt" (Bystanders & Zangara), "Gun Song" (Czolgosz, Booth, Guiteau, Moore), "Ballad of Czolgosz" (Balladeer & Fairgoers), "Unworthy of Your Love" (Hinckley & Fromme), "The Ballad of Guiteau" (Guiteau & Balladeer), "Another National Anthem" (Czolgosz, Booth, Hinckley, Fromme, Zangara, Guiteau, Moore, Byck, Balladeer), "November 22, 1963" (Booth, Oswald, Guiteau, Czolgosz, Byck, Hinckley, Fromme, Moore, Zangara), Final Sequence: "You Can Close the New York Stock Exchange"/"Everybody's" (Booth, Czolgosz, Moore, Guiteau, Zangara, Byck, Hinckley, Fromme, Oswald). It was critically panned, but it sold out. However, the country was not politically ready for this show.

It next played at the SIGNATURE THEATRE, Arlington, Va., 8/20/92–10/3/92. DIRECTOR/CHOREOGRAPHER: Eric D. Schaeffer; SETS: Lou Stancari. *Cast:* PROPRIETOR: Jason Fulmer; CZOLGOSZ: Richard Potter; HINCKLEY: Wallace Acton; GUITEAU: Sean Baldwin; ZANGARA: Gregg

'E: Suzanne Dennis; MOORE: Donna
DEER: Michael Sharp; EMMA: Judy

AREHOUSE, London, 10/29/92–
on had a new number: "Some-
ely before the finale. Henry
R: Sam Mendes; SETS/COS-
Pyant; MUSICAL DIRECTOR:
ard. *Cast:* PROPRIETOR: Paul Bent-
INCKLEY: Michael Cantwell; GUITEAU:
RA: Paul Harrhy; FROMME: Cathryn Bradshaw;
D; BOOTH: David Firth; BALLADEER: Anthony Bar-
evin Walton; EMMA: Sue Kelvin; GARFIELD: Kevin Wal-
NE: Gareth Snook; FORD: Paul Bentley; OSWALD: Gareth
K; BYSTANDERS: Paul Bentley, Michelle Fine, Sue Kelvin, Gareth
nook, Kevin Walton.

It tried again, this time for Broadway, in 2001. It was to have begun previews 11/1/01 for a 11/29/01 opening at the Music Box but, with its content, the 9/11/01 crisis meant it had to be yanked. The stars were to have been Neil Patrick Harris, Denis O'Hare, Raul Esparza (as Zangara), Becky Ann Baker, Mary Catherine Garrison.

BERKSHIRE THEATRE FESTIVAL, Stockbridge, Mass., 8/6/03–8/29/03.

DIRECTOR: Timothy Douglas; CHOREOGRAPHERS: Susan Dibble & Timothy Douglas; MUSICAL DIRECTOR: Ken Clark. *Cast:* CZOLGOSZ: Andrew Michael Neiman; HINCKLEY: Eric Loscheider; GUITEAU: Aric Martin; ZANGARA: Jonathan Kay; BYCK: Kasey Mahaffy; FROMME: Jill Michael; MOORE: Megan Ofsowitz; BOOTH: Michael Baker; BALLADEER/OSWALD: Joe Jung.

FREUD PLAYHOUSE, UCLA, Los Angeles, 9/15/03. A one-night concert version, part of the *Reprise!* series. DIRECTOR: David Lee; MUSICAL DIRECTOR: Steve Orich. *Cast:* Patrick Cassidy, Annie Golden, Lyn Greene, Anthony Crivello, Harry Groener, John Mahoney, Kevin Chamberlin, Kevin Earley, Ben Platt.

On the way to Broadway, John Dossett was going to play Czolgosz, but he stayed in the Broadway run of *Gypsy*. Broadway previews were postponed from 3/19/04 to 3/26/04, and then to 3/31/04 due to construction in the theatre. On 3/10/04 it was announced that the limited Broadway run would extend from 5/30/04 to 6/20/04, then to 7/4/04, then to 9/12/04.

The Broadway Run. STUDIO 54, 4/22/04–7/18/04. Previews from 3/31/04. 26 previews. Limited run of 101 PERFORMANCES. PRESENTED BY the Roundabout Theatre Company; MUSIC/LYRICS: Stephen Sondheim; BOOK: John Weidman; BASED ON an idea by Charles S. Gilbert Jr.; DIRECTOR: Joe Mantello; CHOREOGRAPHER: Jonathan Butterell; SETS: Robert Brill; COSTUMES: Susan Hilferty; LIGHTING: Peggy Eisenhauer & Jules Fisher; SOUND: Dan Moses Schreier; MUSICAL DIRECTOR: Paul Gemignani, *Nicholas Archer* (from 6/15/04); ORCHESTRATIONS: Michael Starobin; NEW CAST RECORDING made on 6/7/04, and released on PS Classics on 8/3/04. It included "Something Just Broke"; PRESS: Boneau/Bryan-Brown; CASTING: Jim Carnahan; ASSOCIATE ARTISTIC DIRECTOR: Scott Ellis; GENERAL MANAGER: Sydney Davolos; COMPANY MANAGER: Nicole Larson; PRODUCTION STAGE MANAGER: William Joseph Barnes; STAGE MANAGER: Jon Krause. *Cast:* THE PROPRIETOR: Marc Kudisch ☆ (until 6/13/04), *John Schiappa* (from 6/15/04); LEON CZOLGOSZ: James Barbour ☆; JOHN HINCKLEY: Alexander Gemignani ☆; CHARLES GUITEAU: Denis O'Hare ☆; GIUSEPPE "JOE" ZANGARA: Jeffrey Kuhn ☆; SAMUEL BYCK: Mario Cantone ☆; LYNETTE "SQUEAKY" FROMME: Mary Catherine Garrison ☆; SARAH JANE MOORE: Becky Ann Baker ☆; JOHN WILKES BOOTH: Michael Cerveris ☆; BALLADEER: Neil Patrick Harris ☆; DAVID HEROLD: Brandon Wardell; EMMA GOLDMAN: Anne L. Nathan; JAMES BLAINE: James Clow; PRESIDENT JAMES GARFIELD: Merwin Foard; BILLY: Eamon Foley; PRESIDENT GERALD FORD: James Clow; LEE HARVEY OSWALD: Neil Patrick Harris ☆; ENSEMBLE: James Clow, Merwin Foard, Eamon Foley, Kendra Kassebaum, Anne L. Nathan, Brandon Wardell. *Understudies:* Moore: Anne L. Nathan; Fromme: Kendra Kassebaum; Booth/Guiteau: James Clow; Czolgosz/Byck: Merwin Foard; Proprietor: Merwin Foard; Hinckley: Brandon Wardell; Balladeer/Zangara: Brandon Wardell. *Swings:* Ken Krugman, Sally Wilfert, Chris Peluso. *Orchestra:* KEYBOARDS: Nicholas Michael Archer & Paul

Ford; FLUTE/PICCOLO: Dennis Anderson & Scott Schachter; CLARINETS: Dennis Anderson, Andrew Shreeves, Scott Schachter, Mark Thrasher; SOPRANO SAX/HARMONICA: Dennis Anderson; OBOE/ENGLISH HORN/ALTO SAX: Andrew Shreeves; BASS CLARINET/E FLAT CLARINET/TENOR SAX: Scott Schachter; BASSOON/BARITONE SAX: Mark Thrasher; TRUMPETS: Dominic Derasse & Phil Granger; CORNET: Dominic Derasse; FLUGELHORN: Phil Granger; FRENCH HORN: Ronald Sell; TROMBONE/EUPHONIUM: Bruce Eidem; GUITARS/BANJO/MANDOLIN: Scott Kuney; BASS/ELECTRIC BASS: John Beal; DRUMS/PERCUSSION: Larry Lelli. "Everybody's Got the Right" (Proprietor, Czolgosz, Guiteau, Fromme, Byck, Booth, Zangara, Hinckley, Moore), "The Ballad of Booth" (Balladeer & Booth), "How I Saved Roosevelt" (Zangara & Ensemble), "Gun Song" (Czolgosz, Booth, Guiteau, Moore), "The Ballad of Czolgosz" (Balladeer & Ensemble), "Unworthy of Your Love" (Hinckley & Fromme), "The Ballad of Guiteau" (Guiteau & Balladeer), "Another National Anthem" (Proprietor, Czolgosz, Booth, Hinckley, Fromme, Zangara, Moore, Guiteau, Byck, Balladeer, Ensemble), "Something Just Broke" (Ensemble), "Everybody's Got the Right" (reprise) (Moore, Byck, Czolgosz, Zangara, Fromme, Hinckley, Oswald, Guiteau, Booth).

The show was the big winner at the 2004 Tony Awards, winning for revival of a musical [sic — the Tony Award committee ruled it to be a revival], director of a musical, lighting, orchestrations, and for Michael Cerveris. It was also nominated for sets, and for Denis O'Hare. Due to bad business, it was announced on 7/7/04 that the show would finally close early on 7/18/04.

40. *Avenue Q*

A *Sesame Street* parody, with puppets and humans discussing issues such as love, money, race, jury duty. "Contains full puppet nudity. Not suitable for children." Set in an outer borough of New York City, in the present.

Before Broadway. In 1998 Jeff Marks and Robert Lopez met and began working on the concept at the BMI — Lehman Engel Musical Theatre Workshop in New York City. They were not sure at first if it was going to be a 45-minute TV pilot or a stage musical.

Avenue Q: Children's Television for Twentysomethings had two York Theatre Company readings on 5/8/00. DIRECTOR: Seth Goldstein. Four puppeteers from *Sesame Street*: Rick Lyon, Stephanie D'Abruzzo, John Tartaglia, Lara MacLean. *Cast:* Brian Yorkey, Ann Harada, Amanda Green. It was such a success that there were two more readings on 5/30/00, free and open to the public. It had the same crew and cast as for the original readings. By 6/01 it was aiming at Broadway.

Then it ran at the DINA MERRILL THEATRE, at the Eugene O'Neill Theatre Conference, Waterford, Conn, 8/10/02, 8/11/02, 8/15/02, and 8/17/02. *Cast:* Rick Lyon, John Tartaglia, Stephanie D'Abruzzo, Lara MacLean, Amanda Green, Ann Harada, Jordan Gelber.

It had its world premiere at the VINEYARD THEATRE, NYC, 3/13/03–5/11/03. Previews from 2/20/03. PRESENTED BY the Vineyard Theatre & New Group. It had the same basic crew as for the later Broadway run, except SOUND: Brett Jarvis. *Cast:* Ann Harada, Natalie Venetia Belcon, Jordan Gelber, Stephanie D'Abruzzo, Rick Lyon, John Tartaglia. Rick Lyon fell during the 2/25/03 preview and the performance of the following night was canceled. He returned on 2/27/03. The 3/12/03 preview was canceled due to a cast member's family emergency. It resumed on 3/13/03. On 5/8/03 Natalie Venetia Belcon injured her ankle during a performance. The show won several Off Broadway awards, and then moved to Broadway. The number "Tear it up and Throw it Away" was cut before Broadway previews.

The Broadway Run. JOHN GOLDEN THEATRE, 7/31/03–. 22 previews from 7/11/03. PRESENTED BY Kevin McCollum, Robyn Goodman, Jeffrey Seller, Vineyard Theatre, The New Group; MUSIC/LYRICS/CONCEIVED BY: Robert Lopez & Jeff Marks; BOOK: Jeff Whitty; DIRECTOR: Jason Moore; CHOREOGRAPHER: Ken Roberson; SETS: Anna Louizos; COSTUMES: Mirena Rada; LIGHTING: Frances Aronson; SOUND: ACME Sound Partners; PUPPETS: Rick Lyon; MUSICAL SUPERVISOR: Stephen Oremus; ORCHESTRATIONS/ARRANGEMENTS: Stephen Oremus; MUSI-

CAL DIRECTOR/INCIDENTAL MUSIC: Gary Adler; CAST RECORDING on RCA Victor, recorded on 8/10/03, and released on 10/7/03; PRESS: Sam Rudy Media Relations; CASTING: Cindy Tolan; ANIMATION DESIGNER: Robert Lopez; GENERAL MANAGER: John S. Corker; COMPANY MANAGER: Mary K. Witte; PRODUCTION STAGE MANAGER: Evan Ensign; STAGE MANAGER: Christine M. Daly; ASSISTANT STAGE MANAGER: Aymee Garcia. *Cast*: PRINCETON/ROD: John Tartaglia, *Barrett Foa* (during Mr. Tartaglia's vacation, 8/5/04–8/14/04), *John Tartaglia* (until 1/30/05), *Barrett Foa* (from 2/1/05); BRIAN: Jordan Gelber; KATE MONSTER/LUCY T. SLUT, ETC: Stephanie D'Abruzzo; NICKY/TREKKIE MONSTER, ETC: Rick Lyon; CHRISTMAS EVE: Ann Harada, *Ann Sanders* (during Miss Harada's pregnancy leave), *Ann Harada* (from 1/25/05); GARY COLEMAN: Natalie Venetia Belcon; MRS. THISTLETWAT, ETC: Jennifer Barnhart; BAD IDEA BEARS: Jennifer Barnhart & Rick Lyon; ENSEMBLE: Jodi Eichelberger & Peter Linz, *Barrett Foa* (from 12/26/03). *Understudies*: Kate/Lucy: Jen Barnhart & Aymee Garcia; Nicky: Jodi Eichelberger; Trekkie Monster/Bear, etc: Jodi Eichelberger & Peter Linz; Gary: Carmen Ruby Floyd, *Chandra Wilson, Jasmin Walker*; Mrs. T: Aymee Garcia; Princeton/Rod/Nicky/Trekkie: Jodi Eichelberger & Peter Linz, *Barrett Foa* (from 12/26/03); Brian: Peter Linz; Christmas Eve: Erin Quill, *Ann Sanders*; Bear: Jodi Eichelberger, Peter Linz, Aymee Garcia. *Band*: KEYBOARD: Mark Hartman; REEDS: Patience Higgins; DRUMS: Michael Croiter; BASS: Maryann McSweeney; GUITARS: Brian Koonin. *Act I*: "The Avenue Q Theme" (Company), Opening (Company), "What Do You Do with a B.A. in English?"/"It Sucks to Be Me," "If You Were Gay" (Nicky & Rod), "Purpose" (Princeton), "Everyone's a Little Bit Racist" (Princeton, Kate, Gary, Brian, Christmas Eve), "The Internet is for Porn" (Kate, Trekkie Monster, Men), "A Mix Tape" (Kate & Princeton), "I'm Not Wearing Underwear Today" (Brian), "Special" (Lucy), "You Can Be as Loud as the Hell You Want (When You're Making Love)" (Gary & Bad Idea Bears), "Fantasies Come True" (Rod & Kate), "My Girlfriend, Who Lives in Canada" (Rod), "There's a Fine, Fine Line" (Kate). *Act II*: "There is Life Outside Your Apartment" (Brian & Company), "The More You Ruv Someone" (Christmas Eve & Kate), "Schadenfreude" (Gary & Nicky), "I Wish I Could Go Back to College" (Kate, Nicky, Princeton), "The Money Song" (Nicky, Princeton, Gary, Christmas Eve, Brian, Trekkie Monster), "For Now" (Company).

It opened to rave reviews. The show missed a performance due to the 8/14/03 power blackout. On 12/14/03 a leak sprung in the mezzanine ceiling and some plaster fell at the end of Act I. Act II was delayed by five minutes. The show won Tonys for musical, book of a musical, original score written for the theatre, and was also nominated for director of a musical, and for John Tartaglia and Stephanie D'Abruzzo. The production recouped its initial investment.

After Broadway. There was no tour. Instead the show had a long-term gig in Las Vegas.

41. *Baby*

The story is of three pregnancies on a college campus and the effect this has on each relationship. Set in the present, March through November. Alan — a dean — and his wife, Arlene, are in their forties, and now their three daughters are in college and they are alone for the first time; track coach Nick and his wife Pam are in their thirties and have been trying for two years; unmarried students Lizzie and Danny have just started living together. Arlene decides to keep hers, but confronts Alan with the thought that they've only functioned as a married couple by having children. This revelation is good for their marriage. Pam is actually not pregnant, and she and Nick find they are fine just by themselves. Lizzie agrees to marry Danny and they have the child. Film projections of fetuses were used.

Before Broadway. Susan Yankowitz and Ted Tally failed to come up with a libretto that appealed to the producers, so they hired Sybille Pearson. Cut songs included: "The Bear, The Tiger, The Hamster, The Mole," "Fathers of Fathers," "I Wouldn't Go Back," "Like a Baby,"

and "Patterns" (this last, sung by Arlene, was re-instated for the cast album, and for the subsequent tour and other regional productions). However, most of these were used in *Closer than Ever* (see the appendix).

The Broadway Run. ETHEL BARRYMORE THEATRE, 12/4/83–7/1/84. 35 previews. 241 PERFORMANCES. A Freydberg/Bloch production, PRESENTED BY James B. Freydberg & Ivan Bloch, Kenneth — John Productions (Kenneth D. Greenblatt & John J. Pomerantz), and Suzanne J. Schwartz, in association with Manuscript Productions; MUSIC: David Shire; LYRICS: Richard Maltby Jr.; BOOK: Sybille Pearson; BASED ON a story developed with Susan Yankowitz; DIRECTOR: Richard Maltby Jr.; CHOREOGRAPHER: Wayne Cilento; SETS: John Lee Beatty; COSTUMES: Jennifer von Mayrhauser; LIGHTING: Pat Collins; SOUND: Jack Mann; FILM DESIGNER: John Pieplow; FILM SEQUENCES BY: Lennart Nilsson, Bo G. Erickson, Carl O. Lofman, Swedish Television; MUSICAL DIRECTOR: Peter Howard; ORCHESTRATIONS: Jonathan Tunick; CAST RECORDING on Jay; PRESS: Jacksina & Freedman; CASTING: Johnson — Liff; GENERAL MANAGERS: Fremont Associates/Barbara Darwall; PRODUCTION STAGE MANAGER: Peter B. Mumford; STAGE MANAGER: Gary M. Zabinski; ASSISTANT STAGE MANAGER: Dana Sherman. *Cast:* LIZZIE FIELDS: Liz Callaway; DANNY HOOPER: Todd Graff, *Lon Hoyt*; ARLENE MACNALLY: Beth Fowler; ALAN MACNALLY: James Congdon; PAM SAKARIAN: Catherine Cox; NICK SAKARIAN: Martin Vidnovic; NURSE: Barbara Gilbert; DOCTOR: John Jellison, *Joe Warfield*; MR. WEISS: Philip Hoffman; DEAN WEBBER: Dennis Warning; MR. HART: Dennis Warning; INTERN: Lon Hoyt, *Michael Brian*; 1ST WOMAN: Judith Thiergaard, *Alaina Warren Zachary*; 2ND WOMAN: Lisa Robinson, *Susan Goodman*; 3RD WOMAN: Kirsti Carnahan; 4TH WOMAN: Barbara Gilbert; 5TH WOMAN: Judith Thiergaard, *Alaina Warren Zachary*; 6TH WOMAN: Kim Criswell; TOWNSPEOPLE: Kirsti Carnahan, Kim Criswell, Barbara Gilbert, Philip Hoffman, Lon Hoyt, John Jellison, Lisa Robinson, Judith Thiergaard, Dennis Warning. *Understudies*: Lizzie: Kirsti Carnahan; Danny: Lon Hoyt; Arlene: Judith Thiergaard; Alan: John Jellison; Pam: Lisa Robinson; Nick: Philip Hoffman; Doctor: Michael Waldron. *Swings*: Judith Bliss & Michael Waldron. *Act I*: MARCH TO EARLY APRIL: *Scene 1* A college town: "We Start Today" (Danny & Lizzie; Alan & Arlene; Nick & Pam; People in the Town); EARLY APRIL: *Scene 2* Danny & Lizzie's apartment: "What Could Be Better?" (Danny & Lizzie); *Scene 3* Alan & Arlene's bedroom: "The Plaza Song" (Alan & Arlene); *Scene 4* Nick & Pam's bedroom: "Baby, Baby, Baby" (Nick & Pam; Alan & Arlene; Danny & Lizzie); MID–APRIL: *Scene 5* A doctor's waiting-room: "I Want it All" (Pam, Lizzie, Arlene); *Scene 6* The track: "At Night She Comes Home to Me" (Nick & Danny); *Scene 7* On the campus: "What Could Be Better?" (reprise) (Danny & Lizzie); EARLY MAY: *Scene 8* A doctor's office; *Scene 9* A baseball field: "Fatherhood Blues" (Danny, Alan, Nick, Weiss, Webber); *Scene 10* Alan & Arlene's bedroom; MID–MAY: *Scene 11* A bus station; Alan & Arlene's house; *Scene 12* Nick & Pam's bedroom: "Romance" (Nick & Pam), "I Chose Right" (Danny); EARLY JUNE: *Scene 13* Graduation: "We Start Today" (reprise) (Ensemble); MID–JULY: *Scene 14* Danny & Lizzie's apartment: "The Story Goes On" (Lizzie). *Act II*: LATE AUGUST: *Scene 1* The town: "The Ladies Singin' Their Song" (Lizzie & Women in the Town); EARLY SEPTEMBER: *Scene 2* A doctor's office; *Scene 3* On the campus: "Baby, Baby, Baby" (reprise) (Arlene); *Scene 4* Nick & Pam's bedroom: "Romance" (reprise) (Nick & Pam); *Scene 5* Alan & Arlene's porch: "Easier to Love" (Alan); MID–SEPTEMBER: *Scene 6* Danny & Lizzie's apartment: "Two People in Love" (Danny & Lizzie); MID–OCTOBER: *Scene 7* Nick & Pam's bedroom: "With You" (Nick & Pam); *Scene 8* Alan & Arlene's porch: "And What if We Had Loved Like That" (Alan & Arlene); MID–NOVEMBER: *Scene 9* All three bedrooms: "We Start Today" (reprise) (Danny & Lizzie; Nick & Pam; Alan & Arlene), "The Story Goes On" (reprise) (Company).

Reviews were somewhat divided, but mostly good. The show cost $2,750,000. It received Tony Nominations for musical, score, book, direction of a musical, choreography, and for Todd Graff and Liz Callaway.

After Broadway. After Broadway it was much revised by the authors. *Baby* is often done in regional and stock theatres. The Roundabout Theatre Company began considering it in 1999, and it got a reading with them that year. DIRECTOR: Richard Maltby Jr. There was a second reading in 2002. DIRECTOR: Charles Randolph-Wright. *Cast:* La Chanze. By late 2002 plans for the 2003–04 Broadway season were being discussed, with Roundabout to produce, Charles Randolph-Wright to direct, and La Chanze to star, but it fell through.

A revised and updated version had public readings at New Jersey Performing Arts Center, Newark, 10/15/03 & 10/18/03. It was part of a series of staged readings called *Other Stages.* DIRECTOR: Mark S. Hoebee; MUSICAL DIRECTOR: Eugene Gwozdz. *Cast:* LIZZIE: Nikki James; DANNY: Robb Sapp; ARLENE: Victoria Clark; ALAN: Michael Rupert; PAM: Brandi Chavonne Massey; NICK: Norm Lewis; ENSEMBLE: Lenny Wolpe, Jordan Leeds, Blake Ginther, Becky Gulsvig, Rosena Hill, Deborah Tranelli.

Then it had a run at the PAPER MILL PLAYHOUSE (the state theatre of New Jersey), 3/31/04–5/9/04. DIRECTOR: Mark S. Hoebee. *Cast:* PAM: La Chanze [Julia Murney was going to take this role]; NICK: Norm Lewis; ARLENE: Carolee Carmello [Victoria Clark was going to take this role]; LIZZIE: Moeisha McGill; DANNY: Chad Kimball; ALAN: Michael Rupert; ALSO WITH: Bill E. Dietrich, Rosena Hill, Lenny Wolpe. Broadway plans were being discussed.

42. *Bajour*

Johnny, a Gypsy king, returns to New York, looking to bring new blood to his tribe by buying his son Steve a bride from the richer Newark tribe who, he hopes, can pull of a big bajour (Romany word meaning "swindle"). Anthropology student Emily is looking for a tribe to study for her Ph.D thesis, and coerces Lou into helping her join Johnny's. Johnny puts a down payment on Anyanka, who is attracted to Steve. She tells Johnny about her plot to pull a bajour on her own father so she can get the money that Johnny needs to buy her. The victim of the bajour turns out to be Emily's sweet old mother; Anyanka convinces her that her late husband's insurance money is cursed and that Anyanka will remove the curse once the money is in her hands. Anyanka gets $10,000 from Emily's mother, and uses some of it to buy herself for Steve, whom she marries. She gives her father the empty purse, returns the rest of the money to Emily and goes off with Johnny and his tribe.

Before Broadway. This was going to be a show with book by Mike Stewart, music and lyrics by Charles Strouse & Lee Adams, and direction and choreography by Gower Champion, but that never happened. Producer Ed Padula tried to get Carol Burnett to play Emily. The show tried out in Boston and Philadelphia, to divided reviews. It suffered somewhat from being too soon after *Fiddler on the Roof.*

The Broadway Run. SHUBERT THEATRE, 11/23/64–5/8/65; LUNT–FONTANNE THEATRE, 5/10/65–6/12/65. Previews from 11/18/64. Total of 232 PERFORMANCES. PRESENTED BY Carroll Masterson, Harris Masterson, Edward Padula, Norman Twain; MUSIC/LYRICS: Walter Marks; BOOK: Ernest Kinoy (based on his book, and somewhat suggested by the *New Yorker* stories "The Gypsy Women" and "The King of the Gypsies," by Joseph Mitchell); DIRECTOR: Lawrence Kasha; CHOREOGRAPHER: Peter Gennaro; SETS: Oliver Smith; COSTUMES: Freddy Wittop; LIGHTING: Peggy Clark; MUSICAL DIRECTOR/VOCAL ARRANGEMENTS: Lehman Engel; ORCHESTRATIONS: Mort Lindsey; DANCE MUSIC ARRANGEMENTS: Richard De Benedictis; CAST RECORDING on Columbia, made on 11/29/64; PRESS: Seymour Krawitz, Merle Debuskey, Ted Goldsmith; GENERAL MANAGER: Frank Hopkins & Sherman Gross; COMPANY MANAGER: Frank Hopkins; STAGE MANAGER: Tony Manzi; ASSISTANT STAGE MANAGER: Ralph Farnworth. *Cast:* RENTING AGENT: Dick Ensslen; COCKEYE JOHNNY DEMBO: Herschel Bernardi; VANNO: Sal Lombardo; LOOPA: Antonia Rey; 1ST PATROLMAN: Harry Danner; PLAINCLOTHESMAN: Harry Goz; 2ND PATROLMAN: Paul Sorvino; 3RD PATROLMAN: Robert Kristen; LT. LOU MCNIALL: Robert Burr; EMILY KIRSTEN: Nancy Dussault, *Virginia Martin* (during Miss Dussault's illness, 2/8/65–2/27/65); MRS. HELENE KIRSTEN (MOMMA): Mae Questel; ROSA: Asya; MITYA: Vito Durante; FRANKIE: Terry Violino; STEVE: Gus Trikonis; THE KING OF NEWARK: Herbert Edelman, *Pierre Epstein* (from 5/17/65); ANYANKA: Chita Rivera; MARFA: Jeanne Tanzy; OLGA: Carmen

Morales; CHAIRLADY: Lucie Lancaster; WAITER: Harry Danner; J. ARNOLD FOSTER: Ralph Farnworth; DANCERS: Asya, Eileen Barbaris, Michael Bennett, Connie Burnett, John Cashman, Betsy Dickerson, Vito Durante, Gene Foote, Bick Goss, Fernando Grahal, Kazimir Kokich, Marc Maskin, Stan Mazin, Carmen Morales, Carolyn Morris, Leland Palmer, Don Rehg, Geri Seignious, Terry Violino, Billi Vitali; SINGERS: Anita Alpert, Harry Danner, Mariana Doro, Dick Ensslen, Peter Falzone, Ralph Farnworth, Harry Goz, Liza Howell, Robert Kristen, Urylee Leonardos, Evy Love, Madeline Miller, Eugene Morgan, Jessica Quinn, Jeanne Repp, Paul Sorvino. *Understudies:* Anyanka: Carolyn Morris; Emily: Madeline Miller; Johnny: Herb Edelman, *Pierre Epstein* (from 5/17/65); Lou: Paul Sorvino; Helene: Lucie Lancaster; Steve: Stan Mazin; Newark: Ralph Farnworth; Loopa: Jeanne Repp; Chairlady: Mariana Doro; Vanno: Peter Falzone; Marfa: Evy Love. *Act I: Scene 1* The empty store: "Move Over, New York" (Johnny & the Dembeschti); *Scene 2* The city; *Scene 3* The Pickpocket and Confidence Squad: "Where is the Tribe for Me?" (Emily); *Scene 4* Emily's bedroom; *Scene 5* The backyard: "The Haggle" (Anyanka, Steve, Dembeschti Men, Movya Men), "Love-Line" (Anyanka); *Scene 6* In front of the store; *Scene 7* The store (now the ofisa): "Words, Words, Words" (Emily & Johnny); *Scene 8* In front of the store; *Scene 9* The ofisa: "Mean" (Anyanka); *Scene 10* An Urban Renewal site: "Must it Be Love?" (Emily); *Scene 11* The ofisa: "Bajour" (Anyanka, Emily, Johnny, the Dembeschti). *Act II: Scene 1* The backyard: "Soon" (Anyanka, Steve, the Dembeschti); *Scene 2* Momma's kitchen; *Scene 3* The backyard: "I Can" (Anyanka & Emily); *Scene 4* The Pickpocket and Confidence Squad: "Living Simply" (Lou, Emily, Patrolmen); *Scene 5* The Guggenheim Museum; *Scene 6* Central Park: "Honest Man" (Johnny & Newark); *Scene 7* Momma's kitchen: "Guarantees" (Momma), "Love is a Chance" (Emily); *Scene 8* The ofisa: "The Sew-Up" (Anyanka, Momma, Dembeschti Women); *Scene 9* An Urban Renewal site; *Scene 10* The empty store; *Scene 11* The New Jersey Flats; Finale ("Move Over, America") (The Dembeschti).

Reviews were mixed, but generally good. During the run a phone number was advertised and callers got a cast member discussing the show and singing a part of one of the musical numbers. The show lost more than its initial investment of $480,000. It received Tony nominations for choreography, and for Nancy Dussault.

43. *Baker Street*

A Holmesian musical adventure. It begins when someone shoots at Holmes through the window of his Baker Street flat, in gaslit, fogbound London, and ends when Holmes returns from the dead and recovers the Queen's jewels. The individual stories, upon which the musical is based, were tied together by Queen Victoria's 1897 Diamond Jubilee, during which Moriarty is planning to steal the Crown Jewels.

Before Broadway. Since the late 1950s Jerome Coopersmith had been writing the libretto. Alex Cohen agreed to produce, and brought in Marian Grudeff and Ray Jessel to write the score. In 1963, as director, Hal Prince replaced Josh Logan, who in turn had replaced Michael Langham. This was Mr. Prince's first big musical directing job. Alex Cohen wanted George Rose to play Dr. Watson, but Hal Prince wanted Peter Sallis. In mid–August 1964 Hal Prince hired Lee Becker as choreographer, after Bob Fosse had turned it down (he wanted to co-direct) and others, such as Onna White, Don Saddler, and Danny Daniels had not got the job. Mr. Prince liked only two of the songs and, after a poor try out, he brought in Jerry Bock and Sheldon Harnick to write four new songs, at $5,000 per song plus one per cent of the royalties. Their song "Buffalo Belle" was not used, neither were Grudeff & Jessel's "Baker Street March" and "A Veritable Work of Art." The show cost $630,000. *Baker Street* was Tommy Tune's New York debut.

The Broadway Run. BROADWAY THEATRE, 2/16/65–10/30/65; MARTIN BECK THEATRE, 10/31/65–11/14/65. 6 previews from 2/10/65. Total of 313 PERFORMANCES. PRESENTED BY Alexander H. Cohen, in association with Gabriel Katzka; MUSIC/LYRICS: Marian Grudeff & Raymond Jessel, except when noted below as being "by Bock & Harnick" (i.e. Jerry Bock & Sheldon Harnick, who were not credited); BOOK: Jerome Coopersmith; BASED ON the 1891 story *A Scandal in Bohemia* and on other adventures of Sherlock Holmes, by Sir Arthur Conan Doyle: *The Empty House, The Final Problem,* and *A Study in Scarlet*; DIRECTOR: Harold Prince; CHOREOGRAPHER: Lee Becker Theodore; DIAMOND JUBILEE PARADE BY Bil Baird's Marionettes; SETS: Oliver Smith; COSTUMES: Motley; LIGHTING: Jean Rosenthal; MUSICAL DIRECTOR: Harold Hastings; ORCHESTRATIONS: Don Walker; DANCE MUSIC ARRANGEMENTS: John Morris; PRESS: James D. Proctor, Louise Weiner, Don Grant; PRODUCTION ASSOCIATE: Hildy Parks; GENERAL MANAGER: Roy A. Somlyo; COMPANY MANAGER: Seymour Herscher; PRODUCTION STAGE MANAGER: Ruth Mitchell; STAGE MANAGERS: Jake Hamilton & Nicholas Rinaldi. *Cast:* CAPTAIN GREGG: Patrick Horgan (5); DR. WATSON: Peter Sallis (4); MRS. HUDSON: Paddy Edwards (7); SHERLOCK HOLMES: Fritz Weaver (1) ☆; INSPECTOR LESTRADE: Daniel Keyes (9); IRENE ADLER: Inga Swenson (2) ☆; DAISY: Virginia Vestoff; BAXTER: Martin Wolfson (8); WIGGINS, LEADER OF THE BAKER STREET IRREGULARS: Teddy Green (6); (FOUR) OTHER BAKER STREET IRREGULARS: DUCKBELLOWS: Bert Michaels; NIPPER: Sal Pernice; PERKINS: George Lee; MACIPPER: Mark Jude Sheil; MURILLO: Jay Norman (10); THE THREE KILLERS: Avind Harum, Tommy Tune, Christopher Walken; TAVERN SINGER: Gwenn Lewis; PROFESSOR MORIARTY: Martin Gabel (3) ☆; DANCERS: Sara Lee Barber, Barbara Blair, Lois Castle, John Grigas, Gwenn Lewis, Diana Saunders; SINGERS: Martin Ambrose, Frank Bouley, Jack Dabdoub, Gay Edmond, Judie Elkins, Maria Graziano, Horace Guittard, Peter Johl, Mara Landi, Hal Norman, Vera Walton. *Understudies:* Irene: Virginia Vestoff; Moriarty: Jack Dabdoub; Watson: Hal Norman; Mrs. Hudson: Mara Landi; Baxter: Martin Ambrose; Gregg: Horace Guittard. *Act I: Prologue:* Baker Street; *Scene 1* The Baker street flat: "It's So Simple" (Holmes, Watson, Gregg, Lestrade); *Scene 2* The stage of the Theatre Royal: "I'm in London Again" (by Bock & Harnick) (Irene); *Scene 3* Backstage at the Theatre Royal; *Scene 4* An alley in Baker Street: "Leave it to Us, Guv" (the Irregulars); *Scene 5* Irene's flat: "Letters" (Irene); *Scene 6* The Baker Street flat: "Cold, Clear World" (by Bock & Harnick) (Holmes), "Finding Words for Spring" (Irene), "What a Night This is Going to Be" (Holmes, Irene, Watson, Daisy); *Scene 7* The London Underworld: "London Underworld" (ballet) (Company); *Scene 8* Moriarty's ship: "I Shall Miss You (Holmes)" (by Bock & Harnick) (Moriarty). *Act II: Scene 1* A street in London: "Roof Space" (the Irregulars); *Scene 2* Moriarty's ship: "A Married Man" (Watson), "I'd Do it Again" (Irene); *Scene 3* Interior of a carriage: "Pursuit" (Holmes); *Scene 4* The Cliffs of Dover; *Scene 5* A part of London; *Scene 6* The Baker Street flat; *Scene 7* A hall in London: "Jewelry" (Baxter & Criminals); *Scene 8* Baker Street.

The critics were all divided on the show. Hal Prince had compromised on the theatre — he had wanted a more intimate one (the 1,100 seat Broadhurst) than the Broadway Theatre which Alex Cohen booked (1,800 seats), so the show had had to be expanded, and this was, perhaps, the main reason it failed. However, toward the end of its run it moved to the Martin Beck, where it played much better in the smaller theatre. It wound up being the longest-running play about Sherlock Holmes ever produced up to that time (William Gillette played Holmes on Broadway in 1899–1900. There were other productions in 1902, 1905, 1910, 1915, 1928, 1929. Basil Rathbone played him in a new play in 1953, and it ran only 3 performances). Set designer Oliver Smith won a special Tony for his entire year's work (which included *Baker Street*). The show was also nominated for book, costumes, and for Inga Swenson.

After Broadway. YORK THEATRE COMPANY, 1/19/01–1/21/01. 5 PERFORMANCES. Part of the *Musicals in Mufti* series. It had a re-worked book, and all of the Bock — Harnick songs were taken out. Marian Grudeff and Raymond Jessel were there. DIRECTOR: Richard Sabellico. *Cast:* HOLMES: Simon Jones; IRENE: Barbara Walsh [Dee Hoty was going to play the role]; MORIARTY: Randall Duk Kim.

44. *Bal Negre*

A music and dance revue of Caribbean voodoo exotica. Essentially a reprise of *Tropical Revue* and *Carib Song*.

The Broadway Run. BELASCO THEATRE, 11/7/46–12/22/46. 52 PERFORMANCES. PRESENTED BY Nelson L. Gross, in association with Daniel Melnick; DEVISED BY/DIRECTOR/CHOREOGRAPHER: Katherine Dunham; COSTUMES/LIGHT: John Pratt; MUSICAL DIRECTOR: Gilberto Valdes; PRESS: Campbell B. Casad; GENERAL MANAGER: Robert Milford; COMPANY MANAGER: Rube Bernstein; STAGE MANAGER: Maury Yaffe. *Cast:* Katherine Dunham (1) ☆ and the Dunham Company: Lenwood Morris, Lucille Ellis, Wilbert Bradley, Vanoye Aikens, Gloria Mitchell, Ronnie Aul, Richardena Jackson, Eddy Clay, Dolores Harper, Jesse Hawkins, Eartha Kitt, Othella Strozier, Lawaune Ingram, Syvilla Fort (guest), Byron Cuttler, Roxie Foster, James Alexander, Eugene Robinson; The Sans-Souci Singers: Miriam Burton, Eartha Kitt, Jean-Leon Destine, Mary Lewis (later known as Mary Rio Lewis), Rosalie King, Ricardo Morrison, Gordon Simpson; *Drummers*: La Rosa Estrada, Julio Mendez, Candido Vicenty. *Act I*: OVERTURE: Ylenko-Ylembe (vocal & orchestral combination that emphasizes unrestrained Afro-Cuban themes) (m: Gilberto Valdes) (Eartha, Jean-Leon, Miriam, Sans-Souci Singers); Congo Paillette (Haitian corn-sorting ritual, based on a native air) (Miss Dunham, Lenwood, Company) [from *Carib Song*]. *Part I*. MOTIVOS: "Rhumba" (m: Gilberto Valdes) (Lucille, Eartha, Othella); "Son" (Cuban slave lament) (Jesse) [from *Tropical Revue*]. POSSESSED DANCER: Dolores Harper; "Nanigo" (m: Gilberto Valdes) (La Rosa, Vanoye, Company); "Choro" (19th-century Brazilian quadrille) (m: Vadico Gogliano) (Gloria, Richardena, Wilbert, Ronnie) [from *Tropical Revue*]; "La Comparsa" (m: Ernesto Lecuona) (James, Byron, Vanoye, Miss Dunham) (alone in the deserted streets in the early morning hours after carnival, a woman encounters three men. She believes one may be her husband). *Part II*. Haitian Roadside (m: Paquita Anderson & Gilberto Valdes): "Soleil, O" (invocation) (Jean-Leon & Male Quartet); "Apollon" (carnival meringue) (Jean-Leon); "Choucoune" (voc arr: Reginald Beane) (Miss Dunham) (on the dusty roads of Haiti, many things happen in the late afternoon. PEDDLER WITH THE GUITAR: Candido Vicenty; OTHER PEDDLERS: La Rosa Estrada, Byron Cuttler, Julio Mendez, James Alexander; TRAVELING PRIEST: Jean-Leon Destine; MARKET GIRLS: Lawaune Ingram & Gloria Mitchell; CARNIVAL KINGS: Lenwood Morris & Jean-Leon Destine; CHACOON: Katherine Dunham; MARKET PEOPLE & WAYSIDE TRAVELERS. *Part III*. Shango (Ritual & Dance) (m: Baldwin Bergerson) [from *Carib Song*, complete with Jo Mielziner sets]. THE SHANGO PRIEST: La Rosa Estrada; THE BOY POSSESSED BY A SNAKE: Jean-Leon Destine; LEADERS OF THE SHANGO DANCERS: Lucille Ellis & Eddy Clay. *Act II*: "L'Ag'Ya" (m: Robert Sanders, from an original story by Katherine Dunham. The scene is Vauclin, tiny 18th-century fishing village in Martinique. Front curtain by Charles Sebree) [from *Tropical Revue*]. LOULOUSE: Katherine Dunham; ALCIDE: Vanoye Aikens; JULOT: Wilbert Bradley; ROI ZOMBIE: Lenwood Morris; PORTERESSES/VENDORS/FISHERMEN/TOWNSPEOPLE. *Act III*: *Part I*. NOSTALGIA. Ragtime Medley (mus arr/orch: Billy Butler) (voc arr: Reginald Beane) (adviser: Tom Fletcher): "Chong," "Under the Bamboo Tree," "Ragtime Cowboy," "Oh, You Beautiful Doll," "Alexander's Ragtime Band" (sung by Rosalie & Sans-Souci Singers), The Waltz, Foxtrot, Ballin' the Jack, Tango, Maxixe, Turkey Trot (danced by Lucille, Lenwood, Company); Blues (m: Floyd Smith) (Miss Dunham's Gown by Leopold Kobrin); "Flaming Youth, 1927" (m: Brad Gowans) (sung by Rosalie) [from *Tropical Revue*]. KANSAS CITY WOMAN: Lucille Ellis. Charleston, Black Bottom, Mooch, Fishtail, Snake Hips (danced by Lawaune, Gilbert, Company). *Part II*. Finale (Sans Souci Singers & the Dunham Company): Havana—1910 (m: Mercedes Navarro) [from *Tropical Revue*]: "Para Que Tu Veas" (m: Bobby Capo) (sung by Jean-Leon) [from *Tropical Revue*]. ENTERTAINER: Katherine Dunham; TWO LADY TOURISTS: Richardena Jackson & Dolores Harper. As with some other Katherine Dunham shows, this was not reviewed by the *New York Times*.

After Broadway. TOUR. After Broadway it toured the USA and Mexico in 1947. In 1948 the tour went transcontinental. Katherine Dunham and her troupe later toured with *A Caribbean Rhapsody*. The first tour was 1948–49, in London (at the Prince of Wales Theatre) and in Paris. DIRECTOR: Paul Erikson; CHOREOGRAPHER: Katherine Dunham; SETS/COSTUMES: John Pratt; LIGHTING: Dale Wasserman; MUSICAL DIRECTOR: Bobby Howell. *Cast*: Katherine Dunham, Lucille Ellis, Dolores Harper, Richardena Jackson, Rosalie King, Eartha Kitt, Othella Strozier, Roxie Foster, Julie Robinson, Anna Smith, Jacqueline Walcott,

Lenwood Morris (also ballet master), Vanoye Aikens, James Alexander, Jesse Hawkins, Wilbert Bradley, Julio Mendez, La Rosa Estrada, Candido Vicenty, James Davis, John Lei, Gordon Simpson, Esteban Larraura. The world tour continued—South America (50–51); Europe & North Africa (52–53); USA & Mexico (53); Germany (54); South America (54–55); Mexico (55); Los Angeles and New York (55–56); Australia and New Zealand (56–57); Far East (58); Europe, Near East, Argentina (59–60).

Katherine Dunham and Her Company were back on Broadway, at the BROADWAY THEATRE, 4/19/50–5/20/50. 38 PERFORMANCES. It did several of the familiar numbers; and again, 11/22/55–12/77/55. 32 PERFORMANCES. Same theatre.

45. *Ballroom*

A musical version of the TV drama. An aging couple—she runs a junk shop, he's a mailman—meet and find love at the Stardust Ballroom. Set in the present, in the Bronx. No intermission.

The Broadway Run. MAJESTIC THEATRE, 12/14/78–3/24/79. 11 previews. 116 PERFORMANCES. PRESENTED BY Michael Bennett, in association with Bob Avian, Bernard Gersten, Susan MacNair; MUSIC: Billy Goldenberg; LYRICS: Alan & Marilyn Bergman; BOOK: Jerome Kass (with doctoring by Larry Gelbart); BASED ON the 1975 TV film *The Queen of the Stardust Ballroom*, by Jerome Kass (uncredited), drawn from the life of the author's mother; DIRECTOR: Michael Bennett; CHOREOGRAPHERS: Michael Bennett & Bob Avian; SETS: Robin Wagner; COSTUMES: Theoni V. Aldredge; LIGHTING: Tharon Musser; SOUND: Otts Munderloh; MUSICAL DIRECTOR: Don Jennings; ORCHESTRATIONS: Jonathan Tunick; CAST RECORDING on Columbia; PRESS: Merle Debuskey, Leo Stern, William Schelble; CASTING: Shirley Rich, Mimi Obler, Joe Nelson; GENERAL MANAGER: Maurice Schaded; COMPANY MANAGER: Sally Campbell; PRODUCTION STAGE MANAGER: Jeff Hamlin; STAGE MANAGER: David Taylor; ASSISTANT STAGE MANAGER: Pat Trott. **Cast:** THE FAMILY: BEA ASHER: Dorothy Loudon (1) ✰; HELEN, HER SISTER-IN-LAW: Sally-Jane Heit (6); JACK, HER BROTHER-IN-LAW: John Hallow; DIANE, HER DAUGHTER: Dorothy Danner; DAVID, HER SON: Peter Alzado; AT THE STARDUST BALLROOM: ALFRED ROSSI: Vincent Gardenia (2) ✰; MARLENE: Lynn Roberts (10); NATHAN BRICKER: Bernie Knee (7); ANGIE: Patricia Drylie (4); JOHNNY "LIGHTFEET": Howard Parker (9); MARTHA: Barbara Erwin; PETEY: Gene Kelton; SHIRLEY: Liz Sheridan; PAUL: Michael Vita; "SCOOTER": Danny Carroll; ELEANOR: Jayne Turner; PAULINE KRIM: Janet Stewart White; FAYE: Roberta Haze; HARRY "THE NOODLE": Victor Griffin (5); MARIE: Adriana Keathley; EMILY: Mary Ann Niles (8); MARIO: Terry Violino; ANITRA: Svetlana McLee Grody; CARL: David Evans; MARGARET: Mavis Ray; THOMAS: Peter Gladke; BILL: Rudy Tronto (11); BALLROOM REGULARS: Marilyn Cooper, Dick Corrigan, Bud Fleming, Carol Flemming, Mickey Gunnersen, Alfred Karl, Dorothy D. Lister, John J. Martin, Joe Milan, Frank Pietri; CUSTOMERS AT BEA'S STORE: NATALIE: Marilyn Cooper (3); ESTELLE: Roberta Haze; KATHY: Carol Flemming. **Understudies**: Bea: Liz Sheridan; Al: John J. Martin; Jack: Joe Milan; Scooter: Rudy Tronto; Angie: Mary Ann Niles; Martha/Emily/Shirley: Adriana Keathley; Diane: Carol Flemming; Helen/Marlene: Marilyn Cooper; Lightfeet: Gene Kelton; Eleanor: Roberta Haze; Pauline: Jayne Turner; David: Alfred Karl; Nathan: Michael Vita. **Swings**: Kathie Dalton & Ken Urmston. **Scene 1** Bea's junk shop; **Scene 2** Outside the Stardust Ballroom: "A Terrific Band and a Real Nice Crowd" (Bea); **Scene 3** Stardust Ballroom: "A Song for Dancin'" (Sung by Marlene & Nathan) (Danced by The Regulars), "One by One" (Sung by Marlene & Nathan) (Danced by Angie, Lightfeet, the Regulars), "The Dance Montage" (Danced by the Regulars), "Dreams" (Marlene), "Somebody Did All Right for Herself (Tonight)" (Bea); **Scene 4** Bea's living room; **Scene 5** Stardust Ballroom: "The Tango Contest" (Danced by Emily & Mario, Bea & Al, Martha & Petey, Anitra & Carl, Shirley & Paul, Margaret & Thomas, Marie & Harry), "Goodnight is Not Goodbye" (Sung by Marlene & Harry) (Danced by the Regulars); **Scene 6** Bea's living room; **Scene 7** Bea's junk store; **Scene 8** Stardust Ballroom: "I've Been Waiting All My Life" (Sung by Nathan) (Danced by the Regulars), "I Love to Dance" (Bea & Al); **Scene 9** Bea's living room; **Scene 10** Stardust Ballroom: "More of the Same" (Sung by Marlene & Nathan) (Danced by the Regulars); **Scene 11** Outside the Ballroom; **Scene 12** Bea's living room: "Fifty Percent" (Bea); **Scene 13** Stardust Ballroom: "The Stardust Waltz" (Danced by the Regulars), "I Wish You a Waltz" (Bea).

Critics were completely divided; the show failed. It lost $2.2 million. It won a Tony for choreography, and was also nominated for musical, book, direction of a musical, costumes, lighting, and for Vince Gardenia and Dorothy Loudon.

46. *Barefoot Boy with Cheek*

A musical comedy caricature of non-academic phases of campus life, at the University of Minnesota. Yetta is a Communist student trying to infect the campus with Stalinism. Asa is a dumb freshman who gets Clothilde in the end.

The Broadway Run. MARTIN BECK THEATRE, 4/3/47–7/5/47. 108 PERFORMANCES. PRESENTED BY George Abbott; MUSIC: Sidney Lippman; LYRICS: Sylvia Dee; BOOK: Max Shulman (based on his 1943 novel of the same name); DIRECTOR: George Abbott; CHOREOGRAPHER: Richard Barstow; SETS/LIGHTING: Jo Mielziner; COSTUMES: Alvin Colt; MUSICAL DIRECTOR: Milton Rosenstock; ORCHESTRATIONS: Philip Lang; VOCAL ARRANGEMENTS: Hugh Martin; PRESS: Richard Maney & Ned Armstrong; GENERAL MANAGER: Charles Harris; GENERAL STAGE MANAGER: Robert E. Griffith; STAGE MANAGERS: Daniel Sattler & Fred Hearn. **Cast:** ROGER HAILFELLOW: Jack Williams (8); SHYSTER FISCAL: Red Buttons (3) ✰, *Joshua Shelley*; VAN VARSITY: Ben Murphy; CHARLIE CONVERTIBLE: Loren Welch; FRESHMAN: Patrick Kingdon; ASA HEARTHRUG: Billy Redfield (2) ✰; EINO FFLLIIKKIINNENN: Benjamin Miller; NOBLESSE OBLIGE: Billie Lou Watt (6); CLOTHILDE PFEFFERKORN: Ellen Hanley (4); YETTA SAMOVAR: Nancy Walker (1) ✰; PROFESSOR SCHULTZ: Philip Coolidge (5); PEGGY HEPP: Shirley Van (7); KERMIT McDERMOTT: Jerry Austin (9); BORIS FIVEYEARPLAN: Solen Burry; PLAYWRIGHT: Marten Sameth; BARTENDER: James Lane; MUSKIE PIKE: Tommy Farrell (10); 1ST BAND MEMBER: Harris Gondell; 2ND BAND MEMBER: Nathaniel Frey; DANCERS: Jean Marie Caples, Leonard Claret, Douglas Deane, June Graham, Marybly Harwood, Ray Kirchner, John Laverty, Louisa Lewis, Marcia Maier, David Neuman, Audrey Peters, Tommy Randall, Doris York; SINGERS: Betty Abbott, Adrienne Aye, James Bowie, Harvey Braun, Dean Campbell, Mary Lee Carrell, Carole Coleman, Robert Edwin, Beverly Fite, Nell Foster, Nat Frey, Harris Gondell, Marion Kohler, Gay Laurence, John Leslie, Abbe Marshall, Ellen Martin, Ray Morrissey, Robert Paul Neukum, Alfred Porter, Walter Rinner, Marten Sameth, Jean Sincere, Pamela Ward. **Act I**: **Scene 1** Alpha Cholera fraternity house; **Scene 2** College corridor; **Scene 3** Classroom; **Scene 4** Corridor; **Scene 5** Campus Publications office; **Scene 6** The Sty; **Scene 7** Street; **Scene 8** The Knoll; **Scene 9** Street; **Scene 10** Alpha Cholera fraternity house. **Act II**: **Scene 1** Alpha Cholera fraternity house; **Scene 2** Street; **Scene 3** The Knoll; **Scene 4** Polling place; **Scene 5** Alpha Cholera fraternity house. **Act I**: "(Here's) A Toast to Alpha Cholera" (Fraternity Men), "We Feel Our Man is Definitely You" (Shyster, Roger, Fraternity Men), "The Legendary Eino Fflliikkiinnenn" (Eino, Asa, Fraternity Men); "(It's) Too Nice a Day to Go to School" (Kermit, Peggy, Charlie, Van, Students). SPECIALTY DANCE: June Graham & Leonard Claret. PUPPY LOVE: Ellen Martin & John Laverty; "I Knew I'd Know" (Clothilde); "I'll Turn a Little Cog" (Yetta & Asa). Sung by Loren Welch, Ben Murphy, John Leslie, Bob Neukum, Students. Danced by June Graham, Marybly Harwood, Leonard Claret, Douglas Deane, Ray Kirchner; "Who Do You Think You Are?" (Kermit, Asa, Students), "Everything Leads Right Back to Love" (Clothilde & Asa), "Little Yetta's Gonna Get a Man" (Yetta); "Alice in Boogieland" (Muskie, Peggy, Shyster, Roger). QUARTET: Beverly Fite, Harvey Braun, Dean Campbell, Betty Abbott. Danced by Students. DANCE SPECIALTY: Shirley Van & Leonard Claret. **Act II**: "(Promise We'll Still Be Sweethearts) After Graduation Day" (Charlie & Students), "There's a Lot of Things You Can Do with Two (But Not with Three)" (Yetta, Shyster, Noblesse, Roger, Asa, Muskie, Leonard Claret, Douglas Deane, Marybly Harwood, Students), "The Story of Carrot" (Asa & Eino), "When You are Eighteen" (Clothilde), "Star of the North Star State" (Students), "I Knew I'd Know" (reprise) (Clothilde), "It Couldn't Be Done (But We Did It)" (Entire Company).

It got good Broadway reviews.

47. *Barnum*

Set all over America and the major world capitals, 1835–1880. The story of legendary showman/circus proprietor P.T. Barnum, "the Prince of Humbug." Told as a three-ring circus with the ringmaster announcing each act. Jugglers, acrobats, papier mache elephants and a band marched up the aisles of the theatre. Chairy wants to live a quiet life in the suburbs. Jenny, "the Swedish Nightingale," is one of Barnum's acts and has an affair with him. The hero sang and danced, walked across the stage on a tightrope, rode a unicycle and jumped off a trampoline onto a high balcony.

Before Broadway. Originally David Merrick was going to produce, but withdrew to do *Forty-Second Street*. Mike Stewart briefly contemplated producing with Cy Coleman, but in the end Off Broadway producer Judy Gordon came in with Mr. Coleman. They auditioned the show for Irvin and Kenneth Feld, producers of Ringling Brothers and Barnum and Bailey Circus (a descendant of Barnum's original circus), and the money was obtained.

The Broadway Run. ST. JAMES THEATRE, 4/30/80–5/16/82. 26 previews. 854 PERFORMANCES. PRESENTED BY Judy Gordon, Cy Coleman, Maurice Rosenfeld, Lois F. Rosenfeld, in association with Irvin Feld & Kenneth Feld; MUSIC: Cy Coleman; LYRICS: Michael Stewart; BOOK: Mark Bramble; SUGGESTED BY events in life of Phineas Taylor Barnum, the great showman (1810–1891), of Barnum & Bailey fame; DIRECTOR/CHOREOGRAPHER: Joe Layton; SETS: David Mitchell; COSTUMES: Theoni V. Aldredge; LIGHTING: Craig Miller; ASSISTANT LIGHTING: Mary Jo Dondlinger; SOUND: Otts Munderloh; MUSICAL DIRECTOR: Peter Howard; ORCHESTRATIONS: Hershy Kay; VOCAL ARRANGEMENTS: Cy Coleman & Jeremy Stone; CAST RECORDING on CBS Masterworks; PRESS: David Powers, *Tom Trenkle* (added by 81–82); CASTING: Howard Feuer & Jeremy Ritzer; MAGIC CREATOR: Bradley Steven-Fields; GENERAL MANAGER: James Walsh; COMPANY MANAGER: Susan Bell; PRODUCTION STAGE MANAGER: Mary Porter Hall; STAGE MANAGER: Marc Schlackman, *Bethe Ward* (added by 80–81); ASSISTANT STAGE MANAGER: Michael Mann, *John Beven & Fred Feldt*. **Cast:** PRE CURTAIN ENTERTAINERS: Commencing one-half hour before the show: Mr. Bradley Steven-Fields, *R.J. Lewis* (by 6/80). With tours through the Exhibition of Wonders by: Miss Catherine Carr, *Barbara Nadel* (by 80–81), *Mary Testa* (from 80–81). And Diversions in the Theatre by: Mr. Andy Teirstein, Miss Barbara Nadel, Miss Mary Testa, Mr. Bruce Robertson (*Fred Garbo Garver & Dirk Lumbard*), Mr. Steven Michael. PHINEAS TAYLOR BARNUM: Jim Dale (1) ☆, *Tony Orlando* (5/5/81–5/25/81), *Jim Dale* (from 5/26/81), *Mike Burstyn* (from 10/13/81); CHAIRY BARNUM: Glenn Close (2), *Catherine Cox* (from 3/3/81), *SuEllen Estey* (1/19/82–1/26/82), *Catherine Cox, Deborah Reagan* (from 3/9/82); RINGMASTER: William C. Witter, *Terrence V. Mann* (from 4/14/81), *Kelly Walters* (from 11/17/81); CHESTER LYMAN: Terrence V. Mann, *R.J. Lewis* (from 4/14/81), *R. Robert Melvin*; JOICE HETH: Terri White (4), *Lillias White* (from 4/14/81); AMOS SCUDDER: Kelly Walters, *Richard Gervais*; LADY PLATE-BALANCER: Catherine Carr, *Missy Whitchurch*; LADY JUGGLER: Barbara Nadel, *Mary Testa, Andrea Wright*; BATON TWIRLER: Sophie Schwab; CHIEF BRICKLAYER: Edward T. Jacobs, *Navarre Matlovsky* (stood in 6/80 & 7/80), *Fred Garbo Garver, Navarre Matlovsky*; WHITE-FACED CLOWN: Andy Teirstein, *Marshall Coid*; SHERWOOD STRATTON: Dirk Lumbard, *R.J. Lewis*; MRS. SHERWOOD STRATTON: Sophie Schwab, *Andrea Wright*; TOM THUMB: Leonard John Crofoot (5); SUSAN B. ANTHONY: Karen Trott; JULIUS GOLDSCHMIDT: William C. Witter (6), *Terrence V. Mann* (from 3/14/81), *Kelly Walters*; JENNY LIND: Marianne Tatum (3), *SuEllen Estey* (1/26/82–2/1/82), *Marianne Tatum, Catherine Gaines* (stood in); ONE-MAN BAND: Steven Michael; WILTON: Bruce Robertson, *Kelly Walters* (stood in), *R.J. Lewis*; EDGAR TEMPLETON: Kelly

Walters; HUMBERT MORRISSEY: Terrence V. Mann, *R.J. Lewis* (from 4/14/81), *R. Robert Melvin*; LADY AERIALIST: Robbi Morgan, *Colleen Flynn*; JAMES A. BAILEY: William C. Witter, *Terrence V. Mann* (from 4/14/81), *Kelly Walters*; PIANISTS: Karen Gustafson, Peter Phillips (gone by 81–82), *Ted Kociolek* (added by 80–81 but gone by 811–82), *Gregory J. Dlugos* (added by 81–82). **Standbys:** Barnum: Harvey Evans, *Jess Richards*; Chairy/Jenny: SuEllen Estey. **Understudies:** Barnum: Terrence V. Mann; Chairy: Sophie Schwab, *Karen Trott*; Jenny: Sophie Schwab, *Andrea Wright*; Lyman: Bruce Robertson & Dirk Lumbard, *R.J. Lewis* & Fred Feldt; Bailey: Terrence V. Mann, *Dirk Lumbard, Michael Harris*; Ringmaster: Terrence V. Mann, *Michael Harris*; Goldschmidt: Dirk Lumbard, *Michael Harris*; Morrissey: Dirk Lumbard, *Fred Feldt*; Joice: Mary Testa; Tom Thumb: Edward T. Jacobs, *Fred Garbo Garver, Fred Feldt*; Mrs. Stratton/Susan B. Anthony: Barbara Nadel; Scudder: Leonard John Crofoot, *Michael Harris*; Templeton: Leonard John Crofoot, *Michael Harris, Dirk Lumbard*; Wilton: Kelly Walters, *Navarre Matlovsky*; Stratton: Terrence V. Mann, *R.J. Lewis, Fred Feldt*. **Ensemble:** Bradley Steven-Fields, Mary Testa, Navarre Matlovksy, *Fred Feldt, Colleen Flynn, Jerry Mitchell, Paula Grider*. **Musicians:** SAXOPHONES: Jack Kripl, Dave Hopkins, Frank Perowsky, Al Hunt, Ray Shanfield; TRUMPETS: Victor Paz, Peter Hyde, Laurie Frink; TROMBONES: Dennis Elliot, Joe Petrizzo, George Flynn; TUBA: John Stevens; BASS: Bruce Samuels; BANJO: Dick Frank; DRUMS: John Redsecker; PERCUSSION: Dan Druckman; VIOLIN: Richard Henrickson; CELLO: Edith Wint. **Act I:** "There is a Sucker Born Ev'ry Minute" (Barnum), "Thank God I'm Old" (Joice & Tambourine Players), "The Colors of My Life" (Barnum, then Chairy), "One Brick at a Time" (Chairy, Barnum, Bricklayers), "Museum Song" (Barnum), "I Like Your Style" (Barnum & Chairy), "Bigger isn't Better" (Tom), "Love Makes Such Fools of Us All" (Jenny), "Out There" (Barnum). **Act II:** "Come Follow the Band" (Potomac Marching Band & Washingtonians), "Black and White" (Chairy, Choir, Blues Singer, Barnum, Citizens of Bridgeport), "The Colors of My Life" (reprise) (Barnum & Chairy), "The Prince of Humbug" (Barnum), "Join the Circus" (Bailey, Circus Performers, Barnum), "There is a Sucker Born Ev'ry Minute" (reprise) (Barnum).

All reviews were favorable. The show won Tonys for sets, costumes, and for Jim Dale, and was also nominated for musical, book, direction of a musical, choreography, lighting, and for Glenn Close.

After Broadway. TOUR. Opened on 5/12/81, at the Saenger Center, New Orleans, and closed on 8/22/81, at the Fisher Theatre, Detroit. MUSICAL DIRECTOR: Robert Billig. **Cast:** BARNUM: Stacy Keach; CHAIRY: Dee Hoty; JENNY: Catherine Gaines; JOICE: Terri White; RINGMASTER/BAILEY/GOLDSCHMIDT: Gabriel Barre.

TOUR. Opened on 12/16/81, at the Golden Gate Theatre, San Francisco, and closed on 4/4/82, at the Pantages Theatre, Los Angeles. MUSICAL DIRECTOR: Ross Allen. **Cast:** BARNUM: Jim Dale (Terrence V. Mann played the role for one performance a week); CHAIRY: Glenn Close; RINGMASTER/BAILEY/GOLDSCHMIDT: Terrence V. Mann; JENNY: Catherine Gaines; JOICE: Terri White; TOM: Ray Roderick.

TOUR. Opened on 8/5/82, at the Palace Theatre, Columbus, Ohio. PRESENTED BY Tom Mallow, in association with James Janek; MUSICAL DIRECTOR: Ross Allen. **Cast:** BARNUM: Harvey Evans; CHAIRY: Jan Pessano; TOM: Leonard John Crofoot; JENNY: Kathleen Marsh.

LONDON PALLADIUM, 6/11/81. 655 PERFORMANCES. **Cast:** BARNUM: Michael Crawford (he won an Olivier Award and great acclaim); CHAIRY: Deborah Grant; JENNY: Sarah Payne; RINGMASTER/BAILEY/GOLDSCHMIDT: William C. Witter; TOM: Christopher Beck; JOICE: Jennie McGustie.

DOMINION THEATRE, London. 1992. **Cast:** BARNUM: Paul Nicholas; CHAIRY: Anne Wood.

48. *The Barrier*

Musical drama, or opera, set in the living-room at Albamar, Thomas Norwood's plantation in a rural Georgia community, on a hot summer day. Norwood has several children by his black housekeeper Cora, including the rebellious Bert, who considers himself the equal of whites, and who strangles his father, flees, is tracked down by a lynch mob, then commits suicide by shooting himself. William is the elder son.

Before Broadway. It was first produced at the BRANDER MATTHEWS THEATRE, in Columbia University, NYC, 1/18/50–1/28/50. 10 PERFORMANCES.

The Broadway Run. BROADHURST THEATRE, 11/2/50–11/4/50. 4 PERFORMANCES. PRESENTED BY Michael Myerberg & Joel Spector; MUSIC: Jan Meyerowitz; LYRICS/BOOK: Langston Hughes (based on his 1935 drama *Mulatto*); DIRECTOR: Doris Humphrey; CHOREOGRAPHERS: Charles Weidman & Doris Humphrey; SETS: H.A. (Heinz) Condell; CONDUCTOR: Herbert Zipper; PRESS: J. Charles Gilbert; COMPANY MANAGER: Leonard Field; STAGE MANAGERS: John Paul & Victor Thorley. *Cast:* WILLIAM: Lorenzo Herrera; SALLY: Charlotte Holloman; LIVONIA: Dolores Bowman; MAID: Reri Grist; HOUSEMAN: John Diggs; SAM: Laurence Watson; TALBOT: Victor Thorley; COL. THOMAS NORWOOD: Lawrence Tibbett (1); CORA LEWIS: Muriel Rahn (2); FRED HIGGINS: Richard Dennis; BERT: Wilton Clary (3); PLANTATION STOREKEEPER: Robert Tankersley; UNDERTAKER: Jesse Jacobs; UNDERTAKER'S ASSISTANT: Stuart Hodes. DANCE SEQUENCE: YOUNG NORWOOD: Lawrence Tibbett (singer), Marc Breaux (dancer); YOUNG CORA: Charlotte Holloman (singer), Josephine Keene (dancer) [end of dance sequence]; THE BRIDE: Helene Ellis. *Act I*: noon: "September Sunlight" (William & Sally), "City Theme" (Livonia), "But, Colonel Tom" (Cora & Norwood), "I Just Wanted to Tell You Goodbye" (Sally & Norwood), "Little Girl Goodbye" (Negroes), "You Should Have Married Again" (Fred), "Help Me, Lawd" (Cora & William), "It's a Wonderful Day" (Bert), "You Are Not Your Father's Son" (Cora & Bert). *Act II*: *Scene 1* late afternoon: "Flesh of My Flesh, Bone of My Bone" (Norwood), "Trio" (Cora, Bert, Norwood), "My Father's Own House" (Norwood, Bert, Cora), "Damn You, Colonel Tom!" (Cora); *Scene 2* that night: "I Don't Want to Die" (Sam), "The First Time I Was Yours in the Dark" (Cora), "And from the Earth a Sweetness Rose" (Young Cora & Young Norwood), "Go to Sleep" (Young Cora), Finale: "Mercy, Lawd" (reprise) (Cora & Bert).

This was the Broadway debut of Lawrence Tibbett. Reviews were unfavorable.

49. *The Beast in Me*

A musical revue.

The Broadway Run. PLYMOUTH THEATRE, 5/16/63–5/18/63. 3 previews from 5/12/63. 4 PERFORMANCES. PRESENTED BY Bonard Productions (Helen G. Bonfils & Haila Stoddard). MUSIC: Don Elliott; LYRICS/BOOK: James Costigan; ADAPTED BY James Costigan from *Fables for Our Time*, by James Thurber; CONCEPT: Haila Stoddard; DIRECTOR: John Lehne; CHOREOGRAPHER: John Butler; SETS/LIGHTING: Jean Rosenthal; COSTUMES: Leo Van Witsen (based on designs by Andre Warhol); MUSICAL DIRECTOR: Don Elliott; CONDUCTOR: Lehman Engel; ORCHESTRATIONS: Bill Byers; DANCE MUSIC ARRANGEMENTS: Judd Woldin; FEATURING: Don Elliott & His Orchestra; PRESS: Dorothy Ross & Richard O'Brien; GENERAL MANAGER: Morton Gottlieb; COMPANY MANAGER: Max Allentuck; PRODUCTION STAGE MANAGER: Warren Crane; STAGE MANAGER: Joseph Dooley; ASSISTANT STAGE MANAGER: Douglas Clarke. *Act I*: *Scene 1* There's a Beast in Everybody (Entire Company): "Percussion" (Entire Company); *Scene 2* The Sea and the Shore: GIBBOUS FEMALE: Kaye Ballard; GIBBOUS MALE: Richard Hayes. "So Beautiful" (Gibbous Female & Male); *Scene 3* The Lover and His Lass: MRS. HIPPO: Kaye Ballard; HIPPO: Richard Hayes; MRS. PARROT: Allyn Ann McLerie; PARROT: Bert Convy; GIRL: Nancy Haywood. "You're Delicious" (Mrs. Parrot & Parrot); *Scene 4* The Lady of the Legs: TOURIST: Richard Hayes; FROG: Allyn Ann McLerie; RESTAURATEUR: James Costigan. "J'ai" (Frog & Restaurateur); *Scene 5* Tea for One: BRIDE: Kaye Ballard; GROOM: Richard Hayes. "I Owe Ohio" (Entire Company); *Scene 6* The Wolf Who Went Places: PROFESSOR: Richard Hayes; WOLF: Bert Convy; WOLFESS: Allyn Ann McLerie. "Go, Go, Go" (Wolf); *Scene 7* The Unicorn in the Garden: MAN: James Costigan; WIFE: Kaye Ballard; DR. CLISBIE: Richard Hayes; POLICEMAN: Bert Convy; NYMPHS: Allyn Ann McLerie & Nancy Haywood. "Breakfast" (Wife & Man), "Eat Your Nice Lily, Unicorn" (Man & Clisbie), "Bacchanale" (Entire Company). *Act II*: *Scene 1* The Foolhardy Mouse

and the Cautious Cat: POUNCETTA: Allyn Ann McLerie; MERVYN: James Costigan; RING LEADER: Richard Hayes; THE GANG: Kaye Ballard, Bert Convy, Nancy Haywood. "Glorious Cheese" (Entire Company), "Calypso Kitty" (Mervyn); *Scene 2* A Moment With Mandy: MANDY: Kaye Ballard; DADDY: Bert Convy. "Why?" (Mandy & Daddy); *Scene 3* The Moth and the Star: OLD MOTH: James Costigan; MOTHER MOTH: Allyn Ann McLerie; FATHER MOTH: Richard Hayes; *Scene 4* The Stork Who Married a Dumb Wife: CIGARETTE GIRL: Allyn Ann McLerie; SPOUSE: Kaye Ballard; STORK: Richard Hayes; THE GIRL: Nancy Haywood; MYSTERIOUS STRANGER: Bert Convy; WAITER: James Costigan. "What Do You Say?" (Stork & Girl), "When I'm Alone" (Spouse & Mysterious Stranger); *Scene 5* The Shore and the Sea: EVANGELIST: Kaye Ballard; SCHOLARLY LEMMING: James Costigan; CONGREGATION: Allyn Ann McLerie, Nancy Haywood, Richard Hayes, Bert Convy. "Hallelujah" (Evangelist & Entire Company).

Some sketches were interchanged, so the order may be different on some programs. Broadway reviews were mixed.

50. *Beauty and the Beast*

A wicked witch turns a prince into a beast, and his household staff into objects. He can only be returned to human if he loves and is loved.

Before Broadway. There have been several musicals and ballets with this title, and based on the same story. This one began when Disney CEO Michael Eisner saw Jerry Orbach (Beast) and Paige O'Hara (Belle) perform musical highlights from the film *Beauty and the Beast* as part of an awards presentation in New York City. He determined to bring it to the musical stage, and enlisted the aid of producer W. McTyre, director Rob Roth, set designer Stan Meyer, and costume designer Ann Hould-Ward. This was Disney's first venture into stage musicals. It tried out at Theatre Under the Stars, Houston, from 11/27/93.

The Broadway Run. PALACE THEATRE, 4/18/94–9/5/99. 46 previews from 3/9/94. 2,250 PERFORMANCES; LUNT—FONTANNE THEATRE, 11/12/99–. PRESENTED BY Walt Disney Productions; MUSIC: Alan Menken; LYRICS: Howard Ashman & Tim Rice; BOOK: Linda Woolverton (an expanded, live-action version of her screenplay for the 1991 Walt Disney animated film musical, with additional songs); DIRECTOR: Robert Jess Roth; CHOREOGRAPHER: Matt West; SETS: Stan Meyer; COSTUMES: Ann Hould-Ward; PROSTHETICS: John Dods & Kate Chittenden; LIGHTING: Natasha Katz; SOUND: T. Richard Fitzgerald, *Jonathan Deans (from 11/12/99)*; ILLUSIONS: Jim Steinmeyer & John Gaughan; MUSICAL SUPERVISOR/VOCAL ARRANGEMENTS: David Friedman; MUSICAL DIRECTOR/INCIDENTAL ARRANGEMENTS: Michael Kosarin; ORCHESTRATIONS: Danny Troob; ADDITIONAL ORCHESTRATIONS: Michael Starobin; DANCE MUSIC ARRANGEMENTS: Glen Kelly; CAST RECORDING on Walt Disney Records; PRESS: Boneau/Bryan-Brown; CASTING: Jay Binder; GENERAL MANAGER: Dodger Productions; COMPANY MANAGER: Kim Sellon, *Mark Rozzano*; PRODUCTION STAGE MANAGER: James Harker, *John Brigleb*; STAGE MANAGERS: John M. Atherlay, Pat Sosnow, Kim Vernace, *M.A. Howard, Jill Larmett, James Harker*. **Cast:** ENCHANTRESS: Wendy Oliver, *Lisa Mayer, Sarah Solie Shannon*; PROLOGUE NARRATOR VOICE: David Ogden Stiers; YOUNG PRINCE: Harrison Beal, *Tom Pardoe (by 95–96), Michael Lang, James Tabeek*; BEAST: Terrence Mann (2) ☆, *Jeff McCarthy (from 94–95), Steve Blanchard (from 95–96), Jeff McCarthy (by 96–97), Chuck Wagner (from 96–97), James Barbour (from 96–97), Steve Blanchard (from 11/12/99), William Michals, Steve Blanchard (by 00–01 and until 2/15/04), Jeff McCarthy (2/17/04–4/11/04), Steve Blanchard (from 4/13/04)*; BELLE: Susan Egan (1) ☆, *Sarah Uriarte (from 94–95), Christianne Tisdale (from 95–96), Kerry Butler (from 96), Deborah Gibson (9/24/97–6/28/98), Kim Huber (from 6/30/98), Toni Braxton (from 9/9/98 — her official opening was 10/1/98 — until 2/28/99), Andrea McArdle (3/3/99–3/00), Sarah Litzsinger (3/00–8/4/02), Ann Sanders (8/6/02–9/29/02), Jamie-Lynn Sigler (10/1/02–2/9/03), Sarah Litzsinger (2/11/03–4/13/03), Megan McGinnis (4/15/03–2/15/04), Christy Carlson Romano (2/17/04–9/12/04), Brooke Tansley (from 9/14/04)*; BOOKSELLER: Skip Harris, *Glenn Rainey, David E. Liddell*; LEFOU: Kenny Raskin (10), *Harrison Beal (by 95–96), Jamie Torcellini (by 98–99), Jeffrey Howard*

Schecter, Jay Brian Winnick (from 11/12/99), *Gerard McIsaac* (by 00–01), *Jeff Skowran* (by 3/01), *Brad Aspel* (by 8/01 & until 11/12/02), *Steve Lavner* (from 11/13/02), *Aldrin Gonzalez*; GASTON: Burke Moses (3), *Marc Kudisch* (from 94–95), *Christopher Monteleone* (during Mr. Kudisch's vacation, 7/97–8/97), *Steve Blanchard* (by 4/98 & until 9/5/99), *Patrick Ryan Sullivan* (from 11/12/99), *Christopher Sieber* (by 3/01), *William Michals, Chris Hoch* (from 12/10/02), *Grant Norman*; THREE SILLY GIRLS: Sarah Solie Shannon, Paige Price (*Alisa Klein* by 95–96), Linda Talcott (later known as Linda Talcott Lee). *Jennifer Cody.* 1996–2001 list: *Lauren Goler-Kosarin, Pam Klinger,* Linda Talcott Lee. *Amanda Watkins.* 3/14/02 list: *Lauren Goler-Kosarin, Jennifer Marcum,* Linda Talcott-Lee. 9/03 list: *Jennifer Marcum, Tia Marie Zorne* (from 3/03), *Lauren Goler-Kosarin*; MAURICE: Tom Bosley (11), *MacIntyre Dixon* (from 94–95), *Tom Bosley* (from 94–95), *Kurt Knudson* (from 94–95), *Tim Jerome* (from 96–97), *J.B. Adams* (from 11/12/99), *Glenn Rainey, J.B. Adams* (by 00–01), *Jamie Ross*; WOLVES: Robert H. Fowler (*Billy Sprague Jr.*) & Jennifer Hampton. *Michael Lang, Michelle Mallardi, Sarah Solie Shannon*; COGSWORTH: Heath Lamberts (6), *Peter Bartlett* (from 95–96), *Gibby Brand* (by 96–97), *Patrick Page* (by 98–99), *John Christopher Jones, Jeff Brooks* (from 11/12/99); LUMIERE: Gary Beach (4), *Lee Roy Reams* (from 94–95), *Patrick Quinn* (from 95–96), *Gary Beach* (from 3/12/97), *Meshach Taylor* (by 98–99 and until 2/28/99), *Patrick Page* (from 3/3/99), *David DeVries* (by 00–01), *Paul Schoeffler* (3/21/01–5/13/01), *Patrick Page* (until 8/12/01), *Bryan Batt* (8/14/01–5/5/01), *Rob Lorey* (during Mr. Batt's absence for knee surgery, 5/7/02–7/9/02), *David DeVries* (from 11/13/02), *Peter Flynn, David DeVries*; BABETTE: Stacey Logan (8), *Pamela Winslow* (from 96–97), *Leslie Castay* (during Miss Winslow's vacation, 7/97; then permanently by 98–99, until 9/5/99), *Pam Klinger, Louisa Kendrick, Jennifer Shrader, Pam Klinger* (from 11/12/99); MRS. POTTS: Beth Fowler (5), *Cass Morgan* (from 94–95), *Beth Fowler* (from 95–96 to 9/5/99), *Beth McVey* (during Miss Fowler's vacation, 4/97), *Leslie Castay, Barbara Marineau* (from 11/12/99), *Beth Fowler* (from 9/12/01), *Cass Morgan* (until 2/15/04), *Alma Cuervo* (from 2/17/04); CHIP: Brian Press (9). By 95–96 the role was alternated between *Andrew Keenan-Bolger* (replaced by *Matthew Dotzman*) & *Patrick Lavery* (replaced by 96–97 by *Joseph Di Concetto*); then by 98–99 by *Jonathan Andrew Bleicher*; then from 11/12/99 by *Ricky Ashley*). Later alternating couples: by March 2001 *Harrison Chad* & *Jonathan Press* (replaced by 8/01 by *William Ullrich*); *Zachary Grill* (replaced by *Adam Casner who was gone by 9/12/03*) & *Nicholas Jonas* (gone by 9/12/03); *Jeremy Bergman* (gone by 9/12/03) & *Joey Caraviglio. Sean Curley* (alternate), *Henry Hodges & Alex Rutherford* (*Matthew Gumley*); MADAME DE LA GRANDE BOUCHE/WARDROBE: Eleanor Glockner (7), *Judith Moore* (by 00–01), *Mary Stout, Sherry Anderson* (from 10/29/02), *Mary Stout, Marguerite Willbanks*; SALT: Robert H. Fowler, *Billy Sprague Jr.*; PEPPER: Joseph Savant, *Brek Williams*; DOORMAT: Michael Lang, *James Tabeek*; CHEESEGRATER: Karl duHoffmann, *Kevin M. Burrows, Denny Paschall*; MONSIEUR D'ARQUE: Gordon Stanley, *Skip Harris, Glenn Rainey, David Spangenthal*; TOWNSPEOPLE/ ENCHANTED OBJECTS: Joan Barber (gone by 96–97), Roxane Barlow (gone by 96–97), Harrison Beal (gone by 96–97), Michael Demby-Cain (gone by 96–97), Kate Dowe (gone by 96–97, but back by 11/12/99), David Elder (gone by 96–97), Merwin Foard (gone by 96–97), Gregorey Garrison, Jack Hayes (gone by 96–97), Kim Huber (gone by 96–97), Elmore James, Rob Lorey, Patrick Loy (gone by 96–97), Barbara Marineau (gone by 96–97), Joanne McHugh (gone by 96–97), Anna McNeely, Bill Nabel, Wendy Oliver (gone by 99), Vince Pesce (gone by 96–97), Paige Price (gone by 96–97), Sarah Solie Shannon (gone by 99), Gordon Stanley (gone by 99; *Glenn Rainey*), Linda Talcott (later known as Linda Talcott Lee), Wysandria Woolsey (gone by 99). New by 94–95: *Ana Maria Andricain, Kevin Berdini, Andrea Burns, Christophe Caballero, Sally Mae Dunn, Barbara Folts, Alisa Klein, Beth McVey, Tom Pardoe* (*Michael Lang, James Tabeek*), *Joseph Savant* (*Brek Williams*), *Matthew Shepard, Steven Sofia, David A. Wood*. New by 96–97: *Steven Ted Beckler, Terri Furr, Lauren Goler-Kosarin, Ellen Hoffman, Pam Klinger, Ken McMullen, Raymond Sage*. Later replacements: *Kevin M. Burrows, Karl duHoffmann* (*Denny Paschall*), *Stacia Fernandez, Robert H. Fowler* (*Billy Sprague Jr.*), *Jerry Godfrey, Jennifer Hampton, Robin Lewis, Lisa Mayer, Angela Piccini, Graham Rowat, Rachel Ulanet, Amanda Watkins. Karl Christian, David E. Liddell, William Paul Michals, Christopher Monteleone, Ann Sanders, Daria Lynn Scatton, Marguerite Shannon* (*Ann*

Arvia), *Gina Carlette, Michelle Mallardi, John Salvatore, Marguerite Willbanks, Tia Marie Zorne.* **Standby**: Beast: Chuck Wagner (94–95). **Understudies**: Beast: David Elder (94–95), *William Paul Michaels, Steven Ted Beckler, Steve Blanchard, Graham Rowat, Christopher Monteleone, Brek Williams*; Belle: Kim Huber (94–95), Paige Price (94–95), *Barbara Folts, Ana Maria Andricain, Andrea Burns, Sarah Litzsinger* (2000–01), *Michelle Mallardi, Ann Sanders*; Enchantress/Silly Girls: Kate Dowe & Alisa Klein (94–95), *Barbara Folts, Carol Lee Meadows, Daria Lynn Scatton*); Young Prince: Gregorey Garrison & Dan Mojica (94–95), *Joseph Favalora, Karl Christian, David E. Liddell*; Gaston: Merwin Foard & Chuck Wagner (94–95), *William Paul Michaels, Steven Ted Beckler, Graham Rowat, Christopher Monteleone, Brek Williams*; Lefou: Harrison Beal & Vince Pesce (94–95), *Joseph Favalora, Michael Lang, Karl Christian, David E. Liddell, James Tabeek*; Cogsworth/Maurice: Bill Nabel (1994–2003), Gordon Stanley (94–95), *Glenn Rainey*; Lumiere: Bill Nabel (1994–2003), *Gordon Stanley* (94–95), *Rob Lorey, Billy Sprague Jr.*; Babette: Joanne McHugh & Sarah Solie Shannon (1994–2003), *Lauren Goler-Kosarin, Carol Lee Meadows, Jennifer Marcum*; Mrs. Potts: Barbara Marineau & Anna McNeely (94–95), *Beth McVey, Stacia Fernandez, Marguerite Shannon, Ann Arvia, Marguerite Willbanks*; Madame de la Grande Bouche: Barbara Marineau (94–95), Anna McNeely (1994–2000), *Stacia Fernandez, Marguerite Shannon, Ann Arvia*; Cheesegrater/Doormat/Pepper/Salt: *Joseph Favalora, Gregorey Garrison, Karl Christian, David E. Liddell*; Chip: Linda Talcott (94–95); D'Arque: Rob Lorey (94–95), *Bill Nabel, Kevin Berdini*; Bookseller: *Rob Lorey, Karl Christian, David E. Liddell.* **Swings**: Alisa Klein (94–95), Dan Mojica (94–95), Kate Dowe (94–95, but back by 11/12/99), Gregorey Garrison (94–95), Rob Lorey (94–95), Joan Barber (94–96). *Joseph Favalora, Barbara Folts, Carol Lee Meadows, Rachel Ulanet, Wendy Oliver, Karl Christian, Robin Lewis, David E. Liddell, Daria Lynn Scatton, Gina Carlette, John Salvatore.* **Orchestra**: CONCERTMASTER: Belinda Whitney; VIOLINS: Cenovia Cummins, Ann Labin, Evan Johnson, George Wozniak, Jean "Rudy" Perrault; CELLI: Caryl Paisner & Joseph Kimura; BASS: Jeffrey Carney; FLUTE: Katherine Fink; OBOE: Vicki Bodner; CLARINETS: Alva Hunt & KeriAnn K. DiBari; BASSOON: Marc Goldberg; TRUMPETS: Neil Balm & Tony Kadleck; FRENCH HORNS: Jeffrey Lang, Anthony Cecere, Glen Estrin; BASS TROMBONE: Paul Faulise; DRUMS: John Redsecker; PERCUSSION: Joseph Passaro; HARP: Stacey Shames; KEYBOARDS: Kathy Sommer & Glen Kelly. **Act I**: Overture (Orchestra); Prologue ("The Enchantress"), "Belle" (Belle, Gaston, Lefou, Silly Girls, Townspeople), "No Matter What" * (Maurice & Belle), "No Matter What" * (reprise) (Maurice), "Me" * (Gaston & Belle), "Belle" (reprise) (Belle), "Home" * (Belle), "Home" * (reprise) (Mrs. Potts), "Gaston" (Lefou, Gaston, Silly Girls, Tavern Patrons), "Gaston" (reprise) (Gaston & Lefou), "How Long Must This Go On?" * (Beast), "Be Our Guest" (Lumiere, Mrs. Potts, Cogsworth, Wardrobe, Chip, Babette, Enchanted Objects) [the big hit], "If I Can't Love Her" * (Beast). **Act II**: Entr'acte/Wolf Chase, "Something There" (Belle, Beast, Lumiere, Mrs. Potts, Cogsworth), "Human Again" (Lumiere, Wardrobe, Cogsworth, Mrs. Potts, Babette, Chip, Enchanted Objects), "Maison des Lunes" (Gaston, Lefou, D'Arque), "Beauty and the Beast" (Mrs. Potts) [a hit], "If I Can't Love Her" * (reprise) (Beast), "A Change in Me" * (Belle) [this number was introduced on 9/9/98 when Toni Braxton took over the role], "The Mob Song" (Gaston, Lefou, D'Arque, Townspeople), "The Battle" (Company), "Transformation" * (Beast & Belle), "Beauty and the Beast" (reprise) (Company).

Musical numbers asterisked had lyrics by Tim Rice. The others are by Howard Ashman (who died in 1991), who had written the movie score.

It had a capital investment of $11.9 million. When it opened it broke Broadway's all-time single-day sales record. Reviews were divided, mostly negative. It won a Tony for costumes, and was also nominated for musical, score, book, direction of a musical, lighting, and for Gary Beach, Susan Egan, and Terrence Mann. The choreography new to the London production was introduced into the Broadway run when Deborah Gibson came aboard as Belle, in 1997. On 7/7/98 it became the longest-ever running show in the history of the Palace Theatre (1,762 performances). By early 3/99 there were rumors that the show might move to another theatre, probably the smaller Lunt-Fontanne (*Titanic* was sinking there), in order to accommodate the incoming *Aida*. On 8/4/99 it played its 2,213th performance, eclipsing the original run of *Oklahoma!*, to become the 17th-longest-running Broadway show of all time. It closed on 9/5/99, and re-opened 11/12/99 (i.e. it was not a transfer). It got a smaller, tighter cast. On 3/1/00, with 2,378 performances, it surpassed *Annie* as the 14th-longest-running Broadway show of all time. On 8/4/02, with 3,389 performances, it became the 8th-longest-running Broadway show of all time, of all types. On 10/30/02, with 3,487 performances, it surpassed the original run of *Forty-Second Street* to become the 7th-longest running show in Broadway history. More than five million people had seen it on Broadway by that time. It missed a performance due to the 8/14/03 power blackout. It had its 4,000th performance on 1/27/04, and on 4/21/04 it passed *Miss Saigon* to become the 6th-longest running Broadway musical of all time.

After Broadway. LOS ANGELES. Opened on 4/12/95, at the SHUBERT THEATRE, Century City, and won several awards. There were rumors that the show was going to close on 7/7/96 and that many of the players would go to Toronto and dispossess the Canadian actors of their roles in the Canadian production. However, the L.A. run ended 9/29/96, after 25 previews & 615 PERFORMANCES (it earned $56 million). *Cast*: BELLE: Susan Egan, *Yvette Lawrence* (from 3/27/96), *Danyelle Bossardet*; BEAST: Terrence Mann, *James Barbour* (from 8/1/95); LEFOU: Jaime Torcellini; GASTON: Burke Moses, *Stephen Bishop* (from 12/26/96); MAURICE: Tom Bosley; COGSWORTH: Fred Applegate, *Gibby Brand* (from 4/26/96); LUMIERE: Gary Beach; BABETTE: Heather Lee; MRS. POTTS: Beth Fowler, *Jeanne Lehman* (from 9/26/95).

PRINCESS OF WALES THEATRE, Toronto. Opened on 8/8/95. *Cast*: BEAST: Chuck Wagner; BELLE: Kerry Butler, *Melissa Thomson* (from 96); GASTON: Dan Chameroy (until 6/9/96); LUMIERE: Andre Therien (until 6/9/96); MADAME DE LA GRANDE BOUCHE: Jo-Anne Kirwan-Clark (until 6/9/96); BABETTE: Elizabeth Beeler (until 6/9/96); COGSWORTH: Paul Brown (until 6/9/96).

AUSTRALIAN PRODUCTION. MELBOURNE, 1995. This was the Australian premiere. After Melbourne, it went to Sydney. *Cast*: BELLE: Rachael Beck, *Sharon Millerchip*; BEAST: Michael Cormick; GASTON: Hugh Jackman, *Scott Irwin*.

TOUR. Opened on 11/15/95 (previews from 11/7/95), at Minneapolis. It set records in many places, and closed on 3/7/99. *Cast*: BELLE: Kim Huber, *Erin Dilly* (from 2/11/98); BEAST: Frederick C. Inkley, *Roger Befeler*; LUMIERE: Patrick Page, *David DeVries, Gary Beach, David DeVries*; LEFOU: Dan Sklar, *Jeffrey Howard Schecter, Aldrin Gonzalez*; GASTON: Tony Lawson; MAURICE: Grant Cowan; COGSWORTH: Jeff Brooks; BABETTE: Leslie Castay, *Mindy Paige Davis* (from 2/15/97), *Heather Lee*; MRS. POTTS: Betsy Joslyn, *Barbara Marineau* (from 7/2/97).

La bella y la bestia. TEATRO ORFEON, Mexico City. The first Spanish-language production of this show). 5/8/97–5/98. DIRECTOR: Keith Batten; CHOREOGRAPHER: Dan Mojica; MUSICAL DIRECTOR: Michael Kosarin. *Cast*: Lolita Cortes, Robert Blandon. It was sold out right to the end (tickets were the most costly ever seen at a Mexican musical up to that time). It went to the OPERA THEATRE, BUENOS AIRES, 11/26/98. *Cast*: Marisol Otero, Juan Rodo.

DOMINION THEATRE, London, 5/13/97–12/11/99. Previews from 4/29/97. The 2000-seat Dominion was reconstructed to house the show, which won an Olivier Award for best musical, and broke all box-office records. In this production was added new choreography which later formed part of the subsequent Broadway performances. The London show cost 10 million pounds ($16.5 million), the most expensive in London's history. It had a 40-member cast, 25-member orchestra, more than 200 costumes, and a great set. Director, choreographer, costume and set designers were the same as for Broadway. *Cast*: BEAST: Alasdair Harvey; BELLE: Julie-Alanah Brighten; GASTON: Burke Moses; LUMIERE: Derek Griffiths; COGSMITH: Barry James; MRS. POTTS: Mary Millar; MAURICE: Norman Rossington; GRANDE BOUCHE: Di Botcher.

TOUR. Opened on 9/7/99, at Tulsa. Closed 8/4/03. During the tour it ran at the Kennedy Center, 4/26/01–5/14/01 (previews from 4/24/01). *Cast*: BEAST: Grant Norman, *Roger Befeler*; BELLE: Susan Owen, *Danyelle Bossardet, Jennifer Shrader*; LEFOU: Michael Raine, *Brad Aspel, Aldrin Gonzales*; GASTON: Chris Hoch, *Edward Staudenmayer, Marc G. Dalio*; MAURICE: Ron Lee Savin; COGSWORTH: John Alban Coughlan, *Ron Bagden, Tom Aulino, Andrew Boyar*; LUMIERE: Ron Wis-

niski, *Jay Russell*; BABETTE: Jennifer Shrader, *Louisa Kendrick, Sally Ann Tumas, Tracy Generalovich*; MRS. POTTS: Janet MacEwen, *Mary Jo McConnell*.

51. *Beg, Borrow or Steal*

A musical satire about the beat generation. It even had a Zen-Buddhist ballet. Set in a run-down section of a monster American city, in the 1950s.

Before Broadway. David Doyle replaced Billy Matthews as director before Broadway, but Mr. Matthews retained the credit "staged by." The numbers "You Would Like Him," "Love is No Laughing Matter," "It Ain't Gonna Be Easy," "The Avalon Ballroom," "Goin' Home Blues," "It's Never Been Done Before," and "Love is No Laughing Matter" were all cut.

The Broadway Run. MARTIN BECK THEATRE, 2/10/60–2/13/60. 5 PERFORMANCES. PRESENTED BY Eddie Bracken, in association with Carroll & Harris Masterson; MUSIC: Leon Pober; LYRICS/BOOK: Bud Freeman; BASED ON the unpublished story "Steal—A Disc Jockey's Handbook," by Marvin Seiger & Bud Freeman; DIRECTOR: David Doyle; STAGED BY Billy Matthews; CHOREOGRAPHER: Peter Hamilton; SETS/COSTUMES/LIGHTING: Carter Morningstar; MUSICAL DIRECTOR: Hal Hidey; ORCHESTRATIONS: Peter Matz & Hal Hidey; PRESS: Harry Davies & Irvin Dorfman; GENERAL MANAGER: Al Goldin; COMPANY MANAGER: Jack Potter; STAGE MANAGERS: Bob Paschall, Joseph Dooley, Bruce Blaine. *Cast:* MRS. PLONSKY: Jean Bruno; JUNIOR: Biff McGuire (4); OLLIE: Estelle Parsons; PHIL: Betty Rhodes; JUDY: Karen Sargent; CLARA: Betty Garrett (2); PISTOL: Eddie Bracken (3); RAFE: Larry Parks (1); JASON: Roy Stuart; ETHEL: Bernice Massi; LOVERS: Mary Sullivan & Del Hanley; MODERN DANCE LEADER: Sally Lee; DANCE CLASS: Carmen Morales, Garold Gardner, Ellen Halpin, Willard Nagel; RUG HOOKER: Michael Davis; POTTERY GIRL: Colleen Corkrey; BAR GIRL: Esther Horrocks; KNITTERS: Fran Leone & Keith Willis; PAINTER: Tom Hester; CHESS PLAYERS: Michel Stuart & Arthur Whitfield; FLAMENCO DANCERS: Adriana Keathley & Harold Da Silva; GUITARIST: Fred Kimbrough; KIBITZER: Mara Wirt; POET: John Tormey; POETRY LOVERS: Shelia Dee, Georgia Kennedy, Virginia Barnes; SCULPTOR: Chuck Arnett; MODEL: Beti Seay; MOBILE ARTIST: Lucinda Stevens; FRIEDA: Claiborne Cary; PATRIOT: Jack Drummond; SAM LEE HOWARD: Richard Armbruster; MUSCLE: Bill Linton; KOPPISCH: Richard Woods; BLANDING: David Doyle (5). *Standbys*: Clara: Cris Kane; Koppisch/Blanding: Bruce Blaine. *Understudies*: Rafe: Richard Armbruster; Junior/Pistol: Jack Drummond; Ethel: Colleen Corkrey; Jason: Del Hanley; Ollie/Mrs. Plonsky: Lucinda Stevens; Judy/Phil: Sally Lee. *Act I*: *Scene 1* The street; *Scene 2* The store; *Scene 3* The street; *Scene 4* The pit; *Scene 5* The park; *Scene 6* The street; *Scene 7* The pit; *Scene 8* Rafe's attic; *Scene 9* The store; *Scene 10* The street; *Scene 11* The pad; *Scene 12* The pit. *Act II*: *Scene 1* The office; six months later; *Scene 2* The street; *Scene 3* Chez pit; *Scene 4* The office; *Scene 5* The street; *Scene 6* The pad; *Scene 7* Chez pit; *Scene 8* The street; *Scene 9* The store. *Act I*: "Some Little People" (Ensemble), "Rootless" (Junior), "What Are We Gonna Do Tonight?" (Ollie, Phil, Judy), "Poetry and All That Jazz" (Frieda & Ensemble), "Don't Stand Too Close to the Picture" (Rafe, Clara, Ensemble), "Beg, Borrow or Steal" (recitative) (Rafe), "Beg, Borrow or Steal" (Rafe), "No One Knows Me" (Clara), "Zen is When" (Pistol, Junior, Ethel, Jason); Ballet (danced by Ensemble). Soloist: Colleen Corkrey; The Lovers: Carmen Morales & Arthur Whitfield; "Clara" (Junior), "You've Got Something to Say" (Rafe & Clara), "You've Got Something to Say" (reprise) (Rafe, Clara, Pistol, Junior, Company). *Act II*: "Presenting Clara Spencer" (Clara, assisted by Keith Willis, Michael Stuart, Chuck Arnett, Harold Da Silva, Willard Nagel, Garold Gardner, Arthur Whitfield), "I Can't Stop Talking" (Clara & Junior), "It's All in Your Mind" (Rafe & Clara), "In Time" (Junior), "Think" (Clara), "Little People" (Pistol & Company) (danced by Keith Willis, Sally Lee, Michael Stuart), "Rafesville, U.S.A." (Ethel & Jason), "Beg, Borrow or Steal" (reprise) (Rafe & Ensemble), "Let's Be Strangers Again" (Clara & Junior), "Little People" (reprise) (Entire Company).

It was mostly panned by reviewers.

52. *Beggar's Holiday*

The John Gay play *Beggar's Opera*, updated to 20th-century American gangsters. Mac, leader of a gang of blacks and whites in New York City, gets in trouble through two master crooks, Peachum and Lockit. He jilts several attractive women, and is about to be sent to the electric chair when he is pardoned.

Before Broadway. Lena Horne turned down the lead in this show which began pre–Broadway tryouts as *Twilight Alley*. John Houseman and Nicholas Ray were directing at that stage. Mr. Houseman quit during the Boston tryout, George Abbott was brought in, and a week before the show went to Broadway he had Nicholas Ray fire Libby Holman (then playing Jenny), who'd had a relationship with Mr. Ray. Then Mr. Abbott fired Mr. Ray.

The Broadway Run. BROADWAY THEATRE, 12/26/46–3/29/47. 111 PERFORMANCES. PRESENTED BY Perry Watkins & John R. Sheppard Jr.; MUSIC: Duke Ellington; LYRICS/BOOK: John Latouche; BASED ON the 1728 British play *The Beggar's Opera*, by John Gay; DIRECTOR: Nicholas Ray; CHOREOGRAPHER: Valerie Bettis; SETS: Oliver Smith; COSTUMES: Walter Florell; TECHNICAL SUPERVISOR/LIGHTING: Peggy Clark; MUSICAL DIRECTOR: Max Meth; ORCHESTRATIONS SUPERVISOR: Billy Strayhorn; VOCAL ARRANGEMENTS: Crane Calder; PRESS: Loretta Val-Mery; GENERAL MANAGER: Leo Rose; COMPANY MANAGER: Otto Hartman; STAGE MANAGER: Frank Coletti. *Cast:* THE BEGGAR: Alfred Drake [role cut during run]; THE PURSUED: Tommy Gomez; COP: Archie Savage; POLICEMEN: Herbert Ross & Lucas Hoving; PLAINCLOTHESMAN: Albert Popwell; THE LOOKOUT (FIRST GIRL): Marjorie Belle [Marjorie Belle later became Marge Champion]; MACHEATH (MAC): Alfred Drake (1); THE COCOA GIRL: Marie Bryant; JENNY DIVER: Bernice Parks (3); DOLLY TRULL: Lavina Nielsen; BETTY DOXY: Leonne Hall, *Margaret Wilson*; TAWDRY AUDREY: Tommie Moore; MRS. TRAPES: Doris Goodwin; ANNIE COAXER: Royce Wallace; BABY MILDRED: Claire Hale; MINUTE LOU: Nina Korda; TRIXY TURNER: Malka Farber; BESSIE BUNS: Elmira Jones-Bey; FLORA, THE HARPY: Enid Williams; THE HORN: Bill Dillard; HIGHBINDER: Jack Bittner; O'HEISTER: Gordon Nelson; THE DRUNK: Perry Bruskin [this character became known as The Foot during the run]; GUNSEL: Archie Savage; FINGERSMITH: Stanley Carlson; STRIP: Lucas Hoving; MOOCH: Perry Bruskin; THE EYE: Pan Theodore; WIRE BOY: Paul Godkin; THE OTHER EYE: Tommy Gomez; SLAM: Albert Popwell; THE CASER: Douglas Henderson; TWO CUSTOMERS: Gordon Nelson & Hy Anzell; THE KNIFE: Lewis Charles [this character became known as A Drunk during the run]; BARTENDER: Herbert Ross; CARELESS LOVE: Avon Long (5); POLLY PEACHUM: Jet MacDonald (4); BLACK MARKETEER: Gordon Nelson; MRS. PEACHUM: Dorothy Johnson; HAMILTON PEACHUM: Zero Mostel (2); CHIEF LOCKIT: Rollin Smith; LUCY LOCKIT: Mildred Smith; BLENKINSOP: Pan Theodore; THE GIRL: Marjorie Belle; THE BOY: Paul Godkin; THE DANCERS: Paul Godkin & Marjorie Belle, Malka Farber, Tommy Gomez, Doris Goodwin, Claire Hale, Lucas Hoving, Elmira Jones-Bey, Lavina Nielsen, Albert Popwell, Herbert Ross, Archie Savage, Royce Wallace, Enid Williams; MAC'S GANG: Jack Bittner, Perry Bruskin, Stanley Carlson, Lewis Charles, Bill Dillard, Gordon Nelson. *Act I:* ***Scene 1*** Exterior of Miss Jenny's; ***Scene 2*** Interior of Miss Jenny's; ***Scene 3*** Outside Miss Jenny's; ***Scene 4*** At Hamilton Peachum's; ***Scene 5*** A street; ***Scene 6*** A hobo jungle; two days later. *Act II:* ***Scene 1*** The street; ***Scene 2*** Chief Lockit's office; ***Scene 3*** The jail; ***Scene 4*** The street; ***Scene 5*** Jenny's bedroom; ***Scene 6*** Under the bridge; Scene 7 Finale. *Act I:* "The Chase" (dance) (The Pursued, Bartender, Strip), "When You Go Down by Miss Jenny's" (Citizens & Girls), "I've Got Me" (Mac), "TNT" (Cocoa Girl), "Take Love Easy" (Jenny), "(I) Wanna Be Bad" (Careless Love), "Rooster Man" (Jenny) [dropped during the run], "When I Walk with You" (Polly & Mac), Wedding Ballet, "I've Got Me" (reprise) (Lookout), "Inbetween" (Lucy) [dropped during the run], "The Scrimmage of Life" (Mr. & Mrs. Peachum), "Ore from a Goldmine" (Mr. & Mrs. Peachum), Finaletto (Polly, Mr. & Mrs. Peachum), "When I Walk with You" (reprise) (Mac & Polly), "Tooth and Claw" (Mac's Gang), "Maybe I Should Change My Ways" (Mac), "(On) the Wrong Side of the Railroad Tracks" (Cocoa Girl, Careless Love, The Horn), "Tomorrow Mountain" (Mac & Company). *Act*

II: "Chorus of Citizens" (dance) (Ensemble), "Girls Want a Hero" [replaced with a reprise of "Tooth and Claw" (Peachum & Reporters) during the run], "Lullaby for Junior" (Jenny), "Quarrel for Three" (Polly, Lucy, Mac), "Fol-de-rol-rol" (dance) (Mac), "Brown Penny" (lyric based on a poem by W.B. Yeats) (Lucy) [dropped during the run], "Women, Women, Women" (Prisoners), "Women, Women, Women" (reprise) (Cocoa Girl & Careless Love), "When I Walk with You" (reprise) (Mac), Ballet, "The Hunted" (dance) (Mac), Finale (Mac, Jenny, Polly, Lucy, Company).

Broadway reviews were mostly bad, but there were one or two raves. John Chapman, of the *Daily News*, called it the most interesting musical since *Porgy and Bess*. It flopped on Broadway. It had a racially mixed cast, and was the first Broadway musical to have an interracial romance. When Alfred Drake kissed Jet McDonald many members of each audience walked out. The show cost $325,000.

After Broadway. THE REVISED VERSION. 10/1/99–10/3/99. PRESENTED BY The York Theatre Company, as part of their Off Broadway ***Musicals in Mufti*** series. This had been the only significant revival of *Beggar's Holiday* to that date. REVISED BOOK: Dale Wasserman; DIRECTOR: Kent Gash; MUSICAL SUPERVISOR: Luther Henderson; MUSICAL DIRECTOR: Leonard Oxley. *Cast:* MACHEATH: Jerry Dixon; FLORA: Lana Gordon; MISS JENNY: Pamela Isaacs; CAPT. LOCKIT: Kenneth Kantor; LUCY: La Chanze; WIREBOY: Jesse Means; COZY COOL: Cheryl Monroe; HIGHBINDER: Joe Langworth; MRS. PEACHUM/DOLLY DIDDLE: Amy Jo Phillips; MR. PEACHUM: Ken Prymus; SNEAKY PETE: Glenn Turner; POLLY: Tami Swartz. In a post-production discussion Mildred Smith Hepburn (Lucy in the 1946 production), Luther Henderson, and Marge Champion (also in the original cast) took part.

MILL VALLEY, California. Opened on 9/7/04. This was the revised version. DIRECTOR: Lee Sankowich; CHOREOGRAPHER: Richard Gibbs; NEW ORCHESTRATIONS: Donald York. It was aiming for Broadway.

53. *Bells Are Ringing*

Set in New York City in 1956. Ella, who at one time worked for the Bonjour Tristesse Brassiere Factory, now works for Susanswerphone, a telephone answering service owned by Sue. Contrary to company policy, she gets involved in the lives of her clients, one of whom is handsome playboy playwright, Jeffrey, to whom she is "Mom," a little old lady. Others are Sandor, a bookie (having a relationship with Sue), Kitchell, a songwriting dentist, and Blake, a would-be actor with a Brando fixation. Jeff has writer's block, and Ella, posing as a girl named Melisande, agrees to meet him and help him overcome this. They fall in love and at a social party she is made to feel out of place and leaves him. He finally finds her. Sandor is operating a telephone bookmaking system, involving names of musical pieces as code. Ella, not knowing what's going on, changes one of the symphony numbers because she feels it is an error, and results for the bookie are disastrous.

Before Broadway. Betty Comden, Adolph Green and Judy Holliday had been a nightclub act in the 1940s before they went their separate ways. Comden and Green were now looking for a show for Judy. After weeks of racking their brains, they came up with the answering service idea. They went along to Mr. Green's own answering service, expecting it to be a great office with hundreds of secretaries, but found a little dingy office with a fat old lady, and a dog peeing in the corner. Miss Holliday and Syd Chaplin (Charlie's son) were an item at the time, and Judy insisted on casting him. Despite Jerome Robbins's reluctant agreement on this, Mr. Chaplin wowed the critics out of town, and threatened to steal the show from the blonde star (this was Judy's first star billing on Broadway, and marked her return to the stage after years in Hollywood). So, the songwriters wrote a new finale song for her. It had been "The Party's Over," but they wrote "I'm Going Back," so that the audience would side with her at the end.

The Broadway Run. SHUBERT THEATRE, 11/29/56–12/13/58; ALVIN THEATRE, 12/15/58–3/7/59. Total of 924 PERFORMANCES. PRESENTED BY the Theatre Guild; MUSIC: Jule Styne; LYRICS/BOOK: Betty Comden

& Adolph Green; DIRECTOR: Jerome Robbins; ASSISTANT DIRECTOR: Gerald Freedman; CHOREOGRAPHER: Jerome Robbins & Bob Fosse; SETS/COSTUMES: Raoul Pene du Bois; ASSISTANT SETS/ASSISTANT COSTUMES: Willa Kim & Waldo Angelo; LIGHTING: Peggy Clark; MUSICAL DIRECTOR: Milton Rosenstock; ORCHESTRATIONS: Robert Russell Bennett; VOCAL DIRECTORS/VOCAL ARRANGEMENTS: Herbert Greene & Buster Davis; DANCE MUSIC ARRANGEMENTS/INCIDENTAL SCORING: John Morris; PRESS: John L. Toohey & Max Gendel (*Dick Weaver*), Alfred H. Tamarin, *Nat Dorfman*; CASTING: Ruth Frankenstein; PRODUCTION SUPERVISOR: Jerome Whyte; GENERAL MANAGER: Peter Davis; GENERAL STAGE MANAGER: Charles Atkin, *Billy Matthews*; STAGE MANAGER: Ruth Mitchell, *Fred* Smith; ASSISTANT STAGE MANAGER: Paul Davis, *Joseph Dooley*. **Cast:** SUE: Jean Stapleton (3), *Alice Pearce*; GWYNNE: Pat Wilkes (10); ELLA PETERSON: Judy Holliday (1) ☆, *Betty Garrett* (during Miss Holliday's vacation for two weeks in 1957); CARL: Peter Gennaro (8), *Buzz Miller, Frank Derbas*; INSPECTOR BARNES: Dort Clark (5); FRANCIS: Jack Weston (12), *Heywood Hale Broun, Ralph Roberts*; SANDOR: Eddie Lawrence (4); JEFF MOSS: Sydney Chaplin (2), *Larry Parks* (during Mr. Chaplin's two-week vacation, 1957), *Hal Linden* (from 6/30/58); LARRY HASTINGS: George S. Irving (7), *Paul Lipson*; TELEPHONE MAN: Eddie Heim, *Philip Nasta*; LUDWIG SMILEY: Frank Milton (13), *Steve Roland*; CHARLES BESSEMER: Frank Green [role cut during run]; DR. KITCHELL: Bernie West (9); BLAKE BARTON: Frank Aletter (6); ANOTHER ACTOR: Frank Green, *Doria Avila, Frank Derbas*; JOEY: Tom O'Steen, *Scott Hunter, Mitchell Nutick*; OLGA: Norma Doggett (14), *Donna Sanders*; MAN FROM THE CORVELLO MOB: John Perkins, *Vincent Beck*; OTHER MAN: Kasimir Kokich, *Louis Kosman*; CAROL: Ellen Ray (11), *Beryl Towbin, Carmen Gutierrez*; PAUL ARNOLD: Steve Roland; MICHELLE: Michelle Reiner; MASTER OF CEREMONIES: Eddie Heim, *Philip Nasta*; SINGER AT NIGHT CLUB: Frank Green, *David McDaniel, Mark Tully*; WAITER: Ed Thompson, *Benjamin Raisen, Marc Leon*; MAITRE D': David McDaniel, *Joe Flynn, Richard Hermany, Jack Rains, Paul Merrill*; POLICE OFFICER: Gordon Woodburn, *Paul Michael, Edmund Walenta*; MADAME GRIMALDI: Donna Sanders; MRS. MALLET: Jeannine Masterson, *Louise Woods*; DANCING GIRLS: Norma Doggett (gone by 57–58), Phyllis Dorne (gone by 57–58), Patti Karr (gone by 57–58), Barbara Newman (gone by 57–58), Nancy Perkins, Marsha Rivers (left in 58), Beryl Towbin (gone by 57–58), Anne Wallace, *Jain Fairfax, Diana Hunter, Sigyn Lund, Rae McLean, Frances Martin, Louisa Cabot, Marian Hunter*; DANCING BOYS: Doria Avila, Frank Derbas (gone by 57–58), Don Emmons, Eddie Heim, Kaz Kokich (*Louis Kosman*), Tom O'Steen (*Scott Hunter, Mitchell Nutick*), Willy Sumner, Ben Vargas (gone by 57–58), Billy Wilson (gone by 57–58), *Philip Nasta, Dale Moreda, Ernest Parham, William Miller, Alan Peterson, Adolph Sambognia*; SINGING GIRLS: Pam Abbott (gone by 57–58), Joanne Birks, Urylee Leonardos (left in 58), Jeannine Masterson, Michelle Reiner, Donna Sanders, *Shirley Chester, Adrienne Angel, Louise Woods, Joan Elliott, Mary Ellen Schimmel*; SINGING BOYS: Frank Green (*Bob Roman*), Marc Leon, David McDaniel (*Mark Tully*), Paul Michael, Julian Patrick, Steve Roland (gone by 57–58), Ed Thompson (gone by 57–58), Gordon Woodburn (gone by 57–58), *Ralph Farnworth, Joe Flynn, Jack Rains, Benjamin Raisen, Michael Davis, Ripple Lewis, Paul Merrill, Edmund Walenta*. **Standbys:** Ella: Marge Redmond, *Phyllis Newman, June Ericson, Lynne Stuart*. **Understudies:** Sandor: George S. Irving, *Paul Lipson*); Sue: Michelle Reiner; Gwynne: Beryl Towbin, *Adrienne Angel, Frances Martin*; Barnes/Smiley/Larry: Gordon Woodburn, *Steve Roland, Paul Michael*; Francis: Willy Sumner, *Mitchell Nutick*; Olga: Jeannine Masterson, *Jain Fairfax*; Paul: Frank Green, *Julian Patrick, Bob Roman*; Man from Mob: Steve Roland, *Paul Michael, Louis Kosman*; Jeff: Hal Linden, *Vincent Beck*; Blake: *David McDaniel, Mark Tully*; Carl: *Doria Avila, Frank Derbas*; Carol: *Gwenn Lewis, Jain Fairfax, Barbara Newman*; Kitchell: *Heywood Hale Broun, Frank Milton, Marc Leon*. **Act I**: Overture (Orchestra); *Opening*: "Bells Are Ringing" (Susanswerphone advertisement) (Telephone Girls); *Scene 1* Office of Susanswerphone; late afternoon: "It's a Perfect Relationship" (Ella); *Scene 2* Jeff Moss's living room: "On My Own" (Jeff & Dancers) [this number was called "Independent" in the 2001 revival], "You've Got to Do It" (Jeff); *Scene 3* An alley; at night: "It's a Simple Little System" (Sandor & Ensemble); *Scene 4* The office; early morning; *Scene 5* A street in front of the office: "Is it a Crime?" (Ella) [in the 2001 revival this number was re-positioned to

the penultimate song of Act I, and sung by Ella, Barnes, Francis]; *Scene 6* Jeff Moss's living room: "(It's) Better than a Dream" (Ella & Jeff) [this number was new for the second season]; *Scene 7* A street; *Scene 8* A subway car: "Hello, Hello, There!" (Ella, Jeff, Ensemble) [in the 2001 revival it was Smiley, Ella, Jeff, Ensemble]; *Scene 9* A street: "I Met a Girl" (Jeff & Ensemble); *Scene 10* Dr. Kitchell's office; *Scene 11* A street; *Scene 12* A drugstore; *Scene 13* A street; *Scene 14* The office; a week later; *Scene 15* Jeff Moss's living room: "Long Before I Knew You" (Jeff & Ella) [a hit]. **Act II**: Entr'acte (Orchestra); *Scene 1* The office; the next night: "Mu-Cha-Cha" (Ella & Carl), Dance (Carol, Carl, Dancing Ensemble) [in the 2001 revival it was by Carl, Ella, Gwynne, Dancers]; *Scene 2* The park: "Just in Time" (Jeff, Ella, Ensemble) [a big hit]; *Scene 3* Larry Hastings' penthouse: "Drop that Name" (Ensemble, with Ella), "The Party's Over" (Ella) [the big hit]; *Scene 4* The *Crying Gypsy* Café: "Salzburg" (Sue & Sandor); *Scene 5* The *Pyramid* Night Club: "The Midas Touch" (Singer, Boys & Girls) [in the 2001 revival it was by Kitchell & Dancers]; *Scene 6* On the Bay Ridge subway platform: "Long Before I Knew You" (reprise) (Jeff) [not in the 2001 revival]; *Scene 7* The office: "I'm Goin' Back" (Ella), Finale (Company).

Broadway reviews were mostly terrific. The production was budgeted at $360,000, and built up advance Broadway sales of over a million, finally making over $5 million at the box office. Frances Martin, who Hal Linden had married the month before he took over as Jeff, was a chorus girl in the show. Judy Holliday and Syd Chaplin won Tonys, and the show was also nominated for choreography and musical. A year into the run Comden and Green wrote a new song, "Better than a Dream," and put it into the show. It was thus added to the score, and was in the movie as well.

After Broadway. COLISEUM, London, 11/14/57–7/26/58. 292 PERFORMANCES. DIRECTOR: Gerald Freedman; CHOREOGRAPHER: Robert Tucker; Musical DIRECTOR: Reginald Burston. **Cast:** ELLA: Janet Blair, *Julie Wilson*; JEFF: George Gaynes; GWYNNE: Allyn McLerie (Miss McLerie was at that time married to George Gaynes), *Leander Fedden*; SUE: Jean St. Clair; CARL: Harry Naughton; BARNES: Donald Stewart; SANDOR: Eddie Molloy; LARRY: Robert Henderson; MICHELLE: Rita Cameron; KITCHELL: Alexander Dore; PAUL: Lewis Henry; BLAKE: Franklin Fox; FRANCIS: C. Denier Warren; LUDWIG: Arthur Wilman, *Leighton Camden*; OLGA: Shelagh Aldrich; MAN FROM MOB: Alister Williamson, *Bill Clothier*; MC: Richard Owens.

MEXICO CITY, 1958. *Ring, Ring, Llama el Amor.* DIRECTOR: Luis de Llano Palmer. **Cast:** Silvia Pinal.

TOUR. Opened on 3/10/59, at the National Theatre, Washington, DC. MUSICAL DIRECTOR: Samuel Matlovsky. **Cast:** ELLA: Judy Holliday; JEFF: Hal Linden; SUE: Alice Pearce; GWYNNE: Sally Brown; MME GRIMALDI/OLGA: Donna Sanders; BARNES: Dort Clark; SANDOR: Eddie Lawrence; KITCHELL: Bernie West; CARL: Frank Derbas; BLAKE: Frank Aletter; PAUL: Steve Roland; FRANCIS: Ralph Roberts; LARRY: Paul Lipson; JOEY: Mitchell Nutick; MAN FROM MOB: Vincent Beck; CAROL: Barbara Newman; MICHELLE: Michelle Reiner. It kept in "Better than a Dream."

THE MOVIE. 1960. DIRECTOR: Vincente Minnelli. Two new numbers were added: "Better than a Dream" and "Do it Yourself," and five were dropped. The "Mu-Cha-Cha" dance was shortened. **Cast:** ELLA: Judy Holliday; JEFFREY: Dean Martin; LARRY: Fred Clark; J. OTTO PRANTZ: Eddie Foy Jr.; SUE: Jean Stapleton; GWYNNE: Ruth Storey; BARNES: Dort Clark; BLAKE: Frank Gorshin; KITCHELL: Bernie West; FRANCIS: Ralph Roberts; OLGA: Valerie Allen.

GOODSPEED OPERA HOUSE, Conn., 1990. DIRECTOR: Sue Lawless; CHOREOGRAPHER: Rob Marshall; SETS: James Noone; MUSICAL DIRECTOR: Don Jones; ADDITIONAL ORCHESTRATIONS: Don Jones & Wendy E. Bobbitt. **Cast:** ELLA: Lynne Wintersteller; JEFF: Anthony Cummings; KITCHELL: Gabor Morea; SUE: Liz Otto; SANDOR: Ron Wisniski; ALSO WITH: Casey Nicholaw.

54. *Bells Are Ringing (Broadway revival)*

The set had an expressive plexiglass skyline.

Before Broadway. This revival began at the KENNEDY CENTER,

Washington, DC, 7/16/98–7/19/98, as part of the *Words and Music* series. DIRECTOR: Tina Landau; CHOREOGRAPHER: Jeff Calhoun. **Cast**: ELLA: Faith Prince; SUE: Joyce Van Patten; JEFF: Alan Campbell. By 9/99 it was being planned to take it to Broadway. Although there were slight revisions to the original 1956 Broadway production here and there, this was not a revised revival. The Pasadena Playhouse tryout, beginning 11/3/00, was canceled. There was an open press rehearsal 1/31/01. It tried out at the Palace Theatre, Stamford, Conn., 2/20/01–2/25/01. On Broadway it was originally to have opened at the Broadway Theatre, but in 11/00 they went for the Plymouth Theatre.

The Broadway Run. PLYMOUTH THEATRE, 4/12/01–6/10/01. 35 previews from 3/13/01. 69 PERFORMANCES. PRESENTED BY Mitchell Maxwell, Mark Balsam, Victoria Maxwell, Robert Barandes, Richard Bernstein, Mark Goldberg, Anthony R. Russo, James L. Simon, in association with Fred H. Krones, Allen M. Shore, Momentum Productions; MUSIC: Jule Styne; LYRICS/BOOK: Betty Comden & Adolph Green; DIRECTOR: Tina Landau; CHOREOGRAPHER: Jeff Calhoun; SETS: Riccardo Hernandez; COSTUMES: David C. Woolard; LIGHTING: Donald Holder; SOUND: Acme Sound Partners; MUSICAL DIRECTOR/VOCAL ARRANGEMENTS: David Evans; ORCHESTRATIONS: Don Sebesky; DANCE MUSIC ARRANGEMENTS: Mark Hummel; INCIDENTAL MUSIC: David Evans & Mark Hummel; NEW CAST RECORDING on Fynsworth Alley (it was going to be recorded on 3/26/01, then on 4/23/01, on the DRG label, but instead it was recorded on 5/14/01 and released on 6/26/01 on Fynsworth Alley; PRESS: Barlow — Hartman Public Relations; CASTING: Stephanie Klapper & Susan Lovell; GENERAL MANAGER: Robert V. Straus; COMPANY MANAGER: Bruce Kagel; PRODUCTION STAGE MANAGER: Erica Schwartz; STAGE MANAGER: James Latus; ASSISTANT STAGE MANAGER: Richard Rauscher. **Cast:** TV ANNOUNCER: Shane Kirkpatrick; TELEPHONE GIRLS: Caitlin Carter, Joan Hess, Emily Hsu, Alice Rietveld; SUE: Beth Fowler (4); GWYNNE: Angela Robinson; ELLA PETERSON: Faith Prince (1) ✩; CARL: Julio Agustin; INSPECTOR BARNES: Robert Ari (6); FRANCIS: Jeffrey Bean (7); SANDOR: David Garrison (3); JEFF MOSS: Marc Kudisch (2) ✩; LARRY HASTINGS: David Brummel; LOUIE: Greg Reuter; LUDWIG SMILEY: Lawrence Clayton; CHARLIE BESSEMER: Josh Rhodes; DR. KITCHELL: Martin Moran (5); BLAKE BARTON: Darren Ritchie; JOEY: Shane Kirkpatrick; PADDY, THE STREET SWEEPER: Roy Harcourt; MRS. SIMMS: Joan Hess; OLGA: Caitlin Carter; MEN FROM THE CORVELLO MOB: David Brummel & Greg Reuter; MRS. MALLET: Joan Hess; MAID: Linda Romoff; PAUL ARNOLD: Lawrence Clayton; BRIDGETTE: Joan Hess; MAN ON STREET/WAITER: Josh Rhodes; MADAME GRIMALDI: Joanne Baum; ENSEMBLE: Julio Agustin, Joanne Baum, David Brummel, Caitlin Carter, Lawrence Clayton, Roy Harcourt, Joan Hess, Emily Hsu, Shane Kirkpatrick, Greg Reuter, Josh Rhodes, Alice Rietveld, Darren Ritchie, Angela Robinson, Linda Romoff; DANCERS: Caitlin Carter, Roy Harcourt, Joan Hess, Emily Hsu, Shane Kirkpatrick, Greg Reuter, Josh Rhodes. **Understudies**: Ella: Linda Romoff & Joan Hess; Jeff: Josh Rhodes; Sue: Joanne Baum & Joan Hess; Blake: Shane Kirkpatrick, James Hadley, Marc Oka; Sandor: David Brummel & Lawrence Clayton; Barnes: Lawrence Clayton; Larry: Lawrence Clayton, James Hadley, Marc Oka; Kitchell: Greg Reuter; Francis: Shane Kirkpatrick; Carl: Roy Harcourt, James Hadley, Marc Oka; Ludwig/Paul: James Hadley & Marc Oka; Gwynne/Olga: Stacey Harris & Kelly Sullivan. **Swings**: James Hadley, Kelly Sullivan, Marc Oka, Stacey Harris. **Orchestra**: VIOLINS: Robert Lawrence & Maura Giannini; VIOLA: Jill Jaffe; CELLO: Scott Ballantyne; WOODWINDS: Steven Kenyon, Kenneth Dybisz, Daniel Block, Ronald Jannelli; TRUMPETS: Stu Satalof & Bruce Staelens; TROMBONE: Clinton Sharman; FRENCH HORN: Peter Gordon; BASS: Louis Bruno; PERCUSSION: Rick Rosenzweig; KEYBOARDS: Joseph Baker.

It got very divided reviews, but a bad one from the *New York Times* killed it. By 6/4/01 it was known that the show was closing. It was capitalized at $5.8 million. It received Tony nominations for revival of a musical and for Faith Prince.

55. *Ben Franklin in Paris*

Ben travels to Paris in 1776–1777 to gain recognition for the American Revolution. The four women he romanced during his trip became one (Diane) for this musical.

Before Broadway. For Diane the producers wanted Simone Signoret, then Arlene Dahl, then Danielle Darrieux, but Ulla Sallert (a baroness in real life, and the queen of Swedish musical theatre), was brought in, even though her English was questionable. Noel Willman was to have directed, but was replaced by Michael Kidd during rehearsals. Mr. Kidd also replaced choreographer Herbert Ross. During Philadelphia tryouts Jerry Herman wrote two new songs (see song list). Jacqueline Mayro was replaced by Susan Watson just before previews began in New York. Bob Preston shaved his head for the part — he was playing a man in his 70s.

The Broadway Run. LUNT—FONTANNE THEATRE, 10/27/64– 5/1/65. 13 previews from 10/7/64. 215 PERFORMANCES. PRESENTED BY George W. George & Frank Granat; MUSIC: Mark Sandrich Jr.; LYRICS/BOOK: Sidney Michaels; ADDITIONAL MUSIC/ADDITIONAL LYRICS: Jerry Herman; BASED PARTLY ON Benjamin Franklin's aphorisms; DIRECTOR/CHOREOGRAPHER: Michael Kidd; SETS: Oliver Smith; COSTUMES: Motley; LIGHTING: Jack Brown; MUSICAL DIRECTOR/VOCAL ARRANGEMENTS: Donald Pippin; ORCHESTRATIONS: Philip J. Lang; DANCE MUSIC ARRANGEMENTS/INCIDENTAL MUSIC: Roger Adams; CAST RECORDING on Capitol; PRESS: Lee Solters, Harvey B. Sabinson, David Powers; GENERAL MANAGER: Edward H. Davis; COMPANY MANAGER: George Oshrin; PRODUCTION STAGE MANAGER: William Dodds; STAGE MANAGER: Ben Janney; ASSISTANT STAGE MANAGER: John Hallow. **Cast:** CAPTAIN WICKES: Sam Greene; BENJAMIN FRANKLIN: Robert Preston (1); TEMPLE FRANKLIN: Franklin Kiser (4); BENJAMIN FRANKLIN "BENNY" BACHE: Jerry Schaefer; FOOTMAN: Anthony Falco; LOUIS XVI: Oliver Clark; VERGENNES: Art Bartow; TURGOT: Clifford Fearl; MME LA COMTESSE DIANE DE VOBRILLAC: Ulla Sallert (2); BRITISH GRENADIER: Roger Le Page; DAVID LORD STORMONT: Byron Webster; FRENCH SOLDIER: Ron Schwinn; PIERRE CARON DE BEAUMARCHAIS: Bob Kaliban; JACQUES FINQUE: John Taliaferro; THE ARTIST: John Keatts [role cut during previews]; LITTLE BOY: Stuart Getz; PEDRO COUNT DE ARANDA: Jack Fletcher; BOOKSELLER: Herb Mazzini; JANINE NICOLET: Susan Watson (3), *Rita Gardner* (from 11/30/64); ABBE DE MORELLET: Herb Mazzini; SPANISH AIDE-DE-CAMP: Kip Andrews; SPANISH SOLDIER: Art Matthews; SPANISH AMBASSADOR'S DAUGHTER: Suzanne France; YVONNE: Lauren Jones; SINGERS: Art Bartow, Barbara Bossert, Mona Crawford, Anthony Falco, Clifford Fearl, Hilda Harris, John Keatts, Art Matthews, Anita Maye, Herb Mazzini, Caroline Parks, John Taliaferro; DANCERS: Kip Andrews, Diane Ball, Marilyn Charles, Jean Eliot, Suzanne France, Ellen Graff, Lauren Jones, Roger Le Page, George Ramos, Eddie Roll, Sandy Roveta, Rec Russell, Ron Schwinn, Lou Zeldis. **Understudies**: Ben: Sam Greene; Diane: Caroline Parks; Janine: Sandy Roveta; Temple: Roger Le Page; Beaumarchais: Eddie Roll; Stormont/Pedro/Louis/Wickes: John Hallow; Benny: Stuart Getz. **Act I**: *Prologue* At sea aboard the S.S. *Reprisal*; "We Sail the Seas" (American Sailors); *Scene 1* The docks: "I Invented Myself" (Ben & Company); *Scene 2* Versailles: "Too Charming" (by Jerry Herman) (Ben & Diane); [during previews Scene 3 was set on A Paris street]; *Scene 3* Ben's house [this was Scene 4 during previews]: "Whatever Became of Old Temple?" (Temple), "Half the Battle" (Ben, Benny, Temple, Beaumarchais); *Scene 4* The park [this was Scene 5 during previews]: "A Balloon is Ascending" (Company) [this number was dropped during the run]; *Scene 5* Sky over Paris [this was Scene 6 during previews]: "To Be Alone with You" (by Jerry Herman) (Ben, Diane, Company); *Scene 6* The Pont Neuf [this was Scene 7 during previews]: "You're in Paris" (Janine, Temple, Company); *Scene 7* Paris Town [this was Scene 8 during previews]; [during previews Scene 9 was set on the Pont Neuf]; *Scene 8* Ben's house [this was Scene 10 during previews]: "How Laughable it Is" (Diane); *Scene 9* The vineyards [this was Scene 11 during previews]: "Hic Haec Hoc" (Monks), "God Bless the Human Elbow" (Ben, Pedro, Marchais, Monks). **Act II**: *Scene 1* The Spanish Embassy: "When I Dance with the Person I Love" (Janine); [during previews Scene 2 was set on A Paris street]; *Scene 2* Versailles [this was Scene 3 during previews]; *Scene 3* Diane's house [this was Scene 4 during previews]: "Diane Is" (Ben), "Look for Small Pleasures" (Ben & Diane); *Scene 4* Ben's house [this was Scene 5 during previews]: "I Love the Ladies" (Ben, Wickes, Beaumarchais, Temple, Sailors); *Scene 5* Versailles [this was Scene 6 during previews]: "To Be Alone with You" (reprise) (Ben).

It got divided Broadway reviews. It lasted as long as it did because of advance sales. However, it lacked spark, and the story was outdated. It received a Tony nomination for book.

56. *The Best Little Whorehouse Goes Public*

Sequel to *The Best Little Whorehouse in Texas*. Mona is brought out of retirement to run a brothel in Vegas.

The Broadway Run. LUNT—FONTANNE THEATRE, 5/10/94–5/21/94. 29 previews from 4/14/94. 16 PERFORMANCES. PRESENTED BY Stevie Phillips & MCA/Universal; MUSIC/LYRICS: Carol Hall; BOOK: Larry L. King & Peter Masterson; DIRECTORS: Peter Masterson & Tommy Tune; ASSOCIATE DIRECTOR: Philip Oesterman; CHOREOGRAPHERS: Jeff Calhoun & Tommy Tune; ASSOCIATE CHOREOGRAPHER: Niki Harris; SETS: John Arnone; COSTUMES: Bob Mackie; LIGHTING: Jules Fisher & Peggy Eisenhauer; SOUND: Tony Meola; MUSICAL SUPERVISOR/VOCAL & DANCE MUSIC ARRANGEMENTS: Wally Harper; MUSICAL DIRECTOR/VOCAL DIRECTOR: Karl Jurman; ORCHESTRATIONS: Peter Matz; MUSICAL ADVISER: Robert Billig; CAST RECORDING on Varese Sarabande; PRESS: Jeffrey Richards Associates; CASTING: Stuart Howard & Amy Schecter; GENERAL MANAGERS: Dodgers Productions; COMPANY MANAGER: Lauren Singer; PRODUCTION STAGE MANAGER: Arturo E. Porazzi; STAGE MANAGER: Bonnie L. Becker; ASSISTANT STAGE MANAGER: Kimberly Russell. *Cast:* SHOWROOM HEADLINER: Troy Britton Johnson; SHOWROOM PATRONS: Gerry Burkhardt, Laurel Lynn Collins, Sally Mae Dunn, Tom Flagg, Joe Hart, Don Johanson, Mark Manley, Mary Frances McCatty, Casey Nicholaw, Louise Ruck, William Ryall, Shaver Tillitt, Jillana Urbina, Richard Vida, Theara J. Ward; STREET WHORES: Pamela Everett, Ganine Giorgione, Amy N. Heggins, Lainie Sakakura, Christina Youngman; RALPH J. BOSTICK: Danny Rutigliano; COMEDIAN: Jim David; LAS VEGAS LEGENDS: Gerry Burkhardt, Laurel Lynn Collins, Sally Mae Dunn, Don Johanson, Mary Frances McCatty, William Ryall, Theara J. Ward; IRS DIRECTOR: Kevin Cooney; SCHMIDT, HIS ASSISTANT: David Doty; TERRI CLARK: Gina Torres; MONA STANGLEY: Dee Hoty (1) ☆; CLIENT OF WHOREHOUSE: Joe Hart; SAM DALLAS: Scott Holmes (2); B.S. BULLEHIT: David Doty; SENATOR A. HARRY HARDAST: Ronn Carroll; LOTTA LOVINGOOD: Pamela Everett; PRESIDENT OF THE USA: David Doty; HIS HAIRDRESSER: Jim David; WORKING GIRLS: Laurel Lynn Collins, Sally Mae Dunn, Pamela Everett, Ganine Giorgione, Amy N. Heggins, Mary Frances McCatty, Louise Ruck, Lainie Sakakura, Jillana Urbina, Theara J. Ward, Christina Youngman; WALL STREET WOLVES: Gerry Burkhardt, Tom Flagg, Joe Hart, Don Johanson, Troy Britton Johnson, Mark Manley, Casey Nicholaw, Danny Rutigliano, William Ryall, Shaver Tillitt, Richard Vida; PIT VOCALISTS: Nancy LaMott, Ryan Perry, Susannah Blinkoff. *Standbys*: Mona: Lauren Mitchell; Sam: J. Mark McVey; *Understudies*: IRS/Hardast: Joe Hart; Schmidt: Danny Rutigliano; Comedian: Gerry Burkhardt; Terri: Laurel Lynn Collins; Swings: Niki Harris & Vincent D'Elia. *Orchestra*: WOODWINDS: Raymond Beckenstein, Dale Kleps, Edward Zuhlke, Vincent Della Rocca, Wally Kane; TRUMPETS: Robert Millikan, Larry Lunetta, David Rogers; TROMBONES: John Fedchok, Sonny Russo, Vincent Fanuele; VIOLINS: Mary Rowell, Andrew Stein, Paul Woodiel, Melanie Baker; CELLO: Bruce Wang; KEYBOARDS: Karl Jurman & Donald Rebic; GUITARS: Jay Berliner & Steven Bargonetti; BASS: John Burr; PERCUSSION: Ronald Zito & James Saporito; HARP: Lise Nadeau. *Act I*: *Prologue* The showroom, Las Vegas: "Let the Devil Take Us" (Las Vegas Legends, Showroom Patrons, Street Whores, Bostick); *Scene 1* Conference room, IRS, Washington, DC; *Scene 2* Cactus Motel, somewhere in Texas: "Nothin' Like a Picture Show" (Mona), "I'm Leavin' Texas" (Mona & Texans); *Scene 3* In the shadows of the Washington Monument; *Scene 4* In the kitchen of the whorehouse, Nevada: "It's Been a While" (Sam & Mona); *Scene 5* The parlor of the whorehouse; and Wall Street, New York: "Brand New Start" (Sam, Mona, Terri, IRS Director, Schmidt, Working Girls, Wall Street Wolves). *Act II*: *Scene 1* On the Information Highway: "The Smut Song" ("Down and Dirty") (Hardast), "Call Me" (Mona, Girls, Couch Potatoes); *Scene 2* Air Force One, on the tarmac, LAX; *Scene 3* IRS Director's Georgetown home; *Scene 4* Sam Dallas's apartment, Washington, DC: "Change in Me"

(Sam); *Scene 5* An IRS corridor; *Scene 6* The hearing: "Here for the Hearing" (Ladies & Senators); *Scene 7* Larry King Live: "Piece of the Pie" (Mona, Sam, Ladies); *Scene 8* Sam Dallas's dressing room, Washington, DC: "Change in Me" (reprise) (Sam); *Scene 9* The Stallion Fields Whorehouse, Nevada; *Scene 10* The steps of our nation's Capitol: "If We Open Our Eyes" (Company).

Broadway reviews were terrible. The show lost $7 million, and was one of the most disastrous flop-sequels. Dee Hoty was nominated for a Tony.

57. *The Best Little Whorehouse in Texas*

For obvious reasons this show is generally referred to as *Best Little Whorehouse*. Ever since the 1840s a whorehouse had been operating in the small Texas town of La Grange. It was called the Chicken Ranch because in the early days chickens and other livestock would often be used as barter for services rendered by the girls. Another story is that in 1915 Jessie Williams bought an old farmhouse on 12 acres near La Grange, which ran smoothly for 50 years as a whorehouse which got the name The Chicken Ranch during the Great Depression. In 1960 Edna Milton bought it from Jessie's estate and remodeled it. Finally, in 1973, at the insistence of a right-wing radio broadcaster, Marvin Zindler (Melvin Thorpe in the musical), the Chicken Ranch was closed, despite protestations from the local citizens that went all the way up to the Governor. This musical depicts the last days of this institution. Mona is the madam, and Ed Earl is the straight-talking sheriff, her former lover, who must close it down.

Before Broadway. Larry L. King, Texas journalist, wrote a *Playboy* article about the Chicken Ranch. Pete Masterson, a fellow Texan then acting on Broadway in *That Championship Season*, read the piece, and conceived the idea of a straight play with a strong statement for women. He showed the article to his friend, another fellow Texan, songwriter Carol Hall, who thought it would make a great musical. She introduced Mr. Masterson to Mr. King, and, although reluctant to have it transformed into a musical, Mr. King finally collaborated on the book with Mr. Masterson.

WORKSHOP PRODUCTION. ACTORS STUDIO, 10/20/77–11/6/77. 12 PERFORMANCES. PRESENTED BY Jay Cohen; DIRECTOR: Pete Masterson; CHOREOGRAPHER: Christopher "Spider" Duncan; SETS: Kert Lundell; COSTUMES: Jane Trapnell; MUSICAL DIRECTOR: George Schneider. *Cast:* MONA: Carlin Glynn [Pete Masterson's wife]; SHERIFF: Henderson Forsythe; THORPE: Clint Allmon; SHY: Joan Ellis; SLICK DUDE: K.C. Kelly; TV ANNOUNCER: Larry L. King; ALSO WITH: Susan Mansur, Gil Rogers, Ed Setrakian, Marta Sanders.

THE ENTERMEDIA RUN. Universal Studios producer Stevie Philips saw the workshop and, on behalf of her company, agreed to mount the show Off Broadway, at the Entermedia Theatre. Miss Phillips agreed that if it was successful Off Broadway she would arrange to have it go to Broadway, in exchange for the film rights. At this point Tommy Tune, another Texan, came on board as choreographer and co-director. ENTERMEDIA THEATRE, 4/17/78–6/11/78. 64 PERFORMANCES. At first the *New York Times* refused to carry ads for the show because of the title, and there were several other protests from church-groups. First-night reviewers covered the show, and it got great notices. It had the same crew as for the later Broadway run, except COMPANY MANAGER: Steven Suskin. *Cast:* RIO GRANDE BAND LEADER: Craig Chambers; RIO GRANDE BAND: Peter Blue, Chris Laird, Ben Brogdon, Lynn Frazier, Ernie Reed; GIRLS: Lisa Brown, Carol Chambers, Donna King, Susan Mansur, Louise Quick-Bowen, Debra Zalkind; COWBOYS: Jay Bursky, Bradley Clayton King, Michael Scott, Paul Ukena Jr.; FARMER/MELVIN P. THORPE: Clint Allmon; SHY KID: Gerry Burkhardt; MISS WULLA JEAN: Edna Milton [Miss Milton was the last owner of the Chicken Ranch in real life, and she took the role to Broadway]; TRAVELING SALESMAN/SCRUGGS/GOVERNOR: Jay Garner; SLICK DUDE/SOUNDMAN: Cameron Burke; TV COLORMAN: Jay Garner [character cut before Broadway]; AMBER: Pamela Blair; SHY: Joan Ellis; JEWEL: Delores Hall; MONA STANGLEY: Carlin

Glynn; (EIGHT) GIRLS AT MISS MONA'S: LINDA LOU: Donna King; DAWN: Lisa Brown; GINGER: Louise Quick-Bowen; BEATRICE: Jan Merchant; TADDY JO: Carol Chambers; RUBY RAE: Becky Gelke; ELOISE: Marta Sanders; DURLA: Debra Zalkind; LEROY SLINEY: Bradley Clayton King; STAGE MANAGER/CAMERAMAN: Tom Cashin; ANGEL IMOGENE CHARLENE: Lisa Brown [this character became Angelette Imogene Charlene]; AGGIE # 1: Cameron Burke [this character was also known as the Ukrainian Place Kicker]; AGGIE # 7: Gerry Burkhardt; AGGIE # 11: Jay Bursky; AGGIE # 12: Tom Cashin (specialty dance); AGGIE # 17: James Rich; AGGIE # 21: Paul Ukena Jr.; AGGIE # 71: Michael Scott; AGGIE # 77: Bradley Clayton King; SHERIFF ED EARL DODD: Henderson Forsythe; MAYOR RUFUS POINDEXTER: J. Frank Lucas; SENATOR WINGWOAH: J. Frank Lucas; EDSEL MACKEY: Don Crabtree; COKEMAN: Don Crabtree [role cut during this run]; DOATSEY MAE: Susan Mansur; TV ANNOUNCER: Larry L. King; REPORTER # 1: Susan Mansur; REPORTER # 2: Paul Ukena Jr.; REPORTER # 3: Michael Scott; GOVERNOR'S AIDE: Jay Bursky; CHOIR: Jay Burksy, Becky Gelke, Delores Hall, Jan Merchant, James Rich, Marta Sanders; THE DOGETTES: Gerry Burkhardt, Jay Bursky, Michael Scott, Paul Ukena Jr.; MELVIN THORPE SINGERS: Becky Gelke, Bradley Clayton King, Susan Mansur, Jay Merchant, James Rich, Marta Sanders; TOWNSPEOPLE: Carol Chambers, Bradley Clayton King, Edna Milton, James Rich, Marta Sanders; ANGELETTES: Louise Quick-Bowen, Becky Gelke, Donna King, Debra Zalkind, Jan Merchant; PHOTOGRAPHERS: Michael Scott, Paul Ukena Jr., James Rich, Jay Burksy. ***Alternate Dancers***: Monica Tiller, Jerry Yoder, Gena Ramsel.

Cameron Burke was killed in a bicycle accident between the Entermedia run and Broadway, and was replaced by K.C. Kelly. Bradley Clayton King was Larry L. King's son.

The Broadway Run. FORTY-SIXTH STREET THEATRE, 6/19/78–3/27/82. 1,576 PERFORMANCES. EUGENE O'NEILL THEATRE, 5/31/82–7/24/82. 9 previews. 63 PERFORMANCES. PRESENTED BY Universal Pictures (Stevie Phillips); MUSIC/LYRICS: Carol Hall; BOOK: Larry L. King & Peter Masterson; Based on the 1974 *Playboy* article by Larry L. King; DIRECTORS: Peter Masterson & Tommy Tune; CHOREOGRAPHER: Tommy Tune; ASSOCIATE CHOREOGRAPHER: Thommie Walsh; SETS: Marjorie Kellogg; COSTUMES: Ann Roth; LIGHTING: Dennis Parichy; SOUND: John Venable; MUSICAL SUPERVISOR/MUSICAL DIRECTOR/VOCAL ARRANGEMENTS: Robert Billig; CONDUCTOR: *Pete Blue* (by 79–80); CAST RECORDING on MCA; PRESS: Jeffrey Richards Associates; GENERAL MANAGERS: Jack Schlissel & Jay Kingwill; COMPANY MANAGER: *Leonard A. Mulhern* (79–80); PRODUCTION STAGE MANAGER: Paul J. Phillips; STAGE MANAGER: Jay Schlossberg-Cohen, *Gerry Burkhardt* (at the Eugene O'Neill); ASSISTANT STAGE MANAGER: Nancy Lynch, *Louise Quick* (at the Eugene O'Neill). **Cast:** RIO GRANDE BAND: Craig Chambers (band leader, guitar, narrator), Ben Brogdon (gone by 79–80), Lynn Frazier (gone by 79–80), Jim Haber (gone by 79–80), Michael Holleman (gone by 82), Ernie Reed (gone by 82), (all 11th billed), *Racine Romaguera* (bass, by 79–80), *Harvey Shapiro* (steel guitar, by 79–80), *Pete Blue* (piano, by 80–81), *Chuck Zeuren* (drums, by 80–81), *Marty Laster* (fiddle, by 80–81); GIRLS: Lisa Brown (gone by 79–80), Carol Chambers (gone by 79–80), Donna King, Susan Mansur (gone by 79–80), Louise Quick-Bowen (gone by 79–80), Debra Zalkind (gone by 79–80), *Monica Tiller* (by 79–80), *Karen Sutherland* (by 79–80), *Becky Gelke* (by 79–80), *Nancy Lynch* (by 79–80), *Valerie Leigh Bixler* (by 80–81), *Rebecca Seay* (by 80–81). At the Eugene O'Neill: *Merilee Magnuson, Mimi Bessette, Ruth Gottschall, Valerie Leigh Bixler*; COWBOYS: Jay Bursky (gone by 82), Bradley Clayton King (*Gene O'Neill* from 78–79 & gone by 82), Michael Scott (gone by 79–80; *Beau Gravitte* from 79–80; *Beau Allen* by 79–80), Paul Ukena Jr. (*Peter Heuchling* by 78–79; *Stephen McNaughton* from 78–79 & gone by 82), *Stephen Bray* (by 79–80 & gone by 82), *Don Bernhardt* (at the Eugene O'Neill), *Michael Boyd* (at the Eugene O'Neill); FARMER: Clinton Allmon, *Andy Parker* (at the Eugene O'Neill); SHY KID: Gerry Burkhardt, *Eric Aaron* (at the Eugene O'Neill); MISS WULLA JEAN: Edna Milton, *Debra Zalkind* (from 78–79), *Louise Quick* (at the Eugene O'Neill); TRAVELING SALESMAN: Jay Garner (6), *Tom Avera* (8/6/79–8/13/79), *Jay Garner, Patrick Hamilton* (5) (from 5/80); SLICK DUDE: K.C. Kelly, *Gene O'Neil* (from 79–80), *Paul Ukena Jr.* (from 80–81), *Roger Berdahl* (from 80–81); CHOIR: Jay Bursky (gone by 82), Becky Gelke (gone by 79–80), Edwina Lewis (gone by 82), Jan Merchant (gone by 82), James Rich (gone by 79–80), Marta Sanders

(gone by 79–80), *Diana Broderick* (by 79–80), *Candace Tovar* (by 79–80 & gone by 82)), *Peter Heuchling* (by 79–80 & gone by 82). At the Eugene O'Neill: *George Dvorsky, Merilyn J. Johnson, Clare Fields, Don Bernhardt, Karen Sutherland*; AMBER: Pamela Blair (4), *Gena Ramsel* (from 8/78), *Tina Johnson* (from 79–80), *Susann Fletcher* (9) (at the Eugene O'Neill) [the character's name was changed to Angel during the first Broadway season]; SHY: Joan Ellis (9), *Cheryl Ebarb* (11) (from 78–79); JEWEL: Delores Hall (3) ☆, *Merilyn J. Johnson* (12/21/81–1/18/82), *Delores Hall*; MONA STANGLEY: Carlin Glynn (2) ☆, *Carol Hall* (during Miss Glynn's vacation, 1/1/79–1/8/79), *Bobbi Jo Lathan* (during Miss Glynn's vacation, 8/6/79–8/20/79), *Fannie Flagg* (from 5/12/80), *Candace Tovar* (from 11/24/80), *Anita Morris* (from 11/16/81), *Carlin Glynn* (from 3/10/82, and again at the Eugene O'Neill, where she was 1st billed); HER (EIGHT) GIRLS: LINDA LOU: Donna King, *Valerie Leigh Bixler* (from 80–81); DAWN: Lisa Brown, *Monica Tiller* (from 78–79), *Mimi Bessette* (12) (at the Eugene O'Neill); GINGER: Louise Quick-Bowen, *Becky Gelke* (from 79–80), *Rebecca Seay* (from 80–81), *Roxie Lucas* (10) (at the Eugene O'Neill); BEATRICE: Jan Merchant, *Clare Fields* (from 80–81); TADDY JO: Carol Chambers, *Jill Cook* (from 78–79), *Karen Sutherland* (by 80–81), *Merilee Magnuson* (at the Eugene O'Neill); RUBY RAE: Becky Gelke, *Candace Tovar* (from 79–80), *Susann Fletcher* (from 80–81), *Diana Broderick* (at the Eugene O'Neill); ELOISE: Marta Sanders, *Diana Broderick* (from 78–79), *Karen Sutherland* (at the Eugene O'Neill); DURLA: Debra Zalkind, *Ruth Gottschall* (at the Eugene O'Neill); LEROY SLINEY: Bradley Clayton King, *Gene O'Neill* (from 78–79), *Stephen Bray* (by 80–81), *Roger Berdahl* (at the Eugene O'Neill); THE DOGETTES: Gerry Burkhardt (gone by 82), Jay Bursky (gone by 82), Michael Scott (gone by 80–81), Paul Ukena Jr. (gone by 80–81), *Peter Heuchling* (by 79–80 & gone by 82), *Beau Gravitte* (by 79–80 & gone by 80–81), *Andy Parker* (by 80–81), *Don Bernhardt* (at the Eugene O'Neill), *Joel Anderson* (at the Eugene O'Neill), *George Dvorsky* (at the Eugene O'Neill); MELVIN P. THORPE: Clinton Allmon (5); SOUNDMAN: K.C. Kelly, *Gene O'Neill* (from 79–80), *Paul Ukena Jr.* (from 80–81), *Roger Berdahl* (from 80–81); STAGE MANAGER: Tom Cashin, *Thomas Griffith* (from 80–81) [role not at the Eugene O'Neill]; MELVIN THORPE SINGERS: Bradley Clayton King (*Robin Haynes* gone by 79–80), Becky Gelke (gone by 79–80), Susan Mansur (gone by 79–80; *Carol Chambers*), Jan Merchant (gone by 82), James Rich (gone by 79–80), Marta Sanders (*Diana Broderick* from 78–79), *Candace Tovar* (by 79–80 & gone by 82), *Beau Allen* (by 79–80), *Karen Sutherland* (by 79–80), *Stephen Bray* (by 79–80 & gone by 82), *Susann Fletcher* (by 80–81 & gone by 82), *Clare Fields* (by 80–81), *Eric Aaron* (at the Eugene O'Neill), *Merilee Magnuson* (at the Eugene O'Neill); SHERIFF ED EARL DODD: Henderson Forsythe (1) ☆, *Larry L. King* (during Mr. Forsythe's vacation, 1/15/79–1/29/79), *Gil Rogers* (2) (from 8/4/80); CAMERAMAN: Tom Cashin, *Thomas Griffith* (from 80–81), *Eric Aaron* (at the Eugene O'Neill); C.J. SCRUGGS: Jay Garner (6), *Tom Avera* (8/6/79–8/13/79), *Jay Garner, Patrick Hamilton* (5) (from 5/80); MAYOR RUFUS POINDEXTER: J. Frank Lucas (7); EDSEL MACKEY: Don Crabtree (8), *John Newton* (from 79–80), *Robert Moyer* (7) (at the Eugene O'Neill); DOATSEY MAE: Susan Mansur (10), *Carol Hall* (1/1/79–1/8/79), *Susan Mansur, Bobbi Jo Lathan* (from 79–80), *Candace Tovar, Becky Gelke* (8) (from 11/24/80); TOWNSPEOPLE: Carol Chambers, Bradley Clayton King (*Robin Haynes*), Edna Milton (*Debra Zalkind*), James Rich, Marta Sanders. At the Eugene O'Neill: *Beau Allen, Karen Sutherland, Patti D'Beck, Clare Fields, Eric Aaron, Merilee Magnuson, Stephen Bray, Diana Broderick, Jill Cook, Jan Merchant, Gene O'Neill, Paul Ukena Jr.*; TV ANNOUNCER: Larry L. King; ANGELETTE IMOGENE CHARLENE: Lisa Brown, *Monica Tiller* (from 78–79), *Mimi Bessette* (12) (at the Eugene O'Neill); ANGELETTES: Louise Quick-Bowen (*Carol Chambers* gone by 80), Becky Gelke (gone by 80), Donna King (gone by 80), Jan Merchant (gone by 80), Debra Zalkind (gone by 82), *Susann Fletcher* (gone by 82), *Diana Broderick, Karen Sutherland, Valerie Leigh Bixler, Merilee Magnuson* (at the Eugene O'Neill), *Ruth Gottschall* (at the Eugene O'Neill); CHIP BREWSTER: Jay Garner (6), *Tom Avera* (8/6/79–8/13/79), *Jay Garner, Patrick Hamilton* (5) (from 5/80); SENATOR WINGWOAH: J. Frank Lucas (7); AGGIE # 21: Paul Ukena Jr., *Peter Heuchling* (by 79–80), *Stephen McNaughton, Eric Aaron* (at the Eugene O'Neill); AGGIE # 71: Michael Scott, *Beau Gravitte* (by 79–80), *Beau Allen* (by 80–81); AGGIE # 11: Jay Bursky (gone by 82), *Joel Anderson* (at the Eugene O'Neill); UKRAINIAN PLACEKICKER (AGGIE # 1): K.C. Kelly, *Roger Berdahl* (at the Eugene

O'Neill) [this role became the Scandinavian Placekicker during the run, but he is referred to as the Scandahoovian Placekicker in the libretto]; AGGIE # 17: James Rich, *Stephen Bray, Paul Ukena Jr., Michael Boyd* (at the Eugene O'Neill); AGGIE # 7: Gerry Burkhardt (gone by 82), *Don Bernhardt* (at the Eugene O'Neill); AGGIE # 12 (specialty dance): Tom Cashin, *Thomas Griffith* (from 80–81), *George Dvorsky* (at the Eugene O'Neill); AGGIE # 77: Bradley Clayton King, *Robin Haynes, Gene O'Neill, Andy Parker* (from 80–81); PHOTOGRAPHERS: Michael Scott (*Beau Gravitte* by 79–80; *Beau Allen* by 80–81), Paul Ukena Jr. (*Peter Heuchling* by 79–80; *Stephen McNaughton; Eric Aaron* at the Eugene O'Neill), James Rich (*Stephen Bray; Paul Ukena Jr.*; *Michael Boyd* at the Eugene O'Neill), Jay Bursky (*Don Bernhardt* at the Eugene O'Neill); REPORTER 1: Susan Mansur, *Bobbi Jo Lathan* (by 79–80), *Becky Gelke* (by 80–81); REPORTER 2: Paul Ukena Jr., *Peter Heuchling* (by 79–80), *Stephen McNaughton, Eric Aaron* (at the Eugene O'Neill); GOVERNOR'S AIDE: Jay Bursky, *Joel Anderson* (at the Eugene O'Neill); GOVERNOR: Jay Garner (6), *Tom Avera* (8/6/79–8/13/79), *Jay Garner, Patrick Hamilton* (5) (from 5/80); REPORTER 3: Michael Scott, *Beau Gravitte* (by 79–80), *Beau Allen* (by 80–81). ***Understudies***: Mona: Susan Mansur (78–79), *Bobbi Jo Lathan* (79–80), *Becky Gelke* (80–82); Sheriff: J. Frank Lucas (78), *Don Crabtree* (78–79), *Gil Rogers* (79–80), *Robert Moyer* (at the Eugene O'Neill); Scruggs/Mayor/Senator: Don Crabtree (78–79), *John Newton* (79–82), *Robert Moyer* (at the Eugene O'Neill); Ginger: Gena Ramsel (78), *Becky Gelke* (78–79), *Diana Broderick* (79–82), *Ruth Gottschall* (at the Eugene O'Neill); Doatsey Mae: Jan Merchant (78–80), *Rebecca Seay* (80–81), *Roxie Lucas* (at the Eugene O'Neill); Shy: Lisa Brown (78–79), *Candace Tovar* (79–80), *Rebecca Seay* (80–81), *Clare Fields* (at the Eugene O'Neill); Governor: Don Crabtree (78), *Gerry Burkhardt* (78–82); Thorpe: Gerry Burkhardt (78–82), *Roger Berdahl* (at the Eugene O'Neill); Angel: Gena Ramsel (78–79), *Monica Tiller* (79–82), *Mimi Bessette* (at the Eugene O'Neill); Jewel: Edwina Lewis (78–81), *Merilyn J. Johnson* (at the Eugene O'Neill); Mackey: Paul Ukena Jr. (78–79), *Ernie Reed* (by 79–80), *Roger Berdahl* (80–82); Narrator: *Ernie Reed* (79–80), *Roger Berdahl* (80–82), *Andy Parker* (at the Eugene O'Neill); Dawn: Monica Tiller (78–79), *Laura Ackerman* (79–80), *Karen Sutherland* (80–82); Bandleader: Paul Ukena Jr. (gone by 80–81). ***Alternates***: Gena Ramsel (*Laura Ackerman* 78–80), Jerry Yoder (78–80), Monica Tiller (78–79), *Steve McNaughton* (80–81), *Patti D'Beck* (80–82).

Note: unless an actor/actress has an end date to their role, they also played it at the Eugene O'Neill in 1982. **Act I**: ***Prologue*** (Rio Grande Band); ***Scene 1*** The parlor of the Chicken Ranch; 1930s: "20 Fans" (Mona, Girls, Cowboys, Farmer, Shy Kid, Wulla Jean, Traveling Salesman, Slick Dude, Choir); ***Scene 2*** The porch and parlor of the Chicken Ranch; 1970s: "A Li'l Ole Bitty Pissant Country Place" (Mona & Girls); ***Scene 3*** The porch and parlor of the Chicken House; 1970s: "Girl, You're a Woman" (Mona, Shy, Jewel, Girls); ***Scene 4*** The Melvin P. Thorpe TV Show: "Watch Dog Theme" (Thorpe & Dogettes), "Texas Has a Whorehouse in It" (Thorpe, Thorpe Singers, Dogettes); ***Scene 5*** A hallway at the Chicken Ranch; ***Scene 6*** A parlor of the Chicken Ranch: "24 Hours of Lovin'" (Jewel & Girls); ***Scene 7*** The Courthouse steps, Gilbert, Texas: "Watch Dog Theme" (reprise) (Dogettes), "Texas Has a Whorehouse in It" (reprise) (Thorpe, Dogettes, Mayor, Scruggs, Edsel, Doatsey Mae, Church Lady, Convent Lady, Townspeople); ***Scene 8*** The *Texas Twinkle* cafe: "Doatsey Mae" (Doatsey Mae); ***Scene 9*** The Texas Aggie Angelettes at the football game: "Angelette March" (Imogene Charlene & Angelettes); ***Scene 10*** The locker room; after the game, and on the way to the Chicken Ranch: "The Aggie Song" (Aggies) [After the play re-opened at the Eugene O'Neill, this is where it ended. i.e. Scenes 11 and 12 were dropped]; ***Scene 11*** The parlor of the Chicken Ranch; ***Scene 12*** The porch of the Chicken Ranch; later that night — the raid: "Bus from Amarillo" (Mona) [Amber sang this in pre–Broadway days; it was shifted from Act I to the last new number of Act II during the Broadway run]. **Act II**: ***Scene 1*** The porch of the Chicken Ranch; immediately following, and at the State Capitol: "The Sidestep" (Governor, Governor's Aide, Wingwoah, Reporters, Thorpe, Dogettes, Thorpe Singers); ***Scene 2*** The porch of the Chicken Ranch: "No Lies" (Mona, Jewel, Girls); ***Scene 3*** The interior of the sheriff's office: "Good Old Girl" (Sheriff & Aggies); ***Scene 4*** The parlor of the Chicken Ranch: "Hard Candy Christmas" (Amber, Linda Lou, Ginger, Dawn, Ruby Rae, Beatrice), "Hard Candy Christmas" (reprise) (Girls), "Bus from Amarillo" [this was the new position of

this number when the play re-opened at the Eugene O'Neill]; ***Scene 5*** The porch of the Chicken Ranch: Finale (Company).

The show won Tony Awards for Henderson Forsythe and Carlin Glynn, and was nominated for musical, book, direction of musical, choreography, and for Joan Ellis. The Broadway Run ended due to a dispute with the Musicians' Union, and the show went to the Colonial Theatre, Boston, where it was labeled a new production, even though it was the same crew and cast. On 5/31/82 this production wound up going back to Broadway's Eugene O'Neill Theatre.

After Broadway. TOUR. Opened on 2/25/79 in Houston. *Cast:* ANGEL: Francie Mendenhall; JEWEL: Jacqueline Teamer; MONA: Marietta Marich, *June Terry*; SHERIFF: William Hardy, *Glenn Holtzman* (from 8/79), *Richard Kennedy* (from 5/80); THORPE: Larry Hovis, *Kevin Cooney*; GOVERNOR: Patrick Hamilton; DOATSEY MAE: Peggy Byers.

TOUR. Opened on 10/2/79, at the Shubert Theatre, Boston, and closed on 1/11/81, at the Pantages Theatre, Los Angeles. *Cast:* NARRATOR: Bradley Clayton King; COWBOYS: Beau Allen & Davis Gaines; FARMER: Andy Parker; SHY KID: Jeff Calhoun; MISS WULLA JEAN: Roxie Lucas; ANGEL: Rebecca Ann Seay; JEWEL: Merilyn J. Johnson; MONA: Alexis Smith; LINDA LOU: Valerie Leigh Bixler; GINGER: Ruth Gottschall; ELOISE: Karen Tamburelli; DURLA: Deborah Magid; THORPE: Larry Hovis; SHERIFF: William Hardy; DOATSEY MAE: Barbara Marineau; GOVERNOR: Tom Avera, *Jay Garner* (from 5/80). The band was now the Texas Tally Wackers.

TOUR. Opened on 6/9/80, at the Civic Auditorium, Jacksonville, Fla. *Cast:* MONA: June Terry; THORPE: Kevin Cooney; SHERIFF: Richard Kennedy, *William Larsen*.

TOUR. Opened on 11/17/80, at the Playhouse, Wilmington, Del., and closed on 6/27/82, at the Opera House, Lexington, Ky. MUSICAL DIRECTOR: Guy Strobel. CAST: MONA: Francie Mendenhall, Darleigh Miller; SHERIFF: Christopher Wynkoop; TV ANNOUNCER: Larry L. King.

THEATRE ROYAL, Drury Lane, London. Opened on 2/26/81. CAST: ANGEL: Betsy Brantley; JEWEL: Miquel Brown; MONA: Carlin Glynn; THORPE: Nigel Pegram; SHERIFF: Henderson Forsythe; DOATSEY MAE: Sheila Brand; GOVERNOR: Fred Evans.

THE MOVIE. 1982. *Cast:* Dolly Parton, Burt Reynolds. It had a few new songs. It failed.

TOURING REVIVAL. Opened on 2/14/01 (date put back from 1/01) at the Oakdale Center, Wallingford, Conn. Rehearsals from 1/8/01 in Manhattan. 1 preview on 2/13/01. It played 30 cities. This was a revised version. The book was trimmed, it had more dancing, and the curtain-call hoedown was now bigger. The one new musical number, the ballad "A Friend to Me" (by Carol Hall), closed the show. PRESENTED BY Manny Kladitis, Mitch Leigh, Lee Marshall, and Clear Channel Entertainment, in association with Jon B. Platt; DIRECTOR/CHOREOGRAPHER: Thommie Walsh; SETS: Marjorie Kellogg; COSTUMES: Dona Granata; COSTUMES FOR ANN-MARGRET: Bob Mackie; LIGHTING: Ken Billington & Jason Kantrowitz; MUSICAL DIRECTOR: Keith Lawrence; NEW CAST RECORDING on Fynsworth Alley, made on 6/4/01, and released on 7/10/01. *Cast:* ANGEL: Terri Dixon; SHY: Jen Celene Little; JEWEL: Avery Sommers; MONA: Ann-Margret; THORPE: Rod Donahue; SHERIFF: Gary Sandy [he was hand-picked by Ann-Margret]; MAYOR/WINGWOAH: Matt Landers; MACKEY: Hal Davis; DOATSEY MAE: Roxie Lucas; GOVERNOR: Ed Dixon. Ann-Margret, in her legitimate stage debut, fell in 12/00, and opening night appeared with a cast on her hand. In 2/01, in Schenectady, shows were canceled because her mother was ill. The show took a vacation 12/16/01–1/7/02.

58. *Big*

About a 12-year-old boy who wants to be big, and becomes a 30-year-old, physically at least. Set in New Jersey & New York City.

Before Broadway. Auditions began in spring 1995. The show tried out at the Fisher Theatre, Detroit, on 2/14/96 (one preview on 2/13/96). Then it laid off for a month for re-writes (by the time it arrived on Broadway it had nine numbers that were either new or re-written). Crista Moore's number "I'll Think About it Later" was cut, and replaced with

"Here We Go Again"; "Thirteen" was re-written as "Can't Wait," with completely new lyrics; "Big" (the title number and Daniel Jenkins' first song in the show) was cut, and replaced with "This isn't Me" (although the cast and crew continued to refer to it as the number formerly known as "Big"); the song in Josh's loft, "Isn't it Magic," was cut, and replaced with "Stars, Stars, Stars"; "Fun" had its score altered. Considering "Big" was cut, the Act II reprise of that number was now called "When You're Big." The Act I ending was a musical scene, "Your Wish is Granted." It was changed to a full-fledged finale called "Cross the Line." "Dishing at the Dance," in Act I, set at the Tavern on the Green, was replaced with "Tavern Foxtrot." The ballet "Skateboard Romance," in Act II, was expanded. During this period Dan Jenkins had to have knee surgery.

The Broadway Run. SHUBERT THEATRE, 4/28/96–10/13/96. 23 previews from 4/8/96. 193 PERFORMANCES. PRESENTED BY James B. Freydberg, Kenneth Feld, Laurence Mark, Kenneth D. Greenblatt, in association with FAO Schwartz Fifth Avenue; MUSIC: David Shire; LYRICS: Richard Maltby Jr.; BOOK: John Weidman; BASED ON the 1988 Tom Hanks movie of the same name, written by Gary Ross & Anne Spielberg; DIRECTOR: Mike Ockrent; CHOREOGRAPHER: Susan Stroman; SETS: Robin Wagner; COSTUMES: William Ivey Long; LIGHTING: Paul Gallo; SOUND: Steve Canyon Kennedy; MUSICAL DIRECTOR: Paul Gemignani; ORCHESTRATIONS: Douglas Besterman; DANCE MUSIC ARRANGEMENTS: David Krane; ELECTRONIC MUSIC DESIGN: Brian Besterman; ADDITIONAL VOCAL ARRANGEMENTS: Patrick Brady; CAST RECORDING on Universal; PRESS: Boneau/Bryan-Brown; CASTING: Johnson—Liff; MAGIC CONSULTANT: Charles Reynolds; GENERAL MANAGEMENT: Fremont Associates; COMPANY MANAGER: Steven Chaikelson; PRODUCTION STAGE MANAGER: Steven Zweigbaum; STAGE MANAGER: Clifford Schwartz; ASSISTANT STAGE MANAGERS: Tamlyn Freund & Ara Marx. *Cast:* CYNTHIA BENSON: Lizzy Mack; YOUNG JOSH: Patrick Levis (7); TIFFANY: Samantha Robyn Lee; MAGGIE: Lori Aine Bennett; MRS. BASKIN: Barbara Walsh (4); MR. BASKIN: John Sloman; MR. KOPECKI: Ray Wills; BILLY: Brett Tabisel (6); MRS. KOPECKI: Donna Lee Marshall; CARNIVAL MAN: Clent Bowers; DEREK: Alex Sanchez; ZOLTAR: Zoltar; VOICE OF ZOLTAR: Michel Bell; JOSH BASKIN: Daniel Jenkins (1) ✩; PANHANDLER: Ray Wills; ARCADE MAN: Frank Mastrone; DERELICT: John Sloman; MATCHLESS: Frank Vlastnik; PAUL: Gene Weygandt (5); SUSAN: Crista Moore (2) ✩; MACMILLAN: Jon Cypher (3) ✩; STARFIGHTER: Brandon Espinoza; FAO SALES EXECUTIVE: Joan Barber; BIRNBAUM: Frank Vlastnik; LIPTON: Frank Mastrone; BARRETT: Clent Bowers; MISS WATSON: Jan Neuberger; DEATHSTARETTES: Joyce Chittick & CJay Hardy; LARRY JOHNSON: John Sloman; NICK: Ray Wills; TOM: John Sloman; DIANE: Donna Lee Marshall; ABIGAIL: Jill Matson; SKATEPHONE: Spencer Liff; KID WITH WALKMAN: Enrico Rodriguez; SKATEBOARD ROMEO: Graham Bowen; PARENTS/SHOPPERS/EXECUTIVES/OFFICE STAFF: Joan Barber, Clent Bowers, Joyce Chittick, CJay Hardy, Donna Lee Marshall, Frank Mastrone, Jill Matson, Jan Neuberger, Alex Sanchez, John Sloman, Frank Vlastnik, Ray Wills; THE BIG KIDS: Lori Aine Bennett, Graham Bowen, Brandon Espinoza, Samantha Robyn Lee, Spencer Liff, Lizzy Mack, Enrico Rodriguez. *Understudies:* Young Josh: Graham Bowen & Spencer Liff; Mrs. Baskin: Joan Barber & Donna Lee Marshall; Susan: Jill Matson & Donna Lee Marshall; Billy: Brandon Espinoza & Graham Bowen; Josh: Stacey Todd Holt & Frank Vlastnik; Paul: Ray Wills & Frank Mastrone; Nick/Tom: Frank Mastrone; MacMillan: Clent Bowers & Frank Mastrone. *Swings:* Stacey Todd Holt, Joseph Medeiros, Corinne Melancon, Kari Pickler. *Orchestra:* VIOLINS: Suzanne Ornstein & Xin Zhao; VIOLA: Richard Brice; CELLO: Clay Ruede; BASS: Charles Bargeron; WOODWINDS: Albert Regni, John Moses, Dennis Anderson, Eric Weidman, John Campo; FRENCH HORNS: Ronald Sell & Michael Ishii; TRUMPETS: Joe Mosello, Danny Cahn, Dave Brown; TROMBONES: Bruce Eidem & Dean Plank; KEYBOARDS: Nicholas Archer, Brian Besterman, Patrick Brady; GUITAR: Andrew Schwartz; DRUMS: Paul Pizzuti; PERCUSSION: Thad Wheeler. *Act I:* *Scene 1* The Neighborhood, New Jersey: "Can't Wait" (Young Josh, Mrs. Baskin, Billy, Kids, Parents), "Talk to Her" (Billy & Young Josh), "The Carnival" (Company); *Scene 2* The Baskin home: "This isn't Me" (Josh); *Scene 3* Port Authority Bus Terminal: "I Want to Go Home" (Josh); *Scene 4* FAO Schwartz: "The Time of Your Life" (Kids), "Fun" (MacMillan, Josh, Company); *Scene 5* The offices of MacMillan Toys: "Dr. Deathstar" (Deathstarettes), "Josh's Welcome" (Susan, Paul, Executives), "Here We Go Again"

(Susan); *Scene 6* Josh's loft: "Stars, Stars, Stars" (Josh & Susan); *Scene 7* A New York restaurant: "Tavern Foxtrot" (Paul & Company), "Cross the Line" (Josh, Kids, Company). *Act II:* *Scene 1* The mall: "It's Time" (Billy & Kids), "Stop, Time" (Mrs. Baskin), "Happy Birthday, Josh" (Kids); *Scene 2* Susan's office: "Dancing All the Time" (Susan), "I Want to Know" (Young Josh); *Scene 3* The offices of MacMillan Toys: "Coffee Black" (Josh, MacMillan, Miss Watson, Birnbaum, Barrett, Lipton, Executives, Staff); *Scene 4* An Eastside apartment: "The Real Thing" (Nick, Tom, Diane, Abigail); *Scene 5* The roof terrace: "One Special Man" (Susan); *Scene 6* The neighborhood: "When You're Big" (Josh), "Skateboard Romance" (Kids); *Scene 7* A warehouse: "I Want to Go Home/Stars, Stars, Stars" (reprise) (Josh & Susan).

Broadway reviews were very divided (but it did get a rave from the *New York Times*). It was noticeably not nominated for a best musical Tony, and this caused a bit of a stir, as well as hurting the show. However, the producers were big about it. Tony nominations: score, book, choreography, Brett Tabisel, Crista Moore. Closing notices were posted on 9/27/96, and the show lost its entire $10.3 million investment, making it one of Broadway's biggest financial disasters of all time. Expected to be the big hit of the 95–96 season, it came up against the phenomenon of adult musicals *Rent* and *Bring in 'da Noise*, and some other shows which, almost overnight, transformed the face of Broadway musicals, leaving *Big* looking out of touch. Barbara Isenberg wrote a book, *Making it Big: The Diary of a Broadway Musical*, which was released in 11/96.

After Broadway. REVISED TOURING REVIVAL. On 3/10/97 Eric D. Schaeffer met with the creative crew, and re-wrote it, going back to an older, simpler, concept that included earlier versions of some of the songs. This revised production was presented as a 40-week, 33-city, national tour by PACE Theatrical Group & Magicworks Entertainment. A tour of a flop Broadway musical is rare. It opened on 9/26/97, at the Playhouse Theatre, Wilmington, Del. DIRECTOR: Eric D. Schaeffer; CHOREOGRAPHER: Karma Camp; SETS: Zack Brown; COSTUMES: William Ivey Long; LIGHTING: Ken Billington; SOUND: Peter Fitzgerald; MUSICAL DIRECTOR: Don Pippin. *Cast:* JOSH: Jim Newman; SUSAN: Jacquelyn Piro; MACMILLAN: Ron Holgate; PAUL: Nick Cokas; BILLY: Brett Tabisel, *Alex Brumel* (from 3/3/98); YOUNG JOSH: Joseph Medeiros, *Travis Greisler* (from 4/14/98); CYNTHIA: Demaree Alexander; MRS. BASKIN: Judy McLane; CHORUS: Dale Hensley, John Hoshko, Dana Lynn Mauro, Kelley Swaim, Leslie Stevens. "Talk to Her" (revised)/"The Carnival," "Say Good Morning to Mom," "Port Authority Shuffle," "Big Boys," "Time of Your Life," "Fun" (revised), "Welcome to Macmillan Toys," "My Secretary's in Love," "Let's Not Move Too Fast," "Do You Want to Play Games?," "Stars, Stars, Stars," "Little Susan Lawrence," "Cross the Line," "Outta Here," "Stop Time," "Dancing All the Time," "I Want to Know," "Coffee Black" (revised), "The Real Thing," "When You're Big," "We're Gonna Be Fine."

59. *Big Deal*

Set in the 1930s on the South Side of Chicago. Charley, an unsuccessful boxer, teams up with four other guys to rob a pawnshop. But they tunnel through the wrong wall. Charley decides to go straight. Lilly is the maid who holds the keys to the apartment next to the pawnshop.

Before Broadway. Bob Fosse had acquired the stage rights to the movie in 1959. Throughout the 1960s and 70s he would return to it briefly, and even interested Stephen Sondheim for a while. In 1969 he planned a film musical, with the locale switched to Tijuana, but it fell through. In 1983 he dug it out again and switched the locale to Chicago. Stuart Ostrow, the producer at that time, asked Peter Allen to write some songs, and he did write two for it before the show was postponed. Mr. Allen, figuring he was the songwriter for a show that would eventually be produced, wrote two more songs, and then found out in the newspapers that the show was back on and he was but one of six songwriters planned. So he backed out. One of Mr. Allen's songs found its way into *Legs Diamond*. After this, Bob Fosse decided to use standard vintage songs, which became very expensive (paying for the rights). He also decided to use an almost all black cast. In spring 1985 it went through backers' auditions, and in November Mr. Fosse began casting. In 12/85 it went into rehearsals. Over 800 dancers auditioned in four days. On 2/12/86 it opened for tryouts at the Shubert, Boston, to divided reviews. Not only was the production having health problems, Fosse was too. Herb Gardner & Steve Tesich were brought in to doctor the book. Budgeted at $4 million, it actually cost $5.4 million to make (although some sources say closer to $7 million) and was performed on an almost bare stage, with a skeletal set of platforms, scaffolding & staircases. In the early stages of production there was a 3rd Narrator, played by former Miss America Vanessa Williams, but it was decided that two were enough.

The Broadway Run. BROADWAY THEATRE, 4/10/86–6/8/86. 7 previews. 70 PERFORMANCES. PRESENTED BY The Shubert Organization, Roger Berlind, Jerome Minskoff, in association with Jonathan Farkas; MUSIC/LYRICS: various composers; BOOK: Bob Fosse; BASED ON the 1958 Italian film *I soliti ignoti* (known in English as *Big Deal*, or *Big Deal on Madonna Street*); DIRECTOR/CHOREOGRAPHER: Bob Fosse; SETS: Peter Larkin; COSTUMES: Patricia Zipprodt; LIGHTING/EXECUTIVE PRODUCER: Jules Fisher; SOUND: Abe Jacob; CONDUCTOR/ARRANGEMENTS: Gordon Lowry Harrell; ORCHESTRATIONS: Ralph Burns; PRESS: Fred Nathan Company; CASTING: Howard Feuer; GENERAL MANAGEMENT: Joseph Harris Associates; COMPANY MANAGER: Steven H. David; PRODUCTION STAGE MANAGER: Phil Friedman; STAGE MANAGER: Perry Cline & Barry Kearsley; ASSISTANT STAGE MANAGERS: Kenneth Hanson & Randall Whitescarver. *Cast:* LILLY: Loretta Devine (2) ☆; 1ST NARRATOR: Wayne Cilento (4); 2ND NARRATOR: Bruce Anthony Davis (5); KOKOMO: Gary Chapman (10); OTIS: Alde Lewis Jr. (7); CHARLEY: Cleavant Derricks (1) ☆; PEARL: Valarie Pettiford (11); SLICK: Larry Marshall (6); SUNNYBOY: Mel Johnson Jr. (9); WILLIE: Alan Weeks (3) ☆; JUDGE & BANDLEADER: Bernard J. Marsh (13); BAND SINGER: Valarie Pettiford (11); PHOEBE: Desiree Coleman (8); DANCIN' DAN: Gary Chapman (10); 1ST SHADOW: Valarie Pettiford (11); 2ND SHADOW: Barbara Yeager (12); LITTLE WILLIE: Roumel Reaux; ANNOUNCER: Candace Tovar; DANCERS: Ciscoe Bruton II, Lloyd Culbreath, Kim Darwin, Cady Huffman, Amelia Marshall, Frank Mastrocola, Stephanie Pope, Roumel Reaux, George Russell, Candace Tovar. *Dance Alternates*: Bryant Baldwin, Diana Laurenson, Vince Cole. *Standbys*: Sunnyboy/Judge/Bandleader: James Stovall; Charley/Slick: Byron Utley. *Understudies*: Willie: Lloyd Culbreath; 1st Narrator: Frank Mastrocola; 2nd Narrator: Bryant Baldwin; Kokomo: Kenneth Hanson; Phoebe: Amelia Marshall; Otis: Roumel Reaux; Dancin' Dan: Roumel Reaux & Ciscoe Bruton II; Lilly: Stephanie Pope; Shadows: Stephanie Pope & Kim Darwin; Pearl: Cady Huffman; Sunnyboy: Vince Cole. *On-Stage Band*: DRUMS: Brian Brake; PIANO: Leonard Oxley; CLARINET: William Shadel; TRUMPET: Joe Mosello; BASS: Earl May; TROMBONE: Britt Woodman. *Act I: Scene 1* Prologue "Life is Just a Bowl of Cherries" (m: Ray Henderson; l: B.G. "Buddy" De Sylva & Lew Brown) [from *George White's Scandals of 1931*] (Lilly), "For No Good Reason at All" (m/l: Abel Baer, Sam M. Lewis, Joseph Young) (Narrators); *Scene 2* Locker room & fight arena: "Charley My Boy" (m/l: Gus Kahn & Ted Fiorito) (Charley); *Scene 3* The Judge's chambers: "I've Got a Feelin' You're Foolin'" (m: Nacio Herb Brown; l: Arthur Freed) [from the movie *Broadway Melody of 1936*] (Kokomo, Charley, Judge, Narrators); *Scene 4* Prison yard: "Ain't We Got Fun" (m: Richard Whiting; l: Gus Kahn & Raymond Egan) (Prisoners); *Scene 5* Gem Theatre: "For No Good Reason at All" (reprise) (Narrators & Dancers); *Scene 6* The men's room at the Gem Theatre; *Scene 7* A camera store; *Scene 8* Cottage Grove Avenue: "Chicago" (m/l: Fred Fisher) (Narrators); *Scene 9* Pool hall: "Pick Yourself Up" (m: Jerome Kern; l: Dorothy Fields) [from the movie *Swing Time*] (Charley, Willie, Slick, Sunnyboy, Otis); *Scene 10* Cottage Grove Avenue: "I'm Just Wild About Harry" (m: Eubie Blake; l: Noble Sissle) [from *Shuffle Along*] (Lilly); *Scene 11* Paradise Ballroom: "Beat Me Daddy Eight to the Bar" (m/l: Don Raye, Hughie Prince, Eleanor Sheehy) (Bandleader, Band, Dancers), "The Music Goes Round and Round" (m: Edward Farley & Michael Riley; l: Red Hodgson) (Bandleader & Band); *Scene 12* Alley Outside Dancehall: "Life is Just a Bowl of Cherries" (reprise) (Lilly). *Act II: Scene 1* Prologue "Now's the Time to Fall in Love" (m/l: Al Sherman & Al Lewis) (Narrators & Dancers); *Scene 2* Slick's apartment: "Ain't She Sweet" (m: Milton Ager; l: Jack Yellen) (Sunnyboy, Phoebe, Narrators, Dancers); *Scene 3* Willie's house: "Everybody Loves My Baby" (m/l: Jack Palmer & Spencer Williams) (Willie & Narrators), "Me and My Shadow" (m: Al Jolson &

Dave Dreyer; l: Billy Rose) (Dancin' Dan & Shadows); *Scene 4* A pawnshop; *Scene 5* Slick's apartment: "Love is Just Around the Corner" (m: Lewis E. Gensler; l: Leo Robin) [from the movie *Here is My Heart*] (Narrators); *Scene 6* Charley's room; *Scene 7* Lilly's rented room: "Just a Gigolo" (m: Leonello Casucci; original German lyrics: Julius Brammer; English lyrics: Irving Caesar) (Bandleader & Charley), "Who's Your Little Who-Zis?" (m: Hal Goering & Ben Birnie; l: Walter Hirsch) (Bandleader & Bandsinger); *Scene 8* Refreshment stand of Gem Theatre; *Scene 9* Lilly's rented room: "Yes Sir, That's My Baby" (m: Walter Donaldson; l: Gus Kahn) (Charley), "Button up Your Overcoat" (m: Ray Henderson; l: B.G. "Buddy" DeSylva & Lew Brown) [from *Follow Thru*] (Lilly); *Scene 10* The robbery; *Scene 11* The fantasies: "Daddy, You've Been a Mother to Me" (m/l: Fred Fisher) (Willie & Little Willie), "Hold Tight, Hold Tight" (m/l: Leonard Ware, Willie Spottswood, Ed Robinson, Ben Smith, Sidney Bechet) (Otis & Ladies), "Happy Days Are Here Again" (m: Milton Ager; l: Jack Yellen) [from the movie *Chasing Rainbows*] (Slick, Phoebe, Sunnyboy, Company), "I'm Sitting on Top of the World" (m: Ray Henderson; l: Samuel L. Lewis, Joseph Young, Ray Henderson) (Charley & Company); *Scene 12* A street: "Life is Just a Bowl of Cherries" (reprise) (Lilly).

Broadway reviews were not good. It won a Tony for choreography, and was nominated for musical, book, direction of a musical, and for Cleavant Derricks.

60. *Big River*

Along the Mississippi River Valley sometime in the 1840s. Sub-titled: *The Adventures of Huckleberry Finn*. About Huck Finn's river-raft odyssey down the Mississippi, from Hannibal, Mo., to Hillsboro, Ark., in company with runaway slave Jim.

Before Broadway. Although the adventures of Huck and Tom had been told many times on TV and movies, and even on stage as a straight play in 1931, it had never been done as a Broadway musical — at least not presented. In 1950 Kurt Weill and Maxwell Anderson had tried one — *Huckleberry Finn* (see appendix) — but it remained unfinished at the time of Mr. Weill's death. Another project that never got beyond the planning stages was a film musical started by Alan Jay Lerner and Burton Lane, to star Gene Kelly and Danny Kaye as the two con men Huck meets on his trip down the Mississippi. In 1957 the Phoenix Theatre (Off Broadway) presented *Livin' the Life* (see appendix), a musical based on Mark Twain's stories. It wasn't until 1982, when husband and wife Rocco and Heidi Landesman went to see country singer/songwriter Roger Miller performing at the Lone Star Café, NY, that things started to happen. They determined to produce a show that Mr. Miller would write, and *Huck Finn* was Mrs. Landesman's favorite book. William Hauptman was hired to write the libretto of what was then called *Huck Finn*, and Robert Brustein, who had taught both Mr. Hauptman and Mr. Landesman at Yale, put the musical (now renamed *Big River*) on the schedule of the AMERICAN REPERTORY THEATRE in Cambridge, Mass., where it had its world premiere 2/17/84. It came perilously close to opening time and Mr. Miller hadn't written a word of the score. Robert Brustein wanted to can Miller and hire Carly Simon or James Taylor, but Rocco Landesman diplomatically guided Mr. Miller into the score. Eight songs formed the score at Cambridge. DIRECTOR: Des McAnuff; SETS: Heidi Landesman; COSTUMES: Patricia McGourty; LIGHTING: James F. Ingalls; SOUND: Randolph C. Head; MUSICAL DIRECTOR/ORCHESTRATIONS/VOCAL ARRANGEMENTS: Michael S. Roth. *Cast:* Nina Bernstein, John Bottoms, Sandy Brown, Thomas Derrah, Mark Driscoll, Ben Evett, Jeremy Geidt, Ben Halley Jr., Robert Joy, Jerome Kilty, Maren MacDonald, Harry S. Murphy, Marianne Owen, Tony Shalhoub, Alison Taylor.

In the summer 1984 it ran at La Jolla Playhouse, Calif. (where Des McAnuff was artistic director), during which time further adjustments were made to the book, and new songs added by Roger Miller.

The Broadway Run. EUGENE O'NEILL THEATRE, 4/25/85–9/20/87. 50 previews. 1,005 PERFORMANCES. PRESENTED BY Rocco Landesman, Heidi Landesman, Rick Steiner, M. Anthony Fisher, Dodger Productions; MUSIC/LYRICS: Roger Miller; BOOK: William Hauptman;

ADAPTED FROM the 1885 novel *The Adventures of Huckleberry Finn*, by Mark Twain; DIRECTOR: Des McAnuff; CHOREOGRAPHER: Janet Watson; SETS: Heidi Landesman; COSTUMES: Patricia McGourty; LIGHTING: Richard Riddell; SOUND: Otts Munderloh; MUSICAL SUPERVISOR: Danny Troob; MUSICAL DIRECTOR/VOCAL ARRANGEMENTS: Linda Twine; ORCHESTRATIONS: Steven Margoshes & Danny Troob; DANCE & INCIDENTAL MUSIC: John Richard Lewis; PRESS: Solters/Roskin/Friedman; CASTING: Stanley Sable & Jason La Padura; GENERAL MANAGER: David Strong Warner; COMPANY MANAGER: Sandra Carlson, *Jill Hurwitz* (added by 85–86); PRODUCTION STAGE MANAGER: Frank Hartenstein; STAGE MANAGER: Steven Adler, *Peter Glazer* (from 85–86), *Steven Adler* (from 86–87); ASSISTANT STAGE MANAGER: Marianne Cane, *Neal Jones* (from 85–86), *Jon Ehrlich & James Dawson* (both from 86–87). *Act I:* IN ST. PETERSBURG, MO.; LATER ON THE ILLINOIS SHORE AND JACKSON'S ISLAND: MARK TWAIN: Gordon Connell, *Robert Sevra* (during Mr. Connell's vacation, 86–87); HUCKLEBERRY FINN: Daniel H. Jenkins, *Martin Moran* (from 4/7/86), *Romain Fruge* (86), *Brian Lane Green* (from 10/21/86), *Jon Ehrlich* (from 4/21/87); WIDOW DOUGLAS: Susan Browning; MISS WATSON: Evalyn Baron, *Karen Looze* (from 85–86); JIM: Ron Richardson, *Larry Riley* (from 2/21/86), *George Merritt* (from 6/1/86); TOM SAWYER: John Short, *Clint Allen* (from 8/22/85), *Roger Bart* (from 4/7/87); BEN ROGERS: William Youmans, *Patrick Breen* (from 85–86), *Russ Jolly* (from 85–86), *Neal Jones* (from 86–87); JO HARPER: Andi Henig; SIMON: Aramis Estevez; DICK: Michael Brian, *Adam Bryant* (from 86–87); PAP FINN: John Goodman, *Leo Burmester* (from 9/3/85), *John Connolly* (from 85–86), *Roger Miller* (from 11/11/86), *Graham Pollock* (from 12/9/86); JUDGE THATCHER: Ralph Byers; WOMAN IN SHANTY: Evalyn Baron, *Karen Looze* (from 85–86); ON THE RIVER, SOUTH OF ST. LOUIS: SLAVES & OVERSEERS ON A FLATBOAT: Carol Dennis (*Carol Woods* from 85–86, *Kecia Lewis-Evans* from 86–87), Elmore James, Jennifer Leigh Warren, Franz Jones, Aramis Estevez, John Goodman (*Leo Burmester* from 9/3/85, *John Connolly* from 85–86, *Roger Miller* from 11/11/86, *Graham Pollock* from 12/9/86), William Youmans (*Patrick Breen* from 85–86, *Russ Jolly* from 85–86, *Neal Jones* from 86–87), Michael Brian; ON THE RIVER, NEAR CAIRO, ILL.: THREE MEN ON A SKIFF: Ralph Byers, Reathel Bean (*Gary Holcombe* from 85–86, *Larry Raiken* from 86–87), Elmore James; ON THE RIVERBANK IN KENTUCKY: THE KING: Bob Gunton, *Michael McCarty* (from 7/8/86); THE DUKE: Rene Auberjonois, *Russell Leib* (from 9/2/85), *Brent Spiner* (from 10/8/85), *Ken Jenkins* (from 1/7/86), *Stephen Mellor* (from 9/2/85), *Ken Jenkins* (from 86–87); SOLDIERS/CITIZENS: Company. *Act II:* IN BRICKTOWN, ARK.: HANK: William Youmans, *Patrick Breen* (from 85–86), *Russ Jolly* (from 85–86), *Neal Jones* (from 86–87); ANDY: Michael Brian; LAFE: Reathel Bean, *Gary Holcombe* (from 85–86), *Larry Raiken* (from 86–87); TOWNSPEOPLE: Company; IN HILLSBORO, ARK.: YOUNG FOOL: William Youmans, *Patrick Breen* (from 85–86), *Russ Jolly* (from 85–86), *Neal Jones* (from 86–87); MARY JANE WILKES: Patti Cohenour, *Karla De Vito* (from 7/9/85), *Patti Cohenour* (from 9/3/85), *Marin Mazzie* (from 10/15/85); SUSAN WILKES: Peggy Harmon; JOANNA WILKES, A HARE LIP: Andi Henig; BILL, A SERVANT: Franz Jones; COUNSELOR ROBINSON: Reathel Bean, *Gary Holcombe* (from 85–86), *Larry Raiken* (from 86–87); ALICE, A SLAVE: Carol Dennis, *Carol Woods* (from 85–86), *Kecia Lewis-Evans* (from 86–87); ALICE'S DAUGHTER: Jennifer Leigh Warren; MOURNERS/MOB: Company; SHERIFF BELL: John Goodman, *Leo Burmester* (from 9/3/85), *John Connolly* (from 85–86), *Roger Miller* (from 11/11/86), *Graham Pollock* (from 12/9/86); HARVEY WILKES: Ralph Byers; MAN IN THE CROWD: Michael Brian; HARMONIA PLAYER: Evalyn Baron, *Karen Looze* (from 85–86); ON A FARM NEAR HILLSBORO: SALLY PHELPS: Susan Browning; SILAS PHELPS: Ralph Byers; DOCTOR: Gordon Connell, *Robert Sevra* (during Mr. Connell's vacation, 86–87); HIRED HANDS: Reathel Bean (*Gary Holcombe* from 85–86, *Larry Raiken* from 86–87), Michael Brian, John Goodman (*Leo Burmester* from 9/3/85, *John Connolly* from 85–86, *Roger Miller* from 11/11/86, *Graham Pollock* from 12/9/86). *Understudies:* Jim: Elmore James (85), *George Merritt* (85–86), *Jimmy Lockett* (86–87); Huck: Andrew Hill Newman (85), *Romain Fruge* (85–86), *Elmore James* (85–86), *Harry L. Burney III* (from 85–86), *Neal Jones* (85–86), *Skip Lackey* (86–87); King: William McClary; Duke: William McClary (85–87), *Larry Raiken* (86–87). Ensemble: Peggy Harmon (85 & 86–87), George Merritt (85–86), Andrew Hill Newman (85), Romain Fruge (85–87), Susan Glaze (85–86), Neal Jones (85–86),

Linda Kerns (85–87), Elmore James (85–86; *Harry L. Burney III* from 85–86 & gone by 86–87), William McClary (85–87), Robert Sevra (85–87), *Skip Lackey* (86–87), *Jimmy Lockett* (86–87), *Yvonne Over* (86–87), Jane Seaman. *Musicians:* HARMONICA: Don Brooks; GUITARS: John Guth & Scott Kuney; BANJO: John Guth; FIDDLE: Kenny Kosek; TROMBONE: Bruce Bonvissuto; DRUMS: Vinnie Johnson; BASS: Jeffrey Ganz; TRUMPET: Lowell J. Hershey; WOODWIND: Robert Steen; PIANO: Linda Twine. *Act I: Scene 1* The Widow Douglas's home in St. Petersburg, Missouri: "Do Ya Wanna Go to Heaven?" (Company); *Scene 2* A cave by the river: "The Boys" (Tom & Gang), "Waiting for the Light to Shine" (Huck); *Scene 3* The Widow Douglas's home; *Scene 4* A cabin on the Illinois shore: "Guv'ment" (Pap); *Scene 5* The cabin; Jackson's Island: "Hand for the Hog" (Tom), "I, Huckleberry, Me" (Huck); *Scene 6* A cabin on the Missouri shore; a raft on the river: "Muddy Water" (Jim & Huck); *Scene 7* On the raft in the moonlight, approaching Cairo, Illinois: "Crossing Over" (Slaves & Overseer), "River in the Rain" (Huck & Jim); *Scene 8* On the riverbank in Kentucky; on the raft downriver: "When the Sun Goes Down in the South" (Duke, King, Huck). *Act II: Scene 1* On the raft in Tennessee; *Scene 2* In Bricktown, Arkansas: "The Royal Nonesuch" (Duke & Company); *Scene 3* On the raft in a nearby cove: "Worlds Apart" (Jim & Huck); *Scene 4* In Hillsboro, Ark.; the Wilkes's farm near Hillsboro: "Arkansas" (Young Fool), "How Blest We Are" (Alice's Daughter & Company), "You Oughta Be Here with Me" (Mary Jane, Susan, Joanna); *Scene 5* Next day at the farm: "How Blest We Are" (reprise) (Company), "Leaving's Not the Only Way to Go" (Mary Jane, Jim, Huck); *Scene 6* The farm; the cemetery; *Scene 7* To the shore and the raft: "Waiting for the Light to Shine" (reprise) (Huck); *Scene 8* A country road; the Phelps' farm near Hillsboro: "Free at Last" (Jim); *Scene 9* The Phelps farm, that night; the raft; *Scene 10* The Phelps farm: "River in the Rain" (reprise) (Huck & Jim), "Muddy Water" (reprise) (Company).

Broadway reviews were divided. The show won Tonys for musical, score, book, direction of a musical, sets, light, and for Ron Richardson, and was also nominated for costumes, and for Rene Auberjonois and Daniel Jenkins.

After Broadway. TOUR: Opened on 3/4/86, in Chicago. **Cast**: HUCK: Brian Lane Green; JIM: Ron Richardson; DUKE: Richard Levine; KING: Michael McCarty; TOM: Roger Bart; MARY JANE: Jessie Janet Richards.

TOUR. Opened on 7/11/87, at the Playhouse Square Center State Theatre, Cleveland. DIRECTOR: Michael Greig; MUSICAL DIRECTOR: Michael Rafter. **Cast**: HUCK: Romain Fruge, *Robert Lambert* (from 4/25/88); TOM: Barry Lee; MARK TWAIN: Kevin Cooney, *Jordan Bowers*; JIM: Michael Edward-Stevens; MARY JANE: Carolee Carmello, *Jessie Janet Richards*; DUKE: Michael Calkins; KING: Walker Joyce.

61. *Big River (Broadway revival)*

Also known as: *Big River: the Adventures of Huckleberry Finn.* This was a re-staged revival using deaf, hearing and hard of hearing actors. Songs and dialogue are often sung and signed with actors doubling as characters — one speaking and singing, and one signing.

Before Broadway. This revival originated at DEAF WEST THEATRE, then on to the MARK TAPER FORUM, Los Angeles, 11/13/02–12/29/02. It had the same basic credits as for the subsequent Broadway run, except: SOUND: Jon Gottlieb & Philip G. Alan. **Cast**: JUDGE: Chuck Baird; ALICE'S DAUGHTER: Michelle A. Banks; JIM: Rufus Bonds Jr.; PREACHER: Gibby Brand; TOM: Michael Davis; MISS WATSON/SALLY: Phyllis Frelich; HUCK: Tyrone Giordano; PAP/KING: Lyle Kanouse; VOICE OF TOM/JOE: Rod Keller; WIDOW DOUGLAS/VOICE OF SALLY: Carol Kline; PAP/DUKE: Troy Kotsur; BEN: Jarret LeMaster; VOICE OF DUKE: William Martinez; DICK: Ryan Schlecht; ALICE: Gwen Stewart; VOICE OF MISS WATSON/MARY JANE: Melissa Van Der Schyff; TWAIN/VOICE OF HUCK: Scott Waara; JOANNA: Alexandria Wailes. **Musicians**: Steven Landau, John David, Tom Christensen, Richard Greene, Scott Higgins.

The Broadway Run. AMERICAN AIRLINES THEATRE, 7/24/03–9/21/03. 28 previews from 7/1/03. Limited run of 67 PERFORMANCES.

PRESENTED BY the Roundabout Theatre Company & Deaf West Theatre, in association with Center Theatre Group/Mark Taper Forum; MUSIC/LYRICS: Roger Miller; BOOK: William Hauptman; ADAPTED FROM the novel by Mark Twain; DIRECTOR/CHOREOGRAPHER: Jeff Calhoun; ASSOCIATE DIRECTOR/ASSOCIATE CHOREOGRAPHER: Coy Middlebrook; SETS: Ray Klausen; COSTUMES: David R. Zyla; LIGHTING: Michael Gilliam; SOUND: Peter Fitzgerald; MUSICAL DIRECTOR/SPECIAL MUSICAL ARRANGEMENTS: Steven Landau; PRESS: Boneau/Bryan-Brown; CASTING: Jim Carnahan; GENERAL MANAGER: Don-Scott Cooper; COMPANY MANAGER: Jean Haring; PRODUCTION STAGE MANAGER: Peter Hanson; STAGE MANAGER: C. Scott Crawford. *Cast*: MARK TWAIN: Daniel H. Jenkins; HUCKLEBERRY FINN: Tyrone Giordano, (voice: Daniel H. Jenkins); JIM: Michael McElroy; TOM SAWYER: Michael Arden; WIDOW DOUGLAS: Gina Ferrall; BEN ROGERS/ANDY/RONALD ROBINSON: Scott Barnhardt; MISS WATSON: Phyllis Frelich, (voice: Melissa Van Der Schyff); SALLY PHELPS: Phyllis Frelich, (voice: Gina Ferrall); MARY JANE WILKES: Melissa Van Der Schyff; JO HARPER/LAFE/DONALD ROBINSON: Rod Keller; JUDGE THATCHER: Iosif Schneiderman, *Drew McVety* (voice: Walter Charles); PAP FINN: Troy Kotsur, (voice: Lyle Kanouse); JOANNA WILKES, A HARE-LIP: Alexandria Wailes, (voice: Melissa Van Der Schyff); PREACHER/DOCTOR: Walter Charles; THE KING: Lyle Kanouse; THE DUKE: Troy Kotsur, (voice: Walter Charles); HARVEY WILKES: Iosif Schneiderman, *Drew McVety* (voice: Drew McVety); DICK SIMON/HANK: Ryan Schlecht, (voice: Drew McVety); SILAS PHELPS: Iosif Schnederman, *Troy Kotsur* (voice: Lyle Kanouse); ALICE, THE WILKES' SLAVE: Gwen Stewart; ALICE'S DAUGHTER: Christina Ellison Dunams, (voice: Gwen Stewart); SLAVES: Gwen Stewart & Christina Ellison Dunams; YOUNG FOOL/SHERIFF BELL: Ryan Schlecht, (voice: Scott Barnhardt); 1ST MAN: Iosif Schneiderman, *Guthrie Nutter* (voice: Walter Charles); 2ND MAN: Drew McVety; ENSEMBLE: Michael Arden, Scott Barnhardt, Walter Charles, Christina Ellison Dunams, Gina Ferrall, Phyllis Frelich, Lyle Kanouse, Rod Keller, Troy Kotsur, Drew McVety, Ryan Schlecht, Iosif Schneiderman (*Guthrie Nutter*), Gwen Stewart, Melissa Van Der Schyff, Alexandria Wailes. **Understudies**: Twain: Drew McVety; Huck: Guthrie Nutter & Ryan Schlecht; Joanna/Mary Jane/Widow Douglas: Catherine Brunell; Miss Watson/Sally: Alexandra Wailes; Jim/Slaves: David Aron Damane; Tom: Rod Keller; Andy/Ben/Donald/Jo/Lafe/Ronald: Kevin Massey; Dick/1st Man/Hank/Harvey/Judge/Sheriff/Young Fool: Guthrie Nutter; Duke/Silas: Ryan Schlecht; Pap: Guthrie Nutter, Ryan Schlecht, George McDaniel; Doctor/King/2nd Man: George McDaniel. **Musicians**: PIANO: Steven Landau; BANJO/GUITAR/DOBRO: Gordon Titcomb & Greg Utzig; HARMONICA: Gordon Titcomb; MANDOLINS/FIDDLE: Gordon Titcomb, Greg Utzig, Cenovia Cummins; ACOUSTIC BASS: Dave Phillips; PERCUSSION/DULCIMER: Frank Pagano.

Reviews were very good. The show missed a Broadway performance due to the 8/14/03 power blackout. It extended its closing date from 9/14/03 to 9/21/03. It received Tony nominations for revival of a musical, and for Michael McElroy.

After Broadway. The first touring company opened on 6/11/04, at the Curran Theatre, San Francisco, and closed in 6/05. It included Japan. DIRECTOR/CHOREOGRAPHER: Jeff Calhoun. *Cast*: Tyrone Giordano, Daniel Jenkins, Michael McElroy.

The first tour being so popular, the second touring company was opened in order to fulfill the contracted 12-week stint at Ford's Theatre, Washington, DC that the first tour couldn't make.

62. *Billion Dollar Baby*

"A musical play of the terrific 20s," with gangsters & gold-diggers, set in 1928–1929. Maribelle, tired of humdrum Staten Island life, attacks the 1920s. Engaged to Champ, a marathon dancer, she leaves him for Dapper, the wealthy gangster & night-club owner, but instead falls for his bodyguard, Rocky. Rocky kills Dapper, and is believed dead himself. Maribelle marries M.M., a billionaire, and just avoids the 1929 stock market crash. The character of Georgia was based on Texas Guinan.

The Broadway Run. ALVIN THEATRE, 12/21/45–6/29/46. 219 PER-FORMANCES. PRESENTED BY Paul Feigay & Oliver Smith; MUSIC/ORCHESTRATIONS: Morton Gould; LYRICS/BOOK: Betty Comden & Adolph Green; DIRECTOR: George Abbott; CHOREOGRAPHER: Jerome Robbins; ASSISTANT CHOREOGRAPHER: Anita Alvarez; SETS: Oliver Smith; COSTUMES: Irene Sharaff; TECHNICAL DIRECTOR: Peggy Clark; LIGHTING: George Schaff; MUSICAL DIRECTOR: Max Goberman; ADDITIONAL ORCHESTRATIONS: Philip J. Lang & Allan Small; REHEARSAL PIANIST: Trude Rittman; PRESS: Karl Bernstein; TECHNICAL ADVISER ON MARATHONS: June Havoc; GENERAL MANAGER: Charles Harris; STAGE MANAGER: Robert E. Griffith; ASSISTANT STAGE MANAGERS: Dan Sattler & Beverly Hume. *Cast*: MA JONES: Emily Ross (9); PA JONES: William David; ESME: Shirley Van (7); NEIGHBORS: Maria Harriton, Edward Hodge, Howard Lenters, Douglas Deane, Helen Gallagher, Beverly Hosier; CHAMP WATSON: Danny Daniels (6); PHOTOGRAPHER: Anthony Reed; REPORTER: Alan Gilbert; MARIBELLE JONES: Joan McCracken (2); NEWSBOYS: Douglas Jones (*Stefan Gierasch*) & Richard Thomas; MASTER OF CEREMONIES: Richard Sanford, *David Thomas, Thomas Hume*; MISS TEXAS: Althea Elder, *Jacqueline Dodge*; MISS CALIFORNIA: Virginia Gorski; MISS FLORIDA: Peggy Anne Ellis; MISS OKLAHOMA: Beth Shea; MISS VIRGINIA: Beverly Hosier; MISS INDIANA: Joan Mann; MISS LOUISIANA: Future Fulton; MISS MASSACHUSETTS: Doris Hollingsworth; MISS VERMONT: Thelma Stevens; MISS SOUTH DAKOTA: Lyn Gammon; MISS KENTUCKY: Betty Saunders; GEORGIA MOTLEY: Mitzi Green (1); DREAM HEROES: Jim Mitchell, Fred Hearn, Bill Skipper; VIOLIN PLAYER: Tony Gardell; JERRY BONANZA: Don De Leo (8) (alternated with Harry Gary); CHARLESTON: COP: Arthur Partington; THREE FLAPPERS: Virginia Gorski, Helen Gallagher, Lorraine Todd; RICH GIRL: Joan Mann; PLAYBOY: Fred Hearn; A TIMID GIRL: Ann Hutchinson; GOOD TIME CHARLIE: Bill Skipper; COLLEGIATES: Virginia Poe & Douglas Deane; YOUNGER GENERATION: Bill Sumner & Maria Harriton; OLDER GENERATION: Jacqueline Dodge & Joe Landis; TWO GANGSTERS: Lucas Aco & Allan Waine; TWO BOOTLEGGERS: Anthony Reed & Alan Gilbert [end of Charleston section]; DAPPER WELCH: David Burns (4); ROCKY BARTON: William Tabbert (3); CIGARETTE GIRL: Jeri Archer; WAITER: David Thomas; M.M. MONTAGUE: Robert Chisholm (5); MARATHON MC: Alan Gilbert; CHORINES: Joan Mann, Lorraine Todd, Virginia Gorski, Virginia Poe, Helen Gallagher, Maria Harriton; COMIC: Douglas Deane; DANNY: Tony Gardell; J.C. CREASY: Horace Cooper; ART LEFFENBUSH: Eddie Hodge; RODNEY GENDER: Richard Sanford, *Stuart Langley, Thomas Hume*; WATCHMAN: Robert Edwin; A LIFE WITH ROCKY: THE WEALTHY ONES: Jacqueline Dodge & Douglas Deane; ROCKY (WHO DANCES): James Mitchell (10); TWO COPS: Joe Landis & Allan Waine; PASSERBY: Arthur Partington; BARTENDER: Fred Hearn; TWO THUGS: Lucas Aco & Bill Sumner; THEIR MOLLS: Joan Mann & Lorraine Todd; LEADER OF THUGS: Bill Skipper [end of A Life with Rocky section]; POLICEMAN: Howard Lenters; DANCERS: Lucas Aco, Douglas Deane, Jacqueline Dodge, Helen Gallagher, Virginia Gorski, Maria Harriton, Fred Hearn, Ann Hutchinson, Joe Landis, Cecille Mann, Joan Mann, Arthur Partington, Virginia Poe, Bill Sumner, Lorraine Todd, Allan Waine; SINGERS: Jeri Archer, Tony Caffaro, Peggy Anne Ellis, Future Fulton, Lyn Gammon, Tony Gardell, Doris Hollingsworth, Beverly Hosier, Philip La Torre, Robert Morrissey, Franklin Powell, Anthony Reed, Betty Saunders, Beth Shea, Thelma Stevens, David Thomas, Sydney Wylie. **Understudy**: Maribelle: Virginia Gibson. *Act I*: *Scene 1* Staten Island living room; *Scene 2* Atlantic City boardwalk: "Million Dollar Smile" ("Billion Dollar Baby") (The Radio), "Who's Gonna Be the Winner?" (Maribelle, Miss Texas, Miss Virginia, Miss Kentucky, Miss Massachusetts, Bathing Beauties); *Scene 3* Staten Island living room: "(Make My) Dreams Come True" (dance) (Maribelle & Dream Heroes); *Scene 4* Staten Island Ferry; *Scene 5* Front of speakeasy: "Charleston" (comedy ballet); *Scene 6* Chez Georgia: "Broadway Blossom" (Georgia), "(Speaking of) Pals" (Dapper, Jerry, Waiter, Violin Player, Rocky, Ensemble); *Scene 7* Georgia's dressing room: "There I'd Be" (Georgia & M.M.); *Scene 8* Staten Island living room: "One Track Mind" (danced by Esme & Champ); *Scene 9* Street; *Scene 10* Dapper's apartment: "Bad Timing" (Rocky & Maribelle); *Scene 11* The Marathon: "The Marathoners" (dance) (Dance Ensemble); *Scene 12* Dapper's apartment; *Scene 13* Backstage of the Jollities; *Scene 14* Onstage Jollities: "A Lovely Girl (is Like a Bird)" (featuring the sketch "Murder at the Jollities") (Georgia, Maribelle, The Jollities Beauties). *Act II*: *Scene 1* A funeral: "Funeral Procession" (dance) (The Mob); *Scene 2* Porch of the Plaza Hotel, Palm Beach: "Havin' a Time" (Georgia); *Scene 3* Entrance to Marathon; *Scene 4* The Marathon: "Marathon Dance" (dance) (Champ); *Scene 5* Entrance to Marathon: "Faithless" (M.M. & Maribelle); *Scene 6* Maribelle's bedroom: "I'm Sure of Your Love" (Rocky), "A Life with Rocky" (dance) (Maribelle. For the rest of the dancers see cast list above); *Scene 7* Church vestry; *Scene 8* Wedding, 1928–29: "The Wedding" (dance).

Broadway reviews were divided, but mostly good to very good. The show won Donaldson Awards for director, and choreographer; Joan McCracken won two — for supporting actress and female dancer. **After Broadway.** ST. PETER'S CHURCH, NYC, 9/25/98–9/27/98. PRESENTED BY the York Theatre Company. It was part of the *Musicals in Mufti* series. DIRECTOR: B.T. McNicholl; CHOREOGRAPHER: Mark Esposito; MUSICAL DIRECTOR: Michael Lavine. **Cast**: ANNOUNCER/DAPPER: Michael McCormick; HARRY JELLYROLL: Casey Nicholaw; MA: Kay Walbye; ROCKY/REPORTER: Marc Kudisch; PA/JERRY: Charles Pistone; MARIBELLE: Kristin Chenoweth; CHAMP: James Darrah; ESME: Darcie Roberts; GEORGIA: Debbie Gravitte; MISS VIRGINIA: Susan Owen; MISS TEXAS: Lesley Blumenthal; MONTAGUE: Richard B. Shull.

63. *Billy*

Billy Budd as a 90-minute musical with no intermission. Set aboard a man o'war in 1796.

Before Broadway. The Billy Budd story had been produced as a straight play on Broadway at the BILTMORE THEATRE, 2/10/51. 105 PERFORMANCES. PRESENTED BY Chandler Cowles & Anthony Brady Farrell. **Cast**: BILLY: Charles Nolte; CLAGGART: Torin Thatcher. More important, Benjamin Britten wrote a fantastically successful 1951 opera, *Billy Budd.*

The story was filmed (straight) in 1962, as *Billy Budd*. PRODUCER/CO-WRITER/DIRECTOR: Peter Ustinov. **Cast**: BILLY: Terence Stamp; CLAGGART: Robert Ryan; VERE: Peter Ustinov; DANSKER: Melvyn Douglas.

The 1969 musical, formerly called *Billy-Be-Dam,'* was refused admission into the Billy Rose Theatre with that title, so it shortened it. **The Broadway Run.** BILLY ROSE THEATRE, 3/22/69. 21 previews. 1 PERFORMANCE. A Vanark Enterprises production, PRESENTED BY Bruce W. Stark, in association with Joseph H. Shoctor; MUSIC/LYRICS: Ron Dante & Gene Allan; BOOK: Stephen Glassman; SUGGESTED BY Herman Melville's novella *Billy Budd*, posthumously published in 1924; DIRECTOR: Arthur A. Seidelman; CHOREOGRAPHER: Grover Dale; SETS: Ming Cho Lee; COSTUMES: Theoni V. Aldredge; LIGHTING: Martin Aronstein; SOUND: Jack Shearing, Admins Ltd; MUSICAL DIRECTOR: Jack Lee; SPECIAL ARRANGEMENTS/INCIDENTAL MUSIC: Wally Harper; ORCHESTRATIONS/VOCAL ARRANGEMENTS: Ronald Frangipane; DANCE MUSIC ARRANGEMENTS: Coleridge-Taylor Perkinson; CAST RECORDING on ABC; PRESS: Harvey B. Sabinson, Lee Solters, David Powers; CASTING: Hilda Guarrera; GENERAL MANAGEMENT: Allentuck, Azenberg & Wolsk; COMPANY MANAGER: Peter Neufeld; PRODUCTION STAGE MANAGER: Frank Rembach; STAGE MANAGER: Tom Porter; ASSISTANT STAGE MANAGERS: Simm Landres & Pascual Vaquer. **Cast**: OFFICERS: CAPT. EDWARD VERE: Laurence Naismith (1) ✩; LT. WILLIAM RADCLIFFE: William Countryman (9); LT. ROGER MORDANT: Michael Tartel; JOHN CLAGGART, MASTER-AT-ARMS: John Devlin (3) ✩; CPL. JOHN BERNARD: Simm Landres; MARINE CORPORALS: Laried Montgomery & Danny Villa; SEAMEN: BILLY BUDD: Robert Salvio (4) ✩; DANSKER: John Beal (2) ✩; WHISKERS: Dolph Sweet (5); CAMPBELL: George Marcy (8); BOSCOMBE: Alan Weeks (7); BOYER: Igors Gavon (10); GILBERT: Al Cohen; DONALD TAFF: Peter De Maio; RAWLEY: Danny Carroll; JOHN THORP: Joseph Della Sorte; STAFFORD: Bill Schustik; FALLON: Pascual Vaquer; SMITHY: Howard Girven; STOKER: Laried Montgomery; RUSH: Steven Boockvor; POTTER: Christopher Chadman; ROPER: Michael Peters; MARSTEN: Tim Ramirez; HARKER: Ron Tassone; SEEGER: Frank De Sal; GRIMER: De Wayne Oliver; and: MOLLY: Barbara Monte (6). **Standbys**: Billy: Robert Berdeen; Molly: Susan Hufford. **Understudies**: Vere: Dolph Sweet; Dansker: Danny Carroll; Claggart: William Countryman; Whiskers: Igors Gavon; Boscombe: Howard Girven; Campbell/Boyer: Peter De Maio; Radcliffe: Michael Tartel; Taff/Thorp/Raw-

ley: Pascual Vaquer; Stafford: Joseph Della Sorte. **Swing Dancer**: Tony Stevens. Prelude, "Molly" (Billy), "Chanty" (Stafford, Fallon, Smithy, Stoker), "Watch Out for Claggart/Work" (Boscombe, Claggart, Crew), "Shaking Hands with the Wind" (Billy), "Whiskers' Dance" (Whiskers & Crew), "Billy" (Molly & Billy), "It Ain't Us Who Make the Wars" (Campbell & Crew), "The Bridge to Nowhere" (Vere), "It Ain't Us Who Make the Wars" (reprise) (Crew) [added during previews], "There in the Dark/Afraid" (Claggart & Billy) [this replaced "The Night and the Sea" (Billy & Claggart)], "Whiskers' Dance" (reprise) (Whiskers, Billy, Fallon, Taff, Thorp) [dropped for Broadway], "In the Arms of a Stranger" (Dansker), "The Fiddlers' Green" (Billy, Thorp, Boyer, Taff, Crew) [before opening night this was sung by Whiskers, Campbell, Boyer, Stoker, Rawley, Gilbert], "Molly" (reprise) (Molly) [this replaced "My Captain" (Vere & Billy)], "Requiem" (Billy).

This was Grover Dale's Broadway debut as choreographer, and he got the few raves in a show otherwise roundly panned (Ming Cho Lee, sets, got the others, and Robert Salvio, as Billy, got good notices). The show received Tony nominations for choreography and sets.

64. *The Billy Barnes People*

This musical revue was a follow-up to *The Billy Barnes Revue.* **The Broadway Run.** ROYALE THEATRE, 6/13/61–6/17/61. 7 PERFORMANCES. PRESENTED BY John Pool; MUSIC/LYRICS: Billy Barnes; SKETCHES/DIRECTOR: Bob Rodgers; CARTOONS: William Box; SETS: Spencer Davies; COSTUMES: Grady Hunt; MUSICAL SUPERVISOR/ARRANGEMENTS: Ray Henderson; PRESS: Bill Doll; GENERAL MANAGER: C. Edwin Knill; COMPANY MANAGER: George Oshrin; STAGE MANAGERS: Allen Kramer & Lee Mason. **Act I: Scene 1** "If it Wasn't for People" (Entire Company); *Scene 2* "There's Nothing Wrong with Our Values" (Joyce Jameson, Patti Regan, Dave Ketchum, Dick Patterson); *Scene 3* Vegas Revisited: BARKER: Jack Grinnage; STATUE: Jackie Joseph; CHORUS GIRL: Patti Regan; HERMAN HEPPLEWHITE: Dave Ketchum; FELLAS: Dick Patterson & Jack Grinnage; OPERA DIVA: Jo Anne Worley; *Scene 4* "Don't Bother" (Jackie Joseph & Ken Berry); *Scene 5* I Wrote a Book: AUTHORESS: Joyce Jameson; FANS: Jo Anne Worley & Dick Patterson; *Scene 6* "If it Makes You Happy" (The Syndicate Song): THE BOSS: Dave Ketchum; HIS GIRL: Jackie Joseph; THE BOYS: Jack Grinnage & Ken Berry; *Scene 7* "Damn-Alot" (parody of *Camelot*, in the style of Brendan Behan): INTRODUCED BY: Jack Grinnage; GUENEVERE: Patti Regan; MORGAN O'FEY: Joyce Jameson; KING ARTHUR: Dave Ketchum; LANCELOT: Dick Patterson; *Scene 8* "What Do We Have to Hold on To?" (Jo Anne Worley); *Scene 9* "I Like You": ROMANTIC COUPLE: Jackie Joseph & Ken Berry; NEUROTIC COUPLE: Jo Anne Worley & Jack Grinnage; SOPHISTICATED COUPLE: Joyce Jameson & Dick Patterson; *Scene 10* "Before and After" (Dave Ketchum & Dick Patterson); *Scene 11* "Let's Get Drunk" (Ken Berry); *Scene 12* "It's Not Easy": ETHEL: Patti Regan; JANET: Joyce Jameson; ADELE: Jo Anne Worley; SCENE 13 The Speech Teacher: TEACHER: Dick Patterson (5); CLIENT: Jack Grinnage; *Scene 14* "The Matinee" (Entire Company). **Act II: Scene 1** "If it Wasn't for People" (reprise) (Jack Grinnage): THE COUCH: Jackie Joseph & Dick Patterson; THE BALCONY: Jo Anne Worley & Dave Ketchum; BUS STOP: Patti Regan & Ken Berry; *Scene 2* Liberated Woman: SALLY O'TOOLE: Joyce Jameson; JOHNNY, HER BOY FRIEND: Jack Grinnage; NARRATOR: Dick Patterson; *Scene 3* "What Do We Have to Hold on To?" (reprise) (Jo Anne Worley); *Scene 4* "The End?" (Dick Patterson, Ken Berry, Dave Ketchum); *Scene 5* Alice: ALICE: Jackie Joseph; FELICIA FASHION: Patti Regan; MARTY MARKET: Dick Patterson; HOUSEWIFE: Jo Anne Worley; MRS. KARR: Joyce Jameson; MR. KARR: Ken Berry; MR. BIG BUSINESS SR.: Dave Ketchum; MR. BIG BUSINESS JR.: Jack Grinnage; *Scene 6* Grauman's Chinese (Dick Patterson, Patti Regan, Ken Berry); *Scene 7* "Second Best" (Joyce Jameson); *Scene 8* "What Do We Have to Hold on To?" (reprise) (Jo Anne Worley); *Scene 9* "Dolls" (Dave Ketchum, Dick Patterson, Patti Regan); *Scene 10* "Where is the Clown?" (Joyce Jameson & Ken Berry); *Scene 11* "Marital Infidelity" (Entire Company); *Scene 12* "I Like You" (reprise) (Entire Company).

Broadway reviews mostly disastrous. On the first night the show opened 45 minutes late due to a power failure.

After Broadway. In 1962 there was a West Coast version, *Billy Barnes L.A.*, with Joyce Jameson and Ken Berry, with musical numbers: "Does Anybody Here Love Me?," "Where Was the Music?" (both written by Billy Barnes).

65. *Billy Barnes Revue*

Before Broadway. This musical revue was first presented at the LAS PALMAS THEATRE, Hollywood, on 10/15/58. Then, it was produced Off Broadway, by George Eckstein, in association with Bob Reese, at the YORK PLAYHOUSE, 6/9/59. 64 PERFORMANCES. It had the same basic cast and crew as for the subsequent Broadway run, except PRESS: Bill Doll & Maurice Turet; COMPANY MANAGER: Harold Kusell; STAGE MANAGER: Allen Kramer. Between the time of its run at the York to the time it arrived on Broadway, various changes were made to the sketches and musical numbers. New ones added were: "Whatever," "City of the Angels," "A Dissertation on Transportation," "Callas Tonight" and "Whatever Happened To?" "Tyler My Boy," and "Blocks" were switched from Act II to Act I. As for "Callas Tonight" it came immediately before "The Vamp and Friends," but was dropped Before Broadway.

The Broadway Run. JOHN GOLDEN THEATRE, 8/4/59–9/26/59; LYCEUM THEATRE, 9/28/59–10/17/59). Total of 87 PERFORMANCES. PRESENTED BY George Eckstein, George Cayley, George Brandt, Samuel J. Friedman; MUSIC/LYRICS/MUSICAL DIRECTOR: Billy Barnes; SKETCHES/DIALOG/DIRECTOR: Bob Rodgers; SETS: Glenn Holse; COSTUMES: Peggy Morrison & Berman Costume Company; LIGHTING: Peggy Clark; AT PIANOS: Billy Barnes & Armin Hoffman; PRESS: Samuel J. Friedman; COMPANY MANAGER: Benjamin Rothman; STAGE MANAGER: Howard Ostroff. *Act I*: *Scene 1* "Do a Revue!" (Company); *Scene 2* "Where Are Your Children?" (Ken Berry, Bert Convy, Jackie Joseph, Ann Guilbert, Patti Regan, Len Weinrib); *Scene 3* "Las Vegas": HERMAN: Bob Rodgers; GIRL WITH HAT: Ann Guilbert; TANYA: Joyce Jameson, *Virginia de Luce*; HER FELLAS: Bert Convy & Ken Berry; *Scene 4* Medic: SURGEON: Len Weinrib; STAFF: Ann Guilbert & Patti Regan; *Scene 5* "Foolin' Ourselves" (Bert Convy & Ken Berry); *Scene 6* Safari a la Marilyn: PAPA: Len Weinrib; ARTHUR: Bob Rodgers; MARILYN: Joyce Jameson, *Virginia de Luce*; *Scene 7* The Pembrooke Story: ARTHUR: Ken Berry; EDYTHE: Ann Guilbert; MISS O'BRIEN: Jackie Joseph; JOHN: Bert Convy; PETER: Len Weinrib; *Scene 8* "Whatever" ("Whatever Happened?" No. 1) (Patti Regan); *Scene 9*: "City of the Angels": LILY: Joyce Jameson, *Virginia de Luce*; LOLLY: Ann Guilbert; DOLLY: Jackie Joseph; *Scene 10* "Listen to the Beat!": HOST: Len Weinrib; JACK: Ken Berry; MARY LOU: Ann Guilbert; DEAN: Bert Convy; SARAH: Joyce Jameson, *Virginia de Luce*; THE PROPHET: Len Weinrib; BEATNIKS: Bob Rodgers, Patti Regan, Jackie Joseph; *Scene 11* Home in Mississippi (parody of *Cat on a Hot Tin Roof*): MAGGIE: Patti Regan; BIG DADDY: Len Weinrib; BIG MAMA: Ann Guilbert; BRICK: Bob Rodgers; NO-NECK MONSTERS: Themselves; *Scene 12* "Tyler My Boy" (Bert Convy); *Scene 13* "Whatever Happened" ("Whatever Happened?" No. 2) (Patti Regan); *Scene 14* The Thirties: NARRATOR: Bob Rodgers; PEDDLER: Patti Regan; FRED: Ken Berry; GINGER: Joyce Jameson, *Virginia de Luce*; FORGOTTEN WOMAN: Ann Guilbert; FORGOTTEN MAN: Len Weinrib; SHIRLEY: Joyce Jameson, *Virginia de Luce*; DADDY: Bert Convy; STEP-MOMMY: Patti Regan; GOLD DIGGER: Jackie Joseph; J.N.: Len Weinrib; SAM: Ken Berry; RUBY: Ann Guilbert; DICK: Bert Convy; JEANETTE: Joyce Jameson, *Virginia de Luce*; NELSON: Bob Rodgers. *Act II*: *Scene 1* A Dissertation on Transportation; or, It All Started with the Wheel: PRINCIPAL: Bob Rodgers; PTA PRESIDENT: Joyce Jameson, *Virginia de Luce*; TEACHER: Patti Regan; SWEET LITTLE GIRL: Jackie Joseph; SOUR LITTLE GIRL: Ann Guilbert; TEACHER'S PET: Ken Berry; BULLY: Len Weinrib; BERT CONVY: Bert Convy; *Scene 2* "The Fights": INTRODUCED BY: Ann Guilbert; SHIRLEY: Joyce Jameson, *Virginia de Luce*; HARRY: Bob Rodgers; *Scene 3* The Vamp and Friends: VAMP: Ann Guilbert; CHAMP: Ken Berry; TRAMP: Patti Regan; CAMP: Len Weinrib; *Scene 4* "Blocks": HUSBAND: Bob Rodgers; WIFE: Jackie Joseph; *Scene 5* Hellahahana: NATIVES: Bert Convy, Ken Berry, Joyce Jameson (*Virginia de Luce*), Len Weinrib, Jackie Joseph; TURISTA: Ann Guilbert; *Scene 6* "Whatever Happened To" ("Whatever Happened?" No. 3) (Patti Regan); *Scene 7* World at Large: MODERATOR: Bert Convy. *World at Large No. 1*: ROSABELLE HALEY: Joyce Jameson, *Virginia de Luce*;

WARDEN: Len Weinrib; MATRON: Ann Guilbert. *Station Break*: FIRE PREVENTION QUEEN: Patti Regan. *World at Large No. 2*: MR. LERNSTEIN: Bob Rodgers; CHORAL GROUP: Choral Group. *World at Large Preview*: OED: Ken Berry; JO: Patti Regan; *Scene 8* "(Have I Stayed) Too Long at the Fair" [Joyce Jameson (*Virginia de Luce*)]; *Scene 9* "One of Those Days": POOR SOUL: Len Weinrib; ADS: Bert Convy, Jackie Joseph, Ken Berry; Scene 10 Finale (Company).

The sketch order is listed differently in some different publications. Broadway reviews were generally good.

After Broadway. The show went back Off Broadway, to the CARNEGIE HALL PLAYHOUSE, 10/20/59–11/29/59. 48 PERFORMANCES.

LYRIC THEATRE, Hammersmith, London. It opened on 4/4/60. 24 PERFORMANCES. PRESENTED BY Harold Fielding; CHOREOGRAPHER: Ross Taylor; SETS: Robert Weaver; LIGHTING: John Wyckham. *Cast*: AMERICAN GIRLS: Joyce Jameson, Ann Guilbert, Patti Regan, Jackie Joseph; ENGLISH BOYS: Ronnie Stevens, Ted Rogers, Terence Cooper, Richard Owens.

66. *Black and Blue*

An all-black musical revue, a celebration of American jazz and blues, with a 13-piece orchestra, and lavish sets.

Before Broadway. Argentinean businessmen Orezzoli & Segovia, both living in Paris, came up with the idea of recreating European shows in which expatriate black singers and musicians starred, and in which they did not have to suffer racial prejudice as they had to in the USA at the time. It opened at THEATRE MUSICAL DE PARIS for a limited run of 8 weeks, but remained for the entire season. PRESENTED BY Theatre Musical de Paris Chatelet, Top # 1, Spectacles Lumroso, Spectacles A.L.A.P, in association with Mel Howard; CHOREOGRAPHER: Henry Le Tang. Orchestra members who transferred to Broadway included Bill Easley, Haywood Henry, and 80-year-old Claude Williams. Trumpeter Stephen Furtaldo was replaced by Jake Porter. Billy Butler took a leave from *Anything* Goes to replace Martin Aubert on guitar. During Broadway previews Ruth Brown was sick, and her numbers were sung by Melba Joyce, Carrie Smith and Dakota Staton. Jake Porter and Emory Thompson switched roles. Tina Pratt (hoofer) and Ivery Wheeler (dancer) were dropped before opening night. During previews the Broadway production was budgeted at $8 million.

The Broadway Run. MINSKOFF THEATRE, 1/26/89–1/20/91. 829 PERFORMANCES. The Claudio Segovia — Hector Orezzoli production, PRESENTED BY Mel Howard & Donald K. Donald (i.e. Donald Tarlton); MUSIC/LYRICS: various authors; CONCEIVED BY/DIRECTORS/SETS/COSTUMES/LIGHTING CONCEPTION: Claudio Segovia & Hector Orezzoli; CHOREOGRAPHERS: Cholly Atkins, Henry Le Tang, Frankie Manning, Fayard Nicholas; LIGHTING: Neil Peter Jampolis & Jane Reisman; SOUND: Abe Jacob; MUSICAL SUPERVISOR/ORCHESTRATIONS/ARRANGEMENTS: Sy Johnson; ADDITIONAL ORCHESTRATIONS & ARRANGEMENTS: Luther Henderson; PRESS: P.R. Partners/Marilynn LeVine; CASTING: Julie Hughes & Barry Moss; GENERAL MANAGERS: Norman E. Rothstein, Robert A. Buckley, Julie Crosby; PRODUCTION STAGE MANAGER: Alan Hall; STAGE MANAGER: Ruth E. Rinklin; ASSISTANT STAGE MANAGERS: Jack Gianino & Tamara K. Heeschen. *Cast*: THE SINGERS: Ruth Brown (*LaVern Baker*), Linda Hopkins, Carrie Smith; THE HOOFERS: Bunny Briggs, Ralph Brown, Lon Chaney, Jimmy Slyde, Dianne Walker; THE DANCERS: Frederick J. Boothe, Rashamella Cumbo, Eugene Fleming, Tanya Gibson, Germaine Goodson, Angela Hall, Kyme, Ted Levy, Valerie Macklin, Bernard Manners, Deborah Mitchell, Van Porter, Kevin Ramsey, Ken Roberson, Valerie E. Smith, Melvin Washington; THE YOUNGER GENERATION: Cyd Glover, Savion Glover, Dormeshia Sumbry. *Standbys*: Singers: Melba Joyce; Younger Generation: Tarik Winston. *Musicians*: GUITAR: Billy Butler; CLARINET/SAXOPHONE: Bill Easley & Haywood Henry; TRUMPETS: Emory Thompson, Virgil Jones, Jake Porter; PIANO: Sir Roland Hanna & Leonard Oxley; BASS: Al McKibbon; ALTO SAX: Jerome Richardson; DRUMS: Grady Tate; VIOLIN: Claude Williams; TROMBONE: Britt Woodman. *Act I*: Blues a Capella — "I'm a Woman" (m/l: Cora Taylor & Elias McDaniel) (Linda, Ruth, Carrie), Hoofers a Capella (Jimmy, Bunny, Ralph, Lon, Bernard, Savion,

Ted), "Royal Garden Blues" (m/l: Clarence & Spencer Williams) (Musicians), "St. Louis Blues" (m/l: W.C. Handy) (Ruth & musicians Sir Roland, Haywood, Britt, Jake, Grady, Billy), "Everybody Loves My Baby" (by Jack Palmer & Spencer Williams) (arr/orch: Luther Henderson) (ch: Henry Le Tang) (Dancers), "After You've Gone" (m: Henry Creamer; l: Turner Layton) (ch: Cholly Atkins) (Linda, Bernard, Male Dancers), "If I Can't Sell It, I'll Keep Sittin' on It" (m: Alex Hill; l: Andy Razaf) (Ruth), "I Want a Big Butter and Egg Man" (m/l: Percy Venable & Louis Armstrong) (ch: Fayard Nicholas) (Carrie, with Kevin, Ted, Eugene, and musicians Sir Roland & Jake), "Rhythm is Our Business" (m: Jimmie Lunceford & Saul Chaplin; l: Sammy Cahn) (ch: Henry Le Tang) (Younger Generation), "Mystery Song" (m: Duke Ellington; l: Irving Mills) (Tanya, Rashamella, Valerie E. Smith), "Stompin' at the Savoy" (m: Benny Goodman, Chick Webb, Edgar Sampson; l: Andy Razaf) (Jimmy), "I Gotta Right to Sing the Blues" (m: Harold Arlen; l: Ted Koehler) [from *Earl Carroll's Vanities of 1932*] (Carrie), "Black and Tan Fantasy" (instrumental by Duke Ellington & Bud Miley) (ch: Frankie Manning) (Bunny & Dancers), "Come Sunday" (m/l: Duke Ellington) (Linda), "Daybreak Express" (m: Duke Ellington) (Musicians), "Taint Nobody's Biz ness if I Do" (m: Porter Grainger; l: Everett Robbins) (Ruth & Linda and musician Sir Roland), "That Rhythm Man" (m: Fats Waller & Harry Brooks; l: Andy Razaf) (ch: Henry Le Tang) (arr/orch: Luther Henderson) (Dancers). *Act II*: "Swingin' to Wednesday Night Hop" (by Johnson & Kirk) (ch: Frankie Manning) (Dancers), "I'm Gettin' 'long Alright" (m/l: Bobby Sharp & Charles Singleton) (Linda) [replaced during the run by "Cry Like a Baby" (m: Kirkland; l: Big Maybelle Smith) (Linda)], "Memories of You" (m: Eubie Blake; l: Andy Razaf) [from *Blackbirds of 1930*] (ch: Cholly Atkins) (Dianne, Bernard, Kevin), "Body and Soul" (m: Johnny Green; l: Edward Heyman, Robert Sour, Frank Eyton) [from *Three's a Crowd*] (Ruth), "I'm Confessin' (That I Love You)" (m: A.J. Nieburg; l: Don Dougherty & Ellis Reynolds) (ch: Cholly Atkins) (Kyme, Bernard, Kevin, Fred, Ted, and musicians Claude & Billy), "East St. Louis Toodle-oo" (m: Duke Ellington) (Ralph & Lon), "Am I Blue" (m: Harry Akst; l: Grant Clarke) [from the movie *On With The Show*] (Carrie & musician Claude), "I Can't Give You Anything but Love" (m: Jimmy McHugh; l: Dorothy Fields) [from *Blackbirds of 1928*] (arr/orch: Luther Henderson) (ch: Henry Le Tang) (Angela, Eugene, Dancers), "In a Sentimental Mood" (instrumental by Duke Ellington) (Bunny & musician Jerome), "Black and Blue" (m: Fats Waller & Harry Brooks; l: Andy Razaf) (arr/orch: Luther Henderson) (Ruth, Linda, Carrie, Jimmy, Bunny), Finale (ch: Henry Le Tang) (arr/orch: Luther Henderson) (Younger Generation, Hoofers, Dancers).

Broadway critics raved. The show won Tonys for choreography, costumes, and for Ruth Brown, and was also nominated for musical, direction of a musical, sets, lighting, Linda Hopkins, Bunny Briggs, Savion Glover. There was a TV production in 1993, on PBS. DIRECTOR: Robert Altman.

Blackouts of 1949 see 371

67. *Bless You All*

A musical revue.

The Broadway Run. MARK HELLINGER THEATRE, 12/14/50–2/24/51. 84 PERFORMANCES. PRESENTED BY Herman Levin & Oliver Smith; MUSIC/LYRICS: Harold Rome; SKETCHES: Arnold Auerbach; DIRECTOR: John C. Wilson; CHOREOGRAPHER: Helen Tamiris; ASSISTANT CHOREOGRAPHER: Daniel Nagrin; SETS: Oliver Smith; COSTUMES: Miles White; LIGHTING: Peggy Clark; MUSICAL DIRECTOR/VOCAL ARRANGEMENTS: Lehman Engel; ORCHESTRATIONS: Don Walker; BALLET MUSIC COMPOSED & ARRANGED BY: Mischa & Wesley Portnoff and Don Walker; PRESS: Richard Maney, Frank Goodman, Lewis Harmon; GENERAL MANAGER: Philip Adler; GENERAL STAGE MANAGER: Frank Coletti; STAGE MANAGERS: David Jones & Richard Haas. *Act I: Scene 1* "Bless You All" [performed by comedians Jules Munshin (1) & Mary McCarty (2), singer Pearl Bailey (3), and star dancer Valerie Bettis (4)];

Scene 2 "Do You Know a Better Way to Make a Living?" [sung by Jules Munshin (1) & Show Girls]; *Scene 3* Southern Fried Chekhov (lampooned southern novelists): COLONEL JASPER OGLETHORPE: Garry Davis; EMMALINE, HIS WIFE: Charlene Harris; MARMADUKE, HIS SON: Gordon Edwards; MARYBELLE, HIS DAUGHTER: Mary McCarty (2); THE PUBLISHER: Gene Barry. "Don't Wanna Write About the South" [sung by Mary McCarty (2), Garry Davis, Charlene Harris, Gordon Edwards]; *Scene 4* "I Can Hear it Now" (sung by Jane Harvey): THE POOR GIRL: Dorothy Etheridge; THE POOR BOY: Dick Reed; THE RICH GIRL: Eleanor Boleyn; THE RICH BOY: Donald Saddler; DANCING COUPLES: Carlene Carroll, Sage Fuller, Vera Lee, Ilona Murai, Emy St. Just, Helen Wenzel, Swen Swenson, Joseph Gifford, Philip Nasta, Bertram Ross, John Sandal, Parker Wilson; *Scene 5* "When" [sung by Pearl Bailey (3)]: A BOY: Joe Nash; A GIRL: Elmira Jones-Bey; *Scene 6* Back to Napoli: BENSON: Robert Chisholm; MISS KANE: Charlene Harris; JAROSLAV: Garry Davis; LASZLO: Gene Barry; THE LADIES: Gwenna Lee Smith, Del Parker, Jill Melford, Jeane Williams; ENRICO BONZO: Jules Munshin; THE CHILDREN: Lee Barnett, Billie Kirpich, Clive Dill, Irene Riley, Betsy Holland, Ray Morrissey; *Scene 7* "Little Things (Meant So Much to Me)" [sung by Mary McCarty (2)]; *Scene 8* "A Rose is a Rose" (sung by June Harvey & Byron Palmer): THE ROSE: Valerie Bettis (4); THE MUSICOS: Joseph Gifford, Dick Reed, Bertram Ross; THE MOBILE: Donald Saddler; THE SLEEPING BOY: Joe Nash; A PIECE OF SCULPTURE: Elmira Jones-Bey; THE REVELERS: Ilona Murai, Helen Wenzel, Parker Wilson; *Scene 9* "Love Letter to Manhattan" (sung by romantic tenor Byron Palmer); *Scene 10* TV Over the White House (Blow runs for the 1960 presidency—entirely by TV): ANNOUNCER: Gene Barry; JOSEPH GABRIEL BLOW: Jules Munshin (1); JANE BLOW: Mary McCarty (2); THEIR SON: Lee Barnett. a/ "Love That Man" (Joe & Ensemble); b/ Breakfast With Joe and Jane (Joe, Jane, Son); c/ "Just a Little White House" (Joe, Jane, Son); d/ Somewhere up There (Joe, Jane, Son): GEORGE WASHINGTON: Noel Gordon; ABE LINCOLN: Garry Davis; TEDDY ROOSEVELT: Robert Chisholm; e/ "Voting Blues" (sung by Valerie Bettis); f/ Stop the Politics! (Joe & Jane): MISS STRONG CONSTITUTION: Del Parker; MISS NATURAL RESOURCES: Jeane Williams; MISS INTERNATIONAL PEACE: Kris Nodland; MISS FEDERAL WATER POWER: Gwenna Lee Smith; g/ Finale [Jules Munshin (1) & Entire Ensemble]. *Act II*: *Scene 1* "Summer Dresses" (sung by Byron Palmer & Ensemble): THE MANNEQUIN: Gwenna Lee Smith; MORNING DRESSES: Jeane Williams, Blanche Grady, Sage Fuller, Emy St. Just; COCKTAIL DRESSES: Jill Melford, Gloria Olson, Eleanor Boleyn, Vera Lee, Billie Kirpich; EVENING DRESSES: Kris Nodland, Del Parker, Madelyn Remini, Carlene Carroll, Ilona Murai, Helen Wenzel; STOCK BOYS: Bertram Ross & Swen Swenson; *Scene 2* The Cold War: BILL SLADE: Jules Munshin (1); THE DRUGGIST: Garry Davis; *Scene 3* "Take off the Coat" (sung by Jane Harvey); *Scene 4* The Nobbiest Hobby: AN ART ENTHUSIAST: Jules Munshin (1); A CLERGYMAN: Robert Chisholm; AUNTY: Margaret Wright; DOCTOR SMITH: Noel Gordon; GRANDMA: Charlene Harris; A NURSEMAID: Grace Varik; A GOOD HUMOR MAN: Gene Barry; A DOWAGER: Geraldine Hamburg; AN OLD FISHERMAN: Gordon Edwards; A PRETTY YOUNG GIRL: Eileen Turner; A LIFEGUARD: Ray Morrissey; A SCHOOLGIRL: Irene Riley; BATHERS: The Show Girls; *Scene 5* "The Desert Flame" (ballet) (m: Don Walker): Scene a/ a street in Morocco; Scene b/ a cafe in Morocco; Scene c/ Desert Flame's bedroom; Scene d/ the execution grounds. DESERT FLAME: Valerie Bettis (4); MONSIEUR LE COMANDANT: Parker Wilson; GENDARMES: Joe Gifford, Donald McKayle, Joe Nash, Philip Nasta, Dick Reed, Bertram Ross; PEPE LE KOKO: Richard D'Arcy; HOURIS: Eleanor Boleyn, Dorothy Etheridge, Billie Kirpich, Vera Lee, Ilona Murai, Emy St. Just, Helen Wenzel; THE TEXAN: Donald Saddler; NATIVE DRUMMERS: Joe Comadore & Osborne Smith; THE TORTURERS: John Sandal & Swen Swenson; SINGING HOURIS: Eileen Turner, Grace Varik, Margaret Wright; *Scene 6* Peter and the P.T.A. (sequel to Jean Arthur's *Peter Pan*, in which Peter has trouble flying): MRS. WEATHERBY (PETER): Mary McCarty (2); MR. FOTHERGILL: Garry Davis; WENDY: Lee Barnett; CAPTAIN HOOK: Robert Chisholm; THE PIRATES: Jane Carlyle, Betsy Holland, Dorothy Richards, Fred Bryan, Clive Dill, Kenny Smith, William Sutherland, Norval Tormsen; *Scene 7* "You Never Know What Hit You [When it's Love]" (sung by Pearl Bailey (3)]; *Scene 8* "The Roaring 20s Strike Back" [sung by Jules Munshin (1) & Mary McCarty (2)]; *Scene 9* Finale (Entire Company).

SHOW GIRLS: Blanche Grady, Jill Melford, Kris Nodland, Gloria Olson, Del Parker, Madelyn Remini, Gwenna Lee Smith, Jeane Williams; DANCERS: Eleanor Boleyn, Carlene Carroll, Richard D'Arcy, Dorothy Etheridge, Sage Fuller, Joseph Gifford, Elmira Jones-Bey, Billie Kirpich, Vera Lee, Donald McKayle, Ilona Murai, Joe Nash, Philip Nasta, Richard "Dick" Reed, Bertram Ross, Emy St. Just, Helen Wenzel, John Sandal, Swen Swenson, Parker Wilson; SINGERS: Fred Bryan, Jane Carlyle, Clive Dill, Gordon Edwards, Noel Gordon, Geraldine Hamburg, Betsy Holland, Ray Morrissey, Dorothy Richards, Irene Riley, Kenny Smith, William Sutherland, Norval Tormsen, Eileen Turner, Grace Varik, Margaret Wright.

The show lost $229,000, despite good reviews. It won a Tony for costumes.

68. *Blood Brothers*

One of the great, long-running British musicals, although it didn't catch on in the USA and is largely forgotten there now. Set in and around Liverpool. Twin brothers separated almost at birth, who grow up in homes at opposite ends of the social spectrum. The narrator is never off stage in 87 scenes.

Before Broadway. It first ran at the LIVERPOOL PLAYHOUSE, England, 1/8/83 (11 weeks). DIRECTOR: Chris Bond; SETS/COSTUMES: Andy Greenfield; MUSICAL DIRECTOR: Richard Spanswick. Then it went to the LYRIC THEATRE, LONDON, 4/11/83–10/22/83. Previews from 4/7/83; 224 PERFORMANCES. It won Olivier Awards for best musical and for Barbara Dickson. *Cast*: MRS. JOHNSTONE: Barbara Dickson, *Eithne Brown*; NARRATOR: Andrew Schofield, *Robert McIntosh*; MRS. LYONS: Wendy Murray; MR. LYONS: Alan Leith; MICKEY: George Costigan; EDDIE: Andrew C. Wadsworth; SAMMY: Peter Christian; LINDA: Amanda York, *Kate Fitzgerald*. ENSEMBLE: Oliver Beamish, Ian Burns, Hazel Ellerbe, David Edge.

Bill Kenwright acquired the rights in 1987. It was revamped and opened at the ALBERY THEATRE, London, 7/28/88. It got rave reviews. It moved to the PHOENIX THEATRE, 11/21/91. It extended its run several times, the latest being until 10/29/05. DIRECTOR: Bob Tomson; SETS/COSTUMES: Kate Robertson; LIGHTING: Stanley Osborne-White; MUSICAL DIRECTOR: Charles Miller. *Cast*: MRS. JOHNSTONE: Kiki Dee, *Angela Richards* (89), *Barbara Dickson* (from 11/21/91), *Stephanie Lawrence, Lyn Paul* (97), *Denise Nolan* (99 for 6 months), *Lyn Paul* (03 for a week), *Linda Nolan* (03), *Lyn Paul* (from 9/1/03 for 6 months); MR. LYONS: Warwick Evans; MICKEY: Con O'Neill, *Steve McGann* (89), *Russel Boulter* (90), *Billy Fellows* (91), *Andy Snowden* (99), *Darren Morfitt* (01–02), *Stephen Palfreman*; EDDIE: Phil Hearne, *Robin Hart* (89), *Glenn McReady* (96), *Drew Ashton* (99), *Mark Hutchinson*; NARRATOR: Michael Atkinson, *Mark Jefferies* (89), *Carl* Wayne (10/90–6/96), *Philip Stewart*; MRS. LYONS: Joanne Zorian, *Helen Hobson* (89), *Vivien Parry* (90), *Joanna Munro, Sarah Hay* (99), *Gillian Kirkpatrick* (01–02), *Louisa Lydell* (02–03), *Sarah Hay*. A UK national tour opened in 1996 with Clodagh Rodgers as Mrs. Johnstone.

THE FIRST DUTCH PRODUCTION. STADSSCHOUBURG EINDHOVEN, 1989. This was the first Dutch production of *Geboren Vrienden* (*Born Friends*). Willy Russell, the author, allows a certain latitude in foreign productions. *Cast*: EDDIE: Frank Rigter; MICKEY: Danny de Munk; MEVROUW JONKERS: Joke Bruijs & Angela Groothuizen (the Mrs. Johnstone role); LINDA: Lottie Hellingman; NARRATOR: Tim Meeuws & Paul Kribbe.

The Broadway Run. MUSIC BOX THEATRE, 4/25/93–4/30/95. 13 previews from 4/14/93. 839 PERFORMANCES. PRESENTED BY Bill Kenwright; MUSIC/LYRICS/BOOK: Willy Russell; DIRECTOR: Bill Kenwright & Bob Tomson; no choreography; SETS/COSTUMES: Andy Walmsley; LIGHTING: Joe Atkins; SOUND: Paul Astbury; MUSICAL DIRECTOR: Rick Fox; PRODUCTION MUSICAL DIRECTOR: Rod Edwards; ARRANGEMENTS: Del Newman; PRESS: Philip Rinaldi & Kathy Haberthur; CASTING: Pat McCorkle, Richard Cole, Tim Sutton; GENERAL MANAGER: Stuart Thompson; COMPANY MANAGER: Bruce Klinger; PRODUCTION STAGE MANAGER: Mary Porter Hall; STAGE MANAGER: John Lucas; ASSISTANT STAGE MANAGER: Douglas Weston; REHEARSAL STAGE MANAGER: Jeffrey Markowitz. *Cast:* MRS. JOHNSTONE: Stephanie Lawrence (1) ☆, *Regina*

O'Malley (stood in), *Petula Clark* (from 8/16/93), *Carole King, Regina O'Malley, Helen Reddy*; NARRATOR: Warwick Evans (6), *Richard Cox, Adrian Zmed, Richard Cox, Domenick Allen* (from 2/7/95); MRS. LYONS: Barbara Walsh (5), *Regina O'Malley*; MR. LYONS: Ivar Brogger (7); MICKEY JOHNSTONE: Con O'Neill (2) ☆, *David Cassidy* (from 8/16/93), *Philip Lehl*; EDDIE LYONS: Mark Michael Hutchinson (3), *Shaun Cassidy, Ric Ryder*; SAMMY: James Clow (8), *John Schiappa*; LINDA: Jan Graveson (4), *Shauna Hicks*; PERKINS: Sam Samuelson; DONNA MARIE/MISS JONES: Regina O'Malley, *Kerry Butler, Jodi Jinks*; POLICEMAN/TEACHER/TEDDY BOY: Robin Haynes; BRENDA: Anne Torsiglieri, *Karyn Quackenbush*; ENSEMBLE: Ivar Brogger, Kerry Butler, James Clow, Robin Haynes, Philip Lehl, Regina O'Malley, Sam Samuelson, John Schiappa (*Nick Cokas*), Anne Torsiglieri (*Karyn Quackenbush*), Douglas Weston, Timothy Gulan, Brian d'Arcy James, Gregory Watt. **Understudies**: Mrs. Johnstone: Regina O'Malley, *Susan Tilson*; Mrs. Lyons: Regina O'Malley, *Susan Tilson, Karyn Quackenbush*; Mickey: Philip Lehl; Sammy: John Schiappa, *Robin Haynes, Nick Cokas*; Narrator: John Schiappa, *Nick Cokas*; Eddie: Sam Samuelson, *Philip Lehl, Brian d'Arcy James*; Linda: Anne Torsiglieri, *Kerry Butler, Karyn Quackenbush*; Mr. Lyons: Robin Haynes; Donna Marie: Kerry Butler. **Swings**: *John Soroka, Susan Tilson*. **Orchestra**: KEYBOARDS: Mark Berman; ACOUSTIC & ELECTRIC GUITAR: Robert Kirshoff; ACOUSTIC & ELECTRIC BASS: Bob Renino; DRUMS: Ray Grappone; PERCUSSION: Barry Centanni; REEDS: Mike Migliore & Billy Kerr; TRUMPET/FLUGELHORN: Neil Balm. *Act I*: "Marilyn Monroe" (Mrs. Johnstone), "My Child" (Mrs. Johnstone & Mrs. Lyons), "Easy Terms" (Mrs. Johnstone), "Shoes Upon the Table" (Narrator), "Easy Terms" (reprise) (Mrs. Johnstone), "Kids Game" (Sammy, Linda, Mickey, Ensemble), "Shoes Upon the Table" (reprise) (Narrator), "Shoes Upon the Table" (reprise) (Narrator), "Bright New Day" (Prelude) (Mrs. Johnstone), "Long Sunday Afternoon"/"My Friend" (Mickey & Eddie), "Bright New Day" (Mrs. Johnstone & Full Company). *Act II*: "Marilyn Monroe" (reprise) (Mrs. Johnstone), "Shoes Upon the Table" (reprise) (Narrator), "That Guy" (Mickey & Eddie), "Shoes Upon the Table" (reprise) (Narrator), "I'm Not Saying a Word" (Eddie), "Take a Letter, Miss Jones" (Mr. Lyons, Miss Jones, Ensemble), "Marilyn Monroe" (reprise) (Mrs. Johnstone), "Light Romance" (Mrs. Johnstone & Narrator), "Madman" (Narrator), "Tell Me it's Not True" (Mrs. Johnstone & Full Company).

Broadway reviews were not good. Warwick Evans, Mark Michael Hutchinson, Con O'Neill, Jan Graveson and Stephanie Lawrence all appeared on Broadway with permission of Equity, under an exchange program with British Equity. The show received Tony nominations for musical, book, direction of a musical, and for Con O'Neill, Stephanie Lawrence, Jan Graveson.

After Broadway. TOUR. Opened on 9/6/94, in Dallas. *Cast*: MRS. JOHNSTONE: Petula Clark; NARRATOR: Mark McGrath; MICKEY: David Cassidy; EDDIE: Tif Luckinbill; MRS. LYONS: Priscilla Quinby; LINDA: Yvette Lawrence.

ROYAL ALEXANDRA THEATRE, Toronto, 6/4/96. Previews from 5/30/96. 15-week run. It got mixed reviews. *Cast*: NARRATOR: Michael Burgess; MICKEY: David Cassidy; EDDIE: Mark Hutchinson; MRS. JOHNSTONE: Amy Sky (her professional acting debut); LINDA: Jan Graveson.

TEATRO DE LOS INSURGENTES, Mexico City, 5/14/98. Previews from 5/8/98. This was the Mexican premiere of *Hermanos de Sangre*. DIRECTOR: Jose Luis Ibanez (replacing the scheduled Rene Pereyra); CHOREOGRAPHER: Joan Mondellini. Juliss and her real-life sons Benny and Alejandro Ibana starred, and Aracely Arambula played Linda (replacing the scheduled Gabriela Platas). Originally scheduled for late 10/97, at Teatro Alameda 2, it was delayed by construction, then they switched theatres.

LUXOR THEATRE, Rotterdam. Dutch revival. 12/22/98. DIRECTOR: Eddy Habbema. *Cast*: NARRATOR: Paul Kribbe; MEVROUW JONKERS: Joke Bruijs (for the first two months, then she alternated with Angela Groothuizen); MICKEY: Danny de Munk; EDDIE: Frank Rigter. After Rotterdam it toured through the Netherlands until 6/99.

69. *Bloomer Girl*

Set in the spring of 1861 in Cicero Falls, NY, a small Eastern manufacturing town. Evelina is the sixth daughter of rich hoop-skirt manufacturer Horatio and his wife Serena. All of Evelina's sisters have married successful salesmen in her father's company, and Evi is about to do the same, but she is inspired to rebel against her father's choice of husband, and against his oppressive garments, by her aunt Dolly Bloomer, an advocate of the new style of women's underwear — pantalettes. Dolly was based on real-life women's advocate Amelia Bloomer. Aunt Dolly also publishes *The Lily*, an abolitionist and feminist newspaper, and with Evi's help, aids runaways slaves, one of whom, Pompey, is pursued by his master Jeff Calhoun who, when he meets Evi, falls in love with her. Their political differences separate them at the end of Act I, but they are reunited after the Civil War. Act II also depicts the war through a ballet. Alexander is another slave.

Before Broadway. This was Celeste Holm's first major role. It was a hit from the time it tried out in Philadelphia, where it had the same basic crew as for Broadway, except: GENERAL MANAGER: C.W. Hobbs; COMPANY MANAGER: Eddie Knill; GENERAL STAGE MANAGER: Ward Bishop; STAGE MANAGER: Robert Calley; ASSISTANT STAGE MANAGER: Ralph Sassano (alone). The numbers "Look North" and "Pretty as a Picture" were cut Before Broadway.

The Broadway Run. SHUBERT THEATRE, 10/5/44–4/27/46. 654 PERFORMANCES. PRESENTED BY John C. Wilson, in association with Nat Goldstone; MUSIC: Harold Arlen; LYRICS/DIRECTOR: E.Y. Harburg; BOOK: Sig Herzig & Fred Saidy; BASED ON an unproduced play by Lilith & Dan James; BOOK DIRECTOR: William Schorr; CHOREOGRAPHER: Agnes de Mille; SETS/LIGHTING: Lemuel Ayers; COSTUMES: Miles White; MUSICAL DIRECTOR: Leon Leonardi, *Frank Cork*; ORCHESTRATIONS: Russell Bennett; CAST RECORDING on Decca; PRESS: Willard Keefe & David Tebet; CASTING: William Liebling; GENERAL MANAGER: C. Edwin Knill; COMPANY MANAGER: James Troup; GENERAL STAGE MANAGER: Robert Calley; ASSISTANT STAGE MANAGERS: Ralph Sassano & Richard Haas. *Cast:* SERENA APPLEGATE: Mabel Taliaferro (6); THE (FIVE) APPLEGATE DAUGHTERS: OCTAVIA: Pamela Randell, *Eleanor Jones*; LYDIA: Claudia Jordan; JULIA: Toni Hart, *Janie Janvier*; PHOEBE: Carol MacFarlane, *Arlene Anderson*; DELIA: Nancy Douglass; DAISY: Joan McCracken (3), *Dorothy Jarnac*; HORATIO APPLEGATE: Matt Briggs (7); GUS: John Call; EVELINA APPLEGATE: Celeste Holm (1), *Nanette Fabray*; THE (FIVE) SONS-IN-LAW: JOSHUA DINGLE: Robert Lyon, *Ben Murphy*; HERMAN BRASHER: William Bender, *Feodore Tedick*; EBENEZER MIMMS: Joe E. Marks; WILFRED THRUSH: Vaughn Trinnier; HIRAM CRUMP: Dan Gallagher; DOLLY BLOOMER: Margaret Douglass (2); JEFFERSON CALHOUN: David Brooks (4); PAULA: Lee Barrie, *Mathilda Strazza*; PRUDENCE: Eleanor Jones, *Harriet Hall*; HETTY: Arlene Anderson, *Terry Saunders, Gloria Tromara*; BETTY: Eleanor Winter; HAMILTON CALHOUN: Blaine Cordner; POMPEY: Dooley Wilson (5); SHERIFF QUIMBY: Charles Howard; 1ST DEPUTY: John Byrd; 2ND DEPUTY: Joseph Florestano; 3RD DEPUTY: Ralph Sassano; AUGUSTUS: Hubert Dilworth; ALEXANDER: Richard Huey; STATE OFFICIAL: John Byrd; GOVERNOR NEWTON: Butler Hixon; VOCAL ENSEMBLE: Arlene Anderson (*Terry Saunders, Gloria Tromara*), Lee Barrie (*Mathilda Strazza*), Ray Cook, Joseph Florestano, Alan Gilbert, Eleanor Jones (*Harriet Hall*), Byron Milligan, Alice Richmond, Henry Roberts, Ralph Sassano, Eleanor Winter, *Dorothy Baxter, Florence Berline, Adele Lulince, Brian Otis, Carlos Sherman, Claire Stevens*; DANCERS: Richard D'Arcy, Frank De Winters, Lidija Franklin, Phyllis Gehrig, Arthur Grahl, Theresa Gushurst, Dorothy Hill, Peggy Holmes, Elena Karina, Carmelita Lanza, Betty Low, Joan Mann, James Mitchell, Kathleen O'Brien, Art Partington, Emy St. Just, Jack Starr, William Weber, *Cecile Bergman, John Duane, Jean Faust, Jean Houloose, Lucas Hoving, Jack L. Nagle, Paul Olson, David Reher, Jimmy Russell, John Ward.* *Act I*: Overture (Orchestra); *Scene 1* Conservatory of the Applegate mansion; spring, 1861: "When the Boys Come Home" (Daughters & Sons-in-Law) [in tryouts it was Serena & Daughters], "Evelina" (Jeff & Evelina) [a big hit], "Welcome Hinges" (Serena, Horatio, Evelina, Jeff, Daughters, Sons-in-Law); *Scene 2* The Applegate bathroom; half an hour later: "Farmer's Daughter" (Sons-in-Law); *Scene 3* A former bordello, now the offices of *The Lily*; a few hours later: "(It Was) Good Enough for Grandma" (Evelina, Daisy, Dolly, Suffragettes), "Dance Specialty" (Daisy & Dancers), "The Eagle and Me" (Pompey & Ensemble),

"Right as the Rain" (Jeff & Evelina); *Scene 4* A hedge outside the Applegate estate; the following Saturday afternoon: "T'morra, T'morra" (Daisy); *Scene 5* The Yellow Pavilion (the buyers' pavilion); that evening: "Rakish Young Man with the Whiskers" (Evelina & Ensemble) [in tryouts it was Evelina & Jeff]; *Scene 6* Garden of the Applegate mansion; a few minutes later: "Pretty as a Picture" (Men) [cut for Broadway], Waltz [Dancers — The Waltzers (tryout cast): Lidija Franklin & James Mitchell, Joan Mann, Theresa Gushurst, Kathleen O'Brien, Phyllis Gehrig, Richard Darcy, Arthur Grahl, William Weber, Art Partington], "Style Show Ballet" (Principals & Dancers). *Act II*: Entr'acte (Orchestra); *Scene 1* Village green; next day: "Sunday in Cicero Falls" (Principals & Company); *Scene 2* Corridor of town jail; next morning: "I Got a Song" (Alexander, with Augustus & Pompey), "Lullaby" ("Satin Gown and Silver Shoe") (Evelina); *Scene 3* Stage of Cicero Falls Opera House; that night: "Simon Legree" (Mr. Florestano), "Liza Crossing the Ice" (Phoebe & Ensemble) (danced by Emy St. Just), "I Never Was Borned" (Daisy), "Man for Sale" (Pompey); *Scene 4* Conservatory of the Applegate mansion; morning, a week later: "Civil War Ballet" (Dancers). WOMAN IN BLACK AND RED: Betty Low; GIRL IN ROSE: Lidija Franklin; HER SOLDIER: James Mitchell; "The Eagle and Me" (reprise) (Ensemble), "When the Boys Come Home" (reprise) (Entire Company).

Broadway reviews were divided (several raves, one pan, and some in between). Agnes de Mille's ballet of the women waiting for their husbands to return after the War made a huge impact considering this show was produced during World War II. However, the writers and producers had wanted her to cut it, as they thought it too depressing, but she insisted, and it became a highlight. There was (as in *The King and I* later) a miniature version of Uncle Tom's Cabin inserted. The show made *Life*'s cover story in the 11/6/44 edition — "Broadway Hit: Bloomer Girl." The show won Donaldson Awards for costumes and for Joan McCracken.

After Broadway. TOUR. 1946. It included Boston (from 5/6/46). *Cast*: EVELINA: Nanette Fabray; JEFF: Dick Smart; DAISY: Peggy Campbell; POMPEY: Dooley Wilson. This touring company returned to New York, to CITY CENTER, 1/6/47–2/15/47. 48 PERFORMANCES. Top ticket prices were $2.40. It had the same basic crew, except MUSICAL DIRECTOR: Jerry Arlen. *Cast*: SERENA: Mabel Taliaferro; OCTAVIA: Holly Harris; LYDIA: Ellen Leslie; JULIA: Dorothy Cothran; PHOEBE: Claire Stevens; DELIA: Claire Minter; DAISY: Peggy Campbell; HORATIO: Matt Briggs; GUS: John Call; EVELINA: Nanette Fabray; JOSHUA: Carlos Sherman; HERMAN: William Bender; EBENEZER: Lester Towne; WILFRED: Byron Milligan; HIRAM: Walter Russell; DOLLY: Olive Reeves-Smith; JEFF: Dick Smart; PAULA: Lily Paget; PRUDENCE: Noella Peloquin; HETTY: Alice Ward; HAMILTON/STATE OFFICIAL: John Byrd; POMPEY: Hubert Dilworth; SHERIFF: Joe E. Marks; 1ST DEPUTY: Edward Chappel; 2ND DEPUTY: Ralph Sassano; 3RD DEPUTY: Donald Green; AUGUSTUS: Arthur Lawson; GOVERNOR: Sidney Bassler; DANCERS INCLUDED: Margit De Kova, Emy St. Just, Virginia Bosler, Ruth Mitchell, Susan Stewart, Scott Merrill. On 7/24/49, in Dallas, while Nanette Fabray was starring in the touring company, an insect got lodged in her costume. Miss Fabray had bug phobia, went hysterical & had to be taken to the hospital.

PAPER MILL PLAYHOUSE, New Jersey, 1949. *Cast*: Andzia Kuzak, Stephen Douglass, Peggy Campbell.

NBC TV PRODUCTION. 5/28/56. *Cast*: EVELINA: Barbara Cook; JEFF: Keith Andes.

ST. CLEMENT'S CHURCH THEATRE, NYC (150 seats), 9/7/00–9/24/00. Previews from 8/31/00. This was the first New York revival. PRESENTED BY Cotton Blossom Musicals; DIRECTOR: Alisa Roost. The numbers "Look North" and "Pretty as a Picture," both cut for the original Broadway run, were back for this one. *Cast*: EVELINA: Meghan Maguire; JEFF: Geoff Sullivan; DOLLY: Maryellen Conroy.

CITY CENTER, NYC, 3/22/01–3/25/01. 5 PERFORMANCES. In concert. Part of the *Encores!* series. ADAPTED BY David Ives; DIRECTOR: Brad Rouse; CHOREOGRAPHER: Rob Ashford; SETS: John Lee Beatty; COSTUMES: Toni-Leslie James; LIGHTING: Ken Billington; SOUND: Scott Lehrer. *Cast*: SERENA: Anita Gillette; OCTAVIA: Michele Ragusa; LYDIA: Joy Hermalyn; JULIA: Ann Kittredge; PHOEBE: Teri Hansen; DELIA: Gay Willis; DAISY: Donna Lynne Champlin; HORATIO: Philip Bosco; EVELINA: Kate Jennings Grant; EBENEZER: Eddie Korbich; DOLLY: Kathleen Chalfant; JEFF: Michael Park; POMPEY: Jubilant Sykes; HAMILTON:

Herndon Lackey; BALLET SOLOISTS: Karine Plantadit-Bageot, Nina Goldman, Robert Wersinger, Todd Hunter.

70. *Blossom Time*

Fictionalized account of the life and work of composer Schubert, told in operetta form. Young Franz is a shy man whose career is sponsored by Herr Kranz, a wealthy patron of the arts. Kranz has 3 daughters — Mitzi, Kitzi and Fritzi. Franz falls for Mitzi, and writes a love song for her. In his place, Franz gets handsome Baron Schober to sing the song, and she falls for the baron. Because of his anguish over this Franz is unable to finish his Eighth Symphony (the famous *Unfinished Symphony*), which contains the melody the show's love song was based on. He composes his final masterpiece, the Ave Maria, then dies of broken heart.

Before Broadway. The original ran on Broadway at the AMBASSADOR THEATRE, 9/29/21–7/1/22. 319 PERFORMANCES. It re-opened, at the same venue, on 8/7/22. Then it moved to JOLSON'S 59TH STREET THEATRE, on 10/2/22, and again to the CENTURY THEATRE, on 10/23/22, and closed there on 1/27/23, after a total of 516 PERFORMANCES. PRESENTED BY The Shuberts; DIRECTOR: J.C. Huffman. *Cast*: SCHOBER: Howard Marsh; SCHUBERT: Bertram Peacock; KRANZ: William Danforth; MITZI: Olga Cook; VOGL: Roy Cropper.

On 5/21/23 the Shuberts opened *Blossom Time* in two different Broadway theatres, with the same basic crew for both, but with different casts. DIRECTOR: J.C. Huffman; SETS: Watson Barratt. The first, at the SHUBERT THEATRE, closed on 6/9/23, after 24 PERFORMANCES. *Cast*: SCHUBERT: Hollis Davenny; SCHOBER: Roy Cropper; GRETA: Dorothy Seegar. The second, at the 44TH STREET THEATRE, closed on 6/2/23, after 16 PERFORMANCES. *Cast*: SCHUBERT: Joseph Mendelsohn; SCHOBER: John Clarke; GRETA: Ferne Newell; SHARNTOFF: Gregory Ratoff.

JOLSON'S 59TH STREET THEATRE, 5/19/24–6/7/24. 24 PERFORMANCES. PRESENTED BY the Messrs Shubert. *Cast*: SCHOBER: Howard Marsh; SCHUBERT: Greek Evans; SHARNTOFF: Gregory Ratoff.

JOLSON'S 59TH STREET THEATRE, 3/8/26–3/20/26. 16 PERFORMANCES. DIRECTOR: J.C. Huffman; SETS: Watson Barratt. *Cast*: SCHUBERT: Knight MacGregor.

AMBASSADOR THEATRE, 3/4/31–3/28/31. 29 PERFORMANCES. DIRECTOR: Edward Scanlon. *Cast*: SCHUBERT: John Charles Gilbert.

46TH STREET THEATRE, 12/26/38–1/10/39. 19 PERFORMANCES. PRESENTED BY the Messrs Shubert; DIRECTOR: Edward Scanlon; SETS: Watson Barratt. *Cast*: SCHUBERT: Everett Marshall; MITZI: Mary McCoy; KRANZ: Douglas Leavitt; SCHOBER: Roy Cropper.

The Broadway Run. AMBASSADOR THEATRE, 9/4/43–10/9/43. 47 PERFORMANCES. PRESENTED BY Messrs Shubert; MUSIC: Sigmund Romberg; LYRICS/BOOK: Dorothy Donnelly; the operetta was an adaptation by Miss Donnelly of the Viennese original, *Das Dreimaedlerhaus* (*The Home of Three Girls*) by A.M. Willner & Heinz Reichert, with Sig Romberg's adaptations & augmentations of melodies by Franz Schubert & Heinrich Berthe; the original idea came from Rudolf H. Bartsch's novel *Schwammerl*; DIRECTOR: J.J. Shubert; CHOREOGRAPHER: Carthay; SETS: Watson Barratt; COSTUMES: Stage Costumes, Inc.; MUSICAL DIRECTOR: Pierre de Reeder. *Cast*: FRANZ SCHUBERT: Alexander Gray (1); CHRISTIAN KRANZ, COURT JEWELER: Doug Leavitt; BARON SCHOBER, A VIENNESE SOCIALITE: Roy Cropper (3); COUNT SCHARNTOFF, THE DANISH AMBASSADOR: Robert Chisholm; THE (THREE) DAUGHTERS OF CHRISTIAN KRANZ: MITZI: Barbara Scully (2); FRITZI: Adelaide Bishop, *Monna Montes*; KITZI: Loraine Manners; BELLABRUNA, COUNTESS SHARNTOFF: Helene Arthur; FLOWER GIRL: Helen Thompson, *Adelaide Bishop*; MRS. KRANZ: Zella Russell; GRETA, MAID: Jacqueline Susann; ROSIE, BELLABRUNA'S MAID: Helene Le Berthon; MRS. COBURG, SCHUBERT'S HOUSEKEEPER: Pamela Dow, *Jane Spelvin*; VOGEL, TENOR AT THE ROYAL OPERA: Roy Barnes; VON SCHWINDT, A PAINTER: George Mitchell, *George Beach*; KUPPELWEISER: Nord Cornell; NOVOTNY, A PRIVATE DETECTIVE: Harry K. Morton; DOMEYER, RESTAURANT PROPRIETOR: Walter Johnson; ERKMAN, SUITOR OF FRITZI: George Beach, *Willard Charles Fry*; BINDER: John O'Neill; WAITRESS: Alice Drake;

WAITER: Walter Johnson; PRIMA BALLERINA: Monna Montes; FLOWER GIRLS/BRIDESMAIDS: Gloria Sterling, Marcella Markham, Edith Vincent, Jay Flower, V. Stowe; BALLET GIRLS: Jacqueline Jacoby, Aura Vainio, Virginia Meyer, Mary Grey, Frances Spelz, Greta Borjosen, Lola Balser. *Act I*: Domeyer's restaurant in the Prater in Vienna; twilight in May, 1826: Opening (Emmy, Kuppelweiser, Schwindt, Vogel, Ensemble), "Melody Triste" (Bellabruna & Scharntoff), "Three Little Maids" (Mitzi, Fritzi, Kitzi, Chorus), "Serenade" (Schubert, Kuppelweiser, Vogel, Schober, Schwind), "My Springtime Thou Art" (Schober, Schubert, Vogel, Kuppelweiser, Schwind, Corps de Ballet, Ensemble), "Song of Love" (Schubert & Mitzi), Finale (Entire Company). *Act II*: Drawing-room in the house of Kranz; three months later: "Hark! The Lark" (Entire Ensemble); Interlude Musicale (Schubert & Girls). Ballet a la Degas by Carthay. Danced by Miss Montes; "Love is a Riddle" (Schober, Binder, Erkman, Mitzi, Fritzi, Kitzi), "Let Me Awake" (Bellabruna & Schober), "Tell Me, Daisy" (Mitzi & Schubert), "Only One Love Ever Fills My Heart" (Mitzi & Schober), Finale (Mitzi, Schubert, Schober). *Act III*: Franz Schubert's lodgings; two months later: "Keep it Dark" (Bellabruna, Vogel, Schwind, Kuppelweiser), "(Peace to My) Lonely Heart" (Mitzi & Schubert), Finale (Entire Company).

1943 Broadway reviews were terrible.

After Broadway. There was a post–Broadway tour.

71. *Blue Holiday*

An all-black variety show.

Before Broadway. Originally called *The Wishing Tree*. After the name change, but before it arrived on Broadway, this is how the program looked [information for each scene is as for the actual Broadway run, unless noted otherwise. The designation Scene 1, Scene 2, etc, was not in the program, but is used here merely to facilitate reading. However, Part 1, etc, was in the program. Similarly with the actual Broadway run]: *Part I*: *Scene 1* "Fiji Island"; *Scene 2* Willie Bryant; *Scene 3* Muriel Gaines [cut before Broadway]: "Alley Cat" (calypso), "Three Little Fishes and Five Loaves of Bread" (by Bernie Hanighen), "True Man True" (by Morey Amsterdam); *Scene 4* The Three Poms; *Scene 5* Timmie Rogers; *Scene 6* Mary Lou Williams; *Scene 7* "Voodoo in Haiti" & Chant; *Scene 8* Miss Ethel Waters with Marian Roberts at piano; *Scene 9* The Hall Johnson Choir. *Part II*: *Scene 1* Lillian Fitzgerald: "I Want to Give it All to the Stage" [cut before Broadway], "Blue Holiday"; *Scene 2* Willie Bryant; *Scene 3* Josephine Premice (Haitian songs & dances); *Scene 4* Charles Holland [cut before Broadway]: "That's Where My Heart Will Be" (by Al Moritz), Flower Song from *Carmen*, "Yours is My Heart Alone" (by Franz Lehar); *Scene 5* Miss Ethel Waters in *Mamba's Daughters*; *Scene 6* Josh White (2) (singer): a/ "Outskirts of Town" & "Hard Time Blues," b/ "Evil-Hearted Man," c/ "The House I Live In"; *Scene 7* The Chocolateers; Scene 8 Free and Equal: "Free and Equal Blues" (Entire Company).

When Jed Harris took over from Moe Hack as director before Broadway (Mr. Harris was unbilled), he cut the show by half an hour and re-shaped it.

The Broadway Run. BELASCO THEATRE, 5/21/45–5/26/45. 8 PERFORMANCES. PRESENTED BY Irvin Shapiro & Doris Cole; MUSIC/LYRICS: Al Moritz; ADDITIONAL SONGS: Duke Ellington, E.Y. Harburg, Earl Robinson; DIRECTOR/LIGHTING: Monroe B. Hack; CHOREOGRAPHER: Katherine Dunham; SETS: Perry Watkins; COSTUMES: Kasia; MUSICAL DIRECTOR: Billy Butler; CHORAL DIRECTOR: Hall Johnson; PRESS: Bernard Simon; CASTING: Max Richard; GENERAL MANAGER: Gerald Goode; COMPANY MANAGER: Joseph Moss; GENERAL STAGE MANAGER: Harry Altner; ASSISTANT STAGE MANAGER: J. DeWitt Spencer. *Act I*: *Scene 1* "The Star-Spangled Banner" [Hall Johnson Choir (6)], "Blue Holiday" (by Al Moritz) (sung by Lillian Fitzgerald); *Scene 2* Willie Bryant (3) (master of ceremonies/comedian); *Scene 3* The Three Poms (dancers); *Scene 4* "Voodoo in Haiti" (created & staged by Miss Dunham) [The Katherine Dunham Dancers (5), featuring Josephine Premice]. Chant (ch: Katherine Dunham) [the Hall Johnson Choir (6)]; *Scene 5* Timmie Rogers (4) (comedian); *Scene 6* Miss Ethel Waters (1) ☆ enacts two scenes from her dramatic success *Mamba's Daughters*, by DuBose & Dorothy Heyward, courtesy of Guthrie McClintic): HAGAR:

Ethel Waters; GILLY BLUTON: Willie Bryant; MAMBA: Evelyn Ellis; LISSA: Mildred Smith. "Sleep Time Lullaby" (by Al Moritz) (sung by Miss Waters); *Scene 7* Josh White (2) (singer): "Hard Time Blues" (m/l: Josh White & Warren Cuney), "Evil-Hearted Man" (traditional song, arranged by Josh White), "The House I Live In" (m/l: Lewis Allan & Earl Robinson), "(I'm Gonna Move to the) Outskirts of Town" (m/l: William Weldon, Andy Razaf, Louis Jordan), "One Meat Ball" (m: Lou Singer; l: Hy Zaret); *Scene 8* "Free and Equal Blues" (m: Earl Robinson; l: E.Y. Harburg) (written specially for the election-eve broadcast made for Roosevelt in Nov. 1944 by the Independent Voters Committee of the Arts and Sciences) (Josh White, Timmie Rogers, Hall Johnson Choir). *Act II: Scene 1* "Fiji Island" (created & staged by Miss Dunham) (m: Herbert Kingsley) [Katherine Dunham Dancers (5), featuring Lavinia Williams & Talley Beatty. Roxie Foster danced Miss Williams' part at matinees]; *Scene 2* Mary Lou Williams (7) (jazz pianist): "Limehouse Blues," Duke Ellington Medley: "Mood Indigo," "Sophisticated Lady," "Solitude," Boogie (by Mary Lou Williams); *Scene 3* Josephine Premice: Haitian songs & dances: "Philomene, The Lazy Girl," "Angelico," "Nibo — The Carnival"; *Scene 4* The Hall Johnson Choir (6): choral arrangement by Hall Johnson: "I Got a Mule" (traditional song), "Fare Ye Well" (traditional spiritual), "Saint Louis Blues" (by W.C. Handy); *Scene 5* The Chocolateers (dancers); *Scene 6* Miss Ethel Waters (1) ✫ with Marian Roberts at piano: "Stormy Weather" (m: Harold Arlen; l: Ted Koehler) [from *Cotton Club Parade*, 23rd Edition], "Happiness is a Thing Called Joe" (m: Harold Arlen; l: E.Y. Harburg) [from the movie *Cabin in the Sky*].

The Katherine Dunham Dancers: LEADERS: Lavinia Williams, Talley Beatty, Florence Moriles, Roxie Foster; DRUMMER: Henri Augustine; *Dancers*: Wilbert Bradley, Tempy Fletcher, Jesse Hawkins, Victoria Henderson, Richard James, Eartha Kitt (her Broadway debut), Alveta Hudson, Albert Popwell, Eugene Robinson, Joe Smith, J. DeWitt Spencer, John Weaver, Enid Williams; THE HALL JOHNSON CHOIR: Laura Adamson, James Armstrong, Olive Ball, Mabel Bergen, Maudiva Brown, William Davis, Bessie Guy, Lola Hayes, Violet McDowell, Ruthena Matson, Willie Mays, Massie Patterson, Bertha Powell, George Rayston, Jessie Williams, Robert Woodland.

Due to open on Broadway on 5/18/45, it was late. It was panned by reviewers.

72. *Blues in the Night*

A musical revue. Set in a cheap Chicago hotel, in 1938; three women, a saloon singer, and the music that gets them through the long, lonely night.

Before Broadway. The show premiered Off Broadway, at PLAYHOUSE 46, 3/26/80–5/11/80. 51 PERFORMANCES. PRESENTED BY the Production Company (Norman Rene, artistic director; Samuel Platt, executive director); DIRECTOR: Sheldon Epps; CHOREOGRAPHER: Gregory Hines; COSTUMES: Jeanette Oleska; LIGHTING: Debra J. Kletter; VOCAL & MUSICAL ARRANGEMENTS: Chapman Roberts; PRESS: Clarence Allsopp; PRODUCTION STAGE MANAGER: Consuelo Mira. *Cast*: David Brunetti, Rise Collins, Suzanne M. Henry, Gwen Shepherd. *Act I*: "Blue Blue" (Company); "Four Walls Blues" (David); "Stompin' at the Savoy" (Rise); "New Orleans Hop Scop Blues" (Gwen); "It Makes My Love Come Down" (Women); "Copenhagen" (Suzanne); "Lush Life"/"Sophisticated Lady" (Rise & David); "Take Me for a Buggy Ride" (Gwen); "Willow Weep for Me" (Suzanne); "Kitchen Man" (Gwen); "Take it Right Back" (Women). *Act II*: "Blues in the Night" (Rise & Suzanne); "When a Woman Loves a Man"/"Am I Blue" (Company); "Something to Live For" (Rise); "Reckless Blues" (Suzanne); "Wasted Life Blues" (Gwen); "Baby Doll" (David); "Nobody Knows You When You're Down and Out" (Women); "I Gotta Right to Sing the Blues" (Company); "Blue Blues"/"Blues in the Night" (reprise) (Company).

Ruth Brown played Woman # 3 during Broadway previews.

The Broadway Run. RIALTO THEATRE, 6/2/82–7/18/82. 13 previews from 5/20/82. 53 PERFORMANCES. PRESENTED BY Mitchell Maxwell, Alan J. Schuster, Fred H. Krones, M2 Entertainment; MUSIC/LYRICS: various authors; CONCEIVED BY/DIRECTOR: Sheldon Epps;

CHOREOGRAPHER: Mercedes Ellington; SETS: John Falabella; COSTUMES: David Murin; LIGHTING: Ken Billington; SOUND: Bill Merrill; MUSICAL SUPERVISOR/VOCAL ARRANGEMENTS: Chapman Roberts; MUSICAL DIRECTOR/ORCHESTRATIONS: Chapman Roberts & Sy Johnson; ARRANGEMENTS/ADDITIONAL VOCAL ARRANGEMENTS: Sy Johnson; PRESS: Judy Jacksina, Glenna Freedman, Diane Tomlinson; CASTING: Chapman Roberts & Jim Pitt; GENERAL MANAGEMENT: M2 Entertainment; COMPANY MANAGER: Paul Matwiow; PRODUCTION STAGE MANAGER: Zoya Wyeth; STAGE MANAGER: William D. Buxton Jr.; ASSISTANT STAGE MANAGER: David Brunetti. *Cast*: WOMAN # 1: Leslie Uggams (1) ✫; WOMAN # 2: Debbie Shapiro (3) ✫; WOMAN # 3: Jean Du Shon (2) ✫; SALOON SINGER: Charles Coleman (4). *Standbys*: Women: Ann Duquesnay; Singer: David Brunetti. *Act I*: "Blue Blue" (m/l: Bessie Smith) (Company), "Four-Walls-and-One-Dirty-Window Blues" (m/l: Willard Robison) (Saloon Singer), "I've Got a Date with a Dream" (m: Harry Revel; l: Mack Gordon) [from the movie *My Lucky Star*] (Women # 1 & 2), "These Foolish Things (Remind Me of You)" (m: Harry Link, Jack Strachey; l: Holt Marvell, who was actually Eric Maschwitz) [from the London production of *New Faces*] (Woman # 1) [not on tour or in the 1987 revival], "New Orleans Hop Scop Blues" (m/l: Geo. W. Thomas) (Woman # 3), "It Makes My Love Come Down" (m/l: Bessie Smith) (Women # 1,2,3), "Copenhagen" (m: Charlie Davis; l: Walter Melrose) (Woman # 2) [not on tour or in the 1987 revival], "Stompin' at the Savoy" (by Benny Goodman, Andy Razaf, Edgar Sampson, Chick Webb) (Woman # 2) [only on tour and in 1987 revival], "Takin' a Chance on Love" (by Vernon Duke, John Latouche, Ted Fetter) (Woman # 3) [only on tour and in the 1987 revival], "Lush Life" (by Billy Strayhorn) (Woman # 2) [only on tour and in the 1987 revival], "I'm Just a Lucky So-and-So" (m: Duke Ellington; l: Mack David) [only in the 1987 revival], "Wild Women Don't Have the Blues" (m/l: Ida Cox) (Saloon Singer), "Lover Man" (m/l: Jimmie Davis, Roger "Ram" Ramirez, Jimmy Sherman) (Woman # 1), "Take Me for a Buggy Ride" (m/l: Leola Wilson & Wesley Wilson) (Woman # 3) [not in the 1987 revival], "Willow, Weep for Me" (m/l: Ann Ronell) (Woman # 2), "Kitchen Man" (m/l: Andy Razaf & Alex Belledna) (Woman # 3), "Low" (m/l: Vernon Duke, Milton Drake, Ben Oakland) (Woman # 1) [not in the 1987 revival], "When Your Lover Has Gone" (by A.E. Swan) [only in the 1987 revival], "Take it Right Back" (m/l: H. Grey) (Women # 1,2,3), "Jam Session" [only on tour, and in the 1987 revival, where it opened Act II]. ACT II: "Wild Women Don't Have the Blues" (reprise) (The Band) [not in 1987 revival], "Blues in the Night" (m: Harold Arlen; l: Johnny Mercer) [from the movie of the same name] (Women # 1 & 2), "Dirty-No-Gooder Blues" (m/l: Bessie Smith) (Woman # 3), "When a Woman Loves a Man" (m: Bernard Hanighen & Gordon Jenkins; l: Johnny Mercer) (Saloon Singer), "Am I Blue" (m: Harry Akst; l: Grant Drake) [from the movie *On With The Show*] (Women # 1,2,3), "Rough and Ready Man" (m/l: Alberta Hunter) (Woman # 1), "Reckless Blues" (m/l: Bessie Smith) (Woman # 2), "Wasted Life Blues" (m/l: Bessie Smith) (Woman # 3), "Baby Doll" (m/l: Bessie Smith) (Saloon Singer), "Nobody Knows You When You're Down and Out" (m/l: Jimmy Cox) (voc arr: Sy Johnson) (Women # 1,2,3), "I Gotta Right to Sing the Blues" (m: Harold Arlen; l: Ted Koehler) [from *Earl Carroll's Vanities*, 1932] (Women # 1,2,3), "Blue Blue"/"Blues in the Night" (reprise) (Women # 1,2,3) (in the 1987 revival a reprise of "Four Walls" was here).

Reviews were generally terrible. The production received a Tony nomination for musical.

After Broadway. TOUR. Opened during the 82–83 season. PRESENTED BY Blues Tours. *Cast*: GIRL WITH A DATE: Neva Small; WOMAN OF THE WORLD: Cynthia White; LADY FROM THE ROAD: Della Reese; SALOON SINGER: Clem Moorman. *Standby*: Jean Trevor. It re-opened on 3/4/85, at Blacksburg, Va., and closed on 3/24/85, at Woodlands, Texas. DIRECTOR: Mitchell Maxwell; SETS: Randel Wright; COSTUMES: Patty Greer McGarity; LIGHTING: Doug Kolbo; MUSICAL SUPERVISOR: David Brunetti; MUSICAL DIRECTOR: Clem Moorman. *Cast*: GIRL WITH A DATE: Liz Larsen; WOMAN OF THE WORLD: Eartha Kitt; LADY FROM THE ROAD: Carrie Smith; SALOON SINGER: Clem Moorman.

DONMAR WAREHOUSE, London, 6/12/87–7/19/87; PICCADILLY THEATRE, London, 9/28/87. This production, a new version, won an Olivier Award. In the USA it first played at the MINETTA LANE THEATRE, NYC, 9/16/88–10/23/88. 16 previews from 8/30/88. 45 PERFOR-

MANCES. PRESENTED BY M2 Entertainment & TV Asahi, in association with Joshua Silver & Victoria Maxwell; DIRECTOR: Sheldon Epps; SETS/COSTUMES: Michael Pavelka; LIGHTING: Susan A. White; SOUND: Charles Bugbee III; MUSICAL SUPERVISOR/ARRANGEMENTS/ORCHESTRATIONS: Sy Johnson; MUSICAL DIRECTOR/ADDITIONAL ARRANGEMENTS: David Brunetti. *Cast*: LADY FROM THE ROAD: Carol Woods; WOMAN OF THE WORLD: Brenda Pressley; GIRL WITH A DATE: Leilani Jones; MAN IN THE SALOON: Lawrence Hamilton. *Understudy*: For Mr. Hamilton: C.E. Smith. *Band*: PIANIST: David Brunetti; DRUMS: Keith Copeland; BASS: Fred Hunter; TRUMPET: Virgil Jones; REEDS: Bill Easley.

TOM BRADLEY THEATRE, Los Angeles, 90–91 season. This was the West Coast premiere. DIRECTOR: Sheldon Epps; CHOREOGRAPHER: Patricia Wilcox; SETS/LIGHTING: Douglas D. Smith; MUSICAL DIRECTOR: Perry Hart. *Cast*: Obba Babatunde, Joanne Jackson, Leilani Jones, Freda Payne.

73. *The Body Beautiful*

A mild young man in New York City wants to be a boxer.

Before Broadway. This was Bock & Harnick's first musical as a team. Cut before opening were: "Every Man for Himself," "He's Our Boy," "Hidden in My Heart," "The Manly Art of Self Defense," "Mother, Come and Fight with Me," and "Ooh, Merci Beaucoup."

The Broadway Run. BROADWAY THEATRE, 1/23/58–3/15/58. 60 PERFORMANCES. PRESENTED BY Richard Kollmar & Albert Selden; MUSIC: Jerry Bock; LYRICS: Sheldon Harnick; BOOK: Joseph Stein & Will Glickman; DIRECTOR: George Schaefer; CHOREOGRAPHER: Herbert Ross; SETS/LIGHTING: William & Jean Eckart; COSTUMES: Noel Taylor; MUSICAL DIRECTOR/VOCAL ARRANGEMENTS: Milton Greene; ORCHESTRATIONS: Ted Royal; BALLET MUSIC: Genevieve Pitot; PRESS: Frank Goodman; GENERAL MANAGER: Walter Fried; PRODUCTION STAGE MANAGER: Michael Ellis; STAGE MANAGERS: Paul Leaf & Henry Beckman. *Cast*: DAVE: Jack Warden (2); ALBERT: William Hickey; HARRY: Lonnie Sattin (4); BOB: Steve Forrest (3); ANN: Mindy Carson (1); DOMINIC: Edward Becker; EDDIE: Tom Raskin; RICHIE: Bob Wiensko; FLORENCE: Jane Romano; BOXER: Bill Richards; HANDLER: Knute Sullivan; FRANK: Richard Chitos; NICKY: Tony Atkins; TRAINER: Albert Popwell; BOXER: Bob Wiensko; MARGE: Barbara McNair (5); JANE: Helen Silver; KATHY: Kathie Forman; DANNY: Tommy Halloran; GEORGE: Armand Bonay; ARTIE: Jeff Roberts; JOSH: Alan Weeks; PETE: Richard DeBella; PHIL: Edmund Gaynes; ANNOUNCER: Jack De Lon; REFEREE: Bill Richards; REPORTERS: Mace Barrett, Harry Lee Rogers, Mitchell Nutick, Stanley Papich; GLORIA: Mara Lynn; CAMPBELL: Mark Allen; TWO MEN: Knute Sullivan & Jack DeLon; BEN: Joe Ross; SINGERS: Dorothy Aull, Mace Barrett, Edward Becker, Jack De Lon, Bette Graham, Buzz Halliday, Mary Louise, Brock Peters, Tom Raskin, Joe Ross, Knute Sullivan, Bob Wiensko; DANCERS: Jeanna Belkin, Bob Daley, Ethelyne Dunfee, Shellie Farrell, Patti Karr, Patsi King, Louis Kosman, James McAnany, Ralph McWilliams, Mitchell Nutick, Stanley Papich, Albert Popwell, Nora Reho, Bill Richards, Harry Lee Rogers, Yvonne Othon. *Standby*: Dave: Henry Beckman. *Understudies*: Marge: Mary Louise; Harry: Brock Peters; Bob: Mace Barrett; Ann: Dorothy Aull; Campbell: Knute Sullivan; Florence: Bette Graham; Jane: Buzz Halliday; Gloria: Patti Karr; Frank: Armand Bonay. *Act I*: *Scene 1* Dave Coleman's office & the Gym; *Scene 2* Corridor of the Jersey City Arena; next night; *Scene 3* The Gym; the following day; *Scene 4* The office; *Scene 5* Community Center Playground & nearby street; *Scene 6* Several stadiums; *Scene 7* Another section of the Gym; a few weeks later; *Scene 8* The office; *Scene 9* Dressing rooms in the Hartford Arena; *Scene 10* The Arena. *Act II*: *Scene 1* Summer training camp; a few days later; *Scene 2* Several stadiums; *Scene 3* The office; three months later; *Scene 4* A steam bath; *Scene 5* The street; *Scene 6* Terrace & ballroom of the Stockton home; *Scene 7* Dressing rooms; *Scene 8* A stadium corridor. *Act I*: "Where Are They?" (Dave, Boy Dancers, Boy Singers), "The Body Beautiful" (Ann, with Bob Daley, Louis Kosman, Mitchell Nutick, Bill Richards, Harry Lee Rogers), "Pffft!" (Bob & Albert) [dropped during the run], "Fair Warning" (Marge & Harry, with Dorothy Aull, Bette Graham, Buzz Halliday, Mary Louise, Mace Barrett, Jack DeLon, Tom Raskin, Knute Sullivan), "Leave Well Enough Alone" (Ann) [replaced during the run with "A Relatively Simple Affair" (Ann)], "Blonde Blues" (Dave), Dance (Gloria & Dave), "Uh-Huh, Oh Yeah!" (Nicky, George, Frank, Pete, Phil, Danny, Artie, Josh), "All of These and More" (Ann, Bob, Ensemble), "Nobility" (Edward Becker, Bob Daley, Jack DeLon, Brock Peters, Albert Popwell, Tom Raskin, Knute Sullivan, Bob Wiensko), "The Body Beautiful" (reprise) (Ann). *Act II*: "Summer Is" (Singers & Dancers, with Kathy), "The Honeymoon is Over" (Gloria, Florence, Jane), "Just My Luck" (Ann & The Kids), "All of These and More" (reprise) (Marge & Harry), "Art of Conversation" (Albert, Singers, Dancers), "Gloria" (Dave, Gloria, Dancers), "A Relatively Simple Affair" (Ann & Marge) [during the run this number was shifted to Act I, and a reprise of "A Relatively Simple Affair" (Ann & Gloria) remained here], Finale (Entire Company).

Broadway reviews were luke-warm and divided.

74. *Bombay Dreams*

A love story set in India, it is about the Bombay film industry, or "Bollywood" as it is known. Akaash is a handsome young slum-dweller who dreams of becoming a Bollywood film star, and does, also winning the girl, Priya, the daughter of Madan, a jailed movie director. Kitty is a bitter journalist. Vikram is the lawyer engaged to Priya. JK is the local gang boss. Rani is the big Bollywood female star. Sweetie is a eunuch, secretly in love with Akaash.

Before Broadway. It first ran at the APOLLO VICTORIA THEATRE, LONDON, 6/19/02–6/13/04. Previews from 5/31/02. PRESENTED BY The Really Useful Theatre Company. *Cast*: AKAASH: Reza Jaffrey, *Stephen Rahman Hughes*; PRIYA: Preeya Kalidas, *Zehra Naqvi*; SWEETIE: Raj Ghatak; RANI: Ayesha Dharker, *Sophiya Haque*; KITTY: Shelley King, *Nila Aalia*; JK: Raad Rawi, *Royce Ullah*; MADAN: Dalip Tahil, *Ravin J. Ganatra*; VIKRAM: Ramon Tikaram, *Munir Khairdin*; ANUPAM: Andrew Playfoot; SHANTI: Adlyn Ross. "Bombay Awakes" (Orchestra), "Bombay Dreams" (Ensemble), "Like an Eagle" (additional arrangements: Marius De Vries) (Akaash), "Love's Never Easy" (Sweetie), "Don't Release Me" (Madan), "Happy Endings" (Priya & Madan), "Ooh La La" (Anupam), "Shakalaka Baby" (additional music/lyrics/arrangements: Marius De Vries) (Priya & Akaash) [the big hit], "(Are You Sure You Want to Be) Famous" (Priya & Akaash), "I Could Live" (Akaash), "Only Love" (Priya), "Chaiyya Chaiyya" (Hindi lyrics: Gulzar) (lip-synched by Akaash & Priya to the singing of Sukhwinder Singh & Sapna Awashti) [a hit], "How Many Stars" (Priya & Akaash), "Salaam Bombay" (Akaash & Ensemble), "Closer than Ever" (Priya & Akaash), "Ganesh" (Orchestra), "The Journey Home" (Akaash), "Wedding Qawali" (Punjabi lyrics: Sukhwinder Singh) (sung by Mr. Singh), "Bombay Sleeps" (Orchestra). The show cost $7.25 million and, despite mixed reviews, became a big hit, extending its run and recouping its cost in 13 months. The UK cast album was released in the USA on 8/27/02 by Sony Classical. On 9/30/02 Andrew Lloyd Webber announced that it would be going to Broadway in spring 2004, instead of having a 2003 Canadian tryout. After the show closed in London, it toured the U.K., then returned to a smaller theatre in London in 2005. This new London run had the revised Broadway script.

The Broadway Run. BROADWAY THEATRE, 4/29/04–1/1/05. 31 previews from 3/29/04. 284 PERFORMANCES. Andrew Lloyd Webber's production, PRESENTED BY Waxman Williams Entertainment & TGA Entertainment, in association with Denise Rich & Ralph Williams, H. Thau/M. Cooper/Ad Prods. [Harold Thau & Max Cooper], Scott Prisand & Danny Seraphine, and Independent Presenters Network; MUSIC: A.R. Rahman; LYRICS: Don Black; ADDITIONAL AMERICAN LYRICS: David Yazbek; ORIGINAL BOOK: Meera Syal; NEW AMERICAN BOOK: Meera Syal & Thomas Meehan; BASED ON AN IDEA BY: Shekhar Kapur & Andrew Lloyd Webber; DIRECTOR: Steven Pimlott; CHOREOGRAPHER: Anthony Van Laast; CHOREOGRAPHER OF BOLLYWOOD DANCE SEQUENCES: Farah Khan; SETS/COSTUMES: Mark Thompson; LIGHTING: Hugh Vanstone; SOUND: Mick Potter; MUSICAL SUPERVISOR/ORCHESTRATIONS/VOCAL & INSTRUMENTAL MUSIC ARRANGEMENTS: Paul Bogaev; MUSICAL DIRECTOR/DANCE MUSIC ARRANGEMENTS: James Abbott; ORIGINAL ADDITIONAL MUSIC ARRANGEMENTS: Christopher

Nightingale: PRESS: Barlow — Hartman Public Relations; CASTING: Tara Rubin; GENERAL MANAGEMENT: Charlotte Wilcox Company; COMPANY MANAGER: Susan Bell; PRODUCTION STAGE MANAGER: Bonnie L. Becker; ASSISTANT STAGE MANAGERS: J. Philip Bassett & Charles Underhill. *Cast:* AKAASH: Manu Narayan (1) ✩; EUNUCHS (HIJIRA): Ron Nahass, Bobby Pestka, Darryl Semira, Kirk Torigoe; RAM: Mueen Jahan Ahmad; SALIM: Aalok Mehta; SHANTI: Madhur Jaffrey ✩; SWEETIE: Sriram Ganesan ✩; MUNNA: Neil Jay Shastri (Wednesday matinees; Thursdays; Saturday evenings; Sundays) ✩ & Tanvir Gopal ✩ (Tuesdays; Wednesday evenings; Fridays; Saturday matinees) (alternated); HARD HATS: Suresh John, Gabriel Burrafato; VIKRAM: Deep Katdare ✩; MUMTAAZ: Miriam Laube; PRIYA: Anisha Nagarajan (2) ✩, *Tamyra Gray* (from 11/9/04 for 12 weeks); MADAN: Marvin L. Ishmael ✩; PAGEANT ANNOUNCER: Zahf Paroo; RANI: Ayesha Dharker ✩; POLICEMEN: Zahf Paroo & Gabriel Burrafato; SHAHEEN: Jolly Abraham; KITTY DaSOUZA: Sarah Ripard; CHAIYYA CHAIYYA SOLOIST: Miriam Laube; MOVIE SWEETIE: Darryl Semira; MOVIE SHANTI: Anjali Bhimani; MOVIE AKAASH: Zahf Paroo; LAMENT SINGER: Ian Jutsun; WEDDING QAWALI SINGERS: Ian Jutsun, Zahf Paroo, Gabriel Burrafato; ENSEMBLE (SLUM DWELLERS, BEAUTY PAGEANT CONTESTANTS, TV AND FILM CREW, FEMINIST DEMONSTRATORS, SHAKALAKA, CHAIYYA CHAIYYA, FILM SALAA'M BOMBAY DANCERS AND FISHERMEN): Jolly Abraham, Mueen Jahan Ahman, Aaron J. Albano, Celine Alwyn, Anjali Bhimani, Shane Bland, Gabriel Burrafato, Wendy Calio, Tiffany Michelle Cooper, Sheetal Gandhi, Krystal Kiran Garib, Tania Marie Hakkim (*Gina Philistine*), Dell Howlett, Suresh John, Ian Jutsun, Miriam Laube [replaced Dani Jazzar during previews], Aalok Mehta, Ron Nahass, Michelle Nigalan (*Natasha Tabandera*), Zahf Paroo, Danny Pathan, Bobby Pestka, Kafi Pierre, Sarah Ripard, Rommy Sandhu [came in during previews], Darryl Semira, Kirk Torigoe. *Understudies*: Rani: Jolly Abraham, Anjali Bhimani, Sarah Ripard; Madan: Mueen Jahan Ahmad, Suresh John, Ian Jutsun; Akaash: Aaron J. Albano, Zahf Paroo, Danny Pathan; Shanti: Anjali Bhimani & Sarah Ripard; Sweetie: Shane Bland & Darryl Semira; Vikram: Gabriel Burrafato & Zahf Paroo; Priya: Sheetal Gandhi, Krystal Kiran Garib, Michelle Nagalan (*Natasha Tabandera*). *Swings*: Wilson Mendieta, Lisa Stevens, James R. Whittington, Nicole Winhoffer.

Bombay Dreams Orchestra: CONCERTMASTER: Sylvia D'Avanzo; VIOLINS: Sean Carney, Nina Evtuhov, Pauline Kim, Ming Yeh; VIOLAS: Liuh-Wen Ting & Arthur Dibble; CELLOS: Ted Mook & Roger Shell; FLUTES: Anders Bostrom; OBOE/ENGLISH HORN: Charles Pillow; DRUMS: Ray Grappone; BASS: Randy Landau; KEYBOARDS: Adam Ben-David, Dan Riddle, Ann Gerschefski; ON-STAGE PERCUSSION: Deep Singh & David Sharma. *Act I: Scene 1* Paradise Slum: Overture: "Salaa'm Bombay" (Akaash & Ensemble), "Bollywood" (Akaash & Ensemble); *Scene 2* Shanti and Akaash's home: "Love's Never Easy" (Sweetie, Priya, Ensemble); *Scene 3* The Miss India pageant, backstage; *Scene 4* The Miss India pageant, frontstage: "Lovely, Lovely Ladies" (Rani & Ensemble), "Bhangra" (Akaash, Rani, Ensemble); *Scene 5* The Miss India pageant, backstage; *Scene 6* Film set of *Diamond in the Rough*: "Shakalaka Baby" (Rani, Akaash, Ensemble) (sung by Preeya Kalidas), "I Could Live Here" (Akaash), "Is This Love?" (Priya); *Scene 7* Akaash's new apartment: "Famous" (Madan, Rani, Akaash, Guests); *Scene 8* *Diamond in the Rough* premiere: "Love's Never Easy" (reprise) (Priya & Sweetie). *Act II: Scene 1* The annual Indian film awards: "Chaiyya Chaiyya" (Akaash, Rani, Ensemble); *Scene 2* Akaash's hilltop mansion: "How Many Stars?" (Akaash & Priya); *Scene 3* Film set of *Bombay Dreams*: "Salaa'm Bombay" (reprise) (Rani & Ensemble), "Hero" (Sweetie & Priya); *Scene 4* Paradise Slum; *Scene 5* Outside the Taj Royale Beach Hotel: "Ganesh Procession" (Company); *Scene 6* Juhu Beach: "The Journey Home" (Akaash); *Scene 7* Paradise Slum; *Scene 8* The Taj Royale Beach Hotel: "Wedding Qawali" (Company).

Ayesha Dharker appeared on Broadway as part of a deal between Actors Equity in the USA and Actors Equity in Britain. The show cost $12.5 million. It got mixed reviews. It received Tony nominations for choreography, costumes and orchestrations. In 7/04 it was announced that Janet Jackson had been approached to play Rani when Ayesha Dharker's contract expired. On 12/7/04 the cast learned that the show was going to close after the 1/1/05 evening performance.

After Broadway. By 10/04 a movie was being discussed, and by 12/04 a tour of the Broadway show was being talked about for the 2005–06 season.

75. *The Boy Friend*

A new musical comedy of the 1920s, an affectionate look at musicals in the Roaring Twenties. Polly is an English heiress attending Mme Dubonnet's finishing school on the French Riviera in 1926 when she meets Tony, a young man of noble heritage but posing as a delivery boy. They fall in love, and after some misunderstandings meet again at the Carnival Ball, dressed as Pierrot and Pierrette.

Before Broadway. Oxford-educated songwriter Sandy Wilson was asked, in 1953, to write the music, lyrics and book for a musical interlude at the PLAYERS' THEATRE CLUB, lasting no more than an hour, and to be based on music of the 1920s. It ran there 4/14/53–5/3/53 (3 weeks). DIRECTOR: Vida Hope; CHOREOGRAPHER: John Heawood; SETS/COSTUMES: Reginald Woolley; AT PIANO: Stan Edwards. *Cast*: POLLY: Anne Rogers; TONY: Anthony Hayes; MAISIE: Ann Wakefield; DULCIE: Maria Charles; HORTENSE/LADY BROCKHURST: Violetta; MME DUBONNET: Joan Sterndale Bennett; PERCIVAL: Fred Stone; FAY: Joan Gadsdon; MARCEL: James Thompson; PIERRE: Malcolm Goddard; BOBBY: Larry Drew; BROCKHURST: John Rutland.

It was so popular that it was revised and lengthened, playing again at the PLAYERS' THEATRE CLUB, 10/13/53–11/22/53 (6 weeks), with the same cast and crew. Then it moved to the EMBASSY THEATRE, 12/1/53–1/11/54. Same cast and crew again, except MUSICAL DIRECTOR: Stan Edwards; AT PIANOS: Valda Plucknett & William Blezard. Then it moved, again, to the WYNDHAM'S THEATRE, LONDON, under the management of Players' Ventures Ltd, for a very successful West End run, 1/14/54–2/7/59. 2,084 PERFORMANCES. It had the same crew. The cast recording was on HMV. *Cast*: HORTENSE: Violetta, *Eleanor McCready*; MAISIE: Denise Hirst, *Ann Wakefield, Penelope Newington*; DULCIE: Maria Charles, *Sheila Bernette*; FAY: Joan Gadsdon, *Millicent Martin, Gwendolyn Watts*; NANCY: Juliet Hunt, *Carole Grey, Eleanor McCready*; POLLY: Anne Rogers, *Patricia Webb, Patricia Vivian*; MARCEL: Stephen Warwick, *James Campbell, Ben Aris*; PIERRE: Jack Thomson, *Norman Warwick*; ALPHONSE: Geoffrey Webb, *Kim Grant*; MME DUBONNET: Totti Truman Taylor, *Joan Sterndale Bennett, Betty Huntley Wright*; BOBBY: Larry Drew; PERCIVAL: Hugh Paddick, *Brian Blades*; TONY: Anthony Hayes; BROCKHURST: John Rutland; LADY BROCKHURST: Beryl Cooke; GENDARME: Bill Horsley, *Hugh Forbes*; WAITER: Alan Dudley, *Patrick Newell*; PEPE: Stephen Warwick, *James Campbell, Ben Aris*; LOLITA: Joan Gadsdon, *Millicent Martin, Carole Grey*; CHORUS: Anton Rodgers, Stella Moray. During the run Millicent Martin returned from the Broadway production to take over the London roles of Fay & Lolita.

This was the first successful London musical to move successfully to Broadway since the 1920s. Cy Feuer replaced Vida Hope as director, but was uncredited. The producers barred Miss Hope and Sandy Wilson from rehearsals, hiring detectives to keep them out.

The Broadway Run. ROYALE THEATRE, 9/30/54–11/26/55. 483 PERFORMANCES. The Vida Hope production, PRESENTED BY Cy Feuer & Ernest H. Martin; MUSIC/LYRICS/BOOK: Sandy Wilson; DIRECTOR: Vida Hope; CHOREOGRAPHER: John Heawood; SETS: Feder (based on the London sets by Reginald Woolley); COSTUMES: Robert Mackintosh (based on the London costumes by Reginald Woolley); LIGHTING: Feder; MUSICAL DIRECTOR: Anton Coppola; ORCHESTRATIONS: Ted Royal & Charles L. Cooke; PRESS: Karl Bernstein, Harvey B. Sabinson, Robert Ganshaw; CASTING: Ira Bernstein; COMPANY MANAGER: Michael Goldreyer, *Leon Spachner*; PRODUCTION STAGE MANAGER: David Kanter, *Ira Bernstein*; STAGE MANAGER: Charles Pratt Jr., *Herman Magidson*; ASSISTANT STAGE MANAGER: Marge Ellis. *Cast*: HORTENSE: Paulette Girard; NANCY: Millicent Martin, *Berkely Marsh*; MAISIE: Ann Wakefield; FAY: Stella Claire; DULCIE: Dilys Lay; POLLY BROWNE: Julie Andrews (1), *Jean Bayless*; MARCEL: Joe Milan; ALPHONSE: Buddy Schwab; PIERRE: Jerry Newby; MADAME DUBONNET: Ruth Altman (4); BOBBY VAN HUSEN: Bob Scheerer (5); PERCIVAL BROWNE: Eric Berry (3); TONY: John Hewer (2); PHILIPPE: Jimmy Alex, *John Perri, Vincent Lynne*; MONICA: Berkely Marsh; LORD BROCKHURST: Geoffrey Hibbert; LADY BROCKHURST: Moyna MacGill; SUSANNE: Lyn Connorty [role dropped during run]; CHARLES: Vincent Lynne [role dropped during run]; GUESTS: Mickey Calin [he later became Michael Callan], Phoebe Mackay, Marge Ellis; GENDARME: Douglas Deane; WAITER: Lyn Robert; PEPE: Joe Milan; LOLITA: Stella Claire; ORCHESTRA: Paul McGrane & His Bearcats. **Understudies**: Polly: Ann Wakefield, *Deborah Remsen*; Tony: Douglas Deane; Maisie/Fay: Millicent Martin; Bobby: Jerry Newby; Mme Dubonnet: Rose Inghram; Percival: Leonard Ceeley; Lady Brockhurst: Phoebe Mackay; Lord Brockhurst: Walter Burke, *George Hall*; Hortense: Marge Ellis; Dulcie: Stella Claire, *Millicent Martin*; Nancy: Lyn Connorty, *Berkely Marsh*; Marcel/Pepe: Buddy Schwab; Pierre: Jimmy Alex, *Vincent Lynne*; Alphonse: Jimmy Alex, *John Perri*.

Overture; **Act I**: The Drawing Room of the Villa Caprice, Madame Dubonnet's finishing school on the outskirts of Nice; 1926: "Perfect Young Ladies" (Hortense, Nancy, Maisie, Fay, Dulcie), "The Boy Friend" (Polly, Maisie, Dulcy, Fay, Nancy, Marcel, Pierre, Alphonse, Philippe), "Won't You Charleston with Me?" (Maisie & Bobby), "Fancy Forgetting" (Mme Dubonnet & Percival), "I Could Be Happy with You" (Polly & Tony) (the main song), Finale of Act I: "The Boy Friend" (reprise) (Entire Company). **Act II**: The Plage; that afternoon: "Sur la Plage" (Maisie, Bobby, Fay, Marcel, Dulcy, Alphonse, Nancy, Pierre, Monica, Philippe), "A Room in Bloomsbury" (Polly & Tony), "The You-Don't-Want-to-Play-with-Me Blues" (Mme Dubonnet, Percival, Fay, Dulcie, Nancy, Monica), "Safety in Numbers" (Maisie, Bobby, Marcel, Pierre, Alphonse), Finale of Act II (Entire Company). **Act III**: The terrace of the Café Pataplon; that night: "The Riviera" (Maisie, Bobby, Fay, Marcel, Dulcie, Alphonse, Nancy, Pierre, Monica, Philippe), "It's Never Too Late to Fall in Love" (Lord Brockhurst & Dulcie), "Carnival Tango" (danced by Pepe & Lolita), "Poor Little Pierrette" (Mme Dubonnet & Polly), Finale (Entire Company).

It got great Broadway reviews. Julie Andrews won a Donaldson Award for (Broadway) female debut.

After Broadway. TOUR. Opened on 11/28/55, at the Shubert Theatre, New Haven, and closed on 1/5/57, at the Shubert Theatre, Philadelphia. MUSICAL DIRECTOR: Stanley Lebowsky. **Cast**: POLLY: Jo Ann Bayless; TONY: John Hewer; MME DUBONNET: Ruth Altman, *Gabrielle*; MAISIE: Ann Wakefield; NANCY: Barbara Ann Sharma; FAY: Margery Gray; DULCIE/LOLITA: Millicent Martin; BROCKHURST: Geoffrey Hibbert; LADY BROCKHURST: Phoebe Mackay; WAITER: Douglas Deane, *David Swain*; PEPE/MARCEL: Ronnie Field; MONICA: Inga Rode; PERCIVAL: Eric Berry; BOBBY: Jerry Newby.

DOWNTOWN THEATRE, NYC. Opened 1/25/58. This was the famous Off Broadway revival. PRESENTED BY New Princess Company. It moved to the CHERRY LANE THEATRE on 4/28/58 (with a total of 763 PERFORMANCES for both theatres). DIRECTOR: Gus Schirmer Jr.; CHOREOGRAPHER: Buddy Schwab; SETS/LIGHTING: Charles Brandon; COSTUMES: Joe Crosby; MUSICAL DIRECTOR: Natalie Charlson. **Cast**: POLLY: Ellen McCown; MAISIE: Gerrianne Raphael, *Maureen Bailey*; NANCY: Christina Gillespie, *Judy Devlin*; TONY: Bill Mullikin, *Neal Kenyon*; HORTENSE: Margaret Hall, *Adele Aron*; FAY/LOLITA: Michele Burke, *Nora Bristow*; DULCIE: June Squibb, *Barbara Gilbert*; PEPE/MARCEL: Thom Molinaro, *Jim Pompeii*; PIERRE: Neal Kenyon, *Bill Regan*; MME DUBONNET: Jeanne Beauvais, *Jenny Lou Law, Evelyn Page*; BOBBY: Peter Conlow, *Buddy Schwab*; PERCIVAL: Leon Shaw; BROCKHURST: David Vaughan, *Robert Bardwell*; LADY BROCKHURST: Phoebe Mackay; ALSO WITH: *Emily Cobb* & *Barbara Sharma* (although not in the first season).

PAPER MILL PLAYHOUSE, New Jersey, 1966. DIRECTOR: Geoffrey Webb. **Cast**: Barbara Cook, Sandy Duncan, Isabelle Farrell.

COMEDY THEATRE, London. 11/29/67–10/12/68. 365 PERFORMANCES. This was a famous revival. PRESENTED BY Michael Codron; DIRECTOR: Sandy Wilson; CHOREOGRAPHER: Noel Tovey; MUSICAL DIRECTOR: Grant Hossack. **Cast**: POLLY: Cheryl Kennedy; TONY: Tony Adams; MME DUBONNET: Marion Grimaldi; BROCKHURST: Geoffrey Hibbert; PERCIVAL: Jeremy Hawk; HORTENSE: Louise Dunn; DULCIE: Jacqueline Clark; FAY: Mary Hewin; MAISIE: Frances Barlow; MARCEL: Mark Moser; PIERRE: David Lloyd Jones; LADY BROCKHURST: Celia Helda; LOLITA: Suzanne Kerchiss; PEPE: Noel Tovey; NANCY: Elizabeth Estensen; ALPHONSE: Trevor Jones; BOBBY: Nicholas Bennett; GENDARME: Bruce Heighley; WAITER: Jan Colet.

Divorce Me, Darling! This was the sequel to *The Boy Friend*.

MUSIC/LYRICS/BOOK: Sandy Wilson. It first ran at the PLAYERS' THEATRE CLUB, London, on 12/15/64. It was described as "A musical comedy of the 1930s." Then it moved to the GLOBE THEATRE, London, 2/1/65–4/17/65. 87 PERFORMANCES. DIRECTOR: Steven Vinaver; CHOREOGRAPHER: Harry Naughton, *Buddy Bradley*; SETS: Reginald Woolley; MUSICAL DIRECTOR: Ian MacPherson. It had the same basic characters as in *The Boy Friend*. **Cast**: MADAME K: Joan Sterndale Bennett, *Joan Heal*; HON. POLLY BROCKHURST: Patricia Michael; FAY DE LA FALAISE: Vicky Clayton; MAISIE VAN HUSEN: Anna Sharkey; DULCIE DUBOIS: Maria Charles; NANCY LEBRUN: Jenny Wren; BOBBY VAN HUSEN: Cy Young; MARCEL DE LA FALAISE: Roy Sone; HORTENSE: Violetta; SOLANGE: Rissa Cooper; RAOUL: Nick Norman; LADY BROCKHURST: Joyce Barbour; SIR FREDDY FFOTHERINGTON-FFITCH: Keith Smith; LORD BROCKHURST: Geoffrey Hibbert; PIERRE LEBRUN: Charles Yates; ALPHONSE DUBOIS: Harry Haythorne; HON. TONY BROCKHURST: Philip Gilbert. "Here We Are in Nice Again," "Someone to Dance With," "Challenge Dance," "Whatever Happened to Love?," "Lights! Music!," "Back to Nature," "On the Loose," "Maisie," "Paradise Hotel," "No Harm Done," "Together Again," "Divorce Me, Darling!," "Here Am I (But Where's the Guy?)," "Out of Step," "Fancy Forgetting" (reprised from *The Boy Friend*), "You're Absolutely Me," "Back Where We Started," "Blondes for Danger," "Swing-Time is Here to Stay." This sequel ran in the USA, at THEATRE UNDER THE STARS, Houston, 7/14/84. DIRECTOR: Frank M. Young; CHOREOGRAPHER: Susan Stroman. **Cast**: Lauri Smith, Rosemary Loar. In 1997 it had another run in England, at CHICHESTER. **Cast**: Marti Webb, Ruthie Henshall, Liliane Montevecchi, Kevin Wilson, David Alder, Joan Savage.

76. *The Boy Friend (Broadway revival)*

A new musical number, "It's Nicer in Nice" (Hortense, Dulcie, Fay, Nancy, Marcel, Pierre, Alphonse) was inserted immediately after "A Room in Bloomsbury."

The Broadway Run. AMBASSADOR THEATRE, 4/14/70–7/18/70. 3 previews. 119 PERFORMANCES. PRESENTED BY John Yorke, Don Saxon, Michael Hellerman; MUSIC/LYRICS/BOOK: Sandy Wilson; DIRECTOR: Gus Schirmer; CHOREOGRAPHER: Buddy Schwab; SETS/COSTUMES: Andrew & Margaret Brownfoot; COSTUME SUPERVISOR: Stanley Simmons; LIGHTING/NEW YORK PRODUCTION SUPERVISOR: Tharon Musser; ASSISTANT LIGHTING: Ken Billington; MUSICAL DIRECTOR: Jerry Goldberg; ORCHESTRATIONS: Ted Royal & Charles L. Cooke; CAST RECORDING on Decca; PRESS: Saul Richman, Sy Sandler, Peggy Mitchell; PRODUCTION STAGE MANAGER: Phil Friedman; STAGE MANAGER: Larry Ziegler; ASSISTANT STAGE MANAGER: Eleanore Treiber. **Cast**: HORTENSE: Barbara Andres (9); NANCY: Lesley Secombe (11); MAISIE: Sandy Duncan (2); FAY: Mary Zahn; DULCIE: Simon McQueen (6); POLLY: Judy Carne (1) ☆; MARCEL: Marcelo Gamboa; ALPHONSE: Ken Mitchell; PIERRE: Arthur Faria; MME DUBONNET: Jeanne Beauvais (4); BOBBY VAN HUSEN: Harvey Evans (7); PERCIVAL BROWNE: Leon Shaw (5); TONY: Ronald Young (3); PHILIPPE: Tony Stevens; MONICA: Carol Culver; LORD BROCKHURST: David Vaughan (8); LADY BROCKHURST: Marie Paxton (10); GENDARME: Jeff Richards; WAITER: Tony Stevens; PEPE: Marcelo Gamboa; LOLITA: Mary Zahn. **Understudies**: Polly: Carol Culver; Tony: Jeff Richards; Percival/Brockhurst: Paul Tracey; Madame: Barbara Andres; Bobby/Pepe: Arthur Faria; Dulcie: Lesley Secombe; Lady Brockhurst/Hortense/Fay/Lolita: Eleanore Treiber; Nancy/Maisie: Mimi B. Wallace; Marcel: Arthur Faria & Tony Stevens; Pierre/Alphonse: Tony Stevens.

Broadway reviews were extremely divided, but it was generally unfavorably received. Sandy Duncan was nominated for a Tony.

After Broadway. THE MOVIE. 1972. PRODUCER/WRITER/DIRECTOR: Ken Russell. There were two new numbers (old numbers, actually, but never used in any of the stage productions): "You Are My Lucky Star" (by Nacio Herb Brown & Arthur Freed), and "Any Old Iron" (by Charles Collins, E.A. Shepherd, Fred Terry). CAST: POLLY: Twiggy; TOMMY: Tommy Tune; TONY: Christopher Gable; ALPHONSE: Murray Melvin; HORTENSE: Barbara Windsor; PETER: Brian Murphy.

CHURCHILL THEATRE, Bromley, England, 4/12/84. PRESENTED BY Cameron Mackintosh. Then it went to the ROYAL ALEXANDRA THE-

ATRE, Toronto; then to the OLD VIC, London, 7/18/84–8/18/84; then to MANCHESTER (4 weeks); then to the West End, to the ALBERY THEATRE, London, 9/20/84–2/2/85. 156 PERFORMANCES. DIRECTOR: John Hewett; CHOREOGRAPHER: Dan Siretta. *Cast*: POLLY: Christine McKenna, *Jane Wellman*; MME DUBONNET: Glynis Johns, *Anna Quayle*; PERCIVAL: Derek Waring; BROCKHURST: Peter Bayliss; ALSO WITH: Simon Green, Rosemary Ashe.

BRITISH TOUR. Opened in Plymouth in spring 2003, aimed at the West End. *Cast*: Liliane Montevecchi, Roy Barraclough.

BAY STREET THEATRE, Sag Harbor, Long Island. 8/9/03–8/31/03. Previews from 8/5/03. DIRECTOR: Julie Andrews. *Cast*: POLLY: Meredith Patterson; PERCIVAL: Byron Jennings; HORTENSE: Veanne Cox; LORD BROCKHURST: Tony Roberts; LADY BROCKHURST: Delphi Harrington; TONY: Sean Palmer; MME DUBONNET: Nancy Hess; ALSO WITH: Jenny Fellner, James Nederlander Jr. (cameo role on 8/24/03 — he won the role in a charity auction). The theatre was partly run by Emma Walton, Julie Andrews' daughter. This production had Broadway plans.

GOODSPEED OPERA HOUSE, Conn. 7/8/05–9/18/05. DIRECTOR: Julie Andrews; CHOREOGRAPHER: John De Luca; SETS/COSTUMES: Tony Walton (Miss Andrews' ex-husband). Then it went on a tour, opening at Wilmington, Del. PRESENTED BY Goodspeed Opera House.

77. *The Boy from Oz*

An Australian musical about singer Peter Allen, from his humble beginnings in the Australian outback to international stardom. While gigging at the Hong Kong Hilton in 1964 he brought himself to the attention of Judy Garland, and became her protégé. He was subsequently (but only for a brief while) married to her daughter, Liza Minnelli. Mr. Allen died of AIDS in 1992. He starred in a Broadway flop —*Legs Diamond*.

Before Broadway. *The Boy from* Oz began at HER MAJESTY'S THEATRE, Sydney, on 3/5/98 and got very good reviews. It ran for two years. PRESENTED BY Ben Gannon & Robert Fox; DIRECTOR: Gale Edwards. *Cast*: PETER: Todd McKenney; GREG: Murray Bartlett; JUDY: Chrissie Amphlett; LIZA: Angela Toohey; MARION: Jill Perryman; DEE: Marcus Eyre; CHRIS: Nick Warnford; BOY: Mathew Waters. *Act I*: "Continental American," "When I Get My Name in Lights," "Pretty Keen Teen," "All I Wanted Was the Dream," "Only an Older Woman," "Don't Wish Too Hard," "Sure Thing, Baby," "Quiet Please, There's a Lady on Stage," "I'd Rather Leave While I'm in Love," "Taught by Experts," "Not the Boy Next Door." *Act II*: "Everything Old is New Again," "Best that You Can Do," "Love Don't Need a Reason," "She Loves to Hear the Music," "I Honestly Love You," "I Still Call Australia Home," "Don't Cry Out Loud," "Tenterfield Saddler," "I Go to Rio" (Peter Allen's theme song).

The original (Australian) book was written by Nick Enright, but Martin Sherman came aboard as new (American) librettist in fall 2001. There was a workshop in 4/02. DIRECTOR: Philip Wm McKinley; CHOREOGRAPHER: Joey McKneely; MUSICAL DIRECTOR: Louis St. Louis; GENERAL MANAGER: Albert Poland. *Cast*: PETER ALLEN: Hugh Jackman; LIZA MINNELLI: Ruthie Henshall; JUDY GARLAND: Isabel Keating; MARION WOOLNOUGH: Patti Allison; THE BOY—YOUNG PETER: Mitchel David Federan; MARK HERRON: Adam Karsten; LADY: Shannon Lewis; GEORGE WOOLNOUGH: Mark Manley; DICK WOOLNOUGH/DEE ANTHONY: Michael Mulheren; GREG: Ben Sheaffer; CHRIS BELL: Jeff Skowron; ENSEMBLE: Leslie Alexander, Todd Anderson, Christopher Freeman, Colleen Hawks, Stephanie Kurtzuba, Matt Loehr, Brian J. Marcum, Lynn Sterling, Kellyanne Wilson. This was to have been followed by out-of-town tryouts, then on to Broadway in spring 2003. However, Broadway was delayed until 10/03 (the final fixed date was announced on 10/4/02, a day after it was announced that *Les Miz* was wrapping up at the Imperial on 3/15/03). Hugh Jackman was confirmed in his role by 10/02, but there were grave doubts as to whether he would ever do it, as his star was rapidly rising, and he may no longer be as available. He did, of course, do it. Also in 10/02 Philip Wm McKinley was confirmed as director. Beth Fowler was announced on 1/9/03. Broadway rehearsals began on 7/21/03.

The Broadway Run. IMPERIAL THEATRE, 10/16/03–9/12/04. 32

previews from 9/16/03. 365 performances. PRESENTED BY Ben Gannon & Robert Fox; MUSIC/LYRICS: Peter Allen (unless otherwise stated); ORIGINAL BOOK: Nick Enright; NEW BOOK FOR BROADWAY: Martin Sherman; DIRECTOR: Philip Wm McKinley; SETS: Robin Wagner; CHOREOGRAPHER: Joey McKneely; COSTUMES: William Ivey Long; LIGHTING: Donald Holder; SOUND: ACME Sound Partners; MUSICAL DIRECTOR/INCIDENTAL MUSIC/VOCAL ARRANGEMENTS: Patrick Vaccariello; ORCHESTRATIONS: Michael Gibson; DANCE MUSIC ARRANGEMENTS: Mark Hummel; CAST RECORDING on Decca Broadway, recorded on 10/20/03 and released on 11/18/03; PRESS: Boneau/Bryan-Brown; CASTING: Dave Clemmons Casting, Joseph McConnell; GENERAL MANAGER: Albert Poland; COMPANY MANAGER: Lane Marsh, *Mark D. Shacket*; PRODUCTION STAGE MANAGER: Eileen F. Haggerty; STAGE MANAGER: Richard C. Rauscher; ASSISTANT STAGE MANAGER: Tina M. Newhauser. *Cast*: PETER ALLEN: Hugh Jackman (1) ✩; BOY (YOUNG PETER): Mitchel David Federan (6); MARION WOOLNOUGH, PETER'S MOTHER: Beth Fowler (3); DICK WOOLNOUGH, PETER'S FATHER: Michael Mulheren (7); CHRIS BELL: Timothy A. Fitz-Gerald; JUDY GARLAND: Isabel Keating (4); MARK HERRON: John Hill; LIZA MINNELLI: Stephanie J. Block (2); TRIO: Colleen Hawks, Tari Kelly, Stephanie Kurtzuba, *Heather Laws, Trisha Rapier*; GREG CONNELL, PETER'S PARTNER: Jarrod Emick (5); DEE ANTHONY, MANAGER/PROMOTER: Michael Mulheren (7); ALICE, THE ROCKETTE: Pamela Jordan, *Emily Hsu*; ENSEMBLE: Leslie Alexander, Brad Anderson (*Shane Rhoades*), Kelly Crandall, Naleah Dey, Nicolas Dromard, Timothy A. Fitz-Gerald, Christopher Freeman, Tyler Hanes, Colleen Hawks, John Hill, Pamela Jordan (*Emily Hsu*), Tari Kelly, Stephanie Kurtzuba, Heather Laws, Brian J. Marcum, Jennifer Savelli, Matthew Stocke, *Ramon Flowers, Ashley Amber Haase, Jessica Lea Patty, Nathan Peck, Trisha Rapier*. **Standby**: Peter: Kevin Spirtas. **Understudies**: Peter: John Hill; Greg: Kevin Spirtas, Brad Anderson (*Shane Rhoades*), John Hill; Marion: Leslie Alexander; Liza: Tari Kelly & Heather Laws; Judy: Stephanie Kurtzuba & Heather Laws; Dee/Dick: Matthew Stocke; Boy: P.J. Verhoest; Alice: Kelly Crandall. **Swings**: Todd Anderson & Jessica Hartman.

The Boy from Oz Orchestra: CONCERTMASTER: Sylvia D'Avanzo; VIOLINS: Victor Heifets, Fritz Krakowski, Wende Namkung, Cecelia Hobbs Gardner, Nina Evtuhov; CELLOS: Mairi Dorman & Vivian Israel; LEAD TRUMPET: Jeff Kievit; TRUMPETS: Tino Gagliardi & Earl Gardner; TROMBONES: Clint Sharman & Randy Andos; REEDS: Ted Nash, Ben Kono, Ken Dybisz, Don McGeen; DRUMS: Brian Brake; BASS: Cary Potts; KEYBOARDS: Mark Berman & Jim Laev; GUITARS: J.J. McGeehan; PERCUSSION: Dan McMillan. *Act I*: Overture ["Arthur's Theme" ("Best that You Can Do")/"Not the Boy Next Door" (Peter)]; *Prologue* Peter in concert: "(All) The Lives of Me" (Peter). THE 1950s: *Scene 1* Various locations in Tenterfield, Australia — Peter's grandfather's store; Peter's childhood home; Josie Mann's New England Hotel interior/exterior: "When I Get My Name in Lights" (Boy & Ensemble), "When I Get My Name in Lights" (reprise) (Peter); THE 1960s: *Scene 2* Australian Bandstand television performance: "Love Crazy" (by Peter Allen & Adrienne Anderson) (Chris, Peter, Ensemble); *Scene 3* Hong Kong Hilton hotel: "Waltzing Matilda" (m: Marie Cowan; l: A.B. "Banjo" Paterson) (Peter & Chris), "All I Wanted Was the Dream" (Judy); *Scene 4* A small Chinese bar/Street in Hong Kong/New York City: "Only an Older Woman" (Judy, Peter, Chris, Mark), "Arthur's Theme" ("Best that You Can Do") (by Peter Allen & Carole Bayer Sager, Burt Bacharach, Christopher Cross) (Peter & Liza); *Scene 5* Peter & Liza's apartment: "Don't Wish Too Hard" (by Peter Allen & Carole Bayer Sager) (Judy), "Come Save Me" (Liza & Peter); *Scene 6* Peter & Liza's apartment; months later; *Scene 7* Liza's act: "She Loves to Hear the Music" (by Peter Allen & Carole Bayer Sager) (Liza & Ensemble); *Scene 8* Peter in concert: "Quiet, Please, There's a Lady on Stage" (by Peter Allen & Carole Bayer Sager) (Peter & Judy); THE 1970s: *Scene 9* Peter & Liza's apartment: "I'd Rather Leave While I'm in Love" (by Peter Allen & Carole Bayer Sager) (Liza & Peter); *Scene 10* The New York nightclubs: "Continental American" (by Peter Allen & Carole Bayer Sager) (Peter & Ensemble); *Scene 11* Marion's home: "Not the Boy Next Door" (by Peter Allen & Dean Pitchford) (Peter & Marion). *Act II*: *Scene 1* The *Reno Sweeney* club: "Bi-Coastal" (by Peter Allen, David Foster, Tom Keane) (Peter & Trio); *Scene 2* Peter's apartment: "If You Were Wondering" (Peter & Greg); *Scene 3* Dee's office/The *Copacabana* Club: "Sure Thing, Baby" (Dee,

Greg, Peter, Trio, Male Ensemble); THE 1980S: *Scene 4* Radio City Music Hall; Jan. 15, 1981: "Everything Old is New Again" (by Peter Allen & Carole Bayer Sager) (Peter & Rockettes); *Scene 5* Peter's dressing-room; Radio City: "Everything Old is New Again" (reprise) (Marion, Dee, Greg); *Scene 6* Peter's apartment: "Love Don't Need a Reason" (by Peter Allen, Michael Callen, Marsha Malamet) (Peter & Greg); THE 1990S: *Scene 7* Peter's apartment: "I Honestly Love You" (by Peter Allen & Jeff Barry) (Greg), "You and Me (We Wanted it All)" (by Peter Allen & Carole Bayer Sager) (Liza & Peter); *Scene 8* Marion's home/The Australian concert/Peter in concert: "I Still Call Australia Home" (Peter & Ensemble), "Don't Cry Out Loud" (by Peter Allen & Carole Bayer Sager) (Marion), "Once Before I Go" (Peter) [Peter Allen originally wrote this song for his friend Ann-Margret], Finale: "I Go to Rio" (by Peter Allen & Adrienne Anderson), (Peter & Company), "Tenterfield Saddler" (Peter & Company).

Note: programs stated: "Musical numbers and sequence are subject to change." The one above is for opening night. During the run, Act I Scenes 10 and 11 were cut, and the final number, "Tenterfield Saddler" was cut.

There was an advance sale at the Broadway box-office of $10 million (the show was capitalized at $8.25 million). Hugh Jackman got rave reviews. It was a big money winner from the start. Mr. Jackman never missed a performance up to the time of his vacation, 2/1/04–2/6/04 and 3/28/04–4/2/04. The producers decided not to let Kevin Spirtas, his understudy, stand in for Mr. Jackman, so they closed the show temporarily while the star was out. It won Tonys for Hugh Jackman, and was also nominated for book of a musical, and for Isabel Keating and Beth Fowler. There was talk of replacing Mr. Jackman with Ricky Martin, or Eric McCormack, or Ewan MacGregor, or Robert Downey Jr., but instead, when the players' contracts expired, so did the show. The show recouped its investment.

78. *The Boys from Syracuse*

Two sets of twins cause confusion in Asia Minor. Set in Ephesus, in Ancient Greence. Time: Thursday.

Before Broadway. The original Broadway production ran at the ALVIN THEATRE, 11/23/38–6/10/39. 235 PERFORMANCES. PRODUCER/DIRECTOR: George Abbott; CHOREOGRAPHER: George Balanchine; SETS: Jo Mielziner; COSTUMES: Irene Sharaff; MUSICAL DIRECTOR: Harry Levant; ORCHESTRATIONS: Hans Spialek. **Cast**: ANTIPHOLUS OF SYRACUSE: Eddie Albert; DROMIO OF EPHESUS: Teddy Hart; DROMIO OF SYRACUSE: Jimmy Savo; ADRIANA: Muriel Angelus; TAILOR'S APPRENTICE: Burl Ives; LUCIANA: Marcy Westcott; ANTIPHOLUS OF EPHESUS: Ronald Graham; COURTESAN: Betty Bruce; AEGEON: John O'Shaughnessy; LUCE: Wynn Murray. Overture. *Act I*: "I Had Twins" (Aegeon, Sergeant, Duke, Angelo, Ensemble), "Dear Old Syracuse" (Antipholus of Syracuse & Dromio of Syracuse), "What Can You Do with a Man?" (Luce & Dromio of Ephesus), "Falling in Love with Love" (Adriana), "Falling in Love with Love" (reprise) (Luciana & Maid), "The Shortest Day of the Year" (Antipholus of Ephesus), "The Shortest Day of the Year" (reprise) (Adriana), "This Can't Be Love" (Antipholus of Syracuse & Luciana), "This Can't Be Love" (reprise) (Luciana), "Ladies Choice" (ballet) (Antipholus of Ephesus, 1st Courtesan, Adriana, Fatima, Duke, Merchant of Syracuse, Corporal, Tailor, Galatea, Pygmalion, Amazons). *Act II*: "Ladies of the Evening" (Sergeant & Company), "He and She" (Luce & Dromio of Syracuse), "You Have Cast Your Shadow on the Sea" (Antipholus of Syracuse & Luciana), "Come with Me" (Antipholus of Ephesus, Sergeant, Corporal, Merchant of Ephesus, Angelo, Merchant of Syracuse, Duke), "Big Brother" (Dromio of Ephesus), "Big Brother" (dance) (Dromio of Syracuse & Dromio of Ephesus), "Sing for Your Supper" (Adriana, Luciana, Luce), "Oh, Diogenes!" (1st Courtesan & Company), Finale (Entire Company).

The 1940 movie had two songs in it that were not in the stage production — "Who Are You?" and "The Greeks Have a Word for It." DIRECTOR: A. Edward Sutherland. **Cast**: Allan Jones, Joe Penner, Martha Raye, Rosemary Lane.

The first theatrical recording of the score was not until 1953, with Portia Nelson, Jack Cassidy, Bibi Osterwald, Stanley Prager.

OFF BROADWAY REVIVAL. THEATRE FOUR, 4/15/63–6/28/64. 503 PERFORMANCES. This was a famous revival. PRESENTED BY Richard York; DIRECTOR: Christopher Hewett; CHOREOGRAPHER: Bob Herget; SETS: Herbert Senn & Helen Pond; COSTUMES: Guy Kent; MUSICAL DIRECTOR: Rene Wiegert; ORCHESTRATIONS: Larry Wilcox; BALLET MUSIC: Peter Matz. There was a cast recording. **Cast**: SERGEANT: Gary Oakes; DUKE: Fred Kimbrough; AEGEON: Matthew Tobin, *Emory Bass*; ANTIPHOLUS OF EPHESUS: Clifford David, *Jay Stuart*; DROMIO OF EPHESUS: Rudy Tronto, *Angelo Mango*; TAILOR: Jim Pompeii; ANTIPHOLUS OF SYRACUSE: Stuart Damon, *Gary Oakes, Gene Bua*; DROMIO OF SYRACUSE: Danny Carroll, *Rudy Tronto*; MERCHANT OF SYRACUSE: Richard Colacino; APPRENTICE: Jeane Deeks, *Isabelle Farrell, Mary Ann Niles*; ANGELO: Richard Nieves; CORPORAL: Dom Salinaro; LUCE: Karen Morrow, *Jane A. Johnston*; ADRIANA: Ellen Hanley, *Karen Shepard, Luce Ennis*; LUCIANA: Julienne Marie, *Marie Santell*; MAIDS: Jeane Deeks (*Isabelle Farrell; Mary Ann Niles* in the second season), Betsy Hepburn, Svetlana McLee (*Myrna Aaron*); SORCERER: Matthew Tobin, *Emory Bass*); COURTESANS: Cathryn Damon (*Dorothy Frank, Ann Hodges*), Violetta Landek, Charlene Carter; FATIMA: Zebra Nevins; MERCHANT OF EPHESUS: Jim Pompeii; GALATEA: Violetta Landek; PYGMALION: Richard Nieves; AMAZONS: Charlene Carter, Svetlana McLee (*Myrna Aaron*), Jeane Deeks (*Isabelle Farrell, Mary Ann Niles*). The 1963 U.S. tour of this production opened on 1/8/64, at the Lyric Theatre, Allentown, Pa., and closed on 5/16/64, at Providence, Rhode Island. **Cast**: John Smolko, Martin Ross, Chet Sommers, Eddie Roll, Laurie Franks.

THEATRE ROYAL, Drury Lane, London. Opened on 11/7/63. 100 PERFORMANCES. It was panned. **Cast**: Ronnie Corbett, Bob Monkhouse, Maggie Fitzgibbon, Denis Quilley, Lynn Kennington.

CITY CENTER, NYC, 5/1/97–5/4/97. 5 PERFORMANCES. This was in concert, part of the *Encores!* series. ADAPTED BY: David Ives; DIRECTOR: Susan H. Schulman; CHOREOGRAPHER: Kathleen Marshall; COSTUMES: Toni-Leslie James; LIGHTING: Peter Kaczorowski; CAST recording on DRG. **Cast**: POLICE SERGEANT: Patrick Quinn; DUKE: Allen Fitzpatrick; CORPORAL: John Wilkerson; DROMIO OF EPHESUS: Michael McGrath; ANTIPHOLUS OF EPHESUS: Malcolm Gets; TAILOR/MERCHANT OF EPHESUS: Danny Burstein; ANTIPHOLUS OF SYRACUSE: Davis Gaines; DROMIO OF SYRACUSE: Mario Cantone; MERCHANT OF SYRACUSE/SORCERER: Kevin Ligon; LUCE: Debbie Gravitte; ADRIANA: Rebecca Luker; LUCIANA: Sarah Uriarte Berry; COURTESAN: Julie Halston; FATIMA: Rachel Jones; ANGELO THE GOLDSMITH: Mel Johnson Jr.; SEERESS: Marian Seldes; AEGEON: Tom Aldredge; DANCERS: Sean Grant, Sean Martin Hingston, Darren Lee, Lisa Mayer, Carol Lee Meadows, Aimee Turner. *Act I*: Overture (Orchestra); *Scene 1* A square in Ephesus: "I Had Twins" (Sergeant, Ladies, Men), "Dear Old Syracuse" (Antipholus & Dromio of Syracuse), "What Can You Do with a Man?" (Luce & Dromio of Ephesus); *Scene 2* Inside the house of Antipholus of Ephesus: "Falling in Love with Love" (Adriana, Luciana, Ladies); *Scene 3* A square in Ephesus: "The Shortest Day of the Year" (Antipholus of Ephesus); *Scene 4* Inside the house of Antipholus of Ephesus: "The Shortest Day of the Year" (reprise) (Adriana & Antipholus of Ephesus), "This Can't Be Love" (Antipholus of Syracuse & Luciana); *Scene 5* Street outside the house of Antipholus of Ephesus: Finale Act I: "Let Antipholus In" (Antipholus of Ephesus & Company). *Act II*: Entr'acte (Orchestra); *Scene 1* Outside the Courtesan's house: "Ladies of the Evening" (Courtesan, Sergeant, Ladies, Men); *Scene 2* Street outside the house of Antipholus of Ephesus: "He and She" (Luce & Dromio of Syracuse), "You Have Cast Your Shadow on the Sea" (Antipholus of Syracuse & Luciana); *Scene 3* A square in Ephesus: "Come with Me" (Sergeant, Antipholus of Ephesus, Men), "Big Brother" (Dromio of Ephesus); *Scene 4* The Twins Ballet (Orchestra); *Scene 5* Inside the house of Antipholus of Ephesus: "Sing for Your Supper" (Adriana, Luciana, Luce, Ladies); *Scene 6* A square in Ephesus: "Oh, Diogenes" (Luce, Ladies, Men); *Scene 7* Street outside the temple: Act II Finale: "This Can't Be Love" (Company).

The newly-revised version (the subject of this entry) was workshopped for the Roundabout Theatre in 1999 and 2000. DIRECTOR: Scott Ellis. **Cast**: Chip Zien. It was planned for Broadway for spring 2002, then postponed until the fall. It used numbers from the 1938 original, but added three new ones from other Rodgers & Hart shows: "Everything I've Got Belongs to You" (dropped before Broadway), "You Took Advantage of Me," and "A Lady Must Live." Nicky Silver reduced

George Abbott's original book to a mere outline — only four lines of Mr. Abbott remain. During Broadway previews Mark Lotito (playing the tailor) was injured, and replaced by Joseph Siravo.

The Broadway Run. AMERICAN AIRLINES THEATRE, 8/18/02–10/20/02. 29 previews from 7/25/02. 73 PERFORMANCES. PRESENTED BY the Roundabout Theatre Company; MUSIC: Richard Rodgers; LYRICS: Lorenz Hart; ORIGINAL BOOK: George Abbott; REVISED BOOK: Nicky Silver; BASED ON Shakespeare's *A Comedy of Errors*; DIRECTOR: Scott Ellis; CHOREOGRAPHER: Rob Ashford; SETS: Thomas Lynch; COSTUMES: Martin Pakledinaz; LIGHTING: Donald Holder; SOUND: Brian Ronan; MUSICAL DIRECTOR/VOCAL ARRANGEMENTS: David Loud; ORCHESTRATIONS: Don Sebesky; DANCE MUSIC ARRANGEMENTS: David Krane; PRESS: Boneau/Bryan-Brown; CASTING: Jim Carnahan; GENERAL MANAGER: Sydney Davolos; COMPANY MANAGER: Jean Haring; PRODUCTION STAGE MANAGER: Peter Hanson; STAGE MANAGER: James Mountcastle. **Cast:** A SERGEANT: Fred Inkley; THE DUKE OF EPHESUS: J.C. Montgomery; AEGEON: Walter Charles, *Tom Galantich*; SOLDIER: Davis Kirby; ANTIPHOLUS OF EPHESUS: Tom Hewitt; DROMIO OF EPHESUS: Chip Zien; TAILOR: Joseph Siravo; ANTIPHOLUS OF SYRACUSE: Jonathan Dokuchitz; DROMIO OF SYRACUSE: Lee Wilkof; TAILOR'S APPRENTICE: Kirk McDonald; ANGELO: Jeffrey Broadhurst; LUCE: Toni DiBuono; ADRIANA: Lauren Mitchell; LUCIANA: Erin Dilly; SORCERER: George Hall (until 10/02), *Tripp Hanson*; MADAM: Jackee Harry; COURTESANS: Sara Gettelfinger, Deidre Goodwin, Milena Govich, Teri Hansen, Elizabeth Mills; MERCHANT OF EPHESUS: Scott Robertson; SEERESS: Georgia Engel (uncredited); ENSEMBLE: Sara Gettelfinger, Deidre Goodwin, Milena Govich, Teri Hansen, Tripp Hanson, Elizabeth Mills, Mark Lotito, J.C. Montgomery, Scott Robertson, Allyson Turner. **Standby**: Aegeon/both Antipholuses/Duke: Tom Galantich. **Understudies**: Luce: Sara Gettelfinger; Madam: Deidre Goodwin; Luciana: Milena Govich; Adriana/Luciana: Teri Hansen; Angelo/Merchant/Sorcerer/Tailor/Apprentice; Tripp Hanson; Antipholus of Ephesus: Fred Inkley; both Dromios: Scott Robertson; Sergeant: Joseph Siravo; Courtesans: Allyson Turner. **Orchestra**: VIOLINS: Paul Woodiel, Ella Rutkovsky, Liuh-Wen Ting; REEDS: Eddie Salkin, Jonathan Levine, Andrew Sterman, Mark Thrasher; TRUMPETS: Jon Owens & Matt Peterson; TROMBONE: Charles Gordon; FRENCH HORN: R.J. Kelly; BASS: Brian Cassier; DRUMS/PERCUSSION: Bruce Doctor; KEYBOARD: Ethyl Will. **Act I**: Overture (Orchestra); *Scene 1* The town square: "Hurrah! Hurroo!" ("I Had Twins") Sergeant, Duke, Aegeon, Crowd), "Dear Old Syracuse" (Antipholus & Dromio of Syracuse); *Scene 2* A tailor's shop: "What Can You Do with a Man" (Luce & Dromio of Ephesus); *Scene 3* An Ephesian street corner: "Falling in Love with Love" (Adriana); *Scene 4* The local bordello: "A Lady Must Live" (Courtesans) [new for this production], "The Shortest Day of the Year" (Antipholus of Ephesus & Adriana); *Scene 5* Adriana's home/The streets of Ephesus: "This Can't Be Love" (Antipholus of Syracuse & Luciana), "This Must Be Love" (Antipholus of Syracuse & Luciana). **Act II**: Entr'acte (Orchestra); *Prologue* "You Took Advantage of Me" (Courtesans) [new for this production]; *Scene 1* Adriana's home, East Wing: "He and She" (Luce & Dromio of Ephesus), "You Have Cast Your Shadow on the Sea" (Antipholus of Syracuse); *Scene 2* Ephesus' red light district: "Big Brother" (Dromio of Ephesus & Dromio of Syracuse), "Come with Me" (Sergeant & Policeman); *Scene 3* Adriana's home: "Oh, Diogenes" (Adriana, Luciana, Luce); *Scene 4* The town square: "Hurrah! Hurroo!" (reprise) (Crowd), "Sing for Your Supper" (Madam, Courtesans, Luce, Adriana, Luciana, Crowd), "This Can't Be Love" (reprise) (Company).

Broadway reviews were mixed. George Hall left the show two weeks before the end of the run due to illness, and died 10/21/02, a day after the show ended. He was 85.

79. *Bravo Giovanni*

The competition between two restaurants in Rome, Giovanni's little one and Uriti, the big chain restaurant next door. Giovanni and friends dig a tunnel between the two restaurants, and steal food from Uriti's. Signora Pandolfi is the aging widow.

Before Broadway. The numbers "Baloon, Baloona," "Beside a Bridge (Along the River Tiber)," "Give All Your Love Away," "Here I Am," "It's Love," and "Time (Love Must Have Time)" were all cut before Broadway. Former ballerina Maria Karnilova was married to George Irving. Miss Lee (accent grave over first "e" in Michele — an accent that was subsequently dropped) was only 19.

The Broadway Run. BROADHURST THEATRE, 5/19/62–9/15/62. 3 previews from 5/17/62. 76 PERFORMANCES. PRESENTED BY Philip Rose; MUSIC: Milton Schafer; LYRICS: Ronny Graham; BOOK: A.J. Russell; BASED ON the 1959 novel *The Crime of Giovanni Venturi*, by Howard Shaw; DIRECTOR: Stanley Prager; CHOREOGRAPHER: Carol Haney; ASSISTANT CHOREOGRAPHER: Buzz Miller; DANCE CAPTAIN: Zoya Leporska; SETS/LIGHTING: Robert Randolph; COSTUMES: Ed Wittstein; MUSICAL DIRECTOR/MUSICAL CONTINUITY/VOCAL ARRANGEMENTS: Anton Coppola; ORCHESTRATIONS/ARRANGEMENTS: Robert Ginzler; DANCE MUSIC ARRANGEMENTS & ORCHESTRATIONS: Luther Henderson; CAST RECORDING on Columbia; PRESS: James D. Proctor; GENERAL MANAGER: Walter Fried; PRODUCTION STAGE MANAGER: Samuel Liff; STAGE MANAGER: Gene Perlowin; ASSISTANT STAGE MANAGER: Mike Abel. **Cast:** GIOVANNI VENTURI: Cesare Siepi (1) ☆; SIGNOR BELLARDI: George S. Irving (5); URITI WAITERS: Rico Froehlich, Joe McGrath, Ed Dumont, Barney Johnston; AMEDEO: David Opatoshu (2); FURNITURE DEALER: Harry Davis (9); NINO: Al Sambogna; GINO: Thatcher Clarke; DINO: Buzz Miller (10); MIRANDA: Michele Lee (3); MOSCOLITO: Arnold Soboloff (8); CARLO: Al Lanti (7); SIGNORA PANDOLFI: Maria Karnilova (4); MUSICIANS: Gene Varrone, Nino Banome, Rico Froehlich; NIGHT CLUB MANAGER: Buzz Miller (10); PROFESSOR PANFREDONI: Harry Davis; TROUBADOUR: Gene Varrone; CELESTINA: Lu Leonard (6); HEAD CHEF: Buzz Miller (10); PIZZA MAKER: Gene Varrone (12); SALAD CHEF: Gene Gavin; BAKERS: Nino Banome & Larry Fuller; SOUP COOK: Thatcher Clarke; HELPERS: Alan Peterson, Alvin Beam, Al Sambogna; SIGNORA ELLI: Penny Gaston; LA CONTESSA: Lainie Kazan; SIGNOR BRANCUSI: John Taliaferro; PROFESSOR MUSA: Rico Froehlich (11); BRIGADIERE: Gene Varrone (12); POLICEMAN: Barney Johnston; SINGERS: Jyll Alexander, Norma Donaldson, Ed Dumont, Penny Gaston, Marcia Gilford, Maria Graziano, Tom Head, Barney Johnston, Lainie Kazan, Betty Kent, Ronald Knight, Joe McGrath, Rita Metzger, Richard Park, John Taliaferro; DANCERS: Nino Banome, Ann Barry, Alvin Beam, Thatcher Clarke, Shellie Farrell, Michele Franchi, Larry Fuller, Gene Gavin, Herad Gruhn, Ellen Halpin, Baayork Lee, Alan Peterson, Barbara Richman, Al Sambogna, Nikki Sowinski, Claude Thompson. **Standby**: Giovanni: Kenneth Smith. **Understudies**: Giovanni: Ronald Knight; Amedeo: Harry Davis; Miranda: Marcia Gilford; Pandolfi: Zoya Leporska; Bellardi: Rico Froehlich; Carlo: Nino Banome; Celestina: Rita Metzger; Moscolito: John Taliaferro; Night Club Manager: Thatcher Clarke; Musa: Tom Head. **Act I**: *Scene 1* A piazza in Trastevere, Rome; dawn of a spring day: "Rome" (Giovanni), "Uriti" (Bellardi & Full Ensemble); *Scene 2* Giovanni's restaurant; three weeks later: "Breachy's Law" (Giovanni & Amedeo); *Scene 3* The piazza; the following afternoon: "I'm All I Got" (Miranda); *Scene 4* A fountain in Rome; the following afternoon: "The Argument" (Giovanni & Bellardi); *Scene 5* The tunnel; a few nights later; *Scene 6* A nightclub in Rome; the following morning: "Signora Pandolfi" (Amedeo, Pandolfi, Manager, Musicians), "The Kangaroo" (Pandolfi, Manager, Waiters, Musicians, Kitchen Help) (demonstration of a dance craze); *Scene 7* The tunnel; the following night; *Scene 8* The Etruscan Room in the Villa Giulia Museum; a few days later: "If I Were the Man" (Giovanni), "Steady, Steady" (Miranda); *Scene 9* The tunnel; a few days later: "We Won't Discuss It" (Giovanni & Amedeo); *Scene 10* Giovanni's room; immediately following; *Scene 11* The piazza; late the following Saturday night: "Ah! Camminare" (Troubadour, Giovanni, Entire Company). **Act II**: *Scene 1* The tunnel; noon the following Monday: "Breachy's Law" (reprise) (Giovanni, Amedeo, Pandolfi, Miranda); *Scene 2* A street in Rome; a month later; *Scene 3* The Uriti kitchen; immediately following: "Uriti Kitchen" (Bellardi, Moscolito, Carlo, Head Chef, Pizza Maker, Salad Chef, Bakers, Soup Cook, Helpers); *Scene 4* The street; immediately following: "Virtue Arrivederci!" (Bellardi); *Scene 5* Giovanni's kitchen; a few days later; *Scene 6* The Etruscan Restaurant; six months later: "Bravo, Giovanni" (Giovanni, Bellardi, Singing Ensemble), "One Little World Apart" (Miranda); *Scene 7* Giovanni's room; a few nights later; *Scene 8* The tunnel; lunchtime, the following day: "Connubiality" (Pandolfi &

Amedeo) [replaced during the run by "Jump In" (Pandolfi & Amedeo)]; **Scene 9** The Etruscan Restaurant; immediately following; **Scene 10** The tunnel; immediately following; "Miranda" (Giovanni); **Scene 11** The piazza; immediately following.

Cesare Siepi, the famous Metropolitan Opera bass (a noted Don Giovanni) was miscast (no fault of his). The book was weak and contrived. Carol Haney's choreography was good, especially the kitchen ballet in Act II. Reviews were generally very good. It was nominated for Tonys for choreography, composer/lyricist, and for musical director. The show suspended performances for the summer, 7/14/62–9/6/62; reopened 9/7/62, after Labor Day; and closed for good a week later. It lost $550,000, a fantastic sum in those days.

80. *Brigadoon*

In the 18th century, thanks to minister Mr. Forsyth, a mythical Scottish highland village was saved by the gods from the contamination of civilization. It disappeared off the face of the map, citizens and all, and now re-appears out of the mist into the real world for only one day once every 100 years. To the inhabitants of the village, only a day has gone by. It is during one of these days in the real world that two weary American hunters, Tommy and Jeff, stumble across it. Tommy becomes involved with Fiona. Meg tries unsuccessfully to awaken some sort of sexual impulse in Jeff. A sub-plot creates tension: part of the deal with the gods is that if an inhabitant leaves the village the spell will be broken and the village will disappear forever. Fiona's sister Jean is to be married that day to Charlie, but Harry is insanely in love with her. After the ceremony Harry threatens to flee Brigadoon and thus break the spell. The villagers, including Tommy and Jeff, pursue him until he is killed. Despite learning the truth about the village, Tommy (with Jeff) leaves and returns to the USA. He knows he made the wrong decision, and goes back to Scotland but the village has gone, and won't re-appear for another 100 years. However, his love for Fiona works miracles, and the village makes an irregular re-appearance to take him on board.

Before Broadway. Lerner and Loewe began planning *Brigadoon* at the Algonquin Hotel after the opening night party of their previous Broadway show, *What's Up.* After several producers had turned it down, Cheryl Crawford took it up. It cost only $167,000. Lerner & Loewe had to audition it 58 times to raise the money. A tech rehearsal in New Haven ran so late that the actual rehearsal became opening night. During tryouts, a week later, at the Colonial Theatre, in Boston (the sets on opening night provided nightmares), Sandy Dean was played by Jeff Warren; Frank by Wendell Phillips; and the part of Kate MacQueen (played by Margaret Hunter) was cut.

The Broadway Run. ZIEGFELD THEATRE, 3/13/47–7/31/48. 581 PERFORMANCES. PRESENTED BY Cheryl Crawford; MUSIC: Frederick Loewe; LYRICS/BOOK: Alan Jay Lerner; BASED ON an original 1862 German story *Germelshausen,* by Friedrich Wilhelm Gestacker; DIRECTOR: Robert Lewis; CHOREOGRAPHER: Agnes de Mille; ASSISTANT TO AGNES DE MILLE ON SCOTTISH DANCES: James Jamieson; SETS: Oliver Smith; SET PAINTING SUPERVISOR: Victor Graziano; COSTUMES: David ffolkes; LIGHTING: Peggy Clark; MUSICAL DIRECTOR: Franz Allers; ORCHESTRATIONS: Ted Royal; VOCAL ARRANGEMENTS: Frederick Loewe; DANCE MUSIC ARRANGEMENTS: Trude Rittman; CAST RECORDING on Victor; PRESS: Wolfe Kaufman & Mary Ward; GENERAL MANAGER: John Yorke; PRODUCTION STAGE MANAGER: Ward Bishop; STAGE MANAGERS: Jules Racine & John Herman. **Cast:** TOMMY ALBRIGHT: David Brooks (1), *Hayes Gordon* (alternate); JEFF DOUGLAS: George Keane (5), *Jules Racine* (alternate); ARCHIE BEATON: Elliott Sullivan, *John Paul* (alternate); HARRY BEATON: James Mitchell (6), *Kenneth Le Roy* (alternate), *Albert Ruiz, James Jamieson*; FISHMONGER: Bunty Kelley; ANGUS MACGUFFIE: Walter Scheff, *Jules Racine, John Paul* (alternate); SANDY DEAN: Hayes Gordon, *Jordan Bentley*; ANDREW MACLAREN: Edward Cullen; FIONA MACLAREN: Marion Bell (2), *Virginia Oswald* (alternate), *Priscilla*

Gillette; JEAN MACLAREN: Virginia Bosler, *Phyllis Gehrig* (alternate); MEG BROCKIE: Pamela Britton (3), *Jean Sincere* (alternate), *Susan Johnson*; CHARLIE DALRYMPLE: Lee Sullivan (4), *Jeff Warren* (alternate); MAGGIE ANDERSON: Lidija Franklin, *Ina Kurland* (alternate); MR. LUNDIE: William Hansen; SWORD DANCERS: Roland Guerard (*James White*) & George Drake; FRANK: John Paul; JANE ASHTON: Frances Charles, *Lois Eastman* (alternate); BAGPIPERS: James McFadden & Arthur Horn (*James Roche*); STUART DALRYMPLE: Paul Anderson, *Delbert Anderson, Bill Hogue, R. Chamberlain*; MACGREGOR: Earl Redding; TOWNSFOLK OF BRIGADOON: SINGING GIRLS: Kay Borron, Wanda Cochran, Lois Eastman, Lydia Fredericks, Jeanne Grant, Margaret Hunter, Linda Mason, Virginia Oswald, Eleanore Parker, Shirley Robbins, Faye Elizabeth Smith, Betty Templeton. *Susan Johnson*; SINGING BOYS: Delbert Anderson, Arthur Carroll, Hayes Gordon, Michael Raymond, Mark Kramer, Robert Lussier, Tommy Matthews, Kenny McCord, Earl Redding, John Schmidt, Paul Valin, Jeff Warren; DANCING GIRLS: Anna Friedland, Helen Gallagher, Phyllis Gehrig, Lidija Franklin, Dorothy Hill, Bunty Kelley, Ina Kurland, Olga Lunick, Mary Martinet, Kirsten Valbor; DANCING BOYS: Forrest Bonshire, George Drake, Richard D'Arcy, Roland Guerard, Kenneth Le Roy, Charles McCraw, Stanley Simmons, Allan Waine, William Weber, *Nathan Baker*. **Act I**: *Prologue* "Once in the Highlands" (Chorus); **Scene 1** A forest in the Scottish Highlands; about 5 on a May morning: "Brigadoon" (Chorus) [a hit]; *Interlude* A road in the town of Brigadoon; a few minutes later; **Scene 2** The square of Brigadoon — MacConnachy Square; later that morning: "Down on MacConnachy Square" (Sandy, Meg, Townsfolk), "Waitin' for My Dearie" (Fiona & Girls), "(I'll Go Home With) Bonnie Jean" (dance) (Charlie & Townsfolk, Maggie, Harry & Dancers), "The Heather on the Hill" (Tommy & Fiona) [a big hit], "Down on MacConnachy Square" (reprise) (Townsfolk); **Scene 3** The Brockie open shed; just past noon: "The Love of My Life" (Meg); **Scene 4** The MacLaren house; mid–afternoon: "Jeannie's Packin' Up" (Girls), "Come to Me, Bend to Me" (dance) (Charlie, Jean & Dancers), "Almost Like Being in Love" (Tommy & Fiona) [the big hit]; **Scene 5** Outside the house of Mr. Lundie; immediately following; **Scene 6** Outside the Kirk of Brigadoon; dusk: The Wedding Dance (dance) (Jean, Charlie, Dancers), Sword Dance (dance) (Harry & Dancers). **Act II**: **Scene 1** A forest inside of Brigadoon; later that night: The Chase (Men of Brigadoon); **Scene 2** On the way from the forest; a few minutes later: "There but for You Go I" (Tommy) [a big hit]; **Scene 3** The glen; soon after: "My Mother's Weddin' Day" (Meg & Townsfolk), Funeral Dance (dance) (Maggie), "From This Day On" (Tommy & Fiona); **Scene 4** A bar in New York City; four months later: "Come to Me, Bend to Me" (reprise) (Fiona), "The Heather on the Hill" (reprise) (Fiona), "I'll Go Home with Bonnie Jean" (reprise) (Charlie & Townsfolk), "From This Day On" (reprise) (Fiona & Tommy), "Down on MacConnachy Square" (reprise) (Townsfolk); **Scene 5** The forest (same as Act I, Scene 1); three nights later: Finale.

It got only raves from Broadway critics. George Jean Nathan (in an excellent review, incidentally), accused Alan Jay Lerner of stealing the story from a German legend called *Germelshausen*, and the story based upon it by Friedrich Wilhelm Gerstacker. Lerner reported in his memoirs that Nathan was in love with Marion Bell, the leading lady, and when he found out she was already engaged to Mr. Lerner, Nathan struck back with this charge of plagiarism. However, there can be little doubt that Mr. Nathan was right. It won a Tony Award for choreography, and Donaldson Awards for choreography, sets, costumes, and for Marion Bell (female debut), and James Mitchell (male dancer).

After Broadway. After Broadway the show went on a long, successful tour, and returned to New York, to CITY CENTER, 5/2/50–5/21/50. 24 PERFORMANCES. $3 top ticket prices. It had the same basic crew as for the 1947 original, except MUSICAL DIRECTOR: Ignace Strasfogel. **Cast:** TOMMY: Phil Hanna; JEFF: Peter Turgeon; SANDY: Douglas Rideout; ARCHIE: Thaddeus Clancy; HARRY: James Jamieson; ANGUS/FRANK: Angus Cairns; FIONA: Virginia Oswald; JEAN: Ann Deasy; MEG: Susan Johnson; CHARLIE: Jeff Warren; LUNDIE: Fred Stewart; SWORD DANCERS: Wayne Sheridan & James White; BAGPIPER: James McFadden; JANE: Winifred Ainslee; ENSEMBLE INCLUDED: Sylvia Chaney, Bobra Suitor, Arthur Carroll, Lou Polacek, Stanley Simmons.

HIS MAJESTY'S THEATRE, London, 4/14/49–11/4/50. 684 PERFORMANCES. *Cast* (several characters' names were changed for the London stage only): TOMMY: Philip Hanna, *Bruce Trent*; JEFF: Hiram Sherman, *Lionel Murton*; DONALD RITCHIE: John Rae; HARRY RITCHIE: James Jamieson, *Paddy Stone*; ANGUS MACMONIES: Peter Dyneley; SANDY: Wilfred Johns; ANDREW MACKEITH: Roy Russell; FIONA MACKEITH: Patricia Hughes; JEAN MACKEITH: Bunty Kelley; MEG: Noele Gordon; CHARLIE CAMERON: Bill O'Conner; MAGGIE ABERNETHY: Noelle de Mosa, *Enid Martin*; MR. MURDOCH: Ivor Barnard; SWORD DANCERS: James White & Robert Harrold; PIPERS: David Ross & Robert Hill; FRANK: Freddie Costello, *Milo Lewis, Peter Dyneley*; JANE ASHTON: Janet MacFarlane, *Helen Lorraine*.

THE MOVIE. In the splendid 1954 movie the MacLaren family's name was changed to Campbell. *Cast:* TOMMY: Gene Kelly; JEFF: Van Johnson; HARRY: Hugh Laing; CHARLIE: Jimmy Thompson; ARCHIE: Tudor Owen; MEG: Dody Heath; ANDREW: Albert Sharpe; FIONA: Cyd Charisse; JEAN: Virginia Bosler; LUNDIE: Barry Jones; JANE: Elaine Stewart; DANCER: George Chakiris.

81. *Brigadoon (1957 Broadway revival)*

Before Broadway. This Broadway revival ran first at CITY CENTER, NYC, 3/27/57–4/7/57. 23 PERFORMANCES. Then it moved to the Adelphi Theatre, on Broadway.

The Broadway Run. ADELPHI THEATRE, 4/15/57–5/5/57. Limited run of 24 PERFORMANCES. PRESENTED BY the New York City Center Light Opera Company, by arrangement with the Lowall Corporation; MUSIC: Frederick Loewe; LYRICS/BOOK: Alan Jay Lerner; DIRECTOR: George H. Englund; CHOREOGRAPHER: James Jamieson re-staged Agnes de Mille's choreography; SETS: Oliver Smith; COSTUMES: Paul du Pont; LIGHTING: Peggy Clark; MUSICAL DIRECTOR: Julius Rudel; PRESS: Tom Trenkle; GENERAL MANAGER: Buford Armitage; COMPANY MANAGER: Ed Haas; PRODUCTION STAGE MANAGER: Bernard Gersten; STAGE MANAGER: John Maxtone-Graham; ASSISTANT STAGE MANAGER: Jack Emrek. *Cast:* TOMMY ALBRIGHT: David Atkinson; JEFF DOUGLAS: Scott McKay; ARCHIE BEATON: Elliott Sullivan; HARRY BEATON: Matt Mattox; FISHMONGER: Dorothy Etheridge; ANGUS MACGUFFIE: Guy Gordon; SANDY DEAN: John Dorrin; ANDREW MACLAREN: Russell Gaige; FIONA MACLAREN: Virginia Oswald; JEAN MACLAREN: Virginia Bosler; MEG BROCKIE: Helen Gallagher; CHARLIE DALRYMPLE: Robert Rounseville; MAGGIE ANDERSON: Lidija Franklin; MR. LUNDIE: John C. Becher; SWORD DANCERS: Glenn Olson & Keith Willis; FRANK: Jack Emrek; JANE ASHTON: Sloan Simpson; BAGPIPER: Duncan MacGaskill; SINGERS: Jennie Andrea, Robert Atherton, Don Becker, Norris Brannstrom, June Buckner, Austin Colyer, Marilyn Cooper, Dori Davis, Arthur Dilks, John Dorrin, Julia Gerace, Patricia Hall, Peter Held, Vincent McMahon, Jean Maggio, Maria Martell, Sheila Mathews, William Nahr, Stanley Page, Mary Thompson; DANCERS: Robert Barnett, Jeanna Belkin, Patricia Birch, Anthony Blum, Anne Boley, Jim Brusock, Anne Crowell, Geralyn Donald, Dorothy Etheridge, Walter Georgov, Rosemary Jourdan, Charles McCraw, Glenn Olson, Ray Pointer, Evelyn Taylor, Mona Jo Tritsch, Keith Willis, Emmanuel Winston. *Understudies*: Tommy: Norris Brannstrom; Jeff: Jack Emrek; Fiona: Patricia Hall; Meg: Maria Martell; Jane: Sheila Mathews; Harry: Glenn Olson; Jean: Rosemary Jourdan; Maggie: Dorothy Etheridge; Andrew: John Dorrin; Angus: Stanley Page; Lundie: Guy Gordon; Archie: Robert Atherton; Frank: John Maxtone-Graham.

This revival won a 1958 Tony nomination for sets.

After Broadway. CITY CENTER, NYC, 5/30/62–6/10/62. 16 PERFORMANCES. PRESENTED BY the New York City Center Light Opera Company; DIRECTOR: John Fearnley; CHOREOGRAPHER: Agnes de Mille; ASSISTANT CHOREOGRAPHER: James Jamieson; ART DIRECTOR: Watson Barratt; COSTUMES: Stanley Simmons; LIGHTING: Peggy Clark; MUSICAL DIRECTOR: Julius Rudel; CONDUCTOR: Don Smith. *Cast:* TOMMY: Peter Palmer, *Stephen Douglass* (when Mr. Palmer fell ill); JEFF: Farley Granger; SANDY: Kenny Adams; MEG: Ann Fraser; ARCHIE: Moultrie Patten; HARRY: Edward Villella; ANDREW: Alexander Clark; FIONA: Sally Ann Howes; JEAN: Jenny Workman; ANGUS: Walter Blocher; CHARLIE: Harry David Snow; MAGGIE: Gemze de Lappe; LUNDIE: John C. Becher; FRANK: Felice Orlandi; JANE: Susan Fellows; DANCERS INCLUDED: Lynne Broadbent, Mickey Gunnersen, Lucia Lambert, Vernon Lusby; SINGERS

INCLUDED: John Aman, Ken Ayers, Don Becker, Marvin Goodis, Robert Lenn.

CITY CENTER, NYC, 1/30/63–2/10/63. 16 PERFORMANCES. It had the same crew as for the 1962 production, except ASSISTANT CONDUCTOR: Rene Wiegert. *Cast:* TOMMY: Peter Palmer; JEFF: Russell Nype; SANDY: William Kennedy; MEG: Ann Fraser; ARCHIE: John Carver; HARRY: Edward Villella; ANDREW: Frank Milan; FIONA: Sally Ann Howes; JEAN: Virginia Bosler; ANGUS: Daniel P. Hannafin; CHARLIE: Harry David Snow; MAGGIE: Jenny Workman; LUNDIE: John C. Becher; FRANK: Felice Orlandi; JANE: Kelly Stevens; DANCERS INCLUDED: Virginia Allen, Lucia Lambert, Evelyn Taylor, Toodie Wittmer, Dennis Cole, Loren Hightower, Vernon Lusby; SINGERS INCLUDED: Julie Sargant, Marvin Goodis, Robert Lenn, Herb Surface, Ralph Vucci. Interestingly — not being a Broadway production — it received three 1963 Tony Nominations: direction of a musical, musical direction, and for Sally Ann Howes.

CITY CENTER, NYC, 5/15/63–5/26/63. 15 PERFORMANCES. Same crew as before. *Cast:* TOMMY: Peter Palmer; JEFF: Russell Nype; FIONA: Sally Ann Howes; LUNDIE: John C. Becher; FRANK: Felice Orlandi; MEG: Ann Fraser; HARRY: Edward Villella; CHARLIE: Harry David Snow; MAGGIE: Gemze de Lappe; SANDY: William Kennedy; ARCHIE: John Carver; JEAN: Virginia Bosler; DANCING ENSEMBLE: Loren Hightower, Vernon Lusby, Lucia Lambert, Dennis Cole; SINGING ENSEMBLE: Julie Sargant, Herb Surface, Ralph Vucci.

CITY CENTER, NYC, 12/23/64–1/3/65. 17 PERFORMANCES. It had the same basic crew as for the 1963 run. *Cast:* TOMMY: Peter Palmer; JEFF: Scott McKay; SANDY: Will MacKenzie; MEG: Louise O'Brien; ARCHIE: Earl McDonald; HARRY: Edward Villella, *James Jamieson* (at 3 matinees); ANDREW: Alexander Clark; JEAN: Imelda de Martin; FIONA: Linda Bennett; ANGUS: Daniel Hannafin; CHARLIE: Harry David Snow; MAGGIE: Gemze de Lappe; LUNDIE: Clarence Nordstrom; FRANK: Si Vario; JANE: Sharon Ritchie; SINGERS INCLUDED: William J. Coppola, Glenn Kezer, Bob Neukum; DANCERS INCLUDED: Virginia Allen, Lynne Broadbent, Dennis Cole, Lucia Lambert, Mavis Ray, Toodie Wittmer.

ABC TV PRODUCTION. 10/15/66. CHOREOGRAPHER: Peter Gennaro; ASSISTANT CHOREOGRAPHER: Larry Fuller. *Cast:* TOMMY: Robert Goulet; JEFF: Peter Falk; HARRY: Edward Villella; MEG: Marlyn Mason; FIONA: Sally Ann Howes.

CITY CENTER, NYC, 12/13/67–12/31/67. 1 preview. 23 PERFORMANCES. PRESENTED BY the New York City Center Light Opera Company; DIRECTOR: Gus Schirmer; CHOREOGRAPHERS: Gemze de Lappe & Dennis Cole; COSTUMES: Stanley Simmons; LIGHTING: Peggy Clark; MUSICAL DIRECTOR: Jonathan Anderson. *Cast:* TOMMY: Bill Hayes; JEFF: Russell Nype; SANDY: Henry Lawrence; MEG: Karen Morrow; ARCHIE: Earl McDonald; HARRY: Edward Villella, Frank Andre (alternate); ANDREW: Alexander Clark; JEAN: Sarah Jane Smith; FIONA: Margot Moser; ANGUS: Gordon Cook; CHARLIE: Evan Thomas; MAGGIE: Leslie Franzos; LUNDIE: William Le Massena; FRANK: Paul Adams; JANE: Jeanne Murray Vanderbilt; SINGERS INCLUDED: Chris Callan, Phyllis Bash, Edward Becker, Donald Brassington, Jane Coleman, Marta Heflin, Ken Richards; DANCERS INCLUDED: Paul Berne, Chele Graham, Scott Hunter, Dick Korthaze, Karen Kristin, Lucia Lambert, Bud Spencer, Toodie Wittmer.

82. *Brigadoon (1980 Broadway revival)*

Before Broadway. This Broadway run was part of a touring revival, previously presented in New Orleans, Wolf Trap Farm Park (in Vienna, Virginia), and in Washington, DC. Before Broadway Larry Hansen was replaced by Joseph Kolinski in the cast. John Curry was the ice-skater.

The Broadway Run. MAJESTIC THEATRE, 10/16/80–2/8/81 (closed at a matinee). 8 previews. 133 PERFORMANCES. The Wolf Trap production, PRESENTED BY Zev Bufman & The Shubert Organization; MUSIC: Frederick Loewe; LYRICS/BOOK: Alan Jay Lerner; DIRECTOR: Vivian Matalon; CHOREOGRAPHER: James Jamieson re-created Agnes De Mille's choreography; SETS: Michael J. Hotopp & Paul de Pass; COSTUMES: Stanley Simmons; LIGHTING: Thomas Skelton; SOUND: T. Richard Fitzgerald; MUSICAL DIRECTOR/VOCAL ARRANGEMENTS: Wally Harper; ORCHESTRATIONS: Mack Schlefer & Bill Brohn; PRESS: Fred Nathan &

Louise Weiner Ment; CASTING: Julie Hughes/Barry Moss, Phil Di Maggio; GENERAL MANAGERS: Theatre Now; COMPANY MANAGER: Hans Hortig; PRODUCTION STAGE MANAGER: Joe Lorden; STAGE MANAGER: Jack Gianino; ASSISTANT STAGE MANAGER: David Rosenberg. *Cast:* TOMMY ALBRIGHT: Martin Vidnovic (1) ☆; JEFF DOUGLAS: Mark Zimmerman (8); ANGUS MCGUFFIE: Kenneth Kantor (12); ARCHIE BEATON: Casper Roos (10); SANDY DEAN: Michael Cone; MAGGIE ANDERSON: Marina Eglevsky (5); MEG BROCKIE: Elaine Hausman (7); HARRY BEATON: John Curry (3) ☆; ANDREW MACLAREN: Jack Dabdoub (9); FIONA MACLAREN: Meg Bussert (2) ☆; JEAN MACLAREN: Mollie Smith (11); CHARLIE DALRYMPLE: Stephen Lehew (6); MR. LUNDIE: Frank Hamilton (4); FRANK: Mark Herrier; JANE ASHTON: Betsy Craig; BAGPIPER: Larry Cole; SINGERS: Michael Cone, Betsy Craig, Larry French, Linda Hohenfeld, Michael Hayward-Jones, Joseph Kolinski, Diane Pennington, Cheryl Russell, Linda Wonneberger; DANCERS: Bill Badolato, Cherie Bower, Amy Danis, Tom Fowler, John Giffin, Mickey Gunnersen, Jennifer Henson, David Hughes, Phil La Duca, Elena Malfitano, Susi McCarter, Jerry Mitchell, Eric Nesbitt, Holly Reeve, Dale Robbins, Harry Williams. *Standbys*: Fiona: Linda Wonneberger; Lundie: Jack Dabdoub; Harry: Eric Nesbitt. *Understudies*: Tommy: Mark Zimmerman; Jeff: Mark Herrier; Fiona/Jane: Linda Hohenfeld; Lundie: Casper Roos; Harry: Tom Fowler; Meg: Diane Pennington; Andrew: Casper Roos; Charlie: Joseph Kolinski; Angus/Sandy: Michael Hayward-Jones; Archie: Kenneth Kantor; Frank: Larry French; Jean: Holly Reeve; Maggie: Amy Danis. SWING DANCERS/SINGERS: Randal Harris & Suzi Winson. *Act I*: *Scene 1* A hillside in Scotland: "Once in the Highlands" (Ensemble), "Brigadoon" (Ensemble); *Scene 2* MacConnachy Square: "Down on MacConnachy Square" (Sandy, Meg, Men & Women of Brigadoon), "Waitin' for My Dearie" (Fiona & Girls), "(I'll Go Home With) Bonnie Jean" (Charlie & Men) (danced by Harry, Maggie, Men & Women of Brigadoon); *Scene 3* A hillside in Brigadoon: "The Heather on the Hill" (Tommy & Fiona), Rain Exorcism (Men & Women of Brigadoon); *Scene 4* The Brockie shed: "The Love of My Life" (Meg); *Scene 5* Outside the MacLaren house: "Jeannie's Packin' Up" (danced by Girls), "Come to Me, Bend to Me" (Charlie) (danced by Jean & Girls), "Almost Like Being in Love" (Tommy & Fiona). *Act II*: *Scene 1* Outside Mr. Lundie's house; *Scene 2* The glen: Wedding Dance (led by Jean & Charlie, and danced by Men & Women of Brigadoon), Sword Dance (led by Harry, and danced by Company); *Scene 3* The forest: The Chase (Harry & Men of Brigadoon), "There but for You Go I" (Tommy & Fiona); *Scene 4* Outside the MacLaren house: Steps Stately (danced by Men & Women of Brigadoon), Drunken Reel (danced by Men & Women of Brigadoon), Funeral Dance (danced by Maggie); *Scene 5* A hillside in Scotland: "From This Day On" (Tommy & Fiona), "Brigadoon" (reprise) (Ensemble); *Scene 6* A cocktail bar in New York City, "Come to Me, Bend to Me"/"The Heather on the Hill" (reprise) (Fiona); *Scene 7* A hillside in Scotland: "From This Day On" (reprise) (Tommy), "Brigadoon" (reprise) (Ensemble).

Broadway reviews were good, The show received Tony nominations for reproduction of a play or musical, and for Martin Vidnovic, and Meg Bussert.

After Broadway. VICTORIA PALACE THEATRE, London. The ballet "Come to Me, Bend to Me" was missing. NEW DANCES BY: Tommy Shaw; MUSICAL DIRECTOR: Stuart Calvert; CAST RECORDING on First Night (the first digital recording of *Brigadoon*). *Cast:* Jacinta Mulcahy, Robert Meadmore, Maurice Clarke, Ian Mackenzie Stewart, Robin Nedwell, Donald Jones, Allan Adams, Lesley Mackie, Leonard Maguire, Sorkina Tate, Jo-Anne Sale.

NEW YORK STATE THEATRE, 3/1/86–3/30/86. 40 PERFORMANCES. PRESENTED BY the New York City Opera; DIRECTOR: Gerald Freedman; CHOREOGRAPHER: James Jamieson; SETS/COSTUMES: Desmond Heeley; LIGHTING: Duane Schuler; SOUND: Farrel Becker; CONDUCTOR: Paul Gemignani. *Cast:* TOMMY: Richard White, John Leslie Wolfe (alternate); JEFF: Tony Roberts; MAGGIE: Tinka Gutrick; ARCHIE: William Ledbetter; ANGUS: Don Yule; MEG: Joyce Castle, Marcia Mitzman (alternate); STUART: Robert Brubaker; SANDY: Gregory Moore; HARRY: Luis Perez; ANDREW: David Rae Smith; FIONA: Sheryl Woods, Beverly Lambert (alternate); JEAN: Camille Ross; CHARLIE: Cris Groenendaal, David Eisler (alternate); MR. LUNDIE: James Billings; FRANK: Ralph Bassett; JANE: Alison Bevan.

NEW YORK STATE THEATRE, 11/7/91–11/17/91. 12 PERFORMANCES IN REPERTORY. PRESENTED BY the New York City Opera; DIRECTOR: Gerald Freedman; CHOREOGRAPHER: James Jamieson; SETS/COSTUMES: Desmond Heeley; LIGHTING: Duane Schuler; SOUND: Abe Jacob; CONDUCTOR: Paul Gemignani. *Cast:* TOMMY: John Leslie Wolfe & George Dvorsky; JEFF: Tony Roberts; MAGGIE: Joan Mirabella; ARCHIE: William Ledbetter; ANGUS: Don Yule; MEG: Joyce Castle & Louisa Flaningam; STUART: Richard Byrne; HARRY: Scott Fowler; FIONA: Michele McBride & Elizabeth Walsh; JEAN: Camille de Ganon; CHARLIE: David Eisler & Robert Tate; LUNDIE: Ron Randell.

PAPER MILL PLAYHOUSE, New Jersey, 1994. DIRECTOR: David Holdgrive; CHOREOGRAPHER: Greg Ganakas; MUSICAL DIRECTOR: Jim Coleman. *Cast:* TOMMY: Joseph Mahowald; JEFF: P.J. Benjamin; ARCHIE: Kenneth Kantor; MEG: Leah Hocking; HARRY: Alex Sanchez; FIONA: Lee Merill; JEAN: Tania Philip; CHARLIE: John Clonts; SWORD DANCERS: Eric H. Kaufman & Steve Ochoa; ENSEMBLE INCLUDED: Joy Hermalyn, Alexia Hess, Max Perlman, Dana Stackpole.

NEW YORK STATE THEATRE, 11/13/96–11/24/96. 14 PERFORMANCES. PRESENTED BY the New York City Opera; DIRECTOR: Christian Smith; CHOREOGRAPHER: Gemze de Lappe; SETS/COSTUMES: Desmond Heeley; LIGHTING: Duane Schuler; SOUND: Abe Jacob; CONDUCTOR: John McGlinn. *Cast:* TOMMY: Brent Barrett; JEFF: Sean Donnellan; MAGGIE: Leslie Brown; ARCHIE: William Ledbetter; ANGUS: James Bobick; MEG: Judy Kaye; HARRY: Robert La Fosse; ANDREW: Don Yule; FIONA: Rebecca Luker; JEAN: Elizabeth Ferrell; CHARLIE: George Dyer; LUNDIE: George Hall; JANE: Stacy Lee Tilton. Note: Rebecca Luker, Brent Barrett and Judy Kaye also sang on John McGlinn's 1992 recording.

GOODSPEED OPERA HOUSE, Conn., 4/30/01–6/23/01. Previews from 3/30/01. This was an updated revival, now set in 2001 and 1801 (the original had been in 1947 and 1747). DIRECTOR: Greg Ganakas; LIGHTING: Kirk Bookman; MUSICAL DIRECTOR: Michael O'Flaherty. *Cast:* TOMMY: James Clow (until 6/3/01), *Robert Bartley* (from 6/6/01); JEFF: David Rossmer; ARCHIE: Dale Hensley; MAGGIE: Elizabeth Ferrell; MEG: Lisa Brescia; FIONA: Amanda Serkasevich.

FREUD PLAYHOUSE, UCLA, Calif., 8/18/04–8/29/04. Previews from 8/17/04. Part of the *Reprise!* series. DIRECTOR: Stuart Ross; CHOREOGRAPHER: Lee Martino; MUSICAL DIRECTOR: Gerald Sternbach. *Cast:* TOMMY: Jason Danieley; FIONA: Marin Mazzie; MEG: Deborah Gibson; LUNDIE: Orson Bean.

83. *Bright Lights of 1944*

A musical revue, also called *Bright Lights*.

Before Broadway. Dan Eckley replaced Anthony Brown as director Before Broadway.

The Broadway Run. FORREST THEATRE, 9/16/43–9/18/43. 4 PERFORMANCES. PRESENTED BY Alexander H. Cohen, in association with Martin H. Poll & Joseph Kipness; MUSIC: Jerry Livingston; ADDITIONAL MUSIC: Norman Zeno; LYRICS: Mack David; ADDITIONAL LYRICS: Al Scofield; SKETCHES: Norman Anthony & Charles Sherman; ADDITIONAL DIALOGUE: Joseph Erens; DIRECTOR: Dan Eckley; CHOREOGRAPHER: Truly McGee; SETS/COSTUMES: Perry Watkins; LIGHTING: Albert Alloy; MUSICAL DIRECTOR: Max Meth; ORCHESTRATIONS: Russell Bennett, Hans Spialek, Ted Royal. *Act I*: A book musical, set in Sardi's, where a couple of waiters dream up the idea of doing an intimate musical revue. *Scene 1* Outside Sardi's: COP: John A. Lorenz; OUT OF TOWNER: Cece Eames; *Scene 2* Inside Sardi's: THE BOY: Jere McMahon; THE GIRL: Billie Worth; 1ST WAITER: Joe Smith (2); 2ND WAITER: Charles Dale (2); MR. LEVY: Solen Burry; MR. FARQUARDT: David Leonard; MR. MARQUARDT: Don Roberts. "Haven't We Met Before?" (danced by Billie Worth & Jere McMahon); *Scene 3* James Barton (1): "Damned Ole Jeeter" (m/l: Dick Leibert & George Blake) (parody of Mr. Barton's role of Jeeter in the very long-running Broadway play *Tobacco Road*), "I Can't Give You Anything but Love" (m: Jimmy McHugh; l: Dorothy Fields) [from *Blackbirds of 1928*]; *Scene 4* Inside Sardi's: MR. POTTS: Russell Morrison; MISS CHAMBERS: Elaine Miller; RENEE CARROLL: herself (Sardi's famous real-life stunning hat-check girl); BUDDY CLARK: himself (4). "You'd Better Dance" (danced by Billie Worth & Jere McMahon), "Thoughtless" (sung by Buddy Clark); *Scene 5* Punxsutawney, Pa.: "Don't Forget the Girl from Punxsutawney." Sung by Jayne Manners (a six-foot tall beauty), Royal Guards, Chorus; *Scene 6* The Pest (sketch, by James Barton, who did his drunk act): THE PEST: James Barton (1); GERT: Kathryn Barton [Mrs. James Barton in real life]; CHARLIE: John A. Lorenz; *Scene 7* "That's Broadway!" (m/l: Gene Herbert & Teddy Hall) [sung by Frances Williams (3)]; *Scene 8* John Kirby and his Orchestra; *Scene 9* "We're Having Our Fling" (Entire Company). *Act II*: The intimate musical revue itself. *Scene 1* "Back Bay Beat" [sung by Frances Williams (3), with the John Kirby Orchestra & Dancing Girls]; *Scene 2* The Royal Guards. This was a Quartet: Thomas Gleason, Arthur Barry, John Hamill, Carlton Male; *Scene 3* "Your Face is Your Fortune" (Sung by Buddy Clark (4) & Frances Williams (3); and danced by Jere McMahon, Billie Worth, Dancing Girls]; *Scene 4* "Yes, I Love You Honey" (m/l: James P. Johnson) [sung by James Barton (1), with the John Kirby Orchestra]; *Scene 5* Smith & Dale. Joe Smith & Charles Dale did their decades-old (but still funny) Dr. Kronkite sketch; *Scene 6* "Frankie and Johnny." Sung by Frances Williams (3): FRANKIE: Jayne Manners; JOHNNY: James Barton; NELLIE BLY: Mimi Lynne; Ensemble; *Scene 7* Jere McMahon. Mr. McMahon was a dancer; *Scene 8* The Trio: "A Lick, and a Riff, and a Slow Bounce" (m/l: Norman Zeno & Al Scofield) [performed by Frances Williams (3), Jayne Manners, Billie Worth]; *Scene 9* Finale (Entire Company).

THE DANCING GIRLS: Cece Eames, Betty De Elmo, Darlene Francys, Rose Marie Magrill, Murnai Pins, Janet Joy. JOHN KIRBY'S BAND: Charlie Shavers, Russell Procope, Clyde Hart, William Bailey, William Beason.

Broadway reviews were generally very bad (the *New York Times* didn't review it).

84. *Bring Back Birdie*

Sequel to *Bye, Bye, Birdie*, set 20 years later. Rose and Albert now have teenage children who are rebelling. One runs off to join a cult, while the other joins Filth, a punk-rock group. Albert is offered $20,000 if he can find Birdie (who has dropped out of sight) and bring him back to do a TV show. Albert takes time off from teaching, and finds Birdie, now overweight and mayor of Bent River Junction, Arizona. He also finds Mae, his long-lost mother, in Arizona.

Before Broadway. There were no out-of-town tryouts. During Broadway previews the character of Buddy Jacky (played by Bill Bateman) was dropped, and Lynnda Ferguson was replaced as Rose II by Colleen Zenk. Marcel Forestieri was an Elvis impersonator known as "Little El."

The Broadway Run. MARTIN BECK THEATRE, 3/5/81–3/7/81. 31 previews. 4 PERFORMANCES. PRESENTED BY Lee Guber, Shelly Gross, Slade Brown, in association with Jim Milford; MUSIC: Charles Strouse; LYRICS: Lee Adams; BOOK: Michael Stewart; CONCEIVED BY/DIRECTOR/CHOREOGRAPHER: Joe Layton; SETS: David Mitchell; COSTUMES: Fred Voelpel; LIGHTING: David Hays; SOUND: Otts Munderloh; MUSICAL DIRECTOR/VOCAL ARRANGEMENTS: Mark Hummel; DANCE MUSIC ARRANGEMENTS: Daniel Troob; ORCHESTRAL ARRANGERS: Ralph Burns (supervising orchestrator), Stanley Applebaum, Daniel Troob, Philip J. Lang, Jim Tyler, Gary Anderson, Gerald Alters, Scott Kuney, Coleridge-Taylor Perkinson, Charles Strouse; MUSIC CONSULTANT: Barbara Strouse; PRESS: Solters/Roskin/Friedman; CASTING: Mary Jo Slater; GENERAL MANAGEMENT: Theatre Now; COMPANY MANAGER: Stephen Arnold; PRODUCTION STAGE MANAGER: Nicholas Russiyan; STAGE MANAGER: Tony Manzi; ASSISTANT STAGE MANAGER: Robert O'Rourke. *Cast:* STORYTELLER: Donna Monroe; ALBERT: Donald O'Connor (1) ☆; ROSE: Chita Rivera (2) ☆; MTOBE: Maurice Hines (4); HOGAN: Howard Parker; ALBERT JR.: Evan Seplow (7); JENNY: Robin Morse (6); GARY: Jeb Brown (5); GIRL FRIENDS: Barbara Dare Thomas, Vanessa Bell, Julie Cohen, Christine Langner; PORTER: Frank De Sal (9); GUARD: Howard Parker; SUNNIE: Betsy Friday; TOURIST WITH CAMERA: Bill Bateman; HIS WIFE: Zoya Leporska; SHOPPING BAG LADY: Rebecca Renfroe; INDIAN SQUAW: Janet Wong; INDIAN BRAVE: Larry Hyman; MAE PETERSON (DELORES ZEPOL): Maria Karnilova (3) ☆; MAYOR C.B. "CONRAD BIRDIE" TOWNSEND: Marcel Forestieri (5); EFFIE: Zoya Leporska; MARSHALL: Howard Parker; "FILTH" GROUP: Evan Seplow, Jeb Brown, Cleve Asbury, Leon Evans, Mark Frawley; HOUSE MANAGER: Peter Oliver Norman; CHORUS GIRLS: Betsy Friday, Rebecca Renfroe, Vanessa Bell; ROSE II: Colleen Zenk (10); REV. SUN: Frank De Sal; REPORTERS: Bill Bateman, Donna Monroe, Frank De Sal, Larry Hyman; STREET CLEANER: Frank De Sal; CAMERAMAN: Michael Blevins; STAGE DOOR JOHNNIES: Bill Bateman, Peter Oliver Norman, Cleve Asbury, Frank De Sal; BIRDETTES: Betsy Friday, Rebecca Renfroe, Vanessa Bell; WALTER: Kevin Petitt. *Standbys*: Albert: Howard Parker; Rose: Michon Peacock. *Understudies*: Mae: Zoya Leporska; Mtobe: Peter Oliver Norman; Conrad: Bill Bateman; Albert Jr.: Michael Blevins; Gary: Cleve Asbury; Rose II: Betsy Friday. *Swings*: Donna Ritche & Porter Hudson. *Act I*: *Scene 1* A darkened office: "Twenty Happy Years" (Rose & Albert); *Scene 2* Forest Hills & environs: "Movin' Out" (Jenny, Gary, Kids), "Half of a Couple" (Jenny & Girl Friends); *Scene 3* Peterson kitchen: "I Like What I Do" (Rose); *Scene 4* Port Authority Bus Terminal: "Bring Back Birdie" (Mtobe & Company), "Movin' Out" (reprise) (Kids); *Scene 5* Bent River Junction, Arizona: "Baby You Can Count on Me" (Albert); *Scene 6* El Coyote Club: "A Man Worth Fightin' For" (Rose & Cowboys); *Scene 7* Office of Mayor: "You Can Never Go Back" (Mayor); *Scene 8* University Stadium: "Filth" (Filth), "Back in Showbiz Again" (Albert). *Act II*: *Scene 1* University Stadium: "Middle Age Blues" (Albert); *Scene 2* Rev. Sun's compound: "Inner Peace" (Rose, Rev. Sun, Sunnies); *Scene 3* Office of the Mayor, Main Street, Bent River Junction: "There's a Brand New Beat in Heaven" (Mtobe & The Tucson Tabernacle Choir), "Twenty Happy Years" (reprise) (Albert), "Well, I'm Not!" (Rose); *Scene 4* University Stadium locker room: "When Will Grown-Ups Grow Up?" (Kids), "Middle Age Blues" (reprise) (Albert); *Scene 5* Rose's motel: "Young" (Albert); *Scene 6* Television studio; *Scene 7* The Grammy Show: "(Show Girls) I Love 'em All" (Delores Zepol & Boyfriends), "Bring Back Birdie" (reprise) (Conrad & Birdettes), "Twenty Happy Years" (reprise) (Albert & Rose).

It was unanimously panned on opening night (when Joe Layton and Michael Stewart were absent). At the final Saturday matinee Donald O'Connor (in his Broadway debut) was singing "Middle Age Blues" and forgot the words. He got down on hands and knees, looking to the pit for a prompt. Then he lay down flat on stage and yelled to the conductor, "You sing it. I always hated this song, anyway." Chita Rivera was nominated for a Tony.

85. *Bring in 'da Noise,*
Bring in 'da Funk

A dance musical, subtitled *A Tap/Rap Discourse on the Staying Power of the Beat*. African American history re-told through kinetic fusion of tap dancing and rap. The story begins on slave ships, goes through ragtime and jazz, and the black caricatures of Uncle Tom in Hollywood movies, and finally to a scene in New York where four well-dressed black men attempt and fail to flag down a cab.

Before Broadway. George C. Wolfe, producer of the New York Shakespeare Festival, and Savion Glover, choreographer, created this show Off Broadway, at the NEWMAN THEATRE (part of the Festival's Public Theatre complex) in New York. 11/15/95–1/28/96. 13 previews from 11/3/95. 85 SELL-OUT PERFORMANCES. It had the same basic crew as for the later Broadway run, except COSTUMES: Karen Perry; PRODUCTION STAGE MANAGER: Gwendolyn M. Gilliam. Same cast, except Reg E. Gaines ('da Voice). Then it moved to Broadway.

The Broadway Run. AMBASSADOR THEATRE, 4/25/96–1/10/99. 18 previews from 4/9/96. 1,123 PERFORMANCES. PRESENTED BY the Joseph Papp Public Theatre/New York Shakespeare Festival (George C. Wolfe, producer), by special arrangement with The Shubert Organization; MUSIC: Daryl Waters, Zane Mark, Ann Duquesnay; BOOK: Reg E. Gaines; CONCEIVED BY/DIRECTOR: George C. Wolfe; BASED ON an idea by Savion Glover & George C. Wolfe; CHOREOGRAPHER: Savion Glover;

SETS: Riccardo Hernandez; COSTUMES: Paul Tazewell; LIGHTING: Jules Fisher & Peggy Eisenhauer; SOUND: Dan Moses Schreier; MUSICAL SUPERVISOR/ORCHESTRATIONS: Daryl Waters; MUSICAL DIRECTOR: Zane Mark; VOCAL ARRANGEMENTS: Ann Duquesnay; CAST RECORDING on RCA; PRESS: Carol R. Fineman; CASTING: Jordan Thaler & Heidi Griffiths; COMPANY MANAGER: Kim Sellon; PRODUCTION STAGE MANAGER: Bonnie Panson; STAGE MANAGER: Gwendolyn M. Gilliam; ASSISTANT STAGE MANAGER: Rick Steiger. *Cast:* 'DA BEAT: Savion Glover (1) ☆, *Baakari Wilder* (during Mr. Glover's vacation, 1/10/97–1/21/97; then permanently from 6/27/97), *Savion Glover* (from 12/8/98, for the last 40 performances); HIMSELF: Baakari Wilder (7), *Dule Hill* (from 7/1/97); THEMSELVES: Jimmy Tate (6) (*Jason Samuels* from 7/1/97) & Vincent Bingham (4) (*Omar A. Edwards* from 2/4/97); 'DA VOICE: Jeffrey Wright (3) (until 8/15/97), *Mark Gerald Douglas* (stood in for Mr. Wright, July–7/13/97 then took over permanently), *Curtis McClarin* (from 8/5/97); 'DA SINGER: Ann Duquesnay (2), *Lynette G. DuPre* (stood in for Miss Duquesnay, May–6/15/97; and permanently from 8/5/97), *Tina Fabrique*; THEMSELVES: Jared Crawford (8) & Raymond King (9); 'DA KID: Dule Hill (5), *Jason Samuels* (from 7/1/97), *Marshall L. Davis Jr.* & *Joseph Monroe Webb* (alternates from 9/16/97). *Standbys*: For Miss Duquesnay: Lynette G. DuPre & Mary Bond Davis; For Miss DuPre: Andrea Frierson Toney; For Mr. Wright: Mark Gerald Douglas. *Understudies*: For Mr. Glover: Baakari Wilder; For Miss Duquesnay: Aisha de Haas; For Mr. Wilder: Dule Hill; For Messrs Bingham, Hill, Tate, and Wilder: Omar A. Edwards, Derick K. Grant, Joseph Monroe Webb; For Mr. Crawford & Mr. King: David Peter Chapman. Other replacement understudies: *Jason E. Bernard, Darrell Dove Jr., Dormeshia Sumbry, Sekou Torbert, Larry Wright.* **Musicians**: KEYBOARDS: Zane Mark & Lafayette Harris; REEDS: Zane Paul; TRUMPET: David Rogers; GUITAR/HARMONICA: Vince Henry; BASS: Luico Hopper; DRUMS: Leroy Clouden.

Program: *Act I*: IN 'DA BEGINNING: "Bring in 'da Noise, Bring in 'da Funk" (Company), "The Door (to Isle Goree)" (Jeffrey), "Slave Ships" (Ann & Savion); SOM'THIN' FROM NUTHIN': "Som'thin' from Nuthin'"/"The Circle Stomp" (Baakari, Dule, Jimmy, Vince, Ann, Jeffrey), "The Pan Handlers" (Jared & Ray); URBANIZATION: "The Lynching Blues" (Baakari, Ann, Company), "Chicago Bound" (Savion, Ann, Company), "Shifting Sounds" (Jeffrey), "Industrialization" (Savion, Baakari, Jimmy, Vince, Jared, Ray), "The Chicago Riot Rag" (Savion, Baakari, Jimmy, Vince, Jared), "I Got the Beat"/"Dark Tower" (Ann, Jeffrey, Company). "The Whirligig Stomp" (Company). *Act II*: WHERE'S THE BEAT?: THE MAN (THE VOICE): Jimmy & Vince; UNCLE HUCK-A-BUCK: Baakari; LI'L DAHLIN': Savion; THE CHANTEUSE: Ann; THE KID: Dule; THE BUCKET DRUMMERS: Jared & Ray. "Now That's Tap" (Grin & Flash), "The Uncle Huck-a-Buck Song" (Uncle Huck-a-Buck, Li'l Dahlin,' Company), "Kid Go!" (Kid & Company), "The Lost Beat Swing" (Chanteuse & Company), "Green, Chaney, Buster, Slyde" (Savion); STREET CORNER SYMPHONY: "1956 — Them Conkheads" (Ann & Company), "1967 — Hot Fun" (Ann, Jeffrey, Company), "1977 — Blackout" (Savion, Baakari, Jimmy, Vince), "1987 — Gospel/Hip Hop Rant" (Ann, Jeffrey, Savion); NOISE/FUNK: "Drummin'" (Jared & Raymond), "Taxi" (Savion, Jimmy, Baakari, Vince), "Conversations" (Jared, Raymond, Savion, Jimmy, Baakari, Vince), "Hittin'" (Savion, Baakari, Jimmy, Vince, Jared, Raymond, Jeffrey), "Bring in 'da Noise, Bring in 'da Funk" (reprise) (Company).

Broadway reviews were very good. Until his vacation Savion Glover had not missed a single performance. Then one thing or another kept taking him away, with Baakari Wilder filling in, until he left for good on 6/27/97 (he had been due to leave on 7/20/97). By the middle of 8/97 Ann Duquesnay was the only one of the original cast left. In 9/97 she left for two weeks to do a gig at Rainbow and Stars. On 12/7/98 it was announced that the show would close on 1/10/99. The show won Tonys for direction of a musical, choreography, lighting, and for Ann Duquesnay, and was nominated for musical, score, book, costumes, and for Savion Glover.

After Broadway. TOUR. Opened on 9/30/97, at the Fisher Theatre, Detroit. Financed by the Public Theatre. DIRECTOR: George C. Wolfe; CHOREOGRAPHER: Derick K. Grant; MUSICAL DIRECTOR: Richard Cummings. *Cast*: 'DA BEAT: Derick K. Grant, *Jimmy Tate, Sean C. Fielder*; 'DA SINGER: Vickilyn Reynolds, *Debra Byrd*; 'DA VOICE:

Dominique Kelley, Jimmy Tate, Christopher A. Scott, Thomas Silcott; 'DA KID: David Peter Chapman, Denis J. Dove, B. Jason Young, *Christopher A. Scott*.

TOURING REVIVAL. Opened on 8/21/02, at the Alliance Theatre, Atlanta. PRESENTED BY Aldo Scrofani; DIRECTOR: George C. Wolfe; CHOREOGRAPHER: Savion Glover; SETS: Riccardo Hernandez; COSTUMES: Paul Tazewell; LIGHTING: Jules Fisher & Peggy Eisenhauer; SOUND: Shannon Slaton. CAST: 'DA BEAT: Savion Glover; 'DA SINGER: Lynette DuPre; 'DA VOICE: Thomas Silcott; 'DA KID: Cartier Anthony Williams; DRUMMERS: Jared Crawford & Ray King; ENSEMBLE: Maurice Chestnut, Marshall L. Davis, Dormeshia Sumbry-Edwards.

86. *Broadway Follies*

A vaudeville show of acts recruited internationally.

The Broadway Run. NEDERLANDER THEATRE, 3/15/81. 14 previews. 1 PERFORMANCE. PRESENTED BY Edgar Lansbury, Joseph Beruh, James Nederlander; MUSIC/LYRICS: Walter Marks; MATERIAL FOR ROBERT SHIELDS & LORENE YARNELL WRITTEN BY Robert Shields; CONCEIVED BY/DIRECTOR: Donald Driver; CHOREOGRAPHER: Arthur Faria; SETS: Peter Larkin; COSTUMES: Alvin Colt; LIGHTING: Roger Morgan; SOUND: Abe Jacob; MUSICAL DIRECTOR/VOCAL & DANCE MUSIC ARRANGEMENTS: Marvin Laird; ORCHESTRATIONS: Bill Byers; PRESS: Gifford/Wallace; TALENT CO-ORDINATOR: Gilbert Miller; GENERAL MANAGEMENT: Marvin A. Krauss Associates; COMPANY MANAGER: Sally Campbell; PRODUCTION STAGE MANAGER: Robert V. Straus; STAGE MANAGER: John Actman; ASSISTANT STAGE MANAGER: Joel Tropper. *Cast:* Robert Shields (1) ☆, Tessie O'Shea (3), Milo & Roger (5), Los Malambos (Guido Lopez, Nicolas Sarrea, Hector Diaz) (7), Lorene Yarnell (2) ☆, Michael Davis [i.e. Michael Allen Davis, the juggler] (4), Scott's Royal Boxers (Katherine, George & Tina Scott) (6), Gaylord Maynard & Chief Bearpaw (8). CHORUS: Stephen Bourneuf, Kitty Kuhn, Mark Martino, Nancy Meadows, Brad Miskell, Alice Ann Oakes, Aurelio Padron, R.J. Peters, D'Arcy Phifer, Mark Ruhala, Karen Teti, Suzanne Walker. **Standby**: For Miss O'Shea: Travis Hudson. *Act I*: "Broadway Follies" (Follies Ensemble), Vaudeville (Robert & Lorene), Wonderful U (Boxers & Follies Ensemble), "Piccadilly" (Tessie), The Oasis (Milo & Roger), The Pampas (Los Malambos), The Toyshop (Robert & Lorene), "The Paper Bag Rag" (Tessie & Bud's Paper Bag Band). *Act II*: At Home With the Clinkers (Robert & Lorene), "The Barnyard" (Tessie & Her Chicks), Specialty (Robert), The Saloon (Maynard & Bearpaw), Tap My Way to the Stars (Lorene & Follies Ensemble), The Rest of Michael Davis (Michael), Grand Parade (Company).

The Playbill said "order of vaudeville acts subject to change without notice," which was ironic, considering the show ran only one night. Broadway reviews were disastrous.

87. *A Broadway Musical*

A "musical about a Broadway musical," set in Washington, DC. A cynical white producer takes a serious basketball locker-room drama called *The Final Point,* by a new black author, and turns it into a black musical called *Sneakers.* It flops, so the producer decides to risk all by substituting the lead actor with a black librettist, and taking the show to Broadway. Stan is a Broadway composer.

Before Broadway. It began at THEATRE OF THE RIVERSIDE CHURCH, HARLEM, 10/10/78–11/12/78. 26 PERFORMANCES. It had the same basic crew as for the subsequent Broadway run, except DIRECTOR/CHOREOGRAPHER: George Faison; DANCE MUSIC ARRANGEMENTS: Timothy Graphenreed. *Cast*: JAMES LINCOLN: Ron Ferrell; EDDIE BELL: Julius La Rosa; PAUL JOHNSON: Larry Riley; LONNIE WRIGHT: Dan Strayhorn; SCOTT BERNARD: Calvin McRae; STAN HOWARD: Alan Weeks; SID FROMAN: Don Guastaferro; MAGGIE SIMPSON: Helen Gallagher; STEPHANIE BELL: Gwyda DonHowe; SYLVESTER LEE: Larry Marshall; JAMALA KING: Julia Lema; RICHIE TAYLOR: Larry Marshall; LAWYERS: Sydney Anderson & Michael Gallagher; AFRICAN FIGMENT:

Alan Weeks; University Figment: Don Guastaferro; Pleasure Figment: Julia Lema; Stan's Ladies: Maggy Gorrill & Loretta Devine; Shirley Wolfe: Anne Francine; Shirley's Associates: Maris Clement, Sydney Anderson, Jackee Harry. Ensemble: Sydney Anderson, Gwen Arment, Adrian Bailey, Nate Barnett, Shirley Black-Brown, Maris Clement, Don Detrick, Loretta Devine, Michael Gallagher, Maggy Gorrill, Jackee Harry, Leon Jackson, Christina Kumi-Kimball, Michael Kubala, Calvin McRae, Joni Palmer, Karen Peskow, Dan Strayhorn. *Rhythm Section*: Piano/Synthesizers: Tim Stella; Percussion: Kurt Farquhar; Guitar: Ken Sobel; Bass: Tom Barney. *Act I: Prologue* A theatre on Broadway; the present: "Here in the Playbill" (James); *Scene 1* The office of Eddie Bell; two years earlier: "A Broadway Musical" (Eddie, James, Paul, Lonnie, Scott, Stan, Sid, Maggie, Stephanie, Ensemble); *Scene 2* A backers' audition at the Manhattan apartment of Eddie & Stephanie Bell: "I Hurry Home to You" (Eddie & Stephanie); *Scene 3* The rehearsal hall: "The 1934 Hot Chocolate Jazz Babies Revue" (Sylvester, James, Ensemble), "You Only Get One Chance" (Jamala & Dancers), "Lawyers" (Eddie, Sid, Lawyers); *Scene 4* Stan Howard's apartment: "A Wrong Song" (James, Stan, Ladies); *Scene 5* The rehearsal hall: "Who Says You Always Have to Be Happy?" (Maggie & James); *Scene 6* James's apartment: "Who Am I?" (James & Figments); *Scene 7* The rehearsal hall; *Scene 8* The rehearsal hall: "Yenta Power" (Shirley, Associates, Ensemble), "Let Me Sing My Song" (Richie). *Act II: Scene 1* Washington, DC; one week later: "Out-a-Town" (James & Company), "Jokes" (James, Figments, Lonnie, Maggie, Edie, Stephanie, Richie); *Scene 2* The theatre in Washington; the technical run-through; a preview; and out-of-town opening night: "Out-a-Town" (reprise) (Maggie, Lonnie, James, Eddie, Stephanie, Stan, Sid, Richie, Jamala, Ensemble); *Scene 3* A disco in Washington; opening night party: "Goin' to Broadway" (Richie, Jamala, Ensemble), "What We Go Through" (Eddie & Stephanie), "I've Been in Those Shoes" (Maggie & Ensemble); *Scene 4* Eddie's hotel room in Washington: "Don't Tell Me" (Eddie); *Scene 5* The theatre in New York: "Be Like a Basketball and Bounce Right Back" (Maggie, Stephanie, Stan, Sid, Paul, Ensemble); *Scene 6* The New York opening night; the present: "A Broadway Musical" (reprise) (Company).

Between the Riverside run and Broadway, Gower Champion replaced George Faison as director/choreographer (Mr. Champion got billing only as production supervisor; director/choreographer were uncredited, although George Bunt was credited as associate choreographer). In the cast second-billed Helen Gallagher was replaced by Patti Karr (no longer second billed).

The Broadway Run. Lunt—Fontanne Theatre, 12/21/78. 14 previews. 1 performance. Presented by Norman Kean & Garth H. Drabinsky; Music: Charles Strouse; Lyrics: Lee Adams; Book: William F. Brown; Director/Choreographer: uncredited; Associate Choreographer: George Bunt; Sets: Peter Wexler; Costumes: Randy Barcelo; Lighting: John De Santis; Sound: Abe Jacob; Musical Supervisor/Vocal Arrangements: Donald Pippin; Musical Director: Kevin Farrell; Orchestrations: Robert Freedman; Dance Music Arrangements: Donald Johnston; Press: Jeffrey Richards Associates; Casting: Julie Hughes & Barry Moss; Production Supervisor: Gower Champion; General Manager: Marilyn S. Miller; Production Stage Manager: David Rubinstein; Stage Manager: Judy Binus; Assistant Stage Manager: Sherry Cohen. *Cast*: Policeman: Nate Barnett; James Lincoln: Irving Allen Lee (3); Eddie Bell: Warren Berlinger (1); Lonnie Paul: Larry Riley (7); Melinda Bernard: Jackee Harry; Stan Howard: Alan Weeks (4); Maggie Simpson: Patti Karr (5); Stephanie Bell: Gwyda DonHowe (2); Kumi-Kumi: Christina Kumi-Kimball; Smoke & Fire Backup Singers: Maris Clement, Loretta Devine, Jackee Harry; Richie Taylor's Lawyers: Sydney Anderson & Michael Gallagher; Rehearsal Pianist: Gwen Arment; Richie Taylor: Larry Marshall (6); Nathaniel: Nate Barnett; Richie's Secretary: JoAnn Ogawa; Shirley Wolfe: Anne Francine (9); Theatre Party Associates: Sydney Anderson, Maris Clement, Loretta Devine; Male Dancers: Albert Stephenson, Robert Melvin, Martin Rabbett; Sylvester Lee: Tiger Haynes (8); Louie: Reggie Jackson; Jake: Martin Rabbett; Big Jake: Albert Stephenson; Junior: Robert Melvin; Ensemble: Sydney Anderson, Gwen Arment, Nate Barnett, Maris Clement, Prudence Darby, Don Edward Detrick, Loretta Devine, Sharon Ferrol, Michael Gallagher, Scott Geralds, Maggy Gorrill, Jackee Harry, Leon

Jackson, Reggie Jackson, Carleton Jones, Christina Kumi-Kimball, Michael Kubala, Robert Melvin, JoAnn Ogawa, Karen Paskow, Martin Rabbett, Albert Stephenson, Marilynn Winbush, Brad Witsger. *Swing Dancers*: Valarie Pettiford, Calvin McRae. *Act I: Prologue* Times Square; one year ago today: "Broadway, Broadway" (New Kids in Town, Policeman, James); *Scene 1* Eddie Bell's office; the same day: "A Broadway Musical" (Eddie, James, Lonnie, Melinda, Stan, Maggie, Ensemble); *Scene 2* Eddie & Stephanie Bell's Manhattan apartment; six months later; and on the street immediately following: "I Hurry Home to You" (Eddie & Stephanie) [cut before Broadway]; *Scene 3* Stan Howard's apartment; a month later: "Smoke and Fire" (Stan, James, Kumi-Kumi, Ensemble); *Scene 4* A midtown Italian restaurant; one week later: "Lawyers" (Eddie, Stephanie, Richie's Lawyers); *Scene 5* On a stage in a theatre on West 44th Street; a few minutes later: "Yenta Power" (Shirley & Associates), "Let Me Sing My Song" (Richie) [this number was later revised and became the title song in *Dance a Little Closer*], "A Broadway Musical" (reprise) (Eddie, Stephanie, James, Shirley, Maggie, Lonnie, Stan, Ensemble). *Act II: Scene 1* The Federal Theatre, Washington, DC; early one morning, a week later: "The 1934 Hot Chocolate Jazz Babies Revue" (Sylvester, James, Ensemble); *Scene 2* Technical run-through and opening night in Washington: "Let Me Sing My Song" (reprise) (Richie & Friends); *Scene 3* The Federal Theatre; later on opening night: "It's Time for a Cheer-Up Song" (Stan, Maggie, Lonnie, James), "You Gotta Have Dancing" (Maggie, James, Ensemble); *Scene 4* The bar in the Washington Hotel; later: "What You Go Through" (Stephanie & Eddie), "Don't Tell Me" (Eddie), "Together" (James, Eddie, Staff) [this number was later revised as "Dumb Dog," and used in movie version of *Annie*].

It was almost universally panned, and lost $1 million. Gwyda Don-Howe was Norman Kean's wife; in 1988 he murdered her and then jumped to his death.

88. *Brooklyn: The Musical*

An urban fairy tale. A young woman searches for her lost father. Her only clue is her name — Brooklyn. Set on a street corner under the Brooklyn Bridge, in the present. No intermission.

Before Broadway. After a workshop (which featured David Jennings as the Street Singer), it ran at the Denver Civic Theatre, 5/7/03–6/15/03. Previews from 4/30/03. Presented by the Denver Civic Theatre, by arrangement with Mitchell Maxwell, John McDaniel, Victoria Maxwell, City Weeds Productions, Sibling Entertainment, Scott Prisand, and Stephen Leiter; Director/Choreographer: Jeff Calhoun; Sets: Ray Klausen; Costumes: Tobin Ost; Lighting: Michael Gilliam; Sound: Jonathan Deans; Musical Supervisor/Arrangements: John McDaniel; Musical Director: Victor Simonson; Press: Boneau/Bryan-Brown; Casting: Dave Clemmons. *Cast*: Brooklyn: Eden Espinosa; Street Singer: David Jennings; Paradice: Ramona Keller; Faith: Karen Olivo; Also with: Mark Deklin, Lee Morgan.

On 8/16/04 it was announced that Cleavant Derricks would play the Street Singer on Broadway.

The Broadway Run. Plymouth Theatre, 10/21/04–. 27 previews from 9/23/04. Presented by Producers Four, Jeff Calhoun, John McDaniel, Leiter/Levine, Scott Prisand, and Gutterman Productions, in association with Sibling Entertainment; Music/Lyrics: Barri McPherson; Book: Barri McPherson & Mark Schoenfeld; Conceived by: Paula Holt; Director/Choreographer: Jeff Calhoun; Sets: Ray Klausen; Costumes: Tobin Ost; Lighting: Michael Gilliam; Sound: Jonathan Deans & Peter Hylenski; Musical Supervisor/Orchestrations/Arrangements: John McDaniel; Musical Director: James Sampliner; Cast recording made on 10/25/04, and released in late 11/04; Press: Boneau/Bryan-Brown; Casting: Dave Clemmons; General Manager: Ken Denison; Company Manager: Seth Marquette; Production Stage Manager: Kimberly Russell; Stage Manager: Jason Trubitt; Assistant Stage Manager: Thomas J. Gates. *Cast*: City Weeds: Kevin Anderson (*Manoel Felciano* from 2/7/05; *Lee Morgan* from 3/14/05), Cleavant Derricks, Eden Espinosa, Ramona Keller, Karen Olivo; Taylor Collins: Kevin Anderson, *Manoel Felciano* (from 2/7/05), *Lee Mor-*

gan (from 3/14/05); STREET SINGER: Cleavant Derricks (David Jennings was going to play the role, but surgery problems sidelined him); BROOKLYN: Eden Espinosa; PARADICE: Ramona Keller; FAITH: Karen Olivo; VOCALISTS: Manoel Felciano, Caren Lyn Manuel, Haneefah Wood. ***Understudies***: Taylor: Manoel Felciano; Brooklyn/Faith: Caren Lyn Manuel & Julie Reiber; Street Singer: Horace V. Rogers; Paradice: Haneefah Wood. ***Swings***: Julie Reiber & Horace V. Rogers. ***Orchestra***: KEYBOARD 1: James Sampliner; KEYBOARD 2: Daniel A. Weiss; GUITAR 1: John Putnam; GUITAR 2: Gary Sieger; BASS: Irio O'Farrill Jr.; DRUMS: Shannon Ford; REEDS: Jack Bashkow; PERCUSSION: Roger Squitero; CELLO: Clay C. Ruede; SYNTHESIZER PROGRAMMER: Justin A. Malakhow; "Heart Behind These Hands" (City Weeds), "Christmas Makes Me Cry" (Faith & Taylor), "Not a Sound" (City Weeds), "Brooklyn Grew Up" (Brooklyn & City Weeds), "Creating 'Once Upon a Time'" (Brooklyn & Faith), "Once Upon a Time" (Brooklyn & City Weeds), "Superlover" (Paradice & City Weeds), "Brooklyn in the Blood" (Paradice, Brooklyn, City Weeds), "Magic Man" (Streetsinger & City Weeds), "Love Was a Song" (Taylor), "I Never Knew His Name" (Brooklyn), "The Truth" (Taylor, Brooklyn, City Weeds), "Raven" (Paradice), "Sometimes" (Taylor & City Weeds), "Love Me Where I Live" (Paradice & City Weeds), "Love Fell Like Rain" (Brooklyn), "Streetsinger (Brooklyn, Streetsinger, City Weeds), "Heart Behind These Hands" (reprise) (City Weeds).

After the 2/6/05 performance Kevin Anderson disappeared from the show, his whereabouts unknown. His roles were taken by his understudy. Mr. Anderson was due back on 2/19/05, but as from 3/14/05 he took a leave of absence (no return date specified) and Lee Morgan took over his roles.

89. *Bubbling Brown Sugar*

A nostalgic black musical revue. A trio of old Harlem performers take two young couples (one black, one white) back in time to the heyday (1920–1940) of Harlem nightspots such as the Cotton Club, the Savoy Ballroom, and Small's Paradise.

Before Broadway. Rosetta Le Noire, artistic director of AMAS Repertory Theatre, an Off Off Broadway musical theatre in Uptown Manhattan, came up with the idea of presenting a musical revue of the songs of Eubie Blake and Noble Sissle. It ran at AMAS as *Reminiscing with Sissle and Blake.* It had black stars and white supporting players. Loren Mitchell, black historian and author of *Voices of the Black Theatre*, came in to re-shape the show into an overview of the work of many black entertainers of the past. A thin plot line was added. It was designed, partially, to show Harlem as an exciting place, rather than a ghetto. Miss Le Noire's nickname was "Bubbling Brown Sugar." CHURCH OF ST. PAUL & ST. ANDREW, NY, 2/14/75–3/2/75. Limited run of 12 PERFORMANCES. Its title by then was *Bubbling Brown Sugar: A Musical Journey Through Harlem.* DIRECTOR: Bob Cooper; CHOREOGRAPHER: Fred Benjamin; SETS: Gene Fabricatore; COSTUME CO-ORDINATOR: Carol Luiken; LIGHTING: Ian Johnson; MUSICAL DIRECTOR: Danny Holgate. **Cast:** SOPHIE/MRS. ROBERTS: Spence Adams; CHECKERS/RUSTY: Joseph Attles; ELLA/CLUB SINGER: Ethel Beatty; BUD/MC: Thommie Bush; CLUB SINGERS: Ethel Beatty & Sandi Hewitt, Yvette Johnson, Alton Lathrop, Julienne Marshall, Vivian Reed; NEIGHBORS: Sandi Hewitt, Yvette Johnson, Alton Lathrop; STROLLERS: Yvette Johnson & Alton Lathrop; JOHN SAGE/BERT WILLIAMS/DUSTY: Avon Long; IRENE PAIGE: Mary Louise; JUDY: Julienne Marshall; DALE/COUNT: Dale McIntosh; JIM/LUNKY/SINGER: Howard Porter; JOYCE/GEORGIA BROWN: Vivian Reed; MR. ROBERTS/DUTCH/WAITER: Anthony Whitehouse. ***Standby***: For Mary Louise: Emme Kemp. The show then toured for 9 months, in cities such as Washington, DC (at the National Theatre), Chicago, and Philadelphia, before going to Broadway. During that time it grossed over $3 million. Chris Beard left the cast to become part of the rock group The Fifth Dimension, and was replaced by Chip Garnett. Thelma Carpenter was replaced by Josephine Premice just before the Broadway opening.

The Broadway Run. ANTA THEATRE, 3/2/76–12/31/77. 766 PERFORMANCES. The Media House production, PRESENTED BY J. Lloyd Grant, Richard Bell, Robert M. Cooper, Ashton Springer, in association

with Moe Septee, Inc.; MUSIC/LYRICS: various authors; ADDITIONAL ORIGINAL MUSIC: Danny Holgate, Emme Kemp, Lillian Lopez; BOOK: Loften Mitchell; BASED ON a concept by Rosetta Le Noire; DIRECTOR: Robert M. Cooper; CHOREOGRAPHER: Billy Wilson; SETS: Clarke Dunham; COSTUMES: Bernard Johnson; LIGHTING: Barry Arnold; SOUND: Joel S. Fichman; MUSICAL DIRECTOR: Danny Holgate; CHORAL ARRANGEMENTS: Chapman Roberts; CAST RECORDING on H & L Records; PRESS: Max Eisen, Barbara Glenn, Judy Jacksina; GENERAL MANAGER: Ashton Springer; COMPANY MANAGER: Carolyne A. Jones, *Stephanie Austin* (added by 76–77); PRODUCTION STAGE MANAGER: Sam Ellis, *Ron Abbott & Kenneth Hanson* (by 76–77); STAGE MANAGER: E. Lynn Nickerson; ASSISTANT STAGE MANAGER: Anthony Whitehouse. **Cast:** SKIP: Lonnie McNeil, *Clinton Keen*; BILL: Vernon Washington, *David Bryant* (from 6/22/76), *Stanley Ramsey*; RAY: Newton Winters, *Clyde-Jacques Barrett*; CAROLYN: Carolyn Byrd; NORMA: Karen Grannum, *Renee Brailsford*; GENE: Alton Lathrop; HELEN: Dyann Robinson; LAURA: Charlise Harris, *Yolanda Raven*; MARSHA: Vivian Reed (3) ☆, *Ursuline Kairson* (from 2/15/77); TONY: Anthony Whitehouse; IRENE PAIGE: Josephine Premice (2) ☆; JOHN SAGE: Avon Long (1) ☆, *Charles "Honi" Coles* (6/20/77–7/4/77), *Avon Long*; CHECKERS: Joseph Attles (4) ☆, *Jay Flash Riley* (6/20/77–7/4/77), *Joseph Attles*; JIM: Chip Garnett, *Milt Grayson*; ELLA: Ethel Beatty; TIME MAN: Vernon Washington, *David Bryant* (from 6/22/76), *Stanley Ramsey*; WAITER: Anthony Whitehouse; JUDY: Barbara Rubenstein; CHARLIE: Barry Preston, *Denny Shearer*; GOSPEL LADY'S SON: Alton Lathrop; GOSPEL LADY: Carolyn Byrd; YOUNG IRENE: Vivian Reed (3), *Ursuline Kairson* (from 2/15/77); YOUNG SAGE: Newton Winters, *Clyde-Jacques Barrett*; YOUNG CHECKERS: Lonnie McNeil, *Clinton Keen*; NIGHTCLUB SINGER: Carolyn Byrd; THE SOLITUNES: Alton Lathrop, Lonnie McNeil (*Clinton Keen*), Newton Winters (*Clyde-Jacques Barrett*), *Ursuline Kairson* (added by 76–77); NIGHTCLUB SINGER: Chip Garnett, *Milt Grayson*; DUSTY: Joseph Attles, *Jay Flash Riley* (6/20/77–7/4/77), *Joseph Attles*; RUSTY: Avon Long (1), *Charles "Honi" Coles* (6/20/77–7/4/77), *Avon Long*; BUMPY: Vernon Washington, *David Bryant* (from 6/22/76), *Stanley Ramsey*; COUNT: Barry Preston, *Denny Shearer;* DUTCH: Anthony Whitehouse; DUTCH'S GIRL: Barbara Rubenstein; MC: Vernon Washington, *David Bryant* (from 6/22/76), *Stanley Ramsey*; CHORUS: Murphy Cross, Nedra Dixon, Emme Kemp (*Marilyn Johnson*), Stanley Ramsey (*Ira Hawkins*), Amii Stewart & *Susan Edwards*. **Standbys:** Sage: Vernon Washington, *Clebert Ford*. **Understudies:** Irene/Carolyn/Gospel Lady/Female Nightclub Singer: Emme Kemp, *Marilyn Johnson*; Marsha/Young Irene: Karen Grannum, *Carolyn Byrd, Cecelia Norfleet*; Checkers/Dusty: David Bryant, *Clebert Ford*; Bill/Bumpy/mc: David Bryant, *Clyde-Jacques Barrett*; Time Man: David Bryant, *Clyde-Jacques Barrett*; Jim/Male Night Club Singer: Stanley Ramsey, *Ira Hawkins*; Judy/Dutch's Girl: Murphy Cross, *Susan Edwards*; Tony/Charlie/Count/Dutch/Waiter: E. Lynn Nickerson; Helen: Charlise Harris; Ella: Nedra Dixon, *Amii Stewart*; Gene/Gospel Lady's Son: Millard Hurley. **Dance Alternates**: Carol Pennyfeather & Millard Hurley, *Leona Johnson & David Cameron*. **Musicians**: PIANO: Neil Tate; DRUMS: Joseph Marshall; GUITAR/FLUTE: Rudy Stevenson. **Act I: Scene 1** HARLEM TODAY: "Harlem '70" * (m: Danny Holgate; l: Loften Mitchell) (Company), "Bubbling Brown Sugar" * (m: Danny Holgate; l: Lillian Lopez & Emme Kemp) (Company), "(That's) What Harlem is to Me" (m/l: Andy Razaf, Russell Wooding, Paul Denniker) [from *Connie's Hot Chocolates of 1935*] (Josephine), Bill Robinson Specialty (danced by Vernon), "Harlem Sweet Harlem" * (m: Danny Holgate; l: Loften Mitchell) (Company), "(I Ain't Never Done Nothin' to) Nobody" (m/l: Alex Rogers & Bert Williams) (Avon), "Goin' Back in Time" * (m: Danny Holgate) (Vernon). THE REST OF THE ACTION TAKES PLACE IN OLD HARLEM BETWEEN 1920 AND 1940. **Scene 2** A Downtown speakeasy: "Some of These Days" (m/l: Shelton Brooks) (Barbara), "Moving Uptown" * (m: Danny Holgate; l: Loften Mitchell & Emme Kemp) (Vernon); **Scene 3** 125th Street & Seventh Avenue: "Strolling" * (m: Danny Holgate) (Alton, Charlise, Lonnie, Karen, Newton, Dyann); **Scene 4** 135th Street & Lenox Avenue: "I'm Gonna Tell God All My Troubles" (traditional) (Alton), Medley: "His Eye is on the Sparrow" and "Swing Low, Sweet Chariot" (traditional) (Carolyn & Company), "Sweet Georgia Brown" (m/l: Maceo Pinkard, Ben Bernie, Kenneth Casey) (Lonnie, Newton, Vivian), "Honeysuckle Rose" (m: Fats Waller; l: Andy Razaf) [from *Load of Coal*] (Avon & Josephine); **Scene 5** Harlem night spots: "Stormy Monday

Blues" (m/l: Earl "Fatha" Hines, Billy Eckstine, Bob Crowder) (Carolyn), "Rosetta" (m/l: Earl "Fatha" Hines & Henri Woode) (Alton, Lonnie, Newton), "Sophisticated Lady" (m: Duke Ellington; l: Irving Mills & Mitchell Parish) (Chip, Vernon, Dyann) (dance understudy for Dyann: Charlise), "In Honeysuckle Time (When Emaline Said She'd Be Mine)" (m: Eubie Blake; m: Noble Sissle) (from *Shuffle Along*) (Avon & Joseph), "Solitude" (m: Duke Ellington; l: Eddie DeLange & Irving Mills) (Alton, Lonnie, Newton, Vivian); *Scene 6* At the Savoy: "C'mon up to Jive Time" * (m: Danny Holgate) (Vernon), Medley: "Stompin' at the Savoy" (m: Benny Goodman, Edgar Sampson, Chick Webb; l: Andy Razaf) and "Take the 'A' Train" (m/l: Duke Ellington & Billy Strayhorn) (Company). *Act II*: *Scene 1* Lenox Avenue; a few minutes later: "Harlem-Time" * (m: Danny Holgate) (Vernon), "Love Will Find a Way" (m: Eubie Blake; l: Noble Sissle) [from *Shuffle Along*] (Chip & Ethel), "Dutch's Song" * (m/l: Emme Kemp) (Anthony), "Brown Gal" (m/l: Avon Long & Lil Armstrong) (Avon), "Pray for the Lights to Go Out" (m/l: Renton Tunnan & Will Skidmore) (Joseph); *Scene 2* Another street in Harlem: "I Got it Bad (and That Ain't Good)" (m: Duke Ellington; l: Paul Francis Webster) [from *Jump for Joy*] (Ethel), "Harlem Makes Me Feel!" * (m/l: Emme Kemp) (Barry); *Scene 3* Small's Paradise: "Jim Jam Jumpin' Jive" (m/l: Cab Calloway) (Vernon, Lonnie, Newton), "There'll Be Some Changes Made" (m/l: W. Benton Overstreet & Billy Higgins) (Josephine), "God Bless the Child" (m/l: Arthur Herzog Jr. & Billie Holiday) (Vivian) (understudy: Carolyn), "It Don't Mean a Thing" (m: Duke Ellington; l: Irving Mills (Chip, Anthony, Josephine, Company).

Those songs asterisked are new compositions written for this production.

Broadway reviews were mostly excellent. The show received Tony nominations for musical, choreography, and for Vivian Reed.

After Broadway. TOUR. Opened on 6/22/76, at the Shubert Theatre, Chicago, and closed on 10/9/77, at the National Theatre, Washington, DC. *Cast*: BILL/TIME MAN/MC: Charles "Honi" Coles, *Ronald "Smokey" Stevens* (from 8/77); IRENE: Mable Lee, *Marilyn Johnson* (from 8/77); JOHN SAGE/RUSTY: Vernon Washington, *Charles "Honi" Coles* (from 8/77); ELLA: Terry Burrell; RAY/YOUNG SAGE: Robert Melvin; CHECKERS/DUSTY: Jay Flash Riley; CAROLYN/NIGHT CLUB SINGER: Marilyn Johnson, *Sandi Hewitt* (from 8/77); BUMPY: Hugh Hurd; MARSHA/YOUNG IRENE: Ursuline Kairson, *Vivian Reed* (from 2/15/77 for 12 weeks), *Bettye Lavette* (from 8/77); NORMA: Yolanda Graves. "Dutch's Song" was replaced with "Ain't Misbehavin'."

TOUR. Opened on 8/23/77, at Uhlein Hall, Milwaukee, and closed on 4/22/78, at the National Arts Centre, Ottawa. DIRECTOR: Ron Abbott; CHOREOGRAPHY RE-STAGED BY: Dyann Robinson; MUSICAL DIRECTOR: Jeff Laibson. *Cast*: CHECKERS/DUSTY: Bobby Hill; IRENE: Mable Lee; CHARLIE: Tom Tofel; JIM/NIGHTCLUB SINGER: Glover Parham; JOHN SAGE/RUSTY: Richard Brown; MARSHA/YOUNG IRENE: Rhetta Hughes; NORMA: Veda Jackson.

ROYALTY THEATRE, London, 9/77. DIRECTOR/CHOREOGRAPHER: Charles Augins. *Cast*: BILL/TIME MAN/MC: Charles Augins; JOHN SAGE/RUSTY: Billy Daniels; IRENE: Elaine Delmar; CHECKERS/DUSTY: Lon Sattin; MARSHA/YOUNG IRENE: Helen Gelzer.

JOHN HOUSEMAN THEATRE, NYC, 3/31/03. One-night benefit concert. PRESENTED BY AMAS; DIRECTOR: Rajendra Ramoon Maharaj; MUSICAL DIRECTOR: David Alan Bunn. *Cast*: MARSHA: Vivian Reed; ALSO WITH: Ebony Jo-Ann, Chuck Cooper, Darius de Haas, Maurice Hines, Pam Isaacs, Sandra Reaves-Phillips, Sheryl Lee Ralph, James Stovall, Maria Torres, Tamara Tunie, Lillias White, Rob Evan, Carmen Ruby Floyd, Sir James Randolph.

FOX THEATRE, Atlanta, 7/16/04–7/24/04. PRESENTED BY Theater of the Stars, in conjunction with the opening of the 2004 National Black Arts Festival; DIRECTOR/CHOREOGRAPHER: George Faison; SETS: Austin K. Sanderson; MUSICAL DIRECTOR: Ron Metcalfe; ORCHESTRATIONS: Danny Holgate. *Cast*: Diahann Carroll, Clent Bowers, Paige Price, Vernel Bagneris, B.J. Crosby, Debra Walton, Jeffry Denman, Byron Easley, Brad Bradley.

90. *Buck White*

The entire action is set in a meeting hall of the Beautiful Allelujah Days organization. A militant black lecturer arrives to address the meeting organized by this black social organization.

Before Broadway. *Big Time Buck White*, the straight drama on which this musical was based, was originally presented in Watts, Los Angeles, by Ron Rich, and then went Off Broadway, at the VILLAGE SOUTH THEATRE, 12/8/68–3/30/69. 124 PERFORMANCES. PRESENTED BY Zev Bufman, in association with Ron Rich & Leonard Grant; DIRECTOR: Dick Williams. *Cast*: BUCK WHITE: Dick Williams (*Don Pedro Colley*); JIVE: Ron Rich, *Don Sutherland*).

The musical ran originally in San Francisco. PRESENTED BY Mel Goldblatt & Dialogue Black/White Company.

The Broadway Run. GEORGE ABBOTT THEATRE, 12/2/69–12/6/69. 16 previews. 7 PERFORMANCES. PRESENTED BY Zev Bufman, in association with High John Productions (Oscar Brown Jr., Jean Pace, Sivuca); MUSIC/LYRICS/BOOK: Oscar Brown Jr.; ADAPTED BY Oscar Brown Jr. from the 1968 play *Big Time Buck White*, by Joseph Dolan Tuotti; DIRECTORS: Oscar Brown Jr. & Jean Pace; SETS: Edward Burbridge; COSTUMES: Jean Pace; LIGHTING: Martin Aronstein; SOUND: Robert Threlfall; MUSICAL DIRECTOR: Merl Saunders; ORCHESTRATIONS: Mike Terry; MUSICAL ARRANGEMENTS: Mike Terry & Merl Saunders; CAST RECORDING on Buddha; PRESS: Robert Ganshaw & John Prescott; GENERAL MANAGER: Robert Kamlot; COMPANY MANAGER: Irving Cone; PRODUCTION STAGE MANAGER: Martin Gold; ASSISTANT STAGE MANAGER: Van Kirksey. *Cast*: HUNTER: Herschell Burton (2); HONEY MAN: David Moody (3); WEASEL: Ted Ross (5); RUBBER BAND: Charles Weldon (7); JIVE: Ron Rich (4); BIG TIME BUCK WHITE: Muhammad Ali (a/k/a Cassius Clay) (1) ☆; WHITEY: Eugene Smith (6); BLACK MAN: Don Sutherland. **Understudies**: Honey Man/Jive: Don Sutherland; Weasel: Van Kirksey; Rubber Band: Arnold Williams; Whitey: Paul F. Canavan. **Musicians**: ORGAN/PIANO: Merl Saunders; TRUMPET: Virgil Jones; TROMBONE: Britt Woodman; ALTO SAX: Monty Waters; TENOR SAX: Seldon Powell; BARITONE SAX: George Barrow; FLUTES: Selden Powell & George Barrow; GUITAR: Ted Dunbar; BASS: Bob Bushnell; DRUMS: Billy Cobham; CONGA DRUMS: Johnny Pacheco. *Act I*: "Honey Man Song" (Honey Man), "Money, Money, Money" (Weasel & Honey Man), "Nobody Does My Thing" (Hunter), "Step Across That Line" (Rubber Band), "H.N.I.C." (Jive), "Beautiful Allelujah Days" (Jive, Weasel, Hunter, Rubber Band, Honey Man), "Tap the Plate" (Jive, Rubber Band, Honey Man), "Big Time Buck White Chant" (Company). *Act II*: "Big Time Buck White Chant" (reprise) (Buck & Company), "Better Far" (Buck), "We Came in Chains" (Buck & Company), "Black Balloons" (Buck & Company), "Look at Them" (Whitey), "Mighty Whitey" (Buck & Company), "Get Down" (Buck & Company).

Broadway reviews ranged from not very good to terrible.

After Broadway. VILLAGE GATE THEATRE, NYC. 1/10/70–1/18/70. 18 PERFORMANCES. This was Act I only of the Broadway musical.

91. *Buddy*

Also known as *Buddy: the Buddy Holly Story*. The life of the rock 'n roll legend; the show recreates the last concert, in Clear Lake, Iowa, on 2/2/59, just before the fatal air crash.

Before Broadway. It first ran at the THEATRE ROYAL, Plymouth, England, in the summer of 1989. Then it went to the VICTORIA PALACE THEATRE, London, 10/12/89–9/30/95. It recouped its money in the first 15 weeks. It won Olivier Awards for musical and actor in a musical. It moved to the STRAND THEATRE, 10/6/95–3/3/02. DIRECTOR: Rob Bettinson; SETS: Andy Walmsley; COSTUMES: Bill Butler; LIGHTING: Graham McLusky; SOUND: Rick Price. *Cast*: BUDDY: Paul Hipp, *Chip Esten, Alex Bourne, Gus MacGregor* (for the last 6 years); BIG BOPPER: Gareth Marks; NORMAN: Ron Emslie; RITCHIE: Enzo Squillino Jr., *Miguel Ayesa, Alex Paez*. Seven million people saw it in London.

The Broadway Run. SHUBERT THEATRE, 11/4/90–5/19/91. 15 previews from 10/23/90. 225 PERFORMANCES. PRESENTED BY Paul Elliott, Laurie Mansfield, Greg Smith (for International Artistes) & David Mirvish; MUSIC/LYRICS: Charles Hardin "Buddy" Holly & others; BOOK: Alan Janes; FROM AN ORIGINAL IDEA BY Laurie Mansfield; ADDITIONAL MATERIAL/DIRECTOR: Rob Bettinson; MOVEMENT COACH:

Trudy Moffatt; SETS: Andy Walmsley; COSTUMES: Bill Butler & Carolyn Smith; LIGHTING: Graham McLusky; SOUND: Rick Price; MUSICAL DIRECTOR/JINGLES COMPOSER: Paul Jury; MUSIC CONSULTANT: Bruce Welch; CAST RECORDING on Relativity; PRESS: Adrian Bryan-Brown; CASTING: Pierce Casting; GENERAL MANAGER: Dowling Entertainment; COMPANY MANAGER: Mark Johnson; PRODUCTION STAGE MANAGER: Peter B. Mumford; STAGE MANAGER: Gary M. Zabinksi; ASSISTANT STAGE MANAGER: Shirley Third, *David Callander & Kate Riddle*. **Cast** (in order of appearance, by act): ***Act I***: HIPOCKETS DUNCAN: Fred Sanders; JINGLE SINGERS: Jo Lynn Burks, Caren Cole, Liliane Stilwell; THE HAYRIDERS: Melanie Doane (*Christine Elliott*), Kevin Fox, Tom Nash, Steve Steiner, Don Stitt; ENGINEER (KDAV): Philip Anthony; BUDDY HOLLY: Paul Hipp; JOE B. MAULDIN: Bobby Prochaska; JERRY ALLISON: Russ Jolly; BOPPERS & AUTOGRAPH HUNTERS: Jill Hennessey (*Diane Di Lascio*), Paul McQuillan, Ken Triwush; DECCA SESSION MUSICIANS: Kevin Fox, Tom Nash, Ken Triwush, Steve Steiner; DECCA PRODUCER: David Mucci; DECCA ENGINEERS: Paul McQuillan & Don Stitt; NORMAN PETTY: Kurt Ziskie; VI PETTY: Jo Lynn Burks; 4TH CRICKET: Ken Triwush; WCLS DJ: David Mucci; WWOL DJ: Philip Anthony; WDAS DJ: Demo Cates; KPST DJ: Don Stitt; CANDY: Melanie Doane, *Christine Elliott*; COUPLES IN WOODS: Jo Lynn Burks, Caren Cole, Jill Hennessey (*Diane Di Lascio*), Kevin Fox, Liliane Stilwell, Ken Triwush; APOLLO SINGERS: Sandra Caldwell, Denese Matthews, Lorraine Scott (*Adriane Lenox*); APOLLO MUSICIANS: Demo Cates, Alvin Crawford, Jerome Smith Jr., James H. Wiggins Jr.; APOLLO PERFORMER: Jerome Smith Jr.; APOLLO DJ: Don Stitt; MAN AT APOLLO: Demo Cates. ***Act II***: WWOL JINGLE SINGERS: Sandra Caldwell, Lorraine Scott (*Adriane Lenox*), Denese Matthews; MARIA ELENA: Jill Hennessey, *Diane Di Lascio*; MURRAY DEUTCH: Steve Steiner; SHIRLEY: Caren Cole; MARIA ELENA'S AUNT: Liliane Stilwell; ENGLISH DJ: Paul McQuillan; PHOTOGRAPHERS: Members of the Company; PEGGY SUE: Melanie Doane, *Christine Elliott*; KRWP DJ: Kurt Ziskie; CLEARLAKE MC: Don Stitt; CLEARLAKE BAND & BACKUP SINGERS: Members of the Company; BIG BOPPER: David Mucci; DION: Paul McQuillan; THE BELMONTS: Russ Jolly & Tom Nash; RITCHIE VALENS: Philip Anthony; TOMMY: Ken Triwush; MARY LOU SOKOLOF: Caren Cole; JACK DAW: Steve Steiner; THE SNOWBIRDS: Jo Lynn Burks, Caren Cole, Jill Hennessey (*Diane Di Lascio*), Melanie Doane (*Christine Elliott*), Liliane Stilwell. **Understudies**: Buddy: Ken Triwush (alternate); Joe/Cricket: Kevin Fox; Jerry/English dj: Tom Nash; Big Bopper/Hipockets/WCLS dj/Decca Producer/KPST dj/Apollo dj/Clearlake mc: Steve Steiner; Ritchie/Petty/KDAV Engineer/WWOL dj/KRWP dj/Dutch/Daw: Paul McQuillan; Vi/Candy/Peggy Sue/Maria Elena's Aunt; Caren Cole; Man at Apollo/WDAS dj/Apollo Performer: Alvin Crawford; Maria Elena/Jingle Singer/Shirley/Mary Lou: Melanie Doane, *Christine Elliott*. **General Understudy**: Louis Tucci. ***Act I***: ***Scene 1*** Roller rink; ***Scene 2*** Radio station; ***Scene 3*** Home; ***Scene 4*** Recording studio; ***Scene 5*** Home; ***Scene 6*** Recording studio; ***Scene 7*** Apollo Theatre. ***Act II***: ***Scene 1*** Office; ***Scene 2*** Maria's home; ***Scene 3*** Tour; ***Scene 4*** Surf Ballroom. ***Act I***: "Texas Rose" (m/l: Paul Jury), "Flower of My Heart" (m/l: Paul Jury), "Ready Teddy" (m/l: John Marascolo & Robert Blackwell), "That's All Right" (m/l: Arthur Crudup), "That'll Be the Day" (m/l: Jerry Allison, Norman Petty, Buddy Holly), "Blue Days, Black Nights" (m/l: Ben Hall), "Changing All These Changes" (m/l: J. Denny), "Peggy Sue" (m/l: Jerry Allison, Norman Petty, Buddy Holly), "(I'm) Looking for Someone to Love" (m/l: Buddy Holly & Norman Petty), "Mailman Bring Me No More Blues" (m/l: Ruth Roberts, Bill Klatz, Stanley Clayton), "Maybe Baby" (m/l: Charles Hardin & Norman Petty), "Every Day" (m/l: Charles Hardin & Norman Petty), "Sweet Love" (m/l: Paul Jury & Caren Cole), "You Send Me" (m/l: Sam Cooke) [replaced with "(Gonna Make) True Love"], "Not Fade Away" (m/l: Charles Hardin & Norman Petty), "Words of Love" (m/l: Buddy Holly), "Oh Boy" (m/l: Sunny West, Bill Tilghman, Norman Petty). ***Act II***: "Listen to Me" (m/l: Charles Hardin & Norman Petty), "Well, All Right" (m/l: Jerry Allison, Norman Petty, Buddy Holly, Joe B. Mauldin), "It's So Easy (to Fall in Love)" (m/l: Buddy Holly & Norman Petty), "Think it Over" (m/l: Jerry Allison, Buddy Holly, Norman Petty), "True Love Ways" (m/l: Buddy Holly & Norman Petty), "Why Do Fools Fall in Love" (m/l: Frankie Lymon & Morris Levy), "Chantilly Lace" (m/l: J.P. Richardson, AKA The Big Bopper), "Maybe Baby" (reprise), "Peggy Sue Got Married" (m/l: Buddy Holly), "Heartbeat" (m/l: Bob Montgomery

& Norman Petty), "La Bamba" (traditional; adapted by Ritchie Valens), "Raining in My Heart" (m/l: Felice & Boudleaux Bryant), "It Doesn't Matter Any More" (m/l: Paul Anka), "Rave On" (m/l: Sunny West, Bill Tilghman, Norman Petty), "Johnny B. Goode" (m/l: Chuck Berry).

Broadway reviews were divided, but none of them were great. Paul Hipp was nominated for a Tony.

After Broadway. TOUR. Opened on 9/10/91, at Hartford, Conn. **Cast**: BUDDY: Joe Warren Davis.

TOUR. This was the post–Broadway tour, and opened in the 92–93 season. PRESENTED BY Tom Mallow, ATP/Dodger, Pace Theatrical Group. It had the same major crew as for Broadway, except SETS: Andy Walmsley & Michael J. Hotopp; LIGHTING: Ken Billington; SOUND: Rick Price & John Kilgore. **Cast**: BUDDY: Chip Esten; VI: Jo Lynn Burks; MARIA ELENA: Lauree Taradash; PETTY: Robin Haynes; BIG BOPPER: Brian Ruf; JOE: Bobby Prochaska; RITCHIE: Alex Paez; PEGGY SUE: Anastasia Glasheen; HIPOCKETS: Tony Gilbert.

TOUR. This successful tour opened on 12/7/99, at the Shubert Theatre, Boston, and closed on 9/3/00, in St. Paul, Minn. PRESENTED BY the Ordway Center & Bob Alwine; DIRECTOR: Paul Mills. **Cast**: BUDDY: Val Zeiler; MARIA ELENA: Victoria Stilwell; BIG BOPPER: Travis Turpin; RITCHIE: Rob Langeder.

UK TOUR. Opened in 9/02, at the THEATRE ROYAL, Plymouth. **Cast**: BUDDY: Gus MacGregor; BIG BOPPER: Jaymz Denning; RITCHIE: Ricky Rojas.

92. *But Never Jam Today*

Alice's 16th birthday party at a disco.

Before Broadway. It began at CITY CENTER on 4/23/69. 1 PERFORMANCE. It formed part of *Black Expo '69*, the first comprehensive entertainment series of black performing artists and companies. It was the second in the series of shows, the others being: *The Afro-American Folkloric Troupe*, *The New York Jazz Sextet*; *Ambrose and the Thetans*; *Dance Caravan*; *Jazzmobile*; and *Soul and Gospel Show*. The series closed 4/27/69, after a limited run of 8 performances. *But Never Jam Today* credits: MUSIC: Gershon Kingsley; ADDITIONAL MUSIC/LYRICS: Robert Larimer; DIRECTOR: Vinnette Carroll; CHOREOGRAPHER: Talley Beatty; SETS: Donald Padgett; COSTUMES: K.T. Fries; LIGHTING: Marshall Williams; GOSPEL ARRANGEMENTS: Alex Bradford; DRUMS: Danny Barrajanos; STAGE MANAGER: Joseph M. Diaz. **Cast**: ALICE: Marie Thomas; WHITE RABBIT: Tommy Pinnock; CATERPILLAR: Marvin Camillo; BLACK QUEEN: Joseph Perry; CHESHIRE CAT: Lola Holman; FIRST COOK: Verna Gillis; SECOND COOK: Winston Savage; DUCHESS: Cynthia Towns; MAD HATTER: Sherman Hemsley; MARCH HARE: Thelma Drayton; DORMOUSE: Wai Ching Ho; WHITE QUEEN: Cynthia Towns; TWO OF SPADES: Lola Holman; FIVE OF SPADES: Alex Alexander; SEVEN OF SPADES: Sherman Hemsley; QUEEN OF HEARTS: Alex Alexander; KING OF HEARTS: Sterling Roberts; KNAVE OF HEARTS: Burt Rodriguez; GRYPHON: Lola Holman; HUMPTY DUMPTY: Marvin Camillo; MOCK TURTLE: Alex Alexander; HERALD: Danny Barrajanos; MEMBERS OF THE JURY: Dance Corps; CITIZENS OF WONDERLAND: Angel Caballero, Johnny Harris, Ernest Holly. DANCERS: Charles Augins, Glenn Brooks, Annette Brown, Delores Brown, Matt Cameron, Hope Clarke, Jacquelynne Curry, Trina Frazier, Joan Peters, Gail Reese, Danny Sloan, Andy Torres. ***Act I***: ***Scene 1*** Alice by the River; ***Scene 2*** Dance of the Alices; ***Scene 3*** Advice from a caterpillar; ***Scene 4*** Black Queen; ***Scene 5*** The Duchess's nursery; ***Scene 6*** A mad tea party; ***Scene 7*** Alice and the White Queen; ***Scene 8*** The croquet game; ***Scene 9*** Humpty Dumpty; ***Scene 10*** The Mock Turtle story; ***Scene 11*** Queen Alice.

By 1978 it was known as *Alice*, and was headed for Broadway (it never made it, at least not for another year). It had a limited run at the FORREST THEATRE, Philadelphia, 5/31/78–6/11/78. Previews 5/23/78–5/30/78. PRESENTED BY Mike Nichols & Lewis Allen, in association with the Urban Arts Corps & Anita MacShane; MUSIC/LYRICS: Micki Grant; BOOK/CONCEIVED BY/DIRECTOR: Vinnette Carroll; CHOREOGRAPHER: Talley Beatty; SETS: Douglas W. Schmidt; COSTUMES: Nancy Potts; LIGHTING: Jennifer Tipton; SOUND: Abe Jacob; MUSICAL DIRECTOR: Joyce Brown. **Cast**: CHARLIE: Charlene Harris; CATERPILLAR/TWEEDLEDUM: Cleavant Derricks; BARTENDER/MUSHROOM:

Alberta Bradford; GRYPH/GRYPHON: Thomas Pinnock; WAITRESS: Marilynn Winbush; CARPENTER/TWEEDLEDEE: Clinton Derricks-Carroll; CHAUFFEUR/BLACK KNIGHT: Douglas Houston; DUCHESS: Jane White; LILY WHITE/WHITE QUEEN: Alice Ghostley; BLACK KNIGHT'S HORSE: Clinton Derricks-Carroll; WHITE KING/WHITE KNIGHT: Hamilton Camp; WHITE KNIGHT'S HORSE: Cleavant Derricks; PRIMA: Roumel Reaux; SECUNDA: Clif De Raita; TERTIA: Christopher Deane; REGINA/BLACK QUEEN: Paula Kelly; ALICE: Debbie Allen; RONNIE: Ronald Dunham; FISH: Clinton Derricks-Carroll & Cleavant Derricks; ERIC/CHESHIRE CAT/MOCK TURTLE: Jeffrey Anderson-Gunter; COOKS: Alberta Bradford, Cleavant Derricks, Clinton Derricks-Carroll, Charlene Harris, Douglas Houston, Thomas Pinnock, Roumel Reaux; CHESHIRE CAT'S GIRLS: Brenda Braxton, Linda James, Juanita Grace Tyler, Kiki Shepard. OTHERS: Adrian Bailey, Roslyn Burrough, Nora M. Cole, Ralph Farrington, Maggy Gorrill, Linda James, Dwayne Phelps, Charles Wynn. "Disco," "Hall of Mirrors Ballet," "Father William," "Chess," "Workin' for the Man," "I Am Real," "Children Are," "Everybody's Mad," "Alice," "Fun and Games," "It's Lonely," "Lobster Rock," "Consider."

On 8/23/78 it was produced again by the Urban Arts Corps, for 12 PERFORMANCES. DIRECTOR: Vinnette Carroll; CHOREOGRAPHER: Talley Beatty; SETS: Mart Kappell; LIGHTING: Jeffrey Schissler. **Cast**: Clinton Derricks-Carroll, Cleavant Derricks, Marilynn Winbush, Reginald VelJohnson.

The Broadway Run. LONGACRE THEATRE, 7/31/79–8/5/79. 9 previews. 8 PERFORMANCES. PRESENTED BY Arch Nadler, Anita MacShane, Urban Arts Theatre; MUSIC: Bert Keyes & Bob Larimer; LYRICS: Bob Larimer; BOOK: Vinnette Carroll & Bob Larimer; DEVISED BY/DIRECTOR: Vinnette Carroll; AN AFRO-AMERICAN ADAPTATION of Lewis Carroll's *Alice's Adventures in Wonderland and Through the Looking Glass*; CHOREOGRAPHER: Talley Beatty; SETS/COSTUMES: William Schroder; LIGHTING: Ken Billington; SOUND: T. Richard Fitzgerald; MUSICAL DIRECTOR/INCIDENTAL MUSIC: Donald Johnston; ORCHESTRATIONS: Bert Keyes; SPECIAL ORCHESTRATIONS: H.B. Barnum & Larry Blank; ADDITIONAL ORCHESTRATIONS: Gary Anderson, Walt Levinsky, Dick Loeb; DANCE MUSIC ARRANGEMENTS: H.B. Barnum; CHORAL ARRANGEMENTS/VOCAL PREPARATION: Cleavant Derricks; PRESS: Alpert & LeVine; GENERAL MANAGER: McCann & Nugent; COMPANY MANAGER: James Kimo Gerald; PRODUCTION STAGE MANAGER: Robert L. Borod; STAGE MANAGER: Robert Charles; ASSISTANT STAGE MANAGER: Gerard Campbell. **Cast**: ALICE: Marilynn Winbush; CATERPILLAR: Cleavant Derricks; PERSONA NON GRATA: Lynne Thigpen; MUSHROOMS: Brenda Braxton, Clayton Strange, Sharon K. Brooks, Garry Q. Lewis, Celestine De Saussure, Jeffrey Anderson-Gunter; THE BLACK QUEEN: Lynne Lifton-Allen; THE WHITE RABBIT: Jeffrey Anderson-Gunter; THE DUCHESS: Reginald VelJohnson; THE CHESHIRE CAT: Jeffrey Anderson-Gunter; COOKS: Cleavant Derricks, Sheila Ellis, Celestine De Saussure; THE MAD HATTER: Jai Oscar St. John; THE MARCH HARE: Sheila Ellis; THE DORMOUSE: Celestine De Saussure; THE WHITE QUEEN: Charlene Harris; HUMPTY-DUMPTY: Reginald VelJohnson; TWEEDLEDUM: Jai Oscar St. John; TWEEDLEDEE: Cleavant Derricks; TWO OF SPADES: Jai Oscar St. John; FIVE OF SPADES: Sheila Ellis; SEVEN OF SPADES: Cleavant Derricks; QUEEN OF HEARTS: Charlene Harris; KING OF HEARTS: Reginald VelJohnson; GUARDS: Clayton Strange & Garry Q. Lewis; THE MOCK TURTLE: Jeffrey Anderson-Gunter. **Act I**: *Scene 1* Down the rabbit hole; *Scene 2* Interview with a caterpillar (Square 1); *Scene 3* The Black Queen (Square 2); *Scene 4* The kitchen of the Duchess (Square 3); *Scene 5* The Cheshire Cat; *Scene 6* A mad party (Square 4); *Scene 7* The White Queen (Square 5); *Scene 8* Humpty Dumpty; *Scene 9* Tweedledum and Tweedledee (Square 6). **Act II**: *Scene 1* The Queen of Hearts' croquet ground; *Scene 2* The Queen's dungeon; *Scene 3* The Mock Turtle (Square 7); *Scene 4* The Queen's dungeon; *Scene 5* An examination (Square 8); *Scene 6* Alice's reward; *Scene 7* The daydream ends. **Act I**: "Curiouser and Curiouser" (Alice); "Twinkle, Twinkle Little Star" (Caterpillar, Persona Non Grata, Company); "Long Live the Queen" (Black Queen & Alice); "A Real Life Lullaby" (Duchess & Cooks); "The More I See People" (Cheshire Cat); "My Little Room" (Alice); "But Never Jam Today" (White Queen & Alice); "Riding for a Fall" (Persona Non Grata, Humpty Dumpty, Alice); "All the Same to Me" (Tweedledum & Tweedledee); "I've Got My Orders" (Alice). **Act II**: "God Could Give Me Anything" (Two, Five, Seven of Spades); "But Never Jam Today" (reprise) (Company & Persona Non Grata); "I Like to Win" (Alice); "And They All Call the Hatter Mad" (Persona Non Grata); "Jumping from Rock to Rock" (Mock Turtle, Alice, Company); "They" (Two, Five, Seven of Spades); "Long Live the Queen" (reprise) (Company); "I've Got My Orders" (reprise) (Alice & Company).

Broadway reviews were not good.

93. *Buttrio Square*

Set in the spring and fall of 1946. A Northeast Italian hamlet needs one more citizen to qualify as an incorporated village. Marisa, daughter of the baron who owns the village, becomes pregnant, which must be kept a secret because the father of the child is an American, Captain Steve, who has married Marisa in spite of the fact that fraternization between the Italians and the occupying GIs is forbidden. Childless Pappa Mario, the village baker and would-be mayor, is led to believe that his own wife is pregnant. A comic subplot revolves around Terry Patterson who is really a girl who wants to become a WAC but who, because of her name, has been accidentally designated as a GI and she can't correct the error.

Before Broadway. During rehearsals a post-dated check written to cover the Equity bond required of all productions, bounced, and Equity stepped in and halted rehearsals. Boston and Philadelphia tryouts were canceled when a major backer withdrew. Eugene Loring replaced Dale Wasserman as director. The Broadway opening date was postponed. There was a $20,000 shortage going into the final stretch before opening. 50 members of the cast and company formed a syndicate and gave $200 each, and Marti Stevens, a singer in a small role, and daughter of Hollywood executive Nicholas Schenck, put up $10,000.

The Broadway Run. NEW CENTURY THEATRE, 10/14/52–10/18/52. 7 PERFORMANCES. PRESENTED BY Gen Genovese & Edward Woods; MUSIC: Arthur Jones & Fred Stamer; LYRICS: Gen Genovese; BOOK: Billy Gilbert & Gen Genovese; FROM THE PLAY BY Hal Cranton, based on a story by Gen Genovese; DIRECTOR/CHOREOGRAPHER: Eugene Loring; SETS/LIGHTING: Samuel Leve; COSTUMES: Sal Anthony; MUSICAL DIRECTOR/CHORAL DIRECTOR/CHORAL ARRANGEMENTS: Maurice Levine; ORCHESTRATIONS: Don Walker; DANCE MUSIC COMPOSER & ARRANGER: Roger Adams; PRESS: Bill Doll, Stanley Brody, Robert Ganshaw, Robert Ullman; COMPANY MANAGER: Paul Groll; STAGE MANAGERS: David Kanter, J. Myles Putnam, Bruce Laffey. **Cast**: MICHELINO: David Kurlan; PADRE: Vincent Barbi; ANGELA: Rina Falcone; MARIA: Joan Morton; ELISABETTA: Ann Needham; DOMINIC: Lionel Ames; BARON D'ALESSANDRO: Ernest Sarracino; ROCCO: Ferdinand Hilt; VITTORIO: James McCracken; CASSIO: Orville Sherman; PIETRO: Ted Thurston; EMELIA: Jane Harven; FRANCESCA: Marie Gibson; PAPPA MARIO: Billy Gilbert (1); NORINA: Charlotte Jones; CARLO: Henry Hamilton; SERGEANT McKENZIE: Walter Black; CAPTAIN STEVE DICKSON: Lawrence Brooks (2); PRIVATE POOLE: James Tarbutton; TABULATOR: Leon Daniels; MARISA D'ALESSANDRO: Lois Hunt (3); PRIVATE BURNS: Joe Mantell; CORPORAL GOWER: Al Checco; PRIVATE WHITFIELD: George Reeder; PRIVATE WEBSTER: Donn Driver; TERRY PATTERSON: Susan Johnson (4); JOAN WELLINGTON: Marti Stevens; CHILDREN: Barbara Karen, Babs Wood, Darryl Richard; DANCING GROUP: Estelle Aza, Alvin Beam, James Capp, Bettina Dearborn, Marcella Dodge, Donn Driver, George Foster, Loren Hightower, Vera Lee, Zoya Leporsky, Rudy Mattise, Joan Morton, Ann Needham, Greg O'Brien, Ann Olchoff, George Reeder, Lewis Schaw, Sandra Zell, Beatrice Ruth; SINGING GROUP: Lionel Ames, Vincent Barbi, Sara Bettis, Joyce Carol, Ann DeBella, Rina Falcone, Marie Gibson, Robert Gilson, Henry Hamilton, Gene Hollman, Mike King, Henry Lawrence, James McCracken, Iona Noble, Noella Peloquin, Jan Scott, Joanne Spiller, Ted Thurston, Joseph Tocci. **Understudies**: Mario: Ernest Sarracino; Joan: Sara Bettis; Dominic/Mackenzie: Henry Hamilton. **Act I**: *Scene 1* On the road to the village; *Scene 2* In Buttrio Square. **Act II**: *Scene 1* In the GI barracks; several months later; *Scene 2* In Buttrio Square; *Scene 3*

In Mario's bakeshop; *Scene 4* In Buttrio Square. *Act I*: Opening (Michelino, Padre, D'Alessandro, Rocco, Village Dancers, Singers), "Every Day is a Holiday" (Steve & Villagers), "Let's Make it Forever" (Steve & Marisa), "I'll Tell the World" (Marisa), "No Place Like This Country" (m: Arthur Jones) (Steve & GIs), "Take it Away" (m: Roger Adams) (GIs & Village Girls), "Get Me Out" (Terry), "I'm Gonna Be a Pop" (Mario & Villagers), "One is a Lonely Number" (Steve & Village Dancers), "One is a Lonely Number" (reprise) (Marisa), "Tarantula" (Villagers). *Act II*: "Get Me Out" (reprise) (Terry), "Love Swept Like a Storm" (Vittorio, Village Singers, Dancers), "Fraternization Ballet" (Gower, Padre, Villagers), "I Keep Telling Myself" (m: Arthur Jones) (Terry), "More and More" (Steve & Marisa), "You're Mine, All Mine" (Terry & Cassio), Finale (Entire Company).

It was universally panned, but Susan Johnson got praise.

94. *By Jeeves*

A musical entertainment. Set in a church hall, later to represent a London flat and the house and grounds of Totley Towers; this very evening. Jeeves is a very organized English butler. Bertram ("Bertie") Wooster is his bumbling, accident-prone employer. Honoria is Bertie's ex-fiancee; Bingo is in love with Honoria; Bassett is a magistrate, Madeline is his daughter, and Stiffy is his ward; Gussie is in love with Madeline; Stinker is in love with Stiffy; and Cyrus is a Yankee guest. It opens in the church hall, where Bertie is about to give a banjo recital. But Jeeves steals his banjo, forcing Bertie to improvise with a dizzy tale of romantic entanglements and mistaken identities.

Before Broadway. The first incarnation of this musical was known as *Jeeves*, and first ran at the BRISTOL HIPPODROME, England, 3/20/75–4/5/75; then as *By Jeeves* at HER MAJESTY'S THEATRE, London, 4/22/75–5/24/75. Previews from 4/11/75. 38 PERFORMANCES. This was Andrew Lloyd Webber's only failure. DIRECTOR: Eric Thompson; CHOREOGRAPHER: Christopher Bruce; SETS/COSTUMES: Voytek; MUSICAL DIRECTOR: Anthony Bowles. *Cast*: BERTIE: David Hemmings; JEEVES: Michael Aldridge; SIR RODERICK SPODE: John Turner; STIFFY: Debbie Bowen; MADELINE: Gabrielle Drake; HONORIA: Angela Easterling; STINKER: Gordon Clyde; BASSETT: Bill Wallis; GUSSIE: Christopher Good; BINGO: David Wood; CHORUS INCLUDED: Elaine Paige. "The Code of the Woosters," "Travel Hopefully," "Female of the Species," "Today," "When Love Arrives," "Jeeves is Past His Peak," "Half a Moment," "S.P.O.D.E.," "Eulalie," "Summer Day," "Banjo Boy," "A False Start," "That Was Nearly Us," "Deadlier than the Male," "The Hallo Song," "By Jeeves," "What Have You Got to Say, Jeeves?," "It's a Pig," "Wizard Rainbow Banjo Mix," "Love Maze," "Wooster Will Entertain You."

The idea was revived at the STEPHEN JOSEPH THEATRE, Scarborough, Yorkshire, 5/1/96–6/1/96. It got good reviews. It was so revised from the 1975 failure that Alan Ayckbourn described it as a "15th cousin, 10 times removed" of his original musical *Jeeves*. It went to the DUKE OF YORK'S THEATRE, London, 7/2/96. The theatre was transformed to an in-the-round space, to maintain the atmosphere of a show being produced in a village hall. There were 12 songs, 12 players and minimal scenery. It got divided reviews. It was recorded on Polydor. "Half a Moment" was the hit. DIRECTOR: Alan Ayckbourn; CHOREOGRAPHER: Sheila Carter. *Cast*: BERTIE: Steven Pacey; JEEVES: Malcolm Sinclair; ALSO WITH: Nicolas Colicos, Robert Austin, Diana Morrison. Later in 1996 the production moved to the LYRIC THEATRE.

Broadway was discussed as early as 1996. In fact the GOODSPEED OPERA HOUSE, in Connecticut, had for some time been discussing an option with Andrew Lloyd Webber of bringing it over, and it did, indeed, run there, 11/7/96–1/19/97 (rehearsals from 9/24/96; previews from 10/17/96; closing date extended from 12/12/96). It had the same basic crew as for the subsequent Broadway run. *Cast*: JEEVES: Richard Kline; BERTIE: John Scherer; HONORIA: Donna Lynne Champlin; BINGO: Randy Redd; BASSETT: Merwin Goldsmith; MADELINE: Nancy Anderson; GUSSIE: Kevin Ligon; STIFFY: Emily Loesser; STINKER: Ian Knauer; CYRUS: Jonathan Stewart; OZZIE NUTLEDGE: Michael O'Flaherty; ALSO

WITH: Tom Ford, Molly Renfroe, Court Whisman. "The Code of the Woosters" (Bertie); "Travel Hopefully—Part I" (Bertie & Jeeves); "That Was Nearly Us" (Honoria & Bertie); "Love's Maze" (Stiffy, Bertie, Gardener); "The Hallo Song" (Bertie, with Budge & Gussie); "By Jeeves" (Bertie, with Bingo & Gussie); "When Love Arrives" (Bertie, with Madeline); "What Have You Got to Say?" (Bertie, with Jeeves); "Half a Moment" (Harold & Stiffy); "It's a Pig" (Honoria & Madeline, with Bertie); "Banjo Boy" (Bertie, with Company). The opening song "Code of the Woosters" was subsequently re-worked by Messrs Ayckbourn and Lloyd Webber, and after new verses (but keeping the same refrain) it emerged as a new version of "Wooster Will Entertain You." This new song was later (by 11/96) inserted into the London production as well. The Goodspeed production moved to the GEFFEN THEATRE, Los Angeles (without Richard Kline), 3/4/97–4/6/97. Then to the KENNEDY CENTER, Washington, DC, 6/4/97–8/31/97.

As early as 3/97 a Broadway move after the Kennedy Center was being talked about, with the Circle in the Square Uptown being the likely theatre. It did not happen. By 8/97 it was rumored that it would tour, with Broadway as one of its stops. By 12/98 the Goodspeed version was being rumored as a definite for the 98–99 Broadway season, but they couldn't get a theatre (they needed a small, intimate Broadway house, such as the Helen Hayes). Then a regional production was talked about, followed by a Broadway move in spring 2000. But none of that happened either. It finally re-appeared at the O'REILLY THEATRE, Pittsburgh, 2/9/01–3/4/01 (previews from 2/1/01), where it was presented in collaboration with the Goodspeed Opera House. It had the same basic crew as it had always had, except MUSICAL SUPERVISOR: Michael O'Flaherty; MUSICAL DIRECTOR: F. Wade Russo. It had the same cast as for the later Broadway run, except BASSETT: Heath Lamberts. There had been some more musical changes, and re-writes to the lyrics. Andrew Lloyd Webber attended the rehearsal of 1/31/01, as well as the dress rehearsal.

By 2/01 the Helen Hayes was being mentioned again as the Broadway venue for spring 2001. Coming up at the Helen Hayes, however, was Hershey Felder doing his one-man show *George Gershwin Alone;* despite a personal call from Andrew Lloyd Webber offering Mr. Felder a London theatre instead, Mr. Felder did in fact play the Helen Hayes, and *By Jeeves* remained homeless. After Pittsburgh the show went to Toronto to be filmed in a studio, and to make a cast recording. Ideas of Broadway were put off until fall 2001. On 6/13/01 a Broadway opening date of 11/01 was announced. On 8/6/01 the Helen Hayes was finally announced as the theatre, previews to begin on 10/17/01, with an opening date of 10/28/01. Previews were brought forward to 10/16/01. By 8/20/01 John Scherer and Martin Jarvis were being rumored for the leads. After the 9/11 attack on New York City, the show lost its two primary backers on 9/18/01, and it was postponed indefinitely. However, by 9/20/01 Andrew Lloyd Webber had found new angels, and the show was on again, same dates. On 9/25/01 John Scherer, Martin Jarvis, and the rest of the cast were confirmed in their roles. The show was to have a limited engagement through 2/3/02, unless audiences really loved it, in which case it would go to an open run. Sam Tsoutsouvas replaced Heath Lamberts in the cast. The Pittsburgh cast recording (done in Toronto) was released by Decca Broadway on 10/16/01.

The Broadway Run. HELEN HAYES THEATRE, 10/28/01–12/30/01. 16 previews from 10/16/01. 72 PERFORMANCES. PRESENTED BY Goodspeed Musicals; MUSIC: Andrew Lloyd Webber; LYRICS/BOOK/DIRECTOR: Alan Ayckbourn; BASED ON the *Jeeves* stories, by P.G. Wodehouse; CHOREOGRAPHER: Sheila Carter; SETS: Roger Glossop; COSTUMES: Louise Belson; LIGHTING: Mick Hughes; SOUND: Richard Ryan; MUSICAL SUPERVISOR/MUSICAL DIRECTOR: Michael O'Flaherty; ARRANGEMENTS: David Cullen & Andrew Lloyd Webber; PRESS: Barlow—Hartman Public Relations; CASTING: Sarah Hughes & Warren Pincus; GENERAL MANAGEMENT: Charlotte Wilcox Company; COMPANY MANAGER: Bruce Kagel; PRODUCTION STAGE MANAGER: Daniel S. Rosokoff; STAGE MANAGER: Nancy Elizabeth Vest; ASSISTANT STAGE MANAGER: Jamison Stern. *Cast:* BERTIE WOOSTER: John Scherer (1); JEEVES: Martin Jarvis (2); HONORIA GLOSSOP: Donna Lynne Champlin; BINGO LITTLE: Don Stephenson; GUSSIE FINK-NOTTLE: James Kall; SIR WATKYN BASSETT: Sam Tsoutsouvas; MADELINE BASSETT: Becky Watson; STIFFY BYNG: Emily Loesser, *Ana Maria Andricain*; HAROLD "STINKER" PINKER: Ian Knauer; CYRUS

BUDGE III (JUNIOR): Steve Wilson; OTHER PERSONAGES: Tom Ford, Molly Renfroe, Court Whisman. *Understudies*: Wooster/Bingo/Gussie: Tom Ford & Jamison Stern; Stiffy/Madeline/Honoria: Cristin Mortenson & Molly Renfroe; Jeeves/Budge/Bassett/Stinker: David Edwards & Court Whisman. Swings: Cristin Mortenson & Jamison Stern.

BY JEEVES *Orchestra*: REEDS: Eddie Salkin; GUITAR: Jack Cavari; DRUMS/PERCUSSION: Brad Flickinger; BASS: Brian Cassier; KEYBOARD: F. Wade Russo; PIANO: Michael O'Flaherty. *Act I*: "A False Start" (Bertie), "Never Fear" (Bertie & Jeeves), "Travel Hopefully" (Bertie & Bingo), "That Was Nearly Us" (Honoria & Bertie), "Love's Maze" (Stiffy, Bertie, Company), "The Hallo Song" (Bertie, Budgie, Gussie). *Act II*: "By Jeeves" (Bertie, Bingo, Gussie), "When Love Arrives" (Bertie, with Madeline), "What Have You Got to Say, Jeeves?" (Bertie & Jeeves), "Half a Moment" (Harold & Stiffy), "It's a Pig!" (Honoria, Madeline, Bassett, Gussie, Bertie), "Banjo Boy" (Company), "The Wizard Rainbow Finale" (Company).

Broadway reviews were divided, mostly negative. On 11/27/01 closing notices were posted.

95. *By the Beautiful Sea*

Set in Coney Island, in 1907. Lottie is a big-hearted, middle-aged vaudevillian who operates a theatrical boarding house in Coney Island. She has her eye on Shakespearian actor Dennis, but just as she wins him over, his long-lost daughter, Betsy, appears. Ruby is the black housemaid; Half-Note is her 9-year-old son. Desperate for cash Lottie takes a parachute jump for $1,000.

Before Broadway. During tryouts Richard France replaced Ray Malone. Marshall Jamison, recommended by Josh Logan, replaced Charles Walter as director, and Helen Tamiris (assisted by Daniel Nagrin) replaced Donald Saddler as choreographer.

The Broadway Run. MAJESTIC THEATRE, 4/8/54–10/1/54; IMPERIAL THEATRE, 10/4/54–11/27/54. Total of 270 PERFORMANCES. PRESENTED BY Robert Fryer & Lawrence Carr; MUSIC: Arthur Schwartz; LYRICS: Dorothy Fields; BOOK: Herbert & Dorothy Fields; DIRECTOR: Marshall Jamison; CHOREOGRAPHER: Helen Tamiris; ASSISTANT CHOREOGRAPHER: Daniel Nagrin; PIANIST FOR HELEN TAMIRIS: Edward Johnson; SETS/LIGHTING: Jo Mielziner; COSTUMES: Irene Sharaff; MUSICAL DIRECTOR/VOCAL ARRANGEMENTS: Jay Blackton; ORCHESTRATIONS: Robert Russell Bennett; PRESS: Marian Byram, Phyllis Perlman, David Powers; GENERAL MANAGER: Jack Schlissel; PRODUCTION STAGE MANAGER: Samuel Liff; STAGE MANAGER: Len Bedsow; ASSISTANT STAGE MANAGER: Charles Millang. *Cast:* QUARTET: John Dennis, Reid Shelton, Ray Hyson, Larry Laurence; ACROBATS: Ray Kirchner & Rex Cooper; CORA BELMONT: Mary Harmon; MOLLY BELMONT: Cindy Robbins; LILLIAN BELMONT: Gloria Smith; RUBY MONK: Mae Barnes (4); MRS. KOCH: Edith True Case; CARL GIBSON: Cameron Prud'homme (3); LOTTIE GIBSON: Shirley Booth (1); HALF-NOTE: Robert Jennings; DIABOLO: Thomas Gleason; BABY BETSY BUSCH: Carol Leigh; MICKEY POWERS: Richard France (5), *Larry Howard*; DENNIS EMERY: Wilbur Evans (2); FLORA BUSCH: Anne Francine; WILLIE SLATER: Warde Donovan; LENNY: Larry Howard, *Eddie Heim*; SIDNEY: Eddie Roll; MR. CURTIS: Paul Reed, *Frederic Downs* [on 5/17/54 this role became known as Barker]; BURT MAYER: Larry Laurence; VIOLA: Gaby Monet; DANCERS: Cathryn Damon (Principal Dancer), Rex Cooper, Dorothy Donau, Lillian Donau, Pat Ferrier, Bob Haddad, Larry Howard (*Eddie Heim*), Ray Kirchner, Arthur Partington, Victor Reilley, Eddie Roll, Sigyn, Mona Tritsch, *John Nola*; SINGERS: JohnDennis, Warde Donovan, Suzanne Easter, Lola Fisher, Thomas Gleason, Ray Hyson, Franklin Kennedy, Larry Laurence, George Lenz, Colleen O'Connor, Pat Roe, Reid Shelton, Jean Sincere, Libi Staiger. *Understudies*: Lottie: Jean Sincere; Dennis: Warde Donovan; Baby Betsy: Cindy Robbins; Carl: Paul Reed, *Frederic Downs*; Ruby: Miriam Burton; Mickey: Larry Howard, *Eddie Heim*; Half-Note: Vincent McLeod; Mr. Curtis: Thomas Gleason; Mrs. Koch: Lola Fisher; Flora: Libi Staiger; For Miss Damon: Lillian Donau.

Note: Lillian & Dorothy Donau later changed their name to D'Honau. *Act I*: *Scene 1* Backyard of Lottie Gibson's Coney Island boarding house: "Mona from Arizona" (Quartet), "The Sea Song" ("By the Beautiful Sea") (Lottie, Boarders, Neighbors); *Scene 1a* Inside the boarding house: "The Sea Song" (reprise) (Lottie); *Scene 2* Seaside street in Coney Island: "Old Enough to Love" (Mickey, to Betsy); *Scene 3* The Midway at Coney Island: "Coney Island Boat" (Lottie, Half-Note, Visitors)/"In the Good Old Summertime" (m: George Evans; l: Ren Shields) [the latter was an old 1902 number]; *Scene 4* The Old Mill (a tunnel of love boat trip): "Alone Too Long" (Dennis); *Scene 5* Backyard of Lottie Gibson's boarding house: "Happy Habit" (Ruby); *Scene 6* The Midway at Coney Island: "Good Time Charlie" (sung by Mickey, Lenny, Sidney, The Belmont Sisters). SPORTS: Male Dancers; SPICY PICTURES: THE VENDOR: Larry Laurence; WICKED WOMEN: Sigyn, Lillian Donau, Cathryn Damon; Iceman and Wife (ballet): Arthur Partington & Pat Ferrier: SERPENTINA SAL: Gaby Monet; FINALE: Dancing Company; *Scene 7* Seaside street in Coney Island: "Good Time Charlie" (reprise) (Mickey, Lenny, Sidney, The Belmont Sisters); *Scene 8* Bedroom of Lottie Gibson's boarding house: "I'd Rather Wake up by Myself" (Lottie); *Scene 9* The Pavilion of Fun; the Fourth of July: "Hooray for George the Third" (Diabolo, Libi Staiger, Visitors). *Act II*: *Scene 1* The backyard of Lottie Gibson's boarding house: "(If the Devil Answers) Hang Up!" (Ruby, Boarders, Neighbors), "Alone Too Long" (reprise) (Lottie), "More Love than Your Love" (Dennis, to Lottie); *Scene 2* Montage of vaudeville acts on the bill, stage of the Brighton Beach theatre: 1. The Three Clowns; 2. A Lady in Red; 3. Butterfly Wings. "Lottie Gibson Specialty" ("Please Don't Send Me Down a Baby Brother") (Lottie); *Scene 3* Dreamland Casino: "Throw the Anchor Away" (The Belmont Sisters, with Larry Laurence & Arthur Partington), Dance (Viola, Arthur Partington, Mickey, Rex Cooper, Patrons), "More Love than Your Love" (reprise) (Dennis); *Scene 4* Lottie's bedroom: "Happy Habit" (reprise) (Lottie); *Scene 5* Seaside street in Coney Island: "Old Enough to Love" (reprise) (Mickey & Betsy); *Scene 6* Dreamland Casino: "I'd Rather Wake up by Myself" (reprise) (Lottie), Finale (Entire Company).

Broadway reviews were middle of the road, mixed and divided. Shirley Booth got raves and won a Donaldson Award.

After Broadway. LAMBS THEATRE, NYC, 6/16/99–6/27/99. 15 PERFORMANCES. This was a staged concert reading, part of the *Musicals Tonight!* series. DIRECTOR: Thomas Mills; MUSICAL DIRECTOR: Michael Lavine. Cast: LOTTIE: KT Sullivan; EMERY: Sam Freed; BETSY: Marisa Bela; FLORA: Louisa Flaningam; RUBY: Amy Jo Phillips; MICKEY: Perry Laylon Ojeda; BELMONT SISTERS: Randi Megibow, Brooke Moriber, Lisa Trader.

96. *Bye, Bye, Birdie*

Birdie is an Elvis-type rock 'n roll idol. Albert, a former teacher and now Conrad's manager, and Rose, Albert's secretary, struggle to come up with one last song for Birdie before he's drafted, so they can marry, retire and lead a normal life with Albert as an English teacher. They contrive a publicity stunt whereby the winner of a national Conrad Birdie Fan Club competition gets to kiss Conrad goodbye on the *Ed Sullivan Show* just before he's drafted. The lucky winner is Kim, from Sweet Apple, Ohio. Albert, Rose and Conrad all descend on Sweet Apple for the telecast. This upsets some of the townsfolk (the older ones) and delights the teenagers and mothers. Complications involve Kim's jealous boyfriend Hugo, and her exasperated father. Mae, Albert's mother, tries to wreck his relationship with Rose, because she fears she'll lose his support.

Before Broadway. The idea was Edward Padula's. It was first written as a libretto in 1957, as *Let's Go Steady*, a regular teenage musical. Mr. Padula had been stage manager for actor Maurice Evans. Mr. Evans had optioned the property, and then dropped it. Mr. Padula took it up. Elvis being drafted gave the story a focus that it needed, and that's when the new (new in more ways than one) librettist Mike Stewart came on board with the Conrad Birdie angle. It tried out in Philadelphia. The numbers "All Woman," "Older and Wiser" and "There Comes a Time" were cut Before Broadway.

The Broadway Run. MARTIN BECK THEATRE, 4/14/60–10/22/60;

FIFTY-FOURTH STREET THEATRE, 10/24/60–1/14/61; SHUBERT THEATRE, 1/16/61–10/7/61). Total of 607 PERFORMANCES. PRESENTED BY Edward Padula, in association with L. Slade Brown; MUSIC: Charles Strouse; LYRICS: Lee Adams; ADDITIONAL SCORING: Elliot Lawrence; BOOK: Michael Stewart; FROM the unproduced libretto *Let's Go Steady*, by Warren Miller & Raphael Milian; DIRECTOR/CHOREOGRAPHER: Gower Champion; SETS: Robert Randolph; COSTUMES: Miles White; LIGHTING: Peggy Clark; MUSICAL DIRECTOR: Elliot Lawrence, *Sherman Frank*; ORCHESTRATIONS: Robert Ginzler; DANCE MUSIC ARRANGEMENTS: John Morris; PRESS: Reuben Rabinovitch; GENERAL MANAGER: Robert Rapport; COMPANY MANAGER: *Michael Goldreyer*; PRODUCTION STAGE MANAGER: Michael Thoma; STAGE MANAGER: Elsa Walden; ASSISTANT STAGE MANAGER: Edward Nayor, *Fred Kimbrough*. **Cast:** ALBERT PETERSON: Dick Van Dyke (2), *Gene Rayburn*; ROSE GRANT: Chita Rivera (1), *Gretchen Wyler*; (SEVENTEEN) TEENAGERS: HELEN: Karin Wolfe, *Marilyn Siskin*; NANCY: Marissa Mason, *Lori Rogers*; ALICE: Sharon Lerit; MARGIE ANN: Louise Quick; PENELOPE ANN: Lada Edmund; DEBORAH SUE: Jessica Albright; SUZIE: Lynn Bowin; LINDA: Judy Keirn; CAROL: Penny Ann Green, *Beth Howland*; MARTHA LOUISE: Vicki Belmonte; HAROLD: Michael Vita; KARL: Jerry Dodge; HARVEY: Dean Stolber, *Bob Mariano*; HENRY: Ed Kresley; ARTHUR: Bob Spencer; FREDDIE: Tracy Everitt; PEYTON: Gary Howe; URSULA MERKLE: Barbara Doherty, *Jacqueline Mayro*; KIM MACAFEE: Susan Watson, *Karin Wolfe, Nancy Tribush*; MRS. MACAFEE: Marijane Maricle; MR. MACAFEE: Paul Lynde (4); TEEN TRIO: Louise Quick, Jessica Albright, Vicki Belmonte; SAD GIRL: Sharon Lerit; ANOTHER SAD GIRL: Karin Wolfe, *Marilyn Siskin*; MAE PETERSON: Kay Medford (3); REPORTERS: Lee Howard, Jim Sisco, Don Farnworth (*Bill Joyce*), John Coyle; ELLSWORTH "CONRAD" BIRDIE: Dick Gautier (5); GUITAR MAN: Kenny Burrell; CONDUCTOR: Kasimir Kokich; CHEERLEADERS: Judy Keirn & Lynn Bowin; MAYOR: Allen Knowles; MAYOR'S WIFE: Amelia Haas; HUGO PEABODY: Michael J. Pollard; RANDOLPH MACAFEE: Johnny Borden; MRS. MERKLE: Pat McEnnis; OLD WOMAN: Dori Davis; NEIGHBORS: Amelia Haas, Jeannine Masterson, Ed Becker, Oran Osburn, George Blackwell, Lee Howard (dropped by 60–61); MR. HENKEL: Charles Nelson Reilly; GLORIA RASPUTIN: Norma Richardson; ED SULLIVAN'S VOICE: Will Jordan; TV STAGE MANAGER: Tony Mordente, *Ed Kresley*; CHARLES F. MAUDE: George Blackwell; BAR CUSTOMERS: Lee Howard & Oran Osburn [roles added by 60–61]; DISH WASHER: Ed Becker [role added by 60–61]; SHRINERS: Allen Knowles, John Coyle, Dick Crowley, Don Farnworth (*Bill Joyce*), Bud Fleming, Kasimir Kokich, Jim Sisco. **Standby**: Rose: Patti Karr, *Carmen Alvarez*. **Understudies**: Albert: Charles Nelson Reilly; Birdie: Tony Mordente, *Ed Kresley*; Mae: Pat McEnnis; Mr. McAfee/Mr. Henkel: Lee Howard; Hugo/Randolph: Dean Stolber, *Bob Mariano*; Kim: Vickie Belmonte; Mayor: Don Farnworth, *Bill Joyce*; Harvey: Bob Spencer; Maude: Ed Becker; Ursula: Jessica Albright; Mrs. McAfee: Jeannine Masterson; Mrs. Merkle: Amelia Haas; TV Stage Manager: Ed Kresley, *Michael Vita*; Gloria: Lyn Bowin; "How to Kill a Man" ballet: Bud Fleming. **Swing Couple**: Ed Kresley & Penny Ann Green (*Beth Howland*). **Act I: Prologue** Overture (Orchestra); **Scene 1** Office of Almaelou Music, New York: "An English Teacher" (Rose & Albert); **Scene 2** Sweet Apple, Ohio: "The Telephone Hour" (Sweet Apple Kids); **Scene 3** McAfee home, Sweet Apple: "How Lovely to Be a Woman" (Kim); **Scene 4** Pennsylvania Station, New York: "We Love You, Conrad!" (Teen Trio), "Put on a Happy Face" (Albert & the Two Sad Girls) [the big hit] [originally written for a revue at Green Mansions, a resort in the Adirondacks], "Normal American Boy" (Rose, Albert, Chorus); **Scene 5** Railroad station, Sweet Apple: "One Boy (One Girl)" (Kim, Deborah, Sue, Alice), "One Boy (One Girl)" (reprise) (Rose); **Scene 6** Courthouse steps, Sweet Apple: "Honestly Sincere" (Conrad & Townspeople); **Scene 7** McAfee home, Sweet Apple: "Hymn for a Sunday Evening" (Mr. & Mrs. McAfee, Kim, Randolph, Neighbors); **Scene 8** Stage, Central Movie Theatre, Sweet Apple; **Scene 9** Backstage office, Central Movie Theatre, Sweet Apple: "How to Kill a Man" (ballet) (Rose, Albert, Company); **Scene 10** Stage, Central Movie Theatre, Sweet Apple: "One Last Kiss" (Conrad & Company). **Act II: Prologue** "The World at Large" (Orchestra); **Scene 1** McAfee home, Sweet Apple: "What Did I Ever See in Him?" (Rose & Kim); **Scene 2** Street outside McAfee home: "A Lot of Livin' to Do" (Conrad, Kim, Teenagers); **Scene 3** McAfee's back door: "Kids!" (Mr. & Mrs. McAfee); **Scene 4** Maude's Roadside Retreat: "Baby,

Talk to Me" (Albert & Quartet); **Scene 5** Private dining room, Maude's Roadside Retreat: "Shriners' Ballet" (Rose & Shriners); **Scene 6** Back door, Maude's Roadside Retreat: "Kids!" (reprise) (Mr. & Mrs. McAfee, Randolph, Townspeople); **Scene 7** The Ice House: "Spanish Rose" (Rose); **Scene 8** Railroad station, Sweet Apple: "Rosie" (Albert & Rose).

It got unanimous raves except for Brooks Atkinson of the *New York Times*. The phenomenon (i.e. rock 'n roll) that this musical satirized was over by 1960, so it went from being a topical spoof to an historical piece. It was a surprise hit with little ballyhoo, and made Dick Van Dyke a star. It won Tonys for musical, choreography, director of a musical, and for Dick Van Dyke, and was also nominated for sets (musical), and musical director, and for Chita Rivera and Dick Gautier. When it started to sag, Mike Stewart and Gower Champion dreamed up the idea of an all-black cast replacement, headed by Sammy Davis Jr. and Diahann Carroll, but it never happened (it did, later, though, with *Hello, Dolly!*). There was a sequel (see *Bring Back Birdie*).

After Broadway. TOUR. Opened on 4/24/61, at the Curran Theatre, San Francisco, and closed on 3/17/62, at the Orpheum Theatre, Minneapolis. MUSICAL DIRECTOR: Jack Havener. **Cast:** ALBERT: Bill Hayes; ROSE: Elaine Dunn; MAE: Joan Blondell, Pat McEnnis (relieved Miss Blondell during the first season); BIRDIE: Jesse Pearson; VOICE OF ED SULLIVAN: Will Jordan; KIM: Karin Wolfe.

TOUR. Opened on 10/9/61, at the Shubert Theatre, Boston, and closed on 3/31/62, at the Forrest Theatre, Philadelphia. MUSICAL DIRECTOR: Shepard Coleman. **Cast:** ALBERT: Dick Patterson; ROSE: Gretchen Wyler; HELEN: Kay Cole; MARGIE ANN: Louise Quick; DEBORAH SUE: Bonnie Schon; MARTHA LOUISE: E.J. Peaker; KARL: John Mineo; KIM: Nancy Tribush; MR. McAFEE: Ned Wertimer; MAE: Kay Medford; CONRAD: Dick Gautier; ED SULLIVAN'S VOICE: Ed Sullivan's Voice [sic].

HER MAJESTY'S THEATRE, London, 6/15/61. 268 PERFORMANCES. It got great reviews. CHOREOGRAPHER: Tony Mordente (Chita Rivera's husband); MUSICAL DIRECTOR: Alyn Ainsworth. Lyricist Lee Adams made a few changes to the lyrics, to make sense to English audiences. CAST RECORDING on Philips. **Cast:** ALBERT: Peter Marshall; ROSE: Chita Rivera; BIRDIE: Marty Wilde; MR. McAFEE: Robert Nichols; KIM: Sylvia Tysick; MAE: Angela Baddeley; HUGO: Clive Endersby; REPORTER: Ed Bishop.

PAPER MILL PLAYHOUSE, New Jersey, 1962. DIRECTOR: Duane Camp. **Cast:** Chita Rivera, Tom Poston, Selma Diamond.

THE MOVIE. 1963. DIRECTOR: George Sidney. **Cast:** ALBERT: Dick Van Dyke; ROSIE DE LEON: Janet Leigh; KIM: Ann-Margret; MAE: Maureen Stapleton; HUGO: Bobby Rydell; CONRAD: Jesse Pearson; HIMSELF: Ed Sullivan; MR. AND MRS. McAFEE: Paul Lynde & Mary La Roche; MAYOR: Frank Albertson.

TOURING REVIVAL. Opened in St. Louis, then went to Long Beach, Calif., 5/9/91. Kennedy Center, 12/25/91–1/26/92. It was very successful. PRESENTED BY Barry & Fran Weissler, and Pace Theatrical Group; DIRECTOR: Gene Saks; CHOREOGRAPHER: Ed Kresley; SETS: Peter Larkin; COSTUMES: Robert Mackintosh; LIGHTING: Peggy Eisenhauer; SOUND: Peter Fitzgerald; MUSICAL DIRECTOR: Michael Biagi. **Cast:** ALBERT: Tommy Tune; ROSE: Ann Reinking, *Lenora Nemetz*; BIRDIE: Marc Kudisch; DORIS/GLORIA: Belle Calaway; MAE: Marilyn Cooper; KIM: Susan Egan; HUGO: Steve Zahn. There were two new songs — "One Giant Step" and "He's Mine," in that order, one after the other, as the last two before "Rosie."

1995 TV PRODUCTION. DIRECTOR: Jerry Zaks. **Cast:** Jason Alexander, Vanessa Williams, Tyne Daly, Marc Kudisch, Sally Mayes. "Let's Settle Down" was a new number.

TOUR. Opened on 1/17/98, at Long Beach, Calif., and closed on 5/17/98, in Honolulu. PRESENTED BY Encore Attractions. **Cast:** ALBERT: Chuck Ragsdale; BIRDIE: Casey Marshall; KIM: Krista Pigotti; MR. McAFEE: Troy Donahue.

CITY CENTER, NYC, 5/6/04–5/10/04. Part of the *Encores!* series. This was to celebrate the 60th anniversary of City Center. This production was not connected to the planned 2005 Broadway revival. ADAPTED TO CONCERT FORM BY: David Ives; DIRECTOR: Jerry Zaks; CHOREOGRAPHER: Casey Nicholaw; [Kathleen Marshall had been scheduled as director/choreographer, but had bowed out to make a TV movie]; MUSICAL DIRECTOR: Rob Fisher. **Cast:** ALBERT: Daniel Jenkins; ROSIE: Karen Ziemba; CONRAD: William Robert Gaynor; MR. McAFEE: Walter Bobbie; KIM: Jessica Grove; HUGO: Keith Nobbs; MRS. McAFEE: Victoria Clark.

THE NEW MOVIE. 2004. ADAPTED BY: Stuart Blumberg; DIRECTOR: Jon Chu.

PLANNED BROADWAY REVIVAL. 2005. It was scheduled to play first at the Kennedy Center. PRESENTED BY Manny Kladitis. However, the Kennedy Center run was scrubbed.

97. *Cabaret*

The *Kit Kat Klub*, a sleazy Berlin nightclub, in 1929–30. At the opening, just before New Year's Eve, the audience is faced not with a curtain but with a huge mirror. Then the androgynous master of ceremonies (the mc) enters (a new character, based on one Hal Prince had seen in a German nightclub; it was Hal Prince's idea to have the mc unify the action) and welcomes everyone. British fun-loving, amoral Sally, who is the star there, has an affair with American writer Clifford (he was British in the stories), but breaks it off when she becomes pregnant. She has an abortion. Cliff's landlady, Fraulein Schneider is having a relationship with a Jewish fruit vendor, Herr Schultz. The Fraulein realizes she may lose her license if she marries a Jew. Ernst is a crooked Nazi who introduces Clifford to Sally. Fraulein Kost is another of Fraulein Schneider's tenants, and she brings in sailors.

Before Broadway. Hal Prince and Don Black separately came up with the idea of musicalizing *I Am a Camera*, or, rather, as it turned out, the stories of Christopher Isherwood. Mr. Black's first choice of librettist was Hugh Wheeler, but when that didn't work out he commissioned Sandy Wilson (creator of *The Boy Friend*) to write the book and score. Julie Andrews turned down the role of Sally. In 11/63 Sandy Wilson brought the libretto and the completed two-thirds of the score to Don Black in New York, but Mr. Black suggested someone else write the book. Mr. Black was having problems securing the rights to the property from John Van Druten's estate. One evening Sandy Wilson ran into Hal Prince and over dinner let him know he was working on the Isherwood project. Mr. Prince was also working on a version on which he had engaged Joe Masteroff as librettist (Mr. Masteroff had written the first version of the book in the summer of 1963), and he asked if Sandy Wilson would play his score to Prince and Masteroff to see how they felt about it. They didn't like it, feeling that it needed a darker, more Germanic, perhaps Kurt Weill-Lotte Lenya feel to it. Sandy Wilson disappeared, as did Don Black. Hal Prince secured the rights. John Kander and Fred Ebb wanted Liza Minnelli for the role, but Hal Prince felt that because she wasn't British, and because she sang too well, she would be wrong for the part (and he still thinks so, even after the film, which did star Miss Minnelli). The songwriters wrote 37 numbers, but only 15 were used. The production went on hold for a while in 1965, then opened in Boston for tryouts, but did not do well there. The show was capitalized at $500,000. The sets were revolutionary.

The Broadway Run. BROADHURST THEATRE, 11/20/66–3/4/67; IMPERIAL THEATRE, 3/7/67–10/2/68; BROADWAY THEATRE, 10/7/68–9/6/69. 21 previews from 11/2/66. Total of 1,165 PERFORMANCES. PRESENTED BY Harold Prince, in association with Ruth Mitchell; MUSIC: John Kander; LYRICS: Fred Ebb; BOOK: Joe Masteroff; BASED ON the 1951 drama *I Am a Camera*, by John Van Druten, and starring Julie Harris, and which in turn was based on the novellas comprising *The Berlin Stories*, i.e. *The Last of Mr. Norris* and *Goodbye to Berlin*, by Christopher Isherwood; DIRECTOR: Harold Prince; CHOREOGRAPHER: Ron Field; SETS: Boris Aronson; COSTUMES: Patricia Zipprodt; LIGHTING: Jean Rosenthal; MUSICAL DIRECTOR: Harold Hastings, *Michael Forman* (by 68–69); ORCHESTRATIONS: Don Walker; DANCE MUSIC ARRANGEMENTS: David Baker; CAST RECORDING on Columbia; PRESS: Mary Bryant, Ellen Levene (*Leslie Coven* by 67–68; *David Rothenberg* by 68–69), Bob Pasolli; CASTING: Shirley Rich; GENERAL MANAGER: Carl Fisher; COMPANY MANAGER: Warren O'Hara; PRODUCTION STAGE MANAGER: Ruth Mitchell; STAGE MANAGER: James Bronson, *Ed Aldridge* (by 68–69); ASSISTANT STAGE MANAGER: Nicholas G. Ronaldi, *Ed Aldridge* (by 68), *Tom Stone* by 68–69). **Cast:** THE MC: Joel Grey (5) (Mr.

Grey's name was raised above the title as one of the stars from 4/21/67), *Danny Meehan* (9/11/67–9/25/67), *Joel Grey, Martin Ross* (from 1/1/68); CLIFFORD BRADSHAW: Bert Convy (3) ☆, *John Cunningham* (relieved Mr. Convy in 67–68, and took over permanently from 7/30/68), *Ken Kercheval* (from 8/26/68), *Larry Kert* (from 12/9/68), *Alfred Toigo* (from 6/3/69); ERNST LUDWIG: Edward Winter (7), *George Reinholt* (from 67–68); CUSTOMS OFFICIAL: Howard Kahl; FRAULEIN SCHNEIDER: Lotte Lenya (4) ☆, *Peg Murray* (during Miss Lenya's absence, 3/6/67–3/18/67, and also during Miss Lenya's 2nd vacation, 2/12/68–2/26/68), *Signe Hasso* (during another of Miss Lenya's vacations in 67–68), *Despo* (during Miss Lenya's third vacation in 67–68, and again during her much longer absence, 6/10/68–10/7/68), *Susan Willis* (took over from Miss Lenya on 6/3/69); HERR SCHULTZ: Jack Gilford (2) ☆, *George Voskovec* (from 6/10/68); FRAULEIN KOST: Peg Murray (6), *Mara Landi* (while Miss Murray was standing in for Miss Lenya), *Rhoda Gemignani* (from 68–69); TELEPHONE GIRL: Tresha Kelly; KIT KAT BAND: Maryann Burns, Janice Mink, Nancy Powers, Viola Smith; MAITRE D': Frank Bouley; MAX: John Herbert; BARTENDER: Ray Baron, *Ken Sherber* (from 68–69); SALLY BOWLES: Jill Haworth (1) ☆, *Penny Fuller* (during Miss Haworth's vacation in 67–68), *Anita Gillette* (from 11/4/68), *Tandy Cronyn* (from 6/30/69), *Melissa Hart* (from 7/28/69); TWO LADIES: Mary Ehara & Rita O'Connor (*Bonnie Walker* by 68–69); GERMAN SAILORS: Bruce Becker (*Ray Chabeau* from 67–68, *Curtis Hood* from 68–69), Steven Boockvor, Roger Briant (*Ralph Nelson* from 68–69), Edward Nolfi (*Tod Miller* from 68–69; *Bill Allsbrook* from 68–69), *Doug Spingler*; FRAU WENDEL: Mara Landi, *Lorraine Serabian* (from 68–69), *Chevi Colton* (from 68–69), *Erica Yohn* (from 68–69); HERR WENDEL: Eugene Morgan; FRAU KRUGER: Miriam Lehmann-Haupt [role cut by 68–69]; HERR ERDMANN: Sol Frieder; (EIGHT) KIT KAT KITTENS: MARIA: Pat Gosling, *Joan Paige* (from 68–69); LULU: Lynn Winn, *Susanne Carroll* (from 67–68); ROSIE: Bonnie Walker, *Sandra Brewer* (from 67–68), *Chele Graham* (from 68–69); FRITZIE: Marianne Selbert, *Lenora Nemetz* (from 68–69); TEXAS: Kathie Dalton; FRENCHIE: Barbara Alston, *Sandy McPherson* (from 68–69); MARLENE: Carol Perea [new role by 67–68]; HULDA: Bonnie Walker [new role by 67–68], *Fran Storey* (from 68–69), *Carol Petri* (from 68–69); BOBBY: Jere Admire, *Michael Toles* (from 68–69); VICTOR: Bert Michaels, *Robert Scherkenbach* (from 68–69); GRETA: Jayme Mylroie; FELIX: Robert Sharp, *Ray Baron* (from 68–69). **Standbys:** Sally: Penny Fuller, *Judy MacMurdo*; Schneider: *Despo* (by 68–69). **Understudies:** Sally: Jayme Mylroie, *Anita Gillette*; Schultz: Sol Frieder; Clifford: Edward Winter, *George Reinholt*; Schneider: Peg Murray; mc: Bert Michaels, *Robert Scherkenbach*; Kost: Mara Landi, *Chevi Colton*; Ernst: John Herbert. **Act I: Scene 1** The Kit Kat Klub: "Wilkommen" (mc & Company); **Scene 2** Aboard a European railway train; **Scene 3** Fraulein Schneider's flat: "So What?" (Schneider); **Scene 4** The Kit Kat Klub; New Year's Eve, 1930: "Don't Tell Mama" (Sally & Girls), "The Telephone Song" (Company); **Scene 5** Cliff's room: "Perfectly Marvelous" (Cliff & Sally); **Scene 6** The Kit Kat Klub: "Two Ladies" (mc & Two Ladies); **Scene 7** Fraulein Schneider's living room: "It Couldn't Please Me More" (Schneider & Schultz); **Scene 8** The Kit Kat Klub: "Tomorrow Belongs to Me" (mc, 1st Waiter, Waiters); **Scene 9** Cliff's room: "Why Should I Wake Up?" (Cliff & Sally); **Scene 10** The Kit Kat Klub: "The Money Song" (mc, Girls, Fat Bankers); **Scene 11** Fraulein Schneider's living room and Fraulein Kost's room: "Married" (Schneider & Schultz); **Scene 12** Herr Schultz's fruit shop: "Meeskite" (Schultz), "Tomorrow Belongs to Me" (reprise) (Kost, Ernst, Guests). **Act II:** Entr'acte (Girl Orchestra); **Scene 1** The Kit Kat Klub: "If You Could See Her" (mc & Girls); **Scene 2** Herr Schultz's shop: "Married" (reprise) (Schneider & Schultz); **Scene 3** The Kit Kat Klub: "If You Could See Her" (reprise) (mc & Bobby); **Scene 4** Cliff's room: "What Would You Do?" (Schneider); **Scene 5** The Kit Kat Klub: "Cabaret" (Sally); **Scene 6** Cliff's room; **Scene 7** A railroad compartment, then the Kit Kat Klub: Finale (Cliff, Sally, Schneider, Shultz, mc, Company)

The show got great Broadway reviews. It won Tony Awards for musical, composer & lyricist, direction of a musical, choreography, sets, costumes, and for Joel Grey and Peg Murray, and also nominated were Jack Gilford, Edward Winter and Lotte Lenya. It was a very influential musical. It made a star of Joel Grey.

After Broadway. TOUR. Opened on 12/26/67, at the Shubert Theatre, New Haven, and ran for 19 months. MUSICAL DIRECTOR: Joseph

Lewis. *Cast:* MC: Robert Salvio, *Charles Abbott* (from 10/30/68); CLIFFORD: Gene Rupert; SCHNEIDER: Signe Hasso; SCHULTZ: Leo Fuchs; SALLY: Melissa Hart.

TOUR. Opened on 8/19/69, at the State Fair Music Hall, Dallas, and closed on 5/23/70, at Columbus, Ohio, after 112 cities. MUSICAL DIRECTOR: Gilbert Bowers. *Cast:* MC: Jay Fox; CLIFFORD: Franklin Kiser; SCHNEIDER: Alexandra Damien; SCHULTZ: Woody Romoff; SALLY: Tandy Cronyn.

PALACE THEATRE, London. Opened 2/28/68. 316 PERFORMANCES. *Cast:* MC: Barry Dennen; CLIFFORD: Kevin Colson; SCHNEIDER: Lila Kedrova, *Thelma Ruby* (from 8/28/68); SCHULTZ: Peter Sallis; SALLY: Judi Dench.

PAPER MILL PLAYHOUSE, New Jersey, 1969. DIRECTOR: Fred Ebb. *Cast:* Martin Ross, Melissa Hart, John Cunningham.

THE MOVIE. Allied Artists optioned the movie rights in 1969 for $1.5 million. Several directors turned it down, including Gene Kelly and Billy Wilder. It had a new story line by Jay Presson Allen. Sally was now American and Clifford was back to being British (as he had been in the original stories). Two new songs were added by Kander & Ebb: "Maybe This Time" and "Mein Herr." DIRECTOR: Bob Fosse. *Cast:* MC: Joel Grey; CLIFFORD: Michael York; SALLY: Liza Minnelli; ALSO WITH: Marisa Berenson. The film won eight Oscars, including Bob Fosse, Joel Grey and Liza Minnelli.

STRAND THEATRE, London, 1986. This run was part of a UK tour that began in 1985. DIRECTOR/CHOREOGRAPHER: Gillian Lynne. *Cast:* MC: Wayne Sleep; SCHNEIDER: Vivienne Martin; SALLY: Kelly Hunter; ALSO WITH: Oscar Quitak.

98. *Cabaret (1987 Broadway revival)*

Before Broadway. When approached by Barry & Fran Weissler to direct a revival of *Cabaret*, Hal Prince jumped at the chance. He'd always wanted to get it more right than it had been in 1966. Joel Grey was better this time around. Cliff was now bisexual. The number "I Don't Care (Much)" (Schneider), which had been cut from the original, was newly introduced into the Act II *Kit Kat Klub* scene by the mc, between "What Would You Do?" and "Cabaret." "Why Should I Wake Up?" was replaced by "Don't Go" (also known as "Sally, Stay"), sung by Cliff. "Meeskite" was cut. This revival was designed as a tour opening on 2/28/87, at the Playhouse, Wilmington, Delaware, then going to cities such as Miami, Chicago, Los Angeles, and San Francisco, and finally to Broadway. It was the same cast and crew for the tour and the Broadway run. The Broadway opening date of 10/29/87 was brought forward to 10/22/87.

The Broadway Run. IMPERIAL THEATRE, 10/22/87–2/7/88; MINSKOFF THEATRE, 2/9/88–6/4/88. 19 previews. Total of 262 PERFORMANCES. PRESENTED BY Barry Weissler & Fran Weissler, in association with Phil Witt; MUSIC: John Kander; LYRICS: Fred Ebb; BOOK: Joe Masteroff; BASED ON *I Am a Camera*, by John Van Druten, which, in turn, was based on Christopher Isherwood's novellas; DIRECTOR: Harold Prince; ASSISTANT DIRECTOR: Ruth Mitchell; CHOREOGRAPHER: Ron Field; SETS: David Chapman re-produced Boris Aronson's original sets; SET CONSULTANT: Lisa Aronson; COSTUMES: Patricia Zipprodt; LIGHTING: Marc B. Weiss; SOUND: Otts Munderloh; MUSICAL SUPERVISOR: Donald Pippin; MUSICAL DIRECTOR: Donald Chan; ORIGINAL ORCHESTRATIONS: Don Walker; ADDITIONAL ORCHESTRATIONS: Michael Gibson; DANCE MUSIC ARRANGEMENTS: Ronald Melrose; PRESS: Fred Nathan Company; GENERAL MANAGERS: Kevmar Productions; COMPANY MANAGER: Robert H. Wallner; PRODUCTION STAGE MANAGER: Scott Faris; STAGE MANAGER: Robert Kellogg; ASSISTANT STAGE MANAGER: Bonnie Walker. *Cast:* THE MC: Joel Grey (1) ☆; CLIFFORD BRADSHAW: Gregg Edelman (5); ERNST LUDWIG: David Staller (6); CUSTOMS OFFICER: David Vosburgh; FRAULEIN SCHNEIDER: Regina Resnik (3), *Peg Murray* (during Miss Resnik's illness); FRAULEIN KOST: Nora Mae Lyng (7); HERR SCHULTZ: Werner Klemperer (4); TELEPHONE GIRL: Ruth Gottschall; SALLY BOWLES: Alyson Reed (2) ☆, *Mary Munger* (from 5/17/88); GIRL ORCHESTRA: TENOR SAX: Sheila Cooper; DRUMS: Barbara Merjan; TROMBONE: Panchali Null; PIANO: Eve Potfora; TWO LADIES: Ruth Gottschall & Sharon Lawrence; MAITRE D': David Vosburgh; MAX: Jon Vandertholen; KISSING COUPLE: Mark Dovey & Sharon

Lawrence; GERMAN SAILORS: Jim Wolfe, Mark Dovey, Gregory Schanuel; KIT KAT GIRLS: Laurie Crochet, Noreen Evans, Caitlin Larsen, Sharon Lawrence, Mary Rotella; FIRST WAITER: Stan Chandler; BOBBY: Michelan Sisti; VICTOR: Lars Rosager; ENSEMBLE: Stan Chandler, Laurie Crochet, Bill Derifield, Mark Dovey, Noreen Evans, Karen Fraction, Laurie Franks, Ruth Gottschall, Caitlin Larsen, Sharon Lawrence, Mary Munger, Panchali Null, Steve Potfora, Lars Rosager, Mary Rotella, Gregory Schanuel, Michelan Sisti, Jon Vandertholen, David Vosburgh, Jim Wolfe. *Understudies:* mc: Michelan Sisti; SALLY: Mary Munger; SCHNEIDER: Laurie Franks; SCHULTZ: David Vosburgh; CLIFFORD/ERNST: Jon Vandertholen; KOST: Caitlin Larsen. *Swings:* Candy Cook, Aurelio Padron, Linda Goodrich. *Orchestra:* KEYBOARDS: Fred Barton; TRUMPETS: Jim Sedlar & Dave Rogers; TROMBONES: Porter Poindexter & Jim Miller; FRENCH HORN: Richard Price; WOODWINDS: Al Bloch, Samson Giat, Ken Adams, Ken Berger, Robert Keller; DRUMS: John Gates; BASS: Ray Kilday; CONCERTMASTER: Elliot Rosoff; VIOLINS: Kathy Livolsi, Elene Dumitrescu, Al Cavaliere, Max Tarr; VIOLAS: Susan Follari & Richard Spencer; CELLI: Ellen Hassman & Marisol Espada; BANJO: Vin Bell.

Most Broadway reviews were good. The show received Tony nominations for revival, and for Werner Klemperer, Regina Resnik, and Alyson Reed.

After Broadway the show continued on tour, re-opening on 9/27/88, in St. Louis. *Cast:* MC: Joel Grey; SALLY: Nancy Ringham; CLIFF: Brian Sutherland; SCHNEIDER: Marcia Lewis; SCHULTZ: Michael Allinson; ERNST: John Leslie Wolfe; KOST: Dorothy Stanley.

99. *Cabaret (1998 Broadway revival)*

This was a new, revised version. The numbers "Meeskite" and "The Telephone Song" were cut.

Before Broadway. It played first at the DONMAR WAREHOUSE, London, where it opened in 12/93. It became the hit of the London season. DIRECTOR: Sam Mendes; CHOREOGRAPHER: Matthew Bourne; SETS: Sue Blane. *Cast:* MC: Alan Cumming; SCHNEIDER: Sara Kestelman; SALLY: Jane Horrocks.

In the USA this production was originally due to play at the Off Broadway 350-seat Supper Club, in 2/97, but it never happened. The old Club Expo disco, in the former Henry Miller's Theatre on West 43rd Street, was re-vamped and re-named specifically for this show, as the Kit Kat Klub, with 500 seats (thus qualifying as a Broadway theatre), set in an environmental theatre style, with the audience feeling that they were part of a cabaret. On 9/22/97 Natasha Richardson and Alan Cumming were announced for the lead roles. On 12/4/97 Ron Rifkin and Mary Louise Wilson were announced in their roles. Rehearsals began on 12/8/97. The official Broadway opening date was put back from 1/20/98 to 3/15/98, then finally to 3/19/98.

The Broadway Run. KIT KAT KLUB, 3/19/98–11/8/98; STUDIO 54, 11/12/98–1/4/04. 37 previews from 2/13/98. Total of 2,378 PERFORMANCES. PRESENTED BY The Roundabout Theatre Company; MUSIC: John Kander; LYRICS: Fred Ebb; ORIGINAL & REVISED BOOK: Joe Masteroff; BASED ON Christopher Isherwood's novellas; DIRECTORS: Sam Mendes & Rob Marshall; CHOREOGRAPHER: Rob Marshall; ASSOCIATE CHOREOGRAPHER: Cynthia Onrubia; SET & KLUB DESIGN: Robert Brill; COSTUMES: William Ivey Long; LIGHTING: Peggy Eisenhauer & Mike Baldassari; SOUND: Brian Ronan; MUSICAL DIRECTOR: Patrick Vaccariello; NEW ORCHESTRATIONS: Michael Gibson; DANCE MUSIC ARRANGEMENTS: David Krane & David Baker; INCIDENTAL MUSIC: David Krane; NEW CAST RECORDING on RCA, released on 6/30/98; PRESS: Boneau/Bryan-Brown; CASTING: McCorkle Casting; GENERAL MANAGER: *Sydney Davolos*; COMPANY MANAGER: Denys Baker; PRODUCTION STAGE MANAGER: *Richard Hester, Peter Wolf, Tom Bartlett*; STAGE MANAGER: Peter Hanson, *Jon Krause*. *Cast:* THE MC: Alan Cumming (until 9/13/98), *Robert Sella* (9/15/98–11/29/98), *Alan Cumming* (12/1/98–12/14/98), *Vance Avery* (12/15/98–12/18/98), *Alan Cumming* (12/19/98–6/6/99), *Vance Avery* (1/19/99–1/21/99), *Alan Cumming* (1/22/99–6/6/99), *Michael C. Hall* (from 6/8/99), *Vance Avery* (during Mr. Hall's vacation, 10/99, and again, stood 7/00–8/00, and again in 10/00), *Matt McGrath* (10/17/00–10/13/01), *Vance Avery* (10/14/01–

10/25/01), *Raul Esparza* (10/26/01–4/28/02), *John Stamos* (4/29/02–9/8/02), *Raul Esparza* (from 9/9/02), *Neil Patrick Harris* (1/3/03–5/25/03), *Vance Avery, Jon Secada* (6/6/03–10/12/03), *Adam Pascal* (from 10/17/03); KIT KAT GIRLS: ROSIE: Christina Pawl, *Heather Laws* (from 3/00); LULU: Erin Hill, *Victoria Lecta Cave* (from 6/98), *Alison Ewing* (from 5/00), *Milena Govich* (from 10/00); FRENCHIE: Joyce Chittick, Nicole Van Giesen (from 5/99), *Linda Romoff* (from 2/00), *Amanda Watkins* (from 12/00); TEXAS: Leenya Rideout, *Tamra Hayden* (from 12/99), *Penny Ayn Maas* (from 6/00); FRITZIE: Michele Pawk (until 5/2/99), *Victoria Clark* (from 5/4/99), *Candy Buckley, Penny Ayn Maas, Jane Summerhays, Liz McConahay* (by 5/03); HELGA: Kristin Olness, *Laura Sheehy* (from 8/00); (FOUR) KIT KAT BOYS: BOBBY: Michael O'Donnell; VICTOR: Brian Duguay, *Michael Curry* (from 8/00); HANS: Bill Szobody, *Richard Costa* (from 9/98), *Thomas Cannizzaro*; HERMAN: Fred Rose, *Maurice Villa-Lobos*; SALLY BOWLES: Natasha Richardson, *Jennifer Jason Leigh* (8/20/98–2/28/99), *Mary McCormack* (from 3/2/99), *Susan Egan* (from 6/17/99), *Linda Romoff* (during Miss Egan's injury), *Susan Egan* (from 8/12/99), *Linda Romoff* (during Miss Egan's vacation, 2/1/00–2/20/00), *Susan Egan* (2/22/00–5/28/00), *Linda Romoff* (5/29/00–6/1/00), *Joely Fisher* (6/2/00–7/30/00), *Lea Thompson* (8/2/00–11/19/00), *Katie Finneran* (from 11/21/00), *Gina Gershon* (1/19/01–6/17/01), *Kate Shindle* (6/19/01–7/1/01), *Brooke Shields* (7/6/01–10/28/01), *Gina Gershon* (10/30/01–12/2/01), *Milena Govich* (12/3/01–12/17/01), *Molly Ringwald* (12/18/01–4/28/02), *Jane Leeves* (4/29/02–7/14/02), *Heather Laws* (from 7/15/02), *Molly Ringwald* (from 8/6/02), *Heather Laws* (1/27/03–2/9/03), *Deborah Gibson* (from 2/21/03), *Melina Kanakeredes* (6/27/03–8/31/03), *Susan Egan* (from 9/1/03 until the end of the run), *Katrina Yaukey* (stood in 10/27/03–11/2/03, and intermittently thereafter); CLIFFORD BRADSHAW: John Benjamin Hickey (until 2/28/99), *Boyd Gaines* (3/2/99–7/27/99), *Brian Duguay* (7/28/99–7/29/99), *Michael Hayden* (from 7/30/99), *Matthew Greer* (from 1/19/01), *Rick Holmes* (from 4/29/02); ERNST LUDWIG: Denis O'Hare (until 5/2/99), *Michael Stuhlbarg* (from 5/4/99), *Martin Moran* (from 11/9/99), *Peter Benson* (1/19/01–10/27/03), *Martin Moran* (from 10/27/03); CUSTOMS OFFICIAL/MAX: Fred Rose, *Maurice Villa-Lobos*; FRAULEIN SCHNEIDER: Mary Louise Wilson, *Blair Brown* (8/20/98–5/2/99), *Carole Shelley* (5/4/99–3/23/02), *Polly Bergen* (3/25/02–9/8/02), *Carole Shelley* (9/9/02–2/16/03), *Alma Cuervo* (from 2/17/03), *Mariette Hartley* (3/7/03–8/31/03), *Alma Cuervo* (9/1/03–9/21/03), *Blair Brown* (from 9/22/03); FRAULEIN KOST: Michele Pawk (until 5/2/99), *Victoria Clark* (from 5/4/99), *Candy Buckley* (from 6/00), *Jane Summerhays* (from 3/7/03), *Liz McConahay* (by 5/03); RUDY: Bill Szobody, *Richard Costa* (from 9/98), *Thomas Cannizzaro*; HERR SCHULTZ: Ron Rifkin (until 5/2/99), *Scott Robertson* (stood in for Mr. Rifkin), *Laurence Luckinbill* (from 5/4/99), *Dick Latessa* (from 11/9/99), *Larry Keith* (from 4/01), *Hal Linden* (from 4/29/02), *Hal Robinson, Tom Bosley* (12/13/02–9/21/03), *Tony Roberts* (from 9/22/03); GORILLA: Joyce Chittick, *Christina Pawl, Linda Romoff*, Laura Sheehy; BOY SOPRANO (RECORDING): Alex Bowen. ***Standbys***: Sally: Heather Laws; Ernst: Maurice Villa-Lobos; mc: Michael O'Donnell; Kost: Heather Laws & Penny Ayn Maas; Schneider: Maureen Moore & Barbara Andres. ***Understudies***: Sally: Linda Romoff, *Alison Ewing, Joyce Chittick, Victoria Lecta Cave*; Clifford: Brian Duguay, *Michael O'Donnell*; Ernst: Fred Rose, *Manoel Felciano*; mc: Vance Avery, *Michael Arnold*; Kost: Erin Hill, *Alison Ewing, Leenya Rideout, Victoria Lecta Cave*; Schneider: Taina Elg, *Barbara Andres* (from 9/98), *Maureen Moore*; Schultz: Bruce Katzman, *Scott Robertson* (from 9/98), *Gordon Stanley* (from 4/01); Victor: Brian Duguay. ***Swings***: Vance Avery, Linda Romoff (*Erin Hill* from 2/00; Katrina Yaukey from 3/00), *Manoel Felciano (Maurice Villa-Lobos* from 11/99), *Susan Taylor* (from 8/98; *Penny Ayn Maas* from 2/99; *Alyssa Stec* from 1/00; *Stacey Sipowicz* from 4/01), *Michael Arnold* (from 3/99—*Jeff Siebert* from 9/99), *David Finch, Lori Eure, Joshua Judge, Jennifer Werner*. ***Act I***: "Wilkommen" (mc & The Kit Kat Klub), "So What" (Schneider), "Don't Tell Mama" (Sally & The Kit Kat Girls), "Mein Herr" [from the movie—newly inserted. It replaced "The Telephone Song"], "Perfectly Marvelous" (Clifford & Sally), "Two Ladies" (mc, Lulu, Bobby), "It Couldn't Please Me More" (Schneider & Schultz), "Tomorrow Belongs to Me" (mc), "Maybe This Time" (Sally) [from the movie—newly inserted. It replaced "Why Should I Wake Up?"], "Money" (The Money Song), "Married" (Schneider & Schultz), "Tomorrow Belongs to Me" (reprise) (Kost, Ludwig, Company). ***Act II***:

Entr'acte; "Kick Line" (dance) {The Kit Kat Klub), "Married" (reprise) (Schultz), "If You Could See Her" (mc & Frenchie), "What Would You Do?" (Schneider), "I Don't Care Much" (mc) [from the movie—newly inserted], "Cabaret" (Sally), Finale (Company).

Broadway reviews were excellent. The show won Tonys for revival of a musical, and for Alan Cumming, Natasha Richardson, and Ron Rifkin, and was also nominated for direction of a musical, choreography, costumes, lighting, orchestrations, and for Mary Louise Wilson. The problem with the small theatre, especially after the successful Tony night, was that the show couldn't make a real profit, and began to look around for a larger venue. Indeed, as far back as 5/98 Studio 54 was being considered as a place to move to. A nearby construction accident, on 7/21/98, at the Conde Nast building at 4 Times Square, devastated the area and forced the closure of *Cabaret* for 35 performances, making it lose $1.5 million. It resumed at the Kit Kat Klub on 8/20/98, with a partially new cast. In 11/98 it made the move to Studio 54 amid lawsuits brought by the owners of the Kit Kat Klub's building. The cost of renovating Studio 54 was about $1.2 million. The scheduled re-opening date was 11/12/98, then 11/13/98, and finally 11/14/98. On 9/30/99, at a special afternoon performance, Vanna White played Sally in the opening number. Polly Bergen was originally scheduled to play Fraulein Schneider only until 6/23/02, but her run was extended until 9/9/02. Neil Patrick Harris extended his run as the mc to 5/11/03, then to 5/25/03 (he had been scheduled to leave on 4/27/03). Susan Egan was going to leave the cast on 10/26/03, and her understudy Katrina Yaukey was going to replace her on 10/27/03, but Miss Egan extended her contract to the end of the run. In 12/02 it was announced that *Cabaret* would be closing in the fall of 2003, to make way for Steve Sondheim's *Assassins*. *Cabaret* was not affected by the musicians union strike in 3/03 because it was on a different contract, but it did miss a performance on 8/14/03 due to the power blackout. Tom Bosley extended his run from 8/31/03 to 9/21/03. On 8/27/03 the closing date was announced as 11/2/04, but by 10/03 that closing date had been extended to 1/4/04 (in order to beat the run of the original *Annie*).

After Broadway. TOUR. Opened on 3/3/99, in Los Angeles. Previews from 2/23/99. PRESENTED BY SFX Theatrical Group, Eric & Scott Nederlander, and Jujamcyn Productions. ***Cast:*** MC: Norbert Leo Butz, *Jon Peterson* (from 1/2/00); CLIFFORD: Rick Holmes, *Jay Goede* (from 10/16/99), *Hank Stratton* (from 1/23/01); ERNST: Andy Taylor, *Drew McVety* (from 10/16/99); SCHNEIDER: Barbara Andres, *Alma Cuervo* (from 9/4/99), *Cass Morgan* (from 3/00), *Alma Cuervo* (from 5/00), *Barbara Andres* (from 6/8/01); SCHULTZ: Dick Latessa, *Hal Robinson* (from 9/4/99); KOST/FRITZIE: Jeanine Morick, *Lenora Nemetz* (from 2/20/00); SALLY: Teri Hatcher, *Joely Fisher* (9/8/99–3/19/00), *Alison Ewing* (3/20/00–3/27/00), *Lea Thompson* (3/28/00–7/9/00), *Kate Shindle* (7/11/00–1/21/01), *Andrea McArdle* (from 1/23/01). **Understudy**: Sally: Alison Ewing.

100. *Cafe Crown*

Set in the early 1930s. Hymie, a busboy at Café Crown (modeled on Café Royale, where Yiddish theatre performers used to congregate), on the corner of Second Avenue and 12th Street, New York City, dreams of backing a Broadway show. Sam is a Second Avenue theatrical patriarch, based on the Yiddish Theatre star Jacob Adler. Mme Cole is his wife. Dr. Gilbert is a dentist from Buffalo who tries unsuccessfully to marry into the theatrical clan.

Before Broadway. This musical was based on a straight play of the same name that originally ran on Broadway at the CORT THEATRE, 1/23/42–5/23/42. 141 PERFORMANCES. DIRECTOR: Elia Kazan; SETS: Boris Aronson. ***Cast:*** HYMIE: Sam Jaffe; SAM: Jay Adler; WALTER: Whitner Bissell; TOPLITZ: Eduard Franz; LESTER FREED: Sam Wanamaker; DAVID: Morris Carnovsky. This straight play would be revived on Broadway by the New York Shakespeare Festival at the BROOKS ATKINSON THEATRE, 2/18/89–3/26/89. 45 PERFORMANCES. DIRECTOR: Martin Charnin. ***Cast:*** Eli Wallach, Anne Jackson, Walter Bobbie, Marilyn Cooper, Bob Dishy, Carl Don.

As for the Broadway musical, before it got to New York Theo Bikel replaced Joseph Schildkraut, who died on 1/21/64.

The Broadway Run. MARTIN BECK THEATRE, 4/17/64–4/18/64. 30

previews from 3/21/64. 3 PERFORMANCES. PRESENTED BY Philip Rose with Swanlee; MUSIC/DANCE MUSIC ARRANGEMENTS: Albert Hague; LYRICS: Marty Brill; BOOK: Hy Kraft; BASED ON Hy Kraft's 1942 comedy of the same name; DIRECTOR: Jerome Eskow; CHOREOGRAPHER: Ronald Field; SETS/LIGHTING: Samuel Leve; COSTUMES: Ruth Morley; MUSICAL DIRECTOR/VOCAL ARRANGEMENTS: Gershon Kingsley; ORCHESTRATIONS: Hershy Kay; ADDITIONAL ORCHESTRATIONS: Bill Stegmeyer, Jack Andrews, Jay Brower; PRESS: Merle Debuskey, Seymour Krawitz, Madi Ross; GENERAL MANAGER: Walter Fried; COMPANY MANAGER: Sam Handelsman; PRODUCTION STAGE MANAGER: Leonard Auerbach; STAGE MANAGER: Mortimer Halpern; ASSISTANT STAGE MANAGERS: Norman Shelly & Edwin Bruce. *Cast:* DR. IRVING GILBERT: Alan Alda (5); MR. MORRIS: Ted Thurston; NATHAN, THE WAITER: Norman Shelly; MME COLE: Brenda Lewis (3); BLOOM, THE FIDDLER: Joe Ross; 1ST WOMAN: Shirley Leinwand; 2ND WOMAN: Fay Reed; 3RD WOMAN: Stephanie Winters; PASSERBY: Ken Richards; MR. EDELMAN: Keith Kaldenberg; MRS. EDELMAN: Ann Marisse; BECK: Roy Stuart; RUBIN: Robert Penn; KAPLAN: Val Avery; MRS. PERLMAN: Francine Beers; MR. TOPLITZ: Martin Wolfson (6); MENDEL POLAN: Wood Romoff; IDA POLAN: Renee Orin; HYMIE, THE BUSBOY: Sam Levene (1); NORMA ROBERTS: Monte Amundsen (7); DAVID COLE: Tommy Rall (4); LIPSKY: Michael Vale; SHIP'S CAPTAIN: John Anania; PETTY OFFICER: Val Avery; SARAH: Betty Aberlin; SAMUEL COLE: Theodore Bikel (2); BURTON: Edwin Bruce; SINGERS: Betty Aberlin, Bonnie Brody, Shirley Leinwand, Ann Marisse, Marilyn Murphy, Fay Reed, Ken Richards, John Wheeler, Stephanie Winters; DANCERS: Bob Avian, Ean Benjamin, Luigi Gasparinetti, Cheryl Kilgren, Patsi King, Betty Rosebrock, Geri Spinner, Keith Stewart, Terry Violino, Bonnie Walker. *Act I: Scene 1* The street: "You're a Stranger in This Neighborhood" (Gilbert & Company); *Scene 2* Cafe Crown: "What's the Matter with Buffalo?" (Hymie, Gilbert, Ensemble), "All Those Years" (David & Norma); *Scene 3* The stage of Lipsky's Theatre — Act I: "Au Revoir Poland — Hello New York!" (Mme Cole & The Lipsky Theatre Ensemble); *Scene 4* Mme Cole's dressing room: "Make the Most of Spring" (Mme Cole); *Scene 5* Cafe Crown: "So Long as it isn't Shakespeare" (Hymie & Sam), "A Lifetime Love" (Sam & Mme Cole); *Scene 6* The street: "I'm Gonna Move" (David); *Scene 7* The stage of Lipsky's Theatre —*Act II:* "A Mother's Heart" (Mme Cole, Sarah, The Lipsky Theatre Ensemble), "On This Wedding Day" (Mme Cole & Wedding Guests). *Act II: Scene 1* The street: "What's Gonna Be Tomorrow" (Company); *Scene 2* Cafe Crown: "A Man Must Have Something to Live For" (Sam & Ensemble), "That's the Life for Me" (Hymie, Samuel, Mme Cole, Company), "A Lifetime Love" (reprise) (David & Norma); *Scene 3* The stage of Lipsky's Theatre: "King Lear Ballet" (Sam, David, Ensemble); *Scene 4* Cafe Crown: "Magical Things in Life" (Hymie, Sam, Ensemble), "That's the Life for Me" (reprise) (Hymie, Sam, Mme Cole, Gilbert, Ensemble); *Scene 5* The street: "A Man Must Have Something to Live For" (reprise) (Company). Broadway reviewers panned it, and it flopped.

101. *La Cage aux Folles*

Set in summer in St. Tropez, at the present time. Georges, a relatively conservative middle-aged transvestite, is the owner of the drag-queen nightclub *La Cage aux Folles*; his male lover of over 20 years, the flamboyant Albin, is the star (known on stage as Zaza). Jean-Michel, Georges's son from an affair in the distant past, has fallen in love with the daughter of Dindon, a right-wing morals crusader. The son brings his fiancee, Anne, and her family home to meet Georges, so Albin disguises himself as George's wife, and that's where the fun starts. The notorious dancers at the club are known as Les Cagelles (including two actual actresses). Francis is the manager of the nightclub. Jacob is a house "maid."

Before Broadway. The straight play (upon which the musical was based) was a big hit in Paris. Producer Allan Carr saw it there in 1976, and wanted to buy the U.S. rights in order to make a movie with Jack Lemmon and Tony Curtis. However, David Merrick, who had been interested in it for the last three years, already had an option, and he

intended it as a vehicle for Zero Mostel. That fell through, and then British producer Michael White optioned it. But he dropped it too, at which point Mr. Carr seized the opportunity, and with a movie in mind found, to his bemusement, that a film had already been made (1978, a French-Italian co-production, directed by Edouard Molinaro, and so successful that it spawned two sequels). At that point Mr. Carr decided to do a stage musical. It was announced that the title would be *Queen of Basin Street*, that it would be set in New Orleans, and that the director would be Mike Nichols, the choreographer Tommy Tune, and with a score by Maury Yeston and libretto by Jay Presson Allen. None of this worked out, though. Harvey Fierstein wrote the new libretto while traveling on the subway between his home in Brooklyn to perform in *Torch Song Trilogy*, for which he had just won Tonys for acting and writing. A reluctant Arthur Laurents directed; however, he went for the humanity in the script rather than for the cheap gags.

The Broadway Run. PALACE THEATRE, 8/21/83–11/15/87. 15 previews. 1,761 PERFORMANCES. PRESENTED BY Allan Carr, with Kenneth D. Greenblatt, Marvin A. Krauss, Stewart F. Lane, James M. Nederlander, Martin Richards, and Barry Brown & Fritz Holt, in association with Jonathan Farkas, John J. Pomerantz, Martin Heinfling; MUSIC/LYRICS: Jerry Herman; BOOK: Harvey Fierstein; BASED ON the play of the same name by Jean Poiret, and on the film; DIRECTOR: Arthur Laurents; CHOREOGRAPHER: Scott Salmon; SETS: David Mitchell; COSTUMES: Theoni V. Aldredge; LIGHTING: Jules Fisher; SOUND: Peter J. Fitzgerald; MUSICAL DIRECTOR/VOCAL ARRANGEMENTS: Donald Pippin; ORCHESTRATIONS: Jim Tyler; DANCE MUSIC ARRANGEMENTS: Gordon Lowry Harrell; CAST recording on RCA; PRESS: Shirley E. Herz; CASTING: Pulvino & Howard (Stuart Howard alone by 86–87); GENERAL MANAGER: Marvin A. Krauss; COMPANY MANAGERS: Allan Williams & Nina Skriloff; PRODUCTION STAGE MANAGER: Fritz Holt; STAGE MANAGER: James Pentecost, *Jay Adler* (from 86–87); ASSISTANT STAGE MANAGER: David Caine. *Cast:* GEORGES: Gene Barry (2) ☆, *Jamie Ross* (during Mr. Barry's vacations, 2/20/84–2/26/84 & from 7/16/84), *Keith Michell* (from 8/13/84), *Van Johnson* (from 1/7/85), *Steeve Arlen* (from 11/12/85), *Tom Urich* (during Mr. Arlen's vacation, 7/22/86–7/29/86), *Peter Marshall* (from 2/17/87), *Mace Barrett* (from 11/19/87); LES CAGELLES: CHANTAL: David Cahn, *Frank Di Pasquale* (from 84–85); MONIQUE: Dennis Callahan; DERMAH: Frank Di Pasquale, *K. Craig Innes* (from 84–85), *Kyle White* (from 85–86), *Keith Allen* (from 86–87); NICOLE: John Dolf, *Eric Underwood* (from 84–85), *John Dolf* (from 85–86), *Eric Underwood* (by 86–87); HANNA: David Engel; MERCEDES: David Evans, *Drew Geraci* (from 84–85), *David Evans* (by 85–86); BITELLE: Linda Haberman, *Lynn Faro* (from 85–86); LO SINGH: Eric Lamp, *David Klatt* (from 84–85), *Eric Lamp* (from 85–86); ODETTE: Dan O'Grady; ANGELIQUE: Deborah Phelan, *Shannon Lee Jones* (from 85–86); PHAEDRA: David Scala; CLO-CLO: Sam Singhaus [end of Les Cagelles]; FRANCIS: Brian Kelly (10), *Robert Brubach* (from 85–86); JACOB: William Thomas Jr. (7), *Pi Douglass* (during Mr. Thomas's vacation, 84–85, and permanently by 85–86), *Darrell Carey* (from 85–86), *David Jackson* (from 86–87); ALBIN ("ZAZA"): George Hearn (1) ☆, *Walter Charles* (during Mr. Hearn's illness, 83–84), *Keene Curtis* (during Mr. Hearn's vacation, 10/8/84–10/22/84), *Walter Charles* (from 8/19/85), *Jack Davison* (during Mr. Charles's vacation 7/15/86–7/22/86), *Keene Curtis* (from 2/17/87), *Lee Roy Reams* (from 11/19/87); JEAN-MICHEL: John Weiner (4); ANNE: Leslie Stevens (6), *Jennifer Smith* (from 84–85), *Juliette Kurth* (from 85–86); JACQUELINE: Elizabeth Parrish (5); RENAUD: Walter Charles (9), *Jack Davison* (from 5/84), *Mace Barrett* (from 86–87); (EIGHT) ST. TROPEZ TOWNSPEOPLE: MME RENAUD: Sydney Anderson; PAULETTE: Betsy Craig, *Suzanne Ishee* (from 86–87); HERCULE: Jack Neubeck, *Rex Hays* (from 86–87); ETIENNE: Jay Pierce; BABETTE: Marie Santell; COLETTE: Jennifer Smith, *Pamela Cecil* (from 84–85); TABARRO: Mark Waldrop; PEPE: Ken Ward, *Thom Sesma* (from 83–84), *David Jackson* (from 85–86), *David Klatt* (from 86–87); EDOUARD DINDON: Jay Garner (3); MARIE DINDON: Merle Louise (8), *Darcy Pulliam* (from 86–87). **Understudies:** Georges: Walter Charles (83), *Jamie Ross* (83–85), *Tom Urich* (86–87); Albin/Dindon: Walter Charles (83–84), *Jack Davison* (84–86), *Mace Barrett* (86–87); Jean-Michel/Hercule/Tabarro/Chantal/Hanna/Mercedes/Dermah: Drew Geraci (83–87); Jacob: Ken Ward (83–84), *Thom Sesma* (84–85), *David Jackson* (85–87); Photographer: Drew Geraci (83–86), *David Klatt* (83–87), *Bob Brubach* (83–84); Mme Dindon: Betsy Craig (83–86), *Suzanne Ishee* (86–87), Jacqueline: Sydney Anderson (83–87), Francis: Bob Brubach (83–84), *Frank Di Pasquale* (84–87), Etienne/Pepe/Phaedra: Bob Brubach (83–84), *David Klatt* (84–87), Renaud: Jack Neubeck (83–86), *Rex Hays* (86–87); Anne/Mme Renaud/Paulette/Babette/Colette/Angelique: Jan Leigh Herndon (83–87). **Swing Performers**: Bob Brubach (*David Klatt* from 83–84), Drew Geraci, Jan Leigh Herndon, Leslie Simons. **Act I**: Overture (Orchestra); **Scene 1** Outside, then inside, the club *La Cage aux Folles*; late afternoon: "We Are What We Are" (Les Cagelles); **Scene 2** The apartment of Georges and Albin; onstage at *La Cage aux Folles*: "A Little More Mascara" (Albin & Friends) [melody taken from "Beautiful," a number in Jerry Herman's 1961 Off Broadway flop, *Madame Aphrodite*); **Scene 3** Offstage at *La Cage aux Folles*; the apartment: "With Anne on My Arm" (Jean-Michel), "With You on My Arm" (Georges & Albin); **Scene 4** The Promenade and a cafe in St. Tropez: "The Promenade" (Townspeople), "Song on the Sand" (Georges); **Scene 5** Offstage and onstage at *La Cage aux Folles*: "La Cage aux Folles" (Albin & Les Cagelles); **Scene 6** Offstage and onstage at *La Cage aux Folles*: "I Am What I Am" (Albin). **Act II**: Entr'acte (Orchestra); **Scene 1** The Promenade and the cafe in St. Tropez: "Song on the Sand" (reprise) (Georges & Albin), "Masculinity" (Georges, Albin, Townspeople); **Scene 2** The apartment: "Look Over There" (Georges), "Cocktail Counterpoint" (Georges, Dindon, Mme Dindon, Jacob); **Scene 3** *Chez Jacqueline*, an elegant restaurant: "The Best of Times" (Albin, Jacqueline, Patrons); **Scene 4** The apartment; the club *La Cage aux Folles*: "Look Over There" (reprise) (Jean-Michel), Grand Finale (Company).

Reviews were generally great, and the show was a hit. It was Broadway's first gay musical. The production cost $5 million. 130,000 copies of the original cast album sold in the first month. The show won Tonys for musical, score, book, director of a musical, costumes, and for George Hearn, and was also nominated for choreography, lighting, and for Gene Barry.

After Broadway. TOUR. Opened on 6/10/84, at the Golden Gate Theatre, San Francisco. MUSICAL DIRECTOR: Larry Blank. **Cast**: ALBIN: Walter Charles; GEORGES: Keith Michell, *Gene Barry* (from 9/13/84); ANGELIQUE: Cady Huffman; DUCLOS: Steeve Arlen (the Renaud character renamed for this tour); JEAN-MICHEL: Joseph Breen; ANNE: Mollie Smith; DINDON: Robert Burr; JACQUELINE: Carol Teitel; BABETTE: Amelia Haas; BITELLE: Lynn Faro; ODETTE: Kyle White; NICOLE: Eric Underwood; FRANCIS: Bob Brubach; JACOB: Darrell Carey; POPPIE: Bradd Wong. **Understudies**: Georges: Steeve Arlen; Mme Dindon: Amelia Haas.

TOUR. Previewed on 12/26/84, in New Orleans; opened on 12/27/84, at the Theatre for Performing Arts, Miami Beach. MUSICAL DIRECTOR: Donald W. Chan. **Cast**: ALBIN: Keene Curtis; GEORGES: Peter Marshall; RENAUD: Mace Barrett; JACOB: Ronald Dennis; JEAN-MICHEL: Peter Reardon; ANNE: Juliette Kurth, *Lynn Rose*; DINDON: Bob Carroll; JACQUELINE: Le Clanche du Rand; MME RENAUD: Melody Jones. **Understudies**: Georges/Albin: Mace Barrett.

TOUR. Opened on 8/4/87, at the Music Hall, Dallas. MUSICAL DIRECTOR: Randy Booth. **Cast**: GEORGES: Larry Kert; ALBIN: Harvey Evans.

LONDON PALLADIUM. Opened on 5/7/86. 301 PERFORMANCES. DIRECTOR: Arthur Laurents. **Cast**: ALBIN: George Hearn; GEORGES: Denis Quilley.

10TH-ANNIVERSARY TOUR. Opened 12/29/93, at the Shubert Theatre, Boston. PRESENTED BY Don Gregory & Saul Kaufman; DIRECTOR/CHOREOGRAPHER: Chet Walker; COSTUMES: Tom Augustine; LIGHTING: Tom Sturge; MUSICAL DIRECTOR: James May. **Cast**: ALBIN: Lee Roy Reams; GEORGES: Walter Charles; JEAN-MICHEL: Robert Lambert; NICOLE: Michael Quinn; JACQUELINE: Susan Cella; RENAUD: Jim Madden; ETIENNE/TABARRO: Dale Hensley.

THEATRE MOGADOR, Paris. Opened on 10/1/99. French premiere (of the American musical). DIRECTOR: Alain Marcel. **Cast**: ALBIN: Patrick Rocca; GEORGES/RENATO: Bernard Alane.

102. *La Cage aux Folles (Broadway revival)*

This revival was set in the present day, rather than in the 1980s, as the original had been (although, of course, back then

it WAS the present day). For this revival Jerry Herman wrote some new lyrics for Georges in the number "With Anne on My Arm" (in the original this number had been by Jean-Michel only), and there were some new lines in the book, but aside from that it was pretty much the same show—no cuts, and no new songs. The entr'acte was now by Georges & Albin, and Jean-Michel and Anne were now added to the number "Cocktail Counterpoint."

Before Broadway. On 6/24/04 the Marquis Theatre was booked. Rehearsals began in the summer of 2004, followed by out-of-town tryouts. On 8/18/04 the two leads were formally announced. The start date of Broadway previews was put back from 11/7/04 to 11/10/04, then to 11/11/04. Daniel Davis was out of previews for a few days as from 11/26/04 due to throat problems, and his understudy, John Hillner stood in.

The Broadway Run. MARQUIS THEATRE, 12/9/04–. Previews from 11/11/04. PRESENTED BY James L. Nederlander, Clear Channel Entertainment, Kenneth Greenblatt, Terry Allen Kramer, Martin Richards; MUSIC/LYRICS: Jerry Herman, BOOK: Harvey Fierstein, BASED ON the play of the same name by Jean Poiret, and on the film; DIRECTOR: Jerry Zaks; CHOREOGRAPHER: Jerry Mitchell; SETS: Scott Pask; COSTUMES: William Ivey Long; LIGHTING: Donald Holder; SOUND: Peter Fitzgerald; MUSICAL DIRECTOR: Patrick Vaccariello; ORCHESTRATIONS: Jim Tyler; ADDITIONAL ORCHESTRATIONS: Larry Blank; VOCAL ARRANGEMENTS: Donald Pippin; DANCE MUSIC ARRANGEMENTS: David Krane; PRESS: Barlow   Hartman Public Relations; CASTING: Jim Carnahan; GENERAL MANAGEMENT: 101 Productions; COMPANY MANAGER: Penelope Daulton; PRODUCTION STAGE MANAGER: Steven Beckler; STAGE MANAGER: Michael Pule; ASSISTANT STAGE MANAGER: Travis Milliken. **Cast:** GEORGES: Daniel Davis (2) ☆; LES CAGELLES: CHANTAL: T. Oliver Reid; MONIQUE: Christopher Freeman; DERMAH: Eric Otte; NICOLE: Nathan Peck; HANNA: Brad Musgrove; MERCEDES: Josh Walden; BITELLE: Joey Dudding; LO SINGH: Jermaine R. Rembert; ODETTE: Charlie Sutton; ANGELIQUE: Andy Pellick; PHAEDRA: Will Taylor; CLO-CLO: Paul Canaan [end of Les Cagelles]; FRANCIS: John Shuman (8); JACOB: Michael Benjamin Washington (9); ALBIN: Gary Beach (1) ☆; JEAN-MICHEL: Gavin Creel (3); ANNE: Angela Gaylor (4); JACQUELINE: Ruth Williamson (5); ST. TROPEZ TOWNSPEOPLE: M. RENAUD/TABARRO: Merwin Foard; MME RENAUD: Dorothy Stanley; PAULETTE: Emma Zaks; HERCULE: Joey Dudding; ETIENNE: John Hillner; BABETTE: Dale Hensley; COLETTE: Patty Goble; FISHERMAN: Adrian Bailey [end of Townspeople] [during previews there were two Fishermen — played by Adrian Bailey & Dale Hensley]; EDOUARD DINDON: Michael Mulheren (6); MME MARIE DINDON: Linda Balgord (7). **Standby**: Bryan Batt. **Understudies**: Albin: Bryan Batt & Dale Hensley; Georges: John Hillner; Jean-Michel: Joey Dudding & Will Taylor; Anne: Leah Horowitz & Emma Zaks; Jacqueline/Mme Dindon: Patty Goble & Dorothy Stanley; Dindon: Merwin Foard & John Hillner; Francis: Adrian Bailey & John Hillner; Jacob: Adrian Bailey & T. Oliver Reid. **Swings**: Clark Johnsen, Paul McGill, Leah Horowitz. **Orchestra**: CONCERTMASTER: Paul Woodiel; VIOLINS: Mary Whitaker, Victor Heifets, Dana Ianculovici; CELLI: Peter Prosser & Vivian Israel; LEAD TRUMPET: Jeff Kievit; TRUMPETS: Trevor Neumann & Earl Gardner; TROMBONES: Michael Seltzer & Randy Andos; FRENCH HORN: Roger Wendt; REEDS: Ted Nash, Ben Kono, David Young, Ron Jannelli; DRUM: Ron Tierno; PERCUSSION: Dan McMillan; BASS: Bill Sloat; KEYBOARD 1/ACCORDION: Jim Laev; KEYBOARD 2: Maggie Torre; GUITAR/BANJO: J.J. McGeehan.

Reviews were good. The production cost $9 million.

After Broadway. As early as 12/04 Martin Richards had been planning the movie version of the stage musical.

103. *Call Me Madam*

Sally is a Perle Mesta–type socialite (Mrs. Mesta was a friend of la Merman) who is lady minister to Lichtenburg, although the program said "the play is laid in two mythical countries. One is called Lichtenburg. The other the United States of America." It went on to say that "neither the character of Mrs. Sally Adams nor Miss Ethel Merman, resembles any other person alive or dead." Cosmo, the Prime Minister, is Mrs. Adams's love interest, a nobleman, who Sally charms with her no-nonsense approach to diplomatics. Kenneth is the embassy's pompous Harvard grad press agent who falls in love with Princess Maria. Sally chats on the phone frequently with President Truman. She is finally recalled because of her disregard for protocol, and her use of American slang, which shocks the people of Lichtenburg.

Before Broadway. Howard Lindsay and Ethel Merman happened to be vacationing separately at the Broadmoor in Colorado Springs when the writer came up with the idea for the show. Certain numbers were not used: "For the Very First Time" (published separately in 1952), "Anthem for Presentation Theme" and "Our Day of Independence." "You're Just in Love" got seven encores at the first tryout performance in Boston. "Mister Monotony" (cut from the 1949 Broadway show *Miss Liberty*) and "Free" were cut from Act II in Boston, and replaced with "Something to Dance About" and "You're Just in Love" ("Free" was later given new lyrics by Irving Berlin and turned up as "Snow" in the 1954 film *White Christmas;* "Mister Monotony" finally showed up on Broadway in *Jerome Robbins' Broadway* in 1979).

The Broadway Run. IMPERIAL THEATRE, 10/12/50–5/3/52. 644 PERFORMANCES. PRESENTED BY Leland Hayward; MUSIC/LYRICS: Irving Berlin; BOOK: Howard Lindsay & Russel Crouse; SUGGESTED BY the 1949 appointment of Washington hostess Perle Mesta as Ambassador to Luxembourg by President Harry Truman; DIRECTOR: George Abbott; CHOREOGRAPHER: Jerome Robbins; SETS/COSTUMES: Raoul Pene du Bois; MISS MERMAN'S DRESSES: Mainbocher; MUSICAL DIRECTOR: Jay Blackton; ORCHESTRATIONS: Don Walker; ADDITIONAL ORCHESTRATIONS: Joe Glover; DANCE MUSIC ARRANGEMENTS: Genevieve Pitot & Jesse Meeker; CAST RECORDING on RCA; PRESS: Leo Freedman, Abner D. Klipstein, Robert Ullman; GENERAL MANAGER: Herman Bernstein; COMPANY MANAGER: Carl Fisher; PRODUCTION STAGE MANAGER: Robert E. Griffith; STAGE MANAGER: Don Hershey & Stowe Phelps; ASSISTANT STAGE MANAGERS: Fred Hearn & Harold S. Prince [however, although Hal Prince was set to be asm, he was drafted into the Army and never got to work on it]. *Cast:* MRS. SALLY ADAMS: Ethel Merman (1); SECRETARY OF STATE: Geoffrey Lumb; SUPREME COURT JUSTICE: Owen Coll; CONGRESSMAN WILKINS: Pat Harrington; HENRY GIBSON: William David; KENNETH GIBSON: Russell Nype (4); SENATOR GALLAGHER: Ralph Chambers; SECRETARY TO MRS. ADAMS: Jeanne Bal; BUTLER: William Hail; SENATOR BROCKBANK: Jay Velie; COSMO CONSTANTINE: Paul Lukas (2); PEMBERTON MAXWELL: Alan Hewitt (3); CLERK: Stowe Phelps; HUGO TANTINNIN: E.A. Krumschmidt; SEBASTIAN SEBASTIAN: Henry Lascoe; PRINCESS MARIA: Galina Talva (5); COURT CHAMBERLAIN: William David; A MAID: Lily Paget; GRAND DUCHESS SOPHIA: Lilia Skala; GRAND DUKE OTTO: Owen Coll; PRINCIPAL DANCERS: Tommy Rall, Muriel Bentley, Arthur Partington, Norma Kaiser, *Conchita del Rivero* [i.e. Chita Rivera; from 1952]; THE "POTATO BUGS": Ollie Engebretson & Richard Fjellman; SINGERS: Rae Abruzzo, Jeanne Bal, Aristide Bartis, Trudy De Luz, Lydia Fredericks, Nathaniel Frey, Estelle Gardner, William Hail, Albert Linville, Ruth McVayne, Lily Paget, Noella Peloquin, Robert Penn, Tom Rieder, John Sheehan, Stanley Simmonds, Ray Stephens, Helene Whitney, *Jane Carlyle, Joy Carroll, Robert Patterson, Will Scholz*; DANCERS: Shellie Farrell, Nina Frenkin, Patricia Hammerlee, Fred Hearn, Barbara Heath, Norma Kaiser, Allen Knowles, Kenneth Le Roy, Virginia Le Roy, Ralph Linn, Douglas Moppert, Arthur Partington, Bobby Tucker, Kirsten Valbor, William Weslow, *Dolores Goodman, Eric Kristen, Gene Myers, Edward Pfeiffer*. **Standbys:** Sally: Nancy Andrews & Elaine Stritch. **Understudies:** Secretary of State/Justice: *Robert Patterson* (in the second season); Otto/Wilkins: Stanley Simmonds; Henry/Chamberlain: Robert Penn; Kenneth: Stowe Phelps; Gallagher: William Hail; Secretary to Sally: Lydia Fredericks; Brockbank: Fred Hearn; Cosmo: Tom Rieder; Sebastian/Hugo: Will Scholz; Maria: Jeanne Bal; Maid/Sophie: Rae Abruzzo.

Note: Irving Fisher, an actor who looked like Harry Truman, took a bow every curtain call. However, he was not in the cast. *Act I*: Overture (Orchestra); *Scene 1* Washington, DC—Office of the Secretary of State: "Mrs. Sally Adams" (Opening Chorus & Dance); *Scene 2* Sally's living-room in Washington: "The Hostess with the Mostes' on the Ball" (Sally) [a hit], "The Hostess with the Mostes' on the Ball (encore), "The Washington Square Dance" (Sally & Company); *Scene 3* Public Square in Lichtenburg: "(Old) Lichtenburg" (Cosmo & Singers); *Scene 4* Reception room in the American Embassy; *Scene 5* Public Square in Lichtenburg: "Can You Use Any Money Today?" (Sally), "Marrying for Love" (Cosmo & Sally); *Scene 6* The Lichtenburg Fair: "(Dance to the Music of) The Ocarina" (Maria, Bobby Tucker, Potato Bugs), "It's a Lovely Day Today" (Kenneth & Maria) a big hit], "It's a Lovely Day Today" (reprise) (Kenneth & Chorus), "It's a Lovely Day Today" (reprise) (Kenneth & Maria); *Scene 7* A corridor in the Palace; *Scene 8* Sally's sitting-room in the Embassy: "The Best Thing for You (Would Be Me)" (Sally & Cosmo), Finale Act I: "Can You Use Any Money Today" (reprise) (Sally). *Act II*: Entr'acte; *Scene 1* The Public Square: Opening: "(Old) Lichtenburg" (reprise) (Cosmo & Chorus); *Scene 2* The Embassy garden: "Something to Dance About" (Sally, Principal Dancers, Company), "Something to Dance About" (reprise), "Once Upon a Time Today" (Kenneth); *Scene 3* The Public Square: "They Like Ike" (Wilkins, Gallagher, Brockbank), "It's a Lovely Day Today" (reprise) (Kenneth & Maria); *Scene 4* Sally's sitting-room in the Embassy: "You're Just in Love" (Sally & Kenneth) [the big hit] [originally sung in Act I, it was moved here before opening night], "The Best Thing for You" (reprise) (Sally), "It's a Lovely Day Today" (reprise) (Kenneth & Maria); *Scene 5* Sally's living-room in Washington: "Mrs. Sally Adams" (reprise) (Chorus), Finale: "You're Just in Love" (reprise) (Sally & Chorus).

Broadway reviews were mostly raves. $7.20 top seat prices; advance sale of nearly $1 million—a record to that time. On opening night people were offering up to $200 a seat, but no one was selling. Ethel Merman, Russell Nype, and the composer all won 1951 Tonys, and Pete Feller won a 1952 Tony for best stage technician. The show was financed by RCA, who released the original cast album, of course, but ironically with Dinah Shore singing—not Merman (Miss Merman was under exclusive contract to Decca Records, but Decca did release a competing LP, with Miss Merman and Dick Haymes). "I Like Ike" (based on "They Like Ike") became Eisenhower's campaign song for the 1952 presidential election. This was Irving Berlin's last successful score.

After Broadway. TOUR. Opened on 5/5/52, at the National Theatre, Washington, DC, and closed on 4/18/53, at the Shubert Theatre, Chicago. MUSICAL DIRECTOR: Phil Ingalls. *Cast*: SALLY: Ethel Merman (for the initial Washington engagement; *Elaine Stritch*); SECRETARY OF STATE: Fairfax Burgher; JUSTICE: Owen Coll; WILKINS: Pat Harrington; HENRY: William David; KENNETH: David Daniels; GALLAGHER: Ralph Chambers; SALLY'S SECRETARY: Jo Francis; BUTLER: William Hail; BROCKBANK: Jay Velie; COSMO: Kent Smith; MAXWELL: Alexander Clark; CLERK: Stanley Simmonds; HUGO: Will Scholz; SEBASTIAN: Cliff Dunstan; MARIA: Galina Talva; CHAMBERLAIN: William David; MAID: Jo Ann O'Connell; SOPHIA: Frances Clark; OTTO: Owen Coll; PRINCIPAL DANCERS: Tommy Rall, Muriel Bentley, Arthur Partington, Norma Kaiser, *Conchita del Rivero* [i.e. Chita Rivera]; POTATO BUGS: Ollie Englebretson & Richard Fjellman.

COLISEUM, London, 3/15/52–5/16/53. 486 PERFORMANCES. PRESENTED BY Jack Hylton; DIRECTOR: Richard Bird; CHOREOGRAPHER: George Carden; MUSICAL DIRECTOR: Cyril Ornadel. *Cast*: SALLY: Billie Worth, *Jean Brampton*; COSMO: Anton Walbrook; SECRETARY OF STATE: Robert Henderson; JUSTICE: Mayne Linton; KENNETH: Jeff Warren; BROCKBANK: Arthur Lowe; MAXWELL: Donald Burr, *Glen Burns*; MARIA: Shani Wallis, *Gillian Moran*; PRINCIPAL DANCERS: George Carden & Olga Roberts.

THE MOVIE. 1953. Included a 1913 Berlin song "That International Rag." *Cast*: SALLY: Ethel Merman; KENNETH: Donald O'Connor; COSMO: George Sanders; MARIA: Vera-Ellen; MAXWELL: Billy De Wolfe; HUGO: Helmut Dantine; TANTINNIN: Walter Slezak; SOPHIA: Lilia Skala.

Irving Berlin wrote new songs for a never-produced (partly because it was already horribly outdated) 1967 TV production—"Call Me Madam," "We Still Like Ike," "You Got to Be Way Out to Be Way In."

CITY CENTER, NYC, 2/16/95–9/18/95. 4 PERFORMANCES IN CONCERT. Part of the *Encores!* series. ADAPTED BY Charles Repole & Bill Russell; DIRECTOR: Charles Repole; CHOREOGRAPHER: Kathleen Marshall; SETS: John Lee Beatty; LIGHTING: Richard Pilbrow & Dawn Chiang;

MUSICAL DIRECTOR: Rob Fisher; CAST RECORDING on DRG. **Cast**: SALLY: Tyne Daly; SOPHIA: Jane Connell; GALLAGHER: Ken Page; BROCKBANK: MacIntyre Dixon; KENNETH: Lewis Cleale; WILKINS: Christopher Durang; GIBSON: John Leslie Wolfe; COSMO: Walter Charles; MAXWELL: Peter Bartlett; SEBASTIAN: Simon Jones; MARIA: Melissa Errico (she stole the show); OTTO: Gordon Connell; ENSEMBLE: Colleen Fitzpatrick, John Clonts, Michael Hayward-Jones, Dale Hensley, David Masenheimer, Beth McVey, Angelo Fraboni, Amy Heggins, JoAnn M. Hunter, Mary Ann Lamb, Darren Lee.

GOODSPEED OPERA HOUSE, Conn., 4/19/04–7/3/04. Previews from 5/16/04. DIRECTOR/CHOREOGRAPHER: James Brennan; SETS: Howard Jones; COSTUMES: Gail Baldoni; LIGHTING: David F. Segal; MUSICAL DIRECTOR: Michael O'Flaherty; ORCHESTRATIONS: Dan DeLange. **Cast**: SALLY: Kim Criswell; MARIA: Catherine Brunell; KENNETH: Zachary Halley; COSMO: David Hess; MAXWELL: Stephen Temperley.

104. *Call Me Mister*

A musical revue, portraying the foibles of army life, and the experiences of soldiers returning to civilian life after World War II. The players all performed in uniform, until the end, when they all paraded in the latest fashions.

Before Broadway. The cast comprised ex-servicemen and USO entertainers, including Betty Garrett, the only performer to have featured billing. The producer, Melvyn Douglas, had directed the Army's Entertainment Production Unit in the Far East during World War II. Corporal Harold Rome and Sgt Arnold Auerbach had contributed songs to this Unit. After the War Mr. Douglas put on this revue and went in search of the two writers. Herman Levin was a lawyer and Harold Rome's financial manager.

The Broadway Run. NATIONAL THEATRE, 4/18/46–7/19/47; MAJESTIC THEATRE, 7/21/47–10/4/47; PLYMOUTH THEATRE, 10/6/47–1/10/48. Total of 734 PERFORMANCES. PRESENTED BY Melvyn Douglas & Herman Levin; MUSIC/LYRICS: Harold Rome; SKETCHES: Arnold Auerbach; ADDITIONAL SKETCHES: Arnold B. Horwitt; DIRECTOR: Robert H. Gordon; CHOREOGRAPHER: John Wray; SETS: Lester Polakov; COSTUMES: Grace Houston; LIGHTING: Carlton Winckler; MUSICAL DIRECTOR/CHORAL ARRANGEMENTS: Lehman Engel; MUSICAL ARRANGEMENTS: Ben Ludlow; ASSISTANT MUSICAL ARRANGEMENTS: Charles Huffine & Julian Work; PRESS: Bernard Simon & Dorothy Ross; GENERAL MANAGER: Phil Adler; PRODUCTION STAGE MANAGER: B.D. Kranz; ASSISTANT STAGE MANAGERS: Steve Allison & David Kanter. *Act I*: *Scene 1* Opening Number: SERGEANT: Jules Munshin (2), *Jack C. Carter*; SOLDIERS: Bill Callahan (3), Harry Clark, Chandler Cowles, Ward Garner, George Hall, Alan Manson, Danny Scholl, Lawrence Winters (4); SAILORS: Robert Baird, Alex Dunaeff, Henry Lawrence, Sid Lawson, William Mende, Edward Silkman, Alvis A. Tinnin, Eugene Tobin; CANTEEN GIRLS: Bettye Durrence, Kate Friedlich, Shellie Filkins, Darcy Gardener, Betty Lorraine, Rae MacGregor, Patricia Penso, Evelyn Shaw, *Diane Marshe*; MARINES: Joe Calvan, Fred Danielli, Tommy Knox, Howard Malone, David Nillo, Roy Ross, Kevin Smith, Glenn Turnbull, *Jay Lloyd*. Song: "The Jodie Chant" [Jules Munshin (2) (*Jack C. Carter*)]. Note: when Jules Munshin left in 46–47, his special material (see below) was replaced by the sketch "America's Square Table of the Air" (or "Round Table of the Air"), which then became the 1st scene. **Cast**: ANNOUNCER: Carl Reiner; LT-GEN THOMAS JUDSON: Ralph Stanley; REAR-ADM FRANK A. MOONEY: George Irving; GEN K.B. JONES: Harry Clark; *Scene 2* Goin' Home Train: EX GIS: Bill Callahan (3), Harry Clark, Chandler Cowles, Ward Garner, George Hall, Alan Manson, David Nillo, Danny Scholl, Lawrence Winters, Robert Baird, Henry Lawrence, Sid Lawson, William Mende, Edward Silkman, Alvis A. Tinnin, Eugene Tobin, Glenn Turnbull, Joe Calvan, Fred Danielli, Alex Dunaeff, Tommy Knox, Roy Ross, *James Young, Jay Lloyd*. Song: "Goin' Home Train" [Lawrence Winters (4)]; *Scene 3* Welcome Home. Comedy. Parents of a returning soldier are worried that their son has become psychotic, but he's actually fine. It's the parents who are going nuts with worry. BILL WILSON: Glenn Turnbull; A SOLDIER: Harry Clark; MR. CHARLES WILSON: George Irving; MRS. JOSEPHINE WILSON: Betty Gar-

rett (1) ☆, *Jane Kean*; LOTTIE: Evelyn Shaw; WALLY WILSON: Joe Calvan; *Scene 4* Love Story. Chapter I — Three Thousand Miles Apart: THE BOY: Danny Scholl; HIS MATES: Robert Baird, Henry Lawrence, Sid Lawson, William Mende, Edward Silkman, Alvis A. Tinnin, Eugene Tobin. *James Young*; THE GIRL: Paula Bane; HER CO-WORKERS: Joan Bartels, Virginia Davis, Ruth Feist, Betty Gilpatrick, Bruce Howard, Margery Oldroyd, Doris Parker, Paula Purnell, *Jessie Armour*. Song: "(You've Always Been) Along with Me" (Danny Scholl & Paula Bane); *Scene 5* The Army Way. Pvt Revere tries to re-enact famous ride of his namesake, but has to go through too much red tape. SAM: Alan Manson; SOLDIER: Tommy Knox; CAPT BAINES: George Irving; PAUL REVERE: George Hall; MASTER SERGEANT: Harry Clark; CORPORAL: Bill Callahan (3); DENTAL OFFICER: Sid Lawson; INSURANCE OFFICER: Glenn Turnbull; HYGIENE OFFICER: Roy Ross; *Scene 6* Surplus Blues. Bemoans fate of canteen waitress who has no one left to serve. A WAITRESS: Betty Garrett (1) ☆, *Jane Kean*. Song: "(Poor Little) Surplus Me" [Betty Garrett (1) ☆]; *Scene 7* Love Story: Chapter II — He Remembers: THE BOY: Danny Scholl; BALLET: THE GIRL: Maria Karnilova; THE BOY: David Nillo; POP HIGGINS: Glenn Turnbull; 1ST COUPLE: Betty Lorraine & Howard Malone; 2ND COUPLE: Kate Friedlich & Fred Danielli; TRIO: Shellie Filkins, Patricia Penso, Joe Calvan. Song: "The Drugstore Song" (Danny Scholl); *Scene 8* Off We Go. Co-written with Arnold B. Horwitt. Typical infantryman imagines life of the Air Corps to be easy after seeing too many movies. TED: Roy Ross; LOU: George Irving; MULVEY: Harry Clark; GROVER: Jules Munshin (2), *Jack C. Carter*; DOVER: Alan Manson; STOVER: George Hall; MENU GIRL: Margery Oldroyd; CANAPE GIRL: Betty Gilpatrick; CIGARETTE GIRL: Joan Bartels; MAC: Sid Lawson; MERRYWEATHER: Chandler Cowles; PLOVER: Glenn Turnbull; GENERAL: Ward Garner; *Scene 9* The Red Ball Express. A man who drove for the famed Red Ball Express in Normandy during the War, and is now unable to get a job as a truck driver in the USA because he is black. TRUCK DRIVER: Lawrence Winters (4); OTHER TRUCK DRIVERS: Robert Baird, William Mende, Edward Silkman, Alvis A. Tinnin; FOREMAN: Roy Ross. Song: "Red Ball Express" [Lawrence Winters (4)]; *Scene 10* Military Life: THE SAILOR: Harry Clark; THE SOLDIER: Chandler Cowles; THE MARINE: Jules Munshin (2), *Jack C. Carter*; THE WAVE: Betty Garrett (1) ☆, *Jane Kean*; THE WAC: Betty Gilpatrick; THE TENDERNECK: Evelyn Shaw. Song: "Military Life" ("The Jerk Song") [Harry Clark, Chandler Cowles, Jules Munshin (2) (*Jack C. Carter*), Betty Garrett (1) ☆ (*Jane Kean*), Betty Gilpatrick, Evelyn Shaw]; *Scene 11* Call Me Mister: THE MARINE: Bill Callahan (3); FLOORWALKER: Jules Munshin (2), *Jack C. Carter*; CUSTOMERS: Betty Garrett (1) ☆ (*Jane Kean*) & Betty Lou Holland; SALES CLERKS: Robert Baird, Joan Bartels, Virginia Davis, Ruth Feist, Betty Gilpatrick, Bruce Howard, George Irving, Henry Lawrence, Sid Lawson, William Mende, Margery Oldroyd, Doris Parker, Paula Purnell, Edward Silkman, Alvis A. Tinnin, Eugene Tobin, *Jessie Armour, James Young*; UNDERWEAR MODELS: Bettye Durrence, Shellie Filkins, Rae MacGregor, Patricia Penso. *Diane Marshe*; THE WACs: Kate Friedlich, Darcy Gardener, Betty Lorraine, Evelyn Shaw; THE GIs: Joe Calvan, Tommy Knox, Howard Malone, Roy Ross; THE CIVILIANS: Fred Danielli, Alex Dunaeff, Kevin Smith, Peter Fara, *Jay Lloyd*. Song: "Call Me Mister" [Bill Callahan (3)]. *Act II*: Entr'acte; *Scene 1* Yuletide, Park Avenue. Park Avenue family sings its gratitude to prominent business houses where the family has shopped for Christmas. THE GRANDMOTHER: Betty Garrett (1) ☆, *Jane Kean*; THE BUTLER: William Mende; THE UNCLE: George Irving; THE SISTER: Margery Oldroyd; HER HUSBAND: Eugene Tobin; THE BROTHER: Robert Baird; HIS WIFE: Betty Gilpatrick; THE FATHER: Edward Silkman; THE MOTHER: Virginia Davis; THE YOUNG SISTER: Betty Lou Holland; THE LIEUTENANT J.G.: Chandler Cowles. Song: "Yuletide, Park Avenue" [Betty Garrett (1) ☆ (*Jane Kean*), Chandler Cowles, Betty Lou Holland, George Irving, William Mende]; *Scene 2* Jules Munshin (special material — see Act I opening number); *Scene 3* Love Story: Chapter III — She Dreams: THE GIRL: Paula Bane; BALLET: THE GIRL: Maria Karnilova; THE BOY: David Nillo; THE GIRLS: Kate Friedlich, Shellie Filkins, Darcy Gardener, Betty Lorraine, Rae MacGregor, Patricia Penso; THE BOYS: Joe Calvan, Fred Danielli, Alex Dunaeff, Howard Malone, Roy Ross. Song: "When We Meet Again" (Paula Bane); *Scene 4* Once Over Lightly (co-written with Arnold B. Horwitt): MIKE: Jules Munshin (2), *Jack C. Carter*; TED: Ward Garner; BARBER: Harry Clark. Song: "The Face on the Dime." Emotional tribute to FDR [sung by A MAN: Lawrence Winters (4); *Scene 5* A Home of Our Own. Dealt with housing shortages. MRS. WINTHROP: Betty Garrett (1) ☆, *Jane Kean*; ARTHUR BENSON: Sid Lawson; A SOLDIER: Alan Manson; A YOUNG HUSBAND: George Irving; A YOUNG WIFE: Betty Gilpatrick; A CAPTAIN: Chandler Cowles; LUCILLE: Betty Lou Holland; BILL: Bill Callahan (3); LUCILLE'S MOTHER: Virginia Davis; LUCILLE'S FATHER: Harry Clark; APPLICANTS: Robert Baird, Joan Bartels, Ruth Feist, Bruce Howard, Henry Lawrence, William Mende, Margery Oldroyd, Doris Parker, Paula Purnell, Edward Silkman, Alvis A. Tinnin, Eugene Tobin, *Jessie Armour, James Young*. Song: "A Home of Our Own" [Bill Callahan (3) & Betty Holland]; *Scene 6* Dance Specialty [Betty Lou Holland & Bill Callahan (3)]; *Scene 7* Love Story: Chapter IV — Together: THE GIRL: Paula Bane; THE BOY: Danny Scholl. Song: "His Old Man" (Paula Bane & Danny Scholl); *Scene 8* South America, Take it Away: THE HOSTESS: Betty Garrett (1) ☆, *Jane Kean*; HER PARTNERS: Chandler Cowles, Fred Danielli, Howard Malone, Alan Manson. Song: "South America, Take it Away" [Betty Garrett (1) ☆ (*Jane Kean*) as a canteen hostess tired of the samba craze (the big hit)]; *Scene 9* South Wind. Ruthless Southern senators try to work out ways to exploit returning servicemen for their votes. SENATOR BURBLE: Jules Munshin (2), *Jack C. Carter*; REPRESENTATIVE SNIDE: Harry Clark; REPRESENTATIVE GUMBLE: George Hall; SENATOR DIBBLE: George Irving; GI JOE: Chandler Cowles. Song: "The Senators' Song" (Harry Clark, George Hall, Jules Munshin (2) (*Jack C. Carter*); *Scene 10* Finale: THE VETERAN: Chandler Cowles. Song: "Call Me Mister" (reprise) (Entire Company).

The show was a big hit with mostly rave reviews. It won Donaldson Awards for Betty Garrett and Jules Munshin (male debut).

After Broadway. TOUR. While it was still running on Broadway a national tour began rehearsals on 10/29/46, then went out very successfully across the country for over a year. *Cast*: Jane & Betty Kean, Bob Fosse, Carl Reiner, Buddy Hackett, Edmund Lyndeck, Howard Morris, Mary Ann Niles (she married Fosse while tour was in Chicago in 1947).

THE MOVIE. 1951. It had a plot: Dan Dailey leaving his post in Japan to be with his wife, a USO entertainer played by Betty Grable. Only three songs of Harold Rome's were left for the film

105. *Camelot*

Set in and around Camelot, a long time ago. Guenevere arrives at Camelot to become Arthur's queen. He doesn't go out to meet her, and she avoids the welcoming parties, but they finally meet and fall in love. Merlyn, Arthur's tutor, is lured away by the spirit Nimue. Arthur has learned the value of peace from Merlyn, and established the Knights of the Round Table. Lancelot comes from France and is not a hit with the queen or the knights. King Pellinore also arrives and temporarily gives up his search for the Questing Beast to join the Round Table. Lancelot jousts with three knights — Dinadan, Sagramore and Lionel. He beats the first two but delivers a mortal blow to Lionel. However, with his faith, he brings him back to life. Lancelot falls in love with Guenevere, which torments him because of his loyalty to Arthur, so he goes off on quests for two years. When he returns the king invests him with knighthood of the Round Table. Arthur has found out about Lancelot and Guenevere, but keeps quiet for the good of Camelot. Mordred, Arthur's illegitimate son, arrives and tries to dishonor his father in an attempt to gain the throne for himself. Mordred arranges for his aunt, Morgan Le Fay, to trap Arthur in the forest for a night, and the knights become restless for battle. Lancelot visits Guenevere in her room and Mordred bursts in with group of knights, accuses Lancelot of treason, but Lancelot escapes. Guenevere is sentenced to burn at the stake, but is rescued by Lancelot and taken to France. Arthur prepares to make war on Lancelot, but just before the battle he meets Lancelot and Guenevere and forgives them. Moments before the battle begins

he discovers a young stowaway, Tom, who wants to be a knight. Arthur knights him and sends him back to England to carry on the Arthurian legend.

Before Broadway. This show was originally called *Jenny Kiss'd Me*. Fritz Loewe had a heart attack on 2/17/59, and retired, making *Camelot* his last musical. Adrian, the costume designer, after working on the show for three months, died in 9/59, and was replaced by Tony Duquette. Laurence Harvey auditioned unsuccessfully for the role of Lancelot. The show was 4½ hours long when it opened in Toronto, where Alan Jay Lerner suffered a severe hemorrhage (bleeding ulcer) and was out of commission for two weeks. On the very day he was released from hospital (10/14/60), Moss Hart had a heart attack. Lerner had promised Hart there would be no new director, so while Hart was recuperating, Lerner directed (but received no credit). This caused a rift between Mr. Lerner and Mr. Loewe (who wanted a new director). The number "Face to Face" was cut in Boston, during further tryouts.

The Broadway Run. MAJESTIC THEATRE, 12/3/60–1/5/63. 2 previews from 12/1/60. 873 PERFORMANCES. PRESENTED BY Alan Jay Lerner, Frederick Loewe, Moss Hart; MUSIC: Frederick Loewe; LYRICS/BOOK: Alan Jay Lerner; BASED ON the 1958 chronicle *The Once and Future King*, by T.H. White; DIRECTOR: Moss Hart (with uncredited Alan Jay Lerner); CHOREOGRAPHER: Hanya Holm; SETS: Oliver Smith; COSTUMES: Adrian, and Tony Duquette; LIGHTING: Feder; SOUND: Jack Mitnick; MUSICAL DIRECTOR: Franz Allers; ORCHESTRATIONS: Robert Russell Bennett & Philip J. Lang; DANCE MUSIC & CHORAL ARRANGEMENTS: Trude Rittman; PRESS: Richard Maney & Martin Shwartz; ASSISTANT TO THE PRODUCER: Stone Widney; GENERAL MANAGER: C. Edwin Knill; COMPANY MANAGER: *Charles Gnys* (by 61–62); PRODUCTION STAGE MANAGER: Robert Downing; STAGE MANAGERS: Edward Preston, Bernard Hart, Jonathan Anderson (Mr. Anderson was gone by 61–62). *Cast:* SIR DINADAN: John Cullum, *Robert Peterson*; SIR LIONEL: Bruce Yarnell, *Jack Dabdoub*; MERLYN: David Hurst, *Louis Turenne, Michael Clarke-Laurence*; KING ARTHUR: Richard Burton (1), *John Cullum* (stood in 4 times), *William Squire* (from 9/25/61); QUEEN GUENEVERE: Julie Andrews (2), *Patricia Bredin* (from 4/16/62), *Janet Pavek* (from 7/9/62), *Kathryn Grayson* (from 10/22/62), *Janet Pavek*; NIMUE: Marjorie Smith, *Mary Sue Berry*; A PAGE: Leland Mayforth; LANCELOT DU LAC: Robert Goulet (5), *Robert Peterson* (from 10/8/62); DAP: Michael Clarke-Laurence, *Byron Webster, Tom Head*; KING PELLINORE: Robert Coote (4), *Arthur Treacher* (from 10/8/62), *Byron Webster*; CLARIUS: Richard Kuch, *Gene GeBauer, Don Strong*; LADY ANNE: Christina Gillespie, *Adriana Keathley, Judith Hastings*; A LADY (LADY SYBIL): Leesa Troy; SIR SAGRAMORE: James Gannon, *Peter Deign, Robert Neukum*; A PAGE: Peter de Vise, *Tommy Long, Richard Mills*; HERALD: John Starkweather, *Jerry Bowers, Joe Nelson*; LADY CATHERINE: Virginia Allen; MORDRED: Roddy McDowall (3), *John Cullum* (stood in sometimes), *Christopher Cary*; SIR OZANNA: Michael Kermoyan, *Robert Peterson*; SIR GWILLIAM: Jack Dabdoub, *Robert Peterson, John Starkweather*; MORGAN LE FAY: M'el Dowd, *Madeleine Sherwood, Tani Seitz*; TOM OF WARWICK: Robin Stewart, *Steve Curry, Royston Thomas, Tommy Long*; LADY JANE: Judith Hastings [new role by 61–62]; SIR COLGREVANCE: Don Stewart, *Donald Maloof* [new role by 61–62]; SIR CASTOR OF CORNWALL: Frank Bouley [new role by 61–62]; SCOTTISH KNIGHT: Paul Huddleston [new role created during run]; SINGERS: Joan August, Mary Sue Berry, Frank Bouley, Marnell Bruce (gone by 61–62), Jack Dabdoub, James Gannon, Murray Goldkind (gone by 61–62), Judy Hastings, Warren Hays (gone by 61–62), Paul Huddleston (gone by 61–62), Benita James (gone by 61–62), Michael Kermoyan, Donald Maloof (gone by 61–62), Larry Mitchell (gone by 61–62), Paul Richards, Marjorie Smith, Sheila Swenson, John Taliaferro (gone by 61–62), Leesa Troy, Dorothy White, *Elizabeth Lamkin, Janet Hayes, Daniel P. Hannafin, Jack Irwin, Jack McMinn, Robert Neukum, Philip Rash, George Ritner, Don Stewart, Jack Eddleman, Robert Mackie, Tom Head, Robert Peterson*; DANCERS: Virginia Allen, Judi Allinson (gone by 61–62), Laurie Archer (gone by 61–62), Jerry Bowers, Carlene Carroll, Joan Coddington, Peter Deign, Randy Doney (gone by 61–62), Richard Englund (gone by 61–62), Richard Gain (gone by 61–62), Gene GeBauer (*Don Strong*), Katia Geleznova, Adriana Keathley, James Kirby, Richard Kuch, Dawn Mitchell, Joe Nelson (gone by 61–62), Paul Olson, Claudia Schroeder (gone by 61–62), Beti Seay (gone by 61–62), John

Starkweather, Jimmy Tarbutton, *Kathie Dalton, Phyllis Lear, Joan Volkman, Toodie Wittmer, Richard Lyle, Frank Piper, Loren Hightower, Lowell Purvis, Evelyn Taylor*; HORSE: Jerry Bowers & Don Strong [new role by 61–62]. **Standby**: Guenevere: Inga Swenson, *Janet Pavek*. **Understudies**: Arthur: John Cullum, *Louis Turenne*; Guenevere: Mary Millar, *Leesa Troy, Helena Scott, Jan Moody*; Morgan: Leesa Troy; Lionel: Jack Dabdoub, *Donald Maloof, Don Stewart, Robert Peterson*; Mordred: Paul Richards, *John Cullum, Jack Eddleman, Garold Gardner*; Lancelot: Bruce Yarnell, *James Gannon, Robert Peterson*; Pellinore: Michael Clarke-Laurence, *Byron Webster*; Merlyn: Michael Clarke-Laurence, *Jack Dabdoub*; Dap: Frank Bouley, *Jonathan Anderson, George Ritner*; Dinadan: Larry Mitchell, *John Starkweather*; Nimue: Mary Sue Berry; Tom: Peter de Vise, *Richard Mills, Tommy Long*; Anne: Judy Hastings; Herald: Jonathan Anderson, *George Ritner, Jerry Bowers*. **Act I: Scene 1** A hilltop, near Camelot; a long time ago: "I Wonder What the King is Doing Tonight" (Arthur), "The Simple Joys of Maidenhood" (Guenevere), "Camelot" (Arthur & Guenevere); **Scene 2** Near Camelot; immediately following: "Follow Me" (Nimue); **Scene 3** Arthur's study; five years later: "Camelot" (reprise) Arthur & Guenevere) [added after the opening]; **Scene 4** A roadside near Camelot; a few months later: "C'est Moi" (Lancelot); **Scene 5** A park near the castle; immediately following: "The Lusty Month of May" (Guenevere & Ensemble); "(Then You May) Take Me to the Fair" (Guenevere, Dinadan, Sagramore, Lionel) [this number was dropped after the opening]; **Scene 6** A terrace of the castle; a few weeks later: "How to Handle a Woman" (Arthur); **Scene 7** The tents outside the jousting field; a few days later: **Scene 8** The grandstand of the field: "The Jousts" (Arthur, Guenevere, Ensemble); **Scene 9** The tents outside the jousting field; immediately following [after the opening this scene became The terrace; immediately following]: "Before I Gaze at You Again" (Guenevere); **Scene 10** The terrace; two years later [during the run this scene was dropped]; **Scene 11** The corridor leading to the great hall; immediately following; **Scene 12** The great hall; immediately following. **Act II: Scene 1** The castle garden; a few years later: Madrigal (Court Dancers & Musicians), "If Ever I Would Leave You" (Lancelot), "The Seven Deadly Virtues" (Mordred); **Scene 2** The terrace; a few weeks later: "What Do the Simple Folk Do?" (Guenevere & Arthur); **Scene 3** Near the forest of Morgan Le Fey; a few days later; **Scene 4** The forest of Morgan le Fey; immediately following: "The Persuasion" (Mordred & Morgan Le Fay); **Scene 5** Corridor; that night: "Fie on Goodness!" (The Knights) [dropped after the opening]; **Scene 6** The Queen's bedchamber; immediately following: "I Loved You Once in Silence" (Guenevere); **Scene 7** Camelot; several days later: "Guenevere" (Ensemble); **Scene 8** A battlefield near Joyous Gard; a few weeks later: Finale: "Camelot" (reprise) (Arthur).

Broadway reviews were divided, but there was a huge advance sale at the box office, naturally, given the names involved (in fact, it was biggest advance sale in Broadway history up to that time, probably well over $3 million, while pre–Broadway costs had amounted to about $500,000). The Broadway reviews hurt the show though, until Ed Sullivan did 20 minutes of *Camelot* on TV. That turned the tide. Sets and costumes were highly praised. The book was its problem. Not a great musical, but one of President Kennedy's favorites. However, with its advance sales, it didn't matter very much—it couldn't fail commercially. After the opening the producers cut a further 25 minutes from the show. There were several other illnesses. Moss Hart died on 12/20/61. The show won Tonys for sets (musical), costumes (musical), musical director, and for Richard Burton. Julie Andrews was nominated.

After Broadway. TOUR. It opened on 1/8/63, at the Fisher Theatre, Detroit, and was successful. MUSICAL DIRECTOR: Dobbs Franks. **Cast**: ARTHUR: William Squire, *Louis Hayward* (from 3/18/63), *George Wallace* (from 2/10/64); GUENEVERE: Kathryn Grayson, *Anne Jeffreys* (from 3/29/64); LANCELOT: Robert Peterson; MORGAN: Jan Moody; PELLINORE: Arthur Treacher; MERLYN: Byron Webster; CATHERINE: Ginny Gagnon; MORDRED: Chris Cary.

TOUR. Opened on 10/3/63, at the Masonic Temple, Scranton, Pa., and closed on 5/16/64, at the Playhouse Theatre, Wilmington, Del. PRESENTED BY Henry Guettel & Arthur Cantor; DIRECTOR: Lawrence Kasha; MUSICAL DIRECTOR: John Anderson & Edward Simons. **Cast**: ARTHUR: Biff McGuire; GUENEVERE: Jeannie Carson; PELLINORE: Melville Cooper, *Arthur Treacher* (from 1/8/63); DINADAN: George Hearn; LANCELOT:

Sean Garrison; MERLYN: Gwyllum Evans; MORDRED: Brendan Burke. The tour re-opened, ran for a while and closed on 12/19/64. The partially new cast included: ARTHUR: George Wallace; GUENEVERE: Jan Moody; LANCELOT: Igors Gavon; PELLINORE: Melville Cooper; MERLYN: Gwyllum Evans; DINADAN: George Hearn; MORDRED: Brendan Burke.

ADELAIDE, South Australia, 10/63. PRESENTED BY J.C. Williamson's. This was a slightly revised version, with new sets and costumes by John Truscott. Two numbers cut from the original Broadway production after opening night—"Fie on Goodness!" (which now opened Act II) and "(Then You May) Take Me to the Fair"—were re-instated. There was some innovative choreography by Betty Pounder. The young lad, Tom, who appears at the end, was now identified as Thomas Malory, who wrote *Morte d'Arthur*. It was Australia's most expensive musical to that date. DIRECTOR: Raymond Westwell. **Cast**: ARTHUR: Paul Daneman; GUENEVERE: Jacquelyn McKeever; LANCELOT: Tom Larson; MORDRED: John Ewing; PELLINORE: Desmond Walter-Ellis; MORGAN: Bettina Welch. This version went on to play at the THEATRE ROYAL, DRURY LANE, London, from 8/19/64. 518 PERFORMANCES. **Cast**: ARTHUR: Laurence Harvey, *Paul Daneman*; GUENEVERE: Elizabeth Larner; LANCELOT: Barry Kent; ALSO WITH: Nicky Henson, Moyra Fraser, Miles Malleson, Josephine Gordon, Cardew Robinson, Kit Williams.

PAPER MILL PLAYHOUSE, New Jersey, 1964. DIRECTOR: Stone Widney. **Cast**: ARTHUR: John Cullum; GUENEVERE: Margot Moser; LANCELOT: Stuart Damon.

THE MOVIE. 1967. DIRECTOR: Josh Logan. The movie cost $15 million. **Cast**: ARTHUR: Richard Harris; GUENEVERE: Vanessa Redgrave; LANCELOT: Franco Nero (singing dubbed by Gene Merlino); MORDRED: David Hemmings

TOURING REVIVAL. 2/1/74–4/9/74. 51 cities. **Cast**: ARTHUR: John Raitt.

106. *Camelot (1981 Broadway revival)*

Before Broadway. The 1980 touring revival came to the NEW YORK STATE THEATRE, 7/8/80–8/23/80. 6 previews from 7/2/80. 56 PERFORMANCES. It had the same basic crew as for the Winter Garden list (see this entry, below), except PRESS: Seymour Krawitz, Patricia McLean Krawitz, Joel W. Dein; COMPANY MANAGER: James Awe; STAGE MANAGER: Jonathan Weiss; ASSISTANT STAGE MANAGER: Cathy Rice. **Tour cast**: ARTHUR: Richard Burton; SAGRAMORE: Andy McAvin; MERLYN: James Valentine; GUENEVERE: Christine Ebersole; DINADAN: William Parry; NIMUE: Jeanne Caryl; LANCELOT: Richard Muenz; MORDRED: Robert Fox; DAP: Robert Molnar; FRIAR: James Valentine; LADY ANNE: Nora Brennan; SYBIL: Deborah Magid; LIONEL: William James; PELLINORE: Paxton Whitehead; HORRID: Bob; LIONEL'S SQUIRE: Davis Gaines; SAGRAMORE'S SQUIRE: Steve Osborn; DINADAN'S SQUIRE: Herndon Lackey; KNIGHTS OF THE INVESTITURE: Ken Henley, Gary Jaketic, Jack Starkey, Ronald Bennett Stratton; TOM: Thor Fields; KNIGHTS/LORDS/LADIES: Nora Brennan, Jeanne Caryl, Melanie Clements, Stephanie Conlow, Van Craig, John Deyle, Debra Dickinson, Richard Dodd, Cecil Fulfer, Davis Gaines, Lisa Ann Grant, Ken Henley, John Herrera, Gary Jaketic, William James, Kelby Kirk, Herndon Lackey, Andy McAvin, Laura McCarthy, Deborah Magid, Robert Molnar, Steve Osborn, Patrice Pickering, Janelle Price, Nancy Rieth, Patrick Rogers, Deborah Roshe, D. Paul Shannon, Jack Starkey, Ronald Bennett Stratton, Sally Ann Swarm, Sally Williams. **Alternates**: Lynn Keeton & Richard Maxon. **Understudies**: Arthur: William Parry; Guenevere: Janelle Price; Lancelot: Gary Jaketic; Pellinore: James Valentine; Mordred: Andy McAvin; Merlyn: Robert Molnar; Nimue: Deborah Magid; Dinadan: D. Paul Shannon & Herndon Lackey; Sagramore: Herndon Lackey; Lionel: John Deyle; Dap: John Herrera. It was basically panned by the critics. On 7/10/80 Richard Burton became ill during the performance. He had been taking medicine for bursitis. He had to be replaced by William Parry, his understudy. Mr. Burton only agreed to do the show for about $60,000 a week, but he was already headed toward oblivion, and it showed (he would die 8/5/84, aged 58). The production received $1,200,000 in insurance. After this limited New York State Theatre run (for which the production won a 1981 Tony nomination for best reproduction, and Paxton Whitehead also received a nomination), it went on tour again, beginning at Chicago's Arie Crown Theatre on 8/26/80, then playing in Dallas from 9/30/80. In 3/81 Mr. Burton had to be hospitalized for back problems, and was replaced by William Parry on 3/17/81, then by Richard Harris on 5/13/81. On 6/4/81 there were several cast replacements: Christine Ebersole by Meg Bussert; Deborah Magid by Patrice Pickering; Paxton Whitehead by Barrie Ingham; Bob by Daisy; Davis Gaines by Steve Osborn; Steve Osborn by Randy Morgan; Herndon Lackey by Craig Mason; and Robert Fox by Albert Insinnia. Michael James Fisher played the 2nd Friar. On 9/25/81 William Parry replaced Richard Harris as Arthur, and on 10/5/81 Richard Backus replaced Albert Insinnia as Mordred. Then the tour went to Broadway.

The Broadway Run. WINTER GARDEN THEATRE, 11/15/81–1/2/82. 15 previews. Limited run of 57 PERFORMANCES. A Dome/Cutler — Herman production, PRESENTED BY Mike Merrick & Don Gregory; MUSIC: Frederick Loewe; LYRICS/BOOK: Alan Jay Lerner; BASED ON *The Once and Future King*, by T.H. White; DIRECTOR: Frank Dunlop; CHOREOGRAPHER: Buddy Schwab; SETS/COSTUMES: Desmond Heeley; LIGHTING: Thomas Skelton; SOUND: John McClure; MUSICAL DIRECTOR: Franz Allers; ORCHESTRATIONS: Robert Russell Bennett & Phil Lang; PRESS: Seymour Krawitz, Patricia McLean Krawitz, Janet Tom; CASTING: Julie Hughes & Barry Moss; ARTISTIC CONSULTANT: Stone Widney; GENERAL MANAGER: Arthur Anagostou; COMPANY MANAGER: Carl Sawyer; PRODUCTION STAGE MANAGER: Alan Hall; STAGE MANAGER: Steven Adler; ASSISTANT STAGE MANAGER: Sally Ann Swarm. *Cast:* KING ARTHUR: Richard Harris (1) ✩; SIR SAGRAMORE: Andy McAvin; MERLYN: James Valentine (5); GUENEVERE: Meg Bussert (2) ✩; SIR DINADAN: William Parry (7); NIMUE: Jeanne Caryl; LANCELOT DU LAC: Richard Muenz (3) ✩; MORDRED: Richard Backus (6); DAP: Robert Molnar; FRIAR: Vincenzo Prestia; LADY ANNE: Sally Williams; LADY SYBIL: Patrice Pickering; SIR LIONEL: William James; KING PELLINORE: Barrie Ingham (4) ✩; HORRID: Daisy; SIR LIONEL'S SQUIRE: Steve Osborn; SIR SAGRAMORE'S SQUIRE: Randy Morgan; SIR DINADAN'S SQUIRE: Richard Maxon; KNIGHTS OF THE INVESTITURE: Bruce Sherman, Jack Starkey, Ken Henley, Ronald Bennett Stratton; TOM: Thor Fields (8); KNIGHTS, LORDS AND LADIES OF THE COURT: Elaine Barnes, Marie Berry, Bjarne Buchtrup, Jeanne Caryl, Melanie Clements, John Deyle, Debra Dickinson, Kathy Flynn-McGrath, Ken Henley, William James, Norb Joerder, Kelby Kirk, Dale Kristien, Lorraine Lazarus, Lauren Lipson, Craig Mason, Richard Maxon, Andy McAvin, Robert Molnar, Randy Morgan, Ann Neville, Steve Osborn, Patrice Pickering, Joel Sager, Mariellen Sereduke, D. Paul Shannon, Bruce Sherman, Jack Starkey, Ronald Bennett Stratton, Nicki Wood. *Understudies:* Arthur: William Parry; Guenevere: Debra Dickinson; Lancelot: Bruce Sherman; Pellinore: James Valentine; Mordred: Andy McAvin; Merlyn: Robert Molnar; Nimue: Sally Williams; Dinadan: D. Paul Shannon & Craig Mason; Lionel: John Deyle; Sagramore: Craig Mason; Dap: Steve Osborn; Tom: Joel Sager. *Alternates:* Ellyn Arons & Gary Wales.

Note: the character of Morgan Le Fay was dropped. *Act I: Prologue* A battlefield near Joyous Gard; a long time ago: "Guenevere" (Ensemble); *Scene 1* A hilltop near Camelot; eight years earlier: "I Wonder What the King is Doing Tonight" (Arthur), "The Simple Joys of Maidenhood" (Guenevere), "Camelot" (Arthur & Guenevere), "Follow Me" (Nimue); *Scene 2* Arthur's study; five years later: "Camelot" (reprise) (Arthur & Guenevere); *Scene 3* A roadside near Camelot; a few months later: "C'est Moi" (Lancelot); *Scene 4* A park near the castle; immediately following: "The Lusty Month of May" (Guenevere & Ensemble); *Scene 5* A terrace of the castle; two months later: "How to Handle a Woman" (Arthur); *Scene 6* The jousting fields; the next day: "The Jousts" (Arthur, Guenevere, Ensemble); *Scene 7* The terrace; early evening of that day: "Before I Gaze at You Again" (Guenevere); *Scene 8* The great hall; immediately following. *Act II: Prologue* The castle garden; a few years later; *Scene 1* A cloister on the castle grounds; immediately following: "If Ever I Would Leave You" (Lancelot), "The Seven Deadly Virtues" (Mordred); *Scene 2* The terrace; a few weeks later: "What Do the Simple Folk Do?" (Guenevere & Arthur), "Fie on Goodness!" (Mordred & Knights); *Scene 3* The forest; the following day; *Scene 4* The Queen's bedchamber; immediately following: "I Loved You Once in Silence" (Guenevere); *Scene 5* Camelot; a month later: "Guenevere" (reprise) (Ensemble); *Scene 6* A battlefield near Joyous Gard; a few weeks later: "Camelot (reprise) (Arthur).

On Broadway this touring revival was panned. After this limited run the tour began again, at Buffalo, on 2/11/82. The tour lasted almost 3 years altogether.

After Broadway. LONDON. 11/23/82. *Cast:* ARTHUR: Richard Harris; GUENEVERE: Fiona Fullerton; LANCELOT: Robert Meadmore; PELLINORE: Robin Bailey; MORDRED: Michael Howe.

TOUR. Opened on 5/15/84, at the Orpheum Theatre, Boston, and closed on 9/9/84, at the Auditorium, Denver. PRESENTED BY Jamar Productions; DEVISED BY/DIRECTOR: Richard Harris; CHOREOGRAPHER: Norb Joerder; SETS: Tom Barnes; LIGHTING: Ruth Roberts; MUSICAL DIRECTOR: Terry James. *Cast:* ARTHUR: Richard Harris; GUENEVERE: Betsy Joslyn; LANCELOT: Richard Muenz; SAGRAMORE: Andy McAvin; NIMUE/LADY SYBIL: Linda Milani; MORDRED: Mark Martino; LADY MARGARET: Marcia Brushingham.

TOUR. Opened on 6/4/85, in Minneapolis, and closed on 12/7/86, in Hershey, Pa. PRESENTED BY King Arthur Productions; DIRECTOR: Richard Harris. It had the same basic crew as for the Jamar tour of the year before. *Cast:* ARTHUR: Richard Harris; GUENEVERE: Martha Traverse, *Elizabeth Williams*; LANCELOT: Chip Huddleston, *Bob Cuccioli*; MERLYN/PELLINORE: James Valentine; MORDRED: Andy McAvin, *Chris Pender*; DINADAN: Patrick Godfrey, *Dennis Skerik*; TOM/YOUNG ARTHUR: William Thomas Bookmyer; SAGRAMORE: Greg Busch, *William Solo*; MUSICIAN/SIR CASTOR: Dean G. Watts; NIMUE/SYBIL: Marcia Brushingham; LADY ANNE: Mary Gaebler, *Tracey Moore*; SIR LIONEL: William James, *J.C. Sheets*; DAP/TURQUINE: Robert Ousley; SPRITE/COURT DANCER: Norb Joerder; HORRID: Sean Sable Belvedere; JESTER: Chris Pender, *Frank Maio*.

107. *Camelot (1993 Broadway revival)*

Before Broadway. This revival was part of a national tour that opened at the Fisher Theatre, Detroit, on 9/8/92. The tour cast and crew were basically the same as for the Broadway run, except MORDRED: Kenneth Boys; TOM OF WARWICK: Justin March. Stephanie Park was replaced by *Karen Longwell* in the chorus.

The Broadway Run. GERSHWIN THEATRE, 6/21/93–8/7/93. 4 previews from 6/17/93. 56 PERFORMANCES. PRESENTED BY Music Fair Productions; MUSIC: Frederick Loewe; LYRICS/BOOK: Alan Jay Lerner; BASED ON the 1958 chronicle *The Once and Future King*, by T.H. White; DIRECTOR/CHOREOGRAPHER: Norbert Joerder; SETS/LIGHTING: Neil Peter Jampolis; COSTUMES: Franne Lee; SOUND: Tom Morse; MUSICAL DIRECTOR: John Visser; PRESS: Jeffrey Richards Associates; CASTING: Sherie L. Seff; GENERAL MANAGEMENT: Marvin A. Krauss Associates; COMPANY MANAGER: Ken Myers; PRODUCTION STAGE MANAGER: Martin Gold; STAGE MANAGER: John C. McNamara; ASSISTANT STAGE MANAGER: William James. *Cast:* SIR DINADAN: Richard Smith; SIR LIONEL: Virl Andrick; MERLYN: James Valentine (7); KING ARTHUR: Robert Goulet (1) ✩; SIR SAGRAMORE: Cedric D. Cannon; LADY ANNE: Jean Mahlmann; GUENEVERE: Patricia Kies (2) ✩; NIMUE: Vanessa Shaw; LANCELOT DU LAC: Steve Blanchard (3) ✩; DAP: Newton R. Gilchrist; PELLINORE: James Valentine (4) ✩; MORDRED: Tucker McCrady (5) ✩; TOM OF WARWICK: Chris Van Strander (6) ✩; ENSEMBLE: Virl Andrick, Steve Asciolla, GregBrown, Cedric D. Cannon, Ben Starr Coates, William Thomas Evans, Newton R. Gilchrist, Lisa Guignard, Theresa Hudson, Brian Jeffrey Hurst, Donald Ives, Ted Keegan, Karen Longwell, Jean Mahlmann, Raymond Sage, Barbara Scanlon, Vanessa Shaw, Richard Smith, Verda Lee Tudor, Kimberly Wells. *Understudies:* Arthur: Richard Smith; Guenevere: Barbara Scanlon; Lancelot: Brian Jeffrey Hurst; Merlyn: Newton R. Gilchrist; Pellinore: Steve Asciolla; Mordred: Ted Keegan; Tom/Sagramore: Michael J. Novin; Dinadan: William Thomas Evans; Lionel: Ben Starr Coates; Anne: Theresa Hudson; Nimue: Verda Lee Tudor; Dap: Raymond Sage. *Swings:* Tina Belis & Michael J. Novin. *Orchestra:* TRUMPET 1: Dominic De; TRUMPET 2: Bud Burridge; TRUMPET 3: Dale Kirkland; BASS TROMBONE: Nathan Durham; FRENCH HORN 1: Glen Estrin; FRENCH HORN 2: Kathy Canfield; FLUTE/PICCOLO: Helen Campo; CLARINET: William Shadel; B-FLAT & E-FLAT CLARINETS: Mitchell Estrin; OBOE/ENGLISH HORN: David Kosoff; BASSOON: George Morera; HARP: Pattee Cohen; BASS: Joseph Russo; CONCERTMASTER (VIOLIN 1): Yuval Waldman; VIOLIN 2: Paul Woodiel; VIO-

LIN 3: Nina Simon; VIOLIN 4: Lesa Terry; VIOLA 1: Judy Witmer; VIOLA 2: Richard Spencer; CELLO 1: Jennifer Langham; CELLO 2: Marisol Espada; DRUMS/PERCUSSION: Kenneth Canty; SYNTHESIZER: Milton Granger. *Act I*: *Scene 1* A hilltop near Camelot; a long time ago: "I Wonder What the King is Doing Tonight" (Arthur), "The Simple Joys of Maidenhood" (Guenevere), "Camelot" (Arthur & Guenevere), "Camelot" (reprise) (Arthur & Guenevere); *Scene 2* The forest; immediately following: "Follow Me" (Nimue); *Scene 3* Arthur's study; five years later: "Camelot" (reprise) (Arthur & Guenevere); *Scene 4* A roadside near Camelot; a few months later: "C'est Moi" (Lancelot); *Scene 5* A park near the castle: "The Lusty Month of May" (Guenevere & Ensemble); *Scene 6* Arthur's study; a few weeks later: "How to Handle a Woman" (Arthur); *Scene 7* The grandstand of the jousting field: "The Jousts" (Arthur, Guenevere, Ensemble); *Scene 8* Arthur's study: "Before I Gaze at You Again" (Guenevere); *Scene 9* The Great Hall. *Act II*: *Scene 1* The castle; a few years later: "The Madrigal" (Court Dancers & Musicians), "If Ever I Would Leave You" (Lancelot), "The Seven Deadly Virtues" (Mordred); *Scene 2* The catacombs; a few weeks later: "Fie on Goodness!" (Mordred & Knights); *Scene 3* Arthur's study: "What Do the Simple Folk Do?" (Guenevere & Arthur); *Scene 4* The forest; the next day; *Scene 5* The Queen's bedchamber; the following morning: "I Loved You Once in Silence" (Guenevere); *Scene 6* The castle; immediately following: "Guenevere" (Ensemble); *Scene 7* A battlefield in France; a few weeks later: "Camelot" (reprise) (Arthur).

Broadway reviews were bad.

After Broadway. PAPER MILL PLAYHOUSE, New Jersey. Previews from 4/2/03. Closed 5/18/03. DIRECTOR: Robert Johanson; SETS: Michael Anania. *Cast*: ARTHUR: Brent Barrett; GUENEVERE: Glory Crampton; LANCELOT: Matt Bogart; PELLINORE/MERLYN: George S. Irving; MORDRED: Barrett Foa; DINADAN: Christopher Carl; MORGAN: Tara Lynn Khaler; NIMUE: Diane Phelan.

ARENA STAGE, Washington, DC, 11/21/03–1/4/04. Previews from 11/14/03. DIRECTOR: Molly Smith. *Cast*: ARTHUR: Steven Skybell; GUENEVERE: Kate Suber; LANCELOT: Matt Bogart.

PLANNED BROADWAY REVIVAL. This began as a national touring revival in 2004. It was a re-shaped production. The role of Morgan Le Fay was re-instated. PRESENTED BY Anita Waxman, Elizabeth Williams, Tom McCoy; DIRECTOR: Glenn Casale; CHOREOGRAPHER: Patti Colombo. By Jan. 2004 Jim Carnahan was casting, and there were rumors about the Broadway gig: the Roundabout Theatre Company was to produce; Edward Hall was to direct; Paul Bogaev was to be musical director; and Liam Neeson was to be Arthur. It was aiming for Broadway first in 2004, then for the spring of 2005, then the fall of 2005.

REGENTS PARK OPEN AIR THEATRE, London, 7/23/04–9/4/04. Previews from 7/20/04. DIRECTOR: Ian Talbot; CHOREOGRAPHER: Gillian Gregory; MUSICAL DIRECTOR: Catherine Jayes. *Cast*: ARTHUR: Daniel Flynn; GUENEVERE: Lauren Ward; PELLINORE: Russ Abbott; LANCELOT: Matt Rawle.

TOUR. Opened at the Fox Theatre, Atlanta, 7/27/04–8/1/04, then on with the tour. PRESENTED BY Theater of the Stars; DIRECTOR/CHOREOGRAPHER: Norb Joerder; ASSOCIATE CHOREOGRAPHER: Lisa Guignard; LIGHTING: John McLain; MUSICAL DIRECTOR: John Visser. *Cast*: ARTHUR: Robert Goulet; GUENEVERE: Teri Hansen; LANCELOT: Nat Chandler; PELLINORE/MERLYN: James Valentine; MORDRED: Keith Merrill.

108. *Can-Can*

Set in Paris in 1893. Aristide, a puritanical young Parisian magistrate, is out to ban the can-can, but falls in love with Pistache, beautiful owner of the *Bal du Paradis* night club where it is performed by laundresses Pistache hires. In the end Aristide defends the can-can in court. A subplot involves Claudine's romances with Boris, a Bulgarian sculptor, and a suave art critic, Hilaire. The show curtain (in place while the overture played) was a detailed map of Paris.

Before Broadway. The producers, Feuer & Martin, approached Abe Burrows and asked if he would do a book based on the ass-baring dance, the can-can of Paris in the 1890s, and told him that Cole Porter would be doing the score. A researcher dug up a lot of information about fin-de-siecle Paris, and Abe Burrows wrote the libretto. The producers wanted Carol Channing, but she was about to go to London to do the West End run of *Gentlemen Prefer Blondes*. However, Ernest Martin had seen the French musical comedy star Lilo, in Paris, and hired her. Peter Cookson was making his stage musical debut. Chita Rivera auditioned for the role of Claudine. It tried out at the Shubert Theatre, Philadelphia from 3/23/53. Several numbers were cut — "The Law," "I Shall Positively Pay You Next Monday," "A Man Must His Honor Defend," "Nothing to Do but Work," "Laundry Scene," "Her Heart Was in Her Work," "Who Said Gay Paree?," "What a Fair Thing is a Woman," "Am I in Love?," "To Think that This Could Happen to Me," "I Do," "If Only You Could Love Me," "When Love Comes to Call." Pembroke Davenport was replaced as musical director by Milt Rosenstock for saying crude things about Cole Porter in the great man's presence.

The Broadway Run. SHUBERT THEATRE, 5/7/53–6/25/55. 892 PERFORMANCES. PRESENTED BY Cy Feuer & Ernest H. Martin; MUSIC/LYRICS: Cole Porter; BOOK/DIRECTOR: Abe Burrows; CHOREOGRAPHER: Michael Kidd; SETS/LIGHTING: Jo Mielziner; COSTUMES: Motley; MUSICAL DIRECTOR: Milton Rosenstock; ORCHESTRATIONS: Philip J. Lang; ADDITIONAL ORCHESTRATIONS: Robert Noelneter; DANCE MUSIC ARRANGEMENTS: Genevieve Pitot; PRESS: Karl Bernstein & Harvey B. Sabinson, *Robert Ganshaw*; CASTING: Ira Bernstein; COMPANY MANAGER: Joseph Harris, *Joseph Shea*; PRODUCTION STAGE MANAGER: Henri Caubisens; STAGE MANAGER: Herman Magidson, *Andy Anderson*; ASSISTANT STAGE MANAGER: David Collyer, *Norman Weise*. *Cast*: BAILIFF: David Collyer, *Norman Fontaine*; REGISTRAR: Michael Cavallaro [role cut by 54–55]; POLICEMEN: Joe Cusanelli, Jon Silo, Arthur Rubin, Ralph Beaumont (*Joe Milan*), Michael De Marco, Socrates Birsky, *Ben Raisen*, *Kayton Nesbitt, Charles Basile, Bill Miller*; JUDGE PAUL BARRIERE: C.K. Alexander; COURT PRESIDENT, HENRI MARCEAU: David Thomas; JUDGE ARISTIDE FORESTIER: Peter Cookson (2), *Norwood Smith*; CLAUDINE: Gwen Verdon (4), *Joan Holloway*; GABRIELLE: Mary Anne Cohan, *Ruth Schoeni, Bernice Massi, Gail Adams*; MARIE: Beverly Purvin, *Basha Regis, Deborah Remsen*; CELESTINE: Jean Kraemer; HILAIRE JUSSAC: Erik Rhodes (5); BORIS ADZINIDZINADZE: Hans Conried (3), *George S. Irving*; HERCULE: Robert Penn, *Clarence Hoffman*; THEOPHILE: Phil Leeds, *Jon Silo*; ETIENNE: Richard Purdy; WAITER: Clarence Hoffman, *Norman Weise*; LA MOME PISTACHE: Lilo (1), *Rita Dimitri*; 2ND WAITER: Ferdinand Hilt; CAFE WAITER: Jon Silo, *Michael Cavallaro*; CAFE CUSTOMER: Joe Cusanelli, *Norman Fontaine*; JAILER: Deedee Wood [role cut by 54–55]; MODEL: Pat Turner, *Ruth Vernon, Marcella Dodge*; MIMI: Dania Krupska, *Ann Sparkman* [role cut by 54–55]; CUSTOMERS: Sheila Arnold (*Beverly Tassoni, Mary Jane Doerr*), David Thomas, Ferdinand Hilt; DOCTOR: Michael Cavallaro; SECOND: Arthur Rubin, *Kayton Nesbitt*; PROSECUTOR: Ferdinand Hilt; DANCERS: Meredith Baylis (gone by 53–54), Ralph Beaumont (*Joe Milan*), Socrates Birsky, Michael De Marco (gone by 54–55), Shelah Hackett (gone by 54–55), Ina Hahn (*Lynn Bernay*), Dania Krupska (gone by 53–54), Al Lanti (gone by 54–55), Vera Lee (*Eleanore Treiber*), Bert May (gone by 54–55), Tom Panko, Arthur Partington (gone by 53–54), Eddie Phillips (gone by 54–55), Michael Scrittorale (gone by 54–55), Beverly Tassoni (gone by 54–55), Pat Turner (*Ann Sparkman*), Ruth Vernon (gone by 54–55), Deedee Wood (gone by 54–55), *Mary Jane Doerr, Marcella Dodge, Duncan Noble, Barbara Allen, Doria Avila, Charles Basile, James Capp, Dorothy Dushock, Edmund Gasper, Penny Ann Green, Jane Hennessy, Ray Kirchner, Hugh Lambert, Martha Mathes, Joyce McConnell, Bill Miller, John Nola, Peter Saul, Babs Warden, Conchita del Rivero* [i.e. Chita Rivera], *Ronnie Landry, Julie Murlowe, Janyce Ann Wagner*. **Standbys**: Pistache: Guylaine Guy & Rita Dimitri. **Understudies**: Forestier/Jussac: Ferdinand Hilt; Claudine: Shelah Hackett & Ina Hahn, *Eleanore Treiber, Deedee Wood*; Boris: Phil Leeds, *Jon Silo*; Theophile: Jon Silo, *Kayton Nesbitt*; Barriere: David Collyer, *Ben Raisen*; Etienne: Michael Cavallaro; Hercule: Clarence Hoffman, *Ben Raisen*; Model: Marcella Dodge, *Eleanore Treiber, Lynn Bernay*. *Act I*: *Prologue*; *Scene 1* Police Correctional Court, Paris; 1893: "Maidens Typical of France" (Laundresses); *Scene 2* A street in Montmartre — exterior of Bal du Paradis; *Scene 3* Montmartre — Interior of Bal du Paradis: "Never Give Anything Away" (Pistache); *Scene 4* Pistache's office: "C'est Magnifique" (Pistache & Aristide) [a hit]; *Scene 5* Interior — Bal du Paradis: "Quadrille" (dance) (Claudine, Laundresses &

Friends, with Bert May); *Scene 6* Sidewalk cafe (tabac) — exterior of Bal du Paradis: "Come Along with Me" (Jussac & Boris); *Scene 7* A jail: "Live and Let Live" (Pistache), "I Am in Love" (Aristide) [a hit]; *Scene 8* The atelier (artist's studio): "If You Loved Me Truly" (Boris, Claudine, Theophile, Hercule, Etienne, Gabrielle, Celestine, Marie); *Scene 9* The street — exterior Bal du Paradis; *Scene 10* Interior — Bal du Paradis — the Quatr'Arts Ball: "Montmart'" (Singing Ensemble), "The Garden of Eden" (ballet) [the show-stopper]: EVE: Gwen Verdon; INCHWORMS: Ina Hahn (*Lynn Bernay*) & Socrates Birsky; FLAMINGOS: Shelah Hackett (*Mary Jane Doerr*) & Arthur Partington (*Ronnie Landry*); KANGAROOS: Beverly Tassoni & Michael Scrittorale; PENGUINS: Eddie Phillips & Deedee Wood; SEA HORSES: Ruth Vernon (*Marcella Dodge*) & Tom Panko; FROGS: Vera Lee (*Eleanore Treiber*) & Al Lanti; LEOPARDS: Pat Turner (*Ann Sparkman*) & Ralph Beaumont (*Joe Milan*); SNAKE: Bert May; "Allez Vous-En (Go Away)" (Pistache) [a hit]. *Act II*: *Scene 1* The atelier (artist's studio): "Never, Never Be an Artist" (Boris, Theophile, Etienne, Model); *Scene 2* The cafe (tabac exterior): "It's All Right with Me" (Aristide) [a hit], "Every Man is a Stupid Man" (Pistache); *Scene 3* La Blanchisserie: "The Apaches" (dance) (Claudine & Dancers, with Ralph Beaumont); *Scene 4* A Paris street; *Scene 5* Rooftop of La Blanchisserie: "I Love Paris" (Pistache) (Pistache) [a big hit], "C'est Magnifique" (reprise) (Pistache & Aristide); *Scene 6* A jail; *Scene 7* Court d'Assizes: "Can-Can" (Pistache, Claudine, Laundresses), Finale (Entire Company).

On Broadway opening night Gwen Verdon stopped the show twice with her dancing, especially the "Garden of Eden" sequence. On one occasion she'd gone to her dressing room, was getting changed, and the calls for her to re-appear forced her to come back on stage in her bath robe. The critics were unkind to the story and the score, but loved the choreography and Miss Verdon (this was the show that made her a star, which really annoyed the actual star, Lilo). The show won Tonys for choreography and for Gwen Verdon. This became Cole Porter's second-longest-running musical after *Kiss Me, Kate*.

After Broadway. COLISEUM, London, 10/14/54–9/24/55. 394 PERFORMANCES. DIRECTOR: Jerome Whyte; CHOREOGRAPHER: Deirdre Vivian; MUSICAL DIRECTOR: Charles Prentice. *Cast*: ARISTIDE: Edmund Hockridge, *Desmond Ainsworth*; CLAUDINE: Gillian Lynne; PAUL: Peter Swanwick; PISTACHE: Irene Hilda; HERCULE: Vincent Charles; BORIS: Alfred Marks; HILAIRE: George Gee; CELESTINE: Joy Turpin; THEOPHILE: Warren Mitchell; HENRI: George Pastell; DANCERS: Jean Muir, Judy Collins, Barbara Ferris, Aleta Morrison.

TOUR. Opened on 6/25/55, at the National Theatre, Washington, DC. MUSICAL DIRECTOR: Stanley Lebowsky. *Cast*: PISTACHE: Rita Dimitri; ARISTIDE: John Tyers; CLAUDINE: Ronnie Cunningham; HILAIRE: Ferdinand Hilt; BAILIFF/CAFE CUSTOMER: Norman Fontaine; BORIS: George S. Irving; 2ND POLICEMAN/2ND WAITER: Kayton Nesbitt; DOCTOR/CAFE WAITER: Michael Cavallaro; ETIENNE: Richard Purdy; CELESTINE: Loni Nelson; BARRIERE: Robert Eckles; MARCEAU: Lewis Brooks; GABRIELLE: Jeannine Masterson; HERCULE: Clarence Hoffman; THEOPHILE: Jon Silo; MODEL: Marcella Dodge. The roles of the Jailer and the Registrar were re-instated for this tour. Several members of the Broadway chorus were also on this tour.

THE MOVIE. 1960. DIRECTOR: Walter Lang; CHOREOGRAPHER: Hermes Pan. It had a somewhat changed story. Additional Cole Porter songs were added, notably "Let's Do It," "Just One of Those Things" and "You Do Something to Me." *Cast*: FRANCOIS DURNAIS: Frank Sinatra (a new character); SIMONE PISTACHE: Shirley MacLaine; PAUL BARRIERE: Maurice Chevalier; PHILIPPE FORRESTIER, THE OFFICIAL, FRANCOIS' RIVAL FOR THE HAND OF SIMONE: Louis Jourdan; CLAUDINE: Juliet Prowse.

HUDSON CELEBRATION THEATRE IN CENTRAL PARK, 8/25/59–8/30/59. 6 PERFORMANCES. PRESENTED BY Jean Dalrymple; PRODUCERS: Barron Polan & Lenny Debin; DIRECTOR: Billy Matthews; CHOREOGRAPHER: Peter Hamilton; SETS: Edward D. Stone; STAGE DECOR: Duane McKinney; LIGHTING: Abe Feder; CONDUCTOR: Rene Wiegert. *Cast*: PISTACHE: Genevieve; CLAUDINE: Pat Turner; ARISTIDE: David Atkinson; BARRIERE: Harry Stockwell; BORIS: Gabriel Dell; DOCTOR: Joe Rocco; HILAIRE: Erik Rhodes; ETIENNE: Emory Bass; CAFE WAITER: Ralph Vucci; THEOPHILE: Dick O'Neill.

CITY CENTER, NYC, 5/16/62–5/27/62. 16 PERFORMANCES. "Every Man is a Stupid Man" was dropped for this production. PRESENTED BY the New York City Center Light Opera Company; DIRECTOR: Gus Schirmer Jr.; CHOREOGRAPHER: Ellen Ray; SETS/LIGHTING: Helen Pond; MUSICAL DIRECTOR: James Leon. *Cast*: BAILIFF/CAFE WAITER: Phil Roth; POLICEMEN: George Del Monte & Darrell Sandeen; BARRIERE: Warne Schreiner; MARCEAU/DOCTOR: Charles Reynolds; ARISTIDE: George Gaynes; CLAUDINE: Mara Lynn; GABRIELLE: Maggie Worth; MARIE: Lillian D'Honau; CELESTINE: Marilyn D'Honau; HILAIRE: Ferdinand Hilt; BORIS: Gabriel Dell; HERCULE: Iggie Wolfington; THEOPHILE: Bob Dishy; PISTACHE: Genevieve; 2ND WAITER: Darrell Sandeen; MODEL: Betty Hyatt Linton; MIMI: Dorothy D'Honau; DANCERS: Peter Gladke, Sterling Clark, Victor Duntiere, David Lober, Louise Quick, Alice Shanahan.

ROYAL ALEXANDRA THEATRE, Toronto, 7/27/65–8/8/65. *Cast*: PISTACHE: Lilo; ARISTIDE: Webb Tilton.

UNITARIAN CHURCH OF ALL SOULS, NYC, 4/11/75–4/19/75. 5 PERFORMANCES. PRESENTED BY Dorothy Harris & Howard Van Der Meulen; DIRECTOR/CHOREOGRAPHER: Jeffrey K. Neill; SETS: Robert Edmonds; COSTUMES: Charles Roeder; MUSICAL DIRECTOR: Wendell Kindberg. *Cast*: PISTACHE: Mary Lynn Metternich; ARISTIDE: Bob Sikso; CLAUDINE: Kathleen W. Gray; ETIENNE: Tran William Rhodes; VARIOUS ROLES: Don Madison & Norb Joerder. The entire score was heard on stage (all the numbers that had been cut from the 1953 Broadway production were put back in): "Maidens Typical of France," "The Law," "I Do," "What a Fair Thing is a Woman," "Never Give Anything Away," "C'est Magnifique," "Quadrille," "Her Heart Was in Her Work," "Come Along with Me," "Live and Let Live," "I Am in Love," "If You Loved Me Truly," "Garden of Eden Ballet," "Montmart'," "Allez-vous-en," "Never, Never Be an Artist," "It's All Right with Me," "Every Man is a Stupid Man," "Apache Specialty," "A Man Must His Honor Defend," "I Love Paris," "To Think that This Could Happen to Me," "Can-Can," Finale.

109. *Can-Can (Broadway revival)*

The numbers "To Think that This Could Happen to Me," "When Love Comes to Call," and "Who Said Gay Paree?" were cut, as they had been in 1953. Joe Cusanelli had been in the original 1953 production, as had co-producer Arthur Rubin.

The Broadway Run. MINSKOFF THEATRE, 4/30/81–5/3/81. 16 previews. 5 PERFORMANCES. PRESENTED BY James M. Nederlander, Arthur Rubin, Jerome Minskoff, Stewart F. Lane, Carole J. Shorenstein, Charles D. Kelman; MUSIC/LYRICS: Cole Porter; REVISED BOOK/DIRECTOR: Abe Burrows; CHOREOGRAPHER: Roland Petit; SETS: David Mitchell; COSTUMES: Franca Squarciapino; COSTUME SUPERVISOR: Patricia Adshead; LIGHTING: Thomas Skelton; SOUND: Larry Spurgeon; MUSICAL DIRECTOR/VOCAL ARRANGEMENTS: Stanley Lebowsky; ORCHESTRATIONS: Philip J. Lang; DANCE MUSIC ARRANGEMENTS/NEW DANCE MUSIC: Donald York; PRESS: The Merlin Group; CASTING: The Nederlander Organization; GENERAL MANAGEMENT: Marvin A. Krauss Associates; COMPANY MANAGER: Duke Kant; PRODUCTION STAGE MANAGER: Mortimer Halpern; STAGE MANAGER: Nate Barnett; ASSISTANT STAGE MANAGER: Sherry Lambert. *Cast:* POLICEMEN: Tommy Breslin, John Remme, John Dolf, Dennis Batutis, Kevin McCready; BAILIFF: Joseph Cusanelli; JUDGE PAUL BARRIERE: David Brooks (6); HENRI MARCEAU, COURT PRESIDENT: Tom Batten; JUDGE ARISTIDE FORESTIER: Ron Husmann (2) ☆; CLAUDINE: Pamela Sousa (5); HILAIRE JUSSAC: Swen Swenson (4); BORIS ADZINIDZINADZE: Avery Schreiber (3) ☆; WAITER: John Remme; LA MOME PISTACHE: Zizi Jeanmaire (1) ☆; HERCULE: Michael Dantuono (8); THEOPHILE: Mitchell Greenberg (9); ETIENNE: Tommy Breslin (7); PHOTOGRAPHER: James Dunne; TABAC WAITER: Joseph Cusanelli; MONARCHIST: Tom Batten; JAIL GUARD: John Remme; MODEL: Deborah Carlson; GARDEN OF EDEN BALLET (see below); MIMI: Donna King; APACHE LEADER: Luigi Bonino; PATRONS: Nealey Gilbert & Dennis Batutis; PROSECUTOR: Tom Batten; CHIEF JUSTICE: Joseph Cusanelli; ENSEMBLE: Darrell Barnett, Dennis Batutis, Deborah Carlson, Pam Cecil, John Dolf, James Dunne, Edyie Fleming, Nealey Gilbert, Linda Haberman, Nancy Hess, Brenda Holmes, James Horvath, Donna King, Manette La Chance, Steven La Chance, Kevin McCready, Meredith

McIver, Gail Pennington, Rosemary Rado, Daryl Richardson, Gregory Schanuel, Linda von Germer. *Understudies*: Aristide: Michael Dantuono; Boris: Mitchell Greenberg; Claudine: Donna King; Barriere: Tom Batten; Hercule: Joe Cusanelli; Theophile: John Remme. *Swings*: Kim Noor & Bob Renny. *Act I*: *Scene 1* "Maidens Typical of France" (Girls), "Maidens Typical of France" (reprise) (Girls & Court Personnel); *Scene 3* "Never Give Anything Away" (Pistache & Girls); *Scene 4* "C'est Magnifique" (Pistache & Aristide); *Scene 5* "Quadrille Dance" (Girls & Men); *Scene 6* "Come Along with Me" (Hilaire & Claudine), "Come Along with Me" (reprise) (Boris); *Scene 7* "Live and Let Live" (Pistache), "I Am in Love" (Aristide); *Scene 10* "Montmartre" (Company), "The Garden of Eden Ballet" (Pistache, Girls, Men): ADAM: Darrell Barnett; EVE: Pamela Sousa (5); THE SNAKE: Zizi Jeanmaire, Dennis Batutis, James Horvath, Steven La Chance, Kevin McCready; "Allez-Vous En" (Pistache). *Act II*: *Scene 1* "Never, Never Be an Artist" (Artists, Boris, Aristide); *Scene 2* "It's All Right with Me" (Aristide, Mimi, Girls); *Scene 3* "Apache Dance" (Girls & Men); *Scene 5* "I Love Paris" (Pistache), "C'est Magnifique" (reprise) (Aristide & Pistache); *Scene 7* "Can-Can" (Pistache, Girls, Men), Finale (Full Company).

Note: the scene breakdown is basically as in the 1953 original production. Only the differences are listed here.

This revival was panned on Broadway. It received Tony nominations for choreography, sets, and costumes.

After Broadway. STRAND THEATRE, London, 1988. With a new book based on the movie. MUSICAL DIRECTOR: Grant Hossack; CAST RECORDING on Virgin. *Cast*: Milo O'Shea, Bernard Alane, Donna McKechnie, Peter Durkin, Janie Dee, Norman Warwick.

TOURING REVIVAL. 1988. PRESENTED BY Nicholas Howey, Kenneth H. Gentry, Dallett Norris, The Troika Company, in association with Columbia Artists Theatrical; DIRECTOR: Dallett Norris; CHOREOGRAPHER: Alan Johnson; MUSICAL DIRECTOR: Hampton F. King Jr. *Cast*: PISTACHE: Chita Rivera; ARISTIDE: Ron Holgate; MODEL: Jacquey Maltby; LAUNDRESSES: Radio City Music Hall Rockettes; PAUL/HERCULE: Mark Basile.

GOODSPEED OPERA HOUSE, Connecticut, 1995. REVISED BOOK/ DIRECTOR: Martin Charnin; CHOREOGRAPHER: Michele Assaf; LIGHTING: Ken Billington. *Cast*: PISTACHE: Silvia Aruj; CLAUDINE: Jamie Chandler-Torns; ALSO WITH: Ed Dixon, Jim Borstelmann, Jennifer Lamberts, Jamie Ross, Todd Thurston.

CITY CENTER, NYC, 2/12/04–2/15/04. Part of the *Encores!* series. DIRECTOR: Lonny Price. *Cast*: PISTACHE: Patti LuPone; ALSO WITH: Michael Nouri, Charlotte d'Amboise, Reg Rogers, Paul Schoeffler, Caitlin Carter, David Costabile.

110. *Candide*

A satirical operetta. The adventures of German youth Candide and his romance with minor princess Cunegonde. Maximilian, Cunegonde's vain brother, was not named in Voltaire's book.

Before Broadway. There was a dance drama version of *Candide* at the BOOTH THEATRE, on Broadway, 5/15/33–5/20/33. 8 PERFORMANCES. In 2 acts, 4 scenes and an interlude. PRESENTED BY Michael Myerberg. COMPOSERS/MUSICAL ARRANGEMENTS: Genevieve Pitot & John Coleman; CONCEIVED BY/ADAPTED BY/DIRECTOR/ARRANGEMENTS: Charles Weidman; NARRATIVE: Ian Wolfe; COSTUMES: Pauline Lawrence. *Cast*: CANDIDE: Charles Weidman; MC/DON FERNANDO/JUDGE/FATE: Jose Limon; CUNEGONDE: Eleanor King; PANGLOSS: John Glenn.

It was Lillian Hellman's idea to re-work this story as a modern day expression of anti–McCarthyism. Leonard Bernstein joined her in the fall of 1953, but wanted to expand it into a musical, which is what happened, and Miss Hellman wrote the libretto (the only one she ever wrote). Leonard Bernstein began work on the music in 1/54, and in 6/54 he and his wife Felicia Montealegre wrote the lyric for "I Am Easily Assimilated" (Mrs. Bernstein actually writing Spanish dialogue heard in this song). Then John Latouche was brought in as lyricist. Sol Hurok was approached to be the producer, but wasn't interested. In 12/54 John Latouche was fired (he would die of a heart attack on 8/7/56), and var-

ious other lyricists were approached — Dorothy Parker, E.Y. Harburg, and James Agee. In 1/55 Ethel Linder Reiner became producer. Dorothy Parker finished the lyrics to the only song she wrote for the show — "Venetian Gavotte" (or rather, part of it). In 7/55 Tyrone Guthrie agreed to direct (Gene Kelly and Rene Clair had both been considered). In 12/55 Richard Wilbur took over as lyricist. Edie Adams refused the role of Cunegonde in favor of the show *Li'l Abner*. Tryouts began at the Colonial Theatre, Boston, on 10/29/56, for 3 weeks. It got divided reviews. 5th-billed Carmen Mathews (as the Contessa) was dropped. Then it tried out for a further week in New Haven. Voltaire's character Paquette had her role considerably reduced for the musical, and Cacombo, another major character, was dropped. There was choreography in this show, but very little dancing.

The Broadway Run. MARTIN BECK THEATRE, 12/1/56–2/2/57. 73 PERFORMANCES. PRESENTED BY Ethel Linder Reiner, in association with Lester Osterman Jr.; MUSIC: Leonard Bernstein; LYRICS: Richard Wilbur; OTHER LYRICS: John Latouche, Dorothy Parker, Leonard Bernstein (uncredited), Lillian Hellman (uncredited); BOOK: Lillian Hellman; BASED ON the 1759 satire of the same name by Voltaire (he disavowed it); DIRECTOR: Tyrone Guthrie; ASSISTANT DIRECTOR: Tom Brown; CHOREOGRAPHER: Wallace Seibert; SETS: Oliver Smith; COSTUMES: Irene Sharaff; LIGHTING: Paul Morrison; MUSICAL DIRECTOR: Samuel Krachmalnick; ORCHESTRATIONS: Leonard Bernstein & Hershy Kay; CAST RECORDING on Columbia, made on 12/9/56; PRESS: Ben Washer & Howard Newman; COMPANY MANAGER: Joseph Moss; PRODUCTION STAGE MANAGER: Peter Zeisler; STAGE MANAGER: Jack Merigold & Joseph Bernard. *Act I*: *Scene 1* Westphalia. Candide about to be married to beautiful Cunegonde. Pangloss, Candide's teacher, expounds his famous optimistic philosophy, to the effect that all is for the best in the best of all possible worlds. The wedding is about to take place when war breaks out between Westphalia and Hesse. Westphalia is destroyed and Cunegonde is killed. DR. PANGLOSS: Max Adrian (1); CUNEGONDE: Barbara Cook (3); CANDIDE: Robert Rounseville (2); BARON: Robert Mesrobian; MAXIMILIAN: Louis Edmonds; KING OF HESSE: Conrad Bain; HESSE'S GENERAL: Norman Roland. Ensemble: "The Best of All Possible Worlds" (l: Wilbur) (Candide, Pangloss, Cunegonde, Chorus), Duet: "Oh, Happy We" (l: Wilbur) (Candide & Cunegonde), Song: "It Must Be So" (l: Wilbur) (Candide); *Scene 1a* Candide Travels to Lisbon. CANDIDE: Robert Rounseville (2); MAN: Boris Aplon; WOMAN: Doris Okerson; DUTCH LADY: Margaret Roy; DUTCH MAN: Tony Drake; ATHEIST: Robert Rue; *Scene 2* Lisbon. In a public square the Infant Casmira, a deranged mystic kept in a cage in a caravan of an Arab conjuror, predicts dire happenings. The Inquisition appears, in the person of two ancient inquisitors and their lawyer, and many citizens are tried and sentenced to hang, including Candide and Pangloss. An earthquake intervenes, killing Pangloss; Candide just escapes. ARAB CONJUROR: Robert Barry; CANDIDE: Robert Rounseville (2); INFANT CASMIRA: Maria Novotna; LAWYER: William Chapman; VERY, VERY OLD INQUISITOR: Conrad Bain; VERY OLD INQUISITOR: Charles Aschmann; JUNKMAN: Robert Cosden; WINE-SELLER: Stanley Grover; BEAR: Charles Morrell; BEAR MAN: Robert Rue; ALCHEMIST: Charles Aschmann; GROCERY LADY: Margaret Roy. "Lisbon Sequence" (l: Bernstein) (Infant Casmira, Conjuror, Chorus); *Scene 2a* Candide Travels to Paris. He wrestles with himself and his Panglossian philosophy. BEGGARS: Margaret Roy, Robert Cosden, Thomas Pyle; CANDIDE: Robert Rounseville (2); FRENCH LADY: Maud Scheerer. Song: "It Must Be Me" (l: Wilbur) (Candide); *Scene 3* Paris. Cunegonde turns up, alive after all, now a whore in a house shared by a Marquis and a Sultan, with Old Lady as her duenna. There is a party going on. In a duel Candide kills the Marquis and the Sultan, and flees with Cunegonde and Old Lady. OLD LADY: Irra Petina (4); MARQUIS MILTON: Boris Aplon; SULTAN MILTON: Joseph Bernard; CUNEGONDE: Barbara Cook (1); CANDIDE: Robert Rounseville (2); PILGRIM FATHER: Robert Rue. "Mazurka" (Orchestra), Aria: "Glitter and Be Gay" (l: Wilbur) (Cunegonde), Duet: "You Were Dead, You Know" (l: Latouche/Wilbur) (Candide & Cunegonde); *Scene 3a* They sail with a band of Pilgrims to the New World. PILGRIM FATHER: Robert Rue; PILGRIM MOTHER: Dorothy Krebill; CUNEGONDE: Barbara Cook (3); OLD LADY: Irra Petina (4); CANDIDE: Robert Rounseville (2); CAPTAIN: Conrad Bain. "Pilgrim's Procession" (l: Wilbur) (Pilgrims); *Scene 4* Buenos Aires. They are brought to the Governor's palace, where all except Cundegonde and Old Lady are enslaved. A streetcleaner, Martin (Pangloss's double), warns Candide of a bad future. Cunegonde agrees to live with the Governor; Candide escapes and goes looking for Eldorado. MARTIN: Max Adrian (1); CAPTAIN: Conrad Bain; PILGRIM FATHER: Robert Rue; CANDIDE: Robert Rounseville (2); CUNEGONDE: Barbara Cook (3); OLD LADY: Irra Petina (4); MAXIMILIAN: Louis Edmonds; GOVERNOR OF BUENOS AIRES: William Olvis; OFFICERS: George Blackwell, Tony Drake, Thomas Pyle; MARTIN: Max Adrian (1). Serenade: "My Love" (l: Latouche/Wilbur) (Governor, Cunegonde, Old Lady), Tango: "I Am Easily Assimilated" (l: Bernstein & his wife, Felicia Montealegre) (Old Lady, Officers played by George Blackwell & Thomas Pyle, Cunegonde, Chorus), "Quartet Finale" (l: Wilbur) (Candide, Cunegonde, Governor, Old Lady). *Act II*: *Scene 1* Buenos Aires. The two ladies begin to act up because of the heat, and the Governor plans to get rid of them. Candide returns rich from Eldorado, looking for Cunegonde, but the Governor has them tied up in a sack in a boat in the harbor. The Governor tells him they have gone to Europe. Candide buys a leaky old vessel from the Governor and as the Governor and his people watch from the terrace, Candide's ship sets sail and almost immediately sinks. Trio: "Quiet" (l: Wilbur) (Cunegonde, Governor, Old Lady), Ballad: "Eldorado" (l: Latouche) (Candide & Chorus), Schottische: "Bon Voyage" (l: Wilbur) (Governor & Chorus); *Scene 1a* Candide Travels to Venice. He and Martin have been rescued from the sinking ship, and are floating in the ocean on a raft. Martin is eaten by a shark, and Pangloss miraculously appears and reinforces his philosophy on Candide. CANDIDE: Robert Rounseville (2); MARTIN/PANGLOSS: Max Adrian (1); *Scene 2* Venice. In a luxurious palazzo, Cunegonde turns up as a scrubwoman, and Old Lady as a woman of fashion. Candide is swindled out of his remaining money. FERONE: William Chapman; MADAME SOFRONIA: Irra Petina (4); DUCHESS: Maud Scheerer; BAZZINI, PREFECT OF POLICE: Norman Roland; PRINCE IVAN: Robert Mesrobian; SCRUB LADY: Barbara Cook (3); CANDIDE: Robert Rounseville (2); DR. PANGLOSS: Max Adrian (1); SULTAN MILTON: Joseph Bernard; MARQUIS MILTON: Boris Aplon; DUKE OF NAPLES: Charles Aschmann; CROUPIER: Robert Barry; LADY CUTELY: Dori Davis; LADY TOOTHLY: George Blackwell; LADY SOOTHLY: Fred Jones; LADY RICHMOND: Thomas Pyle. Waltz: "What's the Use" (l: Wilbur/Bernstein) (Old Lady, Bazzini, Ferone, Prince Ivan, Chorus), "Gavotte" (l: Parker) (Old Lady, Candide, Pangloss, Cunegonde); *Scene 3* Westphalia. Candide, disillusioned, returns to Westphalia. Cunegonde, Pangloss and Old Lady appear, and within them the spark of optimism still flickers. Candide tells them he has had enough of their philosophy, and that the only way is to try to make some sense of life, to make one's garden grow. MAXIMILIAN: Louis Edmonds; CUNEGONDE: Barbara Cook (3); CANDIDE: Robert Rounseville (2); OLD LADY: Irra Petina (4); DR. PANGLOSS: Max Adrian (1). Finale: "Make Our Garden Grow" (l: Wilbur) (Company).

The music for all the numbers was provided by Leonard Bernstein, so only the lyricists are mentioned in parentheses after the number's title (sometimes it's Mr. Bernstein himself).

SINGERS: Peggyann Alderman, Charles Aschmann, Robert Barry, George Blackwell, Dori Davis, Jack DeLon, Tony Drake, Naomi Farr, Stanley Grover, Fred Jones, Mollie Knight, Dorothy Krebill, Vivian Laurence, Henry Lawrence, Robert Mesrobian, Lois Monroe, Doris Okerson, Thomas Pyle, Margaret Roy, Robert Rue, Mara Shorr, Dorothy White; DANCERS: Alvin Beam, Charles Czarny, Marvin Gordon, Carmen Gutierrez, Charles Morrell, Frances Noble, Liane Plane, Gloria Stevens. STANDBY: Cunegonde: Margot Moser. UNDERSTUDIES: Candide: Stanley Grover; Old Lady: Dorothy Krebill; Governor: Tony Drake.

Reviews were generally excellent. The show caused a lot of excitement, but was wrong for the times, and failed; the libretto was too heavy. However, the score was great, and achieved much acclaim at the time. Business was picking up substantially when it was canceled. It received Tony Nominations for musical, sets, costumes, musical direction, and for Irra Petina. On 1/26/57 Leonard Bernstein conducted the New York Philharmonic in the first concert performance of the Overture to *Candide*. Over the years the legend of the musical *Candide* (as heard on the original cast album) grew until it was ready to do a revival.

After Broadway. CONCERT VERSION. The seven-week tour opened in 9/58 at Bucks County Playhouse, Pa. PRESENTED BY Lester Osterman

& Hillard Elkins; REVISED BOOK: Michael Stewart; DIRECTOR: David Alexander; SETS/LIGHTING: W. Broderick Hackett & David Hale Hand; MUSICAL DIRECTOR: Samuel Krachmalnick. **Cast:** CANDIDE: Robert Rounseville; CUNEGONDE: Mary Costa; OLD LADY: Irra Petina; PANGLOSS/MARTIN: Martyn Green; ALSO WITH: Lee Bergere, Jack Matthew, Jeanne Beauvais, Ralston Hill. Overture: *Act I*: *Scene I* "Best of All Possible Words" (Pangloss & Company), "Oh, Happy We" (Candide & Cunegonde), "It Must be So" (Candide), "Dear Boy" (Pangloss & Beggars); *Scene 2* "Lisbon Sequence" (Company); Scene 2A "It Must Be Me" (Candide); *Scene 3* "Glitter and Be Gay" (Cunegonde), "You Were Dead, You Know" (Candide & Cunegonde); *Scene 3A* "Pilgrims' Procession" (Pilgrims); *Scene 4* "I Am Easily Assimilated" (Old Lady & Company), "I Am Easily Assimilated" (reprise) (Old Lady & Cunegonde), "Quartet Finale" (Cunegonde, Candide, Old Lady, Governor). *Act II*: Entr'acte (Orchestra); *Scene 1* "Eldorado" (Candide), "Bon Voyage" (Governor & Company); *Scene 2* "I Am Easily Assimilated" (reprise) (Old Lady & Cunegonde), "What's the Use?" (Old Lady, Ferrone, Prefect, Extortionist); *Scene 3* Finale: "Make Our Garden Grow" (Entire Company).

LONDON PRODUCTION. In the fall of 1958 Lillian Hellman and Michael Stewart began working on revisions for the London production. It ran at the SAVILLE THEATRE, 4/30/59–6/20/59. 60 PERFORMANCES. The numbers "My Love" and "Quiet" were dropped, and a new number — "We Are Women" — was written. PRESENTED BY Linnit & Dunfee; REVISED BOOK: Michael Stewart; DIRECTOR: Robert Lewis (with new staging); CHOREOGRAPHER: Jack Cole; SETS/COSTUMES: Osbert Lancaster; LIGHTING: Michael Northen; MUSICAL DIRECTOR: Alexander Faris. **Cast:** CANDIDE: Denis Quilley; CUNEGONDE: Mary Costa; MAXIMILIAN: Dennis Stephenson; PANGLOSS/MARTIN: Laurence Naismith; OLD LADY: Edith Coates; GOVERNOR: Ron Moody; SULTAN: James Cairncross; MARQUIS: Victor Spinetti. *Act I*: Ensemble: "Best of All Possible Worlds" (Pangloss & Chorus), Duet: "Oh Happy We" (Candide & Cunegonde), Song: "It Must be So" (Candide), Ensemble: "Oh, What a Day for a Holiday" (Inquisitors & Chorus), Song: "It Must Be Me" (Candide), Mazurka: "Paris Waltz" (Orchestra), Aria: "Glitter and Be Gay" (Cunegonde), Duet: "You Were Dead, You Know" (Candide & Cunegonde), Ensemble: "Pilgrims' Procession" (Pilgrims), Tango: "I Am Easily Assimilated" (Old Lady, Cunegonde, Chorus), Quartet: "Quartet Finale" (Cunegonde, Candide, Old Lady, Governor). *Act II*: Ballad: "Eldorado" (Candide & Chorus), Duet: "We Are Women" (Cunegonde & Old Lady), Schottische: "Bon Voyage" (Governor & Chorus), Waltz: "What's the Use?" (Old Lady, Sultan, Chief of Police, Extortionist, Chorus), Duet: "I've Got Troubles" (Old Lady & Cunegonde), Finale: "Make Our Garden Grow" (Candide, Cunegonde, Company).

SHELDON PATINKIN'S VERSION. In 1967 Sheldon Patinkin's newly conceived and re-written version ran as an outdoor summer concert in GRANT PARK, CHICAGO, with spoken narration. Mr. Patinkin is Mandy Patinkin's cousin. Another concert version of this revision ran at PHILHARMONIC HALL, 11/10/68. 1 PERFORMANCE. It was dedicated to Leonard Bernstein's 50th birthday. The number "Nothing More than This" (cut from the 1956 version), was re-instated. **Cast:** VOLTAIRE/PANGLOSS/NARRATOR: Alan Arkin; CANDIDE: David Watson; CUNEGONDE: Madeline Kahn; OLD LADY: Irra Petina; GOVERNOR: William Lewis.

TOUR. A full-scale touring production of this version opened on 7/6/71, at the Curran Theatre, San Francisco. It ran at the Kennedy Center, Washington, DC, 10/26/71–11/13/71 (32 performances). This ended the tour. It failed to go to Broadway. There was a new song: "Words, Words, Words" ("Martin's Laughing Song"). PRESENTED BY Edwin Lester's Civic Light Opera; DIRECTOR: Sheldon Patinkin; CHOREOGRAPHER: Michael Smuin; SETS: Oliver Smith; COSTUMES: Freddy Wittop; LIGHTING: Peggy Clark; MUSICAL DIRECTOR: Maurice Peress. **Cast:** CANDIDE: Frank Porretta; CUNEGONDE: Mary Costa (Barbara Meister alternate); PANGLOSS/MARTIN: Douglas Campbell; OLD LADY: Rae Allen; ALSO WITH: Damita Jo Freeman, Robert Klein, Bob Bakanic, Lucy Andonian, Clifford Fearl, Autris Paige, Casper Roos.

111. *Candide (1974 Broadway revival)*

Before Broadway. This revival was first produced Off Broadway by Robert Kalfin of the Chelsea Theatre Center, and is known as the Chelsea

Version. Mr. Kalfin got Hal Prince to direct, and Mr. Prince came up with the idea of using several stages to represent different locations of the story. Lillian Hellman declined to re-write her original book, but she did grant rights to Hal Prince to re-do the book, provided none of her original material was used. Hugh Wheeler wrote the new book, emphasizing the comic elements, and Steve Sondheim wrote some new lyrics. Set designer Eugene Lee remodeled the theatre to accommodate the multilevel environmental playing space with ramps, catwalks, platforms, drawbridges and trapdoors. The audience sat on bleachers and stools interspersed throughout the set. Hal Prince wanted Jerry Orbach as Pangloss/Voltaire, but he was unavailable. He also wanted Nancy Walker as the Old Lady, but she wasn't interested. Rehearsals began 10/21/73, in Brooklyn. It ran in the 4th-floor 180-seat theatre at the BROOKLYN ACADEMY OF MUSIC, 12/21/73–1/20/74. Limited run of 48 PERFORMANCES (including previews, which began on 12/11/73). It cost $100,000 to produce, and sold out. Then it moved to Broadway, where it was capitalized at $450,000. The Broadway Theatre was remodeled for the flexible staging, with 10 different playing spaces, some amid the audience. In this revival scenes overlap and are played simultaneously. The show ran 1 hour and 57 minutes, with no intermission. The Constantinople scene was new to this production.

The Broadway Run. BROADWAY THEATRE, 3/10/74–1/4/76. Previews from 3/5/74. 740 PERFORMANCES. PRESENTED BY Chelsea Theatre Center of Brooklyn (Robert Kalfin, artistic director; Michael David, executive director; Burl Hash, productions DIRECTOR), in conjunction with Harold Prince & Ruth Mitchell; MUSIC: Leonard Bernstein; LYRICS/BOOK: see the 1956 Broadway production for details; ADDITIONAL LYRICS: Stephen Sondheim & John Latouche; NEW BOOK: Hugh Wheeler; DIRECTOR: Harold Prince; CHOREOGRAPHER: Patricia Birch; SETS/COSTUMES: Eugene & Franne Lee; LIGHTING: Tharon Musser; SOUND: Robert Maybaum; MUSICAL DIRECTOR: John Mauceri, *Paul Gemignani*; ORCHESTRATIONS: Hershy Kay; PRESS: Betty Lee Hunt Associates; PRODUCTION SUPERVISOR: Ruth Mitchell; GENERAL MANAGER: Howard Haines; PRODUCTION STAGE MANAGER: James Doolan; FIRST ASSISTANT STAGE MANAGER: Errol Selsby; SECOND ASSISTANT STAGE MANAGER: Carlos Gorbea. **Cast:** VOLTAIRE/DR. PANGLOSS/GOVERNOR/HOST/SAGE: Lewis J. Stadlen (1) ☆, *Charles Kimbrough* (from 1/20/75); CHINESE COOLIE/ROSARY VENDOR/LION: Jim Corti; CANDIDE: Mark Baker, *Kelly Walters* (from 9/17/75); HUNTSMAN/1ST RECRUITING OFFICER/EUNUCH: David Horwitz; PAQUETTE: Deborah St. Darr, *Paula Cinko* (from 9/75); BARONESS/HARPSICHORDIST/STEEL DRUMMER: Mary-Pat Green; BARON/GRAND INQUISITOR/SLAVE DRIVER/CAPTAIN: Joe Palmieri; CUNEGONDE: Maureen Brennan, Kathryn Ritter (Wednesday & Saturday matinees); MAXIMILIAN: Sam Freed; SERVANT: Robert Henderson; 2ND RECRUITING OFFICER: Peter Vogt; PENITENTES: Gail Boggs (*Lisa Wilkinson*), Lynne Gannaway, Mary-Pat Green, Kelly Walters; ARISTOCRATS: Peter Vogt, Carolann Page, Carlos Gorbea, Becky McSpadden, Kathryn Ritter, Jeff Keller; BULGARIAN SOLDIERS/COWS: Carlos Gorbea & Kelly Walters; WESTPHALIAN SOLDIERS: Jim Corti & Chip Garnett; AGENTS OF THE INQUISITION: David Horwitz, Chip Garnett, Robert Henderson; THE OLD LADY: June Gable, *Niki Flacks* (from 7/3/75), *Joanne Jonas* (from 9/75); PRIESTS: Jim Corti & David Horwitz; SPANISH DONS: Jim Corti, David Horwitz, Robert Henderson; SAILORS: Jim Corti, David Horwitz, Robert Henderson, Carlos Gorbea, Kelly Walters; GUESTS: Jim Corti, Joe Palmieri, Chip Garnett, Jeff Keller; WHORES: Gail Boggs (*Lisa Wilkinson*), Kathryn Ritter; HOURIS: Gail Boggs (*Lisa Wilkinson*), Lynne Gannaway, Becky McSpadden, Mary-Pat Green, Kathryn Ritter; CARTAGENIANS: Lynne Gannaway, Peter Vogt, Renee Semes, Jeff Keller, Becky McSpadden, Carolann Page, Kelly Walters, David Horwitz, Robert Henderson; FRUIT VENDOR/PYGMY: Carlos Gorbea; GOVERNOR'S AIDE: Chip Garnett; RICH JEW/JUDGE/MAN IN BLACK/GERMAN/BOTANIST: Jeff Keller; PIRATES: Chip Garnett & Jeff Keller; LADY WITH KNITTING/1ST SHEEP: Renee Semes; 2ND SHEEP: Carolann Page, *Becky McSpadden*. **Understudies:** Candide: Kelly Walters; Voltaire/Pangloss/Governor/Host/Sage: Sam Freed; Cunegonde: Kathryn Ritter; Maximilian: Robert Henderson; 1st Recruiting Officer/Agent/Eunuch/Huntsman/Priest/Sailor/Don: Jeff Keller; Old Lady: Renee Semes; Paquette: Lynne Gannaway; Baron/Grand Inquisitor/Slave Driver/Captain/Guest: Peter Vogt; Rich Jew/Judge/Man in Black/Pirate/German/Botanist/Guest/Cow: Chip Garnett; Cartagenians: Chip

Garnett & Jeff Keller. **Swing Girl:** Rhoda Butler [she became Rhoda Butler Blank], *Lisa Wilkinson, Holly Shunaman*. **Musicians** (for 1973 Off Broadway): PIANO: Tom Pierson, Joseph D. Lewis, Albin Konopka; TROMBONE: O.T. Myers; CELLO: David Cella; PERCUSSION: Rick Cohen; DOUBLE BASS: Dennis Masuzzo; VIOLIN/VIOLA: Ruth Millhouse & Yuval Waldman; TRUMPETS: Grant Keast & Scott Wharton; CLARINETS: Charles O'Kane, Phil Bashor, Virginia Hourigan. BASS CLARINET/SAX: Phil Bashor; OBOE/BASSOON: Virginia Hourigan; FLUTE/PICCOLO/ALTO RECORDER: Charles O'Kane. *Scene 1* Voltaire's bedroom; *Scene 2* A forest glade: "Life is Happiness Indeed" (l: Stephen Sondheim) (Candide, Cunegonde, Maximilian, Paquette) [a new number, but using Leonard Bernstein's music from the original "Gavotte" in Act II]; *Scene 3* The baroness's boudoir: "Life is Happiness Indeed" (continued); *Scene 4* The baronial garden: "Life is Happiness Indeed" (continued); *Scene 5* Maximilian's bedroom: "Life is Happiness Indeed" (continued); *Scene 6* The castle schoolroom: "The Best of All Possible Worlds" (Pangloss, Candide, Cunegonde, Maximilian, Paquette); *Scene 7* The baronial orchard: "Oh Happy We" (Candide & Cunegonde); *Scene 8* The baronial banquet hall; *Scene 9* A desolate heath in Westphalia: "It Must Be So" (Candide); *Scene 10* The baronial chapel: "O Miserere" (l: Stephen Sondheim) [Miss Page, Miss Gannaway, Miss Boggs, Mr. Henderson (Chip Garnett)]; *Scene 11* A meadow by moonlight; *Scene 12* The battlefield: "Oh Happy We" (reprise) (Candide & Cunegonde); *Scene 13* A village square; *Scene 14* A bedchamber in the Jew's palace: "Glitter and Be Gay" (Cunegonde); *Scene 15* A destroyed fishing village; *Scene 16* The central square in Lisbon: "Auto-da-Fe (What a Day!)" (l: Stephen Sondheim) (Company) [this was a new number], "This World" ("Candide's Lament") (l: Stephen Sondheim) (Candide) [this was a new number]; *Scene 17* A room in a Lisbon palace: "You Were Dead, You Know" (Candide & Cunegonde); *Scene 18* A room in the inn outside Cadiz; *Scene 19* The Central Plaza at Cadiz: "I Am Easily Assimilated" (Old Lady & Spanish Dons), "I Am Easily Assimilated" (reprise) (Old Lady, Candide, Cunegonde); *Scene 20* The Grand Plaza, at Cartagena, Colombia; *Scene 21* The slave market at Cartagena: "My Love" (Pangloss); *Scene 22* A ship at sea; *Scene 23* The Cathedral of the Jesuits at Montevideo: "Alleluia" (Company); *Scene 24* Eldorado: "Sheep's Song" (l: Stephen Sondheim) (Sheep, Lion, Paquette, Candide); *Scene 25* The rocky shore: "Sheep's Song" (continued); *Scene 26* A clearing in the jungle: "Sheep's Song" (continued); *Scene 27* The Grand Plaza, Cartagena; *Scene 28* The dock at Cartagena: "Bon Voyage" (Schottische) (Governor & Company); *Scene 29* A desert island: "The Best of All Possible Worlds" (reprise) (Old Lady, Candide, Paquette, Sheep); *Scene 30* A hall in a palace in Constantinople: "You Were Dead, You Know" (reprise) (Candide & Cunegonde); *Scene 31* A street outside the palace; *Scene 32* The Cave of the Wisest Man in the World; *Scene 33* Candide's farm: "Make Our Garden Grow" (Company).

The show opened on Broadway at a matinee. It got rave notices. It cost $65,000 a week to run, but lost $310,000 of its initial investment, partly because the remodeling of the theatre cut down on the number of seats available (from 1,700 to 900), and also because the musicians' union demanded that 25 of their members be hired when only 13 were necessary for the show. The complex set prohibited a national tour, which might have recouped the loss. It won Tonys for book, direction of a musical, sets, and costumes, and a Special Tony (which led to the establishment of the Best Revival category in 1977). Also nominated were Lewis J. Stadlen, Mark Baker, Maureen Brennan, and June Gable.

After Broadway. *Candide* SUITE. This was a 50-minute performance piece for vocal soloists, chorus and orchestra, arranged by John Mauceri. It had its world premiere at the FREDERIC MANN AUDITORIUM, Tel-Aviv, on 4/9/77. CONDUCTOR: John Mauceri; PERFORMED BY: The Indiana University Chamber Opera Theatre. *Part I*: Overture, "Oh Happy We," "Wedding Procession and Chorale," "Candide Begins His Travels," "It Must Be So," "Paris Waltz," "Glitter and Be Gay," "You Were Dead, You Know," "Pilgrims' Procession," "My Love" (Governor's Serenade). *Part II*: "I Am Easily Assimilated," "Candide's Return from Eldorado," "Bon Voyage," "Into the Raft," "Money Money," "What's the Use?," "Return to Westphalia," "Make Our Garden Grow." During the Bernstein Festival at the BARBICAN CENTRE, LONDON, 4/29/86–5/11/86, John Mauceri conducted the London Symphony Orchestra in the UK premiere of this arrangement.

HAL PRINCE'S OPERA HOUSE VERSION. This was the 1974 production, revised by Hugh Wheeler and Hal Prince. Leonard Bernstein revised his music, with the help of John Mauceri and Hershy Kay. Hugh Wheeler revised the book. Scenes overlap and are played simultaneously It ran at the NEW YORK STATE THEATRE, 10/13/82–11/2/82. 7 PERFORMANCES IN REPERTORY. Its second engagement was 10/16/83–10/30/83. 5 PERFORMANCES IN REPERTORY. Its third engagement was 7/18/84–7/22/84. 7 PERFORMANCES. Its fourth engagement was 7/1/86–7/6/86. 8 PERFORMANCES. Its fifth engagement was 11/11/86–11/16/86. 8 PERFORMANCES. Its sixth engagement was 7/18/89–9/10/89. 14 PERFORMANCES. PRESENTED BY the New York City Opera; DIRECTOR: Harold Prince; STAGE DIRECTOR: *Arthur Masella* (for the 2nd engagement), *Arthur Masella & Albert Sherman* (for the 3rd engagement), *Arthur Masella* (for the 4th & 5th engagements), *Albert Sherman* (for the 6th engagement); CHOREOGRAPHER: Patricia Birch; SETS: Clarke Dunham; COSTUMES: Judith Dolan; LIGHTING: Ken Billington; CONDUCTOR: John Mauceri, *Scott Bergeson* (for the 2nd engagement), *John Mauceri* (for the 3rd engagement), *Scott Bergeson* (for the 4th, 5th & 6th engagements); ADDITIONAL ORCHESTRATIONS: *John Mauceri* (from the 4th engagement on); ORCHESTRATIONS: Leonard Bernstein & Hershy Kay. **Cast:** VOLTAIRE/PANGLOSS/BUSINESSMAN/GOVERNOR/2ND GAMBLER (POLICE CHIEF)/SAGE: John Lankston; CANDIDE: David Eisler, *Cris Groenendaal* (for the 2nd engagement), *David Eisler* (for the 3rd, 4th & 5th engagements), *Mark Beudert* (for the 6th engagement); HUNTSMAN: Don Yule; PAQUETTE: Deborah Darr, *Maris Clement* (for the 2nd engagement), *Deborah Darr* (for the 3rd, 4th & 5th engagements), *Maris Clement* (for the 6th engagement); BARONESS/CALLIOPE PLAYER: Bonnie Kirk, *Carol Sparrow* (for the 3rd engagement), *Ruth Golden* (for the 4th & 5th engagements), *Christine Meadows* (for the 6th engagement); BARON/GRAND INQUISITOR/SLAVE DRIVER/PASHA-PREFECT: Jack Harrold, *Richard McKee* (for the 6th engagement); CUNEGONDE: Erie Mills, *Claudette Peterson* (for the 2nd engagement), *Leigh Munro* (for the 3rd engagement), *Erie Mills* (for the 4th & 5th engagements), *Cyndia Sieden* (for the 6th engagement); MAXIMILIAN: Scott Reeve, *James Javore* (for the 6th engagement); MAXIMILIAN'S SERVANT/DON ISSACHAR THE JEW/JUDGE/FATHER BERNARD/1ST GAMBLER: James Billings; BULGARIAN SOLDIERS: Don Yule & James Billings; WESTPHALIAN SOLDIERS: Andy Roth (*Andy Ferrell* for the 2nd engagement; *Scott Evans* for the 3rd engagement; *Andy Roth* for the 4th & 5th engagements; *Jose Traba* for the 6th engagement) & William Ledbetter; HERESY AGENT: Ralph Bassett; INQUISITION AGENTS: Gary Dietrich & William Poplasky (*William Selissen* for the 2nd engagement; *Michael Martorano* for the 3rd engagement; *Douglas Hamilton* for the 4th & 5th engagements; *Kirk Griffith* for the 6th engagement); OLD LADY: Muriel Costa-Greenspon; DONS: Robert Estner (*Vasilis Iracledes* for the 2nd, 3rd, 4th & 5th engagements; *Daniel Albert* for the 6th engagement), Andy Roth (*Brian Kaman* for the 2nd engagement; *Scott Evans* for the 3rd, 4th & 5th engagements; *William Ward* for the 6th engagement), Michael Rubino (*Richard Smith* for the 3rd, 4th & 5th engagements; *Joey R. Smith* for the 6th engagement), Don Yule, William Ledbetter, Ralph Bassett; GOVERNOR'S AIDE: Andy Roth, *Andy Ferrell* (for the 2nd engagement), *Scott Evans* (for the 3rd engagement), *Andy Roth* (for the 4th & 5th engagements), *Daniel Albert* (for the 6th engagement); SAILORS: Gary Dietrich, William Poplasky (*William Selissen* for the 2nd engagement; *Michael Martorano* for the 3rd engagement; *Douglas Hamilton* for the 4th & 5th engagements; *Kirk Griffith* for the 6th engagement), Andy Roth (*Andy Ferrell* for the 2nd engagement; *Scott Evans* for the 3rd engagement; *Andy Roth* for the 4th & 5th engagements; *Jose Traba* for the 6th engagement), Jeffrey Smith (*Travis Wright* for the 2nd & 3rd engagements; *Scott Evans* for the 4th & 5th engagements; *Daniel Albert* for the 6th engagement); PIRATES: John Henry Thomas & William Ledbetter; PINK SHEEP: Ivy Austin (*Andrea Green* for the 6th engagement) & Rhoda Butler (*Susan Delery-Whedon* for the 3rd engagement; *Rhoda Butler* for the 4th & 5th engagements; *Karen Ziemba* for the 6th engagement); LION: James Sergi, *Robert Brubaker* (for the 2nd, 3rd, 4th & 5th engagements), *Michael Willson* (for the 6th engagement). **Act I:** *Scene 1* Dr. Voltaire's Traveling Freak Show; *Scene 2* The castle and gardens; *Scene 3* A desolate heath; *Scene 4* The baronial chapel; *Scene 5* A meadow by moonlight and the battlefield; *Scene 6* Cunegonde's room; *Scene 7* Destroyed village; *Scene 8* Central square in Lisbon; *Scene 9* A Lisbon street; *Scene 10* Cunegonde's room; *Scene 11* A room in the inn at Cadiz; *Scene 12* Central plaza at Cadiz. **Act II:**

Scene 1 Plaza Grande, Cartagena; *Scene 2* A ship at sea; *Scene 3* Montevideo Cathedral; *Scene 4* A jungle; *Scene 5* Eldorado and a jungle; *Scene 6* A jungle and sheep meadow; *Scene 7* Ballroom in Cartagena and the dock; *Scene 8* A desert island; *Scene 9* A hall in the palace; *Scene 10* The Cave of the Wisest Man; *Scene 11* Candide's farm. **Act I:** "Life is Happiness Indeed" (Candide, Cunegonde, Maximilian, Paquette), "The Best of All Possible Worlds" (Pangloss, Candide, Cunegonde, Maximilian, Paquette), "Oh Happy We" (Candide & Cunegonde), "It Must Be So" (Candide), "Glitter and Be Gay" (Cunegonde), "Dear Boy" (Pangloss & Men's Chorus), "Auto-da-Fe" (What a Day) (Company), "Candide's Lament" (Candide), "You Were Dead, You Know" (Candide & Cunegonde), "I Am Easily Assimilated" (Old Lady & Dons), Quartet Finale (Candide, Cunegonde, Old Lady, Governor). **Act II:** "Ballad of the New World" (Candide & Chorus), "My Love" (Governor & Maximilian), "Alleluia" (Maximilian, Cunegonde, Governor, Chorus), "Sheep Song" (Pink Sheep, Lion, Paquette, Candide, Chorus), "Bon Voyage" (Governor & Company), "Quiet" (Old Lady, Paquette, Candide), "The Best of All Possible Worlds" (reprise) (Old Lady, Candide, Paquette), "What's the Use" (Pasha-Prefect, 1st & 2nd Gamblers), "You Were Dead, You Know" (reprise) (Candide & Cunegonde), "Make Our Garden Grow" (Company). It was very successful and became part of the New York City Opera's repertoire. The second engagement opened at a matinee. This version was recorded in 5/85 at Manhattan Center. It was broadcast live on PBS, 11/12/86. The 6th engagement (in 1989) closed at a matinee. On 11/26/94 Hal Prince directed the Lyric Opera of Chicago in this version.

THE MILLER/WELLS VERSION. Hugh Wheeler's book was somewhat re-written by the directors Jonathan Miller and John Wells (Mr. Wheeler having died). There was a new eight-minute Lisbon sequence. Paquette was now built up into a lead, and Infant Casmira and Arab Conjuror were gone. It was filmed for BBC-TV. Performed by the Scottish Opera. It opened at the THEATRE ROYAL, Glasgow, on 5/19/88, and moved to the OLD VIC, London, 12/1/88–1/7/89 (34 PERFORMANCES). CHOREOGRAPHER: Anthony Van Laast; SETS/COSTUMES: Richard Hudson; MUSICAL DIRECTOR: John Mauceri (for 5 performances), *Justin Brown*. **Cast:** VOLTAIRE/PANGLOSS/CACAMBO/MAN: Nickolas Grace; CANDIDE: Mark Beudert; PAQUETTE: Gaynor Miles; BARONESS: Elaine McKillop; BARON: Leon Greene; CUNEGONDE: Andrea Bolton, *Rosemary Ashe & Marilyn Hill-Smith* (alternated in London); MAXIMILIAN: Mark Tinkler; DON ISSACHAR: Howard Goorney; OLD LADY: Ann Howard, *Patricia Routledge* (in London); GOVERNOR: David Hillman. **Act I:** "Life is Happiness Indeed" (Voltaire & Company), "The Best of All Possible Worlds" (Pangloss, Candide, Cunegonde, Maximilian, Paquette), "Oh Happy We" (Candide & Cunegonde), "It Must be So" (Candide), "Battle Chorale" (Voltaire & Company), "Candide's Lament" (Candide), "Dear Boy" (Pangloss), "Auto-da-Fe" (Company), "It Must Be Me" (Candide), "The Paris Waltz" (Company), "Glitter and Be Gay" (Cunegonde, with Old Lady), "You Were Dead, You Know" (Candide & Cunegonde), "I Am Easily Assimilated" (Old Lady, Candide, Cunegonde, Ensemble), "To the New World" (Quartet Finale) (Candide, Cunegonde, Old Lady, Captain). **Act II:** Entr'acte (Orchestra), Opening (Ensemble), "My Love" (Governor, Cunegonde, Maximilian), "We Are Women" (Cunegonde & Old Lady), "Alleluia" (Ensemble), "The Ballad of Eldorado" (Candide & Ensemble), "Laughing Song" ("Words, Words, Words") (Martin), "Bon Voyage" (Governor & Ensemble), "Money, Money" (Ensemble), "Pass it Along" (What's the Use?") (Old Lady, Ragostki, Max, Gambler, Ensemble), "Venice Gavotte" (Old Lady, Candide, Cunegonde, Pangloss), "Nothing More than This" (Candide); "Universal Good" (Ensemble), "Make Our Garden Grow" (Company).

THE FINAL REVISED VERSION. In 1989 Leonard Bernstein conducted the London Symphony Orchestra and Chorus in two concert performances of *Candide* at the BARBICAN CENTRE. This version is called The Final Revised Version. The cast and orchestra recorded at Abbey Road Studios, 12/15/89–12/18/89. It won a 1991 Grammy Award. This version made its U.S. debut in the LORETTO-HILTON THEATRE, St. Louis, 5/21/94. PRESENTED BY the Opera Theatre of St. Louis; DIRECTOR: Colin Graham; CHOREOGRAPHER: Victoria Morgan; SETS: Emanuele Lazzati; CONDUCTOR: Stephen Lord; ORIGINAL ORCHESTRATIONS: Leonard Bernstein & Hershy Kay; ADDITIONAL ORCHESTRATIONS: John Mauceri. **Cast:** VOLTAIRE/PANGLOSS/MARTIN/CACAMBO: John Stephens; CAN-

DIDE: Kevin Anderson; PAQUETTE: Suzanne Balaes; CUNEGONDE: Constance Hauman; MAXIMILIAN: Steven Combs; BARONESS/OLD LADY: Josepha Gayer; BARON: Brad Cresswell. The West Coast premiere of the Final Revised Version opened on 11/8/95, at the AHMANSON THEATRE, Los Angeles. PRESENTED BY The Center Theatre Group; DIRECTOR: Gordon Davidson; CHOREOGRAPHER: Yehuda Hyman; SETS: Peter Wexler; COSTUMES: Lewis Brown; LIGHTING: Tharon Musser. *Cast:* Nancy Dussault, William Schallert, David Thome.

112. *Candide (1997 Broadway revival)*

This was basically Hal Prince's Opera House version, with some minor changes.

The Broadway Run. GERSHWIN THEATRE, 4/29/97–7/27/97. 11 previews from 4/19/97. 103 PERFORMANCES. PRESENTED BY Livent (U.S.); MUSIC: Leonard Bernstein; LYRICS/BOOK: see the original 1956 production for details; DIRECTOR: Harold Prince; CHOREOGRAPHER: Patricia Birch; SETS: Clarke Dunham; COSTUMES: Judith Dolan; LIGHTING: Ken Billington; SOUND: Jonathan Deans; MUSICAL SUPERVISOR/MUSICAL DIRECTOR: Eric Stern; ORIGINAL ORCHESTRATIONS: Leonard Bernstein & Hershy Kay; ADDITIONAL ORCHESTRATIONS/MUSICAL CONTINUITY: John Mauceri; CAST RECORDING on RCA Victor, made on 5/19/97 & 5/20/97, and released 7/29/97; PRESS: Mary Bryant & Wayne Wolfe; CASTING: Beth Russell & Arnold J. Mungioli; GENERAL MANAGER: Frank P. Scardino; COMPANY MANAGER: Jim Brandeberry; STAGE MANAGER: Bonnie Panson; ASSISTANT STAGE MANAGER: Robbie Young. *Cast:* VOLTAIRE: Jim Dale (1) ✳; CANDIDE: Jason Danieley (6); HUNTSMAN: Seth Malkin; PAQUETTE: Stacey Logan (5); BARONESS VON THUNDER: Julie Johnson, *Melissa Hart*; BARON VON THUNDER: Mal Z. Lawrence (8); CUNEGONDE: Harolyn Blackwell (3) ✳ & Glenda Balkan (7) (at certain performances); MAXIMILIAN: Brent Barrett (4); HUGO, MAXIMILIAN'S SERVANT: Arte Johnson (9); OLD LADY: Andrea Martin (2) ✳; DR. PANGLOSS: Jim Dale (1) ✳; RADU, A BULGARIAN SOLDIER: Arte Johnson (9); 2ND BULGARIAN SOLDIER: Paul Harman; DON ISSACHAR, THE RICH JEW: Arte Johnson (9); GRAND INQUISITOR: Mal Z. Lawrence (8); HERESY AGENT: David Girolmo; JUDGE GOMEZ: Arte Johnson (9); BUSINESSMAN: Jim Dale (1) ✳; GOVERNOR: Jim Dale (1) ✳; GOVERNOR'S AIDE: Allen Hidalgo; COLUMBO, A SLAVE DRIVER: Mal Z. Lawrence (8); FATHER BERNARD: Arte Johnson (9); SHEEP ONE: Nanne Puritz; SHEEP TWO: D'Vorah Bailey; LION: Seth Malkin; PASHA-PREFECT OF CONSTANTINOPLE: Mal Z. Lawrence (8); TURHAN BEY, A CONSTANTINOPLE GAMBLER: Arte Johnson (9), *Avery Saltzman* (from 7/97); 2ND GAMBLER (POLICE CHIEF): Jim Dale (1) ✳; SAGE: Jim Dale (1) ✳; ENSEMBLE: D'Vorah Bailey, Mary Kate Boulware, Diana Brownstone, Alvin Crawford, Christopher F. Davis, Sherrita Duran, Deanna Dys, David Girolmo, Paul Harman, Joy Hermalyn, Allen Hidalgo, Wendy Hilliard, Elizabeth Jimenez, Julie Johnson, Ken Krugman, Chad Larget, Shannon Lewis, Seth Malkin, Andrew Pacho, Nanne Puritz, Owen Taylor, Eric Van Hoven. **Standby:** For Jim Dale: John Lankston. **Understudies:** For Jim Dale: Mal Z. Lawrence & Paul Harman; Candide: Chad Larget & Eric Van Hoven; Cunegonde: Nanne Puritz & Mary Kate Boulware; Paquette: Shannon Lewis & Nanne Puritz; Sheep: Mary Kate Boulware, Rachel Coloff, Diana Brownstone; Old Lady: Julie Johnson & Joy Hermalyn; Baroness: Joy Hermalyn & Rachel Coloff; Maximilian: Ken Krugman & Seth Malkin; For Mal Z. Lawrence/Arte Johnson: Ken Krugman & Seth Malkin; For Arte Johnson: David Girolmo & Paul Harman; Bulgarian/Heresy Agent: Matthew Aibel; Huntsman/Lion: Alvin Crawford & Joseph P. McDonnell. **Swings:** Matthew Aibel, Rachel Coloff, Joseph P. McDonnell, Starla Pace. **Orchestra:** CONCERTMASTER: Erica Kiesewetter; VIOLINS: Elizabeth Lim, Aloysia Friedmann, Elizabeth Chang, John Connelly, Laura Frautschi; VIOLAS: Sarah Adams & Shelley Holland-Moritz; CELLI: Adam Grabois & Roger Shell; BASS: Judith Sugarman; FLUTES: Brian Miller & Laura Conwesser; CLARINETS: Steven Hartman & Maryl Abt; OBOE: Robert Ingliss; BASSOON: Jeffrey Marchand; TRUMPETS: Carl Albach & John Dent; FRENCH HORNS: Chris Komer & Leise Anscheutz Paer; TROMBONES: Dick Clark & Ken Finn; TUBA: Marcus Rojas; HARP: Grace Paradise; PERCUSSION: Paul Hostetter, James Preiss, Tom Partington. *Act I:* Overture; "Life is Happiness Indeed" (Voltaire,

Candide, Cunegonde, Maximilian, Paquette), "The Best of All Possible Worlds" (Pangloss, Candide, Cunegonde, Maximilian, Paquette, Ensemble), "Oh Happy We" (Candide & Cunegonde), "It Must be So" (Candide), "Westphalian Chorale" (Ensemble), "Glitter and be Gay" (Cunegonde), "Auto-da-Fe" (Full Company), "Candide's Lament" (Candide), "You Were Dead, You Know" (Candide & Cunegonde), "I Am Easily Assimilated" (Old Lady, Dons, Company), "Quartet Finale" (Candide, Cunegonde, Business Man, Old Lady, Ensemble). *Act II:* "Ballad of the New World" (Candide & Ensemble), "My Love" (Governor & Maximilian), "Alleluia" (Ensemble), "Sheep Song" (Sheep, Lion, Paquette), "Bon Voyage" (Governor & Ensemble), "Quiet" (Old Lady, Candide, Paquette), "The Best of All Possible Worlds" (reprise) (Candide, Paquette, Old Lady, Sheep), "What's the Use?" (Pasha-Prefect, Turhan Bey, Police Chief, Ensemble), "You Were Dead, You Know" (reprise) (Candide & Cunegonde), "Make Our Garden Grow" (Full Company).

Reviews were divided. The show won a Tony for costumes, and was nominated for revival of a musical, and for Jim Dale and Andrea Martin. A planned post–Broadway tour never happened.

After Broadway. THE JOHN CAIRD VERSION. LAURENCE OLIVIER THEATRE, London, 4/13/99–1/25/00. Previews from 4/6/99. PRESENTED BY The Royal National Theatre; ADAPTED BY/DIRECTOR: John Caird; CHOREOGRAPHER: Peter Darling; SETS: John Napier; COSTUMES: John Napier & Elise Napier; MUSICAL DIRECTOR: Mark W. Dorrell; ORCHESTRATIONS: Bruce Coughlin; CAST RECORDING made in 10/99, at Angel Studios, Islington. *Cast:* VOLTAIRE/PANGLOSS: Simon Russell Beale; CANDIDE: Daniel Evans; CUNEGONDE: Alex Kelly; OLD WOMAN: Beverley Klein; MAXIMILIAN/AGENT: Simon Day; BARON/MARTIN: Denis Quilley; BARONESS: Myra Sands. This version had new characters: James the Anabaptist, Tzar Ivan, Charles Edward, Paraguayan Girl, The King and Queen of Eldorado, Theodore of Corsica, Vanderdendur, Hermann Augustus. Overture (Orchestra); *Act I:* "Voltaire Chorale" (Company), "Life is Happiness Indeed" (Candide), "Life is Happiness Unending" (Candide, Maximilian, Cunegonde, Paquette), "The Best of All Possible Worlds" (Pangloss, Candide, Cunegonde, Maximilian, Paquette), "Universal Good" (Pangloss, Candide, Cunegonde, Maximilian, Paquette), "Oh, Happy We" (Candide & Cunegonde), "It Must Be So" (Candide) [not on cast album], "Candide's Lament" (Candide), "Dear Boy" (Pangloss & Company), "The Paris Waltz" (Orchestra), "Glitter and Be Gay" (Cunegonde), "Auto-da-Fe" (Grand Inquisitor, Inquisitors, Company), "You Were Dead, You Know" (Candide & Cunegonde), "I Am Easily Assimilated" (Old Woman & Company), "Quartet Finale" (Candide, Cunegonde, Old Woman, Cacambo, Company). *Act II:* "We Are Women" (Old Woman & Cunegonde), "My Love" (Governor & Cunegonde), "Alleluia" (Pilgrims) [not on cast album], "The Ballad of Eldorado" (Voltaire, Candide, Cacambo, King, Queen, Company), "Bon Voyage" (Vanderdendur & Company), "It Must Be Me" (Candide), "Words, Words, Words" (Martin), "Money, Money, Money" (Women of Venice), "The Venice Gavotte" (Old Woman, Cunegonde, Candide, Pangloss, Company), "Nothing More than This" (Candide), "What's the Use?" (Cacambo, Paquette, Old Woman, Maximilian, Pangloss, Martin, Company), "The King's Barcarolle" (Stanislaus, Ivan, Charles Edward, Achmet, Hermann Augustus, Theodore, Candide), "Universal Good" (reprise) (Candide & Company), "Make Our Garden Grow" (Candide, Cunegonde, Company).

2005 REVIVAL. NEW YORK STATE THEATRE, 3/4/05–3/19/05. This was the Harold Prince production, PRESENTED BY the New York City Opera. DIRECTOR: Arthur Masella; CHOREOGRAPHER: Patricia Birch; SETS: Clarke Dunham; COSTUMES: Judith Dolan; LIGHTING: Ken Billington; SOUND: Abe Jacob. *Cast:* PANGLOSS: John Cullum; OLD LADY: Judy Kaye; PAQUETTE: Stacey Logan; CUNEGONDE: Anna Christy & Georgia Jarman; CANDIDE: Keith Jameson & William Ferguson; MAXIMILIAN: Kyle Pfortmiller; ALSO WITH: William Ledbetter, Gina Ferrall, Robert Ousley, Christopher Jackson, Nanne Puritz, John Paul Almon, Eric Michael Gillett, Peter Samuel, Deborah Lew.

113. *Canterbury Tales*

Ribald musical comedy, concerning a four-day pilgrimage to Canterbury Cathedral in spring during the late 1300s. The action passes between the Tabard Inn in London and Canterbury Cathedral. The music is in the modern popular idiom, with a Chaucerian flavor.

Before Broadway. It opened at the PHOENIX THEATRE, London, on 3/21/68. 2,080 PERFORMANCES. It was the hit of the London year. DIRECTORS: Vlado Habunek & Martin Starkie; CHOREOGRAPHER: David Drew; SETS: Derek Cousins; COSTUMES: Loudon Sainthill; MUSICAL DIRECTOR: Gordon Rose, *John White, Arthur Tatler, Denys Rawson*; CAST RECORDING on Decca. **Cast**: STEWARD: Wilfred Brambell; ALISON: Gay Soper; CLERK: Billy Boyle; SQUIRE: Nicky Henson; PRIORESS: Pamela Charles, *Patricia Bredin, Marion Grimaldi*; KNIGHT: Trevor Baxter; NUN: Nancy Nevinson, *Jean Challis*; WIFE OF BATH: Jessie Evans; MILLER: Kenneth J. Warren; HOST: Michael Logan. In London The Nun's Priest's Tale came after the Miller's Tale, but was dropped when the show came to Broadway.

The Broadway Run. EUGENE O'NEILL THEATRE, 2/3/69–5/18/69. 5 previews. 122 PERFORMANCES. PRESENTED BY Management Three Productions Ltd (Jerry Weintraub & Martin Kummer) & Frank Productions, Inc. (Frank Loesser & Allen B. Whitehead), by arrangement with Classic Presentations Ltd; MUSIC/ORCHESTRATIONS: Richard Hill & John "Jack" Hawkins; LYRICS: Nevill Coghill; BOOK: Martin Starkie & Nevill Coghill; BASED ON Nevill Coghill's translation of Chaucer; DIRECTOR: Martin Starkie; CHOREOGRAPHER: Sammy Bayes; SETS: Derek Cousins; SET SUPERVISOR: Richard Seger; COSTUMES: Loudon Sainthill; LIGHTING: Jules Fisher; MUSICAL DIRECTOR/VOCAL & DANCE MUSIC ARRANGEMENTS: Oscar Kosarin; CAST RECORDING on Capitol; PRESS: Lee Solters, Harvey B. Sabinson, Jay Russell; CASTING: Esther Feinerman; GENERAL MANAGER: James B. McKenzie; COMPANY MANAGER: Ralph Roseman; PRODUCTION STAGE MANAGER: Elizabeth Caldwell; STAGE MANAGER: Wade Miller; ASSISTANT STAGE MANAGER: Roger Franklin. *Act I*: OVERTURE (Chaucer & Company). THE PILGRIMS: CHAUCER: Martyn Green (3) ✫; HOST: Edwin Steffe (10); MILLER: Roy Cooper (4); WIFE OF BATH: Hermione Baddeley (2) ✫; COOK: David Thomas (16); MERCHANT: Leon Shaw (12); KNIGHT: Reid Shelton (13); STEWARD: George Rose (1) ✫; PRIORESS: Ann Gardner (7); NUN: Evelyn Page (8), *Mary Jo Catlett*; PRIEST: Garnett Smith (11); CLERK OF OXFORD: Bruce Hyde (9); SQUIRE: Ed Evanko (5); FRIAR: Richard Ensslen (14); PARDONER: Garnett Smith (11); SUMMONER: Bert Michaels (15); THE SWEETHEART: Sandy Duncan (6). "Song of Welcome" ("Welcome Song") (Host & Company), "Good Night Hymn" (Company), "Canterbury Day" (Company), "Pilgrim Riding Music" (Company). THE MILLER'S TALE: NICHOLAS: Ed Evanko (5); ALISON: Sandy Duncan (6); CARPENTER: George Rose (1) ✫; ABSALON: Bruce Hyde (9); GERVASE: Roy Cooper (4); ROBIN: Terry Eno; PARISHIONERS: Mary Jo Catlett (*Eleanor Bergquist*) & Suzan Sidney. "I Have a Noble Cock" (Nicholas) [this song is fairly closely translated from the medieval "I have a gentil cock"], "Darling, Let Me Teach You How to Kiss" (Absalon), "There's the Moon" (Nicholas & Alison), "It Depends on What You're At" (Wife of Bath, Nun, Company), "Love Will Conquer All" (Prioress, Village Girl [Suzan Sidney], Company). THE STEWARD'S TALE: MILLER: Roy Cooper (4); MILLER'S WIFE: Evelyn Page (8), *Mary Jo Catlett*; MOLLY: Sandy Duncan (6); ALAN: Ed Evanko (5); JOHN: Bruce Hyde (9). "Beer is Best" (Miller, Miller's Wife, Alan, John, Molly), "Canterbury Day" (reprise) (Company). *Act II*: "Come on and Marry Me, Honey" (Wife of Bath & Company), "Mug Dance" (Company), "Where Are the Girls of Yesterday?" (Host & Company) (danced by Alison, May, Molly). THE MERCHANT'S TALE: JANUARY: George Rose (1) ✫; JUSTINUS: Martyn Green (3) ✫; PLACEBO: Garnett Smith (11); MAY: Sandy Duncan (6); DAMIAN: Ed Evanko (5); PLUTO: Roy Cooper (4); PROSERPINA: Ann Gardner (7); DUENNA: Evelyn Page (8), *Mary Jo Catlett*; PAGE: Tod Miller; BRIDESMAIDS: Patricia Michaels, Marianne Selbert, Karen Kristin, Joyce Maret; ATTENDANTS: Terry Eno, Tod Miller, Gene Myers, Ron Schwinn, Jack Fletcher. "Hymen, Hymen" (Company), "If She Has Never Loved Before" (January), "I'll Give My Love a Ring" (Damian & May), "Pear Tree Quintet" (Damian, January, Pluto, Proserpina, May), "I Am All a-Blaze" (Squire), "Love Pas de Deux" (Pilgrim [Ron Schwinn] & Village Girl [Marianne Selbert]). THE WIFE OF BATH'S TALE: KING: Reid Shelton (13); QUEEN: Ann Gardner (7); OLD WOMAN: Hermione Baddeley (2) ✫; YOUNG KNIGHT: Bruce Hyde (9); EXECUTIONER: Roger Franklin;

COURTIERS: Terry Eno, Ron Schwinn, Tod Miller, Gene Myers; COURT LADIES: Karen Kristin, Marianne Selbert, Joyce Maret, Patricia Michaels; HOUSEWIFE: Mary Jo Catlett; SWEETHEART: Sandy Duncan (6). "What Do Women Want?" (Young Knight & Court Ladies), "April Song" (Company), "Love Will Conquer All" (reprise) (Prioress, Village Girl [Suzan Sidney], Company).

OTHER PILGRIMS/WORKMEN: Terry Eno, Jack Fletcher, Tod Miller, Gene Myers, Ron Schwinn, David Thomas (16); VILLAGE GIRLS: Mary Jo Catlett (*Eleanor Bergquist*), Betsy Dickerson, Karen Kristin, Joyce Maret, Patricia Michaels, Marianne Selbert, Suzan Sidney. **Understudies**: Steward/Carpenter/January: Garnett Smith; Wife of Bath/Old Woman: Evelyn Page, *Mary Jo Catlett*; Chaucer/Justinus: David Thomas; Prioress/Proserpina/Queen: Patricia Michaels; Host: Roger Franklin; Miller/Gervase/Pluto: Dick Ensslen; Nun/Miller's Wife/Duenna: Mary Jo Catlett, *Eleanor Bergquist*; Merchant: Reid Shelton; Clerk/Absalon/John/Young Knight: Terry Eno; Knight/King: Leon Shaw; Squire/Nicholas/Alan/Damian: Jack Fletcher: Summoner: Gene Myers; Sweetheart/Alison/Molly: Karen Kristin; Robin: Tod Miller; Priest/Pardoner/Friar/Placebo: Ron Schwinn.

Broadway reviews were very divided. It was Sandy Duncan's Broadway debut. Frank Loesser, one of the producers, died on 7/28/69, shortly after the show closed at the 5/18/69 matinee. The show won a Tony for costumes, and was also nominated for choreography, sets, and for Sandy Duncan.

After Broadway. TOUR. Opened on 12/29/69, at the Playhouse Theatre, Wilmington, Del., and closed on 4/11/70, at the National Theatre, Washington, DC. PRESENTED BY Hal James; DIRECTOR: James Hammerstein; CHOREOGRAPHER: Tommy Tune; SETS: C. Murawski (redesigned the sets); LIGHTING: Neil Peter Jampolis; MUSICAL DIRECTOR: Richard Parrinello. **Cast**: CHAUCER: Martyn Green; KNIGHT: Reid Shelton; NUN: Mary Jo Catlett; STEWARD/CARPENTER: Ray Walston; WIFE OF BATH: Constance Carpenter; SQUIRE/NICHOLAS: Walter McGinn; CLERK/ABSALON: Terry Eno; PRIORESS: Luce Ennis; MILLER: Patrick Hines; ALISON: Louisa Flaningam. The Nun's Priest's Tale (which had been in the original London production) was re-instated after The Miller's Tale. The number "Chanticleer" (Company) was re-instated with it.

More Canterbury Tales. A piece by the same authors, *More Canterbury Tales*, made up of parts from *Canterbury Tales*, and using some new material, opened up at HER MAJESTY'S THEATRE, Melbourne, Australia, on 10/23/76.

SHAFTESBURY THEATRE, London, 4/24/79–7/27/79. This was a revival of the 1968 original. PRESENTED BY Chanticleer Productions; DIRECTOR: Martin Starkie; CHOREOGRAPHER: Hugh Halliday; SETS: Derek Cousins; COSTUMES: Loudon Sainthill; MUSICAL DIRECTOR: Denys Rawson. **Cast**: HOST: Michael Logan; CHAUCER: Dudley Owen; PRIORESS: Anna Sharkey; MILLER: Percy Herbert; ALISON: Susan Beagley; WIFE OF BATH: Jessie Evans.

114. *Canterbury Tales (Broadway revival)*

Before Broadway. This was an independent revival that began as an Equity Library Theatre production at the MASTER THEATRE, 11/29/79–12/23/79. 30 PERFORMANCES. It had the same crew as for the subsequent Broadway run, except STAGE MANAGER: Sarah Hayden; ASSISTANT STAGE MANAGER: Betsy Nicholson. It had the same cast too, except KNIGHT: David Asher; NUN: Melanie Vaughan (*K.K. Preece* before transfer)

The Broadway Run. RIALTO THEATRE, 2/12/80–2/24/80. 4 previews from 2/8/80. 16 PERFORMANCES. PRESENTED BY Burry Fredrik & Bruce Schwartz, through special arrangement with Music Theatre International; MUSIC: Richard Hill & John "Jack" Hawkins; LYRICS: Nevill Coghill; BOOK: Martin Starkie & Nevill Coghill; BASED ON Nevill Coghill's translation of Chaucer; DIRECTOR: Robert Johanson; CHOREOGRAPHER: Randy Hugill; SETS: Michael Anania; COSTUMES: Sigrid Insull; LIGHTING: Gregg Marriner; MUSICAL DIRECTOR/VOCAL ARRANGEMENTS: John Kroner; PRESS: Shirley Herz, Jan Greenberg, Sam Rudy; GENERAL MANAGER: David Lawlor; PRODUCTION STAGE MANAGER: M.R. Jacobs; STAGE MANAGER: Jim R. Sprague; ASSISTANT STAGE MANAGER: David Asher. **Cast:** THE PILGRIMS: CHAUCER: Earl McCar-

roll; KNIGHT: Robert Stoeckle; SQUIRE: Robert Tetirick; YEOMAN: Andy Ferrell; PRIORESS: Mimi Sherwin; NUN: K.K. Preece; FRIAR: Andrew Traines; MERCHANT: Vance Mizelle; CLERK: Richard Stillman; COOK: Polly Pen; MILLER: Win Atkins; STEWARD: Ted Houck Jr.; WIFE OF BATH: Maureen Sadusk; SUMMONER: Kelly Walters; PARDONER: Martin Walsh; HOST: George Maguire; THE SWEETHEART: Krista Neumann. THE MILLER'S TALE: NICHOLAS: Robert Tetirick; ALISON: Krista Neumann; CARPENTER: Ted Houck Jr.; ABSALON: Kelly Walters; GERVASE: Vance Mizelle; ROBIN: Richard Stillman. THE STEWARD'S TALE: MILLER: Win Atkins; MILLER'S WIFE: Polly Pen; MOLLY: Kaylyn Dillehay; ALAN: Kelly Walters; JOHN: Andy Ferrell; HORSE: Richard Stillman & Robert Tetirick. THE MERCHANT'S TALE: JANUARY: Earl McCarroll; JUSTINUS: Andrew Traines; PLACEBO: Ted Houck Jr.; MAY: Tricia Witham; DAMIAN: Robert Tetirick; PLUTO: George Maguire; PROSERPINA: K.K. Preece; DUENNA: Polly Pen; PAGE: Richard Stillman. THE WIFE OF BATH'S TALE: KING ARTHUR: Andy Ferrell; GUENEVERE: Kaylyn Dillehay; OLD WOMAN: Maureen Sadusk; EXECUTIONER: Martin Walsh; SWEETHEART: Krista Neumann. *Understudies*: Damian/Executioner/Justinus: David Asher; Host/Knight/Squire: David Asher; Pardoner/Friar/Pluto/Nicholas: David Asher; Clerk/Robin/Page: Andy Ferrell; Horse: David Asher & Andy Ferrell; Chaucer/January: George Maguire; Molly/Alison/May: Kim Morgan; Cook/Guenevere/Sweetheart/Miller's Wife/Duenna: Kim Morgan; Nun/Prioress/Proserpina: Polly Pen; Wife of Bath/Old Woman: K.K. Preece; Yeoman/Summoner/John: Richard Stillman; King Arthur/Absalon/Alan: Richard Stillman; Steward/Carpenter/Placebo: Martin Walsh; Merchant/Miller: Andrew Traines. *Orchestra*: PERCUSSION: William Strauss; BASS: Zev Katz; TRUMPETS: Robert Sayer & Joseph Schufle; TROMBONE: Steven Calia; KEYBOARD: John Kroner; GUITAR: Robert Felstein. *Act I*: *Prologue* (Chaucer & Company); *Scene 1* Tabard Inn: "Welcome Song" (Host & Company), "Goodnight Hymn" (Company), "Canterbury Day" (Company); *Scene 2* On the road: "Horse Ride" (Company); *Scene 3* The Miller's Tale (with the Carpenter; his young wife Alison; the noble Nicholas; the lovesick Absalon; the blacksmith Gervase; and the clumsy servant Robin): "I Have a Noble Cock" (Nicholas), "There's the Moon" (Nicholas & Alison), "Darling, Let Me Teach You How to Kiss" (Absalon); *Scene 4* On the road: "It Depends on What You're At" (Wife of Bath, Nun, Company); *Scene 5* The Steward's Tale (with the Miller & his Wife; their daughter Molly; the young swains Alan & John; and their Horse): "Beer is Best" (Miller, Miller's Wife, Molly, Alan, John); *Scene 6* The road: "Love Will Conquer All" (Prioress, Nun, Company), "Canterbury Day" (reprise) (Company). *Act II*: *Scene 1* The road: "Come on and Marry Me, Honey" (Wife of Bath & Company), "Where Are the Girls of Yesterday?" (sung by Host) (danced by Alison, May, Molly); *Scene 2* The Merchant's Tale (with old January and his virgin bride May; the lords Placebo & Justinus; the lovelorn Damian; the clumsy Page; the wise Duenna; and Pluto and Proserpina, god and goddess of the Underworld): "April Song" (Company), "If She Has Never Loved Before" (January & May), "I'll Give My Love a Ring" (Damian & May), "Pear Tree Sextet" (January, May, Damian, Pluto, Proserpina, Merchant); *Scene 3* The Wife of Bath's Tale (with King Arthur & Queen Guenevere; the Knight; an Old Woman; the Executioner; and the Sweetheart: "What Do Women Most Desire?" (Knight & Ladies), "I Am All Ablaze" (sung by Knight to Sweetheart) (danced by Arthur & Guenevere); *Scene 4* Canterbury: "Love Will Conquer All" (Prioress, Nun, Company).
Reviews were generally not good.

115. *The Capeman*

A musical drama. Based on a true incident in the life of Salvador Agron, known as "The Capeman," a 16-year-old Puerto Rican gangster from Queens who, in 1959, killed two teenagers in a New York playground in the infamous Hell's Kitchen district. He was sentenced to the electric chair, the youngest person ever to be accorded this honor, but his sentence was commuted to life. While in prison he underwent a religious conversion, and became a poet. After 21 years in prison he was released by Governor Nelson Rockefeller, and died in 1986. Set in Puerto Rico, NYC, and the Arizona desert, 1949–79. Tony Hernandez, known as The Umbrella Man, was Sal's accomplice.

Before Broadway. In 1996 the show was workshopped twice. The first workshop was directed by Susana Tubert. In the summer of 1996 Eric Simonson replaced Miss Tubert, and he directed the second workshop in 12/96. Choreographer Mark Morris found the workshop to be undisciplined, and in late 1/97 found himself replacing Eric Simonson as director. Paul Simon wrote 36 songs for this show, and on 11/18/97 a CD sampler was released, "Songs From *The Capeman*." The scheduled Broadway opening date of fall 1997 was put back. There was no out-of-town tryout. During Broadway previews it was rumored that Nicholas Hytner was coming aboard as the new director, but instead Jerry Zaks came in to help Mark Morris with the direction, and Joey McKneely came in to help Mr. Morris with the choreography. James Lada, assistant director, left before Broadway. The show was shortened by half an hour. The official opening date was put back from 1/8/98 to 1/29/98.

The Broadway Run. MARQUIS THEATRE, 1/29/98–3/28/98. 59 previews from 12/1/97. 68 PERFORMANCES. PRESENTED BY Plenaro Productions (Dan Klores, Brad Grey, Edgar Dobie), James L. Nederlander, in association with Dreamworks Records & King World Productions; MUSIC: Paul Simon; LYRICS/BOOK: Paul Simon & Derek Walcott; DIRECTOR/CHOREOGRAPHER: Mark Morris; ADDITIONAL CHOREOGRAPHY: Joey McKneely; SETS/COSTUMES: Bob Crowley; LIGHTING: Natasha Katz; SOUND: Peter J. Fitzgerald; MUSICAL DIRECTOR: Oscar Hernandez; ORCHESTRATIONS: Stanley Silverman; CAST RECORDING on Dreamworks (unreleased); PRESS: Boneau/Bryan-Brown; CASTING: Bernard Telsey; GENERAL MANAGEMENT: Nina Lannan Associates; COMPANY MANAGER: Devin M. Keudell; STAGE MANAGERS: Malcolm Ewen, Fredric H. Orner, Valerie Lau-Kee Lai. *Cast*: SALVADOR AGRON (AGES 36 TO 42): Ruben Blades; CARLOS APACHE: Julio Monge; ANGEL SOTO: Raymond Rodriguez; FRENCHY CORDERO: Ray Rodriguez-Rosa; BABU CHARLIE CRUZ: Lugo; TONY HERNANDEZ: Renoly Santiago; SAL AGRON (AGES 16 TO 20): Marc Anthony; ESMERALDA AGRON, SAL'S MOTHER: Ednita Nazario; SANTERO: Ray de la Paz [during previews Nestor Sanchez played this role, as well as that of Lazarus]; LAZARUS: Nestor Sanchez; CARMEN: Claudette Sierra [role cut during previews]; YOLANDA: Natascia A. Diaz; REV. GONZALEZ: Philip Hernandez; AUREA AGRON (AGES 17 TO 43): Michelle Rios; BERNADETTE: Sophia Salguero; COOKIE: Elan; DOO-WOP GROUP: Milton Cardona, Ray de la Paz, Myrna Lynn Gomila, Roger Mazzeo, Frank Negron, Yassmin Alers, Kia Joy Goodwin; MRS. YOUNG: Cass Morgan; MRS. KRZESINSKI: Luba Mason; WAHZINAK: Sara Ramirez; 1ST INMATE: John Lathan; VIRGIL, A GUARD: Stephen Lee Anderson; THE WARDEN: John Jellison; LUIS: Jose Joaquin Garcia; MC: Ray de la Paz; SALVI AGRON, AGE 7: Evan Jay Newman; AUREA AGRON, AGE 8: Tara Ann Villanueva; CHILDREN'S CHOIR: Evan Jay Newman, Sebastian Perez, Khalid Rivera, Amanda A. Vacharat, Tara Ann Villanueva; ENSEMBLE: Yassmin Alers, Stephen Lee Anderson, Milton Cardona, Rene M. Ceballos, Tony Chiroldes, Ray de la Paz, Elan, Jose Joaquin Garcia, Myrna Lynn Gomila, Kia Joy Goodwin, Elise Hernandez, John Jellison, John Lathan, Lugo, Luba Mason, Roger Mazzeo, Claudia Montiel, Marisol Morales, Frank Negron, Evan Jay Newman, Sebastian Perez, Mark Price, Sara Ramirez, Khalid Rivera, Ray Rodriguez-Rosa, Raymond Rodriguez, Ramon Saldana, Claudette Sierra, Amanda A. Vacharat, Tara Ann Villanueva. *Understudies*: Salvador/mc: Jose Joaquin Garcia; Carlos: Jason Martinez & Raymond Rodriguez; Sal/Tony: Lugo & Jason Martinez; Angel/Frenchie/Babu Charlie: Jason Martinez & Mark Price; Bernadette: Yassmin Alers & Kia Joy Goodwin; Yolanda/Aurea: Yassmin Alers & Lada Boder; Cookie: Myrna Lynn Gomilla & Kia Joy Goodwin; Mrs. Young: Lada Boder & Rene Ceballos; Mrs. Krzesinski/Wahzinak: Lada Boder; Lazarus: Stephen Lee Anderson & Ray de la Paz; Inmate: Ray de la Paz; Warden: Tony Chiroldes & Osborn Focht; Rev: Ramon Saldana & Ray de la Paz; Esmeralda: Rene Ceballos; Salvi, age 7: Sebastian Perez; Aurea, age 8: Amanda A. Vacharat; Carmen: Elise Hernandez & Marisol Morales [role cut during previews]; Virgil: Roger Mazzeo & Osborn Focht. *Swings*: Lada Boder, Osborn Focht, Jason Martinez. *Act I*: NEW YORK CITY—1979: "El Coqui" (Children's Choir & Salvador) [cut during previews], "Mama, It's Sal" (Salvador) [new during previews], "Puerto Rican Day Parade" [this number shifted to Act II before Broadway opening—see below],

"Born in Puerto Rico" (Salvador, Sal, Carlos, Angel, Frenchy, Baby Charlie, Tony, Rev. Gonzalez, Lazarus). PUERTO RICO—EARLY 1950S: "In Mayaguez" (Salvador, Esmeralda, Nuns, Children), "Carmen" (Esmeralda) [this was a cut down version of the song; during previews it was sung by Esmeralda & Carmen. The original was recorded on the cast album], "The Santero" (Lazarus, Esmeralda, Celebrants), "Chimes" (Esmeralda), "Christmas in the Mountains" (Three Kings, Carmen, Esmeralda, Guests) [cut during previews, but recorded on cast album]. NEW YORK CITY—1959: "Satin Summer Nights" (Sal, Bernadette, Cookie, Tony, Doo-Wop Group), "Bernadette" (Sal, Bernadette, Doo-Wop Group), "The Vampires" (Tony, Sal, Carlos, Angel, Frenchy, Baby Charlie, Doo-Wop Group), "Shopliftin' Clothes" (Sal, Tony, Sales Clerks, Carlos, Doo-Wop Group), "Dance to a Dream" (Carlos, Yolanda, Bernadette, Sal), "Quality" (Bernadette, Yolanda, Cookie, Sal, Salvador, Doo-Wop Group), "Manhunt" (Salvador, Carlos, Sal, Tony, Ensemble), "Can I Forgive Him" (Esmeralda), "Adios Hermanos" (Sal, Salvador, Aurea, Tony, Bernadette, Yolanda, Lazarus, Ensemble). NEW YORK CITY—1962 [this scene shifted to Act I Scene 1 for Broadway]: "Jesus es mi Senor" [this number shifted to Act II for Broadway]. *Act II*: "Christmas in the Mountains" (instrumental introduction). NEW YORK CITY—1962 [new position for this scene]: "Jesus es Mi Senor" (Congregants, Rev. Gonzalez, Esmeralda, Aurea, Bernadette, Yolanda, Lazarus) [new position for this number]. NEW YORK CITY—1963: "Sunday Afternoon" (Esmeralda). VARIOUS PRISONS IN NEW YORK STATE, 1963–1976: "Time is an Ocean" (Sal, Salvador, Esmeralda). FISHKILL PRISON, 1976–1977: "Wahzinak's First Letter" (Wahzinak), "Killer Wants to Go to College" (1st Inmate, Warden, Inmates), "Virgil" (Virgil & Warden), "Wahzinak's Letter Duet" (Salvador & Wahzinak), "My Only Defense" (Sal) [this number and the preceding one were the other way around during previews], "Virgil and the Warden" (Virgil, Salvador, Warden), "Manhunt" (instrumental" [cut during previews], "Trailways Bus" (Lazarus, Wahzinak, Salvador, Border Patrolman) [this number was cut during previews]. THE DESERT, ARIZONA; 1977: "Trailways Bus" (instrumental) [inserted here for Broadway], "The Mission" (Salvador, Salvi, Young Aurea, Esmeralda) [cut early during previews], "El Malecon" (Esmeralda), "Children's Chimes" (Salvi, Young Aurea, Rev. Gonzalez, Orphans) [number cut during previews], "You Fucked up My Life" (Angel, Babu Charlie, Sal, Tony, Frenchy, Salvador, Doo-Wop Group), "Lazarus"/"Last Drop of Blood" (Lazarus, Salvador, Mrs. Young, Ensemble), "Wahzinak's Last Letter" (Wahzinak). NEW YORK CITY—1979: "El Coqui" (Children's Choir & Salvador) [during previews this was a reprise], "Puerto Rican Day Parade" (Parade Singers & Ensemble) [new position for this number], "Tony Hernandez" (Salvador & Tony), "Carlos and Yolanda" (mc, Aurea, Salvador, Carlos, Yolanda, Ensemble), "Sal's Last Song" (Salvador & Esmeralda), "Esmeralda's Dream" (Esmeralda, Sal, Doo-Wop Group).

On opening night, the families of Agron's victims picketed the theatre. Broadway reviews were almost universally negative, and it lost nearly all of its $11 million investment. On closing night Paul Simon addressed the audience, and draped himself in the Puerto Rican flag. The show received Tony nominations for score, sets, and orchestrations

116. *Carib Song*

A musical tragedy, done in Pidgin English. Set in a small West Indian village. The Woman, a corn farmer's wife, being pursued by the Fisherman, gives the Husband the runaround and suffers the usual revenge. The word "Shango" means John the Baptist, and is a religious ritual combining old African elements and Catholic ones.

The Broadway Run. ADELPHI THEATRE, 9/27/45–10/27/45. 36 PERFORMANCES. PRESENTED BY George Stanton; MUSIC/DIRECTOR OF THE SINGING ENSEMBLE: Baldwin "Beau" Bergersen; LYRICS/BOOK: William Archibald; DIRECTORS: Katherine Dunham & Mary Hunter; BOOK DIRECTOR: Mary Hunter; CHOREOGRAPHER: Katherine Dunham; SETS/LIGHTING: Jo Mielziner; COSTUMES: Motley; MUSICAL DIRECTOR: Pembroke Davenport; ORCHESTRATIONS: Ted Royal; PRESS: Karl Bernstein & Martha Dreiblatt; GENERAL MANAGER: Jesse Long; STAGE MANAGER: William Lilling. *Cast:* THE SINGER: Harriett Jackson; THE

FRIENDS: Eulabel Riley & Mary Lewis [she later became Mary Rio Lewis]; THE FAT WOMAN: Mable Sanford Lewis; THE TALL WOMAN: Mercedes Gilbert; THE HUSBAND: William Franklin; THE FISHERMAN: Avon Long; THE WOMAN: Katherine Dunham; THE FISHWOMAN: Elsie Benjamin; THE MADRAS SELLER: Byron Cuttler; THE SHANGO PRIEST: La Rosa Estrada; THE BOY POSSESSED BY A SNAKE: Tommy Gomez; LEADERS OF THE SHANGO DANCERS: Vanoye Aikens & Lucille Ellis; THE VILLAGE FRIENDS: James Alexander, Eddy Clay, Norman Coker, Byron Cuttler, John Diggs, Lucille Ellis, Roxie Foster, Jesse Hawkins, Lauwane Ingram, Richardena Jackson, Eartha Kitt, Ora Leak, Mary Lewis, Julio Mendez, Gloria Mitchell, Lenwood Morris, Eulabel Riley, Eugene Lee Robinson, Priscilla Stevens, William C. Smith, Charles Welch, Enid Williams; THE KATHERINE DUNHAM DANCERS: Lucille Ellis, Lenwood Morris, Tommy Gomez, Vanoye Aikens, Lawaune Ingram, Richardena Jackson, Gloria Mitchell, Ora Leak, Eddy Clay, Byron Cuttler, James Alexander, Roxie Foster, Eugene Lee Robinson, Eartha Kitt, Jesse Hawkins, Enid Williams; NATIVE DRUMMERS: La Rosa Estrada, Julio Mendez, Norman Coker; SINGING ENSEMBLE: Mary Lewis, Eulabel Riley, Priscilla Stevens, John Diggs, William C. Smith, Charles Welch. *Act I*: *Scene 1* The wake: "Go Sit by the Body" (chant) (Company), "Legba" (dance) (Mr. Welch & Company), "This Woman" (Husband, Mr. Smith, Mr. Welch, Company); *Scene 2* Early morning by the river: "Water Movin' Slow" (Husband); *Scene 3* The new house: "Basket, Make a Basket" (Miss Dunham) (danced by Miss Ellis, Miss Ingram, Miss Jackson, Mr. Gomez, Mr. Morris, Mr. Aikens. Sung by Miss Kitt, Girl Singers, Male Singers, Mr. Hawkins); *Scene 4* The corn sorting: "Congo Paillette" (dance) (Woman & Company), "Woman is a Rascal" (Fisherman, Mr. Smith, Mr. Welch); *Scene 5* The lie: "A Girl She Can't Remain" (Woman, Shango Priest, Madras Seller, Mr. Alexander); *Scene 6* The road to the Shango; *Scene 7* The Shango: Shango Ritual (Shango Priest, Boy Possessed by Snake, Woman, Fisherman, Male Leader of Shango Dancers, Company). *Act II—* Three months later: *Scene 1* Market. Dry season: "Market Song" (dance) (Fat Woman & Company), "Sleep Baby, Don't Cry" (The Singer), "Things Remembered" (Woman, Miss Ellis, Miss Jackson, Miss Leak, Mr. Estrada, Miss Ingram, Mr. Aikens, Miss Mitchell, Mr. Morris); *Scene 2* "Today I is So Happy" (Husband), "Can't Stop the Sea" (Mr. Diggs); *Scene 3* The forest at night: Forest at Night (Woman & Messrs Morris, Aikens, Alexander, Cuttler, Gomez); *Scene 4* "Go to Church, Sunday": "You Know, O Lord" (Husband), "Go to Church Sunday" (Company); *Scene 5* "Wash Clothes, Monday": "Go Down to the River" (Girl Singers & Fat Woman), Washerwomen Dance (Dunham Girl Dancers), "Oh, Lonely One" (Woman & The Singer); *Scene 6* The rain comes.

The show got divided reviews. It lost $150,000.

117. *Caribbean Carnival*

Pamela Ward (the only white performer in cast) played a photographer trying to get into a voodoo ceremony in Trinidad, and guided by a native policeman (played by Sam Manning). Claude Marchant & the dancers did voodoo numbers. The Duke of Iron (real name: Cecil Anderson) was then New York's leading calypso singer.

Before Broadway. Originally called *S.S. Calypso*, then *Calypso*, then *Bongo*, this revue was the first ever calypso musical. It tried out in Philadelphia and Boston, and its Broadway opening date had to be put back from 11/28/47 due to a labor dispute. Several numbers were cut: "Ice Cream Brick" (Miss Premice), "Ugly Woman" (Duke), "Matilda" (Duke), "Peas and Rice" (Smith Kids), "When You're Dead You Don't Know," "Love Sweet Love."

The Broadway Run. INTERNATIONAL THEATRE, 12/5/47–12/13/47. 11 PERFORMANCES. PRESENTED BY Adolph Thenstead; MUSIC/LYRICS: Samuel L. Manning & Adolph Thenstead; BOOK: uncredited; DIRECTOR: Samuel L. Manning; ASSOCIATE DIRECTOR: Col. John J. Hirshman; CHOREOGRAPHERS: Pearl Primus & Claude Marchant; SETS: Herbert Brodkin; COSTUMES: Lou Eisele; MUSICAL DIRECTOR/ORCHESTRATIONS: Ken Macomber; DRUM RHYTHMS: Mario Castillo; PRESS: Bill Doll & Dick Williams; GENERAL MANAGER: Rex Connor; COMPANY MANAGER:

Sam C. Brin; GENERAL STAGE MANAGER: Pat Leonard. *Act I*: Overture: "Fantasia Calypso" (Orchestra); *Scene 1* Carnival in Trinidad: SERGEANT SQUASHIE: Sam Manning (5); PRESS PHOTOGRAPHER: Pamela Ward (7); A NATIVE: Eddie Talifferro. *Scene 2* Duke of Iron (4), Josephine Premice (2), Peggy Watson, Eddie Talifferro. Songs: "America, the Great," "Marabella" (each year the carnival spirit takes possession of everyone on the quaint little island of Trinidad, and the population swarms to the public places to make merry — and say just what they have been thinking about their neighbors, through the age-old medium of Calypso, as in the case of Marabella), "Pretty"; *Scene 3* Native Songs (Smith Kids) (6) (boy and girl singers); *Scene 4* The Claude Marchant Dance Group (ch: Claude Marchant) [featuring Claude Marchant (3) & Billie Allen; also with Jacqueline Hairston, Marjorie James, Donald Curtis, James Brown]. Native dances. "Enlloro" ("Voodoo Moon") (m: Morales-Blanco), "Canto de las Palmas" ("Chant of the Palms") (m: Paquita Anderson); *Scene 5* Trio Cubana (8); *Scene 6* Bribe for an Officer [Sam Manning (5) & Pamela Ward (7)]; *Scene 7* Firefly Dance (fireflies of the Bayou, scattered by a bat, return in friendliness) (Miss Eloise Hill & Dancers); *Scene 8* Comedy Skit: Love in the Dark. "Love, Love, Love"; *Scene 9* "Anything Goes When You Sing Calypso" [Pamela Ward (7)]; *Scene 10* Market Scene: a/ Smith Kids (6), b/ Washerwoman, c/ "Stone Cold Dead in the Market" [Duke of Iron (4)], d/ Claude Marchant (3) & Group; Finale. *Act II*: *Scene 1* "Rookombay" ("Voodoo Night") [Pearl Primus (1)], "Don't Stop the Carnival" (Calypso) (Company); *Scene 2* "Hold 'em, Joe" (Calypso): FAT WOMAN: Peggy Watson; DONKEY: Alex Young; SINGERS: Smith Kids (6); CALYPSO DANCERS: Gem Bolling, Dorothy Graham, Eloise Hill, Curtis James, Andre King, Paul Meeres, Lillie Pearce, Charles Queenan, Bernard Taylor, Mildred Thomas, Alex Young; Gregory Felix & The Caribbean Calypso Band; *Scene 3* "Rookombay" ("Voodoo Night") (Shango — an interpretation of an old legend) (chant music: Duke of Iron) (ch: Pearl Primus): SERPENT TOTEM: Curtis James; GUARDS: Alex Young, Curtis James, Padjet Fredericks; SINGER: Fred Thomas; SHANGO WOMAN: Pearl Primus (1); DANCERS: Gem Bolling, Dorothy Graham, Eloise Hill, Lillie Pearce, Mildred Thomas, Curtis James, Andre King, Charles Queenan, Alex Young, Padjet Fredericks; CHORUS: Helen Carr, Clara Hubbard, Dorothy Macdavid, Wahnetta San, Fannie Turner, Clifton Gray, Louis Sterling, Fred Thomas; *Scene 4* "Cleaning Up Song" (Helen Carr, Fred Thomas, Company); *Scene 5* "Tease for Two" (Gem Bolling & Curtis James); *Scene 6* "Tamboule" (Stick Fight) (Alex Young & Curtis James); *Scene 7* Exultation: SHANGO WOMAN: Pearl Primus (1); *Scene 8* At Bay (m: Camilla de Leon): GUARDS: Alex Young, Curtis James, Padjet Fredericks; SHANGO WOMAN: Pearl Primus (1); *Scene 9* Celebration: WOMEN POSSESSED: Eloise Hill & Dorothy Graham; MAN POSSESSED: Charles Queenan; SHANGO WOMAN: Pearl Primus (1); DRUMMERS: Alphonse Cimber, Bernard Taylor, Paul Meeres; *Scene 10* Sam Manning (5) & Pamela Ward (7); *Scene 12* Native Café Scene [Josephine Premice (2) & Entire Company].

ENSEMBLE: Clifton Gray, Clara Hubbard, William Johnson, Dorothy Macdavid, Louis Sterling, Jerry Meeres, Wahnetta San, Helen Tinsley, Fannie Turner.

Broadway reviews were mostly terrible. There was a tour, with Claude Marchant

118. *Carmelina*

During the War there was a romance between an American soldier and an Italian girl. Twenty years later, three ex–GIs find that they've all been paying child support to the same child in Southern Italy. Set in 1961, somewhere in Italy.

Before Broadway. Alan Jay Lerner started this one, then asked Joseph Stein to join him. It had two tryouts, but made few changes; Maurice Levine was replaced as musical director by Don Jennings (Mr. Levine's vocal arrangements were left in). It ran at the Kennedy Center, Washington, DC, 3/7/79–3/24/79.

The Broadway Run. ST. JAMES THEATRE, 4/8/79–4/21/79. 11 previews. 17 PERFORMANCES. A Whitehead — Stevens production, PRESENTED BY Roger L. Stevens, J.W. Fisher, Joan Cullman, Jujamcyn Productions; MUSIC: Burton Lane; LYRICS: Alan Jay Lerner; BOOK: Alan Jay Lerner &

Joseph Stein; BASED ON the 1968 movie *Buona Sera, Mrs. Campbell* (uncredited, and denied by Alan Jay Lerner); DIRECTOR: Jose Ferrer; CHOREOGRAPHER: Peter Gennaro; SETS: Oliver Smith; COSTUMES: Donald Brooks; LIGHTING: Feder; SOUND: John McClure; MUSICAL DIRECTOR: Don Jennings; ORCHESTRATIONS: Hershy Kay; VOCAL ARRANGEMENTS: Maurice Levine; DANCE MUSIC ARRANGEMENTS: David Krane; PRESS: Jeffrey Richards; CASTING: Terry Fay; ASSISTANT TO ALAN JAY LERNER: Jenifer Lerner; GENERAL MANAGER: Oscar E. Olesen; COMPANY MANAGER: David Hedges; PRODUCTION STAGE MANAGER: William Dodds; STAGE MANAGER: Jay Adler; ASSISTANT STAGE MANAGER: Donnis Honeycutt. **Cast:** BELLINI: Marc Jordan (11); MAYOR NUNZIO MANZONI: Gonzalo Madurga (9); VITTORIO BRUNO: Cesare Siepi (2) ✫; ROSA: Grace Keagy (7); SALVATORE: Ian Towers; SIGNORA CARMELINA CAMPBELL: Georgia Brown (1) ✫; SIGNORA BERNARDI: Judy Sabo; ROBERTO BONAFACCIO: Joseph D'Angerio (10); FATHER TOMMASO: Frank Bouley; GIA CAMPBELL: Josie de Guzman (8); WALTER BRADDOCK: Gordon Ramsey (4); STEVE KARZINSKI: Howard Ross (5); CARLTON SMITH: John Michael King (3); FLO BRADDOCK: Virginia Martin (6); MILDRED KARZINSKI: Kita Bouroff; KATHERINE SMITH: Caryl Tenney; FATHER FEDERICO: David E. Thomas (12); ENSEMBLE: Frank Bouley, Kita Bouroff, Kathryn Carter, Karen Di Bianco, Spence Ford, Ramon Galindo, Liza Gennaro, Laura Klein, Michael Lane, Morgan Richardson, Judy Sabo, Charles Spoerri, Caryl Tenney, David E. Thomas, Ian Michael Towers, Kevin Wilson, Lee Winston. **Standby:** Carmelina: Lorraine Serabian. **Understudies:** Vittorio: Howard Ross; Braddock/Smith: Frank Bouley; Gia: Debra Matthews; Roberto: Michael Rivera; Rosa/Mildred/Katherine: Judy Sabo; Manzoni: Marc Jordan; Karzinski/Bellini: Charles Spoerri; Flo: Kita Bouroff. **Swing Dancers**: Debra Matthews & Michael Rivera. *Act I*: *Scene 1* The piazza of San Forino; "It's Time for a Love Song" (Vittorio), "Why Him?" (Carmelina & Vittorio), "I Must Have Her" (Vittorio); *Scene 2* In Carmelina's house; a short time later: "Someone in April" (Carmelina) [the melody for this song was written for *On a Clear Day You Can See Forever*], "Signora Campbell" (Rosa, Carmelina, Father Tommaso, Mayor, Townspeople); *Scene 3* The piazza; the wee hours of the following morning: "Love Before Breakfast" (Carmelina & Vittorio); *Scene 4* The piazza; late morning, the following day: "Yankee Doodles Are Coming to Town" (Townspeople); *Scene 5* Carmelina's house; a short time later: *Scene 6* The piazza; later: "One More Walk Around the Garden" (Braddock, Karzinski, Smith), "All that He'd Want Me to Be" (Gia & Friends); *Scene 7* Carmelina's house; late that night: "It's Time for a Love Song" (reprise) (Vittorio). *Act II*: *Scene 1* The piazza; early the following morning: "Carmelina" (Vittorio), "The Image of Me" (Braddock, Karzinski, Smith); *Scene 2* Carmelina's house; immediately following; *Scene 3* A church; *Scene 4* Carmelina's house; immediately following: "I'm a Woman" (Carmelina); *Scene 5* The piazza; immediately following: "The Image of You" (Flo & Braddock), "It's Time for a Love Song" (reprise) (Carmelina).

It got bad reviews on Broadway, and closed at a loss of over $1 million. A recording was done after the show, but Cesare Siepi refused any part in it. His role (at that recording) was taken by Paul Sorvino. It has been said that the show failed because of its direction more than anything else. It received a Tony nomination for score.

After Broadway. The YORK THEATRE COMPANY staged a revised revival (now called *Someone in April*), as part of the *Musicals in Mufti* stage-reading series. 9/20/96–9/22/96. 5 PERFORMANCES. ADDITIONAL LYRICS: Barry Harman; DIRECTOR: Michael Leeds; MUSICAL DIRECTOR: Barry Levitt. **Cast**: CARMELINA: Debbie Gravitte; VITTORIO: P.J. Benjamin; CARLETON: Allen Fitzpatrick; WALTER: Daniel Marcus; MAYOR: David Brummel; FLO: Rebecca Judd; STEVE: Tom Flagg; GIA: Gretchen Weiss. "Prayer/Carmelina," "Why Him?," "Someone in April," "Signora Campbell," "You're a Woman," "Love Me Tomorrow," "One More Walk Around the Garden," "All that I Dreamed He Would Be," "It's Time for a Love Song," "The Image of Me," "I Will Kill Her," "Sorry as I Am," "The Image of You," Finale.

119. *Carmen Jones*

Carmen, a worker in a parachute factory in the South, during World War II, is arrested when, because of her flirtations, she gets into a fight with one of the other girls, and stabs her. She is placed in the custody of MP corporal Joe, who protects the factory. She seduces him at Billy Pastor's Café, he leaves his girl Cindy Lou, and goes AWOL as they fly to Chicago. Here Husky, a prizefighter, is to fight Poncho, a Latin American champion. Carmen goes for Husky, but Joe goes after her, killing her with a knife outside the sports stadium, and then killing himself, as we hear the crowd inside the stadium cheering for Husky. Oscar Hammerstein's English rendition updated the story from a Spanish cigarette factory, and Don Jose the soldier became Joe, but Mr. Hammerstein kept to the score faithfully, except that he changed the order of a few songs. Bizet's Spanish gypsies became blacks, the inn a night club, the smugglers' den a black country club, and the bullring a prize ring. The matador Escamillo, Don Jose's successful rival for Carmen, became the boxer Husky. The recitatives between arias were cut in favor of spoken dialogue. Cindy Lou (Micaela in the original) is a country girl who loves Joe.

Before Broadway. In 1934 Oscar Hammerstein II was listening to a concert version of Bizet's opera *Carmen* when it occurred to him that if the words were easily understood it would be more enjoyable to audiences. He thought it might make a good movie, and it might have, but with its racial content it couldn't have been produced in the 1930s. Before *Oklahoma!* Mr. Hammerstein began writing *Carmen Jones*. In re-doing the opera he adhered as closely as possible to the original form. All the melodies, with a few minor exceptions, are sung in their accustomed order. After *Oklahoma!* Mr. Hammerstein sent it out to several producers, who all turned it down. Max Gordon was going to produce, but didn't renew his option on the property, and Billy Rose stepped in. Because of the demands on the performers, two sets of leads were cast, one for evenings and one for matinees. Most of the actors in the all-black cast were making their professional debuts (Muriel Smith, in the lead, was a Philadelphia camera store clerk in real life. Luther Saxon was a checker in the Philadelphia Navy Yard. Glenn Bryant was a New York policeman). It tried out at the Erlanger, Philadelphia, for three weeks, then went to the Boston Opera House for 2½ weeks.

The Broadway Run. BROADWAY THEATRE, 12/2/43–2/10/45. 503 PERFORMANCES. PRESENTED BY Billy Rose; MUSIC: Georges Bizet; LYRICS/BOOK: Oscar Hammerstein II; BASED ON Henri Meilhac & Ludovic Halevy's 1875 operatic libretto for Bizet's *Carmen*, a libretto which in turn was based on the 1845 novel *Carmen*, by Prosper Merimee; DIRECTOR/LIGHTING: Hassard Short; BOOK DIRECTOR: Charles Friedman; CHOREOGRAPHER: Eugene Loring; SETS: Howard Bay; COSTUMES: Raoul Pene du Bois; MUSICAL DIRECTOR: Joseph Littau; NEW ORCHESTRAL ARRANGEMENTS: Robert Russell Bennett; CHORAL DIRECTOR: Robert Shaw; CAST RECORDING on Decca; DIRECTOR OF PUBLICITY: Wolfe Kaufman; TALENT SCOUT: John Hammond Jr.; GENERAL MANAGER: Robert Milford; PRODUCTION STAGE MANAGER: B.D. Kranz; ASSISTANT STAGE MANAGERS: David Morton & Wilson Williams. **Cast:** CORPORAL MORRELL: Napoleon Reed, Robert Clarke (Wednesday & Saturday matinees); FOREMAN: Robert Clarke, George Willis (matinees); CINDY LOU: Carlotta Franzell (4), Elton J. Warren (matinees); SERGEANT BROWN: Jack Carr; JOE: Luther Saxon (2), Napoleon Reed (matinees); CARMEN JONES: Muriel Smith (1), Muriel Rahn (matinees); SALLY: Sibol Cain; T-BONE: Edward Roche; TOUGH KID: William Jones; DRUMMER: Cozy Cole; BARTENDER: Melvin Howard; WAITER: Edward Christopher; FRANKIE: June Hawkins; MYRT: Jessica Russell; RUM: Edward Lee Tyler; DINK: Dick Montgomery; HUSKY MILLER: Glenn Bryant (3); MR. HIGGINS: P. Jay Sidney; MISS HIGGINS: Fredye Marshall; PHOTOGRAPHER: Alford Pierre; CARD PLAYERS: Urylee Leonardos, Ethel White, Sibol Cain; DANCING GIRL IN *Cuba Libre Club*: Ruth Crumpton; PONCHO: William Dillard; DANCING BOXERS: Sheldon B. Hoskins & Randolph Sawyer; BULLET HEAD: Melvin Howard; REFEREE: Tony Fleming Jr.; SOLDIERS: Robert Clarke, William Woolfolk, George Willis, Elijah Hodges, *Randall Steplight*; BOY: J. Flashe Riley; GIRL: Royce Wallace; CHILDREN: E. Drayton, L. Drayton, Melvin Duncan, Oliver Hamilton, James Holman, Gilbert Irvis, David Lee, Carlos Van Putten, Delano Vanterpool, LeRoy Westfall, *Albert Bailey, Robert Bailey, Richard*

Granady, Joe Green, William Jones, Arthur Rames, Robert Smith; DANCERS: Valerie Black, Al Bledger, Tony Fleming Jr., Posie Flowers, J. Prioreau Gray, Frank Green, Erona Harris, Mabel Hart, Sheldon B. Hoskins, Richard James, Rhoda Johnson, Dorothy McNichols, Vera McNichols, Frank Neal, Betty Nichols, Joseph Noble, Bill O'Neil, Evelyn Pilcher, J. Flashe Riley, Edith Ross, Randolph Sawyer, Randolph Scott, Royce Wallace, Dorothy Williams. *Edward Christopher, Carmencita Romero, Daniel Lloyd, Audrey Graham*; ENSEMBLE: Lee Allen, Viola Anderson, William Archer, Willie May Bourne, Miriam Burton, Oliver Busch, Sibol Cain, Robert Clarke, Clarisse Crawford, Ruth Crumpton, William Davis, Richard de Vaultier, Edwina Divers, Anne Dixon, George Dosher, Marguerite Duncan, Awilda Frasier, Mary Graham, Elijah Hodges, Melvin Howard, Clarence Jones, Elsie Kennedy, Urylee Leonardos, Fredye Marshall, Maithe Marshall, Alford Pierre, Bertha Powell, Fred Randall, Chauncey Reynolds, Edward Roche, Mildred Saffold, Randall Steplight, Andrew Taylor, Harold Taylor, Ethel White, Mattie Washington, George Willis, Robert Woodland, *Howard Carter, Hubert Dilworth, Theresa Merritt, Vivienne Mussenden, Inez Matthews, Audrey Vanterpool*. **Act I: Scene 1** Outside a parachute factory near a Southern town: Opening Scene (Morrell, Cindy Lou, Workmen), "Lif' 'em up and Put 'em Down" (Street Boys), "Honey Gal of Mine" (Workers), "Good Luck, Mr. Flyin' Man!" (Female Chorus, Singers, Dancers), "Dat's Love" (Carmen & Chorus) (based on "Habanera"), "You Talk Jus' Like My Maw" (Joe & Cindy Lou), "Murder — Murder!" (Female Chorus), Finale of Scene 1 (Carmen, Joe, Brown, Sally, Chorus); *Entr'Scene* "Carmen Jones is Goin' to Jail" (Children); **Scene 2** A nearby roadside; immediately after: "Dere's a Cafe on de Corner" (Carmen & Joe) (based on "Seguidilla"); **Scene 3** Billy Pastor's cafe; three weeks later: "Beat Out Dat Rhythm on a Drum" (Frankie, Drummer, Chorus), "Stan' up an' Fight (Until You Hear de Bell)" (Husky & Chorus) (based on "The Toreador Song"), "Whizzin' Away Along de Track" (Rum, Dink, Frankie, Myrt, Carmen), "Dis Flower" (Joe), "If You Would Only Come Away" (Carmen & Joe), Finale of Act I. **Act II: Scene 1** Terrace of the Meadowlawn Country Club, South Side of Chicago; two weeks later: "De Cards Don' Lie" (Frankie, Myrt, Female Chorus), "Dat Ol' Boy" (Carmen), "Poncho, de Panther from Brazil" (Frankie, Myrt, Husky, Rum, Chorus), "Ballet Divertissement" ("Dance Roma Suite") (ballet), "My Joe" (Cindy Lou), Finale of Scene 1 (Carmen, Joe, Cindy Lou, Husky, Rum, Dink, Frankie, Myrt); **Scene 2a** Outside a sports stadium; one week later: "Git Yer Program for de Big Fight" (Chorus); **Scene 2b** The Stadium: "(Dat's) Our Man" (Chorus), Finale.

On Broadway opening night it got raves. Billy Rose came in for a lot of kudos, as did sets, costumes, writers, and cast. The show won Donaldson Awards for musical, composer (Bizet), lyrics, director, sets, and costumes.

After Broadway. TOUR. After Broadway the show toured, returning twice to CITY CENTER, both times with the same crew as for the 1943 Broadway run, except MUSICAL DIRECTOR: David Mordecai. The first time was 5/2/45–5/19/45. 21 PERFORMANCES. **Cast:** MORRELL: Robert Clarke; FOREMAN: George Willis; CINDY LOU: Elton J. Warren & Carlotta Franzell; BROWN: Jack Carr; JOE: Le Vern Hutcherson & Napoleon Reed; CARMEN: Muriel Smith & Inez Matthews; SALLY: Sibol Cain; T-BONE: Edward Roche; TOUGH KID: Carlos Van Putten; DRUMMER: Cozy Cole; BARTENDER: Maithe Marshall; WAITER: Edward Christopher; FRANKIE: Theresa Merritt; MYRT: June Hawkins, *Ruth Crumpton*; RUM: John Bubbles; DINK: Ford Buck; BOY: Bill O'Neil; GIRL: Erona Harris; HUSKY: Glenn Bryant; DANCING GIRL: Audrey Vanterpool; PONCHO: Elijah Hodges; BULLET HEAD: Lee Allen.

The second time at CITY CENTER it ran 4/7/46–5/4/46. 32 PERFORMANCES. **Cast:** MORRELL: Robert Clarke; FOREMAN/BULLET HEAD: George Willis; CINDY LOU: Elton J. Warren & Coreania Hayman; BROWN/MR. HIGGINS: Jack Carr; JOE: Napoleon Reed & Le Vern Hutcherson; CARMEN: Urylee Leonardos & Muriel Smith; SALLY: Sibol Cain; T-BONE: Edward Roche; TOUGH KID: James May; DRUMMER: Oliver Coleman; BARTENDER: Andrew J. Taylor; WAITERS: Edward Christopher & Richard de Vaultier; FRANKIE: Theresa Merritt; MYRT: Ruth Crumpton; RUM: John Bubbles; DINK: Ford Buck; HUSKY: Glenn Bryant; MISS HIGGINS: Fredye Marshall; PHOTOGRAPHER: Harold Taylor; CARD PLAYERS: Fredye Marshall, Doryce Brown, Sibol Cain; DANCING GIRL: Audrey Vanterpool; PONCHO: Frank Palmer; DANCING BOX-

ERS: Sheldon B. Hoskins & Randall Sawyer; BOY: Bill O'Neil; GIRL: Erona Harris; SOLDIERS: Robert Clarke, Randall Steplight, George Willis, Elijah Hodges.

THE MOVIE. 1954. DIRECTOR: Otto Preminger. *Cast*: CARMEN: Dorothy Dandridge (Marilyn Horne dubbed her singing); JOE: Harry Belafonte (Le Vern Hutcherson dubbed his singing); CINDY LOU: Olga James; FRANKIE: Pearl Bailey; MYRT: Diahann Carroll; RUM: Roy Glenn; BROWN: Brock Peters; T-BONE: Sandy Lewis; HUSKY: Joe Adams; DINK: Nick Stewart.

CITY CENTER, NYC, 5/31/56–6/17/56. 22 PERFORMANCES. PRESENTED BY the New York City Center Light Opera Company; DIRECTOR: William Hammerstein; CHOREOGRAPHER: Onna White; SETS/LIGHTING: Howard Bay; COSTUME SUPERVISOR: Stanley Simmons; MUSICAL DIRECTOR: Julius Rudel; MUSICAL ADAPTATION: Robert Russell Bennett. *Cast*: CINDY LOU: Reri Grist; BROWN: Walter P. Brown; JOE: William DuPree; CARMEN: Muriel Smith; SALLY: Glory Van Scott; DRUMMER: Cozy Cole; FRANKIE: Delores Martin; MYRT: Audrey Vanterpool; RUM: Joseph James; DINK: John Buie; HUSKY: Jimmy Randolph; HIGGINS: Clyde Turner; DANCERS INCLUDED: Arthur Mitchell, Erona Harris, Billy Wilson (his New York dancing debut), Charles Queenan, Joe Nash.

HUDSON CELEBRATION THEATRE IN CENTRAL PARK, 8/17/59–8/23/59. 7 PERFORMANCES. PRESENTED BY Jean Dalrymple; PRODUCERS: Stanley Prager & James Hammerstein; DIRECTOR: William Hammerstein; CHOREOGRAPHER: Alvin Ailey; SETS: Edward D. Stone; DECOR: Duane McKinney; COSTUMES: Raoul Pene du Bois; LIGHTING: Feder; MUSICAL DIRECTOR: Samuel Krachmalnick. *Cast*: CARMEN: Ethel Ayler & Audrey Vanterpool; JOE: William DuPree & William Baker; BROWN: Herbert Stubbs; SALLY: Jackie Walcott; HUSKY: Jimmy Randolph; FRANKIE: Doris Galiber; MYRT: Mary Louise; RUM: Walter P. Brown.

OLD VIC, London, 4/15/91. Successful revival. DIRECTOR: Simon Callow. CAST RECORDING on EMI. Wilhelmenia Fernandez won an Olivier Award. *Cast*: CARMEN: Wilhelmenia Fernandez, *Patti Boulaye*; RUM: Clive Rowe; ALSO WITH: Damon Evans, Sharon Benson, Michael Austin. It then toured the UK, 6/94–12/94, then went to Japan in 1995.

YORK THEATRE COMPANY, 1/26/01–1/28/01. Part of the *Musicals in Mufti* series. DIRECTOR: Harold Scott; SETS: James Morgan; MUSICAL DIRECTOR: Jack Lee. *Cast*: CARMEN: Suzzanne Douglas; JOE: Jason Raize; HUSKY: Timothy Robert Blevins; MYRT: Tanesha Marie; FRANKIE: Nora Cole; RUM: David Jackson; CINDY LOU: Anika Noni Rose; DINK: Glenn Turner; BROWN: Jonathan Earl Peck.

KENNEDY CENTER, Washington, DC, 11/15/02–11/17/02. A semi-staged production, with a twist on the original. PRESENTED BY Roman Terleckyj; DIRECTOR/CHOREOGRAPHER: Baayork Lee (replacing Debbie Allen); COSTUMES: Oscar de la Renta; LIGHTING: Richard Winkler; Placido Domingo conducted the National Symphony Orchestra. *Cast*: CARMEN: Vanessa Williams; JOE: Tom Randle; CINDY LOU: Harolyn Blackwell; HUSKY: Gregg Baker; MYRTLE: Roberta Laws.

120. *Carnival!*

The audience enters the theatre to find the curtain already up and the stage bare, except for a simple backdrop of a country setting (this was suggested by Helen Deutsch, the original librettist). The lights dim, suggesting pre-dawn, and the weary French carnival roustabouts come on, setting up their seedy tents and wagons, as the main theme—"Love Makes the World Go Round"—sounds out from Jacquot's wheezing concertina. This took the place of the more traditional overture. Lili, an orphan from the town of Mira, joins the carnival (it belongs to a friend of her late father), falls for the egotistical Marco the Magician, and befriends the show's puppets, handled by Paul, a bitter puppeteer who is lame due to an accident. Paul falls in love with Lili, but can only express his feelings for her through the puppets. When he speaks to her direct, he just rages and shouts. Puppets included: Carrot Top, Horrible Henry, Renardo, and Marguerite

(all played by Jerry Orbach in the original). Lili finds that Marco has long been involved in an affair with his assistant, Rosalie, and not wishing to compete, she decides to leave the circus, stopping to say goodbye to her puppet friends, who plead with her to stay. Then she realizes that she loves Paul.

Before Broadway. *Lili* was the first movie musical to be adapted for the Broadway stage. Previously announced with the title *Carrot Top*. Like *Carousel*, it began without an overture. Unfortunately, the great hit from the movie—"Hi-Lili, Hi-Lili, Hi-Lo"—couldn't be used (but it would be re-instated for a later, Mexican, production). There was tension between librettist Helen Deutsch and Gower Champion, and Miss Deutsch quit, to be replaced by Michael Stewart. Kaye Ballard turned down the lead in a touring company of *Gypsy* to do *Carnival!*

The Broadway Run. IMPERIAL THEATRE, 4/13/61–12/15/62; WINTER GARDEN THEATRE, 12/21/62–1/5/63. 2 previews on 4/12/61. Total of 719 PERFORMANCES. PRESENTED BY David Merrick; MUSIC/LYRICS: Bob Merrill; BOOK: Michael Stewart; BASED ON the 1953 MGM movie *Lili* (starring Leslie Caron as Lili Daurier, Mel Ferrer as Paul Berthalet, Jean Pierre Aumont as Marc, Zsa Zsa Gabor as Rosalie, and Kurt Kasznar as Jacquot), written by Helen Deutsch, and itself based on the 1950 magazine story *The Man Who Hated People* by Paul Gallico); DIRECTOR/CHOREOGRAPHER: Gower Champion; SETS/LIGHTING: Will Steven Armstrong; COSTUMES: Freddy Wittop; PUPPET CREATOR & SUPERVISOR: Tom Tichenor; MAGIC & ILLUSION DESIGNER & SUPERVISOR: Roy Benson; MUSICAL DIRECTOR/VOCAL ARRANGEMENTS: Saul Schechtman; ORCHESTRATIONS: Philip J. Lang; DANCE MUSIC ARRANGEMENTS: Peter Howard; CAST RECORDING on MGM; PRESS: Harvey B. Sabinson & David Powers; CASTING: Michael Shurtleff; GENERAL MANAGER: Jack Schlissel; COMPANY MANAGER: Richard Grayson; STAGE MANAGER: Charles Blackwell; ASSISTANT STAGE MANAGER: Pat Tolson, *C.K. Alexander*. *Cast*: JACQUOT: Pierre Olaf (4), *Rudy Tronto*; MR. SCHLEGEL: Henry Lascoe; GROBERT: Will Lee; ROUSTABOUTS: George Marcy, Tony Gomez, Johnny Nola, Buff Shurr; CYCLIST: Bob Murray; MIGUELITO: George Marcy; DOG TRAINER: Paul Sydell; WARDROBE MISTRESS: Carvel Carter, *Walda Kerr*; HAREM GIRLS: Nicole Barth, Iva March, Beti Seay; BEAR GIRL: Jennifer Billingsley, *Sigyn*; PRINCESS OLGA: Luba Lisa, *Adriane Rogers*; BAND: C.B. Bernard & Peter Lombard; STILT WALKER: Dean Crane; JUGGLERS: The Martin Brothers; CLOWNS: Bob Dixon & Harry Lee Rogers; STRONGMAN: Pat Tolson, *Gene Bigelow*; GLADYS ZUWICKI: Mary Ann Niles; GLORIA ZUWICKI: Christina Bartel, *Carvel Carter*; GYPSY: Anita Gillette, *Paula Lloyd*, *Wendy Waring*; MARCO THE MAGNIFICENT: James Mitchell (2), *Jonathan Lucas*; THE INCOMPARABLE ROSALIE: Kaye Ballard (3), *Jane Kean* (from 7/23/62), *Kaye Ballard* (from 8/13/62), *Dell Brownlee*; GRETA SCHLEGEL: June Meshonek; LILI: Anna Maria Alberghetti (1), *Anita Gillette* & *Julia Migenes* (both during Miss Alberghetti's hospitalization, from 8/61), *Susan Watson, Wendy Waring, Mimi Turque, Carla Alberghetti* (from 11/19/62), *Anna Maria Alberghetti*; PAUL BERTHALET: Jerry Orbach (5), *Ed Ames*; BLUE BIRDS: Nicole Barth, Jennifer Billingsley (*Sigyn*), Iva March, Beti Seay; AERIALIST: Dean Crane; DR. GLASS: Igors Gavon. **Standby**: Lili: Wendy Waring. **Understudies**: Lili: Anita Gillette, *Mimi Turque*; Rosalie: Carvel Carter, *Maureen McNally, Christina Bartel, Dell Brownlee*; Marco: George Marcy, *Buff Shurr* (only after James Mitchell had left); *Marco Gomez*; Paul: Igors Gavon; Jacquot: Buff Shurr, *Michel Moinot*; Schlegel/Grobert: Woody Romoff, *C.K. Alexander*; Olga: Paula Lloyd; Glass: Peter Lombard; Roustabouts: Alvin Beam, *Doria Avila*. Act I: Opening "Love Makes the World Go Round" (also called "Theme from *Carnival!*") (instrumental); *Scene 1* The carnival area on the outskirts of a town in Southern Europe: "Direct from Vienna" (piano selections) (Rosalie, Schlegel, Carnival People), "A Very Nice Man" (Lili); *Scene 2* The puppet booth: "Fairyland" (Carrot Top & Puppets), "I've Got to Find a Reason" (Paul), "Mira" ("Can You Imagine That?") (Lili), "Sword, Rose and Cape" (Marco & Roustabouts); *Scene 3* Inside Schlegel's office: "Humming" (Rosalie & Schlegel); *Scene 4* The carnival area: "Yes, My Heart" (Lili & Roustabouts); *Scene 5* The carnival area: "Everybody Likes You" (Paul); *Scene 6* Interior of main tent: "Magic, Magic" (Marco, Rosalie, Lili), "Tanz mit Mir" (Blue Birds), Carnival Ballet (Lili, Carnival People, Townspeople); *Scene 7* Carnival area at night, near the puppet booth: "Mira" (reprise) (Lili), "Love Makes the World Go Round" (also called "Theme

from *Carnival!*") (reprise) (Lili & Puppets) [the big hit]. ***Act II*: *Scene 1***
The midway: "Yum, Ticky (Ticky, Tum, Tum)" (Lili & Puppets), "The
Rich" (Lili & Puppets), "Love Makes the World Go Round" (also called
"Theme from *Carnival!*") (reprise) (Lili & Puppets), "Beautiful Candy"
(Lili, Puppets, Vendors), "Her Face" (Paul), "Grand Imperial Cirque de
Paris" (Jacquot & Carnival People); ***Scene 2*** The trailer camp: "I Hate
Him" (reprise of "Her Face") (Lili & Paul); ***Scene 3*** Outside main tent,
the puppet booth, the carnival area: "Grand Imperial Cirque de Paris"
(reprise) (Carnival People), "Always Always You" (Marco & Rosalie),
"She's My Love" (Paul).

It got mostly rave notices on Broadway. It won Tonys for sets, and
for Anna Maria Alberghetti, and was also nominated for musical, producers of a musical, book, direction of a musical, and for Pierre Olaf.
MGM largely financed *Carnival!*, but due to a dispute with David Merrick, the film of *Carnival!* was never made.

After Broadway. Tour. Opened on 12/7/61, at the Auditorium,
Rochester, NY. Musical Director: Gilbert Stevens, *Oscar Kosarin*.
Cast: Lili: Susan Watson, *Anna Maria Alberghetti*; Paul: Ed Ames, *Jerry
Orbach, Johnny Haymer* (from 12/7/61), *Michel Moinot*; Rosalie: Jo Anne
Worley; Marco: Jonathan Lucas.

Tour. Opened on 10/18/62, at the Bushnell Theatre, Hartford,
Conn. Presented by Lee Guber, Frank Ford, Shelly Gross; Director:
Charles Blackwell; Choreographer: Buff Shurr; Musical Director:
Jerry Goldberg. **Cast**: Lili: Carla Alberghetti, *Anna Maria Alberghetti*
(from 11/21/62), *Elaine Malbin*; Paul: David Daniels, *Ed Ames*; Rosalie:
Madge Cameron; Glass: William J. Coppola.

Lyric Theatre, London. Opened on 2/8/63. 34 performances.
It failed partly due to bad press. Presented by H.M. Tennent; Direc-
tor: Lucia Victor; Choreographer: Doria Avila. **Cast**: Lili: Sally
Logan; Paul: Michael Maurel; Grobert: Reg Lever; Marco: James
Mitchell; Rosalie: Shirley Sands; Gladys: Julia Sutton; Schlegel: Peter
Bayliss; Jacquot: Bob Harris.

Mineola Playhouse, NY. Opened 1/28/64. Liza Minnelli, then a
minor and recovering from kidney problems, went on as Lili despite
strenuous objections from her mother, Judy Garland. Director: Rudy
Tronto. **Cast**: Liza Minnelli, David Daniels, Scott Merrill. This production moved to the Paper Mill Playhouse, New Jersey, 2/11/64.

City Center, NYC, 12/12/68–1/5/69. 2 previews. 30 per-
formances. This was the first New York City revival of *Carnival!*
Presented by the New York City Center Light Opera Company; Direc-
tor: Gus Schirmer; Choreographer: John Nola; Assistant Chore-
ographers: Mary Ann Niles & Jerry Fries; Costumes: Harry Curtis;
Lighting: Feder; Musical Director: Peter Howard; Puppets: Richard
Barclay. **Cast**: Jacquot: Pierre Olaf; Schlegel: Carmine Caridi; Olga:
Dorothy D'Honau; Stilt Walker/Aerialist: Dean Crane; Jugglers:
The Martin Brothers; Gladys: Mary Ann Niles; Gloria: Christina Bar-
tel; Marco: Richard France; Rosalie: Karen Morrow; Lili: Victoria
Mallory; Paul: Leon Bibb; Glass: Robert L. Hultman.

Equity Library Theatre, NYC, 11/3/77–11/20/77. 22 perfor-
mances. Director: Susan Schulman; Choreographer: Steven Gelfer;
Musical Director: James Fradrich. **Cast**: Lili: Sue Anne Gershenson;
Paul: Ross Petty; Jacquot: Jack Hoffman; Olga: Jill Cook; Marco:
Joel Craig; Magic Girl: Kaylyn Dillehay; Schlegel: Carl Don; Glass:
Steven Gelfer; Fire Eater: Elmore James; Rosalie: Laura Kenyon.

St. Peter's Church, NYC, 3/31/93–5/2/93. 34 performances.
Presented by the York Theatre Company; Director/Choreogra-
pher: Pamela Hunt. **Cast**: Lili: Glory Crampton; Paul: Robert Michael
Baker.

Pasadena Playhouse, Calif., 10/19/98. One-night concert. Director: Susan Watson; Musical Director: Jeff Rizzo. On 2/17/98 an ill,
depressed Bob Merrill had shot himself in the head.

City Center, NYC, 2/7/02–2/10/02. 5 performances. Part of
the *Encores!* series (their most successful one yet, beating the 2001 reading of *Hair*). Adapted to concert form: Wendy Wasserstein; Direc-
tor/Choreographer: Kathleen Marshall; Set Consultant: John Lee
Beatty; Musical Director: Rob Fisher. **Cast**: Lili: Anne Hathaway;
Paul: Brian Stokes Mitchell; Marco: Douglas Sills; Schlegel: David
Margulies; Rosalie: Debbie Gravitte; Jacquot: David Costabile.

Disney bought the rights to *Carnival!* in 12/98, and on 1/29/99 held
a reading to determine whether they would do something with the prop-

erty or not (they didn't). **Cast**: Lili: Sarah Uriarte Berry; Marco: Billy
Zane; Rosalie: Michele Pawk; Paul: Peter Gallagher; Jacquot: B.D.
Wong; Glass: Peter Benson; Also with: Lewis J. Stadlen. In 2002 Julian
Schlossberg bought the rights, with a view to bringing it back to Broad-
way in 2003, then when that year didn't pan out, 2004 or 2005. Thomas
Meehan was scheduled to re-write the libretto. However those plans fell
through too.

121. *Carnival in Flanders*

A Spanish duke descends on the peaceful Flanders town of
Flacksenburg in 1616. The mayor decides to play dead, hoping the
Spanish will go away. But the Duke sees Cornelia, the mayor's
pretty wife, and decides to stay and court her, watched, of course,
by the "dead" mayor.

Before Broadway. Harold Arlen was to be have been the com-
poser/lyricist originally, but that fell through. William Gaxton, set to play
the mayor, left before first rehearsals, and was replaced by Walter Abel.
After the Philadelphia tryout, which did not go well, co-librettist George
Oppenheimer (Herbert Fields was the other) was fired, and Dorothy
Fields was brought in to help her brother. They wrote a whole new Act
I, then left. Edwin Lester, head of Los Angeles and San Francisco Civic
Light Operas, had made a deal in which he was going to present *Carni-
val in Flanders* before it went to Broadway. Now he tried to back out,
claiming the show was too racy. But he was forced to take it (he was try-
ing to book *Hazel Flagg*). Before the show went to California, Bretaigne
Windust, the director, was fired, and Preston Sturges was brought in as
new director/librettist. Helen Tamiris replaced Jack Cole as choreographer, and Walter Abel was replaced by Roy Roberts in the cast. Dolores
Gray's part got bigger at every stage of the proceedings (according to
some, she was a tyrant). Nancy Bonnie Shnapier had her role cut. Bob
& Dolores Hope were investors, as were Bing Crosby and the Champions (Marge and Gower). The numbers "Unaccustomed as I Am" and
"Small Things" were cut before Broadway.

The Broadway Run. New Century Theatre, 9/8/53–9/12/53. 6
performances. Presented by Paula Stone & Mike Sloane, in associa-
tion with Johnny Burke & James Van Heusen; Music: James Van
Heusen; Lyrics: Johnny Burke; Book/Director: Preston Sturges;
Based on the 1935 movie *La kermesse heroique*, written by Charles Spaak,
Jacques Feyder, Bernard Zimmer; Choreographer: Helen Tamiris;
Sets: Oliver Smith; Costumes: Lucinda Ballard; Musical Director:
Harold Hastings; Orchestrations: Don Walker; Vocal Arrange-
ments: Elie Siegmeister; Press: Karl Bernstein, Harvey Sabinson, Robert
Ganshaw; General Manager: Samuel H. Schwartz; Production
Stage Manager: Fred Hebert; Stage Managers: Dennis Murray & Al
Checco. **Cast:** Siska: Pat Stanley (4); Jan Breughel: Kevin Scott; Tai-
lor: Paul Reed; Butcher: Paul Lipson; Barber: Bobby Vail; Innkeeper:
Lee Goodman; Mayor: Roy Roberts (3); Cornelia, the Mayor's Wife:
Dolores Gray (1); Martha: Dolores Kempner; Courier: Matt Mattox;
Mourning Women: Sandra Devlin, Julie Marlowe, Lorna Del Maestro;
1st Officer: Ray Mason; 2nd Officer: George Martin; 3rd Officer:
Jimmy Alex; The Duke: John Raitt (2); 1st Citizen: Wesley Swails; 2nd
Citizen: Norman Weise; Lisa: Jean Bradley; Katherine: Undine For-
rest; Orderly: William Noble; Dancers: Jimmy Alex, John Aristedes,
Harry Day, Lorna Del Maestro, Sandra Devlin, Pat Ferrier, Ronnie Field,
Skeet Guenther, Patti Karkalits, Mary Alice Kubes, Julie Marlowe,
George Martin, Greg O'Brien, Paul Olson, Richard Reed, Emy St. Just,
Billie Shane, Michael Spaeth, Elfrieda Zeiger; Singers: Lee Barry, Jean
Bradley, Fred Bryan, Bill Conlon, Jeanine Cowles, Undine Forrest,
Stokely Gray, Dolores Kempner, Mara Landi, William Noble, Mary
Stanton, Dick Stewart, Wesley Swails, Gloria Van Dorpe, Norman Weise.
Standby: Cornelia: Susan Johnson. ***Act I***: "Ring the Bell" (Mayor,
Butcher, Barber, Tailor, Innkeeper, Jan, Siska, Ensemble), "The Very
Necessary You" (Jan & Siska), "It's a Fine Old Institution" (Cornelia),
"I'm One of Your Admirers" (Cornelia), "The Plundering of the Town"
(Cornelia, Courier, 2nd Officer, Emy St. Just, John Aristedes, Julie Mar-
lowe, Ensemble), "The Stronger Sex" (Cornelia), "The Sudden Thrill"
(Duke), "It's an Old Spanish Custom" (Cornelia & Duke), "A Seventeen-

ble). *Act II*: "You're Dead!" (Mayor, Butcher, Barber, Innkeeper, Tailor), "(Here's That) Rainy Day" (Cornelia) [the hit], "Take the Word of a Gentleman" (Duke); "The Carnival Ballet": THE VIRGIN: Emy St. Just; THE BATS: Greg O'Brien & Paul Olson; THE MONK: John Aristedes; THE GOAT: Harry Day; THE YOUNGEST ONE: Pat Stanley; THE PLUMED SWAINS: Jimmy Alex, Ronnie Field, Skeet Guenther, Michael Spaeth, George Martin, Richard Reed; THE SEVEN VIRGINS: Sandra Devlin, Lorna Del Maestro, Pat Ferrier, Julie Marlowe, Patti Karkalits, Mary Alice Kubes, Elfrieda Zeiger; THE SPANISH TRIO: Matt Mattox, George Martin, Jimmy Alex, Singers of the Town; "(For) a Moment of Your Love" (Cornelia & Duke), "How Far Can a Lady Go?" (Cornelia), "It's a Fine Old Institution" (reprise) (Cornelia).

Dolores Gray got rave reviews but otherwise the show was basically panned. In the cast was Ronnie Field, who later became the famous Broadway director/choreographer Ron Field. Miss Gray won a Tony (the shortest-ever Tony Award–winning run)

122. *Caroline, or Change*

An intimate musical that was really an opera. Set in Lake Charles, Louisiana, in Nov. and Dec. 1963, just before and during the assassination of President Kennedy, and as the Civil Rights movement is about to explode. It tells of the relationship between Caroline, a 39-year-old black maid and her employers, the Gellmans, a white Jewish family. It also shows her internal conflicts, and those conflicts within her community. Within her own family Caroline is divorced, one of her sons is away in Vietnam, and Emmie is rebellious. The Gellmans consist of the father, his new wife Rose, and the man's eight-year-old son, Noah (whose mother recently died). Rose is from a progressive Manhattan family, and tries to get along with Noah, who already has a close relationship with Caroline. Rose, with her regard for money, is appalled by Noah's habit of leaving change in his pockets. In order to teach him a lesson, she tells Caroline to keep the change, which is unwittingly patronizing and another source of the maid's anger and frustration. Caroline spends most of her time in the Gellmans' dank basement, washing, drying and ironing clothes, and her closest friends are the washer, the dryer, the radio, and the Moon, all of whom sing to her.

Before Broadway. Written with Tonya Pinkins in mind as the star. Work on the show began in 2001. It was going to be part of the Public Theatre's 2002–03 season (it was originally commissioned and developed by LuEsther Lab, the Public's new play development program), but it wasn't ready, and was delayed a year. The two producers put in a million dollars. Previews at the Public were put back a day. It first ran at the NEWMAN THEATRE (part of the Public Theatre), 11/30/03–2/1/04. Previews from 10/29/03. PRESENTED BY Carole Shorenstein Hays & Frederick DeMann. Aside from the producers, the cast and crew was pretty much the same as for the subsequent Broadway run. It got divided reviews. By early 12/03 there was talk of it going to Broadway, and a major push developed to get it there, to the Eugene O'Neill in 2/04 (later revised to 4/04). In mid-Jan. 2004, after considerable speculation, it was announced that it would, indeed, make the transfer. It extended its run at the Public to 1/4/04, then to 2/1/04. It cost an additional $5 million to get it to Broadway. The beginning of Broadway previews was put forward a day to 4/12/04, but then went back to 4/13/04.

The Broadway Run. EUGENE O'NEILL THEATRE, 5/2/04–8/29/04. 23 previews from 4/13/04. 136 PERFORMANCES. PRESENTED BY Carole Shorenstein Hays, HBO Films, Jujamcyn Theatres, Freddy DeMann, Scott Rudin, Ruth Hendel/Elisabeth Morten/Cheryl Wiesenfeld, Fox Theatricals/Jennifer Manocherian/Jane Bergere, Roger Berlind, Clear Channel Entertainment, Joan Cullman, Greg Holland/Scott Nederlander, Margo Lion, Daryl Roth, and Frederick Zollo/Jeffrey Sine, in association with The Public Theatre; MUSIC: Jeanine Tesori; LYRICS/BOOK: Tony Kushner; DIRECTOR: George C. Wolfe; CHOREOGRAPHER: Hope

Clarke; SETS: Riccardo Hernandez; COSTUMES: Paul Tazewell; LIGHTING: Jules Fisher & Peggy Eisenhauer; SOUND: Jon Weston; MUSICAL SUPERVISOR: Kimberly Grigsby; MUSICAL DIRECTOR: Linda Twine; ORCHESTRATIONS: Rick Bassett, Joseph Joubert, Buryl Red; CAST RECORDING on Hollywood Records; made on 4/26/04 and released on 6/29/04; PRESS: Boneau/Bryan-Brown; CASTING: Jordan Thaler/Heidi Griffiths; GENERAL MANAGEMENT: Stuart Thompson Productions: PRODUCTION STAGE MANAGER: Rick Steiger; STAGE MANAGER: Lisa Dawn Cave; ASSISTANT STAGE MANAGER: Kevin Bertolacci. *Cast:* CAROLINE THIBODEAUX: Tonya Pinkins (1) ☆; THE WASHING MACHINE: Capathia Jenkins (voice); THE RADIO: Tracy Nicole Chapman, Marva Hicks, Brandi Chavonne Massey [Ramona Keller before Broadway]; NOAH: Harrison Chad; THE DRYER: Chuck Cooper (voice); GRANDMA GELLMAN: Alice Playten; GRANDPA GELLMAN: Reathel Bean; ROSE STOPNICK GELLMAN: Veanne Cox; STUART GELLMAN: David Costabile; DOTTY MOFFETT, ANOTHER MAID: Chandra Wilson; THE MOON: Aisha de Haas (voice) [Adriane Lenox before Broadway]; THE BUS: Chuck Cooper (voice); CAROLINE'S (THREE) CHILDREN: EMMIE THIBODEAUX: Anika Noni Rose; JACKIE THIBODEAUX: Leon G. Thomas III [Kevin Tate before Broadway]; JOE THIBODEAUX: Marcus Carl Franklin; MR. STOPNICK: Larry Keith; *Standbys*: Noah: Sy Adamowsky; Emmie: Shannon Antalan; Radio: Shannon Antalan & Vanessa Jones (before Broadway also Brandi Chavonne Massey & Ledisi), *Tanesha Gary*; Rose/Grandma: Sue Goodman; Grandpa/Mr. Stopnick: John Jellison (Donald Grody before Broadway); Stuart: Adam Heller; Dotty/The Moon: Vanessa Jones; Caroline: Adriane Lenox, *Cheryl Alexander*; Dryer/Bus: Milton Craig Nealy; Jackie/Joe: Corwin Tuggles (Chevon Rutty before Broadway); Washing Machine: Ledisi (before Broadway). *Orchestra*: VIOLINS: Paul Woodiel & Christopher Cardona; VIOLA: David Creswell; CELLO: Anja Wood; REEDS: Paul Garment & Stephen Wisner; GUITARS: Steve Bargonetti; BASS: Benjamin Franklin Brown; KEYBOARDS: Matthew Sklar; PERCUSSION: John Clancy & Shane Shanahan. *Act I*: *Scene 1* Washer/Dryer: "16 Feet Beneath the Sea" (Caroline & Washing Machine), "The Radio" (Radio), "Laundry Quintet" (Radio, Caroline, Washing Machine), "Noah Down the Stairs" (Noah), "The Cigarette" (Caroline, Noah, Washing Machine), "Laundry Finish" (Radio), "The Dryer" (Dryer & Radio), "I Got Four Kids" (Caroline, Dryer, Washing Machine); *Scene 2* Cabbage: "Caroline, There's Extra Food" (Rose, Caroline, Grandma, Grandpa, Noah), "There is No God, Noah" (Stuart), "Rose Stopnick Can Cook" (Grandma, Grandpa, Stuart, Rose, Caroline, Noah); *Scene 3* Long-distance: "Long Distance" (Rose); *Scene 4* Moon change: "Dotty and Caroline" (Dotty, Caroline, Moon), "Moon Change" (Moon), "Moon Trio" (Moon, Dotty, Caroline), "The Bus" (Bus), "That Can't Be" (Dotty, Caroline, Moon), "Noah and Rose" (Noah & Rose), "Inside/Outside" (Moon, Noah, Rose), "JFK" (Grandma, Grandpa, Dotty, Moon, Noah); *Scene 5* Duets: "No One Waitin'" (Radio, Emmie, Caroline), "'night, Mama" (Emmie), "Gonna Pass Me a Law" (Caroline & Noah), "Noah Go to Sleep" (Caroline & Noah); *Scene 6* The bleach cup: "Noah Has a Problem" (Caroline & Rose), "Stuart and Noah" (Stuart, Noah, Caroline), "Quarter in the Bleach Cup" (Noah, Caroline, Washing Machine), "Caroline Takes My Money Home" (Noah, Caroline, Emmie, Jackie, Joe), "Roosevelt Petrucious Coleslaw" (Noah, Emmie, Jackie, Joe, Caroline). *Act II*: *Scene 7* Ironing: "Santa Comin,' Caroline" (Radio & Washing Machine), "Little Reward" (Washing Machine, Caroline, Radio), "1943" (Caroline, Radio, Washing Machine), "Mr. Gellman's Shirt" (Rose & Caroline), "Oooh Child" (Washing Machine & Radio), "Rose Recovers" (Rose, Caroline, Dryer); *Scene 8* The Chanukah party: "I Saw Three Ships" (Jackie, Joe, Emmie, Caroline), "Chanukah Party" (Stuart, Noah, Rose, Grandma, Grandpa, Mr. Stopnick), "Dotty and Emmie" (Dotty, Emmie, Caroline), "I Don't Want My Child to Hear That" (Caroline, Mr. Stopnick, Grandma, Grandpa, Rose), "Mr. Stopnick and Emmie" (Emmie, Mr. Stopnick, Caroline, Rose), "Kitchen Fight" (Dotty, Emmie, Caroline); *Scene 9* The Twenty-dollar bill: "A Twenty Dollar Bill and Why" (Noah, Rose, Mr. Stopnick, Grandma, Grandpa, Washing Machine, Caroline), "Caroline and Noah Fight" (Noah, Caroline, Dryer); *Scene 10* Aftermath; *Scene 11* Lot's wife: "Lot's Wife" (Caroline); *Scene 12* How Long Has This Been Going On?: "Salty Teardrops" (Radio), "Why Does Our House Have a Basement?" (Noah, Rose, Washing Machine), "Underwater" (Caroline & Noah); *Epilogue*.

The 5/14/04 performance was canceled because the theatre's sprinkler system malfunctioned, causing a small flood on stage. Anika Noni Rose won a Tony, and the show was also nominated for musical, original score written for a musical, book of a musical, director of a musical, and for Tonya Pinkins. On 8/5/04 it was announced that it would be closing on 8/29/04.

After Broadway. On 9/16/04 it was announced that the show would make its West Coast premiere at the AHMANSON THEATRE, Los Angeles, 11/04–12/26/04. Previews from 11/6/04. From there it went on to the CURRAN THEATRE, San Francisco, 1/18/05–2/20/05. Previews from 1/14/05. PRESENTED BY Carole Shorenstein Hays and Scott E. Nederlander, in association with Gordon Davidson and the Ahmanson and Berkeley Repertory Theatre. It had the same basic crew as for Broadway. **Cast**: CAROLINE: Tonya Pinkins; WASHING MACHINE: Capathia Jenkins (voice); NOAH: Sy Adamowsky; GRANDMA: Alice Playten; GRANDPA: Reathel Bean; ROSE: Veanne Cox; STUART: David Costabile; MOON: Aisha de Haas (voice); EMMIE: Anika Noni Rose; JACKIE: Leon G. Thomas III; JOE: Corwin Tuggles; MR. STOPNICK: Larry Keith; ALSO WITH: Tracy Nicole Chapman, Cicily Daniels, Marva Hicks, Paula Newsome, Benjamin Mall, Kenna Ramsey, Michael A. Shepperd, Renn Woods.

123. *Carousel*

The plot of *Liliom*, the play upon which the musical is based, concerns Liliom, a nasty carnival barker who has an affair with Julie, a shopgirl. When she becomes pregnant, he attempts a robbery in order to be able to pay for the child. However, the robbery is thwarted, and he commits suicide, and is taken to purgatory by two celestial policemen. He must remain there for 15 years, and at the end of that time is allowed back to Earth by the Starkeeper to perform one good deed, so he can get to Heaven. Back on Earth he attempts to give his daughter a star he has stolen from heaven. When she refuses to take it he slaps her in frustration, and is re-consigned to Purgatory. Rodgers and Hammerstein kept the story of *Liliom*, but changed the setting from 1920s Budapest to a New England fishing village in the period 1873–1888, and the name of the lead from Liliom to Billy Bigelow. He and Julie marry before he dies, and the musical has a happy ending. He encourages his daughter, Louise, to have confidence in herself as he reprises "You'll Never Walk Alone," and for this good deed is allowed into Heaven. Mrs. Mullin is the jealous would-be object of Billy's affection. Jigger, a disreputable sailor, is his accomplice in the robbery. Julie's friend, Carrie, is in love with Mr. Snow.

Before Broadway. *Liliom*, the Molnar fantasy upon which *Carousel* was based, had been produced in the USA for the first time by the THEATRE GUILD on 4/21/21, starring Joseph Schildkraut and Eva Le Gallienne. On 10/26/32 Eva Le Gallienne revived *Liliom* at the CIVIC REPERTORY THEATRE, again with Joseph Schildkraut. On 3/25/40 Vinton Freedley's Broadway revival of *Liliom* starred Ingrid Bergman & Burgess Meredith (Elia Kazan was also in the cast), at the FORTY-FOURTH STREET THEATRE. Theresa Helburn of the Theatre Guild had the idea of making the Liliom story into a musical, and took it to Rodgers and Hammerstein. Ferenc Molnar had already rejected both Puccini and George Gershwin as adapters of his play, but he accepted R & H based on what he had seen them do with *Oklahoma! Carousel* eliminated the overture (the usual medley of tunes) altogether, and replaced it with a pantomimed scene accompanied by a single melody ("Carousel Waltz"). Vivian Vance was scheduled to play Mrs. Mullin, but was fired at the insistence of Agnes de Mille. The show opened in New Haven, which is where the scene in the home of Mr. and Mrs. God was cut; during the try out in Boston, the actual characters Mr. and Mrs. God (or He and She, as they were also known), played by Russell Collins and Kathleen Comegys respectively) were cut and replaced by the Starkeeper, Billy's guardian angel and adviser (played by Russell Collins). The Minister

(also played by Russell Collins) was cut too (but put back in before Broadway).

The Broadway Run. MAJESTIC THEATRE, 4/19/45–5/24/47. 890 PERFORMANCES. PRESENTED BY the Theatre Guild, with Richard Rodgers & Oscar Hammerstein II; MUSIC: Richard Rodgers; LYRICS/BOOK: Oscar Hammerstein II; Based on the 1921 play *Liliom*, by Ferenc Molnar, which had been adapted by Benjamin F. Glazer; DIRECTOR: Rouben Mamoulian; CHOREOGRAPHER: Agnes de Mille; SETS/LIGHTING: Jo Mielziner; COSTUMES: Miles White; MUSICAL DIRECTOR: Joseph Littau; ORCHESTRATIONS: Don Walker; BALLET PIANO ARRANGEMENTS: Trude Rittman; PRESS: Alfred H. Tamarin, *Joseph Heidt & Peggy Phillips*; PRODUCTION SUPERVISORS: Lawrence Langner & Theresa Helburn; COMPANY MANAGER: John H. Potter, *Andy Anderson*; GENERAL STAGE MANAGER: Andy Anderson; STAGE MANAGER: John Fearnley, *Paul Crabtree*; ASSISTANT STAGE MANAGER: Herman Magidson. **Cast:** CARRIE PIPPERIDGE: Jean Darling (4); JULIE JORDAN: Jan Clayton (2), *Iva Withers*; MRS. MULLIN: Jean Casto (7), *Effie Afton* (alternated with Miss Casto in 45–46); BILLY BIGELOW: John Raitt (1), *Harold Keel* [later known as Howard Keel] (by 8/45), *John Raitt*; BESSIE: Mimi Strongin; JESSIE: Jimsey Somers [character dropped in 45–46]; JUGGLER: Lew Foldes, *Walter Hull*; 1ST POLICEMAN: Robert Byrn; DAVID BASCOMBE: Franklyn Fox; NETTIE FOWLER: Christine Johnson (6), *Mimi Cabanne* (alternated with Miss Johnson in 45–46); JUNE GIRL: Pearl Lang; ENOCH SNOW: Eric Mattson (3); JIGGER CRAIGIN: Murvyn Vye (5); HANNAH BENTLEY: Annabelle Lyon (10); BOATSWAIN: Peter Birch (9); ARMINY LIVERMORE: Connie Baxter; PENNY SINCLAIR: Marilyn Merkt; JENNIE SANBORN: Joan Keenan; VIRGINIA FRAZER: Ginna Moise; SUSAN PETERS: Suzanne TaFel; JONATHAN CHASE: Richard H. Gordon, *Louis Freed*; 2ND POLICEMAN: Lawrence Evers; CAPTAIN: Blake Ritter; 1ST HEAVENLY FRIEND (BROTHER JOSHUA): Jay Velie; 2ND HEAVENLY FRIEND: Tom McDuffie [character dropped by 8/45]; STARKEEPER: Russell Collins, *Calvin Thomas*; LOUISE: Bambi Linn (8); LOUISE'S FRIENDS: Kathleen Comegys & Ralph Tucker; JIMMY (CARNIVAL BOY): Robert Pagent (11); ENOCH SNOW JR.: Ralph Linn; PRINCIPAL: Lester Freedman, *Robert Byrn*; DR. SELDON, THE MINISTER: Russell Collins, *Calvin Thomas* [role cut by 8/45]; DANCERS: David Adhar, Tom Avera, Diane Chadwick, Margaret Cuddy, Margaretta de Valera, Andrea Downing (*Fern Whitney*), Larry Evers, Lynn Joelson, Sonia Joroff, Pearl Lang, Lee Lauterbur, Ralph Linn, Tony Matthews, Ruth Miller, Ernest Richman (*Kenneth Le Roy, Robert Tucker*), Elena Salamatova, Marjorie Svetlik, Polly Welch, *William Lundy, Frank Marasco, David Raher*; SINGERS: Connie Baxter, Joseph Bell, Robert Byrn, Anne Calvert, Martha Carver, Neil Chirico, Josephine Collins, Tom Duffey (gone by 8/45), Louis Freed, Lester Freedman, Richard H. Gordon, John Harrold (gone by 8/45), Joan Keenan, Charles Leighton, Marilyn Merkt, Beatrice Miller, Ginna Moise, Blake Ritter, Suzanne TaFel, Gordon Taylor, Verlyn Webb, Glory Wills, Iva Withers, *Thomas Lo Monaco*. **Prelude**: An amusement park on the New England coast; in May: Grand Opening (Orchestra), Waltz Suite: "Carousel" ("Carousel Waltz") (Orchestra); **Act I: Scene 1** A tree-lined path along the shore; a few minutes later: "You're a Queer One, Julie Jordan" (Carrie & Julie), "(When I Marry) Mister Snow" (Carrie), "If I Loved You" (Billy & Julie); **Scene 2** Nettie Fowler's spa on the ocean front; in June: "June is Bustin' Out All Over" (Nettie, Carrie, Ensemble) [a hit], Dance (Dancing Ensemble, led by Pearl Lang), "(When I Marry) Mr. Snow" (reprise) (Carrie, Mr. Snow, Girls), "When the Children Are Asleep" (Mr. Snow & Carrie), "Blow High, Blow Low" (Jigger, Billy, Male Chorus), Hornpipe Dance (led by Annabelle Lyon & Peter Birch), "Soliloquy" ("My Boy Bill"/"My Little Girl") (Billy) [the first song written for the show], **Act I Finale:** "June is Bustin' Out All Over" (reprise) (Company). **Act II: Scene 1** On an island across the bay; that night: "(This was a) Real Nice Clambake" (Carrie, Nettie, Julie, Mr. Snow, Ensemble) [this song had originally been "It Was a Real Nice Hayride," a number dropped from *Oklahoma!*], "Geraniums in the Winder"/"Stonecutters Cut it on the Stone" (Mr. Snow), "There's Nothing So Bad for a Woman" (Jigger & Ensemble), "What's the Use of Wond'rin'?" (Julie & Girls); **Scene 2** Mainland waterfront; an hour later: "You'll Never Walk Alone" (Nettie) [the big hit]; **Scene 3** Up there: "The Highest Judge of All" (Billy); **Scene 4** Down here, on a beach; 15 years later: "On the Beach" ("Billy Makes a Journey") (ballet): LOUISE: Bambi Lynn; A YOUNGER MISS SNOW: Annabelle Lyon; THE BROTHERS AND SISTERS SNOW: Margaretta de Valera, Lynn Joelson, Sonia Joroff,

Polly Welch, Diane Chadwick; BADLY BROUGHT UP BOYS: Ralph Linn & Ernest Richman (*Kenneth Le Roy*); A YOUNG MAN LIKE BILLY: Robert Pagent; A CARNIVAL WOMAN: Pearl Lang; MEMBERS OF THE CARNIVAL TROUPE: Robert Pagent, Pearl Lang, Beth Nichols, Lawrence Evers, Elena Solamatova, William Lundy, Marjory Svetlik, Robert Tucker, Fern Whitney, Frank Marasco; **Scene 5** Outside Julie's cottage: "If I Loved You" (reprise) (Billy); **Scene 6** Outside a schoolhouse; same day: "You'll Never Walk Alone" (reprise) (Entire Company), Finale.

Note: In some productions (i.e. the 1954 City Center production) the prelude is counted as Scene 1, and therefore Scene 1 becomes Scene 2, and Scene 2 becomes Scene 3.

On Broadway opening night Richard Rodgers, who had injured his back, was forced to watch the show in a stretcher from behind the curtains. Critics only raved (well, the rather unusual Wilella Waldorf, of the *Post*, was bored, but she knew she was wrong). During the run Jan Clayton left *Carousel*, at the suggestion of Rodgers and Hammerstein, in order to star in their revival of *Showboat*. *Carousel* was Mr. Rodgers' favorite of all the musicals he did with Oc Hammerstein. It won Donaldson Awards for musical, composer, lyrics, book, director, choreographer, John Raitt (actor), Bambi Lynn (female dancer), and Peter Birch (male dancer). It also won the New York Drama Critics' Circle Award for best play (it was the first musical ever to win for this category. The next year separate categories would be introduced—for American Play, Foreign Play, and Musical). Note: Tonys hadn't been introduced yet.

124. *Carousel (1949 return to Broadway)*

Before Broadway. After the original Broadway run the show had gone on tour for 21 months, then returned to New York, first to City Center, then back to Broadway (at the Majestic). It ran at CITY CENTER, 1/25/49–2/20/49. 16 PERFORMANCES. It had the same cast and crew as for the subsequent Broadway return run.

The Broadway Run. MAJESTIC THEATRE, 2/22/49–3/5/49. 32 PERFORMANCES. It was the same basic crew as for the 1945 Broadway production, except for: MUSICAL DIRECTOR: Frederick Dvonch. *Cast:* CARRIE PIPPERIDGE: Margot Moser; JULIE JORDAN: Iva Withers, Jean Rogers (alternate); MRS. MULLIN: Louise Larrabee; BILLY BIGELOW: Stephen Douglass, Warren Harr (alternate); 1ST POLICEMAN: Kenneth Knapp; DAVID BASCOMBE: Ross Chetwynd; NETTIE FOWLER: Christine Johnson; JUNE GIRL: Mavis Ray; ENOCH SNOW: Eric Mattson; JIGGER CRAIGIN: Mario De Laval; HANNAH: Dusty Worrall; BOATSWAIN: Kenneth MacKenzie; ARMINY: Bobra Suitor; PENNY: Evelyne Ross; JENNIE: Audrey Sabetti; VIRGINIA: Jean Rogers; SUSAN: Ruth Devorin; 2ND POLICEMAN: Richmond Page; CAPTAIN: Warren Harr; HEAVENLY FRIEND (BROTHER JOSHUA): Jay Velie; STARKEEPER: Calvin Thomas; LOUISE: Diane Keith; CARNIVAL BOY: Kenneth MacKenzie; ENOCH SNOW JR.: Anthony Aleo; PRINCIPAL: Kenneth Knapp; SINGERS: Lonna Phillips, Jean Rogers, Edith Fitch, Evelyne Ross, Audrey Sabetti, Grace Bruns, Bobra Suitor, Ruth Devorin, Robert Davis, Richmond Page, Jerry Lucas, Warren Harr, Kenneth E. Knapp, Joseph Milly, Charles Scott, Anthony Aleo, Charles E. Wood Jr.; DANCERS: Karl Krauter, Lila Popper, Hazel Patterson, Shirley Andahazy, Jan Burroughs, Mildred Ferguson, Virginia Harris, Hilda Wagner, Meredith Baylis, Yolanda Novak, Lorand Andahazy, Stanley Herbert, Hubert Bland, Raymond Dorian, Joseph Camiolo, Martin Schneider, Marvin Krauter.

After Broadway. THEATRE ROYAL, DRURY LANE, London, 6/7/50–10/13/51. 567 PERFORMANCES. DIRECTOR/CHOREOGRAPHER: Jerome Whyte; MUSICAL DIRECTOR: Reginald Burston. *Cast:* CARRIE: Margot Moser, *Beryl Foley, June Powell, Dorothy Laroque*; JULIE: Iva Withers, *Laverne Burden, Beryl Foley*; MRS. MULLIN: Marjorie Mars; BILLY: Stephen Douglass, *Edmund Hockridge, Kenneth Sandford*; NETTIE: Marion Ross, *Valetta Iacopi*; MR. SNOW: Eric Mattson; JIGGER: Morgan Davies; BOATSWAIN: Robert Pagent, *Robert Stevenson*; ARMINY: Dorothy Laroque; STARKEEPER: William Sherwood; LOUISE: Bambi Linn.

PAPER MILL PLAYHOUSE, New Jersey, 1952. *Cast:* Stephen Douglass, Mary O'Fallon.

CITY CENTER, NYC, 6/2/54–8/8/54. 79 PERFORMANCES. DIRECTOR: William Hammerstein; CHOREOGRAPHER: Robert Pagent; SETS: Oliver Smith; COSTUMES: John Boyt; LIGHTING: Jean Rosenthal; MUSI-

CAL DIRECTOR: Julius Rudel; PRODUCTION STAGE MANAGER: Lucia Victor. *Cast:* CARRIE: Barbara Cook; JULIE: Jo Sullivan; MRS. MULLIN: Winifred Heidt [Karen Ziemba's grandmother in real life]; BILLY: Chris Robinson; 1ST POLICEMAN/PRINCIPAL: Russell Goodwin; BASCOMBE: Stanley Carlson; NETTIE: Jean Handzlik; JUNE GIRL: Mavis Ray; MR. SNOW: Don Blackey; JIGGER: John Conte; HANNAH: Dusty Worrall; BOATSWAIN/CARNIVAL BOY: Robert Pagent; ARMINY: Marilyn Bladd; 2ND POLICEMAN: William W. Reynolds; CAPTAIN: Boris Aplon; HEAVENLY FRIEND: Jay Velie; STARKEEPER: Daniel Reed; LOUISE: Bambi Linn; ENOCH JR.: James Martindale.

THE MOVIE. 1956. *Cast:* CARRIE: Barbara Ruick; JULIE: Shirley Jones; MRS. MULLIN: Audrey Christie; BILLY: Gordon MacRae; MR. SNOW: Robert Rounseville; JIGGER: Cameron Mitchell; HEAVENLY FRIEND: William Le Massena; STARKEEPER: Gene Lockhart; LOUISE: Susan Luckey.

CITY CENTER, NYC, 9/11/57–9/29/57. 24 PERFORMANCES. DIRECTOR: John Fearnley; CHOREOGRAPHER: Robert Pagent; SETS: Oliver Smith; COSTUMES: Florence Klotz; LIGHTING: Peggy Clark; MUSICAL DIRECTOR: Julius Rudel. *Cast:* CARRIE: Pat Stanley; JULIE: Barbara Cook; MRS. MULLIN: Kay Medford; BILLY: Howard Keel; 1ST POLICEMAN: Evans Thornton; BASCOMBE: Robert Eckles; GIRL WITH BEAR: Elisa Monte; NETTIE: Marie Powers; JUNE GIRL: Evelyn Taylor; MR. SNOW: Russell Nype; JIGGER: James Mitchell; HANNAH: Joan Eheman; BOATSWAIN/CARNIVAL BOY: Bob Pagent; 2ND POLICEMAN: James E. Gannon; CAPTAIN: Sam Kirkham; HEAVENLY FRIEND: Leo Lucker; STARKEEPER: Victor Moore; LOUISE: Bambi Linn; ENOCH JR.: Larry Fuller; PRINCIPAL: Bruce Baggett; CHORUS INCLUDED: Basha Regis, Jack Eddleman, Vincent B. McMahon, Patricia Birch, Dorothy Etheridge, Mickey Gunnersen, Kiki Minor, Bob Neukum, Bob St. Clair, Jeanne Shea, Gerald M. Teijelo Jr. This production, despite being a City Center run, was nominated for a Tony, for sets.

CURRAN THEATRE, San Francisco. Opened on 4/22/63. PRESENTED BY Edwin Lester and his San Francisco Civic Light Opera Association; DIRECTOR: Edward Greenberg; CHOREOGRAPHER: Gemze de Lappe; MUSICAL DIRECTOR: Louis Adrian. *Cast:* CARRIE: Pat Stanley; JULIE: Jan Clayton; BILLY: John Raitt; MR. SNOW: Frank Porretta; JIGGER: Gerald Price; HANNAH: Dusty Worrall; STARKEEPER: Don Beddoe.

NEW YORK STATE THEATRE, 8/10/65–9/18/65. 47 PERFORMANCES. PRESENTED BY Music Theatre of Lincoln Center; DIRECTOR: Edward Greenberg; CHOREOGRAPHER: Gemze de Lappe; SETS: Paul C. McGuire; COSTUMES: Stanley Simmons; LIGHTING: Peter Hunt; MUSICAL DIRECTOR: Franz Allers. *Cast:* CARRIE: Susan Watson; JULIE: Eileen Christy; MRS. MULLIN: Benay Venuta; BILLY: John Raitt; BASCOMBE: Ralston Hill; NETTIE: Katherine Hilgenberg; MR. SNOW: Reid Shelton; JIGGER: Jerry Orbach; HANNAH: Jenny Workman; ARMINY: Dixie Carter; CAPTAIN/PRINCIPAL: John Dorrin; STARKEEPER: Edward Everett Horton; LOUISE: Linda Howe; SINGERS INCLUDED: Ronn Carroll, Cathy Corkill, Laried Montgomery, Bob Neukum; DANCERS INCLUDED: Dennis Cole, Victor Duntiere, Lucia Lambert, Toodie Wittmer. This production got great reviews. The show then went on tour. It opened on 9/20/65, at the Shubert Theatre, Cincinnati, and closed on 2/5/66, at the Shubert Theatre, Boston. The tour had the same basic crew, except PRESS: John L. Toohey. It had the same cast except BILLY: Harve Presnell; CARRIE: Dran Seitz.

CITY CENTER, NYC, 12/15/66–1/1/67. 2 previews. 22 PERFORMANCES. DIRECTOR: Gus Schirmer; CHOREOGRAPHER: Gemze de Lappe; SETS: Paul C. McGuire; COSTUMES: Stanley Simmons; LIGHTING: Feder; MUSICAL DIRECTOR: Jonathan Anderson. *Cast:* CARRIE: Nancy Dussault; JULIE: Constance Towers; MRS. MULLIN: Louise Larrabee; BILLY: Bruce Yarnell; NETTIE: Patricia Neway; MR. SNOW: Jack De Lon; JIGGER: Michael Kermoyan; HANNAH: Jenny Workman; BOATSWAIN/CARNIVAL BOY: Darrell Notara; HEAVENLY FRIEND: Jay Velie; STARKEEPER: Parker Fennelly; LOUISE: Sandy Duncan; ENOCH JR.: Dennis Cole; SINGERS INCLUDED: Paul Adams, Gene Albano, Darrell Askey, Phyllis Bash, Austin Colyer, Marvin Goodis, Laried Montgomery, Estella Munson, Maggie Task; DANCERS INCLUDED: Carol Flemming, Mickey Gunnersen, Curtis Hood, Lucia Lambert, Vernon Wendorf, Toodie Wittmer. **Understudies:** Billy: Nolan Van Way; Mrs. Mullin: Betty Hyatt Linton; Julie: Estella Munson.

TV PRODUCTION. ABC, 5/7/67. *Cast:* CARRIE: Marlyn Mason; BILLY: Robert Goulet; JULIE: Mary Grover.

JONES BEACH THEATRE, NY, 6/22/73–9/2/73. 74 PERFORMANCES. PRESENTED BY Guy Lombardo; DIRECTOR: John Fearnley; CHOREOGRAPHER: Robert Pagent; COSTUMES: Winn Morton; LIGHTING: Peggy Clark. *Cast:* CARRIE: Bonnie Franklin; JULIE: Barbara Meister; MRS. MULLIN: Mary Ellen Ashley; BILLY: John Cullum; MR. SNOW: Reid Shelton; JIGGER: Alfred Toigo; HEAVENLY FRIEND: John Stewart; STARKEEPER: Jay Velie; CHORUS INCLUDED: Mickey Gunnersen, Sherry Lambert, Dixie Stewart, Lani Sundsten, Sal Provenza, Ralph Vucci. *Understudy:* BILLY: John Stewart.

KENNEDY CENTER, Washington, DC, 6/14/86–7/19/86. CHOREOGRAPHER: Peter Martins. *Cast:* JULIE: Katharine Buffaloe; BILLY: Tom Wopat.

125. *Carousel (1994 Broadway revival)*

Before Broadway. This revival began in London, where it opened at the ROYAL NATIONAL THEATRE, on 12/10/92, for a limited run. It moved to the SHAFTESBURY THEATRE on 9/10/93. PRESENTED BY Cameron Mackintosh; DIRECTOR: Nicholas Hytner; CHOREOGRAPHER: Sir Kenneth Macmillan; SETS: Bob Crowley; CAST RECORDING on First Night. *Cast:* CARRIE: Janie Dee, *Katrina Murphy*; JULIE: Joanna Riding; BILLY: Michael Hayden, *Hal Fowler*; NETTIE: Meg Johnson.

Then it went to Broadway, where the sets were re-designed specifically for the Vivian Beaumont. The number "The Highest Judge of All" was dropped.

The Broadway Run. VIVIAN BEAUMONT THEATRE, 3/24/94–1/17/95. 46 previews from 2/18/94. 322 PERFORMANCES. PRESENTED BY Lincoln Center Theatre, by arrangement with The Royal National Theatre, Cameron Mackintosh, and the Rodgers & Hammerstein Organization; DIRECTOR: Nicholas Hytner; CHOREOGRAPHER: Jane Elliott (staged Sir Kenneth Macmillan's London choreography); SETS/COSTUMES: Bob Crowley; LIGHTING: Paul Pyant; SOUND: Steve Canyon Kennedy; MUSICAL DIRECTOR: Eric Stern; NEW ORCHESTRATIONS: William David Brohn; BROADWAY CAST recording on Broadway Angel; PRESS: Merle Debuskey; CASTING: Daniel Swee; GENERAL MANAGER: Steven C. Callahan; COMPANY MANAGER: Edward J. Nelson; PRODUCTION STAGE MANAGER: Peter von Mayrhauser; STAGE MANAGER: Michael J. Passaro; ASSISTANT STAGE MANAGER: Valerie Lau-Kee Lai. *Cast:* CARRIE PIPPERIDGE: Audra Ann McDonald; JULIE JORDAN: Sally Murphy; MRS. MULLIN: Kate Buddeke; BILLY BIGELOW: Michael Hayden, *Marcus Lovett, James Barbour* (from 12/94); POLICEMEN: Taye Diggs & Tony Capone; DAVID BASCOMBE: Robert Breuler, *Peter Maloney*; NETTIE FOWLER: Shirley Verrett; ENOCH SNOW: Eddie Korbich, *Darius de Haas*; JIGGER CRAIGIN: Fisher Stevens, *David Warshofsky*; INNKEEPER: Rebecca Eichenberger; CAPTAIN: Brian d'Arcy James; HEAVENLY FRIEND: Lauren Ward; STARKEEPER: Jeff Weiss; LOUISE: Sandra Brown, *Dana Stackpole, Sandra Brown*; LOUISE'S FRIENDS: Robert Cary, Glen Harris, Steven Ochoa, Michael O'Donnell, Alexies Sanchez, Rocker Verastique; FAIRGROUND BOY: Jon Marshall Sharp, *Robert Conn* (during Mr. Sharp's vacation); ENOCH SNOW JR.: Duane Boutte; MARGARET SNOW: Lovette George; OTHER SNOW CHILDREN: Philipp Lee Carabuena, Cece Cortes, Lyn Nagel, Cindy Robinson, Tiffany Sampson, Tse-Mach Washington; PRINCIPAL: Brian d'Arcy James; DR. SELDON: Jeff Weiss; ROBERT ALLEN: Steven Ochoa; HANNAH BENTLEY: Cindy Robinson; PETER BENTLEY JR.: Tony Capone; ABBIE CHASE: Natascia A. Diaz; CHARLIE "CHIP" CHASE: Alexies Sanchez; JONATHAN CHASE: Robert Cary; VIRGINIA FRAZER: Rebecca Eichenberger; BUDDY HAMLIN: Devin Richards; CYRUS HAMLIN: Taye Diggs; ARMINY LIVERMORE: Paula Newsome; HUDSON LIVERMORE: Brian d'Arcy James; WILLIAM OSGOOD: Rocker Verastique; ORRIN PEESLEY: Duane Boutte; SUSAN PETERS: Linda Gabler; MYRTLE ROBBINS: Lacey Hornkohl; ELLA SANBORN: Alexia Hess; JENNY SANBORN: Lauren Ward; MARTHA SEWELL: Keri Lee; LIZA SINCLAIR: Endaylyn Taylor-Shellman; PENNY SINCLAIR: Lovette George; HENRY SEARS: Jeffrey James; ABNER SPERRY: Michael O'Donnell; BEN SPERRY: Glen Harris; SADIE SPERRY: Dana Stackpole. *Understudies:* Billy: Duane Boutte & Tony Capone; Julie: Lauren Ward & Cindy Robinson; Carrie: Paula Newsome & Lovette George; Nettie: Paula Newsome & Rebecca Eichenberger; Mrs. Mullin: Endaylyn Taylor-Shellman & Rebecca Eichenberger; Bascombe: Brian d'Arcy James & Devin Richards;

Jigger: Taye Diggs & Brian d'Arcy James; Mr. Snow: Brian d'Arcy James & Thomas Titone; Starkeeper: Robert Breuler & Devin Richards; Louise: Dana Stackpole, Jennifer Alexander, Donna Rubin; Fairground Boy: Glen Harris & Alexies Sanchez. *Swings:* Robert Cary, Lisa Mayer, Donna Rubin, Thomas Titone, Reggie Valdez. *Orchestra:* WOODWINDS: Diva Goodfriend-Koven, Charles Wilson, Josh Siegel, Virgil Blackwell, Ethan Bauch; HORNS: Paul Riggio, Christopher Costanzi, Janet Lantz; TRUMPETS: John Frosk & Darryl Shaw; TROMBONES: Ed Neumeister & David Bargeron; HARP: Beth Robinson; PERCUSSION: Susan Evans; VIOLINS: Alicia Edelberg, Maura Giannini, Susan Lorentsen, Heidi Stubner, Martha Mott-Gale, Janine Kam-Lal, Blair Lawhead; VIOLAS: John Dexter & Richard Spencer; CELLI: Matthias Naegele, Beverly Lauridsen, Eileen Folson; BASS: Richard Sarpola.

Critics mostly raved. It won Tony Awards for revival of a musical, director, choreography, sets, and for Audra Ann McDonald.

After Broadway. TOUR. Opened on 2/2/96, at the Music Hall, Houston. Previews from 1/30/96. Played in 17 cities. PRESENTED BY Columbia Artists Management, Center Theatre Group, Jujamcyn Theatre Productions, and Theatre Under the Stars, in association with The Troika Organization & PACE Theatrical Group; DIRECTOR: Nicholas Hytner; CHOREOGRAPHER: Kenneth Macmillan; SETS: Bob Crowley; MUSICAL DIRECTOR: Kevin Farrell. *Cast:* CARRIE: Sherry D. Boone, *Katie Hugo* (from 2/18/97); JULIE: Sarah Uriarte, *Jennifer Laura Thompson* (from 11/13/96); BILLY: Patrick Wilson; NETTIE: Rebecca Eichenberger, *Patricia Phillips* (from 12/25/96); MR. SNOW: Sean Palmer, *Jesse Means II* (from 2/18/97); JIGGER: Brett Rickaby; ALSO WITH: Kate Buddeke, Dana Stackpole, Duane Boutte, Heather McFadden, George Merrick, Rommy Sandhu.

PAPER MILL PLAYHOUSE, New Jersey, 6/1/01–7/15/01. Previews from 5/30/01. DIRECTOR: Robert Johanson; CHOREOGRAPHER: Robert La Fosse; SETS: Michael Anania; LIGHTING: F. Mitchell Dana; MUSICAL DIRECTOR: Tom Helm. *Cast:* CARRIE: Christiane Noll; JULIE: Glory Crampton; BILLY: Matt Bogart; MR. SNOW: Brandon Jovanovich [Robert Evan had been the first choice]; JIGGER: Jim Newman; STARKEEPER: Eddie Bracken [opening night was Mr. Bracken's 15,000th career stage performance].

ISAAC STERN AUDITORIUM, Carnegie Hall, 6/6/02 (one night benefit concert). Part of the series *Richard Rodgers: a Centennial Celebration.* DIRECTOR: Walter Bobbie; CONDUCTOR OF THE ORCHESTRA OF ST. LUKE'S: Leonard Slatkin; MUSICAL CONSULTANT/CHORAL DIRECTOR: Ben Whitely. *Cast:* CARRIE: Lauren Ward; JULIE: Audra McDonald; MRS. MULLIN: Blythe Danner; BILLY: Hugh Jackman; NETTIE: Judy Kaye; MR. SNOW: Jason Danieley; JIGGER: Norbert Leo Butz; STARKEEPER: Philip Bosco; LOUISE: Eden Riegel; SPECIAL GUEST: John Raitt.

ROYAL FESTIVAL HALL, London. 6/02. Concert. *Cast:* JULIE: Emily Loesser; BILLY: Spencer McLaren; STARKEEPER: Julian Glover.

126. *Carrie*

It opens in the high-school gym, where twenty or so girls are doing aerobics under the guidance of Miss Gardner. The girls take showers in their underwear — and with no water, as part of the set. Carrie has her first period — on stage!, and is taunted by the other girls for her ignorance of this phenomenon. Carrie's mother, Margaret, is a religious fanatic. Sue is a good girl who regrets taunting Carrie, and Chris is a bad girl who hates Carrie. Miss Gardner helps Carrie believe that one day she will find love. The "Night Spot" is a gathering-place for the students. Sue persuades nice boyfriend Tommy to take Carrie to the prom, but Margaret forbids Carrie to go (that's how Carrie was conceived), and Carrie's hands burst into flame. Billy and Chris slaughter pigs for blood that will humiliate Carrie. Carrie prepares for the prom, and we find she is telekinetic. At the prom Billy pours a bucket of blood over Carrie's head. Then Margaret stabs Carrie, but Carrie kills her mother by touching her.

Before Broadway. There had been the famous 1976 straight film, written by Lawrence D. Cohen from Stephen King's book, and directed by Brian De Palma. Betty Buckley played the gym teacher. It took seven years from the conception of the stage musical by Michael Gore and Lawrence Cohen to the time it hit Broadway. In 8/84 a workshop of Act I was presented at 890 BROADWAY. *Cast*: CARRIE: Annie Golden; MARGARET: Maureen McGovern; MISS GARDNER: Laurie Beechman; SUE: Laura Dean; CHRIS: Liz Callaway; TOMMY: Todd Graff; BILLY: Peter Neptune. It was announced to be having a Broadway opening in the fall of 1986, to be produced by Barry & Fran Weissler and Fred Zollo. But they couldn't find the money, and eventually it was taken up by West German producer Friedrich Kurz, who had produced *Cats* in West Berlin, and who would later do *Starlight Express* in the same place. Kurz arranged for a co-production with the Royal Shakespeare Company in London. That organization's artistic director, Terry Hands, came aboard as director. Debbie Allen (from *Fame* fame) came in as choreographer. By special arrangement with Equity in both Britain and the USA the cast was half American and half British. The crew was equally divided also. Its first brief (but sold out) tryout opened 3/1/88 at the Royal Shakespeare Company's mainstage theatre at STRATFORD-UPON-AVON, where Barbara Cook (as Margaret) quit (at the end of the run) after being almost decapitated on stage by the set. Reviews were terrible; the RSC came under fire for using subsidized funds to mount a Broadway tryout (even though Herr Kurz supplied most of the money). Harold Wheeler was brought in to re-orchestrate the score. CBS, who had an investment in the show, pulled out about this time, and the show almost closed. Then it went to Broadway. The Broadway preview opening date was postponed several times.

The Broadway Run. VIRGINIA THEATRE, 5/12/88–5/15/88. 16 previews from 4/28/88. 5 PERFORMANCES. The Friedrich Kurz/Royal Shakespeare Company production, PRESENTED BY Friedrich Kurz, in association with Whitecap Productions & Martin Barandes; MUSIC: Michael Gore; LYRICS: Dean Pitchford; BOOK: Lawrence D. Cohen; BASED ON the 1974 novel of the same name by Stephen King; DIRECTOR/LIGHTING: Terry Hands; CHOREOGRAPHER: Debbie Allen; SETS: Ralph Koltai; COSTUMES: Alexander Reid; SOUND: Martin Levan; MUSICAL SUPERVISOR: Harold Wheeler; MUSICAL DIRECTOR: Paul Schwartz; ORCHESTRATIONS: Anders Eljas, Harold Wheeler, Michael Starobin; PRESS: PMK Public Relation/Jim Baldassare; CASTING: Lyons/Isaacson; GENERAL MANAGEMENT: Waissman & Buckley; STAGE MANAGERS: Joe Lorden, Jeremy Sturt, Jack Gianino; ASSISTANT STAGE MANAGER: Ed Fitzgerald. *Cast*: MARGARET WHITE: Betty Buckley; CARRIE WHITE: Linzi Hateley; CHRIS: Charlotte d'Amboise; TOMMY: Paul Gyngell; MISS GARDNER: Darlene Love; BILLY: Gene Anthony Ray; SUE: Sally Ann Triplett; ENSEMBLE: JAMIE: Jamie Beth Chandler; CATHY: Catherine Doffey; MICHELE: Michele du Verney; SHELLEY: Michelle Hodgson; ROSE: Rosemarie Jackson; KELLY: Kelly Littlefield; MADDY: Madeleine Loftin; MICHELLE: Michelle Nelson; MARY ANN: Mary Ann Ocdy; SQUEEZIE: Suzanne Maria Thomas; GARY: Gary Co-Burn; KEVIN: Kevin Coyne; DAVID: David Danns; MATTHEW: Matthew Dickens; ERIC: Eric Gilliom; KENNY: Kenny Linden; JOEY: Joey McKneely; MARK: Mark Santoro; CHRIS: Christopher Solari; SCOTT: Scott Wise. *Standbys*: Margaret: Audrey Lavine; Miss Gardner: Lillias White. *Understudies*: Carrie: Rosemarie Jackson; Sue: Catherine Doffey & Jamie Beth Chandler; Chris: Mary Ann Oedy; Billy: Christopher Solari & David Danns; Tommy: Matthew Dickens & Kenny Linden. *Swing Dancers*: Mary Ann Lamb & Darryl Eric Tribble. *Orchestra*: ALTO SAX: William Kerr; TENOR SAXES: Robert Steen & Kenneth Dybisz; TRUMPETS: Scott De Ogburn, David L. Brown, Philip Granger; FRENCH HORN: David W. Smith; TROMBONE: Birch Johnson; BASS TROMBONE: John C. Gale; VIOLINS: Katsuko Esaki, Martin Agee, Karl Kawahara, Carol Pool; VIOLAS: Jenny Hansen & Richard Spencer; CELLI: Diane Chaplin & Francesca Vansaco; KEYBOARDS: Keith Phillips & Greg Dlugos; GUITAR: Andy Schwartz; ELECTRIC BASS: Stuart Woods; DRUMS: Brian Brake; PERCUSSION: Thad Wheeler. *Act I: Prologue* The gymnasium": In" (Miss Gardner & Girls); *Scene 1* The showers: "Dream On" (Girls & Carrie); *Scene 2* The locker room: "Carrie" (Carrie); *Scene 3* The White home: "Open Your Heart" (Margaret & Carrie), "And Eve Was Weak" (Margaret & Carrie); *Scene 4* The drive-in: "Don't Waste the Moon" (Sue, Tommy, Chris, Billy, Girls, Boys); *Scene 5* The White home: "Evening Prayers" (Carrie & Margaret); *Scene 6* The gymnasium: "Unsuspecting Hearts" (Miss Gardner & Carrie); *Scene 7* The "Night Spot": "Do Me

a Favor" (Sue, Tommy, Chris, Billy, Girls, Boys); *Scene 8* The White home: "I Remember How Those Boys Could Dance" (Margaret). *Act II*: *Scene 1* The pig farm: "Out for Blood" (Chris, Billy, Boys); *Scene 2* The gymnasium: "It Hurts to Be Strong" (Sue); *Scene 3* Carrie's room: "I'm Not Alone" (Carrie), "When There's No One" (Margaret); *Scene 4* The prom: "Wotta Night!" (Girls & Boys), "Unsuspecting Hearts" (reprise) (Miss Gardner & Carrie), "Heaven" (Tommy, Sue, Miss Gardner, Carrie, Margaret, Girls, Boys), "Alma Mater" (Girls, Boys, Miss Gardner), "The Destruction" (Carrie); *Scene 5* Epilogue: "Carrie" (reprise) (Margaret).

With the exception of Clive Barnes in *The Post*, the show was panned. Raves were the only things that could have saved it, as there was no money left to keep it going until it found an audience. It lost $8 million, the most expensive flop to that date (Jujamcyn Theatres invested $1 million). It had a lot of good things in it, however. Betty Buckley, for one; some of the music was great; the mother and daughter scenes; and it was never dull.

After Broadway. In 2002 Bryan Fuller wrote a TV script of the straight story. *Cast*: Angela Bettis.

Erik Jackson wanted to re-stage the musical, but was talked out of it. Instead, he went back to Stephen King's novel, and wrote a new stage adaptation, a black comedy (not a musical). In 2003 it got an Off Broadway production with THEATRE COUTURE, starring drag-artist Sherry Vine. DIRECTOR: Josh Rosenzweig; SETS/LIGHTING: Kevin Adams.

127. *Catch a Star!*

An intimate musical revue, an early vehicle for several people who would later make it big.

The Broadway Run. PLYMOUTH THEATRE, 9/6/55–9/24/55. 23 PERFORMANCES. PRESENTED BY Sy Kleinman; MUSIC/LYRICS/SKETCHES: various writers; ADDITIONAL MATERIAL: Lee Adams; CONCEIVED BY: Ray Golden; SKETCH DIRECTOR: Danny Simon; CHOREOGRAPHER: Lee Sherman; SETS: Ralph Alswang; COSTUMES: Thomas Becher; MUSICAL DIRECTOR/ORCHESTRATIONS: Milton Greene; BALLET MUSIC COMPOSED BY: Herb Schutz; PRESS: Karl Bernstein & Harvey Sabinson; PRODUCTION SUPERVISOR: Ray Golden; CO-ORDINATOR: Robert Nesbitt; GENERAL MANAGER: Arthur Klein; PRODUCTION STAGE MANAGER: Gene Perlowin; STAGE MANAGERS: John Foster & Bill Smillie. *Act I*: *Scene 1* Prologue: "Catch a Star!" (m: Sammy Fain; l: Paul Francis Webster). Sung by Wayne Sherwood; *Scene 2* "Everybody Wants to Be in Show Business" (m: Phil Charig; l: Ray Golden & Bud Burston): PRODUCER: David Burns (2); STAGE DOORMAN: Jack Wakefield; THIEF: Denny Desmond, *Carl Jeffrey*; POLICEMAN: Wayne Sherwood; MAGICIAN: Calvin Holt; MAGICIAN'S ASSISTANT: Rhoda Kerns; MODEL: Undine Forrest; WOMAN WITH BABY CARRIAGE: Kay Malone; AMBULANCE ATTENDANTS: Carl Jeffrey (*Denny Desmond*) & Marc Breaux; PATIENT: Mickey Calin; CHORUS GIRLS: Lillian D'Honau & Sigyn; WAITRESS: Helen Halpin; SECRETARIES: Louise Golden & Elaine Dunn; CHARITY COLLECTOR: Kay Kingston; *Scene 3* New Styles in Acting (by Danny Simon): PRODUCER: David Burns (2); SECRETARY: Carol Field [this role was added during the run]; MILITARY PILOT: Jack Wakefield; TENNIS PLAYER: Sonny Sparks, *Denny Desmond*; STAGE MANAGER: Denny Desmond [this role became The Professor during the run, played by *Sonny Sparks*]; THE INGENUE: Pat Carroll (1); *Scene 4* "A Little Traveling Music" (m: Hal Borne; l: Paul Francis Webster & Ray Golden): THE TRAVELER: Elaine Dunn (3); THREE IMPROPER BOSTONIANS: Louise Golden, Sigyn, Lillian D'Honau; *Scene 5* Matinee Idles (by Danny & Neil Simon): a group of gossipy women playgoers and a long-suffering male at a matinee performance of *Damn Yankees*: HAWKER: Denny Desmond; PETE: Wayne Sherwood; MAN: Jack Wakefield; TRIXIE: Pat Carroll (1); DOROTHY: Helen Halpin; MARTHA: Carol Field; LUCILLE: Undine Forrest; HAZEL: Rhoda Kerns; HARRIETT: Kay Malone; FLORENCE: Kay Kingston; ACTOR: Denny Desmond, *Sonny Sparks*; ACTRESS: Lillian D'Honau; *Scene 6* "One Hour Ahead of the Posse" (m: Phil Charig; l: Ray Golden & Dave Ormont): KILLER: Wayne Sherwood; GIRL: Lillian D'Honau; SHERIFF: Marc Breaux; POSSE: Calvin Holt, Carl Jeffrey, Mickey Calin, Denny Desmond; FOLK SINGERS: Carol Field, Rhoda Kerns, Kay Malone; *Scene 7* And Then I Wrote (by Danny & Neil Simon): HARRY: Jack Wakefield; KITTY: Helen Halpin; MAX

DILLINGBERT: David Burns (2); GUS: Marc Breaux; LABONZA: Sonny Sparks; PHOEBE: Undine Forrest; CUSTOMER: Denny Desmond; *Scene 8* "Las Vegas" (m: Sy Kleinman; l: Ray Golden; add l: Lee Adams): GIRL: Pat Carroll (1); BELLHOPS: Wayne Sherwood, Carl Jeffrey, Mickey Calin, Denny Desmond; *Scene 9* "To Be or Not to Be in Love" (m: Phil Charig; l: Ray Golden, Danny Shapiro, Milton Pascal): GIRL: Trude Adams; BOY: Marc Breaux; *Scene 10* "The Story of Alice" (m: Jerry Bock; l: Larry Holofcener): QUARTET: Helen Halpin, Wayne Sherwood, Calvin Holt, Undine Forrest; *Scene 11* Room for Rent (by Danny & Neil Simon): SOUTHERN BELLE: Pat Carroll (1); 1ST MAN: David Burns (2); 1ST ROOMER: Jack Wakefield; 2ND ROOMER: Sonny Sparks; 3RD ROOMER: Lynne Bretonn, *Kay Kingston*; 4TH ROOMER: Kay Malone [role cut during the run]; 2ND MAN: Wayne Sherwood; TRUCK DRIVER: Denny Desmond [role cut during the run]; *Scene 12* "What a Song Can Do" (m/l: Bernie Wayne & Lee Morris). Sung by Helen Halpin; *Scene 13* "Carnival in Court" (m: Jay Navarre; l: Ray Golden & I.A.L. Diamond): TOWN CRIER: David Burns (2); BAILIFF: Calvin Holt; TWO GIRLS: Sigyn & Louise Golden; JUDGE: Jack Wakefield; PLAINTIFF: Helen Halpin; DEFENDANT: Sonny Sparks; PRIVATE EYE: Marc Breaux; PRIVATE EYE'S WIFE: Elaine Dunn (3); CO-RESPONDENT: Pat Carroll (1); THREE BELLES: Lillian D'Honau, Undine Forrest, Kay Malone; TWO SAILORS: Mickey Calin & Denny Desmond; BASKETMAN: Wayne Sherwood; BASKETWOMAN: Carol Field. *Act II*: *Scene 1* Theatre Piece: THREE MALE DANCERS: Marc Breaux, Carl Jeffrey (*Mickey Calin*), Calvin Holt; THREE FEMALE DANCERS: Sigyn, Elaine Dunn, Louise Golden; THREE CHARACTERS: Wayne Sherwood, Mickey Calin, Carol Field [during the run these roles were reduced to one—Character, played by *Carl Jeffrey*]; GLAMOUR GIRLS: Undine Forrest, Kay Malone, Rhoda Kerns, Lillian D'Honau (Harlequin); *Scene 2* Arty (by Danny & Neil Simon): after Paddy Chayefsky's 1955 play *Marty;* a stubborn mother is determined to get her reluctant son a wife: MOM: Pat Carroll (1); ARTY: Jack Wakefield; 1ST MAN: Denny Desmond; 2ND MAN: Sonny Sparks; *Scene 3* "Twist My Arm" (m: Sammy Fain; l: Paul Francis Webster): Girl: Elaine Dunn (3); Boy: Marc Breaux; *Scene 4* "New Hollywood Plots" (m: Sammy Fain; l: Paul Francis Webster). Performed by: David Burns, Denny Desmond, Calvin Holt [this song was dropped during the run]; *Scene 5* "Foreign Cars" (m/l: Norman Martin). Sung by Trude Adams; *Scene 6* "Gruntled" (m/l: Phil Charig, Ray Golden, Sy Kleinman): GIRL: Helen Halpin; BOY: Denny Desmond; THREE COUPLES: Marc Breaux & Elaine Dunn, Calvin Holt & Lillian D'Honau, Mickey Calin & Sigyn; *Scene 7* Matrimonial Agency (by Danny & Neil Simon): FIRST WOMAN: Undine Forrest; SECOND WOMAN: Kay Malone; ADRIAN: David Burns (2); FIRST SHOPPER: Kay Kingston; FIRST MAN: Mickey Calin; MRS. ENNIS: Pat Carroll (1); MISS B.: Carol Field; THE FRENCHMAN: Marc Breaux; THE REJECT: Jack Wakefield; THE BODY: Sonny Sparks; *Scene 8* "Fly Little Heart" (m: Jerry Bock; l: Larry Holofcener): GIRL: Elaine Dunn (3), "Bachelor Hoedown" (m: Jerry Bock; l: Larry Holofcener). Performed by: Elaine Dunn, Marc Breaux, Sigyn, Louise Golden, Carol Field, Lillian D'Honau, Rhoda Kerns, Mickey Calin, Calvin Holt, Denny Desmond, Carl Jeffrey, Wayne Sherwood; *Scene 9* Gift of the Magi (by Mike Stewart): Performed by Pat Carroll; *Scene 10* "Boffola" (m: Phil Charig; l: Danny Shapiro, Milton Pascal, Ray Golden). Performed by the Entire Cast.

Broadway reviews were divided, nothing really bad, nothing really good. Pat Carroll was nominated for a Tony. Mickey Calin, who was in the cast, would become the movie actor Michael Callan; and Carl Jeffrey would become Carl Jablonski.

128. *Cats*

There was not much of a libretto, and no spoken dialogue. Cats cavort around a junkyard in elaborate costumes, singing and dancing. Jellicle Cats are special mainly because they can be reincarnated. Every year, in their junkyard, they get together, under Old Deuteronomy, the oldest and wisest cat, to decide who is going to be the next to go up the Heavyside Layer, a celestial holding bay for Jellicles about to be born again. Each cat tells his or her own story, putting forward their cases. Jennyanydots, the

humble Gumbie Cat, is a housekeeper who, dormant during the day, at night teaches music, crocheting and tatting to the mice, and keeps the cockroaches in line. Rum Tum Tugger is a rock 'n roll cat, an Elvis-type, a ladies' cat. Grizabella, once a glamour cat until she left the junkyard to see what the real world was like, is now an aging, fading hooker, desperate to be born again, but she is rejected by the cats. Bustopher is a fat-cat, a dignified highliver, 25 pounds and still putting it on. He has a cane and white spats. The evil Macavity is lurking nearby, and then his cat-burglar henchmen, Mungojerrie and Rumpleteazer (Cockney crooks in the London version), arrive. They are chased away. Then Old Deuteronomy arrives. Munkustrap, a gray tabby, puts on a play for him, *The Battle of the Pekes and Pollicles*, about dogs barking at each other until Rumpus Cat arrives to break it up. Then they have the Jellicle Ball. Victoria does her dance solo, and then Grizabella comes again, and is again rejected. Jellylorum brings out Gus, a retired stage star, now old and thin, and with palsy. He remembers one of his favorite plays, *Growltiger's Last Stand*, in which he was a pirate, the Terror of the Thames. Genghis and his Siamese cats take his ship and force him to walk the plank. After the pirate play Skimbleshanks tells how he runs everything for the humans on the Sleeping Car Express. Then Macavity kidnaps Old Deuteronomy. Mr. Mistoffolees, a magic cat, brings him back, and Grizabella is the one awarded a place this year to the Heavyside Layer. She ascends on a giant tire to the upper reaches of the theatre, to the tune of "Memory."

Before Broadway. In 1977 Andrew Lloyd Webber began setting T.S. Eliot's poems to music for the amusement of his friends. His intention became to present the show as a one-act musical, to be coupled with *Tell Me on a Sunday*, a one-woman song recital that eventually became the song half of *Song and Dance* (q.v.). It wasn't long before the poems in Eliot's book were exhausted, so Mr. Lloyd Webber chose other Eliot works. Then, as the show expanded into a full evening's entertainment, Trevor Nunn and Richard Stilgoe wrote new lyrics. Valerie Eliot, the poet's widow, gave Andrew Lloyd Webber a previously unpublished fragment of her husband's work, "Rhapsody on a Windy Night" which, with other Eliot poems of his "Prufrock" period, was transformed into the song "Memory" (a popular hit for Barbra Streisand and Judy Collins).

THE LONDON RUN. *Cats* was Andrew Lloyd Webber's first hit without his former partner Tim Rice, and it was this show that made him the pre-eminent name in Western theatre. Judi Dench broke her ankle in rehearsals in the role of Grizabella, and Elaine Paige came in instead. It ran at the NEW LONDON THEATRE, 5/11/81–5/11/02. 8,950 PERFORMANCES. DIRECTOR: Trevor Nunn; CHOREOGRAPHER: Gillian Lynne; SETS/COSTUMES: John Napier; MUSICAL DIRECTOR: David Firman, Tony Stenson, Mike Stanley. **Cast** (with characters arranged alphabetically): ADMETUS: Steven Wayne, *Phillip Devonshire* (by 3/86), *Sandy Strallen* (by 2/87), *Andrew Norman* (by 2/90), *Frank Thompson* (by 11/91), *Bryn Walters* (by 5/92), *Sean Kingsley* (by 6/94), *Richard Armitage* (10/94–5/95), *Alastair Bull* (95–10/96), *Peter Van Dosselaer* (10/96–2/97), *Steven-John Tokaya* (4/97–10/97), *Andrew Wright* (10/97–10/98), *Jeron Mosselman* (10/98–4/99), *Kenny Linden* (4/99–10/00), *Philip Michael* (from 10/00), *Kenny Linden* (from 4/01) [role not on Broadway]; ALONZO: Roland Alexander, *Nigel Spencer* (by 5/82), *Roland Alexander* (by 2/83), *Patrick Wood* (by 9/83), *Sean Kay* (by 5/85), *Hugh Spight* (by 3/86), *Richard Cuerden* (by 2/87), *Calvin Cornwall* (by 8/88), *Neil Johnson* (by 11/91), *Warren Carlyle* (by 11/92), *Steven Houghton* (by 5/93), *Simon Street* (by 6/94), *Nunzio Lombardo* (from 4/95), *Jason Gardiner* (from 4/97), *Patrick Kiens* (by 9/98), *Tristan Temple* (by 7/99), *Sebastian Rose* (from 10/99), *Chris Jarvis* (from 10/01); ASPARAGUS/GROWLTIGER: Stephen Tate, *Michael Sanderson* (by 7/84), *David Hitchen* (by 3/86), *Michael Sanderson* (by 2/87), *Paul Bentley* (by 8/88), *Michael Sanderson* (by 4/89), *Mark Wynter* (by 2/90), *Rory Campbell* (by 11/92), *Tony Timberlake* (by 8/94), *Fenton Gray* (by 11/95), *Tony Timberlake* (from 10/96), *James Barron* (from 4/97), *Michael Cantwell* (by 9/98), *Gareth Snook* (by 12/99), *Peter*

Polycarpou (from 10/01), *Gareth Snook* (from 3/02); BILL BAILEY: Peter Barry, *Michael Sundin* (by 5/82), *Ian Gant* (by 7/84), *Derek Joshua Cullen* (by 2/87), *Adrian Edmeades* (by 8/88), *Darren McGarry* (by 2/90), *Drew Varley* (by 11/91), *Stori James* (by 11/92), *Daniel Crossley* (from 10/94), *Damien Delaney* (by 11/95), *Ross Finnie* (from 10/97), *Christopher Crompton* (from 10/98), *Joe Ryan* (from 4/99), *Nick Crossley* (from 4/15/00), *Joe Ryan* (by 2/00), *Nick Crossley* (by 5/00), *Samuel Hall* (from 4/01, for 3 weeks), *Paul Channon* (from late 4/01), *Joe Ryan* (from 5/01), *Robert Foley* (from 10/01) [in the US this role was known as Tumblebrutus]; BOMBALURINA: Geraldine Gardner, *Beverley Kay* (by 2/83), *Femi Taylor* (by 7/84), *Nicola Kimber* (by 3/86), *Heather Robbins* (by 6/87), *Nadia Strahan* (from 88), *Janie Dee* by (2/90), *Helen Way* (by 11/91), *Donna King* (by 11/92), *Deborah Steel* (by 5/93), *Vanessa Leagh-Hicks* (by 6/94), *Becca Parker* (by 11/95), *Sally Taylor* (from 4/97), *Heather Douglas* (by 7/99), *Julie Barnes* (from 10/00), *Alexis Owen Hobbs* (from 10/01); CARBUCKETTY: David Baxter, *Luke Baxter* (by 5/82); [this character was cut between 7/84 and 3/86]; *Phillip Harrison* (by 3/86), *Simon Horrill* (by 2/87), *Douglas Howes* (by 6/87), *Japheth Myers* (by 8/88), *Geoffrey Garratt* (by 1/89), *Douglas Howes* (by 2/90), *Jonathan Craig* (by 11/91), *Nick Searle* (by 5/92), *Michael Aaron Peth* (by 5/93), *Ian Meeson* (by 6/94), *Sandy Rass* (from 4/95), *Karl Morgan* (by 11/95), *Richard Roe* (from 10/96), *Michiel Verkoren* (by 9/98), *Clifford Stein* (from 4/99), *Robert Hamilton* (from 10/99), *Mark John Richardson* (by 2/00), *Robert Hamilton* (from 4/15/00), *Mark John Richardson* (from 10/00), *Jye Frasca* (from 4/01); CASSANDRA: Seeta Indrani, *Diana Choy* (by 5/82), *Jane Devonshire* (by 2/83), *Nadia Strahan* (by 8/88), *Amanda Rickard* (by 1/89), *Michelle Hodgson* (by 2/90), *Caroline Ephgrave* (by 11/91), *Louise Davidson* (by 5/92), *Deborah Shrimpton* (by 6/94), *Rachel Williams* (by 11/95), *Maggie Chadwick* [alias Connell] (from 10/96), *Nina Radetic* (from 4/97), *Emma Tunmore* (from 4/99), *Julie Barnes* (from 10/99), *Candice Evans* (from 10/00), *Tiffany Graves* (from 10/01); CORICOPAT/GILBERT: Donald Waugh, *Richard Lloyd-King* (by 5/82), *Danny John-Jules* (by 9/83), *Nolan Frederick* (from 84), *Simon Marlow* (by 11/85), *Peter Challis* (by 3/86), *Colin Charles* (by 2/87), *Japheth Myers* (by 1/89), *Derek Joshua Cullen* (by 2/90), *Douglas Franklin* (by 11/91), *Chris Copeland* (by 5/93), *David Olton* (from 4/95), *Robert Yeal* (by 11/95), *Richard Reynard* (from 10/97), *Michiel Verkoren* (from 4/99), *Chris Huston* (by 12/99), *Michiel Verkoren* (by 2/00), *Chris Huston* (by 5/00), *Oliver Tydman* (from 4/01) [the role of Gilbert, the Siamese cat enemy in "Growltiger's Last Stand," became Genghis on Broadway, and subsequently all over the world, including London—but not in Germany or Japan]; DEMETER: Sharon Lee Hill, *Jayne Draper* (by 2/83), *Kim Leeson* (by 7/84), *Erin Lordan* (by 5/85), *Jacqui Harman* (by 3/86), *Kim Leeson* (by 2/87), *Aeva May* (87), *Liz Love* (87), *Linda Mae Brewer* (by 6/87), *Alexandra Worrall* (by 2/90), *Liz Curnick* (by 11/91), *Rebecca Thornhill* (by 5/92), *Angela Heneghan* [alias Tyers] (by 5/93), *Dawn Spence* (by 6/94), *Louise Fribo* (10/94–4/95), *Michele Hooper* (from 4/95), *Barbara King* (by 11/95), *Jo Bingham* (from 4/97), *Suzanne Heyne* (by 9/98), *Wendy Kitching* (from 4/99), *Barbara King* (from 10/00); ELECTRA: Anita Pashley, *Jayne Draper* (by 5/82), *Jane Watts* (83), *Sally Dewhurst* (by 2/83); [the character was cut during the 84–85 season]; *Julie-Ann Marsh* (by 5/85), *Jackie Crawford* (by 2/87), *Robin Cleaver* (by 8/88), *Wendy Kitching* (by 10/91), *Leah-Sue Morland* (by 5/92), *Sarah-Jane Honeywell* (by 5/93), *Charlotte Peck* (4/95), *Nicola Lee Owens* (from 4/95), *Ellie Tyrrell* (by 11/95), *Agnes Vandrepote* (from 4/97), *Leah-Sue Morland* (by 12/97), *Agnes Vandrepote* (by 9/98), *Julie Carlton* (by 12/99) [a role not on Broadway]; ETCETERA: Julie Edmett, *Julie Horner* (by 7/82), *Cathy Cordez* (by 9/83), *Fiona Alexander* (by 10/85), *Marsha Bland* (by 8/88), *Jocelyn Vodovoz Cook* (by 2/90), *Jo Bingham* (by 11/91), *Beata Alfoldi* (by 5/92), *Scarlett O'Neal* (by 5/93), *Chellie Michaels* (by 6/94), *Charlotte Peck* (from 4/95), *Lucie Fentum* (by 11/95), *Sandra Kater* (from 10/96), *Cheryl McAvoy* (4/97–98), *Annalisa Rossi* (by 9/98), *Lucie Fentum* (from 4/99), *Emma Buckle* (by 12/99), *Sarah-Jane Honeywell* (from 4/01); GEORGE: John Chester, *Geoff Davids* (by 5/82), *Wayne Fowkes* (by 12/83), *Steven Wayne* (by 2/87) [a role not on Broadway. It was cut from the London production in 10/00]; GRIZABELLA: Elaine Paige, *Angela Richards* (by 5/82), *Marti Webb* (by 9/83), *Carol Nielsson* (by 7/84), *Anita Harris* (by 5/85), *Verity Ann Meldrum* (from 2/87), *Sharon Benson* (by 12/87), *Ria Jones* (by 1/89), *Jacqui Scott* (by 11/91), *Clare Burt* (by 12/93), *Rosemarie Ford* (by 11/95), *Diane Langton* (by 8/96), *Lindsey Danvers* (10/96–10/97), *Stephanie Lawrence*

(from 10/97), *Sally Ann Triplett* (by 9/98), *Chrissie Hammond* (from 10/99); JELLYLORUM/GRIDDLEBONE: Susan Jane Tanner, *Nina Caie* (by 5/82), *Sally Bentley* (by 7/84), *Ann Woodfield* (by 8/88), *Betsy Marrion* (by 1/89), *Grace Kinirons* (by 2/90), *Iren Bartok* (by 10/91), *Liz Izen* (by 5/92), *Felicity Goodson* (by 6/94), *Carrie Ellis* (by 12/94), *Betsy Marrion* (by 11/95), *Catrin Darnell* (by 2/97), *Niki Ankara* (by 7/99), *Sara West* (by 12/99), *Ulrika Butts* (by 10/99), *Sara West* (from 4/15/00), *Rebecca Lock* (from 10/00), *Louisa Shaw* (from 11/01); JEMIMA: Sarah Brightman, *Jane Wellman* (by 2/83), *Taffy Taylor* (by 7/84), *Tessa Pritchard* (by 11/85), *Nikki Belsher* (by 2/87), *Ruthie Henshall* (by 12/87), *Siobhan Coebly* (by 2/90), *Lisa Waddingham* (by 11/91), *Katherine Whittard* (by 5/92), *Kimberly Partridge* (by 12/93), *Katie Knight-Adams* (by 11/95), *Louise Fribo* (from 10/96), *Sandra Kater* (from 4/97), *Veerle Casteleyn* (by 9/98 & until 10/23/99), *Alexandra Jay* (by 12/99), *Lindsey Wise* (from 10/00–10/01), *Caroline Bagnall* (from 10/01) [in the U.S. this role was known as Sillabub]; JENNYANYDOTS: Myra Sands, *Ann Emery* (by 2/83), *Myra Sands* (by 2/87), *Kim Winfield* (by 6/87), *Valda Aviks* (by 87–88), *Judith Street* (by 8/88), *Sonia Swaby* (by 1/89), *Louisa Shaw* (by 11/91), *Norma Atallah* (by 5/92), *Lindsey Dawson* (by 5/93), *Louisa Shaw* (by 12/93), *Stephanie Johns* (from 4/95), *Susie McKenna* (from 10/96), *Ulrika Butts* (by 9/98), *Kerry Washington* (10/99–4/00), *Catherine Terry* (from 4/15/00), *Kerry Washington* (from 4/01), *Susie Fenwick* (from 10/01); MACAVITY: John Thornton, *Richard Pettyfer* (by 2/83), *Wayne Fowkes* (by 7/84), *Peter Challis* (by 3/86), *Sandy Strallen* (by 2/87), *Andrew Norman* (by 2/90), *Frank Thompson* (by 10/91), *Bryn Walters* (by 5/92), *Simon Street* (by 93–94), *Richard Armitage* (by 6/94), *Alastair Bull* (by 4/95), *Peter Van Dosselaer* (10/96–2/97), *Steven-John Tokaya* (from 4/97), *Andrew Wright* (from 10/97), *Jeron Mosselman* (by 9/98), *Kenny Linden* (from 4/99), *Philip Michael* (from 10/000), *Kenny Linden* (from 4/01); MUNGOJERRIE: John Thornton, *Richard Pettyfer* (by 2/83), *Luke Baxter* (by 7/84), *Steven Wayne* (by 3/86), *Jimmy Johnston* (by 2/87), *Scott Sherrin* (by 8/88), *Shaun Henson* (by 10/91), *Nick Searle* (by 5/93), *Jason Parmenter* (by 6/94), *Ian Meeson* (from 4/95), *Christian Storm* (by 11/95), *Drew Varley* (from 10/96), *Nick Searle* (by 9/98), *Matthew Cross* (by 12/99), *Nick Searle* (from 4/15/00), *Matthew Cross* (by 5/00), *Adrian Edmeades* (from 4/01); MUNKUSTRAP: Jeff Shankley, *David Burt* (by 5/82), *Jeff Shankley* (by 9/83), *Lance Aston* (by 7/84), *Patrick Wood* (by 11/85), *Gary Martin* (by 12/87), *Vincent Leigh* (by 11/91), *Peter Bishop* (by 5/92), *Steven Houghton* (by 6/94), *Andrew Halliday* (from 4/95), *David Malek* (by 11/95), *Jean-Luc "Jack" Rebaldi* (from 4/97), *David Ashley* (from 4/99), *Jack Rebaldi* (4/00—for a few weeks during Mr. Ashley's injury), *David Ashley* (4/00–10/01), *Jack Rebaldi* (from 10/01); OLD DEUTERONOMY: Brian Blessed, *John Turner* (by late 83), *Donald Francke* (by 3/86), *Junix Inosian* (10/94–4/95), *Jeff Leyton* (from 4/95), *John Rawnsley* (by 11/95), *Bruce Graham* (from 4/97), *Nicholas Pound* (by 9/98), *Mark McKerracher* (by 12/99), *Nicholas Pound* (by 2/00), *Mark McKerracher* (by 5/00), *Dave Willetts* (from 4/01), *Junix Inosian* (10/01–5/02); QUAXO/MR. MISTOFFOLEES: Wayne Sleep, *Graham Fletcher* (by 5/82), *Kim Reeder* (by 2/83), *Miguel Godreau* (84), *Machael de Souter* (by 7/84), *Graham Fletcher* (by 10/85), *Guy-Paul Ruolt* (by 11/91), *Luke Baxter* (by 5/92), *Thomas Paton* (by 6/94), *Fergus Logan* (by 11/95), *Gen Horiuchi* (by 9/98), *Campbell McKenzie* (from 10/99), *Jacob Brent* (from 4/01), *Benjamin Tyrrell* (from 10/01) [the role of Quaxo, the black cat, was not on Broadway]; RUMPLETEAZER: Bonnie Langford, *Jilly Mack* (by 7/82), *Bonnie Langford* (by 9/83), *Sally Dewhurst* (by 7/84), *Cathy Cordez* (by 10/85), *Anna-Jane Casey* (by 8/88), *Barbara King* (by 11/91), *Jo Bingham* (by 5/92), *Leah-Sue Morland* (by 5/93), *Vikki Coote* (by 6/94), *Zoe Smith* (by 11/95), *Joann Gibb* (from 10/96), *Sushu Kune* (by 9/98), *Marilyn Wulff* (by 12/99), *Sasha Kane* (by 2/00), *Marilyn Wulff* (by 5/00), *Lynsey Britton* (from 4/01); RUM TUM TUGGER: Paul Nicholas, *Richard Lloyd-King* (by 9/83), *Allan Love* (by 5/85), *Richard Lloyd-King* (by 3/86), *Christopher Howard* (by 11/91), *Keith Burns* (by 12/93), *John Partridge* (from 4/95), *Richard Lloyd-King* (from 4/96–10/96), *Tee Jaye Jenkins* (2/97–9/98), *Kofi Missah* (from 9/98), *David Shannon* (from 10/99), *Tom Lucas* (by 12/99), *David Shannon* (by 2/00), *Tom Lucas* (by 5/00), *John Partridge* (from 4/01); RUMPUS: Steven Wayne* (by 11/91), *Sebastian Rose* (from 10/00), *Chris Jarvis* (from 10/01) [a role added during the run, but not on Broadway]; SKIMBLESHANKS: Kenn Wells, *Richard Pettyfer* (by 5/82), *Kenn Wells* (by 2/83), *Neil Fitzwilliam* (by 7/84), *Jon Peterson* (by 11/85), *Daire O'Dunlaing* (by

2/87), *Adam Matalon* (by 12/87), *Japheth Myers* (by 2/90), *Geoffrey Garratt* (by 10/91), *Jon Peterson* (by 5/92), *Shaun Henson* (by 6/94), *Jimmy Johnston* (by 11/95), *Jon Peterson* (from late 96), *Nigel Garton* (from late 96), *Matthew Gould* (from 4/99), *Ross Finnie* (from 10/00); TANTOMILE: Femi Taylor, *Rosita Yarboy* (by 5/82), *Heather Lea Gerdes* (by 7/84), *Amanda Abbs* (by 5/85), *Louisa MacAlpine* (by 2/87), *Amanda Courtney-Davies* (by 8/88), *Diana Manou* (by 2/90), *Samantha Biddulph* (91), *Kaye E. Brown* (by 10/91), *Karen McSween* (by 5/93), *Cassie Cowan* (by 6/94), *Tee Soo-Chan* (from 4/95), *Samantha Biddulph* (by 11/95), *Beth Robson* (by 9/98), *Rachel Mooney* (by 12/99), *Beth Robson* (by 2/00), *Rachel Mooney* (from 4/15/00), *Helen Harper* (from 4/01); VICTOR: Steven Wayne, *Chris Beeching* (by 5/82), *Christopher Molloy* (by 2/83), *Ken-Michael Stafford* (by 10/91), *Jimmy Johnston* (by 5/92), *Matthew Gould* (by 6/94), *John Stacey* (from 4/95), *Carl Anthony* (by 4/96), *Richard Woodford* (from 10/96), *Zeph* (from 10/97), *Spencer Stafford* (by 9/98), *Neil Reynolds* (from 10/99), *Jason Gardiner* (from 4/01), *Matthew Atwell* (from 10/01) [this role, a blue-gray tomkitten, was added during the run. It did not go to Broadway]; VICTORIA: Finola Hughes, *Jacqui Harman* (by 5/82), *Cherida Langford* (by 3/86), *Amanda Courtney-Davies* (by 2/90), *Marina Stevenson* (by 10/91), *Phyllida Crowley-Smith* (by 5/92), *Sandra Kater* (by 6/94), *Marina Stevenson* (by 11/95), *Sarah Soetaert* (from 10/97), *Emma Harris* [later known as Emma Kerslake] (from 10/99), *Sorrell Thomas* (from 10/01); CATS CHORUS: Jeni Evans (*Meryl Richardson* by 5/82 & gone by 7/84), Nick Hamilton (gone by 3/86), Stephen Hill (*Wayne Fowkes* by 9/83 & gone by 7/84), Nicola Kimber (*Philippa Boulter* by 7/82 & gone by 7/84). *Sinitta Renett* (by 9/83 & gone by 7/84), *Tim Flannigan* (by 7/84 — *Michael Reinhard* by 11/85 & gone by 3/86), *Phillip Harrison* (by 7/84 & gone by 3/86), *Kim Winfield* (by 7/84 & gone by 6/87), *Phillip Devonshire* (by 7/84 & gone by 3/86), *Corinne Barton* (by 7/84; *Debbie Lee London* by 5/85 & gone by 3/86), *Liz Love* (by 3/86 & gone by 8/88), *James Skeggs* (by 3/86 & gone by 2/87), *Lucy Shepherd* (by 3/86 & gone by 8/88), *Stephen Mear* (by 2/87 & gone by 8/88), *Rory McDermott* (by 2/87 & gone by 8/88), *Duncan Macvicar* (by 6/87 & gone by 2/90), *Peter Johnston* (by 6/87 & gone by 8/88), *Cathy Cordez* (by 8/88 & gone by 2/90), *Geoff Garratt* (by 8/88 & gone by 1/89), *Hilton Jones* (by 8/88 & gone by 2/90), *Jacqui Harman* (by 8/88 & gone by 11/91), *Diana Manou* (by 8/88 & gone by 2/90), *Nicola Keen* (by 2/90 & gone by 11/91), *David Olton* (by 2/90 & gone by 11/91), *Caroline Dillon* (by 2/90 & gone by 11/91), *Connor Byrne* (by 2/90 & gone by 11/91), *Mitch Sebastian* (by 2/90 & gone by 11/91), *Samantha Biddulph* (by 11/91 & gone by 5/92), *Joanne Evans* (by 11/91 & gone by 5/93), *Beth Robson* (by 11/91 & gone by 5/92; then again by 6/94 & gone again by 11/95), *James Davies* (by 11/91 & gone by 5/93), *Aidan Treays* (by 11/91 & gone by 10/92), *Robert Yeal* (by 11/91; *Frank Thompson* by 5/92 & gone by 5/93), *Corrie Helen Davies* (by 5/92 & gone by 6/94), *Sarah Hadland* (by 5/92 & gone by 5/93), *Adam Richard Jones* (by 5/93 & gone by 6/94), *Dennis Lupien* (by 5/93 & gone by 6/94), *Scarlett O'Neal* (by 5/93 & gone by 6/94), *Alistair-David Smith* (by 5/93; *Ben Garner* by 5/95 & gone by 2/97), *Donna Winwood* (by 5/93 & gone by 6/94), *Helen Anker* (by 6/94 & gone by 5/95), *Suzy Bloom* (by 6/94 & gone by 5/95), *Carl Parris* (by 6/94 & gone by 11/95), *Tommy Sliiden* (by 6/94 & gone by 11/95), *Belle Dowson* (by 5/95 & gone by 11/95), *Rebecca Parker* (by 5/95 & moved into the role of Bombalurina by 11/95), *Jude Barry* (by 11/95 & gone by 2/97), *Dan Chamberlain* (by 11/95 & gone by 2/97), *Joann Gibb* (by 11/95 & gone by 2/97), *David Lucas* (by 11/95 & gone by 4/97), *Leah-Sue Morland* (by 11/95; *Veerle Casteleyn* by 12/97 & gone by 7/99), *Damian Jackson* (by 2/97; *Steven-John Tokaya* by 12/97 & gone by 7/99), *Ellis Van Laarhoven* (by 2/97 & gone by 4/97), *Lucy Middleton* (by 2/97 & gone by 7/99), *Robert Hamilton* (by 4/97 & gone by 7/99), *Todd Talbot* (by 4/97 & gone by 7/99), *Samuel Hall* (by 7/99 & gone by 10/00), *Mark Johns* (by 7/99 & gone by 12/99), *Sarah Keeton* (by 7/99 & gone by 12/99; back by 2/00 & gone by 5/00), *Patrick Kiens* (by 7/99 & gone by 12/99), *Brenda Moore* (by 7/99 & gone by 10/00), *Ellie Tyrrell* (by 7/99 & gone by 12/99; back by 2/00 & gone by 5/00), *Helen Baker* (by 12/99 & gone by 2/00; back by 5/00; *Summer V. Strallen* by 10/01), *Clinton Brown* (by 12/99 & gone by 2/00; back by 5/00), *Julia Hinchcliffe* (by 12/99 & gone by 2/00; back by 5/00 & gone by 10/00), *Thomas Paton* (by 12/99 & gone by 2/00; back by 5/00; *Joe Ryan* by 10/01), *Cameron Leigh* (by 12/99 & gone by 2/00; back by 5/00 & gone by 10/00), *Simon Coulthard* (by 2/00 & gone by 5/00), *Ben Harley* (by

2/00 & gone by 5/00), *Kit Benjamin* (by 2/00 & gone by 5/00), *Stori James* (by 10/00), *Rebecca Louis* (by 10/00), *Kate Tydman* (by 10/00), *Peter Van Dosselaer* (by 10/00; Andrew Wright by 5/01), *Emma Woods* (by 10/00). Note: at the beginning the characters of Bill Bailey, Electra, Etcetera, and Admetus were all grouped together as Kittens, and were not named individually. London opening night had a bomb scare, and the theatre had to evacuate. Reviews were not great. On 5/12/89 it became London's longest-running musical ever, with 3,358 performances, beating *Jesus Christ Superstar*. It ran 21 years, closing on its birthday, then went on a tour of the U.K.

The Broadway Run. WINTER GARDEN THEATRE, 10/7/82–9/10/00. 16 previews from 9/23/82. 7,485 PERFORMANCES. PRESENTED BY Cameron Mackintosh, The Really Useful Company, David Geffen, The Shubert Organization; MUSIC: Andrew Lloyd Webber; LYRICS: T.S. Eliot (unless otherwise stated); BASED ON the collection of verse for children, *Old Possum's Book of Practical Cats*, by T.S. Eliot ("Possum" was one of Eliot's nicknames), which he first circulated among friends, then had published in 1939; DIRECTOR: Trevor Nunn; ASSOCIATE DIRECTOR/CHOREOGRAPHER: Gillian Lynne; SETS/COSTUMES: John Napier; LIGHTING: David Hersey; SOUND: Martin Levan; MUSICAL DIRECTOR: Rene Wiegert (82–87), *Jack Gaughan* (86–89), *Ethyl Will* (89–90), *Sue Anderson* (89–91), *Edward G. Robinson* (91–97), *Patrick Vaccariello* (95–97), *Mark McLaren* (by 98–99); PRODUCTION MUSICAL DIRECTOR: Stanley Lebowsky (82–90), *David Caddick* (86–93); ORCHESTRATIONS: David Cullen & Andrew Lloyd Webber; CAST RECORDING on Geffen; PRESS: Fred Nathan & Associates (*Bill Evans & Associates* by 97–98, *Viator Associates*) & Johnson — Liff; GENERAL MANAGERS: Gatchell & Neufeld; COMPANY MANAGER: James G. Mennen, *J. Anthony Magner*; PRODUCTION STAGE MANAGER: David Taylor, *Sally J. Greenhut* [later Jacobs] (84–91), *David O'Brien*; STAGE MANAGER: Lani Sundsten, Jeff Lee, *Donald Walters* (87–88), *Sherry Cohen* (by 87–88 & gone by 88–89), *Dan Hild* (88–91), *Peggy Peterson* (88–98), *Peter Wolf*; ASSISTANT STAGE MANAGER: Sally J. Greenhut [later Jacobs], *Suzanne Viverito* (91–98), *Tom Taylor* (91–98), *Andrew Feigen*. **Cast** (basically in amphibolical order): ALONZO: Hector Jaime Mercado, *Scott Wise* (by 2/84), *Hector Jaime Mercado* (by 3/84), *Brian Sutherland* (by 6/84), *Scott Taylor* (by 9/86), *General McArthur Hambrick* (by 11/91), *Michael Koeting* (by 2/92), *Scott Taylor* (by 3/92), *Stephen M. Reed* (by 9/92), *Randy Wojcik* (by 3/93), *Angelo H. Fraboni* (by 10/93), *Hans Kriefall* (from 4/24/95), *Jonathan Stahl* (by 9/99), *Lenny Daniel* (from 11/1/99); BUSTOPHER JONES/ASPARAGUS/GROWLTIGER: Stephen Hanan [he later became Stephen Mo Hanan], *Timothy Jerome* (by 2/84), *Gregg Edelman* (by 1/86), *Bill Carmichael* (by 12/86), *Stephen Hanan* (by 7/88), *Paul Harman* (by 1/89), *Dale Hensley* (by 1/90), *John Dewar* (by 11/90), *Jeffrey Clonts* (by 11/91), *Joel Briel* (by 6/94), *Jeffrey Clonts* (from 7/94), *Joel Briel* (by 12/94), *Richard Poole* (from 12/12/94), *Michael Brian*, *Daniel Eli Friedman* (from 4/14/97), *Michael Brian* (from 6/8/98), *Craig Ricks* (by 7/99), *John Dewar* (from 8/21/99) [By 89–90 these three roles were being billed as Gus/Growltiger/Bustopher, but by 93–94 they were back to the original billing]; BOMBALURINA: Donna King, *Marlene Danielle* (from 1/9/84), *Karen Curlee* (by 7/90), *Marlene Danielle* (by 8/90), *Rachelle Rak* (during Miss Danielle's vacation, 7/97–10/97), *Marlene Danielle* (from 10/3/97), *Jill Nicklaus* (by 11/99), *Marlene Danielle* (by 12/99), *Amy L. Hamel* (12/99–1/00, during Miss Danielle's injury), *Marlene Danielle* (from 1/00); CARBUCKETTY/GENGHIS: Steven Gelfer, *Ray Roderick* (by 7/86) [the Carbucketty role was cut at the 10/87 updating of the show, and the role of Genghis went to Mungojerrie]; CASSANDRA: Rene Ceballos, *Christina Kumi-Kimball* (by 1/83), *Nora Brennan*, *Charlotte d'Amboise* (by 9/84), *Jessica Northrup* (by 8/85), *Roberta Stiehm* (from 8/86), *Julietta Marcelli* (from 7/87), *Leigh Webster* (by 9/89), *Darlene Wilson* (by 10/90), *Leigh Webster* (by 5/93), *Darlene Wilson* (by 6/93), *Colleen Dunn* (by 9/93), *Amy N. Heggins* (by 10/93), *Sara Henry* (by 4/94), *Leigh Webster* (by 93–94), *Sara Henry* (by 93–94), *Amy N. Heggins* (by 11/94), *Sara Henry* (by 12/94), *Ida Gilliams* [AKA Ida Henry] (from 5/22/95), *Meg Gillentine* (by 2/97), *Stephanie Lang* (by 8/98), *Meg Gillentine* (by 10/98), *Lynne Morrissey* [AKA Lynne Marie Calamia] (from 7/5/99), *Amy L. Hamel* (by 3/00), *Melissa Rae Mahon* (from 3/10/00); CORICOPAT: Rene Clemente, *Guillermo Gonzales* (by 10/83), *Joe Antony Cavise* (from 3/84), *Johnny Anzalone* (by 6/87), *Devanand N. Janki* (by 10/91), *Johnny Anzalone* (from 2/92), *Cholsu Kim* (by 11/92), *James Hadley* (by 2/94), *David E. Liddell* (by 1/95), *James Hadley* (from 3/20/95), *Steve Ochoa* (by 9/96), *Billy Johnstone* (from 4/97), *Paul A. Brown* (by 6/98), *Billy Johnstone* (by 7/98), *Ramon Flowers* (by 4/99), *Billy Johnstone* (by 9/99); DEMETER: Wendy Edmead, *Marlene Danielle* (by 10/83), *Jane Bodle* (by 2/84), *Patricia Ruck* (by 7/86), *Beth Swearingen* (by 10/88), *Brenda Braxton* (from 5/90), *Meera Popkin* (by 3/92), *Mercedes Perez* (by 5/92), *Betsy Chang* (by 1/94), *Mercedes Perez* (from 6/17/94), *Mamie Duncan-Gibbs* (by 8/96), *Emily Hsu* (by 10/96), *Susan Lamontagne* (by 8/97), *Amanda Watkins* (by 9/97), *Jill Nicklaus* (by 6/98), *Amanda Watkins* (by 10/98), *Celina Carvajal* (from 5/17/99), *Amy L. Hamel* (by 2/00), *Celina Carvajal* (by 3/00), *Gayle Holsman* (from 7/10/00); ETCETERA: Christine Langner, *Paige Dana* (from 3/84) [role cut at 10/87 update]; GRIZABELLA: Betty Buckley, *Laurie Beechman* (from 4/9/84), *Loni Ackerman* (from 9/5/88), *Heidi Stallings* (by 8/91), *Laurie Beechman* (by 10/91), *Lillias White* (by 12/91), *Laurie Beechman* (by 6/92), *Diane Fratantoni* (by 8/92), *Liz Callaway* (by 11/92), *Laurie Beechman* (by 1/93), *Liz Callaway* (by 5/93), *Heidi Stallings* (during Miss Callaway's vacation, 5/93), *Liz Callaway* (5/3/93–4/23/97), *Heidi Stallings* & *Sally Ann Swarm* (alternated), *Laurie Beechman* (5/16–9/14/97), *Liz Callaway* (from 9/22/97), *Linda Balgord* (by 7/98), *Liz Callaway* (by 10/98), *Linda Balgord* (by 4/99); JELLYLORUM/GRIDDLEBONE: Bonnie Simmons, *Nina Hennessey* (from 6/22/92), *Jean Arbeiter* (by 5/98), *Susan Somerville* (by 11/99), *Jean Arbeiter* (by 12/99); JENNYANYDOTS: Anna McNeely, *Marcy De Gonge* (from 4/89), *Susan Powers* (by 5/89), *Cindy Benson* (by 9/89), *Susan Powers* (by 5/91), *Cindy Benson* (by 6/91), *Rose McGuire* (by 11/91), *Carol Dilley* (by 9/93), *Susan Powers* (by 8/94), *Carol Dilley* (from 8/22/94), *Sharon Wheatley* (from 6/21/99); MR. MISTOFFOLEES: Timothy Scott, *Herman W. Sebek* (from 4/84), *Jamie Torcellini* (by 11/84), *Herman W. Sebek* (by 1/85), *Michael Scott Gregory* (by 6/85), *Barry K. Bernal* (by 1/86), *Don Johanson* (by 7/86), *Kevin Poe* (by 2/88), *Todd Lester* (by 4/89), *Michael Barriskill* (from 4/89), *Michael Arnold* (by 1/90), *Todd Lester* (by 12/90), *Gen Horiuchi* (by 3/91), *Kevin Poe* (by 7/91), *Gen Horiuchi* (by 10/91), *Kevin Poe* (by 1/92), *Gen Horiuchi* (by 3/92), *Kevin Poe* (by 8/92), *Gen Horiuchi* (by 10/92), *Lindsay Chambers* (by 1/93), *Gen Horiuchi* (by 8/93), *Lindsay Chambers* (by 10/93), *Gen Horiuchi* (from 3/18/95), *Steve Ochoa* (by 12/95), *Gen Horiuchi* (by 4/96), *Jacob Brent* (by 9/96), *Christopher Gattelli* (by 4/99), *Jacob Brent* (9/27–12/19/99), *Julius Sermonia* (from 12/28/99); MUNGOJERRIE/GENGHIS: Rene Clemente, *Guillermo Gonzales* (by 10/83), *Joe Antony Cavise* (from 3/84), *Johnny Anzalone* (by 7/87); the roles of Coricopat & Mungojerrie were given to two different actors as from the 10/87 update; *Ray Roderick* (from 10/87), *Todd Lester* (by 11/91), *Roger Kachel* (from 5/11/92), *John Vincent Leggio* (by 11/99), *Roger Kachel* (by 12/99) [as for the role of Genghis, see note above, under Carbucketty]; MUNKUSTRAP: Harry Groener, *Claude R. Tessier* (by 3/84), *Mark Fotopoulos* (by 12/86), *Rob Marshall* (by 6/87), *Robert Amirante* (by 10/87), *Greg Minahan* (by 2/90), *Bryan Batt* (by 7/91), *Robert Amirante* (by 8/92), *Bryan Batt* (by 9/92), *Dan McCoy* (by 1/93), *Keith Bernardo* (from 9/20/93), *Michael Gruber* (by 7/96), *Matt Farnsworth* (by 5/97), *Michael Gruber* (from 6/97), *Abe Sylvia* (by 4/98), *Michael Gruber* (from 5/10/99), *Jeffry Denman* (from 9/13/99); OLD DEUTERONOMY: Ken Page, *Kevin Marcum* (by 6/84), *Clent Bowers* (by 6/86), *Larry Small* (by 12/87), *Ken Prymus* (by 5/91), *Larry Small* (by 7/91), *Ken Prymus* (by 9/91), *Jimmy Lockett* (from 7/97), *Ken Prymus* (from 8/97), *Jimmy Lockett* (by 4/98); PLATO/MACAVITY/RUMPUS CAT: Kenneth Ard, *Scott Wise* (by 10/83), *Kenneth Ard* (by 2/84), *Scott Wise* (by 3/84), *Brian Andrews* (85), *Jamie Patterson* (by 8/85), *Randy Wojcik* (by 2/90), *Robb Edward Morris* (by 9/92), *Jim T. Ruttman* (by 11/94), *Philip Michael Baskerville* (by 4/95), *Karl Wahl* (from 5/20/96), *Rick Gonzales* (by 9/96), *Jim T. Ruttman* (by 10/96), *Jaymes Hodges* (by 11/96), *Karl Wahl* (by 12/96), *Philip Michael Baskerville* (from 4/97), *Angelo H. Fraboni* (by 3/98), *Steve Geary* (by 3/98), *Angelo H. Fraboni* (by 11/98), *Steve Geary* (by 4/99), *Keith Edward Wilson* (from 5/17/99); POUNCIVAL: Herman W. Sebek, *Ramon Galindo* (4/84–8/85), *Robert Montano* (from 8/85), *John Joseph Festa* (by 11/87), *Devanand N. Janki* (by 2/92), *Joey Pizzi* (by 9/92), *Devanand N. Janki* (by 10/92), *Joey Pizzi* (by 5/93), *Devanand N. Janki* (by 11/93), *Marty Benn* (during Mr. Janki's illness, 93–94), *Jacob Brent* (from 10/24/94), *Christopher Gattelli* (by 9/96), *Paul A. Brown* (by 7/98), *Joey Gyondla* (by 4/99), *Christopher Gattelli* (by 7/99 and left 1/16/00), *Jon-Erik Goldberg* (from 1/17/00); THE RUM TUM TUGGER: Terrence V. Mann, *Jamie Rocco* (from 10/84), *Terrence V. Mann* (from 3/25/85), *Rick Sparks* (by 9/85),

Steve Yudson (by 2/87), *Frank Mastrocola* (by 3/88), *Bradford Minkoff* (by 4/92), *B.K. Kennelly* (by 4/93), *David Hibbard* (from 9/20/93), *Stephen M. Reed* (by 9/96), *Ron De Vito* (by 10/96), *Abe Sylvia* (by 5/97), *David Hibbard* (from 6/97), *Stephen Bienskie* (by 4/99); RUMPLETEAZER: Christine Langner, *Paige Dana* (from 3/84), *Kristi Lynes* (by 4/89), *Donna Pompei* (by 6/90), *Kristi Lynes* (by 7/90), *Christine De Vito* (by 5/93), *Jennifer Cody* (by 6/94), *Jeanine Meyers* (by 9/94), *Kristi Sperling* (from 9/19/94), *Maria Jo Ralabate* (from 4/1/96), *Dana Solimando* (by 8/97), *Maria Jo Ralabate* (by 9/97), *Tesha Buss* (by 11/98), *Maria Jo Ralabate* (from 7/10/00); SILLABUB: Whitney Kershaw, *Denise Di Renzo* (by 4/84), *Teresa De Zarn* (by 6/86), *Susan Santoro* (by 4/88), *Dana Walker* (by 5/89), *Michelle Schumacher* (by 1/90), *Lisa Mayer* (by 10/90), *Joyce Chittick* (by 8/92), *Lisa Mayer* (by 10/92), *Jeanine Meyers* (by 11/93), *Bethany Samuelson* (from 8/8/94), *Alaine Kashian* (by 7/95), *Bethany Samuelson* (by 9/95), *Alaine Kashian* (by 10/96), *Bethany Samuelson* (by 1/98), *Maria Jo Ralabate* (by 11/98), *Jessica Dillan* (from 7/10/00) [in the UK this role was known as Jemima]; SKIMBLESHANKS: Reed Jones, *Michael Scott Gregory* (by 3/84), *Robert Burnett* (by 6/85), *Reed Jones*, *Richard Stafford* (by 10/88), *Eric Scott Kincaid* (by 1/90), *Michael Scott Gregory* (by 8/90), *George Smyros* (by 9/91), *Eric Scott Kincaid* (from 6/3/94), *Owen Taylor* (by 11/97), *Jon-Paul Christensen* (from 6/28/99), *James Hadley* (from 3/27/00); TANTOMILE: Janet L. Hubert, *Sundy Leigh Leake* (by 6/83), *Lisa Dawn Cave* (by 1/89), *April Nixon* (by 10/90), *Michelle Artigas* (by 10/91), *Lynn Sterling* (by 12/92), *Michelle Artigas* (by 3/93), *Jill Nicklaus* (from 12/19/94), *Silvia Aruj* (from 3/97), *Jill Nicklaus* (from 4/97), *Silvia Aruj* (by 9/97), *Jill Nicklaus* (by 10/97), *Silvia Aruj* (by 11/97), *Jill Nicklaus* (by 12/97), *Silvia Aruj* (by 1/98), *Amy L. Hamel* (by 4/00); TUMBLEBRUTUS: Robert Hoshour, *Jay Poindexter* (by 9/84), *Randy Bettis* (by 8/90), *Joey Pizzi* (by 1/92), *John Vincent Leggio* (by 8/92), *Michael Giacobbe* (by 3/93), *Marc Ellis Holland* (by 5/93), *Andrew Pacho* (by 10/93), *Marc Ellis Holland* (by 12/93), *Levensky Smith* (from 8/29/94), *Randy Bettis* (by 9/96), *Andrew Hubbard* (by 5/98), *Patrick Mullaney* (by 11/98), *John Vincent Leggio* (by 1/99), *Patrick Mullaney* (by 11/99), *Mark Moreau* (by 1/00), *Patrick Mullaney* (by 4/00) [in the UK this role was known as Bill Bailey]; VICTORIA: Cynthia Onrubia, *Valerie C. Wright* by (9/84), *Claudia Shell* (by 9/85), *Kayoko Yoshioka* (by 1/94), *Nadine Isenegger* (from 7/25/94), *Missy Lay Zimmer* (by 2/98), *Melissa Miller* (by 9/99), *Missy Lay Zimmer* (by 12/99), *Melissa Hathway* (by 3/00), *Missy Lay Zimmer* (by 4/00), *Melissa Hathway* (from 7/10/00). CATS CHORUS: 1ST MEMBER: Walter Charles, *Erick Devine* (by 6/83), *Bill Nolte* (by 6/85), *Jay Aubrey Jones* (by 6/86), *Peter Samuel* (by 9/94), *Kelly Briggs* (by 4/97), *Kurt von Schmittou* (by 4/99). 2ND MEMBER: Susan Powers, *Sally Ann Swarm* (by 5/91), *Susan Powers* (by 6/91), *Jacqueline Reilly* (by 8/94), *Susan Powers* (by 9/94), *Susan Somerville* (by 11/97), *Jeanne Montano* (by 11/99), *Susan Somerville* (by 12/99). 3RD MEMBER: Carol Richards, *Colleen Fitzpatrick* (by 1/84), *Janene Lovullo* (by 10/84), *Brenda Pressley* (by 9/85), *Heidi Stallings* (by 9/88), *Rosemary Loar* (by 8/91), *Heidi Stallings* (by 10/91), *Jessica Hendy* (by 5/99), *Jennifer Allen* (by 8/99), *Heidi Stallings* (by 9/99), *Jessica Hendy* (by 1/00), *Heidi Stallings* (by 4/00); 4TH MEMBER: Joel Robertson, *Michael DeVries* (by 4/88), *Bryan Landrine* (by 2/89), *Lee Lobenhofer* (by 3/90), *Joel Briel* (by 7/90), *Lee Lobenhofer* (by 6/94), *Joel Briel* (by 7/94), *Frank Mastrone* (by 2/95), *Joel Briel* (by 4/95). In 1987, the role of Rumpleteazer was shifted in order of appearance to a position immediately after Pouncival, and various other orders of appearance were shifted over the course of the run. SWINGS: Rene Ceballos, Whitney Kershaw (gone by 86–87), Marlene Danielle (*Deborah Henry* by 10/83, *Roberta Stiehm* by 4/86, *Karen Curlee* by 8/86 & gone by 7/88, *N. Elaine Wiggins* by 8/88, *Darlene Wilson* by 3/90, *Lynn Shuck* by 10/90, *Rebecca Timms* by 12/92, *Sarah Solie Shannon* by 1/93, *Lynn Sterling* by 9/93, *Larissa Thurston* by 4/97), Diane Fratantoni (gone by 12/83, *Valerie Wright* from 4/84, *Lily-Lee Wong* by 9/84, *Amy Splitt* by 2/95, *Alaine Kashian* by 5/95, *Lisa Mayer* by 7/95, *Alaine Kashian* by 9/95, *Amy Splitt* by 7/96, *Dana Solimando* by 4/98, *Melissa Miller* by 6/98, *Amy Splitt* by 4/99, *Melissa Miller* by 12/99, *Carolyn Ockert* by 3/00, *Melissa Hathway* by 4/00, *Tamera Shepherd* from 7/10/00), Rusty Hack (gone by 6/87, *Wade Laboissonniere* from 11/87, *Rusty Mowery* by 6/93, *Marty Benn* by 8/94, *Rusty Mowery* by 9/94 & gone by 3/98, *Joey Gyondla* from 7/99 & gone by 9/99, *Matthew Vargo* from 2/00), Bob Morrisey (*Claude R. Tessier* by 12/83, *Jack Magradey* by 3/84, *Stephen Dahlem* by 7/95, *Michael Ehlers* by 10/96, *Bobby Miranda* by 5/97, *Abe Sylvia* by 6/97, *Jon-Paul Christensen* by 10/97, *Craig Waletzko* by 10/98), *Jane Bodle* (added by 1/83, *Denise Di Renzo* by 2/84, *Dodie Pettit* by 4/84, *Jessica Molaskey* by 12/87, *Mimi Wyche* by 3/88 & gone by 9/88, *Jessica Molaskey* from 12/88, *Marcy De Gonge* by 4/89 & gone by 3/92, *Sally Ann Swarm* from 4/92, *Susan Somerville* by 5/95 & gone by 11/97 but not replaced), *Nora Brennan* (added by 1/83, *Rebecca Timms* by 2/87 & gone by 6/91, *Dawn Marie Church* from 4/92, *Naomi Reddin* by 8/93 & gone by 9/93, *Sally Ann Swarm* from 6/97), *Greg Minahan* (added by 1/83, *Bubba Dean Rambo* by 12/83 & gone by 5/84, *Mark Frawley* from 6/84, *Marc Hunter* by 11/85 & gone by 7/88, *John Aller* from 8/88 & gone by 2/91, *Joe Locarro* from 5/91 and gone by 10/92, *Mark Santoro* from 12/93 and gone by 2/94, *Joe Locarro* from 5/94, *Matthew Vargo* by 9/96, *Billy Sprague Jr.* by 4/99), *Scott Wise* (added by 6/83, *Brian Andrews* by 10/83, *David Liddell* by 6/93, *Owen Taylor* by 1/94, *Jon-Paul Christensen* by 7/96, *Mark Moreau* by 1/98, *Jon-Paul Christensen* by 7/99, *David Spangenthal* who was gone by 7/00 but not replaced), *Rene Clemente* (added by 10/83, *Greg Minahan* by 1/87 & gone by 1/90, *John Vincent Leggio* from 2/90 & gone by 8/92, *Kevin Berdini* from 9/92, *Angelo H. Fraboni* by 4/93, *Douglas Graham* by 10/93 & gone by 5/94, *David Liddell* from 6/94 & gone by 1/95 but back by 2/95, *Jonathan Taylor* by 6/96, *Susan Santoro* (added by 11/87, *Suzanne Viverito* by 4/88, *Leigh Webster* by 6/92, *Suzanne Viverito* by 2/93), *Richard Stafford* (added by 3/90 and gone by 2/91, *Bobby Miranda* from 9/97 & gone by 1/98 but not replaced), *Joey Pizzi* (added by 10/90 and gone by 1/92, *Michael Arnold* from 6/92, *Jim Raposa* by 11/92 & gone by 6/94 but back by 2/95, and gone again by 7/95, *Angel Caban* from 9/95), *Felicia Farone* (added by 5/91 and gone by 3/92, *Michelle Schumacher* from 4/92 and gone by 1/93 but not replaced), *Paige Dana* (86–87), *Scott Taylor* (86–92), *Juliette Marcelli* (86–87), *Robert Montano* (86–87), *Johnny Anzalone* (86–92), *Jamie Patterson* (87–88), *John Joseph Festa* (87–89, 90–91), *Beth Swearingen* (88–89), *Lisa Dawn Cave* (89–91), *Brenda Braxton* (90–91), *Mercedes Perez* (91–95), *Randy Wojcik* (91–95), *Dev Janki* (91–95), *Roger Kachel* (91–92; 96–99), *Colleen Dunn* (93–95), *James Hadley* (93–95), *Amy N. Heggins* (93–95), *B.K. Kennelly* (93–95), *Cholsu Kim* (93–95), *Naomi Naughton* (95–96), *Hector Jaime Mercado*, *Brian Sutherland*, *Jill Nicklaus* (96–99), *Carol Dilley* (96–99), *Christopher Gatelli* (96–99), *Hans Kriefall* (96–99), *Steve Ochoa* (96–97), *Ida Gilliams* (96–97), *Billy Johnstone* (97–99), *Philip Michael Baskerville* (97–99). Others over the years: *Janet L. Hubert, Herman W. Sebek, Mark Frawley, Robert Hoshour, Steve Barton, Steven Gelfer, Sundy Leigh Leake, Christine Langner, Guillermo Gonzalez, Joe Antony Cavise, Michael Scott Gregory*. **Part I**: When Cats are Maddened by the Midnight Dance: "*Cats*"–Overture (instrumental); ***Prologue*** "Jellicle Songs for Jellicle Cats" (add l: Trevor Nunn & Richard Stilgoe) (Company); ***Scene 1*** "The Naming of Cats" (Company); ***Scene 2*** "The Invitation to the Jellicle Ball" (Victoria & Mistoffolees); ***Scene 3*** "The Old Gumbie Cat" (Jennyanydots, Cassandra, Bombalurina, Jellylorum) [the middle verse of the London production was cut for Broadway]; ***Scene 4*** "The Rum Tum Tugger" (Rum Tum Tugger); ***Scene 5*** "Grizabella, the Glamour Cat" (Grizabella, Demeter, Bombalurina); ***Scene 6*** "Bustopher Jones: The Cat About Town" (Bustopher, Jennyanydots, Jellylorum, Bombalurina); ***Scene 7*** "Mungojerrie and Rumpleteazer" (Mistoffolees, Mungojerrie, Rumpleteazer); ***Scene 8*** "Old Deuteronomy" (Munkustrap, Rum Tum Tugger, Old Deuteronomy) [the last verse of the London production was cut for Broadway]; ***Scene 9*** "The Awefull Battle of the Pekes and Pollicles" together with "The Marching Songs of the Pollicle Dogs" (Munkustrap & The Rumpus Cat); ***Scene 10*** "The Jellicle Ball" (Company); ***Scene 11*** "Memory" (Grizabella) (add l: Trevor Nunn) [the big hit, and slightly different to the London version]. **Part II**: Why Will the Summer Day Delay — When Will Time Flow Away: Entr'acte; ***Scene 12*** "The Moments of Happiness" (Old Deuteronomy & Tantomile); ***Scene 13*** "Gus: The Theatre Cat" (Jellylorum & Asparagus); ***Scene 14*** "Growltiger's Last Stand" [Growltiger played by Gus; Griddlebone played by Jellylorum; The Crew: Tumblebrutus, the bosun played by Alonzo; Grumbuskin, the mate played by Munkustrap; Rum Tum Tigger played by himself; Skimbleshanks played by himself; Mistoffolees played by himself; Genghis played by Carbucketty (subsequently by Mungustrap). "In quella tepida notte" (Growltiger & Griddlebone) [this Italian aria, based on Puccini's *Girl of the Golden West*, replaced "The Ballad of Billy McCaw," which had been here during the London run. Eventually this

aria replaced "Billy McCaw" in all productions of *Cats*, even in the London run]; ***Scene 15*** "Skimbleshanks: The Railway Cat" (Skimbleshanks); ***Scene 16*** "Macavity: The Mystery Cat" (Demeter, Bombalurina, Alonzo, Macavity, Munkustrap); ***Scene 17*** "Mr. Mistoffolees" (Mistoffolees & Rum Tum Tugger); ***Scene 18*** "Memory" (reprise) (Victoria & Grizabella); ***Scene 19*** "The Journey to the Heavyside Layer" (Company); ***Scene 20*** "The Ad-Dressing of Cats" (Old Deuteronomy).

Andrew Lloyd Webber wanted Hal Prince to produce the Broadway show, but he turned it down. The show cost $3.9 million to produce. Broadway advance sales were between $6.2 and 6.3 million. The top ticket price was $40. On its first day the show took in $206,230. Reviews were mixed. It won Tony Awards for musical, score, book, direction of a musical, costumes, lighting, and for Betty Buckley, and was also nominated for choreography, sets, and for Harry Groener and Stephen Hanan. In 10/87 the show was updated. By the 95–96 season only two of the original 36 cast members were still with the show. On 1/30/96 David Hibbard, playing Rum Tum Tugger, tried too hard to get audience member Evelyn Amato, an unemployed office worker, involved in the show. She sued *Cats* for $6 million. On 10/14/96 the show overtook *Oh! Calcutta!* to become the second-longest-running show in Broadway history. On 6/19/97 it played its 6,138th performance, thus becoming the longest-running Broadway show (of any description) of all time (overtaking *A Chorus Line*). On that day there was a special performance to mark the occasion. Laurie Beechman, who had been diagnosed with ovarian cancer in 1989, was invited back by Andrew Lloyd Webber to play Grizabella again in time for this special day. The show was going to close on 6/25/00, but the run was extended to 9/10/00.

After Broadway. MADACH THEATRE, Budapest. Opened on 3/25/83, in repertory. This production had only 18 cats.

TOKYO, 11/11/83–11/10/84. After Tokyo the production began a tour around Japan, which, on and off, ran for years (the longest-running musical ever in Japan). In Japanese productions Sillabub and Jemima are two different characters (Sillabub was the Broadway version of London's Jemima).

THEATER AN DER WIEN, Vienna. Opened in 11/83. **Cast**: BOMBALURINA: Ute Lemper; JENNY FLECKENREICH/GRIDDLEBONE: Valda Ariks; MISTO: Valentin Baraian; MUNGOJERRIE: Gregory Jones; MUNKUSTRAP: Steve Barton; POUNCIVAL: Robert Montano. In 8/87 the production toured to East Berlin for a limited run. On 5/20/88 it went on a 10-day tour of Russia. The Vienna production closed in 10/88 and moved to the RAIMUND THEATER, 11/88–9/24/90.

U.S. NATIONAL TOUR # 1. Opened on 12/21/83 at the Shubert Theatre, Boston, and closed on 11/8/87. This was a "slow tour" (i.e. big cities only). MUSICAL DIRECTOR: Stanley Lebowsky (*Kristen Blodgette, Ross Allen, Tony Geralis, Jack Gaughan*) & Thomas Helm. **Cast**: ALONZO/RUMPUS CAT: Jamie Patterson, *Fred Anderson* (by 11/85), *Ken Nagy* (by 7/87); ASPARAGUS/BUSTOPHER/GROWLTIGER: Sal Mistretta, *John Dewar* (by 11/84), *Bill Carmichael* (by 6/86), *Frank Mastrone* (by 3/87); BOMBALURINA: Cindi Klinger, *Nora Brennan* (by 3/87); CASSANDRA: Charlotte d'Amboise, *Jessica Northrup* (by 11/84), *Kim Noor* (by 11/85); CORICOPAT: Allen Hidalgo, *Bob Amore* (by 11/85), *Eric Kaufman* (by 3/87); DEMETER: Pamela Blasetti, *Dorothy Tancredi* (by 12/84), *Diana Kavilis* (by 6/86); GRIZABELLA: Laurie Beechman, *Diane Fratantoni* (from 2/23/84), *Janene Lovullo* (by 11/85); JELLYLORUM/GRIDDLEBONE: Jennifer Butt, *Victoria Clark* (by 10/86), *Jessica Molaskey* (by 3/87); JENNYANYDOTS: Cindy Benson, *Sally Ann Swarm* (by 6/86); MISTOFFOLEES: Jamie Torcellini, *Barry K. Bernal* (by 12/84), *Marvin Engran* (by 7/85), *Mark Esposito* (by 11/85), *Roger Kachel* (by 5/87); MUNGOJERRIE: Ray Roderick, *Todd Lester* (by 11/85), *Roger Kachel* (by 3/87), *Bill Brassea* (by 5/87); MUNKUSTRAP: Mark Dovey, *Scott Dainton* (by 11/84), *Joe Locarro* (by 10/86); OLD DEUTERONOMY: Kevin Marcum, *Calvin E. Remsberg* (by 5/84); PLATO/MACAVITY: Russell Warfield, *Gordan Cragg* (by 10/86), *Fred Anderson* (by 8/87); POUNCIVAL: Barry K. Bernal, *Todd Lester* (by 11/84), *Brian Jay* (by 1/85), *Daniel Jamison* (by 3/87); RUM TUM TUGGER: Rich Hebert, *Paul Mack* (by 7/85), *David McDonald* (by 12/85), *Douglas Graham* (by 10/86); RUMPLETEAZER: Kelli Ann McNally, *Christine Langner* (by 10/86), *Andrea Karas* (by 3/87); SILLABUB: Tina Decker, *Joanne Baum* (by 6/86); SKIMBLESHANKS: Anthony Wigas, *Willie Rosario* (by 11/85), *Danny Rounds* (by 6/86), *Eric Scott Kincaid* (by 3/87); TAN-

TOMILE: Tori Brenno, *Stephanie McConlough* (by 11/84), *Patricia Forestier* (by 6/86); TUMBLEBRUTUS: Thomas McManus, *Mark Esposito* (by 5/84), *Tony Jaeger* (by 11/85); VICTORIA: Susan Zaquirre; CATS CHORUS: 1ST MEMBER: John Dewar, *Peter Kevoian* (by 11/84), *Bill Carmichael* (by 7/85), *R.F. Daley* (by 6/86); 2ND MEMBER: Janene Lovullo, *Anna Maria Gutierrez* (by 11/84), *Raissa Katona* (by 3/87); 3RD MEMBER: Calvin E. Remsberg, *Bill Nolte* (by 5/84), *Clent Bowers* (by 7/85), *Richard Poole* (by 6/86), *Skip Harris* (by 3/87); 4TH MEMBER: Susanna Wells, *Sally Ann Swarm* (by 11/85), *Victoria Clark* (by 6/86 and gone by 10/86), *Kirsti Carnahan* (by 3/87).

U.S. NATIONAL TOUR # 2. Opened on 1/13/85 at the Shubert Theatre, Los Angeles, and closed there, on 11/30/86. This tour gave rise to U.S. National Tour # 4 (# 3 had already begun). MUSICAL DIRECTOR: Martin Levan. *Cast:* ALONZO/RUMPUSCAT: Darryl Yeager; BOMBALURINA: Edyie Fleming; CASSANDRA: Leigh Webster; CORICOPAT: Serge Rodnunsky, *Marc C. Oka* (by 10/86); DEMETER: Sheri Cowart, *April Ortiz* (by 4/86); GRIZABELLA: Kim Criswell, *Sandy Edgerton* (by 10/86); GUS/BJ/GROWLTIGER: Norman Large, *Peter Kevoian* (by 4/86); JELLYLORUM/GRIDDLEBONE: Sally Spencer, *Linden Waddell* (by 10/86); JENNYANYDOTS: Marsha Merchant, *Beth Cloninger* (by 10/86); MISTOFFOLEES: George de la Pena, *Jamie Torcellini* (by 4/86); MUNGOJERRIE: Don Johanson, *Roger Kachel* (by 10/86); MUNKUSTRAP: Mark Morales; OLD DEUTERONOMY: George Anthony Bell; PLATO/MACAVITY: Jedd Adkins; POUNCIVAL: Phineas Newborn III, *Rick Pessagno* (by 10/86); RUM TUM TUGGER: Michael Alan-Ross, *Gregory Donaldson* (by 4/86), *Steve Yudson* (by 10/86); RUMPLETEAZER: Kristi Lynes, *Cathy Carson* (by 10/86); SILLABUB: Kathleen Dawson, *Susan Carr George* (85), *Karen Babcock* (by 10/86); SKIMBLESHANKS: Thom Keeling; TANTOMILE: Andrea Gibbs-Muldoon; TUMBLEBRUTUS: Kenneth Jezek, *David Reitman* (by 4/86); VICTORIA: J. Kathleen Lamb.

ELGIN THEATRE, Toronto, 3/85–3/15/87. 1st Canadian tour, 6/87–1/88; 2nd Canadian tour, 6/88–9/88; 3rd Canadian tour, 1/89–8/89.

SYDNEY, 7/27/85–8/1/87. *Cast:* BOMBALURINA: Kerry Woods; GRIZABELLA: Debbie Byrne; MISTOFFOLEES: David Atkins; OLD DEUTERONOMY: John Wood; SILLABUB: Anita Louise Combe. HER MAJESTY'S THEATRE, Melbourne, 10/10/87–12/88. *Cast:* BOMBALURINA: Femi Taylor; MUNKUSTRAP: Richard Pettyfer; OLD DEUTERONOMY: John Wood; PLATO/MACAVITY: Sean Hingston. The tour played: Festival Theatre, Adelaide, 2/18/89–4/29/89; His Majesty's Theatre, Perth, 5/6/89–7/29/89; Civic Centre, Newcastle, 8/9/89–8/26/89; Lyric Theatre, Brisbane, 9/2/89–10/28/89; Aotea Centre, Auckland, NZ, 11/11/89–1/12/90.

DET NORSK THEATER, Oslo, 11/9/85–1/87.

OPERETTENHAUS HAMBURG. Opened on 4/18/86.

U.S. NATIONAL TOUR # 3. Also known as the First Bus & Truck Tour. Opened on 9/14/86 at West Point, NY, and closed on 8/28/88. MUSICAL DIRECTOR: Edward G. Robinson, *Jay Alger*. *Cast:* ALONZO/RUMPUS CAT: Philip Mollet, *Stephen Moore* (by 6/87), *Jeff Siebert* (by 8/87); BOMBALURINA: Aja Major, *Kari Nicolaisen* (by 3/87), *Andrea Gibbs-Muldoon* (by 4/87); CASSANDRA: Aimee Turner, *Spence Ford* (by 3/88), *Kim Noor*; DEMETER: Deborah Geneviere, *Jennifer Smith* (by 3/88); GRIZABELLA: Leslie Ellis, *Heidi Stallings* (by 4/88); GUS/BJ/GROWLTIGER: Richard Poole; JELLYLORUM/GRIDDLEBONE: Joanna Beck; JENNYANYDOTS: Mary Corcoran, *Cathy Susan Pyles* (by 4/87); MISTOFFOLEES: Randy Slovacek; MUNGOJERRIE: Michael O'Steen, *Bill Brassea* (by 12/87); MUNKUSTRAP: Randy Clements; OLD DEUTERONOMY: Larry Small, *Bill Nolte* (by 11/87); PLATO/MACAVITY: David Roberts; POUNCIVAL: Matt Zarley, *Robert Bianca* (by 3/88); RUM TUM TUGGER: Andy Spangler, *Brian "B.K." Kennelly* (by 9/87); RUMPLETEAZER: Beth Swearingen, *Kari Nicolaisen* (by 10/87), *Donna M. Pompei* (by 11/87); SILLABUB: Christine Toy, *Nikki Rene* (by 7/87), *Beth Swearingen* (by 10/87), *Christine Toy* (by 4/88); SKIMBLESHANKS: Jonathan Cerullo; TUMBLEBRUTUS: Anthony Bova, *Fred Tallaksen* (by 12/87); VICTORIA: JoAnn M. Hunter, *Michele Humphrey* (by 3/88).

KAUPUNGIN TEATTERI, Helsinki, 9/86–12/88.

U.S. NATIONAL TOUR # 4. Also known as the Second Bus & Truck Tour, it came out of U.S. National Tour # 2 (which only played in Los Angeles — see above). Opened on 3/31/87 in New Haven, and closed on 12/19/99 in East Lansing, Michigan. On 7/7/99 it achieved the 5,000-performance mark in Chattanooga, and on 11/18/97 overtook the original *Oklahoma!* tour to become the longest-running tour in history (10 years 6 months 2 weeks). DIRECTOR: David Taylor; CHOREOGRAPHERS: T. Michael Reed & Richard Stafford; MUSICAL DIRECTOR: Jack Gaughan, *Michael Huffman*. *Cast:* ALONZO/RUMPUS CAT: General McArthur Hambrick, *Michael Koetting* (by 11/90), *William Patrick Dunne* (from 12/91), *Jim T. Ruttman* (stood in for Mr. Dunne in 11/93), *William Patrick Dunne* (from 10/93), *Rudd Anderson* (from 6/6/95), *Jonathan Stahl* (by 9/97), *Alan Bennett* (by 3/98), *Scott Carlyle* (from 9/8/98), *Alan Bennett* (from 10/10/98), *Matt Rivera* (from 3/23/98); BOMBALURINA: Wendy Walter, *Helen Frank* (by 12/87), *Wendy Walter* (by 3/91), *Helen Frank* (by 7/91), *Wendy Walter* (by 1/93), *Helen Frank* (by 6/94), *Lori Longstreth* (from 9/26/95), *Courtney Young* (from 10/1/96), *Jeannie Abolt* (by 9/97), *Parisa Ross* (from 9/1/98); BUSTOPHER/ASPARAGUS/GROWLTIGER: Jeffrey Clonts, *Lee Lobenhofer* (by 3/89), *Bryan Landrine* (by 3/90), *Alex Santoriello* (by 7/91), *James Hindman* (by 4/92), *Buddy Crutchfield* (by 1/93), *Richard Poole* (by 10/93), *William R. Park* (by 2/95), *Andy Gale* (from 7/11/95), *Lee Lobenhofer* (by 10/95), *Andy Gale* (by 12/95), *Bart Shatto* (from 3/12/96), *Brian Noonan* (from 10/1/96), *Daniel Eli Friedman* (from 4/14/97), *Craig Ricks* (by 11/97), *Kelly Briggs* (from 3/16/99); CASSANDRA: Paula-Marie Benedetti, *Darlene Wilson* (by 12/87), *Linda May* (by 11/88), *Elizabeth Mills* (by 2/91), *Linda May* (by 12/91), *Laura Quinn* (by 8/92), *Linda May* (by 9/92), *Laura Quinn* (by 12/92), *Linda May* (by 1/93), *Laura Quinn* (by 5/93), *Leigh Webster* (by 6/94), *Laura Quinn* (by 7/94), *Stephanie Lang* (by 10/94), *Izabela Lekic* (from 5/16/96), *Tamlyn Brooke Shusterman* (by 7/97), *Jennifer Paige Chambers* (by 11/97), *Carrie Kenneally* (from 2/1/99), *Jennifer Paige Chambers* (from 3/2/99), *Naomi Kakuk* (from 4/6/99); DEMETER: Patricia Everett, *Helen Frank* (by 9/87), *Felicia Farone* (by 12/87), *Sylvia Dohi* (by 8/88), *N. Elaine Wiggins* (by 3/90), *Susan Lamontagne* (by 2/95), *J. Kathleen Lamb* (by 4/95), *Susan Lamontagne* (from 6/6/95), *Jennifer Lynn Letteleir* (from 10/3/95), *Jeanine Meyers* (from 6/18/96), *Amy Hamel* (by 7/97), *Celina Carvajal* (by 9/98), *Amy Hamel* (from 5/11/99), *Carol Schuberg* (from 10/26/99); GRIZABELLA: Donna Lee Marshall, *Rosemary Loar* (by 6/27/87), *Jan Horvath* (by 4/90), *Donna Lee Marshall* (by 2/91), *Natalie Toro* (by 8/92), *Mary Gutzi* (by 4/93), *Jeri Sager* (by 10/94), *Natalie Toro* (from 3/24/97), *Carter Calvert* (by 4/98), *Linda Balgord* (from 9/22/98), *Jessica Hendy* (from 10/20/98), *Jodie Langel* (by 11/98), *Renee Veneziale* (from 8/10/99); JELLYLORUM/GRIDDLEBONE: Lindsay Dyett, *Alice Lynn* (by 8/88), *Mary Ringstad* (by 3/92), *Leslie Castay* (by 4/92), *Linda Strasser* (by 1/93), *Patty Goble* (by 2/94), *Jean Arbeiter* (by 2/95), *Kris Koop* (from 12/26/95), *Jeanne Montano* (by 3/98), *Kris Koop* (from 2/1/99); JENNYANYDOTS: Robin Boudreau, *Linda Leonard* (by 10/88), *Alice C. DeChant* (by 12/89); MISTOFFOLEES: Eddie Buffum, *Joey Pizzi* by 10/89, *Vince Pesce* by 8/90, *John Joseph Festa* by 2/92, *Christopher Gattelli* by 1/93, *Joey Gyondla* by 6/93, *Joseph Favalora* by 4/95, *Randy Andre Davis* from 3/12/96, *Brian Barry* from 6/9/98, *Julius Sermonia* from 2/1/99; MUNGOJERRIE: Jack Noseworthy, *John Vincent Leggio* (by 7/88), *Todd Lester* (by 2/89), *John Vincent Leggio* (by 3/89), *Enrique Segura* (by 10/89), *Roger Kachel* (by 7/90), *Enrique Segura* (by 9/90), *Dennis Glasscock* (by 12/91), *Michael Koetting* (by 3/92), *Dennis Glasscock* (by 4/92), *Gavan Palmer* (by 12/92), *Ned Hannah* (by 2/95), *Billy Johnstone* (from 5/16/95), *Gavan Palmer* (from 5/28/96), *Jeff Lagace* (by 9/97), *David Petro* (from 4/19/99); MUNKUSTRAP: Dan McCoy, *Paul Clausen* (by 4/89), *Frank Cruz* (by 10/89), *Bryan Batt* (by 2/91), *Michael Ehlers* (by 7/91), *Kevin McCready* (by 1/92), *Robert Amirante* (by 12/92), *Randy Clements* (by 2/95), *Michael Sangiovanni* (from 6/18/96), *James Patterson* (by 12/17/96), *Jason Gillman* (by 9/97), *Kip Driver* (from 6/23/98), *Bobby Miranda* (from 1/12/98), *Paul Clausen* (from 2/1/99); OLD DEUTERONOMY: Richard Nickol, *Francis Ruivivar* (by 4/89), *Daniel Marcus* (by 6/90), *Bill Lindner* (by 7/91), *Robert Du Sold* (by 8/92), *Jimmy Lockett* (by 1/93), *John Treacy Egan* (by 10/93), *Larry Small* (by 6/94), *John Treacy Egan* (by 7/94), *Doug Eskew* (by 10/95), *Craig A. Benham* (from 5/19/98), *Stephen Carter-Hicks* (from 11/16/99 & closed tour); PLATO/MACAVITY: David Reitman, *T. Michael Dalton* (by 9/87), *Randy B. Wojcik* (by 3/88), *Jim T. Ruttman* (by 3/90), *Taylor Wicker* (by 4/93), *Stephen Bertles* (by 2/95), *Taylor Wicker* (by 4/95), *Chadwick T. Adams* (from 2/23/99); POUNCIVAL: Marc C. Oka, *Joey Pizzi* (by 7/88), *Daniel Wright* (by 10/89), *Joseph Favalora* (by 11/91), *Randy Andre Davis* (by 4/95), *Joey Gyondla*, *Christopher Burks* (from 3/12/96), *Michael Barriskill* (from 4/19/96), *Brian Barry* (by 9/97), *David Rosales* (by 11/97), *Jon-Erik Goldberg* (from 3/16/99); RUM TUM TUG-

GER: Steven Bland, *Bradford Minkoff* (by 3/88), *B.K. Kennelly* (by 4/90), *Bradford Minkoff* (by 7/91), *Timothy Smith* (by 2/92), *David Hibbard* (by 8/92), *Hunter Foster* (by 10/93), *Rohn Seykell* (by 11/93), *Ron De Vito* (by 7/94), *J. Robert Spencer* (from 5/16/95), *Robert Bartley* (from 6/18/96), *David Villella* (from 12/17/96), *Andy Karl* (by 3/98), *Kevin Loreque* (from 4/27/99); RUMPLETEAZER: Nancy Melius, *Kristi Lynes* (by 7/88), *Karen Webster* (by 3/89), *Lori Lynch* (by 12/91), *Jennifer Cody* (by 12/92), *Maria Jo Ralabate* (by 4/94), *Dana Solimando* (from 9/15/95), *Amy Shure* (from 4/28/97), *Michele Tibbitts* (by 7/97), *Renee Bonadio* (from 1/12/99), *Dina Lyn Margolin* (from 10/18/99); SILLABUB: Leslie Trayer, *Amelia Marshall* (by 2/88), *Holly Cruz* (by 8/88), *Michelle Kelly* (by 12/90), *Joyce Chittick* (by 12/91), *Bethany Samuelson* (by 8/92), *Joyce Chittick* (by 12/92), *Bethany Samuelson* (by 1/93), *Lanene Charters* (by 2/94), *Carolyn J. Ockert* (from 10/28/96), *Christie McCall* (by 9/97), *Claci Miller* (from 3/23/99); SKIMBLESHANKS: Kevin Winkler, *John Scherer* (by 3/88), *Craig A. Meyer* (by 7/88), *Danny Rounds* (by 2/89), *Gary Mendelson* (by 3/90), *Carmen Yurich* (by 12/90), *Mickey Nugent* (by 6/94), *Blair Bybee* (by 4/95), *Josh Prince* (from 12/31/96), *David W. Eggers* (by 9/97), *Jon-Paul Christensen* (by 1/98), *Michael Etzwiler* (from 5/5/98), *Ryan Shepherd* (from 3/16/99), *Shaun R. Parry* (from 9/6/99); TUMBLEBRUTUS: Robert Torres, *Leon Taylor* (by 9/87), *Randy Bettis* (by 6/27/87), *Andrew Currie* (by 3/90), *Jay Poindexter* (by 9/90), *Marc Ellis Holland* (by 11/91), *Leon Taylor* (by 6/92), *Marc Ellis Holland* (by 8/92), *Joseph Favalora, Tim Hunter* (by 4/93), *Mark R. Moreau* (from 10/28/96), *Angelo Rivera* (from 1/6/98); VICTORIA: J. Kathleen Lamb, *Natasha Davidson* (by 3/88), *Tricia Mitchell* (by 9/90), *J. Kathleen Lamb* (9/23/90–9/30/90), *Tricia Mitchell* (from 10/90), *Natasha Davidson* (by 7/91), *Tricia Mitchell* (by 10/91), *Natasha Davidson* (by 10/93), *Tricia Mitchell* (by 11/93), *Kirstie Tice* (by 4/94), *Joyce Chittick* (from 7/11/95), *Melissa Miller* (from 11/14/95), *Missy Lay Zimmer* (from 10/15/96), *Melissa Miller* (by 9/97), *Alicia Richardson* (by 3/98), *Jessica Dillan* (from 1/12/99). Note: the characters of Coricopat and Tantomile were not on this tour.

CARRE THEATRE, Amsterdam, 7/18/87–11/87 and 8/18/88–10/88 (return engagement). **Cast**: DR. DIAVOLO: Kevin Poe.

CHINA THEATRE, Stockholm, 9/11/87–12/88. The next Swedish production of any note would be a short run at GOTHENBURG, in 9/89.

THEATRE DE PARIS, France, 2/23/89–4/29/90.

U.K. TOUR. WINTER GARDENS, Blackpool, 5/5/89–11/4/89; EDINBURGH, 11/16/89–1/13/90; THE POINT, Dublin, 3/20/90–5/19/90 (the tour ended here). **Cast**: ADMETUS/MACAVITY: Jon Sebastian; ALONZO: John Partridge; BOMBALURINA: Rosemarie Ford; GRIZABELLA: Marti Webb; JEMIMA: Lisa Waddingham; JENNYANYDOTS: Louisa Shaw; MUNGOJERRIE: Adrian Edmeades; MUNKUSTRAP: Peter Bishop; QUAXO/MISTOFFOLEES: Luke Baxter; SKIMBLESHANKS: Geoff Garratt; TANTOMILE: Samantha Biddulph; VICTORIA: Marina Stevenson.

SILVIA PINAL THEATRE, Mexico City, 4/23/91–9/2/92. The production then ran at GUADALAJARA, 10/2/92–11/1/92.

ABB MUSICAL THEATRE, Zurich. Opened 8/9/91.

U.K. TOUR. Opened in 1992.

ARGENTINA. BUENOS AIRES, 6/1/93–11/30/93. **Cast**: BOMBALURINA: Silvia Aruj.

U.S. NATIONAL TOUR # 5. Opened on 7/1/01 in Atlantic City in an abbreviated 105-minute form. It left there on 8/18/01 to go to its first proper full-production stop on the tour, The Belk Theatre, Charlotte, NC, on 8/22/01. **Cast**: ALONZO/RUMPUS: Ronnie Nelson; BUSTOPHER/GUS/GROWLTIGER: William Hartery; BOMBALURINA: Sharon Hunnycutt; CASSANDRA: Tina Moye; DEMETER: Jessica Lea Patty; GRIZABELLA: Gretchen Goldsworthy; JELLYLORUM/GRIDDLEBONE: Wendi Bergamini; JENNYANYDOTS: Julie Garnye; MISTOFFOLEES: McCree O'Kelley; MUNGOJERRIE: Bryce Bermingham; MUNKUSTRAP: Grant Turner; OLD DEUTERONOMY: Jarrett Ali Boyd; PLATO/MACAVITY: Everett Taylor; POUNCIVAL: David A. Blonn; RUM TUM TUGGER: Stan Stanley; RUMPLETEAZER: Emily Haag, Pamela Rainey; SILLABUB: Sara Schudde, Katie Wanner; SKIMBLESHANKS: John Sechrist, Warren Freeman; TUMBLEBRUTUS: Brad Barnes, Brian Collier; VICTORIA: Shylo Smith.

CAPE TOWN. Opened in 12/01. In 2002 the production was in Pretoria.

U.K. TOUR. Opened in 2/03, in Plymouth. By mid–2004 this tour was rumored to be coming back to London, for another West End run, starring Elaine Paige, Bonnie Langford, and Wayne Cilento. The New London Theatre was rumored as the house, but by 2/05 the Cambridge was more strongly favored, after the closure there of *Jerry Springer—The Opera*.

ITALY. Italy finally got a production, due to open 2001, but delayed until 2003.

WALNUT STREET THEATRE, Philadelphia, 11/17/04–1/9/05. Previews from 11/9/04. This was a new staging, and included the little-heard song "The Ballad of Billy Mccaw." DIRECTOR: Richard Stafford; NEW SETS: Peter Barbieri. **Cast**: OLD DEUTERONOMY: Ken Prymus; GRIZABELLA: Katie O'Shaughnessy.

Cats' names in other countries. The characters have different names in certain productions throughout the world (although the title of the show itself has never been translated). A (non-exhaustive) list is: ADMETUS: Amadeus in Mexico; ALONZO: Sambal in Belgium, Cattivo in Finland, Jubalong in Norway; ASPARAGUS: Abrikoos in Belgium & Netherlands; BOMBALURINA: Bomballerien in Belgium & Netherlands, Bomfallerina in Norway; BUSTOPHER JONES: Macoco Cue in Argentina, Ghiselbert Smit in Belgium, Kerhonen B. in Finland, Gastrofar George in Hungary, Gordoceles Cruz in Mexico, Bastian Bull in Norway, Adlige Karl in Sweden; CARBUCKETTY: Klorigar in Norway; CASSANDRA: Merade in Norway; CORICOPAT: Wageschrick in Belgium, Coricompas in Latin America; DEMETER: Hamletra in Norway, Jokasta in Sweden; ELECTRA: Pusine in Norway; ETCETERA: Mirza in Mexico, Huralia in Norway; GENGHIS: Djangus in Belgium, Hongbong in Finland, Tarsan in Norway; GRIDDLEBONE: Lady Kylkiluu in Finland, Chatelune in France, Golfatriz in Latin America, Grillebein in Norway, Silkeseben in Sweden; GRIZABELLA: Misabella in Finland, Siam Ella in Norway, Mirabella in Sweden; GROWLTIGER: Snauwtijger in Belgium, Matamore in France, Tigrunon in Latin America, Morr Tiger in Sweden; JELLYLORUM: Antimakassa in Belgium, Agilorum in Latin America, Jadakatt in Norway; JENNYANYDOTS: Jenny Fleckenreich in Austria, Spikkelpikkelmies in Belgium, Amelie Ron Ron in France, Jenny Fleckenfell in Germany, Gumbie-Katze in Germany & Austria, Gimb-Gomb in Hungary, Lengelingela in Hungary, Bombonachona in Latin America, Annepanneflekk in Norway, Stijfselkat in Netherlands, Vickiprickitass in Sweden; MACAVITY: Van Zonderan in Belgium, Sam Mitzegel in Hungary, Nefastulo in Latin America, Makkentass in Norway; MISTOFFOLEES: Dr. Diavolo in Belgium & Netherlands, Micifustofeles in Latin America, Metrofeliz in Norway, Filurifax in Sweden; MUNGOJERRIE: Lorrenjopie in Belgium, Ben Mickering in Hungary, Pingurriento in Latin America, Burma Harry in Norway, Gycklar Jerry in Sweden; MUNKUSTRAP: Snorrescha in Belgium & Netherlands; OLD DEUTERONOMY: Gatuzalem in Argentina & Mexico, Mister Old Csendbelenn in Hungary, Profetikus in Norway; PLATO: Potefar in Norway; POUNCIVAL: Surripus in Norway; QUAXO: Xinix in Switzerland; RUM TUM TUGGER: Tuk Stuk Rukker in Belgium, Rocky Tam Tam in France, Micsel Rumli in Hungary, Pon Roc Terco in Latin America, Rom Tom Tapper in Norway, Ram Tam Trassell in Sweden; RUMPLETEAZER: Scharrlenellis in Belgium, Mindlevery in Hungary, Rampentussa in Norway, Rumpenstumpen in Sweden; RUMPUSCAT: Branie Kat in Belgium, Chat Rivari in France, Ron Rovarkatt in Norway, Slim Slagsmalkatt in Sweden; Sillabub: Sylvani in Belgium; SKIMBLESHANKS: Anelkauw in Belgium, Toppa-Roy in Finland, Edgar in France, Elvis Tren in Hungary, Mirringo in Latin America, Lokosjekk in Norway; TANTOMILE: Mijleschrok in Belgium; Tumblebrutus: Rymy-Edward in Finland; VICTORIA: Kvitlinga in Norway.

Cats took in over $2 billion worldwide & over 50 million people saw it. Performed in 11 languages, in 26 countries, and over 300 cities.

129. *Celebration*

In 2 acts and 18 scenes. An experimental musical fable. An orphan is in battle over a girl named Angel with the richest man in the Western World and manufacturer of things artificial, evil Edgar Allan Rich (based on David Merrick). Orphan wins the fight and the girl. Set on a platform on New Years Eve. It is an allegory of winter passing and spring coming.

Before Broadway. Tom Jones and Harvey Schmidt worked on this show for eight years. In 1961 it was announced as a show in the making called *Ratfink*, and was about a character called James J. Ratfink. Cheryl Crawford of the Theatre Guild was going to produce. By 1968 it had been re-worked and was now called *Celebration*, and Miss Crawford produced, first at Jones & Schmidt's Portfolio Studio. The show cost $125,000, and the producers raised twice that much.

The Broadway Run. AMBASSADOR THEATRE, 1/22/69–4/26/69. 13 previews. 109 PERFORMANCES. A "Portfolio Production" (Tom Jones & Harvey Schmidt) PRESENTED BY Cheryl Crawford & Richard Chandler; MUSIC: Harvey Schmidt; LYRICS/BOOK/DIRECTOR: Tom Jones; CHOREOGRAPHER: Vernon Lusby; SETS/COSTUMES/LIGHTING: Ed Wittstein; SOUND: Jim Limberg; MUSICAL DIRECTOR: Rod Derefinko; ORCHESTRATIONS: Jim Tyler; CAST RECORDING on Capitol; PRESS: Harvey B. Sabinson, Lee Solters, David Powers; GENERAL MANAGER: Arthur Waxman; PRODUCTION STAGE MANAGER: May Muth; STAGE MANAGER: Robert Schear; ASSISTANT STAGE MANAGER: John Boni. *Cast:* POTEMKIN: Keith Charles (3); ORPHAN: Michael Glenn-Smith (4); ANGEL: Susan Watson (1); RICH: Ted Thurston (2); REVELERS: Glenn Bastian, Cindi Bulak, Stephan de Ghelder, Leah Horen, Patricia Lens, Norman Mathews, Frank Newell, Pamela Peadon, Felix Rice, Sally Riggs, Gary Wales, Hal Watters. *Standbys:* Rich: David Sabin; Potemkin: John Boni. *Understudies:* Orphan: Hal Watters; Angel: Pamela Peadon; Revelers: Tip Kelley & Nina Trasoff. *Percussion Ensemble:* KEYBOARDS: Rod Derefinko, Clay Fullum, Paulette Haupt; PERCUSSION: Dennis Glick, Leon Oxman, Cholli Simons; HARP: Kathryn Easter; GUITAR: Jack Hotop; BASS: Sam Bruno. *Act I:* "Celebration" (Potemkin & Revelers), "Orphan in the Storm" (Orphan & Revelers), "Survive" (Potemkin & Revelers), "Somebody" (Angel & Hittites), "Bored" (Rich), "My Garden" (Orphan & Revelers), "Where Did it Go?" (Rich & Sycophants), "Love Song" (Angel, Potemkin, Rich, Orphan, Revelers), "To the Garden" (Everyone). *Act II:* "I'm Glad to See You've Got What You Want" (Angel & Orphan), "It's You Who Makes Me Young" (Rich & Revelers), "Not My Problem" (Potemkin & Machines), "Fifty Million Years Ago" (Orphan), "The Beautician Ballet" (Rich & Revelers), "Saturnalia" (Potemkin & Revelers), "Under the Tree" (Angel & Animals), "Winter and Summer" (Everyone), Finale: "Celebration" (reprise) (Everyone).

It got bad reviews, partly because its style was already outdated, and partly because it was too intimate a show to be presented at the Ambassador.

After Broadway. PORTFOLIO STUDIO, 1/31/75–2/23/75. 12 PERFORMANCES. DIRECTOR/CHOREOGRAPHER: Vernon Lusby; MUSICAL DIRECTOR: Ken Collins (i.e. Tom Jones); SETS: Ed Wittstein. *Cast:* BOY: Michael Glenn-Smith; POTEMKIN: Gene Foote; ANGEL: Virginia Gregory; RICH: Ted Thurston.

YORK THEATRE COMPANY, 1/12/01–1/24/01. Part of the *Musicals in Mufti* series. *Cast:* POTEMKIN: Keith Charles; ALSO WITH: Kate Dawson, John Treacy Egan, Michael Halling, Natasha Harper, Kenneth Kantor, Jodie Langel, Jeremiah Miller, M. Kathryn Quinlan.

130. *Charlie and Algernon*

"A very special Broadway musical," with no intermission. Charlie is a brain-damaged sweeper at a bakery, with an IQ of 68, and Algernon is a white mouse. Scientific experiments shoot their IQs up dramatically. Charlie can now read *War and Peace* in one night. However, success is temporary, and Charlie begins to regress. Set in Brooklyn and Manhattan.

Before Broadway. Daniel Keyes' short story rapidly became a sci-fi classic. Sterling Silliphant adapted it for *CBS Playhouse* in 1961 as *The Two Worlds of Charly Gordon*, and later adapted his TV play into the 1968 movie *Charly*, starring Cliff Robertson, who won an Oscar. As a stage play, playwright David Rogers was commissioned by the Dramatists Play Service to dramatize the story, and this became the musical *Flowers for Algernon*, which played first as a tryout at the CITADEL, Edmonton, Canada, in 12/78, and which led to the London opening at QUEEN'S THEATRE, 6/14/79. 29 PERFORMANCES. However, despite raves for star Michael Crawford, it flopped. DIRECTOR: Peter Coe. *Cast:* CHARLY GOR-

DON: Michael Crawford; ALICE KINNIAN: Cheryl Kennedy; ALSO WITH: Aubrey Woods, Ralph Nosseck. On 3/8/80 the Dramatists Play Service arranged for the Folger Theatre Group to present a revised version as part of their two-play season at KENNEDY CENTER, Washington, DC. Same crew as for subsequent Broadway run, except DIRECTOR: Louis W. Scheeder. Now called *Charlie and Algernon* (note the change in the spelling of "Charlie"). *Cast:* CHARLIE: P.J. Benjamin; ALICE: Sandy Faison; MOTHER: Julienne Marie; FATHER: Bruce Ed Morrow; LITTLE CHARLIE: Anthony J.C. Paolillo & John Edward Mueller; MRS. DONNER: Nancy Franklin; FRANK: Timothy Meyers; DR. STRAUSS: Chev Rodgers; LITA: Loida Santos; DR. NEMUR: Robert Sevra. It re-opened on 8/4/80 at the TERRACE THEATRE, and from there went to Broadway.

The Broadway Run. HELEN HAYES THEATRE, 9/14/80–9/28/80. 12 previews. 17 PERFORMANCES. PRESENTED BY The John F. Kennedy Center for the Performing Arts, Isobel Robins Konecky, The Fisher Theatre Foundation, Folger Theatre Group (Michael Sheehan & Louis W. Scheeder); MUSIC: Charles Strouse; LYRICS/BOOK: David Rogers; BASED ON the 1959 short story *Flowers for Algernon*, by Daniel Keyes, which first appeared in *The Magazine of Fantasy and Science Fiction*; DIRECTOR: Louis W. Scheeder; CHOREOGRAPHER: Virginia Freeman; SETS: Kate Edmunds; COSTUMES: Jess Goldstein; LIGHTING: Hugh Lester; SOUND: William H. Clements; MUSICAL DIRECTOR: Liza Redfield; ASSISTANT CONDUCTOR/ADDITIONAL VOCAL ARRANGEMENTS: Tom Fay; ORCHESTRATIONS: Philip J. Lang; PRESS: Alpert/LeVine; CASTING: Terry Fay; GENERAL MANAGEMENT: Theatre Now; COMPANY MANAGER: Michael Lonergan; PRODUCTION STAGE MANAGER: Martha Knight; STAGE MANAGER: Peter Dowling; ASSISTANT STAGE MANAGER: P'nenah Goldstein. *Cast:* CHARLIE: P.J. Benjamin (1); ALICE KINNIAN: Sandy Faison (2); DR. STRAUSS: Edward Earle (3); DR. NEMUR: Robert Sevra (4); MRS. DONNER: Nancy Franklin (5); LITA: Loida Santos (8); FRANK: Patrick Jude (6); CHARLIE'S MOTHER: Julienne Marie (7); LITTLE CHARLIE: Matthew Duda (10); CHARLIE'S FATHER: Michael Vita (9). *Standbys:* Charlie/Nemur/Father: Phillip Alan Witt; Strauss/Frank: Michael Vita; Mrs. Donner/Lita/Mother: Sydney Anderson; Little Charlie: R.D. Robb.

"Have I the Right" (Alice, Nemur, Strauss), "I Got a Friend" (Charlie), "I Got a Friend" (reprise) (Charlie & Alice), "Some Bright Morning" (Nemur, Charlie, Strauss, Alice), "Jelly Donuts and Chocolate Cake" (Mrs. Donner, Lita, Frank), "Hey Look at Me" (Charlie & Alice), "Reading" (Charlie & Alice), "No Surprises" (Alice), "Midnight Riding" (Frank & Lita), "Dream Safe with Me" (Charlie's Mother), "Not Another Day Like This" (Charlie's Mother & Father), "Somebody New" (Mrs. Donner & Charlie), "I Can't Tell You" (Charlie), "Now" (Charlie & Alice), "Charlie and Algernon" (Charlie) [the favorite song], "The Maze" (Charlie), "Whatever Time There Is" (Alice & Charlie), "Everything Was Perfect" (Strauss & Nemur), "Charlie" (Charlie), "I Really Loved You" (Charlie), "Whatever Time There Is" (reprise) (Alice).

On Broadway it was pretty much panned. It received a Tony nomination for score.

131. *Chauve-Souris 1943*

This was the fifth edition of the late Nikita Balieff's Russian revue.

Before Broadway. The first Chauve-Souris ("The Bat Theatre of Moscow"—"chauve-souris" means the animal the "bat" in French) was originally organized in a cellar by members of the Moscow Art Theatre for their own amusement. During the Russian Revolution the Chauve-Souris was re-organized in Paris by refugees from the Stanislavsky company, notably comic Nikita Balieff, who owned a restaurant in Paris which he called the *Chauve-Souris*. He was the host of this review, and he then took it out to the Parisian stage, then to London, and finally to Broadway. The first Broadway edition of the *Chauve-Souris* revues was presented by Morris Gest & F. Ray Comstock at the 49TH STREET THEATRE, 2/1/22. 520 PERFORMANCES. There were later *Chauve-Souris* revues—1923, 1925, 1927, 1931, and the final one, in 1943.

The Broadway Run. ROYALE THEATRE, 8/12/43–8/21/43. 12 PERFORMANCES. PRESENTED BY Leon Greanin, by arrangement with Mme Nikita Balieff; COMPILED BY/ MUSICAL DIRECTOR/MUSICAL ARRANGEMENTS: Gleb Yellin; ENGLISH LYRICS: Irving Florman; DEVISED BY/

SUPERVISED BY: Leon Greanin; DIRECTOR: Michel Michon; COMEDY DIRECTOR: Michael Dalmatoff; CHOREOGRAPHER: Vecheslav Swoboda & Boris Romanoff; SETS/COSTUMES: Serge Soudeikine. *Cast:* Leon Greanin (1) ☆ (mc—taking over from the late M. Balieff), Marusia Sava (principal singer) (2), Zinaida Alvers (3), Vera Pavlovska (4), Tatiana Pobers (5), Zhenia (Jeanne) Soudeikina (6), Dania Krupska (7), Georgiana Bannister (8), Norma Slavina (9), Georges Doubrovsky (10), Michael Dalmatoff (11), Simeon Karavaeff (impersonator) (12), Michel Michon (13), Arkady (Arcadi) Stoyanovsky (14), Jack Gansert (15), Vladimir Lazarev (16), Leo Resnickoff (17), Arsen Tarpoff (18), Leo Vlassoff (19), Nicolas Dontzoff (20), Georges Yurka (21), Florence Berline, Cyprienne Gabelman, Audrey Keane, Blanche Sanborska, Fern Sironi, Norma Slavina, Olga Nicolaeva, Nicolas Yourovsky, Lev Xanoff, Sergei Zdanoff. *Act I:* Overture, from Russian classics; *Scene 1* Russian Shawls. Songs of Babi, with greetings from Russia. l: Michel Michon. Misses Sava, Alvers, Bannister, Pavlovska, Pobers. Solo sung by Zhenia Soudeikina; *Scene 2* The Parade of the Wooden Soldiers. m: Leon Jessel. Setting: Serge Soudeikine, after M. Narbout. Messrs Stoyanovsky & Gansert. Misses Berline, Gabelman, Keane, Krupska, Sanborska, Sironi, Slavina; *Scene 3* Victory Parade. Messrs Dalmatoff, Dontzoff, Doubrovsky, Resnickoff, Tarpoff, Vlassoff, Yurka; *Scene 4* Song of the Flea (m: Modest Moussorgsky). MEPHISTOPHELES: Georges Doubrovsky; *Scene 5* Trepak. Folk dance (ch: Boris Romanoff). Misses Gabelman, Keane, Krupska, Sanborska, Sironi. Messrs Karavaeff & Gansert; *Scene 6* Love in the Ranks. The Daughter of the Regiment in Old St. Petersburg. (m: Alexei Archangelsky. Staged by Boris Romanoff. set/cos: Serge Soudeikine, after Nicola Benois). THE DAUGHTER OF THE REGIMENT: Vera Pavlovska; THE CORPORAL: Arcadi Stoyanovsky; THE LIEUTENANT: Arsen Tarpoff; THE CAPTAIN: Michel Michon; THE MAJOR: Georges Doubrovsky; THE GENERAL: Michael Dalmatoff; *Scene 7* The Nightingale. m: Alexander Alabieff-Liszt. ch: Vecheslav Swoboda. Danced by Norma Slavina; *Scene 8* The WAC and the Sniper. m/l for "Sniper Song" by Irving Florman. Staged by Ruthanna Boris. THE AMERICAN WAC: Georgiana Bannister; THE RUSSIAN SNIPER: Vera Pavlovska; *Scene 9* Hobo-Genius Chorus in 4F. Messrs Doubrovsky, Dontzoff, Karavaeff, Michon, Resnickoff, Stoyanovsky, Tarpoff, Vlassoff, Yurka, under the leadership of Michael Dalmatoff; *Scene 10* Song of *Chauve-Souris 1943.* Sung by Vera Pavlovska; *Scene 11* Harvest Festival. Inspired by contemporary Russian composers. ch: Vecheslav Swoboda. (a) Song of the Fields (m: Lev Knipper); (b) United Nations (m: Dimitri Shostakovich). Sung by Zinaida Alvers & Georges Doubrovsky; (c) Balalaikas (m: H. Dounaevsky); (d) Oh, My Heart! (m: H. Dounaevsky). Sung by Marusia Sava; (e) Strolling Home (m: Vladimir Zakharoff); (f) Electric Lights Come to the Village (m: Dimitri Shostakovich & Vladimir Zakharoff). Sung by Zhenia Soudeikina. Misses Sava, Alvers, Bannister, Berline, Gabelman, Keane, Krupska, Pavlovska, Pobers, Sanborska, Sironi, Slavina, Soudeikina, Nicolaeva. Messrs Dalmatoff, Doubrovsky, Dontzoff, Gansert, Karavaeff, Lazarev, Michon, Resnickoff, Stoyanovsky, Tarpoff, Vlassoff, Yurka, Yourovsky, Xanoff, Zdanoff. *Act II:* *Scene 1* The Gypsies. Original Gypsy romances. Songs arr: Mme Nastia Poliakova. Set in a villa at the turn of the century, with an elegant mistress and master listening to the music of an invited band of gypsies. CHORUS LEADER: Michael Dalmatoff. 1ST GYPSY SOLOIST: Marusia Sava; 2ND GYPSY SOLOIST: Zinaida Alvers; 3RD GYPSY SOLOIST: Tatiana Pobers; MINSTREL: Michel Michon; HUSSAR: Georges Doubrovsky; GYPSIES: Misses Bannister, Soudeikina, Gabelman, Berline. Messrs Resnickoff, Dontzoff, Tarpoff, Vlassoff, Yurka; *Scene 2* Polka. ch: Vecheslav Swoboda. Miss Keane, Miss Slavina, Mr. Gansert; *Scene 3* Romances of Tchaikovsky. PETER ILICH TCHAIKOVSKY: Michel Michon. Duet sung by Zinaida Alvers & Vera Pavlovska; *Scene 4* Katinka's Birthday. Katinka is Sweet Sixteen. l: Michon & Robbins. Katinka's Polka by Boris Romanoff. KATINKA: Dania Krupska; MOTHER: Jeanne Soudeikina; FATHER: Leo Vlassoff; AUNT: Georgiana Bannister; BRIDEGROOM: Arsen Tarpoff; UNCLE: Arcadi Stoyanovsky; PORTRAIT: Georges Doubrovsky; STATUE: Michel Michon; LITTLE BROTHER: Blanche Sanborska; *Scene 5* A Russian Sailor in New York. In English. THE SAILOR: Simeon Karavaeff (he did impressions of Ray Bolger & Al Jolson); *Scene 6* Night Idyll. Staged by Mme Elena Balieff. Setting by Serge Soudeikine, after Nicholas Remisoff. THE GIRL: Marusia Sava; THE BOY: Arcadi Stoyanovsky; MUSICAL ECHOES: Jeanne Soudeikina, Georgiana Bannister, Simeon Kar-

avaeff, Leo Resnickoff—ACCORDIONIST: Nicolas Dontzoff; GUITARIST: Georges Yurka; *Scene 7* Wedding in Ukraine. Original Ukrainian folk songs & dances. ch for Hopak by Boris Romanoff. BRIDE: Vera Pavlovska; GROOM: Vladimir Lazarev; MOTHER: Jeanne Soudeikina; FATHER: Michael Dalmatoff; 1ST BEST MAN: Simeon Karavaeff; 2ND BEST MAN: Michel Michon; PRIEST: Georges Doubrovsky; BRIDESMAIDS/NEIGHBORS/FRIENDS/GUESTS: Entire Company.

It was an outdated concept by this time, and got terrible reviews. M. Greanin, the mc, was no Balieff. It was also hampered by strictures imposed on Broadway musicals by the president of the American Federation of Musicians, James Caesar Petrillo, so much so that what was on the program wasn't necessarily what audience saw (or rather, heard). And, most of the show was in Russian.

132. *Chess*

A musical about a chess match between the Russian champion and the American challenger (who was based on Bobby Fischer), intermingled with a love story in which both are rivals. An allegory of the Cold War. The Russian defects to the West. There is minimal dialog.

Before Broadway. It was conceived by Tim Rice in 1984. Made as a concept record album, with the London Symphony Orchestra, and featuring Elaine Paige, Barbara Dickson, Denis Quilley, Murray Head, Tommy Korberg, Bjorn Skifs (it sold over a million copies) before it became a stage production. Tim Rice failed to interest his partner Andrew Lloyd Webber, but it ran at the PRINCE EDWARD THEATRE, London, 5/14/86. 1,029 PERFORMANCES. *Cast*: FLORENCE: Elaine Paige; THE AMERICAN: Murray Head; SVETLANA: Barbara Dickson. It was revised for Broadway, made more conventionally dramatic. On 1/22/86 it was reported that Michael Bennett had withdrawn as director due to angina. He was replaced by Trevor Nunn.

The Broadway Run. IMPERIAL THEATRE, 4/28/88–6/25/88. 17 previews. 68 PERFORMANCES. PRESENTED BY The Shubert Organization, 3 Knights, Ltd. (Benny Andersson, Tim Rice, Bjorn Ulvaeus), Robert Fox, Ltd.; MUSIC: Benny Andersson & Bjorn Ulvaeus; LYRICS: Tim Rice; BOOK: Richard Nelson; BASED ON an idea by Tim Rice; DIRECTOR: Trevor Nunn; CHOREOGRAPHER: Lynne Taylor-Corbett; SETS: Robin Wagner; COSTUMES: Theoni V. Aldredge; LIGHTING: David Hersey; SOUND: Andrew Bruce; MUSICAL SUPERVISOR/MUSICAL DIRECTOR: Paul Bogaev; ORCHESTRATIONS/ARRANGEMENTS: Anders Eljas; CAST RECORDING on RCA Victor; PRESS: Bill Evans & Associates; CASTING: Johnson—Liff & Zerman; GENERAL MANAGEMENT: Gatchell & Neufeld; PRODUCTION STAGE MANAGER: Alan Hall; STAGE MANAGERS: Jake Bell, Zane Weiner, Ruth E. Rinklin. *Cast:* GREGOR VASSEY: Neal Ben-Ari; YOUNG FLORENCE: Gina Gallagher; FREDDIE TRUMPER: Philip Casnoff (3) ☆; FLORENCE VASSEY: Judy Kuhn (1) ☆; ANATOLY SERGIEVSKY: David Carroll (2) ☆; ALEXANDER MOLOKOV: Harry Goz (7); NICKOLAI: Kurt Johns; WALTER: Dennis Parlato (4); ARBITER: Paul Harman (6); SVETLANA: Marcia Mitzman (5); JOE, EMBASSY OFFICIAL: Richard Muenz; HAROLD, EMBASSY OFFICIAL: Eric Johnson; ENSEMBLE: John Aller, Neal Ben-Ari, Suzanne Briar, Steve Clemente, Katherine Lynne Condit, Ann Crumb, David Cryer, R.F. Daley, Deborah Geneviere, Kurt Johns, Eric Johnson, Paul Laureano, Rosemary Loar, Judy McLane, Jessica Molaskey, Richard Muenz, Kip Niven, Francis Ruivivar, Alex Santoriello, Wysandria Woolsey. *Understudies:* Florence: Ann Crumb & Judy McLane; Svetlana: Ann Crumb & Wysandria Woolsey; Anatoly: Richard Muenz & Paul Harman; Freddie: Kurt Johns; Molokov: David Cryer; Walter: Kip Niven; Arbiter: Alex Santoriello; Young Florence: Chrystal Pennington. *Swings*: Karen Babcock & Craig Wells. *Orchestra*: CONCERTMASTER: Sanford Allen; VIOLINS: Dale Stuckenbruck, Jue Yao, Sandra Billingslea, Stanley Hunte, Katherine Livolsi; CELLI: Mark Shuman & Roberta Cooper; FLUTES: David Weiss, Charles Millard, Edward Zuhlke; PICCOLO: David Weiss; CLARINETS: David Weiss, Charles Millard, Peter Simmons; OBOE/ENGLISH HORN: Edward Zuhlke; BASS CLARINET: Charles Millard; BASSOON/BARITONE SAX: Peter Simmons; TRUMPETS/FLUGELHORNS: James Hynes, Richard Hammett, David Rogers; PICCOLO TRUMPET: James Hynes; TROMBONE: Clint Sharman; BASS

TROMBONE: Richard Blanc; FRENCH HORN: Russell Rizner; KEYBOARDS: Steven Margoshes, Robert Gustafson, John Mahoney; DRUMS: Ted Oldakowski; BASS: Hugh Mason; GUITAR: Kevin Kuhn; PERCUSSION: Nicholas Cerrato. *Act I*: *Prologue* Budapest, Hungary, 1956: "(The Story of) Chess" (Gregor). BANGKOK, THAILAND; THE PRESENT TIME: *Scene 1* A large meeting room in the Bangkok Hilton Hotel: "Press Conference" (What a Scene, What a Joy) (Freddie, Florence, Reporters); *Scene 2* Hotel hallway and Anatoly's hotel suite: "Where I Want to Be" (Anatoly); *Scene 3* Freddie's suite: "How Many Women?" (Argument) (Florence & Freddie), "The Russian and Molokov" (Anatoly & Molokov) [this number was added for the tour]; *Scene 4* The Chess trade show: "Merchandisers' Song" (Walter & Merchandisers), "US Versus USSR" (Molokov, American & Soviet Delegates); *Scene 5* The Chess Board Arena, and later, elevators and Anatoly's office: "Chess Hymn" (Arbiter & Company), Quartet ("A Model of Decorum and Tranquility") (Molokov, Florence, Arbiter, Anatoly); *Scene 6* Freddie's suite: "You Want to Lose Your Only Friend?" (Florence & Freddie), "Someone Else's Story" (Florence); *Scene 7* The streets of Bangkok: "One Night in Bangkok" (Freddie & Company); *Scene 8* The Generous Sole Restaurant, and terrace: "Terrace Duet" (Florence & Anatoly), "Who'd Ever Think It?" (Freddie & Florence) [this number was added for the tour]; *Scene 9* The Chess Board Arena, and later, Florence's hotel room: "So, You Got What You Want" (Freddie & Florence); *Scene 10* Underground parking square below the arena; *Scene 11* A small baggage room in the airport, and later, a concourse in the airport: "(Nobody's on) Nobody's Side" (Florence), "The Reporters" (Ensemble) [this number was added for the tour], "Anthem" (Anatoly). *Act II*: *Prologue* Kennedy Airport, New York; eight weeks later [this prologue was dropped after the opening]: "Arbiter's Song" (Arbiter & Company) [dropped after the opening]. BUDAPEST, HUNGARY: *Scene 1* Budapest; eight weeks later: "Hungarian Folk Song" (Company); *Scene 2* A chapel of a large cathedral: "Heaven Help My Heart" (Florence); *Scene 3* Freddie's suite: "No Contest" (Winning) (Freddie & Walter); *Scene 4* A walk along the Danube outside the hotel after dinner: "You and I" (Anatoly, Florence, Svetlana); *Scene 5* Svetlana's hotel room: "You and I" (continued) (Anatoly, Florence, Svetlana); *Scene 6* Outside the Chess Arena building: "A Whole New Board Game" (Freddie); *Scene 7* The lobby of the Chess Arena: "Let's Work Together" (Walter & Molokov); *Scene 8* An elegant restaurant: "I Know Him So Well" (Florence & Svetlana); *Scene 9* Freddie's suite: "Pity the Child" (Freddie); *Scene 10* The walk along the Danube: "Lullaby" ("Apukad Eros Kezen") (Gregor & Florence); *Scene 11* Anatoly's dressing room: "Endgame" (Anatoly, Freddie, Company); *Scene 12* A room at the Budapest airport, and later, a hangar: "You and I" (reprise) (Anatoly & Florence), "Anthem" (reprise) (Florence) [for the tour this reprise was replaced by a reprise of "Someone Else's Story" (Florence)].

Bad reviews and friction between Trevor Nunn and Tim Rice killed the show. It lost $6 million. David Carroll and Judy Kuhn were nominated for Tonys.

After Broadway. TOUR. Opened on 1/9/90, at the Jackie Gleason Theatre, Miami. PRESENTED BY Tom Mallow, William H. Kessler Jr., Michael M. Weatherly, Robert R. Larsen, and PACE Theatrical Group; REVISED BOOK: Robert Coe; DIRECTOR: Des McAnuff; NEW CHOREOGRAPHY: Peter Anastos; ADDITIONAL CHOREOGRAPHY: Wayne Cilento; NEW SETS: David Mitchell; NEW COSTUMES: Susan Hilferty; NEW LIGHTING: Ken Billington; NEW SOUND: Gary Stocker; MUSICAL SUPERVISORS/ADDITIONAL ORCHESTRATIONS: Steven Margoshes & Danny Troob; MUSICAL DIRECTOR: Jonny Bowden; MUSICAL CONSULTANT: Paul Bogaev. *Cast*: ARBITER: Ken Ard; FREDDIE: Stephen Bogardus; WALTER: Gregory Jbara; FLORENCE: Carolee Carmello; MOLOKOV: David Hurst; ANATOLY: John Herrera; SVETLANA: Barbara Walsh; CHORUS: Timm Fujii, Philip Hernandez, Thomas James O'Leary, Carol Denise Smith, Vernon Spencer, Nephi Jay Wimmer. The song order was quite changed.

PAPER MILL PLAYHOUSE, New Jersey, 1991. DIRECTOR/CHOREOGRAPHER: Rob Marshall; SETS: Michael Anania. *Cast*: WALTER: P.J. Benjamin; SVETLANA: Susan Dawn Carson; MOLOKOV: David Cryer; ARBITER: John De Luca; FLORENCE: Judy McLane; ANATOLY: Keith Rice; TV INTERVIEWER: Donna Pompei.

MASTER THEATRE, NYC. The abridged & somewhat revised version. 2/1/92–4/12/92. 4 previews from 1/29/92. 83 PERFORMANCES. PRE-SENTED BY Artists' Perspective; DIRECTOR: David Taylor; CHOREOGRAPHER: Madeline Paul; MUSICAL DIRECTOR/NEW ORCHESTRATIONS: Phil Reno. The settings were Merano (Italy) and Bangkok, in 1972 & 1973. *Cast*: FLORENCE: Kathleen Rowe McAllen; ANATOLY: J. Mark McVey; FREDDIE: Ray Walker; ARBITER: Patrick Jude; SVETLANA: Jan Horvath; MOLOKOV: Bob Frisch; ALSO WITH: Ric Ryder, Rebecca Timms. *Act I*: Merano, Italy, 1972. *Prologue* (Arbiter); *Scene 1* Merano: "Merano" (Arbiter, Freddie, Ensemble); *Scene 2* Anatoly's hotel room: "Where I Want to Be" (Molokov, Svetlana, Anatoly, Ensemble); *Scene 3* Freddie's hotel room: "How Many Women?" (Florence & Freddie); *Scene 4* The tournament arena: "US Versus USSR" (Ensemble). "Arbiter's Song" (Arbiter & Ensemble), "Chess Game # 1" (Orchestra), "A Model of Decorum and Tranquility" (Molokov, Florence, Arbiter, Anatoly), "Chess Hymn" (Molokov, Florence, Arbiter, Anatoly); *Scene 5* Anatoly's hotel room: "Someone Else's Story" (Svetlana); *Scene 6* Freddie's hotel room: "The American and Florence"/"Nobody's on Nobody's Side" (Florence & Ensemble); *Scene 7* The hotel lobby: "The Merchandisers' Song" (Freddie & Ensemble); *Scene 8* Mountain top meeting: "Mountain Top Duet" (Florence & Anatoly), "Who'd Ever Guess It?" (Freddie); *Scene 9* The tournament arena: "Chess Game # 2" (Orchestra), "Florence Quits" (Freddie & Florence), "Pity the Child" (Freddie), "Where I Want to Be" (reprise) (Anatoly & Florence), "Embassy Lament," "Anthem" (Anatoly). *Act II*: Bangkok, Thailand; one year later. *Prologue* (Arbiter); *Scene 1* Bangkok: "One Night in Bangkok" (Arbiter & Ensemble); *Scene 2* Anatoly & Florence's hotel room: "Heaven Help My Heart" (Florence), "Argument" (Florence & Anatoly); *Scene 3* Molokov's hotel room: "The Confrontation" (Anatoly, Molokov, Svetlana); *Scene 4* The hotel lobby: "No Contest" (Anatoly & Freddie); *Scene 5* Florence & Svetlana's balconies: "I Know Him So Well" (Florence & Svetlana); *Scene 6* The deal: "The Deal" (Company); *Scene 7* The tournament arena: "Endgame" (Company), "You and I"/Epilogue (Florence & Anatoly).

TWO-CITY TOURING REVIVAL. 1/28/00–2/6/00, Wilmington, Del; 2/8/00–2/13/00, Bushnell, Hartford, Conn. DIRECTOR: Bill Castellino. *Cast*: FREDDIE: Carl Brad Drummer; FLORENCE: Kim Lindsay; ANATOLY: Philip Hernandez; SVETLANA: Kirsti Carnahan; MOLOKOV: David Brummel; WALTER: Mark McGrath; ARBITER: David Masenheimer.

JOHN HOUSEMAN THEATRE, NYC. All-star benefit concert, conceived in 2000 by Robert Evan, and PRESENTED BY Neil Berg & Robert Evan in association with Eric Krebs & Overland Entertainment, and performed on two Sundays, 5/10/00 & 5/17/00, proceeds going to Broadway Cares/Equity Fights AIDS (it raised $39,400). Certain songs were sung by different characters than in the original, in order to balance the concert version. DIRECTOR: Philip Hoffman; MUSICAL DIRECTOR: Neil Berg. *Cast*: ANATOLY: Robert Evan; FLORENCE: Christiane Noll; SVETLANA: Alice Ripley; MOLOKOV: Raymond Jaramillo McLeod; ARBITER: Danny Zolli; NARRATOR: Michael Cerveris; FREDDIE: Brian d'Arcy James (on 5/10/00) and *Dave Clemmons* on 5/17/00.

In 11/99 Tim Rice & Bjorn Ulvaeus began planning a Broadway revival for the 2000–2001 season. It didn't happen, although by 10/03 there was new talk of a Broadway revival.

NEW AMSTERDAM THEATRE, NYC, 9/22/03. Much-acclaimed one-night benefit concert for the Actors Fund of America. PRESENTED BY Seth Rudetsky; DIRECTOR: Peter Flynn; SETS: Paul Weimer; MUSICAL DIRECTOR: Seth Rudetsky. Barbara Cook introduced it. *Cast*: THE AMERICAN: Adam Pascal; SVETLANA: Sutton Foster (Lara Fabian was going to play this role); FLORENCE: Julia Murney; MOLOKOV: Norm Lewis; WALTER: Jonathan Dokuchitz; ARBITER: Raul Esparza; ALSO WITH: Yassmin Alers, Kristine Bendul, Stephen Bienskie, John Bolton, Stacey Lynn Brass, Stephanie D'Abruzzo, John Treacy Egan, Barrett Foa, Laurie Gamache, Ann Harada, Adam Hunter, Audrey Klinger, Nicole Ruth Snelson, Schele Williams, Wysandria Woolsey, Matt Zarley.

133. *Chicago*

A "musical vaudeville." Staged like a vaudeville show, each scene announced by an mc & performed like an individual act, including stripping, ventriloquism and female impersonation. A very dark and cynical musical. Set in Chicago in the late 1920s. Roxie, a showgirl, murders her unfaithful lover, Fred, and, thanks to Billy, a razzle dazzle attorney, is acquitted, and ends up as a vaudeville headliner with another "scintillating sinner," Velma. Amos is Roxie's husband. There were several other cases of ladies having murdered men and being on trial at the same time. These are represented by the other murderesses in the Cook County Jail — Annie, June, Hunyak, Liz, and Mona. Velma was based on the real-life Belva Gaertner, also acquitted at the trial. Hunyak was a Hungarian prisoner who uttered only two words, "Not Guilty," many times. Mama was the jailhouse matron. Mary Sunshine was a drag role. Kitty is the new "star," who after killing Harry, steals Roxie's thunder. Martin Harrison is the assistant D.A. Aaron is Hunyak's lawyer.

Before Broadway. Maurine Watkins was a cub reporter for the *Chicago Tribune* when she landed a series of exclusive interviews with a stripper, Beulah Annan, who had shot her boyfriend in the back on 4/3/24. The newspaper stories gained public sympathy for the stripper, and she was acquitted. The straight play *Chicago* opened on 12/30/26. 172 PERFORMANCES. PRESENTED BY Sam H. Harris; WRITER: Maurine Dallas Watkins; DIRECTOR: George Abbott. *Cast:* ROXIE: Francine Larrimore; VELMA: Juliette Crosby; BILLY: Edward Willis; AMOS: Charles Halton; LIZ: Dorothy Stickney.

It was filmed straight in 1927, by Cecil B. de Mille, starring Phyllis Haver. It was filmed straight again in 1942 as *Roxie Hart*. DIRECTOR: William Wellman. *Cast:* ROXIE: Ginger Rogers; BILLY: Adolphe Menjou.

By 1956 Maurine Watkins was living as a recluse with her mother in Florida. The two ladies were making a living writing greeting cards for Hallmark. Producers Robert Fryer and Lawrence Carr wanted the rights to the play, in order to do a musical starring Gwen Verdon, and to be directed by Bob Fosse. Miss Watkins, now a born-again Christian, felt that it was a frivolous idea, and refused to release the rights. In 1969 she died, and her mother sold the rights to Fryer & Carr, and Fosse & Verdon. In 1973 Bob Fosse finally began work on *Chicago*, and hired John Kander and Fred Ebb to write the score. In private life Bob Fosse and Gwen Verdon had separated in 1971, but were still able and willing to work together. Lawrence Carr had died by the time *Chicago* began rehearsals on 10/26/74, and was replaced by James Cresson. There was a delay when Bob Fosse had two heart attacks, but he finally brought the show into tryouts in Philadelphia, where it was panned by the critics. Actually the show seen in Philly was less than half of what was later seen on Broadway — there was that much post-tryout revision. David Rounds was originally 3rd-featured on the cast list, but his role was dropped.

The Broadway Run. FORTY-SIXTH STREET THEATRE, 6/3/75–8/27/77. 24 previews from 5/12/75. 898 PERFORMANCES. PRESENTED BY Robert Fryer & James Cresson, in association with Martin Richards, Joseph Harris and Ira Bernstein; MUSIC: John Kander; LYRICS: Fred Ebb; BOOK: Fred Ebb & Bob Fosse (with Herb Gardner); BASED ON the 1926 satirical play *Chicago*, by Maurine Dallas Watkins; DIRECTOR/CHOREOGRAPHER: Bob Fosse; ASSOCIATE DIRECTOR: Stuart Ostrow; ASSISTANT TO THE DIRECTOR: Kathryn Doby; SETS: Tony Walton; COSTUMES: Patricia Zipprodt; LIGHTING: Jules Fisher; SOUND: Abe Jacob; SOUND ENGINEER: Otts Munderloh; MUSICAL DIRECTOR: Stanley Lebowsky; ORCHESTRATIONS: Ralph Burns; DANCE MUSIC ARRANGEMENTS: Peter Howard; CAST RECORDING on Arista; PRESS: The Merlin Group; CASTING: Michael Shurtleff; GENERAL MANAGERS: Joseph Harris & Ira Bernstein; PRODUCTION STAGE MANAGER: Phil Friedman, *Ed Aldridge*; STAGE MANAGERS: Robert Corpora, Craig Jacobs, Paul Phillips; ASSISTANT STAGE MANAGER: Nick Malekos, *Jay S. Hoffman*. *Cast:* VELMA KELLY: Chita Rivera (2) ☆, *Lenora Nemetz* (from 7/28/76); ROXIE HART: Gwen Verdon (1) ☆, *Lenora Nemetz* (during Miss Verdon's minor throat surgery, from 7/30/75), *Liza Minnelli* (from 8/8/75, during Miss Verdon's same absence. Miss Verdon resumed performances on 9/15/75), *Ann Reinking* (from 2/7/77); FRED CASELY: Christopher Chadman, *Gary Gendell*; SERGEANT FOGARTY: Richard Korthaze; AMOS HART: Barney Martin (4), *Rex Everhart* (2/20/76–2/28/76), *Barney Martin* (from 3/1/76), *Rex Everhart* (from 9/76), *Richard Korthaze* (from 8/77); LIZ: Cheryl Clark,

Carla Farnsworth; ANNIE: Michon Peacock, *Joan Bell* (from 5/10/76); JUNE: Candy Brown, *Karen G. Burke, Sally Neal*; HUNYAK: Graciela Daniele, *Sandra Brewer, Candace Tovar*; MONA: Pamela Sousa, *Debra Lyman* (from 12/76); MARTIN HARRISON: Michael Vita, *Jerry Yoder*; MATRON "MAMA" MORTON: Mary McCarty (5), *Alaina Reed* (from 1/10/77), *Georgia Creighton* (from 7/77); BILLY FLYNN: Jerry Orbach (3) ☆, *Steve Elmore* (during Mr. Orbach's vacation); MARY SUNSHINE: M. O'Haughey (6); GO-TO-HELL KITTY: Charlene Ryan, *Fern Fitzgerald* (from 3/76), *Gena Ramsel*; HARRY: Paul Solen, *Ron Schwinn*; AARON: Gene Foote, *Laurent Giroux, Jeremy Blanton*; THE JUDGE: Ron Schwinn, *David Kottke*; COURT CLERK: Gary Gendell, *Ross Miles*; THE BAND: Sy Berger, Harry Di Vito, Hank Freedman, Karen Gustafson, John Monaco, Anthony Pagano, Tony Posk, Waymon Reed, James Sedlar, Charles Spies, William Stanley, Art Wagner, Frank Wess. *Standbys:* Roxie: Lenora Nemetz, Candace Tovar; Matron: Laura Waterbury; Mary Sunshine: Marsha Bagwell; Billy: Steve Elmore. *Understudies:* Mary: Georgia Creighton; Velma: Michon Peacock, Elaine Cancilla; Amos: Richard Korthaze; Billy: Mace Barrett. *Dance Alternates:* Hank Brunjes & Monica Tiller. *Act I:* *Scene 1* Opening: the Hart bedroom: "All That Jazz" (Velma & Company); *Scene 2* The bedroom; three hours later: "Funny Honey" (Roxie); *Scene 3* Limbo: "Cell Block Tango" (Velma & Girls); *Scene 4* Limbo: "When You're Good to Mama" (Matron); *Scene 5* The jail; *Scene 6* The visitors' area: "Tap Dance" (Roxie, Amos, Boys); *Scene 7* Limbo: "All I Care About" (Billy & Girls); *Scene 8* Billy's office: "A Little Bit of Good" (Mary), "We Both Reached for the Gun" (Billy, Roxie, Mary, Company); *Scene 9* Limbo: "Roxie" (Roxie & Boys); *Scene 10* In the jail; *Scene 11* Limbo, and Roxie's cell: "I Can't Do it Alone" (Velma), "Chicago After Midnight" (The Band); *Scene 12* Limbo, and a bedroom, somewhere in Chicago; *Scene 13* The jail: "My Own Best Friend" (Roxie & Velma). *Act II:* Entr'acte (The Band); *Scene 1* The jail: "I Know a Girl" (Velma), "Me and My Baby" (Roxie, Fred, Aaron); *Scene 2* Limbo: "Mister Cellophane" (Amos); *Scene 3* The jail: "When Velma Takes the Stand" (Velma & Boys); *Scene 4* An anteroom in the courthouse; *Scene 5* The anteroom of the courthouse; March 9: "Razzle Dazzle" (Billy & Company); *Scene 6* The courtroom: *Scene 7* A room in the jail: "Class" (Velma & Matron); *Scene 8* The courtroom; *Scene 9* The courtroom: "Nowadays" (Roxie), "Nowadays" (reprise) (Roxie & Velma), "R.S.V.P." (Roxie & Velma), "Keep it Hot" (Roxie & Velma).

Reviews were very divided. There were no hit songs from the show. Gwen Verdon received 10 per cent of the box-office gross. On 8/8/75 Liza Minnelli stepped in for Miss Verdon when the latter was in the hospital having minor throat surgery. Miss Minnelli would be in the show until mid–September. She had had only six days to learn the role and rehearse it before going on. The show received Tony nominations for musical, score, book, direction of a musical, choreography, sets, costumes, lighting, and for Jerry Orbach, Chita Rivera and Gwen Verdon; however, that year Michael Bennett's *A Chorus Line* ran away with all the Tonys.

After Broadway. TOUR. Opened on 8/29/77, in St. Louis. Then it went to the Colonial Theatre, Boston, 9/12/77. MUSICAL DIRECTOR: Arthur Wagner. *Cast:* VELMA: Carolyn Kirsch, *Chita Rivera* (from 4/4/78); ROXIE: Penny Worth, *Gwen Verdon* (from 4/4/78); AMOS: Rex Everhart, *Haskell Gordon*; LIZ: Carla Farnsworth; HUNYAK: Susan Stroman; MATRON: Edye Byrde; BILLY: Jerry Orbach; MARY SUNSHINE: M. O'Haughey; KITTY: Karen Tamburelli; AARON: Jeremy Blanton, *Jon Engstrom*. DANCE ALTERNATE: Ron Schwinn.

CRUCIBLE THEATRE, Sheffield, England, then THE CAMBRIDGE THEATRE, London, 4/10/79. 13 previews. 590 PERFORMANCES. *Cast:* VELMA: Jenny Logan; ROXIE: Antonia Ellis; BILLY: Ben Cross.

SYDNEY, Australia. 1981. *Cast:* VELMA: Geraldine Turner; ROXIE: Nancye Hayes; AMOS: George Spartels; MATRON: Judi Connelli; BILLY: Terence Donovan; MARY SUNSHINE: J.P. Webster.

THEATER DES WESTERNS, Berlin, 1988. *Cast:* Katja Ebstein, Gaye MacFarlane.

134. *Chicago (Broadway revival)*

Before Broadway. This revival began in concert form, 5/2/96–5/4/96. 4 performances. It was part of the *Encores!* series at CITY CEN-

TER. The number "Chicago After Midnight" was cut. "R.S.V.P." and "Keep it Hot" were replaced with "Hot Honey Rag" (original choreography by Bob Fosse) (Roxie & Velma), which now came after "Nowadays" but which had been placed at the end of Act I in the *Encores!* production. It had the same basic crew as for the subsequent Broadway run. It had the same cast except JUNE: Lisa Leguillou and KITTY: Mary Ellen Stuart. Then it moved to Broadway, the only one of the *Encores!* series to do so.

The Broadway Run. RICHARD RODGERS THEATRE, 11/14/96–2/9/97; SHUBERT THEATRE, 2/11/97–1/26/03; AMBASSADOR THEATRE, 1/29/03–. 25 previews from 10/23/96. PRESENTED BY Barry & Fran Weissler, in association with Kardana Productions & PACE Theatrical Group; MUSIC: John Kander; LYRICS: Fred Ebb; BOOK: Fred Ebb & Bob Fosse (with Herb Gardner); SCRIPT ADAPTATION: David Thompson; BASED ON the 1926 play *Chicago*, by Maurine Dallas Watkins; DIRECTOR: Walter Bobbie; CHOREOGRAPHER: Ann Reinking (in the style of Bob Fosse); SETS: John Lee Beatty; COSTUMES: William Ivey Long; LIGHTING: Ken Billington; SOUND: Scott Lehrer; MUSICAL DIRECTOR: Rob Fisher, *Rob Bowman*; ORCHESTRATIONS: Ralph Burns; DANCE MUSIC ARRANGEMENTS: Peter Howard; NEW CAST RECORDING on RCA, made on 11/25/96, and released on 1/18/97; PRESS: The Pete Sanders Group; CASTING: Jay Binder; GENERAL MANAGERS: Darwell Associates; COMPANY MANAGER: Scott A. Moore, *Jim Brandeberry*; PRODUCTION STAGE MANAGER: Clifford Schwartz; STAGE MANAGER: Terrence J. Witter; ASSISTANT STAGE MANAGER: Mindy Farbrother. *Cast:* VELMA KELLY: Bebe Neuwirth (2) ☆, *Nancy Hess (during Miss Neuwirth's vacation, 7/1/97–7/13/97, and again 1/11/98–1/25/98), Ute Lemper (9/8/98–1/9/99), Nancy Hess (from 1/9/99), Bebe Neuwirth (1/14/99–1/24/99), Ute Lemper (1/26/99–2/9/99), Nancy Hess, Bebe Neuwirth (2/20/99–4/4/99), Ute Lemper (from 4/6/99), Nancy Hess (4/99–5/16/99), Mamie Duncan-Gibbs (5/18/99–5/23/99), Ruthie Henshall (5/25/99–10/99), Mamie Duncan-Gibbs (10/26/99–1/16/00), Bebe Neuwirth (1/18/00–3/22/00), Mamie Duncan-Gibbs (during Miss Neuwirth's absence, 2/24/00–2/29/00), Donna Marie Asbury (from 3/23/00), Sharon Lawrence (from 4/11/00), Mamie Duncan-Gibbs (until 7/16/00), Donna Marie Asbury (7/18/00–7/19/00), Vicki Lewis (from 7/20/00), Jasmine Guy (from 9/5/00), Bebe Neuwirth (1/10/01–3/11/01), Donna Marie Asbury, Deidre Goodwin, Vicki Lewis (4/27/01–6/21/01), Deidre Goodwin (from 6/29/01), Roxanne Carrasco, Anna Montanaro (7/9/01–9/4/01), Roxanne Carrasco, Deidre Goodwin (from 9/14/01), Donna Marie Asbury, Roxanne Carrasco (from 1/13/02), Deidre Goodwin (from 3/18/02), Stephanie Pope (6/4/02–9/14/02), Roxanne Carrasco, Caroline O'Connor (11/8/02–3/2/03), Brenda Braxton (from 3/3/03), Deidre Goodwin (6/24/03–10/5/03), Reva Rice (10/7/03–12/28/03), Roxanne Carrasco (12/29/03–1/4/04), Donna Marie Asbury, Brenda Braxton (from 1/12/04), Pia Douwes (4/8/04–5/16/04), Brenda Braxton (from 5/16/04), Terra C. McLeod (from 7/27/04), Donna Marie Asbury (2/14/05–2/20/05), Brenda Braxton (from 2/21/05)*; ROXIE HART: Ann Reinking (1) ☆ (until 6/22/97), *Nancy Hess (on 12/7/96, when Miss Reinking's mother died, and again during Miss Reinking's ankle injury, 3/18/97–4/13/97; when Miss Reinking came back, Nancy Hess alternated with her), Marilu Henner (from 6/24/97, but she injured her foot that very day), Nancy Hess (6/25/97, for 2 performances), Marilu Henner (6/26/97–3/22/98), Karen Ziemba (from 3/24/98), Belle Calaway (5/25/99–5/31/99), Karen Ziemba (6/1/99–6/9/99), Charlotte d'Amboise (6/10/99–8/11/99), Sandy Duncan (8/12/99–8/20/99), Nancy Hess (8/20/99–8/23/99), Belle Calaway (from 8/24/99), Sandy Duncan (by 9/99 & until 1/16/00), Belle Calaway (1/18/00–3/22/00), Charlotte d'Amboise (from 3/23/00), Belle Calaway (1/19/01–5/6/01), Nana Visitor (from 5/8/01), Petra Nielsen (from 10/8/01), Nana Visitor (from 11/19/01), Belle Calaway (from 1/13/02), Denise Van Outen (3/18/02–4/28/02), Belle Calaway (from 4/22/02), Bianca Marroquin (6/18/02–7/7/02), Belle Calaway, Amy Spanger (8/6/02–9/10/02), Charlotte D'Amboise (9/17/02–1/19/03), Belle Calaway (from 1/20/03), Tracy Shayne (4/15/03–7/10/03), Melanie Griffith (7/11/03–10/5/03), Charlotte d'Amboise (10/7/03–12/14/03), Bianca Marroquin (12/15/03–1/4/04), Charlotte d'Amboise (12/29/03–1/4/04), Gretchen Mol (1/5/04–2/29/04), Charlotte d'Amboise (3/1/04–6/12/04), Tracy Shayne (6/13/04–6/21/04), Paige Davis (6/22/04–8/8/04), Charlotte d'Amboise (8/10/04–12/12/04; Miss d'Amboise had been scheduled to depart on 11/28/04), Tracy Shayne (12/13/04–1/2/05), Charlotte d'Am-*

boise; FRED CASELY: Michael Berresse, *Gregory Mitchell, Gregory Butler*; SERGEANT FOGARTY: Michael Kubala, *Luis Perez, Michael Kubala*; AMOS HART: Joel Grey (4) ☆ (until 1/11/98), *John Mineo (during Mr. Grey's vacation, July–7/29/97), Ernie Sabella (during Mr. Grey's vacation, 10/18/97–11/9/97, and then permanently from 1/13/98), Joel Grey (from 7/2/98, for 4 weeks), Tom McGowan (from 7/30/98), P.J. Benjamin, Ernie Sabella (from 11/23/99), P.J. Benjamin, Tom McGowan (from 00–01), Ray Bokhour (from 7/30/01), P.J. Benjamin (from 8/13/01), Rob Bartlett (7/9/02–9/15/02), P.J. Benjamin, Rob Bartlett (11/4/02–1/19/03), P.J. Benjamin (from 3/3/03), Rob Bartlett (from 8/10/03 for 10 performances during Mr. Benjamin's vacation), P.J. Benjamin (until 12/14/03), John Mineo, P.J. Benjamin, Ray Bokhour (by 7/04), P.J. Benjamin (by 8/04), Ray Bokhour (1/10/05–5/22/05)*; LIZ: Denise Faye, *Lisa Leguillou (from 8/97), Michelle Marie Robinson (by 98–99), Sharon Moore, Dana Moore*; ANNIE: Mamie Duncan-Gibbs, *Roxanne Carrasco, Paige Davis, Deidre Goodwin, Suzanne Harrer, Rosa Curry, Mamie Duncan-Gibbs (from 1/14/02), Roxanne Carrasco*; JUNE: Mary Ann Lamb, *Amy Spanger (by 98–99), Deidre Goodwin, Roxanne Carrasco, Donna Marie Asbury, Kristy Richmond (from 1/29/03)*; HUNYAK: Tina Paul, *Kristy Richmond, Darlene Wilson (by 98–99), Mindy Cooper, Jennifer West*; MONA: Caitlin Carter, *Jennifer West, Jennifer Frankel, Michelle DeJean (from 1/29/03)*; MATRON "MAMA" MORTON: Marcia Lewis (5) (until 1/24/99), *Roz Ryan (from 1/26/99), Marcia Lewis (from 3/27/99), Roz Ryan (during Miss Lewis's absences, from 7/27/99 & again, 4/15/00–5/4/00), Jennifer Holliday (6/18/01–8/25/01), Marcia Lewis (from 8/27/01), Roz Ryan (from 11/16/01), Michele Pawk (from 1/14/02), Alix Korey (from 3/4/02), Roz Ryan (from 7/30/02), B.J. Crosby (from 3/3/03), Angie Stone (from 4/14/03), Camille Saviola (6/10/03–12/14/03), Debbie Gravitte (12/15/03–3/14/04), Roz Ryan (3/15/04–9/12/04); Anne L. Nathan (from 9/13/04), Carol Woods (1/31/05–2/20/05), Anne L. Nathan (from 2/21/05)*; BILLY FLYNN: James Naughton (3) ☆, *Gregory Jbara (from 6/24/97), James Naughton (9/2/97–12/21/97), Hinton Battle (from 12/23/97), Alan Thicke (from 9/30/98), Michael Berresse (from 1/5/00), Brent Barrett, Robert Urich (from 1/11/00), Clarke Peters (from 2/1/00), Brent Barrett (from 2/15/00), Clarke Peters (until 4/8/01), Chuck Cooper (from 4/12/01), Alan Thicke (6/25/01–7/1/01), Brent Barrett (from 7/2/01), Chuck Cooper (from 8/27/01), George Hamilton (11/21/01–1/02), Eric Jordan Young (from 1/18/02), Lou Gossett (from 2/02 for 6 performances), Eric Jordan Young, Ron Raines (3/25/02–5/19/02), Eric Jordan Young, George Hamilton (6/4/02–7/28/02), Michael C. Hall (7/30/02–9/10/02), Destan Owens, Taye Diggs, Billy Zane (11/8/02–1/19/03), Kevin Richardson (1/20/03–3/9/03), Clarke Peters (from 3/17/03), Gregory Harrison (from 5/6/03), Brent Barrett (6/2/03–12/14/03), Patrick Swayze (12/15/03–12/28/03), Michael Kubala (12/29/03–1/4/04), James Naughton (1/6/04–1/25/04), Norm Lewis (2/2/04–3/21/04), Christopher Sieber (3/22/04–5/2/04), Tom Wopat (5/6/04–6/16/04), Christopher Sieber (6/17/04–8/1/04), Marti Pellew (8/3/04–9/5/04), Wayne Brady (9/9/04–12/4/04), Tom Wopat (12/7/04–12/19/04), Brent Barrett (1/4/05–3/50/5, and again 3/14/05–3/20/05)*; MARY SUNSHINE: D. Sabella (6) [this was David Sabella, Ernie's brother], *J. Loeffenholz, R. Bean, A. Saunders, J. Maldonado, D. Sabella (from 9/97), R. Bean, A. Saunders (from 1/2/02), R. Bean (from 1/14/02), M. Agnes (1/29/03–3/23/03), R. Bean (until 7/18/04), D. Sabella (3/24/03–5/18/03), R. Bean (5/17/04–7/18/04), D. Sabella-Mills (7/20/04–11/28/04), R. Lowe*; GO-TO-HELL KITTY: Leigh Zimmerman, *Mary Ann Hermansen, Michelle Potterf*; HARRY: Rocker Verastique, *Gregory Mitchell (stood in for Mr. Verastique in 8/97), Sebastian La Cause, Dan LoBuono, James Mitchell, Shawn Emamjomeh*; AARON: David Warren-Gibson, *Mark Bove, Gregory Butler, David Warren-Gibson (from 1/29/03), Greg Reuter*; JUDGE: Jim Borstelmann, *Gregory Butler, Timothy J. Alex, Marc Calamia, Eric Jordan Young, Denis Jones, Bernard Dotson*; MARTIN HARRISON: Bruce Anthony Davis, *Randy Slovacek (10/15/98–11/30/98), Denis Jones, Greg Graham, Marc Calamia, Bernard Dotson, Gary Kilmer*; DOCTOR: Bruce Anthony Davis, *Denis Jones, Greg Graham, Marc Calamia, Bernard Dotson*; COURT CLERK/BAILIFF: John Mineo, *Jack Hayes, John Mineo, Mark Anthony Taylor, John Mineo*; JURY: Luis Perez, Michael Kubala, Shawn Emamjomeh. STANDBYS: Velma: Nancy Hess; Roxie: Nancy Hess, Tracy Shayne (*Belle Calaway*). UNDERSTUDIES: Velma: Mamie Duncan-Gibbs (96–02), *Amy Spanger (98–02), Donna Marie Asbury (from 98)*; Roxie: *Caitlin Carter (97–02), Mary Ann Lamb (97–98), Amy Spanger (98–02), Donna Marie*

Asbury (98–02), *Tracy Shayne*; Mama: Mamie Duncan-Gibbs (96–02), *Michelle M. Robinson* (96–02), *Deidre Goodwin* (98–02), *Belle Calaway*; Amos: John Mineo (96–98, 01–04), *Denis Jones* (97–02), *Michael Kubala* (98–02), *Randy Slovacek* (98–02); Billy: Michael Berresse (96–02), *Luis Perez* (96–02), *Michael Kubala* (98–02), *Gregory Butler* (98–02), *Eric Jordan Young, Destan Owens*; Mary Sunshine: J. Loeffelholz (96–04), *A. Saunders*; Fred: Luis Perez (96–02), *Denis Jones* (97–02), *Eric L. Christian* (98–02), *Rocker Verastique* (98–02), *Gregory Butler* (98–02), *Mark Anthony Taylor* (98–02), *Sebastian La Cause* (98–02). Swings: Mindy Cooper, Luis Perez, *Michelle M. Robinson, Christine Brooks, Gregory Butler, Rosa Curry, Michelle DeJean, David Eggers, Shawn Emamjomeh, Gabriela Garcia, JoAnn M. Hunter, Denis Jones, James Patric Moran, Jeff Shade, Mark Price, Greg Reuter, Dante Sciarra, Lillie Kae Stevens, Mark Anthony Taylor, Jennifer West, Sharon Moore, Jennifer Frankel, Gary Kilmer*. **Orchestra:** WOODWINDS: Seymour Red Press, Kenneth Hitchcock, Richard Centalonza; TRUMPETS: John Frosk & Darryl Shaw; TROMBONES: Dave Bargeron & Bruce Bonvissuto; PIANOS: Leslie Stifelman & Jeffrey Saver; ACCORDION: Jeffrey Saver; BANJO: Jay Berliner; BASS/TUBA: Ronald Raffio; VIOLIN: Marilyn Reynolds; DRUMS/PERCUSSION: Ronald Zito.

The show got very good reviews. It won Tonys for musical revival, direction of a musical, choreography, lighting, and for James Naughton and Bebe Neuwirth, and was also nominated for costumes, and for Marcia Lewis. The show had to leave the Richard Rodgers to make way for the incoming *Steel Pier*. Ute Lemper unexpectedly walked out of her Broadway role as Velma after the third number ("A Cell Block Tango") of the 1/9/99 matinee, due to laryngitis. Nancy Hess was out shopping, and got beeped. Within 40 minutes she was on stage, in costume (but no makeup) and got a standing ovation. Miss Lemper returned a couple of weeks later. Bebe Neuwirth stepped in as her replacement as a favor to the producers and writers. Sandy Duncan's arrival as Roxie was delayed when she broke her foot in rehearsals during the "Roxie Company" tour she was on. She finally came aboard on 8/12/99, but on 8/20/99 she injured her foot again during the "Roxie" number, and she did not perform Act II. Understudy Nancy Hess went on for her. Bob Urich, scheduled for the role of Billy for six weeks from 1/5/00, cut short his stay on Broadway. A few years later he was dead, at 55. In the summer of 2001 Marcia Lewis took off ten weeks to marry Nashville businessman Fred Bryan. From then on she was sometimes billed as Marcia Lewis Bryan. Like all Broadway shows *Chicago* was hard hit by the attack on New York City on 9/11/01, and in order to keep it going the cast and crew agreed to a pay cut of 25 per cent for a few weeks. George Hamilton was scheduled to play Billy from 11/12/01–2/17/02, but he was late starting because he wasn't ready. His new date of 11/19/01 couldn't be met either, because he was sick, so he didn't start until 11/21/01. He had to quit two weeks early due to injury. He came back later. Lou Gossett, who had been scheduled to play Billy 2/18/02–4/7/02, not only started late (2/20/02) but had to cut short his stay due to asthma. *Chicago* became the 2nd-longest-running Broadway revival (behind *Oh! Calcutta!*). Amy Spanger was the new wife of Michael C. Hall. Taye Diggs was due to come in as Billy on 9/19/02, but postponed until 9/24/02, then postponed again. Marti Pellew was meant to play Billy in 3/03, but the musicians' strike canceled that, and Clarke Peters played it instead. *Chicago* had to leave the Shubert to make way for the incoming revival of *Gypsy*. After the hugely successful movie of the stage musical came out at the end of 2002, Broadway box-office sales rose sharply. The Monday, 3/10/03 performance was canceled due to the musicians' strike. In 3/03 rumors began that Melanie Griffith would play Roxie (which she did). The show missed a performance due to the 8/14/03 power blackout. Melanie Griffith postponed her exit from 9/28/03 to 10/5/03, and Brent Barrett postponed his from 9/28/03 to 12/14/03. This revival had its 3,000th performance on 2/2/04. Richard Chamberlain was rumored as Billy Flynn in early 2004 but it never happened. On 9/11/04 Fred Ebb died, aged 76. Lights dimmed on Broadway on 9/14/04. Wayne Brady extended his run as Billy from 11/28/04 to 12/4/04. On 1/6/05, with its 3,389th performance, this revival of *Chicago* passed the original run of *Grease* to become the 10th-longest-running musical in Broadway history. Brent Barrett extended his run from 1/30/05 to 2/13/05, and then again to 2/27/05, and yet again to 3/5/05.

After Broadway. FIRST TOUR. Known as the "Roxie Company."

Opened on 3/25/97, at the Aronoff Theatre, Cincinnati. It ran in Washington, DC from 4/16/97. There was a six-week hiatus from 8/22/99. The tour closed on 4/30/00, at Springfield, Illinois. PRESENTED BY Fran & Barry Weissler; MUSICAL DIRECTOR: Rob Bowman. Sandy Duncan broke her foot during rehearsals, and Ann Reinking stepped in. **Cast:** VELMA: Jasmine Guy, *Janine LaManna, Jasmine Guy* (until late 2/98), *Lisa Leguillou* (from 2/26/98), *Donna Marie Asbury, Stephanie Pope*, Jasmine Guy (from 7/7/98), *Stephanie Pope* (from 7/14/98), *Mamie Duncan-Gibbs* (from 1/12/99), *Deidre Goodwin* (from 2/16/99), *Ruthie Henshall* (4/22/99–5/16/99), *Deidre Goodwin* (5/18/99–5/30/99), *Ruthie Henshall* (from 6/1/99), *Donna Marie Asbury* (from 10/12/99), *Vicki Lewis* (from 11/16/99), *Roxanne Carrasco* (from 1/4/00), *Vicki Lewis* (from 3/14/00), *Roxanne Carrasco* (from 3/21/00); ROXIE: Charlotte d'Amboise, *Belle Calaway* (from 4/97 during Miss d'Amboise's knee injury soon after tour opened), *Charlotte d'Amboise* (from 2/26/98), *Belle Calaway, Charlotte d'Amboise, Belle Calaway* (from 4/25/99), *Ann Reinking* (from 4/27/99), *Karen Ziemba* (until 5/23/99), *Belle Calaway* (from 6/1/99), *Sandy Duncan* (7/13/99–8/1/99), *Belle Calaway* (from 8/3/99), *Nana Visitor* (from 11/16/99), *Tracy Shayne* (from 1/4/00); FRED: Rick Pessagno; FOGARTY: Eric Jordan Young; AMOS: Ron Orbach, *Michael Tucci, Bruce Winant* (from 12/22/98), *Ray Bokhour* (from 10/19/00), *P.J. Benjamin* (from 4/4/00); LIZ: Sharon Moore; ANNIE: Deidre Goodwin; JUNE: Janine LaManna; HUNYAK: Belle Calaway; MONA: Mary MacLeod; MAMA: Carol Woods, *Lea De Laria* (from 4/10/98), *Avery Sommers, Carol Woods* (from 8/4/98); BILLY: Obba Babatunde (2/26/98–late 3/98), *Alan Thicke* (from late 3/98), *Michael Berresse* (from 8/18/98), *Alan Thicke* (from 8/25/98), *Michael Berresse, Alan Thicke* (9/22/98 –9/26/98), *Michael Berresse* (from 9/27/98), *Destan Owens* (from 10/13/98), *Alan Thicke* (from 10/27/98), *Destan Owens* (from 1/26/99), *Adrian Zmed* (2/16/99–8/4/99), *Hal Linden* (8/6/99–8/16/99), *Gregory Jbara* (8/17/99–8/22/99), *Robert Urich* (10/19/99–1/25/00), *Lloyd Culbreath* (from 1/4/00), *Alan Thicke* (from 1/18/00), *Lloyd Culbreath* (from 2/29/00), *Alan Thicke* (from 3/14/00), *Clarke Peters* (from 3/21/00); MARY: M.E. Spencer [i.e. Mark Spencer], *D.C. Levine, M.E. Spencer* (from 7/7/98), *R. Bean* (from 7/28/98), *A. Saunders* (from 10/13/98), *R. Bean* (from 10/20/98), *J. Maldonado* (from 10/27/98), *J. Roberson* (from 2/9/99), *M. von Essen* [i.e. Max von Essen] (from 5/12/99), *J. Maldonado* (from 10/12/99), *M. Agnes* [i.e. Mark Agnes] (from 1/4/00); KITTY: Angie L. Schworer; HARRY: Gregory Butler; AARON: Marc Calamia; MARTIN: Mark C. Reis; BAILIFF: Mark Price; JURY: Mark Arvin. **Understudy**: Roxie: Belle Calaway.

ADELPHI THEATRE, London. Opened on 11/18/97. Previews from 10/28/97. DIRECTOR: Walter Bobbie. There was a cast recording. **Cast:** VELMA: Ute Lemper, *Nicola Hughes, Frederike Haas* (in 6/99 & /99), *Valarie Pettiford, Anna Jane Casey, Annette McLaughlin, Leigh Zimmerman* (in 11/01), *Anna Jane Casey* (3/18–11/16/02), *Tiffany Graves, Ruthie Henshall* (from 2003 until 11/1/03), *Tiffany Graves* (from 11/3/03), *Anna Jane Casey*; ROXIE: Ruthie Henshall, *Maria Friedman, Anna Montanaro* (in 6/99 & 7/99), *Chita Rivera* (from 8/16/99; her rehearsals began 7/28/99), *Josefina Gabrielle, Petra Nielsen, Denise Van Outen* (until 11/26/01), *Claire Sweeney* (from 12/3/01), *Anita Louise Combe* (3/18/02–4/28/02), *Denise Van Outen* (from 4/29/02), *Anita Louise Combe* (until 11/16/02), *Linzi Hateley, Frances Ruffelle* (from 9/8/03), *Rebecca Thornhill, Jennifer Ellison* (from 9/20/04), *Josefina Gabrielle* (from 12/13/04), *Brooke Shields* (from spring 2005); AMOS: Nigel Planer, *Joel Grey* (8/17/98–11/7/98), *Norman Pace, Les Dennis, George Layton, Clive Rowe* (1/21/02–7/20/02), *Barry James, Paul Rider* (until 11/16/02), *Norman Pace* (from 3/24/03), *Paul Baker* (from 9/8/03); MAMA: Meg Johnson, *Alison Moyet, Sue Kelvin* (3/18/02–6/1/02), *Susannah Fellows* (until 8/11/01), *Chrissie Hammond* (until 11/16/02), *Gaby Roslin* (11/18/02–3/8/03), *Zee Asha* (from 3/24/03), *Anita Dobson* (from 9/8/03), *Gaby Roslin* (from 12/1/03 for 8 weeks), *Sharon D. Clarke*; BILLY: Henry Goodman, *Clarke Peters, Calvin Cornwall, Michael Siberry, John Diedrich, Sacha Distel, Neil McCaul, Marti Pellew* (from 6/10/02), *Michael Greco* (from 11/1/02), *Rolf Saxion* (from 3/24/03), *Kevin Richardson* (from 9/22/03 for 6 weeks), *Alex Bourne* (from 11/3/03), *David Hasselhoff* (from 7/16/04), *John Barrowman* (from 9/20/04), *Michael French* (from 12/13/04); MARY: C. Shirvell [i.e. Charles Shirvell]. The London show got rave reviews, and was nominated for seven Olivier Awards (a record; it won two — for musical and for Ute Lemper).

SECOND TOUR. Known as the "Velma Company." Opened on

12/12/97, at Fort Myers & Tampa, Florida. It ran in Chicago and Toronto, then the Mandalay Bay & Resort, Las Vegas (a venue which was opened by this show), 3/11/99–2/27/00. Previews from 3/3/99. 416 performances. The tour played more than 890 performances in toto. PRESENTED BY Barry & Fran Weissler; MUSICAL DIRECTOR: Jack Gaughan. *Cast:* VELMA: Stephanie Pope, *Jasmine Guy, Stephanie Pope (7/7/98–7/14/98), Khandi Alexander (from 8/4/98), Donna Marie Asbury (from 9/29/98), Stephanie Pope (from 2/2/99), Ute Lemper (from 2/19/99), Stephanie Pope (from 4/5/99), Mamie Duncan-Gibbs (from 8/3/99), Jasmine Guy (from 8/24/99), Marianne McCord (from 12/22/99), Vicki Lewis (from 1/3/00);* ROXIE: Karen Ziemba, *Nancy Hess, Charlotte d'Amboise, Amy Spanger (from 11/10/98), Charlotte d'Amboise (from 11/24/98), Amy Spanger (from 12/1/98), Chita Rivera (from 3/3/99 and left 7/4/99 for London tour), Marilu Henner (7/6/99–8/27/99), Charlotte d'Amboise (from 8/29/99), Marilu Henner (from 12/12/99), Nana Visitor (from 1/3/00);* FRED: Gregory Mitchell, *Rick Pessagno, Dan LoBuono;* FOGARTY: Gerry McIntyre; AMOS: Ernie Sabella, *Tom McGowan, Ron Orbach, Tom McGowan, Ron Orbach, P.J. Benjamin (from 11/10/98), Joel Grey (from 12/1/98), P.J. Benjamin (from 12/29/98), Ernie Sabella (from 2/2/99), Michael Tucci (from 8/24/99), P.J. Benjamin (from 1/3/00);* LIZ: Wendy Edmead; ANNIE: Paige Davis, *Kathryn Mowat Murphy;* HUNYAK: Cheryl Clark, *Jillana Urbina;* MONA: Dana Moore; MAMA: Avery Sommers, *Marcia Lewis (from 2/2/99), Roz Ryan (from 7/27/99 and closed tour);* BILLY: Brent Barrett, *Michael Berresse (from 11/3/98), Brent Barrett (from 11/24/98), Michael Berresse (from 12/1/98), Ben Vereen (2/18/99–8/29/99), Hal Linden (from 8/31/99), Gregory Jbara (from 1/3/00), Clarke Peters, Gregory Jbara (closed tour);* MARY: D.C. Levine, *M.E. Spencer* [i.e. Mark Spencer], *D. Sabella (from 9/7/99);* KITTY: Sandahl Bergman, *Leslie Bell, Nicole Bridgewater;* AARON: Gerry McIntyre, *Randy Slovacek;* DOCTOR: Darren Lee. **Understudy**: Roxie: Paige Davis (for Chita Rivera).

AUSTRALIAN TOUR. Opened on 7/4/98, at Her Majesty's Theatre, Melbourne. It also ran from 2/17/00 at the Lyric Theatre, Brisbane. There was a cast recording. *Cast:* VELMA: Caroline O'Connor, *Sharon Millerchip;* ROXIE: Chelsea Gibb; FRED: Mark Hodge, *Gerry Symonds;* FOGARTY: Wayne Scott Kermond, *Dale Pengelly;* AMOS: Anthony Weigh, *Glenn Butcher;* LIZ: Jude Barry, *Christine Tan;* ANNIE: Caroline Kasper, *Renae Berry;* JUNE: Kelly Aykers, *Natalie Bassingthwaighte;* HUNYAK: Nicola Humphrey, *Nicci Hope;* MONA: Chloe Dallimore; MAMA: Caroline Gillmer, *Maria Mercedes;* BILLY: John Diedrich, *Simon Burke;* MARY: D.P. Taylor; KITTY: Tia Jordan, *Caroline Mooney;* HARRY: Christopher Horsey, *Adam Williams;* AARON: Stephen Davison; JUDGE: Wayne Scott Kermond, *Keith Wright;* MARTIN: Troy Phillips, *Aaron Farley;* DOCTOR: Jason Lawrence Coleman, *Thomas Thanassi;* COURT CLERK: Cameron Mitchell, *Thomas Thanassi;* JURY: Christopher Horsey, *Dale Pengelly.*

THEATER AM WIEN, Vienna, 9/23/98–1/6/99; RONACHER THEATER, until 4/20/99. Then it went on to SWITZERLAND, and then THEATER DES WESTERNS, Berlin, 9/25/99–4/11/00. PRESENTED BY Vereinigten Buehnen Wien; DIRECTOR: Scott Faris; MUSICAL DIRECTOR: Caspar Richter. There was a live cast recording on the Reverso label (the longest of all the *Chicago* recordings, at 79 minutes). *Cast:* VELMA: Anna Montanaro; ROXIE: Frederike Haas; BILLY: Rainhard Fendrich; MAMA: Isabel Weicken; AMOS: Leon Van Leeuwenberg.

BEATRIX THEATER, Utrecht, Netherlands. Opened on 5/9/99. Previews from 4/28/99. PRESENTED BY Joop Van Den Ende; DUTCH TRANSLATION: Seth Gaaikema; MUSICAL DIRECTOR: Rene op den Camp. The song "Razzle-Dazzle" was renamed "Hocus Pocus." *Cast:* VELMA: Pia Douwes; ROXIE: Simone Kleinsma; AMOS: Sergi-Henri Valcke; MAMA: Marjolijn Touw; BILLY: Tony Neef.

DUSSELDORF. Opened in the fall of 2001. *Cast:* VELMA: Anna Montanaro; ROXIE: Anne Mandrella; AMOS: Leon Van Leeuwenberg; MAMA: Isabel Weicken; BILLY: Nikolas Gerdell.

MOSCOW. Opened on 10/4/02. This production was in Russian. DIRECTOR: Scott Faris; CHOREOGRAPHER: Gary Chryst. *Cast:* ROXIE: Anastasia Stotskaya; VELMA: Lika Rulla; BILLY: Philip Kirkorov; MAMA: Lolita; MARY SUNSHINE: Ya. Z.

THE MOVIE MUSICAL. Released at Christmas 2002. Kander & Ebb wrote a new song for the film—"I Move On." WRITER: Bill Condon; DIRECTOR: Rob Marshall; LIGHTING: Jules Fisher & Peggy Eisenhauer. *Cast:* ROXIE: Renee Zellweger; VELMA: Catherine Zeta Jones; BILLY: Richard Gere; AMOS: John C. Reilly; FRED: Dominic West; MARY: Chris-

tine Baranski; MAMA: Queen Latifah; CAMEO ROLE: Chita Rivera. It cost $45 million and was a fantastic success, being nominated for 13 Oscars.

TOUR. Opened at the National Theatre, Washington, DC, 6/11/03–6/29/03. Previews from 6/10/03. Then it went on with the rest of the tour. It played the Golden Gate, San Francisco, 8/5/03–8/24/03. The tour was put together in order to capitalize on the great success of the film. DIRECTOR: Walter Bobbie. It had performers from the Broadway and film versions. *Cast:* ROXIE: Bianca Marroquin; VELMA: Brenda Braxton; MAMA: Roz Ryan, *Marcia Lewis Bryan (from 8/4/03);* BILLY: Gregory Harrison, *Kevin Richardson (8/5/03–8/24/03);* AMOS: Ray Bokhour; MARY SUNSHINE: R. Bean; ALSO WITH: Caitlin Carter, Mamie Duncan-Gibbs, Lloyd Culbreath, Bernard Dotson, Kevin Neil McCready. After a hiatus the tour re-opened, at the Civic Center, San Diego, 12/30/03. *Cast:* ROXIE: Bianca Marroquin; VELMA: Reva Rice; BILLY: Patrick Swayze, *Tom Wopat (from 1/27/04);* MAMA: Carol Woods. Then it went to the Pantages Theatre, Los Angeles, 1/7/04–1/18/04, and from 1/27/04 continued with the tour. After another brief hiatus it re-opened again, on 8/3/04–8/8/04, at the Tampa Bay Performing Arts Center. *Cast:* ROXIE: Bianca Marroquin; VELMA: Brenda Braxton (until 2/05); BILLY: Gregory Harrison, *Wayne Brady (from 2/1/05; for the Pantages Theatre, L.A. stint only; he had been booked until 2/20/05, but came down with vocal strain), Gregory Harrison (from 2/05);* MAMA: Carol Woods, *Patti LaBelle (2/1/05–2/20/05, for the Pantages Theatre, L.A. stint only);* AMOS: Ray Bokhour.

CASINO DE PARIS. Opened on 3/3/04. This production was in French. DIRECTOR: Scott Faris; CHOREOGRAPHER: Gary Chryst. *Cast:* *Velma:* Terra Ciccotosto [she later became Terra C. McLeod]; ROXIE: Veronic DiCaire; BILLY: Stephane Rousseau.

135. *The Chocolate Soldier*

An operetta. Bumerli is a cowardly Swiss Army chef who carries chocolate in his holsters instead of guns. When he finds his cook wagon is in the direct line of enemy fire he flees the battlefield and in an attempt to avoid capture by the Bulgarians he climbs a trellis into the bedroom of Nadina, the fiancee of war hero Alexius. Nadina shelters Bumerli and later helps him escape. He returns a year later to find her, and save her from her loveless marriage.

Before Broadway. This is a list of the main early New York productions of The Chocolate Soldier (there is a London one in there as well). The ranks of some officers varied with different productions.

LYRIC THEATRE, 9/13/09. 296 PERFORMANCES. PRESENTED BY F.C. Whitney; CHOREOGRAPHER: Al Holbrook. *Cast:* NADINA: Ida Brooks Hunt; BUMMERLI [sic]: Jack Gardner.

CENTURY THEATRE, 12/12/21–2/18/22. 83 PERFORMANCES. PRESENTED BY The Shuberts. *Cast:* NADINA POPOFF: Tessa Kosta; LT BUMERLI: Donald Brian; MASCHA: Virginia O'Brien.

JOLSON'S 59TH STREET THEATRE, 1/27/30–2/15/30. 25 PERFORMANCES. PRESENTED BY Jolson Light Opera Company; DIRECTOR: Milton Aborn; MUSICAL DIRECTOR: Louis Kroll. *Cast:* NADINA: Alice McKenzie; BUMMERLI: Charles Purcell.

ERLANGERS THEATRE, 9/21/31–10/3/31. 16 PERFORMANCES. PRESENTED BY the New York Civic Light Opera Company; DIRECTOR: Milton Aborn; MUSICAL DIRECTOR: Louis Kroll. *Cast:* NADINA: Vivienne Segal; BUMMERLI: Charles Purcell; CAPT. MASSAKROFF: Detmar Poppen.

ST. JAMES THEATRE, 5/2/34–5/12/34. 13 PERFORMANCES. PRESENTED BY the Knickerbocker Light Opera Company; PRODUCERS: Charles Purcell & Donald Brian; DIRECTOR: Alonzo Price. *Cast:* NADINA: Bernice Claire; LT BUMMERLI: Charles Purcell & Donald Brian; CAPT. MASSAKROFF: Detmar Poppen.

SHAFTESBURY THEATRE, London, 8/40–9/40.

CARNEGIE HALL, 6/23/42–7/12/42. 24 PERFORMANCES. PRESENTED BY Joseph S. Tushinsky & Hans Bartsch; DIRECTOR: John Pierce; BOOK DIRECTOR: Jose Ruben; SETS: E.B. Dunkel Studios; COSTUMES: Paul Dupont; MUSICAL DIRECTOR: Joseph S. Tushinsky. *Cast:* NADINA: Helen Gleason; LT BUMMERLI: Allan Jones; AURELIA: Frances Comstock; CAPT. MASSAKROFF: Detmar Poppen; MASCHA: Doris Patston. The numbers "Never Was There Such a Lover" and "Chocolate Soldier" were dropped for this production.

It was filmed in 1941. The movie had the same title, and some of the songs from *The Chocolate Soldier*, but the plot was that of Ferenc Molnar's *The Guardsman*. DIRECTOR: Roy Del Ruth. *Cast*: Nelson Eddy, Rise Stevens.

The Broadway Run. NEW CENTURY THEATRE, 3/12/47–5/10/47. 69 PERFORMANCES. PRESENTED BY J.H. Del Bondio & Hans Bartsch, for the Delvan Company; MUSIC: Oscar Straus; LYRICS/BOOK: Rudolph Bernauer & Leopold Jacobson (as originally translated from *Der tapfere Soldat* into English by Stanislaus Stange); REVISED BOOK: Guy Bolton & Bernard Hanighen; ADDITIONAL LYRICS: Bernard Hanighen; BASED ON the 1894 play *Arms and the Man*, by George Bernard Shaw; DIRECTOR: Felix Brentano; CHOREOGRAPHER: George Balanchine; SETS: Jo Mielziner; COSTUMES: Lucinda Ballard; MUSICAL DIRECTOR/ORCHESTRATIONS: Jay Blackton; PRESS: Tom Weatherly; COMPANY MANAGER: Edward Haas; GENERAL STAGE MANAGER: Edward Brinkmann; STAGE MANAGER: Rudy Brooks; ASSISTANT STAGE MANAGER: Karl Sittler. *Cast*: NADINA: Frances McCann (3); MASCHA: Gloria Hamilton (5); AURELIA: Muriel O'Malley (6); CAPT. BUMERLI: Keith Andes (2); GEN. MASSAKROFF: Henry Calvin (8); COL. POPOFF: Billy Gilbert (1); MAJ. ALEXIUS SPIRIDOFF: Ernest McChesney (4); STEFAN, A SERVANT: Michael Mann; KATRINA, A SERVANT: Anna Wiman; PREMIERE DANSEUSE: Mary Ellen Moylan (7); PREMIER DANCER: Francisco Moncion (9); LADIES OF THE ENSEMBLE: Elizabeth Bockoven, Eileen Coffman, Catherine Chambers, Peggy Ferris, Adah Friley, Lucy Hillary, Frances Joslyn, Jeanne Koumrian, Josephine Lambert, Terry Saunders, Grace Varik, Evelyn Wick; GENTLEMEN OF THE ENSEMBLE: Jack Anderson, John Duffy, Craig Reynolds, Walter Kelvin, Allan Lowell, Richard Monte, Richmond Page, Harvey Sauber, Stan Simmonds, Karl Sittler, King Taylor, Bill E. Thompson; LADIES OF THE BALLET: Barbara Heath, Lillian Lenase, Eleanor Miller, Virginia Poe, Yvonne Tibor, Anna Wiman, Marjorie Winters; GENTLEMEN OF THE BALLET: Hubert Bland, Harold Haskin, Brooks Jackson, Michael Mann, Shaun O'Brien, George Reich, Walter Stane. Overture (Orchestra); *Act I*: Nadina's bedroom in Popoff's house, situated in a small town in Bulgaria; autumn, 19th century: "We Are Marching Through the Night" (Gentlemen of the Ensemble), "Lonely Women" (Nadina, Aurelia, Mascha), "My Hero" (Nadina), "The Chocolate Soldier" (Nadina & Bumerli), "Sympathy" (Bumerli & Nadina), "Seek the Spy" (Massakroff, Nadina, Mascha, Aurelia, Bumerli, Gentlemen of the Ensemble), Finale of Act I (Aurelia, Mascha, Nadina). Entr'acte (Orchestra). *Act II*: The courtyard of the Popoff house; an afternoon in spring, a year later: "Bulgaria Victorious" (The Singing Ensembles), "Thank the Lord the War is Over" (Alexius, Mascha, Popoff, Aurelia, Singing Ensemble), "Slavic Dance" * (Premier Danseuse, Premier Dancer, Corps de Ballet), "After Today" * (Alexius & Nadina), "Forgive" (Nadina & Bumerli), "Tale of the Coat" (Popoff, Nadina, Aurelia, Mascha, Alexius, Bumerli), "Falling in Love" (Bumerli & Nadina), Finale of Act II (Entire Company). Entr'acte (Orchestra). *Act III*: The place — the same; that evening: "Waltz Ballet" (Premiere Danseuse, Premier Dancer, Corps de Ballet), "Just a Connoisseur" * (Popoff, Karl Sittler, Jack Anderson, Eileen Coffman, Terry Saunders, Barbara Heath, Marjorie Winters), "The Letter Song" (Nadina & Popoff), "After Today" * (reprise)/"That Would Be Lovely" (Alexius & Mascha), "After Today Gala Polka" * (Premiere Danseuse, Premier Dancer, Corps de Ballet), Finale (Entire Company).

Note: Asterisked numbers were arranged and adapted by Jay Blackton from Oscar Straus's melodies.

Four other Straus numbers were interpolated into the 1947 production that were not in the original. G.B. Shaw was not happy with the musicalized version. The Broadway critics were completely divided. Lucinda Ballard won a 1947 Tony for costumes (actually it was for her entire year of work).

After Broadway. GOODSPEED OPERA HOUSE, Conn., 1990. MUSICAL ADAPTATIONS/MUSICAL DIRECTOR: Albin Konopka; NEW LYRICS: Ted Drachman; NEW BOOK/DIRECTOR: Larry Carpenter; CHOREOGRAPHER: Daniel Pelzig; SETS: James Leonard Joy; COSTUMES: John Falabella; ORCHESTRATIONS: Larry Moore. *Cast*: BLUNTSCHLI: Paul Ukena Jr.; CATHERINE: Susan Cella; CAPT. MASSAKROFF: Richard Malone; MASCHA: Joanna Glushak; RAINA: Victoria Clark; LOUKA: Anna Bess Lank; PETKOFF: Kurt Knudson; SERGIUS: Max Robinson; STEPHEN: Robert Torres; ALSO WITH: Deborah Geneviere, Jonathan Cerullo,

Stephen Lloyd Webber. *Act I*: Overture, "We Are Marching Through the Night," "We Too Are Lonely," "We Are Hunting Down the Foe," "When You Haven't Got a Man," "Melodrama," "Say Good Night," "My Hero," "Chocolate Soldier," "Sympathy," "Seek the Spy," "Tiralala." *Act II*: Entr'acte; "Our Heroes Come," "Thank the Lord the War is Over," "Never Was There Such a Lover," "Tale of a Coat," "Bluntschli's Prayer," "Bulgarian Ballet," "Falling in Love," "Letter Song," Finale.

45TH STREET THEATRE, 3/29/05–4/10/05. Part of the *Musicals Tonight!* series. DIRECTOR: Thomas Mills; MUSICAL DIRECTOR: James Stenborg. *Cast*: POPOFF: George S. Irving; NADINA: Morgan James (for 12 performances) and Rena Stober (for 4 performances); BUMMERLI: Paul Jason Green; AURELIA: Neva Rae Powers; MASCHA: Lisa Trader.

136. *A Chorus Line*

A musical with no intermission. Set at an audition in "this theatre" in 1975. The stage is bare, except for tall, rotating mirrors. The actors are in rehearsal costumes until the finale. An honest concept musical, owing a debt to *Cabaret*, *Company*, and *Follies*. Zach (rarely seen, and based on Michael Bennett), is a sadistic cool-headed director, looking for a cast of eight dancers out of 17 hopefuls, one of whom is his ex-mistress, the former featured dancer Cassie, now down on her luck. Another is Sheila, streetsmart but vulnerable; Diana had once failed a method acting class; Val is voluptuous via silicone; Paul is a pathetic drag queen. The musical is basically a series of vignettes dealing with the hopes, fears, frustrations, insecurities of the "gypsies" (hopeful chorus dancers who contribute so much to a show but who receive so little notice), and because this appealed to anyone who has ever stood in line waiting for a job of any sort, the show struck a sympathetic note with audiences. Don was based on Andy Bew, Ron Kuhlman and Michael Bennett; Maggie on Donna McKechnie and Kay Cole; Mike on Wayne Cilento; Connie on Baayork Lee; Greg on Chris Chadman and Michel Stuart; Cassie on Donna McKechnie and Leland Palmer; Sheila on Carole Bishop; Bobby on Thommie Walsh; Bebe on Michon Peacock and Nancy Lane; Judy on Trish Garland; Richie on Ron Dennis and Candy Brown [sic]; Al on Steve Boockvor; Kristine on Denise Boockvor; Val on Pam Blair and Mitzi Hamilton; Mark on Cameron (Rick) Mason; Paul on Nicholas Dante; Diana on Priscilla Lopez; Larry on Bob Avian and Michael Bennett.

Before Broadway. In 1974 dancers Michon Peacock and Tony Stevens, depressed after the closure during Broadway previews of *Rachael Lily Rosenbloom*, determined to do something to improve the lot of the Broadway chorus performer. They contacted Michael Bennett with the idea of doing a show about the chorus. On 1/18/74 24 chorus performers stayed up all night in a session conducted by Mr. Bennett in a rented studio, talking about their experiences in the line, and Mr. Bennett taped 30 hours of it (the 22 dancers got $1 each for their stories). Mr. Bennett and one of the chorus performers, Nicholas Dante (also a writer), began to fashion a show. The number "Who Am I?" was cut at this stage. Mr. Bennett asked Joe Papp of the New York Shakespeare Festival to sponsor a workshop of the musical (it became two workshops, actually, the first in 8/74–9/74, and the 2nd in 1/75–2/75). It was first shown at a running time of 4 hours 20 minutes, but this was reduced to two hours by the time it went into previews Off Broadway, at the ESTELLE R. NEWMAN THEATRE (one of the stages at the Shakespeare Festival's Public Theatre), on 4/16/75, at a $10 top ticket price. It officially opened there 5/21/75, at which point all the New York critics came except Walter Kerr. They gave it a unanimous rave. At a time when tryouts in Philadelphia, Boston, New Haven, Detroit, Baltimore, Washington DC, etc, were becoming too costly, this method of staging a workshop before a non-paying audience was a major breakthrough in stage musical production. The production had the same basic crew as for Broadway, except SOUND: Roger Jay; PRESS: Merle Debuskey, Bob Ullman, Norman L.

Berman; GENERAL MANAGER: David Black; STAGE MANAGERS: Jeff Hamlin & Frank Hartenstein. It had the same cast as for Broadway opening night. The understudies were too, except Mike: Don Percassi; Diana: Judy Beebe & Carole Schweid; Val/Judy: Crissy Wilzak; Al: Scott Allen. The show closed 7/13/75, after 101 PERFORMANCES. Then it went to Broadway.

The Broadway Run. SHUBERT THEATRE, 10/19/75–4/28/90. Previews from 7/25/75. 6,137 PERFORMANCES. The New York Shakespeare Festival production, PRESENTED BY Joseph Papp, in association with Plum Productions (Michael Bennett); MUSIC: Marvin Hamlisch; LYRICS: Edward Kleban; BOOK: James Kirkwood & Nicholas Dante (with jokes by Neil Simon); SUGGESTED BY events in the lives of various participants in the show's development (uncredited but remunerated); CONCEIVED BY/DIRECTOR: Michael Bennett; CHOREOGRAPHERS: Michael Bennett & Bob Avian; SETS: Robin Wagner; COSTUMES: Theoni V. Aldredge; LIGHTING: Tharon Musser; SOUND: Abe Jacob; MUSICAL DIRECTOR: Donald Pippin (75–79), *Robert Rogers* (79–86), *Jerry Goldberg* (by 86–87); ORCHESTRATIONS: Bill Byers, Hershy Kay, Jonathan Tunick; VOCAL ARRANGEMENTS: Donald Pippin; REHEARSAL PIANIST: Fran Liebergall; OFF BROADWAY CAST RECORDING on Columbia, made on 6/3/75; PRESS: Merle Debuskey; CASTING: Rosemarie Tichler; GENERAL MANAGER: Robert Kamlot (until 1985), *Laurel Ann Wilson* (83–86); COMPANY MANAGER: Patricia Carney (75–76), *Harris Goldman* (76–79), *Bob Mac-Donald* (78–86), *Mitchell Weiss* (85–86), *Robert Reilly* (87–88); PRODUCTION STAGE MANAGER: Jeff Hamlin (75–76), *Joe Calvan* (76–77), *Wendy Mansfield* (77–85), *Robert Amirante* (85–87), *Fraser Ellis* (87–90); STAGE MANAGER: Frank Hartenstein (75–76), *Peter von Mayrhauser* (76–78), *Tom Porter* (78–90); ASSISTANT STAGE MANAGER: Scott Allen (75–76), *Zane Weiner* (76–77), *Danny Ruvolo* (76–78), *Jon Michael Richardson* (78–81), *James Beaumont* (78–80), *Morris Freed* (80–89), *Bradley Jones* (81–85), *Ronald Stafford* (83–90). **Cast** (in alphabetical order by the original actor): ROY: Scott Allen, *Danny Ruvolo* (from 8/76), *Scott Allen* (from 1/77), *Danny Ruvolo* (from 2/77), *Dean Badolato* (by 78–79), *Dennis Daniels* (from 79–80), *Philip Perry* (from 80–81), *Don Mirault* (from 80–81), *Evan Pappas* (from 81–82), *Drew Geraci* (from 82–83), *Evan Pappas* (from 82–83), *Tommy Re* (from 85–86), *Dale Stotts* (from 87–88), *Matt Pedersen* (by 89–90); KRISTINE URICH: Renee Baughman, *Cookie Vasquez* (from 4/26/76), *Deborah Geffner* (from 10/76), *P.J. Mann* (from 9/78), *Deborah Geffner* (from 1/79), *Christine Barker* (from 3/79), *Kerry Casserly* (from 8/81), *Christine Barker* (from 10/81), *Kerry Casserly* (from 84–85), *Flynn McMichaels* (from 6/29/87), *Cynthia Fleming* (by 89–90); SHEILA BRYANT: Carole Bishop (name changed to Kelly Bishop 3/76), *Kathrynann Wright* (from 8/76), *Bebe Neuwirth* (from 6/80), *Susan Danielle* (from 3/81), *Jan Leigh Herndon* (from 9/82), *Jane Summerhays* (from 9/82), *Susan Danielle* (from 83–84), *Kelly Bishop* (from 3/84), *Kathrynann Wright* (from 4/84), *Susan Danielle* (from 9/84), *Cynthia Fleming* (from 11/86), *Dana Moore* (from 11/16/87), *Susan Danielle* (from 3/27/89); VAL CLARK: Pamela Blair, *Barbara Monte-Britton* (from 4/26/76), *Karen Jablons* (from 10/76), *Mitzi Hamilton* (from 3/1/77), *Karen Jablons* (from 12/77), *Mitzi Hamilton* (from 3/78), *Gail Mae Ferguson* (78), *Lois Englund* (from 7/78), *Deborah Henry* (from 10/79), *Mitzi Hamilton* (from 1/80), *Deborah Henry* (from 2/80), *Mitzi Hamilton* (from 5/80), *Joanna Zercher* (from 6/81), *Mitzi Hamilton* (from 7/81), *Wanda Richert, DeLys Lively-Mekka* (from 85–86), *Wanda Richert* (from 11/88), *Diana Kavilis* (from 2/20/89); MIKE COSTA: Wayne Cilento, *Don Correia* (from 76–77), *Jim Litten* (from 6/77), *Jeff Hyslop* (from 1/79), *Don Correia* (from 6/79), *Buddy Balou'* (from 6/80), *Carey Scott Lowenstein* (from 7/81), *Scott Wise* (from 7/82), *Danny Herman* (from 4/83), *Don Correia* (from 7/84), *J. Richard Hart* (from 8/84), *Danny Herman* (from 85–86), *Charles McGowan* (from 85–86), *Mark Bove* (from 85–86), *Tommy Re* (from 7/30/87), *Kelly Patterson* (from 9/14/87), *Danny Herman* (from 87–88), *Michael Gruber* (from 1/16/89); BUTCH BARTON: Chuck Cissel, *Edward Love* (from 10/76), *Larry G. Bailey* (from 76–77), *Ken Rogers* (from 77–78), *Michael Dean* (from 78–79), *Kevin Chinn* (by 79–80), *Roscoe Gilliam* (from 80–81), *Michael-Pierre Dean* (from 85–86), *Kevin Chinn* (from 88–89), *Glenn Turner* (from 88–89), *Kevyn Morrow* (by 89–90); LARRY: Clive Clerk, *Jeff Weinberg* (from 10/76), *Clive Clerk* (from 1/77), *Adam Grammis* (from 2/77), *Paul Charles* (from 12/77), *R.J. Peters* (from 3/79), *T. Michael Reed* (from 11/79), *Michael Day Pitts* (from 3/80), *Donn Simione* (from 4/81), *J.*

Richard Hart (from 7/81), *Scott Plank* (from 9/82), *Brad Jeffries* (from 11/82), *J. Richard Hart* (from 8/83), *Jim Litten* (from 7/84), *Danny Herman* (from 85–86), *J. Richard Hart* (from 85–86), *Kevin Neil McCready* (from 88–89); MAGGIE WINSLOW: Kay Cole, *Lauree Berger* (from 4/26/76), *Donna Drake* (from 2/77), *Christina Saffran* (from 3/78), *Donna Drake* (from 4/78), *Christina Saffran* (from 7/78), *Betty Lynd* (from 6/5/79), *Marcia Lynn Watkins* (from 8/79), *Pam Klinger* (from 9/81), *Ann Heinricher* (from 8/84), *Pam Klinger* (from 84–85), *Dorothy Tancredi* (from 12/23/87; she became Dorothy Dybisz from 88–89), *Michele Pigliavento* (from 1/16/89), *Susan Santoro* (from 4/21/89); RICHIE WALTERS: Ronald Dennis, *Winston DeWitt Hemsley* (from 4/26/76), *Edward Love* (from 6/77), *A. William Perkins* (from 12/77 — his name changed to Wellington Perkins 6/78), *Larry G. Bailey* (from 1/79), *Carleton T. Jones* (from 3/80), *Ralph Glenmore* (from 6/80), *Kevin Chinn* (from 1/81), *Reggie Phoenix* (from 10/83), *Eugene Fleming* (from 9/84), *Gordon Owens* (from 3/85), *Bruce Anthony Davis* (from 12/86), *Gordon Owens* (from 2/20/89); TRICIA: Donna Drake, *Jo Speros* (from 10/76), *Cynthia Carrillo Onrubia* (from 4/77), *Diane Fratantoni* (by 79–80), *Karen Curlee* (from 82–83), *Kiel Junius* (from 82–83), *Robin Lyon* (from 83–84); TOM: Brandt Edwards, *Timothy Smith* (from 10/76), *Tim Cassidy* (from 12/76), *Rene Clemente* (from 2/77), *Cameron Mason* (from 77), *Anthony Inneo* (from 77–78), *Jon Michael Richardson* (from 78–79), *Claude Tessier* (from 79–80), *Tim Millett* (from 79–80), *Stephen Crenshaw* (from 80–81), *James Young* (from 80–81), *Frank Kliegel* (from 82–83), *Carlos Lopez* (from 88–89); JUDY TURNER: Patricia Garland, *Sandahl Bergman* (from 4/26/76), *Murphy Cross* (from 12/77), *Victoria Tabaka* (from 11/78), *Joanna Zercher* (from 7/79), *Angelique Ilo* (from 8/79), *Jannet Horsley* (from 9/80 — her name changed to Jannet Moranz 2/81), *Melissa Randel* (from 12/81), *Angelique Ilo* (from 85–86), *Trish Ramish* (from 2/87), *Cindi Klinger* (from 11/23/87), *Julie Tussey* (from 87–88), *Cindi Klinger* (by 88–89), *Angelique Ilo* (from 4/24/89); LOIS DILETTENTE: Carolyn Kirsch, *Vicki Frederick* (from 4/26/76), *Pamela Sousa* (from 12/76), *Cheryl Clark* (from 1/77), *Patti D'Beck* (from 4/77), *Julie Pars* (from 77–78), *Gail Mae Ferguson* (from 78–79), *Bebe Neuwirth* (from 79–80), *Tracy Shayne* (from 79–80), *Ann Louise Schaut* (from 80–81), *Catherine Cooper* (from 81–82), *Laurie Gamache* (from 82–83), *Cynthia Fleming* (from 85–86), *Cindi Klinger* (from 86–87), *Julie Tussey* (by 88–89); DON KERR: Ron Kuhlman, *David Thome* (from 4/26/76), *Dennis Edenfield* (from 3/80), *Michael Weir* (from 8/81), *Michael Danek* (from 10/81), *Randy Clements* (from 11/82), *Michael Danek* (from 12/82), *Keith Bernardo* (by 89–90); BEBE BENZENHEIMER: Nancy Lane, *Gillian Scalici* (from 4/26/76), *Rene Ceballos* (from 9/77), *Karen Meister* (from 1/78), *Rene Ceballos* (from 3/81), *Pamela Ann Wilson* (from 1/82), *Tracy Shayne* (from 85–86), *Karen Ziemba* (from 2/29/88), *Beth Swearingen* (from 88–89), *Christine Maglione* (from 88–89); CONNIE WONG: Baayork Lee, *Lauren Kayahara* (from 4/26/76), *Janet Wong* (from 2/77), *Cynthia Carrillo Onrubia* (from 11/79), *Janet Wong* (from 12/79), *Lauren Tom* (from 10/80), *Lily-Lee Wong* (from 10/81), *Sachi Shimizu* (from 11/83), *Lauren Tom* (from 4/84), *Sachi Shimizu;* DIANA MORALES: Priscilla Lopez, *Barbara Luna* (from 4/26/76), *Carole Schweid* (from 5/7/76), *Rebecca York* (from 8/76), *Loida Iglesias* (from 12/76), *Chris Bocchino* (from 10/79), *Diane Fratantoni* (from 9/79), *Chris Bocchino* (from 9/79), *Gay Marshall* (from 7/80), *Chris Bocchino* (from 8/80), *Dorothy Tancredi* (from 3/82), *Diane Fratantoni* (from 6/82), *Kay Cole* (from 8/82), *Roxann Cabalero* (from 10/82), *Gay Marshall* (from 11/82), *Roxann Cabalero* (from 1/83), *Loida Santos* (formerly Loida Iglesias) (from 3/83), *Roxann Cabalero* (from 85–86), *Gay Marshall* (from 85–86), *Roxann Cabalero* (from 85–86), *Mercedes Perez* (from 10/86), *Denise Di Renzo* (from 2/15/88), *Arminae Azarian* (from 2/13/89), *Roxann Biggs* (formerly Roxann Cabalero) (by 89–90); ZACH: Robert LuPone, *Joe Bennett* (4/26/76–9/76), *Eivind Harum* (from 10/76), *Robert LuPone* (from 1/31/77), *Kurt Johnson* (from 5/77), *Clive Clerk* (from 7/77), *Kurt Johnson* (from 8/77), *Anthony Inneo* (from 8/78), *Eivind Harum* (from 10/78), *Scott Pearson* (from 8/79), *Tim Millett* (from 3/81), *David Thome* (from 81–82), *Tim Millett* (from 81–82), *Steve Boockvor* (from 8/23/82), *Eivind Harum* (from 7/83), *Robert LuPone* (from 3/19/86), *Eivind Harum* (from 85–86), *Robert LuPone* (from 1/19/88), *Scott Pearson* (from 2/29/88), *Robert LuPone* (from 4/7/88), *Randy Clements* (from 9/9/88), *Robert LuPone* (from 11/21/88), *Eivind Harum* (by 89–90); MARK ANTHONY: Cameron Mason, *Brandt Edwards* (stood in, 9/76), *Paul Charles* (from 10/76),

Timothy Scott (from 12/77), *R.J. Peters* (from 4/78), *Timothy Wahrer* (from 3/79), *Dennis Daniels* (from 5/80), *Timothy Wahrer* (from 6/80), *Gregory Brock* (from 8/80), *Danny Herman* (from 5/81), *Fraser Ellis* (from 11/82), *Danny Herman* (from 12/82), *Chris Marshall* (from 4/83), *Gib Jones* (from 85–86), *Andrew Grose* (from 11/86), *Matt Zarley* (from 8/8/88), *Jack Noseworthy* (from 2/21/90); CASSIE FERGUSON: Donna McKechnie, *Ann Reinking* (from 4/26/76), *Donna McKechnie* (from 9/27/76), *Ann Reinking* (from 11/29/76), *Pamela Sousa* (from 1/77), *Vicki Frederick* (from 19/77), *Pamela Sousa* (from 11/14/77), *Candace Tovar* (from 1/78), *Pamela Sousa* (from 3/78), *Cheryl Clark* (from 12/78), *Deborah Henry* (from 10/80), *Cheryl Clark* (from 81–82), *Pamela Sousa* (from 11/81), *Cheryl Clark* (from 10/83), *Wanda Richert* (from 6/84), *Angelique Ilo* (from 10/84), *Wanda Richert* (from 11/84), *Angelique Ilo* (from 7/86), *Donna McKechnie* (from 9/1/86), *Laurie Gamache* (from 5/18/87); AL DE LUCA: Don Percassi, *Bill Nabel* (from 4/26/76), *John Mineo* (from 2/77), *Ben Lokey* (from 4/77), *Don Percassi* (from 7/77), *Jim Corti* (from 1/79), *Donn Simione* (from 9/79), *James Warren* (from 5/80 — his name changed to James Young 9/80), *Jerry Colker* (from 5/81), *Scott Plank* (from 11/82), *Buddy Balou'* (from 3/83), *Mark Bove* (from 85–86), *Kevin Neil McCready* (from 85–86), *Tommy Re* (from 9/17/87), *Stephen Bourneuf* (from 3/27/89), *Tommy Re* (by 89–90); FRANK: Michael Serrecchia, *Tim Cassidy* (from 2/77), *Claude Tessier* (from 78–79), *Michael Day Pitts* (from 79–80), *Troy Garza* (from 79–80), *Philip C. Perry* (from 80–81), *Fraser Ellis* (from 82–83), *William Mead* (from 87–88); GREG GARDNER: Michel Stuart, *Justin Ross* (from 4/26/76), *Danny Weathers* (from 6/78), *Ronald A. NaVarre* (from 9/82), *Michael Day Pitts* (from 83–84), *Justin Ross* (from 10/83), *Danny Weathers* (from 8/84), *Bradley Jones* (from 85–86), *Ronald A. NaVarre* (from 3/23/89), *Doug Friedman* (by 89–90); BOBBY MILLS III: Thomas J. "Thommie" Walsh, *Christopher Chadman* (from 6/77), *Ron Kurowski* (from 1/78), *Tim Cassidy* (from 11/78), *Ronald Stafford* (from 3/79), *Michael Gorman* (from 8/80), *Matt West* (from 9/80), *Ron Kurowski* (from 8/84); PAUL SAN MARCO: Sammy Williams, *George Pesaturo* (from 4/26/76), *Danny Ruvolo* (from 76–77), *Rene Clemente* (from 2/78), *Timothy Wahrer* (from 9/81), *Rene Clemente* (from 10/81), *Tommy Aguilar* (from 5/82), *Sammy Williams* (from 10/19/83), *Wayne Meledandri* (from 1/85), *Drew Geraci* (from 6/10/88); VICKI VICKERS: Crissy Wilzak, *Carol Marik* (from 77–78), *Angelique Ilo* (from 78–79), *Joanna Zercher* (from 79–80), *Tracy Shayne* (from 81–82), *Terri Lombardozzi* (from 81–82), *Peggy Parten* (from 81–82), *Ann Louise Schaut* (from 82–83), *Cynthia Fleming* (from 84–85), *Trish Ramish* (from 85–86), *Laureen Valuch Piper* (from 86–87), *Cindi Klinger* (from 87–88), *Cynthia Fleming* (from 87–88), *Paula Leggett* (by 89–90). **New roles added during the run**: AUDRE: *Fern Fitzgerald* [role added in 76; dropped by 79–80]; RICK: Cameron Mason, *David Fredericks* (from 76–77) [role added in 76; dropped by 79–80]; JARAD: *John Mineo, Troy Garza* (from 77–78), *T. Michael Reed* (by 79–80), *Morris Freed* (from 80–81), *Troy Garza* (from 81–82) [role added in 76]; BARBARA: *Patti D'Beck* (76–78) [role new by 76–77; dropped by 79–80]; AGNES: *Betty Lynd* (by 78–79) [role new by 78–79; dropped by 80–81]; ED: *Mark Fotopoulos* (77–78), *Jon Michael Richardson* (from 78–79), *Kevin Backstrom* (from 81–82), *Morris Freed* (from 81–82), *Tom Kosis* (from 88–89), *Joe Langworth* (by 89–90) [role new by 77–78]; LINDA: *Diane Fratantoni* (by 78–79), *Diane Duncan* (by 79–80), *Tracy Shayne* (from 80–81), *Karen Curlee* (from 81–82), *Tracy Shayne* (from 81–82), *Catherine Cooper* (from 82–83), *Laureen Valuch Piper* (from 84–85), *Laurie Gamache* (from 86–87), *Dana Moore* (from 87–88), *Wanda Richert* (from 87–88), *Niki Harris* (from 87–88), *Dana Moore* (by 89–90) [role new by 78–79]; SAM: *Steve Riley* (77–79), *James Beaumont* (by 79–80), *Troy Garza* (from 80–81), *John Dolf* (from 81–82), *Sam Piperato* (from 82–83), *Tommy Re* (from 84–85), *Evan Pappas* (from 85–86), *Gary Chryst* (from 85–86), *Frank Kliegel* (from 88–89) [role new by 77–78; renamed DOUGLAS by 84–85]; JENNY: *Candace Tovar* (77–79), *Jannet Horsley* (by 79–80), *Catherine Cooper* (from 80–81), *Kathleen Moore* (from 81–82), *Thia Fadel* (from 81–82), *Tracy Shayne* (from 82–83), *Candace Tovar* [role new by 77–78; dropped by 83–84]; RALPH: *Dennis Parlato* (by 78–79), *T. Michael Reed* (from 80–81), *Bradley Jones* (from 81–82), *Robert Amirante* (from 85–86), *Fraser Ellis* (from 87–88) [role new by 78–79; renamed HERMAN from 85–86]; HILARY: *Karen Ziemba* (82–83), *Roxann Cabalero* (from 83–84), *Cynthia Onrubia* (from 84–85), *Roxann Cabalero* (from 84–85), *Tracy Shayne* (from 85–86), *Karen Curlee* (from 85–86), *Dorothy*

Tancredi (from 86–87), *Arminae Azarian* (from 87–88), *Kathleen Moore* (from 88–89), *Donna M. Pompei* (from 88–89) [role new by 82–83]. **Understudies**: Don: Brandt Edwards (75–76), *Tim Cassidy* (76–78), *Tim Millett* (79–80), *Dennis Parlato* (79–80), *Don Mirault* (80–81), *Philip C. Perry* (80–82), *Fraser Ellis* (82–90), *Brad Jeffries* (82–83), *Frank Kliegel* (82–90), *Matt Pedersen* (89–90); Greg: Michael Serrecchia (75–77), *Tim Cassidy* (76–78), *Danny Ruvolo* (76–78), *Jon Michael Richardson* (78–81), *Claude Tessier* (78–79), *Michael Day Pitts* (79–80), *Bradley Jones* (81–85), *James Young* (81–82 — he was formerly James Warren), *Troy Garza* (84–90), *Tommy Re* (84–88), *Robert Amirante* (85–87), *William Mead* (87–90); Bobby: Michael Serrecchia (75–77), *Tim Cassidy* (76–78), *Danny Ruvolo* (76–78), *Claude Tessier* (78–79), *Jon Michael Richardson* (79–81), *Bradley Jones* (81–85, 87–88), *Fraser Ellis* (82–90), *Frank Kliegel* (82–90), *Sam Piperato* (82–84); Val: Crissy Wilzak (75–77), *Murphy Cross* (77–78), *Julie Pars* (78), *Betty Lynd* (78–80), *Catherine Cooper* (80–84), *Diane Fratantoni* (78–82), *Joanna Zercher* (79–81), *Kiel Junius* (82–83), *Pamela Ann Wilson* (82–85), *Robin Lyon* (83–90), *Laureen Valuch Piper* (84–87), *Julie Tussey* (87–90), *Donna M. Pompei* (89–90); Judy: Crissy Wilzak (75–77), *Carol Marik* (77–78), *Julie Pars* (78), *Diane Duncan* (79–80), *Jannet Horsley* (79–80), *Joanna Zercher* (79–81), *Ann Louise Schaut* (80–81, 82–84), *Thia Fadel* (81–82), *Peggy Parten* (81–82), *Laurie Gamache* (82–85, 86–87), *Pamela Ann Wilson* (82–85), *Cynthia Fleming* (84–88), *Cindi Klinger* (86–87), *Paula Leggett* (89–90), *Dana Moore* (89–90); Kristine: Donna Drake (75–77), *Crissy Wilzak* (76–77), *Julie Pars* (77–78), *Angelique Ilo* (78–79), *Diane Duncan* (79–80), *Betty Lynd* (78–80), *Jannet Horsley* (79–80), *Joanna Zercher* (79–81), *Ann Louise Schaut* (80–81, 82–84), *Peggy Parten* (81–82), *Laurie Gamache* (82–85, 86–87), *Cynthia Fleming* (84–88), *Karen Curlee* (85–86), *Trish Ramish* (85–86), *Julie Tussey* (87–90), *Paula Leggett* (89–90); Zach: Clive Clerk (75–77), *Anthony Inneo* (77–78), *David Thome* (78–79), *Tim Millett* (79–80), *Dennis Parlato* (79–80), *James Warren* (79–80 — he was later James Young), *Don Mirault* (80–81), *Michael Danek* (81–88), *James Young* (81–82 — he was formerly James Warren), *Brad Jeffries* (82–83), *Frank Kliegel* (82–90), *J. Richard Hart* (84–86, 87–88), *Robert Amirante* (85–87), *Kevin Neil McCready* (89–90); Diana: Carole Schweid (75–76), *Patti D'Beck* (76–77, 78–79), *Cynthia Carrillo Onrubia* (77–78), *Diane Fratantoni* (78–82), *Tracy Shayne* (79–83, 85–87), *Karen Ziemba* (82–83), *Roxann Cabalero* (83–85), *Robin Lyon* (83–90), *Karen Curlee* (85–86), *Dorothy Tancredi* (86–87), *Arminae Azarian* (87–88), *Diana Kavilis* (89–90), *Donna M. Pompei* (89–90); Bebe: Carole Schweid (75–76), *Patti D'Beck* (76–77, 78–79), *Cynthia Carrillo Onrubia* (77–78), *Diane Fratantoni* (78–82), *Tracy Shayne* (79–83), *Dorothy Tancredi* (81–82), *Karen Ziemba* (82–83), *Laurie Gamache* (83–85, 86–87), *Robin Lyon* (83–90), *Roxann Cabalero* (84–85), *Karen Curlee* (85–86), *Cynthia Fleming* (86–87), *Dorothy Tancredi* (86–87), *Arminae Azarian* (87–88), *Donna M. Pompei* (89–90); Tricia/Vicki/Lois: *Patti D'Beck* (76–77); Maggie: Donna Drake (76–77), *Cynthia Carrillo Onrubia* (76–78), *Diane Fratantoni* (78–82), *Betty Lynd* (78–80), *Tracy Shayne* (79–83, 85–87), *Dorothy Tancredi* (81–82), *Kiel Junius* (82–83), *Karen Ziemba* (82–83), *Roxann Cabalero* (83–85), *Robin Lyon* (83–90), *Karen Curlee* (85–86), *Dorothy Tancredi* (86–87), *Arminae Azarian* (87–88), *Donna M. Pompei* (89–90); Connie: Donna Drake, *Cynthia Carrillo Onrubia* (76–78), *Diane Fratantoni* (78–82), *Betty Lynd* (78–80), *Kiel Junius* (82–83), *Roxann Cabalero* (83–86), *Tracy Shayne* (85–87), *Arminae Azarian* (87–88), *Donna M. Pompei* (89–90); Sheila: Carolyn Kirsch (75–76), *Fern Fitzgerald* (76–77), *Deborah Geffner* (76–77), *Carol Marik* (77–78), *Candace Tovar* (77–78), *Gail Mae Ferguson* (78–79), *Jannet Horsley* (79–80), *Marcia Lynn Watkins* (78–80), *Catherine Cooper* (80–84), *Jannet Moranz* (80–81 — she was formerly Jannet Horsley), *Joanna Zercher* (79–81), *Thia Fadel* (81–82), *Ann Louise Schaut* (82–84), *Cynthia Fleming* (84–88), *Laurie Gamache* (86–87), *Laureen Valuch Piper* (84–87), *Cindi Klinger* (86–87), *Wanda Richert* (87–88), *Paula Leggett* (89–90), *Dana Moore* (89–90); Richie: Chuck Cissel (75–77), *Larry G. Bailey* (76–77), *Ken Rogers* (77–78), *Michael Dean* (78–79), *Kevin Chinn* (79–80), *Roscoe Gilliam* (80–84), *Michael-Pierre Dean* (85–88), *Kevyn Morrow* (89–90); Cassie: Carolyn Kirsch (75–76), *Vicki Frederick* (76), *Sandahl Bergman* (76–77), *Patti D'Beck* (77–79), *Candace Tovar* (77–78), *Gail Mae Ferguson* (78–79), *Deborah Henry* (79–80), *Bebe Neuwirth* (79–80), *Angelique Ilo* (79–80, 85–86, 89–90), *Rene Ceballos* (80–81), *Catherine Cooper* (80–84), *Ann Louise*

Schaut (80–81, 82–84), *Thia Fadel* (81–82), *Laurie Gamache* (82–85, 86–87), *Karen Ziemba* (82–83), *Cynthia Fleming* (84–88), *Dana Moore* (87–88), *Wanda Richert* (87–88), *Diana Kavilis* (89–90); Mark: Brandt Edwards (75–76), *David Fredericks* (76–77), *Danny Ruvolo* (76–78), *Mark Fotopoulos* (77–78), *James Beaumont* (78–80), *Morris Freed* (80–88), *Troy Garza* (78–84), *Philip C. Perry* (80–82), *John Dolf* (81–82), *Fraser Ellis* (82–90), *Evan Pappas* (82–85), *Sam Piperato* (82–83), *Joe Langworth* (89–90), *Carlos Lopez* (89–90); Larry: Michael Serrecchia (75–77), *David Fredericks* (76–77), *Danny Ruvolo* (76–78), *Mark Fotopoulos* (77–78), *James Beaumont* (78–80), *Troy Garza* (78–90), *Tim Millett* (79–80), *John Dolf* (81–82), *Evan Pappas* (81–85), *Sam Piperato* (82–84), *Tommy Re* (84–87), *Gary Chryst* (85–88), *Kevin Neil McCready* (87–88), *Joe Langworth* (89–90), *Matt Pedersen* (89–90); Mike: John Mineo (75–77), *Danny Ruvolo* (76–78), *Troy Garza* (77–80, 81–90), *Dean Badolato* (78–79), *Dennis Daniels* (79–80), *Dennis Edenfield* (79–80), *Jerry Colker* (80–82), *Dennis Edenfield* (80–81), *J. Richard Hart* (80–82, 83–84, 85–88), *Danny Herman* (80–82), *John Dolf* (81–82), *James Young* (81–82), *Sam Piperato* (83–84), *Jim Litten* (84–85), *Tommy Re* (84–87), *William Mead* (87–90), *Carlos Lopez* (89–90), *Matt Pedersen* (89–90); Al: John Mineo (75–77), *Danny Ruvolo* (76–78), *Steve Riley* (77–78), *Dean Badolato* (78–79), *Claude Tessier* (78–79), *Dennis Daniels* (79–80), *Dennis Parlato* (79–80), *Buddy Balou'* (80–81), *Troy Garza* (78–84, 85–90), *J. Richard Hart* (80–82), *Don Mirault* (80–81), *Philip C. Perry* (80–82), *Evan Pappas* (81–85), *James Young* (81–82), *Tommy Re* (84–87), *Kevin Neil McCready* (87–88), *William Mead* (87–90), *Matt Pedersen* (89–90), *Carlos Lopez* (89–90); Paul: Chuck Cissel (76–77), *Rene Clemente* (76–77), *Troy Garza* (77–86, 87–90), *James Beaumont* (78–80), *Jim Corti* (78–79), *Timothy Wahrer* (78–79), *Evan Pappas* (81–85), *Gary Chryst* (85–88), *Carlos Lopez* (89–90). **Orchestra**: KEYBOARDS: Fran Liebergall; GUITARS: George Davis; BASS GUITAR: Roland Wilson; UPRIGHT BASS: Jaime Austria; HARP: Bernice Horowitz; DRUMS: Allen Herman, *Earl Williams*; PERCUSSION: Benjamin Herman; REEDS: Joseph Maggio, Buzz Brauner, Norman Wells, Marvin Roth; TRUMPETS: Bob Millikan, James Morreale, Al Mattaliano; TROMBONES: Vincent Forchetti & Gordon Early Anderson; BASS TROMBONE: Blaise Turi. "I Hope I Get It" ("Who Am I, Anyway? Am I My Own Resume?") (Company), "I Can Do That" (Mike), "And …" (Bobby, Richie, Val, Judy), "At the Ballet" (Sheila, Bebe, Maggie), "Sing!" (Kristine & Al); Montage: Part 1—"Hello 12, Hello 13, Hello Love" (Company); Part 2 —"Nothing" (Diana); Part 3—"Mother" (Company); Part 4—"Monster Montage" (Judy, Greg, Richie, Company); "Dance: 10; Looks: 3" ("Tits and Ass") (Val), "The Music and the Mirror" (Cassie), "One" (Company), "The Tap Combination" (Company), "What I Did for Love" (Diana & Company), "One" (reprise) (Company), Finale: Bows.

It opened on Broadway following the musicians' strike, and Walter Kerr reviewed it, also with a rave. The show won a Pulitzer Prize for drama. It also won the New York Drama Critics' Circle award for best musical while still Off Broadway. It won a Special Theatre World Award for every member of the creative staff and original cast; and it won 1976 Tonys for musical, score, book, direction of a musical, choreography, lighting, and for Donna McKechnie, Kelly Bishop, and Sammy Williams; it was also nominated for costumes, and for Priscilla Lopez and Robert LuPone. On 9/29/83 the Broadway production celebrated 3,389 performances, passing *Grease* to make it the longest-running Broadway musical of all time up to then. 332 members of the original, national and international companies appeared on stage for the curtain call on this occasion, directed by Michael Bennett. He and Donna McKechnie were married and divorced during the run. The show sold 1,125,000 original cast albums during the run. In 1984 it won a Special Tony Award for being the longest-running Broadway musical.

After Broadway. INTERNATIONAL TOURING COMPANY. Opened at the Royal Alexandra Theatre, Toronto, on 5/6/76. Previews from 5/3/76. MUSICAL DIRECTOR: Ray Cook, *Larry Blank, Sherman Frank*; GENERAL MANAGER: Emanuel Azenberg. The tour went from Toronto to London on 7/22/76 (see below). A London cast took over and the International Tour went to the USA, to Baltimore, on 2/13/77. Previews from 2/9/77. It closed at the Shubert Theatre, Chicago, on 5/29/83. **Cast**: PAUL: Tommy Aguilar, *Rene Clemente, Guillermo Gonzalez, Phillip Riccobuono, Wayne Meledandri*; KRISTINE: Christine Barker, *P.J. Mann, Hilary Fields, Peggy Parten, Laurie Gamache*; VICKI: Nancy Dafgek, *Judy Burns, Niki

Harris, Ann Heinricher, Karen Giombetti, Laureen Valuch Piper*; TOM: Mark Dovey, *Ronald Stafford, Steve Belin, Brian Kelly, Drew Geraci, J. Richard Hart*; MAGGIE: Jean Fraser, *Betty Lynd, Pam Cecil, Ann Heinricher, Robin Lyon*; VAL: Mitzi Hamilton, *Karen Jablons* (from 3/1/77), *Pamela Blair* (from 11/77), *Patti Colombo, Deborah Henry, Lisa Embs, Mitzi Hamilton, Lois Englund*; MIKE: Jeff Hyslop, *Troy Garza, C.J. McCaffrey, Rob Draper, Brian Kelly, John Dolf*; FRANK: *Troy Garza, Robert Warners, Matt West, Kevin Backstrom, Michael Ian-Lerner*; ZACH: Eivind Harum, *Clive Clerk* (from 8/77), *Buddy Vest, Ed Nolfi, David Thome, Eivind Harum*; DIANA: Loida Iglesias, *Gina Paglia, Diane Fratantoni, Rita Rehn, Mary Lou Crivello*; BEBE: Miriam Welch, *Susan Claire* (from 2/77), *Teresa Rossomando, Debra Pigliavento, Zoe Vonder Haar, Helen Frank*; MARK: Timothy Scott, *Scott Geralds, Gregory Brock, J. Thomas Smith*; BUTCH: Ken Rogers, *Eric Riley, Kevyn Morrow, Reggie A. Phoenix*; RICHIE: William Perkins, *Millard Hurley, Reggie Mack, Gordon Owens, Woodrow Thompson*; BOBBY: Ron Kurowski, *Ronald Stafford, Michael Gorman, Ron Kurowski*; JARAD: Michael Austin, *Alex MacKay*; GREG: Andy Keyser, *Mark Dovey, Ronald Stafford, Larry Blum, James Warren, Denny Martin Flinn, Robert Amirante*; LARRY: T. Michael Reed, *Ronald Stafford* (from 4/77), *John Fogarty, R.J. Peters, John Addis*; SHEILA: Jane Summerhays, *Judy Burns, Susan Danielle, Lisa Carlson*; DON: Ronald Young, *Brandt Edwards, Barry Thomas, Tim Millett, Matt West, Cory Hawkins, Randy Clements*; CASSIE: Sandy Roveta, *Pamela Sousa, Deborah Henry* (from 11/77), *Alyson Reed, Tina Paul, Angelique Ilo*; LOIS: Wendy Mansfield, *Bebe Neuwirth, Peggy Parten, Kerry Kennedy, Kimberly Dawn Smith*; AL: Don Percassi, *Steve Baumann, Donn Simione, Evan Pappas*; ROY: Donn Simione, *Karis Christensen*; RHODA: Lauren Goler; KEVIN: Christopher Gregory; TRICIA: Nancy Wood, *Kari Nicolaisen*; CONNIE: Jennifer Ann Lee, *Cherylene Lee, Sachi Shimizu*; JOE: Tommy Re; CYNTHIA: Leigh Webster; JUDY: Yvette Matthews, *Murphy Cross, Joanna Zercher*.

NATIONAL TOUR. Opened at the Curran Theatre, San Francisco, on 5/11/76. Previews from 5/6/76. Then it moved to Los Angeles, 7/1/76–1/7/78. Then to Chicago, where it closed on 12/2/78. It then went on the road. The tour closed in Montreal, on 9/14/80. It then became a bus and truck tour, opening again at Schenectady, NY, 9/18/80, and finally closing in Pittsburgh, on 10/3/82. MUSICAL DIRECTOR: Arthur Rubinstein, *Tom Hancock*. **Cast**: KRISTINE: Renee Baughman, *Cookie Vasquez* (from 10/76), *Kerry Casserly, Kathy Flynn-McGrath* (last season); VAL: Pamela Blair, *Mitzi Hamilton* (from 12/77), *Lois Englund, Pamela Ann Wilson, Laureen Valuch Piper* (last season); ROY: Tim Cassidy, *Timothy Smith, Noel Craig, Tony Parise, John Salvatore, Philip Mollet* (last season); MARK: Paul Charles, *Jimmy Roddy* (from 10/76), *R.J. Peters, James Beaumont* (from 4/78), *Morris Freed, Scott Plank, Brian Andrews, Fraser Ellis* (last season); MAGGIE: Kay Cole, *Donna Drake* (from 10/76), *Lisa Donaldson* (from 2/77), *Christina Saffran, Marcia Lynn Watkins, Stephanie Eley, Karen Ziemba* (last season); MIKE: Don Correia, *William Mead, Rob Draper, Jamie Torcellini, Kevin Blair* (last season); RICHIE: Ronald Dennis, *Larry G. Bailey* (from 1/78), *Rudy Lowe, Ralph Glenmore, Eugene Fleming, Raymond Flowers* (last season); JUDY: Patricia Garland, *Victoria Tabaka, Joanna Zercher, Jannet Horsley, Thia Fadel, Leigh Webster* (last season); GREG: Michel Stuart, *Andy Keyser* (from 10/76), *Mark Dovey, Stephen Moore, John De Luca, Joseph Rich* (last season); DON: Ron Kuhlman, *Dennis Edenfield* (from 10/76), *Tom Fowler, Dennis Edenfield, Michael Danek, Frank Kliegel* (last season); BEBE: Nancy Lane, *Trudy Bayne, Rise Clemmer, Tracy Shayne, Kathleen Moore, Helen Frank* (last season); CONNIE: Baayork Lee, *Lauren Kayahara* (from 2/77), *Sachi Shimizu* (last season); DIANA: Priscilla Lopez, *Chris Bocchino* (from 10/76), *Gay Marshall, Alison Gertner, Mary Lou Crivello* (last season); ZACH: Robert LuPone, *Joe Bennett* (from 10/76), *Anthony S. Teague, Alec Teague, Scott Pearson* (last season); CASSIE: Donna McKechnie, *Ann Reinking* (from 9/27/76), *Vicki Frederick* (from 11/29/76), *Pamela Peadon* (from 2/9/77), *Pamela Sousa* (from 1/78), *Cheryl Clark* (from 3/78), *Wanda Richert* (from 12/78), *Catherine Cooper, Cilda Schaur* (last season); VICKIE: Mary Ann O'Reilly, *Deborah Henry, Denise De Renzo, Susie Fenner, Terri Lombardozzi, Ann Louise Schaut* (last season); BOBBY: Scott Pearson, *Michael Austin* (from 4/77), *Matt West, Jim T. Ruttman* (last season); AL: Don Percassi, *Jack Karcher, Jeffory Robinson, James Bontempo, Jack Karcher, Frank Kosik* (last season); SHEILA: Charlene Ryan, *Kelly Bishop* (during Miss Ryan's illness), *Fern Fitzgerald, Charlene Ryan, Jane Summerhays, Sally Benoit, Rita O'Connor, Penelope Richards, Sheryll Fager-Jones* (last season); LARRY: Roy Smith, *Keith Keen, Calvin McRae, Roy Smith, Marshall Hagins, John Addis* (last season); BUTCH: Sam Tampoya, *Dennis Birchall, Glenn Ferrugiari, Daniel Dee, Phineas Newborn III* (last season); TOM: Danny Taylor, *Michael Lane, Rick Conant*; FRANK: Claude R. Tessier, *Jim Wolfe, Jack Magradey, Brad Moranz, Conley Schnaterbeck, Seth Walsh* (last season); PAUL: Sammy Williams, *Tommy Aguilar, Stephen Crenshaw, Sammy Williams, Willy Falk* (last season); LOIS: Carolyn Kirsch, *Lee Wilson, Tina Paul, Catherine Cooper, Jan Horn Adams, Mary Ann Hay* (last season); TRICIA: Rebecca York, *Linda Dangcil, Laura Klein, Karen Maris Pisani, Kari Nicolaisen* (last season).

THEATRE ROYAL, DRURY LANE, London. Opened on 7/22/76. 11 previews from 7/17/76. This was the International Touring Company from Montreal. When this company returned to North America, a London-based cast took over. Elizabeth Seal was originally cast as the new Cassie, but Michael Bennett felt her dancing was not up to par, and on 1/18/77 British Equity authorized Donna McKechnie to fill in for a month until a permanent — British — replacement could be found. Two days later they reversed this decision, and Mr. Bennett was forced to close the show temporarily. It re-opened on 1/24/77, with the London-based cast, and ran a total of 901 PERFORMANCES. The London-based cast (from 1/24/77) included: ROY: Gerry Davis, *Thom Booker*; KRISTINE: Vicki Spencer; SHEILA: Geraldine Gardner, *Wendy Baldock*; VAL: Linda Williams; MIKE: Michael Howe; BUTCH: Richard Lloyd-King, *Okon Jones*; LARRY: Jack Gunn; MAGGIE: Veronica Page; RICHIE: Roy Gayle; TRICIA: Nicki Croyden, *Sharon Lee Hill*; TOM: Ronald Stafford, *Kenn Oldfield, Peter Lowry*; JUDY: Judy Gridley; LOIS: Jo-Ann Robinson, *Carla Webb, Loraine Hart, Rachel Izen, Thorey Mountain*; DON: Lance Aston; BEBE: Susan Claire; CONNIE: Cherry Gillespie, *Liz Bagley*; DIANA: Diane Langton, *Tracie Hart*; ZACH: Jean-Pierre Cassel, *Geoffrey Webb*; MARK: Peter Barry; CASSIE: Petra Siniawski; AL: Jeffrey Shankley; FRANK: John Chester; GREG: Stephen Tate, *Christopher Molly*; BOBBY: Leslie Meadows, *Martin Baker*; PAUL: Michael Staniforth, *Graham Turner*; VICKI: Olivia Breeze, *Jenny Lyons, Juliette Naylor*.

THE MOVIE. 1985. PRODUCERS: Cy Feuer & Ernest H. Martin; DIRECTOR: Richard Attenborough. The number "Hello Twelve" was replaced with "Surprise, Surprise," and "The Music and the Mirror" by "Let Me Dance for You" (i.e. two new songs). "Sing!" was cut. *Cast*: ZACH: Michael Douglas; CASSIE: Alyson Reed; ALSO WITH: Gregg Burge, Nicole Fosse, Vicki Frederick.

PAPER MILL PLAYHOUSE, New Jersey, 1990. DIRECTOR/CHOREOGRAPHER: Baayork Lee; SETS: Michael Anania; COSTUMES: Jose M. Rivera; LIGHTING: Marilyn Rennagel. *Cast*: BEBE: Mindy Cooper; TOM: Scott Coppola; ZACH: Michael Danek; VICKI: Linda Gabler; CONNIE: Lyd-Lyd Gaston; MARK: Aldrin Gonzales; JUDY: Kelly Groninger; SHEILA: Jan Leigh Herndon; ROY: David La Duca; CASSIE: Jane Lanier; LOIS: Paula Leggett; BOBBY: Robert Longbottom; MIKE: Matt Zarley; FRANK: Michael Paternostro; TRICIA: Joanne McHugh.

TOUR. Opened during the 1990–91 season. PRESENTED BY Robert L. Young, Richard Martini, and Albert Nocciolino; RE-STAGED BY: Baayork Lee; LIGHTING: Richard Winkler; SOUND: Abe Jacob; MUSICAL DIRECTOR: Joseph Klein. *Cast*: AL: Buddy Balou,' *Frank Kosik*; SHEILA: Gail Benedict; JUDY: Janie Casserly; BUTCH: Kevin Chinn; ZACH: Randy Clements; DON: Michael Danek; ROY: Morris Freed; CASSIE: Laurie Gamache; DIANA: Deborah Geneviere; BOBBY: Michael Gorman; VICKI: Diana Kavilis; MAGGIE: Julie Pappas; BEBE: Beth Swearingen.

TOURING REVIVAL. Opened at the State Theatre, Minneapolis, on 9/24/96. Played 50 cities. PRESENTED BY PACE Theatricals Group; DIRECTOR/CHOREOGRAPHER: Baayork Lee. *Cast*: CASSIE: Jilly Slyter; BOBBY: John Salvatore; ZACH: Mark Martino; DIANA: Cindy Marchionda; RICHIE: Randy Donaldson; SHEILA: Michelle Bruckner; MAGGIE: Charlene Carr; VAL: Kimberly Dawn Neumann; PAUL: Luis Villabon.

PAPER MILL PLAYHOUSE, New Jersey, 9/7/01–10/14/01. It played here as the culmination of a short tour. DIRECTOR/CHOREOGRAPHER: Baayork Lee; MUSICAL DIRECTOR: Fran Liebergall. Several members of the 1975 original cast attended opening night at the Paper Mill — Clive Clerk, Kelly Bishop, Priscilla Lopez, Thommie Walsh, Sammy Williams, Pamela Blair, Scott Allen, Baayork Lee, and Donna Drake. Cast: Michele Tibbitts, Mark Bove, Caitlin Carter, Nadine Isenegger, Jenifer Lewis.

2006 BROADWAY REVIVAL. By early Jan. 2005 plans were announced for a Broadway revival to open 9/21/06. This production, with a cost estimated at a rather low $7–8 million, would be produced by John Breglio, directed by Bob Avian, choreographed by Mr. Avian and Baayork Lee, and with sets by Robin Wagner. It would have tryouts at the Curran Theatre, San Francisco in the late summer of 2006.

137. *Christine*

An imitation of *The King and I*. An Irishwoman arrives in the little town of Akbarabad, India to find that her daughter, married to Indian doctor, Rashil, has died in childbirth. Christine blames India, but is eventually drawn to the doctor. Set in the present.

Before Broadway. It was the first time a Nobel Prize winner (Pearl Buck) had written the libretto for a Broadway musical. Miss Buck did write the libretto, but so did Charles Peck. Miss Buck claimed she hardly knew Mr. Peck, and demanded his name be removed from the credits. Mr. Peck had written an outline and treatment, it seems, that Miss Buck never used. Then the show played Philadelphia, to lousy reviews, and Mr. Peck was brought back in to re-write Miss Buck's book. Jerome Chodorov, the director, was replaced by Cy Feuer, but neither director wanted his name on the playbill. Christine's nationality was changed from English to Irish during the tryout. The numbers "Happy is the Word" and "I Love Him" were dropped during the tryout.

The Broadway Run. FORTY-SIXTH STREET THEATRE, 4/28/60–5/7/60. 12 PERFORMANCES. PRESENTED BY Oscar S. Lerman & Martin B. Cohen, in association with Walter Cohen; MUSIC: Sammy Fain; LYRICS: Paul Francis Webster; BOOK: Pearl S. Buck & Charles K. Peck Jr.; ADAPTED FROM the 1945 novel *My Indian Family*, by Hilda Wernher; DIRECTOR: Cy Feuer; CHOREOGRAPHER: Hanya Holm; SETS/LIGHTING: Jo Mielziner; COSTUMES: Alvin Colt; MUSICAL DIRECTOR: Jay Blackton; ORCHESTRATIONS: Philip J. Lang; VOCAL & DANCE MUSIC ARRANGEMENTS: Trude Rittman; CONSULTANT ON INDIAN COSTUMES: Bhaskar; PRESS: Frank Goodman, Ben Washer, Leo Stern; GENERAL MANAGER: Charles Harrow; COMPANY MANAGER: Irving Squires; PRODUCTION STAGE MANAGER: Charles Atkin; STAGE MANAGERS: Fred Smith & Stuart Fleming. *Cast:* BEGGAR: Joseph Crawford; SERVANTS TO DR. SINGH: Arthur Tookoyan, Tony Gardell, John Anania; AUNTIE: Nancy Andrews (3); UNCLE: Phil Leeds (4); RAINATH: Bhaskar; JAYA: Leslye Hunter; RAJENDRA: Augie Rios; KRISHNA: Steve Curry; MOHAN ROY: Jonathan Morris; SERVANT TO MOHAN ROY: Nicholas Bianchi; STATION MASTER: Louis Polacek; SITA ROY: Janet Pavek; LADY CHRISTINE FITZSIMONS: Maureen O'Hara (1); DR. RASHIL SINGH: Morley Meredith (2); DR. MACGOWAN: Daniel Keyes; THE MATCHMAKER: Barbara Webb; THE PROSPECTIVE BRIDES: TARA: Mai-Lan; LAKSHMI: Jinja; AMORA: Laurie Archer; THE TWINS: Anjali Devi & Sasha [end of the Brides]; CHILDREN OF THE TOWN: Donna Lynn, Jan Rhodes, Luis Hernandez; THE PRIEST: John Anania; DANCERS: Laurie Archer, Sandra Bowman, Anjali Devi, Vito Durante, Jinja, Dino Laudicino, Mai-Lan, Joseph Nelson, Alan Peterson, Joe Rocco, Jonalee Sanford, Sasha, Gil Schwartz; SINGERS: John Anania, Bea Barrett, Nicholas Bianchi, Diana Corto, Joseph Crawford, Marceline Decker, Tony Gardell, Josephine Lang, Jen Nelson, Louis Polacek, Arthur Tookoyan, Barbara Webb. *Standby:* Sita Roy: Christine Matthews. *Understudies:* Christine: Jen Nelson; Dr. Singh: Arthur Tookoyan; Auntie: Bea Barrett; Uncle: John Anania; Mohan Roy: Nicholas Bianchi; Sita Roy: Diana Corto; Rainath: Joe Rocco; Rajendra/Krishna: Luis Hernandez; Jaya: Donna Lynn. *Act I*: *Scene 1* The railroad station in Akbarabad; *Scene 2* The study in Dr. Rashil Singh's home; *Scene 3* Outside the clinic; *Scene 4* The living room; six days later; *Scene 5* The veranda; two months later; *Scene 6* The living room; *Scene 7* The veranda; *Scene 8* The drawing room; *Scene 9* The clinic; *Scene 10* The city square. *Act II*: *Scene 1* The veranda at Rashil's house; *Scene 2* An open plain; *Scene 3* A shrine; *Scene 4* The living room; *Scene 5* The veranda; *Scene 6* The drawing room; *Scene 7* The veranda; *Scene 8* Mohan Roy's home. *Act I*: "Welcome Song" (Auntie, Uncle, Rainath, Children, Chorus), "My Indian Family" (Christine), "A Doctor's Soliloquy" (Rashil), "UNICEF Song" (The Children), "My Little Lost Girl" (Christine & Rashil), "I'm Just a Little Sparrow" (Jaya, Auntie, Rainath, Servants, Children), "We're Just a Pair of Sparrows" (Christine & Jaya), Cobra Ritual Dance (Rainath & Dancers), "How to Pick a Man a Wife" (Auntie & Uncle), "The Lovely Girls of Akbarabad" (Matchmaker & Chorus), "Room in My Heart" (Christine), "The Divali Festival" (Rainath, Dancers, Singers), "I Never Meant to Fall in Love" (Christine & Rashil). *Act II*: "Freedom Can Be a Most Uncomfortable Thing" (Auntie & Friends), "Ireland Was Never Like This" (Christine & Dancers), "He Loves Her" (Sita), "Christine" (Rashil), "Room in My Heart" (reprise) (Christine), "Freedom Can be a Most Uncomfortable Thing" (reprise) (Auntie & Uncle); Dance: Kathak Plate Dance (Rainath & Girls), Kathakali (Dancing Boys), Bharatha Natyan (Rainath, Dancing Girls, Dancing Boys), "The Woman I Was Before" (Christine), "A Doctor's Soliloquy" (reprise) (Christine & Rashil), "I Never Meant to Fall in Love" (reprise) (Rashil & Christine), Finale.

It was Maureen O'Hara's Broadway debut, and not much of one. Bhaskar got the best critical notice in the show, the overall Broadway reviews being terrible

138. *Chronicle of a Death Foretold*

A dance musical (no song numbers listed). No intermission. Set in an isolated Latin American town, past and present. The story moves back and forth in time, to examine a murder, its causes & consequences.

Before Broadway. The production, and the workshop leading up to it, were part of Lincoln Center Theatre's New Collaboration series, sponsored by Philip Morris. It was the theatre's 55th production. **The Broadway Run.** PLYMOUTH THEATRE, 6/15/95–7/16/95. 30 previews from 5/18/95. 37 PERFORMANCES. PRESENTED BY Lincoln Center Theatre, by arrangement with INTAR Hispanic American Arts Center; MUSIC/ARRANGEMENTS: Bob Telson; ADDITIONAL MATERIAL: Michael John LaChiusa; ADAPTED BY Graciela Daniele & Jim Lewis from the novel by Gabriel Garcia Marquez; CONCEIVED BY/DIRECTOR/CHOREOGRAPHER: Graciela Daniele; SETS: Christopher Barreca; COSTUMES: Toni-Leslie James; LIGHTING: Jules Fisher & Beverly Emmons; SOUND: Tony Meola; MUSICAL DIRECTOR/DANCE MUSIC ARRANGEMENTS: Steve Sandberg; PRESS: Merle Debuskey; CASTING: Daniel Swee; GENERAL STAGE MANAGER: Steven C. Callahan; COMPANY MANAGER: Florie Seery & Edward J. Nelson; PRODUCTION STAGE MANAGER: Leslie Loeb; STAGE MANAGERS: Valerie Lau-Kee, Robert Castro. **Cast:** SANTIAGO NASAR: George de la Pena; CRISTO, HIS FRIEND: Julio Monge; PLACIDA, SANTIAGO'S MOTHER: Yolande Bavan; VICTORIA, THE COOK: Myra Lucretia Taylor; DIVINA, HER DAUGHTER: Monica McSwain; ANGELA VICARIO: Saundra Santiago; PURA VICARIO, HER MOTHER: Ivonne Coll; PABLO VICARIO, ANGELA'S BROTHER: Luis Perez; PEDRO VICARIO, ANGELA'S BROTHER: Gregory Mitchell; BAYARDO SAN ROMAN: Alexandre Proia; CLOTILDE, THE BODEGA KEEPER: Tonya Pinkins; FLORA, SANTIAGO'S FIANCEE: Lisa Leguillou; FAUSTINO, A BUTCHER: Lazaro Perez; XIUS, A WIDOWER: Norberto Kerner; COLONEL APONTE: Nelson Roberto Landrieu; FATHER AMADOR: Jaime Tirelli; MARGOT, A NOVICE: Rene M. Ceballos; MARIA: Denise Faye. **Understudies**: Santiago: Julio Monge & Edgard Gallardo; Cristo/Pablo/Pedro/Bayardo: Colton Green & Edgard Gallardo; Aponte: Edgard Gallardo & Eduard de Soto; Faustino/Xius: Colton Green & Eduard de Soto; Placida/Angela: Susan Pilar & Marina Chapa; Victoria/Clotilde: Susan Pilar & Eyan Williams; Divina: Marina Chapa; Pura: Rene Ceballos & Eyan Williams; Flora: Marina Chapa & Marianne Filali; Margot/Maria: Eyan Williams & Marianne Filali; Amador: Nelson Roberto Landrieu & Eduard de Soto. **Orchestra**: PIANO/SYNTHESIZER: Steve Sandberg & Bob Telson; ACOUSTIC & ELECTRIC BASSES: Gary Haase; GUITAR: Dominic Kanza; TROMBONE: Dan Reagan; ACCORDION: Yury Lemeshev; PERCUSSION: Roger Squitero & Cyro Baptista; DRUMS: Leroy Clouden.

Broadway reviews were divided, mostly negative, but they were not unkind. It received Tony nominations for musical, book, and choreography

139. *Chu Chem*

Although it was billed as a play with music, it really was a musical. A Zen Buddhist-Hebrew musical comedy in English,

billed as "the first Chinese-Jewish musical." The original 1966 musical was a play within a play, really. Three western actors join a Chinese troupe to enact a story, as follows: Chu Chem, a scholar and wanderer journeys to Kaifeng Fu with his wife Rose and daughter Lotte in order to find traces of the Jews who migrated there 300 years before, and also to find a husband for Lotte. Prince Eagle wants to make Lotte one of his concubines, but Lotte is a very liberated young woman and will not have this. The prince abdicates, and gets rid of his harem, and Chu Chem finds that the Jews assimilated and were not, for once, persecuted. For the 1988–89 revival, the play-within-a-play concept was done away with, as was Rose's role. Greater emphasis was placed on the relationship between Lotte and the Prince.

Before Broadway. Ted Allan, the librettist, was inspired to write the book when he visited Kaifeng Fu, China, and learned of the Jews who had migrated there in the 10th century. The original musical production, by Cheryl Crawford & Mitch Leigh, ran 11/15/66–11/19/66 at the NEW LOCUST, PHILADELPHIA, and never made it to Broadway. DIRECTOR: Albert Marre; CHOREOGRAPHER: Jack Cole; SETS/LIGHTING: Howard Bay; COSTUMES: Willa Kim & Howard Bay; MUSICAL DIRECTOR: Howard Cable; DANCE & VOCAL ARRANGEMENTS: Neil Warner. **Cast**: ROSE: Molly Picon, *Henrietta Jacobson* (from 11/14/66); CHU CHEM: Menasha Skulnik; PRINCE EAGLE: James Shigeta; MONGOL LORD HOO HAH: Jack Cole; LOTTE: Marcia Rodd; PRINCE EAGLE'S BROTHER: Robert Ito; THE PROMPTER: Yuki Shimoda; CHERRY STONE: Virginia Wing; HOO HAH'S HENCHMEN: Buzz Miller & J.C. McCord; THE ELDER: Khigh Dhiegh; ROSE: Henrietta Jacobson; PINK CLOUD: Reiko Sato; BLACK CLOUD BRIDE: Tisa Chang; CHILD: Tracey Michele Lee (this was Michele Lee); PRINCE EAGLE'S BODYGUARD: Man Mountain Dean Jr. **Standby**: Chu Chem: Lou Gilbert. The Prince halted the show for the 15-minute intermission, and two sumo wrestlers (not real — one of them was American wrestler Man Mountain Dean) entertained the audience. Top-billed Molly Picon had her part cut and was not happy. She walked out twice during rehearsals and previews; the second time for good, to be replaced by Henrietta Jacobson who, at one point during opening night in Philadelphia turned to the audience and said, "There was a song here, but you'll be better off without it." The individual scenes and musical numbers were not identified as such at the request of the authors, because they wanted to create a casual impression almost of improvisation. The show canceled its scheduled Broadway opening at the George Abbott Theatre.

The 1989 production began in 1988, at the JEWISH REPERTORY THEATRE, on East 14th Street. PRESENTED BY Ted Allan & Mitch Leigh. It had the same crew as for the subsequent Broadway run, except CHOREOGRAPHER: Rosalind Newman; STAGE MANAGER: Gregg Fletcher. Same cast except PRINCE: Thom Sesma; and the role of Izu-Lo-Yeh (played by Marc C. Oka) was cut for Broadway. The name of the character Tsu-Hoke was changed to Shu-Wo. A good review from the *New York Times* third-string critic inspired Mitch Leigh to take it to Broadway. The number "The Wise" was dropped for Broadway. Other numbers not used were: "Chu Chem," "Empty Yourself," "It's Not the Truth," "A Lovely Place," "My Only Love," "One at a Time."

The Broadway Run. RITZ THEATRE, 4/7/89–5/14/89. 24 previews from 3/17/89. 44 PERFORMANCES. The Jewish Repertory Theatre production, PRESENTED BY The Mitch Leigh Company & William D. Rollnick; MUSIC: Mitch Leigh; LYRICS: Jim Haines & Jack Wohl; BOOK/CONCEPT: Ted Allan; DIRECTOR: Albert Marre; SETS: Robert Mitchell; COSTUMES: Kenneth M. Yount; LIGHTING: Jason Sturm; SOUND: Gary M. Stocker; MUSICAL DIRECTOR/VOCAL DIRECTOR: Don James; ORCHESTRATIONS: Michael Gibson; PRESS: Shirley Herz Associates; CASTING: Stephanie Klapper; GENERAL MANAGEMENT: Niko Associates; PRODUCTION STAGE MANAGER: Geraldine Teagarden; STAGE MANAGER: Larry Smith; ASSISTANT STAGE MANAGER: David Stoll. **Cast:** THE ORIENTAL COMPANY: THE PRINCE: Kevin Gray (3), *Thom Sesma*; THE ELDER: Alvin Lum (5); HONG-HO, THE GOVERNOR: Chev Rodgers (8); THE PRINCE'S BROTHER: Hechter Ubarry (9); DAF-AH-DIL: Zoie Lam (6); THE PROMPTER: Timm Fujii (7); NA-MI: Simone Gee; LEI-AN: Keelee Seetoo; SHU-WO: Kenji Nakao; HO-KE: Jason Ma; NU-WO:

Paul Nakauchi; CHUEH-WU: Nephi Jay Wimmer; GUARD: Nephi Jay Wimmer; CONCUBINES: Zoie Lam, Simone Gee, Keelee Seetoo; VILLAGERS: Zoie Lam, Simone Gee, Keelee Seetoo, Kenji Nakao, Jason Ma, Paul Nakauchi; PROPMEN: Kenji Nakao, Jason Ma, Paul Nakauchi, Nephi Jay Wimmer; THE WESTERNERS: CHU CHEM: Mark Zeller (1) ☆; LOTTE: Emily Zacharias (2) ☆, *Mary Munger*; YAKOB: Irving Burton (4). **Standbys**: Chu Chem/Yakob/Hong-Ho: Michael Ingram; Lotte: Mary Munger. **Understudies**: Prince/Prince's Brother: Paul Nakauchi; Elder: Nephi Jay Wimmer; Prompter/Guard: Jason Ma; Daf-ah-Dil: Simone Gee; Na-Mi/Lei-An/Concubines/Ladies: Christine Toy; Propmen: David Stoll. **Band**: KEYBOARD 1: Don Jones; KEYBOARD 2: Brett Alan Sommer; WIND SYNTHESIZER: Bill Meade; ELECTRIC BASS: Ray Kilday; GUITAR SYNTHESIZER: Kevin Kuhn. **Act I**: "Orient Yourself" (Oriental Company), "What Happened, What?" (Chu Chem & Yakob), "Welcome" (Villagers), "You'll Have to Change" (Lotte), "Love Is" (Prince), "I'll Talk to Her" (Chu Chem, Prince, Prince's Brother), "Shame on You" (Chu Chem, Prince, Concubines), "It Must be Good for Me" (Lotte), "I'll Talk to Her" (reprise) (Chu Chem), "You'll Have to Change" (reprise) (Prince), "The River" (Lotte, Prince, Propmen), "We Dwell in Our Hearts" (Chu Chem, Lotte, Prince), "Goodbye Love" [not in previews; added for Broadway]. **Act II**: "Re-Orient Yourself" (Oriental Company), "What Happened, What?" (reprise) (Yakob), "I Once Believed (in Nothing but Beliefs)" (Lotte), "It's Possible" (Chu Chem), "Our Kind of War" (Company), "Boom!" (Hong Ho), Finale (Company).

Reviews were mostly terrible, and the show ran on Broadway at a big loss for two months.

140. *City of Angels*

Witty spoof of detective movies of the late 1940s, in Los Angeles. The story revolves around such a movie being made. The writer of that movie, Stine, is pitted against his creation, the gumshoe Stone, as the former is preparing his movie script. Michael Blakemore came up with the idea of splitting the stage into two halves. On one side was the black & white world of movie detective Stone, as he cracks his case, and the other half was the color world of the real-life Hollywood of Stine, as he wrote and re-wrote his screenplay. Characters in the real and fictional settings parallel each other. Oolie is Stone's secretary.

Before Broadway. Cy Coleman wanted to do a show about the 1940s, and approached Larry Gelbart, who came up with a private-eye show called *Death is for Suckers*. David Zippel joined the team at this point, and Mr. Gelbart expanded on his libretto, now called *Double Exposure*. The collaborators communicated by fax and Federal Express, as Mr. Gelbart was in L.A., and Zippel & Coleman were in New York. There were nine weeks of rehearsals.

The Broadway Run. VIRGINIA THEATRE, 12/11/89–1/19/92. 24 previews. 878 PERFORMANCES. PRESENTED BY Nick Vanoff, Roger Berlind, Jujamcyn Theatres, Suntory International Corporation, The Shubert Organization; MUSIC: Cy Coleman; LYRICS: David Zippel; BOOK: Larry Gelbart; DIRECTOR: Michael Blakemore; CHOREOGRAPHER: Walter Painter; SETS: Robin Wagner; COSTUMES: Florence Klotz; LIGHTING: Paul Gallo; SOUND: Peter Fitzgerald & Bernard Fox; MUSICAL DIRECTOR: Gordon Lowry Harrell; ORCHESTRATIONS: Billy Byers; VOCAL ARRANGEMENTS: Cy Coleman & Yaron Gershovsky; CAST RECORDING on Columbia; PRESS: Bill Evans & Associates; CASTING: Johnson — Liff & Zerman; GENERAL MANAGER: Ralph Roseman; COMPANY MANAGER: Susan Gustafson; PRODUCTION STAGE MANAGER: Steven Zweigbaum; STAGE MANAGER: Brian Meister; ASSISTANT STAGE MANAGER: Matthew Mundinger. **Cast: Movie Cast**: STONE: James Naughton, *Tom Wopat* (from 12/31/90), *Franc Luz, Tom Galantich, Joel Higgins* (from 8/27/91); ORDERLIES: James Hindman & Tom Galantich; OOLIE: Randy Graff, *Susan Terry* (from 12/31/90), *Carolee Carmello* (from 10/10/91); ALAURA KINGSLEY: Dee Hoty, *Beverly Leech, Jan Maxwell, Linda Thorson*; BIG SIX: Herschel Sparber; SONNY: Raymond Xifo; JIMMY POWERS: Scott Waara,

Bob Walton; ANGEL CITY FOUR: Peter Davis, Amy Jane London, Gary Kahn, Jackie Presti; MUNOZ: Shawn Elliott; OFFICER PASCO: Tom Galantich; BOBBI: Kay McClelland, *Donna Bullock*; IRWIN S. IRVING: Rene Auberjonois, *Charles Levin, Richard Kline* (from 4/23/91); PETER KINGSLEY: Doug Tompos; MARGARET: Susan Terry, *Carolee Carmello* (from 12/31/90), *Elizabeth Ward*; LUTHER KINGSLEY: Keith Perry; DR. MANDRIL: James Cahill, *George Taylor*; MALLORY KINGSLEY: Rachel York, *Karen Fineman*; MAHONEY: James Hindman; YAMATO: Alvin Lum; COMMISSIONER GAINES: Evan Thompson, *Christopher Wynkoop*; MARGIE (MADAME): Eleanor Glockner; BOOTSIE: Jacquey Maltby. **Hollywood Cast**: STINE: Gregg Edelman, *James Hindman* (during Mr. Edelman's vacation, 90–91), *Michael Rupert* (from 12/31/90); BUDDY FIDLER: Rene Auberjonois, *Charles Levin, Richard Kline* (from 4/23/91); SHOESHINE: Evan Thompson, *Christopher Wynkoop*; GABBY, STINE'S WIFE: Kay McClelland, *Donna Bullock*; BARBER: James Cahill, *George Taylor*; DONNA: Randy Graff, *Susan Terry* (from 12/31/90), *Carolee Carmello* (from 10/10/91); ANNA (MASSEUSE): Eleanor Glockner; JIMMY POWERS: Scott Waara, *Bob Walton, Sal Viviano*; ANGEL CITY FOUR: Peter Davis, Amy Jane London, Gary Kahn, Jackie Presti; CARLA HAYWOOD: Dee Hoty, *Beverly Leech, Jan Maxwell, Linda Thorson*; DEL DACOSTA: James Hindman; PANCHO VARGAS: Shawn Elliott; WERNER KRIEGLER: Keith Perry; GERALD PIERCE: Doug Tompos; AVRIL RAINES: Rachel York, *Karen Fineman*; GENE: Tom Galantich; CINEMATOGRAPHER: Alvin Lum; STAND-IN: Susan Terry, *Carolee Carmello, Elizabeth Ward*; HAIRDRESSER: Eleanor Glockner; STUDIO COPS: Herschel Sparber & Raymond Xifo. **Understudies**: Stone/Powers: Tom Galantich; Stine/Munoz: James Hindman; Buddy/Irving/Sonny: James Hindman (89–92), *William Linton* (90–92); Alaura/Carla: Jan Maxwell & Susan Terry (89), *Carolee Carmello* (89–90), *Elizabeth Ward* (90–92); Gabby/Bobbi: Susan Terry (89), *Carolee Carmello* (89–90), *Elizabeth Ward* (90–92); Oolie/Donna/Mallory/Anna/Margie/Hairdresser: Jacquey Maltby; Luther/Werner/Mandril/Big Six: Evan Thompson (89–90), *William Linton* (90–92), *Christopher Wynkoop* (90–92); Barber/Orderly/DaCosta/Gaines/Gene/Mahoney/Pasco/Peter/Gerald: Marcus Neville (89–92), *Alvin Lum* (89–90), *William Linton* (90–92), *Marcus Neville* (90–92); Margaret/Bootsie: Chrissy Faith (89–90), *Millie Whiteside* (90–92), Angel City Four/Swings: Chrissy Faith (89–90), *Millie Whiteside* (90–92), Marcus Neville (89–92); Jan Maxwell. **Orchestra**: KEYBOARDS: Kathy Sommer & Lee Musiker; DRUMS: Dave Ratajczak; BASS: Dave Fink; GUITAR: Bob Rose; PERCUSSION: Charles Descarfino; TRUMPETS: Byron Stripling, Glenn Drewes, Dave Rogers; TROMBONES: Jim Pugh, Sy Berger, George Flynn; FRENCH HORN: Peter Gordon; REEDS: Mike Migliore, Ed Salkin, Bob Steen, Ken Hitchcock, John Campo; CONCERTMISTRESS: Belinda Whitney; VIOLINS: Cenovia Cummins & Carl Kawahara; CELLO: Astrid Schween. **Act I**: **Prelude** Theme from *City of Angels* (Angel City Four & Studio Orchestra); **Scene 1** L.A. County Hospital; **Scene 2** Stone's office; one week earlier: "Double Talk" (Stone & Alaura); **Scene 3** Writer's cell, Master Pictures Studio; **Scene 4** Buddy Fidler's office: "Double Talk" (reprise) (Buddy & Stine); **Scene 5** Stone's office; **Scene 6** Stine's bedroom, the Garden of Allah: "What You Don't Know About Women" (Gabby & Oolie); **Scene 7** Stone's bungalow: "Ya Gotta Look Out for Yourself" (Powers & Angel City Four); **Scene 8** Buddy's office: "The Buddy System" (Buddy & Donna); **Scene 9** Stone's bungalow; **Scene 10** The Blue Note (a cocktail lounge): "With Every Breath I Take" (Bobbi); **Scene 11** Bobbi's dressing room; **Scene 12** Writer's cell; **Scene 13** The Kingsley Mansion; **Scene 14** The solarium: "The Tennis Song" (Stone & Alaura); **Scene 15** The search: "Everybody's Gotta Be Somewhere" (Stone & Angel City Four); **Scene 16** Stone's bungalow: "Lost and Found" (Mallory); **Scene 17** Donna's bedroom; **Scene 18** Stone's bungalow; **Scene 19** L.A. County Morgue; **Scene 20** Buddy's office; **Scene 21** The morgue: "All You Have to Do is Wait" (Munoz, Yamato, Mahoney, Pasco), "You're Nothing without Me" (Stine & Stone). **Act II**: **Scene 1** A recording studio: "Stay with Me" (Powers & Angel City Four); **Scene 2** A Bel Air bedroom; **Scene 3** L.A. County Jail; **Scene 4** Oolie's bedroom: "You Can Always Count on Me" (Oolie); **Scene 5** Donna's bedroom: "You Can Always Count on Me" (reprise) (Donna); **Scene 6** A Bel Air garden; **Scene 7** Buddy's study; **Scene 8** The jail; **Scene 9** Buddy's study; **Scene 10** Alaura's bedroom: "Alaura's Theme" (instrumental); **Scene 11** Buddy's office; **Scene 12** Stine's apartment, New York: "It Needs Work" (Gabby); **Scene 13** The Red Room: "L.A. Blues" (instrumental),

"With Every Breath I Take" (reprise) (Stone & Bobbi); *Scene 14* The Kingsley solarium; *Scene 15* Writer's cell: "Funny" (Stine); *Scene 16* A sound stage, Master Pictures Studio: "I'm Nothing without You" (a reprise of "You're Nothing without Me" (Stone, Stine, Gabby).

Reviews were mostly favorable. The show won Tonys for musical, score, book, set, and for James Naughton and Randy Graff. It was also nominated for direction of a musical, costumes, lighting, and for Gregg Edelman and Rene Auberjonois.

After Broadway. TOUR. Opened on 6/4/91, at the Shubert Theatre, Los Angeles. *Cast*: STONE: James Naughton, *Jeff McCarthy, Barry Williams*; STINE: Stephen Bogardus, *Jordan Leeds*; BOBBIE/GABBY: Leslie Denniston; OOLIE/DONNA: Randy Graff, *Betsy Joslyn, Catherine Cox*; ALAURA: Lauren Mitchell; BUDDY'S NEPHEW/MAHONEY/ORDERLY: Jordan Leeds; JIMMY: Bob Walton; BARBER/MANDRIL: Doug Carfrae; CINEMATOGRAPHER/CORONER: Alvin Ing; IRVING/BUDDY: Charles Levin; LUTHER/KRIEGLER: Jack Manning.

PRINCE OF WALES THEATRE, London, 3/30/93. DIRECTOR: Michael Blakemore. *Cast*: STINE: Martin Smith; STONE: Roger Allam; CARLA: Susannah Fellows; JIMMY: Maurice Clarke; DONNA: Hayden Gwynne; GABBY: Fiona Hendley; BUDDY: Henry Goodman; MUNOZ: David Schofield.

MCCALLUM THEATRE, Palm Desert, Calif., 2/20/03–2/23/03. In concert. Produced with the co-operation of the authors. DIRECTOR: Joe Leonardo. *Cast*: BUDDY: Hal Linden; STONE: Burke Moses; ALAURA/ CARLA: Marguerite MacIntyre; STINE: R.F. Daley; DONNA/OOLIE: Barbara Passolt; BOBBI/GABBY: Tami Tappan Damaino.

141. *The Civil War*

An American musical event. Also called *The Civil War: Our Story in Song*.

Before Broadway. The show began as a concept album (actually a CD), which after several delays was finally released by Atlantic Records on 9/1/98 (in Houston anyway; the national release was 10/27/98), just before the world premiere at the Alley Theatre, in Houston. The CD featured the following songs (with artists in parentheses): "Brother, My Brother" (Michael Lanning), "By the Sword"/"Sons of Dixie" (Broadway All-Stars), "Tell My Father" (Kevin Sharp), "Missing You, My Bill" (Deana Carter), "Freedom's Child" (Hootie & the Blowfish), "Virginia" (Gene Miller), "Oh, Be Joyful!" (Broadway All-Stars), "Father, How Long?" (Michel Bell), "I Never Knew His Name" (Linda Eder), "Old Gray Coat" (Trace Adkins), "Five Boys" (Betty Buckley), "River Jordan" (BeBe Winans), "Honor of Your Name" (Tisha Yearwood), "Sarah" (Carl Anderson), "I'll Never Pass This Way Again" (Tracy Lawrence), "Northbound Train" (John Popper & Friends), "Last Waltz for Dixie" (John Berry), "The Glory" (Michael Lanning, Gene Miller, Linda Eder, Orchestra, Choir, Broadway All-Stars), "How Many Devils" (Broadway All-Stars), "Greenback" (Dr. John), "With These Hands" (Bryan White & Amy Grant), "Candle in the Window" (Linda Eder), "Regimental Drummer" (Michael English), "Judgment Day" (Shiloh), "The Day the Sun Stood Still" (Travis Tritt), "Someday" (Patti LaBelle). Narration: Charlie Daniels (Narrator), James Garner (Lincoln), Danny Glover (Frederick Douglass), Ellen Burstyn (The Maid), Maya Angelou (The Voice of Slavery).

ALLEY THEATRE, Houston, 9/16/98–11/1/98. Rehearsals for the Alley (the Alley had commissioned this musical) had begun on 8/11/98, and previews ran 9/8/98–9/15/98. This Alley run was considered a regional production, not a pre–Broadway tryout. The sub-title was changed from *An American Musical* to *Our Story in Song*. DIRECTOR: Nick Corley; CHOREOGRAPHER: George Faison; SETS: Douglas W. Schmidt; COSTUMES: Mark Wendland; LIGHTING: Howell Binkley; SOUND: Karl Richardson; ORCHESTRATIONS: Kim Scharnberg; MUSICAL SUPERVISOR: Jason Howland; VOCAL DIRECTOR: Dave Clemmons. *Cast*: THE CIVILIANS: SARAH: Irene Molloy; NURSE HANNA ROPES: Linda Eder; MRS. LYDIA BIXBY/VIOLET: Beth Leavel; FELL: Jesse Lenat; MABEL: Hope Harris. THE ENSLAVED: CLAYTON: Michel Bell; BENJAMIN: Lawrence Clayton; DOUGLASS: Keith Byron Kirk; THOMAS: Wayne Pretlow; BESSIE: Cheryl Freeman; HOPE: Capathia Jenkins; LIZA: Cassandra White. UNION ARMY: LOCHRAN: Michael Lanning; MCEWEN: Gilles Chiasson;

NATHANIEL TAYLOR: Matt Bogart; HORATIO TAYLOR: Ron Sharpe; CHARLES SPENCER: Bart Shatto; BYRON: Royal Reed; BARTHOLOMEW PATRICK ANDERSON: David Bryant. CONFEDERATE ARMY: PIERCE: Gene Miller; STEWART: David Lutken; BARKSDALE: Kim Strauss; FRANKLIN: Dave Clemmons; STEVENS: Jim Price; SAM WELLES: John Sawyer; BEAUREGARD: Timothy Browning. PIT SINGERS: David Michael Felty, Hope Harris, Christopher Roberts. It was revised again. *Act I*: "Brother, My Brother" (Lochran), "By the Sword"/"Sons of Dixie" (Union & Confederate Soldiers), "Tell My Father" (Taylor), "Freedom's Child" (Douglass & the Enslaved), "Missing You (My Bill)" (Sarah), "Virginia" (Pierce), "The Peculiar Institution" (The Enslaved), "If Prayin' Were Horses" (The Tolers), "Greenback" (Autolycus, Violet, Mabel), "Judgment Day" (Pierce, Lochran, Union & Confederate Soldiers), "The Day the Sun Stood Still" (Barksdale), "I Never Knew His Name" (Hannah), "Father, How Long" (Clayton), "River Jordan" (Reynolds & the Enslaved). *Act II*: "I'll Never Pass This Way Again" (Stewart), "How Many Devils" (Union & Confederate Soldiers), "Five Boys" (Mrs. Bixby), "Candle in the Window" (Hope Jackson & Hannah), "Someday" (Bessie & the Enslaved), "The Honor of Your Name" (Sarah), "Northbound Train" (Lochran), "Last Waltz for Dixie" (Pierce & Company), "The Glory" (Lochran, Pierce, the Angel, Company).

It tried out in New Haven, 2/17/99–3/7/99. 1 preview on 2/16/99. DIRECTOR: Jerry Zaks (he had been announced as director back in 10/98). These numbers were cut during tryouts: "Brother, My Brother," "An Angel's Lullaby," "I Never Knew His Name," "The Day the Sun Stood Still," and "Five Boys."

The Broadway Run. ST. JAMES THEATRE, 4/22/99–6/13/99. 35 previews from 3/23/99. 61 PERFORMANCES. PRESENTED BY Pierre Cossette & PACE Theatrical Group/SFX Entertainment, and Bomurwil Productions, Kathleen Raitt, Jujamcyn Theatres; MUSIC: Frank Wildhorn; LYRICS: Jack Murphy; BOOK: Gregory Boyd & Frank Wildhorn; INSPIRED BY many voices: Sojourner Truth & Abraham Lincoln; Walt Whitman, Sullivan Ballou, Frederick Douglass; Hannah Ropes & R.E. Lee; Henry Kyd Douglas (2nd Virginia) & Henry Pearson (6th New Hampshire), among others; DIRECTOR: Jerry Zaks; CHOREOGRAPHER: Luis Perez; BATTLES: David Leong; SETS: Douglas W. Schmidt; COSTUMES: William Ivey Long; LIGHTING: Paul Gallo; SOUND: Karl Richardson; MUSICAL SUPERVISOR: Jason Howland; MUSICAL DIRECTOR: Jeff Lams; ORCHESTRATIONS: Kim Scharnberg; VOCAL DIRECTOR: Dave Clemmons; PRESS: Echo New York, Norman Zagier; CASTING: Dave Clemmons & Lynne Bond; GENERAL MANAGEMENT: 101 Productions; COMPANY MANAGER: David Auster; STAGE MANAGER: Rick Steiger; ASSISTANT STAGE MANAGER: Jason Brouillard. *Cast*: UNION ARMY: CAPTAIN EMMETT LOCHRAN: Michael Lanning; SERGEANT PATRICK ANDERSON: Rod Weber; SERGEANT BYRON RICHARDSON: Royal Reed; CORPORAL WILLIAM MCEWEN: Gilles Chiasson; PRIVATE CONRAD BOCK: Ron Sharpe; PRIVATE ELMORE HOTCHKISS: Bart Shatto; PRIVATE NATHANIEL TAYLOR: John Sawyer. CONFEDERATE ARMY: CAPTAIN BILLY PIERCE: Gene Miller; SERGEANT VIRGIL FRANKLIN: Dave Clemmons; CORPORAL JOHN BEAUREGARD: Mike Eldred; CORPORAL HENRY STEWART: David M. Lutken; PRIVATE DARIUS BARKSDALE: Anthony Galde; PRIVATE CYRUS STEVENS: Jim Price; PRIVATE SAM TAYLOR: Matt Bogart. OTHERS IN CAST: FREDERICK DOUGLASS: Keith Byron Kirk; CLAYTON TOLER, A SLAVE: Michel Bell; BESSIE TOLER, HIS WIFE: Cheryl Freeman; BENJAMIN REYNOLDS, A SLAVE: Lawrence Clayton; EXTER THOMAS: Wayne W. Pretlow; HARRIET JACKSON: Capathia Jenkins; LIZA HUGHES: Cassandra White; AUTOLYCUS FELL, A PIMP: Leo Burmester; AUCTIONEER'S ASSISTANT: Dave Clemmons; SARAH MCEWEN, WILLIAM'S WIFE: Irene Molloy; VIOLET, A PROSTITUTE: Hope Harris; MABEL: Beth Leavel; MRS. BIXBY: Beth Leavel; NURSE: Hope Harris; VOICE OF PRESIDENT LINCOLN: David M. Lutken; PIT SINGERS: David Michael Felty, Monique Midgette, Raun Ruffin, Hope Harris. *Understudies*: Lochran/ Autolycus: David M. Lutken & Jim Price; McEwen: Mike Eldred & Ron Sharpe; Pierce: Mike Eldred & Royal Reed; Sam: Royal Reed & Ron Sharpe; Bessie: Capathia Jenkins & Monique Midgette; Douglass/Toler/ Reynolds: Wayne W. Pretlow & Raun Ruffin; Harriet: Cassandra White & Monique Midgette; Sarah: Kristine Fraelich & Hope Harris; Violet/Mabel: Kristine Fraelich; Mrs. Bixby: Hope Harris & Kristine Fraelich. *Swings*: David Michael Felty, Monique Midgette, Chris Roberts, Raun Ruffin. *Musicians*: PIANO: Jeff Lams; KEYBOARD: John

Korba; GUITARS: Scott Kuney, Jon Herington, Gordon Titcomb; BASS: Bill Holcomb; DRUMS: Warren Odze; HARMONICA: Michael Rubin; TROMBONE: Birch Johnson; TRUMPET: Wayne duMaine; WOODWINDS: Charlie Pillow; VIOLIN: Carol Sharar; CELLO: Laura Bontrager; PERCUSSION: Roger Squitero. *Act I*: "A House Divided" (The Citizens), "Freedom's Child" (Douglass & the Other Abolitionists), "By the Sword/Sons of Dixie" (The Armies), "Tell My Father" (Sam), "The Peculiar Institution" (The Enslaved), "If Prayin' Were Horses" (Toler & Bessie), "Greenback" (Autolycus, Mabel, Violet), "Missing You (My Bill)" (Sarah), "Judgment Day" (Pierce, Lochran, Sam, Armies), "Father, How Long?" (Toler), "Someday" (Harriet, Bessie, Others), "I'll Never Pass This Way Again" (Stewart), "How Many Devils?" (The Armies). *Act II*: "Virginia" (Pierce), "Candle in the Window" (Harriet), "Oh! Be Joyful!" (Autolycus, Richardson, Bock, Hotchkiss), "You Picked the Wrong Day, Mister" ("The Hospital") (Mrs. Bixby, Nurse, Union Soldiers, Toler), "If Prayin' Were Horses" (reprise) (Toler & Bessie), "River Jordan" (Reynolds & Others), "Sarah" (McEwen), "The Honor of Your Name" (Sarah), "Greenback" (reprise) (Autolycus & Violet), "Northbound Train" (Lochran), "Last Waltz for Dixie" (Pierce & Confederate Soldiers), "The Glory" (Lochran, Douglass, Reynolds, Full Company).

On Broadway it got bad reviews. On 6/8/99 closing notices were posted. It received Tony nominations for musical and score.

After Broadway. The Post-Broadway national tour was revised again, with a new concept. One leading player, the Union Captain, was played in alternate cities by Larry Gatlin and John Schneider. Aside from that the cast would play no set roles. The tour began rehearsals on 12/6/99, and, after sneak preview in Charleston, SC, on 1/13/00, it opened in Cincinnati, 1/18/00. PRESENTED BY Networks; DIRECTOR: Stephen Rayne; CHOREOGRAPHER: Ken Roberson; LIGHTING: Howell Binkley. *Cast*: Michael Lanning, Keith Byron Kirk, Mike Eldred, Bart Shatto, John Ayers, Dan Cooney, Royal Reed, Christopher Roberts, BeBe Winans. The songs were in a different order, and added were: "Brother, My Brother," "Old Gray Coat," "I Never Knew His Name," and "The Day the Sun Stood Still." The tour ended 6/25/00, at the Buell Theatre, Denver; then it resumed on 2/27/01, at the Paramount Theatre, Seattle.

142. *A Class Act*

A revue about Ed Kleban, the difficult, cranky, even neurotic, but charming man who wrote the lyrics to *A Chorus Line*. Set on the stage of the Shubert Theatre, and other locations, between Ed's graduation from college in 1955 and 1988, the year after his death of cancer, age 48. It starts in 1988. Taking existing unpublished music and lyrics by Ed (about 100 songs, all told, which he willed to his friends), writers Linda Kline and Lonny Price developed a piece that "tells the story of a man who discovers that fulfillment isn't measured by success; it's defined by what you do for love." The rest of the cast play his songwriting pals, friends & lovers. Sophie, who was from the Bronx, was his best friend; her character was based on various people, mostly National Public Radio's Susan Stamberg. Lucy has often been rumored to be based on Linda Kline, but she hotly denies this. Mona is a sexpot. Lehman was Ed's mentor.

Before Broadway. Linda Kline, Ed's long-time companion (they met in 1978), had been committed for some time since his death to bringing his unpublished work to light. She and Lonny Price began developing the piece in 1995, as a fictional version of the BMI Musical Theatre Workshop where Ed had been member and teacher. At the third Musical Theatre Works reading Marty Bell, the producer, was in the audience, and he changed the focus of the show to a life of Ed Kleban. It was originally produced by Manhattan Theatre Club, in association with Musical Theatre Works (headed by Lonny Price), and played at the MTC's STAGE II. Ed had, more than anything professionally, wanted to be remembered as both composer and lyricist, not just as the man who wrote the lyrics for *A Chorus Line* (Marvin Hamlisch wrote the music for that one). Lonny Price stepped into the role of Ed at the last minute.

42 previews began on 10/3/00, and it opened on 11/9/00 (a date pushed back from 10/31/00 so the show could be refined more). It had the same basic crew credits as for the subsequent Broadway production, except CHOREOGRAPHER: Scott Wise (with some help from Marguerite Derricks, who eventually replaced Mr. Wise); LIGHTING: Kevin Adams; MUSICAL DIRECTOR: Todd Ellison. *Cast*: ED: Lonny Price; LUCY: Carolee Carmello; ENGEL: Jonathan Freeman; SOPHIE: Randy Graff; FELICIA: Julia Murney; MONA: Nancy Kathryn Anderson; BOBBY/MICHAEL: David Hibbard; CHARLEY/MARVIN: Ray Wills. On 11/13/00 RCA Victor recorded the sell-out show for a 2/20/01 release. On 11/16/00 rumors began of a Broadway move to the Ambassador, and on 11/17/00 these were confirmed. However, there were a few problems keeping the cast intact. Carolee Carmello was five months pregnant by 11/00, and Julia Murney had a conflicting schedule beginning in 1/01. The MTC closing date was extended from 12/3/00 to 12/10/00 (it ran for 38 PERFORMANCES). Broadway rehearsals began 1/01. On 1/3/01 the Broadway cast was announced, and an official opening date of 3/12/01 (on 2/14/01 it was brought forward a day, to 3/11/01). The show had been slightly revised since the MTC production. For example, two songs were deleted, and another ("Don't Do it Again") added. In order to adapt Ed's songs for a narrative, the creators enlisted Brian Stein and Glenn Slater to write additional lyrics.

The Broadway Run. AMBASSADOR THEATRE, 3/11/01–6/10/01. 30 previews from 2/14/01. 105 PERFORMANCES. The Manhattan Theatre Club production, PRESENTED BY Marty Bell, Chase Mishkin, Arielle Tepper, in association with Robyn Goodman & Tokyo Broadcasting System/Kumiko Yoshii; MUSIC/LYRICS: Edward Kleban; BOOK: Linda Kline & Lonny Price; ADDITIONAL LYRICS: Brian Stein & Glenn Slater; ADDITIONAL MATERIAL: David Wolf; DIRECTOR: Lonny Price; CHOREOGRAPHER: Marguerite Derricks; SETS: James Noone; COSTUMES: Carrie Robbins; LIGHTING: Kevin Adams; SOUND: Acme Sound Partners; MUSICAL DIRECTOR/ADDITIONAL ARRANGEMENTS: David Loud; ORCHESTRATIONS: Larry Hochman; VOCAL ARRANGEMENTS/DANCE & INCIDENTAL MUSIC: Todd Ellison; CAST RECORDING on RCA Victor; PRESS: Richard Kornberg; CASTING: Jay Binder; GENERAL MANAGER: Donald Frantz; COMPANY MANAGER: Richard Biederman; PRODUCTION STAGE MANAGER: Jeffrey M. Markowitz; STAGE MANAGER: Heather Fields; ASSISTANT STAGE MANAGER: Jamie Chandler-Torns. *Cast:* LUCY: Donna Bullock; BOBBY/MICHAEL BENNETT, ET AL: David Hibbard; ED KLEBAN: Lonny Price (1), *Danny Burstein* (the standby; he went on about 6 times for Mr. Price), *Adam Heller* (went on 6/2/01 evening & 6/3/01 matinee, and again on 6/5/01, when Lonny Price was in hospital and Danny Burstein had a broken leg); FELICIA: Sara Ramirez; LEHMAN ENGEL: Patrick Quinn; CHARLEY/MARVIN HAMLISCH, ET AL: Jeff Blumenkrantz; MONA: Nancy Anderson (until 6/3/01), *Michele Ragusa* (from 6/01); SOPHIE: Randy Graff (2). **Standbys**: Ed: Danny Burstein, *Adam Heller*; Lehman: Danny Burstein & Jonathan Hadley; Bobby/Charley: Jonathan Hadley; Mona: Jamie Chandler-Torns; Lucy/Sophie/Felicia: Ann Van Cleave. UNDERSTUDY: Lehman: Adam Heller. **Orchestra**: KEYBOARDS: David Loud & Dan Riddle; WOODWINDS: Eddie Salkin & William Sneddon; TRUMPETS: Hollis Burridge & Matthew Peterson; TROMBONE: Patrick Hallaran; DRUMS: Peter Grant; BASS: Ray Kilday. *Act I*: *Scene 1* The Shubert Theatre; 1988: "Light on My Feet" (written in early 1980s; add l: Brian Stein) (Ed & Company); *Scene 2* Hillside Hospital; 1958: "The Fountain in the Garden" (written for *Gallery*, a show that never went beyond readings & workshops) (Company), "One More Beautiful Song" (written in the mid–1980s for *Musical Comedy*) (Ed & Sophie); *Scene 3* The Shubert Theatre; 1988; *Scene 4* The BMI Musical Theatre Workshop; 1966: "Fridays at Four" (from *Musical Comedy*) (Company), "Bobby's Song" (Bobby), "Charm Song" (written in early 1970s)(Lehman & Company), "Paris Through the Window" (inspired by a Chagal painting) (from *Gallery*) (add l: Glenn Slater) (Ed, Bobby, Charley); *Scene 5* Ed's apartment; 1966: "Mona" (written in early 1980s; inspired by the painting *The Mona Lisa*) (Mona), "Making up Ways" (Ed) [dropped before Broadway]; *Scene 6* Recording studio/Columbia Records; 1966–1971: "Under Separate Cover" (written for *Subject to Change*, an unproduced musical in the early 1970s about divorce, with book by Peter Stone) (Lucy, Ed, Sophie), "Don't Do it Again" (a spec song for the musical version of Neil Simon film *The Heartbreak Kid*. One of Ed's last songs. Mr. Simon didn't hire him) (Felicia & Ed), "Gauguin's

Shoes" (written in the early 1970s; inspired by the Van Gogh painting of Gauguin's shoes) (from *Gallery*) (Ed & Company), "Don't Do it Again" (reprise) (Lehman); *Scene 7* Outside the Royal Alexandra Theatre, Toronto; 1972: "Follow Your Star" (from an unproduced musical version of the 1922 movie comedy *Merton of the Movies*) (Sophie & Ed). *Act II*: *Scene 1* The Shubert Theatre; 1988: Manhattan, 1973: "Better" (from *Merton of the Movies*. Barbra Streisand recorded it, but it was cut from album) (Ed & Company) [it had previously been used in Phyllis Newman's 1979 one-woman Off Broadway revue *The Madwoman of Central Park West*]; *Scene 2* Sophie's laboratory; 1973: "Scintillating Sophie" (a very early Kleban song) (Ed), "The Next Best Thing to Love" (written for Michael Bennett's last musical, *Scandal*, which Mr. Kleban quit) (Sophie); *Scene 3* Central Park; 1973; *Scene 4* Michael Bennett's studio; 1973: "Broadway Boogie Woogie" (inspired by a Mondrian painting at the Museum of Modern Art) (Lucy); *Scene 5* The Public Theatre; 1974–1975: "*A Chorus Line* Excerpt" (from *A Chorus Line*, the famous 1975 Michael Bennett musical; excerpts from the numbers "At the Ballet," "One," and "What I Did for Love"); *Scene 6* Manhattan; 1975–1985: "Better"(reprise) (Ed & Company), "I Choose You" (from *Subject to Change*) (Ed & Lucy), "The Nightmare" (Ed); *Scene 7* Sophie's laboratory; 1985: "Say Something Funny" (from *Merton of the Movies*) (Company); *Scene 8* The BMI Musical Theatre Workshop; 1986: "I Won't Be There" (Ed), "When the Dawn Breaks" (Ed) [dropped before Broadway]; *Scene 9* St. Vincent's Hospital; 1987: "Self Portrait" (written in 1981; from *Gallery*) (Ed); *Scene 10* The Shubert Theatre; 1988: "Self Portrait" (reprise) (Company).

It got mixed reviews. The decision to make it a show without "stars" proved costly. By early 5/01, with a constantly low box-office, the producers were looking for stars to replace the leads. If the show were to survive, Nancy Anderson and Lonny Price had to be replaced with "names." Randy Graff was to stay. Jason Alexander was one of the names rumored. Nancy Anderson left on 6/3/01 for another project anyway. On 5/18/01 standby Danny Burstein was injured in a softball accident, and Lonny Price was without a standby for a week, until Adam Heller came in. Also on 5/18/01 a 5/20/01 closing date was rumored, despite no notices having been posted. Also on that date Michele Ragusa was announced as Nancy Anderson's replacement as Mona. By early June Lonny Price was suffering from a perforated colon, and although he missed some performances he was present at the Tonys on 6/3/01. Ed's dream to remembered as composer/musician came real, posthumously, as he was nominated for best score at the 2001 Tonys. Other nominations: musical, book, orchestrations, and Randy Graff. On 6/5/01 a closing date of 6/10 was announced.

After Broadway. PASADENA PLAYHOUSE, 5/3/02–6/16/02 (the original dates were to have been 7/7/02–8/11/02, with previews from 6/28/02). This was the West Coast premiere. DIRECTOR: Lonny Price; CHOREOGRAPHER: Marguerite Derricks; SETS: James Noone; COSTUMES: Carrie Robbins; LIGHTING: Kevin Adams. *Cast:* LUCY: Donna Bullock; ED: Robert Picardo; ENGEL: Lenny Wolpe; BOBBY/MICHAEL: Andrew Palermo; FELICIA: Nikki Crawford; SOPHIE: Luba Mason; MONA: Michelle Duffy; CHARLEY/MARVIN: Will Jude. *Standby*: Craig A. Meyer.

The Pasadena Playhouse production ran at the AKASAKA ACT THEATRE, Tokyo, 7/12/02–7/28/02. PRESENTED BY Tokyo Broadcasting System/Kumiko Yoshii; DIRECTOR: Lonny Price. It had most of the original Broadway cast, except SOPHIE: Michele Pawk; MONA: Michelle Duffy.

STUDIO THEATRE, Washington, DC, 5/14/03–6/22/03. DIRECTOR: Serge Seiden; MUSICAL DIRECTOR: George Fulginiti-Shakar. *Cast*: ED: Bobby Smith; BOBBY: Tony Capone; SOPHIE: Roseanne Medina; FELICIA: Mia Whang; MONA: Cathy Carey; ENGEL: Leo Erickson; CHARLEY/MARVIN: Eric Sutton.

143. *Cleavage*

Close to where the heart is. The pursuit of love, by various couples, young and old.

Before Broadway. Presented very successfully in BILOXI, HOUSTON and NEW ORLEANS by Up Front Productions (Braxton Glasgow III,

William J. O'Brien III, and David E. Fite) who also produced the cast album.

The Broadway Run. PLAYHOUSE THEATRE, 6/23/82. 6 previews. 1 PERFORMANCE. PRESENTED BY Up Front Productions; MUSIC/LYRICS: Buddy Sheffield; BOOK: Buddy & David Sheffield; DIRECTOR: Rita Baker; CHOREOGRAPHER: Alton Geno; SET SUPERVISORS/COSTUMES/LIGHTING: Michael Hotopp & Paul de Pass; SETS: Morris Taylor; COSTUMES: James M. Miller; SOUND: Theodore Jacobi; CONDUCTOR/ARRANGEMENTS: Keith Thompson; PRESS: Susan L. Schulman; GENERAL MANAGEMENT: Theatre Now; ASSISTANT COMPANY MANAGER: Kathryn Frawley; PRODUCTION STAGE MANAGER: Gary Ware; STAGE MANAGER: Arlene Grayson. *Cast:* Daniel David, Tom Elias, Mark Fite, Terese Gargiulo, Marsha Trigg Miller, Jay Rogers, Sharon Scruggs, Dick Sheffield, Pattie Tierce. *Orchestra*: KEYBOARDS: Keith Thompson; PIANO/SYNTHESIZER: Philip Fortbenberry; BASS: Jeff Myers; DRUMS: Howard Joines. *Act I*: "Cleavage" (Ensemble), "Puberty" (Mark & Ensemble), "Only Love" (Sharon & Dan), "Surprise Me" (Terese), "Reprise Me" (Terese & Mark), "Boys Will Be Girls" (Jay & Dancers), "Give Me an And" (Marsha & Dancers), "Just Another Song" (Mark), "Believe in Me, or I'll Be Leavin' You" (Pattie & Dick). *Act II*: "The Thrill of the Chase" (Tom, Mark, Dan), "Lead 'em Around by the Nose" (Marsha, Pattie, Terese), "Sawing a Couple in Half" (Jay), "Only Love" (reprise) (Terese), "Bringing up Badger" (Dan & Ensemble), "Voices of the Children" (Ensemble), "All the Lovely Ladies" (Tom), "Living in Sin" (Tom, Pattie, Ensemble), Finale (Ensemble).

144. *Coco*

The story begins in the late fall of 1953, and ends in the late spring of 1954, a period of time when Coco has been in retirement for 15 years. The action takes place in the Maison Chanel, on rue Cambon, Paris — either in the salon, the apartment above, or in Coco's memory. She makes a flop comeback when she re-opens her salon. She goes bankrupt but four department stores in the USA save her — Bloomingdales, Saks, Ohrbach's, and Best. Her life is revealed in a series of flashbacks. The finale featured a fashion show of Coco's designs from 1918 to 1939.

Before Broadway. It took Freddie Brisson years to convince Coco Chanel to have her story musicalized for the Broadway stage. It also took a long time to convince Alan Jay Lerner to do the show, but he finally signed on in 1965, after his *On a Clear Day You Can See Forever* opened on the Broadway stage. Frederick Loewe was asked many times to collaborate with Mr. Lerner, but he never wanted in. There was talk of producer Brisson's wife, Rosalind Russell, playing Coco, but she apparently didn't like Lerner's script. When Miss Chanel learned that Miss Hepburn was going to play her, she was very excited, until she learned that the Hepburn in question was Katherine and not Audrey. Also, Miss Chanel was severely disappointed when Alan Jay Lerner decided to present the story of Coco Chanel as an older woman, rather than her story in the 1920s and 30s which is what had been agreed upon between Mr. Lerner and herself. Paramount funded *Coco* entirely, to the tune of $900,000, including a record $160,000 of Cecil Beaton costumes. Rehearsals began 9/29/69. It was a 2½ hour production, with Kate on the set all but 12 minutes. The complex and unwieldy revolving set prohibited out of town tryouts. The number "Someone on Your Side" was cut before Broadway.

The Broadway Run. MARK HELLINGER THEATRE, 12/18/69–10/3/70. 40 previews. 332 PERFORMANCES. PRESENTED BY Frederick Brisson for Brisson Productions, and Montfort Productions (Alan Jay Lerner); MUSIC: Andre Previn; LYRICS/BOOK: Alan Jay Lerner; BASED ON the life of couturiere Gabrielle "Coco" Chanel (1883–1971); DIRECTOR: Michael Benthall (with help from Michael Bennett); CHOREOGRAPHER: Michael Bennett; ASSOCIATE CHOREOGRAPHER: Bob Avian; ASSISTANT CHOREOGRAPHER: Graciela Daniele; SETS/COSTUMES: Cecil Beaton; LIGHTING: Thomas Skelton; FILM SEQUENCES produced by Milton Olshin and directed by Fred Lemoine; MUSICAL DIRECTOR: Robert Emmett Dolan; ORCHESTRATIONS: Hershy Kay; DANCE MUSIC CONTINUITY: Harold Wheeler; CAST RECORDING on Paramount; PRESS: Lee Solters, Harvey

B. Sabinson, Leo Stern, Edie Kean; PRODUCTION SUPERVISOR: Stone Widney; GENERAL MANAGER: Ben Rosenberg; COMPANY MANAGER: Ralph Roseman; PRODUCTION STAGE MANAGER: Jerry Adler; STAGE MANAGER: Edward Preston; ASSISTANT STAGE MANAGER: Robert L. Borod. *Cast:* GABRIELLE "COCO" CHANEL: Katharine Hepburn (1) ✩, (until 8/1/70), *Danielle Darrieux* (from 8/3/70); LOUIS GREFF: George Rose (2); PIGNOL: Jeanne Arnold (6); HELENE: Maggie Task; SEBASTIAN BAYE: Rene Auberjonois (5); ARMAND: Al DeSio; ALBERT: Jack Beaber; DOCATON: Eve March; GEORGES: David Holliday (4); LOUBLAYE: Gene Varrone; VARNE: Shirley Potter; MARIE: Margot Travers; JEANINE: Rita O'Connor; CLAIRE: Graciela Daniele; JULIETTE: Lynn Winn; MADELAINE: Carolyn Kirsch; LUCILLE: Diane Phillips; COLETTE: Rosemarie Heyer; SIMONE: Charlene Ryan; SOLANGE: Suzanne Rogers; NOELLE: Gale Dixon (3), *Suzanne Rogers* (from 9/28/70); DR. PETITJEAN: Richard Woods; CLAUDE: David Thomas; THE (FOUR) BUYERS: DWIGHT BERKWIT, OHRBACH'S: Will B. Able; EUGENE BERNSTONE, SAKS: Robert Fitch; RONNY GINSBORN, BLOOMINGDALE'S: Chad Block; PHIL ROSENBERRY, BEST: Dan Siretta; LAPIDUS: Gene Varrone; NADINE: Leslie Daniel. ON FILM: GRAND DUKE ALEXANDROVITCH: Bob Avian; GRAND DUKE'S VOICE: Jack Dabdoub; CHARLES, DUKE OF GLENALLEN: Michael Allinson; JULIAN LESAGE: Paul Dumont; PAPA: Jon Cypher [end of film sequence]. MODELS/SEAMSTRESSES/CUSTOMERS/FITTERS/ETC: Vicki Allen, Oscar Antony, Karin Baker, Roy Barry, Kathy Bartosh, Kathie Dalton, Alice Glenn, Maureen Hopkins, William James, Linda Jorgens, Tresha Kelly, Nancy Killmer (a seamstress), Richard Marr (a lawyer), Jan Metternich, Maralyn Miles, JoAnn Ogawa, Don Percassi, Jean Preece, Ann Reinking, Skiles Ricketts, Marianne Selbert, Pamela Serpe, Gerald Teijelo, Bonnie Walker. *Standby:* Coco: Joan Copeland. *Act I:* Overture (Orchestra); *Scene 1* The salon: "But That's the Way You Are" (Alex) [this number was dropped when Danielle Darrieux took over as Coco], "The World Belongs to the Young" (Coco, Greff, Sebastian, Pignol, Company), "Let's Go Home" (Georges); *Scene 2* The apartment: "Mademoiselle Cliche de Paris" (Coco), "On the Corner of the Rue Cambon" (Coco), "The Money Rings Out Like Freedom" (Coco & Ensemble); *Scene 3* The salon: "A Brand New Dress" (Noelle); *Scene 4* The dressing room: "A Woman is How She Loves" (Georges); *Scene 5* The apartment: "Gabrielle" (Papa), "Coco" (Coco); *Scene 6* The salon: "The Preparation" (Coco & Company). *Act II:* Entr'acte; *Scene 1* The salon: "Fiasco" (Sebastian & Simon), "When Your Lover Says Goodbye" (Greff), "Coco" (reprise) (Coco); *Scene 2* The apartment: "Ohrbach's, Bloomingdale's, Best & Saks" (The Buyers), "Ohrbach's, Bloomingdale's, Best & Saks" (reprise) (Coco & Ensemble); *Scene 3* The salon: "Always Mademoiselle" (Coco & Mannequins).

It had the largest box-office advance in Broadway history, and was the first Broadway show to charge $15 per evening performance (but it may have been worth it just to hear Miss Hepburn say "shit!" as her first word in Act II). The show was panned on Broadway. This was Ann Reinking's first talking part on Broadway (which consisted of the line: "You better get your sundial fixed"). Miss Hepburn quit after nine months (as per her contract), and was replaced by Danielle Darrieux, who couldn't sustain it, and business fell of drastically. Coco Chanel never saw the show about herself. It won Tonys for costumes and for Rene Auberjonois, and was also nominated for musical, direction of a musical, choreography, and for Katharine Hepburn and George Rose. Paramount paid $2.75 million for the film rights, but it was never made.

After Broadway. TOUR. Opened on 1/11/71, at the Public Music Hall, Cleveland, and closed on 6/26/71, at the Dorothy Chandler Pavilion, Los Angeles. Coco Chanel died the day before the opening. Several characters were either dropped, added, re-named or shifted about in order. Many said this was a better production than Broadway. *Cast:* COCO: Katherine Hepburn; LOUIS: George Rose; ARMAND: Al DeSio; PIGNOL: Jeanne Arnold; PETITJEAN: Richard Woods; DWIGHT: Will B. Able; GRAND DUKE: Bob Avian; GRAND DUKE'S VOICE: Jack Dabdoub; CHARLES: Michael Allinson; LUCILLE: Diane Phillips; SIMONE: Charlene Ryan; HELENE: Joan Shea; SEBASTIAN: Daniel Davis; GEORGES: Don Chastain; ADRIENNE: Sandahl Bergman; NOELLE: Lana Shaw, *Gale Dixon*; ZIZI: Graziella. *Understudy:* Zizi: Sandahl Bergman.

TOUR. Ginger Rogers headed a tour, with 8 cities on the schedule, in the fall of 1971. She refused to say the infamous four-letter word.

145. *Come Summer*

Set in the towns and surrounding countryside along the Connecticut River, in New England, during the peddlers' season (early spring to late fall) of 1840, just before the factories took over. A traveling peddler's career is faced with extinction by the Industrial Revolution.

Before Broadway. It tried out in Boston. Burt Shevelove came in to help with direction and libretto. The number "How Much is Far Away" was cut.

The Broadway Run. LUNT—FONTANNE THEATRE, 3/18/69–3/22/69. 14 previews. 7 PERFORMANCES. PRESENTED BY Albert W. Selden & Hal James; MUSIC: David Baker; LYRICS: Will Holt; BOOK: Will Holt (book doctored by Burt Shevelove); BASED ON the 1954 novel *Rainbow on the Road*, by Esther Forbes; DIRECTOR: Agnes de Mille (helped by Burt Shevelove); CHOREOGRAPHER: Agnes de Mille; SETS: Oliver Smith; COSTUMES: Stanley Simmons; LIGHTING: Thomas Skelton; SOUND: Ernest Peters; MUSICAL DIRECTOR: Milton Rosenstock; ORCHESTRATIONS: Carlyle Hall; DANCE MUSIC ARRANGEMENTS: David Baker & John Berkman; VOCAL ARRANGEMENTS/MUSICAL CONTINUITY: Trude Rittman; PRESS: Merle Debuskey, Violet Welles, Faith Geer; CASTING: Wendy Mackenzie; GENERAL MANAGER: Walter Fried; COMPANY MANAGER: G. Warren McClane; PRODUCTION STAGE MANAGER: Phil Friedman; STAGE MANAGER: Frank Hamilton; ASSISTANT STAGE MANAGER: James Albright & Doug Hunt. *Cast:* PHINEAS SHARP: Ray Bolger (1) ✩; NATHANIEL BURNAP: William Cottrell (6); JUDE SCRIBNER: David Cryer (2); DORINDA PRATT: Margaret Hamilton (5); LABE PRATT: John Gerstad (8); SUBMIT "MITTY" PRATT: Cathryn Damon (3); MRS. MESERVE: Dorothy Sands; EMMA FAUCETT: Barbara Sharma (4); FRANCIS FAUCETT: William Le Massena (7); DANCING CHARACTERS: LOVERS: Evelyn Taylor & David Evans; HEAD LOGGER: William Glassman [end of dance sequence]; THE POPULACE: James Albright, Paul Berne, Marcia Brushingham, Bjarne Buchtrup, Dennis Cole, Leonard John Crofoot, Harry Endicott, David Evans, Ellen Everett, William Glassman, Sunny Hannum, Walter Hook, Del Horstmann, Doug Hunt, John Johann, Lucia Lambert, Mary Ann Rydzeski, Lana Sloniger, Sarah Jane Smith, Britt Swanson, Jeanette Williamson, Toodie Wittmer, Jenny Workman. *Standbys:* Phineas: Ben Kapen; Emma/Mitty: Tanny McDonald; Dorinda: Dorothy Sands. *Understudies:* Jude: David Evans; Mitty: Lana Sloniger; Mrs. Meserve: Mary Ann Rydzeski; Faucett: Del Horstmann; Labe: Doug Hunt; Burnap: Walter Hook. *Act I:* "Good Time Charlie" (Phineas & Peddlers), "Think Spring" (Phineas, Jude, Populace), "Wild Birds Calling" (Jude & Mitty), "Goodbye, My Bachelor" (Phineas), "Fine, Thank You, Fine" (Emma), "Road to Hampton" (Emma), "Come Summer" (Phineas, Jude, Emma, Mitty, Visions of Lovers), "Let Me Be" (Mitty & Jude), "Feather in My Shoe" (Phineas), "The Loggers' Song" (Phineas, Jude, Loggers, Populace). *Act II:* "Jude's Holler" (Jude & Populace), "Faucett Falls Fancy" (Phineas & Populace), "Rockin'" (Emma & Jude), "Skin and Bones" (Phineas), "Moonglade" (Phineas, Jude, Mitty, Emma, Dorinda, Labe, Faucett, Populace), "Women" (Mitty), "No" (Phineas & Populace), "So Much World" (Jude).

It got bad Broadway reviews. A problem was Ray Bolger. He was outdated and unnecessary to the plot. He bitterly denounced the critics at the final call. It was his last Broadway show. It was Agnes de Mille's last, too.

146. *Comin' Uptown*

All-black version of Dickens novel. Set in Harlem at present time. Scrooge as modern Harlem slum landlord.

Before Broadway. During Broadway previews this was the scene-by-scene breakdown (where the performers are the same as in the Broadway run they are not repeated here). *Act I:* *Scene 1* Harlem—125th Street: "Christmas is Comin' Uptown"; *Scene 2* Scrooge's office: "Somebody's Gotta Be the Heavy"; *Scene 3* 125th Street: "Christmas is Comin' Uptown" (reprise) (Christmas Shoppers); *Scene 4* Scrooge's bedroom: "Now I Lay Me Down to Sleep," "Get Your Act Together," "Lifeline"

Scene 5 A street in Harlem: "What Better Time for Love"; *Scene 6* Harlem Baptist Church: "It Won't Be Long"; *Scene 7* A street in Harlem: "What I'm Gonna Do for You" (Scrooge), "What Better Time for Love" (reprise) (Scrooge & Young Mary); *Scene 8* Scrooge's bedroom: "Get Down, Brother, Get Down"; *Scene 9* Outside the Cratchit house: "Sing a Christmas Song" (Carolers); *Scene 10* The Cratchit dining-room: "Sing a Christmas Song" (reprise), "What Better Time for Love" (reprise); *Scene 11* Outside the Cratchit house: "Have I Finally Found My Heart?" *Act II*: *Scene 1* Scrooge's bedroom: "Nobody Really Do," "Goin,' Gone"; *Scene 2* A street in Harlem: "Get Down, Brother, Get Down" (reprise); *Scene 3* Cemetery: "One Way Ticket to Hell," "Nobody Really Do" (reprise); *Scene 4* Scrooge's bedroom: "Born Again"; *Scene 5* The Cratchit dining-room: "Born Again" (reprise).

The Broadway Run. WINTER GARDEN THEATRE, 12/20/79–1/27/80. 19 previews. 45 PERFORMANCES. PRESENTED BY Ridgely Bullock & Albert W. Selden, in association with Columbia Pictures; MUSIC/ORCHESTRATIONS/VOCAL ARRANGEMENTS: Garry Sherman; LYRICS: Peter Udell; BOOK: Philip Rose & Peter Udell; BASED ON the 1843 novel *A Christmas Carol*, by Charles Dickens; DIRECTOR: Philip Rose; CHOREOGRAPHER: Michael Peters; SETS: Robin Wagner; ASSISTANT SETS: Adrianne Lobel; COSTUMES: Ann Emonts; LIGHTING: Gilbert V. Hemsley Jr.; SOUND: Jack Shearing; MUSICAL DIRECTOR/ADDITIONAL CHORAL ARRANGEMENTS: Howard Roberts; DANCE MUSIC ARRANGEMENTS: Timothy Graphenreed; SPECIAL DRUM ARRANGEMENTS: Scott Schreer; PRESS: Merle Debuskey & Leo Stern; CASTING: Lynda Watson; GENERAL MANAGER: Jay Kingwill; COMPANY MANAGER: Louise M. Bayer; PRODUCTION STAGE MANAGER: Mortimer Halpern; STAGE MANAGER: Nate Barnett; ASSISTANT STAGE MANAGER: Lisa Blackwell. **Cast:** SALVATION ARMY TRIO: Deborah Lynn Bridges (6), Deborah Burrell (7), Jenifer Lewis (8); SHOPPERS (HARLEM RESIDENTS): Kevin Babb, Shirley Black-Brown, Roslyn Burrough, Barbara Christopher, Duane Davis, Ronald Dunham, Milton Grayson, Linda James, Kevin Jeff, Carol Lynn Maillard, Allison R. Manson, Esther Marrow, Frances Lee Morgan, Raymond Patterson, Vernal Polson, Glori Sauve, Eric Sawyer, Kiki Shepard, Faruma Williams, Ned Wright; SCROOGE: Gregory Hines (1) ☆; BOB CRATCHIT: John Russell (9); MRS. CRATCHIT: Virginia McKinzie (11); TENANT'S REPRESENTATIVE: Larry Marshall; MARY, RECREATION CENTER DIRECTOR: Saundra McClain; MINISTER: Robert Jackson; MARLEY: Tiger Haynes (5); CHRISTMAS PAST: Larry Marshall (2); TRIO: Deborah Lynn Bridges, Deborah Burrell, Jenifer Lewis; TIME: Frances Lee Morgan; MARY (YOUNGER): Loretta Devine (10); YOUNG SCROOGE: Duane Davis; HIS ASSISTANT: Vernal Polson; REVEREND BYRD: Ned Wright; GOSPEL SINGER: Esther Marrow (12); DEACON: John Russell; DEACON'S WIFE: Virginia McKinzie (11); CHRISTMAS PRESENT: Saundra McClain (4); CRATCHIT DAUGHTERS: Shirley Black-Brown & Allison R. Manson; MARTHA CRATCHIT: Carol Lynn Maillard (13); TINY TIM: Kevin Babb; CHRISTMAS FUTURE: Robert Jackson (3). **Understudies**: Scrooge: Larry Marshall; Marley: Ned Wright; Christmas Past: Otis Sallid; Christmas Present/Mrs. Cratchit: Glori Sauve; Christmas Future: Kevin Jeff; Young Mary: Carol Lynn Maillard. **Swings**: Prudence Darby & Otis Sallid. *Act I*: *Scene 1* Harlem—125th Street; "Christmas is Comin' Uptown" (Christmas Shoppers, Trio, Scrooge); *Scene 2* Scrooge's office: "Somebody's Gotta Be the Heavy" (Scrooge); *Scene 3* Scrooge's bedroom: "Now I Lay Me Down to Sleep" (Scrooge), "Get Your Act Together" (Marley), "Lifeline" (orchestrated by Willie Strickland) (Christmas Past & Trio); *Scene 4* A street in Harlem: "What Better Time for Love" (Scrooge & Young Mary); *Scene 5* Harlem Baptist Church: "It Won't Be Long" (Gospel Singer & Congregation); *Scene 6* Scrooge's bedroom: "Get Down, Brother, Get Down" (Christmas Present & The Presents); *Scene 7* The Cratchit dining room: "Sing a Christmas Song" (Cratchit Family & Carolers), "What Better Time for Love" (reprise) (Tiny Tim & Family); *Scene 8* Outside the Cratchit house: "Have I Finally Found My Heart?" (Scrooge). *Act II*: *Scene 1* Scrooge's bedroom: "Nobody Really Do" (Christmas Future & Trio), "Goin,' Gone" (Christmas Future); *Scene 2* A cemetery: "Get Down, Brother, Get Down" (reprise) (Cratchit Family & Mourners); *Scene 3* Another cemetery: "One Way Ticket to Hell" (Trio), "Nobody Really Do" (reprise) (Christmas Future & Trio); *Scene 4* Scrooge's bedroom: "Born Again" (Scrooge); *Scene 5* The Cratchit dining room: "Born Again" (reprise) (Scrooge & Company).

The show opened on Broadway to generally bad reviews, although Gregory Hines came in for a lot of raves and a Tony nomination

147. *Company*

Set in New York City, now. An adult, revolutionary musical, about the pros and cons of matrimony. The show had several characters talking or singing at the same time but not together. The libretto read like a movie script. Five separate stories of marriage connected by a single character, Robert, a bachelor, who influences, and is influenced by, his "good and crazy" married friends. His 35th birthday acts as a framework for the plot. Boris Aronson's highly-acclaimed cage-like skeletal Plexiglas and chrome setting made use of stairways, two elevators, and projections. There was a 12-minute intermission.

Before Broadway. Actor George Furth wrote a collection of 11 one-act plays and called them *Company*. Some of them were about marriages he had known in Southern California. As such, *Company* was planned for Broadway in the fall of 1968. Philip Mandelker and Porter Van Zandt owned the rights. George Morrison was going to direct, and Kim Stanley would play all 11 wives. However, they couldn't raise the money, and in 1/69 George Furth called his friend Steve Sondheim for advice. Sondheim suggested that Hal Prince might be interested. Mr. Prince saw them as a collective musical reflecting how life in a big city influences various couples. Mr. Sondheim was then working on a musical called *The Girls Upstairs*, with James Goldman, and rehearsals for that one were scheduled to begin in fall 1970 (this show, which was never made, had originated in the mid–1960s; the producers then were David Merrick & Leland Hayward). They all planned, therefore, to follow that with *Company* in spring 1971. The trick with *Company* was to find a suitable form for it, a structure that would be suitable for audiences. Only two of Mr. Furth's plays were used as they were, and he revised three more. Some of the unused material was used later in the play *Twigs*. The project was originally announced, in 4/69, as *Threes*, the new Harold Prince musical, to star Anthony Perkins. Tony Perkins never did the show, and neither did Kim Stanley, who had been announced as leading lady. From 5/69 to 7/69 Prince, Sondheim and Furth worked on the show. Boris Aronson was hired to do the sets. Hal Prince had already hired theatres in Boston and New York for spring 1970, and planned the beginning of rehearsals for 2/71. The role of Joanne was written for Elaine Stritch, and she was duly cast. At the beginning of 7/69 Steve Sondheim called Hal Prince (who was then in Germany directing the movie *Something for Everyone*) and told him about the problems that were besetting *The Girls Upstairs*. The producer, Stuart Ostrow, quit, and director Joseph Hardy wanted more re-writes, and Mr. Sondheim wanted Mr. Prince to postpone *Company* (as it was now called) so that he (Sondheim) could get a handle on *The Girl Upstairs*. Mr. Prince refused, but Mr. Sondheim had been working too long on *The Girl Upstairs* to let it go that lightly. Mr. Prince then compromised, and told him to start work on *Company*, and that after *Company* was done, he would produce *The Girls Upstairs* himself. In short order Mr. Sondheim delivered three new songs to Mr. Prince in Germany, one of them being "Company," the title song. Michael Bennett was hired as choreographer. The show took six weeks to rehearse. It tried out in Boston, where reviews were divided. "Happily Ever After" was cut during the last week of the Boston tryout, and replaced by a new song written by Mr. Sondheim—"Being Alive." "Marry Me a Little" was also cut.

The Broadway Run. ALVIN THEATRE, 4/26/70–1/1/72. 16 previews. 690 PERFORMANCES. PRESENTED BY Harold Prince, in association with Ruth Mitchell; MUSIC/LYRICS: Stephen Sondheim; BOOK: George Furth; DIRECTOR: Harold Prince; CHOREOGRAPHER: Michael Bennett; ASSOCIATE CHOREOGRAPHER: Bob Avian; SETS: Boris Aronson; COSTUMES: D.D. Ryan; LIGHTING: Robert Ornbo; SOUND: Jack Mann; MUSICAL DIRECTOR: Harold Hastings, *Arthur Wagner*; ORCHESTRATIONS: Jonathan Tunick; DANCE MUSIC ARRANGEMENTS: Wally Harper; CAST RECORDING on Columbia; PRESS: Mary Bryant & Meg Gordean, *Stanley F. Kaminsky & Sadie Stein*; CASTING: Joanna Merlin; PRODUCTION

SUPERVISOR: Ruth Mitchell; GENERAL MANAGER: Carl Fisher; COMPANY MANAGER: John Caruso; PRODUCTION STAGE MANAGER: James Bronson, *Ben Strobach*; STAGE MANAGER: Fritz Holt, *Bob Burland*; ASSISTANT STAGE MANAGER: George Martin. *Cast:* ROBERT: Dean Jones (1) ☆, *Larry Kert* (from 5/29/70), *John Cunningham* (during Mr. Kert's illness, 2/71), *Kenneth Cory* (during Mr. Kert's absence until 8/23/71), *Gary Krawford* (from 12/27/71); SARAH: Barbara Barrie (2), *Audre Johnston* (from 7/1/71), *Cynthia Harris* (from 7/12/71); HARRY: Charles Kimbrough (7), *Charles Braswell* (from 3/29/71), *Kenneth Kimmins* (from 5/13/71); SUSAN: Merle Louise (14), *Alice Cannon* (from 10/5/70), *Charlotte Frazier* (from 3/29/71); PETER: John Cunningham (5), *James O'Sullivan* (during the time Mr. Cunningham was playing the lead, 2/71), *Kenneth Cory* (from 4/26/71); JENNY: Teri Ralston (6), *Jane A. Johnston* (from 5/13/71), *Teri Ralston* (from 10/25/71); DAVID: George Coe (4), *Lee Goodman* (from 3/29/71), *George Wallace* (from 5/13/71), *Lee Goodman* (from 10/25/71); AMY: Beth Howland (12), *Marian Hailey* (from 5/13/71), *Beth Howland* (from 10/25/71); PAUL: Steve Elmore (11); JOANNE: Elaine Stritch (3), *Jane Russell* (from 5/13/71), *Vivian Blaine* (from 11/1/71); LARRY: Charles Braswell (9), *Stanley Grover* (from 3/29/71); MARTA: Pamela Myers (13), *Annie McGreevey* (from 5/13/71); KATHY: Donna McKechnie (8), *Brenda Thomson* (from 5/13/71), *Priscilla Lopez* (from 10/25/71); APRIL: Susan Browning (10), *Carol Richards* (from 12/71); VOCAL MINORITY: Cathy Corkill, Carol Gelfand, Marilyn Saunders, Dona D. Vaughn. **Standbys**: For Dean Jones: Larry Kert; For Larry Kert: *Kenneth Cory*; For Elaine Stritch: Jessica James; For Jane Russell: *Sandra Deel*. **Understudies**: Robert: John Cunningham; Peter: James O'Sullivan; Paul/David: James O'Sullivan, *Robert Carle*; Larry/Harry: Bob Roman; Kathy: Virginia Sandifur, *Priscilla Lopez*; April: Virginia Sandifur, *Charlotte Frazier*; Susan: Alice Cannon; Jenny: Alice Cannon, *Charlotte Frazier*; Marta: Alice Cannon, *Marilyn Saunders* (by 70–71); Amy/Sarah: Audre Johnston. *Act I*: *Scene 1* Robert's apartment: "Company" (Robert & Company); *Scene 2* Sarah and Harry's living room: "The Little Things You Do Together" (Joanne & Company), "Sorry—Grateful" (Harry, David, Larry); *Scene 3* Peter and Susan's terrace; *Scene 4* Jenny and David's den/playroom: "You Could Drive a Person Crazy" (Kathy, April, Marta), "Have I Got a Girl for You" (Larry, Peter, Paul, David, Harry), "Someone is Waiting" (Robert); *Scene 5* A park bench: "Another Hundred People" (Marta); *Scene 6* Amy's kitchen: "Getting Married Today" (Amy, Paul, Jenny, Company). *Act II*: *Scene 1* Robert's apartment; as in Act I Scene 1: "Side by Side by Side" (Robert & Company), "What Would We Do without You?" (Robert & Company); *Scene 2* Robert's apartment; later: "Poor Baby" (Sarah, Jenny, Susan, Amy, Joanne), "Tick Tock" (instrumental; dance mus arr: David Shire) (Danced by Kathy), "Barcelona" (Robert & April); *Scene 3* Peter and Susan's terrace; *Scene 4* A private night club: "The Ladies Who Lunch" (Joanne) [the showstopper], "Being Alive" (Robert); *Scene 5* Robert's apartment.

The show, capitalized at $550,000, opened on Broadway to mostly great reviews. Dean Jones, the lead, left two weeks after opening night (it wasn't hepatitis, as the publicity said, but depression brought on by the anti-marriage theme of the play; Mr. Jones was going through a painful divorce at the time) to be replaced by Larry Kert, the actor most people remember in the role of Robert. Hal Prince persuaded the Tony Awards committee to accept the eligibility of Mr. Kert for a Tony, even though he was not the original player. [Hal Prince knew Dean Jones was going to leave the show, even before it opened, and promised the actor that he would allow him to quit in return for two weeks worth of great performances, which the actor delivered]. This musical established Steve Sondheim as a major songwriting force on Broadway, and it was also the beginning of the famous Prince—Sondheim partnership that would last for six shows over 11 years (they had worked together before, but not as partners), or seven shows over 33 years if you include *Bounce*. Although this production of *Company* rarely played to more than 60 percent houses, it made a profit. It was nominated for 15 Tonys (a record); it won for musical, producer, score, lyrics, book, direction of a musical, and sets, and was also nominated for choreography, lighting, and for Pamela Myers, Larry Kert, Charles Kimbrough, Susan Browning, Elaine Stritch, and Barbara Barrie.

After Broadway. TOUR. Opened on 5/20/71, at the Ahmanson Theatre, Los Angeles, and closed on 5/20/72, at the National Theatre, Washington, DC, after 86 cities. MUSICAL DIRECTORS: Jonathan Anderson & Richard Kaufman. *Cast*: ROBERT: George Chakiris, *Allen Case* (from 1/10/72), *Gary Krawford*; SARAH: Marti Stevens, *Barbara Broughton* (from 12/71); HARRY: Charles Braswell, *Bernie McInerney*; SUSAN: Milly Ericson, *Ann Johnson*; PETER: Gary Krawford, *Johnny Stewart*; JENNY: Teri Ralston, *Jane A. Johnston* (from 10/25/71); DAVID: Lee Goodman, *George Wallace* (from 10/25/71); AMY: Beth Howland, *Marian Hailey* (from 10/25/71), *Tandy Cronyn*; PAUL: Del Hinkley; JOANNE: Elaine Stritch, *Julie Wilson* (from 12/28/71); LARRY: Robert Goss, *Nolan Van Way* (from 12/71); MARTA: Pamela Myers, *Louisa Flaningam*; KATHY: Donna McKechnie, *Carolyn Kirsch, Susan Plantt* (from 8/71); APRIL: Bobbi Jordan, *Rolly Fanton*; VOCAL MINORITY: Barbara Broughton, Carolyn Kirsch, Mary Roche, Marilyn Saunders, *Sindy Hawke, Leilani Johnson*. **Understudy**: Susan/Jenny/April: Preshy Marker.

HER MAJESTY'S THEATRE, London, 1/18/72. 344 PERFORMANCES. PRESENTED BY Harold Prince & Richard Pilbrow; MUSICAL DIRECTOR: Gareth Davies. The rest of the crew was the same as for Broadway. *Cast* (on 4/10/72 a mostly London-based cast took over): ROBERT: Larry Kert, *Eric Flynn* (for the last two months of the run); SARAH: Marti Stevens; HARRY: Kenneth Kimmins, *Robert Colman* (from 4/10/72); SUSAN: Joy Franz, *Connie Booth* (from 4/10/72); PETER: J.T. Cromwell, *Philip Hinton* (from 4/10/72); JENNY: Teri Ralston, *Barbara Tracey* (from 4/10/72); DAVID: Lee Goodman, *Paul Tracey* (from 4/10/72); AMY: Beth Howland, *Dilys Watling* (from 4/10/72), *Gracie Luck* [i.e. Susan Kramer] (for the last two months of the run); PAUL: Steve Elmore, *Richard Owens* (from 4/10/72); JOANNE: Elaine Stritch, *Marti Stevens* (for the last two months of the run); LARRY: Robert Goss, *Eric Flynn* (from 4/10/72); MARTA: Annie McGreevey, *Julia Sutton* (from 4/10/72); KATHY: Donna McKechnie, *Antonia Ellis* (from 4/10/72); APRIL: Carol Richards, *Julia McKenzie* (from 3/6/72).

EQUITY LIBRARY THEATRE, NYC, 5/4/78–5/28/78. 30 PERFORMANCES. DIRECTOR: Robert Nigro; CHOREOGRAPHER: Randy Hugill; SETS: Richard B. Williams; COSTUMES: Mimi Maxmen; LIGHTING: Victor En Yu Tan; MUSICAL DIRECTOR: Eric Stern. *Cast*: ROBERT: Albert Harris; SARAH: Janet MacKenzie; HARRY: Richard Kevlin-Bell; SUSAN: Joy Bond; PETER: Bob Morrisey; JENNY: Becky McSpadden; DAVID: Lenny Wolpe; AMY: Lauren White; PAUL: Michael Hirsch; JOANNE: Renee Roy; LARRY: Edward Penn; MARTA: Paige O'Hara; KATHY: Gillian Scalici; APRIL: Valerie Beaman; VOCAL MINORITY: Alexa Grant, Maureen McNamara, Linda Nenno, Christine Ranck, Patricia Roark, Lynda Karen Smith.

QUEENS THEATER-IN-THE-PARK, NY. 3/8/80–3/30/80. PRESENTED BY Playwrights Horizons; DIRECTOR: Andre Ernotte; CHOREOGRAPHER: Theodore Pappas. *Cast*: Peter Evans, Christine Baranski, Patricia Richardson, Diane Findlay, Cynthia Crumlish, Walter Bobbie, Sheilah Rae, Tony Blake, James Seymour, Jane Galloway, Randall Easterbrook, Conrad McLaren, Mary Testa, Sonja Stuart.

CHURCH OF THE HEAVENLY REST, NY. 10/23/87–11/14/87. 20 PERFORMANCES. PRESENTED BY the York Theatre Company; DIRECTOR: Susan H. Schulman; CHOREOGRAPHER: Michael Lichtefeld; MUSICAL DIRECTOR: David Krane. *Cast*: ROBERT: David Carroll; SARAH: Susan Elizabeth Scott; HARRY: Lenny Wolpe; SUSAN: Debra Dickinson; PETER: Michael Elich; JENNY: Jeanne Lehman; DAVID: John P. Connolly; AMY: Judith Blazer; PAUL: Robert Michael Baker; JOANNE: Barbara Andres; LARRY: Kip Niven; MARTA: Liz Larsen; KATHY: Louise Hickey; APRIL: Donna English.

Company: the Original Cast in Concert. VIVIAN BEAUMONT THEATRE, 4/11/93–4/12/93. 2 PERFORMANCES. PRESENTED BY Broadway Cares/Equity Fights AIDS, Barry Brown/New York Magazine, in association with Lincoln Center Theatre; DIRECTOR: Barry Brown; CHOREOGRAPHER: George Martin; LIGHTING: Natasha Katz; SOUND: Jon Weston; MUSICAL DIRECTOR: John McDaniel; ORCHESTRATIONS: Jonathan Tunick. The sets were Thomas Lynch's from *My Favorite Year*. The original 1970 cast (see above) except LARRY: Stanley Grover; HOST: Patti LuPone. The Vocal Minority was the same, except that Eileen Barnett replaced Carol Gelfand.

148. *Company (Broadway revival)*

The musical numbers were the same as for the 1970 production, except that the previously cut "Marry Me a Little" (sung by Robert at the end of Act I) was added. This production was outdated before it began.

The Broadway Run. CRITERION CENTER STAGE RIGHT, 10/5/95–12/3/95. 43 previews from 8/30/95. 68 PERFORMANCES. The Roundabout Theatre Company production, PRESENTED BY the Nederlander Organization & Kardana Productions (John Hart); MUSIC/LYRICS: Stephen Sondheim; BOOK: George Furth; DIRECTOR: Scott Ellis; CHOREOGRAPHER: Rob Marshall; SETS: Tony Walton; COSTUMES: William Ivey Long; LIGHTING: Peter Kaczorowski; SOUND: Tony Meola; MUSICAL DIRECTOR: David Loud; ORCHESTRATIONS RE-PRODUCED BY: Jonathan Tunick; NEW CAST RECORDING on Angel; PRESS: Boneau/Bryan—Brown; CASTING: Pat McCorkle; PRODUCTION STAGE MANAGER: Lori M. Doyle; STAGE MANAGER: Matthew T. Mundinger. *Cast*: ROBERT: Boyd Gaines, *James Clow, Boyd Gaines*; SARAH: Kate Burton; HARRY: Robert Westenberg; SUSAN: Patricia Ben Peterson; PETER: Jonathan Dokuchitz; JENNY: Diana Canova; DAVID: John Hillner; AMY: Veanne Cox; PAUL: Danny Burstein; JOANNE: Debra Monk; LARRY: Timothy Landfield; MARTA: La Chanze; KATHY: Charlotte d'Amboise; APRIL: Jane Krakowski. *Standbys*: Robert: James Clow; Peter/Paul: James Clow & Bob Kirsch; Harry/Danny/Larry: Andy Umberger; Susan/Jenny/Marta: Colleen Fitzpatrick; April: Colleen Fitzpatrick & Nancy Hess; Amy/Kathy: Nancy Hess. *Orchestra*: PIANO: David Loud; KEYBOARDS: James Moore; WOODWINDS: Les Scott, Dennis Anderson, John Winder; TRUMPET: Stu Satalof; TROMBONE: Bruce Bonvissuto; BASS: Robert Renino; PERCUSSION: Bruce Doctor.

After the show received divided reviews the Nederlanders dropped out. Boyd Gaines got laryngitis and James Clow stepped in. The remaining producer, John Hart, wanted to move the show to a larger Broadway house—the Brooks Atkinson—and with a new leading man, Michael Rupert, but the director wanted to keep Boyd Gaines. The Brooks Atkinson was announced as the new venue, to begin 12/10/95 (later postponed to 12/19/95). Auditions were held for a replacement actor. Boyd Gaines returned to performances on 11/14/95, then John Hart dropped out (so there was now no producer) and on 11/16/95 plans for the move to the Brooks Atkinson (where advance sales were only $100,000) fell through. There had been a possibility of an Off Broadway run, but that fell through too. It received Tony nominations for revival of a musical, and for Veanne Cox.

After Broadway. DONMAR WAREHOUSE, London, 12/13/95–3/2/96. Previews from 12/1/95; ALBERY THEATRE, 3/13/96–6/29/96. Previews from 3/7/96. DIRECTOR: Sam Mendes; CHOREOGRAPHER: Jonathan Butterell; SETS: Mark Thompson; LIGHTING: Paul Pyant; SOUND: John A. Leonard; ORCHESTRATIONS: Jonathan Tunick. *Cast*: ROBERT: Adrian Lester; SARAH: Rebecca Front; HARRY: Clive Rowe; SUSAN: Clare Burt; PETER: Gareth Snook; JENNY: Liza Sadovy; DAVID: Teddy Kempner; AMY: Sophie Thompson; PAUL: Michael Simkins; JOANNE: Sheila Gish; LARRY: Paul Bentley; MARTA: Anna Francolini; KATHY: Kiran Hocking; APRIL: Hannah James. The show won Olivier Awards for Sam Mendes, Adrian Lester and Sheila Gish. This production was shown on BBC2, on 3/1/97.

TOUR. A brief, East Coast, touring revival opened on 9/28/99, at the Performing Arts Center, Raleigh, NC, the first tour to use George Furth's revised book from the Roundabout's 1995 revival in New York. PRESENTED BY Jeffrey Finn Productions; DIRECTOR/CHOREOGRAPHER: Mark S. Hoebee; SETS: John Farrell. *Cast*: BOBBY: Tom Galantich; LARRY: David Brummel; MARTA: Andrea Burns, *Denise Summerford*; JENNY: Karen Culp; AMY: Shauna Hicks; DAVID: Michael Licata; PAUL: David Lowenstein; SUSAN: Patricia Ben Peterson; PETER: Peter Reardon; KATHY: Rachael Warren; SARAH: Lynne Wintersteller; JOANNE: Emily Zacharias; APRIL: Dana Lynn Mauro; HARRY: Mark McGrath.

KENNEDY CENTER, Washington, DC, 5/17/02–6/29/02. This was the second in *The Sondheim Celebration* series. *Cast*: BOBBY: John Barrowman; JOANNE: Lynn Redgrave; SUSAN: Christy Baron; PAUL: Matt Bogart; SARAH: Keira Naughton; AMY: Alice Ripley; JENNY: Emily Skinner; MARTA: Marcy Harriell; KATHERINE: Elizabeth Zins; LARRY: Jerry Lanning; HARRY: David Pittu; APRIL: Kim Director; DAVID: Marc Vietor; PETER: Dan Cooney.

149. *Concert Varieties*

A composite concert hall/vaudeville revue, or variety show.

The Broadway Run. ZIEGFELD THEATRE, 6/1/45–6/28/45. 36 PERFORMANCES. PRESENTED BY Billy Rose; MUSIC: various composers; DIRECTOR: Billy Rose; TECHNICAL DIRECTOR: Carlton Winckler; MUSICAL DIRECTOR: Pembroke Davenport; PRESS: Tom Van Dyke; COMPANY MANAGER: John Tuerk; GENERAL STAGE MANAGER: Frank Hall; STAGE MANAGER: George Hunter. *Act I*: Deems Taylor (1). mc, explains: *Scene 1* The Salici Puppets; *Scene 2* Eddie Mayehoff (3). Comedian, playing a business executive chomping on a cigar; *Scene 3* Rosario & Antonio, male/female dance couple, dancing to "Caprice Espagnol," by Nikolay Rimsky-Korsakoff; *Scene 4* Nestor Chayres, Mexican lyric tenor; *Scene 5* Rosario & Antonio dancing to "Dansa Ritual del Fuego," from Manuel de Falla's *El amor brujo*; *Scene 6* Imogene Coca (4). Striptease impersonation and impressions of Pola Negri, Clara Bow & Lana Turner, and also singing a song; *Scene 7* Jerome Robbins's ballet "Interplay." mus: ("American Concertette," a short piano concerto which had premiered in April 1943 by Jose Iturbi and the NBC Symphony) by Morton Gould; décor/cos: Carl Kent. 1. Free Play. Jerome Robbins (6) and his company [John Kriza, Michael Kidd, Erik Kristen, Janet Reed, Muriel Bentley, Roszika Sabo (courtesy of Ballet Theatre), Bettina Rosay]. 2. Horse Play. Jerome Robbins. 3. By Play. Janet Reed & John Kriza. 4. Team Play. Full Company. *Act II*: *Scene 8* Katherine Dunham and Her Dance Company (5) (Vanoye Aikens, Talley Beatty, Eddy Clay, LaVerne French, Tommy Gomez, Lenwood Morris, Roger Ohardieno, Lucille Ellis, Syvilla Fort, Dolores Harper, Richardena Jackson, Ora Leak, Gloria Mitchell): Callate (Brazil) (m: Candido Vicenty) (Miss Dunham & Messrs Vicenty, Aikens, Ohardieno, Clay); Rhumba (Mexico) (m: Harl MacDonald) (Miss Dunham, Mr. Beatty, Ensemble); Tropics (Martinique) (m: Paquita Anderson); Drummers: Candido Vicenty, La Rosa Estrada, Julio Mendez. *Scene 9* Routines: "Dance Divertissement." Imogene Coca & William Archibald danced a burlesque version of Debussy's "L'apres-midi d'un faun"; *Scene 10* Albert Ammons (piano), Pete Johnson (piano) & Big Sid Catlett (drums). Jazz trio; *Scene 11* Zero Mostel (2). Played Italian opera singer Mosteli, then after interplay with the mc, played a senator exhorting his constituents. Then he played a coffee percolator; *Scene 12* Rosario & Antonio appeared for the finale in two dances—"Jota de la Dolores" & "Canasteros de Triana" (Flirtation Dance)—with music by (respectively) Tomas Breton & Curritos-Matos-Villacanos. MUSICAL DIRECTOR: Silvio Masciarelli; GUITARIST: G. Villarino; *Scene 13* Finale.

Broadway reviews were mixed and middle-of-the-road.

150. *A Connecticut Yankee*

Martin gets hit on the head by his fiancee in a hotel room in Hartford, Conn. He dreams of being a stranger at the court of King Arthur, and becomes the confidant of the king by industrializing the realm. On waking he realizes he is about to marry the wrong girl, and turns to Alisande's modern day double, Alice.

Before Broadway. The original musical ran on Broadway, at the VANDERBILT THEATRE, 11/3/27–10/27/28. 418 PERFORMANCES. CAST: MARTIN: William Gaxton; ALICE: Constance Carpenter. This version was filmed (straight) in 1931. DIRECTOR: David Butler. *Cast*: HANK: Will Rogers; ALISANDE: Maureen O'Sullivan; MORGAN: Myrna Loy.

The 1943 revival was done to keep Larry Hart alive. He wrote six new songs to replace four old ones (i.e. "A Ladies' Home Companion," "Nothing's Wrong," "The Sandwich Men," and "Evelyn, What Do You Say?").

The Broadway Run. MARTIN BECK THEATRE, 11/17/43–3/11/44. 135 PERFORMANCES. PRESENTED BY Richard Rodgers; MUSIC: Richard Rodgers; LYRICS: Lorenz Hart; BOOK: Herbert Fields; a new musical adaptation of the 1889 novel *A Connecticut Yankee in King Arthur's Court*, by Mark Twain; DIRECTOR: John C. Wilson; CHOREOGRAPHERS: William Holbrooke & Al White Jr.; SETS/COSTUMES/LIGHTING: Nat Karson; ASSISTANT TO NAT KARSON: Peggy Clark; CONSULTING SOUND

ENGINEER: Saki Oura; MUSICAL DIRECTOR: George Hirst; ORCHESTRATIONS: Don Walker; VOCAL ARRANGEMENTS: Buck (i.e. Clay) Warnick; CAST RECORDING on Decca; PRESS: Ben Kornzweig; GENERAL MANAGER: Morris Jacobs; COMPANY MANAGER: Irving Cooper; GENERAL STAGE MANAGER: Ed Scanlon; STAGE MANAGER: Mortimer O'Brien. *Cast:* IN HARTFORD: LT. (J.G.) KENNETH KAY, USN: Robert Byrn; JUDGE THURSTON MERRILL: John Cherry; ADMIRAL ARTHUR K. ARTHUR, USN: Robert Chisholm; ENSIGN GERALD LAKE, USN: Chester Stratton (5); ENSIGN ALLAN GWYNN, USN: Jere McMahon; LT. MARTIN BARRETT, USN: Dick Foran (2); CAPT. LAWRENCE LAKE, USN: Stuart Casey; LT. FAY MERRILL, WAVE: Vivienne Segal (1); CORP. ALICE COURTLEIGH, WAC: Julie Warren (3). IN CAMELOT: SIR KAY, THE SENESCHAL: Robert Byrn; MARTIN: Dick Foran (2); THE DEMOISELLE ALISANDE LA COURTELLOISE (SANDY): Julie Warren (3); ARTHUR, KING OF BRITAIN: Robert Chisholm; MERLIN: John Cherry; QUEEN GUINEVERE: Katherine Anderson; SIR LAUNCELOT OF THE LAKE: Stuart Casey; SIR GALAHAD, HIS SON: Chester Stratton (5); ANGELA, HAND-MAIDEN TO MORGAN: Mimi Berry; QUEEN MORGAN LE FAY: Vivienne Segal (1); SIR GAWAIN: Jere McMahon; Mistress Evelyn la Rondelle: Vera-Ellen (4) [end of Camelot sequence]. DANCING GIRLS: Dorothy Blute, Carole Burke, Eleanor Eberle, Bee Farnum, Virginia Gorski, Janet Joy, Rose Marie Magrill, Frances Martone, Mary McDonnell, Beth Nichols, Murnai Pins, Dorothy Poplar, Joyce Ring, Rosemary Sankey, Helen Vent, Violetta Weems, Doris York; DANCING BOYS: Tad Bruce, Buster Burnell, Pittman Corry, Frank de Winters, Bob Gari, William Hunter, Hal Loman, William Lundy, Jack Lyons; SINGING GIRLS: Marjorie Cowen, Toni Hart, Linda Mason, Martha Emma Watson; SINGING BOYS: Lester Freedman, Vincent Henry, Craig Holden, Wayne McIntyre. *Prologue* A banquet hall of a hotel in Hartford, 1943. voc arr: Buck Warnick. "This is My Night to Howl" (Fay & Ensemble) [not in the 1927 original, which had "A Ladies' Home Companion" (Fay, Principals, Ensemble) here], "My Heart Stood Still" (Martin & Sandy) [the most popular tune]; *Act I*: *Scene 1* On the road to Camelot, 543 A.D.: "Thou Swell" (Martin & Sandy); *Scene 2* Courtyard of King Arthur's castle: "At the Round Table" (Company), "On a Desert Island (With Thee)" (Galahad, Evelyn, Gawain, Ensemble), "To Keep My Love Alive" (Morgan) [the showstopper] [not in the 1927 original], "My Heart Stood Still" (reprise) (Martin & Sandy), Finale; *Act II*: *Scene 1* Corridor of the Royal Factory; three months later: "Ye Lunchtime Follies" (dance) (Galahad & Ensemble) [not in the 1927 original, which had Opening (Ensemble) here], "Can't You Do a Friend a Favor?" (Morgan & Martin) [not in the 1927 original, which had "Nothing's Wrong" (Sandy) here], "Thou Swell" (reprise) (Martin & Sandy) [this reprise was new to this production], "I Feel at Home with You" (Galahad, Evelyn, Gawain, Ensemble); *Scene 2* On the road from Camelot: "You Always Love the Same Girl" (Martin & Arthur) [not in the 1927 original, which had "The Sandwich Men" here]; *Scene 3* The palace of Queen Morgan Le Fay: "Camelot is Learning Fast/The Camelot Samba" (Gawain & Ensemble) [not in the 1927 original, which had "Evelyn, What Did You Say?" here]; *Epilogue* Same as Prologue, 1943: Finale (Company).

On opening night, Larry Hart, on his last binge, was ejected from the Martin Beck for disrupting the performance (standing at the back of the theatre, he was singing along with Vivienne Segal during "To Keep My Love Alive"). He died of pneumonia five days later. Reviews of the show were basically favorable.

After Broadway. THE MOVIE. 1949. The score, by Johnny Burke & Jimmy Van Heusen, included: "Busy Doin' Nothin'," "Once and for Always," "When is Sometime," "When You Stub Your Toe on the Moon," "Twixt Myself and Me." In the story Hank is a blacksmith. DIRECTOR: Tay Garnett. *Cast:* HANK MARTIN: Bing Crosby; ALISANDE: Rhonda Fleming; ARTHUR: Cedric Hardwicke; SAGRAMORE: William Bendix; LANCELOT: Henry Wilcoxon; MERLIN: Murvyn Vye

ALL SOULS FELLOWSHIP HALL, NY, 5/9/86–5/25/86. 16 PERFORMANCES. The modern part of the setting was updated to the New Haven Hilton Hotel in 1986; Martin was now a professor. The character of Allan Gwynn/Sir Gawain was cut, and several new ones added. PRESENTED BY All Souls Players; DIRECTOR/CHOREOGRAPHER: Jeffrey K. Neill; SETS: Norb Joerder; MUSICAL DIRECTOR/ADDITIONAL ORCHESTRATIONS: Wendell Kindberg. *Cast:* PROF. MARTIN BARRETT: Donald Brooks; PROF. MERVIN ROSS: Jeff Paul (this had been the Merrill char-

acter); PROF. ALBERT KAY: Tim McKanic (the Lt. Kay character); PROF. GERALD GARETH: Norb Joerder (the Ensign Lake character); PROF. ARTHUR PENGRASS: William Walters (the Arthur K. Arthur character); PROF. LAWRENCE LAKE: Bob Cuccioli; ALICE CARTER: Anne Fisher (the Alice Courtleigh character); FAY ROSS: Patricia Moline (the Fay Merrill character); PROF. BORENSTEIN/SIR BORS: Brian Bowman; PROF. GEOFFREY/SIR GEOFFREY: Lawrence Raben; PROF. COLBY/SIR GOLGRIM: Andy Thain; PROF. TRACY/SIR TRISTAN: Kevin J. Usher; PROF. SEAGRAM/SIR SAGRAMORE: Eric Walden; PROF. DUNHILL/SIR DINIDIAN: Mark Wilkening; GUINEVERE: Margaret Benczak; EVELYN: Carol Leigh Stevens; ANGELINA/ANGELA: Marlene Greene.

CITY CENTER, NYC, 2/8/01–2/11/01. 5 PERFORMANCES. Part of the *Encores!* series of concert-style readings. ADAPTED BY David Ives; DIRECTOR: Susan H. Schulman; CHOREOGRAPHER: Rob Ashford; SETS: John Lee Beatty; COSTUMES: Toni-Leslie James; LIGHTING: Natasha Katz; SOUND: Scott Lehrer. *Cast:* ARTHUR PENDRAGOS/KING ARTHUR: Henry Gibson; GERALD GARETH/SIR GALAHAD: Sean Martin Hingston; MARTIN BARRETT (THE YANKEE): Steven Sutcliffe; ALBERT KAY/SIR KAY: Mark Lotito; FAY MORGAN/MORGAN LE FAY: Christine Ebersole; EVELYN LANE/DAME EVELYN: Nancy Lemenager; ALICE CARTER/ALISANDE: Judy Blazer; ANGELA/MAID ANGELA: Megan Sikora; HENRY MERLE/MERLIN: Peter Bartlett; SIR LAUNCELOT: Ron Leibman; GUINEVERE: Jessica Walter; DANCERS INCLUDED: Robert M. Armitage, Vance Avery, David Eggers, Matt Lashey.

HERBST THEATRE, San Francisco. 42nd Street Moon produced an *Encores!*-type concert staged reading (with scripts in hand) of *A Connecticut Yankee in King Arthur's Court* (the same show as the 1943 Broadway one, but with the longer title). 8/21/02–8/25/02. DIRECTOR: Greg McKellan. It used the original 1943 orchestrations with full orchestra (Aaron Gandy conductor). *Cast:* MARTIN BARRETT, A PLAYBOY: Davis Gaines.

151. *The Conquering Hero*

A young man, Woodrow, son of a war hero, always wanted to be a marine. He enlists for World War II, but chronic hay fever gets him discharged immediately. Ashamed to go home, he hooks up with a bunch of marines from the jungles of Guadalcanal, who see to it that he returns to his home town a hero.

Before Broadway. Bob Fosse created the show and took it to producer Robert Whitehead. Mr. Fosse was the original director/choreographer. The first tryouts were chaotic, and after negative reviews at the second tryouts, at the National Theatre, Washington, DC, Fosse was fired, partly because the producers felt that a battle scene he had staged made the soldiers look effeminate. Leading lady Cherry Davis was replaced by Kay Brown, and Mr. Whitehead asked Dick Shawn if he would come in and replace Tom Poston. Mr. Shawn refused, so they went on with Tom. Although he had been dismissed, Bob Fosse, against his attorney Jack Peralman's advice to remove his dances from the production, agreed to the use of his dances, on the condition that his two major ballets be used intact or not at all. Robert Whitehead then hired Todd Bolender to "supervise" the dances, and Albie Marre to direct the show as it staggered to Broadway, so Fosse went to arbitration. He won his case — 8 months after the demise of the show. He asked for token damages, and was awarded 6 cents. No credits are given for director or choreographer in the program. This legal award eventually led to the 1976 Copyright Act protecting a choreographer's work. The numbers "Eight Weight Lifters," "I Had Big Plans" and "Past the Age of Innocence" were all cut. The non-profit organization, ANTA, had taken a second mortgage on their theatre, and invested $100,000 in the show.

The Broadway Run. ANTA THEATRE, 1/16/61–1/21/61. 8 PERFORMANCES. PRESENTED BY ANTA (Robert Whitehead, vice-president & Roger L. Stevens, treasurer), by special arrangement with Emka, Ltd; MUSIC: Moose Charlap; LYRICS: Norman Gimbel; BOOK: Larry Gelbart; BASED ON the 1944 movie *Hail, the Conquering Hero*, written and directed by Preston Sturges; CONCEIVED BY: Bob Fosse; DIRECTOR/CHOREOGRAPHER: uncredited; SETS: Jean Rosenthal & William Pitkin; COSTUMES: Patton Campbell; LIGHTING: Jean Rosenthal; MUSICAL

DIRECTOR/CHORAL ARRANGEMENTS: Sherman Frank; ORCHESTRATIONS/ARRANGEMENTS: Robert Ginzler & Sid Ramin; DANCE MUSIC ARRANGEMENTS: Fred Werner; CAST RECORDING on RCA Victor; PRESS: Barry Hyams & Edith L. Kean; GENERAL MANAGER: Oscar Olesen; COMPANY MANAGER: Irving Cooper; PRODUCTION STAGE MANAGER: Phil Friedman; STAGE MANAGER: Walter Rinner; ASSISTANT STAGE MANAGER: Bob Kaliban & Frank Hamilton. *Cast:* DOORMAN: Lee Barry; PFC. DOYLE: Walter Farrell; PFC. O'DELL: Bob Dixon; CPL. GANZ: Bill McDonald; PFC. PASCO: Bernie Meyer; SGT. MURDOCK: Lionel Stander (2); NIGHTCLUB PERFORMER: Marilyn Stark; MASTER OF CEREMONIES: Bob Kaliban; WAITER: Erik Kristen; NIGHTCLUB MANAGER: William Le Massena; WOODROW TRUESMITH: Tom Poston (1) ☆; MP: Burt Bier; BARTENDER: Samye Van; A GENERAL: T.J. Halligan; CONDUCTOR: Don Morgan; MAYOR NOBLE: Fred Stewart (5); JUDGE CALLAN: William LeMassena; FORREST NOBLE: John McMartin; WHITEMAN: Bob Kaliban; MRS. NOBLE: Edith Gresham; REVEREND COX: Geoffrey Bryant; SUE ANNE BARNES: Jane Mason (4); RONNIE: Richard Buckley; MRS. TRUESMITH: Elizabeth Kerr; LIBBY CALLAN: Kay Brown (3); GENE: Kenny Kealy; DOC JOHNSON: T.J. Halligan; THE ENEMY CAPTAIN: John Aristedes; EFFIE: Brina Dexter; DANCERS: John Aristedes, Margery Beddow, Marlene Dell, Shellie Farrell, Pat Ferrier, William Guske, Kathe Howard, Reby Howells, Betty Hyatt Linton, Dick Korthaze, Erik Kristen, Dale Moreda, James Senn, Michel Stuart; SINGERS: Lee Barry, Burt Bier, Shirley Chester, Tony Craig, Georgia Creighton, Brina Dexter, Charlotte Frazier, Marianne Gale, Ed Mastin, Don Morgan, Charles Rule, Marilyn Stark. *Understudies*: Woodrow: Bob Kaliban; Libby: Charlotte Frazier & Pat Ferrier; Sue Anne: Margery Beddow; Murdock: T.J. Halligan; Mayor: William Le Massena; Mrs. Truesmith: Edith Gresham; Pasco: Lee Barry; Doyle: Burt Bier; O'Dell: Erik Kristen; Ganz: Richard Korthaze; Gene: Richard Buckley; Mrs. Noble: Georgia Creighton; Forrest: Ed Mastin; Callan/Johnson/Cox: Frank Hamilton; Dancing Woodrow: James Senn. *Act I*: *Scene 1* The *Chez Victory* club: "Girls! Girls!" (Doorman & The Marines), "Five Shots of Whiskey" (Murdock, O'Dell, Doyle, Ganz, Pasco); *Scene 2* The train; *Scene 3* The station at Hillsdale: "Hail, the Conquering Hero!" (Woodrow & Company), "Must Be Given to You" (Company); *Scene 4* The Truesmith porch: "Wonderful, Marvelous You" (Woodrow, Libby, Gene); *Scene 5* The church: "Truth" (Company), "Won't You Marry Me?" (Libby); *Scene 6* The Truesmith house; *Scene 7* The river bank: "The River Bank" (Sue Anne & Woodrow); *Scene 8* Woodrow's room: "Only Rainbows" (Woodrow, O'Dell, Doyle, Ganz); *Scene 9* The campaign: "The Campaign" (Woodrow & Ensemble). *Act II*: *Scene 1* The election: *Scene 2* The town hall: "One Mother Each" (Murdock, O'Dell, Doyle, Ganz, Pasco), "Must Be Given to You" (reprise) (Company); *Scene 3* The house: "I'm Beautiful" (Libby & The Marines); *Scene 4* The railroad station: "Rough Times" (Libby & Gene); *Scene 5* The Mayor's office: "Yours, All Yours" (Woodrow, Sue Anne, Ensemble); *Scene 6* The town hall; *Scene 7* The station: "Won't You Marry Me?" (reprise) (Woodrow), "Hail, the Conquering Hero!" (reprise) (Entire Company), "Only Rainbows" (reprise) (Entire Company).

Reviews were very divided.

152. *The Consul*

An opera, or "a musical drama" (as Gian-Carlo Menotti called it). Set in a large city somewhere in Europe during the Cold War, where displaced persons are hampered by red tape. A hunted revolutionary, John, denied a visa, escapes from the secret police and flees to the mountains, saying he will not cross the frontier until his wife Magda has her exit visa; Magda's baby and John's mother die of poverty and despair as she attempts to get a visa from the (unseen) consul (via his inflexible secretary). The professorial Mr. Kofner; an Italian peasant, Anna; Vera; Nika; a foreign woman; these are all others waiting in the consul's soulless waiting room. In fact after Magda's enormously long wait to get in to see the consul, the door opens and she sees that the previous interviewee is the chief police agent who has been trying to force her to reveal the names of her husband's friends. The callous delay and interminable red tape, and the knowledge that if her husband comes back to get her he will be killed, force Magda to commit suicide by sticking her head in a gas oven (after asking God's pardon). The irony is that John does come for her, and is captured. Another irony is that the secretary is finally moved by Magda's pleas and becomes her ally — too late. A Mabel Mercer record is a recurring theme throughout, and plays in a café across the street from the apartment. Assan is a glass-cutter who relays messages to Magda from her husband.

Before Broadway. It tried out at the Shubert Theatre, Philadelphia, from 3/1/50. Vera Brynner was Yul's sister.

The Broadway Run. ETHEL BARRYMORE THEATRE, 3/15/50– 11/4/50. 269 PERFORMANCES. PRESENTED BY Chandler Cowles & Efrem Zimbalist Jr.; MUSIC/LYRICS/BOOK: Gian-Carlo Menotti; DIRECTOR: Gian-Carlo Menotti; DREAMS CHOREOGRAPHER: John Butler; SETS: Horace Armistead; COSTUMES: Grace Houston; LIGHTING: Jean Rosenthal; MUSICAL DIRECTOR: Lehman Engel; MUSICAL CO-ORDINATOR: Thomas Schippers; CAST RECORDING on Decca, directed by Gian-Carlo Menotti. Faye Elizabeth Smith took over the role of Vera for the recording; PRESS: George & Dorothy Ross, Madelin Blitzstein; GENERAL MANAGER: Chandos Sweet; GENERAL STAGE MANAGER: David Kanter; STAGE MANAGER: Charles Pratt Jr. *Cast:* JOHN SOREL: Cornell MacNeil, *Russell George*; MAGDA SOREL: Patricia Neway (2), Vera Brynner (Monday evenings & Wednesday matinees — *Bruni Falcon*); THE MOTHER: Marie Powers (1), *Lydia Summers*; CHIEF POLICE AGENT: Leon Lishner; 1ST POLICE AGENT: Chester Watson; 2ND POLICE AGENT: Donald Blackey; THE SECRETARY: Gloria Lane; MR. KOFNER: George Jongeyans, *David Aiken*; THE FOREIGN WOMAN: Maria Marlo; ANNA GOMEZ: Maria Andreassi; VERA BORONELL: Lydia Summers, *Georgeanna Bourdon*; NIKA MAGADOFF, THE MAGICIAN: Andrew McKinley, *Norman Kelley*; ASSAN: Francis Monachino; VOICE ON THE RECORD: Mabel Mercer. STANDBYS: John: Russell George; Secretary/Vera: Faye Elizabeth Smith, *Rosemary Kuhlmann*; Foreign Woman/Anna: Jeanne Grant. Understudies: Mother: Lydia Summers; Chief Agent/Kofner/Assan: Chester Watson; Nika: Donald Blackey, *Roger Schmidt*. *Act I*: *Scene 1* The Sorel apartment; early morning: "Tu Reviendras" ("Now, O Lips, Say Goodbye") (John, Magda, Mother); *Scene 2* The consulate; later the same day: "In Endless Waiting Rooms the Hour Stands Still" (Vera, Anna, Magda, Magadoff, Kofner). *Act II*: *Scene 1* The home; in the evening; one month later: "I Shall Find for You Shells and Stars" (also known as "Lullaby," or "Sleep, My Love") (Magda); *Scene 2* The consulate; a few days later: "Oh, What a Lovely Dance" (Applicants in consulate), "To This We've Come" (Magda). *Act III*: *Scene 1* The consulate; later afternoon; several days later: "Oh, Those Faces!" ("All the Documents Must Be Signed") (Secretary); *Scene 2* The home; that night: "Lo, Death's Frontiers Are Open; All Aboard!" (Company).

It got great reviews. It was very topical, and thus has become dated. It won a Pulitzer Prize for Music, and a Tony Award for musical direction. It also won Donaldson Awards for musical, composer, lyrics, book, director, and for Patricia Neway and Gloria Lane.

After Broadway. CAMBRIDGE THEATRE, London, 2/7/51–4/21/51. 84 PERFORMANCES. *Cast:* JOHN: Russell George; MAGDA: Patricia Neway; MOTHER: Marie Powers; CHIEF: Leon Lishner; 1ST AGENT: Noel Coleman; 2ND AGENT: John Oxley; SECRETARY: Gloria Lane; KOFNER: David Aiken; FOREIGN WOMAN: Maria Marlo; ANNA: Maria Paradiso; VERA: Elinor Warren; NIKA: Norman Kelley; ASSAN: Francis Monachino. This production was televised by the BBC in 1951.

CITY CENTER, NYC, 10/8/52–10/29/52. 3 PERFORMANCES IN REPERTORY. PRESENTED BY the New York City Opera Company. It had the same basic crew as for the 1950 Broadway production. *Cast:* JOHN: Richard Torigi; MAGDA: Patricia Neway; MOTHER: Mary Kreste; AGENT: Emile Renan; PLAINCLOTHESMEN: Charles Kuestner & Thomas Powell; SECRETARY: Gloria Lane; KOFNER: Jon Geyans [i.e. George Jongeyans, who later became George Gaynes]; FOREIGN WOMAN: Maria Marlo; ANNA: Vilma Georgiou; VERA: Edith Evans; NIKA: Norman Kelley; ASSAN: Arthur Newman.

SADLERS WELLS, London. There were three notable runs of *The Consul* here in the mid–50s. The first engagement ran 11/11/54–1/10/55.

9 PERFORMANCES. The second engagement ran 2/3/56–2/16/56. 3 PER-FORMANCES. The third engagement ran 9/28/57–10/16/57. 5 PERFOR-MANCES. *Cast:* JOHN: John Probyn; MAGDA: Amy Shuard; MOTHER: Olwen Price; AGENT: Denis Dowling, *Harold Blackburn* (took over during the 1st engagement, and played it for the 2nd & 3rd engagements also); SECRETARY: Anna Pollak; KOFNER: Stanley Clarkson; FOREIGN WOMAN: Marjorie Shires, *Judith Pierce* (2nd engagement), *Ava June* (3rd engagement); ANNA: Helen Hillier, *Sheila Hardy* (2nd engagement), *Helen Hillier* (3rd engagement); VERA: Elisabeth Robinson, *Patricia Johnson* (2nd & 3rd engagements); NIKA: Rowland Jones.

CANADIAN TV PRODUCTION. 1959. DIRECTOR: Gian-Carlo Menotti. *Cast:* MAGDA: Patricia Neway; CHIEF AGENT: Leon Lishner; FOREIGN WOMAN: Maria Marlo.

CITY CENTER, NYC, 2/14/60–2/21/60. 2 PERFORMANCES IN REPERTORY. PRESENTED BY the New York City Opera; DIRECTOR/CHOREOGRAPHER: Gian-Carlo Menotti; SETS/COSTUMES: Horace Armistead; LIGHTING: Jean Rosenthal; CONDUCTOR: Werner Torkanowsky; MAGIC SEQUENCES: Fred Keating. *Cast:* JOHN: Chester Ludgin; MAGDA: Patricia Neway; MOTHER: Evelyn Sachs; AGENT: Joshua Hecht; PLAINCLOTHESMEN: William Zachariasen & Sam Kirkham; SECRETARY: Regina Sarfaty; KOFNER: Arnold Voketaitis; FOREIGN WOMAN: Maria Marlo; ANNA: Maria Di Gerlando; VERA: Ruth Kobart; NIKA: Jack Harrold; ASSAN: Dan Merriman.

CITY CENTER, NYC, 3/28/62–4/8/62. 4 PERFORMANCES IN REPERTORY. PRESENTED BY the New York City Opera; DIRECTOR: Roger Englander; SETS/COSTUMES: Horace Armistead; CONDUCTOR: Werner Torkanowsky. *Cast:* JOHN: Richard Fredricks; MAGDA: Patricia Neway; MOTHER: Evelyn Sachs; AGENT: William Chapman; PLAINCLOTHESMEN: Glenn Dowlen & Norman Grohan; SECRETARY: Marija Kova; KOFNER: George Gaynes; FOREIGN WOMAN: Maria Marlo; ANNA: Mary Le Sawyer; VERA: Teresa Racz; NIKA: Norman Kelley; ASSAN: Fredric Milstein.

NEW YORK STATE THEATRE, 3/17/66–3/23/66. 3 PERFORMANCES IN REPERTORY. PRESENTED BY the New York City Opera; DIRECTOR: Gian-Carlo Menotti; SETS/COSTUMES: Horace Armistead; CONDUCTOR: Vincent La Selva. *Cast:* JOHN: Sherrill Milnes; MAGDA: Patricia Neway; MOTHER: Evelyn Sachs; AGENT: Herbert Beattie; PLAINCLOTHESMEN: Philip Erickson & Richard Park; SECRETARY: Beverly Evans; KOFNER: David Smith; FOREIGN WOMAN: Elisabeth Carron; ANNA: Ludmilla Azova; VERA: Elisabeth Farmer; NIKA: Gene Bullard; ASSAN: Jack Bittner.

NEW YORK STATE THEATRE, 10/6/66–10/30/66. 2 PERFORMANCES IN REPERTORY. PRESENTED BY the New York City Opera; DIRECTOR: Gian-Carlo Menotti; SETS/COSTUMES: Horace Armistead; CONDUCTOR: Charles Wilson. *Cast:* JOHN: David Clatworthy; MAGDA: Patricia Neway; MOTHER: Evelyn Sachs; AGENT: Joseph Fair; PLAINCLOTHESMEN: Philip Erickson & Richard Park; SECRETARY: Beverly Evans; KOFNER: David Smith; FOREIGN WOMAN: Julia Migenes; ANNA: LaVergne Monette; VERA: Charlotte Povia; NIKA: Gene Bullard; ASSAN: Jack Bittner.

NEW YORK STATE THEATRE, 3/27/74–4/28/74. 4 PERFORMANCES IN REPERTORY. Return engagement, 3/22/75–4/6/75. 2 PERFORMANCES IN REPERTORY. Italics indicate for the return engagement in 1975. PRESENTED BY the New York City Opera; DIRECTOR: Gian-Carlo Menotti, *Francis Rizzo*; SETS: Horace Armistead; CONDUCTOR: Christophe Keene. *Cast:* JOHN: John Darrenkamp; MAGDA: Olivia Stapp; MOTHER: Muriel Costa-Greenspon; AGENT: Edward Pierson; PLAINCLOTHESMEN: Jack Sims & Ray Van Orden (*Tom Barrett*); SECRETARY: Sandra Walker; KOFNER: Don Yule; FOREIGN WOMAN: Judith De Rosa; ANNA: Barbara Hocher; NIKA: Nico Castel, *John Lankston*; VERA: Virginia Brobyn, *Sophia Steffan*; ASSAN: William Ledbetter.

The Consul has been produced on TV many times more recently, one of the notable occasions being an airing of the 1977 stage production at the Spoleto Festival, in Charleston, SC.

153. *Contact*

A two-hour "dance play," in three short parts, each part representing a short story. The musical numbers were a recorded soundtrack. Michael Wylie is suicidal. The Girl in the Yellow Dress is mysterious and elusive, the object of Michael's desire. The wife is a repressed Italian housewife, circa 1950s, who escapes her life through dance fantasies. The title comes from Michael's ability to make "contact" with other people through dance.

Before Broadway. Susan Stroman was in a dance club one night and saw a mysterious woman in a yellow dress dancing with different partners throughout the night. She felt that someone's life would be changed by this (Miss Stroman's was). The show was first announced in 11/98, by Miss Stroman. In 1/99 it was workshopped at Lincoln Center, and then opened there as an Off Broadway show at the MITZI E. NEWHOUSE THEATRE (downstairs at Lincoln Center), on 10/7/99. Previews from 9/9/99. It got a great review in the *New York Times*, and sold out. Soon after opening night there was talk of a Broadway move, and the Vivian Beaumont (upstairs at Lincoln Center) seemed the natural house. After 101 PERFORMANCES it closed at the Mitzi Newhouse on 1/2/00 (its closing date had been extended from 11/28/99), and re-opened at the Beaumont. Broadway previews began on 3/2/00 (the date had been brought forward from 3/9/00).

The Broadway Run. VIVIAN BEAUMONT THEATRE, 3/30/00–9/1/02. 31 previews from 3/2/00. 1,009 PERFORMANCES. PRESENTED BY the Lincoln Center Theatre Company; WRITER: John Weidman; DEVISED BY: Susan Stroman & John Weidman; DIRECTOR/CHOREOGRAPHER: Susan Stroman; ASSOCIATE DIRECTORS: Graciela Daniele, Gerald Gutierrez, Nicholas Hytner, Daniel Sullivan; SETS: Thomas Lynch; COSTUMES: William Ivey Long; LIGHTING: Peter Kaczorowski; SOUND: Scott Stauffer; CAST RECORDING on RCA, released on 3/6/01; PRESS: Philip Rinaldi; CASTING: Johnson — Liff Associates & Tara Rubin Casting; GENERAL MANAGER: Steven C. Callahan; COMPANY MANAGER: Adam Siegel, *Gillian Roth*; PRODUCTION STAGE MANAGER: Thom Widmann; ASSISTANT STAGE MANAGERS: Scott A. Fagant & Lisa Iacucci. *Cast:* SERVANT: Sean Martin Hingston; ARISTOCRAT: Scott Taylor; GIRL ON THE SWING: Stephanie Michels, *Joanne Manning* (from 1/29/02); HUSBAND: Jason Antoon, *Danny Mastrogiorgio* (from 3/9/01); WIFE: Karen Ziemba (until 9/2/01), *Charlotte d'Amboise* (from 9/4/01); HEADWAITER: David MacGillivray; BUSBOY: Rocker Verastique; WAITERS: Scott Taylor & Robert Wersinger; RESTAURANT PATRONS: Tome Cousin, Nina Goldman, Peter Gregus, Dana Stackpole (*Gigi Chavoshi*); UNCLE VINNIE: Sean Martin Hingston; PHOTOGRAPHER: Pascale Faye; CIGARETTE GIRL: Shannon Hammons; MICHAEL WILEY: Boyd Gaines (until 9/2/01), *D.W. Moffett* (9/4/01–3/3/02), *John Bolton* (3/5/02–3/17/02), *Alan Campbell* (from 3/19/02); GIRL IN YELLOW DRESS: Deborah Yates (until 9/2/01), *Colleen Dunn* (from 9/4/01); BARTENDER: Jason Antoon, *Danny Mastrogiorgio* (from 3/01); JACK: Jack Hayes; JOE: Robert Wersinger; JOHNNY: Sean Martin Hingston; VOICE MESSAGES: Jason Antoon, *Danny Mastrogiorgio* (from 3/01); CLUBGOERS: Tome Cousin, Pascale Faye, Nina Goldman, Peter Gregus (occasionally relieved by Andy *Blankenbuehler*), Shannon Hammons, Stephanie Michels (*Joanne Manning*), Mayumi Miguel, Dana Stackpole (*Gigi Chavoshi*), Scott Taylor, Rocker Verastique. **Standbys**: Michael: John Bolton; Girl in Yellow Dress: Holly Cruikshank, *Shannon Lewis*. **Understudies**: Michael: Scott Taylor; Husband: John Bolton, Peter Gregus, Stacey Todd Holt, *Danny Herman*; Wife: Holly Cruikshank, Nina Goldman, Angelique Ilo, *Shannon Lewis*; Girl on Swing: Holly Cruikshank, Shannon Hammons, Joanne Manning, *Angelique Ilo, Leeanna Smith, Shannon Lewis*; Girl in Yellow Dress: Joanne Manning, *Shannon Hammons*; Frenchmen: John Bolton, Steve Geary, Stacey Todd Holt, Robert Wersinger, *Danny Herman, Rod McCune, David Gomez*; Bartender: John Bolton, Stacey Todd Holt, *Peter Gregus, Danny Herman*; Headwaiter: Steve Geary, Scott Taylor, Rocker Verastique, *Robert M. Armitage, Adam Zotovich, David Gomez*. **Swings**: Steve Geary, Stacey Todd Holt, Angelique Ilo, Joanne Manning, *Robert M. Armitage, Danny Herman, Leeanna Smith, Kelly Sullivan, Adam Zotovich, David Gomez, Rod McCune*. **Act I**: PART I: Swinging. A forest glade, 1767. A servant, an aristocrat, a girl on a swing: "My Heart Stood Still" (m: Richard Rodgers; l: Lorenz Hart; performed by Stephane Grappelli); PART II: Did You Move? An Italian restaurant, Queens, 1954. A wife, a husband, a headwaiter, busboy, waiters, restaurant patrons, Uncle Vinnie, photographer, cigarette girl: "Anitra's Dance" (from *Peer Gynt Suite No. 1*, by Edvard Grieg; performed by the New York Philharmonic–Leonard Bernstein, conductor), "Waltz Eugene" (from

Eugene Onegin, Op. 24, by Edvard Grieg performed by the New York Philharmonic–Leonard Bernstein, conductor), "La Farandole" (from *L'Arlesienne Suite No. 2,* by Edvard Grieg; performed by the New York Philharmonic — Leonard Bernstein, conductor), "O Mio Babbino Caro" (by Giacomo Puccini; performed by Andre Kostelanetz & His Orchestra). *Act II*: PART III: Contact: *Scene 1* New York City, 1999 — Awards ceremony. Michael Wiley (an advertising executive), a bartender, a girl in a yellow dress, Jack, Joe, Johnny, Clubgoers, voice messages: "You're Nobody 'til Somebody Loves You" (m/l: Russ Morgan, Larry Stock, James Cavanaugh; performed by Dean Martin) [note: when it came time to do the cast recording, RCA couldn't get permission to include this number, so Boyd Gaines did a full-orchestra version of it for the album], "Powerful Stuff" (m/l: Wally Wilson, Michael Henderson, Robert S. Field; performed by the Fabulous Thunderbirds); *Scene 2* Michael's apartment; *Scene 3* The streets of New York; the club: "Put a Lid on It" (m: Tom Maxwell; performed by Squirrel Nut Zippers), "Sweet Lorraine" (m/l: Clifford Burwell & Mitchell Parish; performed by Stephane Grappelli), "Runaround Sue" (m/l: Ernie Maresca & Dion Di Mucci; performed by Dion), "Beyond the Sea" (m: Charles Trenet & Jack Lawrence; performed by Royal Crown Revue — Arte Butler, conductor); *Scene 4* Michael's apartment; *Scene 5* The club: "See What I Mean?" (m: J. Chapman; performed by Al Cooper & His Savoy Sultans), "Simply Irresistible" (music written & performed by Robert Palmer), "Do You Wanna Dance?" (m/l: Bobby Freeman) (performed by the Beach Boys), "Topsy" (m: William Edgar Battle & Eddie Durham) (performed by the Royal Crown Revue); *Scene 6* Michael's apartment: "You're Nobody 'til Somebody Loves You" (reprise); *Scene 7* The club: "Sing Sing Sing" (m: Louis Prima) (arranged & performed by Benny Goodman), "Christopher Columbus" (m/l: Andy Razaf) (performed by Benny Goodman), "Moondance" (music written & performed by Van Morrison); *Scene 8* Michael's apartment: "Sweet Lorraine" (reprise).

Reviews were very good. Because it had no original score (it just used old recordings) there was doubt that the Tony committee would recognize it as a musical — but they did, despite strenuous objections from the Musicians' Union. In fact, not only did the 2000 Tonys recognize it, it won for best musical (also for choreography, and for Boyd Gaines and Karen Ziemba). It was also nominated for direction of a musical, book, and for Deborah Yates. PBS broadcast the last performance as part of the *Live from Lincoln Center* series.

After Broadway. TOUR. It was announced on 3/24/00 that the tour would open in the fall of 2000. But it began on 5/22/01 (previews from 5/15/01), at the Curran Theatre, San Francisco. Then it went to the Ahmanson Theatre, Los Angeles, 6/29/01–9/1/01, then continued with the tour. The tour closed on 6/02, in Dallas. *Cast*: GIRL IN SWING: Mindy Franzese Wild; SERVANT: Keith Kuhl; ARISTOCRAT: Andrew Asnes, *Dan Sutcliffe*; MICHAEL: Alan Campbell, *Daniel McDonald* (from 3/19/02); GIRL IN YELLOW DRESS: Holly Cruikshank, *Deborah Yates* (for three cities, 5/7/02–6/16/02); WIFE: Meg Howrey; HUSBAND: Adam Dannheiser; HEADWAITER: Gary Franco; BUSBOY: Adam Zotovich; ALSO WITH: Donna Dunmire, Stacey Todd Holt, Danielle Jolie, Joanne Manning, Leeanna Smith, Julius Sermonia. It opened again, at the Canon Theatre, Toronto, 11/5/02–12/17/02. *Cast*: GIRL: Colleen Dunn; WIFE: Meg Howrey; MICHAEL: Daniel McDonald; HUSBAND: Adam Dannheiser.

QUEEN'S THEATRE, London, 10/23/02–5/10/03. Previews from 10/3/03. It was first announced for spring 2002. DIRECTOR: Susan Stroman (her West End directing debut). *Cast*: GIRL: Leigh Zimmerman; MICHAEL: Michael Praed; WIFE: Sarah Wildor; ALSO WITH: Craig Urbani, Spencer Soloman. The closing date was extended from 2/22/03 to 5/31/03, but it closed early.

THE MOVIE. Focused on the last section of the musical. It was scheduled to be made in 2003, but had to be put off until after Susan Stroman finished filming *The Producers*. PRODUCER: Laurence Mark; WRITER: John Weidman; DIRECTOR: Susan Stroman (this was to have been her movie directing debut).

turbance. She becomes entangled in her night stick and fur stole; she battles a modern "womb chair"; and creates havoc in the Holland Tunnel.

Before Broadway. Nancy Walker's husband was David Craig. During the Philadelphia tryout Joan Blondell was replaced by Benay Venuta, and director Marc Daniels by Burt Shevelove, even though Mr. Daniels retained credit. Most of Anna Sokolow's choreography was re-done by Bob Fosse, who came to the show late; he took credit for only one dance ("Baby's Baby"). It played New Haven, 9/13/57–9/21/57.

The Broadway Run. MARTIN BECK THEATRE, 10/17/57–11/16/57. 36 PERFORMANCES. PRESENTED BY Lyn Austin & Thomas Noyes, in association with Anderson Lawler; MUSIC: David Baker; LYRICS: David Craig; BOOK: Ellen Violett & David Craig; DIRECTOR: Marc Daniels; CHOREOGRAPHER: Anna Sokolow (with Bob Fosse); ASSISTANT CHOREOGRAPHER: Donald McKayle; SETS: William & Jean Eckart; COSTUMES: Alvin Colt; MUSICAL DIRECTOR/VOCAL ARRANGEMENTS: Maurice Levine; ORCHESTRATIONS: Ralph Burns; DANCE MUSIC ARRANGEMENTS: John Morris; PRESS: Barry Hyams; GENERAL MANAGER: Richard Horner; COMPANY MANAGER: Norman Maibaum; PRODUCTION STAGE MANAGER: Jean Barrere; STAGE MANAGERS: Harry Young & Beau Tilden. *Cast*: 1ST EXPERT: Byron Mitchell; 2ND EXPERT: David Gold; 3RD EXPERT: Stanley Papich; 4TH EXPERT: Jeff Duncan; 5TH EXPERT: John Dorrin; 6TH EXPERT: Kevin Carlisle; 7TH EXPERT: Bob Roman; 8TH EXPERT: Sam Greene; KATEY O'SHEA: Nancy Walker (1); COMMISSIONER: Beau Tilden; CAPTAIN: Alan Bunce (5); SERGEANT: Bruce MacKay; ETHEL POTTS: Michele Burke; MARY POTTS: Evelyn Russell; ESTELLE O'SHEA, KATEY'S MOTHER: Benay Venuta (2); MRS. ZIMMER: Alice Nunn; MR. MORPHKY: Michael Roberts; MRS. MORPHKY: Doreen McLean; PIGGY: Byron Mitchell; BRAWN: Norma Douglas (6); BRAINS: Peter Conlow (7); BOY: Stanley Papich; PRINCIPAL: Alice Pearce (4); INSTRUCTOR: Clyde Turner; GEORGE: Dick Williams (3); LIMEY: Hank Jones; SLAM: Doug Rogers; PROFESSOR: Ernie Furtado; TRAINTIME: Frank Rehak; SLAM'S GIRL: Elmarie Wendel; LIMEY'S WIFE: Elton J. Warren; PROFESSOR'S GIRL: Bette Graham; ROOKIE COPS: Sam Greene, Michael Roberts, John Dorrin, Bob Roman, Nat Wright, Larry Mitchell, Jack Moore; RODERICK: David Gold; POLICEWOMEN: Dorothy Aull, Joy Lane, Bette Graham; WOMAN IN THE WINDOW: Joy Lane; GUARD: Michael Roberts; DANCERS: Shawneequa Baker, Eve Beck, Kevin Carlisle, Judith Coy, Anita Dencks, Jeff Duncan, Kate Friedlich, David Gold, Ellen Hubel, Donald McKayle, Jack Moore, Willard Nagel, Stanley Papich, Harold Pierson, Coco Ramirez, Tina Ramirez, Ella Thompson; SINGERS: Dorothy Aull, John Dorrin, Laurie Franks, Bette Graham, Sam Green, Buzz Halliday, Joy Lane, Bruce Mackay, Byron Mitchell, Larry Mitchell, Michael Roberts, Bob Roman, Joanne Spiller, Clyde Turner, Elton Warren, Elmarie Wendel, Nat Wright. *Understudies*: Katey: Dorothy Aull; Estelle: Doreen McLean; George: Doug Rogers; Principal: Alice Nunn; Captain: Michael Roberts; Brawn: Buzz Halliday; Brains: Kevin Carlisle; Mary/Ethel: Joanne Spiller. *Act I*: "Career Guidance" (Career Guides & Katey), "Wearing of the Blue" (Katey & Company), "I Need All the Help I Can Get" (Katey), "Cool Combo Mambo" (The Kids), "You Walked Out" (George), "Cool Credo" (George, Katey, Combo, Bandannies, Kids), "Bringing up Daughter" (Estelle) (this number replaced "La Vie Boheme"), "Don't Look Now" (Katey, George, Dancers), "Baby's Baby" (dance ch: Bob Fosse) (Brawn, Brains, Shawneequa Baker, Coco Ramirez, Tina Ramirez), "You Walked Out" (reprise) (Katey). *Act II*: "Call the Police" (Katey & Policewomen), "Unmistakable Sign" (Katey & Estelle), "Why Her?" (George), "Me and Love" (Katey), Remember the Dancing (dance sequence) (Company), "Hong Kong" (Estelle & Company), "Argentine Tango" (Principal & Captain), "Sweet William" (Estelle & Company), "Don't Look Now" (reprise) (George), "Little Woman" (Katey), Finale: "Call the Police" (reprise) (Entire Company).

Broadway reviews were bad.

154. *Copper and Brass*

Set in and around Manhattan. Katey is a policewoman who falls for a jazz musician she meets while investigating a noise dis-

155. *Copperfield*

Before Broadway. In the ensemble Cleve Asbury was replaced by David Ray Bartee before Broadway opening night

The Broadway Run. ANTA THEATRE, 4/16/81–4/26/81. 26 previews from 3/25/81. 13 PERFORMANCES. A Dome production, PRESENTED BY Don Gregory & Mike Merrick; MUSIC/LYRICS/BOOK: Al Kasha & Joel Hirschhorn; BASED ON the 1850 novel *David Copperfield*, by Charles Dickens; DIRECTOR/CHOREOGRAPHER: Rob Iscove; SETS: Tony Straiges; COSTUMES: John David Ridge; LIGHTING: Ken Billington; SOUND: John McClure; MUSICAL DIRECTOR/VOCAL ARRANGEMENTS: Larry Blank; ORCHESTRATIONS: Irwin Kostal; DANCE MUSIC ARRANGEMENTS/INCIDENTAL MUSIC: Donald Johnston; PRESS: Seymour Krawitz, Patricia Krawitz, Warren Knowlton; CASTING: Julie Hughes & Barry Moss; COMPANY MANAGER: Martin Cohen; PRODUCTION STAGE MANAGER: Peter Lawrence; STAGE MANAGER: Jim Woolley; ASSISTANT STAGE MANAGER: Edward Isser & Sarah Whitham. *Cast:* DR. CHILIP: Richard Warren Pugh; PEGGOTTY: Mary Stout; NURSE: Katharine Buffaloe; AUNT BETSEY TROTWOOD: Carmen Mathews (4) ✩; YOUNG DAVID: Evan Richards (7) ✩; CLARA COPPERFIELD: Pamela McLernon; MR. MURDSTONE: Michael Connolly (6) ✩; JANE MURDSTONE: Maris Clement; MR. MICAWBER: George S. Irving (8) ✩; BOOTMAKER: David Horwitz; BUTCHER: Bruce Sherman; BAKER: Richard Warren Pugh; MRS. MICAWBER: Linda Poser; VICTORIA: Spence Ford; VANESSA: Dana Moore; CONSTABLE: Michael Danek; MICK WALKER: Gary Munch; MEALY POTATOES: Brian Quinn; BILLY MOWCHER: Christian Slater; MR. QUINION: Ralph Braun; MR. DICK: Lenny Wolpe; JANET: Darleigh Miller; ADULT DAVID: Brian Matthews (1) ✩; MRS. HEEP: Beulah Garrick; URIAH HEEP: Barrie Ingham (3) ✩; MR. WICKFIELD: Keith Perry; AGNES WICKFIELD: Leslie Denniston (2) ✩; DORA SPENLOW: Mary Mastrantonio (5) ✩; JULIA MILLS: Katharine Buffaloe; TICKET TAKER: Michael Gorman; ENSEMBLE: David Ray Bartee, Ralph Braun, Katharine Buffaloe, Maris Clement, Michael Danek, Spence Ford, Michael Gorman, David Horwitz, Pamela McLernon, Darleigh Miller, Dana Moore, Gary Munch, Keith Perry, Linda Poser, Richard Warren Pugh, Brian Quinn, Lynne Savage, Bruce Sherman, Claude Tessier, Missy Whitchurch. *Understudies*: Young David: Christian Slater; Aunt Betsey: Linda Poser; Murdstone: Ralph Braun; Peggotty: Missy Whitchurch; Uriah: Keith Perry; Micawber: Lenny Wolpe; Mr. Dick: Richard Warren Pugh; Mrs. Heep: Katharine Buffaloe; Dora: Pamela McLernon; Adult David: David Horwitz; Agnes: Darleigh Miller. *Swing Dancers*: Heather Lee Gerdes & Daniel Dee. *Act I: Scene 1* A stormy December night, 1812; the drawing room of the Copperfield cottage in Blunderstone, Suffolk: "I Don't Want a Boy" (Aunt Betsey, Peggotty, Ensemble); *Scene 2* An afternoon in Autumn, 1822; the garden of the Copperfield cottage: "Mama, Don't Get Married" (Young David, Clara, Peggotty); *Scene 3* The following spring; the drawing room of the Copperfield cottage; *Scene 4* 6:30 in the morning; the Murdstone & Grinby Warehouse: "Copperfield" ("The Bottle Song") (Young David, Quinion, Mealy Potatoes, Billy, Mick, Ensemble); *Scene 5* Mid-afternoon, the following summer; a London street near the Micawber home, and inside the Micawber home: "Something Will Turn Up" (Micawber, Young David, Creditors, Ensemble), "Something Will Turn Up" (reprise) (Micawber, Young David, Micawber Family); *Scene 6* Immediately following, on the road to Dover: "Anyone" (Young David); *Scene 7* A few days later; Aunt Betsey Trotwood's country house in Dover; *Scene 8* A week later; on the road near Aunt Betsey's house; *Scene 9* Immediately following; the parlor of Aunt Betsey's house: "Here's a Book" (Aunt Betsey, Mr. Dick, Young David). 10 years later: "Here's a Book" (reprise) (Aunt Betsey, Mr. Dick, David); *Scene 10* A week later; Mr. Wickfield's sitting room in London: "'umble" (Uriah & Mrs. Heep); *Scene 11* The following Sunday; Southwark Fair: "The Circle Waltz" (David, Dora, Agnes, Ensemble). *Act II: Scene 1* Several months later; Mr. Wickfield's office: "Up the Ladder" (Uriah & Micawber), "I Wish He Knew" (Agnes); *Scene 2* Outside the church: "The Lights of London" (David, Dora, Company); *Scene 3* Several months later; Mr. Wickfield's sitting room: "'umble" (reprise) (Uriah); *Scene 4* Several weeks later; the home of David and Dora Copperfield: "I Wish He Knew" (reprise) (Agnes); *Scene 5* A street near the Wickfield house: "Something Will Turn Up" (reprise) (Micawber & David); *Scene 6* The office of Wickfield & Heep: "Villainy is the Matter" (David, Uriah, Micawber, Agnes, Aunt Betsey, Mr. Dick, Mrs. Heep, Peggotty, Mrs. Micawber); *Scene 7* The home of David and Dora Copperfield: "With the One I Love" (David); *Scene 8* One year later; the London Docks: "Something Will Turn Up" (reprise) (Micawber & Ensemble), "Anyone" (reprise) (David & Agnes).

It got very bad Broadway reviews, and closed at the 4/26/81 matinee. It received a Tony nomination for score.

156. *Courtin' Time*

Set in Maine in 1898 (the original play had been set in England). When his daughters leave him to get married, a farmer, Samuel, without benefit of courting, proposes to three women, all of whom turn him down. He finally courts his housekeeper, Araminta.

Before Broadway. Walter Huston was the original lead but he died during the early stages of production, and was replaced by Lloyd Nolan. It opened in Philadelphia, but Mr. Nolan had voice problems and left. Alfred Drake took over for the rest of the Philly run, then Joe E. Brown took over. The number "A Man Never Married a Wife" was cut.

The Broadway Run. NATIONAL THEATRE, 6/13/51–6/30/51; ROYALE THEATRE, 7/2/51–7/14/51. TOTAL OF 37 PERFORMANCES. PRESENTED BY James Russo & Michael Ellis, in association with Alexander H. Cohen; MUSIC/MUSICAL & VOCAL ARRANGEMENTS: Don Walker; LYRICS: Jack Lawrence; BOOK: William Roos; BASED ON the 1924 British comedy *The Farmer's Wife*, by Eden Phillpotts; DIRECTOR: Alfred Drake; CHOREOGRAPHER: George Balanchine; DANCE CAPTAIN: Audrey Keane; SETS/LIGHTING: Ralph Alswang; COSTUMES: Saul Bolasni; MUSICAL DIRECTOR: Bill Jonson; PRESS: Samuel J. Friedman & Maurice Turet; COMPANY MANAGER: Clifford Hayman; STAGE MANAGERS: James Gelb, Joseph Olney, John Padovano. *Cast:* NELL RILLING: Gloria Patrice; CATHY RILLING: Gloria Hamilton; LAURA: Mary O'Fallon; GEORGE MULLINS: Peter Conlow; SAMUEL RILLING: Joe E. Brown (1); CARL STEVENS: Theodor Uppman; FRED LAWSON: David E. Thomas; ARAMINTA: Billie Worth (2); HARRIET HEARN: Effie Afton; MR. HEARN: Joseph Sweeney; THERESA TAPPER: Carmen Mathews; LOUISA WINDEATT: Katherine Anderson; POLLY: May Muth; SADIE: Rosemary Kuhlmann; MILLIE: Teddy Tavenner; LARRY WALTON: Earl William; THE BRAT: Patricia Poole; SINGING ENSEMBLE: Walter Brandin, Michael T. Carolan, Betty Jane Cocho, Peggy Gavan, Glynn Hill, Joan Keenan, John Michael King, Michael Kingsley, Rosemary Kuhlmann, May Muth, Mary O'Fallon, Charles Rule, Robert Strobel, John Taliaferro, Teddy Tavenner, Lawrence Weber; DANCING ENSEMBLE: Edward Andrews, Hubert Bland, Patricia Casey, Peter Deign, Audrey Keane, William Maguire, Mary Martinet, Patricia Poole, Frances Sorenson, Elsa Van Horne, Lou Yetter, Charles Zulkeski. *Act I: Scene 1* Samuel Rilling's farm, Maine, 1898; *Scene 2* Louisa Windeatt's apiary; *Scene 3* The parlor of the Rilling home; *Scene 4* The post office and general store; *Scene 5* Theresa Tapper's garden. *Act II: Scene 1* Samuel Rilling's farm; *Scene 2* The Rilling kitchen; *Scene 3* The road to the station; *Scene 4* The railroad station. *Act I:* "Today at Your House, Tomorrow at Mine" (Sam, Carl, Fred, George, Male Ensemble) (danced by Nell, George, Ensemble), "Fixin' for a Long, Cold Winter" (Sam & Araminta), "Araminta to Herself" (Araminta), "An Old-Fashioned Glimmer in Your Eye" (Araminta, Cathy, Girls), "Goodbye, Dear Friend, Goodbye" (Cathy & Larry), "The Wishbone Song" (Araminta, Cathy, Larry, Nell, George, Carl, Ensemble), "Smile Awhile" (Araminta), "The Wishbone Song" (reprise) (danced by Nell & George), "Too Much Trouble" (Sam), "Choose Your Partner" (Nell, Cathy, Larry, Carl, Singing Ensemble) (danced by Nell, George, Ensemble), "I Do, He Doesn't" (Araminta), "Golden Moment" (Theresa & Sam) [the showstopper], "I Do, He Doesn't" (reprise) (Araminta). *Act II:* "Johnny Ride the Sky" (Carl, Cathy, Singing Ensemble), "Johnny and the Puckwudgies" (ballet): AT THE CONCERT GRAND: Dorothea Freitag; JOHNNY-RIDE-THE-SKY: Peter Conlow; ALSO WITH: Gloria Patrice & Dancing Ensemble. Note: Puckwudgies are Maine pixies often accused of tampering with the weather; "The Sensible Thing to Do" (Araminta & Larry), "The Wishbone Song" (reprise) (Araminta, Cathy, Larry, Nell, George), "Masculinity" (Louisa, Theresa, Harriet), "Maine Will Remember the Maine" (Larry, Carl, Mr. Hearn, Male Ensemble), "Heart in Hand" (Sam & Araminta), Finale (Entire Company).

Broadway reviews were divided, but good for Joe E. Brown and Billie Worth. Carmen Matthews stole the show.

157. *The Cradle Will Rock*

"A play in music." Set in Steeltown, USA, on the night of a union drive. A grim parable dealing with the struggle for union recognition in a steel town. Noble union organizer Larry does battle against the powerful and corrupt Mr. Mister who owns everything and everyone in town. Larry eventually leads the workers to victory.

Before Broadway. The original was the controversial proletarian propaganda "play in music" (actually a musical drama) starring Will Geer and Howard Da Silva, a WPA Federal Theatre 891 project, in a style similar to that of Kurt Weill. PRESENTED BY John Houseman, Orson Welles, and Sam H. Grisman; DIRECTOR: Orson Welles. It had been due to open at the Maxine Elliott Theatre, but due to political pressure it was banned by Federal Theatre officials and canceled at the last minute, on 6/15/37, after one dress rehearsal. Orson Welles, determined to put it on, secured the VENICE THEATRE (which later became the Century Theatre), and the play opened there 6/16/37, and the actors — who were forbidden by their union to appear on any stage — played the parts from their seats in various parts of the theatre, while the show's creator Marc Blitzstein provided accompaniment on a tinny piano. 19 PERFORMANCES; it closed 7/1/37. **Cast:** THE MOLL: Olive Stanton; REV. SALVATION: Edward Hemmer; DRUGGIST: John Adair; PRESIDENT PREXIE: Hansford Wilson; MR. MISTER: Will Geer; MRS. MISTER: Peggy Coudray; JUNIOR MISTER/PROF. TRIXIE: Hiram Sherman; SISTER MISTER: Dulce Fox; LARRY: Howard Da Silva; ELLA HAMMER: Blanche Collins; CHORUS INCLUDED: Henry Kolker, Paula Laurence. Then from 12/5/37 until after Christmas it was shown every Sunday evening at the MERCURY THEATRE. 4 PERFORMANCES. Sponsored by Sam H. Grisman, it moved to the WINDSOR THEATRE, 1/3/38, on a bare stage with Marc Blitzstein still on piano. Same cast, except: MR. MISTER: Ralph McBane; PRESIDENT PREXY [sic]: Le Roi Operti; and the new roles: CLERK/REPORTER/PROF. MAMIE: Marc Blitzstein; COP: Robert Farnsworth; REV. SALVATION: Charles Niemeyer. The chorus was reduced. On 2/28/38 it moved to the MERCURY THEATRE again, and closed there, 4/9/38. A TOTAL OF 108 PERFORMANCES.

In 1939 Leonard Bernstein, then an undergraduate at Harvard, put on a BOSTON production of the piece.

On 11/24/47 & 11/25/47 the play was successfully presented at CITY CENTER by Leonard Bernstein and the New York City Symphony in orchestral form. This production moved to Broadway 12/26/47. For the transfer Alfred Drake took over from Howard Da Silva, Vivian Vance from Shirley Booth, and Harold Patrick from Robert Chisholm.

The Broadway Run. MANSFIELD THEATRE, 12/26/47–1/11/48; BROADWAY THEATRE, 1/28/48–2/7/48. TOTAL OF 34 PERFORMANCES. PRESENTED BY Michael Myerberg; MUSIC/LYRICS/BOOK: Marc Blitzstein; DIRECTOR: Howard Da Silva; CONDUCTOR: Leonard Bernstein (first three performances), *Howard Shanet*; CHORAL DIRECTOR: Maurice Levine; PRESS: Richard Maney & Reuben Rabinovitch, *David Lipsky & Philip Bloom* (from 1/28/48); GENERAL MANAGER: Matilda Stanton, *Samuel Funt* (from 1/28/48); STAGE MANAGER: Virginia Downing. **Cast:** MOLL: Estelle Loring; GENT: Edward S. Bryce; DICK: Jesse White; COP: Taggart Casey; REVEREND SALVATION: Harold Patrick; EDITOR DAILY: Brooks Dunbar; YASHA: Jack Albertson; DAUBER: Chandler Cowles; PRESIDENT PREXY: Howard Blaine; PROFESSOR TRIXIE: Leslie Litomy; PROFESSOR MAMIE: Edmund Hewitt; PROFESSOR SCOOT: Ray Fry; DOCTOR SPECIALIST: Robert Pierson; HARRY DRUGGIST: David Thomas (5); MR. MISTER: Will Geer (3); MRS. MISTER: Vivian Vance (2); JUNIOR MISTER: Dennis King Jr.; SISTER MISTER: Jo Hurt; STEVE: Stephen West Downer; SADIE POLOCK: Marie Leidal; GUS POLOCK: Walter Scheff; BUGS: Edward S. Bryce; LARRY FOREMAN: Alfred Drake (1), *Edward S. Bryce* (from 1/28/48); ELLA HAMMER: Muriel Smith (4); ATTENDANT'S VOICE: Hazel Shermet; 1ST REPORTER: Rex Coston; 2ND REPORTER: Gil Houston; CLERK: Leonard Bernstein (5) (for the first three performances), *Howard Shanet*; CHORUS: Lucretia Anderson, Robert Burr, John Fleming, Michael Pollock, Germaine Poulin, Napoleon Reed, Gwen Ward. *Act I*: *Scene 1* Streetcorner: "I'm Checking Home Now" ("Moll's Song") (Moll), "So That's the Way" (Moll); *Scene 2* Nightcourt — Come to the Rescue: "Hurry up and Telephone" (Liberty Com-

mittee); *Scene 3* Mission: "Hard Times" (Mrs. Mister), Chorale, Choral-variation (Mrs. Mister, Rev. Salvation, Ensemble); *Scene 4* Lawn of Mr. Mister's home: "Croon Spoon" (Junior & Sister), "The Freedom of the Press" (Mr. Mister & Daily), "Let's Do Something" (Junior & Sister), "Honolulu" (Junior, Sister, Mr. Mister, Daily); *Scene 5* Drugstore (Druggist, Steve, Bugs): "Summer Weather" (Druggist, Steve, Bugs), "Gus and Sadie Love Song" (Gus & Sadie); *Scene 6* Hotel Lobby: "The Rich" (Yasha & Dauber), "Ah, There You Are" (Mrs. Mister), "Art for Art's Sake" (Yasha, Dauber, Mrs. Mister). *Act II* (only from re-opening on 1/28/48) [the original 1937 production opened without an intermission, but by the time it moved to the Windsor it had one — also after Scene 6]: *Scene 7* Nightcourt: "Nickel Under The Foot" (Moll), "Leaflets" (Larry), "The Cradle Will Rock" (Larry); *Scene 8* Faculty Room (Mr. Mister, Prexie, Trixie, Scoot): "Lovely Morning" (Prexy, Mr. Mister), "Triple Flank Maneuver" (Mamie), "Do I Have to Say?" (Scoot), "Listen, Fellas" (Trixie); *Scene 9* Dr. Specialist's office: "Joe Worker" (Ella); *Scene 10* Nightcourt: "Stuck Like a Sandwich" (Larry & Liberty Committee), "Ex-Foreman" (Larry & Mr. Mister), "Polyphonic" (Larry, Mr. Mister, Moll, Druggist, Liberty Committee), Finale: "The Cradle Will Rock" (reprise) (Ensemble).

Whatever effect the original had by virtue of its intimacy and immediacy was destroyed in this big Broadway production. Broadway reviews were totally divided. After running 21 performances at the Mansfield, Michael Myerberg relinquished his rights to David Lowe, who re-opened it at the Broadway for another 13 performances.

After Broadway. CITY CENTER, NYC, 2/11/60–2/21/60. 4 PERFORMANCES IN REPERTORY. PRESENTED BY the New York City Opera; DIRECTOR: Howard Da Silva; CHOREOGRAPHER: Billy Parsons; SETS: David Hays; COSTUMES: Ruth Morley; CONDUCTOR: Lehman Engel. **Cast:** MOLL: Tammy Grimes; GENT: Seth Riggs; DICK: Arnold Voketaitis; COP: Dan Merriman; REV. SALVATION: Kenneth Smith; DAILY: Jack Harrold; YASHA: Michael Wager; DAUBER: Chandler Cowles; PREXY: John Macurdy; TRIXIE: Philip Bruns; MAMIE: Maurice Stern; SCOOT: Howard Fried; SPECIALIST: Joshua Hecht; DRUGGIST: William Griffis; CLERK: Lehman Engel; MR. MISTER: Craig Timberlake; MRS. MISTER: Ruth Kobart; JUNIOR: Keith Kaldenberg; SISTER: Nancy Dussault; STEVE: Frank Porretta; SADIE: Sophie Ginn; GUS: Robert Kerns; BUGS: George Del Monte; LARRY: David Atkinson; ELLA: Jane Johnston; REPORTERS: Seth Riggs & William Zachariasen.

THEATRE FOUR, 11/8/64–1/17/65. 82 PERFORMANCES. PRESENTED BY Robert S. Fishko, John A. Prescott, David Rubinstein; DIRECTOR: Howard Da Silva; CHOREOGRAPHER: Rhoda Levine; MUSICAL DIRECTOR: Gershon Kingsley; MUSICAL CONSULTANT: Leonard Bernstein. **Cast:** LARRY: Jerry Orbach; ELLA: Micki Grant; MR. MISTER: Gordon B. Clarke; MRS. MISTER: Nancy Andrews; SISTER MISTER: Rita Gardner, *Kay Cole*; JUNIOR MISTER: Joe Bova; CLERK: Gershon Kingsley.

AMERICAN PLACE THEATRE, 5/9/83–5/29/83. 3 previews. 24 PERFORMANCES. PRODUCER/DIRECTOR/DELIVERED PROLOGUE: John Houseman; CHOREOGRAPHER: Patricia Birch; MUSICAL DIRECTOR: Michael Barrett. **Cast** (some of John Houseman's Acting Company alumni): MOLL/SISTER: Patti LuPone; GENT/EDITOR: Tom Robbins; MRS. MISTER: Mary Lou Rosato; DICK/JUNIOR MISTER: Hank Stram; COP/GUS: Casey Biggs; SALVATION/TRIXIE: James Harper; YASHA: Gerald Gutierrez; DAUBER/LARRY: Randle Mell; PREXY: Paul Walker; MAMIE/DRUGGIST: Brian Reddy; SPECIALIST/BUGS: Charles Shaw-Robinson; CLERK: Michael Barrett; MR. MISTER: David Schramm; STEVE/SCOOT/REPORTER # 1: Daniel Corcoran; SADIE/REPORTER # 3: Laura Hicks; ELLA: Michele Denise Woods; REPORTER # 2: Susan Rosenstock. It ran again, at the DOUGLAS FAIRBANKS THEATRE, 7/12/83–8/14/83. 40 PERFORMANCES. It had the same cast and crew, minus Patricia Birch & Patti LuPone.

OLD VIC THEATRE, London, 8/14/85–9/7/85. **Cast:** Patti LuPone.

THE MOVIE. There has been no film of the musical, as such. But in 1999 Tim Robbins wrote and directed a movie with the same title, in which the story of the famous 1938 opening was told (among many other political and social events of the day). **Cast:** MARC BLITZSTEIN: Hank Azaria; JOHN HOUSEMAN: Cary Elwes; ORSON WELLES: Angus MacFadyen; CHERRY JONES: Hallie Flanagan; NELSON ROCKEFELLER: John Cusack

158. *Cranks*

A small British musical revue. Tony Newley's stage debut.

Before Broadway. NEW WATERGATE THEATRE, London, 12/19/55; ST. MARTIN'S THEATRE, 3/1/56–5/26/56; DUCHESS THEATRE, 5/28/56–7/7/56; LYRIC THEATRE, Hammersmith, 7/9/56–9/15/56. TOTAL OF 223 PERFORMANCES. Cast recording on EMI. It had the same cast as for Broadway.

The Broadway Run. BIJOU THEATRE, 11/26/56–12/29/56. 40 PERFORMANCES. PRESENTED BY Richard Charlton & John Krimsky; MUSIC: John Addison; LYRICS/SKETCHES/DIRECTOR: John Cranko; SETS/LIGHTING: Paul Morrison; DECOR: John Piper; MUSICAL DIRECTOR: Anthony Bowles; ARRANGEMENTS: John Addison, Anthony Bowles, Dave Goldberg; PRESS: Richard Maney, Michel Mok, Martin Shwartz, Lila Glaser; GENERAL MANAGER: Richard Horner; COMPANY MANAGER: Joseph C. Cohen; STAGE MANAGER: Jack Woods. *Cast:* Hugh Bryant (1), Anthony Newley (3), Annie Ross (2), Gilbert Vernon (4). *The "Cranks" Chamber Group*: PIANO: Anthony Bowles (Irving Schlein alternate); HARPSICHORD: Philip Ingalls; HARP: Assunta Dell'Aquila (Eugene Bianco alternate); CLARINET: J. Morton; BASS: Bill Feinbloom. The order of numbers would change, as it did in London. *Part I*: "Who's Who" (piano selections), "Adrift," "Man's Burden" [sometimes "Tra La La" was here], "Where Has Tom Gone?," "Boo to a Goose" [sometimes "Cold Comfort" was here], "Lullaby" (piano selections), "Broadminded," "Waiting Room," "Bats," "Passacaglia" [sometimes "Boo to a Goose" was here], "Who is it Always There?," "Gloves," "This is the Sign," "Present for Gilbert" [sometimes "Chiromancy" was here], "Sea Song," "Valse Anglaise" (piano selections). *Part II*: "Tra La La" [sometimes "Telephone Tango" was here], "Don't Let Him Know You" (piano selections), "Chiromancy" [sometimes "Sea Song" was here], "L'Apres-Midi de Gilbert," "I'm the Boy You Should Say Yes To" [sometimes "Present for Gilbert" was here], "Metamorphosis" [sometimes "Elisabeth" was here], "Would You Let Me Know?," "Arthur, Son of Martha," "Blue," "Elisabeth" [sometimes "I'm the Boy You Should Say Yes To" was here], "Cove in Hove" [sometimes "Metamorphosis" was here] [sometimes "Would You Let Me Know?" was in this space], "Dirge," "Telephone Tango" [sometimes "Arthur, Son of Martha" was here], "Goodnight."

Broadway reviews were divided, but mostly unfavorable.

After Broadway. *New Cranks*, a sequel, ran at the LYRIC THEATRE, Hammersmith, London, from 4/26/60. 39 PERFORMANCES. PRESENTED BY Spur Productions, in association with Jack Waller; MUSIC: David Lee; LYRICS/BOOK/DIRECTOR: John Cranko; SETS: Carl Toms; LIGHTING: William Bundy; CAST RECORDING on HMV. CAST: Yolanda, Bernard Cribbins, Gillian Lynne, Johnny Wade, Carole Shelley, Billy Wilson. "Black and White Cha-Cha," "Names," "Soft Soap," "It Will Never Work Out," "Public Library," "Big Day with You," "Shadow Girl," "Equation," "Little Hours," "Black and White Waltz," "Black and White Bounce," "Pure in Mind," "Psychological Approach," "Jumbo Mambo," "Hole in the Head," "Hands off My Heart," "Other People — Ugh!," "Black and White Blues," "Shadow Love"

159. *Crazy for You*

Bobby, a spoiled New York playboy and would-be performer, is sent out west by his overbearing rich mother to foreclose on one of her hick town theatres in Deadrock, Nevada, that's losing money, and falls in love with the postmistress, Polly, who is also the daughter of the man who has the mortgage on the theatre (Bobby also has an overbearing fiancee back home). He saves the theatre by importing the Zangler Follies (they rescued a college in the original *Girl Crazy*). *Crazy For You* had all the hits from *Girl Crazy*, plus others.

Girl Crazy, upon which this musical was based, had been filmed in 1932, starring Bert Wheeler; in 1943, with Mickey Rooney, Judy Garland & Nancy Walker; and in 1966, as *When the Boys Meet the Girls*, with Connie Francis, Harve Presnell, Louis Armstrong, and Liberace. Roger Horchow, a millionaire in the mail-order catalogue business, sold his business to Neiman — Marcus for $117 million (other figures are often quoted), and set about realizing his life-long dream of presenting a Gershwin musical on Broadway. His favorite score was *Girl Crazy*, and with his partner, Elizabeth Williams, he contacted British director Mike Ockrent, who had revamped *Me and My Girl*. Mr. Ockrent agreed, if the book were re-written. Ken Ludwig was a Washington lawyer turned playwright, and he re-wrote the libretto (this had been authorized by the Gershwin estate, who also allowed the team access to many songs in the Gershwin canon, including several lost numbers unearthed in 1982 in a Secaucus, NJ warehouse). It tried out in Washington, but didn't do too well.

The Broadway Run. SHUBERT THEATRE, 2/19/92–1/7/96. 21 previews from 1/31/92. 1,622 PERFORMANCES. PRESENTED BY Roger Horchow & Elizabeth Williams, by arrangement with Tams-Witmark Music Library; MUSIC: George Gershwin; LYRICS: Ira Gershwin; ADDITIONAL LYRICS: Gus Kahn & Desmond Carter; BOOK: Ken Ludwig; INSPIRED BY the original 1930 book of *Girl Crazy*, by Guy Bolton & John McGowan; CONCEIVED BY: Ken Ludwig & Mike Ockrent; DIRECTOR: Mike Ockrent; CHOREOGRAPHER: Susan Stroman; SETS: Robin Wagner; COSTUMES: William Ivey Long; LIGHTING: Paul Gallo; SOUND: Otts Munderloh; MUSICAL DIRECTOR: Paul Gemignani; ORCHESTRATIONS: William David Brohn & Sid Ramin; DANCE MUSIC & INCIDENTAL ARRANGEMENTS: Peter Howard; CAST RECORDING on Broadway Angel; PRESS: Bill Evans & Associates; CASTING: Julie Hughes & Barry Moss; GENERAL MANAGEMENT: Gatchell & Neufeld; COMPANY MANAGER: Abbie M. Strassler, *Jeffrey M. Wilson* (in 94), *Richard Biederman* (from 94–95); PRODUCTION STAGE MANAGER: Steven Zweigbaum (gone by 94–95), *John Bonanni* & *Mindy Farbrother*; ASSISTANT STAGE MANAGER: Christine Stump. *Cast:* TESS: Beth Leavel (8), *Melinda Buckley* (from 94–95); PATSY: Stacey Logan (11), *Jill Matson* (from 93–94), *Rebecca Downing* (from 94–95), *Joan Leslie Simms*; BOBBY CHILD: Harry Groener (1) ☆, *James Brennan* (from 1/2/95); BELA ZANGLER: Bruce Adler (5), *John Jellison* (by 94–95), *Bruce Adler* (from 94–95), *Sandy Edgerton* (from 94–95); SHEILA: Judine Hawkins Richard; MITZI: Paula Leggett, *Wendy Waring* (by 93–94); SUSIE: Ida Henry [Ida Gilliams], *Angie L. Schworer* (from 94–95); LOUISE: Jean Marie, *Renee Robertson* (from 93–94); BETSY: Penny Ayn Maas, *Angie L. Schworer* (by 94–95), *Leigh Zimmerman* (from 94–95); MARGIE: Salome Mazard, *Kimberly Hester* (by 94–95); VERA: Louise Ruck, *Shannon Lewis* (by 94–95); ELAINE: Pamela Everett, *Elizabeth Mills* (from 93–94), *Paula Leggett Chase* (by 94–95), *Elizabeth Mills* (from 94–95); IRENE ROTH: Michele Pawk (4), *Kay McClelland* (from 93–94), *Sandy Edgerton, Kay McClelland, Sandy Edgerton, Pia Zadora* (from 8/16/95); MOTHER: Jane Connell (7), *Ann B. Davis* (from 8/16/95); PERKINS: Gerry Burkhardt, *James Young* (from 93–94); THE (THREE) MANHATTAN RHYTHM KINGS (12): MOOSE: Brian M. Nalepka, *Gary Douglas* (from 93–94); MINGO: Tripp Hanson, *Branch Woodman* (from 93–94); SAM: Hal Shane, *Michael Duran* (from 93–94), *Alan Gilbert* (from 94–95); JUNIOR: Casey Nicholaw, *John M. Wiltberger* (from 93–94); CUSTUS: Gerry Burkhardt, *James Young* (from 93–94); PETE: Fred Anderson, *James Doberman* (from 94–95); JIMMY: Michael Kubala; BILLY: Ray Roderick; WYATT: Jeffrey Lee Broadhurst, *Robert Ashford* (from 93–94), *Sean Martin Hingston* (by 94–95), *Stephen Reed* (from 94–95); HARRY: Joel Goodness; POLLY BAKER: Jodi Benson (2) ☆, *Karen Ziemba* (from 3/15/94); EVERETT BAKER: Ronn Carroll (6), *Carleton Carpenter* (from 93–94), *Roger Horchow* (from 94–95), *Carleton Carpenter* (from 94–95), *John Jellison* (from 94–95), *Al Checco* (from 94–95), *John Jellison* (from 94–95); LANK HAWKINS: John Hillner (3), *Daren Kelly* (from 8/95); EUGENE: Stephen Temperley (9); PATRICIA: Amelia White (10), *Colleen Smith Wallnau* (by 94–95); ENSEMBLE: Fred Anderson (*James Doberman*), Jeffrey Lee Broadhurst (*Robert Ashford, Sean Martin Hingston, Stephen Reed*), Gerry Burkhardt (*James Young*), Pamela Everett (*Elizabeth Mills*), Joel Goodness, Tripp Hanson (*Branch Woodman*), Ida Henry (*Angie L. Schworer*), Michael Kubala, Paula Leggett (*Wendy Waring*), Stacey Logan (*Jill Matson, Rebecca Downing, Joan Leslie Simms*), Penny Ayn Maas (*Angie L. Schworer, Leigh Zimmerman*), Jean Marie (*Renee Robertson*), Salome Mazard (*Kimberly Hester*), Brian M. Nalepka (*Gary Douglas*), Casey Nicholaw (*John M. Wiltberger*), Judine Hawkins Richard, Ray Roderick, Louise Ruck (*Shannon Lewis*), Hal Shane (*Michael Duran, Alan Gilbert*). *Understudies*: Bobby/Lank: Michael Kubala (92–94), *James Young* (94–96); Bela: Michael Kubala

(92–94), *John Jellison* (92–94), *James Young* (94–96); Polly: Beth Leavel (92–94), *Jill Matson* (94–96), *Darcie Roberts* (from 94); Irene: Jessica Molaskey (92), *Paula Leggett* (92–94), *Wendy Waring* (94–96), *Darcie Roberts* (from 94); Patricia: Jessica Molaskey (92), *Angelique Ilo* (92–96), *Darcie Roberts*; Everett: Gerry Burkhardt (92–94), *John Jellison* (92–94), *James Young* (94–96), *Michael Duran* (94–96); Mother: Amelia White (92–94), *Colleen Smith Wallnau* (94–96); Tess: Paula Leggett (92), *Ida Henry* (AKA Ida Gilliams) (92–94), *Darcie Roberts* (from 94); Eugene: Casey Nicholaw (92–94), *John Jellison* (92–94), *John M. Wiltberger*; Patsy: Penny Ayn Maas (92–94), *Elizabeth Mills, Angie L. Schwarer*. General Standby: Karen Culp. **Swings**: Ken Lundie, Chris Peterson, Maryellen Scilla, *William Alan Coats, Angelique Ilo, Scott Taylor, Leigh-Anne Wencker, Mary Lee DeWitt, Chris Peterson, Bobby Smith*. **Orchestra**: CONCERTMASTER: Suzanne Ornstein, *Michael Roth;* VIOLINS: Martin Agee, Ann Leathers, Aloysia Friedmann, Laura Corcos, John Connelly; CELLI: Deborah Assael & Scott Ballantine (*Roger Shell*); BASS: Charles Bargeron; WOODWINDS: Les Scott (*Dave Tofani),* John Moses, Andrew Drelles, Charles Millard, John Campo (*Mark Thrasher*); HORNS: Ronald Sell & Michael Ishii (*Peter Schoettler & Kelly Dent*); TRUMPETS: Wilmer Wise & David Brown; TROMBONES: Bruce Eidem & Dean Plank; KEYBOARDS: Pam Drews Phillips (*Keith Phillips*); DRUMS: Paul Pizzuti; PERCUSSION: Thad Wheeler (*Hank Jaramillo*); GUITAR/BANJO: Andy Schwartz. **Act I: Scene 1** Backstage at the Zangler Theatre, New York City; in the 1930s: "K-ra-zy for You" [from the 1928 musical *Treasure Girl*] (Bobby); **Scene 2** 42nd Street, outside the theatre: "I Can't Be Bothered Now" [from the 1937 movie *A Damsel in Distress*] (Bobby & Girls); **Scene 3** Main Street, Deadrock, Nevada: "Bidin' My Time" [from the 1930 musical *Girl Crazy*] (Mingo, Moose, Sam), "Things Are Looking Up" [from the 1937 movie *A Damsel in Distress*] (Bobby); **Scene 4** Lank's saloon: "Could You Use Me?" [from the 1930 musical *Girl Crazy*] (Bobby & Polly); **Scene 5** In the desert: "Shall We Dance?" [from the 1937 movie *Shall We Dance?*] (Bobby & Polly); **Scene 6** The Gaiety Theatre; **Scene 7** Main Street, Deadrock; three days later: Entrance to Nevada (Company), "Someone to Watch Over Me" [from the 1926 musical *Oh, Kay!*] (Polly); **Scene 8** The lobby of the Gaiety Theatre; two weeks later; **Scene 9** The stage of the Gaiety Theatre: "Slap that Bass" (orch: Sid Ramin) [from the 1937 movie *Shall We Dance?*] (Bobby, Moose, Tess, Patsy, Company), "Embraceable You" [from the 1930 musical *Girl Crazy*] (Polly & Bobby); **Scene 10** The Gaiety Theatre dressing rooms; opening night: "Tonight's the Night" (l: Ira Gershwin & Gus Kahn) [previously unused] (Company); **Scene 11** Main Street, Deadrock: "I Got Rhythm" [from the 1930 musical *Girl Crazy*] (Polly & Company). **Act II: Scene 1** Lank's saloon; later that evening: "The Real American Folk Song (is a Rag)" [from the 1918 musical *Ladies First*] (Mingo, Moose, Sam), "What Causes That?" [from the 1928 musical *Treasure Girl*] (Bobby & Bela); **Scene 2** Lank's saloon; the next morning: "Naughty Baby" (add l: Desmond Carter) [previously unused] (Irene, Lank, Boys); **Scene 3** The Gaiety Theatre, backstage; **Scene 4** The auditorium of the Gaiety Theatre: "Stiff Upper Lip" [from the 1937 movie *A Damsel in Distress*] (Bobby, Polly, Eugene, Patricia, Company), "They Can't Take That Away from Me" [from the 1937 movie *Shall We Dance?*] (Bobby), "But Not for Me" [from the 1930 musical *Girl Crazy*] (Polly); **Scene 5** New York; six weeks later: "Nice Work if You Can Get It" [from the 1937 movie *A Damsel in Distress*] (Bobby & Girls); **Scene 6** Main Street, Deadrock; six days later: Finale (Company).

All numbers were written by the Gershwins. Sometimes other people were involved as well, and these are noted. "Naughty Baby," "Tonight's the Night" and "What Causes That" were three of the songs found in the New Jersey warehouse.

Broadway reviews were great. The show won Tonys for musical, choreography, and costumes, and was also nominated for book, direction of a musical, lighting, and for Harry Groener, Jodi Benson, and Bruce Adler. Even though it was still making a profit, the show was kicked out of the Shubert to make way for *Big*.

After Broadway. PRINCE OF WALES THEATRE, London, 3/3/93. **Cast**: Ruthie Henshall, Kirby Ward. It won Olivier Awards for best musical, and for Susan Stroman's choreography, and was a huge hit. Fiona Benjamin, who understudied Polly for 18 months, finally went on, and then opened the UK tour.

TOUR. Opened on 5/13/93, at the Music Hall, Dallas. Previews from 5/11/93. **Cast**: BOBBY: James Brennan, *Kirby Ward*; POLLY: Karen Ziemba, *Crista Moore, Beverly Ward*; MOTHER: Lenka Peterson, *Ann B. Davis*; EVERETT: Carleton Carpenter, *Al Checco, Raymond Thorne*; IRENE: Kay McClelland, *Belle Calaway, Riette Burdick*; BELA: Stuart Zagnit, *Paul Keith*; LANK: Chris Coucill, *Daren Kelly*; TESS: Cathy Susan Pyles; EUGENE: Geoffrey Wade, *John Curless*; PATSY: Sally Boyett, *Joan Leslie Simms*; ENSEMBLE: Nora Brennan, Ron De Vito, Bill Brassea, Angie L. Schworer, Heather Douglas. The role of Patricia (played by Jeanette Landis) was cut during the tour.

GERMANY. After two tryouts at the Schiller Theater, Berlin, 6/10/96 & 6/15/96, it went to DEUTSCHES SCHAUSPIELHAUS, Hamburg, 6/24/96–8/18/96. PRESENTED BY Wolfgang Boksch; DIRECTOR: John Neville Andrews. It used the sets from the recently closed London production.

MELBOURNE, Australia, 11/28/97 (strictly limited run). **Cast**: BOBBY: Philip Gould; POLLY: Fiona Benjamin.

PAPER MILL PLAYHOUSE, New Jersey, 4/14/98–5/30/98. DIRECTOR: James Brennan; CHOREOGRAPHER: Angelique Ilo; SOUND: Craig Cassidy; MUSICAL DIRECTOR: Tom Helm. **Cast**: ZANGLER: Bruce Adler; MOTHER: Jane Connell; EVERETT: Larry Linville; POLLY: Stacey Logan; BOBBY: Jim Walton; LOUISE: Jean Marie; MINGO: Scott Willis; HARRY: Matt Lashey.

TEATRO SAN RAFAEL, Mexico City, 5/7/98. First Spanish version of *Loco Por Ti*. DIRECTOR: Rafael Perrin; CHOREOGRAPHERS: Ana Maria Collado & Jose Posadas. **Cast**: BOBBY: Manuel Landeta; POLLY: Lisset; ZANGLER: Eugenio Montessoro; IRENE: Simone Brook; MOTHER: Angelita Castani; EVERETT: Jorge Pais; TESS: Nitzi Arellano.

160. *Cry for Us All*

Also known as *Who to Love*. No intermission. Set in Irish Brooklyn over a five-day period around May 1, 1890; it deals with politics. Quinn is the corrupt Brooklyn mayor who rising young Irish politician Matt, leader of Brooklyn's 6th Ward and owner of the Court Cafe (on the corner of Court Street and Fifth Place) is trying to overthrow, but instead Matt and his delicate wife are destroyed, when details of Matt's previous love affair are made public. Set in Matt's cafe, the street outside, the bar and the back room of the cafe, and also in the Haggerty Parlor, which adjoins it. The action also moves to the street outside Ag Hogan's flat, and to the Printers' Church in Lower Fulton Street, and to the Boardwalk in Seagate.

Before Broadway. *Hogan's Goat*, on which it was based, ran Off Broadway, at the AMERICAN PLACE THEATRE, 11/11/65. 607 PERFORMANCES. Mitch Leigh came up with the idea to make the play into a musical. It tried out in New Haven and Boston, with Joan Diener's role growing in size all the time. Its name changed to *Who to Love*, then back to *Cry For Us All*. John Reardon quit, and was replaced by Steve Arlen just before rehearsals. The part of Josie Finn (played by Margot Moser) was cut.

The Broadway Run. BROADHURST THEATRE, 4/8/70–4/15/70. 18 previews. 9 PERFORMANCES. PRESENTED BY Mitch Leigh, in association with C. Gerald Goldsmith; MUSIC: Mitch Leigh; LYRICS: William Alfred & Phyllis Robinson; BOOK: William Alfred & Albert Marre; BASED ON the 1965 verse-drama *Hogan's Goat*, by William Alfred; DIRECTOR: Albert Marre; CHOREOGRAPHER: Todd Bolender; SETS/LIGHTING: Howard Bay; COSTUMES: Robert Fletcher; SOUND: Jo Donohue; MUSICAL SUPERVISOR: Sam Pottle; MUSICAL DIRECTOR: Herbert Grossman; ORCHESTRATIONS: Carlyle Hall (of Music Makers, Inc.); CAST RECORDING on Project 3 Records; PRESS: Harvey B. Sabinson, Lee Solters, Ted Goldsmith, Sandra Manley; GENERAL MANAGER: Edward H. Davis; COMPANY MANAGER: J. Ross Stewart; PRODUCTION STAGE MANAGER: James S. Gelb; STAGE MANAGER: Bob Burland; ASSISTANT STAGE MANAGER: Jim Stevenson & Bill Dance. **Cast**: THREE STREET RATS: MIGGSY: Scott Jacoby (15); FLYLEGS: Darel Glaser (16); CABBAGE: Todd Jones (17); MATT STANTON: Steve Arlen (3) ☆; KATHLEEN STANTON, HIS WIFE: Joan Diener (1) ☆; EDWARD QUINN, MAYOR OF BROOKLYN: Robert Weede (2) ☆; PETEY BOYLE, A HANGER-ON OF QUINN'S: Tommy Rall (4) ☆; BESSIE

LEGG, A BACK-ROOM GIRL: Helen Gallagher (5); MARIA HAGGERTY, THE STANTONS' HOUSEKEEPER: Dolores Wilson (6); JOHN "BLACK JACK" HAGGERTY, HER HUSBAND AND ASSISTANT WARD LEADER: Paul Ukena (9); JAMES "PALSY" MURPHY, BOSS OF BROOKLYN: Edwin Steffe (7); FATHER STANISLAUS COYNE, PASTOR OF ST. MARY STAR OF THE SEA: William Griffis (8); STATE SENATOR THOMAS WALSH: Jay Stuart (10); MORTYEEN O'BRIEN, THE FIRE COMMISSIONER: Charles Rule (20); PETER MULLIGAN, CHIEF CLERK OF THE POLICE DEPARTMENT: John Ferrante (19); FATHER MALONEY, PRIEST OF THE PRINTERS' CHURCH: Elliott Savage (11); THE CRUELTY MAN: Taylor Reed (12); MRS. TERESA TUOHY: Fran Stevens (13); FIONA QUIGLEY, A FACTORY GIRL: Elaine Cancilla (14); JACK O'BANION, A REPORTER FOR THE *Brooklyn Eagle*: Jack Trussel (21); MRS. MORTYEEN O'BRIEN: Dora Rinehart (22); ALOYSIUS "WISHY" DOYLE, BARTENDER OF THE COURT CAFE: Bill Dance (23); MUTTON EGAN, 13 YEARS OLD: Ronnie Douglas (18). *Standbys*: Kathleen: Willi Burke; Petey/Coyne/Haggerty/Maloney: Ted Forlow. *Understudies*: Matt: Jay Stuart; Quinn: Ed Steffe; Bessie: Elaine Cancilla; Maria: Fran Stevens; Murphy/O'Brien: Taylor Reed; Street Rats: Ronnie Douglas; Walsh/Mulligan: Jack Trussel; Cruelty Man/Doyle: Jim Stevenson. *Scene 1* Tuesday evening: "See No Evil" (Street Rats), "The End of My Race" (Matt), "How Are Ya Since?" (Kathleen, Matt, Constituents); *Scene 2* Wednesday morning: "The Mayor's Chair" (Quinn), "The Cruelty Man" (Street Rats); *Scene 3* Wednesday evening: "The Verandah Waltz" (Kathleen & Matt); *Scene 4* Thursday evening: "Home Free All" (Matt, Street Rats, Constituents), "The Broken Heart, or the Wages of Sin" (Street Rats), "The Confessional" (Matt & Maloney), "Who to Love if Not a Stranger?" (Kathleen); *Scene 5* Friday evening: "Cry for Us All" (Petey & Mourners); *Scene 6* Later Friday evening: "Swing Your Bag" (Bessie), "Call in to Her" (Kathleen & Matt), "That Slavery is Love" (Kathleen); *Scene 7* Saturday afternoon: "I Lost It" (Street Rats); *Scene 8* Saturday night: "Aggie, Oh Aggie" (Quinn); *Scene 9* Sunday afternoon: "The Leg of the Duck" (Petey), "This Cornucopian Land" (Matt & Constituents), "How Are Ya Since?" (reprise) (Kathleen & Quinn), "The Broken Heart, or The Wages of Sin" (reprise) (Street Rats); *Scene 10* Sunday evening: "Cry for Us All" (reprise) (Constituents).

Broadway reviews were terrible. It received Tony nominations for sets, and for Robert Weede.

161. *Cyrano*

Set in France in 1640 and 1654. The musical shows great respect for Rostand's original work, and never dominates it.

Before Broadway. Rostand's straight play was first performed on 12/27/97 at the THEATRE DE LA PORTE DE SAINT-MARTIN, Paris. The straight play was to be done many times in the USA, from Broadway to the smallest theaters. A musical version, *Cyrano de Bergerac*, was produced by the Shuberts in 1932, but never got to Broadway; this was revised in 1939 by Vernon Duke as *The Vagabond Hero*, but it never made Broadway either. In 1959 a college musical, *Cyrano de Bergerac*, was produced, starring Dick Cavett and Carrie Nye. One of the numbers, "Autumn," was the first song ever written together by David Shire and Richard Maltby Jr. In the 1960s David Merrick announced a Cyrano musical to star Christopher Plummer, with a score by Anthony Newley and Leslie Bricusse, but it never happened. Incidentally, Mr. Plummer did star in the 1962 straight play *Cyrano de Bergerac*. A 1973 summer stock tryout of a version by Robert Wright & Chet Forrest, *A Song for Cyrano*, with Jose Ferrer, also never made it to New York (see appendix).

In 1971 novelist Anthony Burgess adapted it and it ran at the GUTHRIE THEATRE, Minneapolis. Rather than remount it, Mr. Burgess & director Michael Langham turned it into a musical, which they presented, in its world premiere, at the GUTHRIE THEATRE, 1/23/73. 24 PERFORMANCES. DIRECTOR: Michael Langham; CHOREOGRAPHER: Rhoda Levine; SETS: John Jensen; COSTUMES: Desmond Heeley; LIGHTING: Gilbert V. Hemsley Jr.; MUSICAL DIRECTOR: Joseph Klein; ORCHESTRATIONS: Eddie Sauter. *Cast*: THEATRE CARETAKER: Shawn McGill; DOORMAN: Joseph Della Sorte; FOODSELLER: Tovah Feldshuh; NOBLEMAN: Michael Vita; PICKPOCKET/MONK: Geoff Garland; PICKPOCKET'S APPRENTICE: James Richardson; CITIZEN: Richard Curnock; CITIZEN'S

SON: Tim Nissen; 1ST MARQUIS: Alexander Orfaly; 2ND MARQUIS: William Tynan; LIGNIERE/JOURNALIST: Arnold Soboloff; CHRISTIAN DE NEUVILLETTE: Mark Lamos; MADAME AUBRY/LISE: Betty Leighton; MADAME DE GUEMENE: Janet McCall; BARTHENOIDE/SISTER CLAIRE: Patricia Roos; FELIXERIE: Judith Ross; URIMEDONTE: Mary Straten; RAGUENEAU: Bruce MacKay; LE BRET: James Blendick; ROXANA: Leigh Beery; SISTER MARTHE/ROXANA'S CHAPERONE: Anita Dangler; COUNT DE GUICHE: Louis Turenne; VISCOUNT DE VALVERT: J. Kenneth Campbell; ACTORS: Anthony Inneo & Neil Jones; ACTRESSES: Dee Martin & Jill Rose; MONTFLEURY/SPANISH OFFICER: Patrick Hines; CYRANO DE BERGERAC: Christopher Plummer; JODELET: Michael Goodwin; CANDLE LIGHTERS/MUSKETEERS/BAKERY STAFF/BOYS/POETS/GASCON CADETS/SPANISH SOLDIERS/NUNS/PAGES, ETC: Paul Berget, J. Kenneth Campbell, Richard Curnock, Joseph Della Sorte, Tovah Feldshuh, Geoff Garland, Michael Goodwin, Patrick Hines, Anthony Inneo, Neil Jones, Christopher Klein, Janet McCall, Shawn McGill, Dee Martin, Tim Nissen, Michael Nolan, Alex Orfaly, James Richardson, Patricia Roos, Jill Rose, Judith Ross, Mary Straten, Donovan Sylvest, Paul Thompson, Michael Tynan, Michael Vita. It got great reviews in Boston, during its next tryouts. Michael Langham was replaced as director by Michael Kidd.

The Broadway Run. PALACE THEATRE, 5/13/73–6/23/73. 5 previews from 5/9/73. 49 PERFORMANCES. PRESENTED BY Richard Gregson & APJAC International; MUSIC: Michael J. Lewis; LYRICS/BOOK: Anthony Burgess; BASED ON Anthony Burgess's 1971 adaptation of the 1897 French drama *Cyrano de Bergerac*, by Edmond Rostand; DIRECTOR: Michael Kidd; CHOREOGRAPHER: Michael Kidd (uncredited); DUELING: Patrick Crean & Erik Fredricksen; SETS: John Jensen; COSTUMES: Desmond Heeley; LIGHTING: Gilbert V. Hemsley Jr.; SOUND: Abe Jacob; MUSICAL DIRECTOR: Thomas Pierson; ORCHESTRATIONS: Philip J. Lang; INCIDENTAL MUSICAL ARRANGEMENTS: Clay Fullum; CAST RECORDING on A & M; PRESS: Gifford/Wallace; GENERAL MANAGER: Victor Samrock; COMPANY MANAGER: James Awe; PRODUCTION STAGE MANAGER: Robert D. Currie; STAGE MANAGERS: Christopher Kelly & Lani Ball. *Cast:* CANDLE LIGHTERS: Paul Berget & Anthony Inneo; DOORMAN: Bob Heath; FOODSELLER: Tovah Feldshuh; MARQUIS IN YELLOW: Danny Villa; MUSKETEER: Michael Nolan; CAVALRYMAN: Donavan Sylvest; PICKPOCKET: Geoff Garland; CITIZEN: James Richardson; CITIZEN'S BROTHER: Tim Nissen; MARQUIS IN RED: Alexander Orfaly; MARQUIS IN BEIGE: Joel Craig; RAGUENEAU, A BAKER AND POET: Arnold Soboloff (7); CHRISTIAN DE NEUVILLETTE: Mark Lamos (3); MADAME AUBRY: Betty Leighton; (FOUR) LADIES OF THE FRENCH ACADEMY: MADAME DE GUEMENE: Janet McCall; BARTHENOIDE: Patricia Roos; FELIXERIE: Mimi Wallace; URIMEDONTE: Mary Straten; LE BRET, CAPTAIN OF THE GASCONS: James Blendick (4); ROXANA: Leigh Beery (2); ROXANA'S DUENNA: Anita Dangler; COUNT DE GUICHE, ROXANA'S GUARDIAN: Louis Turenne (6); VISCOUNT DE VALVERT: J. Kenneth Campbell; ACTORS: Anthony Inneo & Richard Schneider; ACTRESSES: Vicki Frederick & Jill Rose; JODELET, A FARCEUR: Michael Goodwin; MONTFLEURY, A ROMANTIC TRAGEDIAN: Patrick Hines (5); CYRANO DE BERGERAC: Christopher Plummer (1) ☆; LISE, RAGUENEAU'S WIFE: Betty Leighton; BOYS AFTER PIES: Tim Nissen & Paul Berget; BAKERY STAFF: J. Kenneth Campbell, Geoff Garland, Janet McCall, Michael Nolan, James Richardson, Patricia Roos, Mary Straten; GASCON CADETS AND SOLDIERS: J. Kenneth Campbell, Joel Craig, Michael Goodwin, Bob Heath, Anthony Inneo, Gale McNeeley, Michael Nolan, James Richardson, Richard Schneider, Donovan Sylvest, Danny Villa; THEOPHRASTE RENAUDOT: George Spelvin; CYRANO'S PAGES: Paul Berget & Tim Nissen; CAPUCINE MONK: Geoff Garland; SISTER MARGUERITE: Betty Leighton; SISTER MARTHE: Anita Dangler; SISTER CLAIRE: Patricia Roos; NUNS: Tovah Feldshuh, Vicki Frederick, Janet McCall, Jill Rose, Mary Straten, Mimi Wallace. *Understudies*: Roxana: Janet McCall; Le Bret: William Metzo; de Guiche: William Metzo & Alex Orfaly; Duenna: Betty Leighton; de Valvert: Anthony Inneo.

Note: George Spelvin, who played Renaudot, is not the actor's real name. It is a nom de guerre used on Broadway to denote an actor in more than one role. So, we don't know who played this role.

Part I: Scene 1 A theatre, Paris; 1640: "Cyrano's Nose" (Nose Song) (Cyrano), "La France, La France" (Company), "Tell Her" (Le Bret & Cyrano), "From Now Till Forever" (Cyrano & Company), "Bergerac" (Cyrano & Roxana); *Scene 2* Ragueneau's Bakery, Paris: "Pocapdedious"

(Cadets), "No, Thank You" (Cyrano), "From Now Till Forever" (reprise) (Cyrano & Christian). *Part II*: *Scene 3* The balcony of Roxana's house, Paris: "Roxana" (Christian & Company), "It's She and it's Me" (Christian), "You Have Made Me Love" (Roxana), "Thither, Thother, Thide of Thee" (Cyrano); *Scene 4* A battle camp near Arras: "Pocapdedious" (reprise) (Le Bret & Cadets), "Paris Cuisine" (Cyrano, Le Bret, Cadets); *Scene 5* A convent, Paris; 14 years later: "Love is Not Love" (Roxana), "Autumn Carol" (Roxana & Nuns), "I Never Loved You" (Cyrano).

Broadway reviews were very bad, but Chris Plummer himself got raves (and won a Tony Award). Leigh Beery was nominated for a Tony. The show lost all its $500,000 cost, half of which had been put up by A & M Records.

After Broadway. 10/12/01–10/14/01. PRESENTED BY the York Theatre Company, as part of the *Musicals in Mufti* series. DIRECTOR: Michael Montel. **Cast**: ROXANA: Sherry D. Boone; DE GUICHE: Peter Flynn; DUENNA: Melissa Hart; RAGUENEAU: Kenneth Kantor; MONTFLEURY: J. Brandon Savage; LE BRET: Alan Souza; CYRANO: David Staller; CHRISTIAN: Jim Stanek.

162. *Cyrano — The Musical*

Before Broadway. First produced in AMSTERDAM, Netherlands, 9/17/92. There was a cast recording. **Cast**: CYRANO: Bill Van Dijk.

The Broadway Run. NEIL SIMON THEATRE, 11/21/93–3/20/94. 38 previews from 10/19/93. 137 PERFORMANCES. PRESENTED BY Joop Van Den Ende, in association with Peter T. Kulok; MUSIC: Ad Van Dijk; LYRICS/BOOK: Koen Van Dijk; ENGLISH LYRICS: Peter Reeves; ADDITIONAL ENGLISH LYRICS: Sheldon Harnick; BASED ON the play by Edmond Rostand; DIRECTOR: Eddy Habbema; ASSOCIATE DIRECTOR: Eleanor Fazan; SETS: Paul Gallis; ASSOCIATE SETS: Duke Durfee; COSTUMES: Yan Tax; ASSOCIATE COSTUMES: Marcia K. McDonald; LIGHTING: Reinier Tweebeeke; ASSOCIATE LIGHTING: Brian Nason; SOUND: Rogier Van Rossum; ASSOCIATE SOUND: Steve Canyon Kennedy; MUSICAL DIRECTOR: Constantine Kitsopoulos; ORCHESTRATIONS: Don Sebesky & Tony Cox; No Broadway cast recording; PRESS: Merle Frimark & Marc Thibodeau; CASTING: Julie Hughes & Barry Moss; GENERAL MANAGEMENT: Peter T. Kulok Enterprises; PRODUCTION STAGE MANAGER: Bob Borod; STAGE MANAGER: David John O'Brien; ASSISTANT STAGE MANAGERS: Ira Mont & Jon Krause. **Cast**: MAN: Geoffrey Blaisdell, Tom Polum (matinees); LE BRET: Paul Schoeffler (6); RAGUENEAU: Ed Dixon (5); CHRISTIAN: Paul Anthony Stewart (3); DE GUICHE: Timothy Nolen (4); *Geoffrey* Blaisdell; ROXANE: Anne Runolfsson (2); VALVERT: Adam Pelty; CHAPERONE: Joy Hermalyn; MONTFLEURY: Mark Agnes; CYRANO: Bill Van Dijk (1) (*Timothy Nolen*), Jordan Bennett (Wednesday evenings & Saturday matinees—*Robert Guillaume* from 3/8/94; CAPTAIN DE CASTEL JALOUX: Geoffrey Blaisdell, Tom Polum (matinees); MOTHER SUPERIOR: Elizabeth Acosta; NOVICE: Michele Ragusa; ENSEMBLE: OPERA AUDIENCE, CADETS, PRECIEUSES, CHEFS, WAITRESSES, NUNS: Elizabeth Acosta, Mark Agnes, Carina Andersson, Christopher Eaton Bailey, James Barbour, Geoffrey Blaisdell, Michelle Dawson, Jeff Gardner, Daniel Guzman, Joy Hermalyn, Bjorn Johnson, Peter Lockyer, Stuart Marland, Kerry O'Malley, Adam Pelty, Tom Polum, Michele Ragusa, Sam Scalamoni, Robin Skye, Tami Tappan, Ann Van Cleave, Charles West, *Joanne Lessner, Michael Christopher Moore, Debra Wiseman*. **Understudies**: Cyrano: Sam Scalamoni; Roxane: Tami Tappan & Michelle Dawson; Christian: Peter Lockyer & James Barbour; de Guiche: Geoffrey Blaisdell; Ragueneau: Stuart Marland; Le Bret: Jeff Gardner. **Swings**: Ted Keegan, Rose McGuire, Christian Nova. **Orchestra**: KEYBOARDS: Ethyl Will & Milton Granger; BASS: Jeff Carney; GUITAR: Scott Kuney; PERCUSSION: Lou Oddo & Dean Witten; TRUMPET: Neil Balm; TROMBONES: Richard Clark & Nathan Durham; FRENCH HORNS: Peter Gordon & Katherine Canfield; WOODWINDS: Brian Miller, Lynn Cohen, Richard Shapiro, Donald McGeen; CONCERTMISTRESS: Belinda Whitney; VIOLIN: Rob Shaw; VIOLA: Rachel Evans; CELLO: Alvin McCall. **Act I**: PARIS, 1640: Prologue (Man, Le Bret, Ragueneau, Ensemble), "Opera, Opera" (Ensemble), "Aria" (Montfleury, Cyrano, Ensemble), "One Fragment of a Moment" (Christian & Roxane), "Confrontation" (Ensemble), "The Duel" (Cyrano & Ensemble), "Where's All This Anger Coming From?" (Le Bret & Cyrano), "Loving

Her" (Cyrano & Christian), "A Message from Roxane" (Chaperone & Cyrano), "Ragueneau's Patisserie" (Ragueneau, Chefs, Waitresses), "Roxane's Confession" (Roxane & Cyrano), "What a Reward" (De Guiche, Le Bret, Ragueneau), "Hate Me" (Cyrano), "Courage Makes a Man" (Cadets & Captain), "Cyrano's Story" (Cyrano & Christian), "A Letter for Roxane" (Cyrano & Christian), "I Have No Words" (Christian), "Two Musketeers" (Cyrano & Christian), "An Evening Made for Lovers" (Ensemble), "Balcony Scene" (Roxane, Christian, Cyrano), "Poetry" (Cyrano & Roxane), "Moonsong" (Cyrano), "Stay with Me!" (Ensemble). **Act II**: A BESIEGED CAMP NEAR ARRAS, A FEW MONTHS LATER: "Every Day, Every Night" (Cyrano, Christian, Roxane, Cadets), "A White Sash" (De Guiche, Cyrano, Cadets), "When I Write" (Cyrano), "Two Musketeers" (reprise) (Christian & Cyrano), "Rhyming Menu" (Roxane, Ragueneau, Ensemble), "Even Then" (Roxane), "Tell Her Now" (Christian & Cyrano), "The Evening" (Cyrano & Cadets), "Even Then" (reprise) (Roxane & Cyrano), "The Battle" (Ensemble), "Everything You Wrote" (Roxane). PARIS, SEVEN YEARS LATER: "He Loves to Make Us Laugh" (Nuns & Mother Superior), "A Visit from de Guiche" (De Guiche, Roxane, Mother Superior), "Opera, Opera" (reprise) (Ensemble), "An Old Wound"/"The Letter"/"Moonsong" (reprise) (Cyrano & Roxane).

This was the first and only Dutch musical to play Broadway, where reviews were not good. Bill Van Dijk appeared with special permission of Equity. The show received Tony nominations for musical, score, book, and costumes.

After Broadway. FREILICHTSPIELE, Schwaebisch Hall, near Stuttgart, 7/28/99–8/15/99. In repertory. Previews from 7/18/99. This was the German premiere. TRANSLATOR: Curt Werner; DIRECTOR: Helmut Schorlemmer; MUSICAL DIRECTOR: Scott Lawton. **Cast**: CYRANO: Reinhard Brussmann; ROXANE: Sonia McDonald; CHRISTIAN: Martin Berger.

FRANK WILDHORN'S VERSION. MUSIC: Frank Wildhorn; LYRICS/BOOK: Leslie Bricusse. Douglas Sills was the star they had in mind, and indeed he sang the role on a demo done in 2004, as the script was in its early stages. In 2/05 Mr. Wildhorn signed a contact with Bill Kenwright in England, for the show to open in Birmingham in 2006, then go on to London

163. *Damn Yankees*

A modern version of the Faust story. Sometime in the future, Joe Boyd, a fat, bald, middle-aged real estate salesman in Washington, DC, an avid fan of his home town baseball team, after seeing them lose, says he'd sell his soul to see the Senators win the pennant and beat those "damn Yankees" (meaning the unbeatable New York Yankees). At that moment Mr. Applegate appears (really the devil), identifiable by red socks and his ability to pluck cigarettes out of thin air. Applegate offers to transform Joe into a young baseball phenom — in exchange for his soul at the end of the season. Joe agrees, but with an escape clause that he can, at a certain date, be restored to his former self to rejoin his wife and live out the rest of his life normally. The devil agrees. So, Joe becomes the 22-year old Joe Hardy, joins the Senators, becomes their star long-ball hitter (with a .460 average) and takes them all the way to second place in the American League. However, Applegate is a Yankees fan, and when Hardy finds that he is planning sabotage, he invokes the escape clause. But the devil sends him the sensational Lola (in reality a 172-year-old witch who had originally sold her soul to Applegate because she was the ugliest girl in Providence, Rhode Island), but Hardy rejects her. But Lola falls in love with Hardy and helps him beat the Yankees. Joe then returns to his normal self, just as he's making the big catch that will put the Senators into the World Series. Smokey the catcher was based on Yogi Berra, real life legend. Sister was a nosey neighbor and avid Senators fan. Van Buren was the team manager, and Welch was the owner.

Before Broadway. Albert Taylor of the William Morris Agency brought the project to George Abbott's attention, and he agreed to direct, provided Freddie Brisson, Hal Prince and Bobby Griffith produce. So, just a few weeks after the opening of *The Pajama Game*, the same crew got together to make *Damn Yankees*. Mitzi Gaynor and Zizi Jeanmaire both turned down the role of Lola. It was easy to raise the money, with

155 backers. There were many changes in the book and score during out-of-town tryouts — one third of the numbers were cut. Gwen Verdon was given more songs and an earlier entrance. It was the first time Bob Fosse and Gwen Verdon had worked together. The big worry was that plays about baseball don't work — and they don't, on or off Broadway, never have, never will — this was the only one. Mr. Abbott said the reason was because you can't show the diamond. On 4/1/55, during rehearsals in New Haven tryouts, a curtain fell, and landed on Gwen Verdon's head, giving her scalp lacerations.

The Broadway Run. FORTY-SIXTH STREET THEATRE, 5/5/55–5/4/57; ADELPHI THEATRE, 5/7/57–10/19/57. Total of 1,019 PERFORMANCES. PRESENTED BY Frederick Brisson, Robert E. Griffith and Harold S. Prince, in association with Albert B. Taylor; MUSIC/LYRICS: Richard Adler & Jerry Ross; BOOK: George Abbott & Douglass Wallop (Richard Bissell helped, but is uncredited); Based on the 1954 novel *The Year the Yankees Lost the Pennant*, by Douglass Wallop; DIRECTOR: George Abbott; CHOREOGRAPHER: Bob Fosse; SETS/COSTUMES: William & Jean Eckart; MUSICAL DIRECTOR: Harold Hastings, *George Hirst* (by 56–57); ORCHESTRATIONS: Don Walker; DANCE MUSIC ARRANGEMENTS: Roger Adams; PRESS: Reuben Rabinovitch & Howard Newman, *Helen Richards*; GENERAL MANAGER: Carl Fisher; COMPANY MANAGER: Richard Horner; PRODUCTION STAGE MANAGER: James Hammerstein; STAGE MANAGER: Fred Hearn; ASSISTANT STAGE MANAGER: Robert Evans, *Daniel Sattler*. **Cast:** MEG BOYD: Shannon Bolin (5), *Charlotte Fairchild*; JOE: Robert Shafer; APPLEGATE: Ray Walston (3), *Nathaniel Frey* (from 56–57), *Howard Caine* (from 56–57); SISTER: Jean Stapleton, *Anita Webb* (from 56–57); DORIS: Elizabeth Howell; JOE HARDY: Stephen Douglass (2); HENRY: Al Lanti, *William Joyce* (55–56), *George Lake* (from 56–57); SOHOVIK: Eddie Phillips, *Bob Fosse* (stood in one night when Mr. Phillips was out), *Kenneth Le Roy* (from 56–57); SMOKEY, THE CATCHER: Nathaniel Frey, *Bill McDonald* (from 56–57); VERNON: Albert Linville, *Sam Greene* (from 56–57); VAN BUREN: Russ Brown (4), *Marty May* (from 55–56), *Russ Brown* (from 56–57), *Al Lanti* (from 56–57); ROCKY: Jimmie Komack, *Bob Dishy* (from 55–56), *Don Rogers* (from 56–57); GLORIA THORPE: Rae Allen, *Sally Brown* (from 56–57); TEENAGER: Cherry Davis; LYNCH: Del Horstmann; WELCH: Richard Bishop, *William Adams* (from 55–56); LOLA: Gwen Verdon (1), *Sheila Bond* (for two weeks in 55–56), *Gretchen Wyler* (from 56–57), *Devra Korwin* (from 56–57); MISS WESTON: Janie Janvier, *Barbara Williams* (during Miss Janvier's absence in 54–55); GUARD: George Marcy; COMMISSIONER: Del Horstmann; POSTMASTER: Albert Linville, *Sam Greene* (from 56–57); DANCERS: Betty Carr (gone by 56–57), Robert Evans, Timmy Everett (gone by 55–56), Patricia Ferrier (gone by 55–56), Marlyn Greer (gone by 55–56), William Joyce (gone by 56–57), Harvey Jung (gone by 56–57), Marie Kolin, Al Lanti (gone by 56–57), Svetlana McLee (gone by 55–56), George Marcy (gone by 55–56), Julie Marlowe (gone by 55–56), Eddie Phillips (gone by 56–57), Mark Ward. 55–56 replacements: *Jean Caples* (gone by 56–57), *Margot Feldman, Penny Ann Green, Devra Kline* (gone by 56–57), *Louis Johnson, George Lake, Charles Morrell, Lynn Ross.* 56–57 replacements: *Ellen Beach, Alan Johnson, Sandy Leeds, Janyce Ann Wagner, Sally Willis.* Later replacement: *Lee Becker*; SINGERS: Frank Bouley, Fred Bryan, Cherry Davis, Jeanne Grant (gone by 56–57), Janet Hayes, Del Horstmann, Janie Janvier, Joan Keenan, Albert Linville (gone by 56–57), Susan Lovell (gone by 56–57), Ralph Lowe (gone by 56–57), Ralph Strane (*Don Rogers* by 55–56). 56–57 replacements: *Lee Barry, Sam Greene, Earl Muron, Dorothy Richards, Barbara Williams*; CHILDREN: Ronn Cummins & Jackie Scholle, *Jackie Wayne* (by 55–56 was the only child). **Understudies:** Joe Hardy: Ralph Lowe, *Frank Bouley* (by 56–57); Lola: Betty Carr, *Margot Feldman* (by 56–57); Applegate: Nat Frey, *Bill McDonald* (by 56–57); Meg: Janet Hayes; Sister: Joan Keenan; Van Buren: Al Lanti, *Bill McDonald* (by 56–57); Welch: Albert Linville; Doris: Janie Janvier; Joe Boyd: Fred Bryan; Gloria: *Susan Lovell* (by 55–56), *Janie Janvier* (by 56–57); Rocky: Ralph Strane, *Don Rogers* (only after Jimmie Komack left), *Earl Muron* (by 56–57); Smokey: *William Joyce* (by 55–56), *Sam Greene* (by 56–57); Sohovik: *Bob Evans* (by 55–56 & still throughout 56–57), *Tucker Smith* (by 56–57); Mambo Dancer: *Al Lanti* (by 55–56). **Act I: Scene 1** Joe & Meg Boyd's front porch and living room, just outside Washington: "Six Months Out of Every Year" (Meg, Joe, Baseball Fans, Baseball Widows), "Goodbye, Old Girl" (Joe Boyd), "Goodbye, Old Girl" (reprise) (Joe Hardy); **Scene 2** A corridor under the stands of the Washington Senators' baseball park: "Heart" (Van Buren, Rocky, Smokey, Vernon) [a big hit]; **Scene 3** The dugout of the Washington Senators' baseball park: "Shoeless Joe from Hannibal, Mo." (Gloria & Baseball Players); **Scene 4** A billboard near the ballpark; **Scene 5** Welch's office: "A Man Doesn't Know" (Joe Hardy); **Scene 6** A bench in front of the Joe Hardy billboard: "A Little Brains — A Little Talent" (Lola); **Scene 7** Meg's house: "A Man Doesn't Know" (reprise) (Joe Hardy, Meg, Lola); **Scene 8** Corridor at the ballpark; **Scene 9** The locker room: "Whatever Lola Wants (Lola Gets)" (Lola) [the big hit]; **Scene 10** In front of the black curtain: "Not Meg" (Applegate & Gossips) [cut after the first night and replaced with the reprise of "Heart" that had been in Act II Scene 1]; **Scene 11** The stage of the hotel ballroom: "Who's Got the Pain?" (danced as a mambo by Lola & Sohovik. Staged by Mr. Fosse & Miss Verdon), "The American League" (The Downtown Fan Club) [dropped shortly after opening night]. **Act II: Scene 1** The Senators' locker room: "The Game" (Rocky, Smokey, Baseball Players), "Heart" (reprise) (Sister, Children, Teenager) [shortly after opening night this reprise was moved to Act I Scene 10]; **Scene 2** A park at dusk: "Near to You" (Joe Hardy, Meg, Joe Boyd); **Scene 3** Applegate's apartment: "Those Were (The Good Old Days)" (Applegate); **Scene 4** Baseball Commissioner's hearing room; **Scene 5** A bench; **Scene 6** A night club: "Two Lost Souls" (Lola, Joe Hardy, Guys & Dolls); **Scene 7** The Joe Hardy billboard; **Scene 8** The billboard; **Scene 9** The dugout and stands; **Scene 10** Corridor at ballpark; **Scene 11** Meg's house: "A Man Doesn't Know" (reprise) (Meg & Joe Boyd).

Broadway reviews were mostly raves. After the first night a few changes were made. "Not Meg" was dropped, another number was moved from Act II to Act I, and Lola now ended the show as a beautiful girl, instead of an old hag. The show now ran 20 minutes shorter, which was much better. The producers asked Walter Kerr to come back and review it again. He did, and liked it even better. However, the fans didn't exactly pour in (the show cost $33,000 a week to run) until the advertising posters of Gwen Verdon changed her attire from baseball uniform to corset. The show won Tonys for musical, choreography, musical direction, and for Gwen Verdon, Ray Walston and Russ Brown. It also won a Special Tony for stage tech (Harry Green), and was nominated for Stephen Douglass and Rae Allen. Jerry Ross died of respiratory illness 6 months after it opened. The show returned 263 per cent on its investment.

After Broadway. TOUR. Opened on 1/21/56, at the Shubert Theatre, New Haven, and closed on 5/18/57, at the Royal Alexandra Theatre, Toronto. MUSICAL DIRECTOR: William Parson. **Cast:** MEG: Rosemary Kuhlmann, *Charlotte Fairchild*; JOE BOYD: Joe Hill; APPLEGATE: Bobby Clark, *Ray Walston, Bobby Clark* (for the last month); JOE HARDY: Allen Case, *Ralph Lowe*; VAN BUREN: Sid Stone, *Horace McMahon* (from the last season); GLORIA: Jo Hurt, *Joyce Barker*; LYNCH: Jay Flynn; LOLA: Sherry O'Neill, *Devra Korwin*. **Understudy:** Meg: Charlotte Fairchild.

TOUR. Opened on 1/18/58, at The Mosque, Altoona, and closed on 5/10/58, at the Paramount Theatre, Omaha. CHOREOGRAPHER: Zoya Leporska; MUSICAL DIRECTOR: George Hirst. **Cast:** MEG: Charlotte Fairchild; JOE BOYD: Joe Hill; APPLEGATE: Leon Janney; JOE HARDY: Ralph Lowe; SMOKEY: Charles Reynolds; VERNON: Roger Franklin; VAN BUREN: Al Lanti; GLORIA: Sally Brown; LYNCH/COMMISSIONER: Larry Mitchell; LOLA: Devra Korwin; CHORUS INCLUDED: Beth Howland, Cy Young.

THE MOVIE. 1958. DIRECTORS: George Abbott & Stanley Donen. Everyone in the cast had been in the Broadway run, except Tab Hunter (as Joe Hardy). Bob Fosse appeared as a mambo dancer. There was a new song: "There's Something About an Empty Chair."

COLISEUM, London. Opened on 3/28/57. 861 PERFORMANCES. DIRECTOR: James Hammerstein; CHOREOGRAPHER: Zoya Leporska; PRODUCTION SUPERVISOR: Jerome Whyte; MUSICAL DIRECTOR: Robert Lowe. **Cast:** MEG: Betty Paul; JOE BOYD: Phil Vickers; APPLEGATE: Bill Kerr; SISTER: Mavis Villiers; DORIS: Christine Bocca; JOE HARDY: Ivor Emmanuel; SMOKEY: Ed Devereaux; VERNON: Robert Crane; VAN BUREN: Donald Stewart; GLORIA: Judy Bruce; WELCH: Robert Henderson; LOLA: Belita, *Elizabeth Seal*; SINGERS INCLUDED: Terry Donovan, Roy Lees.

NBC TV PRODUCTION. 4/8/67. *Cast:* Jerry Lanning, Lee Remick, Phil Silvers, Linda Lavin, Jim Backus, Ray Middleton.

JONES BEACH THEATRE, NY, 6/30/81–9/6/81. 56 PERFORMANCES. DIRECTOR/CHOREOGRAPHER: Frank Wagner; SETS/COSTUMES: Robert Fletcher; LIGHTING: Marc B. Weiss; MUSICAL DIRECTOR: Joseph Klein. *Cast:* MEG: Julienne Marie; JOE BOYD: Paul Merrill; APPLEGATE: Eddie Bracken; JOE HARDY: Joe Namath; SOHOVIK: Anthony Inneo; GLORIA: Alyson Reed; WELCH: Thomas Ruisinger; CHORUS INCLUDED: Bill Badolato, Mimi Quillin, Mary Leigh Stahl.

PAPER MILL PLAYHOUSE, New Jersey, 1986. DIRECTOR: George Abbott; CHOREOGRAPHER: Michael Shawn; SETS: Michael Anania. *Cast:* Orson Bean, Davis Gaines, Alyson Reed.

164. *Damn Yankees (1994 Broadway revival)*

Before Broadway. This revised version was re-tooled by Jack O'Brien, with the approval of George Abbott. It opened on 10/5/93, at the OLD GLOBE THEATRE, San Diego. George Abbott (then 106 years old) and Richard Adler were both at opening night in San Diego. It had the same crew as for the subsequent Broadway run, and the same cast, except JOE HARDY: Jere Shea; LEONARD: Jim Borstelmann (role cut before Broadway); STUBBS: Scott Robertson (he would play Del on Broadway), FLASH: Bruce Anthony Davis (he would play Henry on Broadway); KITTY: Julia Gregory.

The Broadway Run. MARQUIS THEATRE, 3/3/94–8/6/95. 35 previews from 2/14/94. 510 PERFORMANCES. PRESENTED BY Mitchell Maxwell, PolyGram Diversified (Theatrical) Entertainment, Dan Markley, Kevin McCollum, Victoria Maxwell, Fred H. Krones, Andrea Nasher, The Frankel — Viertel — Baruch Group, Paula Heil Fisher, and Julie Ross, in association with Jon B. Platt, Alan J. Schuster, and Peter Breger; MUSIC: Richard Adler & Jerry Ross; ORIGINAL BOOK: George Abbott & Douglass Wallop; REVISED BOOK: Jack O'Brien; BASED ON the 1954 novel *The Year the Yankees Lost the Pennant*, by Douglass Wallop; DIRECTOR: Jack O'Brien; CHOREOGRAPHER: Rob Marshall; ASSISTANT CHOREOGRAPHER: Kathleen Marshall; SETS: Douglas W. Schmidt; COSTUMES: David C. Woolard; LIGHTING: David F. Segal; SOUND: Jonathan Deans; MUSICAL SUPERVISOR/VOCAL ARRANGEMENTS/MUSIC CONTINUITY: James Raitt; ORCHESTRATIONS: Douglas Besterman; DANCE MUSIC ARRANGEMENTS: Tom Fay; ADDITIONAL DANCE MUSIC ARRANGEMENTS: David Krane; NEW CAST RECORDING made on 3/7/94 & 3/14/94, at the Hit Factory, Studio One, NYC; PRESS: Cromarty & Company; CASTING: Jay Binder; GENERAL MANAGER: Charlotte W. Wilcox; COMPANY MANAGER: Robb Lady, *Bruce Kagel* (from 3/12/95); PRODUCTION STAGE MANAGER: Douglas Pagliotti, *Maureen F. Gibson* (from 3/12/95); STAGE MANAGER: Cosmo P. Hanson; ASSISTANT STAGE MANAGER: James Mountcastle. *Cast:* VOICE OF NARRATOR: Gregory Jbara [new role from 3/12/95]; MEG BOYD: Linda Stephens (7); JOE BOYD: Dennis Kelly (4); SISTER: Susan Mansur (12); GLORIA THORPE: Vicki Lewis (6), *Liz Larsen* (from 3/12/95); APPLEGATE: Victor Garber (2) ☆ (until 12/31/94), *Jerry Lewis* (1) ☆ (from 3/12/95); JOE HARDY: Jarrod Emick (3), Jason Workman, Jarrod Emick, Eric Kunze; THE SENATORS: ROCKY: Scott Wise (8), *Rod McCune*; SMOKEY: Jeff Blumenkrantz (10), *Mark Chmiel*; SOHOVIK: Gregory Jbara (9), *Louis D. Giovannetti*; MICKEY: John Ganun, *Troy Britton Johnson, Christopher Monteleone*; VERNON: Joey Pizzi; DEL: Scott Robertson, *Allen Fitzpatrick*; OZZIE: Michael Winther, *John Bolton, Michael Winther*; BUBBA: Cory English, *Bill Brassea*; HENRY: Bruce Anthony Davis; BOMBER: Michael Berresse, *Robb Edward Morris, David Elder* [end of Senators]; BENNY VAN BUREN: Dick Latessa (5); STADIUM P.A. ANNOUNCER: John Bolton [new role from 3/12/95]; BETTY: Paula Leggett Chase, *Penny Ayn Maas*; DONNA: Nancy Ticotin, *Malinda Shaffer*; KITTY: Cynthia Onrubia, *Karen Babcock*; LULU: Meg Bussert, *Roxie Lucas* [new role written in after opening night]; RITA: Amy Ryder, *Meg Bussert*; HI-TONES: Penny Ayn Maas, Cynthia Onrubia, Malinda Shaffer [new roles from 3/12/95]; AD EXECUTIVE: Scott Robertson [new role from 3/12/95]; PHOTOGRAPHER: Amy Ryder, *Meg Bussert, Roxie Lucas*; LO-TONES: John Bolton, David Elder, Troy Britton Johnson [new roles from 3/12/95]; WELCH: Terrence P. Currier (11); LOLA: Bebe Neuwirth (1) ☆, *Nancy*

Ticotin, Charlotte d'Amboise (2) ☆ (from 3/12/95); STADIUM VOICE: Mel Allen [new role from 3/12/95]; PLAY-BY-PLAY ANNOUNCER: John Bolton [new role from 3/12/95]; VOICE OF TV SPORTSCASTER: Mark Chmiel [new role from 3/12/95]. *Standbys:* Lola: Valerie Wright; Applegate: Patrick Quinn. Understudies: Lola: Nancy Ticotin, *Malinda Shaffer*; Joe Hardy: Michael Berresse & John Ganun, *David Elder, Christopher Monteleone, Troy Britton Johnson*; Meg: Paula Leggett Chase, *Meg Bussert*; Sister: Amy Ryder, *Roxie Lucas, Karen Babcock*; Joe Boyd/Van Buren/Welch: Scott Robertson, *Allen Fitzpatrick*; Gloria: Robyn Peterman, *Linda Gabler, Malinda Shaffer*. SWINGS: Mark Santoro, Robyn Peterman (*Linda Gabler*), David A. Wood, Rod McCune. **Orchestra:** REEDS: Lawrence Feldman, Kenneth Hitchcock (*Edward Joffe*), William Meade, Richard Centalonza, Roger Rosenberg (*Frank Santagata*); TRUMPETS: David Stahl, Danny Cahn, Steve Guttman; TROMBONES: Keith O'Quinn (*Randall Andos*) & Dale Kirkland; BASS TROMBONE: Jack Schatz; FRENCH HORN: Ann Yarbrough; CONCERTMASTER: Marti Sweet; VIOLINS: David Niwa (*Elizabeth Chang*), Carlos Villa, Rebekah Johnson; CELLO: Sarah Carter; HARP: Kathryn Easter; BASS: Ronald Raffio; DRUMS: Raymond Marchica, Martin Fischer; PERCUSSION: Ian Finkel; PIANO: David Chase, Robert Hirschhorn; KEYBOARD 2: Nancy Blair Wolfe. **Act I:** Overture; "Six Months Out of Every Year" (Meg, Joe Boyd, Sister, Gloria, Husbands, Wives), "Goodbye, Old Girl" (Joe Boyd & Joe Hardy), "Blooper Ballet" (Senators) [a new instrumental number], "Heart" (Van Buren & Senators), "Shoeless Joe from Hannibal, Mo." (Gloria & Senators), "Shoeless Joe from Hannibal, Mo." (reprise) (Gloria, Joe Hardy, Ensemble), "A Little Brains, a Little Talent" (Lola), "A Man Doesn't Know" (Meg & Joe Hardy), "Whatever Lola Wants (Lola Gets)" (Lola). **Act II:** Entr'acte; "Who's Got the Pain?" (Lola & Senators), "The Game" (Senators), "Near to You" (Meg, Joe Hardy, Joe Boyd), "Those Were the Good Old Days" (Applegate), "Two Lost Souls" (Lola & Applegate), "A Man Doesn't Know" (reprise) (Meg & Joe Boyd), Finale: "Heart" (reprise) (Company).

Broadway reviews were very good. Jarrod Emick won a Tony, and the show was also nominated for revival, choreography, and for Victor Garber. After 342 performances the show went on hiatus 1/1/95–2/28/95, and officially re-opened 3/12/95 after an additional 16 previews.

After Broadway. TOUR. Opened on 9/25/95, at the Eisenhower Hall, West Point, NY. Previews from 9/22/95. PRESENTED BY Workin' Man Films & PACE Theatrical Group; DIRECTOR: Jack O'Brien; CHOREOGRAPHER: James Raitt; MUSICAL DIRECTOR: Robert Hirschhorn. *Cast:* MEG: Susan Bigelow, *Joy Franz*; JOE BOYD: Dennis Kelly; SISTER: Amy Ryder, *Julie Prosser* (from 3/26/96); APPLEGATE: Jerry Lewis [he played it 616 times on tour]; JOE HARDY: David Elder, *John-Michael Flate*; VAN BUREN: Joseph R. Sicari; GLORIA: Linda Gabler, *Ellen Grosso*; LOLA: Valerie Wright, *April Nixon*; ALSO WITH: Jamie Ross, Mark Chmiel, Louis D. Giovannetti, Ned Hannah, Karen Babcock, Bill Brassea, Bruce Anthony Davis, Mark Esposito, Rod McCune. The tour included a stint at the Kennedy Center, 12/10/96–1/12/97. After playing 50 cities, the tour went to the ADELPHI THEATRE, London, 6/4/97–8/9/97. Previews from 5/29/97. There was a fuss when PolyGram, who had invested nearly a million dollars in the Broadway revival, sued producer Mitchell Maxwell, saying that his misuse of the money to boost the tour at the expense of the Broadway production, and that the two-month hiatus in the Broadway run in Jan. & Feb. 1995 in order to get Jerry Lewis ready for his role, had eaten up most of the $830,000 reserve fund which should have gone to the investors. Jerry Lewis was being paid $100,000 a week — too much for the tour. In London it went on hiatus for a month, so Jerry could host the Telethon on TV, and it was to have moved from the Adelphi to the Savoy on 10/16/97, with Mr. Lewis still starring but with an otherwise all–British cast, and from there on to Berlin and Paris. Then it was to return to Broadway. A movie, with and directed by Jerry Lewis, was being talked about. However, the tour was canceled in 10/97.

ARENA THEATRE, Houston, 3/21/00–4/2/00. PRESENTED BY Theatre Under the Stars; DIRECTOR: Bick Goss; CHOREOGRAPHER: John MacInnis; SETS: John Farrell; COSTUMES: David C. Woolard; LIGHTING: Kirk Bookman; SOUND: Beth Berkeley. *Cast:* MEG: Louisa Flaningam; JOE BOYD: Vincent Smith; APPLEGATE: Tony Randall; JOE HARDY: Jarrod Emick; VAN BUREN: Joel Blum; GLORIA: Beth Leavel; WELCH: Bill Hardy; LOLA: Jill Powell.

165. *Dance a Little Closer*

The action, updated from the eve of World War II of Robert Sherwood's original play *Idiot's Delight*, takes place in the "avoidable future" in the Barclay-Palace Hotel on a hillside in the Austrian Alps, during a confrontation between NATO and Soviet forces that could lead to World War III. The lead female was changed from an American showgirl pretending to be a Russian countess to one pretending to be a British lady. The man she's traveling with is changed from a munitions manufacturer to a Kissinger-like, Austrian-born American diplomat. Lounge entertainer Harry (his last name was changed from Van to Aikens for this musical) is stranded on New Years Eve in the Barclay when the conflict begins and the border is closed. Cynthia is staying at the same hotel. Harry recognizes her as a girl he slept with ten years before in a Ramada Inn in Omaha.

Before Broadway. Liz Robertson, the star, was Alan Jay Lerner's eighth wife. The show had a workshop at 890 Broadway, then went straight into Broadway previews, during which word soon got around that it was a dud, and it acquired the nickname *Close a Little Faster*. In fact, a 500-person opening-night party was canceled the day before the show opened.

The Broadway Run. MINSKOFF THEATRE, 5/11/83. 27 previews. 1 PERFORMANCE. PRESENTED BY Frederick Brisson, Jerome Minskoff, James Nederlander, The John F. Kennedy Center; MUSIC: Charles Strouse; LYRICS/BOOK/DIRECTOR: Alan Jay Lerner; BASED ON the 1936 Pulitzer Prize–winning play *Idiot's Delight*, by Robert E. Sherwood; CHOREOGRAPHER: Billy Wilson; SKATING CHOREOGRAPHER: Blair Hammond; SETS: David Mitchell; COSTUMES: Donald Brooks; LIGHTING: Thomas Skelton; SOUND: John McClure; MUSICAL DIRECTOR: Peter Howard; ORCHESTRATIONS: Jonathan Tunick; DANCE MUSIC ARRANGEMENTS: Glen Kelly; PRESS: Jeffrey Richards Associates; PRODUCTION SUPERVISOR: Stone Widney; GENERAL MANAGER: Joseph P. Harris Associates; COMPANY MANAGER: Mitzi Harder; PRODUCTION STAGE MANAGER: Alan Hall; STAGE MANAGER: Steven Adler; ASSISTANT STAGE MANAGER: Dianne Trulock. *Cast:* ROGER BUTTERFIELD: Don Chastain; HARRY AIKENS: Len Cariou (1) ✫; THE (THREE) DELIGHTS: SHIRLEY: Diane Pennington; BEBE: Cheryl Howard; ELAINE: Alyson Reed; JOHANNES HARTOG: David Sabin; CONTESSA CARLA PIRIANNO: Elizabeth Hubbard; CAPTAIN MUELLER: Noel Craig; CHARLES CASTLETON: Brent Barrett; EDWARD DUNLOP: Jeff Keller; BELLBOY: Philip Mollet; WAITER: Brian Sutherland; REVEREND OLIVER BOYLE: I.M. Hobson; HESTER BOYLE: Joyce Worsley; HEINRICH HALLOWAY: Joseph Kolinski [this character is erroneously called Heinrich Walter in several sources]; CYNTHIA BROOKFIELD-BAILEY: Liz Robertson (2) ✫; DR. JOSEF WINKLER: George Rose (3) ✫; PAS DE DEUX: HARRY'S DOUBLE: Brian Sutherland; CYNTHIA'S DOUBLE: Robin Stephens [end of Pas de Deux sequence]; RINK ATTENDANT: James Fatta; ICE SKATER: Colleen Ashton; VIOLINIST: James Fatta; HARRY, HARRY, HARRY, HARRY: Peter Wandel, Philip Mollet, Brian Sutherland, James Fatta; HOTEL GUESTS: Colleen Ashton, Candy Cook, Mary Dale, James Fatta, Philip Mollet, Linda Poser, Robin Stephens, Brian Sutherland, Peter Wandel. *Standby*: David Sabin. *Understudies*: Harry: Don Chastain; Cynthia: Elizabeth Hubbard; Contessa/Hester: Linda Poser; Mueller: Philip Mollet; Halloway/Charles/Edward: Brian Sutherland; Elaine: Colleen Ashton; Shirley: Candy Cook; Hartog: Reuben Singer; Bebe: Joanne Genelle; Waiter: Peter Wandel. *Swings*: Joanne Genelle & Mark LaManna. *Act I*: *Scene 1* The nightclub of the Barclay-Palace Hotel; New Year's Eve, shortly before midnight: "It Never Would've Worked" (Harry & Delights), "Happy, Happy New Year" (Harry, Delights, Guests); *Scene 2* The main entrance lounge of the hotel; 2 a.m. that night: "No Man is Worth It" (Cynthia), "What Are You Going to Do About It?" (Harry & Halloway); *Scene 3* The Winkler suite; later that night: "A Woman Who Thinks I'm Wonderful" (Winkler); *Scene 3a* Harry's memory: "Pas de Deux" (Harry's Double & Cynthia's Double); *Scene 4* A bedroom in a midwestern hotel; ten years earlier: "There's Never Been Anything Like Us" (Harry), "Another Life" (Cynthia); *Scene 5* The skating rink at the hotel; New Year's Day morning: "Why Can't the World Go and Leave Us Alone?" (Charles & Edward), "He Always Comes Home to Me" (Cynthia & Harry); *Scene 6* The nightclub of the hotel; that evening: "I Got a New Girl" (Harry

& Delights), "Dance a Little Closer" [a re-hashing of Strouse & Adams' "Let Me Sing My Song," from their 1978 flop *A Broadway Musical*] (Harry, Cynthia, Guests), "There's Always One You Can't Forget" (Harry). *Act II*: *Scene 1* The main entrance lounge of the hotel; the following morning: "Homesick" (Delights), "Mad" (Harry & Delights), "I Don't Know" (Harry, Boyle, Contessa, Delights, Charles, Edward, Cynthia), "Auf Wiedersehen" (Winkler), "I Never Want to See You Again" (Harry); *Scene 2* Cynthia's memory: "On Top of the World" (Cynthia & Men); *Scene 3* The main entrance lounge of the hotel; immediately following: "I Got a New Girl" (reprise) (Harry & Cynthia), "Dance a Little Closer" (reprise) (Harry & Cynthia).

The show was universally panned.

166. *Dance Me a Song*

An intimate revue.

The Broadway Run. ROYALE THEATRE, 1/20/50–2/18/50. 35 PERFORMANCES. PRESENTED BY Dwight Deere Wiman, in association with Robert Ross; MUSIC/LYRICS: James Shelton; ADDITIONAL MUSIC/LYRICS: Herman Hupfeld, Albert Hague, Maurice Valency, Bud Gregg; SKETCHES: Jimmy Kirkwood & Lee Goodman, George Oppenheimer & Vincente Minnelli, Marya Mannes, Robert Anderson, James Shelton & Wally Cox; DIRECTOR: James Shelton; CHOREOGRAPHER: Robert Sidney; SETS/LIGHTING: Jo Mielziner; COSTUMES: Irene Sharaff; MUSICAL DIRECTOR: Tony Cabot; ORCHESTRATIONS: Robert Russell Bennett; PRESS: Tom Weatherly; STAGE MANAGERS: John E. Sola, Tony Albert, Robert B. Sola. *Act I*: *Scene 1* A Pair for Tonight (by James Shelton; based on an idea by Jo Mielziner): MAN: Tony Albert; WIFE: Cynthia Rogers; TAXI DRIVER: Donald Saddler; DRILLER: Cliff Ferre; PHONE MAN: Scott Merrill; *Scene 2* Average Family: COOK: Babe Hines; SON-IN-LAW: Erik Rhodes (3); GRANDMOTHER: Marion Lorne; SISTER KATE: Ann Thomas; MOTHER: Tina Prescott; UNCLE: Wally Cox (4); SONS: Alan Ross, Jimmy Kirkwood (5), Bob Scheerer (2); DOG: Silver; *Scene 3* "It's the Weather" (sung by Biff McGuire, Tina Prescott, Bob Fosse (6), Cliff Ferre, Scott Merrill, Mary Ann Niles (6), Francine Bond) (danced by Fosse & Niles (6), Donald Saddler, June Graham; supported by Carmina Cansino, Francine Bond, Marian Horosko, Dusty McCaffrey, Scott Merrill, Douglas Moppert); *Scene 4* She's No Lady (by James Shelton & Cynthia Rogers) (a woman demonstrates self-defense techniques): JUDOEE: Biff McGuire; JUDOER: Ann Thomas; *Scene 5* A Woman's Place: SALESMAN: Erik Rhodes (3); SLEEPING BEAUTY: June Graham. Note: after opening this sketch was replaced with: Inspection (by Wally Cox): PFC: Wally Cox (4); *Scene 6* "Glee Club" (sung by Heidi Krall, Ann Thomas, Francine Bond, Cynthia Rogers, Wally Cox (4), Alan Ross, Erik Rhodes (3), Biff McGuire, Jimmy Kirkwood (5), Scott Merrill); *Scene 7* "Strange New Look." Danced & sung by: FARMER: Biff McGuire; NELLIE: Joan McCracken (1); CITY SLICKER: Bob Scheerer (2); *Scene 8* Buck and Bobbie (by Lee Goodman & Jimmy Kirkwood) (burlesque satire on children's radio horror programs): BUCK: Lee Goodman (5); BOBBIE: Joe Kirkwood (5); SECRETARY: Ann Thomas; *Scene 9* "I'm the Girl" (sung by Hope Foye); *Scene 10* The Lunts Are the Lunts Are the Lunts (by Robert Anderson) (how the Lunts might succeed as actors even by reading the phone book): ALFRED: Alan Ross; LYNN: Joan McCracken (1); *Scene 11* "Matilda." Sung & danced by: MATILDA: June Graham; HILDA: Mary Ann Niles; BUTLER: Bob Scheerer (2); SERVANTS: Francine Bond, Marilyn Gennaro, Carmina Cansino, Marian Horosko, Scott Merrill, Douglas Moppert, Don Little, Dusty McCaffrey; *Scene 12* "Love" (sung by Babe Hines); *Scene 13* Documentary (narration written by James Shelton; m: Bud Gregg; monologue written by Wally Cox) (spoof of slum life as shown in documentaries) (Wally Cox was a monologist from the night clubs who talked about a dumb soda-jerk named Dufo): NARRATOR: Erik Rhodes (3); DUFO'S FRIEND: Wally Cox (4); GIRL: Tina Prescott; DUFO: Bob Fosse (6); POLICEMAN: Scott Merrill; A WOMAN: Hope Foye; CHILDREN: Francine Bond, Marilyn Gennaro, Dusty McCaffrey; DRUNKARD: Donald Saddler; CORA COX: Cynthia Rogers. *Act II*: *Scene 1* "One is a Lonely Number" (m: Albert Hague; l: Maurice Valency) (mirror dance): GIRL: Heidi Krall; BOY: Alan Ross; The Company; *Scene 2* Texas: GIRL: Ann Thomas; TWO COWBOYS: Bob Scheerer (2) & Cliff Ferre; *Scene 3* "The Folks at Home" (sketch by

George Oppenheimer & Vincente Minnelli. Song of the same name by James Shelton) Marion is an antique dealer in a crumbling mansion surrounded by ghouls and demons): MAD SCIENTIST: Joe Kirkwood (5); IDIOT SERVANT: Wally Cox (4); VAMPIRE: Tina Prescott; MAD PROFESSOR: Erik Rhodes (3); FRANKENSTEIN: Biff McGuire; CRONE: Lee Goodman (5); MARION: Marion Lorne; HARPO MARX: Bob Fosse (6); HIGHBOY: Robert B. Sola; BLONDE MAIDEN: Marian Horosko; GEORGE WASHINGTON: Dusty McCaffrey; MR. McINTOSH: Douglas Moppert; *Scene 4* "My Little Dog Has Ego" (m/l: Herman Hupfeld): BOY: Bob Scheerer (2); DOG: Silver; *Scene 5* The Board Meeting (by Marya Mannes): CHAIRMAN: Erik Rhodes (3); MASON: Alan Ross; BATES: Cliff Ferre; TILPIN: Biff McGuire; KNIGHT: Joe Kirkwood (5); A VISITOR: Scott Merrill. Note: this sketch was replaced after opening with Operation Columbus (by Lee Goodman & Jimmy Kirkwood): COLONEL: Lee Goodman (5); MERRIWEATHER: Wally Cox (4); ABERCROMBIE: Joe Kirkwood (5); PILOTS: Scott Merrill & Don Saddler; *Scene 6* "Lilac Wine" (sung by Hope Foye) (danced by June Graham & Don Saddler); *Scene 7* "Paper!" (ballet): NEWSPAPER BOY: Biff McGuire; GIRL: Joan McCracken (1); THE RAKE: Cliff Ferre; BOY FRIEND: Donald Saddler; The Company; *Scene 8* Hello from Hollywood [written & performed by Kirkwood & Goodman (5)]; *Scene 9* "How Little Adam Knew." Sung & danced by: THE SERPENT: Tina Prescott; EVE: Mary Ann Niles (6); ADAM: Bob Fosse (6); *Scene 9* It's His Money (by Wally Cox): COUNTERMAN: Wally Cox (4); CUSTOMER: Biff McGuire; OWNER: Donald Saddler; *Scene 10* "Dance Me a Song." Sung & danced by: THE BOYS: Cliff Ferre, Bob Fosse (6), Bob Scheerer (2); THE GIRL: Joan McCracken (1); The Company; *Scene 11* Finale (Company).

DANCING ENSEMBLE: Francine Bond, Carmina Cansino, Marilyn Gennaro, June Graham, Marian Horosko, Don Little, Dusty McCaffrey, Scott Merrill, Douglas Moppert. *Understudies*: For Marion Lorne, Ann Thomas & Joan McCracken's songs: Cynthia Rogers; For Joan McCracken's dances: June Graham; For Cynthia Rogers: Carmina Cansino; For Biff McGuire: Scott Merrill; For Bob Scheerer's Dances: Don Little & Dusty McCaffrey.

Broadway reviews were divided, mostly unfavorable. This was the show in which Wally Cox came to the fore as a comedian. He won a Donaldson Award.

167. *Dance of the Vampires*

Set in a graveyard near a Carpathian village with an unpronounceable name (Lower Belabartokovich), three nights before Halloween, in the year 1880-something. Sarah (a beautiful village girl and Alfred's girlfriend) and her friends Zsa Zsa and Nadja are picking mushrooms when they discover the castle of Count von Krolock. A professor/vampire killer and his stupid assistant struggle to save the innkeeper's daughter from becoming Queen of the Vampires. Herbert is the Count's gay vampire son; Abronsius is absent-minded; the innkeeper is Jewish, a parody of Tevye in *Fiddler on the Roof*; Magda is busty and lusty; Rebecca is the large, buffo, unsatisfied, griping village spouse of the innkeeper.

Before Broadway. Michael Kunze, a German, wrote the lyrics and libretto in English first, to aid Jim Steinman in writing the music; then he translated it into German. Rehearsals began on 7/21/97 and it first opened on 10/4/97, as *Tanz der Vampire*, at the RAIMUND THEATER, VIENNA. PRESENTED BY the Vereinigte Buehnen Wien GmbH, in association with Roman Polanski, Andrew Braunsberg & Rudi Klausnitzer; PRODUCERS: The Stella Company; DIRECTOR: Roman Polanski. *Cast*: KROLOCK: Steve Barton; ALFRED: Aris Sas; SARAH: Cornelia Zenz; ABRONSIUS: Gernot Kranner. On opening night Gene Gutowski, who had produced the 1967 film, was there. Broadway producers Barry & Fran Weissler canceled their place in the audience at the last moment. The show got good reviews. It ran until 1/00, and cost $7 million (U.S.) It won six German IMAGE awards. The cast recording was released on 2/28/98. Jim Steinman came in for a bit of flak for re-cycling his old Bonnie Tyler hit "Total Eclipse of the Heart" as "Totale Finsternis" (he was in a hurry). But the song worked. He had originally (and coincidentally)

written it as "Vampires in Love" for another vampire show (and it was this original title that he used when the show went to Broadway). In 10/97 Andrew Braunsberg told the *New York Times* that he hoped to bring the show to Broadway in late 1998 (that had always been the idea, although there was, for a while, the option of presenting it in London's West End first) but it didn't happened, partly because director Polanski was still wanted in the USA on a charge of statutory rape (a charge he has always denied). Mr. Polanski had fled the USA in 1977. By late 2/98 Steve Barton was being touted for the lead on Broadway, whenever a Broadway run was to happen. There were workshops in 4/01 and 5/01 at Chelsea Studios, NYC. CAST: Steve Barton, William Youmans, Tom Alan Robbins, Bertilla Baker, Sarah Uriarte, Kate Shindle, Jason Wooten, Ken Jennings. Steve Barton died, however, and by 8/13/01 Michael Crawford was being touted as the lead, with John Caird as director (to be aided by Jim Steinman). Michael Crawford is rumored to have been paid close to 20 million pounds for the show, making him the highest-paid theatre star in history. He was confirmed in the role on 8/23/01. The new, heavily re-worked, Broadway show was a book musical, whereas the original Austrian production was sung through (i.e. no, or at most, a few lines only of, spoken dialog). There were also many changes made by Jim Steinman to the music, and many changes in the construction of the musical. The plan was to bring it to Broadway for previews in 3/02, with the official opening on 4/11/02, then later to take it to Los Angeles, then to London. But on 10/5/01 it was announced that the Broadway opening was being postponed until 10/24/02, due to the impracticalities of planning successfully after the 9/11/01 massacre. On 12/20/01 it was announced that John Caird was out as director, and that the sole director was rumored to be John Rando (who was, indeed, confirmed on 4/30/02). By 4/02 Rene Auberjonois had been offered Abronsius, and was in negotiations. He was confirmed on 6/20/02. On 6/5/02 Max von Essen and Mandy Gonzalez were confirmed. On 6/26/02 Julia Murney and Asa Somers were added. On 7/23/02 Ron Orbach was announced in his role. On 7/30/02 it was announced that Julia Murney was out (she was replaced by Leah Hocking). There was a press preview on 9/18/02. Broadway previews began on 10/16/02 (delayed from 10/14/02), and the opening night was delayed from 11/21/02 to 12/9/02 because director John Rando had to be in Texas with his mother, who was recovering from open-heart surgery. Mr. Rando was back by 11/11/02. The production was capitalized at $12 million.

The Broadway Run. MINSKOFF THEATRE, 12/9/02–1/25/03. 61 previews from 10/16/02. 56 PERFORMANCES. PRESENTED BY Bob Boyett, USA Ostar Theatricals, Andrew Braunsberg, Lawrence Horowitz, Michael Gardner, Roy Furman, Lexington Road Productions, David Sonenberg; MUSIC/ENGLISH LYRICS: Jim Steinman; ADDITIONAL LYRICS: Don Black; ORIGINAL GERMAN LYRICS & BOOK: Michael Kunze; ADAPTED for Broadway by David Ives, Jim Steinman & Michael Kunze; BASED ON the 1967 British film *The Fearless Vampire Killers*, directed by Roman Polanski (it was originally called *Dance with the Vampires*), and starring Sharon Tate & Mr. Polanski (as Alfred); DIRECTOR: John Rando; CHOREOGRAPHER: John Carrafa; SETS: David Gallo; COSTUMES: Ann Hould-Ward; LIGHTING: Ken Billington; SOUND: Richard Ryan; MUSICAL SUPERVISOR/VOCAL & DANCE MUSIC ARRANGEMENTS: Michael Reed; MUSICAL DIRECTOR: Patrick Vaccariello; ORCHESTRATIONS: Steve Margoshes; ADDITIONAL DANCE MUSIC ARRANGEMENTS: Michael Dansicker; CAST RECORDING on Interscope; PRESS: Barlow — Hartman; CASTING: Telsey Casting; GENERAL MANAGEMENT: 101 Productions; COMPANY MANAGER: Elie Landau; PRODUCTION STAGE MANAGER: Bonnie Panson; STAGE MANAGER: Michael J. Passaro; ASSISTANT STAGE MANAGERS: Jason Brouillard & Bryan Scott Clark. **Cast:** SARAH: Mandy Gonzalez; NADJA: E. Alyssa Claar; ZSA ZSA: Erin Leigh Peck; COUNT VON KROLOCK: Michael Crawford; MADAM VON KROLOCK: Dame Edith Shorthouse; CHAGAL: Ron Orbach; REBECCA: Liz McCartney; MAGDA: Leah Hocking; BORIS: Mark Price; PROFESSOR ABRONSIUS: Rene Auberjonois; ALFRED: Max von Essen; HERBERT: Asa Somers, *Doug Storm* (from 12/17/02); DREAM VAMPIRE: Edgar Godineaux; DREAM SARAH: Jennifer Savelli; DREAM ALFRED: Jonathan Sharp; ENSEMBLE: David Benoit, Lindsay Dunn, Jocelyn Dowling, Edgar Godineaux, Ashley Amber Haase, Derric Harris, Robin Irwin, Terace Jones, Larry Keigwin, Brendan King, Heather McFadden, Raymond McLeod, Andy Pellick, Joye Ross, Solange Sandy, Jennifer Savelli, Jonathan Sharp, Doug Storm,

Jenny-Lynn Suckling, Jason Wooten. *Standby*: Krolock/Abronsius: Robert Evan. *Understudies*: Krolock/Abronsius: Timothy Warmen; Chagal: David Benoit & Raymond McLeod; Sarah: Alyssa Claar & Sara Schmidt; Rebecca: Robin Irwin & Jenny-Lynn Suckling; Nadja/Zsa Zsa: Heather McFadden & Sara Schmidt; Magda: Jenny-Lynn Suckling; Alfred/Boris/Herbert: Doug Storm & Jason Wooten. *Swings*: Sara Schmidt, Nathan Peck, Kerin Hubbard, Timothy Warmen. *Orchestra*: CONCERTMASTER: Ann Labin; VIOLINS: Maura Giannini, Victor Heifets, Dana Ianculovici, Fritz Krakowski, Wende Namkung; CELLI: Peter Prosser, Danny Miller, Eileen Folson; LEAD TRUMPET: Tom Hoyt; TRUMPET: Larry Lunetta; BASS TROMBONE: Morris Kainuma; FRENCH HORNS: Roger Wendt, Kelly Dent, Theo Primis; FLUTE/PICCOLO: Helen Campo; OBOE/ENGLISH HORN: Tuck Lee; REEDS: Dennis Anderson; DRUMS: Ray Marchica; BASS: Dave Kuhn; KEYBOARD 1: Adam Ben-David; KEYBOARDS: T.O. Sterrett & Jim Laev; GUITAR: J.J. McGeehan; PERCUSSION: David Rozenblatt. *Act I*: Overture (Orchestra); *Scene 1* A graveyard in the woods: "Angels Arise" (Sarah, Nadja, Zsa), "God Has Left the Building" (Vampires, Sarah, Nadja, Zsa Zsa), "Original Sin" (Krolock, Sarah, Vampires); *Scene 2* An inn: "Garlic" (Chagal, Rebecca, Magda, Boris, Peasants), "Logic" (Abronsius, with Alfred, Chagal, Magda, Rebecca); *Scene 3* Sarah's room, upstairs at the inn: "There's Never Been a Night Like This" (Alfred, Sarah, Chagal, Rebecca, Magda, Abronsius), "Don't Leave Daddy" (Chagal), "The Invitation" (Krolock, Sarah, Nadja, Zsa), "A Good Nightmare Comes So Rarely," "The Devil May Care (But I Don't)," "Sometimes We Need the Boogeyman"; *Scene 4* Outside the inn; next day: "Death is Such an Odd Thing" (Rebecca & Magda); *Scene 5* Outside the inn; that evening: "Braver than We Are" (Sarah & Alfred), "Red Boots Ballet" (Sarah, Dancers, Krolock), "Say a Prayer" (Company); Scene 6 The castle gate: "Say a Prayer" (continued) (Company), "Come with Me" (Krolock). *Act II*: *Scene 1* The great room: "Vampires in Love" (Sarah, Krolock, Vampires); *Scene 2* A hall in the castle: The Library: "Books, Books, Books" (Abronsius & Krolock); The Bed: "Carpe Nostrum" (Company); "For Sarah" (Alfred); *Scene 3* The search through the castle: "Something to Kill (Our Time)" (Vampires); *Scene 4* The crypt of the von Krolock: "Death is Such an Odd Thing" (reprise) (Rebecca, Magda, Chagal); *Scene 5* Herbert's room: "When Love is Inside You" (Alfred & Herbert); *Scene 6* Sarah's room: *Scene 7* The castle graveyard: "Eternity" (Vampires), "Confession of a Vampire" (Krolock); *Scene 8* The ballroom: "The Ball: The Minuet" (Abronsius, Alfred, Herbert, Boris, Vampires), "Never Be Enough" (Krolock & Vampires), "Read My Apocalypse" (Krolock); *Scene 9* The wilderness: "Braver than We Are" (reprise) (Sarah & Alfred); *Scene 10* Finale: "The Dance of the Vampires" (Company).

The show opened to bad reviews.

168. *Dancin'*

A musical entertainment, the first Broadway musical to do away with book and original score. The emphasis was on dancing. So, it was more like a revue.

Before Broadway. It was budgeted at $600,000, and that sum was all raised in 24 hours. It wasn't always going to be a book-less musical. At first there was to be a slight story connecting the dancing episodes, and Bob Fosse asked Frank Loesser to write a libretto. When Mr. Loesser turned him down, he asked Fred Ebb. But, finally, Fosse brought in Herb Gardner and Paddy Chayefsky to write the few spoken words, the introduction, and the prefaces to some of the numbers. For the eight leading women's roles Fosse auditioned 800 dancers. It tried out in Boston. The Shuberts demanded that Fosse cut "Welcome to the City" (depicting the pornographic blandishments a tourist can be bombarded with on arriving in New York) and "The Dream Barre" (where a young male dance student elaborately fantasizes about a young woman in his class, played by Ann Reinking). He cut the first, but not the second. There was difficulty in getting insurance for Mr. Fosse after his heart attacks, but Lloyds of London finally covered him until opening night on Broadway.

The Broadway Run. BROADHURST THEATRE, 3/27/78–11/29/80; AMBASSADOR THEATRE, 12/4/80–6/27/82. 13 previews. Total of 1,774 PERFORMANCES. PRESENTED BY Jules Fisher, The Shubert Organization,

Columbia Pictures (and Bob Fosse); MUSIC/LYRICS: various authors; CONCEIVED BY: Bob Fosse (uncredited); DIRECTOR/CHOREOGRAPHER: Bob Fosse; ASSISTANT DIRECTORS: Kathryn Doby & Christopher Chadman; ASSISTANT CHOREOGRAPHERS: Kathryn Doby, Christopher Chadman, Gwen Verdon; SETS: Peter Larkin; COSTUMES: Willa Kim; LIGHTING: Jules Fisher; SOUND: Abe Jacob; CONDUCTOR/ARRANGEMENTS: Gordon Lowry Harrell; ORCHESTRATIONS: Ralph Burns; PRESS: Merle Debuskey; GENERAL MANAGER: Marvin A. Krauss; COMPANY MANAGER: G. Warren McClane, *Sue Frost* (added by 81–82); PRODUCTION STAGE MANAGER: Phil Friedman; STAGE MANAGER: Perry Cline (78–79), *Peter von Mayrhauser* (from 79–80); ASSISTANT STAGE MANAGER: Richard Korthaze, *Patrick Ballard* (added by 78–79), *Peter B. Mumford* (added by 80–81), *Karen Defaces* (added by 80–81). *Cast*: Gail Benedict (*Janet Wilber* from 5/13/80), Sandahl Bergman (*P.J. Mann* (from 3/20/79), Karen G. Burke (*Wendy Edmead* from 11/2/78), Rene Ceballos (*Barbara Yeager* from 3/11/80), Christopher Chadman (*Gary Flannery* from 1/30/79; *Christopher Chadman* from 4/17/79; *Michael Kubala* from 5/8/79), Wayne Cilento (*Michael Ricardo* from 7/3/79; *Timothy Scott* from 12/4/79; *Chet Walker* from 12/31/79), Jill Cook (*Eileen Casey* from 5/8/79), Gregory B. Drotar (*Ross Miles* from 5/30/78, at which point Mr. Drotar became an alternate; *Gregory B. Drotar* from 7/24/78, when Ross Miles left because he had been injured so many times; *Clif De Raita* from 3/13/79), Vicki Frederick (*Christine Colby* from 7/4/78), Linda Haberman (*Terri Treas* from 6/10/79), Richard Korthaze, Edward Love (*Bruce Anthony Davis* from 1/26/79), John Mineo (*Michael Ricardo* from 3/4/80), Ann Reinking (*Vicki Frederick* from 9/12/78; *Ann Reinking* during Miss Frederick's absence, 1/2/79–1/16/79, and again, permanently, from 2/27/79; *Gail Mae Ferguson* from 12/31/79), Blane Savage (*David Warren-Gibson* from 7/24/78; *Robert Warners* from 11/22/79), Charles Ward (*James Dunne* from 3/27/79; *Robert La Fosse*— no relation to Bob Fosse — from 7/24/79; *James Dunne* from 9/4/79; *Gary Chryst* from 10/30/79; *Hinton Battle* from 5/27/80). *Alternates*: Christine Colby (*Valerie-Jean Miller* from 77–78), William Whitener (*David Warren-Gibson* from 78–79), *Zelda Pulliam* (78–79), *Eugene Little* (78–79), *Anita Ehrler* (78–79), *Chet Walker* (78–79), *Shanna Reed* (78–79), *Michael Kubala* (78–79), *Deborah Phelan* (78–79). 79–80 list: *Valerie-Jean Miller, David Warren-Gibson, Gregory B. Drotar, James Dunne, Eileen Casey, Deborah Phelan, Bryan Nicholas, Laurent Giroux, Katherine Meloche, Beth Shorter, James Horvath, Bill Hastings*. By 80–81 the cast had been replaced. Joan De Luca, Lisa Embs, Bill Hastings, Edmund La Fosse, Dana Moore (gone by 5/31/81), Stephen Moore, Mary-Ann Neu, Cynthia Onrubia, Adrian Rosario, Beth Shorter, Laurie Dawn Skinner (gone by 5/31/81), *Lydia Abarca, Alyson Reed*. New 81–82 cast: Penny Fekany (gone by 5/31/82), Laurent Giroux (gone by 5/31/82), Jodi Moccia (gone by 5/31/82), Keith Keen (gone by 5/31/82), Gayle Samuels (gone by 5/31/82), Ciscoe Bruton, Lloyd Culbreath, Spence Ford, Bebe Neuwirth, Alison Sherve, Sharon Brooks, David Thome, *Charles Ward, Kathrynnann Wright, Laurie Dawn Skinner, Dana Moore*. *Act I*: *Scene 1* Opening: "Prologue (Hot August Night)" (m/l: Neil Diamond) (Mr. Cilento, Mr. Mineo, Company), "Crunchy Granola Suite" (m/l: Neil Diamond) (Mr. Cilento, Mr. Mineo, Company); *Scene 2* Recollections of an Old Dancer: "Mr. Bojangles" (m/l: Jerry Jeff Walker). MR. BOJANGLES: Mr. Chadman; MR. BOJANGLES' YOUNG SPIRIT: Mr. Drotar; SINGER: Mr. Cilento; Alternate for Mr. Chadman: Mr. Korthaze; Alternate for Mr. Drotar: Mr. Whitener; Alternate for Mr. Cilento: Mr. Love; *Scene 3* The Dream Barre: Boy & girl fall in love at the barre: "Chaconne" (transcription from Bach's Sonata for Violin Solo No. 4). A BOY: Mr. Ward; A GIRL: Miss Reinking; BALLET MASTER: Mr. Korthaze; Alternate for Mr. Ward: Mr. Whitener; Alternate for Miss Reinking: Miss Frederick; Alternate for Mr. Whitener: Mr. Drotar; *Scene 4* Percussion: (used only percussion instruments): Part 1: Misses Ceballos, Frederick, Haberman. Alternate: Miss Colby; Part II: Mr. Chadman, Mr. Cilento, Mr. Mineo. Alternate: Mr. Savage; Part III: Misses Bergman, Benedict, Burke, Cook, Mr. Drotar, Mr. Love, Miss Reinking, Mr. Savage. Alternates: Miss Colby, Mr. Whitener; Part IV: "Ionisation" (m: Edgar Varese) (Mr. Ward. Alternate: Mr. Whitener) [this number was replaced during run by "Percussion 4," written by Gordon Lowry Harrell]. *Act II*: *Scene 1* Dancin' Man: tribute to Fred Astaire, with the company in white suits and straw hats: "I Wanna be a Dancin' Man" (m: Harry Warren; l: Johnny Mercer) [from the movie *The Belle of New York*] (Company); *Scene 2* Three in One: "Big Noise From Winnetka" (m/l: Bob Haggart, Ray Bauduc, Gil Rodin, Bob Crosby) (Miss Burke, Mr. Cilento, Miss Cook. Alternate: Miss Benedict); **Scene 3** Joint Endeavor: "If it Feels Good, Let it Ride" (m/l: Carole Bayer Sager & Melissa Manchester). PAS DE DEUX: Miss Frederick & Mr. Ward; Miss Ceballos & Mr. Drotar; Miss Bergman & Mr. Savage. Alternates: Miss Colby, Miss Haberman, Miss Burke, Mr. Drotar; "Easy" (m/l: Carole Bayer Sager & Melissa Manchester) (Miss Reinking. Singers: Messrs Chadman, Cilento, Love, Mineo. Alternate Singer: Miss Benedict); **Scene 4** A Manic Depressive's Lament: (blues number): "I've-Got-Them-Feeling-Too-Good-Today Blues" (m/l: Jerry Leiber & Mike Stoller) (Mr. Love. Alternate: Miss Cook); **Scene 5** Fourteen Feet: seven dancers stepping into nailed-down shoes and swaying and swinging without moving their feet: "Was Dog a Doughnut" (m/l: Cat Stevens) (Miss Bergman, Mr. Chadman, Mr. Cilento, Mr. Drotar, Miss Frederick, Miss Reinking, Mr. Savage. Alternates: Miss Colby, Mr. Whitener). **Act III**: **Scene 1** Benny's Number: a tribute to Benny Goodman. Dedicated "For Gwen and Jack. The latter would have hated it" [i.e. Gwen Verdon, Fosse's long-time partner, and Jack Cole, his mentor]: "Sing Sing Sing" (m: Louis Prima). Part I: Company; Part II: TROMBONE SOLO: Miss Frederick, Mr. Savage, Mr. Ward. Alternates: Miss Haberman & Mr. Drotar; TRUMPET SOLO: Miss Reinking. Alternate: Miss Bergman; CLARINET SOLO: Company; PIANO SOLO: Mr. Cilento & Mr. Mineo. Alternate: Miss Cook; **Scene 2** The Female Star Spot: "Here You Come Again" (m/l: Barry Mann & Cynthia Weil) (Misses Bergman, Burke, Ceballos, Frederick. Alternate: Miss Benedict); **Scene 3** AMERICA: "(I'm a) Yankee Doodle Dandy" (by George M. Cohan) [from *Little Johnny Jones*] (Company), "Gary Owen" (Miss Benedict, Miss Haberman, Mr. Drotar. Alternates: Miss Colby, Mr. Whitener), "American Women" ("Stout Hearted Men") (m: Sigmund Romberg; l: Oscar Hammerstein II) [from *The New Moon*] (Misses Bergman, Frederick, Reinking. Alternate: Miss Haberman), "Under the Double Eagle" (Messrs Cilento, Mineo, Savage. Alternate: Mr. Whitener), "Dixie" (Miss Burke & Mr. Love), "When Johnny Comes Marching Home" (Miss Reinking. Alternate: Miss Frederick), "Rally Round the Flag" (Miss Ceballos. Alternate: Miss Bergman), "Pack up Your Troubles in Your Old Kit Bag and Smile, Smile, Smile" (m: Felix Powell; l: George Asaf) (Miss Frederick, Miss Benedict, Mr. Mineo. Alternate: Miss Benedict), "The Stars and Stripes Forever" (by John Philip Sousa) (Mr. Ward. Alternate: Mr. Whitener), "Yankee Doodle Disco" (ch: Mr. Chadman) (Company); **Scene 4** Improvisation: "Dancin'" (m: Ralph Burns) (Company).

Broadway reviews were very divided. Ann Reinking got the most attention (she was in several numbers) and was terrific. The show was a big hit. It won Tonys for choreography and lighting, and was also nominated for musical, direction of a musical, costumes, and for Wayne Cilento and Ann Reinking. In 11/79 Ann Reinking left after injuring her knee backstage.

After Broadway. TOUR. Opened on 4/19/79, at the Shubert Theatre, Chicago, and closed on 5/18/80, at the Saenger, New Orleans. CHOREOGRAPHERS: Kathryn Doby & Christopher Chadman; PRODUCTION SUPERVISOR: Gwen Verdon. **Cast**: Hinton Battle, Sandahl Bergman, Stuart Carey, Gary Chapman, Anita Ehrler, Gary Flannery, Vicki Frederick, Bick Goss, Keith Keen, Frank Mastrocola, Valerie-Jean Miller, Cynthia Onrubia, Valarie Pettiford, Timothy Scott, Charles Ward, Alison Williams, Barbara Yeager, *Russell Chambers, Andre de la Roche, Cecily Douglas, Lois Englund, Penny Fekany, Manette La Chance, Steve La Chance, Fred C. Mann III, Zelda Pulliam, Laurie Dawn Skinner, Rima Vetter.* **Alternates included**: *James Horvath, Katherine Meloche.*

TOUR. Opened on 7/29/80, at the Performing Arts Center, Milwaukee. Last stop was the Theatre Royal, Drury Lane, London, 11/14/83–1/28/84. PRESENTED BY Tom Mallow & James Janek; DIRECTOR/CHOREOGRAPHER: Gail Benedict; MUSICAL DIRECTOR: Jack Jeffers, *Milton Setzer, Randy Booth.* "The Dream Barre" was cut. **Cast**: Jim Corti, Peggy Parten, Ronald Dunham, Willie Rosario.

At his death, on 9/23/87, Bob Fosse had been working on *Dancin' Too*, the follow-up. But it never got made.

169. *Dangerous Games*

This show consisted largely of dances and dance characterizations. The first part, *Tango*, is set in an Argentine brothel, and

concerns male sexuality in its rougher stages. *Orfeo* is a version of the Orpheus story, and was dedicated to the "desaparecidos" (those who vanished during the military rules of Argentina and other countries). It is told through the eyes of Aurora, a young girl whose parents have "been disappeared." Pursued by the same man who kidnapped her parents, she manages to escape, and falls asleep. She dreams she must confront the truth to be free of the nightmare.

Before Broadway. What would be the first half of this show, *Tango*, originally ran Off Off Broadway in 1987, as *Tango Apasionado. Orfeo* (what would be the second half) originally ran regionally, at La Jolla Playhouse, the Spoleto Festival in Charleston, and the American Music Theatre Festival, Philadelphia.

The Broadway Run. NEDERLANDER THEATRE, 10/19/89–10/21/89. 12 previews. 4 PERFORMANCES. PRESENTED BY Jules Fisher, James M. Nederlander, and Arthur Rubin, in association with Mary Kantor; MUSIC: Astor Piazzolla; LYRICS: William Finn; BOOK/CONCEIVED BY/DIRECTOR: Jim Lewis & Graciela Daniele; CHOREOGRAPHERS: Graciela Daniele & Tina Paul; FIGHT DIRECTORS: Luis Perez (*Tango*) & B.H. Barry (*Orfeo*); SETS: Tony Straiges; COSTUMES: Patricia Zipprodt; LIGHTING: Peggy Eisenhauer; SOUND: Otts Munderloh; MUSICAL DIRECTOR: James Kowal; ARRANGEMENTS: James Kowal & Rodolfo Alchourron; PRESS: Shirley Herz Associates; CASTING: Brian Chavanne & Julie Mossberg; GENERAL MANAGERS: Marvin A. Krauss & Joey Parnes; COMPANY MANAGER: Beth Fremgen; PRODUCTION STAGE MANAGER: Robert Mark Kalfin; STAGE MANAGER: Paula Gray. **Cast: *Tango***: DELIA, THE MADAME: Dana Moore; THE MEN: FELIPE: Philip Jerry; RICARDO: Richard Amaro; CARLOS: Ken Ard; THE WOMEN: RENATA: Rene Ceballos; DIANA: Diana Laurenson; MARIA: Malinda Shaffer; ADRIANA: Adrienne Hurd-Sharlein; THE BROTHERS: JUAN: John Mineo; GREGORIO: Gregory Mitchell, Luis Perez (Wednesday & Saturday matinees); CRISTINA, THE NEW WHORE: Tina Paul, Elizabeth Mozer (Wednesday & Saturday matinees); *Orfeo*: ORFEO: Gregory Mitchell, Luis Perez (Wednesday & Saturday matinees); DICHA: Rene Ceballos; AURORA, A CHILD: Danyelle Weaver; PLUTON: Ken Ard; NORA/LASCIVIA: Tina Paul, Elizabeth Mozer (Wednesday & Saturday matinees); ANTARES/ALTIVO: John Mineo; MIRA/CODICIA: Dana Moore; LYRAE/LA GULA: Malinda Shaffer; CLEO/ENVIDIA: Diana Laurenson; ALBERIO/IRA: Marc Villa; URSULA/MALICIA: Adrienne Hurd-Sharlein; LEON/MENTIRA: Philip Jerry; ARTURO/CHARON/PEREZ: Richard Amaro; BAMBOO PLAYER: Adrian Brito. **Understudies**: Men: Marc Villa, Frank Cava; Pluton: Marc Villa; Diana/Maria/Cleo/Envidia/Lyrae/La Gula: Adrienne Hurd-Sharlein; Christina/Nora/Lascivia: Elizabeth Mozer; Renata/Adriana/Delia/Ursula/Malicia/Mira/Codicia: Mamie Duncan-Gibbs; Juan: Richard Amaro; Gregorio/Orfeo: Luis Perez; Dicha: Dana Moore; Nora/Lascivia: Melinda Shaffer; Orfeo: Philip Jerry; Arturo/Charon/Perez: Frank Cava; Leon/Mentira/Antares: Frank Cava; Altivo/Alberio/Ira: Frank Cava; Cristina: Diana Laurenson; Aurora: Nicole Leach. **Swings**: Frank Cava & Mamie Duncan-Gibbs. **The Quintet**: GUITAR: Rodolfo Alchourron; BASS/BAMBOO FLUTE: Jorge Alfano; BANDONEON: Miguel Arrabal; VIOLIN: Jon Kass; PIANO: James Kowal; OFFSTAGE VOCALS: Rene Ceballos.

Reviews were terrible. The show received a Tony nomination for choreography.

170. *Darling of the Day*

Set in London, 1905–1906. Farll is a famous painter who detests the phoney art-world society. When his butler dies he trades places with him in order "to get out of this world alive." Alice, a nice widow, has been corresponding with the butler, and meets Farll in his butler guise. Farll's dealer eventually discovers evidence that his most successful client is actually alive.

Before Broadway. Originally called *Alice Chalice*, with a libretto by Keith Waterhouse and Willis Hall, its name was changed to *The Great Adventure* before rehearsals. Peter Wood was announced as director, and Geraldine Page as star. But E.Y. Harburg, the lyricist, did not like the personnel, so S.N. Behrman wrote a new book, and Albert Marre came on board as director. Mr. Behrman was replaced as librettist by Nunnally Johnson, and Steven Vinaver came in as new director. Still before rehearsals Mr. Vinaver was fired, replaced by Albie Marre, then re-hired. It tried out in Toronto first, as *Darling of the Day*, but got bad reviews. Then it went to the Shubert, Boston, as *Married Alive!*, and after bad reviews there also, Noel Willman was brought in to direct. Roger O. Hirson was brought in to revise the book, and Nunnally Johnson removed his name from the credits, vowing he would never again write for Broadway, as he had only made $10,000 total from his libretti for *Breakfast at Tiffany's* (which wasn't used), *Henry, Sweet, Henry*, and *Darling of the Day*. Pete Gennaro was set to choreograph, but was replaced by Lee Becker Theodore. The show got ready to go to Broadway, with its title back to *Darling of the Day*.

The Broadway Run. GEORGE ABBOTT THEATRE, 1/27/68–2/24/68. 4 previews from 1/20/68. 33 PERFORMANCES. PRESENTED BY the Theatre Guild & Joel Schenker; MUSIC: Jule Styne; LYRICS: E.Y. Harburg; BOOK: uncredited; BASED ON the 1913 comedy *The Great Adventure*, by Arnold Bennett, from his 1908 novel *Buried Alive*; DIRECTOR: Noel Willman; CHOREOGRAPHER: Lee Theodore; SETS: Oliver Smith; COSTUMES: Raoul Pene du Bois; LIGHTING: Peggy Clark; MUSICAL SUPERVISOR: Lilette Hindin; MUSICAL DIRECTOR/VOCAL ARRANGEMENTS: Buster Davis; ORCHESTRATIONS: Ralph Burns; DANCE MUSIC ARRANGEMENTS: Trude Rittman; CAST RECORDING on RCA Victor; PRESS: Arthur Cantor & Arthur Solomon; CASTING: Ruth Kramer; GENERAL MANAGER: Victor Samrock; COMPANY MANAGER: Ralph Roseman; PRODUCTION STAGE MANAGER: Phil Friedman; STAGE MANAGERS: Michael Sinclair & Phil King. **Cast:** OXFORD: Peter Woodthorpe (4) ✲; PRIAM FARLL: Vincent Price (1) ✲; HENRY LEEK: Charles Welch (11); OLD GENTLEMAN: Carl Nicholas; LADY VALE: Brenda Forbes (3) ✲; CABBY: Ross Miles; DOCTOR: Leo Leyden (8); ALICE CHALLICE: Patricia Routledge (2) ✲; DAPHNE: Joy Nichols (10); ALF: Teddy Green (5); BERT: Marc Jordan (9); ROSALIND: Beth Howland; SYDNEY: Reid Klein; ATTENDANT: Larry Brucker; FRAME MAKER: Paul Eichel; DUNCAN: Mitchell Jason (7); EQUERRY: John Aman; THE KING: Charles Gerald; CONSTABLE: John Aman; MRS. LEEK: Camila Ashland (12); CURATES: Herb Wilson & Fred Siretta; PENNINGTON: Michael Lewis (6); JUDGE: Leo Leyden (8); SINGERS: John Aman, Larry Brucker, Paul Eichel, Marian Haraldson, Reid Klein, Carl Nicholas, Kay Oslin, Jeannette Seibert, Maggie Task, Maggie Worth, Albert Zimmerman; DANCERS: Bonnie Ano, Christopher Chadman, Reby Howells, Beth Howland, George Lee, Jim May, Ross Miles, Fred Siretta, Georgianne Thon, Phyllis Wallach, Denise Winston, Herb Wilson. **Standbys**: Priam: Mitchell Jason; Alice: Joy Nichols. **Understudies**: Lady Vale: Jeannette Seibert; Oxford: Michael Lewis; Alf: Ross Miles; Duncan/Pennington: Charles Gerald; Doctor: Zale Kessler; Daphne: Maggie Worth; Leek: Marc Jordan; Bert: Charles Welch; Mrs. Leek: Maggie Task; King: Paul Eichel. ***Act I***: *Scene 1* Oxford's Art Gallery, London: "Mad for Art" (Art Lovers), "He's a Genius" (Oxford, Priam, Henry); *Scene 2* Farll's London house: "To Get Out of This World Alive" (Priam); *Scene 3* The pub in Putney: "It's Enough to Make a Lady Fall in Love" (Alice, Alf, Bert, Putney Friends); *Scene 4* Farll's London house; *Scene 5* London street: "A Gentleman's Gentleman" (Alice, Alf, Bert, Priam, Duncan, Bystanders); *Scene 6* Paradise Villa, Putney: "Double Soliloquy" (Priam & Alice), "Let's See What Happens" (Alice & Priam); *Scene 7* Oxford's salon: "Panache" (Oxford & Lady Vale); *Scene 8* The Thames river bank: "I've Got a Rainbow Working for Me" (Priam, Putney, Friends); *Scene 9* Paradise Villa, Putney: "Money, Money, Money" (Alf, Bert, Sydney), "That Something Extra Special" (Alice), "Money, Money, Money" (reprise) (Alf, Bert, Sydney). ***Act II***: *Scene 1* Oxford's salon; *Scene 2* Paradise Villa garden: "What Makes a Marriage Merry?" (Alice, Priam, Alf, Bert, Daphne, Rosalind), "He's a Genius" (reprise) (Oxford & Assistants); *Scene 3* Putney High Street; *Scene 4* The pub: "Not on Your Nellie" (Alice, Alf, Bert, Putney Friends), "(Under the) Sunset Tree" (Priam & Alice); *Scene 5* The courtroom: "Butler in the Abbey" (Priam & Courtroom), "Not on Your Nellie" (reprise) (Entire Company).

Broadway reviews were very divided, mostly good. But audiences stayed away. The initial investment was $500,000 and the show lost $750,000, the costliest Broadway failure to that date. Vincent Price should not have been cast in a musical. Patricia Routledge got nothing but raves (and a Tony), as did Styne & Harburg.

After Broadway. YORK THEATRE COMPANY, 9/11/98–9/13/98. Part of the *Musicals in Mufti* series. DIRECTOR: Michael Montel; MUSICAL DIRECTOR: Bruce Coyle. There were revisions not heard in the Broadway run. **Cast**: FARLL: Simon Jones; ALICE: Nancy Opel; LADY VALE: Charlotte Moore; OXFORD: Stephen Mo Hanan; ALF: Randy Redd. "He's a Genius," "To Get Out of This World Alive," "It's Enough to Make a Lady Fall in Love," "A Gentleman's Gentleman," "Putney-on-the-Thames," "Double Soliloquy," "Let's See What Happens," "Panache," "That Stranger in Your Eyes," "A Little Extra Shilling," "Daubs," "What Makes a Marriage Merry?," "Not on Your Nellie," "Under the Sunset Tree," "Butler in the Abbey," Finale.

YORK THEATRE COMPANY, 4/15/05–4/17/05. Again, part of the *Musicals in Mufti* series. ADAPTED BY Erick Haagensen.

171. *The Day Before Spring*

Set in New York City, and at Harrison University campus and environs, at the present time. The action takes place within 24 hours in a day — and night — in June. About the 10-year college reunion of a class of 1935, including Peter and his wife of ten years, Katherine. They meet Alex with whom Katherine would have eloped if the car hadn't broken down. Alex is now a novelist. His new best-seller, called *The Day Before Spring*, tells of what life would have been like if they had eloped. Now Alex and Katherine consider trying it again. The statues of Freud, Voltaire and Plato come to life to advise Katherine. They do run off, but the car breaks down again. Peter catches up with them, but eventually Peter runs off with uninhibited Christopher. It's not an unhappy ending. Gerald was Alex's secretary/valet/handyman.

Before Broadway. Lerner and Loewe wanted Marion Bell for the lead, but she was booked [in 1947 Miss Bell became the second of eight Mrs. Lerners, but they were divorced two years later].

The Broadway Run. NATIONAL THEATRE, 11/22/45–4/14/46. 167 PERFORMANCES. PRESENTED BY John C. Wilson; MUSIC/VOCAL ARRANGEMENTS: Frederick Loewe; LYRICS/BOOK: Alan Jay Lerner; DIRECTOR: John Wilson; Book DIRECTOR: Edward Padula; CHOREOGRAPHER/BALLET DIRECTOR: Anthony Tudor; SETS: Robert Davison; COSTUMES: Miles White; MUSICAL DIRECTOR: Maurice Abravanel; ORCHESTRATIONS: Harold Byrns; PRESS: Willard Keefe & David Tebet; CASTING: Richard LaMarr; GENERAL MANAGER: C. Edwin Knill; GENERAL STAGE MANAGER: Ward Bishop; STAGE MANAGER: John Sola; ASSISTANT STAGE MANAGER: Richard Haas. **Cast:** KATHERINE TOWNSEND: Irene Manning (1); PETER TOWNSEND: John Archer (3); BILL TOMPKINS: Bert Freed; MAY TOMPKINS: Lucille Benson; ALEX MAITLAND: Bill Johnson (2); MARIE: Karol Loraine; LUCILLE: Bette Anderson; LEONORE: Lucille Floetman; MARJORIE: Estelle Loring; SUSAN: Arlouine Goodjohn; ANNE: Betty Jean Smythe; HORN-RIMMED HORTENSE: Mattlyn Gevurtz; GERALD BARKER: Tom Helmore (5); JOE MCDONALD: Don Mayo; HARRY SCOTT: Robert Field; EDDIE WARREN: Dwight Marfield; CHRISTOPHER RANDOLPH: Patricia Marshall (4); KATHERINE (IN THE BOOK): Mary Ellen Moylan (7); ALEX (IN THE BOOK): Hugh Laing (6); VOLTAIRE: Paul Best; PLATO: Ralph Glover; FREUD: Hermann Leopoldi; VOCAL ENSEMBLE: Nina Dean, Arlouine Goodjohn, Karol Loraine, Estelle Loring, Bette Anderson, Lucille Floetman, Shirley Dean, Robert Lussier, Kenny McCord, Paul Mario, Tommy Matthews, Betty Jean Smythe, Alfred Sukey, Ernest Taylor, Bernard Tunis, Jeffrey Warren; DANCERS: Richard Astor, Bruce Cartwright, Ronny Chetwood, Janice M. Cioffi, Mattlyn Gevurtz, Erik Kristen, Jack Miller, Isabel Mirrow, June Morris, Eva Soltesz, Eleanore Treiber, Sonja Tyven, Frank Westbrook. ***Act I***: *Scene 1* The Townsends' apartment, New York City: "The Day Before Spring" (Katherine), The Invitation (Bill); *Scene 2* Harrison: "God's Green World" (Alex & Ensemble). A GIRL: Eleanor Treiber; A BOY: Ronny Chetwood; ANOTHER BOY: Jack Miller; "You Haven't Changed at All" (Katherine & Alex); *Scene 3* A path near Harrison: "My Love is a Married Man" (Christopher); *Scene 4* Rotunda of Harrison library: "The Day Before Spring" (reprise) (Katherine & Alex), Ballet of the Book According to Alex: KATHERINE: Mary Ellen Moylan; ALEX: Hugh Laing;

Scene 5 A corridor: Katherine Receives Advice (dance) (Freud, Plato, Voltaire); *Scene 6* Harrison: Finale (Katherine & Ensemble). *Act II*: *Scene 1* A Harrison resident house: "Friends to the End" (Bill, Joe, Harry, Gerald, Alumni), "A Jug of Wine" (Christopher); The Book (narrated by Peter): "I Love You This Morning" (Katherine, Alex, Ensemble), "The Day Before Spring" (reprise) (Alex & Katherine); "Where's My Wife?" (Peter & Ensemble); *Scene 2* The roadside: "This is My Holiday" (Katherine); Ballet of the Book According to Gerald: KATHERINE: Mary Ellen Moylan; ALEX: Hugh Laing; *Scene 3* Harrison: Finale (Principals & Company).

It got very divided Broadway reviews. Tom Helmore won a Donaldson Award. $250,000 was paid for the film rights, but the film wasn't made.

After Broadway. THEATRE 1010, NYC, 6/26/90–7/10/90. 12 PERFORMANCES. PRESENTED BY Bandwagon; DIRECTOR/CHOREOGRAPHER: Dania Krupska; MUSICAL DIRECTOR: Steven Gross. **Cast**: KATHARINE: Rebecca Hoodwin; PETER: Michael Harrington; ALEX: Gerald Sell; GERALD: James A. Zemarel.

172. *A Day in Hollywood/ A Night in the Ukraine*

Before Broadway. It began at the NEW END THEATRE, London, 1/15/79. Previews from 1/10/79. PRESENTED BY Buddy Dalton & Richard Jackson; DIRECTOR: Ian Davidson; SETS/COSTUMES: Barry Parman; MUSICAL DIRECTOR: Frank Lazarus. **Cast**: MRS. PAVLENKO: Paddy O'Neil; CARLO: Frank Lazarus; GINO: Sheila Steafel; SERGE B. SAMOVAR: John Bay; NINA: Maureen Scott; CONSTANTINE: John Glover; MASCHA: Alexandra Sebastian. It then moved to the MAYFAIR THEATRE, London, 3/28/79–9/15/79. 168 PERFORMANCES. PRESENTED BY Danny O'Donovan, Helen Montagu, Michael Winner. The rest of the cast and crew were the same. Jerry Herman wrote three new songs for the Broadway transfer, and Tommy Tune re-staged it.

The Broadway Run. JOHN GOLDEN THEATRE, 5/1/80–6/14/80; ROYALE THEATRE, 6/17/80–9/27/81. 9 previews. Total of 588 PERFORMANCES. PRESENTED BY Alexander H. Cohen & Hildy Parks; ORIGINAL MUSIC: Frank Lazarus; ORIGINAL LYRICS & BOOK: Dick Vosburgh; ADDITIONAL MUSIC & LYRICS: Jerry Herman; VINTAGE SONGS featured music by Richard Whiting, Hoagy Carmichael, Frank Loesser, E.Y. Harburg, Harold Arlen; *A Night in the Ukraine* is loosely based on Chekhov's 1888 playlet *The Bear*; DIRECTOR: Tommy Tune; CHOREOGRAPHERS: Tommy Tune & Thommie Walsh; SETS: Tony Walton; COSTUMES: Michel Stuart; LIGHTING: Beverly Emmons; SOUND DESIGNER: Otts Munderloh; SOUND ENGINEER: H. Anthony Meola; MUSICAL DIRECTOR/VOCAL & DANCE MUSIC ARRANGEMENTS: Wally Harper; CAST RECORDING on DRG; PRESS: Alpert/LeVine; CASTING: Meg Simon; GENERAL MANAGER: Roy A. Somlyo; COMPANY MANAGER: Charles Willard, *Joel Wyman*; PRODUCTION STAGE MANAGER: Thomas Kelly; STAGE MANAGER: Christopher A. Cohen; ASSISTANT STAGE MANAGER: Jack Magradey.

A DAY IN HOLLYWOOD. A musical cabaret revue; a take-off of old Hollywood musicals and stars. Set in the lobby of Grauman's Chinese Theatre in Hollywood. A group of six actors dressed as ushers glide in and out of the theatre to perform excerpts from movie song-and-dance extravaganzas. **Cast:** USHER: Frank Lazarus (3); ALSO WITH: Priscilla Lopez (1), David Garrison (2) (*Brad Moranz*), Niki Harris (7), Stephen James (4) (*John Sloman*), Peggy Hewett (5) (*Celia Tackaberry*), Kate Draper (6), Albert Stephenson (8).

"Just Go to the Movies" (m/l: Jerry Herman) (Company), "Famous Feet" (Niki & Albert) (the feet of Dick Powell & Ruby Keeler; Chaplin; Sonja Henie on ice; Tom Mix; Judy Garland; Dracula; Dorothy Lamour; Al Jolson; Mickey & Minnie Mouse, are impersonated from the thigh down) [the big number]; "I Love a Film Cliche" (m: Trevor Lyttleton; add m: Frank Lazarus; l: Dick Vosburgh) (Frank); "Nelson" (m/l: Jerry Herman) (Peggy); "The Best in the World" (by Jerry Herman) (Priscilla); "It All Comes Out of the Piano" (m: Frank Lazarus; l: Dick Vosburgh & Mr. Lazarus) (Frank): "Two Sleepy People" (by Hoagy

Carmichael & Frank Loesser), "Over the Rainbow" (m: Harold Arlen; l: E.Y. Harburg), "Hooray for Hollywood" (m: Richard A. Whiting; l: Johnny Mercer), "Easy to Love" (by Cole Porter), "Cocktails for Two" (by Sam Coslow & Arthur Johnston), "It All Comes Out of the Piano" (reprise), Richard Whiting Medley (m: Richard A. Whiting) (Company): "Ain't We Got Fun" (l: Raymond Egan & Gus Kahn), "Too Marvelous for Words" (l: Johnny Mercer) (from the movie *Ready, Willing and Able*), "Japanese Sandman" (l: Raymond Egan), "On the Good Ship *Lollipop*" (l: Sidney Clare) [from the movie *Bright Eyes*], "Double Trouble" (m: Ralph Rainger & Richard A. Whiting; l: Leo Robin) [from the movie *The Big Broadcast of 1936*], "Louise" (l: Leo Robin) [from the movie *Innocents of Paris*] (Company), "Sleepy Time Gal" (m: Ange Lorenzo & Richard A. Whiting; l: Joseph R. Alden & Raymond B. Egan), "Beyond the Blue Horizon" (m: Richard A. Whiting & Frankie Harling; l: Leo Robin) [from the movie *Monte Carlo*] [end of the Richard Whiting medley]; "Thanks for the Memory" (m: Ralph Rainger; l: Leo Robin) (Stephen & Kate), "Another Memory" (Stephen & Kate), "Doin' the Production Code" (lyr only — by Vosburgh) (Chorus), "A Night in the Ukraine" (The Chorus invites audience to their next production, i.e. *A Night in the Ukraine*) [end of "It All Comes Out of the Piano" sequence].

A NIGHT IN THE UKRAINE. Set in the morning room of the Pavlenko residence in the Ukraine before the Revolution. A take-off on Chekhov's *The Bear*, as it might well have been performed by the Marx Brothers if they had done it. Carlo is the piano-playing Chico character and Gino is the mute, girl-chasing Harpo character. They both work on the grounds of the residence, and Groucho is Serge, a shyster lawyer. A couple of lovers croon a ballad, and there is Mrs. Pavlenko, a dowager like Margaret Dumont in the Marx Brothers films. **Cast:** MRS. NATASHA PAVLENKO, A RICH WIDOW: Peggy Hewett (5), *Celia Tackaberry*; CARLO, HER ITALIAN FOOTMAN: Frank Lazarus (3); GINO, HER GARDENER: Priscilla Lopez (1); SERGE B. SAMOVAR, A MOSCOW LAWYER: David Garrison (2), *Brad Moranz*; NINA, MRS. PAVLENKO'S DAUGHTER: Kate Draper (6); CONSTANTINE, A COACHMAN: Stephen James (4), *John Sloman*; MASHA, THE MAID: Niki Harris (7); SASCHA, A MANSERVANT: Albert Stephenson (8). **Standbys:** For David Garrison: Mitchell Greenberg, *Brad Moranz*; For Frank Lazarus: Mitchell Greenberg. **Understudies:** For Frank Lazarus: Brooks Baldwin; For Brad Moranz: Mark Fotopoulos & Brooks Baldwin; For Priscilla Lopez/Kate Draper: Tudi Roach; For Niki Harris: Karen Harvey; For John Sloman/Albert Stephenson/Stephen James: Jack Magradey; For Peggy Hewett: Celia Tackaberry; For Celia Tackaberry: Elizabeth Hansen.

"Samovar the Lawyer" (Samovar & Carlo), "Just Like That" (Nina), "Just Like That" (reprise) (Nina & Constantine), "Again" (Nina), Gino's Harp Solo (Instrumental) (Gino), "A Duel! A Duel!" (Mrs. Pavlenko & Samovar), "Natasha" (Samovar), "A Night in the Ukraine" (reprise) (Company).

It got great Broadway reviews. It won Tonys for choreography and for Priscilla Lopez, and was also nominated for musical, score, book, direction of a musical, sets, lighting, and for David Garrison. The Marx Brothers sued the production for infringement of copyright, and in 10/81 a federal court ruled that the authors were guilty of "unauthorized appropriation" of the image and persona of the Marx Brothers, and stated that their heirs were entitled to monetary damages. The case was settled out of court.

After Broadway. TOUR. Opened on 12/1/81, in Toronto. **Cast:** Evalyn Baron, Jill Cook, Mary D'Arcy, Richard Haskin, Jeff Keller, Frank Lazarus, Patricia Lockery, Brad Moranz.

173. *Dear World*

Set in Paris, in an early spring. The Countess Aurelia has gone mad because she let the love of her life get away. Her underground home is about to be destroyed by the world's largest corporation, which is looking for oil deposits beneath Paris. So, she sets out to destroy them. She then goes off to conquer a new tomorrow morning.

Before Broadway. *The Madwoman of Chaillot* was done as a straight play at the BELASCO THEATRE, 12/27/48. 369 PERFORMANCES; and at CITY CENTER, 6/13/50. 17 PERFORMANCES. Over the years Jerry Herman had unsuccessfully tried to option it for a musical (he had played the deaf-mute in a college production at the University of Miami). The rights were held by Michel Legrand and Richard Wilbur, who had even written an unproduced musical of their own, with Maurice Valency as librettist. Finally Mr. Herman secured the rights. Angela Lansbury signed a two-year contract. During tryouts first-time director Lucia Victor clashed with Miss Lansbury and was soon replaced by Peter Glenville, who in turn was replaced by Joe Layton. Boston reviews were negative, and rumors started to fly that Miss Lansbury wanted the show to close there and then. *Women's Wear Daily* printed these rumors, and Alex Cohen, the producer, sued them. In the cast Michael Kermoyan was replaced by William Larsen. Donald Saddler was replaced as choreographer by Joe Layton, and dance music arranger John Morris by Dorothea Freitag. The numbers "I Like Me" and "Through the Bottom of the Glass" were cut, and the title song was shifted from being toward the end of Act II to being the finale of Act I. The original opening date of 12/26/68 had to be put back until 2/69. Joe Masteroff came in to doctor the book, but the show was getting worse.

The Broadway Run. MARK HELLINGER THEATRE, 2/6/69–5/31/69. 49 previews from 12/18/68. 132 PERFORMANCES. PRESENTED BY Alexander H. Cohen; MUSIC/LYRICS: Jerry Herman; BOOK: Jerome Lawrence & Robert E. Lee (book doctored by Joe Masteroff); BASED ON the 1948 Broadway play *The Madwoman of Chaillot*, Maurice Valency's adaptation of Jean Giraudoux's posthumously produced 1945 play *La Folle de Chaillot*; DIRECTOR/CHOREOGRAPHER: Joe Layton; ASSISTANTS TO JOE LAYTON: Jay Norman & Wakefield Poole; SETS: Oliver Smith; COSTUMES: Freddy Wittop; LIGHTING: Jean Rosenthal; SOUND: Robert Threlfall; MUSICAL DIRECTOR/VOCAL ARRANGEMENTS: Donald Pippin; ORCHESTRATIONS: Philip J. Lang; DANCE & INCIDENTAL MUSIC ARRANGEMENTS: Dorothea Freitag; CAST RECORDING on Columbia; PRESS: James D. Proctor & Ted Goldsmith; CASTING: Linda Otto; ASSOCIATE PRODUCER: Hildy Parks; GENERAL MANAGER: Roy A. Somlyo; COMPANY MANAGER: Seymour Herscher; STAGE MANAGER: Robert L. Borod; ASSISTANT STAGE MANAGER: Sal Pernice. *Cast:* CHAIRMAN OF THE BOARD: William Larsen (7); THE CORPORATION (BOARD MEMBERS): Clifford Fearl, Charles Karel, Zale Kessler, Charles Welch, *Jack Davison*; PROSPECTOR: Joe Masiell; JULIAN: Kurt Peterson (5); NINA: Pamela Hall (6); WAITER: Gene Varrone; DOORMAN: Michael Davis; BUSBOY: Ty McConnell; JUGGLER: Ted Agress; DEAF-MUTE: Miguel Godreau (8); PEDDLER: John Taliaferro; COUNTESS AURELIA, THE MADWOMAN OF CHAILLOT: Angela Lansbury (1) ☆; THE SEWERMAN: Milo O'Shea (2), *Zale Kessler* (from 4/16/69); GABRIELLE, THE MADWOMAN OF MONTMARTRE: Jane Connell (3); CONSTANCE, THE MADWOMAN OF THE FLEA MARKET: Carmen Mathews (4); PEOPLE OF PARIS: Nicole Barth, Bruce Becker, Tony Brealond, Jane Coleman, Jack Davison, Jacque Dean, Richard Dodd, John Grigas, Marian Haraldson, Tony Juliano, Gene Kelton, Carolyn Kirsch, Urylee Leonardos, Larry Merritt, Ruth Ramsey, Orrin Reiley, Patsy Sabline, Connie Simmons, Margot Travers, Mary Zahn. **Standbys:** Gabrielle/Constance: Camila Ashland; Aurelia: M'el Dowd. **Understudies:** Sewerman: Zale Kessler; Chairman: Clifford Fearl; Prospector/Doorman: Larry Merritt; Julian: Ty McConnell; Nina/Housewife: Merrill Leighton; Deaf-Mute/Busboy/Juggler: Gene Kelton; Peddler: Charles Karel; Waiter: Jack Davison; Flower Girl: Barbara Blair. **Swings:** Barbara Blair, Merrill Leighton, Joe Nelson. *Act I: Scene 1* The luxurious bateau of the chairman of the board, afloat on the Seine: "The Spring of Next Year" (Chairman, Prospector, Corporation); *Scene 2* The Cafe Francais and a slice of surrounding Chaillot: "Each Tomorrow Morning" (Aurelia & Company), "I Don't Want to Know" (Aurelia), "I've Never Said I Love You" (Nina); *Scene 3* The sewers underneath Paris: "Garbage" (Sewerman, Aurelia, Gabrielle, Constance, Company), "I Don't Want to Know" (ballet) (Entire Company), "Dear World" (Aurelia & Company). *Act II: Scene 1* The countess's apartment underneath the Cafe Francais: "Kiss Her Now" (Aurelia); The Tea Party: "Memory" (Constance), "Pearls" (Aurelia & Gabrielle), "Dickie" (Gabrielle), "Voices" (Constance), "Thoughts" (Aurelia) [end of the Tea Party sequence]; "And I Was Beautiful" (Aurelia); *Scene 2* A street in Chaillot in the rain: "Each Tomorrow Morning"

(reprise) (Julian); *Scene 3* The flea market (marche aux pouces) at midnight: "One Person" (Aurelia & Company); *Scene 4* The countess's apartment; the park at Colombes: Finale (Entire Company).

On Broadway it got terrible reviews, and lost $750,000. While the score was great, the production was not good, and the book was problematic. Angela Lansbury won a Tony, and the show was also nominated for sets.

After Broadway. TOMMY THOMPSON'S REVISED VERSION. David "Tommy" Thompson revised the book, adapting it more into the spirit of the original (straight) play. There was a reading in 4/98 by the Roundabout Theatre Company (rehearsals from 3/30/98). DIRECTOR: Scott Ellis. *Cast:* AURELIA: Chita Rivera; GABRIELLE: Debra Monk; CONSTANCE: Madeline Kahn; NINA: Audra McDonald; SEWERMAN: Alfred Molina. It intended to go to Broadway in the 1999–2000 season, as a 30th-Anniversary production, but it never happened. Late in 1999 the Goodspeed Opera House (in Connecticut) received a grant of $75,000 from the National Endowment for the Arts, to develop the version revised by Mr. Thompson. Jerry Herman became involved. Rehearsals were from 10/24/00. It ran at the GOODSPEED, 11/16/00–12/10/00. DIRECTOR: Richard Sabellico; CHOREOGRAPHER: Jennifer Paulson Lee; SETS: James Morgan; COSTUMES: Suzy Benzinger; LIGHTING: Mary Jo Dondlinger; MUSICAL DIRECTOR: Darren R. Cohen; ORCHESTRATIONS/ADDITIONAL ARRANGEMENTS: Christopher Jahnke. *Cast:* AURELIA: Sally Ann Howes (Chita Rivera had been rumored for the role); CONSTANCE: Diane J. Findlay; JULIAN: Ben Sheaffer; SERGEANT: Jon Vandertholen; GABRIELLE: Georgia Engel; SEWERMAN: Guy Stroman. The show now opened with "A Sensible Woman." This number, and two other new ones used in this production—"(It's Really) Rather Rugged to Be Rich" and "Just a Little Bit More"—had all been written by Mr. Herman just after the 1969 Broadway run ended. "Through the Bottom of the Glass" (cut from the 1969 original), was here restored. "One Person" (which had ended Act I at the 1998 reading) was now cut.

Tommy Thompson revised it yet again, with Jerry Herman and Philip Himberg (artistic director of the Sundance Theatre, Utah). It ran at the ECCLES STAGE, SUNDANCE VILLAGE, 7/6/00–8/17/00. Previews from 6/29/00. DIRECTOR: Philip Himberg; CHOREOGRAPHER: Peter Anastos; SETS: Neil Patel; MUSICAL DIRECTOR: Ryan Murphy; ORCHESTRATIONS: Christopher Jahnke. *Cast:* AURELIA: Maureen McGovern; CONSTANCE: Joan Barber; SEWERMAN: Max Robinson; PROSPECTOR: Jim Pitts. The show opened with "A Sensible Woman"; "Rugged to Be Rich" was re-written as "Have a Little Pity on the Rich"; "One Person" was back in, now ending Act I; and "Through the Bottom of the Glass" was cut. At one point Jerry Herman, out of frustration with the way it was developing, wanted to cut the title song, and re-name the show *Tomorrow Morning*, but he was prevailed upon not to.

LAWRENCE & LEE'S REVISED VERSION. After the original 1969 run had ended, and again in 1991, Jerome Lawrence & Robert E. Lee revised their script, deleting the title song. Their new version was finally produced in concert by 42nd Street Moon, in SAN FRANCISCO, 9/8/00–9/24/00. Previews from 9/6/00. DIRECTOR: Greg McKellan; MUSICAL DIRECTOR: Dave Dobrusky. *Cast:* AURELIA: Meg Mackay. It restored two songs cut from the 1969 Broadway run—"Just a Little Bit More" and "Through the Bottom of the Glass" (Nina). The song order was changed and the title song (now re-instated) went from Aurelia to Julian. This revised version is not related to Tommy Thompson's revised version.

174. *The Desert Song*

North Africa, 1925. Revolts are going on against the French. The plot was also influenced by Lawrence of Arabia and by the Sheikh movies starring Rudolph Valentino. French woman Margot is abducted into the Sahara by the mysterious Red Shadow, masked leader of the rebellious Riffs. To everyone's surprise he turns out to be Pierre, the simpering son of the French governor of Morocco.

Before Broadway. The original production of this operetta opened on Broadway at the CASINO, 11/30/26. It moved to the CENTURY THEATRE, 10/10/27, and then to the IMPERIAL THEATRE, 11/2/27, where it closed, 1/7/28. Total of 471 PERFORMANCES. It had been called *Lady Fair* during tryouts. PRESENTED BY Laurence Schwab & Frank Mandel; BOOK

DIRECTOR: Arthur Hurley; MUSICAL DIRECTOR: Oscar Bradley. *Cast*: PIERRE/RED SHADOW: Robert Halliday; MARGOT: Vivienne Segal.

Harry Welchman played the Red Shadow in London in 1927.

It was filmed in 1929, the first all-talking, all-singing operetta to come to the big screen. DIRECTOR: Roy Del Ruth. *Cast*: John Boles, Carlotta King, Myrna Loy. It was re-made in 1943, with an anti–Nazi theme. DIRECTOR: Robert Florey. *Cast*: Dennis Morgan, Irene Manning, Bruce Cabot.

The 1945 Los Angeles Civic Light Opera presentation, produced by Russell Lewis & Howard Young, went east to CITY CENTER, NYC, 1/8/46–2/16/46. 45 PERFORMANCES. DIRECTOR: Sterling Holloway; CHOREOGRAPHER: Aida Broadbent; SETS: Boris Aronson; LIGHTING: Nels Petersen; MUSICAL DIRECTOR: Waldemar Guterson. *Cast*: MINDAR: Edward Wellman; SID EL-KAR: Richard Charles; OMAR: Jack Saunders; PIERRE/RED SHADOW: Walter Cassell, *Harry Stockwell*; KIDD: Jack Goode; PAUL: Wilton Clary; SGT LA VERGNE: Joseph Claudio; AZURI: Clarissa; EDITH: Tamara Page; SUSAN: Sherry O'Neill; MARGOT: Dorothy Sandlin; GEN. BIRABEAU: Lester Matthews; CLEMENTINA: Jean Bartel; ALI BEN ALI: George Burnson. *Act I*: "High on a Hill," "The Riff Song," "Margot," "I'll Be a Buoyant Girl," "Why Did We Marry Soldiers?," "French Military Marching Song," "Romance," "Then You Will Know," "I Want a Kiss," "Tropics," "The Desert Song," "Morocco Dance of Marriage," "The Desert Song" (reprise). *Act II*: "My Little Castagnette," "Song of the Brass Key," Spanish Dance, "One Good Boy Gone Wrong," "Eastern and Western Love," "Let Love Go," "One Flower Grows Alone in Your Garden," "One Alone," En Route a la Bain, "The Sabre Song," Finalette, "Farewell," Opening of Scene 5, "Tropics" (reprise), Finale.

Warners did one movie re-make too many, in 1953. The Red Shadow was no longer referred to by that name, because of the prevailing anti–Communist attitude at the time. *Cast*: PAUL BONNARD/ EL KHOBAR: Gordon MacRae; MARGOT: Kathryn Grayson; CAPT. FONTAINE: Steve Cochran; YOUSSEFF: Raymond Massey; BENJY KIDD: Dick Wesson; AZURI: Allyn Ann McLerie (she did a notable houri dance); GEN. BIRABEAU: Ray Collins; HASSAN: Paul Picerni; MINDAR: Frank De Kova; LACHMED: William Conrad.

PALACE THEATRE, London, 1967. *Cast*: John Hanson, Patricia Michael. Over the years, in the UK, Mr. Hanson made the role of the Red Shadow his own.

The Broadway Run. URIS THEATRE, 9/5/73–9/16/73. 1 preview on 9/4/73. 15 PERFORMANCES. The "Lehman Engel" production, PRESENTED BY Moe Septee, in association with Jack L. Wolgin & Victor H. Potamkin; MUSIC: Sigmund Romberg; LYRICS: Otto Harbach & Oscar Hammerstein II; ADDITIONAL LYRICS: Edward Smith; BOOK: Otto Harbach, Oscar Hammerstein II, Frank Mandel; DIRECTOR: Henry Butler; CHOREOGRAPHER: David Nillo; SETS/LIGHTING: Clarke Dunham; COSTUMES: Sara Brook; MUSICAL DIRECTOR: Al Cavaliere; DANCE MUSIC ARRANGEMENTS: Dorothea Freitag; PRESS: Ellen Levene, Betty Lee Hunt Associates; GENERAL MANAGEMENT: Gatchell & Neufeld; COMPANY MANAGER: James Mennen; PRODUCTION STAGE MANAGER: Lee Murray; STAGE MANAGER: Patricia Drylie; ASSISTANT STAGE MANAGER: Austin Colyer. *Cast:* MINDAR: Nicholas Scarpinati; SID EL-KAR: John Ribecchi; HADJI: Dick Ensslen; PALACE GUARD: Frederick G. Sampson III; HASSI: Mandingo Shaka; NERI: Ruby Greene Aspinall; PIERRE BIRABEAU/THE RED SHADOW: David Cryer (1) ☆; BENJAMIN KIDD: Jerry Dodge (3) ☆, *Austin Colyer*; CAPT. PAUL FONTAINE: Stanley Grover (5) ☆; LT. DAVERGNE: Kent Cottam; SGT. BOUSSAC: William Leyerle; AZURI: Gloria Rossi; AZURI DANCING GIRLS: Kita Bouroff, Lana Caradimas, Urylee Leonardos, Jane Lucas, Sandra Mannis, Dundi Wright; EDITH: Osceola Davis; SUSAN: Britt Swanson; GEN. BIRABEAU: Shepperd Strudwick (4) ☆, *David Vogel*; MARGOT BONVALET: Chris Callan (6), Caryl Jeanne Tenney (alternated on Wednesday & Saturday matinees); CLEMENTINA: Gloria Zaglool; ALI BEN ALI: Michael Kermoyan (2); ENSEMBLE: Ruby Greene Aspinall, Marsha Bagwell, Rita Oney Best, Kita Bouroff, Lana Caradimas, Jacqueline Clark, Donald Coleman, Bill Collins, Austin Colyer, Kent Cottam, Osceola Davis, Ronald De Felice, Dennis Dohman, Dick Ensslen, Karen Ford, Bonnie Hinson, Urylee Leonardos, Rona Leslie, William Leyerle, Jane Lucas, Sandra Mannis, Berdeen E. Pigorsh, Frederick G. Sampson III, Nicholas Scarpinati, Peter Schroeder, Brenda Schaffer, Arthur Shaffer, Anthony Tamburello, David

Vogel, David Weatherspoon, Dundi Wright. *Understudies*: Red Shadow/Pierre: Stanley Grover; Margot: Gloria Zaglool; Gen. Birabeau: David Vogel; Ali/Hadji: Anthony Tamburello; Paul: Peter Schroeder; Sid el-Kar: Ronald De Felice; Benjamin: Austin Colyer; Susan: Rita Oney Best; Azuri: Kita Bouroff; Clementina: Bonnie Hinson; Mindar: Bill Collins; Hassi: Frederick G. Sampson III; Neri: Karen Ford; Davergne: Dennis Dohman; Guard: Donald Coleman. *Act I*: *Scene 1* Retreat of the Red Shadow in the Riff Mountains; evening: Prelude: "The Feasting Song" (Sid el-Kar & Riffs), "The Riff Song" (Red Shadow, Sid el-Kar, Riffs), "Feasting Song" (reprise) (Sid el-Kar & Riffs), "The Riff Song" (reprise) (Red Shadow & Sid el-Kar), "Margot" (Paul & Soldiers); *Scene 2* Garden outside General Birabeau's villa; before dawn next day: "Has Anybody Seen My Bennie?" (new l: Edward Smith) (Susan) [this replaced "I'll Be a Buoyant Girl" (Susan), which had been here in the 1926 original]; *Scene 3* Drawing room in Gen. Birabeau's villa; a few minutes later: "Why Did We Marry Soldiers?" (French Girls), "French Military Marching Song" (Margot, French Girls, Soldiers), "Romance" (Margot & French Girls), "Then You Will Know" (Margot, Pierre, Ensemble), "I Want a Kiss" (Margot, Pierre, Paul, Ensemble), "It" (new l: Edward Smith) (Bennie & Susan), "The Desert Song" (Red Shadow & Margot), "Azuri Dance" (Azuri & Azuri Girls), "Soft as a Pigeon" (Sid el-Kar, Paul, Ensemble), "The Desert Song" (reprise) (Red Shadow, Margot, Ensemble). *Act II*: Entr'acte; *Scene 1* The harem of Ali Ben Ali; afternoon of the following day: "My Little Castagnette" (Clementina & Spanish Girls), "Song of the Brass Key" (Clementina & Spanish Girls), "One Good Boy Gone Wrong" (new l: Edward Smith) (Bennie & Clementina); Eastern and Western Love: "Let Love Go" (Ali & Male Ensemble), "One Flower (Grows Alone) in Your Garden" (Sid el-Kar & Male Ensemble), "One Alone" (Red Shadow, Sid el-Kar, Ali, Male Ensemble); *Scene 2* The corridor to the bath; a few minutes later; *Scene 3* The room of the Silken Couch; a few minutes later: "The Sabre Song" (Margot & Red Shadow), "The Desert Song" (reprise) (Margot & Red Shadow); *Scene 4* The edge of the desert; the following morning, half an hour before dawn: "One Alone" (reprise) (Red Shadow & Male Ensemble); *Scene 5* A room in Gen. Birabeau's villa; two days later: "The Desert Song" (reprise) (Margot), "It" (reprise) (Bennie & Susan) [during the run of the original 1926 production, this number had replaced "Let's Have a Love Affair"], "Dance of Triumph" ("As We Are Drinking") (Azuri), "One Alone" (reprise) (Pierre & Margot).

The 1973 Broadway run was part of a road tour. On Broadway it opened to generally bad reviews.

After Broadway. EASTSIDE PLAYHOUSE, 10/22/80–11/23/80. 35 PERFORMANCES. PRESENTED BY the Light Opera of Manhattan; DIRECTOR/MUSICAL DIRECTOR: William Mount-Burke; CHOREOGRAPHER: Jerry Gotham; LIGHTING: Peggy Clark. *Cast*: PIERRE: Gary Ridley; MARGOT: Mary Jennings; PAUL: Aaron Wood; LT. LA VERGNE: Richard Perry; GEN. BIRABEAU: Raymond Allen. *Act I*: Prelude & Opening Chorus: "Feasting Song" (Riffs); *Scene 1* The retreat of the Red Shadow in the Riff Mountains; evening: (Red Shadow, Riffs, Sid el-Kar), "Feasting Song" (reprise) (Riffs), "The Riff Song" (reprise) (Red Shadow & Sid el-Kar), "Margot" (Paul & Soldiers), Scene 1 Finale; *Scene 2* A room in General Birabeau's house; the same evening: Opening Chorus: "Why Did We Marry Soldiers?" (Soldiers' Wives & Ensemble), "Oh, Girls, Girls, Girls" (Margot & Ensemble), "Romance" (Margot & Girls), Duet: "Then You Will Know" (Margot & Pierre), Trio & Chorus: "I Want a Kiss" (Margot, Paul, Pierre, Ensemble), Duet: "It" (Susan, Bennie, Girls), Duet: "The Desert Song" (Margot & Red Shadow), Act 1 Finale: "Won't You Wish Us Luck" (Margot, Paul, Pierre, Ensemble). *Act II*: Entr'acte; *Scene 1* The harem of Ali Ben Ali; afternoon of the following day; Eastern and Western Love (Red Shadow, Sid el-Kar, Ali, Men): "Let Love Go," "One Flower in Your Garden," "One Alone," "The Sabre Song" (Margot & Red Shadow); *Scene 2* A corridor; a few minutes later; *Scene 3* The Room of the Silken Couch; a few minutes later: *Scene 3* Finaletto: "You Love Me" (Margot & Red Shadow); *Scene 4* Edge of the desert; the following morning, half an hour before dawn: "Farewell" (Red Shadow & Men); *Scene 5* Courtyard of General Birabeau's house; two days later: Scene 5 Opening: "All Hail to the General" (Margot, Paul, Birabeau, Girls), "It" (reprise) (Susan & Bennie), Finale: "One Alone" (reprise) (Margot & Red Shadow).

NEW YORK STATE THEATRE, 8/25/87–9/6/87. 16 PERFORMANCES IN REPERTORY. PRESENTED BY the New York City Opera; NEWLY ADAPTED

LYRICS & BOOK/DIRECTOR/CHOREOGRAPHER: Robert Johanson; SETS: Michael Anania; COSTUMES: Suzanne Mess; LIGHTING: Mark W. Stanley; MUSICAL DIRECTOR: Jim Coleman. **Cast**: SID EL-KAR: Michael Cousins & John Stewart; HASSI: Kenneth Kantor; HADJI: William Ledbetter; NERI/CLEMENTINA: Joyce Campana; RED SHADOW/PIERRE: Richard White; BENJAMIN: Philip William McKinley; AZURI: Louise Hickey; PAUL: Theodore Baerg & Cris Groenendaal; SGT LAVERGNE: David Frye; SUSAN: Lillian Graff; EDITH: Paula Hostetter; GEN. BIRABEAU: David Rae Smith; MARGOT: Linda Michele & Jane Thorngren; ALI BEN ALI: Raymond Bazemore; NOGI: Robert Brubaker. This production was first shown at the Paper Mill Playhouse, in New Jersey. **Act I**: **Scene 1** Retreat of the "Red Shadow" in the Riff Mountains: "High on a Hill" (Sid el-Kar & Riffs), "The Riff Song" (Red Shadow & Riffs), "My Margot" (Paul & Soldiers); **Scene 2** Near the desert, outside Gen. Birabeau's house: "Why Did We Marry Soldiers?" (Susan & Women); **Scene 3** The garden of Gen. Birabeau's home; the same day: "French Military Marching Song" (Margot & Company), "Romance" (Margot & Women), "I Want a Kiss" (Margot & Paul), "It" (Benjamin & Susan), "The Desert Song" (Red Shadow & Margot), Finale Act I; **Act II**: **Scene 1** The Great Hall of Ali Ben Ali; the following day: "Song of the Brass Key" (Clementina & Harem Girls), "One Good Boy Gone Wrong" (Benjamin & Clementina), "Eastern Western Love" (Ali & Sid el-Kar), "One Alone" (Red Shadow & Men); **Scene 2** The Room of the Silken Couch: "The Sabre Song" (Margot), "The Desert Song" (reprise) (Red Shadow & Margot); **Scene 3** The edge of the desert: "One Alone" (reprise) (Red Shadow, Margot, Sid el-Kar, Paul, Ali, Men); Scene 4 Back at Gen. Birabeau's; two nights later: "It" (reprise) (Benjamin & Susan), "Dance of Triumph" (Azuri), Finale Act II (Company). This production ran again, same venue, 8/29/89–9/3/89. 7 PERFORMANCES. It had the same basic crew except that Sharon Halley co-choreographed and James Allen Gahres was the conductor. It had the same cast, except: SID EL-KAR: Michael Cousins; HASSI: Erick Devine; PAUL: Louis Otey; GEN. BIRABEAU: Ron Parady; MARGOT: Michele McBride. The character of Nogi was dropped.

LIGHT OPERA OF MANHATTAN, 3/16/88–4/10/88. 28 PERFORMANCES. DIRECTORS: Raymond Allen & Jerry Gotham; LIGHTING: Peggy Clark. **Cast**: PIERRE: Hans Tester; MARGOT: Kathryn Radcliffe.

175. *Destry Rides Again*

A western musical set in the violent frontier town of Bottleneck at the end of the 19th century. Frenchy is the peppery saloon entertainer, and Destry is the violence-hating sheriff who doesn't carry a gun. They wind up together at the end. The whipcracking dance performed by Kent's Gang was one of the major highlights.

Before Broadway. There had been no previous stage productions, but there had been three movies, notably the 1939 version. This was Andy Griffith's only stage musical. John Ireland was replaced by Scott Brady before Broadway. Various numbers were cut: "A Good, Good Thing," "(You're) a Handy Thing to Have Around the House," "The Sunshine Song," "Swap Her for a Mule," and "Let's Talk About a Woman" (originally written for, and cut from, *Fanny*).

The Broadway Run. IMPERIAL THEATRE, 4/23/59–6/18/60. 472 PERFORMANCES. PRESENTED BY David Merrick, in association with Max Brown, by arrangement with Universal Pictures; MUSIC/LYRICS: Harold Rome; ASSISTANT MUSIC & LYRICS: Karen Gustafson; BOOK: Leonard Gershe; BASED ON the 1930 novel of the same name by Frederick Faust (using his usual pseudonym of Max Brand), and on the 1939 movie starring James Stewart & Marlene Dietrich; DIRECTOR/CHOREOGRAPHER: Michael Kidd; ASSISTANT DIRECTORS/ASSISTANT CHOREOGRAPHERS: Deedee Wood, Marc Breaux, Shelah Hackett; SETS: Oliver Smith; COSTUMES: Alvin Colt; LIGHTING: Jean Rosenthal; MUSICAL DIRECTOR/VOCAL ARRANGEMENTS: Lehman Engel; ORCHESTRATIONS: Philip J. Lang; DANCE MUSIC ARRANGEMENTS: Genevieve Pitot; PRESS: Harvey B. Sabinson, David Powers, Bud Westman; GENERAL MANAGER: Jack Schlissel; COMPANY MANAGER: Joe Roth; GENERAL STAGE MANAGER: Leonard Patrick; STAGE MANAGER: Ben Janney; ASSISTANT STAGE MANAGER: Neil Laurence. **Cast**: PROLOGUE: Don Crabtree, David London, Lanier Davis, Nolan Van Way, *Jack Sevier, Robert McClure*; BARTENDER:

Ray Mason; FRENCHY: Dolores Gray (2); WASH: Jack Prince (4); SHERIFF KEOGH: Oran Osburn, *John Conant*; KENT'S GANG (THREE MEMBERS): GYP WATSON: Marc Breaux; BUGS WATSON: Swen Swenson; ROCKWELL: George Reeder; MAYOR SLADE: Don McHenry; CLAGGETT: Don Crabtree; KENT: Scott Brady (3), *Art Lund*; CHLOE: Libi Staiger (5); ROSE LOVEJOY: Elizabeth Watts; JACK TYNDALL: Nolan Van Way; THOMAS JEFFERSON "TOM" DESTRY JR.: Andy Griffith (1), *Don Crabtree* (for 2 weeks); STAGE DRIVER: Chad Block; MING LI: Reiko Sato, *Diane Kim*; MRS. CLAGGETT: May Muth; BAILEY: Ray Mason; CLARA: Rosetta Le Noire; DIMPLES: Sharon Shore; ROSE LOVEJOY GIRLS: Lynne Broadbent, Joan Broderick, Shelah Hackett, Reiko Sato, Sharon Shore, Carol Stevens; FRENCHY'S GIRLS: Shelly Chaplan, Lillian D'Honau, Maureen Hopkins, Bettye Jenkins, Jillana, Andrina Miller, Shirley Nelson, Adriane Rogers, Carol Warner; COWBOYS: Jack Beaber, Chad Block, Mel Davidson, Al Lanti, Ken Malone, Frank Pietri, John Ray, Larry Roquemore, Merritt Thompson, *Joe Blatt, Jeff Duncan, Peter Saul*; TOWNSPEOPLE: Don Crabtree, Lanier Davis, Ralph Farnworth, Maria Graziano, Betty Kent, David London, Ray Mason, Sheila Mathews, May Muth, Oran Osburn (*John Conant*), Nolan Van Way, *Evelyn Joyce, Robert McClure, Anthony Saverino, Jack Sevier*. **Understudies**: Destry: Don Crabtree; Frenchy: Libi Staiger. **Act I**: **Scene 1** The Last Chance Saloon: "Bottleneck" (Patrons of the Last Chance Saloon), "Ladies" (Frenchy & Girls), "Hoop-de-Dingle" (Wash & Patrons of the Saloon); **Scene 2** The same: "Tomorrow Morning" (Destry); **Scene 3** A street: "Ballad of the Gun" (Destry & Wash); **Scene 4** A corral: "The Social" (Townspeople & Kent's Gang); **Scene 5** Frenchy's house: "I Know Your Kind" (Frenchy), "I Hate Him" (Frenchy); **Scene 6** Paradise Alley: "(Rose Lovejoy of) Paradise Alley" (Cowboys & The Rose Lovejoy Girls), "Anyone Would Love You" (Destry & Frenchy); **Scene 7** A road in Bottleneck: "Once Knew a Fella" (Destry, Wash, Friends); **Scene 8** The Last Chance Saloon: "Every Once in a While" (Kent's Gang, Cowboys, Saloon Girls), "Fair Warning" (Frenchy). **Act II**: **Scene 1** Outside the jailhouse: "Are You Ready, Gyp Watson?" (Gyp's Friends), "Not Guilty" (The Jury), "Only Time Will Tell" (Destry), "Respectability" (Rose Lovejoy & Girls); **Scene 2** Frenchy's house: "(That) Ring on the Finger" (Frenchy & Girls), "Once Knew a Fella" (reprise) (Destry & Frenchy), "I Say Hello" (Frenchy); **Scene 3** The Sheriff's office: **Scene 4** The Last Chance Saloon: Finale: "Ballad of the Gun" (reprise) (Chorus).

Broadway reviews were excellent. The show won a Tony for choreography, and was also nominated for direction of a musical, and for Dolores Gray and Andy Griffith.

After Broadway. TOUR. Opened on 7/31/60, at the Riviera, Las Vegas, and closed on 1/28/61, at the O'Keefe, Toronto. "Respectability" was dropped for this tour. MUSICAL DIRECTOR: John Passaretti. **Cast**: DESTRY: Gene Barry, *John Raitt, Stephen Douglass*; FRENCHY: Monique Van Vooren, *Anne Jeffreys, Gretchen Wyler*; WASH: Tom Tully, *Edward Atienza*; KENT: Philip Reed, *Warde Donovan*; CLARA: Alyce Elizabeth Webb; DIMPLES: Lynne Broadbent; MAYOR: Edmund Lyndeck, *Alan MacAteer*. **Understudy**: Frenchy: Marie Bernard.

PAPER MILL PLAYHOUSE, New Jersey, 1961. CAST: Yvonne de Carlo, Ted Scott, John Frederick.

DONMAR WAREHOUSE, London, 9/30/82. 40 PERFORMANCES. This was a scaled-down version, and it had other changes too. DIRECTOR: Robert Walker; MUSICAL DIRECTOR: Chris Walker; CAST RECORDING on TER. **Cast**: DESTRY: Alfred Molina; FRENCHY: Jill Gascoigne; CHLOE: Nicola Blackman; MAYOR: Ram John Holder.

ST. PETER'S CHURCH, NYC, 9/24/99–9/26/99. 5 PERFORMANCES. PRESENTED BY the York Theatre Company, as part of the *Musicals in Mufti* series (in which actors were on stage with script in hand and in street clothes). DIRECTOR: Pamela Hunt. **Cast**: DESTRY: Jim Newman; CLARA: Patti Mariano; WASH: Bill Buell; KENT: Gary Lynch; ROSE: Celia Tackaberry; FRENCHY: Sharon Scruggs (Alison Fraser had been scheduled to play this role); GYP: Jack Doyle; BUGS: William Thomas Evans.

176. *Different Times*

Episodes spread over several generations of a troubled American family, from 1905 through the Prohibition era, to World War II and the present.

The Broadway Run. ANTA THEATRE, 5/1/72–5/20/72. 9 previews from 4/24/72. 24 PERFORMANCES. PRESENTED BY Bowman Productions Inc. (Arthur C. Twitchell Jr., president), in association with William L. Witt & William J. Gumperz; MUSIC/LYRICS/BOOK/DIRECTOR: Michael Brown; CHOREOGRAPHER: Tod Jackson; SETS/COSTUMES: David Guthrie; LIGHTING: Martin Aronstein; AUDIO: Jack Shearing; MUSICAL DIRECTOR/DANCE MUSIC & VOCAL ARRANGEMENTS: Rene Wiegert; ORCHESTRATIONS: Norman Paris, Arthur Harris, Ted Simons; PRESS: David Powers & Michael Ewell; GENERAL MANAGER: Virginia Snow; PRODUCTION STAGE MANAGER: Jack Timmers; STAGE MANAGER: Mary Porter Hall; ASSISTANT STAGE MANAGER: Terry Nicholson. *Cast:* STEPHEN ADAMS LEVY: Sam Stoneburger; MARGARET ADAMS: Barbara Williams; GREGORY ADAMS: Jamie Ross; MRS. DANIEL WEBSTER HEPPLEWHITE: Mary Jo Catlett; MRS. HEPPLEWHITE'S MOTHER: Patti Karr; NELLE HARPER: Joyce Nolen; LARRY LAWRENCE LEVY: Joe Masiell; ANGELA ADAMS: Candace Cooke; DOUGHBOYS: Terry Nicholson, Ronnie De Marco, David K. Thome; OFFICER: Ronald Young; MARIANNE: Dorothy Frank; COLUMBIA: Karin Baker; THE KAISER: Mary Jo Catlett; ELSIE: Mary Bracken Phillips; BOBBY: Ronald Young; MARILYN: Dorothy Frank; THE HAZELNUTS: Candace Cooke, Dorothy Frank, Karin Baker, Joyce Nolen; HAZEL HUGHES: Mary Jo Catlett; LADY FFENGER: Mary Jo Catlett; HATTIE: Dorothy Frank; PAULINE: Candace Cooke; MAE VERNE: Karin Baker; THE KEYNOTERS: Terry Nicholson, Mary Bracken Phillips, David K. Thome, Ronald Young; KIMBERLEY "KIM" LANGLEY: Patti Karr; MRS. CALLAHAN: Mary Jo Catlett; ABIGAIL: Mary Bracken Phillips; JOSIE: Mary Jo Catlett; FRANK GONZALES: Ronald Young; JOE: Terry Nicholson; DON: David K. Thome; MEL: Ronnie De Marco; STAN: Joe Masiell; LINDA: Dorothy Frank. *Understudies:* Stephen: Jamie Ross; Marilyn: Karin Baker; Mother/Kimberley/Lady Ffenger/Margaret: Dorothy Frank; Abigail: Candace Cooke; Mrs. Hepplewhite/Hazel: Patti Karr; Frank/Bobby: Terry Nicholson; Mrs. Callahan: Barbara Williams; Elsie/Josie/Angela/Marianne/Kaiser; Joyce Nolen; Columbia/Hattie/Pauline/Mae/Verne; Joyce Nolen; Gregory/Larry: Ronald Young. *Prologue* 1970; *Act I: Scene 1* 1905; the fair in Portland, Ore.; *Scene 2* 1905; a hotel room in Portland; *Scene 3* 1915; a street in Boston; *Scene 4* 1917; a hotel room in Boston; *Scene 5* 1917; a theatre stage; *Scene 6* 1924–1929; a speakeasy in Boston; *Scene 7* 1929; the Gregory Adams house in Boston; *Scene 8* 1933; the Bijou Ballroom in Bayonne. *Act II: Scene 1* 1942; Ffenger Hall, London; *Scene 2* 1942; a street in London; *Scene 3* 1942; the Gregory Adams house in Boston; *Scene 4* 1963; the Stephen Adams house in Mt. Kisco, and Stephen's office in Manhattan; *Scene 5* 1965; Abigail's room in Manhattan; *Scene 6* 1968; an art gallery; *Scene 7* 1970; Central Park; *Epilogue* 1970. *Act I:* "Different Times" (Stephen), "Seeing the Sights" (People of 1905), "The Spirit is Moving" (Margaret & People of 1905), "Here's Momma" (Margaret), "Everything in the World Has a Place" (Gregory & Margaret), "I Wish I Didn't Love Him" (Margaret), "Forward into Tomorrow" (Mrs. Hepplewhite & Suffragettes), "You're Perfect" (Angela), "Marianne" (Officer, Doughboys, Marianne, Columbia, Kaiser), "Daddy, Daddy" (Hazelnuts), "I Feel Grand" (Hazel & Hazelnuts), "Sock Life in the Eye" (Larry), "I'm Not Through" (Larry & Marathon Dancers). *Act II:* "I Miss Him" (Hattie, Pauline, Mae Verne), "One More Time" (Kim & Keynoters), "Here's Momma" (reprise) (Stephen), "I Dreamed About Roses" (Stephen, Kim, USO Guests), "I Wish I Didn't Love Her" (Gregory), "The Words I Never Said" (Stephen & Kim), "The Life of a Woman" (Kim), "Here's Momma" (reprise) (Kim & Momma's Poppas), "He Smiles" (Abigail & Josie), "Genuine Plastic" (Stephen & Gallery Guests), "Thanks a Lot" (Frank, Abigail, Friends), "When They Start Again" (Abigail & Frank), "Different Times" (reprise) (Stephen), "The Spirit is Moving" (reprise) (Company).

Broadway reviews were mixed.

177. *Do Black Patent Leather Shoes Really Reflect Up?*

The Broadway Run. ALVIN THEATRE, 5/27/82–5/30/82. 15 previews. 5 PERFORMANCES. PRESENTED BY Mavin Productions, Libby Adler Mages & Daniel A. Golman; MUSIC/LYRICS: James Quinn & Alaric Jans;

BOOK: John R. Powers (based on his novel of the same name); DIRECTOR: Mike Nussbaum; CHOREOGRAPHER: Thommie Walsh; SETS: James Maronek; COSTUMES: Nancy Potts; LIGHTING: Marilyn Rennagel; SOUND: Richard Fitzgerald; MUSICAL SUPERVISOR/ORCHESTRATIONS: Jeremy Jay Dryer; MUSICAL DIRECTOR/VOCAL ARRANGEMENTS: Larry Hochman; DANCE MUSIC ARRANGEMENTS: Peter Larson; PRESS: Fred Nathan & Associates; CASTING: Professional Casting Associates; GENERAL MANAGEMENT: Richard Horner Associates; COMPANY MANAGER: Bruce Birkenhead; PRODUCTION STAGE MANAGER: Mortimer Halpern; STAGE MANAGER: Mitchell Lemsky; ASSISTANT STAGE MANAGER: Carol Estey. *Cast:* EDDIE RYAN: Russ Thacker (1); SECRETARY: Amy Miller; BECKY BAKOWSKI: Maureen Moore (3); SISTER MELANIE: Amy Miller; SISTER LEE: Ellen Crawford; FATHER O'REILLY: Robert Fitch (2); VIRGINIA LEAR: Vicki Lewis; FELIX LINDOR: Don Stitt; MIKE DEPKI: Peter Heuchling; NANCY RALANSKY: Karen Tamburrelli; MARY KENNY: Christine Gradl; LOUIE SCHLANG: Jason Graae; SISTER HELEN: Elizabeth Hansen; SISTER MONICA MARIE: Catherine Fries. *Understudies:* Eddie/Felix/Louie: Russ Billingsley; Father/Mike: Orrin Reiley; Becky/Nancy/Mary: Catherine Fries; Lee/Helen: Amy Miller; Secretary/Monica Marie/Melanie/Virginia: Carol Estey. *Act I:* Elementary School: *Scene 1* St. Bastion's School; the present: "Get Ready, Eddie" (Company); *Scene 2* Second grade at St. Bastion's: "The Greatest Gift" (Sister Helen & Kids); *Scene 3* Confession at St. Bastion's Church; *Scene 4* The playground—fifth grade: "It's the Nuns" (Kids & Nuns), "Little Fat Girls" (Becky & Eddie); *Scene 5* Fifth grade at St. Bastion's: "Cookie Cutters" (Sister Lee & Becky); *Scene 6* Confession at St. Bastion's Church: "Patron Saints" (O'Reilly, Eddie, Kids, Nuns); *Scene 7* Eighth grade at St. Bastion's: "Private Parts" (O'Reilly, Eddie, Kids, Nuns) [cut before Broadway opening night], "How Far is Too Far" (Nancy, Girls, Boys), Finale Act I (Company). *Act II:* High School: *Scene 1* The Freshman Mixer in the gym at St. Patrick Bremmer High School for Boys: "Doowah, Doo-wee" (Louie & Company), "I Must Be in Love" (Eddie); *Scene 2* The front yard of Becky's house; a year later: "Friends, the Best of" (Becky & Eddie); *Scene 3* Confession at St. Bastion's Church; *Scene 4* The Parish Bazaar; senior year [during previews this scene was The athletic fields of St. Patrick Bremmer and St. Ann's High Schools]: "Mad Bombers and Prom Queens" (Felix, Virginia, Kids); *Scene 5* The night of the Senior Prom: "Late Bloomer" and Prom Montage (Eddie & Kids); *Scene 6* Becky's hospital room: "Friends, the Best of" (reprise) (Becky & Eddie); *Scene 7* The present: "Thank God" (Company).

Broadway reviews were awful.

178. *Do I Hear a Waltz?*

The only teaming of Richard Rodgers with his late partner Hammerstein's protégé Sondheim. The musical followed the original play very closely. Leona, a lonely, aging secretary touring in Venice, has an intense but doomed affair with married antique seller Di Rossi. The Yaegers are fellow guests at the pensione where Leona is staying.

Before Broadway. In 1958 Arthur Laurents asked Rodgers and Hammerstein if they would like to do a musical of his 1952 stage play *The Time of the Cuckoo*, but it was too soon after the original. However it had been filmed (straight) in 1955, as *Summertime*, with Katharine Hepburn (as Jane Hudson), Rossano Brazzi (as Renato Di Rossi), Isa Miranda (as Signora Fiorina), Darren McGavin (as Eddie Jaeger), and Mari Aldon (as Phyl Jaeger). Finally, after Oscar Hammerstein's death, Richard Rodgers produced it alone, as a stage musical, *Do I Hear a Waltz?* Originally there was to have been no dancing in the show, but the rather sad story did need movement to jolly it along, and it got dance. The first choices for Leona were Florence Henderson and Anne Bancroft. Just before the New Haven tryout (1/30/65–2/13/65) things got very tense. John Dexter, the director, insulted Elizabeth Allen, the star, and from that moment she hardly spoke to him. Dick Rodgers didn't get on with Steve Sondheim. Herb Ross replaced Wakefield Poole as choreographer, but Mr. Poole retained some sort of billing (see below). In Boston, Mr. Rodgers found that the rest of the creative staff were making changes without consulting him. The number "Two by Two by Two" was cut in

Boston; and "Everybody Loves Leona" and "Perhaps" were also cut during tryouts.

The Broadway Run. FORTY-SIXTH STREET THEATRE, 3/18/65–9/25/65. 1 preview on 3/17/65. 220 PERFORMANCES. PRESENTED BY Richard Rodgers, by arrangement with AML Enterprises; MUSIC: Richard Rodgers; LYRICS: Stephen Sondheim; BOOK: Arthur Laurents (based on his 1952 play *The Time of the Cuckoo*, starring Shirley Booth); DIRECTOR: John Dexter; CHOREOGRAPHER: Herbert Ross; CHOREOGRAPHIC ASSOCIATE: Wakefield Poole; SETS/COSTUMES: Beni Montresor; LIGHTING: Jules Fisher; MUSICAL DIRECTOR: Frederick Dvonch; ORCHESTRATIONS: Ralph Burns; DANCE MUSIC ARRANGEMENTS: Richard De Benedictis; CAST RECORDING on Columbia; PRESS: Frank Goodman, Martin Shwartz, Paul Solomon; CASTING: Edward A. Blum; PRODUCTION SUPERVISOR: Jerome Whyte; GENERAL MANAGER: Morris Jacobs; COMPANY MANAGER: Maurice Winters; PRODUCTION STAGE MANAGER: Jean Barrere; STAGE MANAGER: Harry Young; ASSISTANT STAGE MANAGER: Harry Clark. **Cast:** LEONA SAMISH: Elizabeth Allen (1) ✩; MAURO: Christopher Votos; SIGNORA FIORIA: Carol Bruce (3); EDDIE YAEGER: Stuart Damon (6); JENNIFER YAEGER: Julienne Marie (5); MRS. MCILHENNY: Madeleine Sherwood (4); MR. MCILHENNY: Jack Manning (8); GIOVANNA, THE MAID: Fleury D'Antonakis (7); VITO: James Dybas; RENATO DI ROSSI: Sergio Franchi (2) ✩; MAN ON BRIDGE: Michael Lamont, *Steve Jacobs*; MRS. VICTORIA HASLAM: Helon Blount; SINGERS: Darrell J. Askey, Syndee Balaber, Bill Berrian, Helon Blount, Rudy Challenger, Pat Kelly, Liz Lamkin, Michael Lamont (*Frank Dyan*), James Luisi, Jack Murray, Carl Nicholas, Candida Pilla, Casper Roos, Bernice Saunders, Liza Stuart; DANCERS: Jere Admire, Bob Bishop, Wayne De Rammelaere, Steve Jacobs, Sandy Leeds, Joe Nelson, Janice Peta, Walter Stratton, Nancy Van Rijn, Mary Zahn, *Diana Baffa*. **Standby**: Leona: Mitzie Welch. **Understudies**: Di Rossi: James Luisi; Mr. McIlhenny: Casper Roos, *Harry Clark*; Giovanna: Candida Pilla; Vito: Michael Lamont, *Frank Dyan*; Jennifer: Liza Stuart; Eddie: Bill Berrian; Mauro: Mathew Loscalzo. **Act I**: Overture (Orchestra); *Scene 1* Venice: "Someone Woke Up" (Leona); *Scene 2* Garden of Pensione Fioria; evening: "This Week Americans" (Fioria), "What Do We Do? We Fly!" (Leona, the McIlhennys, Eddie, Jennifer); *Scene 3* Di Rossi's shop; the next day: "Someone Like You" (Di Rossi), "Bargaining" (Di Rossi); *Scene 4* Piazza San Marco; the same evening: "Here We Are Again" [(Leona, Vito, Ragazzi (Steve Jacobs, Sandy Leeds, Joe Nelson, Nancy Van Rijn, Mary Zahn)]; *Scene 5* Interior of Pensione Fioria; the following day: "Thinking" (Di Rossi & Leona), "Here We Are Again" (reprise) (Giovanna, Fioria, Eddie, The McIlhennys); *Scene 6* Garden of Pensione Fioria; immediately afterwards: "No Understand" (Fioria, Eddie, Giovanna), "Take the Moment" (Di Rossi). **Act II**: *Scene 1* Facade of Pensione Fioria; the same night: "Moon in My Window" (Jennifer, Fioria, Leona); *Scene 2* Outside the Garden of Pensione Fioria; the next evening: "We're Gonna be All Right" (Eddie & Jennifer), "Do I Hear a Waltz?" (Leona & Company); *Scene 3* The Piazza; the following morning: "Stay" (Di Rossi); *Scene 4* Garden of Pensione Fioria; that night: "Perfectly Lovely Couple" (Leona, Di Rossi, the McIlhennys, Jennifer, Eddie, Giovanna, Fioria); *Scene 5* Garden of Pensione Fioria; the next morning: "Last Week Americans" (Fioria) [cut before Broadway], "Thank You So Much" (Di Rossi & Leona), Finale (Company).

Broadway reviews were divided. It received Tony Nominations for composer & lyricist, sets, and for Elizabeth Allen.

After Broadway. PAPER MILL PLAYHOUSE, New Jersey, 1966. DIRECTOR: Stone Widney. **Cast:** LEONA: Dorothy Collins; DI ROSSI: Ron Holgate.

EQUITY LIBRARY THEATRE, NYC, 3/6/75–3/23/75. 22 PERFORMANCES. The number "Last Week Americans" (not in the 1965 Broadway run) was inserted as the penultimate number in this revival. DIRECTOR: Dolores Ferraro; CHOREOGRAPHER: Peter J. Humphrey; SETS: James L. Joy; MUSICAL DIRECTOR: Jim Coleman. **Cast:** LEONA: Rosalind Harris; DI ROSSI: Donald Craig; VITO: Steven Gelfer.

GEORGE STREET PLAYHOUSE, New Jersey, 10/13/99–11/14/99. 3 previews from 10/9/99. REVISED BY: Arthur Laurents. Steve Sondheim also revised and added some lyrics, and restored "Everybody Love Leona." The number "Bargaining" was cut. DIRECTOR: David Saint; SETS: James Youmans; COSTUMES: Theoni V. Aldredge; LIGHTING: Howell Binkley; MUSICAL DIRECTOR: Sean Patrick Flahaven. **Cast:** LEONA: Penny Fuller;

DI ROSSI: Charles Cioffi; FIORIA: Lynn Cohen; MAURO: Nicholas Cutro; MRS. MCILHENNY: Luce Ennis.

PASADENA PLAYHOUSE, 7/6/01–8/19/01. This was the revised 1999 version. DIRECTOR: David Lee; CAST RECORDING on Fynsworth Alley. **Cast:** LEONA: Alyson Reed; DI ROSSI: Anthony Crivello; FIORIA: Carol Lawrence.

179. *Do, Re, Mi*

Set in New York, New Jersey, and Washington, DC. A satire on the music industry. Hubie is a pushy would-be big shot who persuades three retired slot machine gangsters (Fatso, Skin and Brains) to muscle in on the juke box racket. He fails in this, but does turn a waitress (Tilda) into a singing star. Kay is his long-suffering wife.

Before Broadway. Two songs were cut: "She Doesn't Understand Me" and "Life's Not That Simple."

The Broadway Run. ST. JAMES THEATRE, 12/26/60–12/16/61; 54TH STREET THEATRE, 12/25/61–1/13/62. Total of 400 PERFORMANCES. PRESENTED BY David Merrick; MUSIC: Jule Styne; LYRICS: Betty Comden & Adolph Green; BOOK/DIRECTOR: Garson Kanin (based on his 1955 novella of the same name); ASSOCIATE DIRECTOR: William Hammerstein; CHOREOGRAPHERS: Marc Breaux & Deedee Wood; SETS: Boris Aronson; ASSISTANT SETS: Lisa Jalowetz & Ming Cho Lee; COSTUMES: Irene Sharaff; ASSISTANT COSTUMES: Florence Klotz; COIFFURES: Michel Kazan; LIGHTING: Al Alloy; SOUND: Richard H. Ranger; MUSICAL DIRECTOR: Lehman Engel; ORCHESTRATIONS: Luther Henderson; VOCAL DIRECTOR/VOCAL ARRANGEMENTS: Buster Davis; DANCE MUSIC ARRANGEMENTS: David Baker; CAST RECORDING on RCA Victor; PRESS: Bill Doll; CASTING: Michael Shurtleff; GENERAL MANAGER: Jack Schlissel; COMPANY MANAGER: Vince McKnight; GENERAL STAGE MANAGER: Bernard Gersten; STAGE MANAGER: May Muth; ASSISTANT STAGE MANAGER: Bob McClure, *Allan Stevenson*. **Cast:** THE CASA GIRLS: Marilyn Allwyn, Diane Ball, Sandra Devlin, Regina Groves, Nancy Van Rijn, Carol Stevens, Dean Taliaferro, *Lynne Broadbent, Wendy Nickerson*; THE DANCE TEAM: Patti Karr (*Shirley Nelson*) & Ray Kirchner; KAY CRAM: Nancy Walker (2); HUBERT "HUBIE" CRAM: Phil Silvers (1) ✩; A WAITER: Frank Derbas, *Bill Richards*; JOHN HENRY WHEELER: John Reardon (3); THE SWINGERS: Betty Kent, Donna Sanders, Suzanne Shaw; THE HEAD-WAITER: Marc Jordan; FATSO O'REAR: George Mathews (5); SKIN DEMOPOULOS: George Givot (6); BRAINS BERMAN: David Burns (4); THELMA BERMAN: Marilyn Child, *Sandra Devlin*; THE INTERVIEWER: David Gold; THE PHOTOGRAPHER: Stuart Hodes; WHEELER'S SECRETARIES: Carol Stevens & Dean Taliaferro; JAMES RUSSELL LOWELL IV: Chad Block (10); THE SUMO STUDENT: Ray Kirchner; TILDA MULLEN: Nancy Dussault (7); WOLFIE: Al Nesor (9); MARSHA DENKLER: Carolyn Ragaini, *Laine Roberts*; LOU: Steve Roland; GRETCHEN: Betty Kent; THE RECORDING ENGINEER: Albert Linville; THE MAITRE D': Bob McClure; THE ANIMAL GIRLS: Marilyn Allwyn, Diane Ball, Sandra Devlin, Regina Groves, Patti Karr, Nancy Van Rijn, Carol Stevens, Dean Taliaferro, *Lynne Broadbent, Gail Johnston, Wendy Nickerson*; MOE SHTARKER: Al Lewis (8); THE COMMENTATORS: Bob McClure & Allan Stevenson, *Seth Riggs*; SENATOR ROGERS: Albert Linville; SENATOR REDFIELD: Edward Grace; THE CHIEF COUNSEL: Steve Roland; FATSO'S LAWYER: Marc Jordan; BRAINS' LAWYER: Pat Tolson, *Frank Derbas, Bill Richards*; THE PUBLIC: Marilyn Allwyn, Doria Avila, Diane Ball, Frank Derbas, Sandra Devlin, David Gold, Edward Grace, Regina Groves, Stuart Hodes, Curtis Hood, Daniel Jasinski, Marc Jordan, Betty Kent, Ray Kirchner, Barbara Lang, Josephine Lang, Bob McClure, Ken Malone, Jim Marley, James Moore, Dawn Nickerson, Ed Pfeiffer, Carolyn Ragaini, Steve Roland, Donna Sanders, Suzanne Shaw, Carol Stevens, Liza Stuart, Dean Taliaferro, Pat Tolson, Nancy Van Rijn, Richard Young, *Lynne Broadbent, Gail Johnston, Alan Kirk, Jack Mette, Don Morgan, Shirley Nelson, Wendy Nickerson, Bill Richards, Roy Smith, Wally Strauss*. **Standby**: Hubert: Joshua Shelley, *Bernie West*. **Understudies**: Kay: Marilyn Child, *Patti Karr*; Wheeler: Seth Riggs; Tilda: Liza Stuart, *Dawn Nickerson*; Fatso: Al Lewis; Brains/Shtarker: Al Nesor; Skin: Albert Linville; Wolfie: Marc Jordan; Lowell: David Gold. **Act I**: *Scene*

1 The Casacabana, New York City; now: "Waiting, Waiting" (Kay), "All You Need is a Quarter" (The Swingers); *Scene 2* Hubie & Kay's bedroom: "Take a Job" (Hubie & Kay); *Scene 3* Fatso's ice cream parlor: "The Juke Box Hop" (dance) (Fatso's Customers) [after the opening this number became "The Juke Box Twist"]; *Scene 4* Brains' chicken farm: "It's Legitimate" (Hubie, Fatso, Brains, Skin, The Loaders); *Scene 4a* A box at Hialeah; *Scene 4b* A street; *Scene 5* John Henry Wheeler's office: "I Know About Love" (Wheeler); *Scene 6* The Zen Pancake Parlor; *Scene 7* The Music Enterprise Associates, Inc.: The Auditions (Marsha, Lou, Gretchen); *Scene 8* The Zen Pancake Parlor: "Cry Like the Wind" (Tilda), "Ambition" (Hubie & Tilda); *Scene 9* All over town: "Success" (Tilda Mullen Fans, Tilda, Hubie, Fatso, Brains, Skin); *Scene 10* A recording studio: "Fireworks" (Tilda & Wheeler); *Scene 11* The Imperial Room: "What's New at the Zoo" (Tilda & Animal Girls), "Asking for You" (Wheeler), "The Late, Late Show" (Hubie). *Act II: Scene 1* Hubie & Kay's bedroom: "Adventure" (Hubie & Kay); *Scene 2* John Henry Wheeler's office: "Make Someone Happy" (Wheeler & Tilda); *Scene 3* The Music Enterprise Associates, Inc.: "Don't Be Ashamed of a Teardrop" (Hubie, Fatso, Brains, Skin) [dropped soon after opening]; *Scene 4* The city: The Juke Box Trouble (dance) (Shtarker, Cohorts, Company); *Scene 5* A hearing room in the Senate Office Building, Washington, DC: "V.I.P." (The Public & Hubie), "All of My Life" (Hubie), Finale (Hubie, Kay, Company).

On Broadway it opened to mostly rave reviews. The show vacationed 7/24/61–8/19/61, and re-opened on 8/21/61. The show received Tony nominations for musical, director of a musical, and for Phil Silvers, Nancy Walker and Nancy Dussault.

After Broadway. PRINCE OF WALES THEATRE, London, 10/12/61. 169 PERFORMANCES. PRESENTED BY H.M. Tennent & Leslie A. Macdonnell, in association with Bernard Delfont; DIRECTOR: Bernard Gersten; MUSICAL DIRECTOR: Burt Rhodes. **Cast**: HUBIE: Max Bygraves [his first musical comedy]; KAY: Maggie Fitzgibbon; WHEELER: Steve Arlen; FATSO: Danny Green; GIRLS: Prunella Ransome & Jenny Till.

TOUR. Opened on 1/16/62, at the O'Keefe, Toronto, and closed on 3/19/62, at the Fisher Theatre, Detroit. MUSICAL DIRECTOR: Oscar Kosarin. Certain actors reprised their Broadway roles on this tour: Phil Silvers, Nancy Walker, David Burns, John Reardon, Laine Roberts, Nancy Dussault. The rest of the cast included: FATSO: Bern Hoffman; WOLFIE: Danny Meehan.

CITY CENTER, NYC, 5/6/99–5/9/99. 5 PERFORMANCES. Part of *Encores!* series. ADAPTED: David Ives; DIRECTOR: John Rando; CHOREOGRAPHER: Randy Skinner; SETS: John Lee Beatty; COSTUMES: David C. Woolard; LIGHTING: Ken Billington; GUEST MUSICAL DIRECTOR: Paul Gemignani; CAST RECORDING on DRG. **Cast**: KAY: Randy Graff; HUBIE: Nathan Lane; WAITER: Blake Hammond; JOHN: Brian Stokes Mitchell; MC: Brad Oscar; SWINGERS: Leslie Castay, Colleen Fitzpatrick, Ann Kittredge; FATSO: Lee Wilkof; BRAINS: Lewis J. Stadlen; SKIN: Stephen DeRosa; PHOTOGRAPHER: John Herrera; REPORTER: Patricia Ben Peterson; MARSHA: Marilyn Cooper; IRVING: Gerry Vichi; GRETCHEN: Tovah Feldshuh; TILDA: Heather Headley; MOE: Michael Mulheren; CHIEF COUNSEL: Michael X. Martin; ANIMAL GIRLS: Amy Heggins, Nancy Lemenager, Carol Lee Meadows, Michelle O'Steen, Greta Martin, Tamlyn Brooke Shusterman; DANCERS: Brad Aspel, Vince Pesce, Josh Prince, Noah Racey. *Act I*: Overture (Orchestra); *Scene 1* The Casacabana: "Waiting" (Kay), "All You Need is a Quarter" (Swingers); *Scene 2* Hubie & Kay's apartment: "Take a Job" (Hubie & Kay), "Waiting" (reprise) (Kay); *Scene 3* Fatso's Ice Cream Parlor: "All You Need is a Quarter" (reprise) (Swingers & Dancers); *Scene 4* The Music Enterprise Associates, Inc., office: "It's Legitimate" (Hubie, Kay, Brains, Skin, Men); *Scene 5* John Henry Wheeler's office: "I Know About Love" (Wheeler); *Scene 6* The Music Enterprise Associates, Inc., office: The Auditions (Marsha, Irving, Gretchen); *Scene 7* The Zen Pancake Parlor: "Cry Like the Wind" (Tilda), "Ambition" (Hubie & Tilda); *Scene 8* All over town: Juke Box Montage (Hubie, Tilda, Singers, Dancers); *Scene 9* A recording studio: "Fireworks" (Wheeler & Tilda); *Scene 10* The Imperial Room: "What's New at the Zoo" (Tilda & Animal Girls), "Asking for You" (Wheeler), "The Late, Late Show" (Hubie). *Act II*: Entr'acte (Orchestra); *Scene 1* Hubie & Kay's apartment: "Adventure" (Hubie & Kay); *Scene 2* John Henry Wheeler's office: "Make Someone Happy" (Wheeler & Tilda); *Scene 3* The Music Enterprise Associates,

Inc., office: "Adventure" (reprise) (Kay); *Scene 4* The city: "Investigation — Prelude: Trouble (Moe, Singers, Dancers); *Scene 5* A hearing room in the Senate Office Building: Investigation — "Who is Mr. Big?" (Fatso, Brains, Skin, Singers, Dancers), Investigation — "He's a V.I.P." (Hubie, Singers, Dancers), "All of My Life" (Hubie), Finale (Kay, Hubie, Company).

180. *Doctor Jazz*

Set between 1917 and the 1920s. A black girl singer-dancer goes from Harlem to Broadway under the guidance of a white manager, and at the price of her own happiness. The background was the rise of jazz in New Orleans, Chicago and other places, told in the story of a young man with a horn. Jazz songs of the early part of the 20th century were mixed with original compositions by Buster Davis. There was a partially-nude brothel scene.

Before Broadway. Star Loni Zoe Ackerman (Cyma Rubin's daughter) quit during rehearsals because her part had been diminished. Freda Payne was replaced by Lola Falana, and Frank Owens by Jack Landron. There was no tryout; it went straight to Broadway previews. Librettist Paul Carter Harrison (who had revised Buster Davis's original book prior to rehearsal) was fired, and the book re-written again, this time by Joseph Stein. Director Donald McKayle was replaced by John Berry (who took the credit of "entire production supervised by"). Fourth-billed star Joan Copeland also quit when her part was reduced and all her singing eliminated, and was replaced by Peggy Pope (who lost star status). Then the money ran out, and the show almost closed in previews. Gary Giddens wrote an unfavorable review of the show in the *New York* magazine, before the show had even opened.

The Broadway Run. WINTER GARDEN THEATRE, 3/19/75–3/22/75. 42 previews. 5 PERFORMANCES. A Pyxidium production, PRESENTED BY Cyma Rubin; MUSIC/LYRICS: Buster Davis; BOOK: Paul Carter Harrison (his name was finally removed before Broadway) & Buster Davis (book doctored by Joseph Stein); CONCEIVED BY/MUSICAL DIRECTOR/VOCAL ARRANGEMENTS: Buster Davis; DIRECTOR/CHOREOGRAPHER: Donald McKayle; SETS/COSTUMES: Raoul Pene du Bois; LIGHTING: Feder; SOUND: Abe Jacob; MASTER SOUNDMAN: Otts Munderloh; ASSOCIATE MUSICAL DIRECTOR: Joyce Brown; PRINCIPAL ORCHESTRATOR/DANCE MUSIC ARRANGEMENTS/INCIDENTAL MUSIC COMPOSER: Luther Henderson; ASSOCIATE ORCHESTRATORS: Dick Hyman & Sy Oliver; PRESS: David Powers & Jeff Richards; PRODUCTION SUPERVISOR: John Berry; GENERAL MANAGER: C. Edwin Knill; COMPANY MANAGER: James Mennen; PRODUCTION STAGE MANAGER: Michael Turque; STAGE MANAGER: Marnel Sumner; ASSISTANT STAGE MANAGER: Harrison Avery. **Cast**: STEVE ANDERSON: Bobby Van (1) ☆; SPASM BAND: Quitman D. Fludd III, Bruce Heath, Hector Jaime Mercado, Jeff Veazey; JONATHAN JACKSON JR.: Jack Landron (5); HENRY: Paul Eichel; HARRIET LEE: Peggy Pope (4); GEORGIA SHERIDAN: Lillian Hayman (3) ☆; EDNA MAE SHERIDAN: Lola Falana (2) ☆; GEORGIA'S GIRLS: Bonita Jackson, Michele Simmons, Annie Joe Edwards; HARRIET'S GIRLS: Gail Benedict, Sarah Coleman, Maggy Gorrill, Kitty Jones, Diana Mirras, Sally Neal, Yolanda R. Raven, Catherine Rice; LEAD DANCER: Hector Jaime Mercado (6); THE GROUP: Bruce Heath, Bonita Jackson, Sally Neal, Yolanda R. Raven, Michele Simmons; RUDY: Paul Eichel; PETE: Eron Tabor; HARRY: Paul Eichel; DANCERS: Gail Benedict, Quitman D. Fludd III, Maggy Gorrill, Bob Heath, Bruce Heath, David Hodo, Bonita Jackson, Michael Lichtefeld, Hector Jaime Mercado, Diana Mirras, Sally Neal, Yolanda R. Raven, Catherine Rice, Michele Simmons, Dan Strayhorn, Jeff Veazey; SINGERS: James Braet, Annie Joe Edwards, Paul Eichel, Marian Haraldson, Evelyn McCauley, Eron Tabor; SHOWGIRLS: Sarah Coleman & Kitty Jones; ONSTAGE MUSICIANS: George Davis Jr., Dennis Drury, John Gill, Vince Giordano, Haywood Henry, Danny Moore, Sam Pilafian, Candy Ross, Bob Stewart, Allan Vache, Warren Vache Jr., Earl Williams, Francis Williams. *Understudies*: Steve: Eron Tabor; Edna Mae: Sally Neal; Georgia: Annie Joe Edwards; Harriet: Evelyn McCauley; Jonathan: Quitman D. Fludd III. SWING DANCERS: Marshall Blake & JoAnn Ogawa. *Act I: Scene 1* A brothel quarter in New Orleans; 1917: "Doctor Jazz" (m/l: King Oliver

& Howard Melrose) (Steve, Musicians, Spasm Band), "We've Got Connections" (Steve, Georgia, Harriet); *Scene 2* The street; *Scene 3* Georgia's salon: "Georgia Shows 'em How" (Georgia & Her Girls); *Scene 4* Harriet's boudoir; *Scene 5* The street: "Cleopatra Had a Jazz Band" (m: J.L. Morgan; l: Jack Coogan) (Steve & Ballyhoo Band), "Juba Dance" (Edna Mae & Spasm Band); *Scene 6* Georgia's garden; *Scene 7* The Palace of Pleasure: "Charleston Rag" (m: Eubie Blake) (Jonathan's Band & Harriet's Girls), "I've Got Elgin Watch Movements in My Hips" (Edna Mae), "Blues My Naughty Sweetie Gave to Me" (m/l: Charles McCarron, Arthur Swanstrom, Carey Morgan) (Ballyhoo Band); *Scene 8* Shanghai Theatre: "Good-Time Flat Blues" (m/l: Armand J. Piron) (Georgia); *Scene 9* Harriet's office; *Scene 10* Shanghai Theatre stage: "Evolution Papa" (Edna Mae, Lead Dancer, Troupe); *Scene 11* Backstage: "Rehearsal Tap" (Group), "Blues My Naughty Sweetie Gave to Me" (reprise) (Steve), "I Love It" (m: Harry von Tilzer; l: E. Ray Goetz) (Edna Mae); *Scene 12* Harriet's office: "Anywhere the Wind Blows" (Steve). *Act II*: *Scene 1* The dressing-room — the Lenox Club; *Scene 2* The Lenox Club: "Those Sheik-of-Araby Blues" (Singers & Dancers), "Look Out for Lil" (Edna Mae & Dancers); *Scene 3* The dressing-room; *Scene 4* In front of a New York theatre: "Swanee Strut" (Steve); *Scene 5* Dressing-room, a New York theatre; *Scene 6* On stage: "All I Want is My Black Baby Back" (Edna Mae); *Scene 7* Dressing-room: "Everybody Leaves You" (Steve); *Scene 8* On stage: "Free and Easy" (Edna Mae & Company), "I Love It" (reprise) (Steve & Edna Mae).

Broadway reviews were awful, but Lola Falana got good mentions. It received Tony nominations for choreography, costumes, and for Lola Falana.

181. *A Doll's Life*

The musical opens in 1982, as a company rehearses the final scene of Ibsen's *A Doll's House*. After the scene, the actress, Betsy (also played by Betsy Joslyn, as the director of the play is also played by George Hearn), disappears in a time warp into the year 1879 and becomes Nora of that year. The musical then attempts to tell the story of what happens to Nora after she slams the door on eight years of marriage to Torvald at the end of *A Doll's House*. Realizing she is in an inferior position as a wife, and unable to cope with that, Nora leaves her children and Torvald, and sets out in life alone. She works as a dishwasher, meets Johann, a lawyer, who helps her and falls in love with her. She moves in with Otto, a composer, but leaves him when she finds he is not treating her as an equal. She educates herself, leads a rebellion in a cannery, and is jailed. Johann introduces her to Eric, the cannery owner, and she trades her favors for better conditions for the workers. Eric gives her jewels and she pawns these, setting out on the road to independent wealth. With Johann's help she soon becomes the head of a perfume empire, but she turns down Johann's offer of marriage to return to her children. She has made it in a man's world in four years, and now feels that she and Torvald can meet on equal terms.

Before Broadway. In 1980 Betty Comden and Adolph Green approached Hal Prince to see if he would produce their idea. They all worked on the script for the next two years. Rehearsals began on 4/19/82, and Edmund Lyndeck replaced Giorgio Tozzi. The tryout was from 6/15/82, at the Ahmanson Theatre, Los Angeles, after a week of rehearsals and 4 previews there, and got negative reviews and lost money during its 10-week run, despite the fact that tickets had been pre-sold as part of the Civic Light Opera subscription series. The L.A. run was cut short by two weeks.

The Broadway Run. MARK HELLINGER THEATRE, 9/23/82–9/26/82. 18 previews from 9/8/82. 5 PERFORMANCES. PRESENTED BY James M. Nederlander, Sidney L. Shlenker, Warner Theatre Productions, Joseph Harris, Mary Lea Johnson, Martin Richards, Robert Fryer, in association with Harold Prince; MUSIC: Larry Grossman; LYRICS/

BOOK/CONCEIVED BY: Betty Comden & Adolph Green; BASED ON the play *Nora*, by Henrick Ibsen; DIRECTOR: Harold Prince; CHOREOGRAPHER: Larry Fuller; SETS: Timothy O'Brien & Tazeena Firth; COSTUMES: Florence Klotz; LIGHTING: Ken Billington; SOUND: Jack Mann; MUSICAL DIRECTOR: Paul Gemignani; ASSISTANT MUSICAL DIRECTOR: Tom Fay; ORCHESTRATIONS: Bill Byers; CAST RECORDING on RCA; PRESS: Mary Bryant & Becky Flora; CASTING: Joanna Merlin; GENERAL MANAGER: Howard Haines; PRODUCTION STAGE MANAGER: Beverley Randolph; STAGE MANAGER: Richard Evans; ASSISTANT STAGE MANAGER: Steven Kelley. *Cast*: NORA HELMER: Betsy Joslyn (2) ☆; ACTOR/TORVALD HELMER/JOHAN BLECKER: George Hearn (1) ☆; OTTO BERNICK: Peter Gallagher (3); ERIC DIDRICKSON: Edmund Lyndeck (4); ASTRID KLEMNACHT: Barbara Lang (5); AUDITION SINGERS: Penny Orloff, Norman A. Large, David Vosburgh, Paul Straney; CONDUCTOR/GUSTAFSON/ESCAMILLO/LOKI/MR. ZETTERLING: Norman A. Large (7); STAGE HAND/DR. BERG/AMBASSADOR: David Vosburgh (10); STAGE MANAGER/HAMSUN/PETERSEN/WARDEN/NILSON: Michael Vita (8); DOWAGER: Diane Armistead; MUSICIANS: Gordon Bovinet & Larry Small; MR. KLOSTER: Gordon Bovinet; CAMILLA FORRESTER: Willi Burke (9); ASSISTANT STAGE MANAGER/HELGA: Patti Cohenour; SELMA/JACQUELINE: Penny Orloff (6); PRISON GUARDS: John Corsaut & David Cale Johnson; HELMER'S MAID/WAITRESS: Carol Lurie; WAITERS: Larry Small & Paul Straney; MULLER: Paul Straney; MAID/WIDOW: Olga Talyn; IVAR: Jim Wagg; EMMY: Kimberly Stern; BOB: David Seaman; WOMAN IN WHITE: Lisa Peters; WOMAN IN RED: Teri Gill; WOMAN IN BLACK: Patricia Parker; MAN IN BLACK: David Evans. *Understudies*: Nora: Patti Cohenour; Actor/Torvald/Johan/Eric: Norman A. Large; Otto: Larry Small; Astrid: Willi Burke; Jacqueline/Selma/Audition Singer: Olga Talyn & Sisu Raiken; For Messrs Large, Vosburgh, Vita, and Man in Black: Kevin Marcum; Camilla: Patricia Parker; Woman in Red: Lisa Peters; Ivar/Emmy/Bob: Katie Ertmann. *Swings*: Sisu Raiken & Kevin Marcum. *Act I*: *Scene 1* A rehearsal of Ibsen's *A Doll's House* — 1982: Prologue (Nora & Company); *Scene 2* The train: "A Woman Alone" (Nora, Otto, Conductor, Company); *Scene 3* The Cafe Europa: "Letter to the Children" (Nora), "New Year's Eve" (Eric, Johann, Berg, Gustafson); *Scene 4* Street outside the Cafe Europa; *Scene 5* Otto's room: "Stay with Me, Nora" (Otto & Nora); *Scene 6* Backstage at the Opera; *Scene 7* An opera reading — the opera audition: "Arrival" (Astrid & Company), *Loki and Baldur* (Otto & Singers), "You Interest Me" (Johann), "Departure" (Astrid & Company); *Scene 8* Otto's room: "Letter from Klemnacht" (Astrid), "Learn to Be Lonely" (Nora); *Scene 9* Cannery: "Rats and Mice and Fish" (Women); *Scene 10* Prison: "Jailer, Jailer"/"Letter to the Children" (reprise) (Nora & Women); *Scene 11* The Opera House: Excerpts from *Loki and Baldur* (Company), "Rare Wines" (Eric & Nora). *Act II*: *Scene 1* Eric's bedroom: "No More Mornings" (Nora); *Scene 2* Billiard room: "There She Is" (Johan, Eric, Otto), "Power" (Nora); *Scene 3* Billiard room; the next morning: "Letter to the Children" (reprise) (Nora), "At Last" (Johan); *Scene 4* The Grand Cafe; spring, fall, winter: "The Grand Cafe" (Company); *Scene 5* The living room: Finale (Company).

Broadway reviews were terrible. The show lost $4 million (the original $3 million investment increased to cover the L.A. losses). After the Shuberts had refused to invest, James Nederlander had become the main investor, contributing a million of the original investment, and a further third of the additional costs accrued during the tryouts. Hal Prince also put up a third of that million, as well as making guarantees against future losses. The show received Tony nominations for book, and for George Hearn.

After Broadway. In spring 1994 the York Theatre Company staged a revival, as part of their *Musicals in Mufti* series. This turned into a revised, full-fledged York Theatre Company production at ST. PETER'S CHURCH, 12/13/94–1/22/95. 8 previews. 34 PERFORMANCES. DIRECTOR: Robert Brink; SETS: James Morgan; COSTUMES: Patricia Adshead; LIGHTING: Mary Jo Dondlinger; SOUND: Jim Van Bergen; MUSICAL DIRECTOR: David Kirshenbaum. *Cast*: HAMSUN/KARL/GUEST: Paul Blankenship; JAILER/AMBASSADOR: Paul Blankenship; POWER PATRON: Paul Blankenship; BLECKER: Tom Galantich; RESPECTABLE WOMAN/GUEST: Catherine Anne Gale; CANNERY GIRL/JACQUEL LE BEAU: Catherine Anne Gale; NORA: Jill Geddes; SINGER/SECRETARY: Tamra Hayden; CAMILLA: Tamra Hayden; JAILED WOMAN/HELGA/BRIDGIT: Tamra Hayden; OTTO: Jeff Herbst; TORVALD: Seth Jones; PIMP/GUSTAFSON/

Michael Klashman; CALL BOY: Michael Klashman; LOKI/KLOSTER: Michael Klashman; WAITRESS/SELMA: Eileen McNamara; BERTA: Eileen McNamara; CONDUCTOR/BERG/PETERSON: Howard Pinhasik; MULLER/ZETTERLING: Howard Pinhasik; ERIC: Paul Schoeffler; ASTRID KLEMNACHT: Robin Skye; LADIES OF THE EVENING: Jennifer Laura Thompson & Tamra Hayden. "What Now?," "A Woman Alone," "Letter to the Children," "Arrival in Christiania," "New Year's Eve," "Stay with Me, Nora," "Arrival," "Loki and Baldur," "You Interest Me," "Departure," "Letter from Klemnacht," "Learn to Be Lonely," "Rats and Mice and Fish," "Jailer, Jailer," "Rare Wines," "You Puzzle Me," "No More Mornings," "There She Is," "Power," "At Last," "Can't You Hear I'm Making Love to You?."

182. *Donnybrook!*

American John Enright (Sean Thornton in the movie *The Quiet Man*, upon which this musical was based) returns to the Irish village of Innisfree where he had been born, and falls in love with Ellen Roc (Mary Kate in the movie), the fiery sister of local squire Will Danaher. John wants to buy the house ("White O'Morn") that he was born in, but so does Danaher. Danaher will not give his blessing to the marriage of John with Ellen Roe. John is a former boxer who killed a man in the ring, and now will not fight anyone under any circumstances. Mikeen is the local Mr. Fixit. Kathy is the wealthy widow and tavern keeper.

Before Broadway. Among the backers of this show were Hal Prince, Bobby Griffith & Freddie Brisson, all of whom had once employed Fred Hebert (a producer of this show) as stage manager. The first choices for the role of Ellen Roe were Rhonda Fleming and Joan Diener, but the part went to unknown Kipp Hamilton, who, however, was replaced less than a week before the Philadelphia previews by Joan Fagan. The number "If it isn't Everything" was cut before rehearsals began, and "Dowdling" during the Washington, DC tryout.

The Broadway Run. FORTY-SIXTH STREET THEATRE, 5/18/61–7/15/61. 2 previews on 5/17/61. 68 PERFORMANCES. PRESENTED BY Fred Hebert & David Kapp; MUSIC/LYRICS: Johnny Burke; BOOK: Robert E. McEnroe; BASED ON the short story *The Quiet Man*, by Maurice Walsh, and on the 1950 John Ford movie of the same name, with a screenplay by Frank S. Nugent, and starring John Wayne, Maureen O'Hara, Victor McLaglen and Barry Fitzgerald; DIRECTOR/CHOREOGRAPHER: Jack Cole; SETS/COSTUMES: Rouben Ter-Arutunian; LIGHTING: Klaus Holm; MUSICAL DIRECTOR/VOCAL ARRANGEMENTS: Clay Warnick; ORCHESTRATIONS/ARRANGEMENTS: Robert Ginzler; BALLET MUSIC ARRANGEMENTS & ORCHESTRATIONS: Laurence Rosenthal; PRESS: Sol Jacobson, Lewis Harmon, Maxine Keith, Mary Bryant; GENERAL MANAGER: Ben Rosenberg; COMPANY MANAGER: Richard Seader; PRODUCTION STAGE MANAGER: Frank Coletti; STAGE MANAGER: Dan Brennan; ASSISTANT STAGE MANAGER: John Ford. *Cast:* WILLIE O'BANTIE: Bruce MacKay; MATTHEW GILBANE: James Gannon; GAVIN COLLINS: Al DeSio; OLD MAN TOOMEY: Clarence Nordstrom; TIM O'CONNELL: Darrell J. Askey; WILL DANAHER: Philip Bosco (5); ELLEN ROE DANAHER: Joan Fagan (3); ESME GILLIE, A BARMAID: Marissa Mason [she later became Mary Burke]; SADIE McINTY: Sibyl Bowan; BIRDY MONYHAN: Grace Carney; MIKEEN FLYNN: Eddie Foy Jr. (1); JOHN ENRIGHT: Art Lund (2); FATHER FINUCANE: Charles C. Welch; AN IRISH BOY: Eddie Ericksen; JAMIE, A BARTENDER: George Harwell; KATHY CAREY: Susan Johnson (4); PRINCIPAL DANCER: Norman Maen; SINGERS: Darrell J. Askey, Georgia Creighton, Eddie Ericksen, John Ford, Nancy Foster, Charlotte Frazier, George Harwell, Dee Harless, Georgia Kennedy, Bob Murdock, Maudeen O'Sullivan, Charles Rule; DANCERS: John Aristedes, Gloria Ann Bowen, Judy Dunford, Robert Evans, Larry Fuller, Mickey Gunnersen, William Guske, David Lober, George Martin, Marissa Mason, Carol Sherman, Suanne Shirley, Keith Stewart, Pamela Wood. **Understudies:** Finucane: John Ford; Enright: James Gannon; Mikeen: Charles C. Welch; Sadie/Birdy: Dee Harless; Will: Bruce MacKay; Kathy: Sibyl Bowan; Ellen: Nancy Foster. *Act I: Scene 1* Overture (An Irish Boy, Enright, Sadie, Birdy, Finucane, Ellen Roe, Dancing Ensemble) [Enright was added to this number during the run]; *Scene 2* Kitchen of Will Dana-

her's house: "Sez I" (Ellen, Toomey, O'Bantie, Gilbane, Gavin, O'Connell); *Scene 3* The countryside: "Sez I" (concluded); *Scene 4* Outside "White O'Morn" cottage; *Scene 5* Carey's Pub: "The Day the Snow is Meltin'" (An Irish Boy), "Sad Was the Day" (Kathy & Ensemble), "Donnybrook!" (Ensemble); *Scene 6* The countryside [during the run this scene became The interior of "White O'Morn"]: "The Day the Snow is Meltin'" (reprise) (An Irish Boy, Gavin, O'Connell, Enright) [An Irish Boy was dropped from this number during the run]; *Scene 7* The interior of Enright's cottage [during the run this scene became A street on the edge of Innisfree]: "Ellen Roe" (Enright); *Scene 8* The church: "Sunday Morning" (Ensemble): "(I Could Hate) The Loveable Irish" (Enright & Finucane); *Scene 9* Kathy's sitting room; the Irish countryside: "I Wouldn't Bet One Penny" (Kathy & Flynn); *Scene 10* Kitchen of Will Danaher's house: "He Makes Me Feel I'm Lovely" (Ellen); *Scene 11* Danaher's backyard [during the run this scene became The Courting]: "The Courting" (Ensemble), "I Have My Own Way" (Enright & Ellen); *Scene 12* The Danaher parlor: "A Toast to the Bride" (Toomey & Ensemble). *Act II: Scene 1* The low road: "Wisha Wurra" (Flynn, Toomey, O'Bantie, Gilbane, Gavin); *Scene 2* The interior of "White O'Morn" cottage; *Scene 3* The high road: "Wisha Wurra" (reprise) (Flynn, Toomey, O'Bantie, Gilbane, Gavin) [this reprise was added during the run], "He Makes Me Feel I'm Lovely" (reprise) (Ellen); *Scene 4* The interior of "White O'Morn" cottage: "A Quiet Life" (Enright); *Scene 5* Carey's Pub: "Mr. Flynn" (Kathie, Sadie, Birdy), "Hornpipe Dance" [dropped during the run], "Dee-lightful is the Word" (Flynn & Kathy); *Scene 6* The churchyard: "For My Own" (Ellen & Enright); *Scene 7* The interior of "White O'Morn" cottage; *Scene 8* Railway station; *Scene 9* Danaher's field; *Scene 10* The interior of "White O'Morn" cottage: Finale: "Sez I" (reprise) (Will, Enright, Ensemble).

Broadway reviews were mostly excellent.

183. *Don't Get God Started*

A musical revue; a gospel musical with skits emphasizing moral & religious values, interspersed with gospel songs.

The Broadway Run. LONGACRE THEATRE, 10/29/87–1/10/88. 86 PERFORMANCES. PRESENTED BY Barry Hankerson & Jeffrey Day Sharp; MUSIC/LYRICS: Marvin Winans; BOOK: Ron Milner; STORY/IDEA DEVELOPMENT: Ron Milner & Barry Hankerson; DIRECTOR: Ron Milner; ADDITIONAL STAGING: Conni Marie Brazelton; SETS: Llewellen Harrison; COSTUMES: Victoria Shaffer; LIGHTING: Shirley Prendergast; SOUND: Scott Marcellus; MUSICAL DIRECTOR: Steven Ford; VOCAL & MUSICAL ARRANGEMENTS/MUSIC CONSULTANT: Ronald Winans; PRESS: Jeffrey Richards Associates; CASTING: Reuben Cannon & Associates; GENERAL MANAGEMENT: Marvin A. Krauss Associates; COMPANY MANAGER: Kathryn Frawley; PRODUCTION STAGE MANAGER: Keeth Wallace; ASSISTANT STAGE MANAGER: Louis M. Mellini III. *Cast:* FEMALE LEAD VOCALIST: Vanessa Bell Armstrong (3); WISE OLD MAN/THE REVEREND: Ernie Banks (6); CLAUDETTE/SISTER NEEDLOVE: Conni Marie Brazelton (7); WISE OLD WOMAN: Marilyn Coleman (5); JACK/SILK: Giancarlo Esposito (1); SYLVIA/BARBARA ANN: Chip Fields (2); MALE LEAD VOCALIST: Marvin "BeBe" Winans (4), *Ronald Winans* (alternate); ROBERT/LAWRENCE/BUZZ: Marvin Wright-Bey (8); CHOIR: Donald Albert, Margaret Bell, Susan Dawn Carson, Victor Trent Cook, Starletta DuPois (*Carol Lynn Maillard*), Patty Heaton, Keith Laws, Andrea McClurkin, Donnie McClurkin, Nadine Middlebrooks Norwood, Stefone Pet'tis, Sylvia Simmons, Monique Williams, Angie Winans (left during run), Debbie Winans (left during run), Ronald Wyche (left during run). ***Understudies:*** Female Vocalist: Margaret Bell, *Kathi Walker*; Claudette/Needlove/Old Woman/Sylvia/Barbara Ann: Starletta DuPois, *Carol Lynn Maillard*; Male Vocalist: Donald Albert, *Donnie McClurkin* (added during run); Robert/Lawrence/Buzz: Donald Albert; Jack/Silk/Old Man/Reverend: Ronald Wyche, *Marvin Wright-Bey*. Swings: *Stefone Pett'is* & *Nadine Middlebrooks Norwood*. **Musicians:** KEYBOARDS: Steven Ford & Anthony Walker; PIANO: Evelyn Curenton; SYNTHESIZER: Willard Meeks; LEAD GUITAR: George Bell; BASS: Jeau Frierson; DRUMS/TYMPANI: Garfield Williams; SOPRANO & TENOR SAX: Willie Williams; RHYTHM GUITAR: Fred Cooper. *Act I:* "Cry Loud (Lift Your Voice Like a Trumpet)" (Vanessa & Be Be), "Slipping Away from You" (Vanessa & Be Be), "After Looking for Love" (Vanessa), "Change Your Nature" (Be Be), "What's Wrong with Our Love" (Vanessa & Be Be), "Don't Turn Your Back" (Vanessa), "Turn Us Again" (Vanessa & Be Be). *Act II*: "Abide with Me" (Hymn) (Be Be), "Let the Healing Begin" (Vanessa, Be Be, Choir), "Renew My Mind" (Choir), "Denied Stone" (Vanessa & Be Be), "He'll Make it Alright" (Choir), "Can I Build My Home in You"/"Bring Back the Days of Yea and Nay" (Vanessa & Be Be), "Always" (Vanessa), "Millions" (Marilyn & Ernie), "I Made It" (Vanessa & Be Be), "Still in Love with You" (Be Be), "It's Alright Now" (Choir).

Reviews were not great.

184. *Don't Play Us Cheap*

A coupla days before tomorrow; here. A musical fantasy, all in fun, about a pair of inefficient demons intruding into a Saturday night Harlem family party. Set in Miss Maybell's apartment.

The Broadway Run. Ethel Barrymore Theatre, 5/16/72–10/1/72. Previews from 5/12/72. 164 performances. Presented by Melvin Van Peebles; Music/Lyrics/Book/Director: Melvin Van Peebles; Sets: Kert Lundell; Costumes: Bernard Johnson; Lighting: Martin Aronstein; Sound Operator: John Cycon; Sound Consultant: Lou Gonzalez; Musical Supervisor: Harold Wheeler; Cast recording on Stax; Press: Michael Alpert & Arthur Rubine; General Manager: Eugene Wolsk & Emanuel Azenberg; Company Manager: David Payne; Production Stage Manager: Charles Blackwell; Stage Manager: Charles Briggs; Assistant Stage Manager: Jerry Lawes. *Cast:* Mr. Percy: Thomas Anderson; Mrs. Washington: Joshie Jo Armstead; Harold Johnson, Rat: Nate Barnett; Mr. Johnson, Cockroach: Frank Carey; Mr. Bowser: Robert Dunn; Earnestine: Rhetta Hughes; Trinity: Joe Keyes Jr., *David Connell*; Mrs. Bowser: Mabel King; David: Avon Long; Mr. Washington: Geo. "Ooppee" McCurn; Miss Maybell: Esther Rolle, *Theresa Merritt*; Mrs. Johnson: Jay Vanleer. *Musicians*: Piano: Harold Wheeler; Bass: Bob Bushnell; Guitar: George Davis; Drums: Earl Williams. *Act I*: "Some Days it Seems that it Just Don't Even Pay to Get Out of Bed" (Rat & Cockroach), "Break That Party" (David & Trinity), "8-Day Week" (Mr. Percy & Company), "Saturday Night" (Company), "I'm a Bad Character" (Trinity & Company), "You Cut up the Clothes in the Closet of My Dreams" (Mrs. Washington), "It Makes No Difference" (Miss Maybell & Company), "Quittin' Time" (Mr. Washington & Company). *Act II*: "Ain't Love Grand" (Earnestine & Company), "The Book of Life" (Mr. Bowser & Company), Quartet: "Ain't Love Grand" (reprise) (Earnestine), "Know Your Business" (Miss Maybell), "Big Future" (The Johnsons), "Break That Party" (reprise) (David & Trinity), "Feast on Me" (Mrs. Bowser & Company), "The Phoney Game" (David & Company), "(If You See a Devil) Smash Him" (Company).

Reviews were mixed. The show received Tony nominations for book, and for Avon Long.

After Broadway. Melvin Van Peebles made a movie of the play in 1972.

185. *Doonesbury*

Set at a graduation weekend in the late spring of the present time, in Walden, an off-off campus house of a New England college. Duke buys the commune supposedly to establish a drug rehab center but really plans to turn it into a vacation condo complex.

Before Broadway. Garry Trudeau took a year off from his comic strip to be involved in this. It cost $2 million (funded mostly by Universal Pictures).

The Broadway Run. Biltmore Theatre, 11/21/83–2/19/84. 21 previews. 104 performances. Presented by James Walsh, in association with Universal Pictures; Music/Orchestrations: Elizabeth Swados; Lyrics/Book: Garry Trudeau (based on his *Doonesbury* comic strip); Director: Jacques Levy; Choreographer: Margo Sappington; Sets:

Peter Larkin; Costumes: Patricia McGourty; Lighting: Beverly Emmons; Sound: Tom Morse; Musical Director/Arrangements: Jeff Waxman; Press: Jeffrey Richards Associates; Casting: Juliet Taylor; Puppets: Edward G. Christie; General Manager: James Walsh; Company Manager: Susan Bell; Production Stage Manager: Warren Crane; Stage Managers: Deborah Clelland & Scott Evans. *Cast:* Roland: Reathel Bean; Mike Doonesbury: Ralph Bruneau; Mark: Mark Linn-Baker; B.D.: Keith Szarabajka; Boopsie: Laura Dean; Zonker: Albert Macklin; Duke: Gary Beach; Honey: Lauren Tom; J.J.: Kate Burton; Joanie: Barbara Andres; Provost: Peter Shawn; Voice of Pres. Reagan: Reathel Bean. *Understudies*: Mike/Mark/B.D./Provost: Max Cantor; Duke/Roland: Peter Shawn; Zonker: Scott Evans; Boopsie/J.J.: Eve Bennett-Gordon; Joanie: Deborah Darr; Honey: Janet Wong.

Note: All cast members play multiple roles (so says the tour note).

Musicians: Keyboards: Jeff Waxman & Steve Skinner; Drums/Percussion: David Sawyer; Bass Guitar: Seth Glassman. *Act I*: *Scene 1* Walden—living-room: "Graduation" (Roland, Mike, B.D., Boopsie, Mark, Zonker), "Just One Night" (Mike); *Scene 2* Walden—back porch: "I Came to Tan" (Zonker & Ensemble); *Scene 3* Los Angeles County Courtroom: "Guilty" (Duke & Ensemble); *Scene 4* Walden—living-room: "I Can Have it All" (Boopsie & Ensemble); *Scene 5* Los Angeles County Courtroom; *Scene 6* Walden—living-room: "Get Together" (J.J. & Mike); *Scene 7* WBBY radio station: "Baby Boom Boogie Boy" (Mark, Roland, Ensemble); *Scene 8* Walden—living-room: "Another Memorable Meal" (Mike, B.D., Boopsie, Mark, Zonker, J.J., Joanie). *Act II*: *Scene 1* Walden—living-room: "Just a House" (Ensemble); *Scene 2* Walden—front yard: "Complicated Man" (Honey & Boopsie); *Scene 3* Walden Puddle: "Real Estate" (Duke & Zonker); *Scene 4* Walden—living-room: "Mother" (J.J. & Joanie), "It's the Right Time to Be Rich" (B.D. & Roland), "Muffy and the Topsiders" (Boopsie, Mike, Mark, Zonker), "Just One Night" (reprise) (Mike & J.J.); *Scene 5* Commencement Exercises: "Graduation" (reprise) (Ensemble).

Reviews were middle-of-the-road.

After Broadway. Tour. Opened on 10/12/84, at the Warner Theatre, Washington, DC, and closed on 11/11/84, at the Wilshire Theatre, Los Angeles. It had the same basic crew as for Broadway, but the cast was all different: Doonesbury: Gregg Edelman; Boopsie: Marin Mazzie; Mark: Stuart Bloom; Roland: Hal Robinson; B.D.: Mark T. Fairchild; Zonker: Martin Moran; Duke: Paul Kandel; Honey: Elizabeth Sung; J.J.: Julie Boyd; Joanie: Laura Gardner.

186. *Dracula: The Musical*

The classic vampire story, set in Europe toward the end of the Victorian era. It has flying vampires and many other technical effects. There was also nudity.

Before Broadway. It played in an earlier version at La Jolla Playhouse, Calif., 10/21/01–11/25/01. Previews from 10/13/01 (date put back from 10/9/01). Director: Des McAnuff; Choreographer: Mindy Cooper; Sets: John Arnone; Costumes: Catherine Zuber; Lighting: Howell Binkley; Sound: ACME Sound Partners; Musical Director/Vocal Arrangements/Incidental Music: Constantine Kitsopoulos; Assistant Musical Director: Ethyl Will; Orchestrations: Michael Starobin & Doug Besterman; Casting: Dave Clemmons; Production Stage Manager: Frank Hartenstein; Stage Manager: Kelly Martindale. *Cast*: Dracula: Tom Hewitt; Lucy: Amy Rutberg; Mina: Jenn Morse; Van Helsing: Tom Flynn; Jack: Joe Cassidy; Holmwood: Chris Hoch; Quincey: Lee Morgan; Renfield: William Youmans; Jonathan: Tom Stuart; Child: Michael Cullen & Angelo Scolari; 1st Vampire: Jodi Stevens; 2nd Vampire: Jenny-Lynn Suckling; 3rd Vampire: Emily Kosloski; Ensemble: Margaret Ann Gates, Emily Kosloski, Guy LeMonnier, Lynnette Marrero, Tracy Miller, Jodi Stevens, Jenny-Lynn Suckling, Sara Tobin. *Understudy*: Dracula: Guy LeMonnier.

It was workshopped 12/10/03–12/16/03. Director: Des McAnuff.

Originally John Arnone had been scheduled to be the set designer, Michael Starobin was going to do orchestrations, and Len Cariou was going to play Van Helsing, but they were all replaced. Mr. Cariou was replaced by Hinton Battle as Van Helsing, but during rehearsals Mr. Battle was replaced by Stephen McKinley Henderson. The show was due to begin previews on 7/12/04, then 7/19/04, then, because it needed more time for tech rehearsals, to 7/26/04. However, on that date a waterpipe burst at the Belasco, so preview opening night was put off until 7/28/04, then 7/29/04. The 7/29/04 date was canceled, so it actually began previews on 7/30/04. Opening date too was put back from 8/5/04 to 8/16/04, then on 7/22/04 the producers announced a new official opening date of 8/19/04.

The Broadway Run. BELASCO THEATRE, 8/19/04–1/2/05. Previews from 7/30/04. PRESENTED BY Dodger Stage Holding & Joop Van Den Ende, in association with Clear Channel Entertainment; MUSIC: Frank Wildhorn; LYRICS/BOOK: Don Black & Christopher Hampton; BASED ON the 1897 novel by Bram Stoker; DIRECTOR: Des McAnuff; CHOREOGRAPHER: Mindy Cooper; PERIOD MOVEMENT CONSULTANT: Elizabeth Keen; SETS: Heidi Ettinger; COSTUMES: Catherine Zuber; LIGHTING: Howell Binkley; SOUND: Acme Sound Partners; MUSICAL DIRECTOR/MUSICAL & VOCAL ARRANGEMENTS: Constantine Kitsopoulos; ORCHESTRATIONS: Doug Besterman; SPECIAL EFFECTS: Flying by Foy; AERIAL STAGING: Rob Besserer; PRESS: Boneau/Bryan-Brown; CASTING: Dave Clemmons; COMPANY MANAGER: Sandra Carlson; PRODUCTION STAGE MANAGER: Frank Hartenstein; STAGE MANAGER: Kelly Martindale; ASSISTANT STAGE MANAGERS: Alex Lyu Volckhausen & Mark Gordon. *Cast:* JONATHAN HARKER: Darren Ritchie (4); DRACULA: Tom Hewitt (1) ☆; MINA MURRAY: Melissa Errico (2) ☆, *Elizabeth Loyacano* (stood in from 9/7/04–10/14/04 while Miss Errico was out with vocal cord strain); 1ST VAMPIRE (Tuesdays; Wednesday evenings; Fridays; Saturday evenings): Tracy Miller; 1ST VAMPIRE (Wednesday matinees; Thursdays; Saturday matinees; Sunday matinees): Jenifer Foote; 2ND VAMPIRE (Tuesdays; Wednesday evenings; Fridays; Saturday evenings): Celina Carvajal; 2ND VAMPIRE (Wednesday matinees; Thursdays; Saturday matinees; Sunday matinees): Elizabeth Loyacano; 3RD VAMPIRE (Tuesdays; Wednesday evenings; Fridays; Saturday evenings): Pamela Jordan; 3RD VAMPIRE (Wednesday matinees; Thursdays; Saturday matinees; Sunday matinees): Melissa Fagan; RENFELD: Don Stephenson (3); JACK SEWARD: Shonn Wiley (8); LUCY WESTENRA: Kelli O'Hara (5); QUINCEY MORRIS: Bart Shatto (7); ARTHUR HOLMWOOD: Chris Hoch (6); ABRAHAM VAN HELSING: Stephen McKinley Henderson (9); CHILD (Tuesdays; Wednesday evenings; Fridays; Saturday evenings): Matthew Nardozzi; Child (Wednesday matinees; Thursdays; Saturday matinees; Sunday matinees): Michael Herwitz; ENSEMBLE: Celina Carvajal, Melissa Fagan, Jenifer Foote, Pamela Jordan, Elizabeth Loyacano, Tracy Miller, Graham Rowat. *Standby*: Dracula/Van Helsing/Quincey: Chuck Wagner. *Understudies*: Dracula/Van Helsing: Graham Rowat; Lucy: Celina Carvajal & Megan Sikora; Mina: Elizabeth Loyacano & Megan Sikora; Renfield: Chris Hoch & Graham Rowat; Holmwood/Jack: Anthony Holds & Bart Shatto; Jonathan: Shonn Wiley & Anthony Holds; Quincey: Anthony Holds. *Swings*: Anthony Holds & Megan Sikora. *Orchestra*: REEDS: Rick Heckman; CELLO: Chungsun Kim; PERCUSSION: Barbara Merjan; KEY I: Karl Mansfield; KEY II: Ethyl Will; KEY III: Constantine Kitsopoulos. *Act I*: Prelude (Jonathan), "A Quiet Life" (Dracula), "Over Whitby Bay" (Jonathan & Mina), "Forever Young" (1st, 2nd & 3rd Vampires), "Fresh Blood" (Dracula), "The Master's Song" (Renfield & Jack), "How Do You Choose?" (Lucy, Mina, Quincey, Jack, Holmwood, Company), "The Mist" (Lucy), "Modern World" (Company), "A Perfect Life" (Mina), "The Weddings" (Company), "Prayer for the Dead" (Company), "Life After Life" (Dracula & Lucy). *Act II*: "The Heart is Slow to Learn" (Mina), "The Master's Song" (reprise) (Renfield & Dracula), "If I Could Fly" (Mina), "There's Always a Tomorrow" (Dracula & Mina), "Deep in the Darkest Night" (Van Helsing, Quincey, Holmwood, Jack, Jonathan, Mina), "Before the Summer Ends" (Jonathan), "All is Dark"/"Life After Life (reprise) (Dracula & Mina), "Finale (Dracula & Mina).

Broadway reviews were not good. Melissa Errico missed the 9/7/04 matinee due to strained vocal cords, then took off both performances on 9/8/04. She was expected back for the next performance, but didn't make it back until 10/14/04. People simply did not come, and on 12/7/04 the cast was informed that the show would be closing on 1/2/05. The production lost millions of dollars. No record label wanted to do a cast recording.

187. *Drat! The Cat!*

A musical burlesque-fantasy spoof. Alice is a cat burglar (literally—she dresses as a cat while she steals jewels) who is really a rebellious heiress, and Bob is a bumbling cop assigned to track her down. Set in the latter part of the 19th century, in New York City and environs, in the spring. Alice volunteers to assist Bob, and he falls in love with her at first sight. He unwittingly tips her off to valuable items. Alice can never remember his name. She frames him for the thefts and then asks him to run away with her. At Bob's trial, Alice confesses, and is placed in his custody. The orchestra was on stage, on an elevated bandstand, and they also played background roles.

Before Broadway. Herman Levin began this project in the early 1960s, but abandoned it. It was then picked up by Jerry Adler and Norman Rosemont. Joey Heatherton was cast as the star, but when she objected to the casting of Elliott Gould, she was fired (Mr. Gould was then married to Barbra Streisand, who had provided $50,000 of the $500,000 capitalization). While it was trying out in Philadelphia third-billed star Eddie Foy Jr. (who was playing the fathers of both Bob and Alice) left the show, and was replaced by Jack Fletcher (who lost star billing) and David Gold. At that stage it was still called *Cat and Mouse*. Philly reviews were not good, and the show moved prematurely to Broadway.

The Broadway Run. MARTIN BECK THEATRE, 10/10/65–10/16/65. 11 previews from 9/30/65. 8 PERFORMANCES. A "Rogo Production" (Norman Rosemont & Robert Goulet), PRESENTED BY Jerry Adler & Norman Rosemont; MUSIC: Milton Schafer; LYRICS/BOOK: Ira Levin; DIRECTOR/CHOREOGRAPHER: Joe Layton; SETS/LIGHTING: David Hays; COSTUMES: Fred Voelpel; MUSICAL DIRECTOR/VOCAL ARRANGEMENTS: Herbert Grossman; ORCHESTRATIONS: Hershy Kay & Clare Grundman; DANCE MUSIC ARRANGEMENTS: Genevieve Pitot; CAST RECORDING on Columbia; PRESS: Mike Merrick Company; GENERAL MANAGER: Phil Adler; COMPANY MANAGER: Sam M. Handelsman; PRODUCTION STAGE MANAGER: George Thorn; STAGE MANAGER: Tom Porter; ASSISTANT STAGE MANAGERS: Bob Borod & Robert E. Maxwell Jr. *Cast:* THE MAYOR: Alfred Spindelman; Pincer, SUPERINTENDENT OF POLICE: Charles Durning (5); MALLET, CHIEF OF DETECTIVES: Gene Varrone (7); ROGER "BULLDOG" PUREFOY, FORMER CHIEF OF DETECTIVES: David Gold; KATE PUREFOY, HIS WIFE: Lu Leonard (6); THE DOCTOR: Leo Bloom; EMMA, A PATROLWOMAN: Sandy Ellen; BOB PUREFOY, THE PUREFOYS' SON, A PATROLMAN: Elliott Gould (2) ☆; THE VAN GUILDERS' BUTLER: Harry Naughton; MATILDA VAN GUILDER, A SOCIALITE: Jane Connell (3); LUCIUS VAN GUILDER, HER HUSBAND, A MILLIONAIRE: Jack Fletcher (4); ALICE VAN GUILDER, THEIR DAUGHTER: Lesley Ann Warren (1) ☆; THE MAID: Jacque Dean; THE MINISTER: Al Lanti; THE MAYOR'S WIFE: Marian Haraldson; JULIETTA ONDERDONCK, A DOWAGER FROM BOSTON: Mariana Doro; THE JUDGE: David Gold; THE PROSECUTOR: Leo Bloom; PATROLMEN: Leo Bloom, Ralph Farnworth, Ian Garry, David Gold, Barney Johnston, Al Lanti, William Lutz, George Marcy, Larry Moss, Harry Naughton, Ronald Pare, James Powers, Dan Siretta, Bill Starr; OTHERS IN THE ENSEMBLE: Jeri Barto, Lillian Bozinoff, Margery Gray, Beth Howland, Nancy Lynch, Carmen Morales, Meg Walter, Mary Zahn. *Act I*: *Scene 1* Various places in New York City: "Drat! The Cat!" (Citizens, Patrolmen, Mayor, Pincer, Mallet); *Scene 2* A bedroom in the Purefoys' flat: "My Son, Uphold the Law" (Roger & Patrolmen); *Scene 3* Lucius Van Guilder's study and counting room: "Holmes and Watson" (Alice & Bob), "She Touched Me" (Bob) [a hit]; *Scene 4* Alice Van Guilder's boudoir and a secret chamber: "Wild and Reckless" (Alice); *Scene 5* The Purefoys' kitchen: "She's Roses" (Bob & Kate); *Scene 6* Pier Fourteen: "Ignoble Theft of the Idol's Eyes" (Cat, Patrolmen, Attendants of the Idol). PROPERTY MEN: Jeri Barto, William Lutz, Larry Moss; WARRIORS: Ian Garry, George Marcy, Harry Naughton, Ronald Pare; GEISHAS: Nancy Lynch, Carmen Morales, Mary Zahn; LION: Bill Starr; HIGH PRIEST: David Gold; CANTOR: Gene Varrone; *Scene 7* Van Guilder's study and the garden: "Dancing with Alice" (Bob, Alice, Mr. & Mrs. Van Guilder, Guests), "Drat! The Cat!" (reprise) (Mr. & Mrs. Van Guilder, Guests); *Scene 8* The Van Guilders' cellar: "Purefoy's Lament" (Bob). *Act II*: *Scene 1* Police Headquarters: "A Pox Upon the Traitor's Brow" (Pincer, Mallet, Emma, Patrolmen); *Scene 2* The cellar: "Deep in Your Heart" (Bob); *Scene 3* Van Guilder's study: "Let's Go" (Alice & Bob), "It's Your Fault" (Mr. & Mrs. Van Guilder); *Scene 4* The woods north of the city: "Wild and Reckless" (reprise) (Bob); *Scene 5* Various places in the city: "The Upside-Down Thief" (ballet) (Bob, Citizens, Patrolmen, Kate). TENORS: Ralph Farnworth & Gene Varrone; CONCERT-GOERS: Lillian Bozinoff, David Gold, Marian Haraldson, James Powers, Meg Walter; SOPRANO: Mariana Doro; MAYOR'S COMPANION: Margery Gray; PATROLMEN: Ian Garry, Al Lanti, Ronald Pare, Dan Siretta, Bill Starr; *Scene 6* The woods and the city: "Today is a Day for a Band to Play" (Pincer, Mallet, Emma, Patrolmen, Citizens), "She Touched Me" (reprise) (Bob & Alice); *Scene 7* Van Guilder's study: "I Like Him" (Alice); *Scene 8* A courtroom: "Justice Triumphant" (Entire Company), "Today is a Day for a Band to Play" (reprise) (Entire Company).

Opening night was moved from Saturday to Sunday so Miss Streisand could attend on her night off from *Funny Girl*. Broadway reviews were divided. Lesley Ann Warren, making her Broadway debut at age 19, was a smash hit. The show received a Tony nomination for sets. Barbra Streisand recorded two numbers: "He Touched Me" ("She Touched Me" in the show, of course) and "I Like Him." A recording was made in the 1980s from a live tape made at the time of the show.

188. *Dream: The Johnny Mercer Musical*

A musical revue, inspired by the lyrics of Johnny Mercer. This was not the first musical tribute to Mr. Mercer (see *One For My Baby: Johnny Mercer* in the appendix).

Before Broadway. This show began at the TENNESSEE REPERTORY THEATRE, Nashville. There was an open Broadway rehearsal on 2/27/97.

The Broadway Run. ROYALE THEATRE, 4/3/97–7/6/97. 24 previews from 3/11/97. 109 PERFORMANCES. PRESENTED BY Louise Westergaard, Mark Schwartz, Bob Cuillo, Roger Dean, Obie Bailey, Stephen O'Neil, Abraham Salaman; MUSIC: various composers; LYRICS: Johnny Mercer; CONCEIVED BY: Louise Westergaard & Jack Wrangler; DIRECTOR/CHOREOGRAPHER: Wayne Cilento; SETS: David Mitchell; COSTUMES: Ann Hould-Ward; LIGHTING: Ken Billington; SOUND: Peter Fitzgerald; MUSICAL SUPERVISOR: Donald Pippin; MUSICAL DIRECTOR: Bryan Louiselle; VOCAL ARRANGEMENTS: Donald Pippin & Bryan Louiselle; ORCHESTRATIONS: Dick Lieb; ADDITIONAL ORCHESTRATIONS: Jack Cortner & Torrie Zito; DANCE MUSIC ARRANGEMENTS: Jeanine Tesori; PRESS: Susan L. Schulman; CASTING: Julie Hughes & Barry Moss; MERCER VISUALIZATION BY: Jack Wrangler; GENERAL MANAGER: Ralph Roseman; COMPANY MANAGER: Joka Kops; PRODUCTION STAGE MANAGER: Diane DiVita; STAGE MANAGER: Tripp Phillips; ASSISTANT STAGE MANAGER: Jack Gianino & Rachel Swenson. *Cast:* Lesley Ann Warren (1) ☆, The John Pizzarelli Trio [Guitar/Banjo: John Pizzarelli (2) ☆; Piano: Ray Kennedy; Bass: Martin Pizzarelli], Margaret Whiting (3) ☆, Brooks Ashmanskas, Jonathan Dokuchitz, Charles McGowan, Jessica Molaskey, Darcie Roberts, Todd Bailey, Angelo Fraboni, Amy Heggins, Jennifer Lamberts, Nancy Lemenager, Susan Misner, Kevyn Morrow, Timothy Edward Smith. *Standbys*: For Lesley Ann Warren: Jane Summerhays, *Mary Ellen Stuart* (from 4/97); For Margaret Whiting: Denise Lor. *Understudies*: Jeffry Denman, Jody Ripplinger, Bill Szobody, Deborah Yates. *Orchestra*: TRUMPETS: Robert Millikan, Larry Lunetta, Jon Owens; TROMBONES: John Fedchok, Rock Ciccarone, George Gesslein; REEDS: Andrew Sterman, Daniel M. Block, Scott Schachter, Dennis C. Anderson, Robert Eldridge; FRENCH HORNS: Katie Dennis & Javier Gandara; HARP: Nancy Brennand; BASS: Peter Donovan; GUITAR: Robbie Kirshoff; DRUMS: Tony Tedesco; PERCUSSION: Ed Shea; PIANO: Grant Sturiale. *Act I*: *Scene 1* Savannah — The Age of Innocence: "Dream" (m: Johnny Mercer) (Darcie, Jessica, Nancy, Company), "Lazybones" (m: Hoagy Carmichael) (Amy, Kevyn, John, Company), "On Behalf of the Traveling Salesmen" (m: Walter Donaldson) (Brooks & Timothy), "Pardon My Southern Accent" (m: Matt Malneck) (Lesley Ann), "You Must Have Been a Beautiful Baby" (m: Harry Warren) [from the movie *Hard to Get*] (Charles & Darcie), "Have You Got Any Castles, Baby?" (m:

Richard Whiting) [from the movie *Varsity Show*] (Jonathan, Lesley Ann, Company), "Goody Goody" (m: Matt Malneck) (Lesley Ann & Company), "Skylark" (m: Hoagy Carmichael) (Jessica), "The Dixieland Band" (m: Bernie Hanighen) (John & Company); *Scene 2* Magnificent Obsession — The Age of Decadence: "(I Had Myself a) True Love"/"I Wonder What Became of Me" (m: Harold Arlen) [both from *St. Louis Woman*] (Lesley Ann & Darcie), "Jamboree Jones Jive" (m: Johnny Mercer) (John Pizzarelli Trio & Company), "Fools Rush In" (m: Rube Bloom) (John Pizzarelli Trio & Company), "Come Rain or Come Shine" (m: Harold Arlen) [from *St. Louis Woman*] (Brooks), "Out of This World" (m: Harold Arlen) [from the movie of the same name] (Darcie), "I Remember You" (m: Victor Schertzinger) [from the movie *The Fleet's In*] (Jessica), "Blues in the Night" (m: Harold Arlen) [from the movie of the same name] (Lesley Ann), "One for My Baby" (m: Harold Arlen) [from the movie *The Sky's the Limit*] (Margaret); *Scene 3* Rainbow Room: "You Were Never Lovelier" (m: Jerome Kern) [from the movie of the same name] (John), "Satin Doll" (m: Billy Strayhorn & Duke Ellington) (Susan & Men), "I'm Old Fashioned" (m: Jerome Kern) [from the movie *You Were Never Lovelier*] (Darcie & Jonathan), "Dearly Beloved" (m: Jerome Kern) [from the movie *You Were Never Lovelier*] (Jonathan & Darcie), "This Time the Dream's on Me" (m: Harold Arlen) [from the movie *Blues in the Night*] (John, Lesley Ann, Margaret), "Something's Gotta Give" (m: Johnny Mercer) [from the movie *Daddy Long Legs*] (Jessica), "Too Marvelous for Words" (m: Richard Whiting) [from the movie *Ready, Willing and Able*] (Charles & Company). *Act II*: *Scene 1* Hollywood Canteen: "I Thought About You" (m: James Van Heusen) (John), "And the Angels Sing" (m: Ziggy Elman) (Orchestra), "The Fleet's In" (m: Victor Schertzinger) [from the movie of the same name] (Men), "G.I. Jive" (m: Johnny Mercer) (Lesley Ann, Jessica, Nancy, "I'm Doin' it for Defense" (m: Harold Arlen) [from the movie *Star Spangled Rhythm*] (Darcie), "Tangerine" (m: Victor Schertzinger) [from the movie *The Fleet's In*] (Brooks & Company), "Day In, Day Out" (m: Rube Bloom) (Margaret), "Jeepers Creepers" (m: Harry Warren) [from the movie *Going Places*] (John Pizzarelli Trio), "That Old Black Magic" (m: Harold Arlen) [from the movie *Star Spangled Rhythm*] (Lesley Ann), "Laura" (m: David Raksin) [from the movie of the same name] (Jonathan), "You Go Your Way" (m: Johnny Mercer) (Company), "My Shining Hour" (m: Harold Arlen) [from the movie *The Sky's the Limit*] (Margaret & Company); *Scene 2* Academy Awards: "Hooray for Hollywood" (m: Richard Whiting) [from the movie *Hollywood Hotel*] (Brooks, Angelo, Kevyn, Timothy), "(You've Gotta) Ac-cent-u-ate the Positive" (m: Harold Arlen) [from the movie *Here Come the Waves*] (Brooks, Angelo, Kevyn, Timothy, Nancy), "In the Cool, Cool, Cool of the Evening" (m: Hoagy Carmichael) [from the movie *Here Comes the Groom*] (Margaret & John Pizzarelli Trio), "Charade"/"Days of Wine and Roses" (m: Henry Mancini) [from the two movies of the same names] (Jonathan, Jessica, Company), "Moon River" (m: Henry Mancini) [from the movie *Breakfast at Tiffany's*] (Lesley Ann), "On the Atchison, Topeka and the Santa Fe" (m: Harry Warren) [from the movie *The Harvey Girls*] (Company).

Reviews were bad, and it lost money from the start. On 7/1/97 it was announced that it would close on 7/6/97. It received a Tony nomination for choreography.

189. *Dream with Music*

A musical fantasy in which Dinah, who has been writing soap operas until she's sick of them, dreams she is Scheherazade, with 1001 Arabian Nights stories to tell to the Sultan (Robert in her other life, where he is her boss). Michael is an attractive war correspondent (Aladdin in the dream). Dinah's secretary becomes Jasmin.

Before Broadway. Wolcott Gibbs & Franklin P. Adams were first approached to write it but finally turned it down. Joy Hodges replaced June Knight. Lois & Lucille Barnes were known as the Barnes Twins. Dorothy Kilgallen was married to Dick Kollmar. Vera Zorina was married to George Balanchine.

The Broadway Run. MAJESTIC THEATRE, 5/18/44–6/10/44. 28

PERFORMANCES. PRESENTED BY Richard Kollmar; MUSIC: Clay Warnick (based on several composers—Saint-Saens' Violin Concerto in B Minor, Rimsky-Korsakov's *Scheherazade*, Schubert's Ninth Symphony, Beethoven's Seventh Symphony, Weber's *Oberon*, Grieg's Piano Concerto, Beethoven's First Symphony, Borodin's *Prince Igor*, Moussorgsky's *Night on Bald Mountain*, Wagner's *Ride of the Valkyries*, Chopin's Twenty-four Preludes, Gluck's *Ballet Suite*, Schumann's Piano Concerto, Dvorak's *New World Symphony*, Haydn's First Symphony, Tchaikovsky's *Nutcracker Suite*); LYRICS: Edward Eager; BOOK: Sidney Sheldon, Dorothy Kilgallen, Ben Roberts; DIRECTOR: Richard Kollmar; CHOREOGRAPHER: George Balanchine; TAP CHOREOGRAPHY ROUTINES: Henry Le Tang; SETS: Stewart Chaney; COSTUMES: Miles White; SOUND CONSULTANT: Saki Oura; MUSICAL DIRECTOR: Max Meth; ORCHESTRAL ARRANGEMENTS: Russell Bennett, Hans Spialek, Ted Royal, Clay Warnick; VOCAL ARRANGEMENTS: Clay Warnick; PRESS: Reuben Rabinovitch; GENERAL MANAGER: Leo Rose; STAGE MANAGER: George Hunter; ASSISTANT STAGE MANAGER: Frank Milton. **Cast:** IN REALITY: ELLA: Betty Allen (5); MARIAN: Joy Hodges (3) ☆; DINAH: Vera Zorina (1) ☆; WESTERN UNION BOY: Alex Rotov (10); MICHAEL: Ronald Graham (2) ☆; ROBERT: Robert Brink (4). IN THE DREAM: SCHEHERAZADE: Vera Zorina (1) ☆; JASMIN: Joy Hodges (3) ☆; SULTAN: Robert Brink (4); WAZIR: Alex Rotov (10); MISPAH: Marcella Howard; HISPAH: Janie Janvier; RISPAH: Lois Barnes (13); TISPAH: Lucille Barnes (13); FISPAH: Jane Hetherington; KISPAH: Donna Devel; ALADDIN: Ronald Graham (2) ☆; RUG MERCHANT: Ray Cook; PERFUME MERCHANT: Robert Beam; FAKIR: Michael Kozak; CANDY SALESMAN: Bill Jones; MUSICAL INSTRUMENT MERCHANT: John Panter; SNAKE CHARMER: Byron Milligan; SAND DIVINER: Ralph Bunker (7); SINBAD: Leonard Elliott (6); MRS. SINBAD: Betty Allen (5); GENIE: Dave Ballard; GUARDS: Jerry Ross, Larry Evers, Bill Weber, Parker Wilson; THE LITTLE ONE: Dorothy Babb; THE BLONDE ONE: Dee Turnell; 1ST HOT ONE: Sunny Rice; 2ND HOT ONE: Dixie Roberts; THE SLENDER ONE: Mavis Mims; THE TALL ONE: Dolores Milan; THE ONE WITH THE PUG NOSE: Tari Vance; THE TWINS: Lois and Lucille Barnes (13); DAY: Peter Birch (9); NIGHT: Sunny Rice; MRS. PANDA: Dixie Roberts; MR. PANDA: Ralph Bunker (7); LION: Peter Birch (9); RABBIT: Donna Devel; MR. OWL: Byron Milligan; MRS. OWL: Marcella Howard; UNICORN: Bill Jones; MRS. LION: Janie Janvier; PENGUIN: Bill Weber; WOLF: Ray Cook; ERMINE: Lucille Barnes (13); LAMB: Dorothy Babb; I.J.: Robert Beam; MRS. FOX: Jane Hetherington; LEOPARD: Lois Barnes (13); MONKEY: Jerry Ross (12); TIGER: Michael Kozak; MOUSE: Buddy Douglas (8); ALADDIN'S AIDE: Bill Weber; CHINESE MASSEUR: Jerry Ross (12) [end of Dream sequence]; TAP SPECIALISTS: Sunny Rice, Mavis Mims, Dixie Roberts, Dorothy Babb, Tari Vince, Dolores Milan; CORPS DE BALLET: Jacqueline Cezanne, Betty Claire, Dorothy De Molina, Larry Evers, Georgia Hiden, Carmelita Lanza, Margaret Murray, Jerry Ross, Toni Stuart, Dee Turnell, Bill Weber, Parker Wilson; SINGERS: Lois Barnes, Lucille Barnes, Robert Beam, Ray Cook, Donna Devel, Jane Hetherington, Marcella Howard, Janie Janvier, Bill Jones, Michael Kozak, Byron Milligan, John C. Panter; THE CARYATIDS: Mae Francis, Beatrice Griffith, Roseler Jones, Rosemary Mitchell, Gladys Pollard, Bonita Purdue. *Act I: Scene 1* Dinah's apartment; *Scene 2* The palace of Shariar, King of the Indies; *Scene 3* A street in the bazaars of Baghdad; *Scene 4* Sinbad's garden; *Scene 5* A corridor at Sinbad's house; *Scene 6* The Magic Carpet; *Scene 7* In the clouds. *Act II: Scene 1* Aladdin's forest—China; *Scene 2* Aladdin's game preserve; *Scene 3* The corridor at Sinbad's house; *Scene 4* Aladdin's palace; *Scene 5* The corridor at Sinbad's house; *Scene 6* The palace of Shariar; *Scene 7* Dinah's apartment. *Act I:* Scheherazade's Dance (Vera Zorina & Singing Ensemble), "Be Glad You're Alive" (Joy Hodges & Singing Ensemble; Mr. Rotov, Mr. Birch, Dancing Ensemble), "I'm Afraid I'm in Love (with You)" (Mr. Brink), "Baby, Don't Count on Me" (Mr. Graham & Singing Ensemble), "Give, Sinbad, Give" (Mr. Elliott & Singing Ensemble), "I'll Take the Solo" (Miss Allen, Tap Specialty Girls, Barnes Twins, Ballet), "Love at Second Sight" (Joy Hodges & Mr. Brink), "Relax and Enjoy It!" (Vera Zorina, Joy Hodges, Mr. Brink, Miss Allen, Mr. Elliott), "Come with Me" (Mr. Graham & Vera Zorina), "Battle of the Genie" (Mr. Rotov, Mr. Ballard, Mr. Evers, Mr. Ross, Mr. Weber, Mr. Wilson), "Mr. and Mrs. Wrong" (Miss Allen & Mr. Elliott), "Ballet in the Clouds" (Vera Zorina, Mr. Birch, Sunny Rice, Corps de Ballet, Singing Ensemble). *Act II:* "The Lion and the Lamb" (Miss Devel & Ensemble), "Mouse Meets

Girl" (Vera Zorina & Mr. Douglas), "Baby, Don't Count on Me" (reprise) (Sunny Rice), "Love at Second Sight" (reprise) (Joy Hodges), "The Moon Song" (Mr. Graham), "Woman Against the World" (Vera Zorina, Mr. Ross, Barnes Twins, Tap Specialty Girls, Singing Girls), "The Ballet" (Mr. Elliott), "Dinah's Nightmare" (Entire Company).

Opening night was a disaster, with people missing cues, and lighting going wrong. Reviews were terrible, and it lost $240,000. One night the wire supporting Vera Zorina broke as she stepped from the magic carpet, and she crashed to the stage.

190. *Dreamgirls*

The story takes place between 1962 at the Apollo in Harlem, and 1972 in Hollywood, and is loosely based on the story of the all-girl singing group the Supremes (uncredited). The Dreamettes (later called the Dreams, and later still Deena Jones and the Dreams) is a Motown girl group, originally comprising Effie (the lead), Deena, and Lorrell. Effie is dumpy and awkward, but has a tremendous voice. Curtis, their manager (and Effie's former lover) replaces her as the lead with the more glamorous Deena because she doesn't fit the image they want to present. In real life Florence Ballard was replaced by Diana Ross for much the same reasons. Eventually Effie is fired from the group altogether, and replaced by Michelle. Effie overcomes the rejection, and becomes famous in her own right. Unfortunately, Miss Ballard faded into obscurity and died aged 32.

Before Broadway. Originally called *One Night Only*, when it was directed by Tom Eyen as a workshop at the New York Shakespeare Festival. At that point Nell Carter was playing Effie. Miss Carter dropped out to pursue a TV career, and Tom Eyen & Henry Krieger (the composer) auditioned the show for Michael Bennett in the hopes of getting a Bennett-sponsored workshop at the latter's new theatre and rehearsal complex, 890 Studios. There were three subsequent workshops at 890 Studios, and several script revisions. At one point Effie was a nurse employed by a wise-cracking senior citizen played by Estelle Getty. Michael Bennett took over direction from Tom Eyen, and took the show through its difficult Boston tryout (where it got raves) to success on the Broadway stage. Before Broadway the name of the show was changed to *Big Dreams*, then *Dream Girls*, and finally *Dreamgirls*.

The Broadway Run. IMPERIAL THEATRE, 12/20/81–8/11/85. 1,522 PERFORMANCES. PRESENTED BY Michael Bennett, Bob Avian, Geffen Records (David Geffen) & The Shubert Organization; MUSIC: Henry Krieger; LYRICS/BOOK: Tom Eyen; DIRECTOR: Michael Bennett; CHOREOGRAPHERS: Michael Bennett & Michael Peters; SETS: Robin Wagner; COSTUMES: Theoni V. Aldredge; ASSISTANT COSTUMES: Suzy Benzinger; LIGHTING: Tharon Musser; SOUND: Otts Munderloh; MUSICAL SUPERVISOR/ORCHESTRATIONS: Harold Wheeler; MUSICAL DIRECTOR: Yolanda Segovia, *Paul Gemignani* (added by 82–83); VOCAL ARRANGEMENTS: Cleavant Derricks; CAST RECORDING on Geffen; PRESS: Merle Debuskey & Diane Judge; CASTING: Olaiya & Johnson—Liff Associates; GENERAL MANAGEMENT: Marvin A. Krauss Associates; PRODUCTION STAGE MANAGER: Jeff Hamlin; STAGE MANAGER: Zane Weiner; ASSISTANT STAGE MANAGER: Jacqueline Yancey (81–82), *Frank Di Filia & Jake Bell*. **Cast:** THE STEPP SISTERS: Deborah Burrell (*Terry Burrell* from 82–83), Vanessa Bell (*Graciela Simpson* from 83–84), Tenita Jordan (*Rhetta Hughes* from 82–83; *Gina Taylor* from 83–84), Brenda Pressley; CHARLENE: Cheryl Alexander, *Khandi Alexander* (from 83–84), *Adriane Lenox* (from 84–85); JOANNE: Linda Lloyd, *Ethel Beatty* (from 82–83), *Johnnie Teamer* (from 84–85); MARTY: Vondie Curtis-Hall; CURTIS TAYLOR JR.: Ben Harney, *Vondie Curtis-Hall* (during Mr. Harney's vacation, 82–83), *Weyman Thompson* (from 6/5/84), *Ben Harney* (from 8/84); DEENA JONES: Sheryl Lee Ralph ☆, *Linda Leilani Brown* (during Miss Ralph's vacation, 11/83, and again permanently from 6/5/84), *Deborah Burrell* (from 84–85); THE MC: Larry Stewart, *Leon Summers Jr.* (from 83–84); TINY JOE DIXON: Joe Lynn; LORRELL ROBINSON: Loretta Devine ☆, *Cheryl Alexander* (for one week in lieu of Miss Devine, and again, during vacation, 82–83), *Adriane Lenox* (from 83–84), *Teresa Burrell* (from 6/5/84),

Loretta Devine (from 10/9/84); C.C. WHITE: Obba Babatunde ☆, *Tony Franklin* (from 1/84), *Wellington Perkins* (from 83–84), *Lawrence Clayton* (from 9/84); EFFIE MELODY WHITE: Jennifer Holliday ☆, *Sheila Ellis* (during Miss Holliday's illness, 81–82), *Vanessa Townsell* (from 12/6/82), *Julia McGirt* (from 9/83), *Roz Ryan* (from 6/5/84); LITTLE ALBERT & THE TRU-TONES: Wellington Perkins, Charles Bernard, Jamie Patterson, Charles Randolph-Wright, Weyman Thompson (*Eric Riley* from 82–83); JAMES THUNDER EARLY: Cleavant Derricks ☆, *Hinton Battle* (during Mr. Derricks' vacation, 82–83, and permanently from 7/25/83), *Clinton Derricks-Carroll* (from 83), *Cleavant Derricks* (from 11/83), *David Alan Grier* (from 83–84), *Cleavant Derricks* (from 84–85); EDNA BURKE: Sheila Ellis, *Julia McGirt* (from 82–83), *Allison Williams* (from 83–84); THE JAMES EARLY BAND: Charles Bernard, Jamie Patterson, Wellington Perkins, Scott Plank (*Hal Miller* from 82–83 & gone by 83–84), Charles Randolph-Wright, Weyman Thompson (*Eric Riley* from 82–83), *Frank Mastrocola* (by 82–83), *Richie Abanes* (by 83–84), *Barry Bruce* (by 83–84), *Bobby Daye* (by 83–84), *Sean Walker* (by 83–84), *Gordon Owens* (by 84–85), *Christopher Gregory* (by 84–85), *Thomas Scott Gordon* (by 84–85); WAYNE: Tony Franklin, *Wellington Perkins* (from 83–84), *Eric Riley* (from 83–84); DAVE AND THE SWEETHEARTS: Paul Binotto (relieved by *Richard Poole* for 82–83 vacation; *Ray Benson* took over in 84–85), Candy Darling, Stephanie Eley (*Carol Logen* from 81–82; *Nina Hennessey* from 83–84); FRANK, PRESS AGENT: David Thome, *Buddy Vest* (from 82–83); MICHELLE MORRIS: Deborah Burrell, *Teresa Burrell* (from 3/83), *Ethel Beatty* (during Terry Burrell's absence, 3/84–4/84), *Brenda Pressley* (from 6/5/84), *Teresa Burrell* (from 10/84); JERRY, NIGHTCLUB OWNER: Joe Lynn; THE FIVE TUXEDOS: Charles Bernard, Jamie Patterson, Charles Randolph-Wright, Larry Stewart, Weyman Thompson (*Eric Riley* from 82–83); LES STYLE: Cheryl Alexander (*Khandi Alexander* from 83–84), Tenita Jordan (*Rhetta Hughes* from 82–83; *Mary Denise Bentley* by 83–84), Linda Lloyd (*Ethel Beatty* from 82–83; *Allison Williams* from 83–84), Brenda Pressley; FILM EXECUTIVES: Paul Binotto (relieved during 82–83 vacation by *Richard Poole*; *Ray Benson* took over in 84–85), Scott Plank (*Hal Miller* from 82–83), Weyman Thompson (*Eric Riley* from 82–83); MR. MORGAN: Larry Stewart, *Leon Summers Jr.* (from 83–84); ENSEMBLE (ANNOUNCERS, FANS, REPORTERS, STAGEHANDS, PARTY GUESTS, PHOTOGRAPHERS, ETC): Cheryl Alexander (*Khandi Alexander* by 83–84; *Adriane Lenox* by 84–85), Phylicia Ayers-Allen (*Mary Denise Bentley* from 81–82), Vanessa Bell (*Graciela Simpson* from 83–84), Charles Bernard (became a swing by 83–84 & was gone by 84–85), Paul Binotto (relieved during 82–83 vacation by *Richard Poole*; he was gone by 84–85), Candy Darling, Ronald Dunham, Stephanie Eley (*Carol Logen* from 81–82; *Nina Hennessey* from 83–84), Sheila Ellis (*Julia McGirt* from 82–83 & gone by 83–84), Tenita Jordan (*Rhetta Hughes* from 82–83; *Gina Taylor* from 83–84), Linda Lloyd (*Ethel Beatty* from 82–83; *Johnnie Teamer* by 84–85), Joe Lynn, Frank Mastrocola (gone by 83–84), Jamie Patterson (gone by 83–84), Wellington Perkins (gone by 83–84), Scott Plank (*Hal Miller* from 82–83), Brenda Pressley, David Thome (*Buddy Vest* from 82–83), Charles Randolph-Wright (gone by 83–84), Larry Stewart (*Leon Summers Jr.* from 83–84), Weyman Thompson (*Eric Riley* from 82–83), *Richie Abanes* (new by 83–84 and gone by 84–85), *Barry Bruce* (new by 83–84), *Bobby Daye* (new by 83–84 and gone by 84–85), *Christopher Gregory* (new by 83–84), *Sean Walker* (new by 83–84 & gone by 84–85), *Abe Clark* (new by 84–85), *Thomas Scott Gordon* (new by 84–85), *Gordon Owens* (new by 84–85), *Kecia Lewis* (new by 84–85). **Understudies**: Deena: Phylicia Ayers-Allen, *Ethel Beatty* (82–84), *Terry Burrell* (82–83), *Brenda Pressley* (83–85), *Johnnie Teamer* (84–85); Effie: Sheila Ellis, *Julia McGirt* (82–83), *Brenda Pressley* (82–85), *Roz Ryan* (83–84), *Kecia Lewis* (84–85); Lorrell: Cheryl Alexander (81–83), *Rhetta Hughes* (82–83), *Terry Burrell* (83–85), *Adriane Lenox* (84–85); Michelle: Linda Lloyd (81–82), *Ethel Beatty* (82–84), *Brenda Pressley* (82–85), *Johnnie Teamer* (84–85); Curtis: Vondie Curtis-Hall (81–85), *Tony Franklin* (83–84); *Larry Stewart* (84–85); Early: Larry Stewart (81–83, 84–85), *Tony Franklin* (83–84), *Phillip Gilmore* (84–85); C.C.: Tony Franklin (81–83), *Wellington Perkins* (83–85), *Gordon Owens* (84–85); Marty: Milton Craig Nealy (81–84), *Leon Summers Jr.* (84–85), *Larry Stewart* (84–85); Jerry: Milton Craig Nealy (81–83), *Frank Mastrocola* (82–83), *Hal Miller* (83–85); Wayne: Weyman Thompson (81–82), *Eric Riley* (82–83, 84–85), *Charles Bernard* (84–85), *Gordon Owens* (84–85); Frank: Scott Plank (81–82), *Hal Miller* (82–85), *Charles Bernard, Frank Di Filia* (84–85); mc: *Milton Craig Nealy*

(82–84), *Wellington Perkins* (82–83), *Abe Clark* (84–85); Joe: *Charles Bernard* (82–83, 84–85); Morgan: *Milton Craig Neely* (83–84), *Abe Clark* (84–85); Dave: *Hal Miller* (83–85). **Swings**: Brenda Braxton (81–85), Milton Craig Nealy (81–82), *Allison Williams* (83–85), *Charles Bernard* (83–85), *Phillip Gilmore* (84–85). **Rhythm Section**: KEYBOARDS: Myles Chase; DRUMS: Brian Brake; BASS: Tinker Barfield; GUITARS: Andy Schwartz & Peter Strode. **Act I**: The early 1960s: **Scene 1** The Apollo Theatre: "I'm Looking for Something" (Stepp Sisters), "Goin' Downtown" (Little Albert & Tru-Tones), "Takin' the Long Way Home" (Tiny Joe), "Move" ("You're Steppin' on My Heart") (Dreamettes), "Fake Your Way to the Top" (Jimmy Early, Early Band, Dreamettes), "Cadillac Car" (Curtis, Jimmy, C.C., Marty, Company); **Scene 2** On the road: "Cadillac Car" (reprise) (Company); **Scene 3** A recording studio: "Cadillac Car" (reprise) (Company); **Scene 4** Limbo: "Cadillac Car" (reprise) (Dave & Sweethearts), "Steppin' to the Bad Side" (Curtis, C.C., Jimmy, Wayne, Dreamettes, Company); **Scene 5** A hotel in St. Louis: "Party, Party" (Company); **Scene 6** Miami: "I Want You Baby" (Jimmy & Dreamettes); **Scene 7** Dressing room in the Atlantic Hotel: "Family" (C.C., Curtis, Jimmy, Deena, Lorrell); **Scene 8** Cleveland: "Dreamgirls" (Dreams), "Press Conference" (Company), "Only the Beginning" (Curtis, Deena, Effie); **Scene 9** A TV studio: "Heavy" (Dreams); **Scene 10** San Francisco: "Heavy" (reprise) (Dreams & Curtis); **Scene 11** Las Vegas (backstage): "It's All Over" (Curtis, Effie, Deena, Lorrell, C.C., Michelle, Jimmy), "And I Am Telling You I'm Not Going" (Effie) (Effie); **Scene 12** Las Vegas (on stage), "Love Love You Baby" (Dreams). **Act II**: The early 1970s: **Scene 1** Las Vegas Hilton: "Dreams Medley" (Deena & the Dreams, Company) [number cut by 83–84]; **Scene 2** Chicago nightclub: "I Am Changing" (Effie); **Scene 3** *Vogue* Magazine photo call: "One More Picture, Please" (Company), "When I First Saw You" (Curtis & Deena); **Scene 4** National Democratic fundraiser: "Got to Be Good Times" (Five Tuxedos), "Ain't No Party" (Lorrell & Jimmy), "I Meant You No Harm" (Jimmy), "Quintette" (Deena, Lorrell, C.C., Michelle, Jimmy), "The Rap" (Jimmy, C.C., Marty, Curtis, Frank, Lorrell, Company); **Scene 5** A Chicago recording studio: "I Miss You, Old Friend" (Effie, Marty, C.C., Les Style), "One Night Only" (Effie); **Scene 6** Los Angeles: "One Night Only" (reprise) (Deena & the Dreams, Company); **Scene 7** Chicago: "I'm Somebody" (Deena & the Dreams), "Faith in Myself" (Effie); **Scene 8** New York: "Hard to Say Goodbye, My Love" (Deena & the Dreams), "Dreamgirls" (reprise) (Deena & the Dreams, Effie).

Broadway reviews were very divided. Jennifer Holliday, then only 21, got raves, as did the sets. The show cost $3.5 million, easily the most expensive Broadway show seen to that date. It won Tonys for book, choreography, and lighting, and for Cleavant Derricks, Ben Harney, and Jennifer Holliday. It was also nominated for musical, score, direction of a musical, sets, costumes, and for Obba Babatunde and Sheryl Lee Ralph. On 6/20/83 certain changes that had been made to the Los Angeles production were incorporated into the Broadway production — the first number of Act II was re-done, and seven minutes of Act II were cut.

After Broadway. LOS ANGELES PRODUCTION. Actually called a tour, it opened on 3/20/83, at the Shubert Theatre, Los Angeles. **Cast**: DEENA: Linda Leilani Brown; MC/MORGAN: Ron Richardson; JOE/NIGHTCLUB OWNER: Roy L. Jones; EFFIE: Jennifer Holliday, *Lillias White* (from 12/6/83); LORRELL: Arnetia Walker; CURTIS: Larry Riley; MARTY: Weyman Thompson; JOANNE: Susan Beaubian; CHARLENE: Betty K. Bynum; C.C.: Lawrence Clayton; EARLY: Clinton Derricks-Carroll; EDNA: Edwina Lewis; MICHELLE: Deborah Burrell; ALSO WITH: Johnnie Teamer, Abe Clark, Gordon J. Owens, Thomas Scott Gordon. **Understudies**: Effie: Lillias White; Early: Ron Richardson.

191. *Dreamgirls (Broadway revival)*

Before Broadway. This Broadway revival was part of a new international touring company which had opened on 10/8/85, at the Performing Arts Center, Providence, Rhode Island. "Dreams Medley" was replaced with a reprise of "Dreamgirls" (Dreams & Company). In 86–87, in Tokyo, top tickets were $93. The **original touring cast** included: STEPP SISTERS: Rhetta Hughes, Johnnie Teamer (*R. LaChanze Sapp*), Lauren Velez (*Loraine Velez*), LueCinda Ramseur (*Susan Beaubian*);

CHARLENE: Yvette Louise Cason; JOANNE: Susan Beaubian, *Lynda McConnell*; MARTY: Larry Stewart, *Roy L. Jones*; CURTIS: Weyman Thompson, *Obba Babatunde, Weyman Thompson*; DEENA: Deborah Burrell, *Alisa Gyse*; MC: Vernon Spencer; TINY JOE: Roy L. Jones, *Nat Morris, Leonard Piggee*; LORRELL: Arnetia Walker; C.C.: Lawrence Clayton, *Kevyn Morrow*; EFFIE: Lillias White, Sharon Brown (alternate); LITTLE ALBERT & THE TRU-TONES: Bobby Daye, Robert Clater, Matthew Dickens, Germaine Edwards, Robert Fowler; EARLY: Herbert L. Rawlings Jr.; EDNA: Fuschia Walker; JAMES EARLY BAND: Robert Clater, Bobby Daye, Matthew Dickens, Germaine Edwards, Robert Fowler, David Thome; WAYNE: Milton Craig Nealy; DAVE & THE SWEETHEARTS: Stephen Bourneuf, Shirley Tripp, Loraine Velez; FRANK: Tim Cassidy; DWIGHT: David Thome; TV STAGE MANAGER: Stephen Bourneuf; MICHELLE: LueCinda Ramseur, *Susan Beaubian*; JERRY: Leonard Piggee; CARL: Robert Fowler; THE FIVE TUXEDOS: Robert Clater, Bobby Daye, Matthew Dickens, Germaine Edwards, Robert Fowler; LES STYLE: Yvette Louise Cason, Rhetta Hughes, Lynda McConnell, R. LaChanze Sapp; FILM EXECUTIVES: Matthew Dickens, Robert Fowler, David Thome; MORGAN: Vernon Spencer; GUARD: Leonard Piggee.

The Broadway Run. AMBASSADOR THEATRE, 6/28/87–11/29/87. 7 previews. 177 PERFORMANCES. The Michael Bennett production, PRESENTED BY Marvin A. Krauss & Irving Siders; MUSIC: Henry Krieger; LYRICS/BOOK: Tom Eyen; DIRECTOR: Michael Bennett; CHOREOGRAPHERS: Michael Bennett & Michael Peters; SETS: Robin Wagner; COSTUMES: Theoni V. Aldredge; LIGHTING: Tharon Musser; SOUND: Otts Munderloh; MUSICAL SUPERVISOR/ORCHESTRATIONS: Harold Wheeler; MUSICAL DIRECTOR: Marc Falcone, *Yolanda Segovia*; VOCAL ARRANGEMENTS: Cleavant Derricks; PRESS: The Fred Nathan Company; CASTING: Johnson — Liff; PRODUCTION SUPERVISOR: Bob Avian; GENERAL MANAGEMENT: Marvin A. Krauss Associates; COMPANY MANAGER: Allan Williams; PRODUCTION STAGE MANAGER: Peter B. Mumford; STAGE MANAGER: Thomas A. Bartlett & Robert B. Gould. *Cast:* THE STEPP SISTERS: Susan Beaubian, Rhetta Hughes, R. LaChanze Sapp, Loraine Velez; CHARLENE: Yvette Louise Cason; JOANNE: Lynda McConnell; MARTY: Roy L. Jones; CURTIS TAYLOR JR.: Weyman Thompson; DEENA JONES: Alisa Gyse; THE MC: Vernon Spencer; TINY JOE DIXON: Leonard Piggee; LORRELL ROBINSON: Arnetia Walker; C.C. WHITE: Kevyn Morrow; EFFIE MELODY WHITE: Lillias White, *Sharon Brown* (from 10/27/87); LITTLE ALBERT AND THE TRU-TONES: Bobby Daye, Robert Clater (*Harold Perrineau*), Matthew Dickens, Germaine Edwards, Robert Fowler; JAMES THUNDER EARLY: Herbert L. Rawlings Jr.; EDNA BURKE: Fuschia Walker; JAMES EARLY BAND: Robert Clater (*Harold Perrineau*), Bobby Daye, Matthew Dickens, Germaine Edwards, Robert Fowler, David Thome (*Stephen Terrell*); WAYNE: Milton Craig Nealy; DAVE & THE SWEETHEARTS: Stephen Bourneuf, Shirley Tripp, Loraine Velez; FRANK, A PRESS AGENT: Tim Cassidy; DWIGHT, A TV DIRECTOR: David Thome, *Stephen Terrell*; TV STAGE MANAGER: Stephen Bourneuf; MICHELLE MORRIS: Susan Beaubian; JERRY, A NIGHTCLUB OWNER: Leonard Piggee; CARL, A PIANO PLAYER: Robert Fowler; THE FIVE TUXEDOS: Robert Clater (*Harold Perrineau*), Bobby Daye, Matthew Dickens, Germaine Edwards, Robert Fowler; LES STYLE: Yvette Louise Cason, Rhetta Hughes, Lynda McConnell, R. LaChanze Sapp; FILM EXECUTIVES: Matthew Dickens, Robert Fowler, David Thome (*Stephen Terrell*); MR. MORGAN: Vernon Spencer; SECURITY GUARD: Leonard Piggee; ANNOUNCERS/REPORTERS/STAGE HANDS/PARTY GUESTS/PHOTOGRAPHERS, ETC: Stephen Bourneuf, Yvette Louise Cason, Tim Cassidy, Robert Clater (*Harold Perrineau*), Bobby Daye, Matthew Dickens, Germaine Edwards, Robert Fowler, Rhetta Hughes, Lynda McConnell, Milton Craig Nealy, Leonard Piggee, R. LaChanze Sapp, Vernon Spencer, David Thome (*Stephen Terrell*), Shirley Tripp, Fuschia Walker. *Understudies*: Effie: Yvette Louise Cason, Arnetia Walker, Fuschia Walker; Deena: Susan Beaubian, Lynda McConnell, R. LaChanze Sapp; Lorrell: Susan Beaubian, Brenda Braxton, Rhetta Hughes; Michelle: Lynda McConnell, R. LaChanze Sapp; Curtis: Milton Craig Nealy; Early/mc: Phillip Gilmore & Milton Craig Nealy; C.C.: Bobby Daye & Matthew Dickens; Marty: Milton Craig Nealy, Leonard Piggee, Vernon Spencer; Wayne/Dwight: Robert Clater (*Harold Perrineau*) & Phillip Gilmore; Frank: David Thome (*Stephen Terrell*) & Darryl Eric Tribble; Jerry: Milton Craig Nealy & Vernon Spencer; Dave: Tim Cassidy; Morgan: Phillip Gilmore; Charlene/Joanne/Edna/Sweethearts: Brenda Braxton & Gra-

ciela Simpson; Tiny Joe/Carl/Security Guard: Phillip Gilmore & Darryl Eric Tribble; Stage Manager: Phillip Gilmore, *Tim Cassidy*. **Swings**: Brenda Braxton, Graciela Simpson, Phillip Gilmore, Darryl Eric Tribble. *Musicians*: PIANO I: Myles Chase; PIANO II: David Rhodes, *Thomas W. Coppola*; BASS: Jeff Myers; DRUMS: Steve Singer; GUITAR: Jeff Sigman; PERCUSSION: Gary Seligson; REED I: Lee Secard, *Vincent Della Rocca*; REED II: Glen Berger, *Dennis Anderson*; REED III: Patience Higgins; TRUMPET I: Scott De Ogburn; TRUMPET II: Grant Manhart, *Glenn Drewes*; TRUMPET III: Jeff Conrad; TROMBONE I: Kevin Haines; TROMBONE II: John Hahn.

On Broadway it got better reviews that the first production had. Michael Bennett died (7/2/87, in Tucson) while the show was playing. The show received a Tony nomination for revival.

After Broadway. TOURING REVIVAL. Opened on 9/30/97, at Providence, Rhode Island, to divided reviews. PRESENTED BY Irving Siders & Marvin Krauss, in association with Mitch Leigh, Albert Nocciolino & James M. Nederlander; DIRECTOR/CHOREOGRAPHER: Tony Stevens; SETS: Robin Wagner; COSTUMES: Theoni V. Aldridge; SOUND: Otts Munderloh; MUSICAL SUPERVISOR: Keith Levenson. Book, music and lyrics were all unchanged. Jennifer Holliday was announced for the role of Effie, but couldn't come to terms. *Cast*: EFFIE: Roz White, *B.J. Crosby* (from 1/13/98); DEENA: La Tanya Hall; EARLY: Kevin-Anthony; C.C.: Gary E. Vincent; CURTIS: Brian Everat Chandler; MARTY: Darrin Lamont Byrd; LORRELL: Tonya Dixon; MICHELLE: Kimberly JaJuan; ALSO WITH: Ronald Cadet Bastine, Heidi Blickenstaff, Teri Furr. In 12/97 Tony Stevens left to do a *Dreamgirls* in Germany, and the producers brought in Robert Clater to carry on with direction and choreography. During the tour Roz White was replaced in Baltimore because she apparently had difficulty getting through the show's main number — "And I Am Telling You I'm Not Going." From the outset this tour had had Broadway hopes for 4/98, but there was no theatre available, and plans were put back to 10/98, and then to 1999, then became dormant. The tour closed as planned, in Wallingford, Conn., 5/3/98.

THE MOVIE. It was planned in 1998, by Warner Bros. Joel Schumacher was to have directed, and David Geffen to produce, at a cost of $35 million, but it never happened. However, by 1/05 it was announced that Bill Condon had written the first draft of a screenplay, and it was intended to go into production in the late summer or early fall of 2005, with Laurence Mark, David Geffen and Warner Bros producing.

FORD CENTER FOR THE PERFORMING ARTS, 9/24/01. This was a one-night 20th-Anniversary Benefit for the Actors' Fund of America (who produced), a choreographed concert staging, but not in costume, and some actors held scripts. Audra McDonald held hers for a while, then threw it away. ARTISTIC PRODUCER/MUSICAL DIRECTOR: Seth Rudetsky; DIRECTORS/CHOREOGRAPHERS: Brenda Braxton & Danny Herman; SET CONSULTANT: Michael Brown; LIGHTING: Paul Gallo; SOUND: Peter Fitzgerald. Nonesuch Records recorded it, and released it as a two-disk set on 11/20/01. The benefit raised $1,090,100. *Cast*: LORRELL: Heather Headley; DEENA: Audra McDonald; EFFIE: Audra McDonald, Heather Headley, Lillias White; C.C.: Darius de Haas; CURTIS: Norm Lewis; EARLY: Billy Porter; MARTY: James Stovall; MICHELLE: Tamara Tunie; TINY JOE: Adrian Bailey; DWIGHT: John Bolton; DAVE: Paul Castree; WAYNE: Bobby Daye; CHARLENE: Aisha de Haas; FILM EXECUTIVES: Malcolm Gets, Patrick Wilson, Brad Oscar (Adam Pascal was going to play a film executive, but it didn't happen); ANNOUNCER: E. Lynn Harris; JOANNE: Adriane Lenox; JERRY: Brian Stokes Mitchell; PHOTOGRAPHER: Orfeh; MORGAN/MC: Lee Summers; FRANK: Eric Woodall; VARIOUS ROLES: Andre Garner; SWEETHEARTS: Emily Skinner & Alice Ripley; ENSEMBLE: Jason Opsahl.

PLANNED BROADWAY REVIVAL. Scott Sanders saw the 2001 benefit at the Ford Center for the Performing Arts and became interested in reviving the show on Broadway. In 2003 his company, Creative Battery, acquired the rights, and plans for a spring 2004 Broadway production started. It never happened.

THREE-CITY TOUR ON THE WEST COAST. Opened at San Jose, California, 1/9/04–1/25/04 (rehearsals from 12/15/03); then to Sacramento, 1/28/04–2/8/04; then to Seattle, 2/10/04–2/29/04. PRESENTED BY the California Musical Theatre of Sacramento, the American Musical Theatre of San Jose, and the 5th Avenue Theatre of Seattle; DIRECTOR: Mark S. Hoebee; CHOREOGRAPHER: Brenda Braxton; Robin Wagner's sets and

Theoni V. Aldredge's costumes were used; LIGHTING: Tom Sturge. *Cast*: EFFIE: Frenchie Davis; MARTY: Regi Davis; C.C.: Andre Garner; MICHELLE: Rosena M. Hill; CURTIS: David Jennings; LORRELL: Ramona Keller; WAYNE: Christopher L. Morgan; DEENA: Angela Robinson; EARLY: Harrison White.

2004 REVIVAL. PRESENTED BY the Pittsburgh Civic Light Orchestra, 8/10/04–8/22/04. DIRECTOR: Robert Clater; CHOREOGRAPHER: Lesia Kaye; MUSICAL DIRECTOR: Craig Barna. *Cast*: EFFIE: Frenchie Davis; CURTIS: Norm Lewis; DEENA: Vanita Harbour; LORRELL: Montego Glover; EARLY: Billy Porter; C.C.: Ron Kellum; MARTY: Michael Demby-Cain; MICHELLE: Manoly Farrell.

Drood see 479

192. *The Duchess Misbehaves*

Woonsocket, a timid little sign painter in a department store, is hit on the head by some thieves who are stealing Goya's painting of the (nude) Duchess of Alba, and dreams he is Francisco Goya pursuing the Duchess in the 18th century. He paints the duchess in the nude, and is pursued vengefully by the Duchess's husband. The duchess has a mole on her thigh, and the artist tries desperately to find another woman who has such a mole, who can pass as the model. The story was built around the incident of Goya painting a nude Duchess of Alba. Other than this fact, there is nothing historically accurate about this "frolicsome musical comedy," aside from the use of a few 18th-century names.

Before Broadway. On 1/31/46, only a few weeks before opening, Jackie Gleason sprained his ankle on stage (some say deliberately), and missed two tryout performances. He returned on 2/1/46. On 2/11/46 he quit the show, and two nights later, Joey Faye opened for him. Paula Laurence replaced Luella Gear. George Tapps replaced John Wray as choreographer.

The Broadway Run. ADELPHI THEATRE, 2/13/46–2/16/46. 5 PERFORMANCES. PRESENTED BY A.P. Waxman; MUSIC: Dr. Frank Black; LYRICS/BOOK: Gladys Shelley; ADDITIONAL DIALOGUE: Joe Bigelow; DIRECTOR: Martin Manulis; GENERAL STAGE DIRECTOR: Frank W. Shea; CHOREOGRAPHER: George Tapps; SETS: A. A. Ostrander; COSTUMES: Willa Kim; LIGHTING: Carlton Winckler; MUSICAL DIRECTOR: Charles Sanford; ORCHESTRATIONS: Don Walker; VOCAL ARRANGEMENTS: Clay Warnick; PRODUCTION SUPERVISOR: Chet O'Brien; PRESS: Michael Goldreyer; GENERAL MANAGER: Ben A. Boyar; COMPANY MANAGER: Joseph N. Grossman; STAGE MANAGER: Alfred Morse. *Cast:* IN CARLTON'S DEPARTMENT STORE: WOMAN: Grace Hayle; FRANCHOT: Buddy Ferraro; 1ST SISTER: Elena Boyd; 2ND SISTER: Mildred Boyd; 3RD SISTER: Edith Boyd; BUTTERFLY: Penny Edwards; PAUL: Larry Douglas; FITZGERALD: James MacColl; WOONSOCKET: Joey Faye (4); 1ST GIRL: Gail Adams; 2ND GIRL: Ethel Madsen; MISS KIESTER: Paula Laurence (3); CRYSTAL SHALIMAR: Audrey Christie (1); REPORTER: Al Downing; NEVILLE GOLDGLITTER: Philip Tonge. IN SPAIN: PABLO: Larry Douglas; AMBER: Grace Hayle; GOYA: Joey Faye (4); MODEL: Joanne Jaap; ROBERTO: James MacColl; DUCHESS OF ALBA: Audrey Christie (1); MARIPOSA: Penny Edwards; BARBER: Paul Marten; MANICURIST: Joanne Jaap; TAILOR: Ken Martin; ASSISTANT TAILOR: Bernie Williams; MESSENGER: Buddy Ferraro; 1ST STUDENT: Victor Clarke; 2ND STUDENT: Jess Randolph; DUKE OF ALBA: Philip Tonge; LADIES-IN-WAITING: The Boyd Triplets; QUEEN OF SPAIN: Paula Laurence (3); A MODEL: Norma Kohane; MATADOR: George Tapps (2); JOSE: Al Downing; DANCER: Mata Monteria; THE WOMAN: Jean Handzlik; HER MAN: George Tapps; MAGICIAN: Ken Martin; ASSISTANT MAGICIAN: Buddy Ferraro [end of "In Spain" sequence]; MODELS: Joanne Jaap, Norma Kohane, Ann Miller, Lillian Moore; SINGING GIRLS: Gail Adams, Adele Lulince, Ethel Madsen, Jane Riehl; SINGING BOYS: Victor Clark, Vincent Henry, Jerry O'Rourke, Jess Randolph; DANCING GIRLS: Jane Atwood, Trudy Cirrito, Theo Denis, Helen Devlin, Gertrude Gibbons, Eleanore Gregory, Freddie Grey, Janet Joy, Beverly Joyce, Mary Jane Kersey, Anna Konstance, Dorothy Matthews, Marilyn Pendry; DANCING BOYS: Dan Karry, Walter Koremin, Paul Marten, Anthony Starman, Merritt Thompson, Bernie Williams. *Act I*: *Scene 1* The Art Section of Carlton's Department Store:

"Art" (Fitzgerald) (danced by George Tapps & Ensemble); *Scene 2* Goya's studio in Spain: "(You Are) My Only Romance" (Pablo, Singing Girls, Dancing Girls), "Broad Minded" (Goya & Showgirls), "I Hate Myself in the Morning" (Duchess & Students), "Men" (Queen & Ladies in Waiting); *Scene 3* Street in Madrid: "Couldn't Be More in Love" (Pablo & Mariposa); *Scene 4* Outside the Fiesta grounds: "Dance of the Matador" (dance number to the music of Manuel de Falla's "Ritual Fire Dance") (George Tapps), "Ole, Ole" (Goya & Ensemble), "Katie Did in Madrid" (Duchess, Singers, Dancing Boys & Girls). *Act II*: *Scene 1* Public square, Madrid: "Morning in Madrid" (Entire Ensemble); "Lost": THE WOMAN: Jean Handzlik; HER MAN: George Tapps; "Honeymoon is Over" (Pablo, Mariposa, Dancers); *Scene 2* Side street: "Nuts" (Duchess), "Fair Weather Friends" (Pablo & Mariposa); *Scene 3* Goya's studio: "The Nightmare" (Goya, Queen, Duchess, Dancers, Singers); *Scene 4* Carlton's Department Store: "Art" (reprise) (Entire Company).

It was mercilessly panned by the critics, and lost $230,000.

193. *Dude*

Also called *Dude—the Highway Life*. From the same crew who brought us *Hair*. An unruly rock musical in which Billy Hill (known as Dude) is a man searching the universe for meaning (rather like the audience searched this musical). Dude represents Everyman, and is tempted by the forces of evil. God is represented by # 33. He and Bread, Suzie Moon, Mother Earth and the Shubert Angels, compete with the forces of evil—Zero (the Devil, perhaps?), Nero, Esso, Extra, and Sissy, for Dude's soul. Good finally wins, and Dude is given back his innocence.

Before Broadway. Two weeks into rehearsals it was found that 23-year old Kevin Geer, who was playing the lead, couldn't sing, and he was replaced by 11-year old Ralph Carter. However, some lyrics Ralph had to sing didn't seem right coming from a child, so the role of Dude was split into two—the younger Dude (played by Ralph) and the older Dude (played by Nat Morris). Broadway previews were halted for three days while choreographer Louis Falco was replaced by Tom O'Horgan, and director Rocco Bufano by Tom O'Horgan [sic]. Michael Dunn, who had been the third-billed co-star (playing the 1,000 year old man), had his part cut, and the nudity went as well. Several numbers were cut: "Brooks Atkinson/"New York Lies" (Rags & Shubert Angels), "You Should Be" (# 33), "If it Doesn't Belong to You" (# 33), "The Lone Ranger" (# 33 & Zero), "Heaven's Angels" (Theatre Wings), "Boo on You" (Shubert Angels," "Eieio-Eieio" (Eieio), "Sad" (Zero), "Children/ Children" (Rags & Shubert Angels), and "Birds of the Air" (Rags & Shubert Angels). Late in previews the producers threatened to close unless Gerry Ragni made it more comprehensible. He never did. The Broadway Theatre was totally reconstructed inside and out, as theatre-in-the-round, and the actors roamed to every corner and flew overhead. Audience seats were allocated by different sections: the best seats, at $7, were in "The Foot Hills." Other sections were: "Trees," "Mountains," and "Valleys."

The Broadway Run. BROADWAY THEATRE, 10/9/72–10/21/72. 16 previews from 9/11/72. 16 PERFORMANCES. PRESENTED BY Adela & Peter Holzer; MUSIC: Galt MacDermot; LYRICS/BOOK: Gerome Ragni; DIRECTOR: Tom O'Horgan; CHOREOGRAPHER: Tom O'Horgan (uncredited); SETS: Eugene Lee, Roger Morgan, Franne Lee; COSTUMES: Randy Barcelo; MUSICAL DIRECTOR: Thomas Pierson; ORCHESTRATIONS/MUSICAL ARRANGEMENTS: Horace Ott; CAST RECORDING on Columbia; PRESS: Michael Alpert, Marianne Persson; GENERAL MANAGER: George W. Thorn & Leonard A. Mulhern; PRODUCTION STAGE MANAGER: Michael Maurer; STAGE MANAGER: Robert Currie; ASSISTANT STAGE MANAGER: Robert Vandergriff. *Cast:* THE THEATRE STARS: # 33: Allan Nicholls (4); RAGS: Michael Dunn [cut during previews]; DUDE (AS A BOY): Ralph Carter (6); MOTHER EARTH: Salome Bey (3); BREAD: Delores Hall (5); THE SHUBERT ANGELS: Karen-Maria Faatz, Katie Field, Helen Jennings, David Kruger, Cary Mark, Mark Perman, Aida Random, Lynn Reynolds; THE THEATRE WINGS: HERO: Alan Braunstein; HALO: Sandra Loys Toder; ECHO: Dawn Johnson; SOLO: Michael Jason; REBA, DUDE'S MOM: Rae Allen (2) ☆; HAROLD, DUDE'S DAD: William

Redfield (1) ☆; SUZIE MOON: Nell Carter (8); ZERO: James Patrick Farrell III; NERO: Leata Galloway; SISSY: David Lasley; ELECTRIC BILL: Jim Turner; SHADOW: Dale Soules; SHADE: Barbara Monte-Britton; ESSO: Bobby Alessi; EXTRA: Billy Alessi; MEADOW: Michael Meadows; WORLD WAR WON: Michael Antonio [cut during previews]; WORLD WAR TOO: Georgianna Holmes; NONAME: Carol Estey; TEXACO: Dennis Simpson; DUDE (AS A MAN): Nat Morris (7); EIEIO (# 12): Robin McNamara [cut during previews]. *Act I*: Overture (# 33 & Company), "Theatre/Theatre" (# 33, Theatre Wings, Shubert Angels), "A-Stage" (# 33), "The Mountains"/"I Know Your Name" (Mother Earth & Theatre Wings), "Pears and Peaches" (Mother Earth & Shubert Angels), "Eat It" (Pioneers), "Wah Wah Wah" (Suzie Moon), "Suzie Moon" (Suzie Moon), "Y.O.U." (Dude as a child), "I Love My Boo Boo" (# 33, Suzie Moon, Bread, Mother Earth), "Hum Drum Life" (Halo, Hero, Shadow, Meadow), "Who's It?" (Dude, Shubert Angels, Theatre Wings), "Talk to Me About Love" (Dude as a child & Zero), "Goodbyes, Living a Life at Home" (Reba), "I'm Small" (Hero), "You Can't Do Nothing About It" (Nero), "The Handsomest Man" (Sissy), "Electric Prophet" (Electric Bill), "No-One" (Mother Earth). *Act II*: "Who Will Be the Children" (Shubert Angels), "Go Holy Ghost" (Shubert Angels), "A Song to Sing" (Dude, Bread, Nero, Sissy, Theatre Wings, Shubert Angels), "A Dawn" (Hero, Halo, Theatre Wings), "The Days of This Life" (Esso, Extra, Dude, Zero), "I Never Knew" (Mother Earth), "Air Male" (Theatre Wings), "Undo" (Bread), "The Earth" (Harold & Reba), "My Darling I Love You March" (Theatre Wings & Shubert Angels), "So Long, Dude" (Theatre Wings), "Dude, All Dude" (Theatre Wings & Shubert Angels), "Peace Peace" (Shubert Angels), "Jesus Hi" (Shubert Angels), "Baby Breath" (Mother Earth, Bread, # 33, Theatre Wings, Shubert Angels), "Sweet Dreams" (# 33 & Company).

Note: The order of musical numbers varied during the run.

They hoped it would be another *Hair*, but it flopped and was panned mercilessly. It lost a million dollars.

Duke Ellingon's Sophisticated Ladies see 651

194. *Earl of Ruston*

A country rocker in one act. Set in Ruston, Louisiana.

The Broadway Run. BILLY ROSE THEATRE, 5/5/71–5/8/71. 4 previews from 4/26/71. 5 PERFORMANCES. PRESENTED BY David Black; MUSIC: Peter Link, with C.C. Courtney & Ragan Courtney; LYRICS/BOOK: C.C. Courtney & Ragan Courtney; BASED ON the true story of the Courtneys' cousin, Earl Woods, an eccentric who lived some of his life in mental institutions and who died young; DIRECTOR: C.C. Courtney; SETS/LIGHTING: Neil Peter Jampolis; SOUND: Charles Bellin; CAST RECORDING on Capitol; PRESS: Betty Lee Hunt Associates; GENERAL MANAGER: Jose Vega; COMPANY MANAGER: R. Tyler Gatchell Jr.; STAGE MANAGER: Alvarez Kelly; ASSISTANT STAGE MANAGER: Errol Courtney. *Cast:* EARL: C.C. Courtney & Ragan Courtney; LEDA PEARL CRUMP: Jean Waldo Beck; LEECY R. WOODS MOORE: Herself; SHERIFF: Leon Medica; MR. TURNER: Bootsie Normand; REV. REYNOLDS: Chip McDonald; DOCTOR: Bobby Thomas; ERNESTINE: Lynda Lawley; MARY LEE WOODS: Bonnie Guidry; PIANIST: John Bergeron. Standby: For Messrs Courtney: Terry Mace. *Music* played by Goatleg: LEAD GUITAR: Henry "Bootsie" Normand; RHYTHM GUITAR: Chip McDonald; BASS GUITAR: Leon Medica; DRUMS: Bobby Thomas. "Just Your Old Friend," "Earl is Crazy," "The Guitar Song," "(It's) Easy to Be Lonely," "Standing," "Der Blues" (traditional), "Probably" (m: C.C. Courtney & Ragan Courtney), "Mama, Earl Done Ate the Toothpaste Again" (m: C.C. Courtney), "Silver's Theme," "Mama, Mama, Mama," "I've Been Sent Back to the First Grade" (m: C.C. Courtney), "The Revival," "My Name is Leda Pearl" (m: C.C. Courtney), "Insane Poontang" (m: C.C. Courtney & Ragan Courtney), "You Still Love Me" (m: C.C. Courtney), "Earl Was Ahead."

Note: All music by Peter Link unless stated otherwise.

The show got bad reviews. The studio cast album featured Yolande Bavan, Joe Morton, Boni Enten, C.C. Courtney, Marta Heflin, Peter Link, Annie Rachel, Ragan Courtney. It also featured the number "R.U.S.T.O.N.."

195. *Early to Bed*

A farce, a "fairy tale for grown-ups." A pre-war California college track team thinks that the *Angry Pigeon*, in Martinique, is a girls' seminary, and selects the annex of this bordello as their training quarters. Madame Rowena is the owner. Also making the same mistake are El Magnifico (a retired, penniless bullfighter who had known Rowena very well when she was a school teacher) and his son Pablo, who is brought in when Lois, the nightclub ingénue, runs him down with her car (thus beginning a relationship). The Mayor, a regular visitor, is not mistaken.

Before Broadway. The show opened for tryouts in Boston, on 5/24/43, and the bordello was changed to a casino (but only for puritanical Boston).

The Broadway Run. BROADHURST THEATRE, 6/17/43–5/13/44. 382 PERFORMANCES. PRESENTED BY Richard Kollmar; MUSIC: Thomas "Fats" Waller; LYRICS/BOOK: George Marion Jr.; DIRECTOR: Richard Kollmar; CHOREOGRAPHER: Robert Alton; SETS: George Jenkins; COSTUMES: Miles White; CONSULTING SOUND ENGINEER: Saki Oura; MUSICAL DIRECTOR: Archie Bleyer; ORCHESTRATIONS: Don Walker; VOCAL ARRANGEMENTS: Buck Warnick; SPECIAL BALLET MUSIC COMPOSED & ARRANGED BY: Baldwin "Beau" Bergersen; PRESS: Jean Dalrymple; PRODUCTION SUPERVISOR: Alfred Bloomingdale; STAGE MANAGER: Tom Powers; ASSISTANT STAGE MANAGER: George Hunter. *Cast:* OPAL: Ruth Webb (13); BARTENDER: Anthony Blair; O'CONNOR: John Lund (14); GARDENER: David Bethea; GENDARME: Maurice Ellis; LILY-ANN: Jeni LeGon (7), *Muriel Gaines* (stood in); MAYOR: Ralph Bunker (9); MARCELLA: Louise Jarvis; PAULINE: Choo Choo Johnson, *Josine Cagle*; INTERLUDE: Peggy Cordrey; JESSICA: Mary Small (3); EUPHENIA: Virginia McGraw [role added during the run]; BUTCH: Eleanor Boleyn; DUCHESS: Helen Bennett, *Toni Stuart*; MINERVA: Honey Murray (role cut during the run); CADDY: Harold Cromer; MADAME ROWENA: Muriel Angelus (1); ISABELLA: Angela Greene, *Helen Bennett*; POOCH: Bob Howard (4); PABLO: George Zoritch (5); EL MAGNIFICO: Richard Kollmar (2); LOIS: Jane Deering (6); WILBUR: Jimmy Gardiner, *George Hunter*, COACH: George Baxter (10), *Eddie Mayehoff*; EILEEN: Jane Kean (8); PHOEBE: Elinor Troy [role added during run]; CHARLOTTE: Charlotte Maye (12); BURT: Burt Harger (11); NAOMI: Evelyn Ward; CHARLES: Charles Kraft; JUNIOR: Harrison Muller; ADMIRAL SAINT-CASSETTE: Franklyn Fox (15), *Earle MacVeigh*; DANCER: James Starbuck; RADIO REPRESENTATION OF PRESIDENT ROOSEVELT'S VOICE: Dean Murphy; PIGEONS: Deanna Benmore, Helen Bennett, Eleanor Boleyn, Marianne Cude (gone by 1/2/44), Kay Dowd (gone by 1/2/44), Marge Ellis, Claire Loring, Virginia McGraw, Dolores Milan, Olive Nicolson, Helen Osborne, June Reynolds, Olga Roberts, Isabel Rolfe (gone by 1/2/44), Jean Scott, Toni Stuart, Evelyn Ward, *Dorothy Bennett* (by 1/2/44), *Trude Burke* (by 1/2/44), *Anna Konstance* (by 1/2/44); TRACK TEAM: Andrew Gray (gone by 1/2/44), George Hunter, Thomas Kenny, Charles Kraft, John Martin, Bill Julian (gone by 1/2/44), Harrison Muller, Phil Clavadetscher (gone by 1/2/44), Jack Wilkins, *Tom Powers* (by 1/2/44), Robert Trout (by 1/2/44). **Understudy**: Lily-Ann: Muriel Gaines. *Act I*: *Scene 1* A Bar in New York City; *Scene 2* Villa of the *Angry Pigeon*, Martinique; daybreak; *Scene 3* A corridor; later that morning; *Scene 4* Bedroom of the Royal Suite; *Scene 5* The *Angry Pigeon*; still later that morning. *Act II*: *Scene 1* Again the Bar, in New York City; *Scene 2* Corridor of the *Angry Pigeon*; that afternoon; *Scene 3* The *Angry Pigeon*; that evening; *Scene 4* Tradesmen's Entrance to the *Angry Pigeon*; later that night; *Scene 5* The *Angry Pigeon*; later that afternoon [changed during the run to "the following day"]. *Act I*: "A Girl Who Doesn't Ripple When She Bends" (Jessica, Minerva [later Euphenia], Girls, Caddy), "There's a Man in My Life" (Rowena), "Me and My Old-World Charm" (El Magnifico), "Supple Couple" (Jessica, Lily-Ann, Pooch, El Magnifico), "Slightly Less than Wonderful" (Lois & Pablo), "Slightly Less than Wonderful" (reprise) (Lily-Ann, Pooch, Caddy, Gardener, Gendarme), "This is So Nice (It Must Be Illegal)" (Rowena & El Magnifico), "Hi-De-Ho High (in Harlem)" (Pooch, Lily-Ann, Caddy, Gardener, Gendarme, Naomi, Junior, Ensemble), "The Ladies Who Sing with a Band" (Jessica, Rowena, Eileen, Lois): "Jim," "You Made Me Love You," "Love is the Sweetest Thing," "Wanting You," "Love Me or Leave Me," "All of Me," "Love, Your Magic Spell is Everywhere," "That Old Black Magic," "I Want My Mama," "Oh, Johnny, Oh," "What is This Thing Called Love?" [the end of the "Ladies Who Sing with a Band" sequence], "There's Yes in the Air (in Martinique)" (El Magnifico, Jessica, Eileen, Lois, Pablo, Burt, Charlotte, Ensemble). **Act II**: "Get Away Young Man" (Eileen, Junior, Charles, Wilbur, Ensemble), "Long Time No Song" (El Magnifico & Rowena), "Early to Bed" (Jessica, Lois, Pablo, Burt, Charlotte, Caddy, Ensemble), "There's a Man in My Life" (reprise) (Rowena), "When the Nylons Bloom Again" (Pooch & Lily-Ann), Finale (Entire Company).

Broadway reviews were very divided (a couple of raves among them). The unusual mechanized set came in for a lot of notice. Fats Waller died during the run. The original programs gave no director credit; Dick Kollmar's name was only added during the run.

196. *The Education of H*Y*M*A*N K*A*P*L*A*N*

Set in the Lower East Side of New York City, 1919–1920. Hyman is an eager little immigrant through Ellis Island who hopes to start up a tailor's shop with his clever classmate Rose. Yissel, whose family had given Rose money to come to America, is the villain contracted back in the old country to marry Rose. The asterisks in the title are the way the already patriotic Hyman's tailor shop sign reads, and represent the stars of the Union flag. Hyman is arrested as an anarchist, and threatened with deportation, but he is saved by the intercession of night school teacher Professor Parkhill. The setting was changed from the Chicago of the original stories.

Before Broadway. Actress Donna McKechnie couldn't find work, and begged choreographer Jaime Rogers for a chance to work on this show. He created a part for her (this phone call was played out by Miss McKechnie in *A Chorus Line* some years later). The show previewed at the Erlanger Theatre, Philadelphia, on 3/2/68 and 3/3/68, and tried out 3/4/68–3/23/68. Too few people came, and the run was cut short.

The Broadway Run. ALVIN THEATRE, 4/4/68–4/27/68. 12 previews from 3/28/68. 28 PERFORMANCES. PRESENTED BY Andre Goulston & Jack Farren, and Stephen Mellow; MUSIC/LYRICS: Paul Nassau & Oscar Brand; BOOK: Benjamin Bernard Zavin; BASED ON the 1937 *New Yorker* stories by Leonard Q. Ross (aka Leo Rosten); CONCEIVED BY: Paul Nassau & Oscar Brand; DIRECTOR: George Abbott; CHOREOGRAPHER: Jaime Rogers; SETS: William & Jean Eckart; COSTUMES: Winn Morton; LIGHTING: Martin Aronstein; MUSICAL DIRECTOR/VOCAL ARRANGEMENTS: Julian Stein; ORCHESTRATIONS: Larry Wilcox; DANCE MUSIC ARRANGEMENTS: Lee Holdridge; PRESS: Harvey B. Sabinson, Lee Solters, Leo Stern, Edie Kean; GENERAL MANAGER: Norman Maibaum; COMPANY MANAGER: Al Jones; PRODUCTION STAGE MANAGER: Edward Preston; STAGE MANAGER: Edward Julien; ASSISTANT STAGE MANAGER: Wally Engelhardt & Jack Fletcher. **Cast:** JIMMY: Stephen Bolster (14); PUSHCART VENDOR: Dick Ensslen (16); OLD CLOTHES MAN: Cyril Murkin; KATHY MCKENNA: Donna McKechnie (10); SAM PINSKY: Nathaniel Frey (3); REUBEN PLONSKY: David Gold (9); GIOVANNI PASTORA: Dick Latessa (7); MRS. MOSKOWITZ: Honey Sanders (6); SARAH MOSKOWITZ: Susan Camber (18); MR. PARKHILL: Gary Krawford (4); FANNY GIDWITZ: Maggie Task; ROSE MITNICK: Barbara Minkus (2); HYMAN KAPLAN: Tom Bosley (1) ☆; EILEEN HIGBY: Dorothy Emmerson (11); MARIE VITALE: Beryl Towbin (8); MRS. MITNICK: Mimi Sloan (12); OFFICER CALLAHAN: Wally Engelhardt (15); YISSEL FISHBEIN: Hal Linden (5); GUARD: David Ellin (17); JUDGE MAHON: Rufus Smith (13); DANCERS: Pamela Barlow, Mickie Bier, Susan Camber, Joanne Di Vito, Andrea Duda, Takeshi Hamagaki, Yanco Inone, Lee Lund, Pat Matera, Kuniko Narai, Barry Preston, George Ramos, Steven Ross, Eileen

Woliner; SINGERS: Edward Becker, Alice Cannon, Martha Danielle, David Ellin, Jack Fletcher, Trudy Wallace. **Understudies**: Hyman: Hal Linden; Rose: Alice Cannon; Yissel/Sam: David Ellin; Mrs. Mitnick/Mrs. Moskowitz: Maggie Task; Reuben: Pat Matera; Giovanni: Dick Ensslen; Parkhill: Stephen Bolster; Jimmy: Jack Fletcher; Kathy: Lee Lund; Judge: Wally Engelhardt; Callahan: Rufus Smith; Sarah: Joanne Di Vito. **Act I**: *Scene 1* A street on the Lower East Side: "Strange New World" (Parkhill); *Scene 2* Mr. Parkhill's classroom: "OOOO-EEEE" (Kaplan, Rose, Parkhill, Students); *Scene 3* teachers' room: "A Dedicated Teacher" ("Teachers on Parade") (Higby, Miss Vitale, Parkhill); *Scene 4* Mr. Parkhill's classroom: "Lieben Dich" (Kaplan), "Loving You" (Rose); *Scene 5* Rose Mitnick's apartment: "The Day I Met Your Father" (Mrs. Mitnick); *Scene 6* A street: "Anything is Possible" (Kaplan, Students, Dancers, Singers); *Scene 7* Mr. Parkhill's classroom; *Scene 8* A street: "Spring in the City" (Kathy, Pastora, Plonsky, Pinsky, Mrs. Moskowitz, Fanny, Dancers, Singers). **Act II**: *Scene 1* Kaplan's flat: "An Old Fashioned Husband" (Fishbein); *Scene 2* Mr. Parkhill's classroom: "Julius Caesar" ("Shakespeare") (Kaplan); *Scene 3* Ellis Island Deportation Room: "I Never Felt Better in My Life" (Kaplan, Dancers, Singers); *Scene 4* Judge Mahon's chambers; *Scene 5* Hyman Kaplan's shop: "When Will I Learn" (Rose) [the showstopper]; *Scene 6* A street in front of the school: "All American" (Pinsky & Students); *Scene 7* A U.S. courtroom.

Broadway reviews were divided. As the opening night audience was coming back in for Act II, Mayor Lindsay rushed out of the theatre to quell a potential riot in Harlem. The rest of the audience heard that Martin Luther King had just been assassinated. This put a damper on the show. This was George Abbott's 110th Broadway production.

After Broadway. AMERICAN JEWISH THEATRE, 3/25/89–5/21/89. 11 previews. 67 PERFORMANCES. It was a small production. The musical numbers varied somewhat from the original: "The Adult Class" was the opening number; and the second number in Act II was now called "Shakespeare." DIRECTOR: Lonny Price; ASSISTANT DIRECTOR: Daisy Prince; COSTUMES: Gail Cooper-Hecht; LIGHTING: Betsy Adams; MUSICAL DIRECTOR: Nicholas Levin. **Cast**: HYMAN: Jack Hallett; ROSE: Laura Patinkin; YISSEL/PLONSKY: Neil Ben Ari.

197. *Eubie!*

A musical revue. 23 numbers written by Eubie Blake (1883–1983) and Noble Sissle, between 1899 and 1958. Ten are from *Shuffle Along*.

Before Broadway. It first ran at THEATRE OFF PARK, New York, from 2/2/78. 12 PERFORMANCES. However, it was very different then, basically a revival of *Shuffle Along*. Before Broadway Billy Wilson replaced Dana Manno as choreographer.

The Broadway Run. AMBASSADOR THEATRE, 9/20/78–10/7/79. 7 previews. 439 PERFORMANCES. PRESENTED BY Ashton Springer, in association with Frank C. Pierson & Jay J. Cohen; MUSIC: Eubie Blake & (uncredited) Noble Sissle; LYRICS: Noble Sissle, Andy Razaf, F. E. Miller, Jim Europe & (uncredited) Eubie Blake; DEVISED BY/DIRECTOR: Julianne Boyd; CHOREOGRAPHER: Billy Wilson; TAP CHOREOGRAPHER: Henry Le Tang; SETS: Karl Eigsti; COSTUMES: Bernard Johnson; LIGHTING: William Mintzer; SOUND: Lou Gonzalez; MUSICAL SUPERVISOR/ARRANGEMENTS: Danny Holgate; MUSICAL DIRECTOR: Vicki Carter; ORCHESTRATIONS/ASSISTANT TO THE MUSICAL SUPERVISOR: Neal Tate; CHORAL ARRANGEMENTS: Chapman Roberts; CAST RECORDING on Warner Brothers; PRESS: Max Eisen; GENERAL MANAGEMENT: Theatre Management Associates; COMPANY MANAGER: Robert Ossenfort; PRODUCTION STAGE MANAGER: Donald Christy, *Clinton Turner Davis*; STAGE MANAGER: Harrison Avery, *Kimako*; ASSISTANT STAGE MANAGER: Kellie Williams, *Terry Burrell, David Jackson*. **Cast:** Ethel Beatty (*Deborah Burrell* from 3/79), Terry Burrell (*Gail Nelson* from 7/79), Lynnie Godfrey (*Jenifer Lewis* from 9/79), Gregory Hines, Maurice Hines (*Winston DeWitt Hemsley* from 7/79), Lonnie McNeil (*David Jackson* from 9/79), Janet Powell, Alaina Reed, Leslie Dockery, Mel Johnson Jr., Marion Ramsey (*Jenifer Lewis*), Jeffrey V. Thompson. **Understudies**: Men: David Jackson, Bernard J. Marsh, Skip Cunningham, Nathan Jennings. Women: Deborah Burrell, Andrea Frierson, Jenifer Lewis, Carol Lynn Maillard, Gail Nelson. *Musicians*: PIANO: Vicki Carter & Frank Anderson; GUITAR/HARMONICA/BANJO: Rudy Stevenson; DRUMS: Percy Brice; BASS/TUBA: Gregory Maker; FLUGELHORN: Ernest Royal & E.V. Perry; LEAD TRUMPET: Ernest Royal; TRUMPET: E.V. Perry; TROMBONE: Arthur Hamilton; SAX/CLARINET: Zane Paul; FLUTE: Rudy Stevenson & Zane Paul. *Act I*: *Prologue*: "Goodnight Angeline" (from *Shuffle Along*) (1919) (l: Noble Sissle & James Reese "Jim" Europe) (Company), "Charleston Rag" (1899) (Company) [end of Prologue]; "Shuffle Along" [from *Shuffle Along*] (1921) (Company), "In Honeysuckle Time" [from *Shuffle Along*] (1921) (Lonnie, Janet, Company), "I'm Just Wild About Harry" [from *Shuffle Along*] (1921) (Janet, Maurice, Lynnie, Marion, Ethel) [Blake's most famous song], "Baltimore Buzz" [from *Shuffle Along*] (1921) (mime staged by Dana Manno) (Lonnie, Janet, Jeffrey, Mel, Gregory, Leslie), "Daddy (Won't You Please Come Home)" [from *Shuffle Along*] (1921) (ch: Julianne Boyd) (Lynnie), "There's a Million Little Cupids in the Sky" [cut from *The Chocolate Dandies*] (1924) (Maurice, Lonnie, Gregory, Ethel, Mel, Jeffrey, Marion, Janet, Leslie, Alaina), "I'm a Great Big Baby" [from *Tan Manhattan*] (1940) (l: Andy Razaf) (Jeffrey), "My Handy Man Ain't Handy No More" [from *Blackbirds of 1930*] (1930) (l: Andy Razaf) (Alaina & Mel), "Low Down Blues" [from *Shuffle Along*] (1921) (Gregory), "Gee, I Wish I Had Someone to Rock Me in the Cradle of Love" (1919) (duet arrangement by Vicki Carter) (Ethel), "I'm Just Simply Full of Jazz" [from *Shuffle Along*] (1919) (Company). *Act II*: "High Steppin' Days" (1921–l: Johnny Brandon, 1978) (Company), "Dixie Moon" (1924) (dance) [from *The Chocolate Dandies*] (Mel, the Hines Brothers, Company), "Weary" [from *Tan Manhattan*] (1940) (l: Andy Razaf) (Terry & Company), "Roll, Jordan" [from *Blackbirds of 1930*] (1930) (l: Andy Razaf) (Alaina, Terry, Janet, Company), "Memories of You" [from *Blackbirds of 1930*] (1930) (l: Andy Razaf) (Ethel), "If You've Never Been Vamped by a Brownskin, (You've Never Been Vamped at All)" [from *Shuffle Along*] (1921) (Marion, Mel, Lynnie, Gregory, Jeffrey, Leslie, Janet, Maurice, Lonnie), "You Got to Git the Gittin' While the Gittin's Good" (1956 — l: F.E. Miller) (Maurice), "Oriental Blues" (1921) [from *Shuffle Along*] (Jeffrey, Ethel, Leslie, Janet, Marion), "I'm Craving for That Kind of Love" [from *Shuffle Along*] (1921) (ch: Julianne Boyd) (instrumental written by Blake & Sissle) (Lynnie), "Hot Feet" (1958) (Gregory solo dance), "Goodnight Angeline" (reprise) (voc arr: Vicki Carter) (Ethel, Mel, Lonnie, Janet), Finale (Company).

Note: All songs have music by Eubie Blake. All songs have lyrics by Noble Sissle, unless marked otherwise.

The show opened on Broadway to very good reviews. It received Tony nominations for score, choreography, and for Gregory Hines.

After Broadway. TOUR. Opened on 1/9/79, in Milwaukee. *Cast*: Robert Anderson, Danny Beard, Chris Calloway, Millie Foster, Ron Gattis, Gail Nelson, Karen Ragland.

TOUR. Opened in 8/79, in Huntsville, Ala., and closed in 3/80, in Providence, Rhode Island. PRESENTED BY Tom Mallow; MUSICAL DIRECTOR: William "Gregg" Hunter. *Cast*: Susan Beaubian, Cab Calloway, Keith Alan Davis, Tony Franklin, Jackee Harry, Marva Hicks, Donna Patrice Ingram, Bernard Manners, Robert Melvin, Francine Claudia Moore, Keith Rozie, Deborah Lynn Sharpe, Roderick Spencer Sibert, Vernon Spencer.

POST-BROADWAY TOUR. Opened on 12/28/79, in Los Angeles. *Cast*: Terry Burrell, Leslie Dockery, Winston DeWitt Hemsley, David Jackson, Jenifer Lewis, Bernard J. Marsh, Gail Nelson.

198. *Evita*

Eva Peron (born Eva Duarte) (1919–1952), the glamorous second wife of Argentine dictator Juan Peron, rose from poverty in the village of Junin, to become a model, then a movie actress, and then the most powerful woman in Latin America. The show covers the period 1934 to her death, and opens with her death of cancer. She was called a saint by some, and a devil by others. In one scene Peron's rise to power is shown by five generals playing musical chairs. Che is used as narrator, observer and commentator, along the lines of a Greek chorus. Eva was made tougher for

Broadway than she had been in London. There was a cast of 48. While the London production was being assembled, set designers told Hal Prince that something was missing from the set, something important they couldn't put their finger on. Shortly after that Mr. Prince was in Mexico City and saw the murals by Diego Rivera and Siqueiros. That was the answer, big murals flanking the proscenium, depicting a range of Argentine peasant types.

Before Broadway. In the early 1950s Lillian Hellman and Leonard Bernstein had tried working on an opera based on the life of Eva Peron, but nothing came of it. In 1973 Tim Rice was listening to his car radio when he heard the tail-end of a docu-drama about Eva. Interested, he researched her life, and approached his partner, Andrew Lloyd Webber, about doing a musical on the subject. Mr. Lloyd Webber was reluctant because Eva was too controversial a figure, and, more importantly, perhaps, Mr. Lloyd Webber wanted to finish his current *Jeeves* project with Tim Rice. Rice bowed out of *Jeeves*, and Mr. Lloyd Webber finished it with Alan Ayckbourn, while Mr. Rice went to Argentina to do further research into Eva. *Jeeves* failed miserably in London, and Andrew Lloyd Webber then joined Tim Rice on *Evita*. They produced an LP first (as they had with *Jesus Christ Superstar* and *Joseph and the Amazing Technicolor Dreamcoat*) before putting on the show. Julie Covington sang the title role. Others on the album were Colm Wilkinson, Paul Jones, and Barbara Dickson. The authors took a demo of this album (recorded by the London Symphony Orchestra and some singers) to Hal Prince, who listened to it in his Mallorca home. He liked it, offered to direct, and wrote them a letter of suggestions. They were somewhat intimidated by his letter, and backed off. The album was then released, and became a No. 1 hit all over Europe. "Don't Cry for Me, Argentina" was the big hit single from the album. It was more than a year before they came back to Mr. Prince in New York, asking if he wanted to direct the musical in London. But he was committed for 1½ years, so they waited for him.

THE LONDON RUN. On 3/23/77 *Variety* announced that Lloyd Webber & Rice were going to turn their LP into a musical. On 12/14/77 *Variety* announced that Hal Prince was in London, casting for the role of Eva. Elaine Paige got the role after Julie Covington turned it down. The show cost a staggering (by British standards, anyway) 400,000 pounds. It rehearsed for 3½ weeks and then had 9 previews from 6/12/78. It opened officially on 6/21/78, at the PRINCE EDWARD THEATRE, to rave reviews, and ran 2,900 PERFORMANCES. CHOREOGRAPHER: Larry Fuller; SETS/COSTUMES: Timothy O'Brien & Tazeena Firth; MUSICAL DIRECTOR: Anthony Bowles, *David Caddick, Denys Rawson, John Owen Edwards*. *Cast*: EVA: Elaine Page, *Marti Webb, Stephanie Lawrence* (in 1983), *Siobhan McCarthy, Jacquey Chappell, Kathryn Evans*; CHE: David Essex (for a couple of months), *Gary Bond, Mark Ryan, Martin Smith, Jimmy Kean*; PERON: Joss Ackland, *John Turner, Oz Clarke, Daniel Ben-Zali*; PERON'S MISTRESS: Siobhan McCarthy, *Janet Shaw, Kelly Hunter, Lindy Brill, Jackie Ekers*; MAGALDI: Mark Ryan, *David Burt, Clifton Todd*.

THE U.S. PREMIERE. DOROTHY CHANDLER PAVILION, Los Angeles, on 5/8/79. It had the same cast and crew as for the subsequent Broadway run. It then ran in San Francisco. Raquel Welch, Meryl Streep and Faye Dunaway all wanted the role.

The Broadway Run. BROADWAY THEATRE, 9/25/79–6/25/83. 17 previews. 1,567 PERFORMANCES. PRESENTED BY Robert Stigwood, in association with David Land; MUSIC: Andrew Lloyd Webber; LYRICS: Tim Rice; no book credit as there is no spoken dialog; DIRECTOR: Harold Prince; CHOREOGRAPHER: Larry Fuller; SETS/COSTUMES: Timothy O'Brien & Tazeena Firth; LIGHTING: David Hersey; SOUND: Abe Jacob; MUSICAL SUPERVISOR: Paul Gemignani; MUSICAL DIRECTOR: Rene Wiegert, *Paul Gemignani* (80–82), *Edward Strauss* (82–83), *Jack Gaughan* (82–83); ORCHESTRATIONS: Hershy Kay & Andrew Lloyd Webber; CAST RECORDING on MCA; PRESS: Mary Bryant; PRODUCTION ASSOCIATES: Tim Rice & Andrew Lloyd Webber; GENERAL MANAGER: Howard Haines; COMPANY MANAGER: John Caruso; PRODUCTION STAGE MANAGER: George Martin; STAGE MANAGER: John Grigas; ASSISTANT STAGE MANAGERS: Andy Cadiff & Carlos Gorbea, *John-David Wilder & Kenneth W. Urmston*. *Cast*: EVA: Patti LuPone (1) ☆, *Derin Altay* (from 1/12/81), *Loni Ackerman* (from 4/5/82), *Florence Lacey* (from

5/30/83); EVA (AT MATINEES): Terri Klausner (Wednesdays & Saturdays), *Nancy Opel* (from 10/80), *Pamela Blake* (from 5/25/83); CHE: Mandy Patinkin (2) ☆, *James Stein* (from 10/20/80), *Anthony Crivello* (from 4/5/82), *Scott Holmes* (from 4/5/83), *James Sbano*; JUAN PERON: Bob Gunton (3) ☆, *David Cryer* (from 10/20/80), *Robert Frisch*, *Jack Neubeck*; PERON'S MISTRESS: Jane Ohringer (5), *Cynthia Hunt* (from 80–81); MAGALDI: Mark Syers (4), *James Whitson* (from 80–81); PEOPLE OF ARGENTINA: Seda Azarian (gone by 81–82), Dennis Birchall, Peppi Borza (gone by 80–81), Tom Carder (gone by 81–82), Robin Cleaver (gone by 80–81), Anny De Gange, Mark East (gone by 81–82), Teri Gill (gone by 81–82), Carlos Gorbea (gone by 80–81), Pat Gorman (gone by 80–81), Rex David Hays (*Robert Frisch* by 80–81; *David Green* by 82–83), Terri Klausner (gone by 80–81), Michael Lichtefeld (gone by 80–81), Carol Lugenbeal (*Amy Niles* by 80–81), Paula Lynn (gone by 80–81), Morgan MacKay (gone by 80–81), Peter Marinos (gone by 80–81), Sal Mistretta (gone by 80–81), Bill Nabel (gone by 80–81), Jack Neubeck (*Michael Licata* by 82–83), Marcia O'Brien, Nancy Opel (gone by 82–83), Davia Sacks, James Sbano (*Paul Harman* by 82–83), David Staller, Michelle Stubbs (gone by 82–83), Robert Tanna (gone by 80–81), Clarence Teeters (gone by 80–81), Susan Terry (gone by 82–83), Philip Tracy (gone by 82–83), David Vosburgh (gone by 80–81), Mark Waldrop (gone by 82–83), Sandra Wheeler (gone by 81–82), Brad Witsger (gone by 81– 82), John Leslie Wood (gone by 80–81), Nancy Wood (gone by 80– 81), John Yost. 80–81 replacements: *Susan Cella, Frank Cruz, Kim Darwin, Scott Fless, Carole Garcia, Michael Hayward-Jones, Robert Henderson, Ken Hilliard, Dawn Perry* (gone by 82–83), *Martie Ramm* (gone by 81–82), *Morgan Richardson, Wilfredo Suarez, Ian Michael Towers* (gone by 82–83), *Kenneth W. Urmston.* 81–82 replacements: *Al DeCristo, Robert Heitzinger* (gone by 82–83), *Robert Logan, Joanie O'Neill* (gone by 82–83), *Cassie Rand, Drusilla Ross, Claude Tessier, Leslie Tinnaro.* 82–83 replacements: *Pamela Blake, Patti D'Beck, Gregg Edelman, Barry Gorbar, Barbara Hartman, Lois Hayes, John Herrera, David Horwitz, Robert Kellett, David King, Deborah Lasday, Ivson Polk, Claudia Asbury, Donald Craig, Keith Keen*; CHILDREN: Fritz Collester, Bridget Francis, Simone Francis, Matthew McKeon, Tobrina Van Buskirk. 1980 replacements: *Megan Forste, Nicole Francis, Michael Pastryk, Christopher Wooten.* 80–81 replacements: *Lilo Grunwald, Colette Sena Heyman.* 81–82 replacement: *Tammy Amerson.* 82–83 replacements: *Sam Conte, Bradley Kane, Teddy Moran,* Johanna Hickey, Ward Saxton. **Understudies**: Eva: Nancy Opel (79–80), *Susan Cella* (80–83); Che: Tom Carder (79–81), James Sbano (79–82), *Paul Harman* (82–83), *John Herrera* (82), *Al DeCristo* (82–83); Peron: Rex David Hays (79–80), *Robert Frisch* (80–82), *David Green* (82–83); Magaldi: Sal Mistretta (79–80), *Jack Neubeck* (79–82), *Michael Licata* (82–83); Peron's Mistress: Nancy Wood, *Carol Lugenbeal, Amy Niles* (79–83). **Act I**: "A Cinema in Buenos Aires, July 26, 1952" (Company), "Requiem for Evita" (Company), "Oh, What a Circus" (Che & Company), "On This Night of a Thousand Stars" (Magaldi), "Eva, Beware of the City" (Magaldi, Eva, Family), "Buenos Aires" (Eva & Dancers), "Goodnight and Thank You" (Che, Eva, Lovers), "The Art of the Possible" (Peron, Eva, Colonels), "Charity Concert" (Company), "I'd Be Surprisingly Good for You" (Eva & Peron), "Another Suitcase in Another Hall" (Mistress), "Peron's Latest Flame" (Che, Eva, Company), "A New Argentina" (Eva, Peron, Che, Company). **Act II**: Entr'acte (Orchestra); "On the Balcony of the Casa Rosada" (Peron, Che, Company), "Don't Cry for Me, Argentina" (Eva) [the big hit], "High Flying Adored" (Che & Eva), "Rainbow High" (Eva & Dressers), "Rainbow Tour" (Che, Eva, Peron, Peronists), "The Actress Hasn't Learned (the Lines You'd Like to Hear)" (Eva, Che, Company), "And the Money Kept Rolling In (and Out)" (Che & Company), "Santa Evita" (Children & Workers), "Waltz for Eva and Che" (Eva & Che), "She is a Diamond" (Peron & Officers), "Dice are Rolling" (Peron & Eva), "Eva's Final Broadcast" (Eva & Che), "Montage" (Company), "Lament" (Eva & Che).

Broadway reviews were divided, mostly bad. Patti LuPone had 14 costume changes in each performance, as well as four separate wigs. She left the run on 1/1/81, and found it difficult to get work thereafter, being typecast as a blonde dictator. 3.5 million original cast albums were sold. The show won Tonys for musical, score, book, direction of a musical, lighting, and for Patti LuPone and Mandy Patinkin, and was also nominated for choreography, sets, costumes, and for Bob Gunton.

After Broadway. TOUR. Opened on 1/13/80, at the Shubert Theatre, Los Angeles, and closed on 3/27/83, at the Orpheum Theatre, Minneapolis. MUSICAL DIRECTOR: Arthur Rubinstein. **Cast**: EVA: Loni Ackerman, *Derin Altay* (from 4/5/82); EVA, IN MATINEES: Valerie Perri, *Derin Altay, Pamela Blake* (from 1/10/81), *Joy Lober, Florence Lacey*; CHE: Scott Holmes, *R. Michael Baker*; PERON: Jon Cypher, *David Brummel* (from 3/82), *Robb Alton*; MAGALDI: Sal Mistretta, *Mark Syers, David Dannehl*; PERON'S MISTRESS: Kelli James, *Jill Geddes*; CHORUS INCLUDED: Ken Urmston. **Understudies**: Eva: Sheri Cowart & Iris Revson.

AUSTRALIAN TOUR. Adelaide Festival Theatre, 4/30/80; Perth Entertainment Centre, 6/11/80; Her Majesty's Theatre, Sydney, 2/14/81–9/26/81. **Cast**: EVA: Jennifer Murphy, *Marietta Rupps, Gaye MacFarlane, Michelle Breeze, Patti LuPone* (from 5/16/81), *Karyn O'Neill* (from 8/17/81); CHE: John O'May; PERON: Peter Carroll; MAGALDI: Tony Alvarez; PERON'S MISTRESS: Laura Mitchell.

TOUR. Opened on 9/30/80, at the Shubert Theatre, Chicago. MUSICAL DIRECTOR: Jack Gaughan. **Cast**: EVA: Valerie Perri, *Nancy Opel*; EVA, IN MATINEES: Joy Lober; CHE: John Herrera, *Anthony Crivello, R. Michael Baker* (from 4/3/82); PERON: Robb Alton; MAGALDI: Peter Marinos, *David Dannehl*; PERON'S MISTRESS: Cynthia Simpson, *Jamie Dawn Gangi*; CHORUS INCLUDED: Larry Devon & Gregg Edelman. **Understudy**: Che: Anthony Crivello.

TEATRO FERROCARRILERO, Mexico City. Opened on 6/22/81, and ran for 1½ years. The famous song in Spanish is "No llores por mi, Argentina." DIRECTOR: Hal Prince. **Cast**: EVA: Rocio Banquells.

TOUR. Opened on 2/28/82, at the Masonic Temple, Detroit. MUSICAL DIRECTOR: Kevin Farrell. **Cast**: EVA: Florence Lacey, *Patricia Hemenway*; EVA, IN MATINEES: Patricia Hemenway, *Donna Marie Elio*; CHE: Tim Bowman; PERON: John Leslie Wolfe; MAGALDI: Vincent Pirillo; PERON'S MISTRESS: Patricia Ludd; CHORUS INCLUDED: R. Michael Baker, Mark Dovey, Joanna Glushak.

PAPER MILL PLAYHOUSE, New Jersey, 1984. DIRECTOR: Frank Marino; CHOREOGRAPHER: Sam Viverito; MUSICAL DIRECTOR: Pam Drews. **Cast**: EVA: Loni Ackerman; PERON: David Brummel; CHE: John Herrera.

TOUR. Opened on 8/3/92, in Indianapolis. **Cast**: EVA: Valerie Perri; CHE: John Herrera; PERON: David Brummel; MAGALDI: Sal Mistretta; PERON'S MISTRESS: Jennifer Rae Beck.

TOUR. Opened on 12/27/93, at the Cashman Center, Las Vegas. PRESENTED BY Robert L. Young & PACE Theatrical Group; DIRECTOR/CHOREOGRAPHER: Larry Fuller. **Cast**: EVA: Donna Marie Asbury, Marla Schaffel (alternate); CHE: Daniel C. Cooney; PERON: David Brummel; MAGALDI: Frank Mastrone; PERON'S MISTRESS: Elisa Sagardia; TANGO COUPLE: David Roberts & Tara Tyrrell; ENSEMBLE INCLUDED: Mark Dovey, Scott Hayward, R. Kim Jordan.

THE MOVIE. 1996. At one time Oliver Stone was to direct, with Meryl Streep as Eva, then Madonna got the role. The movie included the song "The Lady's Got Potential" (Che), which had been cut from the original stage production. WRITER/DIRECTOR: Alan Parker; CHOREOGRAPHER: Darius Khondji. **Cast**: EVA: Madonna; PERON: Jonathan Pryce; CHE: Antonio Banderas; MAGALDI: Jimmy Nail.

By 2/97 there was talk of Broadway revival, but it never happened.

TEATRO SILVIA PINAL, Mexico City. This revival was postponed from Aug. to 10/19/97 because of set and lighting difficulties, and it finally opened on 12/18/97. Previews from 12/11/97. PRESENTED BY Mario Palacios, Jorge Berlanga, and Rocio Banquells; LYRICS ADAPTED INTO SPANISH BY: Marco Villafan; DIRECTOR/CHOREOGRAPHER: Larry Fuller; SETS: Chris Nass; COSTUMES: Nuria Marroqui; LIGHTING: Richard Winkler; SOUND: Abe Jacob; MUSICAL DIRECTOR: Jorge Neri; CAST RECORDING made in late 1/98. **Cast**: EVA: Rocio Banquells; PERON: Jose Lavat (it was going to be played by Julio Aleman); CHE: Luis Gatica; MAGALDI: Sergio Acosta; PERON'S MISTRESS: Perla Aguilar.

TOURING REVIVAL. The major 20th anniversary tour was being discussed by 2/98; it opened on 11/6/98, at the Masonic Temple, Detroit, and closed on 7/4/99, in Boston. PRESENTED BY Manny Kladitis, MagicWorks Entertainment, PACE Theatrical Group; DIRECTOR/CHOREOGRAPHER: Larry Fuller; SETS/COSTUMES: Timothy O'Brien. A lot of the score was re-orchestrated, and some choreography was re-done. **Cast**: EVA: Natalie Toro (Ana Maria Andricain played it Tuesday evenings and Saturday & Sunday matinees); PERON: Raymond Jaramillo McLeod;

CHE: Raul Esparza; MAGALDI: Tom Flynn; PERON'S MISTRESS: Angela Covington; ENSEMBLE INCLUDED: Charles Bergell, Kevin Bernard, Kathryn Blake, Sterling Clark, Bill E. Dietrich. It was scheduled to reach Broadway in the fall of 1999, but never made it.

WALNUT STREET THEATRE, Philadelphia, 5/14/03–7/6/03. Previews from 5/6/03. This was a new production, with a new visual concept, a departure from Hal Prince's staging, but with script and score unchanged. DIRECTOR: Bruce Lumpkin; CHOREOGRAPHER: Richard Stafford; SETS: John Farrell; MUSICAL DIRECTOR: Louis F. Goldberg. *Cast*: EVA: Ana Maria Andricain (Krissy Fraelich at certain performances); CHE: Jeffrey Coon; PERON: Scott Holmes; MAGALDI: Vincent D'Elia; PERON'S MISTRESS: Christina DeCicco.

HELEN HAYES THEATRE, Nyack, NY. 10/18/03–11/2/03. This production had a few lyric changes. *Cast*: EVA: Felicia Finley; PERON: David Brummel; CHE: Frank Baiocchi; PERON'S MISTRESS: Claudia Koziner; MAGALDI: Vincent D'Elia. This production first ran at the Ogunquit Playhouse, Maine.

TOURING REVIVAL. Andrew Lloyd Webber and Cameron Mackintosh got together in early 2004 to plan a big revival for 2005. The Equity tour opened at the Colonial Theatre, Boston, 11/2/04–11/14/04. PRESENTED BY Troika Entertainment; DIRECTOR: Larry Fuller; SUPERVISOR: Harold Prince. *Cast*: EVA: Kathy Voytko.

199. *Fade Out— Fade In*

An usherette becomes a movie star in the mid–1930s.

Before Broadway. One of the three 1964 musicals produced by Lester Osterman and Jule Styne, and financed by ABC — Paramount (see *High Spirits* for more details). Originally called *A Girl to Remember*. It was scheduled to arrive on Broadway on 11/23/63, but had to be (seriously) delayed due to Carol Burnett's pregnancy. It tried out in Boston 4/29/64–5/16/64, before going to Broadway.

The Broadway Run. MARK HELLINGER THEATRE, 5/26/64–4/17/65. 6 previews from 5/20/64. 271 PERFORMANCES. PRESENTED BY Lester Osterman & Jule Styne (with ABC — Paramount); MUSIC: Jule Styne; LYRICS/BOOK: Betty Comden & Adolph Green; DIRECTOR: George Abbott; CHOREOGRAPHER: Ernest Flatt; SETS/LIGHTING: William & Jean Eckart; COSTUMES: Donald Brooks; MUSICAL DIRECTOR: Colin Romoff, *John Berkman* (when it re-opened); ORCHESTRATIONS: Ralph Burns & Ray Ellis; ORCHESTRATIONS FOR "L.Z. IN QUEST OF HIS YOUTH": Robert Prince; VOCAL ARRANGEMENTS: Buster Davis; ASSISTANT VOCAL ARRANGER: Marvin Hamlisch; DANCE MUSIC ARRANGEMENTS: Richard De Benedictis; CAST RECORDING on ABC — Paramount; PRESS: Harvey B. Sabinson, Lee Solters, David Powers; CASTING: Judith Abbott; SMAXIE'S TRAINER: John Flino; GENERAL MANAGER: Richard Horner; COMPANY MANAGER: Leonard Soloway; PRODUCTION STAGE MANAGER: John Allen; STAGE MANAGERS: William Krot & Nicholas A.B. Gray; ASSISTANT STAGE MANAGER: Dan Resin. *Cast*: BYRON PRONG: Jack Cassidy (2), *Dick Shawn*; TEENAGERS: Jodi Perselle & Judy Newman [roles cut for re-opening]; WOMAN: Diana Ede [role cut for re-opening]; MAN: Darrell J. Askey [role cut for re-opening]; AUTOGRAPH KIDS: Roger Allan Raby & Charlene Mehl; HELGA SIXTREES: Judy Cassmore, *Alice Glenn* (from 6/22/64); POPS: Frank Tweddell; ROSCOE: Bob Neukum; BILLY VESPERS: Glenn Kezer, *Paul Michael*; LYMAN: John Dorrin; HOPE SPRINGFIELD: Carol Burnett (1); REX: Darrell J. Askey, *Barney Johnston*; CHAUFFEUR: William Louther, *John Richardson*; 1ST GIRL: Wendy Taylor, *Trish Dwelley*; 1ST COWBOY EXTRA: Stephen Elmore, *David Cryer*; 2ND COWBOY EXTRA: Fred Cline [role cut for re-opening]; GANGSTER EXTRA: Gene Varrone; RALPH GOVERNOR: Mitchell Jason (6); RUDOLF GOVERNOR: Dick Patterson (5); NEPHEWS: GEORGE GOVERNOR: Howard Kahl, *Paul Eichel*; FRANK GOVERNOR: John Dorrin; HAROLD GOVERNOR: Gene Varrone; ARNOLD GOVERNOR: Stephen Elmore, *David Cryer*; WAITERS: Fred Cline (*Stephen Elmore*), Richard Frisch, Roger Allan Raby; PUBLICITY MEN: Sean Allen & Darrell J. Askey (*Dean Doss & Barney Johnston*); CONVICTS: Gene Kelton, Ed Pfeiffer, William Louther (*John Richardson*), James von Weiss & Ed Pfeiffer (*Bill Starr & Jerry Gotham*); MYRA MAY MELROSE: Virginia Payne (8); SEAMSTRESS: Diane Arnold; MISS MALLORY: Jo Tract [role cut for re-opening]; CUSTER CORKLEY: Dan Resin; APPROVAL: Smaxie [role cut for re-

opening]; PHOTOGRAPHER: Sean Allen [role cut for re-opening]; MAX WELCH: Richard Frisch; LOU WILLIAMS: Tiger Haynes (9); DORA DAILEY: Aileen Poe; LIONEL Z. GOVERNOR: Lou Jacobi (3); DR. ANTON TRAURIG: Reuben Singer (7); GLORIA CURRIE: Tina Louise (4), *Judy Cassmore* (from 6/22/64); MADAME BARRYMORE: Penny Egleston; SINGERS: Sean Allen, Jackie Alloway, Darrell J. Askey, Fred Cline, John Dorrin, Trish Dwelley, Stephen Elmore, Richard Frisch, Howard Kahl, Carolyn Kemp, Betty Kent, Glenn Kezer, Mari Nettum, Bob Neukum, Roger Allan Raby, Jo Tract (*Dell Brownlee*), Gene Varrone. RE-OPENING SINGERS: Trish Dwelley, Steve Elmore, Richard Frisch, Carolyn Kemp, Mari Nettum, Roger Allan Raby, Dell Brownlee, Gene Varrone, *Terri Baker, David Cryer, Dean Doss, Paul Eichel, Barney Johnston, Bobbi Lange*; LEAD DANCER: Don Crichton; DANCERS: Virginia Allen, Diane Arnold, Judy Cassmore, Diana Ede, Ernie Horvath, Gene Kelton, William Louther (*John Richardson*), Charlene Mehl, Judy Newman, Jodi Perselle, Ed Pfeiffer, Carolsue Shaer, Patricia Sigris, Roy Smith, Bill Stanton, Wendy Taylor, James von Weiss. RE-OPENING DANCERS: Virginia Allen, Diane Arnold, Diana Ede, Gene Kelton, John Richardson, Charlene Mehl, Judy Newman, Jodi Perselle, Carolsue Shaer, Patricia Sigris, *Lynne Broadbent, Alice Glenn, Jerry Gotham, Buddy Spencer, Bill Starr, Ron Tassone, Michael Toles*. **Understudies**: Hope: Carolyn Kemp, Mitzie Welch (gone by re-opening); Byron: Gene Varrone, *Mitchell Gregg*; Rudolf: Don Crichton; Ralph: Steve Elmore; Gloria: Judy Cassmore, Terri Baker; Anton: Richard Frisch; Lou: William Louther, John Richardson; Dora: Jo Tract, *Dell Brownlee*; Myra Mae: Mari Nettum; Custer: Fred Cline, *Steve Elmore*; L.Z.: *Paul Michael* (for the re-opening); Approval: Maxie.

Note: In the cast, and for understudies, replacements are those who took over the roles for the re-opening of 2/15/65 (unless otherwise stated). **Act I**: *Scene 1* In front of Grauman's Chinese Theatre [scene dropped for re-opening]: "Oh, Those Thirties" (Byron) [this number was cut for the re-opening]; *Scene 2* The gate–F.F.F. Studio: "It's Good to Be Back Home" (Hope & Ensemble); *Scene 3* On the lot: *Scene 4* Executive dining room: "Fear" (Rudolf, Ralph, Nephews), "Fear" (reprise) (Byron & Nephews); *Scene 5* Wardrobe department: "Call Me Savage" (Hope & Rudolf), "The Usher from the Mezzanine" (Hope); *Scene 6* On the set; *Scene 7* Dora Dailey: "My Heart is Like a Violin" (Byron) [new number, added for the re-opening]; *Scene 8* Dr. Traurig's office — Vienna; *Scene 9* On the set: "I'm with You" (Hope, Byron, Lead Dancer, Violin Girls, Bow Boys), "The Usher from the Mezzanine" (reprise) (Hope & Ensemble) [replaced for the re-opening by a new number, "Notice Me" (Rudolph)]; *Scene 10* Executive dining room: "My Fortune is My Face" (Byron); *Scene 11* The bungalow: "Lila Tremaine" (Hope), "A Girl to Remember" (Hope) [new number, added for the re-opening]. **Act II**: *Scene 1* The gate — F.F.F. Studio [scene dropped for re-opening]: "Go Home, Train!" (Hope) [cut not long after the original opening, and replaced with "Everybody Loves a Winner"); *Scene 2* Dora Dailey: *Scene 3* Wardrobe department: "Close Harmony" (L.Z., Byron, Gloria, Nephews); *Scene 4* A street: "You Mustn't Be Discouraged" (Hope & Lou); *Scene 5* L.Z.'s office: "The Dangerous Age" (L.Z.), "L.Z. in Quest of His Youth" (L.Z., Gloria, Lead Dancer, Ensemble); *Scene 6* On the set: "The Fiddler and the Fighter" Finale (Byron & Ensemble), "Fade Out — Fade In" (Hope & Rudolf); *Scene 7* In front of Grauman's Chinese Theatre; *Scene 8* In front of Grauman's Chinese Theatre.

Reviews were good. Seven weeks after the Broadway opening, Carol Burnett was injured in a taxi accident, and suffered whiplash. She missed more than 25 performances, and box-office receipts fell drastically. Meanwhile Miss Burnett's first TV series, *The Entertainers*, began showing on CBS, and *Fade Out— Fade In*'s producer, Lester Osterman, demanded she not appear in the TV show if she was too ill to appear in his Broadway show. She countered by claiming that Mr. Osterman was trying to destroy her career by impugning her personal and professional integrity. Miss Burnett, clearly unhappy with the Broadway show, tried to buy her way out for $500,000, but failed. Then, on 10/17/64, she went into the hospital for injuries she claimed she'd received while starring in *Once Upon a Mattress* several years before. *Fade Out— Fade In* struggled along without her for a month, and was then forced to close on 11/14/64, after 199 performances. On 11/18/64 Messrs Styne and Osterman gave a press conference in which they said that Miss Burnett's injuries had in fact been sustained while filming a strenuous sequence for her TV show, and they blamed her for the closing of the Broadway show and for not letting them know when she'd be back. Miss Burnett did acknowledge wanting to leave the show, but accused the producers of harassing her. It went to arbitration with Actors' Equity, and Miss Burnett was forced to return to Broadway after she was de-hospitalized. The show re-opened on 2/15/65 with a slightly altered book and some new songs. Some of the roles had been cut and the order of some had been re-arranged. It ran another 72 performances, then closed for good. Jack Cassidy was nominated for a Tony.

After Broadway. YORK THEATRE COMPANY, 9/12/97–9/14/97. Part of the *Musicals in Mufti* series.

200. *Falsettos*

Neurotic, bisexual Marvin leaves his wife Trina and son Jason to have a life with his friend Whizzer. Later Trina marries Marvin's psychiatrist Mendel. Whizzer leaves Marvin, then they reconcile. As Whizzer is dying of AIDS, Jason holds his bar mitzvah in Whizzer's hospital room. There were three Off Broadway musicals without intermissions about bisexual Marvin—*March of the Falsettos; In Trousers;* and *Falsettoland,* all with music & lyrics by William Finn. The Broadway production of *Falsettos* was a combination of the two successful ones—*March of the Falsettos* and *Falsettoland.*

Before Broadway. *In Trousers* was presented by PLAYWRIGHTS HORIZONS, 12/8/78, as part of their Musical Theatre Workshop series. It had a full production from 2/21/79. 28 PERFORMANCES. DIRECTOR: William Finn; CHOREOGRAPHER: Marta Renzi; SETS: Donato Moreno; LIGHTING: Annie Wrightson; MUSICAL DIRECTOR/ORCHESTRATIONS: Michael Starobin. *Cast*: Alison Fraser, Joanna Green, Mary Testa, Chip Zien. Then it ran Off Broadway, at SECOND STAGE, 2/22/81–3/1/81. 15 PERFORMANCES. DIRECTOR: Judith Swift; CHOREOGRAPHER: Sharon Kinney; SETS: Nancy Winters; LIGHTING: Victor En Yu Tan. *Cast*: MARVIN: Jay O. Sanders; HIS WIFE: Kate Dezina; MISS GOLDBERG, HIS TEACHER: Alaina Reed; HIS HIGH SCHOOL SWEETHEART: Karen Jablons. "I Can't Sleep," "A Helluva Day," "How Marvin Eats His Breakfast," "My High School Sweetheart," "Set Those Sails," "I Swear I Won't Ever Again," "Rit Tit Tat," "I Am Wearing a Hat," "Marvin's Giddy Seizures," "A Breakfast Over Sugar," "I'm Breaking Down," "Whizzer Brown," "The Rape of Miss Goldberg," "Mommy Dear Has Dropped Dead in Her Sleep," "Nausea Before the Game," "Love Me for What I Am," "How America Got Its Name," "Marvin Takes a Victory Shower," "Another Sleepless Night," "Goodnight." PROMENADE THEATRE, 3/26/85–4/7/85. 16 previews. 16 PERFORMANCES. PRESENTED BY Roger Berlind, Franklin R. Levy, and Gregory Harrison; DIRECTOR: Matt Casella; SETS: Santo Loquasto; COSTUMES: Madeline Ann Graneto; LIGHTING: Marilyn Rennagel; SOUND: Tom Morse; MUSICAL DIRECTOR: Roy Leake Jr.; ORCHESTRATIONS: Michael Starobin. *Cast*: MARVIN: Tony Cummings; HIS WIFE: Catherine Cox; HIS HIGH SCHOOL SWEETHEART: Sherry Hursey; MISS GOLDBERG: Kathy Garrick. *Understudies*: For Miss Cox/Miss Hursey: Carol Dilley; For Miss Garrick: Mary Bond Davis. *Musicians*: PIANO: Sande Campbell; TRUMPET: Laurie A. Frink; DRUMS: John Harvey; WOODWINDS: Robert J. Magnuson & Ralph Olson; SYNTHESIZERS: Edward Strauss. "I Can't Sleep" (Marvin & Ladies), "Time to Wake Up" (Wife), "I Have a Family" (Marvin), "How Marvin Eats His Breakfast" (Marvin & Ladies), "Marvin's Giddy Seizures I" (Sweetheart), "My High School Sweetheart" (Sweetheart & Company), "Set Those Sails" (Teacher & Ladies), "I Swear I Won't Ever Again" (Marvin), "High School Ladies at Five O'clock" (Sweetheart & Ladies), "The Rape of Miss Goldberg" (Marvin & Teacher), "Love Me for What I Am" (Marvin & Wife), "I Am Wearing a Hat" (Sweetheart & Teacher), "Wedding Song" (Company), "Three Seconds" (Marvin), "How the Body Falls Apart" (Ladies), "I Feel Him Slipping Away" (Wife & Ladies), "Whizzer Going Down" (Marvin), "Marvin's Giddy Seizures II" (Company), "I'm Breaking Down" (Wife), "Packing Up" (Marvin), "Breakfast Over Sugar" (Marvin & Wife), "How America Got Its Name" (Sweetheart, Teacher, Marvin), "Time to Wake Up" (reprise) (Wife), "Another Sleepless Night" (Company), "Goodnight/No Hard Feelings" (Company).

March of the Falsettos was originally produced Off Off Broadway, at PLAYWRIGHTS HORIZONS, 4/4/81. Previews from 3/27/81. It moved Off

Broadway, to the WESTSIDE ARTS THEATRE, 5/20/81–9/26/81. 170 PERFORMANCES. PRESENTED BY Playwrights Horizons; DIRECTOR: James Lapine; LIGHTING: Frances Aronson; MUSICAL DIRECTOR: Michael Lee Stockler; ORCHESTRATIONS: Michael Starobin. *Cast*: MARVIN: Michael Rupert; TRINA: Alison Fraser; JASON: James Kushner; WHIZZER: Stephen Bogardus; MENDEL: Chip Zien. The Playwrights Horizons production ran again at WESTSIDE ARTS/CHERYL CRAWFORD THEATRE, 11/9/81–1/31/82. Previews from 10/13/81. 128 PERFORMANCES. PRESENTED BY Mary Lea Johnson, Francine LeFrak, Martin Richards & Warner Theatre Productions; DIRECTOR: James Lapine; CAST RECORDING on DRG. *Cast*: MARVIN: Michael Rupert; TRINA: Alison Fraser; JASON: Gregg Phillips; WHIZZER: Brent Barrett; MENDEL: Chip Zien. *Understudies*: Ralph Bruneau, Emily Grinspan, James Kushner. "Four Jews in a Room Bitching" (Company), "A Tight-Knit Family" (Marvin), "Love is Blind" (Trina, Mendel, Company), "The Thrill of First Love" (Marvin & Whizzer), "Marvin at the Psychiatrist" [a three-part mini-opera] (Marvin, Mendel, Jason), "My Father's a Homo" (Jason), "Everyone Tells Jason to See a Psychiatrist" (Company), "This Had Better Come to a Stop" (Company), "Please Come to My House" (Trina, Mendel, Jason), "Jason's Therapy" (Jason, Mendel, Company), "A Marriage Proposal" (Mendel), "A Tight-Knit Family" (reprise) (Marvin & Mendel), "Trina's Song" (Trina), "March of the Falsettos" (Men), "The Chess Game" (Marvin & Whizzer), "Making a Home" (Trina, Mendel, Whizzer), "The Games I Play" (Whizzer), "Marvin Hits Trina" (Company), "I Never Wanted to Love You" (Company), "Father to Son" (Marvin & Jason). In London it ran at the ALBERY THEATRE, 3/24/87–4/13/87.

Falsettoland, a sequel to *March of the Falsettos,* and the third play in the Marvin trilogy, ran, without intermission, at PLAYWRIGHTS HORIZONS, 6/28/90–8/12/90. 23 previews from 6/8/90. 54 PERFORMANCES. PRESENTED BY Maurice Rosenfield, Lois F. Rosenfield, with Steven Suskin; DIRECTOR: James Lapine; SETS: Douglas Stein; COSTUMES: Franne Lee; LIGHTING: Nancy Schertler; SOUND: Scott Lehrer; MUSICAL DIRECTOR: Michael Starobin. *Cast*: MENDEL: Chip Zien; MARVIN: Michael Rupert; JASON: Danny Gerard; WHIZZER: Stephen Bogardus; TRINA: Faith Prince; DR. CHARLOTTE: Heather MacRae; CORDELIA: Janet Metz. *Understudies*: Tim Ewing & Ellen Zachos. *Musicians*: PIANO: Michael Starobin; SYNTHESIZER: James Kowal; DRUMS/PERCUSSION: Glenn Rhian. *Scene 1* "Falsettoland" (Company), "About Time" (Marvin), "Year of the Child" (Charlotte, Cordelia, Marvin, Trina, Mendel, Jason); *Scene 2* "Miracle of Judaism" (Jason); *Scene 3* "The Baseball Game" (Company); *Scene 4* "A Day in Falsettoland," Mendel at Work (Mendel), Trina and Mendel's house (Trina & Mendel), Dr. Charlotte and Cordelia's house (Charlotte & Cordelia), Racquetball court (Marvin & Whizzer); *Scene 5* "Planning the Bar Mitzvah" (Jason, Trina, Mendel, Marvin); *Scene 6* "Everyone Hates His Parents" (Mendel & Jason); *Scene 7* "What More Can I Say?" (Marvin); *Scene 8* "Something Bad is Happening" (Charlotte & Cordelia); *Scene 9* "More Racquetball" (Marvin & Whizzer); *Scene 10* "Holding to the Ground" (Trina); *Scene 11* "Days Like This" (Marvin, Whizzer, Cordelia, Trina, Mendel, Jason, Charlotte); *Scene 12* "Canceling the Bar Mitzvah" (Trina, Mendel, Jason); *Scene 13* "Unlikely Lovers" (Marvin, Whizzer, Cordelia, Charlotte); *Scene 14* "Another Miracle of Judaism" (Jason); *Scene 15* "You Gotta Die Sometime" (Whizzer); *Scene 16* "Jason's Bar Mitzvah" (Jason, Whizzer, Marvin, Trina, Mendel, Cordelia, Charlotte); *Scene 17* "What Would I Do?" (Marvin & Whizzer). DRG recorded this one too. The production moved to the LUCILLE LORTEL THEATRE (also Off Broadway), 9/14/90–1/27/91. 4 previews. 161 PERFORMANCES. It had the same basic cast, except MENDEL: Lonny Price. Michael Rupert was replaced by Scott Waara during the run, and Danny Gerard by Jebby Handwerger.

The Broadway Run. JOHN GOLDEN THEATRE, 4/29/92–6/27/93. 23 previews from 4/8/92. 487 PERFORMANCES. PRESENTED BY Barry & Fran Weissler, in association with James & Maureen O'Sullivan Cushing & Masakazu Shibaoka, Broadway Pacific; MUSIC/LYRICS: William Finn; BOOK: William Finn & James Lapine; DIRECTOR: James Lapine; SETS: Douglas Stein; COSTUMES: Ann Hould-Ward; LIGHTING: Frances Aronson; SOUND: Peter Fitzgerald; MUSICAL DIRECTOR: Scott Frankel; ARRANGEMENTS: Michael Starobin; CAST RECORDING on DRG; PRESS: Pete Sanders Group; CASTING: Wendy Ettinger, Stuart Howard, Amy Schecter, Stephanie Diozzi; GENERAL MANAGER: Barbara Darwall; COMPANY MANAGER: Kim Sellon; STAGE MANAGER: Karen Armstrong. *Cast*:

MARVIN: Michael Rupert (1), *Adrian Zmed, Michael Rupert, Mandy Patinkin* (from 1/15/93), *Gregg Edelman* (from 6/1/93); WHIZZER BROWN: Stephen Bogardus (2), *Sean McDermott* (from 4/12/93), *Sal Viviano*; MENDEL: Chip Zien (3), *Jason Graae* (from 6/4/93); JASON: Jonathan Kaplan (7), *Sivan Cotel* (from 10/15/92); JASON (AT WEDNESDAY & SATURDAY MATINEES): Andrew Harrison Leeds (8), *Jeffrey Landman*; TRINA: Barbara Walsh (4), *Randy Graff* (from 4/12/93); CHARLOTTE: Heather MacRae (5); CORDELIA: Carolee Carmello (6), *Maureen Moore* (from 9/15/92). **Understudies**: Philip Hoffman, John Ruess, Maureen Moore, Susan Goodman. By 92–93: *Sal Viviano, Jordan Leeds, Jay Montgomery*. **Musicians**: PIANO: Scott Frankel; SYNTHESIZER: Ted Sperling; PERCUSSION: Greg Landes; FLUTE/OBOE/CLARINET/ALTO SAX: Rick Heckman. **Act I**: 1979: "Four Jews in a Room Bitching" (Whizzer, Marvin, Jason, Mendel), "A Tight-Knit Family" (Marvin & Mendel), "Love is Blind" (Marvin, Jason, Whizzer, Mendel, Trina), "Thrill of First Love" (Marvin & Whizzer), "Marvin at the Psychiatrist" [a three-part mini-opera] (Jason, Mendel, Whizzer, Marvin), "My Father's a Homo" (Jason), "Everyone Tells Jason to See a Psychiatrist" (Jason, Marvin, Trina, Whizzer), "This Had Better Come to a Stop" (Marvin, Whizzer, Jason, Trina, Mendel), "I'm Breaking Down" (Trina), "Please Come to My House" (Trina, Mendel, Jason), "Jason's Therapy" (Mendel, Trina, Whizzer, Marvin, Jason), "A Marriage Proposal" (Mendel, Tina, Jason), "A Tight-Knit Family" (reprise) (Marvin & Mendel), "Trina's Song" (Trina), "March of the Falsettos" (Mendel, Marvin, Jason, Whizzer), "Trina's Song" (reprise) (Trina), "The Chess Game" (Marvin & Whizzer), "Making a Home" (Mendel, Jason, Trina, Whizzer), "The Games I Play" (Whizzer), "Marvin Hits Trina" ("Marvin Goes Crazy") (Marvin, Mendel, Jason, Trina, Whizzer), "I Never Wanted to Love You" (Marvin, Mendel, Jason, Trina, Whizzer), "Father to Son" (Marvin & Jason). **Act II**: 1981: "Welcome to Falsettoland" (Company), "The Year of the Child" (Company), "Miracle of Judaism" (Company), "Sitting Watching Jason (Play Baseball)" (Company), "A Day in Falsettoland" (Company), "Racquetball: How Was Your Day?" (Company), "The Fight" (Jason, Marvin, Trina, Mendel), "Everyone Hates His Parents" (Mendel, Jason, Marvin, Trina), "What More Can I Say" (Marvin & Whizzer), "Something Bad is Happening" (Charlotte & Cordelia), "Second Racquetball" (Marvin & Whizzer), "Holding to the Ground" (Trina), "Days Like This I Almost Believe in God" (Company), "Canceling the Bar Mitzvah" (Jason, Mendel, Trina), "Unlikely Lovers" (Marvin, Whizzer, Charlotte, Cordelia), "Another Miracle of Judaism" (Jason), "Something Bad is Happening" (reprise) (Marvin & Charlotte), "You Gotta Die Sometime" (Whizzer), "Jason's Bar Mitzvah" (Company), "What Would I Do?" (Marvin & Whizzer).

Broadway reviews were mostly good. The show won Tonys for score and book, and was also nominated for musical, direction of a musical, and for Michael Rupert, Jonathan Kaplan, and Barbara Walsh.

After Broadway. TOUR. Opened in the 92–93 season, and ran in Fort Lauderdale, Palm Beach, Pittsburgh, and Stamford, Conn. MUSICAL DIRECTOR: Ben Whiteley. **Cast**: MARVIN: Adrian Zmed; WHIZZER: Ray Walker; TRINA: Carolee Carmello; CHARLOTTE: Barbara Marineau; CORDELIA: Yvette Lawrence; JASON: Jeffrey Landman; MENDEL: Stuart Zagnit.

TOUR. Also opened during the 92–93 season. **Cast**: MARVIN: Gregg Edelman; WHIZZER: Peter Reardon, *Stephen Bogardus*; MENDEL: Adam Heller; JASON: Jonathan Kaplan, *Sivan Cotel*; JASON (AT MATINEES): Ramzi Khalaf, *Brett Tabisel*; TRINA: Carolee Carmello; CHARLOTTE: Barbara Marineau, *Heather MacRae*; CORDELIA: Jessica Molaskey, *Julie Prosser*. **Standbys** (93–94 season): Gary Moss, Jay Montgomery, Dana Moore. This tour resumed in spring 1994. MUSICAL DIRECTOR: Ben Whiteley. **Cast**: MARVIN: John Herrera; WHIZZER: Peter Reardon; MENDEL: Adam Heller; JASON: Brett Tabisel; TRINA: Barbara Walsh; CHARLOTTE: Heather MacRae; CORDELIA: Julie Prosser.

Falsettos has been produced in several places over the years since 1992. Playwrights Horizons presented a weekend of reunion concert performances in 1/03. **Cast**: TRINA: Alison Fraser; MENDEL: Chip Zien; MARVIN: Michael Rupert.

SKIRBALL CULTURAL CENTER, 5/28/03–6/1/03. PRESENTED BY Los Angeles Theatre Works, as part of *The Play's the Thing* series; DIRECTOR: John Rubinstein. **Cast**: Michael Rupert, Chip Zien, Stephen Bogardus, Faith Prince, Amy Pietz, Asher Book.

The various components have also been produced separately. For example, *Falsettoland*. DIM SUM, NY, 7/9/98–8/18/98. 5 previews. 29 PERFORMANCES. PRESENTED BY National Asian American Theatre Company; DIRECTOR: Alan Muraoka. **Cast**: TRINA: Ann Harada; DR. CHARLOTTE: Christine Toy; MARVIN: Jason Ma; WHIZZER: Welly Yang.

201. *A Family Affair*

Set in Chicago and its suburbs, in the present time. About Sally and Jerry, a young Jewish couple, and their wedding plans from the time of the engagement to the wedding itself. But they come up against Sally's bachelor uncle guardian, Alfie, and Jerry's parents, Morris and Tilly, who develop a war among themselves.

Before Broadway. In early 1961 Leland Hayward bought the rights to the show, which he planned to produce with Jerome Robbins. Mr. Robbins was to have been director/choreographer, and Gertrude Berg was to have starred, but the project fell through. Next, lawyer Andrew Siff optioned the property, and, after Hal Prince had turned him down as director because he felt the story was too predictable, Mr. Siff hired Word Baker. It was capitalized at $350,000, and United Artists was the major investor. After tryouts opened at the Erlanger Theatre, Philadelphia on 12/23/61, during which *Variety* called it a kosher version of *Father of the Bride*, and other unkind things were said about it, Mr. Siff wanted to close and cancel the scheduled Broadway opening date. As a last resort, Mr. Siff called Gower Champion, Jerry Robbins and George Abbott, to see if they could come in and help. They couldn't, so Mr. Siff asked Hal Prince back, and Mr. Prince came to Philly to see the show. With less than three weeks to go before Broadway, with no money to work with, with no more audience to see it in Philly, Mr. Prince was fighting long odds. On top of that he had never directed before. But, encouraged by his old mentor Mr. Abbott, on 1/5/62 Hal Prince became the director. At that point Bob Herget was called in to replace John Butler as choreographer (even though Mr. Butler retained credit — Mr. Herget was credited with "musical staging"). Hal Prince put back the Broadway opening date from 1/23/62 to 1/27/62, and insisted on total authority to get the show done. He had trouble with Shelley Berman, but it was nothing he couldn't handle. On 1/18/62 Mr. Prince added three new scenes and re-staged a whole number. Other huge, wholesale changes were made, to the script, lyrics, and sets. Two numbers were cut — "Milwaukee" and "Mamie in the Afternoon" (later re-written for *The Act*, as "Arthur in the Afternoon"). Then the production went to New York, but it wasn't a success (Hal Prince never thought it could be). This was John Kander's first show as composer.

The Broadway Run. BILLY ROSE THEATRE, 1/27/62–3/25/62. 5 previews from 1/24/62. 65 PERFORMANCES. PRESENTED BY Andrew Siff; MUSIC: John Kander; LYRICS: John Kander & James Goldman; BOOK: James Goldman & William Goldman; DIRECTOR: Harold Prince; CHOREOGRAPHER: John Butler; MUSICAL NUMBERS STAGED BY: Bob Herget; SETS/LIGHTING: David Hays; COSTUMES: Robert Fletcher; MUSICAL DIRECTOR/VOCAL ARRANGEMENTS: Stanley Lebowsky; ORCHESTRATIONS: Robert Ginzler; DANCE MUSIC ARRANGEMENTS: Gerald Alters; CAST RECORDING on United Artists; PRESS: Harvey B. Sabinson, Lila Glaser, David Powers; GENERAL MANAGER: Joseph Harris; COMPANY MANAGER: Ira Bernstein; PRODUCTION STAGE MANAGER: Richard Evans; STAGE MANAGER: James Bronson; ASSISTANT STAGE MANAGER: Geoffrey Brown. **Cast**: SALLY NATHAN: Rita Gardner (5); GERRY SIEGAL: Larry Kert (4); ALFIE NATHAN: Shelley Berman (1); MORRIS SIEGAL: Morris Carnovsky (3); TILLY SIEGAL: Eileen Heckart (2), *Carol Bruce*; MRS. FORSYTHE: Paula Trueman; MOTHER LEDERER: Lulu Bates; BABS SANDITZ: Beryl Towbin; SELMA SIEGAL: Barbara Ann Walters; CINDY: Joan Lowe; JENNY STONE: Cathryn Damon; IRMA: Kelli Scott; WILMA: Linda Lavin; BETTY JANE: Carolsue Shaer; MARIE ROSE: Judy West; CRYING DAUGHTER: Linda Lavin; MOTHER: Alice Nunn; CHRISTOPHER SANDITZ: Randy Garfield; MR. WEAVER: Jack De Lon; WOLFGANG DEMOTT: Sam Greene; KENWOOD SANDITZ: Bill McDonald; MORTON LEDERER: Ferdinand Hilt; BERNICE LEDERER: Lynne Charnay; MILTON LEDERER: Bill Linton; HELENE LEDERER: Yettanda Enelow; SIMON LEDERER: Don Crabtree; EMIL LEDERER: Ed Becker; BIG SADIE

LEDERER: Jean Bruno; LITTLE SADIE LEDERER: Maggie Task; SPORTS ANNOUNCER: Sam Greene; MISS LUMPE: Bibi Osterwald; HARRY LATZ: Gino Conforti; FIFI OF PARIS: Linda Lavin; BRASH GIRL: Charlene Carter; QUIET GIRL: Linda Lavin; STOP & SHOP ANSWERING SERVICE: Alice Nunn; SINGERS: Eddie Becker, Theodora Brandon, Jean Bruno, Yettanda Enelow, Sam Greene, Linda Lavin, Gary Leatherman, Ripple Lewis, Alice Nunn, Kelli Scott, Maggie Task, Barbara Ann Walters; DANCERS: Tommy Abbott, Robert Bishop, Charlene Carter, Jeremy Ives, Bob La Crosse, Carolsue Shaer, Judy West. ***Understudies***: Alfie: Bill Linton; Tilly: Lynn Charnay; Morris: Ferdinand Hilt; Gerry/Harry: Gary Leatherman; Sally: Kelli Scott; Miss Lumpe: Alice Nunn; Mother Lederer: Jean Bruno; Weaver/Milton: Ripple Lewis; Mrs. Forsythe: Barbara Ann Walters; Jenny: Joan Lowe; Kenwood: Gino Conforti; Babs: Linda Lavin; Christopher: Ken Kealy; Morton: Sam Greene. ***Act I***: "Anything for You" (Gerry & Sally), "Beautiful" (Alfie), "Beautiful" (reprise) (Tilly), "My Son, the Lawyer" (Tilly, Mother Lederer, Babs, Ladies), "Every Girl Wants to Get Married" (Sally & Babs), "Right Girls" (staged by John Butler) (Alfie, Mr. Weaver, Gentlemen of the Gym), "Kalua Bay" (staged by John Butler) (Tilly & Morris), "There's a Room in My House" (Gerry & Sally), "Siegal Marching Song" (Football Game) (Babs & Her Family), "Nathan Marching Song" (Football Game) (Alfie & His Friends), "Harmony" (Miss Lumpe, Mr. Weaver, Harry Fifi). ***Act II***: "Now, Morris" (Morris), "Wonderful Party" (Gerry & Kenny), "Revenge" (staged by John Butler) (Alfie & The Voices), "Summer is Over" (Tilly), "Harmony" (reprise) (Alfie, Tilly, Miss Lumpe, Their Staffs), "I'm Worse than Anybody" (Tilly, Morris, Alfie), "What I Say Goes" (Gerry), "The Wedding" (Everybody).

Reviews were very divided. The production lost $420,000.

After Broadway. YORK THEATRE COMPANY, 1/24/03–1/26/03. In concert; part of the *Musicals in Mufti* series. DIRECTOR: Richard Sabellico (Jay Binder had been announced); MUSICAL DIRECTOR: John Mulcahy. **Cast**: TILLY: Alix Korey; JERRY: Blade Hackler (Josh Prince had been announced); SALLY: Leslie Kritzer; MORRIS: David Margulies; ALFIE: Richard Ziman; WEAVER: Eddie Korbich; MISS LUMPE: Nora Mae Lyng; HARRY: Charlie Marcus; JENNY: Kate Suber.

202. *Fanny*

Life on the waterfront of Old Marseilles, not so long ago. Panisse (a rich sail maker) and Cesar (a local waterfront café owner) are old cronies. Cesar's son, Marius, is in love with Fanny (daughter of fish-stall keeper Honorine), but follows his dream and sails away to sea leaving behind a pregnant Fanny. Panisse marries the girl in order to save her honor, and acts as father to her son. When Marius returns he is persuaded by Cesar to give up his claim on the child. A few years later Panisse dictates a letter on his deathbed, asking that Marius marry Fanny. Claudine and Claudette are identical twins, friends of Fanny's. Other friends of Fanny's are: Nanette, Mimi, Marie, Michellette. The Admiral is an eccentric waterfront character. Escartifique is the ferry boat captain. Monsieur Brun is the customs inspector recently returned from Paris.

Before Broadway. This was the first of 27 Broadway musicals produced by former St. Louis lawyer David Merrick, who had acquired the rights to the three Pagnol plays, *Marius, Fanny,* and *Cesar,* after several trips to France to persuade M. Pagnol to sell. Mr. Merrick hired Josh Logan to direct and to write the book and also to get Rodgers & Hammerstein to do the score. However, those giants wanted to produce too, so they turned him down. Mr. Merrick then went after Alan Jay Lerner and Burton Lane, but they were unavailable, so he went with Harold Rome. Josh Logan had translated from the French all three plays, then condensed them into one, while leaving room for musical numbers. He chose S.N. Behrman, famous playwright, to help him. This was Behrman's only stage musical credit. Logan cracked up under the pressure of not only doing all this, but simultaneously directing the pre-Broadway tryout of *Kind Sir* (a straight play), as well as negotiating for the rights to James A. Michener's *Sayonara.* Helen Tamiris replaced James

Starbuck as choreographer. The show tried out at the Shubert Theatre, Boston, 10/12/54–10/30/54. The ending was changed at Oscar Hammerstein's suggestion.

The Broadway Run. MAJESTIC THEATRE, 11/4/54–12/1/56; BELASCO THEATRE, 12/4/56–12/16/56. Total of 888 PERFORMANCES. PRESENTED BY David Merrick & Joshua Logan; MUSIC/LYRICS: Harold Rome; BOOK: S.N. Behrman & Joshua Logan; BASED ON Marcel Pagnol's French movie trilogy *Marius* (1931), *Fanny* (1932), and *Cesar* (1936); DIRECTOR: Joshua Logan; CHOREOGRAPHER: Helen Tamiris; SETS/LIGHTING: Jo Mielziner; COSTUMES: Alvin Colt; MUSICAL DIRECTOR/VOCAL ARRANGEMENTS: Lehman Engel; CONDUCTOR: Pembroke Davenport; ORCHESTRAL ARRANGEMENTS: Philip J. Lang; BALLET MUSIC/MUSICAL CONTINUITY: Trude Rittman; PRESS: Dick Weaver, *Max Eisen, Robert Hector;* CASTING: Martin Baum & Abe Newborn; GENERAL MANAGER: Jack Schlissel; PRODUCTION STAGE MANAGER: Kermit Kegley, *David Kanter;* STAGE MANAGER: Beau Tilden, *Charles Blackwell;* ASSISTANT STAGE MANAGER: Charles Blackwell, *Tom Gleason, Kevin Scott.* **Cast**: ARAB RUG SELLER: Mohammed el-Bakkar [this role became Arab Singer during the run]; MARIUS: William Tabbert (4), *Jack Washburn;* FANNY CABANIS: Florence Henderson (3), *June Roselle;* MAORI VENDOR: Katherine Graves; LACE VENDOR: Betty Carr, *Lindsay Kirkpatrick, Betty Zollinger;* CUSTOMERS: Toni Wheelis (*Ruth Kuzub*), Lindsay Kirkpatrick, Dolores Smith, Margaret Baxter (as the Oyster Fancier); CLAUDINE: Tani Seitz, *Phyllis Dorne, Lynne Broadbent;* CLAUDETTE: Dran Seitz, *Eloise Milton, Melinda Miles;* CHARLES: Wally Strauss; CHARLES'S FRIENDS: Bill Pope, Dean Crane, Ronald Cecill (*Stanley Papich, Jack Beaber*), Michael De Marco; NANETTE: Norma Doggett; MIMI: Carolyn Maye, *Janet Pavek;* MARIE: Ellen Matthews, *Sybil Scotford;* MICHELLETTE: Jane House, *Ellen McCown;* PANISSE: Walter Slezak (2), *Billy Gilbert;* SAILOR: Herb Banke, *Don Braswell;* THE ADMIRAL: Gerald Price; MOROCCAN DRUMMER: Charles Blackwell [this role is also seen as Colonial Soldier]; 2ND MATE: Henry Michel; FISHERMAN: Steve Wiland, *Don Cerulli;* SAILMAKER: Jack Washburn, *Kevin Scott;* FISH-STALL WOMAN: Florence Dunlap, *Dulcie Cooper;* AN ARAB: Michael Scrittorale; CESAR: Ezio Pinza (1), *Lawrence Tibbett;* HONORINE: Edna Preston; ESCARTIFIQUE: Alan Carney, *Henry Lascoe;* M. BRUN: Don McHenry; ARAB DANCING GIRL: Nejla Ates, *Shawnee Smith;* NUN: Ruth Schumacher, *Patricia Finch* (from 55–56); CESARIO: Lloyd Reese, *Gary Wright, Kippy* Campbell; BUTLER: Mike Mason, *Warren Galjour;* MAID: Patricia Finch, *Lindsay Kirkpatrick;* GARAGE OWNER: Tom Gleason; PRIEST: Ray Dorian, *Stanley Papich, Jack Beaber;* ACOLYTES: Gary Wright & Daniel Labeille, *Stanley Vincent & Barry Clifford.* UNDERSTUDIES: Marius: Jack Washburn, *Kevin Scott;* Honorine: Florence Dunlap, *Dulcie Cooper;* Cesario: Daniel Labeille, *Barry Clifford;* Cesar/Escartifique: *Henry Michel;* Panisse: *C.K. Alexander, Alan Carney, Henry Lascoe;* Fanny: *Janet Pavek;* Arab Dancing Girl: *Dolores Smith;* Brun/Admiral: *Tom Gleason;* Rug Seller: *Charles Blackwell;* Fishwife: *Pat Finch;* Garage Owner: *Bill Pope.* ***Act I***: ***Scene 1*** The waterfront of Marseilles: "Never Too Late for Love" (Panisse & Ensemble), "Cold Cream Jar Song" (Panisse), "Octopus Song" (The Admiral), "Restless Heart" (Marius & Male Ensemble), "Does He Know?" (Fanny & Marius) [added after the opening], "Why Be Afraid to Dance?" (sung by Cesar) (danced by Cesar, Marius, Fanny, Ensemble), "Never Too Late for Love" (reprise) (Cesar, Panisse, Honorine); ***Scene 2*** Hakim's cellar: "Shika, Shika" (Arab Dancing Girl, Rug Seller, Ensemble); ***Scene 3*** Cesar's bar: "Welcome Home" (Cesar), "I Like You" (Marius & Cesar), "I Have to Tell You" (Fanny), "Fanny" (Marius); ***Scene 4*** The dock: Montage (Fanny, Marius, Cesar, Ensemble): The Lovers, The Sailing; ***Scene 5*** Cesar's bar; ***Scene 6*** Honorine's kiosk: "Oysters, Cockles and Mussels" (Ensemble); ***Scene 7*** Panisse's sail shop: "Panisse and Son" (Panisse); ***Scene 8*** The wedding: "Wedding Dance" (dance number) (danced by Moroccan Drummer & Ensemble); ***Scene 9*** The waterfront of Marseilles: First Act Finale (Ensemble). ***Act II***: ***Scene 1*** The nursery: "Birthday Song" (Fanny, Honorine, Ensemble); ***Scene 2*** Panisse's living room: "To My Wife" (Panisse), "The Thought of You" (Marius & Fanny), "Love is a Very Light Thing" (Cesar), "Other Hands, Other Hearts" (Fanny, Cesar, Marius), "Fanny" (reprise) (Cesar, Fanny, Marius); ***Scene 3*** Three vignettes: Montage (dance number) (danced by the Ensemble); ***Scene 4*** Cesario's room: "Be Kind to Your Parents" (Fanny & Cesario); ***Scene 5*** The circus: "Cesario's Party" (Cirque Francois) ACROBATS: Charles Blackwell, Michael De Marco, Ray Dorian, Bill Pope,

Toni Wheelis (*Sybil Scotford* from 55–56). *Michael Gugleotti* played the Solo Acrobat as a replacement; PONY: Wally Strauss; PONY'S TRAINER: Steve Wiland, *Don Cerulli* (from 55–56); TRAINED SEALS: Dran & Tani Seitz, *Lynne Broadbent & Eloise Milton* (from 55–56); LIVING STATUES: Betty Carr, Ronald Cecill (*Jack Beaber*), Norma Doggett, Ray Dorian, Ellen Matthews, Dolores Smith, *Ruth Kuzub, Michael Scrittorale*; CLOWNS: Herb Banke (*Don Braswell* from 55–56), Mike Mason (*Warren Galjour* from 55–56), Henry Michel, Jack Washburn (*Kevin Scott* from 55–56); Finale—AERIALIST: Dean Crane`& Ensemble; *Scene 6* A garage in Toulon; *Scene 7* Panisse's bedroom: "Welcome Home" (reprise) (Cesar & Panisse), Finale.

Broadway reviews were somewhat divided, mostly good. Nejla Ates caused quite a stir with her (lack of) costume. After the opening the order of songs in Act I was changed somewhat, and "Does He Know?" was added. In 1956 the show was forced to leave Broadway's largest theatre (the Majestic) for one of the small ones (the Belasco) due to *Happy Hunting* coming in. *Fanny* was Ezio Pinza's last production (he died 5/9/57). Walter Slezak won a Tony.

After Broadway. THEATRE ROYAL, DRURY LANE, London, 11/15/56–9/14/57. 347 PERFORMANCES. DIRECTOR: William Hammerstein; CHOREOGRAPHER: Onna White; SETS/COSTUMES: Georges Wakhevitch; MUSICAL DIRECTOR: Michael Collins. **Cast**: PANISSE: Robert Morley (his first musical), *Colin Cunningham*; FANNY: Janet Pavek, *Doreen Duke, Shelagh Aldrich*; CESAR: Ian Wallace; ADMIRAL: Michael Gough; HONORINE: Mona Washbourne, *Janet Joye*; MARIUS: Kevin Scott; BRUN: Julian Orchard; ESCARTIFIQUE: C. Denier Warren; ARAB DANCING GIRL: Hameda; SIMONE: Shelagh Aldrich.

TOUR. Opened on 12/25/56, at the Shubert Theatre, Boston, and closed on 5/25/57, at the Hanna Theatre, Cleveland. MUSICAL DIRECTOR: Pembroke Davenport. **Cast**: FANNY: June Roselle; PANISSE: Billy Gilbert; MARIUS: Jack Washburn; CESAR: Italo Tajo; HONORINE: Edna Preston; CESARIO: Carson Woods; BRUN: Don McHenry; ARAB DANCING GIRL: Nejla Ates; BUTLER/SAILMAKER/SAILOR: John Guarnieri; NUN: Marion Lauer; MARIE: Sybil Scotford; MICHELLETTE: Laurie Franks; ESCARTIFIQUE: Alan Carney; COLONIAL SOLDIER: Charles Blackwell; ADMIRAL: Gerald Price, *Ted Beniades*. Doretta Morrow played Fanny on the West Coast tour, and had a new number "Every Night" early in Act I.

THE MOVIE. 1961. PRODUCER/DIRECTOR: Joshua Logan. Shot in Marseilles, but without songs. **Cast**: FANNY: Leslie Caron; PANISSE: Maurice Chevalier; CESAR: Charles Boyer; MARIUS: Horst Buchholz; ESCARTIFIQUE: Salvatore Baccaloni; BRUN: Lionel Jeffries; HONORINE: Georgette Anys.

PAPER MILL PLAYHOUSE, New Jersey, 1989. DIRECTOR: Robert Johanson; CHOREOGRAPHER: Sharon Halley; SETS: Michael Anania. **Cast**: FANNY: Teri Bibb; CESAR: Jose Ferrer; PANISSE: George S. Irving; MARIUS: John Leone; ESCARTIFIQUE: KC Wilson; AYAH: Valerie Cutko; HONORINE: Karen Shallo.

THEATRE AT ST. PETER'S, NYC, 3/26/04–3/28/04. PRESENTED BY the York Theatre Company, as part of their *Musicals in Mufti series*; DIRECTOR: Michael Montel; MUSICAL DIRECTOR: Andrew Gerle. **Cast**: Matt Bogart, David Pittu, David Schramm, Martin Vidnovic.

203. *Fearless Frank*

Set in 1921 in Nice and in the memory of Frank Harris. The literary life and many loves of Frank Harris (1855–1931). The musical has no connection to the 1967 movie of the same name, starring Jon Voight.

Before Broadway. Dan Crawford, American landlord of the KING'S HEAD THEATRE CLUB, Islington, London, suggested that Andrew Davies do a musical of his (Mr. Davies') TV play. He did, and it ran there, 5/31/79. Previews from 5/23/79. 52 PERFORMANCES. DIRECTOR: Robert Gillespie; CHOREOGRAPHER: Fred Peters; SETS: Martin E. Tilley; COSTUMES: Maggie Smith; MUSICAL DIRECTOR: Peter Hodgkinson. **Cast** (in the same order given below for the Broadway list): Bill Stewart, Tony Scannell, Mary Chilton, Carol Cleveland, Nigel Bennett, Mandy More, Oliver Pierre, Nichola McAuliffe.

The Broadway Run. PRINCESS THEATRE, 6/15/80–6/25/80. 13 previews. 12 PERFORMANCES. PRESENTED BY David Black & Robert Fabian, in association with Oscar Lewenstein & Theodore P. Donahue Jr.; MUSIC: Dave Brown; LYRICS/BOOK: Andrew Davies (based on his TV play of 10/78, starring Leonard Rossiter & Susan Penhaligon); DIRECTOR: Robert Gillespie; CHOREOGRAPHER: Michael Vernon; SETS: Martin Tilley; COSTUMES: Carrie F. Robbins; LIGHTING: Ruth Roberts; MUSICAL DIRECTOR/ADDITIONAL ARRANGEMENTS: Michael Rose; ORCHESTRATIONS: Michael Reed; PRESS: Hunt/Pucci Associates; CASTING: Mary Jo Slater; GENERAL MANAGEMENT: Theatre Now; PRODUCTION STAGE MANAGER: Larry Forde; STAGE MANAGER: Steven Beckler; ASSISTANT STAGE MANAGER: Ralph Bruneau. **Cast**: FRANK HARRIS: Niall Toibin (1) ✩; FRENCH WAITER: Alex Wipf (7); HEADMASTER: Alex Wipf (7); KENDRICK: Alex Wipf (7); LORD FOLKESTONE: Alex Wipf (7); WHISTLER: Alex Wipf [role cut during previews]; SECRETARY: Valerie Mahaffey (5); SCHOOLGIRL: Valerie Mahaffey (5); JESSIE: Valerie Mahaffey (5); LILLY: Valerie Mahaffey (5); NELLIE: Kristen Meadows (6); KATE: Kristen Meadows (6); LAURA: Kristen Meadows (6); TOBIN: Steve Burney (8); WHITEHOUSE: Steve Burney (8); SMITH/CHAPMAN: Steve Burney (8); OSCAR WILDE: Steve Burney [role cut during previews]; NURSEMAID/ACTRESS: Ann Hodapp (4); BOOTBLACK/TOPSY: Ann Hodapp (4); NEWSBOY/ENID: Ann Hodapp (4); COWBOY/CARLYLE: Oliver Pierre (2); MR. CLAPTON/DE MAUPASSANT: Oliver Pierre (2); DOWSON: Oliver Pierre [role cut during previews]; MRS. MAYHEW/MRS. CLAPTON/MRS. CLAYTON: Evalyn Baron (3); SCHOOLBOYS/NEW YORKERS/HOTEL GUESTS: Company; COWBOYS/COWS/INDIANS: Company; A CROWD/NEWSBOYS: Company; STROLLERS/OPERA CHORUS: Company; HARRIS DETRACTORS/HARRIS PRAISERS: Company. **Understudies**: For Mr. Wipf/Mr. Burney: Ralph Bruneau; For Miss Mahaffey/Miss Hodapp: Valerie Beaman; For Miss Meadows/Miss Baron: Susan Elizabeth Scott. **Act I**: "The Man Who Made His Life into a Work of Art" (Mr. Toibin & Girls), "Nora, the Nursemaid's Door" (Miss Mahaffey) [added during previews], "The Examination Song, or Get Me on That Boat" (Messrs Wipf, Burney, Toibin), "Halted at the Very Gates of Paradise–a Song of Frustration" (Mr. Toibin & Girls), "Come and Help Yourself to America, or Frank in the Melting Pot" (Company), "Dandy Night Clerk, or How to Get On in the Hotel Trade" (Company), "Riding the Range — a Song of the Old West" (Company), "Oh, Catch Me, Mr. Harris, 'cause I'm Falling for You" (Miss Meadows, Miss Hodapp, Miss Mahaffey, Miss Baron, Mr. Toibin), "The Greatest Man of All" (Mr. Toibin & Company). **Act II**: "My Poor Wee Lassic — a Scottish Lament" (Mr. Pierre), "My Own, or True Love at Last" (Mr. Toibin, Miss Meadows, Miss Baron, Mr. Pierre) [added during previews], "Evening News — a Song of Success" (Company), "Le Maitre de la Conte, or Maupassant Tells All" (Mr. Pierre), "Oh, Mr. Harris, You're a Naughty, Naughty Man!" (Mr. Toibin & Miss Baron), "Great Men, Great Days, or The King of the Cafe Royal" (Mr. Toibin) [added during previews], "Free Speech, Free Thought, Free Love" (Miss Hodapp, Mr. Toibin, Company), "Mr. Harris, It's All Over Now!" (Mr. Toibin & Company), "Fearless Frank" (Company).

Broadway reviews were disastrous.

204. *Fiddler on the Roof*

The trials and tribulations of Tevye, the milkman in the Jewish Orthodox village of Anatevka, in Tsarist Russia of 1905. The story opens (without overture) with the cast extolling the virtues of "Tradition," a fiddler sitting precariously on a roof, and Tevye explaining that the people of Anatevka are like the fiddler, they also live precariously. Tevye introduces the townsfolk. Then things begin to change. Three of Tevye's five daughters (he had seven in the original Sholem Aleichem stories) marry against custom. Tzeitel, the eldest, marries Motel, a poor tailor, after Tevye has promised her to Lazar Wolf, the well-to-do, middle-aged butcher. Hodel, the second daughter, marries Perchik, a revolutionary student, and follows him to Siberia. Chava, the third daughter, marries a gentile, and is cut off by Tevye. Men even dance with women at one of the ceremonies. Near the final curtain a government official announces that the town will be destroyed in a pogrom and every Jew must leave the country. Tevye and what is left of his family hope for a new life in America.

Before Broadway. *Tevye the Dairyman* was a Yiddish Theatre non-musical production in 1935, and was filmed in 1939. It was optioned in 11/49, by Rodgers & Hammerstein, with a view to doing a musical using some unpublished numbers by Jerome Kern, but the project never took off. In 8/50 Mike Todd optioned it, but, again, it didn't happen. In London *Tevie der Milchiger*, a straight play, opened at the WINTER GARDEN, 4/1/57. Chewel Buzgan adapted it, directed, and played Tevie. Another straight play, *Tevye and His Daughters*, was done at CARNEGIE HALL PLAYHOUSE, 9/16/57–11/17/57. 72 PERFORMANCES. WRITER: Arnold Perl; DIRECTOR: Howard Da Silva. **Cast:** TEVYE: Mike Kellin; GOLDE: Ann Vita Berger.

As for the famous musical, Rodgers & Hammerstein turned down an offer to write it. In 1960 Jerry Bock, Sheldon Harnick & Joseph Stein wanted to adapt the novel *Wandering Star*, by Sholem Aleichem, but they went for his stories about Tevye instead. By 1961 they had written *Tevye and His Daughters* as a musical, and approached Harold Prince to produce. He turned them down; he felt the only person to direct was Jerome Robbins, but Mr. Robbins was working on *Funny Girl* at the time. So the project was shelved, with Bock & Harnick going to work on *She Loves Me* (with Mr. Prince), and Mr. Stein on his comedy *Enter Laughing*. But the three creators continued to look for a producer for their Russian story. Saint Subber and Fred Coe both optioned it, but failed to raise the money. Jerry Robbins finally came aboard as director/choreographer, and Hal Prince joined Fred Coe as producer, but then bought him out, and became sole producer. Just before rehearsals began (in 6/64) the title was changed to *Fiddler on the Roof*; Hal Prince was inspired by the Chagall painting which depicts a fiddler soaring over a small Eastern European town. Other titles considered were: *Tevye*, *The Old Country*, and *Where Papa Came From*. For the lead Danny Kaye was suggested, and also Alan King, Danny Thomas, Tom Bosley, Howard Da Silva, and Julius La Rosa, but Hal Prince wanted Zero Mostel, and Mr. Mostel was signed — but would agree only to a 9-month contract. The show tried out in Detroit during the summer of 1964, during a newspaper strike (so there were no local reviews). It cost $375,000 and did very well during its four weeks in Detroit, despite a lousy review by *Variety*. Then it went to Washington, DC, where it sold out and got great reviews. The number "As Much as That" (Perchik), which opened Act II, was cut at this point. "Dear, Sweet Sewing Machine" (Motel), was also cut, and "Letters from America" was merged into "Anatevka."

The Broadway Run. IMPERIAL THEATRE, 9/22/64–2/25/67; MAJESTIC THEATRE, 2/27/67–12/12/70; BROADWAY THEATRE, 12/14/70–7/2/72. Previews from 9/17/64. Total of 3,242 PERFORMANCES. PRESENTED BY Harold Prince, by special permission of Crown Publishers, Arnold Perl, the Estate of Olga Rabinowitz; MUSIC: Jerry Bock; LYRICS: Sheldon Harnick; BOOK: Joseph Stein; BASED ON the 1894 short story collection *Tevye and His Daughters*, by Sholem Aleichem; DIRECTOR/CHOREOGRAPHER: Jerome Robbins; ASSISTANT CHOREOGRAPHER: Tommy Abbott; SETS: Boris Aronson; ASSISTANT SETS: Lisa Jalowetz [i.e. Mrs. Aronson]; COSTUMES: Patricia Zipprodt; LIGHTING: Jean Rosenthal; MUSICAL DIRECTOR/VOCAL ARRANGEMENTS: Milton Greene; ORCHESTRATIONS: Don Walker; DANCE MUSIC ARRANGEMENTS: Betty Walberg; CAST RECORDING on RCA Victor; PRESS: Sol Jacobson, Lewis Harmon, Earl Butler (*Faith Geer* by 65–66 & gone by 67–68), *Ruth Smuckler* (by 71–72); CASTING: Shirley Rich & Jack Leigh; GENERAL MANAGER: Carl Fisher; COMPANY MANAGER: Clarence Jacobson, *Warren O'Hara* (by 70–71); PRODUCTION STAGE MANAGER: Ruth Mitchell; STAGE MANAGER: Robert D. Currie, *Edmund Baylies* (by 65–66), *Ed Aldridge* (by 69–70), *Paul Waigner* (by 70–71); ASSISTANT STAGE MANAGER: James Bronson, *Edward Preston* (by 67–68), *Jay Jacobson* (by 69–70), *David Wolf* (by 69–70), *Steve Bohn* (by 71–72). **Cast:** TEVYE, A DAIRYMAN: Zero Mostel (1), *Luther Adler* (during Mr. Mostel's vacation, 1/18/65–1/30/65, and then permanently from 8/15/65), *Herschel Bernardi* (from 11/8/65), *Harry Goz* (during Mr. Bernardi's vacation, 66–67, and during his month-long illness, 8/14/67–9/18/67, and permanently from 11/6/67), *Jerry Jarrett* (from 5/12/69), *Harry Goz* (from 9/8/69), *Jerry Jarrett* (from 1/5/70), *Paul Lipson* (from 1/19/70), *Jerry Jarrett* (during Mr. Lipson's vacations, 10/12/70–10/19/70 & 10/11/71–10/18/71), *Jan Peerce* (from 12/14/71), *Paul Lipson* (from 5/2/72); GOLDE, HIS WIFE: Maria Karnilova (2), *Helen Verbit* (during Miss Karnilova's absence, 6/26/67–7/17/67), *Martha Schlamme* (from 4/9/68), *Dolores Wilson*

(from 7/1/68), *Rae Allen* (from 7/15/68), *Peg Murray* (from 6/30/69), *Mimi Randolph* (during Miss Murray's absence, 8/30/70–9/14/70), *Laura Stuart* (during Miss Murray's absences, 12/21/70–2/1/71, and again, from 10/71), *Mimi Randolph* (from 12/14/71) *Peg Murray* (from 5/2/72); HIS (FIVE) DAUGHTERS: TZEITEL: Joanna Merlin (4), *Ann Marisse* (from 5/24/65), *Joanna Merlin* (from 10/66), *Bette Midler* (from 2/67), *Rosalind Harris* (from 2/70), *Judith Smiley* (from 5/5/70), *Mimi Turque* (from 9/9/70); HODEL: Julia Migenes (7), *Mimi Turque* (from 4/67), *Adrienne Barbeau* (from 10/68), *Susan Hufford* (from 11/2/70); CHAVA: Tanya Everett (10), *Peggy Longo* (from 6/69 — Miss Longo became Peggy Atkinson); SHPRINTZE: Marilyn Rogers, *Peggy Longo* (from 9/66), *Faye Menken* (from 6/69), *Leslie Silvia* (from 70–71), *Jill Harmon* (from 2/8/72); BIELKE: Linda Ross, *Pia Zadora* (from 64–65), *Leslie Silvia* (from 6/69), *Pamela Greene* (from 70–71); YENTE, A MATCHMAKER: Beatrice Arthur (3), *Florence Stanley* (from 6/65), *Ruth Jaroslow* (from 8/19/71); MOTEL KAMZOIL, A TAILOR: Austin Pendleton (5), *Leonard Frey* (from 8/65), *David Garfield* (from 3/67), *Peter Marklin* (from 6/2/70); PERCHIK, A STUDENT: Bert Convy (6), *Leonard Frey* (from 64–65), *Gordon Gray* (from 8/65), *Richard Morse* (by 67–68), *Michael Zaslow* (from 4/71); LAZAR WOLF, A BUTCHER: Michael Granger (8), *Paul Lipson* (from 8/65), *Paul Marin* (by 67–68), *Harry Goz* (from 7/67), *Boris Aplon* (from 8/67); MORDCHA, AN INNKEEPER: Zvee Scooler, *Fyvush Finkel* (during Mr. Scooler's vacation during 70–71); RABBI: Gluck Sandor, *Sol Frieder* (from 69–70); MENDEL, HIS SON: Leonard Frey, *Dan Jasin* (from 64–65), *Ken Le Roy* (from 65–66), *Larry Ross* (by 67–68), *James McDonald* (from 69–70); AVRAM, A BOOKSELLER: Paul Lipson, *Harry Goz* (from 65–66), *Dutch Miller* (by 67–68), *Joe Cusanelli* (from 67–68), *Jerry Jarrett* (from 68–69), *Reuben Schafer* (from 68–69), *Jerry Jarrett* (from 69–70), *Mitchell Jason, Ronald C. Moore* (from 71–72), *Jerry Jarrett*; NACHUM, A BEGGAR: Maurice Edwards, *David Masters* (from 67), *Reuben Schafer* (from 69–70); GRANDMA TZEITEL, GOLDE'S GRANDMOTHER: Sue Babel, *Duane Bodin* (from 65–66), *Jan Myers* (from 67–68), *Anna Perez* (from 69–70), *Faye Menken* (from 70–71); FRUMA-SARAH, LAZAR WOLF'S FIRST WIFE: Carol Sawyer, *Ann C. Davies* (from 67–68), *Marta Heflin* (from 68–69), *Harriet Slaughter* (from 69–70); CONSTABLE: Joseph Sullivan (9), *Ross Gifford* (by 69–70); FYEDKA, A YOUNG MAN: Joe Ponazecki, *Don Atkinson* (from 65–66), *John-Henry Sauvaige* (from 69–70), *Don Lawrence* (from 70–71), *Michael Petro* (from 70–71); SASHA, HIS FRIEND: Robert Berdeen (11), *Samuel Ratcliffe* (by 68–69), *Don Lawrence* (from 69–70), *John-Henry Sauvaige* (by early 70), *Fred Weiss* (by 70–71), *Wallace Munro* (by 71–72); SHANDEL, MOTEL'S MOTHER: Helen Verbit, *Laura Stuart* (from 68–69), *Elaine Kussack* (from 69–70), *Laura Stuart* (from 70–71); THE FIDDLER: Gino Conforti, *Ken Le Roy* (from 64–65), *Sammy Bayes* (from 65–66), *Ken Le Roy* (from 67), *Marc Scott* (from 70–71); VILLAGERS: SHLOIME, THE BAGEL MAN: John C. Attle, *Dan Tylor* (by 68–69); YITZUK, THE STREET SWEEPER: Sammy Bayes, *Pat Matera* (by 66–67), *Marc Scott* (by 67–68), *Glen McClaskey* (by 70–71); CHAIM, THE FISHMONGER: Lorenzo Bianco, *Bill Bugh*; DUVIDEL, THE SELTZER MAN: Duane Bodin, *Ben Gillespie* (by 67–68); SURCHA: Sarah Felcher, *Maralyn Nell* (from 69–70); LABEL, THE WOODSMAN: Tony Gardell; HERSHEL, THE POT SELLER: Louis Genevrino, *Victor Pieran* (by 66–67); YANKEL, THE GROCER: Ross Gifford; SCHMERIL, THE BAKER: Dan Jasin (also known as Dan Jasinsky), *Peter de Nicola* (by 70–71), *Carlos Gorbea* (by 71–72); FREDEL: Sandra Kazan, *Victoria Wyndham* (from 65–66), *Marta Heflin* (by 67–68), *Harriet Slaughter* (by 68–69), *Gretchen Evans* (from 69–70), *Rosalind Harris, Tanny McDonald*; YAKOV, THE KNIFE SELLER: Thom Koutsoukos, *Allan Gruet* (by 68–69), *John Bartholomew* (by 70–71), *Ed Linderman* (by 71–72); BLUMA: Helen Verbit, *Jane Bergere* (65–66), *Jan Myers* (by 67–68), *Anna Perez* (from 69–70), *Lee Arthur* (by 70–71); BERILLE: Sharon Lerit, *Jennie Lou Blackton* (from 65–66), *Adrienne Barbeau* (by 67–68), *Christine Jacobs* (by 68–69), *Felice Camargo*; MIRALA: Sylvia Mann, *Naomi Riseman* (by 65–66), *Charlet Oberley* (by 67–68); SIMA: Peff Modelski, *Judith Doren* (by 66–67), *Carolyn Mignini* (by 68–69), *Jill Harmon* (from 69–70); RIVKA: Irene Paris, *Ann C. Davies* (by 66–67), *Bette Midler* (from 11/66), *Ann Tell* (by 67–68); MOISHE, THE COBBLER: Charles Rule, *Del Franklin* (by 67–68), *Roger Brown* (by 71–72); ANYA: Roberta Senn, *Sue Babel, Phyllis Wallach* (by 65–66), *Susan Feldon* (by 67–68), *Phyllis Wallach* (by 68–69), *Faye Menken* (by 70–71); YUSSEL, THE HATMAKER: Mitch Thomas, *Mel Auston* (by 66–67), *Allan Byrns* (by 68–69), *Roger Briant* (by 70–71), *Kenneth Henley* (by

71–72); VLADIMIR: Tom Abbott, *Kip Andrews* (by 65–66), *Frank Coppola* (by 67–68), *Ronn Steiman* (from 69–70), *Bill Bugh* (by 70–71), *Myron Curtis* (70), *Barry Ball* (by 71–72). OTHER VILLAGERS: Robert D. Currie & Carol Sawyer. STANDBYS: Tevye: Mitchell Jason (70). ***Understudies***: Tevye: Paul Lipson, *Harry Goz* (by 66–67), *Joe Cusanelli* (by 67–68), *Jerry Jarrett* (by 69–70); Lazar: Paul Lipson, *Harry Goz* (by 65–66), *Joe Cusanelli* (by 67–68), *Jerry Jarrett* (by 68–69), *Reuben Schafer* (from 68–69), *Dan Tylor* (from 68–69), *Jerry Jarrett* (by 69–70); Tzeitel: Irene Paris, *Ann C. Davies* (by 66–67), *Bette Midler, Marta Heflin* (by 68–69), *Gretchen Evans* (by 69–70), *Rosalind Harris* (70); Fruma-Sarah: Irene Paris, *Ann C. Davies* (by 66–67), *Bette Midler, Judith Doren* (by 67–68), *Harriet Slaughter* (by 68–69), *Gretchen Evans* (by 69–70), *Rosalind Harris* (70); Hodel: Sandy Kazan, *Victoria Wyndham* (by 66–67), *Adrienne Barbeau* (by 67–68), *Christine Jacobs* (by 68–69), *Tanny McDonald*; Chava: Sharon Lerit, *Jennie Lee Blackton* (by 66–67), *Peggy Longo* (by 67–68), *Jill Harmon* (by 69–70), *Felice Camargo*; Perchik: Leonard Frey, *Thom Koutsoukos* (by 65–66), *Allan Gruet* (by 68–69), *John Bartholomew* (by 70–71), *Ed Linderman* (by 71–72); Motel: Leonard Frey, *John C. Attle* (by 65–66), *Larry Ross* (by 68–69), *James McDonald* (by 70–71); Fyedka: Robert Berdeen, *Samuel Ratcliffe* (by 68–69), *John-Henry Sauvaige, Don Lawrence* (by 69–70), *Fred Weiss* (by 70–71), *Bill Bugh* (by 71–72); Shprintze/Bielke: Sue Babel, *Phyllis Wallach* (by 65–66), *Judith Doren* (by 67–68), *Phyllis Wallach* (by 68–69), *Faye Menken* (by 70–71); Rabbi: Maurice Edwards, *David Masters* (by 66–67), *Reuben Schafer* (by 68–69); Avram: Maurice Edwards, *David Masters* (by 66–67), *Reuben Schafer* (by 68–69); Mendel: Danny Jasin, *Peter de Nicola* (by 70–71), *Glen McClaskey* (by 71–72); Nachum: John C. Attle, *Dan Tylor* (by 69–70); Constable: Ross Gifford; Fiddler: Sammy Bayes, *Larry Ross, Pat Matera* (by 66–67), *Marc Scott* (by 67–68), *Roger Briant* (by 70–71), *Carlos Gorbea* (by 71–72); Mordcha: Thom Koutsoukos, *Tony Gardell*; Grandma Tzeitel: Sylvia Mann, *Jane Bergere* (by 66–67), *Marta Heflin* (by 67–68), *Phyllis Wallach* (by 68–69), *Lee Arthur* (by 70–71); Golde/Yente: Helen Verbit (by 65–66), *Laura Stuart* (by 68–69), *Elaine Kussack* (by 69–70), *Laura Stuart* (by 70–71); Shandel: *Charlet Oberley* (by 67–68). **Act I: Prologue** "Tradition" (Tevye & Villagers); **Scene 1** The kitchen of Tevye's house: "Matchmaker, Matchmaker" (Tzeitel, Hodel, Chava) [a hit]; **Scene 2** The exterior of Tevye's house: "If I Were a Rich Man" (Tevye) [the big hit]; **Scene 3** The interior of Tevye's house: "Sabbath Prayer" (Tevye, Golde, Villagers); **Scene 4** The inn; the following evening: "To Life" (Tevye, Lazar, Mcn); **Scene 5** The street outside the inn; **Scene 6** The exterior of Tevye's house: "Tradition" (reprise) (Tevye's Monologue) (Tevye), "Miracle of Miracles" (Motel); **Scene 7** Tevye's bedroom: "The Tailor, Motel Kamzoil" (The Dream) (Tevye, Golde, Grandma Tzeitel, Fruma-Sarah, Villagers); **Scene 8** The village street and the interior of Motel's tailor shop; **Scene 9** Part of Tevye's yard; night: "Sunrise, Sunset" (Tevye, Golde, Villagers) [a bit hit], "Wedding Dance" (Villagers) (incorporated the ballet "Bottle Dance" (Yussel, Hershel, Shloime, Duvidel); **Scene 10** The entire yard of Tevye's house. **Act II: Scene 1** The exterior of Tevye's house: "Now I Have Everything" (Perchik & Hodel), "Tradition" (reprise) (Tevye's Rebuttal) (Tevye), "Do You Love Me?" (Tevye & Golde) [a hit]; **Scene 2** The village street: "I Just Heard" (The Rumor) (Yente & Villagers); **Scene 3** The exterior of the railroad station: "Far from the Home I Love" (Hodel); **Scene 4** The village street; some months later; **Scene 5** Motel's tailor shop: **Scene 6** A road; late afternoon: "Chavaleh" (Tevye); **Scene 7** Tevye's barn: "Anatevka" (Tevye, Golde, Yente, Lazar, Mendel, Avram) [originally called "A Little Bit of This"]; **Scene 8** Outside Tevye's house: Epilogue (Entire Company).

After the show got very good Broadway reviews, Zero Mostel stopped playing Tevye as the creators had made him, and started playing Zero Mostel. The show won Tonys for musical, producer of a musical, composer & lyricist, book, director of a musical, choreography, costumes, and for Zero Mostel and Maria Karnilova. It was also nominated for sets. On 7/21/71 it overtook *Hello, Dolly!* as Broadway's longest-running musical, with 2,845 performances. On 6/17/72, with 3,225 performances, it became the longest running Broadway show ever, of any type, when it passed *Life With Father* (*Fiddler* lost the record on 12/8/79, to *Grease*). It closed at the 7/2/72 matinee.

After Broadway. TOUR. Tried out from 4/11/66, in San Diego. It opened on 4/19/66, at the Music Center, Los Angeles, and closed on 1/17/70, at the Shubert Theatre, Philadelphia. MUSICAL DIRECTOR: Joseph D. Lewis, *Herbert Schutz* (by 68–69). **Cast**: TEVYE: Luther Adler, Paul Lipson (alternate. He did matinees only from 9/20/67, and all performances from 10/9/67), *Theo Bikel* (from 12/28/67), *Paul Lipson* (from 7/2/68), *Harry Goz* (from 3/70); GOLDE: Dolores Wilson, *Mimi Randolph* (from 4/2/68); SHPRINTZE: Renee Tetro, *Erica Greene*; BIELKE: Maureen Polye, *Ilene Karnow, Pamela Greene*; CHAVA: Kelly Wood, *Marsha Meyers, Elizabeth Hale*; YENTE: Ruth Jaroslow, *Lois Zetter, Jennie Ventriss* (from 7/68), *Marise Counsell*; TZEITEL: Felice Camargo, *Kathleen Noser, Leona Evans* (from 7/68), *Susan Lehman, Gretchen Evans*; HODEL: Royce Lenelle, *Barbara Coggin* (from 7/68), *Chris Callan*; MOTEL: David Garfield, *Stanley Soble* (from 3/67), *Peter Marklin* (from 7/68); PERCHIK: Joseph Masiell, *Virgil Curry, Keith Baker*; MORDCHA: Fyvush Finkel; MENDEL: Stanley Soble, *Lewis J. Stadlen, James McDonald, Lewis J. Stadlen*; LAZAR: Paul Lipson, Maurice Brenner (alternate), *Joe Cusanelli, Merwin Goldsmith, Bob Carroll*; RABBI: Baruch Lumet, *Will Albert* (in the last season); FIDDLER: Al DeSio, *Ross DiVito, Mark Stone*; GRANDMA: Tanny McDonald, *Enid Hart*.

HER MAJESTY'S THEATRE, London, 2/16/67. 2,030 PERFORMANCES. **Cast**: TEVYE: Topol, *Alfie Bass* (from 2/68), *Lex Goudsmit* (from 8/69), *Alfie Bass* (from 2/70); GOLDE: Miriam Karlin, *Avis Bunnage* (from 2/68), *Hy Hazell* (from 8/69), *Avis Bunnage* (from 5/11/70); TZEITEL: Rosemary Nichols, *Norma Dunbar* (from 2/68); YENTE: Cynthia Grenville; MOTEL: Jonathan Lynn, *Jeff L'Cise* (from 5/68); PERCHIK: Sandor Eles, *Harvey Sokolov* (from 5/68); HODEL: Linda Gardner, *Dilys Watling* (from 8/67).

TOUR. It opened on 8/27/68, at the Dallas State Fair Music Hall, and closed in 7/69, at San Francisco. MUSICAL DIRECTOR: Glen Clugston. **Cast**: TEVYE: Joe Cusanelli, *Harry Goz*; GOLDE: Susan Willis; GRANDMA: Fannie Cusanelli; PERCHIK: Richard Balin; VILLAGERS: Frankie Darrow, Clifford Lipson, Ann Reinking. The tour re-opened on 12/27/69, at Dade County Auditorium, Miami. MUSICAL DIRECTOR: Harold Glick. **Cast**: TEVYE: Bob Carroll (temporarily replaced by *Harry Goz & Robert Merrill*); GOLDE: Elaine Kussack, *Fritzi Burr*; GRANDMA: Fannie Cusanelli, *Bess Meisler*.

THE MOVIE. 1971. Isaac Stern provided the violin playing. The film, which cost United Artists $2 million to buy the rights to, was a mistake. "Tevye's Dream" replaced "The Tailor, Motel Kamzoil." **Cast**: TEVYE: Topol; GOLDE: Norma Crane; YENTE: Molly Picon; MOTEL: Leonard Frey.

JONES BEACH THEATRE, NY, 6/27/74–9/1/74. 67 PERFORMANCES. DIRECTOR: John Fearnley; CHOREOGRAPHER: Robert Pagent; SETS: John W. Keck; COSTUMES: Winn Morton; LIGHTING: Thomas Skelton; MUSICAL DIRECTOR: Jay Blackton; RELIGIOUS CONSULTANT: Zvee Scooler; PRODUCTION STAGE MANAGER: Mortimer Halpern. **Cast**: TEVYE: Norman Atkins; GOLDE: Geraldine Brooks; YENTE: Honey Sanders; AVRAM: Lee Cass; LAZAR: Ted Thurston; TZEITEL/GRANDMA: Sherry Lambert; HODEL: Christine Andreas; SHPRINTZE: Christine Miller; BIELKE: Celeste Miller; CHAVA: Robin Hoff; MOTEL: Bruce Adler; FYEDKA: Bjarne Buchtrup; PERCHIK: Richard Ianni; SASHA: Barry Ball; SHANDEL: Jeanne Grant; FRUMA-SARAH: Barbara Cowley; CONSTABLE: Stan Page; FIDDLER: Geoffrey Webb; NACHUM: Tony Slez; RABBI: Zvee Scooler; MENDEL: David Ellin; MORDCHA: Ralph Vucci; YOSEL [i.e. Yussel, the hatmaker]: Robert Monteil; CHORUS: Mickey Gunnersen, Frank Mastrocola, James Braet, Doris Galiber.

TOUR. Played 68 cities 1/21/75–4/21/75. **Cast**: Bob Carroll.

205. *Fiddler on the Roof (1976 Broadway revival)*

This Broadway run was part of a national tour. "I Just Heard" was not in this production.

The Broadway Run. WINTER GARDEN THEATRE, 12/28/76–5/21/77. 1 preview. Limited run of 167 PERFORMANCES. PRESENTED BY The Shubert Organization & Nederlander Producing Company of America & The John F. Kennedy Center for the Performing Arts, in association with Theatre Now, by special permission of Arnold Perl; MUSIC: Jerry Bock; LYRICS: Sheldon Harnick; BOOK: Joseph Stein; BASED ON

Sholem Aleichem's 1894 short story collection *Tevye and His Daughters*; DIRECTOR: Ruth Mitchell re-produced Jerome Robbins's original staging; CHOREOGRAPHER: Tommy Abbott re-produced Jerome Robbins's original choreography; SETS: Boris Aronson; COSTUMES: Patricia Zipprodt; LIGHTING: Ken Billington; MUSICAL DIRECTOR: Milton Rosenstock; ORCHESTRATIONS: Don Walker; VOCAL ARRANGEMENTS: Milton Greene; DANCE MUSIC ARRANGEMENTS: Betty Walberg; PRESS: Betty Lee Hunt & Maria Cristina Pucci; GENERAL MANAGEMENT: Theatre Now; COMPANY MANAGER: Robb Lady; PRODUCTION STAGE MANAGER: Kenneth Porter; STAGE MANAGER: Tobias Mostel; ASSISTANT STAGE MANAGER: Val Mayer. *Cast:* TEVYE, A DAIRYMAN: Zero Mostel (1) ☆, *Paul Lipson* (during Mr. Mostel's illness); GOLDE, HIS WIFE: Thelma Lee (2); HIS (FIVE) DAUGHTERS: TZEITEL: Elizabeth Hale; HODEL: Christopher Callan; CHAVA: Nancy Tompkins; SHPRINTZE: Davia Sacks; BIELKE: Tiffany Bogart; YENTE, A MATCHMAKER: Ruth Jaroslow (3); MOTEL KAMZOIL, A TAILOR: Irwin Pearl; PERCHIK, A STUDENT: Jeff Keller, *Patrick Quinn*; MORDCHA, AN INNKEEPER: Leon Spelman; LAZAR WOLF, A BUTCHER: Paul Lipson (4); RABBI: Charles Mayer; MENDEL, HIS SON: Paul A. Corman; AVRAM, A BOOKSELLER: Merrill Plaskow II; NACHUM, A BEGGAR: David Masters; GRANDMA TZEITEL, GOLDE'S GRANDMOTHER: Duane Bodin; FRUMA-SARAH, LAZAR WOLF'S FIRST WIFE: Joyce Martin; CONSTABLE: Alexander Orfaly; FYEDKA, A YOUNG MAN: Rick Friesen; SHANDEL, MOTEL'S MOTHER: Jeanne Grant; BOTTLE DANCERS: Tog Richards, Myron Curtis, Matthew Inge, Wallace Munro; THE FIDDLER: Sammy Bayes; VILLAGERS: SHLOIME, A BAGEL MAN: Matthew Inge; YITZUK, A STREETSWEEPER: Don Tull; CHAIM, A FISHMONGER: Glen McClaskey; DUVIDEL, A SELTZER MAN: Wallace Munro; SURCHA: Lynn Archer; LABEL: Tog Richards; SCHMERIL: David Horwitz; YAKOV, A KNIFE SELLER: Patrick Quinn; HERSHEL: Myron Curtis; FREDEL: Hope Katcher; BLUMA: Debra Timmons; MIRALA: Maureen Sadusk; SIMA: Lynn Archer; RIVKA: Joyce Martin; YUSSEL, A HATTER: Duane Bodin; VLADIMER: Robert L. Hultman; SASHA, FYEDKA'S FRIEND: Wallace Munro; BASCHA: Shelley Wolf; PINAHAS: Neal Thompson; IGOR: Lorenzo Bianco; LIFSHA: Annette Pirrone; BARUCH: John Kirshy. **Standby**: Tevye: Paul Lipson. **Understudies**: Golde: Jeanne Grant; Motel: Paul A. Corman; Yente: Lynn Archer; Tzeitel/Fruma-Sarah: Hope Katcher; Chava/Shprintze/Bielke: Debra Timmons; Lazar: Leon Spelman; Rabbi/Avram: David Masters; Perchik/Fyedka: Patrick Quinn; Hodel: Nancy Tompkins; Mendel: Matthew Inge; Constable: Glen McClaskey; Mordcha: Merrill Plaskow II; Beggar: Tog Richards; Grandma: Wallace Munro; Fiddler: Neal Thompson. **Swing Dancers**: Vito Durante & Adele Paige.

It opened to great reviews. Four months after his last performance, Zero died, on 9/8/77.

After Broadway. NEW YORK STATE THEATRE, 7/9/81–8/23/81. 3 previews. 53 PERFORMANCES. It got great reviews. The main crew differed from the 1976 Broadway run as follows: PRESENTED BY Eugene V. Wolsk & James M. Nederlander; LIGHTING: Ken Billington; MUSICAL SUPERVISOR: Kevin Farrell; MUSICAL DIRECTOR: Richard Vitzhum. *Cast*: TEVYE: Herschel Bernardi; GOLDE: Maria Karnilova; TZEITEL: Lori Ada Jaroslow; HODEL: Donalyn Petrucci; CHAVA: Liz Larsen; SHPRINTZE: Susan Sheppard; BIELKE: Eydie Alyson, *Kathy St. George*; YENTE: Ruth Jaroslow; MOTEL: Michelan Sisti; PERCHIK: James Werner; LAZAR: Paul Lipson; MORDCHA: Fyvush Finkel; RABBI: Alvin Myerovich; MENDEL: Ken Le Roy; AVRAM: Tog Richards; NACHUM: Ralph Vucci; GRANDMA TZEITEL: Susan Sheppard; FRUMA-SARAH: Joyce Martin; CONSTABLE: Paul E. Hart; FYEDKA: Joel Robertson; SHANDEL: Bess Meisler; FIDDLER: Jay Fox; YUSSEL: Stephen Wright, *Lawrence R. Leritz*; VILLAGERS: Bradford Dunaway, Jimmy Ferraro, Michael Fogarty, Margo F. Gruber, Michael Lane, Mark Manley, Elaine Manzel, Joyce Martin, Bess Meisler, Robert Parola, Thomas Scalise, Charles Spoerri, Marsha Tamaroff, Susan Tilson, Timothy Tobin, Stephen Wright, Robert Yacko. *Lawrence R. Leritz, Stephen Minning*. **Standby**: Tevye: Paul Lipson. **Understudies**: Golde/Yente: Bess Meisler; Lazar: Fy Finkel; Hodel: Susan Tilson; Fyedka: Robert Yacko, Timothy Tobin, Steve Minning; Perchik: Robert Yacko; Avram/Mordcha: Tog Richards; Nachum: Vito Durante; Constable: Charles Spoerri; Fruma-Sarah: Margo F. Gruber; Motel: Stephen Wright & Lawrence R. Leritz. **Swing Dancers**: Frank Colardo & Debra Timmons. Herschel Bernardi was nominated for a Tony.

206. *Fiddler on the Roof (1990 Broadway revival)*

Before Broadway. This Broadway run was part of a tour which had begun in San Francisco on 6/26/89. Namco Booking handled the tour. The tour had the same basic crew as for the Broadway run, except SOUND: Christopher "Kit" Bond; MUSICAL SUPERVISOR/CONDUCTOR: Kevin Farrell. Likewise the cast, except GOLDE: Marcia Rodd; FYEDKA: Mark Damon; LAZAR: Joel Kramer; MORDCHA: Bob Carroll; NACHUM: James F. Brandt; AVRAM: David Masters; RUSSIAN TENOR: Brad Little; OTHER VILLAGERS: Gerry Burkhardt & Jeffrey Wilkins; ALTERNATE VILLAGERS: James Horvath, Lori Ada Jaroslow, Laura Patinkin, Gary John La Rosa. Only Todd Heughens and Joanne Borts in the chorus went on to Broadway. Bob Carroll was understudy for Tevye, and Irma Rogers for Golde.

The Broadway Run. GERSHWIN THEATRE, 11/18/90–6/16/91. 18 previews from 11/3/90. 241 PERFORMANCES. PRESENTED BY Barry Weissler, Fran Weissler, PACE Theatrical Group, in association with C. Itoh & Company/Tokyo Broadcasting System International, A. Deshe (Pashanel); MUSIC: Jerry Bock; LYRICS: Sheldon Harnick; BOOK: Joseph Stein; BASED ON Sholem Aleichem's 1894 short story collection *Tevye and His Daughters*; DIRECTOR: Ruth Mitchell re-produced Jerome Robbins's original staging; CHOREOGRAPHER: Sammy Dallas Bayes re-produced Jerome Robbins's original choreography; SETS: Boris Aronson; ORIGINAL COSTUMES: Patricia Zipprodt; LIGHTING: Ken Billington; SOUND: Peter J. Fitzgerald; MUSICAL DIRECTOR/VOCAL ARRANGEMENTS: Milton Greene; ORCHESTRATIONS: Don Walker; PRESS: Shirley Herz Associates; CASTING: Stuart Howard & Amy Schecter; GENERAL MANAGERS: Charlotte Wilcox & Connie Weinstein; COMPANY MANAGER: Connie Weinstein; PRODUCTION STAGE MANAGER: Martin Gold; STAGE MANAGER: David John O'Brien. *Cast:* TEVYE, A DAIRYMAN: Topol (1), *Mark Zeller* (during Topol's vacation); GOLDE, HIS WIFE: Marcia Lewis; HIS (FIVE) DAUGHTERS: TZEITEL: Sharon Lawrence; HODEL: Tia Riebling; CHAVA: Jennifer Prescott; SHPRINTZE: Kathy St. George; BIELKE: Judy Dodd; MOTEL KAMZOIL, A TAILOR: Jack Kenny; PERCHIK, A STUDENT: Gary Schwartz; FYEDKA, A YOUNG MAN: Ron Bohmer; LAZAR WOLF, A BUTCHER: Mark Zeller; MORDCHA, AN INNKEEPER: David Masters; NACHUM, A BEGGAR: Michael J. Farina; YENTE, A MATCHMAKER: Ruth Jaroslow; RABBI: Jerry Matz; AVRAM, A BOOKSELLER: Jerry Jarrett; CONSTABLE: Mike O'Carroll; MENDEL, THE RABBI'S SON: David Pevsner; THE FIDDLER: Stephen Wright; GRANDMA TZEITEL, GOLDE'S GRANDMOTHER: Kathy St. George; FRUMA-SARAH, LAZAR WOLF'S FIRST WIFE: Jeri Sager; SHANDEL, MOTEL'S MOTHER: Panchali Null; BOTTLE DANCERS: Kenneth M. Daigle, David Enriquez, Craig Gahnz, Keith Keen; RUSSIAN DANCERS: Brian Arsenault, Michael Berresse, Brian Henry; OTHER VILLAGERS: Joanne Borts, Stacey Lynn Brass, Lisa Cartmell, David Enriquez, Todd Heughens, Marty Ross, Beth Thompson, Lou Williford. **Standby**: Tevye: Mark Zeller. **Understudies**: Golde/Yente: Lou Williford; Tzeitel: Lisa Cartmell; Hodel: Beth Thompson; Chava/Shprintze/Bielke: Stacey Lynn Brass; Motel: David Pevsner; Lazar: Mike O'Carroll; Perchik: Keith Keen; Fyedka: Brian Henry; Rabbi: David Masters; Mendel: Todd Heughens; Fiddler: David Enriquez; Constable/Avram/Mordcha: Marty Ross; Nachum: Newton Cole; Grandma: Judy Dodd. **Swings**: Chris Jamison & Newton Cole.

The show got great reviews. It won a Tony for revival, and Topol was nominated.

After Broadway. TOUR. Opened on 10/24/00, in Detroit. *Cast*: TEVYE: Theodore Bikel; GOLDE: Susan Cella, *Maureen Silliman* (from 12/9/01); LAZAR: John Preece; YENTE: Miriam Babin, *Mimi Bensinger* (from 1/15/02); CHAVA: Dana Lynn Caruso, *Sara Schmidt* (from 4/17/01); PERCHIK: Daniel Cooney, *Jonathan Hadley* (from 11/16/01); FYEDKA: Brad Drummer, *Justin Patterson* (from 5/28/01), *Brad Drummer* (from 11/16/01); HODEL: Tamra Hayden, *Rachel Jones* (from 11/16/01); MOTEL: Michael Innucci; TZEITEL: Eileen Tepper.

207. *Fiddler on the Roof (2004 Broadway revival)*

Before Broadway. This revival was announced on 12/13/02. By early 2003 Matthew Warchus had withdrawn as director, as had choreographer Kathleen Marshall. The Broadway date of fall 2003 was put back to early 2004. On 7/23/03 David Leveaux was officially confirmed as the new director. Broadway previews were put back from 1/16/03 to 1/17/03. Randy Graff was in negotiations for the role of Golde by 9/03. David Rockwell was going to do the sets, but Tom Pye did them instead. On 11/17/03 it was announced that the preview opening date was put back to 1/23/04 and the official opening date from 2/12/04 to 2/26/04. Rehearsals began on 12/1/03. There were 40 in the cast. "Topsy Turvy" was a new number recently written by Bock & Harnick for Yente & Villagers, to replace "The Rumor" in Act II. "The Rumor" had really only been there to cover a scene change. Larry Hochman orchestrated the new number. On 2/17/04, during Broadway previews, Nancy Opel replaced Barbara Barrie as Yente.

The Broadway Run. MINSKOFF THEATRE, 2/26/04–. 36 previews from 1/23/04. PRESENTED BY James L. Nederlander, Stewart F. Lane/ Bonnie Comley, Harbor Entertainment. Terry Allen Kramer, Bob Boyett/ Lawrence Horowitz, Clear Channel Entertainment; MUSIC: Jerry Bock; LYRICS: Sheldon Harnick; BOOK: Joseph Stein; BASED ON Sholem Aleichem's 1894 collection of stories, *Tevye and His Daughters*; DIRECTOR: David Leveaux; CHOREOGRAPHER: Jonathan Butterell; SETS: Tom Pye; COSTUMES; Vicki Mortimer; LIGHTING: Brian MacDevitt; SOUND: ACME Sound Partners; MUSICAL DIRECTOR: Kevin Stites; ORCHESTRATIONS: Don Walker; ADDITIONAL ORCHESTRATIONS: Larry Hochman; NEW CAST RECORDING, the most complete yet, on PS Classics, recorded 4/26/04, in Manhattan, and released on 6/8/04; PRESS: Barlow—Hartman Public Relations; CASTING: Jim Carnahan; GENERAL MANAGEMENT: 101 Productions; COMPANY MANAGER: Bruce Klinger; PRODUCTION STAGE MANAGER: David John O'Brien; STAGE MANAGER: Jenny Dewar; ASSISTANT STAGE MANAGER: Matthew Aaron Stern. *Cast:* TEVYE'S FAMILY: TEVYE, THE DAIRYMAN: Alfred Molina (1) ☆ (until 1/2/05), *Mark Lotito* (on 1/3/05), *Harvey Fierstein* (from 1/4/05); GOLDE, HIS WIFE: Randy Graff (2), *Marsha Waterbury* (on 1/3/05), *Andrea Martin* (from 1/4/05); HIS (FIVE) DAUGHTERS: TZEITEL: Sally Murphy; HODEL: Laura Michelle Kelly (until 6/10/04; she was off to play Mary Poppins in London), *Laura Shoop* (from 6/11/04); CHAVA: Tricia Paoluccio; SHPRINTZE: Lea Michele; BIELKE: Molly Ephraim, *Betsy Hogg* (from 8/3/04) [end of family sequence]; YENTE, THE MATCHMAKER: Nancy Opel (3); PAPAS: LAZAR WOLF, THE BUTCHER: David Wohl; RABBI: Yusef Bulos; MORDCHA, THE INNKEEPER: Philip Hoffman; AVRAM, THE BOOKSELLER: Mark Lotito; JAKOV: David Rossmer; CHAIM: Bruce Winant; MAMAS: SHANDEL, MOTEL'S MOTHER: Barbara Tirrell; MIRALA: Marsha Waterbury; FREDEL: Rita Harvey; RIVKA: Joy Hermalyn; SONS: MOTEL KAMZOIL, THE TAILOR: John Cariani (until 3/13/05), *Peter Matthew Smith* (from 3/21/05); PERCHIK, A STUDENT: Robert Petkoff (until 2/13/05), *Paul Anthony Stewart* (from 2/15/05); MENDEL, THE RABBI'S SON: Chris Ghelfi, *Roger Rosen* (stood in); YUSSEL, THE HATTER: Enrique Brown; YITZUK, THE STREET SWEEPER: Randy Bobish; LABEL, THE WOODSMAN: Jeff Lewis; SHLOIME, THE BAGEL MAN: Francis Toumbakaris; (TWO) DAUGHTERS: ANYA: Melissa Bohon; SURCHA: Haviland Stillwell; NACHUM, THE BEGGAR: Thomas Titone; FIDDLER: Nick Danielson; BOY: Michael Tommer; CONSTABLE: Stephen Lee Anderson; (FIVE) RUSSIANS: FYEDKA, A YOUNG MAN: David Ayers (until 1/05); SASHA, FYEDKA'S FRIEND: Jonathan Sharp; VLADEK: Stephen Ward Billeisen; VLADIMIR: Keith Kuhl; BORIS: Craig Ramsay; GRANDMA TZEITEL, GOLDE'S GRANDMOTHER: Haviland Stillwell; FRUMA-SARAH: Joy Hermalyn; BOTTLE DANCERS: Jeff Lewis, Francis Toumbakaris, Chris Ghelfi, Randy Bobish, Enrique Brown, *Ben Hartley*. **Understudies**: Tevye/Lazar: Philip Hoffman & Mark Lotito; Golde: Barbara Tirrell & Marsha Waterbury; Yente: Joy Hermalyn & Barbara Tirrell; Tzeitel: Rita Harvey & Gina Lamparella; Hoddel: Rita Harvey & Haviland Stillwell; Chava: Melissa Bohon & Lea Michele; Shprintze/Bielke: Melissa Bohon & Haviland Stillwell; Motel: Jeff Lewis & David Rossmer; Perchik: David Rossmer & Randy Bobish; Fyedka: Stephen Ward Billeisen & Jonathan Sharp; Constable: Mark Lotito & Bruce Winant; Fiddler: Antoine Silverman & David Rossmer; Rabbi/Mordcha: Tom Titone & Bruce Winant; Mendel: Randy Bobish & Roger Rosen; Grandma Tzeitel/Fruma-Sarah: Gina Lamparella; Boy: Sean Curley. *Orchestra*: CONCERTMASTER: Martin Agee; VIOLINS: Cenovia Cummins, Conrad Harris, Heidi Stubner, Antoine Silverman; VIOLAS: Debra Shufelt & Maxine Roach; CELLOS: Peter Sachon & Charles duChateau; LEAD TRUMPET: Wayne duMaine;

TRUMPETS: Tim Schadt & Joseph Reardon; TROMBONES/EUPHONIUM: Lia Albrecht; FLUTES: Brian Miller, Andrew Sterman, Martha Hyde; OBOE: Matthew Dine; CLARINETS: Andrew Sterman & Martha Hyde; BASSOON: Marc Goldberg; FRENCH HORNS: Larry DiBello & Peter Schoettler; DRUMS/PERCUSSION: Billy Miller; BASS: Peter Donovan; ACCORDION/CELESTE: Elaine Lord; GUITAR/MANDOLIN/LUTE: Greg Utzig.

On opening night, minutes before the curtain, Jerome Robbins' 91-year-old sister, Sonia Cullinen, died of a heart attack. The show got mixed reviews, and received Tony nominations for revival of a musical, sets, lighting, orchestrations, and for Alfred Molina and John Cariani.

208. *The Fig Leaves Are Falling*

Harry, a husband in Larchmont, NY, with nice wife Lillian and two attractive teenage children, suddenly decides to break loose and go off for a fling with a 24-year old girl named Pookie, founder of the Sexual Freedom League.

Before Broadway. Three months before rehearsals director Jack Klugman left and went to Hollywood. The show tried out in Philadelphia, and that's when the bad rumors started. George Abbott replaced Mr. Klugman. 3rd-billed star Jules Munshin was replaced by understudy Kenneth Kimmins (who lost star status). The show filled the vacant spot at Broadhurst that had been scheduled by the never-to-be-produced Bernstein-Sondheim show *A Pray for Blecht*. Before Broadway Scene 9 was The Stones' living room, and there were two more scenes: *Scene 10* Limbo: "Did I Ever Really Live?" (Harry); *Scene 11* The Stones' living room: "All of My Laughter" (reprise) (Harry). These two scenes were dropped and the songs re-allocated. The numbers "Juggling" and "My Aunt Minnie" were dropped. During Broadway previews, George Abbott took the number "All of My Laughter" away from Pookie and gave it to Lillian.

The Broadway Run. BROADHURST THEATRE, 1/2/69–1/4/69. 17 previews. 4 PERFORMANCES. PRESENTED BY Joseph Harris, Lawrence Carr, and John Bowab, in association with Harris Associates, Inc. & Levin-Townsend Enterprises, Inc.; MUSIC: Albert Hague; LYRICS/BOOK: Allan Sherman; DIRECTOR: George Abbott; CHOREOGRAPHER: Eddie Gasper; SETS: William & Jean Eckart; COSTUMES: Robert Mackintosh; LIGHTING: Tharon Musser; ASSISTANT LIGHTING: Ken Billington; MUSICAL DIRECTOR: Abba Bogin; CONDUCTOR/DANCE MUSIC ARRANGEMENTS: Jack Lee; ORCHESTRATIONS: Manny Albam; CAST RECORDING on RCA Victor; PRESS: David Lipsky, Lisa Lipsky, Marian Graham; GENERAL MANAGER: Joseph P. Harris; COMPANY MANAGER: Richard Grayson; PRODUCTION STAGE MANAGER: Terence Little; STAGE MANAGER: Wally Engelhardt; ASSISTANT STAGE MANAGER: Lathan Sanford. *Cast:* HARRY STONE: Barry Nelson (1) ☆; LILLIAN STONE: Dorothy Loudon (2) ☆; POOKIE CHAPMAN: Jenny O'Hara (4); MR. MITTLEMAN: Jay Barney (5); HODGEKINS: Joe McGrath; REV. WALTERS: Darrell Sandeen; GELB: Frank DeSal; MILDRED: Jean Even; GRACE: Mara Landi; MIMSY: Marilyne Mason (12); CHARLEY MONTGOMERY: Kenneth Kimmins (3); MARTY: Patrick Spohn; MOTHER-IN-LAW: Helon Blount (8); BILLY: David Cassidy (7); CECELIA: Louise Quick (6); LE ROY: Alan Weeks (9); QUEEN VICTORIA: Frank De Sal (11); MARY, QUEEN OF SCOTS: Anna Pagan (10); ELIZABETH MARSDEN: Pat Trott; MAO-TSE: John Joy; MARLENE: Jean Even; CYNTHIA: Jocelyn McKay; TOUGH GUY: Lathan Sanford; DANCERS: Frank De Sal, Pi Douglass, Jean Even, Mary Jane Houdina, John Mcdeiros, Michael Misita, Renata Powers, Sally Ransone, Charlene Ryan, Lathan Sanford, Patrick Spohn, Tony Stevens, Pat Trott; SINGERS: Edmund Gaynes, John Joy, Sherry Lambert, Mara Landi, Joe McGrath, Jocelyn McKay, Rosemary McNamara, Anna Pagan, Darrell Sandeen, Alan Weeks. *Standbys*: Lillian: Ellen Hanley; Harry/Charley: Jack Drummond. *Understudies*: Cecelia: Sherry Lambert; Billy: Edmund Gaynes; Pookie: Marilyne Mason; Le Roy: Pi Douglass; Mittleman: Patrick Spohn; Mother-in-Law: Mara Landi; Mimsy: Jocelyn McKay; Mary, Queen of Scots: Mary Jane Houdina; Queen Victoria: Tony Stevens. *Act I: Prologue*: "All is Well in Larchmont" (Choir); *Scene 1* The Stones' living room in Larchmont: "Not Tonight" (Lillian) [before Broadway "What Did We Do Wrong?" was in this spot; then "Lillian"

(Company)]; *Scene 2* Limbo: "Like Yours" (Pookie & Wall Streeters); *Scene 3* Harry's office: "The Fig Leaves Are Falling" (Pookie & Harry) [before Broadway "All of My Laughter" (Pookie & Harry) was here]; *Scene 4* The park: "Give Me a Cause" (Protestors); *Scene 5* Harry's office: "Today I Saw a Rose" (Harry); *Scene 6* The Stones' living room (off to Europe): "We" (Lillian); *Scene 7* The Stones' living room: "For Our Sake" (Billy & Cecelia); *Scene 8* Limbo; *Scene 9* The love-in in park: "Light One Candle" (Le Roy, Queen Victoria, Mary Queen of Scots, Hippies, Yippies, etc); *Scene 10* Limbo: "Oh, Boy" (Choir); *Scene 11* The Stones' bedroom (nightmare). *Act II: Scene 1* The Fig Leaves Are Falling: "The Fig Leaves are Falling" (reprise) (The Boys Club) [before Broadway this was the first time this song was heard, i.e. it was not a reprise]; *Scene 2* Limbo; *Scene 3* The Stones' living room: "For the Rest of My Life" (Lillian); *Scene 4* The theatre: "I Like It" (Harry & Pookie); *Scene 5* Limbo: "All My Laughter" (Lillian) [before Broadway "Broken Heart" (dance) (Lillian) was in the spot]; *Scene 6* Charley's apartment; *Scene 7* Pookie's pad: "Did I Ever Really Live?" (Harry), "Old Fashioned Song" (Charley & Ensemble), "Lillian, Lillian, Lillian" (Lillian, Cecelia, Billy); *Scene 8* Limbo; *Scene 9* The colorful living room: the ending (?).

Reviews were mostly a disaster, but Dorothy Loudon got very good notices. She got her first Tony nomination. This was the show in which Harry and Pookie raffle off a chicken to the audience.

After Broadway. *Hello Muddah, Hello Fadduh*, a series of vignettes inspired by the late Allan Sherman, ran Off Broadway, at CIRCLE IN THE SQUARE DOWNTOWN, 11/24/92–6/27/93. It used two songs from *The Fig Leaves Are Falling*—"Like Yours" and "Did I Ever Really Live?."

209. *Finian's Rainbow*

Humorous musical fantasy with satire and social significance. Finian, an Irishman from Glocca Morra, "borrows" a pot of gold from Og, the leprechaun. He has heard that the US government buries gold in the ground at Fort Knox, and he thinks they do that to make the money grow. So Finian, with his dreamy daughter Sharon, comes to Rainbow Valley, in the mythical southern state of Missitucky, buys land from some sharecroppers, and buries his pot in the ground near Fort Knox. Sharon falls in love with Woody (leader of the sharecroppers), whose sister Susan the Silent is a deaf mute. Woody, a champion of labor, and himself a laborer, can't get into a union and therefore can't work; he reluctantly falls for Sharon. Og arrives, looking for his gold, and much to his surprise finds himself falling in love with Susan and becoming mortal. Rumors begin circulating that the soil in Rainbow Valley is filled with gold, and Senator Rawkins, a southern bigot, tries to steal the land belonging to Finian and the sharecroppers. The gold can grant three wishes. One is that the senator becomes a black evangelist; Susan can suddenly speak; and the sharecroppers retain their land once they find that they have overspent thinking the land is strewn with gold. The land Finian has buried the gold in turns out to be tobacco-rich soil. Og becomes human and finds happiness with Susan. Woody and Sharon are united; Finian and the sharecroppers will become rich on tobacco.

Before Broadway. E.Y. Harburg had various ideas he wanted to satirize in straight plays (i.e. not musicals): an economic system that requires gold reserves to be buried at Fort Knox; southern American racial bigotry — he had the idea of a Theodore Bilbo-type of senator who becomes black overnight and thus becomes subject to the very laws he's behind; and finally the story of a leprechaun and three wishes. He eventually decided to combine all these ideas and make a musical. The role of Finian was difficult to cast. The producers wanted Barry Fitzgerald, but he was so tied up with movie commitments that he couldn't entertain the idea, as much as he might have liked to. Through Ria Mooney, former principal of the acting school at Abbey Theatre in Dublin, they found Albert Sharpe, who flew to New York, auditioned, and got the role (his Broadway debut). This was choreographer Michael Kidd's Broadway

debut (his right name was Milton Greenwald). His choreography was one of the first on Broadway to feature blacks and whites dancing together (but see also *On the Town*). The show tried out at the Shubert Theatre, Boston, from 10/18/46.

The Broadway Run. FORTY-SIXTH STREET THEATRE, 1/10/47–10/2/48. 725 PERFORMANCES. PRESENTED BY Lee Sabinson & William R. Katzell; MUSIC: Burton Lane; LYRICS: E.Y. Harburg; BOOK: E.Y. Harburg & Fred Saidy; DIRECTOR: Bretaigne Windust; CHOREOGRAPHER: Michael Kidd; SETS/LIGHTING: Jo Mielziner; COSTUMES: Eleanor Goldsmith; MUSICAL DIRECTOR: Milton Rosenstock, *Max Meth*; ORCHESTRATIONS: Robert Russell Bennett & Don Walker; DANCE MUSIC ARRANGEMENTS: Trude Rittman; VOCAL ARRANGEMENTS: Lyn Murray; CAST RECORDING on Columbia; PRESS: Samuel J. Friedman; GENERAL MANAGER: Charles Harris; COMPANY MANAGER: Michael Goldreyer; PRODUCTION STAGE MANAGER: James Gelb; STAGE MANAGER: James Russo; ASSISTANT STAGE MANAGER: Michael Ellis, *George Charles*; 2ND ASSISTANT STAGE MANAGER: Jerry Laws. **Cast:** SUNNY (HARMONICA PLAYER): Sonny Terry; BUZZ COLLINS: Eddie Bruce; SHERIFF: Tom McElhany; 1ST SHARECROPPER: Alan Gilbert, *Larry Stuart* (alternate); 2ND SHARECROPPER: Robert Eric Carlson, *Brayton Lewis*; SUSAN MAHONEY: Anita Alvarez (5), *Pearl Lang* (alternate), *Beryl Kaye*; HENRY: Augustus Smith Jr., *James Grimes*; FINIAN McLONERGAN: Albert Sharpe (2), *James N. O'Neill, Patrick J. Kelly, Ian Martin, Patrick J. Kelly* (alternate), *Joe Yule*; SHARON McLONERGAN: Ella Logan (1), *Dorothy Claire, Nan Wynn*; WOODY MAHONEY: Donald Richards (3); 3RD SHARECROPPER: Ralph Waldo Cummings, *Maude Simmons*; OG (A LEPRECHAUN): David Wayne (4), *Harry Townes* (alternate), *Philip Truex*; HOWARD: William Greaves; SENATOR BILLBOARD RAWKINS: Robert Pitkin; 1ST GEOLOGIST: Lucas Aco; 2ND GEOLOGIST: Nathaniel Dickerson, *William McDaniel*; SINGER: Dolores Martin, *Sheila Guyse* [during her tenure this role became the 5th Sharecropper]; DIANE: Diane Woods, *Mary Dawson*; JANE: Jane Earle, *Norma Jane Marlowe*; JOHN THE PREACHER: Roland Skinner; 4TH SHARECROPPER: Maude Simmons, *William Scully, Gene Tobin*; MR. ROBUST: Arthur Tell; MR. SHEARS: Royal Dano; 1ST PASSION PILGRIM GOSPELER: Jerry Laws; 2ND PASSION PILGRIM GOSPELER: Lorenzo Fuller, *Coyal McMahan*; 3RD PASSION PILGRIM GOSPELER: Louis Sharp; 1ST DEPUTY: Michael Ellis, *George Charles, Charles J. Davis*; 2ND DEPUTY: Robert Eric Carlson, *Brayton Lewis*; 3RD DEPUTY: Harry Day, *Louis Yetter*; TOURISTS: Gerry Simpson (*Eleanor Winter*) & Harry Day (*Louis Yetter*) [roles created during run]; HONEY LOU: Elayne Richards [role created during the run]; OTHER CHILDREN: Norma Jane Marlowe (*James Grimes*) & Elayne Richards (*Regina Jouvin*); THE LYNN MURRAY SINGERS (6): Arlene Anderson, Connie Baxter, Carroll Brooks, Robert Eric Carlson (*Brayton Lewis*), Ralph Waldo Cummings, Nathaniel Dickerson (*William McDaniel*), Alan Gilbert (*Larry Stuart*), Theodore Hines, Lyn Joi, Mimi Kelly, Dolores Martin, Marijane Maricle, Morty Rappe, Maude Simmons, William Scully (*Gene Tobin*), Roland Skinner, *Bette Anderson, Eve Lynn, Helen Stanton, Margaret Tynes, Eleanor Winter* (captain of singing chorus), *Charles Dayton* (*Thomas Rieder*); DANCING GIRLS: Freda Flier, Annabelle Gold, Eleanore Gregory, Erona Harris, Ann Hutchinson, Anna Mitten, Kathleen Stanford, Lavinia Williams, *Cyprienne Gabel* (this is Cyprienne Gabelman), *Vera McNichols, Dorothy Tucker, Edythe Udane, Peggy Murray, Betty Nichols, Onna White*; DANCING BOYS: Lucas Aco, Harry Day, Daniel Lloyd, J.C. McCord, Frank Neal, Arthur Partington, James Flashe Riley, Don Weissmuller, *Robert Billheimer, Kenneth Davis, Jack Nagle, David Newman, Roger Ohardieno, Eddie Phillips, Albert Popwell, Gene Wilson, Parker Wilson, Louis Yetter*. **Understudies:** Finian: *P.J. Kelly, James O'Neill*; Susan: Eleanore Gregory; Woody: Larry Stuart; Og: *Philip Truex, Charles J. Davis*; 1st Geologist: *George Charles, Charles J. Davis*; Howard/2nd Geologist: Theodore Hines; Robust: *Brayton Lewis*; Henry: James Grimes; Buzz/Rawkins: Arthur Tell; John/1st Gospeler/3rd Gospeler: Coyal McMahan; Sheriff: Royal Dano; 1st Sharecropper/2nd Sharecropper/1st Deputy/Shears: Charles Dayton, *Thomas Rieder*; 3rd Sharecropper: *Bertha Powell*. **Act I: Scene 1** The Meetin' Place. Rainbow Valley, Missitucky: "This Time of the Year" (Singing Ensemble), Dance (Susan & Dancing Ensemble), "How are Things in Glocca Morra?" (Sharon) [the big hit], "Look to the Rainbow" (Sharon & Singing Ensemble), Dance (Dance Ensemble); **Scene 2** The same; that night: "Old Devil Moon" (Sharon & Woody) [a hit]; **Scene 3** The colonial estate of Senator Billboard Rawkins; the next morning; **Scene 4** The

Meetin' Place; following day: "How Are Things in Glocca Morra?" (reprise) (Sharon), "Something Sort of Grandish" (Sharon & Og), "If This isn't Love" (Sharon, Woody, Singing Ensemble), Dance (Susan & Dance Ensemble), "Something Sort of Grandish" (reprise) (Og); *Scene 5* A path in the woods; *Scene 6* The Meetin' Place; next morning: "Necessity" (Singer & Singing Girls), "(That) Great Come-and-Get-It Day" (Sharon, Woody, Singing Ensemble) [danced by the Dance Ensemble]. *Act II: Scene 1* Rainbow Valley; a few weeks later: "When the Idle Poor Become the Idle Rich": Dance (Susan & Dance Ensemble), Song (Sharon & Singing Ensemble), "Old Devil Moon" (reprise) (Sharon & Woody), "Dance of the Golden Crock" (Susan, accompanied by Sonny Terry); *Scene 2* A wooded section of the hills: "Fiddle Faddle" (Og), "The Begat" (Rawkins, Three Passion Pilgrim Gospelers); *Scene 3* The Meetin' Place: "Look to the Rainbow" (reprise) (Sharon, Woody, Singing Ensemble); *Scene 4* Just before dawn: "When I'm Not Near the Girl I Love" (Og & Susan), "If This isn't Love" (reprise) (Entire Ensemble), Finale: "How are Things in Glocca Morra?" (reprise) (Sharon & Entire Company).

Broadway reviewers mostly raved. The show won 1947 Tony Awards for choreography, and for David Wayne, and a 1948 Tony Award for musical direction (Max Meth). It also won Donaldson Awards for musical, and book, and for David Wayne (actor & supporting actor), Albert Sharpe (male debut), and Carmen Alvarez (female dancer). Ella Logan, very unhappy with the show from the beginning because the producers wouldn't give her the size of billing she wanted (they maintained that all the performances were of equal value), was out 2/4/47–2/9/47 with a throat problem. On 5/31/47 she quit, and audiences still kept coming.

After Broadway. PALACE THEATRE, London, 10/21/47–12/6/47. 53 PERFORMANCES. PRESENTED BY Emile Littler; DIRECTOR: James Gelb; MUSICAL DIRECTOR: Phil Green. *Cast:* SUSAN: Beryl Kaye; FINIAN: Patrick J. Kelly; SHARON: Beryl Seton; WOODY: Alan Gilbert; OG: Alfie Bass; RAWKINS: Frank Royde; DANCERS INCLUDED: Albert Popwell.

CITY CENTER, NYC, 5/18/55–5/29/55. 15 PERFORMANCES. PRESENTED BY the New York City Center Light Opera Company; DIRECTOR: William Hammerstein; CHOREOGRAPHER: Onna White; SETS: Howard Bay; COSTUMES: Alvin Colt; MUSICAL DIRECTOR: Frederick Dvonch; CONDUCTOR: Julius Rudel; ORCHESTRATIONS: Robert Russell Bennett & Don Walker; PRODUCTION STAGE MANAGER: Bernard Gersten. *Cast:* BUZZ COLLINS: Eddie Bruce; SHERIFF: Jack Bryan; 1ST SHARECROPPER: Evans Thornton; 2ND SHARECROPPER: Seth Riggs; SUSAN: Anita Alvarez; HENRY: Michael Gilford; 3RD SHARECROPPER: Rosetta Le Noire; FINIAN: Will Mahoney; SHARON: Helen Gallagher; WOODY: Merv Griffin; OG: Donn Driver; HOWARD: Terry Carter; RAWKINS: Frank Borgman; 1ST GEOLOGIST: Walter P. Brown; 2ND GEOLOGIST/3RD DEPUTY: Emory Knight; DIANE: Lynn-Rose Kohan; HONEY LOU: Jonelle Allen; JOHN THE PREACHER: Rodester Timmons; ROBUST: Oggie Small; SHEARS: James Elward; 1ST DEPUTY: Howard Lear; DANCERS INCLUDED: Jay J. Riley, Charles Queenan, Erona Harris, Mary Martinet, Tom Panko; SINGERS INCLUDED: Clifford Fearl, Bob Rippy, Murray Vines. Rare for Off Broadway, this production received a 1956 Tony Nomination for Will Mahoney.

210. *Finian's Rainbow (Broadway revival)*

Before Broadway. This revival began with a run at CITY CENTER, 4/27/60–5/8/60. 15 PERFORMANCES. The crew and cast were the same as for the Broadway transfer, except: SUSAN: Carmen Gutierrez; SHEARS: Cris Alexander; SHERIFF: Judson Morgan. The singers John Boni, Hugh Dilworth, Don Grey, and Marnell Higley were dropped, as were dancers Marilyn Allwyn, Gene Gavin, Ellen Halpin, Mavis Ray, and Jaime Juan Rogers. Singer Don Grilley was added for Broadway.

The Broadway Run. FORTY-SIXTH STREET THEATRE, 5/23/60–6/1/60. 12 PERFORMANCES. The New York City Center Light Opera Company production, PRESENTED BY Robert Fryer & Lawrence Carr, with John F. Herman & Theatrical Interests Plan; MUSIC: Burton Lane; LYRICS: E.Y. Harburg; BOOK: E.Y. Harburg & Fred Saidy; DIRECTOR: Herbert Ross; CHOREOGRAPHERS: Herbert Ross & Peter Conlow;

SETS/LIGHTING: Howard Bay; COSTUMES: Stanley Simmons; MUSICAL DIRECTOR: Max Meth; ORCHESTRATIONS: Robert Russell Bennett & Don Walker; PRESS: Tom Trenkle; PRODUCTION STAGE MANAGER: Herman Shapiro; STAGE MANAGER: Chet O'Brien. *Cast:* BUZZ COLLINS: Eddie Bruce; SHERIFF: Tom McElhany; 1ST SHARECROPPER: John McCurry; 2ND SHARECROPPER: Knute Sullivan; SUSAN MAHONEY: Anita Alvarez; HENRY: Michael Darden; MAUDE: Carol Brice; FINIAN MCLONERGAN: Bobby Howes; SHARON MCLONERGAN: Jeannie Carson; SAM: Arthur Garrison; WOODY MAHONEY: Biff McGuire; OG (A LEPRECHAUN): Howard Morris; SENATOR BILLBOARD RAWKINS: Sorrell Booke; 1ST GEOLOGIST: Barney Johnston; 2ND GEOLOGIST: Robert Guillaume; HOWARD: Jim McMillan; DIANE: Patti Austin; MR. ROBUST: Edgar Daniels; MR. SHEARS: Joe Ross; 1ST PASSION PILGRIM GOSPELER: Jerry Laws; 2ND PASSION PILGRIM GOSPELER: Bill Glover; 3RD PASSION PILGRIM GOSPELER: Tiger Haynes; 1ST DEPUTY: Don Grey; 2ND DEPUTY: Larry Mitchell; SINGING ENSEMBLE: Issa Arnal, Nan Courtney, Bill Glover, Don Grilley, Robert Guillaume, Tiger Haynes, Barney Johnston, Jerry Laws, Mary Louise, John McCurry, Larry Mitchell, Lispet Nelson, Stephanie Reynolds, Knute Sullivan, Alyce Elizabeth Webb, Beverley Jane Welch; DANCING ENSEMBLE: Julius C. Fields, Jerry Fries, Loren Hightower, Nat Horne, Ronald Lee, Sally Lee, Diane McDaniel, Carmen Morales, Paul Olson, Wakefield Poole, Sandra Roveta, Ron Schwinn, Jacqueline Walcott, Myrna White.

Broadway reviews were either raves or close to it.

After Broadway. CITY CENTER, NYC, 4/5/67–4/23/67. 23 PERFORMANCES. Part of City Center's spring season of three musical revivals (the others were *The Sound of Music* and *Wonderful Town*). PRESENTED BY The New York City Center Light Opera Company; DIRECTOR: Gus Schirmer; CHOREOGRAPHER: Betty Hyatt Linton; SETS: Howard Bay; COSTUMES: Frank Thompson; LIGHTING: Peggy Clark; MUSICAL DIRECTOR: Jonathan Anderson. *Cast:* BUZZ: Ronn Carroll; 1ST SHARECROPPER: John Dorrin; 2ND SHARECROPPER: Laried Montgomery; SUSAN: Sandy Duncan; MAUDE: Carol Brice; FINIAN: Frank McHugh; SHARON: Nancy Dussault; WOODY: Stanley Grover; OG: Len Gochman; RAWKINS: Howard I. Smith; HOWARD: Jim McMillan; DIANE: Ellen Hansen; ROBUST: Austin Colyer; SHEARS: Paul Adams; 1ST GOSPELER: Jerry Laws; 2ND GOSPELER: Tiger Haynes; 3RD GOSPELER: John McCurry; SINGERS INCLUDED: Mary Falconer, Ernestine Jackson, Joyce McDonald, Garrett Morris, Grant Spradling, Dixie Stewart, Alyce Elizabeth Webb; DANCERS INCLUDED: Bjarne Buchtrup, Joanne De Vito, Garold Gardner, Bob La Crosse, Joy Serio, Ronald B. Stratton, Toodie Wittmer, Mary Zahn.

THE MOVIE. *Finian's Rainbow* was not filmed until 1968 because of its racial content. DIRECTOR: Francis Ford Coppola. *Cast:* SHERIFF: Dolph Sweet; SHARECROPPER: Brenda Arnau; SUSAN: Barbara Hancock; FINIAN: Fred Astaire; SHARON: Petula Clark; WOODY: Don Francks; OG: Tommy Steele; JUDGE RAWKINS: Keenan Wynn; HOWARD: Al Freeman Jr.

JONES BEACH THEATRE, NY, 7/4/77–9/4/77. 58 PERFORMANCES. PRESENTED BY Guy Lombardo; DIRECTOR: John Fearnley; CHOREOGRAPHER: Robert Pagent; SETS: John W. Keck; COSTUMES: Winn Morton; MUSICAL DIRECTOR: Jay Blackton. *Cast:* BUZZ: Alan North; SHERIFF: John Dorrin; SUSAN: Gail Benedict; MAUDE: Phyllis A. Bash; FINIAN: Christopher Hewett; SHARON: Beth Fowler; WOODY: Stanley Grover; OG: Charles Repole; RAWKINS: Ronn Carroll; HOWARD: Clyde Williams; ROBUST: Ralph Vucci; MR. SHEARS: Lee Cass; CHORUS INCLUDED: Dixie Stewart, Mickey Gunnersen, Dale Muchmore.

GOODSPEED OPERA HOUSE, Conn., 4/25/97–7/4/97. Previews from 4/2/97. DIRECTOR: Gabriel Barre; CHOREOGRAPHER: Jennifer Paulson Lee; SETS: James Youmans; MUSICAL DIRECTOR: Michael O'Flaherty. *Cast:* FINIAN: James Judy; SHARON: Erin Dilly; OG: Robert Creighton.

1999 REVIVAL. The score had a reprise or two added, but no cut songs (although songs were now in a different, more logical, order). Finian now sung "Look to the Rainbow." It began as a reading in 5/3/99, in New York City. PRESENTED BY Rodger Hess; REVISED BOOK: Peter Stone (he had discussed the revisions with Burton Lane before Mr. Lane died on 1/5/97); DIRECTOR: Lonny Price; CULTURAL ADVISER: Ossie Davis (making sure the ethnic references were okay). *Reading Cast:* FINIAN: Jim Norton [Robert Morse had been scheduled, but had had to bow out]; WOODY: Patrick Wilson; OG: Denis O'Hare; RAWKINS: Austin Pendleton. Then it went on to two full "pre–Broadway productions," one in Miami, and the next in Cleveland. It got very good reviews at both venues. COCONUT GROVE PLAYHOUSE, Miami, 10/23/99–11/21/99. Rehearsals began in late 8/99. Previews from 10/12/99; PALACE THEATRE, Cleveland, 12/1/99–12/12/99. Previews from 11/30/99. DIRECTOR: Lonny Price; CHOREOGRAPHER: Marguerite Derricks; SETS: Loren Sherman; COSTUMES: Paul Tazewell. *Cast:* SHARON: Kate Jennings Grant; OG: Denis O'Hare; RAWKINS: Austin Pendleton; WOODY: J. Robert Spencer; SUSAN: Tina Ou; FINIAN: Brian Murray; BUZZ: Don Stephenson; HONEY LOU: Terri White. Aiming for a Broadway berth in the spring of 2000, it waited for a theatre to open up, but that didn't happen, and show was postponed until the fall of 2000. It now planned to spend the summer at the Ahmanson Theatre, Los Angeles (a space had become available), 7/23/00–9/3/00. Previews from 7/12/00. By now James Noone was doing the sets. Partly because investors were nervous about the racist themes, the producer Rodger Hess couldn't find the money for either L.A. or Broadway, and the project collapsed.

HUDSON THEATRE, 6/2/03. This was a one-night concert, a benefit for the Irish Repertory Theatre of New York City (it was not related to the 1999 revival). Lauren Bacall hosted the evening. ADAPTED BY/DIRECTOR: Charlotte Moore. *Cast:* FINIAN: John Cullum; SHARON: Melissa Errico; OG: Denis O'Hare.

A similar benefit was held, also at the IRISH REP, 4/15/04–7/11/04 (closing date extended from 5/30/04). Previews from 4/6/04. SETS: James Morgan; COSTUMES: David Toser; LIGHTING: Mary Jo Dondlinger; CAST RECORDING on Sh-K-Boom, made on 6/7/04. *Cast:* FINIAN: Jonathan Freeman; NARRATOR: David Staller; SHARON: Melissa Errico (until 5/9/04), *Kerry O'Malley* (from 5/12/04); OG: Malcolm Gets (until 5/30/04), *Chad Kimball* (from 6/1/04); WOODY: Max von Essen (until 6/6/04), *Kevin Kern* (from 6/8/04); RAWKINS: John Sloman.

211. *Fiorello!*

Fiorello La Guardia (1882–1947) was the famous and popular pugnacious reforming mayor of New York City, 1934–1946. Act I is set in New York City, shortly before World War I. It opens with a bare stage, except for a small desk with the mayor behind it, reading on the radio *Dick Tracy* and *Little Orphan Annie* to the children of the city during a newspaper strike. "The Little Flower" (a translation of his Italian name; he was also half Jewish) ended the reign of the Tammany Hall bosses. The musical covers the period 1914–33, from his beginnings as a Greenwich Village lawyer, through his election to Congress under Marino's mentorship, his service as an airman in World War I (we see newsreel film of this war), his first unsuccessful mayoral bid against Tammany boss Jimmy Walker (Fiorello has quarreled with Marino by this time, and thus lost his support), and his second, successful, try at Walker (under the sponsorship of Judge Seabury). He meets his first wife, Trieste-born Thea (then leader of the sweatshop workers), while she is arrested on the trumped-up charge of soliciting during the strike. He defends her. She later becomes ill and dies. His second campaign coincides with his second marriage, to his faithful secretary, Marie. Act II is ten years later, and Marino is now supporting Fiorello again. Dora was a girl picketer and Marie's friend, who defied Floyd the cop and then married him. Morris was La Guardia's faithful office manager and assistant.

Before Broadway. Arthur Penn (the original director) came up with the idea, and suggested it to Hal Prince one day at the Coffee House Club. Mr. Prince and Bobby Griffith agreed to produce it, and it was done with the approval of Marie, La Guardia's widow. Arthur Penn did not like Jerome Weidman's libretto, thinking it too light, but the producers disagreed, and Mr. Penn left, but kept a one percent author's interest. George Abbott was then brought in to direct and re-work the libretto with Mr. Weidman. They shifted the emphasis from the first wife to the second. Mr. Weidman had done some lyrics, and wanted to do all

of them, but the producers realized the need to look elsewhere. Jerry Bock was hired for the music, and Stephen Sondheim was approached for the lyrics. But Sondheim turned it down, Sheldon Harnick took it, and thus began the famous Bock — Harnick relationship. Many changes were made during the out-of-town tryouts in New Haven (good reviews) and Philadelphia. Musical numbers were cut:–"The Business is Fundamentally Sound," "Temporarily Unemployed," "Till the Bootlegger Comes," "Trieste," and "Where do I Go from Here?"; and new ones were added. "Little Tin Box" was written on the road only two weeks before the Broadway opening. Eli Wallach and Mickey Rooney were considered for the lead, but unknown Tom Bosley looked so much like the mayor. He hardly sang at all.

The Broadway Run. BROADHURST THEATRE, 11/23/59–5/6/61; BROADWAY THEATRE, 5/9/61–10/28/61. Total of 796 PERFORMANCES. PRESENTED BY Robert E. Griffith & Harold S. Prince; MUSIC: Jerry Bock; LYRICS: Sheldon Harnick; BOOK: Jerome Weidman & George Abbott; DIRECTOR: George Abbott; CHOREOGRAPHER: Peter Gennaro; SETS/COSTUMES/LIGHTING: William & Jean Eckart; ASSISTANT COSTUMES: Patton Campbell; FILM FOOTAGE EDITED BY: Aram Boyajian; MUSICAL DIRECTOR: Hal Hastings; ORCHESTRATIONS: Irwin Kostal; DANCE MUSIC ARRANGEMENTS: Jack Elliott; PRESS: Sol Jacobson, Lewis Harmon, Jack Toohey, Mary Bryant; CASTING: Judith Abbott; GENERAL MANAGER: Carl Fisher; PRODUCTION STAGE MANAGER: Ruth Mitchell; STAGE MANAGER: Bert Wood; ASSISTANT STAGE MANAGER: Paul J. Phillips. *Cast:* ANNOUNCER: Del Horstmann; FIORELLO LA GUARDIA: Tom Bosley (1); NEIL, LAW CLERK: Bob Holiday; MORRIS: Nathaniel Frey (7); MRS. POMERANTZ: Helen Verbit; MR. LOPEZ: H.F. Green, *Tony Gardell*; MR. ZAPPATELLA: David Collyer; DORA: Pat Stanley (5), *Patricia Harty, Margery Gray*; MARIE: Patricia Wilson (2), *Mary Roche*; BEN MARINO: Howard Da Silva (4), *Russ Brown, Marty May*; ED PETERSON, DEALER: Del Horstmann, *Stanley Simmonds, Charles Aschmann*; 2ND PLAYER: Stanley Simmonds, *Del Horstmann*; 3RD PLAYER: Michael Quinn; 4TH PLAYER: Ron Husmann, *Alan Sanderson*; 5TH PLAYER: David London; 6TH PLAYER: Julian Patrick; SEEDY MAN: Joseph Toner; 1ST HECKLER: Bob Bernard, *Merritt Thompson*; 2ND HECKLER: Michael Scrittorale; 3RD HECKLER: James Maher; 4TH HECKLER: Joseph Toner; NINA: Pat Turner, *Lynda Lynch*; FLOYD MCDUFF, A COP: Mark Dawson (6); SOPHIE: Lynn Ross, *Pat Cooper*; THEA: Ellen Hanley (3), *Willi Burke*; SECRETARY: Mara Landi; SENATOR: Rufus Smith [new role for 60–61 season]; COMMISSIONER: Frederic Downs, *Michael Quinn*; POLITICIAN: H.F. Green, *Tony Gardell*; FRANKIE SCARPINI: Michael Scrittorale; MITZI TRAVERS: Eileen Rodgers, *Joy Nichols*; FLORENCE: Deedy Irwin, *Mara Landi, Beverly Dixon*; REPORTER: Julian Patrick; 1ST MAN: Scott Hunter; 2ND MAN: Michael Scrittorale; TOUGH MAN: David London; DERBY: Bob Bernard, *Merritt Thompson*; FRANTIC: Stanley Simmonds [role cut by 60–61]; JUDGE CARTER: Joseph Toner [role cut by 60–61]; SINGERS: David Collyer, Barbara Gilbert (*Barbara Hammerstein*), Del Horstmann, Ron Husmann (*Alan Sanderson*), Deedy Irwin (gone by 60–61), Mara Landi, David London, Julian Patrick, Ginny Perlowin, Patsy Peterson (*Mary Roche*), Silver Saundors; DANCERS: Bob Bernard (gone by 60–61), Elaine Cancilla, Charlene Carter (gone by 60–61), Ellen Harris (gone by 60–61), Patricia Harty (gone by 60–61), Scott Hunter, Bob La Crosse, Lynda Lynch, Jim Maher, Gregg Owen, Lowell Purvis, Dellas Rennie (gone by 60–61), Lynn Ross (gone by 60–61), Michael Scrittorale, Dan Siretta, Pat Turner (gone by 60–61). *Jeanna Belkin, Pat Cooper, Jean Eliot, Kaarlyn Kitch, Diane McDaniel, Genii Prior, Beatrice Salten, Merritt Thompson*. **Standby**: Fiorello: Harvey Lembeck, *Sorrell Booke*. **Understudies**: Marie: Eileen Rodgers, *Joy Nichols*; Thea: Ginny Perlowin; Dora: Pat Harty, *Kaarlyn Kitch*; Ben: David Collyer; Morris: *David Collyer* (by 60–61); Mitzi: Patsy Peterson, Mara *Landi*; Neil: Ron Husmann, *Alan Sanderson*; Mrs. Pomerantz: Mara Landi; Floyd: *Rufus Smith* (by 60–61); Poker Players: Jack McMinn, *Jack Matthew*. **Act I**: *Prologue* A studio at Radio Station WNYC; sometime in the 1930s; *Scene 1* Fiorello's law offices in Greenwich Village: "On the Side of the Angels" (Neil, Morris, Marie); *Scene 2* Main room of the Ben Marino Association; the same day: "Politics and Poker" (Ben & Politicians); *Scene 3* A street outside strike headquarters; the same day: "Unfair" (Fiorello, Dora, Girls); *Scene 4* Fiorello's law offices; immediately following: "Marie's Law" (Marie & Morris); *Scene 5* Three street corners; 1916: "The Name's La Guardia" (Fiorello & Company); *Scene 6* A street near the Ben

Marino Association; right after election day: "The Bum Won" (Ben & Politicians); *Scene 7* The roof of a Greenwich Village tenement building; 1917: "I Love a Cop" (Dora); *Scene 8* Fiorello's office: Congressional Office building, Washington; shortly after the preceding scene; *Scene 9* A street near the Ben Marino Association; a few weeks later: "I Love a Cop" (reprise) (Dora & Floyd); *Scene 10* Main room and yard of the Ben Marino Association; immediately after the preceding scene: "Till Tomorrow" (Thea, Fiorello, Marie, Morris, Company); *Scene 11* A Pathe news screening; various times during 1917 & 1918; *Scene 11a* Gangplank of a troopship for soldiers returning from overseas; sometime after the Armistice: "Home Again" (Company). *Act II: Scene 1* The La Guardia home; 1929: "When Did I Fall in Love?" (Thea); *Scene 2* The terrace of Floyd & Dora McDuff's penthouse apartment; shortly after the preceding scene: "Gentleman Jimmy" (Mitzi & Dancing Girls); *Scene 3* Fiorello's law office; the following week; *Scene 4* The corner of Madison Avenue & 105th Street; that night; *Scene 5* Fiorello's law office; later that night; *Scene 6* A street near Fiorello's law office; election night, 1929; radio announcement: "Gentleman Jimmy" (reprise) (Company), "The Name's La Guardia" (reprise); *Scene 7* The main room of the Ben Marino Association; 1933: "Little Tin Box" (Ben & Politicians), "The Very Next Man" (Marie), "Politics and Poker" (reprise) (Ben & Politicians); *Scene 8* Fiorello's law office; the next morning: "The Very Next Man" (reprise) (Marie), Finale: "The Name's La Guardia" (reprise) (Politicians).

Broadway reviewers mostly raved. The show was capitalized at $300,000. It was hurt by an eight-day Actors' Equity strike in spring 1960. It won a Pulitzer Prize for Drama (the third musical to win, after *Of Thee I Sing* and *South Pacific*), and Tonys for: musical, director of a musical, supporting actor [sic] (Tom Bosley). Howard Da Silva was nominated, as were choreography, musical direction, and sets (musical).

After Broadway. TOUR. Opened on 8/8/60, at the State Fair Music Hall, Dallas, and closed on 3/31/62, at the Erlanger Theatre, Philadelphia. MUSICAL DIRECTOR: George S. Hirst. **Cast:** FIORELLO: Bob Carroll; THEA: Jen Nelson; MARIE: Charlotte Fairchild; DORA: Zeme North, *Jayme Mylroie*; BEN: Rudy Bond, *Sam Kirkham*; MITZI: Rosemary O'Reilly.

CITY CENTER, NYC, 6/13/62–6/24/62. 16 PERFORMANCES. For this production Act I Scene 11a became Act II Scene 1, complete with the song "Home Again." The previously cut number "Where Do I Go from Here?" (Marie), was re-instated, in Act II Scene 6. PRESENTED BY the New York City Center Light Opera Company; DIRECTOR: Dania Krupska; CHOREOGRAPHER: Kevin Carlisle; SETS/LIGHTING: Walter & Jean Eckart; COSTUME SUPERVISOR: Joseph Codori; MUSICAL DIRECTOR: Jay Blackton. **Cast:** ANNOUNCER/ED: Del Horstmann; FIORELLO: Sorrell Booke; NEIL: Richard France; MORRIS: Paul Lipson; MRS. POMERANTZ: Helen Verbit; MR. LOPEZ: Tony Gardell; DORA: Dody Goodman; MARIE: Barbara Williams; BEN: Art Lund; SEEDY MAN: Terry Violino; 5TH PLAYER: Ned Wright; 2ND PLAYER/SENATOR: Feodore Tedick; 4TH PLAYER: Walter P. Brown; 1ST HECKLER/FRANKIE: Mike Scrittorale; 3RD HECKLER/DRUNK/ FRANTIC: Louis Kosman; NINA: Jeanna Belkin; FLOYD: Dort Clark; THEA: Lola Fisher; WASHINGTON SECRETARY: Mary Louise; MITZI: Sheila Smith; FLORENCE: Maggie Worth; SINGERS INCLUDED: Rosalind Cash, Doreese DuQuan, Maura K. Wedge; DANCERS INCLUDED: Margery J. Beddow, Louise Ferrand, Jere Admire, Sterling Clark, Paul R. Roman.

PAPER MILL PLAYHOUSE, New Jersey, 1962. DIRECTOR: Howard Da Silva. **Cast:** FIORELLO: Tom Bosley; MARIE: Patricia Wilson.

PICCADILLY THEATRE, London, 10/8/62. 56 PERFORMANCES. PRESENTED BY Donald Albery (for Donmar Productions) in association with Oscar Lewenstein, by arrangement with Harold Prince; DIRECTOR: Val May; CHOREOGRAPHER: Peter Wright; SETS: Graham Barlow; COSTUMES: Alan Barrett & Audrey Price; LIGHTING: Ian Albery; MUSICAL DIRECTOR: Marcus Dods; ORCHESTRATIONS: Eric Rogers & Burt Rhodes. **Cast:** FIORELLO: Derek Smith; THEA: Marion Grimaldi; MITZI: Patricia Michael; MARIE: Nicolette Roeg; DORA: Bridget Armstrong; NEIL: Peter Bourne; BEN: Peter Reeves.

GOODSPEED OPERA HOUSE, Conn., 85–86 season. DIRECTOR: Gerald Gutierrez; CHOREOGRAPHER: Peter Gennaro.

CITY CENTER, NYC, 2/9/94–2/12/94. 4 PERFORMANCES. This was the first of City Center's *Encores!* series. DIRECTOR: Walter Bobbie; CHOREOGRAPHER: Christopher Chadman; SETS: John Lee Beatty; MUSICAL DIRECTOR: Rob Fisher. **Cast:** FIORELLO: Jerry Zaks; MARIE: Faith Prince; BEN: Philip Bosco; MRS. POMERANTZ: Marilyn Cooper; DORA:

Liz Callaway; MORRIS: Adam Arkin; NEIL: Gregg Edelman; MR. LOPEZ: Joaquin Romaguera; POLITICAL HACK: Mike Burstyn; MITZI: Donna McKechnie; WALK-ON PART: Ed Koch, former NYC mayor.

On 10/29/01 & 10/30/01 the Plays by Players Festival of American Plays presented a concert performance. DIRECTOR: Kristine Lewis. Sheldon Harnick attended. CAST: FIORELLO: John Martello; THEA: Celia Gentry; MARIE: Deborah Thomas Shull; BEN: Clark Gesner; MITZI: Lesley Sara Carroll; VARIOUS ROLES: Bill Richert.

Hizzoner! A non-musical about Fiorello, ran at the LONGACRE THEATRE, Broadway, 2/24/89–3/5/89. 13 previews. 12 PERFORMANCES. WRITER: Paul Shyre. **Cast:** Tony Lo Bianco.

212. *The Firebrand of Florence*

The rivalry (and not only for the love of Angela, a model) between silversmith Cellini and the Duke. Set in Florence and Paris, 1535. Cellini kills a man and is saved from execution by the Duchess. Finally Cellini allows the Duke to have Angela.

Before Broadway. *The Firebrand* (a straight play) originally ran in New York, 10/15/24. 261 PERFORMANCES. **Cast:** DUKE: Frank Morgan; CELLINI: Joseph Schildkraut.

In 1928 a musical version, **The Dagger and the Rose**, closed in Atlantic City before reaching Broadway. PRESENTED BY Horace Liveright & Otto Kahn (the banker); MUSIC: Eugene Berton; LYRICS: Edward Eliscu; BOOK: Isobelle Leighton.

As for the 1945 Broadway musical, Kurt Weill wrote it to boost the flagging career of his wife Lotte Lenya. Ira Gershwin insisted (unsuccessfully) on Kitty Carlisle. Mr. Weill wanted Don Ameche as Cellini, and Walter Slezak as the Duke, but had to make do. In fact he did get Mr. Slezak, but Melville Cooper eventually played the role. Max Gordon wanted Wilbur Evans and then Alfred Drake for Cellini, and Susanna Foster for Angela, but also had to make do. The show was called *Much Ado About Love* during tryouts (it had previously been called *It Happened in Florence* and *Make Way for Love*). George S. Kaufman helped during tryouts.

The Broadway Run. ALVIN THEATRE, 3/22/45–4/28/45. 43 PERFORMANCES. PRESENTED BY Max Gordon; MUSIC/ORCHESTRATIONS/ ARRANGEMENTS: Kurt Weill; LYRICS: Ira Gershwin; BOOK: Edwin Justus Mayer & Ira Gershwin; BASED ON the 1924 comedy *The Firebrand*, by Edwin Justus Mayer; DIRECTOR: John Murray Anderson; BOOK DIRECTOR: John Haggott; CHOREOGRAPHER/SINGING ENSEMBLES: Catherine Littlefield; SETS/LIGHTING: Jo Mielziner; COSTUMES: Raoul Pene du Bois; ASSISTANT COSTUMES: Willa Kim; MUSICAL DIRECTOR/SELECTED & TRAINED SINGING ENSEMBLE: Maurice Abravanel; PRESS: Nat Dorfman; PRODUCTION ASSISTANT: Arnold Saint Subber; GENERAL MANAGER: Ben A. Boyar; COMPANY MANAGER: Rube Bernstein; GENERAL STAGE MANAGER: William McFadden; ASSISTANT STAGE MANAGERS: Richard Phelan & Mildred Sherman. **Cast:** HANGMAN: Randolph Symonette; TARTMAN: Don Marshall; SOUVENIR MAN: Bert Freed; MAFFIO: Boyd Heathen; ARLECCHINO: Jean Guelis (aka John Guelis) (6); COLUMBINA: Norma Gentner; PIERROT: Eric Kristen; FLOMINA: Diane Meroff; PANTALONE: Hubert Bland; FIORINETTA: Mary Alice Bingham; GELFOMINO: Kenneth Le Roy; ROSANIA: Mary Grey; DOTTORE: William Vaux; MAGISTRATE: Marion Green; BENVENUTO CELLINI: Earl Wrightson (2); APPRENTICES: John "Jack" Cassidy, Lynn Alden, Walter Rinner, Frank Stevens; CAPTAIN OF THE GUARD: Charles Sheldon; OTTAVIANO: Ferdi Hoffman (5); ASCANIO: James Dobson; EMELIA: Gloria Story (8); ANGELA: Beverly Tyler (3); MARQUIS: Paul Best (7); DUKE: Melville Cooper (1); PAGE: Billy Williams; DUCHESS: Lotte Lenya (4); DUCHESS' SEDAN CHAIR BEARERS: George McDonald & Walter Korman; MAJOR-DOMO: Walter Graf; CLERK OF THE COURT: Alan Noel; MODELS: LEONARDO DA VINCI MODEL: Yvonne Heap; TITIAN MODEL: Doris Blake; BOTTICELLI MODEL: Marya Iverson; RAPHAEL MODEL: Gedda Petry; VERONESE MODEL: Rose Marie Elliott; BRONZINO MODEL: Perdita Chandler; SOLDIERS/PROMENADERS/COURTIERS: Edwin Alberian, Jimmy Allison, Suzie Baker, Joan Bartels, Lisa Bert, Ray Bessmer, Angela Carabella, Tony Coffaro, Jean Crone, Gay English, Donna Gardner, John Henson, Frances Joslyn, Julie Jefferson, Thomas Lo Monaco, Ralph Lee,

Paul Mario, Lily Paget, Eric Sander, Gayne Sullivan, Frank Stevens, William Sutherland, Stephanie Turash, Evelyn Ward. *Act I*: *Scene 1* A public square in Florence: "Song of the Hangman" ("One Man's Death is Another Man's Living") (Hangman & His Two Assistants), Civic Song: "Come to Florence" (Hangman & Choral Ensemble, Arlecchino, Columbina, Commedia dell'Arte Dancers), Aria: "My Lords and Ladies" (Cellini, Apprentices, Choral Ensemble), Farewell Song: "There Was Life, There Was Love, There Was Laughter" (Cellini & Choral Ensemble); *Scene 2* Before the standards of Florence; *Scene 3* Cellini's workshop: Love Song: "You're Far Too Near Me" (Angela & Cellini), The Duke's Song: "Alessandro the Wise" (Duke & Choral Ensemble), Finaletto: "I Am Happy Here" (Duke, Ottaviano, Cellini, Angela, Marquis, Emelia, Choral Ensemble); *Scene 4* The city gates: The Duchess's Song: "Sing Me Not a Ballad" (Duchess & Four Courtiers); *Scene 5* The garden of the Summer Palace: Madrigal: "When the Duchess is Away" (Captain of the Guard, Duke, Emelia, Choral Ensemble), Love Song: "There'll Be Life, Love and Laughter" (Cellini & Angela), Trio: "I Know Where There's a Cozy Nook" (Duke, Angela, Cellini), Night Music: "The Night Time is No Time for Thinking" (Emelia, Duke, Angela, Choral Ensemble), Tarantella: "Dizzily, Busily" (Emelia, Choral Ensemble, Arlecchino, Columbina, Commedia dell'Arte Dancers), Finale (Entire Company). *Act II*: *Scene 1* Cellini's workshop: "You're Far Too Near Me" (reprise) (Angela & Cellini), Cavatina: "The Little Naked Boy" (Angela & Female Choral Ensemble), Letter Song: "My Dear Benvenuto" (Cellini & Angela); *Scene 2* Outside the City Palace gates: March of the Soldiers of the Duchy: "Just in Case" (Captain of the Guard & Soldiers of the Duchy); *Scene 3* A loggia in the City Palace: Ode: "A Rhyme for Angela" (Duke, Poets, Ladies in Waiting); *Scene 4* The standards of Florence; *Scene 5* The Grand Council Chamber of the Palace: Procession (Vendors, Hangman, Apprentices, Models, Clerks), Chant of Law and Order: "The World is Full of Villains" (Clerks, Magistrates, Duke, Choral Ensemble), Trial by Music: "You Have to Do What You Do Do" (Cellini, Duke, Marquis, Duchess, Ottaviano, Magistrate, Choral Ensemble), Duet: "Love is My Enemy" (Cellini & Angela), "The Little Naked Boy" (reprise) (Duchess & Angela); *Scene 6* Before the standards of France; *Scene 7* The palace of the King of France: Civic Song: "Come to Paris" (Marquis, two Ladies of Paris, Choral Ensemble), Finale: a/ Gigue (Commedia dell'Arte Dancers); b/ Saraband (Choral Ensemble); c/ "There'll Be Life, Love and Laughter" (reprise) (Entire Ensemble).

Broadway reviewers mostly panned it, although Howard Barnes gave it a rave in the *Herald Tribune*. Nobody came to see it, and it lost $225,000.

213. *The First*

This musical dramatizes the actual events in the life of Jackie Robinson (1919–1972) that occurred between Aug. 1945 and Sept. 1947. Some characters have been created, and some chronology and situations have been altered. Jack was the first major league baseball player to break the color bar. Branch Rickey was president of the Brooklyn Dodgers.

Before Broadway. The idea was TV critic Joel Siegel's, in 1979. In 1980 he approached Martin Charnin. Most of it was written by the time they approached Jack's widow, Rachel, who not only wouldn't go along with it, she called her lawyer. However, after five months Martin Charnin talked her into it. David Huddleston replaced Darren McGavin when the latter quit because his part had been reduced. There were no tryouts; it went straight into Broadway previews, where so many changes took place that it hardly looked like the same show on Broadway opening night. The following characters and actors were cut during Broadway previews: NOONAN: George D. Wallace; EUNICE: Patricia Drylie; FROG: Bill Buell (9); BROOKLYN TRAINER: Stephen Crain; REDS FANS: Sam Stoneburner & Stephen Crain; DODGER FANS: Steven Boockvor, Stephen Crain, Kim Criswell, Tom Griffith, Margaret LaMee, Bob Morrisey; MINISTERS: Rodney Saulsberry, Michael Edward-Stevens, Paul Cook'Tartt. This was the scene-by-scene breakdown during previews: *Act I*: *Scene 1* Noonan's Bar in Brooklyn; October 1946: "Bums" (Noonan,

Eunice, Huey, Frog, Sorrentino, Fans); *Scene 2* Gallagher's Restaurant, West 52nd Street, New York: "Jack Roosevelt Robinson" (Rickey & Durocher); *Scene 3* The third base line in Comiskey Park, Chicago; *Scene 4* The locker room of the Kansas City Monarchs, in Chicago: "The National Pastime" (Cool Minnie, Jackie, Junkyard, Monarchs); *Scene 5* Union Station, Chicago: "Will We Ever Know Each Other" (Jackie & Rachel); *Scene 6* Branch Rickey's office, 215 Montague St., Brooklyn: "The First" (Jackie); *Scene 7* The Havana training camp of the Brooklyn Dodgers: "Bloat" (Durocher, Reporters, Dodgers); *Scene 8* Outside a ballpark, Jacksonville, Fla.: "Southern Hospitality" (Jackie, Rachel, Fans); *Scene 9* A roadhouse, Route 27, Richmond, Va.: "It Ain't Gonna Work!" (Higgins, Sukeforth, Dodgers), "The Brooklyn Dodger Strike" (Rickey & Durocher); *Scene 10* Branch Rickey's office: "Jack Roosevelt Robinson" (reprise) (Rickey), "The First" (reprise) (Rachel). *Act II*: *Scene 1* Noonan's Bar; April 1947: "Is This Year Next Year?" (Noona, Eunice, Huey, Frog, Sorrentino); *Scene 2* Behind first base, Crosley Field, Cincinnati: "You Do-Do-Do-It Good!" (Cool Minnie, Jackie, Monarchs, Ruby, Opal); *Scene 3* The Dodger locker room, Shibe Park, Philadelphia: "Is This Year Next Year?" (reprise) (Rickey, Holmes, Reporters, Sukeforth, Dodgers); *Scene 4* Behind third base, the Polo Grounds, New York City: "There Are Days and There Are Days" (Rachel); *Scene 5* The front porch of a farmhouse, outside St. Louis: "It's a Beginning" (Jackie, Rickey, Rachel); *Scene 6* Outside Ebbets Field: "The Opera Ain't Over" (Noonan, Regulars, Dodgers, Rickey, Hilda, Fans); *Scene 7* Inside Ebbets Field.

The Broadway Run. MARTIN BECK THEATRE, 11/17/81–12/12/81. 33 previews. 37 PERFORMANCES. PRESENTED BY Zev Bufman, Neil Bogart, Michael Harvey, and Peter A. Bobley; MUSIC: Bob Brush; LYRICS: Martin Charnin; BOOK: Joel Siegel (with Martin Charnin); DIRECTOR: Martin Charnin; CHOREOGRAPHER: Alan Johnson; SETS: David Chapman; COSTUMES: Carrie Robbins; LIGHTING: Marc B. Weiss; SOUND: Louis Shapiro; MUSICAL SUPERVISOR/ORCHESTRATIONS/DANCE MUSIC ARRANGEMENTS: Luther Henderson; CONDUCTOR: Mark Hummel; VOCAL ARRANGEMENTS: Joyce Brown; PRESS: Fred Nathan & Associates; CASTING: Meg Simon & Fran Kumin; CONSULTANT: Rachel Robinson (Jackie's widow); GENERAL MANAGEMENT: Gatchell & Neufeld; COMPANY MANAGER: James G. Mennen; PRODUCTION STAGE MANAGER: Peter Lawrence; STAGE MANAGER: Jim Woolley; ASSISTANT STAGE MANAGERS: David Blackwell & Sarah Whitham. **Cast:** *Act I*: PATSY, THE BARTENDER: Bill Buell (9); LEO DUROCHER: Trey Wilson (6); CLYDE SUKEFORTH: Ray Gill (13); POWERS: Sam Stoneburner; THURMAN, *Brooklyn Eagle* PHOTOGRAPHER: Thomas Griffith; BRANCH RICKEY: David Huddleston (1); CANNON: Jack Hallett (8); TOMMY HOLMES: Stephen Crain; SORRENTINO, A BUS BOY: Paul Forrest (12); (THREE) PEOPLE AT BAR: BARTENDER: D. Peter Samuel; SOLDIER: Bob Morrisey (14); GIRL: Kim Criswell; JACKIE ROBINSON: David Alan Grier (3); 3RD BASEMAN: Steven Bland; JUNKYARD JONES: Luther Fontaine (11); CATCHER: Michael Edward-Stevens; JO-JO: Rodney Saulsberry; UMPIRE: Paul Forrest (12); COOL MINNIE EDWARDS: Clent Bowers (4); SOFTBALL: Paul Cook'Tartt; BUCKY: Michael Edward-Stevens; EQUIPMENT MANAGER: Steven Bland; REDCAP: Michael Edward-Stevens; RACHEL ISUM: Lonette McKee (2); PASSENGERS: Margaret LaMee, Sam Stoneburner, Rodney Saulsberry, Janet Hubert, Thomas Griffith, Kim Criswell, Steven Bland, Bob Morrisey, Stephen Crain, Boncellia Lewis; CUBAN REPORTERS: Rodney Saulsberry & Steven Bland; SWANEE RIVERS: Steven Boockvor (10); CASEY HIGGINS: Court Miller (5); HATRACK HARRIS: D. Peter Samuel; PEE WEE REESE: Bob Morrisey (14); EDDIE STANKY: Stephen Crain; DODGER COACHES: Jack Hallett & Bill Buell; DODGER ROOKIE: Thomas Griffith; TRAINER: Paul Forrest (12); FANS: Boncellia Lewis, Steven Bland, Michael Edward-Stevens, Janet Hubert, Rodney Saulsberry; SHERIFF: Jack Hallett (8). *Act II*: HUEY, A FAN: Jack Hallett (8); PHILADELPHIA REPORTERS: Paul Forrest & Jack Hallett; BRIAN WATERHOUSE: Bill Buell (9); OPAL (ON THE LEFT): Janet Hubert; RUBY (ON THE RIGHT): Boncellia Lewis; DODGER WIVES: Kim Criswell & Margaret LaMee; VOICE OF RED BARBER: Himself (7); HILDA CHESTER: Kim Criswell; PITTSBURGH PIRATES: Stephen Crain & Thomas Griffith. **Standby:** Rickey: George D. Wallace. **Understudies:** Jackie: Rodney Saulsberry; Rachel/ Cool Minnie's Girl: Jackie Lowe; Cool Minnie: Paul Cook'Tartt; Junkyard: Michael Edward-Stevens; Eunice/Hilda: Margaret LaMee; Clyde: Bill Buell; Casey: Steven Boockvor; Pee Wee Reese: Stephen Crain.

Swings: Neil Klein, Edward Love, Jackie Lowe, Margaret LaMee. *Musicians*: WOODWINDS: William Slapin, Edward Salkin, Robert Magnuson, Mauricio Smith, Frank Santagata; TRUMPETS: Francis Bunny, Jimmy Owens, Leo Ball; TROMBONES: Jim Pugh, Keith O'Quinn, Garfield Fobbs; PERCUSSION: Richard Brown; HORN: Greg Williams; CELLO: Anne Callahan; DRUMS: Dennis Mackrel; GUITAR: Bernard Grobman; PIANO: Donald Sosin; BASS: William Stanley. *Prologue* On the playing field. *Act I: Scene 1* Gallagher's Restaurant, West 52nd St., New York: "Jack Roosevelt Robinson" (Rickey, Durocher, Sukeforth); *Scene 2* The third base line, Comiskey Park, Chicago: "Dancin' off Third" (Jackie, Junkyard, The Monarchs); *Scene 3* The locker room of the Kansas City Monarchs in Chicago: "The National Pastime" (Cool Minnie, Jackie, Junkyard, The Monarchs); *Scene 4* Union Station, Chicago: "Will We Ever Know Each Other?" (Jackie & Rachel); *Scene 5* Branch Rickey's office, 215 Montague St., Brooklyn: "The First" (Jackie); *Scene 6* The Havana training camp of the Brooklyn Dodgers: "Bloat" (Durocher, Reporters, The Dodgers); *Scene 7* Outside a ballpark, Jacksonville, Fla.: "The First" (reprise) (Jackie); *Scene 8* The locker room: "It Ain't Gonna Work!" (Higgins & The Dodgers), "The Brooklyn Dodger Strike" (Rickey & Durocher); *Scene 9* Branch Rickey's office: "Jack Roosevelt Robinson" (reprise) (Rickey), "The First" (reprise) (Rachel); *Scene 10* The playing field. *Act II: Scene 1* Behind first base, the Polo Grounds, New York: "You Do-Do-Do-It Good!" (Cool Minnie, Jackie, Junkyard, The Monarchs, Ruby, Opal); *Scene 2* The Dodger locker room, Shibe Park, Philadelphia: "Is This Year Next Year?" (Powers & The Reporters, Rickey, Sukeforth, The Dodgers); *Scene 3* Behind third base, Ebbets Field: "There Are Days and There Are Days" (Rachel); *Scene 4* The front porch of a farmhouse, outside of St. Louis: "It's a Beginning" (Rickey & Jackie); *Scene 5* Outside Ebbets Field: "The Opera Ain't Over" (Hilda & The Fans, Jackie & The Dodgers, Rachel, Rickey); *Scene 6* Inside Ebbets Field; the bottom of the seventh; *Scene 7* Inside Ebbets Field; the top of the ninth.

Broadway reviews were divided, mostly bad. As Douglas Watt put it, "a baseball story that never got to first base." It received Tony nominations for book, direction of a musical, and for David Alan Grier.

214. *First Impressions*

Set in the Hertfordshire village of Longbourn, in 1813. The home of the Bennets, Mr. Bennet, his busy wife, and their five unmarried daughters. Mrs. Bennet's aim in life is to see the girls well married. Two rich men are coming to live at nearby Netherfield Hall — Bingley and Darcy. Bingley immediately falls for Jane, but an intense dislike grows up between strong-willed Elizabeth and Darcy, partly because Darcy is such a class-conscious prig. Elizabeth is more attracted to the dashing Wickham, who Darcy hates. Gradually Darcy starts falling for Elizabeth. Mr. Bennet's cousin, Mr. Collins, to whom the Bennet estate is entailed, arrives at Longbourn with the idea of marrying one of the daughters, and decides upon Elizabeth, who rejects him out of hand. Elizabeth starts to fall for Darcy now, but they hear Mrs. Bennet boasting of how she has won Jane a good match, and Darcy, fearing the same has been planned for him, withdraws. Collins marries Charlotte, Elizabeth's friend, and Collins and Charlotte invite Mrs. Bennet and Elizabeth to visit another old snob, Collins's patroness Lady Catherine de Bourgh, who is also Darcy's aunt. Darcy coldly asks Elizabeth to marry him, but she rejects him, and upbraids him for his bad behavior toward Wickham. Lydia, the fourth daughter, runs off with Wickham, who has now come into an inheritance. There is also a history of bad blood between Darcy and Wickham. Elizabeth and Darcy overcome their pride and prejudice based on first impressions. The front curtain opened like a fan during the overture, then disappeared into the flies.

Before Broadway. Before rehearsals the show was called *A Perfect Evening*; it opened in New Haven on 2/2/59, and then played in Philadelphia, before going to Broadway. Polly Bergen replaced a pregnant Gisele MacKenzie. The New Haven tryouts were reviewed favorably, but were divided in Philadelphia. In Philly Hiram Sherman had a difference of opinion with Abe Burrows, and was replaced by Christopher Hewett. The numbers "Goodbye, Kind Sir, Goodbye," "Silly Brats and Rum" and "Not Like Me" were cut before Broadway.

The Broadway Run. ALVIN THEATRE, 3/19/59–5/30/59. 92 PERFORMANCES. PRESENTED BY George Gilbert & Edward Specter Productions, with the assistance of the Jule Styne Organization; MUSIC/LYRICS: Robert Goldman, Glenn Paxton, George Weiss; BOOK/DIRECTOR: Abe Burrows; BASED ON the 1813 novel *Pride and Prejudice* (the title of which was originally going to be *First Impressions*), by Jane Austen, and on the 1935 dramatization, by Helen Jerome (which had been the basis for the 1940 movie); CHOREOGRAPHER: Jonathan Lucas; ASSISTANT CHOREOGRAPHER: Stuart Hodes; SETS: Peter Larkin; COSTUMES: Alvin Colt; LIGHTING: Charles Elson; MUSICAL DIRECTOR: Frederick Dvonch; ORCHESTRATIONS: Don Walker; ASSISTANT ORCHESTRATOR: Robert Ginzler; DANCE MUSIC ARRANGEMENTS: John Morris; VOCAL DIRECTOR/VOCAL ARRANGEMENTS: Buster Davis; PRESS: John L. Toohey; GENERAL MANAGER: Sylvia Herscher; PRODUCTION STAGE MANAGER: Phil Friedman; STAGE MANAGER: Fred Smith; ASSISTANT STAGE MANAGER: Jim Cavanaugh. *Cast:* MR. BENNET: Laurie Main; MARY BENNET: Lois Bewley; MRS. BENNET: Hermione Gingold (3); LYDIA BENNET: Lynn Ross; KITTY BENNET: Lauri Peters; JANE BENNET: Phyllis Newman (5); MAID: Beverley Jane Welch; ELIZABETH BENNET: Polly Bergen (1), *Ellen Hanley*; LADY LUCAS: Sibyl Bowan; CHARLOTTE LUCAS: Ellen Hanley; CAROLINE BINGLEY: Marti Stevens; CHARLES BINGLEY: Donald Madden (6); FITZWILLIAM DARCY: Farley Granger (2); COACHMEN: Garrett Lewis & John Starkweather; CAPTAIN WICKHAM: James Mitchell (4); LIEUTENANT DENNY: Bill Carter; LIEUTENANT ROCKINGHAM: Stuart Hodes; SIR WILLIAM LUCAS: Richard Bengali; BUTLER: Norman Fredericks; MR. STUBBS: Casper Roos; WILLIAMS: Jay Stern; MR. COLLINS: Christopher Hewett (7); BUTLER AT ROSINGS: John Starkweather; LADY CATHERINE DE BOURGH: Mary Finney; LADY ANNE: Martha Mathes; DANCERS: Arlene Avril, Alvin Beam, Jim Corbett, Stuart Fleming, Richard Gain, Janise Gardner, Sally Gura, Stuart Hodes, Harriet Leigh, Garrett Lewis, Martha Mathes, Dorothy Jeanne Mattis, Wendy Nickerson, John Starkweather; SINGERS: Adrienne Angel, Suzie Baker, Stuart Damon, Norman Fredericks, Marian Haraldson, Warren Hays, Jeannine Masterson, Louise Pearl, Casper Roos, Tony Rossi, Jay Stern, Beverley Jane Welch. *Understudies:* Elizabeth: Ellen Hanley; Mrs. Bennet: Sibyl Bowan; Wickham: Stuart Hodes; Collins: Laurie Main; Lady Catherine: Suzie Baker; Jane: Adrienne Angel; Charles: Stuart Damon; Lady Lucas: Marian Haraldson; Lydia: Janise Gardner; Caroline: Jeannine Masterson; Denny: Jim Corbett; Charlotte: Louise Pearl; Mr. Bennet: Richard Bengal; Mary: Martha Mathes; Kitty: Dorothy Jeanne Mattis. *Act I:* Overture (Orchestra); *Scene 1* Longbourn: "Five Daughters" (Mrs. Bennet), "I'm Me" (Elizabeth & Sisters); *Scene 2* A road in Meryton: "Have You Heard the News" (Mrs. Bennet & Townspeople); *Scene 3* The assembly at Meryton: Polka: the Assembly Dance (Townspeople & Officers), "A Perfect Evening" (Darcy & Elizabeth); *Scene 4* Longbourn: "As Long as There's a Mother" (Mrs. Bennet, Jane, Mary, Lydia, Kitty); *Scene 5* Netherfield Hall: "Jane" (Bingley & Darcy) [added during the run], "Love Will Find Out the Way" (Elizabeth), "Gentlemen Don't Fall Wildly in Love" (Darcy); *Scene 6* Longbourn: "Fragrant Flowers" (Collins & Elizabeth); *Scene 7* The garden at Netherfield Hall: "I Feel Sorry for the Girl" (Jane & Bingley); *Scene 8* The lawn at Netherfield Hall: "I Suddenly Find it Agreeable" (Elizabeth & Darcy), "This Really isn't Me" (Elizabeth); *Scene 9* Longbourn: Finaletto: "As Long as There's a Mother" (reprise) (Mrs. Bennet, Mary, Lydia, Kitty, Jane). *Act II: Scene 1* A church in Kent: "Wasn't it a Simply Lovely Wedding?" (Elizabeth, Mrs. Bennet, Charlotte, Collins, Ensemble); *Scene 2* Rosings, home of Lady Catherine de Bourgh, in Kent: "A House in Town" (Mrs. Bennet), "The Heart Has Won the Game" (Darcy), "I'm Me" (reprise) (Elizabeth); *Scene 3* A street in Meryton: (Brighton) Dance (Wickham, Lydia, Officers); *Scene 4* Longbourn; *Scene 5* Longbourn: "Let's Fetch the Carriage" (Elizabeth & Mrs. Bennet); *Scene 6* Netherfield Hall: "The Heart Has Won the Game" (reprise) (Darcy & Elizabeth), Finale: "Love Will Find Out the Way" (reprise) (Company).

Reviews were divided, mostly unfavorable. Several things went wrong with this show. The score wasn't good (even though Jule Styne is "said to have contributed"). Hermione Gingold, known for her aversion to Jane Austen (but despite getting raves during tryouts), shouldn't have played the role if she felt that way. It came across. After six weeks Polly Bergen was rushed to the hospital with "tubal pregnancy," and Ellen Hanley took over. The show lost nearly all its $300,000 investment.

After Broadway. ENGLAND, 1971. PRESENTED BY Birmingham Repertory Theatre. *Cast*: MRS. BENNET: Patricia Routledge.

RIVERDALE COMMUNITY THEATRE, at the Neighborhood House (Off Broadway), 11/10/72–11/25/72. 6 PERFORMANCES. DIRECTOR/ CHOREOGRAPHER: Jeffrey K. Neill. *Cast*: ELIZABETH: Meredith Kelly; KITTY: Ann Travolta; DARCY: Ward Smith. Three songs were added: "It's the Thing to Do," "So This is How it Is," and "Not Like Me," and "Jane" was also included.

215. *Five Guys Named Moe*

Five guys perform the music of Louis Jordan (1908–75). A lovelorn man, Nomax, is listening to his radio, when suddenly, out of his set, explode The Five Moes. They set about educating Nomax in the ways of women and love, and how to repair his relationship with Lorraine.

Before Broadway. Cameron Mackintosh discovered the revue playing at THEATRE ROYAL, STRATFORD EAST, a small East End theatre in London (where the show had opened 10/12/90), and brought it to the West End, where it opened at the LYRIC THEATRE. DIRECTOR/CHORE-OGRAPHER: Charles Augins. In 1991 it won an Olivier for best entertainment. *Cast*: Clarke Peters, Paul J. Medford, Kenny Andrews, Peter Alex Newton, Omar Okai, Dig Wayne.

The Broadway Run. EUGENE O'NEILL THEATRE, 4/8/92–5/2/93. 19 previews from 3/20/92. 445 PERFORMANCES. PRESENTED BY Cameron Mackintosh; MUSIC/LYRICS: Louis Jordan and others; BOOK: Clarke Peters; DIRECTOR/CHOREOGRAPHER: Charles Augins; SETS: Tim Goodchild; COSTUMES: Noel Howard; LIGHTING: Andrew Bridge; SOUND: Tony Meola/Autograph; MUSICAL SUPERVISOR: Chapman Roberts & Reginald Royal; MUSICAL DIRECTOR: Reginald Royal; ORCHESTRATIONS: Neil McArthur; VOCAL ARRANGEMENTS: Chapman Roberts; CAST RECORDING on Columbia; PRESS: The Publicity Office; CASTING: Johnson — Liff & Zerman; GENERAL MANAGER: Alan Wasser; COMPANY MANAGER: Michael Sanfilippo; PRODUCTION STAGE MANAGER: Marybeth Abel; STAGE MANAGERS: Gwendolyn M. Gilliam & Roumel Reaux. *Cast*: NOMAX: Jerry Dixon, *Weyman Thompson* (from 12/92); BIG MOE: Doug Eskew; FOUR-EYED MOE: Milton Craig Nealy; NO MOE: Kevin Ramsey; EAT MOE: Jeffrey D. Sams; LITTLE MOE: Glenn Turner. *Understudies*: Nomax: Phillip Gilmore; Big Moe: Michael-Leon Wooley; Eat Moe: Phillip Gilmore & Michael-Leon Wooley; Four-Eyed Moe: Phillip Gilmore & W. Ellis Porter; No Moe/Little Moe: W. Ellis Porter. *The Band*: PIANO: Reginald Royal; BASS: Luico Hopper; DRUMS: Brian Kirk; TRUMPET/FLUGELHORN: Reggie Pittman; TROMBONE: Gregory Charles Royal; SAX/CLARINET: Mark Grose. *Act I*: "Early in the Morning" (m/l: LJ, Leo Hickman, Dallas Bartley), "Five Guys Named Moe" (m/l: Larry Wynn & Jerry Breslen), "Beware, Brother, Beware" (m/l: Morry Lasco, Dick Adams, Fleecie Moore), "I Like 'em Fat Like That" ("Ooh, It Must Be Jelly 'cos Jam Don' Shake Like That") (m/l: Claude Demetriou, LJ, J. Mayo Williams), "Messy Bessy" (m/l: Jon Hendricks), "Pettin' and Pokin'" (m/l: Lora Lee), "Life is So Peculiar" (m: Jimmy Van Heusen; l: Johnny Burke) [from the movie *Mr. Music*], "I Know What I've Got" (m/l: Sid Robin & LJ), "Azure Te" (m/l: Bill Davis & Don Wolf), "Safe, Sane and Single" (m/l: Johnny Lange, Hy Heath, LJ), "Push Ka Pi Shi Pie" (m/l: Joe Willoughby, LJ, Dr. Walt Merrick). *Act II*: "Push Ka Pi Shi Pie" (instrumental reprise), "Saturday Night Fish Fry" (m/l: Ellis Walsh & LJ), "What's the Use of Gettin' Sober?" (m/l: Busby Meyers), "If I Had Any Sense" (m/l: Rose Marie McCoy & Charles Singleton), "Dad Gum Your Hide, Boy" (m/l: Browley Bri), The Cabaret: "Five Guys Named Moe" (reprise), "Let the Good Times Roll" (m/l: Fleecie Moore & Sam Theard), "Reet, Petite and Gone" (m/l: Spencer Lee & LJ), "Caldonia" (m/l: Claude Moine & Fleecie Moore), "(There) Ain't

Nobody Here but Us Chickens" (m/l: Joan Whitney & Alex Kramer), "Don't Let the Sun Catch You Crying" (m/l: Jo Greene), "Choo Choo Ch'Boogie" (m/l: Vaughn Horton, Denver Darling, Milton Gabler), "Look Out Sister" (m/l: Sid Robin & LJ) [end of Cabaret sequence], Medley: "Hurry Home" (m/l: Joseph Meyer, Buddy Bernier, Robert Emmerich), "Is You or Is You Ain't My Baby?" (m/l: Sil Austin & LJ) [from the movie *Follow the Boys*], "Don't Let the Sun Catch You Crying" (reprise) [end of Medley], "Five Guys Named Moe" (reprise).

Note: LJ means Louis Jordan.

During each Broadway performance hundreds of leaflets were showered on the audience from the stage and balcony, with the words to "Push Ka Pi Shi Pie" on them, so the audience could help Nomax. Later the actors led a conga line to the bar. Broadway reviews were divided. The show received Tony nominations for musical and book.

After Broadway. AHMANSON THEATRE, Los Angeles, 7/7/93. PRESENTED BY the Center Theatre Group. *Cast*: EAT MOE: Kevyn Brackett; BIG MOE: Doug Eskew; FOUR-EYED MOE: Milton Craig Nealy; LITTLE MOE: Jeffrey Polk; NOMAX: Kirk Taylor; NO MOE: Keith Tyrone.

216. *The Five O'clock Girl*

Set in New York City in the 1920s. Poor girl and rich boy.

Before Broadway. The original, also seen as *The 5 O'clock Girl*, opened at the 44TH STREET THEATRE, 10/10/27. It moved on 4/16/28 to the SHUBERT THEATRE, and closed there on 6/2/28. Total of 280 PERFORMANCES. PRESENTED BY Philip Goodman; DIRECTOR: Philip Goodman; SETS: Norman Bel Geddes. *Cast*: PAT: Mary Eaton; GERRY: Oscar Shaw; SUE: Pert Kelton; MADAME ROSALIE: Vehrah Verba.

The revised revival first ran at the GOODSPEED OPERA HOUSE, in Connecticut, in 1979, and again in 1980, before going to Broadway in 1981.

The Broadway Run. HELEN HAYES THEATRE, 1/28/81–2/8/81. 7 previews. 7 PERFORMANCES. PRESENTED BY Rodger H. Hess, by arrangement with Tams-Witmark Music Library; MUSIC/LYRICS: Bert Kalmar & Harry Ruby; BOOK: Guy Bolton & Fred Thompson; DIRECTOR: Sue Lawless; CHOREOGRAPHER: Dan Siretta; SETS: John Lee Beatty; COSTUMES: Nanzi Adzima; LIGHTING: Craig Miller; SOUND: Richard Fitzgerald; MUSICAL DIRECTOR: Lynn Crigler; ORCHESTRATIONS/DANCE MUSIC ARRANGEMENTS: Russell Warner; MUSIC RESEARCH CONSULTANT: Alfred Simon; PRESS: Shirley Herz Associates; GENERAL MANAGEMENT: Theatre Now; PRODUCTION STAGE MANAGER: John J. Bonanni; STAGE MANAGER: Peter Weicker; ASSISTANT STAGE MANAGER: Danute Debney. *Cast*: MADAME IRENE: Sheila Smith (6); HUDGINS, MR. BROOKS' VALET: Ted Pugh (4); SUSAN "SUE" SNOW: Pat Stanley (2); PATRICIA "PAT" BROWN: Lisby Larson (1); GERALD "GERRY" BROOKS: Roger Rathburn (3); RONNIE WEBB: Barry Preston (5); CORA WAINWRIGHT: Dee Hoty (8); JASPER COBB: Timothy Wallace (7); JEANIE: Teri Corcoran; PETE, THE WAITER: James Homan; RODNEY, MADAME IRENE'S ESCORT: Richard Ruth; SAM: Rodney Pridgen; ETHEL/MOLLY, THE MAID: Annette Michelle; ELSIE: Lora Jeanne Martens; BUNNIE: Jean McLaughlin; POLLY: Debra Grimm; MAISIE: Carla Farnsworth-Webb; JULES, THE MAITRE D': Jonathan Aronson; DETECTIVE: G. Brandon Allen; BOBBY, POLICEMAN: Gary Kirsch. *Understudies*: Sue: Jean McLaughlin; Pat: Lora Jeanne Martens; Cora: Carla Farnsworth-Webb; Gerry: Richard Ruth; Ronnie: Jonathan Aronson; Mme Irene: Teri Corcoran; Hudgins: Timothy Wallace; Jasper: G. Brandon Allen. *Swings*: Danute Debney & Robert Rabin. *Act I*: Overture (Orchestra); *Scene 1* A block party near Beekman Place, New York City: "In the Old Neighborhood" (Irene & Ensemble); *Scene 2* On the telephone: "Keep Romance Alive" * [from the movie *Hips, Hips, Hooray*] (Telephone Girls), "Thinking of You" (Pat & Gerry) [the big hit from the 1927 production]; *Scene 3* Gerry's apartment: "I'm One Little Party" (Ronnie & Female Ensemble), "Up in the Clouds" (Pat, Gerry, Ensemble), "My Sunny Tennessee" * [from *Midnight Rounders of 1921*] (Herman Ruby) (Jasper & Female Ensemble), "Any Little Thing" (Sue & Hudgins); *Scene 4* The Snowflake Cleaners; *Scene 5* The Kit Kat Club: "Manhattan Walk" * [from *Good Boy*] (Herbert Stothart) (Irene, Ronnie, Cora, Jasper, Ensemble). *Act II*: Entr'acte (Orchestra); *Scene 1* Outside the Field and Stream Hotel, Southampton, Long Island: "Long Island Low Down" * [from *Animal Crackers*] (Irene

& Ensemble), "Who Did? You Did!" (Pat & Gerry), "Any Little Thing" (reprise) (Sue); *Scene 2* The Snowflake Cleaners: "Nevertheless (I'm in Love with You)" * (Sue & Hudgins); *Scene 3* A street in New York: "All Alone Monday" * [from *The Ramblers*] (Gerry); *Scene 4* Roof garden between the apartments of Gerry and Ronnie: "Dancing the Devil Away" * (from *Lucky*) (Otto Harbach) (Ronnie & Ensemble); *Scene 5* The church: "Up in the Clouds" (reprise) (Pat & Gerry), Finale (Company).

Note: this revival cut some of the original, 1927, songs, and added the Kalmar—Ruby songs indicated in the list by an asterisk, with any additional collaborators in parentheses (i.e. the parenthesized person is in addition to Bert Kalmar & Harry Ruby).

Reviews were divided. The production closed at the 2/8/81 matinee.

217. *Flahooley*

Set in Capsulanti, USA, where "the nation's biggest toy-coon," B.G. Bigelow, runs B.G. Bigelow, Inc., the greatest toy factory in the world. Sylvester, a puppet designer in the Puppet Laboratory there, is in love with his model Sandy, who can hear the puppets talk. As Sylvester is about to present his new laughing Christmas doll, Flahooley, to the board, the Arabs appear. Their magic lamp has lost the power to produce a genie, and they've run out of oil in Arabia. They ask Bigelow to fix the lamp. He does, mostly because he's interested in Princess Najla. Sylvester is given the job of fixing the lamp, and he finds that when rubbed by Fla-hooley's hand, the genie appears. A competitor has stolen the Fla-hooley idea and put out a cheaper model. Sylvester wishes every child could have a Flahooley doll, and his wish comes true. Thus there is no more market, and business is ruined for Bigelow. In the second act the genie escapes but Sandy finds him in New York, where he agrees to become a year-round Santa Claus. Bigelow and Najla get married. Note: the word "flahooley" means "flighty," or "whimsical" and is also used in the book *The Three Wishes of Jamie McRuin*, upon which the musical *Three Wishes for Jamie* was based.

Before Broadway. Originally called *Toyland*. Harold Arlen, and then Burton Lane were scheduled to do the music. During tryouts in New Haven and then Philadelphia, the show got rave reviews. Daniel Mann became involved with the direction in Philadelphia. This was Barbara Cook's first Broadway appearance.

The Broadway Run. BROADHURST THEATRE, 5/14/51–6/17/51. 40 PERFORMANCES. PRESENTED BY Cheryl Crawford, in association with E.Y. Harburg & Fred Saidy; MUSIC: Sammy Fain; LYRICS: E.Y. Harburg; BOOK/DIRECTORS: E.Y. Harburg & Fred Saidy; SPECIAL MATERIAL FOR YMA SUMAC: Moises Vivanco; CHOREOGRAPHER: Helen Tamiris; SETS/LIGHTING: Howard Bay; COSTUMES: David ffolkes; MUSICAL DIRECTOR/CHORAL DIRECTOR/CHORAL NUMBERS ARRANGED BY: Maurice Levine; ORCHESTRATIONS: Ted Royal; DANCE MUSIC ARRANGEMENTS: Freda Miller; CAST RECORDING made on 5/27/51; PRESS: Wolfe Kaufman, Abner D. Klipstein, Merle Debuskey; GENERAL MANAGER: John Yorke; STAGE MANAGERS: Perry Bruskin, Clifford Fearl, Andy Anderson. *Cast:* A MARCH OF TIME VOICE: Stanley Carlson; CLYDE: Bil Baird; MIRABELLE: Cora Baird; SANDY: Barbara Cook (6); SYLVESTER: Jerome Courtland (3); GRISELDA: Fay De Witt; SWITCHBOARD OPERATORS: Vicki Barrett, Jane Fischer, Urylee Leonardos, Laurel Shelby, Tafi Towers, Anneliese Widman; K.T. PETTIGREW: Edith Atwater (4); BOARD OF DIRECTORS (SIX MEMBERS): QUIMSY: Stanley Carlson; PEABODY: Ted Thurston; EVANS: Rowan Tudor; FARQUARSON: Richard Temple; LOVINGHAM: Andrew Aprea; HASTINGS: Edgar Thompson; VOICE ON THE P.A.: Tafi Towers; B.G. BIGELOW: Ernest Truex (1); MISS BUCKLEY: Marilyn Ross; CLAYFOOT TROWBRIDGE: Rowan Tudor; FOWZI (THE YOUNGER ARAB): Nehemiah Persoff; EL-AKBAR (THE ELDER ARAB): Louis Nye; PRINCESS NAJLA: Yma Sumac (2); BUYERS: Lee Ballard, Ray Cook, Clifford Fearl, Laurel Shelby, Franklin T. Syme; ABOU BEN ATOM: Irwin Corey (5); ELSA BULLINGER: Lulu Bates; CITIZENS OF CAPSULANTI: Ray Cook, Clifford Fearl, Sheldon Ossosky, Norval Tormsen; ARABS: Andrew Aprea,

Stanley Carlson, Ted Thurston, Rowan Tudor; DOCTOR SMITH: Franklin T. Syme; NURSE: Laurel Shelby; FLAHOOLEY: Elizabeth Logue; RADIO VOICE: Edgar Thompson; SINGERS: Andrew Aprea, John Anderson, Vicki Barrett, Lewis Bolyard, Ray Cook, Carol Donn, Clifford Fearl, Urylee Leonardos, Laurel Shelby, Lois Shearer, Franklin T. Syme, Edgar Thompson, Norval Tormsen, Tafi Towers; DANCERS: Sara Aman, Jane Fischer, Normand Maxon, Joe Nash, Sheldon Ossosky, James M. Tarbutton, Anneliese Widman; MARIONETTE OPERATORS: Bil Baird, Cora Baird, Carl Harms, Franz Fazakas; PUPPETS: Bil Baird Marionettes (7); PUPPET SINGING VOICES: MIRABELLE: Lois Shearer; CINDERELLA: Lois Shearer; POODLE: Lois Shearer; CLYDE: John Anderson; F.D.R.: John Anderson; HEN: Carol Donn; RHINO: Ted Thurston; CAT: Fay De Witt; LINCOLN: Stanley Carlson; LION: Franz Fazakas; TOM PAYNE: Carl Harms. *Act I: Prologue*; *Scene 1* B.G. Bigelow, Inc.: "You Too Can Be a Puppet" (Puppet Singers), "Here's to Your Illusions" (Sandy & Sylvester); *Scene 2* A section of the puppet laboratory; *Scene 3* "Telephone Switchboard Scene"; *Scene 4* The boardroom; *Scene 5* Bigelow's Toyland Bazaar: "B.G. Bigelow, Inc." (Executives & Personnel), Demonstration Dances (Sara Aman, Joe Nash, Sheldon Ossosky, Anneliese Widman, Jane Fischer, Vicki Barrett), "Najla's Lament" ("Najla's Song") (Najla), "Who Says There Ain't No Santa Claus" (Sylvester, Sandy, Executives, Personnel); *Scene 6* The Bigelow Hall of Fame (Showroom to you): "Flahooley" (sung & danced by Griselda, Miss Buckley, Executives, Personnel). Danced by the Toy Band: BIG DRUM: Joe Nash; CLARINET: James M. Tarbutton; ACCORDION: John Anderson; TUBA: Sheldon Ossosky; GLOCKENSPIEL: Normand Maxon; *Scene 7* The puppet laboratory: "The World is Your Balloon" (Sandy, Sylvester, Puppet Singing Company), "He's Only Wonderful" (Sandy & Sylvester); *Scene 8* "Najla's Song of Joy"/"Arabian for 'Get Happy'" (Najla, Abou, Fowzi, El-Akbar); *Scene 9* Bigelow's inner sanctum: "Inner-Office Scene," "Jump, Little Chillun'" (Ensemble). *Act II: Scene 1* B.G. Bigelow, Inc.: "Consternation," "No More Flahooleys" (Ensemble); *Scene 2* City Hall square: "Spirit of Capsulanti" (sung & danced by Miss Buckley & Townspeople), "Happy Hunting" (Elsa, Miss Buckley, Griselda, Townspeople); *Scene 3* B.G. Bigelow, Inc.; *Scene 4* Bigelow's Bagdad: "Birds"/"Enchantment" (Najla), "Scheherezade" (Arabs & Executives); *Scene 5* Hospital waiting-room; *Scene 6* Abou's hospital room: "Come Back, Little Genie" (Sandy); *Scene 7* "Sing the Merry" (Griselda, John Anderson, Clifford Fearl, Ray Cook, Norval Tormsen, Dr. Smith, Lewis Bolyard); *Scene 8* Main Street, Capsulanti: Finale (Entire Company).

Broadway reviews were divided, and the show's anti-capitalistic sentiments were unfortunately timed (America was involved in the Korean War), and the show was seen as unpatriotic, and that killed the show more than anything. It is also remembered as being strongly and openly anti–McCarthy.

After Broadway. After Broadway it was revised, and re-named *A Little Doll Laughed*, then *Jollyanna*. Most of the political and social comments had now disappeared. It had a limited four-week run at the CURRAN THEATRE, San Francisco, from 8/11/52, PRESENTED BY Edwin Lester's Civic Light Opera Company, San Francisco. DIRECTOR: Jack Donohue; CHOREOGRAPHERS: Jack Donohue & Jack Cole. *Cast:* PENNY: Mitzi Gaynor (this was the old Sandy role); BIGELOW: Bobby Clark; SYLVESTER: John Beal. A new character, Diana (Bigelow's secretary) was added, and the story now centered around the love triangle between Sylvester and the two girls. "B.G. Bigelow, Inc.," "Cinderella" (m: Fain; l: Harburg), "The World is Your Balloon," "Jollyanna" (m: William Friml; l: Harburg), "Bigelow" (recitative), "You Too Can Be a Puppet," "A Little Bit of Magic" (m: Burton Lane; l: Harburg), "Jump, Chillun', Jump," "What's Gonna Happen?" (m: Lane; l: Harburg), "Come Back, Little Genie," "Scheherezade Interlude" (m: Rimsky-Korsakov; l: Harburg), "How Lucky Can You Get?" (m: Fain; l: Harburg), "The Springtime Cometh." It was scheduled to return to Broadway, but never made it. In 1953 Yip Harburg revised it again, slightly, and he and William Friml wrote "Bigelow's Entrance" to replace the recitative. "How Lucky Can You Get?" was dropped. But it never went anywhere.

ST. CLEMENT'S, NY, 9/10/98–9/26/98. A revival using Poko Puppets as part of the International Puppet Festival. It restored some material cut before the 1951 production got to Broadway, and was a combination of pre–Broadway and Broadway drafts. ADAPTED/DIRECTOR: Alisa

Roost; CHOREOGRAPHER: Al Joyal; MUSICAL DIRECTOR/ORCHESTRATIONS: Peter E. Jones. **Cast**: SANDY STAR: April Allen; EDNA: Roxy Becker; B.G. BIGELOW: Christopher Budinich; KT: Natalie Buster; ELSA BUNDSHLAGER: Tiffany M. Card; LILLIAN: Laura Case; SYLVESTER CLOUD: Mark Cortale; DR. JONES: Mimi Ferraro; FARQUARSON: Bill Grainer; CLAYFOOT: Alex Greenshields; ABOU BEN ATOM: Clay Hansen; LIZ: Diann Hinson; THELMA: Virginia Holland; ERMA: Amber Lynch; FLAHOOLEY: Lisa Rudin; ARAB/THREE-HEADED TROLL: Alan Semok; QUIMSY: Morgan Sills; NAJLA: Carol Tammen; MIRABELLE: Cheryl Walsh; TUFFLES: J. Michael Zally. "You Too Can be a Puppet," "Here's to Your Illusions," "B.G. Bigelow, Inc.," "Song of Joy," "Do I Hear a Reindeer?," "He's Only Wonderful," "Flahooley," "The World is Your Balloon," "Jump, Little Chillun'," "No More Flahooleys," "The Spirit of Capsulanti," "Happy Hunting," "Scheherezade," "Birdsong"/"Come Back, Little Genie," "The Springtime Cometh," "Sing the Merry," Finale.

218. *Flora, the Red Menace*

Set 1933–35, in New York City. Flora, a spunky young girl just out of school, is looking for a job as a fashion designer, and is conned into joining the Young Communist League by her boyfriend, commercial artist Harry.

Before Broadway. Hal Prince invited John Kander and Fred Ebb to write the show—their first together as the great songwriting team of Kander & Ebb. Mr. Prince asked Garson Kanin to adapt Lester Atwell's book as a libretto, but Mr. Kanin turned him down, and suggested Bob Russell, who wrote it with Barbra Streisand in mind. Mr. Russell came up with the title, but he wasn't up to the libretto, so George Abbott was called in (and to direct as well; he saw Eydie Gorme as the star). However, Mr. Abbott was in Florida, and wouldn't come north, so he directed from a distance, and this is one of the reasons for the show's failure. On 4/10/65 it finished its New Haven tryout, where it had been well-received, and five days later opened at the Colonial Theatre, Boston, where it ran 2½ weeks and was also well-received. Then to New York. This was Liza Minnelli's Broadway debut.

The Broadway Run. ALVIN THEATRE, 5/11/65–7/24/65. 7 previews from 5/4/65. 87 PERFORMANCES. PRESENTED BY Harold Prince; MUSIC: John Kander; LYRICS: Fred Ebb; BOOK: George Abbott & Robert Russell; BASED ON the 1963 novel *Love is Just Around the Corner*, by Lester Atwell; DIRECTOR: George Abbott; CHOREOGRAPHER: Lee Theodore; SETS: William & Jean Eckart; COSTUMES: Donald Brooks; LIGHTING: Tharon Musser; MUSICAL DIRECTOR: Hal Hastings; ORCHESTRATIONS: Don Walker; DANCE MUSIC ARRANGEMENTS: David Baker; CAST RECORDING on RCA Victor, recorded two days before the opening on Broadway; PRESS: Mary Bryant; PRODUCTION SUPERVISOR: Ruth Mitchell; GENERAL MANAGER: Carl Fisher; PRODUCTION STAGE MANAGER: John Allen; STAGE MANAGER: Frank Gero; ASSISTANT STAGE MANAGER: Bob Bernard. **Cast**: FDR'S VOICE: Art Carney; APPLE SELLER: J. Vernon Oaks; PENCIL SELLER: Clark Morgan; POLICEMAN: Daniel P. Hannafin; BROKER: Henry LeClair; 4TH MAN: John Taliaferro; WOMAN: Anne C. Russell; 5TH MAN: Anthony Falco; 6TH MAN: Les Freed; 7TH MAN: Robert Fitch; SCHOOL PRINCIPAL: Abbie Todd; FLORA MESZAROS: Liza Minnelli (1); HARRY TOUKARIAN: Bob Dishy (2); LILLY: Anne C. Russell; ARTISTS: Les Freed, John Taliaferro, J. Vernon Oaks, Diane McAfee, Anthony Falco, Marie Santell; COMRADE GALKA: Louis Guss (10); COMRADE ADA: Mary Louise Wilson (3); COMRADE JACKSON: Clark Morgan; COMRADE CHARLOTTE: Cathryn Damon (4); ELSA: Stephanie Hill (6); THE LADY: Dortha Duckworth (8); MR. WEISS: Joe E. Marks (9); BRONCO SMALLWOOD: James Cresson (7); JOE: Danny Carroll; KATIE: Marie Santell; MR. REARSON: Gordon Dilworth; MR. STANLEY: Robert Kaye (5); LULU: Jamie Donnelly; MAGGIE: Elaine Cancilla; DANCERS: Harry Bell, Elaine Cancilla, Ciya Challis, Barbara Doherty, Judith Doren, Robert Fitch, Marcelo Gamboa, Ellen Graff, Charles Kalan, James McArdle, Mary Ann Niles, Neil J. Schwartz, Phyllis Wallach; SINGERS: Barbara Christopher, Jamie Donnelly, Anthony Falco, Les Freed, Daniel P. Hannafin, Henry LeClair, Diane McAfee, J. Vernon Oaks, John Taliaferro, Abbie Todd. **Understudies**: Flora: Jamie Donnelly; Harry: Danny Carroll; Ada: Anne C. Russell; Charlotte: Elaine

Cancilla; Stanley: J. Vernon Oaks; The Lady: Abbie Todd; Elsa: Marie Santell; Galka: Gordon Dilworth; Bronco: Bob Fitch; Weiss: Henry LeClair; Joe: Charles Kalan. *Act I*: Overture; *Scene 1* A street in New York and the High School of Commercial Art, New York City; 1933: Prologue (Ensemble), "Unafraid" (Flora, Students, Ensemble); *Scene 2* The advertising office at Garrett & Mellick's Department Store: "All I Need (is One Good Break)" (Flora, Harry, Artists); *Scene 3* The park: "Not Every Day of the Week" (Flora & Harry); *Scene 4* Flora's studio: "All I Need is One Good Break" (reprise) (Flora, Elsa, The Lady), "Sign Here" (Harry); *Scene 5* The party meeting: "The Flame" (Ada, Harry, Comrades); *Scene 6* Flora's studio: "Palomino Pal" (The Lady & Cowboy); *Scene 7* Mr. Stanley's office at Garrett & Mellick's Department Store: "A Quiet Thing" (Flora); *Scene 8* Flora's studio: "Hello, Waves" (Harry & Flora); *Scene 9* Union Square and the street in front of Harry's House: "Dear Love" (Flora & Ensemble). *Act II*: *Scene 1* Harry's apartment: "Express Yourself" (Charlotte & Harry); *Scene 2* The park: "Knock, Knock" (Ada & Cowboy); *Scene 3* Flora's studio: Comrade Charlotte's Ballet ("The Tree of Life") (Charlotte, Ada, Harry, Ensemble): TRUNK: Neil J. Schwartz (a fat ballerino); VINE: Robert Fitch; SPIRIT OF REVOLUTION: Mary Ann Niles; *Scene 4* Mr. Stanley's office at Garrett & Mellick's Department Store: "Sing Happy" (Flora); *Scene 5* Flora's studio: "You Are You" (Weiss & Elsa, Flora, Stanley, Lulu, Katie, Joe), Finale (Entire Company).

Broadway reviews were divided. Liza Minnelli, in her Broadway debut, won a Tony. The show was capitalized at $400,000, and lost almost all of it.

After Broadway. VINEYARD THEATRE, NYC, 11/30/87–1/23/88. 46 PERFORMANCES. It had a tiny orchestra. It was presented as a play within a play being performed by the Federal Theatre Project. NEW BOOK: David Thompson; DIRECTOR: Scott Ellis; CHOREOGRAPHER: Susan Stroman; SETS: Michael J. Hotopp; COSTUMES: Lindsay W. Davis; NEW CAST RECORDING on TER. **Cast**: FLORA: Veanne Cox; HARRY: Peter Frechette; CHARLOTTE: Lyn Greene; STANLEY: David Ossian; WEISS: Ray DeMattis; MAGGIE: Maggy Gorrill; ELSA: B.J. Jefferson; WILLY: Eddie Korbich; KENNY: Dirk Lumbard. *Act I*: Prologue: "Unafraid" (Flora & Company), "Street Song I" (Company), "The Kid Herself" (Flora & Artists), "All I Need is One Good Break" (Katie, Maggie, Elsa, Mr. Weiss, Willie), "Not Every Day of the Week" (Harry & Flora), "Street Song II" (Company), "Sign Here" (Harry & Maggie), "Street Song III" (Company), "A Quiet Thing" (Mr. Stanley & Flora), "The Flame" (Charlotte & Communists), "Not Every Day of the Week" (reprise) (Harry & Flora), "Street Song IV" (Company), "Dear Love" (Flora & Company). *Act II*: "Keepin' it Hot" (Maggie), "Street Song V" (Company), "Express Yourself" (Charlotte), "Where Did Everybody Go?" (Harry, Flora, Charlotte), "Street Song VI" (Company), "You Are You" (Mr. Weiss, Elsa, Flora), "The Joke" (Harry & Crowd), "A Quiet Thing" (reprise) (Willie), "Sing Happy" (Flora), Closing Scene (Willie & Flora).

219. *Flower Drum Song*

Chinese immigrants in San Francisco's Chinatown today (1958), and the social differences between Americans and Chinese, but most specifically the conflict between retaining the old Chinese ways and assimilating into American culture. The household of Wang Chi Yang is having problems adjusting. Mr. Wang is a Chinese gentleman of the old school; his eldest son Wang Ta is caught between two cultures; his second son, Wang San, is entirely Americanized; his sister-in-law, Madam Liang, is enthusiastically studying up for American citizenship. Sammy Fong, owner of the Celestial Bar, has a mail order bride arriving from China, but he is in love with someone else, and succeeds in selling the contract to old Mr. Wang. He introduces Mei Li, the "picture bride," and her father Dr. Li, to the Wangs, and she charms them with her flower drum song. Wang Ta asks the girlfriend of his choice, brassy nightclub singer Linda, if she will marry him, and she says yes. Mei Li finally meets Wang Ta and likes him. Madam Liang becomes a citizen. Wang Ta introduces Linda and announces his engagement, much to the dismay of Mr. Wang and also of Mei Li, who thought she was being set up for Wang Ta. Sammy turns up and it transpires that Linda is the girl he is in love with. Linda works at Sammy's bar, and he invites the Wangs to the bar. Linda tells Helen, her seamstress, that she is quitting to marry Wang Ta. Helen has silently loved Wang Ta for years, and is crushed. The Wangs are horrified by what they find at the bar—strippers, rowdy songs, Frankie, a rather bold mc, etc. Wang Ta has started to fall in love with Mei Li now, and he is confused. He turns to Helen for comfort. Sammy has proposed successfully to Linda by now, but the Chinese organization The Three Family Association demands that Sammy marry Mei Li, as was originally contracted for. Mei Li works it out at the end. Oc Hammerstein referred to it as a sort of Chinese *Life with Father*.

Before Broadway. Joseph Fields had read the novel about the conflicts between first and second generation Chinese-American families (C.Y. Lee's novel was the first written by a Chinese-American to be published by a major publishing house, and became a best-seller). He bought the rights, and took it to Rodgers & Hammerstein to see if they wanted to do a musical of it. Fields & Hammerstein shifted the emphasis from Wang Chi Yang, the patriarch, to a romantic triangle involving Wang Ta, Mei Li and Linda. They added the character of Sammy. It opened at the Shubert Theatre, Boston, on 10/27/58, before going to Broadway. It was Gene Kelly's only directing job in the theatre, and Carol Haney's first job as choreographer. Of the actors few were Chinese. Pat Suzuki and Miyoshi Umeki were Japanese; Ed Kenney was Hawaiian; Juanita Hall was black. Sammy was originally to have been played by Larry Storch, but during the Boston tryouts he was replaced by Larry Blyden (real life husband of Carol Haney), but Mr. Blyden agreed to take the role only if he could have a big musical number. However, it was the first Broadway show to star and feature Asian-American actors. The numbers "My Best Love" and "She is Beautiful" were cut before Broadway ("My Best Love" wound up in the 1993 production of *Cinderella*—see appendix, and later in the 2002 revival of *Flower Drum Song*).

The Broadway Run. ST. JAMES THEATRE, 12/1/58–5/7/60. 602 PERFORMANCES. PRESENTED BY Richard Rodgers & Oscar Hammerstein II, in association with Joseph Fields; MUSIC: Richard Rodgers; LYRICS: Oscar Hammerstein II; BOOK: Oscar Hammerstein II & Joseph Fields; BASED ON the 1957 novel of the same name, by Chin Y. Lee; DIRECTOR: Gene Kelly; CHOREOGRAPHER: Carol Haney; SETS: Oliver Smith; COSTUMES: Irene Sharaff; ASSISTANT COSTUMES: Florence Klotz; LIGHTING: Peggy Clark; MUSICAL DIRECTOR: Salvatore Dell'Isola; ORCHESTRATIONS: Robert Russell Bennett; DANCE MUSIC ARRANGEMENTS: Luther Henderson Jr.; CAST RECORDING on Columbia; PRESS: Michel Mok, Sol Jacobson, Lewis Harmon; CASTING: Edward Blum; PRODUCTION SUPERVISOR: Jerome Whyte; GENERAL MANAGER: Morris Jacobs; COMPANY MANAGER: Maurice Winters; GENERAL STAGE MANAGER: James Hammerstein; STAGE MANAGERS: Ted Hammerstein & Fred Hearn. **Cast:** MADAM LIANG: Juanita Hall (4); LIU MA: Rose Quong; WANG SAN: Patrick Adiarte; WANG TA: Ed Kenney (6); WANG CHI YANG: Keye Luke (5); SAMMY FONG: Larry Blyden (3); DR. LI: Conrad Yama; MEI LI: Miyoshi Umeki (1), *Cely Carrillo* (stood in); LINDA LOW: Pat Suzuki (2); MR. LUNG, THE TAILOR: Harry Shaw Lowe; MR. HUAN: Jon Lee; HELEN CHAO: Arabella Hong (7); PROFESSOR CHENG: Peter Chan; FRANKIE WING: Jack Soo; HEAD WAITER: George Young; NIGHT CLUB SINGER: Anita Ellis; DR. LU FONG: Chao Li; MADAM FONG: Eileen Nakamura; CHILDREN: Luis Robert Hernandez, Susan Lynn Kikuchi, Linda Ribuca, Yvonne Ribuca; DANCING ENSEMBLE: Jose Ahumada, Fumi Akimoto, Paula Chin, Victor Duntiere, Helen Funai, Pat Griffith, Mary Huie, Marion Jim, Betty Kawamura, Baayork Lee, George Li, David Lober, Robert Lorca, Wonci Lui, George Minami, Jo Anne Miya, Denise Quan, Vicki Racimo, Shawnee Smith, Maureen Tiongco, David Toguri, Mabel Wing, Yuriko, George Young, *Yoshiko Kazutani, Carolyn Okada, Yin Sun.* **Standby:** Mei Li: Cely Carrillo. **Understudies:** Wang Ta: Jon Lee; Linda: Anita Ellis (Yin Sun was 2nd understudy); Wang Chi Yang: Conrad Yama, *Chao Li*; Dr. Li: Chao Li; Helen: Anita Ellis; Sammy: Jack

Soo; Liu Ma: Eileen Nakamura; Madam Fong: Rose Quong; Wang San: George Minami; Dr. Lu Fong: Peter Chan; Frankie: George Young. **Act I**: Overture (Orchestra); **Scene 1** The living room in the house of Master Wang Chi Yang: "You are Beautiful" (Wang Ta & Madam Liang), "A Hundred Million Miracles" (Mei Li, Dr. Li, Wang Chi Yang, Madam Liang, Liu Ma); **Scene 2** A hill overlooking San Francisco Bay: "I Enjoy Being a Girl" (Linda & Dancers) [the hit]; **Scene 3** The Wang living room: "I Am Going to Like it Here" (Mei Li); **Scene 4** Wang Chi Yang's bedroom: "Like a God" (Wang Ta); **Scene 5** The garden of the Wang house: "Chop Suey" (Madam Liang, Wang San, Ensemble), "Don't Marry Me" (Sammy & Mei Li), "Grant Avenue" (Linda & Ensemble); **Scene 6** Linda's dressing room in the Celestial Bar: "Love, Look Away" (Helen); **Scene 7** The Celestial Bar: "Fan Tan Fannie" (Night Club Singer & Girls) [show stopper], "Gliding Through My Memoree" (Frankie & Girls), Act I Finale: "Grant Avenue" (reprise) (Entire Company). **Act II**: Entr'acte (Orchestra); **Scene 1** Helen Chao's room: Ballet: WANG TA: Ed Kenney; MEI LI: Yuriko; LINDA LOW: Jo Anne Miya (*Denise Quan*); DANCERS; "Love, Look Away" (reprise) (Helen); **Scene 2** The Wang living room: "The Other Generation" (Madam Liang & Wang Chi Yang); **Scene 3** Sammy Fong's penthouse apartment: "Sunday" (Linda & Sammy) [a hit]; **Scene 4** The Three Family Association: "The Other Generation" (reprise) (Wang San & Children); **Scene 5** Sammy Fong's penthouse apartment; **Scene 6** Grant Avenue, San Francisco's Chinatown: "Wedding Parade" (Mei Li & Dancers); **Scene 7** The Three Family Association: Finale: "A Hundred Million Miracles" (reprise) (Entire Company).

It had an advance sale of $1.5 million. Reviews were generally great. The show won a Tony for musical direction, and was nominated for musical, choreography, costumes, and for Larry Blyden and Miyoshi Umeki.

After Broadway. PALACE THEATRE, London, 3/24/60. 464 PERFORMANCES. PRESENTED BY Williamson Music; DIRECTOR: Jerome Whyte; CHOREOGRAPHER: Deirdre Vivian. **Cast:** LINDA: Yama Saki; LINDA IN BALlet: Naomi Kimura; MEI LI: Yau Shan Tung; MEI LI IN BALLET: Sonya Hana; FRANKIE: Leon Thau; HEAD WAITER: David Toguri; SAMMY: Tim Herbert; WANG CHI YANG: George Pastell; WANG SAN: George Minami Jr.; WANG TA: Kevin Scot; NIGHT CLUB SINGER: Ruth Silvestre.

TOUR. Opened on 5/10/60, at the Riviera Theatre, Detroit, and toured for 1½ years. MUSICAL DIRECTOR: Robert Stanley. **Cast:** MADAM LIANG: Juanita Hall, *Nancy Andrews*; WANG TA: Ed Kenney, *Jon Lee, Alvin Ing*; WANG CHI YANG: Keye Luke, *Chao Li*; MR. LUNG: Harry Shaw Lowe; MR. HUAN: Jon Lee; CHILDREN: Linda & Yvonne Ribuca and Luis Robert Hernandez; LINDA: Elaine Dunn, *Arlene Fontana*; SAMMY: Jack Soo; HELEN: Suzanne Lake; MEI LI: Cely Carrillo; DR. LI: Chao Li; WANG SAN: Gene Castle; PROFESSOR CHENG: Khigh Dhiegh; COMMODORE LOW: Bill Sugihara.

PAPER MILL PLAYHOUSE, New Jersey, 1961. DIRECTOR: James Hammerstein. **Cast:** Yin Sun, Larry Leung.

THE MOVIE. 1961. DIRECTOR: Henry Koster. This was the first major Hollywood movie to star and feature Asian-American actors. **Cast:** LINDA: Nancy Kwan (singing dubbed by B.J. Baker); WANG TA: James Shigeta; AUNTIE: Juanita Hall; SAMMY: Jack Soo; MEI LI: Miyoshi Umeki; WANG CHI YANG: Benson Fong; HELEN: Reiko Sato (singing dubbed by Marilyn Horne); WANG SAN: Patrick Adiarte; FRANKIE: Victor Sen Yung; DR. LI: Kam Tong (singing dubbed by John Dodson).

ROYAL ALEXANDRA THEATRE, Toronto, 8/24/65–9/5/65. **Cast:** Larry Leung, Franceska Kae.

220. *Flower Drum Song (Broadway revival)*

This was the first major revival of *Flower Drum Song*. It was now set in 1960. The slightly revised plot, with an Asian-American perspective, now has Mei Li as an apprentice in a Chinese opera company, who flees to America, in the late 1950s, when her father, a Chinese opera master, is persecuted by the Communist government. She arrives in San Francisco, and finds work in a run-down Chinese opera house, where the patriarch, Master Wang, struggles to keep the old traditions alive, while his American-born son, Ta, dreams of converting the space into a Western-style nightclub. Ta's wish comes true, with help of leggy singer Linda and her agent Madame Liang. It becomes the very popular Club Chop Suey. The older-generation figures were also re-conceived. Chao provided the love-interest conflict for Mei Li.

Before Broadway. David Henry Hwang had been a fan of the show for years. In 1998 he approached Jamie Hammerstein, Mary Rodgers, and Theodore S. Chapin (of the Rodgers & Hammerstein Organization) for permission to do a revised version with a new book, and they gave him the okay. Mr. Hwang consulted with the original novelist, C.Y. Lee. Bobby Longbottom came in as director/choreographer by 4/99, and on 5/27/99 there was a private reading at the Juilliard School, NYC, which he directed. Money for this reading was put up by Jujamcyn Theatres and the R & H Organization. On 10/5/99 there was an industry reading, backed by the R & H Organization. A production was scheduled for the Ahmanson Theatre, Los Angeles, 4/15/01–6/10/01, but in 12/00 it was canceled through lack of funds. It was rescued, and finally made its debut at the non-profit MARK TAPER FORUM, Los Angeles, on 10/14/01. Previews from 10/4/01. It extended its 12/2/01 closing date to 2/3/02. DIRECTOR/CHOREOGRAPHER: Robert Longbottom. *Cast*: MEI LI: Lea Salonga (she quit 12/2/01, and was replaced by *Jennifer Paz*); TA: Jose Llana; CHIN: Alvin Ing; LINDA: Sandra Allen; WANG: Tzi Ma; HARVARD: Allen Liu; MADAME LIANG: Jodi Long; CHAO: Ronald M. Banks; ALSO WITH: Eric Chan, Vivian Eng, Blythe Matsui, Chloe Stewart, Kim Varhola, Christine Yasunaga. The numbers "The Other Generation" and "Sunday" were cut (but "Sunday" was re-instated). One number was added—"The Next Time it Happens" (from *Pipe Dream*), but that was also dropped in time for Broadway. "My Best Love" (cut from the original) was re-instated. Some dance numbers were expanded between the L.A. tryout and Broadway. On 4/11/02 the Broadway venue and dates were confirmed. Jose Llana was confirmed in his role on 7/3/02. On 9/3/01 C.Y. Lee's novel was re-issued by Penguin Books, with an introduction by David Henry Hwang. There was a press preview of the show on 9/4/02.

The Broadway Run. VIRGINIA THEATRE, 10/17/02–3/16/03. 26 previews from 9/23/02. 172 PERFORMANCES. PRESENTED BY Benjamin Mordecai, Michael A. Jenkins, Waxman Williams Entertainment, Center Theatre Group/Mark Taper Forum/Gordon Davidson/Charles Dillingham, with Robert G. Bartner, Stephanie McClelland, Judith Resnick, Robert Dragotta/Temple Gill/Marcia Roberts, and by arrangement with the Rodgers & Hammerstein Organization; MUSIC: Richard Rodgers; LYRICS: Oscar Hammerstein II; ORIGINAL BOOK: Oscar Hammerstein II & Joseph Fields; NEW BOOK: David Henry Hwang; BASED ON the 1957 novel of the same name, by Chin Y. Lee; DIRECTOR/CHOREOGRAPHER: Robert Longbottom; SETS: Robin Wagner; COSTUMES: Gregg Barnes; LIGHTING: Natasha Katz; SOUND: ACME Sound Partners; MUSICAL DIRECTOR/VOCAL & DANCE MUSIC ARRANGEMENTS/ADAPTED MUSIC: David Chase; ORCHESTRATIONS: Don Sebesky; NEW CAST RECORDING on DRG, made on 10/21/00, and released on 1/7/03; PRESS: Boneau/Bryan-Brown; CASTING: Tara Rubin Casting & Amy Lieberman; GENERAL MANAGEMENT: Nina Lannan Associates; COMPANY MANAGER: David R. Calhoun; PRODUCTION STAGE MANAGER: Perry Cline; STAGE MANAGER: Rebecca C. Monroe; ASSISTANT STAGE MANAGER: Tom Kosis. *Cast:* MEI LI: Lea Salonga (1) ☆; MASTER WANG: Randall Duk Kim (3); CHIN: Alvin Ing (6) [new character]; TA: Jose Llana (4); HARVARD: Allen Liu (7); LINDA LOW: Sandra Allen (5); MADAM LIANG: Jodi Long (2); CHAO: Hoon Lee (8) [new character]; CHINESE GIRL: Ma-Anne Dionisio; CHINESE OPERA COMPANY/IMMIGRANTS/NIGHTCLUB PERFORMERS/FACTORY WORKERS/WEDDING PARTY/CITIZENS OF CHINATOWN: Rich Ceraulo, Eric Chan, Marcus Choi (fight captain), Emily Hsu, Telly Leung, J. Elaine Marcos, Daniel May, Marc Oka (dance captain), Lainie Sakakura, Yuka Takara, Kim Varhola, Ericka Yang. *Standby*: Chin/Wang: Raul Aranas. *Understudies*: Ta: Rich Ceraulo, Hoon Lee, Telly Leung; Chin: Eric Chan; Chao: Marcus Choi; Mei Li: Ma-Anne Dionisio & Yuka Takara; Linda: Emily Hsu; Harvard: Marc Oka, *Daniel May*; Mme Liang: Kim Varhola; Wang: *Hoon Lee*. SWINGS: Susan Ancheta (*Sally Wong*) & Robert Tatad (*Bobby Pestka*). *Orchestra*: VIOLINS: Claire Chan, Julius Rene Wirth, Mineko Yajima; VIOLA: Julius Rene Wirth; CELLO/ERHU: Clay C. Ruede; WOODWINDS: Richard A. Heck-

man, Ronald Jannelli, Chuck Wilson; TRUMPETS: Christian Jaudes & Stu Satalof; TROMBONE: Jack Schatz; HORN: Russ Rizner; GUITAR/PIPA: Andrew Schwartz; MANDOLIN: Mineko Yajima; FLUTES/BAMBOO FLUTES/DIZI: Janet A. Axelrod; BASS: Lou Bruno; KEYBOARDS: David Evans; DRUMS: Raymond Grappone; PERCUSSION: Howard Joines. *Act I*: Prologue: "A Hundred Million Miracles" (Mei Li & Company), "I Am Going to Like it Here" (Mei Li), "I Enjoy Being a Girl" (Linda & Company), "You Are Beautiful" (Ta & Mei Li), "Grant Avenue" (Madam Liang & Company), "Sunday" (Ta), "Fan Tan Fannie" (Linda & Company), "Gliding Through My Memoree" (Wang & Company). *Act II*: "Chop Suey" (Wang & Company), "My Best Love" (Chin), "Don't Marry Me" (Madam Liang & Wang), "Love, Look Away" (Mei Li), "Like a God" (Ta), Finale: "A Hundred Million Miracles" (reprise) (Company).

Reviews were terrible for the production, but good for the cast and score. On 2/21/03 closing notices were posted for 3/16/03. It was the first Broadway musical to cancel its Friday 3/7/03 evening performance due to the musicians' strike of 3/7/03–3/9/03. There was doubt as to whether it would re-open, but it did, on 3/11/03, but closed as scheduled. It received Tony nominations for book, choreography and costumes.

After Broadway. A limited tour opened at the Fair Park Music Hall, Dallas, 9/16/03, then went to Seattle's 5th Avenue Theatre, and also played Sacramento and Houston. DIRECTOR/CHOREOGRAPHER: Tom Kosis. *Cast*: TA: Jose Llana; MEI LI: Yuka Takara; LINDA: Emily Hsu; CHIN: Alvin Ing.

An international tour was to open in New Zealand in early 2004, but was canceled due to the SARS scare.

221. *Folies Bergere*

A musical revue, in French. A collection of songs, dances and showgirls from the famous Parisian revue, with 15 tons of scenery and 1,200 costumes.

The Broadway Run. BROADWAY THEATRE, 6/2/64–11/14/64. 11 previews from 5/20/64. 191 PERFORMANCES. Stephen W. Sharmat, in association with Robert J. Purdom, PRESENTED the Arthur Lesser production of Paul Derval's original; MUSIC: Henri Betti; ADDITIONAL MUSIC: Philippe Gerard (and Georges Ulmer); CONCEIVED BY/DIRECTOR/SETS/COSTUMES: Michel Gyarmathy; CHOREOGRAPHER: George Reich; FOLIES BERGERE ATELIERS DIRECTED BY: Mme Paul Derval; MUSICAL DIRECTOR: Jo Basile; PRESS: Arthur Cantor, Tony Geiss, Artie Solomon, Angela Nardelli; GENERAL MANAGERS: Joseph Harris & Arthur Rubin; COMPANY MANAGER: Bill Levine; PRODUCTION STAGE MANAGER: Terence Little; STAGE MANAGER: Peter Stern. *Act I*: *Scene 1* Bonjour de Paris: "Foll' de Broadway" (Nicole Croisille (7), Dancers, Demoiselles, Mannequins), "Ta Ra Ra" [Marion Conrad (9) (*Linda Jorgens*)], "Bonjour Folies" [Liliane Montevecchi (3)]; *Scene 2* Can-Can (Gerry Atkins & Dancers); *Scene 3* Georges Ulmer (2) (songs and impressions): "Pigalle" (m/l: Georges Ulmer, Konyn, Newman), Parody of a flamenco song; *Scene 4* Souper Fin (Monique Carraz, Dominique Chevallier, Andree Hechner, Simone Massix, Jean Moussy, Don Wallwork); *Scene 5* Chopin [Françoise Castel (11) & Demoiselles]; *Scene 6* Paul Sydell & Suzy (6) (acrobatic dog act); *Scene 7* Variete de Danses: Charleston (Nicole Croisille (7) & Dancers), "C'est toi l'plus beau" (tango) [Liliane Montevecchi (3) & Vassili Sulic (8)], Paris Panam (Demoiselles), Paris Swing: "Ca c'est Panam" (by J. Ledru) [Liliane Montevecchi (3)], Les Mains [Françoise Gres (11) & Dancers]; *Scene 8* Georges Ulmer (2) (songs and impressions); *Scene 9* Cleopatra [Liliane Montevecchi (3), Vassili Sulic (8), Dancers, Demoiselles, Mannequins]; *Scene 10* Les Hoganas (Gert Karlsson, Bende Hoganas, Egon Hoganas) (4) (slack wire trio); *Scene 11* A toute a l'heure (The Company). *Act II*: *Scene 1* Texas de France [Françoise Gres (11) & Dancers]; *Scene 2* Georges Ulmer (2) (songs): "Darling, Be Careful" (La Trapeziste) (m/l: Georges Ulmer); *Scene 3* "Mariage" (Françoise Castel & Singers): "Hymne a l'amour" (Dancers, Demoiselles, Mannequins); *Scene 4* The Trotter Brothers (5) (puppetry); *Scene 5* "Gondole a Venise" (Dany Latour); *Scene 6* Georges Ulmer (2) (songs); *Scene 7* Neige [Marion Conrad (9) (*Linda Jorgens*), Vassili Sulic (8), Dancers]; *Scene 8* Patachou (1): "Paris boheme" (m/l:

Philippe Gerard), "Mon menage a moi" (m/l: Constantin Glanzbug), "What Now My Love" (Eh, maintenant?) (m/l: Gilbert Becaud), "I Wish You Love" (Que reste-t-il de nos amours?) (m/l: Charles Trenet; English l: Albert Beach), "My Man" (Mon Homme) (m: Maurice Yvain; French l: Albert Willemetz & Jacques Charles; English l: Channing Pollock); *Scene 9* Finale: "La musique" (m/l: Drejac & Gerard) (Company).

ALSO WITH: Edmee Redouin (10).

THE COMPANY OF LES FOLIES BERGERE: DANCERS: Gerry Atkins, Marisa Barbaria, Sara Lee Barber, Flavio Bennati, Francis Ciampi, Anik David, Dorothy D'Honau, Claude Duvernoy, Diane Fox, Françoise Gres, Ralf Harmer, Nancy Herselin, Marcella Hude, Yvonne Meister, Gordana Pechitch, Don Wallwork, Pamela Wellman, Diana West; LES DEMOISELLES DES FOLIES: Dominique Chevallier, Nicole Gille, Margo Hamilton, Andree Hechner, Margareta Lindblum, Mary Luger, Mikki Maher, Anna Page, Irene Peterson, Judy Tickner, Isabel Wardrop, Elizabeth West; MANNEQUINS: Marion Barker, Sara Brocket, Monique Carraz, Françoise Castel, Charlotte Di Sica, Francesca Fontaine, Lyn Hobart, Dale Humphries, Dany Latour, Simone Massix, Jean Moussy, Andree Peny, Veronica Pierce, Nancy Walker.

Liliane Montevecchi was, in real life, a Folies star for years. Broadway reviews were great. The number "Cypres" (Michele Hardy, Flavio Bennati, Demoiselles) was added to Act I during the run. Marion Conrad was replaced by *Linda Jorgens* from 10/9/64, after a dispute about the scantiness of her costume.

222. *Follies*

The plot revolves around a theatre, Weismann's Follies, which is being torn down. Weismann (a fictional version of Florenz Ziegfeld) throws a reunion party for old Follies performers. The show deals with the reality of life as opposed to the unreality of the theatre, a theme explored principally through the lives of two couples, the upper-class, unhappy Phyllis and Ben and the middle-class, unhappy Sally and Buddy. The show also depicted these people as they were in their youth. Pretense is finally stripped away in a final "Loveland" sequence. There is no intermission.

Before Broadway. Originally called *The Girls Upstairs*, it was a backstage murder mystery involving two men dating the two girls in the dressing-room upstairs. It was actually conceived by Jim Goldman and Steve Sondheim as early as 1965 (Mr. Goldman was inspired by a newspaper story about a reunion of old Ziegfeld Girls), and by the end of that year the first draft of the book was done, and five songs. It was optioned by David Merrick and Leland Hayward, but they did nothing with it beyond asking John Dexter to direct. The creators approached Hal Prince to produce, but he didn't like it. In 1969 it was optioned again, by Stuart Ostrow, and a new draft done. Joseph Hardy was brought in to direct, and it was due to go into rehearsals by the end of 1969. The next part of the story is told under *Company* (qv). Finally Hal Prince took it on, and it was revised again (perhaps for the 13th time since 1965) and re-named *Follies*. Mr. Prince asked Michael Bennett to come in as choreographer, but Mr. Bennett wanted to direct, so they agreed to be co-directors. The show was capitalized at $800,000 ($60,000 was returned to the investors as unneeded). The first four weeks of rehearsals were held at the American Theatre Lab (Jerome Robbins' dance studio), and the final two weeks at Feller Scenic Studio, in the Bronx. It ran at the Colonial Theatre, Boston, 2/24/71–3/20/71. Reviews were divided. Jon Cypher was replaced by John McMartin. Paul Gemignani replaced Hal Hastings as musical director (even though Mr. Hastings gets credit). The number "Can That Boy Fox Trot!" was replaced during Boston tryouts with "I'm Still Here." Other cut numbers were: "All Things Bright and Beautiful," "Little White House," "Uptown, Downtown," and "Who Could Be Blue?." During Broadway previews Hal Prince tried out Michael Bennett's idea of having 2 acts, separated during "Who's That Woman?," but it didn't work. During the last week of previews, Gene Nelson's nine-year-old son was hit by a truck and went into a coma (he eventually recovered). In addition to this, Mr. Nelson also tore a leg muscle.

The Broadway Run. WINTER GARDEN THEATRE, 4/4/71–7/1/72.

12 previews from 3/24/71. 521 PERFORMANCES. PRESENTED BY Harold Prince, in association with Ruth Mitchell; MUSIC/LYRICS: Stephen Sondheim; BOOK: James Goldman; DIRECTORS: Harold Prince & Michael Bennett; CHOREOGRAPHER: Michael Bennett; ASSOCIATE CHOREOGRAPHER: Bob Avian; ASSISTANT CHOREOGRAPHERS: Graciela Daniele & Mary Jane Houdina; SETS: Boris Aronson; COSTUMES: Florence Klotz; LIGHTING: Tharon Musser; SOUND: Jack Mann; MUSICAL DIRECTOR: Harold Hastings; ORCHESTRATIONS: Jonathan Tunick; DANCE MUSIC ARRANGEMENTS: John Berkman; CAST RECORDING on Capitol/Angel; PRESS: Mary Bryant, Stanley F. Kaminsky, Sadie Stein; CASTING: Joanna Merlin; PRODUCTION SUPERVISOR: Ruth Mitchell; PRODUCTION ASSISTANT: Theodore S. "Ted" Chapin; GENERAL MANAGER: Carl Fisher; PRODUCTION STAGE MANAGER: Fritz Holt; STAGE MANAGER: George Martin; ASSISTANT STAGE MANAGER: John Grigas & Donald Weissmuller. *Cast:* MAJOR-DOMO: Dick Latessa (16), *Joseph Nelson*; SALLY DURANT PLUMMER: Dorothy Collins (3) ☆; YOUNG SALLY: Marti Rolph (19); CHRISTINE CRANE: Ethel Barrymore Colt (10), *Terry Saunders* (from 7/7/71), *Jan Clayton* (from 2/27/72) [until just before Broadway opening night this character had been called Christian Donovan]; WILLY WHEELER: Fred Kelly, *Donald Weissmuller*; STELLA DEEMS: Mary McCarty (7); MAX DEEMS: John J. Martin (15); HEIDI SCHILLER: Justine Johnston (14); CHAUFFEUR: John Grigas; MEREDITH LANE: Sheila Smith (12), *Marion Marlowe* (from 1/29/72), *Terry Saunders* (4/24/72–5/16/72), *Marion Marlowe*; CHET RICHARDS: Peter Walker; ROSCOE: Michael Bartlett (11); DEE DEE WEST: Helon Blount; SANDRA DONOVAN: Sonja Levkova; HATTIE WALKER: Ethel Shutta (8); YOUNG HATTIE: Mary Jane Houdina, *Jacqueline Payne*; EMILY WHITMAN: Marcie Stringer (23), *Camila Ashland*; THEODORE WHITMAN: Charles Welch (22), *Dick Latessa, Ted Lawrie*; VINCENT: Victor Griffin; VANESSA: Jayne Turner; YOUNG VINCENT: Michael Misita; YOUNG VANESSA: Graciela Daniele, *Margot Travers*; SOLANGE LAFITTE: Fifi d'Orsay (6); CARLOTTA CAMPION: Yvonne de Carlo (5) ☆; PHYLLIS ROGERS STONE: Alexis Smith (1) ☆; BENJAMIN STONE: John McMartin (4) ☆; YOUNG PHYLLIS: Virginia Sandifur (20), *Alexandra Borrie*; YOUNG BEN: Kurt Peterson (18), *John Johann* (from 8/23/71); BUDDY PLUMMER: Gene Nelson (2) ☆; YOUNG BUDDY: Harvey Evans (17); DMITRI WEISMANN: Arnold Moss (9), *Edwin Steffe*; KEVIN: Ralph Nelson, *Christopher Nelson, David Roman, Roy Barry*; YOUNG STELLA: Julie Pars; YOUNG HEIDI: Victoria Mallory (21), *Marti Rolph*; PARTY MUSICIANS: Taft Jordan, Aaron Bell, Charles Spies (*John Blowers*), Robert Curtis; SHOWGIRLS: Suzanne Briggs, Trudy Carson, Kathie Dalton, Ursula Maschmeyer, Linda Perkins, Margot Travers, *Jennifer Nairn-Smith & Susanna Clemm, Rosemary Shevlin*; SINGERS/DANCERS: Roy Barry, Steve Boockvor, Graciela Daniele, Mary Jane Houdina (*Jacqueline Payne*), Michael Misita, Joseph Nelson, Ralph Nelson (gone by 71–72), Rita O'Connor (gone by 71–72), Julie Pars, Suzanne Rogers, Ken Urmston, Donald Weissmuller, *Denise Pence, Rita Rudner, Joel Craig, David Roman, Patricia Garland, Sonja Levkova, Peter Walker*. **Standbys**: Carlotta/Phyllis: Sheila Smith, *Marion Marlowe*; Solange: Sheila Smith; Buddy: Ted Lawrie; Sally: Jan Clayton; Weismann: Ed Steffe (Mr. Steffe was 13th billed, even though he was Arnold Moss's standby), *Fred Kelly* (standby for Mr. Steffe). **Understudies**: Solange: Marion Marlowe, *Sonja Levkova* (2nd understudy by 71–72); Buddy: Dick Latessa; Sally: Ethel Barrymore Colt; Heidi: Ethel Barrymore Colt, *Jan Clayton*; Ben: Peter Walker; Christine/Hattie/Stella: Helon Blount; Theodore/Major Domo: Fred Kelly; Vincent: Don Weissmuller; Vanessa: Sonja Levkova; Young Sally: *Victoria Mallory* (by 71–72); Young Phyllis: *Suzanne Rogers* (by 71–72); Young Ben: *Ken Urmston* (by 71–72).

"Prologue/Overture" (Company), "Beautiful Girls" (Roscoe & Company), "Don't Look at Me" (Sally & Ben), "Waiting for the Girls Upstairs" (Buddy, Ben, Phyllis, Sally, Young Buddy, Young Ben, Young Phyllis, Young Sally), "(Listen to the) Rain on the Roof" (Emily & Theodore) [cut from the album], "Ah, Paris!" (Solange), "Broadway Baby" (Hattie), "The Road You Didn't Take" (Ben), "Bolero d'Amour" (danced by Vincent & Vanessa) [cut from the album], "In Buddy's Eyes" (Sally), "Who's That Woman?" (Stella & Ladies), "I'm Still Here" (Carlotta), "Too Many Mornings" (Ben & Sally), "The Right Girl" (Buddy), "One More Kiss" (Heidi & Young Heidi) [recorded, but not released on record until 1992], "Could I Leave You?" (Phyllis), LOVELAND: 1. The Folly of Love: "Loveland" (Ensemble) [cut from the album]. THE SPIRIT OF FIRST LOVE: Kathie Dalton; THE SPIRIT OF YOUNG LOVE: Margot

Travers; THE SPIRIT OF TRUE LOVE: Suzanne Briggs; THE SPIRIT OF PURE LOVE: Trudy Carson; THE SPIRIT OF ROMANTIC LOVE: Linda Perkins; THE SPIRIT OF ETERNAL LOVE: Ursula Maschmeyer; 2. The Folly of Youth (scene: a bower in Loveland): "You're Gonna Love Tomorrow" (Young Ben & Young Phyllis), "Love Will See Us Through" (Young Buddy & Young Sally); 3. Buddy's Folly (scene: a thoroughfare in Loveland): "The God-Why-Don't-You-Love-Me Blues" ("Buddy's Blues") (Buddy, with Suzanne Rogers & Rita O'Connor); 4. Sally's Folly (scene: a boudoir in Loveland): "Losing My Mind" (Sally); 5. Phyllis's Folly (scene: a honky-tonk in Loveland): "The Story of Lucy and Jessie" (sung by Phyllis; danced by Phyllis & Men); 6. Ben's Folly (scene: a supper club in Loveland): "Live, Laugh, Love" (sung by Ben; danced by Ben & Dancing Ensemble) [written during the last week of rehearsals].

Broadway reviews were mostly very good, but in the end the show was let down by the thinness of the story and the over-artiness of the production. It confused too many people. Martin Gottfried, then the *New York Times* critic, coined the term "concept musical" to describe *Follies*. The show won Tonys for score, direction of a musical, choreography, sets, costumes, lighting, and for Alexis Smith. It was also nominated for musical, book, and for Dorothy Collins and Gene Nelson. Capitol Records squeezed the original cast recording into a 56-minute single album, thus losing forever half an hour of the show (see above for numbers cut). In addition, most of the remaining songs were shaved down to fit the album. In 1992 a CD was issued of the original cast recording, plus a number that had never been released—"One More Kiss." In 2002 Knopf published Ted Chapin's book about the original 1971 production, in which he had been a production assistant.

After Broadway. TOUR. After running for a week at the Muny, St. Louis, in 7/72, it ran 7/22/72, at the Shubert Theatre, Century City, Calif. (this was the first show to play this theatre), 7/22/72–10/1/72. Most of the crew was the same as for Broadway. *Cast*: MAJOR DOMO: Joseph Nelson; SALLY: Dorothy Collins, *Janet Blair* (from 9/72); YOUNG SALLY: Marti Rolph; CHRISTINE: Jan Clayton; WILLY: Joel Craig; STELLA: Mary McCarty; MAX: Keith Kaldenberg; HEIDI: Justine Johnston; CHAUFFEUR: John Grigas; MEREDITH: Terry Saunders; ROSCOE: Michael Bartlett; ROSCOE'S DAUGHTER: Candace Cooke; DEE DEE: Helon Blount; HATTIE: Ethel Shutta; YOUNG HATTIE: Jacqueline Payne; EMILY: Camila Ashland; THEODORE: Ted Lawrie; VINCENT: Patrick Spohn; VANESSA: Jayne Turner; YOUNG VINCENT: David Evans; YOUNG VANESSA: Margot Travers; SOLANGE: Fifi D'Orsay; CARLOTTA: Yvonne de Carlo; PHYLLIS: Alexis Smith; BEN: John McMartin, *Edward Winter* (from 9/72); YOUNG PHYLLIS: Suzanne Rogers; YOUNG BEN: Kurt Peterson; BUDDY: Gene Nelson; YOUNG BUDDY: Harvey Evans; DMITRI WEISMANN: Edwin Steffe; YOUNG HEIDI: Marti Rolph; KEVIN: Roy Barry; SHOWGIRLS INCLUDED: Sandahl Bergman. Reviews were great, but business was poor, partly because there was no subscription audience yet built up. The show closed on 10/1/72 and the rest of the tour was canceled, by which time the whole show, Broadway and tour, had lost $685,000 of the $700,000 (finally) invested in it, and Hal Prince lost several long-term investors.

SUMMER STOCK TOUR. 1973. *Cast*: PHYLLIS: Vivian Blaine, *Julie Wilson*; SALLY: Jane Kean; CARLOTTA: Julie Wilson; SOLANGE: Hildegarde; ALSO WITH: Robert Alda.

ALL-STAR CONCERT VERSION. Lincoln Center's AVERY FISHER HALL, 1985. This was the complete show, with its 22 songs, and was designed to remedy the hopelessly cut 1971 recorded version (RCA Red Seal Records recorded this new one). The New York Philharmonic, conducted by Paul Gemignani, played music. PRESENTED BY Thomas Z. Shepard; DIRECTOR: Herbert Ross. *Cast*: WEISMANN/SPOKE NARRATIVE TRANSITIONS: Andre Gregory; ROSCOE: Arthur Rubin; SALLY: Barbara Cook; BEN: George Hearn; BUDDY: Mandy Patinkin; PHYLLIS: Lee Remick; YOUNG BUDDY: Jim Walton; YOUNG BEN: Howard McGillin; YOUNG PHYLLIS: Daisy Prince; YOUNG SALLY: Liz Callaway; EMILY: Betty Comden; THEODORE: Adolph Green; SOLANGE: Liliane Montevecchi; HATTIE: Elaine Stritch; STELLA: Phyllis Newman; CARLOTTA: Carol Burnett; HEIDI: Licia Albanese; YOUNG HEIDI: Erie Mills; CHORUS: Ronn Carroll, Susan Cella, Robert Henderson, Frank Kopyc, Marti Morris, Ted Sperling, Susan Terry, Sandra Wheeler. It was filmed for TV.

MANCHESTER, 1985. The European, and British, premiere. *Cast*: Kevin Colson, Josephine Blake, Mary Millar, Meg Johnson.

SHAFTESBURY THEATRE, London, 7/21/87–2/4/89. 644 PERFORMANCES. Revived (by Cameron Mackintosh) and revised (by James Goldman) in the show's first ever West End production. Steve Sondheim dropped four songs for this new production and added five—"Ah, But Underneath" (replacing "The Story of Lucy and Jessie"), "Country House" (a Ben—Phyllis duet replacing Ben's solo "The Road You Didn't Take"), "Loveland" (a new, better one, replacing the old song of the same name), and "Make the Most of Your Music" (replacing "Live, Laugh, Love"). A new sequence, "Social Dancing" (Company), opened Act II (there were now two acts, the first ending with "Too Many Mornings"). After "Make the Most of Your Music" (the final number listed on the program) there were two reprises—"You're Gonna Love Tomorrow"/ "Love Will See Us Through" (Young Buddy, Young Sally, Young Phyllis, Young Ben) and "Beautiful Girls" (Company), the latter forming the finale. Hal Prince was not involved, in this production, which won an Olivier Award for best musical. DIRECTOR: Mike Ockrent; CHOREOGRAPHER: Bob Avian; SETS/COSTUMES: Maria Bjornson; LIGHTING: Mark Henderson; SOUND: Andrew Bruce; MUSICAL DIRECTOR: Martin Koch; NEW CAST RECORDING on First Night Records. *Cast*: PHYLLIS: Diana Rigg, *Millicent Martin*; BEN: Daniel Massey; SALLY: Julia McKenzie; CARLOTTA: Dolores Gray, *Eartha Kitt*; BUDDY: David Healy; STELLA: Lynda Baron, *Meg Johnson*; BILLIE & WALLY WHITMAN: Pearl Carr & Teddy Johnson; SOLANGE: Maria Charles; HATTIE: Margaret Courtenay, *Hope Jackman*; HEIDI: Adele Leigh, *Eileen Page*; WEISMANN: Leonard Sachs, *Harold Kasket*.

MICHIGAN OPERA, 1988. *Cast*: PHYLLIS: Juliet Prowse; SALLY: Nancy Dussault; CARLOTTA: Edie Adams.

LONG BEACH CIVIC LIGHT OPERA, 1990. This was the production in which Susan Johnson resumed her musical stage career. *Cast*: PHYLLIS: Juliet Prowse; SALLY: Shani Wallis; CARLOTTA: Karen Morrow; STELLA: Susan Johnson; SOLANGE: Denise Darcel; HEIDI: Yma Sumac; ALSO WITH: Dorothy Lamour.

THEATER DES WESTERNS, Berlin, 1991. *Cast*: PHYLLIS: Daniela Ziegler; CARLOTTA: Eartha Kitt; ALSO WITH: The Kessler Twins.

BRIGHTON, England, 1993. Benefit concert. *Cast*: Rosemary Ashe, Mary Millar, Josephine Blake, Glyn Kerslake, Caroline O'Connor.

AUSTRALIA, 1995. Although it never had a full-fledged professional production in Australia, the Melbourne Festival of the Arts had a 3-concert performance.

THEATRE UNDER THE STARS, Houston. 3/24/95–4/9/95; FIFTH AVENUE THEATRE, Seattle, 4/25/95–5/14/95. DIRECTOR: Charles Abbott; CHOREOGRAPHER: Mary Jane Houdina; MUSICAL DIRECTOR: Robert Lindner. *Cast*: PHYLLIS: Constance Towers (Juliet Prowse was too ill to play the role); SALLY: Judy Kaye; SOLANGE: Denise Darcel; HEIDI: Edie Adams; HATTIE: Maxene Andrews; YOUNG BUDDY: Brian d'Arcy James; BEN: Walter Charles; BILLIE & WALLY: Virginia Mayo & Billy Barnes; YOUNG BEN: James Clow; STELLA: Kelly Britt; BUDDY: John-Charles Kelly.

THEATRE ROYAL, DRURY LANE, London, 12/96. Concert version. Aired on BBC2 in 2/97. *Cast*: PHYLLIS: Donna McKechnie; SALLY: Julia McKenzie; BEN: Denis Quilley; BUDDY: Ron Moody; BILLIE & WALLY: Pearl Carr & Teddy Johnson; ALSO WITH: Joan Savage, Libby Morris, Angela Richards, Elizabeth Seal.

PAPER MILL PLAYHOUSE, New Jersey, 4/15/98–5/31/98. There were a few script changes for this production; it also used "Ah, But Underneath" rather than "The Story of Lucy and Jessie," and it had an intermission. The choreography also reproduced Michael Bennett's work on "Who's That Woman?." The dance team of Vanessa & Vincent were combined into the roles of Emily & Theodore, to create two characters instead of four. A recording, under the supervision of Stephen Sondheim, was done by TVT Records in New York City on 6/1/98, and released on 11/3/98. DIRECTOR: Robert Johanson; CHOREOGRAPHER: Jerry Mitchell; SETS: Michael Anania; COSTUMES: Gregg Barnes; LIGHTING: Mark Stanley; MUSICAL DIRECTORS: Jim Coleman & Tom Helm. *Cast*: WEISMANN: Eddie Bracken; CARLOTTA: Ann Miller; SALLY: Donna McKechnie; PHYLLIS: Dee Hoty; BENJAMIN: Laurence Guittard; BUDDY: Tony Roberts; THEODORE: Donald Saddler; STELLA: Phyllis Newman; EMILY: Natalie Mosco; SOLANGE: Liliane Montevecchi; SANDRA: Laura Kenyon; YOUNG BEN: Michael Gruber; YOUNG DEE DEE: Karen Lifshey; YOUNG EMILY: Pascale Faye; YOUNG CARLOTTA: Jillana Urbina; HATTIE: Kaye

Ballard; HEIDI: Carol Skarimbas; YOUNG PHYLLIS: Meredith Patterson; YOUNG SALLY: Danette Holden; YOUNG BUDDY: Billy Hartung. It looked as if it might transfer to Broadway, produced by Roger Berlind, but by 7/8/98, despite raised money, these hopes had been dashed, partly because it would have been too expensive, with all the stars, but also (strangely) because librettist James Goldman's wife, Bobby, who controlled Mr. Goldman's interests in the musical, apparently did not want it to go to Broadway, and it may be that Mr. Goldman himself was unhappy with the show. This caused great annoyance among cast and crew. Mr. Goldman died on 10/28/98.

SYDNEY, 1998. Three-concert performance. DIRECTOR: Stephen Helper; MUSICAL DIRECTOR: Tommy Tycho. **Cast**: Terence Donovan, Ron Haddrick, Judi Connelli, Jill Perryman, Toni Lamond, Leonie Page, Todd McKenney.

223. *Follies (Broadway revival)*

This time there were 2 acts. "Too Many Mornings" ended Act I. "Bolero d'Amour" was now revised as "Danse d'Amour."

Before Broadway. On 7/7/99 the Roundabout Theatre, in New York, expressed an interest in reviving *Follies* (this was unrelated to the Paper Mill Playhouse production of 1998, incidentally). By 1/00 Matthew Warchus was in discussions to direct. On 1/24/00 Stephen Sondheim and Bobby Goldman announced that a new New York production was not a certainty, yet on 3/24/00 it was announced that the Roundabout would be presenting it at their American Airlines Theatre in spring 2001, with Matthew Warchus directing. By 8/3/00 various stars were being rumored: Judith Ivey (Sally), Jean Smart (Phyllis), Dan Butler (Buddy), and Gregory Harrison (Ben). The American Airlines Theatre was still a possibility, but the Belasco was now being more strongly rumored. By 8/25/00 Treat Williams was being offered a role, and previews were tentatively set to begin on 3/6/01, with early an April opening in 2001. Also on 8/25/00 Kathleen Marshall was announced as choreographer, and other stars were being rumored: Betty Garrett, Karen Ziemba and Polly Bergen. Ann Miller would not be in it, due to salary issues. In fact, Karen Ziemba had been asked to audition, but had not complied due to other scheduling. The Belasco was looking stronger all the time, and the American Airlines Theatre was now out. On 9/11/00 Treat Williams was confirmed as Buddy. On 9/18/00 the Belasco was confirmed, and the main crew members were all announced. Also, Judith Ivey and Gregory Harrison were both confirmed (however, no contracts had been signed with any of the players yet). On 10/13/00 Blythe Danner, Polly Bergen, Marge Champion, Betty Garrett, Larry Keith (as Weismann), Joan Roberts, Donald Saddler, and Carol Woods were all confirmed. Previews were now set for 3/8/01, and 4/5/01 for opening date. On 12/20/00 Larry Keith was out of the show. On 1/11/01 Jane White was announced in her role and Louis Zorich in his (as Weismann), as well as the rest of the cast. It was also announced that the show would now run through 9/30/01 (this date was extended from 7/14/01). On 2/8/01 Erin Dilly replaced the scheduled Kate Jennings Grant as Young Phyllis. The Belasco was transformed into the crumbling Weismann Theatre on the eve of its demolition.

The Broadway Run. BELASCO THEATRE, 4/5/01–7/14/01. 31 previews from 3/8/01. 117 PERFORMANCES. PRESENTED by the Roundabout Theatre Company; MUSIC/LYRICS: Stephen Sondheim; BOOK: James Goldman; DIRECTOR: Matthew Warchus; CHOREOGRAPHER: Kathleen Marshall; SETS: Mark Thompson; COSTUMES: Theoni V. Aldredge; LIGHTING: Hugh Vanstone; SOUND: Jonathan Deans; MUSICAL SUPERVISOR/CONDUCTOR: Eric Stern; ORCHESTRATIONS: Jonathan Tunick; ORIGINAL DANCE MUSIC ARRANGEMENTS: John Berkman; ADDITIONAL DANCE MUSIC ARRANGEMENTS: David Chase; PRESS: The Publicity Office; CASTING: Jim Carnahan, Amy Christopher, Todd Lundquist, Jeremy Rich, Justin Rose; GENERAL MANAGER: Sydney Davolos; COMPANY MANAGER: Denys Baker; PRODUCTION STAGE MANAGER: Peter Hanson; STAGE MANAGER: Karen Moore; ASSISTANT STAGE MANAGER: James Marr. **Cast:** DMITRI WEISMANN: Louis Zorich, *Tom Brennan*; SHOWGIRLS: Jessica Leigh Brown, Colleen Dunn, Amy Heggins, Wendy Waring; SALLY DURANT PLUMMER: Judith Ivey ✩; SANDRA CRANE: Nancy Ringham; DEE DEE WEST: Dorothy Stanley; STELLA DEEMS: Carol

Woods; SAM DEEMS: Peter Cormican; SOLANGE LaFITTE: Jane White; ROSCOE: Larry Raiken; HEIDI SCHILLER: Joan Roberts, *Marni Nixon*; EMILY WHITMAN: Marge Champion; THEODORE WHITMAN: Donald Saddler; CARLOTTA CAMPION: Polly Bergen; HATTIE WALKER: Betty Garrett; PHYLLIS ROGERS STONE: Blythe Danner ✩; BENJAMIN STONE: Gregory Harrison ✩; BUDDY PLUMMER: Treat Williams ✩; YOUNG PHYLLIS: Erin Dilly, *Kelli O'Hara*; YOUNG SALLY: Lauren Ward; YOUNG DEE DEE: Roxane Barlow; YOUNG EMILY: Carol Bentley; YOUNG CARLOTTA: Sally Mae Dunn; YOUNG SANDRA: Dottie Earle; YOUNG SOLANGE: Jacqueline Hendy; YOUNG HEIDI: Brooke Sunny Moriber; YOUNG HATTIE: Kelli O'Hara, *Emily Rabon-Hall*; YOUNG STELLA: Allyson Tucker; YOUNG ROSCOE: Aldrin Gonzales, *Randy Slovacek*; YOUNG BEN: Richard Roland; YOUNG BUDDY: Joey Sorge; YOUNG THEODORE: Rod McCune, *Noah Racey*; KEVIN: Stephen Campanella; BUDDY'S BLUES GIRLS: "MARGIE": Roxane Barlow; "SALLY": Jessica Leigh Brown; ENSEMBLE: Roxane Barlow, Carole Bentley, Jessica Leigh Brown, Stephen Campanella, Colleen Dunn, Sally Mae Dunn, Dottie Earle, Aldrin Gonzales (*Randy Slovacek*), Amy Heggins, Jacqueline Hendy, Rod McCune (*Noah Racey*), Kelli O'Hara (*Emily Rabon-Hall*), T. Oliver Reid, Alex Sanchez, Allyson Tucker, Matt Wall, Wendy Waring, *Joe Langworth*. **Standbys**: Heidi/Sandra/Dee Dee: Joan Barber; Ben/Buddy/Theodore: Don Correia, *Michael Scott*. **Understudies**: Heidi: Joan Marshall; Phyllis/Emily: Dorothy Stanley; Stella/Carlotta: Dorothy Stanley, *Joan Marshall*; Sally: Nancy Ringham; Hattie/Solange: Nancy Ringham, *Joan Marshall*; Young Phyllis/Young Sally/Young Heidi: Kelli O'Hara, *Emily Rabon-Hall*; Weismann/Roscoe: Peter Cormican; Young Ben/Young Buddy: Matt Wall. **Swings**: Jeffrey Hankinson, Nadine Isenegger, Parisa Ross. **Orchestra**: PIANO: Eric Stern; WOODWINDS: Les Scott, Rick Heckman, John Campo; TRUMPETS: Bob Millikan & Jon Owens; TROMBONE: Randy Andos; PERCUSSION: Billy Miller; CONCERTMASTER: Martin Agee; VIOLIN II: Cenovia Cummins; VIOLA: Debra Shufelt; CELLO: Roger Shell; HARP: Beth Robinson; BASS: Brian Cassier.

Broadway reviews and audience reaction were both very divided. On 6/6/01 it was announced that the show would close earlier than expected, on 7/14/01 (the originally-scheduled closing date). Part of the reason for the failure of this production was the cheap-looking sets. The show received Tony nominations for revival of a musical, costumes, and orchestrations, and for Polly Bergen and Blythe Danner.

After Broadway. WADSWORTH THEATRE, Los Angeles, 6/15/02–6/23/02. This was a concert, part of the *Reprise!* series. DIRECTOR: Arthur Allan Seidelman. **Cast**: BEN: Bob Gunton (replaced the scheduled Hal Linden in 5/02), WEISMANN: Tom Bosley; PHYLLIS: Patty Duke; CARLOTTA: Donna McKechnie; VANESSA: Carol Lawrence; THEODORE: Jack Carter; SALLY: Vikki Carr; BUDDY: Harry Groener; HATTIE: Carole Cook; ROSCOE: Ken Page; SOLANGE: Amanda McBroom; STELLA: Liz Torres; VINCENT: Grover Dale; CHRISTINE: Carol Swarbrick; HEIDI: Justine Johnston; DEE DEE: Stella Stevens; EMILY: Mary Jo Catlett; YOUNG PHYLLIS: Tia Riebling; YOUNG BEN: Kevin Earley.

ROYAL FESTIVAL HALL, London, 8/6/02–8/31/02. Previews from 8/3/02. Limited run of 32 PERFORMANCES. This was the first proper revival in London since 1987. PRESENTED BY RFH & Raymond Gubay; DIRECTOR: Paul Kerryson; CHOREOGRAPHER: David Needham; SETS: Paul Farnsworth; MUSICAL DIRECTOR: Julian Kelly. **Cast:** BUDDY: Henry Goodman; SALLY: Kathryn Evans; PHYLLIS: Louise Gold; CARLOTTA: Diane Langton; BEN: David Durham (Clarke Peters was scheduled but he canceled); STELLA: Shezwae Powell; HATTIE: Joan Savage; SOLANGE: Anna Nicholas; EMILY: Myra Sands; MARGIE: Tiffany Graves; MAX: Nick Hamilton; WEISMANN: Russell Dixon; HEIDI: Julia Goss; THEODORE: Tony Kemp.

224. *Follow the Girls*

A burlesque disguised as a book musical that turned into one of the longest-running Broadway shows of the 1940s. Bubbles is a big-hearted stripper who contributes to the war effort by entertaining sailors at the Spotlight Canteen, in Great Neck, Long Island. Her overweight fiancé, Goofy, who has been classified as 4-f, attempts to get into the canteen, which is off-limits to civilians. He makes several attempts, including disguising himself as a WAVE; an elderly officer makes a date with him. He also tries it as a British sailor. The opening had chorus boys dressed as soldiers, sailors and marines. Viskinova is the greatest ballet dancer in the world, but they suspect her of being a spy. However, Phyllis is the real spy. Banner fancies Bubbles, and Goofy kidnaps him.

Before Broadway. This was Guy Bolton's last musical. Irina Baronova was of the Russian Ballet. This was Gertrude Niesen's only book musical, and it made her a star. The show tried out in Boston.

The Broadway Run. NEW CENTURY THEATRE, 4/8/44–6/12/44; FORTY-FOURTH STREET THEATRE, 6/14/44–6/2/45; BROADHURST THEATRE, 6/5/45–5/18/46. Total of 882 PERFORMANCES. PRESENTED BY Dave Wolper, in association with Albert Borde; MUSIC/LYRICS: Dan Shapiro, Milton Pascal, Phil Charig; BOOK: Guy Bolton & Eddie Davis; ADDITIONAL DIALOGUE: Fred Thompson; DEVISED BY: Harry Delmar; DIRECTOR: Harry Delmar (helped by Fred Thompson); CHOREOGRAPHER: Catherine Littlefield; ASSISTANT CHOREOGRAPHER: Dorothie Littlefield; SETS/LIGHTING: Howard Bay; COSTUMES: Lou Eisele; SOUND CONSULTANT: Saki Oura; MUSICAL DIRECTOR: Will Irwin; ORCHESTRATIONS: Joe Glover, Charles Cooke, Van Cleeve, Walter Paul, Bob Haggart, Julian Work, George Leeman, Ernie Watson, Cornell Tannassy; VOCAL ARRANGEMENTS: Bobby Tucker; PRESS: Zac Freedman, *Ivan Black*; GENERAL MANAGER: Thomas B. Bodkin; STAGE MANAGER: Edward Scanlon, *Paul E. Porter*; ASSISTANT STAGE MANAGERS: Frank Kreig & Robert Kirland (*Charles Conaway Jr.*). **Cast:** YOKEL SAILOR: Bill Tabbert, *Henry Tatler*; DOORMAN: Ernest Goodhart; 1ST GIRL FAN: Terry Kelly, *Ruth Rathbun*; 2ND GIRL FAN: Rae MacGregor [role cut during the run]; BOB MONROE: Frank Parker (2), *John Barry*; ANNA VISKINOVA: Irina Baronova (3); GOOFY GALE: Jackie Gleason (4), *Fred Leary*; SEAMAN PENNYWHISTLE: Frank Kreig; PEGGY BAKER: Dorothy Keller (9), *Jo Ann Whitney*; SAILOR VAL: Val Valentinoff; CATHERINE PEPBURN: Geraldine Stroock [she was later re-named Geraldine Brooks] [role cut during the run]; MARINE: Charles Conaway Jr., *Robert Kirland*; BUBBLES LaMARR: Gertrude Niesen (1); CIGARETTE GIRL: Kathryn Lazell [role cut during the run]; SPUD DOOLITTLE: Tim Herbert (6), *Al Norman*; DINKY RILEY: Buster West (5), *Ross Wyse Jr.*; PHYLLIS BRENT: Toni Gilman (10), *Marie Windsor, Karen Stevens*; DAN DALEY: Robert Tower, *Bill Herne*; PETTY OFFICER BANNER: Lee Davis (11), *Richard Dana*; SHORE PATROL: Ernest Goodhart [role cut during the run]; CAPTAIN HAWKINS: Walter Long (12); ARCHIE SMITH: Frank Kreig; WAITER: Frank Greco; FELIX CHARREL: Val Valentinoff (8); OFFICER FLANAGAN: George Spaulding; FLIRTATIOUS MISS: Del Parker, *June Mann, Ann Mace*; DANCE TEAM IN CANTEEN: The Di Gatanos (Jane & Adam Di Gatano) (7); SHOWGIRLS: Ruth Joseph, Dorothea Pinto, Norma Amigo, Joan Myles, Del Parker (*June Mann, Ann Mace*), Dorothy Wygal, June Sitarr, Kay Crespi, *Caroline Biddle, Jiggs St. Clair, Phyllis Manning, Dana Steadley*; SINGING MEN: Bernard Kovler, Robert Thomas, Bill Tabbert, Richard Harvey, Frank Touhey, Larry Lieberman, Larry Mayo, George Lambrose, John O'Neill, George Marten, *Ernest Anderson, Bill Herne, Arthur Ulisse*; DANCING GIRLS: Lillian Moore, Rae MacGregor, Ruth Rathbun (*Maureen Cunningham, Ruth Rathbun*), Renee Russell, Kathryn Lazell, Ruthe Reed, Nancy Newton, Mitzi Perry, Lee Mayer, Virginia Harriot, Virginia Conrad, Edna Ryan, Terry Kelly, Sherri Phillips, Myra Weldon, Patricia Martin, Merritta Moore, *Daurine Andrews, Alice Anthony, Cookie Conklin, Jessie Fullum, Myra Green, Marion Harvey, Lorraine Latham, Ruth Mitchell, Randee Sanford, Gisella Svetlik, Joan Vohs, Georgina Yeager*; DANCING BOYS: Roy Andrews, Dave Pullman, Francois Brouillard, George J. Sabo Jr., Ben Piazza, Bob Emmett (*Johnny Lane*), Walter Hastings, Ray Hamilton, Arthur Randy, Danny Aiello, Albert Bahr, Don Miraglia, Erik Kristen, Henry Tatler, Ken Tibbetts (*Dick Ericson*), Herbert Ross, *William Campbell, Ted Cona, Michael Conrad, Fred De Winter, Jim Elsegood, Edwin Feder, Jack Foley, William Hunter, Joseph Paz, Peter Thomas, George Thornton*. *Act I*: *Scene 1* Outside Spotlight Canteen; evening in August 1943; *Scene 2* Inside Spotlight Canteen; same evening; *Scene 3* Outside Naval Training Station, Great Neck, Long Island; next day; *Scene 4* Trophy room, Great Neck estate. *Act II*: *Scene 1* Flower garden, Great Neck estate; *Scene 2* Room in house; midnight; *Scene 3* Navy Park, Great Neck; next day; *Scene 4* Good ship *Lady Luck;* 4 weeks later; *Scene 5* Inside Spotlight Canteen; next night. *Act I*: "At the Spotlight Canteen" (Soldiers, Sailors, Marines), "Where You Are" (Bob & Anna), "You Don't Dance" (Peggy, Sailor Val, Boys & Girls), "Strip Flips Hip" (Bubbles & Boys) [dropped during the run], "Thanks for a Lousy Evening" (Spud, Peggy, Dinky), "You're Perf" (Bub-

bles, Goofy, Boys & Girls), Dance (Anna), "Twelve O'clock and All is Well" (Bubbles), "Out for No Good" (Dinky), Dance (Peggy), "You Don't Dance" (waltz reprise) (Boys & Girls), Dance (the Di Gitanos), "Where You Are" (reprise) (Bob & Anna), Flamingo Dance (ballet) (Anna), "Follow the Girls" (Bubbles & Entire Company). *Act II*: "John Paul Jones" (Bob, Boys & Girls), Dance (Sailor Val, Boys & Girls), "Where You Are" (reprise) (Bob & Anna), "I Wanna Get Married" (Bubbles & Bridesmaids) [the big hit], "Today Will Be Yesterday Tomorrow" (Bob & Marines), "You're Perf" (reprise) (Boys & Girls), Dance (Anna), "(I'm Gonna Hang My Hat on) A Tree that Grows in Brooklyn" (Bubbles, Goofy, Spud, Dinky), Finale (Entire Company).

There was tension between Niesen and Gleason (when the show opened Jackie Gleason was 4th billed, but after it immediately became clear that audiences and critics loved him he was quickly promoted to 2nd billed). Niesen considered Gleason unprofessional, and wanted him fired, partly because he was always cracking her up onstage with ad libs. It was also the first production at the re-opened and re-furbished Jolson's 59th Street Theatre, re-named the Century (often referred to as the New Century). Reviews included three favorable, three raves, and two pans. The chorus members demanded a $10 dollar raise over and above the $50 a week they were already making. Management refused, and the chorines quit. On 2/25/46 the producers hired 24 new members. Certain changes were made in the characters during the run (aside from the ones mentioned in the cast list): the first performer on stage was changed from Yokel Sailor to a new character, the Country Hick (played by Jeffrey Warren). The Yokel Sailor was re-positioned on the cast list between Marine and Bubbles; the role of Anna Viskinova was replaced with Betty Deleaninnion (played by Jane Arden); the dual role of Pennywhistle & Smith (played by Frank Kreig) was reduced to only one — Pennywhistle. During the run at the Broadhurst Dave Wolper quit, and Albert Borde became sole producer.

After Broadway. PALACE THEATRE, Manchester, England; Liverpool & Blackpool; HIS MAJESTY'S THEATRE, London, 10/25/45–2/22/47. 572 PERFORMANCES. PRESENTED BY Jack Hylton; DIRECTOR: Fred Grey; CHOREOGRAPHER: Jack Billings; MUSICAL DIRECTOR: Freddie Bretherton. *Cast*: GOOFY: Arthur Askey; BUBBLES: Evelyn Dall; BOB: Hugh French, *William O'Conner*; BETTY: Wendy Toye, *Pamela Kay*; ALSO WITH: Vic Marlowe, Jackie Billings.

225. *Footloose*

Set somewhere in the heartland of America in the recent past. The Midwestern town of Bomont has banned dancing because it (and drinking) was the cause of the town losing four of its brightest kids in an accident after a dance. Ren (Kevin Bacon's role in the movie upon which this musical is based), a young Chicago man who has lost his father, moves to this town. He fights the ban. He also likes the daughter of the reverend who had the ban put in force. This stage musical kept all the hit songs from the movie, and added nine new ones. It had a cast of 37.

Before Broadway. In 1993 Dodger Endemol Productions approached Walter Bobbie with the idea of directing a stage musical of the famous movie (which had an immensely successful sound track). It was first announced on 1/31/97, as a spring or summer 1998 Broadway production, with a tour to follow. There were readings and re-writes. On 6/9/97 it was announced that Madison Square Garden (5,000 seats) would be the theatre, and that Walter Bobbie would direct. That day a 5-week workshop began at 890 STUDIOS, NY, led by Tom Snow, Dean Pitchford and Walter Bobbie, with 30 actors, which culminated in 3 PERFORMANCES for the public. *Cast*: Jeremy Kushnier, Stacy Francis, Martin Vidnovic, Dee Hoty, John Deyle, Tom Plotkin. A.C. Ciulla was hired as choreographer, and at that time the plan was to try out at Theatre Under the Stars, Houston, in 5/98, then to go to Dallas, then Seattle, and finally Madison Square Garden. Then the new plan was to play first at Orange County Performing Arts Center, Costa Mesa, Calif., 7/14/98–7/19/98, then on to the Buell Theatre, Denver, 7/21/98–8/2/98. These plans changed too. The third plan was to try out at the Kennedy Center, Washington, DC, in 10/98. By this time Madison Square Garden was out as a New York venue for the show, and the Richard Rodgers Theatre was in. The Kennedy Center dates were brought forward to 8/29/98–9/20/98 (previews from 8/25/98). On 7/28/98 there was a press rehearsal at 890 Studios. Martin Vidnovic played Rev. Moore during the first part of the Kennedy Center tryouts, but then left. They said it was "voice problems," but there was probably more to it. He was replaced by understudy Stephen Lee Anderson, and there was a debate about whether they should look for another "name." However, Mr. Anderson stayed with the role. On 9/23/98 it was announced that Jeff Calhoun was being brought in to help rookie Ciulla with the choreography. Broadway previews began on 10/6/98 (date put back from 10/1/98, then 10/2/98, then 10/1/98 again, due to loading-in problems at the new venue). The preview of 10/7/98 was canceled to give the show more rehearsal time. The number "Still Rockin'" was cut during previews.

The Broadway Run. RICHARD RODGERS THEATRE, 10/22/98–7/2/00. 18 previews from 10/6/98. 708 PERFORMANCES. PRESENTED BY Dodger Endemol Theatricals, through special arrangement with the Rodgers & Hammerstein Organization; MUSIC: Tom Snow (except where mentioned below); LYRICS: Dean Pitchford; BOOK: Dean Pitchford & Walter Bobbie; BASED ON the 1984 Paramount movie of the same name, with screenplay & lyrics by Dean Pitchford, other lyrics by Tom Snow, and starring Kevin Bacon and Sarah Jessica Parker; DIRECTOR: Walter Bobbie; CHOREOGRAPHER: A.C. Ciulla; ADDITIONAL CHOREOGRAPHY: Jeff Calhoun (unbilled); SETS: John Lee Beatty; COSTUMES: Toni-Leslie James; LIGHTING: Ken Billington; SOUND: Tony Meola; MUSICAL SUPERVISOR/MUSICAL DIRECTOR/VOCAL ARRANGEMENTS: Doug Katsaros; ORCHESTRATIONS: Danny Troob; DANCE MUSIC ARRANGEMENTS: Joe Baker; CAST recording on Q Records, made on 11/2/98, at The Hit Factory, NY, and released on 12/16/99 (although some stores in New York got it on 2/8/99); PRESS: Boneau/Bryan-Brown; CASTING: Julie Hughes & Barry Moss; COMPANY MANAGER: Sandra Carlson; PRODUCTION STAGE MANAGER: Steven Beckler; STAGE MANAGER: Dale Kaufman; ASSISTANT STAGE MANAGER: J. Philip Bassett.

Cast: REN MCCORMACK: Jeremy Kushnier (3) ☆, *Jason Wooten*; ETHEL MCCORMACK, HIS MOTHER: Catherine Cox [later known as Catherine Cox-Evans] (7); REV. SHAW MOORE: Stephen Lee Anderson (1) ☆, *John Hillner*; VI MOORE, HIS WIFE: Dee Hoty (2) ☆; ARIEL MOORE: Jennifer Laura Thompson (4) ☆; LULU WARNICKER: Catherine Campbell; WES WARNICKER: Adam Lefevre; ELEANOR DUNBAR/DOREEN: Donna Lee Marshall; COACH DUNBAR: John Hillner, *Robert Boles, Darrin Baker*; RUSTY: Stacy Francis (5), *Anika Noni Rose*; URLEEN: Kathy Deitch, *Jennifer Gambatese*; WENDY JO: Rosalind Brown, *Katie Harvey*; CHUCK CRANSTON: Billy Hartung (8); LYLE: Jim Ambler; TRAVIS: Bryant Carroll; COP/COUNTRY FIDDLER: Nick Sullivan; BETTY BLAST/IRENE: Robin Baxter; WILLARD HEWITT: Tom Plotkin (6); PRINCIPAL CLERK/SALOON KEEPER: John Deyle; JETER/COWBOY BOB: Artie Harris, *Jamie Gustis*; BICKLE: Hunter Foster, *Michael Seelbach, Jason Wooten*; GARVIN: Paul Castree, *Sean Dooley*; ENSEMBLE: Billy Angell, Angela Brydon, Paul Castree, Hunter Foster, Kristen Leigh Gorski, Artie Harris, Sean Haythe, Lori Holmes, Daniel Karaty, Katharine Leonard, Mark Myars, JoAnna Ross, Serena Soffer, Ron Todorowski, *Bradley Jay Madison, Matthew Morrison, Casey Miles Good, Carolyn Ockert, Tanya Nieves, Karl Wahl*. **Understudies**: Ren: Hunter Foster & Jim Ambler, *Jason Wooten*; Chuck: Hunter Foster & Jim Ambler, *Casey Miles Good*; Coach: Hunter Foster, John Hillner, Rick Crom, *Sean Haythe*; Rev. Moore: John Hillner & Rick Crom, *Robert Boles, Darrin Baker*; Wes/Principal/Saloon Keeper: Nick Sullivan, John Hillner, Rick Crom; Cop/Fiddler: Sean Haythe, John Hillner, Rick Crom, *Nick Sullivan*; Vi: Susan Bigelow & Donna Lee Marshall; Ethel: Susan Bigelow & Jeanine Meyers, *Donna Lee Marshall*; Lulu: Susan Bigelow & Jeanine Meyers; Eleanor: Susan Bigelow & Jeanine Meyers, *Lori Holmes*; Betty/Irene: Donna Lee Marshall & Orfeh; Ariel: Katharine Leonard & Jeanine Meyers, *Jennifer Gambatese, Teresa Marie Sanchez*; Urleen: Katherine Leonard & Jeanine Meyers, *Teresa Marie Sanchez*; Willard: Artie Harris & Paul Castree, *Bryant Carroll & Sean Dooley*; Rusty: Lori Holmes & Orfeh, *Teresa Marie Sanchez*; Wendy Jo: Kristen Leigh Gorski & Orfeh, *Meredith Akins*; Travis/Lyle: Ben Cameron & Jamie Gustis. **Swings**: Ben Cameron, Paige Hinton, Sean Haythe, Jeanine Meyers, Orfeh, *Asmeret Grebremichael, Andrew Hubbard, Meredith Akins, Jason Davies, Teresa Marie Sanchez*. **Orchestra**: GUITARS: John Benthal & Bob Rose; DRUMS: Clint de Ganon; BASS:

Vince Fay; KEYBOARDS: Doug Katsaros & Joseph Baker; REEDS: Tim Ries; VIOLIN: Kenny Kosek; CELLO: Stephanie Cummins; PERCUSSION: Mark Sherman. *Act I: Scene 1* City of Chicago: "Footloose" (m: Kenny Loggins; l: Dean Pitchford & Kenny Loggins) (Ren & Company); Town of Bomont—church: "On Any Sunday" * (Shaw & Company); *Scene 2* Church yard; *Scene 3* Burger Blast Restaurant: "The Girl Gets Around" (m: Sammy Hagar) (Chuck, Ariel, Travis, Lyle); *Scene 4* High school hallway: "I Can't Stand Still" * (Ren); *Scene 5* Street corner; Principal's office; Warnicker home: "Somebody's Eyes" (Rusty, Wendy Jo, Urleen, Company); *Scene 6* Moore home: "Learning to Be Silent" * (Vi & Ethel); *Scene 7* Burger Blast Restaurant: "Holding Out for a Hero" (m: Jim Steinman) (Ariel, Rusty, Wendy Jo, Urleen); *Scene 8* Plans of Bomont; *Scene 9* Moore home: "Somebody's Eyes" (reprise) (Rusty, Wendy Jo, Urleen), "Heaven Help Me" (Shaw); *Scene 10* High school gymnasium: "I'm Free" (m: Kenny Loggins)/"Heaven Help Me" (reprise)/"On Any Sunday" (reprise) (Ren, Shaw, Company). *Act II: Scene 1* The *Bar-B-Q* Country & Western Bar: "Let's Make Believe We're in Love" * (Irene & the Country Kickers), "Let's Hear it for the Boy" (Rusty & Company); *Scene 2* Moore home: "Can You Find it in Your Heart?" * (Vi); *Scene 3* Lot behind the Feed and Fuel: "Mama Says" * (Willard & the Boys); *Scene 4* The Potawney Bridge: "Almost Paradise" (m: Eric Carmen) (Ren & Ariel); *Scene 5* Bomont Town Hall: "Dancing is Not a Crime" * (Ren & the Boys); *Scene 6* Church: "I Confess" * (Shaw), "On Any Sunday" (reprise) (Company); *Scene 7* Church yard: "Can You Find it in Your Heart?" (reprise) (Shaw); *Scene 8* High school gymnasium: "Footloose" (reprise) (Company).

Note: Asterisked numbers means new for this production, and not in the 1984 movie.

Broadway reviews were mostly bad, but teenage girls (and others) kept it running. The number "The Footloose Five" (a Boyband version of "Footloose"/"Let's Hear it for the Boys") was added during the run. The show received Tony nominations for score, book, choreography, and for Dee Hoty.

After Broadway. TOUR. An unusual move was to have the first national tour open at the Allen Theatre, Cleveland, on 12/15/98, less than two months after the Broadway opening. Normally a tour would begin much later after the Broadway opening, say a year or more, or indeed, after the Broadway run had finished. This new move reflected and catered to the fact that people in the provinces wanted a show while it was hot, without necessarily coming to Broadway to see it (sounds simple now, but the actual implementation of touring a new Broadway show was a pretty new concept then). The tour ended on 1/30/00, at the Shubert Theatre, Chicago. DIRECTOR: Walter Bobbie. **Cast:** REN: Joe Machota; ARIEL: Niki Scalera, *Teresa Marie Sanchez* (from 12/14/99); REV. MOORE: Daren Kelly; VI: Mary Gordon Murray, *Jana Robbins* (from 9/21/99); ETHEL: Marsha Waterbury, *Eileen Barnett* (from 8/6/99); RUSTY: Stephanie St. James; WENDY JO: Katie Harvey; URLEEN: Andrea McCormack; CHUCK: Richard H. Blake, *Matthew Morrison* (from 6/21/99); WILLARD: Christian Borle, *Luther Creek* (from 12/14/99); TRAVIS: Andrew Wright; LULU: Tina Johnson; WES: Steve Luker.

THEATRE ROYAL, Plymouth, England, 2/5/04–2/14/04; then a tour of the U.K. then, perhaps, the West End. **Cast:** REN: Chris Jarvis; REV. MOORE: Oliver Tobias; VI: Marilyn Cutts; ARIEL: Rachael Wooding.

226. *Forever Tango*

A dance revue, featuring popular Argentinean songs, and tracing the history and form of the once-forbidden tango, the famous dance that originated in the Argentinean bordellos of the 1880s. It had an on-stage orchestra.

Before Broadway. Luis Bravo created the show in 1990, and that year took it to the West Coast, where it played in eight cities, beginning with San Diego, and including Santa Ana, Sacramento, and Los Angeles. The show returned to the West Coast in 1994, first to Beverly Hills, then it had a 92-week run at THEATRE ON THE SQUARE, San Francisco, from 8/94 to 5/26/96. Then it went to Europe, Japan, and came back for a U.S. tour before going to Broadway.

The Broadway Run. WALTER KERR THEATRE, 6/19/97–4/5/98. 4

previews from 6/16/97; MARQUIS THEATRE, 4/15/98–8/2/98. Total of 453 PERFORMANCES. PRESENTED BY Steven Baruch, Richard Frankel, Thomas Viertel, Marc Routh, Jujamcyn, and Interamerica, Inc; CREATOR/DIRECTOR/LIGHTING: Luis Bravo; CHOREOGRAPHERS: the Dancers; COSTUMES: Argemira Affonso; SOUND: Tom Craft; MUSICAL DIRECTOR/ARRANGEMENTS: Lisandro Adrover; CAST RECORDING on RCA Victor, released on 2/24/98; PRESS: Boneau/Bryan-Brown; GENERAL MANAGEMENT: Richard Frankel Productions; COMPANY MANAGER: Miguel Barreiro; STAGE MANAGER: Jorge Gonzalez. *Cast:* SINGER: Carlos Morel; DANCERS: Miriam Larici, Diego Di Falco, Luis Castro & Claudia Mendoza, Carlos Gavito & Marcela Duran, Jorge Torres & Karina Piazza, Carlos Vera & Laura Marcarie, Guillermo Merlo & Cecilia Saia, Gabriel Ortega & Sandra Bootz, Pedro Calveyra & Nora Robles, Carolina Zokalski. *Musicians*: BANDONEONS: Lisandro Adrover, Hector del Curto, Carlos Niesi, Victor Lavallen; VIOLINS: Humberto Ridolfi & Rodion Boshoer; VIOLA: Oscar Hasbun; CELLO: Dino Quarleri; BASS; Silvio Acosta; PIANO: Fernando Marzan; KEYBOARD: Mario Araolaza. *Program*: *Act I*: "Preludio del bandoneon y la noche" (conceived by Luis Bravo) (Miss Larici & Mr. Di Falco), Overture (m: Lisandro Adrover) (Orchestra), "El suburbio" (1880s bordello scene), "A los amigos" (m: Armando Pontier) (Orchestra), "Derecho viejo" (m: E. Arolas) (Miss Piazza & Mr. Torres), "El dia que me quieras" (m/l: C. Gardel & A. Lepera) (sung by Mr. Morel), "La mariposa" (m: O. Pugliese) (Miss Marcarie & Mr. Vera), "Comme il faut" (m: E. Arolas) (Miss Bootz & Mr. Ortega), "Berretin" (m: P. Laurenz) (Orchestra), "La tablada" (m: F. Canaro) (Miss Mendoza & Mr. Castro), "Milongueando en el '40" (m: Armando Pontier) (Miss Saia & Mr. Merlo), "S.V.P." (m: Astor Piazzolla) (Miss Duran & Mr. Gavito), "Responso" (m: A. Troilo) (Orchestra), "Azabache" (m: E.M. Fracini) (Company). *Act II*: "Tanguera" (m: M. Mores) (Miss Robles & Mr. Calveyra), "A Evaristo Carriego" (m: E. Rovira) (Miss Duran & Mr. Gavito), "Payadora" (m: J. Plaza) (Orchestra), "Quejas de bandoneon" (m: J. de Dios Filiberto) (Miss Marcarie & Mr. Vera), "Gallo ciego" (m: A. Bardi) (Miss Piazza & Mr. Torres), "Balada para un loco" (m: Astor Piazzolla; l: H. Ferrer) (sung by Mr. Morel), "La Cumparsita" (m: G.H. Matos Rodriguez) (Miss Saia & Mr. Merlo, Miss Piazza & Mr. Torres, Miss Duran & Mr. Gavito), "Jealousy" (m: Jacob Gade) (Orchestra), "Felicia" (m: E. Saborido) (Miss Mendoza & Mr. Castro), "Adios Nonino" (m: Astor Piazzolla) (Orchestra) [Nonino was Mr. Piazzolla's late father; this piece was written for, and first played at, his funeral], "Libertango" (m: Astor Piazzolla) (Miss Saia & Mr. Merlo), "Romance del bandoneon y la noche: *Tus ojos de cielo*" (m: Liandro Adrover; conceived by Luis Bravo) (Miss Larici & Mr. Di Falco), Finale: "Lo que vendra" (m: Astor Piazzolla) (Company).

It got very good reviews, and extended its limited run (which was meant to end on 8/9/97), and again, until it became an open-ended run. After 332 performances, the show went on hiatus 4/5/98–4/15/98 while it transferred in order to make way for *The Beauty Queen of Leenane*, which was coming into the Walter Kerr. The 6/27/98 performance had to be canceled because of a power outage at the Marquis Theatre. The cast was nominated for a Tony.

After Broadway. TOUR. Began on 4/17/98, at the Playhouse, Wilmington, Del. It spent the summer and fall of 1999 in Asia. Sometimes two companies were on tour simultaneously. It was back at Theatre on the Square, San Francisco, for a holiday visit, 12/20/00–12/31/00. *Cast*: Carlos Vera, Laura Marcarie, Carlos Gavito, Marcela Duran, Luis Castro, Claudia Mendoza, Cesar Coelho, Karina Piazza, Oscar Mandagaran, Natalie Hills, Sandra Bootz, Gabriel Ortega, Jorge Torres, Guillermina Quiroga.

227. *Forever Tango (Broadway revival)*

The Broadway Run. SHUBERT THEATRE, 7/24/04–8/29/04; 9/28/04–11/28/04. 6 previews from 7/20/04. 114 PERFORMANCES. PRESENTED BY Jack Utsick & BACI Worldwide; CONCEIVED BY/DIRECTOR: Luis Bravo; CHOREOGRAPHERS: the Dancers; LIGHTING: Luis Bravo & Argemira Affonso; SOUND: Mike Miller; ORCHESTRA DIRECTOR: Victor Lavallen; PRESS: Richard Kornberg & Associates and Richard Miramontez; GENERAL MANAGER: Mary-Evelyn Card; COMPANY MANAGER: Oscar Lequizamon. *Cast:* SINGER: Miguel Velazquez; DANCERS: Veron-

ica Gardella, Natalia Hills, Francisco Forquera, Claudio Gonzalez, Marcelo Bernadaz, Marcela Duran, Jorge Torres, Alejandra Gutty, Carlos Vera, Laura Marcarie, Melina Brufman, Gabriel Ortega, Sandra Bootz, Guillermina Quiroga, Juan Paulo Horvath. *Musicians*: BANDONEONS: Victor Lavallen, Santos Maggi, Jorge Trivisonno, Carlos Niesi; VIOLINS: Rodion Boshoer & Abraham Becker; VIOLA: Alexander Sechkin; CELLO: Patricio Villarejo; BASS: Pablo Motta; PIANO: Jorge Vernieri; KEYBOARDS: Gustavo Casenave.

It was due to close at the Shubert on 8/29/04, but, again, proved so popular that it extended its run, re-opening, after a hiatus, at the Shubert on 9/28/04 (date put back from 9/21/04).

228. *Forty-Second Street*

Also called *42nd Street*. "The song and dance fable of Broadway." Set during 1933 in New York City and Philadelphia. Chorus girl Peggy, from Allentown, Pa., steps in when leading lady Dorothy breaks ankle in *Pretty Lady*. Peggy then becomes a star herself.

Before Broadway. *42nd Street*, the classic Hollywood movie musical. 1933. WRITERS: James Seymour & Rian James; DIRECTOR: Lloyd Bacon. *Cast*: JULIAN MARSH: Warner Baxter; PEGGY: Ruby Keeler; PAT DENNING: George Brent; BILLY: Dick Powell; DOROTHY: Bebe Daniels; ANYTIME ANNIE: Ginger Rogers.

In 1978 Michael Stewart and Mark Bramble were watching the movie in the Carnegie Hall Cinema, and felt the world was ready for a Broadway musical version. In fact, they wished they were doing it then, instead of the show they were really working on — *The Grand Tour*. They wrote the book (or as producer David Merrick called it for a while "lead-ins and crossovers" — which confusion probably cost the librettists a Tony, as the award panel didn't know what "lead-ins and crossovers" were — and neither did anyone else), got the rights, and asked Jerry Herman if he would write the score, but he refused, saying that you couldn't do away with the great songs in the movie. As there were only five songs in the movie, they took four of them, and added nine Harry Warren songs from other shows (seven of which were also written with Al Dubin), and asked David Merrick if he would produce it. Mr. Merrick had problems getting financing, so he did it himself. There were three small investors already, and he bought them out. He ran up $2.4 million in costs. It tried out at the Kennedy Center, Washington, DC, 6/21/80–7/27/80, but didn't look good. Gower Champion was dreadfully ill (no one knew how ill), and had been since 1974, and couldn't fix the problems. Mr. Merrick got advice from Joe Layton and Ron Field, but the show was still in poor shape when it moved into the Winter Garden, on Broadway. Previews were postponed as the show continued to rehearse. People didn't know what was going on. The opening date was re-scheduled and re-scheduled again. Mr. Merrick told people that he was waiting for God to tell him when to open, but in truth he was buying time and publicity because his show was in trouble and his new sets hadn't been built yet (the old ones wouldn't work, as had been proved in Washington). David Merrick canceled one of the Broadway previews altogether when he learned that an uninvited critic was in the audience.

The Broadway Run. WINTER GARDEN THEATRE, 8/25/80–3/29/81; MAJESTIC THEATRE, 3/30/81–4/5/87; ST. JAMES THEATRE, 4/7/87–1/8/89. 6 previews. Total of 3,486 PERFORMANCES. PRESENTED BY David Merrick; MUSIC: Harry Warren; LYRICS: Al Dubin (unless otherwise marked in the song list); ADDITIONAL LYRICS: Johnny Mercer & Mort Dixon; LEAD-INS & CROSSOVERS (I.E. BOOK): Michael Stewart & Mark Bramble; BASED ON the 1932 novel of the same name by Bradford Ropes, and on the classic 1933 movie musical; DIRECTOR/CHOREOGRAPHER: Gower Champion; DANCE ASSISTANTS: Karin Baker & Randy Skinner; SETS: Robin Wagner; COSTUMES: Theoni V. Aldredge; LIGHTING: Tharon Musser; SOUND: Richard Fitzgerald; MUSICAL DIRECTOR: John Lesko (81–82), *Philip Fradkin* (82–86), *Eileen La Grange* (85–86), *Donald Johnston* (by 86–87); ORCHESTRATIONS: Philip J. Lang; VOCAL ARRANGEMENTS: John Lesko; DANCE MUSIC ARRANGEMENTS: Donald Johnston; CAST RECORDING on RCA; PRESS: Fred Nathan (80), Louise Weiner Ment (80), Solters/Roskin/Friedman (80–86), Joshua Ellis

(80–88), Milly Schoenbaum, Bud Westman, Kevin Patterson, *Warren Knowlton* (82–83), *David Le Shay* (82–83), *Cindy Valk* (84–86), *Adrian Bryan-Brown* (84–88), *Keith Sherman* (84–85), *Jackie Green* (84–88), *Jim Sapp* (85–86), *Bill Shuttleworth* (85–88), *Leo Stern* (86–87), *Susanne Tighe* (86–88); CASTING: Feuer & Ritzer, *Julie Hughes & Barry Moss* (by 86–87); GENERAL MANAGER: Helen L. Nickerson, *Leo K. Cohen* (85–87); COMPANY MANAGER: Louise M. Bayer (gone by 86–87), *Marcia K. Goldberg* (85–88); PRODUCTION STAGE MANAGER: Steve Zweigbaum; STAGE MANAGER: Arturo E. Porazzi, *Jack Timmers* (85–88); ASSISTANT STAGE MANAGERS: Jane E. Neufeld, Barry Kearsley, Debra Pigliavento, *Janet Friedman* (83–86), *Dennis Angulo* (83–88), *Harold Goldfaden* (85–88), *Michael Pule* (86–88). ***Cast:*** ANDY LEE: Danny Carroll; OSCAR: Robert Colston; MAC: Stan Page; ANNIE: Karen Prunczik, *Clare Leach* (from 81–82), *Billye Kersey* (from 83–84), *Dorothy Stanley* (from 83–84), *Beth Leavel* (from 84–85); MAGGIE JONES: Carole Cook (6), *Charlotte Fairchild* (during Miss Cook's vacation, 81–82), *Sheila Smith* (during Miss Cook's vacation, 81–82), *Peggy Cass* (from 9/81), *Carol Swarbrick* (from 82–83), *Jessica James* (from 10/4/82), *Peggy Cass* (from 84–85), *Marie Lillo* (from 85–86), *Denise Lor* (from 86–87), *Bobo Lewis* (from 7/21/87); BERT BARRY: Joseph Bova (5); BILLY LAWLOR: Lee Roy Reams (4), *Ken Prescott* (during Mr. Reams' vacation, 81–82), *James Brennan* (from 12/13/83), *Lee Roy Reams* (from 1/8/85), *Jim Walton* (from 7/22/86), *Lee Roy Reams* (from 9/3/86), *Jim Walton* (from 10/20/87); PEGGY SAWYER: Wanda Richert (3), *Nancy Sinclair* (from 10/15/80), *Karen Prunczik* (from 10/20/80), *Wanda Richert* (from 10/25/80), *Mary Cadorette* (from 81–82), *Gail Benedict* (from 81–82), *Lisa Brown* (from 7/26/82), *Karen Ziemba* (from 11/15/83), *Gail Benedict* (from 83–84), *Lisa Brown* (from 3/85), *Clare Leach* (from 84–85), *Cathy Wydner* (7/22/85–9/16/85), *Clare Leach* (from 9/17/86); LORRAINE: Ginny King, *Gail Lohla* (from 81–82), *Marla Singer* (from 84–85), *Neva Leigh* (from 85–86); PHYLLIS: Jeri Kansas, *Barbara Mandra* (from 81–82), *Gail Pennington* (from 83–84), *Jeri Kansas* (from 84–85); JULIAN MARSH: Jerry Orbach (2) ✩ *Stephen G. Arlen* during Mr. Orbach's vacation, 81–82), *Steve Elmore* (from 1/15/85), *Jerry Orbach* (left 4/7/85 after 1,929 performances), *Don Chastain* (from 4/85), *Jamie Ross* (from 10/29/85), *Barry Nelson* (from 7/22/86), *Jamie Ross* (from 9/2/86), *Barry Nelson* (during Mr. Ross's vacation); DOROTHY BROCK: Tammy Grimes (1) ✩, *Charlotte Fairchild* (during Miss Grimes' vacation, 81–82), *Sheila Smith* (during Miss Grimes' vacation, 81–82), *Millicent Martin* (from 10/28/81), *Elizabeth Allen* (from 4/26/82), *Millicent Martin* (from 9/6/83), *Anne Rogers* (from 12/13/83), *Millicent Martin* (from 12/84), *Louise Troy* (from 12/17/85), *Dolores Gray* (from 6/17/86), *Elizabeth Allen* (from 1/20/87); ABNER DILLON: Don Crabtree, *Stan Page* (from 84–85), *Don Crabtree* (from 85–86); PAT DENNING: James Congdon, *Stephen G. Arlen* (from 81–82), *Jered Holmes* (from 82–83), *Steve Elmore* (from 82–83), *Michael Dantuono* (from 87–88); THUGS: Stan Page & Ron Schwinn; DOCTOR: Stan Page, *Bill Nabel* (from 84–85), *Stan Page* (from 85–86); ENSEMBLE: Carole Banninger, Steve Belin (gone by 82–83), Robin Black (gone by 81–82), Joel Blum (gone by 83–84), Mary Cadorette (gone by 83–84), Ronny De Vito, Denise Di Renzo (gone by 81–82), Mark Dovey (gone by 82–83), Rob Draper, Brandt Edwards, Jon Engstrom (gone by 81–82), Sharon Ferrol (gone by 83–84), Cathy Greco, Dawn Herbert (gone by 81–82), Christine Jacobsen (gone by 83–84 but back by 86–87), Jeri Kansas (gone by 81–82 but back by 86–87), Ginny King (gone by 81–82), Terri Ann Kundrat (gone by 85–86), Shan Martin (gone by 83–84), Beth McVey (gone by 81–82), Maureen Mellon, Sandra Menhart (gone by 83–84), Bill Nabel, Tony Parise (gone by 81–82), Don Percassi, Jean Preece (gone by 81–82), Vicki Regan (gone by 81–82), Lars Rosager (gone by 86–87), Linda Sabatelli, Nikki Sahagen (gone by 83–84), Ron Schwinn, Yveline Semeria (gone by 86–87), Alison Sherve (gone by 81–82 but back by 83–84 & gone by 84–85), Robin Stephens (gone by 83–84), David Storey (gone by 82–83), Karen Tamburrelli (gone by 81–82). 81–82 replacements: *Doreen Alderman* (gone by 83–84), *Dennis Angulo* (gone by 86–87), *Pam Cecil* (gone by 84–85), *Kim Morgan Greene* (gone by 83–84), *Jack Karcher* (gone by 85–86), *Billye Kersey, Karen Klump* (gone by 86–87), *Neva Leigh, Gail Lohla* (gone by 84–85), *Barbara Mandra* (gone by 82–83), *Michael Ricardo* (gone by 86–87), *Maryellen Scilla* (gone by 83–84). 82–83 replacements: *Dennis Batutis, Ken Mitchell.* 83–84 replacements: *Paula Joy Belis* (gone by 85–86 but back by 86–87), *Gail Benedict* (gone by 84–85), *Yvonne Dutton* (gone

by 84–85), *Mark Frawley* (gone by 84–85), *K. Craig Innes* (gone by 84–85), *Gwendolyn Miller* (gone by 86–87), *Beth Myatt* (gone by 84–85), *Sheila O'Connor* (gone by 85–86), *Gail Pennington* (gone by 84–85), *Rosemary Rado, Pamela S. Scott, Roger Spivy* (gone by 84–85), *Cynthia Thole* (gone by 84–85). 84–85 replacements: *Diane Abrams* (gone by 86–87), *Jeffrey Cornell* (gone by 86–87), *Judy Ehrlich, Jennifer Hammond* (gone by 85–86), *Elisa Heinsohn* (gone by 86–87), *Tony Parise* (gone by 85–86), *Marla Singer* (gone by 85–86), *J. Thomas Smith, Michael Steuber* (gone by 86–87), *Susanne Leslie Sullivan, Vickie Taylor.* 85–86 replacements: *Carla Earle* (gone by 86–87), *Suzie Jary, Mia Malm* (gone by 86–87), *Brenda Pipik* (gone by 86–87), *Karen Sorensen, Mary Chris Wall.* 86–87 replacements: *Susan Banks, Kelly Crafton, David Fredericks, Christine Jacobsen, Bobby Longbottom, Chris Lucas, Anne Rutter, Jeanna Schweppe, David Schwing.* **Understudies**: Dorothy: Leila Martin (80–81), *Sheila Smith* (81–83), *Charlotte Fairchild* (81–83), *Elaine Cancilla* (82–83), *Connie Day* (83–88), *Karen Sorensen* (85–88); Maggie: Leila Martin (80–81), *Sheila Smith* (81–83), *Charlotte Fairchild* (81–83), *Elaine Cancilla* (82–83), *Connie Day* (83–88), *Beth Leavel* (85–86); Marsh: James Congdon (80–81), *Stephen G. Arlen* (81–83), *Steve Elmore* (82–88), *Stan Page* (83–88); Peggy: Nancy Sinclair (80–81), *Mary Cadorette* (80–83), *Nikki Sahagen* (81–83), *Pam Cecil* (83–84), *Vickie Taylor* (84–88), *Debra Ann Draper* (85–88); Billy: Joel Blum (80–83), *Rob Draper* (83–88), *Dennis Angulo* (84–88); Bert/Mac: Bill Nabel (81–88), *Ron Schwinn* (83–88); Andy: Don Percassi (80–88), *Ron Schwinn* (86–88); Abner: Stan Page (80–88); Pat: Stan Page (80–88), *Brandt Edwards* (86–88); Annie: Karen Tamburrelli (80–81), *Barbara Mandra* (81–83), *Billye Kersey* (82–88), *Linda Sabatelli* (83–88); Oscar: Donald Johnston (80–81), *Bernie Leighton* (81–88); Phyllis/Lorraine: *Debra Pigliavento* (81–83), *Lorraine Person* (81–83), *Lizzie Moran* (83–88), *Debra Ann Draper* (83–88). ENSEMBLE: Lorraine Person (80–83), Rick Pessagno (80–81), *Yvonne Dutton* (81–83), *Jon Engstrom* (81–83), *Christopher Lucas* (81–84), *Kelli McNally* (81–83), *Lizzie Moran* (81–88), *Debra Pigliavento* (81–83), *Debra Ann Draper* (83–88), *Patrice McConachie* (83–85), *Ida Gilliams* [by 84–85 known as Ida Henry] (83–85), *Dennis Angulo* (83–88), *Rick Conant* (84–85), *Brenda Pipik* (85–88), *Doug Okerson* (85–86), *John Salvatore* (86–88). **Act I**: *Scene 1* Stage at the 42nd Street Theatre, New York City: "Audition" (Andy & Ensemble), "Young and Healthy" (Billy & Peggy) [song from the movie], "Shadow Waltz" [from the movie *Golddiggers of 1933*] (Maggie, Dorothy, Girls), "Shadow Waltz" (reprise) (Dorothy); *Scene 2* The *Gypsy Tea Kettle* restaurant: "Go into Your Dance" [from the 1935 movie of the same name] (Maggie, Peggy, Annie, Peggy, Andy, Lorraine, Phyllis); *Scene 3* Stage of the 42nd Street Theatre: "You're Getting to Be a Habit with Me" (Dorothy, Billy, Peggy, Ensemble) [song from the movie]; *Scene 4* Dorothy Brock's dressing-room; *Scene 5* Stage of the 42nd Street Theatre: "Getting Out of Town" (l: Mort Dixon) [from the movie *Laugh Parade*] (Pat, Bert, Maggie, Annie, Dorothy, Ensemble); *Scene 6* Arch Street Theatre, Philadelphia: "Dames" [from the 1934 movie of the same name] (Billy & Ensemble); *Scene 7* Regency Club & Dorothy's suite at Hotel Stratford: "I Know Now" [from the 1937 movie *The Singing Marine*] (Dorothy); *Scene 8* Arch Street Theatre; opening night of *Pretty Lady*: "I Know Now" (reprise) (Billy & Girls), "We're in the Money" ("The Gold Diggers' Song") [from the movie *Golddiggers of 1933*] (Annie, Peggy, Lorraine, Phyllis, Billy, Ensemble), Act I Finale (Dorothy, Peggy, Full Company). **Act II**: *Scene 1* Outside Dorothy Brock's dressing-room; 10 minutes later [in the 2001 revival it was a backstage corridor at the Arch Street Theatre; 15 minutes later]; *Scene 2* Dressing-rooms at the Arch Street Theatre: "(There's a) Sunny Side to Every Situation" (l: Johnny Mercer) [from the 1938 movie *Hard to Get*] (Annie & Ensemble); *Scene 3* Stage of the Arch Street Theatre; *Scene 4* Broad Street Station, Philadelphia: "Lullaby of Broadway" [from the movie *Golddiggers of 1935*] (Marsh & Full Company); *Scene 5* Stage of the 42nd Street Theatre; *Scene 6* Peggy's dressing-room: "About a Quarter to Nine" [from the movie *Go Into Your Dance*] (Dorothy & Peggy); *Scene 7* Opening night of *Pretty Lady*, 42nd Street Theatre: "*Pretty Lady* Overture" (Orchestra), "Shuffle off to Buffalo" (Annie, Bert, Maggie, Girls) [from the movie], "Forty-Second Street" (Peggy, Billy, Ensemble) [song from the movie]; Scene 8 Backstage: "Forty-Second Street" (reprise) (Marsh), Finale (Full Company).

It finally opened to great reviews, but with a lot of sadness — Gower

Champion died the afternoon of opening night. David Merrick had to announce his death. It came as a shock to everyone, perhaps especially Wanda Richert (who was playing Peggy), Gower's girlfriend. When the show opened, the top ticket price was $30, a record. By Oct. 1980 it was $50. On 10/15/80 Wanda Richert became ill, and understudy Nancy Sinclair went on—for 5 days, then quit. Karen Prunczik had to go on for her. The show won Tonys for musical and choreography, and was nominated for book, direction of a musical, costumes, lighting, and for Lee Roy Reams and Wanda Richert. At the time of his death, Gower Champion was set to do another musical, *Sayonara*, that never got done.

After Broadway. TOUR. Opened on 1/1/83, at the Lyric Opera House, Chicago. DIRECTOR: Lucia Victor; CHOREOGRAPHERS: Karin Baker & Randy Skinner; MUSICAL DIRECTOR: Stephen Bates. *Cast*: MARSH: Ron Holgate; DOROTHY: Elizabeth Allen, *Millicent Martin* (from 4/26/83); MAGGIE: Bibi Osterwald; MAC/DOCTOR/THUG: Igors Gavon; PEGGY: Nancy Sinclair, *Karen Prunczik, Nancy Sinclair*; BILLY: Jim Walton; BERT: William Linton; ABNER: Brooks Morton; CHORUS INCLUDED: Cynthia Thole. **Standby**: Dorothy/Maggie: Kelly Britt. The tour re-opened at the Forrest Theatre, Philadelphia, on 11/13/83 (previews from 11/9/83), and closed on 7/26/86, at the Queen Elizabeth Theatre, Vancouver. *Cast*: MARSH: Barry Nelson; DOROTHY: Dolores Gray; PEGGY: Clare Leach, *Gail Benedict*; MAGGIE: Bibi Osterwald, *Denise Lor*; BILLY: Jim Walton, *Lee Roy Reams* (from 12/13/83), *Jim Walton*; BERT: Don Potter.

TOUR. Opened on 2/10/84, at the Shubert Theatre, Los Angeles. Previews from 2/3/84. *Cast*: MARSH: Jon Cypher; DOROTHY: Millicent Martin; PEGGY: Nana Visitor; MAGGIE: Carole Cook; BILLY: Lee Roy Reams; BERT: Matthew Tobin.

THEATRE ROYAL, DRURY LANE, London, 8/8/84. Successful run. *Cast*: MARSH: James Laurenson; PEGGY: Clare Leach; BILLY: Michael Howe; MAGGIE: Margaret Courtenay; BERT: Hugh Futcher.

TOUR. Opened on 2/24/85, at the Golden Gate Theatre, San Francisco, and closed in 1986. MUSICAL DIRECTOR: Jack Gaughan. *Cast*: MARSH: Gary Marshall; MAGGIE: Bibi Osterwald; DOROTHY: Elizabeth Allen.

PAPER MILL PLAYHOUSE, New Jersey, 1989. DIRECTOR/CHOREOGRAPHER: Lee Roy Reams; SETS: Robin Wagner. *Cast*: MARSH: Tom Urich; DOROTHY: Joy Franz; BILLY: John Scherer; PEGGY: Cathy Wydner; PAT DENNING: Patrick Hamilton; ENSEMBLE: Gillian Ferrigno, Mia Malm, Maryellen Scilla, Luke Stallins, Mary Wanamaker.

229. *Forty-Second Street* (*Broadway revival*)

Before Broadway. Plans for this revival began in 1997. David Merrick was going to produce, but bowed out due to ill health. Manny Kladitis took over. It was scheduled for Broadway in the 1997–98 season, then put off until 2000, and finally made it in 2001. Auditions began on 12/12/00. On 1/10/01 Mary Testa and Jonathan Freeman were confirmed in their roles; on 1/18/01 so were Michael Cumpsty and Christine Ebersole; and on 1/31/01 so were Kate Levering and David Elder. There was a press preview at Radio City Music Hall, on 3/7/01.

The Broadway Run. FORD CENTER FOR THE PERFORMING ARTS, 5/2/01–1/2/05. 31 previews from 4/4/01. 1,556 PERFORMANCES. PRESENTED BY Dodger Theatricals, Joop Van Den Ende, Stage Holding; MUSIC: Harry Warren; LYRICS: Al Dubin; ADDITIONAL LYRICS: Johnny Mercer & Mort Dixon; BOOK: Michael Stewart & Mark Bramble; BASED ON the novel by Bradford Ropes; DIRECTOR: Mark Bramble; CHOREOGRAPHER: Randy Skinner; SETS: Douglas W. Schmidt; COSTUMES: Roger Kirk; LIGHTING: Paul Gallo; SOUND: Peter Fitzgerald; MUSICAL DIRECTOR: Todd Ellison; ORIGINAL ORCHESTRATIONS: Philip J. Lang; MUSICAL ADAPTATION/DANCE MUSIC ARRANGEMENTS/ADDITIONAL ORCHESTRATIONS/ADDITIONAL VOCAL ARRANGEMENTS: Donald Johnston; NEW CAST RECORDING on Q Records, made on 5/7/01; PRESS: Boneau/Bryan-Brown; CASTING: Jay Binder, Mark Brandon, Laura Stanczyk, Sarah Prosser; HISTORICAL RESEARCH: Megan Bramble; COMPANY MANAGER: Sandra Carlson; PRODUCTION STAGE MANAGER: Frank Hartenstein, *Karen Armstrong, Arturo E. Porazzi*; STAGE MANAGER: Karen Armstrong,

Tripp Phillips; ASSISTANT STAGE MANAGERS: Tripp Phillips & Laura Brown MacKinnon, *Janet Friedman, Adam John Hunter, Zoya Kachadurian, Patsy Lyons*. **Cast:** ANDY LEE: Michael Arnold (8), *Brad Aspel, Chris Clay*; OSCAR: Billy Stritch (3), *George Beck*; MAC: Allen Fitzpatrick (12), *Steve Luker*; ANYTIME ANNIE: Mylinda Hull (9), *Amy Dolan* (from 6/11/02), *Celina Carvajal, Alana Salvatore*; DIANE: Tamlyn Brooke Shusterman, *Erin Crouch, Merritt Tyler Hawkins*; MAGGIE JONES: Mary Testa (5), *Karen Murphy, Patti Mariano*; BERT BARRY: Jonathan Freeman (6), *Joel Newsome, Bob Walton, Frank Root*; BILLY LAWLOR: David Elder (7); PEGGY SAWYER: Kate Levering (4) (until 8/18/01), *Meredith Patterson* (8/19/01–8/18/02). Miss Patterson had gone on for Miss Levering briefly earlier in 2001), *Kate Levering* (from 8/30/02), *Nadine Isenegger*; PHYLLIS: Catherine Wreford, *Angela Kahle*; LORRAINE: Megan Sikora, *Kelly Sheehan*; JULIAN MARSH: Michael Cumpsty (1) ☆ (until 5/26/02), *Michael Dantuono* (5/28/02–6/20/02), *Tom Wopat* (6/21/02 –6/22/02), *Michael Dantuono* (6/24/02–7/7/02), *Tom Wopat* (7/9/02–8/10/03), *Michael Dantuono* (8/12/03–8/14/03), *Patrick Ryan Sullivan* (from 8/15/03), *Patrick Cassidy* (from 5/7/04); DOROTHY BROCK: Christine Ebersole (2) ☆ (until 12/31/01), *Beth Leavel* (from 1/2/02), *Christine Ebersole* (3/12/02–6/9/02), *Beth Leavel* (from 6/11/02), *Shirley Jones* (5/7/04–8/8/04), *Blair Ross* (from 8/10/04); ABNER DILLON: Michael McCarty (10), *Richard Pruitt*; PAT DENNING: Richard Muenz (11), *Michael Dantuono*; WAITERS: Brad Aspel (*Joel Newsome*), Mike Warshaw, Shonn Wiley; THUGS: Allen Fitzpatrick (*Steve Luker*) & Jerry Tellier; DOCTOR: Allen Fitzpatrick, *Steve Luker*; ETHEL: Amy Dolan, *Susan Haefner*; ENSEMBLE: Brad Aspel (*Joel Newsome*), Becky Bersteler, Randy Bobish, Chris Clay, Michael Clowers, Maryam Myika Day, Alexander de Jong, Amy Dolan, Isabelle Flaschmann, Jennifer Jones, Dontee Kiehn, Renee Klapmeyer, Jessica Kostival, Keirsten Kupiec, Todd Lattimore, Melissa Rae Mahon, Michael Malone, Jennifer Marquardt, Meredith Patterson, Darin Phelps, Wendy Rosoff, Megan Schenck, Kelly Sheehan, Tamlyn Brooke Shusterman (*Erin Crouch*), Megan Sikora, Jennifer Stetor, Erin Stoddard, Yasuko Tamaki, Jonathan Taylor, Jerry Tellier, Elisa Van Duyne, Erika Vaughn, Mike Warshaw, Merrill West, Shonn Wiley, Catherine Wreford, *Joni Michelle Schenck, Brad DeLima, Regan Kays, Matt Lashey, Natalie King, Sarah Misiano, Alison Levenberg, Eric Sciotto, Cindy Shadel, Josh Walden, Nikki Williams, Kevin Worley, Will Armstrong, Angie Everett, Emily Fletcher, Kristin Gaetz, Melissa Giattino, Susan Haefner, Kolina Janneck, Sarah L. Johnson, Amy F. Karlein, Alison Levenberg, Alison Paterson, Wes Pope, Jenifer Leigh Schwerer, Vanessa Sonon, Will Taylor, Ericka Yang, Nikki Della Penta, Kelli Barclay, Jeremy Benton, Sarah Brians, Brad Hampton, Jennifer Jones, Jessica Kostival, Gavin Lodge, Jennifer Marquardt, Tony Palomino, Kristyn D. Smith*. **Standby**: Dorothy/Maggie: Beth Leavel (13), *Dorothy Stanley*. **Understudies**: Dorothy: Jessica Kostival; Maggie: Amy Dolan; Marsh: Richard Muenz, Jerry Tellier, Michael Dantuono; Peggy: Meredith Patterson & Erin Stoddard, *Joni Michelle Schenck*; Bert: Brad Aspel, *Steve Luker*; Billy: Shonn Wiley; Pat: Allen Fitzpatrick & Jerry Tellier; Abner: Allen Fitzpatrick, *Steve Luker*; Andy: Brad Aspel & Randy Bobish, *Joel Newsome, Eric Sciotto*; Annie: Becky Berstler & Amy Dolan; Lorraine: Erin Stoddard; Phyllis: Elisa Van Duyne; Mac/Doctor/Thug: Darin Phelps & Luke Walrath; Diane: Renee Klapmeyer. **Swings**: Kelli Barclay, Melissa Giattino, Brian J. Marcum, Luke Walrath, *Sarah Brians, Callie Carter, Nikki Della Penta, Carol Kjellman, Todd Lattimore, Sarah McLellan, Josh Walden*. Partial Swings: Becky Berstler, Isabelle Flaschmann, Jerry Tellier, Elisa Van Duyne, Merrill West, *Kevin B. Worley*. *42nd Street Orchestra*: WOODWINDS: Michael Migliore, Ken Hitchcock, Dave Pietro, Tom Christensen, Roger Rosenberg, Andrew Drelles, Tim Ries; TRUMPETS: Joe Mosello, Ravi Best, Barry Danielian, Dave Ballou; TROMBONES: Mark Patterson, Steve Armour, Mike Christianson; FRENCH HORNS: Theresa MacDonnell, Leise Anscheutz, Michael Ishii; BASS: John Arbo; GUITAR: Scott Kuney; HARP: Victoria Drake; DRUMS: Tony Tedesco; PERCUSSION: Kory Grossman; PIANO: Fred Lassen. *Act I*: Overture (Orchestra); *Scene 1* "Audition" (Andy & Ensemble), "Young and Healthy" (Billy & Peggy), "Shadow Waltz" (Maggie, Dorothy, Ensemble); *Scene 2* "Go into Your Dance" (Maggie, Annie, Peggy, Phyllis, Lorraine, Andy); *Scene 3* "You're Getting to Be a Habit with Me" (Dorothy, Billy, Peggy, Ensemble); *Scene 5* "Getting Out of Town" (Full Company); *Scene 6* "Dames" (Billy & Men), "Keep Young and Beautiful" (Maggie, Bert, Girls), "Dames" (continued) (Full Company); *Scene 7* "I Only Have Eyes for You" [from the movie *Dames*] (Dorothy); *Scene*

8 "I Only Have Eyes for You" (reprise) (Billy & Girls), "We're in the Money" ("The Gold Diggers' Song") (Annie, Peggy, Lorraine, Phyllis, Billy, Ensemble), Act One Finale (Dorothy & Company). *Act II*: Entr'acte (Orchestra); *Scene 2* "(There's a) Sunny Side to Every Situation" (Annie & Ensemble); *Scene 4* "Lullaby of Broadway" (Marsh & Full Company), "Getting Out of Town" (reprise) (Bert, Maggie, Full Company); *Scene 5* "Montage" (Marsh, Andy, Peggy, Ensemble); *Scene 6* "About a Quarter to Nine" (Dorothy & Peggy); *Scene 7* "*Pretty Lady* Overture" (Orchestra), "With Plenty of Money and You" [from the movie *Golddiggers of 1937*] (Peggy & Men), "Shuffle off to Buffalo" (Bert, Maggie, Annie, Girls), "42nd Street" (Peggy, Billy, Ensemble); *Scene 8* "42nd Street" (reprise) (Marsh), Finale (Full Company).

Note: scenes and numbers were as for the 1980 Broadway production, unless where stated.

Broadway reviews were good. The show won Tony awards for revival of a musical, and for Christine Ebersole, and was also nominated for direction of a musical, choreography, sets, costumes, lighting, and for Kate Levering and Mary Testa. On 12/31/01 Christine Ebersole went on a 10-week leave. The show missed the 8/14/03 performance due to the big power blackout. On 3/3/04 the closing date was announced for 10 months away. When Shirley Jones and her son Patrick Cassidy took over the roles of Dorothy and Julian respectively, it was the first time that a mother and son had starred in a Broadway musical together. Miss Jones extended her run from 8/1/04 to 8/8/04, and Mr. Cassidy stayed on until the end. The production recouped its investment just before it closed.

After Broadway. TOUR. This was a scaled-down but "enhanced" production (in the sets mostly). It began rehearsals on 7/8/02, and opened on 8/4/02, at the Starlight Theatre, Kansas City. *Cast*: PEGGY: Catherine Wreford; MARSH: Patrick Ryan Sullivan; DOROTHY: Blair Ross; MAGGIE: Patti Mariano; BILLY: Robert Spring; BERT: Frank Root.

MDM (MOSCOW YOUTH PALACE), 10/11/02–12/31/02. 91 PERFORMANCES. Rehearsals began in late 8/02. This production was a hybrid of the 1980 and 2001 Broadway productions. It was the first English-language production in Russia of a major Broadway musical. It was due to close in the summer of 2003, but because of terrorism in Russia it closed early. PRESENTED BY Troika; DIRECTOR/CHOREOGRAPHER: Randy Skinner; MUSICAL DIRECTOR: Stephen Bates. *Cast*: PEGGY: Meredith Patterson; BILLY: Shonn Wiley; ANDY: John Wescott; ANYTIME ANNIE: Kelly Shook.

230. *Fosse*

Also called *Fosse: A Celebration in Song and Dance*. A musical revue, a dance that celebrates the Bob Fosse style of choreography, with two 10-minute intermissions. It was conceived as a group piece, not as a star vehicle, even though there were two stars and a few featured players.

Before Broadway. Ann Reinking (one of Bob Fosse's major protégées) was the main driving force behind this show. In 1996 Livent acquired worldwide rights to Fosse's choreography (it would be their last production to come out before they were stricken with financial problems they couldn't escape). From 7/29/96 a 4-week workshop was held at York University, Toronto, with 26 dancers led by Gwen Verdon and Chet Walker (another Fosse protégé). The show was, at that time, called *Bob Fosse: The Dancing Man*. Its first Broadway tryout was at the Ford Center for the Performing Arts, Toronto, from 7/16/98. Then it played at the Colonial Theatre, Boston, 9/8/98–9/27/98 (press date was 9/10/98). The third tryout was at the Ahmanson Theatre, Los Angeles, 10/21/98–12/6/98 (previews from 10/9/98 — opening night was put back from 10/19/98). The number "Beat Me Daddy Eight to the Bar" was cut during tryouts.

The Broadway Run. BROADHURST THEATRE, 1/14/99–8/25/01. 22 previews 12/26/98–1/13/99. 1,093 PERFORMANCES. PRESENTED BY Livent (U.S.) (in 9/99 Livent became SFX Entertainment Group); CONCEIVED BY: Richard Maltby Jr., Chet Walker, Ann Reinking; DIRECTORS: Richard Maltby Jr. & Ann Reinking; CHOREOGRAPHERS: Chet Walker & Ann Reinking re-created Bob Fosse's choreography; DANCE RECON-

STRUCTIONS: Brad Musgrove & Lainie Sakakura; SETS/COSTUMES: Santo Loquasto; LIGHTING: Andrew Bridge; SOUND: Jonathan Deans; MUSICAL SUPERVISOR/ARRANGEMENTS: Gordon Lowry Harrell; MUSICAL DIRECTOR: Patrick S. Brady; ORCHESTRATIONS: Ralph Burns & Douglas Besterman; CAST RECORDING on RCA Victor, made 1/24/99–1/25/99, and released on 4/13/99; PRESS: Mary Bryant/Wayne Wolfe; CASTING: Arnold J. Mungioli, *Stuart Howard, Howard Meltzer, Amy Schecter*; ARTISTIC ADVISER: Gwen Verdon; GENERAL MANAGER: Frank P. Scardino; COMPANY MANAGER: Steve Quinn; PRODUCTION STAGE MANAGER: Mary Porter Hall, *Marybeth Abel*; STAGE MANAGER: Lori Lundquist; ASSISTANT STAGE MANAGER: Mary Harwell, *Brad Musgrove, Bryan Landrine*. *Cast:* Valarie Pettiford (1) (until 7/18/99, *Reva Rice* from 7/20/99, *Rachelle Rak, Stephanie Pope* 8/24/99–1/21/01, *Angel Creeks* 1/21/01–1/25/01, *Ben Vereen* 1/26/01–4/1/01, *Eugene Fleming, Ben Vereen* from 5/28/01), Jane Lanier (2) (until 7/18/99; replaced by ensemble members), Eugene Fleming, Desmond Richardson (until 9/99, *Scott Jovovich, Keith Roberts* 1/18/00–2/13/00, *Julio Bocca* from 2/15/00, *Keith Roberts* from 4/11/00, *Desmond Richardson* 6/27/00–7/9/00, *Keith Roberts* from 7/11/00), Sergio Trujillo, Kim Morgan Greene, Mary Ann Lamb, Dana Moore, Elizabeth Parkinson, Scott Wise (until spring 2001), Julio Agustin, Brad Anderson, Andy Blankenbuehler, Marc Calamia, Holly Cruikshank, Lisa Gajda, Scott Jovovich, Christopher R. Kirby, Dede La Barre, Shannon Lewis, Mary MacLeod, Brad Musgrove, Michael Paternostro, Rachelle Rak, Lainie Sakakura, Alex Sanchez. ***Replacements***: *Ann Reinking* (3/2/01–4/27/01; 7/2/01–7/01; 8/17/01–8/18/01–3 performances), *Bebe Neuwirth* (4/9/01–5/27/01) (she & Miss Reinking were the co-stars; after Miss Reinking left, on 4/27/01, Miss Neuwirth was sole headliner), *Ken Alan, Mark Arvin* (he was in L.A. in 1998), *Ashley Bachner, Lynne Calamia, J.P. Christensen, Dilys Croman, Rich Delancy, Byron Easley, Parker Esse, Aaron Felske, Meg Gillentine, Greg Graham, Francesca Harper, Suzanne Harrer, Anne Hawthorne, Curtis Holbrook, Terace Jones, James Kinney, Lorin Latarro, Robin Lewis, Edward Liang, Julio Monge, Sharon Moore, Kathryn Mowat Murphy, Jill Nicklaus, Mark C. Reis, Tracy Terstriep* (in L.A. in 1978). ***Swings***: Bill Burns, Susan Lamontagne, Deborah Leamy, Sean Gregory Palmer, Josh Rhodes, J. Kathleen Watkins, *Mark C. Reis, Suzanne Harrer, Francesca Harper, Robin Lewis, Christopher Windom, J.P. Christensen*. ***Orchestra***: WOODWINDS: Ed Joffe, Dale Kleps, Bill Easley, Walt Weiskopf, Allen Won; TRUMPETS: Craig Johnson, Scott Wendholt, Don Downs, Glenn Drewes; TROMBONES: Jim Pugh, Keith O'Quinn, Jeff Nelson; TUBA: Jeff Nelson; SYNTHESIZERS: Jon Werking, Seth Farber, Ethyl Will; GUITAR: David Spinozza; BASS: Mike Hall; DRUMS: Perry Cavari; PERCUSSION: Jim Saporito. ***Act I: Prologue***: "Life is Just a Bowl of Cherries" (m: Ray Henderson; l: Lew Brown & B.G. "Buddy" De Sylva) [from *George White's Scandals*, 1931; used in *Big Deal*, 1986] (performed by Miss Pettiford) [this number was later allocated to Mr. Vereen], "Fosse's World" (m: Gordon Lowry Harrell, including "Calypso," by Mr. Harrell, and "Snake in the Grass," by Frederick Loewe [from the motion picture *The Little Prince*, 1974]. Dance elements inspired by *The Little Prince* and signature Fosse styles which appeared in *The Little Prince*, and in *Damn Yankees, New Girl in Town, Redhead, Little Me, How to Succeed in Business Without Really Trying, Little Me, Sweet Charity, Cabaret*, and *Chicago*) (staged by Ann Reinking) (performed by Mr. Musgrove, Miss Lanier, and the Entire Company), "Bye Bye Blackbird" (m: Ray Henderson; l: Mort Dixon) [from the TV special *Liza with a Z*, 1972] (performed by Miss Pettiford, Messrs Agustin, Blankenbuehler & Calamia, Miss Cruikshank, Miss Gajda, Mr. Jovovich, Miss La Barre, Miss Lamb, Miss Lewis, Miss MacLeod, Miss Moore, Miss Parkinson, Mr. Paternostro, Miss Rak, Mr. Richardson, Miss Sakakura, Mr. Trujillo); ***Part I***: "From the Edge" (m: Gordon Lowry Harrell) [from *Dancin'*, 1978] (performed by Messrs Anderson, Kirby, Sanchez), "Percussion 4" (m: Gordon Lowry Harrell) [from *Dancin'*, 1978] (performed by Mr. Richardson), "Big Spender" (m: Cy Coleman; l: Dorothy Fields) [from *Sweet Charity*, 1966] (performed by Miss Pettiford, Miss Lanier, Miss Greene, Miss La Barre, Miss Lamb, Miss Lewis, Miss MacLeod, Miss Moore, Miss Parkinson, Miss Rak] "Crunchy Granola Suite" (m/l: Neil Diamond) [from *Dancin'*, 1978] (performed by Mr. Agustin, Mr. Calamia, Miss Cruikshank, Miss Gajda, Mr. Jovovich, Mr. Kirby, Miss La Barre, Miss Lamb, Miss Lewis, Miss MacLeod, Miss Parkinson, Mr. Paternostro, Mr. Richardson, Miss Sakakura, Mr. Sanchez) (sung by Mr. Anderson & Mr. Fleming); ***Part***

II: Transition: "Hooray for Hollywood" (m: Richard Whiting; l: Johnny Mercer), "From This Moment On" (m/l: Cole Porter) [from the motion picture *Kiss Me, Kate*, 1953] (the first 45 seconds of film choreography by Bob Fosse) (originally danced by Bob Fosse & Carol Haney) (performed by Miss Lamb & Mr. Blankenbuehler, and at matinees by Miss Sakakura and Mr. Blankenbuehler), "Alley Dance" [from the motion picture *My Sister Eileen*, 1955], "Got No Room for Mr. Gloom" (m: Jule Styne; l: Leo Robin) (originally danced by Bob Fosse & Tommy Rall) (performed by Scott Wise & Scott Jovovich, and at matinees by Brad Musgrove & Scott Jovovich), Transition (dance elements inspired by *Redhead*, 1959) (music for "Walking the Cat," by Patrick S. Brady) (staged by Ann Reinking) (performed by the Company), "I Wanna Be a Dancin' Man" (m: Harry Warren; l: Johnny Mercer) [from the 1951 Fred Astaire movie *The Belle of New York;* used in *Dancin'*, 1978] (dedicated to Fred Astaire) (performed by Mr. Fleming, Miss Pettiford, Miss Lanier, Mr. Wise and Mr. Anderson, Mr. Blankenbuehler, Mr. Calamia, Miss Gajda, Miss Greene, Mr. Kirby, Miss Lamb, Miss Lewis, Miss MacLeod, Miss Moore, Mr. Musgrove, Miss Parkinson, Mr. Sanchez, Mr. Trujillo; FIRST INTERMISSION. *Act II*: *Part III*: "Shoeless Joe from Hannibal, Mo." (m/l: . Richard Adler & Jerry Ross) [from *Damn Yankees*, 1955] (performed by Messrs Agustin, Anderson, Blankenbuehler, Calamia, Fleming, Kirby, Sanchez, Trujillo, Paternostro, Wise): PITCHER: Alex Sanchez; BATTERS: Brad Anderson & Scott Wise; BUNTER: Julio Agustin [this was cut during the show's final year], Transition (dance elements inspired by *New Girl in Town*, 1958) (performed by Mr. Sanchez), Nightclubs: The Dance team of Bob Fosse & Mary Ann Niles: "Dancing in the Dark" (m: Arthur Schwartz; l: Howard Dietz), "I Love a Piano" (m/l: Irving Berlin) [from *Stop! Look! Listen!*, 1916] (dance elements inspired by Fosse/Niles or Fosse appearances on such TV shows as *Your Hit Parade*, 1950; *The Morey Amsterdam Show*, 1949; *The Colgate Comedy Hour*, 1951; *The Burns and Allen Show*, 1950; the motion picture *The Affairs of Dobie Gillis*, 1953; TV shows such as *Cavalcade of Stars*, 1951; and *The Ed Sullivan Show*, 1956) (mus arr: Patrick S. Brady) (staged by Ann Reinking) (performed by Mr. Wise; Miss Parkinson & Mr. Jovovich; Miss Sakakura & Mr. Blankenbuehler; Miss Lanier, Mr. Paternostro, & Mr. Sanchez; Messrs Agustin, Anderson, Calamia, Miss Cruikshank, Miss La Barre, Miss Lamb, Miss MacLeod, & Mr. Trujillo) (sung by Miss Lewis & Miss Rak) [end of Nightclubs sequence], "Steam Heat" (m/l: Richard Adler & Jerry Ross) [from *The Pajama Game*, 1954] (Miss Lanier, Mr. Paternostro, Mr. Sanchez), "I Gotcha" (m/l: Joseph Arrington Jr. [Joe Tex]) [from the TV special *Liza with a Z*, 1972] (performed by Miss Lewis, Mr. Musgrove, Mr. Kirby), "Rich Man's Frug" (by Cy Coleman) [from *Sweet Charity*, 1966]: Part I: The Aloof; Part II: The Heavyweight; Part III: The Big Finish (performed by Miss Gajda; Mr. Musgrove & Mr. Blankenbuehler; Messrs Agustin, Anderson, Calamia, Miss Cruikshank, Mr. Jovovich, Mr. Kirby, Miss La Barre, Miss Lewis, Miss MacLeod, Miss Rak, Miss Sakakura, Mr. Trujillo) [end of "Rich Man's Frug" sequence], Transition (music: "Silky Thoughts," by Patrick S. Brady), "Cool Hand Luke" (m: Lalo Schifrin) [from *The Bob Hope TV Special*, Oct. 1968] (ch for Gwen Verdon, with Lee Roy Reams & Buddy Vest) (performed by Miss Parkinson, Mr. Richardson, Mr. Kirby), Transition: "Big Noise from Winnetka" (m: Ray Bauduc & Bob Haggart; l: Bob Crosby & Gil Rodin) [used in *Dancin'*, 1978], "Dancin' Dan" ("Me and My Shadow") (m: Dave Dreyer & Al Jolson; l: Billy Rose) [used in *Big Deal*, 1986] (performed by Mr. Fleming, Miss Greene, Miss Moore), "Nowadays" and "The Hot Honey Rag" (m: John Kander; l: Fred Ebb) [from the revival of *Chicago*, 1996] (performed by Miss Pettiford & Miss Lanier); SECOND INTERMISSION. *Act III*: *Part IV*: "Glory" (m/l: Stephen Schwartz) [from *Pippin*, 1972] (performed by Messrs Kirby, Agustin, Anderson, Blankenbuehler, Calamia, Jovovich, Miss Lamb, Mr. Musgrove, Miss Parkinson, Mr. Paternostro, Miss Sakakura, Mr. Sanchez) (sung by Mr. Fleming), "Manson Trio" (m/l: Stephen Schwartz) [from *Pippin*, 1972] (performed by Mr. Fleming, Miss La Barre, Miss MacLeod), "Mein Herr" (m: John Kander; l: Fred Ebb) [from the motion picture *Cabaret*, 1972] (performed by Miss Pettiford, and Miss Cruikshank, Miss Gajda, Miss Greene, Miss Lewis, Miss Moore, Miss Rak), "Take off with Us–Three Pas de Deux" (m: Stanley R. Lebowsky; l: Frederick K. Tobias) [from the motion picture *All That Jazz*, 1979] (performed by Mr. Calamia & Miss Sakakura; Miss Lamb & Miss Parkinson; Mr. Musgrove & Mr. Richardson), "Razzle Dazzle" (m: John Kan-

der; l: Fred Ebb) [from *Chicago*, 1975] (performed by Mr. Wise, Miss Greene, Miss Moore), "Who's Sorry Now?" (m: Harry Ruby; l: Ted Snyder & Bert Kalmar) [used in the motion picture *All That Jazz*, 1979] (performed by Miss Cruikshank, Miss Gajda, Miss La Barre, Miss Lamb, Miss Lewis, Miss MacLeod, Miss Parkinson, Miss Rak, Miss Sakakura), "There'll Be Some Changes Made" (m: W. Benton Overstreet; l: Billy Higgins) [used in the motion picture *All That Jazz*, 1979] (performed by Miss Lanier, Miss Greene, Miss Moore), "Mr. Bojangles" (by Jerry Jeff Walker) [from *Dancin'*, 1978] (sung by Mr. Blankenbuehler): MR. BOJANGLES: Sergio Trujillo; THE SPIRIT: Desmond Richardson; "Life is Just a Bowl of Cherries" (reprise) (performed by Miss Pettiford). PART V: Finale: Benny Goodman's "Sing, Sing, Sing" (by Louis Prima) [used in *Dancin'*, 1978]/"Christopher Columbus" (which interpolates) (m/l: Andy Razaf & Leon Berry) (performed by the Entire Company): DRUMS: Perry Cavari; BASS: Mike Hall; TROMBONE SOLO: Played by Jim Pugh, and danced by Miss Cruikshank, Mr. Kirby, Mr. Richardson; TRUMPET SOLO: Played by Glenn Drewes, and danced by Miss Parkinson; CLARINET SOLO: Played by Walt Weiskopf, and danced by Miss Pettiford, Miss Lanier, Miss MacLeod, Miss Moore, Miss Greene, Miss Lamb, Miss Rak, Messrs Agustin, Anderson, Calamia, Kirby, Sanchez, Trujillo, Paternostro; PIANO SOLO: Played by Jon Werking, and danced by Mr. Wise & Mr. Fleming.

Broadway reviews were divided. The show won Tonys for musical, lighting, and orchestrations, and was also nominated for direction of a musical, costumes, and for Desmond Richardson, Valarie Pettiford, and Scott Wise. Reva Rice left the cast to go on tour with the show. Ann Reinking joined the cast on 3/2/01, and was scheduled to play until 4/29/01, but cut her stint short (her last performance was on 4/27/01). Whereas Bebe Neuwirth was scheduled to come in on 4/3/01, but didn't make it until 4/9/01. She was scheduled to leave 4/27/01, but instead stayed until 5/27/01. The show changed somewhat over the course of its long run. Ben Vereen brought with him two numbers from *Pippin*— "Glory" and "Manson Trio." There was talk also of "Magic to Do," but it didn't make it into the show. The show opened in 3 acts, but changed to 2 acts on 1/25/00. When Scott Wise left the show the number "Shoeless Joe from Hannibal, Mo." was cut (it was re-instated for the particular performance in 8/01 that was filmed by PBS). Closing notices were posted on 5/29/01, and it was going to close on 9/1/01 (which would have made it a run of 1,100 performances), but it closed on 8/25/01 because of the incoming show *Dance of Death*. Ann Reinking made a curtain speech at the final performance.

After Broadway. TOUR. Opened on 9/22/99 (previews from 9/14), at the Ford Center for the Performing Arts — Oriental Theatre, Chicago. It had a cast of 28 (there were 32 in the Broadway cast). It also had 2 acts, instead of 3, and a "pause" between old acts II & III (a change that would later go into effect on Broadway itself). It also cut "Shoeless Joe from Hannibal, Mo.," "Hot Honey Rag" and "Nowadays." It was due to leave Chicago on 12/5/99 and go to Toronto, but instead canceled the Canadian gig, and stayed in Chicago until 1/8/00, then went to Pittsburgh. The tour included a stint at the Kennedy Center, Washington, DC, 12/6/00–12/31/00. After a 7-week trip to Japan, it resumed in the USA on 10/7/01, and finally closed on 2/17/02, at the New Jersey Performing Arts Center, Newark. *Cast*: Reva Rice (the star), Linda Bowen (featured performer), Julio Monge (featured performer), Greg Reuter, April Nixon (featured performer), Terace Jones (featured performer), Ken Alan (*Mark Swanhart* from 4/12/99), Sara Gettelfinger (*LaMae Caparas* from 2/1/00), Shawn Ku (*James Kinney* from 12/20/99), Matt Loehr.

PRINCE OF WALES THEATRE, London. 2/8/00–1/6/01. Previews from 1/24/00. DIRECTORS: Richard Maltby Jr. & Ann Reinking; CHOREOGRAPHER: Chet Walker. *Cast*: Nicola Hughes, Neil Johnson.

INTERNATIONAL TOUR. Opened 10/29/03, at the Empire Theatre, Liverpool, England, then on with the tour of Europe. *Cast*: Claire Sweeney (*Ruthie Henshall* from 11/24/03).

PBS TV. On 1/23/02 PBS aired, on *Great Performances* series, an evening's performance of *Fosse* (one of the three that Ann Reinking & Ben Vereen did together, in 8/01). They called the program "From Broadway: *Fosse*." "Shoeless Joe from Hannibal, Mo." was re-inserted into the production that night. Ben Vereen & Ann Reinking sang "Bye Bye Blackbird." In the PBS show "Steam Heat" was performed by Meg Gillentine, Julio Monge and Josh Rhodes.

231. *Four Saints in Three Acts*

An opera.

Before Broadway. It premiered on 5/20/33, at Ann Arbor, Mich., in concert. The first staged performance was at Hartford, Conn., on 2/8/34, with an all-black cast. On Broadway it ran at the 44th Street Theatre, 2/20/34–3/17/34. 32 performances; and again at the same venue, 4/2/34–4/14/34. 16 performances. Presented by Harry Moses and the Friends and Enemies of Modern Music; Musical Director: Alexander Smallens; Choral Director: Eva Jessye. *Cast:* St. Ignatius: Edward Matthews; St. Theresa I: Beatrice Robinson Wayne; St. Theresa II: Bruce Howard; Commere: Altonell Hines; Compere: Abner Dorsey; Female Saint: Assotta Marshall. Louise Crane presented it at Town Hall, 5/27/41, using most of the 1934 performers.

The Broadway Run. Broadway Theatre, 4/16/52–4/27/52. 15 performances. Presented by ANTA, in association with Ethel Linder Reiner; Music/Artistic Director/Musical Director: Virgil Thomson; Book: Gertrude Stein; Book Director: Maurice Grosser; Choreographer: William Dollar; Sets/Costumes: Paul Morrison (after the original models by Florine Stettheimer); Associate Conductor/Choral Director: William Jonson; Press: Barry Hyams & Robert Hector; Company Manager: Leon Spachner; Stage Managers: Seymour Milbert, Thomas Anderson, Jesse Williams. *Cast:* St. Stephen: Clyde Turner; St. Settlement: Martha Flowers; St. Plan: Calvin Dash; St. Sara: Doris Mayes; Commere: Altonell Hines; Compere: Elwood Smith; St. Theresa I: Inez Matthews (1); St. Theresa II: Betty Lou Allen; St. Ignatius: Edward Matthews (2); St. Cecelia: Leontyne Price; St. Electra: Ida Johnson; St. Jan: George Goodman; St. Chavez: Rawn Spearman (3); St. Eustace: Charles Colman; St. Vincent: Rayfield du Bard; Male Saints: Rayfield du Bard, George Goodman, Charles Colman, William Hughes, Hugh Hurd, Kelsey Pharr, George Royston, Jesse Williams, Nat Wright, Ned Wright, James Young, Curtis Hawkins; Female Saints: Adelaide Boatner, Yvonne Cummings, Billie Daniel, Gloria Davy, Olga James, Ida Johnson, Vera Little, Mary Robbs, Dorothy Ross, Mae Williams, Gloria Wynder; Dancers: Billie Allen, Robert Curtis, Carolyn Jorrin, Louis Johnson, Arthur Mitchell, Helen Taitt.

Prelude: A narrative of Prepare for Saints. *Act I*: Avila; St. Theresa half indoors and half out of doors. *Act II*: Might it be mountains if it were not Barcelona. *Act III*: Barcelona; St. Ignatius and One of Two Liberally. *Act IV*: The Saints and Sisters re-assembled and re-enacting why they went away to stay.

The show got generally favorable reviews.

After Broadway. New York State Theatre, 8/1/96–8/3/96. 4 performances. A Houston Grand Opera production, presented by Lincoln Center Festival 96; New Concept/Director/Sets: Robert Wilson; Costumes: Francesco Clemente; Lighting: Jennifer Tipton & Robert Wilson; Conductor: Dennis Russell Davies. *Cast:* Commere: Marietta Simpson; Compere: Wilbur Pauley; St. Theresa I: Ashley Putnam; St. Theresa II: Suzanna Guzman; St. Ignatius: Sanford Sylvan. *Prelude*: A choral introduction to all the Saints. Act I: On the steps of Avila Cathedral. "A Pageant, or Sunday School entertainment." *Act II*: A garden party in the country near Barcelona. *Act III*: A monastery garden on the coast near Barcelona. *Act IV*: The Saints in heaven.

232. *Foxy*

Set in Dawson City and elsewhere in the Klondike, about the time of the 1896 gold rush. Foxy Jim Fox tells his three prospector friends that he's discovered gold in the Klondike, and they desert him to catch the first steamboat. To get his revenge Foxy and his friend, con artist Doc, set in motion a scheme whereby Foxy will pretend to be very rich and very ill, and the prospectors will cater to Foxy's every whim in the hopes of sharing his last will and testament.

Before Broadway. It began at the Palace Grand Theatre, Dawson City, Yukon. 7/2/62–8/18/62. 43 performances. Produced by Robert Whitehead & Stanley Gilkey for the Dawson City Festival Foundation, in association with the Canadian Theatre Exchange. They had been invited to open the 1962 Canadian Gold Rush Festival. Beatrice Lillie introduced the show on opening night. It played to largely empty houses (the theatre was hard to get to). Robert Whitehead would quit in order to form the Repertory Theatre of Lincoln Center. Director: Robert Lewis; Choreographer: Matt Mattox; Sets/Costumes/Lighting: Ben Edwards; Musical Director: Joseph Lewis; Orchestrations: Eddie Sauter; Press: Sol Jacobson; Stage Manager: William King. *Cast:* Doc: Larry Blyden; Foxy: Bert Lahr; Bedrock: Ralph Dunn; Buzzard: Edward Greenhalgh; Shortcut: Jack Bittner; Drunk: Tony Kraber; Mountie: Bill Becker; Brandy: Buzz Halliday; Celia: Kit Smythe; Stirling: Scott Merrill; Rottingham: Robin Craven; Ben: Bill Hayes; Chorus: Jean Hilzinger, Michele Karaty, Nina Armagh, Joan Jaffe, Audrey Saxon, Mary Ann Corrigan, Will Parkins, Jerry Blair, Todd Butler, John Waller, Jerry Michael, Fred Jayne.

Billy Rose was the original producer of the Broadway run, but after he and the director clashed, David Merrick took it on. Mr. Merrick threatened to close in Detroit, where Jerome Robbins had been helping out, but when his investors threatened to sue, he carried on with it.

The Broadway Run. Ziegfeld Theatre, 2/16/64–4/18/64. 72 performances. Presented by David Merrick; Music: Robert Emmett Dolan; Lyrics: Johnny Mercer; Book: Ian McLellan Hunter & Ring Lardner Jr.; Suggested by the 1606 satirical play *Volpone*, by Ben Jonson; Director: Robert Lewis; Choreographer: Jack Cole; Sets/Lighting: Robert Randolph; Costumes: Robert Fletcher; Musical Director/Vocal Arrangements: Donald Pippin; Orchestrations: Edward Sauter & Hal Schaefer; Dance Music Arrangements: Hal Schaefer; Press: Lee Solters, Harvey B. Sabinson, David Powers, Bob Ullman; General Manager: Jack Schlissel; Company Manager: Emanuel Azenberg; Production Stage Manager: Perry Bruskin; Stage Manager: Henry Velez; Assistant Stage Manager: John Hallow. *Cast:* Doc Mosk, a confidence man: Larry Blyden (2); Foxy, a veteran prospector: Bert Lahr (1); Foxy's (three) partners: Bedrock: Robert H. Harris (7); Buzzard: Edward Greenhalgh; Shortcut: Gerald Hiken (6); Drunk: Tony Kraber; Mountie: John Hallow; Brandy, a saloon-keeper in her early thirties: Cathryn Damon (4); Oliver: Will Parkins; Celia, a girl in her twenties: Julienne Marie (3); 1st Prospector: Newt Sullivan; 2nd Prospector: Eddie James; 3rd Prospector: Herb Fields; Inspector Stirling, the voice of authority in Dawson: David Rounds; 1st Eskimo: John Waller; 2nd Eskimo: John Aristedes; Lord Rottingham, British aristocrat-adventurer: Anthony Kemble-Cooper (8); Clergyman: John Taliaferro; Ben, Bedrock's son: John Davidson (5); Laurette: Mary Ann Corrigan; Marie: Constance Meng; Bellboy: John Taliaferro; Prospectors: John Aristedes, Carlos Bas, Charles Cagle, George Del Monte, Lang Des Jardins, Herbert Fields, Tim Harum, Lee Howard, Eddie James, John Keatts, Robert La Crosse, Will Parkins, Newt Sullivan, John Taliaferro, John Waller; Saloon Girls: Helen Baisley, Mary Ann Corrigan, Virginia Craig, Judith Dunford, Alice Glenn, Marlena Lustik, Ethel Martin, Constance Meng, Nancy Myers, Shelly Rann, Suanne Shirley, June Eve Story, Susan Terry. **Standby:** Foxy: Loney Lewis. **Understudies:** Doc: David Rounds; Celia: Constance Meng; Ben: John Keatts; Brandy: Virginia Craig; Bedrock/Buzzard/Shortcut: Tony Kraber; Stirling: John Hallow. *Act I: Scene 1* Trading post, Alaska; *Scene 2* Brandy's saloon; *Scene 3* Buzzard's cabin; *Scene 4* Buzzard's cabin; *Scene 5* Steamboat landing; *Scene 6* Buzzard's cabin; *Scene 7* Brandy's saloon. *Act II: Scene 1* Outside the hotel; *Scene 2* Hotel room; *Scene 3* Outside the hotel; *Scene 4* Buzzard's cabin; *Scene 5* Front Street—saloon; *Scene 6* Brandy's office; *Scene 7* Brandy's saloon. *Act I:* Prologue (Doc), "Share and Share Alike" (Bedrock, Buzzard, Shortcut) [dropped for Broadway], "A Child of the Wild" (Foxy) [dropped for Broadway], "Share and Share Alike" (reprise) [Bedrock, Buzzard, Shortcut] [dropped for Broadway], "Many Ways to Skin a Cat" (Foxy & Doc), "Rollin' in Gold" (Brandy & Ensemble), "My Weight in Gold" (Celia) [added after the Dawson City run], "Money isn't Everything" (Foxy, Doc, Bedrock, Shortcut, Buzzard, Ensemble), "Larceny and Love" (Brandy & Doc), "Many Ways to Skin a Cat" (reprise) (Foxy & Doc) [dropped for Broadway], "(S.S. *Commodore*) *Ebenezer McAfee III*" (Ensemble), "Talk to Me, Baby" (Celia & Doc) [this replaced Celia & Ben's number here: "The Power of Love," and Ben's reprise of it that came immediately after it],

"(This is) My Night to Howl" (Shortcut, Ben, Ensemble) [this replaced Brandy & Celia's number here: "Take it from a Lady"], "Bon Vivant" (Foxy & Ensemble) [the showstopper, with Bert Lahr posing as an English lord, dressed in a mauve suit, deerstalker hat and yellow gaiters], Finale Act I (Ensemble), "(S.S. *Commodore) Ebenezer McAfee III* (reprise) [dropped for Broadway]. *Act II*: Entr'acte; Opening Dance (Ensemble), "It's Easy When You Know How" (Doc) [this replaced Celia & Ensemble's number here: "Life's Darkest Moment"], "Run, Run, Run Cinderella" (Celia) [added after the Dawson City run], "Talk to Me, Baby" (reprise) (Ben) [hit song] [this replaced Ben's reprise of "Life's Darkest Moment"], "I'm Way Ahead of the Game" (Brandy & Doc) [this replaced Brandy & Doc's number here: "Till it Goes Outta Style"], "A Case of Rape" (Celia, Ben, Ensemble) [this replaced Stirling & Ensemble's number here: "The Letter of the Law"], "In Loving Memory" (Foxy, Doc, Bedrock, Shortcut, Buzzard, Ensemble), Finale (Foxy, Doc, Ensemble).

The Broadway production was Bert Lahr's last stage appearance, and he fought constantly with the writers (who hated his improvs), with Robert Lewis, the director (who couldn't control him), and with his co-star Larry Blyden (who wanted changes in the script). On opening night David Merrick sold his 30 per cent interest in the show to Billy Rose for $10,000, and went off to make *Hello, Dolly!* Billy Rose owned the Ziegfeld, where *Foxy* was playing. Reviews for Bert Lahr were great, but divided for the show. Mr. Lahr won a Tony, and Julienne Marie was nominated. The show lost $400,000 in Dawson City, and another $350,000 on Broadway.

After Broadway. 14TH STREET Y, NYC, 12/5/00–12/17/00. 16 PERFORMANCES. Concert. Part of the *Musicals Tonight!* series. PRESENTED BY Mel Miller; DIRECTOR: Thomas Mills; MUSICAL DIRECTOR: Robert Felstein. *Cast*: FOXY: Rudy Roberson; BRANDY: Jessica Frankel; CELIA: Natasha Harper; DOC: Rob Lorey; BEDROCK: David Sabella; SHORTCUT: Jay Brian Winnick. Prologue, "Respectability," "Many Ways to Skin a Cat," "Rollin' in Gold," "Money isn't Everything," "Larceny and Love," "S.S. *Commodore Ebenezer McAfee III*," "The Honeymoon is Over," "Talk to Me, Baby," "My Night to Howl," "Bon Vivant," "It's Easy When You Know How," "Run, Run, Cinderella," "I'm Way Ahead of the Game," "The Letter of the Law," "In Loving Memory," Finale.

233. *Frank Merriwell (or Honor Challenged)*

Set in about 1896. The play opens with students of Fardale College awaiting the arrival by train of Frank, a high-minded and heroic college student. Three girls march in with placards proclaiming Fardale "unfair to women." Manuel is a Spanish spy. Burt Standish's novels and short stories about Frank Merriwell were very popular.

The Broadway Run. LONGACRE THEATRE, 4/24/71. 7 previews from 4/19/71. 1 PERFORMANCE. PRESENTED BY Sandy Farber & Stanley Barnett, in association with Nate Friedman; MUSIC/LYRICS: Skip Redwine & Larry Frank; BOOK: Skip Redwine, Larry Frank, Heywood Gould; BASED ON the 1896 dime novel *Frank Merriwell, or First Days at Farwell*, by Burt L. Standish (i.e. William Gilbert Patten); DIRECTOR/CHOREOGRAPHER: Neal Kenyon; SETS: Tom John; COSTUMES: Frank Thompson; LIGHTING: John Gleason; SOUND CONSULTANTS: Sound Associates; MUSICAL DIRECTOR/VOCAL ARRANGEMENTS: Jack Lee; ORCHESTRATIONS: Arnold Goland; CONDUCTOR/DANCE MUSIC ARRANGEMENTS: Jack Holmes; PRESS: Seymour Krawitz, Martin Shwartz, Patricia McLean Krawitz; GENERAL MANAGER: Elias Goldin; COMPANY MANAGER: Barry Hoffman; PRODUCTION STAGE MANAGER: Don Lamb; STAGE MANAGER: James Bernardi. *Cast*: CLYDE: J.J. Jepson; NED: Larry Ross; HUGH: Walter Bobbie (2); BELINDA BELLE SNODD: Neva Small (5); SNELLA JEAN: Lori Cesar; UNA MARIE: Ellie Smith; PROF. BURRAGE: Thomas Ruisinger; MRS. SNODD: Liz Sheridan (4); ESTHER CARMICHAEL: Jennifer Williams; BART HODGE: Peter Shawn; TAD JONES: Gary Keith Steven; FRANK MERRIWELL: Larry Ellis (1); INZA BURRAGE: Linda Donovan; MANUEL: Bill Hinnant (3). *Part I*: *Chapter 1* The Blow of a Coward — Fardale train station: "There's No School Like Our School" (Students & Local Girls), "Howdy, Mr. Sunshine" (Frank &

Tad); *Chapter 2* Death at the Picnic — The picnic grounds: "Prim and Proper" (Students & Local Girls), "Inza" (Frank); *Chapter 3* Explosion in Tunnel G — Fardale Caves; *Chapter 4* War! — Mrs. Snodd's boarding house: "Look for the Happiness Ahead" (Frank & All); *Chapter 5* The Spanish Spy — Professor's laboratory; *Chapter 6* By Fair Means or Foul — Mrs. Snodd's boarding house: "I'd Be Crazy to Be Crazy Over You" (Belinda Belle & Bart); *Chapter 7* Terror at the Junction — The picnic grounds: "Now it's Fall" (Students), "The Fallin'-Out-of-Love Rag" (Belinda Belle, Students, Local Girls), Frank; *Part II*: *Chapter 1* A Hatred Grows — The picnic grounds: "Frank, Frank, Frank" (All); *Chapter 2* Waterloo — On the campus: "In Real Life" (Frank), "The Broadway of My Heart" (Professor & Mrs. Snodd); *Chapter 3* Into the Enemy's Hands — The picnic grounds: "Winter's Here" (Students), "The Pure in Heart" (Frank & All), "I Must Be Crazy" (Belinda Belle), "Don't Turn His Picture to the Wall" (Tad, Students, Local Girls); *Chapter 4* Frank is Missing — Burrage front porch; *Chapter 5* Death by Dynamite — Fardale Caves: "Manuel Your Friend" (Manuel), "The Pure in Heart" (reprise) (Fran & All), Finale: "Look for the Happiness Ahead"(reprise) (All).

The show was panned on Broadway, although Bill Hinnant got good reviews.

After Broadway. CLEVELAND PLAY HOUSE, Ohio, 12/25/71. 36 PERFORMANCES. DIRECTOR: George Touliatos. *Cast*: John Everson, William Watson.

234. *The Frogs*

A 405 B.C. comedy. The time is the present. The place is Ancient Greece. A debate between Aeschylus and Euripides to determine who is the greater artist. The winner returns to earth with Dionysos in order to save civilization.

Before Broadway. It began at YALE REP, 5/20/74. It had a limited run of 15 PERFORMANCES. At that stage it was a special 40-minute one-act comedy musical performed in the swimming pool at Yale. MUSIC/LYRICS: Stephen Sondheim; BASED ON Aristophanes' comedy; FREELY ADAPTED BY/DIRECTOR: Burt Shevelove; the words of William Shakespeare & George Bernard Shaw were selected and arranged from their works by Michael Feingold (the musical is a contest between Shakespeare and Shaw, to see which one is better; Aristophanes had Aeschylus & Euripides); CHOREOGRAPHER: Carmen de Lavallade; SETS: Michael H. Yeargan; COSTUMES: Jeanne Button; MUSICAL DIRECTOR: Don Jennings; ORCHESTRATIONS: Jonathan Tunick. *Cast*: DIONYSOS: Larry Blyden; XANTHIAS: Michael Vale; CHARON: Charles Levin; PLUTO: Jerome Dempsey; SHAKESPEARE: Jeremy Geidt; SHAW: Anthony Holland; CHORUS: Dan Desmond, Ron Recasner, Alvin Epstein, Carmen de Lavallade, Stephen R. Lawson, Alma Cuervo, Christopher Durang, Meryl Streep, Sigourney Weaver. Fanfare, "Prologue: Invocation and Instructions to the Audience," Traveling Music, "Parados: The Frogs," "Hymons: Evoe!," Dialogue: Pluto," "Parabasis: It's Only a Play!," "Dialogue: That Was Some Banquet!," "Evoe for the Dead," "Invocation to the Muses," "Fear No More," "Exodos: The Sound of Poets."

CHICAGO, 1988. PRESENTED BY Pegasus Players.

OLD BRENTFORD SWIMMING POOL, London, from 7/24/90. *Cast*: Richard Zajdlic, Bob Husson, John Sheppard, Geoff Saunders, Rory Johnstone.

It was due to be performed at the National Theatre, London in 11/02, in concert, but had to be canceled because a fully-staged production was scheduled in New York in 2003.

An unrelated production was due to run at Truman College, 4/8/04–5/25/04, again produced by the non–Equity Pegasus Players, but they canceled due to the conflict with the Lincoln Center production, and replaced it with *Anyone Can Whistle*.

As for the Lincoln Center production — the subject of this entry. After a successful concert version of The Frogs on 5/22/02, Nathan Lane approached Steve Sondheim about doing a new version. Mr. Lane himself expanded the show and re-wrote about four-fifths of Burt Shevelove's original book. A reading was done at Lincoln Center Theatre in 1/03, with Nathan Lane. DIRECTOR/CHOREOGRAPHER: Susan Stroman. Broadway previews were scheduled to begin on 6/17/04, but that date was put back to 6/22/04, and the opening date was put back from 7/15/04 to 7/22/04. Steve Sondheim wrote six new songs for this production. During Broadway previews the length of the show was trimmed from almost three hours. On 7/11/04, only a few days before the show officially opened on Broadway, it was announced that Roger Bart had replaced Chris Kattan. Xanthias' role was being diminished, and Mr. Kattan got upset, and was fired. Understudy Timothy Gulan went on from 7/12/04 while Mr. Bart was rehearsing his role. Mr. Bart became Xanthias on 7/15/04.

The Broadway Run. VIVIAN BEAUMONT THEATRE, 7/22/04–10/9/04. 34 previews from 6/22/04. PRESENTED BY Lincoln Center Theatre, in association with Bob Boyett; MUSIC/LYRICS: Stephen Sondheim; ORIGINAL BOOK: Burt Shevelove; NEW BOOK: Nathan Lane; FREELY ADAPTED from Aristophanes' comedy by Burt Shevelove, and even more freely by Nathan Lane; DIRECTOR/CHOREOGRAPHER: Susan Stroman; ASSOCIATE DIRECTOR/ASSOCIATE CHOREOGRAPHER: Tara Young; SETS: Giles Cadle; COSTUMES: William Ivey Long; LIGHTING: Kenneth Posner; SOUND: Scott Lehrer; MUSICAL DIRECTOR: Paul Gemignani; ORCHESTRATIONS: Jonathan Tunick; DANCE MUSIC ARRANGEMENTS: Glen Kelly; CAST RECORDING: on PS Classics, made on 10/12/04 and released on 1/25/05; PRESS: Philip Rinaldi; CASTING: Tara Rubin; PUPPET DESIGN: Martin P. Robinson; AERIAL DESIGN: Antigravity, Inc.; GENERAL MANAGER: Adam Siegel; COMPANY MANAGER: Matthew Markoff; STAGE MANAGER: Thom Widmann; ASSISTANT STAGE MANAGERS: Scott Taylor Rollison & Sarah Marie Elliot. *Cast:* DIONYSOS: Nathan Lane, *Timothy Gulan* (stood in, 9/1/04); XANTHIAS, THE SLAVE: Roger Bart; HERAKLES: Burke Moses; CHARON/AEAKOS: John Byner; PLUTO: Peter Bartlett; GEORGE BERNARD SHAW: Daniel Davis; WILLIAM SHAKESPEARE: Michael Siberry; A GREEK CHORUS/A SPLASH OF FROGS/A REVEL OF DIONYSIANS: Ryan L. Ball, Bryn Dowling, Rebecca Eichenberger, Meg Gillentine, Pia C. Glenn, Tyler Hanes, Francesca Harper, Rod Harrelson, Jessica Howard, Naomi Kakuk, Kenway Hon Wai K Kua, Luke Longacre, David Lowenstein, Kathy Voytko, Steve Wilson, Jay Brian Winnick; FIRE BELLY BOUNCING FROGS: Ryan L. Ball & Luke Longacre; THREE GRACES: Meg Gillentine, Jessica Howard, Naomi Kakuk; HANDMAIDEN CHARISMA: Bryn Dowling; VIRILLA, THE AMAZON: Pia G. Glenn; ARIADNE: Kathy Voytko; PLUTO'S HELLRAISERS: Bryn Dowling, Meg Gillentine, Francesca Harper, Jessica Howard, Naomi Kakuk; SHAVIANS: Rebecca Eichenberger, Meg Gillentine, Tyler Hanes, Francesca Harper, David Lowenstein, Jay Brian Winnick. *Understudies:* Dionysos/Xanthias: Timothy Gulan & Jay Brian Winnick; Ariadne/Charisma: Meg Gillentine & Mia Price; Herakles: Ryan L. Ball & Steve Wilson; Shaw/Shakespeare: Steve Wilson & Eric Michael Gillett; Pluto: Eric Michael Gillett & Timothy Gulan; Virilla: Meg Gillentine & Francesca Harper; Charon/Aeakos: David Lowenstein & Jay Brian Winnick. *Swings:* James Brown III, Eric Michael Gillett, Timothy Gulan, Joanne Manning, Mia Price. *The Orchestra:* CONCERTMISTRESS: Marilyn Reynolds; VIOLIN: Mineko Yajima; VIOLA: Richard Brice; CELLO: Deborah Sepe; 1ST CLARINET: Les Scott; 2ND CLARINET: Eric Weidman; 1ST BASSOON: Tom Sefcovic; 2ND BASSOON: Gili Sharett; 1ST TRUMPET: Dominic Derasse; 2ND TRUMPET: Phil Granger; 1ST TROMBONE: Richard Clark; 2ND TROMBONE: Mike Boschen; BASS TROMBONE: Dean Plank; PIANO: AnnBritt duChateau; HARP: Jennifer Hoult; BASS: John Beal; DRUMS: Paul Pizzuti; PERCUSSION: Paul Pizzuti & Thad Wheeler. *Act I:* **Prologue** Onstage at the Vivian Beaumont: Invocation and Instructions to the Audience (1st Actor, 2nd Actor, Greek Chorus); *Scene 1* Ancient Greece: "I Love to Travel" (Dionysos, Xanthias, Greek Chorus); *Scene 2* The house of Herakles: "Dress Big" (Herakles, Dionysos, Xanthias); *Scene 3* The banks of the River Styx: "I Love to Travel" (reprise) (Dionysos & Xanthias), "All Aboard" (Charon); *Scene 4* On the River Styx: "Ariadne" (Dionysos), "The Frogs" (Dionysos, A Splash of Frogs, Fire Belly Bouncing Frogs). *Act II:* *Scene 1* On the River Styx; *Scene 2* On the shore of Hades; *Scene 3* A myrtle grove in Hades: Hymn to Dionysos (Three Graces, Dionysians, Dionysos, Xanthias); *Scene 4* Outside the palace of Pluto; *Scene 5* The palace of Pluto: "Hades" (Pluto & The Hellraisers), "It's Only a Play" (Greek Chorus); *Scene 6* Outside the palace of Pluto; *Scene 7* Outside the palace of Pluto: "Shaw" (Dionysos, Shaw, Shavians), "All Aboard" (reprise) (Charon), "Fear No More" (lyrics from Shakespeare's *Cymbeline*) (Shakespeare); *Scene 8* Return from Hades: Hymn to Dionysos (reprise) (Greek Chorus), Final Instructions to the Audience (Dionysos & Company).

Broadway reviews were mixed. The show was originally going to run until 10/3/04, but extended to 10/9/04. During the 9/1/04 matinee Nathan Lane was injured in Act I, and had to be replaced for the rest of that performance, and for the evening performance, by Timothy Gulan. In 1/05 the Tony Awards Committee ruled it a new musical.

235. *From A to Z*

A musical revue. It was the Broadway debut of Jerry Herman, Fred Ebb, and Woody Allen.

Before Broadway. The Mastersons, Houston oil millionaires (Harris was Pete Masterson's cousin) replaced Anthony Brady Farrell as producers.

The Broadway Run. PLYMOUTH THEATRE, 4/20/60–5/7/60. 21 PERFORMANCES. PRESENTED BY Carroll & Harris Masterson; MUSIC/LYRICS/SKETCHES: various authors; DIRECTOR: Christopher Hewett; CHOREOGRAPHER: Ray Harrison; SETS/COSTUMES/LIGHTING: Fred Voelpel; MUSICAL DIRECTOR/VOCAL ARRANGEMENTS: Milton Greene; ORCHESTRATIONS: Jay Brower & Jonathan Tunick; DANCE MUSIC ARRANGEMENTS: Jack Holmes; PRESS: Irvin Dorfman & Jane Randall; GENERAL MANAGER: Al Goldin; PRODUCTION STAGE MANAGER: Fred Hearn; STAGE MANAGER: Joseph Olney; ASSISTANT STAGE MANAGER: Edwin Aldridge. *Act I: A.* "Best Gold" (m/l: Jerry Herman) [Hermione Gingold (1), Nora Kovach (5), Kelly Brown (6), Michael Fesco, Doug Spingler, Beryl Towbin, Virginia Vestoff, Stuart Damon, Paula Stewart (7)]; *B.* Bardolatry [Louise Hoff (4) & Elliott Reid (2)]; *C.* "Pill Parade" (m/l: Jay Thompson): NARRATOR: Alvin Epstein (3); AVERAGE MAN: Kelly Brown (6); VITAMINS: Michael Fesco & Doug Spingler; BENZABANG: Beryl Towbin; PILLTOWN: Virginia Vestoff; SEXAPHINE: Nora Kovach (5); ONE MORE PILL: Isabelle Farrell; *D.* "Togetherness" (m/l: Dickson Hughes & Everett Sloane): GRANDMOTHER: Hermione Gingold (1); FATHER: Elliott Reid (2); MOTHER: Louise Hoff (4); DAUGHTER: Paula Stewart (7); SON: Stuart Damon; *E.* Psychological Warfare (by Woody Allen): SERGEANT: Alvin Epstein (3); PRIVATES: Larry Hovis & Doug Spingler; ENEMY: Bob Dishy; MEDICS: Stuart Damon & Michael Fesco; *F.* "Balloons" (m/l: Jack Holmes) [Nora Kovach (5), Kelly Brown (6), Michael Fesco, Doug Spingler, Beryl Towbin, Virginia Vestoff]; *G.* Music Talk [Hermione Gingold (1)]; *H.* "Hire a Guy" (m: Mary Rodgers; l: Marshall Barer): THE STAR: Louise Hoff (4); THE DIRECTOR: Elliott Reid (2); THE WRITER: Stuart Damon; PATSY: Bob Dishy; *I.* "Interlude" (m: Jack Holmes): LADIES: Beryl Towbin, Virginia Vestoff, Isabelle Farrell; GENTLEMEN: Kelly Brown (6), Michael Fesco, Doug Spingler; A STRANGER: Nora Kovach (5); A MAN: Stuart Damon; *J.* Hit Parade (by Woody Allen): GIRL: Hermione Gingold (1); BOY: Alvin Epstein (3); *K.* Conventional Behavior [Elliott Reid (2)]; *L.* "I Said to Love" (m: Paul Klein; l: Fred Ebb) [Louise Hoff (4)]; *M.* Winter in Palm Springs (by Herbert Farjeon): COLONEL SPICER: Alvin Epstein (3); MRS. TWICEOVER: Hermione Gingold (1); ALICE: Beryl Towbin; *N.* "Charlie" (m: Norman Martin; l: Fred Ebb) [Paula Stewart (7)]; *O.* "The Sound of Schmaltz" (m: William Dyer; l: Don Parks) (spoof of *The Sound of Music.* We find the heroine under a mountain tree with one leg in the air. She sings her way into the hearts of seven young monsters, children of Baron von Klaptrap, to whom she becomes nanny). *Cast of Characters:* HEAD NANNY: Louise Hoff (4); NANNIES: Nora Kovach (5), Beryl Towbin, Virginia Vestoff, Isabelle Farrell; ALICE CADWALLADER-SMITH: Hermione Gingold (1); BARON VON KLAPTRAP: Elliott Reid (2); CHILDREN: Kelly Brown (6), Alvin Epstein (3), Michael Fesco, Doug Spingler, Stuart Damon, Bob Dishy, Paula Stewart (7). *Synopsis of Scenes:* 1. The offices of "International Nannies, Ltd." (with an interlude in Central Park); 2. The von Klaptrap nursery; 3. Baron von Klaptrap's apartment; 4. The von Klaptrap living room. *Act II: P.* "Grand Jury Jump" (m: Paul Klein; l: Fred Ebb) [Nora Kovach (5), Paula Stewart (7), Beryl Towbin, Virginia Vestoff, Isabelle Farrell, Kelly Brown (6), Stuart Damon, Michael Fesco, Doug Spingler, Larry Hovis]; *Q.* "South American Way" (m: Norman Martin; l: Mr. Martin & Fred Ebb) [Alvin Epstein (3) & Bob Dishy]; *R.* Snapshots (by Herbert Farjeon): SHE: Hermione Gingold (1); HE: Elliott Reid (2); *S.* "Time Step" (m: Paul Klein; l: Fred Ebb) [Kelly Brown (6)]; *T.* Bobo [Elliott Reid (2)]; *U.* "Queen of Song" (m/l: Eric Maschwitz & Jack Strachey) [Hermione Gingold (1)]; *V.* Surprise Party (by Woody Allen) (two young men at a party where all the girls look like

Groucho Marx, except one, who looks like Harpo): FRED: Bob Dishy; HARRY: Kelly Brown (6); MYRNA: Louise Hoff (4); LINDA: Beryl Towbin; RUTHIE: Nora Kovach (5); RITA: Isabelle Farrell; VIRGINIA: Virginia Vestoff; BLONDE: Paula Stewart (7); *W.* "Countermelody" (m: Mary Rodgers & Jay Thompson; l: Marshall Barer) [Paula Stewart (7) & Stuart Damon]. Note: during tryouts this replaced On the Beach (devised by Mark Epstein & Christopher Hewett) (performed by Alvin Epstein); *X.* Park Meeting (by Nina Warner Hook): GOVERNESS: Hermione Gingold (1); WOMAN: Louise Hoff (4); *Y.* "Red Shoes" (m: Jack Holmes): INTRODUCED BY: Bob Dishy; DANCED BY: Isabelle Farrell, Kelly Brown (6) [dropped during tryouts], Michael Fesco, Larry Hovis, Doug Spingler, Beryl Towbin, Virginia Vestoff; *Z.* "Four for the Road" (m: Paul Klein; l: Lee Goldsmith & Fred Ebb) [Hermione Gingold (1)]; & "What Next?" (m: Charles Zwar; l: Alan Melville) (Company).

It got very bad reviews.

236. *The Full Monty*

The British movie upon which the American stage musical was based was set in Sheffield. The musical transfers the action to Buffalo, NY. Six out-of-work blue collar workers decide to pay a few bills by stripping. "The Full Monty" is reputed to be a British expression, indicating "all the way." Jerry is the brains, and wants to impress his son. The names of the characters were Americanized for the stage musical. A few characters were added (i.e. they were not in the movie): Keno, a gay stripper, and the boys' many-times-married rehearsal pianist, Jeanette. Dave is overweight, and his sensitivity over this problem is causing havoc with his marriage. Harold is a former mill supervisor, who can't tell his wife he's lost his job.

Before Broadway. New Zealanders Anthony McCarten and Stephen Sinclair wrote the straight comedy *Ladies Night!* First performed in New Zealand in 1987, it became the biggest box-office hit ever in that country. In 1997, when the British movie *The Full Monty* became so successful, the writers of *Ladies Night!*, which had a story very similar to that of the film, unsuccessfully sued the producers of the film for $200 million (i.e. all the profits). *Ladies Night!* was put on at the NEW YORKER THEATRE, Toronto, again as a straight play, but this time called *A Live Full Monty*. However, 20th–Century Fox asked them not to use the term "Full Monty" in the title, as the film studio owned the rights. The show closed on 1/31/99. There was more to come from *Ladies Night!*.

The Full Monty, as a stage musical version of the movie, premiered at THE OLD GLOBE, San Diego, 6/1/00–7/9/00. Previews from 5/23/00. It got good reviews, and set box-office records. The closing date was extended from 7/2/00 to 7/9/00. Florence Stanley was originally going to play Jeanette, but Kathleen Freeman stepped in at the last moment. Nathan was played by Adam Covalt & Thomas Michael Fiss. The Reg Willoughby character was at that stage called Carroll Crosby (the name was changed during this stint). The cast and crew were the same as for the subsequent Broadway run, except SOUND: Jeff Ladman. After a sneak preview on 9/12/00, it began Broadway previews on 9/25/00 (date pushed forward from 9/26/00).

The Broadway Run. EUGENE O'NEILL THEATRE, 10/26/00–9/1/02. 36 previews from 9/25/00. 769 PERFORMANCES. PRESENTED BY Fox Searchlight Pictures, Lindsey Law, Thomas Hall; MUSIC/LYRICS: David Yazbek; BOOK: Terrence McNally; BASED ON the 1997 British movie of the same name, written by Simon Beaufoy; DIRECTOR: Jack O'Brien; CHOREOGRAPHER: Jerry Mitchell; SETS: John Arnone; COSTUMES: Robert Morgan; LIGHTING: Howell Binkley; SOUND: Tom Clark; MUSICAL DIRECTOR/VOCAL & INCIDENTAL MUSIC ARRANGEMENTS: Ted Sperling; ORCHESTRATIONS: Harold Wheeler; DANCE MUSIC ARRANGEMENTS: Zane Mark; CAST RECORDING on RCA, made on 10/30/00, and released on 12/12/00; PRESS: Barlow — Hartman Public Relations; CASTING: Liz Woodman; GENERAL MANAGER: The Charlotte Wilcox Company; COMPANY MANAGER: Dave Harris, *Matthew Markoff*; PRODUCTION STAGE MANAGER: Nancy Harrington; STAGE MANAGER: Julie Baldauff, *Steven R. Gruse*; ASSISTANT STAGE MANAGER: Matthew Aaron

Stern. ***Cast:*** GEORGIE BUKATINSKY: Annie Golden; BUDDY "KENO" WALSH: Denis Jones; REG WILLOUGHBY: Todd Weeks, *Sal Viviano (from 8/20/01)*; JERRY LUKOWSKI: Patrick Wilson (until 11/4/01), *Will Chase (from 11/6/01)*; DAVE BUKATINSKY: John Ellison Conlee, *Daniel Stewart Sherman (from 11/20/01)*; MALCOLM MACGREGOR: Jason Danieley, *Jay Douglas, Danny Gurwin (from 11/20/01)*; ETHAN GIRARD: Romain Fruge, *Chris Diamantopoulos (from 11/20/01)*; NATHAN LUKOWSKI: Thomas Michael Fiss (Tuesdays; Wednesday evenings; Fridays; Saturday matinees), Nicholas Cutro (Mondays; Wednesday matinees; Thursdays; Saturday evenings); NATHAN ALTERNATES: Connor Paolo & Aaron Nutter, *Dennis Michael Hall*; SUSAN HERSHEY: Laura Marie Duncan, *Heidi Blickenstaff (12/01–3/02), Lori Chase*; JOANIE LISH: Jannie Jones; ESTELLE GENOVESE: Liz McConahay, *Sloan Just*; PAM LUKOWSKI: Lisa Datz, *Carol Linnea Johnson*; TEDDY SLAUGHTER: Angelo Fraboni, *James Moye*; MOLLY MACGREGOR: Patti Perkins; HAROLD NICHOLS: Marcus Neville, *Steven Skybell (from 11/20/01)*; VICKI NICHOLS: Emily Skinner, *Andrea Burns (from 4/16/02)*; JEANETTE BURMEISTER: Kathleen Freeman (her last performance was on 8/18/01), *Jane Connell (during Miss Freeman's vacation, from 7/15/01), Patti Perkins (8/20/01–8/24/01), Jane Connell (from 8/25/01)*; NOAH T. "HORSE" SIMMONS: Andre De Shields, *Larry Marshall (from 11/20/01)*; POLICE SERGEANT/MOVING MAN: C.E. Smith; SOCIAL WORKER: Jannie Jones; MINISTER: Jay Douglas, *Kevin M. Burrows*; TONY GIORDANO: Jimmy Smagula. ***Understudies***: Georgie: Laura Marie Duncan, Jannie Jones, Sue-Anne Morrow, *Sloan Just*; Estelle: Laura Marie Duncan & Sue-Anne Morrow, *Sarah Zimmerman, Lori Chase*; Pam: Laura Marie Duncan & Sue-Anne Morrow, *Sarah Zimmerman*; Vicki: Liz McConahay, Laura Marie Duncan, *Heidi Blickenstaff, Lori Chase*; Keno: Angelo Fraboni, *Jay Douglas*; Jerry: Jay Douglas & Matthew Stocke; Malcolm: Jay Douglas & Jason Opsahl; Ethan: Denis Jones & Jason Opsahl; Jeanette: Patti Perkins, *Lori Chase*; Harold: Todd Weeks, *Matthew Stocke*; Dave: Jimmy Smagula; Horse: C.E. Smith & Ronald Wyche. ***Swings***: Sue-Anne Morrow, Jason Opsahl, Matthew Stocke, Ronald Wyche, *Kate Baldwin, Julie Foldesi, Patti Mariano, James Moye, Courtney Young, Leigh Zimmerman*. ***Orchestra***: REEDS: Lino Gomez & Paul Varcesi; TRUMPETS: Bob Millikan & Kevin Batchelor; TROMBONES: Michael Boschen & Herb Besson; KEYBOARDS: Dan Lipton & Zane Mark; GUITAR: Steve Bargonetti; BASS: Chris Smylie; DRUMS: Dean Sharenow; PERCUSSION: Howard Joines. *Act I*: Overture (Orchestra), "Scrap" (Jerry, Dave, Malcolm, Ethan, Reg, Men), "It's a Woman's World" (Georgie, Susan, Joanie, Estelle), "Man" (Jerry & Dave), "Big-Ass Rock" (Jerry, Dave, Malcolm), "Life with Harold" (Vicki), "Big Black Man" (Horse & The Guys), "You Rule My World" (Dave & Harold), "Michael Jordan's Ball" (The Guys). *Act II*: Entr'acte (Orchestra); "Jeanette's Showbiz Number" ("Things Could Be Better") (Jeanette & The Guys), "Breeze off the River" (Jerry), "The Goods" (The Guys & The Women), "You Walk with Me" (Malcolm & Ethan), "You Rule My World" (reprise) (Georgie & Vicki), "Let it Go" (The Guys & Company).

Unfortunately (in that it got great reviews) it came up against *The Producers* in the 2001 Tony stakes. It was nominated for musical, score, book, direction of a musical, choreography, orchestrations, and for John Ellison Conlee, Andre De Shields, Kathleen Freeman, and Patrick Wilson. Kathleen Freeman died on 8/23/01. Like all other New York shows it was hard hit by the terrorist attack on NYC on 9/11/01. The cast and crew agreed to a 25 per cent pay cut for a couple of weeks, to enable the show to continue. The actors who left the Broadway cast in 11/01 went to London. On 7/10/02 the cast was told that the show was going into its final weeks (this was announced publicly the following day). The Broadway production recouped its $7.5 million investment. It closed at a special matinee. Kathleen Freeman won a Theatre World Award for her part in the show.

After Broadway. TOUR. Opened on 6/6/01 (date put back from 5/22/01), to good reviews, at the Elgin, Toronto. PRESENTED BY Fox Searchlight Pictures, Lindsay Law, and Thomas Hill, in association with Ed & David Mirvish. The tour closed prematurely on 10/27/01, at the Shubert Theatre, Chicago. ***Cast:*** JERRY: Rod Weber, *Christian Anderson, Will Chase*; JEANETTE: Kaye Ballard, *Carol Woods, Jane Connell*; VICKI: Andrea Burns; ETHAN: Chris Diamantopoulos, *Christopher J. Hanke*; GEORGIE: Susann Fletcher; MALCOLM: Danny Gurwin, *Geoffrey Nauffts, Leo Daignault*; PAM: Carol Linnea Johnson; NOAH: Larry Marshall, *Cleavant Derricks, Milton Craig Nealy*; DAVE: Daniel Stewart Sherman, *Michael J. Todaro*; HAROLD: Steven Skybell, *Robert Westenberg*; NATHAN: Brett Murray & Bret Fox; TONY: Erick Buckley; JOANIE: Kimberly Harris; POLICE SERGEANT: Milton Craig Nealy; ALSO WITH: Heidi Blickenstaff, Don Burroughs, Kevin M. Burrows, Julie Foldesi, Patti Mariano, Dana Meller, James Moye, Ryan Perry. *Swings*: David Patrick Ford, Brad Sharp, David A. White.

TEATRO BRANCACCIO, Rome, 12/4/01. DIRECTOR: Gigi Proietti. *Cast*: JERRY: Giampiero Ingrassia; DAVE: Rodolfo Lagana. There was an Italian tour.

PRINCE OF WALES THEATRE, London. 3/12/02–11/23/02. Previews from 2/27/02). It got rave reviews. Jerry Hall was in the opening night audience. DIRECTOR: Jack O'Brien; CHOREOGRAPHER: Jerry Mitchell. *Cast*: JERRY: Jarrod Emick, *Ben Richards* (from 9/2/02); JEANETTE: Dora Bryan, *Lynda Baron*; ETHAN: Romain Fruge, *Paul Keating* (from 9/2/02); DAVE: John Ellison Conlee, *David Ganly* (from 9/2/02); MALCOLM: Jason Danieley, *Samuel James* (from 9/2/02); NOAH: Andre De Shields, *Cornell John* (from 9/2/02); HAROLD: Marcus Neville, *Tony Timberlake* (from 9/2/02).

TOUR. Opened at the Ahmanson Theatre, Los Angeles, on 4/24/02. Previews from 4/16/02. PRESENTED BY Kevin McCollum, Jeffrey Seller, Albert Nocciolino; DIRECTOR: Jack O'Brien. *Cast*: JERRY: Christian Anderson; NOAH: Cleavant Derricks; HAROLD: Robert Westenberg; JEANETTE: Carol Woods; KENO: Aaron Lohr; GEORGIE: Jennifer Naimo; REG: Dale Hensley; DAVE: Michael J. Todaro; MALCOLM: Geoffrey Nauffts; ETHAN: Christopher Hanke; NATHAN: Bret Fox & Brett Murray; SUSAN: Victoria Matlock; JOANIE: Kimberly Harris; PAM: Whitney Allen; ESTELLE GENOVESE: Paige DuBois Wolff; MOLLY: Diana Pappas; VICKI: Heidi Blickenstaff; TEDDY: Troy Britton Johnson; SERGEANT: Milton Craig Nealy; MINISTER: Leo Daignault; TONY: Erick Buckley. *Swings*: David Patrick Ford, Christine Hudman, Brad Sharp, David A. White. This tour went to Japan in 8/02, and closed on 6/29/03, at the Ordway, St. Paul, Minn., for summer hiatus, and re-opened 9/2/03, at The Centre, Vancouver.

Ladies Night! Ladies Night! re-surfaced at the COMEDIA THEATRE, Paris, with additional French material by Jacques Collard. It was a big hit, as it had been in Rome, and it won a Moliere Award. It was scheduled to run until 9/15/02, but an off-stage fist-fight between the two leading players, Pierre Corsso (as Manu) and Christian Mulot (as Steph), led to it closing early. Lisette Malidon was also in the cast.

237. *Funny Girl*

About Fanny Brice's rise to stardom, from her childhood, through her discovery by impresario Florenz Ziegfeld, her triumphs in the Ziegfeld Follies, her infatuation with and stormy marriage to gambler and con man Nicky Arnstein, and the break-up of the marriage after Nick has served time in prison. In fact, the opening scene has Fanny in her dressing room backstage at the New Amsterdam Theatre, waiting for Nick who has just got out of prison. She reminisces about her past, starting with her childhood in New York's Lower East Side. She is not pretty, but she is determined to break into showbiz. She auditions unsuccessfully for Kenny, manager of a music hall, but when she sings "I'm the Greatest Star" for vaudevillian hoofer Eddie Ryan, he agrees to coach her. He eventually hires her and she becomes a hit singing "Cornet Man." Nick comes backstage to pay off a debt to Eddie, and meets Fanny. Then she gets an offer from Flo Ziegfeld to appear in his Follies show. She is a success, and Nick comes backstage to congratulate her. She takes him to a Henry Street block party her mother, Mrs. Brice, is throwing to celebrate her success. She has already fallen in love with Nick, but he goes off to Kentucky and they don't meet again until Baltimore, where Fanny is on tour with the Follies. Nick takes her to dinner in a very high-class place and makes love to her. The next day she decides to give up her career and follow Nick, come what may. Act II opens with Nick and Fanny married, and she soon returns

to the stage in a new edition of Follies. She invests in Nick's new casino, but it fails, and he eventually embezzles money in a Wall Street securities deal, and goes to prison for 18 months. Back to the present, and Nick enters. They both realize that the marriage could never be a happy one, and she now determines to go after success. She and Arnstein were divorced. The show does not cover Fanny's Hollywood, radio and TV successes, especially the latter two in which she became a household name playing Baby Snooks. Her third husband was Billy Rose.

Before Broadway. Producer Ray Stark was married to Fanny Brice's daughter, Fran (originally Frances Arnstein), and, even before his mother-in-law died in 1951, he wanted to do a movie biopic of her. In 1960 Isobel Lennart wrote a screenplay called *My Man*. Mr. Stark couldn't sell it to Hollywood, so he went to Broadway with the show as a musical. *Variety* announced on 12/21/60 that Mary Martin would star as Fanny Brice, in a musical to be produced either in the 1961–62 season, or 62–63. David Merrick was to have produced it, and Jerome Robbins was the original director. It was Merrick who suggested the title *Funny Girl*. Until then it had been announced variously as *A Very Special Person*, *My Man*, and *The Luckiest People*. Mary Martin turned down the lead to do *Jennie*. Carol Burnett, Shirley MacLaine, and Eydie Gorme had all been considered also. Fran Stark wanted Anne Bancroft. After seeing Barbra Streisand at the Bon Soir nightclub, Jerry Robbins and Jule Styne insisted on her as the lead. On 12/12/63 Ray Stark confirmed that he had bought out David Merrick's interest and was going to proceed alone. Jerry Robbins left too, to be replaced by Bob Fosse. After seven months (and after casting Miss Streisand), Mr. Fosse quit too, to be replaced by Sidney Lumet, and finally by Garson Kanin. Jule Styne and Stephen Sondheim were offered the score, but Mr. Sondheim didn't want to do just lyrics anymore, so Bob Merrill came on board with Mr. Styne. Apparently Mr. Styne wrote 50 songs for the show. None of the famous Fanny Brice songs were included in the musical—"Rose of Washington Square," "My Man" (m: Maurice Yvain; English l: Channing Pollock), "Second Hand Rose," "I'm an Indian." This was Ray Stark's decision, and it avoided the trap of Miss Streisand becoming merely a Fanny impersonator. Out-of-town tryouts were strenuous, and lasted 15 weeks, with a lot of major script revisions. When the show opened in Boston it was too long, and had Act II troubles. At least five numbers were cut during tryouts: "A Helluva Group," "It's Home," "Took a Little Time," "Sleep Now, Baby Bunting," and "Absent Minded Me." Jerome Robbins later came back to help doctor the show, at which point Garson Kanin quit. The number "People" was a big hit for Barbra Streisand even before the show opened on Broadway. Opening night was postponed five times (the original opening date was going to be 2/13/64), while previews were extended so the crew could work out the problems.

The Broadway Run. WINTER GARDEN THEATRE, 3/26/64–3/12/66; MAJESTIC THEATRE, 3/14/66–11/26/66; BROADWAY THEATRE, 11/28/66–7/1/67. 17 previews from 3/10/64. Total of 1,348 PERFORMANCES. PRESENTED BY Ray Stark, in association with Seven Arts Productions; MUSIC: Jule Styne; LYRICS: Bob Merrill; BOOK: Isobel Lennart; BASED ON Isobel Lennart's unproduced screenplay of the life story of comedienne Fanny Brice (1891–1951); DIRECTOR: Garson Kanin; ASSOCIATE DIRECTOR: Lawrence Kasha; CHOREOGRAPHER: Carol Haney; SETS/LIGHTING: Robert Randolph; COSTUMES: Irene Sharaff; MUSICAL DIRECTOR: Milton Rosenstock, *Paul Cianci* (by 65–66); ORCHESTRATIONS: Ralph Burns; ASSISTANT ARRANGER: Marvin Hamlisch; DANCE MUSIC ORCHESTRATIONS: Luther Henderson; VOCAL ARRANGEMENTS: Buster Davis; CAST RECORDING on Capitol; PRESS: Frank Goodman (*Martin Shwartz* by 64–65), Walter Alford (*Paul Solomon* by 64–65, *Arlene Gordon* by 65–66), *Henry Luhrmann* (by 66–67); PRODUCTION SUPERVISOR: Jerome Robbins; GENERAL MANAGER: Al Goldin; COMPANY MANAGER: John Larson; PRODUCTION STAGE MANAGER: Richard Evans, *William O'Brien* (from 65–66); STAGE MANAGER: Tom Stone, *Daniel Broun* (from 65–66); ASSISTANT STAGE MANAGERS: Joseph Dooley & Robert Howard, *Bill Letters*. *Cast:* FANNY BRICE: Barbra Streisand (1), *Mimi Hines* (from 12/27/65); JOHN, STAGE MANAGER: Robert Howard; EMMA: Royce Wallace; MRS. ROSE BRICE: Kay Medford (3), *Fritzi Burr* (from 65–66); MRS. STRAKOSH: Jean Stapleton, *Paula Laurence* (during

Miss Stapleton's vacation in 64–65), *Fritzi Burr* (from 64–65), *Beulah Garrick* (from 65–66), *Elizabeth Moore* (from 66–67); MRS. MEEKER: Lydia S. Fredericks, *Barbara Ann Walters* (from 65–66), *Sheila Dowling, Karen Ford* (from 66); MRS. O'MALLEY: Joyce O'Neil, *Jeanne McLaren* (from 65–66), *Stephanie Reynolds* (in 67); TOM KEENEY: Joseph Macaulay; EDDIE RYAN: Danny Meehan (4), *Lee Allen* (from 64–65), *Phil Ford* (from 12/27/65); HECKIE: Victor R. Helou, *Richard Ianni* (from 64–65), *Victor R. Helou* (from 65–66), *Ken Richards* (in 67); WORKMEN: Robert Howard & Robert Henson (*Albert Zimmerman* from 65–66; *Hal Norman* from 67); SNUB TAYLOR: Buzz Miller, *Larry Fuller, Bud Spencer* (in 67); TROMBONE SMITTY: Blair Hammond, *Ted Sprague* (from 65–66), *Bud Spencer, John Nola* (in 67); FIVE FINGER FINNEY: Alan E. Weeks, *John D. Richardson* (in 67); TRUMPET SOLOIST: Dick Perry; BUBBLES: Shellie Farrell; POLLY: Joan Lowe; MAUDE: Ellen Halpin, *Edie Cowan* (from 65–66), *Shirley Nelson* (in 67); NICK ARNSTEIN: Sydney Chaplin (2), *George Reeder, Johnny Desmond* (from 7/5/65), *George Reeder* (for 6 weeks in 66–67), *Johnny Desmond*; 1ST SHOWGIRL: Sharon Vaughn, *Joan Cory* (from 65–66), *Barbara Rhoades* (by 66–67), *Virginia Kerr* (in 67); 2ND SHOWGIRL: Diana Lee Nielsen, *Lynette Bennett* (from 65–66); STAGE DIRECTOR: Marc Jordan, *Jim Ray-James* (in 67), *Richard Miller*; FLORENCE ZIEGFELD JR.: Roger De Koven, *Alan Manson* (from 64–65), *William Larsen*; MIMSEY: Sharon Vaughn, *Joan Cory* (from 65–66), *Barbara Rhoades, Virginia Kerr* (in 67); ZIEGFELD TENOR: John Lankston, *Larry Brucker* (from 65–66); ZIEGFELD LEAD DANCER: George Reeder; ADOLPH: John Lankston, *Larry Brucker* (from 65–66); MRS. NADLER: Rose Randolf; PAUL: Larry Fuller, *John Nola* (from 65–66); CATHY: Joan Cory, *Lynette Bennett* (in 67); VERA: Lainie Kazan, *Donna Monroe* (from 65–66); JENNY: Diane Coupe, *Linda Jorgens* (from 65–66), *Lynette Bennett* (in 67); BEN: Buzz Miller; MR. RENALDI: Marc Jordan, *Jim Ray-James* (in 67), *Richard Miller*; MIKE HALSEY: Robert Howard; REPORTERS: Blair Hammond, Albert Zimmerman, Alan Peterson, Victor R. Helou, Stephanie Reynolds; SHOWGIRLS: Prudence Adams (*Barbara London* from 64–65 & gone by 66–67), Joan Cory, Diane Coupe (*Linda Jorgens* from 65–66), Lainie Kazan (*Donna Monroe* from 65–66), Diane Lee Nielsen (*Lynette Bennett* from 65–66), Sharon Vaughn & Rosemarie Yellen (*Virginia Kerr & Barbara Rhoades* from 65–66); SINGERS: Lydia S. Fredericks (*Barbara Ann Walters* from 65–66, *Sheila Dowling, Karen Ford* by 66–67), Victor R. Helou, Robert Henson, Robert Howard, Marc Jordan (*Jim Ray-James* by 66–67; *Richard Miller*), John Lankston (*Larry Brucker* from 65–66), Mary Louise (*Harriet Lawyer* by 66–67), Jeanne McLaren, Joyce O'Neil (gone by 65–66), Rose Randolf, Stephanie Reynolds, Albert Zimmerman. 65–66 replacement: *Janet Moody-Morris* (*Joan Bryant* by 66–67), *Richard Ianni* (in 67); DANCERS: Jose Ahumada (gone by 65–66), Edie Cowan, Christine Dalsey (*Pat Dalsey* from 65–66), Shellie Farrell, Bud Fleming (gone by 66–67), Larry Fuller (*Bud Spencer* by 65–66, *Robert Avian, Jim Smock* by 66–67), Ellen Halpin (gone by 66–67), Blair Hammond (*Ted Sprague* from 65–66), Rosemary Jelincic (*Rosemarie Barre* from 65–66), Karen Kristin (gone by 66–67), Joan Lowe, John Nola, Alan Peterson (gone by 65–66), Alan E. Weeks. 65–66 replacements: *Billy Brandon* (gone by 66–67), *Terry Violino* (gone by 66–67). 66–67 replacements: *Shirley Nelson, Michael Loman, David Moffatt, Gerry Dalton, Ted Sprague* (again). **Understudies**: Fanny: Lainie Kazan, *Linda Gerard* (by 65–66); Nick: George Reeder; Rose: Beulah Garrick; Eddie: Bud Fleming, *Jim Ray-James*; Mrs. Strakosh: Lydia S. Fredericks, *Barbara Ann Walters* (by 65–66), *Sheila Dowling, Karen Ford* (by 66–67); Ziegfeld: *Marc Jordan* (by 65–66), *Albert Zimmerman* (by 66–67); Tom: *Robert Howard* (by 65–66); Emma: *Janet Moody-Morris* (by 65–66), *Joan Bryant* by 66–67; Snub: *Bud Spencer* (by 65–66), *Robert Avian, Jimmy Smock* (by 66–67); Lead dancer: *Ted Sprague* (by 65–66). **Act I**: Overture (Orchestra); *Scene 1* backstage, Fanny's dressing room; about 1910: "If a Girl isn't Pretty" (Mrs. Strakosh, Mrs. Brice, Eddie Ryan, People); *Scene 2* Keeney's Music Hall, backstage: "If a Girl isn't Pretty" (concluded); *Scene 3* In front of Keeney's Music Hall: "I'm the Greatest Star" (Fanny); *Scene 4* A backyard in Fanny's neighborhood; 6 a.m.; *Scene 5* Keeney's Music Hall, on stage: "Cornet Man" (Fanny, Snub Taylor, Keeney Chorus); *Scene 6* Keeney's Music Hall, backstage and the chorus dressing room immediately following; *Scene 7* Mrs. Brice's kitchen; months later: "Who Taught Her Everything?" (Mrs. Brice & Eddie); *Scene 8* The New York Theatre, backstage; *Scene 9* On the stage of the New York Theatre, the grand finale of the Ziegfeld Follies: "(His Love Makes Me) Beautiful" (Tenor, Ziegfeld Girls, Fanny); *Scene 10* In front of the Follies curtain; immediately following: "I Want to Be Seen with You Tonight" (Nick & Fanny); *Scene 11* Outside the house at 24 Henry Street: "Henry Street" (Henry Street Neighbors), "People" (Fanny) [a big hit]; *Scene 12* The interior of Mrs. Brice's saloon; *Scene 13* A private dining room in Baltimore: "You Are Woman, (I Am Man)" (Nick & Fanny); *Scene 14* The Baltimore Railroad Terminal: "Don't Rain on My Parade" (Fanny) [the big hit]. **Act II**: Entr'acte (Orchestra); *Scene 1* The Arnstein Long Island mansion, unfurnished and at night: "Sadie, Sadie" (Fanny & Friends); *Scene 2* Mrs. Brice's saloon: "Find Yourself a Man" (Mrs. Strakosh, Mrs. Brice, Eddie); *Scene 3* The New Amsterdam Theatre, backstage; around 1920: "Rat-Tat-Tat-Tat" (Ziegfeld Company & Fanny); *Scene 4* The New Amsterdam Theatre, on stage: "Rat-Tat-Tat-Tat" (concluded); *Scene 5* Fanny's dressing room; immediately following: "Who Are You Now?" (Fanny); *Scene 6* The study of the Arnstein house; *Scene 7* The New Amsterdam Theatre, a bare stage rehearsal: "The Music that Makes Me Dance" (Fanny); *Scene 8* The New Amsterdam Theatre, backstage, Fanny's dressing room: "Don't Rain on My Parade" (reprise) (Fanny), Finale.

It finally opened to great reviews. Carol Haney, the choreographer, died on 5/10/64, aged 39, after contracting pneumonia in London while staging the London production of *She Loves Me*. When Barbra Streisand suffered from laryngitis, her understudy, Lainie Kazan, got a lot of praise. Syd Chaplin, feuding with Barbra Streisand and Ray Stark, bought his way out of his contract on 6/19/65, for $90,000. He was replaced by Johnny Desmond, and the critics reviewed the show again. Mimi Hines, who succeeded Miss Streisand on 12/27/65, and Phil Ford, who succeeded Danny Meehan as Eddie, were married. The show received Tony nominations for musical, producer of a musical, composer & lyricist, choreography, and for Sydney Chaplin, Barbra Streisand, Danny Meehan, and Kay Medford.

After Broadway. TOUR. Opened on 10/8/65, at the State Fair, Dallas, and closed on 10/29/66, at the Orpheum Theatre, Madison, Wisc. PRESENTED BY Martin Tahse; CHOREOGRAPHER: Larry Fuller; COSTUMES: Stanley Simmons; MUSICAL DIRECTOR: Jack Lee. **Cast**: FANNY: Marilyn Michaels; NICK: Anthony George; MRS. BRICE: Lillian Roth, *Nancy Andrews*; MRS. STRAKOSH: Dena Dietrich; EDDIE: Danny Carroll; BUBBLES: Mary Jane Houdina; POLLY: Marybeth Kurdock.

PRINCE OF WALES THEATRE, London, 4/13/66–7/16/66. 109 PERFORMANCES. The run ended early because Barbra Streisand was pregnant. CHOREOGRAPHER: Larry Fuller. **Cast**: FANNY: Barbra Streisand; NICK: Michael Craig. **Understudy**: Fanny: Lisa Shane (she sometimes stood in for the star).

THE MOVIE. 1968. PRODUCER: Ray Stark; DIRECTOR: William Wyler. The song list was: "I'm the Greatest Star," "If a Girl isn't Pretty," "Roller Skate Rag," "I'd Rather Be Blue Over You," "Beautiful," "People," "You Are Woman," "Don't Rain on My Parade," "Sadie, Sadie," "The Swan," "Funny Girl," "My Man." **Cast**: FANNY: Barbra Streisand (she won an Oscar); NICK: Omar Sharif; ROSE PRICE: Kay Medford; GEORGIA JAMES: Ann Francis; ZIEGFELD: Walter Pidgeon; EDDIE: Lee Allen; MRS. STRAKOSH: Mae Questel. Barbra Streisand made a 1975 movie sequel, *Funny Lady*.

TOUR. Opened on 10/20/68, in Durham, NH, and closed on 3/31/69, at Lynchburg, Va., after 90 cities. PRESENTED BY Michael Mann Productions, in association with Circle Six, by arrangement with Tams-Witmark; DIRECTOR: Michael Mann; CHOREOGRAPHER: Nancy Mann; SETS: Tom Barnes; MUSICAL DIRECTOR: Walter Janes. **Cast**: FANNY: Carmen Natiku & Evalyn Baron; NICK: Wally Russell.

TOUR. Opened on 10/1/96, Pittsburgh. Played 30 cities. PRESENTED BY Greg Young. The tour ended prematurely in Green Bay, Wisc., after Denver canceled its gig (the Denver boys caught a glimpse and didn't like what they saw). **Cast**: FANNY: Debbie Gibson; NICK: Robert Westenberg.

PAPER MILL PLAYHOUSE, New Jersey, 4/01–5/20/01. Previews from 4/4/01. This revival had been in the works since 3/00. The number "My Man" was not in the score. DIRECTOR: Robert Johanson; CHOREOGRAPHER: Michael Lichtefeld; SETS: Michael Anania; COSTUMES: David Murin; MUSICAL DIRECTOR: Tom Helm. **Cast**: FANNY: Leslie Kritzer; NICK: Robert Cuccioli; ZIEGFELD: Bob Dorian.

SUNDANCE THEATRE, Utah, 6/30/02–9/1/02. DIRECTOR: Philip

Himberg; CHOREOGRAPHER: Peter Anastos. *Cast*: FANNY: Judith Blazer; NICK: Michael Nouri.

NEW AMSTERDAM THEATRE, Broadway, 9/23/02. Much-celebrated one-night only concert, PRESENTED BY Seth Rudetsky, to benefit the Actors Fund of America, with several Broadway leading ladies playing Fanny and singing different songs. Ticket prices were $75–$2,500 (cheaper seats sold out first). DIRECTOR: Peter Flynn; CHOREOGRAPHERS: Dev Janki & Robert Tatad. *Cast*: FANNY (see below); NICK: Peter Gallagher; MRS. BRICE: Kaye Ballard; MRS. STRAKOSH: Marcia Lewis; EDDIE RYAN: John Scherer; ZIEGFELD: Len Cariou; JOHN/DIRECTOR: John Bolton; EMMA: Adriane Lenox; MRS. O'MALLEY: Kristine Zbornik; MRS. MEEKER: Christine Pedi; KEENEY: Gary Beach; PAUL: Brad Oscar; RENALDI: Richard Kind; ENSEMBLE: Sam Harris, Stephanie Mills, Robin Byrd, Phyllis Newman, Liz Smith, Mary Birdson, Bill Burns, Stacey Todd Holt, Brad Musgrove, Michelle Potterf, Michael Serapiglia, Peter Gregus, Paul Castree, Laurie Gamache, Deidre Goodwin, Rusty Reynolds, Ric Ryder. This was the list of songs (with the particular Fanny singing in parentheses):.

Whoopi Goldberg (she was the first Fanny up, in a non-singing role), "I'm the Greatest Star" (Sutton Foster), "Cornet Man" (Idina Menzel), "Nicky Arnstein # 1" (Ricki Lake), "His Love Makes Me Beautiful" (Kristin Chenoweth, with Jason Danieley & Streisand impersonator Stephen Brinberg, and others in drag — Varla Jean Merman, Edie, and Michael Benjamin Washington), "I Want to Be Seen with You Tonight" (La Chanze), "People" (Julia Murney), "You Are Woman (I Am Man)" (Ana Gasteyer), "Don't Rain on My Parade" (Lillias White), "Sadie, Sadie" (Jane Krakowski), "Rat-Tat-Tat-Tat" (Bebe Neuwirth), "Who Are You Now?" (Judy Kuhn), "Funny Girl" (Andrea Martin), "The Music that Makes Me Dance" (Carolee Carmello), Whoopi Goldberg (she was also the last Fanny up, again in a non-singing role). OTHER FANNYS: Spencer Kayden, Alice Playten (unbilled, in the 2nd half). Certain Fannys signed up but canceled before the night: Megan Mullally, Audra McDonald, Donna Murphy, Marissa Jaret Winokur, Rosie O'Donnell, Christine Ebersole. Certain Ensemble members also canceled: Aisha de Haas, Shannon Hammons.

238. *A Funny Thing Happened on the Way to the Forum*

A musical farce, set in continuous action in a street in Ancient Rome, 200 years before the Christian era, on a day in spring. There are three houses on this street, owned by Senex (a lascivious slave-owner), Marcus Lycus (a pimp), and Erronius (a doddering old man who for 20 years has been looking for his stolen son and daughter). Pseudolus is Hero's slave trying to secure his freedom by a series of comic machinations. Hero sees the Cretan virgin Philia in Lycus's house and falls in love with her. Pseudolus offers to acquire her for him in exchange for his freedom. However, Philia has already been sold to Captain Miles Gloriosus, and although she is in love with Hero, she insists that she must be married to Miles. Meanwhile, Senex, Hero's father, also falls in love with Philia, and Philia thinks Senex is Miles. Miles returns and cannot find his bride. When he learns that Pseudolus is behind her disappearance, he is ready to kill the slave. Pseudolus asks if he can say one word in his defense, and Miles agrees. The word is "Intermission!," and the curtain comes down for the end of Act I. In Act II Pseudolus tells Miles that Philia died, and has a fellow slave, the nervous Hysterium, dress up as the dead girl. However, when Miles gives her a kiss, Hysterium rushes out of the house. At that moment Erronius comes back, and discovers that Miles and Philia are both wearing identical jewelry, and thus are his long lost son and daughter. Philia is then able to marry Hero; Miles claims two courtesans, the Gemini, and Pseudolus gains his freedom. The production used only one stage set and no change of costumes.

Before Broadway. While he was at Yale before World War II Richard O'Connell conceived the idea of doing a musical based on Plautus's works. He wrote the music, and fellow student Burt Shevelove wrote the lyrics, and the musical was produced to thunderous applause. One of the songs was called "A Couple of Greeks on a Roman Holiday." Later, during the War, while Mr. Shevelove was resident director of the Yale Dramat, the club did a musical called *When in Rome*, loosely based on Plautus's *Miles Gloriosus* and *Pseudolus*. In 1957 Stephen Sondheim agreed to do the score for a book written by Burt Shevelove & Larry Gelbart, based on Plautus. The librettists came up with an entirely new plot (there wasn't much to Plautus's plots at the best of times). In 1958, with the first draft finished, Mr. Sondheim asked Jerome Robbins to become director/choreographer. Mr. Robbins liked the idea, which was then called *A Scenario for Vaudevillians*. Leland Hayward was going to produce, but backed out, and then Sondheim and Robbins got involved in *Gypsy*. Sondheim offered the Plautus musical (by now called *The Roman Comedy*) to Hal Prince & Bobby Griffith to produce, but they turned it down. David Merrick then optioned it for $4,000, and Jerry Robbins dropped out, as he and Merrick did not get on (after working together on *Gypsy*). Then the writers returned Mr. Merrick's option money to him, and Jerry Robbins came back on board, but he insisted that Hal Prince produce. Mr. Prince agreed (this was his first solo production after the death of Bobby Griffith, who died after having agreed to produce with Mr. Prince), and sent the script to Phil Silvers, for whom it had been written. Mr. Silvers turned it down, as did other stars. The American Theatre Society was offered an involvement, but turned it down. Then Jerry Robbins quit again. It was Steve Sondheim's first effort as composer-lyricist. In 1962 Hal Prince shelved it while he did a non-musical (*Take Her, She's Mine*). When he returned Milton Berle was set to play Pseudolus, but his demands were too high and he dropped out. Zero Mostel replaced him in 12/61, which worried the authors, as they wanted him to play Lycus. This led to tension on the production. The show had now been re-named. George Abbott, who had replaced Jerry Robbins as director, and who had cut many subplots and trimmed down the script, said that if Zero didn't play the lead he would quit. It didn't work during tryouts in New Haven (which began on 3/31/62), so the subplots were restored. In the cast Karen Black and Pat Fox were replaced by Preshy Marker and Brian Davies (at an earlier stage Barbara Harris and Joel Grey had auditioned, unsuccessfully, for these two roles). In Washington DC's National Theatre the show opened with a benefit performance for government officials. On this and succeeding nights audience response was terrible, with many walking out at many performances. Steve Sondheim suggested they bring back Jerome Robbins as play doctor, and Hal Prince agreed. Mr. Robbins's presence was rather tricky as he had named names at the House Un-American Activities Commission some years before, and one of those names had been Jack Gilford's wife (Jack was playing Hysterium). Zero Mostel had also been blacklisted as a communist. So there was a lot of tension, but it worked out. Mr. Robbins replaced the opening number "Love is in the Air" with a new number Mr. Sondheim wrote — "Comedy Tonight," so that audiences would be laughing from the start, rather than being set up for a light romance and then being disappointed when they got a farce instead (Mr. Sondheim had, before "Love is in the Air," written "Invocation" as the opening number, but Abbott & Prince had gone with "Love is in the Air." "Invocation" was later used in Mr. Sondheim's *Frogs*). Other songs cut were: "Your Eyes are Blue," "The Echo Song" (used in the 1972 production), "I Do Like You," "The Gaggle of Geese," "I, Miles Gloriosus," and "There's Something About a War." Jack Cole choreographed what few dances there were (there was no dance chorus).

The Broadway Run. ALVIN THEATRE, 5/8/62–3/7/64; MARK HELLINGER THEATRE, 3/9/64–5/9/64; MAJESTIC THEATRE, 5/12/64–8/29/64. 8 previews from 5/1/62. 964 PERFORMANCES. PRESENTED BY Harold Prince; MUSIC/LYRICS: Stephen Sondheim; BOOK: Burt Shevelove & Larry Gelbart; BASED ON the Roman plays of Titus Maccius Plautus (254–184 BC); DIRECTOR: George Abbott (with an uncredited Jerome Robbins); CHOREOGRAPHER: Jack Cole (with an uncredited Jerome Robbins); SETS/COSTUMES: Tony Walton; LIGHTING: Jean Rosenthal; MUSICAL DIRECTOR: Harold Hastings, *Arthur Wagner*; ORCHESTRATIONS: Irwin Kostal & Sid Ramin; DANCE MUSIC ARRANGEMENTS: Hal Schaefer; ADDITIONAL DANCE MUSIC ARRANGEMENTS: Betty

Walberg; CAST RECORDING on Capitol; PRESS: Sol Jacobson, Lewis Harmon, Mary Bryant (*Earl Butler* by 63–64); CASTING: Judith Abbott; GENERAL MANAGER: Carl Fisher; COMPANY MANAGER: *Clarence Jacobson* (by 63–64); PRODUCTION STAGE MANAGER: Ruth Mitchell; STAGE MANAGER: James Bronson, *George Martin* (added by 63–64). *Cast:* PROLOGUS, AN ACTOR: Zero Mostel (1), *Jerry Lester* (during Mr. Mostel's vacations, 12/17/62–12/23/62, and 10/21/63–11/4/63), *Dick Shawn* (from 2/64); THE PROTEANS: Eddie Phillips (9), George Reeder (10) (*Ron Ross* from 63–64), David Evans (11), *George Martin*; SENEX, A CITIZEN OF ROME: David Burns (5), *Frank McHugh* (from 10/21/63); DOMINA, HIS WIFE: Ruth Kobart (6); HERO, HIS SON: Brian Davies (6), *Harry David Snow* (from 63–64); HYSTERIUM, SLAVE TO SENEX & DOMINA: Jack Gilford (4), *Lee Goodman*; MARCUS LYCUS, A DEALER IN COURTESANS: John Carradine (3), *Danny Dayton* (8/19/63–9/2/63), *John Carradine, Erik Rhodes* (from 9/9/63); PSEUDOLUS, SLAVE TO HERO: Zero Mostel (1) ✰, *Jerry Lester* (during Mr. Mostel's vacations, 12/17/62–12/22/62, and 10/21/63–11/4/63), *Dick Shawn* (from 2/64); TINTINNABULA, A COURTESAN: Roberta Keith, *Ethel Martin* (from 63–64); PANACEA, A COURTESAN: Lucienne Bridou, *Barbara London* (from 63–64); THE GEMINAE, COURTESANS: Lisa James & Judy Alexander (*Lisa Ackerman* from 63–64); VIBRATA, A COURTESAN: Myrna White, *Sally Neal* (from 63–64); GYMNASIA, A COURTESAN: Gloria Kristy; PHILIA, A SLAVE GIRL (VIRGIN): Preshy Marker (7); ERRONIUS, A CITIZEN OF ROME: Raymond Walburn (2), *Horace Cooper* (from 63–64); MILES GLORIOSUS, A WARRIOR: Ronald Holgate (8). **Standbys:** Philia: Marie Santell; Domina: Julia Ross; Prologus/Pseudolus/Senex/Hysterium/Erronius: Coley Worth, *Danny Worth*. **Understudies:** Gymnasia: Lucienne Bridou, *Julia Ross*; Miles: George Reeder; Hero: David Evans; Courtesans: Roberta Keith, *Diane Coupe, Mary Burr*; Proteans: George Martin. *Act I:* "Comedy Tonight" (Prologus, Proteans, Company), "Love I Hear" (Hero), "Free" (Pseudolus & Hero), "The House of Marcus Lycus" (Lycus, Pseudolus, Courtesans), "Lovely" (Hero & Philia), "Pretty Little Picture" (Pseudolus, Hero, Philia), "Everybody Ought to Have a Maid" (Senex, Pseudolus, Hysterium, Lycus), "I'm Calm" (Hysterium), "Impossible" (Senex & Hero), "Bring Me My Bride" (Miles, Pseudolus, Courtesans, Proteans). *Act II:* "That Dirty Old Man" (Domina), "That'll Show Him" (Philia), "Lovely" (reprise) (Pseudolus & Hysterium), "Funeral Sequence and Dance" (Pseudolus, Miles, Courtesans, Proteans), "Comedy Tonight" (reprise) (Company).

The show, capitalized at $300,000, opened at $240,000. It had an advance sale of only $40,000, partly due to opening late in the season. It opened after 11 complete re-writes. It got generally great Broadway reviews. After opening night, Zero Mostel began ad-libbing mercilessly. It won Tonys for musical, producer of a musical, book, director of a musical, and for Zero Mostel and David Burns. Jack Gilford and Ruth Kobart were nominated. On 11/7/63, Zero, then on a diet, forgot to eat, and collapsed during intermission. He couldn't complete the performance.

After Broadway. LONDON. Opened on 10/3/63. 762 PERFORMANCES. PRESENTED BY Hal Prince, Tony Walton, and Richard Pilbrow; DIRECTOR: George Abbott; CHOREOGRAPHER: George Martin; SETS: Tony Walton; LIGHTING: Jean Rosenthal; MUSICAL DIRECTOR: Alyn Ainsworth; LONDON CAST RECORDING on HMV. *Cast:* PSEUDOLUS: Frankie Howerd (Mr. Howerd later starred in the TV series *Up Pompeii*, which was based on this musical), SENEX: Monsewer Eddie Grey; DOMINA: Linda Gray; HERO: John Rye; HYSTERIUM: Kenneth Connor; LYCUS: Jon Pertwee; PHILIA: Isla Blair; PROTEANS: Ben Aris, George Giles, Malcolm McDonald; ERRONIUS: Robertson Hare; MILES: Leon Greene.

TOUR. Opened on 12/25/63, at the Forrest Theatre, Philadelphia, and closed on 8/31/64, at the Shubert Theatre, Chicago. MUSICAL DIRECTOR: Joseph D. Lewis. *Cast:* PSEUDOLUS: Jerry Lester; LYCUS: Erik Rhodes; MILES: Adair McGowan, *Robert Brooks* (from 5/29/64); SENEX: Paul Hartman; HYSTERIUM: Arnold Stang, *Gil Lamb*; ERRONIUS: Edward Everett Horton; PHILIA: Donna McKechnie; TINTINNABULA: Tisa Chang; DOMINA: Justine Johnston.

PAPER MILL PLAYHOUSE, New Jersey, 1965. DIRECTOR: Jack Gilford. *Cast:* Dom De Luise, Jack Gilford.

THE MOVIE. 1966. DIRECTOR: Richard Lester. Several songs were dropped. *Cast:* PSEUDOLUS: Zero Mostel; LYCUS: Phil Silvers; HYSTERIUM: Jack Gilford; ERRONIUS: Buster Keaton; HERO: Michael Craw-

ford; SENEX: Michael Hordern; PHILIA: Annette Andre; MILES: Leon Greene; DOMINA: Patricia Jessel; GYMNASIA: Inga Neilsen; VIBRATA: Myrna White; THE GEMINAE: Jennifer & Susan Baker.

239. *A Funny Thing Happened on the Way to the Forum (1972 Broadway revival)*

Before Broadway. This revival began at the Center Theatre Group's AHMANSON THEATRE, Los Angeles, 10/13/71–11/20/71. 47 PERFORMANCES. The book was slightly re-written, and for some reason Steve Sondheim took out two good numbers and replaced them with weaker ones. "That'll Show Him" (from Act II) was replaced with a number cut from the original production — "Echo Song" (Philia & Hero) before the production started, and "Pretty Little Picture" (from Act I) was replaced after the Ahmanson production with a new song — "Farewell" (sung by Domina). Burt Shevelove re-staged the show. "The House of Marcus Lycus" was revised as a solo for Lycus. *Cast:* PSEUDOLUS: Phil Silvers; SENEX: Lew Parker; DOMINA: Nancy Walker; HERO: John Hansen; HYSTERIUM: Larry Blyden; LYCUS: Carl Ballantine; ERRONIUS: Reginald Owen; MILES: Carl Lindstrom; TINTINNABULA: Ann Jillian; PANACEA: Gloria Mills; GEMINAE: Trish Mahoney & Sonja Haney; VIBRATA: Keita Keita; GYMNASIA: Charlene Ryan; PHILIA: Pamela Hall; PROTEANS: Marc Breaux, Marc Wilder, Joe Ross. Nancy Walker, unable to go east for the Broadway run, was replaced by Lizabeth Pritchett. Jack Lee was replaced by Milton Rosenstock as musical director for Broadway. It was hard to get funding for Broadway.

The Broadway Run. LUNT-FONTANNE THEATRE, 3/30/72–8/12/72. 3 previews from 3/28/72. 156 PERFORMANCES. A Larry Blyden production, PRESENTED BY David Black, in association with Seymour Vall & Henry Honeckman; MUSIC/LYRICS: Stephen Sondheim; BOOK: Burt Shevelove & Larry Gelbart; BASED ON the plays of Plautus (254–184 BC); DIRECTOR: Burt Shevelove; CHOREOGRAPHER: Ralph Beaumont; SETS: James Trittipo; COSTUMES: Noel Taylor; LIGHTING: H.R. Poindexter; MUSICAL DIRECTOR/VOCAL DIRECTOR: Milton Rosenstock; ORCHESTRATIONS: Irwin Kostal & Sid Ramin; DANCE MUSIC ARRANGEMENTS: Hal Schaefer; ADDITIONAL DANCE MUSIC ARRANGEMENTS: Richard De Benedictis; PRESS: Betty Lee Hunt Associates; GENERAL MANAGEMENT: Eugene Wolsk & Emanuel Azenberg; STAGE MANAGER: Scott Jackson; ASSISTANT STAGE MANAGER: Patrick Spohn. *Cast:* PROLOGUS: Phil Silvers (1), *John Bentley* (from 7/24/72), *Tom Poston* (from 8/1/72); SENEX, A ROMAN CITIZEN: Jack Collins (went on for regular performer, Lew Parker, on opening night), *Lew Parker* (3), *Mort Marshall*; DOMINA, HIS WIFE: Lizabeth Pritchett (6); HERO, HIS SON: John Hansen (8); HYSTERIUM: Larry Blyden (2); PSEUDOLUS: Phil Silvers (1) ✰, *John Bentley* (from 7/24/72), *Tom Poston* (from 8/1/72); MARCUS LYCUS: Carl Ballantine (4); ERRONIUS: Reginald Owen (5); MILES GLORIOSUS: Carl Lindstrom (9); TINTINNABULA: Lauren Lucas (16); PANACEA: Barbara Brown (14); THE GEMINAE: Trish Mahoney (18) & Sonja Haney (15); VIBRATA: Keita Keita (17); GYMNASIA: Charlene Ryan (13); PHILIA: Pamela Hall (7); THE PROTEANS: Joe Ross (10), Bill Starr (11), Chad Block (12). **Understudies:** Hysterium: Joe Ross; Domina/Tintinnabula/Geminae: Patti Karr; Vibrata/Gymnasia: Patti Karr; Hero: Bill Starr; Miles: Chad Block; Proteans: Patrick Spohn; Philia: Barbara Brown.

Despite great reviews, the show died. Phil Silvers and Larry Blyden won Tonys, and the show won a 1972 Special Tony for becoming the longest-running Broadway musical of all time. It was also nominated for direction of a musical. Phil Silvers played the role with glasses, and on 8/1/72 had a minor stroke. Tom Poston stepped in for the last 11 days before the show wrapped up. Hal Prince believes this production was not as good as the original.

After Broadway. PAPER MILL PLAYHOUSE, New Jersey, 1976. DIRECTOR: Sue Lawless. *Cast:* Eddie Bracken, Coley Worth, Lizabeth Pritchett.

TOURING REVIVAL. Opened on 3/2/87, at the Shubert Theatre, New Haven. PRESENTED BY Guber/Gross/Young Productions; DIRECTOR: George Martin; CHOREOGRAPHER: Ethel Martin; SETS: Michael Bottari

& Ronald Case; COSTUMES: Gail Cooper-Hecht; LIGHTING: Richard Winkler; SOUND: Abe Jacob; MUSICAL DIRECTOR: Sherman Frank. **Cast**: PSEUDOLUS: Mickey Rooney; HYSTERIUM: Lenny Wolpe; MILES: Michael Dantuono; PHILIA: Jennifer Lee Andrews; TINTINNABULA: Zoie Lam; LYCUS: Mitchell Greenberg; HERO: Bob Walton; SENEX: Robert Nichols; DOMINA: Marsha Bagwell.

YORK THEATRE COMPANY, 3/22/91–4/28/91. 26 PERFORMANCES. DIRECTOR/CHOREOGRAPHER: Pamela Hunt; SETS: James Morgan; COSTUMES: Beba Shamash; LIGHTING: Mary Jo Dondlinger; MUSICAL DIRECTOR: Lynn Crigler. **Cast**: PSEUDOLUS: Jack Cirillo; HYSTERIUM: Jason Graae; SENEX: John Remme; DOMINA: Chris Callan; HERO: Jeffrey Herbst; ERRONIUS: Jim Harder; MILES: Ken Parks; VIBRATA: Valerie Macklin.

240. *A Funny Thing Happened on the Way to the Forum (1996 Broadway revival)*

Before Broadway. The number "Pretty Little Picture" was cut. There was a press preview on 3/4/96.

The Broadway Run. ST. JAMES THEATRE, 4/18/96–1/4/98. 36 previews from 3/18/96. 715 PERFORMANCES. PRESENTED BY Jujamcyn Theatres, Scott Rudin/Paramount Pictures, The Viertel — Baruch — Frankel Group, Roger Berlind, Dodger Productions; MUSIC/LYRICS: Stephen Sondheim; BOOK: Burt Shevelove & Larry Gelbart; BASED ON the plays of Plautus (254–184 BC); DIRECTOR: Jerry Zaks; CHOREOGRAPHER: Rob Marshall; SETS/COSTUMES: Tony Walton; LIGHTING: Paul Gallo; SOUND: Tony Meola; MUSICAL SUPERVISOR: Edward Strauss; ORCHESTRATIONS: Jonathan Tunick; DANCE MUSIC ARRANGEMENTS: David Chase; NEW CAST RECORDING on Broadway Angel; PRESS: Boncau/Bryan-Brown; CASTING: Johnson — Liff; GENERAL MANAGEMENT: Dodger Productions; COMPANY MANAGER: Marcia Goldberg; PRODUCTION STAGE MANAGER: Arthur Gaffin; STAGE MANAGER: Michael Pule; ASSISTANT STAGE MANAGER: John F. Sullivan. **Cast:** PROLOGUS: Nathan Lane (1), *Bob Amaral* (9/2/96–9/7/96, during Mr. Lane's vacation, and again on 9/18/96, during Mr. Lane's throat illness), *Whoopi Goldberg* (2/11/97–7/13/97), *David Alan Grier* (7/15/97–11/30/97), *Bob Amaral* (from 12/2/97); THE PROTEANS: Brad Aspel, Cory English, Ray Roderick; HERO: Jim Stanek (9); PHILIA: Jessica Boevers (7); SENEX: Lewis J. Stadlen (3), *Dick Latessa* (from 3/97), *Robert Fitch* (from 9/97); DOMINA: Mary Testa (6) (until 7/13/97), *Gina Ferrall, Mary Testa* (from 9/97); HYSTERIUM: Mark Linn-Baker (2), *Ross Lehman*; MARCUS LYCUS: Ernie Sabella (4), *Bob Amaral*; PSEUDOLUS: Nathan Lane (1) ☆, *Bob Amaral* (9/2/96–9/7/96, during Mr. Lane's vacation, and again, on 9/18/96, during Mr. Lane's throat illness), *Whoopi Goldberg* (2/11/97–7/13/97), *David Alan Grier* (7/15/97–11/30/97), *Bob Amaral* (from 12/2/97); TINTINNABULA: Pamela Everett; PANACEA: Leigh Zimmerman, *Holly Cruikshank*; THE GEMINAE: Susan Misner (*Tara Nicole*) & Lori Werner; VIBRATA: Mary Ann Lamb, Pascale Faye, Carol Lee Meadows; GYMNASIA: Stephanie Pope, *Kena Tangi Dorsey*; ERRONIUS: William Duell (5); MILES GLORIOSUS: Cris Groenendaal (8). **Standby:** Pseudolus/Prologus: Bob Amaral. **Understudies:** Hysterium: Bob Amaral & Patrick Garner; Lycus: Bob Amaral, Kenneth Kantor, Patrick Garner; Hero: Cory English & Kevin Kraft; Philia: Jennifer Rosin; Senex: MacIntyre Dixon & Kenneth Kantor, *David Rogers*; Miles: Kenneth Kantor; Erronius: MacIntyre Dixon & Patrick Garner; Domina: Ruth Gottschall; Gymnasia: Leigh Zimmerman, *Holly Cruikshank*. **Swings**: Michael Arnold, Kevin Kraft, Kristin Willits, *Shannon Hammons, George Smyros, Aimee Turner*. **Orchestra**: WOODWINDS: Les Scott, Seymour Red Press, Virgil Blackwell, Ed Zuhlke, John Winder; TRUMPETS: Stu Satalof, Larry Lunetta, Kamau Adilifu; TROMBONES: Bruce Bonvissuto & Jack Schatz; FRENCH HORN: Paul Riggio; PERCUSSION: Glenn Rhian & Rick Kivnick; BASS: Lou Bruno; KEYBOARDS: Larry Yurman; HARP: Beth Robinson; VIOLINS: Ronald Oakland, Alexander Vselensky, Katsuko Esaki, Maura Giannini, Melanie Baker; CELLI: Scott Ballantyne & Jeffrey Szabo.

Broadway reviews were generally excellent. The show won Tonys for direction of a musical, and for Nathan Lane, and was nominated for revival of a musical, and for Lewis J. Stadlen. This was the third Broadway pro-

duction of *Forum*, and the third time the leading actor had won a Tony. In 9/96, during Nathan Lane's absence for a week, box-office receipts plummeted by $350,000. After the 10/9/96 matinee it was announced that Whoopi Goldberg would be taking over from Nathan Lane for 20 weeks. Steve Sondheim wrote some new lyrics for her in the number "Free," and there were a few minor script changes to accommodate her playing Pseudolus as a female. In addition, "The House of Marcus Lycus" was re-staged. When Whoopi debuted on 2/6/97 her boyfriend Frank Langella was in the audience, as were Glenn Close and Timothy Dalton. The producers asked critics to wait three weeks before reviewing the new casting, which they did, on 3/6/97. Rumors had been around since 6/5/97 that either David Alan Grier or Chris Elliot was going to replace Whoopi in the role, and Mr. Grier came in on 7/15/97 (Miss Goldberg was going to leave on 6/29/97, but her run was extended to 7/13/97). The next rumor was who was going to replace Mr. Grier when he left on 11/16/97. Carol Burnett was mentioned, and on 9/12/97 the return of Whoopi was mooted, but, as it happened Mr. Grier's role was extended to 11/30/97, and understudy Bob Amaral took over until the end of the run.

After Broadway. TOUR. Comedian Rip Taylor had already been chosen by 11/97 to star in the tour which would begin in Bloomsburg, Pa., on 10/11/98, produced by Michael Vergoff & Park Avenue Theatrical Group. However, in 7/98 Mr. Taylor was replaced by Jo Anne Worley. But, Miss Worley wanted to travel with her two little dogs; she couldn't find a plane that would take them, so Rip Taylor came back.

MEXICO. The original two Mexican productions had used the title *Amor al Reves es Roma (Amor Spelled Backwards is Roma)*. The second Mexican revival opened on 4/30/98, at the HIDALGO THEATRE, Mexico City. DIRECTOR: Manuel Castillo. Midget comedienne Maria Elena Saldana was scheduled to play the lead, but instead comedian Alejandro Suarez did. The new name of this production was *En Roma el Amor es Broma (In Rome, Love is a Joke)*.

OPEN AIR THEATRE, Regents Park, London, 7/23/99–8/31/99. Previews from 7/20/99. DIRECTOR: Ian Talbot; SETS/COSTUMES: Paul Farnsworth. **Cast**: PSEUDOLUS: Roy Hudd; DOMINA: Susie Blake.

NATIONAL THEATRE, London. 7/9/04. Previews from 6/28/04. DIRECTOR: Edward Hall; CHOREOGRAPHER: Rob Ashford; SETS: Julian Crouch; COSTUMES: Kevin Pollard; LIGHTING: Paul Anderson; SOUND: Paul Groothuis; MUSICAL SUPERVISOR/MUSICAL DIRECTOR: Martin Lowe; ORCHESTRATIONS: Michael Starobin. **Cast**: PSEUDOLUS: Desmond Barrit; DOMINA: Isla Blair; GYMNASIA: Tiffany Graves; SENEX: Sam Kelly; HERO: Vince Leigh; PHILIA: Caroline Sheen; HYSTERIUM: Hamish McColl; ERRONIUS: Harry Towb; MILES: Philip Quast; MARCUS LYCUS: David Schneider; VIBRATA: Michelle Lukes.

241. *Gantry*

About hell-fire revivalist preacher, Elmer Gantry.

Before Broadway. The show went straight into Broadway previews; there were no out-of-town tryouts. It was the last show at the 1,434 seat George Abbott Theatre.

The Broadway Run. GEORGE ABBOTT THEATRE, 2/14/70. 32 previews. 1 PERFORMANCE. PRESENTED BY Joseph Cates & Jerry Schlossberg; MUSIC: Stanley Lebowsky; LYRICS: Fred Tobias; BOOK: Peter Bellwood; ADAPTED FROM the 1927 novel *Elmer Gantry*, by Sinclair Lewis, and from the 1960 movie made from it, starring Burt Lancaster; DIRECTOR/CHOREOGRAPHER: Onna White; ASSISTANT CHOREOGRAPHER: Patrick Cummings; SETS: Robin Wagner; COSTUMES: Ann Roth; LIGHTING: Jules Fisher; SOUND: Robert V. Cox; MUSICAL DIRECTOR: Arthur Rubinstein; ORCHESTRATIONS: Jim Tyler; VOCAL ARRANGEMENTS: Stanley Lebowsky; DANCE MUSIC ARRANGEMENTS: Dorothea Freitag; CAST RECORDING on RCA; PRESS: David Powers; GENERAL MANAGERS: Robert Weiner & Nelle Nugent; PRODUCTION STAGE MANAGER: Ben Janney; STAGE MANAGER: William Letters; ASSISTANT STAGE MANAGER: Mary Porter Hall. **Cast:** BILL MORGAN: Tom Batten (5); SISTER DORETHA: Dorothea Freitag; ADELBERTA SHOUP: Gloria Hodes; SISTER SHARON FALCONER: Rita Moreno (2) ☆; ELMER GANTRY: Robert Shaw (1) ☆; JIM LEFFERTS: Wayne Tippit (3); GEORGE F. BABBITT: Ted Thurston (4); REV. GARRISON: Kenneth Bridges; TROSPER: Bob Gorman (7); GUNCH: David Sabin (9); PROUT: Zale Kessler (8); REV. TOOMIS: David Hooks (6); ARCHITECT: Robert Donahue; PHO-

TOGRAPHER: James N. Maher; DEAF MAN: J. Michael Bloom; HIS WIFE: Beth Fowler; TOWNSPEOPLE/REVIVAL TROUPE/STUDENTS/WORKMEN: Chuck Beard, J. Michael Bloom, Kenneth Bridges, Patrick Cummings, Robert Donahue, Sandy Ellen, Carol Estey, Beth Fowler, Gloria Hodes, Keith Kaldenberg, Clyde Laurents, Robert Lenn, James N. Maher, Kathleen Robey, Dixie Stewart, Diane Tarleton, Maralyn Thoma, Terry Violino, Mimi Wallace. *Understudies*: Sharon: Beth Fowler; Lefferts: Kenneth Bridges; Babbitt: David Sabin; Morgan/Toomis/Garrison: Robert F. Donahue; Gunch/Trosper: Keith Kaldenberg; Prout: J. Michael Bloom; Adelberta: Diane Tarleton; Deaf Man: Robert Lenn; Deaf Man's Wife: Dixie Stewart; Woman Possessed by the Devil: Mimi Wallace. *Act I: Scene 1* Revival tent, Shelton, Ill.; *Scene 2* Train; *Scene 3* Revival tent, Fargo, ND; *Scene 4* Revival tent, Page City, Kans.; *Scene 5* Sister Sharon's dressing room; *Scene 6* Revival tent—McAllaster, Kans.; *Scene 7* Sister Sharon's hotel suite, Chicago. *Act II: Scene 1* Revival tent, Chicago; *Scene 2* Revival tent grounds; *Scene 3* A warehouse in Chicago; *Scene 4* Revival tent; *Scene 5* The office of the Church Board; *Scene 6* The Tabernacle office; *Scene 7* Outside the "Waters of Jordan" Tabernacle. *Act I*: "Wave a Hand" (Morgan & Troupe); Gantry Gets the Call: "He Was There" (Gantry, Troupe, Townspeople), "Play Ball with the Lord" (Gantry, Troupe, Townspeople) [end of "Gantry Gets the Call" sequence]; "Katie Jonas" (Sharon), "Thanks, Sweet Jesus!" (Gantry & Townspeople), "Someone I've Already Found" (Gantry), "He's Never Too Busy" (Sharon, Gantry, Morgan, Adelberta, Troupe), "We're Sharin' Sharon" (Gantry). *Act II*: "We Can All Give Love" (Sharon, Adelberta, Townspeople), "Foresight" (Babbitt, Gunch, Trosper, Prout), "These Four Walls" (Sharon), "Show Him the Way" (Gantry & Townspeople), "The Promise of What I Could Be" (Gantry), "Gantry's Reaction" (Gantry), "We're Sharin' Sharon" (reprise) (Gantry).

Broadway reviews were mostly bad.

After Broadway. WORLD PREMIERE. FORD'S THEATRE, Washington, DC, 2/10/88–6/17/88. This was a re-vamped version. PRESENTED BY Joseph Cates; MUSIC: Mel Marvin; LYRICS: Bob Satuloff, John Bishop, David H. Bell; BOOK: John Bishop; DIRECTOR: David H. Bell. *Cast:* GANTRY: Casey Biggs; SHARON: Sharon Scruggs.

LA JOLLA PLAYHOUSE, 10/15/91–12/8/91. This was the re-vamped version. DIRECTOR: Des McAnuff; CHOREOGRAPHER: Marcia Milgrom Dodge; SETS: Heidi Landesman; MUSICAL DIRECTOR: Ted Sperling; ORCHESTRATIONS: Michael Gibson. *Cast:* GANTRY: Mark Harelik; SHARON: Sharon Scruggs; ALSO WITH: Michael Mulheren, Lynette DuPre, Jennifer Leigh Warren, Judith Moore, Darlene Love, Juliet Lambert.

MARRIOTT'S LINCOLNSHIRE THEATRE, Illinois, 2/4/98–3/22/98. Previews from 1/28/98. This was the re-vamped version. *Cast:* Tom Zemon, Kerry O'Malley.

242. *The Gay Life*

Anatol is a rake. Liesl, a shy girl, has been in love with him since childhood. He abandons his ways when he finds himself in love with her. Set in Vienna and Carlsbad in 1904.

Before Broadway. This was the first show ever to try out at the Fisher Theatre, Detroit. Until tryouts Anita Gillette had opened the show by jumping off a bridge, a scene that, along with her part, was cut. Gerry Freedman was replaced by Herbert Ross as director, although Mr. Freedman retained credit. Cut during tryouts were the numbers "Come Away," "Don't Drink the Water," "The Gay Life," "A Girl Like That," "I Lost the Love of Anatol," "I Love a Wedding," "If it Hadn't Been for You," "Just What I Wanted," and "Vignettes." Lucinda Ballard was Howard Dietz's wife.

The Broadway Run. SHUBERT THEATRE, 11/18/61–2/24/62. 3 previews from 11/16/61. 113 PERFORMANCES. PRESENTED BY Kermit Bloomgarden; MUSIC: Arthur Schwartz; LYRICS: Howard Dietz; BOOK: Fay & Michael Kanin; BASED ON the 1893 play *The Affairs of Anatol*, by Arthur Schnitzler; DIRECTOR: Gerald Freedman; CHOREOGRAPHER: Herbert Ross; SETS: Oliver Smith; COSTUMES: Lucinda Ballard; ASSISTANT COSTUMES: Florence Klotz; LIGHTING: Jean Rosenthal; MAGICAL ILLUSIONS CREATED & DESIGNED BY: Jack Adams; MUSICAL DIRECTOR/VOCAL ARRANGEMENTS: Herbert Greene; ASSOCIATE CONDUCTOR: Karen Gustafson; ORCHESTRATIONS: Don Walker; DANCE MUSIC

ARRANGEMENTS: Robert Starer; PRESS: Dick Weaver; CASTING: Lillian Stein; GENERAL MANAGER: Max Allentuck; COMPANY MANAGER: Milton Pollack; PRODUCTION STAGE MANAGER: Kermit Kegley; STAGE MANAGER: Cliff Cothren; ASSISTANT STAGE MANAGERS: Charles McDaniel & Rico Froehlich. *Cast:* MAX: Jules Munshin (3); USHER: Sterling Clark; ANATOL: Walter Chiari (1); FRANZ: Leonard Elliott; HELENE: Jeanne Bal (6); LIESL BRANDEL: Barbara Cook (2); HERR BRANDEL: Loring Smith (4); FRAU BRANDEL: Lu Leonard; MIMI: Yvonne Constant (7); PROPRIETOR: Michael Quinn; THE GREAT GASTON: Jack Adams; OTTO: Rico Froehlich; WAITERS: Ted Lambrinos & Russell Goodwin; ANNA: Joanne Spiller; GRANDMOTHER: Aura Vainio; PHOTOGRAPHER: Gerald Teijelo, *Ben Gillespie*; DOORMAN: Rico Froehlich; HEADWAITER: Carl Nicholas; WAITERS: Hal Norman & Ted Lambrinos; MAGDA: Elizabeth Allen (5); SINGERS: Ken Ayers, Loyce Baker, Joan Bishop, June Card, Luce Ennis, Russell Goodwin, Jeanne Grant, Tony La Russo, Ted Lambrinos, Carl Nicholas, Hal Norman, Carole O'Hara, Michael Quinn, Nancy Radcliffe, Joanne Spiller; DANCERS: Kip Andrews, Karoly Barta, Bonnie Brandon, Carolyn Clark, Sterling Clark, Thatcher Clarke, Marion Fels, Carol Flemming, Leslie Franzos, Bettye Jenkins, Patrick King, Ray Kirchner, Louis Kosman, Doris Ortiz, Michel Stuart, Gerald Teijelo (*Ben Gillespie*), Eleanore Treiber, Aura Vainio, Jenny Workman, *Vernon Wendorf.* **Standby**: Anatol: Stephen Elliott. *Understudies*: Liesl: Luce Ennis, *June Card*; Brandel: Michael Quinn; Frau Brandel: Joanne Spiller; Mimi: June Card, *Leslie Franzos*; Anna/Helene: Nancy Radcliffe; Franz/Gaston: Rico Froehlich; Magda: *Nancy Radcliffe*. *Act I: Scene 1* Vienna; 1904. A church: "What a Charming Couple" (Ensemble) [dropped soon after the opening]; *Scene 2* Anatol's apartment: "Why Go Anywhere at All?" (Helene) [dropped soon after the opening]; *Scene 3* Carlsbad. A pavilion: "Bring Your Darling Daughter" (Max & Ensemble), "Now I'm Ready for a Frau" (Anatol & Max), "Frau Ballet" (Shy Girl, Tennis Girl, Mountain Climbers, Girl on Horseback); *Scene 4* Terrace of the Brandel suite in Carlsbad: "Magic Moment" (Liesl), "Who Can? You Can!" (Anatol & Liesl); *Scene 5* The casino in Carlsbad: "Oh, Mein Liebchen" (Ensemble), Liebchen Waltz (Jenny Workman, Leslie Franzos, Thatcher Clarke, Aura Vainio, Louis Kosman, Sterling Clark, Ensemble), "The Label on the Bottle" (sung by Liesl; danced by Louis Kosman, Ray Kirchner, Michel Stuart) [cut soon after the opening]; *Scene 6* A street in Vienna; Christmas Eve: "This Kind of a Girl" (Anatol & Liesl); *Scene 7* A private room at Sacher's Restaurant: "The Bloom is off the Rose" (Max & Male Ensemble); *Scene 8* The Brandel living room: "Who Can? You Can" (reprise) (Ensemble), "Now I'm Ready for a Frau" (reprise) (Anatol), "Magic Moment" (reprise) (Liesl). *Act II: Scene 1* Sacher's Restaurant. Anatol's bachelor party: "I'm Glad I'm Single" (Max & Male Ensemble); NURSEMAID: Leslie Franzos; ANATOL, THE BOY: Sterling Clark; STRONG MAN: Louis Kosman; CELESTINA: Marion Fels; MAGDA: Jenny Workman; ANATOL, THE MAN: Ray Kirchner; THIRD SWAN FROM THE LEFT: Eleanore Treiber; HELENE: Aura Vainio; MIMI: Bonnie Brandon; "I'm Glad I'm Single" (reprise) (Male Ensemble), "Now I'm Ready for a Frau" (reprise) (Anatol & Max); *Scene 2* Anatol's apartment: "Something You Never Had Before" (Liesl); *Scene 3* The Brandel living room: "You Will Never Be Lonely" (Frau Brandel, Herr Brandel, Ensemble); *Scene 4* A street. Liesl's bedroom: "You're Not the Type" (Anatol & Liesl); *Scene 5* Outside the Paprikas Cafe; *Scene 6* The Paprikas Cafe: "Come a-Wandering with Me" (Magda & Male Dancers); *Scene 7* Anatol's apartment: "Magic Moment" (reprise) (Liesl) [added during the run], "I Never Had a Chance" (Anatol), "I Wouldn't Marry You" (Liesl), "For the First Time" (Anatol).

Broadway reviews were mostly very good. There were major revisions just after the opening. It was now decided not to tell the story as a flashback. The show won a Tony Award for costumes, and was also nominated for sets, musical direction, and for Elizabeth Allen.

After Broadway. When the show's music was finally published in 1986, it was as *The High Life*. Using this new title (since the original run, the term "gay" had taken a new turn in the English language), it ran Off Broadway at the MAZUR THEATRE, 4/23/93–4/25/93. 4 PERFORMANCES. Part of the *Musicals in Concert* series. DIRECTOR: B.T. McNicholl; CHOREOGRAPHER: Courtney Conner; MUSICAL DIRECTOR: James Stenborg. *Cast:* ANATOL: Michael Licata; LIESL: Leslie Beauvais; MAX: Russell Goldberg; BRANDEL: Clark Gesner.

243. *Gentlemen Prefer Blondes*

Set in 1924. Blonde Lorelei and brunette friend Dorothy are on leave from the Follies, and go to Paris on the *Ile de France*, courtesy of Lorelei's generous fiancé, button tycoon Gus. Dorothy, tired of Prohibition, is eager to get going, but Lorelei is sad at leaving Gus. Out at sea she has feeling that Gus might have left her, and that she must get a new sugar daddy. She tells Dorothy her life story, and urges her to stop having so much fun and to try to improve herself. Lorelei finds Henry, a rich Philadelphia bachelor, and his giddy mother, and brings him together with Dorothy. When everyone leaves, Gloria, a dancer, uses Lorelei's suite for a practice room. Lorelei arranges to buy a diamond tiara from Lady Beekman, borrowing the $5,000 necessary from Sir Francis Beekman during a flirtation. In Paris Dorothy and Henry fall in love, and Lorelei finds Gage, a zipper manufacturer. Lady Beekman finds out how Dorothy got the money for the tiara, and sets French lawyers after her. Mr. Esmond arrives to check up on Lorelei, and finds her entertaining Gage. Lorelei makes her debut in a nightclub. All ends happily back in the USA.

Before Broadway. Anita Loos sent her original story to friends George Jean Nathan and H.L. Mencken, editors of *The Smart Set*. They turned it down, but recommended Ray Long, editor of *Cosmopolitan*, who took it, but never published it. So far it was considered not to have enough substance, even though it was very likeable. Later it was published by Henry Sell, editor of *Harper's Bazaar*, in which it was a sensation. It was published all over the world. It became a straight play (written by Miss Loos and John Emerson) in 1926, starring June Walker as Lorelei; and a movie starring June Taylor. Florenz Ziegfeld wanted to do a musical of it around the same time, but it never happened. Over the years John C. Wilson had tried to get Miss Loos involved in a stage musical of the show, but she was too busy. Finally, in 1949, during a return cruise from Europe, music publisher Jack Robbins suggested to producer Herman Levin that he do a musical version. On his return to New York, Mr. Levin bought the rights, and assigned Joe Fields to work with Miss Loos on the book. She didn't like Mr. Fields, and in the end had him banished from the project. She then wrote the new script based on a 10-page outline provided by Billy Rose (uncredited). Until Rodgers & Hammerstein and Josh Logan and Leland Hayward all put in $5,000 each, financing was impossible to find. As for the role of Lorelei, various actresses were mentioned — Ethel Merman, June Havoc, Betty Hutton, Celeste Holm, Doris Day, Dolores Gray, Janet Blair, Gertrude Niesen, Vivian Blaine. This was Carol Channing's first major starring role. It tried out for 2½ weeks in Philadelphia, where it got raves. A dangerous acrobatic dance number was cut at this stage.

The Broadway Run. ZIEGFELD THEATRE, 12/8/49–9/15/51. 740 PERFORMANCES. PRESENTED BY Herman Levin & Oliver Smith; MUSIC: Jule Styne; LYRICS: Leo Robin; BOOK: Joseph Fields & Anita Loos; BASED ON Anita Loos' 1926 volume of sketches of the same name about gold digger Lorelei Lee, which in turn had originally been a series of articles in the magazine *Harper's Bazaar*; DIRECTOR: John C. Wilson; CHOREOGRAPHER: Agnes de Mille; ASSISTANT CHOREOGRAPHER: Dania Krupska; SETS: Oliver Smith; COSTUMES: Miles White; LIGHTING: Peggy Clark; MUSICAL DIRECTOR: Milton Rosenstock, *Max Meth*; ARRANGEMENTS: Don Walker; DANCE MUSIC ARRANGEMENTS: Trude Rittman; VOCAL ARRANGEMENTS/VOCAL DIRECTOR: Hugh Martin; CAST RECORDING on Columbia; PRESS: Richard Maney, Frank Goodman, Peggy Phillips, *Sol Jacobson*; GENERAL MANAGER: Philip Adler; COMPANY MANAGER: Alex Cohen; GENERAL STAGE MANAGER: Frank Coletti; STAGE MANAGER: Samuel Liff, *Jerry Adler*; ASSISTANT STAGE MANAGER: Richard Smith, *Richard Haas*. **Cast:** DOROTHY SHAW: Yvonne Adair (2); A STEWARD: Jerry Craig, *Bob Burkhardt*; LORELEI LEE: Carol Channing (1), *Bibi Osterwald* (during Miss Channing's illness); GUS ESMOND: Jack McCauley (3); THE OLYMPIC TEAM: FRANK: Robert Cooper; GEORGE: Eddie Weston; SUN BATHERS: Pat Donohue & Marjorie Winters (*Pam Donohue & June Kirby*); LADY PHYLLIS BEEKMAN: Reta Shaw; SIR FRAN-

CIS BEEKMAN: Rex Evans; MRS. ELLA SPOFFORD: Alice Pearce (5); DECK STEWARDS: Bob Burkhardt & Shelton Lewis (*Jack Gray & Jay Harnick*); HENRY SPOFFORD: Eric Brotherson (4); AN OLYMPIC: Curt Stafford; JOSEPHUS GAGE: George S. Irving (6); DECK WALKERS: Fran Keegan & Junior Standish (*Rise Drake*); BILL, A DANCER: Peter Birch; GLORIA STARK: Anita Alvarez, *Evelyn Taylor*; PIERRE, A STEWARD: Bob Neukum; JOE: Rex Cooper; SAM: Bill Bradley, *James White*; CHARLIE: Charles Basile; TAXI DRIVER: Kazimir Kokic; LEON, A VALET: Peter Holmes; ROBERT LEMANTEUR: Mort Marshall; LOUIS LEMANTEUR, HIS SON: Howard Morris; A FLOWER GIRL: Nicole France, *Ann Collins*; MAITRE D'HOTEL: Crandall Diehl; MIMI: Judy Sinclair; ZIZI: Hope Zee, *Angela Castle*; DANCE TEAM: Charles "Honi" Coles & Cholly Atkins; THE TENOR: William Krach; POLICEMAN: William Diehl, *Jack Gray*; HEAD WAITER: Kazimir Kokic; MR. ESMOND SR.: Irving Mitchell; SHOW GIRLS: Pat Donohue (*Pam Donohue*), Anna Rita Duffy, Fran Keegan, Annette Kohl, Junior Standish (*Rise Drake*), Marjorie Winters (*June Kirby*), Pat Gaston, Brik Tone; SINGING ENSEMBLE: Bob Burkhardt (*Jack Gray*), Angela Castle, Joan Coburn (gone by 50–51), Jerry Craig (gone by 50–51), William Diehl (gone by 50–51), William Krach, Shelton Lewis (*Jay Harnick*), Ellen McCown, Candy Montgomery (gone by 50–51), Bob Neukum, Judy Sinclair, Curt Stafford, Lucille Udovick (gone by 50–51), David Vogel (gone by 50–51), Beverly Jane Weston (gone by 50–51), Hope Zee (gone by 50–51), *Doris Hollingsworth, Kathy Collin, Ruth Webb, Sara Dillon, Sue Hight, Bob Trehy, Heber Cannon, Beth Douglas*; DANCING ENSEMBLE: Suzanne Ames (gone by 50–51), Charles Basile, Florence Baum, Bill Bradley (*James White*), Rex Cooper, Robert Cooper, Crandall Diehl, Nicole France (*Ann Collins*), Aristide J. Ginoulias, Pauline Goddard (gone by 50–51), Peter Holmes, Patty Ann Jackson, Alicia Krug (gone by 50–51), John Laverty (gone by 50–51), Mary Martinet, Caren Preiss, Evelyn Taylor (gone by 50–51), Norma Thornton (gone by 50–51), Polly Ward, Prue Ward (gone by 50–51), Eddie Weston, Helen Wood (gone by 50–51), *Ann Sparkman, Georgine Darcy, Meredith Baylis, Carol Cole, Marcella Dodge, Martha Mathes, Sherry McCutcheon, Glenn Olson*. **Understudies:** Henry: George S. Irving; Gage: Curt Stafford; Dorothy: Joan Coburn; Gloria: Evelyn Taylor, *Polly Ward*; Taxi Driver: Bill Bradley, *James White*; Lorelei: *Bibi Osterwald;* Gus Sr.: *Crandall Diehl*; Robert: William Diehl, *Howard Morris*; Louis: *Eddie Weston*; Mr. Esmond: *George S. Irving*; Bill: *Rex Cooper*; Phyllis: Lucille Udovick; Ella: Alicia Krug. **Act I:** Overture (Orchestra); *Scene 1* The French Line pier in New York; a midnight sailing: "It's High Time" (Dorothy & Ensemble), "Bye Bye Baby" (Gus & Lorelei) [a hit], "Bye Bye Baby" (reprise) (Gus & Ensemble); *Scene 2* The sun deck of the *Ile de France*; third day out: "A Little Girl from Little Rock" (Lorelei) [a hit], "I Love What I'm Doing" (Dorothy), Dance (Bill, Dorothy, Ensemble); *Scene 3* The boat deck; the same day; *Scene 4* Lorelei's suite on the *Ile de France*; later that day: "Just a Kiss Apart" (Henry), The Practice Scherzo (dance interlude) (Gloria), "It's Delightful Down in Chile" (Sir Francis, Lorelei, Show Girls, Male Ensemble); *Scene 5* Paris. The Place Vendome; one week later: "Sunshine" (Henry & Dorothy); *Scene 6* Champs de Mars. Under the Eiffel Tower; same day: "In the Champ de Mars" (Ensemble), Dance (Gloria & Kaz Kokic); *Scene 7* The Place Vendome; later that day: "Sunshine" (reprise) (Ensemble); *Scene 8* The Ritz Hotel in Paris. Lorelei's suite; that evening: "I'm a'Tingle, I'm a'Glow" (Gage), "House on Rittenhouse Square" (Dorothy) [not on cast album], "You Say You Care" (Henry), Finaletto (Lorelei & Ensemble). **Act II:** *Scene 1* The Pre-Catelan in the Bois; the same evening: "Bye Bye Baby" (reprise) (Dancing Ensemble), "Mamie is Mimi" (Gloria, Dance Team), "Coquette" (Tenor & Show Girls) [not on cast album]; *Scene 2* A street in Paris; later that evening: "Diamonds Are a Girl's Best Friend" (Lorelei) [a big hit]; *Scene 3* The Ritz Hotel in Paris. Lorelei's suite; 3 o'clock the next morning: "You Say You Care" (reprise) (Dorothy & Henry), "Gentlemen Prefer Blondes" (Lorelei & Gus), "Homesick Blues" (Lorelei, Dorothy, Gus, Henry, Mrs. Spofford, Gage); *Scene 4* The Central Park Casino, New York; ten days later: "Keeping Cool with Coolidge" (Dorothy, Bill, Ensemble), "Button Up with Esmond" (Lorelei, Show Girls, Ensemble) [not on cast album], Finale: reprises of: "Gentlemen Prefer Blondes" (Lorelei, Gus, Ensemble) and "Bye Bye Baby" (Entire Company).

It opened on Broadway to a record advance sale of over $600,000. Broadway reviewers raved, with the exception of Richard Watts in the

Post, who made a mistake. From 4/30/51, for two weeks, an exhausted Carol Channing was out, replaced by Bibi Osterwald. The show won Donaldson Awards for sets, costumes, and for female dancer (Anita Alvarez).

After Broadway. Tour. Opened on 9/20/51, at the Palace Theatre, Chicago. Musical Director: Jay Chernis. *Cast*: Lorelei: Carol Channing; Dorothy: Yvonne Adair, *Shirl Conway*; Gus: Jack McCauley; Lady Beekman: Reta Shaw; Henry: Eric Brotherson; Olympic: Curt Stafford; Gloria: Anita Alvarez, *Dorothy Etheridge*; Pierre: Bob Neukum; Head Waiter/Taxi Driver: Kaz Kokic; Dance Team: Charles "Honi" Coles & Cholly Atkins; Frank: Ronnie Field; Beekman: Robert Chisholm; Ella: Mary Finney; Gage: Morley Meredith; Louis: Don Raebern, *Frank Milton*.

The Movie. 1953. The movie had some new songs by Hoagy Carmichael — e.g. "Ain't There Anyone Here for Love?." Choreographer: Jack Cole. *Cast*: Lorelei: Marilyn Monroe; Dorothy: Jane Russell; Beekman: Charles Coburn; Gus: Tommy Noonan; Henry: George Winslow.

Princes Theatre, London, 8/20/62; Strand Theatre, 11/7/62. Total of 223 performances. Director: Henry Kaplan; Choreographer: Ralph Beaumont; Musical Director: Alyn Ainsworth. *Cast*: Lorelei: Dora Bryan; Dorothy: Anne Hart; Henry: Robin Palmer; Gus: Donald Stewart; Fifi: Irene Claire; Gloria: Valerie Walsh; Gage: Michael Malnick; Robert: John Heawood; Mrs. Spofford: Bessie Love; Lady Beekman: Totti Truman Taylor; Sir Francis: Guy Middleton.

In 1974 Carol Channing played Lorelei in *Lorelei* (qv).

244. Gentlemen Prefer Blondes (Broadway revival)

This was a revised version, with the musical program rearranged and using dialogue from the 1953 movie. It was now set in 1926.

Before Broadway. This revised revival was first produced by the Goodspeed Opera House, in Connecticut, as part of their 1994–95 season. The production had the same cast and crew as for the subsequent Broadway run.

The Broadway Run. Lyceum Theatre, 4/10/95–4/30/95. 16 previews from 3/28/95. 24 performances. Presented by the National Actors Theatre (Tony Randall, founder & artistic director), in association with the Goodspeed Opera House (Michael P. Price, exec producer), by arrangement with Tams-Witmark Music Library; Music: Jule Styne; Lyrics: Leo Robin; Book: Anita Loos & Joseph Fields; Based on the 1926 volume of sketches by Anita Loos; Director: Charles Repole; Choreographer: Michael Lichtefeld; Sets/Costumes: Eduardo Sicangco; Lighting: Kirk Bookman; Sound: T. Richard Fitzgerald; Musical Supervisor/Vocal Arrangements: Michael O'Flaherty; Musical Director: Andrew Wilder; Orchestrations: Douglas Besterman; Dance Music Arrangements: Gordon Lowry Harrell; Press: Springer Associates; Casting: Warren Pincus; General Management: Niko Associates; Company Manager: Erich Hamner; Production Stage Manager: Donna Cooper Hilton; Stage Manager: Kathy J. Faul. *Cast*: Dorothy Shaw: Karen Prunzik [formerly Prunczik]; Lorelei Lee: KT Sullivan; Gus Esmond: Allen Fitzpatrick; Lady Phyllis Beekman: Carol Swarbrick; Sir Francis Beekman: David Ponting; Mrs. Ella Spofford: Susan Rush; Henry Spofford: George Dvorsky; Josephus Gage: Jamie Ross; Steward: Dick Decareau; Frank: Craig Waletzko; George: Ken Nagy; Mime: Joe Bowerman; Robert Lemanteur: Craig Waletzko; Louie Lemanteur: John Hoshko; Tango Couples: Paula Grider & Joe Bowerman; Lisa Hanna & Ken Nagy; Lorinda Santos & Richard Costa; Park Casino Trio: Angela Bond, John Hoshko, Craig Waletzko; Mr. Esmond Sr.: Dick Decareau; Ensemble: Angela Bond, Joe Bowerman, Richard Costa, Paula Grider, Lisa Hanna, Bryan S. Haynes, John Hoshko, Ken Nagy, Wendy Roberts, Lorinda Santos, Craig Waletzko. *Understudies*: Lorelei/Mrs. Spofford/Lady Beekman: Angela Bond; Dorothy: Lisa Hanna; Gus/Mr. Edmonds Sr./Steward: John Hoshko; Josephus/Francis: Dick Decareau; Henry:

Craig Waletzko; Mime: Ken Nagy. *Swings*: Melissa Bell & Marty McDonough. *Orchestra*: Keyboards: Michael O'Flaherty & Andrew Wilder; Reeds: Dennis Anderson & John Campo; Trumpet: David Rogers; Trombone: Larry Farrell; Guitar: Greg Utzig; Percussion: Brad Flickinger. *Act I*: Overture (Orchestra); *Scene 1* Onstage and backstage at Club Purgatory, New York City: Opening (Dorothy & Men), "It's High Time" (Lorelei & Dorothy); *Scene 2* The French Line pier in New York; midnight sailing: "It's High Time" (reprise) (Company), "Bye Bye Baby" (Gus, Lorelei, Company); *Scene 3* The Sun Deck of the *Ile de France*; three days out: "(I'm Just a) Little Girl from Little Rock" (Lorelei), "I'm a'Tingle, I'm a'Glow" (Gage, Lorelei, Dorothy, Mrs. Spofford), "I Love What I'm Doing" (Dorothy & Olympic Men); *Scene 4* Lorelei's suite on the *Ile de France*; later that day: "Just a Kiss Apart" (Henry & Dorothy), "It's Delightful Down in Chile" (Sir Francis & Lorelei); *Scene 5* Paris: Sunshine Montage (Mime & Company); *Scene 6* Lorelei's suite at the Ritz in Paris; evening: "I'm a'Tingle, I'm a'Glow" (reprise) (Gage & Company), Finale Act I (Lorelei). *Act II*: Entr'acte; *Scene 1* Onstage at the Club Cocteau in Paris; the next evening: "Mamie is Mimi" (Dorothy & Company); *Scene 2* Dorothy's dressing room backstage; immediately following: "Diamonds Are a Girl's Best Friend" (Lorelei); *Scene 3* Streets of Paris, in front of the Cafe Rouge: "A Ride on a Rainbow" (Henry, Dorothy, Tango Couples); *Scene 4* Lorelei's suite; 3 a.m.: "Gentlemen Prefer Blondes" (Lorelei & Gus), "Homesick" (Gus, Lorelei, Dorothy, Henry, Mrs. Spofford, Gage); *Scene 5* The Central Park Casino, New York; ten days later: "I Love What I'm Doing" (reprise) (trio), "You Say You Care" (Trio), "Keeping Cool with Coolidge" (Company), Finale Act II (Company).

Broadway reviews were terrible.

After Broadway. Open Air Theatre, Regents Park, London, 7/23/98–9/1/98. Previews from 7/21/98. Director: Ian Talbot. *Cast*: Lorelei: Sara Crowe; Gus: Clive Rowe; Dorothy: Debby Bishop.

245. George M!

Also known as *Yankee Doodle Dandy*. Set between 1878 and 1937. Based on the life of George M. Cohan, from his birth in Providence, Rhode Island, to his Broadway triumph as President Roosevelt in *I'd Rather Be Right* (1937), the only musical in which he appeared that he did not himself write.

Before Broadway. Mike Stewart wrote the first libretto, an outline really, and his sister Fran Pascal and her husband did the rest.

The Broadway Run. Palace Theatre, 4/10/68–4/26/69. 8 previews. 427 performances. Presented by David Black, Konrad Matthaei, Lorin E. Price; Music/Lyrics: George M. Cohan (with revisions by Mary Cohan); Book: Michael Stewart, John & Fran Pascal; Suggested by the life of George M. Cohan (1878–1942); Director/Choreographer: Joe Layton; Sets: Tom John; Costumes: Freddy Wittop; Lighting: Martin Aronstein; Sound: Jackie Shearing; Musical Supervisor: Laurence Rosenthal; Musical Director/Vocal Arrangements: Jay Blackton; Orchestrations: Philip J. Lang; Cast recording on Columbia; Press: Frank Goodman, Martin Shwartz, Abby Hirsch; Casting: Carol Cappelletti; General Management: Allentuck, Azenberg, Wolsk; Company Manager: R. Tyler Gatchell Jr.; Stage Manager: Tony Manzi; Assistant Stage Manager: Lee Welling. *Cast*: Dog Trainers: Loni Ackerman & James Dybas; Living Statues: Jonelle Allen, Karin Baker, Roger Braun, Kathie Savage; Fay Templeton: Jacqueline Alloway (7); 1st Little Girl: Susan Batson; Dr. Webb: Roger Braun; Louis Behman: Danny Carroll; Jerry Cohan: Jerry Dodge (3); Ethel Levey: Jamie Donnelly (6); George M. Cohan: Joel Grey (1) ☆, *Jerry Dodge* (12/16/68–12/23/68), *Joel Grey*; Nellie Cohan: Betty Ann Grove (2); Stagehand at Providence Grande Theatre: James Dybas; Wardrobe Lady: Jacqueline Alloway; Designer's Assistant: Alan Weeks; Sam Harris: Harvey Evans; Secretary in Cohan & Harris' Office: Jonelle Allen; Piano Player in Cohan & Harris's Office: Scotty Salmon; Rose, Fay's Maid: Loni Ackerman; Freddie, Fay Templeton's Manager: Danny Carroll (9); Ma Templeton: Angela Martin; Secretary: Jonelle Allen; Congressman Burkhardt: James Dybas; Mayor: Roger Braun; Judge

ANSPACHER: John Mineo; ALDERMAN HAILEY: Ronald Young; LITTLE GIRL IN FAY TEMPLETON SCENE: Susan Batson; 2ND LITTLE GIRL: Patti Mariano; VENTRILOQUIST: Angela Martin; ARCHIE THE DRUMMER: John Mineo; BELL RINGERS: Danny Carroll, Ronald Young, Scotty Salmon, Harvey Evans; VIOLINIST: Harvey Evans (8); AGNES NOLAN: Jill O'Hara (4), *Sheila Sullivan* (from 8/26/68), *Deborah Deeble* (from 12/30/68); JOSIE COHAN: Bernadette Peters (5), *Patti Mariano* (from 8/26/68); 1ST PIANIST: Scotty Salmon; 2ND PIANIST: Loni Ackerman; MADAME GRIMALDI: Janie Sell; LOUIE: James Dybas; DRAPER: John Mineo; DRAPER'S ASSISTANT: Jacqueline Alloway; E.F. ALBEE: Roger Braun; ACTOR IN STRIKE SCENE: James Dybas; BEN: Roger Braun; MAN ON STREET: John Mineo; VENDOR: Danny Carroll; PUSHCART GIRLS: Karin Baker & Kathie Savage; BOY IN PUSHCART: Bill Brandon; WILLIE IN "POPULARITY:" Gene Castle; DOCKHAND: John Mineo; SHIP'S CAPTAIN: Ronald Young; SAILOR: Alan Weeks; 1ST POLICEMAN IN "NELLIE KELLY:" John Mineo; ACCORDIONIST IN "HARRIGAN:" Ronald Young; DIRECTOR OF "I'D RATHER BE RIGHT:" Ronald Young; WALT, STAGE MANAGER OF "I'D RATHER BE RIGHT:" Gene Castle (10); MRS. RED DEER: Susan Batson; MRS. BAKER: Janie Sell; FRANKIE: Alan Weeks; ACROBATS: Bill Brandon, Scotty Salmon, Patti Mariano; SHARPSHOOTER: Gene Castle; SHARPSHOOTER'S ASSISTANT: Susan Batson; BUCK AND WINGER: Alan Weeks; SAXOPHONIST: Ronald Young; FLAMETHROWER'S ASSISTANT: Janie Sell; FLAMETHROWER: Ronald Young; VOICE IN RECORDING: George M. Cohan; VOICES OF THE FOUR COHANS: Edie Cowan, Darryl Hickman, Linda Larson, Ted Pritchard. **Understudies**: George: Jerry Dodge; Josie: Patti Mariano; Jerry: Danny Carroll; Nellie/Agnes: Karin Baker; Ethel: Kathie Savage; Albee: Bill Brandon; Sam/Behman/Willie: John Mineo; Fay: Jonelle Allen; Mme Grimaldi: Angela Martin; Director: Roger Braun; Walt: James Dybas. **Swing Girl**: Katherine Hull. **Act I: Scene 1** Prologue: Overture; **Scene 2** Providence, Rhode Island; 1878; **Scene 3** Onstage, Columbia Theatre, Cedar Rapids; 1897: "Musical Moon" [from *The Little Millionaire*] (Jerry & Nellie), "Oh, You Wonderful Boy" [from *The Little Millionaire*, but revised] (Josie), "All Aboard for Broadway" [from *George Washington Jr.*] (George, then Four Cohans); **Scene 4** Street in Cedar Rapids: "Musical Comedy Man" [from *The Honeymooners*, but revised] (Four Cohans & Full Company); **Scene 5** Madame Grimaldi's boarding house; **Scene 6** En route to New York: "All Aboard for Broadway" (reprise) (Four Cohans & Full Company); **Scene 7** Adams Street Theatre, various other theatres, New York; 1901–1903: "I Was Born in Virginia" [from *George Washington Jr.*] (Ethel), "Twentieth Century Love" [from *The Merry Malones*] (Four Cohans & Ethel); **Scene 8** General area, New York, then in front of Savoy Theatre: "My Town" (George); **Scene 9** Stage of Liberty Theatre, New York: "Billie" [from *Billie*] (Agnes), "Push Me Along In My Pushcart" [from the 1906 revival of *The Governor's Son*] (Ethel & Pushcart Girls), "(A Ring to the Name of) Rose" [from *The Rose of Rosie O'Reilly*] (Josie & Bell Ringers), "Popularity" ("The Man Who Owns Broadway") (Willie & Full Company), "Give My Regards to Broadway" [from *Little Johnny Jones*] (George & Full Company). **Act II**: Entr'acte (Orchestra); **Scene 1** Office of Cohan & Harris, Fay Templeton's apartment: "Forty-Five Minutes from Broadway" [from *Forty Five Minutes from Broadway*] (George, then Rose), "So Long, Mary" [from *Forty Five Minutes from Broadway*] (George, Sam, then Rose, Freddie, Ma Templeton), "Down by the Erie (Canal)" [from *Hello, Broadway*] (Secretary, Politicians, Little Girl, then Full Company); **Scene 2** Onstage, New Amsterdam Theatre; New Years Eve, 1906: "Mary ('s a Grand Old Name)" [from *Forty Five Minutes from Broadway*] (Fay); **Scene 3** Rector's Restaurant; Jan. 1, 1907: "All Our Friends" [a revised version of "They're All My Boys" from *Little Nellie Kelly*] (Sam & Full Company); **Scene 4** Street outside Rector's; next morning; **Scene 5** The years till 1919: "Yankee Doodle Dandy" [based on "Yankee Doodle Boy" from *Little Johnny Jones*] (George & Full Company), "Nellie Kelly, I Love You" [from *Little Nellie Kelly*] (George & Full Company), "Harrigan" [from *Fifty Miles from Boston*] (George & Full Company), "Over There" (George & Full Company), "You're a Grand Old Flag" [from *George Washington Jr.*] (George & Full Company); **Scene 6** The years till 1937: "The City" [montage of "The Man Who Owns Broadway" from *The Man Who Owns Broadway*] (Full Company); **Scene 7** Midtown New York; Feb. 1937; **Scene 8** Stage of the Alvin Theatre: "I'd Rather Be Right" [from *I'd Rather Be Right*] (m: Richard Rodgers; l: Lorenz Hart) (George & Company), "Give My Regards to Broadway" (reprise) (George); **Scene 9** Epilogue (Full Company) [with the exception of the Cohan recording at the end, this Epilogue was dropped during the run], "Dancing Our Worries Away" [from *Little Nellie Kelly*, but revised], "The Great Easter Sunday Parade," "Hannah's a Hummer" [from *The Wise Guy*], "Barnum and Bailey Rag" [from *Hello, Broadway*], "The Belle of the Barbers' Ball" [from *Cohan and Harris Minstrels*], "The American Ragtime" [from *The American Idea*], "All in the Wearing" [from *Little Nellie Kelly*], "I Want to Hear a Yankee Doodle Tune" [from *Mother Goose*], Recording at end of epilogue, by George M. Cohan (The Four Cohans).

Note: in some programs the Prologue is not counted as Scene 1 (i.e. it is listed just as Prologue), and Providence, R.I. becomes Scene 1. Similarly, the Epilogue is not always counted as Act II Scene 9 (i.e. it is listed as just Epilogue).

The show opened to very divided reviews. It was Clive Barnes's first rave for a musical in the eight months he had been the *New York Times* critic. It was too late to be eligible for that season's Tony Awards, and by next year (1969) had been almost shunted into history, winning only for choreography. Joel Grey was nominated.

After Broadway. TOUR. Opened on 5/8/69, at the Curran Theatre, San Francisco. PRESENTED BY James & Joseph Nederlander, George M. Steinbrenner III, with Elizabeth Ireland McCann; MUSICAL DIRECTOR: Jack Lee. Instead of the number "Musical Comedy Man" it had "The Four of Us" (based on "The Two of Us" from *Billie*). **Cast**: GEORGE: Joel Grey, *Darryl Hickman* (from 10/21/69); NELLIE: Betty Ann Grove; FAY: Jacqueline Alloway; JERRY: Jerry Dodge; LOUIS: Gerard Brentte; WILLIE/WALT: Gene Castle; JOSIE: Jennifer Williams; AGNES: Pamela Peadon; ARCHIE: John Mineo. Several other actors reprised their Broadway roles.

TOUR. Opened on 9/25/70, at KRNT, Des Moines, and closed on 4/10/71, at the Civic Opera House, Chicago. PRESENTED BY Tom Mallow; DIRECTOR: Billy Matthews; CHOREOGRAPHER: Robert Pagent; SETS: Leo B. Meyer; LIGHTING: Ralph Alswang; MUSICAL DIRECTOR: Milton Setzer. **Cast**: GEORGE: Tony Tanner.

NBC-TV PRESENTATION, 9/12/70. Actually a rehearsal for the show, so the actors played themselves as well as the characters. Only Joel Grey and Bernadette Peters reprised their Broadway roles.

GOODSPEED OPERA HOUSE, Conn., 7/28/00–10/7/00. Previews from 7/7/00. DIRECTOR: Greg Ganakas; CHOREOGRAPHER: Randy Skinner; SETS: Howard Jones; MUSICAL DIRECTOR: Michael O'Flaherty. John Blum was to have played George, but he injured his foot during rehearsals. **Cast**: GEORGE: John Scherer (*Stacey Todd Holt*); JERRY: Frank Root; NELLIE: Dorothy Stanley; JOSIE: Liz Pearce; ALBEE/SAM HARRIS: Dale Hensley; MME GRIMALDI/MA TEMPLETON: Nancy Johnston; ETHEL: Jennifer Smith; AGNES: Tia Speros; FAY: Jennifer Goode; WALT: Shonn Wiley.

246. *Georgy*

Set in the "Swinging London" of the 1960s. Two roommates: Meredith, a glamorous bitch, and Georgy, a dowdy but lovable teacher. Jos makes Meredith pregnant, but falls for Georgy. The movie hit song "Georgy Girl" was not in this musical.

Before Broadway. Myra Carter's role was written out during tryouts. The numbers "Electric Windows," "Fog-Out," and "This Time Tomorrow" were all cut.

The Broadway Run. WINTER GARDEN THEATRE, 2/26/70–2/28/70. 7 previews. 4 PERFORMANCES. PRESENTED BY Fred Coe, in association with Joseph P. Harris & Ira Bernstein; MUSIC: George Fischoff; LYRICS: Carole Bayer; BOOK: Tom Mankiewicz; BASED ON the 1966 British movie *Georgy Girl*, written by Margaret Forster & Peter Nichols (starring Lynn Redgrave), which in turn was based on Margaret Forster's 1966 novel *Georgy Girl*; DIRECTOR: Peter Hunt; CHOREOGRAPHER: Howard Jeffrey; ASSISTANT CHOREOGRAPHER: Michael Shawn; SETS/LIGHTING: Jo Mielziner; COSTUMES: Patricia Zipprodt; AUDIO DESIGN: Robert Liftin; MUSICAL DIRECTOR/VOCAL ARRANGEMENTS: Elliot Lawrence; ORCHESTRATIONS: Eddie Sauter; DANCE MUSIC ARRANGEMENTS: Marvin Laird; CAST RECORDING on Bell; PRESS: Karl Bernstein & Dan Langan; CASTING: Marion Dougherty Associates; MAGICAL TECHNICAL ADVISER: Jack Adams; GENERAL MANAGERS: Joseph P. Harris & Ira Bernstein; COMPANY MANAGER: Sam Pagliaro; STAGE MAN-

AGER: Philip Mandelker; ASSISTANT STAGE MANAGERS: James Haire & Lynn Montgomery. *Cast*: GEORGY: Dilys Watling (1) *; CHILDREN: Kelley Boa, Mona Daleo, Jackie Paris, Donna Sands, Jill Streisant, Dewey Golkin, Jeffrey Golkin, Anthony Marciona, Roger Morgan, Johnny Welch; JAMES LEAMINGTON: Stephen Elliott (4) *; TED: Louis Beachner (5); MEREDITH: Melissa Hart (3) *; PEG: Helena Carroll (6); JOS: John Castle (2) *; PETER: Richard Quarry; HEALTH OFFICER: Cynthia Latham (7); SINGERS: Susan Goeppinger, Del Horstmann, Don Jay, Geoff Lyon, Regina Lynn; PARTY GUESTS/LONDONERS, ETC: Rick Atwell, Kathryn Doby, Pi Douglass, Sherry Durham, Arthur Faria, Patricia Garland, Charlie Goeddertz, Margot Head, Mary Jane Houdina, Neil Jones, Jane Karel, Barbara Monte-Britton, Michon Peacock, Sal Pernice, Richard Quarry, Allan Sobek, Tony Stevens, Mary Zahn. *Understudies*: Georgy: Carol Prandis; Meredith: Barbara Monte-Britton; James/ Ted: John O'Leary; Peg/Health Officer: Myra Carter; Peter: Allan Sobek. *Act I*: *Scene 1* A playground: "Howdjadoo" (Georgy & Children); *Scene 2* Georgy & Meredith's flat: "Make it Happen Now" (Georgy); *Scene 3* A street: "Ol' Pease Puddin'" (Jos & Georgy); *Scene 4* The flat: "Just for the Ride" (Meredith & Men), "So What?" (Georgy); *Scene 5* James Leamington's house: "Georgy" (James); *Scene 6* The flat: "A Baby (Mrs. Jones)" & "Howdjadoo" (reprise) (Georgy, Jos, Meredith); *Scene 7* London streets; *Scene 8* James Leamington's house; *Scene 9* The flat: "That's How it Is" (Georgy & James); *Scene 10* A street; *Scene 11* Apollo Cinema, Piccadilly Circus: "There's a Comin' Together" (Jos, Georgy, Chorus). *Act II*: *Scene 1* The flat: "Something Special" (Georgy & Jos), "Half of Me" (Georgy); *Scene 2* A street: "Gettin' Back to Me" (Meredith); *Scene 3* James Leamington's house: "Sweet Memory" (Ted, James, Chorus), "Georgy" (reprise) (James); *Scene 4* The flat: "Life's a Holiday" (Jos & Georgy), "Make it Happen Now" (reprise) (Georgy); *Scene 5* A playground: Finale: "There's a Comin' Together" (reprise) (Company).

Broadway reviews were mostly unfavorable. Part of the reason for the failure of this show was that one couldn't buy Dilys Watling as dowdy. Miss Watling and Melissa Hart were both nominated for Tony Awards. Carol Bayer became Carol Bayer Sager.

After Broadway. Revised revival by WINGS THEATRE COMPANY, 7/16/91–8/9/91. 16 PERFORMANCES. The numbers "Howdjadoo?" and "Something Special" were dropped; "Life's a Holiday" was replaced by new number—"Toy Balloon." DIRECTOR: Morgan La Vere; CHOREOGRAPHER: Schellie Archbold; SETS: Vicki R. Davis; MUSICAL DIRECTOR: Darren R. Cohen. *Cast*: GEORGY: Meghan Duffy; JAMES: Jon Lutz; TED: Bill Wheeler.

247. *The Gershwins' Fascinating Rhythm*

Also seen as *Fascinatin' Rhythm*. A 90-minute musical revue, with no intermission. A collage of George and Ira Gershwin songs; a sexy, modern take on their classic music.

Before Broadway. This show was first produced in 1997, in HARTFORD, Conn., by the Hartford Stage Company, quite a different version, not yet developed into what it would later become. It won great acclaim. It had more songs than the final version (which had 27). The Arizona Theatre Company produced it, again to great acclaim, in TUCSON, 12/11/98–12/26/98. Previews from 12/5/98. They produced it again, at the HERBERGER THEATRE, Phoenix, 1/1/99–1/24/99. It was the company's biggest money-maker. *Arizona cast*: Kena Dorsey, David Elder, Romain Fruge, Chris Ghelfi, Jillian, Karen Lifshey, Brian J. Marcum, Jill Nicklaus, Sara Ramirez, Scott Spahr. On 1/10/99 David Elder fell during a performance of "Our Love is Here to Stay," and injured his knee. After an intermission, he carried on, and for the next few days, with someone else doing the dancing part, but finally had to leave the show for surgery on 1/14/99.

The Broadway Run. LONGACRE THEATRE, 4/25/99–5/9/99. 27 previews from 4/2/99. 17 PERFORMANCES. PRESENTED BY Music Makers, Inc., Columbia Artists, and Manny Kladitis, in association with Magicworks/SFX Entertainment & Jerry Frankel; MUSIC: George Gershwin; LYRICS: Ira Gershwin; CONCEIVED FOR THE STAGE BY Mark Lamos & Mel

Marvin; SOURCE MATERIAL BY Deena Rosenberg; DIRECTOR: Mark Lamos; CHOREOGRAPHER: David Marques; SETS: Michael Yeargan; COSTUMES: Paul Tazewell; LIGHTING: Peggy Eisenhauer; SOUND: Abe Jacob; MUSICAL SUPERVISOR/MUSICAL DIRECTOR: Cynthia Kortman; ORCHESTRATIONS: Larry Hochman; ADDITIONAL ORCHESTRATIONS: Jack Cortner, Jay Dryer, Gary Fagin, Joe Gianono, Ned Ginsburg; MUSICAL & VOCAL ARRANGEMENTS: Mel Marvin; ADDITIONAL MUSICAL & VOCAL ARRANGEMENTS: Paul J. Ascenzo & Joseph Church; PRESS: Boneau/ Bryan-Brown; CASTING: Bernard Telsey; GENERAL MANAGEMENT: Niko Associates; COMPANY MANAGER: James Lawson; PRODUCTION STAGE MANAGER: Alan Hall; STAGE MANAGER: Ruth E. Rinklin; ASSISTANT STAGE MANAGER: Tracy Burns. *Cast*: Michael Berresse, Darius de Haas, Adriane Lenox, Orfeh, Sara Ramirez, Patrick Wilson, Chris Ghelfi, Tim Hunter, Karen Lifshey, Jill Nicklaus. *Swings*: Brian J. Marcum, Kenya Unique Massey. *Orchestra*: REED 1: Dennis Anderson; REED 2: Ed Salkin; REED 3: Frank Santagata; TRUMPET 1: Danny Cahn; TRUMPET 2: Bud Burridge; TROMBONE: Randy Andos; KEYBOARD 1: Mark Berman; KEYBOARD 2: Paul J. Ascenzo; GUITAR: Greg Skaff; BASS: Jeff Ganz; DRUMS: Gary Seligson; PERCUSSION: Paul Hostetter. "Fascinating Rhythm" [from *Lady, Be Good!*] (Company), "I've Got a Crush on You" [from *Treasure Girl*, and subsequently used in *Strike Up the Band*] (Sara & Michael), "Oh, Lady, Be Good!" * [from *Lady, Be Good!*] (Darius), "High Hat" [from *Funny Face*] (Patrick & Sara), "Clap Yo' Hands" [from *Oh, Kay!*] (Orfeh & Company), "(My) Cousin in Milwaukee/The Lorelei" [from *Pardon My English*] (Adriane & Orfeh), "The Man I Love" [dropped from *Strike Up the Band*]/"Soon" [from *Strike Up the Band*] (Sara & Patrick), "Love is Here to Stay" (pas de deux) † (Jill & Michael), "Little Jazz Bird" † [from *Lady, Be Good!*] (Darius), "Isn't it a Pity" [from *Pardon My English*] (Sara & Karen), "I Love to Rhyme" [from the movie *Goldwyn Follies*], "Blah, Blah, Blah" [from the movie *Delicious*], "I Got Rhythm" * [from *Girl Crazy*] (Michael & Company), "Embraceable You" * [from *Girl Crazy*] (Patrick, Chris, Tim, Karen, Jill), "Let's Call the Whole Thing Off" [from the movie *Shall We Dance*] (Darius & Orfeh), "Nice Work if You Can Get It" [from the movie *A Damsel in Distress*] (Adriane), "But Not for Me" [from *Girl Crazy*] (Patrick), "Just Another Rhumba" † [an unused song from the movie *Goldwyn Follies*] (Sara & Michael), "Someone to Watch Over Me" [from *Oh, Kay!*] (Darius, Karen, Orfeh, Sara, Patrick), "The Half-of-it-Dearie Blues" * [from *Lady, Be Good!*] (Adriane), "Love is Here to Stay" [from the movie *Goldwyn Follies*] (Sara), "How Long Has This Been Going On" [from *Rosalie*] (Patrick), "Home Blues" (l: Ira Gershwin & Gus Kahn) [from *Show Girl*] (set to the Homesickness Theme from the movie *An American in Paris*) (Sara & Patrick), "Who Cares" (from *Of Thee I Sing*) (Michael & Company), "They Can't Take That Away from Me" [from the movie *Shall We Dance*] (Company), "Hang on to Me" [from *Lady, Be Good!*] (Company).

Note: * means musical arrangement by Paul J. Ascenzo; † means musical arrangement by Joseph Church.

Broadway reviews were not good, and provisional closing notices were posted on 5/4/99.

248. *Gigi*

Set mostly in Paris in May 1901. Gigi is a young girl raised by Mamita, her grandmother, and Alicia, her great-aunt, to follow the family tradition of becoming a courtesan. Gaston is an eligible bachelor who scandalizes Gigi's family by proposing marriage to her; Honore is Gaston's worldly grandfather.

Before Broadway. The straight Broadway comedy ran 11/24/51– 5/31/52. 217 PERFORMANCES. *Cast*: GIGI: Audrey Hepburn.

The musical was Lerner & Loewe's first stage collaboration since *Camelot* in 1960. Edwin Lester, of the Los Angeles & San Francisco Civic Light Operas, had been asking Lerner & Loewe for years to do a stage version of their Hollywood musical *Gigi* (directed by Vincente Minnelli, and starring Leslie Caron as Gigi; Maurice Chevalier as Honore; Louis Jourdan as Gaston; Hermione Gingold as Mme Alvarez; and Eva Gabor as Liane, and which won 8 Oscars). In 1971, when the two were working on the movie *The Little Prince* (not released until 1974), Fritz Loewe finally agreed to do the stage musical. The major problem was that they couldn't find a

Gigi. Katharine Hepburn found one for them — Terese Stevens, a 20-year-old actress then playing in a London rock version of *Carmen.* Terry wasn't right, and was replaced by Karin Wolfe, her understudy, and that didn't work either. The show opened in California, and toured the country for six months before going to Broadway. In Detroit Joseph Hardy was replaced as director by Alan Jay Lerner himself, despite which Mr. Hardy retained credit.

The Broadway Run. URIS THEATRE, 11/13/73–2/10/74. 7 previews from 11/7/73. 103 PERFORMANCES. Edwin Lester's Los Angeles & San Francisco Civic Light Opera production, PRESENTED BY Saint Subber; MUSIC: Frederick Loewe; LYRICS/BOOK: Alan Jay Lerner; BASED ON the 1958 movie musical, which in turn was based on the 1944 novella by Colette and the 1951 Broadway dramatization by Anita Loos; DIRECTOR: Joseph Hardy; CHOREOGRAPHER: Onna White; SETS: Oliver Smith; COSTUMES: Oliver Messel; LIGHTING: Thomas Skelton; SOUND: Thomas Fitzgerald; MUSICAL DIRECTOR: Ross Reimueller; ORCHESTRATIONS: Irwin Kostal; DANCE MUSIC ARRANGEMENTS: Trude Rittman; CAST recording on RCA; PRESS: Martin Shwartz & Ben Washer; GENERAL MANAGER: C. Edwin Knill; COMPANY MANAGER: James Turner; PRODUCTION STAGE MANAGER: M. William Lettich; STAGE MANAGER: Howard Chitjian. *Cast:* HONORE LACHAILLES: Alfred Drake (1) ☆; GASTON LACHAILLES: Daniel Massey (4) ☆; LIANE D'EXELMANS: Sandahl Bergman (9); INEZ ALVAREZ (MAMITA): Maria Karnilova (3) ☆; GIGI: Karin Wolfe (5); AUNT ALICIA: Agnes Moorehead (2) ☆, *Louise Kirtland, Arlene Francis* (from 1/24/74); CHARLES, HER BUTLER: Gordon de Vol; HEAD WAITER/RECEPTIONIST: Joe Ross (7); TELEPHONE INSTALLER/MAITRE D': Joe Ross (7); TWO WAITERS: Leonard John Crofoot & Thomas Stanton; LIANE'S DANCE PARTNER: Thomas Anthony; AN ARTIST: Patrick Spohn, *Andy Bew*; A COUNT: Joel Pressman; SANDOMIR: Randy Di Grazio; DANCING TEACHER: Gregory Drotar; MANUEL: Truman Gaige (8); MAITRE DU FRESNE: George Gaynes (6), *Richard Woods*; MAITRE DUCLOS: Howard Chitjian (10), *John Dorrin*; TWO LAW CLERKS: Leonard John Crofoot & Thomas Stanton; LITTLE GIRLS: Patricia Daly & Jill Turnbull; ENSEMBLE: Thomas Anthony, Alvin Beam, Russ Beasley, Robyn Blair, Leonard John Crofoot, Gordon de Vol, Randy Di Grazio, John Dorrin, Gregory Drotar, Janice Eckhart, Margit Haut, Andy Keyser, Beverly Kopels, Diane Lauridsen, Merilee Magnuson, Kelley Maxwell, Vickie Patik, Joel Pressman, Patrick Spohn, Thomas Stanton, Cherie Suzanne, Marie Tillmanns, Sallie True, *Judy Cummings, Clyde Laurents, Jean McLaughlin, Susan Plantt*. *Standbys:* Gigi: Patricia Arnell, *Hallie Scott*; Honore: Larry Keith, *George Gaynes*; Mamita/Alicia: Louise Kirtland. *Understudies:* Gaston: Gordon de Vol; Du Fresne/Manuel: John Dorrin; Liane: Marie Tillmanns; For Joe Ross: Joel Pressman. *Swing Dancer*: Bjarne Buchtrup. *Act I*: Overture (Orchestra); *Scene 1* The Pre-Catelan Restaurant in the Bois, Paris; a September afternoon, 1900: "Thank Heaven for Little Girls" (Honore) [the big hit, at least it was back in 1958, when the movie was out], "It's a Bore" (Honore & Gaston); *Scene 2* Mamita's apartment; immediately following; *Scene 3* Aunt Alicia's apartment; immediately following: "The Earth and Other Minor Things" * (Gigi); *Scene 4* The restaurant of the Eiffel Tower; evening: "Paris is Paris Again" * (Honore & Ensemble), "She's Not Thinking of Me" ("Waltz at Maxim's") (Gaston); *Scene 5a* Alicia's apartment; midday, the following day; *Scene 5b* Apartment of Honore Lachailles; simultaneously; *Scene 5c* Alicia's apartment; as before; *Scene 5d* Honore's dressing room; as before: "It's a Bore" (reprise) (Honore, Gaston, Manuel, Alicia) [this song was spread out over the entire four parts of Scene 5]; *Scene 6* Mamita's apartment; two weeks later: "The Night They Invented Champagne" (Gigi, Gaston, Mamita); *Scene 7a* The lobby of the Grand Hotel, Trouville; the following afternoon: "I Remember it Well" (Honore & Mamita) [from *Love Life*]; *Scene 7b* The beach at Trouville: "I Never Want to Go Home Again" * (Gigi & Ensemble). *Act II*: *Scene 1* Mamita's apartment; early afternoon, three weeks later; *Scene 2* The street outside Mamita's apartment; immediately following: "Gigi" (Gaston); *Scene 3* The office of Maitre Du Fresne; a day or two later: "The Contract" * (Alicia, Mamita, Duclos, Du Fresne) [the big new song]; *Scene 4* Mamita's apartment; the following day; *Scene 5* A street cafe; an hour later: "I'm Glad I'm Not Young Anymore" (Honore); *Scene 6* Mamita's apartment; later that day: "In This Wide, Wide World" * (Gigi); *Scene 7* Maxim's; that night; *Scene 8* Mamita's apartment; immediately following: "Thank Heaven for Little Girls" (reprise) (Honore), Finale (Company).

Note: those songs asterisked were newly written for this stage musical, i.e. they were not in the 1958 movie.

Broadway reviews were divided, and, despite its long pre–Broadway tour, still lost more than half its investment of $800,000. It failed partly because its star was no Leslie Caron, and partly because the story was now outdated. It won a Tony for score, and was nominated for sets, costumes, and for Alfred Drake.

After Broadway. TOUR. 1984–85. *Cast:* HONORE: Louis Jourdan (lip-synched); MAMITA: Taina Elg; ALICIA: Betsy Palmer; GIGI: Lisa Howard (her professional debut); GASTON: Tom Hewitt.

LYRIC THEATRE, London, 9/17/85. This production was much more intimate than the Broadway one. DIRECTOR: John Dexter; CAST RECORDING on First Night. *Cast:* GIGI: Amanda Waring; ALICIA: Beryl Reid; MAMITA: Sian Phillips; GASTON: Geoffrey Burridge; HONORE: Jean-Pierre Aumont.

EQUITY LIBRARY THEATRE, NYC, 5/11/89–6/4/89. 32 PERFORMANCES. DIRECTOR: Gerard Alessandrini; CHOREOGRAPHER: John Carrafa; MUSICAL DIRECTOR: Paul Johnson. "The Earth and Other Minor Things" was replaced by "I Don't Understand the Parisians," and the new number, "The Telephone Installer Song" now ended Act I. *Cast:* GIGI: Pamela Shafer; HONORE: Russell Costen; ALICIA: Lynette Bennett; VICTOR: Kevin Brunner; JACQUES: Jonathan Cerullo; GASTON: Bob Cuccioli.

PAPER MILL PLAYHOUSE, New Jersey, 11/3/96–12/15/96. DIRECTOR: Robert Johanson; CHOREOGRAPHER: Sharon Halley; SETS: Michael Anania; COSTUMES: Gregg Barnes; LIGHTING: Tim Hunter; MUSICAL DIRECTOR: Wendy Bobbitt. *Cast*: HONORE: Gavin MacLeod; ALICIA: Liliane Montevecchi; MAMITA: Anne Rogers; GIGI: Glory Crampton.

THEATRE UNDER THE STARS, Houston, 1/17/98–2/1/98. Previews from 1/15/98. DIRECTOR: Bruce Lumpkin; MUSICAL DIRECTOR: Wayne Green. *Cast:* HONORE: Gavin MacLeod; ALICIA: Liliane Montevecchi; MAMITA: Anne Rogers; GIGI: Linnea Dakin; GASTON: Alberto Stevens.

249. *The Girl from Nantucket*

Michael, a housepainter, uses binoculars to watch Betty, the girl across the street, and gets a job painting the outside sills of her bathroom window, but he is mistakenly commissioned to do murals for a museum in Nantucket. He can't do the job, of course, so Betty, an art student, does the job for him.

Before Broadway. The number "That's How I Know that I'm in Love" was cut during tryouts. Billy Lynn replaced star James Barton, and Adelaide Bishop replaced Evelyn Wyckoff. Eugene von Grona was dance director and Val Raset was ballet director, but by Broadway opening night Val Raset was choreographing the whole show. It had a cast of 80.

The Broadway Run. ADELPHI THEATRE, 11/8/45–11/17/45. 12 PERFORMANCES. PRESENTED BY Henry Adrian; MUSIC/VOCAL & ORCHESTRAL ARRANGEMENTS: Jacques Belasco; LYRICS: Kay Twomey; ADDITIONAL MUSIC & LYRICS: Hughie Prince & Dick Rogers; BOOK: Paul Stamford & Harold M. Sherman; ADDITIONAL DIALOGUE: Hi Cooper; BASED ON a story by Fred Thompson & Berne Giler; DIRECTOR: Henry Adrian; BOOK DIRECTOR: Edward Clarke Lilley; CHOREOGRAPHER: Val Raset; SETS/LIGHTING: Albert Johnson; COSTUMES: Lou Eisele; MUSICAL DIRECTOR: Harry Levant; ADDITIONAL ARRANGEMENTS: Ted Royal; PRESS: Marjorie Barkentin; COMPANY MANAGER: George Zorn; GENERAL STAGE MANAGER: R.O. Brooks; STAGE MANAGER: Tony Ferreira. *Cast:* MICHAEL NICOLSON: Bob Kennedy (4); BETTY ELLIS: Adelaide Bishop (evenings), Pat McClarney (matinees); TOM ANDREWS: George L. Headley; ANN ELLIS: Marion Niles (8) (this was Mary Ann Niles); DODEY ELLIS: Jane Kean (3); KEZIAH GETCHEL: Helen Raymond (5); JUDGE PELEG: John Robb; CAPTAIN MATTHEW ELLIS: Billy Lynn (2); DICK OLIVER: Jack Durant (1); ENRICO NICOLETTI: Richard Clemens; CORNELIUS B. VAN WINKLER: Norman Roland [character cut before Broadway]; THE CORPORATION (THE FOUR BUCCANEERS): John Panter, Don Cortez, Joseph Cunneff, Paul Shiers; ROY/CALEB/SEVERAL OTHER FELLOWS: Johnny Eager; MARY: Connie Sheldon; DANCE SPECIALISTS: Kim & Kathy Gaynes (6), Rapps & Tapps; SOLO DANCER: Tom Ladd (7); THE NANTUCKET GUIDES: Claire Weidener, Deanne Benmore, Marilyn Pendry, Mary Bernice Brady, Madeleine Detry, Gloria Evans, Lee Joyce, Zelda Allen, Fran Celia, Kay Popp, Louise Harris, Arleen Frank, Sylvia Mehler; THE VACATIONISTS: Bettina Thayer, Ruth Vrana, Jeanne North, Geraldine Willier, Harriet Pegors, Linda Hayes; THE TOWNS-

FOLK: Jean D'Arcy, Doris Claire, Rita Rallis, Lee Dennis, Vicky Raaf, Jerry Daily, Sherry Stevens, Francis Pruitt, Temple Texas, Norma Hetzler, Panette Piper, Francis Kiernan, Allan Waine, Mischa Pompianov, Randolf Hughes; THE FISHERMEN: Erno Czako, Gerald Scima, Robert Vaden, Neal Towner, Jack Riley, T.C. Jones, Terry Dawson. *Act I: Prologue* An apartment house in New York City. *Act I: Scene 1* Office of the Nantucket Steamship Company; *Scene 2* Nantucket pier; *Scene 3* Mike and Dick's apartment in New York City; *Scene 4* Nantucket pier; *Scene 5* Whalers' bar; *Scene 6* Outside the Nantucket Museum; a week later; *Scene 7* Inside the museum; the following night [during tryouts this scene was Keziah's beach home; the following night]; *Scene 8* Old Nantucket [this scene was added during tryouts]. *Act II: Scene 1* Nantucket pier; the following day; *Scene 2* Mike and Dick's bungalow in Nantucket; *Scene 3* Keziah's beach home [during tryouts this scene was Outside the museum]; *Scene 4* Outside the museum [during tryouts this scene was Old Nantucket]; *Scene 5* Inside the museum; *Scene 6* Nantucket Square. *Act I:* "I Want to See More of You" (Betty & Michael), "Take the Steamer to Nantucket" (Vacationists & Guides) (dance specialty by Kim & Kathy Gaynes, Ann), "What's He Like?" (Betty, Dodey, Girls), "What's a Sailor Got?" (Ellis & Ensemble), "Magnificent Failure" (m/l: Hughie Prince & Dick Rogers) (arr: Sam Medoff) (Dick), "Hurray for Nicoletti" (l: Kay Twomey & Burt Milton) (Dick & Entire Ensemble) (dance specialty by Ann, Rapps & Tapps), "When a Hick Chick Meets a City Slicker" (l: Burt Milton) (Dodey & Dick), "Your Fatal Fascination" (Betty, Michael, Kim & Kathy Gaynes, Ann, Ensemble), "Let's Do and Say We Didn't" (m/l: Hughie Prince & Dick Rogers; arr: Sam Medoff) (Dodey & Girls), "Nothing Matters" (Mary & Girls) (dance specialty by Rapps & Tapps), "Sons of the Sea" (Tom & Fishermen), "Whalers' Ballet — A Page from Old Nantucket" (long ballet) (monologue written by Mary Carroll and spoken by Tom): THE SEA: Kathy Gaynes; THE WHALE: Kim Gaynes; TOM, THE FISHERMAN: Tom Ladd. *Act II:* "Isn't it a Lovely View" (Betty & Vacationists), "Isn't it a Lovely View" (reprise) (Betty), "From Morning Till Night" (Betty & Michael), "I Love That Boy" (Dodey & Dick), "From Morning Till Night" (reprise) (Michael), "Hammock in the Blue" (Betty, Michael, Ensemble), "The Captain and His Lady" [cut before Broadway], "Boukra Fill Mish Mish" (Ellis, Tom Ladd, Ensemble), Dance Specialty (Dick & Ellis), Reprise, Finale.

The show was universally panned by the critics. It lost $365,000.

250. *The Girl in Pink Tights*

A musical extravaganza. Historically, a fire at the Academy of Music in New York left a ballet company stranded, and as a goodwill gesture as much as anything, Charles M. Barras integrated the ballet into his production *The Black Crook*, then playing at Niblo's Garden, thus making *The Black Crook* the first ever Broadway musical (so some history books say). This musical calls the play *The Red Devil*, and the focus is on Lisette, a French ballerina with the show.

Before Broadway. It was originally conceived as an MGM movie with Leslie Caron and Gene Kelly, but it was never made. This was Sig Romberg's last score (he died on 7/10/51, three years before the Broadway opening; the score was completed by Don Walker). It opened for tryouts on 1/25/54, at the Shubert Theatre, New Haven, for one week only. Then to Philadelphia, where leading man David Brooks was replaced by David Atkinson.

The Broadway Run. MARK HELLINGER THEATRE, 3/5/54–6/12/54. 115 PERFORMANCES. PRESENTED BY Shepard Traube, in association with Anthony Brady Farrell; MUSIC: Sigmund Romberg; LYRICS: Leo Robin; BOOK: Jerome Chodorov & Joseph Fields; DIRECTOR: Shepard Traube; CHOREOGRAPHER: Agnes de Mille; ASSISTANT CHOREOGRAPHER: Dania Krupska; SETS/LIGHTING: Eldon Elder; COSTUMES: Miles White; MUSICAL DIRECTOR/CHORAL DIRECTOR: Sylvan Levin; DEVELOPED MUSIC/ORCHESTRATIONS: Don Walker; BALLET MUSIC ARRANGEMENTS: Trude Rittman; PRESS: George Ross & Madelin Blitzstein; GENERAL MANAGER: J.H. Del Bondio; PRODUCTION STAGE MANAGER: Bill Ross; STAGE MANAGER: Bruce Savan; ASSISTANT STAGE MANAGER: Perry Bruskin. *Cast*: BORIS: Joshua Shelley; VOLODYA KUZENTSOV: Alexandre Kalioujny (5); LISETTE GERVAIS: Jeanmaire (1); MAESTRO GALLO: Charles Goldner (2);

LOTTA LESLIE: Brenda Lewis (3); CLYDE HALLAM: David Atkinson (4); EDDINGTON: David Aiken; HATTIE HOPKINS: Dania Krupska; VAN BEUREN: Robert Smith; BRITISH TARS: Tom Rieder & John Taliaferro; POLICEMAN: John Stamford; NEWSPAPER BOY: Maurice Hines; SHOE SHINE BOY: Gregory Hines; MIKE: Kalem Kermoyan (he became Michael Kermoyan); BRUCE: John Stamford; NELLIE: Lydia Fredericks; HOLLISTER: Ray Mason; SIMONE: Katia Geleznova; MIMI: Eva Rubinstein; LUCETTE: Lynne Marcus; ODETTE: Nancy King; GISELE: Lila Popper; PAULETTE: Mickey Gunnersen; FIRE CHIEFS: Ted Thurston & John Taliaferro; JENNY: Jenny Workman; BLANCHETTE: Beryl Towbin; EMILE: Ted Thurston; SOMMELIER: John Taliaferro; GYPSY VIOLINIST: Douglas Rideout; SINGERS: David Aiken, Herbert Banke, Robert Driscoll, Lydia Fredericks, Jane House, Deedy Irwin, Kalem Kermoyan, Peggy Kinard, Ray Mason, Marni Nixon, Stas Pajenski, Michelle Reiner, Douglas Rideout, Tom Rieder, James Schlader, Joanne Spiller, John Stamford, John Taliaferro, Ted Thurston, Beverly Weston; DANCERS: Harry Asmus, Meredith Baylis, Joan Bowman, Katia Geleznova, Mickey Gunnersen, Mary Haywood, Rhoda Kerns, Nancy King, Louis Kosman, Lynne Marcus, Julie Marlowe, Ellen Matthews, Paul Olson, Lila Popper, Eva Rubinstein, Dorothy Scott, Beverly Simms, Edward Stinnett, Beryl Towbin, Diana Turner, William Weslow, Jenny Workman. *Understudies*: Lisette: Dania Krupska; Gallo: Ted Thurston; Lotta: Michelle Reiner; Clyde: Ray Mason; Volodya: William Weslow; Van Beuren/Mike: Tom Rieder; Hattie: Marni Nixon; Boris: Perry Bruskin; Eddington: Douglas Rideout; Blanchette: Rhoda Kerns; Hollister: James Schlader; Emile/Fire Chief: John Stamford; Violinist: Robert Driscoll; Bruce/Policeman: Herb Banke. *Act I: Scene 1* A rehearsal hall at the Academy of Music: Ballet Class (danced by the French Ballet Company): LISETTE: Jeanmaire; VOLODYA: Alexandre Kalioujny; SOLOISTS: Diana Turner, William Weslow, Lynne Marcus, Harry Asmus, Beverly Simms, Paul Olson, Dorothy Scott, Edward Stinnett; *Scene 2* A street near the Academy of Music and Niblo's Garden: "That Naughty Show from Gay Paree" (Singing Ensemble); *Scene 3* Outside the Academy of Music and Niblo's Garden: "Lost in Loveliness" (Clyde). LISETTE: Jeanmaire; 1ST LOVER: Paul Olson; 2ND LOVER: Harry Asmus; LOVERS: Edward Stinnett & Louis Kosman; *Scene 4* A street near the theatrical district: "I Promised Their Mothers" (Gallo); *Scene 5* Bowling Green: "Up in the Elevated Railway" (sung & danced by Lisette, Clyde, Volodya, Hattie, Shoe Shine Boy, Newspaper Boy, Singing Ensemble), "In Paris and in Love" (Clyde & Lisette); *Scene 6* The stage at Niblo's Garden: "You've Got to Be a Little Crazy" (Lotta, Nellie, Mike, Bruce); *Scene 7* A corridor at the Academy of Music: "(When I Am) Free to Love" (Lisette); *Scene 8* The stage at the Academy of Music; three days later: Pas de Deux (danced by Lisette & Volodya); *Scene 9* A street: "Out of the Way"/"Roll Out the Hose, Boys" (Members of Singing Ensemble); *Scene 10* In front of the Academy of Music: First Act Finale (Entire Company). *Act II: Scene 1* A pier at Battery Park; a week later: "My Heart Won't Say Goodbye" (Clyde, Lisette, Singing Ensemble), "We're All in the Same Boat" (sung & danced by Entire Company); *Scene 2* A theatrical costumer's; two weeks later: "Lost in Loveliness" (reprise) (Clyde); *Scene 3* The stage at Niblo's Garden: Bacchanale (Danced by the French Ballet Company): DIONYSIUS: Alexandre Kalioujny; THE WAYWARD NYMPH: Jenny Workman; NYMPHS: Meredith Baylis, Joan Bowman, Dorothy Scott, Beverly Simms, Diana Turner; SATYRS: Harry Asmus, Paul Olson, Edward Stinnett, William Weslow; MESSENGER: Beryl Towbin; ATTENDANTS: Maurice Hines & Gregory Hines; "My Heart Won't say Goodbye" (reprise) (Lotta), "Love is the Funniest Thing" (Lotta & Gallo); *Scene 4* A private dining room at the Hotel Brevoort; *Scene 5* A corridor backstage at Niblo's Garden; *Scene 6* Clyde's dressing room: "(When I Am) Free to Love" (reprise) (Lisette); *Scene 7* The final scene of *The Soul of Dick the Renegade* ("The Bill is Due! It Must be Paid"), "The Cardinal's Guard Are We" (Lotta & Members of Singing Ensemble), "Going to the Devil" (Lisette) [added during the run]; Grand Imperial Ballet (danced by the Ballet Company): LUCIFER: Alexandre Kalioujny; HECATE: Jeanmaire; DEVILS: Harry Asmus, Paul Olson, Edward Stinnett, William Weslow; EVIL SPIRITS: Katia Geleznova, Lynne Marcus, Dorothy Scott, Beverly Simms; BATS: Mary Heyward, Meredith Baylis, Joan Bowman, Julia Marlowe, Lila Popper, Diane Turner; DANCING BATLETS: Nancy King, Ellen Matthews, Eva Rubinstein, Jenny Workman; BATLETS: Mickey Gunnersen, Rhoda Kerns, Beryl Towbin; ATTENDANTS: Maurice Hines & Gregory Hines; Finale Act II (Entire Company).

Broadway reviews were generally unfavorable, but Jeanmaire got universal raves.

251. *The Girl Who Came to Supper*

Set in London 6/21/1911–6/22/1911, just prior to and during the coronation of George V. Chorus girl Mary, from Milwaukee, meets the prince regent of the small Balkan country of Carpathia, and is invited to dine at his embassy. The regent only wants to get her into bed, but eventually falls in love with her after she manages to make peace between him and his estranged son. Whereas Terence Rattigan's original straight play was set exclusively in the royal suite at the embassy, the musical opened up scenes to include St. Martin's Lane, Trafalgar Square, Westminster Abbey, and backstage at Mary's show. Also, the prince's wife became his mother for the musical, he became a widower, adultery was no longer an issue, and his son now became King of Carpathia.

Before Broadway. In 1953 *The Sleeping Prince* ran as a straight play in London, with Laurence Olivier and Vivien Leigh. On Broadway it starred Michael Redgrave and Barbara Bel Geddes. The musical version, *The Girl Who Came to Supper*, was backed by CBS. Rex Harrison and Chris Plummer were early choices for the role of the prince regent. The show tried out in Boston, where reviews were tremendous. It wasn't so good at the next stop, Toronto. During further tryouts in Philadelphia, where reviews were favorable, President Kennedy was assassinated, so the number "Long Live the King (If He Can)" was yanked. Noel Coward re-wrote his old song "Countess Mitzi" (from his 1938 show *Operette*) into a new number, "My Family Tree," to replace it. Other numbers cut before Broadway were: "Come Be My True Love," "Hey, Nonny-No," "If Only Mrs. Applejohn Were Here," "Just People," "Life without Love," "Put Not Your Trust in Princes," "Time Will Tell (originally written for the unfinished *Later Than Spring*), and "What's the Matter with a Nice Beef Stew?" This was the last show with a Noel Coward score, and the only one never performed in London (despite a rumor that it was going to open at the Theatre Royal, Drury Lane).

The Broadway Run. BROADWAY THEATRE, 12/8/63–3/14/64. 4 previews from 12/5/63. 112 PERFORMANCES. PRESENTED BY Herman Levin; MUSIC/LYRICS: Noel Coward; BOOK: Harry Kurnitz; BASED ON the movie *The Prince and the Showgirl*, which in turn was based on the 1953 comedy *The Sleeping Prince*, by Terence Rattigan (which had been written to honor Queen Elizabeth's coronation that year); DIRECTOR/CHOREOGRAPHER: Joe Layton; SETS: Oliver Smith; COSTUMES: Irene Sharaff; LIGHTING: Peggy Clark; MUSICAL DIRECTOR/VOCAL ARRANGEMENTS: Jay Blackton; ORCHESTRATIONS: Robert Russell Bennett; DANCE MUSIC ARRANGEMENTS: Genevieve Pitot; CAST RECORDING on Columbia; PRESS: Richard Maney & Martin Shwartz; GENERAL MANAGER: Philip Adler; COMPANY MANAGER: S.M. Handelsman; PRODUCTION STAGE MANAGER: Samuel Liff; STAGE MANAGER: Jerry Adler; ASSISTANT STAGE MANAGER: Marnel Sumner & Geoffrey Johnson. *Cast*: JESSIE MAYNARD: Marian Haraldson; MARY MORGAN: Florence Henderson (2); TONY MORELLI: Jack Eddleman; MR. GRIMES: Peter Pagan; VIOLETTA VINES: Maggie Worth; PETER NORTHBROOK: Roderick Cook (5); COLONEL HOFMANN: Chris Gampel; THE GRAND DUKE CHARLES, PRINCE REGENT OF CARPATHIA: Jose Ferrer (1); 1ST GIRL: Donna Monroe; 2ND GIRL: Ruth Shepard; MAJOR-DOMO: Carey Nairnes; KING NICOLAS III OF CARPATHIA: Sean Scully; SIMKA: Murray Adler; QUEEN MOTHER: Irene Browne (3); ADA COCKLE: Tessie O'Shea (4); BARONESS BRUNHEIM: Lucie Lancaster; LADY SUNNINGDALE: Ilona Murai; DANCERS: Ivan Allen, Julie Drake, Robert Fitch, Sheila Forbes, Jose Gutierrez, Peter Holmes, Jami Landi, Sandy Leeds, Nancy Lynch, Carmen Morales, Ilona Murai, Scott Ray, Paul Reid Roman, Mari Shelton, Dan Siretta, Gloria Smith, Mike Toles, Mary Zahn; SINGERS: Jeremy Brown, Kellie Brytt, Jack Eddleman, John Felton, Carol Glade, Del Hanley, Marian Haraldson, Barney Johnston, Elaine Labour, Art Matthews, Donna Monroe, Bruce Payton, Jack Rains, Ruth Shepard, Mitchell Taylor, Maggie Worth. *Standbys*: Prince: David Brooks; Mary:

Dran Seitz. *Understudies*: Prince: Jack Eddleman; Queen Mother: Lucie Lancaster; Ada: Kellie Brytt; Northbrook: Peter Pagan; Nicolas: Mike Toles; Hofmann: Robert Fitch; Grimes: Barney Johnston; Baroness: Elaine Labour; Major-Domo: Jose Gutierrez. *Act I*: *Scene 1* Backstage at the Majestic Theatre: "Swing Song" (Jessie, Tony, Ensemble), "Yasni Kozkolai" (Carpathian National Anthem) (Ensemble), "My Family Tree" (Prince Regent, Northbrook, Regent's Aides); *Scene 2* A dressing room, backstage: "I've Been Invited to a Party" (Mary); *Scene 3* Backstage: Waltz (Ensemble), "I've Been Invited to a Party" (reprise) (Mary); *Scene 4* The Regent's apartment, Carpathian Embassy, Belgrave Square: "When Foreign Princes Come to Visit Us" (Major-Domo & Footmen), "Sir or Ma'am" (Northbrook), "Soliloquies" (Prince Regent & Mary), "Lonely" (Prince Regent); *Scene 5* St. Martin's Lane; *Scene 6* Trafalgar Square: "London (is a Little Bit of All Right)" (Ada, Nicolas, Ensemble), "What Ho, Mrs. Brisket" (Ada, Nicolas, Ensemble), "Don't Take Our Charlie for the Army" (Ada, Nicolas, Ensemble), "Saturday Night at the Rose & Crown" (Ada, Nicolas, Ensemble); *Scene 7* St. Martin's Lane: "London (is a Little Bit of All Right)" (reprise) (Ada); *Scene 8* The regent's apartment; the next morning: "Here and Now" (Mary), "I've Been Invited to a Party" (reprise) (Mary); *Scene 9* The Great Hall of the Embassy: "Soliloquies" (reprise) (Prince Regent & Mary). *Act II*: *Scene 1* Westminster Abbey: "Coronation Chorale" (Mary, Prince Regent, Principals, Ensemble); *Scene 2* The Regent's apartment: "How Do You Do, Middle Age?" (Prince Regent); *Scene 3* A drawing room, Carpathian Embassy: "Here and Now" (reprise) (Mary); *Scene 4* The Foreign Office Ball: "The Stingaree" (dance) (Prince Regent, Lady Sunningdale, Ensemble), "Curt, Clear and Concise" (Prince Regent & Northbrook), Tango (dance) (Prince Regent, Mary, Dancing Ensemble); *Scene 5* St. Martin's Lane: The Coconut Girl (sung by Mary): "Welcome to Pootzie Van Doyle," "The Coconut Girl," "Paddy MacNeil and His Automobile," "Swing Song" (reprise), "Six Lilies of the Valley," "The Walla Walla Boola" [end of the Coconut Girl sequence]; *Scene 6* The Regent's apartment; after the ball: "This Time it's True Love" (Mary); *Scene 7* The Regent's apartment; the next morning: "This Time it's True Love" (reprise) (Prince Regent), "I'll Remember Her" (Prince Regent).

Broadway reviews were generally favorable. This was Florence Henderson's only starring role on Broadway, and she got raves, as did Tessie O'Shea, who really stole the show with her cockney numbers. During the run Joe Ferrer flew to Puerto Rico one Saturday night to visit his wife, Rosie Clooney, and couldn't get back into New York because snow had closed the airports. His understudy, David Brooks, couldn't get into town either, so the show had to be canceled that night, losing about $10,000. The show failed because it was too much like *My Fair Lady*. Tessie O'Shea won a Tony Award, and the show was nominated for book and costumes.

After Broadway. YORK THEATRE COMPANY, 9/17/99–9/19/99. 5 PERFORMANCES. This was a staged reading, part of the York's *Musicals in Mufti* series. DIRECTOR: Michael Montel. *Cast*: QUEEN MOTHER: Celeste Holm; PRINCE: Simon Jones; MARY: Nancy Anderson; ADA: Evalyn Baron; NORTHBROOK: Stephen Mo Hanan.

252. *The Girls Against the Boys*

A musical revue.

Before Broadway. The numbers "Crossover," "Here it Comes Again, Spring," and "Lolita" were all cut.

The Broadway Run. ALVIN THEATRE, 11/2/59–11/14/59. 16 PERFORMANCES. PRESENTED BY Albert Selden; MUSIC: Richard Lewine; ADDITIONAL MUSIC: Albert Hague; LYRICS/SKETCHES MOSTLY BY: Arnold B. Horwitt; SKETCH DIRECTOR: Aaron Ruben; CHOREOGRAPHER: Boris Runanin; SETS/LIGHTING: Ralph Alswang; COSTUMES: Sal Anthony; MUSICAL DIRECTOR: Irving Actman; ORCHESTRATIONS: Sid Ramin & Robert Ginzler; DANCE MUSIC ARRANGEMENTS: John Morris; PRESS: Arthur Cantor & Tony Geiss; GENERAL MANAGER: Walter Fried; COMPANY MANAGER: Abe Cohen; STAGE MANAGERS: Paul Leaf, Sterling Mace, Jim Smock. *Cast*: PRINCIPALS: Bert Lahr (1), Nancy Walker (2), Shelley Berman (3), Dick Van Dyke (4), Joy Nichols, Imelda De Martin, Richard France, June L. Walker, Maureen Bailey, Buzz Halliday,

Mace Barrett. SUPPORTING PLAYERS: Caroljane Abney, Sandra Devlin, Ray Pointer, Noel Schwartz, Martin Charnin, Bob Roman, Cy Young, Jo Anne Tenney, Roger Le Page, Malachi Throne, Mona Pivar, Al Fiorella, Margaret Gathright, Nina Popova, Mitchell Nutick, Beatrice Salten, Jim Sisco, Ellen Graff. **Standbys**: For Bert Lahr & Shelley Berman: Phil Leeds; For Nancy Walker: Dorothy Greener; For Dick Van Dyke: Martin Charnin. **Act I**: **Scene 1** "The Girls Against the Boys" (Dick, Mace, Buzz, Ensemble); **Scene 2** "Rich Butterfly:" HUSBAND: Shelley Berman; WIFE: Nancy Walker; **Scene 3** Can We Save Our Marriage? COUNSELOR: Dick Van Dyke; STELLA: June L. Walker; HARRY: Bert Lahr; **Scene 4** "I Gotta Have You" (Imelda, Richard, Caroljane, Sandra, Ray, Noel); **Scene 5** Home Late (based on an idea by Robert Mott): HUSBAND: Dick Van Dyke; WIFE: Buzz Halliday; **Scene 6** I Remember (Bert Lahr): BUTLER: Mace Barrett; **Scene 7** Assignation: JOCK: Dick Van Dyke; CYNTHIA: Joy Nichols; ESSIE: Nancy Walker; WAITER: Martin Charnin; COUNTERMAN: Ray Pointer; MAN AT CENTER TABLE: Bob Roman; MAX: Noel Schwartz; OTHER PATRONS: Cy Young, Jo Anne Tenney, Roger Le Page, Mal Throne, Mona Pivar, Al Fiorella; **Scene 8** Comic Monologue (Phone Call with Jewish Father) Shelley Berman (written & performed by Shelley Berman); **Scene 9** "Where Did We Go? Out" (Mace, Maureen, Richard, Imelda); **Scene 10** "Too Young to Live" (Bert & Nancy); **Scene 11** "Overspend" (Shelley, Joy, Ensemble). **Act II**: **Scene 1** "Girls and Boys:" OBSERVER: Mace Barrett; MOTHER: Joy Nichols; GROOM: Dick Van Dyke; BRIDE: Imelda De Martin; BEST MAN: Richard France; FATHER: Bob Roman; MAID OF HONOR: Maureen Bailey; BRIDESMAIDS: Mona Pivar, Margaret Gathright, Sandra Devlin, Buzz Halliday; GUESTS: Ensemble; **Scene 2** Nightflight (by Arnold Horwitt & Aaron Ruben): PASSENGER: Bert Lahr; GIRL: Joy Nichols; MAN: Mal Throne; HOSTESS: June L. Walker; MOTHER: Buzz Halliday; FOUR PEOPLE: Mace Barrett, Cy Young, Bob Roman, Nina Popova; **Scene 3** "Light Travelin' Man" (m: Albert Hague) (Shelley & Richard): GIRLS: Sandra Devlin, Caroljane Abney, Margaret Gathright; **Scene 4** He and She: INTRODUCTION: Shelley Berman; HE: Dick Van Dyke; GOAT: Noel Schwartz; SKUNKS: Caroljane Abney & Roger Le Page; RABBITS: Mitchell Nutick & Beatrice Salten; DUCKS: Ray Pointer & Mona Pivar; WOLF: Al Fiorella; LAMB: Jo Anne Tenney; SHE: Nancy Walker; SNAKE: Sandra Devlin; IT: Jim Sisco; **Scene 5** "Old-Fashioned Girl:" DOORMAN: Mal Throne; MONROE FULLER: Bert Lahr; TAWNY: June L. Walker; USHER: Beatrice Salten; TREASURER: Sandra Devlin; MALE DANCER: Roger Le Page; SHOW GIRLS: Buzz Halliday, Margaret Gathright, Caroljane Abney, Jo Anne Tenney, Ellen Graff, Mona Pivar; **Scene 6** Comic Monologue (Phone Call to Girl Friend After a Date) (written & performed by Shelley Berman); **Scene 7** Hostility (by Arnold Horwitt & Aaron Ruben): HUSBAND: Bert Lahr; WIFE: Nancy Walker; **Scene 8** "Nobody Else but You" (m: Albert Hague) (Bert & Nancy); **Scene 9** Finale (Entire Company).

Broadway reviews were generally unfavorable.

253. *Godspell*

A rock musical in 2 acts and 16 scenes. It tells of the last seven days in the life of Jesus, who sports clown makeup and has an "S" on his shirt (for "Superman"). His disciples dress like flower children, and parables are enacted in a modern, frolicsome manner. Godspell is the old way of spelling "Gospel."

Before Broadway. John-Michael Tebelak created it as part of a thesis project while studying for his master's degree at Carnegie-Mellon. After attending Easter services, he was stopped by a policeman and searched for drugs, just because he had long hair. This incident inspired him to write a positive show about the persecution of Christ. After graduation, a theatre professor suggested he do a workshop of it at Ellen Stewart's Off Off Broadway theatre Cafe La Mama. The show, which at that stage was not a musical, featured only a couple of songs written by cast members. Angela Lansbury's younger brother, Edgar, along with Stuart Duncan and Joseph Beruh optioned it, added songs by Stephen Schwartz (who also did musical arrangements and was musical director), and opened it Off Broadway on 5/17/71, at the CHERRY LANE THEATRE (in Greenwich Village), where it was hugely successful. It had the same

crew as for the subsequent Broadway run, except LIGHTING: Lowell B. Achziger; STAGE MANAGER: Nina Faso, *Peter Kean*. **Cast**: JESUS: Stephen Nathan, *Andy Rohrer* (from 5/6/72), *Don Hamilton, Ryan Hilliard, Don Scardino* (from 1/73), *Jeremy Sage* (from 2/74), *Don Scardino, Tom Rolfing* (from 8/74); JUDAS: David Haskell, *Bart Braverman* (from 5/72), *Lloyd Bremseth, Don Scardino, Michael Hoit* (from 4/75); ALSO WITH: Lamar Alford, Joanne Jonas, Robin Lamont, Sonia Manzano, Jeffrey Mylett, Peggy Gordon, Gilmer McCormick, Herb Simon (*Herb Braha*), Delores Hall, Marley Sims, Bob Garrett. **Orchestra**: KEYBOARD: Steve Reinhardt; BASS/GUITAR: Jesse Cuer & Richard Labonti; PERCUSSION: Ricky Shutter. It moved to the PROMENADE THEATRE (operated by Lansbury & Beruh) on 8/10/71. At the fourth anniversary the producers wanted to move it to the Ethel Barrymore Theatre, on Broadway, but a dispute with the authors prevented that. Its Off Broadway run totaled 2,124 PERFORMANCES (the third-longest run in Off Broadway history until then). The show closed on 6/13/76, and moved to Broadway.

MARK TAPER FORUM, Los Angeles, 11/4/71. 54 PERFORMANCES. PRESENTED BY the Center Theatre Group; DIRECTORS: John Michael Tebelak & Nina Faso; SETS: Peter Wexler; COSTUMES: Susan Tsu. **Cast**: Lamar Alford, Roberta Baum, David Haskell, Lynne Thigpen.

TOUR. Opened on 12/11/71, at the Wilbur Theatre, Boston. **Cast**: JESUS: Dan Stone, *Jeffrey F. Weller* (from 8/72); JUDAS: Lloyd Bremseth, *Mark Syers*.

TOUR. Opened on 4/7/72, at Ford's Theatre, Washington, DC. **Cast**: JESUS: Dean Pitchford, *Rune Kaptur*; JUDAS: Irving Lee; ALSO WITH: Bart Braverman, Tony Hoty, Patti Mariano, Lynne Thigpen.

TOUR. Opened on 6/1/72, at the Royal Alexandra Theatre, Toronto. MUSICAL DIRECTOR: Paul Shaffer. **Cast**: JESUS: Victor Garber, *Don Scardino, Gordon Thompson, Eugene Levy* (from 6/1/73); JUDAS: Jerry Salsberg, *Jim Betts* (from 6/1/73); ALSO WITH: Gilda Radner, Martin Short.

TOUR. Opened on 7/18/72, at the Geary Theatre, San Francisco. **Cast**: JESUS: Stacker Thompson, *Stephen Nathan*; JUDAS: Tom Rolfing.

TOUR. Opened on 9/18/72, at the Studebaker Theatre, Chicago. **Cast**: JESUS: Dan Stone, *Richard Gilliland*; JUDAS: Joe Mantegna.

TOUR. Opened on 9/21/72, in Toledo, Ohio, and closed on 8/25/73, after 151 cities. **Cast**: JESUS: Jeremy Sage; JUDAS: Michael Hoit.

TOUR. Opened on 10/27/72, at the Nixon Theatre, Pittsburgh. **Cast**: JESUS: Mark Shera, *Robert Brandon, Tom Rolfing*; JUDAS: Mark Ganzel, *Tom Rolfing, Michael Hoit*.

TOUR. Opened on 9/6/73, at the Masonic Auditorium, Toledo.

TOUR. Opened on 9/10/73, at the Nixon Theatre, Pittsburgh. **Cast**: Tom Rolfing (*Michael Hoit*).

LONDON PRODUCTION. ROUNDHOUSE THEATRE, 11/17/71; WYNDHAM'S THEATRE, 1/26/72. 1,128 PERFORMANCES. CAST RECORDING on Bell. **Cast**: JESUS: David Essex; JOHN THE BAPTIST: Jeremy Irons; ALSO WITH: Julie Covington, Marti Webb, Johanna Cassidy, Gay Soper.

THE MOVIE. 1973. Shot on location in New York City. It included a new song—"Beautiful City." **Cast**: Victor Garber, David Haskell.

The Broadway Run. BROADHURST THEATRE, 6/22/76–9/13/76; PLYMOUTH THEATRE, 9/15/76–1/9/77; AMBASSADOR THEATRE, 1/12/77–9/4/77. Total of 527 PERFORMANCES. PRESENTED BY Edgar Lansbury, Stuart Duncan, Joseph Beruh & The Shubert Organization; MUSIC/NEW LYRICS: Stephen Schwartz (unless otherwise stated); BOOK/CONCEIVED BY/DIRECTOR: John-Michael Tebelak; BASED ON *The Gospel According to St. Matthew*; COSTUMES: Susan Tsu; LIGHTING: Spencer Mosse; SOUND: Robert Minor; MUSICAL DIRECTOR: Steve Reinhardt; CAST RECORDING on Bell; PRESS: Gifford/Wallace, Glenna Freedman, Tom Trenkle; GENERAL MANAGEMENT: Marvin A. Krauss Associates; COMPANY MANAGER: Gail Bell; STAGE MANAGERS: Michael J. Frank & Kitty Rea. **Cast**: JUDAS: Tom Rolfing, *Michael Hoit*; JESUS: Don Scardino, *Jeremy Sage*; ADULTERESS: Elizabeth Lathram; ALSO WITH: Lamar Alford, Laurie Faso, Lois Foraker, Robin Lamont, Bobby Lee, Marley Sims, Valerie Williams, *Tony Hoty, Sonia Manzano, Jo-Ann Washington, Patti Mariano, Marilyn Pasekoff*.

Note: All parts are interchangeable.

Alternates: Kerin Blair, Bob Garrett, Michael Hoit, Kitty Rea. **Band**: KEYBOARD: Paul Shaffer; GUITAR: Mark Zeray; BASS: Chris Warwin; PERCUSSION: Michael Redding. **Act I**: *Prologue*: "Tower of Babble" [not on the album], "Prepare Ye (the Way of the Lord)" (John the

Baptist & Company) [a hit], "Save the People" (Jesus & Company), "Day by Day" (Robin Lamont & Company) [the big hit], "Learn Your Lessons Well" (Marley Sims), "(O) Bless the Lord (My Soul)" (Valerie Williams & Company), "All for the Best" (Jesus & Judas), "All Good Gifts" (Lamar Alford & Company), "Light of the World" (Laurie Faso & Company). *Act II*: Entr'acte: "Learn Your Lessons Well" (reprise) (Lamara Alford & Company), "Turn Back, O Man" (Lois Foraker & Company), "Alas for You" (Jesus, then Company), "By My Side" (m: Peggy Gordon; l: Jay Hamburger) (Adulteress), "We Beseech Thee" (Goats) (Bobby Lee & Company), "Day by Day" (reprise) (Company), "On the Willows" (Band), Finale: "Long Live God" (Jesus, then Company)/"Prepare Ye" (Company).

Reviews were not all that great. The show received a Tony nomination for score.

After Broadway. EQUITY LIBRARY THEATRE, NYC, 1/8/81–2/1/81. 30 PERFORMANCES. DIRECTOR: William Koch. *Cast*: Scott Bakula, Liz Callaway, Jason Graae, Andy Roth, Elizabeth Bruzzese, Bev Larson.

YOUNG VIC THEATRE, London, 6/22/81–7/11/81.

LAMBS THEATRE, NYC, 6/12/88–12/31/88. 15 previews from 5/31. 225 PERFORMANCES. This was the first major New York revival. DIRECTOR: Don Scardino; COSTUMES: David C. Woolard; SOUND: T. Richard Fitzgerald; MUSICAL DIRECTOR: Steven M. Alper. *Cast*: Trini Alvarado, Laura Dean, Eddie Korbich, Harold Perrineau Jr.

A NEW VERSION. VICTORIA THEATRE (a 400-seat theatre in Harlem). This was the first all-black version; it was now set in 21st-century Harlem. Stephen Schwartz & Richard Haase re-arranged the score; "Beautiful City" (from the movie) was inserted. The show initially cost about $30,000. The opening date was put back from early 1/97 in order to accommodate changes suggested by Stephen Schwartz, and it finally opened 2/6/97. Previews from 11/22/96. PRESENTED BY Ron Brown, Jimmy Glover, Richard Haase; DIRECTOR: Richard Haase; CHOREOGRAPHER: Gene Compson; MUSICAL DIRECTOR: Davina Haase. *Cast*: JESUS: Michael Leonard James; JUDAS: Ray Champion; MARY MAGDALENE: N'Tombkhona; ALSO WITH: Adrienne Unae (who replaced LaVern Baker, who was ill). It was not reviewed by a single major newspaper; this caused much complaint from the producers. Peter Marks of the *New York Times* came, saw, and liked, but did not print. However, the show did have a lot of other coverage in several papers. From the beginning it had its eye on a tour and Broadway. By 6/97 a transfer looked very probable. Jermaine Jackson and Ruth Brown had both committed, and Ben Vereen looked very possible. Linda Hopkins was also interested. However, Stephen Schwartz, leery of Broadway, wanted to continue with a lavish production in Harlem. There were also Los Angeles plans. All looked good until Amy Nederlander (and others) started planning a similar all-black version for Broadway for the 1998–99 season (unfortunately, Stephen Schwartz was in this camp too), and this caused much bitter rivalry, complaints of plagiarism, and lawsuit threats. The result was that both productions died.

ANOTHER NEW VERSION. Set in the late 1990s, with new lyrics by Stephen Schwartz, opened at the EXCALIBUR THEATRE, Studio City, Los Angeles. The cast now represented downtown street people of L.A. 2/20/99–4/25/99. PRESENTED BY La Petite Musicale; ADAPTED/DIRECTORS: Gary B. Lamb & William Reilly. *Cast*: JESUS: Rodney Hicks.

THEATRE AT ST. PETER'S CHURCH, NYC, 8/2/00–10/7/00. 18 previews from 7/18/00. 77 PERFORMANCES. This production originated at the Third Eye Repertory in the 1999–2000 season. PRESENTED BY NET Theatrical Productions; DIRECTORS: Shawn Rozsa & R.J. Tolan; CHOREOGRAPHER: Ovi Vargas; SETS: Keven Lock; COSTUMES: William Ivey Long & Bernard Grenier; MUSICAL DIRECTOR: Dan Schachner; NEW CAST RECORDING on Fynsworth Alley. *Cast*: Shoshana Bean, Barrett Foa, Capathia Jenkins, Leslie Kritzer, Chad Kimball.

254. *Going Up*

It is 1919, in Lenox, Mass., at the Gordon Inn. A daring young man pretends to be a pilot, and takes a plane up to impress the girl he loves.

Before Broadway. THE ORIGINAL 1917 RUN. As a musical it was first done on Broadway, at the LIBERTY THEATRE, 12/25/17. 351 PERFORMANCES. It was set in 1917. *Cast*: Frank Craven, Edith Day, Marion Sunshine.

THE NEW PRODUCTION. Tried out at the Goodspeed Opera House, in Connecticut, from 6/22/76. PRESENTED BY Michael P. Price. Although a revival, it was not billed as such in the program (or in the Broadway program), partly because it was revised.

The Broadway Run. JOHN GOLDEN THEATRE, 9/19/76–10/31/76. 4 previews. 49 PERFORMANCES. The Goodspeed Opera House production, PRESENTED BY Ashton Springer, William Callahan, Stephens—Weitzenhoffer Productions (Norman Stephens & Max Weitzenhoffer), in association with Stephen R. Friedman & Irwin Meyer; MUSIC: Louis A. Hirsch; LYRICS/BOOK: Otto Harbach; FOUNDED ON James Montgomery's comedy *The Aviator*, first produced on Broadway on 12/6/1910, and which ran for 44 performances; DIRECTOR: Bill Gile; CHOREOGRAPHER: Dan Siretta; SETS/LIGHTING SUPERVISOR: Edward Haynes; COSTUMES: David Toser; LIGHTING: Peter M. Ehrhardt; MUSICAL DIRECTOR/VOCAL ARRANGEMENTS: Lynn Crigler; MUSICAL ARRANGEMENTS: Russell Warner; PRESS: Max Eisen, Irene Gandy, Barbara Glenn, Judy Jacksina; SPECIAL CONSULTANT: Alfred Simon; GENERAL MANAGEMENT: Theatre Management Associates; COMPANY MANAGER: Gino Giglio; PRODUCTION STAGE MANAGER: Marnel Sumner; STAGE MANAGER: Ron Abbott; ASSISTANT STAGE MANAGER: Larry McMillian. *Cast*: MISS ZONNE: Pat Lysinger; ALEX: Calvin McRae; GUS: Larry Hyman; JOHN GORDON: Stephen Bray; GRACE DOUGLAS: Kimberly Farr; F.H. DOUGLAS: Lee H. Doyle; JULES GAILLARD: Michael Tartel; HOPKINSON BROWN: Walter Bobbie; MADELINE MANNERS: Maureen Brennan; JAMES BROOKS: Noel Craig; ROBERT STREET: Brad Blaisdell; SAM ROBINSON: Ronn Robinson; DWAYNE: James Bontempo; FAYE: Deborah Crowe; HOWELL: Michael Gallagher; ENNIS: Teri Gill; MOLLIE: Barbara McKinley. *Act I: Scene 1* The Gordon Inn lobby; afternoon: "Paging Mr. Street" (Miss Zonne, Gordon, Bellboys, Ensemble), "I Want a Determined Boy" (Madeline, Brown, Four Aviators), "If You Look in Her Eyes" (Grace, Street, Madeline), "Going Up" (Street & Company); *Scene 2* The smoking-room; later that evening: "Hello Frisco" (l: Gene Buck) [from *Ziegfeld Follies of 1915*] (Miss Zonne & Four Aviators), "Down, Up, Left, Right" (Street, Brown, Brooks, Robinson), "Kiss Me" (Grave & Gaillard), "(Everybody Ought to Do) The Tickle Toe" (Grace & Ensemble). *Act II: Scene 1* The terrace; the same evening: "(There's a) Brand New Hero" (Ensemble), "I'll Think of You" (l: Rennold Wolf) [from *The Rainbow Girl*] (Grace & Street), "I'll Think of You" (reprise) (Grace & Street); *Scene 2* An airfield near the Gordon Inn; 6 o'clock, the next afternoon: "Do it for Me" (Madeline & Brown), "My Sumurun Girl" (l: Al Jolson) [from *The Whirl of Society*] (Miss Zonne & Robinson), "Going Up" (reprise) (Company), "Down, Up, Left, Right" (reprise) (Company), "The Tickle Toe" (reprise) (Company), Finale (Company).

Reviews were generally good.

255. *The Golden Apple*

Basically an opera (the spoken word is kept to minimum). A re-working of Homer's *Odyssey* and *Iliad* to a small American town, Angel's Roost, on the edge of Mount Olympus; and in the seaport of Rhododendron, Washington State, 1900–1910. According to Homer, the Golden Apple was a symbol of discord. In this musical Paris is a traveling salesman who makes his rounds by balloon. He flies into Angel's Roost and abducts Menelaus' always-willing wife, Helen. Ulysses has just led his soldiers back from the Spanish-American War, and now feels obliged to go off and retrieve Helen, thus leaving his own wife Penelope for ten years, during which travels he resists various temptations (including the five Sirenettes at Goona-Goona Lagoon), beats Paris in a bare-knuckle fight, and is finally re-united with Penelope. Scene changes were choreographed, and performed in front of the audience.

Before Broadway. It took a few years to find a producer. Cheryl Crawford quit in 1951; Herman Levin in 1952; and Kermit Bloomgarden in 1953. But, it finally ran Off Broadway, at the PHOENIX THEATRE, 3/11/54–4/18/54. 48 PERFORMANCES. It was reviewed there to mostly raves. This show, and *The Threepenny Opera*, were the first two Off Broadway musicals to have a huge impact on theatregoers. It was the first ever Off Broadway show to win a New York Critics' Circle Award for best musical. On 4/20/54 it became the first musical to move from Off Broadway to Broadway. There were some cast changes when it transferred: Shannon Bolin replaced Geraldine Viti; Martha Larrimore replaced Nola Day; Martin Keane replaced Larry Chelsi; and Ed Grace and Bill Nuss were added to the chorus.

The Broadway Run. ALVIN THEATRE, 4/20/54–8/7/54. 125 PERFORMANCES. The Phoenix Theatre production, presented by Alfred de Liagre Jr. & Roger L. Stevens, in association with T. Edward Hambleton & Norris Houghton (both of the Phoenix Theatre); MUSIC: Jerome Moross; LYRICS/BOOK: John Latouche; BASED ON *The Odyssey*, by Homer; DIRECTOR: Norman Lloyd; CHOREOGRAPHER: Hanya Holm; SETS: William & Jean Eckart; COSTUMES: Alvin Colt; LIGHTING: Klaus Holm; MUSICAL DIRECTOR: Hugh Ross; ORCHESTRAL ARRANGEMENTS: Jerome Moross & Hershy Kay; CAST RECORDING on RCA; PRESS: Samuel J. Friedman; GENERAL MANAGER: C. Edwin Knill; COMPANY MANAGER: Thelma Chandler; PRODUCTION STAGE MANAGER: Robert Woods; STAGE MANAGER: Dan Brennan; ASSISTANT STAGE MANAGER: David Hooks. *Cast*: HELEN, A FARMER'S DAUGHTER: Kaye Ballard (3); LOVELY MARS, THE LOCAL MATCHMAKER: Bibi Osterwald (5); MRS. JUNIPER, THE MAYOR'S WIFE: Shannon Bolin, *Charlotte Rae*; MISS MINERVA OLIVER, THE VILLAGE SCHOOLMARM: Portia Nelson (7); MOTHER HARE, THE LOCAL MYSTIC: Martha Larrimore; PENELOPE, ULYSSES' WIFE: Priscilla Gillette (1); MENELAUS, THE OLD SHERIFF: Dean Michener; THE (TWELVE) HEROES: CAPTAIN MARS: Frank Seabolt; AJAX: Marten Sameth; AGAMEMNON: Crandall Diehl; NESTOR: Maurice Edwards; BLUEY: Murray Gitlin; THIRSTY: Don Redlich; SILAS: Peter De Maio; HOMER: Barton Mumaw; DIOMEDE: Robert Flavelle; ACHILLES: Julian Patrick; PATROCLUS: Martin Keane, *Richard Hermany*; DOC MACCAHAN: Gary Gordon; ULYSSES, A VETERAN: Stephen Douglass (2); THERON: David Hooks; MAYOR JUNIPER: Jerry Stiller; PARIS, A TRAVELING SALESMAN: Jonathan Lucas (6); HECTOR CHARYBDIS, MAYOR OF RHODODENDRON: Jack Whiting (4); LOCAL GIRLS: Sara Bettis, Dorothy Etheridge, Nelle Fisher, Dee Harless, Janet Hayes, Lois McCauley, Ann Needham, Joli Roberts, Jere Stevens, Tao Strong, *Helen Ahola, Anneliese Widman, Mitzi Wilson* (last three added during the run); LOCAL BOYS: Santo Anselmo, Bob Gay, Ed Grace, Bill Nuss, Charles Post, Arthur Schoep, *Bob Bakanic* (added during the run). **Standby**: Helen/Lovely Mars/Mrs. Juniper: Geraldine Viti. **Understudies**: Penelope: Janet Hayes; Ulysses: Julian Patrick; Hector: Crandall Diehl; Paris: Barton Mumaw; Minerva: Helen Ahola; Mother Hare: Sara Bettis; Menelaus: Arthur Schoep; For Ann Needham: Tao Strong. **Act I**: The township of Angel's Roost: **Scene 1** In the orchard; **Scene 2** The village green; **Scene 3** The church social; **Scene 4** At Helen's house. **Act II**: **Scene 1** The seaport of Rhododendron; **Scene 2** The main street of Rhododendron; **Scene 3** Back in Angel's Roost. Penelope's home; **Scene 4** The main street again; **Scene 5** The big spree; **Scene 5a** Madame Calypso's parlor; **Scene 5b** The brokerage office of Scylla and Charybdis; **Scene 5c** A waterfront dive; **Scene 5d** The Hall of Science; **Scene 5e** The wrong side of the tracks; **Scene 6** Angel's Roost. In the backyard. **Act I**: "Nothing Ever Happens in Angel's Roost" (Helen, Lovely Mars, Mrs. Juniper, Miss Minerva), "Mother Hare's Séance" (Mother Hare), "My Love is on the Way" (Penelope), "The Heroes Come Home" (Entire Company), "It Was a Glad Adventure" (Ulysses & Heroes), "Come Along, Boys (We're Gonna Raise a Ruckus Tonight)" (Heroes & Ensemble), "(It's the) Going Home Together" (Ulysses & Penelope), "Mother Hare's Prophecy" (Mother Hare, Penelope, Ulysses), "Helen is Always Willing" (Heroes), "The Church Social" (Heroes & Ensemble), "Introducin' Mr. Paris" (Paris & Ensemble), "The Judgment of Paris" (Lovely Mars, Mrs. Juniper, Miss Minerva, Mother Hare, Paris), "Lazy Afternoon" (Helen & Paris) [the big hit], "The Departure for Rhododendron" (Entire Company). **Act II**: "My Picture in the Papers" (Helen, Paris, Male Ensemble), "The Taking of Rhododendron" (Ulysses, Hector, Paris), "Hector's Song" (Hector), "Windflowers" ("When We Were Young") (Penelope), "Store-bought Suit" (Ulysses), "Calypso" (Mrs. Juniper), "Scylla and Charybdis" (Menelaus & Hector), "(By) Goona-Goona (Lagoon)"

(Lovely Mars), "Doomed, Doomed, Doomed" (Miss Minerva), "Circe, Circe" (Martha Larrimore & Ensemble. Danced by Ann Needham), "Ulysses' Soliloquy" (Ulysses), "The Sewing Bee" (Penelope, Helen, Miss Minerva, Mrs. Juniper, Lovely Mars, Suitors, Ulysses), "The Tirade" (Penelope), Finale: "(It's the) Going Home Together" (reprise) (Ulysses & Penelope — this replaced "We've Just Begun" — also by Ulysses & Penelope, which had been the ending for the Off Broadway production. All subsequent productions have had the original Off Broadway ending back again).

Strangely, on Broadway it failed, and lost its investment. Still, it is to this day the favorite musical of so many people. It won Donaldson Awards for musical, lyrics, book, sets, and for male dancer (Jonathan Lucas).

After Broadway. YORK PLAYHOUSE, 2/12/62–5/12/62. 112 PERFORMANCES. PRESENTED BY Dorothy Olim & Gerald Krone; DIRECTOR: Robert Turoff; CHOREOGRAPHER: Nelle Fisher; SETS/COSTUMES: Bill Hargate; LIGHTING: Jules Fisher; MUSICAL DIRECTOR: Philip Fradkin. *Cast*: LOVELY MARS: Jane Connell, *Travis Hudson*; HELEN: Roberta MacDonald; MOTHER HARE: Julia Ross; PARIS: Michael Dominico; PENELOPE: Jan McArt; MRS. JUNIPER: Sylvia Short; MRS. MINERVA OLIVER: Peggy LeRoy; MENELAUS: Gabor Morea; CAPTAIN MARS: Todd Butler; AJAX: Bill Oliver; AGAMEMNON: Scott Ray; NESTOR: Jay Foote; DIOMEDE: John Holmes Jr.; ACHILLES: Stephen Elmore; PATROCLUS: Ken Corday; DOC MACCAHAN: Dick Latessa; ULYSSES: Stan Page; HECTOR CHARYBDIS: Swen Swenson; CHORUS: Lynne E. Albert, Harriet All, Nancy Fenster, Janet McCall, Lois Ann Oakes, Marcia Shaw, Dave Anderson, Buddy Mann, John Philibert, Jerry Powell.

YORK PLAYERS, NY, 11/24/78. 12 PERFORMANCES. DIRECTOR: Janet Hayes. *Cast*: Sara Wiedt, Lulu Downs, Harriet Hill, Michael Hayward-Jones, Peter Boynton, Robert Ray, Robert Stoeckle, Dee Hoty.

YORK THEATRE COMPANY, 3/23/90–4/22/90. 23 PERFORMANCES. DIRECTOR: Charles Kondek; CHOREOGRAPHER: David Holdgrive; MUSICAL DIRECTOR: Lawrence W. Hill. *Cast*: HELEN: Ann Brown; LOVELY MARS: Mimi Wyche; MRS. JUNIPER: Mary Stout; MINERVA: Cynthia Sophiea; MOTHER HARE: Muriel Costa-Greenspon; PENELOPE/CIRCE: Sylvia Rhyne; PATROCLUS: Bryan Batt; ULYSSES: Robert R. McCormick; FIGUREHEAD: Mary Phillips; DOC: Tim Salce; MENELAUS: Gordon Stanley; ALSO WITH: Tim Warmen, Kelly Patterson, Kip Niven.

256. *Golden Boy*

A re-working and updating (now set 1960–1964 in New York City) of the Clifford Odets play, with the boxer now being black (Joe, the protagonist in the straight play, had been an Italian-American violinist turned boxer). In the musical too, Joe started out as a violinist, but was then made into a pianist, and finally a medical student, who chooses boxing for a quick way to overcome racial prejudice. The opening number replaced the traditional overture, with boxers working out in a gym to the sound of percussion. Joe falls for Lorna, mistress of his manager Tom, and they have a doomed affair. But Lorna loves Tom, and Joe drives away, killing himself. Eddie was the nightclub owner who bought Joe's contract. Lopez was his opponent in the big fight.

Before Broadway. The original straight play ran on Broadway at the BELASCO THEATRE, 11/4/37. 250 PERFORMANCES. PRESENTED BY the Group Theatre; DIRECTOR: Harold Clurman. *Cast*: JOE BONAPARTE: Luther Adler; LORNA MOON: Frances Farmer; TOKIO: Art Smith; SIGGIE: Jules [later John] Garfield; MR. CARP: Lee J. Cobb; MR. BONAPARTE: Morris Carnovsky; LEWIS: Howard Da Silva; SAM: Martin Ritt; EDDIE FUSELI: Elia Kazan. There was a later, much better (-remembered) New York run, at ANTA THEATRE, 3/12/52–4/6/52. 56 PERFORMANCES. DIRECTOR: Clifford Odets. *Cast*: JOE: John Garfield; MR. BONAPARTE: Lee J. Cobb; FRANK BONAPARTE: Jack Klugman; EDDIE: Joseph Wiseman, *Joe De Santis*; PEPPER WHITE: Arthur O'Connell; MICKEY: Jack Warden.

For his Broadway debut Hillard Elkins conceived the idea of turning the famous Odets play into a musical. Mr. Odets was hired to do the libretto. However, on 8/14/63 he died of cancer, during the writing, and just about everyone connected with the show set about finishing it. A try-out tour began in Philadelphia, where reviews were not good. They weren't good in Boston, either, and Mr. Elkins asked the advice of Boston critic Elliott Norton, the result of which was that the director, Peter Coe (who had had a violently antagonistic relationship with Sammy Davis), was replaced by Arthur Penn, and Bill Gibson was brought on board to fix the book. It then went to New Haven and Detroit, but still wasn't ready. In Detroit there were race riots, and the interracial relationship on stage between Sammy Davis and Paula Wayne, and Mr. Davis's off-stage marriage to Swedish actress Maj Britt, brought death threats to the two leads. On 10/17/64, three days before the opening, Sammy Davis, who throughout the trying 22 weeks on the road had been suffering from laryngitis, missed the preview matinee at the Majestic, because he was on the edge of a nervous breakdown.

The Broadway Run. MAJESTIC THEATRE, 10/20/64–3/5/66. 25 previews from 9/23/64. 569 PERFORMANCES. An Epic production, PRESENTED BY Hillard Elkins; MUSIC: Charles Strouse; LYRICS: Lee Adams; BOOK: Clifford Odets & William Gibson; BASED ON the 1937 drama *Golden Boy*, by Clifford Odets; DIRECTOR: Arthur Penn; CHOREOGRAPHER: Donald McKayle; ASSISTANT CHOREOGRAPHER: Jaime Rogers; SETS/COSTUMES: Tony Walton; LIGHTING: Tharon Musser; MUSICAL DIRECTOR/ADDITIONAL MUSICAL SCORING: Elliot Lawrence; ORCHESTRATIONS: Ralph Burns; DANCE MUSIC ARRANGEMENTS/FIGHT BALLET MUSIC ASSEMBLER: Dorothea Freitag; CAST recording on Capitol; PRESS: Lee Solters, Harvey B. Sabinson, Harry Nigro; GENERAL MANAGER: Joseph Harris; COMPANY MANAGER: Sam Pagliaro; STAGE MANAGER: Ralph Linn; ASSISTANT STAGE MANAGERS: Vincent Lynne, Bruce W. Stark, Ralph Vucci. **Cast**: TOM MOODY: Kenneth Tobey (4); ROXY GOTTLIEB: Ted Beniades; TOKIO: Charles Welch; JOE WELLINGTON: Sammy Davis Jr. (1); LORNA MOON: Paula Wayne (3), *Sheila Sullivan* (during Miss Wayne's vacation); MR. WELLINGTON: Roy Glenn; ANNA: Jeannette DuBois; RONNIE: Johnny Brown; FRANK: Louis Gossett, *Albert Popwell*; TERRY: Terrin Miles; HOODLUM: Buck Heller; EDDIE SATIN: Billy Daniels (2), *Louis Gossett*; BENNY: Benny Payne; AL: Albert Popwell; LOLA: Lola Falana; LOPEZ: Jaime Rogers; MABEL: Mabel Robinson; LES: Lester Wilson; DRAKE: Don Crabtree; THERESA: Theresa Merritt, *Hilda Harris*; STEVIE: Stephen Taylor [role added during the run]; FIGHT ANNOUNCER: Maxwell Glanville; REPORTER: Bob Daley; DRISCOLL: Ralph Vucci; ENSEMBLE: Bob Daley, Marguerite Delain, Lola Falana, Maxwell Glanville, Buck Heller, Baayork Lee, Theresa Merritt, Robbin Miller, Sally Neal, Benny Payne, Harold Pierson, Albert Popwell, Louise Quick, Mabel Robinson, Amy Rouselle, Kenneth Scott, Stephen Taylor, Ralph Vucci, Lamont Washington, Lester Wilson, *Barbara Charles, Nat Horne*. **Standby**: Lorna: Sheila Sullivan. **Understudies**: Joe: Lamont Washington; Eddie: Lou Gossett; Ronnie/Frank: Albert Popwell; Tom: Don Crabtree; Roxie/Tokio: Ralph Vucci; Mr. Wellington: Maxwell Glanville; Drake/Driscoll: Bob Daley; Terry: Stephen Taylor; Lopez: Harold Pierson, *Buck Heller*; Anna: Amy Rouselle. **Act I**: *Scene 1* A boxers' gymnasium: "Workout" (Boxers); *Scene 2* The Wellington kitchen in Harlem; *Scene 3* Rooftop of the tenement: "Night Song" (Joe); *Scene 4* Tom Moody's office: "Everything's Great" (Tom & Lorna); *Scene 5* A schoolyard playground: "Gimme Some" (Joe & Terry), "Stick Around" (Joe); *Scene 6* A Harlem street: "Don't Forget 127th Street" (Joe, Ronnie, Company); *Scene 7* The Wellington kitchen; *Scene 8* A railroad depot: "Lorna's Here" (Lorna); *Scene 9* The road tour: The Road Tour (Joe, Lorna, Tom, Roxy, Eddie, Tokio, Company), "This is the Life" (Eddie, Joe, Lola, Company); *Scene 10* Joe's dressing room in Madison Square Garden. **Act II**: *Scene 1* A bar: "Golden Boy" (Lorna); *Scene 2* A party at Eddie's penthouse apartment: "While the City Sleeps" (Eddie), "While the City Sleeps" (dance) (Mabel, Lopez, Les), "Colorful" (Joe); *Scene 3* Along the river: "I Want to Be with You" (Joe & Lorna); *Scene 4* Dawn in the park: "Can't You See It?" (Joe); *Scene 5* Tom's office; *Scene 6* 127th Street at night: "No More" (Joe & Company); *Scene 7* The dressing room; *Scene 8* The boxing ring: "The Fight" (Joe & Lopez); *Scene 9* The dressing room; *Scene 10* A Harlem street at night.

On Broadway opening night Sammy Davis wore a body mike, but he fought off his laryngitical ailment. Reviews were mixed. Mr. Davis got injured one evening, and appeared for the last act with a bandaged

ankle. When he missed a performance due to illness, or a week's vacation, box office dropped off to almost nothing. The show's original investment was $575,000, and it lost $120,000 of that. After the show the Society of Stage Directors and Choreographers sued Hillard Elkins, the producer, and won $11,902 in salary adjustments for Donny McKayle, the choreographer. The show received Tony nominations for musical, producer of a musical, choreographer, and for Sammy Davis.

After Broadway. TOUR. Opened on 4/23/68, at the Auditorium, Chicago, and closed there on 5/25/68. Then it went to the London Palladium, where Sammy Davis, then very sick, missed 9 performances. For this tour the book was revised. The numbers "Can't You See It?," "Stick Around," and The Road Tour were all dropped. Other numbers were shifted around—"Colorful" went to Act I Scene 1, after "The Workout;" "No More" was moved to the opening of Act II; "Golden Boy" was moved to Act II Scene 6, which was now Lorna's bedroom. There were new numbers—"Yes I Can" (Joe) now closed Act I; "You're No Brother of Mine" (Joe & Frank) now belonged to Act II Scene 3 (which used to be Act II Scene 2); "The Riot" (Company) was now in Act II Scene 8, which was now A Harlem street; and "What Became of Me?" was the final song, in Act II Scene 11, which was now Madison Square Garden (in the Broadway production there had been only been 10 scenes in the last act). DIRECTOR: Michael Thoma; CHOREOGRAPHER: Jaime Rogers; MUSICAL DIRECTOR: Shepard Coleman. **Cast**: JOE: Sammy Davis; TOM: Mark Dawson; LORNA: Gloria De Haven, *Vivienne Martin* (in London); ANNA: Altovise Gore; EDDIE SATIN: Lonnie Sattin; LOLA: Lola Falana; REPORTER: Dan Frazer; BAAYORK: Baayork Lee; ANNOUNCER: Ben Vereen; FRANK: Al Kirk; CHORUS: Urylee Leonardos, Marcelo Gamboa, Albert Popwell.

LONG WHARF THEATRE, New Haven, Conn., 11/15/00–12/17/00. Previews from 11/8/00. This was a revised version. Charles Strouse made the score more jazzy–Harlem, and wrote some new songs, with lyrics by Mike Glover—"Playing the Game," "Natural African Man," "Yes, Yes, Yes," "Lane's Lament," and "One More Chance." One song from the original was cut—"While the City Sleeps." Mike Glover wrote a new book from the original Odets draft (i.e. before Bill Gibson and everyone else had re-worked it). DIRECTOR: Mike Glover; CHOREOGRAPHER: Willie Rosario; MUSICAL DIRECTOR: George Caldwell. **Cast**: JOE: Rodney Hicks; TOM: Michael Rupert; LORNA: Nana Visitor; EDDIE: Peter Jay Fernandez; MR. BONAPARTE: Doug Eskew; TOKIO: Frank Mastrone; RONNIE: Milton Craig Neely; ANNIE: Harriett D. Foy; FRANK: David St. Louis; DOWNSEY: Marc Damon Johnson.

CITY CENTER, NYC, 3/21/02–3/24/02. 5 PERFORMANCES. Part of the *Encores!* series. ADAPTED BY: Suzan-Lori Parks; DIRECTOR: Walter Bobbie; CHOREOGRAPHER: Wayne Cilento; SETS: John Lee Beatty; COSTUMES: William Ivey Long; LIGHTING: Peter Kaczorowski; MUSICAL DIRECTOR: Rob Fisher. **Cast**: JOE: Alfonso Ribeiro; TOM: William McNulty; LORNA: Anastasia Barzee; TOKIO: Joseph R. Sicari; EDDIE: Norm Lewis; POP: Paul Butler; ALSO WITH: Thursday Farrar, Rob Bartlett, Karine Plantadit-Bageot, Julio Monge, April Nixon, Patrick Wetzel, Vicky Lambert, Terace Jones, Devin Richards.

GREENWICH THEATRE, London, 6/19/03–7/12/03. This was the first London revival. There were two new songs by Charles Strouse—"Winners" and "I'm a Success." CHOREOGRAPHER: Mykal Rand; SETS/COSTUMES: Richard Aylwin. **Cast**: JOE: Jason Pennycooke; LORNA: Sally Ann Triplett; ANNA: Alana Maria; RONNIE: Omar Okai; TOM: Nicolas Colicos; EDDIE: Ray Shell; TOKIO: Charlie Folorunsho; BENTON: Neil Johnson.

257. *Golden Rainbow*

Set in Las Vegas, today (Florida in the original novel). A widower allows his beloved son to grow up too fast and with too little discipline, in a run-down resort hotel.

Before Broadway. Arnold Schulman (who started it all) was fired by the Lawrences (Steve and Eydie were, of course, married) when he suggested they do a book musical of the show rather than a Steve & Eydie nightclub act. Michael Stewart replaced him, but he experienced similar problems, and was replaced by TV-writer Ernest Kinoy. Arthur Storch was replaced as director by Steve Lawrence himself, and Ron Field was replaced as choreographer by Tom Panko (assisted by Onna White). The number "Life's a Gamble" was not used. Broadway previews extended ad nauseam.

The Broadway Run. SHUBERT THEATRE, 2/4/68–11/17/68; GEORGE ABBOTT THEATRE, 12/27/68–1/12/69. 43 previews. Total of 383 PERFORMANCES. A Diplomat production (Steve Lawrence & Eydie Gorme), PRESENTED BY Joseph P. Harris & Ira Bernstein; MUSIC/LYRICS: Walter Marks; ADDITIONAL SCORING/MUSICAL DIRECTOR/VOCAL ARRANGEMENTS: Elliot Lawrence; BOOK: Ernest Kinoy; BASED ON the 1957 comedy *A Hole in the Head*, by Arnold Schulman, which in turn was based on his own 1955 TV play *The Heart's a Forgotten Hotel*; DIRECTOR: Arthur Storch; CHOREOGRAPHER: Tom Panko (with Onna White); SETS/LIGHTING: Robert Randolph; COSTUMES: Alvin Colt; SOUND: Robert Liftin; MUSICAL SUPERVISOR: Don Kirshner; ORCHESTRATIONS: Pat Williams & Jack Andrews; DANCE MUSIC ARRANGEMENTS: Marvin Hamlisch & Luther Henderson; CAST RECORDING on Calendar & distributed by RCA Victor; PRESS: Mike Merrick Company; PRODUCTION STAGE MANAGER: Terence Little; STAGE MANAGER: George Thorn; ASSISTANT STAGE MANAGER: Peter Stern. **Cast**: MR. NOVOTNY: Alan Kass (9); ALLY: Scott Jacoby (4); MR. HAUSKNECHT: Howard Mann (7); ELOISE: Linda Jorgens; LAUNDRYMAN: Charles Karel; HENRY: Will Hussung (6); MR. DIAMOND: Sid Raymond (5); LARRY DAVIS: Steve Lawrence (1) ☆; MRS. MAGRUDER: Fay Sappington (8); LOU GARRITY: Joseph Sirola (3); JEROME STONE: Gene Foote; ROSEMARY GARRITY: Marilyn Cooper (12); GORDON: John Anania; MR. KORNGOLD: Sam Kressen (10); 1ST REPORTER: Charles Karel; 2ND REPORTER: Lanier Davis; LEAD DANCER: Diana Saunders (11); JUDY HARRIS: Eydie Gorme (2) ☆; GEORGIA: Carol Conte; STRIPPER: Thelma Sherr; SAM: Frank Pietri; UMBAWA: Larry Merritt; PERSIAN GIRL: Linda Jorgens; CAT GIRL: Carole Bishop; NEBUCHADNEZZAR: John Anania; VIRGIN: Diana Saunders (11); HERO: Antony De Vecchi; STAGE MANAGER: Charles Karel; VICTOR: Lanier Davis; GAMBLER: Michael Vita; DANCERS: Carole Bishop, Wayne Boyd, Carol Conte, Antony De Vecchi, Susan Donovan, Tina Faye, Gene Foote, Alice Glenn, Blair Hammond, Linda Jorgens, Larry Merritt, Maralyn Miles, Jean Preece, Frank Pietri, Tom Rolla, Michael Shawn, Michael Vita; SHOWGIRLS: Betty Jo Alvies, Bernadette Brooks, Rae Samuels, Thelma Sherr. **Standbys**: Larry: Mace Barrett; Judy: Marilyn Cooper. **Understudies**: Novotny: Gene Foote; Ally: Dewey Golkin; Hausknecht/Diamond/Korngold: John Anania; Eloise: Carole Bishop; Henry: Lanier Davis; Mrs. Magruder: Carol Conte; Garrity: Charles Karel; Rosemary: Tina Faye; Gordon: Frank Pietri. **Act I**: **Scene 1** The Strip, Las Vegas: "Golden Rainbow" (Las Vegans) [replaced shortly after opening by "24 Hours a Day" (Las Vegans)]; **Scene 2** Golden Rainbow lobby: "We Got Us" (Larry & Ally); **Scene 3** The airport: "He Needs Me Now" (Judy); **Scene 4** Golden Rainbow lobby: "Kid" (Larry); **Scene 5** The Algeria Patio Restaurant: "For Once in Your Life" (Judy, Larry, Boys); **Scene 6** Golden Rainbow pantry: "Taking Care of You" (Judy, Ally, Friends); **Scene 7** Golden Rainbow lobby: "I've Gotta Be Me" (Larry) [the big hit]. **Act II**: **Scene 1** Babylon Nightclub: "The Fall of Babylon" (Babylonians); **Scene 2** Backstage: "Taste" (Lou & Friends); **Scene 3** The desert: "Desert Moon" (Larry & Judy), "All in Fun" (Larry & Judy); **Scene 4** Golden Rainbow lobby: "It's You Again" (Judy); **Scene 5** Babylon Casino: "I've Got to Be Me" (reprise) (Larry); **Scene 6** The Golden Rainbow: "How Could I Be So Wrong?" (Judy), "We Got Us" (reprise) (Larry, Judy, Ally), Finale (Entire Company).

It finally opened to an advance box-office of over $1 million. Reviews were not kind. The show received Tony nominations for sets, and for Scott Jacoby.

258. *Goldilocks*

About the silent movie industry. Maggie is a stage actress about to leave the footlights for marriage to wealthy George Randolph Brown. Max, a moviemaker, makes Maggie honor her contract and do the film, thus postponing the marriage. Maggie and Max fall in love, and Brown goes off with Lois, a studio hanger-on.

Before Broadway. Originally it was going to be produced by David Merrick and Jo Mielziner, but they withdrew, and Robert Whitehead took it on. Dolores Gray was first announced for the lead, but Elaine Stritch got it. Barry Sullivan (who had been the original choice, but was unavailable then, replaced Ben Gazzara, who had asked to be released) played the lead in the Philadelphia tryout, but after critics complained about his singing, he was replaced after the Boston tryout by Don Ameche. The numbers "Are We Feeling Any Better?," "A Chance He'll Never Stay," "Come to Me," "Guess Who," "Hello, My Love, Hello," "Little Girls Should Be Seen" and "This is My Last Spring" were all cut before Broadway. It was the first show to play in the newly-named Lunt—Fontanne Theatre (it had been the Globe).

The Broadway Run. LUNT—FONTANNE THEATRE, 10/11/58–2/28/59. 161 PERFORMANCES. The Robert Whitehead production, PRESENTED BY The Producers Theatre (Roger L. Stevens, Robert Whitehead, Robert W. Dowling); MUSIC: Leroy Anderson; LYRICS: Joan Ford, Walter Kerr, Jean Kerr; BOOK: Walter & Jean Kerr; DIRECTOR: Walter Kerr; CHOREOGRAPHER: Agnes de Mille; SETS: Peter Larkin; COSTUMES: Castillo; LIGHTING: Feder; Lehman Engel; ORCHESTRATIONS: Leroy Anderson & Philip J. Lang; DANCE MUSIC ARRANGEMENTS: Laurence Rosenthal; CAST RECORDING: in the late 1980s Sony re-issued it on CD; PRESS: Barry Hyams, Bob Ullman, Lila Glaser; GENERAL MANAGER: Oscar Olesen; COMPANY MANAGER: Richard Horner; PRODUCTION STAGE MANAGER: James Gelb; STAGE MANAGERS: Frederic de Wilde & Jonathan Anderson; ASSISTANT STAGE MANAGER: Beau Tilden. **Cast**: MAGGIE HARRIS: Elaine Stritch (2); CLOWN: Delbert Anderson [role cut before Broadway]; GEORGE RANDOLPH BROWN: Russell Nype (3); MAX GRADY: Don Ameche (1); LOIS LEE: Pat Stanley (4); PETE: Nathaniel Frey (5); ANDY: Richard Armbruster; MAX'S ASSISTANTS: Gene Varrone & Sam Greene; J.C.: Martin Wolfson; BESSIE: Margaret Hamilton (6); DEPUTIES: Del Anderson & Beau Tilden; CHAUFFEUR: Samye Van; SINGERS: Del Anderson, Richard Armbruster, Jane Carlyle, John Carter, Jeanne Grant, Sam Greene, Josanne Lavalle, Sadie McCollum, Rita Noble, Ben Parrish, Rufus Smith, Suzanne Stahl, Gene Varrone; DANCERS: Donald Barton, Patricia Birch, Lynne Broadbent, Kelly Brown, Judith Chazin, Imelda De Martin, Michael Fesco, Loren Hightower, George Jack, Bunty Kelley, Ronald Landry, Margaret Lithander, Carolyn Morris, Ilona Murai, Patti Nestor, David Nillo, Paul Olson, Peter Saul, Ron Stratton, Evelyn Taylor, Diana Turner. **Standbys**: Lois: Jan Norris; Max: Martin Brooks. **Understudies**: George: Sam Greene; Pete: Rufus Smith; Bessie: Jane Carlyle; J.C.: Beau Tilden; Andy/ 1st Assistant: John Carter; 2nd Assistant: Ben Parrish. **Act I**: **Scene 1** Onstage, New York City, 1913 (finale of *Lazy Moon*): "Lazy Moon" (Company); **Scene 2** Maggie's dressing room; immediately following: "Give the Little Lady" (Maggie & Company), "Save a Kiss" (George & Maggie); **Scene 3** Max's lot; next morning: "No One'll Ever Love You" (Maggie & Max); **Scene 4** Outside Max's lot; that evening: "If I Can't Take it with Me" (Pete & Company) [dropped before Broadway]; **Scene 5** Max's lot; four days later: "Who's Been Sitting in My Chair?" (Maggie), Dance (Donald Barton & Maggie), "There Never Was a Woman" (Max); **Scene 6** The Fat Cat Roof Garden; later that night: "The Pussy Foot" (ballet) (Lois & Company): TOM CAT: Kelly Brown; BRUNETTE: Ilona Murai; BLONDE: Lynne Broadbent; **Scene 7** Huckleberry Island; several days later: "Huckleberry Island Ballet" (Company) [this later became "Pirate Orgy"]. **Act II**: **Scene 1** A rest home on the mainland; two days later: "Lady in Waiting" (Lois & George), "Do Be Careful" (dance) (Lois, Kelly Brown, Evelyn Taylor, Company), "The Beast in You" (Maggie), "Shall I Take My Heart and Go?" (George); **Scene 2** Bessie's barn, up the Hudson; that afternoon: "Bad Companions" (Pete, Bessie, Andy, Gene Varrone), "I Can't Be in Love" (Max); **Scene 3** Ballroom, George's town house; that evening: "I Never Know When (to Say When)" (Maggie), "The Town House Maxixe" (dance) (Lois, David Nillo, Company), "Two Years in the Making" (Pete, Bessie, Singers); **Scene 4** Egypt-on-the-Hudson; next morning: "Heart of Stone" (Pyramid Dance) (Ilona Murai & Company).

Broadway reviews were divided, and unspectacular. Pat Stanley and Russell Nype won Tonys, and choreography, costumes and musical direction were nominated. The production lost almost all of its $360,000 investment. The Kerrs hated the show so much they refused ever to talk about it again.

After Broadway. ALL SOULS UNITARIAN CHURCH, 4/16/71–4/24/71. 8 PERFORMANCES; weekends only. PRESENTED BY All Souls Players; PRODUCED BY: Dorothy Harris, Walter Landa, Mary McCartney; DIRECTOR/CHOREOGRAPHER: Jeffrey K. Neill. **Cast**: MAGGIE: Sandy Sprung; MAX: Ed Penn; GEORGE: John York; LOIS: Barbara Coggin; PETE: John Harris; ANDY/CLOWN: Randy Wilson. "Lazy Moon," "Give the Little Lady," "Save a Kiss," "Little Girls Should Be Seen," "Indian Sequence," "No One'll Ever Love You," "Who's Been Sitting in My Chair," "There Never Was a Woman," "The Pussyfoot," "Pirate Sequence," "Are We Feeling Any Better?," "Lady in Waiting," "Silent Movie Ballet," "The Beast in You," "Shall I Take My Heart and Go?," "I Can't Be in Love," "Bad Companions," "Guess Who," "I Never Know When," "Two Years in the Making," "Heart of Stone."

14TH STREET Y, NYC. Concert reading. 6/13/00–6/25/00. 16 PERFORMANCES. Part of the Off Off Broadway *Musicals Tonight!* series. PRESENTED BY Mel Miller; DIRECTOR/CHOREOGRAPHER: Thomas Mills; MUSICAL DIRECTOR: Mark Hartman. **Cast**: BESSIE: Georgia Creighton; PETE: Matthew Ellison; J.C.: Gene Jones; ANDY: Jay Gould; LOIS: Jen Celene Little; MAX: Michael McKenzie; GEORGE: James Patterson; MAGGIE: Cathy Trien. **Act I**: "Lazy Moon," "Give the Little Lady," "Save a Kiss," "No One'll Ever Love You," "If I Can't Take it with Me," "Who's Been Sitting in My Chair," "There Never Was a Woman," "The Pussy Foot," "My Last Spring," Act I Finale. **Act II**: "Come to Me," Opening, "Lady in Waiting," "The Beast in You," "Shall I Take My Heart?," "I Can't Be in Love," "Bad Companions," "I Never Know When," "Two Years in the Making," "Heart of Stone," Finale.

259. *Good News!*

Set in the mid–1930s on and around the co-ed campus of Tait College. Will the star quarterback pass the final exam so he can play in the big game? Connie, the campus brain, reluctantly agrees to help Tom with astronomy, and a romance develops.

Before Broadway. The original opened on Broadway at CHANIN'S 46TH STREET THEATRE, 9/6/27–1/5/29. 551 PERFORMANCES. It was the longest-running musical of the 1920s. PRESENTED BY Laurence Schwab & Frank Mandel; DIRECTOR: Edgar MacGregor. It was set in the 1920s. **Cast**: TOM: John Price Jones; CONNIE: Mary Lawlor; BOBBY: Gus Shy. It was filmed in 1930. DIRECTORS: Nick Grinde & Edgar MacGregor. The numbers "The Best Things in Life Are Free" and "Lucky in Love" were cut. **Cast**: Bessie Love, Stanley Smith, Gus Shy, Mary Lawlor. The 1947 movie re-make featured new material by Betty Comden & Adolph Green (their first screenplay). "Pass That Peace Pipe" was a new song. DIRECTOR: Charles Walters. **Cast**: Peter Lawford, June Allyson, Joan McCracken, Mel Torme.

The 1974 production was quite revised and updated, and kept the original music and lyrics, and added several other songs by De Sylva, Brown and Henderson that were not in the original. "Flaming Youth," "On the Campus," "Baby, What?" were all cut from Act I, and "In the Meantime" was cut from Act II. The long pre–Broadway national tour opened in Philadelphia on 12/7/73, then went to the Colonial Theatre, Boston on 12/17/73. The tour had the same cast as for the subsequent Broadway run, except BILL: John Payne. **Understudy**: Muffin: Buttons. In addition, the song order was somewhat changed. It ran at the Kennedy Center, Washington, DC, 1/30/74–2/16/74, by which time Stubby Kaye had replaced Eddie "Rochester" Anderson. Abe Burrows was replaced by Garry Marshall (as librettist) and by Michael Kidd (as director). Mr. Kidd replaced Don Saddler as choreographer, but Mr. Saddler retained billing. Arthur Faria was replaced as associate choreographer by Gary Menteer. Broadway previews ran on and on, during which leading man John Payne quit, to be replaced by Gene Nelson.

The Broadway Run. ST. JAMES THEATRE, 12/23/74–1/4/75. 51 previews from 11/11/74. 16 PERFORMANCES. PRESENTED BY Harry Rigby & Terry Allen Kramer, in association with Tams-Witmark Music Library; MUSIC/LYRICS: B.G. "Buddy" De Sylva, Lew Brown, Ray Henderson; ORIGINAL BOOK: Laurence Schwab, B.G. "Buddy" De Sylva, Frank Mandel; NEW BOOK: Garry Marshall; ADAPTED BY: Abe Burrows; DIRECTOR: Michael Kidd; CHOREOGRAPHER: Donald Saddler; ASSOCIATE CHOREOGRAPHER: Gary Menteer; SETS: Donald Oenslager; COSTUMES: Donald Brooks; LIGHTING: Tharon Musser; SOUND: Tony Alloy; MUSICAL SUPERVISOR/VOCAL ARRANGEMENTS: Hugh Martin & Timothy Gray; MUSICAL DIRECTOR: Liza Redfield; ORCHESTRATIONS: Philip J. Lang; DANCE & INCIDENTAL MUSIC COMPOSER/ARRANGER: Luther Henderson; PRESS: Henry Luhrman Associates; CASTING: Howard Feuer; GENERAL MANAGERS: Joseph Harris & Ira Bernstein; COMPANY MANAGER: Archie Thomson; PRODUCTION STAGE MANAGER: Phil Friedman; STAGE MANAGER: Craig Jacobs; ASSISTANT STAGE MANAGER: Judy Olsen. **Cast**: BILL JOHNSON: Gene Nelson (2) ☆; TOM MARLOWE: Scott Stevensen (5); BEEF SAUNDERS: Joseph Burke (9); BOBBY RANDALL: Wayne Bryan (8); POOCH KEARNEY: Stubby Kaye (3) ☆; FLO: Rebecca Urich (14); MILLIE: Paula Cinko (13); PAT: Jana Robbins (6); BABE O'DAY: Barbara Lail (7); WINDY: Terry Eno (11); SLATS: Jimmy Brennan (12); SYLVESTER: Tommy Breslin (10); PROFESSOR KENYON: Alice Faye (1) ☆; CONNIE LANE: Marti Rolph (4); MUFFIN: Margaret; COLTON PLAYER: Ernie Pysher (15); HAPPY DAYS QUARTET: Tim Cassidy, Randall Robbins, Scott Stevensen, David Thome; ACROBATS: Lisa Guignard, Mary Ann Lipson, Ernie Pysher, Jeff Spielman; BATON TWIRLERS: Tim Cassidy, Lynda Goodfriend, Lisa Guignard; TAP DANCERS: Terry Eno & Jimmy Brennan; CO-EDS: Paula Cinko, Robin Gerson, Lynda Goodfriend, Lisa Guignard, Anne Kaye, Mary Ann Lipson, Sally O'Donnell, Rebecca Urich, Marcia Lynn Watkins; BOYS: Michael Austin, Jimmy Brennan, Tim Cassidy, Ernie Pysher, Randall Robbins, Jeff Spielman, David Thome. **Understudies**: Prof. Kenyon: Jana Robbins; Bill: Randall Robbins; Pooch: Jimmy Brennan; Connie: Anne Kaye; Tom: Terry Eno; Pat: Paula Cinko; Babe: Rebecca Urich; Bobby: Tommy Breslin; Beef: Ernie Pysher; Millie: Marcia Lynn Watkins; Sylvester: Jimmy Brennan; Flo: Sally O'Donnell; Windy: David Thome; Slats: Tim Cassidy; Muffin: Mini. **Alternates**: Kathel Carson & David Fredericks. **Act I**: Overture (Orchestra & Company), "(He's) a Ladies Man" [from *Follow Thru*] (Pat, Millie, Flo, Students), "The Best Things in Life Are Free" (Prof. Kenyon & Students), "Just Imagine" (Connie, with Pat, Millie, Flo), "Happy Days" * (Tom, Pat, Millie, Flo, Sylvester, Boys), "Button up Your Overcoat" * [from *Follow Thru*] (Bobby & Babe), "Lucky in Love" (Connie, Tom, Students), "You're the Cream in My Coffee" * [from *Hold Everything*] (Prof. Kenyon & Johnson), "Varsity Drag" (Babe & Students), "Together" * (Prof. Kenyon), "Tait Song" * (Johnson, Pooch, Students), "Lucky in Love" (reprise) (Company). **Act II**: "Today's the Day" * (Girls), "Girl of the Pi Beta Phi" (Pat & Girls), "Good News" (Prof. Kenyon, Connie, Students), "(Keep Your) Sunny Side Up" * [from *Sunny Side Up*] (Pooch & Boys), "The Best Things in Life Are Free" (reprise) (Connie & Tom), "Life is Just a Bowl of Cherries" * [from *George White's Scandals of 1931*] (Prof. Kenyon, Connie, Babe) [this number replaced "Never Swat a Fly"], "I Want to Be Bad" * (Prof. Kenyon) [cut before Broadway], "The Professor and the Students" * (Prof. Kenyon, Pooch, Company), Finale (Company).

Note: asterisks indicate songs not in the 1927 production.

It was panned by Broadway reviewers. The show, capitalized at $500,000, went way over budget, and lost $1.25 million.

After Broadway. PAPER MILL PLAYHOUSE, New Jersey, 1977. DIRECTOR: Bill Guske. **Cast**: Virginia Mayo, Bert Parks, Tom Batten, Jill Choder.

NEW REVISION. By Mark Madama & Wayne Bryan. It went on tour in the 93–94 season. DIRECTOR: Mark Madama; CHOREOGRAPHER: Linda Goodrich; SETS: Charles O'Connor; COSTUMES: Peggy J. Kellner; LIGHTING: David Neville; MUSICAL DIRECTOR/ORCHESTRATIONS: Craig Barna. The order of the musical numbers was changed. **Cast**: COACH JOHNSON: Timothy W. Robu; PATRICIA BINGHAM: Jessica Boevers; TOM: Michael Gruber; CONNIE: Kim Huber; PROF. CHARLOTTE KENYON: Linda Michele; POOCH: Steve Frazier; BABE: Ann Morrison; SLATS: Matt Bogart; FLO: Alisa Klein; CORDA: Lauren Kennedy.

260. *The Goodbye Girl*

Set in New York City. The mother of a ten-year-old girl finds herself sharing her apartment with an aspiring actor.

Before Broadway. The director during the Chicago tryout was Gene Saks, and he was replaced by Michael Kidd.

The Broadway Run. MARQUIS THEATRE, 3/4/93–8/15/93. 23 previews from 2/13/93. 188 PERFORMANCES. PRESENTED BY Office Two-One, Gladys Nederlander, Stewart F. Lane, James M. Nederlander, Richard Kagan, and Emanuel Azenberg; MUSIC: Marvin Hamlisch; LYRICS: David Zippel; BOOK: Neil Simon; BASED ON the 1977 movie of the same name, written by Neil Simon; DIRECTOR: Michael Kidd; CHOREOGRAPHER: Graciela Daniele; SETS/COSTUMES: Santo Loquasto; LIGHTING: Tharon Musser; SOUND: Tom Clark; MUSICAL DIRECTOR: Jack Everly; ORCHESTRATIONS: Billy Byers & Torrie Zito; DANCE MUSIC ARRANGEMENTS: Mark Hummel; CAST RECORDING on Columbia; PRESS: Bill Evans & Associates; CASTING: Jay Binder; GENERAL MANAGER: Leonard Soloway; COMPANY MANAGER: Dana Sherman; STAGE MANAGER: Thomas A. Bartlett; ASSISTANT STAGE MANAGER: Greta Minsky. **Cast**: LUCY: Tammy Minoff (10); PAULA: Bernadette Peters (1) ☆, *Betsy Joslyn* (during Miss Peters' illness); BILLY: Scott Wise (9); DONNA: Susann Fletcher (4); JENNA: Cynthia Onrubia (7); CYNTHIA: Erin Torpey (8); MELANIE: Lisa Molina (6); MRS. CROSBY, LANDLADY: Carol Woods (3); ELLIOT: Martin Short (2) ☆; MARK: John Christopher Jones (5); STAGE MANAGER: Darlesia Cearcy; 1ST MAN AT THEATRE: Larry Sousa; WOMAN AT THEATRE: Mary Ann Lamb; 2ND MAN AT THEATRE: Rick Crom; RICHARD III CAST: Barry Bernal, Darlesia Cearcy, Jamie Beth Chandler, Dennis Daniels, Denise Faye, Nancy Hess, Joe Locarro, Rick Manning, Cynthia Onrubia, Linda Talcott, Scott Wise; RICHARD III AUDIENCE: Rick Crom, Ruth Gottschall, Sean Grant, Mary Ann Lamb, Larry Sousa; MARK'S MOTHER: Ruth Gottschall; TV STAGE MANAGER: Rick Crom; RICKY SIMPSON ANNOUNCER: Rick Crom; RICKY SIMPSON: John Christopher Jones (5). **Standbys**: Paula: Betsy Joslyn; Elliot: Michael McGrath. **Understudies**: Paula: Nancy Hess; Elliot/Mark/Ricky: Rick Crom; Lucy: Erin Torpey & Lisa Molina; Mrs. Crosby: Darlesia Cearcy; Donna: Ruth Gottschall; Melanie/Cynthia: Ibijoke Akinola. **Swings**: Ned Hannah & Michele Pigliavento. **Orchestra**: REEDS: Al Regni, Bob Keller, Ed Zuhlke, John Winder; TRUMPETS: Bob Millikan, Danny Cahn, Darryl Shaw; TROMBONE: Keith O'Quinn; BASS TROMBONE: George Flynn; FRENCH HORN: John Clark; DRUMS: Michael Keller; PERCUSSION: Jim Saporito; KEYBOARDS: Lee Musiker & Myles Chase; CONCERTMASTER: Ron Oakland; VIOLINS: Ron Oakland, Janet Hill, Claudia Hafer Tondi, Deborah Wong; CELLI: Alvin McCall, Mark Shuman, Ellen Westerman; BASS: Bill Sloat; HARP: Lise Nadeau. *Act I*: *Scene 1* Paula's apartment: "This is as Good as it Gets" (Paula & Lucy), "No More" (Paula); *Scene 2* A dance studio: "A Beat Behind" (Paula, Billy, Ensemble); *Scene 3* In front of Paula's building: "This is as Good as it Gets" (reprise) (Lucy, Melanie, Cynthia); *Scene 4* Paula's apartment: "My Rules"/"Elliot Garfield Grant" (Elliot & Paula), "Good News, Bad News" (Elliot, Paula, Lucy); *Scene 5* Paula's apartment: "Good News, Bad News" (reprise) (Mrs. Crosby); *Scene 6* An Off Off Broadway theatre; *Scene 7* Central Park: "(Don't Follow in My) Footsteps" (Paula & Lucy); *Scene 8* Paula's apartment: "How Can I Win?" (Paula); *Scene 9* An Off Off Broadway theatre: "Richard Interred" (Elliot, Paula, Lucy, Mark, Mrs. Crosby, Donna, Ensemble). *Act II*: *Scene 1* Paula's apartment: "How Can I Win?" (reprise) (Paula); *Scene 2* Paula's apartment: "Good News, Bad News" (reprise) (Elliot); *Scene 3* The Ricky Simpson Show: "Too Good to Be Bad" (Paula, Donna, Jenna); *Scene 4* Paula's apartment: "2 Good 2 B Bad" (Mrs. Cosby); *Scene 5* Paula's apartment: "Who Would've Thought?" (Paula, Elliot, Lucy, Melanie, Cynthia); *Scene 6* The rooftop of Paula's building: "Paula" (an Improvised Love Song) (Elliot & Paula); *Scene 7* Paula's apartment; *Scene 8* A schoolyard: "Who Would've Thought?" (reprise) (Lucy, Melanie, Cynthia); *Scene 9* The lake in Central Park: "I (Think I) Can Play This Part" (Elliot); *Scene 10* A TV studio: "Jump for Joy" (Paula & Ensemble); *Scene 11* Paula's apartment: "What a Guy" (Paula); *Scene 12* In front of Paula's building: "I'm Outta Here" [this finale was cut during previews].

Broadway reviews were not good. The show received Tony nominations for musical, direction of a musical, choreography, and for Martin Short and Bernadette Peters.

After Broadway. REVISED VERSION IN ENGLAND. Actually, very revised, and scaled-down, with only three of the original songs left in, and seven new songs written by Marvin Hamlisch & Don Black. It tried out to great response in BROMLEY, Kent, in 1997, then came to the ALBERY THEATRE, London, 4/17/97–6/28/97. Previews from 4/14/97. DIRECTOR: Rob Bettinson; SETS: Robert Jones; MUSICAL ARRANGEMENTS: John Cameron; NEW CAST RECORDING on First Night Records. **Cast**: PAULA:

Ann Crumb; ELLIOT: Gary Wilmot; YOUNG LUCY: Dina Tree; MRS. CROSBY: Shezwae Powell. "I'll Take the Sky" (opening number) (replaced "No More"), "Body Talk" (replaced "A Beat Behind"), "Am I Who I Think I Am?" (Elliot & Paula) (ended Act I) (replaced "I Think I Can Play This Part"), "The Future isn't What it Used to Be" (Elliot & Young Lucy), "Do You Want to Be in My Movie?," "If You Break Their Hearts" (Mrs. Crosby), "Get a Life" (replaced "Footsteps"), "Elliot Garfield Grant," "Good News, Bad News," "Who Would've Thought?."

WALNUT STREET THEATRE, Philadelphia. Fall, 1997. **Cast**: Donna McKechnie, Rita Rehn, William Ryall.

TV FILM. Aired on TNT, 1/16/04. DIRECTOR: Richard Benjamin. **Cast**: PAULA MCFADDEN: Patricia Heaton; ELLIOTT GARFIELD: Jeff Daniels; LUCY: Hallie Kate Eisenberg; ALSO WITH: Alan Cumming.

261. *Goodtime Charley*

Set in France between March 6, 1429 and Feb. 28, 1461, with an ineffectual dauphin (Charley) under the thumb of a corrupt general and archbishop. Joan of Arc's belief in Charley eventually inspires him to take command and be a man. The classic line (from Joan): "Well, I sure don't want to burn."

Before Broadway. When originally conceived, it was called *Charley and Joan*. Alan Jay Lerner saw a developmental performance and suggested the new name. When it became apparent that it was going to be a star vehicle for Joel Grey, the production was re-shaped. Three numbers were cut — "Tomorrow's Good Old Days," "All She Can Do is Say No," and "There Goes the Country." The Broadway opening was postponed for two months while Ann Reinking overcame a back injury sustained during a dance in the Broadway musical *Over Here*. She joined the cast of *Goodtime Charley* wearing a back brace.

The Broadway Run. PALACE THEATRE, 3/3/75–5/31/75. 12 previews. 104 PERFORMANCES. PRESENTED BY Max Brown & Byron Goldman, in association with Robert Victor & Stone Widney; MUSIC: Larry Grossman; LYRICS: Hal Hackady; BOOK: Sidney Michaels; SUGGESTED BY events in the life of Charles VII of France (1403–1461) and Joan of Arc (ca. 1412–1431); DIRECTOR: Peter H. Hunt (helped by Bob Fosse); CHOREOGRAPHER: Onna White (she replaced Dennis Nahat); SETS: Rouben Ter-Arutunian; COSTUMES: Willa Kim; LIGHTING: Feder; SOUND: Jack Mann; CONDUCTOR: Arthur B. Rubinstein, *Lawrence J. Blank* (from 5/75); ORCHESTRATIONS: Jonathan Tunick; DANCE MUSIC ARRANGEMENTS: Daniel Troob; INCIDENTAL MUSIC: Arthur B. Rubinstein; CAST RECORDING on RCA; PRESS: Max Eisen, Barbara Glenn, Judy Jacksina; GENERAL MANAGER: Ralph Roseman; COMPANY MANAGER: Ken Myers; STAGE MANAGERS: Bruce W. Stark & Lee Murray. **Cast**: HENRY V: Brad Tyrrell; CHARLES VI: Hal Norman; ISABELLA OF BAVARIA: Grace Keagy (7); QUEEN KATE: Rhoda Butler, *Maureen Maloney*; PHILIP OF BURGUNDY: Charles Rule, *Kenneth Bridges*; YOLANDE: Peggy Cooper; MARIE: Nancy Killmer; POPE: Ed Becker; CHARLEY, THE DAUPHIN: Joel Grey (1) ☆; ARCHBISHOP REGNAULT DE CHARTRES: Jay Garner (6); GENERAL GEORGES DE LA TREMOUILLE: Louis Zorich (4); SERVANTS: George Ramos, Ross Miles, Pat Swayze, Cam Lorendo; AGNES SOREL: Susan Browning (3); JESTERS: Andy Hostettler & Gordon J. Weiss; JOAN OF ARC: Ann Reinking (2); MINGUET, THE PAGE: Richard B. Shull (5); 1ST ENGLISH CAPTAIN: Charles Rule; 2ND ENGLISH CAPTAIN: Hal Norman; 3RD ENGLISH CAPTAIN: Kenneth Bridges; HERALD: Hal Norman; TRIO: Kenneth Bridges, Brad Tyrrell, Ed Becker; LOUIS: Dan Joel; CHEF: Charles Rule; 1ST SOLDIER: Kenneth Bridges; 2ND SOLDIER: Brad Tyrrell; 3RD SOLDIER: Hal Norman; GUARD: Charles Rule; ESTELLE: Kathe Dezina; SINGERS: Ed Becker, Kenneth Bridges, Rhoda Butler, Peggy Cooper, Kathe Dezina, Nancy Killmer, Hal Norman, Charles Rule, Jane Ann Sargia, Brad Tyrrell; DANCERS: Andy Hostettler, Dan Joel, Cam Lorendo, Glen McClaskey, Ross Miles, Tod Miller, Sal Pernice, George Ramos, Pat Swayze, Gordon Weiss, Jerry Yoder. **Standby**: Charley: Austin Pendleton. **Understudies**: Joan: Susan Browning; Agnes: Rhoda Butler; Archbishop: Hal Norman; General: Charles Rule; Isabella: Peggy Cooper; Yolande: Nancy Killmer; Minguet/Henry: Kenneth Bridges; Charles/Philip/Pope: Kenneth Bridges; Kate/Marie/Estelle: Jane Ann Sargia.

The Trio (played by Kenneth Bridges, Brad Tyrrell and Hal Norman) were variously seen as the Citizen Trio, the Soldier Trio, the Peasant Trio, and the Hostile Trio. *Act I: Scene 1* Prologue Charley's nightmare; March 6, 1429: Overture (Orchestra), "History" (Henry V, Charles VI, Isabella, Kate, Philip, Yolande, Marie, Pope, Ensemble); *Scene 2* Charley's bedroom at Chinon; that morning: "Goodtime Charley" (Charley & Ensemble); *Scene 3* Great Hall; immediately after: "Visions and Voices" (Joan); *Scene 4* Charley's study; that evening: "Bits and Pieces" (Charley & Joan), "To Make the Boy a Man" (Joan); *Scene 5* Before a tapestry; immediately after: "Why Can't We All Be Nice?" (Charley & Agnes); *Scene 6* Council Chamber; three weeks later, April: "Born Lover" (Charley); *Scene 7* A nearby grove; twilight: "I Am Going to Love (The Man You're Going to Be)" (Joan); *Scene 8* Castles of the Loire; subsequent weeks: "Castles of the Loire" (m: Arthur B. Rubinstein) (Joan & Soldiers); *Scene 9* Reims Cathedral; late May, 1429: "Coronation" (Charley, Joan, Ensemble). *Act II: Scene 1* A formal garden; late summer: "You Still Have a Long Way to Go" (Joan & Charley); *Scene 2* Chinon courtyard; the following spring: "Merci, Bon Dieu" (Minguet & Agnes); *Scene 3* A bank of the Vienne River; immediately after sunset; *Scene 4* Confession booth; a week later: "Confessional" (General & Archbishop); *Scene 5* Cell in Rouen; May 30, 1431: "One Little Year" (Joan); *Scene 6* Cell and war tent; that same day, simultaneously; *Scene 7* Great Hall; three weeks later; *Scene 8* Epilogue; 32 years later, Feb. 28, 1461: "I Leave the World" (Charley), Finale.

It was panned by the reviewers, but nominated for seven Tony Awards — sets, costumes, lighting, and for Joel Grey, Richard B. Shull, Susan Browning, and Ann Reinking. The show was forced to close for two reasons: Joel Grey was leaving anyway, to do a Paul Newman film, and no suitable replacement could be found; and, Ann Reinking got the flu. The production lost a million dollars, well over the original investment, thanks to consistent operating losses. However, over the years it has become something of a cult.

After Broadway. NEW CONSERVATORY THEATRE, San Francisco, 6/6/96–6/23/96. Concert version. The three cut Broadway songs were re-instated. PRESENTED BY 42nd Street Moon; PRODUCED BY: Greg McKellan & Stephanie Rhoads; DIRECTOR: Greg McKellan. *Cast*: CHARLEY: Bill Fahrner; JOAN: Juliette Morgan; ISABELLA: Lisa Peers.

ARCLIGHT, Manhattan, 9/6/01–9/22/01. Larry Grossman & Hal Hackady added new material. "This isn't Happening" was the new number now ending Act I. PRESENTED BY Tweiss Productions (Eileen B. Weiss & Sharon Weiss); DIRECTOR: Bryan D. Leys; CHOREOGRAPHER: Karen Oster; MUSICAL DIRECTOR: Steve Liebman. *Cast*: CHARLEY: Daniel Reichard; JOAN: Camille Diamond; MINGUET: Ted Bouton; AGNES: Kelli Maguire; ARCHBISHOP: Steve Liebman; GENERAL: Peter Waldren.

262. *Gospel at Colonus*

The Sophocles play interpreted as an evangelical religious ceremony with music.

Before Broadway. It first ran at the BROOKLYN ACADEMY OF MUSIC/CAREY PLAYHOUSE, 11/8/83–11/20/83. 14 PERFORMANCES; and again, same venue, 12/15/83–12/31/83. 16 PERFORMANCES. PRESENTED BY the Brooklyn Academy of Music Next Wave Festival, in association with Liza Lorwin & the Walker Art Center. It had the same basic crew as for the later Broadway production, except SOUND: Otts Munderloh; PRESS: Ellen Lampert, Susan Spier, Jerri Brown; COMPANY MANAGER: Debbie Lepsinger; STAGE MANAGERS: Sal Rasa & Rob Brenner. It had the same cast, except THESEUS: Carl Lumbly. Then it played at the HOUSTON GRAND OPERA, Texas, in 5/84. Then at the ARENA STAGE THEATRE, Washington, DC, in 11/84. It was revised for the AMERICAN MUSIC THEATRE FESTIVAL, CLEVELAND, in 9/85. Then in 1988 it went to Broadway.

The Broadway Run. LUNT—FONTANNE THEATRE, 3/24/88–5/15/88. 15 previews. 61 PERFORMANCES. PRESENTED BY Dodger Productions, Liza Lorwin, Louis Busch Hager, Playhouse Square Center (Cleveland, Ohio), Fifth Avenue Productions (Karen Walter Goodwin & Elizabeth Williams); MUSIC: Bob Telson; LYRICS/BOOK/ADAPTED/DIRECTOR: Lee Breuer; BASED ON the adaptation of Sophocles' *Oedipus at Colonus* in the version by Robert Fitzgerald, and incorporating the

passage from both *Oedipus Rex* and *Antigone*, both by Sophocles, in the versions by Dudley Fitts and Robert Fitzgerald; SETS: Alison Yerxa; COSTUMES: Ghretta Hynd & Alison Yerxa; LIGHTING: Julie Archer; SOUND: David Hewitt, Ron Lorman, Daryl Bornstein; MUSICAL ARRANGEMENTS: Bob Telson; PRESS: The Joshua Ellis Office; COMPANY MANAGER: Douglas C. Baker; PRODUCTION STAGE MANAGER: Peter Glazer; STAGE MANAGER: Susan Green; ASSISTANT STAGE MANAGER: Dwight R.B. Cook. *Cast*: MESSENGER: Morgan Freeman; OEDIPUS: Clarence Fountain and the Five Blind Boys of Alabama (Bobby Butler, James "Jimmy L." Carter, J.T. Clinkscales, Rev. Olice Thomas, Joseph Watson); ANTIGONE: Isabell Monk; THESEUS: Rev. Earl F. Miller; ISMENE: Jevetta Steele & the J.D. Steele Singers (J.D. Steele, Fred Steele, Janice Steele); CREON: Robert Earl Jones; POLYNEICES: Kevin Davis; CHORAGOS: Martin Jacox & J.J. Farley and the Soul Stirrers (Jackie Banks, Ben Odom, Willie Rogers); THE SINGER: Sam Butler Jr.; THE CHOIR SOLOIST: Carolyn Johnson-White; CHORUS: THE INSTITUTIONAL RADIO CHOIR: ALTOS: Betty Cooper, Angie Haddock, Vincent Haddock Jr., Crystal Johnson, Selene Jones, Shellie Jordan, Janet Napper, Pamela Poitier, Arnita Tillman (*O'Jean Lilly*), Candace White; SOPRANOS: Regina Berry, Deborah Britt, Sharon R. Driskill, Lady Peachena Eure, Mary Fischer, Parthea Hill (left during the run), Josie Johnson, Carolyn Johnson-White, Francine Thompkins, Joan Faye Wright (left during the run), *Katie Braan, Ernestine King, Kecia Lewis-Evans*; TENORS: Charles Bellamy, Jim Craven (left during the run), Walter Dixon (left during the run), Hayward Jerome Gregory, Sidney Hull (left during the run), Kevin Jackson, Roscoe Robinson, Billy Steele, Ezekiel Tobby, Carl Williams Jr., Jeff Young, *Londwood Chamberlain, George Cooper*; GUEST CHOIR DIRECTOR: J.D. Steele. **Understudies**: Messenger: Rev. Earl F. Miller & Jim Craven; Oedipus: James Carter; Theseus/Polyneices: Jim Craven; Antigone: Pamela Poitier; Creon: Carl Williams Jr.; The Swinger: Hayward Gregory; Choir Soloist: Parthea Hill; J.D. Steele Singers: Parthea Hill & Billy Steele. **Musicians**: LITTLE VILLAGE: GUITAR: Sam Butler Jr.; DRUMS: Leroy Coudon; ORGAN: Butch Heyward; PIANO/SYNTHESIZER: Bob Telson; TROMBONE: David Sacks; SAXOPHONES: John Hagen; TRUMPET: Chris Royal; BASS: Lincoln Schleifer; ALTO SAX/SLIDE GUITAR: Josh Shneider; HARMONICA: Don Brooks. **Act I**: Welcome and Quotations (Mr. Freeman); Invocation: "Live Where You Can" (Jevetta Steele & Choir); Recapitulation from *Oedipus the King* (Miss Monk & Rev. Miller); Oedipus and Antigone Enter Colonus (Miss Monk & Mr. Freeman); Ode to Colonus: "Fair Colonus" (Mr. Rogers), "Stop! Do Not Go On" (Mr. Butler, Mr. Farley, Soul Stirrers; *Bridge*— Mr. Fountain & Five Blind Boys); Choral Dialogue: "Who is This Man?" (Mr. Jacox & Mr. Freeman); Ismene Comes to Colonus: "How Shall I See You Through My Tears?" (Miss Steele & J.D. Steele Singers), Narrative of Ismene (Miss Monk), Tableau — Polyneices and Eteocles (J.D. Steele & Fred Steele), The Rite (Miss Monk, Mr. Freeman, Mr. Fountain), Tableau — Antigone and Ismene (Janice Steele & Jevetta Steele) [end of Ismene Comes to Colonus sequence]; Dialogue: Chorus Questions Oedipus (Mr. Jacox & Mr. Freeman); The Prayer: "A Voice Foretold" (Mr. Fountain, Five Blind Boys, Mr. Butler); Oedipus is Welcomed to Colonus: Peroration (Rev. Miller), Jubilee: "No, Never" (Mr. Jacox & Soul Stirrers; *Bridge*— Mr. Fountain, Five Blind Boys, Choir, Ensemble); Creon Comes to Colonus and The Seizure of the Daughters (Mr. Jones, Mr. Freeman, Mr. Fountain, Five Blind Boys); Oedipus Curses Creon: Suite, "All My Heart's Desire" (Mr. Fountain, Five Blind Boys, Choir, Mr. Jones, Mr. Freeman); Choral Ode: "Numberless Are the World's Wonders" (J.D. Steele Singers, J.D. Steele, Janice Steele, Choir). **Act II**: Oedipus Laments: "Lift Me Up" (Mr. Fountain & Five Blind Boys); Polyneices' Testimony and Supplication: Oedipus' Curse (Messrs Davis, Freeman, Fountain), "Evil" (Mr. Butler), "You Break My Heart" (J.D. Steele, Fred Steele, Mr. Odom), Poem: *Love Unconquerable* (Mr. Freeman & Mr. Fountain) [end of Polyneices' Testimony and Supplication sequence]; Preaching with Tuned Response (Mr. Freeman & Mr. Fountain); Special Effect: "Ah! Heaven's Height Has Cracked!:" Teachings (Mr. Freeman & Rev. Miller); The Descent of Oedipus: "Oh, Sunlight of No Light" (Mr. Butler), "Eternal Sleep" (Mr. Rogers & Soul Stirrers); Mourning (Miss Monk, Rev. Miller, Jevetta Steele, Janice Steele); Doxology, The Paean: "Lift Him Up" (Choir, Miss Johnson-White); Sermon (Mr. Freeman); Closing Hymn: "Now Let the Weeping Cease" (Mr. Rogers, Soul Stirrers, Choir, Ensemble); Benediction (Mr. Freeman).

Reviews were mixed. The show received a Tony nomination for book.

263. *Got Tu Go Disco*

A rock musical loosely based on the Cinderella story. Poor little girl works in rag trade and wants to go to disco and become ballroom queen.

Before Broadway. Joe Eula replaced John Zodrow as director, and Mr. Eula was, in turn, replaced by Larry Forde. In the cast Patrick Jude replaced Scott Holmes.

The Broadway Run. MINSKOFF THEATRE, 6/25/79–6/30/79. 9 previews. 8 PERFORMANCES. PRESENTED BY Jerry Brandt & Gotta Dance, Inc., in association with Roy Rifkind, Julie Rifkind, Bill Spitalsky, WKTU-Radio 92; MUSIC/LYRICS: various writers; BOOK: John Zodrow; CONCEIVED & CREATED BY: Joe Eula (his billing was removed); BASED ON the fairy tale *Cinderella*; DIRECTOR: Larry Forde; CHOREOGRAPHERS: Jo Jo Smith & Troy Garza; ADDITIONAL CHOREOGRAPHY: George Faison; SETS/PHYSICAL SUPERVISOR: James Hamilton; COSTUMES: Joe Eula; LIGHTING: S.A. Cohen; SOUND: Lenny Will; FILM SEQUENCES: Robert Rabinowitz; MUSICAL SUPERVISOR/MUSICAL DIRECTOR: Kenny Lehman; VOCAL DIRECTORS: Kenny Lehman & Mitch Kerper; CAST RECORDING on Casablanca Records & Filmworks; PRESS: Owen Levy, Valerie Warner, Connie De Nave, Carole Beberfeld; CASTING: TNI Casting (Julie Hughes & Barry Moss); GENERAL MANAGEMENT: Theatre Now; COMPANY MANAGER: Robb Lady; PRODUCTION STAGE MANAGERS: David Piel & Michael Turque; STAGE MANAGER: Arlene Grayson; ASSISTANT STAGE MANAGERS: John Fennesy & Lee Magerman. **Cast:** NARRATOR/VITUS: Joe Masiell (3); CASSETTE: Irene Cara (1); BILLY: Patrick Jude (2); MINNIE: Lisa Raggio (7); CONTACT: Laurie Dawn Skinner (8); ANTWERP: Patti Karr (6); LILA: Jane Holzer (9); CUBBY: Charlie Serrano (10); SNAP-FLASH: Rhetta Hughes (4); PETE: Justin Ross (5); MARC: Marc Benecke (11); SPINNER: Bob Pettie (12); SINGERS: Robin Lynn Beck, Gloria Covington, Gerry Griffin, Jack Magradey, Billy Newton-Davis; DANCERS: Conni Marie Brazelton, Prudence Darby, Ronald Dunham, Miguel Gonz, Christine Jacobsen, Peter Kapetan, Patrick Kinser-Lau, Julia Lema, Bronna Lipton, Mark Manley, Jodi Moccia, Jamie Patterson, Dee Ranzweiler, Adrian Rosario, Willie Rosario, Sue Samuels. **Understudies:** Cassette: Julia Lema; Billy: Billy Newton-Davis; Snap-Flash: Conni Marie Brazelton; Minnie: Dee Ranzweiler; Cubby: Jamie Patterson; Lila: Sue Samuels; Vitus: Patrick Kinser-Lau; Contact: Bronna Lipton; Pete: Ronald Dunham; Marc: Peter Kapetan; Spinner: Miguel Gonz. **Swing Dancer:** Tony Constantine. **Orchestra:** DRUMS: Richie Tannenbaum; GUITARS: Ross Trout & Kenneth Mazur; BASS GUITAR: Norbert Sloley; PERCUSSION: Eddie Colon; CONGAS: Mike Lewis; PIANO: Mitch Kerper & Steve Robbins; SYNTHESIZER: Steve Robbins; ALTO SAX/FLUTE: Jack Kripl; TENOR SAX: Gary Anderson; BARITONE SAX: Roger Rosenberg; VIOLINS: Joanna Jenner, Dan Reed, Roxanne Bergman, Susan Winterbottom, Richard Henrickson, Beth Cohen, Helen Huybrechts; VIOLA: Maureen Gallagher; CELLI: Myron Lutske & Richard Sher; TROMBONE: Bob Smith; TRUMPETS: Greg Ruvolo & Robert Zattola. **Act I: Prologue:** "Puttin' it On" (m/l: Kenny Lehman & Steve Boston; orch: Mr. Lehman) (Ensemble — lead vocalist Robin Lynn Beck); **Scene 1** The Disco Rag Store: "Disco Shuffle" (m/l: Ray Chew, with assistance from Nat Adderley Jr.) (orch: Mr. Chew; voc arr: Mr. Adderley) (Billy & Cassette); **Scene 2** Streets of New York and a bridge in Central Park; **Scene 3** Antwerp's apartment; **Scene 4** Rooftop of Antwerp's apartment: "All I Need" (m/l: Thomas Jones & Wayne Morrison) (orch: Kenny Lehman) (Cassette); **Scene 5** Vitus's office: "It Won't Work" (m/l/orch: John Davis) (Vitus); **Scene 6** Various parts of the Disco Rag Store: "Trust Me" (m/l: Kenny Lehman & Steve Boston) (orch: Mr. Lehman) (Cubby & Contact); **Scene 7** Sidewalk outside the Dream Castle Disco: "In and Out" (m/l: Kenny Lehman & Steve Boston) (orch: Mr. Lehman) (Marc & Company); **Scene 8** The Dream Castle Disco: "Got to Go Disco" (m/l/orch: John Davis) (Ensemble — lead vocalist Billy Newton-Davis), "Pleasure Pusher" (m/l: Eugene Narmore) (orch: Brad Baker) (Pete), "If That Didn't Do, It Can't Be Done" (m/l: Ray Chew, with assistance from Nat Adderley Jr.) (orch: Mr. Chew; voc arr:

Mr. Adderley) (Company). **Act II:** "Inter-Mish-Un" (m/l: Kenny Lehman, Thomas Jones, Wayne Morrison) (orch: Mr. Lehman; mixed by disc jockey Tee Scott) (sung by Billy Newton Davis); **Scene 1** Vitus's office and the city: "Hanging Over and Out" (m/l: Kenny Lehman & Steve Boston) (orch: Mr. Lehman) (Vitus); **Scene 2** Antwerp's apartment, rooftop and a park; **Scene 3** Various parts of the Disco Rag Store: "Chic to Cheap" (m/l: Jerry Powell) (orch: Brad Baker) (Snap-Flash), "Bad, Glad, Good and Had" (m/l/orch: John Davis) (Cassette); **Scene 4** The king and queen's dressing room; **Scene 5** A bridge in Central Park: "Cassie" (m/l: Ray Chew, with assistance from Nat Adderley Jr.) (orch: Mr. Chew; voc arr: Mr. Adderley) (Billy); **Scene 6** The Dream Castle Disco: "Takin' the Light" (m/l: Kenny Lehman, Thomas Jones, Wayne Morrison) (orch: Mr. Lehman) (Cassette, Billy, Ensemble — lead vocalist Gerri Griffin), "Gettin' to the Top" (m/l/orch: John Davis) (Antwerp).

Opening night tickets cost $50. It was unanimously panned by the critics. It was said to be the most expensive show ever produced on Broadway until then (cost $2 million; lost $3 million).

264. *Grand Hotel*

Also called: *Grand Hotel: The Musical.* A theatrical ballet, with no intermission. Set in 1928. The *Grand Hotel* in Berlin is the setting for five disparate people and their stories. Baron von Gaigern is forced to become a jewel thief to pay off his debts; the aging ballerina is losing her talent; the blustering business executive, von Preysing, is losing his empire; the timid clerk, Kringelein, has a fatal disease, and determines to live his last days in luxury; a pretty secretary dreams of going to Hollywood but is saddled with an unwanted pregnancy. The Baron falls in love with the ballerina, instead of stealing her jewels. Raffaela is the ballerina's devoted servant. The story is told in short, fast scenes, with endless movement. The only scenery was a row of chairs and a long pole to suggest a bar. Often two or three scenes would occur simultaneously. Musical numbers did not begin or end in any traditional way, but flowed into dialogue and out again without stopping. Dances of the period commented on the action. Pierre Dulaine and Yvonne Marceau, founders of the American Ballroom Theatre, were added to the cast during the Boston tryouts as an allegorical couple dancing through the intertwining stories.

Before Broadway. It had been a straight Broadway play, 11/13/30. 257 PERFORMANCES, written by W.A. Drake; and a grand 1932 MGM movie (with Garbo, Jack & Lionel Barrymore, Wally Beery, and Joan Crawford), but the first musical staging of the story —*At the Grand*— opened 7/7/58, at the Philharmonic Auditorium, Los Angeles, but failed, and closed on 9/13/58, at the Curran Theatre, San Francisco. Joan Diener played an opera singer, rather than a ballerina, as it better suited her talents. PRESENTED BY Edwin Lester; MUSIC/LYRICS: Robert Wright & George Forrest; BOOK: Luther Davis; DIRECTOR: Albert Marre; CHOREOGRAPHER: Ernest Flatt; SETS: Rouben Ter-Arutunian; GOWNS: Adrian; LIGHTING: Feder; TECHNICAL DIRECTOR: Richard Rodda; MUSICAL DIRECTOR: Jay Blackton; ORCHESTRATIONS: Albert Sendry & Arthur Kay; DANCE & INCIDENTAL MUSIC ARRANGEMENTS: Trude Rittman. **Cast:** KRINGELEIN: Paul Muni; ISOLA PARELLI: Joan Diener; ALSO WITH: Diki Lerner, Truman Gaige, David Opatoshu, John Banner, Donald Lawton, Vladimir Sokoloff, John Van Dreelen, Shevlin Rodgers, Cesare Danova, Neile Adams. "Feeding Time," "End of Aria from *La Saracena*," "Blest?," "A Table with a View," "The Grand Tango," "Isola," "Sophia," "At the Grand," "La Saracena," "We'll Take a Glass Together," "What You Need," "The Bare Necessities," "Crescendo," "Va Bene," "I Waltz Alone," "Press Conference." Between 1958 and 1989 the authors re-wrote the script, and Tommy Tune wanted to do it, but he wanted it totally re-done. He developed the show as a workshop in the lobby of the Hotel Diplomat. During the Boston tryout, half of the Wright/Forrest score was thrown out, and new songs by Maury Yeston were added. In addition, Peter Stone came in to re-work Luther Davis's book.

The Broadway Run. MARTIN BECK THEATRE, 11/12/89–1/27/92;

GERSHWIN THEATRE, 2/3/92–4/26/92. 31 previews from 10/17/89. Total of 1,018 PERFORMANCES. PRESENTED BY Martin Richards, Mary Lea Johnson, Sam Crothers, Sander Jacobs, Kenneth D. Greenblatt, Paramount Pictures, and Jujamcyn Theatres, in association with Patty Grubman & Marvin A. Krauss; MUSIC/LYRICS: Robert Wright & George Forrest; ADDITIONAL MUSIC & LYRICS: Maury Yeston; ADDITIONAL MUSIC/ MUSICAL SUPERVISOR: Wally Harper; BOOK: Luther Davis & (uncredited) Peter Stone; BASED ON the 1927 novel *Menschen im Hotel*, by Vicki Baum, by arrangement with Turner Entertainment, owner of the motion picture of the same title; DIRECTOR/CHOREOGRAPHER: Tommy Tune; ASSOCIATE CHOREOGRAPHER: Jeff Calhoun; SETS: Tony Walton; COSTUMES: Santo Loquasto; LIGHTING: Jules Fisher; SOUND: Otts Munderloh; MUSICAL DIRECTOR/VOCAL DIRECTOR: Jack Lee; ORCHESTRATIONS: Peter Matz; CAST RECORDING on Elektra & RCA Victor; PRESS: The Jacksina Company; CASTING: Julie Hughes & Barry Moss; PRODUCTION ASSOCIATE: Kathleen Raitt; GENERAL MANAGER: Joey Parnes; COMPANY MANAGER: Nina Skriloff, *Steve Winton* (by 91–92); PRODUCTION STAGE MANAGER: Bruce Lumpkin; STAGE MANAGER: David Wolf, *Robert Kellogg;* ASSISTANT STAGE MANAGER: Rob Babbitt. **Cast**: COLONEL DR. OTTERNSCHLAG: John Wylie, *Edmund Lyndeck* (during Mr. Wylie's vacation, 91–92); THE DOORMAN: Charles Mandracchia, *George Dudley* (from 90–91); THE COUNTESS: Yvonne Marceau, *Pascale Faye-Williams* (during Miss Marceau's vacation, 91–92); THE GIGOLO: Pierre Dulaine, *Patrick Taverna* (during Mr. Dulaine's vacation, 91–92); MADAME PEEPEE: Kathi Moss, *Brooks Almy* (from 91–92); ROHNA, THE GRAND CONCIERGE: Rex D. Hays; THE (FOUR) BELLBOYS: Georg Strunk: Ken Jennings; KURT KROENENBERG: Keith Crowningshield, *Carlos Lopez* (from 90–91); HANNS BITTNER: Gerrit de Beer; WILLIBALD, CAPTAIN: J.J. Jepson; ERIK, FRONT DESK: Bob Stillman; THE TELEPHONE OPERATORS: HILDEGARDE BRATTS: Jennifer Lee Andrews, *Lisa Merrill McCord* (during Miss Andrews' illness, 89–90), *Jill Powell* (from 90–91); SIGFRIEDE HOLZHEIM: Suzanne Henderson; WOLFFE BRATTS: Lynnette Perry, *DeLys Lively Mekka* (from 89–90), *Meg Tolin* (from 90–91); THE CHAUFFEUR: Ben George, *Luis Perez* (from 90–91), *Ben George* (by 91–92); ZINNOWITZ, THE LAWYER: Hal Robinson, *Merwin Goldsmith* (from 90–91); GENERAL DIRECTOR PREYSING OF SAXONIA MILLS: Timothy Jerome, *Michael DeVries* (during Mr. Jerome's illness, 89–90), *Merwin Goldsmith* (during Mr. Jerome's vacation, 91–92); FLAEMMCHEN, THE TYPIST: Jane Krakowski, *DeLys Lively-Mekka* (from 90–91), *Lynnette Perry* (from 90–91), *Meg Tolin* (during Miss Perry's vacation, 90–91), *Jill Powell & Meg Tolin* (during Miss Perry's vacation, 91–92); OTTO KRINGELEIN, THE BOOKKEEPER: Michael Jeter, *Chip Zien* (during Mr. Jeter's illness, 89–90), *J.J. Jepson* (from 90–91), *Chip Zien* (from 9/12/90), *Austin Pendleton* (from 91–92); RAFFAELA, THE CONFIDANTE: Karen Akers, *Caitlin Brown* (from 90–91), *Debbie de Coudreaux* (from 91–92), *Valerie Cutko* (from 91–92); SANDOR, IMPRESARIO: Mitchell Jason; VICTOR WITT, COMPANY MANAGER: Michel Moinot; ELIZAVETA GRUSHINSKAYA, BALLERINA: Liliane Montevecchi, *Rene Ceballos* (from 11/12/90), *Tina Paul* (during Miss Ceballos's illness), *Zina Bethune* (from 90–91), *Penny Worth* (during Miss Bethune's vacation, 91–92), *Cyd Charisse* (from 1/92); BARON FELIX VON GAIGERN: David Carroll, *Mark Jacoby* (stood in 5/90), *Brent Barrett* (from 5/8/90), *Rex Smith* (from 5/29/90), *David Carroll* (from 12/2/90), *John Schneider* (from 3/4/91), *Walter Willison* (during Mr. Schneider's illness, 90–91 and during his vacation, 91–92), *Greg Zerkle* (from 91–92); THE JIMMYS: David Jackson & Danny Strayhorn (*Glenn Turner* then *Ken Leigh Rogers* during illness, 91–92, and then replaced by *Michael Demby-Cain* in 91–92); THE (FOUR) SCULLERY WORKERS: ERNST SCHMIDT: Henry Grossman; FRANZ KOHL: William Ryall, *Jerry Ball* (from 90–91), *Abe Reybold* (during Mr. Ball's illness, 91–92); WERNER HOLST: David Elledge, *Michael Piehl* (from 91–92); GUNTHER GUSTAFSSON: Walter Willison, *Abe Reybold* (during Mr. Willison's vacation, 91–92); THE HOTEL COURTESAN: Suzanne Henderson; TOOTSIE: Lynnette Perry, *DeLys Lively-Mekka* (from 89–90), *Meg Tolin* (from 89–90); TRUDE THE MAID: Jennifer Lee Andrews, *Lisa Merrill McCord* (during Miss Andrews' illness, 89–90), *Jill Powell* (from 90–91); THE DETECTIVE: William Ryall, *Jerry Ball* (from 90–91), *David Elledge* (by 91–92), *Jerry Ball* (from 91–92), *Abe Reybold* (from 91–92). **Standbys**: Raffaela: Penny Worth (89–90); Grushinskaya/Peepee: Penny Worth (89–90), *Niki Harris* (90–92); Doctor/Preysing/Baron: Mark Jacoby (89–90), *Brent Barrett* (90). **Understudies**: Sandor: Gerrit de Beer; Zinnowitz: Michael DeVries (89–90), *Jerry Ball* (90–92), *Eivind Harum*

(90–92), *Merwin Goldsmith* (90–91), *Lee Lobenhofer* (90–92), *Greg Zerkle* (91–92); Courtesan: Niki Harris; Witt: Ken Jennings; Otto/Gigolo: J.J. Jepson; Flaemmchen: Lynnette Perry (89–90), *Jill Powell* (90–92), *Meg Tolin* (90–92); Rohna: William Ryall (89–90), *Jerry Ball* (90–92), *David Elledge* (90–92), *Eivind Harum* (90–91); Chauffeur: William Ryall (89–90), *Jerry Ball* (90–92), *David Elledge* (90–92), *Merwin Goldsmith* (90–91), *Lee Lobenhofer* (90–92), *Eivind Harum* (91–92), *Greg Zerkle* (91–92); The Jimmys: Glenn Turner; Doctor: Rex D. Hays; Preysing: Hal Robinson (89–90), *Merwin Goldsmith* (90–92), *Lee Lobenhofer* (90–92), *Greg Zerkle* (91–92); Erik: Keith Crowningshield & Michael DeVries (89–90), *J.J. Jepson* (90–92), *Merwin Goldsmith* (90–91), *Lee Lobenhofer* (90–92), *Eric Bohus* (90–92), *Greg Zerkle* (91–92); Baron: *Brent Barrett* (90), *Walter Willison* (90–92), *Merwin Goldsmith* (90–91), *Lee Lobenhofer* (90–92), *Ben George* (90–92), *Greg Zerkle* (91–92); Kringelein: Chip Zien (89–90), *Ken Jennings* (90–92), *J.J. Jepson* (90–92). **Swings**: Michael DeVries (89–90), Niki Harris (89–92), Glenn Turner (89–92), Eivind Harum (89–92), *Rob Babbitt* (90–92), *Lee Lobenhofer* (90–92), *Eric Bohus* (90–92), *Greg Zerkle* (91–92), *Ken Leigh Rogers* (91–92). **Orchestra**: CONCERTMASTER: Elliot Rosoff; VIOLINS: Erle Grubb, Marion Guest, Ethel Abelson; VIOLAS: Al Brown & Richard Spencer; CELLI: Anne Callahan & Alessandro Benetello; WOODWINDS: Mort Silver, Victor Morosco, Edward Zuhlke, Walter Kane; FRENCH HORN: Sharon Moe; TRUMPETS: Burt Collins, John Bova, Greg Ruvolo; TROMBONE: Arthur Baron; BASS TROMBONE: Alan Raph; BASS: Ray Kilday; PERCUSSION: Beth Ravin; DRUMS: Ronald Zito.

THE PRESENTATION OF THE COMPANY: in which the audience is introduced to the *Grand Hotel's* guests and staff as their lives begin to intertwine in the Grand Parade of life: "The Grand Parade" † (Company); *Scene 1* The Grand Hotel lobby and far below in the scullery: "As it Should Be" * (Baron), "Some Have, Some Have Not" * (Scullery Workers), "At the Grand Hotel" † (Kringelein), "Grand Tango" ("Table with a View") * (Kringelein), "And Life Goes On" (Kringelein); *Scene 2* The Moroccan Coffee Bar: the employees' smoking lounge: "Maybe My Baby Loves Me" (Jimmys); *Scene 3* A corner of the Grand Ballroom: in which Grushinskaya suffers her daily barre: "Fire and Ice" * (Grushinskaya), "Twenty-Two Years" † (Raffaela), "Villa on a Hill" (Raffaela); *Scene 4* The ladies' powder room: in which the Baron and Flaemmchen meet, flirt deliciously and agree to rendezvous: "I Want to Go to Hollywood" † (Flaemmchen); *Scene 5* Men's washroom and the hotel bar: "Everybody's Doing It" † (Preysing), "The Crooked Path" * (Preysing); *Scene 6* The Baron's room: in which the Baron finds himself trapped in a snare set by Algerian villains: "As it Should Be" * (reprise) (Baron); *Scene 7* The Yellow Pavilion: in which the Baron and Flaemmchen complete their tryst. She then dances with the innocent Kringelein who melts in her able arms: "The Grand Foxtrot" ("Trottin' the Fox") ("Who Couldn't Dance with You?") (Kringelein); *Scene 8* The hotel conference room: in which the desperate Preysing throws away his scruples and lies to his stockholders: "The Boston Merger" * (Preysing); *Scene 9* Backstage at the Opera House: in which Grushinskaya collapses in emotional despair: "No Encore" (Grushinskaya; *Scene 10* The financial corner of the hotel lobby: in which the Baron convinces Kringelein that the 1928 American Stock Market is the soundest of all investments; *Scene 11* The roof of the Grand Hotel: in which the Baron uses the cloak of night to prowl the precipice in order to enter Grushinskaya's suite in furtive search of her jewels: "Fire and Ice" * (reprise) (Baron); *Scene 12* Grushinskaya's suite: in which she surprises the thieving Baron only to fall helplessly for his handsome charms. Their initial attraction proves that they were both wrong when they despaired that love can't happen. They are in love: "Love Can't Happen" † (Baron & Grushinskaya); *Scene 13* Raffaela's room: in which the lonely confidante says to her imagined mistress "What she needs is someone strong:" "What She Needs" * (Raffaela); *Scene 14* The hotel conference room and just inside the ever-revolving door: in which sexual pressure is applied in both places; *Scene 15* Raffaela's room: in which her loneliness continues; *Scene 16* Grushinskaya's suite: in which the ballerina rejoices in her new-found love with a "good morning" to the world: "Bonjour Amour" † (Grushinskaya); *Scene 17* The Yellow Pavilion; the hotel bar; the maids' changing room; a room far below the lobby; the Moroccan Coffee Bar; a corner of the lobby: in which the Charleston is danced because all are happy: "The Grand Charleston" ("Happy") (Company), "We'll Take a Glass Together" * (Kringelein);

Scene 18 A cross corridor upstairs in the hotel; the Doctor's room; Preysing's room; Flaemmchen's adjoining room; Kringelein's room; the bedchamber of the Countess and the Gigolo: "I Waltz Alone" * (Doctor), "Roses at the Station" † (Baron); *Scene 19* Grushinskaya's suite; Kringelein's room; Preysing's room: "How Can I Tell Her?" (Raffaela); *Scene 20* The lobby of the Grand Hotel: in which we learn a baby has been born: "As it Should Be" * (reprise) (Company), "And Life Goes On" (reprise) (Company), "Some Have, Some Have Not" * (reprise) (Scullery Workers); The Grand Finale: "The Grand Parade" † (reprise) (Company), "The Grand Waltz" (Company).

Note: * means lyrics revised by Maury Yeston; † means music & lyrics by Mr. Yeston. All other numbers are by Wright & Forrest.

Broadway reviews were divided. The show won Tonys for direction of a musical, choreography, costumes, lighting, and for Michael Jeter. Mr. Jeter's big Charleston number was shown on the Tony Awards telecast and bolstered the box office. The show was also nominated for musical, score, book, sets, and for David Carroll, Jane Krakowski, and Liliane Montevecchi. The staging by Tommy Tune was the main reason for its long success on Broadway, and it made Mr. Tune's name as a director/choreographer. David Carroll left the cast in 5/90, sick with AIDS. He collapsed and died while recording the cast album on 3/11/92. This was Cyd Charisse's Broadway debut.

After Broadway. TOUR. Opened on 11/27/90, at the Tampa Bay Performing Arts Center. As part of the tour it ran at the Kennedy Center, Washington, DC, 12/4/90–1/6/91. MUSICAL DIRECTOR: Michael Biagi. *Cast*: GRUSHINSKAYA: Liliane Montevecchi; BARON: Brent Barrett; KRINGELEIN: Mark Baker; OTTERNSCHLAG: Tony Franciosa; ERIC: Dirk Lumbard; ZINNOWITZ: Erick Devine; PREYSING: KC Wilson; FLAEMMCHEN: DeLys Lively-Mekka; CHORUS: Keith Crowningshield, Rick Stockwell, William Ryall, Abe Reybold, Reggie Phoenix, Corinne Melancon, Barbara Marineau.

WALNUT STREET THEATRE, Philadelphia, 5/19/99–6/27/99. Previews from 5/11/99. DIRECTOR: Bruce Lumpkin; CHOREOGRAPHER: Richard Stafford. *Cast*: KRINGELEIN: Tony Freeman; GRUSHINSKAYA: Natalie Mosco; FLAEMMCHEN: Jill Powell; OTTERNSCHLAG: Edmund Lyndeck; BARON: David Hess. This production then played at the BENEDUM CENTER, Pittsburgh, 7/13/99–7/18/99. PRESENTED BY the Civic Light Opera of Pittsburgh. Same cast and crew.

THEATRE UNDER THE STARS, Houston, 10/12/99–10/14/99. *Cast*: GRUSHINSKAYA: Liliane Montevecchi.

COLONY THEATRE, Burbank, Calif., 10/16/04–11/14/04. Previews from 10/13/04. DIRECTOR: Peter Schneider; SETS: David Potts. *Cast*: KRINGELEIN: Jason Graae; ALSO WITH: Michael McCarty.

DONMAR WAREHOUSE, London, 11/29/04–2/12/05. Previews from 11/19/04. DIRECTOR: Michael Grandage; CHOREOGRAPHER: Adam Cooper; SETS: Christopher Oram; LIGHTING: Hugh Vanstone; SOUND: Terry Jardine; MUSICAL DIRECTOR: Jae Alexander. *Cast*: GRUSHINSKAYA: Mary Elizabeth Mastrantonio; ALSO WITH: Sarah Annis, Gillian Bevan, Martyn Ellis, Daniel Evans, Paul Hazel, David Lucas.

265. *The Grand Tour*

Set between 6/13/40 and 6/18/40, between Paris and the Atlantic Coast of France. Stjerbinsky, an aristocratic and anti-Semitic Polish cavalry colonel, and an ingenious Polish Jew (Jacobowsky) join forces to escape Nazi-occupied France during World War II. Jacobowsky repeatedly saves the colonel, who comes to admire the little Jew. Jacobowsky is attracted to the colonel's wife, and decides to leave on his own "grand tour."

Before Broadway. The original straight play ran on Broadway as *Jacobowsky and the Colonel*, 3/14/44. 417 PERFORMANCES. *Cast*: JACOBOWSKY: Oscar Karlweis. It was filmed in 1958 as *Me and the Colonel*, with Danny Kaye. As for the musical, at first Diana Shumlin was going to produce a musical version of *Jacobowsky and the Colonel*, with that title, music/lyrics by Stan Daniels, book by Leonard Gershe, and cast headed by Alec McCowan and Richard Kiley. But she couldn't get it off the ground, so she called in her friend Mike Stewart, who agreed to mount the show if Jerry Herman came in as songwriter. Gower Champion turned it down as director/choreographer. James Coco and Jerry Orbach were considered for the role of Jacobowsky, before Joel Grey took it. The show tried out in San Francisco, where Tommy Tune came in to try to help the production along. The number "I Want to Live Each Night" was cut before Broadway.

The Broadway Run. PALACE THEATRE, 1/11/79–3/4/79. 18 previews. 61 PERFORMANCES. PRESENTED BY James M. Nederlander, Diana Shumlin, and Jack Schlissel, in association with Carole J. Shorenstein & Stewart F. Lane; MUSIC/LYRICS: Jerry Herman; BOOK: Michael Stewart & Mark Bramble; BASED ON the 1944 comedy *Jacobowsky and the Colonel*, by S.N. Behrman, which was adapted from the Austrian play *Jacobowsky und der Oberst*, by Franz Werfel, which was unproduced in its original version until 1958; DIRECTOR: Gerald Freedman (helped by Tommy Tune); CHOREOGRAPHER: Donald Saddler (helped by Tommy Tune); ASSISTANT CHOREOGRAPHER: Mercedes Ellington; SETS: Ming Cho Lee; ASSISTANT SETS: Adrianne Lobel; COSTUMES: Theoni V. Aldredge; LIGHTING: Martin Aronstein; SOUND: Jack Mann; MUSICAL DIRECTOR: Wally Harper; ORCHESTRATIONS: Philip J. Lang; DANCE MUSIC ARRANGEMENTS: Peter Howard; VOCAL ARRANGEMENTS: Donald Pippin; CAST RECORDING on Columbia; PRESS: Betty Lee Hunt & Maria Cristina Pucci; CASTING: Feuer & Ritzer; GENERAL MANAGERS: Jack Schlissel & Jay Kingwill; PRODUCTION STAGE MANAGER: Mary Porter Hall; STAGE MANAGER: Richard Elkow; ASSISTANT STAGE MANAGERS: Marc Schlackman & Debra Lyman. *Cast*: S.L. JACOBOWSKY: Joel Grey (1) ✩; MME. BOUFFIER: Grace Keagy (8), *Lynne Charnay*; CZIESNO: Jack Karcher; JEANNOT: Mark Waldrop; COL. TADEUSZ BOLESLAV STJERBINSKY: Ron Holgate (2) ✩; SZABUNIEWICZ: Stephen Vinovich (4); CHAUFFEUR: Stan Page; CAPT. MUELLER: George Reinholt (5); MME. VAUCLAIN: Chevi Colton (7); MARIANNE: Florence Lacey (3); CONDUCTOR: Gene Varrone (6); MME. MARVILLE, AN ELEGANT LADY: Travis Hudson (9); A PEASANT WOMAN WITH CHICKENS: Grace Keagy (8), *Lynne Charnay*; JACQUES, THE EJECTED PASSENGER: Bob Morrisey; HUGO THE HUNGARIAN HERCULES: Kenneth Kantor; MME MANZONI: Chevi Colton (7); STILT-WALKER: Jay Pierce; BARGEMAN: Kenneth Kantor; MAN WITH FLOWER IN HIS LAPEL: Jay Stuart (10); PAPA CLAIRON: Jay Pierce; CLAUDINE: Jo Speros; BRIDE'S MOTHER: Grace Keagy (8), *Lynne Charnay*; BRIDE'S FATHER: Gene Varrone (6); BRIDE'S AUNT: Chevi Colton (7); GROOM: Mark Waldrop; BRIDE: Michelle Marshall; COMMISSAIRE OF POLICE: Bob Morrisey; PEDDLER: Stan Page; MOTHER MADELEINE: Travis Hudson (9); SISTER ROLAND: Grace Keagy (8), *Lynne Charnay*; ENSEMBLE (REFUGEES, PARISIANS, TRAIN TRAVELERS, CARNIVAL PERSONNEL, GERMAN SOLDIERS, WEDDING GUESTS, SISTERS OF CHARITY): Bjarne Buchtrup, Carol Dorian, Kenneth Kantor, Jack Karcher, Debra Lyman, Michelle Marshall, Bob Morrisey, Stan Page, Tina Paul, Jay Pierce, Linda Poser, Theresa Rakov, Paul Solen, Jo Speros, Jeff Veazey, Mark Waldrop, Bonnie Young. *Standby*: Jacobowsky: Charles Abbott. *Understudies*: Colonel: Jay Stuart; Marianne/Vauclain/Madeleine: Linda Poser; Szabuniewicz: Kenneth Kantor; Captain: Jack Karcher; Man with Flower: Bob Morrisey; Bride's Aunt: Bronna Lipton; Mmes Marville & Manzoni: Theresa Rakov. *Swing Dancers*: Bronna Lipton & Jeff Richards. *Act I*: *Prologue*: "I'll Be Here Tomorrow" (Jacobowsky); *Scene 1* Square outside the Hotel de la Rose: "For Poland" (Colonel, Mme. Bouffier, Parisians); *Scene 2* Saint-Cyrille: "I Belong Here" (Marianne), "Marianne" (Colonel); *Scene 3* A local train heading west: "We're Almost There" (Marianne, Szabuniewicz, Jacobowsky, Colonel, Mme. Marville, Conductor, Passengers); *Scene 4* Wagons of the Carnival Manzoni: "Marianne" (reprise) (Jacobowsky); *Scene 5* Open spot in the countryside near Rennes: "More and More/Less and Less" (Marianne & Colonel); *Scene 6* Dressing area of the Carnival Manzoni: "One Extraordinary Thing" (Jacobowsky, Marianne, Colonel, Szabuniewicz, Carnival Performers); *Scene 7* Midway of the Carnival Manzoni: "One Extraordinary Thing" (reprise) (Jacobowsky). *Act II*: *Scene 1* A tree-lined canal in the west of France: "Mrs. S.L. Jacobowsky" (Jacobowsky); *Scene 2* Cafe of Papa Clairon at St. Nazaire: "Wedding Conversation" (Jacobowsky & Bride's Father), "Mazeltov" (Bride's Father & Wedding Guests); *Scene 3* A country road near St. Nazaire: "I Think, I Think" (Colonel); *Scene 4* 23 rue Mace: "For Poland" (reprise) (Marianne, Mother Madeleine, Sisters of Charity); *Scene 5* Empty street in St. Nazaire: "You I Like" (Colonel & Jacobowsky); *Scene 6* The Old Wharf at St. Nazaire: "I Belong Here" (reprise) (Marianne), "I'll Be Here Tomorrow" (reprise) (Jacobowsky).

On Broadway it received some favorable reviews, but was mostly panned. It was capitalized at $950,000, and wound up losing $1,457,183. It was going to close earlier than it did, but Joel Grey tore up the closing notice onstage. The show received Tony nominations for score, and for Joel Grey and Ron Holgate.

After Broadway. TOUR. Opened on 3/10/79, in Chicago. *Cast*: JACOBOWSKY: Joel Grey; THE COLONEL: Ron Holgate; MARIANNE: Florence Lacey.

JEWISH REPERTORY THEATRE, 6/14/88. DIRECTOR: Ran Avni; CHOREOGRAPHER: Helen Butleroff; SETS: Jeffrey Schneider; COSTUMES: Karen Hummel; MUSICAL DIRECTOR: Andrew Howard. *Cast*: JACOBOWSKY: Stuart Zagnit; THE COLONEL: Paul Ukena Jr.; VARIOUS ROLES: Ray Wills.

JEWISH REPERTORY THEATRE, 1/23/03, 1/26/03, 1/27/03. 4 PERFORMANCES. In concert form. DIRECTOR: Stuart Zagnit. *Cast*: THE COLONEL: Paul Ukena Jr.; MARIANNE: Kim Lindsay.

266. *The Grass Harp*

A sentimental pastorale of the good old days. The musical tells of spinster sisters Dolly and Verena, at their house in Joy City in the present, and in River Woods in the past. They live with cousin Collin and housekeeper Catherine. Dolly was once good to some gypsies, and they gave her a miracle dropsy cure, which does more than cure dropsy, it seems, and she guards it (and her innocence) from all neighbors and friends. Verena falls for Dr. Ritz from Chicago, and they decide to bottle and sell the cure. But Dolly refuses to give them the recipe. Dolly, Catherine and Collin retreat to a tree house in the woods. Verena finds Ritz has stolen her money and left town, so she joins the others in the tree house. Babylove is a revivalist, preaching love and flowers.

Before Broadway. Truman Capote dramatized his own play in 1952, and it ran on Broadway, at the MARTIN BECK THEATRE, 3/27/52–4/26/52. 36 PERFORMANCES. This was not a musical, but had incidental music by Virgil Thomson. PRESENTED BY Saint Subber & Rita Allen; DIRECTOR: Robert Lewis; SETS/COSTUMES: Cecil Beaton. *Cast*: DOLLY: Mildred Natwick; BABYLOVE: Alice Pearce; VERENA: Ruth Nelson; RITZ: Jonathan Harris; BARBER: Sterling Holloway; COLLIN: Johnny Stewart.

The musical version had its premiere at the TRINITY SQUARE PLAYHOUSE, Providence, Rhode Island, 12/27/66. 17 PERFORMANCES. Reviews were not great. DIRECTOR: Adrian Hall; CHOREOGRAPHER: Zoya Leporska; SETS: Lynn Pecktal; COSTUMES: John Lehmeyer; LIGHTING: Roger Morgan; MUSICAL DIRECTOR: Theodore Saidenberg. *Cast*: DOLLY: Barbara Baxley; BABYLOVE: Elaine Stritch; ALSO WITH: Carol Brice, David Hooks, Carol Bruce, Skip Hinnant, Louis Beachner. Kermit Bloomgarden optioned it for Broadway, and asked Mary Martin to play Dolly, but she refused, seeing herself as Babylove. Mr. Bloomgarden did not pick up the option when it expired, and it was taken up by Messrs Barr, Woodward & Harvey. Ellis Rabb (of the non-profit Association of Producing Artists, or A.P.A.) was set to direct his only Broadway musical. It then got ready to go up to Broadway. The A.P.A., based at the University of Michigan in Ann Arbor, had joined forces with the Off Broadway Phoenix Theatre in 1964, but the new organization became defunct before they could produce *The Grass Harp*. A new group, Theatre 1972, stepped in, and tried it out at the new Power Center for the Performing Arts, at the University of Michigan. Carol Brice was still with the show; new players were Barbara Cook, Ruth Ford, and Celeste Holm (as Babylove). Karen Morrow took over from Celeste Holm, who could not handle the singing requirements. The show was previously called *Yellow Drum*. The number "Brazil" was cut before Broadway.

The Broadway Run. MARTIN BECK THEATRE, 11/2/71–11/6/71. 5 previews from 10/28/71. 7 PERFORMANCES. "The University of Michigan Professional Theatre Program's Production," PRESENTED BY Theater 1972 (Richard Barr, Charles Woodward, Michael Harvey); MUSIC: Claibe Richardson; LYRICS/BOOK: Kenward Elmslie; BASED ON the 1952 Truman Capote play, from his 1951 novella; DIRECTOR: Ellis Rabb; CHOREOGRAPHER: Rhoda Levine; SETS/LIGHTING: James Tilton; COSTUMES: Nancy Potts; MUSICAL DIRECTOR: Theodore Saidenberg; ARRANGE-

MENTS: J. (Billy) Ver Planck; ADDITIONAL ORCHESTRATIONS: Jonathan Tunick & Robert Russell Bennett; DANCE & INCIDENTAL MUSIC: John Berkman; PRESS: Betty Lee Hunt Associates; GENERAL MANAGER: Michael Kasdan; COMPANY MANAGER: Oscar Abraham; PRODUCTION STAGE MANAGER: Bruce A. Hoover; STAGE MANAGER: Charles Kindl; ASSISTANT STAGE MANAGER: Allan Williams. *Cast*: DOLLY TALBO: Barbara Cook (1) ✰; COLLIN TALBO: Russ Thacker (6) ✰; CATHERINE CREEK: Carol Brice (2) ✰; VERENA TALBO: Ruth Ford (4) ✰; MAUDE RIORDAN: Christine Stabile (8); DR. MORRIS RITZ: Max Showalter (5) ✰; JUDGE COOL: John Baragrey (7) ✰; BABYLOVE: Karen Morrow (3) ✰; THE HEAVENLY PRIDE'N JOYS: Kelley Boa, Trudy Bordoff, Colin Duffy, Eva Grant, David Craig Moskin; SHERIFF AMOS LEGRAND: Harvey Vernon (9). STANDBYS: Dolly/Verena: Laurie Franks; Catherine: Alyce Webb; Babylove: Travis Hudson; Collin: Walter Bobbie; Ritz: William Larsen. UNDERSTUDIES: Sheriff: Allan Williams; Judge: Harvey Vernon; Maude: Ann Hodapp. *Scene 1* The Talbo backyard: "Dropsy Cure Weather" (Dolly, Catherine, Collin), "This One Day" (Collin), "This One Day" (dance) (Collin & Maude); *Scene 2* The Talbo house: "Think Big Rich" (Ritz), "If There's Love Enough" (Catherine), "Yellow Drum" (Dolly, Catherine, Collin); *Scene 3* The tree-house in River Woods: "Marry with Me" (Catherine), "I'll Always Be in Love" (Dolly), "Floozies" (Collin), The Babylove Miracle Show: "Call Me Babylove" (Babylove), "Walk into Heaven" (Babylove), "Hang a Little Moolah on the Washline" (Babylove & Pride'n Joys), "Talkin' in Tongues" (Babylove), "Whooshin' Through My Flesh" (Babylove, Catherine, Dolly, Collin, Company) [end of the Babylove Miracle Show sequence], "Walk into Heaven" (reprise) (Babylove), "Something for Nothing" (Ritz); *Scene 4* The jail: "Indian Blues" (Catherine & Company), "Take a Little Sip" (Collin, Dolly, Catherine, Maude, Company); *Scene 5* Joy City: "Yellow Drum" (reprise) (Company), "What Do I Do Now (He's Gone)?" (Verena); *Scene 6* The tree-house: "Pick Youself a Flower" (Babylove & Company), "The Flower Fortune Dance" (Company), "Reach Out" (Dolly & Company).

Broadway reviews were very divided.

After Broadway. YORK PLAYERS (in New York), 11/16/79. DIRECTOR: Janet Hayes Walker. *Cast*: Donna Pelc, Jan Pessano, Carolyn Miller, Ralph David Westfall.

YORK THEATRE COMPANY, spring, 1994. This was the first ever in the York's *Musicals in Mufti* series. DIRECTOR: Randall Hugill. *Cast*: Lynne Wintersteller, Lillias White, Cass Morgan.

NEW CONSERVATORY THEATRE CENTER, San Francisco, 10/29/99–11/14/99. Previews from 10/27/99. A "revisal;" certain revisions were done by Kenward Elmslie and Claibe Richardson. There was a new song—"The Dark Night of the Soul." The number "Brazil" (cut from the original) was restored. PRESENTED BY 42nd Street Moon; DIRECTOR: Greg MacKellan; MUSICAL DIRECTOR: Brandon Adams. *Cast*: DOLLY: Susan Watson; BABYLOVE: Meg MacKay.

REVISED, CONCERT, VERSION. 1/17/03–1/19/03. PRESENTED BY the York Theatre Company; DIRECTOR: James Morgan. Claibe Richardson died on 1/5/03.

267. *Grease*

A new '50s rock 'n' roll musical; a nostalgic parody of the Elvis era. Set at a reunion of the Class of '59 of the fictitious Rydell High School in Chicago. The main plot is the attraction between greaser Danny and prim and proper Sandy, who eventually learns to be a bad girl.

Before Broadway. First produced by amateurs at Kingston Mines community theatre in Chicago, a converted trolley barn. The show was then five hours long.

The Broadway Run. EDEN THEATRE, 2/14/72–6/5/72; BROADHURST THEATRE, 6/7/72–11/21/72; ROYALE THEATRE, 11/23/72–1/27/80; MAJESTIC THEATRE, 2/11/80–4/13/80. Total of 3,388 PERFORMANCES. PRESENTED BY Kenneth Waissman & Maxine Fox, in association with Anthony D'Amato; MUSIC/LYRICS/BOOK: Jim Jacobs & Warren Casey; DIRECTOR: Tom Moore; CHOREOGRAPHER: Patricia Birch; SETS: Douglas W. Schmidt; COSTUMES: Carrie F. Robbins; LIGHTING: Karl Eigsti; SOUND: Bill Merrill, *Jack Shearing* (from 6/7/72); MUSICAL SUPERVISOR: Michael Leonard,

Louis St. Louis (by 76–77); ORCHESTRATIONS: Michael Leonard; MUSICAL DIRECTOR: Louis St. Louis, *Jeremy Stone* (by 76–77); VOCAL ARRANGEMENTS/DANCE MUSIC ARRANGEMENTS: Louis St. Louis; CAST RECORDING on MGM; PRESS: Betty Lee Hunt Associates; GENERAL MANAGEMENT: Theatre Now; COMPANY MANAGER: Leo K. Cohen, Camille Ranson, *Edward H. Davis, Robb Lady, Camille Ranson*; PRODUCTION STAGE MANAGER: Joe Calvan; STAGE MANAGER: A. Robert Altschuler (gone by 77–78), *T. Schuyler Smith* (gone by 77–78), *John Fennesy, Tom Harris* (gone by 77–78), *Larry Forde* (by 74–75 & gone by 77–78), *Paul Bengston* (by 74–75 & gone by 77–78), *John Everson* (by 74–75 & gone by 77–78), *M. William Lettich* (by 74–75 & gone by 77–78), *Lynne Guerra* (by 74–75), *Steve Beckler* (by 76–77), *Michael Martorella* (by 75–76 & gone by 77–78), *Greg Zadikov* (by 77–78), *Scott Holmes* (78–79). **Cast**: MISS LYNCH: Dorothy Leon, *Sudie Bond* (during vacation, 73–74), *Ruth Russell* (by 74–75); PATTY SIMCOX: Ilene Kristen, *Joy Rinaldi* (from 73–74), *Carol Culver* (by 74–75), *Katherine Meloche* (by 76–77), *Foresby Russell* (by 77–78), *JoEla Flood* (by 78–79); EUGENE FLORCZYK: Tom Harris, *Barrey Smith* (from 73–74), *Stephen Van Benschoten* (from 73–74), *Lloyd Alann* (by 74–75), *Randy Powell* (by 77–78); JAN: Garn Stephens, *Alaina Warren, Jamie Donnelly* (from 72–73), *Randee Heller, Rebecca Gilchrist* (by 74–75), *Mimi Kennedy* (by 75–76), *Cynthia Darlow* (by 76–77), *Pippa Pearthree* (by 77–78); MARTY: Katie Hanley, *Meg Bennett* (from 6/7/72), *Denise Nettleton, Marilu Henner* (by 74–75), *Char Fontane* (by 75–76), *Diane Stilwell* (from 8/76), *Sandra Zeeman* (by 77–78); BETTY RIZZO: Adrienne Barbeau, *Elaine Petricoff* (from 3/73), *Randee Heller* (from 5/74), *Karen Dille* (from 12/1/75), *Livia Genise* (by 76), *Judy Kaye* (from 5/10/77), *Lorelle Brina* (by 77–78), *Marcia Mitzman* (from 3/79), *Lisa Orberg* (by 79–80); DOODY: James Canning, *Barry J. Tarallo* (by 74–75), *Bill Vitelli* (by 77–78); ROGER: Walter Bobbie, *Richard Quarry* (from 72–73), *John S. Driver* (from 72–73), *Walter Bobbie* (from 73–74), *Michael Tucci* (by 74–75), *Ray DeMattis* (by 75–76), *Dan Woodard* (by 77–78); KENICKIE: Timothy Meyers, *John Fennesy* (from 72–73), *Jerry Zaks* (from 73–74), *Timothy Meyers* (by 75–76), *Danny Jacobson* (from 12/75), *Michael Tucci* (by 76–77), *Matt Landers, Danny Jacobson, Tom Wiggin* (from 1/80), *Danny Jacobson* (from 4/80); SONNY LATIERRI: Jim Borrelli, *Matt Landers* (by 74–75), *Albert Insinnia* (by 75–76), *David Paymer* (by 76–77); FRENCHY: Marya Small, *Ellen March* (from 73–74), *Joy Rinaldi* (by 74–75), *Jill P. Rose* (by 75–76), *Foresby Russell* (by 76–77), *Peggy Lee Brennan* (by 77–78), *Duffi* (by 78–79); SANDY DUMBROWSKI: Carole Demas, *Ilene Graff* (from 3/73), *Candice Earley* (from 6/17/75), *Robin Lamont* (by 76–77), *Foresby Russell, Andrea Walters* (from 11/77), *Shannon Fanning* (by 77–78); DANNY ZUKO: Barry Bostwick, *Jeff Conaway* (from 6/73), *John Lansing* (from 11/74), *Treat Williams* (from 12/75), *Lloyd Alann* (from 6/14/76), *Treat Williams, Adrian Zmed, Patrick Swayze, Peter Gallagher* (by 77–78), *Frank Piegaro* (by 79–80); VINCE FONTAINE: Don Billett, *Gardner Hayes* (from 6/7/72), *Jim Weston* (from 72–73), *John Holly, Walter Charles* (from 73–74), *Jim Weston* (from 1/76), *Walter Charles, Stephen M. Groff* (by 77–78), *Stan Birnbaum* (by 78–79), *Barry Vigon* (from 1/80); JOHNNY CASINO: Alan Paul, *Bob Garrett* (from 73–74), *Philip Casnoff, Joe Rifici* (by 74–75), *Philip Casnoff* (by 75–76), *Frank Piegaro* (from 75–76); CHA-CHA DIGREGORIO: Kathi Moss, *Robin Vogel* (by 77–78); TEEN ANGEL: Alan Paul, *Bob Garrett* (from 73–74), *Philip Casnoff, Joe Rifici* (by 74–75), *Philip Casnoff* (by 75–76), *Frank Piegaro* (from 75–76). **Understudies**: Danny: Frank Piegaro. Female Roles: Joy Rinaldi (72–75), Alaina Warren (72–75), *Foresby Russell* (72–74), *Ann Travolta* (72–74), *Adele Paige* (73–77), *Shelley Barre* (75–77), *Lori Ada Jaroslow* (77–79), *Linda Nenno* (78–79), *Lesley Berry* (77–78). Male Roles: Jeff Conaway (72–73), Richard Gere (72–73), Daniel Deitch (72–73), *Philip Casnoff* (73–74), *John Everson* (73–74), *Malcolm Groome* (73–74), *John Fennesy* (74–77), *Albert Insinnia* (74–75), *Tony Shultz* (74–75), *Ted Wass* (by 75–77), *Jim Langrall* (76–77), *Greg Zadikov* (76–78), *Barry J. Tarallo* (77–78), *Scott Holmes* (78–79), *Bob Reynolds* (78–79). **Act I**: **Scene 1** Reunion: "Alma Mater" (Miss Lynch, Patty, Eugene), "Alma Mater Parody" (Pink Ladies & Burger Palace Boys); **Scene 2** Cafeteria and school steps: "Summer Nights" (Sandy, Danny, Pink Ladies, Burger Palace Boys), "Those Magic Changes" (Doody, Burger Palace Boys, Pink Ladies); **Scene 3** Pajama party: "Freddy, My Love" (Marty, Jan, Frenchy, Rizzo); **Scene 4** Street Corner: "Greased Lightnin'" (Kenickie & Burger Palace Boys); **Scene 5** Schoolyard; **Scene 6** Park: "Mooning" (Roger & Jan), "Look at Me, I'm Sandra Dee" (Rizzo), "We Go Together" (Pink Ladies & Burger Palace

Boys). **Act II**: **Scene 1** Kids' homes: "Shakin' at the High School Hop" (Entire Company), "It's Rainin' on Prom Night" (Sandy) (Radio Voice: Kathi Moss); **Scene 2** School gym: "Shakin' at the High School Hop" (reprise) (Entire Company), "Born to Hand-Jive" (Johnny Casino & Company); **Scene 3** Front of Burger Palace: "Beauty School Drop-Out" (Teen Angel, Frenchy, Choir); **Scene 4** Drive-In Movie: "Alone at a Drive-In Movie" (Danny & Burger Palace Boys); **Scene 5** Jan's Party: "Rock n' Roll Party Queen" (Doody & Roger), "There Are Worse Things I Could Do" (Rizzo), "Look at Me, I'm Sandra Dee" (reprise) (Sandy); **Scene 6** Burger Palace: "All Choked Up" (Sandy, Danny, Company), Finale: "We Go Together" (reprise) (Entire Company).

Note: The Pink Ladies were: Rizzo, Frenchy, Marty, and Jan; and the Burger Palace Boys were: Kenickie, Doody, Roger, and Sonny.

Cut considerably from its pre–New York days, it opened at the Eden Theatre (formerly the Phoenix) on 2/14/72, to divided reviews. Even though the Eden was an Off Broadway theatre, the cast was paid first-class Broadway rates, and the Tony award committee agreed to look on it as a Broadway production. Kenneth Waissman and Maxine Fox, the producers, were in bad trouble with the show; people weren't flocking in, and the show was in huge debt. Chicago showman Anthony D'Amato bought them out. After 128 performances it moved to a real Broadway theatre. The show received Tony nominations for musical, book, choreography, costumes, and for Barry Bostwick, Timothy Myers, and Adrienne Barbeau. On 12/8/79 it overtook *Fiddler on the Roof* to become the longest-running Broadway show of all time (it was finally beaten by *A Chorus Line*). The show was forced to close prematurely at the 4/13/80 matinee, due to a New York transit strike that had begun on 4/1/80. Even as late as 1/7/05 it was still the 11th-longest-running musical in Broadway history (the revival of *Chicago* overtook it on 1/6/05).

After Broadway. TOUR. Opened on 12/23/72, at the Shubert Theatre, Boston. It closed, and re-opened on 1/22/73, in New Haven. MUSICAL DIRECTOR: Mack Schlefer. **Cast**: DOODY: John Travolta; MARTY: Marilu Henner; RIZZO: Judy Kaye; KENICKIE: Jerry Zaks; DANNY: Jeffrey Conaway, *Barry Bostwick* (from 6/73); JOHNNY: Mike Clifford; VINCE: Walter Charles; SANDY: Pamela Adams, *Candice Earley.*

NEW LONDON THEATRE, London, 6/26/73. 236 PERFORMANCES. **Cast**: SANDY: Stacey Gregg, *Elaine Paige*; DANNY: Richard Gere, *Paul Nicholas*; RIZZO: Jacqui-Ann Carr. **Principal Understudy**: Elaine Paige.

TOUR. Opened on 10/8/73, as a bus-truck tour, and closed on 4/5/74, after 95 cities. On 4/7/74 it was converted to a regular touring company, and opened in Philadelphia. **Cast**: DANNY: John Lansing; SANDY: Marcia McClain; RIZZO: Karren Dille.

TOUR. Opened on 9/1/76, at the Paper Mill Playhouse, NJ; then on to the Shubert, Boston, 10/10/76, and then the rest of the tour. PRESENTED BY Kenneth Waissman & Maxine Fox, in association with Anthony D'Amato; MUSICAL DIRECTOR: Thom Janusz, *Elizabeth Myers*. **Cast**: DOODY: Bill Vitelli; DANNY: Adrian Zmed, *Peter Gallagher, Rex Smith*; JAN: Pippa Pearthree, *Patricia Douglas*; SANDY: Andrea Walters; KENICKIE: Paul Regina Jr.; VINCE: Douglas Barden; MARTY: Char Fontane, *Sandra Zeeman*; RIZZO: Lorelle Brina.

THE MOVIE. 1978. Big success. **Cast**: John Travolta, Olivia Newton-John. Several new songs were added (these would be used in practically all subsequent stage versions, beginning with the 1993 London revival), by writers such as Louis St. Louis, Scott Simon, John Farrar, and Barry Gibb: "Grease," "Hopelessly Devoted to You," "Sandy," "You're the One that I Want." There was a movie sequel, in 1982 — *Grease 2*. DIRECTOR/CHOREOGRAPHER: Patricia Birch. **Cast**: Maxwell Caulfield, Michelle Pfeiffer, Lorna Luft.

TOUR. Opened on 5/1/79, in Boston. **Cast**: DANNY: Rex Smith; SANDY: Mary Murray; RIZZO: Lisa Orberg; KENICKIE: Terry Michos.

DOMINION THEATRE, London, 7/15/93–10/19/96; CAMBRIDGE THEATRE, London, 10/24/96–9/4/99 (where it was replaced by *Great Balls of Fire*). This was the first production to use the songs added for the movie. DIRECTOR: David Gilmore. **Cast**: DANNY: Craig McLachlan, *Shane Richie* (7/23/94–7/12/97), *Luke Goss* (8/97–1/98), *Ian Kelsey* (from 1/26/98), *Darren Day* (from 3/99); SANDY: Debbie Gibson, *Marissa Dunlop, Helen Way, Nikki Worrall* (from 9/98); MARTY: Charlotte Avery, *Kim Leeson* (from 9/98); SONNY: Richard Calkin, *Sebastien Torkia, Sean Oliver*; JOHNNY CASINO: Glenn Carter, *Nigel Francis*; ROGER: Drew Jaymson, *Lee Bright* (from 9/98); TEEN ANGEL: Andrew Kennedy, *Paul*

Gyngell; MISS LYNCH: Myra Sands, *Stephanie Johns*; RIZZO: Sally Ann Triplett, *Emma Dears, Michele Hooper*; GIUSEPPE: Sebastien Torkia; JAN: Liz Ewing, *Leigh-Anne Stone*; VINCE: Gary Martin, *Paul Gyngell*; FRENCHY: Jo Bingham; DOODY: John Combe, *Neil Couperthwaite, Mark Marson*; EUGENE: Aidan Treays, *Ben Stock* (from 9/98); PATTY: Tamzin Outhwaite, *Katherine Fletcher*; KENICKIE: Shane Richie, *Ben Richards, Richard Calkin, Philip Bulcock, Andrew Playfoot, Alex Bourne* (from 9/98); CHA-CHA: Heather Robbins, *Charlotte Gorton*. This production toured the UK from 1997. **Cast**: DANNY: Shane Richie, *Ian Kelsey*.

268. *Grease! (Broadway revival)*

This production had an exclamation point after the title, which the original didn't.

Before Broadway. It began as a tour, on 1/13/94, at the Playhouse, Wilmington, Del. Then it went to Boston, Washington, DC, Seattle, and Costa Mesa, Calif. Then to Broadway. It had the same cast and crew as for the Broadway run.

The Broadway Run. EUGENE O'NEILL THEATRE, 5/11/94–2/23/97; 20 previews from 4/23/94. 1,150 PERFORMANCES, EUGENE O'NEILL THEATRE, 4/8/97–1/25/98. 353 PERFORMANCES. Total of 1,503 PERFORMANCES. The Tommy Tune production, PRESENTED BY Barry & Fran Weissler, Jujamcyn Theatres, in association with PACE Theatrical Group & TV ASAHI; MUSIC/LYRICS/BOOK: Jim Jacobs & Warren Casey; DIRECTOR/CHOREOGRAPHER: Jeff Calhoun; ASSOCIATE CHOREOGRAPHER: Jerry Mitchell; SETS: John Arnone; COSTUMES: Willa Kim; LIGHTING: Howell Binkley; SOUND: Tom Morse; MUSICAL DIRECTOR/VOCAL & DANCE MUSIC ARRANGEMENTS: John McDaniel; ORCHESTRATIONS: Steve Margoshes; NEW CAST RECORDING on RCA Victor; PRESS: Pete Sanders Group; CASTING: Stuart Howard & Amy Schecter; GENERAL MANAGER: Charlotte W. Wilcox; COMPANY MANAGER: Scott A. Moore, *Barbara Darwall* (by 94–95), *Thia Calloway*; PRODUCTION STAGE MANAGER: Craig Jacobs; STAGE MANAGER: Tom Bartlett, *David Hyslop* (by 94–95); ASSISTANT STAGE MANAGER: Scott Mohon. **Cast**: VINCE FONTAINE: Brian Bradley, *Mickey Dolenz* (from 94–95), *Brian Bradley* (from 94–95), *"Cousin" Brucie Morrow* (from 94–95, for 2 weeks), *Joe Piscopo* (from 2/96), *Brian Bradley* (from 96–97), *Nick Santa Maria* (from 96–97), *Brian Bradley, Dave Konig* (from 96–97), *Jeff Conaway* (from 96–97), *Joe Piscopo* (from the re-opening, 4/8/97), *Jeff Conaway* (from 5/6/97, for a few weeks), *Brian Bradley* (from 5/97), *Jeff Conaway* (5/97–8/3/97), *Brian Bradley* (from 8/3/97); MISS LYNCH: Marcia Lewis (5), *Mimi Hines* (from 94–95), *Jo Anne Worley* (from 94–95), *Dody Goodman* (from 95–96), *Marcia Lewis* (from 95–96), *Mimi Hines, Sally Struthers* (from 95–96), *Mimi Hines* (from 96–97 until 4/97), *Marilyn Cooper* (from 4/97); PATTY SIMCOX: Michelle Blakely, *Christine Toy* (from 94–95), *Carrie Ellen Austin* (from 94–95), *Dominique Dawes* (from 12/96, for a month; and from the re-opening, 4/8/97 to 7/97); EUGENE FLORCZYK: Paul Castree; JAN: Heather Stokes, *Marissa Jaret Winokur* (from 95–96); MARTY: Megan Mullally, *Sherie Rene Scott* (from 94–95), *Leah Hocking* (from 94–95), *Deirdre O'Neill* (from 95–96); BETTY RIZZO: Rosie O'Donnell (1), *Maureen McCormick* (from 94–95), *Brooke Shields* (from 94–95), *Joely Fisher* (from 94–95), *Tia Riebling* (from 94–95), *Susan Moniz* (from 95–96), *Jody Watley* (from 95–96), *Debby Boone* (by 96–97), *Sheena Easton* (from 96–97 to 9/23/96), *Tracy Nelson* (from 9/96), *Mackenzie Phillips, Tracy Nelson* (11/26/96–1/97), *Jasmine Guy* (1/97–3/16/97), *Angela Pupello* (from 96–97), *Lucy Lawless* (from 9/2/97; officially from 9/3/97–10/19/97), *Linda Blair* (10/19/97–late 11/97), *Angela Pupello* (from late 11/97); DOODY: Sam Harris (4), *Ray Walker* (from 94–95), *Ty Taylor* (from 95–96), *Ric Ryder* (by 96–97); ROGER: Hunter Foster, *David Josefsberg* (while Mr. Foster was on honeymoon to Jennifer Cody, 8/97–9/97); KENICKIE: Jason Opsahl, *Douglas Crawford* (from 95–96), *Steve Geyer* (by 96–97), *Gregory Cunneen, Steve Geyer* (from 8/19/97); SONNY LATIERRI: Carlos Lopez, *Brad Kane* (from 94–95), *Nick Cavarra* (from 94–95), *Danny Cistone* (from 95–96), *Carlos Lopez* (from 95–96); FRENCHY: Jessica Stone, *Monica Lee Gradischek* (from 94–95), *Beth Lipari* (from 95–96), *Alisa Klein* (by 96–97); SANDY DUMBROWSKI: Susan Wood (3), *Susan Moniz* (from 94–95), *Lacey Hornkohl* (from 95–96), *Kelli Severson* (by 96–97), *Melissa Dye* (from 96–97); DANNY ZUKO: Ricky Paull Goldin (2), *Adrian Zmed*

(from 94–95), *Ricky Paull Goldin* (from 94–95), *Jon Secada* (from 94–95), *Jeff Trachta* (from 95–96), *Joseph Barbara* (from 95–96), *Vincent Tumeo* (from 10/96), *Sean McDermott* (from 96–97), *Joseph Barbara* (during Mr. McDermott's vacation, 12/7/97–12/14/97); "STRAIGHT A"s: Clay Adkins, Patrick Boyd (*Brad Aspel* by 94–95), Denis Jones (*Denny Tarver* by 94–95), *Paul Castree* (added by 94–95); DREAM MOONERS: Patrick Boyd (*Brad Aspel* by 94–95) & Katy Grenfell; HEARTBEATS: Katy Grenfell, Janice Lorraine Holt, Lorna Shane; CHA-CHA DE GREGORIO: Sandra Purpuro, *Jennifer Cody* (from 94–95), *Lesley Jennings* (while Miss Cody was on honeymoon with Hunter Foster, 9/97–9/97); TEEN ANGEL: Billy Porter (6), *Mary Bond Davis* (from 94–95), *Charles Gray* (from 94–95), *Jennifer Holliday* (from 94–95), *Charles Gray* (from 94–95), *Al Jarreau* (from 95–96 to 4/28/96), *Chubby Checker* (from 4/30/96), *Kevin-Anthony* (from 96–97), *Lee Truesdale* (from 96–97), *Darlene Love* (5/6–8/3/97), *Kevin-Anthony* (8/3–9/97), *Billy Porter* (from 9/97), *Andre Garner* (by 11/24/97); ENSEMBLE: Clay Adkins, Melissa Bell (gone by 95–96), Patrick Boyd (*Brad Aspel* by 94–95), H. Hyland Scott II (*Vince D'Elia* from 94), Katy Grenfell, Ned Hannah (gone by 95–96), Janice Lorraine Holt, Denis Jones (*Denny Tarver* by 94–95), Allison Metcalf, Lorna Shane. 94–95 replacements: *Gregory Cunneen, Jeff Edgerton, Connie Ogden*. **Understudies**: Miss Lynch: Patti D'Beck (94–95), *Allison Metcalf* (94–95); Patty: Melissa Bell (94–95); Eugene: Ned Hannah (94), *Jeff Edgerton* (94–95), *Brian-Paul Mendoza* (94–95); Jan: Katy Grenfell (94–95), *Melissa Bell* (94–95); Marty: Allison Metcalf (94–95), *Lorna Shane* (94–95); Rizzo: Sandra Purpuro (94–95), *Lorna Shane* (94–95); Doody/Teen Angel: Clay Adkins (94–95); Roger: Patrick Boyd (94–95), *Paul Castree* (94–95); Kenickie/Danny: H. Hyland Scott II, *Vincent D'Elia* (from 94), Gregory Cunneen (94–95), Hunter Foster (94–95); Vince: H. Hyland Scott II, *Vincent D'Elia* (from 94), Scott Moon (94–95), Jason Opsahl (94–95); Sonny: Denis Jones (94–95), *Brian Loeffler* (94–95), *Brad Aspel* (94–95); Frenchy: Janice Lorraine Holt (94–95), *Carrie Ellen Austin* (94–95); Sandy: Michelle Blakely (94–95), *Jeanna Schweppe* (94–95); Cha-Cha: Lorna Shane (94–95), *Jeanna Schweppe* (94–95). **Swings**: Patti D'Beck, Brian-Paul Mendoza. **The High School Band**: KEYBOARD 1: Steve Marzullo; KEYBOARD 2: Steven Freeman; DRUMS: Norbert Goldberg; TRUMPET: Donald Downs; TROMBONE: Charles Gordon; SAX: Timothy Ries; GUITAR: Alan Cohen; BASS: Vincent Fay; PERCUSSION: Beth Ravin. **Act I: Scene 1** Rydell High: "Alma Mater" (Miss Lynch & Company) [this number was revised as an a cappella version of "We Go Together"], "We Go Together" (Pink Ladies & Burger Palace Boys); **Scene 2** Cafeteria: "Summer Nights" (Sandy, Danny, Pink Ladies, Burger Palace Boys); **Scene 3** School hallway: "Those Magic Changes" (Doody & Company); **Scene 4** Marty's bathroom: "Freddy, My Love" (Marty & Pink Ladies); **Scene 5** Street corner: "Greased Lightin'" (Kenickie & Burger Palace Boys), "Greased Lightnin'" (reprise) (Rizzo & Burger Palace Boys); **Scene 6** Bleachers: "Rydell Fight Song" (Sandy, Patty, Cheerleading Squad); **Scene 7** Schoolyard: "Mooning" (Roger & Jan), "Look at Me, I'm Sandra Dee" (Rizzo); **Scene 8** The lockers: "Since I Don't Have You" (m/l: Joseph Rock, James Beaumont and the Skyliners) (Sandy), "We Go Together" (Company). **Act II: Scene 1** Rydell High boy's gym: "Shakin' at the High School Hop" ("Straight A"s), "It's Raining on Prom Night" (Sandy & "Straight A"s), "Born to Hand-Jive" (Eugene, Miss Lynch, Company); **Scene 2** Outside the Burger Palace: "Beauty School Drop-Out" (Teen Angel, Frenchy, Company); **Scene 3** Twi-Light Drive-In: "Alone at a Drive-In Movie" (Danny); **Scene 4** Rizzo's rec room: "Rock 'n Roll Party Queen" (Doody & Kenickie), "There Are Worse Things I Could Do" (Rizzo), "Look at Me, I'm Sandra Dee" (reprise) (Sandy & Rizzo); **Scene 5** Burger Palace: Finale: "Grease" (Company) [this finale included "All Choked Up"].

Broadway reviews were evenly divided. The show received Tony nominations for revival of a musical, choreography, and for Marcia Lewis. In 6/94 the top ticket price went to $67.50. Joe Piscopo took over as Vince in 2/96, during the bad blizzard. In fact, *Grease!* was the only show running on Broadway that night. Tracy Nelson was due to play Rizzo (again) until 1/12/97, but she cut her Broadway stint short to go on tour. It was announced that *Grease!* would close on 2/23/97, to make way for *Annie*. It had hoped to move to another theatre, as it was still making money. However, on 2/12/97 it was announced that it would keep running at the Eugene O'Neill. *Annie* had now booked into the

Martin Beck, which had become vacant because *Whistle Down the Wind* never made it to Broadway. However, the show did close at the Eugene O'Neill on 2/23/97, and re-opened at the same theatre, on 4/8/97, with a new cast. It was going to close over a dispute with Equity about Lucy Lawless playing Rizzo, and notices were posted on 7/22/97, but taken down on 7/23/97. The New-Zealander had from 9/2/97 been advertised as the upcoming Rizzo, but Equity decided she wasn't a big enough star (Equity's rules were that if an actor was considered an international star, then he/she could appear on Broadway for six months without complications). When the producers threatened to quit, Equity decided Miss Lawless did have the required magnitude. Linda Blair was going to play Rizzo for three months, but she quit early. When it closed it was 2nd-longest-running revival in Broadway history (behind *Oh! Calcutta!*).

After Broadway. TOUR. Opened on 9/19/94, in Syracuse, NY. It had the same basic crew as for the Broadway run, except MUSICAL SUPERVISOR/VOCAL & DANCE MUSIC ARRANGEMENTS: John McDaniel; MUSICAL DIRECTOR: John Samorian. *Cast*: VINCE: Davy Jones, *Mickey Dolenz* [i.e. one member of the Monkees pop group replacing another], *Donnie Most* (from 8/95), *Nick Santa Maria* (from 11/95), *Joe Piscopo* (from 1/96), *Brian Bradley* (from 1/96), *Nick Santa Maria* (from 4/96), *Peter Scolari* (from 11/19/96), *Donnie Most* (11/29–12/1/96), *Peter Scolari* (12/96–1/97), *Brian Bradley* (from 1/97); MISS LYNCH: Sally Struthers, *Dody Goodman* (from 6/95), *Mimi Hines* (from 9/24/95), *Sally Struthers* (from 8/20/96), *Mimi Hines*; SONNY: Danny Cistone, *Tom Richter* (from 8/95), *Stephen Gnojewski*; KENICKIE: Douglas Crawford, *Steve Geyer* (from 10/95), *Douglas Crawford* (from 10/8/95), *Steve Geyer, Christopher Carothers* (from 1/14/97), *Douglas Crawford* (from 4/9/97); FRENCHY: Beth Lipari, *Jennifer Naimo* (from 1/96), *Megan Lawrence* (from 8/6/96), *Beth Lipari* (from 10/8/96), *Alisa Klein*; DOODY: Scott Beck, *Ric Ryder* (from 7/95), *Roy Chicas* (from 4/96); RIZZO: Angela Pupello, *Wendy Springer* (from 8/95), *Angela Pupello* (from 10/95), *Debbie Gibson* (from 11/95), *Mackenzie Phillips* (from 3/96), *Sheena Easton* (from 8/20/96), *Mackenzie Phillips, Jasmine Guy* (from 11/19/96), *Tracy Nelson* (11/29–12/1/96, *Jasmine Guy* (12/96–1/97), *Tracy Nelson* (from 1/6/97), *Sheena Easton* (for two2 weeks in Los Angeles, in 4/97), *Mackenzie Phillips* (for final week in L.A., until 4/27/97); MARTY: Deirdre O'Neill, *Amanda Watkins* (from 8/95), *Cathy Trien*; ROGER: Nick Cavarra, *Erick Buckley* (from 5/95), *David Josefsberg*; JAN: Robin Irwin, *Marissa Jaret Winokur* (from 8/95), *Farah Alvin*; DANNY: Rex Smith, *Jon Secada* (from 6/95), *Adrian Zmed* (from 7/95), *Joseph Barbara* (from 12/3/95), *Adrian Zmed* (from 9/20/96); EUGENE: Christopher Youngsman, *Christopher Carothers* (from 12/95), *Ashton Byrum* (from 2/96), *Christopher Youngsman*; PATTY: Melissa Papp, *Lesley Jennings* (from 9/95), *Leanna Polk* (from 2/96), *Stephanie Seeley* (from 9/5/96); SANDY: Trisha M. Gorman, *Sutton Foster* (from 11/95), *Christiane Noll* (by 11/19/96), *Kelli Severson* (from 1/7/97), *Lacey Hornkohl* (from 3/25/97), *Kelli Severson* (from 4/29/97); CHA-CHA: Jennifer Cody, *Michelle Bombacie* (from 3/95), *Lori Lynch* (from 5/96); TEEN ANGEL: Kevin-Anthony, *Lee Truesdale* (from 9/5/96), *Kevin-Anthony* (from 10/15/96), *Lee Truesdale*.

Over Thanksgiving Weekend (11/29/96–12/1/96) this National Touring Company played 5 performances at City Center while the Broadway company continued at the Eugene O'Neill, thus there were two productions of *Grease!* running in New York City at the same time.

MEXICO CITY, 1995. *Vaselina!* was revived. *Cast*: SANDY: Iran Castillo; DANNY: Alejandro Ibarra.

ITALY. Although there had been a very successful English-language version shown in Italy, the first Italian version of the show (translated by Silvio Testi & Michele Renzullo) opened in Milan, 3/97 (it ran 25 weeks). It then ran in Rome, 4/21/98–7/12/98 (and closed after several extensions). DIRECTOR: Saverio Marconi; CHOREOGRAPHER: Franco Miseria; CAST RECORDING (one of Italy's first) was released on 12/97, by EMI. The show broke box office records. *Cast*: SANDY: Lorella Cuccarini, *Eleanora Russo* (stood in while Miss Cuccarini went to Hollywood to discuss being in the movie *Star Trek: Insurrection*); DANNY: Giampiero Ingrassia; KENICKIE: Michele Carfora; RIZZO: Renata Fusco; TEEN ANGEL: Mal; VINCE: Marco Predolin. **Understudy**: Rizzo: Eleanora Russo. It re-opened in Rome, on 3/10/99, with the same cast as before, except VINCE: Mauro Marino.

AUSTRALIAN TOUR. This was a concert version called *Grease: The Arena Spectacular*. Melbourne, 4/24/98 (it had technical problems opening night); Sydney 5/3/98; Brisbane 5/12/98; Adelaide 5/18/98. PRESENTED BY John Frost; DIRECTOR: David Gilmore. *Cast*: DANNY: Craig McLachlan; RIZZO: Danni Minogue, *Kelly Abbey* (went on when Miss Minogue became ill); SANDY: Jane Scali; TEEN ANGEL: Anthony Warlow; JOHNNY CASINO: Glenn Shorrock; MISS LYNCH: Totti Goldsmith [Olivia Newton-John's niece in real life]. The tour had advance box office receipts so great that a second tour was planned even before the first one had opened. The new tour: Melbourne 6/1/98–6/2/98; Sydney 6/9/98–6/10/98; Brisbane 6/16/98–6/17/98. Gina G was due to replace Danni Minogue for this second tour, but after a week of rehearsals she quit on 8/18/98, so it was decided Kelly Abbey would play Rizzo on the first two legs of the tour (Melbourne & Sydney), while Danni Minogue would return for the last leg, in Brisbane.

LOPE DE VEGA THEATRE, Madrid, 3/17/99. Previews 2/23/99–3/16/99. This show replaced *El Hombre de la Mancha*. The Spanish *Grease* had begun with a concept album called "Grease en Espanol," which sold very well. SPANISH LYRICS: Nacho Artime. The show had over 70 songs, and ran 2 hours 40 minutes. The cast comprised 40 hitherto unknown actors. DIRECTOR: Luis Ramirez; CHOREOGRAPHER: Ramon Oller; MUSICAL DIRECTOR: Alberto Quintero. *Cast*: DANNY: J.G. Gomez; SANDY: Geraldine Larrosa; VINCE/TEEN ANGEL: Carlos Marin; RIZZO: Marta Ribera. After Madrid it toured several Latin American countries. Note: In Mexico the show is known as *Vaselina* (later *Vaselina!*).

PALAIS DES SPORTS, Paris. Christmas, 1999. DIRECTOR: David Gilmore. *Cast*: SANDY: Jodi Carmeli; DANNY: Greg Kohout.

BRITISH TOURING REVIVAL. 2001. Closed mid–Aug. 2002, after a year. As part of the tour it ran at the DOMINION THEATRE, London for two weeks in 10/01; then the CAMBRIDGE THEATRE, London. *Cast*: Craig Urbani, Helen Flaherty.

VICTORIA PALACE THEATRE, London. Opened 10/2/02. Previews from 9/26/02. This show replaced *Kiss Me, Kate*. It was to run until 3/1/03, but extended its closing date. *Cast*: DANNY: Greg Kohout, *Ben Richards* (from 1/8/03), *Craig Urbani* (stood in from 5/12/03 for two weeks); SANDY: Caroline Sheen; TEEN ANGEL: Lee Latchford Evans.

PAPER MILL PLAYHOUSE, New Jersey, 6/6/03–7/27/03. Rehearsals from 5/15/03. Previews from 6/4/03. DIRECTOR: Mark S. Hoebee; CHOREOGRAPHER: Jeffrey Amsden; MUSICAL DIRECTOR: Vicki Carter. *Cast*: DANNY: Andy Karl; SANDY: Jennifer Hope Wills; RIZZO: Leslie Kritzer.

269. *Great to Be Alive!*

Rich divorcee Mrs. Leslie Butterfield buys an old Pennsylvania mansion from shy botanist Woodrow, a descendant of the original owners. The ghosts of all the former residents band together to prevent her from acquiring the mansion. The only people (aside from the audience) who can see the ghosts on stage are virgins, and there aren't many of those. Those that there are are guilty of murdering a priest. Kitty is the head ghost; Carol (Leslie's niece, to whom Leslie is going to give the house) and Vince are the young love interest. The ghosts win in the end.

The Broadway Run. WINTER GARDEN THEATRE, 3/23/50–5/6/50. 52 PERFORMANCES. PRESENTED BY Vinton Freedley, in association with Anderson Lawler & Russell Markert; MUSIC: Abraham Ellstein & Robert Russell Bennett; LYRICS: Walter Bullock; BOOK: Walter Bullock & Sylvia Regan; DIRECTOR: Mary Hunter; CHOREOGRAPHER: Helen Tamiris; SETS/COSTUMES/LIGHTING: Stewart Chaney; MUSICAL DIRECTOR: Max Meth; ORCHESTRATIONS: Robert Russell Bennett & Donald J. Walker; SPECIAL MUSICAL ARRANGEMENTS: Genevieve Pitot; BALLET MUSIC: Abraham Ellstein; VOCAL ARRANGEMENTS: Crane Calder; PRESS: Karl N. Bernstein & Harvey Sabinson; GENERAL MANAGER: Robert Milford; PRODUCTION STAGE MANAGER: B.D. Kranz; STAGE MANAGER: Larry Baker; ASSISTANT STAGE MANAGER: Ted Cappy. *Cast*: BONNIE: Bambi Linn; PRUDENCE: Betty Low; ALBERT: Rod Alexander; JAKE: J.C. McCord; MAYBELLE: Aleen Buchanan; KITTY: Valerie Bettis; CRUMLEIGH: Jay Marshall; BUTCH: Earl Oxford; LESLIE BUTTERFIELD: Vivienne Segal; CAROL: Martha Wright; VINCE: Mark Dawson; WOODROW TWIGG: Stuart Erwin; MIMSEY: Marjorie Peterson; SANDRA: Virginia

Curtis; FREDDIE: Russell Nype; BLODGETT: Lulu Bates; JONATHAN: David Nillo; THE MINISTER: Ken Carroll; O'BRIEN: Don Kennedy; RAFFERTY: Paul Reed; DANCERS: Chuck Brunner, Ted Cappy, Eleanor Fairchild, Roscoe French, Eleanore Gregory, Barbara Heath, Ann Hutchinson, Norma Kaiser, David Nillo, Harry Rogers, Janice Rule, Swen Swenson; SINGERS: Leigh Allen, Jeanne Bal, Fred Bryan, Ken Carroll, Virginia Curtis, Ed Gombos, John Juliano, Ruth McVayne, Joyce Mitchell, Russell Nype, Robert Wallace, Julia Williams. *Act I*: *Scene 1* The reception hall of an old Pennsylvania mansion; before dawn; *Scene 2* Same; a few weeks later; *Scene 3* Exterior of the mansion; *Scene 4* The reception hall; midnight; *Scene 5* Exterior of the mansion; *Scene 6* The reception hall; a moment later. *Act II*: *Scene 1* The garden; afternoon of the same day; *Scene 2* Exterior of the mansion; *Scene 3* The reception hall; later that day; *Scene 4* Exterior of the mansion; *Scene 5* A corner of the library; *Scene 6* Reception hall; midnight; *Scene 7* Exterior of the mansion; *Scene 8* The reception hall; the following morning. *Act I*: "When the Sheets Come Back from the Laundry" (Kitty, Bonnie, Prudence, Maybelle, Albert, Jake, Crumleigh, Dancers), "It's a Long Time Till Tomorrow" (Carol & Vince), "Headin' for a Weddin'" (arr: Genevieve Pitot) (Woodrow, Kitty, Bonnie, Prudence, Maybelle, Albert, Jake, Crumleigh), "Redecorate" (Butch), "What a Day!" (Carol, Vince, Blodgett, Sandra, Freddie, Guests), "Call it Love" (Carol & Vince), "There's Nothing Like It" (Blodgett), "Dreams Ago" (arr: Genevieve Pitot) (Carol & Vince): Waltz (Bonnie & Albert), The Story of Kitty (Kitty, Jonathan, Dancers); "From This Day On" (Entire Company). *Act II*: "Who Done It?" ("The Riddle") (arr: Genevieve Pitot) (Sandra, Freddie, O'Brien, Rafferty, Blodgett, Guests), "Blue Day" (Carol), "That's a Man Every Time" (Leslie, Mimsey, Sandra, Bridesmaids), "You Appeal to Me" (Leslie & Woodrow), "Who Done It?" (reprise) (Blodgett), "Let's Have a Party" (Kitty, Prudence, Jake, Dancers), "Call it Love" (reprise) (carol & Vince), "Thank You, Mrs. Butterfield" (Wedding Guests), Finale (Entire Company).

Reviews were divided and mixed. Rod Alexander married Bambi Lynn on 4/2/50, not long after the opening. They went on to create a nightclub act at the Plaza Hotel in New York City. They split up in 1959.

270. *Greenwillow*

A musical fantasy. A lonely mixed-up boy, Gideon, lives in the mythical and old-fashioned village of Greenwillow, on the Meander River. He wants to stay where he is and marry Dorrie, his summertime love, but is afraid that the curse of his family's "call to wander solitary" will someday make him run off to sail distant seas. Gramma spends most of the show trying to recover a cow from the man she almost married once. The four seasons are covered.

Before Broadway. It was turned down by Lerner & Loewe. It was the first Broadway musical for Tony Perkins and for George Roy Hill. Because big names were involved, it took only three weeks to raise the necessary money. Helon Blount did backers' auditions as Dorrie. As rehearsals were about to begin, George Roy Hill quit as director. He was persuaded to come back, although he and Frank Loesser would have at least one fist fight before the Broadway opening. During Philadelphia tryouts leading lady Zeme North was replaced with Ellen McCown, a cow pancaked on stage, and the numbers "My Beauty," "Heart of Stone," "Bless This Day," "Yes," and "Riddleweed" were cut.

The Broadway Run. ALVIN THEATRE, 3/8/60–5/28/60. 97 PERFORMANCES. PRESENTED BY Robert A. Willey, in association with Frank Productions (Frank Loesser); MUSIC/LYRICS: Frank Loesser; BOOK: Lesser Samuels & Frank Loesser; BASED ON the 1956 novel of the same name, by B.J. Chute [Beatrice Joy Chute]; DIRECTOR: George Roy Hill; CHOREOGRAPHER: Joe Layton; SETS: Peter Larkin; COSTUMES: Alvin Colt; LIGHTING: Feder; SOUND: C. Robert Fine; MUSICAL DIRECTOR: Abba Bogin; ORCHESTRATIONS: Don Walker; CAST RECORDING on RCA; PRESS: Philip Bloom, David Lipsky, Fred Weterick; GENERAL MANAGER: Joseph Harris; PRODUCTION STAGE MANAGER: Terence Little; STAGE MANAGER: Arthur Rubin; ASSISTANT STAGE MANAGER: Ralph Linn.

Cast: JABEZ BRIGGS: John Megna; CLARA CLEGG: Dortha Duckworth (12); MRS. HASTY: Maggie Task; MR. PREEBS: Jordon Howard; MRS. LUNNY: Marie Foster; REVEREND LAPP: William Chapman (5); GRAMMA BRIGGS: Pert Kelton (3); MAIDY: Elaine Swann (9); EMMA: Saralou Cooper (11); GIDEON BRIGGS: Anthony Perkins (1); DORRIE WHITBRED: Ellen McCown (4); AMOS BRIGGS: Bruce MacKay (7); MICAH BRIGGS: Ian Tucker; MARTHA BRIGGS: Lynn Brinker (10); SHEBY BRIGGS: Brenda Harris; THOMAS CLEGG: Lee Cass; REVEREND BIRDSONG: Cecil Kellaway (2); YOUNG CHURCHGOER: Thomas Norden; WILL: David Gold; NELL: Margery Gray; ANDREW: Grover Dale (8); SINGERS: Kenny Adams, Betsy Bridge, Marie Foster, Rico Froehlich, Russell Goodwin, Jordon Howard, Marian Mercer, Carl Nicholas, Virginia Oswald, Bob Roman, Sheila Swenson, Maggie Task, Karen Thorsell; DANCERS: Jere Admire, Don Atkinson, Estelle Aza, Joan Coddington, Ethelyne Dunfee, Richard Englund, David Gold, Margery Gray, Mickey Gunnersen, Patsi King, Jack Leigh, Nancy Van Rijn, Jimmy White. *Standby*: Birdson: Clarence Nordstrom. *Understudies*: Gideon: Grover Dale; Lapp: Rico Froehlich; Dorrie: Karen Thorsell; Gramma/Clara: Marie Foster; Thomas: Jordon Howard; Amos: Russell Goodwin; Maidy/Emma: Marian Mercer; Martha: Maggie Task; Jabez: Thomas Norden; Sheby: Ave Maria Megna; Micah: Edmund Gaines; Mrs. Hasty: Virginia Oswald; Preebs: Bob Roman; Andrew: Ralph Linn; Nell: Patsi King; Will: Jack Leigh. *Act I*: *Scene 1* The square; *Scene 2* Briggs farm; *Scene 3* The mill; *Scene 4* The willow; *Scene 5* The square; *Scene 6* Clegg's farm; *Scene 7* The mill; *Scene 8* Briggs farm; *Scene 9* The church; *Scene 10* The square. *Act II*: *Scene 1* The square; *Scene 2* Briggs farm; *Scene 3* Clegg's house; *Scene 4* The square; *Scene 5* Briggs farm. *Act I*: "A Day Borrowed from Heaven" (Villagers), "A Day Borrowed from Heaven" (reprise) (Gideon), "Dorrie's Wish" (dance) (Dorrie), "The Music of Home" (Amos, Gideon, Villagers), "Gideon Briggs, I Love You" (Gideon & Dorrie), "The Autumn Courting" (dance) (All the Villagers), "The Call to Wander" (Amos), "Summertime Love" (Gideon & Villagers), "Walking Away Whistling" (Dorrie), "The Sermon" (Reverends Lapp & Birdsong), "Could've Been a Ring" (Clegg & Gramma), "Gideon Briggs, I Love You" (reprise) (Dorrie), "Halloweve" (dance) (Young Villagers), "Never Will I Marry" (Gideon), "Greenwillow Christmas" (a carol) (Martha & Villagers). *Act II*: "The Music of Home" (reprise) (Villagers), "Faraway Boy" (Dorrie), "Clang Dang the Bell" (Gideon, Gramma, Martha, Micah, Sheby, Jabez), "What a Blessing (to Know There's a Devil)" (Rev. Birdsong), "He Died Good" (Villagers), "The Spring Courting" (Andrew, Dorrie, Young Villagers), "Summertime Love" (reprise) (Gideon), "What a Blessing" (reprise) (Rev. Birdsong), "The Call" (Gideon), "The Music of Home" (reprise) (All of Greenwillow).

Broadway reviews were not good, but Tony Perkins got raves. It was a rare Frank Loesser flop. The book let it down. There were several Tony nominations—choreography, sets (musical), costumes, stage technician (James Orr), musical direction, and Pert Kelton. It toured with Susan Johnson as Dorrie (replaced on tour by *Helen Blount*), after which Frank Loesser, and then his widow, Jo Sullivan, kept the show out of general circulation for years.

After Broadway. EQUITY LIBRARY THEATRE, NYC, 12/3/70–12/20/70. 22 PERFORMANCES. DIRECTOR: Clinton Atkinson; CHOREOGRAPHER: Deborah Jowitt; SETS: William Puzo; MUSICAL DIRECTOR: Norman Dean; PIANIST: John Williams. *Cast*: GIDEON: John Fennesy; GRAMMA: Mary Jo Catlett; DORRIE: Laurie Hutchinson; BIRDSONG: Bernard Frawley.

NOVA STUDIOS, NYC, 6/3/96. 1 PERFORMANCE. The book was revised by Walter Willison & Douglas Holmes, augmenting the original but using material never used in the original. Lesser Samuels was no longer credited as librettist. PRESENTED BY Jo Sullivan Loesser (Frank Loesser's widow); DIRECTOR: Walter Willison; MUSICAL DIRECTOR: Dennis Buck. *Cast*: GRANNY: Marcia Lewis; BIRDSONG/THOMAS: Jack Eddleman; GIDEON: Andrew Driscoll; DORRIE: Emily Loesser; LAPP: Michael X. Martin; MRS. HASTY/SHADRACH: Joan Barber; LUNNY/AMOS: George Lee Andrews; MARTHA: Joy Hermalyn; CLARA: Karen Murphy. It was re-worked again, and in 2/97 had a workshop done by FLORIDA STATE UNIVERSITY'S SCHOOL OF THEATRE, Tallahassee. The reading cast of 14 included: GRANNY: Marcia Lewis; DORRIE: Emily Loesser; GIDEON: Andy Driscoll. More changes were made after the workshop.

GOLDEN APPLE DINNER THEATRE, Sarasota, Fla, 6/12/97–7/27/97.

Previews from 6/10/97. This was the new, revised, Walter Willison-directed version, now called *Frank Loesser's Greenwillow: The Musical Folktale*. Three Frank Loesser songs were added—"My Beauty" [which the boy sings to his cow; cut before the original *Greenwillow* got to Broadway]; "Truly Loved" [from *Pleasures and Palaces*, and which Martha now sings]; and "House and Garden" [a cut number from the original *The Most Happy Fella*]. CHOREOGRAPHER: Brad Wages; MUSICAL DIRECTOR: Michael Sebastian; PRODUCTION SUPERVISOR: Jo Sullivan. *Cast*: GRANNY: Helen Blount; GIDEON: Andy Driscoll; AMOS: Walter Willison; AGGIE LIKEWISE: Jacquiline Rohrbacker; DORRIE: Maxine Wood; LAPP: Jeffrey Atherton; LITTLE FOX JONES: Douglas Holmes; EMMA: Loraine Sheeler; THOMAS CLEGG: James Pritchett; JACK FINK: Brad Wages. There were Broadway plans for 1998, but they never materialized.

ELLEN ECCLES THEATRE, Logan, Utah, 7/19/97. The Utah Festival Opera Company produced the revised version, on a bigger scale than the Sarasota production, with which it ran partially concurrently. DIRECTOR: Vincent Liotta. *Cast*: GIDEON: Chad McAlester; DORRIE: Carol Chickering; BIRDSONG: Michael Ballam. It was repeated, same venue, the following year.

THEATRE AT ST. PETER'S, NYC, 10/22/04–10/24/04. PRESENTED BY the York Theatre Company, as part of their *Musicals in Mufti* series of staged concert readings. DIRECTOR: Michael Montel; MUSICAL DIRECTOR: Mark Hartman. *Cast*: GIDEON: Joe Machota; DORRIE: Carey Brown; LAPP: David Staller; BIRDSONG: Simon Jones; JABEZ: Jamie Kelton; MARTHA: Lois Hart; CLEGG: Nick Wyman; GRAMMA: Annie Golden.

271. *Grind*

Set in and around Harry Earle's Burlesque Theatre, Chicago, in 1933, during the World's Fair. It is about the lives of black and white strippers, and their associates. Gus is the star comic, and is going blind. He has problems keeping his stooges, and hires Doyle, a derelict and former IRA man haunted by dreams of his wife and child being blown up by a train bomb that he devised. Satin (born Letitia) is the star black stripper in this theatre where black and white acts are strictly segregated. Gus commits suicide.

Before Broadway. Back in 1975 a couple of producers from Universal Studios approached writer Fay Kanin, to see if she would write a screenplay about a bi-racial burlesque house in 1930s Chicago. She wrote *This Must Be the Place*, but the movie never happened. Toward the end of 1982 she told Hal Prince she thought it might make a good Broadway musical. Mr. Prince went for it. Miss Kanin spent the next two years re-writing. Originally it was called *A Century of Progress*, and Kevin Kline and Debbie Allen were announced for the roles of Doyle and Satin. The production was capitalized at $4.75 million. There was a rumor that Bob Fosse had a hand in the choreography, but Hal Prince denied that (Ken Mandelbaum comes flat out and says Fosse staged the number "A New Man"). It tried out to bad reviews in Baltimore in 3/85, during which time the Dramatists Guild suspended the creators of the show (Ellen Fitzhugh, Larry Grossman, Fay Kanin and Hal Prince) for agreeing to a contract that fell below Guild standards.

The Broadway Run. MARK HELLINGER THEATRE, 4/16/85–6/22/85. 25 previews. 79 PERFORMANCES. PRESENTED BY Kenneth D. Greenblatt, John J. Pomerantz, Mary Lea Johnson, Martin Richards, James M. Nederlander, Harold Prince, and Michael Frazier, in association with Susan Madden Samson & Jonathan Farkas; MUSIC: Larry Grossman; LYRICS: Ellen Fitzhugh; BOOK: Fay Kanin; FROM an idea by Alan Handley & Bob Wynn; DIRECTOR: Harold Prince; CHOREOGRAPHER: Lester Wilson; SETS: Clarke Dunham; COSTUMES: Florence Klotz; LIGHTING: Ken Billington; SOUND: Otts Munderloh; MUSICAL DIRECTOR: Paul Gemignani; ORCHESTRATIONS: Bill Byers; ADDITIONAL ORCHESTRATIONS: Jim Tyler & Harold Wheeler; DANCE MUSIC ARRANGEMENTS/ASSISTANT CONDUCTOR: Tom Fay; PRESS: Mary Bryant; EXECUTIVE PRODUCERS: Ruth Mitchell & Sam Crothers; GENERAL MANAGEMENT: Theatre Now; COMPANY MANAGER: Sally Campbell; PRODUCTION STAGE MANAGER: Beverley Randolph; STAGE MANAGER:

Richard Evans; ASSISTANT STAGE MANAGER: William Kirk. *Cast*: LEROY: Ben Vereen (1) ☆, *Obba Babatunde*; HARRY EARLE: Lee Wallace (6); GUS: Stubby Kaye (2) ☆; SOLLY: Joey Faye (5); VERNELLE: Marion Ramsey (11); EARLE'S (FOUR) PEARLS: RUBY: Hope Clarke (14); FLETA: Valarie Pettiford (15); KITTY: Candy Brown (13); LINETTE: Wynonna Smith (12); MAYBELLE: Carol Woods (8); MECHANICAL MAN: Jackie Jay Patterson; KNOCKABOUTS: Leonard John Crofoot, Ray Roderick, Kelly Walters, Steve Owsley, Malcolm Perry; ROMAINE: Sharon Murray (7); SATIN: Leilani Jones (3) ☆; LOUIS, THE STAGE MANAGER: Brian McKay; MIKE, THE DOORMAN: Oscar Stokes; STOOGE: Leonard John Crofoot; DOYLE: Timothy Nolen (4) ☆; GROVER: Donald Acree (10); MRS. FAYE: Ruth Brisbane (9); TOUGHS: Leonard John Crofoot, Ray Roderick, Kelly Walters, Steve Owsley, Malcolm Perry. *Understudies*: Satin: Candy Brown; Leroy: Jackie Jay Patterson; Ruby/Kitty/Vernelle/Fleta/Linette: Gayle Samuels; Doyle/Mike: Brian McKay; Gus/Harry/Solly: Oscar Stokes; Romaine: Dana Lorge; Maybelle: Ruth Brisbane; Mrs. Faye: Carol Woods; Grover: Raymond Hickman; Mechanical Man: Dwight Baxter; Louis: David Reitman. *Swing*: David Reitman. *Act I*: *Scene 1* Backstage: Prologue, "This Must Be the Place" (Company); *Scene 2* Onstage: "Cadava" (Solly, Gus, Romaine); *Scene 3* In the wings; *Scene 4* Onstage: "A Sweet Thing Like Me" (Satin & Earle's Pearls); *Scene 5* The alley next to the theatre: "I Get Myself Out" (Gus); *Scene 6* Girls' dressing room; backstage: "My Daddy Always Taught Me to Share" (Leroy); *Scene 7* The alley: "All Things to One Man" (Satin); *Scene 8* Onstage: "The Line" (Leroy & Earle's Pearls); *Scene 9* The alley: "Katie, My Love" (Doyle); *Scene 10* Backstage: "The Grind" (Gus & Company), "Yes, Ma'am" (Doyle); *Scene 11* Mrs. Fay's kitchen: "Why, Mama, Why?" (Satin & Leroy); *Scene 12* On the street: "This Crazy Place" (Leroy & Company). *Act II*: *Scene 1* Backstage: "From the Ankles Down" (Leroy & Earle's Pearls), "Who is He?" (Satin), "Never Put it in Writing" (Gus), "I Talk, You Talk" (Doyle); *Scene 2* Onstage; *Scene 3* Stage right wing; *Scene 4* Onstage: "Timing" (Romaine & Solly); *Scene 5* Backstage: "These Eyes of Mine" (Maybelle & Company) [the most famous number]; *Scene 6* Backstage: "A New Man" (dance mus arr: Gordon Lowry Harrell) (Leroy); *Scene 7* The alley; *Scene 8* Satin's room: "Down" (Doyle); *Scene 9* Onstage: "A Century of Progress" (Leroy, Satin, Earle's Pearls); *Scene 10* Backstage; *Scene 11* Onstage: Finale (Company).

Broadway reviews were mostly bad; the show lost its huge investment. It won Tonys for costumes, and for Leilani Jones, and was also nominated for musical, score, book, direction of a musical, and sets.

272. *La Grosse Valise*

Basically a follow up to *La Plume de Ma Tante*. Set in customs at Orly Airport, Paris. A clown tries to get his enormous valise through, and when it's opened it spills out a show full of zany sketches and song and dance numbers.

Before Broadway. It played in Paris.

The Broadway Run. FIFTY-FOURTH STREET THEATRE, 12/14/65–12/18/65. 12 previews from 12/2/65. 7 PERFORMANCES. PRESENTED BY Joseph Kipness & Arthur Lesser; MUSIC: Gerard Calvi; LYRICS: Harold Rome; BOOK: Robert Dhery; DEVISED BY: Robert Dhery; DIRECTOR: Robert Dhery; CHOREOGRAPHER: Colette Brosset; ASSOCIATE CHOREOGRAPHER: Tom Panko; SETS/COSTUMES: Jacques Dupont; SETS/COSTUMES SUPERVISED BY: Frederick Fox; LIGHTING: John Gleason; MUSICAL DIRECTOR: Lehman Engel; ASSISTANT MUSICAL DIRECTOR: Karen L. Gustafson; ORCHESTRATIONS: Gerard Calvi; CAST RECORDING on Mercury; PRESS: Arthur Cantor & Arthur Solomon; GENERAL MANAGER: Philip Adler; COMPANY MANAGER: S.M. Handelsman; PRODUCTION STAGE MANAGER: Bob Burland; STAGE MANAGER: Pierre Billon. *Cast*: TRAVELER TO BORDEAUX: Jacques Ebner; ANTOINE, A CUSTOMS INSPECTOR: Michel Modo; SPANISH TOURISTS: Marcelo Gamboa & Diane Coupe; PEPITO, A CUSTOMS INSPECTOR: Guy Grosso; JEAN-LOUP ROUSSEL, ASSISTANT CHIEF OF CUSTOMS: Ronald Fraser; LA FOUILLETTE, AN AIRPORT POLICE OFFICER: Tony Doonan; LA NANA: France Arnell; PHOTOGRAPHERS: Max Vialle & Bernard Gauthron; NICOLAS: Brigitte Valadin; SVATSOU, THE CLOWN (M. CHERI): Victor Spinetti; VLAMINSKY: Guy Bertil; RAOUL: Barry L. Martin; CHIEF OF CUSTOMS: John

Maxim; THE LITTLE PORTER: Bert Michaels; DE WALLEYNE: Sybil Bartrop; BABY'S MAID: Maureen Byrnes; CHEF D'ETAT, A DIPLOMATIC OFFICIAL: Max Vialle; OLD LADY: Rita Charisse; ANDRE: Jean-Michel Mole; BABY: Joyce Jillson; MIREILLE: Mireille Chazal; PEDRALINI, HEAD SCOUT: John Maxim; 1ST SCOUT: George Tregre; BALD MAN: Bernard Gauthron; BERTHOZEAU: Tony Doonan; OTHERS: Diana Baffa, Maureen Byrnes, Diane Coupe, Ronn Forella, Marcelo Gamboa, Pat Gosling, Carolyn Kirsch, Alex MacKay, Bert Michaels, Donna Sanders, George Tregre, Mary Zahn. *Act I*: "La Grosse Valise" (Roussel, Cheri, Nicolas, Company), "A Big One" (Roussel, Antoine, Pepito, Cheri, Nicolas, Company), "C'est Defendu" (Roussel, La Nana, Pepito, Antoine), "Hamburg Waltz" (Principals, Dancing Girls & Boys), "Happy Song" (Roussel, Pepito, Antoine, Chief of Customs), "For You" (Baby), "Sandwich for Two" (Cheri & Nicolas), "La Java" (La Nana, Chief of Customs, Baby, Dancing Girls & Boys), "Xanadu" (La Nana, Cheri, Roussel). *Act II*: "Slippy Sloppy Shoes" (Cheri, Roussel, Dancing Girls & Boys), "Spanish Dance" (Roussel & Mireille), "For You" (reprise) (Roussel & Baby), "Delilah Done Me Wrong" (Cheri, la Nana, Slaves), "Hawaii" (La Nana, Baby, Dancing Girls).

273. *Guys and Dolls*

A musical fable of Broadway, based on Damon Runyon's characters (the musical added some new ones). Nathan, a New York gambler, has been engaged to Adelaide, star attraction at the Hot Box Night Club, for 14 years, but every time they plan to get married, Nathan has to go off to another floating crap game, which Lieutenant Brannigan keeps trying to break up. Things don't look good for wedding bells. Adelaide, "well-known fiancee," over the years has developed a psychosomatic perpetual cold. Nathan bets fellow gambler Sky that he can't make the next girl they see fall in love with him. Sky accepts, and claims he can take any girl to Cuba, and Nathan bets him that he can't take Sarah Brown, local Salvation Army girl, one of the Save-a-Soul Mission of Times Square Salvation Army band. He does.

Before Broadway. Cy Feuer and Ernest H. Martin, the producers, originally wanted a serious musical love story, about a former show-girl who converts to the Salvation Army and preaches to the low-lifes in Times Square. In the original Damon Runyon short story *The Idyll of Miss Sarah Brown*, she falls in love with a gambler, and tries to reform him. Frank Loesser was hired to write the score, and Jo Swerling the book. Mr. Swerling kept to his mandate, but Mr. Loesser's score became more and more light-hearted, a la Runyon. Something had to give, and it was Jo Swerling's book. However, his contract stipulated that he receive primary librettist credit, come what may. After a dozen more librettists (including Peter Lyon) were unsuccessful in coming up with a working book, Abe Burrows came through with a totally new comedy libretto around Frank Loesser's songs, and Mr. Loesser wrote some new songs to go around what Mr. Burrows was writing. Jo Swerling's son claims that Mr. Burrows only polished his father's libretto. The fact that Abe Burrows had never worked on a theatrical hit before caused some consternation among investors — Billy Rose withdrew his money for this reason. A Loesser song that didn't make it into this show was "Standing on the Corner." However, six years later he used it for The Most Happy Fella. The show tried out in two Philadelphia theatres, for three weeks each, to rave reviews and sell-out audiences. This was Isabel Bigley's Broadway debut, and a first musical for Robert Alda (Alan Alda's father) and Vivian Blaine. Sam Levene couldn't sing (he was tone-deaf), so "Travelin' Light" (Sky & Nathan) was cut during tryouts. Other songs cut were "It Feels Like Forever" and "Shango." Sam Levene wound up with only one song, "Sue Me," with Vivian Blaine.

The Broadway Run. FORTY-SIXTH STREET THEATRE, 11/24/50–11/28/53. 1,200 PERFORMANCES. PRESENTED BY Cy Feuer & Ernest H. Martin; MUSIC/LYRICS: Frank Loesser; BOOK: Jo Swerling & Abe Burrows; BASED ON Damon Runyon's 1931 short story *The Idyll of Miss Sarah Brown*, and on other Runyon characters; DIRECTOR: George S. Kaufman; CHOREOGRAPHER: Michael Kidd; ASSISTANT CHOREOGRAPHERS: Onna White & Deedee Wood; SETS/LIGHTING: Jo Mielziner; COSTUMES: Alvin Colt; MUSICAL DIRECTOR: Irving Actman; ORCHESTRATIONS: George Bassman & Ted Royal; VOCAL DIRECTOR & VOCAL ARRANGEMENTS: Herbert Greene; PRESS: Karl Bernstein & Harvey B. Sabinson, *Ted Goldsmith*; CASTING: Ira Bernstein; GENERAL MANAGER: Charles Harris; COMPANY MANAGER: Otto Hartman; PRODUCTION STAGE MANAGER: Henri Caubisens; STAGE MANAGER: James Wicker; ASSISTANT STAGE MANAGER: Marge Ellis. **Cast:** NICELY-NICELY JOHNSON: Stubby Kaye (6), *Jack Prince* (from 52–53); BENNY SOUTHSTREET: Johnny Silver (9), *Al Nesor* (from 52–53); RUSTY CHARLIE: Douglas Deane; SISTER SARAH BROWN: Isabel Bigley (4), *Susan Hight* (from 52–53); ARVIDE ABERNETHY: Pat Rooney Sr. (5); MISSION BAND (THREE MEMBERS): CALVIN: Paul Migan; AGATHA: Margery Oldroyd, *Suzanne Hanson* (from 51–52), *Maria Novotna* (from 52–53), *Jeanne Schlegel* (from 52–53); PRISCILLA: Christine Matsios, *Toni Reynolds* (from 51–52), *Maureen McNalley* (from 52–53); HARRY THE HORSE: Tom Pedi (8), *Del Markee* (from 52–53); LT BRANNIGAN: Paul Reed (10), *Tom Ahearne* (from 51–52); NATHAN DETROIT: Sam Levene (3), *Julie Oshins* (from 52–53); ANGIE THE OX: Tony Gardell; MISS ADELAIDE: Vivian Blaine (2), *Martha Stewart* (during Miss Blaine's vacation in 51–52), *Iva Withers* (from 52–53); SKY MASTERSON: Robert Alda (1), *Norwood Smith* (from 52–53); JOEY BILTMORE: Bern Hoffman; MIMI: Beverly Tassoni, *Ann Sparkman* (from 52–53); GENERAL MATILDA B. CARTWRIGHT: Netta Packer (11); BIG JULE: B.S. Pully (7); DRUNK: Eddie Phillips, *Peter Gennaro* (from 51–52); WAITER: Joe Milan, *Bob Evans* (from 51–52); DANCERS: Wana Allison (gone by 51–52), Forrest Bonshire (gone by 51–52), Geraldine Delaney (gone by 52–53), Barbara Ferguson (gone by 51–52), Pete Gennaro, Lee Joyce (gone by 51–52), Marcia Maier, Joe Milan (*Bob Evans* by 51–52), Eddie Phillips (gone by 51–52), Harry Lee Rogers (gone by 51–52), Buddy Schwab (gone by 51–52), Beverly Tassoni (*Ann Sparkman* by 51–52), Merritt Thompson, Ruth Vernon (gone by 52–53), Onna White. 51–52 replacements: *Jan Kovac* (gone by 52–53), *Jack Konzal* (gone by 52–53), *Al Lanti* (gone by 52–53), *Ralph Linn* (gone by 52–53), *Michael Scrittorale* (gone by 52–53), *Harriet Talbot* (gone by 52–53), *Pat Turner* (gone by 52–53). 52–53 replacements: *Bob Bernard, Lynn Bernay, Gene Carrons, Paul Gannon, Louise Golden, Loretta Moffat, Philip Nasta, Joan Petrone, Kenneth Urmston, Ben Vargas, Marc West, Gretchen Wyler.* Later replacements: *Loretta Rossi, Scott Merrill, Alicia Krug, Donn Driver, Chita Rivera*; SINGERS: Charles Drake (gone by 51–52), Tony Gardell, Bern Hoffman (gone by 51–52), Beverly Lawrence (gone by 52–53), Christine Matsios (*Toni Reynolds* by 51–52; *Maureen McNalley* by 52–53), Carl Nicholas, Don Russell (gone by 51–52), Hal Saunders (gone by 52–53), Earle Styres. 51–52 replacements: Neil Chirico (gone by 52–53), *Tom Rieder* (*Ralph Farnworth* by 52–53). 52–53 replacements: *Jeanne Schlegel, Arthur Ulisse.* **Understudies:** Sky: *Tom Rieder* (from 51–52), *Ralph Farnworth* (from 52–53); Nathan: *Sammy Schwartz* (from 51–52); Sarah: Christine Matsios, *Toni Reynolds* (from 51–52), *Maureen McNalley* (from 52–53); Adelaide: *Beverly Lawrence* (from 51–52), *Gretchen Wyler* (from 52–53); Arvide: *Earle Styres* (from 51–52); Nicely-Nicely/Big Jule: *Bern Hoffman* (from 51–52); Brannigan: *Hal Saunders* (from 51–52); Harry the Horse: *Tony Gardell* (from 51–52); Benny: *Carl Nicholas* (from 51–52); General: *Suzanne Hanson* (from 51–52), *Jeanne Schlegel* (from 52–53), *Maria Novotna.* **Act I: Scene 1** Runyonland (i.e. Broadway): "Runyonland Music" comprising two numbers: "Fugue for Tinhorns" (Nicely-Nicely, Benny, Charlie) [a re-worked version of the earlier "Three-Cornered Tune"] and "Follow the Fold" (Sarah, Arvide, The Mission Band), "The Oldest Established (Permanent Floating Crap Game in New York)" (Nathan, Nicely-Nicely, Benny, Male Chorus) [a hit]; **Scene 2** Interior of the Save-a-Soul Mission: "I'll Know" (Sarah & Sky) [a hit]; **Scene 3** A phone booth; **Scene 4** The Hot Box: "A Bushel and a Peck" (Adelaide & Hot Box Girls) [a big hit], "Adelaide's Lament" (Adelaide) [a hit]; **Scene 5** A street off Broadway: "Guys and Dolls" (Nicely-Nicely & Benny). GUY & DOLL: Pete Gennaro & Beverly Lawrence; **Scene 6** Exterior of the Mission; noon, the next day; **Scene 7** A Broadway sidestreet; **Scene 8** Cathedral Square, in Havana, Cuba: "Havana" (Onna White & Ensemble); **Scene 9** The same; outside Cafe El Cubano; immediately following: "If I Were a Bell" (Sarah) [a hit]; **Scene 10** Exterior of the Mission; 4 a.m, the following morning: "My Time of Day" (Sky) [a hit], "I've Never Been in Love Before" (Sky & Sarah). **Act II: Scene 1** The Hot Box: "Take Back Your Mink" (Adelaide & Hot Box

Girls) [a hit], "Adelaide's Lament" (reprise) (Adelaide); *Scene 2* West 48th Street: "More I Cannot Wish You" (Arvide); *Scene 3* The crap game in the sewer: "The Crapshooters' Dance" (also called "The Crap Game Dance") (Ensemble), "Luck Be a Lady (Tonight)" (Sky & Guys) [a big hit]; *Scene 4* West 48th Street: "Sue Me" (Nathan & Adelaide); *Scene 5* Interior of the Save-a-Soul Mission: "Sit Down, You're Rockin' the Boat" (Nicely-Nicely & Chorus) [a big hit], "Follow the Fold" (reprise) (Mission Meeting Group); *Scene 6* A newsstand in Times Square: "Marry the Man Today" (Adelaide & Sarah); *Scene 7* Return to Runyonland: "Guys and Dolls" (reprise) (Company).

Broadway reviews were all raves. The show won Tony Awards for musical, direction, choreography, and for Robert Alda and Isabel Bigley. It also won Donaldson Awards for musical, composer, lyrics, book, director, female debut (Vivian Blaine), and male debut (Robert Alda). It should have won a Pulitzer Prize, but Abe Burrows' troubles with the House Un-American Activities Commission scared away the award's trustees (Columbia University). The show vacationed 6/27/53–8/24/53. *Guys and Dolls* was the fifth-longest running show of the 1950s, grossing over $12 million.

After Broadway. Tour. Opened on 6/4/51, at the Curran Theatre, San Francisco. MUSICAL DIRECTOR: Samuel Farber. *Cast:* BENNY: Sid Melton; SARAH: Jan Clayton, *Jeanne Bal*; ARVIDE: Ralph Riggs, *Sydney Grant, Bobby Barry*; NATHAN: Julie Oshins, *Sam Schwartz*; ADELAIDE: Pamela Britton; SKY: Allan Jones, *Charles Fredericks*; BIG JULE: Maxie Rosenbloom, *Mike Mazurki*; WAITER: Ralph Beaumont, *Roy Wilson*; CHORUS INCLUDED: Tom Panko, Deedee Wood, Alvin Beam, Eddie Gasper, Ben Vargas, Gretchen Wyler.

The same company began a new tour on 11/30/53, at Ford's Theatre, Baltimore. *Cast:* BENNY: Al Nesor; SARAH: Jan Clayton, *Susan Hight*; ARVIDE: Pat Rooney Sr.; NATHAN: Julie Oshins; ADELAIDE: Pamela Britton, *Iva Withers*; SKY: Allan Jones, *Norwood Smith*; BIG JULE: B.S. Pully.

COLISEUM, London. Opened 5/28/53. 545 PERFORMANCES. *Cast:* NICELY-NICELY: Stubby Kaye, *William Thorburn*; BENNY: Johnny Silver, *Davy Kaye*; CHARLIE: Robert Arden, *Ed Devereaux*; SARAH: Lizbeth Webb; ARVIDE: Ernest Butcher; HARRY: Tom Pedi, *George Margo*; BRANNIGAN: Robert Cawdron; NATHAN: Sam Levene; ANGIE: George Margo, *Vincent Charles*; LIVER LIPS LOUIE: Lou Jacobi, *Jon Farrell* [this was a new character]; ADELAIDE: Vivian Blaine, *Jacqueline James*; SKY: Jerry Wayne, *Edmund Hockridge*; JOEY: Danny Green; MIMI: Joyce Blair, *Mildred Anderton*; GENERAL: Colleen Clifford, *Phyllis Bourke*; BIG JULE: Lew Herbert, *Danny Green*; DRUNK: John Heawood, *John Blysdale*; WAITER: Ed Devereaux, *Edward Monson*; DANCER: Stephanie Voss.

THE MOVIE. 1955. Sam Goldwyn paid a record million dollars for the film rights. This was Marlon Brando's musical debut (Gene Kelly was approached for the role first). The number "A Bushel and a Peck" was replaced by "Pet Me Poppa" and "I've Never Been in Love Before" by "(Your Eyes Are the Eyes of) A Woman in Love" (sung by Brando & Jean Simmons). Both new songs were written by Frank Loesser. *Cast:* NICELY-NICELY: Stubby Kaye; BENNY: Johnny Silver; HARRY: Sheldon Leonard; SARAH: Jean Simmons; ARVIDE: Regis Toomey; BRANNIGAN: Robert Keith; NATHAN: Frank Sinatra; ADELAIDE: Vivian Blaine; SKY: Marlon Brando; BIG JULE: B.S. Pully.

CITY CENTER, NYC, 4/20/55–5/1/55. 15 PERFORMANCES. Return engagement 5/31/55–6/12/55. 16 PERFORMANCES. PRESENTED BY the New York City Center Light Opera Company; DIRECTOR: Philip Mathias; CHOREOGRAPHER: Onna White; COSTUME SUPERVISOR: Frank Spencer; MUSICAL DIRECTOR: Frederick Dvonch; PRODUCTION STAGE MANAGER: Bernard Gersten. *Cast:* NICELY-NICELY: Oggie Small, *John Dorman* (from 5/31/55); BENNY: Al Nesor; CHARLIE: Murray Vines; SARAH: Leila Martin, *Patricia Northrop* (from 5/31/55); ARVIDE: Martin Wolfson; HARRY: Tom Pedi; BRANNIGAN: Tom Ahearne, *Wallace Rooney* (from 5/31/55); NATHAN: Walter Matthau; ANGIE: Ralph Vucci; ADELAIDE: Helen Gallagher, *Judy Johnson* (from 5/31/55); SKY: Ray Shaw; JOEY: Joe Bernard; MIMI: Norma Kaiser; GENERAL: Kate Tomlinson; BIG JULE: Lou Nova; DRUNK: Robert Karl; WAITER: Seth Riggs, *Ralph Vucci* (from 5/31/55); DANCERS INCLUDED: Tommy Panko, Marcia Maier; SINGERS INCLUDED: Clifford Fearl, Bob Rippy, Seth Riggs (*Howard Lear* from 5/31/55). **Understudy:** Sky: Seth Riggs.

HUDSON CELEBRATION THEATRE IN CENTRAL PARK, 7/21/59–

8/2/59. 14 PERFORMANCES. PRESENTED BY Jean Dalrymple; DIRECTOR: Billy Matthews; CHOREOGRAPHER: Peter Conlow; SETS: Edward D. Stone; DECOR: Duane McKinney; COSTUMES: Audre; LIGHTING: Feder; MUSICAL DIRECTOR: Samuel Matlovsky. *Cast:* SARAH: Margot Moser; ARVIDE: Martin Wolfson; ADELAIDE: Iva Withers; NATHAN: Harvey Stone; SKY: Lloyd Bridges; JOEY: Ron Husmann; BIG JULE: Jake La Motta; GENERAL: Claire Waring.

CITY CENTER, NYC, 4/28/65–5/9/65. 15 PERFORMANCES. Part of the City Center spring program of four musicals (the others were: *Kiss Me, Kate*, *South Pacific* & *The Music Man*). Due to post–Castro sensitivities in the USA, Act I Scene 8 (the Havana scene) was now set in San Juan, Puerto Rico, and the accompanying dance was now known as "San Juan." PRESENTED BY the New York City Center Light Opera Company; DIRECTOR: Gus Schirmer Jr.; CHOREOGRAPHER: Ralph Beaumont; SETS: Peter Wolf (he adapted Jo Mielziner's originals); COSTUMES: Frank Thompson; LIGHTING: Peggy Clark; MUSICAL DIRECTOR: Irving Actman. *Cast:* NICELY-NICELY: Jack De Lon; BENNY: Joey Faye; CHARLIE: Ed Becker; SARAH: Anita Gillette; ARVIDE: Clarence Nordstrom; HARRY: Tom Pedi; BRANNIGAN: Frank Campanella; NATHAN: Alan King; ANGIE: Vern Shinnal; ADELAIDE: Sheila MacRae; SKY: Jerry Orbach; JOEY: Ed Becker; MIMI: Ginna Carr; GENERAL: Claire Waring; BIG JULE: Jake La Motta; DRUNK: Stuart Mann; WAITER: Philip Lucas; DANCERS INCLUDED: Dorothy D'Honau, Tina Faye, Shelley Frankel, Leslie Franzos, Altovise Gore, Frank Coppola, Luigi Gasparinetti, Fernando Grahal, Carlos Macri, Mitchell Nutick, Ron Stratton; SINGERS INCLUDED: Ken Ayers, Walter P. Brown, Henry Lawrence, Joy Franz, Jeanne Schlegel, Victor R. Helou, Darrell Sandeen. This production, rare for a non–Broadway run, received a 1965 Tony Nomination for Jerry Orbach.

PAPER MILL PLAYHOUSE, New Jersey, 1965. DIRECTOR: Gus Schirmer. *Cast:* ADELAIDE: Vivian Blaine; NATHAN: Sam Levene; SKY: Norwood Smith.

CITY CENTER, NYC, 6/8/66–6/26/66. 23 PERFORMANCES. A remounting of the 1965 production (same crew), part of City Center's spring season of four Frank Loesser revivals (the others were: *How to Succeed in Business Without Really Trying*, *The Most Happy Fella* and *Where's Charley?*). The character of Joey Biltmore was deleted. This production used "San Juan" instead of the number "Havana." PRESENTED BY the New York City Center Light Opera Company. *Cast:* NICELY-NICELY: Dale Malone; BENNY: Joe Ross; CHARLIE: Ed Becker; SARAH: Barbara Meister; ARVIDE: Clarence Nordstrom; HARRY: Tom Pedi; BRANNINGAN: Frank Campanella; NATHAN: Jan Murray; ANGIE: Roger Brown; ADELAIDE: Vivian Blaine; SKY: Hugh O'Brian; MIMI: Rita O'Connor; GENERAL: Claire Waring; BIG JULE: B.S. Pully; DRUNK: Eddie Phillips; WAITER: Marvin Goodis; DANCERS INCLUDED: Gerard Brentte, Frank Coppola, Marilyn D'Honau, Mercedes Ellington, Altovise Gore, Vito Durante, Bob La Crosse, Carlos Macri, Mitchell Nutick, Rita O'Connor, Dom Salinaro; SINGERS INCLUDED: Dick Ensslen, Joseph Gustern. **Understudies:** Sky: Joe Bellomo; Sarah: Jeanne Frey; Adelaide: Iva Withers.

274. *Guys and Dolls* (1976 Broadway revival)

Before Broadway. This all-black revival ran first at the NATIONAL THEATRE, Washington, DC, from 5/5/76. Danny Holgate was musical supervisor then. Act I Scene 8 (the Havana scene) was still re-set in San Juan, Puerto Rico, but the accompanying dance was now called "El Cafe Felicidad."

The Broadway Run. BROADWAY THEATRE, 7/21/76–2/13/77. 12 previews. 239 PERFORMANCES. PRESENTED BY Moe Septee, in association with Victor H. Potamkin, Frank Enterprises, and Beresford Productions; MUSIC/LYRICS: Frank Loesser; BOOK: Jo Swerling & Abe Burrows; BASED ON Damon Runyon's 1931 short story *The Idyll of Miss Sarah Brown*, and on other Runyon characters; DIRECTOR/CHOREOGRAPHER: Billy Wilson; ASSISTANT TO THE DIRECTOR: Charles Augins; SETS: Tom H. John; COSTUMES: Bernard H. Johnson; LIGHTING: Thomas Skelton; SOUND: Sandy Hacker; MUSICAL DIRECTOR/CHORAL ARRANGEMENTS: Howard Roberts; ORIGINAL ORCHESTRATIONS: George Bassman & Ted Royal;

ARRANGEMENTS/ADDITIONAL ORCHESTRATIONS: Danny Holgate & Horace Ott; CAST RECORDING on Motown; PRESS: Max Eisen, Barbara Glenn, Judith Jacksina; PRODUCTION SUPERVISOR: Abe Burrows; GENERAL MANAGER: Laurel Ann Wilson; COMPANY MANAGER: Donald Tirabassi; PRODUCTION STAGE MANAGER: R. Derek Swire; STAGE MANAGER: Clinton Jackson; ASSISTANT STAGE MANAGER: Bonnie Sue Schloss. *Cast:* NICELY-NICELY JOHNSON: Ken Page (6); BENNY SOUTHSTREET: Christopher Pierre (7); RUSTY CHARLIE: Sterling McQueen; SISTER SARAH BROWN: Ernestine Jackson (3); HARRY THE HORSE: John Russell; LT BRANNINGAN: Clark Morgan; NATHAN DETROIT: Robert Guillaume (2); ANGIE THE OX: Jymie Charles; MISS ADELAIDE: Norma Donaldson (1); SKY MASTERSON: James Randolph (4); ARVIDE ABERNETHY: Emett "Babe" Wallace (8); AGATHA: Irene Datcher; CALVIN: Bardell Conner, *Alvin Davis*; MARTHA: Marion Moore; JOEY BILTMORE: Derrick Bell; MASTER OF CEREMONIES: Andy Torres; WAITER: Derrick Bell; MIMI: Prudence Darby; GENERAL CARTWRIGHT: Edye Byrde (5); BIG JULE: Walter White; DRUNK: Andy Torres; THE GUYS: Derrick Bell, Tony Brealond, Jymie Charles, Bardell Conner (*Alvin Davis*), Nathan Jennings Jr., Bill Mackey, Sterling McQueen, Andy Torres, Eddie Wright Jr.; THE DOLLS: Prudence Darby, Jacquelyn Du Bois, Anna Maria Fowlkes, Helen Gelzer, Julia Lema, Jacqueline Smith-Lee. *Understudies*: Sky: Nathan Jennings Jr.; Sarah: Irene Datcher; Adelaide/General: Helen Gelzer; Arvide: John Russell; Nathan/Nicely-Nicely: Jymie Charles; Benny: Andy Torres; Harry: Bill Mackey; Rusty Charlie: Bill Mackey & Eddie Wright Jr.; Big Jule: Tony Brealond; Agatha/Mimi: Julia Lema; Drunk: Derrick Bell. SWING DANCERS: Alvin Davis & Freda T. Vanterpool (*Brenda Braxton*). *Musicians*: KEYBOARDS: Lea Richardson; PERCUSSION: Herbert Lovelle; CONGAS: Monti Ellison; BASS: John Cartwright.

It opened on Broadway to divided reviews. The show received Tony Nominations for revival, and for Robert Guillaume, and Ernestine Jackson.

After Broadway. Laurence Olivier had planned to do *Guys and Dolls* at the ROYAL NATIONAL THEATRE, London, in 1970, with himself as Nathan, but he had fallen ill. The RNT finally hosted it, from 3/9/82. It was a hit and transferred to the West End, to the PRINCE OF WALES THEATRE. Opened 6/19/85. 354 PERFORMANCES. DIRECTOR: Richard Eyre; CHOREOGRAPHER: David Toguri; SETS: John Gunter; COSTUMES: Sue Blane; LIGHTING: David Hersey; MUSICAL DIRECTOR: Tony Britten; ORCHESTRATIONS: Tony Britten & Terry Davies; CAST RECORDING on MFP, done in 4/82. *Cast:* SARAH: Julie Covington; ADELAIDE: Julia McKenzie, *Imelda Staunton*; NATHAN: Bob Hoskins; SKY: Ian Charleson; ALSO WITH: David Healy, Barry Rutter, Jim Carter.

PAPER MILL PLAYHOUSE, New Jersey, 1984. DIRECTOR: Robert Johanson; CHOREOGRAPHER: Michael Shawn; SETS: Michael Anania; LIGHTING: Frances Aronson; MUSICAL DIRECTOR: Jim Coleman. *Cast:* Jack Carter, Larry Kert, Susan Powell, Lenora Nemetz.

275. *Guys and Dolls* (1992 Broadway revival)

This was the longest-running musical revival in Broadway history.

The Broadway Run. MARTIN BECK THEATRE, 4/14/92–1/8/95. 33 previews from 3/16/92. 1,143 PERFORMANCES. PRESENTED BY Dodger Productions, Roger Berlind, Jujamcyn Theatres/TV ASAHI, Kardana Productions, and the John F. Kennedy Center for the Performing Arts; MUSIC/LYRICS: FRANK LOESSER; BOOK: Jo Swerling & Abe Burrows; Based on Damon Runyon's 1931 short story *The Idyll of Miss Sarah Brown*, and on other Runyon characters; DIRECTOR: Jerry Zaks; CHOREOGRAPHER: Christopher Chadman; SETS: Tony Walton; COSTUMES: William Ivey Long; LIGHTING: Paul Gallo; SOUND: Tony Meola; MUSICAL SUPERVISOR: Edward Strauss, *Lawrence Yurman*; ORIGINAL ORCHESTRATIONS: George Bassman & Ted Royal; NEW ORCHESTRATIONS: Michael Starobin; ORCHESTRATIONS FOR "THE CRAPSHOOTERS' DANCE:" Michael Gibson; DANCE MUSIC ARRANGEMENTS: Mark Hummel; CAST RECORDING on RCA Victor; PRESS: Boneau/Bryan-Brown; CASTING: Johnson—Liff & Zerman & Tara Jayne Rubin; COMPANY MANAGER: Marcia Goldberg; PRODUCTION STAGE MANAGER: Steven Beckler,

Clifford Schwartz; STAGE MANAGER: Clifford Schwartz, *Deborah F. Porazzi*; ASSISTANT STAGE MANAGER: Joe Deer, *David O'Brien*. *Cast:* NICELY-NICELY JOHNSON: Walter Bobbie, *Larry Cahn* (by 93–94); BENNY SOUTHSTREET: J.K. Simmons, *Jeff Brooks* (from 92–93), *Adam Grupper* (by 93–94); RUSTY CHARLIE: Timothy Shew, *Scott Wise* (by 93–94), *Dale Hensley* (from 93–94), *Timothy Shew* (from 93–94); SISTER SARAH BROWN: Josie de Guzman ☆ (3), *Kim Crosby* [Carolyn Mignini played Sarah during previews]; ARVIDE ABERNATHY: John Carpenter, *Conrad McLaren* (from 92–93); AGATHA: Eleanor Glockner, *Susan Rush* (by 93–94), *Louisa Flaningam* (from 93–94); CALVIN: Leslie Feagan; MARTHA: Victoria Clark, *Jennifer Allen* (from 92–93), *Kim Crosby* (by 93–94), *Leslie Castay* (from 93–94); HARRY THE HORSE: Ernie Sabella, *Bob Amaral* (from 93–94); LT. BRANNIGAN: Steve Ryan, *Stephen Mendillo* (from 93–94); NATHAN DETROIT: Nathan Lane (2) ☆, *Adam Arkin* (from 92), *Nathan Lane* (from 92–93), *Jonathan Hadary* (from 5/17/93), *Jamie Farr* (from 3/15/94), *Jeff Brooks* (from 93–94); ANGIE THE OX: Michael Goz, *Michael Brian* (by 93–94), *Michael Goz* (from 93–94); MISS ADELAIDE: Faith Prince (4) ☆, *Jennifer Allen* (by 93–94); SKY MASTERSON: Peter Gallagher (1) ☆, *Tom Wopat* (from 10/12/92), *Burke Moses* (from 4/12/93), *Tom Wopat, Martin Vidnovic* (from 93–94); JOEY BILTMORE: Michael Goz, *Michael Brian* (by 93–94), *Michael Goz* (from 93–94); HOT BOX MC: Stan Page, *Michael Brian* (by 93–94), *Stan Page* (from 93–94); MIMI: Denise Faye, *Tina Marie De Leone* (from 92–93); GEN. MATILDA B. CARTWRIGHT: Ruth Williamson, *Louisa Flaningam* (by 93–94), *Ruth Williamson* (from 93–94); BIG JULE: Herschel Sparber, *Michael Goz* (by 93–94), *Herschel Sparber* (from 93–94), *Ron Holgate* (from 93–94); DRUNK: Robert Michael Baker, *Jere Shea* (from 92–93), *Wade Williams* (by 93–94); WAITER: Kenneth Kantor; HAVANA DANCE SPECIALTY: Sergio Trujillo (*Andy Blankenbuehler* from 93–94; *Jerome Vivona* 1/94–9/94) & Nancy Lemenager [new roles by 92–93]; CRAPSHOOTER DANCE LEAD: Scott Wise, *Darren Lee* (by 93–94), *Kirk Ryder* (from 93–94); GUYS: Robert Michael Baker (*Jere Shea* from 92–93; *Wade Williams* by 93–94), Gary Chryst (gone by 92–93), R.F. Daley, Randy Andre Davis, David Elder (gone by 92–93), Cory English (gone by 92–93), Mark Esposito, Leslie Feagen, Michael Goz (*Michael Brian* from 93–94, *Michael Goz* from 93–94), Kenneth Kantor, Carlos Lopez, John MacInnis, Stan Page, Timothy Shew, Scott Wise (*Darren Lee* by 93–94; *Kirk Ryder* from 93–94). 92–93 replacements: *Randy Bettis, Larry Cahn, Lloyd Culbreath, Aldrin Gonzales, Dale Hensley*. 93–94 replacements: *Michael Paternostro, Joey Pizzi, Sergio Trujillo* (*Andy Blankenbuehler* from 93–94, Jerome Vivona 1/94–9/94), *Steven Sofia;* OTHER DOLLS: Tina Marie De Leone, Denise Faye (gone by 92–93), JoAnn M. Hunter (gone by 92–93), Nancy Lemenager, Greta Martin, Pascale Faye-Williams. 92–93 replacements: *Jennifer Lamberts, Holly Raye*. 93–94 replacements: *Susan Misner, Michelle Chase*. **Understudies**: Nathan: Jeff Brooks & Larry Cahn, *Steve Ryan;* Benny: Jeff Brooks & Larry Cahn, *Michael Brian;* Harry: Jeff Brooks, Larry Cahn, Leslie Feagan; Sky: Robert Michael Baker, *Wade Williams;* Big Jule: Michael Goz, *Kenneth Kantor;* Brannigan: Kenneth Kantor & Timothy Shew, *Stan Page;* Arvide: Stan Page, *Leslie Feagan, Stan Page;* Nicely-Nicely: Timothy Shew, *Michael Brian;* Calvin: Steven Sofia, *Kirk Ryder;* Rusty Charlie: Scott Wise, *R.F. Daley, John MacInnis;* Adelaide: Victoria Clark, *Susann Fletcher, Leah Hocking;* Agatha: Victoria Clark & Denise Faye, *Kim Crosby, Leah Hocking, Michelle Chase;* General: Eleanor Glockner, Susan Rush, Susann Fletcher, Leah Hocking, *Louisa Flaningam;* Mimi: Tina Marie De Leone, *Greta Martin;* Martha: Nancy Lemenager, *Michelle Chase;* Sarah: *Kim Crosby* (by 93–94), *Leah Hocking* (by 93–94); mc: *Jerome Vivona*. **Swings**: Larry Cahn, Susan Misner, Steven Sofia, *Kirk Ryder, Michael Paternostro, Michelle Chase*. **Orchestra**: KEYBOARDS: Lawrence Yurman & Steve Tyler; VIOLINS: Katsuko Esaki, Robert Lawrence, Andrew Stein, Melanie Baker; VIOLA: Juliet Haffner; CELLO: Jeffrey Szabo; BASS: Joseph Bongiorno; PERCUSSION: Glenn Rhian & Eric Kivnick; TRUMPETS: Brian O'Flaherty, Glenn Drewes, Kamau Adilifu; TROMBONES: Bruce Bonvissuto & Earl McIntyre; FRENCH HORN: Roger Wendt; WOODWINDS: Seymour Red Press, Raymond Beckenstein, Dennis Anderson, Robert Steen, Wally Kane.

Broadway reviews were tremendous. The show won Tony Awards for revival, direction of a musical, sets, and for Faith Prince, and was nominated for choreography, lighting, and for Nathan Lane and Josie de Guzman.

After Broadway. BROADWAY NATIONAL TOUR. Opened on 9/15/92, at the Bushnell Theatre, Hartford, Conn., and closed on 7/3/94. One of the stops was the Kennedy Center, Washington, DC, 4/13/93–5/30/93. PRESENTED BY ATP/Dodger, Roger Berlind, Kardana Productions, Tom Mallow, and the Kennedy Center; MUSICAL DIRECTOR: Randy Booth. *Cast:* NICELY-NICELY: Kevin Ligon; SARAH: Patricia Ben Peterson; ARVIDE: MacIntyre Dixon, *Donald Grody*; HARRY: James Dybas; BRANNIGAN: Andy Umberger, *Allen Fitzpatrick*; NATHAN: Lewis J. Stadlen, *David Garrison, Philip LeStrange, Steve Landesberg*; ADELAIDE: Lorna Luft, *Beth McVey*; SKY: Richard Muenz; JOEY: David Hart, *George Dudley*; GENERAL: Joy Franz.

ROYAL NATIONAL THEATRE, London, 12/17/96–11/22/97. The closing date was extended from 3/29/97. This was a revival of the 1982 London production. DIRECTOR: Richard Eyre. *Cast:* NICELY-NICELY: Clive Rowe; SARAH: Joanna Riding; ARVIDE: John Normington; ADELAIDE: Imelda Staunton; NATHAN: Henry Goodman, *Colin Stinton*; SKY: Clarke Peters; BRANNIGAN: Colin Stinton. It got raves. Clive Rowe won an Olivier Award.

Strizzis und Mizzis. METROPOL-THEATER, Vienna, 1997. This was *Guys and Dolls* translated into the Viennese dialect by Dunja Sowinetz and Caroline Koczan. DIRECTOR: Karl Welunschek; MUSICAL DIRECTOR: Walter Lochman. *Cast:* SIGI MEISTER (the Sky role): Karlheinz Hackl; MARIE BRAUN (the Sarah role): Maria Koestlinger; FRAULEIN ADELHEID (the Adelaide role): Gabriele Schuchter; PEPI NOVAK (the Nathan role): Georg Schuchter [Mr. Schuchter was Gabriele's real-life brother].

ARENA STAGE, Washington, DC, 12/29/99–2/20/00. THIS WAS THE 50th-Anniversary revival. DIRECTOR: Charles Randolph-Wright; CHOREOGRAPHER: Ken Roberson; SETS: Thomas Lynch; COSTUMES: Paul Tazewell; LIGHTING: Michael Gilliam; SOUND: Susan R. White. *Cast:* NICELY-NICELY: Wayne W. Pretlow; BENNY: Lawrence Redmond; HARRY: Carlos Lopez; SARAH: Diane Sutherland [formerly Diane Fratantoni]; ARVIDE: Terrence Currier; ADELAIDE: Alexandra Foucard; NATHAN: Maurice Hines; BRANNIGAN: Stephen F. Schmidt; SKY: Brian Sutherland; BIG JULE: Richard J. Pelzman; GENERAL: Donna Migliaccio. A very enthusiastic Jo Sullivan (Frank Loesser's widow) saw the show and suggested a tour that would end on Broadway in 2002. Rehearsals began in 7/01, and after a two-day tryout at the Eisenhower Theatre, West Point, NY, 8/25/01–8/26/01, the tour began a 50-city schedule, at Wolf Trap, Vienna, Va., on 8/28/01, and ended in Casa Manana, Fort Worth, Texas, on 6/9/02. But it never made it to Broadway. The tour was PRESENTED BY: Richard Martini, Jonathan Reinis, Adam Friedson, Allen Spivak, and Albert Nicciolino. It had the same basic crew credits as for the Arena production, except for: SETS: Norbert Kolb; CAST RECORDING on DRG, released on 11/6/01. *Tour cast:* NICELY-NICELY: Clent Bowers; BENNY: Lawrence Redmond; CHARLIE: Michael W. Howell; SARAH: Diane Sutherland; ARVIDE: Tad Ingram; AGATHA: Cathy Carey; HARRY: Carlos Lopez; BRANNIGAN: Paul De Pasquale; NATHAN: Maurice Hines; ANGIE: Ryan Blanchard; ADELAIDE: Alexandra Foucard; SKY: Brian Sutherland; MIMI: Liza Shaller; GENERAL: Donna Migliaccio; BIG JULE: Curt M. Buckler; DRUNK: P.J. Terranova; ENSEMBLE: Tiffany Cooper, Johanna Gerry, David Kent, Jessica Rizzo, Danita Salamida, Scott Schmidt, Keith Lamelle Thomas, Gary E. Vincent.

PAPER MILL PLAYHOUSE, New Jersey. 6/5/04–7/18/04. Previews from 6/2/04. DIRECTOR: Stafford Arima; CHOREOGRAPHER: Patti Wilcox; SETS: Tony Walton; LIGHTING: F. Mitchell Dana; MUSICAL DIRECTOR: Tom Helm. *Cast*: SARAH: Kate Baldwin; SKY: Robert Cuccioli; NATHAN; Michael Mastro; ADELAIDE: Karen Ziemba; BRANNIGAN: Steven Bogard; NICELY-NICELY: Robert Creighton; BIG JULE: Tony Cucci; ARVIDE: Bob Dorian; BENNY: Robert Du Sold. On 6/9/04 the power went out, and that performance had to be canceled.

PICCADILLY THEATRE, London, 6/1/05. Previews from 5/19/05. This was the first new London production in 20 years (new production, that is). It cost 3 million pounds. PRESENTED BY Howard Panter; CHOREOGRAPHER: Rob Ashford. *Cast*: SKY: Ewan MacGregor; NATHAN: Douglas Hodge (Kevin Kline had been talked about for this role); ADELAIDE: Jane Krakowski; SARAH: Jenna Russell (Megan Mullally had been rumored for this role); NICELY-NICELY: Martyn Ellis.

276. *Gypsy*

A musical fable. The story of Gypsy Rose Lee (real name Louise Hovick) and her domineering mother Rose. The story begins in Seattle in the early 1920s, and follows the careers of Rose and her daughters Louise and June as they trudge through every two-bit vaude house in the country, to satisfy Rose's insane drive, which is to make her daughters succeed in showbiz no matter the cost, and also so she won't have to play bingo any more or pay rent. Baby June and Baby Louise are rehearsing for a kiddie show. Rose can't understand how some people can settle for an ordinary life. Moving from Seattle, Rose collects some boys, and Louise and June begin performing as Baby June and her Newsboys. Rose meets Herbie, a likeable candy salesman, who becomes their manager. The years pass. Herbie books them onto the Orpheum Circuit through Mr. Goldstein. Louise receives a lamb as a present. Herbie wants Rose to retire and marry him (Rose has already been married three times), and threatens to leave, but she charms him into staying. The act is regurgitated as Dainty June and Her Farmboys. An important producer offers to take June and make her a star, but Rose refuses. One of the farmboys, Tulsa, elopes with June, and Rose determines to make a star out of June's older, less talented sister Louise instead. Louise performs as a stripper, ultimately becoming Gypsy Rose Lee. The end sees Rose on stage, trying to work out her frustrations and having a breakdown. The plot ends in the early 1930s.

Before Broadway. Both Irving Berlin and Cole Porter turned down the show. Cy Coleman & Carolyn Leigh auditioned as composer & lyricist, with the numbers "(To) Be a Performer!" and "Firefly," but failed. Jerome Robbins wanted Steve Sondheim to do music and Lyrics, but Ethel Merman wanted only an experienced composer to handle the music part, and Jule Styne was brought in. Sondheim reluctantly went with lyrics only, and it did him no harm. John Kander arranged the dance music, a big break for the man who would later become so famous as part of the Kander & Ebb songwriting team. Anne Bancroft was the first choice for the role of Gypsy Rose Lee. Several songs written for the show were not used—"Mama's Talkin' Soft," "Smile, Girls," "(If I Had) Three Wishes for Christmas," "Who Needs Him," "Let's Go to the Movies," "Nice She Ain't," "(Tomorrow's) Mother's Day." On 4/6/59, in Philadelphia, *Gypsy* was performed for the first time, on a bare stage, with no costumes or lights, very little music, and a house full of New York theatre patrons. They stopped the show four times with their applause. On 4/13/59 it began five-week sold-out run in Philly. Then on to Broadway. 18 per cent of the show was owned by its two biggest investors, Max J. Brown and Byron Goldman. Sandra Church was Jule Styne's girlfriend.

The Broadway Run. BROADWAY THEATRE, 5/21/59–7/9/60; IMPERIAL THEATRE, 8/15/60–3/25/61. 2 previews. Total of 702 PERFORMANCES. PRESENTED BY David Merrick & Leland Hayward; MUSIC: Jule Styne; LYRICS: Stephen Sondheim; BOOK: Arthur Laurents; SUGGESTED BY *Gypsy*, the 1957 memoirs of stripper Gypsy Rose Lee (1914–1970); DIRECTOR/CHOREOGRAPHER: Jerome Robbins; ASSISTANT TO THE DIRECTOR: Gerald Freedman; SETS/LIGHTING: Jo Mielziner; COSTUMES: Raoul Pene du Bois; ASSISTANT COSTUMES: Willa Kim; SOUND: Jack Mitnick; MUSICAL DIRECTOR: Milton Rosenstock; ORCHESTRATIONS: Sid Ramin (with Robert Ginzler); DANCE MUSIC ARRANGEMENTS/ REHEARSAL PIANIST: John Kander; ADDITIONAL DANCE MUSIC ARRANGEMENTS: Betty Walberg; PRESS: Frank Goodman & Seymour Krawitz, *Harvey Sabinson, David Powers, Ted Goldsmith*; GENERAL MANAGER: Jack Schlissel; COMPANY MANAGER: Vince McKnight; PRODUCTION STAGE MANAGER: Ruth Mitchell; STAGE MANAGER: Lo Hardin; ASSISTANT STAGE MANAGER: James Bronson, *Eddie Dimond & Robert Tucker*. *Cast*: UNCLE JOCKO: Mort Marshall, *Charles White*; GEORGE: Willy Sumner; ARNOLD (AND HIS GUITAR): John Borden, *Jay Roy*; BALLOON GIRL: Jody Lane, *Patty Brownell*; BABY LOUISE: Karen Moore, *Alice Playten*; BABY JUNE: Jacqueline Mayro, *Jan Tanzy*; MADAME ROSE: Ethel Merman (1), *Jane Romano* (for a week during Miss Merman's illness in 8/59); CHOWSIE, THE DOG: Chowsie; POP: Erv Harmon; NEWSBOYS: Bobby Brownell, Gene Castle (*Jeffrey Allen*), Steve Curry (*Billy Curtis*), Billy Harris, *Jay Roy* (added by 59–60); WEBER: Joe Silver; HERBIE: Jack Klugman (2); LOUISE/GYPSY ROSE: Sandra Church (3), *Julienne Marie*;

JUNE: Lane Bradbury, *Merle Letowt*; TULSA: Paul Wallace; YONKERS: David Winters, *Dick Foster*; ANGIE: Ian Tucker, *Michael Mann*; L.A.: Michael Parks; KRINGELEIN: Loney Lewis; MR. GOLDSTONE: Mort Marshall, *Willy Sumner*; FARMBOYS: Marvin Arnold, Ricky Coll, Don Emmons, Michael Parks, Ian Tucker (*Michael Mann*), Paul Wallace, David Winters (*Harvey Hohnecker*); MISS CRATCHITT: Peg Murray; (SIX) HOLLYWOOD BLONDES: AGNES: Marilyn Cooper; MARJORIE MAY: Patsy Bruder; DOLORES: Marilyn D'Honau; THELMA: Merle Letowt, *Anita Gillette*; EDNA: Joan Petlak; GAIL: Imelda De Martin, *Linda Donovan*; PASTEY: Richard Porter; TESSIE TURA: Maria Karnilova, *Betty Bruce*; MAZEPPA: Faith Dane; CIGAR: Loney Lewis; ELECTRA: Chotzi Foley, *Marsha Rivers, June Squibb*; SHOW GIRLS: Kathryn Albertson, Gloria Kristy (dropped by 59–60), Denise McLaglen, Barbara London, Theda Nelson, Carroll Jo Towers, Marie Wallace; MAID: Marsha Rivers; PHIL: Joe Silver; BOUGERON-COUCHON: George Zima; COW: Willy Sumner & George Zima. **Standbys**: Rose: Jane Romano; Louise: Leila Martin, *Julienne Marie*; Baby June: Ivy Ellen, *Jan Tanzy*. **Understudies**: June: Imelda De Martin, *Anita Gillette*; Kringelein: Joe Silver, *Willy Sumner*; Cigar: Joe Silver; Baby Louise: Jody Lane; Herbie: *Vincent Beck* (not in the first season); Tulsa: *Harvey Hohnecker* (by 59–60); Tessie: *Peg Murray* (by 59–60); Electra: *Marsha Rivers* (by 59–60); Pop/Weber: Sterling Beath. **Act I:** Overture (Orchestra); **Scene 1** Vaudeville theatre stage, Seattle: "May We Entertain You" (Baby Louise & Baby June); **Scene 2** Kitchen of a frame house, Seattle; shortly afterward: "Some People" (Rose); **Scene 3** A car on the road between Seattle and Los Angeles: "Traveling" (instrumental dance number); **Scene 4** Backstage of a vaudeville house, Dallas: "Small World" (Rose & Herbie); **Scene 5** Onstage of a vaudeville theatre, Los Angeles; then Akron, Ohio: Baby June and Her Newsboys (dance) (Baby June & Newsboys); **Scene 6** Two plaster-cracked hotel rooms in Akron: "Mr. Goldstone, I Love You" (Rose & Ensemble), "Little Lamb" (Louise); **Scene 7** A Chinese restaurant in New York City: "You'll Never Get Away from Me" (Rose & Herbie); **Scene 8** The stage of Grantziger's Palace Theatre, New York City: Dainty June and Her Farmboys (dance) (June & Farmboys); **Scene 9** Grantziger's office: "If Momma Was Married" (Louise & June); **Scene 10** A theatre alley outside the stage door of a vaudeville theatre in Buffalo: "All I Need is the Girl" (Tulsa & Louise); **Scene 11** A railroad platform in Omaha, Nebraska: "Everything's Coming up Roses" (Rose) [the big hit] [a revised version of "I'm Betwixt and Between," a song cut from *High Button Shoes*]. **Act II:** **Scene 1** In the Texas desert country; late afternoon: "Madame Rose's Toreadorables" (Louise & Toreadorables) [not recorded on the album], "Together (Wherever We Go)" (Rose, Louise, Herbie); **Scene 2** Backstage of a burlesque house, in Wichita, Kansas: "You Gotta Have a Gimmick" (also known as "You Gotta Get a Gimmick") (Tessie, Mazeppa, Electra); **Scene 3** Backstage corridor; **Scene 4** The dressing room and corridor, Wichita, then Detroit, Philadelphia, Minsky's: "Small World" (reprise) (Rose), "Let Me Entertain You" ("The Strip") (Louise & Company); **Scene 5** Louise's dressing-room; Scene 6 Backstage after the show: "Rose's Turn" (Rose).

It got mostly rave reviews on Broadway. Top price seats were $9.40. In 8/59 Merman burst a blood vessel in her larynx, and her understudy, Jane Romano, went on for a week, to great applause, but diminishing box-office returns. Because of the timing of its opening, the show fell into next year's Tony Awards (i.e. 1960), where it came up against *The Sound of Music*, and lost all eight of the nominated categories — musical, direction of a musical, sets (musical), costumes, musical direction, and Jack Klugman, Ethel Merman, and Sandra Church. This was the last Broadway role that Ethel Merman created.

After Broadway. POST-BROADWAY TOUR. Opened on 3/29/61, at the Auditorium, Rochester, NY, and closed on 12/9/61, at the American Theatre, St. Louis. This was the first show Ethel Merman ever toured with. MUSICAL DIRECTOR: Milton Rosenstock. **Cast**: ROSE: Ethel Merman; HERBIE: Alfred Sandor; LOUISE: Julienne Marie; L.A.: Michael Parks; KRINGELEIN/CIGAR: Loney Lewis; JUNE: Merle Letowt; TESSIE: Betty Bruce; BABY LOUISE: Alice Playten; BABY JUNE: Jan Tanzy; GEORGE/BOUGERON-COUCHON/PART OF COW: George Zima; SHOWGIRL: *Ellen Travolta*.

TOUR. Opened on 9/14/61, at the Shubert Theatre, Detroit, and closed on 1/20/62, at the Hanna Theatre, Cleveland. PRESENTED BY Manny Davis; CHOREOGRAPHER: Michael Mann; MUSICAL DIRECTOR:

Gilbert Stevens. **Cast**: ROSE: Mary McCarty; HERBIE: Joseph Leon; THELMA: Bernadette Peters; HAWAIIAN GIRL: Bernadette Peters, *Dorothy Marie*; LOUISE: Mimi Turque.

PAPER MILL PLAYHOUSE, New Jersey, 1962. DIRECTOR: Gerald Freedman. **Cast**: Julie Wilson, Jo Wilder, Alfred Sandor.

THE MOVIE. 1962. DIRECTOR: Mervyn LeRoy. The only song that was cut was "Together." **Cast**: ROSE: Rosalind Russell (singing partly dubbed by Lisa Kirk); LOUISE: Natalie Wood; HERBIE SOMMERS: Karl Malden; TESSIE: Betty Bruce; KRINGELEIN: Parley Baer; MAZEPPA: Faith Dane; ANGIE: Ian Tucker.

277. *Gypsy* (1974 Broadway revival)

The opening number in this production was "Let Me Entertain You" (Baby June & Baby Louise).

Before Broadway. This Broadway revival began at the PICCADILLY THEATRE, London, 5/29/73. 300 PERFORMANCES. It was the first time the show had ever been seen in London, as Ethel Merman had always refused to travel overseas with a tour. Miss Merman and Angela Lansbury both turned down the role of Rose, and Elaine Stritch was then scheduled to play it. However, the producers (Fritz Holt and Barry M. Brown) couldn't get backing with Stritch's name, so Miss Lansbury finally accepted it. DIRECTOR: Arthur Laurents. **Cast**: ROSE: Angela Lansbury, *Dolores Gray* (when Miss Lansbury left to take the show to Broadway); HERBIE: Barrie Ingham; BABY JUNE: Bonnie Langford; LOUISE: Zan Charisse. The production then came to North America, and did a tour beginning on 3/25/74, at the Royal Alexandra Theatre, Toronto. MUSICAL DIRECTOR: Marc Pressel. The tour included the Kennedy Center, Washington, DC, 8/12/74–8/31/74, then on to Broadway for previews. During the first preview at the Winter Garden, on 9/19/74, there was a bomb scare in the theatre.

The Broadway Run. WINTER GARDEN THEATRE, 9/23/74–1/4/75. 4 previews from 9/19/74. Limited run of 120 PERFORMANCES. PRESENTED BY Barry M. Brown, Edgar Lansbury, Fritz Holt, Joseph Beruh; MUSIC: Jule Styne; LYRICS: Stephen Sondheim; BOOK/DIRECTOR: Arthur Laurents; SUGGESTED BY *Gypsy*, the 1957 memoirs of stripper Gypsy Rose Lee; CHOREOGRAPHER: Robert Tucker re-produced Jerome Robbins' original choreography; SETS/LIGHTING: Robert Randolph; COSTUMES: Raoul Pene du Bois; ANGELA LANSBURY'S COSTUMES: Robert Mackintosh; SOUND: Jack Mann; MUSICAL DIRECTOR: Milton Rosenstock; ORCHESTRATIONS: Sid Ramin & Robert Ginzler; DANCE MUSIC ARRANGEMENTS: John Kander; PRESS: The Merlin Group; CASTING: Amos Abrams; GENERAL MANAGEMENT: Marvin A. Krauss Associates; COMPANY MANAGER: Charles Willard; PRODUCTION STAGE MANAGER: Kathleen A. Sullivan; STAGE MANAGER: Moose Peting; ASSISTANT STAGE MANAGER: Serhij Bohdan. **Cast**: UNCLE JOCKO: John C. Becher; GEORGE: Don Potter; CLARENCE (AND HIS CLASSIC CLARINET): Craig Brown; BALLOON GIRL: Donna Elio; BABY LOUISE: Lisa Peluso; BABY JUNE: Bonnie Langford (8); ROSE: Angela Lansbury (1) ☆; CHOWSIE, THE DOG: Peewee; POP: Ed Riley; NEWSBOYS: Craig Brown, Anthony Marciona, Sean Rule, Mark Santoro; WEBER: Charles Rule; HERBIE: Rex Robbins (2); LOUISE: Zan Charisse (3); JUNE: Maureen Moore (6); TULSA: John Sheridan (7); YONKERS: Steven Gelfer; L.A.: David Lawson; LITTLE ROCK: Jay Smith; SAN DIEGO: Dennis Karr; BOSTON: Serhij Bohdan; KRINGELEIN: John C. Becher; MR. GOLDSTONE: Don Potter; GIGOLO: Edith Ann; WAITRESS: Patricia Richardson; MISS CRATCHITT: Gloria Rossi; HOLLYWOOD BLONDES: Pat Cody, Jinny Kordek, Jan Neuberger, Marilyn Olson, Patricia Richardson; AGNES: Denny Dillon; PASTEY: Richard J. Sabellico; TESSIE TURA: Mary Louise Wilson (4); MAZEPPA: Gloria Rossi (5); CIGAR: John C. Becher; ELECTRA: Sally Cooke; MAID: Bonnie Walker; PHIL: Ed Riley; BOUGERON-COUCHON: Serhij Bohdan. **Standby**: Rose: Mary Louise Wilson. **Understudies**: Louise: Patricia Richardson; Herbie: Ed Riley; June: Jan Neuberger; Baby June/Baby Louise: Donna Elio; Tulsa: Steven Gelfer; Miss Cratchitt: Sally Cooke; Tessie/Mazeppa/Electra: Bonnie Walker; Pop/Weber: Don Potter; Jocko/Cigar: Ed Riley & Don Potter; Kringelein: Charles Rule & Ed Riley; Goldstone: Charles Rule; George: Richard J. Sabellico.

Opening night reviews were mostly raves. Angela Lansbury won a

Tony, and the show was also nominated for direction of a musical, and for Zan Charisse.

After Broadway. MEXICO CITY, 1976. *Cast:* ROSE: Marga Lopez; LOUISE: Claudia Islas. This was a revival. The Mexican version, adapted into Spanish by Jose Luis Ibanez, had first played in Mexico in the 1960s.

PAPER MILL PLAYHOUSE, New Jersey, 1976. DIRECTOR: Bill Guske. *Cast:* ROSE: Dolores Gray.

WOLF TRAP FARM PARK, Vienna, Va., 6/19/78. 8 PERFORMANCES. DIRECTOR: Fritz Holt; CHOREOGRAPHER: Bonnie Walker; SETS: Kenneth Foy; COSTUMES: Sydney Smith; LIGHTING: Charles Collins. *Cast:* Angela Lansbury, Nana, Lew Resseguie.

278. *Gypsy (1989 Broadway revival)*

Before Broadway. This Broadway run was part of a tour that opened in Chattanooga on 5/2/89. It tried out for Broadway at the Kennedy Center, Washington, DC, 8/9/89–9/16/8.

The Broadway Run. ST. JAMES THEATRE, 11/16/89–1/6/91. 23 previews from 10/27/89. 476 PERFORMANCES. PRESENTED BY Barry Weissler, Fran Weissler, Kathy Levin, Barry Brown, in association with Tokyo Broadcasting System International & PACE Theatrical Group; MUSIC: Jule Styne; LYRICS: Stephen Sondheim; BOOK/DIRECTOR: Arthur Laurents; SUGGESTED BY *Gypsy*, the memoirs of stripper Gypsy Rose Lee; CHOREOGRAPHER: Bonnie Walker re-produced Jerome Robbins' original choreography; SETS: Kenneth Foy; COSTUMES: Theoni V. Aldredge; LIGHTING: Natasha Katz; SOUND: Peter J. Fitzgerald; MUSICAL DIRECTOR: Eric Stern; ORCHESTRATIONS: Sid Ramin & Robert Ginzler; DANCE MUSIC ARRANGEMENTS: John Kander; NEW CAST RECORDING on Elektra Nonesuch; PRESS: Shirley Herz Associates; CASTING: Stuart Howard & Amy Schecter; GENERAL MANAGER: Alecia Parker; COMPANY MANAGER: Nancy Nagel Gibbs & Jim Brandeberry; PRODUCTION STAGE MANAGER: Craig Jacobs; STAGE MANAGER: Tom Capps; ASSISTANT STAGE MANAGER: James Bernandi. *Cast:* UNCLE JOCKO: Tony Hoty (12), *Stan Rubin*; GEORGE: John Remme (13), *Victor Raider-Wexler*; CLARENCE: Bobby John Carter; BALLOON GIRL: Jeana Haege; BABY LOUISE: Kristen Mahon (14); BABY JUNE: Christen Tassin (15), *Susan Cremin*; ROSE: Tyne Daly (1) ☆, *Jana Robbins* (2/20/90–2/25/90), *Tyne Daly, Linda Lavin* (from 7/30/90); CHOWSIE, THE DOG: Peewee; POP: Ronn Carroll (9); NEWSBOYS: Demetri Callas, Bobby John Carter, Danny Cistone, Jason Minor; WEBER: Mace Barrett (10), *Richard Levine*; HERBIE: Jonathan Hadary (2), *Jamie Ross* (from 10/30/90); LOUISE: Crista Moore (3); JUNE: Tracy Venner (4); TULSA: Robert Lambert (5); YONKERS: Bruce Moore; L.A.: Craig Waletzko; KANSAS: Ned Hannah, *Paul Geraci*; FLAGSTAFF: Paul Geraci, *Kevin Pettito*; ST. PAUL: Alec Timmerman, *Cory English*; KRINGELEIN: Tony Hoty (12), *Stan Rubin*; MR. GOLDSTONE: John Remme (13), *Victor Raider-Wexler*; MISS CRATCHITT: Barbara Erwin (6); HOLLYWOOD BLONDES: Barbara Folts, Teri Furr, Nancy Melius, Michele Pigliavento, Robin Robinson; AGNES: Lori Ann Mahl; PASTEY: Jim Bracchitta (11), *Jeff Brooks*; TESSIE TURA: Barbara Erwin (6); MAZEPPA: Jana Robbins (8); ELECTRA: Anna McNeely (7); CIGAR: Ronn Carroll (9); MAID: Ginger Prince; PHIL: Mace Barrett (10), *Richard Levine*; BOUGERON-COCHON: Jim Bracchitta (11), *Jeff Brooks*. **Standbys:** Mazeppa/Tessie/Electra/Cratchitt: Ginger Prince; Herbie: Mace Barrett; Rose: Jana Robbins; Louise: Michele Pigliavento. **Understudies:** George/Goldstone: Jim Bracchitta; Pop/Pastey/Bougeron-Cochon: John Remme, *Victor Raider-Wexler*; Weber/Cigar/Phil: Tony Hoty, *Stan Rubin*; Tulsa: Alec Timmerman, *Craig Waletzko*; Agnes/June: Teri Furr; Baby June/Baby Louise: Jeana Haege. **Swings:** Julie Graves, Eric H. Kaufman, *Laurie Crochet, George Smyros*.

Most reviews were great, but there were some dissenters. The show won Tony Awards for revival, and for Tyne Daly. It was also nominated for costumes, and for Jonathan Hadary and Crista Moore.

After Broadway. After Broadway it toured again, returning later in the year to Broadway.

279. *Gypsy (1991 return to Broadway)*

This was the Tyne Daly tour returned to Broadway.
The Broadway Run. MARQUIS THEATRE, 4/28/91–7/28/91. 12 previews from 4/18/91. 105 PERFORMANCES. It had the same basic crew except MUSICAL DIRECTOR: Michael Rafter; COMPANY MANAGER: Scott A. Moore; STAGE MANAGER: James Bernandi; ASSISTANT STAGE MANAGER: Tony Rader. *Cast:* UNCLE JOCKO: Stan Rubin (13); GEORGE: Victor Raider-Wexler (12); CLARENCE: Bobby John Carter; BALLOON GIRL: Jeana Haege; BABY LOUISE: Kristen Mahon (14); BABY JUNE: Susan Cremin (15); ROSE: Tyne Daly (1); CHOWSIE, THE DOG: Chowsie; POP: Ronn Carroll (9); NEWSBOYS: Bobby John Carter, Thomas Fox, Danny Cistone, Tony Yazbeck; WEBER: Richard Levine (10); HERBIE: Jonathan Hadary (2); LOUISE: Crista Moore (3); JUNE: Tracy Venner (4); TULSA: Robert Lambert (5); YONKERS: Bruce Moore; L.A.: Craig Waletzko; KANSAS: Paul Geraci; FLAGSTAFF: Kevin Petitto; ST. PAUL: Cory English; THE COW: Crista Moore, Barbara Folts, Robin Robinson, Cory English, Kevin Petitto; KRINGELEIN: Stan Rubin (13); MR. GOLDSTONE: Victor Raider-Wexler (12); MISS CRATCHITT: Barbara Erwin (6); HOLLYWOOD BLONDES: Teri Furr, Barbara Folts, Michele Pigliavento, Nancy Melius, Robin Robinson; AGNES: Lori Ann Mahl; PASTEY: Jeff Brooks (11); TESSIE TURA: Barbara Erwin (6); MAZEPPA: Jana Robbins (8); ELECTRA: Anna McNeely (7); CIGAR: Ronn Carroll (9); MAID: Ginger Prince; PHIL: Richard Levine (10); BOUGERON-COCHON: Jeff Brooks (11). **Standbys:** Mazeppa/Tessie/Electra/Cratchitt: Ginger Prince; Louise: Michele Pigliavento; Herbie: Richard Levine; Rose: Jana Robbins. **Understudies:** Pop/Bougeron-Cochon: Victor Raider-Wexler; Tulsa: Craig Waletzko; Weber/Cigar/Phil: Stan Rubin; Baby Louise/Baby June: Jeane Haege; Agnes/June: Teri Furr. **Swings:** Laurie Crochet & George Smyros. **Orchestra:** Nicholas Archer, Kenneth Adams, Bruce Bonvissuto, Kenneth Berger, Yari Bond, Pattee Cohen, Alexandra Cook, Andrew Drelles, Nathan Durham, Susan Follari, Philip Granger, Cliff Hardison, William Kerr, Jeffrey Kievit, Dale Kirkland, Byung Kwak, Ann Leathers, Mark Minkler, Suzanne Ornstein, Richard Raffio, Glenn Rhian, William Shadel.

After Broadway. WESTCHESTER BROADWAY THEATRE, Elmsford, NY, 1992. DIRECTOR: Charles Repole; CHOREOGRAPHER: Susan Stroman; SETS/COSTUMES: Michael Bottari & Ron Case. *Cast:* ROSE: Beth Fowler, *Jana Robbins*; HERBIE: Jamie Ross; LOUISE: Jacqulyn Piro; JUNE: Susan Gail Bernstein; TESSIE: Isabelle Farrell; POP/KRINGELEIN: Jerold Goldstein; ALSO WITH: Jason Robert Redford.

CBS TV PRODUCTION. On 12/12/93 RHI Entertainment presented a TV film on CBS. PRODUCER/DIRECTOR: Emile Ardolino. *Cast:* ROSE: Bette Midler; JOCKO: Tony Shalhoub; GEORGE: Sean Sullivan; POP: Ed Asner; HERBIE: Peter Riegert; KRINGELEIN: Keene Curtis; TESSIE: Christine Ebersole.

MEXICAN REVIVAL. TEATRO SILVIA PINAL, Mexico City, 6/25/98. Previews from May. ADAPTED INTO SPANISH BY Jose Luis Ibanez; DIRECTOR: Enrique Reyes; SETS: David Anton. *Cast:* ROSE: Silvia Pinal; HERBIE: Claudio Baez; LOUISE: Alejandra Guzman [in real life Silvia Pinal's daughter] (until 10/18/98, i.e. for the first 100 performances), *Iran Castillo* (from 10/22/98); JUNE: Stephanie Salas [in real life Silvia Pinal's granddaughter], *Maru Duenaz* (until 10/18/98), *Lolita Cortez* (from 10/22/98). The cast recording was released in Spanish in 10/98 with the following tracks: Overtura, "Algunas gentes," "Que casualidad" ("Small World"), "Baby June y los periodiqueros," "Don Eduardo" ("Mr. Goldstone"), "Burrequito" ("Little Lamb"), "No te podras librar de mi," "La bella June y los granjeros," "Si mama se casa," "Solo me falta un amor," "Todo se tine de rosas," "Juntos," "Deberas tener un truco," "El turno de Rose," "Gracias" ("Bows").

PAPER MILL PLAYHOUSE, New Jersey, 9/20/98–10/25/98. Rehearsals from 8/20/98. Previews from 9/9/98. Betty Buckley missed three previews due to vocal problems, and Jana Robbins went on. The production was criticized in some areas, but Miss Buckley got raves. DIRECTOR: Mark Waldrop; CHOREOGRAPHER: Liza Gennaro; SETS: Michael Anania; COSTUMES: Michael Bottari & Ron Case; LIGHTING: Mark Stanley; MUSICAL DIRECTOR: Edward Strauss. *Cast:* ROSE: Betty Buckley (Patti LuPone had been in discussions for the role); HERBIE: Lenny Wolpe; MAZEPPA: Jana Robbins; MISS CRATCHITT/TESSIE: Dorothy Stanley; LOUISE: Deborah Gibson; JUNE: Laura Bell Bundy; TULSA: Joe Machota; ELECTRA: Anna McNeely; L.A.: Brian J. Marcum; MAID: Meredith Patterson. **Standbys:** Rose: Jana Robbins; Mazeppa: Lori Alexander. The production was rumored to be going on to the Royal Alexandra Theatre, Toronto, in the spring of 1999, under the auspices of the Mirvish Brothers, and starring Betty Buckley. But Arthur Laurents refused to release the rights, as he had plans for a "different" version in London (see 2003 Broadway revival, below). So the Paper Mill Playhouse production died here.

280. *Gypsy (2003 Broadway revival)*

Before Broadway. In 1998 Arthur Laurents was planning to do a London version of *Gypsy*, and by 4/00 rumor had it that Bernadette Peters was going to star as Rose. By 10/00 Sam Mendes was being rumored as the director, and by 12/00 Miss Peters herself confirmed it and gave the Royal National as the theatre, with a Broadway run after London. Rehearsals were to begin in London in 1/03, with Jonathan Tunick doing the orchestrations. However, by 2/6/02 the London deal was off, and it was now going to open on Broadway instead. London would now be a long way in the future, if at all. By 6/02 Tammy Blanchard was being rumored as Louise, an on 11/25/02 it was announced that Kate Buddeke had been offered Mazeppa, and on 12/5/02 it was announced that John Dossett had been offered Herbie; he was confirmed on 12/21/02. On 12/23/02 David Burtka and Julie Halston were confirmed. When *Chicago* moved from the Shubert on Broadway, that theatre became available, and the latest revival of *Gypsy* moved in. This version had a live lamb. Rehearsals began on 1/27/03 (a date brought forward from 1/30/03). In early 12/02 Broadway previews were put back from 3/24/03 to 3/31/03, and the opening date was put back from 4/24/03 to 5/1/03. The top ticket price for this show would be $100. Most of the choreography was new. There was some debate about how Jerome Robbins would be credited (only two numbers retained his original choreography—"You Gotta Have a Gimmick" and "All I Need is the Girl"). On 1/29/03 the full cast was announced. Bernadette Peters was out with a cold, 4/21/03–4/23/03, during previews. Maureen Moore stood in on 4/21/03 and 4/22/03, and for the 4/23/03 matinee and evening performances. Miss Peters was back on 4/24/03.

The Broadway Run. SHUBERT THEATRE, 5/1/03–5/30/04. 33 previews from 3/31/03. 451 PERFORMANCES. PRESENTED BY Robert Fox, Ron Kastner, Roger Marino, Michael Watt, Harvey Weinstein, and WWLC; MUSIC: Jule Styne; LYRICS: Stephen Sondheim; BOOK: Arthur Laurents; SUGGESTED BY *Gypsy*, the 1957 memoirs of stripper Gypsy Rose Lee; DIRECTOR: Sam Mendes; CHOREOGRAPHER: Jerome Robbins; ADDITIONAL CHOREOGRAPHY: Jerry Mitchell; SETS/COSTUMES: Anthony Ward; LIGHTING: Jules Fisher & Peggy Eisenhauer; SOUND: ACME Sound Partners; MUSICAL SUPERVISOR: Patrick Vaccariello; MUSICAL DIRECTOR/ADDITIONAL DANCE MUSIC ARRANGEMENTS: Marvin Laird; ORCHESTRATIONS: Sid Ramin & Robert Ginzler; ADDITIONAL ORCHESTRATIONS: Bruce Coughlin; DANCE MUSIC ARRANGEMENTS: John Kander; NEW CAST RECORDING on Angel Records, made 6/22/03–6/23/03; PRESS: Boneau/Bryan-Brown; CASTING: Jim Carnahan; GENERAL MANAGEMENT: Nina Lannan Associates; COMPANY MANAGER: Ken Davenport; 1ST ASSISTANT STAGE MANAGER: Richard Hester; 2ND ASSISTANT STAGE MANAGERS: Jim Woolley & Carrie Meconis. *Cast*: UNCLE JOCKO: Michael McCormick; GEORGIE: Joey Dudding; STAGEHANDS: MacIntyre Dixon & William Parry; CLARENCE (AND HIS CLASSIC CLARINET): Stephen Scott Scarpulla; BALLOON GIRL: Molly Grant Kallins; BABY LOUISE: Addison Timlin; BABY JUNE: Heather Tepe; ROSE: Bernadette Peters (1) *, Maureen Moore* (stood in) ☆; CHOWSIE, THE DOG: Coco; POP: William Parry; CHAUFFEUR: Brooks Ashmanskas; PASSENGER: Michael McCormick; NEWSBOYS: Eamon Foley, Stephen Scott Scarpulla, Jordan Viscomi; WEBER: MacIntyre Dixon; HERBIE: John Dossett (3); LOUISE: Tammy Blanchard (2); JUNE: Kate Reinders; TULSA: David Burtka; YONKERS: Matt Bauer; L.A.: Brandon Espinoza; KANSAS: Benjamin Brooks Cohen; KRINGELEIN: William Parry; HOTEL GUEST: Michael McCormick; MR. GOLDSTONE: Brooks Ashmanskas; WAITRESS: Dontee Kiehn; MISS CRATCHITT: Julie Halston (until 1/24/04), *Gayton Scott* (from 1/26/04); STAGE MANAGER: Brooks Ashmanskas; FARMBOYS: Joey Dudding, Brandon Espinoza, Tim Federle, David Burtka, Matt Bauer, Benjamin Brooks Cohen; COW: Sarah Jayne Jensen & Dontee Kiehn; AGNES: Chandra Lee Schwartz; HOLLYWOOD BLONDES: Jenna Gavigan, Julie Martell, Ginifer King, Dontee Kiehn, Sarah Jayne Jensen; PASTEY: Brooks Ashmanskas; STRIPPER: Cathy Trien; COMICS: MacIntyre Dixon

& William Parry; TESSIE TURA: Heather Lee; MAZEPPA: Kate Buddeke; CIGAR: Michael McCormick; ELECTRA: Julie Halston (until 1/24/04), *Gayton Scott* (from 1/26/04); RENE, THE MAID: Cathy Trien; PHIL: MacIntyre Dixon; BOUGERON-COCHON: Tim Federle; ENSEMBLE: Matt Bauer, Benjamin Brooks Cohen, MacIntyre Dixon, Joey Dudding, Brandon Espinoza, Tim Federle, Eamon Foley, Jenna Gavigan, Sarah Jayne Jensen, Molly Grant Kallins, Dontee Kiehn, Ginifer King, Gina Lamparella, Julie Martell, Stephen Scott Scarpulla, Chandra Lee Schwartz, Cathy Trien, Jordan Viscomi. *Standby*: Rose: Maureen Moore. ***Understudies***: Rose: Cathy Trien; Jocko/Cigar/Hotel Guest: Wally Dunn & Patrick Garner; Passenger/Pop/Kringelein: Wally Dunn & Patrick Garner; Stagehand/Comic: Wally Dunn & Patrick Garner; Herbie: Michael McCormick & William Parry; Goldstone/Pastey/Stage Manager/Chauffeur: Graham Bowen, Wally Dunn, Patrick Garner; Weber/Phil: Wally Dunn & Patrick Garner; June: Jenna Gavigan & Chandra Lee Schwartz; Georgie/Bougeron-Cochon: Graham Bowen; Baby Louise/Clarence/Newsboy: Molly Grant Kallins & Julianna Rose Mauriello; Baby June/Balloon Girl: Alexandra Stevens; Tulsa: Matt Bauer & Tim Federle; Yonkers/L.A./Kansas: Graham Bowen & Joey Dudding; Agnes: Dontee Kiehn & Pamela Remler; Electra/Mazeppa/Cratchitt/Tessie: Gina Lamparella & Cathy Trien; Hollywood Blonde: Gina Lamparella; Louise: Ginifer King & Julie Martell; Cow/Waitress/Stripper/Rene: Gina Lamparella & Pamela Remler. *Swings*: Graham Bowen, Wally Dunn (during previews only), Julianna Rose Mauriello, Pamela Remler (dance captain). *Orchestra*: CONCERTMASTER: Ann Labin; VIOLINS: Maura Giannini & Dana Ianculovici; VIOLA: Richard Brice; CELLI: Peter Prosser & Eileen Folson; HARP: Grace Paradise; LEAD TRUMPET: Chris Jaudes; TRUMPETS: Larry Lunetta & Hollis Burridge; TROMBONES: Bruce Eidem & Michael Seltzer; BASS TROMBONE: Morris Kainuma; FRENCH HORN: Roger Wendt; REEDS: Dennis Anderson, Mort Silver, Ralph Olson, Charles Pillow, Ron Jannelli; DRUMS: Cubby O'Brien; BASS: Bill Ellison; PIANO: Ethyl Will; PERCUSSION: Deane Prouty.

Broadway reviews were mostly good. Bernadette Peters' cold was still plaguing her as the show opened. She was out again 5/5/03–5/8/03, and again on 5/10/03, but she did play 5/9/03. Maureen Moore covered each time. Miss Moore covered again on 7/21/03. The show received Tony nominations for revival of a musical, and for Bernadette Peters, John Dossett, and Tammy Blanchard. It also won a Grammy. A performance was missed on 8/14/03 due to the big power blackout. Bernadette Peters vacationed 9/29/03–10/4/03, and Maureen Moore again stood in. The closing date of 2/28/04 was announced on 2/2/04 due to bad weather in New York, and also to the fact that business was bad. It picked up and the show stayed open until 5/30/04. There was talk of a tour with Bernadette Peters.

After Broadway. ECTOR THEATRE, Odessa, Texas. Limited run, 8/11/05–8/28/05. DIRECTOR: Tony Georges. *Cast*: ROSE: Maria Friedman; LOUISE: Daisy Eagan.

281. *Gypsy Lady*

An operetta set in France about 1900. Alvarado, a handsome actor, is in love with Valerie, whose father, the duke, considers marriage out of the question because of Alvarado's humble background. Alvarado persuades gypsy princess Musetta to impersonate the royal princess and marry Valerie's snobbish brother, Andre. Ballet master Fresco instructs her in impersonation. Musetta's father, Boris, a gypsy chieftain, also poses as royalty. In the end Alvarado falls for Musetta, but she takes her original lover, Sandor. Pettibois is the comic owner of a ballet school. Imri and Roszika were the two dancers.

Before Broadway. It was tried out by Edwin Lester's San Francisco Civic Light Opera Association under title *The Fortune Teller*, at the Curran Theatre, San Francisco, from 7/1/46. It was then brought to New York by Mr. Lester and the Shuberts.

The Broadway Run. NEW CENTURY THEATRE, 9/17/46–11/23/46. 79 PERFORMANCES. PRESENTED BY Edwin Lester; MUSIC: Robert Wright, George Forrest, Victor Herbert; NEW LYRICS/DIRECTORS: Robert Wright & George Forrest; BOOK: Henry Myers; An operetta which, by arrangement with Ella Herbert Bartlett, combined the score of the 1898 musical *The Fortune Teller* (m: Victor Herbert; l: Harry B. Smith) with that of another work by Herbert & Smith—*The Serenade* (1897); MUSICAL ADAPTATIONS/MUSICAL DIRECTOR/ORCHESTRATIONS/CHORAL ARRANGEMENTS: Arthur Kay; VOCAL NUMBERS STAGED BY: Lew Kesler; CHOREOGRAPHER: Aida Broadbent; SETS: Boris Aronson; COSTUMES: Miles White; LIGHTING: Adrian Awan; PRESS: C.P. Greneker, Ben Kornzweig, Lenny Traube; GENERAL MANAGER: Eleanor Pinkham; COMPANY MANAGER: George Leffler; STAGE MANAGER: Kay Hammond. *Cast*: BARON PETTIBOIS: Clarence Derwent (5), *Ralph Herbert*; YVONNE: Kaye Connor; FRESCO: Jack Goode; MUSETTA: Helena Bliss (1); SERGEANT OF GENDARMES: Edmund Dorsay; THE GREAT ALVARADO: John Tyers (3); VALERIE, MARQUISE OF RONCEVALLE: Doreen Wilson; IMRI: Val Valentinoff, *Rem Olmsted*; RUDOLFO: William Bauer; BORIS: Melville Cooper (2), *Billy Gilbert*; ROSZIKA: Patricia Sims; SANDOR: George Britton (4); ANDRE, MARQUIS OF RONCEVALLE: Gilbert Russell; STEPHAN, DUKE OF RONCEVALLE: Joseph Macaulay; THE UNDECIDED MADEMOISELLE: Suzette Meredith; M. GUILBERT ARMAND: Bert Hillner; MAJORDOMO: Harvey Shahan; YOUNG LADIES OF THE ACADEMY/GYPSIES/GUESTS/MAIDS/MANNIKINS: Jeanne Bal, Phyllis Bateman, Mardi Bayne, Betty Brusher, Marydee Buscher, Dorothy Coulter, Beth Alba Cushing, Betty Galavan, Florette Hillier, Rosemary Leisen, Suzette Meredith, Dani Nelson, Bernice Saunders, Nelda Scarsella, Peggy Weakland, Helen Wysatt; GYPSIES/GENTLEMEN/BELLBOYS/WAITERS: James Andrews, George Dempsey, Paul De Poyster, Ray Drakeley, Dean Etmund, Max Hart, Bert Hillner, Elton Howard, William James, Dale Johnson, Richard Scott, Robert Searles, Harvey Shahan, Ray Smith, John Stamford, Stanley Wolfe; DANCING GYPSIES AND BALLET: Barbara Bailey, Lyza Baugher, Donna Biroc, Florence Brundage, Jean Marie Caples, Kathleen Cartmill, Elaine Corbett, Marietta Elliott, Mitzi Gerber, Irene Hall, Judy Landon, Joan Larkin, Betty Orth, Patricia Sims, Betty Slade, Maria Taweel. *Act I*: *Scene 1* Baron Pettibois' Academy of Theatre Arts; an afternoon early in summer: "On a Wonderful Day Like Today" (Young Ladies of the Academy), "The Facts of Life Backstage" (Fresco, Yvonne, Young Ladies), The Serenade: "I Love You, I Adore You" (Alvarado & Valerie), "Interlude" (Musetta & Alvarado), "On a Wonderful Day Like Today" (reprise) (Young Ladies); *Scene 2* The Gypsy camp; at sunset the same day: "Life is a Dirty Business" (Gypsy Men), "My Treasure" (Sandor & Gypsy Men), "Romany Life" (orig l: Harry B. Smith) (Musetta & Gypsies); *Scene 3* The Baron's garden; the next day: "Pantomime" (dance) (Fresco), "The World and I" (Andre, Alvarado, Girls from Paris), "Piff Paff" (Stephan, Valerie, Andre), "Andalusia Bolero" (dance) (Imri, Roszika, Gypsies), "Keepsakes" (Alvarado & Valerie), Finale (Alvarado, Musetta, Pettibois, Fresco, Sandor, Gypsies). *Act II*: *Scene 1* A suite in a Paris hotel; a few weeks later: "Young Lady a la Mode" (Alvarado, Musetta, Fresco, Yvonne, Armand, Bellboys); *Scene 2* Roof of the hotel overlooking Montmartre; same evening: "Springtide" (Andre & Musetta); *Scene 3* Terrace of the Chateau de Roncevalle; a fortnight later: Ballet Divertissement (Ballet Company), "My First Waltz" (Musetta, Andre, Alvarado, Fresco, Ensemble), "Reality" (Boris, Fresco, Pettibois), "Gypsy Love Song" (orig l: Harry B. Smith) (Sandor), "Piff Paff" (reprise) (Stephan, Alvarado, Andre, Valerie, Fresco, Guests); *Scene 4* Cupid's cupola; later that night: "Springtide" (reprise) (Andre), "I Love You, I Adore You" (reprise) (Alvarado); *Scene 5* The road; dawn: Finale: "Romany Life" (reprise) (Ensemble).

Broadway reviews were (mostly) divided between (mostly) pans and a rave.

After Broadway. After it closed on Broadway it ran in London, as *Romany Love*, at HIS MAJESTY'S THEATRE, 3/7/47 (12 weeks). PRESENTED BY Jack Hylton. *Cast*: Melville Cooper, Helena Bliss.

282. *Hair*

An American tribal love-rock musical. Set in New York, mostly in the East Village, at the present time. Claude is a draftee who spends his last civilian hours with a tribe of hippies. The original Shakespeare Festival production ended with toy tanks rolling onto the stage, while the Broadway version, which had

been made much softer in tone, ended with the company singing "Let the Sunshine In." It by no means disapproved of certain subjects in its virtually plot-free story: drugs, sex, homosexuality, inter-racial relations; it dealt in a rather unconservative way with the American flag and Christianity, and attacked Vietnam and pollution.

Before Broadway. *Hair* was first shown Off Broadway as the premiere offering of the Public Theatre (Joe Papp's New York Shakespeare Festival's new quarters, the refurbished Astor Place Library). ANSPACHER THEATRE (part of the Public Theatre), 10/29/67–12/10/67. 15 previews from 10/17/67. It had a $2.50 ticket price. PRESENTED BY The New York Shakespeare Festival; DIRECTOR: Gerald Freedman; SETS: Ming Cho Lee; COSTUMES: Theoni V. Aldredge; LIGHTING: Martin Aronstein; MUSICAL DIRECTOR: John Morris; PRESS: Merle Debuskey; PRODUCTION STAGE MANAGER: Russell McGrath; STAGE MANAGER: Michael Chambers. *Cast:* DIONNE: Jonelle Allen; "DAD:" Ed Crowley; CLAUDE: Walker Daniels; WOOF: Steven Dean; JEANIE: Sally Eaton; "MOM:" Marijane Maricle; SHEILA: Jill O'Hara; CRISSY: Shelley Plimpton; BERGER: Gerome Ragni; HUD: Arnold Wilkerson; SUSAN: Susan Batson; LINDA: Linda Compton; SUZANNAH: Suzannah Evans; LYNDA: Lynda Gudde; LOUISE: Jane Levin; ALMA: Alma Robinson; CHARLIE: Warren Burton; THOMMIE: Thommie Bush; BILL: William Herter; PAUL: Paul Jabara; BOB: Bob Johnson; JIM: Edward Murphy Jr. Note: James Rado was not in the cast. *Act I*: "Red, Blue and White" ("Mom" & "Dad") [cut before Broadway], "Ain't Got No" (Claude, Berger, Woof, Hud, Company), "I Got Life" (Claude & "Mom"), Air (Jeannie, Crissy, Dionne), "Going Down" (Berger & Company), "Hair" (Claude, Berger, Company), "Dead End" (Sheila & Company), "Frank Mills" (Crissy), "Where Do I Go?" (Claude & Company). *Act II*: "Electric Blues" (Suzannah, Linda, Paul), "Easy to Be Hard" (Suzannah, Linda, Paul, Company), "Manchester" (Claude), "White Boys" (Dionne, Susan, Alma), "Black Boys" (Linda, Crissy, Suzannah), "Walking in Space" (Company), "Aquarius" (Company), "Good Morning Starshine" (Sheila & Company), "Exanaplanetooch" (Claude & Sheila) [cut before Broadway], "Climax!" (Sheila) [cut before Broadway].

Michael Butler, a rich Chicago businessman, saw it and decided he wanted to do something with it. After it closed at the Public, Mr. Butler moved the show to a Broadway-area discotheque, THE CHEETAH, 12/22/67–1/28/68. 45 PERFORMANCES. It had a slightly changed cast. Steve Curry replaced Gerome Ragni; Gale Dixon replaced Shelley Plimpton; Suzannah Evans had become Suzannah Norstrand. Mr. Butler then bought the production rights from Joe Papp and hired Tom O'Gorman as director. The script was revised, certain cast and crew members were replaced yet again, and it went to Broadway.

The Broadway Run. BILTMORE THEATRE, 4/29/68–7/1/72. 8 previews from 4/11/68. 1,742 PERFORMANCES. The Natoma production, presented by Michael Butler; MUSIC: Galt McDermot; LYRICS/BOOK: Gerome Ragni & James Rado; DIRECTOR: Tom O'Horgan; DANCE DIRECTOR: Julie Arenal; SETS: Robin Wagner; COSTUMES: Nancy Potts; LIGHTING: Jules Fisher; SOUND: Robert Kiernan; MUSICAL SUPERVISOR: Irving Raymond; MUSICAL DIRECTOR: Galt MacDermot, *Margaret Harris* (by 71–72); CAST RECORDING on RCA Victor; PRESS: Michael F. Goldstein, Inc., *Arthur Cantor & Arthur Solomon*; *David Rothenberg & Mary Bryant* (in 68–69); *Gifford/Wallace* (by 69–70); CASTING: Linda Otto; GENERAL MANAGER: Richard Osorio; COMPANY MANAGER: Virginia Snow, *William Orton* (by 68–69); PRODUCTION STAGE MANAGER: Fred Reinglas, *Neil Phillips* (by 68–69); STAGE MANAGER: Michael Maurer, *Lani Ball, Danny Sullivan, David Hixon* (the last three in 68–69), *Robert D. Currie, Ronald Schaeffer, Robert Goldberg* (the last three in 69–70), *Joe Donovan & Ronald Schaeffer* (both in 70–71); ASSISTANT STAGE MANAGER: Donnie Burks, *Robert Peitscher* (by 68–69). *Cast:* CLAUDE HOOPER BUKOWSKI: James Rado, *Barry McGuire* (from 11/22/68), *Joseph Campbell Butler* (from 1/69), *Ben Vereen* (from 68–69, *Erik Robinson* (from 68–69), *James Rado* (by 5/69), *Robin McNamara* (from 8/69), *Keith Carradine* (from 10/69), *Allan Nicholls* (from 2/70), *Robin McNamara* (from 4/71), *Willie Windsor* (from 71–72); RON: Ronald Dyson [role dropped by 69]; BERGER: Gerome Ragni, *Steve Curry* (from 11/22/68), *Richard Kim Milford* (from 68–69), *Peter Link* (from 68–69, *Oatis Stephens* (from 68–69), *Allan Nicholls, Gerome Ragni* (by

5/69), *Oatis Stephens* (from 2/70), *Larry Marshall, Steve Curry* (from 70–71), *Red Sheppard* (from 12/17/70), *Oatis Stephens* (from 2/71), *Allan Nicholls* (from 4/71), *Steve Curry* (by 71–72), *Roger Cruz* (from 71–72), *Gregory V. Karliss*; WOOF: Steve Curry, *Bert Sommer* (from 68–69), *Keith Carradine* (in 68–69), *Robin McNamara* (from 69–70), *Alan Braunstein* (from 70–71), *Peppy Castro* (from 71–72); HUD: Lamont Washington, *Donnie Burks* (from 68–69), *Larry Marshall* (from 69–70), *Obie Bray* (alternating by 69–70), *Michael Rohn* (from 71–72); SHEILA: Lynn Kellogg, *Diane Keaton* (from 7/68), *Heather MacRae* (from 1/69), *Martha Velez* (in 69), *Melba Moore* (from 10/69), *Victoria Medlin* (from 12/69), *Heather MacRae* (from 6/70), *Victoria Medlin* (from 8/70), *Marta Heflin* (from 3/71), *Beverly Bremers* (from 71–72); JEANIE: Sally Eaton, *Kay Cole* (by 71–72), *Dale Soules* (from 71–72); DIONNE: Melba Moore, *Joan Johnson* (from 69–70), *Delores Hall* (from 70–71), *Zenobia Conkerite* (from 71–72); CRISSY: Shelley Plimpton, *Lillian Wong* (from 69–70), *Shelley Plimpton* (from 70–71), *Debbie Andrews* (by 71–72), *Shelley Plimpton* (from 71–72); 1ST MOTHER: Sally Eaton, *Kay Cole* (by 71–72), *Dale Soules* (from 71–72); 2ND MOTHER: Jonathan Kramer, *Charles O. Lynch* (from 68–69), *Nat Grant* (from 70–71)), *Bobby C. Ferguson* (by 71–72); 3RD MOTHER: Paul Jabara, *Obie Bray* (from 68–69), *Bartholomew Miro Jr.* (in 69), *Charles O. Lynch* (from 70–71), *Bryan Spencer* (by 71–72); 1ST FATHER: Robert I. Rubinsky, *Clifford Lipson* (from 68–69), *Rick Granat* (from 69–70), *Clifford Lipson* (from 70–71); 2ND FATHER: Suzannah Norstrand, *Linda Compton* (from 69), *Debbie Offner* (from 68–69), *Valerie Williams* (from 70–71)); 3RD FATHER: Lamont Washington, *Donnie Burks* (from 68–69), *Larry Marshall* (from 69–70), *Fluffer Hirsch* (by 70–71), *Michael Rhone* (from 71–72); 1ST PRINCIPAL: Robert I. Rubinsky, *Clifford Lipson* (from 68–69), *Rick Granat* (from 69–70), *George Garcia* (from 70–71); 2ND PRINCIPAL: Suzannah Norstrand, *Linda Compton* (from 69), *Debbie Offner* (from 69), *Angie Ortega* (from 70–71); 3RD PRINCIPAL: Lamont Washington, *Donnie Burks* (from 68–69), *Larry Marshall* (from 69–70), *Bobby C. Ferguson* (from 70–71), *Clifford Lipson* (by 71–72), *Gloria Goldman* (from 71–72); TOURIST: Robert I. Rubinsky, *Clifford Lipson* (from 68–69), *John Aman* (from 69–70), *Clifford Lipson* (from 70–71), *Jonathan Johnson* (by 71–72); TOURIST LADY: Jonathan Kramer, *Charles O. Lynch* (relieved Mr. Kramer in 68–69), *Bryan Spencer* (from 70–71); WAITRESS: Diane Keaton, *Natalie Mosco* (from 68–69), *Debbie Offner* (from 69–70), *Valerie Williams* (from 70–71); YOUNG RECRUIT: Jonathan Kramer, *Charles O. Lynch* (from 68–69), *Jonathan Kramer* (from 69–70), *Fluffer Hirsch* (from 70–71), *George Garcia* (by 71–72), *Bobby C. Ferguson* (from 71–72); GENERAL GRANT: Paul Jabara, *Charles O. Lynch* (from 68–69), *Bartholomew Miro Jr.* (in 69), *Rick Granat* (from 69–70), *Charles O. Lynch* (from 70–71), *Clifford Lipson* (from 71–72), *Stephen Fenning*; ABRAHAM LINCOLN: Lorrie Davis, *Valerie Williams* (from 70–71); SERGEANT: Donnie Burks, *Obie Bray* (from 69–70), *Robalee Barnes* (from 70–71), *Larry Marshall* (by 71–72), *Michael Rhone* (from 71–72); PARENTS: Diane Keaton & Robert I. Rubinsky, *Linda Compton & Natalie Mosco* (from 68–69; Miss Mosco was replaced by *Clifford Lipson* by 69–70), *Debbie Offner & Rick Granat* (from 69–70), *Kathrynann Wright & Clifford Lipson* (from 70–71; Mr. Lipson was replaced by *Robert Golden* from 71–72); BOX OFFICE: Steve Gamet; TRIBE: Donnie Burks (gone by 68–69), Lorrie Davis (gone by 70–71), Leata Galloway (gone by 70–71), Steve Gamet (gone by 70–71), Walter Harris (gone by 68–69), Diane Keaton (gone by 68–69), Hiram Keller (gone by 68–69), Marjorie LiPari (gone by 68–69), Emmaretta Marks (gone by 70–71), Natalie Mosco (gone by 69–70), Suzannah Norstrand (gone by 69–70), Robert I. Rubinsky (gone by 68–69). 68–69 replacements: *John Aman* (gone by 70–71), *Beverly Ann* (left in 69), *Carolyn Blakey* (left in 69), *Obie Bray* (gone by 70–71), *Keith Ian Carradine* (gone by 69–70), *Linda Compton* (gone by 69–70), *Denise Delapenha* (gone by 70–71), *Clifford Lipson* (gone by 71–72), *Charles O. Lynch* (gone by 69–70), *Robin McNamara* (left in 69), *Dolores Morris* (gone by 69–70), *Erik Robinson* (gone by 69–70), *Bert Sommer* (gone by 69–70), *Oatis Stephens* (gone by 69–70). Later 69 replacements: *Kay Beckett* (gone by 69–70), *Gene Blythe* (gone by 69–70), *Erroll Booker* (gone by 69–70), *Steve Gillette* (gone by 69–70), *Gerri Griffin* (gone by 69–70), *Bartholomew Miro Jr.* (gone by 69–70), *George Tipton* (gone by 70–71), *Martha Velez* (gone by 69–70), *Helena Walquer* (gone by 69–70). 69–70 replacements: *Hazel Bryant* (gone by 70–71), *Jim Carozzo* (gone by 70–71), *Robin Eaton* (gone by 70–71), *Rick Granat* (gone by 70–71), *Jes-*

sica Harper (gone by 70–71), *Joan Johnson* (gone by 70–71), *Fluffer Hirsch* (gone by 71–72), *Jonathan Kramer* (gone by 70–71), *Holly Near* (gone by 70–71), *Debbie Offner* (gone by 70–71), *Angie Ortega* (gone by 70–71), *George Tipton* (gone by 70–71), *Singer Williams* (gone by 70–71), *Lillian Wong* (gone by 70–71). 70–71 replacements: *Zenobia Conkerite, Bobby C. Ferguson, George Garcia* (gone by 71–72), *Gloria Goldman, Nat Grant* (gone by 71–72), *Delores Hall* (gone by 71–72), *Ursuline Kairson* (gone by 71–72), *Bobby London* (gone by 71–72), *Mary Mendum* (gone by 71–72), *Valerie Williams, Kathrynann Wright*. 71–72 replacements: *Billy Alessi, Marjorie Barnes, Candice Earley, Stephen Fenning, Robert Golden, Ula Hedwig, Jonathan Johnson, Stephanie Parker, Carl Scott, Mary Seymour, Bryan Spencer, George Turner*. STANDBY: Claude: Seth Allen. **Understudies:** Berger: John Aman (by 68–69), *Oatis Stephens* (69), *Jim Carozzo* (by (69–70), *George Garcia* (by 70–71), *Larry Marshall* (by 70–71), *Peppy Castro* (by 71–72), *Robert Golden* (by 71–72); Sheila: Denise Delapenha (68–70), *Jean Glover* (68–69), *Ursuline Kairson* (by 70–71), *Gloria Goldman* (by 70–71 & still there 71–72), *Kathrynann Wright* (by 71–72); Jeanie: Suzannah Norstrand (68–69), *Mary Davis* (68–69), *Lorrie Davis* (69–70), *Angie Ortega* (by 70–71), *Valerie Williams* (by 70–71 & still there 71–72), *Zenobia Conkerite* (by 71–72); Dionne: Dolores Morris (68–69), *Denise Delapenha* (69–70); Crissy: Linda Compton (68–69), *Kay Beckett* (69), *Debbie Offner* (69–70), *Dale Soules* (by 70–71), *Candice Earley* (by 71–72); Claude: Bert Sommer (68–69), *Erik Robinson* (69), *Robin McNamara* (68–69), *Robin Eaton* (69–70), *Alan Braunstein* (by 70–71), *Jonathan Johnson* (by 71–72); Hud: Obie Bray (68–69), *Nat Grant* (by 70–71), *Robalee Barnes* (by 70–71), *George Turner* (by 71–72), *Bobby C. Ferguson* (by 71–72); Woof: Keith Ian Carradine (68–69), *Fluffer Hirsch* (69–71), *Jonathan Johnson* (by 71–72), *Stephen Fenning* (by 71–72). **Musicians:** ELECTRIC PIANO: Galt MacDermot, Neil Tate (alternate); GUITARS: Alan Fontaine, Charlie Brown, Jimmy Lewis; BASS: Jimmy Lewis; CLARINET/SAX: Zane Paul Zacharoff; TRUMPETS: Donald Leight & Eddy Williams; PERCUSSION: Warren Chaisson; DRUMS: Leo Morris; *Later musicians (by 70–71)*: *Margaret Harris, Idris Muhammad*. **Act I**: "Aquarius" (Ron & Company) [Later in the run, and in subsequent productions, the name of the performer was listed] [the big hit], "Donna" (Berger & Company), "Hashish" (Company), "Sodomy" (Woof & Company), "Colored Spade" (Hud & Company), "Manchester (England)" (Claude & Company), "Ain't Got No" (Woof, Hud, Dionne, Berger, Company) [Berger's name was later omitted] [a big hit], "Dead End" (Dionne & three male tribe members) [this number was re-positioned here during the run, and remained here for subsequent productions], "I Believe in Love" (Sheila), "I Got Life" (Claude & Company) [this was the position of this number prior to Broadway opening night. It subsequently shifted position — see below], "Air" (Jeanie, Crissy, Dionne, Company), "Initials" (Company), "I Got Life" (Claude & Company) [this was the new position on Broadway opening night — see above; and also in subsequent productions], "Going Down" (Berger & Company), "Hair" (Claude, Berger, Claude, Company), "My Conviction" (Tourist Lady & Company), "Hung" (Berger & Company) [this was its original position and the original singers], "Dead End" (Sheila & Company) [this was the position of this number prior to Broadway opening night. It was cut for Broadway opening night, but re-instated during the run], "Easy to Be Hard" (Sheila) [this number was re-positioned here by Broadway opening night, before which it was a song for Group, Sheila, Berger], "Hung" (Berger, Woof, Claude, Sheila, Jeanie, Company) [this was the new position on Broadway opening night, and the new singers], "Don't Put it Down" (Berger & Woof) [another male Tribe Member was added as a third singer later–Steve on opening night — and in subsequent productions Hud was also added], "The Flesh Failures" [this number was in this position originally, but was later re-titled "The Flesh," shifted to end of Act II, and reduced to a reprise], "Frank Mills" (Crissy), "Hare-Krishna" (Company) [later called "Be-In"], "Where Do I Go?" (Claude & Company). **Act II**: "Electric Blues" (Suzannah, Leata, Steve, Paul) [this number was later sung by five Tribe Members, always 2 male and two female, and the fifth being of either sex], "Easy to Be Hard" (Suzanna & The Group, Sheila, Berger) [this was the position before Broadway opening night; it was later shifted — see above], "Black Boys" (Diane Keaton, Suzannah Norstrand, Natalie Mosco), "White Boys" (Dionne, Lorri, Emmaretta), "Walking in Space" (Company), "Abie Baby" (Hud, Ron, Sergeant, Abraham Lincoln) [this number was later sung by three men and a woman], "Three-Five-Zero-Zero" (Company) [originally called "Prisoners in Niggertown"], "What a Piece of Work is Man" (with a lyrical assist from Shakespeare) (two male Tribe Members—Ronald & Walter in the original) [originally this number was part of the above number, when that number was known as "Prisoners of Niggertown." Later listed as a separate number], "Good Morning Starshine" (Sheila, Dionne, Company) [later sung by just Sheila & Company] [a big hit], "The Bed" (Company), "You Are Standing on My Bed" (Company) [cut before Broadway], "Exanaplanetooch" [cut before Broadway], "The Flesh" (reprise) (Company) [originally called "The Flesh Failures"–see above], "Let the Sun Shine In" (Claude, Sheila, Dionne, Company) [a big hit].

Michael Butler rushed the Broadway opening to qualify for that year's Tonys (it had been nominated for musical and direction of a musical), only to be told that it was ineligible because it had originated Off Broadway. The rules were changed the following season. The show opened to great reviews. On Broadway James Rado and Jerome Ragni began inserting new material into the musical, and Michael Butler banned them from the set. It was Broadway's first hit rock musical and the fourth-longest-running musical of the 1960s. There was a tiny amount of nudity at the end of Act I (added only after it moved to Broadway), and some bad language, and this caused enormous controversy.

After Broadway. SHAFTESBURY THEATRE, London. Opened on 9/27/68. 1,999 PERFORMANCES. *Cast:* CLAUDE: Paul Nicholas; BERGER: Oliver Tobias. It had a successful run, but only after the UK censor had had his powers cut.

There were several tours in the USA. Certain new songs were added for some of these tours. In Act I: "Kama Sutra" (Company) and "Hello There" (Berger); and in Act II: "Oh, Great God of Power" (Berger & Company).

THE FIRST TOUR. Opened on 11/22/68, at the Aquarius Theatre, Los Angeles. PRESENTED BY Michael Butler, Ken Kragen, Tom Smothers, and Ken Fritz; MUSICAL DIRECTOR: Danny Hurd. *Cast:* CLAUDE: James Rado, *Teddy Neeley*; BERGER: Gerome Ragni, *Ben Vereen*; DELORES: Delores Hall; HUD: Ben Vereen; SHEILA: Jennifer Warren; CRISSY: Kay Cole.

PARIS, 1969. PRESENTED BY Gilbert Marouani; FRENCH LYRICS: Jacques Lanzmann. *Cast:* Julien Clerc.

THE SECOND TOUR. Opened on 8/15/69, at the Geary Theatre, San Francisco. DANCES RE-STAGED BY: Jerry Combs; MUSICAL DIRECTOR: Steve Gillette. *Cast:* CLAUDE: Eron Tabor; BERGER: Bruce Hyde, *Roger Cruz, Philip Thomas*.

THE THIRD TOUR. Opened on 10/13/69, at the Shubert Theatre, Chicago. PRESENTED BY Michael Butler & Paul Butler. *Cast:* CLAUDE: Ken Griffin; BERGER: Robert Golden, *Robert DeLano*; ALSO WITH: Stan Shaw, Valerie Williams, Joe Mantegna.

THE FOURTH TOUR. Opened on 12/3/69, in Las Vegas. *Cast:* CLAUDE: Lyle Kang; BERGER: James Benton.

THE FIFTH TOUR. Opened on 1/12/70, at the Royal Alexandra Theatre, Toronto. PRESENTED BY Michael Butler, in association with Glen Warren Productions; DANCES RE-STAGED BY: Natalie Mosco; MUSICAL DIRECTOR: George Taros. *Cast:* CLAUDE: Doug Barnes, *Clint Ryan*; BERGER: Robin White, *Kid Carson*; SHEILA: Gale Garnett; CRISSY: Rachel Jacobson.

THE SIXTH TOUR. This tour ran into problems. On 2/22/70 it had its first previews at the Wilbur Theatre, Boston. *Cast:* CLAUDE: Paul Fitzgerald; BERGER: Richard Spiegel. The censor was immediately outraged, and on 4/9/70 this tour was banned in Boston by the courts. The producers were told they could continue if they dropped the nudity. They refused and, despite an advance sale of $600,000, closed the show and draped the theatre in black. However, on 5/23/70 the U.S. Supreme Court overturned the Massachusetts Court ruling. The sixth tour reopened on 3/9/71, at the Hanna Theatre, Cleveland, and closed on 9/3/72, in Latham, NY. RE-STAGED BY: Robert Farley; MUSICAL DIRECTOR: Fred Waring Jr. *Cast:* CLAUDE: Del Cunningham & John Jerzog (alternating), *William Swiggard & John David Yarborough*; BERGER: Richard Almack (*Rick Spiegel*) & Doug Rowell (alternating); HUD: *Stan Shaw*; VARIOUS ROLES: Meat Loaf.

THE SEVENTH TOUR. Opened on 4/18/70, at the Moore Theatre,

Seattle. PRESENTED BY Michael Butler, in association with William D. Owens & H.H. Burke Garrett; DIRECTOR: Joe Donovan; CHOREOGRAPHER: Rhonda Oglesby. *Cast:* CLAUDE: Skip Bowe; BERGER: Eric.

THE EIGHTH TOUR. Opened in 6/70, at the Vest Pocket Theatre, Detroit. DIRECTOR: Armand Coullet; CHOREOGRAPHER: Rhonda Oglesby; MUSICAL DIRECTOR: Dennis Smith. *Cast:* CLAUDE: David Patrick Kelly; BERGER: Michael Campbell; ALSO WITH: Meat Loaf.

THE NINTH TOUR. Opened on 1/7/71, at the University Auditorium, Kalamazoo. PRESENTED BY R. Robert Lussier; DIRECTOR: Robert Farley; MUSICAL DIRECTOR: Fred Waring Jr. *Cast:* CLAUDE: Claude Carlsen; BERGER: Richard Spiegel; SHEILA: Candice Earley; HUD: Michael Rhone.

283. *Hair (Broadway revival)*

Before Broadway. Randall Easterbrook replaced B.G. Gibson, who had replaced David Patrick Kelly; Michael Hoit replaced Doug Katsaros; Alaina Reed replaced Trudi Perkins as Dionne; Eva Charney replaced Trudi Perkins as one of the Fathers; as Jeanie only, Iris Rosenkrantz replaced Annie Golden (who went to act in the film version); Kristen Vigard replaced Soni Moreno. Peter Gallagher was in the ensemble, and was understudy for Claude, but left during previews to replace Treat Williams in *Grease*.

The Broadway Run. BILTMORE THEATRE, 10/5/77–11/6/77. 79 previews. 43 PERFORMANCES. PRESENTED BY Michael Butler, in association with K.H. Nezhad; MUSIC: Galt MacDermot; LYRICS/BOOK: Gerome Ragni & James Rado; DIRECTOR: Tom O'Horgan; CHOREOGRAPHER: Julie Arenal; SETS: Robin Wagner; COSTUMES: Nancy Potts; LIGHTING: Jules Fisher; SOUND: Abe Jacob; MUSICAL SUPERVISOR: Earl Shendell; MUSICAL DIRECTOR/VOCAL ARRANGEMENTS: Denzil A. Miller Jr.; MUSICAL ARRANGEMENTS: Galt MacDermot; VOCAL DIRECTOR: Patrick Flynn; PRESS: Gifford/Wallace; CASTING: Mary Jo Slater; GENERAL MANAGER: Eugene V. Wolsk; COMPANY MANAGER: Steven Suskin; PRODUCTION STAGE MANAGER: J. Galen McKinley; STAGE MANAGER: Seth M.M. Sternberg; ASSISTANT STAGE MANAGER: Eva Charney. *Cast:* CLAUDE HOOPER BUKOWSKI: Randall Easterbrook; BERGER: Michael Hoit; WOOF: Scott Thornton; HUD: Cleavant Derricks; SHEILA: Ellen Foley; JEANIE: Iris Rosenkrantz; DIONNE: Alaina Reed; CRISSY: Kristen Vigard; SHOPPING CART LADY: Michael Leslie; MOTHERS: Annie Golden, Louis Mattioli, Perry Arthur; FATHERS: James Rich, Eva Charney, Martha Wingate; PRINCIPALS: Carl Woerner, Michael Leslie, Linda Myers; TOURIST COUPLE: Perry Arthur & Carl Woerner; YOUNG RECRUIT: Perry Arthur; GENERAL GRANT: Carl Woerner; ABRAHAM LINCOLN: Linda Myers; SERGEANT: Byron Utley; PARENTS: Lori Wagner & James Rich; TRIBE: Perry Arthur, Emily Bindiger, Paul Binotto, Eva Charney, Loretta Devine, Doug Katsaros, Michael Leslie, Louis Mattioli, Linda Myers, Raymond Patterson, James Rich, James Sbano, Deborah Van Valkenburgh, Lori Wagner, Doug Wall, Martha Wingate, Carl Woerner, Charlaine Woodard. *Standby:* Crissy: Soni Moreno. *Understudies:* Claude: Scott Thornton; Berger: Doug Katsaros; Sheila: Deborah Van Valkenburgh; Hud: Byron Utley; Dionne: Charlaine Woodard; Woof: James Rich. *Musicians:* ELECTRIC KEYBOARD: Denzil A. Miller Jr. [Kirk Nurock before Broadway]; BASS: Jerry Jemmott; TRUMPETS: Chris Alpert & Richard Hurwitz; BARITONE SAX/REEDS: Danny Bank; ELECTRIC GUITARS: Brian Koonin & Billy Butler; RHYTHM GUITAR: Billy Butler; DRUMS: Rick Cutler; PERCUSSION/HAND DRUMS: Muhammad Abdullah.

Steven Suskin was in 7 of the Broadway previews. This time *Hair* was absolutely panned. It was outdated, and a mistake.

After Broadway. THE MOVIE. 1979. DIRECTOR: Milos Forman; WRITER: Michael Weller. It added a strong plot. *Cast:* Treat Williams, John Savage, Beverly D'Angelo, Annie Golden.

25TH-ANNIVERSARY REVIVAL. OLD VIC THEATRE, London, 1993. *Cast:* GEORGE BERGER: Paul Hipp. *Hair* had long, long passed its time.

NEW FRENCH VERSION. THEATRE MOGADOR, Paris, 3/5/98–4/30/98. PRESENTED BY Jacques Marouani; ADAPTED LYRICS & BOOK: Joelle Angeli; DIRECTOR: Jacques Rosny. Mr. Marouani, the producer, was a cousin of Gilbert Marouani, who had produced the 1969 Paris run. "Good Morning Starshine" became "Bonjour lune d'argent".

TOURING REVIVAL. Opened on 2/22/94, at the Morris A. Mechanic

Theatre, Baltimore. DIRECTOR: James Rado; CHOREOGRAPHER: Joe Donovan; SETS/LIGHTING: Rick Belzer; COSTUMES: Warren Morrill; MUSICAL DIRECTOR: Keith Thompson. This new production had three new songs. *Cast:* CLAUDE: Luther Creek; BERGER: Kent Dalian; WOOF: Sean Jenness; DIONNE: Catrice Joseph.

In 11/99 there was talk of a tour, followed by a New York revival at Madison Square Garden, with Alanis Morisette and Lenny Kravitz, but it never happened.

CITY CENTER, NYC, 5/3/01–5/7/01. 6 PERFORMANCES. Part of the *Encores!* series. This production used material from the 1967 Off Broadway production and the 1968 Broadway production. DIRECTOR/CHOREOGRAPHER: Kathleen Marshall; SETS: John Lee Beatty; COSTUMES: Martin Pakledinaz; LIGHTING: Ken Billington; SOUND: Scott Lehrer. *Cast:* CLAUDE: Luther Creek; BERGER: Tom Plotkin; WOOF: Kevin Cahoon; HUD: Michael McElroy; SHEILA: Idina Menzel; JEANIE: Miriam Shor; DIONNE: Brandi Chavonne Massey; CRISSY: Jessica-Snow Wilson; GRANT: Jesse Tyler Ferguson. There was talk of going to Broadway in 2001–02, but by 6/01 those plans were canceled.

NATIONAL TOURING REVIVAL. Opened in 9/03, at the Wadsworth Theatre, Los Angeles. PRESENTED BY Michael Butler & Bob Emmer; DIRECTOR: Scott Schwartz. This tour was capitalized at $3 million.

THEATRE UNDER THE STARS (TUTS) Houston, 9/9/04–9/26/04. DIRECTOR: Philip Wm McKinley. *Cast:* BERGER: Asa Somers.

NEW AMSTERDAM THEATRE, Broadway, 9/20/04. One-performance, all-star concert, in aid of the Actors' Fund of America. This was their fourth annual benefit concert. It brought in half a million dollars. PRODUCER/MUSICAL DIRECTOR: Seth Rudetsky; DIRECTORS: Dev Janki & Christopher Gattelli. *Cast:* Shoshana Bean, Laura Benanti, Stephen Bienskie, Kathy Brier, Paul Castree, Gavin Creel, Bobby Daye, Aisha de Haas, Darius de Haas, Raul Esparza, Harvey Fierstein, Hunter Foster, Ana Gasteyer, Annie Golden, Ann Harada, Jennifer Hudson, Audrey Klinger, Anika Larsen, Norm Lewis, Michael McKean, Idina Menzel, Julia Murney, Adam Pascal, Billy Porter, Jai Rodriguez, RuPaul, Christopher Sieber, John Tartaglia, Lillias White.

284. *Hairpin Harmony*

Musical farce, set in Lucy's California home, summer afternoon and evening. Baby food manufacturer Howard is looking for a radio feature to advertise his product. Bill, a young press agent, tries to sell him an all-girl 16-member orchestra and its singer, Reenie. Howard refuses to buy until he finds Heller can imitate a baby's voice. Reenie is having a romance with Chet. The Clawson Triplets added a touch of novelty.

Before Broadway. The show's only set was borrowed from *Pie in the Sky*, that ran two years earlier. There were several cast-changes and re-writes during tryouts in Bridgeport, Conn., while the show postponed its opening night several times. The role of the Keeper (played by Scott Moore) was replaced by the Inspector (played by David Leonard). Jean Moore was replaced by Margaret Irving, and Fanette Stalle by Irene Corlett. The third saxophonist, Muriel Burns, was dropped. Director Carl Randall was replaced a week before it opened on Broadway.

The Broadway Run. NATIONAL THEATRE, 10/1/43–10/2/43. 3 PERFORMANCES. PRESENTED BY Harold Orlob; MUSIC/LYRICS/BOOK: Harold Orlob; ADDITIONAL DIALOGUE: Don Witty; DIRECTOR: Dora Maugham; SETS: Donald Oenslager; COSTUMES: Mahieu; LIGHTING: Jeanette Hackett; ORCHESTRATIONS: Arthur Norris; PRESS: Arthur J. Levy; PRODUCTION SUPERVISOR: Mack Hilliard. *Cast:* BILL HELLER: Lennie Kent (2); HOWARD SWIFT: Carlyle Blackwell (1); CHET WARREN: Gil Johnson (4); REENIE FRANTON: Maureen Cannon (3); JACKIE STEVENS: Teri Keane; EVELYN: Karen Conrad; BETTY: Gay Gaynor; JUNE: Barbara Clawson; RUTH: Doris Clawson; SUE: Dorothy Clawson; COBALT & LOOSEKNIT: Smiles & Smiles (a black duo); RACEY CORDAY: Irene Corlett; REV. DR. BROWN: Don Valentine; CAPTAIN BUDDY ROC: Ving Merlin; MRS. LUCY WARREN: Margaret Irving; INSPECTOR: David Leonard; STATE TROOPER: Clair Kramer; CHORUS: *The Hairpin Harmonettes:* PIANO: Rochelle Kritchmer; VIOLINS: Esther Shure & Julia Goldman; VIOLA: Esther Rabiroff; HARP/VIOLA: Suzanne Sprecher; BASS:

Thelma Fitch; DRUMS: Julia Goldman; SAXES: Nadine Winstead & L'Ana Hyams; TRUMPETS: Leona May Smith & Elvira Rohl; TROMBONES: Elaine Fitch. **Act I:** Opening (Hairpin Harmonettes), "Hairpin Harmony" (Reenie & Clawson Triplets), "You're the Reason" (Chet, Reenie, Clawson Triplets, Smiles & Smiles), "What-a-Ya-Say" (Bill, Chet, Reenie, Jackie, Clawson Triplets), "I'm Tickled Pink" (Jackie & Clawson Triplets), "I'm a Butter Hoarder" (Chet), "Without a Sponsor" (Bill & Clawson Triplets) (danced by Evelyn), Tango (Evelyn). **Act II:** Trumpet Solo (Leona May Smith), "You're the Reason" (reprise) (violin solo) (Buddy), Dance (Evelyn), "I Can Be Like Grandpa" (Chet & Reenie), "Without a Sponsor" (reprise) (Reenie & Chet), "That's My Approach to Love" (Jackie & Bill), Violin Solo (Buddy), "Piccaninny Pie" (Smiles & Smiles), "That's My Approach to Love" (reprise) (Jackie, Bill, Clawson Triplets), "What Do the Neighbors Say?" (Reenie, Jackie, Evelyn, Betty, Clawson Triplets), "You're the Reason" (reprise) (Entire Company).

Reviews were terrible, and it was roundly panned. The humor was too offensive for its time, and people left the theatre.

285. *Hairspray*

Set in 1962 in Baltimore. *The Corny Collins Show*, a dance revue, attracts girls. The girl with the biggest hair and best dance moves can become locally famous. Plain (and rather large) Tracy (played in the movie by Ricki Lake) beats reigning queen Amber and now Amber's parents want revenge. Tracy's parents, Edna and Wilbur (played in the movie by Divine & Jerry Stiller) are there to make sure she stays queen. Link is popular and handsome. He falls for Tracy. Maybelle's son Seaweed (who is black) romances Penny (who is white and Tracy's best friend). Motormouth Maybelle is dj on the "Negro Day" segment of *The Corny Collins Show*. The triple role of Prudy/Matron/Gym teacher is also known as The Female Authority Figure, and the multiple role of Spritzer/Pinky/Principal/Guard is also known as The Male Authority Figure.

Before Broadway. Act I was finished by the summer of 2000, when it had its first reading at the New York Theatre Workshop. Kerry Butler was a featured actor. They began casting in Baltimore on 12/6/01. As of that month Jack O'Brien became the new director (replacing Rob Marshall), and a Broadway opening date of 8/02 was announced. On 2/7/02 Marissa Jaret Winokur, Harvey Fierstein and Kerry Butler were announced in their roles. Mr. Fierstein had always been the first choice for the role of Tracy's mother. On 4/30/02 the rest of the cast was announced. On 5/6/02 James Carpinello, who was playing Link, dropped out, and was replaced by his understudy Matthew Morrison. There was a press preview on 5/8/02. Tryouts began at Seattle's Fifth Avenue Theatre on 6/12/02 (previews from 5/30), and got rave reviews, and had only a few minor changes made to it. Ensemble member Linda Hart was promoted to the role of Velma, and John Hill came in as a new ensemble member. The Neil Simon Theatre, on Broadway, expanded its seating to accommodate the expected audience.

The Broadway Run. NEIL SIMON THEATRE, 8/15/02–. 31 previews from 7/18/02. PRESENTED BY Margo Lion, Adam Epstein, The Baruch — Viertel — Routh — Frankel Group, James D. Stern & Douglas L. Meyer, Rick Steiner & Frederic H. Mayerson, SEL & GFO, and New Line Cinema, in association with Clear Channel Entertainment, Allan S. Gordon & Elan V. McAllister, Dede Harris & Kardana — Swinsky Productions, and John & Bonnie Osher; MUSIC/MUSICAL ARRANGEMENTS: Marc Shaiman; LYRICS: Scott Wittman & Marc Shaiman; BOOK: Mark O'Donnell & Thomas Meehan; BASED ON John Waters' 1988 New Line Cinema movie of the same name, which was inspired by the real-life Baltimore TV dance show *The Buddy Deane Show* (1957–64; Mr. Deane died on 7/16/03, aged 78); DIRECTOR: Jack O'Brien; CHOREOGRAPHER: Jerry Mitchell; SETS: David Rockwell; COSTUMES: William Ivey Long; LIGHTING: Kenneth Posner; SOUND: Steve Canyon Kennedy; MUSICAL DIRECTOR: Lon Hoyt; ORCHESTRATIONS: Harold Wheeler; CAST RECORDING on Sony Classical, recorded on 6/30/02 and released in 8/13; PRESS: Richard Kornberg & Don Summa of Richard Kornberg & Associates; CASTING: Bernard Telsey; GENERAL MANAGEMENT: Richard

Frankel Productions/Laura Green; COMPANY MANAGER: Marc Borsak; PRODUCTION STAGE MANAGER: Steven Beckler, *Frank Lombardi*; STAGE MANAGER: J. Philip Bassett; ASSISTANT STAGE MANAGER: Marisha Ploski. **Cast:** TRACY TURNBLAD: Marissa Jaret Winokur (1), *Katy Grenfell* (stood in at various times, notably 1/29/03–1/30/03, and 2/1/03–2/6/03, during Miss Winokur's injury), *Shoshana Bean* (stood in 1/31/03), *Marissa Jaret Winokur* (2/7/03–8/10/03), *Kathy Brier* (8/12/03–5/2/04), *Carly Jibson* (from 5/4/04); TV ANNOUNCER VOICE: John Waters (recorded—uncredited); CORNY COLLINS: Clarke Thorell (until 1/11/04), *Jonathan Dokuchitz* (from 1/13/04); AMBER VON TUSSLE: Laura Bell Bundy (until 7/13/03), *Tracy Jai Edwards* (from 7/15/03), *Jordan Ballard* (from 10/5/04); BRAD: Peter Matthew Smith; TAMMY: Hollie Howard, *Heather Lindell*; FENDER: John Hill (until 6/29/03), *John Jeffrey Martin*; BRENDA: Jennifer Gambatese, *Michelle Kittrell, Alli Mauzey*; SKETCH: Adam Fleming, *Serge Kushnier* (from 2/20/04); SHELLY: Shoshana Bean, *Leslie Kritzer* (from 4/21/04); IQ: Todd Michel Smith; LOU ANN: Katharine Leonard; LINK LARKIN: Matthew Morrison (until 1/11/04), *Richard H. Blake* (from 1/13/04); PRUDY PINGLETON: Jackie Hoffman (until 10/14/04), *Leslie Kritzer & Liz Larsen* (stood in), *Julie Halston*; EDNA TURNBLAD: Harvey Fierstein (2) (until 5/2/04), *Michael McKean* (5/4/04–10/3/04), *Bruce Vilanch* (from 10/5/04); PENNY PINGLETON: Kerry Butler (until 7/13/03), *Jennifer Gambatese* (7/15/03–4/11/04), *Brooke Tansley* (4/13/04), *Jennifer Gambatese* (from 6/15/04); VELMA VON TUSSLE: Linda Hart (until 7/13/03), *Liz Larsen* (during Miss Hart's vacation), *Barbara Walsh* (from 7/15/03); HARRIMAN F. SPRITZER: Joel Vig; WILBUR TURNBLAD: Dick Latessa, *Peter Scolari* (10/28/03–11/2/03 during Mr. Latessa's vacation), *Dick Latessa* (from 11/4/03), *Todd Susman* (during Mr. Latessa's vacation), *Dick Latessa* (until 8/1/04), *Peter Scolari* (from 8/3/04), *Todd Susman* (from 10/5/04); PRINCIPAL: Joel Vig; SEAWEED J. STUBBS: Corey Reynolds (until 7/13/03), *Chester Gregory II* (from 7/15/03); DUANE: Eric Anthony, *Tyrick Wiltez Jones*; GILBERT: Eric Dysart; LORRAINE: Danielle Lee Greaves; THAD: Rashad Naylor, *Tyrick Wiltez Jones*; THE DYNAMITES: Kamilah Martin, Judine Richard, Shayna Steele, *Racquel Roberts, Tracee Beazer*; MR. PINKY: Joel Vig; GYM TEACHER: Jackie Hoffman (until 10/14/04), *Leslie Kritzer & Liz Larsen* (stood in), *Julie Halston*; LITTLE INEZ: Danelle Eugenia Wilson (until 7/15/03), *Aja Maria Johnson* (from 7/19/03); MOTORMOUTH MAYBELLE: Mary Bond Davis; MATRON: Jackie Hoffman (until 10/14/04), *Leslie Kritzer & Liz Larsen* (stood in), *Julie Halston*; GUARD: Joel Vig; BAND: GUITAR: Matthew Morrison; KEYBOARDS: Linda Hart; GLOCKENSPIEL: Joel Vig; HARMONICA: Kerry Butler; DENIZENS OF BALTIMORE: Eric Anthony, Shoshana Bean, Eric Dysart, Adam Fleming, Jennifer Gambatese (*Alli Mauzey*), Danielle Lee Greaves, John Hill (*John Jeffrey Martin*), Jackie Hoffman, Hollie Howard, Katharine Leonard, Kamilah Martin, Rashad Naylor, Judine Richard, Peter Matthew Smith, Todd Michel Smith, Shayna Steele, Joel Vig, *Racquel Roberts*. **Understudies**: Seaweed: Eric Anthony & Eric Dysart; Tracy: Shoshana Bean & Katy Grenfell, *Kathy Brier, Shannon Durig*; Velma: Shoshana Bean, Jackie Hoffman (*Julie Halston*), Liz Larsen; Link: Adam Fleming & John Hill, *Serge Kushnier, John Jeffrey Martin*; Penny: Jenn Gambatese & Hollie Howard, *Brooke Tansley*; Motormouth: Danielle Lee Greaves & Kamilah Martin, *Tracee Beazer*; Edna: David Greenspan & Joel Vig, *J.P. Dougherty*; Wilbur: David Greenspan & Joel Vig; Corny: John Hill & Peter Matthew Smith, *John Jeffrey Martin*; Amber: Hollie Howard & Katharine Leonard, *Brooke Tansley*; Inez: Judine Richard & Shayna Steele; Gym Teacher/Matron: Shoshana Bean, *Danielle Lee Greaves, Liz Larsen*; Prudy: Shoshana Bean & Liz Larsen; Dynamites: *Denosh Bennett, Danielle Lee Greaves, Brooke Tansley, Nicole Powell, Rashad Naylor*; Spritzer/Guard/Pinky/Principal: *J.P. Dougherty & Peter Matthew Smith*. **Swings**: Joshua Bergasse, Greg Graham, Brooke Tansley, *Denosh Bennett, Michelle Kittrell, Abdul Latif, Michael Langoria, Rusty Mowery, Nicole Powell*. **Orchestra:** GUITARS: David Spinozza & Peter Calo; KEYBOARDS: Lon Hoyt, Keith Cotton, Seth Farber; ELECTRIC BASS: Francisco Centeno; DRUMS: Clint de Ganon; PERCUSSION: Walter "Wally" Usiatynski; REEDS: David Marin & Dave Riekenberg; TRUMPETS: Danny Cahn & Birch Johnson; VIOLINS: Rob Shaw & Carol Pool; CELLO: Sarah Hewitt Roth. ***Act I: Prologue*** "Good Morning, Baltimore" (Tracy & Company); ***Scene 1*** TV Station WZZT & Turnblad home: "The Nicest Kids in Town" (Corny & Council Members); ***Scene 2*** At the Vanities: "Mama, I'm a Big Girl Now" (Edna & Tracy, Velma & Amber, Penny & Prudy); ***Scene 3*** TV Station WZZT: "I Can Hear

the Bells" (Tracy), "(The Legend of) Miss Baltimore Crabs" (Velma & Council Members) [the orig number here was "Velma's Cha-Cha"]; ***Scene 4*** Detention; ***Scene 5*** Patterson Park High School gymnasium: "The Madison" (dance) (Corny & Company); ***Scene 6*** WZZT & Turnblad home: "The Nicest Kids in Town" (reprise) (Corny & Council Members), "Positivity" (Wilbur, to Tracy) [cut for Broadway], "The New Girl in Town" (Corny) [cut for Broadway], "It Takes Two" (Link & Tracy); ***Scene 7*** Turnblad home & streets of Baltimore: "Miss Baltimore Crabs" (reprise) (Tracy) [cut for Broadway] [the original number here was "Velma's Cha-cha" (reprise)], "Welcome to the 60s" (Tracy, Edna, Dynamites, Company); ***Scene 8*** Patterson Park playground: "Run and Tell That" (Seaweed); ***Scene 9*** Motormouth Maybelle's record shop: "Run and Tell That" (reprise) (Seaweed, Inez, Company), "Big, Blonde, and Beautiful" (Motormouth, Inez, Tracy, Edna, Wilbur). ***Act II: Scene 1*** Baltimore Women's House of Detention: "The Big Dollhouse" (Women), "Good Morning, Baltimore" (reprise) (Tracy); ***Scene 2*** The Har-De-Har Hut: "(You're) Timeless (to Me)" (Wilbur & Edna); ***Scene 3*** Tracy's jail cell & Penny's bedroom: "Without Love" (Link, Tracy, Seaweed, Penny); ***Scene 4*** Motormouth Maybelle's record shop: "I Know Where I've Been" (Motormouth & Company); ***Scene 5*** The Baltimore Eventorium: "(It's) Hairspray" (Corny & Council Members), "Cooties" (Amber & Council Members), "You Can't Stop the Beat" (Tracy, Link, Penny, Seaweed, Edna, Wilbur, Motormouth, Company).

The show opened to a $12 million advance sale, and took in $1.7 million on its first day, and got good reviews. On 1/29/03 Marissa Jaret Winokur pulled a calf muscle during the Act I number "Mama, I'm a Big Girl Now." After a brief halt she continued for several scenes before bowing out. Katy Grenfell, her understudy, jumped in during the reprise of "The Nicest Kids in Town," and for the next several days she and Shoshana Bean stood in. By early May 2003 it had returned its entire $10.5 million investment. It won Tonys for musical, score, book, direction of a musical, costumes, and for Marissa Jaret Winokur, Harvey Fierstein and Dick Latessa. It was also nominated for choreography, sets, lighting, orchestrations, and for Corey Reynolds. It missed the performance on 8/14/03 due to the New York power blackout. By very early 2004 rumors were that Michael McKean would take over from Harvey Fierstein as Edna, but these rumors proved first untrue, then true. Julie Halston was meant to take over as Prudy from 11/5/04, but for unknown reasons this was delayed.

After Broadway. TOUR. Auditions began on 9/20/02, and rehearsals from 7/28/03 in Manhattan. The tour was launched, appropriately, at the Morris Mechanic Theatre, Baltimore, on 9/9/03. It had the same basic crew as for Broadway. **Cast**: EDNA: Bruce Vilanch (until 7/28/04), *John Pinette* (from 9/7/04); TRACY: Carly Jibson (until 4/11/04), *Keala Settle* (from 4/13/04), *Marissa Jaret Winokur* (7/20/04–9/5/04, while the tour was in Los Angeles); AMBER: Jordan Ballard, *Worth Williams*; PRUDY/MATRON/GYM TEACHER: Joanna Glushak; CORNY: Troy Britton Johnson; SEAWEED: Terron Brooks, Alan Mingo Jr.; VELMA: Susan Cella; MOTORMOUTH: Charlotte Crossley; PENNY: Sandra DeNise, *Chandra Lee Schwartz*; LINK: Austin Miller, *Matthew Morrison* [from 9/25/04; he was scheduled in until 10/24/04, but left early to film *Once Upon a Mattress*]; SPRITZER/PINKY/PRINCIPAL/GUARD: Blake Hammond, *Kenny Morris*; WILBUR: Todd Susman, *Stephen DeRosa*; INEZ: Kianna Underwood, *Shannon Antalan*. **Standby**: Tracy: Keala Settle.

PRINCESS OF WALES THEATRE, Toronto, 5/5/04–11/28/04. Previews from 4/8/04. 264 PERFORMANCES. PRESENTED BY David & Ed Mirvish. **Cast**: TRACY: Vanessa Olivarez; WILBUR: Tom Rooney; EDNA: Jay Brazeau; LINK: Michael Torontow; VELMA: Susan Henley; AMBER: Tara Macri; MOTORMOUTH: Fran Jaye; SEAWEED: Matthew Morgan; CORNY: Paul McQuillan; PENNY: Jennifer Stewart; INEZ: Shennell Campbell.

CAMBRIDGE THEATRE, London, 10/05. Mostly British cast. PRESENTED BY Barry & Fran Weissler, and Clear Channel Entertainment; DIRECTOR: Jack O'Brien; CHOREOGRAPHER: Jerry Mitchell.

LUXOR, Las Vegas, 11/05. 90 minute tab version, no intermission. Presented by Michael Gill & Myron Martin.

THE MOVIE. That is, the movie of the hit stage musical. Planned for 2006. PRODUCERS: Craig Zadan & Neil Meron; SCREENWRITER: Leslie Dixon (replaced Mark O'Donnell and Thomas Meehan); DIRECTOR: Jack O'Brien; CHOREOGRAPHER: Jerry Mitchell. There was early talk of Marissa Jaret Winokur reprising her role of Tracy, but this was just rumor. By 12/04 Harvey Weinstein was the only one of the original cast likely to reprise his role for the film, but by 2/05 even that was gone—John Travolta was the new runner for that role. By 3/05 Billy Crystal was being touted as Wilbur and Aretha Franklin as Motormouth.

286. *Half a Sixpence*

Arthur Kipps is a lively young Cockney apprentice at Shalford's Drapery Emporium in Folkestone, England, at the turn of the 20th century. Ann is his girlfriend, who works as a maid. He gives her half of a sixpence as token of his love. He is forced to enroll in evening class for workers, and falls for his teacher, Helen, but is discouraged by the difference in their social standings. However, he comes into a large inheritance, asks Helen to marry him, she agrees, but he is disheartened by her snobbishness, and returns to Ann, who marries him. However, Ann can't adjust to being rich. Young Walsingham, Helen's brother, swindles him and Kipps and Ann open up a small bookshop, where they find true happiness among their class.

Before Broadway. *Half a Sixpence*, an intimate musical starring (and written for) famous British comedian Tommy Steele, first tried out at the WIMBLEDON THEATRE, on the outskirts of London, from 3/9/63. Then it moved to the West End, to the CAMBRIDGE THEATRE, 3/21/63–10/31/64. 679 PERFORMANCES. PRESENTED BY Harold Fielding; MUSIC/ LYRICS: David Heneker; BOOK: Beverley Cross; BASED ON the 1905 novel *Kipps*, by H.G. Wells; DIRECTOR: John Dexter; CHOREOGRAPHER: Edmund Balin; SETS/COSTUMES: Loudon Sainthill; MUSICAL DIRECTOR: Kenneth Alwyn; DANCE MUSIC ARRANGEMENTS & ORCHESTRATIONS/COMPOSER OF OPENING BALLET MUSIC: Robert Prince; CAST RECORDING on Deram. *Cast:* KIPPS: Tommy Steele; ANN: Marti Webb; HELEN: Anna Barry; VICTORIA: Cheryl Kennedy; CHITTERLOW: James Grout; PEARCE: Anthony Valentine; SHALFORD: Arthur Brough; SID: John Bull; YOUNG WALSINGHAM: Ian White.

It was altered and expanded in the American version, particularly the dance music arrangements (Robert Prince did revisions to his own arrangements). Word Baker (of *The Fantasticks*) was originally hired to direct, but was replaced by Gene Saks in his Broadway debut, just three days before the out-of-town tryouts, which took place from 3/8/65, at the Colonial Theatre, Boston. Previews from 3/6/65. Then it ran for 3 weeks at the O'Keefe, Toronto, from 3/30/65. John Cleese left the Off Broadway revue *Cambridge Circus* so he could be in *Half a Sixpence*. Charlotte Rae was replaced as Mrs. Walsingham before Broadway by Ann Shoemaker. April Shawhan was replaced as Flo by Michele Hardy, who had been playing Kate, and Michele Hardy was replaced by Louise Quick.

The Broadway Run. BROADHURST THEATRE, 4/25/65–7/16/66. 4 previews from 4/15/65. 512 PERFORMANCES. PRESENTED BY Allen-Hodgdon (Lewis Allen & Dana Hodgdon), Stevens Productions (Roger L. Stevens), Harold Fielding, and Harry Rigby (sometimes billed, sometimes not); ORIGINAL MUSIC & LYRICS: David Heneker: LYRICS REVISED FOR BROADWAY BY: Michael Brown; ORIGINAL BOOK: Beverley Cross; BOOK REVISED FOR BROADWAY BY: Hugh Walker; BASED ON the 1905 novel *Kipps*, by H.G. Wells; DIRECTOR: Gene Saks; CHOREOGRAPHER: Onna White; ASSISTANT CHOREOGRAPHER: Tom Panko; SETS/COSTUMES: Loudon Sainthill; LIGHTING: Jules Fisher; MUSICAL DIRECTOR: Stanley Lebowsky; ORCHESTRATIONS: Jim Tyler; REVISED DANCE MUSIC ARRANGEMENTS: Robert Prince; VOCAL ARRANGEMENTS: Buster Davis; CAST RECORDING on RCA Victor; PRESS: Bill Doll & Company; CASTING: Terry Fay; GENERAL MANAGER: Victor Samrock; COMPANY MANAGER: Ben Rosenberg; PRODUCTION STAGE MANAGER: Terence Little, *Joe Calvan* (by 65–66); STAGE MANAGER: Ernest Austin; ASSISTANT STAGE MANAGER: William Larsen, *Stanley Simmonds* (by 65–66). *Cast:* ARTHUR KIPPS: Tommy Steele (1) ☆, *Tony Tanner* (from 3/21/66), *Joel Grey* (during Mr. Tanner's vacation), *Dick Kallman* (from 7/4/66); SID PORNICK: Will MacKenzie (7), *Carl Esser*; BUGGINS: Norman Allen (8); PEARCE: Grover Dale (6), *Larry Roquemore*; CARSHOT: William Larsen,

Stanley Simmonds; FLO: Michele Hardy; EMMA: Reby Howells; KATE: Louise Quick; VICTORIA: Sally Lee; MR. SHALFORD: Mercer McLeod; MRS. WALSINGHAM: Ann Shoemaker, *Jean Cameron*; MRS. BOTTING: Trescott Ripley; ANN PORNICK: Polly James (5), *Rosanna Huffman, Anne Rogers* (from 7/4/66); YOUNG WALSINGHAM: John Cleese (9), *Remak Ramsay*; HELEN WALSINGHAM: Carrie Nye (4), *Gwyda DonHowe*; CHITTERLOW: James Grout (3), *Robert Urquhart, William Larsen*; LAURA: Eleanore Treiber; GIRL STUDENT: Rosanna Huffman, *Jeanne Shea*; BOY STUDENT: Sterling Clark, *Patrick Cummings, Robert Gorman*; PHOTOGRAPHER: Sean Allen; PHOTOGRAPHER'S ASSISTANT: Robert Gorman; 1ST REPORTER: Reid Klein, *Fred Cline*; 2ND REPORTER: Fred Cline, *Jack Knapp*; GWENDOLIN: Ann Rachel, *Henrietta Valor*; MR. WALSINGHAM: Glenn Kezer; DANCERS: Diane Blair, Sterling Clark (*Patrick Cummings*), Lynn Fields (gone by 65–66), Robert Karl (*Bert Michaels*), Alan Peterson, Sally Ransone, Bill Stanton (gone by 65–66), Ron Schwinn, *Kathleen Doherty, Ben Gillespie, Loren Hightower, Alex MacKay, Fabian Stewart, Vernon Wendorf, Denise Winston*; SINGERS: Sean Allen, Fred Cline, Robert Gorman, Rosanna Huffman (*Jeanne Shea*), Glenn Kezer, Reid Klein (*Darrell J. Askey*), John Knapp, Constance Moffit (*Rosalind Ammons*), Max Norman, Carol Richards (*Carol Joplin*), Ann Rachel (*Henrietta Valor*). **Standby:** Kipps: Kenneth Nelson; **Understudies:** Kipps: Grover Dale; Ann: Reby Howells, *Rosanna Huffman, Jeanne Shea*; Helen: Eleanore Treiber; Sid: Ron Schwinn; Buggins: Robert Karl, *Bert Michaels, Ron Schwinn*; Pearce: Sterling Clark, *Patrick Cummings, Sean Allen*; Carshot/Young Walsingham: Jack Knapp; Flo: Reby Howells; Victoria/Laura: Sally Ransone; Emma/Kate: Diane Blair; Shalford: William Larsen, *Stanley Simmonds*; Chitterlow: William Larsen, *Remak Ramsay*; Mrs. Botting: Constance Moffit, *Henrietta Valor*; Mrs. Walsingham: Trescott Ripley; Girl Student: Carol Richards, *Carol Joplin*; Boy Student: Bob Gorman, *Bert Michaels*. **Act I: Scene 1** The Emporium, Folkestone, England; 1900; **Scene 2** The Promenade: "All in the Cause of Economy" (Kipps, Sid, Buggins, Pearce), "Half a Sixpence" (Kipps & Ann) [a hit]; **Scene 3** The Emporium; **Scene 4** The *Hope and Anchor* bar: "Money to Burn (Buy Me a Banjo)" (Kipps, Laura, Men); **Scene 5** The street; **Scene 6** The classroom; **Scene 7** The Emporium; **Scene 8** The Promenade: "A Proper Gentleman" (Kipps, Sid, Buggins, Pearce, Shopgirls), "She's Too Far Above Me" (Kipps); **Scene 9** The old lighthouse: "If the Rain's Got to Fall" (Kipps, Sid, Buggins, Pearce, Shopgirls, Singers, Dancers); **Scene 10** The Military Canal Regatta: "The Old Military Canal" (Singers), "If the Rain's Got to Fall" (reprise) (Singers). **Act II: Scene 1** Mrs. Botting's solarium: "A Proper Gentleman" (reprise) (Kipps, Mrs. Walsingham, Helen, Mrs. Botting, Young Walsingham, Party Guests); **Scene 2** Kitchen: "Long Ago" (Kipps & Ann); **Scene 3** Photographer's studio: "Flash, Bang, Wallop!" (Kipps, Ann, Chitterlow, Mr. Shalford, Pearce, Sid, Buggins, Shopgirls, Singers) [a hit]; **Scene 4** Parlor of rented house: "I Know What I Am" (Ann); **Scene 5** The pier; **Scene 6** The building site: "The Party's on the House" (Kipps, Pearce, Sid, Buggins, Shopgirls, Singers, Dancers), "Half a Sixpence" (reprise) (Kipps & Ann); **Scene 7** The Promenade: "All in the Cause of Economy" (reprise) (Flo, Pearce, Sid, Buggins); **Scene 8** The bookshop: Finale (Entire Company).

It opened on Broadway to mostly very good reviews, especially for Onna White. It received Tony Nominations for musical, producers of a musical, composer & lyricist, book, direction of a musical, choreography, and for Tommy Steele, James Grout, and Carrie Nye. The show lost $100,000 of its original $300,000 investment, but the tours finally made the show a success.

After Broadway. TOUR. The U.S. road company opened on 7/25/66, at the Curran Theatre, San Francisco. MUSICAL DIRECTOR: Carmen Coppola. *Cast:* KIPPS: Dick Kallman; SID: Ron Schwinn; ANN: Anne Rogers, *Ann Wakefield* (from 11/28/66); CHITTERLOW: Roger C. Carmel, *William Le Massena*; LAURA: Eleanore Treiber, *Marion Fels.*

TOUR. A bus-truck touring troupe opened on 8/22/66, and closed on 3/18/67, at the Shubert Theatre, New Haven, after 104 cities. DIRECTOR: Christopher Hewett; MUSICAL DIRECTOR: Glen Clugston. *Cast:* Kenneth Nelson, Alice Cannon, Byron Webster.

THE MOVIE. 1968. DIRECTOR: George Sidney. *Cast:* KIPPS: Tommy Steele; ANN: Julia Foster; HARRY CHITTERLOW: Cyril Ritchard; HELEN: Penelope Horner; PEARCE: Grover Dale.

287. *Hallelujah, Baby!*

Traces the American black musical experience over the course of the 20th century, as personified in Georgina, a talented and determined black girl who struggles from the kitchen to celebrity and affluence (and more freedom) over a period of 60 or so years in which neither she, her doubting mother, her two lovers (one black and one white), or the other characters, age. Clem is Georgina's young man who goes from Pullman porter to black leader. Harvey is a white liberal.

Before Broadway. Originally Lena Horne was going to star, and Arthur Laurents brought it to David Merrick to produce. But Miss Horne dropped out, as did Mr. Merrick. Joseph P. Harris and Ira Bernstein then optioned it, replacing Gene Saks as director with Burt Shevelove. Pete Gennaro was hired as choreographer, and then the new producers (and Mr. Gennaro) dropped out. Helen Jacobson picked it up, and two months later dropped it. Apparently none of these producers liked the countless libretto changes Arthur Laurents was making. Then Al Selden and Hal James took it up, but couldn't raise the money. So, they took on Jane Nusbaum and Harry Rigby as co-producers, and it finally went into rehearsal. Black choreographer Kevin Carlisle was brought in. Allen Case replaced James Rado in the cast.

The Broadway Run. MARTIN BECK THEATRE, 4/26/67–1/13/68. 22 previews from 4/6/67. 293 PERFORMANCES. PRESENTED BY Albert W. Selden & Hal James, Jane C. Nusbaum & Harry Rigby; MUSIC: Jule Styne; LYRICS: Betty Comden & Adolph Green; BOOK: Arthur Laurents; DIRECTOR: Burt Shevelove; CHOREOGRAPHER: Kevin Carlisle; SETS: William & Jean Eckart; COSTUMES: Irene Sharaff; LIGHTING: Tharon Musser; MUSICAL DIRECTOR/VOCAL ARRANGEMENTS: Buster Davis; ORCHESTRATIONS: Peter Matz; DANCE ORCHESTRATIONS: Luther Henderson; CAST RECORDING on Columbia; PRESS: Merle Debuskey, Violet Welles, Faith Geer; GENERAL MANAGERS: Walter Fried & Oscar Olesen; COMPANY MANAGER: James Awe; PRODUCTION STAGE MANAGER: James Gelb; STAGE MANAGER: Ernest Austin; ASSISTANT STAGE MANAGERS: Chad Block & Frank Hamilton. *Cast:* GEORGINA: Leslie Uggams (1) ✫; MOMMA: Lillian Hayman (4); CLEM: Robert Hooks (2) ✫, *Billy Dee Williams* (from 6/26/67), *Robert Hooks* (from 10/23/67); PROVERS: Clifford Allen, Garrett Morris, Kenneth Scott, Alan Weeks; HARVEY: Allen Case (3) ✫; CAPTAIN YANKEE: Justin McDonough; CALHOUN: Lou Angel; MARY: Barbara Sharma (5); MISTER CHARLES: Frank Hamilton; MRS. CHARLES: Marilyn Cooper (6); TIP AND TAP: Winston DeWitt Hemsley (7) & Alan Weeks (8); CUTIES: Hope Clarke, Sandra Lein, Saundra McPherson; PRINCE: Bud Vest; PRINCESS: Carol Flemming; SUGAR DADDY: Darrell Notara; BOUNCER: Chad Block; MISTRESS: Marilyn Cooper (6); MASTER: Darrell Notara; DIRECTOR: Alan Peterson; ETHEL: Marilyn Cooper (6); OFFICIAL: Chad Block; BRENDA: Ann Rachel; TIMMY: Frank Hamilton; GIs: Winston DeWitt Hemsley, Kenneth Scott, Alan Weeks, Clifford Allen; BUS DRIVER: Lou Angel; DOROTHY: Marilyn Cooper (6); MAID: Hope Clarke; ENSEMBLE: Clifford Allen, Barbara Andrews, Lou Angel, Chad Block, Hope Clarke, Norma Donaldson, Carol Flemming, Nat Gales, Maria Hero, Lee Hooper, Alan Johnson, Sandra Lein, Justin McDonough, Saundra McPherson, Garrett Morris, Darrell Notara, Paul Reid Roman, Suzanne Rogers, Kenneth Scott, Ella Thompson, Bud Vest. *Standbys*: Georgina: Norma Donaldson; Momma: Alma Hubbard. *Understudies*: Clem: Nat Gales; Harvey: Justin McDonough; Mary: Suzanne Rogers. *Act I*: INTRODUCTION: Prologue (Georgina); THE 1900S: The kitchen: "Back in the Kitchen" (Momma), "My Own Morning" (Georgina), "The Slice" (Clem & Provers), "When the Weather's Better" (Clem & Georgina) [this number was cut during tryouts], "Farewell, Farewell" (Mr. Calhoun, Betty Lou, Captain Yankee, Georgina, Harvey); THE 1920S: A cabaret: "Feet Do Yo' Stuff" (Georgina, Chorines, Tip & Tap), "Watch My Dust" (Clem) [during the run this number was replaced with "You Ain't Gonna Shake Them Feathers No More" (Clem)], "Hey!" (Georgina) [this number was added during the run], "Smile, Smile" (Clem, Georgina, Momma); THE 1930S: The bread line: "Witches' Brew" ("Double Double") (Georgina, Mary, Ethel, Company), Breadline Dance (Bums), "When the Weather's Better" (reprise) (Harvey & Mary) [this reprise was

dropped during tryouts], "Another Day" (Harvey, Clem, Mary, Georgina), "I Wanted to Change Him" (Georgina) [dropped during run], "Being Good isn't Enough" (Georgina). *Act II*: THE 1940S: An Army camp; outside a night club: Dance Drill (Clem's Drill) (dance) (Tip & Tap, GIs), "Talkin' to Yourself" (Georgina, Clem, Harvey), Limbo Dance (Night Club Patrons); THE 1950S: A night club: "Hallelujah, Baby!" (Georgina, Tip & Tap), "Not Mine" (Harvey), "I Don't Know Where She Got It" (Momma, Clem, Harvey), "Now's the Time" (Georgina); THE 1960S: An apartment: "Now's the Time" (reprise) (Entire Company).

Broadway reviews were very divided. The show won Tony Awards for musical, producers of a musical, composer & lyricist, and for Leslie Uggams and Lillian Hayman; it was also nominated for direction of a musical, choreography, costumes, and for Robert Hooks.

After Broadway. TOUR. The tour re-instated the number "When the Weather's Better," as well as its reprise, both of which had been dropped during tryouts. Also added were some new numbers: "You're Welcome" (Georgina) in the 1920s, after "Watch My Dust" (which was back in, replacing "You Ain't Gonna Shake Them Feathers No More" which had replaced it on Broadway during the run); "Under the Ropes" (Dancers) as the first number in the 1950s; and "Freedom March" (Dancers) as the first song in the 1960s. Also dropped were: "Hey!," Breadline Dance, "I Wanted to Change Him," and Limbo Dance. *Cast:* GEORGINA: Kim Weston; CLEM: Adam Wade; HARVEY: Julius La Rosa; MARY: Bobbi Baird.

The York Theatre Company presented the show in concert, 10/27/00–10/29/00, as part of their *Musicals in Mufti* series. DIRECTOR: Hope Clarke. *Cast:* GEORGINA: Thursday Farrar; MOMMA: Carol Woods.

In 10/03 it came to light that Arthur Laurents and Amanda Green (Adolph Green's daughter) had been revising *Hallelujah, Baby!*, Mr. Laurents updating the book, and bringing Georgina's journey to the present day, and Miss Green adding lyrics. The cast was cut from 20 to nine. A workshop was held in 2/04. CHOREOGRAPHER: Hope Clarke. *Cast:* MOMMA: Leslie Uggams. Then it had a run both at the George Street Playhouse, in New Jersey and at the Arena Stage, in Washington, DC, in the 2004–05 season, with a small Off Broadway run to follow. GEORGE STREET PLAYHOUSE, 10/9/04–11/7/04. Previews from 10/6/04. DIRECTOR: Arthur Laurents: CHOREOGRAPHER: Hope Clarke; SETS: Jerome Sirlin; COSTUMES: Theoni V. Aldredge; LIGHTING: David Lander; SOUND: Shannon Slaton; MUSICAL DIRECTOR: David Alan Bunn. *Cast:* GEORGINA: Suzzanne Douglas; MOMMA: Ann Duquesnay; CLEM: Curtiss I'Cook; HARVEY: Stephen Zinnato; ALSO WITH: Todd Cerveris, Laurie Gamache, Randy Donaldson, Gerry McIntyre, Crystal Noelle.

288. *The Happiest Girl in the World*

An operetta, set in 400 BC, in Athens. Lysistrata leads the women of Athens to withhold sex from their husbands until they agree to stop war.

Before Broadway. Carol Lawrence was originally announced as Lysistrata. The numbers "Excuse My Laughter," "Little Old Gehenna," "Politics," "Simple Serenade," "Strategy," and "When Your Heart is Too Young" were not used. The show tried out in New Haven and Philadelphia, to good reviews. The numbers "Hup-Two-Three" and "Honestly" were cut before Broadway. The show's 3/30/61 Broadway opening was postponed.

The Broadway Run. MARTIN BECK THEATRE, 4/3/61–6/24/61. 97 PERFORMANCES. PRESENTED BY Lee Guber; MUSIC: Jacques Offenbach; LYRICS: E.Y. Harburg; BOOK: Fred Saidy & Henry Myers; ADAPTED BY Jay Gorney, from E.Y. Harburg's adaptation of *Lysistrata*, by Aristophanes, and also based on Bullfinch's stories of Greek mythology; DIRECTOR: Cyril Ritchard; CHOREOGRAPHER: Dania Krupska; SETS/LIGHTING: William & Jean Eckart; COSTUMES: Robert Fletcher; MUSICAL DIRECTOR/VOCAL ARRANGEMENTS: Robert De Cormier; ORCHESTRATIONS: Robert Russell Bennett & Hershy Kay; DANCE MUSIC ARRANGEMENTS: Gerald Alters; PRESS: Bill Doll; GENERAL MANAGER: Marvin A. Krauss; PRODUCTION STAGE MANAGER: Henri Caubisens; STAGE MANAGER:

Herman Magidson; ASSISTANT STAGE MANAGER: Renato Cibelli. **Cast:** 1ST COURIER: Alton Ruff; 2ND COURIER: Ronald B. Stratton; 1ST MINISTER: Ted Thurston; 2ND MINISTER: Don Crabtree; 3RD MINISTER: Richard Winter; CHIEF OF STATE: Cyril Ritchard; A HERALD: Don Atkinson; GENERAL KINESIAS: Bruce Yarnell; PHOEBE: Rita Metzger; LYSISTRATA: Dran Seitz (3); CAPTAIN CRITO: John Napier; JUPITER: Michael Kermoyan; JUNO: Lu Leonard; BACCHUS: Ted Thurston; MERCURY: Don Atkinson; APOLLO: John Napier; NEPTUNE: Richard Winter; APHRODITE: Joy Claussen; PLUTO: Cyril Ritchard (1); DIANA: Janice Rule (2); AMARYLLIS: Joy Claussen; MYRRHINA: Lu Leonard; A HECKLER: Cyril Ritchard; DAPHNE: Norma Donaldson; HECTOR: David Canary; ATARAXOHYMONIDES: John Wheeler; ULYSSES: Richard Winter; SERGEANT: Don Crabtree; A GAY BLADE: Cyril Ritchard; A WINE SMUGGLER: Cyril Ritchard; SENTINEL: Nancy Windsor; THE PIED PIPER OF HAMELIN: Cyril Ritchard; THEODORA: Lainie Kazan; SPARTAN WOMAN: Maura K. Wedge; A PLAYWRIGHT: Cyril Ritchard; RHODOPE: Janice Painchaud; AN AMBASSADOR: Cyril Ritchard; SINGERS: Ellen Berse, David Canary, Joy Claussen, Norma Donaldson, Lainie Kazan, Jeff Killian, Leonora Lanzilotti, Paul Merrill, Rita Metzger, Theodore Morill, Elaine Spaulding, Arthur Tookoyan, Mark Tully, Maura K. Wedge, John Wheeler, Nancy Windsor, Richard Winter; DANCERS: Bill Atkinson, Don Atkinson, Bonnie Brandon, Candace Caldwell, Grant Delaney, Victor Duntiere, Natasha Grishin, Judith Haskell, Lisa James, Gloria Kaye, Louis Kosman, Susan May, Carmen Morales, Janice Painchaud, Alton Ruff, Kenneth Scott, Ron Sequoio, Ron Stratton. **Understudies:** For Mr. Ritchard: Ted Thurston; Diana: Judith Haskell; Kinesias: Michael Kermoyan. *Act I*: *Scene 1* Office of the Chief of State of Athens; *Scene 2* The Rotunda; *Scene 3* The Agora; *Scene 4* Patio of the General's home; *Scene 5* Atop Mount Olympus; *Scene 6* Garden of the general's home; *Scene 7* The Agora; *Scene 8* The patio; *Scene 9* Lysistrata's boudoir. *Act II*: *Scene 1* The public baths; *Scene 2* Outside the Citadel; *Scene 3* The patio; *Scene 4* Steps leading to the Temple of Diana; *Scene 5* The Agora. *Act I*: "The Olympics" (ballet) (Dance Ensemble), "Cheers for the Hero" (Ensemble), "The Glory that is Greece" (Chief of State, Kinesias, Ensemble), "The Happiest Girl in the World" (Lysistrata & Kinesias), "The Greek Marine" (Chief of State, Ministers, Soldiers), "Shall We Say Farewell" (Lysistrata), "Never Be-Devil the Devil" (Pluto), "Whatever That May Be" (Diana & Gods), "Eureka" (Jupiter & Gods), Diana's Arrival in Athens (dance) (Diana), "The Oath" (Lysistrata & Women), "The Happiest Girl in the World" (reprise) (dance) (Lysistrata & Kinesias), "Diana's Transformation" (Pluto, Diana, Two Suitors), "Vive la Virtue!" (Pluto & Diana), "Adrift on a Star" (Lysistrata & Kinesias), "The Happiest Girl in the World" (reprise) (Lysistrata & Kinesias), Finale of Act I (Lysistrata, Kinesias, Ensemble). *Act II*: "That'll Be the Day" (Men), "How Soon, Oh Moon?" (Lysistrata, Sentinel, Women), "Love-Sick Serenade" (Pluto & Myrrhina), "Five Minutes of Spring" (Kinesias, Lysistrata, Diana), "The Greek Marine" (reprise) (Soldiers), "Five Minutes of Spring" (reprise) (Soldiers), "Never Trust a Virgin" (Pluto & Women) [this number also sometimes seen as "Never Trust a Woman"], "Entrance of the Courtesans" (Women), "The Pied Piper's Can-Can" (Pluto & Dancers), "Vive la Virtue!" (reprise) (Pluto & Diana), Finale (Entire Company).

Most reviews were very good. The show received a Tony nomination for choreography.

289. *Happy as Larry*

A musical fantasy. Set anywhere, any time. An Irish tailor, Larry, reminisces to his fellow workers about his grandfather, also named Larry. Grandpa had two wives, one good and one bad, but which was which was the question. With the aid of Irish witchcraft and the Three Fates the tailors are transported back in time to Grandpa's day in Dublin for an eyewitness appraisal of the wives. The tailors are also bent on revenge on the evil wife's doctor-lover who murdered the original Larry 50 years before this spring. Seamus was a mad pharmacist.

Before Broadway. Donagh MacDonagh's straight play first ran at the MERCURY THEATRE, London, 9/18/47; then at the CRITERION THEATRE, 12/16/47–1/31/48. 53 PERFORMANCES. **Cast:** LARRY: Liam Redmond; MRS. LARRY: Anna Burden; SEAMUS: Edward Byrne; DOCTOR:

Fred Johnson; 1ST TAILOR: W.A. Kelly; 2ND TAILOR: Michael Gwynn; 3RD TAILOR: Norman Tyrrell; 4TH TAILOR: Wilfred Brambell. It was Buzz Meredith's idea to turn it into a musical.

The Broadway Run. CORONET THEATRE, 1/6/50–1/7/50. 3 PERFORMANCES. PRESENTED BY Leonard Sillman; MUSIC: Mischa & Wesley Portnoff; LYRICS/BOOK: Donagh MacDonagh (based on his play of the same name); DIRECTOR: Burgess Meredith; CHOREOGRAPHER: Anna Sokolow; SETS/COSTUMES: Motley; MOBILES: Alexander Calder; MUSICAL DIRECTOR: Franz Allers; ORCHESTRATIONS: Rudolph Goehr & Charles Cooke; VOCAL ARRANGEMENTS: Herbert Greene; PRESS: Phillip Bloom, David Lipsky, Michael Gross; GENERAL MANAGER: Al Golden; MANAGERS: Monroe B. "Moe" Hack, Irving Stiber, Kenneth Utt, William Hogue. **Cast:** 1ST TAILOR: Maurice Edwards; 3RD TAILOR: Frank Milton; 4TH TAILOR: Harry Allen; 5TH TAILOR: Henry Calvin; 6TH TAILOR: William Hogue; 7TH TAILOR: Jack Warner; 8TH TAILOR: Fin Olsen; 2ND TAILOR: himself; LARRY: Burgess Meredith; THE WIDOW: Marguerite Piazza; THE GRAVEDIGGER: Ralph Hertz; MRS. LARRY: Barbara Perry; THE DOCTOR: Gene Barry; SEAMUS: Irwin Corey; THE THREE FATES: CLOTHO: Mara Kim; LACHESIS: Diane Sinclair; ATROPOS: Royce Wallace. **Understudies:** Larry: Frank Milton; Widow: Barbara Ashley; Mrs. Larry: Wana Allison. General Understudy: Kenneth Utt. *Act I*: *Scene 1* A casual tailor shop; *Scene 2* A restless graveyard; *Scene 3* Interior, the house of Larry; *Scene 4* Space. *Act II*: *Scene 1* Exterior, the house of Larry; *Scene 2* Interior, the house of Larry; *Scene 3* The tailor shop. *Act I*: "No One Loves Me" (2nd Tailor), "Without a Stitch" (The Tailors), "Now and Then" (Larry), "October" (Widow), "Mrs. Larry, Tell Me This" (Doctor & Mrs. Larry), "A Cup of Tea" (Larry, Mrs. Larry, Widow, Seamus, Doctor), "He's with My Johnny" (Widow), "And So He Died" (The Tailors), "Three Old Ladies from Hades" (Fates), Dance of the Fates (7th Tailor & Fates). *Act II*: "It's Pleasant and Delightful" (Doctor), "The Dirty Dog" (The Tailors), "The Flatulent Ballad" (Seamus), "The Loyalist Wife" (Mrs. Larry), "Oh, Mrs. Larry" (The Tailors & Mrs. Larry), "Give the Doctor the Best in the House" (The Tailors), "The Doctor's Dance" (The Tailors), "Double Murder, Double Death" (5th Tailor & Widow), "He's a Bold Rogue" (Mrs. Larry, Widow, The Tailors), "I Remember Her" (Larry), "The Tobacco Blues" (Widow & Larry), Finale (Larry & The Tailors).

Reviews were awful.

After Broadway. The musical later ran Off Broadway, at the MARTINIQUE THEATRE, 4/25/61–4/30/61. 8 PERFORMANCES. PRESENTED BY Lucille Lortel; DIRECTOR/SETS: Michael Clarke-Laurence; CHOREOGRAPHER: Laurie Archer; COSTUMES: Bette Gifford; LIGHTING: Jack Jackson; MUSICAL DIRECTOR: Brendan Burke. **Cast:** LARRY: Dermot McNamara; MRS. LARRY: Barbara Hayes; GRAVEDIGGER: Brendan Burke; 5TH TAILOR: Bob Kaliban.

290. *Happy End*

Set in Chicago in Dec. 1915 (in the original German book it was Berlin in 1929). Hallelujah Lil, the Saint of South Canal Street, makes a brave attempt to reform the gang led by Bill, the toughest crook in Chicago, and the Lady in Gray. She makes progress but is thrown out of the Salvation Army. But she is so popular that she is re-instated. The gang robs a bank on Christmas Eve.

Before Broadway. Producer Ernst Josef Aufricht asked Bert Brecht & Kurt Weill to write another musical as a sequel to *Die Dreigroschenoper* (*The Threepenny Opera*). They did, in Germany. Dorothy Lane, whose short story Mr. Brecht apparently based his libretto on, was really Elisabeth Hauptmann, Brecht's secretary and sometime collaborator. Mr. Brecht later admitted this, and lost interest in the work. It was produced in Berlin on 9/2/29, starring Peter Lorre, Oscar Homolka, and Helene Weigel. Miss Weigel, Brecht's politically active wife, unexpectedly and unfairly seized the opportunity to make the last act a platform for her views, and the show bombed and was not produced again until early 1958, in Munich. Lotte Lenya did a recording.

THE YALE REP commissioned Michael Feingold to do the American adaptation, and was the first to produce it, on 4/6/72. 22 PERFOR-

MANCES. DIRECTOR: Michael Posnick; SETS/LIGHTING: Raymond C. Recht; COSTUMES: Michael H. Yeargan; MUSICAL DIRECTOR: Thomas Fay. *Cast*: THE GANG: BILL: Stephen Joyce; JIMMY: David Hurst; JOHNNY: James Brick; BOB: Thomas Barbour; SAM: Jeremy Geidt; NAKA-MURA: Alvin Epstein; LADY IN GRAY: Elizabeth Parrish; MIRIAM: Rosemary Stewart; THE SALVATION ARMY: STONE: Nancy Wickwire; JACKSON: John McAndrew; LILLIAN: Stephanie Cotsirilos; SISTER MARY PRITCHARD: Joan Welles; SISTER JANE GRANT: Sara Albertson; BEN: Herb Downer; THE FOLD: Lisa Carling, Dean Lanier Radcliffe, Yannis Simonides; 1ST MAN: Yannis Simonides; 2ND MAN: Bill Gearhart; COP: Paul Schierhorn.

The Chelsea Theater Center/Michael Harvey production ran at the BROOKLYN ACADEMY OF MUSIC, 3/8/77–4/3/77. 32 PERFORMANCES. DIRECTOR: Michael Posnick; the rest of the crew was the same as for the later Broadway run, except GENERAL MANAGER: William Craver. It reran (to divided reviews, but mostly good, some very good) at the BROOKLYN ACADEMY OF MUSIC on 4/12/77–4/30/77. 24 PERFORMANCES. It was now directed by Robert Kalfin (who had taken over only shortly before), and with Meryl Streep and Bob Gunton having taken over from Shirley Knight and Christopher Lloyd (Mr. Lloyd had torn two ligaments, but made it back in time for Broadway) in the leads. Christopher Cara took over from Bob Gunton as Ben. Aside from that it was the same cast as for Broadway.

The Broadway Run. MARTIN BECK THEATRE, 5/7/77–7/10/77. 75 PERFORMANCES. The Chelsea Theatre Center production newly conceived by Robert Kalfin, PRESENTED BY Michael Harvey & the Chelsea Theater Center (Robert Kalfin, artistic director; Michael David, executive director); MUSIC: Kurt Weill; LYRICS/BOOK: Bertolt Brecht (adapted by Michael Feingold); ORIGINAL GERMAN BOOK: Elisabeth Hauptmann (originally and erroneously credited to the fictitious Dorothy Lane); DIRECTOR: Robert Kalfin; CHOREOGRAPHER: Patricia Birch; SETS: Robert U. Taylor; COSTUMES: Carrie F. Robbins; LIGHTING: Jennifer Tipton; SOUND: Leonard Will; MUSICAL DIRECTOR: Roland Gagnon; ASSISTANT MUSICAL DIRECTOR: David Krane; PRESS: Susan Bloch, Sally G. Christiansen, Francis X. Tobin; GENERAL MANAGERS: Jack Schlissel & Jay Kingwill; COMPANY MANAGER: Albert Poland; PRODUCTION STAGE MANAGER: Mark Wright; STAGE MANAGER: Charles Kindl; ASSISTANT STAGE MANAGER: Christopher Cara. *Cast*: THE GANG: BILL CRACKER: Christopher Lloyd (2) ✩; SAM "MAMMY" WURLITZER: Benjamin Rayson (5); DR. NAKAMURA ("THE GOVERNOR"): Tony Azito (6), *Victor Pappas*; JIMMY DEXTER ("THE REVEREND"): John A. Coe; BOB MARKER ("THE PROFESSOR"): Robert Weil (10); JOHNNY FLINT ("BABY FACE"): Raymond J. Barry; A LADY IN GRAY ("THE FLY"): Grayson Hall (3) ✩; MIRIAM, THE BARMAID: Donna Emmanuel; THE ARMY: LT LILLIAN HOLIDAY ("HALLELUJAH LIL"): Meryl Streep (1) ✩, *Janie Sell* (from 6/27/77); MAJOR STONE: Liz Sheridan (4); CAPT. HANNIBAL JACKSON: Joe Grifasi (9); SISTER MARY: Prudence Wright Holmes; SISTER JANE: Alexandra Borrie (7); BROTHER BEN OWENS: Christopher Cara (8); THE FOLD: Kristin Jolliff, Frank Kopyc, Tom Mardirosian, Martha Miller, Victor Pappas; A COP: David Pursley. *Standby*: Bill: Bob Gunton. *Understudies*: Lillian: Alexandra Borrie; Jane: Donna Emmanuel; Miriam/Mary: Kristin Jolliff; Jackson: Frank Kopyc; Baby Face/Cop: Tom Mardirosian; Major/Fly: Martha Miller; Nakamura/Marker: Victor Pappas; Wurlitzer/Dexter: David Pursley; Owens: Christopher Cara. *Musicians*: CLARINETS: Dennis Anderson & Billy Kerr; TENOR SAX/BASS SAX: Dennis Anderson; PERCUSSION: Mark Belair; PIANO: Roland Gagnon; GUITAR/BANJO: Allan Jaffee; TRUMPETS: Grant "Gus" Keast & William Rohdin; FLUTE/ALTO: Billy Kerr; ACCORDION/HARMONIUM: William Schimmel; TROMBONE: Jonathan Taylor. *Prologue* (Company). *Act I*: Bill's Beer Hall; Dec. 22: "The Bilbao Song" (Governor, Baby Face, Bill, Gang), "Lieutenants of the Lord" (Lillian & Army), "March Ahead" (Army), "The Sailors' Tango" (Lillian) [new song for the transfer to Broadway]. *Act II*: The Salvation Army Mission, Canal Street; Dec. 23: "Brother, Give Yourself a Shove" (Army & Fold), "Song of the Big Shot" (Governor), "Don't Be Afraid" (Jane, Army, Fold), "In Our Childhood's Bright Endeavor" (Hannibal), "The Liquor Dealer's Dream" (Hannibal, Governor, Jane, Army, Fold). *Act III*: *Scene 1* The Beer Hall; Dec. 24: "The Mandalay Song" (Sam & Gang), "Surabaya Johnny" (Lillian), "Song of the Big Shot" (reprise) (Bill), "Ballad of the Lily of Hell" (Fly); *Scene 2* The Mission; later that night: "The Happy End" (Finale) (Company).

It opened at a matinee. The show received Tony nominations for musical, score, and book.

291. *Happy Hunting*

Liz Livingstone, a Philadelphia matron, arrives in Monaco and finds that she hasn't been invited to the royal wedding of Prince Rainier and Grace Kelly. She is offended, and decides to arrange a wedding for her daughter that is more royal than the official one about to happen. She meets the Duke of Granada.

Before Broadway. The show tried out in Boston. Actor Gene Wesson was fired during the run, and claimed that Ethel Merman was behind it. Equity looked into it and found no grounds for complaint. Mr. Wesson was censured, and Equity apologized to Miss Merman.

The Broadway Run. MAJESTIC THEATRE, 12/6/56–11/30/57. 413 PERFORMANCES. PRESENTED BY Jo Mielziner; MUSIC: Harold Karr; LYRICS: Matt Dubey; BOOK: Howard Lindsay & Russel Crouse; SUGGESTED BY the 1956 wedding of Princess Grace and Prince Rainier; DIRECTOR: Abe Burrows; CHOREOGRAPHERS: Alex Romero & Bob Herget; SETS/LIGHTING: Jo Mielziner; COSTUMES: Irene Sharaff; MUSICAL DIRECTOR: Jay Blackton; ORCHESTRATIONS: Ted Royal; ADDITIONAL ORCHESTRATIONS: Joe Glover, Don Walker, Seymour Ginzler; DANCE MUSIC DEVISED BY: Roger Adams; CAST RECORDING on RCA Victor; PRESS: Leo Freedman & Abner D. Klipstein; GENERAL MANAGER: Herman Bernstein; COMPANY MANAGER: Emmett R. Callahan; PRODUCTION STAGE MANAGER: Robert Downing; STAGE MANAGERS: John Scott & Lo Hardin. *Cast*: SANFORD "SANDY" STEWART JR.: Gordon Polk (4); MRS. SANFORD STEWART SR.: Olive Templeton; JOSEPH: Mitchell M. Gregg; BETH LIVINGSTONE: Virginia Gibson (3); JACK ADAMS, A REPORTER: Seth Riggs, *Mike Rayhill*; HARRY WATSON, A REPORTER: Gene Wesson; MAN WHO LOOKS LIKE FAROUK: Edward Becker; CHARLEY, A PHOTOGRAPHER: Delbert Anderson, *Carl Nicholas*; LIZ LIVINGSTONE: Ethel Merman (1); PHOTOGRAPHERS: SAM: Clifford Fearl; JOE: John Craig, *Jack K. Rains*; FREDDY: George Martin; WES: Jim Hutchison, *Richard Korthaze*; (THREE) REPORTERS: MARY MILLS: Estelle Parsons; DICK DAVIS: Robert C. Held; BOB GRAYSON: Carl Nicholas; MAUD FOLEY: Mary Finney; POLICE SERGEANT: Marvin Zeller; ARTURO: Leon Belasco; THE DUKE OF GRANADA: Fernando Lamas (2); COUNT CARLOS: Renato Cibelli; WAITER: Don Weissmuller, *Clifford Fearl*; SHIP'S OFFICER: John Leslie; BARMAN: Warren J. Brown; MRS. B.: Florence Dunlap; MRS. D.: Madeleine Clive; MRS. L.: Kelley Stephens; TERENCE, A GROOM: Jim Hutchison, *Marc Scott*; TOM, A GROOM: Eugene Louis; DAISY, THE HORSE: Moe; MR. T., A MEMBER OF THE HUNT: John Leslie; MR. M., A MEMBER OF THE HUNT: Jay Velie; ALBERT, A GROOM: George Martin; MARGARET, A MAID: Mara Landi, *Helene Whitney*; SINGERS: Peggy Acheson, Delbert Anderson, Edward Becker, Marilynn Bradley, Warren J. Brown, David Collyer, John Craig, Jack Dabdoub, Clifford Fearl, Robert C. Held, Deedy Irwin, Jane A. Johnston, Jean Kraemer, Mara Landi, Betty McGuire, Carl Nicholas, Estelle Parsons, Noella Peloquin, Ginny Perlowin, Seth Riggs, Mary Roche, Charles Rule, Kelley Stephens, Dell Warner, Helene Whitney, Mark Zeller; DANCERS: Bob Bakanic, Betty Carr, Alice Clift, Jane Fischer, John Harmon, Jim Hutchison, Roberta Keith, Dick Korthaze, Eugene Louis, Svetlana McLee, George Martin, Jim Moore, Patti Nestor, Wendy Nickerson, Lowell Purvis, Fleur Raup, Sigyn, Don Weissmuller, Roy Wilson. *Understudies*: Duke: Mitchell Gregg; Beth: Jane Fischer; Sandy: Seth Riggs; Maud: Florence Dunlap; Mrs. Stewart: Madeleine Clive; Baron/Arturo: David Collyer; Mesdames B. D, and L: Helene Whitney. *Act I*: Opening (Chorus); *Scene 1* Outside the palace, Monaco: "Postage Stamp Principality" (Tourists & Monegasques), "Don't Tell Me" (Sandy & Beth), "(Gee, But) It's Good to Be Here" (Liz & Reporters); *Scene 2* Liz's suite, Hotel Riviera, Monaco: "Mutual Admiration Society" (Liz & Beth); *Scene 3* Terrace of the hotel: "For Love or Money" (Girls), Bikini Dance (Beth); *Scene 4* Veranda of the Duke's suite, Hotel Riviera: "It's Like a Beautiful Woman" (Duke); *Scene 5* Quai: "Wedding of the Year Blues" (Maud, Harry, Jack, Reporter, Photographers); *Scene 6* In the ship's bar: "Mr. Livingstone" (Liz); *Scene 7* Afterdeck of the ship: "If'n" (Beth, Sandy, Passengers); *Scene 8* In the ship's bar; *Scene 9* Afterdeck of the ship: "This is What I Call Love" (Liz) [replaced during the run by "Just a Moment Ago" (m/l: Kay Thompson) (Liz)]. **Act II**: Entr'acte (Chorus); **Scene 1** Liz's estate, near Philadelphia: "A New-Fangled Tango" (Liz, Beth, Arturo, Guests), "She's Just Another Girl" (Sandy); **Scene 2** The Livingstone stables: "The Game of Love" (Liz) [replaced during the run by "I'm Old Enough to Know Better and Young Enough Not to Care" (m/l: Kay Thompson) (Liz); **Scene 3** Summerhouse, Liz's estate; **Scene 4** The Philadelphia Hunt Club: "Happy Hunting" (Liz, Duke, Members of the Hunt); **Scene 5** Another part of the forest; **Scene 6** Liz's boudoir: "I'm a Funny Dame" (Liz), "This Much I Know" (Duke), "Just Another Guy" (Liz); **Scene 7** The Hunt Ball: "Everyone Who's 'Who's Who'" (Jack, Harry, Footmen), "Mutual Admiration Society" (reprise) (Liz & Duke), Grand Finale (Company).

Reviews were mostly excellent. Ethel Merman and Fernando Lamas did not get on. The show was nominated for a Tony for costumes, as were Ethel Merman, Fernando Lamas and Virginia Gibson.

292. *Happy New Year*

Johnny wants to go off and explore the world and find himself before settling down as a member of the rich Seton family into which he is about to marry. The older Johnny narrates the proceedings. Set on the five floors in the 5th Avenue townhouse of Edward Seton, in New York City.

Before Broadway. It was first produced at the Stratford Festival's AVON THEATRE, Ontario; only rare Cole Porter songs were used. By the time it hit Broadway, several well-known ones had crept in too. The Stratford crew was basically the same as for the subsequent Broadway run, except COSTUMES: Robin Fraser Paye. The Stratford cast was quite different: NARRATOR: Ted Follows; EDWARD SETON: Eric Donkin; NED SETON: David Dunbar; JULIA: Leigh Beery; LINDA: Victoria Snow; JOHNNY: Ed Evanko; MARY/ANNIE: Marylu Moyer; NANCY/MOLLY/MISS MADDEN: Heather Summerhayes; THOMPSON/MARK: Barrie Wood; DIXON/PHILIP: Barry Van Elen; HARRISON/ANDREW: Hank Stinson; FRAZER: William Copeland; CHARLES: Wally Michaels; ROSE: Carol Forte; BRIDGET: Maida Rogerson. "I'm in Love at Last," "To Hell with Everyone but Us," "See for Yourself," "Nervous," "Boy, Oh Boy," "After You, Who?," "Find Me a Primitive Man," "Once Upon a Time," "Let's Make it a Night," "Ours," "Bless the Bride," "Goodbye, Little Dream, Goodbye," "My Lover Loves Me," "When Your Troubles Have Started," "I'm in Love at Last" (reprise). After Stratford William Atherton replaced Ed Evanko as Johnny, and he was replaced by Michael Scott before Broadway.

The Broadway Run. MOROSCO THEATRE, 4/27/80–5/10/80. 27 previews. 17 PERFORMANCES. PRESENTED BY Leonard Soloway, Allan Francis, Hale Matthews, in association with Marble Arch Productions (Lew Grade & Martin Starger); MUSIC/LYRICS: Cole Porter; BOOK/DIRECTOR: Burt Shevelove; SONG EDITOR/MUSICAL DIRECTOR/VOCAL ARRANGEMENTS: Buster Davis; BASED ON the 1928 comedy *Holiday*, by Philip Barry; CHOREOGRAPHER: Donald Saddler; ASSISTANT CHOREOGRAPHER: Mercedes Ellington; SETS: Michael Eagan; COSTUMES: Pierre Balmain; COSTUME SUPERVISOR: John Falabella; LIGHTING: Ken Billington; SOUND: Tom Morse; ASSOCIATE CONDUCTOR/DANCE MUSIC ARRANGEMENTS: Charles H. Coleman; ORCHESTRATIONS: Luther Henderson; ADDITIONAL ORCHESTRATIONS: Daniel Troob; PRESS: Shirley Herz, Jan Greenberg, Sam Rudy; GENERAL MANAGERS: Leonard Soloway & Allan Francis; COMPANY MANAGER: Michael Kasdan; PRODUCTION STAGE MANAGER: Nina Seely; STAGE MANAGER: Zane Weiner; ASSISTANT STAGE MANAGER: Alan Mann. **Cast:** THE NARRATOR: John McMartin (4); EDWARD SETON: William Roerick (6); EDWARD SETON JR. ("NED"): Richard Bekins (5); JULIA SETON: Kimberly Farr (2); LINDA SETON: Leslie Denniston (1); JOHNNY CASE: Michael Scott (3); THE STAFF: FRAZER: Roger Hamilton (7); CHARLES: Morgan Ensminger (8); PATRICK: J. Thomas Smith; GEORGE: Tim Flavin (10); STEVEN: Richard Christopher; VICTOR: Lara Teeter (9); ROSE: Lauren Goler; MAUDE: Mary Sue Finnerty; ANNIE: Bobbie Nord; BRIDGET: Michelle Marshall; MISS MADDEN: Mary Sue Finnerty; SOME OF THE STORK CLUB SET: NANCY: Lauren Goler; MARY: Mary Sue Finnerty; JOAN: Michelle Mar-

shall; GLORIA: Bobbie Nord; THOMPSON: Tim Flavin (10); DIXON: Lara Teeter (9); ANDERSON: Morgan Ensminger (8); HARRISON: Richard Christopher. **Standbys:** Julia: Michelle Marshall; Ned: Lara Teeter; Narrator/Mr. Seton: Roger Hamilton; Frazer/Charles: Ken Mitchell; Staff/Stork Club Set: Terry Rieser & Ken Mitchell. **Act I**: Dec. 1933: "At Long Last Love" [from *You Never Know*, 1938] (Julia, Linda, Ned), "Ridin' High" [from *Red Hot and Blue*, 1936] (Johnny & Julia), "Let's Be Buddies" [from *Panama Hattie*, 1940] (Johnny & Linda), "Boy, Oh, Boy" (l: Burt Shevelove) (Linda), "Easy to Love [from the movie *Born to Dance*, 1936] (Young Men), "You Do Something to Me" [from *Fifty Million Frenchmen*, 1929] (Johnny), "Red Hot and Blue" [from *Red Hot and Blue*, 1936] (Linda, Johnny, Patrick, Stork Club Set), "Once Upon a Time" [from an unproduced musical of the same name] (Ned & Linda). **Act II**: Jan. 1934: "Night and Day" [from *Gay Divorce*, 1932] (Narrator & Johnny), "Let's Make it a Night" [intended for *Silk Stockings*, 1955, but unused] (Linda, Thompson, Dixon), "Ours" [from *Red Hot and Blue*, 1936] (Julia), "After You, Who?" [from *You Never Know*, 1938] (Johnny), "I Am Loved" [from *Out of This World*, 1950] (Julia), "When Your Troubles Have Started" [cut from *Red Hot and Blue* during tryouts, 1936] (Linda & Ned), "Boy, Oh, Boy" (reprise) (Linda), "Once Upon a Time" (reprise) (Ned & Linda). INCIDENTAL MUSIC: "Just One of Those Things," "It's De-Lovely," "Take Me Back to Manhattan," "Make it Another Old-Fashioned, Please," "They Couldn't Compare to You," "You've Got That Thing," "Every Time We Say Goodbye," "Let's Do It," "Where Have You Been?," "Let's Fly Away," "Girls," "What is This Thing Called Love?".

Reviews were mostly bad. Pierre Balmain was nominated for a Tony for costumes.

293. *The Happy Time*

This musical tells the story of the Bonnard family, French Canadian father, Scottish mother, and their son Bibi. Jacques, Bibi's world-weary magazine photographer uncle, a lonely failure, has returned to his family for a brief visit, and appears glamorous to Bibi. Bibi wants to go off and see the world with him, but Grandpere and Jacques convince the lad to stay home. Set in the past in Jacques' studio, and earlier still in his home in a small town in Canada. The show used film projections to set the mood for the live action.

Before Broadway. The original straight comedy of the same name, upon which this musical was based, was PRESENTED BY Rodgers & Hammerstein on Broadway, at the PLYMOUTH THEATRE, 1/24/50. 614 PERFORMANCES. DIRECTOR: Robert Lewis. **Cast:** BIBI: Johnny Stewart; HIS PARENTS: Claude Dauphin & Leora Dana; ALSO WITH: Eva Gabor. It was filmed (straight) in 1952. **Cast:** JACQUES: Charles Boyer; BIBI: Bobby Driscoll; UNCLE DESMOND: Louis Jourdan; SUSAN: Marsha Hunt. David Merrick rejected Sam Taylor's original musical version, and instead mixed an original story with the revised version of an N. Richard Nash play. Julie Gregg replaced Willi Burke before Broadway.

The Broadway Run. BROADWAY THEATRE, 1/18/68–9/28/68. 23 previews from 12/29/67. 286 PERFORMANCES. PRESENTED BY David Merrick; MUSIC: John Kander; LYRICS: Fred Ebb; BOOK: N. Richard Nash; BASED PRIMARILY ON the 1950 comedy which was Samuel Taylor's dramatization of Robert L. Fontaine's 1945 stories; DIRECTOR/CHOREOGRAPHER: Gower Champion; ASSOCIATE CHOREOGRAPHER: Kevin Carlisle; SETS: Peter Wexler; COSTUMES: Freddy Wittop; LIGHTING: Jean Rosenthal; SOUND: Joseph Donohue; PROJECTIONS: Gower Champion; FILM SEQUENCES CREATED BY: Christopher Chapman; FILM TECHNICAL DIRECTOR: Barry O. Gordon; MUSICAL DIRECTOR/VOCAL ARRANGEMENTS: Oscar Kosarin; ORCHESTRATIONS: Don Walker; DANCE & INCIDENTAL MUSIC ARRANGEMENTS: Marvin Laird; CAST recording on RCA Victor; PRESS: Harvey B. Sabinson, Lee Solters, David Powers; CASTING: Mitchell Erickson & Michael Shurtleff; GENERAL MANAGER: Jack Schlissel; COMPANY MANAGER: Fred Cuneo; STAGE MANAGERS: Bob Bernard & Jeff Chambers. **Cast:** JACQUES BONNARD: Robert Goulet (1) ☆; SUZANNE BONNARD: Jeanne Arnold (5); PHILIPPE BONNARD:

George S. Irving (4); BIBI BONNARD: Mike Rupert (7); LOUIS BONNARD: Charles Durning (6); ANNABELLE BONNARD: Kim Freund; GILLIE BONNARD: Julane Stites; NANETTE BONNARD: Connie Simmons; FELICE BONNARD: June Squibb (8); GRANDPERE BONNARD: David Wayne (2) *; THE SIX ANGELS: LIZETTE: Jacki Garland; DORINE: Mary Gail Laverenz; SYLVIE: Tammie Fillhart; MONIQUE: Mary Ann O'Reilly; BELLA: Vicki Powers; GRACE: Susan Sigrist; LAURIE MANNON: Julie Gregg (3); FOUFIE: Jeffrey Golkin; GANACHE: Dallas Johann; STUDENTS OF ST. PIERRE BOYS' SCHOOL: DANCERS: Ron Abshire, Jovanni Anthony, Quin Baird, Andy Bew, Blake Brown, Leonard Crofoot, Ron Crofoot, Wayne Dugger, Jo Giamalva, Dallas Johann, Gene Law, Steve Reinhardt, Jon Simonson, Michael Stearns; SINGERS: Marc Anthony, Alan Blight, George Connolly, Tom De Mastri, Paul Dwyer, Scott Gandert, Eric Hamilton, Gary Hamilton, Jeffrey Hamilton, Kevin Hamilton, Mark Lonergan, Brian Shyer, Brandy Wayne, Teddy Williams, Marc Winters. *Standbys*: Jacques/Philippe: John Gabriel; Grandpere/Louis: Ben Kapen; Suzanne/Felice: Iva Withers. Understudies: Laurie: Vicki Powers; Bibi: Leonard Crofoot. Swing Dancer: Sammy Williams. *Act I*: *Scene 1* Jacques' studio: "The Happy Time" (Jacques & Family); *Scene 2* The Bonnard home: "He's Back" (The Family); *Scene 3* The theatre: "Catch My Garter" (Six Angels), "Tomorrow Morning" (Jacques, Grandpere, Bibi, Six Angels); *Scene 4* Bibi's bedroom: "Please Stay" (Bibi & Jacques), "I Don't Remember You" (Jacques); *Scene 5* The classroom: "St. Pierre" (Glee Club), "I Don't Remember You" (reprise) (Laurie & Jacques); *Scene 6* The schoolyard: "Without Me" (Bibi & Schoolmates); *Scene 7* The Bonnard garden: "The Happy Time" (reprise) (Jacques). *Act II*: *Scene 1* Jacques' studio: "(Walking) Among My Yesterdays" (Jacques); *Scene 2* A street in St. Pierre: "Please Stay" (reprise) (Laurie); *Scene 3* The gymnasium: "The Life of the Party" (Grandpere, Six Angels, Schoolboys); *Scene 4* After the party: "Seeing Things" (Jacques & Laurie); *Scene 5* The schoolyard: Ballet (Bibi, Gillie, Annabelle, Nanette, Schoolboys); *Scene 6* Grandpere's room: "A Certain Girl" (Grandpere, Jacques, Bibi); *Scene 7* Jacques' studio: "Being Alive" (Jacques) [dropped after the opening]; *Scene 8* The school; Bibi's graduation: "St. Pierre" (reprise) (Schoolboys), "The Happy Time" (reprise) (Jacques & Entire Company).

It opened on Broadway to very bad reviews. However, it won Tony Awards for direction of a musical, choreography, and for Robert Goulet, and was also nominated for musical, composer & lyricist, sets, costumes, and for David Wayne, Mike Rupert, and Julie Gregg. It was the first Broadway show to lose a million dollars.

294. *Happy Town*

Set in Back-A-Heap, the only town in Texas without a millionaire. Four Houston trillionaires send their innocent brother Craig to Back-A-Heap, ostensibly to help the town by buying property, but really to obtain the land to exploit a big cave below the town as an oil storage basin.

Before Broadway. Backed by Texas millionaires, it closed after a week's tryout in Boston (beginning 9/9/59), for a complete rewrite. Those in the cast who departed after Boston included Henry Hull (the star), Linda Ross, and Karen Thorsell.

The Broadway Run. FIFTY-FOURTH STREET THEATRE, 10/7/59–10/10/59. 5 PERFORMANCES. PRESENTED BY b & m Productions (Allan A. Buckhantz & Mitchell May); MUSIC: Gordon Duffy; LYRICS: Harry M. Haldane; ADDITIONAL MUSIC & LYRICS: Paul Nassau; BOOK: Harry M. Haldane (uncredited); BOOK ADAPTED BY: Max Hampton; DIRECTOR: Allan A. Buckhantz; CHOREOGRAPHER: Lee Scott; SETS: Curt Nations; COSTUMES: J. Michael Travis; LIGHTING: Paul Morrison; MUSICAL DIRECTOR/VOCAL ARRANGEMENTS: Samuel Krachmalnick; ORCHESTRATIONS: Nicholas Carras; PRESS: Shirley E. Herz; GENERAL MANAGER: John Yorke; PRODUCTION STAGE MANAGER: Lawrence N. Kasha; STAGE MANAGER: Jim Cavanaugh; ASSISTANT STAGE MANAGER: Donald L. Jackson. *Cast:* LINT RICHARDS: George Blackwell; BUB RICHARDS: Bruce MacKay; SIB RICHARDS: George Ives; GLENN RICHARDS: Michael Kermoyan; JANICE DAWSON: Cindy Robbins (3); CRAIG RICHARDS: Biff McGuire (1); CLINT YODER: Tom Williams (9); BOBBIE JO HARTMAN:

Alice Clift; MOLLY BIXBY: Lee Venora (2); JUDGE ED BIXBY: Dick Elliott (6); JIM JOE JAMIESON: Frederic Tozere (7); A REPORTER: Rico Froehlich; PERT HAWKINS: Ralph Dunn (5); CLANEY: Charles May; DOC SPOONER: Will Wright (4); MRS. HAWKINS: Lizabeth Pritchett; SUSAN GREY: Leigh Evans; REVEREND HORNBLOW: Edwin Steffe (8); MULT: Roy Wilson; LUKE GRANGER: Chester Watson; TOWNSWOMEN OF BACK-A-HEAP: Diana Baron, Lillian Bozinoff, Alice Clift, Colleen Corkrey, Dori Davis, Isabelle Farrell, Laurie Franks, Rita Golden, Connie Greco, Marian Haraldson, Marilyn Harris, Judy Keirn, Maxine Kent, Patricia Mount, Robbi Palmer; TOWNSMEN OF BACK-A-HEAP: John Buwen, Bob Daley, Rico Froehlich, James Gannon, George Jack, Danny Joel, Charles May, Jim McAnany, Nixon Miller, Howard Parker, Tom Pocoroba, Stewart Rose, Roy Wilson. *Standbys*: Craig: Stewart Rose; Molly/Janice: Laurie Franks. *Understudies*: Craig/Sib: James Gannon; Molly: Diana Barron; Janice: Alice Clift; Spooner: Michael Kermoyan; Pert: Bruce MacKay; Judge/Lint/Claney: Nixon Miller; Jamieson: George Blackwell; Hornblow/Glenn: Rico Froehlich; Clint: Bob Daley; Mrs. Hawkins: Rita Golden; Bub: Charles May; Susan/Bobbie Jo: Colleen Corkrey; Mult: John Buwen. *Act I*: *Scene 1* A private office in the T.B.A. Exchange: "It isn't Easy" (Janice, Glenn, Bub, Lint, Sib); *Scene 2* Back-A-Heap, Texas, the Main Street; a few hours later: "Celebration!" (Townspeople), "Something Special" (Craig); *Scene 3* Bixby's Super Market; a little later; *Scene 4* The Main Street; immediately following: "The Legend of Black-Eyed Susan Grey" (dance) (Susan & Townspeople), "Opportunity!" (Craig, Hornblow, Mrs. Hawkins, Townspeople), "As Busy as Anyone Can Be" (Clint & Girls); *Scene 5* "Heaven Protect Me!" (Janice & Girls); *Scene 6* The T.B.A. office; a little later; *Scene 7* The Main Street; that evening: "I Feel Like a Brother to You!" (Craig & Molly); *Scene 8* Back-A-Heap Town Hall; immediately following: "Hoedown!" (Townspeople); *Scene 9* The Main Street; immediately following: "I Am What I Am!" (Craig & Molly), "The Beat of a Heart" (Molly), "Mean" (Janice); *Scene 10* Fairgrounds; next morning; *Scene 11* The T.B.A. office: "It isn't Easy" (reprise) (Glenn, Bub, Lint, Sib); *Scene 12* The prairie: "When the Time is Right" (Hornblow). *Act II*: *Scene 1* The Main Street; the next day: "Pick-Me-Up!" (Townspeople); *Scene 2* E Street; immediately following: "I'm Stuck with Love" (Molly); *Scene 3* The TB.A. office; at about the same time: "It isn't Easy" (reprise) (Glenn, Bub, Lint, Sib); *Scene 4* Fairgrounds; two weeks later: "Nothing in Common" (Janice & Molly), "Talkin' 'bout You" (Janice, Clint, Townspeople), "Something Special" (reprise) (Craig & Molly); *Scene 5* A street; immediately following; *Scene 6* The Main Street; *Scene 7* T.B.A. office; *Scene 8* Main Street; later: "Y' Can't Win" (Janice); *Scene 9* Bixby's Super Market; *Scene 10* A street; immediately following; *Scene 11* Town Hall; later: "Opportunity" (reprise) (Entire Company).

The show was universally panned on Broadway. It received a Tony nomination for choreography.

295. *Harrigan 'n Hart*

Harrigan (1845–1911) and Hart (1855–1891) were two New York vaudevillians. The story is set between 1871 (when the two boys teamed up) and 1888 (the team split in 1885). Gerta was Hart's wife, a villainess.

Before Broadway. It originally opened on 7/10/84, as the first production at the Goodspeed Opera House's Norma Terriss Theatre, in Chester, Conn. PRESENTED BY Gerald A. Davis & Warren Pincus; DIRECTOR: Edward Stone; CHOREOGRAPHER: D.J Giagni; SETS: James Leonard Joy; COSTUMES: Ann Hould-Ward; LIGHTING: Marilyn Rennagel; MUSICAL SUPERVISOR/ORCHESTRATIONS/ARRANGEMENTS: John McKinney; MUSICAL DIRECTOR: Michael Skloff. Of the cast only Leslie Cokery, Meredith Murray, and Marianne Tatum did not go with the show to Broadway. Those who appeared on Broadway but not at Goodspeed were: Harry Groener, Merilee Magnuson, Amelia Marshall, Christine Ebersole, and Alison Mann. Joe Layton took over as director for Broadway, with Edward Stone as his assistant, but Mr. Stone quit during rehearsals.

The Broadway Run. LONGACRE THEATRE, 1/31/85–2/3/85. 24 previews. 5 PERFORMANCES. PRESENTED BY Elliot Martin, Arnold Bernhard, The Shubert Organization; NEW MUSIC: Max Showalter; NEW LYRICS: Peter Walker; BOOK: Michael Stewart; SONGS OF THE PERIOD BY Edward Harrigan (lyrics) & David Braham (music); BASED ON biographical material compiled by Nedda Harrigan Logan, and on *The Merry Partners*, by E.J. Kahn Jr.; DIRECTOR: Joe Layton; CHOREOGRAPHER: D.J. Giagni; SETS: David Mitchell; COSTUMES: Ann Hould-Ward; LIGHTING: Richard Nelson; SOUND: Otts Munderloh; MUSICAL SUPERVISOR/ORCHESTRATIONS/ARRANGEMENTS: John McKinney; MUSICAL DIRECTOR: Peter Howard; PRESS: Fred Nathan & Associates; CASTING: Warren Pincus & Marjorie Martin; GENERAL MANAGEMENT: Joseph Harris Associates; COMPANY MANAGER: Mitzi Harder; PRODUCTION STAGE MANAGER: Mary Porter Hall; STAGE MANAGER: Marc Schlackman; ASSISTANT STAGE MANAGER: Rita Calabro. *Cast:* STETSON: Mark Fotopoulos; EDWARD HARRIGAN: Harry Groener (2); TONY HART: Mark Hamill (1); ARCHIE WHITE: Clent Bowers; OLD COLONEL: Cleve Asbury; THE COLONEL'S WIFE: Barbara Moroz; ELEANOR: Roxie Lucas; ANDREW LECOUVRIER: Mark Fotopoulos; MARTIN HANLEY: Oliver Woodall; SAM NICHOLS: Clent Bowers; ALFRED J. DUGAN: Christopher Wells; FELIX BARKER: Clent Bowers; JUDGE: Mark Fotopoulos; ANNIE BRAHAM HARRIGAN: Tudi Roche (5); JOHNNY WILD: Mark Fotopoulos; BILLY GROSS: Cleve Asbury; CHESTER FOX: Kenston Ames; LILY FAY: Merilee Magnuson; ELSIE FAY: Barbara Moroz; ADA LEWIS: Roxie Lucas; MRS. ANNIE YEAMONS: Armelia McQueen (4); JENNIE YEAMONS: Amelia Marshall; HARRY MACK: Christopher Wells; PHOTOGRAPHER: Kenston Ames; JUDGE HILTON: Christopher Wells; NAT GOODWIN: Cleve Asbury; CAPTAIN: Mark Fotopoulos; NEWSBOY: Kenston Ames; NEWSGIRL: Amelia Marshall; BELLE: Barbara Moroz; GERTA GRANVILLE: Christine Ebersole (3); ADELAIDE HARRIGAN: Merilee Magnuson; UNCLE ALBERT: Clent Bowers; NEWSPAPERMAN: Kenston Ames; WILLIAM GILL: Mark Fotopoulos; DOCTOR: Christopher Wells; NURSE: Merilee Magnuson. *Understudies*: Harrigan/Hart: Christopher Wells; Gerta: Merilee Magnuson; Annie: Barbara Moroz; Mrs. Yeamons: Roxie Lucas; Martin/Archie/Felix/Sam/Albert: Michael Gorman. *Swings*: Michael Gorman & Alison Mann. *Orchestra:* TRUMPET: Irving Berger; PERCUSSION: Bruce Doctor; DOUBLE BASS: Bill Ellison; TROMBONE: Jack Gale; BANJO/MANDOLIN: Scott Kuney; VIOLIN: Robert Lawrence; PIANOS: Peter Howard & Michael Skloff; FLUTES/CLARINETS: Robert Steen & David Weiss; OBOE: Robert Steen; ALTO SAX: David Weiss. *Act I: Scene 1* Stetson's American Music Hall, Galesburg, Ill; 1871: "Put Me in My Little Bed" * (Hart), "Wonderful Me" * (Harrigan & Hart); *Scene 2* New York City; *Scene 3* The Theatre Comique: "Mulligan Guard" (Harrigan & Hart) [the "Mulligan Guards" series, satirical but affectionate stories and characters in NY, were their most famous works]; *Scene 4* U.S. Courthouse, Worcester, Mass.: "Put Me in My Little Bed" * (reprise) (Hart); *Scene 5* The Theatre Comique: "I Love to Follow a Band" (Harrigan & Company), "Such an Education Has My Mary Ann" (Harrigan, Hart, Company), "Maggie Murphy's Home" (Annie, Harrigan, Nichols, Company), "McNally's Row of Flats" (Mrs. Yeamons & Company), "Something New, Something Different" * (Harrigan, Hart, Company); *Scene 6* The Theatre Comique: "That's My Partner" * (Harrigan & Hart); *Scene 7* Outside the New Theatre Comique; opening night; *Scene 8* Old Nieuw Amsterdam: "She's Our Gretel" (Harrigan, Hart, Mrs. Yeamons, Company); *Scene 9* A restaurant; later that evening: "What You Need is a Woman" * (Gerta); *Scene 10* The New Theatre Comique: "Knights of the Mystic Star" (Mrs. Yeamons & Company), "Girl of the Mystic Star" (Gerta & Men), "Mulligan Guard" (reprise) (Harrigan & Hart). *Act II: Scene 1* New York City, and the Park Theatre: "Skidmore Fancy Ball" (Nichols, Mack, Wild, Gross), "Sweetest Love" (Ada & Elsie), "The Old Barn Floor" * (Wild, Jennie, Fox, Lily), "Silly Boy" (Gerta, Gross, Mack), "Mulligan Guard" (reprise) (Harrigan, Hart, Company), "We'll Be There" * (Harrigan, Hart, Company); *Scene 2* Harrigan's Tour; 1880 to 1886: "Ada with the Golden Hair" (Annie, Wild, Gross), "That Old Featherbed" (Mack, Fay Sisters), "Sam Johnson's Colored Cakewalk" (Nichols & Jennie), "Dip Me in the Golden Sea" (Harrigan, Mrs. Yeamons, Company), "That's My Partner" * (reprise) (Harrigan); *Scene 3* Backstage, Wallack's Theatre: "I've Come Home to Stay" (Hart), "If I Could Trust Me" * (Hart); *Scene 4* New York City: "Maggie Murphy's Home" (reprise) (Hanley, Lily, Mrs. Yeamons, Ada), "I've Come Home to Stay" (reprise) (Hart & Girls); *Scene 5* New York Hospital: "I Need This One Chance" * (Gerta); *Scene 6* The Park Theatre; March 22, 1888: "I Love to Follow a Band" (reprise) (Annie & Company), "Mulligan Guard" (reprise) (Harrigan, Hart, Mrs. Yeamons), "Something New, Something Different" * (reprise) (Harrigan, Hart, Company).

Note: Asterisked numbers were written by Max Showalter & Peter Walker

Reviews were terrible. The show received a Tony nomination for book.

After Broadway. ST. PETER'S CHURCH, NYC, 9/13/96–9/15/96. 5 PERFORMANCES. PRESENTED BY the York Theatre Company, as part of their *Musicals in Mufti* series. DIRECTOR: William Westbrook; MUSICAL DIRECTOR: David La Marche.

296. *Hayride*

Hillbilly folk musical revue, in 2 acts. An offshoot of the very successful radio program *The Old Dominion Barn Dance*, presented and broadcast every Saturday night from the barn at "Medley Grove" (i.e. the WRVA Theatre, in Richmond, Va.).

Before Broadway. It had an eight-year run in Richmond.

The Broadway Run. FORTY-EIGHTH STREET THEATRE, 9/13/54–10/2/54. 24 PERFORMANCES. PRESENTED BY Barron Howard & Jack Stone; MUSIC/LYRICS/SKETCHES: various authors; SETS: Art Guild, Jack Woodson, Jack Derrenberger; PRESS: Bill Doll & Robert Ullman; COMPANY MANAGER: Clarence Jacobson; STAGE MANAGER: Daniel Pennell & Jennings Robinson. *Program* (not in order): Cousin Joe Maphis (comedian and wizard of stringed instruments) & Rose (i.e. Rose Lee Maphis) [they were known as "Mr. and Mrs. Country Music"] (ballads of the prairie country); Lester Flatt & Earl Scruggs and the Foggy Mountain Boys (Paul Warren, Jake Tulloch, Curly Sechler) (mountain music); The Coon Creek Girls [the three Ledford sisters from Pilot, Kentucky — Lily May, Rosie, and Black-Eyed Susan (whose real name was Minnie Lena)] (songs of the old hill "splinter-kickin'" dances and parties); The Trail Blazers (Ray Smith, Roy Horton, Johnny Newton); Eddy (Texas) Smith; Quincy Snodgrass (comedian); Mary Klick (singer) (songs of the swamp and bayou regions); Zeb Robinson; Sonny Day (accordionist from Kentucky); Fiddlin' Irving; Gene Jenkins (guitarist); Jody Carver (steel guitarist). "Old MacDonald Had a Farm;" "The Blue Tail Fly;" Hank Williams songs, including "Jambalaya;" Stephen Foster songs; "Little Things Mean a Lot" (m/l: Carl Stuzt & Edith Lindeman) [Sunshine Sue (1) (i.e. Mary Arlene Higdon), the "femcee"); "Vegetable Love" (Zag, the Ozark Mountain Boy, who sang lonesome cabinsongs of his native Ozark hills).

Reviews were generally not good.

297. *Hazel Flagg*

A musical satire, set in the 1930s. Hazel, of Stonyhead, Vt., has been working in a watch factory, painting luminous dials, and is told by Dr. Downer that she has radium poisoning and has three weeks to live. When she finds that everything was a mistake, and all is okay, she decides to go to New York anyway, and have a fling, courtesy of *Everywhere* magazine, whose genius editor Laura believes she's granting Hazel's last wish. Hazel finds true love in New York.

Before Broadway. This was Jule Styne's effort to make Helen Gallagher a star. Thomas Mitchell was in a non-singing lead role. The number "Think How Many People Never Find Love" was cut. The show tried out at the Shubert Theatre, Philadelphia, for three weeks beginning 1/12/53.

The Broadway Run. MARK HELLINGER THEATRE, 2/11/53–9/19/53. 190 PERFORMANCES. PRESENTED BY Jule Styne, in association with Anthony Brady Farrell; MUSIC: Jule Styne; LYRICS: Bob Hilliard; BOOK: Ben Hecht; Based on the 1937 Carole Lombard movie *Nothing Sacred*, written by Charles MacArthur & Ben Hecht, which in turn was based on the story *Letter to the Editor*, by James Street; BOOK DIRECTOR: David

Alexander; CHOREOGRAPHER: Robert Alton & Donald Saddler; SETS: Harry Horner; COSTUMES: Miles White; LIGHTING: Harry Horner & James Orr; MUSICAL DIRECTOR: Pembroke Davenport, *Oscar Kosarin*; ORCHESTRATIONS: Don Walker; BALLET MUSIC ARRANGEMENTS: Oscar Kosarin; CHORAL DIRECTOR/CHORAL ARRANGEMENTS: Hugh Martin; PRESS: John L. Toohey, Arthur Cantor, Harriette Gelb; PRODUCTION SUPERVISOR: Robert Alton; GENERAL MANAGER: Rose Goldstein; COMPANY MANAGER: Michael Goldreyer; PRODUCTION STAGE MANAGER: Neil Hartley; STAGE MANAGER: Freddie Nay. *Cast:* AN EDITOR: Dean Campbell; OLEANDER: Jonathan Harris (6); LAURA CAREW: Benay Venuta (3); WALLACE COOK: John Howard (4), *Tony Bavaar*; VERMONT VILLAGERS: Carol Hendricks, B.J. Keating, Joan Morton, Dorothy Love, Laurel Shelby; MR. BILLINGS: Lawrence Weber; MR. JENKINS: Robert Lenn; HAZEL FLAGG: Helen Gallagher (1); DR. DOWNER: Thomas Mitchell (2); MAN ON THE STREET: George Reeder, *Ross Martin*; BELLBOY: Jerry Craig; MAXIMILIAN LAVIAN: John Pelletti (9); FIREMAN: Bill Heyer; MISS WINTERBOTTOM: Betsy Holland; THE MAYOR OF NEW YORK: Jack Whiting (5); WHITEY: Sheree North (8); WILLIE: John Brascia (7); DR. EMIL ENGELHOFER: Ross Martin (10); CHORUS GIRLS: Lori Jon & Virginia Poe; COMMITTEE MEN: Michael Spaeth & John Bartis, *Bill Heyer*; POLICEMAN: Eric Schepard; JUDGE CURLEY: *Richard Bishop* [role added during the run]; TENTH AVENUE MERCHANT: *Ross Martin* [role added during the run]; DANCERS: Estelle Aza, Christopher Brown, Chris Carter, Ronald Cecill, Al Craine, Don Crichton, Marcella Dodge, Lillian Donau, Anna Friedland, Ruby Herndon, Lori Jon, Hugh Lambert, Gerard Leavitt, Sherry McCutcheon, Betty McMillen, Barbara Michaels, Judy Miller, Joan Morton, Margot Myers, Virginia Poe, Eva Ralf, George Reeder, Eric Schepard, Michael Spaeth, Beryl Towbin, Toni Wheelis; SINGERS: John Bartis, Dean Campbell, David Carter, Jerry Craig, Bob Davis, Sara Dillon, Mary Harmon, Carol Hendricks, Bill Heyer, Betsy Holland, Dossie Hollingsworth, B.J. Keating, Robert Lenn, Beverly McFadden, David Randall, Laurel Shelby. *Understudies*: Hazel: Dorothy Love; Downer: Jonathan Harris; Laura: Dossie Hollingsworth; Wallace: Lawrence Weber; Willie: George Reeder; Whitey: Chris Carter. *Act I: Scene 1* Conference room of *Everywhere* Magazine; late afternoon: "A Little More Heart" (Laura, Wallace, Magazine Staff); *Scene 2* Dr. Downer's house; the next day: "The World is Beautiful Today" (Hazel) [replaced during the first part of the run by "My Wild Imagination" (Hazel)], "I'm Glad I'm Leaving" (Hazel); *Scene 3* Railroad depot, Stonyhead; that evening: "The Rutland Bounce" (dance) (Joan Morton, George Reeder, Don Crichton, Villagers); *Scene 4* A New York street; the next day: "Hello, Hazel" (Laura & New Yorkers); *Scene 5* Hazel's New York hotel suite; later that day: "Paris Gown" (ballet) (Hazel, Lavian, Ronald Cecill, Gerard Leavitt, George Reeder, Models, Attendants), "The World is Beautiful Today" (reprise) (Wallace & Editors) [replaced during the first part of the run by "Make the People Cry" (Laura, Oleander, Editors)], "Money Burns a Hole in My Pocket" (Wallace) [number added for re-opening]; *Scene 6* Laura Carew's office; two weeks later: "Ev'ry Street's a Boulevard (in Old New York)" (Mayor) [the big hit]; *Scene 7* Hazel's hotel suite; evening, a week later: "How do You Speak to an Angel?" (Wallace); *Scene 8a* A cross-section of New York City; later that evening: "Autograph Chant" (Autograph Hunters), "I Feel Like I'm Gonna Live Forever" (Hazel); *Scene 8b* Roseland Ballroom: "You're Gonna Dance with Me, Willie" (Hazel, Willie, Company). *Act II: Scene 1* A radio station in the hotel; the next morning: "Who is the Bravest?" (University Glee Club); *Scene 2* Hazel's hotel bedroom; the same morning: "Dream Parade" (ballet) (Hazel & Company) [for the reopening this ballet was replaced by a new ballet, "Champagne and Wedding Cake" (Hazel & Company), choreographed by Don Saddler]; *Scene 3* The same; several hours later; *Scene 4* The Mayor's luncheon; that afternoon: "Salome" (Dancing Girls): SALOME: Sheree North; COWBOY SINGER: Dean Campbell; COWBOY DANCERS: George Reeder & Don Crichton; "Everybody Loves to Take a Bow" (Laura, Mayor, Men); *Scene 5* Under the East River Bridge; later that evening: "Something in the Wind" (Wallace) [number added for re-opening], "Laura de Maupassant" (Hazel); *Scene 6* A barge on the river's edge; a little later: "Autograph Chant" (reprise) (Autograph Hunters); *Scene 7* Finale: "I Feel Like I'm Gonna Live Forever" (reprise) (Company) and "How Do You Speak to an Angel?" (reprise) (Company) [replaced during the first part of the run by "Autograph Chant"].

The show got divided Broadway reviews. After five months it suspended performances on 7/4/53, recouping half its investment of $240,000. After eight weeks it re-opened on 9/1/53, with Tony Bavaar replacing John Howard in the leading man's role. But the show lasted only another two weeks. It won Tony Awards for costumes and for Thomas Mitchell; and Donaldson Awards for Thomas Mitchell, Jack Whiting (in his comeback) and John Brascia (male dancer).

After Broadway. THE MOVIE. 1954. Re-worked as *Living it Up*, with four of the songs. *Cast*: HOMER FLAGG: Jerry Lewis; STEVE: Dean Martin; WALLY COOK: Janet Leigh; MAYOR: Edward Arnold.

298. *Hear! Hear!*

A musical revue, with many songs revolving around the theme of Americana. Lumpy Brannum was famous on TV's *Captain Kangaroo*, as Mr. Greenjeans.

The Broadway Run. ZIEGFELD THEATRE, 9/27/55–10/23/55. 38 PERFORMANCES. PRESENTED BY Fred Waring; SPECIAL SONGS & MATERIAL BY: various writers; LYRICS: Hugh "Lumpy" Brannum; DIRECTOR: Fred Waring; STAGE DIRECTOR: Ray Sax; SETS: Sam Leve; COSTUMES: Jeanne Partington; ORCHESTRA DIRECTOR: Fred Culley; CHORAL DIRECTOR: Jack Best. *Cast:* Fred Waring & All the Pennsylvanians: *Singers*: SOPRANO: Dorothy Arms, Patti Beems, Ruth Best; MEZZO-SOPRANO: Preshy Marker; CONTRALTO: Norma Barnes; ALTO: Norma Douglas; BASS: Jack Best, Ralph Isbell, T.J. Marker; BASS BARITONE: Frank Davis; BARITONE: Joe Marine, Leonard Kranendonk, George Geyer, Bob Kranendonk; TENOR: Eddie Ericksen, Gordon Goodman, Bob Sands, Bill Caniff, George Pilon, Fred Waring Jr. *Players*: ORCHESTRAL DIRECTOR: Fred Culley; PIANO: Hawley Ades; VIOLIN: Jean Eley, Lou Eley, Ben Feldham; VIOLA: Lamar Alsop & Fred Culley; CELLO: Julius Ehrenworth; HARP: Rosalie Randall; STRING BASS: Hugh "Lumpy" Brannum; DRUMS: Poley McClintock & Buss Dillon; CLARINET: Ray Sax, Norman Ronemus, Lou Bode, Mike Doty; SAXOPHONE: Ray Sax, Norman Ronemus, Lou Bode; TRUMPET: Ward Cole, George Guggisberg, Nelson Keller; TROMBONE: Charles Evans & Marvin Long. *Act I: Scene 1* Thanks for Coming: "Your Song" (Your Hosts), "Hear! Hear!" (We! We!); *Scene 2* Let Freedom Sing: "America Our Heritage" (m/l: Helen Steele) (The People), "Where in the World but America" (The People), "Paul Revere's Ride" (The Patriots), "Give Me Your Tired, Your Poor" (m: Irving Berlin; l: Emma Lazarus) [from *Miss Liberty*], "Pledge of Allegiance" (m: Fred Waring) (US); *Scene 3* The Song is the Thing: "Say it with Music" (m/l: Irving Berlin) (Singers & Players), "So Beats My Heart" (m/l: Pat Ballard, Charles Henderson, Tom Waring) (Patti Beems, Singers, Players); *Scene 4* Long Hair, Horse Hair, Cat Gut and Wire: "Hora Staccato" (The No-Sing String Section); *Scene 5* Rock and Roll: "I Want You to Be My Baby" (Joe Marine & the Beat Boys); *Scene 6* Plain and Fancy Folk Songs: "Black is the Color of My True Love's Hair" (Rosalie Randall & Friends), "Across the Wide Missouri" (Bob Kranendonk), "He's Gone Away" (The Girls He Left Behind), "Double Ring Ceremony" (m/l: Buddy Bernier & Phyllis Williams) (Mountain Lovers), "Barefoot" (m/l: Buddy Bernier, Charles Naylor, Hugh "Lumpy" Brannum) (Norma Douglas, Jack Best, Ruth Best, Eddie Ericksen, Preshy Marker, Fred Waring Jr.); *Scene 7* Songs of All Faiths: "No Man is an Island" (The Men), "Come, Come Ye Saints" (Patti Beems, T.J. Marker, Norma Barnes, George Pilon), "I Wonder as I Wander" (m/l: John Jacob Niles) (Dorothy Arms), "Salve Regina" (The Chanters), "Work, for the Night is Coming" (Jean Eley, Rosalie Randall, Marvin Long, Nelson Keller), "Song of Galilee" (The Folks), "God of Our Fathers" (m/l: George William Warren & Daniel Crane Roberts) (arr: Livingston Gearhart); *Scene 8* Negro Spiritual Inspiration: "Deep River" (The Congregation), "The Creation" (m/l: Roy Ringwald & James Weldon Johnson) [Sermon from *God's Trombones*] (Frank Davis), "He's Got the Whole World in His Hands" (The Preacher); *Scene 9* Miniature Mammoth Minstrel Show: "Rampart Street" (Marching Band), "Angels Meet Me at the Crossroads" (The Minstrels), "I'll Be Dar" (Leonard Kranendonk), "(I Dream of) Jeannie with the Light Brown Hair" (m/l: Stephen Foster; arr: Hawley Ades) (Eddie Ericksen), "For Me and My Gal" (m: George W. Meyer; l: Edgar Leslie & E. Ray Goetz) (George Geyer),

"Camptown Races" (Ray Sax), "My Lindy Lou" (Gordon Goodman), "Oh, Susanna" (m/l: Stephen Foster; arr: Hawley Ades) (The Minstrels), "Dixie" (Marching Band). TAKE FIVE (INTERMISSION); Unsung Dixie Interlude [Junior's Jumpin' Jivers (i.e. Fred Waring Jr., Ward Cole, Mike Doty, Lou Bode, Ray Sax, Hawley Ades, Hugh "Lumpy" Brannum, Buss Dillon)]. *Act II*: *Scene 1* Primary Mathematics: "Inchworm" (m/l: Frank Loesser); *Scene 2* Collegiate Conviviality: "A Toast to Michigan" (m/l: Richard Kirk & Louise Elbel) (Convivial Collegians), "A Toast to All Colleges" (same later), "Everybody's Alma Mater" (Alumni Association); *Scene 3* High-Fidelity: "My Old High School" (m/l: Tom Waring) (Joe Marine & Old Grads); *Scene 4* Songs from New Young Pennsylvanians: "Granada" (Bob Sands), "Unchained Melody" (m: Alex North; l: Hy Zaret) (Dorothy Arms), "If I Love You" (m: Richard Rodgers; l: Oscar Hammerstein II) [from *Carousel*] (Patti Beems), "Piano Session" (Title to be announced) (Norma Douglas); *Scene 5* Choral Symphony and Opera: "The Nutcracker Suite" (m: Peter Ilych Tchaikovsky; arr: Johnson — Cunkle — Simeone — Bernier — Waring) (Choral Symphony Orchestra), "Rigoletto" [Swanee River Quartette (i.e. Bob Sands, Preshy Marker, Ralph Isbell, Patti Beems)]; *Scene 6* The Ever-Shining Old Stars: Lou Eley, Jean Eley, Leonard Kranendonk, Joe Marine, Gordon Goodman, Hugh "Lumpy" Brannum, Frank Davis; *Scene 7* Songs You'd Hope to Hear, Hear and See, See: "Dry Bones" (The Singers), "Dancing Tambourines" (m: W.C. Polla; l: Phil Ponce) (The Singers & Players), "Over the Rainbow" (m: Harold Arlen; l: E.Y. Harburg) [from the movie *The Wizard of Oz*] (Everybody Sings), "Dear Old Donegal," "Darktown Strutters Ball" (m/l: Shelton Brooks), "Jesus Walked This Lonesome Valley," "Joshua Fit the Battle of Jericho," "The Happy Wanderer" (Val-De-Ri, Val-De-Ra) (m: Friedrich Wilhelm Moeller; l: Antonia Ridge), "Carry Me Back to Old Virginny," "Way Back Home" (m/l: Al Lewis & Tom Waring), "We'll Go a Long, Long Way Together" (m/l: Jimmy Kennedy & A. Fragna), "With a Song in My Heart" (m: Richard Rodgers; l: Lorenz Hart) [from *Spring is Here*], "You'll Never Walk Alone" (m: Richard Rodgers; l: Oscar Hammerstein II) [from *Carousel*], "Battle Hymn of the Republic" (m/l: Julia Ward Howe), Hear, Hear the People.

After Broadway. Fred Waring later took the show on the road.

299. *Heathen!*

Set in the past (1819) and the present (1972). The basic needs, beliefs and desires of two eras, compared and found similar.

The Broadway Run. BILLY ROSE THEATRE, 5/21/72. 6 previews from 5/13/72. 1 PERFORMANCE. PRESENTED BY Leonard J. Goldberg & Ken Gaston, in association with R. Paul Woodville; MUSIC/LYRICS: Eaton "Bob" Magoon Jr.; BOOK: Robert Helpmann & Eaton "Bob" Magoon Jr.; DIRECTOR: Lucia Victor; CHOREOGRAPHER: Sammy Bayes; ASSOCIATE CHOREOGRAPHER: Dan Siretta; SETS: Jack Brown; COSTUMES: Bruce Harrow; LIGHTING: Paul Sullivan; MUSICAL SUPERVISOR/VOCAL, DANCE & INCIDENTAL MUSIC: Mel Marvin; MUSICAL DIRECTOR: Clay Fullum; ORCHESTRATIONS: Larry Fallon; PRESS: Max Eisen & Milly Schoenbaum; GENERAL MANAGER: Sherman Gross; PRODUCTION STAGE MANAGER: Alan Hall; STAGE MANAGER: Jack B. Craig; ASSISTANT STAGE MANAGER: Karen Kristin. *Cast:* REV. JONATHAN BEACON/JONATHAN: Russ Thacker; KALIALANI/KALIA: Yolande Bavan; MANO'ULA/MANO: Edward Rambeau; THE MUGGERS: Dennis Dennehy, Justis Skae, Sal Pernice; REV. HIRAM BURNHAM: Dan Merriman; HEPSIBAH BURNHAM: Ann Hodges; CHURCH ELDERS: Christopher Barrett, Mary Walling, Michael Serrecchia; KAHA KAI/THE CHANTER: Dennis Dennehy; ALIKA: Mokihana; TOURISTS: Dan Merriman & Ann Hodges; HAWAIIAN BOY: Charles Goeddertz; POLICEMAN: Christopher Barrett; PUEO: Honey Sanders; MOMONA-NUI: Tina Santiago; BOYS IN JAIL: Charles Goeddertz, Michael Serrecchia, Quitman Fludd; THE GIRLS & BOYS OF PAST & PRESENT: Nancy Dafgek, Dennis Dennehy, Randy Di Grazio, Quitman Fludd, Charles Goeddertz, Karen Kristin, Sal Pernice, Michael Serrecchia, Justis Skae, Jaclynn Villamil, Mary Walling. *Understudies*: Jonathan/Kahuna: Christopher Barrett; Mano/Policeman: Dennis Dennehy; Kalia: Karen Kristin; Alika: Honey Sanders. *Act I*: THE PRESENT: a beach by a sea wall, Waikiki: "Paradise" (Jonathan & Beach People); THE PAST: a church in Boston: "The Word of the Lord" (Hiram, Hepsibah, Elders); THE PAST: aboard a ship at sea: "My Sweet Tomorrow" (Rev. Jonathan); THE PAST: Mano'ula's canoe at sea: "A Man among Men" (Mano'ula & Rowers); THE PAST: The Kona shore: "Aloha" (Company), "Kalialani" (Kalialani); THE PRESENT: the beach, Waikiki; THE PAST: a grove near Jonathan's hut: "No Way in Hell" (Rev. Jonathan, Kalialani, Mano'ula); THE PRESENT: Jail in Honolulu; THE PAST: on the edge of the village: "Battle Cry" (Kalialani); THE PAST: The Heiau, a council meeting: "This is Someone I Could Love" (Mano'ula); THE PAST: Mano'ula's compound: "House of Grass" (Mano'ula); PAST AND PRESENT BLEND: "Kava Ceremony" (Company). *Act II*: THE PRESENT: Jail in Honolulu: "For You Brother" (Jonathan & Boys in Jail); THE PAST: the church grounds, dedication ceremony: "Spear Games" (Company), "Christianity" (Company); THE PRESENT: Waikiki Beach bar: "This is Someone I Could Love" (reprise) (Kalia); THE PAST: Mano'ula's compound: "Heathen" (Rev. Jonathan); THE PAST: riding the breakers: "Heathen" (reprise) (Rev. Jonathan & Mano'ula); THE PAST: a corner o the compound: "More Better Go Easy" (Alika); THE PAST: Kalialani's hut; THE PAST: The village under the eruption of Mauna Loa; PAST AND PRESENT BLEND: "Eighth Day" (Company).

It was universally panned. Seven years later producer Leonard J. Goldberg was found murdered in his bedroom, handcuffed and shot in the head, the morning following his 33rd birthday. The other producer, Ken Gaston, died in 1983, aged 41. Bob Magoon was a Hawaiian real-estate man turned songwriter (he had done *13 Daughters*).

300. *Heaven on Earth*

A musical fantasy, a cheap imitation of *Finian's Rainbow*. Set in New York City, on the first day of spring. John, a veteran, is so poor that he lives up a tree in Central Park. He and Mary are befriended by McCarthy, a genial Irish Robin Hood–type of horse-hack driver who is friendly with all the denizens of the Park, including a pixy named Friday who is his silent and admiring secretary (she danced her role). McCarthy arranges a wedding for the lovers, and installs them in a new model Hutton home for their wedding night. Hutton, the builder, has McCarthy and his friends arrested, but relents when McCarthy frightens him by imitating Hollywood stars (this was Peter Lind Hayes's specialty act). Frobisher was the mad housing commissioner.

Before Broadway. Jackie Gleason left during tryouts, and his role was re-written as a female part (for Wynn Murray). The show cost $300,000.

The Broadway Run. NEW CENTURY THEATRE, 9/16/48–9/25/48. 12 PERFORMANCES. PRESENTED BY Monte Proser, in association with Ned C. Litwack; MUSIC: Jay Gorney; LYRICS/BOOK: Barry Trivers; ADDITIONAL LYRICS: Norman Zeno; DIRECTOR/LIGHTING: John Murray Anderson; CHOREOGRAPHER: Nick Castle; SETS/COSTUMES: Raoul Pene du Bois; MUSICAL DIRECTOR: Clay Warnick; MUSICAL ARRANGEMENTS: Russell Bennett & Don Walker; VOCAL DIRECTOR/VOCAL ARRANGEMENTS: Hugh Martin; MUSICAL ADAPTATION FOR DANCES: Alan Morand; PRESS: Bill Doll; PRODUCTION SUPERVISOR: Eddie Dowling; GENERAL MANAGER: Mac Kaplus; COMPANY MANAGER: Joe Moss; GENERAL STAGE MANAGER: Chet O'Brien; STAGE MANAGER: Harry Rogue; ASSISTANT STAGE MANAGER: Alan Bandler. *Cast:* JAMES ALOYSIUS McCARTHY: Peter Lind Hayes (1); FRIDAY: Dorothy Jarnac (5); PUNCHY: Danny Drayson (14); FANNIE FROBISHER: Caren Marsh; FLORABELLE FROBISHER: Ruth Merman; MRS. FROBISHER: Nina Varela; COMMISSIONER FROBISHER: Irwin Corey (4); OFFICER CLABBER: Claude Stroud (6); JOHN BOWERS: Robert Dixon (9); MARY BROOKS: Barbara Nunn (8); THE LOVERS: June Graham (10) & Richard D'Arcy (12); LIEUTENANT SULLIVAN: Wynn Murray (3); OFFICER JONESY: Dorothy Keller (7); OFFICER BLANDINGS: Betty George (16); SAILOR: Billy Parsons (15); H.H. HUTTON: David Burns (2); MAGISTRATE KENNEDY: Dick Bernie (13); SAILOR WITH TRUMPET: Steve Condos (11); OFFICER O'BRIEN: Bert Sheldon; RADIO ENGINEER: Jack Russell; SLIM: Remi Martel; DIPPY: Jack Russell; BUTCH: Bill Hogue; DANCERS: Lisa Ayres, Ernie Di Gennaro, Dante Di Paolo, Harold Drake, Cece Eames, Babette George, Gretchen

Houser, Marguerite James, Ray Johnson, Red Knight, Carol Lee, Dorothy Love, Caren Marsh, Remi Martel, Jack Mattis, Ruth Merman, Don Powell, Frank Reynolds, Gloria Suckling, Alice Swanson, Evelyn Ward, Jack Whitney (17), Jack Wilkins; SINGERS: Dean Campbell, Angela Castle, Julie Curtis, Betty George, John Gray, Pearl Hacker, Bill Hogue, Doug Luther, Ellen McCown, Jean Olds, Dottie Pyren, Jack Russell, Bert Sheldon, Curt Stafford, Lucille Udovick, Vincent Van Lynn. **Act I**: *Scene 1* Central Park; noon; *Scene 2* The Housing Commissioner's office; that afternoon; *Scene 3* Central Park; that afternoon; *Scene 4* The Hutton Home of Tomorrow; that evening. **Act II**: *Scene 1* Central Park; next morning; *Scene 2* A cell block in the Park jail; that morning; *Scene 3* Police Court in the Park jail; that morning; *Scene 4* Fifth Avenue; immediately afterwards; *Scene 5* Interior of Hutton Home; late that day; *Scene 6* Central Park; immediately afterwards. **Act I**: Overture (Orchestra), "In the Back of a Hack" (McCarthy, Betty George, Pearl Hacker, Doug Luther, Dean Campbell), "Anything Can Happen" (Full Company), "(You Are) So Near (and Yet So Far)" (Mary & John), Lovers Dance (Lovers), "Don't Forget to Dream" (McCarthy), "Bench in the Park" (Sullivan, Jonesy, Sailor, Punchy, Dancing Ensemble), "The Letter" (McCarthy dictates a letter to the dancing Friday), "Push a Button in a Hutton" (Hutton, Jack Whitney, Singing & Dancing Ensemble), "Home (is Where the Heart Is)" (Mary, John, Singing Ensemble), "Apple Jack" (voc arr: Bus Davis) (Sullivan, Steve Condos, Jonesy, Friday, Singing & Dancing Ensemble), "Wedding in the Park" (McCarthy, Mary, John), "Heaven on Earth" (Mary, John, Lovers), Finale (Full Company). **Act II**: Entr'acte Music (Orchestra), "What's the Matter with Our City?" (McCarthy & Full Company), "(You Are) So Near (and Yet So Far)" (reprise) (Mary & John), "First Cup of Coffee (in the Morning)" (voc arr: Bus Davis) (Sullivan, Clabber, Jonesy, Steve Condos, Singing & Dancing Ensemble), "Gift Number" (McCarthy, Clabber, Jack Whitney, Quartette, Ensemble), "Musical Tour of the City" (McCarthy & Clabber), Finale (McCarthy & Entire Company).

Reviews were terrible.

301. *Helen Goes to Troy*

An operetta, a free adaptation of the Homeric legend concerned with Helen of Troy, her suitor Paris, and her husband Menelaus.

Before Broadway. Although this production was an adaptation of Max Reinhardt's production of the Offenbach operetta *La Belle Helene*, it was re-orchestrated, and 14 Offenbach numbers from more or less forgotten operettas (*Perichole, Doctor Ox, Le Roi Carotte, Robinson Crusoe, Genevieve de Brabant*) were interpolated. For the Broadway run Erich Wolfgang Korngold added two other numbers: "What Will the Future Say?" (from *The Bridge of Sighs)* and "Love at Last" (based on *Barcarolle* from *The Rhine Nymphs. Barcarolle* had been inserted into *The Tales of Hoffman* after Offenbach's death). Director Herbert Graf took over from Max Reinhardt who, during the making of this musical, died in 1943 at the Gladstone Hotel, in New York. His son Gottfried was one of the librettists.

The Broadway Run. ALVIN THEATRE, 4/24/44–7/16/44. 97 PERFORMANCES. PRESENTED BY Yolanda Mero-Irion for the New Opera Company; MUSIC: Jacques Offenbach; MUSIC RE-ORCHESTRATED & RE-ARRANGED BY: Erich Wolfgang Korngold; LYRICS: Herbert Baker; NEW BOOK: Gottfried Reinhardt & John Meehan Jr.; DIRECTOR: Herbert Graf; DIALOGUE DIRECTOR: Melville Cooper; CHOREOGRAPHER: Leonide Massine; SETS/LIGHTING: Robert Edmond Jones; COSTUMES: Ladislas Czettel; CONDUCTOR: Erich Wolfgang Korngold; CHORAL DIRECTOR: Irving Landau; PRESS: James D. Proctor; GENERAL MANAGER: Norman Pincus; COMPANY MANAGER: Joseph Moss; PRODUCTION STAGE MANAGER: Andy Anderson; STAGE MANAGER: Mortimer O'Brien; ASSISTANT STAGE MANAGER: Herman Magidson. **Cast:** PHILOCOMUS, ASSISTANT SEER: George Rasely (4); CALCHAS, HIGH PRIEST OF JUPITER: Ralph Dumke (3); HELEN, QUEEN OF SPARTA: Jarmila Novotna (1) ☆, Lillian Andersen (matinees); ORESTES, HELEN'S NEPHEW: Donald Buka (6); PARTHENIS, A COURTESAN: Doris Blake; LEILA, ANOTHER COURTESAN: Phyllis Hill; PARIS, PRINCE OF TROY: William Horne (5), Joseph Laderoute (matinees); DISCORDIA, GODDESS OF MISCHIEF: Rose

Inghram; MINERVA, GODDESS OF WISDOM: Doris Blake; JUNO, WIFE OF JUPITER: Rosalind Nadell; VENUS, GODDESS OF LOVE & BEAUTY: Peggy Corday; POLICEMAN: Michael Mann; WHITE WING: John Guelis; AJAX 1, KING OF A SMALL NATION: Jesse White; AJAX 2, ANOTHER KING, HIS TWIN BROTHER: Alfred Porter; MENELAUS, KING OF SPARTA: Ernest Truex (2); AGAMEMNON, ANOTHER KING, MENELAUS' BROTHER: Gordon Dilworth; ACHILLES, ANOTHER KING: Hugh Johnson; LADY-IN-WAITING: Jane Kiser; PREMIERE DANSEUSES: Katia Geleznova, Kathryn Lee, Nancy Mann; PREMIER DANCERS: Michael Mann, John Guelis, George Chaffee; LADIES OF THE ENSEMBLE: Johnsie Bason, Peggy Blatherwick, Louise Fagg, Elizabeth Giacobbe, Eleanor Jones, Nancy Kenyon, Jeanne Stephens, Virginia Beeler, Anne Bolyn, Louise Newton, Maria Orelo, Mathilda Strazza, Betty Tucker, Leona Vanni; GENTLEMEN OF THE ENSEMBLE: Sam Adams, George Crawford, William Golden, John Gould, Vincent Henry, Robert Marco, Edwin Alberian, Paul Campbell, Robert Kirland, Seymour Osborne, Gordon Richards, Irving Strull; BALLET: Galina Razoumova, Lee Lauterbur, Rickey Soma, Edwina Seaver, Jane Kiser, Claire Pasch, Katherine Clark, Ricia Orkina, Nina Frenkin, Nicholas Beriozoff, Sviatoslav Toumine, Todd Bolender, David Adhar, Ricardo Sarroga. **Act I**: *Scenic Overture*: Antiquity Awakes (danced by Michael Mann, John Guelis, Kathryn Lee, Edwina Seaver, Ballet); *Scene 1* The Temple of Jupiter in Sparta: "Come to the Sacrifice" (Philocomus & Chorus), "Where is Love?" (Helen, Ladies-in-Waiting, Ballet), "Tsing-la-la" (Orestes, Calchas, Leila, Parthenis, Philocomus, Chorus, Ballet), "Take My Advice" (Helen & Orestes); *Scene 2* Mount Ida: "The Shepherd Song" (Paris), "The Judgment of Paris" (Paris, Discordia, Minerva, Juno, Venus); *Scene 3* The Temple of Jupiter in Sparta: "What Will the Future Say?" (Calchas); *Scene 4* A street in Sparta: "Extra! Extra!" (Philocomus, Policeman, Chorus, Ballet), Ajax 1 and Ajax 2 (Ajax 1 & Ajax 2), "Sweet Helen" (Helen & Paris); *Scene 5* The Temple of Jupiter in Sparta: Entrance of the Kings (Entire Company), First Finale (Entire Company): Introduction of the Kings, Dance of Procreation, Opera Parody, Go to Naxos. **Act II**: *Prologue to Second Act* (introduced by Discordia); *Scene 1* Helen's bath in the palace: Dance of the Ladies-in-Waiting (Katia Geleznova & Ballet), "Love at Last" (Helen); *Scene 2* King's private banquet hall (Bacchanale), "Bring on the Concubines" (Cast & Chorus), Waltz & Can-Can (Parthenis, Kathryn Lee, Orestes, Ballet), "If Menelaus Only Knew It" (Kings, Calchas, Chorus), Drinking Song and Dance (Paris, Kings, Calchas, Kathryn Lee, Michael Mann, John Guelis, Ballet); *Scene 3* A road near Sparta: Reprise (Menelaus); *Scene 4* Helen's boudoir: "Is it a Dream?" (Helen & Paris); *Scene 5* Outside palace door; *Scene 6* Helen's boudoir: "A Little Chat" (Orestes, Agamemnon, Menelaus, Chorus), "Advice to Husbands" (Helen & Chorus); *Scene 7* Corridor in the palace: Grecian Frieze (ballet) (Entire Company); *Scene 8* Main banquet hall: "Come with Me" (Helen, Paris, Menelaus, Company), Second Finale (Entire Company).

Critics were clearly happy, and gave it very good reviews.

302. *Hello, Dolly!*

Dolly Levi is a take-charge, all-purpose busybody in Yonkers, in the 1880s. She makes her entrance as she glides down the stairs of the Harmonia Gardens Restaurant to be serenaded by the adoring staff of waiters. After mourning the death of her husband, she decides not to let the world pass her by. She returns, engineering matches between several couples. She is, indeed, the matchmaker. She is engaged by pompous Yonkers merchant Vandergelder to find him a mate, but instead she sets her cap for him — and gets him. Along the way she helps two of Vandergelder's clerks, Barnaby and Cornelius, who enjoy a night at Harmonia Gardens with dressmaker Irene and her assistant Minnie Fay. Cornelius and Mrs. Molloy fall in love, and eventually, after firing him, Vandergelder takes Cornelius on as partner.

Before Broadway. It all started in 1835 with a British play called *A Day Well Spent*, by John Oxenford. In 1842 a Viennese variation, *Einen Jux will er sich machen* (*He Wants to Have a Lark*), by Johann Nestroy, was produced. In 1891 *A Trip to Chinatown* played Broadway, and was based on the same story. American playwright Thornton Wilder adapted the European version into *The Merchant of Yonkers*, which opened in New York, as straight play, at the GUILD THEATRE, 12/28/38. 39 PERFORMANCES. DIRECTOR: Max Reinhardt; SETS: Boris Aronson. *Cast:* MRS. LEVI: Jane Cowl; VANDERGELDER: Percy Waram; CORNELIUS: Tom Ewell; BARNABY: John Call; MINNIE FAY: Nydia Westman; MELCHIOR STACK: Joseph Sweeney; ERMENGARDE: Frances Harison; RUDOLPH: Max Willenz; AMBROSE: Bartlett Robinson; MRS. MOLLOY: June Walker.

Thornton Wilder re-wrote *The Merchant of Yonkers*, and called it *The Matchmaker*. The Theatre Guild & David Merrick produced that on Broadway, at the ROYALE THEATRE, 12/5/55–2/2/57. 488 PERFORMANCES. DIRECTOR: Tyrone Guthrie. *Cast:* DOLLY: Ruth Gordon; VANDERGELDER: Loring Smith; ERMENGARDE: Prunella Scales, *Mari Lynn*; BARNABY: Robert Morse [his Broadway debut]. *The Matchmaker* was filmed in 1958, with Shirley MacLaine.

David Merrick decided the time was right for a musical version of *The Matchmaker*, so *Dolly: a Damned Exasperating Woman* was written, with Ethel Merman in mind as star, but she was too tired from a grinding tour of *Gypsy*. Mary Martin and Lucille Ball also turned it down. Hal Prince was approached to direct, but rejected it because he didn't like the score. The title was changed to *Hello, Dolly!* It first tried out from 11/18/63, in Detroit, where it was a disaster (according to Gower Champion). Bob Merrill, Charles Strouse and Lee Adams were brought in to help with the score. Strouse and Adams wrote "Before the Parade Passes By." This was not used. However, Jerry Herman wrote another song, with the same title, which was used, to replace "Penny in My Pocket," which wasn't working. "You're a Damned Exasperating Woman" and "No, a Million Times No" were cut before Broadway. It opened for further tryouts at the National Theatre, Washington, DC, on 12/17/63, and ran there for 4 weeks. Jerry Dodge replaced James Dybas, and 8th-billed Gloria Leroy was replaced by Mary Jo Catlett. Then it went to Broadway.

The Broadway Run. ST. JAMES THEATRE, 1/16/64–12/27/70. 2 previews on 1/15/64. 2,844 PERFORMANCES. A David Merrick-Champion Five, Inc. production. PRESENTED BY David Merrick; MUSIC/LYRICS: Jerry Herman (unless noted below); ADDITIONAL MUSIC & LYRICS: Bob Merrill, Charles Strouse, Lee Adams (all unbilled); BOOK: Michael Stewart; SUGGESTED BY the 1954 farce *The Matchmaker*, by Thornton Wilder, which was based on his own comedy, *The Merchant of Yonkers*, which was produced by the Theatre Guild in 1938; DIRECTOR/CHOREOGRAPHER: Gower Champion, *Lucia Victor* (re-staged the show for the all-black production); ASSISTANT DIRECTOR/ASSISTANT CHOREOGRAPHER: Lucia Victor (until 67); SPECIAL ASSISTANT TO GOWER CHAMPION: Marge Champion; SETS: Oliver Smith; ASSISTANT SETS: Robin Wagner; COSTUMES: Freddy Wittop; LIGHTING: Jean Rosenthal; SOUND: Robert Maybaum, *Charles Bellin* (67–70); MUSICAL DIRECTOR: Shepard Coleman, *Peter Howard* (by 67), *Saul Schechtman* (from the beginning of the all-black production until the end of the run); ORCHESTRATIONS: Philip J. Lang; VOCAL ARRANGEMENTS: Shepard Coleman; DANCE & INCIDENTAL MUSIC ARRANGEMENTS: Peter Howard; CAST recording on RCA Victor; PRESS: Lee Solters, Harvey B. Sabinson, Lila Glaser King, David Powers. Additions for the all-black production: *Leo Stern & Muffy Newman* (*Shirley Herz* by 68–69); CASTING: Joel Erickson; GENERAL MANAGER: Jack Schlissel; COMPANY MANAGER: Richard Highley; GENERAL STAGE MANAGER: *Jack Timmers* (for the all-black production); PRODUCTION STAGE MANAGER: Frank Dudley; STAGE MANAGER: Pat Tolson, *Tony Manzi* (by 67–68), *Bob Bernard* (for the all-black production); ASSISTANT STAGE MANAGER: David Hartman, *E.B. Smith* (for the all-black production), *Robert L. Hultman* (for the Phyllis Diller run). *Cast:* MRS. DOLLY GALLAGHER LEVI: Carol Channing (1), *Ginger Rogers* (from 8/9/65), *Martha Raye* (from 2/27/67), *Betty Grable* (6/12/67–11/5/67), *Bibi Osterwald* (11/6/67–11/9/67, the last 4 performances before Pearl Bailey took over), *Pearl Bailey* (from 11/12/67), *Thelma Carpenter* (Wednesday matinees only, 1/29/69–3/5/69, then she took over from Pearl Bailey for all performances), *Pearl Bailey* (from 7/28/69), *Thelma Carpenter* (stood in for Pearl Bailey, 9/6/69–10/9/69, and then did all matinees until 12/13/69), *Pearl Bailey* (until 12/20/69), *Phyllis Diller* (from 12/26/69), *Ethel Merman* (from 3/28/70); ERNESTINA: Mary Jo Catlett (8), *Patricia Sauers* (by 67), *Mabel King* (from 11/12/67), *Alyce Webb* (from 69 until 12/20/69), *Marcia Lewis* (from 12/26/69); AMBROSE

KEMPER: Igors Gavon (9), *Charles Karel* (from 64–65), *Richard Hermany* (from 65–66), *David Evans* (from late 67), *Roger Lawson* (11/12/67–12/20/69), *Ronald Young* (from 12/26/69), *David Gary* (from 70); HORSE: Jan LaPrade & Bonnie Mathis (*Patti Pappathatos & Elisa De Marko* from 65–66, and Patti Pappathatos was replaced in late 67 by *Debra Lyman*), *Dianne Conway & Barbara Harper* (both from 11/12/67), *Leu Comacho* (replaced Barbara Harper in 68–69), *Beverley Baker & Alice Grant* (69), Patti Pappathatos & Ellen Elias (both from 12/26/69); HORACE VANDERGELDER: David Burns (2), *George Blackwell* (alternate by 65–66), *Max Showalter* (from 3/13/67), *Cab Calloway* (11/12/67–12/20/69), *Richard Deacon* (from 12/26/69), *Jack Goode* (from 3/28/70); ERMENGARDE: Alice Playten (10), *Andrea Bell* (from late 67), *Sherri "Peaches" Brewer* (from 11/12/67), *Edloe* (right name Edloe R. Brown–from 68–69), *Andrea Bell* (from 12/26/69), *Patricia Cope* (from 70); CORNELIUS HACKL: Charles Nelson Reilly (5), *Lawrence Holofcener* (from 65–66), *Gene GeBauer* (alternate by 65–66), *Carleton Carpenter* (from 65–66), *Will MacKenzie* (from 8/9/65), *Richard Hermany* (from late 67), *Jack Crowder* (11/12/67–12/20/69), *Bill Mullikin* (from 12/26/69), *Russell Nype* (from 3/28/70); BARNABY TUCKER: Jerry Dodge (6), *Neil Jones* (alternate by 65–66), *John Mineo* (from 8/66), *Harvey Evans* (from 7/67), *Winston DeWitt Hemsley* (11/12/67–12/20/69), *Danny Lockin* (from 12/26/69); IRENE MOLLOY: Eileen Brennan (3), *Patte Finley* (from 8/9/65), *Joyce Dahl* (alternate by 65–66), *June Helmers* (from 4/67), *Emily Yancy* (from 11/12/67), *Ernestine Jackson* (12/6/69–12/20/69), *June Helmers* (from 12/26/69); MINNIE FAY: Sondra Lee (4), *Alix Elias* (from 4/67), *Leland Palmer* (from 7/67), *Chris Calloway* (from 11/12/67), *Sherri "Peaches" Brewer* (3/68–12/20/69), *Georgia Engel* (from 12/26/69); MRS. ROSE: Amelia Haas, *Yolanda Poropat* (by 67), *Marie Bryant* (from 11/12/67), *Marki Bey* (from 68–69 until 12/20/69), *Joyce Dahl* (from 12/26/69); RUDOLPH: David Hartman, *Dan Merriman* (from 65–66), *Morgan Freeman* (from 11/12/67), *Jimmy Justice* (from 68–69 until 12/20/69), *James Beard* (from 12/26/69); JUDGE: Gordon Connell (7), *Keith Kaldenberg* (alternate by 65–66), *Walter P. Brown* (from 11/12/67), *Burt Bier* (69–12/20/69), *George Blackwell* (from 12/26/69); COURT CLERK: Ken Ayers, *Keith Kaldenberg* (from 65–66), *James Kennon-Wilson* (11/12/67–12/20/69), *Dick Crowley* (from 12/26/69); TOWNSPEOPLE/WAITERS, ETC: Ken Ayers (*KeithKaldenberg* from 65–66 until 11/67), Nicole Barth (gone by 66), Alvin Beam (gone by 65–66), Monica Carter (gone by 67–68), Carvel Carter (gone by 65–66), Joel Craig (gone by 66), Dick Crowley (until 11/67), Hamp Dickens (gone by 64–65), Gene GeBauer (until 11/67), Amelia Haas (gone by 66), Joe Helms (until 11/67), Richard Hermany (gone by 65–66), Neil Jones (gone by 66), Charles Karel (gone by 65–66), Paul Kastl (gone by 65–66), Jan LaPrade (*Patti Pappathatos* from 65–66; *Debra Lyman* from late 67 until 11/67), Joan Buttons Leonard (gone by 66), Jari Lynn (gone by 64–65), Jim Maher (gone by 66), Marilyne Mason (gone by 65–66), Bonnie Mathis (*Elisa De Marko* from 65–66 until 11/67), Joe McWherter (gone by 65–66), John Minco (gone by 66–67), Else Olufsen (gone by 65–66), Randy Phillips (gone by 65–66), Yolanda Poropat (until 11/67, Lowell Purvis (gone by 65–66), Michael Quinn (gone by 65–66), Will Roy (gone by 65–66), Bonnie Schon (until 11/67), Barbara Sharma (gone by 64–65), Mary Ann Snow (until 11/67), Paul Solen (gone by 66–67), Jamie Thomas (gone by 65–66), Pat Trott (until 11/67), Ronnie Young (gone by 65–66). 65–66 replacements: *Paul Berne* (gone by 67–68), *George Blackwell* (until 11/67), *Joyce Dahl* (until 11/67), *David Evans* (until 11/67), *Tony Falco* (until 11/67), *Diane Findlay* (gone by 66–67), *Ian Garry* (gone by 66–67), *Lee Hooper* (gone by 66–67), *Katherine Hull* (gone by 67–68), *Eddie James* (gone by 66–67), *J. David Kirby* (until 11/67), *Ed Mastin* (until 11/67), *Anne Nathan* (gone by 67–68), *Jane Quinn* (gone by 67–68), *Dan Siretta* (gone by 66–67). 66–67 replacements: *Linda Bonem* (until 11/67), *Wayne Boyd* (until 11/67), *Gerard Brentte* (gone by 67–68), *Ben Gillespie* (until 11/67), *Jerry Gotham* (until 11/67), *Jim Hovis* (until 11/67), *Scott Hunter* (until 11/67), *Voight Kempson* (gone by 67–68), *Lee Lund* (gone by 67–68), *Joe McGrath* (until 11/67), *Ellie Rogers* (gone by 67–68), *Pat Stevens* (gone by 67–68). 67–68 replacements (until 11/67): *Eileen Casey, Wayne Dugger, Caryl Hinchee, Kay Oslin, Janice Painchaud, Michael Podwal, Bob Remick, Bettiane Shumska.* The all-black production (from 11/12/67): *Guy Allen, Bryant Baker, Fred Benjamin* (gone by 68–69), *Marki Bey, Edloe R. Brown* (gone by 68–69), *Walter P. Brown, Donald Coleman, Peter Colly, Dianne Conway, Dowlin Davis* (gone by 68–69),

Clifton Davis (gone by 68–69), *Merle Derby, Dolores Easty* (gone by 68–69), *Sargent Faulkner, Larry Ferrell, Julius Fields, Ray Gilbert, Olon Godare* (gone by 68–69), *DeMarest Grey, Lavinia Hamilton, Barbara Harper* (gone by 68–69), *Patti Harris, Lolli Hinton* (gone by 68–69), *Ernestine Jackson, Reginald Jackson, Don Jay, Bob Johnson, James Kennon-Wilson, Laverne Ligon, Peter Norman* (gone by 68–69), *Joni Palmer, Saundra Sharp, E.B. Smith, Freda Turner* (gone by 68–69), *Joe Williams* (gone by 68–69). 68–69 replacements: *Clifford Allen, Beverley Baker, Leu Comacho, Joetta Cherry, Pi Douglass, Eugene Edwards, Alice Grant, Waltye Johnson, Gail Nelson, Jozella Reed, Kenneth Scott, Luke Stover, Melvin Taylor, Freda Vanterpool.* From 12/26/69: *Maggie Benson, Paul Berne, George Blackwell, Ted Bloecher, Wayne Boyd, Monica Carter, Jack Craig, Ron Crofoot, Dick Crowley, Joyce Dahl, Richard Dodd, Mark East, Ellen Elias, David Evans, Ed Goldsmid, Jerry Gotham, Joseph Helms, Gwen Hillier, Lee Hooper, Jim Hovis, Robert L. Hultman, Irma Kingsley, J. David Kirby, Sean Nolan, Alex Orfaly, Janice Painchaud, Patty Pappathatos, Jacqueline Payne, Pat Trott, Elise Warner.* **Standbys**: For Carol Canning: Jo Anne Worley; For Pearl Bailey: *Thelma Carpenter* (by 68–69). **Understudies**: Dolly: *Bibi Osterwald* (for Ginger Rogers/Betty Grable), *Marie Bryant* (for Pearl Bailey), Bibi Osterwald for Phyllis Diller/Ethel Merman); Vandergelder: Gordon Connell (for David Burns/Max Showalter), *George Blackwell* (by 67), *Walter P. Brown* (for Cab Calloway), *Burt Bier* (for Cab Calloway), *Nat Horne* (for Cab Calloway), *George Blackwell* (for Richard Deacon/Jack Goode); Cornelius: Charles Karel (for Charles Nelson Reilly), *Gene GeBauer* (by 66–67), *Richard Hermany* (by 66–67), *Clifton Davis* (for Jack Crowder), *Eugene Edwards* (for Jack Crowder — by 68–69), *Sean Nolan* for Bill Mullikin/Russell Nype); Irene: Mary Ann Snow (for Eileen Brennan), *Joyce Dahl* (by 66–67), *Saundra Sharp* (for Emily Yancy), *Ernestine Jackson* (for Emily Yancy — by 68–69), *Gail Nelson* (for Emily Yancy–by 69), *Joyce Dahl* (for June Helmers); Minnie: Barbara Sharma (for Sondra Lee), *Mary Ann Snow* (by 65–66), *Bonnie Schon* (by 66–67), *Marki Bey* (for Chris Calloway), *Leu Comacho* (for Peaches Brewer), *Patricia Cope* (for Georgia Engel); Barnaby: John Mineo (for Jerry Dodge), *Joe Helms* (by 66–67), *J. David Kirby* (by 66–67), *Olon Godare* (for Winston DeWitt Hemsley), *Larry Ferrell* (for Winston DeWitt Hemsley — by 68–69), *Ed Goldsmid* (for Danny Lockin); Ambrose: Charles Karel (for Igors Gavon), *David Evans* (for Charles Karel & Richard Hermany), *Gene GeBauer* (for David Evans), *Donald Coleman* (for Roger Lawson), *Ted Bloecher* (for Ronald Young & David Gary); Judge: Michael Quinn (for Gordon Connell), *Richard Hermany* (by 65–66), *Keith Kaldenberg* (by 66–67), *Ed Mastin* (by 67), *Don Jay* (for Walter P. Brown), *E.B. Smith* (for Walter P. Brown–by 68–69), *Robert L. Hultman* (for George Blackwell); Ernestina: Amelia Haas, *Yolanda Poropat* (by 66–67), *Laverne Ligon* (for Mabel King), *Elise Warner* (for Marcia Lewis); Mrs. Rose: Jamie Thomas, *Yolanda Poropat* (by 65–66), *Ellie Rogers* (by 66–67); Ermengarde: *Patti Pappathatos* (by 65–66), *Debra Lyman* (by 67), *Edloe R. Brown* (for Peaches Brewer), *Merle Derby* (for Edloe), *Patti Pappathatos* (for Andrea Bell & Patricia Cope); Rudolph: *Ed Mastin* (by 65–66), *Guy Allen* (for Morgan Freeman & Jimmy Justice), *Robert L. Hultman* (for James Beard). **Act I**: **Scene 1** Along Fourth Avenue, New York City; **Scene 2** Grand Central Station: "I Put My Hand In" (Dolly & Company); **Scene 3** A street in Yonkers; **Scene 4** Vandergelder's Hay & Feed Store, Yonkers: "It Takes a Woman" (Vandergelder & the Instant Glee Club), "World, Take Me Back" [added when Ethel Merman took over the role of Dolly in 1970], "Put on Your Sunday Clothes" (Cornelius, Barnaby, Dolly, Ambrose, Ermengarde); **Scene 5** The Yonkers Depot: "Put on Your Sunday Clothes" (reprise) (The People of Yonkers); **Scene 6** Outside Mrs. Molloy's hat shop, Water Street, New York City; **Scene 7** Inside the hat shop: "Ribbons Down My Back" (Mrs. Molloy), "Motherhood (March)" (by Bob Merrill & Jerry Herman) (Dolly, Vandergelder, Mrs. Molloy, Minnie Fay, Cornelius, Barnaby), "Dancing" (Dolly, Cornelius, Barnaby, Minnie Fay, Mrs. Molloy, Dancers); **Scene 8** A quiet street: "Love, Look in My Window" [added when Ethel Merman took over the role of Dolly in 1970]; **Scene 9** Fourteenth Street: "Before the Parade Passes By" (by Jerry Herman, Charles Strouse, Lee Adams) (Dolly, Vandergelder, Company). **Act II**: **Scene 1** In front of the Hoffman House Hotel, on Fifth Avenue: "Elegance" (by Bob Merrill & Jerry Herman) (Mrs. Molloy, Cornelius, Minnie Fay, Barnaby) [originally cut from *New Girl in Town*]; **Scene 2** Outside the Harmonia Gardens Restaurant, on the Battery; **Scene 3** Inside the Harmonia Gardens Restaurant: "The Waiters' Gallop" (Rudolph & Waiters), "Hello, Dolly!" (Dolly, Rudolph, Waiters, Cooks) [big hit]; **Scene 4** Tableaux Vivantes: "Come and Be My Butterfly" (Ambrose, Muses, Nymphs, Flowers, Butterflys) [Note: after the opening this scene became The Polka Contest. The song "Come and Be My Butterfly" was dropped, and replaced with "The Polka Contest" (Ambrose, Ermengarde, Mrs. Molloy, Cornelius, Minnie Fay, Barnaby, Contestants)]; **Scene 5** A Courtroom on Centre Street: "It Only Takes a Moment" (Cornelius, Mrs. Molloy, Prisoners, Policemen), "So Long, Dearie" (Dolly & Vandergelder); **Scene 6** The Hay & Feed Store, Yonkers: "Hello, Dolly!" (reprise) (Dolly & Vandergelder), Finale (Company).

Broadway reviews were tremendous. The show won Tony Awards for musical, producer of a musical, composer & lyricist, book, direction of a musical, choreography, sets, costumes, musical direction, and for Carol Channing. Charles Nelson Reilly was also nominated. It grossed over $60 million and made a profit of $9 million. Songwriter Mack David brought a lawsuit, claiming his 1948 song "Sunflower" was plagiarized for the title song "Hello, Dolly!." He seems to have been right. He settled for over a quarter million dollars. In 1966, while Ginger Rogers was starring there was a transit strike, which crippled the show for a while. Ginger missed only one performance, and Bibi Osterwald, her understudy, went on for her. By 1967 the show had started to sag, so David Merrick made a rather dramatic move — he closed the show on 11/9/67, and re-opened on 11/12/67, with an entirely black cast, starring Pearl Bailey and Cab Calloway. This new cast had already tried out from 10/11/67, at the National Theatre, Washington, DC, to rave reviews. On Broadway it opened to unanimous raves. Carol Channing was in the audience that night, and Pearl Bailey called her up on stage, and the two of them did the title song together. On 12/20/69 (after 889 performances) the all-black company closed to go on tour, and was succeeded on Broadway by a white cast, starring Phyllis Diller, that opened on 12/26/69. This all kept the show going for a while, then it started to sag again. On 3/28/70, not wishing to give up until he had beaten the record for longest running musical on Broadway, Mr. Merrick finally persuaded Ethel Merman to star for the last nine months of the run. This was Merman's last musical. Jerry Herman wrote two new songs for her — "Love, Look in My Window" and "World, Take Me Back" (although she did them, they didn't pass into the *Dolly* canon). On 9/9/70 the show beat *My Fair Lady*'s record run (it was itself overtaken on 7/21/71 by *Fiddler on the Roof*). Thornton Wilder got a weekly check from the box office of $7,000. Including tryouts and road shows, Carol Channing played Dolly 1,272 times, including 640 Broadway performances. Her last show as Dolly was on tour in Houston, on 6/11/67.

After Broadway. TOUR. Opened on 4/9/65, at the Orpheum Theatre, Minneapolis. In 5/65 the tour set a record for grosses in an 8-performance week when it took in $168,790 at the 4,120-seat Dallas State Fair Music Hall. Then it went to Tokyo, Korea, Okinawa, Vietnam (from 10/10/65, for 10 days), and then the Theatre Royal, Drury Lane, London, on 12/2/65 (for 794 performances). MUSICAL DIRECTOR: Jay Blackton. **Cast:** DOLLY: Mary Martin, *Dora Bryan* (from 5/14/66); VANDERGELDER: Loring Smith, *Bernard Spear* (from 5/14/66); CORNELIUS: Carleton Carpenter; BARNABY: Johnny Beecher; IRENE: Marilyn Lovell, *Jill Martin* (from 5/14/66); MINNIE FAY: Coco Ramirez; CHORUS INCLUDED: Bob Avian, Alvin Beam.

TOUR. Carol Channing left the Broadway company, as per her contract, to head the second tour, which opened on 9/7/65, at the Community Concourse, San Diego, and closed on 6/11/67. It broke records everywhere. In Chicago Miss Channing left to make a movie, but returned to the tour in Houston. MUSICAL DIRECTOR: Myron Roman. **Cast:** DOLLY: Carol Channing (until 6/13/66), *Eve Arden, Carol Channing* (from 10/66), *Betty Grable*; VANDERGELDER: Horace McMahon, *Milo Boulton* (from 11/65); CORNELIUS: Garrett Lewis, *Carleton Carpenter* (from 11/65), *Rex Robbins* (from 6/13/66), *Peter Walker* (from 6/67).

TOUR. Opened on 11/3/65, at the Tivoli Theatre, Chattanooga, and closed on 3/23/68, at the Shubert Theatre, Boston. In Denver new stars took over. The tour included Las Vegas for eight weeks (from 8/23/67), where Ginger Rogers and David Burns did eight shows a week and Dorothy Lamour and Max Showalter did the other six. This Vegas stint ended on 10/18/67, and on 10/20/67 Ginger Rogers resumed her regular tour. MUSICAL DIRECTOR: Jay Blackton. **Cast:** DOLLY: Betty Grable,

Ginger Rogers (from 4/19/67), *Dorothy Lamour* (alternate); VAN-DERGELDER: Max Showalter, *David Burns* (from 4/19/67), *Max Showalter* (alternate); IRENE: June Helmers, *Patte Finley, Mari Nettum* (from 3/68); MINNIE FAY: Billie Hayes, *Sondra Lee, Harriet Lynn*; CHORUS INCLUDED: Bob Avian, Alvin Beam.

TOUR. This tour was specifically designed for Dorothy Lamour. It opened on 11/14/67, at Indiana University Auditorium, Bloomington, Indiana. CHOREOGRAPHER: Lucia Victor; MUSICAL DIRECTOR: Gil Bowers. *Cast:* DOLLY: Dorothy Lamour; VANDERGELDER: Eric Brotherson.

TOUR. Martha Raye played Dolly in a special tour for troops overseas.

TOUR. Opened on 12/26/68, and closed on 4/21/69, after 32 cities. *Cast:* DOLLY: Yvonne de Carlo; VANDERGELDER: Don De Leo.

THE MOVIE. 1969. David Merrick sold the film rights for over $2.5 million, plus a percentage of the gross. "I Put My Hand In," the opening number, was replaced by "Just Leave Everything to Me." "Motherhood" was cut, and a new number "Love is Only Love" (rejected from Jerry Herman's stage musical *Mame*) was inserted. DIRECTOR: Gene Kelly. *Cast:* DOLLY: Barbra Streisand; AMBROSE: Tommy Tune; VANDERGELDER: Walter Matthau; ERMENGARDE: Joyce Ames; CORNELIUS: Michael Crawford; BARNABY: Danny Lockin; IRENE: Marianne McAndrew; MINNIE FAY: E.J. Peaker; ORCHESTRA LEADER: Louis Armstrong.

POST-BROADWAY TOUR. Opened on 1/13/70, in Boston, with the all-black cast from Broadway (the Broadway run continued, but with a white cast). On 5/17/70 star Pearl Bailey quit for health reasons, and the tour lost an astonishing amount of money as a result.

ALL-BLACK TOUR. Opened on 5/25/71, at the O'Keefe, Toronto, and closed on 7/24/71, at the San Diego Community Center. Lucia Victor's staging was used. MUSICAL DIRECTOR: Alfonso Cavaliere. *Cast:* DOLLY: Pearl Bailey; VANDERGELDER: Cab Calloway; IRENE: Ernestine Jackson; MINNIE FAY: Marki Bey; COURT CLERK: James Kennon-Wilson; CHORUS INCLUDED: Janice Painchaud, Alton Lathrop.

303. *Hello, Dolly!* (1975 Broadway revival)

This was a brief Broadway visit for another all-black touring company starring Pearl Bailey.

The Broadway Run. MINSKOFF THEATRE, 11/6/75–12/21/75. 3 previews. Limited run of 51 PERFORMANCES. PRESENTED BY Robert Cherin, in association with Theatre Now; MUSIC/LYRICS: Jerry Herman; ADDITIONAL MUSIC & LYRICS: Bob Merrill, Charles Strouse, Lee Adams; BOOK: Michael Stewart; BASED ON Thornton Wilder's play, *The Matchmaker*; DIRECTOR: Lucia Victor; CHOREOGRAPHER: Jack Craig; SETS: Oliver Smith; COSTUME SUPERVISORS: Robert Pusilo, Vida Thomas, Holly Hummel; LIGHTING: John Gleason; MUSICAL DIRECTOR: Al Cavaliere; ORCHESTRATIONS: Philip J. Lang; VOCAL ARRANGEMENTS: Shepard Coleman; DANCE & INCIDENTAL MUSIC ARRANGEMENTS: Peter Howard; PRESS: Betty Lee Hunt Associates; GENERAL MANAGERS: Theatre Now; PRODUCTION STAGE MANAGER: Kenneth Porter; STAGE MANAGER: Robert Vandergriff; ASSISTANT STAGE MANAGER: Richard Maxon. *Cast:* MRS. DOLLY GALLAGHER LEVI: Pearl Bailey (1) ☆; ERNESTINA: Bessye Ruth Scott; AMBROSE KEMPER: Howard Porter; HORSE: Kathy Jennings & Karen Hubbard; HORACE VANDERGELDER: Billy Daniels (2); ERMENGARDE: Karen Hubbard; CORNELIUS HACKL: Terrence Emanuel (4); BARNABY TUCKER: Grenoldo Frazier; IRENE MOLLOY: Mary Louise (3); MINNIE FAY: Chip Fields; MRS. ROSE: Birdie M. Hale; RUDOLPH: Jonathan Wynne; JUDGE: Ted Goodridge; COURT CLERK: Ray Gilbert; TOWNSPEOPLE: Guy Allen, Sally Benoit, Don Coleman, Richard Dodd, Terry Gene, Pat Gideon, Ray Gilbert, Ann Givin, Charles Goeddertz, Ted Goodridge, Birdie M. Hale, Karen Hubbard, Gwen Humble, Clark James, Eulaula Jennings, James Kennon-Wilson, Richard Maxon, Francie Mendenhall, Charles Neal, Howard Porter, Jimmy Rivers, Ken Rogers, Bessye Ruth Scott, Sachi Shimizu, David Staller, Teddy Williams, Jonathan Wynne. *Understudies:* Dolly: Birdie M. Hale; Vandergelder: Ted Goodridge; Irene: Pat Gideon; Cornelius: Jonathan Wynne; Minnie Fay: Gwen Humble; Barnaby: Teddy Williams; Ermengarde: Eulaula Jennings; Mrs. Rose/Ernestina: Lisa Brown; Rudolph/

Judge: Guy Allen; Ambrose: Ken Rogers; Clerk: Don Coleman. **Dance Alternates:** Ron Crofoot & Lisa Brown.

Broadway critics were completely divided.

After Broadway. Immediately after Broadway it went to the Kennedy Center, Washington, DC, 12/30/75–1/24/76.

304. *Hello, Dolly!* (1978 Broadway revival)

This Broadway run was part of a year-and-a-half-long tour which closed on 6/3/79, at the Opera House Theatre, Reno.

The Broadway Run. LUNT-FONTANNE THEATRE, 3/5/78–7/9/78. 5 previews. 147 PERFORMANCES. PRESENTED BY James M. Nederlander & The Houston Grand Opera; MUSIC/LYRICS: Jerry Herman; ADDITIONAL MUSIC & LYRICS: Bob Merrill, Charles Strouse, Lee Adams; BOOK: Michael Stewart; BASED ON Thornton Wilder's comedy, *The Matchmaker*; DIRECTOR: Lucia Victor; CHOREOGRAPHER: Jack Craig; SETS: Oliver Smith; COSTUMES: Freddy Wittop; LIGHTING: Martin Aronstein; SOUND: John Rude; MUSICAL DIRECTOR: John L. De Main; ORCHESTRATIONS: Philip J. Lang; VOCAL ARRANGEMENTS: Shepard Coleman; DANCE & INCIDENTAL MUSIC ARRANGEMENTS: Peter Howard; PRESS: Solters & Roskin; CASTING: TNI Casting (Julie Hughes); PRODUCTION SUPERVISOR: Jerry Herman; GENERAL MANAGERS: Jack Schlissel, Jay Kingwill, Robert Buckley; COMPANY MANAGERS: Morry Efron; PRODUCTION STAGE MANAGER: Pat Tolson; STAGE MANAGER: T.L. Boston; ASSISTANT STAGE MANAGER: Judith Binus. *Cast:* MRS. DOLLY GALLAGHER LEVI: Carol Channing (1) ☆; ERNESTINA: P.J. Nelson (10); AMBROSE KEMPER: Michael C. Booker (9); HORSE: Carole Banninger & Debra Pigliavento; HORACE VANDERGELDER: Eddie Bracken (2) ☆; ERMENGARDE: K.T. Baumann (7); CORNELIUS HACKL: Lee Roy Reams (3); BARNABY TUCKER: Robert Lydiard (5); MINNIE FAY: Alexandra Korey (6); IRENE MOLLOY: Florence Lacey (4); MRS. ROSE: Marilyn Hudgins; RUDOLPH: John Anania (8); JUDGE: Bill Bateman; COURT CLERK: Randolph Riscol; TOWNSPEOPLE/WAITERS, ETC: Diane Abrams, Richard Ammon, Carole Banninger, Bill Bateman, Kyle Cittadin, Ron Crofoot, Don Edward Detrick, Richard Dodd, Rob Draper, David Evans, JoEla Flood, Tom Garrett, Charles Goeddertz, James Homan, Marilyn Hudgins, Alex MacKay, Richard Maxon, Deborah Moldow, Randy Morgan, Janyce Nyman, Jacqueline Payne, Debra Pigliavento, Theresa Rakov, Randolph Riscol, Barbara Ann Thompson, Mark Waldrop. *Understudies:* Vandergelder: John Anania; Cornelius: Michael C. Booker; Irene: Deborah Moldow; Minnie Fay: K.T. Baumann; Barnaby: Kyle Cittadin; Rudolph: Randy Morgan; Ermengarde: Jacqueline Payne; Ernestina: Theresa Rakov; Ambrose: Rob Draper; Mrs. Rose: Barbara Ann Thompson; *Swing Dancers:* Coby Grossbart & Bubba Rambo. *Act I: Scene 1* Along Fourth Avenue, New York City: "I Put My Hand In" (Dolly & Company); *Scene 2* Grand Central Station; *Scene 3* Vandergelder's Hay and Feed Store, Yonkers: "It Takes a Woman" (Vandergelder & The Instant Glee Club), "Put on Your Sunday Clothes" (Cornelius, Barnaby, Dolly, Ambrose, Ermengarde); *Scene 4* The Yonkers Depot: "Put on Your Sunday Clothes" (reprise) (People of Yonkers); *Scene 5* Outside Mrs. Molloy's Hat Shop, Water Street, New York City; *Scene 6* Inside the hat shop: "Ribbons Down My Back" (Mrs. Molloy), "Motherhood" (Dolly, Vandergelder, Mrs. Molloy, Minnie Fay, Cornelius, Barnaby), "Dancing" (Dolly, Cornelius, Barnaby, Minnie Fay, Mrs. Molloy, Dancers); *Scene 7* A quiet street — Ephraim's deserted store; *Scene 8* 14th Street: "Before the Parade Passes By" (Dolly, Vandergelder, Company). *Act II: Scene 1* In front of the Hoffman House Hotel, on Fifth Avenue: "Elegance" (Mrs. Molloy, Cornelius, Minnie Fay, Barnaby); *Scene 2* Outside the Harmonia Gardens Restaurant, on the Battery; *Scene 3* Inside the Harmonia Gardens Restaurant: "The Waiters' Gallop" (Rudolph & Waiters), "Hello, Dolly!" (Dolly, Rudolph, Waiters, Cooks), "The Polka Contest" (Ambrose, Ermengarde, Mrs. Molloy, Cornelius, Minnie Fay, Barnaby, Contestants); *Scene 4* A courtroom on Center Street: "It Only Takes a Moment" (Cornelius, Mrs. Molloy, Prisoners, Policemen), "So Long, Dearie" (Dolly); *Scene 5* The Hay & Feed Store, Yonkers: "Hello, Dolly!" (reprise) (Dolly & Vandergelder), Finale (Company).

Broadway reviews were great. Eddie Bracken was nominated for a Tony.

After Broadway. TOUR. Opened on 4/11/83, at the Auditorium, Rochester, NY. PRESENTED BY James M. Nederlander, Fred Walker, and Charles Lowe Productions; DIRECTOR: Lucia Victor; CHOREOGRAPHER: Terry Lacy; SETS: Gail Cooper-Hecht; MUSICAL DIRECTOR: Terry La Bolt. *Cast:* DOLLY: Carol Channing; VANDERGELDER: Tom Batten; ERMENGARDE: Jane Dorian; CORNELIUS: Davis Gaines; BARNABY: Gary Wright; MINNIE FAY: K.T. Baumann.

305. *Hello, Dolly!* (1995 Broadway revival)

Before Broadway. The Broadway Run was part of a tour that opened on 7/12/94, in Denver. It had the same basic cast and crew as for the Broadway stint, except that a few chorus members were added for Broadway. During the tour Jim Walton stood in for Michael DeVries during his vacation. A new character, Danny, was introduced on this tour, but for Broadway his name was changed to Stanley. The scene and musical number breakdowns were the same as for the 1978 Broadway revival. On 8/16/95, while still on tour, fire destroyed $750,000 worth of sets. Just before Broadway, the show ran at the Kennedy Center, in Washington, DC, 9/12/95–9/18/95.

The Broadway Run. LUNT-FONTANNE THEATRE, 10/19/95–1/28/96. 11 previews from 10/11/95. 116 PERFORMANCES. PRESENTED BY Manny Kladitis, Magic Promotions & Theatricals, PACE Theatrical Group, and Jon B. Platt; MUSIC/LYRICS: Jerry Herman; ADDITIONAL MUSIC & LYRICS: Bob Merrill, Charles Strouse, Lee Adams; BOOK: Michael Stewart; BASED ON Thornton Wilders' comedy, *The Matchmaker*; DIRECTOR/CHOREOGRAPHER: Lee Roy Reams; SETS: Oliver Smith; COSTUMES: Jonathan Bixby; LIGHTING: Ken Billington; SOUND: Peter J. Fitzgerald; MUSICAL SUPERVISOR: Tim Stella; MUSICAL DIRECTOR: Jack Everly; ORIGINAL ORCHESTRATIONS: Philip J. Lang; VOCAL ARRANGEMENTS: Shepard Coleman; DANCE MUSIC ARRANGEMENTS: Peter Howard; NEW CAST RECORDING on Varese Sarabande; PRESS: Boneau/Bryan-Brown; CASTING: Mark Reiner; PRODUCTION SUPERVISOR: Jerry Herman; GENERAL MANAGERS: Niko Associates; COMPANY MANAGER: Brig Berney; PRODUCTION STAGE MANAGER: Thomas P. Carr; STAGE MANAGER: Jim Semmelman; ASSISTANT STAGE MANAGER: John Salvatore. *Cast:* MRS. DOLLY GALLAGHER LEVI: Carol Channing (1) ☆, *Monica M. Wemitt* (4 performances on 11/2/95 and 11/3/95, during Miss Channing's absence due to a stomach bug); ERNESTINA: Monica M. Wemitt (8); AMBROSE KEMPER: James Darrah (7); HORSE: Sharon Moore & Michele Tibbitts; HORACE VANDERGELDER: Jay Garner (2) ☆; ERMENGARDE: Christine De Vito (9); CORNELIUS HACKL: Michael DeVries (3); BARNABY TUCKER: Cory English (5); MINNIE FAY: Lori Ann Mahl (6); IRENE MOLLOY: Florence Lacey (4); MRS. ROSE: Elizabeth Green; RUDOLPH: Steve Pudenz (10); STANLEY: Julian Brightman; JUDGE: Bill Bateman; COURT CLERK: Halden Michaels; TOWNSPEOPLE/WAITERS, ETC: John Bantay, Desta Barbieri, Bill Bateman, Kimberly Bellmann, Bruce Blanchard, Stephen Bourneuf, Julian Brightman, Holly Cruikshank, Simone Gee, Jason Gillman, Milica Govich, Elizabeth Green, Donald Ives, Dan LoBuono, Jim Madden, Halden Michaels, Sharon Moore, Michael Quinn, Robert Randle, Mitch Rosengarten, Mary Setrakian, Clarence M. Sheridan, Randy Slovacek, Roger Preston Smith, Ashley Stover, Michele Tibbitts. *Standby*: Dolly: Florence Lacey. **Understudies:** Vandergelder: Steve Pudenz; Cornelius: Jim Madden; Barnaby: Julian Brightman; Irene: Mary Setrakian; Minnie Fay: Christine De Vito; Ambrose: Dan LoBuono; Ermengarde: Michele Tibbitts; Ernestina: Elizabeth Green; Judge: Halden Michaels; Rudolph/Clerk: Roger Preston Smith; Mrs. Rose: Milica Govich; Stanley: Matthew A. Sipress. SWINGS: Kevin M. Burrows, Jennifer Joan Joy, John Salvatore, Matthew A. Sipress. **Orchestra:** REEDS: Lawrence Feldman, Robert Keller, Bill Meade, Frank Santagata; TRUMPETS: Larry Pyatt, Jeff Parke, David Rogers; TROMBONES: Dale Kirkland & Jack Schatz; CONCERTMASTER: Masako Yanagita; VIOLINS: Ann Labin, Carlos Villa, Debbie Wong, Elizabeth Chang, Claudia Hafer Tondi, Robert Lawrence; CELLI: Daniel Miller & Ellen Westerman; BASS: Jeff Ganz; DRUMS: Joseph

DeLuca; PERCUSSION: Ian Finkel; HARP: Lise Nadeau; GUITAR: Steven Bargonetti; KEYBOARD: Richard Riskin.

The show got only raves from Broadway reviewers. It received a Tony nomination for revival of a musical. After the Broadway run the show went back on tour, this time with Jeanne Lehman as Irene. The tour went on vacation 12/23/96–1/13/97.

After Broadway. *Que Tal, Dolly!* MEXICO CITY, 1996. This was a Mexican revival. *Cast:* DOLLY: Silvia Pinal; VANDERGELDER: Ignacio Lopez Tarso.

306. *Henry, Sweet Henry*

Set in New York City. A lonesome teenager, neglected by her globe-trotting parents, idealizes and chases after, and inadvertently terrorizes, her handsome and sportive bachelor idol, a composer (based on author Nora Johnson's similar crush on pianist Oscar Levant). Mrs. Boyd is Val's adulterous mother. Henry Boyd is Val's father.

Before Broadway. The show tried out in Detroit and Philadelphia. It got great reviews in Philadelphia. The number "Somebody, Someplace" was cut before Broadway.

The Broadway Run. PALACE THEATRE, 10/23/67–12/31/67. 12 previews from 10/12/67. 80 PERFORMANCES. PRESENTED BY Edward Specter Productions & Norman Twain; MUSIC/LYRICS: Bob Merrill; BOOK: Nunnally Johnson; BASED ON the 1958 autobiographical novel *The World of Henry Orient*, by Nora Johnson, and on the 1964 movie, written by Nora Johnson and Nunnally Johnson (Nora's father), and starring Peter Sellers; DIRECTOR: George Roy Hill; CHOREOGRAPHER: Michael Bennett; ASSISTANT CHOREOGRAPHERS: Charlene Mehl & Robert Avian; SETS/LIGHTING: Robert Randolph; COSTUMES: Alvin Colt; LIGHTING: Century Lighting; SOUND: Robert Goble; MUSICAL DIRECTOR/VOCAL ARRANGEMENTS: Shepard Coleman; ORCHESTRATIONS: Eddie Sauter; DANCE MUSIC ARRANGEMENTS: William Goldenberg & Marvin Hamlisch; CAST RECORDING on ABC; PRESS: Harvey Sabinson, Lee Solters, David Powers; GENERAL MANAGER: Sherman Gross; COMPANY MANAGER: Virginia Snow; PRODUCTION STAGE MANAGER: William Dodds; STAGE MANAGER: Harry Clark; ASSISTANT STAGE MANAGER: Neil Jones. *Cast:* KAFRITZ: Alice Playten (6); VALERIE "VAL" BOYD: Robin Wilson (3); MISS COONEY: Barbara Beck; MARIAN "GIL" GILBERT: Neva Small (4); HENRY ORIENT: Don Ameche (1) ☆; STELLA: Louise Lasser (5); MRS. GILBERT: Trudy Wallace; USHERETTE: Julie Sargant; MRS. BOYD: Carol Bruce (2) ☆; RUSS: John Mineo; CAPTAIN KENNETH: George NeJame; HAL: Robert Iscove; POLICEMAN: Gerard Brentte; MR. BOYD: Milo Boulton (7); POLICEMAN: Charles Rule; BIG VAL: K.C. Townsend (8); NORTON SCHOOL STUDENTS: Chris Bocchino, Lori Cesar, Terry Forman, Joyce James, Baayork Lee, Gina Page, Ilene Schatz, Joy Stark, Rebecca Urich, Pia Zadora; KNICKERBOCKER GREYS: Paul Charles, Rob Iscove, Joe Mazzello, Kim Milford, John Mineo, George NeJame, Craig Wineline; ADULT ENSEMBLE: Robert Avian, Barbara Beck, Gerard Brentte, Gene Castle, Robert Fitch, Marvin Goodis, Neil Jones, Maryann Kerrick, Priscilla Lopez, Lee Lund, Laried Montgomery, Charles Rule, Julie Sargant, Mary Ann Snow, Trudy Wallace. *Standbys*: Henry: Joseph Leon; Stella: Leila Martin. Understudies: Mrs. Boyd: Mary Ann Snow; Val: Rebecca Urich; Gil: Pia Zadora; Kafritz: Lori Cesar; Big Val: Maryann Kerrick; Mrs. Gilbert: Barbara Beck. *Act I: Scene 1* A street in New York City: "Academic Fugue" (Company); *Scene 2* Locker room: "In Some Little World" (Val); *Scene 3* Central Park Zoo: "Pillar to Post" (Orient & Stella); *Scene 4* Two bedrooms: "Here I Am" (Val); *Scene 5* Concert hall; *Scene 6* Val's bedroom: "Whereas" (Val & Gil) [dropped after the opening]; *Scene 7* Telephone booths; *Scene 8* Luncheonette: "I Wonder How it Is (to Dance with a Boy)" (Gil & Girls); *Scene 9* Street telephone booth: "Nobody Steps on Kafritz" (Kafritz); *Scene 10* Orient's apartment — exterior and interior: "Henry, Sweet Henry" (Val & Gil), "Woman in Love" (Val & Gil), "The People Watchers" (Company). *Act II: Scene 1* Boyd's living room; *Scene 2* Washington Square: "Weary Near to Dyin'" (Val & Hippies); *Scene 3* Orient's apartment; *Scene 4* Boyd's living room; *Scene 5* Exterior school and locker room: "Poor Little Person" (Kafritz, Girls, Knickerbocker Greys), "I'm Blue Too" (Val

& Gil); *Scene 6* Cocktail bar: "To Be Artistic" (Orient & Mrs. Boyd); *Scene 7* Exterior Orient's apartment; *Scene 8* Boyd's living room; *Scene 9* Orient's bedroom: "Forever" (Orient); *Scene 10* Val's bedroom: "Do You Ever Go to Boston?" (Val); *Finale*: Knickerbocker Grey Happening: "Here I Am" (reprise) (Val).

Thanks in part to Clive Barnes' *New York Times* review, it was not a hit (it got very bad Broadway reviews all the way around). It lost its $400,000 investment. The show received Tony nominations for choreography, and for Alice Playten.

After Broadway. THEATRE AT ST. PETER'S, NYC, 10/8/04–10/10/04. PRESENTED BY the York Theatre Company, as part of their *Musicals in Mufti* series. DIRECTOR: Gordon Greenberg. *Cast*: KAFRITZ: Sara Inbar; VAL: Ann Letscher; MISS COONEY/STELLA/MRS. GILBERT: Miriam Shor; GIL: Katie Adams; HENRY: Mark Nelson; MRS. BOYD: Kaitlin Hopkins; MR. BOYD: Matthew Arkin.

307. *Her First Roman*

Set in Egypt Oct. 48–March 47 BC. The romance between Caesar as an elderly philosopher-warrior and Cleopatra as a barbaric sex-kitten, as imagined by G.B. Shaw.

Before Broadway. Donald McKayle was replaced as choreographer by Kevin Carlisle before rehearsals started. Leslie Caron was the first choice for Cleopatra, but Michael Benthall, the director, went for Leslie Uggams instead. He also hired Richard Kiley. During Boston tryouts Mr. Benthall was replaced as director by Derek Goldby, and Kevin Carlisle was as choreographer by Dania Krupska. The score was changed drastically, with Bock & Harnick adding three new songs, and six Ervin Drake numbers being cut—"When My Back is to the Wall," "Pleasure Him"/"He Pleasures Me," "Parable of the Monkey," "The Wrong Man," "Let Me Lead the Way," and "I Fell in with (Evil Companions)".

The Broadway Run. LUNT—FONTANNE THEATRE, 10/20/68–11/2/68. 21 previews. 17 PERFORMANCES. PRESENTED BY Joseph Cates & Henry Fownes, in association with Warner Bros.—7 Arts; MUSIC/LYRICS/BOOK: Ervin Drake; ADDITIONAL SONGS: Jerry Bock & Sheldon Harnick; BASED ON the 1907 comedy *Caesar and Cleopatra*, by George Bernard Shaw; DIRECTOR: Derek Goldby; CHOREOGRAPHER: Dania Krupska; ASSISTANT CHOREOGRAPHER: Barbara Sharma; SETS/COSTUMES: Michael Annals; LIGHTING: Martin Aronstein; SOUND: Jack Mann; MUSICAL DIRECTOR/DANCE & INCIDENTAL MUSIC ARRANGEMENTS: Peter Howard; ORCHESTRATIONS/VOCAL ARRANGEMENTS: Don Walker; CAST RECORDING on Atlantic; PRESS: Max Eisen, Carl Samrock, Cheryl Sue Dolby; CASTING: Alan Shayne Associates; GENERAL MANAGERS: Robert Weiner & George Thorn; COMPANY MANAGER: Leonard A. Mulhern; PRODUCTION STAGE MANAGER: Ellen Wittman; STAGE MANAGER: George Rondo; ASSISTANT STAGE MANAGER: Philip Cusack. *Cast*: FTATATEETA, CLEOPATRA'S SERVANT: Claudia McNeil (3); RUFIO: Bruce MacKay (4); ROMAN CENTURION: Jack Dabdoub (11); JULIUS CAESAR: Richard Kiley (1) ☆; CLEOPATRA: Leslie Uggams (2) ☆; IRAS: Barbara Sharma (9); CHARMIAN: Diana Corto (10); ACHILLAS: Larry Douglas (8); POTHINUS: Earl Montgomery (6); PTOLEMY: Phillip Graves (12); BRITANNUS: Brooks Morton (7); ROMAN SENTRY: George Blackwell; APOLLODORUS: Cal Bellini (5); PALACE OFFICIAL: Marc Jordan; ROMAN SOLDIERS: John Baylis, Paul Berne, George Blackwell, Gerry Burkhardt, Robert Carle, Gordon Cook, Bill Gibbens, Scott Hunter, Sean Nolan, Doug Spingler, Don StomsVik, Ronald Stratton; EGYPTIANS: Henry Baker, Pamela Barlow, Diana Corto, Marc Jordan, Priscilla Lopez, Sally Neal, George Nestor, Alexander Orfaly, Trina Parks, Suzanne Rogers, Renee Rose, Kenneth Scott, Geri Seignious. *Standbys*: Caesar: Larry Douglas; Ftatateeta: Fran Stevens. *Understudies*: Cleopatra: Diana Corto; Rufio: Jack Dabdoub; Ptolemy: Jason Howard; Britannus: George Blackwell; Centurion: Robert Carle; Achillas: John Baylis; Iras: Priscilla Lopez; Charmian: Geri Seignious; Apollodorus: Gordon Cook; Pothinus: Alex Orfaly. *Swing Girl*: Myrna White. *Swing Boy*: Ron Schwinn. *Act I*: *Prologue*: "What Are We Doing in Egypt?" (Rufio, Centurion, Roman Soldiers); *Scene 1* The Sphinx: "Hail to the Sphinx" (Caesar), "Save Me from Caesar!" (Cleopatra & Caesar); *Scene 2* The Throne Room at Memphis: "Many Young Men from Now" (Cleopatra); *Scene 3* The Council Chamber at Alexandria; *Scene 4* The Queen's chamber: "Ptolemy" (by Bock & Harnick) (Cleopatra & Egyptian Women); *Scene 5* Caesar's chamber: "(Kind) Old Gentleman" (by Bock & Harnick) (Caesar); *Scene 6* A Roman guard room: "Her First Roman" (Rufio, Britannus, Roman Soldiers); *Scene 7* Caesar's chamber: "Magic Carpet" (Cleopatra, Apollodorus, Egyptians); *Scene 8* The lighthouse: "Rome" (Caesar), "The Things We Think We Are" (Caesar, Cleopatra, Britannus, Apollodorus). *Act II*: *Scene 1* A palace garden: "I Cannot Make Him Jealous" (Cleopatra)/"I Can't Help Feeling Jealous" (Caesar)); *Scene 2* The roof of the palace: "The Dangerous Age" (Rufio & Britannus), "In Vino Veritas" (Caesar, Rufio, Britannus, Apollodorus), "Caesar is Wrong" (by Bock & Harnick) (Caesar), "Just for Today" (Cleopatra); *Scene 3* The wharf at Alexandria.

It was almost universally panned on Broadway, and lost $575,000.

After Broadway. In 1993 A 25th-anniversary recording of the original Ervin Drake pre–Broadway score (i.e. no Bock/Harnick songs) was made on Ducy Lee Recordings. *Cast*: CAESAR: Richard Kiley; CLEOPATRA: Leslie Uggams; RUFIO: Ron Raines; FTATATEETA: Brenda Silas-Moore; BRITANNUS: Jack Eddleman; IRAS: Priscilla Lopez. *Act I*: Opening/What Are We Doing in Egypt?" (Roman Soldiers), "Song of the Sphinx" (Caesar), "Save Me from Caesar!" (Cleopatra & Caesar), "Many Young Men from Now" (Cleopatra), "When My Back is to the Wall" (Caesar, Cleopatra, Pothinus, Ptolemy, Egyptians), "Pleasure Him" (Ftatateeta)/"He Pleasures Me" (Cleopatra), "Her First Roman" (Rufio, Britannus, Iras, Chorus), "Magic Carpet" (Cleopatra), "Rome" (Caesar & Roman Soldiers), "The Dangerous Age" (Caesar & Rufio), "The Things We Think We Are" (Caesar, Cleopatra, Rufio, Britannus, Apollodorus). *Act II*: "Her First Roman" (reprise) (Rufio, Britannus, Roman Soldiers), "Parable of the Monkey" (Iras & Handmaidens), "I Cannot Make Him Jealous" (Cleopatra)/"I Can't Help Feeling Jealous" (Caesar), "The Wrong Man" (Cleopatra), "Let Me Lead the Way" (Ftatateeta), "In Vino Veritas" (Caesar, Rufio, Britannus, Apollodorus), "(I Fell in With) Evil Companions" (Rufio, Caesar, Cleopatra, Roman Soldiers), "Just for Today" (Cleopatra), Finale Ultimo (Ensemble).

YORK THEATRE COMPANY, 9/19/97–9/21/97. Part of the *Musicals in Mufti* series. This staged reading used the script of the old pre–Broadway tryout run. DIRECTOR: Alex Dmitriev; MUSICAL DIRECTOR: Steven D. Brown.

308. *Here's Love*

A musical fantasy. Set between Thanksgiving Day and Christmas Day, around New York City. A man really believes he is Santa Claus, and by the end has everyone else believing it too.

Before Broadway. Stuart Ostrow replaced Norman Jewison as director. The number "Dear Mister Santa Claus" ("If Santa Claus Were Crazy") (Children) was cut, as were: "Fa La La, Fa La La," "We Live on the Park," "You Don't Have to Prove it if You Sing It".

The Broadway Run. SHUBERT THEATRE, 10/3/63–7/25/64. 2 previews on 10/2/63. 338 PERFORMANCES. PRESENTED BY Stuart Ostrow; MUSIC/LYRICS/BOOK: Meredith Willson; BASED ON the 1947 movie *Miracle on 34th Street* (screenplay by Valentine Davies), which itself was based on a story by Valentine Davies; DIRECTOR: Stuart Ostrow; CHOREOGRAPHER: Michael Kidd; SETS: William & Jean Eckart; COSTUMES: Alvin Colt; LIGHTING: Tharon Musser; MUSICAL DIRECTOR/VOCAL ARRANGEMENTS/ADDITIONAL SCORING: Elliot Lawrence; ORCHESTRATIONS: Don Walker; DANCE MUSIC ARRANGEMENTS: Peter Howard; CAST RECORDING on Columbia; PRESS: Harvey B. Sabinson, Harry Nigro, David Powers; GENERAL MANAGER: Joseph Harris; PRODUCTION STAGE MANAGER: Terence Little; STAGE MANAGER: Arthur Rubin; ASSISTANT STAGE MANAGER: Ralph Linn. *Cast:* MR. KRIS KRINGLE: Laurence Naismith (3); FRED GAILY: Craig Stevens (2), *Richard Kiley*; SUSAN WALKER: Valerie Lee (5); MARVIN SHELLHAMMER: Fred Gwynne (4); DORIS WALKER: Janis Paige (1), *Lisa Kirk*; CLERKS: Michael Bennett, Gene Kelton, Bill Stanton, Patrick Cummings, Diane Ball, Sandra Roveta, Patti Pappathatos, Elaine Cancilla; R.H. MACY: Paul Reed; HARRY FINFER: Sal Lombardo; MRS. FINFER: Mara Landi; HENDRIKA: Kathy Cody; HENDRIKA'S NEW MOTHER: Suzanne France; MISS CROOK-

SHANK: Reby Howells; MR. PSAWYER: David Doyle, *Dom De Luise*; GOVERNOR: Darrell Sandeen; MAYOR: Hal Norman; MR. GIMBEL: William Griffis; POLICEMAN: Bob McClure; CLARA: Mary Louise, *Ceil Delli*; JUDGE MARTIN GROUP: Cliff Hall; DISTRICT ATTORNEY THOMAS MARA: Larry Douglas; TAMMANY O'HALLORAN: Arthur Rubin, *William Griffis*; NURSE: Leesa Troy; MARINES: John Sharpe, Bob McClure, Darrell Sandeen; GIRL SCOUT LEADER: Mara Landi; BAILIFF: Del Horstmann; MAILMAN: Hal Norman; THOMAS MARA JR.: Ronnie Kroll, *Dewey Golkin*; MURPHY: William Griffis; CHILDREN: Debbie Breen, Kathy Cody, Sal Lombardo, Ronnie Kroll, Terrin Miles; DANCERS: Diane Ball, Michael Bennett, Duane Bodin, Elaine Cancilla, Patrick Cummings, Suzanne France, Reby Howells, Gene Kelton, Baayork Lee, David Lober, Bill Louther, Patti Pappathatos, Sandra Roveta, John Sharpe, Bill Stanton, Carolsue Shaer; SINGERS: Ceil Delli, Penny Gaston, Del Horstmann, Mara Landi, Mary Louise, Bob McClure, Hal Norman, Darrell Sandeen, Leesa Troy. **Understudies**: Doris: Leesa Troy; Fred: Larry Douglas; Kris: William Griffis; Macy: Hal Norman; Shellhammer/Tammany: Bob McClure; Susan: Debbie Breen; Psawyer/Gimbel: Del Horstmann; Judge: William Griffis; D.A.: Darrell Sandeen. **Act I**: Overture (Orchestra); **Scene 1** West 73rd Street; Thanksgiving morning; **Scene 2** Parade assembly area; immediately following; **Scene 3** Along Central Park West; immediately following: "The Big Clown Balloons" (Paradesters); **Scene 4** 34th Street roof; immediately following; **Scene 5** Doris Walker's apartment; that evening: "Arm in Arm" (Doris & Susan), "You Don't Know" (Doris); **Scene 6** Briefing room at Macy's; 3 p.m., the next afternoon: "The Plastic Alligator" (Shellhammer & Clerks); **Scene 7** Macy's Toy Department; elevators; escalator; and into Herald Square; immediately following: "The Bugle" (Kris & Hendrika), "Here's Love" (Kris, Fred, Susan, Customers, Clerks, Employees, Children); **Scene 8** Playground in Central Park; later that afternoon: "My Wish" (Fred & Susan); **Scene 9** Doris Walker's office; in the meantime: "Pine Cones and Holly Berries" ("It's Beginning to Look Like Christmas") (Kris, Doris, Shellhammer); **Scene 10** Fred Gaily's apartment; after work, that day: "Look, Little Girl" (Fred); **Scene 11** On the way to Doris's apartment; immediately following: "Look, Little Girl" (reprise) (Doris); **Scene 12** Store psychologist's office at Macy's; the following Monday morning; **Scene 13** Macy's Toy Department; that evening: "Expect Things to Happen" (Kris); **Scene 14** The Party: "Love, Come Take Me Again" (waltz ballet) (instrumental) (Ballet Corps); **Scene 15** Macy's Toy Department: "Toy Ballet" (Dancers), Finale Act I (Orchestra). **Act II**: Prelude (Orchestra); **Scene 1** Judge Martin Group's chambers; several weeks later; Thursday, Dec. 19, morning; **Scene 2** In isolation at Bellevue; later that day: "Pine Cones and Holly Berries" (reprise) (Kris & Susan); **Scene 3** Fred's apartment; that evening: "She Hadda Go Back" (Fred & The Marines); **Scene 4** A corridor in the New York Supreme Court; 10 o'clock the next morning; **Scene 5** The courtroom; immediately following: "That Man Over There" (Macy), "My State (My Kansas, My Home)" (Doris, Macy, Shellhammer, Tammany, Judge Group); **Scene 6** The courthouse corridor; 3 p.m., the following Tuesday afternoon, Dec. 24: "Nothin' in Common" (Doris); **Scene 7** The courtroom; immediately following: "That Man Over There" (reprise) (Court Personnel & Spectators), Case Dismissed (Company), "Love, Come Take Me Again" (Doris) [added during the run]; **Scene 8** Macy's model living-room display; Christmas Eve, immediately following: Finale Ultimo (Company).

It got generally great Broadway reviews, but missed the boat.

After Broadway. TOUR. Opened on 8/3/64, at the Los Angeles Philharmonic Auditorium, and closed on 12/19/64, at the Curran Theatre, San Francisco. **Cast**: DORIS: Lisa Kirk; KRIS: Laurence Naismith; JUDGE: Cliff Hall; POLICEMAN: Bob McClure; FRED: John Payne; SHELLHAMMER: Bill Hinnant; SUSAN: Diane Higgins; MACY: Howard I. Smith; MARA: Charles Braswell.

GOODSPEED OPERA HOUSE, Conn., 1992. ADAPTED/DIRECTOR: Larry Carpenter; CHOREOGRAPHER: Daniel Pelzig; SETS: James Leonard Joy; COSTUMES: John Falabella; LIGHTING: Craig Miller; MUSICAL DIRECTOR: Mark Mitchell; CONDUCTOR: Wendy Bobbitt. **Cast**: DORIS: Jan Maxwell; MACY: Jerry Lanning; KRIS: Denis Homes.

LARK THEATRE COMPANY, 12/17/01. One-night benefit. It restored the number "Dear Mister Santa Claus." **Cast**: DORIS: Debbie Gravitte; JUDGE/HENDRIKA'S MOTHER/CROOKSHANK: Mary Testa; FRED: James Stovall; KRIS: Chuck Cooper; MACY: Arthur Rubin; SHELLHAMMER: Jeff Blumenkrantz; ALSO WITH: Ann Harada, Robert Creighton, William Michals.

309. *Here's Where I Belong*

Brooding Cal Trask has a rivalry with his father Adam's other son, Aron, who is the favorite. Cal, believing his mother to be dead, finds that she is running a nearby brothel. Aron's girlfriend Abra is drawn to Cal. Lee is the oriental houseboy who raised the Trask boys.

Before Broadway. Previously called *East of Eden*. Mitch Miller got United Artists to put up $500,000 to produce this show (after MCA had backed out). A fire started among the spotlights on opening night of tryouts in Philadelphia, where reviews were bad. Tony Mordente replaced Hanya Holm as choreographer. Alex Gordon (who in reality was novelist Gordon Cotler) replaced Terrence McNally as librettist when Mr. McNally walked out of the show because they were tinkering with his book without his knowledge (that's his story. Mitch Miller's is that Mr. McNally was not doing the re-writes demanded of him). The upshot was that Mr. McNally wanted his name removed from the credits (even though most of the book that was eventually shown was his). Genevieve Pitot was replaced by Arnold Goland as dance music arranger. Norman Leyden and Jonathan Tunick were brought in to assist Glenn Osser on orchestrations.

The Broadway Run. BILLY ROSE THEATRE, 3/3/68. 20 previews from 2/7/68. 1 PERFORMANCE. PRESENTED BY Mitch Miller, in association with United Artists; MUSIC: Robert Waldman; LYRICS: Alfred Uhry; BOOK: Alex Gordon; BASED ON the 1952 novel *East of Eden*, by John Steinbeck; DIRECTOR: Michael Kahn; CHOREOGRAPHER: Tony Mordente; SETS: Ming Cho Lee; COSTUMES: Ruth Morley; LIGHTING: Jules Fisher; SOUND: John Tolbutt; MUSICAL DIRECTOR/VOCAL ARRANGEMENTS: Theodore Saidenberg; ORCHESTRATIONS: Glenn Osser, Norman Leyden, Jonathan Tunick; DANCE MUSIC ARRANGEMENTS: Arnold Goland; CAST RECORDING on United Artists; PRESS: Frank Goodman, Martin Shwartz, Abby Hirsch; CASTING: Michael Shurtleff; GENERAL MANAGERS: Max Allentuck, Manny Azenberg, Gene Wolsk; COMPANY MANAGER: Peter Neufeld; PRODUCTION STAGE MANAGER: William Dodds; STAGE MANAGER: D.W. Koehler; ASSISTANT STAGE MANAGER: Gene Gavin. **Cast:** ADAM TRASK: Paul Rogers (1) ☆; CALEB ("CAL") TRASK: Walter McGinn (3); ARON TRASK: Ken Kercheval (5); LEE: James Coco (4); WILL HAMILTON: Casper Roos (10); MRS. BACON: Bette Henritze (7); MRS. TRIPP: Dena Dietrich (8); MRS. HEINK: Patricia Kelly (9); ABRA BACON: Heather MacRae (6); SCHOOL CHILDREN: Lee Wilson & Tod Miller; MISS IDA: Barbara Webb; RABBIT HOLMAN: Scott Jarvis; FAITH: Graciela Daniele; EVA: Aniko Morgan; DELLA: Dorothy Lister; KATE: Nancy Wickwire (2) ☆; JOE: Joseph Nelson; JUANA: Joetta Cherry; NEWSPAPER MAN: Taylor Reed; BRITISH PURCHASING AGENT: Darrell J. Askey; TOWNSPEOPLE/MEXICAN FIELD WORKERS/DENIZENS OF CASTROVILLE STREET: Darrell Askey, Joetta Cherry, Graciela Daniele, Elisa De Marko, Larry Devon, John Dickerson, Bud Fleming, John William Gardner, Gene Gavin, John Johann, Ray Kirchner, Jane Laughlin, Dorothy Lister, Andy Love, Richard Marr, David McCorkle, Joyce McDonald, Tod Miller, Aniko Morgan, Joan Nelson, Joseph Nelson, Donald Norris, Taylor Reed, Clifford Scott, Joy Serio, Michele Simmons, David Thomas, Barbara Webb, Lee Wilson. **Standby**: Kate: Rita Morley. **Understudies**: Cal: Scott Jarvis; Lee: Taylor Reed; Aron: Tod Miller; Abra: Joan Nelson; Mrs. Bacon: Dena Dietrich; Mrs. Tripp/Mrs. Heink: Joyce McDonald; Will: Richard Marr; Rabbit: John Johann. **Act I**: Prologue: The Trask House, Salinas, Calif., 1915: "We Are What We Are" (Adam, Cal, Lee, Aron), "Cal Gets By" (Cal); **Scene 1** Castroville Street; two years later: "Raising Cain" (Cal & Ensemble); **Scene 2** The Trask house; later that day: "Soft is the Sparrow" (Aron); **Scene 3** Kate's place; immediately following; **Scene 4** The streets of Salinas; immediately following: "Where Have I Been?" (Adam, Lee, Townspeople); **Scene 5** The ice house; several weeks later: "No Time (is a Goodbye Time)" (Cal & Aron), "Progress" (Male Ensemble), "Good Boy" (Cal); **Scene 6** The lettuce fields; six weeks later: Ballet (Cal, Juana, Abra, Dancing Ensemble); **Scene 7** Near the depot; the same day: "Act Like a Lady"

(Abra); ***Scene 8*** The train depot; immediately following: "The Send-Off" (Townspeople); ***Scene 9*** The Trask house; three days later: "Top of the Train" (Adam & Cal); ***Scene 10*** The willow tree; early the next morning: "Waking Up Sun" (Abra & Cal). ***Act II***: ***Scene 1*** Salinas, down-town; two months later: "Pulverize the Kaiser" (Mrs. Bacon, Mrs. Tripp, Mrs. Heink, Townspeople), "Where Have I Been?" (reprise) (Adam); ***Scene 2*** The Salinas Bank; two weeks later: "Good Boy" (reprise) (Cal); ***Scene 3*** Kate's place; the same day: "You're Momma's" (Kate); ***Scene 4*** The willow tree; the next day: "Here's Where I Belong" (Cal & Abra); ***Scene 5*** The Trask house; Thanksgiving dinner: "We're a Home" (Adam, Lee, Aron, Abra); ***Scene 6*** Outside Kate's; immediately following: ***Scene 7*** The Trask house; a few hours later.

It was panned on Broadway. On opening night 19 members of a group called The Oriental Actors of America picketed the show in protest against Jimmy Coco playing a Chinese houseboy.

310. *High Button Shoes*

About author Stephen Longstreet's family in New Brunswick, NJ, in 1913. Floy, a con man, and his assistant Pontdue return to their home town. The Longstreets become interested in Floy, remembering him, as all the others do, as the honest boy he once was. Papa thinks he can help Floy sell some of his land. Mama has hopes that he will marry Fran, who is in love with the star football player at nearby Rutgers. At a big community picnic Floy begins to sell the land, but it is soon discovered to be just worthless swamp. Everyone rushes off to see for themselves. Meanwhile, a lot of sales have been made and Fran is holding the cash. Floy makes a rapid proposal to her, and they flee to Atlantic City. However, Stevie has overheard their plans, and the Longstreets set out in pursuit, aided by some Keystone Kops in Atlantic City. Pontdue steals the money from Floy, and by the time Floy catches up with him, he's lost most of it. Floy returns to New Brunswick and finds that Fran and the football player have got together. With the remaining money Floy bets on Princeton to beat Rutgers in the big ball game, but he loses. However, he immediately sets about to perpetrate a new swindle, but the police arrive, Floy escapes to another town, and everybody is sort of happy, but poorer.

Before Broadway. In 1947 lyricist Sammy Cahn, at home in Hollywood, saw an ad for a new book in the *New York Times* Book Reviews, with a picture of a 1910 family out for a drive in their Model-T. He took the ad to his collaborator, composer Jule Styne, and declared that this was their new musical (it would be Mr. Styne's Broadway debut). Coincidentally, Stephen Longstreet, the author of the book, lived right across the street from Jule Styne, and they all met. Styne & Cahn, although they had done several movie musicals, had only done one stage musical together before this — *Glad to See Ya*, which had closed in Boston during tryouts. Mr. Longstreet adapted his book to a libretto, and George Abbott and Phil Silvers re-wrote that. None of Mr. Longstreet's lines were used in the Broadway production, and he was so disgusted that he quit, and never saw the show until it toured. Vivienne Segal was originally going to play Mama, and had an unbreakable contract for the run of the play. However, Jule Styne saw Nanette Fabray in *Meet the People*, and knew he must have her for the role. Joe Kipness, the producer, told Miss Segal that the numbers "Papa, Won't You Dance with Me" and "I Still Get Jealous" were being cut, so she quit, her main reason for doing the show being to sing those two numbers. Of course, it was a ruse, and the songs stayed in — Miss Segal stayed out. Nanette Fabray, on the other hand, was initially wary of a role that cast her as a mother. The show tried out in Philadelphia, and Phil Silvers was suffering from throat problems. The number "Gone Are the Days" was cut, as was "I'm Betwixt and Between" (later revised as "Everything's Coming up Roses," and used in *Gypsy*).

The Broadway Run. NEW CENTURY THEATRE, 10/9/47–12/20/47; SHUBERT THEATRE, 12/22/47–10/18/48; BROADWAY THEATRE, 10/18/48–

7/2/49. Total of 727 PERFORMANCES. PRESENTED BY Monte Proser & Joseph Kipness; MUSIC/BALLET MUSIC: Jule Styne; LYRICS: Sammy Cahn; BOOK: Stephen Longstreet (based on his 1946 semi-autobiographical novel *The Sisters Liked Them Handsome*); DIRECTOR: George Abbott; ASSISTANT DIRECTOR: Robert Griffith; CHOREOGRAPHER: Jerome Robbins; SETS: Oliver Smith; COSTUMES: Miles White; LIGHTING: Peggy Clark; MUSICAL DIRECTOR: Milton Rosenstock; ORCHESTRATIONS: Philip Lang; VOCAL ARRANGEMENTS: Bob Martin; DANCE MUSIC ARRANGEMENTS: Genevieve Pitot; PRESS: Karl Bernstein; CASTING: Howard Hoyt; GENERAL MANAGER: Jack Small; COMPANY MANAGER: Jesse Long; STAGE MANAGER: George Hunter; ASSISTANT STAGE MANAGER: Richard Smith. **Cast:** HARRISON FLOY: Phil Silvers (1) ☆, *Joey Faye* (alternate, and for several weeks during Mr. Silvers' illness during Nov. & Dec. 1948, then permanently from 5/30/49); MR. PONTDUE: Joey Faye (6), *Jack Diamond* (alternate), *Jack Albertson* (from 5/30/49); UNCLE WILLIE, MAMA'S BROTHER: Paul Godkin, *Donald Saddler*; HENRY LONGSTREET, PAPA: Jack McCauley (3); GENERAL LONGSTREET, GRAMP: Clay Clement (5); STEVIE LONGSTREET: Johnny Stewart; FRAN, MAMA'S SISTER: Lois Lee (7); SARA LONGSTREET, MAMA: Nanette Fabray (2), Carole Coleman (alternate), *Joan Roberts, Carol Stone*; NANCY, THE MAID: Helen Gallagher; HUBERT "OGGLE" OGGLETHORPE: Mark Dawson (4); SHIRLEY SIMPKINS: Carole Coleman, Helene Whitney (alternate); ELMER SIMPKINS: Nathaniel Frey; ELMER SIMPKINS JR.: Donald Harris; COACH: Tom Glennon; MR. ANDERSON: William David, Howard Lenters (alternate); "A Summer Incident:" A BOY AT THE PICNIC: Arthur Partington; HIS PLAYMATE: Sondra Lee; A POPULAR GIRL: Jacqueline Dodge; HER FRIEND: Raul Celada, *Don Weissmuller* [end of the "Summer Incident" sequence]; A BETTING MAN: George Spelvin; ANOTHER BETTING MAN: Howard Lenters, David E. Dubble (alternate); Mack Sennett Ballet: BATHING BEAUTIES: Audrey Peters (*Sue Scott*), Jean Marie Caples, Virginia Gorski (*Evelyn Giles*), June Graham (*Christine Karner*), Elena Lane, Gloria Smith, Eleanore Treiber; LIFE GUARD: Evans Davis; THE TWINS: Toni Stuart (*Louisa Lewis*) & Betty Hyatt (*Kay Lewis*); Fred Hearn & Don Weissmuller; CROOKS: Raul Celada (*Dick Beard, Roy Tobias, Dick Beard*), Jacqueline Dodge, Sondra Lee; CHIEF OF POLICE: William Sumner; COPS: Vincent Carbone, Lenny Claret (*Kenneth Spaulding, George Bockman, Kenneth Spaulding*), Ray Kirchner, Tommy Morton (*Rex Cooper*), William Pierson [end of Mack Sennett Ballet sequence]; CORPS DE BALLET: Jean Marie Caples, Vincent Carbone, Raul Celada (*Dick Beard, Roy Tobias, Dick Beard*), Lenny Claret (Kenneth Spaulding), Evans Davis, Jacqueline Dodge, Virginia Gorski (*Evelyn Giles*), June Graham (*Christine Karner*), Fred Hearn, Betty Hyatt [later known as Betty Hyatt Linton] (*Kay Lewis*), Ray Kirchner, Elena Lane, Sondra Lee, Tommy Morton (*Rex Cooper*), Arthur Partington, Audrey Peters (*Sue Scott*), William Pierson, Gloria Smith, Toni Stuart (*Louisa Lewis*), William Sumner, Eleanore Treiber, Don Weissmuller; SINGERS: Nancy Babcock, Gloria Casper, Edward Cole, Ray Cook, Erno Czako, John Dennis, Nathaniel Frey, Estelle Gardner, Ronnie Hartmann, Neil Harwood, Edward Hayes, Dorothy Karrol, Ben Murphy, Hannah O'Leary, Fay Moore, Helene Whitney.

Note: George Spelvin is not the actor's real name. The name George Spelvin is a nom de guerre, a Broadway tradition denoting an actor in more than one role. So we don't know who played A Betting Man. **Act I**: ***Scene 1*** Kokomo and points east: "He Tried to Make a Dollar" (Ed Cole, Ray Cook, John Dennis, Edward Hayes); ***Scene 2*** Living-room of the Longstreet home, New Brunswick, NJ; early autumn, 1913: "Can't You Just See Yourself (in Love with Me?)" (Oggle & Fran); ***Scene 3*** Redmond Street, New Brunswick: "There's Nothing Like a Model-T" (choral arr: Hugh Martin) (Floy & Company); ***Scene 4*** Near the stadium: "Next to Texas, I Love You" (Oggle & Fran; danced by Girls & Boys), "Security" (Mama, Fran, Singing Girls); ***Scene 5*** The Longstreet living-room: "Tango" (dance) (Nancy & Willie), "Bird Watcher's Song" (Mama & Singing Girls); ***Scene 6*** Road to the picnic: "Get Away for a Day in the Country" (Papa, Stevie, Chorus), "A Summer Incident" (dance) (see cast list above); ***Scene 7*** "Longstreetville:" "Papa, Won't You Dance with Me?" (Mama, Papa, Girls & Boys) [the showstopper], "Can't You Just See Yourself (in Love with Me?)" (Floy & Fran) [cut during the run], Finaletto (Entire Company). **Act II**: ***Scene 1*** Atlantic City — the bathhouses: "On a Sunday by the Sea" (Singers); ***Scene 2*** The beach: "Mack Sennett Ballet" ("Bathing Beauty Ballet") (see cast list above);

Scene 3 The bathhouses; *Scene 4* Redmond Street: "You're My Girl" (Oggle & Fran); *Scene 5* The Longstreet living-room: "I Still Get Jealous (Over You)" (Mama & Papa); *Scene 6* The road: "You're My Boy" (Floy & Pontdue); *Scene 7* The stadium: "Nobody Ever Died for Dear Old Rutgers" (Floy, Oggle, Singing Boys); *Scene 8* The Longstreet garden: "Castle Walk" (Entire Company) (danced by Mama & Papa) [this dance was originally created by Vernon & Irene Castle], "He Tried to Make a Dollar" (reprise) (Entire Company).

Broadway reviews were generally favorable, and Jerome Robbins' 20-minute Mack Sennett ballet was singled out for praise. Mr. Sennett sued the producers for using his name in connection with the ballet, and his name was later removed from the production (even though the ballet remained). Mary Hunter sued, claiming she'd been contracted to direct before George Abbott became available, and was then dropped. She won. There was also a dispute between the producers and Sammy Cahn & Stephen Longstreet over royalties, but this was amicably settled. The show won a Tony for choreography, and Donaldson Awards for musical, direction, choreography, sets, costumes, and for Nanette Fabray (two — for best actress and best supporting actress!), and Jack McCauley. The role of Gramp was eliminated after the Broadway opening, but re-instated in the show's second season. Sammy Cahn took Helen Gallagher out of this show and put her into *Make a Wish*.

After Broadway. TOUR. It was a success. *Cast*: Eddie Foy Jr., Audrey Meadows, Jack Whiting, Ellen Hanley, Frankie Hyers, Harry Fleer.

HIPPODROME, London, 12/22/48–6/11/49. 291 PERFORMANCES. PRESENTED BY Val Parnell; DIRECTOR: Archie Thomson; CHOREOGRAPHER: Fred Hearn; MUSICAL DIRECTOR: Freddie Bretherton. *Cast*: FLOY: Lew Parker; PONTDUE: Tommy Godfrey; NANCY: Joan Heal; HENRY: Sid James; SINGERS INCLUDED: Alma Cogan & Marion Ryan; DANCERS INCLUDED: Nick Dana & Audrey Hepburn.

TV. There was talk of a movie, starring Milton Berle, but it didn't happen. However, there were two TV productions. The first aired on NBC, on 11/24/56. PRODUCER/DIRECTOR: Joseph Cates. *Cast*: FLOY: Hal March; MAMA: Nanette Fabray; PONTDUE: Joey Faye; HENRY: Don Ameche. The second, in 1966, was an abbreviated version (without the Mack Sennett ballet). *Cast*: FLOY: Jack Cassidy; PAPA: Garry Moore; ALSO WITH: Maureen O'Hara, Carol Lawrence.

In 1989 the manic Sennett ballet was re-done as part of *Jerome Robbins' Broadway*. The number "I Still Get Jealous" was included.

RUBICON THEATRE, Ventura, Calif., 5/24/02–6/2/02. It was part of *Lost and Found Concert Series*. DIRECTOR: Bonnie Hellman. *Cast*: FLOY: Jason Graae; FRAN: Susan Egan; PONTDUE: Will Sharpe; MAMA: Cynthia Ferrer; PAPA: Doug Carfrae; HUBERT: Gregg Whitney.

The success of *High Button Shoes* has much to do with the talents of its leads, and for this reason has not been performed much.

311. *The High Rollers Social and Pleasure Club*

A musical revue. Set during Mardi Gras in the club of the title, in New Orleans; there is also a side trip to the Bayou.

The Broadway Run. HELEN HAYES THEATRE, 4/21/92–5/3/92. 18 previews from 4/6/92. 14 PERFORMANCES. PRESENTED BY Judy Gordon, Dennis Grimaldi, Allen M. Shore, and Martin Markinson; MUSIC/LYRICS: various authors, including Allen Toussaint; CONCEIVED BY: Judy Gordon; DIRECTOR/CHOREOGRAPHER: Alan Weeks; SETS: David Mitchell; COSTUMES: Theoni V. Aldredge; LIGHTING: Beverly Emmons; SOUND: Peter J. Fitzgerald; MUSICAL DIRECTOR/ORCHESTRATIONS/MUSICAL ARRANGEMENTS: Allen Toussaint; ASSOCIATE CONDUCTOR: Carl Maultsby; MUSIC ADVISERS: Jerry Wexler & Charles Neville; PRESS: Springer Associates; CASTING: Alan Filderman; GENERAL MANAGEMENT: Brent Peek Productions; COMPANY MANAGER: Kip Makkonen; STAGE MANAGER: David H. Bosboom. *Cast* (in alphabetical order): WONDER BOY # 1: Keith Robert Bennett; QUEEN: Deborah Burrell-Cleveland (2); KING: Lawrence Clayton; JESTER: Eugene Fleming; SORCERER: Michael McElroy; ENCHANTRESS: Vivian Reed (1); PRINCESS: Nikki Rene; WONDER BOY # 2: Tarik Winston; ALSO WITH: Allen Toussaint (3). *Understudies*: Wonder Boys: Bruce Anthony Davis; Jester: Bruce Anthony Davis; Queen/Enchantress/Princess: Mona Wyatt; King/Sorcerer: Frederick J. Boothe. *The High Rollers Band*: BASS: Frank Canino; SAX: Gary Keller; TROMBONE: Joel Helleny; DRUMS: Steve Johns; TRUMPET: Darryl Shaw; GUITAR: Bob Rose; PIANO: Allen Toussaint. *Act I*: 1. "Tu Way Pocky Way" (traditional; arr: The Wild Magnolias, 1974) (Jester), 2. "Open Up" (Band), 3. "Mr. Mardi Gras" (m/l: Allen Toussaint, 1978) (Company), 4. "Piano Solo" (Mr. Toussaint), 5. "Chicken Shack Boogie" (m/l: Lola Ann Callum & Amos Milburn, 1949) (Jester & Company), 6. "Lady Marmalade" (m/l: Kenny Nolan) (Enchantress, Sorcerer, Company), 7. "Don't You Feel My Leg" (m/l: Danny Barker & Blue Lu Barker) (Queen, King, Jester, Sorcerer), 8. "You Can Have My Husband (But Please Don't Mess with My Man)" (m/l: Dorothy La Bostrie, 1963) (Enchantress), 9. "Fun Time" (m/l: Allen Toussaint, 1978) (Wonder Boys), 10. Rock Medley: (Company), "It Will Stand" (m/l: Norman Johnson, 1961), "Mother-in-Law" (m/l: Allen Toussaint, 1961), "Workin' in a Coal Mine" (m/l: Allen Toussaint), "Lipstick Traces (on a Cigarette)" (m/l: Naomi Neville, 1962), "Rockin' Pneumonia" (m/l: Huey P. Smith, 1957), "(Sittin' in) Ya Ya" (m/l: Clarence Lewis, Morgan Robinson, Lee Dorsey), 11. "Feet, Don't Fail Me Now" (m/l: Mad musicians) (Wonder Boys), 12. "Ooh Poo Pa Doo" (m/l: Jessie Hill, 1960) (Jester), 13. "Dance the Night (Away with You)" (m/l: Doc Pomus & Mac Rebennack)/"Such a Night" (m/l: Mac Rebennack) (King & Queen), 14. "All These Things" (m/l: Naomi Neville, 1978) (Enchantress & Sorcerer), 15. "Mellow Sax" (m/l: Roy Montrell) (Princess, Saxophone, Company), 16. "Sea Cruise" (m/l: Huey P. Smith) (Enchantress, Queen, Princess), 17. "Jambalaya" (by Hank Williams, 1952) (Jester & Company). *Act II*: 1. "Tu Way Pocky Way" (reprise) (Jester), 2. "Bourbon Street Parade" (m/l: Paul Barbarin, 1950) (Company), 3. "(Ain't Gonna Give Nobody None of This) Jelly Roll" (1919) (m/l: Spencer & Clarence Williams) (Wonder Boys), 4. "Heebie Jeebie Dance" (m: Boyd Atkins) (Princess, Queen, Enchantress), 5. "I Like it Like That" (m/l: Chris Kenner) (Jester & Company), 6. "Fiyou on the Bayou" (m/l: Arthur Neville, Leo Nocentelli, George Porter Jr., Joseph Modiste, Cyril Neville) (Company), 7. "Marie Leveau" (m/l: Shel Silverstein & Baxter Taylor III) (Enchantress), 8. "Walk on Gilded Splinters" (m/l: Mac Rebennack) (Company), 9. "Black Widow Spider" (m/l: Mac Rebennack) (King), 10. "Tell it Like it Is" (m/l: Lee Diamond & George Davis)/"You're the One" (m/l: Adolph Smith & Cosmo Matassa, 1954) (Queen & King), 11. "Let the Good Times Roll" (m/l: Leonard Lee) (Company), 12. "Challenge Dance" (Jester, King, Sorcerer, Wonder Boys), 13. "Mos Scoscious" (m/l: Mac Rebennack) (Sorcerer & Princess), 14. "We All Need Love" (m/l: Allen Toussaint) (Enchantress), 15. "Tu Way Pocky Way" (reprise) (Jester), 16. "Injuns, Here We Come" (m/l: The Wild Magnolias & Wilson Turbinton, 1974) (Wonder Boy # 1 & Company), 17. "Golden Crown" (m/l: Theodore Dollis, 1974) (Company), 18. "Jockomo" (m/l: James Crawford Jr., 1965) (Company), 19. "Hey Mama" (Company), 20. "(When the) Saints Go Marching In" (Company).

Broadway reviews were mostly bad. Vivian Reed was nominated for a Tony.

312. *High Society*

Set in Oyster Bay, Long Island, during a glorious weekend in June 1938. The plot was as in *The Philadelphia Story*, and the movie *High Society*, except that girl-chasing, gin-swilling Uncle Willie has been added (his marriage was ruined by his addiction to the bottle). Tracy, formerly of Philadelphia and Newport, and now of Oyster Bay, is about to embark on her second high-society marriage, to newly-rich stuffed shirt George Kittredge (her first husband was C.K. Dexter Haven, who still carries a torch for her). Mike, the reporter there to cover the event, gives her reason for pause before the altar. Seth and Margaret are Tracy's estranged parents. Liz is Connor's sidekick photographer. This production used seven of the nine songs from the movie musical *High Society* (1956), and also Cole Porter songs from other sources, and a few others. The two movie songs not used were "Now You Has Jazz" and "Mind if I Make Love to You?"

Before Broadway. It tried out at the AMERICAN CONSERVATORY THEATRE (ACT), San Francisco, 9/10/97–10/12/97. Previews from 9/4/97. It had the same basic crew as for the later Broadway run, except SETS: Judith Dolan; LIGHTING: Christopher Akerlind. It also had the same leading players except CONNOR: Jere Shea; DINAH: Lisbeth Zelle; SETH: Michael Goodwin. *Act I*: "High Society Calypso" (Household Staff), "I Am Loved" [from *Out of This World*] (Tracy & Household Staff), "Ridin' High" (Dexter), "Little One" (Dexter & Dinah), "Who Wants to Be a Millionaire?" (Mike & Liz), "I Love Paris" (Dinah & Tracy), "She's Got That Thing" (Willie & Dexter), "Who Wants to Be a Millionaire" (reprise) (Household Staff), "Once Upon a Time" (Dexter), "I Worship You" [cut from *Fifty Million Frenchmen*] (George), "True Love" (Dexter & Tracy), "I Am Loved" (reprise) (Tracy). *Act II*: "High Society" (Household Staff), "I'm Getting Myself Ready for You" (Willie & Liz), "(It was) Just One of Those Things" (Dexter), "Let's Misbehave" (Tracy, Willie, Company), "You're Sensational" (Mike), "Midsummer Madness" (montage): "Well, Did You Evah!" (Ensemble), "Nobody's Chasing Me" [from *Out of This World*] (Dinah), "Say it with Gin" (Willie), "Why Don't We Try Staying Home?" [cut from *Fifty Million Frenchmen*] (Seth & Margaret) [end of montage], "It's All Right with Me" (Tracy), "He's a Right Guy" (Liz), "(I Love You) Samantha" (Dexter).

The Public Theatre's revival of *On the Town* had been scheduled for the St. James Theatre, on Broadway, but it had to postpone because the production wasn't ready. Broadway previews for *High Society* began on 3/31/98 (date put back from 3/30/98), and many changes were made during previews. Des McAnuff was brought in to help (some say to replace) director Christopher Renshaw, while Wayne Cilento did the same for choreographer Lar Lubovitch (the original choreographer was Christopher d'Amboise). The number "Why Don't We Try Staying Home?" was cut during previews; and "I Worship You" and "I Am Loved" were both cut from Act I. The official opening date was put back from 4/23/98 to 4/27/98.

The Broadway Run. ST. JAMES THEATRE, 4/27/98–8/30/98. 28 previews from 3/31/98. 144 PERFORMANCES. PRESENTED BY Lauren Mitchell & Robert Gailus, Hal Luftig & Richard Samson, Dodger Endemol Theatricals, in association with Bill Haber; MUSIC/LYRICS: Cole Porter; ADDITIONAL LYRICS: Susan Birkenhead; BOOK: Arthur Kopit; BASED ON the 1956 movie of the same name, starring Grace Kelly, which in turn was based on the 1940 movie *The Philadelphia Story*, which was based on Philip Barry's comedy of that name which opened at the Shubert Theatre, Broadway, on 3/28/39, with Katharine Hepburn, Joseph Cotten, Van Heflin, and Shirley Booth; DIRECTOR: Christopher Renshaw; ADDITIONAL DIRECTION: Des McAnuff; CHOREOGRAPHER: Lar Lubovitch; ADDITIONAL CHOREOGRAPHY: Wayne Cilento; SETS: Loy Arcenas; COSTUMES: Jane Greenwood; LIGHTING: Howell Binkley; SOUND: Tony Meola; MUSICAL DIRECTOR: Paul Gemignani; ORCHESTRATIONS: William David Brohn; DANCE MUSIC ARRANGEMENTS: Glen Kelly; CAST RECORDING on DRG, made 8/31/98–9/1/98; PRESS: Boneau/Bryan-Brown; CASTING: Jay Binder; GENERAL MANAGERS: Stuart Thompson & Florie Seery; COMPANY MANAGER: Kimberly Kelley; STAGE MANAGER: Rolt Smith. **Cast:** POLLY, THE DOWNSTAIRS MAID: Jennifer Smith; ARTHUR, THE BUTLER: Glenn Turner; CHESTER, THE HOUSE MAN: Barry Finkel; SUNNY, THE SCULLERY MAID: Kisha Howard; STANLEY, THE HOUSE BOY: Jeff Skowron; PATSY, THE COOK: Betsy Joslyn; PEG, THE UPSTAIRS MAID: Dorothy Stanley; EDMUND, THE MAJOR DOMO: William Ryall; MARGARET LORD: Lisa Banes; DINAH LORD: Anna Kendrick; TRACY SAMANTHA LORD: Melissa Errico; UNCLE WILLIE: John McMartin; C.K. DEXTER HAVEN: Daniel McDonald; MIKE CONNOR: Stephen Bogardus; LIZ IMBRIE: Randy Graff; GEORGE KITTREDGE: Marc Kudisch; SETH LORD: Daniel Gerroll. **Standbys:** Dexter/George/Mike: Richard Muenz; Tracy: Stacey Logan. **Understudies:** Tracy: Sarah Solie Shannon; Margaret/Liz: Dorothy Stanley & Jennifer Smith; Dinah: Holiday Segal; Willie/Seth: William Ryall & Barry Finkel; Mike: Jeff Skowron. **Swings:** Vince Pesce & Sarah Solie Shannon. *Act I*: Scene 1 The Lords' estate: Overture, "High Society" [from the film *High Society*] (new lyrics: Susan Birkenhead) (Household Staff); *Scene 2* Tracy's room: "Ridin' High" [from *Red, Hot and Blue*] (Tracy & Household Staff); *Scene 3* The veranda; breakfast: "(You're) Throwing a Ball Tonight" [from *Panama Hattie*] (new lyrics: Susan Birkenhead) (Margaret, Tracy, Willie, Dinah); *Scene 4* The nursery: "Little One" [from

the film *High Society*] (Dexter & Dinah); *Scene 5* The grounds; arrival of the reporters: "Who Wants to Be a Millionaire?" [from the film *High Society*] (Liz & Mike); *Scene 6* The South Parlor: "I Love Paris" [from *Can-Can*] (Dinah & Tracy); *Scene 7* The Pavilion: "She's Got That Thing" [from *Fifty Million Frenchmen*] (Willie, Dexter, Company); *Scene 8* The swimming pool: "Once Upon a Time" [from *Ever Yours*] (new lyrics: Susan Birkenhead) (Tracy), "True Love" [from the film *High Society*] (Dexter & Tracy). *Act II*: *Scene 1* Uncle Willie's house; very early Sunday morning: "High Society" (reprise) (Household Staff); *Scene 2* Uncle Willie's ballroom: "Let's Misbehave" [from *Paris*] (additional lyrics: Susan Birkenhead) (Tracy, Willie, Company), "I'm Getting Myself Ready for You" [from *The New Yorkers*] (Willie & Liz); *Scene 3* Dexter's house: "Once Upon a Time" (reprise) (Dexter), "(It Was) Just One of Those Things" [from *Jubilee*] (Dexter); *Scene 4* Uncle Willie's kitchen: "Well, Did You Evah!" [from the film *High Society*] (new lyrics: Susan Birkenhead) (Household Staff, Tracy, Willie, Liz); *Scene 5* Uncle Willie's grounds: "You're Sensational" [from the film *High Society*] (Mike), "Say it with Gin" [from *The New Yorkers*] (Willie, to Dexter), "Ridin' High" (reprise) (Margaret); *Scene 6* The Lords' pool: "It's All Right with Me" [from *Can-Can*] (Tracy); *Scene 7* The Lords' garden: "He's a Right Guy" [from *Something for the Boys*] (Liz); *Scene 8* The terrace; the wedding day: "(I Love You) Samantha" [from the film *High Society*] (Dexter), Finale: "True Love" (reprise) (Tracy & Dexter).

Broadway reviews were generally not good. John McMartin and Anna Kendrick were nominated for Tonys.

After Broadway. OPEN AIR THEATRE, Regents Park, London, 7/24/03–9/13/03. DIRECTOR: Ian Talbot. **Cast:** LIZ: Tracie Bennett; MOTHER LORD: Bridget Forsyth; TRACY: Annette McLaughlin; DEXTER: Dale Rapley; MIKE: Hal Fowler.

313. *High Spirits*

"An improbable musical comedy." Madame Arcati is a dizzy spiritualist who brings back the ghost of writer Charles's first wife, Elvira who, in her efforts to take Charles back with her, accidentally causes the death of his current wife, Ruth. Ruth takes revenge by playing some ghostly tricks of her own.

Before Broadway. As early as 1954 Hugh Martin and Timothy Gray had wanted to adapt Noel Coward's play, but they couldn't get permission until 1960. The musical was initially entitled *Faster Than Sound*. It opened in LONDON, in 9/64. 93 PERFORMANCES. CHOREOGRAPHER: Danny Daniels. **Cast:** MADAME ARCATI: Cicely Courtneidge (her last West End role). The Broadway production was one of the three 1964 Broadway musicals financed ($1,000,000 total) by ABC—Paramount and produced by Lester Osterman and Jule Styne. All three failed. There was friction during the Philadelphia tryouts between Noel Coward and Bea Lillie, so Mr. Coward was replaced as director by Gower Champion (who remained uncredited). Mr. Champion also replaced Danny Daniels as choreographer, but likewise Mr. Champion remained uncredited. His most noticeable achievement as far as this show goes was his substitution of blackouts between scenes with visually choreographed scene changes, so the audience didn't get bored between scenes.

The Broadway Run. ALVIN THEATRE, 4/7/64–2/27/65. 14 previews from 3/24/64. 375 PERFORMANCES. PRESENTED BY Lester Osterman & Jule Styne, Robert Fletcher, Richard Horner with ABC-Paramount; MUSIC/LYRICS/BOOK/VOCAL DIRECTORS/MUSICAL ARRANGEMENTS: Hugh Martin & Timothy Gray; BASED ON the 1941 British farce *Blithe Spirit*, by Noel Coward; DIRECTOR: Noel Coward; CHOREOGRAPHER: Danny Daniels; SETS/COSTUMES: Robert Fletcher; TAMMY GRIMES'S COSTUMES: Valentina; LIGHTING: Jules Fisher; SOUND: Jack Tolbutt; MUSICAL DIRECTOR: Fred Werner; ORCHESTRATIONS: Harry Zimmerman; DANCE MUSIC ARRANGEMENTS: William Goldenberg; CAST RECORDING on ABC-Paramount; PRESS: Harvey B. Sabinson, Lee Solters, Leo Stern, David Powers; CASTING: Nicholas Gray; GENERAL MANAGER: Richard Horner; PRODUCTION STAGE MANAGER: Frank Gero; STAGE MANAGER: Bruce Laffey. **Cast:** CHARLES CONDOMINE: Edward Woodward (3); EDITH: Carol Arthur (5); RUTH CONDOMINE: Louise Troy (4); MRS. BRADMAN: Margaret Hall (6); DR. BRADMAN: Lawrence

Keith (7); MADAME ARCATI: Beatrice Lillie (1); ELVIRA: Tammy Grimes (2); BOB: Robert Lenn; BETH: Beth Howland; RUPERT: Gene Castle; SINGERS & DANCERS: Adrienne Angel, Syndee Balaber, Gene Castle, Jerry Craig, Jackie Cronin, Altovise Gore, Judith Haskell, Beth Howland, Jack Kauflin, Bill Kennedy, Al Lanti, Miriam Lawrence, Renee Lee, Robert Lenn, Alex MacKay, Jacqueline Maria, Stan Mazin, Joe McGrath, Don Percassi, Kathy Preston, Sybil Scotford, Tom Thornton, Ronnie Walken [he later became Christopher Walken], Anne Wallace, *Michael Davis, Frank Derbas, Ian Garry, Daniel Joel, Ray Kirchner, Barbara Newman.* **Standbys**: Mme Arcati: Beulah Garrick; Elvira: Iva Withers; Charles: Lawrence Keith; Ruth: Lynne Stuart, *Adrienne Angel.* **Understudies**: Mrs. Bradman: Adrienne Angel; Dr. Bradman: Robert Lenn; Edith: Jacqueline Maria. *Act I*: *Scene 1* The Condomines' living room; *Scene 2* A road on the heath; immediately following; *Scene 3* The Condomines' living room; after dinner; *Scene 4* The Condomines' terrace; the next morning; *Scene 5* The Inner Circle; early that evening; *Scene 6* The Condomines' living room; immediately following; *Scene 7* The Roof Garden of the Grovechester Hotel; immediately following. *Act II*: *Scene 1* The Condomines' living room; immediately following; *Scene 2* Madame Arcati's bedroom; the following morning; *Scene 3* The Condomines' living room; that afternoon; *Scene 4* The Inner Circle; that evening; *Scene 5* The Condomines' living room; several hours later. *Act I*: "Was She Prettier than I?" (Ruth), "The Bicycle Song" (Mme Arcati & Ensemble), "You'd Better Love Me" (Elvira), "Where is the Man I Married?" (Charles & Ruth), "The Sandwich Man" (Bob & Beth), "Go Into Your Trance" (Mme Arcati & Ensemble), "Where is the Man I Married?" (reprise) (Ruth), "Forever and a Day" (Charles & Elvira), "Something Tells Me" (Elvira & Ensemble), "I Know Your Heart" (Charles & Elvira), "Faster than Sound" (Elvira & Ensemble). *Act II*: "If I Gave You" (Charles & Ruth), "Talking to You" (Mme Arcati), "Home Sweet Heaven" (Elvira), "Something is Coming to Tea" (Mme Arcati's Tea Party) (Mme Arcati & Ensemble), "The Exorcism" (Mme Arcati & Ensemble), "What in the World Did You Want?" (Charles, Elvira, Ruth), "Faster than Sound" (reprise) (Entire Company).

Broadway review were unanimously favorable. The show received Tony nominations for musical, composer & lyricist, book, direction of a musical, choreographer, musical direction, and for Beatrice Lillie and Louise Troy.

After Broadway. PAPER MILL PLAYHOUSE, New Jersey, 1965. DIRECTOR: Franklin Lacey. *Cast*: MADAME ARCATI: Bea Lillie.

314. *Hilarities*

A vaudeville revue, also known as *Morey Amsterdam's Hilarities*.

The Broadway Run. ADELPHI THEATRE, 9/9/48–9/18/48. 14 PERFORMANCES. PRESENTED BY Ken Robey & Stan Zucker; MUSIC/LYRICS: Buddy Kaye, Stanley Arnold, Carl Lampl; SKETCHES: Sidney Zelinka, Howard Harris, Morey Amsterdam; CONCEIVED BY: Ken Robey; CHOREOGRAPHER: George Tapps; SCENES: Crayon; MUSICAL DIRECTOR: Ruby Zwerling; SPECIAL MUSICAL ARRANGEMENTS: Elliott Jacoby; PRODUCTION SUPERVISOR: Mervyn Nelson; PRESS: George Ross; GENERAL MANAGER: Paul Groll; STAGE MANAGER: David Kanter. *Act I*: *Scene 1* "Showtime" [Betty Jane Watson (2) (singer), Mitzi Norvello, Larry Douglas (5), Gerald Austen, Connie Stevens, the Calgary Brothers, Enid Williams (black singer), Raul & Eva Reyes (Cuban dancers), Entire Company]; *Scene 2* Your host, Morey Amsterdam (1), and others; *Scene 3* The Man and the Snake (Harold & Lola) (dancers); *Scene 4* The Pitchman (Sid Stone) (comedian); *Scene 5* "Rise and Shine" [Gerald Austen, Connie Stevens, Connie Sawyer (4), Nancy Andrews, Mitzi Norvello, Morey Amsterdam (1)]; *Scene 6* The Holloway Sisters; *Scene 7* Gali Gali; *Scene 8* The Bridegroom [Morey Amsterdam (1), Larry Douglas (5), Gerald Austen, the Calgary Brothers]; *Scene 9* "Where in the World" [Betty Jane Watson (2) (singer), Larry Douglas (5), George Tapps (3) (tap dancer)]; *Scene 10* The Lost Weekend (The Calgary Brothers — i.e. Andre & Steve — acrobats, did a slow-motion drunk scene); *Scene 11* George Tapps (3) (tap dancer), assisted by Victoria Crandall & Moreland Kortkam; *Scene 12* Morey Amsterdam (1) and his cello. *Act II*: *Scene 1* About Pol-itics [Morey Amsterdam (1) & Al Kelly (monologist)]; *Scene 2* "tis the Luck of the Irish" [Betty Jane Watson (2) (singer), Gerald Austen, Nancy Andrews, Mitzi Norvello, Larry Douglas (4), George Tapps (3) (tap dancer), the Holloway Sisters]; *Scene 3* The Herzogs; *Scene 4* Vaudeville Hoofer [George Tapps (3) (tap dancer)]; *Scene 5* Great New Talent (Connie Stevens); *Scene 6* One Man's Menagerie (Gil Maison — animal act; with a punch-drunk St. Bernard and a jitterbugging monkey); *Scene 7* Rio de Janeiro [Nancy Andrews, Gerald Austen, Larry Douglas (5), the Holloway Sisters, Raul & Eva Reyes (Cuban dancers)]; *Scene 8* The Entrance of the Adelphi Theatre [Morey Amsterdam (1) & Entire Company]. ALSO WITH: Mazzone & the Abbott Dancers (tap dancers).

The show was universally panned by the critics.

315. *Hit the Trail*

Set in Virginia City, Nevada, during the gold rush of the late 19th century. An operetta troupe is stranded. Diva Lucy is forced to choose between Clay (her former lover and the company's corrupt manager), and Murph (an honest local banker who gives her money to open a beauty emporium in town).

Before Broadway. Elizabeth Miele had tried for two years to present a stage musical for actress Irra Petina, and finally came up with *On With the Show*, with music by Portuguese composer Frederico Valerio. During the first tryout, in New Haven, Irra Petina sustained an ankle injury. During the next tryout, in Boston, she was not up to the role because of the injury, and her understudy, Vera Brynner (Yul's sister), took over. Miss Brynner wasn't very sure of the role, and one day Miss Miele went backstage and harangued her, which initiated a real dingdong between the two ladies. Miss Brynner was also playing a featured part in the show, and when her one big number was given to Miss Petina, she quit. The choreographer was fired, and cast members threatened to quit, saying that the show needed far more work. The title was changed at the last minute before Broadway.

The Broadway Run. MARK HELLINGER THEATRE, 12/2/54–12/4/54. 4 PERFORMANCES. PRESENTED BY Elizabeth Miele; MUSIC: Frederico Valerio; LYRICS: Elizabeth Miele; BOOK: Frank O'Neill; DIRECTORS: Charles W. Christenberry Jr. & Byrle Cass; CHOREOGRAPHER: Gene Bayliss; SETS/LIGHTING: Leo Kerz; COSTUMES: Michi; MUSICAL DIRECTOR/VOCAL ARRANGEMENTS: Arthur Norris; ORCHESTRATIONS: Don Walker; PRESS: Nat & Irvin Dorfman; GENERAL MANAGER: Ben A. Boyar; PRODUCTION STAGE MANAGER: Neil Hartley; STAGE MANAGERS: Phillip E. Schrager & John Moorehead. *Cast*: JERRY: Donn Driver; JOAN: Diana Drake; WILLIE: Fred Lightner; CLAYTON HARRISON: Paul Valentine (3); LUCY VERNAY: Irra Petina (1); MURPH: Robert Wright (2); AGGIE JULY: Toby Deane; MILLER: Charles G. Martin; WAITERS: Jack Purcell & Rene Miville; DANCERS: Robert Bakanic, Jeanna Belkin, Lois Bewley, Sandy Bozoki, Diane Consoer, Patty Fitzsimmons, Paul Gannon, Nancy Hachenberg, Jack Purcell, Alton Ruff, Buff Shurr, Fred Zoeter; SINGERS: Josephine Annunciata, Paul Brown, Irene Carroll, Peggy Kinard, Michael King, Dolores Micheline, Rene Miville, Robert Price, Michelle Reiner, Martha Rich, James Schlader, Iris Sinding, Flavine Valentine, Lois Van Pelt. **Standby**: Lucy: Eileen Shawley. **Understudies**: Jerry: Buff Shurr; Joan: Martha Rich; Aggie: Michelle Reiner; Miller: James Schlader; Willie: Michael King. *Act I*: *Scene 1* Outside Virginia City: "On with the Show" (Jerry, Joan, Troupers); *Scene 2* Lucy Vernay's dressing room: "Mr. Right" (Lucy), "Dynamic" (Lucy & Murph); *Scene 3* The Blue Sierra Casino: "Blue Sierras" (Aggie & Patrons), "No! No! No!" (Clay), "The Wide Open Spaces" (Clay, Aggie, Joan, Jerry); *Scene 4* A street in Virginia City: "Gold Cannot Buy" (Townspeople), "Remember the Night" (Clay & Lucy), "Tell Me How" (Murph); *Scene 5* The stage of Piper's Opera House: "It Was Destiny" (Aggie & Girls); *Scene 6* A park in Virginia City: "Just a Wonderful Time" (Jerry & Joan); *Scene 7* The Blue Sierra Casino: "Nevada Hoe Down" (Aggie & Patrons). *Act II*: *Scene 1* Emporium (staged by Donn Driver): "New Look Feeling" (Lucy, Jerry, Joan, Patrons), "Set Me Free" (Lucy), "Somehow I've Always Known" (Murph); *Scene 2* Gambling room: "Remember the Night?" (reprise) (Clay); *Scene 3* A street in Virginia City: "(What's) My Fatal Charm" (Clay), "Men are a Pain in the Neck" (Aggie);

Scene 4 The Blue Sierra Casino: "Wherever I May Go" (Lucy); *Scene 5* A street in Virginia City: "Take Your Time" (Jerry & Joan); *Scene 6* The garden behind Murph's house: "Happy Birthday" (Company), "Mr. Right" (reprise) (Lucy & Murph).

It was roundly panned by the critics.

316. *Hold It!*

Set in the present, at Lincoln University. The "leading lady" in the campus show is really Bobby, a male student and ex–GI, who is picked to play the female lead in a Mammoth Pictures movie. However his girl, Jessica, gets the part.

Before Broadway. Anthony B. Farrell invested $300,000, and was very actively involved in the production. During tryouts the character of Dean Hubbell (played by Robert Noe) was cut.

The Broadway Run. NATIONAL THEATRE, 5/5/48–6/12/48. 46 PERFORMANCES. PRESENTED BY Sammy Lambert (and Anthony Brady Farrell); MUSIC: Gerald Marks; LYRICS: Sam Lerner; BOOK: Matt Brooks & Art Arthur; DIRECTOR: Robert E. Perry; CHOREOGRAPHER: Michael Kidd; SETS/LIGHTING: Edward Gilbert; COSTUMES: Julia Sze; MUSICAL DIRECTOR/VOCAL ARRANGEMENTS: Clay Warnick; ORCHESTRATIONS: Hans Spialek & Ted Royal; BALLET MUSIC ARRANGEMENTS: Irma Jurist; PRESS: Bill Doll, Dick Williams, Michael O'Shea; GENERAL MANAGER: William Norton; GENERAL STAGE MANAGER: David Jones; STAGE MANAGERS: Ralph Simone & Willie Torpey. **Cast:** USHERETTES: Wana Allison, Gloria Benson, Janet Bethel, Penny Carroll, Kathryne Mylroie, Helena Schurgot; RODNEY TRENT: Bob Shawley; MRS. SIMPKINS: Ruth Saville; MR. SIMPKINS: Douglas Rutherford; MRS. BLANDISH: Helen Wenzel; MR. BLANDISH: Budd Rogers; "SARGE" DENTON: Larry Douglas (6); BOBBY MANVILLE: Johnny Downs (1); HELEN (STAGE MANAGER): Helen Wenzel; JACK: Jack Warner; CHUCK: Bob Evans; "JUDGE" ROGERS: Kenny Buffett (7); SID: Sid Lawson; JESSICA DALE: Jet MacDonald (3); PAMELA SCOTT: Patricia Wymore (5); MILLIE HENDERSON: Ada Lynne (4); BUDD: Budd Rogers; BERNIE: Bob Bernard; "DINKY" BENNETT: Red Buttons (2); PAUL: Paul Lyday; GEORGE MONOPOLIS: Douglas Chandler (11); PENNY: Penny Carroll; MR. JENKINS: Paul Reed (9); JOE: Tom Bowman; CHARLIE BLAKE: Pat McVey (8); HEADWAITER: Douglas Rutherford; MRS. JOLLOP (HOUSE MOTHER): Ruth Saville; O'BRIEN: Scott Landers; MARTIN: Martin Kraft; REPORTERS: Budd Rogers, Sid Lawson, Helena Schurgot; FELIX DEXTER: John Kane (10); ANNE GREEN: Ruth Saville; SINGING ENSEMBLE: Gloria Benson, Tom Bowman, Penny Carroll, Sid Lawson, Katie Mylroie, Budd Rogers, Helena Schurgot, Frank Stevens; DANCING ENSEMBLE: Onna White (captain), Wana Allison, John Begg, Bob Bernard, Janet Bethel, Robert Cadwallader, Jack Claus, Margit De Kova, Robert Evans, Martin Kraft, Vernon Lusby, Paul Lyday, Barbara McCutcheon, Vera Mallin (*Helen Kramer*), Elena Salamatova, Yvonne Tibor, Helen Wenzel. **Understudies:** Bobby: Jack Stanton; Jessica: Gloria Benson; Dinky: Jack Warner; Millie: Penny Carroll; Sarge: Sid Lawson; Pamela: Helen Wenzel; Judge: Budd Rogers; Monopolis/O'Brien: Ralph Simone; Mr. Jenkins: Martin Kraft; Mr. Blake: Paul Reed; Mrs. Jollop/Anne Green: Wana Allison; Mr. Dexter: Douglas Rutherford; Rodney: Bob Bernard. *Act I: Scene 1* Lobby of Lincoln University auditorium; the present; *Scene 2* Stage of University auditorium; immediately following; *Scene 3* The Tasty Toasty; the following day; *Scene 4* The Campus Walk; nine days later; *Scene 5* The Tasty Toasty; the following day; *Scene 6* The Tasty Toasty; the following evening; *Scene 7* The Campus Walk; same night; *Scene 8* Lobby of the Pink Angel Night Club; later that night. *Act II: Scene 1* Outside of sorority house; later that night; *Scene 2* The sorority dormitory; immediately following; *Scene 3* The Campus Walk; the following afternoon; *Scene 4* The Tasty Toasty; later the same day; *Scene 5* Outside of sorority house; a few minutes later; *Scene 6* Living room of Dexter's hotel suite; that night. *Act I:* Opening (Usherettes), "Heaven Sent" (Sarge, Bobby, Boys), Dance (Dancing Ensemble), "Buck in the Bank" (Bobby, Jessica, Singing Ensemble), Dance (Bobby), "Always You" (Bobby & Jessica), "About Face" (Sarge, Bobby, Dinky, Judge, Dancing Ensemble), Dance (Bobby, Dinky, Judge, Dancing Ensemble), "Fundamental Character" (Millie & Dinky), "Hold It!" (Bobby, Jessica, Dinky, Millie, Pamela, Judge, Singing Ensemble), Dance (Pamela), "Nevermore" (Jessica), "Roll 'em" [Sarge, Jessica, Millie, Pamela, Singing Ensemble) (music for Hollywood sequence by Irma Jurist). *Continued Next Week* (dance): STAR: Jessica; STAND-IN: Millie; DIRECTOR: Sarge; *Operation X* (dance): DOCTOR: Vernon Lusby; PATIENT: Jack Claus; NURSES: Elena Salamatova, Janet Bethel, Wana Allison, Vera Mallin (*Helen Kramer*); *Saga of Roaring Gulch* (dance): THE KID: Jack Warner; THE GAL: Margit De Kova; THE BOSS: Martin Kraft; BARTENDER: Paul Lyday; DANCE HALL GIRLS: Barbara McCutcheon & Yvonne Tibor; COWBOYS: Robert Evans, Robert Cadwallader, Bob Bernard; *Arsenic and Old Araby* (dance): SULTAN: Budd Rogers; FAVORITE: Jessica; OUT OF FAVOR TRIO: Wana Allison, Helen Wenzel, Onna White; OUT OF FAVOR DUO: Margit De Kova & Barbara McCutcheon; VESSEL BEARERS: Elena Salamatova & Yvonne Tibor; MESSAGE BEARERS: Jack Claus & Bob Bernard; ATTENDANTS: Vera Mallin (*Helen Kramer*) & Janet Bethel; SINBAD: Martin Kraft [end of "Roll 'em" sequence]. *Act II:* "(It Was) So Nice Having You" (Millie & Entire Ensemble), Dance (Dancing Ensemble), "Down the Well" (Sarge & Jessica), "You Took Possession of Me" (Pamela & Judge), Dance (Dancing Ensemble), "Always You" (reprise) (Bobby), "Friendly Enemy" (Millie & Dinky), "Hold It!" (reprise) (Entire Company), Finale (Entire Company).

Broadway reviews were divided, but mostly bad. Producer Anthony Brady Farrell had to close it because it wasn't making enough money. However, he bought the Warner Theatre, re-named it the Mark Hellinger, and kept over 20 members of the staff on hold (at over $1,000 a week), intending to put it on at the new theatre. But the re-opening did not happen.

317. *Hollywood Pinafore*

Subtitled *The Lad Who Loved a Salary*. Set in Pinafore Pictures Studio, Hollywood. This is Gilbert and Sullivan transferred to Hollywood and updated. Dick (Dick Deadeye in the original), complete with eye-patch, is a movie agent, and Joe (Sir Joseph Porter in the original) is a Pinafore Pictures executive, head of a huge movie producing unit. Miss Hebe is his secretary. LouHedda is a gossip columnist, known as Little Miss Butter-Up (based on Gilbert & Sullivan's Little Miss Buttercup). Ralph, a screenwriter, represents a group of wage slaves, mostly writers, who wear prison clothes as their regular working uniforms. He is in love with Brenda, a movie star. Bob is a press agent. Mike is a director. The doorman announced the salaries of each person, and of the collie star, Silver Tassels, who made $5,000 a week.

Before Broadway. The idea came to George S. Kaufman when he was playing cards with screenwriter Charles Lederer, who happened to parody some lines from *HMS* Pinafore.

The Broadway Run. ALVIN THEATRE, 5/31/45–7/14/45. 52 PERFORMANCES. PRESENTED BY Max Gordon, in association with Meyer Davis; MUSIC: Sir Arthur Sullivan; REVISED LYRICS/BOOK: George S. Kaufman (with deepest apologies to William S. Gilbert); BASED ON Gilbert & Sullivan's 1878 comic opera HMS Pinafore; DIRECTOR: George S. Kaufman; CHOREOGRAPHER: Douglas Coudy; BALLET CHOREOGRAPHER: Anthony Tudor; SETS/LIGHTING: Jo Mielziner; MODERN COSTUMES: Katherine Kuhn; PERIOD COSTUMES: Mary Percy Schenck; MUSICAL DIRECTOR: George Hirst; BALLET ORCHESTRATIONS: Hans Spialek; ADDITIONAL ORCHESTRATIONS: Stephen Jones; CHORAL ASSISTANT: Silas Engum; PRESS: John Peter Toohey; PRODUCTION SUPERVISOR: Arnold Saint Subber; GENERAL MANAGER: Ben A. Boyar; GENERAL STAGE MANAGER: Yola Miller; STAGE MANAGER: Mort O'Brien. **Cast:** JOSEPH W. PORTER: Victor Moore (2); MIKE CORCORAN: George Rasely; RALPH RACKSTRAW: Gilbert Russell, DICK LIVE-EYE: William Gaxton (1); BRENDA BLOSSOM: Annamary Dickey; LOUHEDDA HOPSONS: Shirley Booth (3); BOB BECKETT: Russ Brown; MISS HEBE: Mary Wickes (4); MISS GLORIA MUNDI: Diana Corday; MISS BEVERLY WILSHIRE: Pamela Randell; LITTLE MISS PEGGY: Ella Mayer; DOORMAN: Dan De Paolo; SECRETARIES: Jackson Jordan, Eleanor Prentiss, Drucilla Strain; GUARD: Ernest Taylor; SINGERS: Viola Essen & the Lynn Murray Singers, Sally

Billings, Florence George, Jane Hansen, Lucy Hillary, Josephine Lambert, Margaret Mckenna, Candace Montgomery, Jeanne North, Annette Sorrell, Mary Williams, Dean Campbell, Harold Cole, Jack Collins, Charles Dubin, Silas Engum, Howard Hoffman, Barry Kent, James Mate, John Mathews, Larry Stuart, Jeffrey Warren; DANCERS: Mary Alice Bingham, Eleanor Boleyn, John Butler, Ronny Chetwood, Helene Constantine, Babs Heath, Stanley Herbert, Virginia Meyer, Ann Newland, Shaun O'Brien, Jack Purcell, Regis Powers. **Understudy**: Ralph: Jeff Warren. **Act I**: morning: "(We Are) Simple Movie Folk" (Company), "(I'm Called) Little Butter-Up" (LouHedda & Company), "When an Agent's Not Engaged in His Employment" ("An Agent's Lot is Not a Happy One") (Dick & Women), "Wherever I Roam"/"A Maid Often Seen" (Ralph & Company), "I'm a Big Director at Pinafore" (Corcoran & Chorus), "Mike, What's the News?" (LouHedda & Corcoran), "Here on the Lot" (Brenda), "Joe Porter's Car is Seen" (Company), "I Am the Monarch of the Joint" (Porter, Hebe, Women), "When I Was a Lad" (Porter & Chorus), "A Writer Fills the Lowest Niche" (Ralph, Bob, Doorman, Writers), "Never Mind the Why and Wherefore" (Dick & Secretaries), "Refrain, Audacious Scribe"/"Proud Lady, Have Your Way" (Brenda, Ralph, Hebe, Chorus), "Can I Survive This (Overbearing)?" (Ralph, Dick, Brenda, Hebe, Bob, Company), "A Writer Fills the Lowest Niche" (reprise) (Company). **Act II**: night: "Fair Moon" (Corcoran), "I Am the Monarch of the Joint" (reprise) (Porter, Hebe, Chorus), Ballet Interlude: "Success Story:" CAMILLE, THE MOVIE HEROINE: Viola Essen; OTHER LITTLE MAIDS: Barbara Heath [also known as Babs Heath] & Helene Constantine; TALENT SCOUT: Regis Powers; HER TRUE LOVE: Ronny Chetwood; TWO MORE BOYS: Shaun O'Brien & Jack Purcell; ARMAND, THE MOVIE HERO: John Butler; DIRECTOR: Stanley Herbert; STUDIO ASSISTANTS: Eleanor Boleyn, Ann Newland, Virginia Meyer [end of ballet interlude], "Hollywood's a Funny Place" (LouHedda & Porter), "To Go Upon the Stage" (Brenda), "He is a Movie Man" (Porter, Dick, Bob, Corcoran, Ralph, Hebe), "Joe Porter, I've Important Information" (Dick & Porter), "Carefully on Tiptoe Stealing" (Brenda, Women, Ralph, Writers, Dick, Corcoran, Hebe, Porter), "Pretty Daughter of Mine" (Corcoran, Ralph, Hebe, Porter, Dick, Chorus), "Farewell My Own" (Ralph, Brenda, Porter, Dick, LouHedda, Hebe, Bob, Company), "The Town I Now Must Shake (LouHedda & Company), Finale Act II: "(We Are) Simple Movie Folk" (reprise) (Company).

Broadway reviews were drastically divided. Some raved about it, some panned it. There was very little in between. Reviews were academic, however, as there was a newspaper strike. There was an icemen's strike too, which meant air-conditioning in Broadway theatres wasn't working, and the Alvin was very hot. In addition to all that bad luck, another Pinafore show had opened on Broadway the week before—*Memphis Bound*.

318. *Home Sweet Homer*

The show concentrated on Odysseus's return home to Ithaka after his 10-year walkabout. Penelope is his long-suffering wife, fending off suitors, and Telemachus is their son. There was no intermission.

Before Broadway. It was originally called *Odyssey*, and it had a cast of 18. It ran at the Kennedy Center, Washington, DC, 12/19/74–1/25/75. 45 PERFORMANCES. This stint kicked off a year-long tour that eventually took it to Broadway. **Cast**: ANTINOUS: Martin Vidnovic; AGELAOS: Greg Bell; KTESIPPOS: Bill Mackey; EURYMACHUS: Michael Mann; LEOKRITOS: Brian Destazio; PIMTEUS: John Gorrin; MELIOS: Jeff Phillips; POLYBOS: Derrick Bell; PENELOPE: Joan Diener; TELEMACHUS: Russ Thacker; ODYSSEUS: Yul Brynner; KALYPSO, A NYMPH: Catherine Lee Smith; NAUSIKAA: Diana Davila; THERAPINA: Christine Uchida; MELANTHO: Cecile Santos; HIPPODAMEIA: P.J. Mann; KING ALKINOOS: Shev Rodgers; KERUX: Garon Douglass; POLYPHEMUS: Ian Sullivan. Mr. & Mrs. Brynner and Mr. & Mrs. Marre (Joan Diener was Mrs. Marre) sued Trader Vic's restaurant in New York in 4/75 for $7.5 million, claiming they had been food poisoned, and that this had affected their work on tour. 5th-billed Catherine Lee Smith's role was written out, as was Agelaos, Penelope's second suitor (played by Greg Bell). However, a new second suitor,

Pilokrates, was written in, and Ian Sullivan, who had played a character named Polyphemus on tour, was slotted into that role. There was a fuss in Boston when the Colonial Theatre, contrary to stipulations, left Joan Diener's name off the marquee. She insisted that the marquee be shrouded in black, leading some theatregoers to believe that Yul Brynner had died. During the Los Angeles gig Erich Segal asked that his name be removed from the credits as lyricist/librettist. It was, although much of his work remained. Albie Marre also removed Billy Wilson as choreographer, and took over that role himself. On the road the show had consistently bad reviews, but did good business. On 8/21/75 Yul Brynner sued to end his contract but backed off in face of a million dollar counter suit threat. In November Roger Stevens threatened to close the show in California, and Yul Brynner threatened to walk out of the show there and then if it wasn't brought to New York. A short while later Erich Segal sued, demanding that the show be closed.

The Broadway Run. PALACE THEATRE, 1/4/76. 11 previews. 1 PERFORMANCE. PRESENTED BY the John F. Kennedy Center for the Performing Arts (Roger L. Stevens, Martin Feinstein, Alex Morr); MUSIC: Mitch Leigh; LYRICS: Charles Burr & Forman Brown; BOOK: Roland Kibbee & Albert Marre; SUGGESTED BY the 9th century BC poem *The Odyssey*, by Homer; DIRECTOR/CHOREOGRAPHER: Albert Marre; SETS/LIGHTING: Howard Bay; COSTUMES: Howard Bay & Ray Diffen; SOUND: Lenny Will; MUSICAL DIRECTOR: Ross Reimueller; ORCHESTRATIONS: Buryl Red; DANCE MUSIC ARRANGEMENTS: Danny Holgate; PRESS: Betty Lee Hunt, Maria Cristina Pucci, Ruth Cage; GENERAL MANAGERS: Eugene Wolsk & Emanuel Azenberg; COMPANY MANAGER: Fred J. Cuneo; STAGE MANAGERS: Patrick Horrigan & Gregory Allen Hirsch. **Cast**: ODYSSEUS: Yul Brynner (1) ☆; PENELOPE, HIS WIFE: Joan Diener (2) ☆; TELEMACHUS, HIS SON: Russ Thacker (3) ☆; PENELOPE'S (EIGHT) SUITORS: ANTINOUS: Martin Vidnovic (5); PILOKRATES: Ian Sullivan (8); KTESIPPOS: Bill Mackey; EURYMACHUS: Daniel Brown; LEOKRITOS: Brian Destazio; PIMTEUS: John Aristedes; MELIOS: Bill Nabel; POLYBOS: Les Freed; KING ALKINOOS: Shev Rodgers (6); NAUSIKAA, HIS DAUGHTER: Diana Davila (4); NAUSIKAA'S (THREE) HANDMAIDENS: THERAPINA: Suzanne Sponsler; MELANTHO: Cecile Santos; HIPPODAMEIA: Christine Uchida; KERUX, THE HERALD: Darel Glaser (9); DEKATI EVDOMI VII: P.J. Mann (7). **Standby**: Penelope: Karen Shepard. **Understudies**: Odysseus: Shev Rodgers; Telemachus: Darel Glaser; Antinous: Daniel Brown; Alkinoos: Ian Sullivan; Nausikaa: Suzanne Sponsler. **Swing**: Linda Byrne. "The Sorceress" (Penelope & Suitors), "The Departure" (Odysseus & Dekati), "Home Sweet Homer" (Odysseus), "The Ball" (Nausikaa & Handmaidens), "How Could I Dare to Dream" (Odysseus & Telemachus), "I Never Imagined Goodbye" (Penelope), "Love is the Prize" (Odysseus), "Penelope's Hand" (Antinous), "He Will Come Home Again" (Telemachus), "Did He Really Think?" (Penelope), "I Was Wrong" (Odysseus), "The Rose" (Penelope), "Tomorrow" (Antinous & Suitors), "The Contest" (Odysseus, Telemachus, Antinous, Suitors).

Broadway critics devastated it, with the exception of Clive Barnes of the *New York Times*, who was only sorry it wasn't good.

319. *Honky Tonk Nights*

About black vaudeville. Sub-titled *How Billy Sampson and company left Hell's Kitchen for the Promised Land and What They Found There*.

The Broadway Run. BILTMORE THEATRE, 8/7/86–8/9/86. 16 previews. 4 PERFORMANCES. PRESENTED BY Edward H. Davis & Allen M. Shore, in association with Marty Feinberg & Schellie Archbold; MUSIC: Michael Valenti; LYRICS/BOOK: Ralph Allen & David Campbell; DIRECTOR/CHOREOGRAPHER: Ernest O. Flatt; SETS: Robert Cothran; COSTUMES: Mardi Philips; LIGHTING: Natasha Katz; SOUND: Jack Mann; MUSICAL DIRECTOR/VOCAL ARRANGEMENTS: George Broderick; ORCHESTRATIONS: Jim Tyler; DANCE MUSIC ARRANGEMENTS: David Krane; PRESS: Mark Goldstaub Public Relations; CASTING: Stuart Howard Associates; MAGIC CONSULTANT: William Veloric; CIRCUS CO-ORDINATOR: Hovey Burgess; PRODUCTION STAGE MANAGER: Larry Forde; STAGE MANAGER: Mark Rubinsky; ASSISTANT STAGE MANAGER: Clifford Schwartz. **Cast**: BARNEY WALKER: Joe Morton (1); BILLY SAMPSON: Ira Hawkins (3); ARMISTEAD

SAMPSON: Danny Strayhorn (5); LILY MEADOWS: Teresa Burrell (2); GEORGE GOOSEBERRY: Reginald VelJohnson (4); RUBY BUSH: Yolanda Graves; IVY VINE: Kyme; COUNTESS AIDA: Susan Beaubian; KITTY STARK: Robin Kersey; MONTGOMERY BOYD: Michael Demby-Cain; WINSTON GREY: Keith Rozie; SPARKS ROBERTS: Lloyd Culbreath; PATRON: Charles Bernard Murray; SAMPSON PHILHARMONIA: George Broderick, Kamau Adilifu, Robert Keller, Gregory Maker, Andrew Stein, John Gale, David Krane, James Sedlar, Quentin White. *Understudies*: Barney: Danny Strayhorn; Billy/George: Keith Rozie; Armistead: Lloyd Culbreath; Lily: Susan Beaubian; Ruby/Countess/Kitty: Julia Lema-Jackson; Ivy: Yolanda Graves; Montgomery/Winston/Sparks: Charles Bernard Murray. *Act I*: Sampson's Music Hall on a winter evening in 1912, in New York City's Hell's Kitchen: Overture, or "The Honky Tonk Nights Rag," or "Professor Walker and His Solo Symphony" (The Sampson Philharmonia), "Honky Tonk Nights" (Sampson & His Company), "Hot and Bothered" (Lily), "Roll with the Punches" (Barney, Armistead, Aida, Ivy, Kitty, Ruby), "Lily of the Alley" (Sampson, Winston, Montgomery, Sparks, Barney, Lily), "Choosing a Husband's a Delicate Thing" (Armistead, Barney, Gooseberry), "Little Dark Bird" (Lily), "Withered Irish Rose" (Barney, Armistead, Gooseberry, Montgomery, Lily), "Tapaholics" (Sparks, Ivy, Montgomery) [this number replaced "A Lush Ballad" (Sampson, with Aida & Ivy)], "Eggs" (Barney & Lily), "(A Ticket to the) Promised Land" (The Sampson Company). *Act II*: The *Promised Land Saloon* in Harlem during the summer of 1922: Overture: "The Promised Land" (The Pyromaniacs), "Stomp the Blues Away" (The Sampson Company), "I've Had It" (Barney & Lily), "The Sampson Beauties" (Ivy, Kitty, Ruby), "The Reform Song" (Barney, Gooseberry, Armistead), "I Took My Time" (Lily), "The Brothers Vendetto" (Barney, Gooseberry, Armistead), "A Man of Many Parts" (Barney), Finale (The Sampson Company).

Broadway reviews were bad.

320. *Hot Spot*

Based on a real-life incident involving the Peace Corps in 1961. Sally is a hygiene teacher in the Peace Corps. As the curtain rises she has already gotten into trouble in three different countries. Now she is in D'hum, the most remote country possible, where she inadvertently stirs up a Communist threat, thus assuring D'hum of U.S. aid. The ruler was the Nadir of D'hum, and the currency was the dreg.

Before Broadway. In 1962 this musical spoof began to take shape. Barbra Streisand was the first choice, but Judy Holliday did it, almost purely for the money. Miss Holliday's character's name was changed from Dulcie to Sally. The show tried out, unsuccessfully, at the National Theatre, Washington, DC., in 2/63. The director, Morton Da Costa, was on a deal that guaranteed him 13.75 per cent of the profits, but before Broadway he had become ill and had to leave. On 2/28/63 the show arrived in Philadelphia for further tryouts, at which point the producers considered replacing Judy Holliday with Carol Channing. Robert Fryer and Martin Charnin both acted as director during this period, until Richard Quine (Judy's choice) took over in his first Broadway show. However he almost immediately quit. Likewise, Arthur Laurents lasted a day. Larry Gelbart was brought in as play doctor, changed a few scenes, then left. Other writers also gave opinions, but otherwise steered clear of the doomed project. Several numbers were cut: "Don't Take My Word for It," "From the Red," "(This) Gallant Girl," "Over," "(Very) Simple People," "You Can Always Count on Us," and "He Needs Somebody." A new number, "Don't Laugh," which was added and was the best thing in the show, was written primarily by Steve Sondheim, a good friend of Mary Rodgers'. "Who Knows" (m: Mary Rodgers & Steve Sondheim; l: Steve Sondheim & Martin Charnin) was also written at this time, but not used (it was, later, in the revue *Hey Love*). The Majestic Theatre became available when Mary Rodgers' father's (Richard Rodgers) new show, *I Picked a Daisy* was postponed. During Broadway previews, from 3/63 (58 previews — one of the longest ever Broadway preview periods; it was scheduled to have 5) Herb Ross took over as director (uncredited). Mr. Ross also took over the choreography from Onna White, and is uncredited for that too. *Hot Spot* postponed its opening four times in order to avoid reviewers, and to take advantage of advance sales.

The Broadway Run. MAJESTIC THEATRE, 4/19/63–5/25/63. 58 previews. 43 PERFORMANCES. PRESENTED BY Robert Fryer & Lawrence Carr, in association with John Herman; MUSIC: Mary Rodgers; LYRICS: Martin Charnin; ADDITIONAL LYRICS: Stephen Sondheim; BOOK: Jack Weinstock & Willie Gilbert (book doctored by Herb Gardner & Larry Gelbart); DIRECTOR: Morton Da Costa (uncredited); CHOREOGRAPHER: Onna White (uncredited); SETS/COSTUMES: Rouben Ter-Arutunian; LIGHTING: John Harvey; MUSICAL DIRECTOR: Milton Rosenstock; ORCHESTRATIONS/ARRANGEMENTS: Luther Henderson & Ralph Burns; DANCE MUSIC/VOCAL ARRANGEMENTS: Trude Rittman & John Morris; CAST RECORDING on Warner Brothers; PRESS: Betty Lee Hunt; GENERAL MANAGER: Joseph Harris; COMPANY MANAGER: Sam Pagliaro; STAGE MANAGERS: Paul Davis, James Cresson, Jonathan Anderson, David Bean. *Cast:* ANDERSON: James Cresson; HENDERSON: Charles Braswell; SALLY HOPWINDER: Judy Holliday (1) *; GEORGE HIGGINS: Conrad Bain; THE PEACE CORPS (THREE MEMBERS): SUE ANN: Mary Louise Wilson (4); HOWARD MASON: Bob McClure; VERNON BREEN: James Moore; HARLEY, THE PILOT: George Furth; DUKE, THE CO-PILOT: James Cresson; THE (THREE) D'HUMIANS: THE NADIR OF D'HUM: Arny Freeman; SHIM: Joseph Bova (3); TWO MINISTERS OF STATE: Jack Dabdoub & Howard Kahl; DEVA: Jack Eddleman; IRAM: Carmen de Lavallade (5); RAMI: Buzz Miller; GABREL SNAPPER: Joseph Campanella (2); SUMNER TUBB SR.: Howard Freeman; MRS. SUMNER TUBB: Virginia Craig; SUMNER TUBB JR.: George Furth; ALLISON KENT: Sheila Smith; GROBANYKOV: Gerald Teijelo; PULSKI: Buzz Miller; ENSEMBLE: Marty Allen, Doria Avila, Jill Bartholomew, Alvin Beam, David Bean, Mary Sue Berry, Frank Bouley, Marnell Bruce, Diane Coupe, Virginia Craig, John Cunningham, Rhett Dennis, Sandra Devlin, Gildo Di Nunzio, Diane Ede, John Herbert, Lee Hooper, Audre Johnston, Jami Landi, Jim McArdle, Gloria Mills, Virginia Oswald, Bill Richards, Dean Taliaferro. STANDBY: Sally/Sue Ann: Marilyn Child. *Understudies:* Snapper: Charles Braswell; Shim: James Moore; Nadir: Conrad Bain; Tubb Sr.: Jack Dabdoub; Grobanykov/Pulski/Rami: Bill Richards. *Act I: Scene 1* The 6:45 report; *Scene 2* Peace Corps headquarters; *Scene 3* National Airport; *Scene 4* In the air over D'hum; *Scene 5* The D'hum Airstrip; *Scene 6* The American Consulate in D'hum; *Scene 7* The market place; *Scene 8* The clinic; *Scene 9* The D'hum Airstrip; *Scene 10* The Palace; *Scene 11* The 6:45 report; *Scene 12* A beauty salon in Washington; *Scene 13* All of D'hum. *Act II: Scene 1* Exterior of Yakacabana; *Scene 2* Interior of Yakacabana; *Scene 3* Moscow; *Scene 4* A street in D'hum; *Scene 5* The back room of the clinic; *Scene 6* Snapper's apartment at the consulate; *Scene 7* Outside the Yakacabana; *Scene 8* The Yakacabana; *Scene 9* The 6:45 report; *Scene 10* The consulate yard; *Scene 11* Peace Corps headquarters. *Act I*: "Don't Laugh" (m: Mary Rodgers & Stephen Sondheim; l: Mr. Sondheim & Martin Charnin) (Sally), "Don't Laugh" (reprise) (Sally & Peace Corps), "Welcome (to Our Country)" (D'humians), "Welcome Dance" (Iram, Rami, James Moore), "This Little Yankee" (Gabrel), "Smiles" (Sally, Deva, John Cunningham, Howard Kahl, Bob McClure, John Herbert, David Bean, Alvin Beam, Buzz Miller), "A Little Trouble (Goes a Long, Long Way)" (Sally, Shim, Nadir, D'humians), "(You'd Like) Nebraska" (Breen & Iram), "Hey, Love" (Sally), "I Had Two Dregs" (Sally, Shim, Tubb Sr., D'humians), "Rich, Rich, Rich" (Shim, Sue Ann, Peace Corps, D'humians). *Act II*: "That's Good–That's Bad" (l: Stephen Sondheim) (Sally), Iram and the Royal D'humian Dancers (dance) (Iram & Dancers), "I Think the World of You" (Sue Ann & Shim), "Gabie" (Sally), "A Matter of Time" (Gabrel & Sally), "Gabie" (reprise) (Gabrel), "Big Meeting Tonight" (Pulski, Grobanykov, Ensemble), Russian Dance at the Yakacabana (Sally, Grobanykov, Pulski), "A Far, Far Better Way" (Sally), "Don't Laugh" (reprise) (Sally, Gabrel, Ensemble).

Note: all numbers were written by Rodgers & Charnin, unless otherwise stated.

It opened on a Friday (no one reads the papers on a Saturday), and was panned. No director or choreographer was listed in the playbill. This was Judy Holliday's last show.

321. *House of Flowers*

Madame Fleur's whorehouse on a Caribbean island has come down with an epidemic of mumps, and is losing business to the rival house owned by Madame Tango. Ottilie has been adopted by Fleur and her name has been changed to Violet. Ottilie has been kept a virgin so Fleur may have an ace in the hole in her old age, but Fleur agrees to loan her out to a favored customer, Jamison, in exchange for money needed to import exotic girls to compete with Madame Tango. A U.S. battleship has arrived on Mardi Gras weekend, and Fleur's only chance is Ottilie, who, however, wants only to marry Royal, a local mountain boy. Fleur tries to have Royal killed (as she did with several husbands), fails, is forgiven, and the young lovers finally win. Tango's entire crew is lured away on a world cruise for a year on Jonas's ship, leaving the island open for Fleur.

Before Broadway. Truman Capote, an habitué of the Port-au-Prince homosexual brothels in Haiti, came up with the idea in 1948, as a short story (introducing the lovers Ottilie and Royal), then converted it into a play with incidental music. However, it became a large-scale musical, for which Mr. Capote wrote the libretto. Much of the collaboration between Harold Arlen and Mr. Capote on the score was done by phone or mail. Harry Belafonte was first mentioned for the role that went to Rawn Spearman, and opera singer Mattawilda Dobbs and Eartha Kitt for the roles that eventually went to Diahann Carroll and Pearl Bailey. The show tried out at the Erlanger Theatre, Philadelphia, 11/24/54–12/18/54. There were backstage problems with the star, Pearl Bailey, who collapsed, claiming she had been given too much new material to learn. Juanita Hall was forced to go on for her, with script in hand. Miss Bailey also clashed violently with English director Peter Brook, and Mr. Brook was replaced by Herb Ross, who also replaced the fired George Balanchine as choreographer (although Mr. Ross was uncredited as director). The role of 4th-billed Josephine Premice was deemed to be too good and was eliminated (as was Miss Premice), and her part was re-apportioned among two other characters. Certain songs that belonged to Diahann Carroll and Juanita Hall went to Pearl Bailey. 7th-billed Jacques Aubuchon was replaced by Ray Walston, who was bumped up to 4th-billed. Dancers Alvin Ailey and Carmen de Lavallade were added. Late in the tryout Otto Preminger helped a little, and Johnny Mercer added some lyrics. "Albertina's Beautiful Hair" was cut before Broadway.

The Broadway Run. ALVIN THEATRE, 12/30/54–5/21/55. 165 PERFORMANCES. PRESENTED BY Saint Subber; MUSIC: Harold Arlen; LYRICS: Truman Capote & Harold Arlen; ADDITIONAL LYRICS: Johnny Mercer & Michael Brown; BOOK: Truman Capote (based on his novella); DIRECTOR: Peter Brook; CHOREOGRAPHER: Herbert Ross; ASSISTANT CHOREOGRAPHER: Geoffrey Holder; SETS/COSTUMES: Oliver Messel; LIGHTING: Jean Rosenthal; MUSICAL DIRECTOR: Jerry Arlen; ORCHESTRATIONS: Ted Royal; DANCE MUSIC ARRANGEMENTS/VOCAL ARRANGEMENTS/REHEARSAL PIANIST: Peter Matz; CAST RECORDING on Columbia; PRESS: Dorothy Ross, Betty Lee Hunt, Shirley Herz; CASTING: Monte Kay; GENERAL MANAGER: C. Edwin Knill; PRODUCTION STAGE MANAGER: Lucia Victor; STAGE MANAGERS: John Barry Ryan & John Scott. *Cast:* TULIP: Dolores Harper; GLADIOLA: Ada Moore; PANSY: Enid Mosier; DO: Winston George Henriques; DON'T: Solomon Earl Green; MOTHER: Miriam Burton; OTTILIE, ALIAS VIOLET: Diahann Carroll (2); MADAME FLEUR: Pearl Bailey (1) ☆; CAPTAIN JONAS: Ray Walston (4), *John Randolph*; MADAME TANGO: Juanita Hall (3); MAMSELLE IBO-LELE: Pearl Reynolds; THE SISTERS MERINGUE: Leu Comacho & Margot Small; MAMSELLE HONOLULU: Mary Mon Toy; MAMSELLE CIGARETTE: Glory Van Scott; ROYAL: Rawn Spearman (6); THE CHAMPION: Geoffrey Holder (7); CHIEF OF POLICE: Don Redman; CARMEN: Carmen de Lavallade; ALVIN: Alvin Ailey; MONSIEUR JAMISON: Dino DiLuca (5); THE HOUNGAN: Frederick O'Neal (8); BARON OF THE CEMETERY: Geoffrey Holder; DUCHESS OF THE SEA: Miriam Burton; STEEL BAND: Michael Alexander, Roderick Clavery, Alphonso Marshall; TOWNSPEOPLE: Joseph Comadore, Hubert Dilworth, Philip Hepburn, Louis Johnson, Mary Louise, Donald McKayle, Audrey Mason (*Cristyne Lawson*), Arthur Mitchell, Walter Nicks, Albert Popwell, Sabu, Herbert Stubbs. *Understudies*: Fleur: Ada Moore; Tango: Miriam Burton; Gladiola/Ottilie: Mary Louise; Pansy: Glory Van Scott; Tango Belles: Audrey Mason, *Cristyne Lawson*; Royal: Herbert Stubbs; Houngan: Hubert Dilworth; Jonas/Jamison: Bill Sharon; Champion: Albert Popwell; Chief of Police: Walter Nicks. *Act I:* Overture (Orchestra); *Scene 1* Maison des Fleurs: "Waitin'" (Pansy, Tulip, Gladiola), "One Man Ain' Quite Enough" (Fleur), "Madame Tango's Tango" (Tango & Tango Belles), "A Sleepin'

Bee" (Ottilie, Pansy, Tulip, Gladiola); *Scene 2* On the way to the cockfight: "Bamboo Cage" (The Champion, Steel Band, Do, Don't, Pansy, Tulip, Gladiola, Tango, Chief of Police, Ensemble); *Scene 3* At the cockfight: "House of Flowers" (Royal & Ottilie); *Scene 4* Maison des Fleurs: "Two Ladies in de Shade of de Banana Tree" (Sung by Pansy & Gladiola. Danced by Carmen, Tulip, Ensemble), "What is a Friend For?" (Fleur); *Scene 5* The Houngan's hut: "A Sleepin' Bee" (reprise) (Ottilie & Royal); *Scene 6* The harbor of the town: "Mardi Gras" (Sung by Mother. Danced by Carmen, Alvin, Ensemble), "I Never Has Seen Snow" (Ottilie). *Act II*: *Scene 1* Maison des Fleurs: "Husband Cage" (Pansy, Tulip, Gladiola, Ensemble), "I'm Gonna Leave off Wearing My Shoes" (Ottilie & Ensemble) [added after opening]; *Scene 2* Madame Fleur's salon: "Has I Let You Down" (Fleur, Pansy, Tulip, Gladiola); *Scene 3* The Houngan's hut: "Voudou" (Houngan & Ensemble) (Banda dance ch: Geoffrey Holder). THE DRUMMERS: Sabu, Joseph Comadore, Michael Alexander, Alphonso Marshall; DUCHESS OF THE SEA: Miriam Burton; OCTOPUS: Albert Popwell; SHARK: Walter Nicks, Arthur Mitchell, Alphonso Marshall; TURTLE: Joseph Comadore & Ensemble; BARON OF THE CEMETERY: Geoffrey Holder; *Scene 4* Madame Tango's salon: "Slide Boy Slide" (sung by Tango & Ensemble. Danced by Alvin & Ensemble); *Scene 5* Madame Fleur's salon: "Don't Like Goodbyes" (Fleur) (this number was replaced during run by new song, "Indoor Girl," with lyrics by Michael Brown); *Scene 6* Maison des Fleurs: "Turtle Song" (Royal, Ottilie, Ensemble), Finale: "Bamboo Cage"/"Two Ladies in de Shade of de Banana Tree" (reprise) (Entire Company).

Broadway reviews were mostly very good. While the show was running Geoffrey Holder married Carmen de Lavallade. Act II was re-structured during the run. Peter Brook was called back to effect these revisions, but Pearl Bailey stated to the press that as Mr. Brook had had nothing to do with the show since mid-way through its Philadelphia tryout, she intended to co-operate with nobody but Herb Ross. The show lost about $215,000 of its $250,000 investment. However, by the time it closed it had built up a cult following, and the theatre was packed for the last week. At the final curtain call Miss Bailey said to the audience, "Where were you when we needed you?" The show won a Tony for sets.

After Broadway. THEATRE DE LYS, NYC, 1/28/68–3/17/68. 57 PERFORMANCES. This was a revised version. PRESENTED BY Saint-Subber, by special arrangement with Lucille Lortel Productions; DIRECTOR: Joseph Hardy; CHOREOGRAPHER: Talley Beatty; SETS: Kert Lundell; COSTUMES: Richard Castler; LIGHTING: Tharon Musser; MUSICAL DIRECTOR: Joseph Rapos; NEW CAST RECORDING on United Artists; GENERAL MANAGER: Eddie Knill. *Cast:* PANSY: Thelma Oliver; FLEUR: Josephine Premice; TANGO: Novella Nelson; OTTILIE: Yolande Bavan; TULIP: Hope Clarke; JAMISON: Tom Helmore; WOMAN: Trina Parks, *Sandra Lein*; MARIA: Carla Pinza; MAN: Walter Raines; HOUNGAN: Charles Moore; CHAMPION: Bob Broadway. This was the revised score (all music by Harold Arlen, and all lyrics by Harold Arlen & Truman Capote, unless otherwise specified): *Act I*: "Two Ladies in de Shade of de Banana Tree" (Pansy & Tulip), "A Sleepin' Bee" (Ottilie, Pansy, Tulip), "Somethin' Cold to Drink" (Fleur), "Smellin' of Vanilla" (Pansy, Tulip, Tango, Company), "House of Flowers" (Royal & Ottilie), "Don't Like Goodbyes" (Ottilie), "Jump de Broom" (m: Arlen; l: Capote) (Houngan & Company). *Act II*: "Waitin'" (Pansy & Tulip), "I Never Has Seen Snow" (Ottilie), "Walk to de Grave" (Houngan & Mourners), "Woman Never Understan'" (Royal), "Madame Tango's Particular Tango" (Tango, Maria, Tulip, Pansy), "What is a Friend For?" (Jamison & Fleur), "A Sleepin' Bee"/"I Never Has Seen Snow" (reprise) (Royal & Ottilie), "Two Ladies in de Shade of de Banana Tree" (reprise) (Fleur, Tulip, Pansy, Company). However, the show failed. The cast was wrong, the show too big for the small stage, and it lost its entire investment. However it was sold for $200,000 to United Artists for a movie that was never made.

BRIEF REVIVAL IN STOCK, 1991. DIRECTOR: Geoffrey Holder. *Cast*: FLEUR: Patti LaBelle.

CITY CENTER, NYC, 2/13/03–2/16/03. 5 PERFORMANCES. Part of the *Encores!* series. ADAPTED BY: Kirsten Childs; DIRECTOR/CHOREOGRAPHER: Kathleen Marshall; MUSICAL DIRECTOR: David Chase. *Cast*: JONAS: Maurice Hines; FLEUR: Tonya Pinkins; TANGO: Armelia McQueen; HOUNGAN: Roscoe Lee Browne; ALSO WITH: Nikki James, Brandon Victor Dixon, Brenda Braxton, Stacy Francis, Alexandra Foucard, Peter Francis James, Desmond Richardson, Wayne Pretlow, Everett Bradley.

322. *How Now, Dow Jones*

A musical comedy set in Manhattan. Kate is the voice of Dow Jones, whose job it is to announce the latest stock market averages. She is engaged to Herbert, but becomes pregnant by the suicidal Charley. Herbert tells Kate he will marry her when the Dow Jones average hits 1000, so Kate announces that it has. Her lie causes a hurricane of buying, followed by a near crash. Charley saves the day by getting the oldest man on Wall Street to buy everything, causing everyone else to buy, and he winds up with Kate. Wingate is a Wall Street tycoon who sets Cynthia up as his mistress and then neglects to visit her.

Before Broadway. It tried out first at New Haven, where reviews were good, then to the Shubert Theatre, Philadelphia, 10/10/67–10/28/67. Here reviews were not good, and George Abbott replaced Arthur Penn as director, and Michael Bennett replaced Gillian Lynne as choreographer, even though her name is on the Broadway credits. Mr. Bennett also brought Tommy Tune to the show. In the cast George Coe was replaced by James Congdon, and the role of Miss Whipple was cut, thereby we lost Madeline Kahn (Miss Kahn was also understudying Brenda Vaccaro). Barnard Hughes was written in after Boston and before Broadway, replacing Ed Steffe. The question mark after the title was cut too.

The Broadway Run. LUNT—FONTANNE THEATRE, 12/7/67–6/15/68. 19 previews from 11/21/67. 220 PERFORMANCES. PRESENTED BY David Merrick, BY ARRANGEMENT WITH Edwin H. Morris & Company; MUSIC: Elmer Bernstein; LYRICS: Carolyn Leigh; BOOK: Max Shulman (helped by George Abbott); BASED ON an original idea by Carolyn Leigh; DIRECTOR: George Abbott; CHOREOGRAPHER: Gillian Lynne; ASSISTANT CHOREOGRAPHER: Tommy Tune; SETS: Oliver Smith; COSTUMES: Robert Mackintosh; LIGHTING: Martin Aronstein; SOUND: Charles Bellin; MUSICAL DIRECTOR/DANCE MUSIC & VOCAL ARRANGEMENTS/INCIDENTAL MUSIC ARRANGEMENTS & CONDUCTOR: Peter Howard; ORCHESTRATIONS: Philip J. Lang; CAST RECORDING on RCA Victor; PRESS: Lee Solters, Harvey B. Sabinson, David Powers; CASTING: Mitchell Erickson; GENERAL MANAGER: Jack Schlissel; COMPANY MANAGER: Richard Highley; PRODUCTION STAGE MANAGER: Charles Blackwell; STAGE MANAGER: Henry Velez; ASSISTANT STAGE MANAGER: Kenneth Porter. **Cast:** CYNTHIA: Brenda Vaccaro (3) ✮; HERBERT: James Congdon (6); BROKER: Joe McGrath; KATE: Marlyn Mason (2) ✮; WINGATE: Hiram Sherman (4), *Barnard Hughes* (from 3/4/68); NICHOLS: Bob Gorman; JUDY EVANS: Patti Davis; WALLY: Alexander Orfaly; CHARLEY: Anthony Roberts (1) ✮; SUE ELLEN: Jennifer Darling (10); BRADBURY: Rex Everhart (9), *Barney Martin* (from 3/4/68); WAITER: Tommy Tune; SENATOR MCFETRIDGE: Barnard Hughes (5), *Ted Tiller* (from 3/4/68); DOW: Stanley Simmonds; JONES: Martin Ambrose; TYCOONS: Frank De Sal, Bob Gorman, John Joy, Alexander Orfaly; LION: Ron Schwinn; CUSTOMERS' MEN: Bob Gorman, Frank De Sal, John Joy, Doug Spingler; DR. GILMAN: Sammy Smith (7); (FOUR) WIDOWS: MRS. RAGOSA: Francesca Smith; MRS. KLEIN: Fran Stevens; MRS. HARRIS: Sally De May; MRS. CALLAHAN: Lucie Lancaster; MRS. MILLHAUSER: Charlotte Jones (8); A.K.: Arthur Hughes (11); DANCERS: Oscar Antony, Linnea Chandler, Joel Conrad, Patricia Cope, Frank De Sal, Lois Etelman, Cyndi Howard, Yanco Inone, Eileen Lawlor, Debra Lyman, Diana Quijano, Sally Ransone, George Ramos, Ron Schwinn, Doug Spindler, Ron L. Steinbeck, Pat Trott; SINGERS: Martin Ambrose, Leigh Curran, Patti Davis, Bill Gibbens, Bob Gorman, Maria Hero, John Joy, Joe McGrath, Jack Murray, Alexander Orfaly, Anna Pagan, Dixie Stewart, Mara Worth. **Standby:** Charley: Lester James. **Understudies:** Kate: Maria Hero; Cynthia: Leigh Curran; Sue Ellen/Widows: Patricia Cope; Wingate: Alex Orfaly; Gilman: Stanley Simmonds; Mrs. Millhauser: Fran Stevens; Bradbury: Martin Ambrose. **Act I: Scene 1** Financial District: "A.B.C." (Cynthia, Tourists, Wall Streeters); **Scene 2** Child's Restaurant: "They Don't Make 'em Like That Any More" (Kate & Cynthia), "Live a Little" (Charley, Kate, New Yorkers), Crazy Night Ballet: "The Pleasure's About to Be Mine" (Charley & Kate); **Scene 3** Wingate's private office: "A Little Investigation" (Wingate, McFetridge, Dow, Jones, Tycoons); **Scene 4** Kate's apartment: "Walk Away" (Kate);

Scene 5 Wall Street; early a.m.; **Scene 6** Wingate & Co., brokers: "Goodbye, Failure, Goodbye" ("Gawk, Tousle, Shucks") (Charley, Customers' Men, Brokers); **Scene 7** Mrs. Millhauser's living room: "Step to the Rear" (Charley, Millhauser, Widows, Ensemble); **Scene 8** Kate's apartment: "Shakespeare Lied" (Kate, Cynthia, Gilman); **Scene 9** Wingate's private office; **Scene 10** Wall Street; **Scene 11** Dow Jones office: "Big Trouble" (Kate). **Act II: Scene 1** New York City: "Credo" ("Rich is Better") (Gilman, Mrs. Klein, Widows, New Yorkers), "One of Those Moments" ("Just for the Moment") (Kate); **Scene 2** Wingate's private office: "Big Trouble" (reprise) (Wingate & Tycoons); **Scene 3** Mrs. Millhauser's living room; **Scene 4** Cynthia's apartment: "He's Here!" (Cynthia) [the show's highlight]; **Scene 5** Financial District: "Panic" (Entire Cast); **Scene 6** Kate's apartment: "Touch and Go" (Charley & Kate) [this replaced "Where You Are" (Charley & Kate) before Broadway]; **Scene 7** Wingate & Co., brokers: Finale: "That's Good Enough for Me" (Entire Cast).

Broadway reviews were mostly terrible. Hiram Sherman won a Tony, and the show was also nominated for composer & lyricist, direction of a musical, and for Anthony Roberts and Brenda Vaccaro.

After Broadway. In concert, 11/8/02–11/10/02. PRESENTED BY the York Theatre Company as part of their *Musicals in Mufti* series. Elmer Bernstein attended the evening performance of 11/9/02. DIRECTOR: Sheryl Keller. *Cast:* CYNTHIA: Kaitlin Hopkins; WINGATE: David Garrison; CHARLEY: Brooks Ashmanskas; SUE ELLEN: Kristin Maloney; GILMAN: Mitchell Greenberg.

323. *How to Succeed in Business Without Really Trying*

For obvious reasons this show is generally referred to as *How to Succeed.* It is a re-vamping of the Horatio Alger, rags-to-riches, story, a satire about making it in corporate America by using any means one can. Set in the new Park Avenue (New York City) office building of the World Wide Wicket Company, Inc., in 1961. About boyish-looking young man J. Pierpont Finch, and his meteoric rise in the company. We see him first as a window washer, studying Shepherd Mead's real-life book of the same name. He goes to work in the company's mail room, under Twimble, and alongside Frump, the presidents' scheming nephew. He is selected as the head mail clerk, but cunningly turns it down so that he can move into an executive position. From then on he schemes and tramples over anyone and everything in his rise to the top. He mercilessly exploits everyone, including Mr. Biggley, the stuffy president of the company, and Hedy, Biggley's girlfriend, until he finally becomes Chairman of the Board, a position previously held by Mr. Womper, himself an ex-window washer. Rosemary is patiently in love with Finch, and Miss Jones is Biggley's secretary.

Before Broadway. Jack Weinstock and Willie Gilbert bought the rights to Shepherd Mead's plotless book, and wrote a script, planning to make a non-musical comedy out of it. They sent it to producers Feuer & Martin who saw it as a musical. Abe Burrows came in and re-wrote the script as a libretto for the musical (that's how it happened, despite program credits listing Messrs Gilbert & Weinstock as co-librettists), and Frank Loesser was drafted to write the score (his last for Broadway). The part of Finch was written for Robert Morse (this was the show that made him a star). Rehearsals began on 8/3/61. Hugh Lambert was replaced during the Philadelphia tryouts by the more experienced Bob Fosse, but Mr. Fosse let Mr. Lambert keep his credit as choreographer. The numbers "I Worry About You," "Organization Man" and "Status" were cut before Broadway.

The Broadway Run. FORTY-SIXTH STREET THEATRE, 10/14/61–3/6/65. 3 previews from 10/12/61. 1,417 PERFORMANCES. PRESENTED BY Cy Feuer & Ernest Martin, in association with Frank Productions (Frank Loesser); MUSIC/LYRICS: Frank Loesser; BOOK: Abe Burrows; BASED ON an unproduced play of the same name by Jack Weinstock & Willie Gilbert, which in turn was based on the 148-page best selling 1952 book

How to Succeed in Business Without Really Trying: a Dastard's Guide to Fame and Fortune, by advertising agency vice-president Shepherd Mead; DIRECTOR: Abe Burrows; CHOREOGRAPHER: Hugh Lambert; MUSICAL STAGING BY: Bob Fosse; SETS/LIGHTING: Robert Randolph; COSTUMES: Robert Fletcher; MUSICAL DIRECTOR: Elliot Lawrence, *Abba Bogin* (by 63–64); ORCHESTRATIONS: Robert Ginzler; ADDITIONAL SCORING: Elliot Lawrence; CAST RECORDING on RCA Victor, made at Webster Hall, NY, 10/22/61; PRESS: Merle Debuskey, Seymour Krawitz, Madi Ross, Judith S. Davidson (gone by 63–64); PRODUCTION STAGE MANAGER: Phil Friedman, *Herman Magidson* (by 62–63); STAGE MANAGER: Lawrence Kasha, *Jeffrey Longe*; ASSISTANT STAGE MANAGERS: Lanier Davis & Stuart Fleming, *Darrell Notara* (added by 62–63). **Cast:** J. PIERPONT FINCH: Robert Morse (1), *Darryl Hickman* (from 10/7/63), *Ronnie Welsh* (from 8/31/64); MILT GATCH: Ray Mason; JENKINS: Robert Kaliban, *Hal England* (from 62–63), *Ronnie Welsh* (from 63–64), *Richard Barclay* (from 63–64); TACKABERRY: David Collyer; PETERSON: Casper Roos; J.B. BIGGLEY: Rudy Vallee (2), *Jeff De Benning* (from 10/19/64); KITTRIDGE: Lanier Davis [new character by 63–64]; ROSEMARY PILKINGTON: Bonnie Scott (3), *Lois Leary* (from 61–62), *Michele Lee* (from 10/8/62), *Suzanne Menke* (from 12/21/64); BERT BRATT: Paul Reed, *Walter Klavun* (from 62–63), *Bruce MacKay* (from 63–64); SMITTY: Claudette Sutherland; BUD FRUMP: Charles Nelson Reilly (5), *Ralph Purdum* (from 9/30/63); MISS JONES: Ruth Kobart, *Leta Bonynge* (from 62–63), *Jean Handzlik*; MR. TWIMBLE: Sammy Smith; HEDY LA RUE: Virginia Martin (4), *Joy Claussen* (from 8/27/62), *Maureen Arthur* (from 8/31/64); 1ST SCRUBWOMAN: Mara Landi, *Virginia Perlowin* (by 63–64), *Carole Lindsey* (from 63–64); 2ND SCRUBWOMAN: Silver Saundors, *Alice Evans* (from 63–64); MISS KRUMHOLTZ: Mara Landi, *Carole Lindsey* (from 63–64); TOYNBEE: Ray Mason; OVINGTON: Lanier Davis; POLICEMAN: Bob Murdock, *Harris Hawkins* (from 63–64); WALLY WOMPER: Sammy Smith; SINGERS: David Collyer, Lanier Davis, Charlotte Frazier (*Nanette Workman* by 63–64, *Anne Nathan* from 64), Bob Kaliban (*Hal England* from 62–63, *Ronnie Welsh* from 63–64; *Richard Barclay* from 63–64), Mara Landi (*Carole Lindsey* from 63–64), Fairfax Mason, Bob Murdock (*Harris Hawkins* by 63–64), Maudeen O'Sullivan (*Georgia Creighton* from 62–63 & gone by 63–64), Casper Roos, Silver Saundors (*Alice Evans* from 63–64). 63–64 replacement: Renee Gorsey. Later replacement: *Randy Phillips*; DANCERS: Caroljane Abney, Nick Andrews, Elaine Cancilla, Madilyn Clark (gone by 62–63), Tracy Everitt (gone by 63–64), Stuart Fleming (gone by 62–63), Suzanne France (gone by 62–63), Richard Korthaze, Donna McKechnie (gone by 63–64), Dale Moreda (gone by 63–64), Darrell Notara, Ellie Somers (gone by 62–63), Merritt Thompson, Rosemarie Yellen (gone by 63–64). 62–63 replacements: *Pat Ferrier* (gone by 63–64), *Mickey Gunnersen, Patrick Heim* (gone by 63–64), *Maralyn Thoma* (gone by 63–64). 63–64 replacements: *Gene Cooper, Don Emmons, Enid Hart, Kaarlyn Kitch, Iva March, Alice Shanahan, Ron Stratton.* Later replacement: *Tod Jackson.* **Understudies:** Finch: Bob Kaliban, *Hal England, Ronnie Welsh, Richard Barclay* (by 63–64), *Len Gochman*; Frump: Bob Kaliban, *Hal England, Richard Barclay* (by 63–64), *Darrell Notara* by 63–64; Rosemary: Charlotte Frazier, *Nanette Workman* (by 63–64), *Anne Nathan* (in 64); Hedy: Fairfax Mason; Smitty: Silver Saundors, *Carole Lindsey* (by 63–64); Bratt: David Collyer; Twimble: Lanier Davis; Miss Jones: Mara Landi, *Alice Evans* (by 63–64); Womper: Casper Roos; J.B.: Walter Klavun. **Act I:** Overture (Orchestra); **Scene 1** Exterior of the World Wide Wicket Company building: "How to (Succeed in Business without Really Trying)" (Finch); **Scene 2** Corridor of the World Wide Wicket Company: "Happy to Keep His Dinner Warm" (Rosemary); **Scene 3** Outer office of the World Wide Wicket Company: "Coffee Break" (Frump, Smitty, Office Staff); **Scene 4** The mail room: "The Company Way" (Finch & Twimble), "The Company Way" (reprise) (Frump, Twimble, Office Staff); **Scene 5** J.B. Biggley's desk; **Scene 6** Corridor of the World Wide Wicket Company: "A Secretary is Not a Toy" (Bratt, Frump, Office Staff); **Scene 7** Elevator landing; home time: "Been a Long Day" (Finch, Rosemary, Smitty), "Been a Long Day" (reprise) (Biggley, Hedy, Frump); **Scene 8** Outer office; on a deserted Saturday morning: "(Grand) Old Ivy" (Finch & Biggley); **Scene 9** Finch's first office; **Scene 10** Plans & Systems office — promotion; **Scene 11** Corridor of the World Wide Wicker Company: "Paris Original" (Rosemary, Smitty, Miss Jones, Secretaries); **Scene 12** On the roof of the World Wide Wicker Company building: "Paris Original"

(continued); **Scene 13** Elevator landing; **Scene 14** J.B. Biggley's office; "Rosemary" (Finch & Rosemary); Finaletto (Finch, Rosemary, Frump). **Act II:** Entr'acte (Orchestra); **Scene 1** Outer office: "Cinderella, Darling" (Rosemary, Smitty, Secretaries); **Scene 2** Finch's new advertising office: "Happy to Keep His Dinner Warm" (reprise) (Rosemary); **Scene 3** J.B. Biggley's office: "(Love from a) Heart of Gold" (Biggley & Hedy); **Scene 4** Men's washroom: "I Believe in You" (Finch, Frump, Bratt, Executives); **Scene 5** J.B. Biggley's office as a board room; **Scene 6** The World Wide Wicket Company television studio: "The Yo Ho Ho" ("The Pirate Dance") (The Jolly Wickets & Wickettes) (choreography by Hugh Lambert) [cut by 63–64, but re-instated for 1995 revival]; **Scene 7** Outer office — wrecked: "I Believe in You" (reprise) (Rosemary); **Scene 8** Elevator landing; **Scene 9** J.B. Biggley's office: "Brotherhood of Man" (Finch, Biggley, Frump, Bratt, Womper, Miss Jones, Office Staff); **Scene 10** Outer office: Finale: "The Company Way" (reprise) (Company).

Broadway reviewers only raved. The show won a Pulitzer Prize (only the fourth ever for a musical). It also won Tony Awards for musical, producers of a musical, book, direction of a musical, musical direction, and for Robert Morse and Charles Nelson Reilly. It was also nominated for composer. It was a smash hit, becoming the fifth-longest running musical ever on Broadway to that time. It grossed over $10.5 million. The show made a profit on its three tours.

After Broadway. TOUR. Opened on 2/4/63, at the Hanna Theatre, Cleveland. MUSICAL DIRECTOR: Fred Werner. *Cast:* FINCH: Dick Kallman, *Ronnie Welsh*; BIGGLEY: Willard Waterman, *Jeff De Benning*; ROSEMARY: Dyan Cannon, *Suzanne Menke*; FRUMP: William Major; HEDY: Maureen Arthur.

TOUR. Opened on 10/14/63, at the Center Theatre, Norfolk, Va. *Cast:* FINCH: Hal England; BIGGLEY: Jeff De Benning; ROSEMARY: Kipp Hamilton; BRATT: Art Barnett; FRUMP: Bill Mullikin; MISS JONES: Maggie Task; HEDY: Sandra O'Neill.

POST-BROADWAY TOUR. Opened on 5/10/65. *Cast:* FINCH: Dick Kallman; BIGGLEY: Jeff De Benning; ROSEMARY: Suzanne Menke; FRUMP: William Major; HEDY: Maureen Arthur.

SHAFTESBURY THEATRE, London, 3/28/63. 520 PERFORMANCES. PRESENTED BY Arthur Lewis; CHOREOGRAPHER: Hugh Lambert. *Cast:* FINCH: Warren Berlinger; PETERSON: Michael Billington; BIGGLEY: Billy De Wolfe; ROSEMARY: Patricia Michael; SMITTY: Josephine Blake; FRUMP: David Knight; TWIMBLE/WOMPER: Bernard Spear; HEDY: Eileen Gourlay.

Comment reussir dans les affaires sans vraiment se fatiguer. THEATRE DE PARIS, 1964. ADAPTED BY: Raymond Castans. It ran 9 months, then toured.

CITY CENTER, NYC, 4/20/66–5/8/66. 23 PERFORMANCES. This was the first major revival, and was part of the City Center Light Opera Company's spring season of four Frank Loesser revivals (the others were *The Most Happy Fella, Where's Charley?* and *Guys and Dolls*). DIRECTOR: Gus Schirmer; SETS: Robert Randolph; COSTUMES: Stanley Simmons; LIGHTING: Peggy Clark; MUSICAL DIRECTOR: Anton Coppola. *Cast:* FINCH: Len Gochman; JENKINS: Austin Colyer; TACKABERRY: Henry Lawrence; BIGGLEY: Billy De Wolfe; ROSEMARY: Sheila Sullivan; BRATT: Art Barnett; SMITTY: Pat McEnnis; FRUMP: Lee Goodman; MISS JONES: Justine Johnston; TWIMBLE/WOMPER: Lou Cutell; HEDY: Betty Linton; DANCERS INCLUDED: Doria Avila, Mickey Gunnersen, Beth Howland, Roger Allan Raby.

THE MOVIE. 1967. Certain numbers were dropped: "Happy to Keep His Dinner Warm," "Cinderella, Darling," "Love from a Heart of Gold," as well as the ballet sequence "The Pirate Ballet." "Paris Original" was only heard in background. PRODUCER/DIRECTOR: David Swift. *Cast:* FINCH: Robert Morse; GATCH: Jeff De Benning; J.B. BAGLEY: Rudy Vallee; ROSEMARY: Michele Lee; BUD: Anthony Teague; MISS JONES: Ruth Kobart; TWIMBLE/WOMPER: Sammy Smith; HEDY: Maureen Arthur.

324. *How to Succeed in Business Without Really Trying (Broadway revival)*

Before Broadway. It tried out at the La Jolla Playhouse, San Diego. It had the same cast and crew as for the subsequent Broadway run, except BIGGLEY: Robert Mandan; SMITTY: Dawn Lewis; TWIMBLE/WOMPER:

Ernie Sabella. The it played at the Kennedy Center, Washington, DC, 1/29/95–2/26/95. The number "Cinderella, Darling" was cut for this revival and replaced with a reprise of "How To" (Smitty, Krumholtz, Women).

The Broadway Run. RICHARD RODGERS THEATRE, 3/23/95–7/14/96. 16 previews from 3/9/95. 548 PERFORMANCES. PRESENTED BY Dodger Productions, Kardana Productions, the John F. Kennedy Center for the Performing Arts, and the Nederlander Organization; MUSIC/LYRICS: Frank Loesser; BOOK: Abe Burrows; BASED ON Shepherd Mead's book; DIRECTOR: Des McAnuff; CHOREOGRAPHER: Wayne Cilento; SETS: John Arnone; COSTUMES: Susan Hilferty; LIGHTING: Howell Binkley; SOUND: Steve Canyon Kennedy; MUSICAL DIRECTOR/VOCAL ARRANGEMENTS/INCIDENTAL MUSIC ARRANGEMENTS: Ted Sperling; ORCHESTRATIONS: Danny Troob; ADDITIONAL ORCHESTRATIONS: David Siegel & Robert Ginzler; DANCE MUSIC ARRANGEMENTS: Jeanine Tesori; NEW CAST RECORDING on RCA Victor; PRESS: Boneau/Bryan-Brown; CASTING: Julie Hughes & Barry Moss; COMPANY MANAGER: Marcia Goldberg; PRODUCTION STAGE MANAGER: Frank Hartenstein; STAGE MANAGER: Diane DiVita; ASSISTANT STAGE MANAGERS: Kimberly Fisk & Glynn Turner. *Cast:* VOICE OF THE NARRATOR: Walter Cronkite (10); J. PIERPONT FINCH: Matthew Broderick (1) ✩, *Martin Moran (during Mr. Broderick's vacations), John Stamos (from 11/13/95), Matthew Broderick (from 3/19/96)*; MILT GATCH: Tom Flynn; JENKINS: Jay Aubrey Jones; DAVIS: William Ryall, *John MacInnis*; BERT BRATT: Jonathan Freeman (5); TACKABERRY: Martin Moran; J.B. BIGGLEY: Ronn Carroll (2), *William Ryall*; ROSEMARY PILKINGTON: Megan Mullally (3), *Jessica Stone (from 1/30/96), Sarah Jessica Parker (from 3/12/96)*; SMITTY: Victoria Clark (6); BUD FRUMP: Jeff Blumenkrantz (4), *Brooks Ashmanskas (from 2/19/96)*; MISS KRUMHOLTZ: Kristi Lynes; OFFICE BOY: Randl Ask, *John Bolton*; SECURITY GUARD: Kevin Bogue; HENCHMEN: Jack Hayes & Jerome Vivona; MISS JONES: Lillias White (9), *Tina Fabrique*; MR. TWIMBLE: Gerry Vichi (8); HEDY LA RUE: Luba Mason (7); TOYNBEE: Tom Flynn; SCRUBWOMEN: Rebecca Holt & Carla Renata Williams; DANCE SOLOIST: Nancy Lemenager, *Susan Misner*; OVINGTON: Randl Ask; TV ANNOUNCER: Randl Ask; WICKETS & WICKETTES: Kevin Bogue, Maria Calabrese, Jack Hayes, Nancy Lemenager (*Susan Misner*), Kristi Lynes, Aiko Nakasone (*JoAnn M. Hunter*), Jerome Vivona, Carla Renata Williams; WALLY WOMPER: Gerry Vichi; ENSEMBLE: Randl Ask (*John Bolton*), Kevin Bogue, Maria Calabrese, Tom Flynn, Jack Hayes, Rebecca Holt, Jay Aubrey Jones, Nancy Lemenager (*Susan Misner*), Martin Moran, Aiko Nakasone (*JoAnn M. Hunter*), William Ryall (*John MacInnis*), Jerome Vivona, Carla Renata Williams. *Understudies:* Finch: Martin Moran & Randl Ask, *John Bolton*; Frump: Randl Ask; Twimble/Womper: Jay Aubrey Jones; Bratt: Tom Flynn; Smitty/Miss Jones: Carla Renata Williams; Hedy: Pamela Gold & Rebecca Holt; Rosemary: Kristi Lynes; Biggley: William Ryall. *Swings:* Jeffry Denman, Tom Flagg, Pamela Gold, *Jerold Goldstein, Andrew Palermo, Jennifer Prescott*. *Orchestra:* CONCERTMASTER: Diane Monroe; VIOLINS: Michael Roth, Rob Shaw, Nam-Sook Lee; CELLI: Adam Grabois & Susannah Chapman; BASS: John Babich; WOODWINDS: Chuck Wilson, Mike Migliore, Rick Heckman, Ken Hitchcock, Roger Rosenberg; TRUMPETS: Byron Stripling, Glenn Drewes, Larry Lunetta; FRENCH HORN: Chris Korner; TROMBONES: Keith O'Quinn & Herb Besson; GUITAR: Scott Kuney; DRUMS: Ray Marchica; PERCUSSION: Bill Hayes; HARP: Grace Paradise.

Broadway reviews were excellent. The show won a Tony Award for Matthew Broderick, and was nominated for revival of a musical, direction of a musical, and choreography.

After Broadway. TOUR. Opened on 5/28/96, at the Mechanic Theatre, Baltimore, and closed on 6/1/97, at De Vos Hall, Grand Rapids, Mich. DIRECTOR: Des McAnuff; ASSOCIATE DIRECTOR: Judy Minor; MUSICAL DIRECTOR: Randy Booth. *Cast:* FINCH: Ralph Macchio; BIGGLEY: Richard Thomsen; ROSEMARY: Shauna Hicks; BRATT: John Deyle; SMITTY: Susann Fletcher; FRUMP: Roger Bart, *Todd Weeks (from 1/19/97)*; MISS JONES: Tina Fabrique; TWIMBLE/WOMPER: Michael Cone; HEDY: Pamela Blair; ALSO WITH: Danny Rutigliano, Lorna Shane, Christopher Mixon, Jessica Sheridan.

325. *The Human Comedy*

An opera, almost entirely in song, set in 1943 in Ithaca, a little town in California. The Macauley family consists of a widowed mother, sis-

ter Bess, and brothers Ulysses, Homer and Marcus. Marcus is away at war, and is killed. His soldier buddy, Tobey, who has heard all about the family, arrives and becomes part of the family. During the show the orchestra was on stage, at the sides.

Before Broadway. William Saroyan originally wrote the story as a screenplay for the 1943 movie of the same name. He was also director of the movie, but was fired, and subsequently wrote the novel of the story which was released just before the movie. The musical played originally Off Broadway, at the ANSPACHER THEATRE (part of the New York Shakespeare Festival's Public Theatre complex), 12/28/83–3/4/84. 8 previews from 12/20/83. 79 PERFORMANCES. It got pretty good reviews. It had the same basic crew as for the subsequent Broadway production, except LIGHTING: Stephen Strawbridge. It had the same cast too, except GIRL: Lisa Kirchner; BOY: Louis Padilla; SOLDIERS: Kenneth Bryan & Michael Wilson (there were only two at that stage); MARCUS/VOICE OF MATTHEW: Don Kehr; TOWNSPEOPLE: Donna Lee Marshall, Grady Mulligan, Vernon Spencer. Walter Hudson replaced Rex Smith in 2/84.

The Broadway Run. ROYALE THEATRE, 4/5/84–4/15/84. 19 previews. 13 PERFORMANCES. The New York Shakespeare Festival production, PRESENTED BY Joseph Papp & The Shubert Organization; MUSIC/MUSICAL DIRECTOR/ORCHESTRATIONS: Galt MacDermot; BOOK: William Dumaresq; FROM the novel of the same name by William Saroyan; DIRECTOR: Wilford Leach; SETS: Bob Shaw; COSTUMES: Rita Ryack; LIGHTING: James F. Ingalls; SOUND: Tom Morse; CAST recording not released until 1998; PRESS: Merle Debuskey, Richard Kornberg, Barbara Carroll, Bruce Campbell; GENERAL MANAGER: Laurel Ann Wilson; COMPANY MANAGER: David Conte; PRODUCTION STAGE MANAGER: Alan Fox; STAGE MANAGER: K. Siobhan Phelan. *Cast:* TRAINMAN: David Lawrence Johnson; ULYSSES MACAULEY: Josh Blake; MRS. KATE MACAULEY: Bonnie Koloc; HOMER MACAULEY: Stephen Geoffreys; BESS MACAULEY: Mary Elizabeth Mastrantonio; HELEN: Anne Marie Bobby; MISS HICKS, TEACHER: Laurie Franks; SPANGLER: Rex Smith; THIEF: Christopher Edmonds; MR. GROGAN: Gordon Connell; FELIX: Daniel Noel; BEAUTIFUL MUSIC: Debra Byrd; MARY ARENA: Caroline Peyton; MEXICAN WOMAN: Olga Merediz; VOICE OF MATTHEW MACAULEY: Grady Mulligan; MARCUS MACAULEY: Don Kehr; TOBEY: Joseph Kolinski; SOLDIERS: Kenneth Bryan, Louis Padilla, Michael Wilson; NEIGHBOR: Kathleen Rowe McAllen; DIANA STEED: Leata Galloway; MINISTER: Walter Hudson; TOWNSPEOPLE: Marc Stephen Del Gatto, Lisa Kirchner, Vernon Spencer, Dan Tramon. *Standby:* Kate: Cass Morgan. *Understudies:* Kate: Lisa Kirchner; Trainman/Felix: Vernon Spencer; Ulysses: Marc Stephen Del Gatto; Mexican Woman: Lisa Kirchner; Homer: Dan Tramon; Bess/Mary: Donna Murphy; Helen/Diana: Kathleen Rowe McAllen; Miss Hicks: Debra Byrd; Marcus: Grady Mulligan; Spangler: Walter Hudson & Grady Mulligan; Thief: Daniel Noel; Grogan: David Vogel; Beautiful Music: David Lawrence Johnson; Tobey: Louis Padilla. *Swing:* David Vogel. *Musicians:* VIOLINS: Joel Derovin & Josh Rodriguez; VIOLA: Gregory Singer; CELLO: Nestor Cybriwsky; DOUBLE BASS: Doug Shear; PERCUSSION: Jimmy Madison; GUITARS: Charles C. Brown III; SAX/CLARINET/FLUTE: Seldon Powell & Allen Won; KEYBOARD: Allen Shawn; TRUMPET/FLUGELHORN: Mac Gollehan; TROMBONE: Eddie Bert. *Act I:* "In a Little Town in California" (Company); *Scene 1* At the train crossing: "Hi Ya, Kid" (Trainman & Ulysses); *Scene 2* At home: "We're a Little Family" (Mrs. Macauley, Homer, Ulysses, Bess); *Scene 3* At school: "The Assyrians" (Helen & Miss Hicks), "Noses" (Homer); *Scene 4* At the telegraph office: "You're a Little Young for the Job" (Spangler & Homer), "I Can Carry a Tune" (Homer), "Happy Birthday" (Homer), "Happy Anniversary" (Homer, Spangler, Mr. Grogan), "I Think the Kid Will Do" (Mr. Grogan & Spangler), "Beautiful Music" (Beautiful Music & Company), "Cocoanut Cream Pie" (Mr. Grogan & Homer), "When I Am Lost" (Homer, Beautiful Music, Company); *Scene 5* Message: "I Said 'Oh, No'" (Bess, Mary, Mexican Woman); *Scene 6* At home: "Daddy Will Not Come Walking Through the Door" (Mrs. Macauley), "The Birds in the Sky" (Bess), "Remember Always to Give" (Mrs. Macauley), "Long Past Sunset" (Voice of Matthew Macauley); *Scene 7* Message: "Don't Tell Me" (Mary, Marcus, Family, Company); *Scene 8* At the telegraph office: "The Fourth Telegram" (Spangler & Mr. Grogan), "Give Me All the Money" (Thief & Spangler); *Scene 9* At home: "Everything is Changed" (Homer & Mrs. Macauley), "The World is Full of Loneliness" (Mrs. Macauley), "Hi Ya,

Kid" (reprise) (Trainman, Ulysses, Company). *Act II*: *Scene 1* At the debarkation center: "How I Love Your Thingamajig" (Soldiers), "Everlasting" (Tobey), "An Orphan I Am" (Tobey), "I'll Tell You About My Family" (Marcus); *Scene 2* At home: "I Wish I Were a Man" (Mary); *Scene 3* War front: "Marcus, My Friend" (Tobey), "My Sister Bess" (Marcus); *Scene 4* Home front: "I've Known a Lot of Guys" (Diana), "Diana" (Spangler); *Scene 5* At war and at home: "Dear Brother" (Homer & Marcus), "The Birds in the Trees"/"A Lot of Men" (Diana & Spangler), "Parting" (Mrs. Macauley, Wives, Sweethearts, Mothers); *Scene 6* At the telegraph office: "Mr. Grogan, Wake Up" (Homer), "Hello, Doc" (Spangler); *Scene 7* In the park: "What Am I Supposed to Do?" (Homer & Spangler); *Scene 8* Home: "Long Past Sunset" (reprise) (Mrs. Macauley & Company), "I'm Home" (Tobey), "Somewhere, Someone" (Bess), "I'll Always Love You" (Mary & Company) [end of Scene 8]; "Hi Ya, Kid" (reprise) (Trainman, Ulysses, Company), "Fathers and Mothers (and You and Me)" (Company).

Reviews were divided. Stephen Geoffreys was nominated for a Tony Award.

After Broadway. ST. PETER'S CHURCH, NYC, 9/26/97–9/28/97. A staged reading, part of the *Musicals in Mufti* series, PRESENTED BY the York Theatre Company.

THERESA LONG THEATRE, NYC, 3/5/03–3/9/03. PRESENTED BY the Marymount Theatre Company; DIRECTOR: Patricia Hoag Simon; CHOREOGRAPHER: Ed Kresley; SETS: Edward Gianfrancesco; MUSICAL DIRECTOR: David John Madore. *Cast*: 35 members of Marymount Manhattan College. The last night of this sold-out fully-staged production was a $100-per-ticket benefit performance for the college, and Galt MacDermot sat in with the orchestra that night.

326. *Hurry, Harry*

Poor little rich boy wants to be happy, trying Greece, Africa, Broadway, sex and fortune-telling.

Before Broadway. Samuel D. Ratcliffe replaced Bill Hinnant in the lead.

The Broadway Run. RITZ THEATRE, 10/12/72–10/13/72. 9 previews from 10/5/72. 2 PERFORMANCES. PRESENTED BY Peter Grad (and David Seltzer, whose name was removed during previews); MUSIC: Bill Weeden; LYRICS: David Finkle; BOOK: Jeremiah Morris, Lee Kalcheim, Susan Perkis; DIRECTOR: Jeremiah Morris; CHOREOGRAPHER: Gerald Teijelo; SETS: Fred Voelpel; COSTUMES: Sara Brook; LIGHTING: Martin Aronstein; MUSICAL SUPERVISOR/ORCHESTRATIONS: Lee Norris; MUSICAL DIRECTOR: Arthur Azenzer; PRESS: Lee Solters, Harvey B. Sabinson, Marilynn LeVine; GENERAL MANAGER: Marvin A. Krauss; COMPANY MANAGER: David Wyler; PRODUCTION STAGE MANAGER: Victor Straus; STAGE MANAGER: Harvey Landa; ASSISTANT STAGE MANAGER: Don Fenwick. *Cast: Act I*: HARRISON "HARRY" FAIRCHILD IV: Samuel D. Ratcliffe (1); HARRISON FAIRCHILD III: Phil Leeds (3); PATIENCE FAIRCHILD: Liz Sheridan (4); MUFFY WEATHERSFORD: Mary Bracken Phillips (2); NICK: Louis Criscuolo (5); MARCO: Jack Landron; STAVOS: Robert Darnell; HELENA: Randee Heller; MAMA: Liz Sheridan; TOWN DRUNK: Phil Leeds; MELINA: Donna Liggitt Forbes; GENESIS: Jack Landron; EXODUS: Robert Darnell; DEUTERONOMY: Louis Criscuolo; DR. KRAUSS: Phil Leeds; WRITERS: Louis Criscuolo, Robert Darnell, Randee Heller, Jack Landron, Liz Sheridan; STARLET: Donna Liggitt Forbes; NATIVES: Robert Darnell, Donna Liggitt Forbes, Liz Sheridan, Randee Heller, Jack Landron; WITCH DOCTOR: Louis Criscuolo; CHIEF: Phil Leeds; *Act II*: DR. KRAUSS: Phil Leeds; STAR: Liz Sheridan; CHORUS BOYS: Louis Criscuolo, Robert Darnell, Jack Landron, Phil Leeds; MUFFY: Mary Bracken Phillips; HARRY: Samuel D. Ratcliffe; GRAND LAMA: Robert Darnell; NOT-SO-GRAND LAMAS: Phil Leeds, Louis Criscuolo, Jack Landron, Donna Liggitt Forbes, Randee Heller, Liz Sheridan; WINSTON: Robert Darnell; GYPSY: Randee Heller; UNCLE LARRY: Phil Leeds; CONGREGATION: Louis Criscuolo, Robert Darnell, Donna Liggitt Forbes, Randee Heller, Jack Landron, Phil Leeds, Liz Sheridan. *Act I*: Overture; *Scene 1* The wedding day: "I'm Gonna" (Harry); *Scene 2* Taverna in Greece: "When a Man Cries" (Nick, Mama, Helena, Marco, Stavos, Town Drunk, Melina); *Scene 3* Airport: "A Trip Through My Mind" (Muffy

& Dead Sea Scrolls); *Scene 4* Psychiatrist's office; *Scene 5* Hollywood: "Life" (Harry & Writers); *Scene 6* Street in Hollywood: "Love Can" (Muffy); *Scene 7* Psychiatrist's office; *Scene 8* Africa: "Africa Speaks" (Natives & Witch Doctor); *Scene 9* Alone in the world: "Somewhere in the Past" (Harry). *Act II*: Entr'acte; *Scene 1* Psychiatrist's office; *Scene 2* Shubert Theatre: "Hurry, Harry" (Star & Chorus Boys); *Scene 3* Psychiatrist's office: "Goodby" (Muffy); *Scene 4* Lamasery; *Scene 5* Psychiatrist's office: "You Won't Be Happy" (Harry & Dr. Krauss); *Scene 6* A street; *Scene 7* Gypsy's store; *Scene 8* Church: "He is My Bag" (Harry & Congregation); *Scene 9* Alone in the world: "Somewhere in the Past" (reprise) (Harry & Muffy); *Scene 10* Beach: Finale.

Broadway reviewers roundly panned it.

327. *I Can Get It for You Wholesale*

A musical play set in the Bronx, and about the garment district in New York.

Before Broadway. Jerome Weidman's novel had been filmed straight, in 1951, with Susan Hayward and Dan Dailey. This stage musical was 19-year-old Barbra Streisand's Broadway debut. She auditioned for the role on 11/24/61. She was almost fired for being late and abrasive. The number "Grab Them While You Can" was cut before Broadway.

The Broadway Run. SHUBERT THEATRE, 3/22/62–9/29/62; BROADWAY THEATRE, 10/1/62–12/8/62. 2 previews on 3/21/62. Total of 300 PERFORMANCES. PRESENTED BY David Merrick; MUSIC/LYRICS: Harold Rome; BOOK: Jerome Weidman (based on his 1937 novel of same name); DIRECTOR: Arthur Laurents; CHOREOGRAPHER: Herbert Ross; SETS/LIGHTING: Will Steven Armstrong; COSTUMES: Theoni V. Aldredge; MUSICAL DIRECTOR/VOCAL ARRANGEMENTS: Lehman Engel; ORCHESTRATIONS: Sid Ramin; DANCE & INCIDENTAL MUSIC ARRANGEMENTS: Peter Howard; PRESS: Harvey B. Sabinson, Lee Solters, David Powers; CASTING: Alan Shayne & Michael Shurtleff; GENERAL MANAGER: Jack Schlissel; COMPANY MANAGER: Gino Giglio, *Vince McKnight*; PRODUCTION STAGE MANAGER: Richard Blofson; STAGE MANAGER: May Muth; ASSISTANT STAGE MANAGER: Robert Schear. *Cast*: MISS MARMELSTEIN: Barbra Streisand (8); MAURICE PULVERMACHER: Jack Kruschen (4), *Martin Wolfson*; MEYER BUSHKIN: Ken Le Roy (6); HARRY BOGEN: Elliott Gould (2); TOOTSIE MALTZ: James Hickman; RUTHIE RIVKIN: Marilyn Cooper (7); MRS. BOGEN: Lillian Roth (1) *; MARTHA MILLS: Sheree North (3); MARIO: William Reilly; MITZI: Barbara Monte; EDDIE: Edward Verso, *Larry Gradus, Eliot Feld*; BLANCHE BUSHKIN: Bambi Linn (9), *Dusty Worrall*; TEDDY ASCH: Harold Lang (5); BUGGO: Kelly Brown; MISS SPRINGER: Pat Turner; VELMA: Francine Bond; LENNY: William Sumner; NORMAN: Stanley Simmonds; MANETTE: Luba Lisa, *Diane Ball, Luba Lisa*; GAIL: Wilma Curley; ROSALINE: Marion Fels, *Louise Lasser, Elly Stone*; NOODLE: Jack Murray, *Ben Gillespie*; SAM: Don Grilley, *Jack Fletcher*; MOXIE: Ed Collins [role cut soon after opening]; SHELDON BUSKIN: Steve Curry; EDITH: Margaret Gathright, *Marion Fels*. STANDBY: Mrs. Bogen: Phoebe Brand. **Understudies**: Sheldon: Larry Gradus & Eliot Feld; Miss Marmelstein: Elly Stone, *Louise Lasser, Susan Lehman*; Maurice/Meyer: Stanley Simmonds; Martha: Wilma Curley; Blanche: Wilma Curley, *Susan Lehman*; Teddy: William Reilly; Harry: Kelly Brown; Ruthie: Francine Bond; Tootsie: *Ed Collins*. *Act I*: *Prologue*: Seventh Avenue, New York City; 1937; *Scene 1* Office of Maurice Pulvermacher, Inc.: "(I'm Not a) Well Man" (Miss Marmelstein & Mr. Pulvermacher); *Scene 2* Seventh Avenue: "The Way Things Are" (Harry); *Scene 3* A Bronx stoop: "When Gemini Meets Capricorn" (Ruthie & Harry); *Scene 4* Mrs. Bogen's kitchen in the Bronx: "Momma, Momma!" (Harry & Mrs. Bogen); *Scene 5* The Club Rio Rhumba: "The Sound of Money" (Harry, Martha, Mitzi, Mario, Eddie); *Scene 6* Mrs. Bogen's kitchen: "Family Way" (Mrs. Bogen, Harry, Ruthie, Teddy, Blanche, Meyer), "Too Soon" (Mrs. Bogen); *Scene 7* A Bronx stoop: "Who Knows?" (Ruthie); *Scene 8* Apex Modes, Inc. [named changed to Acme Modes, Inc. soon after the opening]: "Have I Told You Lately?" (Blanche & Meyer); *Scene 9* Apex Modes showroom [name changed to Acme Modes soon after the opening]: "Ballad of the Garment Trade" (Miss Marmelstein, Ruthie, Blanche, Harry, Teddy, Meyer, Company). *Act II*: *Scene 1* Harry Bogen's penthouse: "A Gift Today" (Sheldon, Harry, Mrs.

Bogen, Blanche, Meyer, Ruthie), Dance (Blanche, Meyer, Sheldon); *Scene 2* Apex Modes, Inc. [named changed to Acme Modes, Inc. soon after the opening]: "Miss Marmelstein" (Miss Marmelstein), "The Sound of Money" (reprise) (Harry); *Scene 3* Apex Modes, Inc. [name changed to Acme Modes, Inc. soon after the opening]: "A Funny Thing Happened (on My Way to Love)" (Ruthie & Harry); *Scene 4* The Club Rio Rhumba: "What's in it for Me?" (Teddy & Martha); *Scene 5* Apex Modes showroom [name changed to Acme Modes soon after the opening]: "What Are They Doing to Us Now?" (Miss Marmelstein, Buggo, Tootsie, Manette, Gail, Springer, Creditors); *Scene 6* Mrs. Bogen's kitchen: "Eat a Little Something" (Mrs. Bogen & Harry); *Scene 7* Office of Maurice Pulvermacher, Inc.: Epilogue (Company); *Scene 8* Seventh Avenue.

Broadway reviews were divided, but la Streisand was noticed in a big way, and received a Tony nomination. Shortly after the show closed she and Elliott Gould married.

After Broadway. TOUR. Opened on 11/12/62. *Cast:* HARRY: Larry Kert; MRS. BOGEN: Fritzi Burr.

AMERICAN JEWISH THEATRE, 2/23/91–4/21/91. 59 PERFORMANCES. This was a revised revival. DIRECTOR/CHOREOGRAPHER: Richard Sabellico; MUSICAL DIRECTOR: Jonny Bowden. *Cast:* MISS MARMELSTEIN: Vicki Lewis; MAURICE/EDDIE: Joel Rooks; MEYER/RAMON: Richard Levine; HARRY: Evan Pappas; TOOTSIE/TEDDY: Jim Bracchitta; RUTHIE: Carolee Carmello; MRS. BOGEN: Patti Karr; MARTHA: Deborah Carlson; BLANCHE: Alix Korey; SHELDON: Sam Brent Riegel. The opening number, "Well Man," was cut.

328. *I Do! I Do!*

Broadway's first two-character book musical. The story covers 50 years of marriage from just before turn of the 20th century. Aside from one or two sequences, the bedroom is the main set.

Before Broadway. *The Fourposter,* upon which *I Do! I Do!* was based, opened as a straight play on Broadway, on 10/24/51. 632 PERFORMANCES. DIRECTOR: Jose Ferrer. *Cast:* Jessica Tandy and Hume Cronyn. In 1963 *The Fourposter* was musicalized as *No Bed of Roses,* and tried out in summer stock. MUSIC/LYRICS: Martin Kalmanoff. *Cast:* Biff McGuire and Jeannie Carson. But it didn't get to Broadway.

I Do! I Do! (not in any way connected to the *No Bed of* Roses production) opened in Boston, where reviews were not good. David Merrick had re-writes from Jule Styne and Comden & Green all ready to thrust onto Tom Jones and Harvey Schmidt who refused to change their material. However four songs were cut before Broadway: "Echoes of the Past," "Spring Cleaning," "Thousands of Flowers," and "What Can I Tell Her?".

The Broadway Run. FORTY-SIXTH STREET THEATRE, 12/5/66–6/15/68. 4 previews from 12/1/66. 561 PERFORMANCES. A David Merrick and Champion-Six, Inc. production, PRESENTED BY David Merrick; MUSIC: Harvey Schmidt; LYRICS/BOOK: Tom Jones; BASED ON the 1951 comedy *The Fourposter,* by Jan de Hartog; DIRECTOR/CHOREOGRAPHER: Gower Champion; ASSISTANT TO THE DIRECTOR: Lucia Victor; SETS: Oliver Smith; COSTUMES: Freddy Wittop; LIGHTING: Jean Rosenthal; MUSICAL DIRECTOR: John Lesko; ORCHESTRATIONS: Philip J. Lang; CAST RECORDING on RCA Victor; PRESS: Harvey B. Sabinson, Lee Solters, Ben Washer (*Jay Russell*); CASTING: Linda Otto & Geoffrey Johnson; GENERAL MANAGER: Jack Schlissel; COMPANY MANAGER: Richard Highley.

STAGE MANAGER: Wade Miller; ASSISTANT STAGE MANAGERS: Robert Avian & Patricia Drylie, *Henry Sutton & Robert Vandergriff.* *Cast:* SHE (AGNES): Mary Martin (1) ☆, Carol Lawrence (matinees only from 10/18/67, then all performances from 12/4/67); HE (MICHAEL): Robert Preston (2) ☆, Gordon MacRae (matinees only from 10/18/67, then all performances from 12/4/67). *Standbys:* For Gordon MacRae: Stephen Douglass; For Carol Lawrence: Dran Hamilton. AT THE TWO PIANOS: Woody Kessler & Albert Mello. *Act I:* their early married life and children. As the years pass Michael becomes a famous author and thinks he has found a new romance. Agnes wins him back: Prologue (Both): "All the Dearly Beloved," "Together Forever" [end of Prologue],

"I Do! I Do!" (Both), "Good Night" (Both), "I Love My Wife" (He), "Something Has Happened" (She), "My Cup Runneth Over" (Both), "Love isn't Everything" (Both), "Nobody's Perfect" (Both), "A Well-Known Fact" (He), "Flaming Agnes" (She), "The Honeymoon is Over" (Both). *Act II:* the children are married, and Agnes finds a new romance with a young poet. Michael wins her back: "Where Are the Snows?" (Both), "When the Kids Get Married" (Both), Another Wedding: "The Father of the Bride" (He), "What is a Woman?" (She) [end of Another Wedding sequence], "Someone Needs Me" (She), "Roll up the Ribbons" (Both), "This House" (Both) (now they are an elderly couple preparing to move into a smaller house).

It had a huge advance sale at the box-office. The show opened on Broadway to excellent reviews. Robert Preston won a Tony, and the show was also nominated for musical, composer & lyricist, direction of a musical, sets, costumes, and for Mary Martin. At the beginning there were no understudies or standbys, so it was too strenuous to do matinees as well. After a few performances had to be canceled when Mary Martin got a cold, it was deemed wise to bring on board Carol Lawrence and Gordon MacRae as matinee players, and to get them ready to take over from the stars when those two went on tour in 1967. Mr. MacRae and Miss Lawrence played both evenings and matinees, but had standbys, who more and more began to appear instead of the stars.

After Broadway. TOUR. Opened on 4/8/68, at the Auditorium, Rochester, NY. MUSICAL DIRECTOR: Mitchell Ayres. *Cast:* Mary Martin and Robert Preston.

TOUR. Opened on 9/11/69, at the Playhouse, Wilmington, Delaware, and closed on 4/11/70, at the Santa Monica Civic Auditorium. DIRECTOR: Lucia Victor; MUSICAL DIRECTOR: Norman Geller. *Cast:* Mimi Hines and Phil Ford.

LONDON, 1968. *Cast:* Anne Rogers and Ian Carmichael.

PAPER MILL PLAYHOUSE, New Jersey, 1968. DIRECTOR: Wade Miller. *Cast:* Dran Hamilton and Stephen Douglass.

TOURING REVIVAL. Opened on 9/21/72; Closed on 11/15/72; Re-opened on 2/25/73; finally closed on 3/27/73. It played a grand total of 90 cities. *Cast:* Lesley Stewart and Don Gilley.

HUNTINGTON HARTFORD THEATRE, Los Angeles. Opened on 6/20/73. 32 PERFORMANCES. *Cast:* Carol Burnett and Rock Hudson.

TOURING REVIVAL. Opened on 7/26/83, at the Dallas Music Hall, and closed on 9/25/83, at the Morris Mechanic Theatre, Baltimore. DIRECTOR/CHOREOGRAPHER: Lucia Victor; SETS: Oliver Smith; COSTUMES: Michael Bottari; MUSICAL DIRECTOR: Gordon O. Browne. *Cast:* Lucie Arnaz and Laurence Luckinbill. **Understudies:** Beth Leavel and Dale Radunz.

JUPITER THEATRE, Florida, 1994. DIRECTOR/CHOREOGRAPHER: Norb Joerder. *Cast:* Lee Meriwether and Tom Urich.

LAMB'S THEATRE, NYC, 3/28/96–5/12/96. 11 previews from 3/19/96. 52 PERFORMANCES. PRESENTED BY Arthur Cantor; DIRECTOR: Will Mackenzie; CHOREOGRAPHER: Janet Watson; SETS: Ed Wittstein; COSTUMES: Suzy Benzinger; LIGHTING: Mary Jo Dondlinger; MUSICAL DIRECTOR: Tim Stella. *Cast:* Karen Ziemba and David Garrison. The show was much praised.

QUEENS THEATRE IN THE PARK (Q-Tip), 3/6/97–3/16/97. DIRECTOR: Christopher Catt. *Cast:* Donna McKechnie and John Hillner.

329. *I Had a Ball*

Matchmaking Coney Island fortune-teller Garside tries to match up two couples. The men choose the wrong girls, and the marriages come to grief.

Before Broadway. This was Buddy Hackett's only Broadway musical. It was Joe Kipness's idea. Lloyd Richards (who would have been the first black American to direct a "white" musical on Broadway) was replaced as director by John Allen (unbilled) after a disagreement with Mr. Kipness in Detroit, where the show tried out and won praise.

The Broadway Run. MARTIN BECK THEATRE, 12/15/64–6/12/65. Previews from 12/8/64. 199 PERFORMANCES. PRESENTED BY Joseph Kipness; MUSIC/LYRICS: Jack Lawrence & Stan Freeman; BOOK: Jerome Chodorov; DIRECTOR: Lloyd Richards; CHOREOGRAPHER: Onna White;

ASSISTANT CHOREOGRAPHER: Tom Panko; SETS/LIGHTING: Will Steven Armstrong; COSTUMES: Ann Roth; TECHNICAL CONSULTANT: Jules Fisher; MUSICAL DIRECTOR/VOCAL ARRANGEMENTS: Pembroke Davenport; ORCHESTRATIONS: Philip J. Lang; DANCE MUSIC ARRANGEMENTS: Luther Henderson; PRESS: Frank Goodman, Ben Kornzweig, Martin Shwartz, Robert Ganshaw, Paul Solomon; GENERAL MANAGER: Philip Adler; COMPANY MANAGER: S.M. Handelsman; PRODUCTION STAGE MANAGER: Mortimer Halpern; STAGE MANAGER: Nathan Caldwell Jr.; ASSISTANT STAGE MANAGERS: Bob Bernard & Marty Allen. **Cast:** GARSIDE: Buddy Hackett (1); STAN THE SHPIELER: Richard Kiley (2); JEANNIE: Karen Morrow (3); THE ALLEY GANG (FOUR MEMBERS): GIMLET: Al Nesor; JOE THE MUZZLER: Jack Wakefield, *Danny Dayton*; MA MALONEY: Rosetta Le Noire; GEORGE OSAKA: Conrad Yama; MOROCCO: Herself; LIFEGUARD: Marty Allen; JIMMY: Nathaniel Jones; OFFICER MILLHAUSER: Ted Thurston; BROOKS: Steve Roland; ADDIE: Luba Lisa; CHILDREN: Sheldon Golomb & Gina Kaye; SINGERS: Miriam Burton, Jacqueline Carol, Jacque Dean, Eugene Edwards, Marilyn Feder, Herbert Fields, Murray Goldkind, Marvin Goodis, Shirley Leinwand, Lispet Nelson, Herb Surface, John Wheeler, *Janet Moody Morris*; DANCERS: Marty Allen, Doria Avila, Bob Bernard, Mary Ehara, Ray Gilbert, Edward J. Heim, Gary Hubler, Scott Hunter, Sandra Lein, Nancy Lynch, Patti Mariano, Alice Shanahan, John Sharpe, June Eve Story, Patti Ann Watson, *Paul Berne, Trudy Carson, Curtis Hood*. **Standby:** Stan/Brooks: Charles Braswell. **Understudies:** Jeannie: Lispet Nelson; Addie/Morocco: June Eve Story; Millhauser/George: John Wheeler; Gimlet: Herb Surface; Ma: Miriam Burton & June Eve Story; Joe: Bob Bernard & Herb Surface. **Act I:** in and around Coney Island on the Fourth of July: "Coney Island, USA" (Joe, Ma, Osaka, Gimlet, Coney Characters, Tourists, Children), "The Other Half of Me" (Stan), "Red-Blooded American Boy" (Brooks & Alley Gang), "(I Got) Everything I Want" (Jeannie), "(Doctor) Freud" (Garside), "Think Beautiful" (Ma, Jeannie, Joe, Osaka, Gimlet, Ensemble), "Addie's at it Again" (Addie, Joe, Osaka, Gimlet), "Faith" (Stan, Alley Gang, Children, Ensemble), "Can it Be Possible?" (Stan, Jeannie, Brooks, Addie, Garside). **Act II:** 60 days later: "The Neighborhood Song" (Alley Gang & Coney Characters), "The Affluent Society" (Stan & Brooks), "Boys, Boys, Boys" (Addie & Lifeguards), "Fickle Finger of Fate" (Stan), "I Had a Ball" (Jeannie, Alley Gang, Morocco, Coney Characters), "Almost" (Jeannie) [dropped during run], "You Deserve Me" (Garside, Brooks, Addie), "You Deserve Me" (reprise) (Garside), "Tunnel of Love Chase" (Garside, Stan, Jeannie, Millhauser, Ensemble).

Broadway reviews were divided. After two months Buddy Hackett began to ad-lib. Luba Lisa was nominated for a Tony.

330. *I Love My Wife*

Set in the present, in Trenton, New Jersey. Two couples, at the suggestion of the husbands, experiment with wife-swapping on Christmas Eve, but everyone is embarrassed and the experiment falls through as the husbands agree "I love my wife." The band (four musicians) was integrated into the cast on stage.

Before Broadway. Gene Saks was the original choice of director, but turned it down. Just before rehearsals were about to begin, Joe Kipness, the producer, lost two-thirds of his capitalization money, and closed the show. Two new producers, Harry Rigby and Terry Allen Kramer, took it over. Ten days into rehearsals, Joe Layton was seriously injured (off the set), and, after a few days was replaced as director by Gene Saks and as choreographer by Onna White. The show tried out in Philadelphia, to terrible reviews and no business. After considering closing again, the producers decided to go for Broadway previews, during which things looked so bad that Harry Rigby sold his share of the production to Terry Allen Kramer's husband just before the show opened.

The Broadway Run. ETHEL BARRYMORE THEATRE, 4/17/77–5/20/79. 7 previews. 857 PERFORMANCES. PRESENTED BY Terry Allen Kramer & Harry Rigby, by arrangement with Joseph Kipness; MUSIC: Cy Coleman; LYRICS/BOOK: Michael Stewart; BASED ON the 1975 French farce *Viens chez moi, j'habite chez une copine*, by Luis Rego & Didier Kaminka; DIRECTOR: Gene Saks; CHOREOGRAPHER: Onna White; SETS:

David Mitchell; COSTUMES: Ron Talsky; LIGHTING: Gilbert V. Hemsley Jr.; SOUND DESIGNER: Lou Gonzalez; SOUND ENGINEER: Peter Fitzgerald; MUSICAL DIRECTOR: John Miller; ARRANGEMENTS: Cy Coleman; CAST RECORDING on Atlantic; PRESS: Henry Luhrman; CASTING: Feuer & Ritzer; GENERAL MANAGERS: Jack Schlissel & Jay Kingwill; ASSISTANT GENERAL MANAGER: Mark Bramble; STAGE MANAGER: Tony Manzi. **Cast:** CLEO: Ilene Graff, *Barbara Sharma* (from 9/4/78), *Maureen Moore* (from 3/6/79, *Hattie Winston* (from 5/1/79); MONICA: Joanna Gleason, *Virginia Sandifur* (from 5/1/78), *Janie Sell* (from 9/4/78), *Marjorie Barnes* (from 5/1/79); WALLY: James Naughton, *James Seymour, Brad Blaisdell, Tom Wopat* (from 7/78), *Dick Smothers* (from 9/4/78), *Larry Riley* (from 5/1/79); STANLEY: Michael Mark; QUENTIN: Joe Saulter; HARVEY: John Miller; NORMAN: Ken Bichel, *Mark Franklin*; ALVIN: Lenny Baker, *James Brennan* (from 2/27/78), *Brad Blaisdell, Lawrence John Moss, Tom Smothers* (from 9/4/78), *Lawrence Hilton-Jacobs* (from 5/1/79). **Understudies**: Quentin: Warren Benbow; Harvey: Michael Mark; Stanley: Michael Sergio; Norman: Joel Mofsenson; Cleo/Monica: Jana Robbins, *Lisby Larson, Mary Murray*; Alvin/Wally: James Brennan, *James Seymour, Walter Bobbie*. **General Standby**: Christine Ebersole. **Act I**: **Scene 1** Harvey's Diner: "We're Still Friends" (Company), "Monica" (Alvin, Monica, Four Guys), "By Threes" (Wally, Alvin, Harvey); **Scene 2** A mover's life: "A Mover's Life" (Alvin & Four Guys); **Scene 3** Alvin and Cleo's apartment: "Love Revolution" (Cleo), "Someone Wonderful I Missed" (Monica & Cleo), "Sexually Free" (Alvin, Cleo, Wally). **Act II**: **Scene 1** Christmas Eve: "Hey There, Good Times" (Harvey, Stanley, Quentin, Norman); **Scene 2** Wally and Monica's apartment: "Lovers on Christmas Eve" (Monica, Wally, Norman), "Scream" (Harvey, Stanley, Quentin, Norman), "Ev'rybody Today is Turning On" (Alvin & Wally), "Married Couple Seeks Married Couple" (Alvin, Cleo, Wally, Monica), "I Love My Wife" (Alvin & Wally).

Opening night was brought forward, so the show would not go head to head with *Annie* and *Side by Side by Sondheim* (both due to open in the next couple of days). Consequently, partly because the critics had no other musicals to go to, it got excellent reviews. Lenny Baker was highly praised and was touted for a great future (however, he died in 1982 of cancer, age 37). The show won Tony Awards for direction of a musical and for Lenny Baker. It was nominated for musical, score, book, and choreography. From 5/1/79 it became an all-black cast.

After Broadway. PRINCE OF WALES THEATRE, London, 10/6/77. 401 PERFORMANCES. **Cast:** WALLY: Ben Cross; ALVIN: Richard Beckinsale; CLEO: Deborah Fallender; MONICA: Liz Robertson.

FOURTH INTERVAL, 5/28/02–6/8/02. DIRECTOR: John Znidarsic; LIGHTING: Scott Clyve; MUSICAL DIRECTOR: Scott Stein. **Cast**: ALVIN: J. Brandon Savage; MONICA: Elizabeth Shaw; CLEO: Julie Beckham; WALLY: Matt Kuehl.

331. *I Remember Mama*

Kathryn Forbes's fictionalized reminiscences of her Norwegian immigrant family and her girlhood in San Francisco. Mama pretends she has a bank account, in order to save her five children from money worries. The eldest daughter, Katrine, is an aspiring writer.

Before Broadway. The original (straight) play, *I Remember Mama*, produced by Rodgers & Hammerstein, ran on Broadway 10/19/44 (714 PERFORMANCES), and is most remembered now for being Marlon Brando's pro stage debut. It was filmed in 1948, with Irene Dunne. Rodgers & Hammerstein contemplated doing a musical version with Charlotte Greenwood and Shirley Jones, but the TV series *I Remember Mama* (1949–1956) was just ending, and they thought it might be overexposed as a story.

A musical adaptation, called *Mama,* and not connected to the Broadway show, ran at the STUDIO ARENA, Buffalo, NY, 1972. MUSIC/LYRICS: John Clifton; BOOK: Neal Du Brock; DIRECTOR: Warren Enters; CHOREOGRAPHER: Tom Panko; SETS: Robert Randolph; COSTUMES: Patton Campbell; MUSICAL DIRECTOR: John L. De Main. **Cast**: MAMA: Celeste Holm; KATRINE: Jill O'Hara; PAPA: Wesley Addy; CHRIS: Michael Kermoyan; FLORENCE DANA MOORHEAD: Marijane Maricle.

This 1979 production was the first musical version of *I Remember Mama* to reach Broadway, and was the first revival of the original 1944 straight play in New York City in any form. It took 323 investors to come up with the $1.25 million necessary to put this musical into production. Half was supplied by Universal Pictures. Martin Charnin was fired the day after bad reviews appeared in the Philadelphia paper during tryouts, and within a week had been replaced by Cy Feuer. The number "When" was cut during tryouts (but restored for the recording). Several other songs were cut: "Maybe Maybe Maybe," "Midsummer Night," "A Most Disagreeable Man," "An Old City Boy at Heart," "A Fam'ly We Will Be," "Such Good Fun." Most of Martin Charnin's lyrics remained, but Raymond Jessel was brought in to write the lyrics for six new songs, two of which—"Where We Came From" and "I Don't Know How" were cut. Also during the Philly tryouts two roles were merged into one. There were two Katrines—one, older, who looked back and narrated, and the young one, who appeared in the actual scenes. Kate Dezina, who played the older one, was fired, and Kristin Vigard, who played the younger one, got a new role created for her (Miss Vigard would ultimately be fired too). Maureen Silliman took over the new combined Katrine role. During Broadway previews Danny Daniels took over from Graciela Daniele as choreographer, several characters were cut, several actors were replaced, and there were several changes to the musical numbers. The actual Broadway opening was postponed twice.

The Broadway Run. MAJESTIC THEATRE, 5/31/79–9/2/79. 40 previews. 108 PERFORMANCES. PRESENTED BY Alexander H. Cohen & Hildy Parks; MUSIC: Richard Rodgers; LYRICS: Martin Charnin; ADDITIONAL LYRICS: Raymond Jessel; BOOK: Thomas Meehan; BASED ON the 1944 Rodgers & Hammerstein-produced comedy of the same name, by John Van Druten, which in turn was adapted from the magazine stories *Mama's Bank Account*, by Kathryn Forbes; DIRECTOR: Cy Feuer; CHOREOGRAPHER: Danny Daniels; SETS: David Mitchell; COSTUMES: Theoni V. Aldredge; LIGHTING: Roger Morgan; SOUND DESIGN: Otts Munderloh; SOUNDMAN: Tony Meola; MUSICAL DIRECTOR/VOCAL ARRANGEMENTS: Jay Blackton; ORCHESTRATIONS: Philip J. Lang; DANCE MUSIC ARRANGEMENTS: Jay Blackton, Allen Cohen, Uel Wade; PRESS: David A. Powers, Barbara Carroll, Martha Mason; CASTING: Meg Simon; GENERAL MANAGER: Roy A. Somlyo; COMPANY MANAGER: Charles Willard & David Hedges; STAGE MANAGER: Robert Bennett; ASSISTANT STAGE MANAGER: Christopher Cohen. *Cast:* KATRINE: Maureen Silliman (7); CHRISTINE: Carrie Horner (14); DAGMAR: Tara Kennedy (13); JOHANNE: Kristen Vigard (11), *Elissa Wolfe*; NILS: Ian Ziering (12) [John Nevitt during previews]; PAPA: George Hearn (3); MAMA: Liv Ullmann (1) ☆; MR. McGUIRE: Dick Ensslen (10); AUNT TRINA: Elizabeth Hubbard (4); MR. HYDE: Francis Bethencourt [role cut during previews]; AUNT JENNY: Dolores Wilson (5), *Grace Keagy*; AUNT SIGRID: Betty Ann Grove (6); MR. PETERSEN: John Dorrin [role cut during previews]; MR. THORKELSON: Armin Shimerman (8); KARIN LARSEN: Marisa Morell [role cut during previews]; MRS. McGUIRE: Donna Monroe [role cut during previews]; ERIC: Steve Boockvor [role cut during previews]; OLAF: Paul Solen [role cut during previews]; UNCLE CHRIS: George S. Irving (2); LUCIE: Janet McCall; NURSE: Sigrid Heath; DOCTOR ANDERSON: Stan Page; DAME SYBIL FITZGIBBONS: Myvanwy Jenn (9); HOTEL MANAGER: Austin Colyer [role cut during previews]; BELLBOYS: Elissa Wolfe & Ian Ziering [roles cut during previews]; STEINER STREET NEIGHBORS: Angela App [dropped during previews], Austin Colyer, John Dorrin, Mickey Gunnersen, Daniel Harnett, Danny Joel, Jan Kasni, Kevin Marcum, Richard Maxon, Marisa Morell, Frank Pietri, Elissa Wolfe. *Understudies*: Mama: Elizabeth Hubbard; Chris: Dick Ensslen; Papa: Stan Page; Aunt Trina: Janet McCall; Aunt Jenny: Myvanwy Jenn; Sigrid: Sigrid Heath [Janet McCall during previews]; Sybil: Janet McCall [Donna Monroe during previews]; Katrine: Kristen Vigard; Mr. Hyde: John Dorrin [role cut during previews]; Johanne/Christine: Elissa Wolfe; Nils: Daniel Harnett [Ian Ziering during previews]; Dagmar: Marisa Morell; McGuire: Austin Colyer; Thorkelson: Arthur Whitfield [Steve Boockvor during previews]. *Alternates*: Cathy Rice & Arthur Whitfield. *Act I: Scene 1* The kitchen and dining room of the Hansen house on Steiner Street, in San Francisco; spring 1910: "I Remember Mama" (Katrine), "A Little Bit More" (l: Ray Jessel) (Mama, Papa, Children), "A Writer Writes at Night" (Katrine & Mama); *Scene 2* The Hansen parlor; 21st of June 1910, evening: "Ev'ry Day (Comes Something Beautiful)" (Mama &

Company), "The Hardangerfjord" (Company), "You Could Not Please Me More" (ch: Graciela Daniele) (Papa & Mama); *Scene 3* The Hansen kitchen; mid–November 1910, early afternoon: "Uncle Chris" (l: Ray Jessel) (Aunts); *Scene 4* The hospital; later that day: *Scene 5* The Hansen kitchen; ten days later, early afternoon: "Easy Come, Easy Go" (l: Ray Jessel) (Chris & Friends); *Scene 6* The Hansen kitchen, early December 1910, a Friday evening: "It is Not the End of the World" (Family). *Act II: Scene 1* The Hansen back porch; spring 1911, evening: "Mama Always Makes it Better" (Children), "Lars, Lars" (l: Ray Jessel) (Mama); *Scene 2* The Hansen kitchen; later that night and the following morning; *Scene 3* The lobby of the Fairmount Hotel; a few hours later: "Fair Trade" (Dame Sybil, Mama, Friends); *Scene 4* Uncle Chris's ranch; mid–May 1911, later afternoon: "It's Going to Be Good to Be Gone" (Chris); *Scene 5* The Hansen kitchen; three days later, evening: "Time" (Mama); *Scene 6* The Hansen parlor; June 1911: "I Remember Mama" (reprise) (Katrine).

Reviews were awful. Martin Charnin suffered a (non-fatal) heart attack in 6/79, during the run, brought on by stress. The show lost $1.5 million. Richard Rodgers, who won a special Tony, died on 12/13/79, four months after his last show (a flop) closed. The show was not recorded until five years later, with only George Hearn and George S. Irving of the original cast participating in it.

332. *If the Shoe Fits*

A spoof set during the Middle Ages in one of those mythical kingdoms known only to writers of musical comedies, in this case the Kingdom of Nicely. The sets were unique, in that they were a large book that popped open and closed (the set builder, T.A. MacDonald, won a 1947 Tony for "intricate construction").

The Broadway Run. NEW CENTURY THEATRE, 12/5/46–12/21/46. 21 PERFORMANCES. PRESENTED BY Leonard Sillman; MUSIC: David Raksin; LYRICS: June Carroll; BOOK: June Carroll, Robert Duke, Leonard Sillman; ADAPTED FROM Perrault's Cinderella story; BOOK DIRECTOR: Eugene S. Bryden; CHOREOGRAPHER: Charles Weidman; TAP CHOREOGRAPHY ROUTINES: Don Liberto; SETS: Edward Gilbert; SET BUILDER: T.A. MacDonald; COSTUMES: Katherine Kuhn; MUSICAL DIRECTOR: Will Irwin; ORCHESTRATIONS: Russell Bennett; ADDITIONAL ORCHESTRATIONS: Ted Royal, Hans Spialek, Walter Paul, Joseph Glover; VOCAL DIRECTOR: Joe Moon; PRESS: Dorothy Ross & Lewis Harmon; PRODUCTION SUPERVISOR: Leonard Sillman; GENERAL MANAGER: Lillian Mills; STAGE MANAGER: T.C. Jones. *Cast:* TOWN CRIER: Robert Penn; SINGING ATTENDANT: Eugene Martin; DANCING ATTENDANT: Billy Vaux; BRODERICK: Jack Williams; ACROBATIC ATTENDANTS: Jane Vinson & Paula Dee; CINDERELLA: Leila Ernst (2); MISTRESS SPRATT: Jody Gilbert; HER DAUGHTERS: DELILAH: Marilyn Day; THAIS: Sherle North; THE BUTCHER BOY: Richard Wentworth; 1ST UNDERTAKER: Don Mayo; 2ND UNDERTAKER: Walter Kattwinkel; LORELEI: Gail Adams; LILITH: Eileen Ayers; 1ST LAWYER: Harvey Braun; 2ND LAWYER: Stanley Simmonds; LADY EVE: Florence Desmond (1); HERMAN: Joe Besser (3); FOUR SPRITES: Fred Bernaski, Vincent Carbone, Allen Knowles, Harry Rogers; 1ST TROUBADOUR: William Rains; 2ND TROUBADOUR: Ray Morrissey; 3RD TROUBADOUR: Richard Wentworth; THEIR ARRANGER: Fin Olsen; MAJOR DOMO: Youka Troubetzkoy; LADY GUINEVERE: Eleanor Jones; LADY PERSEVERE: Dorothy Karrol; DAME CRACKLE: Chloe Owen; THE BAKER: Ray Cook; DAME CRUMPLE: Joyce White; DAME CRINKLE: Jean Olds; PRINCE CHARMING: Edward Dew; WIDOW WILLOW: Adrienne; KATE: Barbara Perry; KING KINDLY: Edward Lambert; HIS MAGNIFICENCE, THE WIZARD: Frank Milton; COURT DANCER: Vincent Carbone; SAILOR: Richard D'Arcy; HIS SWEETHEARTS: Marcia Maier & Marybly Harwood; CORPS DE BALLET: Fred Bernaski, Vincent Carbone, Paula Dee, George Drake, Yvette Fairhill, Jean Harris, Marybly Harwood, Allen Knowles, Marcia Maier, Roy Marshall, Ruth Ostrander, Audrey Peters, Harry Rogers, Gloria Smith, Billy Vaux, Jane Vinson. *Act I: Prologue* (Town Crier); *Scene 1* Town gate: "Start the Ball Rollin'" (sung by Broderick). Danced by Broderick & Corps de Ballet); *Scene 2* Cinderella's kitchen: "I Wish" (Cinderella), "Start the Ball Rollin'" (reprise) (Mistress Spratt & Her Daughters), "I Wish" (reprise) (Cinderella), "In the Morning" (Eve); *Scene 3* Palace gate: "Come and Bring Your Instruments" (Troubadours & Their Arranger); *Scene 4* Ballroom: "Night After Night" (Guinevere) (danced by Kate & Corps de Ballet), "Every Eve" (Prince Charming & King), "With a Wave of My Hand" (Eve & Cinderella). Danced by: GOOD GIRLS: Jean Harris, Marybly Harwood, Audrey Peters; BAD GIRLS: Marcia Maier, Yvette Fairhill, Gloria Smith; *Scene 5* Anteroom of palace: "Am I a Man or a Mouse?" (Herman), "I'm Not Myself Tonight" (Cinderella, Prince Charming, Kate, Eve); *Scene 6* Ballroom: "Three Questions" (Eve, Cinderella, Wizard) (danced by Kate & Court Dancer). *Act II*: Entr'acte; *Scene 1* Town gate: "If the Shoe Fits" (Wizard & Citizens) (danced by the Corps de Ballet); *Scene 2* Cinderella's kitchen: "I Wish" (reprise) (Prince Charming), "In the Morning" (reprise) (Eve, Herman, Cinderella); *Scene 3* Palace gate: "What's the Younger Generation Coming To?" (King & Entourage); *Scene 4* Village street: "Have You Seen the Countess Cindy?" (Prince Charming & Citizens), "This is the End of the Story" (Cinderella) (danced by Sailor, Marcia Maier, Marybly Harwood); *Scene 5* Palace gate: "(But) I Took Another Look" (Kate & Broderick); *Scene 6* Ante-room: "I Want to Go Back to the Bottom of the Garden" (Eve), "This is the End of the Story" (reprise) (Prince Charming & Broderick); *Scene 7* Village street: "My Business Man" (Widow Willow), Finale (Entire Company).

The show was universally panned by the critics. It cost, and lost more than, $300,000.

333. *Illya Darling*

Set in the port of Piraeus, Athens, in the present. An American teacher tries to rescue a popular Greek prostitute from the life she loves.

Before Broadway. This musical was previously called *Never on Sunday*. The production was completely funded by United Artists, with a view to a movie. Jules Dassin replaced John Patrick as librettist before rehearsals. The nine weeks of tryouts in Philadelphia, Toronto and Detroit, were very successful, but stormy, and Kermit Bloomgarden brought in Stephen Sondheim to help with the lyrics, and Joe Anthony to help with direction, but Mr. Dassin and his wife Melina Mercouri wanted nothing to do with them, so they left. When musical director Lehman Engel was fired in Toronto, his assistant, Karen Gustafson, stepped in, and so became the first woman to fill that role at a Broadway musical opening night. This is the show that created such a (positive) fuss when Melina Mercouri stripped down to a tiny bikini.

The Broadway Run. MARK HELLINGER THEATRE, 4/11/67–1/13/68. 22 previews from 3/22/67. 318 PERFORMANCES. PRESENTED BY Kermit Bloomgarden (for Jules Dassin & Melina Mercouri), in association with United Artists; MUSIC: Manos Hadjidakis (helped by Stephen Sondheim); LYRICS: Joe Darion; BOOK: Jules Dassin; BASED ON the 1960 movie *Never on Sunday*, written by Jules Dassin, and starring Melina Mercouri; DIRECTOR: Jules Dassin (helped by Joseph Anthony); CHOREOGRAPHER: Onna White; ASSISTANT CHOREOGRAPHER: Tommy Panko; SETS: Oliver Smith; COSTUMES: Theoni V. Aldredge; LIGHTING: Jean Rosenthal; SOUND: Robert Liftin; MUSICAL DIRECTOR/VOCAL ARRANGEMENTS: Karen Gustafson; ORCHESTRATIONS: Ralph Burns; DANCE MUSIC ARRANGEMENTS: Roger Adams; CAST RECORDING on United Artists; PRESS: James D. Proctor, Max Gendel, Lawrence Belling; GENERAL MANAGER: Max Allentuck; COMPANY MANAGER: Peter Neufeld; PRODUCTION STAGE MANAGER: Don Doherty; STAGE MANAGER: Bert Wood; ASSISTANT STAGE MANAGERS: Jon DeHart & Joe Alfasa. *Cast:* YORGO: Titos Vandis (3); COSTA: Thomas Raskin; WORKMAN: Dom Angelo; TONIO: Nikos Kourkoulos (4); CAPTAIN: Rudy Bond (8); ILLYA: Melina Mercouri (1) ✩; HOMER THRACE: Orson Bean (2) ✩; WAITER: Harold Gary (7); GARBAGE: William Duell; DESPO: Despo (5); MUSICIAN: Joseph Alfasa; LITTLE MAN: Gerrit de Beer; FORWARD SAILOR: Joseph Corby; TIMID SAILOR: Robert La Tourneaux; VASSILY: Joe E. Marks (9); VOULA: Lou Rodgers; KIKI: Sandy Ellen; CASSANDRA: Gloria Lambert; PLAYGOER: Nick Athas; DRAMA CRITIC: Fred Burrell; WIFE: Del Green; NO FACE: Hal Linden (6); BODYGUARDS: Gerrit de Beer & Harry Kalkanis; THE OTHER GIRL: Ann Barry; BOUZOUKI SOLOIST: Harry Lemonopoulos; ENSEMBLE: Martin Allen, Dom Angelo, Nick

Athas, Ann Barry, Edward Becker, Alvin Cohen, Joseph Corby, Lonnie Davis, Gerrit de Beer, Sandy Ellen, Marcelo Gamboa, Louis Genevrino, Del Green, Eileen Joy Haber, Suzanne Horn, Nat Horne, Harry Kalkanis, Robert Karl, Johnny La Motta, Stephen Lardas, Robert La Tourneaux, Urylee Leonardos, Thomas Raskin, Lou Rodgers, Juleste Salve, Arthur Shaffer, Loukas Skipitaris, Bill Starr, Maria Strattin, Mitch Thomas, Terry Violino, *Charles Dunn, Grant Spradling*. **Standby:** Illya: Fleury D'Antonakis. **Understudies:** Homer: Fred Burrell; Yorgo/Captain/No Face: Harold Gary; Tonio: Hal Linden; Despo: Gloria Lambert; Garbage/Vassily: Joe Alfasa. *Act I: Scene 1* A shipyard in Piraeus; *Scene 2* A bouzouki place; *Scene 3* Illya's bedroom; *Scene 4* Outside Illya's house; *Scene 5* Seaside; *Scene 6* Shipyard; *Scene 7* Illya's apartment; *Scene 8* The Acropolis; *Scene 9* The bouzouki place; *Scene 10* Illya's bedroom. *Act II: Scene 1* Illya's apartment; *Scene 2* Outside Illya's house; *Scene 3* Illya's bedroom; *Scene 4* A street in Piraeus; *Scene 5* Illya's apartment; *Scene 6* Street of the Girls; *Scene 7* The bouzouki place; Scene 8 The port. *Act I:* "Po, Po, Po" (Homer & Tonio), Dance (Ensemble), "Zebekiko" (Yorgo), "Piraeus, My Love" (Illya & Men), "Golden Land" (Homer & Ensemble), "Zebebiko" (reprise) (Yorgo), "Love, Love, Love" (Illya) [dropped after opening], "I Think She Needs Me" (Homer), "I'll Never Lay Down Any More" (Despo), "After Love" (Tonio) [dropped after opening], "Birthday Song" (Tonio, Captain, Men), "Medea Tango" (Illya & Men), "Illya Darling" (Illya, Yorgo, Ensemble). *Act II:* "Dear Mr. Schubert" (Illya), "The Lesson" (Illya & Homer), "Never on Sunday" (Illya & Ensemble), "Piraeus, My Love" (reprise) (Illya), "Medea Tango" (reprise) (Tonio), "Heaven Help the Sailors on a Night Like This" (dance) (Illya, Homer, Yorgo, Tonio, Captain, Vassily, Waiter, Ensemble), "Ya Chara (Bye-Bye-Bye)" (Company).

Broadway reviews were very bad. The show received Tony nominations for musical, composer & lyricist, direction of a musical, choreography, and for Nikos Kourkoulos and Melina Mercouri. Manos Hadjidakis refused his nomination, stating that he had had little control over his work. After opening night Act I was revised and shortened.

334. *I'm Solomon*

A musical fable, set in and around Jerusalem in 1,000 BC, from the morning of one day to noon of the next. King Solomon experiences an identity crisis, and wonders if he is respected for himself or for his title. So, he changes places with a look-alike cobbler.

Before Broadway. The 1938 comedy *King Solomon and the Cobbler* was revived as a hit musical at the CAMERI THEATRE, Tel Aviv, in 1964. It also ran at the ALDWYCH THEATRE, London, in 5/67, as part of their World Theatre Season. *I'm Solomon* tried out in New Haven, 3/8/68–3/16/68. A new book had been written by Erich Segal & Anne Croswell, to make it more adult, but before the show hit Broadway Mr. Segal had withdrawn his name, and the name of Dan Almagor appeared in his place. Alexander Argov's music was replaced by that of Ernest Gold. The show opened in Baltimore as *In Someone Else's Sandals*, but later changed to *Solomon/Solomon*, and even later to *King Solomon and the Cobbler*. It had a cast of 60. It opened on Broadway as *I'm Solomon*.

The Broadway Run. MARK HELLINGER THEATRE, 4/23/68–4/27/68. 9 previews from 4/11/68. 7 PERFORMANCES. PRESENTED BY Zvi Kolitz, Solomon Sagall, and Abe Margolies; MUSIC: Ernest Gold; LYRICS: Anne Croswell; BOOK: Anne Croswell & Dan Almagor; AMERICAN ADAPTATION in collaboration with Zvi Kolitz; SPECIAL MATERIAL: David Finkle & Bill Weeden; BASED ON the 1938 Jewish comedy *King Solomon and the Cobbler*, by Sammy Gronemann; DIRECTOR: Michael Benthall; CHOREOGRAPHER: Donald McKayle; SETS: Rouben Ter-Arutunian; COSTUMES: Jane Greenwood; LIGHTS: Martin Aronstein; MUSICAL DIRECTOR/VOCAL ARRANGEMENTS: Gershon Kingsley; ORCHESTRATIONS: Hershy Kay; DANCE MUSIC ARRANGEMENTS: Dorothea Freitag; PRESS: Max Eisen, Cheryl Sue Dolby, Ed Jaffe; GENERAL MANAGER: Al Goldin; COMPANY MANAGER: Oscar Berlin; PRODUCTION STAGE MANAGER: Mortimer Halpern; STAGE MANAGERS: Norman Shelly & Bert Wood. *Cast:* MEIR, THE DRUMMER: Meir Alon; ALI, THE FLUTIST: Al

DeSio; ISSAC, TAVERN KEEPER: John Dorrin; TAVERN DANCER: Sally Neal; YONI, A COBBLER: Dick Shawn (1) ☆; NA'AMA, HIS WIFE: Karen Morrow (3) ☆; YOEL, TEMPLE BUILDING SUPERVISOR: Kenneth Scott; MAGO, ARCHITECT OF THE TEMPLE: Johnny La Motta; LEMECH, A DYER: Eddie Ericksen; AVIVA, A HARLOT: Alice Evans; BRURIA, A HARLOT: Lynn Archer; OFFICER OF THE ROYAL GUARD: Gordon Cook; BEN HESED, COMMANDER OF THE ROYAL GUARD: Paul Reed (6); PRINCESS NOFRIT, SOLOMON'S FAVORITE WIFE: Barbara Webb (7); F'HTAR, HER SLAVE: Mary Barnett (8); KING SOLOMON: Dick Shawn (1) ☆; BATHSHEBA, SOLOMON'S MOTHER: Carmen Mathews (2) ☆; AMBASSADOR: Nat Horne; SOLOMON'S CONCUBINES: Jeri Barto, Connie Burnett, Miriam Ehrenberg, Carol Flemming, Mary Jane Houdina, Nina Janik, Carol Manning, Sally Neal, Martha Pollak, Renee Rose, Joan Tannen, Nina Trasoff, Myrna White; RANOR, AMBASSADOR OF THE QUEEN OF SHEBA: Fred Pinkard (5); AIDE TO RANOR: Garrett Morris; RACHEL, ONE OF SOLOMON'S WIVES: Caryl Tenney; OTHER WIVES: Lynn Archer, Chris Callan, Jacque Dean, Alice Evans, Carol Flemming, Marsha Hastings, Mary Jane Houdina, Sherry Lambert, Carol Manning, Sally Neal, Joan Tannen; MAKEDAH, A MEMBER OF THE QUEEN OF SHEBA'S PARTY: Salome Jens (4); ENSEMBLE (PEOPLE OF JERUSALEM, COURTIERS, GUARDS, SLAVES, CHILDREN, ETHIOPIANS, ETC): Clifford Allen, Meir Alon, Jeri Barto, Connie Burnett, Chris Callan, Al Cohen, Gordon Cook, Nikolas Dante, Jacque Dean, Esteban de Leon, Al DeSio, John Dorrin, Miriam Ehrenberg, Ed Ericksen, Carol Flemming, Stokely Gray, Rodney Griffin, Jerry Grimes, Marsha Hastings, Nat Horne, Mary Jane Houdina, Jason Howard, Nina Janik, Sherry Lambert, John La Motta, Carol Manning, Garrett Morris, Sally Neal, Keith Perry, Martha Pollak, Ken Richards, Renee Rose, Jeffrey Shawn, Clay Taliaferro, Joan Tannen, Caryl Tenney, Nina Trasoff, Kyle Weaver, Bruce Wells, Myrna White. **Standby**: Solomon/Yoni: Alfred Toigo. **Understudies**: Na'ama: Alice Evans; Bathsheba: Lynn Archer; Ranor: Nat Horne; Nofrit: Lynn Archer & Carol Flemming; Makedah: Carol Flemming; Aviva: Joan Tannen; Bruria: Jacque Dean; Rachel: Myrna White; Ben Hesed: John Dorrin; F'htar: Renee Rose; Yoel/Lemech: Garrett Morris; Mago: Al Cohen. DANCER: Martha Pollak. *Act I*: "David and Bathsheba" (Yoni & People of Jerusalem), "Hail the Son of David!" (Solomon, Courtiers, Solomon's Wives), "Preposterous" (Solomon), "Have You Heard?" (People of Jerusalem), "The Citation" (Ben-Hesed), "In Love with a Fool" (Na'ama), "Someone Like Me" (Solomon), "In Someone Else's Sandals" (Yoni, Bathsheba, Slaves, Concubines), "The Three Riddles" (l: Erich Segal) (Ranor, Ben-Hesed, Solomon, People of Jerusalem). *Act II*: "Once in 2.7 Years" (Solomon's Wives), "Have You Ever Been Alone with a King Before?" (m: Bill Weeden; l: David Finkle) (Yoni & Na'ama), "Lord I Am but a Little Child" (Solomon), "I Am What I Am" (Solomon), "Something in His Eyes" (Na'ama), "That Guilty Feeling" (m: Bill Weeden; l: David Finkle) (Yoni), "Time to Let Go" (Bathsheba), "With Your Hand in My Heart" (Yoni, Na'ama, Bathsheba, People of Jerusalem), "Lord I Am but a Little Child" (reprise) (Entire Company).

Broadway reviews were terrible. The production lost over $700,000, one of the two most expensive musical flops to that date (*Darling of the Day* was the other).

335. *Inner City*

Subtitled *A Street Cantata*. A musical pot-pourri of nursery-rhyme parodies about the ironies and miseries of life in decaying inner cities.

The Broadway Run. ETHEL BARRYMORE THEATRE, 12/19/71–3/11/72. 24 previews from 11/29/71. 97 PERFORMANCES. PRESENTED BY Joseph Kipness, Lawrence Kasha, and Tom O'Horgan, in association with RCA Records; MUSIC: Helen Miller; LYRICS: Eve Merriam; BASED ON the book *The Inner City Mother Goose*, by Eve Merriam; CONCEIVED BY/DIRECTOR: Tom O'Horgan; ASSISTANT DIRECTOR: Harvey Milk; SETS: Robin Wagner; COSTUMES: Joseph G. Aulisi; LIGHTING: John Dodd (in association with Jane Reisman); SOUND: Gary Harris; MUSICAL DIRECTOR: Clay Fullum; ORCHESTRATIONS/ARRANGEMENTS: Gordon Lowry Harrell; VOCAL ARRANGEMENTS: Helen Miller; CAST RECORDING on RCA; PRESS: Bill Doll & Company; ASSOCIATE PRO-

DUCERS: Harvey Milk & John M. Nagel; GENERAL MANAGER: Philip Adler; COMPANY MANAGER: Morry Efron; PRODUCTION STAGE MANAGER: Nicholas Russiyan; STAGE MANAGER: Daniel Landau; ASSISTANT STAGE MANAGER: Joe Scott. **Cast:** Joy Garrett, Carl Hall, Delores Hall, Fluffer Hirsch, Linda Hopkins, Paulette Ellen Jones, Larry Marshall, Allan Nicholls, Florence Tarlow (*Gretel Cummings*). **Act I**: *Scene 1* Nub of the Nation: "Fee Fi Fo Fum" (Linda), "Now I Lay Me" (Carl, Delores, Allan), "Locks"/"I Had a Little Teevee" (Fluffer), "Hushabye Baby"/"My Mother Said" (Paulette Ellen), "Diddle Diddle Dumpling"/"Rub a Dub Dub" (Larry), "You'll Find Mice" (Linda), "Ding Dong Bell" (Carl & Cast), "The Brave Old City of New York" (Joy), "Urban Renewal" (Linda), "The Nub of the Nation" (Cast); *Scene 2* Urban Mary: "Mary, Mary" (Cast), "City Life" (Florence), "One Misty Moisty Morning" (Larry), "Jack Be Nimble" (Carl, Fluffer, Larry), "If Wishes Were Horses" (Delores); *Scene 3* Deep in the Night: "One Man"/"Deep in the Night" (Linda); *Scene 4* Take a Tour, Congressman: "Statistics" (Cast), "Twelve Rooftops Leaping" (Cast), "Take a Tour, Congressman" (Cast), "Simple Simon" (Larry, Allan, Cast), "Poverty Program" (Cast), "One, Two" (Carl & Cast), "Tom, Tom" (Allan), "Hickety, Pickety" (Cast), "Half Alive" (arr/orch by Bernie Hoffer) (Delores); *Scene 5* The Spirit of Education: "This is the Way We Go to School" (Cast), "The Spirit of Education" (Florence), "Little Jack Horner" (Cast), "Subway Dream" (Larry), "Christmas is Coming" (Fluffer), "I'm Sorry Says the Machine" (Larry & Cast), "Jeremiah Obadiah" (Larry), "Riddle Song" (Cast), "Shadow of the Sun" (Cast). **Act II**: *Scene 1* Wisdom: "Boys and Girls Come Out to Play" (Cast), "Summer Nights" (Joy, Delores, Paulette Ellen), "Lucy Locket" (Fluffer), "Winter Nights" (Linda & Florence), "Wisdom" (Larry), "The Hooker" (You Make it Your Way) (Joy); *Scene 2* Starlight: "Wino Will"/"Man in the Doorway" (Paulette Ellen), "Starlight Starbright" (Delores), "The Cow Jumped Over the Moon" (Larry), "The Dealer" (You Push it Your Way) (Allan); *Scene 3* Crooked Man: "Taffy" (Carl, Fluffer, Cast), "Numbers" (Larry & Cast), "The Pickpocket" (Carl), "Law and Order" (arr/orch: Horace Ott) (Delores & Cast); *Scene 4* Kindness: "Kindness" (Allan & Cast), "As I Went Over" (Allan), "There Was a Little Man" (Cast), "Who Killed Nobody" (Cast); *Scene 5* If: "It's My Belief" (Linda)', "Street Sermon" (Carl), "The Great If" (Carl), "On This Rock" (Cast), "The Great If" (reprise) (Cast).

Reviews were not good. Linda Hopkins won a Tony.

336. *Inside U.S.A.*

A revue. An itinerary of different parts of the USA. Bea Lillie and Jack Haley were the comic cicerones.

Before Broadway. During tryouts the "Atlanta" sketch was dropped.

The Broadway Run. NEW CENTURY THEATRE, 4/30/48–8/21/48; MAJESTIC THEATRE, 8/23/48–2/19/49. Total of 339 PERFORMANCES. PRESENTED BY Arthur Schwartz; MUSIC: Arthur Schwartz; LYRICS: Howard Dietz; SKETCHES: Arnold Auerbach, Moss Hart, Arnold B. Horwitt; ADDITIONAL SKETCH MATERIAL: Arnold Auerbach; TITLE BASED ON John Gunther's classic book of the same name; SKETCH DIRECTOR: Robert H. Gordon; CHOREOGRAPHER: Helen Tamiris; ASSISTANT CHOREOGRAPHER: Daniel Nagrin; SETS: Lemuel Ayers; COSTUMES for Bea Lillie's "Come, O Come" and We Won't Take it Back:" Eleanor Goldsmith; Miss Lillie's Costumes & Gowns, Costumes for Valerie Bettis and Thelma Carpenter, for "Haunted Heart," the Opening & the Finale: Castillo; MUSICAL DIRECTOR/VOCAL SUPERVISOR: Jay Blackton; ORCHESTRATIONS: Robert Russell Bennett; INCIDENTAL MUSIC FOR DANCES: Genevieve Pitot; PRESS: Nat Dorfman; COMPANY MANAGER: Abe Cohen; PRODUCTION STAGE MANAGER: Alan Anderson; STAGE MANAGER: Randell Henderson; ASSISTANT STAGE MANAGER: Walter N. Kapp. **Act I**: *Scene 1* "Inside U.S.A." (sung by the Entire Company); *Scene 2* "Leave My Pulse Alone." Any Town, Coast-to-Coast. LOTTIE, THE MAID: Estelle Loring; 1ST POLLSTER: Carl Reiner; MRS. JONES: Jane Lawrence; MR. JONES: Jack Haley (2) ☆; 2ND POLLSTER: Lewis Nye; MARY, THE DAUGHTER: Beverlee Bozeman; 3RD POLLSTER: William Le Massena. Scene: The Jones's living-room; *Scene 3* "Come, O Come" ("Come to Pittsburgh"). Pittsburgh (pronounced "Peetsburgh"). Sung by the Pittsburgh Choral Society. CHORAL DIRECTOR: Beatrice Lillie (1) ☆; SINGERS: Jack Haley (2) ☆, Thelma Carpenter, Estelle Loring, John Tyers. A choral society takes on industrial pollution; *Scene 4* "Forty Winks." Miami Beach (by Arnold B. Horwitt & Arnold Auerbach). MR. BEMIS: Jack Haley (2) ☆; HOTEL MANAGER: William Le Massena; BELLBOY: Lewis Nye; PROF. POULTERGEIST: Carl Reiner. Scene: Regal-Plaza Hotel. The many gadgets in the room designed to help a tired guest sleep only keep him awake; *Scene 5* "Blue Grass." Churchill Downs, Kentucky. SUNG BY: Thelma Carpenter; DANCED BY HER BOY FRIEND: Albert Popwell; HIS FRIEND: J.C. McCord; BOOKIES/SPECTATORS/JOCKEYS: Rod Alexander, Talley Beatty, Beverlee Bozeman, Michael Charnley, Ronald Chetwood, Jacqueline Fisher, Bob Hamilton, Holly Harris, Pat Horn, Norma Larkin, Mara Lynn, Dorothy MacNeil, Joan Mann, Nannon Millis, John Mooney, Betty Nichols, Richard Reed, George Reich, Thomas Rieder, Ricky Riccardi, Boris Runanin, Dorothy Scott, Sherry Shadburne, Gloria Stevens, Royce Wallace. A lament of one whose lover has been lost betting on the ponies at the Kentucky Derby; *Scene 6* A Song to Forget. Chillicothe, Ohio (by Arnold Auerbach). MISS TWITCHELL: Beatrice Lillie (1) ☆; FREDERIC CHOPIN: Carl Reiner; A BUTLER: William Le Massena; MME LAPIS DE LAZULI: Beatrice Lillie (1) ☆; FRANZ LISZT: John Tyers; PETER ILYITCH TSCHAIKOWSKY: Lewis Nye. Scene: in front of a movie theatre. A movie fan with delusions of being a Viennese who inspires romantic compositions; *Scene 7* "Rhode Island is Famous for You" [sung by Jack Haley (2) ☆ and Estelle Loring]. About a mermaid on Plymouth Rock; *Scene 8* "Haunted Heart" [the big hit tune]. San Francisco. Sung by John Tyers. Danced by Valerie Bettis, with J.C. McCord, George Reich, Rod Alexander, under the Golden Gate Bridge. Scene: Waterfront; *Scene 9* "Massachusetts Mermaid:" Beatrice Lillie (1) ☆; *Scene 10* A Feller from Indiana: Herb Shriner; *Scene 11* "First Prize at the Fair." Wisconsin. TICKET SELLER: William Le Massena; 1ST COUPLE: Jane Lawrence & Ray Stephens; 2ND COUPLE: Estelle Loring & Jim Hawthorne; 3RD COUPLE: Beatrice Lillie (1) ☆ & Jack Haley (2) ☆; CALLER: Eric Victor; CONTESTANTS & SPECTATORS: Entire Company. Scene: Fair Grounds, Kenosha County. *Act II*: *Scene 1* "At the Mardi Gras" [sung by Beatrice Lillie (1) ☆]. New Orleans. SIX SWAINS: Jack Cassidy, Jim Hawthorne, Alfred Homan, Thomas Rieder, Michael Risk, Raymond Stephens; DANCED BY: Rod Alexander, Talley Beatty, Beverlee Bozeman, Michael Charnley, Ronald Chetwood, Robert Hamilton, Pat Horn, Mara Lynn, Joan Mann, J.C. McCord, Nannon Millis, Betty Nichols, Albert Popwell, Richard Reed, George Reich, Ricky Riccardi, Boris Runanin, Dorothy Scott, Gloria Stevens, Royce Wallace. Bea Lillie is Queen of the Mardi Gras. MASKS BY: John Robert Lloyd; *Scene 2* "School for Waiters" (by Arnold Auerbach; suggested by George S. Kaufman). New York City. GIRL: Joan Mann; MAN: Carl Reiner; PROFESSOR: Jack Haley (2) ☆; HERMAN: Lewis Nye; GIRL DINER: Jane Lawrence; HER ESCORT: William Le Massena; ANOTHER DINER: Carl Reiner; HIS COMPANIONS: Holly Harris & Hilde Palmer; CAPTAIN OF WAITERS: Ronald Chetwood; STUDENT WAITERS: Rod Alexander, Court Fleming, Richard Reed, George Reich, Boris Runanin. Scene: schoolroom for waiters. The Professor teaches waiters how to annoy customers; *Scene 3* "My Gal is Mine Once More" (a Saturday night song for cowboys) (sung by John Tyers). Wyoming. GROOM: John Tyers; BRIDE: Estelle Loring; MINISTER: Carl Reiner; COWBOY WITH ROPE: J.C. McCord; TOWNSPEOPLE: Mary Lou Boyd, Beverlee Bozeman, Jack Cassidy, Jim Hawthorne, Norma Larkin, Mara Lynn, Dorothy MacNeil, Joan Mann, J.C. McCord, John Mooney, Thomas Rieder, Michael Risk, Dorothy Scott, Sherry Shadburne, Raymond Stephens, Gloria Stevens. Scene: a street in Jackson Hole (a rodeo); *Scene 4* "Better Luck Next Time." Just Off Broadway (by Moss Hart). MARY SHELTON: Jane Lawrence; GLADYS, HER MAID: Beatrice Lillie (1) ☆; THE STAGE MANAGER: Randell Henderson. Scene: Miss Shelton's dressing room; opening night. Superstitious Gladys predicts a flop for Mary; *Scene 5* "Tiger Lily." Chicago (a tabloid ballet conceived by Helen Tamiris). TIGER LILY: Valerie Bettis (3); DOCTOR ZILMORE: Eric Victor; DETECTIVES: Rod Alexander, Robert Hamilton, J.C. McCord, Richard Reed; PROSECUTING ATTORNEY: Rod Alexander; DEFENSE ATTORNEY: Ronald Chetwood; JURY: Talley Beatty, Michael Charnley, Robert Hamilton, Joan Mann, J.C. McCord, Boris Runanin; JUDGE: Carl Reiner; NEWSPAPER READERS/SPECTATORS: Beverlee Bozeman, Jack Cassidy, Jacqueline Fisher, Court Fleming, Holly Harris, Jim Hawthorne, Alfred Homan, Pat Horn, Norma Larkin, William Le Massena, Mara Lynn, Nannon Millis, John Mooney, Betty Nichols, Richard Reed, George Reich, Ricky Riccardi, Thomas Rieder, Michael Risk, Dorothy Scott, Sherry Shadburne, Raymond Stephens, Gloria Stevens, Royce Wallace; *Scene 6* "We Won't Take it Back" [sung by Beatrice Lillie (1) ☆ & Jack Haley (2) ☆]. Albuquerque, New Mexico. TOURISTS: Alfred Homan, Jane Lawrence, William Le Massena, Carl Reiner, Lewis Nye, Hilde Palmer. Scene: Railroad station. Two Indians, Bea Lillie ☆ & Jack Haley ☆, refuse to take the country back; *Scene 7* Finale (Entire Company).

Broadway reviews were terrific. Valerie Bettis won Donaldson Awards for best female debut and for best dancer.

After Broadway. TOUR. For the national tour the sketch A Feller from Indiana was replaced with All Over the Map (by Joseph Stein & Will Glickman) featuring Jack Haley.

337. *Into the Light*

The Turin Shroud is tested by scientists, headed by Prescott, who has abandoned his wife and son at home in the USA. The son has an imaginary friend, performed by a mime, who accompanies him everywhere. Set during late summer in Los Alamos, New Mexico.

Before Broadway. The show cost over $3 million, and was raised from religious adherents in a single backers' audition in California. It tried out in Detroit.

The Broadway Run. NEIL SIMON THEATRE, 10/22/86–10/26/86. 14 previews. 6 PERFORMANCES. PRESENTED BY Joseph Z. Nederlander, Richard Kughn, Jerrold Perenchio; MUSIC: Lee Holdridge; LYRICS: John Forster; BOOK: Jeff Tambornino; DIRECTOR: Michael Maurer; CHOREOGRAPHER: Mary Jane Houdina; SETS/LIGHTING: Neil Peter Jampolis; COSTUMES: Karen Roston; SOUND: Jack Mann; LASER DESIGN: Marilyn Lowey; SPECIAL LASER EFFECTS: Laser Media; MUSICAL SUPERVISOR: Stan Sheldone; MUSICAL DIRECTOR: Peter Howard; ORCHESTRATIONS: Ira Hearshen; PRESS: The Jacksina Company; CASTING: Dennis D'Amico; GENERAL MANAGEMENT: Darwall Associates; COMPANY MANAGER: Mitzi Harder; PRODUCTION STAGE MANAGER: William Dodds; STAGE MANAGER: Steven Shaw; ASSISTANT STAGE MANAGER: Paul Reid Roman. *Cast:* FRIEND: Alan Mintz (5); MATHEW PRESCOTT: Danny Gerard (4); KATE PRESCOTT: Susan Bigelow (2); JAMES PRESCOTT: Dean Jones (1) ☆; COLONEL: Ted Forlow; MAJOR: David Young; FATHER FRANK GIRELLA: William Parry (3); PETER VONN: Lenny Wolpe (6); NATHAN GELB: Peter Walker; VIJAY BANNERJEE: Mitchell Greenberg; PHYLLIS TERWILLIGER: Kathryn McAteer; PAUL COOPER: Alan Brasington; DON CESARE: Casper Roos (8); ARCHBISHOP PARISI: Thomas Batten (7); SIGNOR BOCCIARELLI: Gordon Stanley; ENSEMBLE: Deborah Carlson, Valerie de Pena, Michael Duran, Terri Homberg, David Young. *Understudies*: James: Alan Brasington; Friend: Ron Chisholm; Mathew: Michael Marona; Kate: Kathryn McAteer; Peter/Paul: David Young; Girella/Archbishop: Gordon Stanley; Vijay: Michael Duran; Phyllis: Deborah Carlson; Gelb/Bocciarelli: Ted Forlow; Don Cesare: Peter Walker. *Swings*: Cheri Butcher & Ron Chisholm. *Prologue:* "Poltergeists" (Mathew & Kate). *Act I*: *Scene 1* James Prescott's office, and the Prescott home: "Neat/Not Neat" (James, Girella, Kate), "It Can All Be Explained" (James & Girella); *Scene 2* The lab at Los Alamos: "The Data" (James & Team); *Scene 3* The Prescott home; late that night: "A Talk About Time" (James & Kate); *Scene 4* The next morning: "Trading Solos" (Girella, Matthew, Friend); *Scene 5* Turin, Italy — the council chambers of Il Centro di Sindonologia: "Let There Be Light" (James, Don Cesare, Girella, Bocciarelli, Parisi); *Scene 6* The Prescott home: "Wishes" (Mathew); *Scene 7* The airport and lab at Los Alamos: "The Three of Us" (Kate & James), "Rainbow Logic" (James). *Act II*: *Scene 1* Turin, Italy: "Fede, Fede" (Don Cesare, Parisi, Team); *Scene 2* Turin, Italy: "To Measure the Darkness" (James & Kate); *Scene 3* The Prescott home; *Scene 4* The testing room, St. John's Cathedral: "The Testing" (James & Team); *Scene 5* Albergo Excelsiore: "The Rose and I" (Kate); *Scene 6* The testing room: "The Testing" (continued) (James & Team), "To Measure the Darkness" (reprise) (James), "Be There" (James & Mathew). Epilogue: "Into the Light" (Company).

The show got awful reviews.

338. *Into the Woods*

A baker and his sardonic wife must steal various objects from each of the other characters in the musical in order to break the spell of childlessness placed upon them by the wicked Witch. A complex plot connects this story with the traditional stories of Cinderella, Jack and the Beanstalk, Rapunzel, and Little Red Ridinghood. The Three Little Pigs and Rumpelstiltskin were dropped during the early stages of production. In Act I everyone, including the Witch, ends up happily ever after. Act II turns dark, and everybody must pay for their good fortune. The widow of the giant killed by Jack climbs down the beanstalk and wreaks havoc on the kingdom (the moral is "be responsible for your actions").

Before Broadway. It began as a workshop at PLAYWRIGHTS HORIZONS, in 1986, but only with a first draft of the book and half the music & lyrics of Act I. Steve Sondheim originally intended for each character to have his or her own musical style, but this proved too confusing, and the concept was basically dropped. After acquiring the Landesmans as producers, the show opened on 12/4/86, at the OLD GLOBE THEATRE, San Diego, where it got divided reviews from the Los Angeles newspapers. It had the same basic crew as for the subsequent Broadway production, except SOUND: Michael Holten; MUSICAL DIRECTORS: Paul Gemignani & Eric Stern. *Cast*: NARRATOR/STEWARD: John Cunningham; CINDERELLA: Kim Crosby; JACK: Ben Wright; BAKER: Chip Zien; BAKER'S WIFE: Joanna Gleason; CINDERELLA'S STEPMOTHER: Joy Franz; FLORINDA/RAPUNZEL: Kay McClelland; LUCINDA: Lauren Mitchell; JACK'S MOTHER: Barbara Byrne; LITTLE RED RIDINGHOOD: LuAnne Ponce; WOLVES: John Cunningham, Joy Franz, Merle Louise; WITCH: Ellen Foley; MYSTERIOUS MAN/CINDERELLA'S FATHER: George Coe; CINDERELLA'S MOTHER/GRANDMOTHER/GIANT: Merle Louise; RAPUNZEL'S PRINCE: Chuck Wagner; CINDERELLA'S PRINCE: Kenneth Marshall; FOOTMAN: Ric Oquita; SNOW WHITE: Pamela Tomassetti; SLEEPING BEAUTY: Terri Cannicott. After more re-writes and rehearsals it went into Broadway previews. Betty Buckley was replaced by Bernadette Peters at this point.

The Broadway Run. MARTIN BECK THEATRE, 11/5/87–9/3/89. 43 previews. 764 PERFORMANCES. PRESENTED BY Heidi Landesman, Rocco Landesman, Rick Steiner, M. Anthony Fisher, Frederic H. Mayerson, and Jujamcyn Theatres; MUSIC/LYRICS: Stephen Sondheim; BOOK/DIRECTOR: James Lapine; CHOREOGRAPHER: Lar Lubovitch; SETS: Tony Straiges; COSTUMES: Ann Hould-Ward; COSTUMES BASED ON original concepts by Patricia Zipprodt & Ann Hould-Ward; LIGHTING: Richard Nelson; SOUND: Alan Stieb & James Brousseau; MUSICAL DIRECTOR: Paul Gemignani; ORCHESTRATIONS: Jonathan Tunick; MAGIC CONSULTANT: Charles Reynolds; CASTING: Joanna Merlin; PRESS: The Joshua Ellis Office; GENERAL MANAGEMENT: David Strong Warner; COMPANY MANAGER: Sandra Carlson; PRODUCTION STAGE MANAGER: Frank Hartenstein; STAGE MANAGER: Johnna Murray, *Marianne Cane* (from 12/1/88); ASSISTANT STAGE MANAGER: James Dawson, *Karen Armstrong & Donna A. Drake* (added by 88–89). *Cast:* NARRATOR: Tom Aldredge (4) ☆, *Dick Cavett* (during Mr. Aldredge's vacation, 7/19/88–9/13/88); CINDERELLA: Kim Crosby, *Patricia Ben Peterson*; JACK: Ben Wright, *Jeff Blumenkrantz* (during Mr. Wright's vacation, 87–88); BAKER: Chip Zien (3), *Philip Hoffman* (during Mr. Zien's vacation, 87–88); BAKER'S WIFE: Joanna Gleason (2) ☆, *Lauren Mitchell & Kay McClelland* (alternating from 6/28/88), *Mary Gordon Murray* (from 7/19/88), *Cynthia Sikes* (from 11/15/88), *Joanna Gleason* (from 5/23/89), *Kay McClelland* (from 5/27/89); CINDERELLA'S STEPMOTHER: Joy Franz; FLORINDA: Kay McClelland, *Susan Gordon Clark*; LUCINDA: Lauren Mitchell, *Teresa Burrell*; JACK'S MOTHER: Barbara Byrne; LITTLE RED RIDINGHOOD: Danielle Ferland, *Heather Shulman* (during Miss Ferland's vacation), *LuAnne Ponce* (from 9/20/88); WITCH: Bernadette Peters (1) ☆, *Betsy Joslyn* (from 3/29/88), *Phylicia Rashad* (from 4/14/88), *Betsy Joslyn* (from 7/5/88), *Nancy Dussault* (from 12/13/88), *Bernadette Peters* (from 5/23/89), *Nancy Dussault* (from 5/27/89), *Ellen Foley* (from 8/1/89); CINDERELLA'S FATHER: Edmund Lyndeck; CINDERELLA'S MOTHER: Merle Louise; MYSTERIOUS MAN: Tom Aldredge (4) ☆, *Edmund Lyndeck* (during Mr. Aldredge's vacation, 7/19/88–9/13/88); WOLF: Robert Westenberg (5) ☆;

RAPUNZEL: Pamela Winslow, *Marin Mazzie* (from 3/7/89); RAPUNZEL'S PRINCE: Chuck Wagner, *Dean Butler* (from 3/7/89), *Don Goodspeed*; GRANDMOTHER: Merle Louise; CINDERELLA'S PRINCE: Robert Westenberg (5) ☆; STEWARD: Philip Hoffman, *Greg Zerkle* (during Mr. Hoffman's vacation, 87–88), *Adam Grupper*; GIANT: Merle Louise; SNOW WHITE: Jean Kelly, *Heather Shulman, Cindy Robinson*; SLEEPING BEAUTY: Maureen Davis. **Standby:** Narrator/Mysterious Man: Ed Lyndeck. **Understudies:** Jack: Jeff Blumenkrantz & Michael Piontek, *Jonathan Dokuchitz*; Rapunzel's Prince: Jeff Blumenkrantz, Ed Lyndeck, Michael Piontek, *Jonathan Dokuchitz*; Baker/Cinderella's Father: Philip Hoffman & Greg Zerkle, *Adam Grupper, James Judy*; Cinderella's Prince: Michael Piontek, Chuck Wagner, Greg Zerkle, *Dean Butler, Jonathan Dokuchitz, James Judy*; Wolf: Michael Piontek & Chuck Wagner, *Dean Butler, Jonathan Dokuchitz, James Judy*; Steward: Jeff Blumenkrantz & Greg Zerkle, *James Judy*; Baker's Wife: Lauren Mitchell & Kay McClelland, *Jennifer Chatfield*; Stepmother/Jack's Mother/Cinderella's Mother/Grandmother/Giant: Carolyn Marlow, *Judith Moore*; Cinderella: Suzanne Douglas & Pamela Winslow, *Cindy Robinson, Marin Mazzie*; Lucinda/Florinda: Pamela Winslow, *Jennifer Chatfield, Marin Mazzie*; Rapunzel/Red Ridinghood: Maureen Davis & Jean Kelly, *Cindy Robinson*; Witch: Suzanne Douglas & Joy Franz, *Marin Mazzie*; Sleeping Beauty: Suzanne Douglas; Snow White: Maureen Davis; Narrator: Ed Lyndeck, *James Judy*; Mysterious Man: James Judy. **Orchestra:** VIOLIN I/CONCERTMISTRESS: Marilyn Reynolds; VIOLIN II: Laura Corcos; VIOLA I: Karl Bargen; VIOLA II: Maxine Roach; CELLO: Eileen Folson; STANDUP BASS: John Beal; FLUTE: Les Scott; CLARINET: John Moses; BASSOON: John Campo; HORN I: Ron Sell; HORN II: Richard Hagen; TRUMPETS: Wilmer Wise; PIANO: Paul Ford; SYNTHESIZERS: Scott Frankel; PERCUSSION: Robert Ayers. **Act I**: *Scene 1* Prologue: "Into the Woods" (Company); *Scene 2* "Cinderella at the Grave" (Narrator & Company), "Hello, Little Girl" (Wolf & Little Red Ridinghood), "I Guess This is Goodbye" (Jack), "Maybe They're Magic" (Baker's Wife), "I Know Things Now" (Little Red Ridinghood), "A Very Nice Prince" (Cinderella & Baker's Wife), First Midnight; *Scene 3* "Giants in the Sky" (Jack), "Agony" (Cinderella's Prince & Rapunzel's Prince), "Just Like Last Night" [cut before Broadway], "It Takes Two" (Baker & Baker's Wife); *Scene 4* "Stay with Me" (Witch & Rapunzel) (added for Broadway), "On the Steps of the Palace" (Cinderella) [before Broadway this number was known as "Back to the Palace"]; *Scene 5* "Ever After" (Narrator & Company). **Act II**: *Scene 1* Prologue: "So Happy" (Company); *Scene 2* "Agony" (reprise) (Cinderella's Prince & Rapunzel's Prince), "Lament" (Witch), "Any Moment" (Cinderella's Prince & Baker's Wife), "Moments in the Woods" (Baker's Wife) [before Broadway this number was known as "Ready for the Woods"], "Your Fault" (Jack, Baker, Witch, Cinderella, Little Red Ridinghood), "Last Midnight" (Witch) [this number replaced "Boom Crunch!" before Broadway], "No More" (Baker & Mysterious Man), "No One is Alone" (Cinderella, Little Red Ridinghood, Baker, Jack) [this number was added during the run at the Old Globe], Finale: "Children Will Listen" (Witch & Company).

The show built up a $3.7 million advance at the Broadway box-office, largely on the strength of Bernadette Peters' and Steve Sondheim's names. Critics enjoyed it, with the exception of the *New York Times*. The public liked it. It won Tonys for score, book, and for Joanna Gleason, and was also nominated for musical, direction of a musical, choreography, sets, costumes, lighting, and for Robert Westenberg. As with *Sunday in the Park with George*, the original cast reassembled toward the end of the run for videotaping the show for the PBS TV series *American Playhouse*.

After Broadway. TOUR. Opened on 11/22/88, at the Parker Playhouse, Fort Lauderdale. During the run it played at the Kennedy Center, Washington, DC, 6/21/89–7/16/89. The tour closed on 5/13/90, at the Mechanic Theatre, Baltimore. PRESENTED BY Tom Mallow & Pace Theatrical Group; MUSICAL DIRECTOR: Randy Booth. In Act II there were some changes from that of the Broadway production. *Cast*: CINDERELLA: Kathleen Rowe McAllen, *Patricia Ben Peterson, Jill Geddes* (alternate from 3/89); WITCH: Cleo Laine, *Betsy Joslyn* (from 5/89); JACK'S MOTHER: Charlotte Rae, *Nora Mae Lyng* (from 5/89), *Frances Ford*; NARRATOR/MYSTERIOUS MAN: Rex Robbins, *Peter Walker*; BAKER'S WIFE: Mary Gordon Murray, *Judy McLane*; LITTLE RED RIDINGHOOD: Tracy Katz; CINDERELLA'S PRINCE/WOLF: Chuck Wagner, *James Weatherstone*; GRANDMOTHER/GIANT: Nora Mae Lyng, *Barbara Marineau*;

JACK: Robert Duncan McNeill, *Kevin R. Wright*; BAKER: Ray Gill, *Adam Grupper, Marcus Olson*; RAPUNZEL: Marguerite Lowell, *Gay Willis*; RAPUNZEL'S PRINCE: Douglas Sills, *Jonathan Hadley*.

PHOENIX THEATRE, London, 9/25/90. 186 PERFORMANCES. A new number, "Our Little World" (Witch & Rapunzel), was introduced, between "Maybe They're Magic" and "I Know Things Now." *Cast*: Clive Carter, Imelda Staunton, Julia McKenzie, Nicholas Parsons.

BROADWAY THEATRE, Broadway, 11/9/97. 2 PERFORMANCES. This was a 10th-anniversary benefit reunion concert. PRESENTED BY two AIDS-related charities — Friends in Deed and God's Love We Deliver. PRODUCED BY: Mosaic Entertainment; DIRECTOR: James Lapine; SETS: Mitchell Greenberg; COSTUMES: Ann Hould-Ward; MUSICAL DIRECTOR: Paul Gemignani. The score included "Our Little World," the first time the song had been performed on Broadway (it had been introduced for the London production, in 1990). Being a reunion, it had the same basic cast, except WOLF/CINDERELLA'S PRINCE: Chuck Wagner; RAPUNZEL'S PRINCE: Jonathan Dokuchitz; STEWARD: Jeff Blumenkrantz. The role of Snow White was cut. Tickets cost $55–$1,000.

DONMAR WAREHOUSE, London, 11/16/98–2/13/99. Previews from 11/6/98. DIRECTORS: John Crowley & Jonathan Butterell; CHOREOGRAPHER: Jonathan Butterell. *Cast*: BAKER: Nick Holder; WITCH: Clare Burt; NARRATOR: Frank Middlemass; CINDERELLA: Jenna Russell; FLORINDA: Caroline Sheen; BAKER'S WIFE: Sophie Thompson; STEPMOTHER: Louise Davidson.

THEATRE UNDER THE STARS, Houston, 12/4/01–12/16/01. DIRECTOR: Glenn Casale. *Cast*: WITCH: Leslie Uggams; BAKER: Lenny Wolpe; LITTLE RED RIDINGHOOD: Tracy Palladini; CINDERELLA: Kim Huber; BAKER'S WIFE: Mary Gordon Murray; RAPUNZEL: Deanna Julian; CINDERELLA'S PRINCE/WOLF: Christopher Carl; JACK: Daniel Frank Kelly; MYSTERIOUS MAN/NARRATOR: Bill McCauley; RAPUNZEL'S PRINCE: Jeff Barnett; CINDERELLA'S STEPMOTHER: Carol Swarbrick; CINDERELLA'S MOTHER: Kathy Knight; CINDERELLA'S FATHER: James Shaffer.

339. *Into the Woods (Broadway revival)*

This was a re-conceived version. It included the number "Our Little World." The narrator, who in the original had been off to the side, was now brought into the action. The immobile, inanimate cow of the original was now an actor who walked about on all fours (on stilts) (Kate Reinders in Los Angeles; Chad Kimball on Broadway). There were now two wolves instead of one, and the number "Hello, Little Girl" was now sung by the two wolves. The Three Little Pigs, cut from the original, were reinstated. The original had very little dance, but the new version had a lot. There were also other lyric changes in various songs.

Before Broadway. The revival was first announced on 3/2/01, for a Broadway production in the spring of 2002. Broadway plans were confirmed on 5/16/01. On 9/7/01 it was announced that 4/02 was the likely Broadway date. By 9/01 casting and pre-production had begun in earnest. It was decided to try it out in Los Angeles, and by 10/23/01 everyone knew that Vanessa Williams was going to be the Witch in L.A. and on Broadway. Laura Benanti was also being rumored as Cinderella, and Gregg Edelman as her Prince. It did, indeed, try out, in L.A., at the AHMANSON THEATRE, 2/10/02–3/24/02. Previews from 2/1/02. At that stage the show was three hours long. It was cut to 2 hours 45 minutes for Broadway. In L.A. the cast was the same as for the subsequent Broadway production, except for MILKY-WHITE: Kate Reinders. This try-out got great reviews, which dispelled misgivings in certain quarters that a revival was coming too soon after the original. On 4/25/02 a boiler exploded in the eight-story building at 123 West 19th Street, Chelsea, Manhattan, where the costumes for the show were in the shop for repairs and touching up. A floor collapsed, and some of the costumes were destroyed. The cow's head was hurt bad. The building was sealed off, and the costumes that survived were made inaccessible. The crew worked frantically to restore and re-build the missing costumes, and everything worked out well. Opening date was delayed a day, from 4/29/02 to 4/30/02.

The Broadway Run. BROADHURST THEATRE, 4/30/02–12/29/02. 18 previews from 4/13/02. 279 PERFORMANCES. PRESENTED BY Dodger Theatricals, Stage Holding, Joop Van Den Ende, and Theatrical Dreams; MUSIC/LYRICS: Stephen Sondheim; BOOK/DIRECTOR: James Lapine; CHOREOGRAPHER: John Carrafa; SETS: Douglas W. Schmidt; COSTUMES: Susan Hilferty; LIGHTING: Brian McDevitt; SOUND: Dan Moses Schreier; ILLUSIONS DESIGNER: Jim Steinmeyer; MUSICAL DIRECTOR: Paul Gemignani; ORCHESTRATIONS: Jonathan Tunick; CAST RECORDING on Nonesuch, made on 5/6/02, and released on 6/25/02; PRESS: Boneau/Bryan-Brown; JIM Carnahan; GENERAL MANAGERS: Robert C. Strickland & Sally Campbell Morse; COMPANY MANAGER: Kimberly Kelley; STAGE MANAGER: Lisa Dawn Cave; ASSISTANT STAGE MANAGER: Scott Taylor Rollison. *Cast*: BAKER'S WIFE: Kerry O'Malley; BAKER: Stephen DeRosa; WITCH: Vanessa Williams (until 12/22/02), *Linda Mugleston* (stood in), *Tracy Nicole Chapman* (stood in), *Linda Mugleston* (replaced Miss Williams, 12/24/02); NARRATOR/MYSTERIOUS MAN: John McMartin; JACK'S MOTHER: Mary Louise Burke, *Nora Mae Lyng*; RAPUNZEL: Melissa Dye, *Danielle Haben*; RAPUNZEL'S PRINCE: Christopher Sieber; LITTLE RED RIDINGHOOD: Molly V. Ephraim; CINDERELLA: Laura Benanti, *Melissa Dye* (from 10/8/02); JACK: Adam Wylie; CINDERELLA'S PRINCE: Gregg Edelman; CINDERELLA'S STEPMOTHER/GRANNY: Pamela Myers, *Joy Franz*; CINDERELLA'S FATHER: Dennis Kelly; FLORINDA: Tracy Nicole Chapman; STEWARD: Trent Armand Kendall; HORSE: Jennifer Malenke; LUCINDA: Amanda Naughton; MILKY-WHITE: Chad Kimball; WOLVES: Christopher Sieber & Gregg Edelman; GIANT (RECORDED VOICE): Judi Dench. **Understudies**: Narrator/Mysterious Man: Stephen Berger & Dennis Kelly; Cinderella's Prince: Christopher Sieber & Adam Brazier; Baker/Cinderella's Father: Stephen Berger & Trent Armand Kendall; Steward: Stephen Berger & Adam Brazier; Cinderella's Stepmother/Granny: Kristin Carbone; Lucinda: Kristin Carbone, *Alison Walla*; Witch: Tracy Nicole Chapman & Linda Mugleston; Cinderella: Melissa Dye & Kate Reinders, *Alison Walla*; Red Ridinghood: Melissa Dye & Kate Reinders, *Alison Walla*; Rapunzel's Prince/Wolf/Jack: Chad Kimball & Adam Brazier; Florinda: Jennifer Malenke & Kate Reinders, *Alison Walla*; Rapunzel: Jennifer Malenke & Kate Reinders, *Alison Walla*; Milky-White: Jennifer Malenke & Kate Reinders; Jack's Mother: Pamela Myers & Linda Mugleston, *Joy Franz*; Baker's Wife: Amanda Naughton & Linda Mugleston; Horse: Adam Brazier; Stepmother/Granny: Linda Mugleston. **Orchestra:** KEYBOARD 1: Annbritt duChateau; KEYBOARD 2: Mark Mitchell; CONCERTMASTER/VIOLIN 1: Marilyn Reynolds; VIOLIN 2: Mineko Yajima; VIOLA 1: Richard Brice; VIOLA 2: Shelley Holland-Moritz; CELLO: Deborah Assael; BASS: John Beal; FLUTE: Les Scott; CLARINET: Amy Zoloto; BASSOON: John Campo; FRENCH HORN 1: Ron Sell; FRENCH HORN 2: Nancy Billman; TRUMPET: Dominic Derasse; PERCUSSION: Paul Pizzuti.

Broadway reviews were good. The show won Tonys for revival of a musical and lighting, and was also nominated for direction of a musical, choreography, sets, costumes, and for Gregg Edelman, John McMartin, Laura Benanti, and Vanessa Williams. In 10/02 Laura Benanti left under mysterious circumstances, and her understudy, Melissa Dye went on. Some said Miss Benanti was sick, others said she had an injury (it was later revealed to be a herniated disc). Erin Dilley was rumored as the replacement. Vanessa Williams did not perform on Nov. 7, 8, 10, 12, 13, 14, 15, 16, 17, and understudies stood in. On 12/4/02 it was announced that the show would close on 12/29/02. On 5/6/02 a national tour for 2003 was announced, but it never happened.

340. *Irene*

Set in Manhattan and Long Island, in 1919. Irene is a sweet, pure, Irish-American piano tuner (an upholsterer in the original 1919 musical) who is nobody's fool, and who makes good. She is sent to tune the piano at a Long Island home, and there Donald falls in love with her. He persuades his friend, flamboyant male couturier Mme Lucy, to hire her as a socialite. The show is a variation of *Cinderella* and *My Fair Lady*.

Before Broadway. The original musical ran on Broadway, at the VANDERBILT THEATRE, 11/18/19–6/18/21. 675 PERFORMANCES. It was the longest-running musical on Broadway until surpassed by *Pins and Needles* in 1939. PRESENTED BY Carle Carleton & Joe McCarthy; DIRECTOR: Edward Royce. **Cast**: IRENE: Edith Day; DONALD: Walter Regan; MME LUCY: Bobbie Watson. It ran again, at JOLSON'S 59TH STREET THEATRE, 4/2/23–4/14/23. 16 PERFORMANCES. DIRECTOR: Edward Royce. **Cast**: IRENE: Dale Winter. It was filmed in 1940. PRODUCER/DIRECTOR: Herbert Wilcox. **Cast**: Anna Neagle, Ray Milland. It had a run at HIS MAJESTY'S THEATRE, London, 3/21/45–7/28/45. 166 PERFORMANCES. PRESENTED BY Jack Hylton; DIRECTOR: Freddie Grey. **Cast**: IRENE: Pat Taylor; DONALD: Frank Leighton; MME LUCY: Arthur Riscoe. Harry Rigby did the first adaptation of this 1973 revival, but further revisions were done by Joseph Stein and Hugh Wheeler. Billy De Wolfe was set as Mme Lucy, but he got sick, and was replaced by George S. Irving. During Toronto tryouts (which began on 11/28/72) Debbie Reynolds got laryngitis and during one performance acted her part on stage without a word, a synopsis of her scenes being read by John Gielgud, the director. There was some booing from the audience, to which Miss Reynolds said, in a hoarse voice, "I don't have to be here. I could be at home with my seven maids." Next came Philadelphia, where reviews were bad. In 1/73 John Gielgud was replaced by Gower Champion, who got it into better shape by the time it reached Washington, DC, where President Nixon, to the delight of the show's free publicity department, gave it a good review. Broadway opening night was pushed back three times. This was Debbie Reynolds' Broadway debut.

The Broadway Run. MINSKOFF THEATRE, 3/13/73–9/7/74. 13 previews from 3/1/73. 594 PERFORMANCES. PRESENTED BY Harry Rigby, Albert W. Selden, and Jerome Minskoff; MUSIC/LYRICS: various writers; BOOK: Hugh Wheeler & Joseph Stein (from an adaptation by Hugh Wheeler, Harry Rigby, and David Rogers); BASED ON the original play by James Montgomery; DIRECTOR: Gower Champion; CHOREOGRAPHER: Peter Gennaro; DANCE CAPTAIN: Mary Ann Niles; SETS/COSTUMES: Raoul Pene du Bois; DEBBIE REYNOLDS' COSTUMES: Irene Sharaff; JANE POWELL'S COSTUMES: Donald Brooks; LIGHTING: David F. Segal; SOUND: Tony Alloy; MUSICAL DIRECTOR/VOCAL DIRECTOR: Jack Lee; ORCHESTRATIONS: Ralph Burns; DANCE MUSIC ARRANGEMENTS/INCIDENTAL MUSIC/ASSISTANT CONDUCTOR: Wally Harper; CAST RECORDING on Columbia; PRESS: John Springer Associates; CASTING: Wendy Mackenzie; GENERAL MANAGER: Walter Fried; COMPANY MANAGER: G. Warren McClane; PRODUCTION STAGE MANAGER: James Gelb; STAGE MANAGER: Robert Schear; ASSISTANT STAGE MANAGERS: Steven Beckler & Joe Lorden. **Cast:** MRS. O'DARE: Patsy Kelly (2) ☆, *Mary McCarty* (during Miss Kelly's vacation, 8/2/73–8/20/73); JANE BURKE: Janie Sell (8), *Dottie Frank*; HELEN McFUDD: Carmen Alvarez (7), *Patti Karr*; JIMMY O'FLAHERTY: Bruce Lea; IRENE O'DARE: Debbie Reynolds (1) ☆, *Jane Powell* (from 2/6/74), *Patricia Peadon* (during Miss Powell's vacation in 6/74), *Debbie Reynolds* (from 9/2/74); EMMELINE MARSHALL: Ruth Warrick (5) ☆; CLARKSON: Bob Freschi; DONALD MARSHALL: Monte Markham (3) ☆ (until 5/31/73), *Ron Husmann* (from 6/4/73); OZZIE BABSON: Ted Pugh (6); MADAME LUCY: George S. Irving (4) ☆, *Hans Conried* (from 6/27/74); ARABELLA THORNSWORTHY: Kate O'Brady; DEBUTANTES: Meg Bussert, Arlene Columbo, Carrie Fisher, Dorothy Wyn Gehgan (*Judy Endacott*), Marybeth Kurdock (*Trudy Carson*), Frances Ruth Lea, Jeanne Lehman, Kate O'Brady (*Karen Weeden*), Julie Pars, Pamela Peadon, Pat Trott, Sandra Voris, Jeanette Williamson, Penny Worth; NINTH AVENUE FELLAS: Paul Charles, Dennis Edenfield, David Evans, Bob Freschi, John Hamilton, Bruce Lea, Joe Lorden, Bryan Nicholas, Robert Rayow (*Stan Picus*), Dennis Roth, Kenn Scalice (*Gary Gendell*), Ron Schwinn (*Gerard Brennte*), David Steele, Albert Stephenson. **Standbys**: Mrs. O'Dare/Mrs. Marshall: Justine Johnston, *Mary McCarty*; Mme Lucy: Emory Bass. **Understudies**: Irene: Janie Sell, *Dottie Frank, Meg Bussert, Frances Lea*; Donald: John Hamilton, *Donegan Smith*; Jane: Dorothy Wyn Gehgan; Helen: Penny Worth, *Arlene Columbo* (added in second season); Ozzie: Bob Freschi. **Swing Dancers**: Frances Lea, Kenn Scalice (*Gary Gendell*). **Act I: Scene 1** The piano store: "The World Must Be Bigger than an Avenue" (m: Wally Harper; l: Jack Lloyd) (Irene), "What Do You Want to Make Those Eyes at Me For?" (by Howard Johnson, James V. Monaco, Joseph McCarthy) (Chorus) [cut during previews]; **Scene 2** The music room of the Marshall estate: "The Family Tree" * (m: Harry Tierney; l: Joseph McCarthy) (Mrs. Marshall & Debutantes), "Alice Blue Gown" * (m: Harry Tierney;

l: Joseph McCarthy) (Irene), "They Go Wild, Simply Wild, Over Me" (m: Fred Fisher; l: Joseph McCarthy) (Madame Lucy & Debutantes); **Scene 3** Ninth Avenue: "An Irish Girl" (m: Otis Clements; l: Charles Gaynor) (Irene & Company); **Scene 4** Madame Lucy's salon: "Stepping on Butterflies" (m: Wally Harper) (Madame Lucy, Irene, Helen, Jane); **Scene 5** The front of the piano store: "Mother Angel Darling" (m/l: Charles Gaynor) (Irene & Mrs. O'Dare); **Scene 6** The Palais Royale: "The Riviera Rage" (instrumental by Wally Harper) (Irene & Company). **Act II: Scene 1** The Palais Royale: "I'm Always Chasing Rainbows" (m: Harry Carroll: l: Joseph McCarthy) (Irene) [this number was cut during previews, but restored during the run for Jane Powell. However, Debbie Reynolds did record it on the cast album], "The Last Part of Ev'ry Party" * (m: Harry Tierney; l: Joseph McCarthy) (Company), "We're Getting Away with It" * (m: Harry Tierney; l: Joseph McCarthy) (Madame Lucy, Helen, Jane, Ozzie); **Scene 2** The piano store: "Irene" * (m: Harry Tierney; l: Joseph McCarthy) (Irene & Company); **Scene 3** Outside the marquee tent: "The Great Lover Tango" (m: Charles Gaynor; l: Otis Clements) (Donald, Helen, Jane), "You Made Me Love You" (m: James Monaco; l: Joseph McCarthy) [from *The Honeymoon Express*] (Irene & Donald), "You Made Me Love You" (reprise) (Madame Lucy & Mrs. O'Dare); **Scene 4** The Italian garden: Finale (Company).

Note: It was almost a new score from the 1919 original. Only five songs were retained, and those are asterisked.

The show got bad reviews, but it was a commercial sell-out, setting the box-office record for a one-week take ($144,689, beating *Coco*). George S. Irving won a Tony, and she show was also nominated for choreography, and for Debbie Reynolds and Patsy Kelly. Despite its long run, production costs had been so phenomenal that it didn't return any money to the investors. Originally budgeted at $800,000, it shot up to $1,492,000.

After Broadway. TOUR. Opened on 9/13/74, at the Aerie Crown Theatre, Chicago, where it broke box-office records. It closed on 5/3/75, at the Shubert Theatre, Boston. MUSICAL DIRECTOR: Robert Brandzel. **Cast**: IRENE: Debbie Reynolds, *Jane Powell* (from 12/2/74); MRS. O'DARE: Patsy Kelly; EMMELINE: Ruth Warrick, *Constance Carpenter* (from 1/15/75); DONALD: Ron Husmann, *David Holliday*; OZZIE: Ted Pugh, *Ted Richards*; LUCY: Hans Conried, *Lee Wallace* (from 1/27/75); CLARKSON: Albert Stephenson; JIMMY: J.J. Epson; HELEN: Karen Weeden, *Carole Bishop, Kathryn Sandy*; JANE: Penny Worth, *Bette Glenn*.

PAPER MILL PLAYHOUSE, New Jersey, 1975. DIRECTOR: Larry Forde. **Cast**: Nancy Dussault, Bibi Osterwald, Elliott Reid, Marijane Maricle, Ted Pritchard, Paul Dumont.

TOUR. Opened on 10/3/75, and closed on 2/23/76. **Cast**: IRENE: Patsy Kelly, *Virginia Graham, Meg Bussert*.

ADELPHI THEATRE, London, 6/15/76. 974 PERFORMANCES. CAST RECORDING on EMI. **Cast**: IRENE: Julie Anthony (who had starred in the 1973 Australian production as well), *Patricia Michael* (from spring 1977); ALSO WITH: Jon Pertwee, Jessie Evans, Eric Flynn.

SYLVIA & DANNY KAYE PLAYHOUSE, NYC, 9/23/98. A concert version (one night only), to celebrate the 25th anniversary of the 1973 Broadway production. This was a benefit for Gilda's Club (a cancer support service named for Gilda Radner). DIRECTORS: Donald E. Birely & Mike Harmon; CHOREOGRAPHER: Bruce Lea; MUSICAL DIRECTORS: Thom Conroy & Michael Meffe. The cast (several of whom had been in the 1973 production) included: Alix Korey (replaced Beth Fowler before the production), Penny Worth (replaced Emily Skinner before the production), Lee Roy Reams, George S. Irving, Ruth Warrick, Bob Freschi, Mary Stout, Marguerite Shannon.

341. *Irma La Douce*

About a Parisian streetwalker with a heart of gold, and her protector. It opens in the back streets of Pigalle. We meet the gang. A poule, Irma ("the girl who helps all Paris relax — for just a thousand francs, including tax"), falls in love with penniless law student, Nestor. They set up house together, and she goes to work to support him while he studies. But he is jealous of her other clients, so he dons a beard and bowler hat, and becomes M.

Oscar, her exclusive client, at 10,000 francs a shot, which she then gives to Nestor. So, Nestor always has the same 10,000 francs. However, he becomes jealous of M. Oscar and kills him. He is arrested, and sent to Devil's Island, escapes, and returns to Paris to prove his innocence. He is just in time for the birth of his child. All ends happily.

Before Broadway. The original opened at the THEATRE GRAMONT, Paris, on 11/12/56 (it would run there for four years). Prologue, "Because" [not used in London or Broadway], "C'est Polyte-le-Mou," "Me v'la, te v'la," "Avec les anges," "Elle a du chien," "Un cave, un seul, pas exigeant," "Ah, dis donc, dis donc," "To be or not to be," "Le cave a Irma," "Je cherche qui," "L'aventure est morte," "C'est dur a croire qu'il est plus la," "Irma la douce" ("Le pont Caulaincourt"), "Hardi, joli gondolier," "Irma la douce" (reprise), "Y'a qu'Paris pour ca," "Il a raison" ("Il n'a pas tort"), "Ce mec la degomme," "Il est ne le mome a Irma," Epilogue.

Peter Brook saw it in Paris, and approached Monty Norman, who in turn took the idea of doing it in English to newcomers Julian More and David Heneker, and in England it opened at the PAVILION, BOURNEMOUTH, on 6/24/58. It moved to London's West End, to the LYRIC THEATRE, 7/17/58–3/3/62. 1,511 PERFORMANCES. There was no performance on 10/14/58 due to a loss of power in the theatre. PRESENTED BY Donmar Productions & H.M. Tennent Ltd.; DIRECTOR: Peter Brook; CHOREOGRAPHER: John Heawood; SETS/COSTUMES: Rolf Gerard; MUSICAL DIRECTOR: Alexander Faris. *Cast*: IRMA: Elizabeth Seal, *Shani Wallis, Mary Preston*; NESTOR: Keith Michell, *John Neville, Howard Short, Denis Quilley, Gerard Hely*; BOB: Clive Revill, *Joe Melia*; ROBERTO: Ronald Barker, *Harry Goodier, Richard Curnock*; FRANGIPANE: Gary Raymond, *Gerard Hely, David Ritch*; POLICE INSPECTOR: Julian Orchard, *Michael Barrington*.

This was the first book musical on Broadway to have originated in Paris. For Broadway the number "Bravo!" was cut.

The Broadway Run. PLYMOUTH THEATRE, 9/29/60–10/28/61; Alvin Theatre, 10/30/61–12/31/61. 2 previews on 9/28/60. Total of 524 PERFORMANCES. PRESENTED BY David Merrick, in association with Donald Albery & H.M. Tennent, Ltd., and by arrangement with Henry Hall; MUSIC: Marguerite Monnot; LYRICS/BOOK: Alexandre Breffort; ENGLISH LYRICS & BOOK: Julian More, David Heneker, Monty Norman; DIRECTOR: Peter Brook; CHOREOGRAPHER: Onna White; ASSISTANT CHOREOGRAPHER: Tom Panko; SETS/COSTUMES: Rolf Gerard; LIGHTING: Joe Davis; MUSICAL DIRECTOR: Stanley Lebowsky; ASSISTANT MUSICAL DIRECTOR: Don Pippin; ORCHESTRATIONS: Andre Popp; ADDITIONAL ORCHESTRATIONS: Robert Ginzler; VOCAL ARRANGEMENTS: Bert Waller & Stanley Lebowsky; DANCE MUSIC ARRANGEMENTS: John Kander; PRESS: Frank Goodman & Ben Washer; CASTING: Michael Shurtleff & Robert Schear; GENERAL MANAGER: Jack Schlissel; COMPANY MANAGER: Vince McKnight; GENERAL STAGE MANAGER: Ben Janney; STAGE MANAGER: David Clive, *Harold Stone*; ASSISTANT STAGE MANAGERS: John Ray & Angelo Mango. *Cast*: BOB-LE-HOTU, PROPRIETOR OF THE BAR-DES-INQUIETS: Clive Revill (3); IRMA-LA-DOUCE, A POULE: Elizabeth Seal (1) ☆; A CLIENT: Eddie Gasper; JOJO-LES-YEUX-SALES, A MEC: Zack Matalon; ROBERTO-LES-DIAMS, A MEC: Aric Lavie; PERSIL-LE-NOIR, A MEC: Osborne Smith; FRANGIPANE: Stuart Damon; POLYTE-LE-MOU, A MEC: Fred Gwynne, *Vincent Beck*; POLICE INSPECTOR: George S. Irving; NESTOR-LE-FRIPE, A LAW STUDENT: Keith Michell (2) ☆; M. BOUGNE, A BALLROOM OWNER: George Del Monte; COUNSEL FOR THE PROSECUTION: Rico Froehlich; COUNSEL FOR THE DEFENSE: Rudy Tronto; AN USHER: Elliott Gould; AN HONEST MAN: Joe Rocco; COURT GENDARME: Byron Mitchell; 1ST WARDER: Elliott Gould; 2ND WARDER: George Del Monte; 3RD WARDER: Rico Froehlich; A PRIEST: Elliott Gould; A TAX INSPECTOR: Rudy Tronto; GENDARMES/PRISONERS/IRMA'S ADMIRERS: George Del Monte, Michael Fesco, Rico Froehlich, Eddie Gasper, Elliott Gould, Byron Mitchell, Rudy Tronto. *Standby*: Irma: Virginia Vestoff. *Act I*: *Scene 1* Outside the Bar-des-Inquiets, Pigalle: "Valse Milieu" (Bob); *Scene 2* Inside the bar: "Sons of France" (Mecs, Polyte, Police Inspector) [in the London production it was called "Tres Tres Snob"], "The Bridge of Caulaincourt" (Irma & Nestor); *Scene 3* Irma's room: "Our Language of Love" (Irma & Nestor) [the main song]; *Scene 4* The Pont Caulaincourt (Hotel Rapid in the background): "She's Got the Lot" (Police Inspector & Irma's Admirers); *Scene 5* Hotel rapid — bedroom:

"Our Language of Love" (reprise) (Irma); *Scene 6* The bar: "Dis-Donc (Dis-Donc)" (Irma), "Le Grisbi is le Root of le Evil in Man" (Bob, Nestor, Mecs); *Scene 7* Hotel Rapid; *Scene 8* Nestor and Irma's room: "Wreck of a Mec" (Nestor); *Scene 9* Narrow street: "That's a Crime" (Bob, Nestor, Mecs); *Scene 10* The banks of the Seine; *Scene 11* The bar. *Act II*: *Scene 1* A law court: "The Bridge of Caulaincourt" (reprise) (Irma & Nestor); *Scene 2* Prison ship: "From a Prison Cell" (Nestor & Mecs); *Scene 3* Street outside Irma's house: "Irma-la-Douce" (Irma); *Scene 4* Devil's Island: "There is Only One Paris for That"— introducing: *Scene 5* The raft: "The Freedom of the Seas" (Nestor & Mecs), "Storm Ballet" ("Arctic Ballet") (includes "Fever Dance") (Irma & Company); *Scene 6* A Paris street: "There is Only One Paris for That" (reprise) (Nestor & Mecs), "Our Language of Love" (reprise) (Irma); *Scene 7* The police station: "But" (Nestor, Police Inspector, Tax Inspector, Bougne, Polyte); *Scene 8* The street: *Scene 9* Irma's room: Finale: "Christmas Child" (Company).

It got raves, and Elizabeth Seal won a Tony. It was also nominated for musical, direction of a musical, choreography, costumes (musical), musical direction, and for Clive Revill.

After Broadway. TOUR. Opened on 1/4/62, at the Colonial Theatre, Boston. MUSICAL DIRECTOR: Don Pippin. *Cast*: IRMA: Taina Elg; NESTOR: Denis Quilley; BOB: Joseph Bova.

THE MOVIE. 1963. PRODUCER/DIRECTOR: Billy Wilder. All songs were removed, but Andre Previn adapted Marguerite Monnot's music as incidental music (he won an Oscar). *Cast*: NESTOR: Jack Lemmon; IRMA: Shirley MacLaine; HIPPOLYTE: Bruce Yarnell.

PAPER MILL PLAYHOUSE, New Jersey, 1963. DIRECTOR: Don Driver. *Cast*: Genevieve, Gabriel Dell, Igors Gavon.

MEXICO CITY, 1964. *Irma la Dulce*. DIRECTOR: Enrique Rambal. *Cast*: Silvia Pinal.

ITALY. After a successful tour that had begun in 6/97 in Trieste, the new Italian production of *Irma la dolce* (translated by Roberto Cavosi) ran at the TEATRO SISTINA, Rome, 3/17/98–4/12/98. DIRECTOR: Antonio Calenda; CHOREOGRAPHER: Marco Ierva; MUSICAL DIRECTOR: Germano Mazzocchetti. *Cast*: IRMA: Daniela Giovanetti; NESTOR: Fabio Camilli; COUTEAU: Paolo Triestino; BOB: Gian.

VOLKSTHEATER, Vienna, 3/31/98. Previews from 3/28/98. NEW GERMAN LYRICS: Lida Winiewicz; DIRECTOR: J. Michael Fields; MUSICAL DIRECTOR: Bernhard Van Ham. *Cast*: IRMA: Nicole Ansari; NESTOR: Ludwig Hirsch.

342. *Is There Life After High School?*

Adult memories of high school days.

Before Broadway. The world premiere of this show was at HARTFORD, CONN., on 4/10/81. PRESENTED BY the Hartford Stage Company; DIRECTOR: Melvin Bernhardt; CHOREOGRAPHER: Nora Peterson; SETS: John Lee Beatty; COSTUMES: Jess Goldstein; LIGHTING: Spencer Mosse; MUSICAL DIRECTOR/ORCHESTRATIONS: Bruce Coughlin. *Cast*: Raymond Baker, Susan Bigelow, Roger Chapman, Joel Colodner, David Patrick Kelly, Elizabeth Lathram, Michael McCormick, Maureen Silliman. *Act I*: "The Kid Inside," "Things I Learned in High School," "Second Thoughts," "Nothing Really Happened," "Beer," "For Them," "Shove It," "Diary of a Homecoming Queen." *Act II*: "Thousands of Trumpets," "I'm Glad You Didn't Know Me," "Reunion," "The School Song".

The Broadway Run. ETHEL BARRYMORE THEATRE, 5/7/82–5/16/82. 41 previews. 12 PERFORMANCES. PRESENTED BY Clive Davis, Francois de Menil, Harris Maslansky, 20th Century–Fox Theatre Productions; MUSIC/LYRICS: Craig Carnelia; BOOK: Jeffrey Kindley; SUGGESTED BY the book of the same title by Ralph Keyes; DIRECTOR: Robert Nigro; CHOREOGRAPHER: Larry Fuller (name removed from credits by Broadway opening night); SETS: John Lee Beatty; COSTUMES: Carol Oditz; LIGHTING: Beverly Emmons; SOUND: Tom Morse; MUSICAL DIRECTOR/ORCHESTRATIONS: Bruce Coughlin; PRESS: Jeffrey Richards Associates; CASTING: Shirley Rich; GENERAL MANAGER: James Walsh; COMPANY MANAGER: Susan Bell; PRODUCTION STAGE MANAGER: Robert D. Currie; STAGE MANAGER: Bernard Pollock; ASSISTANT STAGE MANAGER: Gerald M. Teijelo Jr. *Cast*: Raymond Baker, Philip Hoffman, Cynthia Carle, David Patrick Kelly, Alma Cuervo, Maureen Silliman,

Sandy Faison, James Widdoes, Harry Groener. *Understudies*: Scott Bakula, Marcus Olson, Lauren White. *Musicians:* ELECTRIC KEYBOARDS: Edward Strauss; DRUMS: James Ogden; GUITARS: Brian Koonin & Scott Kuney; CELLI: Laurence Lenske & Eugene Moye; BASS: Harry Max; PERCUSSION: Eric Cohen. *Act I*: "The Kid Inside" (Company), "Things I Learned in High School" (Mr. Groener), "Second Thoughts" (Mr. Baker, Miss Faison, Mr. Kelly, Miss Silliman, Mr. Widdoes), "Nothing Really Happened" (Miss Cuervo & Women), "Beer" (Messrs Baker, Groener, Kelly), "For Them" (Mr. Hoffman & Company), "Diary of a Homecoming Queen" (Miss Silliman). *Act II*: "Thousands of Trumpets" (Mr. Widdoes & Company). DRUM MAJOR: Harry Groener; "Reunion" (Company), "High School All Over Again" (Mr. Kelly), "Fran and Janie" (Miss Faison & Miss Silliman), "I'm Glad You Didn't Know Me" (Miss Carle & Mr. Hoffman).

It got terrible reviews.

343. *It Ain't Nothin' But the Blues*

A musical revue. A history of the blues from Africa to the present day.

Before Broadway. This show was first produced by the DENVER CENTER THEATRE COMPANY, 3/17/95. It sold out. It had the same basic crew as for the subsequent Broadway run, except SETS: Andrew V. Yelusic; SOUND: David R. White. *Cast*: Mississippi Charles Bevel, Lita Gaithers, Eloise Laws, Chic Street Man (i.e. Charles Streetman), Ron Taylor, Laura Theodore, Dan Wheetman. There was a special production at the CLEVELAND PLAY HOUSE as part of their 1995–96 season, to coincide with the opening of the Rock 'n Roll Hall of Fame in Cleveland. It sold out. Same basic crew as for Broadway, except SETS: Andrew V. Yelusic. *Cast*: Mississippi Charles Bevel, Carter Calvert, Lita Gaithers, Eloise Laws, Chic Street Man, Ron Taylor, Dan Wheetman. It next played at the ARENA STAGE THEATRE, Washington, DC, 11/20/96–1/19/97. It sold out. It had the same basic crew as for the later Broadway run, except SETS: Andrew V. Yelusic; SOUND: Timothy Thompson. It had the same cast as in Cleveland. SAN DIEGO REPERTORY COMPANY produced it, 9/19/98–10/25/98, and this began a national tour (originally scheduled for 9 months). It had the same basic crew and cast as before. It also ran at the ALABAMA SHAKESPEARE FESTIVAL. It first ran in New York at the NEW VICTORY THEATRE, 3/26/99–4/11/99. Previews from 3/17/99. 16 PERFORMANCES. PRESENTED BY New 42nd Street, Inc. PRODUCED BY the Crossroads Theatre Company, in association with the San Diego Repertory Theatre, and the Alabama Shakespeare Festival. Again, it sold out. Certain Act I numbers were dropped after this run: "Gabrielle" (m/l: Dan Wheetman) (Dan & Ron), "Goin' to Louisianne" (m/l: Ron Taylor) (Ron), "How Can I Keep from Singing?" (traditional) (Carter), "Go Tell it on the Mountain" (traditional) (Eloise).

The Broadway Run. VIVIAN BEAUMONT THEATRE, 4/26/99–8/29/99; AMBASSADOR THEATRE, 9/9/99–1/9/00. 5 previews from 4/22/99. Total of 276 PERFORMANCES. The Crossroads Theatre Company, San Diego Repertory Theatre & Alabama Shakespeare Festival production, PRESENTED BY Eric Krebs, Jonathan Reinis, Lawrence Horowitz, Anita Waxman, Elizabeth Williams, CTM Productions, and Anne Squadron, in association with Lincoln Center Theatre; WRITERS: Mississippi Charles Bevel, Lita Gaithers, Randal Myler, Ron Taylor, Dan Wheetman; BASED ON an original idea by Ron Taylor; DIRECTOR: Randal Myler; MOVEMENT: Donald McKayle; SETS: Robin Sanford Roberts; COSTUMES: unbilled; LIGHTING: Don Darnutzer; SOUND: Edward Cosla; MUSICAL DIRECTOR: Dan Wheetman; VOCAL DIRECTOR: Lita Gaithers; CAST RECORDING on MCA, made live at the Vivian Beaumont, 8/26/99 & 27/99, and released in 11/99; PRESS: James L.L. Morrison & Associates; GENERAL MANAGEMENT: Eric Krebs Theatrical Management; COMPANY MANAGER: Bob Reilly; PRODUCTION STAGE MANAGER: Doug Hosney; STAGE MANAGER: Mark C. Sharp. *Cast*: "Mississippi" Charles Bevel (until 8/29/99; *Lawrence Clayton* from 9/9/99), Gretha Boston, Carter Calvert (until 8/29/99; *Christiane Noll* from 9/9/99), Gregory Porter, Eloise Laws (until 8/29/99; *Debra Laws* [Eloise's sister] from 9/9/99; *Ann Duquesnay*), Ron Taylor (until 6/11/99; *C.E. Smith* from 6/11/99, during Mr. Taylor's illness; *Ken Page* from 7/1/99, during latter part of

Mr. Taylor's illness; *Ron Taylor* 8/24/99–8/29/99; *Ken Page* from 9/9/99), Dan Wheetman (until 8/29/99; *Sean McCourt* from 9/9/99). *Understudies*: Gretha/Carter/Eloise: Debra Laws; Ron: C.E. Smith; Others: Cheryl Alexander. *The Band*: BASS: Kevin Cooper; KEYBOARDS: Jim Ehinger; BACKUP VOCALS: Debra Laws; GUITAR: Tony Mathews; SAX/HORNS: Charlie Rhythm; PERCUSSION: Daryll Whitlow. *Act I*: "Odun De" (traditional) (Company), "Niwah Wechi" (Eloise & Company), "Blood Done Signed My Name" (traditional) (Ron & Gretha), "Raise Them up Higher" (traditional) (Mississippi), "Danger Blues" (traditional) (Eloise), "Black Woman" (traditional) (Gregory), "I'm Gonna Do What the Spirit Says Do" (traditional) (Gretha), "I've Been Living with the Blues" (m/l: Sonny Terry & Brownie McGhee) (Company), "Blues Man" (m/l: Z.Z. "Arzelle" Hill) (Ron), "My Home's Across the Blue Ridge Mountains" (traditional) (Carter), "'T' for Texas" (m/l: Jimmie Rodgers) (Dan), "Who Broke the Lock?" (traditional) (Gregory & Mississippi), "My Man Rocks Me" (traditional) (Eloise), "St. Louis Blues" (m/l: W.C. Handy) (Gretha), "Now I'm Gonna Be Bad" (m/l: Dan Wheetman) (Carter), "Walking Blues" (m/l: Robert L. Johnson) (Mississippi), "Come on in My Kitchen" (m/l: Robert L. Johnson) (Gregory), "Cross Road Blues" (m/l: Robert L. Johnson) (Mississippi), "I Know I've Been Changed" (traditional) (Gretha), "Child of the Most High King" (traditional; arr: Ron Taylor) (Ron & Men), "Children, Your Line is Dragging" (traditional; arr: Fisher Thompson Sr.) (Gregory), "Catch on Fire" (traditional; arr: Lita Gaithers) (Company). *Act II*: "Let the Good Times Roll" (m/l: Sam Theard & Fleecie Moore) (Ron), "Sweet Home Chicago" (m/l: Robert L. Johnson) (Gregory & Mississippi), "Wang Dang Doodle" (m/l: Willie Dixon) (Gretha, Carter, Eloise), "Someone Else is Steppin' In" (m/l: Denise La Salle) (Eloise), "Please Don't Stop Him" (m/l: Herb J. Lance & John Wallace; add l/arr: Lita Gaithers) (Gretha), "I'm Your Hoochie Coochie Man" (m/l: Willie Dixon; arr: Ron Taylor) (Ron), "Crawlin' King Snake" (m/l: John Lee Hooker) (Gregory), "Mind Your Own Business" (m/l: Hank Williams) (Dan), "Walking After Midnight" (m: Alan Block; l: Don Hect) (Carter), "I Can't Stop Lovin' You" (m/l: Don Gibson) (Mississippi), "The Thrill is Gone" (m/l: Roy Hawkins & Rick Darnell) (Ron), "I Put a Spell on You" (m/l: Screaming Jay Hawkins) (Eloise), "Fever" (m/l: John Davenport & Eddie Cooley) (Carter), "Candy Man" (traditional) (Dan), "Goodnight, Irene" (m/l: Huddie Ledbetter ["Leadbelly"] & John Lomax; arr: Chic Street Man) (Mississippi & Dan), "Strange Fruit" (m/l: Lewis Allan) (Gretha), "Someday We'll All Be Free" (m/l: Donny Hathaway & Edward Howard; arr by Mississippi Charles Bevel) (Mississippi & Gregory), "Members Only" (m/l: Larry Addison; arr by Ron Taylor) (Company), "Let the Good Times Roll (reprise) (Company).

Broadway reviews were divided, and attendance at the Vivian Beaumont was never much. The show received Tony nominations for musical, book, and for Ron Taylor and Gretha Boston. There was a fuss at the Tonys (the musical had taken the trouble to do two production numbers for the televised awards ceremony, numbers which would give them great publicity; then they were cut when the Tonys program threatened to run overtime). However, because of this lapse, they did get a lot of sympathetic press. On 6/11/99 Ron Taylor had a mild stroke which put him out of the show until 8/24/99 (he had been scheduled to come back on 7/27/99, but wasn't ready). His understudy, C.E. Smith, went on, until he (Mr. Smith) was replaced by Ken Page on 7/1/99 (Mr. Page, scheduled to leave 7/25/99, had to stay on until late August, until Ron Taylor got back). On 7/2/99 it was announced that the show would be leaving the Vivian Beaumont on 8/29/99 and going to the Ambassador on 9/8/99 (it was actually 9/9/99). Ron Taylor left at the end of the Vivian Beaumont run to open up the West Coast production, and Ken Page came back to see out the run at the Ambassador. On 12/3/99 it was announced that the Broadway run would be ending on 1/9/00 (despite the fact that 2/2/00 had been rumored as a closing date), with a national tour to follow.

After Broadway. GEFFEN PLAYHOUSE, Los Angeles, 11/21/99–2/2/00. Previews from 11/13/99. This was the West Coast premiere. It had the same basic crew as for the Broadway run, except COSTUMES: Alex Jaeger; SOUND: Jon Gottlieb. Even before it opened it was a hit, and extended its closing date from 12/19/99 to 2/2/00 (it had to leave then because *Wit* was coming in). *Cast*: Eloise Laws, Ron Taylor, Dan Wheetman, Jewel Tompkins, Billy Valentine, Janiva Magness, Kingsley Leggs, Mark Leroy Jackson.

TOUR. This was a streamlined, 90-minute version (20 minutes had been cut), without an intermission, and ran successfully at the Kennedy Center, Washington, DC, 6/20/00–7/30/00. Then it went to the Fox Theatre, Atlanta, where the tour officially began, on 8/1/00. PRESENTED BY Eric Krebs; DIRECTOR: Randal Myler; MUSICAL DIRECTOR: Jim Ehinger. *Cast:* Mississippi Charles Bevel, Gregory Porter, Carter Calvert, Cheryl Alexander, Michael Mandell (the Ron Taylor role), Charles Weldon, *Debra Laws, Scott Wakefield, Kelli Rabke, Horace V. Rogers.* At the same time the tour made a deal with the 450-seat B.B. King Blues Club & Grill, Manhattan, where, as its base, it would have an open-ended run, six shows a week, Sunday to Wednesday. From Thursday to Saturday the company toured the country and sometimes didn't get back to New York for its nightclub stints (this arrangement was part of the deal, and was something of a first in the annals of the American theatre). It wound up running at B.B. KING'S, 8/28/00–11/12/00. 11 previews from 8/20/00. 37 PERFORMANCES.

344. *"It's a Bird ... It's a Plane ... It's Superman"*

A musical about the famous comic strip character. Sedgwick, a ten-time Nobel Prize–loser and villainous nuclear scientist, forms a plan to gain notoriety — to unmask and overcome Superman, with the help of Max, a *Daily Planet* columnist who resents Lois's attraction to Superman. The chink they find is that Superman needs to be loved. Set in Metropolis, USA, at the present time.

Before Broadway. In 1964 Charles Strouse & Lee Adams and David Newman & Robert Benton got together to write a musical. Benton & Newman came up with the idea of Superman, and all four men wrote the show together. David Merrick was going to produce, but backed out. Hal Prince agreed to produce and direct. At first it was called *It's Superman!* This was the first time Ruth Mitchell had been Hal Prince's co-producer. Until then she'd been his production stage manager. The show opened at the Shubert Theatre, in Philadelphia, on 2/15/66, and got bad reviews. Pat Marand replaced Joan Hotchkiss. Hal Prince had problems with Jack Cassidy.

The Broadway Run. ALVIN THEATRE, 3/29/66–7/17/66. 19 previews from 3/9/66. 129 PERFORMANCES. PRESENTED BY Harold Prince, in association with Ruth Mitchell; MUSIC: Charles Strouse; LYRICS: Lee Adams; BOOK: David Newman & Robert Benton; BASED ON Jerry Siegel & Joe Shuster's comic strip *Superman* (which first appeared in 1938 in *Detective Comics*); DIRECTOR: Harold Prince; CHOREOGRAPHER: Ernest Flatt; SETS/LIGHTING: Robert Randolph; COSTUMES: Florence Klotz; SOUND: Jack Mann; MUSICAL DIRECTOR: Harold Hastings; ORCHESTRATIONS: Eddie Sauter; DANCE MUSIC ARRANGEMENTS: Betty Walberg; CAST RECORDING on Columbia; PRESS: Mary Bryant & Robert Pasolli; CASTING: Shirley Rich; FILMED SEQUENCES BY: MPO Pictures, Inc.; GENERAL MANAGER: Carl Fisher; PRODUCTION STAGE MANAGER: Ruth Mitchell; STAGE MANAGER: Ben Strobach; ASSISTANT STAGE MANAGER: Nicholas G. Rinaldi. *Cast:* SUPERMAN/CLARK KENT: Bob Holiday (2); MAX MENCKEN: Jack Cassidy (1) ☆; LOIS LANE: Patricia Marand (4); PERRY WHITE: Eric Mason; SYDNEY, SECRETARY AT THE *Daily Planet*: Linda Lavin (6); DR. ABNER SEDGWICK: Michael O'Sullivan (3); JIM MORGAN: Don Chastain (5); THE FLYING LINGS: (7): FATHER LING: Jerry Fujikawa; DONG LING: Bill Starr; TAI LING: Murphy James; FAN PO LING: Juleste Salve; MING FOO LING: Michael Gentry; JOE LING: Joseph Gentry; THE SUSPECTS: 1: Les Freed; 2: Dick Miller; 3: Dal Richards; 4: John Grigas; 5: John Smolko; CITIZENS OF METROPOLIS: BYRON, THE BANK GUARD: Eugene Edwards; HARVEY, THE TOUR GUIDE: Bob Scherkenbach, *Dallas Edmunds*; BONNIE, THE MOLL: April Nevins; SUE-ELLEN, THE TEENAGER: Tina Faye; MARNIE, THE MODEL: Judy Newman; GORDON, THE STUDENT: Bick Goss; ANNETTE, THE SECRETARY: Michelle Barry; WANDA, THE WAITRESS: Gay Edmond, *Barbara Christopher*; ROSALIE, THE HIGH SCHOOL GIRL: Marilyne Mason; LESLIE, THE SHOPPER: Jayme Mylroie; CATHY, THE CHILD: Lori Browne; BARBIE, THE RECEPTIONIST: Mara Landi; AL, THE BANK ROBBER: George Bunt; MIL-

TON, THE HOOD: Dallas Edmunds; KEVIN, THE COLLEGE BOY: Roy Smith; WILLIAM, THE EXCHANGE STUDENT: Haruki Fujimoto. **Standby:** Superman: John Smolko, *Seth Riggs.* **Understudies:** Max: Dick Miller, *Mace Barrett*; Sedgwick: Dal Richards, *Anthony Holland*; Lois: Marilyne Mason; Jim: Eric Mason; Sydney: Jayme Mylroie; The Flying Lings: Haruki Fujimoto & Roy Smith; Father Ling: Juleste Salve; *Swing Girl*: Diane McAfee. *Act I:* *Scene 1* Outside the Chase — Metropolis Bank: "Doing Good" (Superman), "We Need Him" (Max, Lois, Clark, Company); *Scene 2* The offices of the *Daily Planet*: "It's Superman" (Lois); *Scene 3* A telephone booth; *Scene 4* The nuclear reactor at Metropolis Institute of Technology: "We Don't Matter at All" (Jim & Lois), "Revenge" (Sedgwick); *Scene 5* The offices of the *Daily Planet*: "The Woman for the Man (Who Has Everything)" (Max), "You've Got Possibilities" (Sydney); *Scene 6* Dr. Sedgwick's study; *Scene 7* The screening room: "What I've Always Wanted" (Lois), "Revenge" (reprise) (Sedgwick); *Scene 8* Dr. Sedgwick's home: "Everything's Easy When You Know How" (The Flying Lings); *Scene 9* The offices of the *Daily Planet*: *Scene 10* Atop City Hall Tower; *Scene 11* The M.I.T. dedication grounds: "It's Super Nice" (Company). *Act II:* *Scene 1* The front page; one week later: "So Long, Big Guy" (Max); *Scene 2* Clark Kent's apartment: "The Strongest Man in the World" (Superman); *Scene 3* A street in Metropolis: "Ooh, Do You Love You!" (Sydney); *Scene 4* Dr. Sedgwick's laboratory: "You've Got What I Need (Baby)" (Max & Sedgwick); *Scene 5* Meanwhile: "It's Superman" (reprise) (Company); *Scene 6* An abandoned power station outside Metropolis; *Scene 7* The power station; next morning: "I'm Not Finished Yet" (Lois), "Pow! Bam! Zonk!" (Superman & The Flying Lings).

The show opened on Broadway with $100,000 advance in sales. Ticket prices ranged from $12 (orchestra) to $2 (balcony). Reviews were mostly favorable. The show received Tony nominations for Jack Cassidy, Michael O'Sullivan, and Patricia Marand. The show failed for three reasons: it had taken 13 months to write, and by the time it came out the pop-art craze, which had barely started when this musical's concept began, had had its run, and the show now seemed a little outdated. It failed partly because *Batman* was running on TV at the time, but mostly because the show was, in effect, really only a cartoon and thus we didn't care about the characters. The show was capitalized at $400,000 (it would lose it all).

After Broadway. GOODSPEED OPERA HOUSE, Conn., 1992. DIRECTOR: Stuart Ross; CHOREOGRAPHER: Michele Assaf; SETS: Neil Peter Jampolis; MUSICAL DIRECTOR: Michael O'Flaherty. *Cast:* CLARK KENT: Gary Jackson; LOIS: Kay McClelland; MAX: Jamie Ross; PERRY: Michael E. Gold; SEDGWICK: Gabriel Barre; SUPERMAN: Himself.

TV. 2/21/75. ABC *Wide World of Entertainment* presented a TV version of the musical, with much of the music cut. *Cast:* CLARK: David Wilson; LOIS: Lesley Ann Warren; SEDGWICK: David Wayne; MAX: Ken Mars; SYDNEY: Loretta Swit.

345. *It's So Nice to Be Civilized*

Set on Sweetbitter Street over a weekend in late summer. The lives and loves of the folks in a city neighborhood.

Before Broadway. This show was first produced as an Off Broadway showcase, by the AMAS REPERTORY COMPANY, 2/22/79–3/11/79. 12 PERFORMANCES. DIRECTOR: Jeffrey Dunn; CHOREOGRAPHER: Fred Benjamin; SETS: Patrick Mann; LIGHTING: Paul Sullivan; COSTUMES: Bill Baldwin; MUSICAL SUPERVISOR/ARRANGEMENTS: Danny Holgate; CHORAL DIRECTOR/ARRANGEMENTS: Chapman Roberts; CONDUCTOR: William "Gregg" Hunter; STAGE MANAGERS: Carolyn Greer & Gwendolyn M. Gilliam. *Cast:* Charles Berry, Karen G. Burke, David Cahn, Claudine Cassan, Jean Cheek, Kevin De Voe, Eugene Edwards, Joey Ginza, Dwayne Grayman, Paul Harman, Sundy Leake, Carol Lynn Maillard, Brenda Mitchell, Ennis Smith, Cassie Stein, Diane Wilson. "Step into My World," "Wake Up Sun," "Subway Rider," "God Help Us," "Who's Gonna Teach the Children?," "Out on the Street," "Welcome Anderson," "Why Can't Me and You?," "When I Rise," "Up Front Behind," "Walkin' the Dog," "I Want to Be Your Congressman," "Everybody's Got a Pitch," "Terrible Tuesday," "Come Back Baby," "Alice,"

"It's So Nice to Be Civilized," "The World Keeps Going Round," "Talking to People," "Old Things," "I've Still Got My Bite," "Look at Us," "Jun-Jub," "Bright Lights," "Like a Lady," "Me and Jesus," "Pass a Little Love Around".

The Broadway Run. MARTIN BECK THEATRE, 6/3/80–6/8/80. 23 previews. 8 PERFORMANCES. PRESENTED BY Jay Julien, Arnon Milchan, and Larry Kalish; MUSIC/LYRICS/BOOK: Micki Grant; DIRECTOR: Frank Corsaro; CHOREOGRAPHER: Mabel Robinson; SETS/VISUALS: Charles E. Hoefler; COSTUMES: Ruth Morley; LIGHTING: Charles E. Hoefler & Ralph Madero; SOUND: Palmer Shannon; MUSICAL DIRECTOR: Coleridge-Taylor Perkinson; ORCHESTRATIONS: Danny Holgate & Neal Tate; CHORAL ARRANGEMENTS: Tasha Thomas; DANCE MUSIC ARRANGEMENTS: Carl Maultsby; PRESS: The Merlin Group; CASTING: June Archibald; GENERAL MANAGER: John Larson; PRODUCTION STAGE MANAGER: Jack Gianino; STAGE MANAGER: Carolyn Greer; ASSISTANT STAGE MANAGER: Paul Harman. **Cast:** SHARKY: Obba Babatunde (3) ✩; MOLLIE: Vivian Reed (2) ✩; LARRY: Larry Stewart; SISSY: Vickie D. Chappell; LUANNE: Carol Lynn Maillard; GRANDMA: Mabel King (1) ✩; MR. ANDERSON: Stephen Pender; BLADE: Dan Strayhorn; REV. WILLIAMS: Eugene Edwards; MOTHER: Deborah Burrell; DANCING BAG LADY: Juanita Grace Tyler; ENSEMBLE: Daria Atanian, Paul Binotto, Sharon K. Brooks, P.L. Brown, Jean Cheek, Vondie Curtis-Hall, Paul Harman, Esther Marrow, Wellington Perkins, Dwayne Phelps, Juanita Grace Tyler. **Understudies**: Grandma: Jean Cheek; Mollie: Esther Marrow; Sharky/Larry/Blade: Vondie Curtis-Hall; LuAnne: Deborah Burrell; Rev. Williams: P.L. Brown; Joe/Anderson: Paul Harman; Bag Lady: Allison Renee Manson; Mother/Sissy: Sharon K. Brooks. **Dance Alternatives:** Renee Manson & Steiv Semien. **Act I:** "Step into My World" (Ensemble), "Keep Your Eye on the Red" (Sharky), "Wake-Up, Sun" (Sharky & Mollie), "Subway Rider" (Ensemble), "God Help Us" (Larry & LuAnne), "Who's Going to Teach the Children?" (Grandma), "Out on the Street" (Ensemble), "Welcome, Mr. Anderson" (Blade & Hawks), "Why Can't Me and You?" (Mr. Anderson), "Why Can't Me and You?" (reprise) (Sissy & Mr. Anderson), "Out on the Street" (reprise) (Ensemble), "When I Rise" (Rev. Williams), "The World Keeps Going Round" (Mollie & Ensemble). **Act II:** "Antiquity" (Ensemble), "I've Still Got My Bite" (Grandma), "Look at Us" (Larry & LuAnne), "Keep Your Eye on the Red" (reprise) (Sharky), "The American Dream" (Mr. Anderson), "Bright Lights" (Mollie), "Step into My World" (reprise) (Sharky & Mollie), "It's So Nice to Be Civilized" (Mr. Anderson, Sissy, Hawks), "Like a Lady" (Mollie), "Pass a Little Love Around" (Ensemble).

Reviews were bad.

346. *Jackpot*

Three marines, Jerry, Winkie and Hank, combine to buy a war bond in a lucky number contest, the prize being $50,000 and Sally Madison, a pretty defense worker. They win. They try to divide her up, but it can't be done. After two hours Hank, the baritone, marries Sally, and the other two get two other girls (Nancy and Sgt. Maguire).

The Broadway Run. Alvin Theatre, 1/13/44–3/11/44. 69 performances. Presented by Vinton Freedley; MUSIC: Vernon Duke; LYRICS: Howard Dietz; BOOK: Guy Bolton, Sidney Sheldon, Ben Roberts; DIRECTOR: Roy Hargrave; CHOREOGRAPHER: Lauretta Jefferson; ASSISTANT CHOREOGRAPHER: Don Liberto; BALLET STAGED BY: Charles Weidman; SETS: Raymond Sovey & Robert Edmond Jones; COSTUMES: Kiviette; SOUND CONSULTANT: Saki Oura; MUSICAL DIRECTOR: Max Meth; ORCHESTRAL ARRANGEMENTS: Hans Spialek, Ted Royal, Russell Bennett, Vernon Duke; VOCAL ARRANGEMENTS: Buck (i.e. Clay) Warnick; PRESS: Karl N. Bernstein; STAGE MANAGER: William Johnson. **Cast:** PEGGY: Althea Elder; BILLIE: Billie Worth; MR. DILL: Morton L. Stevens; BILL BENDER: Ben Lackland; NANCY PARKER: Mary Wickes (5); SALLY MADISON: Nanette Fabray (4); DEXTER DE WOLF: Houston Richards; Edna: Jacqueline Susanne; HEDY: Helena Goudvis; HAWLEY: John Kearny; ASSISTANT BARTENDER: Walter Monroe; JERRY FINCH: Jerry Lester (2); Winkie Cotter: Benny Baker (3); HANK TRIMBLE: Allan Jones (1) ✩; GIRL: Flower Hujer; REPORTER: Bill Jones; TOT PATTERSON: Althea

Elder; SGT. NAYLOR: Wendell Corey; SGT. MAGUIRE: Betty Garrett (6); HELEN WESTCOTT: Frances Robinson; SNIPER: Bob Beam; 1ST MARINE: John Hamil (later Hamill); 2ND MARINE: Bill Jones; Edith: Edith Turgell; ACCORDIONIST: Eva Barcinska; MONICA: Drucilla Strain; PAT: Pat Ogden; BETTY: Betty Stuart; SHERRY: Sherry Shadburne; MARY LOU: Marie Louise Meade; CONNIE: Connie Constant; NURSE: Billie Worth; HOSTESSES: Cece Eames, Virginia Barnes, Diane Chase, Jean Cooke, Billie Dee, Marion Harvey, Marion Lulling, Edith Laumer, Dorothy G. Thomas, Dorothy Matthews, Aileen Reed, Ellen Taylor, Sally Tepley, Edith Turgell, Jeanne C. Tryborn, Lorraine Todd, Georgina E. Yeager; VOCALISTS: Fague Springman, Robert Beam, George Frank, Mario Pichler, Bill Jones, Michael Kozak, Roger E. Miller, John Hamil; OTHER MARINES: Ray Cook, Lawrence Evers, Bob Ferguson, T.C. Jones, Walter Koremin, Jack McCaffrey, Robert Sullivan, Joe Wismak, Frank Westbrook. **Act I:** *Scene 1* Assembly room of the Duff and Dill Engine Corporation; *Scene 2* Hawley's bar; *Scene 3* A broadcasting studio; *Scene 4* Recreation room, Priscilla Manor, Turtle Beach, SC; *Scene 5* A cornfield; *Scene 6* The recreation room. **Act II:** *Scene 1* Garden of the Priscilla Manor; *Scene 2* Bedroom of the bridal suite; *Scene 3* The balcony; *Scene 4* Garden of the Manor; the next day. **Act I:** "The Last Long Mile" (Sally, Peggy, Billie, Factory Workers), "Blind Date" (Sally & Workers), "I Kissed My Girl Goodbye" (Hank & Marines), "A Piece of a Girl" (Hank, Jerry, Winkie), "My Top Sergeant" (Jerry, Maguire, Boys), "Sugar Foot" (Maguire, Nancy, Jerry, Winkie, Ensemble) [Specialty dance—Don Liberto], "I Kissed My Girl Goodbye" (reprise) (Marines), "What Happened?" (Sally & Hank), "Sugar Foot" (reprise) (Maguire, Jerry, Winkie), "Grist for de Mille" (staged by Charles Weidman) (Nancy & Ensemble): Spoof of Agnes de Mille's choreography; COWBOY: Peter Hamilton; NYMPH: Florence Lessing; FLOWER GIRL: Flower Hujer. **Act II:** Opening (Eva Barcinska), "He's Good for Nothing but Me" (staged by Charles Weidman) (Maguire & Ensemble) [Dancers—Don Liberto, Billie Worth, Althea Elder], "What's Mine is Yours" (Jerry & Winkie), "What Happened?" (reprise) (Hank), "It was Nice Knowing You" (Sally & Hank), "Nobody Ever Pins Me Up" (Nancy & Ensemble), "(I've Got a) One Track Mind" (Hank) [Danced by Florence Lessing & Peter Hamilton], "There Are Yanks" (Maguire & Ensemble), Finale (Entire Company).

It was panned. The offensive jokes were taken out after the first week. It lost a lot of money (it cost $170,000).

347. *Jacques Brel Is Alive and Well and Living in Paris*

For obvious reasons this musical entertainment is generally referred to as *Jacques Brel*. It is actually a cabaret revue (with no plot) using adaptations of songs by Belgian composer Jacques Brel.

Before Broadway. THE FIRST AMERICAN PRODUCTION. This was the famous run of *Jacques Brel*, the long run, Off Broadway, at the VILLAGE GATE THEATRE, 1/22/68–7/2/72. 1,847 PERFORMANCES. PRESENTED BY 3W Prods. It had the same crew as for the later Broadway run, except SETS: Henry E. Scott III; STAGE MANAGER: James Nisbet Clark. Jacques Brel attended the production two years after it opened (he had refused to come to the USA in protest over the Vietnam War. He died in 1978, aged 49). To celebrate the fifth year a gala performance was given in CARNEGIE HALL, on 1/25/72. It was Off Broadway's fourth-longest-running show to that time. **Off Broadway Cast:** Elly Stone, *Betty Rhodes* from 7/1/68, *Fleury D'Antonakis* from 7/24/68, *Aileen Fitzpatrick* from 8/20/68, *Elinor Elsworth* from 1/25/69, *Rita Gardner* from 4/1/69, *Joy Franz* from 6/23/70, *Barbara Gutterman* from 11/24/70 [Elly Stone took this role on Broadway]; Mort Shuman, *Robert Guillaume* (from 5/31/68), *Joe Masiell* (from 6/22/68), *Wayne Sherwood* (from 7/16/68), *John C. Attle* (from 8/13/68), *Jack Blackton* (from 10/8/68) [Joe Masiell took this role on Broadway]; Alice Whitfield, *June Gable* (from 5/7/68), *Chevi Colton* (from 7/1/68), *Juanita Franklin* (from 7/8/68), *Amelia Haas* from 7/30/68), *Denise LeBrun* (from 8/20/68), *Sally Cooke* (from 5/11/69), *Teri Ralston* (from 5/27/69), *Margery Cohen* (from 3/10/70), *Henrietta Valor* (from 6/23/70) [Henrietta Valor took this role on Broadway];

Shawn Elliott, *Adam Stevens* (from 7/68), *Stan Porter* (from 8/1/68), *George Ball* (from 8/20/68), *Jack Eddleman* (from 9/17/68) [George Ball took this role on Broadway]. Others who appeared at some time during the run included: J.T. Cromwell (from 5/20/69), Dominic Chianese (from 5/27/69), Michael Johnson (from 5/27/69), Joe Silver (from 6/3/69), Norman Atkins (from 3/3/70), Howard Ross (from 6/16/70), Michael Vita (from 6/23/70), George Lee Andrews (from 12/26/70), Ben Bryant (from 1/9/71), Fran Uditsky (from 5/4/71), Amanda Bruce (from 6/3/71), Ted Lawrie (from 1/11/72), Janet McCall (from 5/13/72). Then it moved to Broadway.

DUCHESS THEATRE, London, 6/3/68. 41 PERFORMANCES. It had the original Off Broadway cast.

THE FIRST TOUR. Opened on 9/12/68, in Chicago. *Cast*: Alice Whitfield, Robert Guillaume, Joe Masiell, Aileen Fitzpatrick.

THE SECOND TOUR. Opened on 11/26/68, in Toronto. *Cast*: Arlene Meadows, Stan Porter, Robert Jeffrey, Judy Lander.

THE THIRD TOUR. Opened on 6/10/69, in Los Angeles. *Cast*: Elly Stone, Robert Guillaume, George Ball, June Gable.

THE FOURTH TOUR. Opened on 6/17/69, in Washington, DC. *Cast*: Fleury D'Antonakis, Stan Porter, John C. Attle, Sally Cooke.

THE FIFTH TOUR. Opened on 9/17/69, in San Francisco. *Cast*: Betty Rhodes, Robert Guillaume, George Ball, Teri Ralston.

THE SIXTH TOUR. Opened on 4/30/70, in Boston. *Cast*: Elly Stone, Stan Porter, Robert Jeffrey, Arlene Meadows, Joe Masiell, Joy Franz.

The Broadway Run. ROYALE THEATRE, 9/15/72–10/28/72. Previews from 9/13/72. Limited run of 51 performances. Presented by Bill Levine; MUSIC: Jacques Brel, Francois Rauber, Gerard Jouannest, Jean Corti; ENGLISH LYRICS/ADDITIONAL MATERIAL: Eric Blau & Mort Shuman; Based on Jacques Brel's lyrics & commentary; PRODUCTION CONCEPT: Eric Blau & Mort Shuman; DIRECTOR: Moni Yakim; SETS: Les Lawrence; COSTUMES: Ilka Suarez; LIGHTING: James Nisbet Clark; MUSICAL DIRECTOR: Mort Shuman; CONDUCTOR/ARRANGEMENTS: Wolfgang Knittel; VOCAL DIRECTOR: Lillian Strongin; Cast recording on Columbia; PRESS: Ivan Black; PRODUCTION SUPERVISOR: Eric Blau; GENERAL MANAGER: Lily Turner; PRODUCTION STAGE MANAGER: Phillip Price; ASSISTANT STAGE MANAGER: Joseph Neal. *Cast*: George Ball (3), Joe Masiell (2) ☆, Elly Stone (1) ☆, Henrietta Valor (4). Alternates: Janet McCall (5), Joseph Neal (6). *Act I*: Overture (Orchestra), "My Childhood" (Company), "Marathon" (by Blau & Brel) (Company), "Alone" (George), "Madeleine" (Company), "I Loved" (by Blau, Shuman, Jouannest) (Elly) [Alice Whitfield sang it Off Broadway], "Mathilde" (Joe), "Bachelor's Dance" (George), "Timid Frieda" (by Blau, Shuman, Brel) (Henrietta), "My Death" (Elly), "Girls and Dogs" (Joe & George), "Jackie" (by Blau, Shuman, Jouannest) (Joe), "The Statue" (George), "Desperate Ones" (by Blau, Shuman, Jouannest) (Company), "Sons of ..." (by Blau, Shuman, Jouannest) (Elly), "(Port of) Amsterdam" (by Blau, Shuman, Brel) (Joe). *Act II*: "The Bulls" (George), "Old Folks" (by Blau, Shuman, Jouannest) (Elly), "Marieke" (Elly), "Brussels" (Henrietta), "Fannette" (by Blau, Shuman, Brel) (George), "Funeral Tango" (Joe), "The Middle Class" (Joe & George), "(No, Love) You're Not Alone" (Elly), "Next" (Joe), "Carousel" ("La Valse a Mille Temps") (Elly), "If We Only Have Love" (by Blau, Shuman, Brel) (Company).

Reviews were divided.

After Broadway. POST-BROADWAY TOUR. Opened on 12/29/72, in Greenville, Pa., and closed on 4/26/73, in Nashville, after 14 cities. PRESENTED BY Wayne Adams. This production was conceived by the entire company, and assembled by Wayne Adams and Paul Plumadore; MUSICAL DIRECTOR: Mark Harelik; ARRANGEMENTS: Mark Harelik & Bill Schneider. *Cast*: Paul Baker, Mark Harelik, Shashi Musso, Dede Washburn.

THE MOVIE. 1975. *Cast:* Jacques Brel, Elly Stone (i.e. Mrs. Eric Blau), Mort Shuman, Joe Masiell.

ASTOR PLACE THEATRE, NYC, 5/17/74–9/1/74. 125 PERFORMANCES. PRESENTED BY 3W Productions & Lily Turner. It had the same basic crew as for the 1972 Broadway production, except SETS/COSTUMES: Don Jensen; LIGHTING: Ian Calderon. *Cast*: Jack Blackton, Barbara Gutterman, Stan Porter, Henrietta Valor (*Nila Greco, Teri Ralston*), Howard Ross (*J.T. Cromwell*), Ann Mortifee.

TOWN HALL, NYC, 2/19/81–3/8/81. 21 PERFORMANCES. PRESENTED BY Lily Turner Attractions; PRODUCTION SUPERVISOR: Eric Blau. *Cast*: Joe Masiell, Sally Cooke, Betty Rhodes, Shawn Elliott.

FIRST CITY, NYC, 5/15/83–6/26/83. 13 previews. 48 PERFORMANCES. PRESENTED BY Pat Productions; DIRECTOR: Eric Blau. *Cast*: Leon Bibb, Betty Rhodes, Joseph Neal, Jacqueline Reilly, J.T. Cromwell, Margery Cohen.

TOWN HALL, NYC, 1/22/88–2/12/88. 7 PERFORMANCES. The International 20th-anniversary production, PRESENTED BY Robin Hoppenstein; DIRECTOR: Elly Stone; CHOREOGRAPHER: Don Jensen; GENERAL MANAGER: Lily Turner. *Cast:* Karen Akers, Shelle Ackerman, Elmore James, Kenny Morris, Aileen Savage, Adam Bryant.

VILLAGE GATE THEATRE, NYC, 10/18/92–2/7/93. Previews from 10/1/92. 131 PERFORMANCES. This was the 25th American anniversary production. DIRECTOR: Elly Stone; MUSICAL DIRECTOR: Annie Lebeaux. *Cast:* Gabriel Barre, Andrea Green, Joseph Neal, Karen Saunders.

348. *Jamaica*

Set in the present. Life and love on mythical Pigeon Island, near Kingston, Jamaica. Poor but handsome fisherman, Koli, is content with idyllic island life. Savannah is his starry-eyed seamstress girlfriend, who wants to go to New York City; she is tempted by slick pearl dealer, Joe, from Harlem, but chooses to remain with Koli after he saves her little brother Quico during a hurricane. Two islanders, Ginger and Cicero, have always wanted to know what it would be like to rule the island, and after the hurricane they get the chance for a short time.

Before Broadway. In order to capitalize on the calypso craze, the producers wanted Harry Belafonte to star, but he became sick. So, Lena Horne, who had already agreed to be in it, was bumped up to star billing and her role expanded until she became the focus instead of the Belafonte role. David Merrick threatened to close in Boston because of the weak book, and Joseph Stein was brought in. The numbers "Sweet Wind Blowin' My Way," and "Whippoorwill" were cut before Broadway. "What Did Noah Do When the Big Wind Came?" (more commonly known as "Noah") was also cut, but re-instated during the Broadway run.

The Broadway Run. IMPERIAL THEATRE, 10/31/57–4/11/59. 558 PERFORMANCES. PRESENTED BY David Merrick; MUSIC: Harold Arlen; LYRICS: E.Y. Harburg; BOOK: E.Y. Harburg & Fred Saidy (with help from Joseph Stein, uncredited); DIRECTOR: Robert Lewis; CHOREOGRAPHER: Jack Cole; SETS: Oliver Smith; COSTUMES: Miles White; LIGHTING: Jean Rosenthal; MUSICAL DIRECTOR/CONTINUITY/VOCAL ARRANGEMENTS: Lehman Engel; ORCHESTRATIONS: Philip J. Lang; DANCE MUSIC/ADDITIONAL VOCAL ARRANGEMENTS: Peter Matz; PRESS: Harvey Sabinson & David Powers; GENERAL MANAGER: Jack Schlissel; COMPANY MANAGER: Vince McKnight; PRODUCTION STAGE MANAGER: Neil Hartley; STAGE MANAGERS: Charles Blackwell, Alan Shatne, James E. Wall. *Cast*: KOLI: Ricardo Montalban (2); QUICO: Augustine Rios; SAVANNAH: Lena Horne (1); GRANDMA OBEAH: Adelaide Hall (3); GINGER: Josephine Premice (4); SNODGRASS: Roy Thompson; HUCKLEBUCK: Hugh Dilworth; ISLAND WOMEN: Ethel Ayler & Adelaide Boatner; THE GOVERNOR: Erik Rhodes; CICERO: Ossie Davis (5); LANCASTER: James E. Wall; 1ST SHIP'S OFFICER: Tony Martinez; 2ND SHIP'S OFFICER: Michael Wright; JOE NASHUA: Joe Adams; DOCK WORKER: Allen Richards; RADIO ANNOUNCER: Alan Shayne; LEAD DANCERS: Alvin Ailey & Cristyne Lawson; ISLANDERS: Ethel Ayler, Adelaide Boatner, George Boreland, Hugh Bryant, Herb Coleman, Jayne Craddock, Hugh Dilworth, Norma Donaldson, Patricia Dunn, Doris Galiber, Frank Glass, Harold Gordon, Lavinia Hamilton, Sandra Hinton, Nat Horne, Albert Johnson, Chailendra Jones, Jim McMillan, Tony Martinez, Audrey Mason, Charles Moore, Sally Neal, Pearl Reynolds, Allen Richards, Christine Spencer, Carolyn Stanford, Claude Thompson, Roy Thompson, Ben Vargas, Jacqueline Walcott, Billy Wilson, Barbara Wright, Michael Wright. **Standbys**: Grandma: Virginia Capers; Joe: Charles Blackwell. **Understudies**: Savannah: Ethel Ayler; Koli: Hugh Bryant & Alan Shayne; Cicero: James E. Wall; Joe: Roy Thompson; Quico: Herb Coleman; Governor: Alan Shayne. *Act I*: *Scene 1* Grandma Obeah's shack; a day in spring: "Savannah" (Koli & Fishermen); *Scene 2* The knoll near Grandma's shack; next day: "Savannah's Wedding Day" (Grandma & Islanders), "Pretty to Walk With" (Savannah), "Push de Button" (Savannah) [the big song], "Incompatibility" (Koli, Quico, Island Men); *Scene 3* Ginger's hut; that evening: "Little Biscuit" (Cicero & Ginger); *Scene 4* Grandma's shack; later that evening: "Cocoanut Sweet" (Grandma & Savannah); *Scene 5* Koli's boat; same night: "Pity de Sunset" (Koli & Savannah); *Scene 6* Dockside; next morning: "(Hooray for de) Yankee Dollar" (Ginger & Islanders), "What Good Does it Do?" (Koli, Cicero, Quico); *Scene 7* The Governor's mansion; a few days later: "Monkey in de Mango Tree" (Koli & Fishermen); *Scene 8* A night club: "Take it Slow, Joe" (Savannah); *Scene 9* The beach; at night: Beach at Night (dance) (Koli & Islanders); *Scene 10* Grandma's shack; early evening: "Ain't it de Truth" (Savannah); *Scene 11* Dockside; next morning. *Act II*: *Scene 1* A bluff on the coast; three days later: "Leave de Atom Alone" (Ginger & Islanders), "Cocoanut Sweet" (reprise) (Savannah); *Scene 2* The Governor's mansion; next afternoon: "For Every Fish" (Grandma & Fishermen), "I Don't Think I'll End it All Today" (Savannah, Koli, Islanders); *Scene 3* A room in the Governor's mansion; a few days later: "Napoleon" (Savannah); *Scene 4* Koli's fish market; next day: "Ain't it de Truth" (reprise) (Savannah & Islanders); *Scene 5* The Governor's mansion; same day: "Savannah" (reprise) (Savannah, Koli, Islanders); *Scene 6* The knoll; later afternoon of the same day.

It had an advance sale of almost $2 million, and got excellent reviews. Yip Harburg refused to attend the opening because, in his mind, they'd done bad things to his libretto. The show closed on 6/28/58 (after 276 performances) for vacation, and re-opened on 8/11/58. Lena Horne stayed for the entire run. It was also notable in that David Merrick forced the stagehands' local union to accept black stagehands. *Jamaica* received Tony nominations for musical, sets, costumes, and for Ricardo Montalban, Ossie Davis, Lena Horne, and Josephine Premice.

After Broadway. York Theatre Company, NY, 4/10/05–4/10/05. One of the *Musicals in Mufti* series, it was also presented as paert of the Harold Arlen centennial Celebration. ADAPTED BY Jeff Hochhauser.

James Clavell's Shogun see 628

349. *James Joyce's The Dead*

Set at the turn of the 20th century, at the Misses Morkans' (two elderly spinsters and their niece) annual Christmas-time party, in Dublin. A dozen friends and relatives show up. It has no intermission.

Before Broadway. In 1987 the story had been filmed straight (although it had songs in it), by John Huston, and starring his daughter Angelica, and Donal McCann.

The musical play (even though Gregory Mosher, the producer, called it a "play with music," it is really a musical play) was first presented for a limited run at PLAYWRIGHTS HORIZONS, 10/28/99–11/28/99. 29 previews from 10/1/99. 40 PERFORMANCES. The presence of Christopher Walken assured a sell-out even before it opened, and the closing date was extended from 11/14/99 to 11/28/99. There were some canceled performances due to illness, but these were made up by additional matinees. It had the same basic credits as for the later Broadway run, except DIRECTORS: Richard Nelson & Jack Hofsis; STAGE MANAGER: Kelley Kirkpatrick. This Off Broadway production won a Lucille Lortel award for best musical. Then it went to Broadway.

The Broadway Run. BELASCO THEATRE, 1/11/00–4/16/00. 32 previews from 12/14/99. 112 PERFORMANCES. The Playwrights Horizons production, PRESENTED BY Gregory Mosher & Arielle Tepper; MUSIC/ORCHESTRATIONS: Shaun Davey; LYRICS: Richard Nelson & Shaun Davey; BOOK/DIRECTOR: Richard Nelson; BASED ON James Joyce's short story *The Dead*, in his book *Dubliners*; CHOREOGRAPHER: Sean Curran; SETS: David Jenkins; COSTUMES: Jane Greenwood; LIGHTING: Jennifer Tipton; SOUND: Scott Lehrer; MUSICAL DIRECTOR: Charles Prince; PRESS: The Publicity Office; CASTING: James Calleri (of Playwrights Horizons) & Mark Bennett (of Hopkins, Smith & Barden); GENERAL MANAGERS: Lynn Landis & Edward J. Nelson; PRODUCTION STAGE MANAGER: Matthew Silver; STAGE MANAGER: Dan da Silva; ASSISTANT STAGE MANAGER: Henry Maiman. *Cast:* THE HOSTESSES: AUNT JULIA MORKAN, A MUSIC TEACHER: Sally Ann Howes; AUNT KATE MORKAN, HER SISTER (ALSO A MUSIC TEACHER): Marni Nixon; MARY JANE MORKAN, THEIR NIECE (ALSO A MUSIC TEACHER): Emily Skinner, *Donna Lynne Champlin*; THE FAMILY: GABRIEL CONROY, JULIA AND KATE'S NEPHEW: Christopher Walken (until 4/2/00), *Stephen Bogardus* (from 4/4/00); GRETTA CONROY, GABRIEL'S WIFE: Blair Brown, *Faith Prince*; THE GUESTS: MR. BROWNE, A FRIEND OF THE AUNTS: Brian Davies, *Rex Robbins*; FREDDY MALINS: Stephen Spinella; MRS. MALINS, FREDDY'S MOTHER: Paddy Croft; MISS MOLLY IVORS: Alice Ripley; BARTELL D'ARCY, AN OPERA SINGER: John Kelly; THE HELP: LILY, THE MAID: Brooke Sunny Moriber, *Angela Christian*; MICHAEL, A MUSIC STUDENT OF MARY JANE'S: Dashiell Eaves; RITA, ANOTHER STUDENT OF MARY JANE'S: Daisy Eagan; CELLIST, A MUSIC STUDENT OF JULIA'S: Daniel Barrett; VIOLINIST, A MUSIC STUDENT OF KATE'S: Louise Owen; GHOST: YOUNG JULIA MORKAN: Daisy Eagan. **Understudies**: Mary Jane/Molly Ivors: Donna Lynne Champlin; Lily/Rita/Young Julia: Angela Christian, *Russell Arden Koplin*; Aunt Julia/Kate/Mrs. Malins: Patricia Kilgarriff; Michael: Brandon Sean Wardell; Gabriel/Freddy: Sean Cullen; Gretta: Anne Runolfsson; Browne/D'Arcy: Gannon McHale. *Orchestra*: PIANO: Deborah Abramson; CELLO: Daniel Barrett; GUITAR: Steve Benson; OBOE/ENGLISH HORN: Jackie Leclair; VIOLIN: Louise Owen; PERCUSSION: Tom Partington; SYNTHESIZER/HARMONIUM: Virginia Pike; FLUTE: Gen Shinkai. *Scene 1* The drawing-room of the Misses Morkans' flat: Prologue (Musicians), "Killarney's Lakes" (Mary Jane, Aunt Kate, Rita), "Kate Kearney" (Michael, Mary Jane, Company), "Parnell's Plight" (Miss Ivors, Michael, Gabriel, Gretta, Company), "Adieu to Ballyshannon" (Gabriel & Gretta), "When Lovely Lady" (Aunt Julia & Aunt Kate), "Three Jolly Pigeons" (Freddy, Mr. Browne, Company), "Goldenhair" (Gretta & Gabriel); *Scene 2* The drawing room arranged for dinner: "Three Graces" (Gabriel & Company), "Naughty Girls" (Aunt Julia, Aunt Kate, Mary Jane, Company), "Wake the Dead" (Freddy & Company); *Scene 3* Aunt Julia's bedroom: "D'Arcy's Aria" (lyr translated into Italian by Ali Davey) (D'Arcy), "Queen of Our Hearts" (Mr. Browne, Freddy, Gabriel, D'Arcy, Michael), "When Lovely Lady" (reprise) (Young Julia & Aunt Julia); *Scene 4* A room in the Gresham Hotel: "Michael Furey" (Gretta), "The Living and the Dead" (Gabriel & Company).

Note: Mary Jane's academy piece and additional arrangements by Deborah Abramson. Note: The lyrics to some of the songs were adapted from, or inspired by, a number of 18th- and 19th-century Irish poems by Oliver Goldsmith, Lady Sydney Morgan, Michael William Balfe, William Allingham, and from an anonymous 19th-century music hall song. Other lyrics were adapted from James Joyce or were original. Other party underscore pieces in Scene 3 derived from works of Thomas Moore.

The show got good reviews. It opened for a limited Broadway run of 10 weeks (80 performances), but it turned into an open run at the haunted Belasco Theatre (David Belasco, the owner who died in 1931, is said to make the occasional appearance). The show won a Tony for book, and was nominated for musical, score, and for Christopher Walken and Stephen Spinella. Just after closing notices were posted Mr. Walken made his last appearance on 4/2/00 before going off on three-week vacation.

After Broadway. AHMANSON THEATRE, Los Angeles, 7/19/00–9/3/00. Previews from 7/11/00. This was the West Coast premiere. *Cast*: GABRIEL: Stephen Bogardus; GRETTA: Faith Prince; FREDDY: Stephen Spinella; MOLLY: Alice Ripley; MARY JANE: Donna Lynne Champlin; RITA/YOUNG JULIA: Russell Arden Koplin; MRS. MALINS: Paddy Croft; D'ARCY: John Kelly; MICHAEL: Brandon Sean Wardell; LILY: Angela Christian; AUNT JULIA: Sally Ann Howes; AUNT KATE: Marni Nixon. Alice Ripley left after L.A. for a role in *The Rocky Horror Show*. It then went to the Kennedy Center, Washington, DC, 10/14/00–11/12/00.

ABELSON AUDITORIUM, Chicago, 11/39/02–12/22/02. Previews from 11/21/02. PRESENTED BY Court Theatres; DIRECTOR: Charles Newell; MUSICAL DIRECTOR: Jeff Lewis. *Cast*: GABRIEL: John Reeger; GRETTA: Paula Scrofano; MOLLY: Hollis Resnik.

350. *Jane Eyre*

Set in England in the 1840s, at Gateshead Hall, Lowood School, Thornfield Hall, and surrounding Yorkshire Moors. A poor governess, a plain woman, learns why she can't marry her mysterious and secretive employer, Rochester. It was underscored throughout (i.e. music ran throughout the complete play). The audience was addressed as "gentle audience." There were 36 set changes. Thornfield Hall burned down eight times a week.

Before Broadway. It was originally workshopped at the MANHATTAN THEATRE CLUB, then in LOS ANGELES. It first had a run at WICHITA CENTER FOR THE ARTS, Kansas, from 12/1/95. 17 PERFORMANCES. DIRECTOR: John Caird. *Cast:* JANE: Marla Schaffel; ROCHESTER: Anthony Crivello. The official pre–Broadway world premiere was at the ROYAL ALEXANDRA THEATRE, Toronto, 12/3/96–2/1/97. Previews from 11/14/96. The production cost $6 million, financed by Mirvish Productions of Toronto (David & Ed Mirvish, who also produced, in association with Janet Robinson & Pam Koslow. Miss Koslow was married to Gregory Hines). DIRECTOR: John Caird; CHOREOGRAPHER: Kelly Robinson; LIGHTING: Chris Parry; SOUND: Tom Clark; VOCAL ARRANGEMENTS: Michael Rafter & Steve Tyler. The rest of the major crew credits were basically the same as for the later Broadway run. It also had the same basic 30-member cast as in Wichita. During this run it was fine-tuned, which meant shortening it to 2 hours and 40 minutes (running time when it finally hit Broadway was 2 hours and 45 minutes), and which meant delaying the 11/22/96 opening to 12/3/96. The production had a 38-foot-deep set created by John Napier. It got divided reviews. The Toronto cast recording came out in 5/97, but had limited release.

It was re-vamped after Toronto, with a smaller cast and stronger orchestrations. By 6/98 it was being scheduled for the Tennessee Repertory Theatre, 9/16/98–10/3/98, with Marla Schaffel, Anthony Crivello and Mary Stout, but on 7/1/98 that gig was canceled. By 6/98 Scott Schwartz had come in as co-director with John Caird. There were two readings at CITY CENTER, NYC, both on 2/19/99, one at noon and the other at 4 pm, and these were effectively rehearsals for the ensuing LA JOLLA PLAYHOUSE run in San Diego. (see below). *Reading cast:* JANE: Marla Schaffel; ROCHESTER: James Barbour; MRS. FAIRFAX: Mary Stout; YOUNG JANE: Anna Kendrick; HELEN: Julia McIlvaine; BLANCHE: Elizabeth De Grazia; JANE'S MOTHER: Jayne Paterson; JANE'S FATHER: Christopher Yates; AMY: Nell Balaban; LOUISA: Rachel Ulanet; ROBERT: Bruce Dow; JOHN REED: Lee Zarrett; MASON: Bill Nolte; MRS. REED: Gina Ferrall; ALSO WITH: Robin Skye, Alyse Wojciechowski. La Jolla previews were to begin 7/6/99, but were postponed to 7/13/99. The official run there was 7/25/99–9/5/99 (closing date extended from 8/29/99). The ensemble telling Jane's story was a holdover from the Toronto production. It had essentially the same crew as for the later. Broadway run, except LIGHTING: Chris Parry. It had the same basic cast too, except HELEN BURNS: Megan Drew; YOUNG JANE: Tiffany Scarritt; MRS. REED/LADY INGRAM: Anne Allgood. *Act I*: "Secrets of the House," "Let Me Be Brave," "Children of God," "Forgiveness," "The Fever," "The Farewell," "Sweet Liberty," "Perfectly Nice," "The Icy Lane," "The Master Returns," "The Governess," "As Good as You," "Sirens," "Society's Best," "Finer Things," "Enchante," "The Pledge," "Secret Soul." *Act II*: "Secrets of the House" (reprise), "Sirens" (reprise), "Painting Her Portrait," "In the Light of the Virgin Morning," "Oh, Sister," "Second Self," "The Chestnut Tree," "Slip of a Girl," "The Wedding," "Wild Boy," "Farewell, Good Angel," "The Fever" (reprise), "Child in the Attic," "Forgiveness". (reprise), "The Voice Across the Moors," "Oh, Sister" (reprise), "Second Self" (reprise), "Brave Enough for Love." The originally scheduled Broadway opening date of 3/16/97 was canceled because no theatre big enough came their way. By mid–1998 a new Broadway date of winter 98–99 was being scheduled, but that fell through too. By 6/99 the final Broadway producers had assembled together, and it was being scheduled for late 1999, but this date was put back to 1/00 while they waited for suitable theatre again. By now it was a very different show to the one it had been in 95–96. Indeed, since the 1999 readings it was new, new songs having been added. It was re-scheduled again, this time for late 4/00. By 1/00 it was still looking for a theatre to get into by 5/3/00, in order to qualify for the Tonys cut-off date, which it finally couldn't make. On 5/18/00 it was announced that it would open for previews at the Brooks Atkinson (a 1926 theatre, originally the Mansfield, and since 1960 known as the Brooks Atkinson, and now renovated and holding 1,044 seats) on 11/8/00 (this date was put back from 11/7/00, due to Election Day), to open officially on 12/3/00, and that James Barbour, Marla Schaffel and Mary Stout were all confirmed in their roles. On 7/7/00 new lighting designers were announced. On 8/31/00 rest of cast was announced. It rehearsed at the New 42nd Street Studios, Manhattan. Broadway previews were re-scheduled for 11/7/00, then put back to 11/8/00 again due to technical delays, then finally they began on 11/9/00. The official opening had to be postponed until 12/10/00 due to fixing the massive computerized scenic carousel.

The Broadway Run. BROOKS ATKINSON THEATRE, 12/10/00–6/10/01. 36 previews from 11/9/00. 210 PERFORMANCES. PRESENTED BY Annette Niemtzow, Janet Robinson, Pamela Koslow, and Margaret McFeeley Golden, in association with Jennifer Manocherian & Carolyn Kim McCarthy; MUSIC/LYRICS: Paul Gordon; BOOK/ADDITIONAL LYRICS: John Caird; BASED ON Charlotte Bronte's 1847 novel of the same name (she used the pseudonym Currer Bell); DIRECTORS: John Caird & Scott Schwartz; CHOREOGRAPHER: Jayne Paterson; SETS: John Napier; COSTUMES: Andreane Neofitou; LIGHTING: Jules Fisher & Peggy Eisenhauer; SOUND: Mark Menard & Tom Clark; MUSICAL DIRECTOR/VOCAL & INCIDENTAL MUSIC ARRANGEMENTS: Steven Tyler; ORCHESTRATIONS: Larry Hochman; CAST RECORDING, made 10/5/00–10/6/00, and released on 11/21/00, on Sony Classical; PRESS: The Publicity Office; CASTING: Johnson — Liff; GENERAL MANAGEMENT: Richards/Climan; COMPANY MANAGER: Diana L. Fairbanks; PRODUCTION STAGE MANAGER: Lori M. Doyle; STAGE MANAGER: Debra A. Acquavella; ASSISTANT STAGE MANAGER: David Sugarman. *Cast:* JANE EYRE: Marla Schaffel (1); YOUNG JANE: Lisa Musser; YOUNG JOHN REED: Lee Zarrett; MRS. REED: Gina Ferrall; MR. BROCKLEHURST: Don Richard; MISS SCATCHERD: Marguerite MacIntyre; MARIGOLD: Mary Stout; HELEN BURNS: Jayne Paterson; SCHOOLGIRLS: Nell Balaban, Andrea Bowen, Elizabeth De Grazia, Bonnie Gleicher, Rita Glynn, Gina Lamparella; MRS. FAIRFAX: Mary Stout (3); ROBERT: Bruce Dow; ADELE: Andrea Bowen; GRACE POOLE: Nell Balaban; EDWARD FAIRFAX ROCHESTER: James Barbour (2); BERTHA: Marguerite MacIntyre; BLANCHE INGRAM: Elizabeth De Grazia; LADY INGRAM: Gina Ferrall; MARY INGRAM: Jayne Paterson; YOUNG LORD INGRAM: Lee Zarrett; MR. ESHTON: Stephen R. Buntrock; AMY ESHTON: Nell Balaban; LOUISA ESHTON: Gina Lamparella; COLONEL DENT: Don Richard; MRS. DENT: Marguerite MacIntyre; RICHARD MASON: Bill Nolte; THE GYPSY: Marje Bubrosa [this is an anagram of James Barbour]; VICAR: Don Richard; ST. JOHN RIVERS: Stephen R. Buntrock. *Understudies*: Jane: Jayne Paterson & Gina Lamparella; Rochester: Stephen R. Buntrock & Bradley Dean; Mrs. Fairfax/Bertha: Sandy Binion; Mrs. Reed: Sandy Binion & Erica Schroeder; Brocklehurst: Bradley Dean & Bruce Dow; Helen: Gina Lamparella & Erica Schroeder; Robert: Lee Zarrett & Bradley Dean; Adele: Rita Glynn & Bonnie Gleicher; Blanche: Gina Lamparella & Nell Balaban; Grace/Louisa: Erica Schroeder & Sandy Binion; Mason: Bruce Dow & Don Richard; Young Jane/Young John: Bonnie Gleicher & Rita Glynn. *Swings*: Sandy Binion, Bradley Dean, Erica Schroeder. *Orchestra:* CONCERTMASTER: Regis Iandiorio; VIOLINS: Rebekah J. Johnson & Mineko Yajima; CELLO: Leo Grinhauz; BASS: Mark Vanderpoel; FLUTE/ALTO FLUTE/PICCOLO/SOPRANO RECORDER: Helen Campo; CLARINET/BASS CLARINET: John J. Moses; OBOE/ENGLISH HORN: Brian Greene; FRENCH HORN: Jerry W. Peel; TRUMPET/FLUGELHORN: Thomas Hoyt; PERCUSSION: William Hayes; KEYBOARDS: David Gursky, Antony Geralis, Steven Withers. *Act I*: "The Orphan" (Jane), "Children of God" (Schoolgirls, Brocklehurst, Mrs. Reed, Scatcherd, Ensemble), "Forgiveness" (Helen, Young Jane, Jane), "The Graveyard" (Jane, Young Jane, Ensemble), "Sweet Liberty" (Jane & Ensemble), "Perfectly Nice" (Mrs. Fairfax, Adele, Jane), "As Good as You" (Rochester), "Secret Soul" (Jane & Rochester), "The Finer Things" (Blanche), "Oh, How You Look in the Light" (Rochester, Blanche, Ensemble), "The Pledge" (Jane & Rochester), "Sirens" (Rochester, Jane, Bertha). *Act II*: "Things Beyond This Earth" (Ensemble), "Painting Her Portrait" (Jane), "In the Light of the Virgin Morning" (Jane & Blanche), "The Gypsy" (Gypsy), "The Proposal" (Jane & Rochester), "Slip of a Girl" (Mrs. Fairfax, Jane, Robert,

Adele), "The Wedding" (Ensemble), "Wild Boy" (Rochester, Jane, Bertha, Ensemble), "Sirens" (reprise) (Jane & Rochester), "Farewell, Good Angel" (Rochester), "My Maker" (Jane & Ensemble), "Forgiveness" (reprise) (Mrs. Reed, Jane, Ensemble), "The Voice Across the Moors" (St. John, Jane, Rochester), "Poor Master" (Mrs. Fairfax & Jane), "Brave Enough for Love" (Jane, Rochester, Ensemble).

The show cost $6.5 million. Reviews were luke-warm. The closing of the show was as dramatic as the opening had been. On 5/14/01 it was announced that the show would close on 5/20/01, then immediately after this announcement it got a reprieve because singer-songwriter Alanis Morissette put in another $150,000, allowing it to run for another week, until 5/27/01. Box-office receipts picked up and they kept it running until 6/10/01 (a date announced on 6/4/01). On 6/8/01 it was videotaped for the archives. It received Tony nominations for musical, score, book, lighting, and for Marla Schaffel.

351. *Jekyll and Hyde*

Good and noble doctor takes potion JH7, loses his inhibitions, and becomes his alter ego, an evil maniac.

Before Broadway. This musical (albeit in slightly different shape back then) was first produced at the Alley Theatre in Houston, Texas, on 5/25/90, but failed to make Broadway. DIRECTOR: Gregory Boyd; CHOREOGRAPHER: Jerry Mitchell; SETS: David Peter Gould; COSTUMES: V. Jane Suttell; LIGHTING: Robert Jared; SOUND: Karl Richardson. **Cast:** CAREW: Edmund Lyndeck; JEKYLL: Chuck Wagner; POOLE: Eddie Korbich; PRINCE MICHAEL: Martin Van Treuren; STRIDE: Bill Nolte; UTTERSON: Philip Hoffman; LISA: Rebecca Spencer; GEN. GLOSSOP: Bob Wrenn; BISHOP: Dave Clemmons; PROOPS: Bob Zolli; LADY BEACONSFIELD: Lee Merrill; SAVAGE: Tug Wilson; NELLIE: Nita Moore; LUCY: Linda Eder.

It was re-vamped, and had another Alley run from 1/25/95. DIRECTOR: Gregory Boyd; CHOREOGRAPHER: Barry McNabb; SETS: Vincent Mountain; COSTUMES: David C. Woolard; LIGHTING: Howell Binkley; SOUND: Karl Richardson & Scott Stauffer; MUSICAL DIRECTOR: Jeremy Roberts; ORCHESTRATIONS: Kim Scharnberg. **Cast:** CONDEMNED PRISONER: Sven Toorvald; JEKYLL/HYDE: Robert Cuccioli; CAREW: Rod Loomis; GABRIEL JOHN UTTERSON: Philip Hoffman; LADY BEACONSFIELD: Sandy Rosenberg; SAVAGE/POOLE/BISSET: Brad Oscar; TWO YOUNG MEN ABOUT TOWN, HUGO CARRUTHERS & THEO DAVENPORT: Bob Wrenn & Rob Evan; BUTLER: James Hadley; SIMON STRIDE: Bill Nolte; ORDERLY TO THE BOARD OF GOVERNORS: William Thomas Evans; PROOPS/SPIDER: Martin Van Treuren; GEN. SIR GEORGE GLOSSOP: Raymond McLeod; BISHOP OF BASINGSTOKE: Dave Clemmons; (NINE) PROSTITUTES: NELLIE: Nita Moore; LUCY HARRIS: Linda Eder; JENNY: Allyson Tucker; LIZZIE: Amy Spanger; MARY: Lauren Goler-Kosarin; NANCY: Mary Jo Mecca; ROSIE: Andie L. Mellom; IVY: Michelle Mallardi; LOTTIE: Judy Glass; NEWSBOY: Amy Spanger; FENWICK: Lenny Daniel. It was due to open on Broadway at the end of 1995, but it was mid–97 before it finally made it to New York. Meanwhile it also had runs at the 5th Avenue Theatre, Seattle and at Theatre Under the Stars (TUTS), Houston. Left behind between the Alley Theatre premiere and Broadway were the numbers "Board of Governors," "Bring on the Men," "Girls of the Night," "Lisa Carew" and "Transformation".

The Broadway Run. PLYMOUTH THEATRE, 4/28/97–1/7/01. 44 previews from 3/21/97. 1,543 PERFORMANCES. The Alley Theatre production, PRESENTED BY PACE Theatrical Group & Fox Theatricals, in association with Jerry Frankel, Magicworks Entertainment, and the Landmark Entertainment Group; MUSIC: Frank Wildhorn; LYRICS/BOOK: Leslie Bricusse; CONCEIVED FOR THE STAGE BY Steve Cuden & Frank Wildhorn; BASED ON the 1886 novella *The Strange Case of Dr. Jekyll and Mr. Hyde*, by Robert Louis Stevenson; DIRECTOR/SETS: Robin Phillips; CHOREOGRAPHER: Joey Pizzi; COSTUMES: Ann Curtis; LIGHTING: Beverly Emmons; SOUND: Karl Richardson & Scott Stauffer; MUSICAL SUPERVISOR: Jeremy Roberts; MUSICAL DIRECTOR: Jason Howland; ORCHESTRATIONS: Kim Scharnberg; VOCAL ARRANGEMENTS: Jason Howland & Ron Melrose; CAST RECORDING on Atlantic; PRESS: Richard Kornberg & Associates; CASTING: Julie Hughes & Barry Moss; GENERAL

MANAGEMENT: Niko Associates; COMPANY MANAGER: Bruce Klinger; STAGE MANAGERS: Maureen F. Gibson & David Hyslop. **Cast:** JOHN UTTERSON: George Merritt; SIR DANVERS CAREW: Barrie Ingham; DR. HENRY JEKYLL: Robert Cuccioli, *Robert Evan (from 1/5/99), Jack Wagner (from 1/25/00), Sebastian Bach (from 6/13/00), David Hasselhoff (from 10/18/00)*; DR. HENRY JEKYLL (AT WEDNESDAY & SATURDAY MATINEES): Robert Evan, *Joseph Mahowald*; OLD MAN IN MENTAL HOSPITAL: David Chaney; MENTAL PATIENTS: David Koch (*John Schiappa*) & Bill E. Dietrich (*Juan Betancur, Rod Weber*); DOCTOR: Donald Grody, *Peter Johl*; ATTENDANTS: Frank Mastrone (*Craig Schulman*) & Charles E. Wallace (*Russell B. Warfield*); NURSES: Emily Scott Skinner (*Sheri Cowart*) & Jodi Stevens (*Kate Shindle*); KATE, A COCKLE SELLER: Leah Hocking, *Kelli O'Hara, Christy Tarr*; ALICE, A SCULLERY MAID: Emily Scott Skinner, *Sheri Cowart, Corinne Melancon*; MOLLY, A FISH GUTTER: Molly Scott Pesce, *Sally Ann Tumas, Rebecca Baxter*; BET, A SCULLERY MAID: Jodi Stevens, *Kate Shindle*; POLLY, A SCRUBBER WOMAN: Bonnie Schon; MIKE, A CLERK: John Treacy Egan; ALBERT, A BARMAN: Frank Mastrone, *Craig Schulman*; DAVEY, A BARROW BOY: David Chaney; NED, A SAILOR: David Koch, *John Schiappa*; BILL, A DOCKER: Bill E. Dietrich, *Juan Betancur, Rod Weber*; JACK, A BEGGAR: Charles E. Wallace, *Russell B. Warfield*; MR. SIMON STRIDE: Raymond Jaramillo McLeod, *Merwin Foard, Robert Jensen*; RUPERT, BISHOP OF BASINGSTOKE: Michael Ingram, *Joel Robertson*; RT HON ARCHIBALD PROOPS: Brad Oscar, *Bill E. Dietrich*; LORD SAVAGE: Martin Van Treuren; LADY BEACONSFIELD: Emily Zacharias, *Corinne Melancon, Rebecca Spencer*; GEN. LORD GLOSSOP: Geoffrey Blaisdell, *Stuart Marland*; EMMA CAREW: Christiane Noll, *Anastasia Barzee, Andrea Rivette (from 1/25/00)*; GENTS: Frank Mastrone (*Craig Schulman*) & Brad Oscar (*Bill E. Dietrich*); MANSERVANT AT SIR DANVERS': David Chaney; UNDER FOOTMAN: Charles E. Wallace, *Russell B. Warfield*; GROOMS: John Treacy Egan & Bill E. Dietrich (*Juan Betancur, Rod Weber*); HOUSEMAIDS: Emily Scott Skinner (*Sheri Cowart, Corinne Melancon*) & Jodi Stevens (*Kate Shindle*); GUINEVERE ("GWINNY"), MANAGERESS OF THE *Red Rat*: Emily Zacharias, *Corinne Melancon, Rebecca Spencer*; LUCY, THE MAIN ATTRACTION AT THE *Red Rat*: Linda Eder, *Luba Mason, Colleen Sexton (from 1/25/00)*; TOUGHS OF THE *Red Rat*: David Koch (*John Schiappa*), Bill E. Dietrich (*Juan Betancur, Rod Weber*), Charles E. Wallace (*Russell B. Warfield*); WHORES: Emily Scott Skinner (*Sheri Cowart, Corinne Melancon*) & Bonnie Schon; SIEGFRIED, PIANIST AT THE *Red Rat*: Geoffrey Blaisdell, *Stuart Marland*; THE SPIDER, PROPRIETOR OF THE *Red Rat*: Martin Van Treuren; SIR DOUGLAS: Michael Ingram, *Joel Robertson*; SIR PETER: Brad Oscar, *Bill E. Dietrich*; LORD G: Donald Grody, *Peter Johl*; POOLE, JEKYLL'S MANSERVANT: Donald Grody, *Peter Johl*; EDWARD HYDE: Robert Cuccioli, *Robert Evan (from 1/5/99), Jack Wagner (from 1/25/00), Sebastian Bach (from 6/13/00), David Hasselhoff (from 10/18/00)*; MR. HYDE (AT WEDNESDAY & SATURDAY MATINEES): Robert Evan, *Joseph Mahowald*; DOG: B.J.; YOUNG GIRL, MANAGED BY GWINNY: Jodi Stevens, *Kate Shindle*; NEWSBOY: Bill E. Dietrich, *Juan Betancur, Rod Weber*; PRIEST AT BISHOP'S FUNERAL: Frank Mastrone, *Craig Schulman*; MR. BISSET, AN APOTHECARY: David Chaney; POLICEMEN: Geoffrey Blaisdell (*Stuart Marland*) & Michael Ingram (*Joel Robertson*); MAITRE D' AT SOCIAL CLUB: David Chaney; DOORMAN AT SOCIAL CLUB: Charles E. Wallace, *Russell B. Warfield*; BARROW BOYS: Michael Ingram (*Joel Robertson*), Brad Oscar (*Bill E. Dietrich*), Geoffrey Blaisdell (*Stuart Marland*); BOY SOPRANO AT WEDDING: Linda Eder, *Luba Mason, Colleen Sexton*; BRIDESMAIDS: Emily Scott Skinner (*Sheri Cowart, Corinne Melancon*) & Jodi Stevens (*Kate Shindle*); PRIEST AT WEDDING: David Chaney; CURATE: Charles E. Wallace, *Russell B. Warfield*; CHOIRBOY: Bill E. Dietrich, *Juan Betancur, Rod Weber*. **Understudies:** Jekyll/Hyde: Frank Mastrone (97–98), Bill E. Dietrich (97–98), *Sebastian Bach, Joseph Mahowald (Wednesday & Saturday matinees), Craig Schulman, Robert Jensen, Juan Betancur, Rod Weber*; Savage/Spider: Frank Mastrone (97–98), *Craig Schulman, Douglas Ladnier, John Schiappa*; Lucy: Leah Hocking (97–98), *Emily Skinner (97–98), Jodi Stevens (97–98), Whitney Allen*; Emma: Leah Hocking (97–98), *Emily Skinner (97–98), Jodi Stevens (97–98), Kate Shindle, Sheri Cowart, Whitney Allen, Christy Tarr*; Utterson: Geoffrey Blaisdell (97–98), *Stuart Marland, Craig Schulman, John Treacy Egan*; Poole: Geoffrey Blaisdell (97–98), *Brad Oscar (97–98), Bill E. Dietrich, Stuart Marland*; Danvers: Martin Van Treuren (97–98), *Donald Grody (97–98), Peter Johl*; Boy Soprano: Emily Skinner, *Sheri Cowart*; Molly: Rebecca Baxter; Alice:

Corinne Melancon; Proops: Bill E. Dietrich (97–98), *Brad Oscar, Juan Betancur, Carmen Yurich, Rod Weber*; Lady Beaconsfield/Guinevere: Bonnie Schon (97–98), *Rebecca Spencer, Corinne Melancon*; Glossop: John Treacy Egan (97–99), *Douglas Ladnier*; Bishop: John Treacy Eagan (97–98), *Craig Schulman, Douglas Ladnier*; Stride: David Koch (97–98), *John Schiappa, Douglas Ladnier*; Kate: Christy Tarr. **Swings**: Paul Hadobas (97–98), Rebecca Spencer (97–98), *William Allen, Whitney Allen, Sheri Cowart, Douglas Ladnier, Colleen Sexton, Carmen Yurich, Rebecca Baxter*. **Act I**: *Scene 1* A London street; *Scene 2* The violent ward, St. Jude's Hospital: "Lost in the Darkness" (Jekyll); *Scene 3* A London square: "Facade" * (Ensemble); *Scene 4* St. Jude's Hospital: "Jekyll's Plea" (Jekyll & Board of Governors); *Scene 5* The sidewalk, Regent's Park: "Facade" (reprise) (Ensemble); *Scene 6* Sir Danvers Carew's home, Regent's Park: "Emma's Reasons" (Stride & Emma), "Take Me as I Am" * (Jekyll & Emma); *Scene 7* Dock side, London's East End: "Facade" (reprise) (Ensemble); *Scene 8* Backstage at the *Red Rat*: "No One Knows Who I Am" (Lucy); *Scene 9* The *Red Rat*: "Good 'n Evil" (Lucy); *Scene 10* Harley Street; *Scene 11* Dr. Jekyll's consulting room: "This is the Moment" * (Jekyll); *Scene 12* Dr. Jekyll's laboratory; *Scene 13* The East End: "Alive" * (Hyde); *Scene 14* Harley Street; *Scene 15* Dr. Jekyll's consulting room; the Carew house: "His Work and Nothing More" * (Jekyll, Utterson, Sir Danvers, Emma); *Scene 16* Dr. Jekyll's consulting room: "Someone Like You" * (Lucy); *Scene 17* The Embankment, Westminster: "Alive" (reprise) (Hyde & Ensemble). **Act II**: *Scene 1* A London street; outside the cathedral; a pharmacy; Harley Street; supper club entrance in the West End; platform at Victoria Station: "Murder, Murder" * (Newsboy & Ensemble); *Scene 2* Dr. Jekyll's laboratory: "Once Upon a Dream" * (Emma), "Obsession" (Jekyll); *Scene 3* The Carew house; the river bank: "In His Eyes" * (Lucy & Emma); *Scene 4* The bridge, London's East End: "(It's a) Dangerous Game" * (Hyde & Lucy); *Scene 5* Dr. Jekyll's laboratory: "The Way Back" (Jekyll); *Scene 6* Lucy's room, above the *Red Rat*: "A New Life" * (Lucy), "Sympathy, Tenderness" (Hyde); *Scene 7* Dr. Jekyll's laboratory: "Lost in the Darkness" (reprise) (Jekyll), "Confrontation" * (Jekyll & Hyde); *Scene 8* Westminster: "Facade" (reprise) (Ensemble); *Scene 9* St. Anne's Church, Westminster: "Dear Lord and Father of Mankind" (Boy Soprano).

Note: Numbers asterisked were also in the 1990 Alley Theatre production.

Broadway reviews were decidedly divided, mostly negative. The show received Tony nominations for book, costumes, lighting, and for Bob Cuccioli. It was taped live during the run, when David Hasselhoff, Andrea Rivette and Colleen Sexton were starring, and HBO showed it on 12/7/00.

After Broadway. TOUR. 4/13/99–4/30/00. This was quite a revised production. New staging, new sets. DIRECTOR: David Warren; CHOREOGRAPHER: Jerry Mitchell; SETS: James Noone. **Cast**: JEKYLL/HYDE: Chuck Wagner; JEKYLL/HYDE (AT MATINEES): Brian Noonan; EMMA: Andrea Rivette, *Kelli O'Hara*; LUCY: Becca Ayers; SIR DANVERS: Dennis Kelly; UTTERSON: James Clow; SAVAGE/SPIDER: Robin Hayes; SIMON: Abe Reybold; PROOPS: David Elledge; LADY BEACONSFIELD: Bertilla Baker; BASIL/BISHOP OF BASINGSTOKE: Roger E. DeWitt. **Prologue**: A London street. **Act I**: *Scene 1* The violent ward, St. Jude's Hospital: "Lost in the Darkness" (Jekyll), "I Need to Know" (Jekyll) [added for this tour]; *Scene 2* A London square: "Facade" (Ensemble); *Scene 3* St. Jude's Hospital: "Board of Governors" (Jekyll's Plea), "Pursue the Truth" (Jekyll & Utterson); *Scene 4* Sir Danvers Carew's home, Regent's Park: "The Engagement Party" (Sir Danvers, Simon, Emma), "Take Me as I Am" (Jekyll & Emma), "Letting Go" (Sir Danvers & Emma); *Scene 5* The *Red Rat*: "Bring on the Men" (Lucy & Ensemble) [added for this tour] [the showstopper]; *Scene 6* Outside Dr. Jekyll's laboratory: "This is the Moment" (Jekyll), "The Transformation" (l: Steve Cuden, Leslie Bricusse, Frank Wildhorn) (Jekyll); *Scene 7* The streets of London: "Alive!" (l: Steve Cuden, Leslie Bricusse, Frank Wildhorn) (Hyde & Lucy); *Scene 8* Jekyll's study: "Sympathy, Tenderness" (Lucy), "Someone Like You" (Lucy); *Scene 9* Shabby street near the *Red Rat*: "Alive!" (reprise) (Hyde). **Act II**: *Scene 1* London montage: "Murder, Murder!" (l: Steve Cuden, Leslie Bricusse, Frank Wildhorn) (Ensemble); *Scene 2* Dr. Jekyll's laboratory: "Once Upon a Dream" (l: Steve Cuden, Leslie Bricusse, Frank Wildhorn) (Emma), "Streak of Madness" (Emma & Jekyll), "In His Eyes" (Lucy & Emma); *Scene 3* Outside the *Red Rat*:

"(It's) a Dangerous Game" (Lucy & Hyde), "Facade" (reprise) (Spider & Ensemble); *Scene 4* Dr. Jekyll's laboratory: "The Way Back" (Jekyll); *Scene 5* Lucy's room, above the *Red Rat*: "A New Life" (Lucy), "Sympathy, Tenderness" (reprise) (Hyde); *Scene 6* Dr. Jekyll's laboratory: "Confrontation" (Jekyll & Hyde); *Scene 7* St. Anne's Church, Westminster: "Facade" (reprise) (Ensemble), "Final Transformation" (Jekyll).

NON-EQUITY TOUR. 9/19/00–5/20/01. **Cast**: JEKYLL/HYDE: Guy LeMonnier; LUCY: Annie Berthiaume; EMMA: Lynn Nielsen.

MAINE STATE THEATRE, Brunswick, Me. 7/16/03–8/2/03. DIRECTOR: Charles Abbott. **Cast**: JEKYLL/HYDE: Todd Alan Johnson; LUCY: Amy Bodnar; EMMA: Kate Fisher.

TOURING CONCERT VERSION. By 2004 there was a somewhat new phenomenon in the stage musical business — touring concert versions. Frank Wildhorn, Leslie Bricusse and Gregory Boyd adapted *Jekyll and Hyde* to this format, and it first ran successfully at the LENAPE REGIONAL PERFORMING ARTS CENTER, in New Jersey. It was then PRESENTED BY Frank Wildhorn, Tom Lazenby and David Hart, at MOHEGAN SUN, Connecticut, for 5 PERFORMANCES, 9/8/04–9/12/04. DIRECTOR: Gregory Boyd; MUSICAL DIRECTOR: Jason Howland; ORCHESTRATIONS: Kim Scharnberg; SOUND: Jeffrey Osborne. **Cast**: JEKYLL/HYDE: Rob Evan; LUCY: Kate Shindle; EMMA: Victoria Matlock [Lauren Kennedy was going to play Emma, but she went into the Hollywood stage production of *The Ten Commandments*].

U.K. TOUR. Opened on 8/24/04, in Eastbourne. **Cast**: JEKYLL/HYDE: Paul Nicholas; LUCY: Louise Dearman; EMMA: Shona Lindsay. A London run followed in early 2005.

352. *Jelly's Last Jam*

The life of Ferdinand Joseph Le Menthe "Jelly Roll" Morton, jazz pioneer. Jelly is summoned to the Jungle Inn, "a lowdown club somewheres 'tween Heaven 'n' Hell" on the last night of his life. In a series of flashbacks led by the Hunnies, the mystical Chimney Man leads Jelly on a review of his life, from his childhood in New Orleans (he was a light-skinned black who often boasted of his French-Creole background and who derided darker blacks) to fame and fortune as bandleader, pianist and songwriter, and finally to his lonely last days. Chimney Man forces Jelly to see that because he has denied his black heritage he has betrayed himself. Finally Jelly embraces his roots in a wild New Orleans–style funeral.

Before Broadway. The idea was Margo Lion's, and she approached Gregory Hines's wife, Pamela Koslow, to be co-producer. It was workshopped as *Mister Jelly Lord*, with Gregory Hines, Lonette McKee, Leilani Jones, and Ben Harney. Luther Henderson adapted Jelly Roll Morton's original music. BOOK: Ken Cavander; DIRECTOR: Stan Latham; CHOREOGRAPHER: Otis Sallid. August Wilson was then hired to re-write the book, and Jerry Zaks to direct. Finally, George C. Wolfe replaced August Wilson, and Susan Birkenhead wrote the lyrics. Jerry Zaks quit to direct *Miss Saigon* (a job that fell through) and Mr. Wolfe became director as well. A second workshop followed, and then a mainstage production (world premiere, 2/24/91) at Mark Taper Forum, Los Angeles, of the show now called *Jelly's Last Jam*, but without Gregory Hines, who didn't like the idea of the inexperienced George C. Wolfe as director. The show was well-received. CHOREOGRAPHER: Hope Clarke; SETS: George Tsypin; COSTUMES: Toni-Leslie James; LIGHTING: James F. Ingalls; SOUND: Jon Gottlieb; CASTING: Stanley Soble. **Cast**: JELLY ROLL MORTON: Obba Babatunde; CHIMNEY MAN: Keith David; HUNNIES: Phyliss Bailey, Patty Holley, Regina Le Vert; MAMAN: Karole Foreman; GRAN MIMI: Freda Payne; ANITA: Tonya Pinkins; MABEL: Leilani Jones; YOUNG JELLY: Robert Barry Fleming; EULALIE: Peggy Blow; ANCESTORS: Timothy Smith, Mary Bond Davis, Gil Pritchett III, Patrick McCollum, Peggy Blow; VIOLA: Phyliss Bailey; AMEDE: Patty Holley; BUDDY BOLDEN: Ruben Santiago-Hudson; BLUES SINGER: Mary Bond Davis; THREE FINGER JAKE: Gil Pritchett III; TOO TIGHT NORA: Deborah L. Sharpe; JACK THE BEAR: Stanley Wayne Mathis; HICK MAN: Gil Pritchett III; HICK WOMAN: Regina Le Vert; GRIEVING WIDOW: Patty Holley; DEAD MAN:

Jerry M. Hawkins; POOL PLAYER: Patrick McCollum; MELROSE BROTH-ERS/AGENTS/GANGSTERS: Timothy Smith & Jerry M. Hawkins; LOOSE LIL AND THE JUNGLE INN JAMMERS: LOOSE LIL: Linda Twine; LI'L MOE: Garnett Brown; HOT DADDY: Richard Grant; TOO SHARP: Jeffrey Clayton; LEFT FOOT: Quentin Dennard; JOE: Karl Vincent; CROWD: Karole Foreman, Freda Payne, Tonya Pinkins, Robert Barry Fleming, Peggy Blow, Timothy Smith, Mary Bond Davis, Gil Pritchett III, Deborah L. Sharpe, Stanley Wayne Mathis, Jerry M. Hawkins, Patrick McCollum, Ruben Santiago-Hudson. It was then workshopped yet again, in New York, this time with Gregory Hines. Changes were constant right up to opening night on Broadway.

The Broadway Run. VIRGINIA THEATRE, 4/26/92–9/5/93. 25 previews from 3/31/92. 569 PERFORMANCES. PRESENTED BY Margo Lion & Pamela Koslow-Hines, in association with PolyGram Diversified Entertainment, 126 Second Avenue Corporation/Hal Luftig, Rodger Hess, Jujamcyn Theatres/TV ASAHI, and Herb Alpert; MUSIC: Jelly Roll Morton (unless otherwise stated); MUSICAL ADAPTATION/ADDITIONAL MUSIC/MUSICAL SUPERVISOR/ORCHESTRATIONS: Luther Henderson; LYRICS: Susan Birkenhead; BOOK/DIRECTOR: George C. Wolfe; CHOREOGRAPHER: Hope Clarke; TAP CHOREOGRAPHERS: Gregory Hines & Ted L. Levy; SETS: Robin Wagner; COSTUMES: Toni-Leslie James; LIGHTING: Jules Fisher; SOUND: Otts Munderloh; MUSICAL DIRECTOR: Linda Twine; CAST RECORDING on Mercury; MASKS/PUPPETS: Barbara Pollitt; PRESS: Richard Kornberg & Associates; CASTING: Hughes/Moss & Stanley Soble; GENERAL MANAGEMENT: David Strong Warner; COMPANY MANAGER: Susan Gustafson; PRODUCTION STAGE MANAGER: Arturo E. Porazzi; STAGE MANAGERS: Bernita Robinson & Bonnie L. Becker. *Cast*: CHIMNEY MAN: Keith David, *Ken Ard* (from 2/9/93), *Ben Vereen* (from 4/8/93); THE HUNNIES: Mamie Duncan-Gibbs, Stephanie Pope, Allison M. Williams; THE CROWD: Ken Ard (*Ken Roberson*), Adrian Bailey, Sherry D. Boone, Brenda Braxton, Mary Bond Davis, Ralph Deaton, Melissa Haizlip, Cee-Cee Harshaw, Ted L. Levy, Stanley Wayne Mathis, Victoria Gabrielle Platt, Gil Pritchett III, Michele M. Robinson; JELLY ROLL MORTON: Gregory Hines, *Brian Mitchell* (from 5/4/93 — this is Brian Stokes Mitchell]; YOUNG JELLY: Savion Glover; SISTERS: Cee-Cee Harshaw, Victoria Gabrielle Platt, Sherry D. Boone; ANCESTORS: Adrian Bailey, Mary Bond Davis, Ralph Deaton, Ann Duquesnay, Melissa Haizlip; MISS MAMIE: Mary Bond Davis; BUDDY BOLDEN: Ruben Santiago-Hudson; TOO-TIGHT NORA: Brenda B. Braxton; THREE-FINGER JAKE: Gil Pritchett III; GRAN MIMI: Ann Duquesnay; JACK THE BEAR: Stanley Wayne Mathis; FOOT-IN-YO-ASS SAM: Ken Ard, *Ken Roberson*; ANITA: Tonya Pinkins, *Phylicia Rashad* (from 5/28/93); MELROSE BROTHERS: Don Johanson & Gordon Joseph Weiss. *Standby*: Jelly: Lawrence Hamilton. *Understudies*: Chimney Man: Ken Ard, *Adrian Bailey*; Young Jelly: Jimmy W. Tate; Anita: Stephanie Pope; Jack the Bear: Ralph Deaton; Buddy: Adrian Bailey; Mimi/Mamie: Clare Bathe; Hunnies: Melissa Haizlip; Melrose Brothers: Bill Brassea. *Swings*: Ken Roberson, Janice Lorraine-Holt, La-Rose Saxon, *Keith L. Thomas, Rosa Curry*. *Jelly's Red Hot Peppers*: DRUMS: Brian Grice; BASS: Ben Brown; BANJO: Steve Bargonetti; TRUMPET: Virgil Jones; TROMBONE: Britt Woodman; CLARINET: Bill Easley. **Act I**: *Scene 1* The jam: "Jelly's Jam" (Hunnies & Crowd), "In My Day" (Jelly & Hunnies); *Scene 2* In the beginning: "The Creole Way" (m: Luther Henderson) (Ancestors, Sisters, Young Jelly), "The Whole World's Waitin' to Sing Your Song" (Jelly, Young Jelly, Street Crowd)/"Street Scene" (m: Luther Henderson) (Jelly, Young Jelly, Street Crowd); *Scene 3* Goin' uptown: "Michigan Water" (Mamie & Buddy), The Banishment: "Get Away, Boy" (Gran Mimi, Young Jelly, Jelly)/"Lonely Boy Blues" (traditional) (Gran Mimi, Young Jelly, Jelly); *Scene 4* The journey to Chicago: "Something More" (Jelly, Jack, Chimney Man, Hunnies, Crowd), "That's How You Jazz" (Jelly, Jack, Dance Hall Crowd); *Scene 5* Chicago!: "The Chicago Stomp" (Jelly, Red Hot Peppers, Chimney Man, Hunnies, Chicago Crowd); *Scene 6* Jelly 'n' Anita: "Play the Music for Me" (Anita), "Lovin' is a Low-Down Blues" (Hunnies); *Scene 7* The Midnite Inn: "Dr. Jazz" (m: King Oliver & Walter Melrose; add lyr: Susan Birkenhead) (Jelly & Crowd). **Act II**: *Scene 1* The Chimney Man takes charge; *Scene 2* The New York suite: "Good Ole New York" (Chimney Man, Hunnies, Jelly, New York Crowd), "Too Late Daddy" (m: Luther Henderson) (Jelly & Harlem Crowd), "That's the Way We Do Things in New Yawk" (Jelly & Melrose Brothers), Jelly's Isolation Dance (Jelly & Young Jelly); *Scene 3*

The last chance: "The Last Chance Blues" (Jelly & Anita); *Scene 4* Central Avenue; *Scene 5* The last rites: "The Last Rites" (m: Luther Henderson & Jelly Roll Morton) (Jelly, Chimney Man, People of his Past).

Broadway reviews were generally very good. The show won Tonys for lighting, and for Gregory Hines and Tonya Pinkins, and was also nominated for musical, score, book, direction of a musical, choreography, sets, costumes, and for Keith David.

After Broadway. TOUR. Opened on 10/25/94. *Cast*: JELLY: Maurice Hines; CHIMNEY MAN: Mel Johnson Jr.; ANITA: Nora Cole; YOUNG JELLY: Savion Glover; JACK: Stanley Wayne Mathis; MAMIE: Cleo King; GRAN MIMI: Freda Payne; BUDDY BOLDEN: Ted L. Levy.

353. *Jennie*

Loosely based on the life of actress Laurette Taylor (1884–1946). Set in 1906, in a small town in South Dakota; in New York City; and in Seattle, Washington. Jennie barnstorms across the country with her husband James, putting on spectacular melodramas. She leaves him, and is given a job by English playwright Christopher. Mary Martin is involved in many melodramatic moments — the opening has her hanging from the limb of a tree over a waterfall (which actually worked), struggling to rescue her baby while being pursued by a bear and a coolie. In the sequence *The Sultan's 50th Bride* she is on a torture wheel and rotated, while singing "Lonely Nights." There was a fire in which James's theatre is destroyed.

Before Broadway. In the 1950s plans were afoot to make the book *Laurette*, by Marguerite Taylor Courtney (daughter of Laurette Taylor) into a musical, but they failed. A Broadway-bound straight play of *Laurette* ran at the SHUBERT THEATRE, New Haven, 9/26/60–10/1/60. DIRECTOR: Jose Quintero; INCIDENTAL MUSIC: Elmer Bernstein. *Cast*: LAURETTE: Judy Holliday; MARGUERITE TAYLOR: Joan Hackett. Laurette Taylor had another child, Dwight, by Charles A. Taylor, the melodrama king. Dwight had also written a book, and it was upon this work that the next attempt at a musical was based. The show was to revolve around Charles Taylor, and Mary Martin was to play seven women in his life, one of them being Laurette. The show was to be called *Blood and Thunder*. S.N. Behrman was to write the libretto. Then they went back to Marguerite Taylor Courtney's book, and Arnold Schulman adapted it, fictionalizing its characters, and calling the show *Jennie*. Mary Martin turned down *Funny Girl* and *Hello, Dolly!* for this one. The show cost $550,000, half of that coming from Richard Halliday (Mary Martin's husband). It tried out at the Colonial Theatre, Boston, where Constance Carpenter, who was playing a friend of Jennie's, was written out. Carol Haney replaced Matt Mattox as choreographer, but didn't take credit. Kevin Kelly of the *Boston Globe*, in his review, said that the score had been poached from composers such as Rodgers & Hammerstein, Meredith Willson, Frank Loesser and Bob Merrill, and Arthur Schwartz sued him. The show then went to Detroit, where leading man Dennis O'Keefe was replaced by George Wallace because he couldn't sing, and because of other problems. Backstage there were fights between star, songwriters, producer and director. Dietz & Schwartz hated Mary Martin and her husband. Mary Martin refused to sing a particular lyric, and Mr. Schwartz threatened to take the matter up with the Dramatists Guild, and he and Howard Dietz were barred from the theatre for a while. Toward the end of the run in Detroit, the Hallidays decided against taking the show to Broadway. However, the advance sales had already reached $1,300,000, and Dietz & Schwartz threatened to sue them for that amount if they didn't go to New York. The show went to New York. Certain numbers were cut before Broadway: "Close Your Eyes," "Dinner is Served," "Femme Fatale," "Jennie," "A Mother Who's Really a Mother," "Night Race," "No Hope for the Human Race," "O'Conner," "On the Other Hand" and "On the *Thomas J. Muldoon*".

The Broadway Run. MAJESTIC THEATRE, 10/17/63–12/28/63. 4 previews from 10/14/63. 82 PERFORMANCES. PRESENTED BY Cheryl Crawford & Richard Halliday, by arrangement with Alan J. Pakula; MUSIC/

LYRICS: Howard Dietz & Arthur Schwartz; BOOK: Arnold Schulman; SUGGESTED BY the 1955 biography *Laurette*, by Marguerite Taylor Courtney; DIRECTOR: Vincent J. Donehue; CHOREOGRAPHER: Matt Mattox; SETS: George Jenkins; COSTUMES: Irene Sharaff; LIGHTING: Jean Rosenthal; MUSICAL DIRECTOR: John Lesko; ORCHESTRATIONS: Philip J. Lang & Robert Russell Bennett; DANCE MUSIC/VOCAL ARRANGEMENTS/INCIDENTAL MUSIC: Trude Rittman; CAST RECORDING on Victor; PRESS: Ben Washer; GENERAL MANAGER: Herman Bernstein; COMPANY MANAGER: Thomas Kilpatrick; PRODUCTION STAGE MANAGER: Randall Brooks; STAGE MANAGERS: Steven Meyer, Paul Bertelsen, Richard Via. *Cast*: JENNIE MALONE: Mary Martin (1) ✩; JAMES O'CONNER: George Wallace (2); BESSIE MAE SUE: Elaine Swann; STELLA: Linda Donovan; SYDNEY HARRIS: Jeremiah Morris (7); FRANK GRANADA: Rico Froehlich; CASEY O'HARRISON: Stephen Elmore; GREGORY HYMAN: Kirby Smith; SHERIFF PUGSLEY: Jay Velie; ABE O'SHAUGHNESSY: Jack De Lon (5); KEVIN O'CONNER: Brian Chapin; LOIS HOUSER: Imelda De Martin (6); O'CONNER'S WARDROBE MISTRESS: Bernice Saunders; DEPUTIES: Martin Ambrose & Oran Osburn; LINDA O'CONNER: Connie Scott (8); NELLIE MALONE: Ethel Shutta (4); DELIVERY MAN: Stephen Elmore; CHARLIE, THE JUICEMAN: Stan Watt; FLOWER GIRL: Debbie Scott; RITA BRADLEY: Diane Coupe; CHRISTOPHER LAWRENCE CROMWELL: Robin Bailey (3); SHINE BOY: Robert Murray; TEDDY: Sean Peters; GENTLEMAN: Jay Velie; STAGE MANAGER: Stan Watt; THE PIANO PLAYER: Woody Kessler; THE PONY: Misty; FIRE CHIEF: Jay Velie; DANCING ENSEMBLE: Sally Ackerman, Diane Coupe, Blair Hammond, Robert Murray, Al Sambogna, Mollie Sterns, Gerald Teijelo; SINGING ENSEMBLE: Martin Ambrose, Steve Elmore, Rico Froehlich, Lispet Nelson, Oran Osburn, Julie Sargant, Bernice Saunders, Sharon Vaughn. *Standbys*: Jennie: Christina Lind; James/Christopher: Jon Cypher, *Webb Tilton*. *Act I*: *Scene 1* The stage of a theatre in a small town in South Dakota; early spring, 1906: "Waitin' for the Evening Train" (Jennie & James), MELODRAMA: *The Mountie Gets His Man*, OR *Chang Lu, King of the White Slavers*: THE EVIL CHANG LU: Kirby Smith; RANDOLPH OF THE ROYAL MOUNTED: George Wallace (2); TWO MISGUIDED COOLIES: LU WONG: Gerald Teijelo; DONG FOO: Robert Murray; OUR MELISSA: Mary Martin (1); THE BEAR: Jeremiah Morris (7); THE WICKED OWNER OF A HOUSE OF ILL-REPUTE: Elaine Swann; A TRAGIC VIRGIN SOLD INTO WHITE SLAVERY: Linda Donovan; A SINFUL WOMAN OF ILL-REPUTE: Sharon Vaughn; A CROUPIER: Stephen Elmore; A WOODSMAN: Rico Froehlich; A PIONEER WOMAN: Julie Sargant; *Scene 2* Backstage immediately after; *Scene 3* The town square; a few minutes later: "When You're Far Away from New York Town" (Abe & Company), "I Still Look at You That Way" (Jennie); *Scene 4* Living room of Nellie Malone's brownstone, New York City; two months later: "When You're Far Away from New York Town" (reprise) (Kevin & Sewing Girls), "For Better or Worse" (Nellie); *Scene 5* Stage door alley, New York City; the next morning: "Born Again" (Jennie, Abe, Company), "Over Here" (Christopher & Jennie); *Scene 6* Exterior, Nellie Malone's brownstone; a few hours later: "Before I Kiss the World Goodbye" (Jennie); *Scene 7* Christopher Lawrence Cromwell's New York town house; eight weeks later: "Sauce Diable" (dance) (Dance Company), "Where You Are" (Christopher & Jennie), "The Jig" (Christopher, Jennie, Company); *Scene 8* The living room of Nellie Malone's brownstone; the following Sunday afternoon: "See Seattle" (James). *Act II*: *Scene 1* Seattle, Washington; several weeks later: "High is Better than Low" (James, Jennie, Company), "The Night May Be Dark" (Jennie & Nellie); *Scene 2* O'Conner's Crystal Palace, backstage; three weeks later: Dance Rehearsal (Harem Girls), "I Believe in Takin' a Chance" (James & Abe); *Scene 3* Several hours later; *Scene 4* On stage; immediately after: "Welcome" (Harem Girls), "Lonely Nights" (Jennie); *Scene 5* Several hours later. MELODRAMA: *The Sultan's 50th Bride*: SULTAN: Kirby Smith; HAREM GIRLS: Diane Coupe, Sally Ackerman, Linda Donovan; GUARDIANS: Gerald Teijelo, Robert Murray, Al Sambogna; EUNUCHS: Blair Hammond & Martin Ambrose; INDIAN FAKIR: Jeremiah Morris (7); SHALAMAR: Mary Martin (1); OMAR: George Wallace (2); SCENE 6 Seattle Railroad Station: "Before I Kiss the World Goodbye" (reprise) (Jennie).

Broadway reviews were not good, and the Hallidays (Richard Halliday and his wife, Mary Martin) didn't attend the opening night party at Sardi's. Mr. Halliday told press that the show had recouped its investment, but this is probably not the case.

354. *Jerome Kern Goes to Hollywood*

A musical revue, a collection of Jerry Kern's numbers from his movies of the 1930s & 1940s.

Before Broadway. This show opened on 5/28/85, at the DONMAR WAREHOUSE, London, as a cabaret musical. CHOREOGRAPHER: Irving Davies. *Cast*: David Kernan, Liz Robertson, Elisabeth Welch, Elaine Delmar.

The Broadway Run. RITZ THEATRE, 1/23/86–2/2/86. 9 previews. 13 PERFORMANCES. PRESENTED BY Arthur Cantor & Bonnie Nelson Schwartz, by arrangement with Peter Wilson & Showpeople; MUSIC: Jerome Kern; LYRICS: various writers; WRITER: Dick Vosburgh; CONCEIVED BY/DIRECTOR: David Kernan; ADDITIONAL STAGING: Irving Davies; SETS: Colin Pigott; COSTUMES: Christine Robinson; LIGHTING: Ken Billington; SOUND: Tony Meola; MUSICAL DIRECTOR: Peter Howard; PRESS: Arthur Cantor Associates (including Ken Mandelbaum); GENERAL MANAGER/COMPANY MANAGER: Harvey Elliott; PRODUCTION STAGE MANAGER: Robert Schear; STAGE MANAGER: Kenneth L. Peck. *Cast:* Elaine Delmar, Liz Robertson, Scott Holmes, Elisabeth Welch. *Standbys:* Jeanne Lehman & Michael Maguire. *Musicians:* SYNTHESIZER: Arnold Gross; BASS: Bruce Samuels; DRUMS: Tony Tedesco; GUITAR: Steve Uscher; CLARINET/FLUTE: Les Scott. *Act I:* "The Song is You" (*Music in the Air*, 1934; OH) (Ensemble), "I've Told Every Little Star" (*Music in the Air*, 1934; OH) (Ensemble), "Let's Begin" (*Roberta*, 1935; Harbach) (Liz), "I Won't Dance" (*Roberta*, 1935; Harbach, Fields, McHugh) (Liz), "Californ-i-ay" (*Can't Help Singing*, 1944; Harburg) (Elaine, Scott, Liz), "I'll Be Hard to Handle" (*Roberta*, 1935; Bernard Dougall) (Liz), "Smoke Gets in Your Eyes" (*Roberta*, 1935; Harbach) (Elisabeth), "Yesterdays" (*Roberta*, 1935; Harbach) (Scott & Elisabeth), "Bojangles of Harlem" (*Swing Time*, 1936; Fields) (Elaine, Scott, Liz), "I'm Old Fashioned" (*You Were Never Lovelier*, 1942; Johnny Mercer) (Elaine), "Dearly Beloved" (*You Were Never Lovelier*, 1942; Johnny Mercer) (Liz), "Make Believe" (*Show Boat*, 1936; OH) (Liz), "Here Comes the Showboat!" (*Show Boat*, 1936; m; Maceo Pinkard; l: Billy Rose) (Elaine, Scott, Liz), "Why Do I Love You?" (*Show Boat*, 1951; OH) (Liz), "I Have the Room Above Her" (*Show Boat*, 1936; OH) (Scott), "I Still Suits Me" (*Show Boat*, 1936; OH) (Scott & Elisabeth), "Daydreaming" (*You Were Never Lovelier*, 1941; Gus Kahn) (Elaine, Scott, Liz), "I Dream Too Much" (*I Dream Too Much*, 1935; Fields) (Elaine, Scott, Liz), "Can I Forget You?" (*High, Wide and Handsome*, 1937; OH) (Elaine, Scott, Liz), "Pick Yourself Up" (*Swing Time*, 1936; Fields) (Elaine & Liz), "She Didn't Say Yes" (*The Cat and the Fiddle*, 1934; Harbach) (Elisabeth), "The Folks Who Live on the Hill" (*High, Wide and Handsome*, 1937; OH) (Scott), "Long Ago and Far Away" (*Cover Girl*, 1944; Ira Gershwin) (Ensemble). *Act II:* "The Show Must Go On" (*Cover Girl*, 1944; Ira Gershwin) (Ensemble), "Don't Ask Me Not to Sing" (*Roberta*, 1935; Harbach) (Scott), "The Way You Look Tonight" (*Swing Time*, 1936; Fields) (Scott), "A Fine Romance" (*Swing Time*, 1936; Fields) (Elaine & Scott), "Lovely to Look At" (*Roberta*, 1935; Fields & McHugh) (Elisabeth), "Just Let Me Look at You" (*Joy of Living*, 1938; Fields) (Liz), "Who?" (*Sunny*, 1930; OH & Harbach) (Ensemble), "Remind Me" (*One Night in the Tropics*, 1940; Fields) (Elaine & Scott), "The Last Time I Saw Paris" (*Lady Be Good*, 1940; OH) (Scott), "Ol' Man River" (*Show Boat*, 1929; OH) (Elaine, Scott, Liz), "Why Was I Born?" (*Sweet Adeline*, 1935; OH) (Elisabeth), "Bill" (*Show Boat*, 1936; OH & P.G. Wodehouse) (Liz), "Can't Help Lovin' Dat Man" (*Show Boat*, 1936; OH) (Elaine), "All the Things You Are" (*Broadway Rhythm*, 1946; OH) (Elaine, Scott, Liz), "I've Told Every Little Star" (reprise) (Elisabeth), "They Didn't Believe Me" (*Till the Clouds Roll By*, 1946; Herbert Reynolds) (Ensemble), "Till the Clouds Roll By" (*Till the Clouds Roll By*, 1946; P.G. Wodehouse) (Ensemble), "Look for the Silver Lining" (*Sally*, 1929; Buddy de Sylva) (Ensemble), "Make Way for Tomorrow" (*Cover Girl*, 1944; Harburg & Ira Gershwin) (Ensemble).

Note: After the title is the movie the song came from, then the year the movie was released in the USA, then the lyricist(s). OH = Oscar Hammerstein II; Harbach = Otto Harbach; Harburg = E.Y. "Yip" Harburg; Fields = Dorothy Fields; McHugh = Jimmy McHugh; All music by Jerome Kern. The performer(s) come(s) last.

The Broadway reviews for the show itself were divided, but Elisabeth Welch got raves and was nominated for a Tony.

After Broadway. KING'S HEAD, Islington, London, 1/5/05. Previews from 12/29/04. This was the 20th-anniversary production, and the show was now called *Kern Goes to Hollywood*. PRESENTED BY Nica Burns; DIRECTOR: David Kernan; CHOREOGRAPHER: David Lee; SETS/COSTUMES: Norman Coates; LIGHTING: Chris Davies; MUSICAL DIRECTORS: Dominic Barlow & Fiz Shapur. *Cast*: Angela Richards, Glyn Kerslake, Sheri Coplan, Jamie Golding.

355. *Jerome Robbins' Broadway*

A musical revue; a look back at the 20-year Broadway career of director/choreographer Jerome Robbins. Aside from film versions of *West Side Story* and *Fiddler on the Roof*, none of his work had been preserved for posterity. Of his 15 Broadway shows the nine excerpted for this Broadway show were: *On the Town* (1944), *Billion Dollar Baby* (1945), *High Button Shoes* (1947), The "Small House of Uncle Thomas" ballet from *The King and I* (1951), *Peter Pan* (1954), *West Side Story* (1957), *Gypsy* (1959), *Fiddler on the Roof* (1964). Also shown were the "Comedy Tonight" number from *A Funny Thing Happened on the Way to the Forum* (1962), which Mr. Robbins created during its out-of-town tryouts but never received program credit for, and "Mr. Monotony," an Irving Berlin song, with Robbins choreography built around it, which had been dropped first from *Miss Liberty* (49) and then from *Call Me Madam* (50). The numbers were held together by the setter (narrator). The cast of 62 is referred to as "The company."

Before Broadway. The rehearsal period extended to 22 weeks, and the show had seven weeks of Broadway previews.

The Broadway Run. IMPERIAL THEATRE, 2/26/89–9/1/90. 55 previews from 1/9/89. 634 PERFORMANCES. PRESENTED BY The Shubert Organization, Roger Berlind, Suntory International, Byron Goldman, and Emanuel Azenberg, in association with PACE Theatrical Group; MUSIC/LYRICS/BOOK: by the original authors (see below); CONCEIVED BY/CHOREOGRAPHER: Jerome Robbins; DIRECTORS: Jerome Robbins & Grover Dale; ASSISTANT CHOREOGRAPHERS: Cynthia Onrubia, Victor Castelli, Jerry Mitchell; CHOREOGRAPHER ON *West Side Story*: Peter Gennaro; DANCE CAPTAINS: Susan Kikuchi & George Russell; FLYING: Foy; PRODUCTION SCENIC DESIGNER: Robin Wagner; ORIGINAL SET CREDITS: Boris Aronson (*Fiddler on the Roof*), Jo Mielziner (*The King and I* and *Gypsy*), Oliver Smith (*On the Town, Billion Dollar Baby, High Button Shoes, West Side Story*), Robin Wagner (*Peter Pan*), Tony Walton (*A Funny Thing Happened on the Way to the Forum*); SUPERVISING COSTUME DESIGNER: Joseph G. Aulisi; ORIGINAL COSTUME CREDITS: Joseph G. Aulisi (*Peter Pan* and *Miss Liberty*), Alvin Colt (*On the Town*), Raoul Pene du Bois (*Gypsy*), Irene Sharaff (*Billion Dollar Baby, The King and I, West Side Story*), Tony Walton (*A Funny Thing Happened on the Way to the Forum*), Miles White (*High Button Shoes*), Patricia Zipprodt (*Fiddler on the Roof*); LIGHTING: Jennifer Tipton; SOUND: Otts Munderloh; MUSICAL DIRECTOR: Paul Gemignani; ORCHESTRATIONS: Sid Ramin & William D. Brohn; PRESS: The Fred Nathan Company; CASTING: Jay Binder; RECONSTRUCTION ASSISTANTS: Richard Caceres (*West Side Story*), Sammy Bayes (*Fiddler on the Roof*), Yuriko (*The King and I*), Kevin Joe Jonson (*High Button Shoes*), Anne Hutchinson Guest ("The Charleston"), George Martin (*A Funny Thing Happened on the Way to the Forum*); GENERAL MANAGER: Leonard Soloway; COMPANY MANAGER: Brian Dunbar; PRODUCTION STAGE MANAGER: Beverley Randolph; STAGE MANAGER: Jim Woolley, *Pamela Singer, Dale Kaufman, Joe Klonicki*. **Act I**: *Overture and Prologue*: THE SETTER: Jason Alexander ✩, *Terrence Mann (from 7/25/89), Tony Roberts (from 1/15/90)*; OVERTURE SINGERS: Michael Lynch (*K. Craig Innes, Alan Arino, Steve Ochoa, Harrison Beal*), Debbie Shapiro (*Karen Mason, Donna Marie Elio, Dorothy Stanley*), Company. UNDERSTUDY: Setter: Tom Robbins. "I'm a Guy Who's Gotta Dance" (m/l: Hugh Martin) [from *Look Ma, I'm Dancin'*], "Papa, Won't You Dance with Me?" (m: Jule Styne; l: Sammy Cahn) [from *High Button Shoes*], "Shall We Dance?" (m: Richard Rodgers; l: Oscar Hammerstein II) [from *The King and I*]; **Excerpts**: **On the Town**:

GABEY: Robert La Fosse ✩, *Scott Fowler, Cleve Asbury, Kipling Houston* (from 4/22/89), *Angelo H. Fraboni, Troy Myers*; CHIP: Scott Wise; OZZIE: Michael Kubala; HILDY: Debbie Shapiro, *Karen Mason, Donna Marie Elio, Dorothy Stanley*; CLAIRE: Mary Ellen Stuart, *Deanna Wells, Maureen Moore, Colleen Fitzpatrick*; DOLORES DOLORES: Nancy Hess; MC: Jason Alexander ✩, *Terrence Mann, Tony Roberts*; 1ST WORKMAN: David Lowenstein; SAILORS/WORKMEN/DANCE-HALL HOSTESSES/PASSERS-BY, ETC: Company; **Understudies**: mc: Tom Robbins; Gabey: Christophe Caballero & Joey McKneely; Chip: Jack Noseworthy & Kelly Patterson; Ozzie: Michael Scott Gregory & Michael Lynch; Hildy: Donna Marie Elio; Ivy: Camille de Ganon; Claire: Nancy Hess; Dolores: Pamela Khoury & Faith Prince; 1st Workman: Tom Robbins. "New York, New York" (m: Leonard Bernstein; l: Betty Comden & Adolph Green), "Sailors on the Town" (m: Leonard Bernstein; l: Betty Comden & Adolph Green), "Ya Got Me" (m: Leonard Bernstein; l: Betty Comden & Adolph Green); **Billion Dollar Baby**: COP: David Lowenstein; DOORMAN: Michael Lynch, *K. Craig Innes, Alan Arino, Steve Ochoa, Harrison Beal*; THREE FLAPPERS: Barbara Yeager (*Nancy Ticotin*), Mary Ann Lamb (*Lisa Leguillou, Lori Werner, Maria Neenan*), JoAnn M. Hunter (*Lyd-Lyd Gaston, Andi Tyler*); SOCIALITES: Jane Lanier (*Lori Werner, Alexia Hess, Maria Neenan*) & Nicholas Garr; A TIMID GIRL: Susann Fletcher; GOOD TIME CHARLIE: Troy Myers; COLLEGIATES: Elaine Wright & Angelo H. Fraboni; YOUNGER GENERATION: Christophe Caballero & Linda Talcott (*Christine De Vito, Mindy Cartwright*); OLDER GENERATION: Barbara Hoon (*Linda Talcott, Mindy Cartwright*) & Scott Fowler (*John MacInnis*); TWO GANGSTERS: Michael Scott Gregory (*Marc Villa, Cleve Asbury, Jack Noseworthy, Ned Hannah*) & Scott Jovovich (*Scott Spahr*); TWO BOOTLEGGERS: Andrew Grose & Julio Monge (*Sergio Trujillo, Tony Caligagan*). "Charleston" (m: Morton Gould; l: Betty Comden & Adolph Green); **A Funny Thing Happened on the Way to the Forum**: PSEUDOLUS: Jason Alexander ✩, *Terrence Mann, Tony Roberts*; 1ST PROTEAN: Scott Wise; 2ND PROTEAN: Joey McKneely, *Steve Ochoa*; 3RD PROTEAN: Michael Kubala; THE COMPANY: Charlotte d'Amboise ✩ (*Nancy Ticotin, Leslie Trayer*), Dorothy Benham, Susann Fletcher, Michael Scott Gregory (*Marc Villa, Cleve Asbury, Jack Noseworthy, Ned Hannah*), Andrew Grose, Robert La Fosse ✩ (*Scott Fowler, Cleve Asbury, Kipling Houston* from 4/22/89, *Angelo H. Fraboni, Troy Myers*), Mary Ann Lamb (*Lisa Leguillou, Lori Werner, Maria Neenan*), David Lowenstein, Michael Lynch (*K. Craig Innes, Alan Arino, Steve Ochoa, Harrison Beal*), Jack Noseworthy, Kelly Patterson (*Cleve Asbury, John MacInnis*), Luis Perez (*Angelo H. Fraboni*), Tom Robbins (*Jeff Gardner, Greg Schanuel*), Greg Schanuel, Debbie Shapiro (*Karen Mason, Donna Marie Elio, Dorothy Stanley*). **Understudies**: Pseudolus: Tom Robbins; 1st Protean: Andrew Grose & Michael Lynch; 2nd Protean: Jack Noseworthy & Kelly Patterson; 3rd Protean: Michael Scott Gregory & David Lowenstein. "Comedy Tonight" (by Stephen Sondheim); **High Button Shoes**: MA: Faith Prince; PA: Jason Alexander. **Understudies**: Ma: Nancy Hess & Mary Ellen Stuart; Pa: Michael Kubala & Tom Robbins. "I Still Get Jealous" (m: Jule Styne; l: Sammy Cahn); **West Side Story**: TONY: Robert La Fosse ✩, *Scott Fowler, Cleve Asbury, Kipling Houston* (from 4/22/89), *Angelo H. Fraboni, Troy Myers*; MARIA: Alexia Hess; RIFF: Scott Wise; BERNARDO: Nicholas Garr; ANITA: Charlotte d'Amboise ✩, *Nancy Ticotin, Leslie Trayer*; ROSALIA: Debbie Shapiro, *Karen Mason, Donna Marie Elio, Dorothy Stanley*; GRAZIELLA: Donna Di Meo; "SOMEWHERE" SOLOIST: Dorothy Benham; 1ST JET: Joey McKneely, *Steve Ochoa*; OTHER JETS: Christophe Caballero, Scott Fowler (*John MacInnis*), Angelo H. Fraboni, Michael Scott Gregory (*Marc Villa, Cleve Asbury, Jack Noseworthy, Ned Hannah*), Andrew Grose, Eric A. Hoisington, Troy Myers, Jack Noseworthy, Kelly Patterson (*Cleve Asbury, John MacInnis*), Greg Schanuel; JET GIRLS: Louise Hickey, Barbara Hoon (*Linda Talcott, Mindy Cartwright*), Mary Ann Lamb (*Lisa Leguillou, Lori Werner, Maria Neenan*), Maria Neenan (*Erin Robbins*), Mary Ellen Stuart (*Deanna Wells, Maureen Moore, Colleen Fitzpatrick*), Linda Talcott (*Christine De Vito, Mindy Cartwright*), Leslie Trayer, Alice Yearsley; THE SHARKS: Jamie Cohen, Mark Esposito, Scott Jovovich (*Scott Spahr*), David Lowenstein, Michael Lynch (*K. Craig Innes, Alan Arino, Steve Ochoa, Harrison Beal*), Julio Monge (*Sergio Trujillo, Tony Caligagan*), Steve Ochoa (*Christophe Caballero*), James Rivera; SHARK GIRLS: Irene Cho (*JoAnn M. Hunter, Ellen Troy*), Donna Marie Elio, Nancy Hess, JoAnn M. Hunter (*Lyd-Lyd Gaston, Andi Tyler*), Renee

Stork, Andi Tyler, Elaine Wright, Barbara Yeager (*Nancy Ticotin*).
Understudies: Maria: JoAnn M. Hunter & Ellen Troy; Tony: Scott
Fowler & Angelo H. Fraboni; Anita: Barbara Yeager; Riff: Andrew Grose
& Kelly Patterson; Graziella: Camille de Ganon; Rosalia: Donna Marie
Elio; "Somewhere" Soloist: Pamela Khoury; 1st Jet: Jeffrey Lee Broad-
hurst, Christophe Caballero, Andrew Grose (1st Jet). Suite of Dances (m:
Leonard Bernstein; l: Stephen Sondheim)—Prologue, "The Dance at
the Gym," "Cool," "A-me-ri-ca," "The Rumble," "Somewhere;" *Act II*:
The King and I: NARRATOR: Barbara Yeager, *Nancy Ticotin*; ELIZA:
Susan Kikuchi, *Lyd-Lyd Gaston*; KING SIMON: Joey McKneely, *Steve Ochoa*;
LITTLE EVA: Linda Talcott, *Christine De Vito, Mindy Cartwright*; TOPSY:
JoAnn M. Hunter, *Lyd-Lyd Gaston, Andi Tyler*; UNCLE THOMAS: Barbara
Hoon, *Linda Talcott, Mindy Cartwright*; ANGEL/GEORGE: Irene Cho,
JoAnn M. Hunter, Ellen Troy; ROYAL DANCERS: Christophe Caballero,
Donna Di Meo, Mark Esposito, Eric A. Hoisington, Maria Neenan (*Erin
Robbins*), Steve Ochoa (*Christophe Caballero*), Renee Stork, Andi Tyler,
Elaine Wright, Alice Yearsley; ROYAL SINGERS: Dorothy Benham, Donna
Marie Elio, Nancy Hess, Louise Hickey, Mary Ellen Stuart (*Deanna
Wells, Maureen Moore, Colleen Fitzpatrick*), Leslie Trayer; PROPMEN:
Jamie Cohen, Scott Fowler (*John MacInnis*), Angelo H. Fraboni, Nicholas
Garr, Scott Jovovich (*Scott Spahr*), James Rivera. **Understudies**: Donna
Marie Elio & Jane Lanier (Narrator), Mindy Cartwright, Donna Di
Meo, Greta Martin (Topsy), Mindy Cartwright (Little Eva), Mindy
Cartwright & Ramon Galindo (Uncle Thomas), Irene Cho & JoAnn M.
Hunter & Ellen Troy (Eliza), Ramon Galindo (Simon), Mindy
Cartwright & Ellen Troy (Angel & George). "The Small House of Uncle
Thomas" (m: Richard Rodgers; l: Oscar Hammerstein II); *Gypsy*: CIGAR:
Jason Alexander ☆, *Terrence Mann, Tony Roberts*; LOUISE: Mary Ann
Lamb, *Lisa Leguillou, Lori Werner, Maria Neenan*; TESSIE: Faith Prince,
Dorothy Stanley; MAZEPPA: Debbie Shapiro, *Karen Mason, Donna Marie
Elio, Dorothy Stanley*; ELECTRA: Susann Fletcher. **Understudies**: Louise:
Maria Neenan & Ellen Troy; Mazeppa: Donna Marie Elio & Pamela
Khoury; Electra: Donna Marie Elio & Mary Ellen Stuart; Tessie: Nancy
Hess & Pamela Khoury; Cigar: Tom Robbins. "You Gotta Have a Gim-
mick" (m: Jule Styne; l: Stephen Sondheim); *Peter Pan*: PETER PAN:
Charlotte d'Amboise ☆, *Nancy Ticotin, Leslie Trayer*; WENDY: Donna Di
Meo; MICHAEL: Linda Talcott, *Christine De Vito, Mindy Cartwright*;
JOHN: Steve Ochoa, *Christophe Caballero*. **Understudies**: Peter: Jack
Noseworthy; Michael: Mindy Cartwright & Barbara Hoon; Wendy:
Ellen Troy & Andi Tyler; John: Jack Noseworthy. "I'm Flying" (m:
Moose Charlap & Jule Styne; l: Carolyn Leigh, Betty Comden, Adolph
Green); *High Button Shoes*: FLOY: Jason Alexander ☆, *Terrence Mann,
Tony Roberts*; PONTDUE: Troy Myers; MA: Faith Prince, *Dorothy Stanley*;
FRAN: Barbara Yeager, *Nancy Ticotin*; UNCLE WILLY: Michael Kubala;
CHIEF OF POLICE: Michael Scott Gregory, *Marc Villa, Cleve Asbury, Jack
Noseworthy, Ned Hannah*; COPS: Mark Esposito, Angelo H. Fraboni,
Andrew Grose, Eric A. Hoisington, Julio Monge (*Sergio Trujillo, Tony
Caligagan*), Greg Schanuel; 1ST BATHING BEAUTY: Louise Hickey; OTHER
BATHING BEAUTIES: Donna Di Meo, Susann Fletcher, JoAnn M. Hunter
(*Lyd-Lyd Gaston, Andi Tyler*), Debbie Shapiro (*Karen Mason, Donna
Marie Elio, Dorothy Stanley*), Renee Stork, Leslie Trayer, Elaine Wright;
LIFE GUARD: Tom Robbins, *Jeff Gardner, Greg Schanuel*; TWINS: Alexia
Hess & Maria Neenan (*Erin Robbins*), Scott Fowler (*John MacInnis*) &
Scott Jovovich (*Scott Spahr*); PAPA CROOK: Scott Wise; MAMA CROOK:
Nancy Hess; BABY CROOK: Linda Talcott, *Christine De Vito, Mindy
Cartwright*; SINGING CHORUS: Dorothy Benham, Christophe Caballero,
Donna Marie Elio, Nicholas Garr, Barbara Hoon (*Linda Talcott, Mindy
Cartwright*), David Lowenstein, Michael Lynch (*K. Craig Innes, Alan
Arino, Steve Ochoa, Harrison Beal*), Jack Noseworthy, Kelly Patterson
(*Cleve Asbury, John MacInnis*), James Rivera, Mary Ellen Stuart (*Deanna
Wells, Maureen Moore, Colleen Fitzpatrick*), Leslie Trayer, Andi Tyler,
Alice Yearsley. **Understudies**: Floy: Tom Robbins; Pa: Michael Kubala
& Tom Robbins; Ma: Nancy Hess & Mary Ellen Stuart; Papa Crook:
Richard Amaro, Jamie Cohen, Michael Lynch; Mama Crook: Camille
de Ganon & Pamela Khoury; Baby Crook: Mindy Cartwright & Bar-
bara Hoon; Uncle Willie: Jeffrey Lee Broadhurst & Gregorey Garrison;
Twins: Camille de Ganon, Carolyn Goor, Ellen Troy; Chief of Police:
Richard Amaro, Jeffrey Lee Broadhurst, Joey McKneely; Life Guards:
Greg Schanuel. "On a Sunday by the Sea" (ballet mus: Jule Styne); *Miss
Liberty/Call Me Madam*: "MISS LIBERTY" SINGER: Debbie Shapiro,

Karen Mason, Donna Marie Elio, Dorothy Stanley; "MR. MONOTONY" 1ST
DANCER: Luis Perez, *Angelo H. Fraboni*; "MR. MONOTONY 2ND DANCER:
Jane Lanier, *Lori Werner, Alexia Hess, Maria Neenan*; "MR. MONOTONY
3RD DANCER: Robert La Fosse ☆, *Scott Fowler, Cleve Asbury, Kipling
Houston* (from 4/22/89), *Angelo H. Fraboni, Troy Myers*. **Understudies**:
1st Dancer: Angelo H. Fraboni; 2nd Dancer: Charlotte d'Amboise ☆ &
Camille de Ganon; 3rd Dancer: Scott Fowler, Scott Jovovich, Kelly Pat-
terson; Singer: Donna Marie Elio. "Mr. Monotony" (by Irving Berlin);
Fiddler on the Roof: TEVYE: Jason Alexander ☆, *Terrence Mann, Tony
Roberts*; GOLDE: Susann Fletcher; MOTEL KAMZOIL: Michael Lynch, *K.
Craig Innes, Alan Arino, Steve Ochoa, Harrison Beal*; TZEITEL: Andi Tyler;
GRANDMA TZEITEL: Barbara Hoon, *Linda Talcott, Mindy Cartwright*;
FRUMA-SARAH: Nancy Hess; LAZAR WOLF: Tom Robbins, *Jeff Gardner,
Greg Schanuel*; RABBI: Troy Myers; FIDDLER: Joey McKneely, *Steve Ochoa*;
BOTTLE DANCERS: Christophe Caballero, Mark Esposito, Scott Jovovich
(*Scott Spahr*), Greg Schanuel; VILLAGERS/WEDDING GUESTS: Company.
Understudies: Golde: Pamela Khoury; Tzeitel: Maria Neenan & Leslie
Trayer; Lazar: Michael Kubala & David Lowenstein; Fruma-Sarah:
Pamela Khoury & Mary Ellen Stuart; Motel: Eric A. Hoisington; Fid-
dler: Michael Scott Gregory; Rabbi: Ramon Galindo; Grandma Tzeitel:
Jack Noseworthy & Linda Talcott. "Tradition" (m: Jerry Bock; l: Shel-
don Harnick), "The Dream" ("Tevye's Dream") (m: Jerry Bock; l: Shel-
don Harnick), "Sunrise, Sunset" (m: Jerry Bock; l: Sheldon Harnick),
"The Wedding Dance" (m: Jerry Bock); **Finale**: from **On the Town**:
GABEY: Robert La Fosse ☆, *Scott Fowler, Cleve Asbury, Kipling Houston*
(from 4/22/89), *Angelo H. Fraboni, Troy Myers*; CHIP: Scott Wise; OZZIE:
Michael Kubala; HILDY: Debbie Shapiro, *Karen Mason, Donna Marie
Elio, Dorothy Stanley*; CLAIRE: Mary Ellen Stuart, *Deanna Wells, Mau-
reen Moore, Colleen Fitzpatrick*; IVY: Alexia Hess; THREE SAILORS:
Christophe Caballero, Kelly Patterson (*Cleve Asbury, John MacInnis*),
Michael Scott Gregory (*Marc Villa, Cleve Asbury, Jack Noseworthy, Ned
Hannah*). **Understudy**: Ivy: Camille de Ganon. "Some Other Time" (m:
Leonard Bernstein; l: Betty Comden & Adolph Green), "New York,
New York" (m: Leonard Bernstein; l: Betty Comden & Adolph Green).
1989–90 replacements: *Bill Burns, Sean Grant* (*Bill Brassea*), *Mark S.
Hoebee, Andrea Leigh-Smith, Stephen Reed, Jim Borstelmann*. **Orchestra**:
CONCERTMASTER: Robert Chausow; VIOLINS: Dale Stuckenbruck, Ann
Leathers, Martin Agee, Miohiso Takada, Carol Pool; PRINCIPAL VIOLA:
Karl Bergen; VIOLA: Sarah Adams; PRINCIPAL CELLO: Lanny Paykin;
CELLO: Roger Shell; BASS: Joseph Bongiorno; WOODWINDS: Les Scott,
Alva Hunt, John Moses, Richard Heckman, John Campo; PRINCIPAL
FRENCH HORN: Ronald Sell; FRENCH HORN: Richard Hagen; LEAD
TRUMPETS: James Hynes & Wilmer Wise; TRUMPETS: Dominic Derasse
& Lorraine Cohen; PRINCIPAL TROMBONE: Jack Gale; TROMBONES:
Bruce Bonvissuto & Dean Plank; DRUM SET: Michael Berkowitz; PER-
CUSSION: Joseph Passaro; KEYBOARD: Pamela Drews.

Despite the then-highest Broadway show ticket price of $55 (later
raised to $60), and one of the biggest budgets ($8.8 million), and an
advance sale of $10 million, and despite rave reviews, it ailed financially
because of such a high production cost. It won Tonys for musical, direction of a musical, lighting, and for Jason Alexander, Scott Wise and
Debbie Shapiro. It was also nominated for Robert La Fosse, Jane Lanier,
Charlotte d'Amboise, Faith Prince. At award time it wasn't certain that
the musical should be considered a revival or a new musical. They
decided on new musical. On 4/2/90 Equity complained that there was
only one black actor in the show.

After Broadway. TOUR. Opened on 10/10/90, at the Shubert Theatre, Los Angeles.

356. *Jerry's Girls*

Originally described as a "musical revue in 2 acts," then,
later, on Broadway, as a "musical entertainment in 2 acts," starring the music and lyrics of Jerry Herman, a compendium of his
songs from stage musicals, movies and other sources.

Before Broadway. This show was first produced Off Off Broadway,
at ONSTAGE THEATRE, 8/17/81–11/11/81. 101 PERFORMANCES. PRESENTED
BY Bosom Buddies Company; DIRECTOR: Larry Alford; CHOREOGRA-

PHER: Sharon Halley; SETS/LIGHTING: Hal Tine; COSTUMES: Bernard Johnson; MUSICAL DIRECTOR: Cheryl Hardwick; VOCAL ARRANGEMENTS: John Visser; PRESS: Ted Hook & Walt Veasey; GENERAL MANAGER: Leonard A. Mulhern; COMPANY MANAGER: Jack Tantleff; STAGE MANAGERS: Gene Bland & Todd Fleischer. *Cast*: Evalyn Baron, Alexandra Korey, Leila Martin, Pauletta Pearson, Jerry Herman.

TOUR. Opened on 2/28/84, at the Royal Poinciana Playhouse, Palm Beach, and closed 7/21/84, at the Kennedy Center, Washington, DC. PRESENTED BY Zev Bufman, Barry Lewis, Miles Wilkin, and the Nederlander Producing Company, in association with Charles Lowe Productions; DIRECTOR: Larry Alford; CHOREOGRAPHER: Sharon Halley; SETS: Hal Tine; COSTUMES: David Dille; LIGHTING: Michael Newton-Brown; SOUND: Peter J. Fitzgerald; MUSICAL SUPERVISOR: Donald Pippin; CONDUCTOR: Janet Glazener; ORCHESTRATIONS: Joseph Gianono & Christopher Bankey; PIANIST: Maida Libkin; PRESS: Charles Cinnamon Associates; CASTING: Mark Reiner; GENERAL MANAGEMENT: Theatre Now; STAGE MANAGER: Patrick Tolson. *Cast*: Carol Channing (who, just three days before had broken her arm in an offstage accident, but still went on in that night's preview), Leslie Uggams, Andrea McArdle, Ellyn Arons, Laura Soltis, Deborah Graham, Suzanne Ishee, Diane Myron, Helena-Joyce Wright. The tour had a slightly different arrangement of songs from the Broadway run, and some numbers that didn't make it to Broadway—"Jerry's Girls" (opening number), "I Wanna Make the World Laugh" [from *Mack and Mabel*], "The Tea Party" [from *Dear World*], and "Gooch's Song" [from *Mame*]. Others were added for Broadway: "It Takes a Woman," "Just Leave Everything to Me," "Take it All Off," "Have a Nice Day," "Dickie," "Voices," "Thoughts," "My Type." On 4/2/84, while the show was playing at Orlando Arts Center, a storm put out the lights. The leading ladies gathered around the piano and sang. On 5/3/84 Carol Channing was in hospital in New Haven, with laryngitis, and performances were canceled. On 5/10/84 Andrea McArdle was knocked out of the show in Toledo with emergency appendectomy, but was back by 6/12/84, when the tour ran at the Kennedy Center, Washington, DC (which is where it closed).

The Broadway Run. ST. JAMES THEATRE, 12/18/85–4/20/86. 14 previews. 139 PERFORMANCES. PRESENTED BY Zev Bufman & Kenneth—John Productions, in association with Agnese/Raibourn; MUSIC/LYRICS: Jerry Herman; CONCEPTS: Larry Alford, Wayne Cilento, Jerry Herman; DIRECTOR: Larry Alford; CHOREOGRAPHER: Wayne Cilento; SETS: Hal Tine; COSTUMES: Florence Klotz; LIGHTING: Tharon Musser; SOUND: Peter Fitzgerald; MUSICAL SUPERVISOR: Donald Pippin; MUSICAL DIRECTOR: Janet Glazener; ORCHESTRATIONS: Christopher Bankey, Joseph Gianono, Jim Tyler; DANCE MUSIC ARRANGEMENTS: Mark Hummel; CASTING: Mark Reiner; PRESS: Shirley Herz Associates; GENERAL MANAGEMENT: Theatre Now; COMPANY MANAGER: Sally Campbell; PRODUCTION STAGE MANAGER: Patrick Horrigan; STAGE MANAGERS: Larry Bussard, Brenna Krupa Holden & Barbara Schneider. *Cast:* Ellyn Arons, Kirsten Childs, Kim Crosby, Anita Ehrler, Terri Homberg, Robin Kersey, Joni Masella, Deborah Phelan, Dorothy Loudon (1) ☆, Leslie Uggams (3) ☆, Chita Rivera (2) ☆ (*Deborah Phelan* for 1 performance, 4/8/86). *Swing*: Jacquey Maltby. ON-STAGE PIANIST: Sue Anderson. *Act I:* "Jerry's Girls" [to the tune of "It's Today" from *Mame*] (Orchestra), "It Takes a Woman" [from *Hello, Dolly!*] (Ellyn, Kirsten, Kim, Anita, Terri, Robin, Joni, Deborah), "It Takes a Woman" (reprise) (Ensemble), "Just Leave Everything to Me" [from the movie *Hello, Dolly!*] (Dorothy), "Put on Your Sunday Clothes" [from *Hello, Dolly!*] (Dorothy & Ensemble), "It Only Takes a Moment" [from *Hello, Dolly!*] (Leslie), "Wherever He Ain't" [from *Mack and Mabel*] (Chita), "We Need a Little Christmas" [from *Mame*] (Ellyn, Kirsten, Kim, Anita, Deborah), "Tap Your Troubles Away" [from *Mack and Mabel*] (Dorothy, Chita, Leslie, Ensemble), "I Won't Send Roses" [from *Mack and Mabel*] (Leslie), Vaudeville Medley: "(Wonderful World of the) Two-a-Day" [from *Parade*] (Dorothy), "Bosom Buddies" [from *Mame*] (Chita & Leslie), "The Man in the Moon" [from *Mame*] (Dorothy), "So Long, Dearie" [from *Hello, Dolly!*] (Chita), "Take it All Off" [written for *Jerry's Girls*] (Kim, Terri, Robin, Joni, Dorothy), "(Wonderful World of the) Two-a-Day" (reprise) (Dorothy, Leslie, Chita, Ensemble) [end of medley], "Shalom" [from *Milk and Honey*] (Leslie), "Milk and Honey" [from *Milk and Honey*] (Leslie, Ellyn, Kirsten, Kim, Terri, Robin, Deborah), "Before the Parade Passes By" [from *Hello, Dolly!*] (Chita), "Have a Nice Day" [from *La Cage aux Folles*]

(Dorothy, Ellyn, Kirsten, Kim, Robin, Joni), "(There's No Tune Like a) Show Tune" [from *Parade*] (Chita & Ensemble), "If He Walked into My Life" [from *Mame*] (Leslie), "Hello, Dolly!" [from *Hello, Dolly!*] (Dorothy, Leslie, Chita, Ensemble). *Act II*: Entr'acte; Movies Medley: "Just Go to the Movies" [from *A Day in Hollywood/A Night in the Ukraine*] (Ellyn, Kirsten, Kim, Terri, Deborah), "Movies Were Movies" [from *Mack and Mabel*] (Leslie), "Look What Happened to Mabel" [from *Mack and Mabel*] (Chita), "Nelson" [from *A Day in Hollywood/A Night in the Ukraine*] (Dorothy), "Just Go to the Movies" (reprise) [end of Movies Medley] (Chita), "I Don't Want to Know" [from *Dear World*] (Chita), "It's Today" [from *Mame*] (Leslie, Ellyn, Kim, Anita, Terri, Robin, Joni, Deborah), "Mame" [from *Mame*] (Dorothy, Ellyn, Kim, Anita, Terri, Robin, Joni, Deborah), "Kiss Her Now" [from *Dear World*] (Leslie & Kirsten), The Tea Party [from *Dear World*]: "Dickie" (Dorothy), "Voices" (Leslie), "Thoughts" (Chita) [end of Tea Party sequence], "Time Heals Everything" [from *Mack and Mabel*] (Dorothy), "That's How Young I Feel" [from *Mame*] (Chita, Anita, Joni), "My Type" [from *Nightcap*] (Dorothy), La Cage aux Folles Medley: "La Cage aux Folles" (Chita, Kirsten, Anita, Terri, Robin, Joni, Deborah), "Song on the Sand" (Dorothy, Kirsten, Terri, Robin, Deborah), "I Am What I Am" (Leslie), "The Best of Times" (Dorothy, Chita, Leslie, Ensemble) [end of La Cage sequence].

Reviews were mostly raves, but there were one or two pans as well. During the Broadway run, on 4/7/86, Chita Rivera broke her leg in a car crash, and was forced out of the show. She was nominated for a Tony Award (for her performance).

After Broadway. *Jerry's Boys*. ALEX THEATRE, Los Angeles, 7/12/02–7/14/02. *Jerry's Boys* was a showcase of Jerry Herman's hits, along with the first public presentation of "Where in the World is My Prince?," a song from his latest show, *Miss Spectacular*. *Cast*: Malcolm Gets, Nancy Dussault, Jerry Herman, The Gay Men's Chorus of Los Angeles.

357. *Jesus Christ Superstar*

A rock opera depicting the last seven days in the life of Jesus Christ, a mortal figure with human weaknesses, as seen through the eyes of Judas. His religiosity is not mentioned, and the Resurrection is not part of the plot. Jesus descended on a butterfly bridge with three chorus girls. Caiaphas and the priests were suspended from a platform made of dinosaur bones.

Before Broadway. This very controversial show was first presented when Andrew Lloyd Webber was 23. It started life as a 45 rpm record, with "I Don't Know How to Love Him" on the A-side, and "Jesus Christ Superstar" on the flip-side. It became a hit in Britain, and led to a double LP in 1970 (not to be confused with the original cast recording), produced by Robert Stigwood, who was manager of Tim Rice and Andrew Lloyd Webber. With backing from MCA a musical was created from all this, the first (but not last) time a show came out of an LP (see also *Evita, Joseph and the Amazing Technicolor Dreamcoat, Chess*). The double album became a big hit in the USA, but not in Britain, and several unauthorized live "concert versions" were produced. Before the Broadway run opened Tito Capobianco was replaced as director by Tom O'Horgan.

The Broadway Run. MARK HELLINGER THEATRE, 10/12/71–6/30/73. 13 previews from 9/29/71. 711 PERFORMANCES. PRESENTED BY Robert Stigwood, in association with MCA, by arrangement with David Land; MUSIC: Andrew Lloyd Webber; LYRICS: Tim Rice; CONCEIVED FOR THE STAGE BY Tom O'Horgan; DIRECTOR: Tom O'Horgan; SETS: Robin Wagner; COSTUMES: Randy Barcelo; LIGHTING: Jules Fisher; SOUND: Abe Jacob; MUSICAL SUPERVISOR: Mel Rodnon; MUSICAL DIRECTOR: Marc Pressel; ORCHESTRATIONS: Andrew Lloyd Webber; CAST RECORDING on Decca, made on 10/15/71, with one new number—"Could We Start Again, Please?," that had not been on the original two-LP set; PRESS: Merle Debuskey & Leo Stern; GENERAL MANAGEMENT: Gatchell & Neufeld; COMPANY MANAGER: John Corkill; STAGE MANAGER: Galen McKinley; ASSISTANT STAGE MANAGERS: Frank Marino, William Schill, Robert W. Pitman. *Cast:* JUDAS ISCARIOT: Ben Vereen (3), *Patrick Jude* (from 7/5/72); JESUS OF NAZARETH: Jeff Fenholt (1),

Dennis Cooley (from 4/2/73); MARY MAGDALENE: Yvonne Elliman (2), *Marta Heflin* (from 4/17/72), *Kathye Dezina* (from 3/12/73); 1ST PRIEST: Alan Braunstein, *Jeffrey Hillock*; 2ND PRIEST: Michael Meadows, *Roger Lawson*; CAIAPHAS: Bob Bingham (6), *Stephen Klein*; ANNAS: Phil Jethro, *William Daniel Grey*; 3RD PRIEST: Steven Bell, *William Parry*; SIMON ZEALOTES: Dennis Buckley, *Reggie Mack, Samuel E. Wright*; PONTIUS PILATE: Barry Dennen (4), *Seth Allen* (from 1/24/72), *W.P. Dremak* (from 7/24/72), *George Mansour* (from 4/23/73); PETER: Michael Jason, *Robert Brandon*; MAID BY THE FIRE: Linda Rios; OLD MAN: Peter Schlosser; KING HEROD: Paul Ainsley (5); SOLDIERS/JUDAS'S TORMENTORS: Tom Stovall (*Dennis Simpson*), Paul Sylvan (*Edward Q. Barton*), Edward Q. Barton (*Alan Blair*), Tony Gardner (*Clifford Lipson*); TORMENTORS AT JUDAS'S DEATH: James Sbano, Clifford Lipson, Dennis Cooley, Doug Lucas (*Victor Vail*); CURED LEPERS: Robin Grean, James Sbano, Laura Michaels, Clifford Lipson, Bonnie Schon, Pi Douglass, Celia Brin, Dennis Cooley; TEMPLE LADIES: Robin Grean (*Christina Putnam*), Laura Michaels (*Penelope Bodry*), Bonnie Schon, Celia Brin, Anita Morris, Kay Cole, Ferne Bork, Denise Delapenha; APOSTLES: James Sbano, Clifford Lipson, Pi Douglass, Dennis Cooley, Willie Windsor, Samuel E. Wright, Robalee Barnes, Doug Lucas (*Victor Vail*), Peter Schlosser; MERCHANTS: James Sbano, Clifford Lipson, Robalee Barnes, Paul Ainsley (5), Michael Jason (*Robert Brandon*), Dennis Buckley (*Reggie Mack*); REPORTERS: Bonnie Schon, Pi Douglass, Anita Morris, Ted Neeley, Kay Cole, Kurt Yaghjian, Margaret Warncke, Willie Windsor, Ferne Bork, Samuel E. Wright, Robalee Barnes, Doug Lucas (*Victor Vail*); APOSTLE WOMEN: Celia Brin, Anita Morris, Kay Cole, Ferne Bork, Denise Delapenha; LEPERS: Anita Morris, Kay Cole, Kurt Yaghjian, Margaret Warncke, Willie Windsor, Ferne Bork, Samuel E. Wright, Denise Delapenha, Robalee Barnes, Doug Lucas (*Victor Vail*), Charlotte Crossley, Cecelia Norfleet, Janet Powell, Ted Neeley, Linda Rios, Michael Jason (*Robert Brandon*), Dennis Buckley (*Reggie Mack*), Peter Schlosser, Paul Ainsley (5); SOUL GIRLS: Charlotte Crossley, Janet Powell, Cecelia Norfleet. *Replacements*: *William Daniel Grey, Shirley Sypert, Christopher Allen, William Parry, Randy Wilson, Roy Bailey, Lynn Gerb, Anthony White, Michael Lamont, Lorraine Feather, Laura Michaels, Dan Gibson, Mark Shannon, Christopher Allen, Randy Wilson, Lynn Gerb, Roy Bailey, Bob Bingham, Martha Deering, Carol Estey, Michael Lamont, Linda Ribbach, Realinda Farrell, DeMarest Grey, William Gestrich, Anthony White.* **Understudies**: Judas: Kurt Yaghjian; Jesus: Ted Neeley & Dennis Cooley; Mary Magdalene: Denise Delapenha; Caiaphas: Peter Schlosser; Pilate: Phil Jethro; Herod: Michael Meadows; Annas: Michael Jason; Simon: Robalee Barnes; Peter: Willie Windsor, *Doug Lucas, Victor Vail*; 1st & 2nd Priest: Clifford Lipson; 3rd Priest: Doug Lucas, *Victor Vail*. **Swing Girl**: Marsha Faye; **Swing Boy**: Nat Morris. **Musicians**: RANDALL'S ISLAND (7th-billed). ELECTRIC GUITAR/ACOUSTIC GUITAR: Elliott Randall; SOPRANO SAX/TENOR SAX/BARITONE SAX/FLUTE/CLARINET: Paul Fleisher; PIANO/ORGAN: Pot Namanworth; DRUMS/PERCUSSION: Allen Herman; BASS GUITAR: Gary King; RHYTHM GUITAR: Jim Miller. Note: the original Randall's Island had been smaller, more compact: GUITAR: Elliott Randall; VOCALS: Sam Wright; DRUMS: Allen Herman; FENDER BASS: Wolf Friedman. It was expanded for Broadway. **Act** I: Overture (Company); "Heaven on Their Minds" (Judas); Bethany; FRIDAY NIGHT: "What's the Buzz" (Jesus, Mary, Apostles, Their Women); "Strange Thing Mystifying" (Judas, Jesus, Apostles, Their Women), "Everything's All Right" (Mary, Judas, Jesus, Apostles, Their Women); Jerusalem: SUNDAY: "This Jesus Must Die" (Caiaphas, Annas, Priests, Company), "Hosanna" (Caiaphas, Jesus, Priests, Company), "Simon Zealotes" (Simon & Company), "Poor Jerusalem" (Jesus); Pontius Pilate's House: MONDAY: "Pilate's Dream" (Pilate), "The Temple" (Jesus & Company), "Everything's All Right" (reprise) (Mary Magdalene & Jesus), "I Don't Know How to Love Him" (Mary Magdalene & Jesus); TUESDAY: "Damned for All Time"/"Blood Money"(Judas, Annas, Caiaphas, Priests). **Act II**: THURSDAY NIGHT: "The Last Supper" (Jesus, Judas, Apostles); The Garden: "I Only Want to Say (Gethsemane)" (Jesus), "The Arrest" (Peter, Jesus, Apostles, Reporters, Caiaphas, Annas), "Peter's Denial" (Maid, Peter, Soldier, Old Man, Mary Magdalene); Pilate's Palace: FRIDAY: "Pilate and Christ" (Pilate, Soldier, Jesus, Company); House of Herod: "King Herod's Song" (Herod), "Could We Start Again, Please?" (Mary & Peter), "Judas' Death" (Judas, Annas, Caiaphas); Pilate's Palace: "Trial Before Pilate" (Pilate, Caiaphas, Jesus, Mob),

"Superstar" (Voice of Judas, Company); Golgotha: "The Crucifixion" (Jesus & Company), "John 19:41" (Orchestra).

Broadway reviews were divided. It received Tony nominations for score, sets, costumes, lighting, and for Ben Vereen.

After Broadway. AMPHITHEATRE, Universal Studios, Los Angeles. Opened on 7/26/72. 77 PERFORMANCES. *Cast*: Ted Neeley, Heather MacRae, Carl Anderson, Bruce Scott.

THEATRE NATIONAL DU PALAIS DE CHAILLOT, Paris, 1972. PRESENTED BY Annie Fargue & Robert Stigwood; DIRECTOR: Victor Spinetti; MUSICAL DIRECTOR: Anthony Bowles. *Cast*: JESUS: Daniel Beretta; JUDAS: Farid Dali; MARY MAGDALENE: Anne-Marie David; ANNAS: Mourad Malki; CAIAPHAS: Bob Bingham; PILATE: Michel Mella; HEROD: Remy Deshauteurs.

PALACE THEATRE, London, 8/9/72–8/23/80. Previews from 7/29/72. 3,358 PERFORMANCES. A smaller, less flashy production than on Broadway. On 10/3/78, with its 2,620th performance, it surpassed *Oliver!* as the longest-running musical on the British stage to that time (in turn, it was superseded by *Cats*). PRESENTED BY Robert Stigwood; DIRECTOR: Jim Sharman; SETS: Brian Thomson; COSTUMES: Gabrielle Falk; ORIGINAL MUSICAL DIRECTOR: Anthony Bowles. *Cast*: JESUS: Paul Nicholas; JUDAS: Stephen Tate, *Colm Wilkinson*; MARY MAGDALENE: Dana Gillespie; PILATE: John Parker; HEROD: Paul Jabara, *Barry James, Terry Wood, Victor Spinetti, Jonathan Kramer*; CHORUS INCLUDED: Elaine Paige, Lionel Morton.

Jesus Christ Superstar has been translated into 11 languages, and staged in over 22 countries.

THE MOVIE. 1973. PRODUCERS: Robert Stigwood & Norman Jewison; MUSIC: Andre Previn; WRITER/DIRECTOR: Norman Jewison. *Cast*: JESUS: Ted Neeley; JUDAS: Carl Anderson; PILATE: Barry Dennen; CAIAPHAS: Bob Bingham; MARY MAGDALENE: Yvonne Elliman; HEROD: Josh Mostel [Zero's son].

358. *Jesus Christ Superstar (1977 Broadway revival)*

This production was staged concert style. Despite that, it is a bona fide Broadway musical entry.

Before Broadway. Broadway was the culmination of a tour that had opened on 1/11/77, at Kalamazoo, Mich., and closed on 4/24/77, at Stratford, Conn. The tour had the same crew as for the subsequent Broadway run, except SETS: Frank Desmond; COSTUMES: Barbara Sabella; STAGE MANAGER: Donald Moss. It had the same cast too, except MARY MAGDALENE: Joy Garrett; SIMON: Shelly Safir; 2ND PRIEST: Garon Douglass; MAID BY FIRE: Joy Kohner; APOSTLES: Kelly St. John, David Cahn, Norman Meister. For Broadway Alan Blair was replaced by D. Bradley Jones, and Mara Joyce by Claudette Washington.

The Broadway Run. LONGACRE THEATRE, 11/23/77–2/12/78. 96 PERFORMANCES. A Mammoth production, PRESENTED BY Hal Zeiger; MUSIC: Andrew Lloyd Webber; LYRICS: Tim Rice; DIRECTOR: William Daniel Grey; CHOREOGRAPHER: Kelly Carrol; SETS/COSTUMES/LIGHTING/SOUND: uncredited; MUSICAL DIRECTOR: Peter Phillips; ORCHESTRATIONS: uncredited; PRESS: Hal Zeiger; COMPANY MANAGER: Manuel L. Levine; PRODUCTION STAGE MANAGER: Chuck Linker; STAGE MANAGER: Rick Ralston; ASSISTANT STAGE MANAGER: Alan Blair. *Cast*: JUDAS ISCARIOT: Patrick Jude; JESUS OF NAZARETH: William Daniel Grey; MARY MAGDALENE: Barbara Niles; 1ST PRIEST: Doug Lucas; 2ND PRIEST: Richard Tolin; CAIAPHAS: Christopher Cable; ANNAS: Steve Schochet; SIMON ZEALOTES: Bobby London; PETER: Randy Martin; PONTIUS PILATE: Randy Wilson; SOLDIERS: D. Bradley Jones & George Bernhard; TORMENTORS: D. Bradley Jones & George Bernhard; SOUL GIRLS: Freida Ann Williams, Claudette Washington, Pauletta Pearson; MAID BY THE FIRE: Celeste Hogan; APOSTLES: Doug Lucas, Richard Tolin, David Cahn, Ken Samuels, Lennie Del Duca; KING HEROD: Mark Syers. **Understudies**: Jesus: Randy Wilson; Judas/Pilate: Steve Schochet; Mary Magdalene: Freida Ann Williams; Caiaphas: Doug Lucas; Chorus: Alan Blair & Kelly Carrol.

After Broadway. PAPER MILL PLAYHOUSE, New Jersey, 1987. DIRECTOR: Robert Johanson; CHOREOGRAPHER: Susan Stroman. *Cast*:

Robert Johanson, James Rocco, Kim Criswell, Robert Cuccioli, George Dvorsky, Judith McCauley, John Sloman.

TOUR. A long anniversary tour, PRESENTED BY Landmark Entertainment Group, Magic Promotions & Theatricals, and TAP Products, opened at Morris A. Mechanic Theatre, Baltimore, on 12/15/92. Previews from 12/12/92. DIRECTOR/CHOREOGRAPHER: Tony Christopher; SETS: Bill Stabile; COSTUMES: David Paulin; LIGHTING: Rick Belzer; SOUND: Jonathan Deans; MUSICAL DIRECTOR: Michael Rapp. *Cast*: JESUS: Ted Neeley; JUDAS: Carl Anderson; MARY MAGDALENE: Leesa Richards, *Irene Cara*; CAIAPHAS: David Bedella; ANNAS: Danny Zolli; SIMON: Steven X. Ward; PILATE: Dennis De Young; PETER: Kevin R. Wright; HEROD: Laurent Giroux. After 112 cities this tour played Off Broadway, at the PARAMOUNT THEATRE, Madison Square Garden, 1/17/95–1/29/95. 16 PERFORMANCES. MUSICAL DIRECTOR: Craig Barna. It had the same basic cast, except HEROD: Douglass Fraser; MARY MAGDALENE: Syreeta Wright; SIMON: Lawrence Clayton; PETER: Mike Eldred. During this short New York run Carl Anderson, playing Judas, got sick, and was replaced by Lawrence Clayton, whose role as Simon went to Robert H. Fowler.

359. *Jesus Christ Superstar (2000 Broadway revival)*

This production ran 2 hours 20 minutes.

Before Broadway. This revival had its origins in a production at NEWCASTLE, England, which then went to London's West End, where it re-opened the LYCEUM THEATRE (the theatre was refurbished for this production), 11/19/96–3/28/98. Previews from 11/12/96. It got good reviews. DIRECTOR: Gale Edwards; CHOREOGRAPHER: Aletta Collins; SETS: John Napier; LIGHTING: David Hersey; MUSICAL SUPERVISOR: Mike Dixon; MUSICAL DIRECTOR: Simon Lee. *Cast*: JESUS: Steve Balsamo (for a year), *Glenn Carter* (closed the show); JUDAS: Zubin Varla, *Ramon Tikaram*; MARY MAGDALENE: Joanna Ampill. Originally there were going to be three North American tryouts — Toronto, Chicago and Boston, but these were scrapped, and the show went straight to Broadway. Auditions were held in New York on 8/20/99. Glenn Carter was announced in his role on 1/14/00. He appeared as part of the deal between British and American Equity Unions. Rehearsals began on 2/14/00. There was a press preview on 3/8/00. Early in Broadway previews Jason Pebworth (as Judas) was replaced by Tony Vincent, who until then was playing Simon. Michael K. Lee stepped in as Simon.

The Broadway Run. FORD CENTER FOR THE PERFORMING ARTS, 4/16/00–9/3/00. 28 previews from 3/23/00. 161 PERFORMANCES. PRESENTED BY The Really Useful Superstar Company & Nederlander Producing Company of America, in association with Terry Allen Kramer; MUSIC: Andrew Lloyd Webber; LYRICS: Tim Rice; DIRECTOR: Gale Edwards; ASSISTANT DIRECTOR: Kevin Moriarty; CHOREOGRAPHER: Anthony Van Laast; SETS: Peter J. Davison; COSTUMES: Roger Kirk; LIGHTING: Mark McCullough; SOUND: Richard Ryan; MUSICAL SUPERVISOR: Simon Lee; MUSICAL DIRECTOR: Patrick Vaccariello; ORCHESTRATIONS: Andrew Lloyd Webber; PRESS: Boneau/Bryan-Brown; CASTING: Johnson — Liff; GENERAL MANAGEMENT: The Charlotte Wilcox Company; COMPANY MANAGER: Susan J. Sampliner; PRODUCTION STAGE MANAGER: Bonnie Panson; STAGE MANAGER: Ira Mont; ASSISTANT STAGE MANAGER: Kenneth J. McGee. *Cast:* JESUS OF NAZARETH: Glenn Carter (1); JUDAS ISCARIOT: Tony Vincent (2), *Manoel Felciano* (during Mr. Vincent's illness); MARY MAGDALENE: Maya Days (3); PONTIUS PILATE: Kevin Gray (4); KING HEROD: Paul Kandel (5); CAIAPHAS: Frederick B. Owens (6); ANNAS: Ray Walker (7); SIMON ZEALOTES: Michael K. Lee (8), *Jason Wooten*; PETER: Rodney Hicks (9); APOSTLES/DISCIPLES: Christian Borle, Lisa Brescia, D'Monroe, Manoel Felciano, Somer Lee Graham, J. Todd Howell, Daniel C. Levine, Anthony Manough, Joseph Melendez, Eric Millegan, Michael Seelbach, Alexander Selma, David St. Louis, Shayna Steele, Max von Essen, Joe Wilson Jr., Andrew Wright, *Bernard Dotson, Jessica Phillips, Adam Simmons, Ray Walker, Ashley Wilkinson*; SOUL GIRLS/DISCIPLES: Merle Dandridge, Deidre Goodwin, Lana Gordon; PRIESTS/GUARDS: Hank Campbell, Devin Richards, Timothy Warmen. *Understudies*: Jesus: Max von Essen; Judas:

Manoel Felciano; Mary Magdalene: Merle Dandridge & Shayna Steele; Pilate: Timothy Warmen; Herod: Adam Simmons & Ray Walker; Caiaphas: Devin Richards & David St. Louis; Annas: Manoel Felciano & Adam Simmons; Simon: Anthony Manough; Peter: Anthony Manough & Andrew Wright. *Swings*: Bernard Dotson, Keenah Reid, Adam Simmons. *Orchestra:* KEYBOARDS: Jim Laev, Mark Berman, T.O. Sterrett; DRUMS: Gary Tillman; BASS: Joe Quigley; GUITARS: Doug Quinn & J.J. McGeehan; PERCUSSION: Howard Joines; TRUMPETS: Bob Millikan, Tino Gagliardi, Lorraine Cohen-Moses; PICCOLO TRUMPETS: Bob Millikan & Tino Gagliardi; FLUGELHORN: Lorraine Cohen-Moses; FRENCH HORNS: Larry Di Bello & Theresa MacDonnell; TROMBONES: Charles Gordon & Bob Suttmann; BASS TROMBONE/TUBA: John Hahn; FLUTE: Gretchen Pusch; & Scott Shachter; PICCOLO: Gretchen Pusch; CLARINET/TENOR SAX: Scott Schachter.

The show got terrible Broadway reviews. It received a Tony nomination for revival of a musical.

After Broadway. TOUR. Opened 11/1/02–11/17/02, at La Mirada Theatre for the Performing Arts, Calif., then went on the rest of the tour. PRESENTED BY Tom McCoy; DIRECTOR: Gale Edwards was not available, so her assistant, Kevin Moriarty, directed; CHOREOGRAPHER: David Wilder; SETS: Peter J. Davison; COSTUMES: Roger Kirk; LIGHTING: Mark McCullough; SOUND: Jon Gottlieb & Phil Allen; MUSICAL DIRECTOR: Craig Barna. *Cast*: JESUS: Sebastian Bach (he was fired in Columbus on 3/28/03), *Eric Kunze* (from 4/15/03); JUDAS: Carl Anderson, *Lawrence Clayton* (from 7/8/03); MARY MAGDALENE: Natalie Toro; PILATE: Stephen Breithaupt; SIMON: Todd Fournier; HEROD: Peter Kevoian, *Barry Dennen*; CAIAPHAS: Lawson Skala; ANNAS: Jeffrey Polk; PETER: James Clow; ALSO WITH: Joan Almedilla, Perry Brown, Dana Solimando.

PBS TV. 4/11/01. *Cast*: JESUS: Glenn Carter; JUDAS: Jerome Pradon; MARY MAGDALENE: Renee Castle; HEROD: Rik Mayall; SIMON: Tony Vincent; CAIAPHAS: Frederick B. Owens.

STUDIO RECORDING, 4/1/03, on Decca Broadway. *Cast*: JESUS: Jeff Fenholt; JUDAS: Ben Vereen; MARY MAGDALENE: Yvonne Elliman.

360. *Jimmy*

Set between 1925 and 1931. A musical play of the life and good times of Mayor Jimmy Walker of New York City. Betty Compton was Jimmy's girlfriend (she had worked for Jack L. Warner in Hollywood; Mr. Warner produced *Jimmy*). Allie was Jimmy's estranged wife. The show featured a raid on a speakeasy by Izzie and Moe (see *Nowhere to Go But Up*).

Before Broadway. This show was previously called *Beau James*. It was Jack Warner's first Broadway production. He had been a friend of Jimmy Walker's. Jack Cassidy was the original choice for Jimmy. It was impressionist Frank Gorshin's Broadway debut. The early book was about the corruption of that period, but in the end it was all toned down. It was this show that pushed *Mame* out of the Winter Garden and into the Broadway Theatre.

The Broadway Run. WINTER GARDEN THEATRE, 10/23/69–1/3/70. 8 previews. 84 PERFORMANCES. PRESENTED BY Jack L. Warner, in association with Don Saxon; MUSIC/LYRICS: Bill & Patti Jacob; BOOK: Melville Shavelson; BASED ON the 1957 movie *Beau James*, written by Jack Rose & Melville Shavelson, and starring Bob Hope, which in turn was based on the 1949 biographical novel by Gene Fowler; DIRECTOR: Joseph Anthony; CHOREOGRAPHER: Peter Gennaro; SETS: Oliver Smith; COSTUMES: W. Robert LaVine; LIGHTING: Peggy Clark; AUDIO ADVISER: Saki Oura; MUSICAL DIRECTOR/VOCAL ARRANGEMENTS: Milton Rosenstock; MUSICAL ARRANGEMENTS: Jack Andrews; DANCE MUSIC ARRANGEMENTS: John Berkman; CAST RECORDING on RCA Victor; PRESS: Marvin Kohn; GENERAL MANAGER: Al Goldin; COMPANY MANAGER: G. Warren McClane; PRODUCTION STAGE MANAGER: William Ross; STAGE MANAGER: Michael Sinclair; ASSISTANT STAGE MANAGERS: Jeanna Belkin & Ellen Wittman. *Cast:* JIMMY WALKER: Frank Gorshin (1) ✩; BONNIE: Cindi Bulak; JIM HINES: Jack Collins (4), *Stanley Simmonds*; AL SMITH: William Griffis (6); ALLIE WALKER: Julie Wilson (3) ✩; FRANCIS XAVIER ALOYSIUS O'TOOLE: Edward Becker; LAWRENCE

HORATIO FINK: Stanley Simmonds; ANTONIO VISCELLI: Paul Forrest; STANISLAUS KAZIMIR WOJCIEZKOWSKI: Henry Lawrence; MRS. AL SMITH: Peggy Hewett; MISS MANHATTAN: Sally Neal; MISS BRONX: Andrea Duda; MISS BROOKLYN: Carol Conte; MISS RICHMOND: Nancy Dalton; MISS QUEENS: Cindi Bulak; STAGE MANAGER: Gary Gendell; BETTY COMPTON: Anita Gillette (2) ☆; TEXAS GUINAN: Dorothy Claire (8); EDWARD DURYEA DOWLING: Larry Douglas (5); WARRINGTON BROCK: Clifford Fearl; CHARLEY HAND: Evan Thompson (9); MOE: Del Horstmann; IZZY: Carl Nicholas; POLICEMAN: Herb Fields; PHOTOGRAPHERS: Andy G. Bew & Tony Stevens; SECRETARY: Barbara Andres; REPORTER: Frank Newell; TAILOR: Carl Nicholas; POLITICIANS: Del Horstmann, Ben Laney, Joe McGrath; GIRL IN FUR COAT: Carol Conte; POLICEMAN: Ben Laney; PASSERBY: Sandi McCreadie; MRS. COMPTON: Sibyl Bowan (7); BAND VOCALIST: Joseph McGrath; PROCESS SERVER: John D. Anthony; DOORMAN: Steven Boockvor; RECORDED IMPERSONATIONS: Dwight Weist; DANCING ENSEMBLE: Andy G. Bew, Steven Boockvor, Cindi Bulak, Christopher Chadman, Carol Conte, Nancy Dalton, Andrea Duda, David Evans, Gary Gendell, Scott Hunter, Saundra McPherson, Sally Neal, Frank Newell, Harold Pierson, Eileen Shannon, Tony Stevens, Monica Tiller, Pat Trott; SINGING ENSEMBLE: Barbara Andres, John D. Anthony, Ed Becker, Austin Colyer, Gini Eastwood, Herb Fields, Paul Forrest, Barbara Gregory, Peggy Hewett, Del Horstmann, Ben Laney, Henry Lawrence, Mary Louise, Sandi McCreadie, Joseph McGrath, Carl Nicholas, Claire Theiss, Roberta Vatske. **Standby**: Jimmy: Danny Meehan. **Understudies**: Betty: Roberta Vatske; Allie/Mrs. Compton: Barbara Andres; Hines: Evan Thompson; Smith: Stanley Simmonds; Texas: Claire Theiss; Charley: Joe McGrath. **Act I: Scene 1** S.S. *Conte Grande;* 1931: "Will You Think of Me Tomorrow?" (Jimmy); **Scene 2** Jimmy's apartment; 1925: "The Little Woman" (Smith, Hines, Jimmy, then Allie & Jimmy); **Scene 3** Tammany Hall; 1925: "The Darlin' of New York" (Hines, Smith, Charley, Allie, Jimmy, Five Lovely Ladies, Campaign Workers), "Five Lovely Ladies" (Jimmy) [a new number developed and added soon after opening]; **Scene 4** Texas Guinan's; 1925: "Oh, Gee!" (Betty), "The Walker Walk" (Texas, Betty, Guinan Girls, Jimmy, Patrons); **Scene 5** Betty's apartment; 1925: "That Old Familiar Ring" (Betty & Jimmy); **Scene 6** The 1925 Victory Celebration: "The Walker Walk" (reprise) (Hines, Politicians, Party Workers); **Scene 7** Allie's bedroom; 1925: "I Only Wanna Laugh" (Allie); SCENE 8 City Hall; 1926: "They Never Proved a Thing" (Jimmy, Hines, Viscelli, Fink, O'Toole, Wojciezkowski, Politicians, Brock, Tailor), "What's Out There for Me?" (Jimmy) [dropped soon after opening]. **Act II: Scene 1** Riverside Drive; 1929: "Riverside Drive" (Jimmy & Strollers); **Scene 2** Betty's new apartment; 1929: "The Squabble Song" (Jimmy & Betty); **Scene 3** Polling booth; 1929; **Scene 4** Central Park Casino; 1929: "Medley" (Band Vocalist), "One in a Million" (Jimmy & Betty); **Scene 5** The street; 1930: "It's a Nice Place to Visit" (Viscelli, Fink, O'Toole, Wojciezkowski, Brock, Girl in Fur Coat, Company); **Scene 6** Betty's dressing room; 1931: "The Charmin' Son-of-a-Bitch" (Allie), "Jimmy" (Betty), "Five Lovely Ladies" (reprise) (Jimmy); **Scene 7** Washington Square; 1931: "Our Jimmy" (Hines, Jimmy, Allie, Hand, Smith, Texas, Five Lovely Ladies, Policemen, Spectators) [inserted here soon after opening]; **Scene 8** City Hall; 1931; **Scene 9** Yankee Stadium; 1931: "Life is a One-Way Street" (Jimmy); **Scene 10** S.S. *Conte Grande*; 1931: Finale (Jimmy & Betty).

It was universally panned. The show lost a million dollars. It received a Tony nomination for costumes.

361. *John Murray Anderson's Almanac*

The Broadway Run. IMPERIAL THEATRE, 12/10/53–6/26/54. 229 PERFORMANCES. PRESENTED BY Michael Grace, Stanley Gilkey, Harry Rigby; MUSIC/LYRICS/SKETCHES: various writers; ENTIRE PRODUCTION DEVISED & DIRECTED BY: John Murray Anderson; SKETCH DIRECTOR: Cyril Ritchard; CHOREOGRAPHER: Donald Saddler; SETS: Raoul Pene du Bois; COSTUMES: Thomas Becher; MUSICAL DIRECTOR/VOCAL ARRANGEMENTS: Buster Davis; ORCHESTRATIONS: Ted Royal; DANCE MUSIC ARRANGEMENTS: Gerald Alters; PRESS: Sol Jacobson & Lewis Harmon; COMPANY MANAGER: Manning Gurian; PRODUCTION STAGE MANAGER: Arthur Barkow; STAGE MANAGER: Perry Bruskin; ASSISTANT

STAGE MANAGER: Dennis Murray, *Wayne Brown*. **Part I: Prologue** "Harlequinade" (m/l: Richard Adler & Jerry Ross). HARLEQUIN: Carleton Carpenter, *Orson Bean*; PUNCINELLO: Harry Mimmo, *Kenneth Urmston*; PIERROT: James Jewell, *Harry Snow, Tony Bavaar;* PIERRETTE: Celia Lipton; COLUMBINE: Nanci Crompton; PIERRETTES: Lee Becker, Imelda De Martin, Dorothy Dushock, Greb Lober, Ilona Murai, Margot Myers, Gwen Neilson, Gloria Smith, *Joan Morton, Toni Wheelis*; PIERROTS: Jimmy Albright, Hank Brunjes, Ronald Cecill, Dean Crane (*Skeet Guenther*), Ralph McWilliams, Gerard Leavitt (*Peter Deign*). **The Almanac**. **Page 1** Sketch: The Coronation. Song: "Queen for a Day" (m/l: Richard Adler & Jerry Ross). THE FOUR QUEENS: Jacqueline Mickles, Colleen Hutchins, Monique Van Vooren, Tina Louise, *Siri*; THE BRIDEGROOMS: Larry Kert, Bob Kole, George Reeder, Jay Harnick, Ronald Cecill, Ralph McWilliams, Hank Brunjes, Gerard Leavitt (*Peter Deign*), George Vosburgh; MISS REINGOLD: Hermione Gingold (1); **Page 2** Sketch: Best Seller. "My Cousin Who?" (by Jean Kerr). DAVID: Billy De Wolfe (2); BUTLERS: Jimmy Albright, Kenneth Urmston, Ronald Cecill, Ralph McWilliams; WITCH DOCTOR: Dean Crane, *Skeet Guenther*; MAIDS: Toni Wheelis & Gwen Neilson; REBECCA: Celia Lipton; LOUISE: Ilona Murai; **Page 3** Teenage: "(You're So Much a) Part of Me" (m/l: Richard Adler & Jerry Ross). The Pierrot of 1953 (sung by Carleton Carpenter). The Pierrette of 1953 (sung by Elaine Dunn); **Page 4** Song: "I Dare to Dream" (m: Michael Grace & Carl Tucker; l: Sammy Gallop) [sung by Polly Bergen (4)]; **Page 5** The Concert Stage: "The Cello" (m: Charles Zwar; l: Leslie Julian-Jones). THE CELLIST: Hermione Gingold (1); **Page 6** Don Brown's Body (by Jean Kerr): A reading of Mickey Spillane, complete with choral chants: MIKE HAMMER: Orson Bean (5); SALLY DUPREY: Kay Medford, *Alice Pearce*; MAN: Carleton Carpenter; CHORUS: Jay Harnick, Colleen Hutchins, Jacqueline Mickles, Tina Louise, Bob Kole, Monique Van Vooren, Siri, George Reeder, Larry Kert, *Joan Morton*; **Page 7** Folklore: "Mark Twain" (by Harry Belafonte) [sung by Harry Belafonte (3)] (guitarist: Millard Thomas) [scene dropped during the run]; **Page 8** Revival: "The Nightingale and the Rose." Adapted by John Murray Anderson from the story by Oscar Wilde. Song: "Nightingale, Bring Me a Rose" (m: Henry Sullivan; l: John Murray Anderson. Sung by James Jewell (*Henry Snow*). THE STORY TELLER: Celia Lipton; THE STUDENT: Dean Crane, *Tony Bavaar*; THE PRINCE: Gerard Leavitt, *Peter Deign*; THE COQUETTE: Margot Myers; THE NIGHTINGALE: Nanci Crompton; GUESTS AT THE BALL: Siri, Monique Van Vooren, Tina Louise, Colleen Hutchins, Greb Lober, Dorothy Dushock, Gloria Smith, Gwen Neilson, Hank Brunjes, Ralph McWilliams, Ronald Cecill, George Reeder, Jimmy Albright, *Larry Kert, George Vosburgh, Toni Wheelis*; **Page 9** European Express (also called Travel) (written by Orford St. John for the London revue *Swinging the Gate*). Sub-titled Tea in Ceylon. Two ladies on the Orient Express, who sip port all the way to Istanbul and get pretty drunk. Mrs. B talks about Ceylon until she finally gets to believe there's no such place. MRS. A: Hermione Gingold (1); MRS. B: Billy De Wolfe (2); **Page 10** "My Love is a Wanderer" (m/l: Bart Howard) [sung by Polly Bergen (4)] [scene dropped during the run]; **Page 11** "Tin Pan Alley" (m: Cy Coleman; l: Joseph McCarthy Jr.): THE SONG PLUGGER: Carleton Carpenter; WITH: Ronald Cecill, Jay Harnick, Larry Kert, Bob Kole. "Mammy Songs:" Ralph McWilliams & Kenneth Urmston; "Rhythm Songs:" George Reeder, Imelda De Martin, Lee Becker, Greb Lober, Dorothy Dushock; "Torch Songs:" Gloria Smith, Ilona Murai, Margot Myers, Hank Brunjes, Gerard Leavitt (*Peter Deign*), Dean Crane (*Tony Bavaar*); "Patriotic Songs:" Elaine Dunn; **Page 12** Commentary (by Orson Bean). Song: "Merry Little Minuet" (m/l: Sheldon Harnick; this had been cut from *Two's Company*). Performed by: Orson Bean (5) [Note: scene dropped during the run]; **Page 13** Sketch: Musicals a la Mode: "Hope You Come Back" (by Sumner Locke-Elliott). Song: "Hope You Come Back" (m/l: Richard Adler & Jerry Ross). MEG: Polly Bergen (4), *Celia Lipton*; BETH: Nanci Crompton; JO: Elaine Dunn; AMY: Hermione Gingold (1); MARMEE: Kay Medford, *Alice Pearce*; LAURIE: Billy De Wolfe (2); FATHER: Orson Bean (5); FRIENDS: Harry Belafonte, James Jewell (*Harry Snow*), Carleton Carpenter, Company. **Part II: Page 1** Ziegfeldiana: "If Every Month Were June" (m: Henry Sullivan; l: John Murray Anderson) [sung by Polly Bergen (4)]. THE SPRING BRIDE: Colleen Hutchins; THE SUMMER BRIDE: Siri; THE AUTUMN BRIDE: Jacqueline Mickles; THE WINTER BRIDE: Monique Van Vooren, *Tina Louise*; THE BOUQUET: Nanci Crompton; THE TRAIN BEARERS: Imelda De Martin,

Lee Becker, Dorothy Dushock, Gwen Neilson; *Page 2* "Which Witch?" (m: Charles Zwar; l: Alan Melville) [sung by Hermione Gingold (1)]; *Page 3* Colour Print: La Loge (Renoir) (by Herbert Farjeon). "Fini" (m/l: Richard Adler & Jerry Ross). [sung by Polly Bergen (4)]. THE MAN IN THE BOX: Jay Harnick; *Page 4* Sketch: "Cartoon" (by Arthur Macrae): 1ST SECRETARY: Kay Medford, *Colleen Hutchins*; 2ND SECRETARY: Colleen Hutchins, *Alice Pearce*; THE NEW MANAGER: Orson Bean (5); *Page 5* Woodcut: "Acorn in the Meadow" (m/l: Richard Adler & Jerry Ross) [sung by Harry Belafonte (3)]; *Page 6* Harry Mimmo: STARRING: Harry Mimmo; THE LADIES: Tina Louise, Jacqueline Mickles, Monique Van Vooren; SEDAN CHAIR BEARERS: Jay Harnick & Larry Kert [scene dropped during the run]; *Page 7* "When Am I Going to Meet Your Mother?" (m/l: Richard Adler & Jerry Ross) [sung & danced by Elaine Dunn & Carleton Carpenter]; *Page 8* Gossip Column: Dinner for One (by Lauri Wylie). The most famous sketch, about a 90-year old grand dame seated alone at the end of a long, elegant dining table. Her decrepit butler sets places also for four of her long-dead admirers, and he takes their place in turn, toasting her, clears the places, then sets them again, toasts again, until finally they're both blotto. He then takes her off staggering to her room. THE LADY: Hermione Gingold (1); THE BUTLER: Billy De Wolfe (2); *Page 9* Commentary. [The Chinese Monologue (American Town) was written by Orson Bean & Phil Green). Performed by: Orson Bean (5); *Page 10* Song: Calypso. "Hold 'em Joe" (written by Harry Thomas—who was actually Harry Belafonte) [sung by Harry Belafonte; danced by Ilona Murai, George Reeder, Gloria Smith, Monique Van Vooren, Colleen Hutchins, Dancers]; *Page 11* Paris '90s: "La Pistachio" (by Billy K. Wells, and adapted for the *Almanac* by Sumner Locke-Elliott). BoBo, the Queen of Montmartre, makes an impression on straitlaced Bostonian Cornelius. BOBO: Hermione Gingold (1); CORNELIUS: Billy De Wolfe (2); FIFI: Kay Medford; *Page 12* Astrology: "The Earth and the Sky" (m/l: John Rox) [sung by Polly Bergen (4)] [added during the run]; *Finale*: Company; *Epilogue*: Hermione Gingold (1).

Note: The "Pages" were not always performed in the order given here (above is opening night order). Indeed, during the run, the order would vary tremendously. In addition, new sketches and songs were added, and others taken away. New sketches over the course of the run included: Health Talk (written & performed by Hermione Gingold); Diplomacy. "Paisan" (m/l: Adler & Ross). THE DIPLOMAT: Harry Mimmo; THE REPORTERS: Imelda De Martin, Lee Becker, Margot Myers, Gloria Smith, Toni Wheelis, Greb Lober, Gwen Neilson, Dorothy Dushock; and Jonathan Winters' Marine Corps sketch. New Songs included: "Elevator" (m/l: Adler & Ross. Sung by Elaine Dunn); "Anema e Core" ("With All My Heart and Soul") (m: Salve Desposito; English l: Mann Curtis & Harry Akst) (sung by Tony Bavaar). THE MINSTREL: Tony Bavaar; THE COUNTESS: Gwen Neilson; COURTIERS: Jay Harnick, Skeets Guenther, Hank Brunjes; and "Flowers" (m/l: Jerry Bock & Sheldon Harnick; performed by Hermione Gingold).

ALMANAC BEAUTIES: Monique Van Vooren, Tina Louise, Colleen Hutchins, Jacqueline Mickles. **Understudies**: For Harry Belafonte: Larry Kert; For Dean Crane/Tony Bavaar: Bob Kole.

Reviews were quite divided, but most were good or very good. Harry Belafonte won a Tony Award and a Donaldson Award; Donaldsons also went to Hermione Gingold and Billy De Wolfe for female and male debuts respectively.

362. *Joseph and the Amazing Technicolor Dreamcoat*

The biblical story about Joseph in Egypt. Joseph is given a splendid multi-colored coat by his father, Jacob. Joseph's eleven brothers are envious and sell him into slavery in Egypt. But his ability to interpret dreams leads him to become the Elvis-type Pharaoh's adviser. The brothers show up years later looking for food, and have to go through Joseph. There is no spoken dialog. Part I is the prologue, and the rest of the story is Part II.

Before Broadway. Andrew Lloyd Webber was only 20 when this show was first produced. Colet Court was a school that fed pupils into the famous British school, St. Paul's, and head of music there was Alan Doggett, who needed something short, morally uplifting, and hopefully with a religious theme for an end-of-term concert. Mr. Doggett knew Andrew Lloyd Webber's parents (Andrew's younger brother was a student there), and knew that Andrew was an up-and-coming composer. *Joseph and the Amazing Technicolor Dreamcoat*, a 15-minute piece, was completed in two months, and premiered at COLET COURT the afternoon of 3/1/68, performed by the St. Paul's Junior School Boys' Choir. Andrew Lloyd Webber wrote the music, and Tim Rice (who was only 23 at the time) wrote the lyrics to fit it. It was well-received. Andrew Lloyd Webber's father (himself a musician) encouraged the development of the show. This "pop cantata" soon became 20 minutes long, and played before 2,500 people at CENTRAL HALL, WESTMINSTER (where Lloyd Webber pere was organist), on 5/12/68. In the audience that night happened to be music critic Derek Jewell, and he gave it a favorable mention in his *Sunday Times* column. On 11/9/68 it was performed at ST. PAUL'S CATHEDRAL. It was performed again at CENTRAL HALL, WESTMINSTER, 1/28/69, by the Joseph Consortium. *Cast*: JOSEPH: David Daltrey; PHARAOH: Tim Rice; ALSO WITH: the Mixed Bag (Malcolm Parry, Terry Saunders, Bryan Watson, John Cook), the Wonderschool Boys' Choir (Alan Doggett, musical director), and the Rameses III Orchestra with Dr. W.S. Lloyd Webber (Grand Organ) and Martin Wilcock (piano). Subsequently the show became a 40-minute production. Its American debut was at the COLLEGE OF THE IMMACULATE CONCEPTION, Douglastown, Long Island, NY, in 5/70. On 8/21/72 the show was mounted very successfully (in tandem with the *Genesis Medieval Mystery Plays*) at the EDINBURGH FESTIVAL, by Frank Dunlop of the Young Vic Company, as part of the *Bible One-Two Looks at the Book of Genesis*. It then played at the HAYMARKET ICE RINK. 10 PERFORMANCES. Then at the YOUNG VIC, 10/16/72–10/28/72. 16 PERFORMANCES. It was, at this stage, still with the *Mystery Plays*. The running time was expanded to 90 minutes, an album of the score was produced, and a British TV version was shown.

It ran at the intimate ROUNDHOUSE, Chalk Farm, London, 11/8/72–12/16/72. 43 PERFORMANCES. It was very controversial, using, as it did, a variety of music styles and interpretations of biblical characters. PRESENTED BY Robert Stigwood (the writers' manager); DIRECTOR: Frank Dunlop; CHOREOGRAPHER: Christopher Bruce; SETS/COSTUMES: Nadine Baylis; MUSICAL DIRECTOR: Alan Doggett; CAST RECORDING on Deram. *Cast*: JACOB'S WIFE: Joan Heal; NARRATOR: Peter Reeves; JOSEPH: Gary Bond; SIMEON/BAKER: Riggs O'Hara; JACOB: Alex McEvoy; REUBEN: Paul Brooke; LEVI: Mason Taylor; GAD: Ian Charleson; DAN: Ian Trigger; ZEBULUN: David Wynn; ASHER: Gordon Waller; ISSACHAR/POTIPHAR: Gavin Reed; PHARAOH: Gordon Waller; BENJAMIN: Jeremy James Taylor; JUDAH/BUTLER: Andrew Robertson; NAPHTALI: Richard Kane. It was a huge success, and soon moved yet again to the ALBERY THEATRE, its first West End showing, 2/17/73–9/16/73. 243 PERFORMANCES. In tandem with *Jacob's Journey* (see appendix). PRESENTED BY Robert Stigwood, in association with Qwertyuiop Productions, Michael White, and Granada, and by arrangement with David Land; DIRECTOR: Frank Dunlop; LIGHTING: Jules Fisher; MUSICAL DIRECTOR: Anthony Bowles. *Cast*: JACOB'S WIFE: Joan Heal; JOSEPH: Gary Bond; SIMEON: Maynard Williams; NAPHTALI: Daniel Shepherd; ISSACHAR: Frank Vincent; ASHER: Sam Cox; GAD/BUTLER: Kevin Williams; BENJAMIN/BAKER: Roy North; JUDAH: Peter Blake; POTIPHAR: Ian Trigger.

It had a limited-run at PLAYHOUSE IN THE PARK, Philadelphia; 12/30/76–1/9/77.

Frank Dunlop re-staged the British Young Vic production Off Broadway, with 2 acts & 18 scenes, at the BROOKLYN ACADEMY OF MUSIC, 12/26/76. Previews from 12/22/76. Limited run of 22 PERFORMANCES. CHOREOGRAPHER: Graciela Daniele; Nadine Baylis's sets & costumes were used; LIGHTING: F. Mitchell Dana; SOUND: Abe Jacob; MUSICAL DIRECTOR: Steve Margoshes. *Cast*: JOSEPH: David-James Carroll; NARRATOR: Cleavon Little; MRS. POTIPHAR: Virginia Martin; BENJAMIN: Leonard John Crofoot; POTIPHAR: Terry Eno; JACOB: Tony Hoty; LADIES: Mary Jane Houdina, Marybeth Kurdock, Jill Streisant; REUBEN: Stuart Pankin; SIMEON: Adam Grammis; ASHER: William Parry; DAN/BAKER: Kurt Yaghjian; GAD/BUTLER: David Patrick Kelly; LEVI:

Paul Kreppel; NAPHTALI: Don Swanson; ISSACHAR: Ron Taylor; ZEBULUN: Craig Schaefer; JUDAH: Robert Rhys; PHARAOH: Jess Pearson; EGYPTIAN/ISHMAELITE: Richard Seer; ALSO WITH: The Brooklyn Boys Chorus.

BROOKLYN ACADEMY OF MUSIC, 12/13/77–1/1/78. 24 PERFORMANCES. It had the same basic crew as the previous run at that venue, except DIRECTOR/CHOREOGRAPHER: Graciela Daniele; SETS: John Pitts; COSTUMES: Dona Granata; MUSICAL DIRECTOR: Glen Roven. *Cast*: NARRATOR: Alan Weeks; JOSEPH: David-James Carroll; REUBEN: Ben Agresti; SIMEON: Denny Martin Flinn; BENJAMIN: Eric Weitz; MRS. POTIPHAR: Marybeth Kurdock; POTIPHAR: Terry Eno; LEVI: Paul Kreppel; NAPHTALI: Don Swanson; DAN/BAKER: Kurt Yaghjian; JUDAH: Robert Rhys; ISSACHAR: Leonard Piggee; GAD/BUTLER: Michael Hoit; ZEBULUN: Craig Schaefer; PHARAOH: William Parry; MOTHERS: Jill Streisant, Marybeth Kurdock, JoAnn Ogawa; JACOB: Tony Hoty.

THE OLNEY THEATRE, Washington, DC, 5/30/78. 21 PERFORMANCES. DIRECTOR/LIGHTING: James D. Waring; SETS: Rolf Beyer; MUSICAL DIRECTOR: Kevin McCarthy. *Cast*: Mark Heckler, Ayl Mack, Tony Gunther, Blaise Corrigan, Steve Le Blanc. It re-opened on 9/12/78. 24 PERFORMANCES.

WESTMINSTER THEATRE, London, 11/27/78–1/17/79. 85 PERFORMANCES. PRESENTED BY Martin Gates; DIRECTOR: Ken Hill; CHOREOGRAPHER: David Thornton; SETS: Saul Radomsky; MUSICAL DIRECTOR: Jack Forsyth. *Cast*: JACOB: Michael Bauer; JOSEPH: Paul Jones; REUBEN: Stan Pretty; LEVI: Robert Lister; NAPHTALI: Ray Scally; SIMEON: Frank Ellis; ISSACHAR: Eric Gething; ASHER/POTIPHAR: Michael Heath; DAN: Terry Matkin; ZEBULUN: Bryan Byrne; GAD: Peter Eden; JUDAH: John Aron; BENJAMIN: Clive Griffin; MRS. POTIPHAR: Audrey Duggan; PHARAOH: Leonard Whiting; NARRATOR: John Golder; LADIES: Francesca Lucy, Jeanna L'Esty, Maggie Ryder.

WESTMINSTER THEATRE, London, 11/1/79–1/19/80. 142 PERFORMANCES. PRESENTED BY Martin Gates; DIRECTOR: Ken Hill; CHOREOGRAPHER: Francesca Lucy; SETS: Saul Radomsky; MUSICAL DIRECTOR: Jack Forsyth. *Cast*: JOSEPH: Paul Jones; REUBEN: Stan Pretty; SIMEON: Frank Ellis; NAPHTALI: Ray Scally; LEVI: Robert Lister; ISSACHAR: Eric Gething; ZEBULUN: Bryan Byrne; GAD: Peter Eden; BENJAMIN: Clive Griffin; JACOB: Philip Summerscales; ASHER: Paul Napier-Burrows; DAN/POTIPHAR: Frank Coda; JUDAH: Ben Kelly; MRS. POTIPHAR: Lisa Westcott; PHARAOH: Maynard Williams; NARRATOR: Clifton Todd; LADIES: Louise Kelly, Carolyn Allen, Francesca Boulter.

VAUDEVILLE THEATRE, London, 12/15/80–3/7/81. PRESENTED BY Bill Kenwright; DIRECTOR: Bill Kenwright; CHOREOGRAPHER: Henry Metcalfe; SETS/COSTUMES: David Terry; MUSICAL DIRECTOR: Keith Hayman. *Cast*: JACOB/POTIPHAR: Peter Lawrence; JOSEPH: Jess Conrad; REUBEN: David O'Brien; SIMEON/BUTLER: Mickie Driver; LEVI: John Ogilvie; NAPHTALI: Oliver Robins; ASHER: Roy Miles; DAN/BAKER: Derek Connell; GAD: Steve Simmonds; ISSACHAR: Hugh Janes; BENJAMIN: John Melvin; ZEBULUN: Lewis Barber; NARRATOR: Leo Andrew; MRS. POTIPHAR: Mandy Demetriou; PHARAOH: Dave Mayberry; LADIES: Tessa Hatts, Jan Revere, Odette Bridgewater.

SADLERS WELLS, London, 12/23/81–2/13/82. 90 PERFORMANCES. It had the same basic crew as at the Vaudeville in 1980. *Cast*: JACOB/POTIPHAR: Peter Lawrence; JOSEPH: Jess Conrad; REUBEN: Henry Metcalfe; SIMEON: Richard Beaumont; LEVI/BAKER: Niall Gavin; NAPHTALI/BUTLER: Mickie Driver; GAD: Eric Danot; BENJAMIN: John Melvin; ZEBULUN: Ashley Keech; MRS. POTIPHAR: Claire Peters; ASHER: Ian Parkin; DAN/FRENCHMAN: Michael Cowie; ISSACHAR: Martyn Knight; NARRATOR: Keith Raymel; PHARAOH: Dave Mayberry; LADIES: Sarah Kimm, Rosalind Ball, Janet Date.

FORD'S THEATRE, Washington, DC, 4/23/80–9/28/80. Previews from 4/13/80. DIRECTOR: James D. Waring; CHOREOGRAPHER: Wayne Cilento. Then it played Off Broadway, at the ENTERMEDIA THEATRE, 11/18/81–1/24/82. 77 PERFORMANCES. It was reviewed here (reviews were very divided). Then it moved to Broadway.

The Broadway Run. ROYALE THEATRE, 1/27/82–9/4/83. 670 PERFORMANCES. PRESENTED BY Zev Bufman, Susan R. Rose, and Melvyn J. Estrin, Sidney Shlenker, Gail Berman, by arrangement with the Robert Stigwood Organisation, and David Land; MUSIC: Andrew Lloyd Web-

ber; LYRICS: Tim Rice; BASED ON the story from the Old Testament; DIALOGUE FOR THE PROLOGUE by Ray Galton & Alan Simpson; DIRECTOR/CHOREOGRAPHER: Tony Tanner; SETS: Karl Eigsti; COSTUMES: Judith Dolan; LIGHTING: Barry Arnold; SOUND: Tom Morse; MUSICAL SUPERVISORS/ORCHESTRATIONS/ARRANGEMENTS: Martin Silvestri & Jeremy Stone; MUSICAL DIRECTOR: David Friedman; CAST RECORDING on Chrysalis; PRESS: Fred Nathan & Associates; CASTING: Meg Simon/ Fran Kumin; GENERAL MANAGEMENT: Theatre Now; COMPANY MANAGER: Helen V. Meier; PRODUCTION STAGE MANAGER: Michael Martorella; STAGE MANAGER: John Fennesy; ASSISTANT STAGE MANAGER: John Ganzer, *Stephen Bourneuf* & *Jerry Bihm*. *Cast*: NARRATOR: Laurie Beechman (2), *Sharon Brown* (from 12/1/82); WOMEN'S CHORUS: Lorraine Barrett, Karen Bogan, Katharine Buffaloe, Lauren Goler (dropped during run), Randon Lo, Joni Masella (dropped during run), Kathleen Rowe McAllen (dropped during run), Renee Warren, *Terry Iten, Rosalyn Rahn, Dorothy Tancredi*; JACOB: Gordon Stanley; REUBEN: Robert P. Hyman; SIMEON: Kenneth Bryan, *James Rich*; LEVI: Steve McNaughton, *Peter Samuel*; NAPHTALI: Charlie Serrano; ISSACHAR: Peter Kapetan, *Eric Aaron*; ASHER: David Asher, *James Rich*; DAN: James Rich, *Richard Hilton*; ZEBULUN: Doug Voet; GAD: Barry Tarallo, *John Ganzer*; BENJAMIN: Philip Carrubba, *Stephen Bourneuf*; JUDAH: Stephen Hope; JOSEPH: Bill Hutton (1), *Doug Voet, Allen Fawcett* (from 6/24/82), *Doug Voet, Andy Gibb* (12/1/82–1/12/83), *Doug Voet* (from 1/13/82), *David Cassidy* (from 3/6/83); ISMAELITES: Tom Carder & David Ardao (*Kenneth Bryan*); POTIPHAR: David Ardao, *Kenneth Bryan*; MRS. POTIPHAR: Randon Lo, *James Rich*; BUTLER: Kenneth Bryan, *Stephen Hope*; BAKER: Barry Tarallo, *John Ganzer*; PHARAOH: Tom Carder; APACHE DANCER: Joni Masella [role dropped during previews]. ***Understudies***: Narrator: Rosalyn Rahn, *Dorothy Tancredi*; Jacob: David Asher, *Michael Howell Deane*; Joseph: Doug Voet, *John Ganzer*; Potiphar: Kenneth Bryan; Pharaoh: James Rich, *Barry Tarallo*. Swings: Rosalyn Rahn, John Ganzer, *Stephen Bourneuf, Michael Howell Deane, Terri Homberg, Joni Masella, James Rich*. **Part I: *Prologue*** "You Are What You Feel" (Narrator). **Part II: Act I:** "Jacob and Sons"/"Joseph's Coat" ("The Coat of Many Colors") (Narrator, Brothers, Jacob, Joseph, Women), "Joseph's Dreams" (Narrator, Joseph, Brothers), "Poor, Poor Joseph" (Narrator, Brothers, Women), "One More Angel in Heaven" (Levi & Brothers), "Potiphar" (Narrator, Women, Mrs. Potiphar, Potiphar, Joseph), "Close Ev'ry Door (to Me)" (Joseph & Women), "Stone the Crows" (Narrator, Pharaoh, Joseph, Women, Men) [this number was replaced during previews with "Go, Go, Go, Joseph" (see immediately below)], "Go, Go, Go, Joseph" (Narrator, Butler, Baker, Male Chorus, Joseph) [during previews this number replaced "Stone the Crows"], "Pharaoh's Story" (Narrator & Women) [during previews this was the first song in Act II]. **Act II:** "Poor, Poor Pharaoh"/ "Song of the King" (Narrator, Pharaoh, Women, Men), "Pharaoh's Dream Explained" (Joseph, Women, Men), "Stone the Crows" (Narrator, Pharaoh, Joseph, Women, Men) [this was a reprise during previews, but on Broadway it was the only time it was done], "Those Canaan Days" (Reuben & Brothers), "The Brothers Came to Egypt"/ "Grovel, Grovel" (Narrator, Brothers, Joseph, Women), "Who's the Thief?" (Joseph, Brothers, Women), "Benjamin Calypso" (Naphtali & Brothers), "Joseph All the Time" (Narrator, Joseph, Brothers, Women), "Jacob in Egypt" (Joseph, Brothers, Women), "Any Dream Will Do" (Joseph & Company), "May I Return to the Beginning" (Company).

Reviews were divided, mostly good. The show received Tony nominations for musical, score, book, direction of a musical, choreography, and for Bill Hutton and Laurie Beechman. On 1/12/83 Andy Gibb, playing Joseph, was fired for missing his performance of that night (the 21st time he had missed a performance out of 51).

After Broadway. WALNUT STREET THEATRE, Philadelphia, 1989. DIRECTOR/CHOREOGRAPHER: Charles Abbott. *Cast*: NARRATOR: Laurie Beechman; JOSEPH: Sal Viviano; JUDAH: Tony Capone; POTIPHAR/ISHMAELITE: Patrick Hamilton; MERMAID: Stephanie Paul; CHORUS INCLUDED: Mercedes Perez & Eileen Tepper.

TOURING REVIVAL. Opened in 6/92. PRESENTED BY Livent; DIRECTOR: Steven Pimlott. *Cast*: JOSEPH: Donny Osmond (he played the role over 1,800 times, until 5/25/97). Sometimes his understudy, Sam Harris, stood in. David Barnhum subsequently played the role.

363. *Joseph and the Amazing Technicolor Dreamcoat (Broadway revival)*

Before Broadway. This revival began with a hugely successful run at the LONDON PALLADIUM, 6/12/91–1/15/94. Previews from 6/1/91. DIRECTOR: Steven Pimlott; CHOREOGRAPHER: Anthony Van Laast; SETS/COSTUMES: Mark Thompson; LIGHTING: Andrew Bridge; SOUND: Martin Levan; MUSICAL DIRECTOR: Michael Dixon; CAST RECORDING released on 8/91. *Cast*: JOSEPH: Jason Donovan, *Phillip Schofield* (during Mr. Donovan's vacation from 1/13/92 and then permanently from 5/25/92), *Darren Day* (for 3 weeks in 5/93), *Phillip Schofield* (until 10/2/93), *Jason Donovan* (10/4/93–1/15/94); NARRATOR: Linzi Hateley; REUBEN: Nicolas Colicos; REUBEN'S WIFE: Megan Kelly; JACOB/POTIPHAR: Aubrey Woods; ISSACHAR/BAKER: Patrick Clancy; GAD/BUTLER: Paul Tomkinson; MRS. POTIPHAR/NAPHTALI'S WIFE: Nadia Strahan; PHARAOH/LEVI: David Easter; SIMEON: Philip Cox; SIMEON'S WIFE: Jacqui Jameson; LEVI'S WIFE: Jocelyn Vodovoz Cook; ASHER: Peter Bishop; ASHER'S WIFE: Elizabeth Renihan; DAN: Connor Byrne; DAN'S WIFE: Sonia Swaby; ZEBULUN: Michael Small; GAD'S WIFE: Caroline Dillon; JUDAH: Johnny Amobi; JUDAH'S WIFE: Amanda Courtney-Davies; BENJAMIN: Jason Moore; BENJAMIN'S WIFE: Robin Cleaver; ISSACHAR'S WIFE: Gael Johnson; NAPHTALI: Mark Frendo; ZEBULUN'S WIFE: Jacqui Harman; APACHE DANCERS: Michael Small & Amanda Courtney-Davis. It re-opened at the APOLLO THEATRE, HAMMERSMITH, 2/27/96. DIRECTOR: Wayne Fowkes. *Cast*: JOSEPH: Phillip Schofield; NARRATOR: Ria Jones. It came to the USA, as a national tour that opened on 2/25/93, at the Pantages Theatre, Hollywood, and closed in 1994, at the Golden State Theatre, San Francisco. It had the same basic crew as for the Broadway run, except MUSICAL DIRECTOR: Paul Bogaev; GENERAL MANAGEMENT: Gatchell & Neufeld. On tour Willy Falk was replaced by Timothy Smith as Asher. George McIntyre was replaced by Gordon Owens, but Mr. McIntyre was back in time for Broadway. Aside from that, and 50 new boys for the choir, the cast was the same too.

The Broadway Run. MINSKOFF THEATRE, 11/10/93–5/29/94. 17 previews from 10/26/93. 231 PERFORMANCES. Andrew Lloyd Webber's new production, PRESENTED BY James M. Nederlander & Terry Allen Kramer; MUSIC: Andrew Lloyd Webber; LYRICS: Tim Rice; DIRECTOR: Steven Pimlott; CHOREOGRAPHER: Anthony Van Laast; SETS/COSTUMES: Mark Thompson; LIGHTING: Andrew Bridge; SOUND: Martin Levan; MUSICAL SUPERVISOR: Michael Reed; MUSICAL DIRECTOR: Patrick Vaccariello; ORCHESTRATIONS: John Cameron; CHILDREN'S CHOIR DIRECTOR: Janet Rothermel; PRESS: Boneau/Bryan-Brown; CASTING: Johnson — Liff; GENERAL MANAGEMENT: The Really Useful Management Company; COMPANY MANAGER: Mark Johnson; PRODUCTION STAGE MANAGER: Jeff Lee; STAGE MANAGER: J.P. Elins; ASSISTANT STAGE MANAGERS: Stephen A. Zorthian, Louise Currie, Patricia F. Feldstein. *Cast*: JOSEPH: Michael Damian (1) ☆; NARRATOR: Kelli Rabke (2); PHARAOH: Robert Torti (4); JACOB: Clifford David (3); BUTLER: Glenn Sneed; BAKER: Bill Nolte; MRS. POTIPHAR: Julie Bond, *Mamie Duncan-Gibbs*; POTIPHAR: Clifford David (3); REUBEN: Marc Kudisch, *Bryan Batt*; SIMEON: Neal Ben-Ari, *Paul Harman;* LEVI: Robert Torti (4); NAPHTALI: Danny Bolero; ISSACHAR: Bill Nolte; ASHER: Timothy Smith; DAN: Joseph Savant; ZEBULUN: Tim Schultheis, *Richard Stafford, Matthew Zarley*; GAD: Glenn Sneed; BENJAMIN: Ty Taylor; JUDAH: Gerry McIntyre; REUBEN'S WIFE: Michelle Murlin, *Jocelyn Vodovoz Cook*; SIMEON'S WIFE: Mindy Franzese; LEVI'S WIFE: Jocelyn Vodovoz Cook, *Malinda Shaffer;* NAPHTALI'S WIFE: Julie Bond, *Mamie Duncan-Gibbs;* ISSACHAR'S WIFE: Jacquie Porter; ASHER'S WIFE: Lisa Akey, *Susan Santoro;* DAN'S WIFE: Sara Miles; ZEBULUN'S WIFE: Diana Brownstone; GAD'S WIFE: Betsy Chang, *Gina Trano;* BENJAMIN'S WIFE: Tina Ou; JUDAH'S WIFE: Susan Carr George, *Kelli Severson;* GURU: Clifford David (3); APACHE DANCERS: Tina Ou & Tim Schultheis (*Richard Stafford, Matthew Zarley)*; CHILDREN'S CHOIRS: Carolabbe Chorus, La Petite Musicale, Long Island Performing Arts Center Choir, William F. Halloran Vocal Ensemble, Blessed Sacrament Chorus of Staten Island, Friends Academy Singers, Public School 39 Chorus, Righteousness Unlimited. *Understudies*: Joseph: Ty Taylor & Matt Zarley; Narrator: Lisa Akey, Susan

Carr George, Kelli Severson, *Susan Santoro*; Jacob/Potiphar/Guru: Bill Nolte & Glenn Sneed; Pharaoh: Marc Kudisch & Joseph Savant, *Bryan Batt*. *Swings*: Ron Kellum, Andrew Makay, Janet Rothermel, Kelli Severson, Gina Trano, Matt Zarley, *Angel Caban, Jennifer Kay Jones*. *Orchestra*: CONCERTMASTER: Sanford Allen; VIOLIN: Sylvia D'Avanzo; VIOLA: Richard Brice; CELLO: Francesca Vanasco; FLUTE/CLARINET/SAX: Andrew Sterman; OBOE/ENGLISH HORN: Edward Zuhlke; FRENCH HORN: Steven Zimmerman; KEYBOARDS: James Abbott, Robert Hirschhorn, Grant Sturiale; GUITARS: Robbie Kirshoff & J.J. McGeehan; BASS: Hugh Mason; DRUMS: Gary Tillman; PERCUSSION: Bill Hayes. *Act I*: *Scene 1* Overture (Orchestra); *Scene 2* Prologue (Narrator); *Scene 3* "Any Dream Will Do" (Joseph & Children); *Scene 4* "Jacob and Sons"/"Joseph's Coat" (Narrator, Brothers, Wives, Children, Jacob, Joseph); *Scene 5* "Joseph's Dreams" (Narrator, Joseph, Brothers, Female Ensemble); *Scene 6* "Poor, Poor Joseph" (Narrator, Brothers, Children); *Scene 7* "One More Angel in Heaven" (Reuben, Reuben's Wife, Narrator, Brothers, Wives, Jacob, Children); *Scene 8* "Potiphar" (Narrator, Ensemble, Mrs. Potiphar, Potiphar, Joseph); *Scene 9* "Close Every Door" (Joseph & Children); *Scene 10* "Go, Go, Go Joseph" (Narrator, Butler, Baker, Ensemble, Joseph, Guru, Children). *Act II*: *Scene 11* Entr'acte (Children); *Scene 12* "Pharaoh Story" (Narrator & Children); *Scene 13* "Poor, Poor Pharaoh"/"Song of the King" (Narrator, Butler, Pharaoh, Children); *Scene 14* "Pharaoh's Dream Explained" (Joseph, Ensemble, Children); *Scene 15* "Stone the Crows" (Narrator, Pharaoh, Children, Joseph, Female, Ensemble); *Scene 16* "Those Canaan Days" (Simeon, Jacob, Brothers, Apache Dancers); *Scene 17* "The Brothers Came to Egypt"/"Grovel, Grovel" (Narrator, Brothers, Joseph, Female Ensemble, Children); *Scene 18* "Who's the Thief" (Joseph, Brothers, Female Ensemble, Children); *Scene 19* "Benjamin Calypso" (Judah, Brothers, Female Ensemble, Children); *Scene 20* "Joseph All the Time" (Narrator, Joseph, Children, Brothers, Female Ensemble); *Scene 21* "Jacob in Egypt" (Narrator, Jacob, Children, Ensemble); *Scene 22* "Any Dream Will Do" (reprise) (Joseph, Narrator, Ensemble, Jacob, Children); *Scene 23* "Close Every Door" (reprise) (Joseph & Children); *Scene 24* "Joseph Megamix" (Company).

Broadway reviews were divided, mostly bad..

After Broadway. TOUR. Opened on 1/13/95, in West Point, NY. *Cast*: JOSEPH: Sam Harris, *Brian Lane Green* (from 2/26/96); NARRATOR: Kristine Fraelich, *Jodie Langel*; JACOB/POTIPHAR/GURU: Russell Leib, *Steve Pudenz* (from 2/25/96); PHARAOH: John Ganun, *Jeffrey Scott Watkins* (from 1/12/96); BUTLER: Glenn Sneed, *Jon Carver*; BAKER: Paul J. Gallagher, *Max Perlman*; MRS. POTIPHAR: Justine DiCostanzo, *Mindy Franzese, Jennifer Werner*.

TOUR. Opened on 5/31/95, in Toronto. MUSICAL DIRECTOR: Kevin Finn. *Cast*: JOSEPH: Donny Osmond, *David Burnham* (from 6/97), *Donny Osmond* (from 1/98); NARRATOR: Kelli James Chase, *Donna Kane* (from 11/12/95), *Kelli James Chase* (from 1/97), *Sarah Litzsinger* (from 1/98); JACOB/POTIPHAR/GURU: James Harms, *Gary Krawford* (from 11/29/95), *James Harms* (from 3/31/96); PHARAOH: Johnny Seaton, *Abe Reybold*; BUTLER: J.C. Montgomery, *Martin Murphy*; BAKER: Erich McMillan-McCall, *Paul J. Gallagher*; MRS. POTIPHAR: Carole Mackereth, *Julia Alicia Fowler* (from 3/31/96), *Carole Mackereth*; ALSO WITH: Stephen R. Buntrock, Alton Fitzgerald White, Jamie Dawn Gangi.

TOURING REVIVAL. Opened on 6/9/99, at the Paper Mill Playhouse, New Jersey, and closed there on 7/25/99. It then went on tour. PRESENTED BY the Paper Mill Playhouse, Troika Entertainment, and the Pittsburgh Light Opera; DIRECTOR: Dallett Norris; SETS: James Fouchard; MUSICAL DIRECTOR: Helen Gregory. *Cast*: NARRATOR: Deborah Gibson; JOSEPH: Patrick Cassidy; BENJAMIN: Jon Osmond; DAN: Michael Osmond; ZEBULUN: Nathan Osborne; GAD: Scott Osmond.

LONDON, 1999. Revival. *Cast*: Nicolas Colicos, Donny Osmond, Patrick Clancy, Christopher Biggins, Maria Friedman, Richard Attenborough, Joan Collins, Robert Torti, Jeff Blumenkrantz, Gerry McIntyre, Peter Challis.

In 1999 PBS filmed a version at Pinewood Studios, England, that was based on the Donny Osmond touring production. It was released on 4/5/00. DIRECTORS: David Mallet & Steven Pimlott. *Cast*: NARRATOR: Maria Friedman; JOSEPH: Donny Osmond; POTIPHAR'S WIFE: Joan Collins; JACOB: Richard Attenborough.

NEW LONDON THEATRE, London. Opened on 3/3/03. This was a

new version, specifically designed for this particular theatre. PRESENTED BY Bill Kenwright; DIRECTOR: Bill Kenwright; CHOREOGRAPHER: Henry Metcalfe; SETS/COSTUMES: Sean Cavanagh; LIGHTING: Nick Richings; MUSICAL DIRECTOR: David Steadman. *Cast*: JOSEPH: Stephen Gately (until 9/13/03), *Lee Waterworth* (9/15/03–10/5/03), *Darren Day* (from 10/6/03); NARRATOR: Vivienne Carlyle; PHARAOH/SIMEON: Trevor Jary; JACOB/POTIPHAR: James Head; NAPHTALI/BAKER: Russell Hicken; ZEBULUN: Brian Graves; LEVI: Lee Waterworth; REUBEN: Philip Burrows; BENJAMIN: John Marques.

MINI-TOUR. Opened 8/24/04–8/29/04, at the Fox Theatre, Atlanta. Then it went on with the tour. PRESENTED BY Theater of the Stars; DIRECTOR/CHOREOGRAPHER: Norb Joerder; MUSICAL DIRECTOR: Michael Biagi. *Cast*: JOSEPH: Jon Secada; NARRATOR: Monica Patton; PHARAOH: Ed Staudenmayer; JACOB/POTIPHAR: Martin Van Treuren.

364. *Jotham Valley*

A story that actually happened. Laid at and near a ranch house in the Sierra country, it covers a period of one week. A feud between two western brothers that threatens not only their lives but the life of their community.

Before Broadway. Certain songs were cut before the opening, and are mentioned in the song list below. One not mentioned was "The Answer Man."

The Broadway Run. FORTY-EIGHTH STREET THEATRE, 2/6/51–2/51; CORONET THEATRE, 2/19/51–3/3/51. Total of 31 PERFORMANCES. The Dr. Buchman Oxford Group (Moral Re-Armament) production, PRESENTED BY Howard Reynolds, in association with Lena Ashwell; MUSIC: Cecil Broadhurst, Frances Hadden, Will Reed; ADDITIONAL MUSIC: Alan Thornhill & George Fraser; LYRICS/BOOK: Cecil Broadhurst; DIRECTORS: Howard Reynolds & Lena Ashwell; CHOREOGRAPHERS: June Day & Christine Nowell; SETS: Erling Roberts; LIGHTING: Louis Fleming; MUSICAL DIRECTORS: Will Reed & George Fraser. *Cast*: NIELSON: Scoville Wishard; "JOTH" JOTHAM: Leland Holland; SPINDLE: Cecil Broadhurst; THE WAGGLE KIDS: David Allen, Valerie Exton, June Day, Tom Kennedy, Christine Nowell; JENNIFER: Ilene Godfrey; MRS. WHIPPLE: Marion Clayton; MISS HUBBARD: Phyllis Konstam; WIDOW WAGGLE: Elsa Purdy; THE FOUR COWHANDS: MOOSE: Dwight Boileau; SLUGGER: Frank McGee; SMOKEY: Ron Roberts; SUNDOWN: Howard Boyd; MART BILLINGS: Bill Stubbs; JACK: Jack Currie; SETH JOTHAM: Dick Stollery; MURRAY WILKINS: Scoville Wishard; WILL: Robert Anderson; THE JUDGE: Eugene Bedford; SARAH: Greta Stollery; TWICKLEHAMPTON SCHOOL GIRLS: Molly Corner, Leone Exton, Valerie Exton, Nancy Hore-Ruthven, Sally Hore-Ruthven, Barbara Jardine, Clare Meynell, Christine Nowell, Rosemary Pinsent, Juliet Rodd; THEIR TEACHER: June Day; JOTHAM VALLEY'S LADIES AID: Carol Ann Beal, Janet Binns, Mary Jane Broadhurst, Marion Clayton, Mabel Curtis, Nancy Curtis, Leone Exton, Phyllis Konstam, Ruth Ridgway, Rea Zimmerman; CHORUS ENSEMBLE: Aage Anderson, Carol Ann Beal, Cyril Beall, Eleanor Crary, Mabel Curtis, Nancy Curtis, Walter & Florence Farmer, Helen Hunter, Vere James, Hope Kitchen, Phyllis Limburg, Ed McRae, Eric Millar, Hugh Nowell, Harold Sack, Norman Schwab, Ivor Sharpe, Frank Sherry, Ben Trotter, Ken Twitchell Jr. *Act I: Scene 1* Jotham's ranch house: "Wonder Why" (Joth), "Nuthin' Like a Celebration" (Neighbors), "(There's a Certain Kind of) Jingle to My Spurs" (Cowhands), "I'm the Luckiest Girl Alive" (Jennifer & Neighbors) [this replaced "Where I'm Belonging" before opening], "When I Point My Finger at My Neighbor" (Spindle & Cowhands), "Nothing's Ever Quite Like This" (Jennifer & Widow Waggle), "Twicklehampton School for Girls" (School Girls), "Have You Heard?" (Mrs. Whipple & Gossip Chorus); *Scene 2* A cafe on a street in town; *Scene 3* The Jotham Reservoir: "(There's a Certain Kind of) Jingle to My Spurs" (reprise) (Cowhands), "Wonder Why" (reprise) (Joth). *Act II: Scene 1* Outside the County Court House; *Scene 2* Widow Waggle's kitchen: "Sorry is a Magic Little Word" [cut before the opening], "When I Grow Up" (The Waggle Kids), "The Omelet Song" (Widow Waggle, The Waggle Kids, Cowhands); *Scene 3* Jotham's ranch house: "Somewhere in the Heart of a Man" (Joth, Spindle, Jennifer), "Change in a Home on the Range"

(Joth & Jennifer), "Look to the Mountains!" (Joth, Jennifer, Neighbors), Finale (The Whole Valley).

365. *A Joyful Noise*

Time: yesterday and today. Place: Macedonia and Nashville, Tennessee. About Shade, a wandering folk minstrel, and his effect on a small hill town in Tennessee. His backup band was called The Motley Crew. Shade is run out of Macedonia by the irate father of Jenny Lee, the girl he loves. When he returns he has become a popular folk-singing idol, but chooses to return to his former existence as an itinerant minstrel.

Before Broadway. Originally called *The Insolent Breed, i*t was going to be produced by Kermit Bloomgarden, from a libretto by John Gerstad. But Mr. Bloomgarden dropped it, and Ed Padula took it up, and aside from producing, he also wrote a new libretto. It tried out in summer tents, and underwent major changes. Before Broadway Mr. Padula's libretto was re-written by Dore Schary, who also took over the direction from Ben Shaktman. Mr. Schary also brought with him $100,000 of RKO's money to help the show, and he also brought along Karen Morrow. Then Schary quit and Michael Bennett and Ed Padula were left with the directing chores. Donna McKechnie had the non-dancing ingénue lead, but she was replaced during Boston tryouts (thanks partly to Kevin Kelly's unkind review of her in the *Globe*) by Teresa Rinaldi, who in turn was replaced by Susan Watson for Broadway. Mitzie Welch was replaced by Gay Edmond, who in turn was replaced by Karen Morrow. James Rado was replaced by Clifford David. Allan Louw was replaced by George Mathews. Jordan Reed, who was also in the cast, was dropped. The Broadway opening night was delayed from 12/10/66 to 12/15/66.

The Broadway Run. MARK HELLINGER THEATRE, 12/15/66–12/24/66. 4 previews from 11/28/66. 12 PERFORMANCES. PRESENTED BY Edward Padula & Slade Brown, in association with Sid Bernstein; MUSIC/LYRICS: Oscar Brand & Paul Nassau; BOOK: Edward Padula (and Dore Schary, whose billing was removed); BASED ON the 1959 novel *The Insolent Breed*, by Borden Deal; DIRECTOR: Edward Padula; CHOREOGRAPHER: Michael Bennett (his solo choreographic debut); ASSISTANT CHOREOGRAPHERS: Leland Palmer & Jo Jo Smith; SETS/LIGHTING: Peter Wexler; COSTUMES: Peter Joseph; MUSICAL DIRECTOR: Rene Wiegert; ORCHESTRATIONS/VOCAL ARRANGEMENTS: William Stegmeyer; DANCE MUSIC: Lee Holdridge; CAST RECORDING on Liberty; PRESS: Sol Jacobson, Lewis Harmon, Shirley Herz; GENERAL MANAGERS: Frank Hopkins & David Lawlor; PRODUCTION STAGE MANAGER: Edward Julien; STAGE MANAGER: Howard Perloff; ASSISTANT STAGE MANAGER: Maxine Fox. *Cast*: SHADE MOTLEY: John Raitt (1) ✩; BROTHER LOCKE: Clifford David (5); WALTER WISHENANT: George Mathews (6); JENNY LEE: Susan Watson (3); SAM FREDRICKSON: Art Wallace (8); MISS JIMMIE: Leland Palmer (7); (FIVE) SAW MILL BOYS AND THE MOTLEY CREW (9): DE WITT: Eric Weissberg; FREDDY: Martin Ambrose; JAYBIRD: Charles Morley; OSCAR: Oatis Stephens; TOMMY: Tommy Tune; BLISS STANLEY: Swen Swenson (2) ✩; STAGE MANAGER: Jack Fletcher; DIRECTOR: Ken Ayers; MARY TEXAS: Karen Morrow (4); BOYS: Paul Charles, Scott Pearson, Alan Peterson, Barry Preston; ANNOUNCER: Jack Mette; BAILEY: Jo Jo Smith; JOHN TOM: Shawn Campbell; ENSEMBLE SINGERS: Ken Ayers, Jack Fletcher, Veronica McCormick, Stuart Mann, Eric Mason, Jack Mette, Jessica Quinn, Darrell Sandeen, Diane Tarleton, Linda Theil, Jamie Thomas; ENSEMBLE DANCERS: Bonnie Ano, Christine Bocchino, Paul Charles, Susan Donovan, Winston DeWitt Hemsley, Baayork Lee, April Nevins, Scott Pearson, Alan Peterson, Diane Phillips, Barry Preston, Steven Ross, Joy Serio, Jo Jo Smith, Melissa Stoneburn, Tommy Tune, Carol Lynn Vasquez. *Understudies*: Shade: Jack Mette; Jenny Lee/Mary Texas: Jamie Thomas; Brother Locke: Jack Fletcher; Walter: Darrell Sandeen; Miss Jimmie: Christine Bocchino; John Tom: Vone O'Fallon; Saw Mill Boys: Tommy Tune. *Act I: Scene 1* A clearing in the hills; *Scene 2* The town square; *Scene 3* A clearing; *Scene 4* The saw mill; *Scene 5* The field; *Scene 6* The top of the valley. *Act II: Scene 1* Backstage, Nashville; *Scene 2* A clearing in Macedonia; *Scene 3* The Grand Ole Opry; *Scene 4* The recording studio; *Scene 5* The state fair; *Scene 6* The town square. *Act I*: "Longtime Traveling" (Shade), "A Joyful Noise" (Shade & Townspeople), "I'm Ready" (Jenny Lee, Miss Jimmie, The Girls), "Spring Time of the Year" (Shade), "I Like to Look My Best" (Shade, Sam, The Saw Mill Boys), "No Talent" (Bliss), "Not Me" (Jenny Lee & Miss Jimmie), "Until Today" (Shade & Jenny Lee), "Swinging a Dance" (Shade & Company), "To the Top" (Bliss & Shade). *Act II*: "I Love Nashville" (Mary Texas & Her Boys), "Whither Thou Goest" (Brother Locke), "We Won't Forget to Write" (Miss Jimmie, Sam, The Saw Mill Boys), Grand Ole Opry: "Ballad Maker" (Shade, Mary Texas, Motley Crew, Ensemble), "Barefoot Gal" (Mary Texas), "Clog Dance" (Dance Ensemble), "Fool's Gold" (Shade, Mary Texas, Motley Crew, Ensemble) [end of Grand Ole Opry sequence], "The Big Guitar" (Bliss), "Love Was" (Jenny Lee), "I Say Yes" (Shade, Motley Crew, Ensemble), "Lord, You Sure Know How to Make a New Day" (Shade), "A Joyful Noise" (reprise) (Shade, Townspeople).

Reviews were divided, but mostly bad. The show received Tony nominations for choreography, and for Susan Watson and Leland Palmer.

366. *Juan Darien: A Carnival Mass*

An experimental music theatre piece, with no intermission. Set in a South American jungle. It used puppets, masked actors and unusual instruments to tell, in the form of a "carnival mass," a folk tale about the effects of savagery on civilization. Mr. Bones, the show's half-jaguar, half-man MC, presents a series of bawdy, scatological puppet interludes called "Tiger Tales" which break up the tension of the story and show man and jaguar as deadly enemies. Horacio Quiroga, on whose stories the play was based, was Uruguayan.

Before Broadway. It was first performed Off Off Broadway, at ST. CLEMENT'S THEATRE, by the Music-Theatre Group, 3/4/88–3/23/88. 21 PERFORMANCES. It had the same basic crew as for the later Broadway run, except LIGHTING: Richard Nelson. *Cast*: Ariel Ashwell, Renee Banks, Willie C. Barnes, Thuli Dumakude, Nicholas Gunn, Andrea Kane, Stephen Kaplin, Lawrence A. Neals Jr., Leonard Petit, Barbara Pollitt, Irene Wiley. It won the Richard Rodgers Award for musicals in development. It ran again at ST. CLEMENT'S THEATRE, 12/26/89–3/3/90. 48 PERFORMANCES. Again, it had the same basic crew, except LIGHTING: Debra Dumas; SOUND: Bob Bielecki. *Cast*: VOCAL SOLOISTS: Lawrence A. Neals Jr. & Jamie Blachly; MOTHER—DANCER & OLD WOMAN: Ariel Ashwell; MOTHER—SINGER: Thuli Dumakude; HUNTER/TOLEDO: Kristofer Batho; MR. BONES/SCHOOLTEACHER: Leonard Petit; SHADOWS: Stephen Kaplin & Company; PUPPET JUAN: Kristofer Batho, Andrea Kane, Stephen Kaplin; JUAN AS A BOY: Lawrence A. Neals Jr. & Jamie Blachly; SCHOOLCHILDREN: Matthew Kimbrough, Nancy Mayans, Irene Wiley; MOTH: Mimi Wyche; DRUNKEN COUPLE: Kristofer Batho & Andrea Kane; CIRCUS TIGERS: Thuli Dumakude, Nancy Mayans, Irene Wiley; CIRCUS BARKER: Matthew Kimbrough; GREEN DWARF: Andrea Kane. *Understudy*: Barbara Pollitt. *Musicians*: KEYBOARDS: Richard Cordova, Richard Martinez, John C. Thomas; PERCUSSION: Geoffrey Gordon & Valerie Naranjo; VIOLIN: Philip Johnson; DIDGERIDOOS: Susan Rawcliffe & John C. Thomas; WIND INSTRUMENTS: Susan Rawcliffe; TRUMPET: John C. Thomas; TUBA: Ray Stewart.

Broadway previews began on 11/6/96 (date pushed back from 10/31/96).

The Broadway Run. VIVIAN BEAUMONT THEATRE, 11/24/96–1/5/97. 20 previews from 11/6/96. 49 PERFORMANCES. PRESENTED BY Lincoln Center Theatre, in association with Music-Theatre Group; MUSIC/LATIN TEXT CHOSEN & ARRANGED BY: Elliot Goldenthal; LYRICS/BOOK: Julie Taymor & Elliot Goldenthal; INSPIRED BY Horacio Quiroga's short story; DIRECTOR/PUPPETS/MASKS: Julie Taymor; MOVEMENT CO-ORDINATOR: Andrea Kane; PUPPET MASTER: Stephen Kaplin; SETS/COSTUMES: G.W. Mercier & Julie Taymor; LIGHTING: Donald Holder; SOUND: Tony Meola; MUSICAL DIRECTOR: Richard Cordova; CAST RECORDING on Sony Classical, released on 10/29/96, with many members of the original cast; PRESS: Philip Rinaldi; CASTING: Jay Binder; GENERAL MANAGER: Steven C. Callahan; COMPANY MANAGER: Edward J. Nelson; STAGE MANAGER: Jeff Lee; ASSISTANT STAGE MANAGER: Elizabeth Burgess & Steve "Doc" Zorthian. *Cast:* PLAGUE VICTIMS: The Company; MOTHER (DANCER): Ariel Ashwell; MOTHER (VOCALIST): Andrea Frierson Toney; HUNTER: Kristofer Batho; MR. BONES: Bruce Turk; SHADOWS: Stephen Kaplin & Company; JUAN (PUPPET): Kristofer Batho, Andrea Kane, Barbara Pollitt; JUAN (BOY): Daniel Hodd; SCHOOLTEACHER: Bruce Turk; SCHOOLCHILDREN: Company; DRUNKEN COUPLE: Kristofer Batho & Andrea Kane; SENOR TOLEDO: Martin Santangelo; CIRCUS TIGERS: Company; CIRCUS BARKER/STREET SINGER: David Toney; OLD WOMAN: Ariel Ashwell; GREEN DWARF: Andrea Kane & Sophia Salguero; MARIE POSA: Sophia Salguero; BALLAD OF RETURN SOLOIST: Irma-Estel La Guerre. *Understudies*: Juan: Khalid Rivera; Mother-Vocalist: Irma-Estel La Guerre; Hunter/Bones/Teacher/Barker/Street Singer: Tom Flynn; Toledo: Kristofer Batho; Mother-Dancer/Old Woman/Marie Posa: Andrea Kane. *Musicians:* KEYBOARDS: Richard Martinez & Bruce Williamson; PERCUSSION: Geoffrey Gordon & Valerie Naranjo; VIOLIN: Svetoslav J. Slavov; WIND INSTRUMENTS: Susan Rawcliffe; DIDGERIDOOS: Susan Rawcliffe & John C. Thomas; TRUMPET: John C. Thomas; TUBA: Ray Stewart. *Prologue:* DARKNESS: a church in the jungle; THE JUNGLE: a hunter shoots a jaguar, leaving the orphaned cub (played by a puppet), which is rescued by a woman whose baby has died of the plague; THE PLAGUE: a village in mourning; A PRAYER ANSWERED: the transformation: the jaguar cub becomes a boy, Juan Darien (played by another puppet); THE NURTURING: Juan's ritual baptism: the mother raises him; NIGHT IN THE VILLAGE; JOURNEY TO SCHOOL: the parting: the mother sends him to school (he is now played by yet another puppet); SCHOOL: discipline; fact; THE MOTHER DIES: leaving him an orphan again (he is now played by a real human); THE CARNIVAL: Juan takes shelter in the tigers' cage of a circus that has come to town; DISCOVERY: suspicion: Toledo, the tiger tamer, suspects Juan for what he is; THE INTERROGATION: schoolroom: Toledo takes Juan to a hypnotist and his earliest memories are revealed; THE TORTURE AND TRANSFORMATION OF JUAN DARIEN: the terrified villagers torture Juan until he turns back into a jaguar. He is left to die at the edge of the jungle; THE JAGUARS' CONGRESS: retribution: Juan is brought back to health by the jaguars who eat the tiger tamer; THE MOTHER'S GRAVE AND THE RETURN TO THE JUNGLE: Juan goes to his mother's grave, where, with his own blood, he writes his name below hers, then returns to the jungle, a jaguar forever; THE JUNGLE. *Prologue:* Agnus Dei (Chorus), Lacrymosa (Chorus, Mother Dancer, Mother Vocalist), Mr. Bones' Fanfare (dance) (Mr. Bones), Jaguar Cub Approach (Mother Dancer & Mother Vocalist), Mr. Bones' Two-Step (dance) (Mr. Bones), The Hunter's Entrance, Gloria (Chorus, Mother Dancer, Mother Vocalist), Initiation, A Round at Midnight, Sanctus (Mother Dancer & Mother Vocalist), School (Juan the Boy), Recordare ("Inter Oves") (Mother Dancer, Mother Vocalist, Juan the Boy, Chorus), Carnaval (Circus Barker), Lullaby (l: Elliot Goldenthal) (Street Singer), Trance (l: Horacio Quiroga) (Juan the Boy), "Dies Irae" (Street Singer, Chorus, Mother Dancer, Mother Vocalist), Lacrymosa II, Retribution, "The Ballad of Return" (Soloist).

Reviews were generally good. The show received Tony nominations for musical, score, direction of a musical, sets, and lighting. The Broadway production was part of Lincoln Center Theatre's New Collaboration series sponsored by the Philip Morris Companies.

367. *Juno*

About the struggle between the IRA and the British. Set in Dublin in 1921. Work-shy Captain Jack spends his time at Foley's Bar. Juno is his long-suffering wife who, with Mary their daughter, supports the family. Johnny is the brooding son who has lost a hand in the fighting. At the beginning Robbie Tancred, an IRA soldier, is shot by the British in the street. The Boyles are informed by lawyer Bentham that they have come into an inheritance. They spend the money that turns out to be an illusion. Bentham leaves Mary pregnant, and Johnny is taken away and killed for betraying Tancred. Captain Jack and his pal Joxer drink themselves into oblivion, and Juno and Mary go off to new life.

Before Broadway. Originally announced as *Daarlin' Man*. Author Sean O'Casey had never seen a musical before he was approached for the rights, which he gave. He also approved music, lyrics and libretto (which diluted a lot of the original dialogue, for the sake of American audiences, but otherwise remained faithful to the play). Tony Richardson was the first director, and made some of the important staging decisions, but he quit before rehearsals, and was replaced by Vincent J. Donehue. It tried out first in Washington, DC, then on 2/4/59 opened for further tryouts at the Shubert Theatre, Boston. Mr. Donehue was fired, and replaced by Jose Ferrer (Mr. Donehue would get billing in the back of the playbill as "assistant to Mr. Ferrer"). In the cast Jean Stapleton replaced Jane Rose. The role of 8th-billed Jack Betts was cut. Several songs were cut before Broadway: "Farewell, Me Butty," "His Own Peculiar Charm," "Ireland's Eye" (dance), "Lament," "Quarrel Song," "and "You're the Girl."

The Broadway Run. Winter Garden Theatre, 3/9/59–3/21/59. 16 performances. Presented by The Playwrights' Company, Oliver Smith, Oliver Rea; Music/Lyrics: Marc Blitzstein; Book: Joseph Stein; Based on the 1924 Irish play, *Juno and the Paycock*, by Sean O'Casey; Director: Jose Ferrer; Choreographer: Agnes de Mille; Sets: Oliver Smith; Costumes: Irene Sharaff; Lighting: Peggy Clark; Musical Director: Robert Emmett Dolan; Orchestrations: Robert Russell Bennett, Marc Blitzstein, Hershy Kay; Press: William Fields, Walter Alford, Reginald Denenholz, Mae Lyons; Associate Producer: Lyn Austin; Company Manager: Emmett R. Callahan; Production Stage Manager: Peter Zeisler; Stage Manager: Randall Brooks; Assistant Stage Manager: Jerry Crews. **Cast**: Mary Boyle: Monte Amundsen (5); Johnny Boyle: Tommy Rall (6); Juno Boyle: Shirley Booth (1) ☆; Jerry Devine: Loren Driscoll (9); Mrs. Madigan: Jean Stapleton (4); Mrs. Brady: Nancy Andrews (8); Mrs. Coyne: Sada Thompson (7); Miss Quinn: Beulah Garrick (12); Charlie Bentham: Earl Hammond; Foley: Arthur Rubin; Sullivan: Rico Froehlich; Michael Brady: Robert Rue; Paddy Coyne: Julian Patrick; "Captain" Jack Boyle: Melvyn Douglas (2) ☆; "Joxer" Daley: Jack MacGowran (3); Molly: Gemze de Lappe (10); "Needle" Nugent: Liam Lenihan; IRA Men: Tom Clancy (13) & Jack Murray; Mrs. Tancred: Clarice Blackburn (11); Mrs. Dwyer: Betty Low; IRA Singer: Robert Hoyem; Furniture Removal Men: George Ritner & Frank Carroll; Policeman: Rico Froehlich; Singers: Frank Carroll, Anne Fielding, Ted Forlow, Rico Froehlich, Cleo Fry, Robert Hoyem, Pat Huddleston, Gail Johnston, Barbara Lockard, Jack Murray, Julian Patrick, George Ritner, Robert Rue, Pat Ruhl, Diana Sennett, Joanne Spiller, James Tushar; Dancers: Chuck Bennett, Sharon Enoch, Ted Forlow, Mickey Gunnersen, Pat Heyes, Curtis Hood, Scott Hunter, Rosemary Jourdan, Eugene Kelton, Annabelle Lyon, James Maher, Enrique Martinez, Howard Parker, Jim Ryan, Glen Tetley, Marjorie Wittmer, Jenny Workman. **Standbys**: Juno: Sandra Kent; Jack Boyle: Walter Kinsella. **Understudies**: Johnny/Charlie: Ted Forlow; Mary: Anne Fielding; Joxer/Nugent: Tom Clancy; Mrs. Madigan/Mrs. Tancred: Joanne Spiller; Jerry: James Tushar; Mrs. Brady: Cleo Fry; Mrs. Coyne/Miss Quinn: Barbara Lockard; Molly: Jenny Workman. **Act I**: *Prologue*: The street in front of the Boyle home; early evening in summer: "We're Alive" (Ensemble); *Scene 1* The Boyle home: "I Wish it So" (Mary), "Song of the Ma" (Juno); *Scene 2* Another street; *Scene 3* The street, and Foley's bar: "We Can Be Proud" (Foley, Sullivan, Michael, Paddy), "Daarlin' Man" (Boyle, Joxer, Ensemble); *Scene 4* A park square: "One Kind Word" (Jerry); *Scene 5* The Boyle home: "Old Sayin's" (Juno & Captain Jack), "What is the Stars?" (Captain Jack & Joxer), "Old Sayin's" (reprise) (Juno & Captain Jack); *Scene 6* Another street: "(You) Poor Thing" (Mrs. Madigan, Mrs. Brady, Mrs. Coyne, Miss Quinn); *Scene 7* A square in the city: "Dublin Night" (ballet) (ballet mus: Trude Rittman & Marc Blitzstein) (Johnny, Molly, Ensemble); *Scene 8* A park square; evening, a few days later: "My True Heart" (Mary & Bentham); *Scene 9* The street: Finale Act I ("On a Day Like This") (Juno, Captain Jack, Ensemble). Jig: Howard Parker & Eugene Kelton; Slip Jig: Glen Tetley; Shillelagh Dance: Curtis Hood, Enrique Martinez, Chuck Bennett, Scott Hunter; Jig: Juno, Captain Jack, Ensemble). **Act II**: *Scene 1* The Boyle home; evening, a few days later: "Bird Upon the Tree" (Juno & Mary); *Scene 2* The yard behind the house: The Party: (a) "Music in the House" (Captain Jack & Ensemble); (b) "It's Not Irish." [Gramophone]: Arthur Rubin; [Quartet]: Foley, Sullivan, Michael, Captain Jack; (c) "The Liffey Waltz:" Ensemble [end of the

Party sequence], "Hymn" (IRA Singer), "Johnny" (ballet) (ballet mus: Marc Blitzstein) (Johnny & Molly); *Scene 3* A street: "You Poor Thing" (reprise) (Mrs. Madigan, Mrs. Brady, Mrs. Coyne, Miss Quinn); *Scene 4* The Boyle home; *Scene 5* A park square: "For Love" (Mary), "One Kind Word" (reprise) (Jerry); *Scene 6* The Boyle home: "Where?" (Juno); *Scene 7* The street and Foley's bar: Finale Act II (Juno, Mary, Captain Jack, Joxer).

Broadway reviews were so-so. *West Side Story*, which had moved from the Winter Garden to make way for *Juno*, moved back to the Winter Garden after *Juno* folded, just after which Monte Amundsen married Tommy Rall.

After Broadway. From 1964 onwards Joseph Stein devoted himself to a satisfactory revision, and approached Hal Prince to produce. But Mr. Prince rejected it. Irish actress Geraldine Fitzgerald and songwriter Richard Maltby Jr. adapted the new version, with Mr. Maltby writing some new lyrics, and Thomas Fay arranging the music for a small orchestra as well as writing the music for one new song. More of Sean O'Casey's original dialogue was brought back, but the ballets were taken out. In 1974 this much-revised version, now called *Daarlin' Juno*, played at the Williamstown Theatre Festival, with Milo O'Shea and Geraldine Fitzgerald in the leads. Director: Arvin Brown. In 1976 *Daarlin' Juno* played at the Long Wharf Theatre, with the same leads and director as in 1974.

Vineyard Theatre, NYC, 10/14/92–11/15/92. 34 performances. This was another revised version, but still called *Juno*. Additional Lyrics: Ellen Fitzhugh; Director: Lonny Price; Choreographer: Joey McKneely; Musical Director: Grant Sturiale. **Cast**: Juno: Anita Gillette; Captain Jack: Dick Latessa; Joxer: Ivar Brogger; Mrs. Coyne: Jeanette Landis; Reilly: Bill Nabel; Mary Doyle: Erin O'Brien; IRA Man: Stephen Lee Anderson; Mrs. Tancred: Tanny McDonald; Nugent: Frank O'Brien. Some songs cut from the original were added here—"His Own Peculiar Charm," "Ireland's Eye," "Farewell, Me Butty".

368. *Kat and the Kings*

Life among the Cape Coloureds of South Africa during apartheid. District Six is the "New Orleans of South Africa," where kids bopped to rock records brought into Cape Town by American sailors. Kat is 17 and thinks he's the best singer and dancer in the district. He and his mixed race doo-wop harmony band, the Cavalla Kings, hit the big time for a short while, but can't surmount the color bar, and they crash. 40 years later Kat is a street shoeshine man, reflecting on his 15 minutes in the sun.

Before Broadway. *Kat and the Kings* began at the Dock Road Theatre, Cape Town, in 9/95. It had many successful runs in South Africa. Then it went to England, where it had a run at the Tricycle Theatre, Kilburn, London, in 1997, and a return engagement, 2/19/98–3/14/98. Then it had a limited run at the Vaudeville Theatre, London, 3/23/98–8/1/98. Previews from 3/18/98. Presented by Paul Elliott, Nick Salmon, and Lee Menzies. **Cast**: Kat: Salie Daniels. It was the first South African musical to run in London since the new South African regime. It won two Olivier Awards. The recording done live at the 6/6/98 performance, and released on 8/10/99 by First Night Records.

The Broadway Run. Cort Theatre, 8/19/99–1/2/00. 15 previews from 8/6/99. 157 performances. Presented by Harriet Newman Leve, Judith & David Rosenbauer, in association with Richard Frankel, Marc Routh, Willette Klausner, Kardana—Swinsky Productions, David Kramer, Taliep Petersen, and Renaye Kramer, by special arrangement with Paul Elliott, Nick Salmon, and Lee Menzies; Music: Taliep Petersen; Lyrics/Book: David Kramer; Created by: David Kramer & Taliep Petersen; Based on the real-life memories of star Salie Daniels, to whom the Broadway production was dedicated; Director: David Kramer; Choreographers: Jody J. Abrahams & Loukmaan Adams; Sets/Costumes: Saul Radomsky; Lighting: Howard Harrison; Sound: Orbital Sound/Sebastian Frost; Musical Supervisor: Gary Hind; Musical Director: Jeff Lams; Arrangements: Taliep Petersen; Press: Helene Davis Publicity; Casting: Binder Casting Associates; General

MANAGERS: Richard Frankel Productions; COMPANY MANAGER: Steven H. David; PRODUCTION STAGE MANAGER: Pat Sosnow; STAGE MANAGER: Paul J. Smith; ASSISTANT STAGE MANAGER: Laurie Goldfeder. **Cast:** KAT DIAMOND: Terry Hector; LUCY DIXON: Kim Louis; YOUNG KAT DIAMOND: Jody J. Abrahams; BINGO: Loukmaan Adams; BALLIE: Junaid Booysen; MAGOO: Alistair Izobell. **Standbys**: Kat: Rudy Roberson; Lucy: Pia Glenn; Ballie/Magoo/Bingo: E. Clayton Cornelius. **Understudy**: Young Kat: Alistair Izobell. **Orchestra:** KEYBOARDS: Jeff Lams; GUITARS: Jerome Harris; BASS: Francisco Centeno; DRUMS: Warren Odze; SAX/FLUTE: Mark Grose; TRUMPET: Ravi Best. **Act I**: Cape Town, South Africa, 1999; and District Six, 1957: Overture (Orchestra), "Memory" (Lucy & The Kings), "American Thing" (Kat & Company), "(My) Lucky Day" (Young Kat & Kat), "Mavis" (Kat, Bingo, Young Kat, Ballie, Magoo), "Boetie Guitar" (Kat & The Kings), "Cavalla Kings" (Lucy & The Kings), "If Your Shoes Don't Shine" (Kat), "Dress to Kill" (Lucy & The Kings), "Shine" (Lucy & The Kings), "The Tafelberg Hotel" (Lucy & The Kings), "Lonely Girl" (Bingo, Magoo, Kat, Young Kat, Ballie), "Josephine" (Ballie & The Kings), "Wild Time" (Company). **Act II**: Cape Town, 1999/1959; Durban, South Africa, 1959: "Happy to Be Nineteen" (Company), "Lonely Girl" (reprise) (Bingo & The Kings), "Oo Wee Bay Bee" (Young Kat & The Kings), "Only if You Have a Dream" (Lucy & Magoo), "The Last Thing You Need" (Young Kat, Bingo, Magoo, Ballie), "Stupid Boy" (Kat); The Claridges Hotel Medley: "Cavalla Kings" (reprise) (The Kings), "The Singing Sensation" (Young Kat, Lucy, The Kings), "The Bell Hop" (Bingo & The Kings), "Blind Date" (Magoo), "Lonely Girl" (reprise) (Lucy & The Kings), "The Invisible Dog" (Bingo & The Kings), "Hey, Baby" (Young Kat & The Kings), "Cavalla Kings" (reprise) (Lucy & The Kings), "Skeleton Dance" (The Kings), "Lagunya" (Bingo, Ballie, Young Kat, Magoo), "Lucky Day" (reprise) (Young Kat & Kat) [end of medley]; Finale: "The Singing Sensation" (reprise) (Young Kat & The Kings), "Hey, Baby" (reprise) (Magoo & The Kings), "We Were Rocking" (Kat & Company), "Lagunya" (reprise) (Bingo & Company), "Wild Time" (reprise) (Company).

The Broadway opening night audience included Cicely Tyson, Ossie Davis, Ruby Dee, Lesley Gore, Spike Lee, Leslie Uggams. Reviews were completely divided.

After Broadway. NETHERLANDS TOUR. Opened on 9/29/99, in Rotterdam, and closed on 11/7/99. DIRECTOR: David Kramer. **Cast:** OLD KAT DIAMOND: Danny Butler; YOUNG KAT: Emraan Adams; MAGOO: Elton Landrew; ALSO WITH: Kurt Herman, Ashley Washing, Tertia Botha.

TRICYCLE THEATRE, Kilburn, 12/16/03–2/8/04. DIRECTOR: David Kramer; SETS/COSTUMES: Saul Radomsky. **Cast:** OLD KAT DIAMOND: Danny Butler; LUCY: Abigail Petersen; YOUNG KAT: Emraan Adams; BINGO: Loukmaan Adams; BALLIE: Munthir Dullisear; MAGOO: Elton Landrew.

369. *Kean*

Edmund Kean (1787–1833), the most famous regency actor, is unable to differentiate between real life and his roles. Set in London.

Before Broadway. Alfred Drake had bought the rights to Sartre's play, with a view to starring in a New York version. They couldn't find funding, so he and his manager, Robert Lantz, turned it into a musical. This was Peter Stone's first musical libretto, and also the first original Wright & Forrest score to reach Broadway (the others, such as *Kismet* and *Song of Norway*, had been adaptations of the works of classical composers). This show was Jack Cole's second effort as director/choreographer. The production was capitalized at over $400,000, mostly by Columbia Records. It opened in Boston; Alfred Drake missed half the run there; and the show got terrific reviews. Then it went to Philadelphia, where things got worse. The numbers "Ado About Kean," "Disorder and Genius," "Inevitable," "Shadow Play," and "Amsterdam" were all cut before Broadway.

The Broadway Run. BROADWAY THEATRE, 11/2/61–1/20/62. 1 preview on 11/1/61. 92 PERFORMANCES. PRESENTED BY Robert Lantz (and Alfred Drake); MUSIC/LYRICS: Robert Wright & George Forrest; BOOK: Peter Stone; BASED ON the 1953 comedy of the same name by Jean-Paul Sartre, which was based on the 1836 play by Alexandre Dumas; DIRECTOR/CHOREOGRAPHER: Jack Cole; SETS/COSTUMES: Ed Wittstein; LIGHTING: John Harvey; MUSICAL DIRECTOR/VOCAL ARRANGEMENTS: Pembroke Davenport; ORCHESTRATIONS: Philip J. Lang; BALLET & INCIDENTAL MUSIC: Elie Siegmeister; CAST RECORDING on Columbia; PRESS: Harvey B. Sabinson, David Powers, Ted Goldsmith; GENERAL MANAGER: Monty Shaff; COMPANY MANAGER: Arthur Waxman; PRODUCTION STAGE MANAGER: Peter Bronte; STAGE MANAGER: Walter Neal; ASSISTANT STAGE MANAGER: Malcolm Marmorstein. **Cast:** CHRISTIE: Alfred DeSio; BARNABY: Christopher Hewett; EDMUND KEAN: Alfred Drake (1) ☆; STAGE MANAGER: Alfred Toigo; BEN: Robert Penn; FRANCIS, AN ACTOR: Arthur Rubin; SOLOMON: Truman Smith; LORD NEVILLE: Roderick Cook; COUNTESS ELENE DE KOEBERG: Joan Weldon (4); LADY AMY GOSWELL: Patricia Cutts (5); COUNT DE KOEBERG: Patrick Waddington; LORD DELMORE: John Lankston; MAJOR-DOMO: Martin Ambrose; PRINCE OF WALES: Oliver Gray (3); ANNA DANBY, ASPIRING ACTRESS: Lee Venora (2); PROP BOY: Eddie Ericksen; SECRETARY: Joseph McGrath; MAXWELL: Larry Shadur; HENCHMAN: Martin Ambrose; POTT: George Harwell; ST. ALBANS: Rene Jarmon; SPARROW: Margaret Gathright; BOLT: Gloria Warner; TIM: Randy Doney; DAVID: John Jordan; PIP: Paul Jordan; PATRICK: Charles Dunn; GUARDS: Larry Shadur & John Wheeler; DANCERS: John Aristedes, Barbara Beck, Johanna Carothers, Lois Castle, Charles Corbett, Kenneth Creel, Randy Doney, Judy Dunford, Larry Fuller, Mickey Gunnersen, Pamela Hayford, Jim Hutchison, Lisa James, Rene Jarmon, Richard Lyle, George Martin, Roger Puckett, Suanne Shirley; SINGERS: Martin Ambrose, Charise Amidon, Charles Dunn, Eddie Ericksen, Nancy Foster, Margaret Gathright, Maggie Goz, George Harwell, John Lankston, Joseph McGrath, Lispet Nelson, Mari Nettum, Larry Shadur, Susan Terry, Alfred Toigo, Gloria Warner, John Wheeler. **Standby**: Kean: Lawrence Brooks. **Understudies**: Anna: Nancy Foster; Prince: Christopher Hewett; Amy/Elene: Mari Nettum; De Koeberg: John Lankston; Neville: Alfred Toigo; Christie: Larry Fuller; Ben: Larry Shadur; Francis: John Wheeler. **Act I**: *Prologue*: Drury Lane Theatre. The stage: "Penny Plain, Twopence Colored" (Christie), "Man and Shadow" (Kean); *Scene 1* The Danish Embassy. A ballroom: "Mayfair Affair" (Elena, Mary, Dancing & Singing Ensemble), "Sweet Danger" (Elena & Kean); *Scene 2* The street. Drury Lane: "Queue at Drury Lane" (Barnaby, Ben, Francis, Ensemble), "King of London" (Barnaby, Ben, Francis, Ensemble); *Scene 3* Drury Lane Theatre. Kean's dressing room: "To Look Upon My Love" (Kean & Solomon), "Let's Improvise" (Kean & Anna), "Elena" (Kean, Francis, Ensemble); *Scene 4* The Danish Embassy. A private room. And Carlton House. A private room: "Social Whirl" (Elena, Amy, Prince, Count) [cut after the opening]; *Scene 5* A street in front of a Thames-side tavern: "The Fog and the Grog" (Barnaby, Ben, Francis, Kean, Ensemble); *Scene 6* The Green Frog. A tavern: Finale Act I (Kean & Ensemble). **Act II**: *Scene 1* Drury Lane Theatre. Kean's dressing room: "Civilized People" (Kean, Anna, Elena), "Service for Service" (Elena & Kean), "Willow, Willow, Willow" (Anna as Desdemona); *Scene 2* Drury Lane Theatre. The stage boxes: "Fracas at Old Drury" (Barnaby, Ben, Francis, Christie, Ensemble), "Chime In" (Christie, Barnaby, Ben, Francis, Ensemble); *Scene 3* The street. Drury Lane; *Scene 4* Kean's house. A drawing room: "Swept Away" (Elena & Kean), "Domesticity" (Anna & Kean) [cut after the opening]; *Scene 5* The street. Drury Lane: "Clown of London" (Ensemble); *Scene 6* Drury Lane. The stage: "Apology?" (Kean).

It finally opened to basically good reviews. Alfred Drake got raves. After five weeks on Broadway, 20 minutes was cut from the length of the show, including two numbers and the bathtub scene. By this time there were over 550 balcony seats going for $1 each, but there were few takers. Alfred Drake was great, but the production couldn't cut it, and Mr. Drake's ill health precipitated the premature closing. Judy Garland recorded the number "Sweet Danger." The show received Tony nominations for musical direction, and for Alfred Drake.

After Broadway. YORK THEATRE COMPANY, 1/14/00–1/16/00. 5 PERFORMANCES. A reading, part of the *Musicals in Mufti* series. Certain numbers were cut, but "Inevitable" (Anna) was restored as the first song in Act II. Peter Stone and Robert Wright attended the performances

(George Forrest had died in 1999). DIRECTOR: Richard Sabellico; MUSICAL DIRECTOR: Fred Barton. *Cast*: KEAN: Walter Willison; ELENE: Susan Watson; ANNA: Christiane Noll; FRANCIS/DANISH AMBASSADOR: Arthur Rubin; PRINCE: Robert Sella; AMY/CAROLINA: Diane J. Findlay; SOLOMON: Douglas Holmes; CHRISTIE/NARRATOR: Jesse Tyler Ferguson; BARNABY: Hans Friedrichs.

370. *Kelly*

Set in the 1880s, in New York City. The real life Steve Brodie (who after his "jump" appeared on Broadway in 1891 in *Money Mad*, in which he jumped off a replica Brooklyn Bridge) became brash teenage busboy Hop Kelly for the musical. Hop has already chickened out of three attempts, and the Bowery gamblers don't like that (will he survive, or won't he? That makes a good bet). The gamblers decide to throw a dummy off in his place, but Hop does make the jump (we don't see it, and that was one of the major problems with the show — there was no visible climax). Sid Crane was a gambler, and Jack Mulligan a world heavyweight boxing champ.

Before Broadway. At first it was called *Never Go There Anymore*. The property was first optioned by Herbert Greene, then by Joseph P. Harris & Ira Bernstein. None of them could get on with the writers. Then Edward Padula optioned it, and signed Richard Harris for the title role, and Lindsay Anderson to direct, but Mr. Padula fired Mr. Anderson, and hired Peter Coe. Richard Harris also disappeared when his contract expired. Gene Kelly, Tommy Sands, and Frank Gorshin were all contemplated for the title role, but then Ed Padula dropped the project. He again cited "extreme differences" with the writers. Then David Susskind and Daniel Melnick took it up, hired Herbert Ross to direct and choreograph, and with backing from Joseph E. Levine, got it into a tryout production in 12/64 in Philadelphia, where audience reaction was terrible. It then went to the Shubert Theatre, Boston, from 1/20/65, where, despite doctoring of the book by David Goodman, reviews were so bad they cut the number of performances to 5, instead of going all the way to 2/6/65, as planned. Leonard Stern & Mel Brooks were invited in to doctor it further, and drastically cut the top-billed role of Ma Kelly (played by Ella Logan, who then quit), and eliminated roles played by Jack Creley and Avery Schreiber. Meanwhile the writers were suing the producers for changing their concept, and thus they were refusing to engage in rewrites. So, the producers brought in a new writer — Jack Segal. Don Francks replaced Roy Castle in the title role. *Oh, What a Lovely War* was forced out of the Broadhurst to make way for *Kelly*.

The Broadway Run. BROADHURST THEATRE, 2/6/65. 7 previews from 2/1/65. 1 PERFORMANCE. PRESENTED BY David Susskind & Daniel Melnick, in association with Joseph E. Levine; MUSIC: Moose Charlap; LYRICS: Eddie Lawrence; ADDITIONAL MUSIC & LYRICS: Jack Segal; BOOK: Eddie Lawrence (book doctored by David Goodman, Leonard Stern, Mel Brooks); SUGGESTED BY Steve Brodie's purported jump off the Brooklyn Bridge on 7/23/1886; DIRECTOR/CHOREOGRAPHER: Herbert Ross; SETS: Oliver Smith; COSTUMES: Freddy Wittop; LIGHTING: Tharon Musser; MUSICAL DIRECTOR: Samuel Matlovsky; ORCHESTRATIONS: Hershy Kay; DANCE MUSIC: Betty Walberg; CAST RECORDING on Columbia; PRESS: Nat Dorfman & Irvin Dorfman, Harold Rand, Marcia Katz; GENERAL MANAGER: Philip Adler; COMPANY MANAGER: Edward Blatt; PRODUCTION STAGE MANAGER: Randall Brooks; STAGE MANAGER: Tom Porter. *Cast*: HOP KELLY: Don Francks (6); DAN KELLY: Wilfred Brambell (1) ✫; JACK MULLIGAN: Mickey Shaughnessy (3) ✫; AUGIE MASTERS: Leon Janney (4) ✫; STICKPIN SIDNEY CRANE: Jesse White (2) ✫; JAMES: Steve Elmore (8); CARRUTHERS: Brandon Maggart (10); FAY CHERRY: Eileen Rodgers (5) ✫; CHARLIE: Josip Elic; SPARKENBROKE, THE BUTLER: Bill Richards; MAYOR TULLY: Hamilton Camp (9); ENGLISHMAN: Thomas Rezarf; ANGELA CRANE: Anita Gillette (7); TOUGH KID: Barbara Monte; THREE TOUGH GUYS: Louis Kosman, Antony De Vecchi, Michael Nestor; SAILOR: James Moore; THE REDHEAD: Lynn Fields; THE RUBE: Sterling Clark; YOUNG GIRL: Hanne Marie Reiner; 1ST YOUNG MAN: Larry Roquemore; 2ND YOUNG MAN:

Paul Charles; THE DRUNK: Ronald B. Stratton; THREE LADIES: Leslie Franzos, Eleanore Treiber, Kathleen Doherty; LOLLYPOP GIRL: Bettye Jenkins; BEGGAR: Bill Richards; BUMS: James Moore, Larry Roquemore, Bill Richards; POLICE CHIEF: J. Vernon Oaks; POLICEMAN: Robert L. Hultman; CHIEF DIGNITARY: Stanley Simmonds; DANCERS: Paul Charles, Sterling Clark, Anthony De Vecchi, Kathleen Doherty, Lynn Fields, Leslie Franzos, Bettye Jenkins, Barbara Monte, Michael Nestor, Hanne Marie Reiner, Bill Richards, Larry Roquemore, Ron Stratton, Eleanore Treiber; SINGERS: Walter P. Brown, Georgia Creighton, Ceil Delli, Steve Elmore, Howard Hartman, Robert L. Hultman, Carol Joplin, Lorene Latine, Donna Monroe, J. Vernon Oaks, Maggie Task, William Wendt. *Understudies*: Hop/Dan: Hamilton Camp; Angela: Carol Joplin; Fay: Georgia Creighton; Mulligan: Bill Richards; Mayor: Stanley Simmonds; Charlie: J. Vernon Oaks; Carruthers: Louis Kosman. *Prologue:* Under the Bridge: "Ode to the Bridge" (Hop). *Act I*: *Scene 1* Along the Bowery: "Six Blocks from the Bridge" (Sid, Mulligan, Augie, Company); *Scene 2* The backroom at Augie Masters' cabaret on the Bowery: "That Old Time Crowd" (Fay & Boys), "Simple Ain't Easy" (Hop & Fay); *Scene 3* The Kelly shack under the Brooklyn Bridge: "I'm Gonna Walk Right up to Her" (Hop & Mulligan); *Scene 4* Sid Crane's mansion — the Oval Room: "A Moment Ago" (Angela & Hop); *Scene 5* Red Hook, Brooklyn: "This is a Tough Neighborhood" (Entire Company), "(I'll) Never Go There Anymore" (Angela & Hop). *Act II*: *Scene 1* The Kelly shack: "Life Can Be Beautiful" (Fay, Dan, Bums), "Everyone Here Loves Kelly" (Fay & Company), "Ballad to a Brute" (Angela & Hop); *Scene 2* Augie Masters' Cabaret: "Heavyweight Champ of the World" (Mulligan & Company); *Scene 3* "Me and the Elements:" "Me and the Elements" (Hop & Dan); *Scene 4* At the foot of the Brooklyn Bridge: "Everyone Here Loves Kelly" (reprise) (Fay & Company); *Scene 5* Below the bridge: *Scene 6* Atop the bridge; *Scene 7* Along the Bowery: "Never Go There Anymore" (reprise) (Angela); *Scene 8* Augie Masters' Cabaret: "Everyone Here Loves Kelly" (reprise) (Entire Company).

It was mercilessly panned, and lost $650,000 (this was 1965!). The only recording of *Kelly* is a demo recorded by the authors and commercially released 15 years later.

After Broadway. YORK THEATRE COMPANY, 9/18/98–9/20/98. Reading, part of the *Musicals in Mufti* series. This production was presented as intended by the creators, prior to the 1965 revisions. DIRECTOR: Donna Kaz; MUSICAL DIRECTOR: John Glaudini. *Cast*: DAN: Paul V. Ames; FRANK JAMES/MAYOR: Sean Dougherty; AUGIE: Michael J. Farina; STICKPIN SID/JESSE JAMES: Terence Goodman; FAY: Cady Huffman; EUSTACE "HOP" KELLY: Brian d'Arcy James; ANGELA: Jennifer Prescott (Mrs. d'Arcy James in real life); CARRUTHERS/MAJ. BROOME: Tom Souhrada; BESS KELLY: Mary Stout; JACK L. MULLIGAN: Pete Van Wagner. "Ode to the Brooklyn Bridge," "Heavyweight Champ of the World," "That Old Time Crowd," "Me and the Elements," "Times that Linger," "This is Augie Masters," "We Got a Deal," "Soliloquy," "Home Again," "Never Go There Anymore," "It Kinda Makes Yuh Wonder," "The Insurance Game," "Go to Sleep Early," "A Man is a Man," "Ballad to a Brute," "Big Town," "Everyone Here Loves Kelly," "Life Can Be Beautiful," Finale.

371. *Ken Murray's Blackouts of 1949*

A nightclub vaudeville revue also known as: *Blackouts of 1949*, and *Ken Murray's Blackouts*.

Before Broadway. *Blackouts of 1942*, a nightclub vaudeville revue starring Marie Wilson and Ken Murray, with music and lyrics by Harry & Pauline Carroll, opened on 6/24/42, at EL CAPITAN THEATRE, Los Angeles. "Say When" was one of the musical numbers. It ran year after year in L.A. until 1949, subtly mutating its title at appropriate times to *Blackouts of 1943*, *Blackouts of 1944*, etc, until it finally got to Broadway in 1949. The reason for the shift east was a TV contract in New York.

The Broadway Run. ZIEGFELD THEATRE, 9/6/49–10/15/49. 51 PERFORMANCES. PRESENTED BY David W. Siegel; CONCEIVED BY/DIRECTOR: Ken Murray; SETS: Ben Tipton; SKY BACKGROUND: Leo Atkinson; GOWNS: Betty Colburn Kreisel; MUSICAL DIRECTOR: Ben Shefter; MUSICAL ARRANGEMENTS: A.M. Courage; PRESS: Bill Doll, Dick Williams,

Michael O'Shea; COMPANY MANAGER: Rube Bernstein; STAGE MANAGER: Stanley Poss. *Act I*: *Scene 1* "Hollywood and Vine" (m/l: Charles Henderson & Royal Foster): MOVIE EXTRA: Joan Morley; WOMAN IN SLACKS: Mabel Hart; TWINS: The Corbett Twins (Jean & JoAnn); PETER, THE HERMIT: Danny Duncan; NEWSBOY: Bob Decker; BROADWAY PLAYBOY: Bob Wollter; MAHARAJAH: Val Grund; PROSPECTOR: Sheldon Disrud; MISS IOWA 1949: Darla Hood; VERONICA: Irene Kaye; PLAZA DOORMAN: Shelton Brooks; BETTE DAVIS: Consuelo Cezon; CHINESE LAUNDRYMAN: Joe Wong; SHOE SHINE BOY: Danny Alexander (he tap-danced while jumping a rope); STROLLING COUPLE: Betsy Ross & Milton Charleston; SAILOR: Robert Hightower; *Scene 2* Now and Then (THE GLAMOURLOVELIES: LoRayne Anderson, Phyllis Applegate, Consuelo Cezon, Bettye Meade, Jean Marshall, Joan Morley, Crystal White, Joy Windsor, The Corbett Twins); *Scene 3* Introducing Your Host — Ken Murray (1) (master of ceremonies); *Scene 4* Pat Williams; *Scene 5* Three Idle Rumors; *Scene 6* Ecstasy in F (Harris & Shore — dance satirists); *Scene 7* Shelton Brooks (black songwriter/singer/pianist): "Some of These Days," "Darktown Strutters Ball;" *Scene 8* Bridal Night: GROOM: Jack Mulhall; BRIDE: Jean Marshall; BELL-HOP: Danny Alexander; BRIDESMAIDS: Irene Kaye, Betsy Ross, Joan Morley; HOTEL GUEST: Ken Murray (1); *Scene 9* Jungle Fantasy with Les Zoris (Claudine Baudin & Robert Gross — French couple) (dance): VOCAL SPECIALTY: The Enchanters (Darla Hood, Bob Decker, Val Grund, Sheldon Disrud, Bob Wollter); DANCE SPECIALTY: Crystal White; JUNGLE MAN: Robert Gross; LEOPARD: Claudine Baudin; GIRLS OF THE FOREST: The Glamourlovelies; *Scene 10* D'Vaughn Pershing (virtuoso pianist/clarinetist); *Scene 11* Charles Nelson (singer); *Scene 12* Burton's Birds (George Burton) (Outstanding bird novelty act, introducing "Bill and Coo," the stars of Ken Murray's Academy Award–winning film of the same name). *Act II*: *Scene 1* Al Mardo — "This shouldn't happen to a man;" *Scene 2* Blackouts Television Newsreel; *Scene 3* "The New Look" (Alphonse Berge, who draped gowns on living models at tremendous speed): MODELS: The Glamourlovelies; MAID: Elizabeth Walters; *Scene 4* Nick Lucas (guitarist/singer); *Scene 5* Owen McGiveney [the world's greatest quick-change artist (the only artist alive offering this type of entertainment) in a page from *Oliver Twist*]. Scene: Sikes' garret; Time: an hour before dawn. Mr. McGiveney as Monks/Nancy/Fagin/Bill Sikes/The Artful Dodger; *Scene 6* Nautical Moments: PIRATES: The Glamourlovelies; LONG JOHN SILVER: Peg Leg Bates (one-legged tap-dancer); *Scene 7* Blackouts of 1949 Sports Parade: ARCHERY: Bettye Meade; ICE-SKATING: Darla Hood; COWGIRL: LoRayne Anderson; GOLF: Joan Morley; BASEBALL: Consuelo Cezon; HUNTING: The Corbett Twins; SKIING: Jean Marshall; SWIMMING: Phyllis Applegate; FISHING: Joy Windsor; *Scene 8* Finale.

ALSO WITH: Dot Remy; THE ELDERLOVELIES: Mabel Butterworth, Rose de Haven, Ethel Getty, Sally Hale, Sue Kelton, Perle Kincaid, Mattie Kennedy, Julia Wright.

Reviews were mostly very good.

372. *The King and I*

Set in and around King Mongkut's palace in Bangkok, Siam, in the early 1860s. It tells of the relationship between the old-fashioned 19th-century Siamese king and Anna Leonowens, the widowed English governess he hires in 1862 to tutor his 67 children; the conflict between traditional Siamese living and the encroachment of western culture. She arrives with her son Louis (there were two children in real life), and gradually becomes indispensable to the knowledge-thirsty king. A diplomat, Ramsey, is to arrive, and the king is anxious to make a good impression, as it is the King's intention to pre-empt Western colonialism of his country by entering, of his own will, full-bore into the modern age. Anna helps him. A subplot involves the relationship between Tuptim, one of the King's wives, and Lun Tha, a servant. They try to elope, but are caught and executed. Anna resolves to leave because of this, but then she learns that the King is dying, and she stays. She then helps the Prince, who has been her charge. In

real life the King died in 1868, succeeded by his son, and Anna lectured around the world. She died in Canada in 1915. The ballet sequence "The Small House of Uncle Thomas" was Harriet Beecher Stowe's *Uncle Tom's Cabin* as seen through eyes of Tuptim.

Before Broadway. Gertrude Lawrence had read Margaret Landon's book and seen the 1946 (straight) film with Irene Dunne and Rex Harrison, and she came up with idea of a musical for herself, and suggested it to Cole Porter, who rejected the idea. Rodgers & Hammerstein, aware as they were of the star's limited singing ability, went with it. Rex Harrison, Alfred Drake and Noel Coward all turned down the subsidiary role of the King (Mr. Drake wanted $5,000 a week, which would have been a record. Incidentally, he did play it while Yul Brynner was on vacation). Mary Martin recommended Yul Brynner, who had starred with her in *Lute Song* a few years earlier. Richard Rodgers, in his memoirs, said about Mr. Brynner at his audition, that he "scowled in our direction, sat down on the stage, and crossed his legs, tailor-fashion, then plunked one whacking chord on his guitar and began to howl in a strange language that no one could understand. He looked savage, he sounded savage, and there was no denying that he projected a feeling of controlled ferocity." Several ballads were dropped during New Haven tryouts because Miss Lawrence's voice couldn't handle them — "Anna and Son Klin," "Waiting," "Who Would Refuse?," "Why? Why? Why?," and "Now You Leave." The number "Getting to Know You," rejected from *South Pacific*, was re-worked and added during the Boston tryout (which began on 3/6/51). Two other songs were added in Boston: "I Have Dreamed" and "Western People Funny." John Van Druten, the director, was replaced by Oscar Hammerstein himself. 4th-billed Murvyn Vye was the original Kralahome, but when his role was cut to next to nothing, he quit, being replaced by John Juliano (who didn't get the same billing). Famous producer Leland Hayward, who was an investor, suggested they close before Broadway, but thanks to Rodgers & Hammerstein he made a good investment on his money instead.

The Broadway Run. ST. JAMES THEATRE, 3/29/51–3/20/54. 1,246 PERFORMANCES. PRESENTED BY Richard Rodgers & Oscar Hammerstein II; MUSIC: Richard Rodgers; LYRICS/BOOK: Oscar Hammerstein II; BASED ON the 1943 biographical novel *Anna and the King of Siam*, by Margaret Landon, which was based on Anna Leonowens' 1870 book *The English Governess at the Siamese Court*; DIRECTOR: John Van Druten; CHOREOGRAPHER: Jerome Robbins; ORIENTAL DANCE CONSULTANT: Michiko; SETS/LIGHTING: Jo Mielziner; COSTUMES: Irene Sharaff; ASSISTANT COSTUMES: Florence Klotz; MUSICAL DIRECTOR: Frederick Dvonch; ORCHESTRATIONS: Robert Russell Bennett; BALLET MUSIC ARRANGEMENTS: Trude Rittman; PRESS: Michel Mok & John L. Toohey; CASTING: John Fearnley; GENERAL MANAGER: Morris Jacobs; COMPANY MANAGER: William G. Norton; STAGE MANAGERS: Jerome Whyte, John Cornell, Ruth Mitchell, *Duane* Camp, *Ed Preston*. **Cast:** CAPTAIN ORTON: Charles Francis, *Leon Shaw* (from 52–53); LOUIS LEONOWENS: Sandy Kennedy, *Ronn Cummins, Michael Allen* (from 52–53); ANNA LEONOWENS: Gertrude Lawrence (1) ✰, *Celeste Holm* (during Miss Lawrence's vacation, 6/28/52–8/11/52), *Constance Carpenter* (from 9/6/52), *Annamary Dickey, Patricia Morison*; THE INTERPRETER: Leonard Graves; THE KRALAHOME: John Juliano; THE KING OF SIAM: Yul Brynner (2), *Alfred Drake* (during Mr. Brynner's 6-week summer vacation in 52); PHRA ALACK: Len Mence; TUPTIM: Doretta Morrow (4), *Stephanie Augustine* (from 51–52), *Suzanne Lake* (stood in); LADY THIANG: Dorothy Sarnoff (3), *Terry Saunders* (from 51–52); PRINCE CHULALONGKORN: Johnny Stewart, *Ronnie Lee* (from 51–52), *Sal Mineo* (from 52–53); PRINCESS YING YAOWALAK: Baayork Lee, *Toby Stevens*; LUN THA: Larry Douglas (5), *Joseph Caruso*; SIR EDWARD RAMSEY: Robin Craven; PRINCESSES & PRINCES: Nora Baez (gone by 51–52), Cristanta Cornejo, Rodolfo Cornejo, Robert Cortazal (gone by 51–52), Andrea Del Rosario, Thomas Griffen (gone by 52–53), Margie James (gone by 51–52), Barbara Luna (gone by 51–52), Alfonso Maribo (gone by 51–52), James Maribo (gone by 51–52), Orlando Rodriguez (gone by 51–52), Corinne St. Denis (gone by 51–52), Bunny Warner. 51–52 replacements: *Carla de Guzman* (gone by 52–53), *Joann Garcia* (gone by 52–53), *Richard Mercado, Patrick Adiarte, Dennis Bonilla, Thomas Bonilla*. 52–53 replacements: *Yvette Cardinoza, Geraldine Lorenti, Laurence Lee, Carol Percy;*

THE ROYAL DANCERS: Jamie Bauer (gone by 52–53), Lee Becker (gone by 52–53), Mary Burr (gone by 51–52), Gemze de Lappe (gone by 51–52), Shellie Farrell (gone by 51–52, but back by 52–53), Marilyn Gennaro, Evelyn Giles (gone by 52–53), Ina Kurland (gone by 52–53), Nancy Lynch, Michiko, Helen Murielle (gone by 52–53), Prue Ward, Dusty Worrall, Yuriko. 51–52 replacements: *Sara Aman, Barbara Luna, Claire Pasch, Corinne St. Denis, Meryl Sargent* (gone by 52–53), *Beryl Towbin* (gone by 52–53). 52–53 replacements: *Barbara Davenport, Joan Fitzmaurice, Rhoda Johannson, Jean Houloose, Mavis Ray, Tao Strong, Bettina Dearborn, Ann Needham, Jacqueline Hairston, Cordelia Ware*; WIVES: Stephanie Augustine (gone by 51–52), Marcia James, Ruth Korda, Suzanne Lake, Gloria Marlowe (gone by 52–53), Carolyn Maye (gone by 51–52), Helen Merritt, Phyllis Wilcox. 51–52 replacements: *Beverly Alleman* (gone by 52–53), *Marie Traficante*. 52–53 replacements: *Julienne Hendricks, Helena Schurgot, Jeanne Grant, Jenny Collins, Ruth Scheoni, Jan Scott*; AMAZONS: Geraldine Hamburg, Maribel Hammer (*Frances Russell* by 51–52), Norma Larkin, Miriam Lawrence; PRIESTS: Duane Camp, Joseph Caruso, Leonard Graves (*Otis Bigelow* from 52–53), Jack Matthew, Ed Preston; SLAVES: Doria Avila, Raul Celada (*Otis Bigelow* from 51–52), Beau Cunningham, Tommy Gomez, *Murray Gitlin*. **Standby**: Anna: Constance Carpenter, *Annamary Dickey* (by 52–53). **Understudies**: King: Leonard Graves, *Ed Preston* (by 51–52), *Leonard Graves* (by 52–53); Thiang: Norma Larkin; Tuptim: Gloria Marlowe, *Suzanne Lake* (by 51–52); Kralahome: Len Mence, *Ed Preston* (by 51–52); Orton/Ramsey: Len Mence, *Leon Shaw* (by 51–52); Lun Tha: Joseph Caruso; Phra Alack: Ed Preston; Interpreter: Jack Matthew; Louis: Herbie Walsh, *Johnny Connoughton* (by 51–52), *Peter Monsen* (by 52–53), *Ronald Batz*; Prince: *Salvatore Mineo* (by 51–52), *Robert Ozores* (by 52–53). **Act I**: **Scene 1** Deck of the *Chow Phya* as it approaches Bangkok: Overture ("Arrival in Bangkok") (Orchestra), "I Whistle a Happy Tune" (Anna & Louis); **Scene 2** A Palace corridor; **Scene 3** The King's study in the Palace: "My Lord and Master" (Tuptim), "Hello, Young Lovers!" (Anna), "The Royal Siamese Children" (instrumental) (danced by Anna, King, His Wives & Children) [by 51–52 this number was known as "The March of the Siamese Children"], "Children Sing, Priests Chant" (Men's Chorus & Children's Chorus); **Scene 4** In the Palace grounds: "A Puzzlement" (King); **Scene 5** The schoolroom: "The Royal Bangkok Academy" (Anna & Pupils) [not on the cast album], "Getting to Know You" (Anna, Wives, Children, Michiko [i.e the actress who plays Angel in the ballet]), "We Kiss in a Shadow" (Tuptim & Lun Tha); **Scene 6** A Palace corridor: "A Puzzlement" (reprise) (Prince Chulalongkorn & Louis); **Scene 7** Anna's bedroom: "Shall I Tell You What I Think of You?" (Anna), "Something Wonderful" (Lady Thiang); **Scene 8** A Palace corridor; **Scene 9** The King's study: First Act Finale (Entire Company). **Act II**: **Scene 1** The schoolroom: "Western People Funny" (Lady Thiang & Wives) [not on the cast album]; **Scene 2** In the Palace grounds: "Dance of Anna and Sir Edward" (instrumental), "I Have Dreamed" (Tuptim, Lun Tha, Orchestra), "Hello, Young Lovers" (reprise) (Anna); **Scene 3** "The Small House of Uncle Thomas" (ballet): NARRATOR: Doretta Morrow, *Stephanie Augustine* (from 51–52); UNCLE THOMAS: Dusty Worrall; TOPSY: Ina Kurland; LITTLE EVA: Shellie Farrell; ELIZA: Yuriko; KING SIMON: Gemze de Lappe, *Jamie Bauer*; ANGEL: Michiko; ROYAL DANCERS: Jamie Bauer, Lee Becker, Mary Burr, Marilyn Gennaro, Evelyn Giles, Margie James, Nancy Lynch, Helen Murielle, Corinne St. Denis, Prue Ward; MUSICIANS: Doria Avila, Raul Celada (*Otis Bigelow* from 51–52), Beau Cunningham, DRUMMER: Tommy Gomez; **Scene 4** The King's study: "Song of the King" (King), "Shall We Dance?" (King & Anna); **Scene 5** In the Palace grounds; **Scene 6** A room in Anna's house; **Scene 7** A Palace corridor; **Scene 8** The King's study: "I Whistle a Happy Tune" (reprise) (Anna), Finale (Entire Company).

Broadway reviews were excellent but (being a Rodgers & Hammerstein musical) somewhat disappointing. The show won Tonys for musical, sets, costumes, and for Gertrude Lawrence and Yul Brynner (as featured actor). It also won Donaldson Awards for choreography, sets, costumes, actor (Yul Brynner), supporting actress (Doretta Morrow). It was the fourth-longest-running Broadway show in the 1950s, and the third-longest musical of all time to that date. On 8/16/52, just after getting back from a long summer vacation, Gertrude Lawrence missed a performance. They said it was due to an adverse reaction to an allergy shot. She died of cancer of the liver on the morning of 9/6/52, and was replaced

by Constance Carpenter. As per Miss Lawrence's wishes, Mr. Brynner was raised from supporting actor to lead, and his billing changed accordingly. On the day of Miss Lawrence's funeral (9/9/52) the show did not go on, and Broadway lights dimmed at 8:30 that night (London's West End dimmed too). On 6/22/53 Yul Brynner returned after an 11-week leave. The show cost $360,000, but by the end of run had brought in over a million dollars. The cast album was only 37 minutes long.

After Broadway. THEATRE ROYAL, DRURY LANE, London, 10/8/53–1/14/56. 946 PERFORMANCES. DIRECTOR: Jerome Whyte; CHOREOGRAPHER: June Graham; MUSICAL DIRECTOR: Reginald Burston; CAST RECORDING on Philips. **Cast**: ANNA: Valerie Hobson, *Eve Lister, Ann Martin*; KING: Herbert Lom, *George Pastell*; THIANG: Muriel Smith; TUPTIM: Doreen Duke, *Julia Shelley*; LUN THA: Jan Muzurus, *Ivor Emmanuel*; ORTON: John Harvey; KRALAHOME: Martin Benson, *James Appleby*; RAMSEY: Ronald Leigh Hunt; ELIZA: Sonya Hana; LOUIS: Roy Grant, *Terence Sharkey, Gerald Smith*.

TOUR. Opened on 3/22/54, at the Community Theatre, Hershey, Pa., and closed on 12/17/55, at the Shubert Theatre, Philadelphia. MUSICAL DIRECTOR: Will Irwin. **Cast**: ANNA: Patricia Morison; KING: Yul Brynner, *Leonard Graves*; KRALAHOME: Leonard Graves, *Alfred Cibelli Jr.*; THIANG: Terry Saunders, *Norma Larkin*; TUPTIM: Suzanne Lake, *Christine Matthews*. **Understudy**: Kralahome: Alfred Cibelli Jr.

CITY CENTER, NYC, 4/18/56–5/6/56. 24 PERFORMANCES. PRESENTED BY the New York City Center Light Opera Company; DIRECTOR: John Fearnley; CHOREOGRAPHER: June Graham; SETS: Jo Mielziner; COSTUMES: Irene Sharaff; LIGHTING: Jean Rosenthal; MUSICAL DIRECTOR: Frederick Dvonch. **Cast**: ORTON: Leon Shaw; LOUIS: Kevin Coughlin; ANNA: Jan Clayton; INTERPRETER: John George; KRALAHOME: Leonard Graves; KING: Zachary Scott; PHRA ALACK: Hubert Bland; LUN THA: Philip Wentworth; TUPTIM/NARRATOR: Christine Matthews; THIANG: Muriel Smith; PRINCE: Patrick Adiarte; YING YAOWALAK: Lynn Kikuchi; RAMSEY: Ben Lackland; UNCLE THOMAS: Bettina Dearborn; LITTLE EVA: Wonci Lui; ELIZA: Yuriko; TOPSY: Alice Uchida; KING SIMON: Marion Jim; ANGEL: Dusty Worrall; ROYAL DANCERS INCLUDED: Dorothy Etheridge, Norma Kaiser, Tao Strong. **Understudy**: King: Leonard Graves.

THE MOVIE. 1956. The numbers "My Lord and Master," "Shall I Tell You What I Think of You?," "Western People Funny" and "I Have Dreamed" were all dropped. **Cast**: KING: Yul Brynner (he won the best actor Oscar); ANNA: Deborah Kerr (singing dubbed by Marni Nixon); TUPTIM: Rita Moreno; LOUIS: Rex Thompson; PRINCE: Patrick Adiarte; UNCLE THOMAS: Dusty Worrall; SPECIALTY DANCER: Gemze de Lappe; LUN THA: Carlos Rivas; KRALAHOME: Martin Benson; THIANG: Terry Saunders; ELIZA: Yuriko.

CITY CENTER, NYC, 5/11/60–5/29/60. 24 PERFORMANCES. It got excellent reviews. PRESENTED BY the New York City Center Light Opera Company; DIRECTOR: John Fearnley; CHOREOGRAPHER: Yuriko; SETS: Jo Mielziner; COSTUME SUPERVISOR: Stanley Simmons; LIGHTING: Klaus Holm; MUSICAL DIRECTOR: Pembroke Davenport. **Cast**: ORTON: Sam Kirkham; LOUIS: Richard Mills; ANNA: Barbara Cook; INTERPRETER/DRUMMER: Murray Gitlin; KRALAHOME: Ted Beniades; KING: Farley Granger; PHRA ALACK: Mark Satow; LUN THA: Seth Riggs; TUPTIM/NARRATOR: Joy Clements; THIANG: Anita Darian; PRINCE: Miki Lamont; YING YAOWALAK: Susan Lynn Kikuchi; RAMSEY: Claude Horton; UNCLE THOMAS: Bettina Dearborn; LITTLE EVA: Wonci Lui; TOPSY: Julie Oser; ELIZA: Yuriko; SIMON: Gemze de Lappe; ANGEL: Marion Jim; CHORUS INCLUDED: Victor Duntiere, Irving Barnes, Ann Marisse.

CITY CENTER, NYC, 6/12/63–6/23/63. 15 PERFORMANCES. PRESENTED BY the New York City Center Light Opera Company; DIRECTOR: John Fearnley; CHOREOGRAPHER: Yuriko; LIGHTING: Peggy Clark; MUSICAL DIRECTOR: Pembroke Davenport. **Cast**: ORTON: Sam Kirkham; LOUIS: Tommy Leap; ANNA: Eileen Brennan; INTERPRETER: Paul Flores; KRALAHOME: Ken Le Roy; KING: Manolo Fabregas; PHRA ALACK: John Garces; LUN THA: L.D. Clements; TUPTIM: Joy Clements; THIANG: Anita Darian; PRINCE: Ramon Caballero; YING YAOWALAK: Lisa Jo Abe; RAMSEY: John D. Seymour; CHORUS INCLUDED: Delfino de Arco, Susan Kikuchi, Ado Sato, Victor Duntiere.

NEW YORK STATE THEATRE, 7/6/64–8/8/64. 40 PERFORMANCES. PRESENTED BY Music Theatre of Lincoln Center; DIRECTOR: Edward Greenberg; CHOREOGRAPHER: Yuriko; SETS: Paul C. McGuire; COS-

TUMES: Irene Sharaff; MUSICAL DIRECTOR: Franz Allers; CAST RECORDING on RCA. **Cast**: ORTON: Fred Miller; LOUIS: James Harvey; ANNA: Rise Stevens; INTERPRETER: Rudy Vejar; KRALAHOME: Michael Kermoyan; KING: Darren McGavin; PHRA ALACK: Stuart Mann; TUPTIM/NARRATOR: Lee Venora; THIANG: Patricia Neway; PRINCE: Barry Rubins; YING YAOWALAK: Gina Kaye; LUN THA: Frank Porretta; RAMSEY: Eric Brotherson; UNCLE THOMAS: Bettina Dearborn; LITTLE EVA: Susan Kikuchi; TOPSY: Paula Chin; ELIZA: Takako Asakawa; KING SIMON: Linda Hodes; ANGEL: Connie Sanchez; DRUMMER: Jim McMillan; CHORUS INCLUDED: Delfino de Arco, Dixie Carter, Victor Duntiere, Julius Fields, Ken Richards, Anthony Saverino. **Standbys**: Anna: Annamary Dickey; King: Michael Kermoyan.

CITY CENTER, NYC, 5/23/68–6/9/68. 23 PERFORMANCES. PRESENTED BY the City Center Light Opera Company; DIRECTOR: John Fearnley; CHOREOGRAPHER: Yuriko reproduced Jerome Robbins' original choreography; SETS: Paul C. McGuire; COSTUMES: Irene Sharaff; COSTUME SUPERVISOR: Frank Thompson; LIGHTING: Feder; MUSICAL DIRECTOR: Jonathan Anderson. **Cast**: ORTON: Sam Kirkham; LOUIS: Eric Hamilton; ANNA: Constance Towers; INTERPRETER; Paul Flores; KRALAHOME: Ted Beniades; KING: Michael Kermoyan; PHRA ALACK: Robert Lenn; LUN THA: Stanley Grover; TUPTIM/NARRATOR: Eleanor Calbes; THIANG: Anita Darian; PRINCE: Michael Thom; YING YAOWALAK: Dana Shimizu; RAMSEY: Christopher Hewett; UNCLE THOMAS: Diane Adler; LITTLE EVA: Wonci Lui; TOPSY: Paula Chin; ELIZA: Yuriko; KING SIMON: Carol Fried; ANGEL: Jaclynn Villamil; DRUMMER: Lazar Dano; BUDDHA: Lawrence Kikuchi; CHORUS INCLUDED: JoAnn Ogawa, Margot Travers, Maggie Worth, Vito Durante, Rachel Ticotin, Nancy Ticotin, Marcus Ticotin. **Standbys**: Anna: Virginia Vestoff; King: Ted Beniades; Kralahome: Paul Flores.

PAPER MILL PLAYHOUSE, New Jersey, 1969. DIRECTOR: Stone Widney. **Cast**: Dorothy Sandlin, Michael Kermoyan, Terry Saunders.

JONES BEACH THEATRE, NY, 6/28/72–9/3/72. 55 PERFORMANCES. PRESENTED BY Guy Lombardo; DIRECTOR: John Fearnley; CHOREOGRAPHER: Yuriko; COSTUMES: Winn Morton; LIGHTING: Peggy Clark; MUSICAL DIRECTOR: Jay Blackton. **Cast**: KING: John Cullum; ANNA: Constance Towers; KRALAHOME: Edmund Lyndeck; INTERPRETER: Paul Flores; LUN THA: John Stewart; TUPTIM: Patricia Arnell; YING YAOWALAK: Cynthia Onrubia; PRINCE: Keenan Shimizu; CHORUS INCLUDED: June Angela, Gene Profanato, Loretta Abbott, Tisa Chang, Doris Galiber, Sherry Lambert, Ric Ornellas.

WOLF TRAP FARM PARK, Vienna, Va., 1972. 6 PERFORMANCES. DIRECTOR: Jerome Eskow. **Cast**: Michael Kermoyan, Roberta Peters.

ADELPHI THEATRE, London, 10/10/73. 263 PERFORMANCES. PRESENTED BY Triumph Theatre Productions. **Cast**: KING: Peter Wyngarde; ANNA: Sally Ann Howes; PRINCE: David Morris. It followed a UK tour.

373. *The King and I* (*1977 Broadway revival*)

Before Broadway. This was the national touring company come to Broadway. Susan Kikuchi is Yuriko's daughter. Marianne Tatum was the original standby for Constance Towers, but was too strong, and was demoted to regular understudy by Yul Brynner a week before previews, and replaced by Margot Moser.

The Broadway Run. URIS THEATRE, 5/2/77–12/30/78. 23 previews. 696 PERFORMANCES. PRESENTED BY Lee Guber & Shelly Gross; MUSIC: Richard Rodgers; LYRICS/BOOK: Oscar Hammerstein II; BASED ON the 1943 biographical novel *Anna and the King of Siam*, by Margaret Landon; DIRECTOR/CHOREOGRAPHER: Yuriko; ASSISTANT TO THE DIRECTOR: Susan Kikuchi; SETS: Peter Wolf; COSTUMES: Stanley Simmons reproduced Irene Sharaff's originals; LIGHTING: Thomas Skelton; SOUND: Richard Fitzgerald; MUSICAL SUPERVISOR: Milton Rosenstock; MUSICAL DIRECTOR: John Lesko; PRESS: Solters & Roskin; CASTING: TNI Casting; GENERAL MANAGEMENT: Theatre Now; COMPANY MANAGER: Robb Lady; PRODUCTION STAGE MANAGER: Ed Preston; STAGE MANAGER: Conwell Worthington; ASSISTANT STAGE MANAGER: Thomas J. Rees. **Cast**: CAPTAIN ORTON: Larry Swansen (9); LOUIS LEONOWENS: Alan Amick (11), *Jason Scott, Thor Fields, Alexander Winter*; ANNA LEON-

OWENS: Constance Towers (2) ☆, *Angela Lansbury (4/11/78–4/30/78) Constance Towers (from 5/2/78)*; THE INTERPRETER: Jae Woo Lee, *Robert Vega (4/11/78–4/30/78)*; THE KRALAHOME: Michael Kermoyan (3), *Jae Woo Lee (4/11/78–4/30/78), Michael Kermoyan (from 5/2/78)*; THE KING: Yul Brynner (1) ☆, *Michael Kermoyan (4/11/78–4/30/78), Yul Brynner (from 5/2/78)*; TUPTIM: June Angela (6); LADY THIANG: Hye-Young Choi (4); PRINCE CHULALONGKORN: Gene Profanato (10); PRINCESS YING YAOWALAK: Julie Woo (14); LUN THA: Martin Vidnovic (5); SIR EDWARD RAMSEY: John Michael King (8), *Donald Symington*; ROYAL DANCERS AND WIVES: Su Applegate, Jessica Chao, Lei-Lynne Doo, Dale Harimoto, Pamela Kalt, Susan Kikuchi, Faye Fujisaki Mar, Sumiko Murashima, Libby Rhodes, Cecile Santos, Hope Sogawa, Mary Ann Teng, Patricia K. Thomas, *Gusti Bogok, Kaipo Daniels, V.V. Matsuoka, Diane Lam, Barrett Hong, Richard R. Perlon, Freda Foh Shen, Patricia Weber, Henry Yu*; PRINCESSES AND PRINCES: Ivan Ho, Clark Huang, Annie Lam, Connie Lam, Jennifer Lam, Paul Siu, Tim Waldrip, Kevan Weber, Kym Weber, Julie Woo, Mary Woo, *Diana Chan, Susana Chan, Jonathan Chin, Julian Hsiang, Xavier Rodrigo, Jamie Wong, Jodrell Dimaculangan*; NURSES AND AMAZONS: Sydney Smith, Marianne Tatum, Patricia K. Thomas, Rebecca West (12), *Pamela Kalt, V.V. Matsuoka, Libby Rhodes, Maggie* Stewart; PRIESTS AND SLAVES: Kaipo Daniels, Barrett Hong, Jae Woo Lee, Ric Ornellas, Simeon Den, Chandra Tanna, Robert Vega, *Richard R. Perlon, Henry Yu*; The following wives perform in the ballet "The Small House of Uncle Thomas" (seven characters): NARRATOR: June Angela (6); UNCLE THOMAS: Jessica Chao, *Gusti Bogok*; TOPSY: Lei-Lynne Doo; LITTLE EVA: Dale Harimoto, *Diane Lam*; ELIZA: Susan Kikuchi (7); KING SIMON: Rebecca West (12); ANGEL: Patricia Weber (13); ROYAL DANCERS: Barrett Hong, Faye Fujisaki Mar, Ric Ornellas, Libby Rhodes, Simeon Den, Cecile Santos, Sydney Smith, Hope Sogawa, Chandra Tanna, Patricia K. Thomas, *Dale Harimoto, Henry Fu*; PROPMEN: Kaipo Daniels, Jae Woo Lee, Thomas J. Rees, Robert Vega, *Ric Ornellas*. **Standbys**: King: Michael Kermoyan; Anna: Margot Moser, *Jo Ann Cunningam (by 77–78)*. **Understudies**: King: *William Kiehl (by 77–78)*; Anna: Marianne Tatum, *Pamela Kalt (added by 77–78)*; Kralahome: Jae Woo Lee; Thiang: Sumiko Murashima; Lun Tha: Robert Vega; Interpreter: Robert Vega, *Kaipo Daniels*; Tuptim: Pamela Kalt, *Freda Foh Shen*; Prince: Ivan Ho, *Xavier Rodrigo*; Louis: Tim Waldrip, *Thor Fields*; Simon: Patricia K. Thomas & Dale Harimoto, *Chandra Tanna*; Angel: Faye Fujisaki Mar; Uncle Thomas: Hope Sogawa; Topsy: Libby Rhodes; Eliza: Diane Lam; Little Eva: Dale Harimoto. **Swings**: Ching Gonzalez, Alis-Elaine Anderson, JoAnn Ogawa (first season only), Mimmee Wong (first season only).

Reviews were good.

After Broadway. After Broadway the tour continued, re-opening on 1/4/79, at Chicago.

LONDON PALLADIUM, 1979. 538 PERFORMANCES. **Cast**: KING: Yul Brynner; ANNA: Virginia McKenna; THIANG: Hye-Young Choi; TUPTIM: June Angela; LUN THA: Marty Rhone; KRALAHOME: John Bennett.

TOUR. Opened 2/15/81, at the Warner Theatre, Washington, DC, and closed on 6/5/83, at the Fox Theatre, San Diego. PRESENTED BY Mitch Leigh; DIRECTOR: Mitch Leigh; CHOREOGRAPHER: Rebecca West; SETS: John J. Moore; COSTUMES: Stanley Simmons; LIGHTING: Ruth Roberts; SOUND: Jack Shearing; MUSICAL DIRECTOR: Lawrence Brown. **Cast**: KING: Yul Brynner; ANNA: Kate Hunter Brown; THIANG: Hye-Young Choi; KRALAHOME: Michael Kermoyan; LUN THA: Sal Provenza; TUPTIM: Patricia Ann Welch; RAMSEY: Edward Crotty; PRINCE: Kevan Weber; ORTON: Morton Banks; LOUIS: Anthony Rapp; ELIZA: Marie Takazawa; INTERPRETER: Jae Woo Lee; SIMON: Rebecca West; YING YAOWALAK: Yvette Laura Martin; UNCLE THOMAS: Hope Sogawa; LITTLE EVA: Evelina Deocares.

TOUR. Opened on 9/13/83, at the Pantages Theatre, Los Angeles. Yul Brynner played the King for the 4,000th time.

374. *The King and I* (*1985 Broadway revival*)

Before Broadway. This Broadway production was part of a tour which had opened on 2/21/84, at the Lyric Theatre, Baltimore. The pre–Broadway part of the tour had the same basic crew as the Broadway run, except SETS: John Jay Moore; MUSICAL DIRECTOR: Lawrence Brown. It had the same cast too, except KRALAHOME: Christopher Wynkoop (he also understudied Yul Brynner); CHULALONGKORN: Douglas Klaif; LUN THA: Thomas Heath. In the chorus Caroline Ann Cabrera took over from Amy Chin, and Jamie Chung from Annie Woo.

The Broadway Run. BROADWAY THEATRE, 1/7/85–6/30/85. 191 PERFORMANCES. PRESENTED BY The Mitch Leigh Company; MUSIC: Richard Rodgers; LYRICS/BOOK: Oscar Hammerstein II; BASED ON the 1943 biographical novel *Anna and the King of Siam*, by Margaret Landon; DIRECTOR: Mitch Leigh; CHOREOGRAPHER: Rebecca West re-produced Jerome Robbins' original choreography; SETS: Peter Wolf; COSTUMES: Stanley Simmmons re-produced Irene Sharaff's originals; LIGHTING: Ruth Roberts; SOUND: Scott Marcellus; MUSICAL DIRECTOR: Richard Parrinello; PRESS: Solters/Roskin/Friedman; CASTING: Mark Reiner; COMPANY MANAGER: Abbie M. Strassler; PRODUCTION STAGE MANAGER: Kenneth L. Peck; STAGE MANAGERS: John M. Galo & Charles Reif. *Cast:* LOUIS LEONOWENS: Jeffrey Bryan Davis (9); CAPTAIN ORTON: Burt Edwards (15); ANNA LEONOWENS: Mary Beth Peil (2) ☆; THE INTERPRETER: Jae Woo Lee (11); THE KRALAHOME: Jonathan Farwell (5); THE KING: Yul Brynner (1) ☆; LEAD ROYAL DANCER: Kathy Lee Brynner (10); LUN THA: Sal Provenza (6); TUPTIM: Patricia Welch (3); LADY THIANG: Irma-Estel LaGuerre (4); PRINCE CHULALONGKORN: Araby Abaya (8); PRINCESS YING YAOWALAK: Yvette Laura Martin (14); FAN DANCER: Patricia Weber (13); SIR EDWARD RAMSEY: Edward Crotty (7); UNCLE THOMAS: Hope Sogawa; LITTLE EVA: Evelina Deocares; TOPSY: Deborah Harada; ELIZA: Kathy Lee Brynner (10); SIMON: Rebecca West (12); ANGEL: Patricia Weber (13); ROYAL DANCERS & WIVES: Marla F. Bingham, Young-Hee Cho, Carolyn DeLany, Evelina Deocares, Deborah Harada, Valerie Lau-Kee, Suzen Murakoshi, Hope Sogawa, Sylvia Yamada; PRINCES & PRINCESSES: Max Barabas, Michael Bulos, Caroline Ann Cabrera, Lisa Chui, Jamie Chung, Mark Damrongsri, Kate Gwon, Tracie Mon-Ting Lee, Michelle Nigalan, Steven Tom, Luke Trainer; NURSES & AMAZONS: Alis-Elaine Anderson, Joyce Campana, Mariann Cook, Janet Jordan; PRIESTS & SLAVES: Cornel Chan, Kaipo Daniels, Gary Bain Domasin, Stanley Earl Harrison, Thomas Heath, Andre Lengyel, Ron Stefan. *Standby*: King: Jonathan Farwell. *Understudies*: Anna: Mariann Cook; Orton: Edward Crotty; Louis: Luke Trainer; Interpreter: Kaipo Daniels; Kralahome: Jae Woo Lee; Tuptim: Carolyn DeLany; Thiang: Joyce Campana; Prince: Michael Bulos; Ying Yaowalak: Tracie Mon-Ting Lee; Lun Tha: Thomas Heath; Ramsey: Burt Edwards; Fan Dancer/Angel: Deborah Harada; Lead Royal Dancer: Evelina Deocares; Eliza: Sylvia Yamada; Simon: Thom Cordeiro Kam; Topsy: Sandy Sueoka; Uncle Thomas: Marla F. Bingham; Eva: Young-Hee Cho. *Swings*: Sandy Sueoka & Thom Cordeiro Kam.

The top Broadway ticket price when the show closed was $75. The last week pulled in a record $605,546. Yul Brynner won a 1985 Special Tony for having played the King a total of 4,525 times in his lifetime. The show won a regular Tony for director of a musical, and Mary Beth Peil was nominated.

After Broadway. As this Broadway run was part of a tour, after Broadway it continued that tour. While on the tour Yul Brynner was forced to quit after his 4,635th lifetime performance as the King, and died three months later, on 10/10/85. Aside from the stage musicals and the movie, he had also starred in a 13-episode CBS TV series *Anna and the King*, with Samantha Eggar. TOUR. Opened on 8/18/89, at the Civic Center, Syracuse, NY, and closed on 3/4/90, at the Orpheum Theatre, San Francisco, never reaching its intended target — Broadway. PRESENTED BY Manny Kladitis, Columbia Artists Management, Concert Productions International, and PACE Theatrical Group; DIRECTOR: Arthur Storch; CHOREOGRAPHER: Patricia Weber; SETS: John Jay Moore; COSTUMES: Stanley Simmons; LIGHTING: Jason Kantrowitz; SOUND: Gary Stocker; MUSICAL SUPERVISOR: Don Pippin; MUSICAL DIRECTOR: Michael D. Biagi. *Cast:* KING: Rudolph Nureyev; ANNA: Liz Robertson; KRALAHOME: Michael Kermoyan; TUPTIM: Suzan Postel; LUN THA: Patrick A'Hearn; INTERPRETER: Kaipo Daniels; LADY THIANG: Irma Estel-La Guerre; PRINCE: Jason Brown; LOUIS: Kenny Lund; ORTON/RAMSEY: Kenneth Garner; YING YAOWALAK: Shana Sueoka-Matos; CHORUS INCLUDED: Michael Hayward-Jones, Sal Mistretta. *Understudies*: King: Michael Kermoyan; Anna: Elizabeth Hansen.

375. *The King and I* (1996 Broadway revival)

Before Broadway. This revival had its origins in Australia, as a national tour, directed by Christopher Renshaw, sets by Brian Thomson, and costumes by Roger Kirk (all as per Broadway). It had some dialog from the 1956 movie in it. Hayley Mills starred as Anna.

The Broadway Run. NEIL SIMON THEATRE, 4/11/96–2/22/98. 27 previews from 3/19/96. 807 PERFORMANCES. PRESENTED BY Dodger Productions, the John F. Kennedy Center for the Performing Arts, James M. Nederlander, Perseus Productions with John Frost & the Adelaide Festival Centre, in association with The Rodgers & Hammerstein Organization; MUSIC: Richard Rodgers; LYRICS/BOOK: Oscar Hammerstein II; BASED ON the 1943 biographical novel *Anna and the King of Siam*, by Margaret Landon; DIRECTOR: Christopher Renshaw; CHOREOGRAPHER: Lar Lubovitch re-produced Jerome Robbins's original choreography, supervised by Susan Kikuchi; SETS: Brian Thomson; COSTUMES: Roger Kirk; LIGHTING: Nigel Levings; SOUND: Tony Meola & Lewis Mead; MUSICAL SUPERVISOR: Eric Stern; MUSICAL DIRECTOR: Michael Rafter; ORIGINAL ORCHESTRATIONS: Robert Russell Bennett; NEW ORCHESTRATIONS: Bruce Coughlin; NEW CAST RECORDING on Varese Sarabande, made on 8/26/96, and released on 9/24/96; PRESS: Boneau/Bryan-Brown; CASTING: Jay Binder; GENERAL MANAGEMENT: David Strong Warner; COMPANY MANAGER: Sandra Carlson; PRODUCTION STAGE MANAGER: Frank Hartenstein; STAGE MANAGER: Karen Armstrong; ASSISTANT STAGE MANAGERS: Kelly Martindale & Donna A. Drake. *Cast:* CAPTAIN ORTON: John Curless (7); LOUIS LEONOWENS: Ryan Hopkins (9), *Matthew Ballinger*; ANNA LEONOWENS: Donna Murphy (1) ☆ (until 3/19/97), *Barbara McCulloh* (during Miss Murphy's vacation, 11/5/96–11/17/96, and again 3/20/97–3/21/97), *Faith Prince* (3/22/97–12/14/97), *Marie Osmond* (from 12/19/97); THE INTERPRETER: Alan Muraoka; THE KRALAHOME: Randall Duk Kim (3); THE KING OF SIAM: Lou Diamond Phillips (2) ☆, *Kevin Gray* (from 6/97); LUN THA: Jose Llana (6) (until 6/29/97), *Benjamin Bryant* (from 7/1/97); TUPTIM: Joohee Choi (5), *Cornilla Luna* (from 3/97), *Joohee Choi* (from 3/24/97); LADY THIANG: Taewon Kim (4); PRINCE CHULALONGKORN: John Chang (10), *R.J. Remo*; FAN DANCER: Kelly Jordan Bit; PRINCESS YING YAOWALAK: Lexine Bondoc; SIR EDWARD RAMSEY: Guy Paul (8), *Graeme Malcolm* (from 6/97); ROYAL WIVES/SLAVES/COURTIERS/GUARDS/MONKS/ENGLISH GUESTS/MARKET PEOPLE: Tito Abeleda, John Bantay (*Zhang Zhenjun*), Camille M. Brown, Benjamin Bryant, Meng-Chen Chang, Kam Cheng, Vivian Eng, Lydia Gaston, Margaret Ann Gates (*Mary Ann McGuinness*), C. Sean Kim, Shawn Ku, Doan Mackenzie, Paolo Montalban, Alan Muraoka, Paul Nakauchi, Tina Ou (*Christine Yasunaga*), Andrew Pacho, Mami Saito, Lainie Sakakura (Royal Dance Soloist—*Kristine Bendul*), Tran T. Thuc Hanh, Carol To, Yolanda Tolentino, Yan Ying, Kayoko Yoshioka, Greg Zane. *Michael Lomeka, Rommel V. Pacson, Khamla Somphanh*; ROYAL CHILDREN: Kelly Jordan Bit, Lexine Bondoc, Kailip Boonrai, Erik Lin-Greenberg, Brandon Marshall Ngai, Kenji Miyata, Amy Y. Tai, Jacqueline Te Lem, Jenna Noelle Ushkowitz, Shelby Rebecca Wong, Jeff G. Yalun. *Travis Feretic, Stephanie La, Cristina Matoto*; "The Small House of Uncle Thomas" (ballet): ELIZA: Yan Ying; SIMON LEGREE: Tito Abeleda; ANGEL GEORGE: Meng-Chen Chang; LITTLE EVA: Tran T. Thuc Hanh; TOPSY: Tina Ou, *Christine Yasunaga*; UNCLE THOMAS: Mami Saito; DOGS: John Bantay (*Zhang Zhenjun*), Doan Mackenzie, Greg Zane; GUARDS: Andrew Pacho, C. Sean Kim, Shawn Ku. *Michael Lomeka*, C. Sean Kim, *Rommel V. Pacson*; PROPMEN: Benjamin Bryant, Paolo Montalban, Alan Muraoka, Paul Nakauchi; ARCHERS: Camille M. Brown, Vivian Eng, Lainie Sakakura (*Kristine Bendul*), Kayoko Yoshioka. *Camille M. Brown, Vivian Eng, Khamla Somphanh*; SINGERS: Kam Cheng, Margaret Ann Gates (*Mary Ann McGuinness*), Carol To, Yolanda Tolentino. *Standby*: King: Raul Aranas. *Understudies*: King: Paul Nakauchi; Anna: Barbara McCulloh, *Kay McClelland*; Kralahome: Paul Nakauchi & Alan Mauraoka; Lun Tha: Benjamin Bryant & Paolo Montalban; Ramsey: John Curless; Tuptim: Kam Cheng & Carol To; Louis: Jonathan Giordano; Orton: Guy Paul; Thiang: Lydia Gaston & Yolanda Tolentino. *Swings*: Jonathan Giordano, Devanand N. Janki, Susan Kikuchi, Joan Tsao. *Partial Swings*: Lydia Gaston & John Bantay. *Orchestra*: FLUTE: Helen Campo;

OBOE: Rich Dallessio; CLARINETS: Jon Manasse, Larry Guy, Anthony Brackett; BASSOON: Kim Laskowski; TRUMPETS: Alec Holten & Chuck Olsen; FRENCH HORNS: Kaitilin Mahoney & Alexandra Cook; TROMBONES: Dick Clark & Jeff Caswell; CONCERTMASTER: Martin Agee; VIOLINS: Roy Lewis, Darryl Kubian, Shinwon Kim; VIOLA: Crystal Garner; CELLI: Stephanie Cummins & Sarah Carter; BASS: Bill Ellison; HARP: Victoria Drake; PERCUSSION: James Baker; KEYBOARD: Cherie Rosen. *Act I*: Overture (Orchestra) [this was shortened], "I Whistle a Happy Tune" (Anna & Louis), "Royal Dance Before the King" [new number; choreography by Lar Lubovitch] (Company), "My Lord and Master" (Tuptim), "Hello, Young Lovers!" (Anna), "March of the Siamese Children" (Children), "A Puzzlement" (King), "The Royal Bangkok Academy" (Anna & Pupils) [in abbreviated form], "Getting to Know You" (Anna, Wives, Children), "We Kiss in a Shadow" (Lun Tha & Tuptim), "A Puzzlement" (reprise) (Prince & Louis) [cut during previews], "Shall I Tell You What I Think of You?" (Anna), "Something Wonderful" (Lady Thiang), Finale to Act One (Company). *Act II*: "Western People Funny" (Lady Thiang & Wives) [cut during previews], "I Have Dreamed" (Lun Tha & Tuptim), "Hello, Young Lovers!" (reprise) (Anna), "The Small House of Uncle Thomas" (Tuptim & Ensemble), "Song of the King" (King & Anna), "Shall We Dance?" (Anna & King), "Procession of the White Elephant" (new number; choreography by Lar Lubovitch) (Company), "I Whistle a Happy Tune" (reprise) (Anna), Finale (Entire Company).

Broadway reviews were great. The show won Tonys for revival of musical, sets, costumes, and for Donna Murphy (the surprise winner, as most people assumed Julie Andrews would win it for *Victor/Victoria*, despite her renunciation of the award). The show was also nominated for direction of a musical, lighting, and for Lou Diamond Phillips and Joohee Choi. Faith Prince took over from Donna Murphy at the matinee of 3/22/97 (a day later than previously scheduled). In late 1997 rumors were rife that Arnold Schwarzenegger was going to replace Kevin Gray as the King, but it never happened. This was Marie Osmond's Broadway debut.

TOUR. Opened on 4/2/97, at the Orpheum Theatre, Minneapolis, and closed there on 4/12/97; it then ran at the Kennedy Center, 4/16/97–5/18/97; then it continued with tour, including Toronto. It toured for 70 weeks. PRESENTED BY Dodger/Endemol Theatricals; DIRECTOR: Christopher Renshaw; CHOREOGRAPHER: Lar Lubovitch used parts of Jerome Robbins's choreography and some of his own; MUSICAL DIRECTOR: Kevin Farrell. *Cast*: ANNA: Hayley Mills, *Marie Osmond*; KING: Vee Talmadge; KRALAHOME: Ernest Abuba (Kralahome, *Mel Duane Gionson*; THIANG: Naomi Itami; TUPTIM: Luzviminda Lor; LUN THA: Timothy Ford Murphy; ROYAL DANCE SOLOIST: Hsin-Ping Chang, *Youn Kim*.

ANIMATED FEATURE FILM. The first ever animated feature of a Rodgers & Hammerstein piece was a cartoon of *The King and I* that came out on 3/19/99 (the soundtrack was released three days earlier). There were some plot changes. WRITERS: Peter Bakalian, Jacqueline Feather, David Seidler; DIRECTOR: Richard Rich. *Voices*: ANNA: Miranda Richardson; ANNA (SINGING VOICE): Christiane Noll; KING: Martin Vidnovic; KRALAHOME: Ian Richardson.

LONDON PALLADIUM, 5/3/00–1/5/02. It was a great success. Performances were canceled 10/23/00–10/25/00 due to technical difficulties. *Cast*: KING: Jason Scott Lee, *Keo Woolford*; ANNA: Elaine Paige, *Josie Lawrence*. **Understudy**: King: Ronobir Lahiri. The U.K. tour opened in 8/02, at the Theatre Royal, Plymouth (it had originally been scheduled to open in Edinburgh, on 4/19/02). *Cast*: ANNA: Marti Webb; KING: Ronobir Lahiri.

PAPER MILL PLAYHOUSE, New Jersey, 4/5/02–5/19/02. Previews from 4/3/02. This was the 51st Anniversary revival. DIRECTOR: Mark S. Hoebee; CHOREOGRAPHER: Susan Kikuchi. *Cast*: KING: Kevin Gray; ANNA: Carolee Carmello; TUPTIM: Margaret Ann Gates; LUN THA: Paolo Montalban.

STRATFORD FESTIVAL, Canada. Opened on 5/27/03. Previews from 4/26/03. It ran in repertory until 11/9/03. It featured new staging by Susan H. Schulman. DIRECTOR: Susan H. Schulman; CHOREOGRAPHER: Michael Lichtefeld; SETS: Debra Hanson; COSTUMES: Roger Kirk; LIGHTING: Kevin Fraser; SOUND: Peter McBoyle; MUSICAL DIRECTOR: Berthold Carriere. *Cast*: ANNA: Lucy Peacock; KING: Victor Talmadge; KRALAHOME: Thom Allison; LUN THA: Charles Azulay.

NATIONAL TOUR. Opened on 6/15/04, at the Benedum Center, Pittsburgh. PRESENTED BY Atlanta Theatre of the Stars/Independent Presenters Network; DIRECTOR: Baayork Lee; CHOREOGRAPHER: Susan Kikuchi; SETS: Kenneth Foy; COSTUMES: Roger Kirk; LIGHTING: John McLain; SOUND: Abe Jacob; MUSICAL DIRECTOR: Kevin Farrell. *Cast*: ANNA: Sandy Duncan (until 12/04), *Stefanie Powers* (1/05–12/05); KING: Martin Vidnovic.

376. *King of Hearts*

Set during one day in Sept. 1918, toward the end of World War I, when the Germans have booby-trapped the French village of Du Temps in order to welcome the arriving Americans. Inhabitants of the town evacuate, and a lone American is sent in to defuse the bombs. He makes his headquarters at the local asylum, and leaves the gates open, thus allowing the inmates to take over the town. In the empty streets and houses they act out their fantasies. The question is, with all the "official" insanity of war raging around them, what is insanity? One inmate imagines he's a circus ringmaster, which allows us to have a circus scene open Act II. In the end the American finds the bombs and elects to remain with the lunatics.

Before Broadway. Born in the summer of 1977 at WESTPORT COUNTRY PLAYHOUSE, Westport, Conn., with book by Steve Tesich, and directed by A.J. Antoon. Robby Benson was the star. After the Westport production, Don Scardino took over from Robby Benson, and Joseph Stein took over the libretto from Steve Tesich. It was totally revamped for Broadway. It tried out in Boston. Harold Themmen was replaced as musical director by Karen Gustafson.

The Broadway Run. MINSKOFF THEATRE, 10/22/78–12/3/78. 6 previews. 48 PERFORMANCES. PRESENTED BY Joseph Kipness & Patty Grubman, in association with Jerome Minskoff; MUSIC: Peter Link; LYRICS: Jacob Brackman; BOOK: Joseph Stein; BASED ON the 1966 French film *Le roi de coeur*, written by Philippe de Broca, Maurice Bessy, and Daniel Boulanger; DIRECTOR/CHOREOGRAPHER: Ron Field; SETS: Santo Loquasto; COSTUMES: Patricia Zipprodt; LIGHTING: Pat Collins; SOUND: Jack Shearing; MUSICAL DIRECTOR: Karen Gustafson; ORCHESTRATIONS: Bill Brohn; DANCE MUSIC ARRANGEMENTS: Dorothea Freitag; PRESS: The Merlin Group; CASTING: Peter Cereghetti; GENERAL MANAGER: Marvin A. Krauss; COMPANY MANAGER: Bob Skerry; PRODUCTION STAGE MANAGER: Janet Beroza; STAGE MANAGER: Clint Jakeman; ASSISTANT STAGE MANAGER: Robert Schear. *Cast*: INMATES: DEMOSTHENES (LE MUET): Gary Morgan (4); MADELEINE (LA MADAME): Millicent Marrin (3); GENEVIEVE (LA COURTISANE): Mirzi Hamilton; SIMONE (LA BALLERINE): Marilyn D'Honau; DAHLIA (LA SERVANTE): Isabelle Farrell; RAOUL (LE PATRON DU CIRQUE): Bob Gunton (5); JEUNEFILLE (LA JEUNE FILLE): Pamela Blair (2); VALERIE (LA FLUTISTE): Neva Rae Powers; JACQUES (LE FERMIER): Rex David Hays; DU BAC (LE MONSEIGNEUR): Michael McCarty; THERESA (LA MAMAN): Maria Guida; ISOLDE (LA CHANTEUSE D'OPERA): Gerrianne Raphael; CLAUDE (LE COIFFEUR): Gordon J. Weiss (6); GUY-LOUIS (LE PETIT GARCON): Timothy Scott; M. CLICHY (LE PHOTOGRAPHE): David Thomas; PHILIPPE (LE MAITRE D'HOTEL): Bryan Nicholas; MARIE-CLAIRE (LA DUCHESSE): Julia Shelley; HENRI (LE DUC): Will Roy; MONSIEUR COCHON (LE PORC): Wilbur; AMERICAN SOLDIERS: PVT. JOHNNY PERKINS: Donald Scardino (1); LT. MCNEILL: Jay Devlin; FRANK: Robert Brubach; STEVE: Harry Fawcett; JOE: John Scoullar; TOM: Jamie Haskins; PHILLIP: Richard Christopher; GERMAN SOLDIERS: HANS: Scott Allen; KAPITAN KOST: Alexander Orfaly; SIEGFRIED: Scott Barnes; FRITZ: Roger Berdahl; KARL: Timothy Wallace; WILLIE: Karl Heist. **Understudies**: Johnny: Harry Fawcett; Madeleine: Gerrianne Raphael; Jeunefille: Neva Rae Powers; Demosthenes/Claude: Timothy Scott; Raoul: Rex David Hays; McNeill: Richard Christopher; Du Bac/Kost/Clichy/Jacques: Timothy Wallace; Henri: Bryan Nicholas; Marie Claire: Marilyn D'Honau; Genevieve/Isolde/Simone: Spence Ford; Valerie/Dahlia/Therese: Spence Ford; Guy-Louis/Philippe: Navarre Matlovsky; American & German Soldiers: Navarre Matlovsky. *Act I*: *Scene 1* Du Temps and the American and

German trenches; *Scene 2* Asylum of Sainte Anne: "A Stain on the Name" (Inmates); *Scene 3* Outside the asylum gate; *Scene 4* The main square of Du Temps: "Deja Vu" (Madeleine), "Promenade" (The Transformation) (Inmates); *Scene 5* Madeleine's establishment: "Turn Around" (Madeleine & Inmates); *Scene 6* Chamber of Love: "Nothing, Only Love" (Jeunefille, Johnny, Madeleine); *Scene 7* Du Temps: "King of Hearts" (Demosthenes, Jeunefille, Raoul, Madeleine, Inmates), "Close Upon the Hour" (Johnny); *Scene 8* American and German trenches; *Scene 9* Roof of the cathedral: "A Brand New Day" (The Coronation) (Du Bac, Johnny, Inmates). *Act II*: *Scene 1* An abandoned circus: "Le Grand Cirque de Provence" (Raoul & Inmates), "Hey, Look at Me, Mrs. Draba" (Johnny); *Scene 2* Outskirts of Du Temps; *Scene 3* German and American trenches: "Going Home Tomorrow" (Soldiers); *Scene 4* The terrace: "Somewhere is Here" (Madeleine), "Nothing, Only Love" (reprise) (Raoul, Madeleine, Jeunefille, Johnny); *Scene 5* Du Temps and No Man's Land: "March, March, March" (Johnny & Inmates), "The Battle" (dance) (Soldiers).

Reviews were bad, except for the look of the piece. Capitalized at $1,100,000, it went way over budget, and lost over $1.8 million, the biggest loss on Broadway to that date. It closed at a matinee. Millicent Martin was nominated for a Tony. This was the last Broadway show that Ron Field directed. Over the years it has gained a cult following.

After Broadway. 14TH STREET Y, NYC, 12/7/99–12/19/99. 16 PERFORMANCES. Part of the *Musicals Tonight!* series. This production used Steve Tesich's original libretto, and restored much of the original material that was altered for the 1978 Broadway production. DIRECTOR: Peter Link; SETS: Gwen Adler; MUSICAL DIRECTOR: Robert Lamont. *Cast*: BISHOP: Jimmy Bennett; JEUNEFILLE: Kerry Butler; GERMAN SOLDIER/MAITRE D': Barrett Foa; DUCHESS: Teri Gibson; THERESE: Samantha Heller; SOLDIER: Michael Hunsaker; GENEVIEVE: T. Doyle Leverett; JOHNNY: Michael Magee; MARIE CLAIRE: Rose McGuire; GUILLOTINE: Tracey Moore; BARBER: Gabor Morea; MADELEINE/MADAME: Shaelynn Parker; SGT. HAMBURGER: Christopher Regan; LT. McFISH/JACQUES: Tom Reidy; SIMONE: Julia Wade; DUKE: Michael Kevin Walsh; DEMOSTHENES: Gordon Joseph Weiss. "Here Comes Mine," "Name of St. Anne's," "Transformation," "Down at Madeleine's," "Nothing, Only Love," "King of Hearts," "Close Upon the Hour," "Coronation Hymn," "With My Friends," "Mrs. Draba," "Now We Need to Cry," "Going Home Tomorrow," "Somewhere is Here," "A Day in Our Life," Finale.

GOODSPEED OPERA HOUSE, Conn., 10/11/02–12/22/02. Previews from 10/4/02. The closing date was extended from 12/15/02. This revival used the original score and libretto (i.e book by Steve Tesich). DIRECTOR: Gabriel Barre (it was going to be Darko Tresnjak); CHOREOGRAPHER: Peggy Hickey; SETS: James Youmans. Johnny Able tries to save a small French village during World War II. *Cast*: JOHNNY ABLE: Joe Farrell; JEUNEFILLE: Vanessa Lemonides; MADELEINE: Melissa Hart; BARBER: Gabor Morea; DUCHESSE: Pamela Burrell.

377. *Kismet*

A musical Arabian night, a costume operetta following the exploits of Hajj, a roguish poet (a beggar in the original play), over an eventful 24-hour period in legendary Baghdad. Hajj's daughter, Marsinah, falls in love with the caliph (disguised as a gardener), and the poet foils and drowns the dastardly wazir and runs off with his attractive wife, Lalume. He then becomes Emir of Baghdad. That's "kismet" ("fate").

Before Broadway. Edwin Lester, head of the Los Angeles and San Francisco Civic Light Operas, who had had a hit with *Song of Norway* in the 1940s, dreamed up the idea of using Borodin's music as the basis for a 1950s musical. It was first produced by Mr. Lester at both of his Californian venues in the summer of 1953, but before Broadway Mr. Lester quit, to be replaced by Charles Lederer. Richard Kiley replaced Glenn Burris as the Caliph. The numbers "Bored" and "My Magic Lamp" were cut. In the cast was Ronnie Field, who would later become Ron Field, the famous choreographer.

The Broadway Run. ZIEGFELD THEATRE, 12/3/53–4/23/55. 583 PERFORMANCES. Edwin Lester's production, PRESENTED BY Charles Led-

erer; MUSIC/LYRICS: Robert Wright & George Forrest; BOOK: Charles Lederer & Luther Davis; BASED ON music by Alexander Borodin, and also on the 1911 play *Kismet*, by Edward Knoblock, that had starred Otis Skinner; DIRECTOR: Albert Marre; CHOREOGRAPHER: Jack Cole; SETS/COSTUMES: Lemuel Ayers; SCENIC ARTIST: Phil Raiguel; LIGHTING: Peggy Clark; MUSICAL DIRECTOR: Louis Adrian, *Maurice Levine* (from 1/24/55); ORCHESTRAL & CHORAL ARRANGEMENTS: Arthur Kay; CHORAL DIRECTOR: Christine Ell & William Ellfeldt; CAST RECORDING on Columbia, made on 12/6/53; PRESS: Barry Hyams & Martin Shwartz; COMPANY MANAGER: Harry Essex; GENERAL STAGE MANAGER: Phil Friedman; STAGE MANAGER: James Wicker; ASSISTANT STAGE MANAGER: Richard Vine. *Cast*: IMAM OF THE MOSQUE: Richard Oneto, *Gerald Cardoni*; MUEZZINS: Gerald Cardoni, Kirby Smith, Ralph Strane, Louis Polacek, *Don Rogers, Arthur Hammond*; DOORMAN: Jack Mei Ling, *Ronnie Field, Stuart Hodes* (1955); 1ST BEGGAR: Earle MacVeigh; 2ND BEGGAR: Robert Lamont; 3RD BEGGAR: Rodolfo Silva, *Ronnie Field*; DERVISHES: Jack Dodds & Marc Wilder, *Don Weissmuller*; OMAR: Philip Coolidge, *Francis Compton*; PUBLIC POET, LATER CALLED HAJJ: Alfred Drake (1), *William Johnson*; MARSINAH, HIS DAUGHTER: Doretta Morrow (2), *Elaine Malbin*; A MERCHANT: Kirby Smith, *Ted Thurston* [this role was later called Taman]; HASSAN-BEN: Hal Hackett, *Clifford Fearl*; JAWAN: Truman Gaige; STREET DANCERS: Florence Lessing & Ethel Martin; AKBAR: Jack Dodds, *Stuart Hodes* (1955); ASSIZ: Marc Wilder, *Ronnie Field*; BANGLE MAN: Richard Oneto, *Loren Driscoll, Gerald Cardoni*; CHIEF POLICEMAN: Tom Charlesworth, Kirby Smith; 2ND POLICEMAN: Hal Hackett; THE WAZIR OF POLICE: Henry Calvin (5); WAZIR'S GUARDS: Stephen Ferry & Steve Reeves, *Al Smith & Mario Lamm*; LALUME: Joan Diener (4), *Julie Wilson*; ATTENDANTS: Mario Lamm & John Weidemann, *Edward Thuren, Steve Reeves*; PRINCESSES OF ABABU: Patricia Dunn, Bonnie Evans, Reiko Sato, *Neile Adams, Prue Ward*; THE CALIPH: Richard Kiley (3), *Richard Oneto* (from 2/54), *Ted Thurston*; SLAVE GIRLS: Carol Ohmart, Joyce Palmer, Sandra Stahl, Lila Jackson. *Jeane Williams, Ingeborg Kjellsen, Joanne Spiller, Ann Flood, Carmen Austin*; A PEDDLER: Earle MacVeigh; A SERVANT: Richard Vine; PRINCESS ZUBBEDIYA OF DAMASCUS: Florence Lessing; AYAH TO ZUBBEDIYA: Lucy Andonian; PRINCESS SAMARIS OF BANGALORE: Beatrice Kraft; AYAH TO SAMARIS: Thelma Dare; STREET WOMEN: Jo Ann O'Connell & Lynne Stuart; PROSECUTOR: Earle MacVeigh; THE WIDOW YUSSEF: Barbara Slate; DIWAN DANCERS: Neile Adams, Jack Dodds, Marc Wilder; SINGERS: Gerald Cardoni, Anita Coulter, Thelma Dare, Lila Jackson, Robert Lamont, Jo Ann O'Connell, Richard Oneto, Louis Polacek, Barbara Slate, Kirby Smith (*Ted Thurston*), Sandra Stahl, Ralph Strane, Lynne Stuart, Erica Twiford, Richard Vine, Doris Yarick, George Yarick, *Ingeborg Kjellsen, Joanne Spiller, Don Rogers, Arthur Hammond, Clifford Fearl, Loren Driscoll, Carmen Austin*; DANCERS: Neile Adams, Patricia Dale, Devra Kline, Pat Lynch, Ania Romaine, Vida Ann Solomon, Roberta Stevenson, Prue Ward, *April Gaskins, Phyllis Gehrig, Nancy Lynch*. **Understudies**: Hajj: Earle MacVeigh; Caliph: Richard Oneto, *Arthur Hammond*; Lalume: Carol Ohmart, *Joanne Spiller*; Marsinah: Jo Ann O'Connell; Wazir: Earle MacVeigh, *Kirby Smith*; Jawan: Kirby Smith; Omar: Richard Vine; Peddler/1st Beggar/Prosecutor/Chief Policeman: Kirby Smith, *Ted Thurston*; Muezzin: Ted Thurston; Hassan-Ben: Clifford Fearl; 2nd Policeman: Gerald Cardoni, *Clifford Fearl*; Akbar/Assiz/Doorman/3rd Beggar: Don Weissmuller; Princesses of Ababu: Neile Adams & Roberta Stevenson; Samaris: Ethel Martin; Ayah to Zubbediya: Doris Yarick. *Act I*: Overture (Orchestra); *Scene 1* A tent just outside the city: "Sands of Time" [from "In the Steppes of Central Asia"] (Imam, Hajj, Marsinah, Muezzins), "Rhymes Have I" [from the last act of "Prince Igor"] (Imam, Hajj, Marsinah, Muezzins), "Fate" [from "Symphony No. 2 in B Minor"] (Hajj); *Scene 2* On the steps of the mosque: "Fate" (reprise) (Hajj); *Scene 3* The Bazaar of the Caravans: "Bazaar of the Caravans" (Street Dancer, Akbar, Assiz, Merchants, Shoppers), "Not Since Nineveh" [from the "Polovetsian Dances"] (Lalume, Wazir, Princesses of Ababu, Akbar, Assiz, Merchants, Shoppers), "Baubles, Bangles and Beads" [from the "D Major String Quartet"] (Marsinah, Bangle Man, Chorus) [a hit]; *Scene 4* A side street; *Scene 5* A corridor in the Wazir's palace: "Stranger in Paradise" [from the "Polovetsian Dances"] (Marsinah & Caliph) [the big hit]; *Scene 6* A street near the bazaar: "He's in Love!" [from the "Polovetsian Dances"] (Hassan-Ben, Chief Policeman, 2nd Policeman, Prosecutor, Princesses of Ababu, Akbar, Assiz, Caliph, Omar); *Scene 7* The throne room of His Exalted Excellency, the Wazir of Police: "Gesticulate" [from "Symphony No. 1"] (Hajj, Lalume, Wazir, Chorus), "Fate" (reprise) (Hajj & The Ladies of the Wazir's Harem). *Act II: Scene 1* Along the route of the Caliph's procession: "Night of My Nights" (from "Night of My Nights") (Caliph & Entourage); *Scene 2* The garden: "Stranger in Paradise" (reprise) (Marsinah), "Baubles, Bangles and Beads" (reprise) (Caliph), "He's in Love" (reprise) (Entourage); *Scene 3* Ante-room to the Wazir's harem: "Was I Wazir" [from the "D Major Quartet"] (Wazir & His Guards, Policemen); *Scene 4* A rooftop pavilion in the wazir's palace: "Rahadlakum" (Hajj, Lalume, Zubbediya, Samaris, Princesses of Ababu, Zubbediya's Ayah, Ladies of the Wazir's Harem), "And This is My Beloved" [from the 3rd movement of the "D Major String Quartet"] (Hajj, Marsinah, Caliph, Wazir) [a hit]; *Scene 5* A corridor in the Wazir's palace: "The Olive Tree" [from the Love Duet from "Prince Igor"] (Hajj); *Scene 6* Ante-room to the wazir's harem; *Scene 7* The ceremonial hall of the Caliph's palace: "Ceremonial of the Caliph's Diwan" (Diwan Dancers) [not on the cast album], "Presentation of Princesses:" a/ Damascus (Zubbediya, Zubbediya's Ayah); b/ Bangalore (*Samaris*, Samaris' Ayah); c/ Ababu (Princesses of Ababu); Finale: "Sands of Time" (reprise) (Hajj, Marsinah, Caliph, Ensemble).

The show opened on Broadway during a newspaper strike, but the sets and the song "Stranger in Paradise" kept the audiences coming. The reviews, when they did come out, were divided, with a couple of raves and a pan among them. The show won Tony Awards for musical, musical director, and for Alfred Drake. It also won Donaldson Awards for composer, director, costumes, and for Alfred Drake. The composer, Alexander Borodin, who won so many awards for this show, had been dead 67 years, and so was unable to receive his awards in person. The show cost $400,000 (Alfred Drake was getting $5,000 a week).

After Broadway. STOLL THEATRE, London, 4/20/55–12/1/56. 676 PERFORMANCES. When the show opened, it was again during a newspaper strike, and again had a long run, and again for same reasons as the Broadway production. PRESENTED BY Jack Hylton; CHOREOGRAPHER: George Martin; MUSICAL DIRECTOR: Cyril Ornadel. *Cast:* POET: Alfred Drake; MARSINAH: Doretta Morrow, *Elizabeth Larner*; HASSAN-BEN: Alister Williamson; STREET DANCEr: Josephine Blake; WAZIR: Paul Whitsun-Jones; LALUME: Joan Diener, *Sheila Bradley*; CALIPH: Peter Grant; SAMARIS: Juliet Prowse; PROSECUTOR: Tudor Evans.

TOUR. Opened on 4/25/55, at the Shubert Theatre, New Haven. MUSICAL DIRECTOR: Maurice Levine. *Cast:* BEGGARS: Earle MacVeigh & Ronnie Field; DERVISHES: Stuart Hodes & Don Weissmuller; OMAR: Francis Compton; POET: William Johnson; MARSINAH: Elaine Malbin; TAMAN/PROSECUTOR: Ted Thurston; HASSAN-BEN: Clifford Fearl; JAWAN: Truman Gaige; AKBAR: Stuart Hodes; ASSIZ: Ronnie Field; CHIEF POLICEMAN: Earle MacVeigh; WAZIR: Kirby Smith; LALUME: Julie Wilson; ATTENDANTS: Steve Reeves & Edward Thuren; PRINCESSES OF ABABU: Neile Adams, Bonnie Evans, Prue Ward; CALIPH: Richard Oneto.

THE MOVIE. There had been a couple of straight movies done of *Kismet*, one starring Ronald Colman. MGM bought the rights to the stage musical, even though they owned the rights to the straight play, and despite the fact that Borodin's music was in the public domain and they could have easily made their own musical. 1955. DIRECTOR: Vincente Minnelli; CHOREOGRAPHER: Jack Cole. *Cast:* OMAR: Monty Woolley; POET: Howard Keel; MARSINAH: Ann Blyth; WAZIR: Sebastian Cabot; LALUME: Dolores Gray; CALIPH: Vic Damone; PRINCESS OF ABABU: Reiko Sato.

PRINCES THEATRE, London, 6/7/57–6/29/57. 29 PERFORMANCES. RE-STAGED BY: Tommy Hayes. *Cast:* POET: Tudor Evans; MARSINAH: Diane Todd; WAZIR: Paul Whitsun-Jones; LALUME: Sheila Bradley; PRINCESSES: Jacqueline Chan, Sandra Hampton, Anna Sharkey; CALIPH: Colin Thomas.

TOUR. Opened on 9/19/55, at Hershey, Pennsylvania. PRESENTED BY Manuel Davis; CONDUCTOR: Michael Kuttner. *Cast:* POET: Earle MacVeigh; MARSINAH: Margot Moser; WAZIR: George Lipton; LALUME: Marthe Errolle; CALIPH: Donald Clarke.

WEST COAST REVIVAL. Opened on 8/6/62, at the Curran Theatre, San Francisco, and closed on 11/10/62, at the Philharmonic Auditorium, Los Angeles. PRESENTED BY Edwin Lester's Los Angeles Civic Light Opera Association; DIRECTOR: Edward Greenberg; CHOREOGRAPHER:

Jack Cole; SETS: Lemuel Ayers; COSTUMES: Frank Thompson; LIGHTING: Peggy Clark; MUSICAL DIRECTOR: Louis Adrian. *Cast:* FIRST BEGGAR: Earle MacVeigh; OMAR: Don Beddoe; POET: Alfred Drake; MARSINAH: Lee Venora; HASSAN-BEN: Kirby Smith; JAWAN: Truman Gaige; WAZIR: Henry Calvin, *Ned Romero*; LALUME: Anne Jeffreys; PRINCESSES: Reiko Sato, Jo Anne Miya, Virginia Ann Lee; CALIPH: Richard Banke. *Understudy*: Wazir: Ned Romero.

NEW YORK STATE THEATRE, 6/22/65–7/31/65. 39 PERFORMANCES. PRESENTED BY Music Theatre of Lincoln Center; DIRECTOR: Edward Greenberg; CHOREOGRAPHER: Jack Cole; SETS: Lemuel Ayers; COSTUMES: Frank Thompson; LIGHTING: Peter Hunt; MUSICAL DIRECTOR: Franz Allers. *Cast:* IMAM/THE BANGLE MAN: Rudy Vejar; MULLAH: Julius Fields; 1ST BEGGAR/PROSECUTOR: Earle MacVeigh; 2ND BEGGAR: Robert Lamont; 3RD BEGGAR: Andre St. Jean; OMAR: Don Beddoe; POET: Alfred Drake; MARSINAH: Lee Venora; HASSAN-BEN: Frank Coleman; JAWAN: Truman Gaige; CHIEF POLICEMAN: Alfred Toigo; WAZIR: Henry Calvin; LALUME: Anne Jeffreys; PRINCESSES: Reiko Sato, Diana Banks, Nancy Roth; CALIPH: Richard Banke; SAMARIS: Beatrice Kraft; SINGERS INCLUDED: Bob Neukum; DANCERS INCLUDED: Joanne Di Vito (her New York debut), Jenny Workman. *Understudy*: Princesses: Joanne Di Vito. The tour of this production opened on 8/2/65, at the O'Keefe, Toronto, and closed on 11/18/65, at the Fisher Theatre, Detroit. The tour had the same cast except MARSINAH: Patricia Welting; LALUME: Patricia Morison.

Timbuktu. In 1978 a revised version called *Timbuktu* ran on Broadway (see under *Timbuktu* in this book).

NEW YORK STATE THEATRE, 10/3/85–11/17/85. 13 PERFORMANCES IN REPERTORY. PRESENTED BY the New York City Opera; DIRECTOR: Frank Corsaro; SETS/COSTUMES: Lawrence Miller; LIGHTING: Mark W. Stanley.

CONDUCTOR: Scott Bergeson. *Cast:* BEGGARS: Don Yule & Robert Brubaker; OMAR: James Billings; POET: Theodore Baerg; MARSINAH: Michele McBride; JAWAN: John Lankston; WAZIR: Richard McKee; LALUME: Joyce Castle; CALIPH: Mark Thomsen. NEW YORK STATE THEATRE, 7/8/86–7/13/86. 8 PERFORMANCES. PRESENTED BY the New York City Opera; DIRECTOR: Frank Corsaro; CHOREOGRAPHER: Randolyn Zinn; SETS/COSTUMES: Lawrence Miller; LIGHTING: Mark W. Stanley; CONDUCTOR: Paul Gemignani. *Cast:* BEGGARS: Don Yule & Robert Brubaker; OMAR: James Billings; POET: Timothy Nolen; MARSINAH: Diana Walker; JAWAN: John Lankston; WAZIR: Jack Harrold; LALUME: Susanne Marsee; CALIPH: Cris Groenendaal.

FREUD PLAYHOUSE, UCLA, California. 1/20/04–2/1/04. In concert, part of the *Reprise* series. DIRECTOR: Arthur Allan Seidelman; CHOREOGRAPHER: Rob Barron. *Cast:* LALUME: Jennifer Leigh Warren; ALSO WITH: Jason Graae, Len Cariou, Anthony Crivello.

378. *Kiss Me, Kate*

A play within a play; set at Ford's Theatre, Baltimore, from 5 pm to midnight during one evening of an out-of-town tryout of a musical version of *Taming of the Shrew* (the title comes from Petruchio's last command in the Shakespeare play). Act I — The cast is assembled for final instructions before opening night. The egotistical producer/lead actor is Fred, playing Petruchio, and his temperamental former wife is Lilli, playing Katharine. Lois is playing Bianca, and Fred is very interested in her. However, Bill, who is playing Lucentio, is Lois's main squeeze. But Bill is irresponsible. He has signed Fred's name to a $10,000 IOU he lost in the "most respectable floating crap game in town." Fred and Lilli patch up their differences as they reminisce about all the shows they've been in together, especially one called *Wunderbar*. Fred sends a bouquet to Lois, but it arrives by mistake for Lilli, and she is overcome with emotion. The play gets underway, and Lilli discovers the truth about the bouquet and threatens to leave the show. However, she is prevented from leaving by the arrival of two gangsters who have come to collect the IOU (Fred has convinced them that only by having Lilli stay with the show can he afford to pay back the debt). Act II — Paul, Fred's dresser, comments on Baltimore weather in the famous Act II opening scene in the alley behind the theatre. The play carries on, and the gangsters, due to a change in the leadership of the mob, tear up the IOU. Lois and Bill and Fred and Lilli all get together in the end the way they should.

Before Broadway. Arnold Saint Subber (as he was then before he dropped the "Arnold" after the opening night of this show), while a stage hand on the 1940 tour of the 1935 Alfred Lunt and Lynn Fontanne revival of *The Taming of the Shrew*, saw that the two stars quarreled constantly off stage, and thus was born the idea of this play-within-a-play (this according to Saint Subber, anyway; the Sam & Bella Spewack estate later vigorously denied the story). Burton Lane was the first choice of composer, but he turned it down. After acquiring Cole Porter, the show took a year to raise the capital (72 investors finally climbed aboard). Aside from the numbers cut (see below) "I'm Afraid, Sweetheart, I Love You," was also dropped. The part of Lilli was rejected in turn by Jarmila Novotna, Mary Martin, Lily Pons and Jeanette MacDonald, and in the end Cole Porter got who he had wanted, Patricia Morison, who had been out of Broadway for ten years. During rehearsals the working title was *Shrew*. From the time it began four-week tryouts at the Shubert Theatre, Philadelphia, on 12/2/48, they knew they had a hit. Choreographer Hanya Holm recorded her work on the Laban notation system and copyrighted it, which was a first.

The Broadway Run. NEW CENTURY THEATRE, 12/30/48–7/28/50; SHUBERT THEATRE, 7/31/50–7/28/51. Total of 1,070 PERFORMANCES. PRESENTED BY Arnold Saint Subber & Lemuel Ayers; MUSIC/LYRICS: Cole Porter; BOOK: Sam & Bella Spewack; BASED partly on the play *The Taming of the Shrew*, by William Shakespeare; DIRECTOR: John C. Wilson; CHOREOGRAPHER: Hanya Holm; SETS/COSTUMES: Lemuel Ayers; LIGHTING: Al Alloy; MUSICAL DIRECTOR/VOCAL ARRANGEMENTS: Pembroke Davenport; CONDUCTOR: John Passaretti; ORCHESTRATIONS: Robert Russell Bennett; INCIDENTAL BALLET MUSIC ARRANGEMENTS: Genevieve Pitot; CAST RECORDING on Columbia; PRESS: George & Dorothy Ross, *Madelin Blitzstein*; GENERAL MANAGER: C. Edwin Knill; PRODUCTION STAGE MANAGER: Ward Bishop; STAGE MANAGER: Don Mayo, *Angus Cairns* (by 50–51); ASSISTANT STAGE MANAGER: Bill Lilling, *Dan Brennan* (by 49–50), *Reed Allyn* (by 50–51). **Cast:** FRED GRAHAM/PETRUCHIO: Alfred Drake (1) ✩, *Keith Andes* (from 50–51), *Ted Scott* (from 50–51); HARRY TREVOR/BAPTISTA: Thomas Hoier; LOIS LANE/BIANCA: Lisa Kirk (4), *Betty Ann Grove* (from 50–51), *Marilyn Day* (from 50–51); RALPH, THE STAGE MANAGER: Don Mayo, *Angus Cairns* (from 50–51); LILLI VANESSI/KATHARINE: Patricia Morison (2) ✩, *Anne Jeffreys* (from 50–51); HATTIE: Annabelle Hill, *Helen Dowdy* (from 49–50); PAUL: Lorenzo Fuller; BILL CALHOUN/LUCENTIO: Harold Lang (3), *Danny Daniels* (from 49–50); 1ST MAN: Harry Clark; 2ND MAN: Jack Diamond; STAGE DOORMAN: Bill Lilling, *Dan Brennan* (from 49–50), *Reed Allyn* (from 50–51); HARRISON HOWELL: Denis Green; SPECIALTY DANCERS: Fred Davis & Eddie Sledge; GREMIO (1ST SUITOR): Edwin Clay; HORTENSIO (2ND SUITOR): Charles Wood; HABERDASHER: John Castello, *Marc Breaux* (from 50–51), *Paul Gannon* (from 50–51); TAILOR: Marc Breaux [role discontinued from 50–51]; SINGING ENSEMBLE: Tom Bole, George Cassidy, Peggy Ferris (gone by 50–51), Herbert Fields, Florence Gault (gone by 49–50), Noel Gordon (gone by 50–51), Gay Laurence (*Joan Kibrig* by 49–50), Allan Lowell, Ethel Madsen (gone by 50–51), Helen Rice, Mathilda Strazza (gone by 50–51), Charles Wood. 49–50 replacements: *Christine Matsios* (gone by 50–51), *Stan Rose*. 50–51 replacements: *Irene McCollum, June Reimer, Grayce Spence, Marian Burke, Mary Montgomery, David Collyer*; DANCERS: Marc Breaux (gone by 50–51), John Castello (gone by 50–51), Ann Dunbar (gone by 49–50), Victor Duntiere (gone by 50–51), Shirley Eckl (gone by 50–51), Jean Houloose (gone by 50–51), Paul Olson (gone by 49–50, but back by 50–51), Ingrid Secretan, Gisella Svetlik (gone by 50–51), Jean Tachau (gone by 49–50), Glen Tetley (gone by 50–51), Rudy Tone (*Nick Vanoff* by 50–51). 49–50 replacements: *Janet Gaylord* (gone by 50–51), *Doreen Oswald, Jean Haas* (gone by 50–51), *Harry Asmus* (gone by 50–51), *Tom Hansen* (gone by 50–51). 50–51 replacements: *Carol Nelson, Jean Goodall, Eve Hebert, Nina Popova, Cynthia Riseley, Keith Willis, Richard Thomas, Paul Gannon, Bill Harris, Harry Jones*. **Standbys:** Fred/Petruchio: Keith

Andes, *Edwin Clay, Ted Scott, Andrew Gainey* (by 50–51). **Understudies:** LILLI/KATHARINE: Peggy Ferris, *Holly Harris* (by 50–51); BILL/LUCENTIO: Rudy Tone, *Nick Vanoff* (by 50–51); LOIS/BIANCA: Gay Laurence, *Joan Kibrig* (by 49–50); Howell: Don Mayo; MEN/GREMIO/RALPH: Noel Gordon; HARRY/BAPTISTA: Allan Lowell; PAUL: Fred Davis; HATTIE: Mathilda Strazza; HORTENSIO: Herb Fields; DOORMAN: George Cassidy; HABERDASHER: Marc Breaux. **Act I:** Overture (Orchestra); *Scene 1* The stage of Ford's Theatre, Baltimore: "Another Op'nin', Another Show" (Hattie & Singing Ensemble) (danced by the Dancing Ensemble); *Scene 2* In the corridor backstage: "Why Can't You Behave?" (Lois, to Bill); *Scene 3* Adjoining dressing rooms of Fred Graham & Lilli Vanessi: "Wunderbar" (Fred & Lilli) [replaced "It was Great Fun the First Time"], "So in Love (Am I)" (Lilli) [replaced "We Shall Never Be Younger"]; *Scene 4* In Padua: "We Open in Venice" (Petruchio, Katharine, Bianca, Lucentio); *Scene 5* Street scene, Padua (piazza): Dance (Dancing Ensemble), "Tom, Dick or Harry" (Bianca, Lucentio, Gremio, Hortensio) [replaced "If Ever Married I'm"], Specialty Dance ("Rose Dance") (Lucentio), "I've Come to Wive it Wealthily in Padua" (Petruchio & Singing Ensemble), "I Hate Men" (Katharine), "Were Thine That Special Face" (sung by Petruchio, and danced by Shirley Eckl & Dancing Girls); *Scene 6* Backstage; *Scene 7* Fred and Lilli's dressing rooms; *Scene 8* Exterior of a church: "Cantiamo d'Amore" ("I Sing of Love") (Lucentio & Singing Ensemble) [not on the original cast album], First Act Finale: "Kiss Me, Kate" (Katharine, Petruchio, Singing Ensemble) [not on the original cast album], Tarantella (dance) (Bianca, Lucentio, Dancing Ensemble). **Act II:** *Scene 1* The theatre alley: "Too Darn Hot" (sung by Paul, and danced by Bill, Lois and Specialty Dancers) [replaced "What Does Your Servant Dream About?"]; *Scene 2* Before the curtain; *Scene 3* Petruchio's house: "Where is the Life that Late I Led?" (Petruchio); *Scene 4* The corridor backstage: "Always True to You (in My Fashion)" (Bianca) [the hit]; *Scene 5* Fred and Lilli's dressing rooms; *Scene 6* The corridor backstage: "Bianca" (Sung by Bill & Singing Girls, and danced by Bill & Dancing Girls), "So in Love (Am I)" (reprise) (Fred) [replaced "A Woman's Career"]; *Scene 7* Before the asbestos curtain: "Brush up Your Shakespeare" (1st Man & 2nd Man); *Scene 8* Baptista's home: "I Am Ashamed that Women Are So Simple" (Katharine), "Pavanne" (dance) (Bianca, Lucentio, Dancing Ensemble) [cut during the run]; *Scene 9* Finale (Petruchio, Katharine, Company).

The opening was a major event. The critics only raved. The show won Tony Awards for musical, producers of a musical, composer & lyricist, book, and costumes; It also won Donaldson Awards for sets, costumes, and for Alfred Drake. In the audience on several occasions was a young Yale man, Roger Horchow, who would later go on to produce the 1999 revival of *Kiss Me, Kate*. During the run Act II Scene 9 was cut and the finale became part of Act II Scene 8. In addition to this there were Act I scene and song shifts (although not in the actual playing order). *Kiss Me, Kate* was the longest-running of any of the Cole Porter musicals, and the fourth-longest running Broadway musical of the 1940s. The show, which was capitalized at $180,000, paid back its investment in a record-breaking 16 weeks.

After Broadway. TOUR. Opened in 1949, and ran almost 2 years. **Cast:** FRED: Keith Andes, *Robert Wright*; LILLI: Anne Jeffreys, *Frances McCann*; LOIS: Julie Wilson, *Betty George*; BILL: Marc Platt. The tour then returned to Broadway in 1952.

379. *Kiss Me, Kate* (1952 return to Broadway)

Before Broadway. After the tour (see above) the show opened for pre–Broadway return tryouts at New Haven on 9/17/51, and finally returned to Broadway.

The Broadway Run. BROADWAY THEATRE, 1/8/52–1/13/52. Limited run of 8 PERFORMANCES. It had the same basic crew as in the 1948 run, except: MUSICAL DIRECTOR: George Hirst; PRODUCTION STAGE MANAGER: Milton Stern; STAGE MANAGERS: Bruce Laffey & Emory Bass. **Cast:** FRED: Robert Wright; HARRY: Nat Burns; LOIS: Marilyn Day; RALPH: Emory Bass; LILLI: Holly Harris; HATTIE: Lillyn Brown; PAUL: Bobby Johnson; BILL: Frank Derbas; CAB DRIVER: Max Hart; STAGE DOORMAN:

Bruce Laffey; 1ST MAN: Hank Henry; 2ND MAN: Sparky Kaye; HARRISON: Lionel Ince; SPECIALTY DANCERS: Charles Cook & Ernest Brown; BIANCA: Marilyn Day; BAPTISTA: Nat Burns; GREMIO: Jim Howard; HORTENSIO: Alfred Homan; LUCENTIO: Frank Derbas; KATHARINE: Holly Harris; PETRUCHIO: Robert Wright; HABERDASHER: Jan Kovac; SINGING ENSEMBLE: Charles Adrian, Emory Bass, Jean Cannon, Sylvia Chaney, Frank Green, Joseph Gregory, Marilyn Hanson, Max Hart, Louise Hoffman, Alfred Homan, Janet Medlin, Pat Sayers, Bobra Suitor, Edward Whitman; DANCERS: Charles Arnett, Doris Atkinson, Esta Beck, Naomi Boneck, Harold Drake, Bill Harris, Albertina Horstmann, Jay Kleindorf, Jan Kovac, Ronald Landry, Claire Mallardy, Julie Marlowe, Florence Miller, Jess Ramirez. *Understudies*: Fred: Jim Howard; Lilli/Lois: Janet Medlin; Bill: Jan Kovac; Harry: Emory Bass; Hattie: Marilyn Hanson; Howell: Edward Whitman; 1st Man: Max Hart; 2nd Man: Frank Green; Stage Doorman: Alfred Homan; Ralph/Hortensio: Joseph Gregory; Gremio: Charles Adrian; Paul: Ernest Brown; Haberdasher: Bill Harris.

After Broadway. COLISEUM, London, 3/8/51–2/23/52. 401 PERFORMANCES. PRESENTED BY Jack Hylton; MUSICAL DIRECTOR: Freddie Bretherton. There was a cast recording. *Cast:* FRED: Bill Johnson; HARRY: Daniel Wherry; LOIS: Julie Wilson, *Valerie Tandy*; RALPH: Ronan O'Casey, *Gordon Mulholland*, LILLI: Patricia Morison, *Helena Bliss, Elizabeth Larner, Helen Jutsen*; PAUL: Archie Savage, *Laurie Lawrence*; HATTIE: Adelaide Hall; STAGE DOORMAN: Peter Bentley; BILL: Walter Long, *George Carden*; 1ST MAN: Danny Green; 2ND MAN: Sid James, *Ronan O'Casey*; HOWELL: Austin Trevor; DANCER: John Williamson.

THE MOVIE. 1953. It was a new 3-D film. It kept the entire score from the stage production, and added a new song, "From This Moment On," the only hit to come from Cole Porter's score for *Out of This World* (it was actually dropped from that Broadway musical prior to Broadway opening night). *Cast:* FRED: Howard Keel; LILLI: Kathryn Grayson; LOIS: Ann Miller; BILL: Tommy Rall; GREMIO: Bobby Van; BAPTISTA: Kurt Kasznar; COLE PORTER: Ron Randell; DANCERS INCLUDED: Bob Fosse, Carol Haney, Jeanne Coyne.

CITY CENTER, NYC, 5/9/56–5/27/56. 23 PERFORMANCES. PRESENTED BY the City Center Light Opera Company; DIRECTOR: Burt Shevelove; CHOREOGRAPHER: Ray Harrison; ASSISTANT CHOREOGRAPHER: Patricia Birch; SETS: Watson Barratt; COSTUMES: Alvin Colt; LIGHTING: Jean Rosenthal; MUSICAL DIRECTOR: Frederick Dvonch. *Cast:* FRED: David Atkinson; HARRY: Harrison Dowd; LOIS: Barbara Ruick; RALPH: Vincent McMahon; LILLI: Kitty Carlisle; HATTIE: Delores Martin; STAGE DOORMAN: Robert Reim; PAUL: Bobby Short; BILL: Richard France; MEN: Al Nesor & Tom Pedi; HOWELL: Ben Lackland; GREMIO: Philip Wentworth; HORTENSIO: Ray Weaver; HABERDASHER: Arthur Mitchell; DANCERS INCLUDED: Patricia Birch, Olga Bergstrom, Dorothy Etheridge, Kate Friedlich, Norma Kaiser, Gene Gavin; SINGERS INCLUDED: Doris Galiber, Louise Pearl.

NBC TV VERSION, 11/20/58. Part of the *Hallmark Hall of Fame* series. *Cast:* FRED: Alfred Drake; LILLI: Patricia Morison.

CITY CENTER, NYC, 5/12/65–5/30/65. 23 PERFORMANCES. Part of the City Center's spring program of four musicals (the others were *Guys and Dolls, South Pacific,* and *The Music Man*). PRESENTED BY the City Center Light Opera Company; DIRECTORS: John Fearnley & Billy Matthews; CHOREOGRAPHER: Hanya Holm; SETS: Robert O'Hearn; COSTUMES: Stanley Simmons; LIGHTING: Peggy Clark; MUSICAL DIRECTOR: Pembroke Davenport; DANCE MUSIC ARRANGEMENTS: Genevieve Pitot. *Cast:* FRED: Bob Wright; HARRY: Alexander Clark; LOIS: Nancy Ames; RALPH: William H. Batchelder; LILLI: Patricia Morison; PAUL: Tiger Haynes; HATTIE: Alyce Elizabeth Webb; BILL: Kelly Brown; MEN: Jesse White & Victor Helou; HOWELL: Royal Beal; GREMIO: William Wendt; HORTENSIO: Stephen John Rydell; HABERDASHER: Loren Hightower; DANCERS INCLUDED: Kiki Minor, Lucia Lambert, Ben Gillespie; SINGERS INCLUDED: Madeline Kahn, Jeanne Shea, Jack L. Fletcher, Maggie Worth. New characters were created for this production — Doctor, Nurses, Messengers, Banker, Truck Driver, Innkeeper, Waiter. Act I Scene 8 was now split into two scenes (as explained below for the 1999 revival). The Act II Scene 8 "Pavanne," which had been cut during the run of the original 1948 production, was re-instated.

STUDIO RECORDING. In 1959 there was a studio recording (i.e. not a stage performance) of *Kiss Me, Kate*, with Alfred Drake, Patricia Morison, Lisa Kirk, and Harold Lang.

OLD VIC THEATRE, London, 1987. DIRECTOR: Adrian Noble; CHOREOGRAPHER: Ron Field; COSTUMES: Liz Da Costa. *Cast:* FRED: Paul Jones; LOIS: Fiona Hendley; BILL: Tim Flavin; LILLI: Nichola McAuliffe.

GOODSPEED OPERA HOUSE, Conn., 4/5/94–7/1/94. DIRECTOR: Ted Pappas; CHOREOGRAPHER: Liza Gennaro; SETS: James Noone; MUSICAL DIRECTOR: Michael O'Flaherty. *Cast:* FRED: Steve Barton; LILLI: Marilyn Caskey; LOIS: Leah Hocking; BILL: Michael Gruber; PAUL: Kevin Bogue; HATTIE: Laura Kenyon; GREMIO: Bob Freschi; CHORUS INCLUDED: Nadine Isenegger.

380. *Kiss Me, Kate* (1999 Broadway revival)

The book was slightly updated. Harrison Howell, Lilli's boyfriend, who was a government adviser in the original (based on Bernard Baruch) is now a chauvinistic military man. This change, wrought by an unknown author (people thought it might be Alfred Uhry at first, but John Guare began to loom larger as a suspect until it became known that it was, indeed, Mr. Guare), was done so at the request of the Spewack estate.

Before Broadway. The idea of doing a Broadway revival of *Kiss Me, Kate* had long been talked about. At one time Mandy Patinkin and Bernadette Peters were being rumored to be starring in a production, and in 1998 Dee Hoty was being touted, but none of these happened. However, in 6/98 Roger Berlind announced his intention of doing it, in the spring of 1999. Michael Blakemore was rumored to be the director of choice. By 9/98 Kevin Kline was being talked about as Fred, but this rumor was quickly dismissed. By 3/29/99 Sharon Lawrence had been offered the role of Lois (she didn't take it, as it happens), and the opening date was put back to the fall of 1999. Kathleen Marshall was confirmed as choreographer, and Michael Blakemore as director. Scott Rudin was one of the producers at that point (he would drop out). Rumors were also now circulating that Marin Mazzie and Brian Stokes Mitchell were going to be the leads (they were confirmed on 6/19/99). Michael Berresse and Amy Spanger were also confirmed in their roles. On 8/10/99 full casting was announced. On 10/7/99 there was an open press rehearsal. Roger Horchow, another of the producers, had vowed he would never produce another Broadway play, but he was inspired by the odd coincidence that his father and his brother had both occupied the very room Cole Porter had occupied at Yale (different years). Roger Horchow himself had been at Yale.

The Broadway Run. MARTIN BECK THEATRE, 11/18/99–12/30/01. 28 previews from 10/25/99. 885 PERFORMANCES. PRESENTED BY Roger Berlind & Roger Horchow, in association with Richard Goodwin & Edwin W. Schloss; MUSIC/LYRICS: Cole Porter; BOOK: Sam & Bella Spewack; BASED PARTLY ON William Shakespeare's *The Taming of the Shrew*; UNCREDITED CONTRIBUTIONS BY: John Guare; DIRECTOR: Michael Blakemore; CHOREOGRAPHER: Kathleen Marshall; SETS: Robin Wagner; COSTUMES: Martin Pakledinaz; LIGHTING: Peter Kaczorowski; SOUND: Tony Meola; MUSICAL DIRECTOR: Paul Gemignani; ORCHESTRATIONS: Don Sebesky; DANCE MUSIC ARRANGEMENTS: David Chase; CAST RECORDING ON DRG, recorded on 11/22/99 and released on 1/25/00 (it did not have "From This Moment On"); PRESS: Boneau/Bryan-Brown; CASTING: Johnson — Liff; GENERAL MANAGEMENT: 101 Productions; COMPANY MANAGER: Ron Gubin; STAGE MANAGER: Ara Marx; ASSISTANT STAGE MANAGER: Elaine Bayless. *Cast:* HATTIE: Adriane Lenox, *Mamie Duncan-Gibbs* (from 2/20/01); PAUL: Stanley Wayne Mathis; RALPH, THE STAGE MANAGER: Eric Michael Gillett; LOIS LANE: Amy Spanger (3) ☆, *JoAnn M. Hunter* (4/24/01–6/17/01), *Janine LaManna* (from 6/19/01); BILL CALHOUN: Michael Berresse (4) ☆, *Kevin Neil McCready, David Elder* (from 9/19/00), *Michael Berresse* (from 12/19/00); LILLI VANESSI: Marin Mazzie (2) ☆ (until 5/27/01), *Carolee Carmello* (from 5/29/01); FRED GRAHAM: Brian Stokes Mitchell (1) ☆ (until 1/28/01), *Burke Moses* (from 1/30/01); DANCE CAPTAIN: Vince Pesce; HARRY TREVOR: John Horton, *Herb Foster*; POPS, THE STAGE DOORMAN: Robert Ousley; CAB DRIVER: Jerome Vivona, *Lee A. Wilkins*;

1ST MAN: Lee Wilkof, *Michael McCormick*; 2ND MAN: Michael Mulheren; HARRISON HOWELL: Ronald Holgate, *Merwin Foard, Walter Charles, Christopher Coucill*; *Taming of the Shrew* PLAYERS: BIANCA: Amy Spanger, *JoAnn M. Hunter* (4/24/01–6/17/01), *Janine LaManna* (from 6/19/01); BAPTISTA: John Horton, *Herb Foster*; GREMIO (1ST SUITOR): Kevin Neil McCready, *Brad Anderson*; HORTENSIO (2ND SUITOR): Darren Lee, *Michael Gruber* (from 4/11/01*)*, *John MacInnis*; LUCENTIO: Michael Berresse, *Kevin Neil McCready, David Elder* (from 9/19/00), *Michael Berresse* (from 12/19/00); KATHARINE: Marin Mazzie (until 5/27/01), *Carolee Carmello* (from 5/29/01); PETRUCHIO: Brian Stokes Mitchell (until 1/28/01), *Burke Moses* (from 1/30/01); NATHANIEL: Jerome Vivona, *Lee A. Wilkins*; GREGORY: Vince Pesce; PHILIP: Blake Hammond, *Kevin Ligon*; HABERDASHER: Michael X. Martin; ENSEMBLE: Eric Michael Gillett, Patty Goble, Blake Hammond, JoAnn M. Hunter, Darren Lee, Nancy Lemenager, Kevin Neil McCready, Michael X. Martin, Carol Lee Meadows, Elizabeth Mills, Linda Mugleston, Robert Ousley, Vince Pesce, Cynthia Sophiea, Jerome Vivona, *Brad Anderson, Lisa Gajda, Michael Gruber, Ashley Hull, Kevin Ligon, Lorin Latarro, Corinne Melancon, John MacInnis*. **Standby**: Fred/Howell: Merwin Foard & Michael X. Martin; **Understudies**: Lilli/Kate: Patty Goble; Lois/Bianca: JoAnn M. Hunter & Nancy Lemenager; Bill/Lucentio: Kevin Neil McCready; Hattie: Cynthia Sophiea, *Corinne Melancon*; Harry/Baptista: Robert Ousley; 1st Man: Blake Hammond; 2nd Man: Blake Hammond & Michael X. Martin; Paul: T. Oliver Reid & Jerome Vivona; Gremio: Jerome Vivona & T. Oliver Reid; Hortensio: Vince Pesce & T. Oliver Reid. **Swings:** Paula Leggett Chase & T. Oliver Reid, *Tripp Hanson, Derric Harris, John MacInnis, Lisa A. Mayer, Marisa Rozek*. **Orchestra:** KEYBOARD: Mark Mitchell; CONCERTMISTRESS: Suzanne Ornstein; VIOLINS: Suzanne Ornstein, Xin Zhao, Richard Brice; VIOLA: Richard Brice; CELLO: Igor Seedrov; WOODWIND # 1: Dennis Anderson; WOODWIND # 2: Eric Weidman; WOODWIND # 3: Charles Pillow; WOODWIND # 4: Don McGeen; TRUMPET # 1: Dominic Derasse; TRUMPET # 2: Larry Lunetta; TROMBONE: Bruce Eidem; FRENCH HORN: Ronald Sell; DRUMS/PERCUSSION/REHEARSAL DRUMMER: Paul Pizzuti; BASS: John Beal. **Act I**: Ford's Theatre, Baltimore; June 1948: *Scene 1* The stage: "Another Op'nin', Another Show" (Hattie & Company) [this opening number was newly conceived — it was interweaved with the overture]; *Scene 2* The backstage corridor: "Why Can't You Behave?" (Lois & Bill); *Scene 3* Fred and Lilli's dressing rooms: "Wunderbar" (Lilli & Fred), "So in Love (Am I)" (Lilli); *Scene 4* Padua: "We Open in Venice" (Petruchio, Katharine, Bianca, Lucentio); *Scene 5* Street in Padua: "Tom, Dick or Harry" (Bianca, Lucentio, Gremio, Hortensio), "I've Come to Wive it Wealthily in Padua" (Petruchio & Men), "I Hate Men" (Katharine), "Were Thine That Special Face" (Petruchio); *Scene 6* The backstage corridor; *Scene 7* Fred and Lilli's dressing rooms; *Scene 8* A country road in Padua: "Cantiamo d'Amore" ("I Sing of Love") (Ensemble); *Scene 9* The church in Padua: "Kiss Me, Kate" (Petruchio, Kate, Singing Ensemble). **Act II**: Immediately following: *Scene 1* The theatre alley: "Too Darn Hot" (Paul & Ensemble); *Scene 2* Before the curtain; *Scene 3* Petruchio's house: "Where is the Life that Late I Led?" (Petruchio); *Scene 4* The backstage corridor: "Always True to You (in My Fashion)" (Bianca); *Scene 5* Fred and Lilli's dressing rooms: "From This Moment On" (Harrison & Lilli) [this number had been in the 1953 film, and had been cut from *Out of This World*]; *Scene 6* The backstage corridor: "Bianca" (Bill & Ensemble), "So in Love (Am I)" (reprise) (Fred); *Scene 7* Before the curtain: "Brush up Your Shakespeare" (1st & 2nd Man); *Scene 8* Baptista's house, Padua: Pavanne (Bianca, Lucentio, Ensemble), "I Am Ashamed that Women Are So Simple" (Katharine), Finale: "Kiss Me, Kate" (reprise) (Company).

Broadway reviews were very good. The show won Tony Awards for revival of a musical, direction of a musical, costumes, orchestrations, and for Brian Stokes Mitchell. It was also nominated for sets, costumes, lighting, and for Lee Wilkof, Michael Mulheren, and Marin Mazzie. When the attack happened on New York City on 9/11/01, it devastated box-office returns on Broadway. *Kiss Me, Kate* told Equity that it was unable to continue without everyone in the production taking a 50 percent pay cut. This show, and others, were taking a 25 percent pay cut, just to survive, but Equity found 50 percent unacceptable. So on 9/19/01 it was announced that the show would close on 9/23/01, three months early. However, a way was found to keep it open. The additional 25 per cent was donated to ticket purchases for rescue workers and others, and this enabled the show to carry on to the end of the year.

After Broadway. TOUR. Opened 6/19/01–7/1/03, at the Shubert Theatre, New Haven; then it went to the Kennedy Center, Washington, DC, 7/3/01–8/5/01; then to the Shubert Theatre, Los Angeles, 8/24/01–10/13/01 (previews from 8/22/01). The tour closed on 6/16/02, at the Blumenthal Arts Center, Charlotte, NC. DIRECTOR: Michael Blakemore; CHOREOGRAPHER: Kathleen Marshall. **Cast:** FRED: Rex Smith; LILLI: Rachel York; LOIS: Nancy Anderson, *Jenny Hill*; BILL: Jim Newman, *Kevin Neil McCready*; HATTIE: Susan Beaubian; HOWELL: Chuck Wagner; PAUL: Randy Donaldson; HARRY: Herman Petras; 1ST MAN: Richard Poe; 2ND MAN: Michael Arkin; ENSEMBLE INCLUDED: John Treacy Egan, Rommy Sandhu.

VICTORIA PALACE THEATRE, London, 10/30/01–8/24/02. Previews from 10/16/01. This was the 1999 Broadway revival come to London, and this London run had the same basic crew as for Broadway. Marin Mazzie and Brian Stokes Mitchell had been rumored for the leads, but on 8/10/01 Miss Mazzie & Brent Barrett were confirmed in the roles. **Cast:** FRED: Brent Barrett; LOIS: Nancy Anderson; BILL: Michael Berresse; LILLI: Marin Mazzie, *Carolee Carmello* (6/3/02–6/29/02), *Rachel York* (from 7/1/02); 1ST MAN: Teddy Kempner; HOWELL: Nicolas Colicos. *Kiss Me, Kate* revived the sagging fortunes of the Victoria Palace. PBS filmed a performance (shown on 2/26/03). On 8/26/02 a full British company was going to take over from the American cast (the show had extended its run until 3/1/03), but instead, in a surprise move, the show closed on 8/24/01. A UK tour was talked about.

381. *Kiss of the Spider Woman*

Also known as: *Kiss of the Spider Woman — the Musical*. Set sometime in the recent past. Molina, a homosexual window dresser, is jailed in South America on a morals charge. His heterosexual cellmate is Valentin, a revolutionary. The warden enlists Molina to get Valentin to reveal the names of his co-revolutionaries. To survive prison life, Molina dreams about Aurora, the Spider Woman, a B-movie star, and he relates her adventures to Valentin.

Before Broadway. THE MOVIE. Not a musical. 1984. **Cast:** VALENTIN ARREGUI: Raul Julia; LUIS MOLINA: William Hurt; SPIDER WOMAN: Sonia Braga.

THE STAGE MUSICAL. It failed in its work-in-progress tryouts (presented by New Musicals) at the PERFORMING ARTS CENTER OF THE STATE UNIVERSITY OF NEW YORK, Purchase, NY, 5/1/90–6/24/90. PRESENTED BY Martin J. "Marty" Bell; DIRECTOR: Harold Prince; CHOREOGRAPHER: Susan Stroman; SETS: Thomas Lynch; COSTUMES: Florence Klotz; LIGHTING: Peter A. Kaczorowski; SOUND: Alan Stieb; MUSICAL DIRECTOR: Donald Chan; ORCHESTRATIONS: Michael Gibson. **Cast:** VALENTIN: Kevin Gray; MARCOS: Philip Hernandez; WARDEN/MONSTER: Harry Goz; ESTEBAN: John Norman Thomas; GUARD: Adam Heller; MOLINA: John Rubinstein; AURORA/SPIDER WOMAN: Lauren Mitchell; SENORA MOLINA: Barbara Andres; MARTA: Lauren Mufson; PIANO PLAYER: Carl Maultsby; ARMANDO: Donn Simione; DRAG QUEEN: Aurelio Padron; GABRIEL: Greg Zerkle; JOSE: Jonathan Brody; JORGE: Forest Dino Ray; ALSO WITH: Bill Christopher-Myers, Karen Giombetti, Ruth Gottschall, Dorie Herndon, David Koch, Rick Manning, Casey Nicholaw, Lorraine Serabian, Wendy Waring, Matt Zarley. **Orchestra:** TRUMPET I: James Sedlar; TRUMPET II: Charles Affelt; TROMBONE I: Joseph Petrizzo; TROMBONE II: James Miller; FRENCH HORN I: Kaitilin Mahoney; FRENCH HORN II: Leise Anscheutz; VIOLA I/VIOLIN I: Mimi Dye; VIOLA II/VIOLIN II: Dan Seidenberg; VIOLA III: Brian Zenone; VIOLA IV: Don Krishnaswami; REED I: Albert Bloch; REED II: Charles Millard; REED III: David Diggs; REED IV: Matthew Bennett; DRUMS: Jay Mattes; PERCUSSION: Ian Finkel; LATIN PERCUSSION: Luther Rix; BASS: Joe Leisa; GUITAR: Robbie Kirshoff; PIANO: David Pogue; SYNTHESIZER: Carl Maultsby; CELLO I: David Berkjamian; CELLO II: Marisol Espada. **Act I**: "Her Name is Aurora" (Molina, Aurora, Company), "Over the Wall I" (Male Ensemble), "Dear One" (Senora Molina, Marta, Valentin, Molina), "Man Overboard" (Aurora & Male Ensemble), "I Do Miracles" (Aurora & Marta), "Over the Wall II" (Male Ensemble), "Every Day" (Armando), "I Don't Know" (Aurora & Molina), "Tango" (Female Ensemble), "You Could Never Shame Me" (Senora Molina), "Letter from a Friend" (Drag Queen), "Letter from Gabriel" (Gabriel), "The Day After That" (Valentin), "She's a Woman" (Molina), "Gimme Love" (Aurora & Company). *Act II*: "Good Clean Fight" (Male Ensemble), "Cookies" (Molina & Valentin), "Never You" (Armando & Aurora), "Mama, It's Me" (Molina), "Over the Wall III" (Male Ensemble), "Kiss of the Spider Woman" (Aurora), "The Day After That" (reprise) (Valentin, Armando, Company), "Over the Wall IV" (Male Ensemble), "Only in the Movies" (Molina, Karen Giombetti, Ruth Gottschall, Dorie Herndon, Wendy Waring). Revised and re-presented by Live Entertainment Corporation of Canada, in Toronto, where it had its world premiere at the St. Lawrence Centre for the Arts' Bluma Appel Theatre, 6/92–8/92.

SHAFTESBURY THEATRE, London. 10/20/92. 390 performance). The main cast was the same as for the subsequent Broadway opening night.

The Broadway Run. BROADHURST THEATRE, 5/3/93–7/1/95. 16 previews from 4/19/93. 906 PERFORMANCES. PRESENTED BY Livent (U.S.); MUSIC: John Kander; LYRICS: Fred Ebb; BOOK: Terrence McNally; BASED ON the novel by Manuel Puig; DIRECTOR: Harold Prince, ASSISTANT DIRECTOR: Ruth Mitchell; CHOREOGRAPHER: Vincent Paterson; ADDITIONAL CHOREOGRAPHY: Rob Marshall; ASSISTANT ADDITIONAL CHOREOGRAPHY: Kathleen Marshall; SETS: Jerome Sirlin; COSTUMES: Florence Klotz; LIGHTING: Howell Binkley; SOUND: Martin Levan; MUSICAL SUPERVISOR/CONDUCTOR: Jeffrey Huard; ORCHESTRATIONS: Michael Gibson; DANCE MUSIC ARRANGEMENTS: David Krane; LONDON CAST RECORDING ON RCA; VANESSA WILLIAMS CAST RECORDING ON Mercury; PRESS: Mary Bryant (U.S.), Norman Zagier (Canada); CASTING: Johnson — Liff & Zerman; GENERAL MANAGER: Frank P. Scardino; COMPANY MANAGER: Jim Brandeberry, *Alan R. Markinson* (by 94–95); PRODUCTION STAGE MANAGER: Beverley Randolph, *Bonnie Panson*; STAGE MANAGER: Clayton Phillips, *Michael Pule*; ASSISTANT STAGE MANAGER: Jonathan Arak. **Cast:** MOLINA: Brent Carver ☆ (2), *Jeff Hyslop, Howard McGillin* (from 6/6/94); WARDEN: Herndon Lackey (5); VALENTIN: Anthony Crivello (3) ☆, *Brian Mitchell* (he later became Brian Stokes Mitchell); ESTEBAN: Philip Hernandez; MARCOS: Michael McCormick; SPIDER WOMAN/AURORA: Chita Rivera ☆ (1), *Carol Lawrence* (during Miss Rivera's vacation), *Vanessa Williams* (from 6/27/94), *Maria Conchita Alonso* (from 3/20/95); AURORA'S MEN: Keith McDaniel (*Gregory Mitchell*), Robert Montano, Dan O'Grady, Raymond Rodriguez, Andre E. Carthen, David Marques, Troy Myers; PRISONERS: Keith McDaniel (*Gregory Mitchell*), Robert Montano, Dan O'Grady, John Norman Thomas (*John Aller*), Jerry Christakos, Aurelio Padron (gone by 93–94), *Andre E. Carthen, David Marques*; MOLINA'S MOTHER: Merle Louise (4), *Mimi Turque*; MARTA: Kirsti Carnahan (6); ESCAPING PRISONER: Colton Green, *Troy Myers*; TORTURED PRISONER: Raymond Rodriguez [during the run this role became singled out as such; before that he was just one of the Prisoners]; RELIGIOUS FANATIC: John Norman Thomas, *Robert Du Sold*; AMNESTY INTERNATIONAL OBSERVER/PRISONER EMILIO: Joshua Finkel, *Bob Stillman, Jeff Bannon*; PRISONER FUENTES: Gary Schwartz, *Vincent D'Elia*; GABRIEL: Jerry Christakos; WINDOW DRESSER AT MONTOYA'S: Aurelio Padron, *Roberto Montano, John Aller*. **Standbys:** Spider Woman/Aurora: Dorothy Stanley, *Nancy Hess*; Marta: Dorothy Stanley, *Judy McLane, Nancy Hess*; Mother: Lorraine Foreman, *Barbara Andres*. **Understudies:** Molina: Joshua Finkel, *Juan Chioran, Bob Stillman*; Valentin: Philip Hernandez & Gary Schwartz; Esteban/Observer: Gary Schwartz, *Vincent D'Elia*; Marcos: John Norman Thomas; Warden: Michael McCormick; Gabriel: Dan O'Grady. **Swing:** Gregory Mitchell, *Richard Montoya, Mark Bove*. **Partial Swing:** Colton Green, *David Marques*. **Orchestra:** 1ST TRUMPET: Jeffrey Kievit; 2ND TRUMPET: Larry Lunetta; TROMBONE: Porter Poindexter; FRENCH HORNS: Katie Dennis & Susan Panny; REED I: Al Hunt; REED II: Mort Silver; REED III: Richard Heckman; REED IV: Ken Berger; BASS: John Babich; DRUMS: John Redsecker; PERCUSSION: Mark Sherman; KEYBOARD I: Jeff Saver; KEYBOARD II: Greg Dlugos; CONCERTMISTRESS/VIOLA I: Susan Follari; VIOLA II: Ann Barak; VIOLA III: Maxine Roach; VIOLA IV: Katherine Sinsabaugh; CELLO: Caryl Paisner. *Act I*: *Prologue* a prison (Spider Woman & Prisoners); *Scene 1* The prison — Molina's cell: "Her Name is Aurora" (Molina, Aurora, Aurora's Men, Prisoners); *Scene 2* The prison: "Over the Wall I" (Prisoners); *Scene 3* Molina and Valentin's cell: "Bluebloods" (Molina), "Dressing Them Up"/"I Draw the Line" (Molina & Valentin), "Dear One" (Molina's Mother, Marta, Valentin, Molina); *Scene 4* The prison: "Over the Wall II" (Prisoners, Molina, Valentin); *Scene 5* The cell: "Where You Are" (Aurora, Aurora's Men, Prisoners); *Scene 6* The prison: "Over the Wall III — Marta" (Valentin & Prisoners); *Scene 7* Warden's office: "Come" (Spider Woman); *Scene 8* The prison; the cell: "I Do Miracles" (Aurora & Marta); *Scene 9* The cell: "Gabriel's Letter"/"My First Woman" (Gabriel & Valentin); *Scene 10* The infirmary: "Morphine Tango" (Orderlies), "You Could Never Shame Me" (Molina's Mother), "A Visit" (Spider Woman & Molina); *Scene 11* The cell: "She's a Woman" (Molina); *Scene 12* Molina's movie; the cell: "Gimme Love" (Aurora, Molina, Aurora's Men); *Act II*: Entr'acte; *Scene 1* The cell: "Russian Movie"/"Good Times" (Aurora, Molina, Valentin), "The Day After That" (Valentin, Families of the Disappeared); *Scene 2* Limbo; Warden's office: "Mama, It's Me" (Molina); *Scene 3* The cell: "Anything for Him" (Spider woman, Molina, Valentin); *Scene 4* Kiss of the Spider Woman: "Kiss of the Spider Woman" (Spider Woman); *Scene 5* The cell: [no song] (Molina, Valentin, Esteban, Marcos); *Scene 6* The prison; Warden's office; Molina's apartment; a park; Molina's mother's apartment: "Over the Wall IV — Lucky Molina" (Warden & Prisoners); *Scene 7* The interrogation room; a theatre: "Only in the Movies" (Molina & the People in His Life).

Broadway reviews were mostly excellent. The show won Tonys for musical, score, book, costumes, and for Brent Carver, Anthony Crivello and Chita Rivera. It was also nominated for direction of a musical, choreography, sets, and lighting. Vanessa Williams replacing Chita Rivera boosted ticket sales up again.

After Broadway. TOUR. Opened on 11/1/94, in Tampa. *Cast*: SPIDER WOMAN: Chita Rivera, *Carol Lawrence, Chita Rivera*; VALENTIN: John Dossett, *Dorian Harewood* (from 8/95); MOLINA: Juan Chioran, *Jeff Hyslop* (from 7/95), *Juan Chioran* (from 8/95); WARDEN: Mark Zimmerman, *Michael McCormick* (from 8/95); MOLINA'S MOTHER: Rita Gardner, *Merle Louise* (from 8/95); MARTA: Juliet Lambert, *Lauren Goler-Kosarin* (from 9/95). As part of the tour it was produced by the Center Theatre Group at the Ahmanson Theatre, Los Angeles. During that stay the cast was: Chita Rivera, Dorian Harewood, Merle Louise, Juan Chioran, Michael McCormick, Lauren Goler-Kosarin, Robert Ashford, Mark Dovey, Joshua Finkel, Todd Hunter, Richard Montoya, Gary Moss, Bonnie Schon, Sergio Trujillo.

382. *Kwamina*

Set in a West African country about to gain its independence from Britain. Kwamina (the name means "Born on Sunday"), son of a tribal chief, returns home to his village from medical training in London and soon clashes with white, African-born doctor, Eve. Kwamina wants to take his people into the modern era, but it's not that easy. A girl of the tribe is betrothed to Kwamina, but she loves another man. When Kwamina's father dies, three others must die with him, according to custom. Kwamina tries desperately to change this and other barbaric customs which are holding his people back, but he is up against the witch doctor, and is expelled from his tribe, and his clinic is destroyed. By this time he is in love with Eve, and the two of them set about teaching new values to the young of the country.

Before Broadway. The show cost $420,000, all of which was put up by South African industrialist John S. Schlesinger. It tried out first in Toronto, where reviews were good. Then it went to Boston, but it was obvious the show had problems, not the least of which was that Richard Adler's marriage to Sally Ann Howes (the leading lady) was breaking up. Tony Richardson was set to direct, but was replaced by Robert Lewis. This was the first time Richard Adler had written both music and lyrics for a show. The number "Happy is the Cricket" was cut before Broadway.

The Broadway Run. FIFTY-FOURTH STREET THEATRE, 10/23/61–11/18/61. 32 PERFORMANCES. PRESENTED BY Alfred de Liagre Jr.; MUSIC/

LYRICS: Richard Adler; BOOK: Robert Alan Aurthur; DIRECTOR: Robert Lewis; CHOREOGRAPHER: Agnes de Mille; SETS/LIGHTING: Will Steven Armstrong; COSTUMES: Motley; MUSICAL DIRECTOR/CHORAL DIRECTOR: Colin Romoff; ORCHESTRATIONS: Sid Ramin & Irwin Kostal; DANCE MUSIC ARRANGEMENTS: John Morris; CAST RECORDING on Capitol, made the day after the show closed; PRESS: Fred Weterich, Frank Goodman, Ben Washer; TECHNICAL CONSULTANT: Albert Opoku; GENERAL MANAGER: C. Edwin Knill; COMPANY MANAGER: Charles Gnys; PRODUCTION STAGE MANAGER: James E. Wall; STAGE MANAGER: Arthur Marlowe; ASSISTANT STAGE MANAGER: William Weaver. *Cast:* OBITSEBI: Brock Peters (3); BLAIR: Norman Barrs; AKO: Robert Guillaume; EVE: Sally Ann Howes (1); NAII: Ethel Ayler; AKUFO: Joseph Attles; KWAMINA (PETER): Terry Carter (2); KOJO: Ainsley Sigmond; CHILDREN: Vaughn Fubler & Renaye Fubler; NANA MWALLA: Rex Evans; ALLA: Rosalie Maxwell; MAMMY TRADER: Lillian Hayman; POLICEMEN: Ronald Platts & Edward Thomas; SINGERS: Issa Arnal, Joseph Crawford, Doreese DuQuan, Scott Gibson, Victoria Harrison, Lillian Hayman, Lee Hooper, Wanza King, Mary Louise, James Lowe, Rosalie Maxwell, John Miles, Clark Morgan, Helen Phillips, Mal Scott, Rawn Spearman, George Tipton, Gordon Watkins, Arthur Wright; DANCERS: Pepsi Bethel, Hope Clarke, Zebedee Collins, Doris de Mendez, Julius Fields, Frank Glass, Altovise Gore, Louis Johnson, Minnie Marshall, Charles Moore, Joan Peters, Ronald Platts, Mike Quashie, Charles Queenan, Lucinda Ransom, Joan Seabrook, Barbara Ann Teer, Glory Van Scott, Philip Stamps, Edward Thomas, Myrna White, Camille Yarbrough; DRUMMERS: Montego Joe & Robert Crowder. *Standby*: Eve: Elizabeth Hubbard. *Understudies*: Kwamina: Rawn Spearman; Naii: Glory Van Scott; Kojo: Vaughn Fubler; Ako: George Tipton; Nana/Okufo/Obitsebi: Clark Morgan; Blair: William Weaver; Alla: Mary Louise; Mammy Trader: Helen Phillips. *Act I: Scene 1*; *Scene 2* "The Cocoa Bean Song" (Ako, Scott Gibson, Gordon Watkins, Company); *Scene 3* "Welcome Home" (Scott Gibson, Mal Scott, Lee Hooper, Mike Quashie, Company): SPEAR DANCERS: Charles Moore & Charles Queenan; FONGA: Joan Seabrook, Barbara Ann Teer, Glory Van Scott, Myrna White; "The Sun is Beginning to Crow" (Company); *Scene 4* "Did You Hear That?" (Eve & Kwamina), "You're as English As" (Eve); *Scene 5* "Seven Sheep, Four Red Shirts, and a Bottle of Gin" (Akufo, Scott Gibson, Charles Queenan, George Tipton, Company); *Scene 6* "Nothing More to Look Forward To" (Ako & Naii), "What's Wrong with Me?" (Eve); *Scene 7* "Something Big" (Kwamina & Company), "Ordinary People" (Eve & Kwamina); *Scene 8* "Mammy Traders" (dance): GIRL WITH PARASOL: Glory Van Scott; ADMIRERS: Charles Moore & Zebedee Collins; Dancers; *Scene 9* "A Man Can Have No Choice" (Obitsebi); *Scene 10* "What Happened to Me Tonight?" (Eve). *Act II: Scene 1* "Naii's Nuptial Dance" (Naii, Hope Clarke, Company), "One Wife" (Mammy Trader, Alla, Issa Arnal, Victoria Harrison, Lee Hooper, Mary Louise, Helen Phillips, Dancers), "Nothing More to Look Forward To" (reprise) (Naii); *Scene 2* "Something Big" (reprise) (Company), "Another Time, Another Place" (Eve); *Scene 3*; *Scene 4*; *Scene 5* Fetish (dance) (Obitsebi): PRIESTS: Zebedee Collins, Frank Glass, Charles Moore, Mike Quashie, Charles Queenan, Philip Stamps [Note: this dance number replaced "I'm Seeing Rainbows" before Broadway].

Broadway reviews were so-so. The voodoo drummer in the show led a ritual backstage designed to kill the critics (it didn't work). Various things killed this show — a weak book, a formula love story, and the fact that 1961 audiences were not prepared to accept such a relationship between a white woman and a black man. The show received Tony Nominations for composer, choreography, and costumes.

La Cage aux Folles see **101** and **102**

La Grosse Valise see **272**

La Plume de Ma Tante see **553**

La Strada see **662**

383. *A Lady Says Yes*

His potency as a prospective lover having been questioned because of the old Florentine superstition that a man whose nose is repaired surgically will suffer in other anatomical areas, Caufield, a young naval officer, dreams on the operating table that he goes back to Venice and China in 1545 to prove the validity of his assertions that he is physically all right. This he does to the satisfaction of Licetta, a courtesan. When he returns to consciousness he wins Ghisella, the hospital nurse. The show featured "thirty lovely ladies of fashion and passion."

Before Broadway. Originally called *A Lady of?* Clayton Ashley was really Dr. Maxwell Maltz, a New York plastic surgeon/playwright (he would try other New York plays later in his career, using his real name). For this musical he supplied most of the money. J.J. Shubert replaced Edgar MacGregor as director. Arthur Gershwin was George and Ira's younger brother, in his only professional outing. This was the stage debut of Carole Landis, blonde movie goddess. Jacqueline Susann later became a writer.

The Broadway Run. BROADHURST THEATRE, 1/10/45–3/25/45. 87 PERFORMANCES. PRESENTED BY J.J. Shubert, in association with Clayton Ashley; MUSIC: Fred Spielman & Arthur Gershwin; LYRICS: Stanley Adams; BOOK: Clayton Ashley; DIRECTOR: J.J. Shubert; CHOREOGRAPHER: Boots McKenna; CHOREOGRAPHY FOR BALLETS: Natalie Kamarova; SETS: Watson Barratt; COSTUMES: Lou Eisele; LIGHTING: William Thomas; MUSICAL DIRECTOR: Ving Merlin; ARRANGEMENTS: Irving Riskin, Paul Shelley, Ralph Lane, Frank Denning, Ving Merlin; PRESS: C.P. Greneker; COMPANY MANAGER: George Oshrin; STAGE MANAGER: Arthur Mayberry; ASSISTANT STAGE MANAGER: J. Edgar Joseph. *Cast:* 1945: 1ST NURSE: Helene Le Berthon (17); LICETTA: Sue Ryan (2); 2ND NURSE: Jackson Jordan (18); 3RD NURSE: Blanche Grady (16); DOCTOR: Jack Albertson (14); SCAPINO: Bobby Morris (4); GHISELLA: Carole Landis (1); CHRISTINE: Christine Ayres (3); HILDEGARDE: Jacqueline Susann (6); LT ANTHONY CAUFIELD, USNR: Arthur Maxwell (5); DR. GASPARE: Earl McDonald (12); ISABELLA: Martha King (7); CAPTAIN GORDON: Pittman Corry (8). 1545: CAPTAIN DESIRI: Pittman Corry (8); FRANCESCA: Helene Le Berthon (17); ROSA: Blanche Grady (16); CARMELA: Jackson Jordan (18); DR. BARTOLI: Jack Albertson (14); ISABELLA: Martha King (7); SCAPINO: Bobby Morris (4); ANTHONY GASPARE: Arthur Maxwell (5); CHRISTINE: Christine Ayres (3); HILDEGARDE: Jacqueline Susann (6); LICETTA: Sue Ryan (2); GASPARE: Earl McDonald (12); KILLER PEPOLI: Fred Catania (15); SECOND: Al Klein (13); PANTALOON: Steve Mills (10); GHISELLA: Carole Landis (1); PAGE BOY: Francelia Schmidt (19); LADIES OF THE ENSEMBLE: Maika Beranova, Doris Brent, Jan Brooks, Jane Cleaveland, Betty Greene, Lola Kendrick, Marguerite Kimball, Pat Leslie, Candace Montgomery, Cecilia Nielsen, Shirley Norman, Olivia Russell, Exilona Savre, Fredi Sears, Tiigra, Eileen K. Upton; DANCERS: Lucas Aco, Jack Allen, Peyton Blowe, Corbett Booth, Bunnie Brady, Fena Cella, Madeleine Detry, Dick Hayes, Sheila Herman, Albertina Horstmann, Jacqueline Jones, Jacqueline Karsh, Carol Keyser, Virginia Lee, Patricia Leith, Jeanne Lewis, Elaine Meredith, Eddie Miller, Cammy O'Brien, Joseph O. Paz, Susan Pearce, Desiree Rockafellow, Francelia Schmidt, Helen Schmidt, Alice Swanson, Eddie Wells; ALSO WITH: Tatiana Grantzeva (9), Ronnie Cunningham (11). *Prologue*: Time: the year 1945; *Scene 1* Waiting room of a hospital: Opening Chorus — "Viva Vitamins" (sung & danced by the Ensemble); *Scene 2* The operating room: A Lesson in Terpsichore (Christine & Scapino). *Act I*: Time: the year 1545: *Scene 1* A street in Venice: "You're the Lord of Any Manor" (sung & danced by the Ensemble), "Take My Heart with You" (sung by Isabella & Anthony; danced by Pittman Corry, Tatiana Grantzeva, Ensemble), "Without a Caress" (Ghisella & Ladies of the Ensemble), "I Wonder Why You Wander" (Licetta, Scapino, Ensemble), "I Don't Care What They Say About Me" (Anthony & Ensemble), "A Hop, a Skip, a Jump, a Look" (Messrs Allen, Blowe, Aco, Booth, Miller, Wells as the Judges); *Scene 2* Ghisella's bedroom: "A Pillow for His Royal Head" (sung by the Six Chambermaids — Misses Cella, Schmidt, Schmidt [sic], Swanson, Meredith, Lee) (danced by Ronnie Cunningham), Dance (Christine Ayres), "Don't Wake Them up Too Soon" (Ghisella & Ladies of the Ensemble), Finaletto (Entire Company).

Act II: Time: the year 1545: *Scene 1* Street in Venice: Opening—Carnival Dance (Pittman Corry, Ronnie Cunningham, Ensemble), "You're More than a Name and an Address" (Ghisella & Anthony), "Brooklyn, U.S.A." (by Will Morrissey) (Licetta) [the show-stopper]; *Scene 2* Garden of the Emperor of China: Chinese Ballet (m: Georges F. Kamaroff): BOY: Pittman Corry; PRINCESS: Tatiana Grantzeva; EMPEROR: Lucas Aco; SLAVE GIRL: Virginia Lee; EXECUTIONER: Al Klein; GONG GIRLS: Francelia Schmidt, Helen Schmidt, Alice Swanson; MONKEYS: Bunnie Brady, Jeanne Lewis, Patricia Leith; COMMENTATOR: Bobby Morris; "I'm Setting My Cap for a Throne" (Ghisella); *Scene 3* Hospital laboratory. Time: the year 1945: "Leave Us Let Things Alone Like They Was" (m: Harold Cohen; l: Bud Burton) (Licetta); *Scene 4* Cannibal Club: "It's the Girl Every Time, It's the Girl" (Anthony & Ladies of the Ensemble); *Scene 5* A garden party, Washington, DC: "You're More than a Name and an Address" (reprise) (Ghisella & Anthony), Finale (Entire Company).

Critics mercilessly panned it.

384. *Laffing Room Only*

A vaudeville revue. Being Olsen & Johnson it had a lot of zaniness and pre-curtain activity. On stage there was even more. Mrs. Roosevelt was caricaturized, and not kindly (ugly mask), as was Tom Dewey, gangbusting New York Governor. The "Harvey" gags (about a rabbit) were current, rampant, and not all that funny. A sailor trying to cross-dress, a pianist with boxing gloves, midgets dressed as babies, and stooges in boxes, dirty jokes and gags (drooping rifles coming to attention again at the sight of a near naked woman), Rodin's "Thinker" on the toilet; seltzer siphons.

Before Broadway. Al Dubin started to write these songs but became ill, and they were finished by Burton Lane.

The Broadway Run. WINTER GARDEN THEATRE, 12/23/44–7/14/45. 232 PERFORMANCES. PRESENTED BY the Messrs Shubert, with Ole Olsen & Chic Johnson; MUSIC/LYRICS: Burton Lane; BOOK: Olsen & Johnson, Eugene Conrad; DIRECTOR: John Murray Anderson; ASSISTANT TO JOHN MURRAY ANDERSON: Arny St. Subber; COMEDY DIRECTOR: Edward Cline; GENERAL DIRECTOR FOR OLSEN & JOHNSON: David Murray; STAGE DIRECTOR: Dennis Murray; CHOREOGRAPHER: Robert Alton; SETS: Stewart Chaney; ASSISTANT TO STEWART CHANEY: Peggy Clark; COSTUMES: Billy Livingston; MUSICAL DIRECTOR: John McManus; ARRANGEMENTS FOR THE GLEE CLUB: Penn Davenport, Ford Ringwald, Robert Shaw; PRESS: C.P. Greneker & Stanley Seiden; PRODUCTION SUPERVISOR: Harry Kaufman; COMPANY MANAGER: George Leffler; STAGE MANAGER: Henning Irgens; ASSISTANT STAGE MANAGER: Cliff Crist. *Before the Show*: IN THE LOBBY: Dippy Diers, Billy (i.e. Willie) West (4), Harry Burns (17); IN THE AUDIENCE: Frank Libuse (2); Overture: THE CONDUCTOR: Frank Libuse (2); STAGE MANAGER: Chas. Senna (21); COMPANY MANAGER: Fred Peters. *Act I*: *Scene 1* The Russian Art Players: ANNA: Catherine Johnson (27); SONYA: Mary La Roche; COUNT DMITRI RESLUVSKY: Robert Breton (15); PRINCE VASILOFF: Bruce Evans (14); *Scene 2* "Hooray for Anywhere." Sung by Pat Brewster (10) & The Glee Club (12) (Lewis Appleton, George Beach, Gerard Bercier, Gene Bone, Francis Cooke, Ruth Cottingham, Burke Esaias, John Ferguson, Jerry Gilbert, Johanna Gillman, Betty Gilpatrick, James Kovach, Allan Leonard, Jocelyn McIntyre, Roger Miller, Fred Peters, Andrew Ratousheff, Roy Russell, Edward Sanders, Otto Simanek, Tommy Thompson). Danced by Frances Henderson (24) & Kenny Buffett (23), with Ray Arnett, May Block, Forrest Bonshire, Jean Bortz, Ronny Chetwood, Lillian Cross, Dotty Dee, Norman Drew, Eloise Farmer, Virginia Gorski, Gae Hess, Penny Holt, Gretchen Houser, Marjorie Johnstone, Lee Joyce, Elana Keller, Eleanor Leaman, Patricia Lenn, Jennie Lewis, J.C. McCord, Marcia Maier, Kenneth Peterson, Jack Pierce, Budd Rogers, Herbert Ross, June Walker, Susan West, Doris York; *Scene 3* Olsen & Johnson (1) ✻; *Scene 4* The White House: GUESTS & TOURISTS: Frank Libuse (2), Margot Brander (6), Pat Brewster (10), Charles O'Donnell, Joe Young (20), Shannon Dean (26), Charles Senna (21), Harry

Burns (17), Stanley Stevens, Ernie D'Amato (22), Billy Young (19), Jean Moorhead (25), Penny Edwards (18), Bruce Evans, Frances Henderson (24), Betty Gilpatrick, Doris York, Lee Joyce, and Olsen & Johnson (1) ✻; *Scene 5* "Go Down to Boston Harbor." Ballet mus: Alan Moran. Sung by Betty Garrett (3). Danced by Kathryn Lee (9), William Archibald (8), J.C. McCord. BRITISH SOLDIERS: Norman Drew, Herbert Ross, Ronny Chetwood, Kenneth Peterson; CONSPIRATORS: Elana Keller & J.C. McCord; GIRL PATRIOTS: Gae Hess, Marcia Maier, Lillian Cross, Eleanor Leaman, Eloise Farmer, Corps de Ballet; GENERAL DUQUESNE: Chic Johnson (1) ✻; *Scene 6* The Russian Art Players: COLONEL: Bruce Evans (14); FIRING SQUAD: Francis Cooke, John Ferguson, Jerry Gilbert; *Scene 7* "The Fakir Dance" (Mata & Hari) (5); *Scene 8* An apartment in 1890: REAL ESTATE AGENT: Ole Olsen (1) ✻; MR. TENANT: Chic Johnson (1) ✻; MRS. TENANT: Ethel Owen (7); MINER: Frank Libuse (2); ALSO WITH: Stanley Stevens, Gus Stevens, John Stevens, Dippy Diers, Jennie Lewis, Andrew Ratousheff, Harry Burns (17), Billy Young (19), Susan West, Bruce Evans (14), Shannon Dean (26), Pat Brewster (10), Charles Senna (21), Ted McGinty (Willie West's dummy), Eddie Vincent with Chico & Coco; *Scene 9* Moments Musicals: HARPIST: Frank Libuse (2); SOPRANO: Margot Brander (6); FLUTIST: Tom McKee (28); CELLIST: Sam Kramer (28) [McKee & Kramer were a team]; *Scene 10* "Stop That Dancing" [the hit]. Sung by Betty Garrett (3). THE SAILOR: William Archibald (8); IN CENTRAL PARK: Penny Holt & Jack Pierce; ON BROADWAY: Eleanor Leaman, Ronny Chetwood, Lillian Cross, Herbert Ross; IN GREENWICH VILLAGE: Frances Henderson, Forrest Bonshire, Gae Hess, J.C. McCord, Marcia Maier; AT *El Morocco*: Penny Edwards (18), Kenny Buffett (23), Marjorie Johnstone, Virginia Gorski, May Block, Dotty Dee; IN HARLEM: Gretchen Houser, Ken Peterson, Ray Arnett, Lee Joyce, The Glee Club & The Corps de Ballet; *Scene 11* Pocatello, Idaho [Ole Olsen (1) ✻, Joe Young (20), Chic Johnson (1) ✻]; *Scene 12* The Russian Art Players; *Scene 13* The Ghost Train (A Night on a Union Pacific Pullman). With Olsen & Johnson (1) ✻, and O'Donnell Blair (13), Ernie D'Amato (22), Billy (i.e. Willie) West (4), Fred Peters, Tom McKee (28), Virginia Barrett (29), Shannon Dean (26), Tom Fletcher, Billy Young (19), Joe Young (20), Jean Moorhead (25), Penny Edwards (18), Susan West, Harry Burns (17), Jennie Lewis, Frances Henderson (24), Pat Brewster (10), Ethel Owen (7), Charles Senna (21), Roy Russell; *Scene 14* "This is as Far as I Go." Sung by Betty Garrett (3), and Ray Arnett, Forrest Bonshire, Ronny Chetwood, Norman Drew, Kenneth Peterson, Jack Pierce, J.C. McCord, Budd Rogers, Herbert Ross; *Scene 15* Willie West & McGinty (4) (ventriloquist); *Scene 16* Stanley Stevens & "Big Boy;" *Scene 17* "Fussin', Feudin' and Fightin'" [the hit song "Feudin' and Fightin'" had lyrics co-written by Al Dubin. Sung by Pat Brewster (10) & The Glee Club (12), and re-introduced into the pop charts in 1947]. Danced by Kathryn Lee (9), William Archibald (8), The Corps de Ballet. MOTHER HATFIELD: Eleanor Leaman; GRANDMOTHER: June Walker; DAUGHTER: Kathryn Lee (9); FATHER: Herbert Ross; UNCLES: Ronny Chetwood & Norman Drew; McCOY SON: William Archibald (8); MAW McCOY: Ethel Owen (7); CHILD: Jean Moorhead (25); NEIGHBORS: Stanley Stevens, Virginia Barrett (29), Billy Young (19); JUDGE: Bruce Evans (14); BRIDEGROOM: Ole Olsen (1) ✻; PAW: Harry Burns (17); BRIDE: Chic Johnson (1) ✻; SONS: Robert Breton (15), Charles Senna (21), Ernie D'Amato (22). "Gotta Get Joy:" The Entire Company. *Intermission*: IN THE BOX: Frank Libuse (2), and Margot Brander (6), Virginia Barrett (29), Andrew Ratousheff, Dippy Diers. *Act II*: *Scene 1* "Got That Good Time Feelin'" (Mississippi). Sung by Ida James (11) & Laffing Room Only Glee Club (12). Danced by: THE BALLERINA: Kathryn Lee (9); THE BEAU: Kenny Buffett (23); THE SUITOR: Ronny Chetwood; And the Corps de Ballet; *Scene 2* The Piano Movers [Olsen & Johnson (1) ✻, O'Donnell Blair (13)]; *Scene 3* Lou Wills Jr. (16); *Scene 4* "Sunny California." Sung by Betty Garrett (3). Danced by: THE HOLLYWOOD STAR: Penny Edwards (18); THE HOLLYWOOD PRODUCER: William Archibald (8); THE CAMERAMAN: Lewis Appleton; CHAUFFEUR: Rhythm Red; AND: The Ensemble, The Olympic Team, Mata & Hari; *Scene 5* In a radio station: A RADIO ANNOUNCER: Ole Olsen (1) ✻; The Glee Club; THE SOUND MAN: Chic Johnson (1) ✻; AND: Ethel Owen (7), Billy Young (19), Joe Young (20), Charles Senna (21), Jean Moorhead (25), Shannon Dean, Jennie Lewis, Andrew Ratousheff, Tom Fletcher, Susan West, Virginia Barrett (29), Bruce Evans (14), Tom McKee (28), Gretchen Houser; *Scene 6* "The Hellzapoppin

Polka." Danced by Virginia Barrett 29), Ruth Cottingham, Jean Moorhead (25), Doris York, Shannon Dean (26), Betty Gilpatrick, Johanna Gillman, Mary La Roche, Jocelyn McIntyre, Penny Holt, Susan West, Jennie Lewis, Frances Henderson (24); *Scene 7* "The Steps of the Capitol." Sung by Betty Garrett (3), Pat Brewster (10), The Glee Club (12).

Broadway reviews ranged from mediocre to dreadful. Audiences (some of them anyway) loved it.

385. *Late Nite Comic*

A love story, with a punch line. The showbiz ambitions of a comedian and a dancer. Set in New York and Las Vegas.

Before Broadway. This show originally ran at the American Musical Theatre, New London, Conn. Before Broadway Tony Stevens replaced Philip Rose as director, but was not credited.

The Broadway Run. RITZ THEATRE, 10/15/87–10/17/87. 16 previews. 4 PERFORMANCES. PRESENTED BY Rory Rosegarten; MUSIC/LYRICS: Brian Gari; BOOK: Allan Knee; DIRECTOR: Philip Rose; CHOREOGRAPHER: Dennis Dennehy; SETS: Clarke Dunham; COSTUMES: Gail Cooper-Hecht; LIGHTING: Ken Billington; SOUND: Abe Jacob; MUSICAL DIRECTOR: Gregory J. Dlugos; ORCHESTRATIONS: Larry Hochman; VOCAL & DANCE MUSIC ARRANGEMENTS: James Raitt; PRESS: Henry Luhrman Associates; CASTING: Lynda Watson; GENERAL MANAGEMENT: Frank Scardino Associates; PRODUCTION STAGE MANAGER: Mortimer Halpern; STAGE MANAGER: Brian A. Kaufman; ASSISTANT STAGE MANAGER: Lorna Littleway. *Cast:* DAVID ACKERMAN: Robert LuPone (1) ☆; CECIL: Patrick Hamilton; CLUB OWNERS: Kim Freshwater, Patrick Hamilton, Michael McAssey, Don Stitt; GABRIELLE: Teresa Tracy (2) ☆; CLARA: Susan Santoro; TANYA: Aja Major; JENNY: Lauren Goler; SUSAN: Pamela Blasetti; KRAZY KORN MC: Patrick Hamilton; DAVID'S ALTER EGO: Mason Roberts; BARTENDERS: Don Stitt & Mason Roberts; BUSBOY: Don Stitt; HOOKERS: Kim Freshwater, Pamela Blasetti, Lauren Goler, Judine Hawkins, Sharon Moore, Susan Santoro; METROPOLITAN BALLERINA: Sharon Moore; MALE DANCER: Mason Roberts; LAS VEGAS MC: Michael McAssey; VOICE OF GOD: Patrick Hamilton; DELILAH: Aja Major; NAT: Mason Roberts; MIKE: Michael McAssey; ENSEMBLE: Pamela Blasetti, Kim Freshwater, Lauren Goler, Patrick Hamilton, Judine Hawkins, Michael McAssey, Aja Major, Sharon Moore, Mason Roberts, Susan Santoro, Don Stitt. *Understudies*: David: Patrick Hamilton; Gabrielle: Susan Santoro. *Swings*: Danielle P. Connell & Barry Finkel. *Orchestra*: KEYBOARDS: Gregory J. Dlugos & Timothy Stella; REED # 1: Bill Meade; REED # 2: Alva Hunt; TRUMPET # 1: Francis Bonny; TRUMPET # 2: Laurence Etkin; FRENCH HORN: Peter Gordon; ELECTRIC BASS/GUITARS: Kevin Kuhn; CELLO: Bruce Wang; PERCUSSION: Ron Tierno. *Act I*: *Scene 1* A piano lounge: "Gabrielle" (David); *Scene 2* Comedy Clubs: "The Best in the Business" (David & Club Owners); *Scene 3* Streets of New York; *Scene 4* David's apartment: "Clara's Dancing School" (Gabrielle & Clara), "This Lady isn't Right for Me" (David, Tanya, Jenny, Susan, Gabrielle); *Scene 5* Streets of New York; *Scene 6* David's apartment; *Scene 7* Streets of New York: "Having Someone" (David & Club Owners); *Scene 8* David's apartment: "Stand-Up" (David); *Scene 9* Street of New York: "The Best in the Business" (reprise) (David); *Scene 10* Krazy Korn Klub: "Late Nite Comic" (David), "Stand-Up" (reprise) (David); *Scene 11* David's apartment: "It Had to Happen Sometime" (David & Gabrielle), "When I Am Movin'" (Gabrielle), "Think Big" (David & David's Alter Ego). *Act II*: *Scene 1* Mr. Ribs' Club; *Scene 2* A hookers' bar: "Relax with Me, Baby" (David, Bartender, Hookers); *Scene 3* Club dressing room; *Scene 4* Bloomingdale's; *Scene 5* Apartment stoop; *Scene 6* Metropolitan Opera House: "Dance" (David, Gabrielle, Ensemble); *Scene 7* Street of New York; *Scene 8* David's apartment; *Scene 9* The comedy circuit: "Late Nite Comic" (reprise) (David); *Scene 10* Las Vegas: "It's Such a Different World" (David Vegas Girls, Vegas Guys), "It Had to Happen Sometime" (reprise) (David & Gabrielle), "Gabrielle" (reprise)/"Yvonne" (David).

Reviews were terrible.

386. *Laugh Time*

The third in a series of vaudeville revue revivals sponsored by Fred Finklehoffe and Paul Small, the others being *Show Time* and *Big Time*, all originating on the West Coast, but *Big Time* not making it to New York.

The Broadway Run. SHUBERT THEATRE, 9/8/43–10/16/43; AMBASSADOR THEATRE, 10/17/43–11/20/43. Total of 126 PERFORMANCES. PRESENTED BY Paul Small & Fred Finklehoffe; MUSICAL DIRECTOR: Lou Forman; Reginald Beane accompanied Ethel Waters on piano. *Act I*: Frank Fay (1) (comedian & mc); Adriana & Charly (trampoline acrobats); Buck & Bubbles (i.e. Ford Lee Buck & John W. Bubbles) (comical dancers); The Bricklayers (Leonard Gautier's trained dog act); The Di Gatanos (Jane & Adam Di Gatano) (ballroom team). *Act II*: Bert Wheeler (3) (comedian) (the sandwich monologue); Ethel Waters (2) (singer): "Cabin in the Sky," "Happiness is a Thing Called Joe," "Am I Blue?," "Stormy Weather," "Heat Wave," "Dinah," "Taking a Chance on Love;" Lucienne & Ashour (apache dancers), Jerri Vance (contortionist). ALSO WITH: Warren Jackson.

The show got great reviews, even though the scenery had been lost coming from the West Coast. It did 12 shows a week, including five matinees and a show on Sunday.

387. *Leader of the Pack*

The life and songs of Ellie Greenwich, whose compositions for female singing groups were an entertainment fixture of the 1960s. Set here and now ... and in the days of beehives and 45s. No intermission.

Before Broadway. It first ran Off Broadway, at the BOTTOM LINE, 1/17/84. During Broadway previews Danny Herman & Jodi Moccia were added to the chorus. The cast then was (in order of appearance): ANGEL MORAN: Annie Golden; GUS: Dennis Bailey; HAROLD: Lon Hoyt; CANDY: Pattie Darcy; DARLENE: Darlene Love; YOUNG ELLIE, 1960s: Dinah Manoff; ROSIE: Zora Rasmussen; SHELLEY: Barbara Yeager; MICKEY: Jasmine Guy; JEFF: Patrick Cassidy; DJ VOICE: Peter Neptune; GINA: Gina Taylor; WAITRESS: Jasmine Guy; LOUNGE SINGER: Pattie Darcy; ELLIE, 1980s: Ellie Greenwich. Back then there were 2 acts (or "sides"); the scene-by-scene breakdown was (the songwriters, of course, are the same, and will not be repeated here, unless the song is not in the song-list above. Likewise, with the characters performing the songs): *Side 1*: *1st Cut* Rehearsal/recording studio; 1980s: "Be My Baby" (Angel & Girls), "Wait 'til My Bobby Gets Home;" *2nd Cut* Levittown, New York; 1960s: "A ... My Name is Ellie," "Jivette Boogie Beat;" *3rd Cut* Brill Building; 1960s: "Why Do Lovers Break Each Other's Hearts?;" *4th Cut* Office; 1960s: "Today I Met the Boy I'm Gonna Marry" (Darlene & Company), "I Want to Love Him So Bad," "And Then He Kissed Me;" *5th Cut* Lovers Lane; 1960s: "Hanky Panky;" *6th Cut* Brill Building; 1960s; *7th Cut* Wedding Scene; 1960s: "Not Too Young (to Get Married)," "Chapel of Love;" *8th Cut* A subway; 1960s: "He's the Kind of Boy You Can't Forget" (Barry) (Jeff, Young Ellie, Company); *9th Cut* Brill Building; 1960s; *10th Cut* Rehearsal/recording studio; 1980s: "Baby I Love You" (Angel & Girls), "Leader of the Pack" (Angel & Girls). *Side 2*: *1st Cut* Rehearsal/recording studio; 1980s: "Keep it Confidential," "A ... My Name is Angel" (written by Ellie Greenwich alone) (Angel & Voice of Ellie); *2nd Cut* Jeff & Ellie's apartment; *3rd Cut* B.M.I. Awards; 1960s: "Dance Craze Number" (Kent) (Girls & Guys), "Do Wah Diddy" (Jeff & Guys), "People Say" (Barry) (Young Ellie); *4th Cut* Chez Smooch; 1960s: "Look of Love," "Look of Love" Pas de Deux (danced by Keith McDaniel & Shirley Black-Brown); *5th Cut* Ellie's apartment; 1960s: "Christmas — Baby Please Come Home;" *6th Cut* Brill Building; 1960s: "Rock of Rages;" *7th Cut* Rehearsal/recording studio; 1980s: "I Can Hear Music" (Angel, Harold, Company), "Da Doo Ron Ron," "What a Guy," "Maybe I Know" (Ellie, Angel, Darlene, Company), "We're Gonnna Make It (After All)" (Ellie, Angel, Gus, Darlene, Company), "River Deep, Mountain High."

The Broadway Run. AMBASSADOR THEATRE, 4/8/85–7/21/85. 52 previews from 3/11/85. 120 PERFORMANCES. PRESENTED BY The Pack (Elizabeth I. McCann, Nelle Nugent, Francine LeFrak, Clive Davis, John Hart Associates, Rodger H. Hess, Richard Kagan); MUSIC/LYRICS: Ellie Greenwich & Friends (George "Shadow" Morton, Jeff Barry, Phil Spector, Tony Powers, Jeff Kent, Ellen Foley); LINER NOTES (i.e. book): Anne Beatts; ADDITIONAL MATERIAL: Jack Heifner; BASED ON an original concept by Melanie Mintz; DIRECTOR/CHOREOGRAPHER: Michael Peters; SETS: Tony Walton; COSTUMES: Robert de Mora; LIGHTING: Pamela Cooper; SOUND: Abe Jacob; MUSICAL DIRECTOR/MUSICAL ADAPTATIONS: Jimmy Vivino; VOCAL ARRANGEMENTS: Marc Shaiman; DANCE MUSIC ARRANGEMENTS: Timothy Graphenreed; CAST RECORDING on Elektra Music Records; PRESS: Solters/Roskin/Friedman; CASTING: Julie Hughes & Barry Moss; GENERAL MANAGEMENT: McCann & Nugent; COMPANY MANAGER: Susan Gustafson; PRODUCTION STAGE MANAGER: William Dodds; STAGE MANAGER: Kenneth Hanson; ASSISTANT STAGE MANAGER: Christopher Gregory. *Cast:* DARLENE LOVE: Darlene Love (6); ANNIE GOLDEN: Annie Golden (5); YOUNG ELLIE GREENWICH (1960s): Dinah Manoff (2); ROSIE, ELLIE'S MOTHER: Zora Rasmussen; SHELLEY: Barbara Yeager; MICKEY: Jasmine Guy; JEFF BARRY: Patrick Cassidy (3); GUS SHARKEY: Dennis Bailey (4); D.J. VOICE: Peter Neptune; WAITRESS: Jasmine Guy; LOUNGE SINGER: Pattie Darcy; DANCE COUPLE: Shirley Black-Brown & Keith McDaniel; GINA: Gina Taylor; ELLIE GREENWICH (1980s): Ellie Greenwich (1); GIRLS & GUYS: Shirley Black-Brown, Pattie Darcy, Christopher Gregory, Jasmine Guy, Danny Herman, Lon Hoyt, Keith McDaniel, Jodi Moccia, Peter Neptune, Zora Rasmussen, Joey Sheck, Gina Taylor, Barbara Yeager. *Understudies:* Young Ellie: Pattie Darcy; Jeff: Peter Neptune; Ellie Greenwich: Zora Rasmussen; Gus: Joey Sheck; Annie: Jasmine Guy; Darlene: Gina Taylor. *Swings*: Lisa Grant & Kevyn Morrow. *Musicians*: GUITARS: Jimmy Vivino & William Washer; DRUMS: Leo Adamian; PIANO: Ed Alstrom; BASS: Dennis Espantman; TRUMPETS: Gary Guzio & Jeff Venho; SAXES: Artie Kaplan, Lennie Pickett, Jimmy Vivino; PERCUSSION: Frank Pagano; TROMBONE: Bob Smith; SYNTHESIZER: Daryl Waters. "Be My Baby" (Barry & Spector) (Annie & Girls), "Wait 'til My Bobby Gets Home" (Barry & Spector) (Darlene & Company), "A ... My Name is Ellie" (Young Ellie), "Jivette Boogie Beat" (Young Ellie, Shelley, Mickey), "Why Do Lovers Break Each Others Hearts" (Powers & Spector) (Darlene & Company), "Today I Met the Boy I'm Gonna Marry" (Powers & Spector) (Darlene & Company), "I Want to Love Him So Bad" (Barry & Spector) (Young Ellie & Girls), "Do Wah Diddy" (Barry) (Jeff), "And Then He Kissed Me" (Barry & Spector) (Young Ellie & Girls), "Hanky Panky" (Barry) (Jeff & Guys), "Not Too Young (to Get Married)" (Barry & Spector) (Darlene & Girls), "Chapel of Love" (Barry & Spector) (Company), "Baby I Love You" (Barry & Spector) (Annie & Girls), "Leader of the Pack" (Barry & Morton) (Annie & Company), "Look of Love" (Barry) (Pattie), "Christmas — Baby, Please Come Home" (Barry & Spector) (Darlene & Girls), "I Can Hear Music" (Barry & Spector) (Jeff, Annie, Pattie, Keith), "Rock of Rages" (Kent) (Young Ellie), "Keep it Confidential" (Kent & Foley) (Gina & Company), "Da Doo Ron Ron" (Barry & Spector) (Ellie & Company), "What a Guy" (Barry & Spector) (Ellie & Company), "Maybe I Know" (Barry) (Ellie, Darlene, Annie, Girls), "River Deep, Mountain High" (Barry & Spector) (Darlene & Company), "We're Gonna Make It (After All)" (Ellie, Darlene, Annie, Company).

Note: All numbers are by Ellie Greenwich. Her co-authors (only last names are given) are in parentheses after the song titles (for a list of these authors, see credits). Sometimes there is no co-author, in which case no writer name appears by the song title.

Reviews were disastrous. The show received a Tony nomination for musical.

After Broadway. TOURING REVIVAL. Opened on 3/16/01, at Wilmington, Del. Originally a book musical, this revised version was (like *Smokey Joe's Café*) a revue, or rather a song-cycle, instead of in story form. There were three new songs: "If You Loved Me Once," "The First Time," and "The Sunshine After the Rain." DIRECTOR: Kurt Stamm; CHOREOGRAPHER: Scott Wise; SETS: Michael Anania. *Cast:* Brenda Braxton, Jewel Thomkins (*Mary Wilson*, of the Supremes, 4/14/01–4/29/01, *Jewel Thomkins* from 5/2/01), Shoshana Bean, Joe Machota, Ric Ryder, David Josefsberg.

388. *Legs Diamond*

Jack "Legs" Diamond is a Prohibition-era Chicago hoofer who becomes a gangster in order to help his entrée into showbiz. Set in and around New York in the 1920s.

Before Broadway. Peter Allen and Charles Suppon began work on the musical in 1983. It was workshopped in 1987. The libretto was much more serious at that stage. DIRECTOR: Robert Allan Ackerman. At that point Harvey Fierstein was brought in to write a new script (Charles Suppon retained credit). Pre-Broadway tryouts were impossible because of the needlessly complex sets. In 8/88 choreographer Michael Shawn was fired, and replaced by Alan Johnson. Mr. Shawn later took the producers to court, claiming he was fired because he had AIDS. They settled out of court on 1/6/90, for $175,000, and Mr. Shawn died in 4/90. Broadway previews were postponed several times, finally beginning in late 10/88, and going for 8 weeks, with enormously bad publicity. Within a week of the start of previews, the role of Legs' wife, Alice (played by Christine Andreas) was cut, then Legs' brother, Eddie (played by Bob Stillman) was dropped.

The Broadway Run. MARK HELLINGER THEATRE, 12/26/88–2/19/89. 72 previews. 64 PERFORMANCES. PRESENTED BY James M. Nederlander, James L. Nederlander, Arthur Rubin, The Entertainment Group, and George M. Steinbrenner III, in association with Jonathan Farkas & Marvin A. Krauss; MUSIC/LYRICS: Peter Allen; BOOK: Harvey Fierstein & Charles Suppon; BASED UPON the 1960 Warner Brothers movie *The Rise and Fall of Legs Diamond*; DIRECTOR: Robert Allan Ackerman; CHOREOGRAPHER: Alan Johnson; SETS: David Mitchell; COSTUMES: Willa Kim; LIGHTING: Jules Fisher; SOUND: Peter J. Fitzgerald; BLACK ART EFFECTS CONSULTANT: Ted Shapiro; MUSICAL DIRECTOR/VOCAL ARRANGEMENTS: Eric Stern; ORCHESTRATIONS: Michael Starobin; DANCE MUSIC ARRANGEMENTS: Mark Hummel; PRESS: Shirley Herz Associates; CASTING: Meg Simon/Fran Kumin; ASSOCIATE PRODUCER: Kathleen Raitt; GENERAL MANAGEMENT: Marvin A. Krauss Associates; COMPANY MANAGER: Nina Skriloff; PRODUCTION STAGE MANAGER: Peter B. Mumford; STAGE MANAGER: Gary M. Zabinski; ASSISTANT STAGE MANAGER: Robert B. Gould. *Cast:* JACK "LEGS" DIAMOND: Peter Allen (1) ☆; CONVICTS: Adrian Bailey, Quin Baird, Frank Cava, Norman Wendall Kauahi, Bobby Moya, Paul Nunes, Keith Tyrone; PRISON GUARDS: Stephen Bourneuf & Rick Manning; MADGE: Brenda Braxton (9); CIGARETTE GIRL: Deanna Dys; BONES: Christian Kauffmann (6); AUGIE: Raymond Serra (5); KIKI ROBERTS: Randall Edwards (3); DEVANE: Pat McNamara (7); HOTSY TOTSY ANNOUNCER: Mike O'Carroll; FLO: Julie Wilson (2); HOTSY TOTSY GIRLS: Carol Ann Baxter, Colleen Dunn, Deanna Dys, Gwendolyn Miller, Wendy Waring; MORAN: Jim Fyfe (8); ARNOLD ROTHSTEIN (A.R.): Joe Silver (4); TROPICABANA ANNOUNCER: James Brandt; TUXEDO DANCERS: Stephen Bourneuf, Jonathan Cerullo, K. Craig Innes, Kevin Weldon; LATIN DANCERS: Adrian Bailey, Frank Cava, Norman Wendall Kauahi, Bobby Moya, Paul Nunes, Keith Tyrone; CHAMPAGNE GIRLS: Carol Ann Baxter & Gwendolyn Miller; SHOWGIRLS: Colleen Dunn & Wendy Waring; GANGSTERS: Quin Baird, Stephen Bourneuf, James Brandt, Jonathan Cerullo, Rick Manning, Bobby Moya, Paul Nunes, Mike O'Carroll; TAXI DANCERS: Frank Cava, K. Craig Innes, Bobby Moya; BOYS FROM BAY RIDGE: Adrian Bailey, Rick Manning, Bobby Moya; MOURNER: Ruth Gottschall; BURLESQUE WOMEN: Gwendolyn Miller & Wendy Waring; BARBER: Mike O'Carroll; CHINESE WAITER: Norman Wendall Kauahi; A.R.'S GANG: Adrian Bailey, Quin Baird, Jonathan Cerullo, Rick Manning, Bobby Moya; JACK'S GANG: Stephen Bourneuf, Frank Cava, K. Craig Innes, Norman Wendall Kauahi, Paul Nunes, Keith Tyrone; POLICEMAN: Paul Nunes; JACK DIAMOND'S SECRETARY: Shelley Wald; FBI MEN: James Brandt & Rick Manning. *Standby*: Legs: Larry Kert. *Understudies:* Flo: Ruth Gottschall; Kiki: Colleen Dunn; A.R./Devane: Mike O'Carroll; Bones: Adrian Bailey; Moran: Frank Cava. *Swings*: Dan O'Grady, Jennifer Rymer, Steven Scionti. *Orchestra*: 1ST TRUMPET: James Sedlar; TRUMPETS: James Hynes & Phil Granger; TROMBONES: Porter Poindexter & James Miller; FRENCH HORN: Russ Rizner; CLARINETS: John Purcell & Charles Millard; FLUTE: Lou Cortelezzi; OBOE: Peter Angelo; BARITONE SAX: Joseph Grimaldi; SYNTHESIZERS: Ronald Melrose & Tim Stella; BASS: Mark Berger; GUITAR: Larry Saltzman;

DRUMS: Glenn Rhian & Bruce Doctor; CONCERTMASTER: Bernard Zeller; VIOLINS: Kathy Livolsi, Al Cavaliere, Frank Wang; VIOLAS: Susan Follari & Richard Spencer; CELLI: Bruce Want & Marisol Espada. *Act 1*: Overture (Orchestra); *Scene 1* Pennsylvania State Prison; 1921: "When I Get My Name in Lights" (Jack, Convicts, Ensemble); *Scene 2* Pennsylvania Station, New York City; *Scene 3* The Hotsy Totsy Club and Grill: "Speakeasy" (Ensemble), "Applause" (Flo & Hotsy Totsy Girls), "Knockers" (Jack & Hotsy Totsy Girls); *Scene 4* The back room of the Hotsy Totsy Club; *Scene 5* Hotsy Totsy Club alley; *Scene 6* The stage of the Tropicabana: "I Was Made for Champagne" (Kiki & Tropicabana Dancers), "Tropicabana Rhumba" (Jack & Kiki); *Scene 7* Times Square: "Sure Thing, Baby" (Jack); *Scene 8* The backroom of the Hotsy Totsy Club: "Speakeasy Christmas" (Hotsy Totsy Dancers), "Charge it to A.R." (A.R., Augie, Moran, Bones, Gangsters); *Scene 9* Flo's office: "Only an Older Woman" (Jack & Flo); *Scene 10* The Hotsy Totsy Club and Grill: "Taxi Dancers' Tango" (Jack & Ensemble); *Scene 11* Taxi dancers' dressing room; *Scene 12* Around New York: "Only Steal from Thieves" (Jack, Kiki, Gangsters); *Scene 13* The Hotsy Totsy Club and Grill: "When I Get My Name in Lights" (reprise) (Jack & Company). *Act II*: Entr'acte (Orchestra); *Scene 1* A funeral parlor: "Cut of the Cards" (Jack & Company); *Scene 2* The streets of New York: "Gangland Chase" (Jack & Gangsters); *Scene 3* The Hotsy Totsy stage and the Tropicabana stage: "Now You See Me, Now You Don't" (Jack, Kiki, Ensemble); *Scene 4* The ladies' powder room of the Hotsy Totsy Club: "The Man Nobody Could Love" (Kiki, Flo, Madge); *Scene 5* The back room of the Hotsy Totsy Club; *Scene 6* The Hotsy Totsy stage: "The Music Went Out of My Life" (Flo); *Scene 7* The Diamond Building: "Say it isn't So" (Jack & Company); *Scene 8* The Hotsy Totsy Club and Grill: "All I Wanted Was the Dream" (Jack).

The show opened on Broadway to a huge advance sale, partly because it was just about the only book musical of the season, certainly during that part of a terrible season for musicals. The show was panned and lost the Nederlanders $5 million. The Mark Hellinger became a church after this show. The production received Tony nominations for choreography, costumes, and for Julie Wilson.

389. *Lend an Ear*

An intimate musical revue. It opened as if its members were rehearsing the material about to come.

Before Broadway. It was first produced in 1941, at Carnegie Tech, Pittsburgh (where William Eythe was a theatre student), and subsequently in summer stock in Cohasset, Mass. Mr. Eythe tried to get it on to Broadway, but the war, and his movie career, interrupted its progress. It ultimately arrived on Broadway, in a much-expanded form, via Los Angeles (where it was produced by Mr. Eythe for $30,000 at Las Palmas Theatre). There were then 21 in the cast. This was Gower Champion's first directing/choreographing job, and Carol Channing's Broadway debut.

The Broadway Run. NATIONAL THEATRE, 12/16/48–2/19/49; BROADHURST THEATRE, 2/22/49–10/8/49; SHUBERT THEATRE, 10/10/49–10/29/49; MANSFIELD THEATRE, 10/31/49–1/21/50. Total of 460 PERFORMANCES. PRESENTED BY William R. Katzell, Franklin Gilbert, William Eythe; MUSIC/LYRICS/SKETCHES: Charles Gaynor; ADDITIONAL SKETCHES: Joseph Stein & Will Glickman; DIRECTOR/CHOREOGRAPHER: Gower Champion; BOOK DIRECTOR: Hal Gerson; ASSISTANT TO THE CHOREOGRAPHER: Marge Champion; SETS/COSTUMES/LIGHTING: Raoul Pene du Bois; MUSICAL DIRECTOR/ADDITIONAL ARRANGEMENTS: George Bauer; ORCHESTRATIONS: Clare Grundman; VOCAL ARRANGEMENTS: Dorothea Freitag; DUO PIANISTS: George Bauer & Dorothea Freitag; PRESS: Samuel J. Friedman, Lewis Harmon, Harvey Sabinson; GENERAL MANAGER: Michael Goldreyer; PRODUCTION STAGE MANAGER: David Kanter; STAGE MANAGER: Peter Lawrence; ASSISTANT STAGE MANAGER: Al Checco, *Raymond Thomas*. *Act I*: *Scene 1* "After Hours" (The Company); *Scene 2* "Give Your Heart a Chance (to Sing):" THE GIRL: Dorothy Babb; THE BOYS: Robert Dixon, Arthur Maxwell, Bob Herget, Tommy Morton, Bob Scheerer (5); *Scene 3* "Neurotic You and Psychopathic Me." Satirized psycho-analysts: THE NURSE: Lee Stacy; THE

PATIENT: Anne Renee Anderson; THE DOCTOR: William Eythe (1); *Scene 4* "I'm Not in Love:" THE BOSS WHO DICTATES: Arthur Maxwell; THE SECRETARY WHO SINGS: Yvonne Adair (3); THE BOSSES WHO DANCE: Gene Nelson (4), Tommy Morton, Bob Scheerer (5); *Scene 5* "Power of the Press." By Joseph Stein & Will Glickman. Satirizing gossip columnists: HUSBAND: George Hall; WIFE: Carol Channing (2); *Scene 6* "Friday Dancing Class." Waltzers Henry & The Girl fall in love: SUNG BY: Gloria Hamilton, Beverly Hosier, Jeanine Smith, Arthur Maxwell, Robert Dixon, Larry Stuart; HENRY JONES: Bob Scheerer (5); HIS MOTHER: Carol Channing (2); HIS FRIENDS: Al Checco & Bob Herget; MISS BRIDEY: Jenny Lou Law; THE GIRL: Dorothy Babb; THE DANCING CLASS: Lee Stacy, Antoinette Guhlke, Nancy Franklin (*Betty Low*), Gene Nelson (4), Bob Herget, Tommy Morton; *Scene 7* "Ballade" (sung by Anne Renee Anderson, with her musical instrument, the "twang"); *Scene 8* "When Someone You Love Loves You" [sung by Robert Dixon & Gloria Hamilton; danced by Antoinette Guhlke & Gene Nelson (4)]; *Scene 9* "The Missing Road Company:" ANNOUNCER: William Eythe (1). "The Gladiola Girl" (written in 1941); an encapsulated mini musical comedy of the mid–20s with flappers and lounge lizards on a Long Island estate where everyone dances the new sensation "The Old Yahoo Step." *Cast of characters:* ROSALIE: Gloria Hamilton; LARRY VAN PATTEN: William Eythe (1); GINGER O'TOOLE: Yvonne Adair (3); SKIDDY TYRES: George Hall; POLICEMAN: Bob Herget; GIRLS: Dorothy Babb, Anne Renee Anderson, Carol Channing (2), Lee Stacy; BOYS: Bob Scheerer (5), Al Checco, Tommy Morton, Arthur Maxwell. Act I: Scene: A garden in Bronxville: a/ "Join Us in a Cup of Tea (Boys)" (Boys & Girls); b/ "Where is the She for You?" (Larry & Girls); c/ "I'll Be True to You" (Rosalie & Larry); d/ "(Doin') The Old Yahoo Step" (Ginger & Chorus); e/ Finaletto (Ginger & Chorus). Act II: Scene: Skiddy's estate on Long Island: a/ Opening: "A Little Game of Tennis" (Boys & Girls); b/ "In Our Teeny Little Weeny Nest (for Two)" (Rosalie & Larry); c/ Finale (Full Company). *Act II*: *Scene 1* "Santo Domingo;" a tourist-eye spoof of a modern village in the West Indies, complete with gunfire. This number had been done straight in Pittsburgh in 1941. THE TRAVEL AGENT: Arthur Maxwell; THE TOURIST: Yvonne Adair (3); SANTO DOMINGANS: The Company; *Scene 2* "I'm on the Lookout" (sung by Gloria Hamilton); *Scene 3* "Three Little Queens of the Silver Screen" (spoof of Mary Pickford, Theda Bara, and *The Perils of Pauline*) [sung by Lee Stacy, Anne Renee Anderson, Carol Channing (2)]; *Scene 4* "Molly O'Reilly" [danced by Bob Scheerer (5) & Dorothy Babb; sung by Jeanine Smith, Gloria Hamilton, Beverly Hosier, Robert Dixon, Arthur Maxwell, Larry Stuart; *Scene 5* "All the World's." Husband & wife moviegoers give impressions of a Laurence Olivier film): ANNOUNCER: Arthur Maxwell; MR. PLAYGOER: William Eythe (1); MRS. PLAYGOER: Carol Channing (2); A BARTENDER: George Hall; *Scene 6* "Who Hit Me?" [sung by Yvonne Adair (3); danced by Gene Nelson (4)]; *Scene 7* "Words without Song." A third-rate opera company has to speak its lines because it can't afford orchestral accompaniment: ANNOUNCER: Arthur Maxwell; THE COUNTESS: Carol Channing (2); MATHILDA: Anne Renee Anderson; ALBERTO: George Hall; THE COUNT: William Eythe (1); THE CHORUS: Antoinette Guhlke, Lee Stacy, Beverly Hosier, Jenny Lou Law, Bob Herget, Al Checco, Tommy Morton, Larry Stuart; *Scene 8* Finale (The Company).

It opened on Broadway to raves, and won a Tony Award and a Donaldson Award, both for choreography. Yvonne Adair also won a Donaldson for best female debut. She and Carol Channing both went on to lead the cast of *Gentlemen Prefer Blondes*, a year later.

After Broadway. RENATA THEATRE, NYC. It closed on 12/6/59, after 94 PERFORMANCES. The program was basically same as the original. PRESENTED BY Jenny Lou Law & Stephan Slane; DIRECTOR: Jenny Lou Law; CHOREOGRAPHER: Bill Hooks; SETS: Warwick Brown; COSTUMES: Marian Lathrop; LIGHTING: Theda Taylor; MUSICAL DIRECTOR: George Bauer; PIANIST/CONDUCTOR: David Hollister. **Cast**: Jenny Lou Law, Elizabeth Allen, Al Checco, Jack Eddleman, Alan Peterson, June Squibb, Jeff Warren, Tom Cahill, Barbara Creed, Robert Fitch, Sherry McCutcheon, Charles Nelson Reilly, Fiddle Viracola, Susan Watson.

MASTER THEATRE, 1969. PRESENTED BY the Equity Library Theatre; DIRECTOR: Sue Lawless; CHOREOGRAPHER: Judith Haskell; SETS/LIGHTING: John A. Baker III; COSTUMES: Pamela Scofield; MUSICAL DIREC-

TOR: James Kay. *Cast*: Maureen Silliman, William J. Coppola, Georgia Engel, Ted Pugh.

Leonard Sillman's New Faces of 1968 *see* 486

Les Miserables *see* 450

390. *Let It Ride!*

Erwin is a meek little man who writes poems for The Modern Greeting Card Company. He discovers he has knack for picking the winner on the horses. A group of shady characters also discover this about him. Flutterby is the horse. Set in New York City.

Before Broadway. The numbers "Best Undressed Girl in Town," "Honest Work," "Love is the Greatest," "Sweet Man," and "Trust Me" were all cut.

The Broadway Run. EUGENE O'NEILL THEATRE, 10/12/61–12/9/61. 1 preview on 10/11/61. 68 PERFORMANCES. PRESENTED BY Joel Spector; MUSIC: Jay Livingston; LYRICS: Jay Livingston & Ray Evans; BOOK: Abram S. Ginnes; ADDITIONAL BOOK MATERIAL: Ronny Graham; BASED ON the 1935 farce *Three Men on a Horse*, written by John Cecil Holm & George Abbott; DIRECTOR: Stanley Prager; CHOREOGRAPHER: Onna White; SETS/LIGHTING: William & Jean Eckart; COSTUMES: Guy Kent; MUSICAL DIRECTOR: Jay Blackton; ORCHESTRATIONS: Raymond Jaimes; DANCE MUSIC ARRANGEMENTS: Billy Goldenberg; VOCAL DIRECTOR: Jerry Packer; PRESS: David Lipsky & Chester Fox; GENERAL MANAGER: Paul Vroom; COMPANY MANAGER: Herb Cherin; PRODUCTION STAGE MANAGER: Terence Little; STAGE MANAGER: John Ford; ASSISTANT STAGE MANAGER: Ralph Linn. *Cast*: ERWIN: George Gobel (1) ⭐; AUDREY: Paula Stewart (4); CARVER: Stanley Grover (5); HARRY: Harold Gary; CHARLIE: Albert Linville; FRANKIE: Larry Alpert (6); MABEL: Barbara Nichols (3) ⭐; PATSY: Sam Levene (2) ⭐; BIRTHDAY GIRLS: Pat Turner, Sandra Devlin, Ann Johnson, Sandy Walsh, Rae McLean, Carol Glade, Sally Lee, Sally Kirk, Barbara Marcon; NICE NOSE BROPHY: Dort Clark; MOTHER: Maggie Worth; CHIEF SCHERMERHORN: Ted Thurston (7); REPULSKI: Stanley Simmonds; FIRST COP: John Ford; ANNOUNCER'S VOICE: Ted Thurston; DANCERS: Ted Adkins, Marty Allen, Robert Bakanic, Rhett Dennis, Sandra Devlin, Bob Evans, Dick Gingrich, Ann Johnson, Sally Kirk, Sally Lee, Jack Leigh, Vernon Lusby, Rae McLean, Barbara Marcon, Pat Turner, Sandra Walsh, Marc West; SINGERS: Helen Baisley, Francine Bond, Austin Colyer, Clifford Fearl, John Ford, Carol Glade, Robert Lenn, Virginia Perlowin, Michael Roberts, Maggie Worth. *Standby*: Erwin: Edwin Bruce. *Understudies*: Patsy: Harold Gary; Carver: Austin Colyer; Frankie: Stanley Simmonds; Mother: Helen Baisley; Repulski/Charlie: John Ford; Audrey: Francine Bond; Mabel: Ginny Perlowin. *Act I*: *Scene 1* Bus; *Scene 2* Main office of Modern Greeting Card Company; *Scene 3* Street outside Hotel Lavillere; *Scene 4* Bar, Hotel Lavillere; *Scene 5* Corridor, Modern Greeting Card Company; *Scene 6* Patsy's party; *Scene 7* Audrey's porch; *Scene 8* Mabel's room. *Act II*: *Scene 1* Opening; *Scene 2* Bar; *Scene 3* Audrey's porch; *Scene 4* Mabel's room; *Scene 5* Rogues' Gallery; *Scene 6* Lineup; *Scene 7* Outside police station; *Scene 8* Erwin's Island; *Scene 9* Bar; *Scene 10* Finale. *Act I*: "Run, Run, Run" (Singers & Dancers), "The Nicest Thing" (Audrey), "Hey Jimmy, Joe, John, Jim, Jack" (Erwin), "Broads Ain't People" (Erwin, Harry, Frankie, Charlie), "Let it Ride" (Patsy, Singers & Dancers), "I'll Learn Ya" (Erwin & Patsy), "Love, Let Me Know" (Audrey & Carver), "Happy Birthday" (Birthday Girls), "Ev'rything Beautiful" (Erwin & Birthday Girls), "Who's Doing What to Erwin?" (Audrey, Chief, Carver, Mother), "I Wouldn't Have Had To" (Mabel). *Act II*: "There's Something About a Horse" (Singers & Dancers), "He Needs You" (Erwin, Frankie, Charlie), "Just an Honest Mistake" (Chief, Repulski, Cops), "His Own Little Island" (Erwin), "If Flutterby Wins" (Erwin, Patsy, Frankie, Charlie, Harry, Hoods), Finale (Entire Company).

Broadway reviews were terrible.

After Broadway. ALL SOULS CHURCH, NYC, 1/31/91–2/17/91. 15 PERFORMANCES. This was a revised revival. PRESENTED BY the All Souls Players; DIRECTOR/CHOREOGRAPHER: Jeffrey K. Neill; MUSICAL DIRECTOR/ARRANGEMENTS: Joyce Hitchcock. *Cast*: ERWIN TROWBRIDGE: David Babbitt; CHIEF/RALPH: Dan Entriken; DAISY/LISA: Robin Fernandez; FENSTER/GIGOLO/GEORGE: John Golterman; WITHERSPOON/JOHN CHARLES: John Golterman; GIRL ON BUS/VIOLET: Susan Hale; SADIE/ALICE: Susan Hale; IRIS/MARLENE: Teressa Hoover; JACK CARVER: Hugh Hysell; GIRL/MIMI/HAZEL/ROZ: Casey Jones; NICE NOSE BROPHY: Jerry Koenig; HERBERT/HENNES/SPANISH SPAM/PATROLMAN FIORI: Robert Laconi; MAN/OSCAR/HOT HORSE HERBIE/DAVIS/MCDONALD: John Lindsay; CHARLIE: Terrence O'Brien; MABEL: Trudi Posey; PATSY POMEROY: Steve Sterner; KROKOVER/JACK O'HEARTS/CAGNEY: Larry Stotz; HARRY THE BARTENDER: William Walters; FRANKIE: Jay Brian Winnick; AUDREY: Wendy Worth; REPULSKI: Bob Zanfini. "Run, Run, Run," "The Nicest Thing," "Sweet Man," "Through the Children's Eyes," "Best Undressed Girl in Town," "Let it Ride," "I'll Learn Ya," "Love, Let Me Know," "Happy Birthday/I Wouldn't Have Had To," "Ev'rything Beautiful," "It Just Didn't Happen That Way," "Who's Doing What to Erwin?," "My Own Little Island," "He Needs You," "Just an Honest Mistake," "If Flutterby Wins," Finale.

LAMB'S THEATRE, NYC, 6/14/98–6/28/98. Previews from 6/11/98. 15 PERFORMANCES. This was a concert version, part of the *Musicals Tonight!* series. Jay Livingston & Ray Evans were there opening night. ADAPTED BY Mel Miller; DIRECTOR: Thomas Mills; MUSICAL DIRECTOR: Mark W. Hartman. *Cast*: AUDREY/MABEL: Robin Baxter; PATSY: E.J. Carroll; CHARLIE: Aaron Ellis; ERWIN: David Gurland; CARVER/NICE NOSE: Gary Lynch; SGT. MOMMASKIND: Wayne Pretlow; FRANKIE: Tom Reidy. "Run, Run, Run," "The Nicest Thing," "Sweet Man," "Through the Children's Eyes," "Broads Ain't People," "Best Undressed Girl in Town," "Let it Ride," "I'll Learn Ya," "Love, Let Me Know," "Ev'rything Beautiful," "I Wouldn't Have Had To," "Who's Doing What to Erwin?," "It Just Didn't Happen That Way," "Honest Work," "His Own Little Island," "He Needs You," "Just an Honest Mistake," "If Flutterby Wins," "There's Something About a Horse."

391. *Let My People Come*

A sexual musical.

Before Broadway. Earl Wilson Jr. was son of Earl Wilson, famous newspaper columnist. Producer Phil Oesterman asked him if he would like to do a revue of songs and sketches dealing with sex, and Mr. Wilson wrote 44 songs in four months, 20 of them used in the show. The show began performances Off Broadway, at Village Gate, on 1/8/74, but never formally opened, Phil Oesterman fearing that negative reviews would kill it. It was, however, reviewed occasionally during the run. It had the same basic crew as for the later Broadway run, except CHOREOGRAPHER: Ian Naylor; LIGHTING: Centaur Productions; MUSICAL ARRANGER/CONDUCTOR: Billy Cunningham; COMPANY MANAGER: Robert H. Wallner; STAGE MANAGERS: Angus Moss (*Andie Wilson Kingwill, Duane F. Mazey*) & Ray Colbert. *Cast*: Christine Andersen, Tobie Columbus, Marty Duffy, Ian Naylor, Daina Darzin, Lorraine Davidson, Alan Evans, Lola Howse, Joe Jones, James Moore, Larry Paulette, Peachena, Jim Rise, Denise Connolley. 1974 replacements: *Ray Colbert, James Morgan, Shezwae Powell, Christine Rubens, Dean Tait, Robin Charin*. 74–75 replacements: *Stephan Burns, Steven Alex-Cole, Carl Deese, Judy Gibson, Jo Anna Lehmann, Edwina Lewis, Jim Rich, Tuesday Summers, Michael Poulos, Joanne Baron*. 75–76 replacements: *James Bryan, Scott Farrell, Yvette Freeman, Bob Jockers, Empress Kilpatrick, Barry Pearl, Rocky Suda, Dean Tait (again), Terri White, Irma Kaye*. The cast recording was made on Libra Records, on 4/29/74. "Give it to Me" (Lorraine), "I'm Gay" (Marty & Joe), "Come in My Mouth" (Tobie), "Dirty Words" (Company), "Linda, Georgina, Marilyn and Me" (Christine Rubens), "I Believe My Body" (Company), "Take Me Home with You" (Larry), "Choir Practice" (Company), "And She Loved Me" (Shezwae & Peachena), "Whatever Turns You On" (Company), "Doesn't Anybody Love Anymore?" (Shezwae), "Let My People Come" (Company). The government tried on occasion to ban it (there was nudity), but it kept going for 1,167 performances, closed on 7/5/76, then moved to Broadway.

The Broadway Run. MOROSCO THEATRE, 7/22/76–10/2/76. 16 previews. 106 PERFORMANCES. PRESENTED BY Phil Oesterman; MUSIC/LYRICS: Earl Wilson Jr.; DIRECTOR: Phil Oesterman; CHOREOGRAPHER: Charles Augins; SETS/PRODUCTION STAGE MANAGER: Duane F. Mazey; SETS/COSTUME SUPERVISOR: Douglas W. Schmidt; LIGHTING: Duane F. Mazey & John Gleason; MUSICAL DIRECTOR/VOCAL ARRANGEMENTS: Norman Bergen; CONDUCTOR: Glen Roven; PRESS: Saul Richman & Fred Nathan; GENERAL MANAGER: Jay Kingwill; COMPANY MANAGER: Mark Bramble; STAGE MANAGER: Robert Walter; ASSISTANT STAGE MANAGER: Bob Blume. **Cast:** Brandy Alexander, Joanne Baron, Dwight Baxter, Pat Cleveland, Lorraine Davidson, Joelle Erasme, Yvette Freeman, Paul Gillespie, Gloria Goldman, Tulane Howard II, Bob Jockers, Empress Kilpatrick, Dianne Legro, Allan Lozito, Bryan Miller, Rod R. Neves, Rozaa, Don Scotti, Sterling Saint-Jacques, Bryan Spencer, Dean Tait, Lori Wagner (left during the run), Charles Whiteside. **Act I:** Opening Number: "Screw" (Company), "Mirror" (Bryan Spencer, Gloria, Pat, Empress, Rod, Lori, Tulane, Joelle, Dean, Pat, Sterling), "Whatever Turns You On" (Company), "Give it to Me" (Lorraine & Lori), "Giving Life" (Empress, Bryan Miller, Pat, Rod, Lori, Joelle, Dean, Pat, Sterling), "The Ad" (Charles), "Fellatio 101" (Allan & Students), "I'm Gay" (Bob, Bryan Miller, Rod, Paul), "Linda, Georgina, Marilyn & Me" (Joanne), "Dirty Words" (Company), "I Believe My Body" (Company). **Act II:** "The Show Business Nobody Knows" (Company), "Take Me Home with You" (Bryan Miller), "Choir Practice" (Allan & Company), "And She Loved Me" (Rozaa, Empress, Lori, Joelle), "Poontang" (Company), "Come in My Mouth" (Empress), "The Cunnilingus Champion of Company C" (Bryan Miller, Pat, Joanne, Charles), "Doesn't Anybody Love Anymore" (Rozaa), "Let My People Come" (Company).

It opened on Broadway against the wishes of the League of Broadway Producers and Theatres, and also against the wishes of Earl Wilson, who requested that his name be removed from the bill. He was upset because he felt Phil Oesterman had distorted his original concept. He brought an injunction, which was not granted. Again, the critics were not invited to a formal opening.

After Broadway. LONDON, 1975. **Cast:** Gil Beresford, Michael Cowie.

392. *Let's Make an Opera*

A musical novelty, really an opera. Some teachers and children create their own opera, about Sammy, a little sweep who gets stuck in a chimney and is rescued by some other children, and hidden from his wicked masters. At the urging of the musical conductor, the audience itself is urged to participate in the singing of some of the songs.

Before Broadway. Benjamin Britten's opera first ran at the ALDEBURGH FESTIVAL, England, on 5/24/48, and again there, on 6/14/49. Then it went to London, where it had a run at the LYRIC THEATRE, HAMMERSMITH, 11/15/49–1/14/50. 63 PERFORMANCES. DIRECTORS: Basil Coleman & Stuart Burge. **Cast** (the first in a series of productions by the English Opera Group): BLACK BOB, THE BRUTAL SWEEPMASTER: Norman Lumsden, *John Highcock*; CLEM, HIS SON & ASSISTANT: Andrew Gold, *Max Worthley*; SAM, THEIR NEW 8-YEAR-OLD SWEEP BOY: John Moules; JOHNNY CROME, AGED 15: Brian Cole; GAY BROOK, AGED 13: Bruce Hines; HUGHIE CROME, AGED 8: Ralph Canham; MISS BAGGOTT, THE HOUSEKEEPER AT IKEN HALL: Gladys Parr, *Anne Wood*; JULIET BROOK, AGED 14: Anne Sharp, *Pamela Petts*; ROWAN, THE NURSERY MAID TO THE WOODBRIDGE COUSINS: Pamela Woolmore, *Dorothy Nash*; SOPHIE BROOK, AGED 10: Monica Garrod; TINA CROME, AGED 8, TWIN TO HUGHIE: Mavis Gardiner.

LYRIC THEATRE, HAMMERSMITH, London, 12/5/50–1/27/51. 63 PERFORMANCES. DIRECTORS: Basil Coleman & Stuart Burge. **Cast:** BLACK BOB: Norman Lumsden, *George Prangell*; CLEM: Andrew Gold; JOHNNY: Patrick Freeman; SAM: Ronald Millar; GAY: Neil Batsford; HUGHIE:

Clive Wyatt; MISS BAGGOTT: Gladys Parr, *Anne Wood*; JULIET: Doreen Orme; ROWAN: Pamela Woolmore, *Dorothy Nash*; TINA: Shirley Eaton; SOPHIE: Monica Garrod.

The Broadway Run. JOHN GOLDEN THEATRE, 12/13/50–12/16/50. 5 PERFORMANCES. PRESENTED BY Peter Lawrence & The Show-of-the-Month Club; MUSIC: Benjamin Britten; LYRICS/BOOK: Eric Crozier; BASED ON Benjamin Britten's 1949 opera *The Little Sweep*; DIRECTOR: Marc Blitzstein; SETS/LIGHTING: Ralph Alswang; COSTUMES: Aline Bernstein; MUSICAL DIRECTOR: Norman Del Mar; PRODUCTION STAGE MANAGER: Mortimer Halpern. **Cast:** THE PLAY: Played by Themselves: Rosalind Nadell, Paul Carter, Claire Richard, Jo Sullivan, Angela Adamides, Frank Catal, Arlyne Frank, Randolph Symonette, Mario Santamaria, Lawrence Young, Rawn Spearman, Norman Del Mar. THE OPERA ("THE LITTLE SWEEP"): BIG BOB: Randolph Symonette; CLEM: Rawn Spearman; SAMMY: Lawrence Young; MISS BAGGOTT: Rosalind Nadell; ROWAN: Arlyne Frank; JULIET BROOK: Jo Sullivan; GAY BROOK: Frank Catal; SOPHIE BROOK: Claire Richard; TINA CROME: Angela Adamides; HUGHIE CROME: Paul Carter; JOHNNY CROME: Mario Santamaria; TOM: Randolph Symonette; ALFRED: Rawn Spearman. **Act I:** The Play: *Scene 1* Rosalind's home; an autumn evening; *Scene 2* Stage of the school auditorium; before dress rehearsal. **Act II:** The Opera ("The Little Sweep"): *Scene 1* Nursery at Iken Hall, England; 1810; a January morning; *Scene 2* A few minutes later; *Scene 3* The following morning.

It got bad Broadway reviews, but Jo Sullivan was favorably noticed.

After Broadway. LYRIC THEATRE, Hammersmith, London, 5/5/51, 5/12/51, 5/19/51. 3 MATINEE PERFORMANCES. DIRECTOR: Basil Coleman. **Cast:** BLACK BOB: George Prangell; CLEM: Andrew Gold; JOHNNY: John Banks; SAM: Derek Mitchell; GAY: Francis Adamson; HUGHIE: Reginald Blowers; MISS BAGGOTT: Gladys Parr; JULIET: Doreen Orme; ROWAN: Pamela Woolmore; TINA: Eileen Grice; SOPHIE: Sally Kiddell.

LYRIC THEATRE, Hammersmith, London, 12/24/51–1/26/52. 40 PERFORMANCES. DIRECTOR: Basil Coleman; CONDUCTORS: Edward Renton & Boyd Neel. **Cast:** BLACK BOB: Ian Wallace; CLEM: Andrew Downie; JOHNNY: Jonathan Carver; SAM: Derek Mitchell, *Victor Budds*; GAY: Richard Tovell; HUGHIE: Reginald Blowers, *Derek Mitchell*; MISS BAGGOTT: Gladys Parr, *Anne Wood*; JULIET: Anne Sharp; ROWAN: Gladys Whitred; TINA: Eileen Grice, *June Stevenson*; SOPHIE: Sally Kiddell, *Monica Garrod*.

SCALA THEATRE, London. 9/22/55–10/1/55. 6 PERFORMANCES. DIRECTOR: Peter Potter. **Cast:** BLACK BOB: Trevor Anthony; CLEM: Maurice Wearmouth, *Leighton Camden*; SAM: David Hemmings, *Michael Ingram*; GAY: Michael Ingram, *James Warren*; MISS BAGGOTT: Gladys Parr; JULIET: Rosemarie Hill; SOPHIE: Marilyn Baker.

COURT THEATRE, London. 12/19/55–1/14/56. 35 PERFORMANCES. DIRECTOR: Peter Potter. **Cast:** BLACK BOB: Trevor Anthony, *David Oddie*; CLEM: Maurice Wearmouth, *Leighton Camden*; JOHNNY: Robin Fairhurst, *Lyn Vaughan, David Hemmings*; SAM: David Hemmings, *Raymond Dring, Michael Ingram*; GAY: Michael Ingram, *James Warren*; HUGHIE: Lyn Vaughan, *Alan Gunter*; MISS BAGGOTT: Gladys Parr, *Nora Ogonovsky*; SOPHIE: Marilyn Baker, *Valerie Cattermole*.

VAUDEVILLE THEATRE, London, 12/26/62. Matinees only.

393. *The Liar*

Set in 16th-century Venice, in spring. The entire action takes place within 24 hours. A young Italian lad's vivid imagination and glib tongue get him into many scrapes with pretty girls and the law.

Before Broadway. On the road Alfred Drake replaced Norris Houghton as director, and in the cast William Eythe replaced Dennis Harrison at the last moment.

The Broadway Run. BROADHURST THEATRE, 5/18/50–5/27/50. 12 PERFORMANCES. PRESENTED BY Dorothy Willard & Thomas Hammond; MUSIC: John Mundy; LYRICS: Edward Eager; BOOK: Edward Eager & Alfred Drake; BASED ON the 1750 Italian comedy *Il Bugiardo*, by Carlo Goldoni; DIRECTOR: Alfred Drake; CHOREOGRAPHER: Hanya Holm; SWORDPLAY CHOREOGRAPHER: Leslie Litomy; SETS/LIGHTING: Donald Oenslager; COSTUMES: Motley; MUSICAL DIRECTOR: Lehman

Engel; ORCHESTRATIONS: Lehman Engel & Ben Ludlow; PRESS: Samuel J. Friedman & Max Eisen; COMPANY MANAGER: Arthur Singer; GENERAL STAGE MANAGER: John E. Sola; STAGE MANAGER: Tony Albert; ASSISTANT STAGE MANAGER: Robert B. Sola. *Cast*: INNKEEPER: Walter F. Appler; INNKEEPER'S WIFE: Jean Handzlik; SERVING WENCH: Lee Wilcox; SERVING MEN: Leonardo Cimino & Martin Balsam; WOMAN AT WINDOW: May Muth; FIORI: Margery Oldroyd; VINO: David Collyer; VEGETABILI: Marybelle Norton; LETTER CARRIER: Leslie Litomy; URCHIN: William Myers; CAPTAIN OF THE VENETIAN GUARDS: Robert Penn; GUARDS: Edward Bryce, William Hogue, Lawrence Weber, Walter Matthau; LELIO BISOGNOSI: William Eythe (1); ARLECCHINO: Joshua Shelley; BRIGHELLA: Russell Collins; FLORINDO PALLIDO: Glenn Burris; ROSAURA BALANZONI: Barbara Moser; BEATRICE BALANZONI: Karen Lindgren; OTTAVIO OSSIMORSI: Stanley Carlson; COLOMBINA: Paula Laurence (3); PANTALONE BOSOGNOSI: Melville Cooper (2); DR. BALANZONI: Philip Coolidge; CLEONICE ANSELMI: Barbara Ashley (4). *Act I*: *Scene 1* The square: "March of the Guards" (Captain & Guards), "The Ladies' Opinion" (Innkeeper's Wife, Woman at Window, Serving Wench, Fiori, Vegetabili), "You've Stolen My Heart" (Florindo), "The Liar's Song" (Lelio & Arlecchino), "Supper Trio" (Lelio, Arlecchino, Ottavio), "Truth" (Colombina, Arlecchino, Lelio, Rosaura, Beatrice); *Scene 2* The inn; *Scene 3* The doctor's house: "Lack-a-Day" (Rosaura & Florindo), "Stop Holding Me Back" (Ottavio & Company); *Scene 4* The square: "What's in a Name?" (Rosaura & Lelio), Finale. *Act II*: *Scene 1* The square: "Women's Work" (m: Lehman Engel) (Colombina, Innkeeper's Wife, Serving Wench, Woman at Window), "Spring" (Colombina & Brighella), "Stomachs and Stomachs" (Arlecchino), "A Jewel of a Duel" (Captain, Rosaura, Beatrice, Colombina, Pantalone, Dr. Balanzoni, Lelio, Arlecchino), "Out of Sight, Out of Mind" (Lelio & Company); *Scene 2* The doctor's house: "Lack-a-Day" (reprise) (Rosaura & Florindo), "A Plot to Catch a Man In" (Company); *Scene 3* The square: "Out of Sight, Out of Mind" (reprise) (Cleonice), "Funeral March" (Company), "'twill Never Be the Same" (Cleonice), Finale.

Broadway reviews were terrible. The show lost $160,000.

394. *The Lieutenant*

A new rock opera, 90 minutes long, with no intermission. The story revolved around the most notorious of the Vietnam War atrocities (at least as committed by Americans). American soldiers, looking for Viet Cong guerrillas, killed 347 civilians at My Lai, and this fanned antiwar sentiment in the USA. In 1971 Lt. William Calley (although he is not named in the musical) was court-martialed and sentenced to life imprisonment. In 1974 his conviction was overturned, and he was released. This was all material for this musical. It opens and closes with the catchy recruiting song, "Join the Army." The action alternates between Vietnam and the USA over a three-year period.

Before Broadway. This show began at Joseph S. Kutzreba's Queens Playhouse.

The Broadway Run. LYCEUM THEATRE, 3/9/75–3/16/75. 7 previews. 9 PERFORMANCES. PRESENTED BY Joseph S. Kutzreba & Spofford J. Beadle; MUSIC/LYRICS/BOOK: Gene Curty, Nitra Scharfman, Chuck Strand; BASED ON events surrounding the 3/16/68 massacre at My Lai, South Vietnam; DIRECTOR: William Martin; CHOREOGRAPHER: Dennis Dennehy; SETS/COSTUMES: Frank J. Boros; LIGHTING: Ian Calderon; SOUND: Bill Merrill; MUSICAL DIRECTOR: Chuck Strand; ARRANGEMENTS: Chuck Strand & Gus Montero; PRESS: Alan Eichler & Marilyn Percy; CASTING: Ruby Theodore; GENERAL MANAGER: Spofford J. Beadle; COMPANY MANAGER: James O'Neill; PRODUCTION STAGE MANAGER: Bruce Hoover; STAGE MANAGER: Philip Moser; ASSISTANT STAGE MANAGER: Marius Hanford. *Cast*: LIEUTENANT: Eddie Mekka (1) ☆; JUDGE: Gene Curty; RECRUITING SERGEANT: Joel Powers; 1ST GENERAL: Chet D'Elia; 2ND GENERAL: Eugene Moose; 3RD GENERAL: Danny Taylor; OCS SERGEANT: Gene Curty; CHAPLAIN: Don McGrath; CAPTAIN: Walt Hunter; SERGEANT "C" COMPANY: Jim Litten; "C" COMPANY: Steven Boockvor, Clark James, Jim-Patrick McMahon, Joseph Pugliese,

Burt Rodriguez, Tom Tofel; G.I.: Tom Tofel; SENATOR: Joel Powers; 1ST CONGRESSMAN: Don McGrath; CLERGYMAN: Jim Litten; 2ND CONGRESSMAN: Burt Rodriguez; 1ST REPORTER: Jim Litten; 2ND REPORTER: Tom Tofel; 3RD REPORTER: Jo Speros; PROSECUTOR: Burt Rodriguez; DEFENSE ATTORNEY: Gordon Grody; NEW RECRUIT: Alan K. Siegel. *Standby*: Defense Attorney: Dan Kruger. *Understudies*: Lieutenant: Joseph Pugliese; Captain: Burt Rodriguez; Defense Attorney/Judge: Walt Hunter; Prosecutor: Gene Curty; Judge/OCS Sergeant: Steve Boockvor; Recruiting Sergeant/Senator/1st Congressman: Danny Taylor; G.I./2nd Congressman: Dan Kruger; 3rd General: Clark James; Male Reporters/Clergyman: Jim-Patrick McMahon; 3rd Reporter: Beth Kennedy; Chaplain: Eugene Moose; New Recruit: Tom Tofel. *Swing Dancer*: Marius Hanford. *Musicians*: RHYTHM GUITAR: John Angelori (Zan Burnham, standby); ORGAN: Alan Bowin (Stephanie Sarafoglu, standby); LEAD GUITAR: Mark Cianfrani (Zan Burnham, standby); DRUMS: Joe Di Carlo (John Angelori, standby); BASS GUITAR: James Marino (John Angelori, standby); PIANO: Chuck Strand (Stephanie Sarafoglu, standby). "The Indictment" (Lieutenant & Judge), "Join the Army" (Lieutenant, Recruiting Sergeant, Recruits), "Look for the Men with Potential" (Generals), "Kill" (OCS Sgt), "I Don't Want to Go Over to Vietnam" (Lieutenant & "C" (Company), "Eulogy" (Chaplain), "At 0700 Tomorrow" (Captain & "C" Company), "Massacre" (Captain, Lieutenant, "C" Company, Vietnamese), "Something's Gone Wrong" (Captain & Lieutenant), "Twenty-Eight" (Generals, Captain, Lieutenant), "Let's Believe in the Captain" (Generals), "Final Report" (1st General), "I Will Make Things Happen" (GI). TWO YEARS LATER: "He Wants to Put the Army in Jail" (Senator, 1st & 2nd Congressmen, Clergyman), "There's No Other Solution" (Generals), "I'm Going Home" (Lieutenant & "C" Company), "We've Chosen You, Lieutenant" (Generals), "The Star of This War" (Reporters & Lieutenant), "On Trial for My Life" (Lieutenant), "The Conscience of a Nation" (Prosecutor), "Damned, No Matter How He Turned" (Defense Attorney), "On Trial for My Life" (reprise) (Lieutenant), "The Verdict" (Judge & Jurors), Finale: "Join the Army" (reprise) (New Recruit, Recruiting Sergeant, Company).

Broadway reviews very divided, with a great one from Clive Barnes of the *New York Times*. The show received Tony nominations for musical, score, book, and for Eddie Mekka.

395. *The Life*

About prostitution on 42nd Street. The time is "Then" (originally the late 1970s to the early 1980s, but re-defined early in pre–Broadway re-writes to 1980).

Before Broadway. This show began Off Broadway, at the WESTBETH THEATRE CENTER, 7/30/90–8/16/90. 12 PERFORMANCES. DIRECTOR/CHOREOGRAPHER: Joe Layton; SETS: Bob Phillips; COSTUMES: Franne Lee; LIGHTING: Nancy Collings; SOUND: Richard Dunning; MUSICAL DIRECTOR: Donald York; STAGE MANAGER: Victor Lukas. *Cast*: BARMAIDS: Heather Wright & Allyson Pimentel; SAM/VENDOR/BUM: Mark Maharry; SCOTTY/POLICE: Stuart Hult; FLEETWOOD: Edwin Louis Battle; JOJO: Stanley W. Mathis; RICK: Jan Mussetter & Enrique Cruz de Jesus; MARY/ANGEL: Lori Fischer; BOBBY: Alde Lewis Jr.; QUEEN: Pamela Isaacs; CHIBA: Percy Cochran Hall III; BULL: Matt Zarley; SONJA: Lillias White; TAFFY: Mamie Duncan-Gibbs; FRENCHY: Laura Berman; LACY: Larry Marshall; CHICHI: Sharon Wilkins; BLACKIE: Guylane Bouchard; TRACY: Degan Everhart; CRYSTAL: D. Drake; PEPA: Lillian Colon; TOYA: Sachi Shimizu; MEMPHIS: Chuck Cooper; SNICKERS: Harold Cromer; SAL/MINISTER: Peter Schankowitz; TONY: Jorge Rios; VOYEUR/CON ED MAN: Kurt Elftman; HARRY: Bill Buell; PRISON MATRON: Jane McPherson. "The Street," "Piece of the Action," "A Lovely Day to Be Outta Jail," "Getting Too Old," "Don't Take Much," "My Body," "Easy Money," "Working Girls," "Reefer Man," "He's No Good," "Hooker's Ball," "Signifyin' Monkey," "Mr. Greed," "My Way or the Highway," "Lucky Me," "Someday," "People Magazine," "Use What You Got," "I'm Leaving You," "We Gotta Go," Finale.

There was an invitation-only reading at the NEW VICTORY THEATRE on 11/7/96. *Cast*: Lillias White, Pam Isaacs, Michael McElroy, Chuck Cooper. In 5/96 a concept album was released by BMG/RCA, featuring Jennifer Holliday, Liza Minnelli, George Burns, Lou Rawls, Joe Williams, Jack Jones, Peggy Lee, Billy Stritch, Bobby Short, and others. The Broadway opening date was originally announced as 4/30/97, but had to be brought forward because another play had already been scheduled to open on Broadway that night — the Roundabout Theatre production of *London Assurance* (the League of American Theatres and Producers discourages more than one Broadway show opening on the same night, for reviewing reasons). Rehearsals took place at the Brooklyn Academy of Music. The number "Was That a Smile?" was cut during Broadway previews.

The Broadway Run. ETHEL BARRYMORE THEATRE, 4/26/97–6/7/98. 22 previews from 4/8/97. 465 PERFORMANCES. PRESENTED BY Roger Berlind, Martin Richards, Cy Coleman, Sam Crothers; MUSIC: Cy Coleman; LYRICS: Ira Gasman; BOOK: David Newman, Ira Gasman, Cy Coleman; BASED ON an original idea by Ira Gasman; DIRECTOR: Michael Blakemore; CHOREOGRAPHER: Joey McKneely; SETS: Robin Wagner; COSTUMES: Martin Pakledinaz; LIGHTING: Richard Pilbrow; SOUND: Peter Fitzgerald; MUSICAL DIRECTOR: Gordon Lowry Harrell; ORCHESTRATIONS: Don Sebesky & Harold Wheeler; DANCE MUSIC ARRANGEMENTS/VOCAL ARRANGEMENTS: Cy Coleman & Doug Katsaros; CAST RECORDING on Sony, made on 5/5/97 and released on 6/3/97; PRESS: The Jacksina Company; CASTING: Julie Hughes & Barry Moss; GENERAL MANAGER: Marvin A. Krauss; COMPANY MANAGER: David Richards & Barbara Crompton; STAGE MANAGER: Ara Marx; ASSISTANT STAGE MANAGER: Rolt Smith. *Cast:* JOJO: Sam Harris (9) (until 10/19/97), *Brian Lane Green*; CARMEN: Lynn Sterling; CHICHI: Sharon Wilkins; FRENCHIE: Katy Grenfell; TRACY: Judine Richard; BOBBY: Mark Bove; ODDJOB: Michael Gregory Gong, *Joshua Bergasse*; SILKY: Rudy Roberson; SLICK: Mark Anthony Taylor, *Christopher F. Davis*; MEMPHIS: Chuck Cooper (4), *James Stovall* (during Mr. Cooper's vacation); APRIL: Felicia Finley, *Kate Levering*; SNICKERS: Gordon Joseph Weiss (8); LACY: Vernel Bagneris (6); QUEEN: Pamela Isaacs (1); SONJA: Lillias White (3); FLEETWOOD: Kevin Ramsey (2); MARY: Bellamy Young (5); DOLL HOUSE DANCER: Stephanie Michels; STREET EVANGELISTS: Judine Richard, Rudy Roberson, Mark Anthony Taylor (*Christopher F. Davis*); COP: Mark Bove; SHOESHINE: Michael Gregory Gong, *Joshua Bergasse*; LOU: Rich Hebert (7); SHATELLIA: Mark Anthony Taylor, *Christopher F. Davis*; ENRIQUE: Rudy Roberson; ENSEMBLE: Mark Bove, Felicia Finley (*Kate Levering*), Chris Ghelfi, Michael Gregory Gong (*Joshua Bergasse*), Katy Grenfell, Stephanie Michels, Judine Richard, Rudy Roberson, Lynn Sterling, Mark Anthony Taylor (*Christopher F. Davis*), Sharon Wilkins, *Rommy Sandhu*. **Understudies**: Jojo/Lou/Snickers: Michael Brian; Queen: Tracy Nicole Chapman & Kimberly Hawthorne, *Heather Brown*; Sonja: Sharon Wilkins; Fleetwood/Memphis: James Stovall, *David Aron Damane*; Silky: James Stovall; Lacy: Rudy Roberson, *David Aron Damane*; Mary: Felicia Finley & Stephanie Michels, *Kate Levering*. **Swing**: Tracy Nicole Chapman, *Carla Renata Williams*. **Orchestra**: GUITAR: David Spinozza; DRUMS: Warren Odze; KEYBOARDS: Mark Berman & Joseph Baker; PERCUSSION: Dave Yee; TRUMPETS: Gregory Gisbert & Hollis Burridge; WOODWINDS: Mike Migliore, Tom Christensen, Dale Kleps. *Act I*: "Check it Out!" (Company), "Use What You Got" (Jojo & Company), "A Lovely Day to Be Outta Jail" (Queen & Sonja), "A Piece of the Action" (Fleetwood), "The Oldest Profession" (Sonja), "Don't Take Much" (Memphis), "Go Home" (Queen & Mary), "You Can't Get to Heaven" (Queen, Sonja, Street Evangelists), "My Body" (Frenchie, Chichi, Tracy, Carmen, Sonja, Queen, April), "Why Don't They Leave Us Alone?" (Oddjob, Bobby, Silky, Slick, Snickers, April, Carmen, Chichi, Frenchie, Queen, Sonja, Tracy), "Easy Money" (Mary, Jojo, Fleetwood), "He's No Good" (Queen), "I'm Leaving You" (Queen), "The Hooker's Ball" (Lacy & Company). *Act II*: "Step Right Up" (Enrique, Slick, Oddjob), "Mr. Greed" (Jojo, Bobby, Enrique, Oddjob, Slick), "My Way or the Highway" (Memphis & Queen), "People Magazine" (Lou & Mary), "We Had a Dream" (Queen), "Use What You Got" (reprise) (Mary, Lou, Jojo), "Someday is for Suckers" (Sonja, Frenchie, April, Shatellia, Carmen, Chichi), "My Friend" (Queen & Sonja), "We Gotta Go" (Fleetwood & Queen), "Check it Out!" (reprise) (Company).

Broadway reviews were very divided, mostly negative. However, the show was nominated for 12 Tonys. Lillias White and Chuck Cooper won. Nominations were: musical, score, book, direction of a musical, choreography, costumes, lighting, orchestrations, Sam Harris, Pamela Isaacs.

396. *Li'l Abner*

Set in the mythical hillbilly community of Dogpatch, USA. Muscular but innocent Li'l Abner is always being pursued by beautiful Daisy Mae, but on a typical day Abner would rather go fishing with his cronies. This is interrupted by an emergency meeting in Cornpone Square, a spot dedicated to the founder of the town, Jubilation T. Cornpone, Dogpatch's incompetent Civil War general. The U.S. government has decided, after years of research, that Dogpatch is the most useless place in the USA, so it plans to test atomic bombs there. The townsfolk are all for moving out, but Mammy (Abner's small, wiry, tyrannical mother), wants to stay put and find something unique about the town which will stop the USA from doing this. She comes up with a tonic called Yokumberry Tonic, made from the Yokumberry Tree, which has made Abner the fine physical specimen he is. They try it on a stranger, the scientist Finsdale, and he too benefits from it. Abner and the scientist set out for Washington to do further tests there on six more Dogpatch men, with great results. Extremely right wing General Bullmoose (who wants to get all the money in the world), offers Abner a million dollars for the tonic's formula, but Abner prefers to donate it to the government. Bullmoose sends in Appassionata to sway Abner. Meanwhile Dogpatch gets ready for Sadie Hawkins Day, where women of the chorus chase prospective husbands. Abner agrees to let himself be caught by Daisy Mae so she can avoid being caught by Earthquake McGoon (the dirtiest wrestler in the world), but instead, by using the evil talents of Evil Eye Fleagle (who casts spells by giving whammies), he is caught by Appassionata. Abner returns to Washington. Daisy Mae feels he is in danger, and a bunch of people from Dogpatch go to Washington to rescue him from a wedding with Appassionata. It transpires that the side effect of the tonic is to remove the desire for love, so the wives of the six men plead to have them put back the way they were. Back in Dogpatch two things are about to happen: the wedding of McGoon and Daisy Mae, and the dropping of an A-Bomb. The inhabitants won't leave without their statue of Cornpone, and as they are moving it, they discover a tablet signed "A. Lincoln," thus designating Dogpatch a national shrine. All ends happily. There were six geese, six chickens (the geese's understudies), three pigs, two dogs and a mule.

Before Broadway. In 1946–47 Rodgers & Hammerstein wanted to do a show based on Al Capp's characters, but they were too busy. Alan Jay Lerner, with Burton Lane (and later with Arthur Schwartz) got as far as a script in 1955, but difficulties in forging a suitable script, as well as his involvement in *My Fair Lady*, got in the way for Mr. Lerner, and it never even got to rehearsal. Paramount Pictures financed the 1956 stage musical effort. Dick Shawn, Andy Griffith, and Elvis Presley were all considered for Abner, but the producers spotted Peter Palmer on the *Ed Sullivan Show*. The show was tried out in Washington, Boston, and then Philadelphia before Broadway.

The Broadway Run. ST. JAMES THEATRE, 11/15/56–7/12/58. 693 PERFORMANCES. PRESENTED BY Norman Panama, Melvin Frank, and Michael Kidd; MUSIC: Gene de Paul; LYRICS: Johnny Mercer; BOOK: Norman Panama & Melvin Frank; BASED ON the comic strip characters created by Al Capp, which first appeared in the *New York Daily Mirror* on 8/12/35, and last appeared in 1977. Mr. Capp got his inspiration for Abner from Henry Fonda's performance in the movie *Trail of the Lonesome Pine*; DIRECTOR/CHOREOGRAPHER: Michael Kidd; ASSISTANT CHOREOGRAPHERS: Marc Breaux & Deedee Wood; SETS/LIGHTING: William & Jean Eckart; ASSISTANT SETS/ASSISTANT LIGHTING: Tharon Musser & William Goodhart; COSTUMES: Alvin Colt; ASSISTANT COSTUMES: Stanley Simmons; MUSICAL DIRECTOR: Lehman Engel, *John Passaretti*; PRODUCTION MUSICAL ASSISTANT: Karen Gustafson; MUSICAL

CONTINUITY/VOCAL ARRANGEMENTS: Lehman Engel; ORCHESTRATIONS: Philip J. Lang; BALLET MUSIC ARRANGEMENTS: Genevieve Pitot; CAST RECORDING on Columbia; PRESS: Harvey B. Sabinson, Max Eisen (*David Powers*), B.J. Westman; GENERAL MANAGER: Joseph Harris; COMPANY MANAGER: Ira Bernstein; PRODUCTION STAGE MANAGER: Terence Little; STAGE MANAGER: Lawrence N. Kasha; ASSISTANT STAGE MANAGER: Lanier Davis. **Cast:** LONESOME POLECAT: Anthony Mordente, *Robert Karl*; HAIRLESS JOE: Chad Block; ROMEO SCRAGG: Marc Breaux; CLEM SCRAGG: James Hurst, *John Craig*; ALF SCRAGG: Anthony Saverino; MOONBEAM MCSWINE: Carmen Alvarez, *Maureen Hopkins*; MARRYIN' SAM: Stubby Kaye (4); EARTHQUAKE MCGOON: Bern Hoffman; DAISY MAE SCRAGG: Edith Adams (1), *Wynne Miller*; LUCIFER "PAPPY" YOKUM: Joe E. Marks; MAMMY YOKUM: Charlotte Rae (5), *Billie Hayes*; LI'L ABNER YOKUM: Peter Palmer (2); CRONIES: Marc Breaux, Ralph Linn (*Chad Block*), Jack Matthew, Robert McClure, George Reeder (*Merritt Thompson*); MAYOR DAWGMEAT: Oran Osburn; SENATOR JACK S. PHOGBOUND: Ted Thurston; DR. RASMUSSEN T. FINSDALE: Stanley Simmonds; GOVERNMENT MAN: Richard Maitland, *Joe Calvan*; AVAILABLE JONES: William Lanteau; STUPEFYIN' JONES: Julie Newmar, *Denise Colette*; COLONEL: George Reeder, *Lanier Davis*; RADIO COMMENTATORS: James Hurst (*John Craig*), Jack Matthew, Robert McClure; PRESIDENT: Lanier Davis; GENERAL BULLMOOSE: Howard St. John (3); SECRETARIES: Lanier Davis, Jack Matthew, Robert McClure, George Reeder (*Merritt Thompson*); APPASSIONATA VON CLIMAX: Tina Louise, *Deedee Wood*; EVIL EYE FLEAGLE: Al Nesor; DR. SMITHBORN: George Reeder, *Chad Block*; DR. KROGMEYER: Ralph Linn, *Anthony Saverino*; DR. SCHLEIFITZ: Marc Breaux; SOFTWICKE (STATE DEPARTMENT MAN): Lanier Davis; 1ST WIFE: Carmen Alvarez, *Maureen Hopkins*; 2ND WIFE: Pat Creighton, *Christy Reeder*; 3RD WIFE: Lillian D'Honau; 4TH WIFE: Bonnie Evans; 5TH WIFE: Hope Holiday; 6TH WIFE: Deedee Wood, *Sharon Shore*; BUTLER: James J. Jeffries, *Robert McClure*; COLONEL: Lanier Davis; SINGERS: Margaret Baxter, Don Braswell (gone by 57–58), Joan Cherof, Pat Creighton (gone by 57–58), Lanier Davis, Joyce Gladmond (gone by 57–58), Hope Holiday, Jane House (gone by 57–58), James Hurst (*John Craig*), Robert McClure, Jack Matthew, Oran Osburn, Louise Pearl (gone by 57–58), George Ritner (gone by 57–58), Anthony Saverino, Jeanette Scovotti (gone by 57–58), *Katherine Williams, Bob Gorman*; DANCERS: Carmen Alvarez (gone by 57–58), Chad Block, Marc Breaux, Grover Dale (gone by 57–58), Lillian D'Honau, Bonnie Evans, Maureen Hopkins, Robert Karl, Barbara Klopfer, Ralph Linn (gone by 57–58), Richard Maitland (*Joe Calvan*), Tony Mordente (gone by 57–58), Tom Panko (gone by 57–58), Christy Peterson (she married George Reeder and became Christy Reeder by 57–58), George Reeder (*Merritt Thompson*), Sharon Shore, Rebecca Vorno (gone by 57–58), Deedee Wood (gone by 57–58), *Valerie Harper, Joan Lindsay, Shirley Nelson, Patti Nestor, Carol Stevens, Joe Calvan, Mel Davidson, John Kessler, John Ray, Larry Roquemore, George Zima*; ENSEMBLE: Jan Gunnar, Lucky Kargo, Mario Lamm, Reed Morgan, Aldo Ventura, Robert Wiensko, *Joe Mauri, Cliff Carnell, Frank Loren, Ken Ackles*. **Understudies:** Daisy Mae: Joyce Gladmond; Abner: James Hurst, *John Craig*; Bullmoose/Earthquake: Oran Osburn; Marryin' Sam: James J. Jeffries, *Jack Prince*; Mammy: Hope Holiday; Appassionata: Deedee Wood, *Sharon Shore*; Pappy: Bobby Barry, *Joe Calvan*; Evil Eye: Robert Karl; Available: Ralph Linn, *Marc Breaux*; Stupefyin': Lillian D'Honau; Phogbound: Lanier Davis & James J. Jeffries; Finsdale/Butler: Lanier Davis. *Act I*: Overture (Orchestra); *Scene 1* Dogpatch, USA: "A Typical Day" (Dogpatchers); *Scene 2* The Yokum cabin; *Scene 3* The fishing hole: "If I Had My Druthers" (Abner & Cronies), "If I Had My Druthers" (reprise) (Daisy Mae); *Scene 4* Cornpone Square: "Jubilation T. Cornpone" (Marryin' Sam & Dogpatchers), "Jubilation T. Cornpone" (encore) (Marryin' Sam & Dogpatchers), "Rag Offen the Bush" (Dogpatchers), Dogpatch Dance (Dogpatchers); *Scene 5* Dogpatch Road: "Namely You" (Daisy Mae & Abner); *Scene 6* Cornpone Square: "Unnecessary Town" (Daisy Mae, Abner, Dogpatchers); *Scene 7* Washington, DC, sequence; *Scene 7a* Government Laboratory; *Scene 7b* The President's office; *Scene 8* General Bullmoose's office: "What's Good for General Bullmoose" (Secretaries); *Scene 9* Dogpatch Road; *Scene 10* Dogpatch: "There's Room Enough for Us" (Dogpatchers) [added during the run], "The Country's in the Very Best of Hands" (Abner & Marryin' Sam), "The Country's in the Very Best of Hands" (encore) (Abner & Marryin' Sam); *Scene 11* Dogpatch Road; *Scene 12*

Dogpatch: "Sadie Hawkins Day" (ballet) (Dogpatchers). *Act II*: Entr'acte (Orchestra); *Scene 1* Government Testing Laboratory, Washington, DC: "Oh, Happy Day" (Finsdale, Smithborn, Krogmeyer, Schleifitz); *Scene 2* The Yokum cabin: "(I'm) Past My Prime" (Daisy Mae & Marryin' Sam), "Love in a Home" (Abner & Daisy Mae); *Scene 3* General Bullmoose's office; *Scene 4* Corridor in Bullmoose's mansion: "Progress is the Root of All Evil" (Bullmoose); *Scene 5* Ballroom in Bullmoose's mansion: "In Society" (also known as "Society Party") (dance) (Guests & Dogpatchers), "Progress is the Root of All Evil" (reprise) (Bullmoose); *Scene 6* Corridor in Bullmoose's mansion; *Scene 7* Government Testing Laboratory, Washington, DC: "Put 'em Back" (Wives); *Scene 8* Cornpone Square: "Namely You" (reprise) (Daisy Mae), "The Matrimonial Stomp" (Marryin' Sam & Dogpatchers), "Put 'em Back" (reprise) (Wives), "The Matrimonial Stomp" (reprise) (Marryin' Sam & Dogpatchers), Finale: "Jubilation T. Cornpone" (reprise) (Entire Company).

Reviews were generally great. Marc Breaux and Deedee Wood met and married during the production. Edie Adams won a 1957 best supporting actress Tony, and the show would also win for choreography. It was nominated for costumes.

After Broadway. TOUR. Opened on 9/1/58, at the Riviera, Las Vegas, and closed on 1/3/59, at the Royal Alexandra Theatre, Toronto. PRESENTED BY Triad Productions; MUSICAL DIRECTOR: John Passaretti. *Cast*: ABNER: Peter Palmer; DAISY MAE: Wynne Miller; EARTHQUAKE: Bern Hoffman; PAPPY: Joe E. Marks; MAMMY: Billie Hayes; STUPEFYIN': Denise Colette; MARRYIN' SAM: Stubby Kaye; DAWGMEAT: Oran Osburn; PHOGBOUND: Ted Thurston; FINSDALE: Stanley Simmonds; AVAILABLE: William Lanteau; MOONBEAM: Maureen Hopkins; LONESOME: Robert Karl; HAIRLESS JOE/SMITHBORN: Chad Block; ROMEO/SCHLEIFITZ: Marc Breaux; CLEM/KROGMEYER: John Craig; ALF: Anthony Saverino; BULLMOOSE: Howard St. John; APPASSIONATA: Deedee Wood; GOVERNMENT MAN: Joe Calvan; COLONEL/PRESIDENT/STATE DEPARTMENT MAN: Lanier Davis; EVIL EYE: Al Nesor; BUTLER: Robert McClure; ALSO WITH: Jack Matthew, Merritt Thompson, Lillian D'Honau, Bonnie Evans, Hope Holiday, Sharon Shore.

THE MOVIE. 1959. *Cast*: ABNER: Peter Palmer; MARRYIN' SAM: Stubby Kaye; DAISY MAE: Leslie Parrish; BULLMOOSE: Howard St. John; EARTHQUAKE: Bern Hoffman; PAPPY: Joe E. Marks; APPASSIONATA: Stella Stevens; MAMMY: Billie Hayes; ROMEO: Robert Strauss; STUPEFYIN': Julie Newmar; EVIL EYE: Al Nesor; PHOGBOUND: Ted Thurston; AVAILABLE: William Lanteau; MOONBEAM: Carmen Alvarez; DAWGMEAT: Alan Carney; GUEST STAR: Jerry Lewis. Like *The Music Man*, this was a very faithful reproduction of the stage musical. You see the movie, and it's like you'd seen the play.

PAPER MILL PLAYHOUSE, New Jersey, 1968. DIRECTOR: James Mitchell. *Cast*: Dagmar, Michael Beirne, Willi Burke.

In 1996 Marshall Maxwell announced plans to produce a revised version, with Tony Curtis as Phogbound/Bullmoose, and to take it on a tour that culminated in a Broadway run. It never happened.

CITY CENTER, NYC, 3/26/98–3/30/98. 6 PERFORMANCES. Adapted & updated by Christopher Durang to concert format. It was part of the *Encores!* series. DIRECTOR: Christopher Ashley; CHOREOGRAPHER: Kathleen Marshall; LIGHTING: Ken Billington; MUSICAL DIRECTOR: Rob Fisher. Peter Palmer was there opening night. *Cast*: MOONBEAM: Cady Huffman; MARRYIN' SAM: Lea De Laria [sic]; EARTHQUAKE: Michael Mulheren; DAISY MAE: Alice Ripley; PAPPY: Dick Latessa; MAMMY: Dana Ivey; ABNER: Burke Moses; MAYOR DAN'L DAWGMEAT/DR. KROGMEYER: Tom Riis Farrell (Rick Crom was going to play these roles); PHOGBOUND: Kevin Chamberlin (Tom Riis Farrell was going to play this role); EVIL EYE/FINSDALE: John Mineo (Jonathan Freeman was going to play Finsdale); AVAILABLE/SCHLEIFITZ: Marcus Neville; STUPEFYIN': Julie Newmar; BULLMOOSE: David Ogden Stiers; APPASSIONATA: Katie Finneran; SMITHBORN: Danny Burstein; CHORUS: Sean Martin Hingston, Nancy Lemenager, Elizabeth Mills, Cynthia Onrubia, Joey Pizzi.

397. *The Lion King*

The story of Simba, the young Lion Prince, and his battle with his uncle Scar, who wanted to oust his brother Mufasa, the powerful Lion King of Pride Rock. Rafiki is the wise baboon; Sarabi is Simba's mother;

Shenzi is a female hyena; Timon is a meerkat; Pumbaa is a warthog; Zazu is a bird; Nala is Simba's friend. It took 17,000 hours to build the puppets and masks for the original production. There were more than 232 puppets in the show.

Before Broadway. As early as 12/95 Disney was looking at making their successful 1994 animated film into a Broadway stage musical. Workshops began in 1996. Auditions for the chorus began on 1/11/97. The show opened for tryouts in the Orpheum Theatre, Minneapolis, on 7/31/97.

The Broadway Run. NEW AMSTERDAM THEATRE, 11/13/97–. 33 previews from 10/15/97. PRESENTED BY Walt Disney Theatrical Productions; MUSIC: Elton John; LYRICS: Tim Rice; ADDITIONAL MUSIC & LYRICS: Lebo M (i.e. Lebo Morake, the South African musician), Mark Mancina, Jay Rifkin, Julie Taymor, Hans Zimmer; BOOK: Roger Allers & Irene Mecchi; BASED ON the 1994 animated Disney film of the same name, written by Irene Mecchi, Jonathan Roberts, Linda Woolverton; DIRECTOR/COSTUMES: Julie Taymor; CHOREOGRAPHER: Garth Fagan; SETS: Richard Hudson; MASK & PUPPET DESIGN: Julie Taymor & Michael Curry; LIGHTING: Donald Holder; SOUND: Tony Meola; MUSICAL DIRECTOR: Joseph Church; ORCHESTRATIONS: Robert Elhai, David Metzger, Bruce Fowler; VOCAL ARRANGEMENTS/CHORAL DIRECTOR: Lebo M; CAST RECORDING on Disney; PRESS: Boneau/Bryan-Brown; CASTING: Jay Binder; COMPANY MANAGER: Steve Chaikelson, *Sammy Ledbetter, Kathryn Frawley & Marshall Jones* (7/10/01–5/5/02), *Dave Ehle* (from 5/6/02); PRODUCTION STAGE MANAGER: Jeff Lee, *Elizabeth Burgess.* **Cast:** RAFIKI: Tsidii LeLoka (4), *Thuli Dumakude* (from 11/11/98), *Sheila* Gibbs (by 00–01), *Nomvula Dlamini*; MUFASA: Samuel E. Wright (2), *Brian Everat Chandler, Samuel E. Wright*; SARABI: Gina Breedlove, *Meena T. Jahi* (from 8/4/98), *Denise Marie Williams* (by 00–01), *Meena T. Jahi, Robin Payne* (on 9/10/03); ZAZU: Geoff Hoyle (3), *Bill Bowers* (from 10/21/98), *Robert Dorfman, Tony Freeman* (by 00–01), *Adam Stein*; SCAR: John Vickery (1), *Tom Hewitt* (from 10/21/98), *Derek Smith* (by 00–01); YOUNG SIMBA: Scott Irby-Ranniar (11), *Mykel Bath, Kai Braithwaite & David Dakota Sanchez* (by now a split role), *Rodney Henry Jr. & Alexander Mitchell, Aaron L. Harris & Robert D. Wright, Danny Fetter* (alternate), *Rajonie Hammond* (alternate from 2/04); YOUNG NALA: Kajuana Shuford (12), *Imani Parks & Ashley Perry* (a split role, 6/98–8/99), *Jordan Puryear, Leovina Charles & Ivana Grace*; SHENZI: Tracy Nicole Chapman (9), *Vanessa A. Jones, Lana Gordon* (from 00–01), *Marlayna Syms*; BANZAI: Stanley Wayne Mathis (8), *Keith Bennett* (from 9/30/98), *Leonard Joseph* (by 00–01), *Curtiss I'Cook*; ED: Kevin Cahoon (10), *Jeff Skowron* (from 10/21/98), *Jeff Gurner, Timothy Gulan* (by 00–01), *Thom Christopher Warren*; TIMON: Max Casella (13), *John E. Brady, Danny Rutigliano* (from 6/16/98), *John E. Brady* (by 00–01), *Danny Rutigliano*; PUMBAA: Tom Alan Robbins (5); SIMBA: Jason Raize (6), *Christopher Jackson* (by 00–01), *Clifton Oliver, Josh Tower*; NALA: Heather Headley (7) (until 7/5/98), *Mary Randle* (from 7/7/98), *Heather Headley* (on 12/7/98, and then permanently from 12/9/98), *Bashirrah Creswell* (on 4/6/00), *Sharon L. Young* (by 00–01), *Kissy Simmons* (from 8/26/03), *Renee Elise Goldsberry*; ENSEMBLE SINGERS: Eugene Barry-Hill, Gina Breedlove, Ntomb'khona Dlamini, Sheila Gibbs, Lindiwe Hlengwa, Christopher Jackson, Vanessa A. Jones, Faca Kulu, Ron Kunene, Lebo M, Philip Dorian McAdoo, Sam McKelton, Anthony Manough, Nandi Morake, Rachel Tecora Tucker, *Andrea Frierson Toney, Nhlanhla Ngema, Leonard Wooldridge, Kristen Dowtin, Adrian Bailey, Brian Everat Chandler, Lindiwe Dlamini, Nomvula Dlamini, Roy Harcourt, Charles Holt, Keswa, Sheryl McCallum, Robin Payne, Remember, Rema Webb, Kenny Redell Williams, Sophian Brown*; ENSEMBLE DANCERS: Camille M. Brown, Iresol Cardona, Mark Allan Davis, Lana Gordon, Timothy Hunter, Michael Joy, Aubrey Lynch II, Karine Plantadit-Bageot, Endalyn Taylor-Shellman, Levensky Smith (*Gary Lewis*), Ashi K. Smythe, Christine Yasunaga, *Felipe Abrigo, Dameka Hayes, Erika LaVonn, Stephanie C. Battle, Ramon Flowers, LaMae, Michelle Dorant, Rod Harrelson, Gregory A. King, Marque Lynch Jr., Abdul Latif, Ian Vincent McGinnis, Ryan Brooke Taylor, Valencia Yearwood, Nelson M. Babassa*; SINGER/DANCER REPLACEMENTS: *Sandy Alvarez, Kylin Brady, Latrisa A. Coleman, Bobby Daye, Christine Hollingsworth, Mpume Sikakane, Torya.* **Standbys:** Scar/Pumbaa: Mark Deklin; Mufasa: Mel Johnson Jr. **Understudies:** Scar: Kevin Bailey, *Derek Smith, Patrick Page, Martin Kildare, Tom Hewitt, Thom Christopher Warren*; Mufasa: Eugene Barry-Hill, Philip Dorian McAdoo, *Alton Fitzgerald White, C.C. Brown, Adrian Bai-*

ley, Frank Wright II, Brian Evaret Chandler; Banzai: Philip Dorian McAdoo, Levensky Smith, Curtis l'Cook, Adrian Bailey, Kenny Redell Williams, Charles Holt; Pumbaa: Philip Dorian McAdoo, Danny Rutigliano, *John E. Brady*; Sarabi: Camille M. Brown, Vanessa A. Jones, *Robin Payne, Sheryl McCallum*; Zazu: Kevin Cahoon, Danny Rutigliano, *Bill Bowers, Tony Freeman, Thom Christopher Warren, John E. Brady*; Timon: Kevin Cahoon, Danny Rutigliano, *Thom Christopher Warren, John E. Brady*; Rafiki: Sheila Gibbs, Rema Webb, Lindiwe Hlengwa, *Marva Hicks, Sheryl McCallum, Mpume Sikakane*; Shenzi: Lana Gordon, Vanessa A. Jones, *Michelle Dorant, Rema Webb, Angelica Edwards Patterson*; Nala: Lindiwe Hlengwa, Sonya Leslie, *Renee Elise Goldsberry, Mary Randle, Camille M. Brown, Rema Webb*; Simba: Timothy Hunter, Christopher Jackson, *Josh Tower, Bobby Daye, Dennis Johnston, Marque Lynch Jr., Rod Harrelson*; Ed: Frank Wright II, *Jeff Skowron, Jeff Gumer, Dennis Johnston*; Young Nala: Jennifer Josephs; Young Simba: Alberto Cruz Jr., *Alexander Mitchell.* Swings: Lindiwe Dlamini, Peter Anthony Moore, Frank Wright II, Sonya Leslie, Nhlanhla Ngema, Rachel Tecora Tucker, *Felicio Gonzales, Tony James, Dennis Johnston, Leonora Stapleton, Marque Lynch Jr., Sheryl McCallum, Bobby Daye, LaMae Caparas, Ramon Flowers.* **Act I: Scene 1** Pride Rock: "Grasslands Chant ("Nants Ingonyama") (by Lebo M)/"Circle of Life" (Rafiki & Ensemble); **Scene 2** Scar's cave; **Scene 3** Rafiki's tree; **Scene 4** The Pridelands: "The Morning Report" (Zazu, Young Simba, Mufasa); **Scene 5** Scar's cave; **Scene 6** The Pridelands: "I Just Can't Wait to Be King" (Young Simba, Young Nala, Zazu, Ensemble); **Scene 7** Elephant graveyard: "Chow Down" (Shenzi, Banzai, Ed); **Scene 8** Under the stars: "They Live in You" (by Mark Mancina, Jay Rifkin, Lebo M) (Mufasa & Ensemble); **Scene 9** Elephant graveyard: "Be Prepared" (Scar, Shenzi, Banzai, Ed, Ensemble); **Scene 10** The Gorge; **Scene 11** Pride Rock: "Be Prepared" (reprise) (Scar & Ensemble); **Scene 12** Rafiki's tree; Scene 13 The desert/the jungle: "Hakuna Matata" (Timon, Pumba, Young Simba, Simba, Ensemble). **Act II:** Entr'acte: "One by One" (by Lebo M) (Ensemble); **Scene 1** Scar's cave: "The Madness of King Scar" (Scar, Zazu, Banzai, Shenzi, Ed, Nala); **Scene 2** The Pridelands: "Shadowland" (m: Lebo M & Hans Zimmer; l: Mark Mancina & Lebo M) (Nala, Rafiki, Ensemble); **Scene 3** The jungle; **Scene 4** Under the stars: "Endless Night" (m: Lebo M, Hans Zimmer, Jay Rifkin; l: Julie Taymor) (Simba & Ensemble); **Scene 5** Rafiki's tree; **Scene 6** The jungle: "Can You Feel the Love Tonight?" (Timon, Pumbaa, Simba, Ensemble), "He Lives in You" (reprise of "They Live in You") (Rafiki, Simba, Ensemble); **Scene 7** Pride Rock: "King of Pride Rock" (m: Hans Zimmer & Lebo M) (Ensemble)/"Circle of Life" (reprise) (Ensemble).

Note: all music by Elton John, and all lyrics by Tim Rice–unless otherwise stated. Rafiki's chants by Tsidii LeLoka. Lioness chant by Lebo M.

Broadway reviews were great. In 7/98 Actors' Equity allowed the South African performers in the show to remain with the Broadway cast indefinitely. Prior to that they had been granted only 20 weeks. However, it was found impossible to find American performers to be trained to replicate the singing styles. The show won Tonys for musical, direction of a musical, choreography, sets, costumes, and lighting. It was the first time a woman director had won a Tony for a Broadway musical. It was also nominated for score, orchestrations, and for Samuel E. Wright, Tsidii LeLoka. The Clintons and Gores attended the 9/14/98 showing. The production missed a performance on 8/14/03 due to the big power blackout.

After Broadway. FILM. *The Lion King II: Simba's Pride* was released on video on 10/7/98. The story picks up where the original left off, and follows Simba's relationship with his daughter.

HARU THEATRE, Tokyo, 12/20/98. PRESENTED BY Shiki Theatrical Company; DIRECTOR: Keita Asari. OSAKA, 4/18/99–1/21/00. 674 PERFORMANCES. FUKUOKA, 4/17/01.

LYCEUM THEATRE, London, 10/19/99. Previews from 9/24/99. It had the same basic crew as for the Broadway run. On 8/21/02 it extended its closing date to 6/29/03, and this date was extended to 9/28/03.

PRINCESS OF WALES THEATRE, Toronto, 4/25/00. Rehearsals from 2/7/00. Previews from 3/30/00. It had a cast of 48. PRESENTED BY Ed & David Mirvish. **Cast:** RAFIKI: Tshidi Manye; SIMBA: Stephen Allerick, *Michael Blake*; MUFASA: Eugene Clark, *Horace V. Rogers*; SCAR: Richard McMillan, *Richard Clarkin*; NALA: Saskia Garel, *Jewelle Blackman*; SARABI: Robin S. Walker; ZAZU: Gerald Isaac; ED: Dean Balkwill;

TIMON: Bill Perry. It was going to close on 9/28/03 due to the SARS scare, but it kept running.

PANTAGES THEATRE, Los Angeles, 10/19/00–1/12/03. Previews from 9/29/00. It extended its run three times, and was the longest-running musical ever at the Pantages. 1.5 million people saw it there. *Cast*: SCAR: John Vickery; TIMON: Danny Rutigliano; MUFASA: Rufus Bonds Jr.; RAFIKI: Fuschia Walker; SIMBA: Clifton Oliver; NALA: Moe Daniels, *Jewl Anguay* (from 10/3/01); ZAZU: William Akey; PUMBAA: Bob Bouchard; SHENZI: Carla Renata Williams; BANZAI: Jeffrey Polk; ED: Price Waldman, *Jim Raposa* (from 12/2/01); SIMBA: Adrian Diamond & KaRonn Henderson; YOUNG NALA: Jasmine Guy & Lisa Tucker. Its next stop was the CADILLAC PALACE THEATRE, Chicago, 5/3/03–11/23/03. Previews from 4/23/03. DIRECTOR: Julie Taymor; CHOREOGRAPHER: Garth Fagan; SETS: Richard Hudson & Julie Taymor; LIGHTING: Donald Holder. CAST: SCAR: Larry Yando; MUFASA: Rufus Bonds Jr.; RAFIKI: Thandi Soni; TIMON: Benjamin Clost; ZAZU: Derek Hasenstab; PUMBAA: Bob Amaral; SIMBA: Brandon Victor Dixon; NALA: Adia Dobbins; BANZAI: Melvin Abston. This production next moved to the ORPHEUM THEATRE, San Francisco, on 1/29/04.

HAMBURG, 12/2/01. This was the first continental European run. PRESENTED BY Stage Holdings (owned by Joop Van Den Ende) & Disney Theatrical Productions.

FIRST NATIONAL TOUR. This was the "Gazelle" tour. It opened on 4/27/02, at the Buell Theatre, Denver. Previews from 4/17/02. *Cast*: SCAR: Patrick Page; MUFASA: Alton Fitzgerald White; RAFIKI: Fredi Walker-Browne, *Futhi Mhlongo*; TIMON: John Plumpis; ZAZU: Jeffrey Binder; PUMBAA: Blake Hammond, *Ben Lipitz*; SARABI: Jean Michelle Greer; BANZAI: James Brown-Orleans; SHENZI: Jacquelyn Renae Hodges; ED: Wayne Pile; SIMBA: Josh Tower, *Alan Mingo Jr.*; NALA: Kissy Simmons (until 8/03); YOUNG SIMBA: Akil L. Luqman & Chris Warren.

SECOND NATIONAL TOUR. This was the "Cheetah" tour. It opened on 4/23/03, in Chicago. *Cast*: RAFIKI: Thandazile A. Soni; MUFASA: Rufus Bonds Jr.; SARABI: Marvette Williams; ZAZU: Derek Hasenstab; SCAR: Larry Yando; BANZAI: Melvin Abston; SHENZI: Shaullanda Lacombe; ED: Brian Sills; TIMON: Benjamin Clost; PUMBAA: Bob Amaral; SIMBA: Brandon Victor Dixon; NALA: Adia Ginneh Dobbins;.

398. *Little Johnny Jones*

Johnny is an American jockey in Britain to win the Derby on his horse Yankee Doodle Dandy. He is accused of throwing the race, and with the help of a private detective finds he has been framed by an American gambler, and clears his name. The idea behind the original 1904 musical was a newspaper article about Tod Sloan, the American jockey living in England.

Before Broadway. The original opened on Broadway at the LIBERTY THEATRE, 11/7/1904. 52 PERFORMANCES. PRESENTED BY Sam Harris; DIRECTOR: George M. Cohan. *Cast*: George M. Cohan, Jerry J. Cohan, Donald Brian, Helen F. Cohan. Then it ran at the NEW YORK THEATRE, 5/8/1905–8/26/1905; and again, same venue, 11/13/1905–12/9/1905. It opened at the ACADEMY OF MUSIC, on 4/22/1907. 16 PERFORMANCES. Warners filmed it in 1923, with Johnny Hines and Wyndham Standing; and in 1929, adapted by Adelaide Heilbron, and directed by Mervyn LeRoy, and starring Eddie Buzzell and Alice Day. The 1982 production (the first recorded revival since those early days) originated at the Goodspeed Opera House, in Connecticut.

The Broadway Run. ALVIN THEATRE, 3/21/82. 29 previews. 1 PERFORMANCE. PRESENTED BY James M. Nederlander, Steven Leber, David Krebs, The John F. Kennedy Center; MUSIC/LYRICS/BOOK: George M. Cohan; ADAPTED BY Alfred Uhry; DIRECTOR: Gerald Gutierrez; CHOREOGRAPHER: Dan Siretta; SETS: Robert Randolph; COSTUMES: David Toser; LIGHTING: Thomas Skelton; SOUND: Abe Jacob; MUSICAL DIRECTOR: Lynn Crigler; ADDITIONAL ORCHESTRATIONS: Eddie Sauter & Mack Schlefer; DANCE MUSIC ARRANGEMENTS: Russell Warner; VOCAL ARRANGEMENTS/ADDITIONAL DANCE MUSIC ARRANGEMENTS: Robert Fisher; MUSIC CONSULTANT: Alfred Simon; PRESS: Fred Nathan; CASTING: Warren Pincus; GENERAL MANAGER: Marvin A. Krauss; ASSISTANT COMPANY MANAGER: Susan B. Frost; PRODUCTION STAGE MANAGER:

Robert V. Straus; STAGE MANAGER: John Actman; ASSISTANT STAGE MANAGER: Earl Aaron Levine. *Cast*: STARTER AT THE HOTEL CECIL: Jack Bittner; ANTHONY ANSTEY, A RACE TRACK MAN: Peter Van Norden (3); FLORABELLE FLY, SOCIETY EDITOR OF THE *San Francisco Searcher*: Jane Galloway (4); TIMOTHY D. MCGEE, ANOTHER RACETRACK MAN: Tom Rolfing (8); GOLDIE GATES, AN AMERICAN COPPER HEIRESS: Maureen Brennan (2); SING-SONG, SPORTS EDITOR, *Peking Gazette*: Bruce Chew; WHITNEY WILSON, THE GREAT UNKNOWN: Ernie Sabella (5); A BELLBOY: Al Micacchion; JOHNNY JONES, AN AMERICAN JOCKEY: Donny Osmond (1) ☆; MRS. KENWORTH, GOLDIE'S AUNT AND GUARDIAN: Anna McNeely (6); ANNOUNCER AT ENGLISH DERBY: Jack Bittner (7); CAPTAIN SQUIRVY: Jack Bittner (7); A NEWSBOY: David Fredericks; AMERICAN BOYS/PORTERS/SAILORS: Richard Dodd, David Fredericks, James Homan, Gary Kirsch, Bobby Longbottom, Al Micacchion, David Monzione, Keith Savage; AMERICAN GIRLS: Colleen Ashton, Teri Corcoran, Susie Fenner, Linda Gradl, Debra Grimm, Lori Lynott, Annette Michelle, Mayme Paul. **Standby**: Johnny: Jamie Torcellini. **Understudies**: Mrs. Kenworth/Florabelle: Colleen Ashton; Goldie: Susie Fenner; Timothy: Gary Kirsch; Anthony/Starter/Announcer: Earl Aaron Levine; Squirvy/Sing-Song/Whitney: Earl Aaron Levine. **Dance Alternates**: Tammy Silva, Jonathan Aronson, Jamie Torcellini. *Act I*: Overture (Orchestra); *Scene 1* Exterior of the Hotel Cecil, London; 1904: "The Cecil in London (Town)" (Starter & Ensemble); *Scene 2* Interior of the Hotel Cecil; immediately following: "Then I'd Be Satisfied with Life" (Anthony), "Yankee Doodle Boy" (Johnny & Ensemble); *Scene 3* Hyde Park; immediately following: "Oh, You Wonderful Boy" [from *The Little Millionaire*, 1911] (Goldie, Florabelle, American Girls); *Scene 4* The British Derby; that afternoon: "The Voice in My Heart" [from *Little Nellie Kelly*, 1922] (Mrs. Kenworth & Ensemble), Finaletto (Company). *Act II*: Entr'acte (Orchestra); *Scene 1* Outside the pier at Southampton; a week later: "Captain of a Ten Day Boat" (Captain & Ensemble); *Scene 2* The pier itself; immediately following: "Goodbye Flo" (Florabelle & Sailors), "Life's a Funny Proposition" (Johnny), "Let's You and I Just Say Goodbye" [from *The Rise of Rosie O'Reilly*, 1923] (Goldie), "Give My Regards to Broadway" (Johnny & Ensemble); *Scene 3* A New York street; two weeks later: "Extra! Extra!" (Newsboys); *Scene 4* Saratoga; the 4th of July: "American Ragtime" [from *The American Idea*, 1908] (Florabelle, Timothy, Johnny, Ensemble), Finale (Company).

Note: program subject to change (ironic considering the show ran for only one performance).

Reviews were terrible.

After Broadway. PLAYHOUSE 91, 6/10/87–11/15/87. 175 PERFORMANCES. This Off Broadway revival was called *Give My Regards to Broadway*. PRESENTED BY the Light Opera of Manhattan; FREELY ADAPTED from the original by Raymond Allen, Todd Ellison, Jerry Gotham; DIRECTORS: Raymond Allen & Jerry Gotham; SETS: Mina Albergo. *Cast*: JOHNNY: Brian Quinn; MRS. ANNETTE KENWORTH: Millie Petroski; FLORABELLE: Fehr Bradley; TIMOTHY: Peder Hansen; MARY DUGAN: Susan Davis Holmes; ANSTEY: Bruce MacKillip. "The Cecil in London Town," "They're All My Friends," "I Want You," "I'm Just a Mademoiselle," "'op in Me 'ansom," "New Yorkers," "Here at the Derby," "Yankee Doodle Dandy," "All Aboard," "Captain of a Ten Day Boat," "Goodbye Flo," "Trio," "Life's a Funny Proposition," "A Girl I Know," "Give My Regards to Broadway," "Why is There a Sunrise," "Mary," Finale.

399. *Little Me*

The rise of a voluptuous, manipulative, egotistical, beauty from Drifters' Row, Venezuela, Illinois, to a Southampton, Long Island, estate. Sid Caesar played all seven men in her life: Noble is an over-achieving teenage snob who loves poor Belle Schlumpfert as much as he can (he says, for example, "considering you're riff-raff, and I'm well-to-do"). Belle loves him but until she attains social position he can't marry her. So she sets out to do just that. Noble studies medicine and law at Harvard and Yale, becomes a flying ace in World War I (he shoots down 46 enemy planes — 27 in the air, 13 on the ground, and 6 in the factory), becomes governor of both North and South Dakota, and is the man with whom Belle, literally, walks off into the sunset at the end of the show. Amos is the 88-year-old decrepit skinflint banker; Val is the flashy but hopelessly untalented French straw-hatted boulevard entertainer; Fred is the hick soldier who marries Belle and who quickly dies (she takes his name and becomes Belle Poitrine): Otto is the dictatorial Prussian Hollywood director rather like Erich von Stroheim (Schniztler is head of Metronome Pictures and kills himself after seeing Belle's latest picture — she is such a bad actress); Cherney is the weak and impoverished ruler of the Duchy of Rosenzweig; and Noble Jr., over achieving, just like his father, studies at both Julliard and Georgia Tech to become a musical engineer. George is Belle's faithful admirer.

Before Broadway. Patrick Dennis's artful spoof on the celebrities who in the late 1950s were beginning to "tell all" in their biographies was re-written by Neil Simon as a vehicle for comedian Sid Caesar, so that the star could show off his peculiar talent for doing many roles. The numbers "Be a Mother," "Doing Time," "Thanks! Don't Mention It" and "Vitabelle" were not used. Bob Fosse had to contend with songwriter Carolyn Leigh, who would try to have him arrested (literally) if he in any way tampered with her songs. The show tried out in Philadelphia. "Smart People Stay Single," "Mama's Little Girl," "Lafayette" and "Gifts of a Second Chance" were cut before Broadway.

The Broadway Run. LUNT—FONTANNE THEATRE, 11/17/62–6/29/63. 3 previews from 11/15/62. 257 PERFORMANCES. PRESENTED BY Cy Feuer & Ernest H. Martin; MUSIC: Cy Coleman; LYRICS: Carolyn Leigh; BOOK: Neil Simon; BASED ON the 1961 spoof novel *Little Me: The Intimate Memoirs of That Great Star of Stage, Screen and Television, Belle Poitrine, as told to Patrick Dennis*, by Patrick Dennis; DIRECTORS: Cy Feuer & Bob Fosse; CHOREOGRAPHER: Bob Fosse; SETS/LIGHTING: Robert Randolph; COSTUMES: Robert Fletcher; MUSICAL DIRECTOR: Charles Sanford; ORCHESTRATIONS: Ralph Burns; DANCE MUSIC ARRANGEMENTS: Fred Werner; VOCAL ARRANGEMENTS: Clay Warnick; CAST RECORDING on RCA; PRESS: Merle Debuskey & Seymour Krawitz; COMPANY MANAGER: Marshall Young, *Arthur Glicksman*; PRODUCTION STAGE MANAGER: Phil Friedman; STAGE MANAGER: William Dodds; ASSISTANT STAGE MANAGER: Robert Merriman. **Cast:** BUTLER: John Anania; PATRICK DENNIS: Peter Turgeon (8); MISS POITRINE, TODAY: Nancy Andrews (3); MOMMA: Adnia Rice (10); BELLE POITRINE: Virginia Martin (2); GEORGE MUSGROVE, AS A BOY: John Sharpe; BRUCEY: James Senn; RAMONA: Else Olufsen; NOBLE EGGLESTON: Sid Caesar (1) *; MRS. EGGLESTON: Nancy Cushman (7); MISS KEPPLEWHITE: Gretchen Cryer, *Barbara Beck*; PINCHLEY JR.: Mickey Deems (9); NURSE: Margery Beddow; AMOS PINCHLEY: Sid Caesar (1) *; KLEEG: Burt Bier; NEWSBOY: Michael Smuin; BERNIE BUCHSBAUM: Joey Faye (5); BENNIE BUCHSBAUM: Mort Marshall (4); DEFENSE LAWYER: Mickey Deems; VAL DU VAL: Sid Caesar (1) *; GEORGE MUSGROVE: Swen Swenson (6); FRED POITRINE: Sid Caesar (1) *; PREACHER: Ken Ayers; GERMAN OFFICER: Mickey Deems (9); GENERAL: Michael Quinn; COURIER: Eddie Gasper; RED CROSS NURSE: Sandra Stahl; STEWARD: David Gold; OTTO SCHNITZLER: Sid Caesar (1) *; SECRETARY: Marcia Gilford; PRODUCTION ASSISTANT: Mickey Deems (9); VICTOR: Marc Jordan; PRINCE CHERNEY: Sid Caesar (1) *; YULNICK: Mickey Deems (9); BABY: Virginia Martin (2); NOBLE EGGLESTON JR.: Sid Caesar (1) *; SINGERS: John Anania, Ken Ayers, Burt Bier, Gretchen Cryer, Marcia Gilford, Harris Hawkins, Marc Jordan, Else Olufsen, Michael Quinn, Sandra Stahl, Lory Stark; DANCERS: Barbara Beck, Margery Beddow, Eddie Gasper, Gene Gavin, David Gold, Reby Howells, James Kirby, Odette Phillips, Dounia Rathbone, James Senn, Barbara Sharma, John Sharpe, Michael Smuin, Michel Stuart, Renata Vaselle. **Understudies:** For Sid Caesar: Mickey Deems; For Mickey Deems: Burt Bier; Belle/Baby: Sandra Stahl; Bernie/Bennie: Marc Jordan; George: David Gold; Mrs. Eggleston: Adnia Rice; Patrick: Ken Ayers; Momma: Marcia Gilford. **Act I:** THE PRESENT: *Scene 1* Belle's estate in Southampton, Long Island: "The Truth" [Belle today (Miss Poitrine), Butler, Servants]. THE PAST: *Scene 2* A tumbledown shack in Drifters' Row, Venezuela, Illinois: "(On the) Other Side of the Tracks" (Belle), "Birthday Party" (The Rich Kids' Rag) (Boys & Girls); *Scene 3* The Egglestons' elegant living room: "I Love You" (Noble & Belle);

Scene 4 Exterior of the Eggleston home: "(On the) Other Side of the Tracks" (reprise) (Belle). THE PRESENT: *Scene 5* Belle's estate. THE PAST: *Scene 6* Interior of a small-town bank: "Deep Down Inside" (Amos, Belle, Pinchley Jr., Poor People). THE PRESENT: *Scene 7* A golf course. THE PAST: *Scene 8* A hotel room in Peoria; *Scene 9* A prison: "(To) Be a Performer!" (Bennie & Bernie) [originally written by Coleman & Leigh as part of a demo when they were trying to get the job of scoring *Gypsy*]; *Scene 10* A courtroom in Chicago; *Scene 11* A stage in Chicago: "(Oh! Dem Doggone) Dimples" (Belle & Police Escort). THE PRESENT: *Scene 12* Belle's estate. THE PAST: *Scene 13* The Skylight roof, Chicago: "(Le Grand) Boom-Boom" (Val & Girls), "I've Got Your Number" (George & Belle — George danced a memorable striptease). THE PRESENT: *Scene 14* Belle's estate. THE PAST: *Scene 15* A small gaily-decorated apartment in Chicago: "Real Live Girl" (Fred); *Scene 16* At the battle front and in Chicago: "Real Live Girl" (reprise) (The Doughboys) [a highlight], "(Le Grand) Boom-Boom" (reprise) (Belle & Howitzers); *Scene 17* A base hospital somewhere in France. **Act II:** THE PRESENT: *Scene 1* Belle's estate. THE PAST: *Scene 2* On board the S.S. *Gigantic*, in the North Atlantic. THE PRESENT: *Scene 3* Belle's estate. THE PAST: *Scene 4* Hollywood; *Scene 5* Belle in Hollywood: "Poor Little Hollywood Star" (Belle); *Scene 6* The office of the Buchsbaum Brothers, Hollywood: "(To) Be a Performer!" (reprise) (Bennie & Bernie); *Scene 7* A biblical movie set. THE PRESENT: *Scene 8* Belle's estate: "Little Me" (Miss Poitrine & Belle). THE PAST: *Scene 9* The casino in Monte Carlo. THE PRESENT: *Scene 10* Belle's estate. THE PAST: *Scene 11* The royal bedchamber of Prince Cherney of Rosenzweig: "The Prince's Farewell" (Goodbye) (Cherney, Doctor, Yulnick, Loyal Subjects). THE PRESENT: *Scene 12* The rumpus room in Belle's estate. THE PAST: *Scene 13* The Dakotas. THE PRESENT: *Scene 14* The rumpus room in Belle's estate: "Here's to Us" (Miss Poitrine & Guests). THE PAST: *Scene 15* The exterior of the house, Belle's estate. THE PRESENT: *Scene 16* Belle's estate; *Scene 17* Belle's estate: Finale (Noble & Belle).

Broadway reviews were generally terrific, but the show failed. Mickey Deems went on for Sid Caesar on 6/12/63, but the next day Mr. Caesar was back. The production never recouped its $400,000 investment. The show won a Tony for choreography, and was nominated for musical, producer of a musical, composer & lyricist, book, director of a musical, costumes, and for Sid Caesar, Swen Swenson, Virginia Martin.

After Broadway. TOUR. Opened on 1/30/64, at the Auditorium, Rochester, NY. MUSICAL DIRECTOR: Charles Sanford. **Cast:** NOBLE, ETC: Sid Caesar; BELLE: Virginia Martin; BELLE, TODAY: Nancy Andrews; GEORGE: Swen Swenson; MOMMA: Alice Nunn; BUTLER: Burt Bier; MRS. EGGLESTON: Edith Gresham; PINCHLEY JR., ETC: H.F. Green; NURSE: Leelyn Palmer (she become Leland Palmer); DANCERS INCLUDED: Kathryn Doby & Leelyn Palmer.

CAMBRIDGE THEATRE, London, 11/18/64. 334 PERFORMANCES. It got great reviews, especially for Bruce Forsyth in the lead. In the audience one night in Dec. 1964 was Judy Garland, then living in London. DIRECTOR: Arthur Lewis; MUSICAL DIRECTOR: Ed Coleman; LONDON CAST RECORDING on DRG (it included "Rich Kids Rag"). **Cast:** NOBLE, ETC: Bruce Forsyth; BELLE: Eileen Gourlay; OLDER BELLE: Avril Angers.

400. *Little Me (1982 Broadway revival)*

This was a revised version; had to be really as there wasn't an actor like Sid Caesar who could tackle all the roles.

The Broadway Run. EUGENE O'NEILL THEATRE, 1/21/82–2/21/82. 30 previews. 36 PERFORMANCES. PRESENTED BY Ron Dante, Wayne Rogers, Steven Leber, David Krebs, McLaughlin, Piven, Inc., Warner Theatre Productions, and Emanuel Azenberg; MUSIC/VOCAL & DANCE MUSIC ARRANGEMENTS: Cy Coleman; LYRICS: Carolyn Leigh; REVISED BOOK: Neil Simon; BASED ON the 1961 spoof novel *Little Me: The Intimate Memoirs of That Great Star of Stage, Screen and Television, Belle Poitrine, as told to Patrick Dennis*, by Patrick Dennis; DIRECTOR: Robert Drivas; CHOREOGRAPHER: Peter Gennaro; SETS/COSTUMES: Tony Walton; LIGHTING: Beverly Emmons; SOUND: Tom Morse; MUSICAL DIRECTOR: Donald York; ORCHESTRATIONS: Harold Wheeler; PRESS: Bill Evans & Associates; CASTING: Marilyn Szatmary; GENERAL MANAGER: Jose

Vega; COMPANY MANAGER: Bruce Birkenhead; STAGE MANAGER: Robert Lo Bianco; ASSISTANT STAGE MANAGER: Lani Sundsten; SECOND ASSISTANT STAGE MANAGER: John Hillner. **Cast: Act I**: ANNOUNCER: Gibby Brand (7); BELLE (TODAY): Jessica James (9); CHARLIE DRAKE: Henry Sutton (5); BELLE POITRINE: Mary Gordon Murray (3) ✰; MOMMA: Mary Small (6); RAMONA: Mary C. Holton; CERINE: Gail Pennington; BRUCE: Brian Quinn; NOBLE EGGLESTON: Victor Garber (2) ✰; FLO EGGLESTON: James Coco (1) ✰; GREENSLEEVES: Henry Sutton (5); MS. KEPPLEWHITE: Maris Clement; PINCHLEY JR.: James Brennan (8); NURSE: Sean Murphy; AMOS PINCHLEY: James Coco (1) ✰; TOWN SPOKESMAN: Henry Sutton (5); COURT CLERK: Stephen Berger; ATTORNEY: Gibby Brand (7); BANDLEADER: Gibby Brand (7); HENCHMEN: Bob Freschi & Stephen Berger; FRANKIE POLO: Don Correia (4); VAL DU VAL: Victor Garber (2) ✰; BOOM BOOM GIRLS: Bebe Neuwirth & Gail Pennington; FRED POITRINE: Victor Garber (2) ✰; BERT: Mark McGrath; SERGEANT: Stephen Berger; PREACHER: Gibby Brand (7); GERMAN SOLDIER: Gibby Brand (7); GENERAL: Gibby Brand (7); RED CROSS NURSE: Andrea Green. **Act II**: CAPTAIN: Bob Freschi; STEWARD: David Cahn; SAILOR I: Brian Quinn; SAILOR II: Mark McGrath; MR. WORST: James Coco (1) ✰; ASSISTANT DIRECTOR: Henry Sutton (5); OTTO SCHNITZLER: James Coco (1) ✰; PHARAOH I: Kevin Winkler; CROUPIER: Henry Sutton (5); DOCTOR: Stephen Berger; YULNICK: Gibby Brand (7); PRINCE CHERNEY: James Coco (1) ✰; BABY BELLE: Mary Gordon Murray (3) ✰; NOBLE JUNIOR: Victor Garber (2) ✰; ENSEMBLE (TOWNSPEOPLE, SKYLIGHT PATRONS, NURSES, SOLDIERS, PASSENGERS, INTERNATIONAL SET, PEASANTS): Stephen Berger, Michael Blevins, David Cahn, Maris Clement, Bob Freschi, Andrea Green, Mary C. Holton, Mark McGrath, Gary Mendelson, Sean Murphy, Bebe Neuwirth, Gail Pennington, Susan Powers, Brian Quinn, Kevin Brooks Winkler. **Understudies**: For James Coco: Gibby Brand; For Victor Garber: Gibby Brand & John Hillner; For Mary Gordon Murray: Susan Powers; For Jessica James: Mary Small; For Don Correia: James Brennan; For Henry Sutton: Bob Freschi; For Mary Small: Maris Clement; For Gibby Brand: Stephen Berger; For James Brennan: John Hillner. **Swings**: John Hillner & Meredith Murray. **Orchestra**: REEDS: Joel Kaye & Rick Centalonza; TRUMPETS: Earl Gardner & Joe Mosello; TROMBONE: Dale Kirkland; PIANO: Barry Gordon; BASS: David Finck; PERCUSSION: Joe Passaro; DRUMS: Luther Rix. **Act I**: **Scene 1** The Casa Manana, Hackensack, New Jersey; this evening. Young Belle's home in Twin Jugs, Illinois; years ago: "Don't Ask a Lady" (Belle today) [a new number], "(On) the Other Side of the Tracks" (Belle); **Scene 2** Noble Eggleston's home on Quality Hill. Belle's shack: "The Rich Kids Rag" (The Birthday Party) (Company), "I Love You" (Noble, Bell, Company), "The Other Side of the Tracks" (reprise) (Belle); **Scene 3** Pinchley's Bank: "Deep Down Inside" (Pinchley, Belle, Company) [choreography by Bob Fosse, recreated from the original production]; **Scene 4** Young Belle's apartment; **Scene 5** The Skylight Roof Cafe: "(Le Grand) Boom-Boom" (Val), "I've Got Your Number" (Frankie); **Scene 6** Young Belle's apartment: "Real Live Girl" (Fred); **Scene 7** Young Belle's apartment; a few months later. In the trenches in Europe in World War I; **Scene 8** A base hospital somewhere in France: "Real Live Girl" (reprise) (Doughboys). **Act II**: **Scene 1** The Casa Manana; tonight. On board ship after World War I: "I Love You" (reprise) (Noble & Belle); **Scene 2** Older Belle recalls her life back in the United States; **Scene 3** The dining room in the castle of Phillip Randolph Worst: "I Wanna Be Yours" (Belle & Worst) [a new number]; **Scene 4** Hollywood set at Paramour Pictures: **Scene 5** Older Belle recalls her life after Hollywood: "Little Me" (Belle today, Belle, Momma); **Scene 6** The casino at Monte Carlo; **Scene 7** Young Belle's apartment; a few months later. In the trenches in Europe in World War I: "Goodbye" (Cherney, Yulnick, Doctor, Company); **Scene 8** Older Belle recalls her life after the Prince's funeral: "Here's to Us" (Belle today & Company); **Scene 9** Outside the house on Quality Hill; **Scene 10** The house on Quality Hill; **Scene 11** The Casa Manana; tonight: Finale (Belle of today & Company).

Reviews were divided. The show received Tony nominations for choreography, and for Victor Garber and Mary Gordon Murray.

After Broadway. PRINCE OF WALES THEATRE, London, 5/30/84. DIRECTOR: John Sharpe. This revival stuck close to the original. **Cast**: Russ Abbott, Lynda Baron, Sheila White.

YORK THEATRE COMPANY, 3/26/92–4/26/92. Previews from 3/20/92. DIRECTOR: Jeffrey B. Moss; CHOREOGRAPHER: Barbara Siman; SETS: James E. Morgan; COSTUMES: Michael Bottari & Ronald Case; MUSICAL DIRECTOR: Leo P. Carusone. **Cast**: Stephen Joseph, Jo Ann Cunningham, Russ Thacker, Ray Wills.

401. *Little Me (1998 Broadway revival)*

Before Broadway. In 1996 this revival was first rumored for the 1997–98 Broadway season, starring Martin Short, and hopefully with Walter Bobbie to direct. Then it was planned for the fall of 1998. Walter Bobbie was still first choice for director. By 1998 Faith Prince was being rumored for the role of Belle (this production combined the two leading lady roles into one), and by 8/98 she was confirmed in her role, as was the rest of the cast. Broadway previews began 10/8/98 (date put back from 9/20/98, then 9/30/98, then 10/6/98, then 10/7/98, due to technical problems). Official opening night was pushed back from 10/29/98 to 11/12/98 (they were going to have it on 11/5/98, but Sandra Bernhard was opening her solo act in another Broadway theatre that night, and Broadway does not want two shows opening the same night). It was Rob Marshall's Broadway debut as director/choreographer. This show was the largest staging in the Roundabout's history to that date (by now the Criterion had been re-designated a Broadway theatre).

The Broadway Run. CRITERION CENTER STAGE RIGHT, 11/12/98–2/7/99. 50 previews from 10/8/99. 101 PERFORMANCES. PRESENTED BY the Roundabout Theatre Company; MUSIC: Cy Coleman; LYRICS: Carolyn Leigh; BOOK: Neil Simon; Based on the 1961 spoof novel *Little Me: The Intimate Memoirs of That Great Star of Stage, Screen and Television, Belle Poitrine, as told to Patrick Dennis*, by Patrick Dennis; DIRECTOR/CHOREOGRAPHER: Rob Marshall; SETS: David Gallo; COSTUMES: Ann Hould-Ward; LIGHTING: Kenneth Posner; SOUND: Brian Ronan; MUSICAL DIRECTOR: David Chase; ORCHESTRATIONS: Harold Wheeler; DANCE MUSIC ARRANGEMENTS: David Krane; CAST RECORDING on Varese Sarabande, made on 2/1/99, and released on 3/9/99; PRESS: Boneau/Bryan-Brown; CASTING: Jim Carnahan; GENERAL MANAGER: Ellen Richard; COMPANY MANAGER: Peilin Chou; PRODUCTION STAGE MANAGER: Perry Cline; STAGE MANAGER: David Sugarman. **Cast:** BELLE: Faith Prince; BELLE'S BOYS: Michael Arnold, Jeffrey Hankinson, Ned Hannah, Denis Jones; MOMMA: Ruth Williamson; RAMONA: Andrea Chamberlain; BRUCE: Michael McGrath; CERINE: Cynthia Onrubia; NOBLE EGGLESTON: Martin Short; MRS. EGGLESTON: Ruth Williamson; GREENSLEEVES: Michael McEachran; MAID: Christine Pedi; LUCKY: Michael Park; MISS KEPPLEWHITE: Christine Pedi; PINCHLEY JR.: Brooks Ashmanskas; NURSE: Kimberly Lyon; AMOS PINCHLEY: Martin Short; KLEEG: Peter Benson; NEWSBOYS: Michael Arnold & Jeffrey Hankinson; BERNIE BUCHSBAUM: Michael McGrath; BENNY BUCHSBAUM: Martin Short; DEFENSE LAWYER: Peter Benson; CHAIN GANG: Michael Arnold, Ned Hannah, Jeffrey Hankinson, Denis Jones; MAITRE D': Peter Benson; BOOM BOOM GIRLS: Kimberly Lyon, Joanne McHugh, Cynthia Onrubia; VAL DU VAL: Martin Short; COLETTE: Roxane Barlow; KITTY: Cynthia Onrubia; SUZIE: Joanne McHugh; ROXANE: Roxane Barlow; CHRISTINE: Christine Pedi; BERT: Michael McGrath; SOLDIER: Denis Jones; FRED POITRINE: Martin Short; SERGEANT: Michael McEachran; PREACHER: Peter Benson; GERMAN SOLDIER: Michael McGrath; GENERAL: Peter Benson; ARMY NURSE: Christine Pedi; CAPTAIN: Peter Benson; STEWARD: Brooks Ashmanskas; 1ST SAILOR: Ned Hannah; 2ND SAILOR: Jeffrey Hankinson; ASSISTANT DIRECTOR: Brooks Ashmanskas; SECRETARY: Christine Pedi; OTTO SCHNIZTLER: Martin Short; MOVIE "KING:" Michael McEachran; VICTOR: Peter Benson; PRINCE CHERNEY: Martin Short; YULNICK: Michael McGrath; CASINO WOMAN: Christine Pedi; DOCTOR: Brooks Ashmanskas; JUSTICES: Denis Jones & Jeffrey Hankinson; THE DRUNK: Martin Short; PARTY GUESTS, RICH KIDS, DRIFTER'S ROW, TOWNSPEOPLE, COURTROOM DANCERS, SKYLIGHT ROOF PATRONS, NURSES, SOLDIERS, MEDICS, PASSENGERS, BIBLICAL SLAVES, CASINO PATRONS, MOURNERS all played by the Company. **Standbys**: For Faith Prince: Jennifer Allen & Stacey Logan. **Understudies**: For Martin Short: Michael McGrath; For Peter Benson: Michael McEachran; For Michael McGrath & Brooks Ashmanskas: Josh Prince; Lucky: Denis Jones; For Christine Pedi: Courtney Young; For Ruth Williamson: Christine Pedi. **Swings**: Joey Pizzi, Josh Prince, Courtney Young. **Orchestra**: KEYBOARDS: David Chase & Robert Berman; TRUMPETS: Danny Cahn

& Glenn Drewes; TROMBONE/TUBA: Jack Schatz; WOODWINDS: Dan Willis & Frank Santagata; DRUMS: Ray Grappone; BASS: Leon Maleson; PERCUSSION: Dave Yee. *Act I*: "Little Me" (newly arranged) (Belle & Belle's Boys), "(On the) Other Side of the Tracks" (Belle), "Rich Kids Rag" (The Birthday Party) (Rich Kids & Noble), "I Love You" (Noble, Belle, Company), "(On the) Other Side of the Tracks" (reprise) (Belle), "Deep Down Inside" (Belle, Pinchley, Company), "(To) Be a Performer" (Benny, Bernie, Belle), "Dimples" (Belle & Chain Gang), "Boom Boom" (Val & Boom Boom Girls), "I've Got Your Number" (Lucky), "Real Live Girl" (Fred), "Real Live Girl" (reprise) (Fred & Soldiers), Finale Act I (Belle). *Act II*: "I Love Sinking You" (Belle, Fred, Company) [this number is a revised version of "I Love You"], "Poor Little Hollywood Star" (Belle), "Goodbye" (Cherney, Yulnick, Company), "Here's to Us" (Belle & Company).

Broadway reviews were divided, leaning toward good, and the performances were sold out. The show, which had a limited run with the option of extensions was first scheduled to close on 12/17/98, then extended to 1/24/99, and then extended again to 2/7/99. A longer run wasn't possible because Marty Short wanted to go back to California to be with his family. It seemed a pity to discontinue a successful show, so the producers began looking at a continuation on the West Coast, in order to accommodate Mr. Short. By 11/98 negotiations were underway for a Los Angeles theatre, possibly the Ahmanson, but it never happened. The Broadway production won a Tony Award for actor in a musical (Mr. Short), and was nominated for revival of a musical, choreography, and orchestrations.

402. *A Little Night Music*

Set in Sweden at the turn of the 20th century; the story follows the affairs of a group of lovers. Actress Desiree wants to settle down with middle-aged lawyer Fredrik, the father of her 13-year-old daughter. Unfortunately, Fredrik is newly married to Anne, a virginal girl of 18, and Desiree is engaged in an affair with jealous, vain and aristocratic dragoon Carl-Magnus, whose wife, Charlotte is suicidal. Fredrik's son, Henrik, is in love with his new stepmother, Anne. Then there is a country weekend party at the mansion of Desiree's mother, Madame Armfeldt, a former courtesan.

Before Broadway. Hal Prince and Stephen Sondheim had discussed doing a show like this as far back as 1957, but at that stage they had in mind *Ring Round the Moon*, by Jean Anouilh. Anouilh did not want this work musicalized however. In 1971, just after *Follies* and *Fiddler on the Roof* closed (7/1/71 and 7/2/71 respectively), the two creators approached M. Anouilh again, with the same results. They then looked at Jean Renoir's film *Les Regles du Jeu* (*Rules of the Game*), and Ingmar Bergman's film *Smiles of a Summer Night*. By this time librettist Hugh Wheeler was involved and ready to write an adaptation. They all went for Bergman's film, and on 12/7/71 the famous Scandinavian director sent a wire giving his approval and the rights. Hermione Gingold really wanted the role of Madame Armfeldt, but because Hal Prince thought she was wrong for the part she had to audition (for the first time in 40 years). She changed Mr. Prince's mind. Len Cariou auditioned for Carl-Magnus, but Mr. Prince cast him as Fredrik. Steve Sondheim composed his unique score all in three-quarter time, but only about half of the 13 waltzes, scherzos, minuets, polonaises and barcaroles were ready by the time rehearsals started. Another unique Sondheim creation was the use of five lieder singers to comment musically on the action, rather than a conventional singing/dancing chorus. A week before rehearsals began, Actors Equity ruled that these singers should be employed under lower-paying chorus contracts, as they had no spoken dialogue, but they refused to sign these contracts, and Hal Prince supported their claim, stating that their roles were just as important as those of the main characters. There was a lot of trouble over this, but eventually Equity agreed after Mr. Prince gave the characters names and listed them in the program. Rehearsals began on 12/10/72, in the American Theatre Laboratory, NY. Out of the 13 completed Sondheim numbers three were cut in the first days of

rehearsals—"Bang!," "Two Fairy Tales," and "My Husband, the Pig." The show played one run-through at Broadway's Shubert Theatre on 1/8/73. Steve Sondheim wrote "Send in the Clowns" only two weeks before the company went for tryouts in Boston (beginning on 2/15/73), where reviews were okay; Garn Stephens was replaced by D'Jamin Bartlett. When the show moved to Broadway, and was in previews, Glynis Johns got intestinal flu, and almost didn't make opening night. Tammy Grimes was considered as her replacement, but Miss Johns pulled through.

The Broadway Run. SHUBERT THEATRE, 2/25/73–9/15/73; MAJESTIC THEATRE, 9/18/73–8/3/74. 12 previews. Total of 601 PERFORMANCES. PRESENTED BY Harold Prince, in association with Ruth Mitchell; MUSIC/LYRICS: Stephen Sondheim; BOOK: Hugh Wheeler; SUGGESTED BY Ingmar Bergman's 1956 film *Sommarnattens leende* (*Smiles of a Summer Night*); DIRECTOR: Harold Prince; CHOREOGRAPHER: Patricia Birch; SETS: Boris Aronson; COSTUMES: Florence Klotz; LIGHTING: Tharon Musser; SOUND: Jack Mann; MUSICAL DIRECTOR: Harold Hastings; ORCHESTRATIONS: Jonathan Tunick; CAST RECORDING on Columbia; PRESS: Mary Bryant, Bill Evans, Laura Waage; CASTING: Joanna Merlin; PRODUCTION SUPERVISOR: Ruth Mitchell; GENERAL MANAGER: Howard Haines; COMPANY MANAGER: Ralph Roseman; PRODUCTION STAGE MANAGER: George Martin; FIRST ASSISTANT STAGE MANAGER: John Grigas; SECOND ASSISTANT STAGE MANAGER: David Wolf. *Cast:* MR. LINDQUIST: Benjamin Rayson (13); MRS. NORDSTROM: Teri Ralston (14), *Joy Franz*; MRS. ANDERSSEN: Barbara Lang (12), *Sherry Mathis*; MR. ERLANSON: Gene Varrone (16); MRS. SEGSTROM: Beth Fowler (15); FREDRIKA ARMFELDT: Judy Kahan (8), *Sheila K. Adams*; MADAME ARMFELDT: Hermione Gingold (3) ☆; FRID, HER BUTLER: George Lee Andrews (10), *Dick Sabol*; HENRIK EGERMAN: Mark Lambert (7); ANNE EGERMAN: Victoria Mallory (4); FREDRIK EGERMAN: Len Cariou (2) ☆, *William Daniels* (from 2/25/74); PETRA, THE MAID: D'Jamin Bartlett (9); DESIREE ARMFELDT: Glynis Johns (1) ☆; MALLA, HER MAID: Despo (11); BERTRAND, A PAGE: Will Sharpe Marshall; COUNT CARL-MAGNUS MALCOLM: Laurence Guittard (5); COUNTESS CHARLOTTE MALCOLM: Patricia Elliott (6); OSA: Sherry Mathis. *Standby*: Fredrik/Count: Len Gochman. *Understudies*: Desiree: Barbara Lang; Madame: Despo; Anne/Fredrika: Sherry Mathis; Countess/Petra: Beth Fowler; Henrik/Frid: Will Sharpe Marshall. *Act I*: Overture (Mr. Lindquist, Mrs. Nordstrom, Mrs. Anderssen, Mr. Erlanson, Mrs. Segstrom—i.e. the Chorus); *Prologue* "Night Waltz" (Company); *Scene 1* The Egerman rooms: "Now" (Fredrik), "Later" (Henrik), "Soon" (Anne, Henrik, Fredrik), "The Glamorous Life" (Fredrika, Desiree, Malla, Mme Armfeldt, Chorus); *Scene 2* Stage of local theatre: "Remember?" (Chorus); *Scene 3* The Egerman rooms: "Remember?" (continued) (Chorus); *Scene 4* Desiree's digs: "You Must Meet My Wife" (Desiree & Fredrik), "Liaisons" (Mme Armfeldt), "In Praise of Women" (Carl-Magnus); *Scene 5* Breakfast room in the Malcolm country house: "In Praise of Women" (continued) (Carl-Magnus); *Scene 6* The Egerman rooms: "Every Day a Little Death" (Charlotte & Anne); *Scene 7* Armfeldt terrace: "A Weekend in the Country" (Company). *Act II*: Entr'acte; *Scene 1* The Armfeldt lawn: "Night Waltz I—The Sun Won't Set" (Chorus); *Scene 2* The other part of the garden: "Night Waltz II—The Sun Sits Low" (Chorus); *Scene 3* Armfeldt terrace: "It Would Have Been Wonderful" (Fredrik & Carl-Magnus); *Scene 4* The dining room: "Perpetual Anticipation" (Mrs. Nordstrom, Mrs. Segstrom, Mrs. Anderssen); *Scene 5* Armfeldt garden; another part of the garden; *Scene 6* Desiree's bedroom: "Send in the Clowns" (Desiree) [the big hit]; *Scene 7* The trees: "The Miller's Son" (Petra); *Scene 8* Armfeldt house and garden: Finale: "Send in the Clowns" (reprise) (Company).

The show opened to very good reviews. It won Tonys for musical, direction of a musical, score, book, costumes, and for Glynis Johns and Patricia Elliott. It was also nominated for sets, lighting, and for Len Cariou, Hermione Gingold, and Laurence Guittard. Ingmar Bergman saw the production in 11/73, and loved it. Musical director Hal Hastings died during the run. [Note: in 1975, after the Broadway run had ended, Judy Collins had a big Grammy–award winning hit in the charts with "Send in the Clowns," and Frank Sinatra and Barbra Streisand also had hits with it].

After Broadway. TOUR. Opened on 2/26/74, at the Forrest Theatre, Philadelphia, and closed on 2/15/75, at the Shubert Theatre,

Boston. MUSICAL DIRECTOR: Richard Parrinello. *Cast*: DESIREE: Jean Simmons; MME ARMFELDT: Margaret Hamilton; FREDRIK: George Lee Andrews; MR. LINDQUIST: Elliott Savage; MRS. SEGSTROM: Karen Zenker; HENRIK: Stephen Lehew; CARL-MAGNUS: Ed Evanko; CHARLOTTE: Andra Akers; ANNE: Virginia Pulos.

ADELPHI THEATRE, London, 4/15/75. 406 PERFORMANCES. This was a big success, and a carbon copy of the original Broadway production. PRESENTED BY Harold Prince, Ruth Mitchell, Frank Milton, Eddie Kulukundis, and Richard Pilbrow, in association with Bernard Delfont; CHOREOGRAPHER: George Martin. *Cast*: DESIREE: Jean Simmons; FREDRIK: Joss Ackland; MME ARMFELDT: Hermione Gingold; CARL-MAGNUS: David Kernan; CHARLOTTE: Maria Aitken; PETRA: Diane Langton; MRS. ANDERSSEN: Liz Robertson.

STUDIO ARENA THEATRE, Buffalo, 3/26/76. 35 PERFORMANCES. DIRECTOR/CHOREOGRAPHER: Tony Tanner. *Cast:* Rosemary Prinz, William Chapman, Paula Laurence.

BUS-TRUCK TOUR. 9/18/76–12/11/76. *Cast:* Julie Wilson.

THE MOVIE. 1978. DIRECTOR: Harold Prince. It did not do well at all. *Cast*: DESIREE: Elizabeth Taylor; FREDRIK: Len Cariou; MME ARMFELDT: Hermione Gingold; ALSO WITH: Diana Rigg.

EQUITY LIBRARY THEATRE, NYC, 5/9/85–6/2/85. 30 PERFORMANCES. DIRECTOR: Susan H. Schulman; SETS: Linda Hacker; MUSICAL DIRECTOR: Phil Reno. *Cast*: DESIREE: Kathryn Hays; CARL-MAGNUS: Patrick Quinn; ANNE: Judith Blazer; CHARLOTTE: Maris Clement; MME ARMFELDT: Avril Gentles; HENRIK: Eddie Korbich; MRS. NORDSTROM: Barbara Scanlon.

NEW YORK STATE THEATRE, 8/3/90–11/7/90. 11 PERFORMANCES IN REPERTORY. This was a major revival, and got rave reviews. PRESENTED BY the New York City Opera; DIRECTOR: Scott Ellis (this helped launch his career); CHOREOGRAPHER: Susan Stroman; SETS: Michael Anania; COSTUMES: Lindsay W. Davis; LIGHTING: Dawn Chiang; SOUND: Abe Jacob; MUSICAL DIRECTOR: Paul Gemignani. *Cast*: MRS. SEGSTROM: Susanne Marsee; FREDRIKA: Danielle Ferland; MME ARMFELDT: Regina Resnik, *Elaine Bonazzi*; FRID: David Comstock; HENRIK: Kevin P. Anderson; ANNE: Beverly Lambert; FREDRIK: George Lee Andrews, *Harlan Foss*; PETRA: Susan Terry; DESIREE: Sally Ann Howes; CARL-MAGNUS: Michael Maguire; CHARLOTTE: Maureen Moore, *Susanne Marsee*. It ran again, same venue, 7/9/91–8/10/91. 7 performances in repertory. It had the same basic crew, and the same cast except MME ARMFELDT: Elaine Bonazzi; PETRA: Joanna Glushak.

AHMANSON THEATRE, Los Angeles, 1991. PRESENTED by the Center Theatre Group; DIRECTOR: Gordon Davidson; CHOREOGRAPHER: Onna White; MUSICAL DIRECTOR: Arthur B. Rubinstein. *Cast*: DESIREE: Lois Nettleton; MME ARMFELDT: Glynis Johns; CHARLOTTE: Marcia Mitzman; PETRA: Kathleen Rowe McAllen; FREDRIK: John McMartin; CARL-MAGNUS: Jeff McCarthy; ALSO WITH: Teri Ralston.

On 10/26/98 it was announced that there might be a Broadway revival in late 4/99. Margo Lion, Fred Zollo, Nick Paleologos, and Jujamcyn Theatres were going to produce, and rehearsals were to begin in late 2/99. Declan Donnellan was going to direct, and Paddy Cunneen was the musical director. On 11/12/98 it was announced that it was postponed to the fall of 1999 because they couldn't find a suitable theatre. Glenn Close, Ann-Margret and Betty Buckley were all being rumored as Desiree, and by early 1/99 Glenn Close was actually in discussions about the project. On 1/14/99 Miss Close revealed she would "absolutely" be playing the part in the fall, but the show never happened, even through rumors persisted for some years. Finally, in mid–2004 plans began again for a 2006 Broadway revival, with Miss Close, but this time with Trevor Nunn directing.

KENNEDY CENTER, Washington, DC, 8/3/02–8/25/02. 1 preview on 8/2/02. Press night was 8/4/02. This was a concert version, part of the *Sondheim Celebration* series, and ran in repertory with *Merrily We Roll Along* & *Passion*. DIRECTOR: Mark Brokaw. *Cast*: DESIREE: Blair Brown; CARL-MAGNUS: Douglas Sills; CHARLOTTE: Randy Graff; FREDRIK: John Dossett; ANNE: Sarah Uriarte Berry; HENRIK: Danny Gurwin; LINDQUIST: Christopher Flint; MME ARMFELDT: Barbara Byrne; PETRA: Natascia Diaz; MRS. NORDSTROM: Siobhan Kolker; MR. ERLANSON: Peter Cormican; FREDRIKA: Kristen Bell.

PAVILION THEATRE, Highland Park, Ill., 8/22/02–8/24/02. Concert version, part of the Ravinia Festival. DIRECTOR: Lonny Price; CON-

DUCTOR: Grant Gershon. *Cast*: DESIREE: Patti LuPone; FREDRIK: George Hearn; MME ARMFELDT: Zoe Caldwell; CARL-MAGNUS: Marc Kudisch; PETRA: Sara Ramirez; HENRIK: John McVeigh; CHARLOTTE: Hollis Resnik; ANNE: Johanna Mckenzie Miller.

NEW YORK STATE THEATRE, 3/7/03–3/29/03. 15 PERFORMANCES, IN REPERTORY. PRESENTED BY the New York City Opera; DIRECTOR: Scott Ellis; CHOREOGRAPHER: Susan Stroman; SETS: Michael Anania; CONDUCTOR: Paul Gemignani. *Cast*: FREDRIK: Jeremy Irons; DESIREE: Juliet Stevenson; MME ARMFELDT: Claire Bloom; CHARLOTTE: Michelle Pawk (Kate Burton had been scheduled for this role); HENRIK: Daniel Gurwin; CARL-MAGNUS: Marc Kudisch; ANNE: Kristin Huxhold; PETRA: Jessica Boevers; FREDRIK: Anna Kendrick; FRID: Quentin Marc.

DOROTHY CHANDLER PAVILION, Los Angeles, 7/7/04–7/31/04. This was the 2003 New York City Opera staging. PRESENTED by the Los Angeles Opera. *Cast*: FREDRIK: Victor Garber (Jeremy Irons was going to play this role, but he pulled out); DESIREE: Judith Ivey (Juliet Stevenson was going to play this role, but she pulled out); MME ARMFELDT: Zoe Caldwell; CHARLOTTE: Michele Pawk; HENRIK: Daniel Gurwin; CARL-MAGNUS: Marc Kudisch; PORTIA: Jessica Boevers; ALSO WITH: Laura Benanti, Stephanie Woodling, Kristen Bell, Joohee Choi, Ashley Rose Orr.

403. *Little Shop of Horrors*

Seymour is a skid-row schlub who works at Mushnik's down-at-heel flower shop. He yearns for the affections of ditzy blonde Audrey who, unfortunately, is stuck on sadistic dentist Orin. Seymour's fortunes change when the strange plant he takes under his care grows into a huge Venus flytrap-like behemoth, winning him media attention, riches, respect, and the love of Audrey. However, the plant, Audrey II, needs human blood in order to survive ("Feed Me!"). The cast decreases in size. The girls of the chorus are based on girl groups of early 1960s.

Before Broadway. First it was a film, Roger Corman's legendary (and awfully bad) "straight" 1960 movie of the same name, which is now most famous, probably, for the presence of the actor who played the small role of the masochistic dental patient. *Cast*: SEYMOUR KRELBOINED: Jonathan Haze; MUSHNIK: Mel Welles; AUDREY FORQUAD: Jackie Joseph; BURTON FOUCH: Dick Miller; WINIFRED KRELBOINED: Myrtle Vail; WILBUR FORCE: Jack Nicholson; VOICE OF AUDREY II: Charles B. Griffith.

After their stage adaptation of Kurt Vonnegut's *God Bless You, Mr. Rosewater*, failed, Alan Menken and Howard Ashman wrote a stage musical of the film *Little Shop of Horrors* in 1982. It ran Off Broadway, at the WPA THEATRE. It moved to the ORPHEUM THEATRE, 7/27/82–11/1/87. 2,209 PERFORMANCES. PRESENTED BY the WPA Theatre, David Geffen, Cameron Mackintosh, The Shubert Organization; MUSIC: Alan Menken; LYRICS/BOOK/DIRECTOR: Howard Ashman; CHOREOGRAPHER: Edie Cowan; SETS: Edward T. Gianfrancesco; SOUND: Otts Munderloh; MUSICAL DIRECTOR: Robert Billig; ORCHESTRATIONS: Robby Merken; CAST RECORDING on Geffen Records; DESIGNER OF THE MAN-EATING PLANT AUDREY II: Martin Robinson (of *The Muppets*). *Cast*: CHIFFON: Marlene Danielle, *Leilani Jones, Suzzanne Douglas, Melodee Savage*; CRYSTAL: *Jennifer Leigh Warren, Tena Wilson*; RONNETTE: Sheila Kay Davis, *Louise Robinson, Deborah Dotson*; GRAVIS MUSHNIK: Hy Anzell, *Fyvush Finkel* (from 3/83); AUDREY: Ellen Greene, *Faith Prince* (from 3/83), *Katherine Meloche, Marsha Skaggs, Eydie Alyson, Annie Golden, Marsha Skaggs*; SEYMOUR: Lee Wilkof, *Brad Moranz* (from 3/83), *Andrew Hill Newman*; DERELICT/AUDREY II MANIPULATION: Martin Robinson, *Anthony B. Asbury* (from 3/83), *Lynn Hippen, William* Szymanski; ORIN BERNSTEIN/SNIP/LUCE/EVERYONE ELSE: Franc Luz, *Robert Frisch, Ken Land*; Audrey II Voice: Ron Taylor. **Standbys**: Audrey: Audrey: Katie Meloche; Mushnik: Fy Finkel; Chiffon/Crystal/Ronnette: Deborah Lynn Sharpe; Seymour, and for Mr. Luz & Mr. Taylor: Brad Moranz; For Martin Robinson: Anthony B. Asbury. **Musicians**: PIANO: Robert Billig; ELECTRONIC KEYBOARDS: Robby Merkin; BASS GUITAR: Steve Gelfand; PERCUSSION: Steve Ferrera. The musical numbers were as for the 2003 Broadway revival.

After the 1982 New York opening, it opened in LOS ANGELES, on 4/27/83. *Cast*: Hy Anzell, Lee Wilkof, Ellen Greene, Martin Robinson. COMEDY THEATRE, London, 10/12/83. 813 PERFORMANCES. DIRECTOR: Howard Ashman; CHOREOGRAPHER: Edie Cowan; SETS: Tim Goodchild; MUSICAL DIRECTOR: Roger Ward. *Cast*: AUDREY: Ellen Greene; SEYMOUR: Barry James; MUSHNIK: Harry Towb; CHIFFON: Nicola Blackman; ALSO WITH: Shezwae Powell.

1986. A movie of the stage musical. *Cast*: AUDREY: Ellen Greene; SEYMOUR: Rick Moranis; ORIN: Steve Martin; MUSHNIK: Vince Gardenia.

The new production was going to appear on Broadway in early 2003, but it was put back to the summer. It tried out at the Actors' Playhouse, Miracle Theatre, Coral Gables, Fla., 5/16/03–6/15/03. Previews 5/7/03–6/15/03. Broadway previews were set to begin 7/22/03, and the show was to open officially on 8/14/03, at the Virginia Theatre, with Connie Grappo directing (the rest of the crew was the same as for the eventual Broadway run). The cast, at that stage, was: OPENING VOICE: Robert Stack (Mr. Stack died 5/14/03, but his voice had already been recorded); AUDREY: Alice Ripley; SEYMOUR KRELBORN: Hunter Foster; MUSHNIK: Lee Wilkof; AUDREY II: Billy Porter; ORIN: Reg Rogers; CRYSTAL: Dioni Michelle Collins; RONNETTE: Moe Daniels; CHIFFON: Moeisha McGill. On 6/2/03 it was announced that the scheduled production had been canceled. The piece couldn't gell. They held on to the Virginia Theatre, and plans were proposed for a newly conceived production to open on Broadway 10/9/03, directed by Jerry Zaks (the previous director, Connie Grappo, was Lee Wilkof's wife). On 6/30/03 it was announced that Kerry Butler had been offered the role of Audrey; on 7/1/03 that Rob Bartlett had been offered Mushnik; on 7/2/03 that Michael-Leon Wooley had been offered Audrey II; and on 7/8/03 that Douglas Sills had been offered Orin. The opening date was brought forward to 10/2/03, then put back to 10/3/03, then back to 10/2/03.

The Broadway Run. VIRGINIA THEATRE, 10/2/03–8/22/04. 40 previews from 8/29/03. 372 PERFORMANCES. PRESENTED BY Marc Routh, Richard Frankel, Thomas Viertel, Steven Baruch, James D. Stern, Douglas L. Meyer, Rick Steiner, John Osher, Bonnie Osher, Simone Genatt Haft, in association with HoriPro, Inc., Tokyo Broadcasting System International, Clear Channel Entertainment, Endgame Entertainment, Zemiro, Morton Swinsky, Michael Fuchs, Judith Marinoff Cohn, Rhoda Mayerson, Frederic H. Mayerson, Amy Danis, Mark Johannes; MUSIC: Alan Menken; LYRICS/BOOK: Howard Ashman; BASED ON the 1960 Roger Corman film, which had a screenplay by Charles Griffith; DIRECTOR: Jerry Zaks; CHOREOGRAPHER: Kathleen Marshall; SETS: Scott Pask; COSTUMES: William Ivey Long; PUPPET DESIGN: The Jim Henson Company & Martin P. Robinson; LIGHTING: Donald Holder; SOUND: T. Richard Fitzgerald; MUSICAL SUPERVISOR/NEW ARRANGEMENTS: Michael Kosarin; MUSICAL DIRECTOR: Henry Aronson; ORCHESTRATIONS: Danny Troob; ORIGINAL VOCAL ARRANGEMENTS: Robert Billig; CAST RECORDING on DRG, made on 9/15/03 and released 10/21/03; PRESS: Barlow — Hartman Public Relations; CASTING: Bernard Telsey; GENERAL MANAGEMENT: Richard Frankel Productions & Jo Porter; COMPANY MANAGER: Sammy Ledbetter; PRODUCTION STAGE MANAGER: Karen Armstrong; STAGE MANAGER: Adam John Hunter; ASSISTANT STAGE MANAGER: Claudia Lynch. *Cast:* PROLOGUE VOICE (RECORDED): Don Morrow; CHIFFON: DeQuina Moore; CRYSTAL: Trisha Jeffrey; RONNETTE: Carla J. Hargrove; MUSHNIK: Rob Bartlett; AUDREY: Kerry Butler (until 6/20/04), *Jessica-Snow Wilson* (from 6/22/04); SEYMOUR: Hunter Foster (until 6/6/04), *Jonathan Rayson* (6/8/04–6/20/04), *Joey Fatone* (from 6/22/04 — he had been scheduled to come in on 6/24/04); DERELICTS/SKID ROW OCCUPANTS: Douglas Sills (until 6/13/04), *Darren Ritchie* 6/15/04–6/20/04; *Jonathan Rayson* 6/22/04–6/27/04; *Robert Evan* from 6/29/04), Anthony Asbury, Bill Remington, Martin P. Robinson, Matt Vogel, Michael-Leon Wooley; AUDREY II PUPPETEERS: Martin P. Robinson, Anthony Asbury, Bill Remington, Matt Vogel; VOICE OF AUDREY II: Michael-Leon Wooley; ORIN SCRIVELLO, D.D.S./BERNSTEIN/SKIP SNIP/MRS. LUCE/EVERYONE ELSE: Douglas Sills (until 6/13/04), *Darren Ritchie* (6/15/04–6/20/04), *Jonathan Rayson* (6/22/04–6/27/04), *Robert Evan* (from 6/29/04). **Understudies**: Chiffon/Crystal/Ronnette: Ta'Rea Campbell, *Dana Dawson*; Mushnik: Ray DeMattis; Voice of Audrey II: Michael James Leslie; Seymour/Orin/Bernstein/Snip/Luce/Everyone Else: Jonathan Rayson & Darren Ritchie; Audrey: Jessica-Snow Wilson. **Prologue**: "Little Shop of Horrors"

(Chiffon, Crystal, Ronnette). *Act I*: *Scene 1* Mushnik's Skid Row Florists: "Skid Row (Downtown)" (Company), "Grow for Me" (Seymour); *Scene 2* Radio Show: "(Don't it Go to Show) Ya Never Know" (Mushnik, Chiffon, Crystal, Ronnette, Seymour), "Somewhere that's Green" (Audrey); *Scene 3* The flower shop: "Closed for Renovations!" (Seymour, Audrey, Mushnik), "Dentist!" (Orin, Chiffon, Crystal, Ronnette), "Mushnik and Son" (Mushnik & Seymour), "Git It!" (Seymour & Audrey II); *Scene 4*: The flower shop: "Now (It's Just the Gas)" (Seymour & Orin). *Act II*: *Scene 1* The flower shop: "Call Back in the Morning" (Seymour & Audrey), "Suddenly, Seymour" (Seymour & Audrey), "Suppertime" (Audrey II); *Scene 2* The flower shop: "The Meek Shall Inherit" (Company); *Scene 3* The flower shop: "Suppertime" (reprise) (Audrey), "Somewhere That's Green" (reprise) (Audrey), Finale: "Don't Feed the Plants" (Company).

Reviews were generally good. Hunter Foster was nominated for a Tony Award. On 7/27/04 it was announced that the show would be closing on 8/22/04.

After Broadway. TOUR. Opened on 8/10/04, at the Music Hall, Dallas. Then it had a long stay at the Ahmanson Theatre, Los Angeles, 8/24/04–10/17/04, then on with the tour. DIRECTOR: Jerry Zaks; CHOREOGRAPHER: Kathleen Marshall. *Cast*: SEYMOUR: Anthony Rapp; AUDREY: Tari Kelly; MUSHNIK: Lenny Wolpe; ORIN: James Moye; VOICE OF AUDREY II: Michael James Leslie; CRYSTAL: Amina Robinson; CHIFFON: Yasmeen Suleiman; RONNETTE: La Tonya Holmes; AUDREY II PUPPETEERS: Paul McGuiness & Michael Latini.

404. *Look Ma, I'm Dancin'!*

Lily, the stage-struck ugly-duckling daughter of a rich Milwaukee brewer, backs the traveling Russo-American Ballet Company in order to get a place in it. She finally takes it over from its Russian impresario, Mr. Plancek, and the thing livens up. Eddie, the arrogant choreographer who is having an affair with Ann, one of the dancers, revises the "Swan Lake" sequence, which Lily performs to thunderous applause from the crowd, pushing her to stardom.

Before Broadway. During tryouts the parts of Shauny O'Shay (played by Bill Shirley) and the Rehearsal Pianist (played by Kathleen Carnes) were cut.

The Broadway Run. ADELPHI THEATRE, 1/29/48–7/10/48. 188 PERFORMANCES. PRESENTED BY George Abbott; MUSIC/LYRICS/VOCAL ARRANGEMENTS: Hugh Martin; BOOK: Jerome Lawrence & Robert E. Lee; CONCEIVED BY/CHOREOGRAPHER: Jerome Robbins; DIRECTOR: George Abbott; SETS: Oliver Smith; ASSISTANT TO OLIVER SMITH: Peggy Clark; COSTUMES: John Pratt; MUSICAL DIRECTOR: Pembroke Davenport; ORCHESTRATIONS: Don Walker; BALLET MUSIC ARRANGEMENTS: Trude Rittman; CAST RECORDING: featured Bill Shirley & Hugh Martin, neither of whom was in the show itself; PRESS: Richard Maney & Frank Goodman; GENERAL MANAGER: Charles Harris; ASSISTANT COMPANY MANAGER: Joe Harris; PRODUCTION STAGE MANAGER: Robert E. Griffith; STAGE MANAGERS: Dan Sattler & Doug Jones. *Cast:* WOTAN: Don Liberto (7); LARRY: Loren Welch (5); DUSTY LEE: Alice Pearce (4), *Marie Foster*; ANN BRUCE: Janet Reed (3); SNOW WHITE: Virginia Gorski (6); EDDIE WINKLER: Harold Lang (2); TOMMY: Tommy Rall (8); *Eric Kristen*; F. PLANCEK: Robert Harris (10); TANYA DRINSKAYA: Katharine Sergava (9); VLADIMIR LUBOFF: Alexander March (11); LILY MALLOY: Nancy Walker (1) ☆, Betty Lou Barto (alternate); MR. GLEEB: James Lane; MR. FERBISH: Eddie Hodge; TANYA'S PARTNER: Raul Celada, *Richard D'Arcy*; BELL BOY: Dean Campbell; STAGE MANAGER: Dan Sattler; SUZY: Sandra Deel (12); MEMBERS OF THE RUSSO-AMERICAN BALLET COMPANY: Margaret Banks, Forrest Bonshire, Mary Broussard, Dean Campbell, Bruce Cartwright, Raul Celada, Leonard Claret, Virginia Conwell, Julie Curtis, Richard D'Arcy, Charles Dickson, Clare Duffy, Nina Frenkin, June Graham, Marybly Harwood, Priscilla Hathaway, Eric Kristen, Ina Kurland, Douglas Luther, Bettye McCormick, Gloria Patrice, James Pollack, Dorothy Pyren, Walter Rinner, Herbert Ross, Marten Sameth, Walter Stane, Gisella Svetlik, Robert Tucker. **Understudies**: Wotan: Forrest Bonshire; Snow White: Gloria Patrice; Lily:

Sandra Deel; Eddie: Lenny Claret; Ann: Maggie Banks; Dusty: Bettye McCormick; Larry: Dean Campbell; Tanya: Nina Frenkin; Luboff: Herb Ross; Plancek: Marten Sameth; Gleeb: Eddie Hodge; Tommy: Eric Kristen; Stage Manager: Walter Rinner. *Act I: Scene 1* Pennsylvania Station, New York City: "(I'm a Guy Who's) Gotta Dance" (Eddie & Company); *Scene 2* On tour; *Scene 3* A rehearsal hall, Joplin, Missouri: "I'm the First Girl (in the Second Row)" (Lily & the Corps de Ballet); *Scene 4* On tour: "I'm Not So Bright" (Larry) (danced by Ann & Eddie); *Scene 5* Hotel room, Amarillo, Texas: "I'm Tired of Texas" (Lily & Company), "Tiny Room" (Larry); *Scene 6* Outside a theatre, Phoenix, Arizona: "The Little Boy Blues" (Snow White & Wotan); *Scene 7* Stage door of the Philharmonic Auditorium, Los Angeles; *Scene 8* Back stage of the Philharmonic; *Scene 9* Stage of the Philharmonic: "Mademoiselle Marie" (ballet) (m: Trude Rittman): MADEMOISELLE MARIE, A YOUNG BRIDE: Nancy Walker; HER BELOVED: Herbert Ross; ATTENDANTS: Virginia Gorski & Gisella Svetlik; MESSENGER: Tommy Rall; INNKEEPER: Eric Kristen; SERVANT: Leonard Claret; JACQUES: Charles Dickson; IGOR: Richard D'Arcy; ADOLPH: Raul Celada; ARCHIE: Forrest Bonshire; SERFS: Leonard Claret, Bruce Cartwright, Ina Kurland, Marybly Harwood, Virginia Conwell; and the Corps de Ballet. *Act II: Scene 1* A railroad platform, Glendale, California; early the next morning: "Jazz" (Wotan, Lily, Company), "The New Look" (Dusty); *Scene 2* A Pullman car: "If You'll Be Mine" (Lily, Dean Campbell, Priscilla Hathaway, Suzy, Larry, Dusty, James Pollack), "Pajama Dance" (Company); *Scene 3* On tour: "Shauny O'Shay" (Snow White & Wotan) [the hit]; *Scene 4* A theatre basement, Des Moines, Iowa: Pas de Deux from *Swan Lake* (music by Tchaikovsky) (Ann & Eddie), "The Two of Us" (Lily, Eddie, Co-workers).

Reviews were mostly bad, although there was a rave or two. Harold Lang won a Donaldson Award for best male dancer. Nancy Walker was often ill, and her sister, Betty Lou Barto (who looked like her, but did not have her talent), stepped in. This was a major reason for the show failing. There were plans for a movie with Betty Hutton, but it never happened.

After Broadway. 14TH STREET Y, NYC, 3/7/00–3/19/00. 16 PERFORMANCES. Part of the *Musicals Tonight!* series. PRESENTED BY Mel Miller; DIRECTOR/CHOREOGRAPHER: Thomas Mills; MUSICAL DIRECTOR: C. Colby Sachs. *Cast*: WOTAN: Julian Brightman; LILY: Jennifer Allen; GINNY: Alli Bivins; FERBISH: Stephen Carter-Hicks; LENNY: Ryan Duncan; EDDIE: Noah Racey; TANYA: Rita Rehn; PLANCEK: Richard Ruiz.

405. *The Look of Love*

A revue, subtitled *The Songs of Burt Bacharach and Hal David*.

Before Broadway. Originally called *What the World Needs Now* (from title of a Bacharach—David song), it was a book musical (with book by Kenny Solms—well, not much of a book), based on an idea by Mr. Solms & Gillian Lynne. It ran at the Old Globe Theatre, in the summer of 1998. DIRECTOR/CHOREOGRAPHER: Gillian Lynne; SETS: Bob Crowley. It had over 30 Bacharach—David numbers. *Cast*: Sutton Foster, Paula Newsome, Lewis Cleale, John Bolton, Jonathan Sharp. The Roundabout picked it up, and planned to do it on Broadway, at Studio 54. However, *Cabaret* was there, and aside from that the project fell through. It was now newly conceived. Ruthie Henshall was rumored to be in it, but she never made it. The first Broadway preview was put back from 4/1/03 to 4/4/03.

The Broadway Run. BROOKS ATKINSON THEATRE, 5/4/03– 6/15/03. 36 previews from 4/4/03. 49 PERFORMANCES. PRESENTED BY the Roundabout Theatre Company; MUSIC: Burt Bacharach; LYRICS: Hal David; CONCEIVED BY: David Thompson, Scott Ellis, David Loud, Ann Reinking; DIRECTOR: Scott Ellis; CHOREOGRAPHER: Ann Reinking; SETS: Derek McLane; COSTUMES: Martin Pakledinaz; LIGHTING: Howell Binkley; SOUND: Brian Ronan; MUSICAL DIRECTOR/ARRANGEMENTS: David Loud; ORCHESTRATIONS: Don Sebesky; PRESS: Boneau/Bryan-Brown; CASTING: Jim Carnahan; GENERAL MANAGEMENT: Richards/Climan; COMPANY MANAGER: Laura Janik Cronin; PRODUCTION STAGE MANAGER: Lori M. Doyle; STAGE MANAGER: Tamlyn Freund Yerkes;

ASSISTANT STAGE MANAGER: Michael Sisolak. *Cast:* Liz Callaway, Kevin Ceballo, Jonathan Dokuchitz, Eugene Fleming, Capathia Jenkins, Janine LaManna, Shannon Lewis, Rachelle Rak, Desmond Richardson. PIT SINGERS: Farah Alvin, Nikki Renee Daniels. *Swings:* Allyson Turner, Eric Jordan Young. *Orchestra:* KEYBOARD # 1: Philip Fortenberry; KEYBOARD # 2: Sue Anschutz; WOODWINDS: Chuck Wilson, Kenneth Dybisz, Mark Thrasher; TRUMPETS: Jon Owens & Matt Peterson; GUITAR: Stephen Benson; BASS: Benjamin Franklin Brown; DRUMS: Dave Ratajczak; PERCUSSION: Bill Hayes; VIOLINS: Paul Woodiel, Ella Rutkovsky, Jonathan Dinklage. *Act I*: "The Look of Love" (Capathia & Entire Company), "(There's) Always Something There to Remind Me" (Eugene, Jonathan, Kevin), "You'll Never Get to Heaven (if You Break My Heart)" (Janine), "I Say a Little Prayer" (Liz, Capathia, Janine), "Promise Her Anything" (Jonathan, Shannon, Rachelle), "I Just Don't Know What to Do with Myself" (Liz), "Raindrops Keep Fallin' on My Head" (Eugene & Desmond), "Are You There (with Another Girl)?" (Capathia), "Another Night" (Janine), "Yo Nunca Volver Amar" ("I'll Never Fall in Love Again") (Kevin & Shannon), "She Likes Basketball" (Eugene), "What's New, Pussycat?" (Shannon, Janine, Rachelle), "Walk on By" (Capathia), "A House is Not a Home" (Jonathan), "One Less Bell to Answer" (Liz). *Act II*: "Casino Royale" (Orchestra, Farah, Nikki Renee), "Wishin' and Hopin'" (Janine, Shannon, Rachelle), "This Guy's in Love with You"/"This Girl's in Love with You" (Eugene & Capathia), "(What's it All About) Alfie?" (Liz), "Trains and Boats and Planes" (Desmond), "Do You Know the Way to San Jose?" (Kevin, Jonathan, Eugene, Desmond), "Twenty-Four Hours from Tulsa" (Rachelle), "Close to You" (Janine & Jonathan), "Anyone Who Had a Heart" (Kevin), "Wives and Lovers" (Shannon, Desmond, Eugene), "Make it Easy on Yourself" (Capathia), "Knowing When to Leave" (Liz), "Promises, Promises" (Liz & Capathia), "What the World Needs Now (is Love)" (Entire Company).

It was a limited run, but extended to 6/29/03. However, it got some bad Broadway reviews and no Tony nominations, and on 6/1/03 announced that it would close on the originally scheduled date of 6/15/03. Burt Bacharach was not involved in this show, and did not particularly like it.

406. *Look to the Lilies*

Mother Maria persuades Homer Smith, a black vagrant and handyman on the run from the police, to build her a chapel in New Mexico. The nuns, being German, call him Mr. Schmidt.

Before Broadway. Previously called *Some Kind of Man*, this was Jule Styne's idea. He wanted Ethel Merman, but Josh Logan insisted on Shirley Booth, who had just exited the long-running TV series *Hazel*. Sammy Davis Jr. was the unanimous choice for Homer, but he wanted too much money, and the role went to Al Freeman Jr., who Josh Logan would later say was difficult to work with. The show did not try out out of town, but went straight into Broadway previews. This was the scene-by-scene breakdown during previews: *Act I*: Overture (Orchestra); *Scene 1* The farm: "Gott is Gut" (Maria & Sisters), "First Class Number One Bum" (Homer); *Scene 2* The farm: "Himmlisher Vater" (Maria & Sisters), "Follow the Lamb!" (Homer, Maria, Sisters), "Don't Talk About God" (Homer), "When I Was Young" (Maria); *Scene 3* Juan's cafe: "Meet My Seester" (Juanita, Rosita, Truckers); *Scene 4* The farm: "One Little Brick at a Time" (Maria & Sisters); *Scene 5* Exterior Juan's cafe: "To Do a Little Good" (Juan & Employees); *Scene 6* The farm: "There Comes a Time" (Homer), "Why Can't He See?" (Maria); *Scene 7* Juan's cafe: "I'd Sure Like to Give it a Shot" (Homer, Juanita, Rosita, Juan, Customers). *Act II*: Entr'acte (Orchestra); *Scene 1* Farmhouse kitchen: "Them and They" (Maria & Sisters); *Scene 2* Courtroom: "Does it Really Matter?" (Homer); *Scene 3* A bus stop: "Look to the Lilies" (Maria & Sisters); *Scene 4* The farm: "I Admire You Very Much, Mr. Schmidt" (Albertine), "Some Kind of Man" (Homer); *Scene 5* Juan's cafe: "Chant" (Homer's Followers); *Scene 6* The farm: "Casamagordo, New Mexico" (Sisters), "Follow the Lamb!" (reprise) (Homer, Maria, Sisters), "One Little Brick at a Time" (reprise) (Homer & Townspeople); *Scene 7* A bus stop: "I, Yes, Me! That's Who" (Maria); *Scene 8* Chapel exterior; *Scene 9* Chapel interior: "I, Yes, Me! That's Who" (reprise) (Homer).

The Broadway Run. Lunt—Fontanne Theatre, 3/29/70–4/19/70. 31 previews. 25 performances. Presented by Edgar Lansbury, Max J. Brown, Richard Lewine, Ralph Nelson; Music: Jule Styne; Lyrics: Sammy Cahn; Book: Leonard Spigelgass; Based on the 1962 movie *Lilies of the Field*, written by James Poe, and starring Sidney Poitier (he won an Oscar), which in turn was based on the novel of the same name by William E. Barrett; Director: Joshua Logan; Choreographer: Joyce Trisler (unbilled); Sets/Lighting: Jo Mielziner; Costumes: Carrie F. Robbins; Audio Design: Robert I. Liftin; Musical Director: Milton Rosenstock; Orchestrations: Larry Wilcox; Dance Music Arrangements: John Morris; Vocal Director/Vocal Arrangements: Buster Davis; Cast recording on Warner Bros; Press: Max Eisen, Warren Pincus, Bob Satuloff; Casting: Michael Shurtleff; General Manager: Joseph Beruh; Company Manager: Jewel Howard; Production Stage Manager: Wade Miller; Stage Manager: Gigi Cascio; Assistant Stage Manager: Gail Bell. **Cast:** Homer Smith: Al Freeman Jr. (2) ☆; Sister Gertrude: Maggie Task (7); Sister Elizabeth: Virginia Craig (8); Sister Agnes: Linda Andrews (9); Mother Maria: Shirley Booth (1) ☆; Sister Albertine: Taina Elg (4); Lady Guitarist: Anita Sheer (11); Juanita: Patti Karr (6); Rosita: Carmen Alvarez (5); Juan Archuleta: Titos Vandis (3); Bartender: Marc Allen III; 1st Policeman: Joe Benjamin; 2nd Policeman: Richard Graham; Senora Perez: Shirley Potter; Senora Gonzalez: Ravah Malmuth; Senora Chavales: Maggie Worth; Courtroom Guards: Paul Eichel & Michael Davis; Judge: Joe Benjamin; District Attorney: Don Prieur; Defense Attorney: Ben Laney; Monsignor O'Hara: Richard Graham (10); Poker Players: Michael Davis, Paul Eichel, Don Prieur; Children: Lori Bellaran, Ray Bellaran; Singers: Tourists: Marian Haraldson & Don Prieur; Bus Girl: Sherri Huff; Local: Suzanne Horn; Jewelry Vendor: Maggie Worth; Indian Barkeep: Marc Allen III; Trucker: Michael Davis; Mexican Bummer: Paul Eichel; Farmer: Tony Falco; Souvenir Salesman: Ben Laney [end of Singers section]; Dancers: Child: Lisa Bellaran; Teeny Bopper: Carol Conte; Indian Waitress: Maria Di Dia; Mexican Wife: Tina Faye; Mexican Girlfriend: Ravah Malmuth; Mexican Hippie: Glenn Brooks; College Student: Harry Endicott; White Suit: Gary Gendell; Ranch Hand: Steven Ross [end of Dancers section]. **Standbys**: Homer: Clifton Davis; Juan: Ted Beniades. **Understudies**: Maria: Maggie Task; Albertine: Shirley Potter; Rosita: Carol Conte; Juanita: Tina Faye; Gertrude/Elizabeth/Agnes: Marian Haraldson; Judge/1st Policeman: Paul Eichel; Monsignor/2nd Policeman: Michael Davis. **Act I: Scene 1** The farm: "Gott is Gut" (Maria & Sisters), "First Class Number One Bum" (Homer); **Scene 2** Farmhouse kitchen: "Himmlisher Vater" (Maria & Sisters), "Follow the Lamb!" (Homer, Maria, Sisters); **Scene 3** Juan's cafe: "Meet My Seester" (Juanita & Rosita); **Scene 4** Farmhouse kitchen: "Don't Talk About God" (Homer), "When I Was Young" (Maria); **Scene 5** The farm; the next morning: "On That Day of Days" (Juanita, Rosita, Children, Townspeople), "You're a Rock" (Homer), "I Am What I Am" (Maria), "I'd Sure Like to Give it a Shot" (Homer); **Scene 6** Juan's cafe: "I'd Sure Like to Give it a Shot" (dance) (Homer, Juanita, Rosita, Customers). **Act II:** Entr'acte; **Scene 1** Farmhouse kitchen: "I Admire You Very Much, Mr. Schmidt" (Albertine); **Scene 2** Courtroom; **Scene 3** A bus stop: "Look to the Lilies" (Maria & Sisters); **Scene 4** The farm: "Some Kind of Man" (Homer); **Scene 5** Near Casamagordo: "Homer's Pitch" (Homer & Townspeople); **Scene 6** Juan's cafe; **Scene 7** The farm: "Casamagordo, New Mexico" (Sisters), "Follow the Lamb!" (reprise) (Homer, Maria, Sisters), "One Little Brick at a Time" (Homer & Townspeople); **Scene 8** A bus stop: "I, Yes Me! That's Who" (Maria); **Scene 9** Chapel exterior: "Prayer" (Townspeople); **Scene 10** Chapel interior: "I, Yes Me! That's Who" (reprise) (Homer).

It opened on Easter Sunday, during a blizzard, and Broadway reviews were divided, mostly bad. Shirley Booth got raves, however. It was her last musical.

407. *Lorelei*

Also known as *Lorelei: or Gentlemen STILL Prefer Blondes*. Set aboard the *Ile de France*, in Paris, and in New York. This was an update of *Gentlemen Prefer Blondes*, with Carol Channing

reprising her 1949 Broadway role as a widow looking back on the 1920s.

Before Broadway. The Broadway production began as an 11-month national try-out tour, which opened on 2/26/73, at the Civic Center Music Hall, Oklahoma City. It ran at the National Theatre, Washington, DC, 5/15/73–6/2/73, by which time Joe Layton had been replaced as director by Betty Comden & Adolph Green, who were in turn replaced by Robert Moore before Broadway. Joe Layton retained the credit of "entire production staged by." Ernie Flatt, who prior to Broadway had merely "additional choreography" credit, was now listed as "choreographer."

The Broadway Run. Palace Theatre, 1/27/74–11/3/74. 11 previews from 1/17/74. 320 performances. A Music Fair Enterprises production, Presented by Lee Guber & Shelly Gross; Music/New Music: Jule Styne; Lyrics: Leo Robin; New Lyrics: Betty Comden & Adolph Green; Original Book: Anita Loos & Joseph Fields; New Book: Kenny Solms & Gail Parent; Based on *Gentlemen Prefer Blondes*, by Anita Loos; Director: Robert Moore (Joe Layton on the pre–Broadway tour); Choreographer: Ernest O. Flatt; Sets: John Conklin; Costumes: Alvin Colt; Carol Channing's Costumes: Ray Aghayan & Bob Mackie; Lighting: John Gleason; Sound: Ray Yowell; Musical Director: Milton Rosenstock; Assistant Musical Director: Robert Stanley; Orchestrations: Philip J. Lang & Don Walker; Dance Music Arrangements: Jay Thompson; Vocal Arrangements: Hugh Martin & Buster Davis; Cast recording on MGM—Verve; Press: Solters/Sabinson/Roskin; General Managers: Joseph Harris & Ira Bernstein; Company Manager: Milton M. Pollack, *David Lawlor*; Production Stage Manager: Ben D. Kranz, *Tom Porter*; Stage Manager: George Boyd (Maxine Sholar-Taylor on the pre–Broadway tour); Assistant Stage Manager: David Neuman, *Jamie Haskins*. **Cast:** Lorelei Lee: Carol Channing (1) ☆; Henry Spofford: Lee Roy Reams (5); Mrs. Ella Spofford: Dody Goodman (2), *Bobo Lewis*; Lord Francis Beekman: Jack Fletcher (7) (Brooks Morton on the pre–Broadway tour); Lady Phyllis Beekman: Jean Bruno (8); Josephus Gage: Brandon Maggart (6); Dorothy Shaw: Tamara Long (3); Gus Esmond: Peter Palmer (4); Bartender: Ray Cox; Frank: Steve Short (David Roman on the pre–Broadway tour); George: Bob Daley, *Gregg Harlan*; Pierre: Ray Cox; Charles: Robert Riker (Ken Ploss on the pre–Broadway tour); Robert Lemanteur: Bob Fitch (9), *Joe Bratcher*; Louis Lemanteur: Ian Tucker (10) (John Mineo on the pre–Broadway tour); Lobster (Un délicieux Pince Rouge!): Brenda Holmes, *Roxanna White* (Gia de Silva on the pre–Broadway tour); Caviar (Un Bon Ouef!): Linda McClure, *Brenda Holmes* (Angela Martin on the pre–Broadway tour); Pheasant (Un Oiseau Dans le Matin!): Aniko Farrell; Salade (A Votre Sante!): Marie Halton, *Kerry McGrath* (Donna Monroe on the pre–Broadway tour); Dessert (Vive la Glace Chaude!): Carol Channing; Maitre d': Willard Beckham (David Roman on the pre–Broadway tour); Simone Duval: Sherrill Harper, *Gena Ramsel*; Tenor: Ken Ploss (on the pre–Broadway tour, but this role was dropped for Broadway); Zizi: Katherine Hull Mineo (on the pre–Broadway tour, but this role was dropped for Broadway); Fifi: Maureen Crockett (on the pre–Broadway tour, but this role was dropped for Broadway); MC: Robert Riker; Announcer: Ray Cox; Engineer: Bob Daley (Ken Sherber on the pre–Broadway tour); Mr. Esmond: David Neuman, *Ray Cox*; Minister: Ray Cox (role dropped for Broadway); Tapsters: Joyce Chapman, Bob Fitch, John Mineo, Ken Ploss (roles dropped for Broadway); Bridesmaids: Aniko Farrell, Marie Halton (*Kerry McGrath*), Sherrill Harper, Linda McClure, *Bonnie Hinson, Roxanna White* [On pre–Broadway tour: Gia de Silva, Anniko Farrell, Angela Martin, Donna Monroe]; Ensemble (Ship's Personnel, Passengers, Tourists, Olympic Team Members, Waiters, Wedding Guests): Willard Beckham, Ray Cox, Bob Daley, Aniko Farrell, Bob Fitch, Joela Flood, Marie Halton, Marian Haraldson, Gregg Harlan, Sherrill Harper, Brenda Holmes, Linda Lee MacArthur, Linda McClure, Wayne Mattson, Jonathan Miele, Susan Ohman, Gena Ramsel, Jeff Richards, Robert Riker, Rick Schneider, Steve Short, Don Swanson, Ian Tucker, Roxanna White, *Joe Bratcher, Paul Eichel, Jamie Haskins, Bonnie Hinson, Randy Hugill, Karen Jablons, Kerry McGrath, Chester Walker* [Pre-Broadway tour ensemble: Chris Bartlett, Joyce Chapman, Ray Cox, Maureen Crockett, Bob Daley, Georgia Dell, Gia de Silva, Aniko Farrell, Bob Fitch, Peggy Marie Haug, Casey Jones, Howard Leonard, Linda Lee MacArthur, Angela Martin, Jonathan Miele, John Mineo, Katherine Hull Minco, Donna Monroe, Richard Natkowski, Ken Ploss, Penny Pritchard, Robert Riker, David Roman, Ken Sherber]. **Understudies**: Lorelei: Sherrill Harper, *Brenda Holmes* (Donna Monroe on the pre–Broadway tour); Dorothy: Gena Ramsel (Angela Martin on the pre–Broadway tour); Ella/Phyllis: Marian Haraldson (Georgia Dell on the pre–Broadway tour); Gus/Gage: Ray Cox (David Roman on the pre–Broadway tour); Henry: Wayne Mattson (Ken Ploss on the pre–Broadway tour); Lord Beekman: David Neuman, *Paul Eichel*; Frank: Jonathan Miele; Louis: Jonathan Miele, *Randy Hugill*; George: Jonathan Miele, *Bob Daley*; Robert: Robert Riker, *Wayne Mattson*; Mr. Esmond: Bob Daley, *Joe Bratcher*. **Act I**: *Prologue* Dockside, New York; 1944: "Looking Back" * (Lorelei); *Scene 1* The pier of the *Ile de France*: "Bye Bye Baby" (Gus, Lorelei, Passengers, Tourists); *Scene 2* The deck of the Ile de France: "(It's) High Time" (Dorothy, Mrs. Spofford, Passengers), "(I'm Just a Little Girl from) Little Rock" (Lorelei), "I'm a-Tingle, I'm a-Glow" [on the tour, but dropped for Broadway]; *Scene 3* Lorelei's suite on the *Ile de France*: "I Love What I'm Doing" (Dorothy), "A Girl Like I" [on the tour, but dropped for Broadway], "Paris, Paris" [on the tour, but dropped for Broadway], "It's Delightful Down in Chile" (Lorelei, Lord Francis, Stewards) [not on the pre–Broadway tour]; *Scene 4* The Eiffel Tower: "I Won't Let You Get Away" * (Henry & Dorothy); *Scene 5* Lorelei's suite, the Ritz Hotel in Paris: "Keeping Cool with Coolidge" (Henry, Dorothy, Mrs. Spofford, Guests), "Men" * (dance supervised by Robert Tucker) (Lorelei). **Act II**: *Scene 1* Pre-Catalin nightclub: "Coquette" (Dorothy, Lorelei, Showgirls), "Mamie is Mimi" (Lorelei, Robert, Louis); *Scene 2* A Paris street: "Diamonds Are a Girl's Best Friend" (Lorelei), "Homesick (Blues)" (Lorelei & Gus); *Scene 3* Lorelei's suite, the Ritz Hotel in Paris [this scene was added for Broadway]: "Miss Lorelei Lee" * (Henry, Dorothy, Mrs. Spofford, Gage, Robert, Louis, Wedding Guests), "(We're Just) a Kiss Apart" [on the tour, but dropped for Broadway]; *Scene 4* On the way home: "Button Up with Esmond" (Lorelei & Bridesmaids); *Scene 5* The Central Park Casino, New York: "Diamonds Are a Girl's Best Friend" (reprise) (Lorelei); EPILOGUE The present: Finale.

Note: all music by Jule Styne. All lyrics by Leo Robin, unless marked with an asterisk, in which case they are new numbers by Comden & Green (with Jule Styne again providing the music).

On Broadway it opened to very good reviews. Carol Channing was nominated for a Tony. The production was capitalized at half a million dollars, but in the end cost about $700,000 to get to Broadway. The show recouped more than half its cost during its pre–Broadway tour. Another $100,000 or so was recouped on Broadway.

408. *Lost in the Stars*

A musical tragedy. Set in the small South African village of Ndotsheni, and in the city of Johannesburg, in the present (1949). It tells a story of racial prejudice and hatred in South Africa. Stephen, an Anglican minister of a Zulu tribe, leaves his quiet home in the hills of Natal, and sets out for Jo'burg to find his wayward son, Absalom, and finds that during an attempted robbery he has accidentally killed the young (white) son of planter James Jarvis, the greatest benefactor of the black race (although still a firm believer in apartheid). While Absalom admits his guilt, and faces the hangman, his companions deny it, and go free. As Absalom is about to die, he is visited by Mr. Jarvis, who admires Absalom for his integrity. The two become friends.

Before Broadway. This was Kurt Weill's last musical. He died of a heart attack on 4/3/50, aged 50. Oscar Hammerstein II's wife, Dorothy, read the novel before it was published, and recommended it to Maxwell Anderson. Paul Robeson turned down the lead.

The Broadway Run. MUSIC BOX THEATRE, 10/30/49–7/1/50. 281 PERFORMANCES. PRESENTED BY The Playwrights' Company (Maxwell Anderson, Elmer Rice, Robert E. Sherwood, Kurt Weill, John F. Wharton); MUSIC/ORCHESTRATIONS/MUSICAL ARRANGEMENTS: Kurt Weill;

LYRICS/BOOK: Maxwell Anderson; BASED ON the 1948 novel *Cry, the Beloved Country*, by Alan Paton; SOME MATERIAL taken from an earlier Kurt Weill—Maxwell Anderson collaboration, the unfinished musical *Ulysses Africanus*; DIRECTOR/PRODUCTION SUPERVISOR: Rouben Mamoulian; CHOREOGRAPHER: LaVerne French; SETS: George Jenkins; JOHANNESBURG SET BACKDROP: Horace Armistead; COSTUMES: Anna Hill Johnstone; MUSICAL DIRECTOR/CHORAL GROUP TRAINED BY: Maurice Levine; CAST RECORDING on Decca; PRESS: William Fields, Walter Alford, Arthur Cantor; CASTING: Rouben Mamoulian & Edward Brinkmann; GENERAL STAGE MANAGER: Andy Anderson; STAGE MANAGER: Edward Brinkmann; ASSISTANT STAGE MANAGER: Roy Allen. *Cast:* LEADER: Frank Roane (7); ANSWERER: Joseph James; NITA: Elayne Richards; GRACE KUMALO: Gertrude Jeannette; STEPHEN KUMALO: Todd Duncan (1); THE YOUNG MAN: LaVerne French; THE YOUNG WOMAN: Mabel Hart; JAMES JARVIS: Leslie Banks (2); EDWARD JARVIS: Judson Rees; ARTHUR JARVIS: John Morley; JOHN KUMALO: Warren Coleman (3); PAULUS: Charles McRae; WILLIAM: Roy Allen; JARED: William C. Smith; ALEX: Herbert Coleman; FOREMAN: Jerome Shaw; MRS. M'KIZE: Georgette Harvey; HLABENI: William Marshall, *Joseph James*; ELAND: Charles Grunwell; LINDA: Sheila Guyse (8); JOHANNES PAFURI: Van Prince; MATTHEW KUMALO: William Greaves (6); ABSALOM KUMALO: Julian Mayfield (5); ROSE: Gloria Smith; IRINA: Inez Matthews (4); POLICEMAN: Robert Byrn; WHITE WOMAN: Biruta Ramoska; WHITE MAN: Mark Kramer; THE GUARD: Jerome Shaw; BURTON: John W. Stanley; THE JUDGE: Guy Spaull; VILLAGER: Robert McFerrin; SINGERS: LaCoste Brown, Robert Byrn, Sibol Cain, Joseph Crawford, Russell George, Alma Hubbard, Joseph James, Mark Kramer, Moses LaMarr, Elen Longone, Robert McFerrin, June McMechen, Paul Mario, Biruta Ramoska, William C. Smith, Christine Spencer, Constance Stokes, Joseph Theard, Lucretia West, *Leon Bibb, Clyde Turner*. **Understudies**: Stephen: William Marshall, *Joseph James*; John: William Marshall, *William C. Smith*; James: Guy Spaull; Irina: Christine Spencer; Absalom: William Greaves; Matthew: Van Prince; Nita: Yvonne Coleman; Grace: Georgette Harvey; Edward: Richard Rhoades; Arthur/Eland/Burton: Jerome Shaw; Linda: Sibol Cain; Johannes: Roy Allen; Judge: John W. Stanley; Mrs. M'Kize: Lucretia West; Alex: William Davidson. **Act I**: *Opening*: "The Hills of Ixopo" (Leader, Answerer, Singers). NDOTSHENI, a small village in South Africa; *Scene 1* Stephen's home: "Thousands of Miles" (Stephen); *Scene 2* Railroad station: "Train to Johannesburg" (Leader & Singers). JOHANNESBURG. *Scene 3* John Kumalo's tobacco shop; *Scene 4* "The Search" (Stephen, Leader, Singers); *Scene 4a* Factory office; *Scene 4b* Mrs. M'Kize's house; *Scene 4c* Hlabeni's house; *Scene 4d* Parole office; *Scene 5* Stephen's Shantytown lodging: "The Little Grey House" (Stephen & Singers); *Scene 6* A dive in Shantytown: "Who'll Buy?" (Linda) (danced by The Young Man & The Young Woman); SCENE 6A A street in Shantytown; *Scene 7* Irina's hut in Shantytown: "Trouble Man" (Irina); *Scene 8* Kitchen in Arthur Jarvis's home: "Murder in Parkwold" (Singers); *Scene 9* Arthur Jarvis's library; *Scene 10* A street in Shantytown: "Fear" (Singers); *Scene 11* Prison; *Scene 12* Stephen's Shantytown lodging: "Lost in the Stars" (Stephen & Singers). **Act II**: *Opening*: "The Wild Justice" (Leader & Singers). JOHANNESBURG. *Scene 1* John Kumalo's tobacco shop; *Scene 2* Stephen's Prayer: "O Tixo, Tixo, Help Me" (Stephen); *Scene 3* Arthur Jarvis's doorway; *Scene 4* Irina's hut in Shantytown: "Stay Well" (Irina); *Scene 5* A courtroom: "The Wild Justice" (reprise) (Singers); *Scene 6* A prison cell: "Cry, the Beloved Country" (Leader & Singers). NDOTSHENI. *Scene 7* Stephen's chapel: "Big Mole" (Alex), "A Bird of Passage" (Stephen); *Scene 8* Stephen's home: "Four O'clock" (Leader & Singers), Finale: "Thousands of Miles" (reprise) (Stephen).

Reviews were divided. Todd Duncan won a Donaldson Award.

After Broadway. In 1958 it became part of repertory of the New York City Opera, who produced it at CITY CENTER, NYC, 4/9/58–5/11/58. 14 PERFORMANCES IN REPERTORY. NEWLY CONCEIVED BY/DIRECTOR/CHOREOGRAPHER: Jose Quintero; SETS/COSTUMES: Andreas Nomikos; LIGHTING: Lee Watson; CONDUCTOR: Julius Rudel. *Cast*: NITA: Patti Austin; GRACE: Rosetta Le Noire; STEPHEN: Lawrence Winters; YOUNG WOMAN: Mary Louise; JAMES JARVIS: Nicholas Joy; EDWARD JARVIS: Chris Snell; ARTHUR JARVIS: John Irving; JOHN: Frederick O'Neal; PAULUS: Emory Richardson; WILLIAM: Lawson Bates; MRS. M'KIZE: Eva Jessye; HLABENI: Garwood Perkins; ELAND: Conrad Bain;

LINDA: Olga James; JOHANNES: Godfrey Cambridge; MATTHEW: Douglas Turner; ABSALOM: Lou Gossett; ROSE: Alyce Webb; IRINA: Shirley Carter; WHITE WOMAN: Naomi Collier.

409. *Lost in the Stars (Broadway revival)*

Before Broadway. This revival tried out at the Kennedy Center, Washington, DC, from 2/19/72. 29 performances.

The Broadway Run. IMPERIAL THEATRE, 4/18/72–5/21/72. 8 previews from 4/12/72. 39 PERFORMANCES. PRESENTED BY Roger L. Stevens & Diana Shumlin for the John F. Kennedy Center for the Performing Arts; MUSIC/ORCHESTRATIONS/MUSICAL ARRANGEMENTS: Kurt Weill; LYRICS/BOOK: Maxwell Anderson; BASED ON the 1948 novel *Cry the Beloved Country*, by Alan Paton; SOME MATERIAL taken from *Ulysses Africanus*, an earlier (unfinished) musical by Kurt Weill & Maxwell Anderson; DIRECTOR: Gene Frankel; CHOREOGRAPHER: Louis Johnson; SETS: Oliver Smith; COSTUMES: Patricia Quinn Stuart; LIGHTING: Paul Sullivan; ASSISTANT LIGHTING: Ken Billington; MUSICAL DIRECTOR: Karen Gustafson; NEW CAST RECORDING on Columbia; PRESS: Seymour Krawitz, Martin Shwartz, Patricia Krawitz; COMPANY MANAGER: David Hedges; PRODUCTION STAGE MANAGER: Frank Hamilton; STAGE MANAGER: Robert Keegan; ASSISTANT STAGE MANAGER: Leonard Hayward. *Cast*: ANSWERER: Lee Hooper; DANCER: Harold Pierson; LEADER: Rod Perry (3); DRUMMER: Babafumi Akunyun; STEPHEN KUMALO: Brock Peters (1) ☆; GRACE KUMALO: Rosetta Le Noire (6); STATIONMASTER: Adam Petroski; THE YOUNG MAN: Sid Marshall; THE YOUNG WOMAN: Ruby Greene Aspinall; ARTHUR JARVIS: Don Fenwick; JAMES JARVIS: Jack Gwillim (2); EDWARD JARVIS: David Jay; MRS. JARVIS: Karen Ford; JOHN KUMALO: Leonard Jackson (5); PAULUS: Leonard Hayward; WILLIAM: Harold Pierson; ALEX: Giancarlo Esposito (10); FOREMAN: Mark Dempsey; MRS. M'KIZE: Alyce Elizabeth Webb; HLABENI: Garrett Saunders; ELAND: Peter Bailey-Britton; LINDA: Marki Bey; JOHANNES PAFURI: Autris Paige; MATTHEW KUMALO: Damon Evans (9); ABSALOM KUMALO: Gilbert Price (4); ROSE: Judy Gibson; IRINA: Margaret Cowie (7); 1ST POLICEMAN: Mark Dempsey; 2ND POLICEMAN: Roy Hausen; SERVANT: Richard Triggs; THE GUARD: Roy Hausen; BURTON: Alexander Reed; JUDGE: Staats Cotsworth (8), *Ian Martin*; MCRAE: Leonard Hayward; SINGERS: Lana Caradimas, Suzanne Cogan, Karen Ford, Aleesa Foster, Ruby Greene Aspinall, Amelia Haas, Edna Husband, Urylee Leonardos, Rona Leslie Pervil, Therman Bailey, Donald Coleman, Raymond Frith, Leonard Hayward, Autris Paige, Mandingo Shaka, Richard Triggs; DANCERS: Michael Harrison, Wayne Stevenson Hayes, Oba-Ya, Michael Oiwake. *Standbys*: Alex: Douglas Grant; Edward: Riley Mills. *Understudies*: Stephen/Leader: Clyde Walker; James/Arthur: Mark Dempsey; Absalom: Harold Pierson; Irina/Linda: Judy Gibson; John: Leonard Hayward; Grace: Lee Hooper; Johannes/Matthew: Sid Marshall; Judge: Adam Petroski; Answerer: Edna Husband; Eland: Alex Reed. *Act I*: *Opening*: "The Hills of Ixopo" (Leader, Answerer, Singers). NDOTSHENI, a small village in South Africa. *Scene 1* Stephen Kumalo's home: "Thousands of Miles" (Stephen); *Scene 2* The railroad station: "Train to Johannesburg" (Leader & Singers). JOHANNESBURG. *Scene 3* John Kumalo's tobacco shop; *Scene 4* "The Search" (Stephen, Leader, Singers): 1/ The factory office; 2/ Mrs. M'Kize's house; 3/ Hlabeni's house; 4/ Parole office; *Scene 5* Stephen's Shantytown lodging: "The Little Grey House" (Stephen & Singers); *Scene 6* A dive in Shantytown; *Scene 7* A street in Shantytown: "Stay Well" (Absalom); *Scene 8* Irina's hut in Shantytown: "Trouble Man" (Irina); *Scene 9* Arthur Jarvis's home: "Murder in Parkwold" (Singers); *Scene 10* A street in Shantytown: "Fear" (Singers); *Scene 11* Prison; *Scene 12* A street in Shantytown: "Lost in the Stars" (Stephen). *Act II*: *Opening*: "The Wild Justice" (Leader & Singers). JOHANNESBURG. *Scene 1* Stephen's Shantytown lodging: "O Tixo, Tixo, Help Me" (Stephen); *Scene 2* Arthur Jarvis's doorway; *Scene 3* The courtroom; *Scene 4* Prison cell: "Cry the Beloved Country" (Leader & Singers). Ndotsheni. *Scene 5* Stephen's chapel: "Big Mole" (Alex); *Scene 6* Stephen Kumalo's home: "Thousands of Miles" (reprise) (Singers).

On Broadway it opened to several raves. Brock Peters and Gilbert Price were nominated for Tony Awards.

After Broadway. THE MOVIE. 1974. *Cast*: Brock Peters, Clifton Davis, Melba Moore.

YORK THEATRE COMPANY, 3/25/88–4/17/88. 16 PERFORMANCES. DIRECTOR: Alex Dmitriev; MUSICAL DIRECTOR: Lawrence W. Hill. *Cast*: STEPHEN: George Merritt; GRACE: Karen Eubanks; MATTHEW: Fred Anderson; JAMES: Dalton Russell Dearborn; LEADER/WILLIAM: Ken Prymus; JOHN: Evan Bell; ABSALOM: Steve Harper; ARTHUR: Lee Lobenhofer.

GOODMAN THEATRE, Chicago, 6/28/93. This production was called *Cry the Beloved Country*. ADAPTED BY/DIRECTOR: Frank Galati; SETS: Loy Arcenas. *Cast*: STEPHEN: Ernest Perry Jr.; GRACE: Cheryl Lynn Bruce; ABSALOM: Darius de Haas; STEPHEN'S FRIEND: Kingsley Leggs; MAFOLO/HLABENI: Dathan B. Williams; MRS. HLATSHWAYOS: Aisha de Haas; ABSALOM'S GIRL: La Chanze.

410. *Louisiana Lady*

Innocent convent-raised Marie-Louise returns on vacation from finishing school to her old family home in New Orleans only to find it being run as a whorehouse by Mme Corday, her mother, who had been forced into this way of life because of debt, and is being controlled by Merluche, a blackmailing slave trader. Marie-Louise falls in love with romantic pirate El Gato.

Before Broadway. The physical production was salvaged from the out-of-town failure *In Gay New Orleans* (see appendix). During tryouts the scene breakdown of Act I was the same as for Broadway, but Act II was: *Scene 1* The parlor; immediately following; *Scene 2* A street; *Scene 3* The Cucacheena Café; *Scene 4* Canal Street; *Scene 5* The gambling room; one hour later; *Scene 6* The garden. The cast was the same except JOE: Patrick Meany; MICHEL: Lou Wills Jr.; CHRISTOPHE: William Downes; MME CORDAY: Olga Baclanova, *Irene Bordoni*; PIERRE: Ken Bond; MERLUCHE: Henry Lascoe. Certain roles during the tryouts were cut for Broadway: CHICO: Michael Landau; MRS. DANFORT: Ann Viola; GEORGE: Ameil Brown. Also cut were the dancing routines of the Hotshots (William Downes & Ameil Brown). The character of Gaston was re-written as Judge Morgan, and Georgette became Genevieve.

The Broadway Run. NEW CENTURY THEATRE, 6/2/47–6/4/47. 4 PERFORMANCES. PRESENTED BY Hall Shelton; MUSIC/LYRICS: Monte Carlo & Alma Sanders; BOOK: Isaac Green Jr. & Eugene Berton; BASED ON the 1927 play *Creoles*, by Samuel Shipman & Kenneth Perkins; DIRECTOR: Edgar J. MacGregor; CHOREOGRAPHER: Felicia Sorel; SETS: Watson Barratt; COSTUMES: Frank Thompson; LIGHT: Leo Kerz; MUSICAL DIRECTOR/CHORAL ARRANGEMENTS: Hilding Anderson; ORCHESTRATIONS: Hans Spialek & Robert Russell Bennett; PRESS: Leo Freedman & June Greenwall; COMPANY MANAGER: Tom Kane; GENERAL STAGE MANAGER: Frank Coletti; STAGE MANAGER: David Jones; ASSISTANT STAGE MANAGER: Charles Conaway. *Cast*: EL GATO: Ray Jacquemont; JOE: Lou Wills Jr.; MICHEL: Val Buttignol; SARAH: Tina Prescott; CORRINE: Ann Lay; GERMAINE: Patti Hall; ANNETTE: Angela Carabella; SUZANNE: Patti Kingsley; YVONNE: Ann Viola; MARIE-LOUISE: Edith Fellows (1); CHARLEY: Howard Blaine; CHRISTOPHE: Bert Wilcox; HUGO: Lee Kerry; GENEVIEVE: Isabella Wilson; MADAME CORDAY: Monica Moore (2); PIERRE: Gil Cass; MARQUET: Robert Kimberly; MERLUCHE: George Baxter; ALPHONSE: Charles Judels (3); CELESTE: Bertha Powell; A DRUNK: George Roberts; HOSKINS: Berton Davis; JANET: Frances Keyes; GOLONDRINA: Victoria Cordova; LT MASON: Patrick Meany; JUDGE MORGAN: Bert Wilcox; SINGING ENSEMBLE: Angela Carabella, Gil Cass, Berton Davis, Ken Emery, Gerald Griffin Jr., Patti Hall, Frances Keyes, Robert Kimberly, Patti Kingsley, Michael Landau, Ann Lay, Patrick Meany, Tina Prescott, George Roberts, Ann Viola, Isabella Wilson; BALLET ENSEMBLE: Daniel Buberniak, Aleta Buttignol, Val Buttignol, Raul Celada, Kenneth Davis, Karlyn DeBoer, Robert DeVoye, Louise Harris, Anzia Kubicek, Tony Matthews, Terry Miele, Nancy Milton, Helen Osborne, Ruth Ostrander, Ralph Williams. *Act I*: *Scene 1* A levee in New Orleans; April 1830; *Scene 2* A study in Miss Browne's Finishing School; Sunday afternoon; *Scene 3* The parlor of the Casino De Luxe of Madame Corday; the following evening; *Scene 4* A garden; *Scene 5* The parlor; a few minutes later. *Act II*: *Scene 1* Canal Street;

Scene 2 The Cucaracha Cafe; *Scene 3* A street; *Scene 4* The garden. **Act I**: "Gold, Women and Laughter" (El Gato & Men), "That's Why I Want to Go Home" (Marie-Louise), "Men About Town" (Mme Corday & Ensemble), "That's Why I Want to Go Home" (reprise) (Marie-Louise), "Just a Bit Naïve" (Marie-Louise & El Gato), "The Cuckoo-Cheena" (Golondrina, Joe, Ensemble), Dance (Helen Osborne, Louise Harris, Tony Matthews, Ensemble), "I Want to Live, I Want to Love" (Marie-Louise), Ballet (Corps de Ballet): CLASSIC TRIO: Ruth Ostrander, Kenneth Davis, Robert DeVoye), "The Night Was All to Blame" (El Gato), "Beware of Lips that Say 'Cherie'" (Mme Corday), "Louisiana's Holiday" (El Gato, Golondrina, Ensemble), Finale Act I (Company). **Act II**: "It's Mardi Gras" (Ensemble & Corps de Ballet), Specialty (Kenneth Davis), "No, No, Mam'selle" (El Gato & Girls), "When You Are Close to Me" (Marie-Louise & El Gato), "When You Are Close to Me" (reprise) (Marie-Louise), Mardi Gras Dance (Joe), "No One Cares for Dreams" (Mme Corday, Ensemble, Ballet), "Mammy's Little Baby" (Celeste), Finale (Company).

On Broadway the critics roundly panned it.

411. *Love Life*

Billed as "a vaudeville" and a "musical fantasy." Susan and Sam, a typical young American couple, remain typical, young and American from the Colonial days to the present. As mechanical and business civilization expands, their love life becomes more complex and difficult. But in the end it all boils down to "Boy Needs Girl and Girl Needs Boy." Johnny and Elizabeth are their children. The show starts with a magician's act, with Sam being levitated and Susan being sawn in half—all of which is symbolic of their lives throughout the play. Vaudeville acts come between each story.

Before Broadway. The number "Susan's Dream" was cut during tryouts.

The Broadway Run. FORTY-SIXTH STREET THEATRE, 10/7/48–5/14/49. 252 PERFORMANCES. PRESENTED BY Cheryl Crawford; MUSIC/ORCHESTRATIONS/ARRANGEMENTS: Kurt Weill; LYRICS/BOOK: Alan Jay Lerner; DIRECTOR: Elia Kazan; CHOREOGRAPHER: Michael Kidd; SETS: Boris Aronson; COSTUMES: Lucinda Ballard; LIGHTING: Peggy Clark; MUSICAL DIRECTOR: Joseph Littau; PRESS: Wolfe Kaufman & Abner D. Klipstein; GENERAL MANAGER: John Yorke; STAGE MANAGERS: Robert Calley, James C. Wicker, Jules Racine. *Part I*: *Act 1* The Magician: 1948. Sam & Susan, helping the Magician with his tricks, try to remember a time when they had a happy marriage. It was 1790: THE MAGICIAN: Jay Marshall; SUSAN: Nanette Fabray (1); SAM: Ray Middleton (2); *Act 2* The Cooper Family. Scene: Outside the Cooper home, Mayville, Connecticut, 1791: MARY JO: Holly Harris; TIM: Evans Thornton; GEORGE CROCKETT: David Thomas; JONATHAN ANDERSON: Gene Tobin; CHARLIE HAMILTON: Victor Clarke; WILL: Mark Kramer; HANK: Robert Byrn; BEN: Lenn Dale; CHILD: Vincent Gugleotti; SAM COOPER: Ray Middleton (2); SUSAN COOPER: Nanette Fabray (1); ELIZABETH COOPER: Cheryl Archer; JOHNNY COOPER: Johnny Stewart. "Who is Samuel Cooper?" (Mary Jo, George, Jonathan, Charlie, Hank, Women), "My Name is Samuel Cooper" (Sam), "Here I'll Stay" (Susan & Sam); *Act 3* Eight Men. Vaudeville: "Progress" [the Go-Getters (David Collyer, Victor Clarke, David Thomas, Robert Byrn, Jules Racine, Gene Tobin, Mark Kramer, Larry Robbins)]; *Act 4* The Farewell. Scene: Outside the Cooper home, Mayville, April 1821: SUSAN: Nanette Fabray (1); ELIZABETH: Cheryl Archer; JOHNNY: Johnny Stewart; SAM: Ray Middleton (2); WALT: Evans Thornton. "I Remember it Well" (Susan & Sam) [later used in *Gigi*], "Green-Up Time" (Susan, Men & Women), "Green-Up Time" (dance) (Arthur Partington & Dancers); *Act 5* Quartette. Vaudeville: "Economics" (Quartette—John Diggs, Joseph James, James Young, William Veasey); *Act 6* The New Baby. Scene: The bedroom of the Cooper home. Sept. 1857: SUSAN: Nanette Fabray (1); SAM: Ray Middleton (2); *Act 7* The Three Tots and a Woman. Vaudeville: THREE TOTS: Rosalie Alter, Vincent Gugleotti, Lenn Dale; TRAPEZE ARTIST: Elly Ardelty; "Mother's Getting Nervous" (Three Tots); *Act 8* My Kind

of Night. Scene: The porch and living room of the Cooper home; the early 1890s: SAM: Ray Middleton (2); ELIZABETH: Cheryl Archer; JOHNNY: Johnny Stewart; SUSAN: Nanette Fabray (1); TWO WOMEN SOLOISTS: Lily Paget & Faye Elizabeth Smith. "My Kind of Night" (Sam), "Women's Club Blues" (Susan & Women); *Act 9* Love Song. Vaudeville: HOBO: Johnny Thompson. "Love Song" (Hobo); *Act 10* The Cruise. Scene: The main dining room of an ocean liner; in the 1920s: ENTERTAINER: Virginia Conwell, *Nina Frenkin*; HARVEY: David Thomas; SAM: Ray Middleton (2); BOYLAN: Victor Clarke; SLADE: Larry Robbins; LEFFCOURT: David Collyer; SUSAN: Nanette Fabray (1); WILLIAM TAYLOR: Lyle Bettger, *Evans Thornton*. "I'm Your Man" (Sam, Slade, Boylan, Harvey, Leffcourt), Finale. *Part II*: *Act 1* Radio Night. Scene: The living room of the Coopers' New York apartment. The present time: SAM: Ray Middleton (2); JOHNNY: Johnny Stewart; ELIZABETH: Cheryl Archer; SUSAN: Nanette Fabray (1); *Act 2* Madrigal Singers. Vaudeville: MADRIGAL LEADER: David Thomas. Modern Madrigal: "Ho, Billy O!" (Madrigal Singers); *Act 3* Farewell Again. The locker room: "I Remember it Well" (reprise) (Sam & Susan), "Is it Him or is it Me?" (Susan); *Act 4* "Punch and Judy Get a Divorce." A bedroom in the Coopers' apartment: PUNCH: Arthur Partington; JUDY: Barbara McCutcheon; LAWYER: Forrest Bonshire; JUDGE: Jules Racine. "Punch and Judy Get a Divorce" (ballet) (Dancers); *Act 5* A Hotel Room: SAM: Ray Middleton (2); BELL HOP: Ed Phillips; CORRESPONDENT: Vida Brown; LAWYER: Frank Westbrook; FLIGHTY PAIR: Shirley Eckl (*Melissa Hayden*) & Ed Phillips; SPEEDY PAIR: Pat Hammerlee & Bill Bradley; CHILD: Virginia Conwell; FATHER: Lenny Claret, *Michael Maule*; MOTHER: Wana Allison. "This is the Life" (Sam); *Act 6* "The Minstrel Show:" INTERLOCUTOR: Victor Clarke; SAM: Ray Middleton (2); SUSAN: Nanette Fabray (1); MISS HOROSCOPE: Holly Harris; MISS MYSTICISM: Carolyn Maye; MR. CYNIC: David Thomas; GIRL: Josephine Lambert; GIRL: Marie Leidal; MISS IDEAL MAN: Sylvia Stahlman; QUARTETTE: John Diggs, Joseph James, James Young, William Veasey. "Here I'll Stay" (reprise) (Boylan), "Minstrel Parade" (Minstrels), "Madame Zuzu" (Miss Horoscope & Miss Mysticism), "Taking No Chances" (Mr. Cynic), "Mr. Right" (Susan & Miss Ideal Man), Finale.

SINGERS: Holly Harris, Josephine Lambert, Peggy Turnley, Marie Leidal, Sylvia Stahlman, Carol Maye, Lily Paget, Dorothea Berthelson, Faye E. Smith, David Collyer, Victor Clarke, David Thomas, Robert Byrn, Evans Thornton, Gene Tobin, Mark Kramer, Larry Robbins; DANCERS: Paula Lloyd, Shirley Eckl (*Melissa Hayden*), Pat Hammerlee, Wana Allison, Virginia Conwell, Barbara McCutcheon, Ed Phillips, Bill Bradley, Frank Westbrook, Arthur Partington, Forrest Bonshire, Lenny Claret (*Michael Maule*), Vida Brown, Robert Tucker. *Understudies*: Susan: Holly Harris; Sam/Hobo/Bill: Evans Thornton; Magician/Walt: Jules Racine; Johnny: Lenn Dale; Elizabeth: Carol O'Donnell; Mike/Madrigal Leader: Victor Clarke; Interlocutor: Robert Byrn; Mr. Cynic: David Collyer; Horoscope/Mysticism/Ideal Man: Wana Allison.

Broadway reviews were divided, with several raves. It lost money. Elia Kazan does not even mention the production in his autobiography *A Life*. Nanette Fabray won a Tony Award.

After Broadway. AMERICAN MUSIC THEATRE FESTIVAL, Philadelphia, 6/6/90. ADAPTED BY: Thomas Babe; DIRECTOR: Barry Harman; MUSICAL DIRECTOR: Robert Kapilow.

THE EUROPEAN PREMIERE. Not until 1/25/96, at LEEDS GRAND THEATRE, England. PRESENTED BY Opera North. DIRECTOR: Caroline Gawn; MUSICAL DIRECTOR: Wyn Davies.

412. *Lovely Ladies, Kind Gentlemen*

Set on Okinawa during a few months in 1946. The book followed the original play very closely. Characters included the long-suffering Col. Purdy. Lotus Blossom was Fisby's love interest.

Before Broadway. *Teahouse of the August Moon*, on which this musical was based, was a straight play, and a monster hit, which opened on Broadway on 10/15/53. 1,027 performances. Because MGM owned the play's title, John Patrick (who wrote the libretto for this musical) used the first four words spoken in the play (by the interpreter Sakini) "Lovely

Ladies, Kind Gentlemen." Before tryouts producer Herman Levin's office was picketed by the Oriental Actors of America, who claimed that not one Asian actor was auditioned for the key role of Sakini (Ken Nelson was white), and that the show had auditioned too few Asians for a cast of over 40. It tried out at the Shubert Theatre, Philadelphia, 8/19/70–9/4/70. 19 performances. David Burns replaced Bernie West during tryouts, and 6th-billed Judy Knaiz left the show. Six songs were cut, and five new ones added.

The Broadway Run. MAJESTIC THEATRE, 12/28/70–1/9/71. 3 previews from 12/26/70. 16 PERFORMANCES. PRESENTED BY Herman Levin; MUSIC/LYRICS: Stan Freeman & Franklin Underwood; BOOK: John Patrick; BASED ON the Pulitzer Prize–winning novel *The Teahouse of the August Moon*, by Vern J. Sneider, and on the famous and multi-award-winning 1953 Broadway comedy therefrom, by John Patrick, and starring David Wayne, and on the movie made from it, starring Marlon Brando; DIRECTOR: Lawrence Kasha; CHOREOGRAPHER: Marc Breaux; SETS: Oliver Smith; COSTUMES: Freddy Wittop; LIGHTING: Thomas Skelton; SOUND: Robert Minor; MUSICAL DIRECTOR/CHORAL ARRANGEMENTS: Theodore Saidenberg; ORCHESTRATIONS: Philip J. Lang; DANCE MUSIC ARRANGEMENTS: Al Mello; PRESS: Martin Shwartz; GENERAL MANAGER: Max Allentuck; COMPANY MANAGER: Joseph M. Grossman; PRODUCTION STAGE MANAGER: Phil Friedman; STAGE MANAGER: Richard Hughes; ASSISTANT STAGE MANAGERS: Robert Corpora & Jim Weston. *Cast:* SAKINI: Kenneth Nelson (1) ✫; MISSIONARY: David Steele; COL. WAINWRIGHT PURDY III: David Burns ✫; SGT. GREGOVICH: Lou Wills (6); CAPT. FISBY: Ron Hussman (2) ✫; OLD LADY: Sachi Shimizu; THE DAUGHTER: Tisa Chang; CHILDREN: June Angela, Gene Profanato, Dana Shimizu; LADY ASTOR: Herself; ANCIENT MAN: Sab Shimono; MR. SEIKO: Alvin Lum; MISS HIGA JIGA: Lori Chinn; MR. OSHIRA: David Thomas; MR. HOKAIDA: Big Lee; LOTUS BLOSSOM: Eleanor Calbes (4) ✫; MR. KEORA: Sab Shimono; CAPT. MCLEAN: Remak Ramsay (5); LOGAN: David Steele; MILLER: James Weston; O'MALLEY: Stephen Bolster; CABOT: Stuart Craig Wood; STOCK: James B. Spann; LIPSHITZ: Kirk Norman; SWENSON: James Hobson; CARDONE: Dennis Roth; MANCINI: Richard Nieves; COLOMBO: Charlie J. Rodriguez; OKINAWANS & AMERICANS: Stephen Bolster, Henry Boyer, Tisa Chang, Paul Charles, Lori Chinn, Barbara Coggin, Christi Curtis, Catherine Dando, Marjory Edson, Charles Goeddertz, James Hobson, J.J. Jepson, Rosalie King, Alvin Lum, Joe Milan, Joan Nelson, Richard Nieves, Sylvia Nolan, Kirk Norman, JoAnn Ogawa, Tim Ramirez, Charlie J. Rodriguez, Steven Ross, Dennis Roth, Sachi Shimizu, Sab Shimono, Susan Sigrist, James B. Spann, David Steele, Sumiko, Ken Urmston, Jim Weston, Stuart Craig Wood. *Understudies*: Sakini: J.J. Jepson; Fisby: Stephen Bolster; Purdy: David Thomas; Lotus: Sumiko; McLean: Jim Weston; Gregovich: James B. Spann; Oshira: Sab Shimono; Hokaida: Alvin Lum. *Act I*: *Scene 1* Okinawa: "With a Snap of My Finger" (Sakini, Okinawans, GIs); *Scene 2* Purdy's office: "Right Hand Man" (Purdy, Sakini, Fisby, GIs); *Scene 3* Outside Purdy's office; *Scene 4* Village square in Tobiki; Fisby's office: "Find Your Own Cricket" (Sakini, Oshira, Higa Jiga, Villagers), "One Side of World" (Sakini); *Scene 5* Outskirts of Tobiki: "Geisha" (Lotus Blossom), "You Say — They Say" (Sakini & Villagers), "This Time" (Fisby); *Scene 6* Purdy & Fisby's office; *Scene 7* Village square in Tobiki; Fisby's office; on the way to Big Koza: "Simple Word" (Lotus Blossom), "Garden Guaracha" (McLean), "Find Your Own Cricket" (reprise) (Sakini & Villagers); *Scene 8* The grove: "Simple Word" (reprise) (Fisby & Lotus Blossom), "If it's Good Enough for Lady Astor" (Fisby, McLean, Sakini, Villagers); *Scene 9* Outskirts of Tobiki: "Batata" (Sakini, Fisby, McLean, Villagers). *Act II*: *Scene 1* The teahouse: "Chaya" (Sakini & Villagers), "Call Me Back" (Fisby, McLean, Sakini) [the showstopper]; *Scene 2* Village street: "Lovely Ladies, Kind Gentlemen" (Sakini); *Scene 3* Fisby's office: "You've Broken a Fine Woman's Heart" (Purdy), "Right Hand Man" (reprise) (Sakini); *Scene 4* Village street; *Scene 5* Village shacks: "One More for the Last One" (Sakini, Gregovich, GIs, Villagers); *Scene 6* The teahouse: "With a Snap of My Fingers" (reprise) (Sakini).

It was mostly panned by the critics, and Clive Barnes's famous "I come to bury *Lovely Ladies, Kind Gentlemen*, not to praise it" review in *New York Times* caused a protest from the producer and cast. The show received Tony nominations for costumes, and for David Burns.

413. *Lute Song*

An Oriental love-story drama with music. About a Chinese married couple, Tsai-Yong and Tchao-ou-Niang. Tsai-Yong goes to the capital to take his civil service exams; because he has read 6,000 books he is appointed chief magistrate and forced to marry Nieou-Chi. He loses contact with his family back in the village, where a famine strikes. Tchao-Ou-Niang's parents die of starvation, and Tchao-ou-Niang is reduced to begging. She even has to sell her hair to raise the money to give Tsai-Yong's parents a decent burial. Then she walks hundreds of miles to the capital, carrying her husband's lute. The kindly princess discovers who she is, and brings the husband and wife together (in the original the women share Tsai-Yong, but Mary Martin had the ending changed, over John Houseman's objections).

Before Broadway. Sidney Howard was crushed by a farm tractor, and died on 8/23/39, just before the release of *Gone with the Wind*, the movie he had written. He had also been working with Will Irwin on a straight theatrical version of *The Lute Song*, which had various non–New York productions. In 1944 film producer John Byram suggested to theatrical producer Michael Myerberg that he make it into stage musical with Mary Martin.

The Broadway Run. PLYMOUTH THEATRE, 2/6/46–6/8/46. 142 PERFORMANCES. PRESENTED BY Michael Myerberg; MUSIC/ORCHESTRATIONS: Raymond Scott; LYRICS: Bernard Hanighen; BOOK: Sidney Howard & Will Irwin; ADAPTED FROM the 5th-century Chinese play *Pi-Pa-Chi* (meaning *Story of a Lute*), by Kao-Tsi-ch'ing; DIRECTOR: John Houseman; CHOREOGRAPHER: Yeichi Nimura; SETS/COSTUMES/LIGHTING: Robert Edmond Jones; MARY MARTIN'S GOWNS: Valentina; MUSICAL DIRECTOR: Eugene Kusmiak; CAST RECORDING on Decca (actually Mary Martin singing only five songs. Yul Brynner is not on the album); PRESS: Richard Maney & Ted Goldsmith; GENERAL MANAGER: Matilda Stanton; COMPANY MANAGER: J. Charles Gilbert; STAGE MANAGER: Jose Vega; ASSISTANT STAGE MANAGER: Millicent Ellis. *Cast:* THE MANAGER, THE HONORABLE CHANG: Clarence Derwent (4); TSAI-YONG, THE HUSBAND: Yul Brynner (2); 1ST PROPERTY MAN: Alberto Vecchio; 2ND PROPERTY MAN: Leslie Rheinfeld; TSAI, THE FATHER: Augustin Duncan (5); MADAME TSAI, THE MOTHER: Mildred Dunnock (6); TCHAO-OU-NIANG, THE WIFE: Mary Martin (1) ✫, *Dolly Haas* (for the last week of the run); PRINCE NIEOU, THE IMPERIAL PRECEPTOR: McKay Morris; PRINCESS NIEOU-CHI, HIS DAUGHTER: Helen Craig (3); SI-TCHUN, A LADY-IN-WAITING: Nancy Davis; WAITING WOMEN: Pamela Wilde & Sydelle Sylvona; HAND MAIDENS: Blanche Zohar & Mary Ann Reeve; YOUEN-KONG, THE STEWARD: Rex O'Malley; A MARRIAGE BROKER: Diane de Brett; A MESSENGER: Jack Amoroso; THE IMPERIAL CHAMBERLAIN: Ralph Clanton, *George Cotton*; THE FOOD COMMISSIONER: Gene Galvin; 1ST CLERK: Max Leavitt, *Charles Leavitt*; 2ND CLERK: Bob Turner; 1ST APPLICANT: Tom Emlyn Williams; 2ND APPLICANT: Michael Blair; IMPERIAL GUARDS: John Robert Lloyd & John High; IMPERIAL ATTENDANTS: Gordon Showalter & Ronald Fletcher (*Edward Crain*); THE GENIE: Ralph Clanton, *George Cotton*; THE WHITE TIGER: Lisa Maslova; THE BLACK APE: Lisan Kay; PHOENIX BIRDS: Lisa Maslova & Lisan Kay; LI-WANG: Max Leavitt, *Charles Leavitt*; PRIEST OF AMIDHA BUDDHA: Tom Emlyn Williams; A BONZE: Gene Galvin; TWO LESSER BONZES: Joseph Camiolo & Leslie Rheinfeld (*Leslie John*); A RICH MAN: Bob Turner; A MERCHANT: John High; A LITTLE BOY: Donald Rose; THE LION: Walter Stane & Alberto Vecchio, *Ronald Fletcher*; CHILDREN: Mary Ann Reeve, Blanche Zohar, Teddy Rose; A SECRETARY: Michael Blair; TRAVELERS ON THE NORTH ROAD, BEGGARS, GUARDS, ATTENDANTS, GODS, ETC: Jack Amoroso, Alan Banks, Mary Burr, Victor Burset, Joseph Camiolo, Jack Cooper, Ronald Fletcher, Arlene Garver, John High, John Robert Lloyd, Lang Page, Bernard Pisarski, Leslie Rheinfeld (*Leslie John*), Gordon Showalter, Walter Stane, Sydelle Sylvona, Alberto Vecchio Pamela Wilde, *Val Buttignol, Edward Crain, Fiora Fontana, Quentin Howard*. *Act I*: *Scene 1* The house of Tsai in the village of Tchin-lieou: Introduction to Act I, "Mountain High, Valley Low" (Tchao-ou-Niang & Tsai-Yong); *Scene 2* The North Road leading to the capital: North Road (dance); *Scene 3* The gate to the Palace of the Voice of Jade: Imperial March (dance); *Scene 4* The house of Tsai in the village of Tchin-lieou: "Monkey See, Monkey Do" ("See the Monkey") (Tchao-ou-Niang), "Where You Are" (Tchao-ou-Niang); *Scene 5* Gardens of the palace of Prince Nieou: Eunuch Scene, Marriage Music (dance). *Act II*: *Scene 1* Gardens of the palace of Prince Nieou: Introduction to Act II, "Willow Tree" (Tsai-Yong) [this number was omitted from the cast album]; *Scene 2* A public granary in the village of Tchin-lieou: Beggars' Music (dance); *Scene 3* Gardens of the palace of Prince Nieou: "Vision Song" (Tchao-ou-Niang & Tsai-Yong); *Scene 4* The house of Tsai in the village of Tchin-lieou; *Scene 5* Market place — Street of the Hair Buyers: Chinese Market Place (dance), Bitter Harvest (dance) (Tchao-ou-Niang); *Scene 6* A burial place in the village of Tchin-lieou: Dirge Song, Genie Music (dance). *Act III*: *Scene 1* In the gardens of the palace of Prince Nieou: Introduction to Act III, Phoenix Dance; *Scene 2* The North Road leading to the capital: "Mountain High, Valley Low" (reprise) (Tchao-ou-Niang); *Scene 3* In the palace; *Scene 4* The Temple of Amidha Buddha: Lion Dance; *Scene 5* A street in the capital: Imperial March (reprise); *Scene 6* The Blue Pavilion in the palace of Prince Nieou: "Lute Song" (Tchao-ou-Niang) [this number was omitted from the cast album].

Broadway reviews were divided, mostly good. Sets and costumes got raves. One of the critics, Louis Kronenberger, said, of Yul Brynner, "he is not much of an actor, and is not up to the frantic demands of the play's most important role." The show won Donaldson Awards for sets, costumes, and for Yul Brynner as most promising newcomer. Nancy Davis, in her Broadway debut, was the daughter of Mary Martin's rather eminent orthopedic surgeon (the star had chronic back problems), and Miss Martin insisted Nancy be hired. John Houseman wanted to fire her during tryouts, but Miss Martin intervened. Miss Davis later married Ronald Reagan.

After Broadway. WINTER GARDEN, London, 10/11/48–10/30/48. 24 PERFORMANCES. PRESENTED & DIRECTED BY Albert de Courville; CHOREOGRAPHER: Lisan Kay; MUSICAL DIRECTOR: Ludo Philipp. **Cast**: TSAI-YONG: Yul Brynner; TSAI: George Manship; TCHAOU-OU-NIANG: Dolly Haas; HANDMAIDENS: Millicent Martin & Virginia Vernon.

CITY CENTER, NYC, 3/12/59–3/22/59. 14 PERFORMANCES. For this production the intermission between Acts I and II was cut out, and the last scene of Act I and the first scene of Act II were merged. PRESENTED BY the New York City Center Light Opera Company; DIRECTOR: John Paul; CHOREOGRAPHER: Yeichi Nimura; ART DIRECTOR: Watson Barratt; SETS/COSTUMES/LIGHTING: Robert Edmond Jones; COSTUME SUPERVISOR: Ruth Morley; MUSICAL DIRECTOR: Sylvan Levin. **Cast**: TSCHANG: Clarence Derwent; TSAI-YONG: Shai-K-Ophir; TSAI: Tonio Selwart; MME TSAI: Estelle Winwood; TCHAOU-OU-NIANG: Dolly Haas; IMPERIAL PRECEPTOR: Philip Bourneuf; HIS DAUGHTER: Leueen McGrath; SI-TCHUN: Rain Winslow; YOUEN-KONG: Joseph Daubenas; MARRIAGE BROKER: Diane de Brett; SWEEPER OF HEAVEN AND EARTH/WHITE TIGER/PHOENIX BIRD/RIBBON SPINNER: Asia (i.e. Asia Mercoolova); IMPERIAL CHAMBERLAIN/GENIE: Donald Symington; FOOD COMMISSIONER/BONZE: Gene Galvin; PRIEST/APPLICANT: Tom Emlyn Williams; CHORUS INCLUDED: Coco Ramirez, Tina Ramirez, Peter Deign, Sheldon Ossosky.

414. *Mack and Mabel*

A musical love story, "the Musical Romance of Mack Sennett's Funny and Fabulous Hollywood." Set in New York and Hollywood between 1911 and 1938, it tells of the growth of the silent movies, and the frustrated love affair between Sennett and Mabel Normand. Mack, now in his late 50s, and out of place in the world of modern film-making, returns to his old sound stage. Then there's a flashback to 1911, and his first studio in Brooklyn. He meets Mabel, and they go off to California. She leaves Mack and turns to drugs, and her career is finally ruined by the scandalous death of director William Desmond Taylor. In this production Mack flew over the audience, suspended by a giant crane, during the number "I Want to Make the World Laugh."

Before Broadway. Leonard Spigelgass and Edwin Lester (head of the San Francisco and Los Angeles Civic Light Opera Companies) came up with the idea in 1971. Jerry Herman worked on the score for a year and then Mr. Spigelgass bowed out, to be replaced as librettist by Mike Stewart. Joseph Kipness came in as producer, but was bought out by David Merrick for 10 per cent of the profits, and Gower Champion was brought on board as director/choreographer. Rehearsals began in Los Angeles, and two days in Mr. Champion fired leading lady Marcia Rodd (Penny Fuller had been announced for this role first), and replaced her with Kelly Garrett, the girl with the great voice he had just heard in *Words and Music* (it took Miss Garrett only a week and a half to get out of *Words and Music*). However, after a week it became apparent that, despite her great voice, Miss Garrett was not suitable for the role in an acting capacity, and she was replaced by Bernadette Peters (this is the vehicle that made Miss Peters a star). Jerry Orbach was set for the role of Mack, but before he signed a contract Robert Preston was chosen instead. Gower Champion's mysterious illness first surfaced during preparation for this show. Rehearsals were postponed, tryouts were shortened. It premiered in San Diego, then it played in Los Angeles and St. Louis, getting good reviews all the way; then at the Kennedy Center, Washington, DC, where it got terrible reviews. David Merrick attempted to replace Gower Champion with Ron Field, but Mike Stewart threatened to withdraw his book if he did. The number "Today I'm Gonna Think About Me" was cut before Broadway.

The Broadway Run. MAJESTIC THEATRE, 10/6/74–11/30/74. 5 previews. 66 PERFORMANCES. PRESENTED BY David Merrick, in association with Edwin H. Morris; MUSIC/LYRICS: Jerry Herman; BOOK: Michael Stewart; BASED ON an idea by Leonard Spigelgass, and suggested by events in the lives of Mack Sennett (1880–1960) and Mabel Normand (1989–1930); DIRECTOR/CHOREOGRAPHER: Gower Champion; SETS: Robin Wagner; COSTUMES: Patricia Zipprodt; LIGHTING: Tharon Musser; SOUND: Otts Munderloh; AUDIO CONSULTANT: Abe Jacob; FILM CO-ORDINATOR: Andy Stein; MUSICAL DIRECTOR/VOCAL ARRANGEMENTS: Donald Pippin; ORCHESTRATIONS: Philip J. Lang; INCIDENTAL & DANCE MUSIC: John Morris; CAST RECORDING on ABC; PRESS: Solters, Sabinson & Roskin; CASTING: Lucia Victor & Howard Feuer; PRODUCTION SUPERVISOR: Lucia Victor; GENERAL MANAGER: Jack Schlissel; ASSISTANT GENERAL MANAGER: Mark Bramble; PRODUCTION STAGE MANAGER: Marnel Sumner; STAGE MANAGER: Tony Manzi; ASSISTANT STAGE MANAGER: Pat Trott. **Cast**: EDDIE, THE WATCHMAN: Stanley Simmonds (11); MACK SENNETT: Robert Preston (1) ✰; LOTTIE AMES: Lisa Kirk (3); ELLA: Nancy Evers (9); FREDDIE: Roger Bigelow; CHARLIE MULDOON: Christopher Murney (6); WALLY: Robert Fitch (10); FRANK WYMAN: Jerry Dodge (5), *Frank Root, Jess Richards*; MABEL NORMAND: Bernadette Peters (2) ✰; MR. KLEINMAN: Tom Batten (7); MR. FOX: Bert Michaels (8); IRIS, THE WARDROBE MISTRESS: Marie Santell; WILLIAM DESMOND TAYLOR: James Mitchell (4); PHYLLIS FOSTER: Cheryl Armstrong; SERGE: Frank Root; THE GRIPS: John Almberg, Roger Bigelow, George Blackwell, Frank Bouley, Gerard Brentte, Lonnie Burr, Chet D'Elia, Igors Gavon, Jonathan Miele, Don Percassi, Frank Root; MACK SENNETT BATHING BEAUTIES: Cheryl Armstrong, Claudia Asbury, Sandahl Bergman, Chrystal Chambers, Nancy Dafgek, Prudence Darby, Elaine Handel, Paula Lynn, Patricia Michaels, Carol Perea, L.J. Rose, Rita Rudner, Marianne Selbert, Jo Speros, Pat Trott, Geordie Withee. **Understudies**: Mack: Igors Gavon; Mabel: Marie Santell; Lottie: Patricia Michaels; Taylor: Roger Bigelow; Wyman: Frank Root (for Mr. Dodge); Muldoon: Lonnie Burr; Kleinman: Frank Bouley; Fox: Jonathan Miele; Ella: L.J. Rose; Wally: Don Percassi; Watchman: George Blackwell; **Swing Dancers**: Helen Butleroff & Richard Maxon. *Scene 1* The Sennett Studios; 1938: "Movies were Movies" (Mack); *Scene 2* The Brooklyn Studio; 1911: "Look What Happened to Mabel" (Mabel, Wally, Charlie, Frank, Grips); *Scene 3* Mack's office, Brooklyn: "Big Time" (Lottie & the Family); *Scene 4* En route to California: "I Won't Send Roses" (Mack), "I Won't Send Roses" (reprise) (Mabel); *Scene 5* Los Angeles; 1912: "I Wanna Make the World Laugh" (Mack & Company); *Scene 6* On the set: "I Wanna Make the World Laugh" (reprise) (Mack & Company); *Scene 7* The Orchid Room of the Hollywood Hotel; 1919: "Wherever He Ain't" (Mabel & Waiters); *Scene 8* On the set: "Hundreds of Girls" (Mack & Bathing Beauties) [AN INTERMISSION WAS ADDED HERE DURING THE RUN]; *Scene 9* Mack's new office; 1923; *Scene 10* The studio; early next morning: "When Mabel Comes into the Room" (Company), "My Heart Leaps Up" (Mack); *Scene 11* A pier, New York: "Time Heals Everything" (Mabel); *Scene 12* Vitagraph Varieties of 1929 and the terrace of William Desmond Taylor's home: "Tap Your Troubles Away" (Lottie & Girls); *Scene 13* Mack's office — then Mabel's home: "I Promise You a Happy Evening" (Mack); *Scene 14* The Sennett Studios; 1938.

Reviews were terrible. The show received Tony Nominations for musical, book, direction of a musical, choreography, sets, costumes, and for Robert Preston and Bernadette Peters. It lost all its $800,000 investment.

After Broadway. 1976 TOUR. This was a revised version, in which the ending was changed to make it happy. DIRECTOR/CHOREOGRAPHER: Ron Field. *Cast:* MACK: David Cryer; MABEL: Lucie Arnaz; ALSO WITH: Tommy Tune (in the Lottie Ames role–but now revamped for a man).

THEATRE ROYAL, DRURY LANE, London. Opened on 2/21/88. In concert. *Cast:* MACK: Denis Quilley; MABEL: Debbie Gravitte; ALSO WITH: Stubby Kaye, George Hearn, Robert Meadmore, Paige O'Hara, Tommy Tune, Frances Ruffelle, Georgia Brown, Jerry Herman (linking songs at the piano), David Jacobs.

In 1988 plans for a fall Broadway revival at the Neil Simon Theatre began with a tryout at the PAPER MILL PLAYHOUSE, in New Jersey. It used the happy ending. However, the producers could not raise the money for Broadway. *Cast:* MACK: George Hearn; MABEL: Ellen Foley.

PICCADILLY THEATRE, London, 11/7/95–6/29/96. 270 PERFORMANCES. This was the revised hit version by Francine Pascal (sister of the original librettist, Michael Stewart). It had a new song — "Mabel and Mack." PRESENTED BY Jon Wilner; CAST RECORDING on EMI. *Cast:* MACK: Howard McGillin; MABEL: Caroline O'Connor; ALSO WITH: Kathryn Evans.

SHEFFIELD, MASS., 6/22/99–7/18/99. Francine Pascal further revised her book. Jerry Herman himself was involved in the staging. There were no new songs, but there was a reprise of "Wherever He Ain't." The show now ended in 1929, with the happier ending. Also Frank and Lottie were more prominent. Frank now sung "When Mabel Comes into the Room," instead of the Night Watchman, and it became clear Frank was based on Frank Capra. PRESENTED BY the Barrington Stage Company; DIRECTOR: Hope Clarke; SETS: Ken Foy.

COSTUMES: Jeff Fender; MUSICAL DIRECTOR: Darren R. Cohen. *Cast:* MACK: Jeff McCarthy; MABEL: Kelli Rabke; LOTTIE: Kathryn Kendall; FATTY: Ric Stoneback; FRANK: Will Erat; TAYLOR/WATCHMAN: Peter Kapetan.

FREUD PLAYHOUSE, UCLA, Los Angeles, 11/8/00–11/19/00. Francine Pascal had again further revised her book (it was now 75 per cent hers), and this production was acclaimed as a "world premiere." "Mabel and Mack" was in this one too. This production was part of the *Reprise!* series. Again, Jerry Herman took an active part in the production. PRESENTED BY Jon Wilner; DIRECTOR: Arthur Allan Seidelman; CHOREOGRAPHER: Dan Siretta; MUSICAL DIRECTOR: Peter Matz. *Cast:* MACK: Douglas Sills; MABEL: Jane Krakowski; LOTTIE: Donna McKechnie.

FAILED BROADWAY ATTEMPT. Jon Wilner planned to produce it on Broadway on 4/23/01, with rehearsals beginning on 3/1/01, and to star Douglas Sills, Jane Krakowski and Donna McKechnie. Again Dan Siretta was to choreograph, and Bill Irwin was to stage the silent Mack Sennett sequences. However, plans were put back to 11/01 because they couldn't find a theatre (Mr. Wilner stated that he had the money in place). Jane Krakowski had to quit, and Caroline O'Connor became the new Mabel. On 6/13/01 a new Broadway date was announced — 1/10/02, with previews to begin in late 12/01, but by 10/01 it was evident that it wasn't going to happen. Jon Wilner was now saying he had only half the money. In 2/02 Mr. Wilner announced he had plans to bring it to the Hobby Center, Houston, in 1/03, this time with Kristin Chenoweth as Mabel, but it was postponed again. In fact, the same crew (Wilner, Seidelman, Siretta, Herman) put on a one-night only benefit production (for Gay Men's Health Crisis) at AVERY FISHER HALL, Lincoln Center, on 3/31/03. MUSICAL DIRECTOR: Donald Pippin. *Cast:* Marissa Jaret Winokur, Brian Stokes Mitchell, Leslie Uggams, Nathan Lane, Donna McKechnie, Michael Feinstein, Debbie Gravitte, Douglas Sills, Radio City Music Hall Rockettes, Uptown Express.

GOODSPEED PRODUCTION. Then in mid–Jan. 2004 it was announced that there may be a production at the GOODSPEED OPERA HOUSE, in Connecticut, 10/27/04–12/12/04 (previews from 10/1/04), with the same basic crew of Arthur Allan Seidelman, Dan Siretta, and Jerry Herman. This was confirmed later in the year. SETS/COSTUMES: Eduardo Sicangco; LIGHTING: Kirk Bookman; MUSICAL DIRECTOR: Michael O'Flaherty; ORCHESTRATIONS: Dan DeLange. *Cast:* MACK: Scott Waara; MABEL: Christiane Noll; LOTTIE: Donna McKechnie; KESSEL: Steve Pudenz; TAYLOR: Gary Lindemann. The production included the numbers "Mabel and Mack" and "Hit 'em on the Head."

415. *Magdalena*

A costume operetta, or musical adventure, with a South American jungle theme set mostly in Colombia, about 1912. Maria, a Muzo Indian of Colombia, and her followers, attempt to obtain justice from General Carabana, a dictatorial and dissipated old spendthrift who owns the local emerald mines in which they work. She leads a strike that brings Carabana back from his good time in Paris. Maria is in love with Pedro, the anti-clerical and lusty bus driver and Mestizo leader of the pagan Indians. Pedro is planning a revolution. Maria is forced into promising to marry the general, but his French mistress, Teresa, a chef, kills him by overfeeding him a delicious meal as she sings "Food for Thought." Pedro is finally converted to Christianity.

Before Broadway. It played first, to great reviews, on the West Coast, with John Arthur playing Lopez. Aside from that the cast and crew were the same as for Broadway. Heitor Villa-Lobos came to New York to work on the score with Wright & Forrest.

The Broadway Run. ZIEGFELD THEATRE, 9/20/48–12/4/48. 88 PERFORMANCES. The Edwin Lester production, PRESENTED BY Homer Curran; BASED ON music by Heitor Villa-Lobos; LYRICS/PATTERN: Robert Wright & George Forrest; BOOK: Frederick Hazlitt Brennan & Homer Curran; DIRECTOR: Jules Dassin; CHOREOGRAPHER: Jack Cole; ASSISTANT TO JACK COLE: Gweneth Verdun (i.e. Gwen Verdon); SETS/LIGHTING: Howard Bay; COSTUMES: Sharaff (i.e. Irene Sharaff); MUSICAL DIRECTOR: Arthur Kay; CHORAL DIRECTOR: Robert Zeller; CAST RECORDING: none, due to the Musicians' Union strike; PRESS: Anthony Buttitta; GENERAL MANAGER: R. Victor Leighton; STAGE MANAGERS: Dan Brennan & Franklin Lacey. *Cast:* PADRE JOSEF: Gerhard Pechner; MANUEL: Peter Fields; SOLIS: Melva Niles; RAMON: Henry Reese; MARIA: Dorothy Sarnoff (3); PEDRO: John Raitt (2); MAJOR BLANCO: Ferdinand Hilt; DOCTOR LOPEZ: Carl Milletaire; GENERAL CARABANA: Hugo Haas (4); CHANTEUSE: Betty Huff; CIGARETTE GIRL: Christine Matsios; ZOGGIE, THE ASTROLOGER: John Schickling; DANSEUSE: Lorraine Miller; MME TERESA: Irra Petina (1); THE OLD ONE: Gene Curtsinger; CHICO: Patrick Kirk; JUAN: Leonard Morganthaler; CONCHITA: Betty Brusher; MAJOR DOMO: Roy Raymond; BAILADORA: Marie Groscup; BAILADOR: Matt Mattox; SINGING GIRLS: Lucy Andonian, Marion Begin, Jean Bishop, Betty Brusher, Trudy De Luz, Sofia Derue, Jeanne Eisen, Vera Ford, Betty Flannagan, Martha Flynn, Audrey Guard, Phyllis Kramer, Gwenn La Kind, Christine Matsios, Theresa Piper, Mary Wood; SINGING BOYS: Ralph Angell, Arthur Brey, Stephen Esail, Kahler Flock, Tommy Gleason, John Huck, Robert Hudson, John King, Ross Lynch, Joe Mazzolini, Roy Raymond, Stanley Rose, Leonard Taylor; DANCING GIRLS: Libby Burke, Rita Charisse, Norma Doggett, Marie Groscup, Judy Landon, Mary Menzies, Lorraine Miller, Joan Morton, Sue Remos; DANCING BOYS: Dale Lefler, Matt Mattox (dance captain), Bill Miller, Verne Miller, Michael Sandin, Michael Scrittorale, Ralph Smith, Paul Steffen, Robert Thompson; CHILDREN: Fred Cuelar, Peter De Bear, Patrick Kirk, Rosarita Varela; SOLDIERS & SERVANTS: Ralph Graves, Robert Meser, Maurice Monte, Arthur Veiga. *Standbys:* Teresa: Vera Brynner; Pedro: Tommy Gleason. *Understudies:* Maria: Melva Niles; Solis: Betty Huff; Padre Josef: Roy Raymond. *Act I: Scene 1* The courtyard of Padre Josef's chapel, near the Magdalena River, Colombia: The Jungle Chapel: Women Weaving (Ensemble & Padre Josef), Petacal (Solis, Ramon, Dancers, Ensemble), "The Seed of God" (Padre Josef, Dancers, Ensemble) [End of Jungle Chapel sequence], "The Omen Bird (Teru Teru)" (Maria, Dancers, Ensemble), "My Bus and I"

(Pedro, Children, Passengers, Muzos), "The Emerald (Song)" (Maria & Pedro); *Scene 2* Private dining room in the Little Black Mouse Café in Paris; two weeks later: "The Civilized People" (Carabana, Danseuse, Zoggie, Habitués & Staff of Teresa's cafe), "Food for Thought" (Teresa & Habitués), Colombia Calls: "Come to Colombia" (Teresa, Carabana, Ensemble), "Plan it by the Planets" (Teresa, Zoggie, Ensemble), "Bon Soir, Paris" (Teresa), "Travel, Travel, Travel" (Teresa, Carabana, Blanco, Zoggie, Ensemble) [End of Colombia Calls sequence]; *Scene 3* Boatlanding at the Muzo village; ten days later: The River Port: "Magdalena" (The Old One), "The Broken Pianolita" (dance) (Matt Mattox, Norma Doggett, Dancers, Indian Youths) [End of River Port sequence], Festival of the River (Maria, Muzos, Pedro, Chivors): "Greeting" (Children), "River Song" (Maria & Muzos), "Pedro Wrecks the Festival" (Chivor Dance) (Dancers) [End of Festival of the River sequence], The Bus Departs: "My Bus and I" (reprise) (Children); *Scene 4* Padre Josef's jungle chapel; that evening: Guarding the Shrine of the Madonna: "The Forbidden Orchid" (Maria & Pedro), "The Theft" (dance) (the Chivors). *Act II*: *Scene 1* At the Singing Tree; a few hours later: "Ceremonial" (dance) (Marie Groscup, Norma Doggett, Danseuse, The Old One, Dancers, Ensemble), "The Singing Tree" (Ramon & Solis), "Lost" (Maria & Pedro), "Freedom!" (Pedro & Muzos); *Scene 2* The kitchen of General Carabana's hacienda; the next afternoon: In the Kitchen (comedy scene): "Teresa Cooks" (Teresa & Carabana); *Scene 3* The terrace of the General's hacienda; that evening: "Vals de Espana" ("A Spanish Waltz") (dance) (Orchestra) (Marie Groscup, Matt Mattox, Carabana's Guests), "The Emerald (Song)" (reprise) (Pedro), "Piece de Resistance" (Teresa, Carabana, Guests); *Scene 4* The floor of a nearby canyon; a few minutes later: "The Broken Bus" (Pedro); *Scene 5* The chapel courtyard; the next morning: The Empty Shrine: "The Emerald (Song)" (reprise) (Maria), Finale: "The Seed of God" (reprise) (Padre Josef, Maria, Pedro, Ramon, Solis, Muzos).

Broadway reviews were completely divided. The show cost $350,000.

After Broadway. Since its New York failure, it has come to be regarded, in some circles, as a classic. It was revived, for one night only, 11/23/87, Off Broadway, at ALICE TULLY HALL. ADAPTED BY Evans Haile & Dona D. Vaughn (Miss Vaughan was also the director, and Mr. Haile produced & conducted the Orchestra of New England). *Cast*: PADRE: Charles Damsel; MARIA: Faith Esham; PEDRO: Kevin Gray; BLANCO: Keith Curran; ZOGGIE: Charles Repole; CARABANA: George Rose; TERESA: Judy Kaye; TRIBAL ELDER: John Raitt; NARRATOR: Simon Jones.

416. *Maggie*

Set during the period 1899 to 1906. Maggie is a plain little Scots girl. She seems to knuckle down to her ambitious and overbearing husband, John. But it is Maggie who has created John — made him into a powerful political figure, step by step. She even writes her husband's parliamentary speeches for him. When he dallies on the primrose path he realizes he needs Maggie more than he does a new romance.

Before Broadway. Odette Myrtil (mother of dance music arranger Roger Adams) replaced Irene Bordoni.

The Broadway Run. NATIONAL THEATRE, 2/18/53–2/21/53. 5 PERFORMANCES. PRESENTED BY Franklin Gilbert & John Fearnley; MUSIC/LYRICS: William Roy; BOOK: Hugh Thomas; BASED ON the 1908 comedy *What Every Woman Knows*, by J.M. Barrie; DIRECTOR: Michael Gordon; CHOREOGRAPHER: June Graham; SETS/COSTUMES: Raoul Pene du Bois; LIGHTING: Peggy Clark; MUSICAL DIRECTOR/CHORAL ARRANGEMENTS: Maurice Levine; ORCHESTRATIONS: Don Walker; DANCE MUSIC ARRANGEMENTS: Dean Fuller; PRESS: Michel Mok & Sol Jacobson; COMPANY MANAGER: Joe Moss; STAGE MANAGERS: J. Myles Putnam, James Hammerstein, Bruce Laffey. *Cast*: ALICK WYLIE: Bramwell Fletcher; JAMES WYLIE: James Broderick; DAVID WYLIE: Frank Maxwell; MAGGIE WYLIE SHAND: Betty Paul (1); JOHN SHAND: Keith Andes (2); PROFESSOR DUBOIS: Henry Hamilton; MRS. MACLAUGHLIN: Jenny Lou Law; MADAME MARSTONNE: Odette Myrtil (3); SYBIL TENTERDON: Celia Lipton; WILLIAMS: Gene Hollmann; VENABLES: John Hoyt; JOHN (IN BAL-

LET): Marc Platt; MAGGIE (IN BALLET): Alicia Krug; SYBIL (IN BALLET): Kathryn Lee; PORTERS: Gene Hollmann, Henry Hamilton, Oran Osburn; CONDUCTOR: Paul Ukena; SINGERS: Robert Busch, John Ford, Henry Hamilton, Gene Hollmann, Marion Lauer, James E. McCracken, Oran Osburn, Jan Scott, Joanne Spiller, Paul Ukena, Gloria Van Dorpe; DANCERS: Adele Aron, J. Corky Geil, Sura Gesben, John George, Alan Howard, Jeanne Jones, Patti Karkalits, Nata Lee, David Nillo, Ruby Ann Saber, Bob St. Clair, Keith Willis. *Standby*: Maggie: Anita Ellis. *Understudies*: John: Robert Busch & Paul Ukena; Alick/Venables: Henry Hamilton; David: Paul Ukena; James: J. Corky Geil; Mme Marstonne/Sybil: Jenny Lou Law. *Act I*: *Scene 1* In the Wylie home in small town near Glasgow; winter, 1899; *Scene 2* Covering the years between 1899 and 1905; *Scene 3* In the lobby of the Bright Heather Hotel, Glasgow; winter, 1905; *Scene 4* Glasgow; the same night; *Scene 5* In the garden of Mme Marstonne's country home; a late afternoon in spring, 1906. *Act II*: *Scene 1* Paddington Station; *Scene 2* John Shand's study; the same day; *Scene 3* Paddington station; later that spring; *Scene 4* In the garden of Mme Marstonne's country home; summer 1906. *Act I*: "I Never Laughed in My Life" (John), "Long and Weary Wait" (John & Maggie), "Thimbleful" (Alick, David, James, John, Maggie), "He's the Man" (John, Singers, Dancers), "What Every Woman Knows" (Maggie), "Any Afternoon About Five" (Mme Marstonne), "Smile for Me" (staged by Paul Godkin) (Maggie), "You Become Me" (Maggie & John), "He's the Man" (reprise) (Company), "It's Only Thirty Years" (Mme Marstonne & Venables), "What Every Woman Knows" (reprise) (Maggie), "The New Me" (ballet) (Maggie, Alick, David, James, Singers, Dancers). *Act II*: "The Train with the Cushioned Seats" (staged by Paul Godkin) (David, Alick, James), "People in Love" (John & Sybil), "Practical" (Maggie), "Charm" (Maggie), "Fun in the Country" (Mme Marstonne), "What Every Woman Knows" (reprise) (Maggie), "Smile for Me" (reprise) (Maggie), "You Become Me" (reprise) (John).

Reviews were divided, mostly bad.

After Broadway. PAPER MILL PLAYHOUSE, New Jersey, 1962. DIRECTOR: Word Baker. *Cast*: Betsy Palmer, Stuart Damon.

417. *Maggie Flynn*

A weak copy of *The Sound of Music* ("The Thank You Song" was an obvious imitation of "Do Re Mi"). Set in various streets in Lower Manhattan in 1863, during the draft protests. Maggie, an Irishwoman, runs an orphanage for children of runaway slaves. She is about to marry a colonel, but is once again drawn to her ne'er-do-well husband, Phineas, who she believed was dead. Despite the fact that the existence of the Meagan Orphan Home, its fate, and all the other events in the show are historically accurate, the characters are essentially fictional.

Before Broadway. This musical was originally called *Beautiful Mrs. Flynn*.

The Broadway Run. ANTA THEATRE, 10/23/68–1/5/69. 6 previews. 81 PERFORMANCES. PRESENTED BY John Bowab, in association with Harris Associates, Inc. & Levin — Townsend Enterprises, Inc; MUSIC/LYRICS: Hugo & Luigi (i.e. Hugo Peretti & Luigi Creatore) and George David Weiss; BOOK: Hugo & Luigi and George David Weiss, in collaboration with Morton Da Costa; BASED ON an idea by John Flaxman, suggested by the 1863 New York Draft Riots; DIRECTOR: Morton Da Costa; CHOREOGRAPHER: Brian MacDonald; SETS: William & Jean Eckart; COSTUMES: W. Robert LaVine; LIGHTING: Tharon Musser; ASSISTANT LIGHTING: Ken Billington; MUSICAL DIRECTOR/VOCAL ARRANGEMENTS: John Lesko; ORCHESTRATIONS: Philip J. Lang; DANCE MUSIC ARRANGEMENTS: Trude Rittman; CAST RECORDING on RCA Victor; PRESS: Harvey B. Sabinson & Lee Solters; CASTING: Paul Phillips; GENERAL MANAGER: Joseph P. Harris; COMPANY MANAGER: Seth Schapiro; PRODUCTION STAGE MANAGER: Terence Little; STAGE MANAGER: Lee Murray; ASSISTANT STAGE MANAGERS: Nick Malekos & Derick Jones. *Cast*: MULLIGAN SERGEANT: David Vosburg; SPRAGUE SERGEANT: Larry Pool; GARIBALDI SERGEANT: James Senn; DONNELLY: Austin Colyer (10); O'MALLEY: George Tregre; 1ST SOLDIER: Roger Bigelow; CARTER: Charles Rule (12); O'BRIAN: Stanley Simmonds (11);

CLANCY: Mario Maroze; TIMMY: William James (5); WALTER: Douglas Grant; MAGGIE FLYNN: Shirley Jones (1) ☆; WILLIAM: Clarence Espinosa; ANDREW: Giancarlo Esposito; ERASMUS: Vincent Esposito; VIOLET: Sharon Brown; HYACINTH: Jewel Hoston; IRIS: Irene Cara; PANSY: Stephanie Mills; CHRYSANTHEMUM: Cheri Welles; MARY O'CLEARY: Jennifer Darling (6); BOB JEFFERSON: Bill Berrian (16); WILL JEFFERSON: Mitch Taylor (17); FIREMAN: Charles Rule (12); OFFICER O'REILLY: Nick Malekos (15); EFFRAM: Peter Norman (7); MOLLY: Hazel Steck (14); MICK: John Stanzel; BELLINI: Robert Mandan (9); ATLAS: Robert Roman (8); PHINEAS: Jack Cassidy (2) ☆; YOUNG GIRL: Kathleen Robey; GOLIATH: Roy Barry; LENA, THE GORILLA: Jim Senn; ACROBATS: George Bunt & Don Bonnell; COL. JOHN FARRADAY: Robert Kaye (3); MRS. VANDERHOFF: Sibyl Bowan (4); MRS. OPDYKE: Jeannette Seibert; 2ND LADY: June Eve Story; MRS. SAVAGE: Sandie Fields; MRS. VAN STOCK: Hazel Steck (14); DEAF LADY: Betty Hyatt Linton (13); CAPT. PIEDMONT: Charles Rule (12); LIEUTENANT: Larry Pool; GENERAL PARKINTON: Robert Mandan (9); SOLDIER ED WATERS: Dallas Johann; TESSIE: Hazel Steck (14); LADIES OF THE EVENING: Reby Howells & Sandie Fields. **Standbys**: Maggie: Marilyn Child; Phineas: Robert Roman. **Understudies**: Mary: Reby Howells; Timmy: Dallas Johann; The Jeffersons/Mulligan/Sprague: Nick Malekos; Jenny: June Eve Story; Mrs. Vanderhoff: Jeannette Seibert; Piedmont/O'Brian: Larry Pool; Bellini/Donnelly: Charles Rule; Mick: George Tregre; Effram: Derick Jones. **Act I**: **Prologue** Streets of New York City; 1863: "(They're) Never Gonna Make Me Fight" (Soldiers, Men from Barlow's, Timmy); **Scene 1** Dormitory & facade of Meagan Orphan Home: "(It's a) Nice Cold Morning" (Maggie & Children); **Scene 2** Barlow's Saloon: "(I Wouldn't Have You) Any Other Way" (Maggie & Saloon Boys); **Scene 3** Christopher Street: "Learn How to Laugh" (Phineas & Townspeople); **Scene 4** Dressing tent: "Maggie Flynn" (Phineas); **Scene 5** Parlor & facade of orphanage: "The Thank You Song" (Maggie, Mary, Children), "Look Around Your Little World" (Farraday & Phineas); **Scene 6** Kitchen of orphanage, and street: "Maggie Flynn" (reprise) (Phineas, Maggie, Children, Saloon Boys); **Scene 7** Kitchen of orphanage: "I Won't Let it Happen Again" (Maggie); **Scene 8** Solarium of Vanderhoff Mansion: "How About a Ball?" (Phineas, Maggie, Mrs. Vanderhoff, Ladies); **Scene 9** Union Army Headquarters and the kitchen: "Pitter Patter" (Phineas), "I Won't Let it Happen Again" (reprise) (Maggie). **Act II**: **Scene 1** Barlow's Saloon and a street: "Never Gonna Make Me Fight" (reprise) (Donnelly, O'Brian, Timmy, Men); **Scene 2** Veranda of the Vanderhoff mansion: "Why Can't I Walk Away?" (Phineas); **Scene 3** The basement of the orphanage: "The Game of War" (Children); **Scene 4** The parlor; **Scene 5** A jail: "Mr. Clown" (Phineas, Maggie, Children, Bums, Ladies of the Evening), "Pitter Patter" (reprise) (Maggie); **Scene 6** The jail office; **Scene 7** Various New York streets: The Riot (dance) (Full Company); **Scene 8** The kitchen and front of the orphanage: "Don't You Think it's Very Nice?" (Maggie, Phineas, Children), "Mr. Clown"/"Maggie Flynn" (reprise) (Maggie & Phineas).

Broadway reviews were divided. Jack Cassidy and Shirley Jones were married, and it was her only Broadway musical lead role for decades. Both stars missed several performances. Jack Cassidy was nominated for a Tony.

After Broadway. EQUITY LIBRARY THEATRE, NYC, 3/4/76–3/21/76. 22 PERFORMANCES. DIRECTOR: William Koch; SETS/LIGHTING: Richard B. Williams; MUSICAL DIRECTOR: Thomas Helm. **Cast**: MAGGIE: Bette Glenn; PHINEAS: Ross Petty; VARIOUS ROLES: Austin Colyer & Nita Novy. "Overture of Coming Attractions," "Cold Morning Montage," "Nice Cold Morning," "Hot Morning Montage," "Any Other Way," "Maggie Flynn," "Learn How to Laugh," "Look Around Your Little World," "Thank You Song," "I Won't Let it Happen Again," "Homeless Children," "How About a Ball?," "They're Never Gonna Make Me Fight," "Pitter Patter," "It Works!," "Why Can't I Walk Away?," "Game of War," "Let's Drink to That," "Mr. Clown150

418. *The Magic Show*

A magic show with music. The hero (Doug, or whoever replaced him) is an up-and-coming magician hired by a seedy night club, *The Passaic Top Hat*, in New Jersey, to replace its worn

out act. The new man (Doug) turns out to be an amazing performer whose illusions are part of this musical's spectacle. Feldman is the hammy and jealous older magician who Doug overshadows. There is no intermission.

The Broadway Run. CORT THEATRE, 5/28/74–12/31/78. 16 previews from 5/16/74. 1,859 PERFORMANCES. PRESENTED BY Edgar Lansbury, Joseph Beruh, and Ivan Reitman; MUSIC/LYRICS: Stephen Schwartz; BOOK: Bob Randall; DIRECTOR/CHOREOGRAPHER: Grover Dale; SETS: David Chapman; COSTUMES: Randy Barcelo; LIGHTING: Richard Nelson; SOUND: Phil Ramone; MUSICAL DIRECTOR: Stephen Reinhardt; DANCE MUSIC ARRANGEMENTS: David Spangler; CAST RECORDING on January Records (only released on 10/20/98); PRESS: Gifford/Wallace; CASTING: Otto & Windsor; MAGIC: Doug Henning; GENERAL MANAGER: Marvin A. Krauss; COMPANY MANAGER: Gary Gunas, *Bob Skerry* (added by 76–77); PRODUCTION STAGE MANAGER: Herb Vogler, *William Dodds* (by 74–75); STAGE MANAGER: John Actman; ASSISTANT STAGE MANAGER: Jay Fox, *Brennan Roberts* (added by 76–77). **Cast**: MANNY: Robert LuPone (7), *Clifford Lipson* (by 74–75); FELDMAN: David Ogden Stiers (4), *Kenneth Kimmins* (from 12/29/74), *Timothy Jerome* (from 7/25/75), *Steve Vinovich* (from 4/14/76), *Rex Robbins* (from 5/23/76), *Kenneth Kimmins* (from 10/27/76), *Tom Mardirosian* (by 77–78), *Nicholas Wyman*; DONNA: Annie McGreevey (6), *Lisa Raggio* (by 75–76), *Cindy Cobitt* (by 77–78); DINA: Cheryl Barnes (5), *Lynne Thigpen* (by 75–76), *Valerie Williams* (by 77–78); CAL: Dale Soules (3), *Dara Norman* (from 10/29/75), *Dale Soules* (by 76), *Gwendolyn Coleman* (by 76–77); DOUG: Doug Henning (1), *Jeffrey Mylett* (during Mr. Henning's vacation, and he played Jeff), *Joseph Abaldo* (during Mr. Henning's vacation, and he played Joe), *Joseph Abaldo* (from 3/30/76), *Doug Henning* (from 7/21/76), *Joseph Abaldo* (from 11/3/76); MIKE: Ronald Stafford (9), *Robert Brubach* (by 76–77); STEVE: Loyd Sannes (10), *T. Michael Reed* (by 74–75), *Christopher Lucas* (by 75–76), *Timothy Wahrer* (by 77–78); CHARMIN: Anita Morris (2), *Loni Ackerman* (from 8/75), *Louisa Flaningam* (from 3/76), *Natalie Mosco* (from 9/12/77), *Rita Rudner*; GOLDFARB: Sam Schacht (8), *Frederick Wessler* (by 77–78). **Understudies**: Doug: Justin Ross, *Jeffrey Mylett* (by 75–76), *Steven Peterman* (76–78); Cal/Donna: Baillie Gerstein, *Nancy Sheehy* (by 77–78); Charmin/Dina: Sharron Miller, *Rita Rudner* (by 77–78); Feldman/Goldfarb: Garnett Smith, *Nicholas Wyman* (by 76–77), *Kevin Marcum* (by 77–78); Mike/Steve: Justin Ross, *Robert Brubach* (by 75–76), *Richard Balestrino* (by 76–77), *Christopher Lucas* (by 77–78); Manny: Jay Fox, *Christopher Lucas* (by 75–76), *Jay Fox* (by 77–78), *Timothy Wahrer* (by 77–78). **Musicians**: KEYBOARDS: Stephen Reinhardt & Paul Shaffer; GUITARS: Brian McCormick & Jerry Wiener; BASS: Steve Manes; DRUMS: Joseph Saulter; PERCUSSION: Charles Birch Jr. "Up to His Old Tricks" (Entire Company), "Solid Silver Platform Shoes" (Dina & Donna), "Lion Tamer" (Cal), "Style" (Feldman & Company), "Charmin's Lament" (Charmin), "Two's Company" (Dina & Donna), "The Goldfarb Variations" (Dina, Feldman, Donna, Manny, Charmin), "Doug's Act" (or "Jeff's Act," etc) (Doug) [in some touring performances there is an intermission here], "A Bit of Villainy" (Feldman, Dina, Donna), "West End Avenue" (Cal), "Sweet, Sweet, Sweet" (Charmin, Manny, Mike, Steve), "Before Your Very Eyes" (Dina, Donna, Feldman).

Broadway reviews were divided, but most agreed it was really Doug Henning's show, and not a musical. It was his tricks that kept the audiences coming. The show received Tony nominations for direction of a musical, and for Doug Henning. It was the fifth-longest running Broadway musical of 1970s.

After Broadway. TOUR. Opened on 12/21/74, at the Wilbur Theatre, Boston. **Cast**: THE MAGICIAN: Peter de Paula; DINA: Signa Joy; MIKE: Richard Balestrino; CAL: Pippa Pearthree; CHARMIN: Hester Lewellen; FELDMAN: Paul Keith. **Standby**: For Mr. de Paula: Joseph Abaldo.

STUDIO ARENA THEATRE, Buffalo, NY, 2/20/76. 37 PERFORMANCES. DIRECTOR: Jay Fox. **Cast**: Joseph Abaldo, Connie Day, Anthony Inneo.

PAPER MILL PLAYHOUSE, New Jersey, 1979. DIRECTOR: Jay Fox. **Cast**: Joseph Abaldo.

Stephen Schwartz wrote the score for a new musical called *Magic to Do*, conceived by Frank Bantolucci & Ernie Zulia. CINCINNATI PLAYHOUSE, 6/29/79. 72 PERFORMANCES. **Cast**: Scott Bakula.

419. *Mail*

A fantasy musical. A writer, returning to his apartment after an absence, reads his piled-up mail, as the letter-writers materialize in song and dance.

Before Broadway. It began at the PASADENA PLAYHOUSE, Los Angeles. DIRECTOR: Andrew Cadiff; CHOREOGRAPHER: Grover Dale; SETS/LIGHTING: Gerry Hariton & Vicki Baral; COSTUMES: George T. Mitchell; SOUND: Jon Gottlieb; MUSICAL DIRECTOR: Henry Aronson. *Cast:* ALEX: Michael Rupert; DANA: Mara Getz; MAX: Robert Mandan; FRANKLIN: Brian Mitchell; SANDI: Jonelle Allen; FEATURED ENSEMBLE: Mary Bond Davis, Robert Loftin, Michele Pawk, Rick Stockwell, Bradd Wong, Kathrynann Wright. Pre-Broadway tryouts were at the Kennedy Center, Washington, DC, 2/13/88–3/19/88.

The Broadway Run. MUSIC BOX THEATRE, 4/14/88–5/14/88. 20 previews. 36 PERFORMANCES. PRESENTED BY Michael Frazier, Susan Dietz, Stephen Wells, The John F. Kennedy Center/ANTA; MUSIC: Michael Rupert; LYRICS/BOOK: Jerry Colker; DIRECTOR: Andrew Cadiff; CHOREOGRAPHER: Grover Dale; SETS: Gerry Hariton & Vicki Baral; COSTUMES: William Ivey Long; LIGHTING: Richard Nelson; SOUND: Tom Morse; MUSICAL SUPERVISOR: Paul Gemignani; MUSICAL DIRECTOR/VOCAL & DANCE MUSIC ARRANGEMENTS: Tom Fay; ORCHESTRATIONS: Michael Gibson; PRESS: The Joshua Ellis Office; CASTING: Eleanor Albano & Susan Chieco; GENERAL MANAGEMENT: Frank Scardino Associates; PRODUCTION STAGE MANAGER: Craig Jacobs; STAGE MANAGERS: Michael F. Wolf & C.C. Cary; ASSISTANT STAGE MANAGER: Larry Collis. *Cast:* ALEX: Michael Rupert (1) ☆; DANA: Mara Getz; RADIO ANNOUNCER: Rick Stockwell; RADIO SINGER: Mary Bond Davis; LIFE EXECS: Alan Muraoka, Robert Loftin, Rick Stockwell; FRANKLIN: Brian Mitchell; SANDI: Antonia Ellis; MAX: Robert Mandan; KATHY SUE BINGER: Michele Pawk; BILLY RAY BINGER: Rick Stockwell; ASSISTANTS: Alan Muraoka & Robert Loftin; POWER LADIES: Louise Hickey & Michele Pawk; MAMA UTILITY: Mary Bond Davis; CON ED MEN: Alan Muraoka, Rick Stockwell, Robert Loftin; DEMOCRATIC PARTY DELEGATE: Michele Pawk; BRUNHILDA: Mary Bond Davis; HUNTER: Rick Stockwell; GYPSY: Louise Hickey; BOY SCOUT: Robert Loftin; IRS AUDITOR: Alan Muraoka; OPERATOR: Mary Bond Davis; CANDI SUWINSKI: Michele Pawk; HARMONY STEINBERG: Louise Hickey; CRATERFACE CALLAHAN: Robert Loftin; TAKEUCHI FUJIMOTO: Alan Muraoka; MR. STANSBURY: Rick Stockwell; LOIS T. WERTSHAFTER: Mary Bond Davis; PITCHMAN: Rick Stockwell; PITCHPEOPLE: Mary Bond Davis, Robert Loftin, Alan Muraoka, Michele Pawk, Rick Stockwell, Louise Hickey. *Understudies*: Alex: Jerry Colker; Dana/Sandi: Michele Pawk; Max: Larry Collis; Franklin: Milton Craig Nealy. *Swings*: Stephen Jay & Rachelle Ottley. *Musicians*: PIANO: Henry Aronson; CELLI: Wendy Brennan & Evalyn Steinboch; WOODWINDS: Vinnie Della Rocca & Dale Kleps; DRUMS: Norbert Goldberg; VIOLIN/VIOLA: Jill Jaffe; GUITAR: Scott Kuney; BASS: Doug Romoff. *Prologue*: A Manhattan apartment; 6:00 a.m., one winter morning: Overture (Orchestra), "Monolithic Madness" (Alex). *Act I*: The same apartment; 11.15 p.m., four months later: "Gone So Long" (Radio Singer), "Hit the Ground Running" (Dana & Alex), "It's Your Life" (LIFE Execs), "Cookin' with Steam" (m: Brian Mitchell & Michael Rupert; l: Jerry Colker) (recorded track arranged & played by Brian Mitchell) (Franklin), "It's Just a Question of Technique" (Sandi & Alex), "It's None of My Business" (Max), "Crazy World" (Dana), "Ambivalent Rag" (Alex), "It's Your Life II" (LIFE Execs), "You Better Get Outta Town" (Kathy Sue, Billy Ray, Assistants), "We're Gonna Turn off Your Juice" (Power Ladies, Mama Utility, Con Ed Men), "The World Set on Fire by a Black and a Jew" (Franklin & Alex), "Where Are You/Where Am I?" (Dana), "Family Ties" (Max), "One Lost Weekend" (Sandi, Alex, Dana), "Junk Mail"/"Disconnected" (Ensemble), "Helplessness at Midnight" (Radio Singer), "What Have You Been Doing for the Past Ten Years?" (Alex & Ensemble), "A Blank Piece of Paper" (Alex). *Act II*: same setting as Act I: "Sweepstakes" (Alex, Pitchman, Pitchpeople), "It's Getting Harder to Love You" (Dana & Pitchwomen), "Publish Your Book" (Sandi, Alex, Pitchpeople), "Ambivalent Rag II" (Alex), "Pages of My Diary" (Dana, Alex, Pitchwomen), "One Step at a Time"/"Ambivalent Rag III" (Alex & Pitchpeople), "Don't Count on It" (Sandi & Alex), "Friends for Life" (Franklin & Alex), "29 Years Ago" (Max & Alex), "Crazy World" (reprise) (Alex), "Sweepstakes" (reprise) (Pitchpeople), "A Blank Piece of Paper" (reprise) (Alex), Finale: "Crazy World" (reprise) (Alex & Dana).

Reviews were mostly terrible.

420. *Make a Wish*

Janette, a young war orphan in Paris, while touring the Louvre, escapes her fellow orphans, and plunges into the ritzy life of the Left Bank. She is tempted by meat packer Frigo, one of the richest men in town, but succumbs to penniless law student Paul. The opening scene was revealed through a gigantic Venetian blind. The highlight was the brilliant "Sale" ballet. Ricky and Poupette are a dance team at the Folies Labiche.

Before Broadway. *The Good Fairy* had been a play starring Helen Hayes, and a movie with Margaret Sullavan. As far as Broadway book musicals go, this was a first for producer Alex Cohen and for choreographer Gower Champion. It tried out for three weeks at the Shubert Theatre, Philadelphia, from 3/12/51. Preston Sturges wrote the first libretto, but quit during the tryout (but he got to retain credit, partly because of his big name), Anita Loos was called in (but that didn't work), and finally Abe Burrows was called in as play doctor, the first of many times in his career that he filled this role. Mr. Burrows wrote an almost entirely new book, and even took over the direction when John C. Wilson became ill late in the tryout. In the cast Le Roi Operti replaced 6th-billed Franklin Pangborn, and dropped a billing, and Phil Leeds was brought in as 6th billed. Marie Bryant was in it in Philadelphia, as were the Sylvia Manon Trio (Sylvia Manon, Ray Borden, Victor Voley), who were in the "Sale" ballet. But they did not make it to Broadway. Melville Cooper was in a non-singing lead role (unusual for a Broadway musical, but by no means unheard-of).

The Broadway Run. WINTER GARDEN THEATRE, 4/18/51–7/14/51. 102 PERFORMANCES. PRESENTED BY Harry Rigby & Jule Styne, in association with Alexander H. Cohen; MUSIC/LYRICS/VOCAL ARRANGEMENTS: Hugh Martin; BOOK: Preston Sturges; BASED ON the 1931 comedy *The Good Fairy*, by Ferenc Molnar; DIRECTOR: John C. Wilson; CHOREOGRAPHER: Gower Champion; SETS/COSTUMES: Raoul Pene du Bois; MUSICAL DIRECTOR: Milton Rosenstock; ORCHESTRATIONS: Phil Lang & Allan Small; VOCAL DIRECTOR: Buster Davis; DANCE MUSIC ARRANGEMENTS: Richard Pribor; PRESS: Willard Keefe & David Tebet; COMPANY MANAGER: Paul Groll; PRODUCTION STAGE MANAGER: Archie Thomson; STAGE MANAGERS: Neil Hartley, Larry Baker, John Barry Ryan Jr. *Cast:* DR. DIDIER: Eda Heinemann; DR. FRANCEL: Phil Leeds (6); JANETTE: Nanette Fabray (1) ☆; RICKY: Harold Lang (3); POUPETTE: Helen Gallagher (5); POLICEMAN: Howard Wendell; MARIUS FRIGO: Melville Cooper (2); PAUL DUMONT: Stephen Douglass (4); THE MADAM: Mary Finney; FELIX LABICHE: Le Roi Operti (7); OLD GENTLEMAN: George Spelvin; SALES MANAGER: Howard Wendell; SINGERS: Dean Campbell, Robert Davis, Edward Gombos, Mary Harmon, Carol Hendricks, David Huenergardt, Anne Humphrey, Janie Janvier, Douglas Luther, Beverly McFadden, Don McKay, Ellen Martin, Michael Mason, Claire Mitchell, Peggy O'Hara, Rica Owen, Robert Shaver, David Vogel; DANCERS: Gene Bayliss, Aleen Buchanan, Dick Crowley, Ray Dorian, Lynn Joelson, Margaret Jeanne, Lida Kochring, John Laverty, Carol Lee, Ernie Preston, Jack Purcell, Charlotte Ray, Richard Reed, Sue Scott, Thelma Tadlock, Norma Thornton, Kenneth Urmston, Ken Whelan.

Note: George Spelvin is not a real name. It is a nom de guerre, used by an actor playing more than one role. So we don't know who played the Old Gentleman here. *Act I: Scene 1* A museum: "The Tour Must Go On" (Dean Campbell, Girls & Boys), "I Wanna Be Good 'n' Bad" (Janette & Girls); *Scene 2* A street: "The Time Step" (Janette, Poupette, Ricky); *Scene 3* Café Victor: "(You're Just) What I Was Warned About" (Janette), "Who Gives a Sou?" (Janette, Paul, Poupette, Ricky); *Scene 4* A street; *Scene 5* A dressing-room; *Scene 6* Folies Labiche curtain: "Folies Labiche Overture" ("Hello, Hello, Hello" (Folies Chorus); *Scene 7* Folies Labiche: "Tonight You Are in Paree" (Janette, Girls & Boys); *Scene 8* Outside of Folies Labiche: "When Does This Feeling Go Away?"

(Paul); *Scene 9* A street: "Suits Me Fine" (Poupette & Ricky); *Scene 10* "The Students Ball" (ballet) (Girls & Boys), "(Meet the Lady Known as) Paris, France" (Entire Company). *Act II*: *Scene 1* A courtyard: "That Face!" (Poupette, Ricky, Girls & Boys); *Scene 2* Hallway of Paul's apartment; *Scene 3* Paul's apartment: "Make a Wish" (Janette); *Scene 4* A street: "I'll Never Make a Frenchman Out of You" (Poupette & Ricky); *Scene 5* Galerie Napoleon department store: "Over and Over" (Janette & Boys), "The Sale" (ballet) (Aleen Buchanan, Ray Dorian, Howard Wendell, Girls & Boys); *Scene 6* A street: "Over and Over" (reprise) (Poupette & Ricky), "Who Gives a Sou?" (reprise) (Janette & Paul); *Scene 7* Mr. Frigo's apartment; *Scene 8* A street: "Take Me Back to Texas with You" (Janette, Poupette, Ricky); *Scene 9* A courtyard: "Suits Me Fine" (reprise) (Girls & Boys), Finale: "Make a Wish" (reprise) (Janette & Entire Company).

Broadway reviews were mixed, with the ballets coming in for raves. It was the first time Nanette Fabray had sole star billing on Broadway. Jule Styne took Helen Gallagher out of this show and put her into *Pal Joey*. Harold Lang won a Donaldson for best male dancer. The show cost $340,000.

421. *Make Mine Manhattan*

A revue. A light-hearted look at Manhattan.

Before Broadway. When Sid Caesar first took the part (at $250 a week), he was booked to do only two of the numbers. He wound up doing 12 (and getting $1,500 a week plus 5 per cent of weekly gross).

The Broadway Run. BROADHURST THEATRE, 1/15/48–1/8/49. 429 PERFORMANCES. PRESENTED BY Joseph M. Hyman; MUSIC: Richard Lewine; LYRICS/SKETCHES: Arnold B. Horwitt (with valued "suggestions" from Moss Hart); ADDITIONAL MATERIAL: Max Liebman, Allan Roberts, Sid Caesar, Peter Barry, David Gregory, Sylvia Rosales; DIRECTOR/LIGHTING: Hassard Short; SKETCH DIRECTOR: Max Liebman; CHOREOGRAPHER: Lee Sherman; SETS: Frederick Fox; COSTUMES: Morton Haack; MUSICAL DIRECTOR: Charles Sanford; ORCHESTRATIONS: Ted Royal; VOCAL SUPERVISOR: Lois Moseley; MUSICAL CONTINUITY FOR DANCES: Mel Pahl; PRESS: Michel Mok; CASTING: Jane Deacy & Maurice La Pue; GENERAL MANAGER: Al Goldin; GENERAL STAGE MANAGER: Don Hershey; STAGE MANAGERS: Sterling Mace & Francis Spencer. *Act I*: *Song*: "Anything Can Happen in New York." Danced by Nelle Fisher (*Ina Kurland*), Hal Loman, and Willis Brunner, Tony Charmoli, Anne Feris, Louise Ferrand, Annabelle Gold, Rhoda Johannson, Wayne Lamb, Betty Lind, Phyllis Mayo, Tommy Morton, Dolores Novins, Skip Randall, Rudy Tone. Sung by Max Showalter, Eleanor Bagley, and Stephanie Augustine, Larry Carr (*Eric Brotherson*), Joy Carroll, Ed Chappel, Jean Jones, Biff McGuire; *Sketch*: "First Avenue Gets Ready." Restaurateur Kelly tries to cater to the whims of U.N. delegates. KELLY: David Burns (2) (*Julie Oshins*) (understudy: Perry Bruskin); MAMIE: Sheila Bond (3); A DELEGATE: Sid Caesar (1); HIS AIDE: Perry Bruskin; ANOTHER DELEGATE: Sid Caesar (1); STILL ANOTHER DELEGATE: Sid Caesar (1); UKRAINIAN: Richard Arnold; SLOVANIAN: Ed Chappel; ROUMANIAN: Joseph Melvin; Scene: Kelly's First Avenue Diner (by Arnold B. Horwitt & Max Liebman); *Ballet*: "Phil the Fiddler:" Sung by Jack Kilty. PHIL: Ray Harrison; PASSERS-BY: Biff McGuire, Dolores Novins, Betty Lind, Anne Feris, Annabelle Gold; BALLROOM DANCERS: Stephanie Augustine, Rhoda Johannson, Phyllis Mayo, Willis Brunner, Skip Randall, Rudy Tone; THE HEROINE: Nelle Fisher (*Ina Kurland*); THE VILLAIN: Tommy Morton; THE HORSES: Tony Charmoli & Hal Loman; THE BILLIONAIRE: Joshua Shelley (5) (understudy: Perry Bruskin); THE LACKEYS: Larry Carr (*Eric Brotherson*), Biff McGuire, Max Showalter; *Song*: "Movie House in Manhattan" (with Eleanor Bagley); *Sketch*: "Any Resemblance …" (Bassett, the *Daily Gazette* editor, seeking a drama critic, brings Jukes in to the office to be interviewed by Blodgett, the publisher, who asks the new man what his qualifications are. Jukes is deaf, blind, and hates the theatre. So, he gets the job. Parody of George Jean Nathan). BLODGETT: Sid Caesar (1); BASSETT: David Burns (2) (*Julie Oshins*) (understudy: Perry Bruskin); JUKES: Joshua Shelley (5) (understudy: Perry Bruskin); *Song*: "Talk to Me." Dance accompaniment by Sheila Bond (3) & Danny Daniels (4) (understudies: Annabelle Gold & Rudy Tone); *Sketch*: "Traftz." Spoof of the menu at

Schrafft's. Joshua Shelley (5); *Song*: "I Don't Know His Name:" THE BOY: Jack Kilty; THE GIRL: Kyle MacDonnell. Scene: Roof-tops in Manhattan; *Song & dance act*: "The Good Old Days" (l: Arnold Horwitt & Ted Fetter). Sid Caesar (1) & David Burns (2) (*Julie Oshins*). THE GIRLS: Sheila Bond (3) & Eleanor Bagley; *Sketch*: "Once Over Lightly." Parody of the hit musical *Allegro*, with the idealistic doctor now a dentist. IN FRONT OF THE THEATRE: David Burns (2) (*Julie Oshins*), Eleanor Bagley, and the dancers; MOTHER: Phyllis Mayo; FATHER: Perry Bruskin; MOTHER-IN-LAW: Jean Jones; GREAT AUNT: Rhoda Johannson; SECOND COUSIN: Eleanor Bagley; HERMAN W. WILLOUGHBY JR.: Sid Caesar (1); BESSIE BRICKER: Sheila Bond (3); NURSE: Nelle Fisher (*Ina Kurland*); PATIENT: Max Showalter; THE CHOIR: Joshua Shelley (5), Jack Kilty, Kyle MacDonnell, Stephanie Augustine, Joy Carroll, Barbara Weaver, Biff McGuire, Ed Chappel, Larry Carr (*Eric Brotherson*); THE DANCERS: Anne Feris, Annabelle Gold, Betty Lind, Dolores Novins, Tony Charmoli, Tommy Morton, Skip Randall, Rudy Tone; *Sketch*: "Penny Gum Machine" (by Allan Roberts, Sid Caesar, Max Liebman). Sid Caesar doing a penny gum machine imitation; *Song*: "Saturday Night in Central Park." Sung by Kyle MacDonnell, Jack Kilty, Eleanor Bagley, Max Showalter, and the singers. Dance variations: Annabelle Gold, Tony Charmoli, Rudy Tone, Hal Loman. Also with Phyllis Mayo, Dolores Novins, Willis Brunner, Sheila Bond (3), Nelle Fisher (*Ina Kurland*), Danny Daniels (4), Ray Harrison. The hit song. INTERMISSION. *Act II*: *Sketch & song*: "Ringalevio." The ensemble dress as street kids: Sung by Joshua Shelley (5) (understudy: Biff McGuire). FIRST RINGLEADER: Tommy Morton; SECOND RINGLEADER: Rudy Tone; SISSY: Danny Daniels (4); and the dancers; *Sketch & song*: "Noises in the Street" (l: Peter Barry, David Gregory, Arnold B. Horwitt). About early morning New York noises: TAXI DRIVER: David Burns (2) (*Julie Oshins*); MILKMAN: Max Showalter; STREET CLEANER: Sid Caesar (1); STREET DIGGER: Perry Bruskin; NEWSBOY: Joshua Shelley (5); Understudy for all roles: Biff McGuire; *Song*: "I Fell in Love with You." Sung by Kyle MacDonnell & Jack Kilty. Danced by Nelle Fisher (*Ina Kurland*) & Ray Harrison. Scene: overlooking the East River; *Dance*: "My Brudder and Me." Dance — Sheila Bond (3) & Danny Daniels (4) [replaced "Take it Back, We're Through" during tryouts]; *Sketch*: "Hollywood Heads East" (15 minute sketch about what life would be like if movies were made in New York instead of Hollywood. Bigelow the director, a former garment manufacturer gets into conversation about the rag trade with Rappaport, the garment manufacturer hired to provide atmosphere on the set). MAYOR O'DWYER: Max Showalter; EDDIE: Joshua Shelley (5); BRUCE BIGELOW: Sid Caesar (1); THE ACTRESS: Kyle MacDonnell; THE ACTOR: Jack Kilty; PHOTOGRAPHER: Biff McGuire; ASSISTANT PHOTOGRAPHER: Perry Bruskin; MAKE-UP GIRL: Stephanie Augustine; MR. RAPPAPORT: David Burns (2) (*Julie Oshins*) (understudy: Perry Bruskin). Scene: a street in Manhattan (by Arnold B. Horwitt & Max Liebman); *Song and dance number*: "Gentleman Friend." Sheila Bond (3), Hal Loman, and the dancers (understudies: Annabelle Gold & Rudy Tone); *Song*: "Subway Song" (boy from 242nd Street, Bronx, whose girlfriend lives at the other end of the line, New Lot's Avenue, Brooklyn): THE BOY: Joshua Shelley (5); THE GIRL: Rhoda Johannson; *Sketch*: "Full Fathom Five" (customer resists sales pitch for a water-resistant "atomic pen," is undressed and thrown into a tank of water): THE SALESMAN: Max Showalter (understudy: Perry Bruskin); THE CUSTOMER: David Burns (2) (*Julie Oshins*); THE MODEL: Jean Jones (understudy: Stephanie Augustine); THE CLERKS: Larry Carr (*Eric Brotherson*), Ed Chappel, Sterling Mace, Biff McGuire. Scene: a pen shop in Manhattan (by Arnold B. Horwitt & Sylvia Rosales); *Sketch and song*: "A Night Out" (by Max Liebman). Sid Caesar (1). Prices have skyrocketed between 1938 and 1948; *Finale*: "Glad to Be Back." Scene: Grand Central Station. The Entire Company.

DANCERS: Willis Brunner, Tony Charmoli, Anne Feris, Annabelle Gold, Rhoda Johannson, Betty Lind, Hal Loman, Phyllis Mayo, Tommy Morton, Marta Nita, Dolores Novins, Skip Randall, Rudy Tone; SINGERS: Stephanie Augustine, Larry Carr (*Eric Brotherson*), Joy Carroll, Ed Chappel, Jean Jones, Biff McGuire, Barbara Weaver. **Understudies:** Betty Lind (for Nelle Fisher), Tony Charmoli (for Ray Harrison).

The show opened to mostly raves. Sid Caesar won a Donaldson Award for male debut.

After Broadway. TOUR. 1948. MUSICAL DIRECTOR: Jerry Arlen. The tour failed. *Cast*: Bert Lahr (in the Sid Caesar role), Jack Albertson,

Jean Jones, Lou Wills Jr., Fosse & Niles (Bob Fosse & his then wife, Mary Ann Niles), Earl William. There was some new material. In Act I: **Sketch**: Doctors Don't Tell (by Matt Brooks), set in a doctor's office in mid–town Manhattan. NURSE: Jean Jones; MR. SMITH: Jack Albertson; DOCTOR: Bert Lahr; **Song**: "Schrafft's" (sung by Bert Lahr); and in Act II: **Sketch**: Income Tax (by David Freedman). HIGGINS: Jack Albertson; GRUNCHER: Bob Gallagher; CLARKSON: Bert Lahr; **Song**: "Song of the Woodman" [from *The Show is On*] (m/l: Harold Arlen & E.Y. Harburg) (sung by Bert Lahr).

422. *Mame*

Set in Mame's apartment at 3 Beekman Place, Manhattan, and at various locales in which she becomes involved from 1928 to 1946. On Dec. 1, 1928 faithful nanny Gooch arrives from Des Moines to deposit her charge, recently orphaned ten-year-old Patrick, to his only living relative, Mame. They are greeted by Ito, Mame's houseboy, and a party is going on in the penthouse apartment, with Mame playing bugle. Patrick likes her immediately. The Knickerbocker Bank, represented by Babcock, is the trustee which stipulates that Mame's late brother's boy should be raised in a conservative way. But Mame has plans for Patrick's education which are anything but conservative. However, Babcock takes the boy to his own alma mater, St. Boniface, in Massachusetts. The stock market crashes, and Mame is broke. She accepts the role of the Moon Lady in a musical starring her friend Vera, and tries several other jobs, including manicurist, where she accidentally stabs wealthy Southern client Beau. Beau wants to marry her, but needs the approval of his mother at Peckerwood, the family plantation. Mame goes to Peckerwood with Patrick. Sally has been engaged to Beau since childhood. However, Mame and Beau get married. Patrick grows up, Beau slips off an alp and dies, and Mame is now wealthy again, and back at Beekman Place. She will now write her memoirs, and Gooch is sent off to Speedo to improve her shorthand to 200 words a minute. Woolsey is the publisher. Mame and Vera reminisce about old times and they decide Gooch must get out and have some fun. They re-do her and she goes out and swings, and gets pregnant. Patrick now has a girlfriend, Gloria, a bit of a square. Mame meets Gloria's parents, Mr. and Mrs. Upson, of Mountebank. There is a party at Mame's apartment, recently decorated by Pegeen, with whom Patrick falls in love. Mame announces that she has bought the plot next to Mountebank as the Beauregard Burnside Memorial Home for Single Mothers, which scandalizes the Upsons. Patrick and Pegeen have a son, Peter, and Mame leaves on a round-the-world trip, first to India.

Before Broadway. This famous musical was originally called *My Best Girl*. It was turned down by Mary Martin and Ethel Merman. After some 40 other actresses were turned down, Angela Lansbury got the part, and it made her a star. Joshua Logan (who also worked on the book originally) was the first director, but he was let go with a 1.5 per cent interest in the show (so he did well), and was replaced by Gene Saks (and his wife Bea Arthur came along as star). The show tried out in Philadelphia; then to Boston. In both places word spread that this would be a hit. Tommy Karaty replaced Randy Kirby just before Broadway.

The Broadway Run. WINTER GARDEN THEATRE, 5/24/66–10/4/69; BROADWAY THEATRE, 10/6/69–1/3/70. 5 previews from 5/18/66. Total of 1,508 PERFORMANCES. PRESENTED BY Fryer, Carr & Harris (Robert Fryer, Lawrence Carr, Sylvia Harris, Joseph Harris); MUSIC/LYRICS: Jerry Herman; BOOK: Jerome Lawrence & Robert E. Lee; BASED ON the 1955 memoir *Auntie Mame*, by Patrick Dennis, and on the 1956 comedy of the same name based on it by Jerome Lawrence & Robert E. Lee, which ran at the Broadhurst Theatre from 10/31/56 (639 performances), starring Rosalind Russell; DIRECTOR: Gene Saks; CHOREOG-

RAPHER: Onna White; ASSISTANT CHOREOGRAPHER: Tom Panko; SETS: William & Jean Eckart; COSTUMES: Robert Mackintosh; LIGHTING: Tharon Musser; AUDIO DESIGNER: Robert Lifrin; MUSICAL DIRECTOR/VOCAL ARRANGEMENTS: Donald Pippin; PRODUCTION MUSICAL DIRECTOR: Shepard Coleman; ORCHESTRATIONS: Philip J. Lang; DANCE MUSIC ARRANGEMENTS: Roger Adams; CAST RECORDING on Columbia; PRESS: David Lipsky, Lisa Lipsky, *Marian Graham* (added by 66–67); GENERAL MANAGER: Joseph P. Harris; COMPANY MANAGER: Richard Grayson; PRODUCTION STAGE MANAGER: Terence Little; STAGE MANAGER: Ralph Linn; ASSISTANT STAGE MANAGER: Delmar Hendricks, *Stan Page & Nancy Lynch* (by 9/66), *Paul Phillips & Edward Becker* (by 68–69). **Cast:** PATRICK DENNIS (AGE 10): Frankie Michaels (5), *Stuart Getz* (from 5/8/67), *David Manning* (from 4/1/68), *Chris Hagan* (from 68–69); AGNES GOOCH: Jane Connell (3), *Helen Gallagher* (from 4/29/68), *Laurie Franks, Marilyn Cooper* (from 12/15/69); VERA CHARLES: Beatrice Arthur (2), *Sheila Smith* (during Miss Arthur's vacation, 3/27/67–4/10/67), *Anne Francine* (from 7/10/67), *Audrey Christie* (from 4/1/68), *Anne Francine* (from 9/23/68), *Sheila Smith* (during Miss Francine's vacation, 68–69), *Helen Gallagher*; MAME DENNIS: Angela Lansbury (1) ☆, *Sheila Smith* (during Miss Lansbury's vacation, 2/13/67–2/27/67), *Celeste Holm* (during Miss Lansbury's vacation, 8/15/67–8/29/67), *Janis Paige* (from 4/1/68), *Jane Morgan* (from 12/2/68), *Ann Miller* (from 5/26/69); RALPH DEVINE: Ron Young, *Henry Brunjes* (from 67–68); BISHOP: Jack Davison, *Casper Roos* (from 67–68); M. LINDSAY WOOLSEY: George Coe (9), *Ray McDonnell* (from 67); ITO: Sab Shimono (11), *Tom Matsusaka* (from 67–68), *Sab Shimono* (from 68–69); DOORMAN: Art Matthews; ELEVATOR BOY: Stan Page, *Ross Miles* (from 68–69); MESSENGER: Bill Stanton, *Gene Kelton* (from 67), *Edward Becker* (from 68–69), *Jim Connor*; DWIGHT BABCOCK: Willard Waterman (4), *Ed Herlihy* (from 67–68), *Willard Waterman* (from 68–69); ART MODEL: Jo Tract; DANCE TEACHER: Johanna Douglas; LEADING MAN: Jack Davison, *Casper Roos* (from 67–68); STAGE MANAGER: Art Matthews; MME. BRANISLOWSKI: Charlotte Jones, *Ruth Jaroslow* (from 67–68), *Tally Brown* (from 68–69), *Honey Sanders*; GREGOR: John Taliaferro, *Edward Becker* (by 68–69), *Jim Connor, Luigi Gasparinetti* (from 68–69); BEAUREGARD JACKSON PICKETT BURNSIDE: Charles Braswell (6), *Randy Phillips* (from 67–68), *Robert R. Kaye* (from 68–69), *John Taliaferro*; UNCLE JEFF: Clifford Fearl, Stan Page (from 68–69), *Casper Roos* (from 68–69); COUSIN FAN: Ruth Ramsey, *Laurie Franks* (from 67–68), *Mary Roche*; SALLY CATO: Margaret Hall (8), *Sheila Smith* (from 67–68), *Margaret Hall* (from 68–69); MOTHER BURNSIDE: Charlotte Jones (10), *Ruth Jaroslaw* (from 67–68), *Tally Brown* (from 68–69), *Honey Sanders*; PATRICK DENNIS (AGED 19–29): Jerry Lanning (7), *Joseph Gallison* (from 67–68), *David Chaney* (from 67–68); JUNIOR BABCOCK: Tommy Karaty (17), *David Chaney* (from 67–68), *Roger Allan Raby* (from 67–68), *Jerry Wyatt* (from 68–69), *Ross Miles*; MRS. UPSON: Johanna Douglas (13); MR. CLAUDE UPSON: John C. Becher (12), *Tom Batten, Clifford Fearl*; GLORIA UPSON: Diana Walker (14), *Laurie Franks* (from 67), *Susan Walther* (from 67–68); PEGEEN RYAN: Diane Coupe (15); PETER DENNIS: Michael Maitland (16), *Danny Snow* (from 67–68), *Shawn McGill* (from 68–69), *Joey Raymond* (from 68–69), *Paris Themmen*; MAME'S FRIENDS: Diana Baffa (gone by 67–68), Jack Blackton (gone by 67–68), David Chaney (gone by 67–68), Pat Cummings (gone by 68–69), Jack Davison (*Casper Roos* from 67–68), Hilda Harris (gone by 67–68), Tommy Karaty (gone by 9/66), Nicole Karol (gone by 67–68), Gene Kelton (gone by 68–69), Nancy Lynch (gone by 67–68), Art Matthews, Ross Miles (gone by 67–68, but back by 68–69), Stan Page (*Jim Connor* by 68–69), Ruth Ramsey (gone by 67–68), Betty Rosebrock (gone by 68–69), Scott Salmon (gone by 66–67), Bella Shalom, Bill Stanton (gone by 66–67), John Taliaferro (gone by 68–69), Jo Tract, Jodi Williams, Kathy Wilson (gone by 68–69). 66–67 replacements: *Henry Brunjes, Tod Miller* (gone by 67–68), *Roy Smith* (gone by 67–68), *Mary Zahn* (gone by 67–68). 67–68 replacements: *Sean Allen* (gone by 68–69), *Diane Blair, Robert Fitch* (gone by 68–69), *Luigi Gasparinetti, Jerri Harris* (gone by 68–69), *Merrill Leighton* (*Mary Roche* by 68–69), *Roger Allan Raby* (gone by 68–69), *Carol Richards* (gone by 68–69), *Eleanore Treiher, Susan Walther, Jerry Wyatt* (*Roland Ireland* by 68–69). 68–69 replacements: *Ronald Bostick, Eileen Casey, Danny Joel, Eric Paynter, Michael Misita, Roger Rathburn, Kathleen Robey, Deirdre Ryan*. Later replacements: *Marilyn Wilber, Ron Young*. **Standby**: Mame: Charlotte Fairchild,

Sheila Smith (by 66–67). **Understudies:** Gooch: Jodi Williams, *Laurie Franks* (by 67–68), *Mary Roche, Ruth Ramsey;* Fan: Jodi Williams, *Merrill Leighton* (by 67–68), *Mary Roche* (by 68–69), *Susan Walther, Marilyn Wilber;* Mrs. Upson: Jodi Williams, *Laurie Franks* (by 68–69), *Mary Roche, Ruth Ramsey;* Babcock: Clifford Fearl, *Casper Roos* (by 68–69); Upson: Clifford Fearl, *Roland Ireland* (by 68–69); Beau: Art Matthews; Older Patrick: Jack Blackton, *Sean Allen* (by 67–68), *John Stewart* (by 68–69), *David Chaney;* Young Patrick: Michael Maitland, *Danny Snow* (by 67–68), *Joey Raymond* (by 68–69), *Paris Themmen;* Sally/Mme. Branislowski: Jo Tract; Lindsay: Jack Davison, *Casper Roos* (by 67–68); Ito: Hilda Harris, *Eleanore Treiber* (by 67–68); Pegeen: Betty Rosebrock, *Carol Richards* (by 68–69), *Eleanore Treiber;* Gloria: Laurie Franks, *Betty Rosebrock* (by 67–68), *Carol Richards* (by 68–69), *Eleanore Treiber;* Gregor: David Chaney, *Casper Roos* (by 68–69), *Luigi Gasparinetti* (by 68–69); Uncle Jeff: Stan Page, *Jim Connor;* Stage Manager: *Stan Page* (by 67–68), *Jerry Wyatt* (by 68–69), *Roland Ireland;* Junior: *David Chaney* (by 66–67), *Pat Cummings* (by 67–68), *Jerry Wyatt* (by 68–69), *Ron Bostick.* **Act I:** Overture (Orchestra); *Scene 1* Somewhere in New York; 1928: "St. Bridget" (Gooch & Young Patrick); *Scene 2* Mame's Apartment: "It's Today" (Mame & All) [the melody of this song came from Jerry Herman's "Show Tune," which had been a number in his 1960 Off Broadway show *Parade*]; *Scene 3* Hallway of Mame's Apartment; *Scene 4* Mame's Bedroom; *Scene 5* Mame's Living Room (and all around New York): "Open a New Window" (Mame & All); *Scene 6* Mame's Apartment; *Scene 7* Shubert Theatre, New Haven: "The Man in the Moon" (Vera, Mame, Moon Maidens), "My Best Girl" (Young Patrick & Mame); *Scene 8* Salon pour Messieurs; *Scene 9* Mame's Apartment: "We Need a Little Christmas" (Mame, Young Patrick, Gooch, Beau, Ito); *Scene 10* Peckerwood: "The Fox Hunt" (Uncle Jeff, Young Patrick, Fan, Mother Burnside, Cousins) [not on the album], "Mame" (Beau & All). **Act II:** *Scene 1* Prep School & College (and Singapore): "Mame" (reprise) ("The Letter") (Young Patrick & Older Patrick), "My Best Girl" (reprise) (Older Patrick); *Scene 2* Mame's Apartment: "Bosom Buddies" (Mame & Vera); *Scene 3* Mame's Apartment; six months later: "Gooch's Song" (Gooch); *Scene 4* Upson Farm: "That's How Young I Feel" (Mame & All), "If He Walked into My Life" (Mame); *Scene 5* Mame's Apartment: "It's Today" (reprise) (Mame & All), "My Best Girl" (reprise) (Older Patrick); *Scene 6* Mame's Apartment; 1946: "Open a New Window" (reprise) (Mame), Finale (Mame & All).

Broadway reviews were divided. The show won Tony Awards for Angela Lansbury, Frankie Michaels and Bea Arthur, and was nominated for musical, composer & lyricist, direction of a musical, choreography, and sets. It became the fifth-longest running Broadway musical of the 1960s. It was forced out of the Winter Garden by the incoming *Jimmy.*

After Broadway. THE CELESTE HOLM TOUR. Opened on 9/28/67, at the Mechanic Theatre, Baltimore. CHOREOGRAPHER: Pat Cummings; MUSICAL DIRECTOR: Myron Roman. **Cast:** YOUNG PATRICK: Shawn McGill; GOOCH: Loretta Swit; VERA: Vicki Cummings; MAME: Celeste Holm; ITO: Arsenio Trinidad; BABCOCK: Wes Addy; DANCE TEACHER/MRS. UPSON: Louise Kirtland; MME BRANISLOWSKI/MOTHER BURNSIDE: Ruth Gillette; BEAU: Robert Kaye; OLDER PATRICK: John Stewart; MR. UPSON: David Huddleston.

THE ANGELA LANSBURY TOUR. Opened on 5/30/68, at the Curran Theatre, San Francisco. PRESENTED BY Fryer, Carr & Harris; MUSICAL DIRECTOR: David Saidenberg. **Cast:** YOUNG PATRICK: Stuart Getz; GOOCH: Jane Connell; VERA: Anne Francine; MAME: Angela Lansbury; BISHOP/LEADING MAN: Jack Davison; ITO: Sab Shimono; BABCOCK: Willard Waterman; MME BRANISLOWSKI/MOTHER BURNSIDE: Tally Brown; BEAU: Charles Braswell; FAN: Ruth Ramsey; SALLY: Cathryn Damon; OLDER PATRICK: Jerry Lanning.

THE SUSAN HAYWARD TOUR. Opened on 12/27/68, at Caesar's Palace, Las Vegas. PRESENTED BY Fryer, Carr & Harris. **Cast:** MAME: Susan Hayward, *Celeste Holm* (from 3/10/69); GOOCH: Loretta Swit; VERA: Delphi Lawrence; ITO: Alvin Y.F. Ing; BABCOCK: Rufus Smith; MME BRANISLOWSKI/MOTHER BURNSIDE/MRS. UPSON: Ruth Gillette.

THE JANET BLAIR TOUR. 1/24/69–5/18/69. Played 16 cities. **Cast:** VERA: Elaine Stritch; MAME: Janet Blair.

THE SHEILA SMITH TOUR. Opened on 9/25/69, at the Bushnell Theatre, Hartford, Conn., and closed on 5/13/70, at the Fisher Theatre, Detroit. PRESENTED BY Lee Guber & Shelly Gross; DIRECTOR: John

Bowab; CHOREOGRAPHER: Diana Baffa; MUSICAL DIRECTOR: William Cox. **Cast:** GOOCH: Isabelle Farrell, *Donna Curtis;* VERA: Sandy Sprung; MAME: Sheila Smith, *Patrice Munsel, Anne Russell;* ITO: Arsenio Trinidad; MME BRANISLOWSKI/MOTHER BURNSIDE/MRS. UPSON: Hazel Steck; BEAU: Brian Moore.

THEATRE ROYAL, DRURY LANE, 2/27/69. 443 PERFORMANCES. PRESENTED BY Harold Fielding; DIRECTOR: Lawrence Kasha; CHOREOGRAPHER: Onna White. A cast recording was never made (although Dora Bryan, who was not in the show itself, did a studio recording). **Cast:** VERA: Margaret Courtenay; MAME: Ginger Rogers, *Juliet Prowse* (during Miss Rogers' 2-week vacation in 8/69); ALSO WITH: Ann Beach, Barry Kent, Gary Warren.

MEXICO, 1972. This was the Mexican premiere. DIRECTOR: Jose Luis Ibanez. **Cast:** MAME: Silvia Pinal; ALSO WITH: Evangelina Elizondo, Fernando Allende, Virma Gonzalez.

THE MOVIE. 1974. **Cast:** GOOCH: Jane Connell; VERA: Bea Arthur; MAME: Lucille Ball; BEAU: Robert Preston; ADULT PATRICK: Bruce Davison. There was a new song for Beau—"Loving You." It was a disappointing film.

423. *Mame (Broadway revival)*

Before Broadway. This revival opened at the Academy of Music in Philadelphia on 7/7/83, kicking off what was going to be a big pre–Broadway tour. However, it died in Philly, and they canceled that town on 7/13/83, and prematurely went straight into Broadway previews with too little promotion or advertising.

The Broadway Run. GERSHWIN THEATRE, 7/24/83–8/28/83. 7 previews from 7/19/83. 41 PERFORMANCES. PRESENTED BY the Mitch Leigh Company; MUSIC/LYRICS: Jerry Herman; BOOK: Jerome Lawrence & Robert E. Lee; BASED ON the 1955 memoir *Auntie Mame*, by Patrick Dennis; DIRECTOR: John Bowab; CHOREOGRAPHER: Diana Baffa-Brill (re-created Onna White's original choreography); SETS: Peter Wolf (reproduced William & Jean Eckart's original sets); COSTUMES: Robert Mackintosh; LIGHTING: Thomas Skelton; SOUND: Christine Voellinger; MUSICAL DIRECTOR: Jim Coleman; ORCHESTRATIONS: Philip J. Lang; VOCAL ARRANGEMENTS: Donald Pippin; PRESS: John A. Prescott; CASTING: Mark Reiner; PRODUCTION SUPERVISOR: Jerry Herman; GENERAL MANAGERS: Niko Entertainment; STAGE MANAGER: Paul Phillips; ASSISTANT STAGE MANAGER: Peter J. Taylor. **Cast:** PATRICK DENNIS (AGED 10): Roshi Handwerger; AGNES GOOCH: Jane Connell; VERA CHARLES: Anne Francine; MAME DENNIS: Angela Lansbury; RALPH DEVINE: Jacob Mark Hopkin; BISHOP: Merwin Foard; M. LINDSAY WOOLSEY: Donald Torres; ITO: Sab Shimono; DOORMAN: Brian McAnally; ELEVATOR BOY: Marshall Hagins; MESSENGER: David Miles; DWIGHT BABCOCK: Willard Waterman; BUBBLES THE CLOWN: Ken Henley; DANCE TEACHER: Louise Kirtland; BIRD DANCERS: Suzanne Ishee & Patrick Sean Murphy; LEADING MAN: Kenneth Kantor; STAGE MANAGER: Richard Poole; MME BRANISLOWSKI: Fran Stevens; GREGOR: Ken Henley; BEAUREGARD JACKSON PICKETT BURNSIDE: Scot Stewart; UNCLE JEFF: Kenneth Kantor; COUSIN FAN: Carol Lurie; SALLY CATO: Barbara Lang; MOTHER BURNSIDE: Fran Stevens; PATRICK DENNIS (AGED 19–29): Byron Nease; JUNIOR BABCOCK: Patrick Sean Murphy; MRS. UPSON: Louise Kirtland; MR. UPSON: John C. Becher; GLORIA UPSON: Michaela Hughes; PEGEEN RYAN: Ellyn Arons; PETER DENNIS: Daniel Mahon; MAME'S FRIENDS: Ellyn Arons, Alyson Bristol, Merwin Foard, Marshall Hagins, Ken Henley, Jacob Mark Hopkin, Michaela Hughes, Suzanne Ishee, Kenneth Kantor, Harry Kingsley, Melinda Koblick, David Loring, Carol Lurie, Brian McAnally, David Miles, Patrick Sean Murphy, Viewma Negromonte, Michele Pigliavento, Richard Poole, Cissy Rebich, Joseph Rich, Mollie Smith. **Understudies:** Patrick: Daniel Mahon; Gooch: Cissy Rebich; Vera: Barbara Lang; Woolsey/Babcock/Upson: Kenneth Kantor; Mme Branislowski/Mother Burnside: Louise Kirtland; Beau: Donald Torres; Sally: Carol Lurie Patrick, 19–29: Merwin Foard; Mrs. Upson: Fran Stevens; Peter: Roshi Handwerger; Ito: Kenneth Kantor & Ken Henley.

Despite great Broadway reviews, it was a flop.

After Broadway. MEXICAN REVIVAL, 1985. **Cast:** PATRICK: Eduardo Palomo; VERA: Maria Rivas; MAME: Silvia Pinal; BEAU: Gustavo Rojo.

In 1989 Miss Pinal got her own theatre in Mexico City, and continued to play Mame there.

TOURING REVIVAL. From 1989. *Cast:* GOOCH: Marsha Kramer; VERA: Gretchen Wyler; MAME: Juliet Prowse.

PAPER MILL PLAYHOUSE, New Jersey, 9/11/99–10/24/99. Previews from 9/8/99. PRESENTED BY Angelo Del Rossi; DIRECTOR: Robert Johanson; CHOREOGRAPHER: Michael Lichtefeld; SETS: Michael Anania; COSTUMES: David Murin; LIGHTING: F. Mitchell Dana; MUSICAL DIRECTOR: Jim Coleman. *Cast:* PATRICK: Paul S. Iacano; GOOCH: Sandy Rosenberg; VERA: Kelly Bishop; MAME: Christine Ebersole; ITO: Tony Romero; BEAU: Dan Schiff, *Jeff McCarthy* (from 10/20/99); PATRICK, 19–29: Ken Barnett; GLORIA: Danette Holden; ENSEMBLE INCLUDED: Susan Cella, Matt Lashey, Melissa Rae Mahon, Regina O'Malley, Peter Cormican. This was the most spectacular staging of *Mame* since the 1966 original. Two performances were canceled on 10/16/99, when Hurricane Floyd hit. Performances resumed on 10/17/99.

HELEN HAYES CENTER, Nyack, New York, 6/17/00–7/9/00. DIRECTOR/CHOREOGRAPHER: Norb Joerder; SETS: Michael Anania; COSTUMES: Kimberly Wick; LIGHTING: Aaron Spivey; SOUND: Peter Fitzgerald; MUSICAL DIRECTOR: William R. Cox. *Cast:* VERA: Diane J. Findlay; MAME: Carol Lawrence.

BROADWAY REVIVAL PLANS. On 10/11/02 the Nederlander Organization announced plans for a 2003 Broadway revival of *Mame*. In 1/03 Jerry Herman confirmed that he and the Nederlanders planned to bring back to Broadway within 5 years his shows *Mame, La Cage aux Folles* and *Hello, Dolly!* 2003 was later amended to 2004–05. First, in spring 2003 a Cleveland run of *Mame* was proposed for spring 2004. By 5/03 Tommy Tune's name was linked to the project. After Cleveland, the Orpheum, Minneapolis, was booked for 8/25/04–9/5/04. Christine Baranski was rumored to be starring. However, in mid 1/04 Jerry Herman himself said that both Cleveland and Minneapolis had been prematurely projected. 2005 was now the proposed year for the new *Mame*.

TV PRODUCTION. It hasn't happened yet. However a TV musical, starring Cher, was being rumored in late 2003, but in 1/04 Jerry Herman himself denied it.

HOLLYWOOD BOWL, 8/1/04. One-night only, all-star concert. DIRECTOR: Gordon Hunt; CHOREOGRAPHER: Kay Cole; SETS: Bradley Kaye; COSTUMES: Lisa Ann Hill; LIGHTING: Casey Cowan. *Cast:* MAME: Michele Lee; VERA: Christine Ebersole [she replaced Jean Smart before the opening]; BEAU: John Schneider; GOOCH: Allyce Beasley; UPSON: Alan Thicke; PEGEEN: Jessica Lindsey.

424. *Mamma Mia*

A musical with a disco beat, featuring the music of Swedish pop group ABBA. On a Greek island 20-year-old Sophie is due to be married. Her mother, Donna, a former singing star, is there, but her father isn't, partly because they don't know who he is. So, Sophie researches her mother's diary and chooses three former lovers as candidates and invites them to the wedding, thinking she'll figure it out when she sees them. Donna is a bit confused about all this.

Before Broadway. It opened to raves at the PRINCE EDWARD THEATRE, London, on 4/6/99. Previews from 3/20/99. It had the same major crew as for the later Broadway run. *Cast:* DONNA: Siobhan McCarthy, *Louise Plowright* (from 3/20/00), *Vivien Parry* (from 2/9/04); SOPHIE: Lisa Stokke, *Julie Atherton* (from 3/20/00), *Amanda Salmon* (3/19/01–3/16/02), *Laura Michelle Kelly* (from 3/18/02), *Alexandra Jay* (from 3/17/03); BILL: Nicolas Colicos, *Rohan Tickell* (from 3/19/01), *Dale Rapley* (from 2/9/04); SAM: Hilton McRae, *Michael Simkins* (3/20/00–3/18/01), *Simon Slater* (from 3/19/01), *Michael Simkins* (from 3/17/03), *Marcus D'Amico* (from 2/9/04); ROSIE: Jenny Galloway, *Lesley Nicol* (3/20/00–3/16/02), *Myra McFadyen* (from 3/18/02), *Lara Mulcahy* (from 2/9/04); LISA: Melissa Gibson, *Gail McKinnon* (3/20/00–3/18/01), *Hayley Tamaddon* (from 3/19/01), *Shona White* (from 3/17/03), *Kelly Price* (from 2/9/04); ALI: Eliza Lumley, *Melissa Gibson* (3/20/00–3/18/01), *Amanda Harrison* (from 3/19/01), *Selina Chilton* (from 3/17/03), *Louise Raven* (from 2/9/04); SKY: Andrew Langtree, *Gareth Bryn* (3/20/00–

3/18/01), *Raza Jeffrey* (3/19/01–3/16/02), *Paul Basleigh* (from 3/18/02 — he had stood in before), *Samuel Board* (from 3/17/03), *Dean Stobbart* (from 2/9/04); TANYA: Louise Plowright, *Louise Gold* (3/20/00–3/16/02), *Susannah Fellows* (from 3/18/02), *Kim Ismay* (from 3/17/03); HARRY: Paul Clarkson, *Craig Pinder* (3/20/00–3/19/01), *Peter Forbes* (from 3/19/01), *Robert Hands* (from 2/9/04); EDDIE: Nigel Harman, *Simon Coulthard* (3/20/00–3/18/01), *Paul Basleigh* (3/19/01–3/16/02), *Grant Anthony* (from 3/18/02); PEPPER: Neal Wright, *Andrew Prosser* (3/20/00–3/18/01), *Adam C. Booth* (from 3/19/01), *Kieran Jay* (from 2/9/04); FATHER ALEXANDRIOS: Tom Magdich, *James Barron* (3/20/00–3/18/01), *Andy Couchman* (from 3/19/01). Jenny Galloway won an Olivier Award. On 8/18/01 it celebrated its 1,000th sell-out performance. The cast recording, on Polydor, was released in 11/99 (and in the USA on 10/19/01). On 5/29/04 the show left the Prince Edward, a week later than had been scheduled, and on 6/3/04 (again, a week later than scheduled) moved into the PRINCE OF WALES THEATRE (both theatres being owned by Sir Cameron Mackintosh), in order to accommodate the incoming show *The Producers*.

It came to North America with the intention of touring, then with the touring company going onto Broadway. However, its first stint on this tour — the ROYAL ALEXANDRA THEATRE, Toronto, which opened on 5/23/00 (previews from 5/11/00) proved so popular that plans had to be revised. A new company would have to be formed for Broadway. Another problem that had to be overcome was that it was originally going to play in Toronto only until 11/4/00, then go off to San Francisco, but it started breaking records in Toronto and didn't stop. So, the run was extended to 12/31/00, and later to 4/1/01, and again to 7/1/01, and yet again to 9/30/01. It would continue to get extensions. However, San Francisco was waiting, so the Toronto cast went south and a new company was formed to continue at the Royal Alex as from 11/7/00. *Toronto cast:* DONNA: Louise Pitre, *Camilla Scott* (from 11/7/00); SOPHIE: Tina Maddigan, *Julie Martell* (from 11/7/00), *Marisa McIntyre* (by 11/02); SKY: Adam Brazier, *Todd Hofley* (by 11/02); SAM: Gary Lynch, *David Keeley, David Mucci* (by 11/02); HARRY: Lee MacDougall, *Laurie Murdoch* (by 11/02); TANYA: Mary Ellen Mahoney, *Nicole Roberts* (by 11/02); BILL: David Mucci, *Andrew Wheeler* (by 11/02); ROSIE: *Martha Reilly* (by 11/02). The Toronto production went to Vancouver, 7/2/03–9/29/03, then re-opened in Toronto on 9/30/03.

The old Toronto cast began performances at the ORPHEUM THEATRE, San Francisco, on 11/15/00. The show closed there on 2/17/01 (extended from 1/7/01), then went on to the Shubert Theatre, Los Angeles, where it opened on 2/26/01 (previews from 2/22). On opening night Louise Pitre got the news that she would be playing the lead on Broadway. The show closed in Los Angeles on 5/12/01 (extended from 4/22/01). Then it went on to the Cadillac Palace Theatre, Chicago on 5/18/01. Even before it arrived in the Windy City it had its run extended from 6/24/01 to 7/7/01. Later it extended again, to 8/11/01. There were two other cities scheduled between Chicago and Broadway — Washington, DC and Boston. However, Washington was canceled. It ran at the Colonial Theatre, Boston, 8/17/01–11/3/01 (extended from 10/28/01), with a new cast (the Chicago cast, i.e. the original North American cast, was getting ready for Broadway). After Boston the tour went to Minneapolis, 11/9/01–12/22/01, then to Detroit, 12/27/01–2/9/02. At that point it split into 2 touring companies — the existing company (now to be called Company No. 1) and Company No. 2. For details of these two tours see the Tours section after the Broadway run. PRINCESS THEATRE, Melbourne, Australia, 6/9/01–6/23/02. 441 PERFORMANCES. LYRIC THEATRE, Brisbane, from 7/5/02; SYDNEY, from 9/28/02. *Cast:* DONNA: Ann Wood; SOPHIE: Natalie O'Donnell; SKY: Jolyon James; TANYA: Rhonda Burchmore; ROSIE: Lara Mulcahy; SAM: Nicholas Eadie; BILL: Peter Hardy; HARRY: Robert Grubb.

As for the Broadway run, in 5/01 David Keeley and Karen Mason were confirmed in their roles, and on 7/25/01 Tina Maddigan and Judy Kaye were both confirmed in theirs. On 8/9/01 the rest of the cast was announced. The Winter Garden (now known as the Cadillac Winter Garden Theatre) and the 10/18/01 date were both announced on 9/8/00. Broadway previews began 10/5/01, and all revenues from the shows on that day, from all productions then going on around the world, were donated to the Red Cross to help the victims of 9/11.

The Broadway Run. CADILLAC WINTER GARDEN THEATRE,

10/18/01–. 14 previews from 10/5/01. Presented by Judy Craymer, Richard East, Bjorn Ulvaeus, for Littlestar, in association with Universal Pictures and David & Ed Mirvish; Music/Lyrics: Benny Andersson & Bjorn Ulvaeus; some songs with Stig Anderson; Additional Material: Martin Koch; Book: Catherine Johnson; Director: Phyllida Lloyd; Choreographer: Anthony Van Laast; Sets/Costumes: Mark Thompson; Lighting: Howard Harrison; Sound: Andrew Bruce & Bobby Aitken; Musical Supervisor/Arrangements: Martin Koch; Musical Director: Edward G. Robinson; Conductor: David Holcenberg; Press: Boneau/Bryan-Brown; Casting: Tara Rubin; Company Manager: Rina L. Saltzman; Production Stage Manager: Andrew Fenton; Stage Managers: Tom Capps, Sherry Cohen, Dean R. Greer. **Cast:** Sophie Sheridan: Tina Maddigan (2), *Somer Lee Graham & Meghann Dreyfuss* (alternated 7/29/02–8/4/02), *Tina Maddigan* (from 8/5/02), *Somer Lee Graham & Meghann Dreyfuss* (alternated 11/26/02–12/2/02), *Tina Maddigan* (from 12/3/02), *Jenny Fellner* (from 10/22/03), *Sara Kramer* (from 10/20/04); Ali: Sara Inbar (10), *Rebecca Kasper* (from 10/22/03); Lisa: Tonya Doran (9), *Keisha T. Fraser* (from 10/22/03); Tanya: Karen Mason (4), *Jeanine Morick* (during Miss Mason's vacation, 6/24/02–6/29/02), *Karen Mason* (from 6/30/02), *Jeanine Morick* (8/5/02–8/7/02), *Karen Mason* (from 8/8/02), *Jeanine Morick* (8/23/02–8/24/02), *Karen Mason* (8/26/02–10/6/02), *Jeanine Morick* (from 10/8/02), *Tamara Bernier* (from 10/22/03), *Judy McLane* (from 10/20/04); Rosie: Judy Kaye (3), *Sandy Rosenberg* (during Miss Kaye's vacation, 8/26/02–8/31/02), *Judy Kaye* (from 9/2/02), *Harriett D. Foy* (from 10/22/03), *Liz McCartney* (from 10/20/04); Donna Sheridan: Louise Pitre (1), *Marsha Waterbury* (7/1/02–7/7/02), *Louise Pitre, Marsha Waterbury* (stood in 8/28/02), *Louise Pitre, Carol Linnea Johnson* (stood in 10/16/02), *Louise Pitre, Carol Linnae Johnson* (during Miss Pitre's vacation 10/21/02–10/28/02), *Louise Pitre* (from 10/29/02), *Carol Linnea Johnson* (stood in for 11/29/02 matinee), *Louise Pitre, Carol Linnea Johnson* (during Miss Pitre's vacation days–3/8/03, 3/9/03, 3/11/03, 3/12/03), *Louise Pitre* (until 10/19/03), *Dee Hoty* (from 10/22/03), *Carolee Carmello* (from 10/20/04); Sky: Joe Machota (5), *Adam Monley & Michael Benjamin Washington* (alternated during Mr. Machota's vacation, 9/2/02–9/10/02), *Joe Machota* (from 9/12/02), *Aaron Staton* (from 10/20/04); Pepper: Mark Price (11), *Jason Weston, Ben Gettinger* (from 10/20/04); Eddie: Michael Benjamin Washington (12), *Albert Guerzon*; Harry Bright: Dean Nolen (8), *Richard Binsley, Michael Winther* (from 10/22/03), *David Beach* (from 10/20/04); Bill Austin: Ken Marks (7), *Tony Carlin & Brent Black* (alternated during Mr. Marks' vacation, 7/29/02–8/4/02), *Ken Marks* (from 8/5/02), *Adam Lefevre, Mark L. Montgomery* (from 10/20/04); Sam Carmichael: David Keeley (6), *Brent Black & Tony Carlin* (alternated during Mr. Keeley's vacation, 7/15/02–/21/02), *David Keeley* (from 7/22/02), *John Hillner* (from 10/22/03), *Daniel McDonald* (from 10/20/04); Father Alexandrios: Bill Carmichael, *Brent Black* (stood in); Ensemble: Meredith Akins, Leslie Alexander, Stephan Alexander, Kim-e J. Balmilero, Robin Baxter (*Sandy Rosenberg*), Brent Black, Tony Carlin, Bill Carmichael, Meghann Dreyfuss, Somer Lee Graham, Kristin McDonald, Adam Monley, Chris Prinzo, Peter Matthew Smith, Yuka Takara, Marsha Waterbury (*Jeanine Morick*), *Kelly Fletcher, Natasha Tabandera, Tom Galantich, Tyler Maynard, Carlos L. Encinias, Carol Linnea Johnson, Darryl Semira* (7/30/02–1/11/04), *David Ayers, Jesse Nager, Sandy Rosenberg.* **Understudies**: Sophie: Meghann Dreyfuss & Somer Lee Graham; Ali: Kim-e J. Balmilero & Kristin McDonald; Lisa: Meredith Akins & Yuka Takara; Donna: Marsha Waterbury, Monique Lund, Carol Linnea Johnson, *Jeanine Morick*; Tanya: Leslie Alexander & Marsha Waterbury, *Jeanine Morick*; Rosie: Robin Baxter & Marsha Waterbury, *Sandy Rosenberg*; Sky: Adam Monley & Peter Matthew Smith, *Michael Benjamin Washington*; Pepper: Stephan Alexander & Jon-Erik Goldberg, *Chris Prinzo*; Eddie: Chris Prinzo & Peter Matthew Smith, *Carlos L. Encinias*; Harry: Tony Carlin & Bill Carmichael, *Tom Galantich*; Bill/Sam: Brent Black & Tony Carlin, *Tom Galantich*; Father: Brent Black & Tony Carlin, *Carlos L. Encinias.* **Swings**: Barrett Foa, Jon-Erik Goldberg, Hollie Howard, Janet Rothermel, *Britt Shubow, Jerad Bontz, Tyler Maynard.* **The Band**: Keyboard 1: David Holcenberg; Keyboard 2: Steve Marzullo; Keyboard 3: Rob Preuss; Keyboard 4: Myles Chase; Guitar 1: Doug Quinn; Guitar 2: Jeff Campbell; Bass: Paul Adamy; Drums: Gary Tillman; Percussion: David Nyberg. *Act 1*: The day before the wedding:

Prologue Overture: "I Have a Dream" (Sophie); *Scene 1* Exterior of taverna: "Honey Honey" (Sophie, Lisa, Ali); *Scene 2* Interior of taverna; lobby (or hallway): "Money, Money, Money" (Donna, Tanya, Rosie); *Scene 3* Same: "Thank You for the Music" (Harry), "Mamma Mia" (Donna, to Sam, Bill, Harry); *Scene 4* Rosie & Tanya's bedroom: "Chiquitita" (Rosie & Tanya, to Donna), "Dancing Queen" (Rosie, Tanya, Donna); *Scene 5* The beach: "Lay All Your Love on Me" (Sophie & Sky); *Scene 6* Interior of taverna; women's hen night party: "Super Trouper" (Donna, Tanya, Rosie), "Gimme! Gimme! Gimme! (A Man After Midnight)" (Female Chorus), "The Name of the Game" (Sophie), "Voulez-Vous" (Chorus). *Act II*: The day of the wedding: Entr'acte; *Scene 1* Sophie's bedroom: "Under Attack" (Sophie); *Scene 2* Kitchen: "One of Us" (Donna & Sam), "S.O.S." (Sam, Donna, Chorus); *Scene 3* The beach: "Does Your Mother Know?" (Tanya & Chorus), "Knowing Me, Knowing You" (Sam); *Scene 4* Donna's bedroom: "Our Last Summer" (Harry & Donna), "Slipping Through My Fingers" (Donna & Sophie); *Scene 5* Interior of taverna: "The Winner Takes it All" (Donna), *Scene 6* Interior of church: "Take a Chance on Me" (Tanya), "I Do, I Do, I Do, I Do, I Do" (Donna, Sam, Chorus); *Scene 7* The reception; *Scene 8* Open countryside: "I Have a Dream" (reprise) (Sophie & Sky).

The show opened with $27 million in advance sales, and recouped its $10 million investment by 5/29/02, after less than 28 weeks, and all that despite bad reviews. It had the highest average ticket price on Broadway ($85.92). It received Tony nominations for musical, book, orchestrations, and for Judy Kaye and Louise Pitre. On 8/6/02 it was announced that Karen Mason would leave the show in early October. The show missed the 8/14/03 performance due to the power blackout. On 3/4/04 it celebrated its 1,000th performance, and had grossed over $144 million. By the end of 2004 the show had grossed over a billion dollars worldwide.

After Broadway. For what led up to the two tours see the section "Before Broadway," above.

Company No. 1. The cast of Company No. 1 (which was also the cast who played in Boston and subsequent dates) included: Donna: Dee Hoty (who had actually taken over in Chicago); Sophie: Michelle Aravena; Sam: Gary P. Lynch; Sky: Adam Brazier, *Ryan Silverman*; Rosie: Gabrielle Jones; Tanya: Mary Ellen Mahoney; Harry: Lee MacDougall, *Mark Zimmerman*; Lisa: Miku Graham, *Karen Burthwright*; Ali: Nicole Fraser, *Emy Baysic*; Eddie: Adam Fleming, *Joe Paparella*; Pepper: Nicholas Dromard, *Mike Erickson*; Bill: Craig Bennett; Alexandrios: Milo Shandel. **Understudy**: Donna: Mary Ellen Mahoney.

Company No. 2. Opened on 2/28/02, at Providence, Rhode Island. **Cast**: Donna: Monique Lund; Sophie: Kristie Marsden; Rosie: Robin Baxter; Bill: Pearce Bunting; Tanya: Ellen Harvey; Harry: James Kall; Sam: Don Noble; Sky: Chris Bolan; Pepper: J.P. Potter. **Understudy**: Sky: J.P. Potter.

Hamburg, 11/3/02. This was the first foreign-language version.

Umi, Tokyo. This was the first show to play this venue. 12/1/02 (rehearsals from 10/14/02). **Cast**: Donna: Chizu Hosaka.

Mandalay Bay, Las Vegas. Opened 2/13/03. **Cast**: Donna: Tina Walsh; Rosie: Jennifer Perry; Tanya: Karole Foreman; Sophie: Jill Paice; Sky: Victor Wallace; Sam: Nick Cokas; Bill: Mark Leydorf; Harry: Michael Piontek; Lisa: Danielle Ferretti; Ali: Courtney Bradshaw; Pepper: Brandon Alameda; Eddie: Felipe Crook.

Seoul, Korea. 1/25/04. In Korean.

Tour. A new international tour opened at The Point, Dublin, 9/9/04–11/6/04. Previews from 9/4/04. Then to the Edinburgh Playhouse, Scotland, 11/12/04–1/29/05; then on to South Africa, then Europe. **Cast**: Donna: Helen Hobson; Tanya: Geraldine Fitzgerald; Rosie: Joanna Munro; Sophie: Emily Dykes; Sam: Cameron Blakely; Harry: John Langley; Bill: Ulrich Wiggers; Sky: Michael Xavier.

Lope de Vega Theatre, Madrid. Opened 11/11/04. This was the first Spanish language production. Songs Translated by: Albert Mas-Griera; Book Translated by: Juan Martinez Moreno; Director: Paul Garrington. **Cast**: Donna: Nina; Sophie: Mariona Castillo; Tanya: Marta Valverde; Rosie: Paula Sebastian; Sky: Leandro Rivera.

Cirkus, Stockholm. 2/12/05. Catherine Johnson's libretto was translated into Swedish by Peter Dalle. Niklas Stranstedt translated ABBA's lyrics into Swedish.

425. *Man of La Mancha*

A musical with no intermission. About Cervantes and his relationship with his fictional hero, Don Quixote. All the characters in the play are imprisoned in a dungeon in Seville at the end of the 16th century, awaiting trial by the Spanish Inquisition for religious offenses. Cervantes' fellow prisoners try to steal his things, including his manuscript of *Don Quixote*, but he persuades the prisoners to hold a mock trial, wherein Cervantes can explain his philosophy by staging a dramatization of his manuscript. He makes himself up to resemble his hero. The entire action takes place there and in various other places in the imagination of the novelist. The prisoners all take roles. The story revolves around the adventures of an old, demented knight bent on restoring chivalry, and his manservant, Sancho Panza. The two come to an inn which the Don is convinced is a castle. He meets Aldonza, a serving-wench and strumpet, whom Don Quixote worships as the virginal Dulcinea and for whom he is prepared to do battle in order to be worthy of knighthood. Aldonza scorns him for his foolishness. At the Don's home, meanwhile, his niece, Antonia, and the Don's housekeeper, and Antonia's fiancé Dr. Carrasco, are asking the padre for help in dealing with the Don's madness. The padre agrees to help them bring the Don back home. After the Don has defended Aldonza against the attack of the muleteers, the innkeeper knights Quixote in a ceremony called The Dubbing. The muleteers then carry Aldonza off anyway and have their way with her. After his first attempt fails, Carrasco disguises himself as the Knight of the Mirrors, challenges Quixote, and forces him to look in the mirror of reality, wherein he sees himself as an old, demented fool. The doctor takes him back home, followed by Aldonza, who has finally been won over by the Don as he lies dying, and she gets to believe in his impossible dream. Back to the dungeon, and the prisoners (including Cervantes himself) are inspired by the story. They return his manuscript and Cervantes goes off to face the Inquisition with a new boldness.

Before Broadway. Writer Dale Wasserman was in Madrid researching for a movie when he read in the newspapers that he was there to do a play about Don Quixote. That was the first he'd heard of this, so he read up on the old fictional hero, and as a result he wrote the TV play *I, Don Quixote* (shown on CBS, 11/9/59, and starring Lee J. Cobb). Mr. Wasserman was then going to do it as a straight play, but Albie Marre came up with the idea of making it into a stage musical. Originally W.H. Auden and Chester Kallman were to have done the lyrics, but Joe Darion finally wrote them. Michael Redgrave was touted as the star, but Richard Kiley finally starred in his most famous role. The show opened at the GOODSPEED OPERA HOUSE, Conn., on 7/24/65. CHOREOGRAPHER: Eddie Roll [there was to be a fuss several productions later over who did or did not choreograph this show]. *Cast:* DON QUIXOTE/CERVANTES: Richard Kiley; SANCHO PANZA: Irving Jacobson; ALDONZA: Joan Diener [Miss Diener was actually Mrs. Marre]; INNKEEPER: Ray Middleton; PADRE: Robert Rounseville; ALSO WITH: Luba Malina, Irwin Corey, Martyn Green.

After its Connecticut beginnings at Goodspeed, it couldn't find a Broadway house, so it opened at ANTA Washington Square Theatre, Greenwich Village, which was really an Off Broadway house, as some critics pointed out, but the Tony committee decided that, despite its venue, *Man of La Mancha* was a Broadway show, partly because all the contracts for the show were Broadway contracts. However, given that ANTA held only 1,115 people, the show was struggling to make a profit, and threatened to go to Broadway, so ANTA re-arranged their contract whereby the show could make an additional weekly profit of $1,500. Roberto Iglesias, the flamenco dancer, was advertised as co-star, but failed to make it through the New York rehearsals.

The Broadway Run. ANTA THEATRE, 11/22/65–3/18/68; MARTIN

BECK THEATRE, 3/20/68–3/1/71; EDEN THEATRE, 3/2/71–5/24/71; MARK HELLINGER THEATRE, 5/26/71–6/26/71. 21 previews from 10/30/65. Total of 2,329 PERFORMANCES. The ANTA—Goodspeed production, PRESENTED BY Albert W. Selden & Hal James; MUSIC: Mitch Leigh; LYRICS: Joe Darion; BOOK: Dale Wasserman; BASED ON Dale Wasserman's 1959 teleplay *I, Don* Quixote; SUGGESTED BY the life and works of Miguel de Cervantes y Saavedra, and especially by his 1615 romance *Don Quixote de la Mancha;* DIRECTOR: Albert Marre; ASSISTANT DIRECTOR/DANCE CAPTAIN: Eddie Roll; CHOREOGRAPHER: Jack Cole; SETS/LIGHTING: Howard Bay; COSTUMES: Howard Bay & Patton Campbell; MUSICAL DIRECTOR: Neil Warner, *R. Bennett Benetsky* (by 68–69); DANCE MUSIC ARRANGEMENTS: Neil Warner; MUSICAL ARRANGEMENTS: Music Makers; CAST RECORDING on Kapp; PRESS: Arthur Cantor, Artie Solomon, Merle Debuskey, Faith Geer, *Violet Welles* (by 66–67 & gone by 69–70); CASTING: Wendy Mackenzie; GENERAL MANAGER: Walter Fried; COMPANY MANAGER: Gino Giglio; PRODUCTION STAGE MANAGER: Marnel Sumner, *James S. Gelb* (by 70–71); STAGE MANAGER: Michael Turque, Martin Newman; ASSISTANT STAGE MANAGERS: Renato Cibelli & Phill Lipman, *Louis Criscuolo* (by 66–67), *Alfred Leberfeld* (by 67–68). *Cast:* DON QUIXOTE/CERVANTES: Richard Kiley (1) ☆, *Jose Ferrer* (for two weeks from 5/28/66), *Richard Kiley, John Cullum* (from 2/24/67), *Jose Ferrer* (from 4/11/67), *David Atkinson* (from 7/14/67), *Hal Holbrook* (from 7/1/68), *Bob Wright* (from 9/23/68), *David Atkinson* (from 9/8/69), *Claudio Brook* (from 9/22/69), *Keith Michell* (from 12/22/69), *Somegoro Ichikawa* (from 3/2/70), *Charles West* (from 5/11/70), *Gideon Singer* (from 9/18/70), *David Atkinson* (from 4/2/71); QUIXOTE/CERVANTES (MATINEES): *Laurence Guittard* (from 5/22/68), *John Cullum* (from 68–69), *David Holliday* (from 10/12/68), *Jack Dabdoub* (from 10/20/69); SANCHO PANZA: Irving Jacobson (3) ☆, *Pierre Olaf* (7/5/66–7/19/66), *Irving Jacobson, Joey Faye* (from 11/1/68), *Tony Martinez* (from 10/69), *Sammy Smith* (from 4/13/70), *Titos Vandis* (from 5/11/70), *Rudy Tronto* (from 11/13/70), *Edmond Varrato* (from 71); CAPTAIN OF THE INQUISITION: Renato Cibelli, *Ray Dash* (by 68–69 he was doing matinees); ALDONZA/DULCINEA: Joan Diener (2) ☆, *Gerrianne Raphael* (for two weeks from 5/28/66), *Joan Diener, Marion Marlowe* (from 1/17/67), *Maura K. Wedge* (from 4/11/67), *Bernice Massi* (from 7/25/67), *Gaylea Byrne* (from 5/5/69), *Emily Yancy* (from 1/21/71); ALDONZA/DULCINEA (MATINEES): Patricia Marand (from 2/68), *Carolyn Maye* (during Miss Marand's absence 3/20/68), *Patricia Marand, Barbara Williams* (from 11/1/68), *Marilyn Child* (from 5/28/69), *Emily Yancy* (from 12/3/69, *Dell Brownlee* (from 1/21/71); THE INNKEEPER: Ray Middleton (4) ☆, *Wilbur Evans* (from 4/11/67), *Ray Middleton* (from 9/19/67), *Jack Dabdoub* (10/5/70–10/19/70), *Ray Middleton;* DR. CARRASCO: Jon Cypher (6), *David Atkinson* (by 67–68), *Laurence Guittard* (from 67–68), *Renato Cibelli* (by 68–69 doing matinees), *David Holliday* (from 68–69), *Timothy Jerome* (from 69–70), *Ian Sullivan* (from 70–71); THE PADRE: Robert Rounseville (5) ☆, *Ralph Farnworth* (7/6/70–7/20/70), *Robert Rounseville;* ANTONIA: Mimi Turque (7), *Dell Brownlee* (by 66–67), *Marcia Gilford* (from 67–68), *Dianne Barton* (from 67–68); THE HOUSEKEEPER: Eleanore Knapp (8), *Rita Metzger* (from 70–71); THE BARBER: Gino Conforti (9), *James Coco* (from 66), *Taylor Reed* (from 67), *Howard Girven* (from 67–68), *Leo Bloom* (from 68–69); PEDRO, HEAD MULETEER: Shev Rodgers (10), *Bruce MacKay* (from 67–68), *Shev Rodgers* (from 68–69), *Carmine Caridi* (from 69–70), *Shev Rodgers* (from 70–71); ANSELMO, A MULETEER: Harry Theyard (11), *Ted Forlow* (from 66), *Wilson Robey* (from 68–69); JOSE, A MULETEER: Eddie Roll, *Will Carter* (from 67), *Bert Michaels* (from 69–70), *Hector Mercado* (from 70–71); JUAN, A MULETEER: John Aristedes, *Mark Ross* (from 67–68), *John Aristedes* (from 68–69), *Robert Rayow* (from 70–71); PACO, A MULETEER: Antony De Vecchi, *Bill Stanton* (from 67–68); TENORIO, A MULETEER: Fernando Grahal, *Carlos Macri* (from 67), *Don Bonnell* (from 69–70), *Robert Rayow* (from 69–70), *Don Bonnell* (from 70–71); ROMERO, A MULETEER: Louis Criscuolo [new role, created by 68–69 & dropped by 69–70]; HORSE: Anthony De Vecchi (*Bill Stanton* by 68–69) & Will Carter (*Bert Michaels* from 69–70; *Hector Mercado* from 70–71 [new role, or roles, created by 66–67, and known by 69–70 as Dancing Horses]; MARIA, THE INNKEEPER'S WIFE: Marceline Decker, *Rita Metzger* (from 67–68), *Louise Armstrong* (from 70–71); HORSES: Leo Bloom & Carmine Caridi (*Shev Rodgers* from 70–71) [this was a new role, or roles, or rather a re-vamped one, added for the last season]; FERMINA, A SLAVEY: Gerrianne Raphael,

Marcia Gilford (from 67–68), *Marcia O'Brien* (from 69–70), *Violet Santangelo* (relieved Miss O'Brien, 69–70), *Marcia O'Brien, Violet Santangelo* (from 70–71), *Heather Golembo* (from 71); GUITARIST: David Serva, *Karl Herreshoff* (from 67), *Stephen Sahlein* (from 68–69); GUARDS & MEN OF THE INQUISITION: Ray Dash, Jonathan Fox (*James Leverett* from 68–69), John Fields, Samye Van, David Matson. 67–68 replacements: *Charles Leipart* (gone by 68–69), *John Fields* (*Angelo Nazzo* from 69–70), *Robert Cromwell* (gone by 68–69). 68–69 replacements: *Toby Tompkins* (*Robert Einenkel* by 69–70; *David Wilder* from 69–70; *Jeff Killion* by 70–71). Other replacements: *Carlton Davis, John Felton, John Rossi, Peter Shire*. **Understudies**: Quixote: David Atkinson (66–67), *Laurence Guittard* (67–68), *Renato Cibelli* (67–71), *David Holliday* (68–69), *Jack Dabdoub* (69–71); Sancho: Will Carter (66–67), *Lou Criscuolo* (67–68), *Eddie Roll* (69–71), *Wilson Robey* (69–71); Aldonza: Gerrianne Raphael (66–67), *Marcia Gilford* (67–69), *Barbara Williams* (68–69), *Emily Yancy* (69–70), *Violet Santangelo* (69–71), *Dell Brownlee* (70–71), *Heather Golembo* (71); Innkeeper: *Bruce MacKay* (67–68), *Renato Cibelli* (67–71), *Stephen Pearlman* (68–69), *Jack Dabdoub* (69–71), *Paul Michael* (69–70), *Shev Rodgers* (70–71); Padre: Ralph Farnworth (66–71), *Wilson Robey* (68–71); Carrasco: Renato Cibelli (66–71), *Al Leberfeld* (68–71), *Harry Theyard*; Pedro: Renato Cibelli (66–71), *Stephen Pearlman* (68–69), *David Wilder* (69–70), *Jeff Killion* (70–71); Barber: Eddie Roll (66–71), *Lou Criscuolo* (67–68), *Ted Forlow* (67–68), *Al Leberfeld* (69–71); Antonia: Dell Brownlee (66–67), *Marcia Gilford* (67–69), *Janet Gaylord* (67–69), *Patricia Lens* (69–70, *Rosemary Harvey* (70–71); Maria: Dell Brownlee (66–67), *Janet Gaylord* (67–69), *Violet Santangelo* (69–71), *Heather Golembo* (71); Fermina: Dell Brownlee (66–67), *Janet Gaylord* (67–69), *Patricia Lens* (69–70), *Rosemary Harvey* (70–71); Housekeeper: Marceline Decker (66–67), *Rita Metzger* (67–70), *Louise Armstrong* (70–71); Captain: Ray Dash (66–71), *Jonathan Fox* (68–69). **Swing Dancer**: *John Gorrin* (68–71). Overture, "I, Don Quixote (Man of La Mancha)" (Quixote, Sancho, Horses), "It's All the Same" (Aldonza & Muleteers), "Dulcinea" (Quixote & Muleteers), "I'm Only Thinking of Him" (Padre, Antonia, Housekeeper, Doctor), "I Really Like Him" (Sancho), "What Does He Want of Me?" (Aldonza), "Little Bird, Little Bird" (Anselmo & Muleteers), "The Barber's Song" (Barber), "Golden Helmet (of Mambrino)" (Quixote, Sancho, Barber, Muleteers), "To Each His Dulcinea (To Every Man His Dream)" (Padre), "The Quest" ("The Impossible Dream") (Quixote) [the big hit], "The Combat" (Quixote, Aldonza, Sancho, Muleteers), "The Dubbing (The Knight of the Woeful Countenance)" (Innkeeper, Aldonza, Sancho), "The Abduction" (Aldonza & Muleteers), Moorish Dance (Ensemble), "Aldonza" (Aldonza), "The Knight of the Mirrors" (Quixote, Knight and His Attendants), "A Little Gossip" (Sancho), "Dulcinea" (reprise) (Aldonza), "I, Don Quixote (Man of La Mancha)" (reprise) (Quixote, Aldonza, Sancho), "The Psalm" (Padre), Finale: "The Quest" ("The Impossible Dream") (reprise) (Entire Company).

Broadway reviews were excellent. The show won Tony Awards for musical, composer & lyricist, direction of a musical, sets, and for Richard Kiley, and was nominated for choreography and costumes. When ANTA was torn down, the show moved to the Martin Beck. Gideon Singer was the first Israeli stage star to play a leading role on Broadway. On 3/2/71 it left Broadway and moved back to the Eden, an Off Broadway house, for a couple of months (this short stay was still a part of its Broadway run, for reasons given above), then it came back to Broadway for the final part of its long run. It was the third-longest running Broadway musical of the 1960s (and by the end of 2002 it was still the 18th-longest running show of any kind in Broadway history).

After Broadway. TOUR. Opened on 9/24/66, *at the* Shubert Theatre, New Haven, and was on the road for 3½ years. MUSICAL DIRECTOR: James Peterson, *Joseph Klein*. **Cast:** QUIXOTE: Jose Ferrer, *Richard Kiley* (from 4/11/67), *Jose Ferrer* (7/17/67–8/7/67), *Richard Kiley, Keith Andes* (from 12/4/67), *Jose Ferrer* (from 9/23/68), *Bob Wright* (from 9/15/69); SANCHO: Harvey Lembeck, *Sammy Smith*; ALDONZA: Maura K. Wedge, *Joan Diener* (from 4/11/67), *Marion Marlowe* (from 7/31/67), *Carolyn Maye* (from 11/7/68); ALDONZA (MATINEES): *Natalie Costa* (from 3/18/67), *Maura K. Wedge* (from 10/15/68); INNKEEPER: Wilbur Evans, *Marvin Brody*; CARRASCO: David Atkinson, *Ian Sullivan*; ANTONIA: Dianne Barton, *Leanna Nelson*; HOUSEKEEPER: Lu Leonard, *Nadine Lewis*; TENORIO: Fernando Grahal, *Ben Vargas*; MOORISH DANCER: Mar-

ilyn Sokol, *Rosemary Harvey*; GUITARIST: David Serva. **Understudy**: Quixote: David Atkinson.

MADRID. Opened on 9/28/66.
TEL AVIV. Opened on 2/7/67. In Hebrew. Starring Gideon Singer
MALMO, Sweden. Opened on 9/1/67.
COPENHAGEN. Opened on 9/15/67.
MELBOURNE. Opened on 9/30/67. Starring Charles West.
BRATISLAVA, Czechoslovakia. Opened on 10/30/67.
HELSINKI. Opened on 12/20/67.
VIENNA. Opened on 1/4/68.
PRAGUE. Opened on 1/24/68.
PICCADILLY THEATRE, London. Opened on 4/25/68. 253 PERFORMANCES. CHOREOGRAPHER: Norman Maen. **Cast:** QUIXOTE: Keith Michell; SANCHO: Bernard Spear; ALDONZA: Joan Diener, *Ruth Silvestre* (from 9/68).
BUENOS AIRES. Opened on 8/14/68.
BERLIN. Opened on 9/10/68.
TOUR. Opened on 9/27/68, and closed on 4/26/69, after playing 110 cities. **Cast:** QUIXOTE: David Atkinson; ALDONZA: Patricia Marand.
BRUSSELS. Opened on 10/4/68.
AMSTERDAM. Opened on 12/21/68.
MEXICO CITY. Opened on 2/18/69. Starring Claudio Brook.
HAMBURG. Opened on 2/20/69.
TOKYO. Opened on 4/4/69. Starring Somegoro Ichikawa.
TOUR. Opened on 9/27/69, and closed on 2/28/70, after playing 60 cities. **Cast:** QUIXOTE: David Atkinson; ALDONZA: Natalie Costa.
OSLO. Opened on 3/16/70.
TOUR. Opened on 11/9/71, at the National Theatre, Washington, DC, and closed on 12/18/71, at the O'Keefe, Toronto. RE-STAGED BY: Antony De Vecchi; MUSICAL DIRECTOR: Joseph Klein. **Cast:** QUIXOTE: Allan Jones; ALDONZA: Gerrianne Raphael; SANCHO: Edmond Varrato; INNKEEPER: Rowan Tudor; PEDRO: Antony De Vecchi.
PARIS. Opened on 12/10/68. TRANSLATED INTO FRENCH BY: Jacques Brel. **Cast:** QUIXOTE: Jacques Brel.
LONDON. Opened on 6/10/69. **Cast:** QUIXOTE: Richard Kiley; SANCHO: Bernard Spear; ALDONZA: Ruth Silvestre; INNKEEPER: Charles West.

426. *Man of La Mancha (1972 Broadway revival)*

The Broadway Run. VIVIAN BEAUMONT THEATRE, 6/22/72–10/21/72. 140 PERFORMANCES. The Albert Marre production, PRESENTED BY Albert W. Selden & Hal James, by arrangement with Lincoln Center; MUSIC: Mitch Leigh; LYRICS: Joe Darion; BOOK: Dale Wasserman; BASED ON the novel by Cervantes; DIRECTOR: Albert Marre; CHOREOGRAPHER: Jack Cole; SETS/LIGHTING: Howard Bay; COSTUMES: Howard Bay & Patton Campbell; MUSICAL DIRECTOR: Joseph Klein; MUSICAL ARRANGEMENTS: Music Makers; DANCE MUSIC ARRANGEMENTS: Neil Warner; PRESS: Gifford/Wallace; COMPANY MANAGER: G. Warren McClane; PRODUCTION STAGE MANAGER: James Gelb; STAGE MANAGER: Patrick Horrigan; ASSISTANT STAGE MANAGERS: Alfred Leberfeld & Joe Lorden. **Cast:** DON QUIXOTE/CERVANTES: Richard Kiley, David Atkinson (Weds & Sat matinees); SANCHO PANZA: Edmond Varrato (for the first two performances), *Irving Jacobson*; CAPTAIN OF THE INQUISITION: Renato Cibelli; ALDONZA: Joan Diener, Gerrianne Raphael (Wednesday & Saturday matinees); INNKEEPER: Jack Dabdoub; DR. CARRASCO: Lee Bergere; PADRE: Robert Rounseville; ANTONIA: Dianne Barton; HOUSEKEEPER: Eleanore Knapp; BARBER: Ted Forlow (for the first two performances), *Edmond Varrato*; PEDRO, HEAD MULETEER: Shev Rodgers;.

ANSELMO: Joe Lorden (for the first two performances), *Ted Forlow*; JOSE, A MULETEER: Hector Mercado; JUAN, A MULETEER: John Aristedes; PACO, A MULETEER: Bill Stanton; TENORIO, A MULETEER: Fernando Grahal; MARIA, INNKEEPER'S WIFE: Rita Metzger; DANCING HORSES: Fernando Grahal & Hector Mercado; HORSES AT THE WELL: Jeff Killion (for the first two performances; *Edmond Varrato*) & Shev Rodgers; FERMINA, MOORISH DANCER: Laura Kenyon; GUITARIST: Stephen Sahlein; GUARDS

AND MEN OF THE INQUISITION: Jeff Killion, David Wasson, Robert Cromwell, William Tatum. *Standby*: Padre: Ronn Carroll. *Understudies*: Quixote: Renato Cibelli; Carrasco: Renato Cibelli, Shev Rodgers, Al Leberfeld; Sancho: Edmond Varrato; Aldonza/Maria: Laura Kenyon; Barber: Ted Forlow & Al Leberfeld; Innkeeper: Shev Rodgers; Antonia/Fermina: Joyce McDonald; Housekeeper: Rita Metzger; Pedro: Jeff Killion; Captain: David Wasson. *Swing Dancer*: Joe Lorden.

Irving Jacobson was to have played Sancho, but an accident kept him out of the production for the first two performances, during which his understudy played it. Edmond Varrato's understudy played the Barber and the Horse for those two performances, and Joe Lorden, the swing, played the part that Ted Forlow should have played. Broadway reviews were generally excellent.

After Broadway. After Broadway the show went on to an overwhelmingly successful tour.

THE MOVIE. 1972. United Artists bought the screen rights for a sum in excess of $2 million. *Cast:* QUIXOTE: Peter O'Toole; SANCHO: James Coco; ALDONZA: Sophia Loren.

TOUR. Opened on 1/15/76, at Kalamazoo, and closed on 4/4/76, at Paramus, NJ. MUSICAL DIRECTOR: Milton Setzer. *Cast:* QUIXOTE: David Atkinson; ALDONZA: Alice Evans; SANCHO: Mark Ross; JOSE: Hector Mercado.

427. *Man of La Mancha* (1977 *Broadway revival*)

Before Broadway. Richard Kiley hand-picked his cast from productions he had worked with. Jack Cole's name was removed from the billing because the producers felt his contribution to the original had been somewhat minor (Eddie Roll had created the choreography during the very original Goodspeed tryout). Cole's estate sued, and lost.

The Broadway Run. PALACE THEATRE, 9/15/77–12/31/77. 3 previews. 124 PERFORMANCES. PRESENTED BY Eugene V. Wolsk (and Mitch Leigh); MUSIC: Mitch Leigh; LYRICS: Joe Darion; BOOK: Dale Wasserman; BASED ON the novel by Cervantes; DIRECTOR/CHOREOGRAPHER: Albert Marre; ORIGINAL CHOREOGRAPHER: Jack Cole (unbilled); SETS/LIGHTING: Howard Bay; COSTUMES: Howard Bay & Patton Campbell; SOUND: Charles Belin; MUSICAL DIRECTOR: Robert Brandzel; MUSICAL ARRANGEMENTS: Music Makers; DANCE MUSIC ARRANGEMENTS: Neil Warner; PRESS: John A. Prescott; CASTING: Kay Vance; PRODUCTION ASSISTANT: Adam Marre; COMPANY MANAGER: Chuck Eisler; PRODUCTION STAGE MANAGER: Patrick Horrigan; STAGE MANAGER: Gregory Allen Hirsch; ASSISTANT STAGE MANAGER: Kay Vance. *Cast:* CERVANTES/DON QUIXOTE: Richard Kiley (1) ☆; SANCHO PANZA: Tony Martinez (3); THE HORSE: Ben Vargas; THE MULE: Hector Mercado; THE INNKEEPER: Bob Wright (5); MARIA, THE INNKEEPER'S WIFE: Marceline Decker; PEDRO, HEAD MULETEER: Chev Rodgers (7); ANSELMO, A MULETEER: Ted Forlow (8); JUAN, A MULETEER: Mark Holliday; TENORIO, A MULETEER: Ben Vargas; PACO, A MULETEER: Antony De Vecchi; JOSE, A MULETEER: Hector Mercado; ALDONZA: Emily Yancy (2); FERMINA, A SLAVEY: Joan Susswein; GUITARIST: Robin Polseno; JORGE, A MULETEER: Edmond Varrato; FERNANDO, A MULETEER: David Wasson; ANTONIA: Harriett Conrad (9); THE HOUSEKEEPER: Margaret Coleman (10); THE PADRE: Taylor Reed (4); DR. CARRASCO: Ian Sullivan (6); THE BARBER: Ted Forlow (8); MOORISH DANCER: Joan Susswein; THE CAPTAIN: Renato Cibelli; GUARDS: Michael St. Paul & David Wasson. *Standby*: Sancho: Edmond Varrato. *Understudies*: Aldonza/Antonia: Joan Susswein; Carrasco: Marshall Borden & David Wasson; Pedro/Tenorio/Horse/Jose/Mule: Antony De Vecchi; Maria/Fermina/Moorish Dancer: Kay Vance; Innkeeper: Renato Cibelli; Padre: Mark Holliday & David Wasson; Anselmo: Edmond Varrato & Mark Holliday; Barber: Edmond Varrato; Housekeeper: Marceline Decker; Captain: Michael St. Paul.

Broadway reviews were divided, but generally favorable.

After Broadway. TOUR. Opened on 2/14/78, in San Francisco. On 8/3/78 it opened at Boston's Music Hall. MUSICAL DIRECTOR: Lawrence Brown. *Cast:* QUIXOTE: Richard Kiley; SANCHO: Tony Martinez; CAPTAIN: Renato Cibelli; ALDONZA: Susan Waldman; INNKEEPER: Bob

Wright; CARRASCO: Ian Sullivan; PADRE: David Wasson; ANTONIA: Frances Roth; HOUSEKEEPER: Marceline Decker; ANSELMO/BARBER: Ted Forlow; PEDRO: Dan Hannafin; JOSE/MULE: Hector Mercado; JUAN: Mark Holliday; PACO: Antony De Vecchi; JORGE: Edmond Varrato; FERNANDO: Sal Provenza; TENORIO/HORSE: Ben Vargas; MARIA: Carolyn Friday; FERMINA: Jane Seaman; GUITARIST: Robert Ferry; GUARDS: Michael St. Paul & David Wasson.

PAPER MILL PLAYHOUSE, NEW JERSEY, 1982. DIRECTOR/CHOREOGRAPHER: Rudy Tronto; SETS/LIGHTING: Howard Bay. *Cast:* Jerome Hines, Bernice Massi.

428. *Man of La Mancha* (1992 *Broadway revival*)

Again, there was no intermission. In this production "Little Bird, Little Bird" was sung by Paco and the Muleteers.

The Broadway Run. MARQUIS THEATRE, 4/24/92–7/26/92. 28 previews from 3/31/92. 108 PERFORMANCES. PRESENTED BY The Mitch Leigh Company; MUSIC: Mitch Leigh; LYRICS: Joe Darion; BOOK: Dale Wasserman; BASED ON the novel by Cervantes; DIRECTOR/CHOREOGRAPHER: Albert Marre; SETS: Howard Bay; COSTUMES: Howard Bay & Patton Campbell; LIGHTING: Gregory Allen Hirsch; SOUND: Jon Weston; MUSICAL DIRECTOR: Brian Salesky; ORCHESTRATIONS: Music Makers; DANCE MUSIC ARRANGEMENTS: Neil Warner; PRESS: Dennis Crowley; CASTING: Richard Shulman; GENERAL MANAGERS: Niko Associates; COMPANY MANAGER: Lynn Landis; PRODUCTION STAGE MANAGER: Patrick Horrigan; STAGE MANAGER: Betsy Nicholson; ASSISTANT STAGE MANAGER: Larry Bussard. *Cast:* CERVANTES/DON QUIXOTE: Raul Julia (1) ☆, *David Holliday, Laurence Guittard* (from 6/30/92); ALDONZA/DULCINEA: Sheena Easton (2) ☆, *Joan Susswein Barber* (during Miss Easton's illness), *Joan Diener* (from 6/30/92); SANCHO: Tony Martinez (3) ☆; GOVERNOR/PEDRO: Chev Rodgers (5); PADRE: David Wasson (6); DR. CARRASCO: Ian Sullivan (8); INNKEEPER: David Holliday (4); ANTONIA: Valerie de Pena; HOUSEKEEPER: Marceline Decker; BARBER: Ted Forlow (7); PACO/MULE: Hechter Ubarry; JUAN/HORSE: Jean-Paul Richard; MANUEL: Luis Perez; TENORIO: Gregory Mitchell; JOSE: Bill Santora; JORGE: Chet D'Elia; MARIA: Tanny McDonald; FERMINA/MOORISH DANCER: Joan Susswein Barber; CAPTAIN OF THE INQUISITION: Jon Vandertholen; GUITARISTS: Robin Polseno & David Serva; GUARDS: Chet D'Elia & Darryl Ferrera. *Understudies*: Cervantes/Quixote/Governor: David Holliday; Aldonza/Antonia/Maria: Joan Susswein Barber; Sancho/Pedro/Barber: Darryl Ferrera; Innkeeper: Chev Rodgers; Carrasco: Jon Vandertholen; Housekeeper/Fermina/Dancer: Tanny McDonald; Mule: Bill Santora; Captain: Jean-Paul Richard. *Swing*: Rick Manning. *Orchestra*: FLUTES: Bill Meade, Lucy Goeres, Helen Campo; CLARINET: Larry Guy; OBOE: David Diggs; BASSOON: Ethan Silverman; TRUMPETS: Rich Raffio & Larry Etkin; TROMBONES: Dennis Elliot, George Moran, Jack Jeffers; FRENCH HORNS: Anne Yarbrough, Will Parker, Sue Panny, Kathy Morse; PERCUSSION: William Trigg, Steve Bartosik, Maya Gunji, David Yee; BASS: Ray Kilday; GUITARS: Robin Polseno, David Serva, Cherie Rosen.

Broadway reviews were bad.

After Broadway. ROYAL ALEXANDRA THEATRE, Toronto, 1993. *Cast:* QUIXOTE: Michael Burgess; ALDONZA: Susan Gilmour (Mrs. Burgess in real life).

TOUR. Opened in 8/96, in Chattanooga. *Cast:* QUIXOTE: Robert Goulet; SANCHO: Darryl Ferrera; CAPTAIN: Michael Licata; ALDONZA: Susan Hoffman; INNKEEPER: William Parcher, *Jack Dabdoub* (from 2/97); CARRASCO: Ian Sullivan; PADRE: David Wasson; ANTONIA: Linda Cameron.

El hombre de la Mancha. Opened at the LOPE DE VEGA THEATRE, Madrid, on 11/13/97. Spain's most successful musical of the time. The Lope de Vega had been a movie house for ten years, then it was renovated as a theatre for musicals and dance. This was the production that re-opened it. PRESENTED BY Luis Ramirez; ADAPTED INTO SPANISH BY: Ignacio Artime; DIRECTOR: Mario Gas; SETS: Gustavo Tambascio; MUSICAL DIRECTOR: Santiago Perez. There was a cast recording. *Cast:* QUIXOTE: Jose Sacristain, Carlos Marin (Fridays & Saturdays); SANCHO:

Juan Manuel Cifuentes; ALDONZA: Paloma San Basilio. On 8/20/98 Mitch Leigh attended, as an invited guest of the producer. Mr. Leigh hoped to bring it to Broadway for five weeks, at the Marquis. It would have been the first American-originated musical to play Broadway in a language other than English. But it never happened. A tour began in 6/98.

GOODSPEED OPERA HOUSE, Conn. (where it all began), 4/28/00–7/1/00. Previews from 4/7/00. DIRECTOR: Gerald Gutierrez; CHOREOGRAPHER: Ramon Oller; SETS: John Lee Beatty; COSTUMES: Catherine Zuber & Fabio Toblini; LIGHTING: Pat Collins; SOUND CONSULTANT: Tony Meola; MUSICAL DIRECTOR: Michael O'Flaherty; ORCHESTRATIONS: Christopher Jahnke. *Cast:* QUIXOTE: Shawn Elliott, *Bill Nolte*; ALDONZA: Nancy Ticotin; SANCHO: Stephen Mo Hanan; INNKEEPER: Don Mayo; CARRASCO: Brent Black; ANTONIA: Michelle Carr; PADRE: Joseph Dellger.

429. *Man of La Mancha* (2002 Broadway revival)

Before Broadway. The revival was announced on 4/19/02. On 6/6/02 Mary Elizabeth Mastrantonio and Ernie Sabella were announced in their roles. Rehearsals began in 8/02. The show tried out 10/8/02–11/10/02, at the National Theatre, Washington, DC (it was going to try out in Boston before Washington, but the Boston gig was canceled). On 10/15/02 it was announced that choreographer Richard Amaro had left for family reasons, and that Luis Perez had taken over. Broadway previews began at the 11/23/02 matinee (put back from 11/19/02).

The Broadway Run. MARTIN BECK THEATRE, 12/5/02–8/31/03. 16 previews from 11/23/02. 304 PERFORMANCES. PRESENTED BY David Stone, Jon B. Platt, Susan Quint Gallin & Sandy Gallin, Seth M. Siegel, and USA Ostar Theatricals, in association with Mary Lu Roffe, Clear Channel Entertainment, Michael Fuchs, JAM Theatricals, Ronald Lee, Paul Libin, Magic Entertainment, James L. Nederlander, James M. Nederlander, Scott Nederlander, Marc Platt, Jonathan Reinis, The Road Company, and Allen Spivak; MUSIC: Mitch Leigh; LYRICS; Joe Darion; BOOK: Dale Wasserman; BASED ON the novel by Cervantes; DIRECTOR: Jonathan Kent; CHOREOGRAPHER: Luis Perez; SETS/COSTUMES: Paul Brown; LIGHTING: Paul Gallo; SOUND: Tony Meola; MUSICAL DIRECTOR: Robert Billig; ORIGINAL ORCHESTRATIONS: Music Makers; ORIGINAL DANCE MUSIC ARRANGEMENTS: Neil Warner; NEW DANCE MUSIC ORCHESTRATIONS: Brian Besterman; NEW DANCE MUSIC ARRANGEMENTS: David Krane; NEW CAST RECORDING on RCA Victor, recorded at Right Track Recording, Manhattan, on 11/14/03, before Broadway previews had even started, and was released 1/7/03; PRESS: The Publicity Office; CASTING: Bernard Telsey; GENERAL MANAGERS: EGS; COMPANY MANAGER: Penelope Daulton; PRODUCTION STAGE MANAGER: Mahlon Kruse; STAGE MANAGERS: Michael John Egan & Bernita Robinson. *Cast:* OPENING DANCER: Wilson Mendieta; OPENING SINGER: Olga Merediz; CERVANTES/DON QUIXOTE: Brian Stokes Mitchell (1) ☆; CAPTAIN OF THE INQUISITION: Frederick B. Owens; SANCHO PANZA: Ernie Sabella (3) ☆; GOVERNOR/INNKEEPER: Don Mayo (6); DUKE/DR. CARRASCO: Stephen Bogardus (5); ALDONZA/DULCINEA: Mary Elizabeth Mastrantonio (2) ☆ (until 6/29/03), *Marin Mazzie* (from 7/1/03); (SEVEN) MULETEERS: QUITO: Andy Blankenbuehler; TENORIO: Timothy J. Alex; JUAN: Thom Sesma; PACO: Dennis Stowe; ANSELMO: Bradley Dean; PEDRO, HEAD MULETEER: Gregory Mitchell; JOSE: Wilson Mendieta; MARIA, INNKEEPER'S WIFE: Michelle Rios; FERMINA: Lorin Latarro; ANTONIA: Natascia Diaz; PADRE: Mark Jacoby (4); HOUSEKEEPER: Olga Merediz; BARBER: Jamie Torcellini; GUARDS: John Herrera & Jimmy Smagula; GYPSY DANCERS: Lorin Latarro & Andy Blankenbuehler; PRISONER: Allyson Tucker; ON-STAGE GUITARIST: Robin Polseno. *Understudies:* Sancho: Jimmy Smagula & Jamie Torcellini; Captain: Timothy J. Alex, Dennis Stowe; Quixote/Cervantes: Bradley Dean & John Herrera; Aldonza/Dulcinea: Natascia Diaz & Allyson Tucker; Padre: Bradley Dean & Jimmy Smagula; Antonia: Lorin Latarro & Allyson Tucker; Duke/Carrasco: John Herrera & Thom Sesma; Governor/Innkeeper: John Herrera & Frederick B. Owens; Fermina/Maria: Jamie Karen; Barber: Carlos Lopez & Jimmy Smagula; Housekeeper: Michelle Rios &

Allyson Tucker. *Swings:* Jamie Karen, Carlos Lopez, Richard Montoya, *Kristine Bendul. Orchestra:* LEAD TRUMPET: Wayne duMaine; TRUMPET: John Dent; TROMBONE: Dale Kirkland; BASS TROMBONE: Douglas Purviance; FRENCH HORNS: Patrick Milando & Eva Conti; FLUTE: Kathleen Nester; OBOE: Blair Tindall; CLARINET: Lino Gomez; BASSOON: Braden Toan; DRUMS: Steve Bartosik; BASS: Randall Landau; GUITARS: Robin Polseno & Cherie Rosen; PERCUSSION: David Yee; TYMPANI: Michael Hinton. "Man of La Mancha" ("I, Don Quixote") (Don Quixote & Sancho), "It's All the Same" (Aldonza & Muleteers), "Dulcinea" (Don Quixote & Muleteers), "I'm Only Thinking of Him" (Antonia, Housekeeper, Padre), "We're Only Thinking of Him" (Carrasco, Antonia, Padre, Housekeeper), "The Missive" (Sancho), "I Really Like Him" (Sancho), "What Does He Want of Me?" (Aldonza), "Little Bird, Little Bird" (Anselmo, Pedro, Muleteers), "Barber's Song" (Barber), "Golden Helmet of Mambrino" (Don Quixote, Sancho, Barber, Padre, Muleteers), "To Each His Dulcinea (To Every Man His Dream)" (Padre), "The Impossible Dream" ("The Quest") (Don Quixote), "The Combat" (Don Quixote, Aldonza, Sancho, Muleteers), "The Dubbing"/"Knight of the Woeful Countenance" (Innkeeper, Don Quixote, Aldonza, Sancho), "The Abduction" (Aldonza, Muleteers, Fermina), "The Impossible Dream" ("The Quest") (reprise) (Don Quixote), "Man of La Mancha" ("I, Don Quixote") (reprise) (Don Quixote), "Gypsy Dance" (Don Quixote, Sancho, Gypsy Dancers, Muleteers), "Aldonza" (Aldonza), "A Little Gossip" (Sancho), "Dulcinea" (reprise) (Aldonza), "The Impossible Dream" ("The Quest") (reprise) (Don Quixote & Aldonza), "Man of La Mancha" ("I, Don Quixote") (reprise) (Don Quixote, Sancho, Aldonza), "The Psalm" (Padre), Finale (Company).

Reviews were very good. The name of the Martin Beck changed to the Al Hirschfeld Theatre, or more popularly the Hirschfeld, on 6/23/03. The show missed the 8/14/03 performance due to the big New York power blackout, but made up the performances by closing after the evening performance rather than the matinee. It received Tony Nominations for revival of a musical, and for Brian Stokes Mitchell and Mary Elizabeth Mastrantonio.

430. *Maria Golovin*

Italian veteran Donato has lost his sight three years earlier, and now lives in a villa with his mother and Agata, a housekeeper who is secretly in love with him. They rent out the upstairs apartment to Maria, who has a cook, chauffeur, three maids and a tutor, Dr. Zuckertanz, for her young son Trottolo. Maria's husband has been a prisoner of war for four years, and she hasn't heard from him all winter. Maria and Donato become involved, and this upsets Agata. It also upsets Donato, because Maria lies about her old flame Aldo in order to protect Donato. The show is full of passion and torment, lies and destructive, insane love. A prisoner of war escapes and hides out in the house. Then Maria's husband is released. Donato thinks he has shot Maria, to save her from being another man's, and he and his mother prepare to leave the country, watched by Maria.

Before Broadway. It was originally commissioned as a TV production by NBC's *Opera Theatre,* but instead it premiered at the U.S. Pavilion of the Brussels World Fair, on 8/20/58. PRESENTED BY Samuel Chotzinoff. It had the same cast as for Broadway, except ZUCKERTANZ: Herbert Handt. It had the same basic crew.

The Broadway Run. MARTIN BECK THEATRE, 11/5/58–11/8/58. 5 PERFORMANCES. PRESENTED BY David Merrick and NBC, in association with Byron Goldman; MUSIC/LYRICS/BOOK/DIRECTOR: Gian-Carlo Menotti; SETS: Rouben Ter-Arutunian; COSTUMES: Helene Pons; LIGHTING: Charles Elson; MUSICAL DIRECTOR: Herbert Grossman; CAST RECORDING on RCA. This recording had the same cast as Broadway, except Genia Las as Agata; PRESS: Harvey Sabinson & David Powers; GENERAL MANAGER: Jack Schlissel; COMPANY MANAGER: Arthur Klein; PRODUCTION STAGE MANAGER: Richard Evans; STAGE MANAGER: Tom Brennan. *Cast:* DONATO: Richard Cross (2); AGATA: Ruth Kobart; DONATO'S MOTHER: Patricia Neway (3); DR. ZUCKERTANZ: Norman

Kelley; MARIA GOLOVIN: Franca Duval (1); TROTTOLO: Lorenzo Muti; THE PRISONER OF WAR: William Chapman (4); SERVANT: John Kuhn. *Act I*: *Scene 1* The living room of a villa in Northern Italy; soon after the end of World War II; early spring; *Scene 2* The living room; a month later. *Act II*: *Scene 1* The terrace of the villa; three months later; midsummer; late afternoon; *Scene 2* The villa; later that day. *Act III*: *Scene 1* The living room; afternoon, early fall; *Scene 2* The terrace; in the evening, a week later; *Scene 3* The villa; past midnight, the same day.

Broadway reviews were divided. There were doubts at the time, and those doubts remain today, as to whether this should be classified as a musical or not. It was Gian-Carlo Menotti's last Broadway show.

After Broadway. CITY CENTER, NYC, 3/30/59–4/23/59. 2 PERFORMANCES IN REPERTORY. PRESENTED BY the New York City Opera Company; DIRECTOR: Kirk Browning; SETS: Rouben Ter-Arutunian; COSTUMES: Ruth Morley; LIGHTING: Lee Watson; CONDUCTOR: Herbert Grossman. **Cast:** DONATO: Richard Cross; AGATA: Regina Sarfaty; MOTHER: Patricia Neway; ZUCKERTANZ: Norman Kelley; MARIA: Ilona Kombrink; TROTTOLO: Craig Sechler; PRISONER OF WAR: Chester Ludgin. NBC's *Opera Theatre* televised this production.

431. *Marie Christine*

A quasi-operatic version of *Medea*. The time moves from the present to the past, or future. The prelude is set in a women's prison in Chicago, in 1899. Louisiana Creole girl Marie Christine is questioned by three prisoners, and she recounts her story, first about her mother, her African heritage and voudon magic, and of Blue Rose Park, on the shore of Lake Pontchartrain. She meets Dante, a sea captain from Chicago whose ship is stranded in Biloxi, and who came to New Orleans to settle a score with a ship's owner. Marie Christine's brothers are Jean, a lawyer, engaged to very proper Beatrice, and Paris, a bon vivant. Marie Christine's servants are scandalized by her affair with a white man, and her brothers demand that she end it. However, she is pregnant; Dante, unaware, prepares to go to Chicago, but only after Marie Christine has caught him flirting with Lisette, who is put under a paralyzing spell by Marie Christine. Dante returns for Marie Christine, and Jean and Paris beat him up. Marie Christine stabs Paris to death; she and Dante flee on his ship. He learns she is pregnant. They spend five years sailing up and down the Atlantic Seaboard; they have two sons, and they all settle in Chicago, and Dante pursues his political ambitions. Magdalena, a saloon owner, entertains the patrons, who include Dante and his mentor, political boss Gates. Dante is running for City Alderman. He has abandoned Marie Christine and is engaged to Helena. Marie Christine kills Helena on her wedding night, and her own children so that Dante will not get them.

Before Broadway. On 3/20/98 it was announced that it would play on Broadway. By 10/98 it was strongly being touted that the star would be Audra McDonald (the writers had Miss McDonald in mind when they wrote it). Miss McDonald was also in two workshops of the musical produced by Graciela Daniele and Jules Fisher. She was finally announced on 5/10/99. On 5/12/99 Mary Testa was announced in her role, and 6/7/99 Darius de Haas in his. Anthony Crivello was rumored as co-star from 7/22/99, and on 9/15/99 Kim Huber was announced in her role. Broadway previews began on 10/28/99 (put back from mid–October). The opening date was put back from 11/99 to 12/2/99.

The Broadway Run. VIVIAN BEAUMONT THEATRE, 12/2/99–1/9/00. 39 previews from 10/28/99. 44 PERFORMANCES. PRESENTED BY Lincoln Center Theatre; MUSIC/LYRICS: Michael John La Chiusa; BASED LOOSELY ON *Medea*, by Euripides; DIRECTOR/CHOREOGRAPHER: Graciela Daniele; SETS: Christopher Barreca; COSTUMES: Toni-Leslie James; LIGHTING: Jules Fisher & Peggy Eisenhauer; SOUND: Scott Stauffer; MUSICAL DIRECTOR: David Evans; ORCHESTRATIONS: Jonathan Tunick; CAST RECORDING on RCA, made on 12/6/99, and released on 4/18/00;

PRESS: Philip Rinaldi, Miller Wright, James A. Babcock; CASTING: Alan Filderman; GENERAL MANAGER: Steven C. Callahan; COMPANY MANAGER: Susan Sampliner; STAGE MANAGER: Arturo E. Porazzi; ASSISTANT STAGE MANAGERS: Alexis Shorter & Casey Aileen Rafter. **Cast:** PRISONER # 1: Jennifer Leigh Warren; PRISONER # 2: Andrea Frierson Toney; PRISONER # 3: Mary Bond Davis; MARIE CHRISTINE L'ADRESE: Audra McDonald, Sherry D. Boone (at Wednesday & Saturday matinees); MARIE CHRISTINE'S MOTHER: Vivian Reed; SERPENT: Donna Dunmire; DANTE KEYES: Anthony Crivello; CELESTE, A MAID: Lovette George; OZELIA, A MAID: Rosena M. Hill; JEAN L'ADRESE: Keith Lee Grant; PARIS L'ADRESE: Darius de Haas; LISETTE, MARIE CHRISTINE'S MAID: Kimberly JaJuan; JOACHIM, A VALET: Andre Garner; OSMOND, A VALET: Jim Weaver; MONSIEUR ST. VINSON: Jim Weaver; MONSIEUR ARCHAMBAUD: Andre Garner; BEATRICE, JEAN'S FIANCEE: Joy Lynn Matthews; CHILDREN: Powers Pleasant, Zachary Thornton, Joshua Walter; MAGDALENA: Mary Testa; PETAL, MAGDALENA'S "DAUGHTER:" Janet Metz; DUCHESS, MAGDALENA'S "DAUGHTER:" Kim Huber; GATES: Shawn Elliott; BARTENDER: Peter Samuel; BAR PATRON: Michael Babin; LEARY: Michael McCormick; MCMAHON: Mark Lotito; ESAU PARKER: Peter Samuel; OLIVIA PARKER: Janet Metz; GRACE PARKER: Kim Huber; OLD DANTE: Michael Babin [role cut during previews]; HELENA, GATES' DAUGHTER: Donna Dunmire; CHAKA (DRUMS): David Pleasant; ENSEMBLE: Franz C. Alderfer, Ana Maria Andricain, Michael Babin, Brent Black, Donna Dunmire, Andre Garner, Lovette George, Rosena M. Hill, Kim Huber, Mark Lotito, Joy Lynn Matthews, Michael McCormick, Janet Metz, Monique Midgette, Peter Samuel, Jim Weaver. **Understudies:** St. Vinson/Archambaud/Valets: Franz C. Alderfer; Helena/Daughters: Ana Maria Andricain; McMahon: Michael Babin; Dante/Bartender: Brent Black; Paris: Andre Garner; Beatrice: Lovette George; Lisette: Rosena M. Hill; Mother: Joy Lynn Matthews; Gates: Michael McCormick; Magdalena: Janet Metz; Maids: Monique Midgette; Leary: Peter Samuel; Jean: Jim Weaver; Prisoners: Lovette George, Joy Lynn Matthews, Monique Midgette. **Orchestra:** KEYBOARDS: David Evans & Lawrence Yurman; WOODWINDS: Steven Kenyon, John Moses, Richard Heckman, John Winder; TRUMPETS: Brian O'Flaherty & Kamau Adilifu; FRENCH HORNS: Peter Gordon & Janet Lantz; VIOLINS: Robert Lawrence & Maura Giannini; VIOLA: Kenneth Burward-Hoy; CELLO: Scott Ballantyne; BASS: Raymond Kilday; PERCUSSION: Raymond Grapppone & Lawrence Spivack; SYNTHESIZER: Lawrence Spivack. **Prelude**: A prison: "Before the Morning" (Women), "Mamzell' Marie" (Company), "Ton Grandpere est le Soleil" (Marie Christine's Mother). **Act I**: 1894 — A park on Lake Pontchartrain, outside of New Orleans; Marie Christine's home on Mandolin Street in New Orleans, and its interiors, as well as its garconniere and ballroom; A pier: "Beautiful" (Marie Christine), "Way Back to Paradise" (Marie Christine & Lisette), "The Map of Your Heart" (Paris, Jean, Marie Christine) [cut during previews], "Storm" (Dante) [added during previews], "To Find a Lover" (Marie Christine & Company), "Nothing Beats Chicago"/"Ocean is Different"/"Danced with a Girl" (Dante) [during previews "The Adventure Never Ends" preceded these three songs], "Tou Mi Mi" (Lisette), "Miracles and Mysteries" (Marie Christine's Mother & Prisoners), "I Don't Hear the Ocean" (Dante & Marie Christine), "Bird Inside the House" (Maids & Valets), "All Eyes Look Upon You" (Jean), "A Month Ago" (Maids), "Danced with a Girl" (reprise) (Dante), "We're Gonna Go to Chicago" (Dante & Marie Christine), "Dansez Calinda" (Lisette), "I Will Give" (Marie Christine & Prisoners), Finale of Act I (Paris & Company). **Act II**: 1899 — A saloon in the First Ward, Chicago; An alleyway; A small house and its interior; Interior of a church: Opening/"I Will Love You" (Prisoners, Dante, Marie Christine), "Cincinnati" (Magdalena & Daughters), "You're Looking at the Man" (Leary, McMahon, Dante, Company), "The Scorpion" (Dante & Marie Christine), "Lover Bring Me Summer" (Olivia & Grace), "Old Dante" (Old Dante) [cut during previews], "Tell Me" (Marie Christine), "Paradise is Burning Down" (Magdalena), "Prison in a Prison" (Marie Christine & Prisoners, Helena, Dante), "Better & Best" (Leary & McMahon), "Good Looking Woman" (Gates, Leary, McMahon), "No Turning Back" (Paris, Mother, Jean, Lisette), "Beautiful" (reprise) (Marie Christine), "A Lovely Wedding" (Magdalena), "I Will Love You" (reprise) (Marie Christine), "Your Name" (Dante), Finale of Act II (Women).

Reviews were divided, but mostly negative. It was going to be a limited run until 1/2/00, but extended until 1/9/00 (*Contact* was due into the Vivian Beaumont in March 2000). The show received Tony nominations for score, book, lighting, orchestrations, and for Audra McDonald.

432. *Marilyn: An American Fable*

Set between 1934 and 1962, in Hollywood and New York City. In the end Marilyn is happily reunited with Joe Di Maggio, and walks off into the sunset with the young Norma Jean. Throughout the play, Marilyn is shadowed by an awkward trio called "Destiny," which comments on her travails and urges her on to glory. This musical should not be confused with *Marilyn* (see appendix).

Before Broadway. During rehearsals Gerolyn Petchel was dismissed, and replaced by Alyson Reed. During Broadway previews director/choreographer Kenny Ortega was replaced by Thommie Walsh (as director) and Baayork Lee (as choreographer), neither of whom took credit; and 45 minutes of the play and several numbers were dropped. This was the scene-by-scene breakdown during previews. If any information is repeated in the actual Broadway scene-by-scene breakdown, then it is not given in this list. *Act I*: *Scene 1* A soundstage, Hollywoodland: "We Are the Ones;" *Scene 2* Under the Hollywood Hills; 1934–42: "Close the Door, Norma" (m/l: Beth Lawrence) (Destiny), "A Single Dream," "Jimmy Jimmy" (Destiny, Norma Jean, Babs, Jim, Pat, Ensemble), "Church Doors;" *Scene 3* The parachute factory; 1945: "Miss Parachute" (m/l: Beth Lawrence & Norman Thalheimer) (Photographer, Madge, Elda, Dottie, Ramona, Virginia); *Scene 4* Overseas: "The Golden Dream" (Soldier); *Scene 5* Agent's home, Hollywood: "Uh-Huh" (m/l: Beth Lawrence & Norman Thalheimer) (Agent); *Scene 6* Studio's executive office: *Scene 7* The soundstage; 1948–53: "Can't Keep My Heart from Racing" (m/l: Beth Lawrence) (Marilyn), "Money, Men and More" (m/l: Jeanne Napoli & Doug Frank) (Marilyn & Men); *Scene 8* A movie balcony; *Scene 9* The soundstage; 1955: "I'll Send You Roses" (m/l: Beth Lawrence & Norman Thalheimer) (Joe & Marilyn), "Church Doors" (reprise) (Destiny); *Scene 10* Marilyn's dressing-room; *Scene 11* Di Maggio's Restaurant: "I'll Send You Roses" (reprise) (Joe & Marilyn); *Scene 12* Premiere night: "It's a Premiere Night," "Stairway Leading Nowhere" (m/l: Jeanne Napoli & Doug Frank) (Marilyn). *Act II*: *Scene 1* Marilyn's bedroom: "We'll Help You Through the Night;" *Scene 2* Soundstage: "Shootin'" (m/l: Beth Lawrence & Norman Thalheimer) (Marilyn & Company), "Run Between the Raindrops," "You Are So Beyond;" *Scene 3* New York City; 1956–60: "In Disguise" (m/l: Doug Frank) (Marilyn, Arthur, Ensemble), "A Special Man" (m/l: Jeanne Napoli & Doug Frank), "Church Doors" (reprise); *Scene 4* New York penthouse: "Don't Hang up the Telephone" (Joe & Marilyn); *Scene 5* New York to Hollywood: "All Roads Lead to Hollywood;" *Scene 6* Soundstage: "My Heart's an Open Door," "Miss Bubbles," "A Single Dream" (reprise).

The Broadway Run. MINSKOFF THEATRE, 11/20/83–12/3/83. 35 previews. 16 PERFORMANCES. PRESENTED BY Malcolm C. Cooke, William May, Dolores Quinton, James H. Kabler III, Joseph DioGuardi, John (Rick) Ricciardelli, Arnold H. Bruck, Tom Kaye, Leo Rosenthal, Harper Sibley, June Curtis and Renee Blau, in association with Jerome Minskoff; MUSIC/LYRICS: various writers; BOOK: Patricia Michaels; DIRECTOR/CHOREOGRAPHER: Kenny Ortega; SETS: Tom H. John; COSTUMES: Joseph G. Aulisi; LIGHTING: Marcia Madeira; SOUND: T. Richard Fitzgerald; MUSICAL SUPERVISOR/MUSICAL DIRECTOR/VOCAL & ORCHESTRAL ARRANGEMENTS: Steven Margoshes; ORCHESTRATIONS: Bill Brohn; ADDITIONAL ORCHESTRATIONS/DANCE MUSIC ARRANGEMENTS: Donald Johnston; ADDITIONAL DANCE MUSIC ARRANGEMENTS: Ronald Melrose; PRESS: Shirley Herz Associates; CASTING: Julie Hughes & Barry Moss; GENERAL MANAGERS: Joseph P. Harris Associates; COMPANY MANAGER: Jean Rocco; PRODUCTION STAGE MANAGER: Steve Zweigbaum; STAGE MANAGER: Arturo E. Porazzi; ASSISTANT STAGE MANAGER: Sherry Cohen. *Cast*: YOUNG NORMA JEAN: Kristi Coombs; DESTINY: Peggie Blue, Michael Kubala, T.A. Stephens; NORMA JEAN/MARILYN MONROE: Alyson Reed (1); JIM DOUGHERTY: George Dvorsky;

BABS: Lise Lang [role cut during previews]; PAT: Debi Monahan; FACTORY GIRLS: MADGE: Dooba Wilkins; ELDA: Melissa Bailey; DOTTIE: Mary Testa; RAMONA: Deborah Dotson; VIRGINIA: Jodi Marzorati; PHOTOGRAPHER: James Haskins; SOLDIER: Mark Ziebell [role cut during previews]; SERVICEMEN: Gary-Michael Davies & Mark Ziebell; AGENT: Mitchell Greenberg; STUDIO HEAD: Alan North; DIRECTOR: Gary-Michael Davies; ASSISTANT DIRECTOR: Ty Crowley; CAMERAMAN: Ed Forsyth; HAIRDRESSER: Deborah Dotson; DESIGNER: Michael Rivera; HEDDA: Mary Testa; LOUELLA: Melissa Bailey; JOE DI MAGGIO: Scott Bakula; SIS: Lise Lang; TOMMY: Willy Falk; JUNIOR: Kevin Cort [role cut during previews]; COACH/COMPANION: Dooba Wilkins; ARTHUR MILLER: Will Gerard; STRASBERG: Steve Schochet; ACTING COACH: Ty Crowley; ENSEMBLE: Melissa Bailey, Eileen Casey, Andrew Charles, Kevin Cort, Ty Crowley, Gary-Michael Davies, Deborah Dotson, Mark Esposito, Ed Forsyth, Marcial Gonzalez, Christine Gradl, Marguerite Lowell, Jodi Marzorati, Debi Monahan, Michael Rivera, Steve Schochet, Mary Testa, Dooba Wilkins, Mark Ziebell. *Understudies*: Destiny: Deborah Dotson, Michael Rivera, Mark Ziebell; Young Norma Jean: Sarah Litzsinger; Norma Jean/Marilyn: Marguerite Lowell; Jim: James Haskins; Photographer: Andrew Charles; Agent/Studio Head: Steve Schochet; Babs/Sis: Christine Gradl; Tommy: Mark Ziebell; Joe: Gary-Michael Davies; Arthur: Mitchell Greenberg. *Swings*: Ivson Polk & Maryellen Scilla. *Act I*: *Scene 1* Under the Hollywood Hills; 1934–1942: "A Single Dream" (m/l: Jeanne Napoli & Doug Frank) (Young Norma Jean & Destiny), "Jimmy Jimmy" (m/l: Jeanne Napoli & Doug Frank) (Destiny, Norma Jean, Jim, Pat, Ensemble), "Church Doors" (m/l: Beth Lawrence & Norman Thalheimer) (Destiny); *Scene 2* The parachute factory; 1945: "Swing Shift" (m/l: Beth Lawrence & Norman Thalheimer) (Factory Girls); *Scene 3* Overseas: "The Golden Dream" (m/l: Beth Lawrence & Norman Thalheimer) (Jim & Servicemen); *Scene 4* Studio's executive office: "When You Run the Show" (by Beth Lawrence & Norman Thalheimer) (Studio Head & Agent); *Scene 5* The soundstage; 1948–1953: "Gossip" (by James Komack & Doug Frank) (Hedda & Louella), "Cold Hard Cash" (m: Wally Harper; l: David Zippel) (Marilyn & Men); *Scene 6* Outside the studio: "I'm a Fan" (m/l: Beth Lawrence & Norman Thalheimer) (Tommy & Sis); *Scene 7* The soundstage; 1955: "Finally" (m/l: Beth Lawrence & Norman Thalheimer) (Joe & Marilyn), "Church Doors" (reprise) (Destiny); *Scene 8* Marilyn's dressing room; *Scene 9* Di Maggio's restaurant; *Scene 10* Premiere night: "It's a Premiere Night" (m/l: Beth Lawrence & Norman Thalheimer) (Company), "A Single Dream" (reprise) (Marilyn). *Act II*: *Scene 1* Marilyn's bedroom: "We'll Help You Through the Night" (m/l: Jeanne Napoli, Dawsen & Turner) (Destiny); *Scene 2* Soundstage: "Run Between the Raindrops" (m/l: Jeanne Napoli & Gary Portnoy) (Marilyn), "You Are So Beyond" (m/l: Jeanne Napoli & Doug Frank) (Tommy); *Scene 3* New York City; 1956–1960: "Cultural Pursuits" (m/l: Doug Frank) (Marilyn, Arthur, Ensemble), "Church Doors" (reprise) (Destiny); *Scene 4* New York penthouse: "Don't Hang up the Telephone" (m/l: Jeanne Napoli & Gary Portnoy) (Joe); *Scene 5* New York to Hollywood: "All Roads Lead to Hollywood" (m/l: Beth Lawrence & Norman Thalheimer) (Marilyn & Company); *Scene 6* Soundstage: "My Heart's an Open Door" (m/l: Beth Lawrence & Norman Thalheimer) (Marilyn & Joe), "Miss Bubbles" (m/l: Jeanne Napoli, Doug Frank, Gary Portnoy) (Marilyn & Men's Ensemble), "The Best of Me" (m/l: Beth Lawrence & Norman Thalheimer) (Marilyn), "A Single Dream" (reprise) (Marilyn), Finale: "We Are the Ones" (m/l: Beth Lawrence & Norman Thalheimer) (Company).

Alyson Reed came in for good Broadway reviews. But that was it.

433. *Marinka*

After watching the 1937 movie, *Mayerling* at a drive-in, some schoolgirls are told by Bradley (the son of Rudolph's coachman) the true story of what happened in that tragedy of 1888, wherein Crown Prince Rudolph of Austria and his mistress, Baroness Vetsera (known as Marinka) both mysteriously died — or did they? This musical has them escaping to a farm in Connecticut. Lobkowitz is the elderly adviser to young Rudolph.

Before Broadway. Originally called *Song of Vienna*. It tried out at the National Theatre, Washington, DC, in 6/45. At that point Jerry Wayne was playing Rudolph. The roles of the Naval Lieutenant and Countess Huebner were not added to the cast until Broadway. Ethel Levey, who cameo'd as Madame Sacher, the famous cigar-smoking Austrian hotelier, was George M. Cohan's first wife.

The Broadway Run. Winter Garden Theatre, 7/18/45–9/29/45; Ethel Barrymore Theatre, 10/1/45–12/8/45. Total of 165 performances. Presented by Jules J. Leventhal & Harry Howard; Music: Emmerich Kalman; Lyrics: George Marion Jr.; Book/Book Directors: George Marion Jr. & Karl Farkas; Inspired by Claude Anet's book *Mayerling*; Director/Lighting: Hassard Short; Choreographer: Albertina Rasch; Sets: Howard Bay; Costumes: Mary Grant; Musical Director: Ray Kavanaugh; Orchestrations: Hans Spialek; Press: James D. Proctor & Frank Goodman; General Manager: Charles Mulligan; Stage Manager: Robert Barre; Assistant Stage Manager: Jack Leslie. **Cast:** Bradley: Romo Vincent (3); Nadine: Ruth Webb, *Ethel Madsen*; Countess von Diefendorfer: Elline Walther, *Helene Arthur*; Bratfisch: Romo Vincent (3); Crown Prince Rudolph: Harry Stockwell (2), *Jerry Wayne*; Count Lobkowitz: Taylor Holmes (5); Naval Lieutenant: Noel Gordon; Count Hoyos: Paul Campbell; Francis: Leonard Elliott (8), *Doodles Weaver*; Tilly: Ronnie Cunningham (9); Marinka: Joan Roberts (1), *Edith Fellows*; Madame Sacher: Ethel Levey (7); Countess Landovska: Luba Malina (4); Waiter: Jack Leslie; Lieutenant Baltatzy: Bob Douglas; Emperor Franz Josef: Reinhold Schunzel (6), *Taylor Holmes, John McKee*; Countess Huebner: Adrienne Gray, *Elline Walther*; Sergeant Negulegul: Michael Barrett; Lieutenant Palafy: Jack Gansert (10), *Charles Laskey*; Ladies of the Ensemble: Suzie Baker (*Doris Elaine Baker*), Ethel Madsen, Jane Riehl, Gloria A. Tromera, Elline Walther, Donna Gardner, Lois Eastman (dropped during the run); Gentlemen of the Ensemble: Jimmy Allison, Paul Campbell (dropped during the run), John "Jack" Cassidy, Richard Clemens, Edwin Craig, Noel Gordon, Lynn Alden, Vincent Henry; Dancing Girls: Tessie Carrano, Muriel Bruenig, Arline DuBois, Phoebe Engels, Marie Fazzin, Albertina Horstmann, Ann Hutchinson, Jeanne Lewis, Thea Lind, Judy Sargent, Natalie Kelpouska, Alla Shishkina, Aura Vainio, Betty Williams, Carol Keyser, Anna Scarpova, *Marina Lvova*; Dancing Boys: Stanley Zompakos, Robert Armstrong, Lee Michael (*Nicholas Beriozoff*), Edmund Howland, Ted Lund, George Albert Tomal, John Begg, Francisco Xavier Ortiz. **Act I: Scene 1** An open-air movie theatre in Connecticut; a June evening, 1945: "One Touch of Vienna" (Bratfisch & Girls); **Scene 2** Gardens of the Imperial Palace of Schoenbrunn; a summer night in 1888: Ballet (Tilly & Ballet Girls), "One Touch of Vienna" (reprise) (Rudolph) [added during the run], "The Cab Song" (Bratfisch, Tilly, Francis), "My Prince Came Riding" (Marinka & Debutantes) [during the run this number and "The Cab Song" were switched in order], "If I Never Waltz Again" (Marinka & Rudolph); **Scene 3** Bratfisch's cab: "The Cab Song" (reprise) (Tilly, Diefendorfer, Debutantes); **Scene 4** Living-room of the lodge at Mayerling: "Turn on the Charm" (Bratfisch), "I Admit" (Rudolph's Narrative) (Rudolph) [added during the run], "One Last Love Song" (Marinka & Rudolph); **Scene 5** A street in Vienna: "Old Man Danube" [based on "Ol' Man River" from *Show Boat*] (Bratfisch & Officers); **Scene 6** The Red Room of the Sacher Restaurant, Vienna: Hungarian Dance (Tilly, Palafy, Dancers), "Czardas" (Countess Landovska & Officers), "Sigh by Night" (Marinka & Rudolph); **Scene 7** The Gardens at Schoenbrunn, 1888: "One Last Love Song" (reprise) (Marinka & Rudolph), "Paletas" (dance) (Palafy & Dancers). **Act II: Scene 1** The Austro-Hungarian border; 1888; **Scene 2** Budapest—a corner of the Parade Grounds: "Treat a Woman Like a Drum" (Marinka, Tilly, Bratfisch, Francis, Palafy), Dance (Ballerinas & Sailors), "When I Auditioned for the Harem of the Shah" (Countess Landovska), "Song" (Rudolph) [added during the run], "Young Man Danube" (Francis, Tilly, Diefendorfer, Palafy, Ensemble); **Scene 3** Gardens of the Imperial Palace of Schoenbrunn: "Turn on the Charm" (reprise) (Marinka & Rudolph) [dropped during the run]; **Scene 4** Mayerling; a January evening, 1889: "Sigh by Night" (reprise) (Marinka & Rudolph); **Scene 5** An open-air movie theatre in Connecticut; a June evening, 1945: Finale (Marinka, Rudolph, Entire Company): a/ "One Last Love Song" (reprise); b/ "One Touch of Vienna" (reprise) [added during the run].

Broadway reviews were divided, mostly bad.

434. *Marlowe*

A rock musical, set in England in 1593. Marlowe, the playwright, is a 16th-century man with a 20th-century mind (so the musical says). Emelia is in love with him and Shakespeare, and is forced to live her life as a boy in order to act in 16th-century England. The story of this drama is essentially true and accurate, except for minor adjustments in time for dramatic purposes.

The Broadway Run. Rialto Theatre, 10/12/81–11/22/81. 8 previews from 10/7/81. 48 performances. A John Annunziato production, co-produced by Robert R. Blume, in association with Billy Gaff & Howard P. Effron, and presented by Tony Conforti; Music/Orchestrations: Jimmy Horowitz; Lyrics: Leo Rost & Jimmy Horowitz; Book: Leo Rost; Director/Choreographer: Don Price; Sets: Cary Chalmers; Costumes: Natalie Walker; Lighting: Mitch Acker & Rick Belzer; Sound: Peter Fitzgerald; Musical Supervisor: Larry Fallon; Musical Director: Kinny Landrum; Vocal Arrangements: Jimmy Horowitz & Patrick Jude; Choral Director: Billy Cunningham; Press: Max Eisen, Alan Eichler, Maria Somma; General Management: Weiler/Miller/Carrellas; Company Manager: Barbara Carrellas; Production Stage Manager: Alisa Adler; Stage Manager: Bo Metzler; Assistant Stage Manager: Tony Berk. **Cast:** Queen Elizabeth I: Margaret Warncke; Audrey Walsingham: Debra Greenfield; Captain Townsend: Steve Hall; Archbishop Parker: Raymond Serra (3); Richard Burbage: John Henry Kurtz; William Shakespeare: Lennie Del Duca Jr.; Emelia Bossano: Lisa Mordente (2) ✩; Christopher Marlowe: Patrick Jude (1) ✩; Ingram Frizer: Robert Rosen; Chorus: Kenneth D. Ard, Marlene Danielle, Renee Dulaney, Teri Gibson, Robert Hoshour, Diane Pennington, Caryn Richmond, Timothy Tobin. **Standby**: Marlowe/Frizer/Parker: James Sbano. **Understudies**: Emelia/Audrey: Diane Pennington; Shakespeare: Robert Hoshour; Queen: Teri Gibson; Burbage: Steve Hall; Townsend: Timothy Tobin. **Swings**: Kathy Jennings & Willie Rosario. **Band**: Piano: Kinny Landrum; Electric Keyboards: Don Rebic; Guitars: John Putnam & Bill Washer; Bass: Chico Rindner; Drums/Percussion: Frank Vilardi. **Act I: Scene 1** Queen Elizabeth's bedchamber; May 28, late morning; **Scene 2** Backstage at the Globe Theatre; a few hours later; **Scene 3** The Mall, near St. James's Palace; during the Jubilee Festival; **Scene 4** Sir Walter Raleigh's observatory; that evening; **Scene 5** The Privy Council Chamber, at St. James's Palace; May 30, morning. **Act II: Scene 1** Eleanor Bull's tavern at Deptford; May 30, early evening; **Scene 2** Deptford waterfront docks; May 30, later that evening; **Scene 3** The courtyard at St. James's Palace; a few days later. **Act I:** Prologue (Chroniclers), "Rocking the Boat" (Parker, Queen, Townsend, Chorus), "Because I'm a Woman" (Emelia, Shakespeare, Burbage), "Live for the Moment" (Marlowe & Company), "Emelia" (Shakespeare & Marlowe), "I'm Coming Round to Your Point of View" (Marlowe & Emelia), "The Ends Justify the Means" (Frizer & Audrey), "Higher than High" (Marlowe, Emelia, Burbage, Shakespeare, Chorus), "Rocking the Boat" (reprise) (Company). **Act II:** Act II Prologue (Chroniclers), "Christopher" (Emelia & Chorus), "So Do I" (Ode to Virginity) (Burbage & Chorus), "Two Lovers" (Emelia), "The Funeral Dirge" (Burbage, Emelia, Shakespeare, Frizer, Townsend, Queen), "Live for the Moment" (reprise) (Marlowe & Emelia), "Emelia" (reprise) (Marlowe & Emelia), "Can't Leave Now" (Marlowe), "Christopher" (reprise) (Emelia, Shakespeare, Company), "The Madrigal Blues" (Marlowe & Company).

Reviews were generally terrible. Lisa Mordente (Chita Rivera's daughter) was nominated for a Tony.

435. *Mask and Gown*

An intimate revue showcasing the talents of famous female impersonator T.C. Jones.

Before Broadway. Thomas Craig Jones, one of the most influential of all the drag artists (he was married to Connie Dickson), and famous for his Tallulah Bankhead and Bette Davis impersonations, was the number one nightclub performer in San Francisco when Leonard

Sillman invited him onto *New Faces of 1956*; that led to *Mask and Gown*.

The Broadway Run. JOHN GOLDEN THEATRE, 9/10/57–10/12/57. 39 PERFORMANCES. PRESENTED BY Leonard Sillman & Bryant Haliday; MUSIC/LYRICS: various writers; CONTINUITY: Ronny Graham & Sidney Carroll; CONCEIVED BY/DIRECTOR: Leonard Sillman; CHOREOGRAPHER: Jim Russell; LIGHTING: Lee Watson; MUSICAL DIRECTOR/ARRANGEMENTS: Dorothea Freitag; CAST RECORDING on RCA; PRESS: Bill Doll, Samuel Friedman, Lorella Val-Mery; PRODUCTION STAGE MANAGER: Peter Pell. **Cast:** Mr. T.C. Jones (1), Betty Carr, Gaby Monet, John Smolko, Rod Strong. **Accompaniment:** PIANOS: Arthur Siegel & Dorothea Freitag; DRUMS: Ralph Roberts. **Act I: Scene 1** "The Circus is Over" (m: Arthur Siegel; l: June Carroll) (John, with T.C., Betty, Gaby, Rod); **Scene 2** T.C. on T.C. (by Sidney Carroll) (T.C.); **Scene 3** T.C. on T.V. ("Your Money or Your Life") (by Ronny Graham) (T.C., with Betty, Gaby, John, Rod); **Scene 4** "Make Friends" (instrumental) (m: Arthur Siegel) (Betty, Gaby, John, Rod); **Scene 5** Catch (short bits by various composers) (T.C., Betty, Gaby, John, Rod); **Scene 6** "Hesitation Waltz" (instrumental) (m: Emile Waldteufel) (Betty & Rod); **Scene 7** "T.C. A Dance" ("Ten Cents a Dance," from *Simple Simon*) (m: Richard Rodgers; l: Lorenz Hart) (T.C.); **Scene 8** Bolero (instrumental) (m: Dorothea Freitag) (Gaby & John); **Scene 9** T.C. on Hollywood (by Leonard Sillman & Everett Marcy) (T.C. & John); **Scene 10** T.C. on Taps Topside ("Don't Give up the Ship," from the movie *Shipmates Forever*) (m: Harry Warren; l: Al Dubin) T.C., Betty, Gaby, John, Rod); **Scene 11** On Their Own: "House of Blue Lights" (m/l: Ronny Graham) (Gaby) [this was changed to "Shakin' the Blues Away" m/l: Irving Berlin], "Shangri-La" (m/l: Ronny Graham), "Speedy Gonzales" (m/l: Ronny Graham) (Betty) [this was changed to "Copper Mood" m/l: Mr. Graham) (Betty), "Chopin Waltz in E Minor" (Rod); **Scene 12** T.C. on Certain Singers (T.C., with Betty, Gaby, John, Rod): "Remind Me" (m: Jerome Kern; l: Dorothy Fields; from the movie *One Night in the Tropics*), "I Cover the Waterfront" (m: Johnny Green; l: Edward Heyman; from the movie of the same name), "How Did He Look?" (m: Abner Silver; l: Gladys Shelley), "New Sounds" (m/l: Ronny Graham). **Act II: Scene 1** Setting the Stage (m: Francesco Scarlatti) (Rod); **Scene 2** T.C.-on-Avon (idea conceived by T.C. Jones) (T.C., with Betty, Gaby, John, Rod): Ethel Merman as Juliet, Marilyn Monroe as Ophelia, Tallulah as Cleopatra, Mae West, Claudette Colbert or Ethel Barrymore as Kate, Bette Davis as Lady Macbeth, Judy Holliday as Portia, Katharine Hepburn as Rosalind; **Scene 3** "You Better Go Now" (m: Irvin Graham; l: Bickley Reichner; from *New Faces of 1936*) (T.C., with Betty, Gaby, John, Rod); **Scene 4** "I'll Be Seeing You" (m: Sammy Fain; l: Irving Kahal; from *Right This Way*) [this song was also used in *New Faces of 1956*]; **Scene 5** T.C. Himself.

Broadway reviews were not good.

After Broadway. TOUR. Opened on 7/21/58, at the Curran Theatre, San Francisco, and closed on 10/4/58, at the Great Northern Theatre, Chicago. The cast and crew were the same as for Broadway.

436. *Me and Bessie*

A musical evening; memories of Bessie Smith evoked in the story of her life, and in songs she sang, in a third-person concept stopping short of actual impersonation of the noted blues singer.

Before Broadway. The idea originated with Linda Hopkins and Mrs. Apostoleris (formerly Lee Rupe of the famous Specialty Records). The world premiere was at the MARK TAPER FORUM, Los Angeles, 10/3/74. 8 PERFORMANCES. It had the same cast, and the same basic crew as for the subsequent Broadway run, except SETS/LIGHTING: Donald Harris; COSTUMES: Terence Tam Soon. It ran again, at the same venue, 4/4/75. 35 PERFORMANCES. MUSICAL DIRECTOR: Tony Berg. In 6/75 it ran at the AMERICAN CONSERVATORY THEATRE, San Francisco.

The Broadway Run. AMBASSADOR THEATRE, 10/22/75–11/29/75; EDISON THEATRE, 12/3/75–12/5/76. Total of 453 PERFORMANCES. The Center Theatre Group/Mark Taper Forum & Lee Apostoleris production, PRESENTED BY Lee Apostoleris; WRITTEN & CONCEIVED BY: Will Holt & Linda Hopkins; DIRECTOR: Robert Greenwald; SPECIAL DANCE SEQUENCES: Lester Wilson; SETS: Donald Harris; COSTUMES: Pete Mene-

fee; LIGHTING: Tharon Musser; SOUND: James Travers; MUSICAL DIRECTOR: Howlett Smith; CAST RECORDING on Columbia; PRESS: The Merlin Group, *Les Schecter Associates*; GENERAL MANAGER: Emanuel Azenberg; PRODUCTION STAGE MANAGER: Martin Herzer; STAGE MANAGER: Bethe Ward, *Lani Sundsten*. **Cast:** BESSIE SMITH: Linda Hopkins (1) ✫; MAN: Lester Wilson (2), *Thomas M. Pollard* (from 11/17/75); WOMAN: Gerri Dean (3). **Standbys:** Man: Thomas M. Pollard, *Larry Low*; Woman: Alfre Woodard. **The Band:** PIANO: Howlett Smith; BASS: Bob Bushnell; DRUMS: Ray Mosca; TROMBONE: Dick Griffin; CLARINET/SAX: Lenny Hambro. **Act I:** "I Feel Good," "God Shall Wipe All Tears Away," "Moan, You Mourners," "New Orleans Hop Scop Blues," "Romance in the Dark" (m/l: Lil Green), "Preach Them Blues" (m/l: Bessie Smith), "A Good Man is Hard to Find" (m/l: Eddie Green), "T'aint Nobody's Bizness if I Do" (m/l: Porter Grainger, Clarence Williams, Graham Prince), "Gimme a Pigfoot" (m/l: Wesley Wilson), "Put it Right Here" (m/l: Porter Grainger), "You've Been a Good Ole Wagon" (m/l: J. Henry), "Trombone Cholly," "Jazzbo Brown," "After You've Gone" (m: Turner Layton; l: Henry Creamer). **Act II:** "There'll Be a Hot Time in the Old Town Tonight" (m/l: Joseph Hayden & Theodore H. Metz), "Empty Bed Blues" (m/l: J.C. Johnson), "Kitchen Man" (m: Alex Belledna; l: Andy Razaf), "Mama Don't 'Low," "Do Your Duty" (m/l: Wesley Wilson), "Fare Thee Well," "Nobody Knows You When You're Down and Out" (m/l: Jimmy Cox), "Trouble" (m/l: D. Akers), "The Man's All Right."

On Broadway it played first at the Ambassador, then, under the auspices of Norman Kean, moved to the Middle Broadway theatre the Edison, where, from 9/24/76 it ran alternately with the 1976 revival of *Oh! Calcutta!* until *Me and Bessie* closed. Broadway reviews were generally good, but reserved.

After Broadway. Tour. Opened on 2/1/77, at the Coconut Grove Playhouse, Miami. PRESENTED BY Norman Kean; LIGHTING: William H. Batchelder; PRESS: Les Schecter & Bill Miller; GENERAL MANAGERS: Maria Di Dia & Jim Fiore; COMPANY MANAGER: Doris Buberl; STAGE MANAGER: Sam Stickler. It had the same cast as for Broadway, except MAN: Thomas M. Pollard. On 3/7/77 the tour re-opened in Los Angeles.

437. *Me and Juliet*

The entire action takes place in and around the theatre where *Me and Juliet* is currently playing. The central story is the romance between chorus girl Jeanie and assistant stage manager Larry, but there is a fly in the ointment — the violently jealous, heavy-drinking electrician, Bob, who is also in love with Jeanie. Betty is determined to win the briskly efficient stage manager Mac, who has vowed never to fraternize with members of his own company. The on-stage romance is between a lad named Me and a lass named Juliet, which parallels the off-stage romances. At the end of Act I Bob drops a sandbag on Jeanie from high above the stage, but misses. In Act II Bob nearly ruins the show, and afterwards seeks out the lovers. There is a fight between him and Larry, and Larry knocks him out. Bob then finds that Larry and Jeanie have married secretly that day, and backs off. Mac is transferred to another show, and now feels able to go for Betty.

Before Broadway. It opened first in Boston, where Rodgers and Hammerstein asked Jerome Robbins to take over as choreographer (he refused). The numbers "Boss, May I Have a Raise?," "Wake Up, Little Theatre," "You're Not Living," and "Meat and Potatoes" were cut. "Me, Who Am I?" was also cut, but the music from it was used in the Opening of *Me and Juliet*. "You Never Had it So Good" was also cut, but was used later, in the 1996 production of *State Fair*. After Boston the show went to Broadway.

The Broadway Run. MAJESTIC THEATRE, 5/28/53–4/3/54. 358 PERFORMANCES. PRESENTED BY Richard Rodgers & Oscar Hammerstein II; MUSIC: Richard Rodgers; LYRICS/BOOK: Oscar Hammerstein II; DIRECTOR: George Abbott; CHOREOGRAPHER: Robert Alton; ASSISTANT CHOREOGRAPHER: Ernest O. Flatt; SETS/LIGHTING: Jo Mielziner; COSTUMES: Irene Sharaff; MUSICAL DIRECTOR: Salvatore Dell'Isola; VOCAL

& ORCHESTRAL ARRANGEMENTS: Don Walker; PRESS: Michel Mok & Peggy Phillips; COMPANY MANAGER: Maurice Winters; STAGE MANAGERS: Charles Atkin, Beau Tilden, James Hammerstein. *Cast:* GEORGE, 2ND ASSISTANT STAGE MANAGER: Randy Hall; SIDNEY, ELECTRICIAN: Edwin Philips; JEANIE, CHORUS SINGER: Isabel Bigley (1); HERBIE, CANDY COUNTER BOY: Jackie Kelk (6); TRIO: CHRIS, REHEARSAL PIANO PLAYER: Barbara Carroll; MILTON, DRUMMER: Herb Wasserman; STU, BASS FIDDLE PLAYER: Joe Shulman; MICHAEL, A CHORUS BOY: Michael King; BOB, ELECTRICIAN: Mark Dawson (5); LARRY, ASSISTANT STAGE MANAGER: Bill Hayes (2); MAC, STAGE MANAGER: Ray Walston (4); MONICA, CHORUS DANCER: Patty Ann Jackson; RUBY, COMPANY MANAGER: Joe Lautner; CHARLIE (ME), FEATURED LEAD: Arthur Maxwell; DARIO, CONDUCTOR: George S. Irving; LILY (JULIET), SINGING PRINCIPAL: Helena Scott; JIM (DON JUAN), PRINCIPAL DANCER: Bob Fortier; SUSIE (CARMEN), PRINCIPAL DANCER: Svetlana McLee; VOICE OF MR. HARRISON, PRODUCER: Henry Hamilton; VOICE OF MISS DAVENPORT, CHOREOGRAPHER: Deborah Remsen; HILDA, AN ASPIRANT FOR A DANCING PART: Norma Thornton; MARCIA, ANOTHER ASPIRANT FOR A DANCING PART: Thelma Tadlock; BETTY, SUCCESSOR TO SUSIE AS PRINCIPAL DANCER: Joan McCracken (3); BUZZ, PRINCIPAL DANCER: Buzz Miller; RALPH, ALLEY DANCER: Ralph Linn; MISS OXFORD, A BIT PLAYER: Gwen Harmon; SADIE, AN USHER: Francine Bond; MILDRED, ANOTHER USHER: Lorraine Havercroft; A THEATRE PATRON: Barbara Lee Smith; ANOTHER THEATRE PATRON: Susan Lovell; DANCING ENSEMBLE: Lance Avant, Francine Bond, Betty Buday, Grant Delaney, John George, Penny Ann Green, Lorraine Havercroft, Patty Ann Jackson, Helene Keller, Jack Konzal, Lucia Lambert, Harriet Leigh, Sonja Lindgren, Ralph Linn, Elizabeth Logue, Shirley MacLaine, Cheryl Parker, Eddie Pfeiffer, Augustin Rodriguez, Dorothy Silverherz, Bob St. Clair, Thelma Tadlock, Norma Thornton, Janyce Ann Wagner, Bill Weber, Rosemary Williams; SINGING ENSEMBLE: Adele Castle, Jack Drummond, John Ford, Henry Hamilton, Gwen Harmon, Richard Hermany, Warren Kemmerling, Michael King, Larry Laurence, Susan Lovell, Theresa Mari, Jack Rains, Georgia Reed, Deborah Remsen, Thelma Scott, Barbara Lee Smith. **Understudies**: Jeanie: Deborah Remsen; Larry: Michael King; Betty: Francine Bond; Mac: Larry Laurence; Bob: Warren Kemmerling; Herbie/Buzz: Ralph Linn; Charlie: Jack Rains; Lily: Georgia Reed; Jim: Lance Avant; Sidney: Jack Drummond; Ruby/Dario: Henry Hamilton; Susie: Thelma Tadlock. *Act I: Scene 1* Backstage: "A Very Special Day" (Jeanie & Trio), "That's the Way it Happens" (Jeanie & Trio), "That's the Way it Happens" (reprise) (Larry), Dance Impromptu (Chorus, George, Trio); *Scene 2* The orchestra pit: Overture to *Me and Juliet* (Dario & Orchestra); *Scene 3* First scene of *Me and Juliet*: Opening of *Me and Juliet* (Lily, Jim, Susie, Charlie), "Marriage-Type Love" (Charlie, Lily, Singers); *Scene 4* The light bridge: "Keep it Gay" (Bob & Chorus); *Scene 5* During the performance of *Me and Juliet*: "Keep it Gay" (reprise) (dance) (Jim & Dance Ensemble); *Scene 6* Backstage: "Keep it Gay" (reprise) (dance) (Betty, Buzz, Dance Ensemble), "The Big Black Giant" (Larry), "No Other Love" (Jeanie & Larry) [the big hit] [the melody had been used previously, as background for the "Beneath the Southern Cross" episode of the NBC-TV series *Victory at Sea*]; *Scene 7* The alley leading to the stage door: Dance (Ralph, Francine, Elizabeth), "The Big Black Giant" (reprise) (Ruby); *Scene 8* Betty's dressing room. "It's Me" (Betty & Jeanie); *Scene 9* The light bridge; *Scene 10* Night club scene in *Me and Juliet* and backstage: First Act Finale of *Me and Juliet* (Lily, Betty, Charlie, Jim, Jeanie, Chorus). *Act II: Scene 1* Downstairs lounge in the theatre: Intermission Talk ("The Theatre is Dying") (Herbie & Chorus); *Scene 2* The bar across the street: "It Feels Good" (Bob); *Scene 3* A second act sequence of *Me and Juliet*: Opening Sequence in Second Act of *Me and Juliet* (Charlie, Jim, Lily, Dancers), "The Baby You Love" (Lily & Dancers), "We Deserve Each Other" (Betty, Jim & Chorus); *Scene 4* Theatre manager's office: "I'm Your Girl" (Jeanie & Larry); *Scene 5* The orchestra pit: The change music of the last scene of *Me and Juliet* (Dario & Orchestra); *Scene 6* Last scene of *Me and Juliet*: Second Act Finale of *Me and Juliet* (Charlie, Lily, Betty, Jim, Chorus); *Scene 7* Backstage: Finale of Our Play (Entire Company). Reviews were not good.

After Broadway. TOUR. Opened on 4/7/54, at the Shubert Theatre, Chicago, and closed there, on 5/29/54. Reprising their Broadway roles were: Randy Hall, Edwin Philips, Michael King, Mark Dawson, Bill Hayes, Ray Walston, Joe Lautner, Arthur Maxwell, George S. Irving, Bob Fortier, Henry Hamilton, Isabel Bigley, Svetlana McLee, Thelma Tadlock, Joan McCracken. Also in the *Cast:* LILY: Shirley Jones; HILDA: Sonja Lindgren.

In 1954 there was rumor that Eddie Fisher and Debbie Reynolds would star in a 90-minute color TV special. This never happened.

MASTER THEATRE, NYC, 5/14/70–5/24/70. 14 PERFORMANCES. PRESENTED BY the Equity Library Theatre; DIRECTOR: Charles Willard; CHOREOGRAPHER: George Bunt; SETS: Jeffrey B. Moss; COSTUMES: Jay Liebman; LIGHTING: Edward Greenberg; MUSICAL DIRECTOR: Thom Janusz; PIANIST: John R. Williams; STAGE MANAGER: Peter Riegert. *Cast:* JEANIE: Susan Blanchard; LARRY: John Johann; BETTY: Patti Mariano; MAC: John Swearingen; BOB: Robert Berdeen.

YORK THEATRE COMPANY, 4/19/02–4/21/02. Part of the *Musicals in Mufti* series. DIRECTOR: Michael Montel. *Cast:* LARRY: Perry Laylon Ojeda; JEANIE: Jessica-Snow Wilson; BETTY: Danica Conners; BOB: Tim Warmen; ALSO WITH: Josh Prince.

438. *Me and My Girl*

Set in the late 1930s in and around Hareford Hall (in Hampshire), Mayfair, and Lambeth. Brash Cockney Bill is found to be the long lost 14th Earl of Hareford. The executors of the previous earl's will try to teach Bill aristocratic ways and insist that he give up Sally, a fishmonger's assistant. The story has a happy ending.

Before Broadway. In 1935 Lupino Lane created a character named Bill Snibson, and came up with the idea of doing a musical revolving around him. He hired Noel Gay to write the score and L. Arthur Rose & Douglas Furber to write the libretto. The new show, *Me and My Girl*, opened at the VICTORIA PALACE THEATRE, London, on 12/16/37. 1,646 PERFORMANCES. *Cast*: Lupino Lane, George Graves. This musical introduced the Lambeth Walk, a dance craze. The show was filmed in 1939. Lupino Lane toured with the show for years, and revived it in London in 1941, and at the VICTORIA PALACE THEATRE, 8/6/45–3/30/46. 304 PERFORMANCES. DIRECTOR: Lupino Lane. *Cast*: BILL: Lupino Lane; PARCHESTER: Wallace Lupino; GERALD: Vernon Kelso; TELEGRAPH BOY: Richard Lupino; BOB: Lauri Lupino Lane. The third London revival was at the WINTER GARDEN, 12/12/49–2/11/50. 75 PERFORMANCES. DIRECTOR: Lupino Lane; MUSICAL DIRECTOR: Harold Brewer. *Cast*: BILL: Lupino Lane; PARCHESTER: Cyril Smith; GERALD: Peter Lupino; SIR JOHN: Austin Melford; BOB: Peter Glaze; SALLY: Polly Ward.

Noel Gay's son, Richard Armitage (Noel Gay's right name was Reginald Armitage), re-presented his father's show at the ADELPHI THEATRE, LONDON, from 2/12/85. Stephen Fry and Mike Ockrent re-wrote the libretto, and two new Gay songs were included. Robert Lindsay and Emma Thompson played the leads. Robert Lindsay won an Olivier Award, as did the musical itself. The show ran eight years in London (3,303 PERFORMANCES), during which time it went to Broadway, and for a tour in Australia.

The Broadway Run. MARQUIS THEATRE, 8/10/86–12/31/89. 11 previews. 1,420 PERFORMANCES. PRESENTED BY Richard Armitage, Terry Allen Kramer, James M. Nederlander, Stage Promotions, Ltd. & Company; MUSIC: Noel Gay; ADDITIONAL MUSIC: Maurice Elwin; LYRICS/BOOK: L. Arthur Rose & Douglas Furber; ADDITIONAL LYRICS: Harry Graham & Ralph Butler; BOOK REVISION: Stephen Fry; CONTRIBUTOR TO THE BOOK REVISION/DIRECTOR: Mike Ockrent; CHOREOGRAPHER: Gillian Gregory; SETS: Martin Johns; COSTUMES: Ann Curtis; LIGHTING: Chris Ellis & Roger Morgan; SOUND: Tom Morse; MUSICAL DIRECTOR: Stanley Lebowsky; ASSOCIATE MUSICAL DIRECTOR: Thomas Helm; ORCHESTRATIONS/DANCE MUSIC ARRANGEMENTS: Chris Walker; PRESS: Jeffrey Richards Associates (including Ken Mandelbaum); CASTING: Howard Feuer; GENERAL MANAGER: Ralph Roseman; COMPANY MANAGER: Robb Lady; PRODUCTION STAGE MANAGER: Steven Zweigbaum; STAGE MANAGER: Arturo E. Porazzi; ASSISTANT STAGE MANAGER: Tracy Crum. *Cast:* LADY JACQUELINE CARSTONE: Jane Summerhays (5), *Dee Hoty* (from 2/23/88), *Lauren Mitchell* (from 9/26/89); THE HON. GERALD BOLINGBROKE: Nick Ullett (6), *Edward Hibbert* (from 10/87), *Nick*

Ullett (from 4/18/88); LORD BATTERSBY: Eric Hutson (12), *Herb Foster* (from 87–88), *Merwin Goldsmith* (from 87–88); LADY BATTERSBY: Justine Johnston (10), *Eleanor Glockner* (from 87–88); STOCKBROKERS: Cleve Asbury (*Bobby Longbottom* from 87–88), Randy Hills, Barry McNabb (*John MacInnis* from 87–88); FOOTMAN: Larry Hansen; HERBERT PARCHESTER: Timothy Jerome (7); SIR JASPER TRING: Leo Leyden (9), *J.B. Adams*; MARIA, DUCHESS OF DENE: Jane Connell (4), *Sylvia O'Brien* (from 1/31/89); SIR JOHN TREMAYNE: George S. Irving (3) ✩, *Jay Garner* (from 1/31/89); CHARLES HEATHERSETT, BUTLER: Thomas Toner (8); BILL SNIBSON: Robert Lindsay (1) ✩, *Jim Dale* (12/16/86–12/23/86), *Robert Lindsay, Jim Dale* (from 6/16/87), *James Brennan* (during Mr. Dale's vacation, 3/1/88–3/15/88), *Jim Dale, James Brennan* (from 1/31/89); SALLY SMITH: Maryann Plunkett (2) ✩, *Ellen Foley* (from 2/23/88), *Judith Blazer* (from 7/4/89); PUB PIANIST: John Spalla; MRS. WORTHINGTON-WORTHINGTON: Gloria Hodes; LADY DISS: Elizabeth Larner (11), *Donna Monroe* (from 87–88); LADY BRIGHTEN/LAMBETH TART: Susan Cella, *Ann Heinricher* (from 87–88); BOB BARKING: Kenneth H. Waller, *J.B. Adams* (from 87–88); TELEGRAPH BOY: Bill Brassea, *Jamie Torcellini* (from 86–87), *John M. Wiltberger* (from 87–88); MRS. BROWN: Elizabeth Larner, *Eleanor Glockner* (from 87–88); CONSTABLE: Eric Johnson, *John Jellison* (from 87–88); ENSEMBLE: Cleve Asbury, Bill Brassea (*Jamie Torcellini* from 86–87; *John M. Wiltberger* from 87–88), Jonathan Brody (gone by 87–88), Frankie Cassady (gone by 87–88), Susan Cella (*Ann Heinricher* from 87–88), Sheri Cowart, Bob Freschi (gone by 87–88), Ann-Marie Gerard (gone by 87–88), Larry Hansen, Michael Hayward-Jones (gone by 87–88), Ida Henry, Randy Hills, Gloria Hodes, K. Craig Innes (gone by 87–88), Eric Johnson (*John Jellison* from 87–88), Barry McNabb (*John MacInnis* from 87–88), Donna Monroe, Barbara Moroz, Cindy Oakes (gone by 87–88), William Ryall (gone by 87–88), John Spalla, Cynthia Thole, Mike Turner (by 87–88 he was known as Michael Turner Cline), Kenneth H. Waller (*J.B. Adams* from 87–88). 87–88 replacements: *Mark Agnes, Gail Benedict, Michael Duran, Nancy Hess, Kenneth Kantor, Wiley Kidd, Bobby Longbottom, Martin Van Treuren, Dana Walker*. **Standbys:** Bil/Gerald: James Brennan; Jacqueline: Gail Benedict. **Understudies:** Gerald: Larry Hansen; Sally: Sheri Cowart; Duchess: Justine Johnston; Sir John: Eric Hutson; Jacquie: Susan Cella; Jasper/Battersby/Heathersett: Kenneth H. Waller; Parchester: John Spalla; Lady Battersby: Elizabeth Larner; Mrs. Brown: Donna Monroe & Barbara Moroz; Lady Brighten/Lady Diss: Barbara Moroz; Constable: Michael Hayward-Jones; Barking: Jonathan Brody. **Swings:** Corinne Melancon & Tony Parise. **Act I: *Prologue*** Mayfair; ***Scene 1*** Hareford Hall, Hampshire: "A Weekend at Hareford" (Ensemble), "Thinking of No One but Me" (m: Gay; l: Furber) (Lady Jacquie & Gerald), "The Family Solicitor" (Parchester & Family), "Me and My Girl" (m: Gay; l: Furber) (Bill & Sally); ***Scene 2*** The kitchen: "An English Gentleman" (Heathersett & Staff); ***Scene 3*** The drawing-room: "You Would if You Could" (m: Gay; l: Furber) (Lady Jacquie & Bill), "Hold My Hand" (m: Elwin & Gay; l: Graham) [from the London production of *Hold My Hand*] (Bill, Sally, Dancers); ***Scene 4*** The Hareford Arms: "Once You Lose Your Heart" (m/l: Gay) (Sally); ***Scene 5*** The terrace: "Preparation Fugue" (Company), "The Lambeth Walk" (m: Gay; l: Furber) (Bill, Sally, Company). **Act II: *Scene 1*** The garden at Hareford Hall; the next afternoon: "The Sun Has Got His Hat On" (m: Gay; l: Butler) (Gerald, Lady Jacquie, Ensemble) [not in the 1937 London production], "Take it on the Chin" (m: Gay; l: Butler) (Sally); ***Scene 2*** The library: "Once You Lose Your Heart" (reprise) (Sally), "Song of Hareford" (Duchess, Bill, Ensemble), "Love Makes the World Go Round" (m/l: Gay) [from the London production of *These Foolish Things*] (Bill & Sir John); ***Scene 3*** Lambeth: "(I'm) Leaning on a Lamp-Post (at the Corner of the Street)" (m/l: Gay) [from the movie *Feather Your Nest*] (Bill & Ensemble) [not in the 1937 London production]; ***Scene 4*** Hareford Hall: Finale (Company).

Note: all musical numbers have music by Noel Gay & lyrics by L. Arthur Rose & Douglas Furber, unless otherwise noted.

Broadway reviews were very good. The show won Tony Awards for choreography, and for Robert Lindsay and Maryann Plunkett. It was also nominated for musical, score, book, direction of a musical, sets, costumes, and for George S. Irving, Timothy Jerome, Jane Summerhays, and Jane Connell. On 1/19/88 the Broadway cast complained to Equity about the freezing working conditions at the new Marquis Theatre (this

show was the first at that theatre). Jim Dale took the first week of 3/88 off as a vacation, but the *New York Times* ads did not tell readers this.

After Broadway. TOUR. Opened on 10/6/87, in San Francisco, and closed in 1989. PRESENTED BY the Noel Gay Organisation, Terry Allen Kramer, James M. Nederlander, and Strada Entertainment; MUSICAL DIRECTORS: Michael D. Biagi & Robert Fisher. **Cast**: BILL: Tim Curry, *James Brennan* (from 10/4/88), *James Young* (from 1/24/89); LADY JACQUELINE: Susan Cella, *Barbara Passolt*; BOLINGBROKE: Nick Ullett, *David Cromwell*; SIR JOHN: Barrie Ingham, *Gary Gage* (from 10/4/88); LADY BATTERSBY: Evelyn Page; LORD BATTERSBY: Ralph Farnworth; PARCHESTER: Walter Charles, *Erick Devine*; TRING: Gordon Connell, *Louis S. Crume*; SALLY: Donna Bullock, *Sheri Cowart* (from 10/4/88); PIANIST: Brad Moranz, *Gregg Kirsopp*; CLARA DAMMING: Lou Williford; TELEGRAPH BOY: Jamie Torcellini, *Don Johanson*; CONSTABLE: Michael Hayward-Jones; MARIA: Ursula Smith, *Lenka Peterson, Sylvia O'Brien*; CHORUS: Cleve Asbury, Gary Barker, Dan Mojica, Ann Neiman, Tina Parise, Linda Paul.

PAPER MILL PLAYHOUSE, New Jersey, 1990. DIRECTOR/CHOREOGRAPHER: Tony Parise; SETS: Michael Anania. **Cast**: BILL: James Brennan; LADY JACQUELINE: Susan Cella; MARIA: Jane Connell; PARCHESTER: John Jellison; SALLY: Judy Blazer; TRING: Leo Leyden; BARKING: Leslie Feagan; TREMAYNE: Thomas Toner; BUTLER: Michael Mulheren.

GOODSPEED OPERA HOUSE, Conn., 5/28/03–7/5/03. Previews from 4/25/03. PRESENTED BY Michael P. Price, for Goodspeed; DIRECTOR: Scott Schwartz; SETS: Anna Louizos; COSTUMES: David C. Woolard; MUSICAL DIRECTOR: Michael O'Flaherty. **Cast**: BILL: Hunter Bell; SALLY: Becky Watson; DUCHESS: Me'l Dowd; LADY JACKIE: Michele Ragusa; HEATHERSETT: Stephen Temperley; BOLINGBROKE: Ian Knauer; PARCHESTER: Ron Wisniski; TREMAYNE: Bob Dorian.

There was to have been a production at the New London Theatre, London, 5/11/04 (previews from 4/29/04), to be presented by Alex Armitage, directed by Rachel Kavanaugh, choreographed by Stephen Mear, and with sets by Peter McKintosh, but it was canceled.

BENEDUM CENTER, Pittsburgh, 8/3/04–8/8/04. PRESENTED BY the Pittsburgh CLO; DIRECTOR: Charles Repole; CHOREOGRAPHER: Alan Coats; MUSICAL DIRECTOR: Tom Helm. **Cast**: BILL: James Brennan; SALLY: Sutton Foster; SIR JOHN: Walter Charles; LADY JACKIE: Ann Kittredge; GERALD: John Hickok; HERBERT: Tim Jerome; MARIA: Eleanor Glockner.

439. *The Me Nobody Knows*

Set in a ghetto of New York. A 13-year-old boy tries heroin; another boy witnesses an elderly black alcoholic picked up by an ambulance; a youngster feels glad his baby brother died because now there'll be more food in the house; and other stories of ghetto life.

Before Broadway. After a tryout in a small theatre in TRENTON, NJ, it opened Off Broadway at the ORPHEUM THEATRE, 5/18/70, with a cast of 13 teenagers, and an ensemble of pros and non-pros. It had the same crew as for the subsequent Broadway run, except PRESS: Samuel J. Friedman, Rod Jacobsen, Jane Friedman. It had the same cast too, except for the understudies: Marion Ramsey, Roy Bailey, Dennis Johnson. It was reviewed that night, and reviews were very divided. It ran 208 PERFORMANCES, then a labor dispute between Actors Equity and Off Broadway theatre managers closed 16 shows, including this one on 11/15/70, and it moved to Broadway. It won Drama Desk and Obie Awards for best musical.

The Broadway Run. HELEN HAYES THEATRE, 12/18/70–8/28/71; LONGACRE THEATRE, 9/15/71–11/14/71. 7 previews. Total of 378 PERFORMANCES. PRESENTED BY Jeff Britton, in association with Sagittarius Productions (Edgar M. Bronfman & Henry S. White); MUSIC: Gary William Friedman; LYRICS: Will Holt (unless otherwise stated); BOOK: Robert H. Livingston & Herb Schapiro; ADDITIONAL LYRICS/ORIGINAL IDEA: Herb Schapiro; BASED ON the 1969 book of the same name, a collection of writings by New York City schoolchildren, edited by teacher Stephen M. Joseph, and subtitled *Voices from the Ghetto*. These kids were mostly blacks and latinos, aged 7–18, who attended public schools in such neighborhoods as Bedford — Stuyvesant, Harlem, Jamaica, Manhattan and the Youth House in the Bronx; ADAPTED BY: Robert H. Livingston & Herb Schapiro; DIRECTOR: Robert H. Livingston; CHOREOGRAPHER: Patricia Birch; SETS/LIGHTING: Clarke Dunham; COSTUMES: Patricia Quinn Stuart; MUSICAL DIRECTOR: Edward Strauss; ORCHESTRATIONS/MUSICAL ARRANGEMENTS: Gary William Friedman; CAST RECORDING on Atlantic; PRESS: Samuel J. Friedman & Louise Weiner Ment; CASTING: Erlinda Zetlin; GENERAL MANAGERS: Malcolm Allen & Jose Vega; PRODUCTION STAGE MANAGER: Martha Knight; STAGE MANAGERS: Jason Travis & G. Dean [i.e. Gerri Dean] (*Leanna Lenhart*). **Cast:** RHODA: Melanie Henderson (8), *Andrea Frierson*; LILLIAN: Laura Michaels (11), *Elaine Petricoff*; CARLOS: Jose Fernandez (6); LILLIE MAE: Irene Cara (4), *Rhonda Alfaro*; BENJAMIN: Douglas Grant (7), *Ralph Carter*; CATHERINE: Beverly Ann Bremers (3), *Julienne Ciukowski* (for 2 weeks); MELBA: Gerri Dean (5); LLOYD: Northern J. Calloway (1), *Damon Evans*; DONALD: Paul Mace (10), *Lenny Bari*; CLOROX: Carl Thoma (12); WILLIAM: Kevin Lindsay (9); NELL: Hattie Winston (2). **Standbys:** Roy Bailey, Lenny Bari, Edloe, Giancarlo Esposito, Elaine Petricoff, *Gerry Kirby, Danny Beard, Marley Sims*. **Orchestra:** SAX/ALTO FLUTE: Edward Daniels; FENDER BASS: Gary Newman; TRUMPET/FLUGELHORN: Richard Williams; DRUMS: James Firzsimon; GUITAR: Jack Cavali; ELECTRIC PIANO/ORGAN: Edward Strauss. **Act I:** "Dream Babies" (l: Herb Schapiro) (Melba), "Light Sings" (l: Herb Schapiro) (William & Company), "This World" (l: Herb Schapiro) (Company), "Numbers" (Company), "What Happens to Life" (Lillian & Lloyd), "Take Hold the Crutch" (Nell & Company), "Flying Milk and Runaway Plates" (Benjamin & Company), "I Love What the Girls Have" (Donald), "How I Feel" (Catherine & Carlos), "If I Had a Million (Dollars)" (Company). **Act II:** "Fugue for Four Girls" (Lillie Mae, Lillian, Catherine, Nell) (the lyric is the poem exactly as the children wrote it), "Rejoice" (Clorox) (the lyric is the poem exactly as the children wrote it), "Sounds" (Nell & Catherine), "The Tree" (Carlos), "Robert, Alvin, Wendell and Jo Jo" (Rhoda, Lillian, Lillie Mae, William), "Jail-Life Walk" (Donald, Lloyd, Clorox), "Something Beautiful" (Rhoda), "Black" (Benjamin, Clorox, Lillie Mae, Lloyd, Melba, Nell, Rhoda, William), "The Horse" (The White Horse) (Lloyd) (the lyric is the poem exactly as the children wrote it), "Let Me Come In" (Company), "War Babies" (Lloyd) (the lyric is the poem exactly as the children wrote it).

The show received Tony nominations for musical, score, lyrics, book, and direction of a musical.

After Broadway. TOUR. Opened on 2/8/71, at the Civic Theatre, Chicago. PRESENTED BY Jeff Britton; MUSICAL DIRECTOR: David Frank. **Cast:** RHODA: Trudy Bordoff; LILLIAN: Tricia Ann Smith; CARLOS: Joe Rifici; LILLIE MAE: Kelly Richardson; BENJAMIN: David Kruger; CATHERINE: Julienne Ciukowski; MELBA: Debra Kelly; LLOYD: Greg Sullivan; DONALD: Tony Michael Pann; CLOROX: Andre de Shields; WILLIAM: Marshaund Chandler; NELL: Jo Ann Brown.

TOUR. Opened on 10/19/71, at the Locust Street Theatre, Philadelphia, and closed there on 11/7/71. PRESENTED BY Moe Septee; MUSICAL DIRECTOR: Milton Setzer. **Cast:** RHODA: Angela Miller; LILLIAN: Shelley Russek; CARLOS: Jon Heron; LILLIE MAE: Toni Lund; BENJAMIN: Michael Malone; CATHERINE: Jill Streisant; MELBA: Judy Gibson; LLOYD: Danny Beard; DONALD: Bobby Lee; CLOROX: Andre de Shields; WILLIAM: Darius Smith; NELL: Louise Heath.

SOUTH STREET THEATRE, 4/5/84–4/15/84. 16 PERFORMANCES. Off Broadway revival. DIRECTOR: Robert H. Livingston; CHOREOGRAPHER: Rael Lamb; SETS/COSTUMES: John Falabella; LIGHTING: Jeff Davis; CONDUCTOR: Jefrey Silverman. **Cast:** RHODA: Sonia Bailey; LILLIAN: Tisha Campbell; CARLOS: Jose Martinez; LILLIE MAE: Kia Joy Goodwin; BENJAMIN: Donald Acree; CATHERINE: Jessie Janet Richards; MELBA: Pamela Harley; LLOYD: Jaison Walker; DONALD: Stephen Fenning; CLOROX: Keith Amos; NELL: Deborah Smith.

On 10/15/03 composer Gary William Friedman announced that after a workshop in Feb. or March 2004, there were plans for a Broadway revival in early 2004, at a small theatre such as the Helen Hayes or the Booth. Tara Fishman was to produce; Maurice Hines was to be director/choreographer; sets by Jerome Sirlin. However Maurice Hines was planning a hip-hop version, so the producer fired him, and canceled the workshops.

VINEYARD THEATRE, NYC, 1/20/05–1/21/05. Staged reading. PRESENTED BY Whitehorse Productions; DIRECTOR: Scott Schwartz. **Cast:** Brooke Moriber, Nicole Lewis, Orlando Torres, Ronny Mercedes, DeQuina Moore, Sabrina Reitman, Rydell Rollins, Chiarra Nivarra, Cedric Sanders, Utkarsh Ambudkar.

440. *Meet Me in St. Louis*

Set in and around the Smith family home (5135 Kensington Ave., St. Louis) from the summer of 1903 to the spring of 1904, and the opening of the Louisiana Purchase Exposition.

Before Broadway. The 1944 movie was directed by Vincente Minnelli. Hugh Martin & Ralph Blane composed only three songs for the film; the rest of the numbers were other people's standards. **Cast:** ESTHER: Judy Garland; TOOTIE: Margaret O'Brien; MRS. ANNE SMITH: Mary Astor; ROSE: Lucille Bremer; LUCILLE: June Lockhart; JOHN: Tom Drake; KATIE, THE MAID: Marjorie Main; GRANDPA: Harry Davenport; AGNES: Joan Carroll. In the summer of 1960 the MUNICIPAL OPERA IN ST. LOUIS mounted a musical staging of the movie. In 1984 Hugh Martin, Ralph Blane, and Hugh Wheeler began revising this stage production for Broadway, but it took a long time to get Ted Turner to give up the movie rights. Five years later it made it to Broadway. The production cost $5 million.

The Broadway Run. GERSHWIN THEATRE, 11/2/89–6/10/90. 16 previews. 253 PERFORMANCES. PRESENTED BY Brickhill — Burke Productions (Joan Brickhill & Louis Burke), Christopher Seabrooke, EPI Products; SONGS: Hugh Martin & Ralph Blane; BOOK: Hugh Wheeler; BASED ON the 1944 MGM movie *Meet Me in St. Louis*, which in turn was based on *The Kensington Stories* (in the *New Yorker*), by Sally Benson; DIRECTOR: Louis Burke; CHOREOGRAPHER: Joan Brickhill; ICE CHOREOGRAPHER: Michael Tokar; SETS/COSTUMES: Keith Anderson; LIGHTING: Ken Billington; SOUND: Alan Stieb & James Brousseau; ANIMATIONS: Michael Sporn; MUSICAL SUPERVISOR: Milton Rosenstock; MUSICAL DIRECTOR: Bruce Pomahac; ORCHESTRATIONS: Michael Gibson; DANCE MUSIC ARRANGEMENTS: James Raitt; VOCAL ARRANGEMENTS: Hugh Martin & Bruce Pomahac; CAST recording on DRG; PRESS: The Joshua Ellis Office; CASTING: Jay Binder; GENERAL MANAGEMENT: Weiler/Miller/Carrellas; PRODUCTION STAGE MANAGER: Robert Bennett; STAGE MANAGER: Jay Adler; ASSISTANT STAGE MANAGERS: Robin Rumpf & Jim Semmelman. **Cast:** LON SMITH: Michael O'Steen, *Christopher Scott*; RANDY TRAVIS: Brian Jay; KATIE, THE MAID: Betty Garrett (4) ✮; MOTORMAN: Jim Semmelman; TOOTIE SMITH: Courtney Peldon (6); MRS. SMITH: Charlotte Moore (3) ✮; GRANDPA PROPHATER: Milo O'Shea (2) ✮; ESTHER SMITH: Donna Kane (5); ROSE SMITH: Juliet Lambert; JOHN TRUITT: Jason Workman; AGNES SMITH: Rachael Graham; MR. ALONZO SMITH: George Hearn (1) ✮; WARREN SHEFFIELD: Peter Reardon, *Kevin Blair*; IDA BOOTHBY: Naomi Reddin; DOUGLAS MOORE: Gregg Whitney; EVE FINLEY: Shauna Hicks; DR. BOND: Gordon Stanley, *Jess Richards*; LUCILLE BALLARD: Karen Culliver, *Rebecca Baxter*; CLINTON A. BADGER: Craig A. Meyer; ENSEMBLE: Kevin Backstrom, Dan Buelow, Victoria Lynn Burton, Karen Culliver, Deanna Dys, H. David Gunderman, Shauna Hicks, K. Craig Innes, Brian Jay, Rachel Jones, Nancy Lemenager, Joanne McHugh, Frank Maio, Carol Lee Meadows, Craig A. Meyer, Christopher Lee Michaels, Ron Morgan, Georga L. Osborne, Rachelle Ottley, Christina Pawl, Naomi Reddin, Carol Schuberg, Jim Semmelman, Ken Shepski, Gordon Stanley, Sean Frank Sullivan, Cynthia Thole, Gregg Whitney, Kyle Whyte, Lee Wilson. **Understudies:** Father/Grandpa: Gordon Stanley; Mrs. Smith: Cynthia Thole; Katie: Georga L. Osborne; John/Motorman: Christopher Lee Michaels; Esther: Shauna Hicks; Tootie/Agnes: Victoria Lynn Burton; Rose/Lucille: Rachelle Ottley; Lon: H. David Gunderman; Warren: Sean Frank Sullivan; Douglas: Ken Shepski. **Orchestra:** KEYBOARDS: Stephen Bates; VIOLINS: Marilyn Reynolds, Katherine Livolsi, Sandra Billingslea, Andrew Stein, Melanie Baker; CELLI: Jeffrey Szabo & Garfield Moore; HARP: Susan Jolles; WOODWINDS: Seymour Red Press, Raymond Beckenstein, Dennis Anderson, Steven Boschi; TRUMPETS: Hollis Burridge, Laurie Frink, Kamau Adilifu; TROMBONES: Santo Russo & Earl McIntyre; FRENCH HORNS: Russell Rizner & Albert Richmond; GUITAR/BANJO: Andrew Schwartz; BASS: Ronald Raffio; DRUMMER: John

Redsecker; PERCUSSION: Eric Kivnick. *Act I*: Overture (Orchestra); *Scene 1* Street outside the Smith family home; summer 1903: "Meet Me in St. Louis" (m: Kerry Mills; orig l: Andrew Sterling; new l: Hugh Martin & Ralph Blane) (Ensemble); *Scene 2* Interior of the Smith home: "Meet Me in St. Louis" (reprise) (Grandpa & Tootie), "The Boy Next Door" (by Hugh Martin & Ralph Blane) (Esther), "Be Anything but a Girl" (Grandpa, Agnes, Tootie); *Scene 3* Lon's Princeton party: "Skip to My Lou" (traditional; new l: Hugh Martin & Ralph Blane) (Rose, Esther, Lon, Douglas, John, Warren, Company), "Under the Bamboo Tree" (written by Bob Cole & J. Rosamund Johnson, and used in the movie) (Esther & Tootie), "Banjos" (Lon & Company); *Scene 4* Preparing for Halloween: "Ghosties and Ghoulies and Things That Go Bump in the Night" (Katie, Agnes, Tootie, Neighborhood Kids), Halloween Ballet (Company); *Scene 5* The girls' bedroom and the Smith home: "Wasn't it Fun?" (Mr. & Mrs. Smith); *Scene 6* Esther's dream: "The Trolley Song" (written by Martin & Blane for the movie) (Esther & Company); *Scene 7* The bedroom again; the next morning. *Act II*: *Scene 1* The frozen pond; before Thanksgiving: "Ice" (Rose, Warren, Douglas, Company) (featured skaters: Rachelle Ottley & Ron Morgan), "Raving Beauty" [from the 1963 revival of *Best Foot Forward*] (Warren, Douglas, Rose); *Scene 2* The Smith home; preparing for Thanksgiving: "A Touch of the Irish" (Katie, Esther, Rose), "You Are for Loving" [from the 1963 revival of *Best Foot Forward*] (John & Esther); *Scene 3* Tree-trimming time: "A Day in New York" (Mr. Smith & Family); *Scene 4* Snowy men; Christmas Eve; *Scene 5* The ball and portico outside: "The Ball" (Grandpa & Company), "Diamonds in the Starlight" (John & Esther); *Scene 6* Back home; later that evening: "Have Yourself a Merry Little Christmas" (written by Martin & Blane for the movie) (Esther); *Scene 7* The Louisiana Purchase Exposition; spring 1904: "Paging Mr. Sousa" (Mr. Smith & Company), Finale (Company).

Broadway reviews were divided. The show received Tony nominations for musical, score, book, and choreography.

After Broadway. TOUR. It was greatly revised. Several numbers were dropped—"Be Anything but a Girl," "Ghosties and Ghoulies," "Halloween Ballet," "Raving Beauty," "A Touch of the Irish," "The Ball," "Diamonds in the Starlight," and "Paging Mr. Sousa." "Banjos" was shifted to Act II Scene 4, and "Wasn't it Fun?" was shifted to Act II Scene 3. Scenes 1 and 7 of Act I were cut, and the ice skating sequence was re-set inside the Smith home. New numbers added for the tour were: in the new Act I Scene 3—"Whenever I'm with You" (Grandpa & Family), and "You Hear a Bell" (Mrs. Smith); and in the new Act I Scene 5—"Over the Bannister" (John). Added to Act II Scene 3 was "What's His Name?" (Katie). **Cast:** GRANDPA: Billy Barnes; MRS. SMITH: Jo Ann Cunningham; JOHN TRUITT: Stuart Larson; KATIE: Barbara Sharma [this tour information comes solely from Richard C. Norton's *A Chronology of American Musical Theater*].

441. *Memphis Bound*

A takeoff on Gilbert & Sullivan in the South, near Calliboga, Tennessee, at the present time. Aunt Mel, black owner of the Mississippi riverboat the *Calliboga Queen*, organizes a troupe of black singers and dancers for a trip down the Mississippi to Memphis, to put on a production of *HMS Pinafore*. However, due to Pops Meriwether's pilot error, long ago the boat had drifted onto a mud-bank, where it got stuck, so to get the money to get the boat off the bank, she has to put on the show right there and then. But her black friends jazz it up, and one of them has stolen the box-office receipts. Pops (based on Gilbert & Sullivan's Sir Joseph Porter) lives in the jail so he doesn't have to marry Mel.

Before Broadway. The show was originally called *Send Me a Sailor*. **The Broadway Run.** BROADWAY THEATRE, 5/24/45–6/9/45; BELASCO THEATRE, 6/11/45–6/23/45. Total of 36 PERFORMANCES. PRESENTED BY John Wildberg; PRODUCED BY Vinton Freedley; MUSIC/LYRICS: Don Walker & Clay Warnick; BOOK: Albert Barker & Sally Benson; ADAPTATION/NEW MUSIC/ORCHESTRATIONS: Don Walker; BASED ON Gilbert & Sullivan's 1878 comic opera *HMS Pinafore* (and also

on their *Trial by Jury*); DIRECTOR: Robert Ross; ASSISTANT DIRECTOR: Eva Jessye; CHOREOGRAPHER: Al White Jr.; SETS/LIGHTING: George Jenkins; COSTUMES: Lucinda Ballard; MUSICAL DIRECTOR: Charles Sanford; ORCHESTRATIONS TO BILL ROBINSON'S DANCES: Ted Royal; VOCAL ARRANGEMENTS: Clay Warnick; ADDITIONAL VOCAL ARRANGEMENTS: Rene de Knight; PRESS: Karl N. Bernstein; PRODUCTION SUPERVISOR: Vinton Freedley; GENERAL MANAGER: Nick Holde; COMPANY MANAGER: Clarence Jacobson; STAGE MANAGER: Paul E. Porter; ASSISTANT STAGE MANAGER: Ruth Mitchell. **Cast:** HECTOR: William C. Smith; MELISSA CARTER (AUNT MEL): Edith Wilson (10); CHLOE: Ann Robinson; ROY BAGGOTT/RALPH RACKSTRAW: Billy Daniels (8); MRS. PARADISE: Ada Brown (7); LILY VALENTINE: Sheila Guys (3) (she later became Sheila Guyse); PENNY PARADISE: Ida James (4); HENNY PARADISE: Thelma Carpenter (5); MR. FINCH: Frank Wilson (9); WINFIELD "WINDY" CARTER/CAPT. CORCORAN: Avon Long (2); PILOT MERIWETHER/ADMIRAL PORTER: Bill "Bojangles" Robinson (1) ☆; TIMMY: Timothy Grace; SHERIFF MCDANIELS: Oscar Plante; EULALIA: Joy Merrimore; SARABELLE: Harriett Jackson; BILL: Charles Welch; GABRIEL: William Dillard; CHERUBS: Georgia Ann Timmons & Marliene Strong; THE DELTA RHYTHM BOYS: Traverse Crawford, Rene De Knight, Carl Jones, Kelsey Pharr, Lee Gaines (6); MEMBERS OF THE CALLIBOGA SOCIAL DRAMA CENTER: Lee Eberle, Ethel White, Joy Merrimore, Eulabel Riley, Nell Plante, Marion Bruce, Harriett Jackson, Mary Lewis, Muriel Watkins, John Diggs, Leslie Gray, William C. Smith, Oscar Plante, Roy White, William Archer, David Perry, Rodester Timmons, Lulling Williams, Charles Welch, Theodore Brown, William Dillard; DANCING GIRLS: Sophie Miller, Louise Patterson, Lula Hill, Bethesta Williamson, Laure Catherell, Mitzi Coleman, Clarice Cook, Eleanor Brown, Mimi Williams, Jacqueline Petty, Jackie Lewis, Joan Cooper, Charlotte Saunders, Libby Parker; DANCING BOYS: Prince Hall, William Chapman, Toni Thompson, Morton Brown, Wilson Young, Abe Moore, Charles Keith, John Smith, Andre Drew; CHILDREN: Georgia Ann Timmons, Jeanne Petti, June Fussell, Marliene Strong, Richard Reed, Neils LeRoy, Timothy Grace, James Worden. *Act I*: *Scene 1* Deck of the *Calliboga Queen*; *Scene 2* A street; *Scene 3* A cell in Calliboga jail; *Scene 4* HMS *Pinafore* aboard the *Calliboga Queen*. *Act II*: *Scene 1* The village square; *Scene 2* The street; *Scene 3* The cell; that night; *Scene 4* The trial; *Scene 5* The cell; next morning; *Scene 6* The street; *Scene 7* Pops Meriwether in the rest of *HMS Pinafore*. *Act I*: "Big Ol' River" (Ensemble), "Stand Around the Band" (Windy, Delta Rhythm Boys, Ensemble), "Old Love (and Brand New Love)" (Roy, Windy, Lily), "Growin' Pains" (Pops), "We Sail the Ocean Blue" (Sailors), "I'm Called Little Buttercup" (Mrs. Paradise & Delta Rhythm Boys), "A Maiden Fair to See" (Ralph & Sailors), "I Am the Captain of the *Pinafore*" (Corcoran & Sailors), "Sorry Her Lot" (Lily, Penny, Henny), "Over the Bright Blue Sea" (Ensemble), "I Am the Monarch of the Sea" (Porter & Ensemble), "The Ruler of the Queen's Navee" (Porter), "The Nightingale, The Moon and I" (Ralph), Finale (Ensemble). *Act II*: "The Gilbert and Sullivan Blues" (Chloe), "Farewell, My Own" (Pops, Roy, The Beer Garden Four), "Fair Moon" (Windy, Delta Rhythm Boys, Ensemble), "Love or Reason" (Lily, Penny, Henny), "Things Are Seldom What They Seem" (Pops & Windy), "Trial by Jury" (Pops, Windy, Aunt Mel, Mr. Finch, Gabriel, Ensemble), "The Nightingale, the Moon and I" (reprise) (Ralph, Lily, Ensemble), "Old Love and Brand New Love" (reprise) (Delta Rhythm Boys & Ensemble), "A-Many Years Ago" (Mrs. Paradise & Delta Rhythm Boys), "Ring the Merry Belles" (based on Gilbert & Sullivan's "Never Mind the Why and Wherefore") (Pops), Finale (Entire Company).

Broadway reviews were divided, with some raves. See also *Hollywood Pinafore*.

442. *Merlin*

Set in the time of sorcery. A queen so evil that she has no name, has a son, Fergus, who she attempts to put on the English throne. The queen is aware that Arthur is the rightful heir and that Merlin the magician is the man who will make Arthur's claim happen, and she attempts to destroy Merlin. Doug Henning, one of the great magicians himself, made a horse and rider disappear on stage; a black panther was turned into a woman; pieces of a suit of armor were transformed into a giant knight.

Before Broadway. The entire cast and crew were obliged to sign secrecy agreements not to reveal any of magician Doug Henning's secrets. Early on during Broadway previews Frank Dunlop was replaced as director by producer Ivan Reitman. Choreographer Ron Field was replaced by Chris Chadman, who was later joined by Billy Wilson. All of Doug Henning's singing was cut, which, some say, was just as well. Previews dragged on for eight weeks, and the opening was canceled three times. Frank Rich of the *New York Times* and Doug Watt of the *Daily News* chose to review it two weeks prior to the latest announced opening date, and this provoked much controversy, even from fellow critic Clive Barnes, then of the *New York Post*. The 2/11/83 preview had to be canceled when a horse and panther needed for the act were stranded in New Jersey during a 20-inch snowfall.

The Broadway Run. MARK HELLINGER THEATRE, 2/13/83–8/7/83. 69 previews. 199 PERFORMANCES. PRESENTED BY Ivan Reitman, Columbia Pictures Stage Productions, Marvin A. Krauss, James M. Nederlander; SONGS/INCIDENTAL MUSIC: Elmer Bernstein; LYRICS: Don Black; BOOK: Richard Levinson & William Link; BASED ON an original concept by Doug Henning & Barbara De Angelis; DIRECTOR: Ivan Reitman; CHOREOGRAPHERS: Christopher Chadman & Billy Wilson; SETS: Robin Wagner; COSTUMES: Theoni V. Aldredge; LIGHTING: Tharon Musser; SOUND: Abe Jacob; MUSICAL DIRECTOR/VOCAL ARRANGEMENTS: David Spear; ORCHESTRATIONS: Larry Wilcox; DANCE MUSIC ARRANGEMENTS: Mark Hummel; PRESS: The Merlin Group; CASTING: Pulvino & Howard; MAGIC ILLUSIONS: Doug Henning; MAGIC CONSULTANT: Charles Reynolds; GENERAL MANAGER: Marvin A. Krauss; PRODUCTION STAGE MANAGER: Jeff Lee; STAGE MANAGER: Bonnie Panson; ASSISTANT STAGE MANAGER: B.J. Allen. **Cast:** OLD MERLIN: George Lee Andrews (7); CREATURES OF THE GLADE: Robin Cleaver, Ramon Galindo, Todd Lester, Claudia Shell, Robert Tanna; YOUNG MERLIN: Christian Slater (9), *Knowl Johnson*; THE WIZARD: Edmund Lyndeck (4); MERLIN: Doug Henning (1) ☆; PHILOMENA: Rebecca Wright (5); THE QUEEN: Chita Rivera (2) ☆; THE QUEEN'S COMPANION: Gregory Mitchell; PRINCE FERGUS: Nathan Lane (3); MERLIN'S VISION: Debby Henning; ARIADNE: Michelle Nicastro (6); ACOLYTE: Alan Brasington (8); EARTH: Peggy Parten; AIR: Robyn Lee, *Andrea Handler*; FIRE: Spence Ford; WATER: Debby Henning; LADIES OF THE COURT: Pat Gorman, Leslie Hicks, Robyn Lee, Peggy Parten, Iris Revson; MANSERVANT: Alan Brasington; OLD SOLDIER: George Lee Andrews (7); ARTHUR: Christian Slater (9), *Knowl Johnson*; LADIES OF THE ENSEMBLE: Robin Cleaver, Spence Ford, Pat Gorman, Andrea Handler, Debby Henning, Leslie Hicks, Sandy Laufer, Robyn Lee, Peggy Parten, Iris Revson, Claudia Shell; MEN OF THE ENSEMBLE: David Asher, Ramon Galindo, Todd Lester, Joe Locarro, Fred C. Mann III, Gregory Mitchell, Andrew Hill Newman, Eric Roach, Robert Tanna, Robert Warners. **Understudies**: Merlin: Andrew Hill Newman; Queen: Sandy Laufer; Fergus: Robert Warners; Wizard: Alan Brasington & David Asher; Old Merlin/Old Soldier: Alan Brasington; Acolyte/Manservant: David Asher; Philomena: Claudia Shell; Ariadne: Leslie Hicks; Young Merlin/Arthur: Ron Meier. **Act I: Scene 1** Merlin's Glade: "It's About Magic" (Old Merlin, Young Merlin, Philomena, Ensemble); **Scene 2** The palace of the Queen: "I Can Make it Happen" (Queen); **Scene 3** The glade: "Beyond My Wildest Dreams" (Ariadne), "Something More" (Merlin & Ariadne); **Scene 4** A crystal grove: "The Elements" (Merlin, Wizard, Ensemble); **Scene 5** A river: "Fergus's Dilemma" (Fergus & Ladies of the Court); **Scene 6** The Hall of the Angels: "Nobody Will Remember Him" (Queen & Wizard). **Act II: Scene 1** A far away village: "Put a Little Magic in Your Life" (Old Merlin, Merlin, Philomena, Ensemble), "He Who Knows the Way" (Wizard); **Scene 2** The palace: "I Can Make it Happen" (reprise) (Queen); **Scene 3** A marsh: "He Who Knows the Way" (reprise) (Wizard); **Scene 4** The palace ramparts: "We Haven't Fought a Battle in Years" (Fergus & Soldiers); **Scene 5** The Queen's dungeon: "Satan Rules" (Queen), "Nobody Will Remember Him" (reprise) (Queen); **Scene 6** On the way to London: "He Who Knows the Way" (reprise) (Merlin, Wizard, Arthur).

They say it was Doug Henning's lack of acting ability that killed the show, and that may be, although one remembers the success of *The Magic Show* a decade earlier, and Doug's Tony nomination for that show. Still, the critics panned *Merlin*. It received Tony nominations for musical, score, book, direction of a musical, and for Chita Rivera.

443. *Merrily We Roll Along*

Three friends, adults who have sold out and betrayed their youthful dreams, look back on what went wrong and how. Franklin, a composer who has become a film producer and recording executive; Charley, a lyricist who has become a Pulitzer Prize–winning playwright — he and Frank are no longer talking; Mary Flynn novelist, now a drunken film critic. The show opens in 1980, with Frank advising the graduating class of Lake Forest Academy (from which he and Charley had graduated in 1955), to accept compromise and face life's values. Then the action moves chronologically backwards, each scene that follows being set earlier in time than the last, and each showing the changes undergone by the trio. It ends in 1955, at Frank and Charley's graduation, as Frank offers his classmates Polonius's advice, "To thine own self be true." Gussie was one of Frank's two wives, but Mary has always loved him. The characters wore sweatshirts with their role or job function written on them, for example: "Ex-Wife," "Charley," "Producer," "Best Friend."

Before Broadway. The original (straight) play opened on Broadway at the MUSIC BOX THEATRE, 9/29/34. 155 PERFORMANCES. Its trick of working backwards in time was a novelty. It began in 1934 and ended in 1916, examining what went wrong with playwright Richard Niles' dreams, and why he sold out. **Cast**: Kenneth MacKenna, Walter Abel, Herbert Steiner, Jessie Royce Landis, and, playing Buddy Murney, Robert E. Griffith (who would later become Hal Prince's partner).

In 1979 Hal Prince's wife, Judy, suggested he do a show about teenagers (with Hal & Judy's children, Charley & Daisy, specifically in mind). While shaving, Mr. Prince came up with the idea of combining this notion with the 1934 Kaufman & Hart comedy *Merrily We Roll Along*. Prince asked Stephen Sondheim to work on the show with him, and he agreed. George Furth re-worked the play, and came up with a virtually new story. Casting was completed by 5/80. By the time rehearsals were due to begin in 12/80 Steve Sondheim had not yet finished the score, and Hal Prince was beset by other commitments, so the show was postponed for almost a year, rehearsals finally beginning on 9/1/81. *Annie* was kicked out of the Alvin to make way for this show, which, without benefit of out of town tryouts, came straight into Broadway previews, during which audiences couldn't understand it, and many walked out. Word of mouth soon got out, and the show was dead in New York before it officially opened (illustrating how important it is to do out of town tryouts). The show was radically revised during previews, but it did no good. James Weissenbach (son of an old friend of Hal Prince's) was replaced in the lead by the more experienced Jim Walton, who had been playing a small role. Ron Field was fired as choreographer because he was saying bad things about the show, and was replaced by Larry Fuller. The numbers "Honey," "Darling," and "The Blob" were all dropped during previews. Opening night was postponed twice.

The Broadway Run. ALVIN THEATRE, 11/16/81–11/28/81. 52 previews from 10/8/81. 16 PERFORMANCES. PRESENTED BY Lord Grade (i.e. Lew Grade), Martin Starger, Robert Fryer, Harold Prince; MUSIC/LYRICS: Stephen Sondheim; BOOK: George Furth; BASED ON the 1934 comedy of the same name by George S. Kaufman & Moss Hart; DIRECTOR: Harold Prince; CHOREOGRAPHER: Larry Fuller; SETS: Eugene Lee; COSTUMES: Judith Dolan; LIGHTING: David Hersey; SOUND: Jack Mann; MUSICAL DIRECTOR: Paul Gemignani; ORCHESTRATIONS: Jonathan Tunick; DANCE MUSIC ARRANGEMENTS: Tom Fay & Arnold Gross; REHEARSAL PIANISTS: Edward Strauss & Tom Fay; CAST RECORDING on RCA, made on 11/29/81; PRESS: Mary Bryant; CASTING: Joanna Merlin; ASSOCIATE PRODUCERS: Ruth Mitchell & Howard Haines; GENERAL MANAGER: Howard Haines; PRODUCTION STAGE MANAGER: Beverley Randolph; STAGE MANAGER: Richard Evans; ASSISTANT STAGE MAN-

AGER: Steve Knox. *Cast:* FRANKLIN SHEPARD: Jim Walton (1) ☆; MARY FLYNN: Ann Morrison (2) ☆; CHARLEY KRINGAS: Lonny Price (3) ☆; GUSSIE CARNEGIE: Terry Finn (6); JOE JOSEPHSON: Jason Alexander (5); BETH SPENCER: Sally Klein (4); FRANKLIN SHEPARD (AGED 43): Geoffrey Horne; JEROME: David Cady; TERRY: Donna Marie Elio; MS. GORDON (KATE): Maryrose Wood; ALEX, TALK-SHOW HOST: Marc Moritz; GWEN WILSON: Tonya Pinkins; TED: David Loud; LES: David Shine; MR. SPENCER: Paul Hyams; MRS. SPENCER: Mary Johansen; MEG: Daisy Prince; RU: Forest D. Ray; CHANNING, THE BARTENDER: Tom Shea; EVELYN: Abby Pogrebin; VALEDICTORIAN: Giancarlo Esposito; GEORGE, THE HEADWAITER: James Bonkovsky; GIRL AUDITIONING: Marianna Allen; NIGHTCLUB WAITRESS: Liz Callaway; PHOTOGRAPHER: Steven Jacob; SOUNDMAN: Clark Sayre; WAITER: Gary Stevens. *Understudies:* Frank/Jerome: David Cady; Mary: Liz Callaway; Charley: David Loud; Joe: James Bonkovsky; Beth: Daisy Prince; Gussie: Marianna Allen. *Swings*: Janie Gleason & Steven Jacob. *Act I: Scene 1* 1980. Lake Forest Academy, Lake Forest, Ill.: "Merrily We Roll Along" (Company); *Scene 2* 1979. Franklin Shepard's house, Bel Air, Calif.: "Rich and Happy" (Frank & Guests); *Scene 3* 1979–1976: "Merrily We Roll Along" (reprise) (Company); *Scene 4* 1975. The Polo Lounge of the Beverly Hills Hotel, Beverly Hills, Calif.: "Like it Was" (Mary); *Scene 5* 1973. A TV studio, New York City: "Franklin Shepard, Inc." (Charley); *Scene 6* 1973–1969: "Merrily We Roll Along" (reprise) (Company); *Scene 7* 1968. Frank's apartment, Central Park West, New York City: "Old Friends" (Frank, Charley, Mary); *Scene 8* 1968–1966: "Merrily We Roll Along" (reprise) (Company); *Scene 9* 1966. Outside a courthouse, Centre Street: "Not a Day Goes By" (Frank), "Now You Know" (Mary & Company). *Act II: Scene 1* 1964. Outside a theatre: "It's a Hit!" (Frank, Mary, Charley, Joe); *Scene 2* 1964–1962: "Merrily We Roll Along" (reprise) (Company); *Scene 3* 1962. Joe & Gussie's apartment, Sutton Place: "Good Thing Going" (Charley & Frank); *Scene 4* 1961: "Merrily We Roll Along" (reprise) (Company); *Scene 5* 1960. A small nightclub in Greenwich Village: "Bobby and Jackie and Jack" (Charley, Beth, Frank, Ted), "Not a Day Goes By" (reprise) (Frank & Mary); *Scene 6* 1959–1957. Frank & Charley's apartment/Joe Josephson's office, Manhattan: "Opening Doors" (Frank, Charley, Mary, Joe, Beth); *Scene 7* 1957. A rooftop on West 110th Street: "Our Time" (Frank, Charley, Mary, Company); *Scene 8* 1955. Lake Forest Academy: "The Hills of Tomorrow" (Company).

It finally opened on Broadway, where it was roundly panned. Frank Sinatra had recorded "Good Thing Going" as a single before the show opened, and Carly Simon was to record an album which contained "Not a Day Goes By." The score was nominated for a Tony.

After Broadway. Several colleges began producing the show soon after its Broadway failure.

LA JOLLA PLAYHOUSE, 6/16/85. 24 PERFORMANCES. This was a major revival, with a very revised book by George Furth. DIRECTOR: James Lapine; CHOREOGRAPHER: Lynne Taylor-Corbett; SETS: Loren Sherman; COSTUMES: Ann Hould-Ward; LIGHTING: Beverly Emmons; SOUND: John Kilgore; MUSICAL DIRECTOR: Michael Starobin. *Cast*: FRANK: John Rubinstein; CHARLEY: Chip Zien; MARY: Heather MacRae; BETH: Marin Mazzie; GUSSIE: Mary Gordon Murray; JOE: Merwin Goldsmith; TERRY: Joy Franz; DORY: Rosalyn Rahn; MEG: Kathleen Rowe McAllen. *Act I*: "Merrily We Roll Along," "That Frank" (new number), "Like it Was" "Franklin Shepard, Inc.," "Old Friends," "Growing Up" (new number), "Not a Day Goes By," "Now You Know." *Act II*: "It's a Hit!," "The Blob," "Growing Up" (reprise), "Good Things Going," "Bobbie and Jackie and Jack," "Not a Day Goes By" (reprise), "Opening Doors," "Our Time."

Ongoing changes were made by George Furth and Stephen Sondheim, and another major revival took place, at the KREEGER THEATRE, Washington, DC., 1/30/90–4/8/90. DIRECTOR: Douglas C. Wager; CHOREOGRAPHER: Marcia Milgrom Dodge; SETS: Douglas Stein; COSTUMES: Ann Hould-Ward; LIGHTING: Allen Lee Hughes; MUSICAL DIRECTOR: Jeffrey Saver. *Cast*: FRANK: Victor Garber; CHARLEY: David Garrison; MARY: Becky Ann Baker; GUSSIE: Mary Gordon Murray; BETH: Marin Mazzie; JOE: Richard Bauer; MEG: Deanna Wells; SCOTTY: Tom Hewitt; TERRY: Ruth Williamson; TYLER: Erick Devine; JEROME: Rufus Bonds Jr.; RUBEN: Thom Sesma; BUNKER: John Dehle.

HAYMARKET THEATRE, Leicester, England, 4/14/92–5/9/92. Previews from 4/10/92. This was the by-now revised show. DIRECTOR: Paul Kerryson; SETS/COSTUMES: Martin Johns; LIGHTING: Chris Ellis; SOUND: Shaun Knowles; MUSICAL DIRECTOR: Julian Kelly. *Cast*: FRANK: Michael Cantwell; MARY: Maria Friedman; CHARLEY: Evan Pappas; BETH: Jacqueline Dankworth; GUSSIE: Louise Gold.

YORK THEATRE COMPANY. The revised version. 5/26/94–7/17/94. 54 PERFORMANCES. DIRECTOR: Susan H. Schulman; CHOREOGRAPHER: Michael Lichtefeld; SETS: James Morgan; COSTUMES: Beba Shamash; LIGHTING: Mary Jo Dondlinger; MUSICAL DIRECTOR: Michael Rafter; ORCHESTRAL ADAPTATIONS FOR THE NEW VERSION: Gordon Lowry Harrell. *Cast*: RU: Danny Burstein; TERRY/SPENCER: Rick Crom; FRANK: Malcolm Gets; CHARLEY: Adam Heller; GUSSIE: Michele Pawk; MARY: Amy Ryder; KT: Christine Toy; DORY/MRS. SPENCER: Cass Morgan; SCOTTY: Adriane Lenox; TYLER: James Hindman; JOSEPH: Paul Harman.

DONMAR WAREHOUSE, London, 12/11/00–3/3/01. 8 previews from 12/1/00. 79 PERFORMANCES. This production won Olivier Awards for best new musical [sic], and for Samantha Spiro and Daniel Evans. DIRECTOR: Michael Grandage; CHOREOGRAPHER: Peter Darling; SETS/COSTUMES: Christopher Oram; LIGHTING: Time Mitchell. *Cast*: MARY: Samantha Spiro; CHARLEY: Daniel Evans; FRANK: Julian Ovenden; BETH: Mary Stockley; GUSSIE: Anna Francolini; JOE: James Millard. *Act I*: "The Hills of Tomorrow" (Company), "Merrily We Roll Along" (Company), "Rich and Happy" (Frank & Guests), "Old Friends" (Mary & Charley), "Like it Was" (Mary), "Franklin Shepard, Inc." (Charley), "Old Friends" (reprise) (Mary, Frank, Charley), "Growing Up" (Part I) (Frank & Gussie), "Growing Up" (Part 2) (Gussie), "Not a Day Goes By" (Beth), "Now You Know" (Mary & Company). *Act II*: "It's a Hit!" (Joe, Frank, Charley, Mary, Beth), "The Blob" (Gussie & Company), "Good Thing Going" (Charley & Frank), "Bobby and Jackie and Jack" (Charley, Beth, Frank, Pianist), "Not a Day Goes By" (reprise) (Beth, Mary, Frank), "Opening Doors" (Frank, Mary, Charley, Joe, Girl Auditioning, Beth), "Our Time" (Frank, Charley, Mary, Company), "The Hills of Tomorrow" (reprise) (Company).

KENNEDY CENTER, Washington, DC, 7/13/02–8/24/02. Previews from 7/12/02. Part of the Stephen Sondheim Celebration. DIRECTOR: Christopher Ashley. *Cast*: CHARLEY: Raul Esparza; MARY: Miriam Shor; GUSSIE: Emily Skinner; FRANK: Michael Hayden; BETH: Anastasia Barzee; JOE: Adam Heller; TERRY: John Jellison; TYLER: Jason Gilbert; JEROME: Keith Byron Kirk; BUNKER: Edgar Godineaux.

LA GUARDIA HIGH SCHOOL OF MUSIC & ART AND PERFORMING ARTS, 9/30/02. Most of the original Broadway cast were in this reunion production for a one night-only benefit. PRESENTED BY Musical Theatre Works; DIRECTOR: Kathleen Marshall; MUSICAL DIRECTOR: Paul Gemignani. HOST: Jason Alexander. The cast finally got together only on 9/27/02, the first time in over 20 years. Sally Klein & Tom Shea couldn't make it. Liz Callaway played Miss Klein's role of Beth.

FREUD PLAYHOUSE, UCLA, Los Angeles, 9/23/02. This was a concert version, part of the *Reprise!* series. DIRECTOR: Arthur Allan Seidelman; CHOREOGRAPHER: Darryl Archibald. *Cast*: FRANKLIN: Kevin Chamberlin; MARY: Lea De Laria; CHARLEY: Hugh Panaro; GUSSIE: Teri Hatcher; BETH: Jean Louisa Kelly; KT: Stella Stevens.

9/03. A reading, with Broadway in mind. PRESENTED BY the Roundabout Theatre Company; DIRECTOR: Matthew Warchus. *Cast*: Gavin Creel, Lauren Ward, Joey Sorge.

444. *The Merry Widow*

Set in Paris. Popoff, ambassador of Marsovia, tries to induce his attaché, Danilo, to marry wealthy widow Sonia in order to aid the country's dwindling finances. Despite reluctance of both parties, they find themselves falling in love.

Before Broadway. The original operetta opened in VIENNA as *Die Lustige Witwe*, on 12/30/05, and ran for more than 300 PERFORMANCES. MUSIC: Franz Lehar; BOOK: Victor Leon & Leo Stein; BASED ON the French play *L'Attaché d'Ambassade*, by Henri Meilhac. Then on to London, where it was a huge success. NEW ENGLISH BOOK: Basil Hood.

In the USA it ran at the NEW AMSTERDAM THEATRE, New York, 10/21/07–10/17/08. 416 PERFORMANCES. This production used the Basil

Hood version of the book. PRESENTED BY Henry W. Savage. NEW ENGLISH LYRICS: Adrian Ross; DIRECTOR: George Marion.

Burlesque of *The Merry Widow*. WEBER'S MUSIC HALL, NYC, 1/2/1908–5/16/1908. 156 PERFORMANCES. *Cast:* BARON COPOFF: Albert Hart; PRINCE DANDILO: Charles J. Ross; CARAMEL DE JOLLIDOG: Peter F. Dailey; DISCH: Joe Weber; RAOUL ST. GROUCHE: W. Douglas Stevenson; MARQUIS CASCARA: Max Scheck. This was revised as *The Merry Widow and the Devil*, and presented by Joe Weber at the WEST END THEATRE, Broadway in 1908–09.

KNICKERBOCKER THEATRE, New York, 9/5/21–10/22/21. 56 PERFORMANCES. DIRECTOR: George Marion. *Cast:* SONIA: Lydia Lipkowska; PRINCE DANILO: Reginald Pasch; POPOFF: Raymond Crane; NATALIE: Dorothy Francis; RAOUL DE ST. BRIOCHE: Ralph Soule.

THE MOVIE. 1925. A filming of the 1921 Knickerbocker Theatre stage production. DIRECTOR: Erich von Stroheim.

JOLSON'S 59TH STREET THEATRE, New York, 12/2/29–12/14/29. 16 PERFORMANCES. DIRECTOR: Milton Aborn; MUSICAL DIRECTOR: Louis Kroll. *Cast:* SONIA: Beppe De Vries; DANILO: Evan Thomas; JOLIDON: Roy Cropper.

ERLANGER'S THEATRE, New York, 9/7/31–10/19/31. 16 PERFORMANCES.

ERLANGER'S THEATRE, New York, 2/22/32–3/5/52. 16 PERFORMANCES. PRESENTED BY the Civic Light Opera Company. DIRECTOR: Milton Aborn; MUSICAL DIRECTOR: Louis Kroll. *Cast:* SONIA: Alice McKenzie; DANILO: Donald Brian; JOLIDON: Roy Cropper.

THE MOVIE. 1934. The classic movie version. DIRECTOR: Ernst Lubitsch. *Cast:* SONIA: Jeanette MacDonald; CAPTAIN DANILO: Maurice Chevalier; POPOFF: Edward Everett Horton.

CARNEGIE HALL, 7/15/42–8/16/42. 39 PERFORMANCES. PRESENTED BY Joseph S. Tushinsky & Hans Bartsch; DIRECTORS/CHOREOGRAPHERS: John Pierce & Felix Brentano; MUSICAL DIRECTOR: Joseph S. Tushinsky. *Cast:* SONIA: Helen Gleason; DANILO: Wilbur Evans.

The Broadway Run. MAJESTIC THEATRE, 8/4/43–5/6/44. 322 PERFORMANCES. PRESENTED BY Yolanda Mero-Irion, for the New Opera Company, by arrangement with Tams-Witmark Music Library; ORIGINAL MUSIC: Franz Lehar; NEW MUSIC: Robert Stolz; ENGLISH LYRICS: Adrian Ross; SPECIAL LYRICS: Robert Gilbert; ORIGINAL GERMAN BOOK (*Die lustige Witwe*): Victor Leon & Leo Stein; ENGLISH BOOK: Basil Hood (uncredited); NEW BOOK: Sidney Sheldon & Ben Roberts; DIRECTOR: Felix Brentano; CHOREOGRAPHER: George Balanchine; SETS: Howard Bay; COSTUMES: Walter Florell; MUSICAL DIRECTOR: Robert Stolz, *Isaac Van Grove*; PRESS: Karl Bernstein; COMPANY MANAGER: Joseph Moss; PRODUCTION STAGE MANAGER: Andy Anderson; STAGE MANAGER: Edward Brinkmann; ASSISTANT STAGE MANAGER: Stanley Zompakos. *Cast:* THE KING: Karl Farkas; BARON POPOFF: Melville Cooper (3); CAMILLE DE JOLIDON: Robert Field; NATALIE: Ruth Matteson; OLGA BARDINI: Etheleyne Holt; GENERAL BARDINI: Ralph Dumke; NOVAKOVICH: Gene Barry, *Alan Vaughan*; GUESTS: Josephine Griffin & Mark Farrington; CASCADA: Alex Alexander; KHADJA: Arnold Spector, *C.K. Alexander, David Morris*; NISH: David Wayne, *Norman Budd*; SONIA SADOYA: Marta Eggerth (2) ✩; PRINCE DANILO: Jan Kiepura (1) ✩; CLO-CLO: Lisette Verea; LO-LO: Wana Allison, *Babs Heath*; FROU-FROU: Bobbie Howell; DO-DO: Babs Heath, *Cyprienne Gabelman*; PREMIERE DANSEUSES: Lubov Roudenko & Milada Mladova; PREMIER DANCER: Chris Volkoff, *Roland Guerard*; GASTON, THE HEAD WAITER: Karl Farkas; LADIES OF THE ENSEMBLE: Janie Janvier, Doris Pape, Biruta Ramoska, Renee Rochelle, Peggy Turnley, Marya Woczeska, Frances Yeend, Marie Fox, Arlene Carmen, Josephine Griffin, Florence McGovern, Irene Jordan; GENTLEMEN OF THE ENSEMBLE: Jerome Cardinale, Frank Finn, John Harrold, Robert LaMarr, Albert Schiller, Nathaniel Sprinzena, Edward Visca, Mark Farrington, Nicholas Torzs, Robert Tower (dropped during run), Alan Vaughan (promoted during run to main cast), Dennis Dengate, *Walter Graf*. BALLET: David Adhar, Wana Allison, Alan Banks, June Graham, Babs Heath, Bobbie Howell, Zoya Leporska, Nicholas Magallanes, Frank Moncion, Jayne Ward, Stanley Zompakos, *Cyprienne Gabelman, Alla Shishkina, Rita Charisse, Jerome Andrews, David Raher, James Starbuck*; LACKEYS: Morgan Kendall, George Buzante, Eddie Dane (Mr. Dane dropped during run).

Note: The character of St. Brioche was not in this production. *Act I: Scene 1* Prologue; *Scene 2* The Marsovian Embassy in Paris; a summer evening in the year 1906: "A Dutiful Wife" (Natalie & Jolidon), "In Marsovia" (Sonia, with Bardini, Cascada, Male Chorus), "Maxim's" (Danilo), Polka (Miss Roudenko & Premier Danseur), Finale of Act I (Danilo, Sonia, Popoff, Bardini, Cascada, Ensemble). *Act II:* Grounds of Sonia's house, near Paris; the following day in the early evening: "Vilia" (Sonia), "Marsovian Dance" (Miss Mladova, Premier Danseur, Corps de Ballet), "Never Give Your Heart Away" (Clo-Clo) [only in the 1957 City Center revival], "The Pavilion" (Danilo), "The Women:" (a) Popoff, Bardini, Jolidon, Nish, Khadja, Novakovich, Cascada; (b) The above, with June Graham (Jayne Ward) & Babs Heath of the Ballet; (c) Misses Griffin, Rochelle, Carmen, Woczeska, Pape, Janvier; "I Love You So" (The Merry Widow Waltz) (Sung by Danilo & Sonia; danced by Miss Mladova, Premiere Danseur, Corps de Ballet; Finale of Act II (Entire Company). *Act III:* Maxim's Restaurant, Paris; later that same evening: "The Girls at Maxim's" (sung by Clo-Clo; danced by Miss Roudenko & Ballet Girls), "Kuiawiak" (m: Henri Wieniawski; l: Walter Eiger & Jan Kiepura; arr: Mr. Kiepura) (Sung in Polish by Danilo), "I Love You So" (reprise) (Danilo & Sonia), Finale (Entire Company).

Broadway reviews were divided. Stars Jan Kiepura and Marta Eggerth were married in real life.

After Broadway. CITY CENTER, NYC, 10/7/44–11/4/44. 32 PERFORMANCES. The number "The Girls at Maxim's" was replaced with a French song, "Ya de la Joie," written and performed by Lisette Verea, and danced by Nina Popova and the Ballet Girls. This run was a return of the 1943 Broadway production, and had the same basic crew, except: MUSICAL DIRECTOR: Fritz Zweig. *Cast:* THE KING: John Harrold; POPOFF: Karl Farkas; JOLIDON: Nils Landin; NATALIE: Xenia Bank; OLGA BARDINI: Lucy Hillary; GENERAL BARDINI: Gordon Dilworth; NOVAKOVICH: Alan Vaughan; CASCADA: Dennis Dengate; KHADJA: Alfred Porter; GUESTS: Connie Clark & Ward Richard; NISH: Norman Budd; SONIA SADOYA: Marta Eggerth; PRINCE DANILO: Jan Kiepura; CLO-CLO: Lisette Verea; LO-LO: Annette Norman; FROU-FROU: Mary Broussard; DO-DO: Babs Heath; MARGOT: Alice Borbus; JOU-JOU: Teddi Sanders; PREMIERE DANSEUSES: Babs Heath & Nina Popova; PREMIER DANCER: Jack Gansert; GASTON: John Harrold; LADIES OF THE ENSEMBLE: Connie Clark, Irene Gans, Leona Vanni, Georgette Rolandez, Maxine Schraeder, Jan Rankin, Doris Parker, Dorothy Ramsay, Katherine Borron, Beatrice Gordon, Mary Rankin; GENTLEMEN OF THE ENSEMBLE: Alfred Morgan, George Karle, Joseph Monte, Ward Richard, Joseph Bellafiore, Louis Fried, Colin Harvey, Stanton Barrett, Jon Carlson; BALLET: Mary Broussard, Teddi Sanders, Alice Borbus, Rita Charisse, Barbara Gaye, Annette Norman, Alice Tisen, Aleks Bird, Jeffrey Longe, Stanley Zompakos, Terry Townes, Ernest Richman, Bruce Laffey, Charles Chartier.

STOLL THEATRE, London, 4/14/52–6/14/52. 72 PERFORMANCES. DIRECTOR: Richard Bird; CHOREOGRAPHER: Dorothy MacAusland; MUSICAL DIRECTOR: Alexander Faris. *Cast:* SONIA: Margaret Mitchell; DANILO: Peter Graves; NISH: Billy Tasker; POPOFF: Jerry Verno; NATALIE: Linda Lee; JOLIDON: Colin Thomas; FROU-FROU: Greta Unger.

THE MOVIE. 1952. CHOREOGRAPHER: Jack Cole. *Cast:* CRYSTAL RADEK: Lana Turner (singing dubbed by Trudy Erwin); COUNT DANILO: Fernando Lamas; BARON POPOFF: Richard Haydn; CAN-CAN DANCER: Gwen Verdon.

CHRISTOPHER HASSALL'S ADAPTATION. This was the first new major adaptation since the 1943 Broadway production, and the first ever radical departure from the original. Christopher Hassall wrote this new operatic adaptation in England in the 1950s, and the opera would run in London pretty much on a yearly basis, usually presented by the Sadlers Wells Opera Company. The new characters were Baron Mirko Zeta, Pontevedrinian ambassador in Paris; Valencienne, his wife; Count Danilo Danilowitsch, secretary of the Pontevedrinian embassy; Hanna Glawari, the widow; Camille de Rosillon; Vicomte Cascada; Raoul de St. Brioche; Bogdanowitsch, Pontevedrinian consul; Sylviane, his wife; Kromow, counsellor; Olga, his wife; Pritschitsch, military attaché; Praskowia, his wife; Njegus, major-domo of the Pontevedrinian embassy [there have been slight variations of these names]. Otto Falvay and Christine von Widmann played the leads in the 1954 London production, and Jan Kiepura and Marta Eggerth in 1955. Thomas Round and June Bronhill became identified with the roles in the late 1950s.

CITY CENTER, NYC, 4/10/57–4/21/57. 15 PERFORMANCES. PRE-

SENTED BY the New York City Center Light Opera Company; DIRECTOR: Felix Brentano; DANCES: Edward Brinkmann; SETS: George Jenkins; COSTUMES: Paul du Pont; LIGHTING: Peggy Clark; MUSICAL DIRECTOR: Michael Kuttner. **Cast**: KING/GASTON: Jose Duval; POPOFF: Melville Cooper; CASCADA: Alex Alexander; NATALIE: Helena Scott; KHADJA: C.K. Alexander; OLGA: Lucy Hillary; BARDINI: George Lipton; NOVAKOVICH: Lewis Brooks; JOLIDON: Jim Hawthorne; GUESTS: Sonja Savig & Casper Roos; NISH: Norman Budd; SONIA: Marta Eggerth; ST. BRIOCHE: Warde Donovan; DANILO: Jan Kiepura; CLO-CLO: Monique Van Vooren; PREMIERE DANSEUSE: Mary Ellen Moylan; PREMIERE DANSEUR: Michael Maule; BALLERINA: Paula Lloyd; DANCERS INCLUDED: Marilyn d'Honau, Charlotte Rae, Scott Hunter, Bob St. Clair.

CITY CENTER, NYC, 10/27/57–11/10/57. 3 PERFORMANCES IN REPERTORY. PRESENTED BY the New York City Opera; DIRECTOR: Glenn Jordan; CHOREOGRAPHER: Robert Joffrey; SETS: George Jenkins; CONDUCTOR: Franz Allers. **Cast**: SONIA: Beverly Sills; DANILO: Robert Rounseville; POPOFF: Hiram Sherman; NATALIE: Peggy Bonini; JOLIDON: William Lewis; ST. BRIOCHE: John Reardon; KHADJA: Arthur Newman; NOVAKOVICH: Richard Wentworth; MME NOVAKOVICH: Lu Leonard.

CITY CENTER, NYC, 10/31/58–11/16/58. 3 PERFORMANCES IN REPERTORY. PRESENTED BY the New York City Opera; DIRECTOR: Michael Pollock; CONDUCTOR: Julius Rudel. **Cast**: SONIA: Beverly Sills; DANILO: John Reardon; POPOFF: Jack Harrold; NATALIE: Helena Scott; JOLIDON: John Alexander; KHADJA: Arthur Newman; NOVAKOVICH: Keith Kaldenberg.

CITY CENTER, NYC, 10/10/59–10/24/59. 4 PERFORMANCES IN REPERTORY. This was a return of the 1958 City Center production. It had the same crew. **Cast**: SONIA: Beverly Bower; DANILO: John Reardon; POPOFF: Jack Harrold; NATALIE: Helena Scott; JOLIDON: Frank Porretta; ST. BRIOCHE: Chester Ludgin; KHADJA: Dan Merriman; MME KHADJA: Dorothy White; NOVAKOVICH: Grant Williams.

CITY CENTER, NYC, 10/21/62–11/11/62. 3 PERFORMANCES IN REPERTORY. PRESENTED BY the New York City Opera; DIRECTOR: Michael Pollock; CHOREOGRAPHER: Thomas Andrew; SETS: George Jenkins; LIGHTING: Jules Fisher; CONDUCTOR: Carl Bamberger. **Cast**: SONIA: Arlene Saunders; DANILO: John Reardon; POPOFF: Jack Harrold; NATALIE: Nancy Foster; JOLIDON: Jon Crain; ST. BRIOCHE: Richard Krause; NOVAKOVICH: Spiro Malas.

CITY CENTER, NYC, 10/13/63–11/10/63. 4 PERFORMANCES IN REPERTORY. Opened at a matinee. This was a return of the 1962 City Center production. It had the same basic crew. **Cast**: SONIA: Arlene Saunders; DANILO: John Reardon; POPOFF: Jack Harrold; NATALIE: Gillian Grey; JOLIDON: Frank Porretta; ST. BRIOCHE: Richard Krause; NOVAKOVICH: R.G. Webb.

MILT LAZARUS'S ADAPTATION. This production originated at Edwin Lester's Civic Opera in Los Angeles, then went to the NEW YORK STATE THEATRE, 8/17/64–9/19/64. 40 PERFORMANCES. PRESENTED BY Music Theatre of Lincoln Center; NEW LYRICS: Forman Brown; REVISED BOOK: Milt Lazarus; DIRECTOR: Edward Greenberg; CHOREOGRAPHER: Zachary Solov; SETS: Rouben Ter-Arutunian; COSTUMES: Rene Hubert; MUSICAL DIRECTOR: Franz Allers. **Cast**: MAJOR DOMO: George Quick; NISH: Sig Arno; BARON POPOFF: Mischa Auer; NATALIE, BARONESS POPOFF: Joan Weldon; CHEVALIER ST. BRIOCHE: Robert Goss; MARQUIS CASCADA: Rudy Vejar; GENERAL NOVAKOVICH: Joseph Leon; COUNSELOR KHADJA: Wood Romoff; SYLVANIE, MME KHADJA: Luce Ennis; OLGA, MME NOVAKOVICH: Marian Haraldson; CAPT. PIERRE JOLIDON: Frank Porretta; SONIA, THE WIDOW: Patrice Munsel; PRINCE DANILO: Bob Wright; GIRLS FROM MAXIM'S: LOLO: Carol Flemming; CLO-CLO: Jean Lee Schoch; DODO: Annette Bachich; MARGOT: Kathy Wilson; JOUJOU: Skiles Ricketts; FROU FROU: Birgitta Kiviniemi; ZOZO: Dixie Carter. **Act I: Scene 1** A corridor at the Marsovian Embassy in Paris, 1905; **Scene 2** The reception hall: "When in France" (St. Brioche, Cascada, Natalie, Olga, Sylvanie, Popoff, Guests), "A Respectable Wife" (Natalie & Jolidon), "Who Knows the Way to My Heart?" (Sonia, St. Brioche, Cascada, Bachelors), "Maxim's" (Danilo & Girls from Maxim's), "Riding on a Carousel" (Sonia & Danilo), Act I Finale (Sonia, Danilo, Ensemble). **Act II**: The garden party at Sonia's villa, just outside Paris; a week later: Marsovian Dance (Dancing Ensemble), "Vilia" (Sonia), "Women" (Popoff, Nish, Novakovich, Khadja, St. Brioche, Cascada), Czardas and Waltz (Sonia, Danilo, Dancing Ensemble), "Romance" (Jolidon &

Natalie), Act II Finale (Sonia, Danilo, Jolidon, Natalie, Ensemble). **Act III**: At Maxim's; later that night: "Girls at Maxim's" (Girls from Maxim's, Waiters, Sonia), "I Love You So" (The Merry Widow Waltz) (Danilo & Sonia), Finale (Entire Company). After this New York stint it went on tour, closing on 1/16/65, at the Chicago Opera House.

CITY CENTER, NYC, 10/10/64–11/1/64. 3 PERFORMANCES IN REPERTORY. This was a return of the 1963 City Center production. It had the same basic crew. **Cast**: SONIA: Nadja Witkowska; DANILO: John Reardon; POPOFF: Jack Harrold; NATALIE: Patricia Welting; JOLIDON: Michele Molese; CASCADA: David Smith; ST. BRIOCHE: Richard Krause; KHADJA: William Ledbetter; MME KHADJA: Charlotte Povia; NOVAKOVICH: Spiro Malas; MME NOVAKOVICH: Beverly Evans; NISH: Coley Worth; CLO-CLO: Helen Guile; SOLO DANCERS: Rochelle Zide & Michael Maule.

CITY CENTER, NYC, 10/2/65–11/14/65. 4 PERFORMANCES IN REPERTORY. PRESENTED BY the New York City Opera; DIRECTOR: Jack Harrold; CHOREOGRAPHER: Thomas Andrew; SETS: George Jenkins; LIGHTING: Jules Fisher; CONDUCTOR: Charles Wilson. **Cast**: SONIA: Eileen Schauler; DANILO: David Smith; POPOFF: Jack Harrold; JOLIDON: John Craig; ST. BRIOCHE: Richard Krause; KHADJA: William Ledbetter; MME NOVAKOVICH: Charlotte Povia.

La viuda alegre. CITY CENTER, NYC, 6/4/74–6/9/74. 7 PERFORMANCES. This was Christopher Hassall's adaptation, but in Spanish. SPANISH VERSION by: Miguel Padilla; DIRECTOR: Miguel de Grandy; LIGHTING: Lawrence Metzler; MUSICAL DIRECTOR: Alfredo Munar. **Cast**: BARON MIRKO ZETA: Miguel de Grandy; OLGA KROMOW: Nydia del Rivero; ANA DE GLAVARI: Georgina Granados; COUNT DANILO: Tomas Alvarez.

NEW YORK STATE THEATRE, 6/22/76–7/3/76. 15 PERFORMANCES. This was the first New York production to use Christopher Hassall's 1950s adaptation. PRESENTED BY Hurok Concerts, in association with the Australian Ballet Foundation; DIRECTOR: Robert Helpmann; CHOREOGRAPHER: Ronald Hynd; SETS/COSTUMES: Desmond Heeley; MUSICAL ADAPTATION/MUSICAL DIRECTOR: John Lanchbery; CONDUCTORS: Alan Barker & Alan Abbott. **Cast**: The Australian Ballet.

ALICE HAMMERSTEIN MATHIAS'S ADAPTATION. The Light Opera of Manhattan produced *The Merry Widow* several times in the 1970s and 1980s, with new English lyrics by Alice Hammerstein Mathias. 12/8/76. CHOREOGRAPHER: Jerry Gotham. **Cast**: DANILO: Julio Rosario & Michael Harrison; SONIA: Jeanne Beauvais; NATALIE: Georgia McEver & Elaine Olbrycht.

SHELDON HARNICK'S ADAPTATION. NEW YORK STATE THEATRE, 4/2/78–4/27/78. 8 PERFORMANCES IN REPERTORY. Return engagement 9/17/78–11/11/78. 6 PERFORMANCES IN REPERTORY. Second return engagement 9/5/79–9/9/78. 7 PERFORMANCES. The San Diego Opera production, PRESENTED BY the New York City Opera. This was a revised version of Christopher Hassall's 1950s adaptation. Tito Capobianco directed the San Diego Opera production which preceded the move to New York. NEW ENGLISH TRANSLATION & DIALOGUE: Ursula Eggers & Joseph de Rugeris; NEW LYRICS: Sheldon Harnick; DIRECTOR: Gigi Denda, *Antoni Jaworski* (for the two return engagements); CHOREOGRAPHER: Gigi Denda, *Jessica Redel* (for the two return engagements); SETS/COSTUMES: Carl Toms; LIGHTING: Ken Billington; CONDUCTOR: Julius Rudel, *Imre Pallo* (for the two return engagements). **Cast** (if there is only one name listed, then that actor played the same role in all three engagements. If there are two names, then the one in italics played it in the second and third engagements. If there are three names, then it is engagements one, two, three, in that order): BARON MIRKO ZETA: David Rae Smith; VALENCIENNE: Glenys Fowles, *Diana Soviero, Marianna Christos*; COUNT DANILO: Alan Titus, *Howard Hensel, Alan Titus*; ANNA GLAWARI: Beverly Sills, *Johanna Meier, Diana Soviero*; CAMILLE DE ROSILLON: Bruce Reed; VICOMTE CASCADA: Harlan Foss; RAOUL ST. BRIOCHE: Howard Hensel, *Alan Kays*; BOGDANOVITCH: John Lankston, *Herbert Hunsberger*; SYLVIANE: Jane Shaulis, *Kathleen Murphy, Jane Shaulis*; KROMOV: William Ledbetter; OLGA: Sandra Walker, *Myrna Reynolds, Penny Orloff*; PRITCHITCH: Jonathan Green, *Louis Perry*; PRASKOVIA: Puli Toro, *Susan Delery-Whedon*; NJEGUS: James Billings; GRISETTES: LOLO: Candace Itow; DODO: Jane Shaulis, *Kathleen Murphy, Jane Shaulis*; JOU-JOU: Sandra Walker, *Myrna Reynolds, Penny Orloff*; FROU-FROU: Toni-Ann Gardella; CLO-CLO: Puli Toro, *Susan Delery-Whedon*; MARGOT: Emilietta Ettlin, *Raven Wilkinson*. *Act I:* At the Petrovenian Embassy, in Paris; 1905: "Thank you for your invitation, Sir" (Cascada, Zeta, Ensemble), "Do listen, please" (Valencienne & Rosillon), "Gentlemen, how kind" (Anna's entrance) (Anna, Cascada, St. Brioche, Men), "Oh Fatherland" (Maxim's) (Danilo), Act I Finale: "Ladies choice!" (Company). *Act II:* At the home of Anna Glawari: "If you'll indulge us" (Dances & Vilia) (Anna & Ensemble), "Heia! See the horseman come" (Anna & Danilo), "Ev'ry woman ..." (Danilo & Men), "I'm often at Maxim's" (Danilo), "Just as a rosebud blossoms" (Valencienne & Rosillon), Act II Finale: "Ha! Ha! Ha!" (Company). *Act III:* At Maxim's: "Here we are: Grisettes and Playgirls" (Grisette Song) (Valencienne & Grisettes), "I'm a loyal native son" (Tres parisien) (Njegus & Ensemble), "Strings are sighing" (Waltz) (Danilo & Anna), Act III Finale: "Oh the study of feminine ways" (Company).

The 1976 LOOM production of Alice Hammerstein Mathias's adaptation ran, 9/20/78–5/27/79. 63 PERFORMANCES IN REPERTORY. DIRECTOR/MUSICAL DIRECTOR: William Mount-Burke; CHOREOGRAPHER: Jerry Gotham; LIGHTING: Peggy Clark. *Cast:* DANILO: Julio Rosario & Gary Ridley; SONIA: Georgia McEver, Jeanne Beauvais, Joan Lader; NOVAKOVICH: Gerard Alessandrini, Tom Olmstead, Robert Berlott, Stephen Bradley.

NEW YORK STATE THEATRE, 9/7/82–11/13/82. 13 PERFORMANCES IN REPERTORY. Return engagement 10/2/83–11/13/83. 6 PERFORMANCES IN REPERTORY. For its first engagement this production interpolated "One Love in a Lifetime" (m: Franz Lehar; orig l: Paul Knepler & Fritz Loehner; new English l: Scott Bergeson) (from *Giuditta*). For its second engagement it interpolated "Girls Were Made to Love and Kiss" (m: Franz Lehar; original German l: Paul Knepler & Bela Jenbach; English l: A.P. Herbert) (from *Paganini*). PRESENTED BY the New York City Opera; DIRECTOR: Bill Gile, *Ronald Bentley* (for the return engagement); CHOREOGRAPHER: Donald Saddler; SETS: Helen Pond & Herbert Senn; COSTUMES: Suzanne Mess; LIGHTING: Gilbert V. Hemsley Jr.; CONDUCTOR: Scott Bergeson, *Eric Knight* (for the return engagement). *Cast* (names in italics are for the return engagement if they differ from the first engagement): POPOFF: Jack Harrold; NATALIE: Susanne Marsee; DE BRIOCHE: William Eichorn; CASCADA: Thomas Jamerson; JOLIDON: Joseph Evans, *Alan Kays*; KHADJA: William Ledbetter; SONIA: Elizabeth Hynes, *Karen Huffstodt*; DANILO: Alan Titus, *Cris Groenendaal*; HEAD WAITER: Robert Brubaker, *Mervin Crook*; JOU-JOU: Candace Itow.

Die lustige Witwe. NEW YORK STATE THEATRE, 4/11/84–4/21/84. 5 PERFORMANCES IN REPERTORY. This production was Christopher Hassall's adaptation, but in German. A Vienna Volksoper production, PRESENTED BY Kazuko Hillyer International; DIRECTOR: Robert Herzl; CHOREOGRAPHER: Gerhard Senft. *Cast:* HANNA GLAWARI: Irjana Irosch; DANILO: Eberhard Waechter.

NEW YORK STATE THEATRE, 8/30/85–11/3/85. 12 PERFORMANCES IN REPERTORY. This was a return engagement of the 1982 and 1983 production. PRESENTED BY the New York City Opera Company; DIRECTOR: Ronald Bentley; SETS: Helen Pond & Herbert Senn; COSTUMES: Suzanne Mess; LIGHTING: Gilbert V. Hemsley Jr.; CONDUCTOR: Imre Pallo. *Cast:* POPOFF: Jack Harrold; NATALIE: Susanne Marsee; KHADJA: William Ledbetter; ST. BRIOCHE: John Lankston; JOLIDON: Mark Thomsen; NISCH: James Billings; SONIA: Leigh Munro; DANILO: Alan Titus; HEAD WAITER: Kevin Crook; JOU-JOU: Candace Itow.

NEW YORK STATE THEATRE, 7/6/88–8/25/88. 5 PERFORMANCES IN REPERTORY. Return engagement 7/8/89–8/1/89. 4 PERFORMANCES IN REPERTORY. This was a new engagement of the 1982, 1983 and 1985 production. PRESENTED BY the New York City Opera Company; DIRECTOR: Ronald Bentley, *Cynthia Edwards* (for the return engagement); CHOREOGRAPHER: Sharon Halley; SETS: Helen Pond & Herbert Senn; COSTUMES: Suzanne Mess; LIGHTING: Ken Tabachnick; CONDUCTOR: Imre Pallo. *Cast:* POPOFF: Richard McKee; NATALIE: Ruth Golden; NOVAKOVICH: John Lankston; KHADJA: Michael Willson; CASCADA: Robert Ferrier; SYLVIANE: Michele McBride, *Lisbeth Lloyd* (for the return engagement); ST. BRIOCHE: Michael Rees Davis, *Richard Byrne* (for the return engagement); OLGA: Joyce Campana; JOLIDON: Paul Austin Kelly; NISCH: James Billings; SONIA: Leigh Munro, *Michele McBride* (for the return engagement); DANILO: Richard White; HEAD WAITER: Jonathan Guss; JOU-JOU: Candace Itow.

ROBERT JOHANSON'S ADAPTATION. PAPERMILL PLAYHOUSE, New Jersey. Opened on 4/3/91. ADAPTED BY: Robert Johanson; NEW ENGLISH LYRICS: Albert Evans; DIRECTOR: Robert Johanson; CHOREOGRAPHER: Sharon Halley; SETS: Michael Anania; COSTUMES: Gregg Barnes; LIGHTING: Mark W. Stanley; SOUND: Abe Jacob; MUSICAL DIRECTOR: Jim Coleman. *Cast:* BARON MIRKO ZETA: Merwin Goldsmith; CASCADA: Joseph Mahowald; ST. BRIOCHE: John Clonts; HANNA: Judy Kaye; COUNT DANILO DANILOVITCH: Richard White; ALSO WITH: Cynthia Thole, Peter Kapetan, Robert Ashford.

Robert Johanson's Paper Mill Playhouse production went on to the NEW YORK STATE THEATRE, 3/26/95–4/22/95. 7 PERFORMANCES. Return engagement 3/23/96–4/19/96. 6 PERFORMANCES IN REPERTORY. PRESENTED BY the New York City Opera. *Cast:* BARON MIRKO ZETA, MARSOVIAN AMBASSADOR TO PARIS: George S. Irving; VALENCIENNE, HIS WIFE: Elizabeth Futral, *Patricia Johnson* (for the return engagement); KROMOV, MARSOVIAN GENERAL: Joseph McKee; OLGA, HIS WIFE: Beth McVey; BOGDANOVITCH, MARSOVIAN CONSUL: John Lankston; SYLVIANE, HIS WIFE: Suzanne Ishee; NJEGUS, AIDE TO BARON ZETA: Robert Creighton; CAMILLE DE ROSILLON, VALENCIENNE'S ADMIRER, A PARISIAN: Carlo Scibelli; VICOMTE CASCADA, AN ELIGIBLE PARISIAN: Jeffrey Lentz, *Matthew Chellis* (for the return engagement); RAOUL DE ST. BRIOCHE, ANOTHER ELIGIBLE PARISIAN: James Dubick, *Shon Sims* (for the return engagement); HANNA, THE WIDOW GLAWARI: Jane Thorngren; COUNT DANILO DANILOVITCH, NEPHEW OF THE KING OF MARSOVIA: Michael Hayes; (SIX) GRISETTES: LOLO: Jean Barber; DODO: Stephanie Godino; JOU-JOU: Christiane Farr, *Julie Stahl* (for the return engagement); FROU-FROU: Kathy Meyer; CLO-CLO: Debbie Fuhrman; MARGOT: Joan Mirabella; YOUNG HANNA: Christiane Farr, *Julie Stahl* (for the return engagement); YOUNG DANILO: John MacInnis, *Marty McDonough* (for the return engagement). *Act I:* The Marsovian Embassy, Paris; early 1900s: "For Marsovia" (Zeta, Valencienne, Cascada, St. Brioche, Rosillon, Parisians), "A Respectable Wife" (Valencienne & Rosillon), "Gentlemen, I Pray" (The Widow's Entrance) (Hanna & Men), "Maxim's" (Danilo, Njegus, Grisettes), "The Quarrel" (Hanna & Danilo), Finale Act I (Hanna, Danilo, Full Company). *Act II:* The garden of Madame Glawari's villa: "Marsovian Dances" (Company), "Vilia" (Hanna & Company), "Women" (Danilo, Zeta, Njegus, Bogdanovitch, Kromov, St. Brioche, Cascada, Rosillon), "Marsovian Dances" (reprise) (Hanna, Danilo, Men), "Romance" (Valencienne & Rosillon), "Summerhouse Quintet" (Hanna, Danilo, Valencienne, Rosillon, Zeta), Finale Act II (Hanna, Danilo, Company). *Act III:* Chez Maxim: "Cakewalk" (Full Company), "Another Frenchman" (Njegus's Song) (Njegus & Women), "I'll Remember" (Valencienne & Rosillon) [from *Giuditta*], "Cancan" (Hanna, Grisettes, Company), "Yours is My Heart" (Danilo) [from *The Land of Smiles*], "The Merry Widow Waltz" (Danilo & Hanna), Finale Act III (Company).

The Merry Widow from Bluegum Creek. DUBBO, Australia, 12/99. Frank Hatherley took the basic story, and gave it new lyrics and libretto. It was set in the first Australian Embassy in Paris in 1901.

445. *Metro*

Before Broadway. Originally presented to packed houses on 1/30/91, at DRAMATYCZNY THEATRE, Warsaw. This was Poland's first musical and first private theatre production since World War II. Work began on it toward the end of 1989. Auditions began that autumn. From the beginning Broadway was the goal of Wiktor Kubiak (the sole producer and organizer). COSTUMES: Ewa Krauze & Magda Maciejewska; LIGHTING: Mietek Koziol. While it was running very successfully in Warsaw for months, getting ready for Broadway, a second cast was assembled, and some of the cast from this second cast — Jaroslaw Derybowski, Katarzyna Skarpetowska (who was only 15), Jaroslaw Janikowski, and Katarzyna Gawel — joined the "American" team. Mr. Kubiak built an acting school in the village of Ojcowek, about 25 miles outside Warsaw, and began work on the American production. In New York, after a competition, Mary Bracken Phillips was chosen to adapt the libretto. The Polish company appeared on Broadway with Equity permission.

The Broadway Run. MINSKOFF THEATRE, 4/16/92–4/26/72. 24 previews from 3/26/92. 13 PERFORMANCES. PRESENTED BY Wiktor Kubiak; MUSIC: Janusz Stoklosa; ORIGINAL LYRICS & BOOK: Agata &

Maryna Miklaszewska; ENGLISH LYRICS: Mary Bracken Phillips; ENGLISH BOOK: Mary Bracken Phillips & Janusz Jozefowicz; DIRECTOR/CHOREOGRAPHER: Janusz Jozefowicz; AMERICAN DANCE SUPERVISOR: Cynthia Onrubia; SETS: Janusz Sosnowski; COSTUMES: Juliet Polcsa & Marie Anne Chiment; LIGHTING: Ken Billington; LASER EFFECTS: Mike Deissler; SOUND: Jaroslaw Regulski; MUSICAL DIRECTOR/VOCAL & ORCHESTRAL ARRANGEMENTS: Janusz Stoklosa; PRESS: Bill Evans & Associates; CASTING: Jay Binder; GENERAL MANAGER: Leonard Soloway; COMPANY MANAGER: Stanley D. Silver; PRODUCTION STAGE MANAGER: Beverley Randolph; STAGE MANAGER: Dale Kaufman; ASSISTANT STAGE MANAGER: Michael Pule. *Cast:* ANKA: Katarzyna Groniec; JAN: Robert Janowski; EDYTA: Edyta Gorniak; MAX: Mariusz Czajka; PHILIP: Olek Krupa, *Janusz Jozefowicz;* VIOLA: Violetta Klimczewska; IWONA: Iwona Runowska; CHORUS: Krzysztof Adamski, Monika Ambroziak, Andrew Appolonow, Jacek Badurek, Alicja Borkowska, Michal Chamera, Pawel Cheda, Magdalena Depczyk, Jaroslaw Derybowski, Wojciech Dmochowski, Malgorzata Duda, Katarzyna Galica, Katarzyna Gawel, Denisa Geislerova, Lidia Groblewska, Piotr Hajduk, Joanna Jagla, Jaroslaw Janikowski, Adam Kamien, Grzegorz Kowalczyk, Andrzej Kubicki, Katarzyna Lewandowska, Barbara Melzer, Michal Milowicz, Radoslaw Natkanski, Polina Oziernych, Marek Palucki, Beata Pawlik, Katarzyna Skarpetowska, Igor Sorine, Ewa Szawlowska, Marc Thomas, Ilona Trybula, Beata Urbanska, Kamila Zapytowska [chorus members played themselves]. *Alternates/Standbys*: Anka: Robyn Griggs; Jan: Rohn Seykell. *Orchestra*: SYNTHESIZER I: Kinny Landrum; SYNTHESIZER II: Ted Baker; TRUMPET I: Jeff Kievit; TRUMPET II: Larry Lunetta; TROMBONE: Dale Kirkland; SAX: Scott Kreitzer; BASS: Vince Fay; PERCUSSION: Mark Sherman; GUITAR: Miroslaw "Carlos" Kaczmarczyk; DRUMS: Radoslaw Macinski; ACCORDION: Wojciech Dmochowski; VIOLIN I: Paul Woodiel; VIOLINS: Francisca Mendoza, Byung Kwak, Nina Simon, Susan Lorentsen, David Tobey; VIOLA I: Susan Follari; VIOLA II: Judy Witmer; VIOLA III: Katherine Sinsabaugh; CELLO I: Jennifer Langham; CELLO II: Eliana Mendoza. *Act I*: *Scene 1* A theatre somewhere in Europe (Philip, Jan, Company): Overture (Orchestra); *Scene 2* A Metro somewhere in Europe: "Metro" (Jan & Company); *Scene 3* The theatre (Klaus, Denisa, Alicja, Duda, Wojtek, Jaga, Basia, Monika, Magda, Max, Philip, Anka, Company): "My Fairy Tale" (singers: Basia, Alicja, Denisa; dancers: Iwona, Lidia, Violetta); *Scene 4* The Metro (Jan & Anka): "But Not Me" (Jan & Company); *Scene 5* The Theatre (Max, Philip, Anka, Company): "Windows" (Anka) (dancer: Iwona); *Scene 6* The Metro (Jan & Anka); *Scene 7* Audition results (Edyta, Piotr, Alicja, Denisa, Monika, Duda, Jaga, Magda, Anka), "That's Life" (Edyta, Anka, Polina) [cut during previews], "Bluezwis" (Jan, Wojtek, Company), "Love Duet" (Anka & Jan); *Scene 8* Tower of Babel: "Tower of Babel" (Company). *Act II*: *Scene 1* The Metro: "Labels" (Company) [cut during previews and replaced with "Benjamin Franklin, In God We Trust" (Jan & Company)]; *Scene 2* Philip's office (Philip & Max); *Scene 3* Abandoned subway station (Anka, Jan, Edyta, Duda, Jaga, Klaus, Alicja, Basia, Wojtek, Duda): "Uciekali" (a Christmas carol) (Jan & Company); *Scene 4* The Metro (Jan, Anka, Philip); *Scene 5* The Metro: "Waiting" (Edyta, Anka, Dancers); *Scene 6* The Metro (Anka, Jan, Max, Philip); *Scene 7* Pieniadze: "Pieniadze" (Company); *Scene 8* The Metro (Edyta, Denisa, Jan, Wojtek, Duda, Basia, Magda, Piotr, Alicja, Grzegorz, Monika, Jaga): "Love Duet II" (Anka & Jan); *Scene 9* The Metro: "Dreams Don't Die" (Anka).

Broadway reviews were not good. The show received a Tony nomination for score.

446. *Mexican Hayride*

Also known as *Michael Todd's Mexican Hayride.* Joe is a numbers racketeer in Mexico on the lam from the FBI and from his wife. At a bullfight, when American girl bullfighter Montana throws the bull's ears to her boyfriend, David, an employee with American Express, the appendages wind up in Joe's lap, and he is mistakenly selected as the "Amigo Americano," or good-will ambassador during the Mexico — America Good Fellowship Week. Joe cheats Montana out of her money, and sets up an ille-

gal numbers racket in Mexico, at the behest of Montana's crooked manager Lombo. Alternately hailed by the people, and trailed by the FBI, he goes from Mexico City to Chepultepec, Xochimilco and Taxco, assuming several disguises, including a Mariachi flute player and a tortilla-vending, cigar-chomping Indian woman with a baby strapped to her back (the baby was a cigar-chewing, glasses-wearing replica of Clark).

Before Broadway. The show was written for Victor Moore and William Gaxton, but they demanded 16 per cent of the gross, and lost out. The following numbers were written for the show, but were unused: "A Humble Hollywood Executive" (Eadie), "It's a Big Night" (Chorus), "It's Just Like the Good Old Days" (Montana & Humphrey), "It's Just Yours" (intended for either Humphrey or David), "Octet" (intended as the Act II finale, for Miguel, Lolita, Montana, David, Dagmar, Eadie, Lombo, Humphrey), "Put a Sack Over Their Heads" (Humphrey), "A Sight-Seeing Tour" (Lombo & Chorus), "That's What You Mean to Me," "I'm Afraid I Love You," "I'm So Glahd to Meet You" [sic] (Montana & Humphrey). These were cut during rehearsals: "We're off for a Hayride in Mexico" (originally the opening number), "He Certainly Kills the Women" (Eadie). The show tried out at the Shubert theatre, Boston, from 12/29/43. The sets and costumes were late in arriving, hence the opening night delay in Boston. When they did arrive they were ruined. Mike Todd got replacements even during times of wartime shortage. One of the musicians died in Mr. Todd's arms during a rehearsal. The following numbers were cut during the Boston tryout: "Hereafter" (Montana & Humphrey; Act I), "It Must Be Fun to Be You" (David, Miguel, Montana: Act I), "Here's a Cheer for Dear Old Ciro's" (Blumenthal & Chorus), "Tequila" (Lolita). A famous huge advertising poster of a reclining girl, executed by pin-up artist Alberto Varga, and which cost $10,000, took 10 days to erect over Broadway.

The Broadway Run. WINTER GARDEN THEATRE, 1/28/44–12/16/44; MAJESTIC THEATRE, 12/18/44–3/17/45. Total of 481 PERFORMANCES. PRESENTED BY Michael Todd; MUSIC/LYRICS: Cole Porter; BOOK: Herbert & Dorothy Fields; DIRECTOR/LIGHTING: Hassard Short; BOOK DIRECTOR: John Kennedy; CHOREOGRAPHER: Paul Hakuna; SETS: George Jenkins; ASSISTANTS TO THE SET DESIGNER: Chase Adams & Peggy Clark; COSTUMES: Mary Grant; MUSICAL DIRECTOR: Harry Levant; ORCHESTRATIONS: Russell Bennett & Ted Royal; CHORAL ARRANGEMENTS: William Parson; CAST RECORDING on Decca; PRESS: Bill Doll; TALENT SCOUT: Harriet Kaplan; COMPANY MANAGER: William G. Norton; GENERAL STAGE MANAGER: Sammy Lambert; STAGE MANAGER: Robert Downing; ASSISTANT STAGE MANAGER: John Scott. *Cast:* MRS. AUGUSTUS ADAMSON: Jean Cleveland; LOMBO CAMPOS: George Givot (3); EADIE JOHNSON: Edith Meisler (9); AUGUSTUS JR.: Eric Roberts (8); MR. AUGUSTUS ADAMSON: William A. Lee; JOE BASCOMBE (ALIAS HUMPHREY FISH): Bobby Clark (1) ☆; MONTANA: June Havoc (2); PICADORS: Horton Henderson & Jerry Sylven; BILLY: Bill Callahan (11); DAGMAR MARSHAK: Luba Malina (5); HENRY A. WALLACE: Byron Halstead; JOSE, HEAD WAITER: Paul Reyes (12); LOLITA CANTINE, A LATIN SINGER: Corinna Mura (6); A.C. BLUMENTHAL: Larry Martin; TILLIE LEEDS: Lois Bolton; LYDIA TODDLE: Virginia Edwards; CAROL, EX-KING OF RUMANIA: Arthur Gondra; MADAME LUPESCU: Dorothy Durkee; MIGUEL CORRERES: Sergio DeKarlo (10); DAVID WINTHROP: Wilbur Evans (4); BOLERO: Alfonso Pedroza; CHIEF OF POLICE: Richard Bengali; LOTTERY BOY: Hank Wolff; MRS. MOLLY WINCOR: Jeanne Shelby; 1ST MERCHANT: Paul Reyes; 2ND MERCHANT: Horton Henderson; 3RD MERCHANT: Ben Hernandez; 4TH MERCHANT: Jerry Sylven; 5TH MERCHANT: Bobby Lane (15); WOMAN VENDOR: Claire Anderson (15); LOTTERY GIRL: Eva Reyes (12); PAUL: Paul Haakon (7); ELEANOR: Eleanor Tennis (14); LILLIAN: Marjorie Leach; SENOR MARTINEZ: David Leonard; SHOW GIRLS: Anita Arden, Cynthia Cavanaugh, Mildred Hughes, Andrea Mann, Nancy Callahan, Martha McKinney, Candy Jones, Gail Banner; SINGING GIRLS: Doris Blake, Jean Cumming, Lydia Fredericks, Perdita Hanson, Barbara Jovne, Rose Marie Patane, Gedda Petry, Naomi Sanders; DANCING GIRLS: Margaret Cuddy, Malka Farber, Marjorie Gaye, Janet Gaylord, Peggy Holmes, Audrey Howell, Dorothy Hyatt, Alicia Krug, Ramona Lang, Dean Mylas, Vera Teatom, Aura Vainio, Betty Williams; DANCING BOYS: Richard Andre, Thor Bassoe, Aleks Bird, Edmund Howland, John Conrad (*Trman Korn*), Joey Gilbert

(*James Lanphier*), Ted Lund, Jimmy Russell, Eric Schepard, Pat Vecchio, Leonard Bushong, Donald Powell; SINGING BOYS: Morton Beck, Danny Leeds, James Mate, Roy Mantelman, Tony Montell, Gar Moore, Armando Sisto, Robert Tavis; MARIACHI PLAYERS: Manuel San Miguel, Frank Guzzardo, Ben Hernandez, Nuncio Di Bocnis, Savino Lucatorto, Sara Mercado; CHILDREN: Jimmy Dutton, Lois Altmark, Hank Wolff, Francine Fernandez; ALSO WITH: Marta Nita (13), Hermanos Williams Trio (16). Overture (Orchestra). *Act I: Scene 1* The Plaza de Toros, Mexico, DF: Entrance of Montana (Principals and Girls & Boys), Dance (dir: Dan Eckley) (Girls & Boys), Dance (dir: Dan Eckley) Bill Callahan); *Scene 2* Bedroom at the Reforma Hotel; *Scene 3* The bar at Ciro's: "Sing to Me, Guitar" (Lolita & Ensemble), Dance (Hermanos Williams Trio), "The Good-Will Movement" (David & Ensemble), Dance (dir: Virginia Johnson & Dan Eckley) (Marta Nita, Bill Callahan, Girls & Boys), "The Good-Will Movement" (reprise) (David & Girls); *Scene 4* A street in the Merced Market: "I Love You" (written in 1918) (David) [the big hit], Dance (Paul & Eleanor), "I Love You" (reprise) (David); *Scene 5* An outdoor corridor of the National Palace: "There Must Be Someone for Me" (Montana); *Scene 6* Terrace of the palace at Chapultepec: "Carlotta" (Lolita & Ensemble), Dance (Girls & Boys), "Girls" (dir: Lew Kessler) (Humphrey & Girls). *Act II*: Entr'acte (Orchestra); *Scene 1* Xochimilco: "What a Crazy Way to Spend Sunday" (Girls & Boys), Dance (Bobby Lane & Claire); *Scene 2* A gas station (on the Paseo de la Reforma): "Abracadabra" (dir: Lew Kessler) (Montana & Boys), "I Love You" (reprise) (David); *Scene 3* Taxco: Dance (Girls & Boys and Mariachi Players), Dance (Paul & Eva Reyes), "Count Your Blessings" (Montana, Humphrey, Lombo); *Scene 4* Terrace of the palace at Chapultepec: Dance (Paul Haakon & Ensemble), Finale (Entire Company).

It opened to mostly raves on Broadway. The top ticket price was $5.50. The show won Donaldson Awards for Bobby Clark, June Havoc, and male dancer (Paul Haakon). It cost about $250,000. On 6/29/44 June Havoc tripped over a prop and broke her knee. Bing Crosby had the big hit, with "I Love You," in 1944, and Jo Stafford and Perry Como also had hits with it the same year.

After Broadway. THE MOVIE. 1948. DIRECTOR: Charles T. Barton. Its plot was modified, and there were no Cole Porter songs in it. *Cast*: JOE BASCOM/HUMPHREY FISH: Lou Costello; HARRY LAMBERT: Bud Abbott; MARY: Virginia Grey; DAGMAR: Luba Malina; DAVID WINTHROP: John Hubbard; MR. CLARKE: Eddie Kane; PROF. GANZMEYER: Fritz Feld; GUS ADAMSON: Frank Fenton.

447. *Michael Todd's Peep Show*

Also known as *Peep Show*. A burlesque revue, featuring the Ladies of the Ensemble. Acts included a male/female acrobatic dancing team covered with gold paint; and ventriloquists.

Before Broadway. The show tried out in Philadelphia. This was Mike Todd's last Broadway show. Bhumibol, one of the composers for this show, was really His Majesty, Prince Chakraband Bhumibol, King of Thailand.

The Broadway Run. WINTER GARDEN THEATRE, 6/28/50–2/25/51. 278 PERFORMANCES. PRESENTED BY Mike Todd; MUSIC/LYRICS: various writers; SKETCHES: Bobby Clark, H.I. Phillips, William Roos, Billy K. Wells; DIRECTOR/LIGHTING: Hassard Short; SKETCH DIRECTOR: Mr. Robert Edwin Clark, Esq. (i.e. Bobby Clark); CHOREOGRAPHER: James Starbuck; SETS: Howard Bay; COSTUMES: Irene Sharaff; MUSICAL DIRECTOR: Clay Warnick; ORCHESTRATIONS: Ken Hopkins & Irwin Kostal; ARRANGEMENTS: Mel Pahl; PRESS: Max Gendel; GENERAL MANAGER: Ben F. Stein; STAGE MANAGERS: Ted Hammerstein, Dick Towers, Charles Wood. *Act I: Scene 1* "The Model Hasn't Changed" (m/l: Harold Rome) [dropped after opening night]. SINGER: Linda Bishop; THE KEY HOLE GIRL: Mary Donn; LADIES OF THE ENSEMBLE; *Scene 2* Street Scene. "Red" Marshall, "Hi Wilberforce" Conley, Jack "Peanuts" Mann, Thomas "Bozo" Snyder, Dick "Gabby" Dana, June Allen, Shannon Dean, Linda Bishop; *Scene 3* "You've Never Been Loved" (m: Sammy Stept; l: Dan Shapiro). Performed by Lina Romay (1), Peiro Brothers (jugglers), Ladies & Gentlemen of the Ensemble; *Scene 4* Friendly Neighbors (by Billy K. Wells): 1ST WIFE: Lina Romay (1); 1ST HUSBAND:

Jack "Peanuts" Mann; 2ND WIFE: Shannon Dean; 2ND HUSBAND: "Red" Marshall; POLICEMAN: Dick "Gabby" Dana; *Scene 5* "Got What it Takes" (m: Sammy Stept; l: Dan Shapiro) [dropped after opening night] (Ladies of the Ensemble); *Scene 6* The Shades of Night [dropped after opening night]; *Scene 7* Minnie: WIFE: Lilly Christine; HUSBAND: "Hi Wilberforce" Conley; 2ND HUSBAND: Dick "Gabby" Dana; DETECTIVE: Ben "Spike" Hamilton; *Scene 8* "Desire" (m: Raymond Scott; l: Walter Mourrant): THE CAT GIRL: Lilly Christine; LADIES OF THE ENSEMBLE; *Scene 9* Clifford Guest & Lester [they left during the run, and their roles were taken over by The Maxwells (Max Kitson & Lou Sachse) and Dick "Gabby" Dana (who was already in the show); *Scene 10* Midway: BARKER: Dick "Gabby" Dana; 1ST RUBE: "Red" Marshall; 2ND RUBE: "Bozo" Snyder; SLICKER: "Peanuts" Mann; 3RD RUBE: "Hi Wilberforce" Conley; PASSERBY: Shannon Dean; JOSEPH PAIGE: "Spike" Hamilton; ALSO WITH: Valarie Wallace, Bettina Edwards, Garry Fleming, James Brock, Frank Reynolds. Note: during the run this sketch was replaced with Lower Eight: CONDUCTOR: Dick Dana; 1ST PASSENGER: "Red" Marshall; 2ND PASSENGER: "Bozo" Snyder; ABSOLM (AND 8 WIVES): A. Albin; CANDY BUTCHER: "Spike" Hamilton; 1ST SAILOR: Charles Chartier; 2ND SAILOR: Larry Villani; 1ST COUPLE: Shannon Dean & Richard Towers; 3RD PASSENGER: "Peanuts" Mann; 2ND COUPLE: "Hi Wilberforce" Conley & Rosemary Williamson; 4TH PASSENGER: Linda Bishop; *Scene 11* Clifford Guest [replaced during run by The Maxwells (see Scene 9)]; *Scene 12* "Ballet Burlesque" (June Allen, Linda Bishop, Ensemble) [dropped after opening night]; *Scene 13* "I Hate a Parade" (m/l: Harold Rome). Sung by "Hi Wilberforce" Conley, "Peanuts" Mann, "Red" Marshall, Dick "Gabby" Dana, "Bozo" Snyder. Danced by Jesus Moll; *Scene 14* "Blue Night" (m: Bhumibol; l: Chakraband & N. Tongyai). Sung by Art Carroll, Ladies & Gentlemen of the Ensemble. THE IDOLS: Myrtill & Pacaud. *Act II*: *Scene 1* "Stay with the Happy People" (m: Jule Styne; l: Bob Hilliard). Sung by Lina Romay (1) & Ensemble; *Scene 2* Love Nest: PROPRIETOR: Dick "Gabby" Dana; WILBUR WINTERBOTTOM: "Hi Wilberforce" Conley; MLLE DAGMAR PEPPER: Lina Romay; BANKER: "Red" Marshall; BUTLER: "Spike" Hamilton. Note: after opening night this sketch was replaced with Dentist: DENTIST: J.P. Mann [i.e. "Peanuts" Mann]; 1ST PATIENT: A. Albin; NURSE: Linda Bishop; 2ND PATIENT: "Red" Marshall; *Scene 3* "Violins from Nowhere" (m: Sammy Fain; l: Herb Magidson). Sung by Art Carroll. With Corrinne & Tito Valdez & Ensemble; *Scene 4* "Pocketful of Dreams" (m/l: Harold Rome). Sung by "Red" Marshall, "Peanuts" Mann, "Bozo" Snyder, "Hi Wilberforce" Conley; *Scene 5* Cocktails at Five (parody of *The Cocktail Party*) (a drunken butler, and paperhangers who glue guests to the wall): MRS. IRVINGTON IRVING: Shannon Dean; BEECHUM, THE BUTLER: "Peanuts" Mann; 1ST PAPERHANGER: "Spike" Hamilton; 2ND PAPERHANGER: "Bozo" Snyder; MR. IRVINGTON IRVING: Dick "Gabby" Dana; WALDO BROMLEY: "Hi Wilberforce" Conley; LYDIA FITZ-HUGH: Linda Bishop; DR. C.C. CHEDDER: "Red" Marshall; GUEST: Clifford Guest; *Scene 6* "Gimme the Shimmy!" (m/l: Harold Rome). SUNG BY: Lina Romay; THE CHARLESTON: Garry Fleming, Ralph Linn, James Brock, Frank Reynolds, Gloria Danyl, Christina Frerichs, Fran Whitney, Lynn Bernay; *Scene 7* The Castle Walk. Danced by Corrinne & Tito Valdez [dropped after opening night]; *Scene 8* The Shimmy. Sung by Lina Romay. Danced by Lilly Christine; *Scene 9* Finale (Entire Company).

ALSO WITH: Les Farceurs; THE PEEPERS: Charlotte Bergmeier, Penny Davidson, Glen Grayson, Bucy, Hegyi, June Kirby, Barbara Leslie, Rosemarie Lynn, Mickey Miller, Mira Stefen, Gwenna Lee Smith, Jeanne Tyler, Rosemary Williamson; LADIES OF THE ENSEMBLE: Jan Arnold, Lisa Ayres, Wendy Bartlett, Lynn Bernay, Gloria Danyl, Audrey Dearden, Bettina Edwards, Christina Frerichs, Carol Hendricks, Frances Krell, Jill Melford, Leila Martin, Ronnie Oatley, Elsie Rhodes, Kaja Sundsten, Jackie Tapp, Mary Thomas, Ruth Vernon, Valarie Wallace, Fern Whitney, Ronan York; GENTLEMEN OF THE CHORUS: Hubert Bland, James Brock, Garry Fleming, Edward Gambos, Vincent Henry, Robert Davis, Ralph Linn, John Juliano, Frank Reynolds.

Broadway reviews were divided. After opening, the Commissioner of Licenses in New York invited Mike Todd to modify certain sketches, striptease numbers (Lilly Christine was the great stripper of New Orleans at that time, and was in partnership here with Jesus Moll as Christine & Moll) and other elements of old-style burlesque, which he did.

448. *Milk and Honey*

Seven American women touring in Israel. Ruth, an attractive widow, still young, meets Phil, a wealthy and retired American contractor living on a kibbutz with his daughter, Barbara, who is married to Israeli farmer David. Phil and Ruth fall in love, but Ruth learns that Phil is married although separated from a wife who refuses to divorce him. They have an affair which ends unhappily, with Ruth returning to the USA not optimistic about Phil's divorce possibilities. On the other hand, the widowed Clara, leader of the touring women, thinks it's time she re-married (she was married to Hymie at one time), and says that a woman should be married to a man who gets her a glass of water in the night if she wants it. Later, in a restaurant, she asks the waiter for a glass of water, and the man sitting at the next table offers her his. Romance blossoms and in the end she marries the man. Subplots involved the hardships overcome by Israeli farmers, and the pride they have in the land. Barbara decides to return to the States, with or without David. David promises to follow her, but knows he would be unhappy in the USA. Phil's unhappy romance with Ruth finally determines Barbara to stay with David. Adi is an Israeli farmer reluctant to marry Zipporah, the girl who will soon give birth to his child. They finally do marry in a ceremony of three couples, because the rabbi is a circuit rider and can't get around to each village every time there's a marriage.

Before Broadway. Originally called *Shalom*, this was Molly Picon's first Broadway musical, and also Jerry Herman's first major Broadway effort. It was also the first hit musical set in Israel. The authors spent some weeks in Israel, researching, and came to the conclusion that, in order to avoid all the music being in a minor key, which it would be if it was Hebrew music, then the story had to revolve around American tourists. It tried out in New Haven, where the number "Give Me a Word" was cut.

The Broadway Run. MARTIN BECK THEATRE, 10/10/61–1/26/63. 1 preview on 10/9/61. 543 PERFORMANCES. PRESENTED BY Gerard Oestreicher; MUSIC/LYRICS: Jerry Herman; BOOK: Don Appell; DIRECTOR: Albert Marre; CHOREOGRAPHER: Donald Saddler; ETHNIC DANCE ADVISER: Juki Arkin; SETS/LIGHTING: Howard Bay; COSTUMES: Miles White; SOUND: Jack Mann; MUSICAL DIRECTOR: Max Goberman, *Theodore Saidenberg*; ORCHESTRATIONS: Hershy Kay & Eddie Sauter; DANCE MUSIC ARRANGEMENTS: Genevieve Pitot; CHORAL ARRANGEMENTS: Robert De Cormier; PRESS: Dick Weaver, Eugene Secunda, Reuben Rabinovitch; CASTING: Louis Criss; GENERAL MANAGER: Philip Adler; COMPANY MANAGER: S.M. Handelsman; PRODUCTION STAGE MANAGER: James S. Gelb; STAGE MANAGER: Burry Fredrik; ASSISTANT STAGE MANAGER: Marnel Sumner, *John Ford*. **Cast:** PORTER: Burt Bier, *George Smiley*; SHEPHERD BOY: Johnny Borden, *Marilyn Stark* (as Shepherd Girl); POLICEMAN: Ronald Holgate, *Gerald Cardoni*; RUTH STEIN: Mimi Benzell (2), *Terry Saunders* (from 12/5/62); PHIL ARKIN: Robert Weede (1); CLARA WEISS: Molly Picon (3), *Hermione Gingold* (from 9/4/62), *Molly Picon*; THE GUIDE: Ellen Berse, *Judith Haskell*; MRS. WEINSTEIN: Addi Negri; MRS. STRAUSS: Dorothy Richardson; MRS. BRESLIN: Rose Lischner; MRS. SEGAL: Diana Goldberg; MRS. KESSLER: Ceil Delli; MRS. PERLMAN: Thelma Pelish, *Marceline Decker*; BARBARA ARKIN: Lanna Saunders; DAVID: Tommy Rall (4); ADI: Juki Arkin, *Marc Hertsens*; ZIPPORAH: Ellen Madison, *Gerrianne Raphael*; CANTORS: Lou Polacek & David London; MAID OF HONOR: Matt Turney, *Mary Hinkson*; WEDDING COUPLES: Jose Gutierrez & Linda Howe (*Penny Ann Green*), Michael Nestor & Jane Zachary, *Jane Meserve, Sybil Scotford, Judith Younger*; CAFE ARAB: Renato Cibelli; MAN OF THE MOSHAV: Art Tookoyan, *Gerald Cardoni*; MR. HOROWITZ: Reuben Singer; ENSEMBLE (HASSIDIM, SOLDIERS, ARABS, TOURISTS, WAITERS, TRADESMEN, FARMERS): Myrna Aaron, Burt Bier (*George Smiley*), Gerald Cardoni, Renato Cibelli, Antony De Vecchi, Marceline Decker, Nina Feinberg, Louis Gasparinetti, Murray Goldkind, Penny Ann Green, Jose Gutierrez, Judith Haskell, Stuart Hodes, Ronald Holgate, Linda Howe, Alex Kotimski,

Urylee Leonardos, David London, Carlos Macri, John Mandia, Terry Marone, Ed Mastin, Susan May, Michael Nestor, Lou Polacek, Eddie Roll, Robert Rue, Dom Salinaro, Sandra Stahl, Marilyn Stark, Walter Stratton, Art Tookoyan, Matt Turney (*Mary Hinkson*), Patti Winston, Jane Zachary, *George Zima, Judith Younger, Ralph Farnworth, Johnny Ford, Ted Forlow, John Grigas, Nancy Haywood, John Smolko, Angela Tobias, Jane Meserve, Bella Shalom*. **Understudies**: Phil: Robert Rue; Clara: Diane Goldberg; David: Ronald Holgate; Zipporah/Shepherd Boy: Penny Ann Green; Horowitz: David London; Adi: Eddie Roll; Mrs. Perlman/Mrs. Segal: Marceline Decker; Mrs. Weinstein/Mrs. Kessler: Terry Marone; Mrs. Breslin/Mrs. Strauss: Sandra Stahl; Ruth: Rose Inghram. *Act I*: *Scene 1* A street in Jerusalem; present time: "Shepherd's Song" (Shepherd Boy & Phil), "Shalom" (Phil & Ruth) [a hit]; *Scene 2* Another street; that night: "Independence Day Hora" (Mrs. Weiss & Company); *Scene 3* A moshav in the desert; a few days later: "Milk and Honey" (David, Adi, Company) [a hit]; *Scene 4* David's house; a week later: "There's No Reason in the World" (Phil), "Chin Up, Ladies" (Mrs. Weiss & The Widows); *Scene 5* The barn: "That Was Yesterday" (Ruth, Phil, David, Adi, Company); *Scene 6* A hill overlooking the valley: "Let's Not Waste a Moment" (Phil); *Scene 7* The wedding: "The Wedding" (Ruth, Phil, Company). *Act II*: *Scene 1* Another part of the moshav; the next morning: "Like a Young Man" (Phil), "I Will Follow You" (David); *Scene 2* The Cafe Hotok, Tel Aviv; the same day: "Hymn to Hymie" (Mrs. Weiss); *Scene 3* A street in Jerusalem; that night: "There's No Reason in the World" (reprise) (Ruth); *Scene 4* Outside Adi's house; a day later: "Milk and Honey" (reprise) (Adi & Company), "As Simple as That" (Ruth & Phil); *Scene 5* The airport, Tel Aviv: "Shalom" (reprise) (Ruth, Phil, Company).

Broadway reviews were favorable. Molly Picon's leaving for several months to make the movie *Come Blow Your Horn* really hurt the box office. The show received Tony nominations for musical, producers of a musical, composer, costumes, and for Molly Picon. The production lost $70,000, and was the first Broadway musical to run over 500 performances and still lose money.

After Broadway. TOUR. Opened on 1/29/63, at the Shubert Theatre, Philadelphia, and closed on 9/7/63, at the Biltmore Theatre, Los Angeles. MUSICAL DIRECTOR: Theodore Saidenberg. Several Broadway cast members reprised: Robert Weede, Molly Picon, Terry Saunders, Diane Goldberg, Tommy Rall, Lou Polacek (now the only cantor), Renato Cibelli, Reuben Singer. Dorothy Richardson now played Mrs. Breslin.

PAPER MILL PLAYHOUSE, New Jersey, 1963. DIRECTOR: Burry Fredrik. **Cast**: Molly Picon, William Chapman.

AMERICAN JEWISH THEATRE, 4/30/94–6/26/94. 59 PERFORMANCES. DIRECTOR: Richard Sabellico. **Cast**: PHIL: Ron Holgate, *Spiro Malas*; RUTH STEIN: Jeanne Lehman; ADI: Avi Hoffman; CLARA: Chevi Colton; MYRA SEGAL: Joanne Bogart; ZIPPORAH PERETS: Lori Wilner; CANTOR/SOL HOROWITZ: Norman Golden; BARBARA KAPLAN: Katy Selverstone; DAVID KAPLAN: James Barbour, *Michael Park*; SELMA KESSLER: Irma Rogers.

449. *Minnie's Boys*

A rollicking new Marx Brothers musical, i.e. based on the early lives of the famous comedians, at a time when their meddling but lovable mother Minnie was encouraging them.

Before Broadway. The first librettist was David Steinberg, who was replaced by Burt Shevelove. Neil Simon was also asked to write the book. Finally it was done by Groucho's son, Arthur Marx and Robert Fisher (who had written for Groucho). It went straight to Broadway previews, missing the out-of-town tryouts. New songs were put in, old ones taken out (including "Empty" and "He Gives Me Love"), and much revision was done. Lawrence Kornfeld was replaced as director by Stanley Prager, and Patricia Birch as choreographer by Marc Breaux. Shelley Winters was not popular with the production staff, and several times threatened to walk out. On one occasion she did, leaving her ill-prepared standby to go on for her.

The Broadway Run. IMPERIAL THEATRE, 3/26/70–5/30/70. 64

previews. 76 PERFORMANCES. PRESENTED BY Arthur Whitelaw, Max J. Brown, and Byron Goldman; MUSIC: Larry Grossman; LYRICS: Hal Hackady; BOOK: Arthur Marx & Robert Fisher; SUGGESTED BY the early lives of the Marx Brothers; DIRECTOR: Stanley Prager; CHOREOGRAPHER: Marc Breaux; SETS: Peter Wexler; COSTUMES: Donald Brooks; LIGHTING: Jules Fisher; MUSICAL DIRECTOR/VOCAL ARRANGEMENTS: John Berkman; ORCHESTRATIONS: Ralph Burns; DANCE MUSIC ARRANGEMENTS/INCIDENTAL MUSIC: Marvin Hamlisch & Peter Howard; CAST RECORDING on RCA; PRESS: Max Eisen, Warren Pincus, Bob Satuloff; CASTING: Larry Goossen; PRODUCTION CONSULTANT: Groucho Marx; GENERAL MANAGER: Marvin A. Krauss; PRODUCTION STAGE MANAGER: Frank Hamilton; STAGE MANAGER: John Andrews; ASSISTANT STAGE MANAGERS: Ci Herzog & Doug Spingler. *Cast:* JULIE MARX (GROUCHO): Lewis J. Stadlen (6); LEONARD MARX (CHICO): Irwin Pearl (8); ADOLPH MARX (HARPO): Daniel Fortus (7); HERBIE MARX (ZEPPO): Alvin Kupperman (9); MILTON MARX (GUMMO): Gary Raucher (10); MRS. FLANAGAN: Jean Bruno; MRS. KRUPNIK: Jacqueline Britt; MINNIE MARX: Shelley Winters (1); SAM (FRENCHIE) MARX: Arny Freeman (2); HOCHMEISTER: Merwin Goldsmith; AL SHEAN: Mort Marshall (3); COP: Doug Spingler; SIDEBARK: Ronn Hansen; ACROBATS: Evelyn Taylor, David Vaughan, George Bunt; CINDY: Marjory Edson; MAXIE: Richard B. Shull (11); TELEGRAPH BOY: Stephen Reinhardt; ROBWELL: Casper Roos; HARPIST: Jean Bruno; THEATRE MANAGER: Gene Ross; E.F. ALBEE: Roland Winters (5); MRS. MCNISH: Julie Kurnitz (4); MURDOCK: Jacqueline Britt; SANDOW THE GREAT: Richard B. Shull; MISS TAJ MAHAL: Lynne Gannaway; MISS WHITE HOUSE: Marjory Edson; MISS EIFFEL TOWER: Vicki Frederick; ENSEMBLE: Jacqueline Britt, Jean Bruno, Bjarne Buchtrup, George Bunt, Dennis Cole, Deede Darnell, Joan B. Duffin, Marjory Edson, Vicki Frederick, Marcelo Gamboa, Lynne Gannaway, Ronn Hansen, Elaine Manzel, Stephen Reinhardt, Casper Roos, Gene Ross, Carole Schweid, William W. Sean, Doug Spingler, Evelyn Taylor, David Vaughan, Toodie Wittmer, Mary Zahn. *Standby:* Minnie: Thelma Lee. *Understudies:* Sam/Al: Merwin Goldsmith; Mrs. McNish: Jacqueline Britt; Groucho/Chico: Gary Raucher; Zeppo: Stephen Reinhardt; Harpo: George Bunt; Gummo: William Sean; Maxie/Albee: Casper Roos; Hochmeister/Sidebark/Robwell: Ci Herzog. *Act I: Scene 1* The street: "Five Growing Boys" (Minnie & Neighbors); *Scene 2* The Marx apartment: "Rich Is" (Al & Marx Family), "More Precious Far" (Julie, Herbie, Adolph, Minnie); *Scene 3* Backstage Nagadoches: "Four Nightingales" (Julie, Herbie, Adolph), "Underneath it All" (Maxie & Girls); *Scene 4* Nagadoches Hotel: "Mama, a Rainbow" (Adolph & Minnie), "You Don't Have to Do it for Me" (Minnie, Julie, Leonard, Adolph, Herbie); *Scene 5* School act; *Scene 6* Onstage: "If You Wind Me Up" (Minnie, Julie, Herbie, Adolph, Leonard); *Scene 7* Backstage Chicago: "Where Was I When They Passed Out Luck?" (Julie, Herbie, Adolph, Leonard). *Act II: Scene 1* Mrs. McNish's boarding house: "The Smell of Christmas" (Julie, Adolph, Herbie, Leonard), "You Remind Me of You" (Julie & Mrs. McNish); *Scene 2* Outside Palace Theatre: "Minnie's Boys Theme—Ninety-Third Street" (Minnie & Company); *Scene 3* Albee's office; *Scene 4* Minnie's Long Island home: "Be Happy" (Minnie, Adolph, Leonard, Herbie, Miltie); *Scene 5* Walnut Street Theatre: "The Act" (Julie, Herbie, Adolph, Leonard, Minnie), Finale (Company).

Broadway reviews were very divided, but there were no raves. It lost about $750,000 on an investment of $550,000.

After Broadway. There were two summer revivals, with Kaye Ballard & Charlotte Rae heading the companies.

JEWISH REPERTORY THEATRE, 11/3/02–11/4/02. This was a concert revival. ADAPTED/DIRECTOR: Walter Willison; MUSICAL DIRECTOR: Fred Barton. *Cast:* Diane J. Findlay, Douglas Holmes, Gary Litton.

450. *Les Miserables*

Naturally, this musical is known as *Les Miz.* There was no spoken dialogue (only singing and music). Set in France 1815–1832. Jean Valjean is released on parole after 19 years on the chain gang, after having stolen a loaf of bread to save the life of a starving child. He finds the yellow ticket-of-leave he must, by law, dis-

play condemns him to be an outcast. The saintly Bishop of Digne is the only one to treat him kindly, but Valjean, embittered by years of hardship, steals some silver from him. He is caught, but the Bishop lies for him, and Valjean starts life anew. We find that eight years later he has changed his name to Monsieur Madeleine, and has become a factory owner and mayor. Fantine, one of his workers, has an illegitimate child, and the foreman throws her out. She becomes a whore, but is saved by Jean. Javert, the policeman, sees Valjean rescue a man pinned under a cart, and realizes he is the old convict 24601 (who has broken his parole). Fantine dies and Valjean promises to look after her daughter, Cosette. Valjean escapes again and Cosette is lodged for five years with the despicable innkeepers, the Thenardiers, who abuse her and indulge their own daughter, Eponine. Valjean rescues her, and takes her to Paris, but is still pursued by Javert. Nine years later there is unrest in Paris, and Javert inadvertently saves Valjean and Cosette from a mob led by the Thenardiers. Gavroche is a street urchin in the city at this time. Marius, a student, has fallen in love with Cosette, but Eponine is in love with Marius. Eponine helps Marius find Cosette. Enjolras, the student leader, incites a riot. Cosette is now in love with Marius. Then the revolution happens, with the barricades. Eponine joins the fight, but is killed, with all the rebels. Javert, overcome by the goodness in Valjean, kills himself. Valjean reveals his past to Cosette before he dies.

Before Broadway. In 1978 French writer Alain Boublil and poet Jean-Marc Natel wrote the lyrics for a musical based on the novel *Les Miserables*. Claude-Michel Schoenberg wrote the music, and they made a recording (or "concept album") which sold well on the Relativity label. Then the libretto was written, and a show was presented at the PALAIS DES SPORTS, Paris. Opened on 9/17/80. 107 PERFORMANCES. *Cast:* JEAN VALJEAN: Maurice Barrier; JAVERT: Jacques Mercier; FANTINE: Rose Laurens; THENARDIER: Yves Dautin; MME THENARDIER: Marie-France Roussel; MARIUS: Richard Dewitte; COSETTE: Fabienne Guyon; YOUNG COSETTE: Maryse Cedolin; ENJOLRAS: Michel Sardou; COMBEFERRE: Salvatore Adamo; GUILLENORMAND: Dominique Tirmont [this character was discontinued]; COURFEYRAC: Claude-Michel Schoenberg; GAVROCHE: Fabrice Bernard; EPONINE: Marie. Cameron Mackintosh, who was brought a copy of the record by a friend in 1981, was the only one outside France who seemed to be enthusiastic, and he wanted to put the show on in London. But he needed it to be adapted to the English-speaking market, and Alain Boublil was not that good in English. So, Mr. Mackintosh asked his good friend Alan Jay Lerner if he would write the English lyrics, but Mr. Lerner felt he wasn't right. In 2/82 Mr. Mackintosh met with Boublil and Schoenberg in Le Bernardin restaurant in Paris, and got the green light for the British production. Mr. Mackintosh got Trevor Nunn to direct, and Mr. Nunn took on John Caird as co-director. James Fenton, drama critic and poet, was taken on as lyricist, but couldn't get the lyrics out quickly enough, so Herbert Kretzmer was brought in to finish the job. By now the production (by Mr. Mackintosh and the Royal Shakespeare Company), which was in its preparation stages, was famous, and actors from all over the world were clamoring for the role of Jean Valjean—Max von Sydow and Topol being but two who were rejected in favor of Irish singer Colm Wilkinson. One week after rehearsals began Patti LuPone got the role of Fantine (she was the first American to play a principal role with the RSC). By 8/85 a rehearsal draft was ready. Then it had its London run.

BARBICAN CENTER (it was this theatre's first production). Previews from 9/30/85. Opened on 10/8/85. 63 PERFORMANCES. Then it moved to the PALACE THEATRE, on 12/4/85, and closed there on 3/27/04, after 18 years and 7,500 PERFORMANCES. Then, it re-opened at the QUEEN'S THEATRE, on 4/3/04, with new sets and a few improvements, and is still running (as of the end of 2004). TRANSLATED FROM THE FRENCH BY: Siobhan Brache. This production had the same choreographer, set designer, lighting designer, and sound designer as for Broadway. MUSICAL SUPERVISOR: John Cameron; MUSICAL DIRECTOR: Martin Koch. *Selected Partial London Cast:* JEAN VALJEAN: Colm Wilkinson, *Hans*

Peter Janssens, Michael Sterling (from 7/29/02), Hans Peter Janssens (from 12/2/02), Jeff Leyton (from 7/28/03); JAVERT: Roger Allam, *Michael McCarthy, Jerome Pradon (from 7/29/02), Michael McCarthy (from 12/2/02);* INNKEEPER'S WIFE: Jill Martin; INNKEEPER: Peter Polycarpou; BISHOP OF DIGNE: Ken Caswell; FANTINE: Patti LuPone, *Carmen Cusack (from 12/10/01), Joanna Ampill (from 7/28/03);* FAUCHELEVENT: Ian Calvin; YOUNG COSETTE: Zoe Hart, Jayne O'Mahony, Joanne Woodcock; MME THENARDIER: Sue Jane Tanner, *Rosemary Ashe (from 7/29/02), Katy Secombe (from 7/28/03);* THENARDIER: Alun Armstrong, *Stephen Tate (from 11/26/01);* YOUNG EPONINE: Danielle Akers, Gillian Brander, Juliette Caton; EPONINE: Frances Ruffelle, *Caroline Sheen (from 11/26/01), Sophia Ragavelas;* MONTPARNASSE: Keith Burns; BRUJON: Dave Willetts; CLAQUESOUS: Colin Marsh; ENJOLRAS: David Burt, *Paul Manuel (from 7/29/02), Oliver Thornton (from 7/28/03);* MARIUS: Michael Ball, *Hadley Fraser (from 7/29/02), Jon Lee (from 7/28/03);* COSETTE: Rebecca Caine, *Sarah Lane (from 11/26/01), Helen French (from 7/29/02), Lydia Griffiths (from 7/28/03);* COMBEFERRE: Paul Leonard; COURFEYRAC: Craig Pinder; JOLY: Christopher Beck; GRANTAIRE: Clive Carter.

It was received in a luke-warm way by the critics, but the public loved it. Patti LuPone won an Olivier. The changes effected for the Broadway score were duly incorporated into the London production during its run.

American Equity objected to an Irishman playing the lead role on Broadway, so Cameron Mackintosh threatened that if Colm Wilkinson did not play the role, the show wouldn't go on. Equity backed down. Mutual Benefit Life Insurance invested $1,125,000. The Broadway production tried out at the Kennedy Center, Washington, DC, 12/27/86–1/17/87. Previews from 12/20/86. It sold out.

The Broadway Run. BROADWAY THEATRE, 3/12/87–10/16/90; IMPERIAL THEATRE, 10/18/90–5/18/03. 11 previews from 2/28/87. Total of 6,680 PERFORMANCES. PRESENTED BY Cameron Mackintosh, in association with the John F. Kennedy Center for the Performing Arts; MUSIC: Claude-Michel Schoenberg; ORCHESTRAL SCORE: John Cameron; ORIGINAL FRENCH LYRICS: Alain Boublil & Jean-Marc Natel; ENGLISH LYRICS: Herbert Kretzmer; ORIGINAL FRENCH BOOK: Alain Boublil & Claude-Michel Schoenberg; ADDITIONAL MATERIAL: James Fenton; BASED ON the classic 1862 French novel of the same name, by Victor Hugo; CONCEIVED BY: Alain Boublil; ADAPTED BY: Trevor Nunn & John Caird; DIRECTORS: Trevor Nunn & John Caird; CHOREOGRAPHER: Kate Flatt; SETS: John Napier; COSTUMES: Andreane Neofitou; LIGHTING: David Hersey; SOUND: Andrew Bruce/Autograph; ASSOCIATE SOUND DESIGNER: *Abe Jacob (87–88);* MUSICAL SUPERVISOR: Robert Billig, *Dale Rieling (from 96–97);* MUSICAL DIRECTOR: Robert Billig, *James May (by 90–91), Jay Alger (91–93), Tom Helm (from 93–94), Dale Rieling (from 96–97);* EXECUTIVE MUSICAL DIRECTOR: David Caddick; CAST RECORDING on Geffen; PRESS: The Fred Nathan Company; CASTING: Johnson—Liff; EXECUTIVE PRODUCERS: Martin McCallum, Richard Jay-Alexander (gone by 91–92), *Peter Lawrence (added by 97–98), David Caddick (98–99);* GENERAL MANAGER: Alan Wasser; COMPANY MANAGER: Gordon G. Forbes, *Mark S. Andrews (by 88–89), Robert Nolan (by 91–92);* PRODUCTION STAGE MANAGER: Sam Stickler; STAGE MANAGERS: Mitchell Lemsky & Fredric Hanson; ASSISTANT STAGE MANAGER: Bill Buxton (87–88), *Marybeth Abel (88–97), Susan L. Derwin (87–88), Deborah Clelland (88–91), Michael John Egan (88–91), Thom Schilling (89–93 & 97–99), Mary Fran Loftus (91–96), Gregg N. Kirsopp (91–94 & 96–99), Brent Peterson (94–96 & 97–99), Bryan Landrine (96–99), Karen Carpenter (98–99).* **Cast:** *Prologue:* 1815, DIGNE: JEAN VALJEAN: Colm Wilkinson (1), *Gary Morris (from 11/30/87), Tim Shew (5/30/88–7/89), William Solo (from 7/3/89), Craig Schulman (from 1/13/90), J. Mark McVey (from 1/22/91), Mark McKerracher (from 11/19/92), Donn Cook (from 92–93), J.C. Sheets (alternate–93), Craig Schulman (from 93–94), J. Mark McVey (from 93–94), David "Dudu" Fisher (from 93–94), Donn Cook (from 93–94), Craig Schulman (by 94–95), Donn Cook (by 95–96), Frederick C. Inkley (from 95–96), Philip Hernandez (from 95–96), Craig Schulman (from 95–96), Robert Evan (from 9/10/96), Ivan Rutherford (from 9/24/96), Robert Marien (from 3/12/97), Ivan Rutherford (Weds matinees & Thurs evenings from 3/12/97, and lead from 9/9/97), Robert Marien (from 12/12/97), Craig Schulman (from 3/3/98), Frederick C. Inkley (9/8/98–9/4/99), Tim Shew (from 9/7/99), J. Mark McVey* *(3/7/00–4/21/01), Ivan Rutherford (from 4/23/01), J. Mark McVey (1/29/02–2/23/03), Randal Keith (from 2/25/03);* JAVERT: Terrence Mann, *Anthony Crivello (from 11/30/87), Norman Large (from 1/18/88), Anthony Crivello (from 3/14/88), Norman Large (from 7/19/88), Herndon Lackey (from 1/17/89), Peter Samuel (from 1/15/90), Robert Westenberg (from 90), Robert Du Sold (from 90–91), Richard Kinsey (from 11/19/92), Chuck Wagner (from 93), Robert Cuccioli (from 93–94), Merwin Foard (from 94–95), David Masenheimer (from 95–96), Christopher Innvar (from 10/15/96), Robert Gallagher (from 12/6/97), Philip Hernandez (10/27/98–9/4/99), Gregg Edelman (9/7/99–10/8/00), David McDonald & Paul Truckey (alternated), Shuler Hensley (10/31/00–11/17/01), Philip Hernandez (from 11/20/01), Joseph Mahowald (from 2002), Philip Hernandez, David Masenheimer (11/4/02–2/2/03), Terrence Mann (2/4/03–5/4/03), Michael McCarthy (from 5/6/03);* CHAIN GANG: MEMBER # 1: Kevin Marcum (died 7/20/87), *Tim Shew, J.C. Sheets (from 88–89), Robert Evan (from 93–94), Dave Clemmons (from 94–95), J.C. Sheets (by 95–96), Charles Bergell (from 96), Pete Herber (from 96), Gary Moss (from 96–97), Stephen Paul Cramer (from 00), Bart Shatto (from 01), Andrew Varela (from 02);* MEMBER # 2: Paul Harman, *Joel Robertson (from 87–88), Robert Du Sold (from 94), Mark Hardy (from 94), Joel Robertson (from 94), Robert Gallagher (by 96–97), Ben Starr Coates (from 97–98), David McDonald (from 97–98), Ben Starr Coates (from 98), Brian Noonan (from 98), David McDonald (from 99), Robert Gallagher (from 00), David McDonald (from 00), Robert Hunt (from 01);* MEMBER # 3: Anthony Crivello, *Stephen Bogardus (by 87–88), Tom Zemon (from 88–89), Alan Osburn (by 91–92), Wade Williams (from 93), Michael X. Martin (by 93–94), Alan Osburn (from 95), J.C. Sheets (by 95–96), Tom Zemon (by 95–96), Paul Truckey (from 97–98), Robert D. Mamanna (from 99), Paul Truckey (from 99), David McDonald (from 01);* MEMBER # 4: John Dewar, *Scott Elliott (from 89), Rohn Seykell (from 89–90), Kevin R. Wright (from 91–92), Matt McClanahan (by 91–92), Kipp Marcus (by 95–96), Scott Hunt (by 96–97), John Capes (from 96–97), Stephen Colella (from 97–98), Hunter Foster (from 97–98), D.B. Bonds (from 98), Dave Hugo, Chris Diamantopoulos (from 98), D.B. Bonds (from 99), David Josefsberg (from 99), Chris Diamantopoulos (from 00), Kevin Kern (from 01), Kevin Odekirk (from 01), Edward Juvier (from 02);* MEMBER # 5: Joseph Kolinski, *Jordan Leeds (from 88–89), Raymond Saar (from 89), Jordan Leeds (from 90), Dann Fink (by 91–92), Michael Berry (from 92–93), John Cudia (by 95–96), Robert Vernon (from 96), John Cudia (from 96), Peter Gunther (from 96), Adam Hunter (by 96–97), D.B. Bonds (from 98), Adam Hunter, Dave Hugo, D.B. Bonds, Christopher Eid (from 99), Roger Seyer (from 00), John Cudia (from 02);* MEMBER # 6: Leo Burmester, *Norman Large (from 87–88), Ed Dixon (from 88–89), Drew Eshelman, Ed Dixon, Adam Heller (from 91), Allen Fitzpatrick (from 92), Ed Dixon (from 92), Drew Eshelman (from 92), Nicholas Wyman (from 3/12/97), J.P. Dougherty (from 99), Nicholas Wyman (from 99);* MEMBER # 7: David Bryant, *Ray Walker (from 87–88), HughPanaro (from 88–89), Matthew Porretta (by 90–91), John Leone (from 91–92), Eric Kunze (by 92–93), Michael Sutherland Lynch (from 92–93), Craig Rubano (from 93–94), Tom Donoghue (from 95–96), Marsh Hanson (from 95–96), Ricky Martin (6/24–9/8/96), Tom Donoghue (from 96–97), Peter Lockyer (from 3/12/97), Stephen Brian Patterson (from 02), Kevin Kern;* MEMBER # 8: Alex Santoriello, *Rene Clemente (from 87–88), Bruce Kuhn (from 87–88), Craig Wells (from 90), Sam Fontana (from 90), Liam O'Brien (by 91–92), Ken Krugman (by 92–93), Stephen Bishop (from 94), Tony Lawson (from 95), Phil Johnson (from 95), Richard Falzone (from 95), Richard Vida (by 95–96), Peter Lockyer (from 96), Kurt Kovalenko (by 96–97), Stephen Colella (from 98), Clif Thorn (from 98), Kurt Kovalenko (from 98), D.B. Bonds, Clif Thorn, Kurt Kovalenko, Darren Ritchie (from 00), Kurt Kovalenko (from 02);* MEMBER # 9: Michael Maguire, *Joseph Kolinksi (from 88–89), Joe Locarro (from 89–90), Joseph Kolinski (from 89–90), Joseph Mahowald (by 91–92), Lawrence Anderson (by 92–93), Ron Bohmer (by 93–94), Gary Mauer (from 95–96), Robert Aaron Tesoro (from 96) Paul Avedisian (from 96–97), Stephen R. Buntrock (from 3/12/97), Gary Mauer (from 99), Stephen R. Buntrock (from 99), Christopher Mark Peterson (from 99), Ben Davis (from 00), Christopher Mark Peterson (from 1/7/02), David Gagnon (from 02), Christopher Mark Peterson (from 02);* FARMER: Jesse Corti, *Jeffrey Clonts (from 88–89), Frank Mastrone (by 91–92), Douglas Webster (by 92–93), Bryan Landrine (by 93–94), John Capes (by 96–97), Stephen Colella (by 98), Clif*

Thorn, Joe Paparella (from 98), *Neal Mayer* (from 99); LABORER: Alex Santoriello, *Rene Clemente* (from 87–88), *Bruce Kuhn* (from 87–88), *Craig Wells* (from 89), *Sam Fontana* (from 90), *Liam O'Brien* (by 91–92), *Ken Krugman* (by 92–93), *Stephen Bishop* (from 94), *Tony Lawson* (from 95), *Phil Johnson* (from 95), *Richard Falzone* (from 95), *Richard Vida* (by 95–96), *Peter Lockyer* (from 96), *Kurt Kovalenko* (by 96–97), *Stephen Colella* (from 98), *Clif Thorn* (from 98), *Kurt Kovalenko* (from 98), D.B. Bonds, Clif Thorn, Kurt Kovalenko, *Darren Ritchie* (from 01), *Kurt Kovalenko* (from 02); INNKEEPER'S WIFE: Susan Goodman, *Deborah Bradshaw* (from 89–90), *Lucille De Cristofaro* (by 90–91), *Ann Arvia* (by 96–97), *Joanna Glushak, Ann Arvia* (by 00–01), *Anne Tolpegin, Ann Arvia*; INNKEEPER: John Norman Thomas, *Merwin Foard* (from 89–90), *Gary Lynch* (by 90–91), *Jeffrey Scott Watkins* (by 96–97), *Andrew Varela* (from 97–98), *Ron Sharpe* (from 00); BISHOP OF DIGNE: Norman Large, *Anthony Crivello* (from 88–89), *Steve Schochet* (from 88–89), *Adam Heller* (from 89–90), *Kevin McGuire* (by 90–91), *Kenny Morris* (by 91–92), *Nicholas S. Saverine* (by 93–94), *Kevin McGuire* (by 95–96), *David McDonald* (by 96–97), *David Benoit* (from 97–98), *David McDonald* (from 98), *David Benoit* (from 99), *Clif Thorn* (from 99), *John Haggerty* (from 99), *David Benoit* (from 00), *Robert Hunt* (from 00), *David Benoit* (from 01); 1ST CONSTABLE: Marcus Lovett, *John Ruess* (from 88–89), *Willy Falk* (from 88–89), *Peter Gutenbein* (from 90), *John Leone* (from 91), *Larry Alexander* (by 91–92), *Ciaran Sheehan* (from 92), *Daniel C. Cooney* (from 92–93), *Tom Donoghue* (from 92–93), *Marsh Hanson* (by 95–96), *Kipp Marcus* (by 96), *Kevin Kern* (from 97), *D.B. Bonds* (from 99), *Kevin Odekirk* (from 00), *David Josefsberg* (from 00), *Kevin Odekirk* (from 01), *Kevin Kern* (from 01); 2ND CONSTABLE: Steve Schochet, *Pete Herber* (from 88–89), *Paul Avedisian* (from 89–90), *Gary Moss* (from 96), *Peter Gunther* (from 96), *Kevin Earley* (from 97–98), *Christopher Mark Peterson* (from 99), *David Gagnon* (from 99), *John-Andrew Clark* (from 02). 1823, MONTREUIL-SUR-MER: FANTINE: Randy Graff, *Maureen Moore* (from 7/19/88), *Susan Dawn Carson* (from 1/17/89), *Laurie Beechman* (from 1/15/90), *Christy Baron* (from 89–90), *Susan Dawn Carson* (from 11/19/92), *Rachel York* (from 91–92), *Donna Kane* (from 92–93), *Andrea McArdle* (from 8/16/93), *Susan Gilmour* (by 94–95), *Debbie Shapiro Gravitte* (from 94–95), *Christy Baron* (from 94–95), *Catherine Hickland* (from 95), *Paige O'Hara* (from 95), *Jacquelyn Piro* (from 95–96), *Melba Moore* (from 1/96), *Susie McGonagle* (from 4/96), *Florence Lacey* (from 9/10/96), *Lisa Capps* (1/28–3/4/97), *Juliet Lambert* (3/12/97–4/15/98), *Lisa Capps* (from 4/15/98), *Juliet Lambert* (from 6/15/98), *Alice Ripley* (from 9/8/98), *Susan Gilmour* (during Miss Ripley's vacation, from 3/9/99), *Alice Ripley* (3/23/99–9/4/99), *Jane Bodle* (9/7/99–4/21/01), *Jacquelyn Piro* (from 4/23/01), *Lauren Kennedy* (11/4/02–3/16/03), *Jayne Paterson* (from 3/18/03); FOREMAN: Paul Harman, *Joel Robertson* (from 87–88), *Robert Du Sold* (from 94), *Mark Hardy* (from 94), *Joel Robertson* (from 94), *Robert Gallagher* (by 96–97), *Ben Starr Coates* (from 97–98), *David McDonald* (from 97–98), *Ben Starr Coates* (from 97–98), *Brian Noonan* (from 98), *David McDonald* (from 99), *Robert Gallagher* (from 00), *David McDonald* (from 00), *Robert Hunt* (from 01); 1ST WORKER: Jesse Corti, *Jeffrey Clonts* (from 88–89), *Frank Mastrone* (by 91–92), *Douglas Webster* (from 92–93), *Bryan Landrine* (by 93–94), *Peter Gunther* (from 95), *Bryan Landrine* (from 96), *Peter Gunther* (from 96), *Robert Evan* (from 96), *Ivan Rutherford* (from 96), *Charles Bergell* (from 96), *Jeffrey Scott Watkins* (by 96–97), *Andrew Varela* (from 97–98), *Ron Sharpe* (from 00); 2ND WORKER: John Dewar, *Scott Elliott* (from 89), *Rohn Seykell* (from 89–90), *Kevin R. Wright* (from 91–92), *Matt McClanahan* (by 91–92), *Kipp Marcus* (by 95–96), *Scott Hunt* (by 96–97), *John Capes* (from 96–97), *Stephen Colella* (from 97–98), *Hunter Foster* (from 97–98), *D.B. Bonds* (from 98), *Dave Hugo, Chris Diamantopoulos* (from 98), *D.B. Bonds* (from 99), *David Josefsberg* (from 99), *Chris Diamantopoulos* (from 00), *Kevin Kern* (from 01), *Kevin Odekirk* (from 01), *Edward Juvier* (from 01); 1ST WOMAN WORKER: Cindy Benson, *Jessica Molaskey* (from 88–89), *Jean Fitzgibbons* (by 91–92), *Liz McCartney* (by 95–96), *Madeleine Doherty* (by 96–97), *Joanna Glushak, Madeleine Doherty, Becky Barta*; 2ND WOMAN WORKER: Marcie Shaw, *Olga Merediz* (by 88–89), *Marcie Shaw* (by 90–91), *Diane Della Piazza* (by 91–92), *Jessica Sheridan* (by 92–93), *Nicola Boyer* (by 93–94), *Jessica Sheridan* (by 95–96), *Megan Lawrence* (by 96–97), *Danielle de Niese* (from 97–98), *Megan Lawrence* (from 97–98), *Jennifer Paz* (from 97–98), *Megan Lawrence* (from 97–98), *Sutton Foster, Catherine Brunell*; 3RD WOMAN WORKER: Jane Bodle, *Cissy Rebich* (from 88–89), *Cissy Lee Cates* (by 90–91), *Connie Kunkle* (by 93–94), *Kristen Behrendt* (by 95–96), *Gina Lamparella* (by 96–97), *Lisa Capps, Gina Lamparella*; 4TH WOMAN WORKER: Joanna Glushak, *Jean Fitzgibbons* (from 88–89), *Madeleine Doherty* (by 90–91), *Diane Della Piazza* (by 93–94), *Madeleine Doherty* (by 94–95), *Erika MacLeod* (by 96–97); FACTORY GIRL: Ann Crumb, *Janene Lovullo* (from 87–88), *Anne Marie Runolfsson* (from 88–89), *Mary Gutzi* (from 89–90), *Jessie Janet Richards* (by 91–92), *Audrey Klinger* (by 95–96), *Alicia Irving* (by 96–97), *Jennifer Zimmerman* (from 97–98), *Holly Jo Crane*; 1ST SAILOR: Joseph Kolinski, *Jordan Leeds* (from 88–89), *Raymond Saar* (from 89), *Jordan Leeds* (from 90), *Dann Fink* (by 91–92), *Michael Berry* (from 92–93), *John Cudia* (by 95–96), *Robert Vernon* (from 96), *John Cudia* (from 96), *Peter Gunther* (from 96), *Adam Hunter* (by 96–97), *D.B. Bonds* (from 98), *Adam Hunter, Dave Hugo, D.B. Bonds, Christopher Eid* (from 99), *Roger Seyer* (from 00), John Cudia (from 02); 2ND SAILOR: Kevin Marcum (died 7/20/87), *Tim Shew* (from 87–88), *William Solo* (from 87–88), *J.C. Sheets* (from 88–89), *Nicholas F. Saverine* (from 93), *Robert Evan* (from 93–94), *Dave Clemmons* (by 94–95), *J.C. Sheets* (by 95–96), *Charles Bergell* (from 96), *Pete Herber* (from 96), *Gary Moss* (by 96–97), *Stephen Paul Cramer* (from 00), *Bart Shatto* (from 01), *Andrew Varela* (from 02); 3RD SAILOR: John Dewar, *Scott Elliott* (from 89), *Rohn Seykell* (from 89–90), *Kevin R. Wright* (from 91–92), *Matt McClanahan* (by 91–92), *Kipp Marcus* (by 95–96), *Scott Hunt* (by 96–97), *John Capes* (from 96–97), *Stephen Colella* (from 97–98), *Hunter Foster* (from 97–98), *D.B. Bonds* (from 98), *Dave Hugo, Chris Diamantopoulos* (from 98), *D.B. Bonds* (from 99), *David Josefsberg* (from 99), *Chris Diamantopoulos* (from 00), *Kevin Kern* (from 01), *Kevin Odekirk* (from 01), *Edward Juvier* (from 02); 1ST WHORE: Susan Goodman, *Deborah Bradshaw* (from 89–90), *Lucille De Cristofaro* (by 90–91), *Ann Arvia* (by 96–97), *Joanna Glushak, Ann Arvia, Anne Tolpegin, Ann Arvia*; 2ND WHORE: Joanna Glushak, *Jean Fitzgibbons* (from 88–89), *Madeleine Doherty* (by 90–91), *Diane Della Piazza* (by 93–94), *Madeleine Doherty* (by 94–95), *Erika MacLeod* (by 96–97); 3RD WHORE: Jane Bodle, *Cissy Rebich* (from 88–89), *Cissy Lee Cates* (by 90–91), *Connie Kunkle* (by 93–94), *Kristen Behrendt* (by 95–96), *Gina Lamparella* (by 96–97), *Lisa Capps, Gina Lamparella*; 4TH WHORE: Ann Crumb, *Janene Lovullo* (from 87–88), *Anne Marie Runolfsson* (from 88–89), *Mary Gutzi* (from 89–90), *Jessie Janet Richards* (by 91–92), *Audrey Klinger* (by 95–96), *Alicia Irving* (by 96–97), *Jennifer Zimmerman* (from 97–98), *Holly Jo Crane*; 5TH WHORE: Frances Ruffelle, *Kelli James* (from 9/15/87), *Natalie Toro* (from 7/88), *Debbie Gibson* (from 1/7/92), *Michele Maika* (from 91–92), *Debbie Gibson* (from 3/2/92), *Brandy Brown* (from 92–93), *Lea Salonga* (from 1/5/93), *Tia Riebling* (from 92–93), *Lea Salonga* (from 93–94), *Sarah Uriarte* (later known as Sarah Uriarte Berry) (from 93–94), *Jessica-Snow Wilson* (from 94–95), *Shanice* (from 94–95), *Jessica-Snow Wilson* (by 95–96), *Christeena Michelle Riggs* (from 95–96), *Sarah Uriarte Berry* (from 3/12/97), *Megan Lawrence* (during Miss Uriarte's two vacations, 97–9/8/97, and again 97–98), *Kerry Butler* (from 98), *Megan Lawrence* (from 99), *Jessica-Snow Wilson* (until 9/12/99), *Rona Figueroa* (9/14–10/99), *Megan Lawrence* (from 10/99), *Jessica Boevers* (from 00), *Catharine Brunell* (from 1/00), *Dana Meller* (from 01), *Diana Kaarina* (from 1/14/02); 6TH WHORE: Judy Kuhn, *Tracy Shayne* (from 87–88), *Jacquelyn Piro* (from 89–90), *Jennifer Lee Andrews* (from 92–93), *Jacquelyn Piro* (from 94), *Jodie Langel* (from 95), *Jennifer Lee Andrews* (from 95), *Dana Meller* (by 95–96), *Tamra Hayden* (by 95–96), *Jennifer Lee Andrews* (from 11/19/96), *Christeena Michelle Riggs* (from 3/12/97), *Tobi Foster* (from 11/6/98), *Sandra Turley* (nee Dudley) (from 2/5/01), *Stephanie Waters* (from 02), *Sandra Turley* (from 02); 7TH WHORE: Gretchen Kingsley-Wiehe, *Betsy True* (by 89–90), *Melissa Anne Davis* (by 90–91), *Sarah E. Litzsinger* (by 91–92), *Jessica-Snow Wilson* (by 93–94), *Shanice* (from 94–95), *Jessica-Snow Wilson* (by 95–96), *Tammy Jacobs* (from 95–96), *Alexandra Foucard* (by 96–97); OLD WOMAN: Cindy Benson, *Jessica Molaskey* (from 88–89), *Jean Fitzgibbons* (by 91–92), *Liz McCartney* (by 95–96), *Madeleine Doherty* (by 96–97), *Joanna Glushak, Madeleine Doherty, Becky Barta*; CRONE: Marcie Shaw, *Olga Merediz* (by 88–89), *Marcie Shaw* (by 90–91), *Diane Della Piazza* (by 91–92), *Jessica Sheridan* (from 92–93), *Nicola Boyer* (by 93–94), *Jessica Sheridan* (by 95–96), *Gina Lamparella* (by 96–97), *Lisa Capps, Gina Lamparella*; PIMP: Steve Schochet, *Adam Heller* (from 89–90), *Bill Carmichael* (from 90), *Kevin McGuire* (from 91), *Kenny Morris* (by 91–92), *Kevin McGuire* (from

93–94), *Nicholas F. Saverine (by 93–94), Kelly Briggs (from 95–96), Kevin McGuire (from 95–96), Peter Gunther (by 96–97), Kevin Earley (from 97–98), Christopher Mark Peterson*; BAMATABOIS: Anthony Crivello, *Stephen Bogardus (from 87–88), Tom Zemon (from 88–89), Alan Osburn (by 91–92), Wade Williams (from 93), Michael X. Martin (by 93–94), Alan Osburn (from 95), J.C. Sheets (by 95–96), Tom Zemon (by 96–97), Paul Truckey (from 97–98), Robert D. Mamanna (from 99), Paul Truckey (from 99), David McDonald (from 01)*; FAUCHELEVENT: Steve Schochet, *Adam Heller (from 89–90), Bill Carmichael (from 90), Kevin McGuire (from 91), Kenny Morris (by 91–92), Kevin McGuire (from 93–94), Nicholas F. Saverine (by 93–94), Kelly Briggs (from 95–96), Kevin McGuire (from 95–96), Jeffrey Scott Watkins (by 96–97), Kipp Marcus (by 97–98), Kevin Kern (from 97–98)*; CHAMPMATHIEU: *Gary Moss (by 96–97)* [new role by 96–97]. 1823, MONTFERMEIL: YOUNG COSETTE: Donna Vivino (alone in 87), *Amy Beth* (alternated 87–88; *Daisy Eagan* from 88–89), Shanelle Workman (alternated 87–89). The three 89–90 alternates were: *Marlo Landry, Eden Riegel, Tamara Robin Spiewack* (later in 89–90 it was: *Eden Riegel, Eliza Harris, Christen Tassin*). The three 91–92 alternates were: *Lacey Chabert, Eliza Harris (Savannah Wise by 92–93), Jessica Scholl*. 95–96 list: *Lea Michele, Crysta Macalush, Kimberly Hannon*. 96–97 list: *Alexis Kalehoff (Lisa Musser* from 97–98, *Danielle Raniere* from 97–98, *Lisa Musser* from 97–98), *Alicia Morton (Christiana Anbri, Alicia Morton, Christiana Anbri), Kimberly Hannon* (dropped by 97–98), *Hana Kitasei (Andrea Bowen* from 97–98, *Netousha N. Harris* from 97–98, *Christiana Anbri, Netousha N. Harris, Christiana Anbri, Cristina Faicco, Ashley Rose Orr* during Miss Faicco's vacation, *Cristina Faicco)*; MADAME THENARDIER: Jennifer Butt, *Evalyn Baron* (from 1/15/90), *Diana Rogers (from 93–94), Gina Ferrall (from 94–95), Tregoney Shepherd (by 96–97), Ann Arvia (from 96–97), Fuschia Walker* [she later became just Fuschia] (3/12/97–7/22/00), *Betsy Joslyn* (from 7/24/00), *Aymee Garcia* (from 02); THENARDIER: Leo Burmester, *Norman Large (from 87–88), Ed Dixon (from 88–89), Drew Eshelman, Ed Dixon, Adam Heller (from 91), Allen Fitzpatrick (from 92), Ed Dixon (from 92), Drew Eshelman (from 92), Nicholas Wyman (from 3/12/97), J.P. Dougherty (from 99), Nicholas Wyman (from 99)*; YOUNG EPONINE: Chrissie McDonald (alone in 87 and gone by 87–88), *Shanelle Workman* (alternated 87–89), *Amy Beth* (alternated 87–88; *Daisy Eagan* from 88–89). The two 89–90 alternates were: *Eden Riegel & Tamara Robin Spiewack*. Later in the season the three were: *Eliza Harris, Eden Riegel, Christen Tassin*. The three 91–92 alternates were: *Lacey Chabert, Eliza Harris (Savannah Wise by 92–93), Jessica Scholl*. 95–96 list: *Lea Michele, Crysta Macalush, Kimberly Hannon*. 96–97 list: *Alexis Kalehoff (Lisa Musser* from 97–98, *Danielle Raniere* from 97–98, *Lisa Musser* from 97–98), *Alicia Morton (Christiana Anbri, Alicia Morton, Christiana Anbri), Kimberly Hannon* (dropped by 97–98), *Hana Kitasei (Andrea Bowen* from 97–98, *Netousha N. Harris* from 97–98, *Christiana Anbri, Netousha N. Harris, Christiana Anbri, Cristina Faicco, Ashley Rose Orr* during Miss Faicco's vacation, *Cristina Faicco)*; DRINKER: Jesse Corti, *Jeffrey Clonts (from 88–89), Frank Mastrone (by 91–92), Douglas Webster (by 92–93), Bryan Landrine (by 93–94), Peter Gunther (from 95), Bryan Landrine (from 96), Peter Gunther (from 96), Robert Evan (from 96), Ivan Rutherford (from 96), Charles Bergell (from 96), Jeffrey Scott Watkins (by 96–97), Andrew Varela (from 97–98), Ron Sharpe (from 00)*; YOUNG COUPLE: MAN: Alex Santoriello, *Rene Clemente (from 87–88), Bruce Kuhn (from 87–88), Craig Wells (from 90), Sam Fontana (from 90), Liam O'Brien (by 91–92), Ken Krugman (by 92–93), Stephen Bishop (from 94), Tony Lawson (from 95), Phil Johnson (from 95), Richard Falzone (from 95), Richard Vida (by 95–96), Adam Hunter (by 96–97), D.B. Bonds, Adam Hunter, Dave Hugo, D.B. Bonds, Christopher Eid*; WOMAN: Gretchen Kingsley-Wiehe, *Betsy True (from 89–90), Melissa Anne Davis (by 90–91), Sarah E. Litzsinger (by 91–92), Jessica-Snow Wilson (by 93–94), Shanice (from 94–95), Jessica Snow–Wilson (by 95–96), Tammy Jacobs (from 95–96), Alexandra Foucard (by 96–97)*; DRUNK: John Norman Thomas, *Merwin Foard, Gary Lynch (by 90–91), Kipp Marcus (by 96–97), Kevin Kern (from 97), D.B. Bonds (from 99), Kevin Odekirk (from 00), David Josefsberg (from 00), Kevin Odekirk (from 00), Kevin Kern (from 01)*; 1ST DINER: Norman Large, *Bruce Kuhn (from 88), Pete Herber (from 88–89), Paul Avedisian (from 89–90), Joseph Kolinski (from 93), Paul Avedisian (from 93), David McDonald by 96–97), David Benoit (from 97–98), David McDonald (from 98), David Benoit (from 99), Clif*

Thorn (from 99), John Haggerty (from 99), David Benoit (from 00), Robert Hunt (from 00), David Benoit (from 01); 2ND DINER: Joanna Glushak, *Jean Fitzgibbons (from 88–89), Madeleine Doherty (from 90–91), Diane Della Piazza (by 93–94), Madeleine Doherty (by 94–95), Erika MacLeod (by 96–97)*; 1ST OTHER DRINKER: Steve Schochet, *Adam Heller (from 89–90), Bill Carmichael (from 90), Kevin McGuire (from 91), Kenny Morris (by 91–92), Kevin McGuire (from 93–94), Nicholas F. Saverine (from 93–94), Kelly Briggs (from 95–96), Kevin McGuire (from 95–96), John Capes (by 96–97), Stephen Colella (by 98), Clif Thorn, Joe Paparella (from 98), Neal Mayer (from 99)*; 2ND OTHER DRINKER: Anthony Crivello, *Stephen Bogardus (from 87–88), Tom Zemon (from 88–89), Alan Osburn (by 91–92), Wade Williams (from 93), Michael X. Martin (by 93–94), Alan Osburn (from 95), J.C. Sheets (by 95–96), Tom Zemon from 95–96, Paul Truckey (from 97–98), Robert D. Mamanna (from 99), David McDonald (from 01)*; 3RD OTHER DRINKER: Kevin Marcum (died 7/20/87), *Tim Shew (from 87–88), William Solo (from 87–88), J.C. Sheets (from 88–89), Nicholas F. Saverine (from 93), Robert Evan (by 93–94), Dave Clemmons (by 94–95), J.C. Sheets (by 95–96), Charles Bergell (from 96), Pete Herber (from 96), Gary Moss (from 96), Peter Gunther (by 96–97), Kevin Earley (from 97–98), Christopher Mark Peterson (from 99), David Gagnon (from 99), John-Andrew Clark (from 02)*; 4TH OTHER DRINKER: Ann Crumb, *Janene Lovullo (from 87–88), Anne Marie Ranulfsson (from 88–89), Mary Gutzi (from 89–90), Jessie Janet Richards (from 91–92)* [role deleted by 95–96]; 5TH OTHER DRINKER: Susan Goodman, *Deborah Bradshaw (from 89–90), Lucille De Cristofaro (by 90–91), Ann Arvia (by 96–97), Joanna Glushak, Ann Arvia, Anne Tolpegin, Ann Arvia*; 6TH OTHER DRINKER: Cindy Benson, *Jessica Molaskey (from 88–89), Jean Fitzgibbons (by 91–92), Liz McCartney (by 95–96), Madeleine Doherty (by 96–97), Joanna Glushak, Madeleine Doherty, Becky Barta*; YOUNG MAN: Joseph Kolinski, *Jordan Leeds (from 88–89), Raymond Saar (from 89), Jordan Leeds (from 90), Dann Fink (by 91–92), Michael Berry (from 92–93), John Cudia (by 95–96), Gary Moss (by 96–97), Stephen Paul Cramer (from 00), Bart Shatto (from 01), Andrew Varela (from 02)*; 1ST YOUNG GIRL: Jane Bodle, *Cissy Rebich (by 88–89), Cissy Lee Cates (by 90–91), Connie Kunkle (by 93–94), Kristen Behrendt (by 95–96), Gina Lamparella (by 96–97), Lisa Capps, Gina Lamparella*; 2ND YOUNG GIRL: Kelli James, *Lisa Ann Grant (by 87–88), Gina Feliccia (by 93–94), Jodie Langel (by 94–95), Dana Meller (by 95–96)*; OLD COUPLE: WOMAN: Marcie Shaw, *Olga Merediz (from 88–89), Marcie Shaw (by 90–91), Diane Della Piazza (by 91–92), Jessica Sheridan (by 92–93), Nicola Boyer (by 93–94), Jessica Sheridan (by 95–96), Megan Lawrence (by 96–97), Danielle de Niese (from 97–98), Megan Lawrence (from 97–98), Jennifer Paz (from 97–98), Megan Lawrence (from 97–98), Sutton Foster, Catherine Brunell*; MAN: John Dewar, *Scott Elliott (from 89), Rohn Seykell (from 89–90), Kevin R. Wright (from 91–92), Matt McClanahan (by 91–92), Kipp Marcus (by 95–96), Scott Hunt (by 96–97), John Capes (from 96–97), Stephen Colella (from 97–98), Hunter Foster (from 97–98), D.B. Bonds (from 98), Dave Hugo, Chris Diamantopoulos (from 98), D.B. Bonds (from 99), David Josefsberg (from 99), Chris Diamantopoulos (from 00), Kevin Kern (from 01), Kevin Odekirk (from 01), Edward Juvier (from 02)*; 1ST TRAVELER: Paul Harman, *Joel Robertson (from 87–88), Robert Du Sold (from 94), Mark Hardy (from 94), Joel Robertson (from 94), Robert Gallagher (by 96–97), Ben Starr Coates (from 97–98), David McDonald (from 97–98), Ben Starr Coates (from 98), Brian Noonan (from 98), David McDonald (from 99), Robert Gallagher (from 00), David McDonald (from 00), Robert Hunt (from 01)*; 2ND TRAVELER: Marcus Lovett, *John Ruess (from 88–89), Willy Falk (from 88–89), Peter Gutenbein (from 90), John Leone (from 91), Larry Alexander (by 91–92), Ciaran Sheehan (from 92), Daniel C. Cooney (from 92–93), Tom Donoghue (by 92–93), Marsh Hanson (by 95–96), Peter Lockyer (from 96), Kurt Kovalenko (by 96–97), Stephen Colella (from 98), Clif Thorn (from 98), Kurt Kovalenko (from 98), D.B. Bonds, Clif Thorn, Kurt Kovalenko, Darren Ritchie (from 01), Kurt Kovalenko (from 02)*. 1832, PARIS: GAVROCHE: Braden Danner, *Danny Gerard (from 87–88)*. By 89–90 the role had two actors alternating: *Alex Dezen & Joey Rigol (Gregory Grant & Brian Press* by 90–91. Mr. Press was replaced by *Tommy J. Michaels)*. 92–93 list: *Brian Press & Michael Shulman*. 93–94 list: *Sean Russell & Brandon Espinoza (Simon Pearl & Michael Zeidman* by 95–96). 96–97 list: *Christopher Trousdale, Alex Strange, Jordan Siwek, Evan Jay Newman*. 97–98 list: *Jordan Siwek (Christopher Win-*

sor from 97–98, *Evan Jay Newman* from 97–98, Cameron Bowen), *Evan Jay Newman* (*Ian Parry* from 97–98; *Patrick J.P. Duffey* from 97–98); OLD BEGGARWOMAN: Susan Goodman, *Deborah Bradshaw* (from 89–90), *Lucille De Cristofaro* (by 90–91), *Madeleine Doherty* (by 96–97), *Joanna Glushak, Madeleine Doherty, Becky Barta*; YOUNG PROSTITUTE: Ann Crumb, *Janene Lovullo* (from 87–88), *Anne Marie Ranulfsson* (from 88–89), *Mary Gutzi* (from 89–90), *Jessie Janet Richards* (by 91–92), *Audrey Klinger* (by 95–96), *Dana Meller* (by 96–97); PIMP: John Norman Thomas, *Merwin Foard* (from 89–90), *Gary Lynch* (by 90–91), *Robert Gallagher* (by 96–97), *Ben Starr Coates* (from 97–98), *David McDonald* (from 97–98), *Ben Starr Coates* (from 98), *Brian Noonan* (from 98), *David McDonald* (from 99), *Robert Gallagher* (from 00), *David McDonald* (from 00), *Robert Hunt* (from 01); EPONINE: Frances Ruffelle, *Kelli James* (from 9/15/87), *Natalie Toro* (from 7/88), *Debbie Gibson* (from 1/7/92), *Michele Maika* (from 91–92), *Debbie Gibson* (from 3/29/92), *Brandy Brown* (from 92–93), *Lea Salonga* (from 1/5/93), *Tia Riebling* (from 93), *Lea Salonga* (from 93–94), *Sarah Uriarte* [later known as Sarah Uriarte Berry] (from 93–94), *Jessica-Snow Wilson* (from 94–95), *Shanice* (from 94–95), *Jessica-Snow Wilson* (by 95–96), *Christeena Michelle Riggs* (from 95–96), *Sarah Uriarte Berry* (from 3/12/97), *Megan Lawrence* (during Miss Uriarte's two vacations, 97–98, and permanently from 6/19/98), *Kerry Butler* (from 12/11/98), *Megan Lawrence* (from 2/25/99), *Rona Figueroa* (during Miss Lawrence's absence to marry Kevin Kern — 6/3/99–6/23/99), *Megan Lawrence* (from 6/24/99), *Jessica-Snow Wilson* (8/31/99–9/12/99), *Rona Figueroa* (9/14/99–10/99), *Megan Lawrence* (from 10/99), *Jessica Boevers* (from 12/7/00), *Catharine Brunell* (from 8/10/00), *Dana Meller* (from 12/13/01), *Diana Kaarina* (from 1/14/02); (THE FOUR MEMBERS OF) THENARDIER'S GANG: MONTPARNASSE: Alex Santoriello, *Rene Clemente* (from 87–88), *Bruce Kuhn* (from 87–88), *Craig Wells* (from 90), *Sam Fontana* (from 90), *Liam O'Brien* (by 91–92), *Ken Krugman* (by 92–93), *Stephen Bishop* (from 94), *Tony Lawson* (from 95), *Phil Johnson* (from 95), *Richard Falzone* (from 95), *Richard Vida* (by 95–96), *David McDonald* (by 96–97), *David Benoit* (from 97–98), *David McDonald* (from 98), *David Benoit* (from 99), *Clif Thorn* (from 99), *John Haggerty* (from 99), *David Benoit* (from 00), *Robert Hunt* (from 00), *David Benoit* (from 01); BABET: Marcus Lovett, *John Ruess* (from 88–89), *Willy Falk* (from 88–89), *Peter Gutenbein* (from 90), *John Leone* (from 91), *Larry Alexander* (by 91–92), *Ciaran Sheehan* (from 92), *Daniel C. Cooney* (from 92–93), *Tom Donoghue* (by 92–93), *Marsh Hanson* (from 95–96), *Peter Lockyer* (from 96), *Kurt Kovalenko* (by 96–97), *Stephen Colella* (from 98), *Clif Thorn* (from 98), *Kurt Kovalenko* (from 98), *D.B. Bonds, Clif Thorn, Kurt Kovalenko, Darren Ritchie* (from 01), *Kurt Kovalenko* (from 02); BRUJON: Kevin Marcum (died 7/20/87), *Tim Shew* (from 87–88), *William Solo* (from 87–88), *J.C. Sheets* (from 88–89), *Nicholas F. Saverine* (from 93), *Robert Evan* (by 93–94), *Dave Clemmons* (by 94–95), *J.C. Sheets* (by 95–96), *Charles Bergell* (from 96), *Pete Herber* (from 96), *Gary Moss* (by 96–97), *Stephen Paul Cramer* (from 00), *Bart Shatto* (from 01), *Andrew Varela* (from 02); CLAQUESOUS: Steve Schochet, *Adam Heller* (from 89–90), *Bill Carmichael* (from 90), *Kevin McGuire* (from 91), *Kenny Morris* (by 91–92), *Kevin McGuire* (from 93–94), *Nicholas F. Saverine* (by 93–94), *Kelly Briggs* (from 95–96), *Kevin McGuire* (by 95–96), *John Capes* (by 96–97), *Stephen Colella* (by 98), *Clif Thorn, Joe Paparella* (from 98), *Neal Mayer* (from 99); ENJOLRAS: Michael Maguire, *Joseph Kolinski* (from 88–89), *Joe Locarro* (from 1/15/90), *Joseph Kolinski* (from 89–90), *Joseph Mahowald* (from 91–92), *Lawrence Anderson* (by 92–93), *Ron Bohmer* (from 93–94), *Gary Mauer* (from 95–96), *Robert Aaron Tesoro* (from 96), *Paul Avedisian* (from 10/29/96), *Stephen R. Buntrock* (from 3/12/97), *Gary Mauer* (from 12/8/98), *Stephen R. Buntrock* (from 4/6/99), *Christopher Mark Peterson* (from 6/21/99), *Ben Davis* (from 9/10/01), *Christopher Mark Peterson* (from 1/7/02), *David Gagnon* (from 02), *Christopher Mark Peterson* (from 02); MARIUS: David Bryant, *Ray Walker* (from 87–88), *Hugh Panaro* (from 88–89), *Matthew Porretta* (by 90–91), *John Leone* (from 91–92), *Erich Kunze* (by 92–93), *Michael Sutherland Lynch* (from 92–93), *Craig Rubano* (from 93–94), *Tom Donoghue* (from 95–96), *Ricky Martin* (6/24–9/8/96), *Tom Donoghue* (from 9/10/96), *Peter Lockyer* (from 3/12/97), *Stephen Brian Patterson* (from 2002), *Kevin Kern* (from 02); COSETTE: Judy Kuhn, *Tracy Shayne* (from 87–88), *Jacquelyn Piro* (from 89–90), *Melissa Anne Davis* (from 91–92), *Jennifer Lee Andrews* (from 92–93), *Jacquelyn Piro* (from 94), *Jodie Langel* (from 95), *Jennifer Lee

Andrews* (from 95), *Tamra Hayden* (by 95–96), *Jennifer Lee Andrews* (from 11/19/96), *Christeena Michelle Riggs* (from 3/12/97), *Tobi Foster* (from 11/6/98), *Sandra Turley* (nee Dudley) (from 2/5/01), *Stephanie Waters* (from 02), *Sandra Turley* (from 02); COMBEFERRE: Paul Harman, *Joel Robertson* (from 87–88), *Robert Du Sold* (from 94), *Mark Hardy* (from 94), *Joel Robertson* (from 94), *Robert Gallagher* (by 96–97), *Ben Starr Coates* (from 97–98), *David McDonald* (from 97–98), *Ben Starr Coates* (from 98), *Brian Noonan* (from 98), *David McDonald* (from 99), *Robert Gallagher* (from 00), *David McDonald* (from 00), *Robert Hunt* (from 01); FEUILLY: Joseph Kolinski, *Jordan Leeds* (from 88–89), *Raymond Saar* (from 89), *Jordan Leeds* (from 90), *Dann Fink* (by 91–92), *Michael Berry* (from 92–93), *John Cudia* (by 95–96), *Robert Vernon* (from 96), *John Cudia* (from 96), *Peter Gunther* (from 96), *Adam Hunter* (by 96–97), *D.B. Bonds* (from 98), *Adam Hunter, Dave Hugo, D.B. Bonds, Christopher Eid* (from 99), *Roger Seyer* (from 00), *John Cudia* (from 02); COURFEYRAC: Jesse Corti, *Jeffrey Clonts* (from 88–89), *Frank Mastrone* (by 91–92), *Douglas Webster* (from 92–93), *Bryan Landrine* (by 93–94), *Peter Gunther* (from 95), *Bryan Landrine* (from 96), *Peter Gunther* (from 96), *Robert Evan* (from 96), *Ivan Rutherford* (from 96), *Charles Bergell* (from 96), *Jeffrey Scott Watkins* (by 96–97), *Andrew Varela* (from 97–98), *Ron Sharpe* (from 00); JOLY: John Dewar, *Scott Elliott* (from 89), *Rohn Seykell* (from 89–90), *Kevin R. Wright* (from 91–92), *Matt McClanahan* (by 91–92), *Kipp Marcus* (by 95–96), *Scott Hunt* (by 96–97), *John Capes* (from 96–97), *Stephen Colella* (from 97–98), *Hunter Foster* (from 97–98), *D.B. Bonds* (from 98), *Dave Hugo, Chris Diamantopoulos* (from 98), *D.B. Bonds* (from 99), *David Josefsberg* (from 99), *Chris Diamantopoulos* (from 00), *Kevin Kern* (from 2001), *Kevin Odekirk* (from 01), *Edward Juvier* (from 01); GRANTAIRE: Anthony Crivello, *Stephen Bogardus* (from 87–88), *Tom Zemon* (from 88–89), *Alan Osburn* (by 91–92), *Wade Williams* (from 93), *Michael X. Martin* (by 93–94), *Alan Osburn* (from 95), *J.C. Sheets* (from 95–96), *Tom Zemon* (by 95–96), *Paul Truckey* (from 97–98), *Robert D. Mamanna* (from 99), *Paul Truckey* (from 99), *David McDonald* (from 01); LESGLES: Norman Large, *Bruce Kuhn* (from 88), *Pete Herber* (from 88–89), *Paul Avedisian* (from 89–90), *Joseph Kolinski* (from 93), *Paul Avedisian* (from 93), *Gary Moss* (from 96), *Peter Gunther* (by 96–97), *Kevin Earley* (from 97–98), *Christopher Mark Peterson* (from 99), *David Gagnon* (from 99), *John-Andrew Clark* (from 02); JEAN PROUVAIRE: John Norman Thomas [he was also known as John Norman], *Merwin Foard* (from 89–90), *Gary Lynch* (by 91–92), *Kipp Marcus* (by 96–97), *Kevin Kern* (from 97 — he was absent 6/3/99–6/23/99 to get married to Megan Lawrence), *D.B. Bonds* (from 99), *Kevin Odekirk* (from 00), *David Josefsberg* (from 00), *Kevin Odekirk* (from 01), *Kevin Kern* (from 01); MAJOR DOMO: Scott Hunt (by 97–98), *Stephen Colella* (from 97–98), *Hunter Foster* (from 97–98), *Dave Hugo, Chris Diamantopoulos* [new role by 97–98]. ***Understudies***: Valjean: Kevin Marcum (87), Paul Harman (87), *Joel Robertson* (87–95), *J.C. Sheets* (91–93), *Kevin McGuire* (91), *Jeffrey Clonts* (91), *Frank Mastrone* (91–92), *Douglas Webster* (92–93), *Bryan Landrine* (93–95), *Nicholas F. Saverine* (93–95), *Dave Clemmons* (94–95), *Gary Moss* (from 96), *Ivan Rutherford* (96–98), *John Capes* (97–98), *Andrew Varela* (from 97); Javert: Anthony Crivello (87), Norman Large (87), *Stephen Bogardus* (87–88), *Bruce Kuhn* (87–91), *Gary Lynch* (91–95), *Tom Zemon* (91, 96–98), *Alan Osburn* (91–93), *Michael X. Martin* (93–95), *Robert Gallagher* (96–98), *David Benoit* (97–98), *David McDonald* (from 97), *Paul Truckey* (from 98); Bishop: Steve Schochet (87–88), *John Dewar* (87–88), *Bruce Kuhn* (87–91), *Paul Avedisian* (91–95), *Gary Moss* (91–92), *Sam Scalamoni* (91), *Bruce Thompson* (92–93), *Joseph Kolinski* (93–95), *Wayne Scherzer* (93–95), *Gregory Brandt* (from 96), *Dave Hugo* (96–98), *Jeffrey Scott Watkins* (from 96); Fantine: Ann Crumb (87), Joanna Glushak (87–91), *Janene Lovullo* (87–88), *Mary Gutzi* (91), *Alice Vienneau* (91), *Jessie Janet Richards* (91–93), *Jean Fitzgibbons* (91–95), *Connie Kunkle* (93–94), *Kerrianne Spellman* (94–95), *Alexandra Foucard* (from 96), *Alicia Irving* (96–98), *Erika MacLeod* (from 96), *Jennifer Zimmerman* (from 97), *Holly Jo Crane* (from 98); Young Cosette: Brandy Brown (87), Chrissie McDonald (87), *Amy Beth* (87–88), *Shanelle Workman* (87–88); Mme. Thenardier: Cindy Benson (87–88), Susan Goodman, (87), *Marcie Shaw* (87–88, 91), *Jessica Molaskey* (91), *Jean Fitzgibbons* (91–95), *Diane Della Piazza* (91–92), *Jessica Sheridan* (92–93), *Nicola Boyer* (from 96), *Ann Arvia* (from 96), *Madeleine Doherty* (from 96), *Joanna Glushak* (from 98), *Anne Tolpegin* (from 98), *Becky Barta* (from 98); Thenardier: John Norman Thomas

(87–88), *Norman Large* (87–91), *Bruce Kuhn* (87–91), *Kevin McGuire* (91), *Sam Fontana* ((91), *Kenny Morris* (91–93), *Liam O'Brien* (91–92), *Ken Krugman* (92–95), *Nicholas F. Saverine* (93–95), *John Capes* (96–98), *David McDonald* (from 96), *David Benoit* (from 97), *Stephen Colella* (from 97), *Joe Paparella* (from 98); Young Eponine: Brandy Brown (87), *Amy Beth* (87–88), *Alexis Kalehoff, Alicia Morton*; Gavroche: R.D. Robb (87), *David Burdick* (87–88), *Lacey Chabert* (91–95), *Gregory Grant* (92–93), *Patrick J.P. Duffey* (98–99); Eponine: Kelli James (87), Gretchen Kingsley-Wiehe (87–88), Jane Bodle (87), *Lisa Ann Grant* (87–93), *Melissa Anne Davis* (91), *Sarah Litzsinger* (91–93), *Gina Felic-cia* (93–94), *Jessica-Snow Wilson* (93–95), *Jodie Langel* (94–95), *Megan Lawrence* (from 96), *Dana Meller* (from 96), *Gina Lamparella* (96–98), *Cathy Nichols* (97–98), *Jennifer Paz* (97–98), *Michelle de Niese* (97–98), *Catherine Brunell* (from 98), *Tobi Foster* (from 98); Enjolras: Joseph Kolinski (87–91), Paul Harman (87), *Jordan Leeds* (87–91), *Paul Avedisian* (91–95), *Dann Fink* (91–92), *Michael Berry* (92–95), *Peter Gunther* (96–98), *Kurt Kovalenko* (96–99), *Kevin Earley* (97–99), *Gregory Brandt* (97–99), *Christopher Mark Peterson* (98–99), *Clif Thorn* (98–99); Mar-ius: Marcus Lovett (87–88), Joseph Kolinski (87–91), *Jordan Leeds* (91), *Rohn Seykell* (91), *John Leone* (91), *Larry Alexander* (91–92), *Matt McClanahan* (91–95), *Tom Donoghue* (92–95), *Scott Hunt* (96–98), *Kipp Marcus* (96–98), *Hunter Foster* (97–99), *Adam Hunter* (97–98), *Kevin Kern* (98–99), *Chris Diamantopoulos* (98–99); Cosette: Gretchen Kings-ley-Wiehe (87–91), Jane Bodle (87–88), *Melissa Anne Davis* (91), *Sarah Litzsinger* (91–93), *Cissy Lee Cates* (91–93), *Gina Feliccia* (93–94), *Jes-sica-Snow Wilson* (93–95), *Jodie Langel* (94–95), *Megan Lawrence* (96–98), *Dana Meller* (from 96), *Gina Lamparella* (from 96), *Cathy Nichols* (from 97), *Jennifer Paz* (97–98), *Michelle de Niese* (97–98). **Swings**: Patrick A'Hearn (87–88), Diane Della Piazza (87), Jordan Leeds (87–88), *Anny De Gange* (87–88), *Nina Hennessey* (87–92), *Sam Scala-moni* (91), *Alice Vienneau* (91), *T. Ryan Barkman* (91–92), *Christa Justus* (91–95), *Gary Moss* (91–92), *Lorraine Goodman* (92–93), *Wayne Scherzer* (92–93, 94–95), *Bruce Thompson* (92–93), *Kerrianne Spellman* (93–95), *Joseph Kolinski* (93–95), *Mark Hardy* (93–94), *Gregory Brandt* (96–99), *Angela De Cicco* (96–99), *Dave Hugo* (96–99), *Cathy Nichols* (96–99), *Jeffrey Scott Watkins* (97–99), *Catherine Brunell* (97–98), *Julia Haubner* (98–99), *Pete Herber* (98–99), *Clif Thorn* (98–99). **Musicians** (list from 3/91): KEYBOARDS: James Laev & Lawrence Yurman; CONCERTMASTER: Mineko Yajima; VIOLINS: Marti Sweet, Marion Pinheiro, Mitchell Stern, Marilyn Reynolds, Sean Carney; VIOLAS: Mitsue Takayama & Brian Zenone; CELLI: Clay Ruede & Batia Lieberman; FLUTE/PICCOLO: Jacqueline Giat; CLARINET/ALTO SAX: Mitchell Weiss; OBOE/ENGLISH HORN: Harriet Orenstein; TRUMPETS/PICCOLO TRUMPETS: David Gale, Robert Zottola, Pete Hyde; FLUGELHORNS: David Gale & Robert Zot-tola; BASS TROMBONE: John Rojak; FRENCH HORNS: Brooks Tillotson & Daniel Culpepper; GUITARS: Brian Koonin; BASS: Lindsey Horner; DRUMS: Michael Hinton; PERCUSSION: Howard Joines. *Prologue* Digne, France; 1815: PROLOGUE (Company): "Work Song" (Valjean, Javert, Pris-oners), Valjean Arrested/Valjean Forgiven (Valjean, Constables, Bishop), "What Have I Done?" ("Soliloquy") (Valjean); "At the End of the Day" (Unemployed & Factory Workers). *Act I*: *Scene 1* Montreuil-sur-Mer; 1823: "I Dreamed a Dream" (Fantine), "Lovely Ladies" (Ladies & Clients), Fantine's Arrest (Javert, Fantine, Bamatabois, Valjean), The Runaway Cart (Valjean, Crowd, Fauchelevent, Javert), "Who Am I?" (The Trial) (Valjean), "Come to Me" (Fantine's Death) (Fantine & Val-jean), Confrontation (Valjean & Javert), "Castle on a Cloud" (Young Cosette), "Master of the House" (Thenardier, Mme Thenardier, Cus-tomers), The Bargain (Thenardier), "Thenardier Waltz (of Treachery)" (The Thenardiers & Valjean); *Scene 2* Montfermeil; 1823: "Look Down" (Gavroche & Beggars), The Robbery (Thenardier & Gang), Javert's Intervention, "Stars" (Javert), Eponine's Errand, "Little People" (Gavroche) [in the London production, but cut for Broadway], "Red and Black" (ABC Cafe) (Enjolras, Marius, Students), "Do You Hear the People Sing?" (Enjolras, Combeferre, Courfeyrac, Feuilly, Chorus); *Scene 3* Paris; 1832: Love Montage: "I Saw Him Once" (Cosette) [cut for Broad-way], "In My Life" (Cosette, Valjean, Marius, Eponine), "A Heart Full of Love" (Cosette, Marius, Eponine) [end of montage], The Attack on Rue Plumet (Thenardier & Gang, Eponine), "One Day More" (Valjean, Marius, Cosette, Eponine, Enjolras, Javert, The Thenardiers). *Act II*: Paris; 1832: Upon These Stones (Building the Barricade), "On My Own"

(Eponine), Upon These Stones (Javert at the Barricade/"Little People") [a reduced version of the London original], First attack (Policemen, Enjolras, Students), "A Little Fall of Rain" (Eponine & Marius), "Drink with Me (to Days Gone By)" (Night of Anguish) (Grantaire, Students, Women, Marius), "Bring Him Home" (Valjean), Dawn of Anguish, Sec-ond Attack (Death of Gavroche), The Final Battle, "Dog Eats Dog" (The Sewers) (Thenardier), "Soliloquy" (Javert's Suicide), "Turning" (Women), "Empty Chairs at Empty Tables" (Marius) [the show stop-per], "Every Day" (Valjean's Confession), "Wedding Chorale" (Guests) [on the weekend of 10/23/98 this sequence was re-choreographed by Kate Flatt], "Beggars at the Feast" (The Thenardiers), Finale (Epilogue): "Do You Hear the People Sing?" (reprise) (Company).

Les Miz opened on Broadway at the top ticket price of $47.50, and on the first day at the box office took in $447,275 (a record, but easily beaten by *Phantom* in 1987). Most critics raved, but there some who were mistaken. It won Tony Awards for musical, score, book, direction of a musical, sets, lighting, and for Michael Maguire and Frances Ruffelle, and was nominated for costumes, and for Colm Wilkinson, Terrence Mann and Judy Kuhn. Kevin Marcum was slated to succeed Mr. Wilkin-son in the lead, but he died on 7/20/87, of acute cocaine intoxication. The show ran so long, and was so popular, it became known as *Les Miz*. On 9/21/96 Mr. Mackintosh happened to view a performance, and men-tioned to Equity executive secretary Alan Eisenberg that some actors were looking too old in their parts. On 9/24/96 Alan Wasser, general manager of the Broadway and touring productions, announced that sev-eral actors would be fired, others would be re-cast in different roles, and others would stay as they were. This caused dismay not only among the cast, but in the theatre world at large. Mr. Eisenberg claimed to be shocked, and probably was. On 10/27/96 the names of the actors were announced. On 11/5/96 Peter Marks of the *New York Times* reviewed it again, and gave it a terrible review, saying it was stale and needed changes. In the end Cameron Mackintosh offered the departing actors a much bet-ter deal than if they had contested the firings legally and won. The com-pany performed its last show on 1/26/97, and on 1/28/97 was replaced with the bus and truck touring company (Tour # 3) of *Les Miz* as an interim measure, until on 3/6/97 (a date put forward from 3/3/97) a 10th-anniversary company began previews, and official performances on 3/12/97. The producers gave away 1,000 free tickets as prizes for this event (winners were chosen on 2/14/97). Aside from the cast changes (in the end, of the 38 cast members in the show as of late 1996, 18 were retained), there were other, structural, changes in the show: a new scene inserted into Act I, and there were minor lyric changes throughout; sets were re-furbished; more than 160 new costumes were designed by Andreane Neofitou; all wigs were new; lighting technology was updated; and there was new sound design by Andrew Bruce. And, the role of Jean Valjean was now played by a lead actor, and an alternate on certain days. Shuler Hensley was due to arrive as the new Javert on 10/24/00, but this was put back a week. It was his Broadway debut. Early in 2001 the running time of 3 hours 20 minutes was cut to 2 hours 58 minutes, to save money. Like all Broadway shows, it was hit hard by the 9/11 attack in 2001, and like several other shows the cast and crew agreed to a 25 per-cent pay cut for a couple of weeks to enable the show to carry on. On 1/5/02 it played its 6,138th performance, beating *A Chorus Line* as the second-longest-running Broadway musical of all time (behind *Cats*). After the 10/2/02 matinee the cast was informed that the show would be closing on 3/15/03, after 6,612 performances — the end of an era. How-ever, on 1/30/03 Cameron Mackintosh announced that this date had been extended to 5/18/03. It would have played a total of 6,684 perfor-mances, but due to the musicians' strike of 3/03 it lost 4 performances. The last performance was by invitation only, at big ticket prices. At the end was a mega finale, with over 300 past and present performers tak-ing part. After the show closed the set went to Berlin, for a production there. On Broadway it grossed over $410 million, and 9.2 million peo-ple saw it. World-wide, by 5/03 it had grossed over $2 billion, and over 50 million people had seen it.

After Broadway. IMPERIAL THEATRE, Tokyo. Opened on 7/13/87.
CAMERI THEATRE, Tel Aviv. Opened on 8/9/87. *Cast:* JEAN VAL-JEAN: Dudu Fisher; JAVERT: Elior Yeini; FANTINE: Riki Gal.
ROCK THEATRE, Vigzinhaz, Budapest. Opened on 8/14/87.
THEATRE ROYAL, Sydney. Opened on 11/27/87.

TOUR. Opened on 12/15/87, at the Shubert Theatre, Boston. Previews from 12/5/87. This tour closed. MUSICAL DIRECTOR: Dale Rieling (by 1990). *Cast:* JEAN VALJEAN: William Solo, *Craig Schulman (from 4/88), J. Mark McVey, Gary Morris, Mark McKerracher;* JAVERT: Herndon Lackey, *Charles Pistone, Robert Du Sold, Richard Kinsey;* INNKEEPER'S WIFE: Deborah Bradshaw, *Ann Arvia;* BISHOP: Kevin McGuire, *Claude R. Tessier, Stephen Frugoli;* FANTINE: Diane Fratantoni, *Ann Crumb, Hollis Resnik, Kathy Taylor, Susan Dawn Carson, Laurie Beechman* (from 1/89), *Susan Gilmour, Anne Ranulfsson;* CRONE: Olga Merediz, *Eydie Alyson;* MME THENARDIER: Victoria Clark, *Rosalyn Rahn;* THENARDIER: Tom Robbins, *Neal Ben-Ari (from 12/5/88), Drew Eshelman;* EPONINE: Renee Veneziale, *Jennifer Naimo, Susan Tilson;* ENJOLRAS: John Herrera, *Joe Locarro, Kurt Johns, Pete Herber, Christopher Yates;* MARIUS: Hugh Panaro, *John Ruess, Peter Gunther;* COSETTE: Tamara Jenkins, *Melissa Errico, Kimberly Behlman;* JOLY: Scott Elliott, *Daniel C. Cooney;* PROUVAIRE: Willy Falk, *J.C. Montgomery.*

NATIONAL THEATRE, Reykjavik. Opened on 12/26/87.

DET NORSKE TEATRET, Oslo. Opened on 3/17/88.

CHUNICHI THEATRE, Nagoya, Japan. Opened on 3/25/88.

TOUR. Opened on 6/1/88, in Los Angeles. Previews from 5/21/88. It went on to San Francisco, where it closed in 12/94. MUSICAL DIRECTOR: John David Scott. *Cast:* JEAN VALJEAN: William Solo, *Jordan Bennett, Rich Hebert, Kevin McGuire, Richard Poole;* JAVERT: Jeff McCarthy, *Richard Kinsey, Tim Bowman;* LABORER: Martin Croft; BISHOP: Kevin McGuire; FANTINE: Elinore O'Connell, *Kelly Ground;* FOREMAN: Bruce Winant; FAUCHELEVENT: Liam O'Brien; MME THENARDIER: Kay Cole, *Gina Ferrall;* THENARDIER: Gary Beach; YOUNG MAN: Dann Fink; EPONINE: Michelle Nicastro, *Michele Maika, Candese Marchese, Misty Cotton;* ENJOLRAS: Greg Blanchard, *Raymond Saar, Craig Oldfather;* MARIUS: Reece Holland, *Peter Gantenbein, Matthew Porretta, John Ruess;* COSETTE: Karen Fineman, *Jacquelyn Piro, Ellen Rockne.*

RAIMUND THEATRE, Vienna. Opened on 9/15/88.

TOUR. This was a 4.2 million dollar bus and truck tour, a complete replica of the Broadway show, and became known as the Broadway National Tour, or the Third National Company. It opened on 11/30/88, at Tampa Bay Performing Arts Center, Festival Hall. Previews from 11/20/88. It closed at the Capitol Theatre, Salt Lake City, 6/15/03, for vacation until 9/03, and re-opened on 9/9/03, at the Fox Theatre, Atlanta. Part of its run was in Toronto, 7/15/98–10/18/98. By the end of 2004 it was the only tour of *Les Miz* running in the USA. TOUR DIRECTORS: John Caird & Trevor Nunn; MUSICAL SUPERVISOR: Dale Rieling; MUSICAL DIRECTOR: Robert S. Gustafson, *R. Andrew Bryan.* *Cast:* JEAN VALJEAN: Gary Barker, *Richard Poole, Brian Lynch, Dave Clemmons, Donn Cook, Craig Schulman, Frederick C. Inkley, William Solo, Ivan Rutherford* (from 10/95), *Robert Evan (from 4/96), Craig Schulman* (Honolulu only, from 9/9/96), *Robert Evan (from 9/30/96), Gregory Calvin Stone (from 3/3/97), Colm Wilkinson* (Toronto only, from 7/15/98), *Ivan Rutherford (from 1/19/99), Randal Keith (from 3/01), Ivan Rutherford, Randal Keith (from 9/9/03);* JAVERT: Peter Samuel, *Paul Schoeffler, David Jordan, Chuck Wagner, Michael X. Martin, Merwin Foard, David Masenheimer, Richard Kinsey, Ron Baker (from 6/95), David McDonald (from 12/95), Robert Longo (from 4/96), David Jordan (from 11/18/96), David Masenheimer (from 1/27/97), Todd Alan Johnson (from 3/31/97), Stephen Bishop (from 8/3/99), Philip Hernandez, Joseph Mahowald, Stephen Tewksbury, James Clowe (from 9/9/03), Stephen Tewksbury, Robert Hunt;* BISHOP: Claude R. Tessier, *Dario Coletta, Kelly Briggs;* FANTINE: Hollis Resnik, *Christy Baron, Lisa Vroman, Donna Keane, Jill Geddes, Alice Ripley, Christy Baron, Anne Torsiglieri, Jacquelyn Piro, Susie McGonagle (from 6/95), Lisa Capps (from 3/96), Laurie Beechman (from 12/16/96), Lisa Capps (from 1/27/97), Catherine Hickland (from 3/10/97), Lisa Capps (from 3/24/97), Holly Jo Crane, Susan Gilmour (from 6/2/98), Joan Almedilla (from 3/2/99), Thursday Farrar, Joan Almedilla, Jayne Paterson (from 10/01), Tonya Dixon;* YOUNG COSETTE/YOUNG EPONINE: Eden Riegel & Tracy Ward (alternating), *Jennifer Elaine Davis & Talaria Haast;* MME THENARDIER: Linda Kerns, *Diana Rogers, Gina Ferrall, Kelly Ebsary, Tregoney Shepherd, Jean Fitzgibbons, Tregoney Shepherd, Aymee Garcia, Jodi Capeless, Cindy Benson (from 9/9/03), Jennifer Butt;* THENARDIER: Paul Ainsley, *J.P. Dougherty, David Benoit, J.P. Dougherty, Michael Hayward-Jones, Michael Kostroff (from 9/9/03), David Benoit;* EPONINE: Michele Maika, *Dana Lynn Caruso, Candese Marchese, Angela Pupello, Jennifer Rae*

Beck, *Sarah Uriarte, Gina Feliccia, Jessica-Snow Wilson, Caren Lyn Manuel, Christeena Michelle Riggs (from 11/95), Dawn Younker (from 2/96), Lea Salonga (in Honolulu only, from 9/9/96), Dawn Younker (from 9/30/96), Andrea McArdle (from 12/16/96), Dawn Younker (from 1/27/97), Rona Figueroa (3/31/97–5/99), Jessica-Snow Wilson (from 5/19/99), Sutton Foster, Diana Kaarina (from 3/21/00), Dina Morishita, Ma-Anne Dionisio, Jessica-Snow Wilson, Nicole Riding, Ma-Anne Dionisio (from 9/9/03), Melissa Lyons;* CLAQUEOUS: Adam Heller, *Kirk Mouser, Joshua Finkel;* ENJOLRAS: Greg Zerkle, *Jerry Christakos, Aloysius Gigl, Christopher Yates, Gary Mauer, Michael Maguire* (Toronto only), *Robert Vernon, Brian Noonan (from 12/95), Brian Herriott (from 9/30/96), Kurt Kovalenko, Michael Todd Cressman, Matthew Shepard (from 12/8/98), Kevin Earley (from 1/19/99), Stephen Tewksbury (from 2/15/00), Dallyn Vail Bayles, John Andrew Clark (from 9/9/03);* MARIUS: Matthew Porretta, *Christopher Pecaro, Gilles Chiasson, Ron Sharpe, Hayden Adams, Tom Donoghue, Andrew Redeker (from 6/95), Rich Affannato (from 8/12/96), Steven Scott Springer, Tim Howard, Stephen Brian Patterson, Scott Hunt, Josh Young (from 9/9/03), Adam Jacobs;* COSETTE: Jacquelyn Piro, *Tamra Hayden, Lisa Vroman, Marian Murphy, Tamra Hayden (by 93), Barbra Russell, Jennifer Rae Beck, Jodie Langel (by 95), Gina Feliccia (by 95), Kate Fisher (from 9/9/96), Regan Thiel, Stephanie Waters (by 00), Sandra Turley* [nee Dudley] (by 02), *Amanda Huddleston, Leslie Henstook;* FEUILLY: Brian Lynch, *Peter Lind Harris, Ron Sharpe;* COURFEYRAC: Jerry Christakos, *Douglas Webster;* JOLY: Rohn Seykell, *Amick Byram, Gilles Chiasson, Ron La Rosa;* GRANTAIRE: Craig Wells, *Alan Osburn, Paul Truckey;* ENSEMBLE: Reed Armstrong, Jeanne Smith, Mercedes Perez, Todd Zamarripa, Brian Lynch, Dave Hugo, Jessica Sheridan.

ROYAL ALEXANDRA THEATRE, Toronto. Opened on 3/15/89. *Cast:* JEAN VALJEAN: Michael Burgess.

AMSTERDAM. Opened on 2/24/91. This was the Dutch version (translated by Seth Gaaikema).

THEATRE MOGADOR, Paris. Opened in 1991. This was the Paris premiere of the famous version. *Cast:* JEAN VALJEAN: Robert Marien.

DUISBURG, Germany, 1/26/96–11/28/99.

ANTWERP. Opened on 5/24/98. Previews from 5/12/98. This was the Belgian version (in the Dutch language, newly translated by Paul Berkenman). DIRECTOR: Ken Caswell. *Cast:* JEAN VALJEAN: Hans Peter Janssens; JAVERT: Jan Danckaert; FANTINE: Hilda Norge; EPONINE: Chadia Cambie; COSETTE: Deborah Dutcher.

DUBLIN. 2/25/99–5/99. *Cast:* JEAN VALJEAN: Colm Wilkinson.

OPÉRA THEATRE, Buenos Aires. Opened on 3/22/00. Previews from 3/14/00. The Spanish-language premiere of *Los Miserables.* PRESENTED BY Cameron Mackintosh. *Cast:* JEAN VALJEAN: Carlos Vittori; JAVERT: Juan Rodo; FANTINE: Elena Roger.

SHANGHAI GRAND THEATRE, China, 6/22/02–7/7/02. This was the first time that a Broadway or West End musical had played in China. It was invited by the Chinese government. It played in English, but with Chinese sub-titles. *Cast:* JEAN VALJEAN: Colm Wilkinson, *Randal Keith* (at some performances); JAVERT: Michael McCarthy; FANTINE: Ria Jones; MME THENARDIER: Aymee Garcia; THENARDIER: J.P. Dougherty; EPONINE: Ma-Anne Dionisio; ENJOLRAS: Christopher Mark Peterson; COSETTE: Sandra Turley. The show then went on to SEOUL, KOREA, minus Mr. Wilkinson. Jayne Paterson played Fantine.

451. *Miss Liberty*

Set in New York and Paris in 1885. It tells of the rivalry between the two big New York newspapers, the *Herald* and the *World,* and their respective owners — James Gordon Bennett and Joseph Pulitzer. The Statue of Liberty is about to be dedicated when Horace, a young photographer (recently fired for ineptitude) discovers in Paris the girl, Monique, he believes to have been Bartholdi's model for the famous statue (in real life it was Bartholdi's mother), and the girl's nutty mother, the Countess. He brings Monique to New York amid much fanfare, then they all discover their error. However Monique has become famous, and Horace chooses her over Maisie, his American girl friend, a *Police Gazette* reporter.

Before Broadway. Playwright Robert E. Sherwood was inspired to write the book by the faces of GIs as they shipped out to Europe during World War II and took a farewell look at the Statue of Liberty. The numbers "The Hon'rable Profession of the Fourth Estate" (a revision of an unpublished number — "Automat Opening" — which was not used for the 1932 musical *Face the Music*), "Finding Work in Paris," "Entrance of the Reporters," and "The Next Time I Fall in Love" were dropped. In the month-long out-of-town tryouts in Philadelphia The *Herald* Reader was played by Rowan Tudor; and the Sharks were Bill Bradley, Allen Knowles, Kazimir Kokic & Robert Pagent. Several numbers were cut: "The Story of Nell and the Police Gazette," "Sing a Song of Sing Sing," "The Pulitzer Prize," "Business for a Good Girl is Bad," and "Mr. Monotony" (originally called "Mrs. Monotony"). The production had to delay its July 4 opening date. This was Robert E. Sherwood's only musical.

The Broadway Run. IMPERIAL THEATRE, 7/15/49–4/8/50. 308 PERFORMANCES. PRESENTED BY Irving Berlin, Robert E. Sherwood, Moss Hart; MUSIC/LYRICS: Irving Berlin; BOOK: Robert E. Sherwood; DIRECTOR: Moss Hart; CHOREOGRAPHER: Jerome Robbins; SETS/LIGHTING: Oliver Smith; COSTUMES: Motley; STAGE TECHNICIAN: Joe Lynn; MUSICAL DIRECTOR/VOCAL ARRANGEMENTS: Jay Blackton; ORCHESTRATIONS: Don Walker; DANCE MUSIC ARRANGEMENTS: Genevieve Pitot; PIANO ARRANGEMENTS: Helmy Kresa; PRESS: William Fields, Walter Alford, Arthur Cantor; GENERAL MANAGER: Victor Samrock; COMPANY MANAGER: Don Hershey; PRODUCTION STAGE MANAGER: Milton Baron; STAGE MANAGER: Terence J. Little; ASSISTANT STAGE MANAGER: Francis Spencer. *Cast:* MAISIE DELL: Mary McCarty (3); *Herald* READER: John Thompson; JAMES GORDON BENNETT: Charles Dingle; HORACE MILLER: Eddie Albert (1), *Billy Redfield*; POLICE CAPTAIN: Evans Thornton; THE MAYOR: Donald McClelland; FRENCH AMBASSADOR: Emile Renan; CARTWRIGHT: Sid Lawson, *Robert Patterson*; JOSEPH PULITZER: Philip Bourneuf; THE SHARKS: Forrest Bonshire, Allen Knowles, Leonard Claret, Robert Pagent, *Erik Kristen, Joe Milan*; BARTHOLDI: Herbert Berghof; THE MODELS: Stephanie Augustine, Trudy De Luz, Marilyn Frechette, *Irene Carroll, Estelle Gardner*; MONIQUE DUPONT: Allyn McLerie (2) (she later became Allyn Ann McLerie); THE BOY: Tommy Rall; THE GIRL: Maria Karnilova; THE ACROBATS: Virginia Conwell, Joseph Milan, Eddie Phillips; STRONG MAN: Kazimir Kokic, *Leonard Claret*; THE COUNTESS: Ethel Griffies (4); A LOVER: Ed Chappel; HIS GIRL: Helene Whitney; A GENDARME: Robert Penn; A LAMPLIGHTER: Johnny V.R. Thompson; ANOTHER LAMPLIGHTER: Tommy Rall; A SOCIALITE: Marilyn Frechette, *Joy Carroll*; AN ACTRESS: Helene Whitney; A MINISTER: Ed Chappel; AN ADMIRAL: Robert Patterson; THE BOYS: Bob Kryl & Ernest Laird; THE MOTHER: Elizabeth Watts; THE POLICEMAN: Evans Thornton; THE BROTHERS: Lewis Bolyard & David Collyer; THE TRAIN: Eddie Phillips, Erik Kristen, Joseph Milan; RECEPTION DELEGATION: Dolores Goodman, Virginia Conwell, Fred Hearn, Bob Tucker, Allen Knowles; A MAID: Gloria Patrice; THE DANDY: Tommy Rall; RUBY: Maria Karnilova; A SAILOR: Eddie Phillips; HIS GIRL: Dolores Goodman (she later became Dody Goodman); RICHARD K. FOX: Donald McClelland; THE JUDGE: Erik Kristen; A POLICEMAN: Robert Patterson; IMMIGRATION OFFICER: Evans Thornton; A BOY: William Calhoun, *Ernest Laird*; SINGERS: Stephanie Augustine, Lewis Bolyard, Irene Carroll, Ed Chappel, David Collyer, Trudy De Luz, Marilyn Frechette, Estelle Gardner, Billy Hogue, Norma Larkin, Sid Lawson, Robert Patterson, Robert Penn, Yolanda Renay, John Sheehan, Evans Thornton, Helene Whitney, *Donald Devor, Lucy Hillary*; DANCERS: Forrest Bonshire, Bill Bradley, Lenny Claret, Virginia Conwell, Coy Dare, Norma Doggett, Dolores Goodman, Patricia Hammerlee, Fred Hearn (dance captain), Norma Kaiser, Allen Knowles, Kazimir Kokic, Erik Kristen, Joe Milan, Robert Pagent, Gloria Patrice, Eddie Phillips, Janice Rule, Tiny Shimp, Bob Tucker, *Kirsten Valbor, Sue Scott*; NEWSBOYS: William Calhoun, Ronald Kane, Bob Kryl, Ernest Laird, Kevin Mathews, Rusty Slocum, *Julius Cappozzoli*. **Understudies**: Horace: Ed Chappel; Monique: Norma Doggett; Maisie: Irene Carroll; Pulitzer: Evans Thornton; Bennett: Donald McClelland; Countess: Elizabeth Watts; Bartholdi: David Collyer; Mayor/Fox: Robert Penn; French Ambassador: Robert Patterson; Male Principal Dancer: Bob Tucker & Eddie Phillips; Female Principal Dancer: Virginia Conwell & Patricia Hammerlee. *Act I*: *Scene 1* Printing House Square; *Scene 2* Bartholdi's studio in Paris; *Scene 3* Bennett's office; *Scene 4* Under a Paris bridge. *Act II*: *Scene 1* Cabin on the RMS *Aurania*; *Scene 2* The waterfront; *Scene 3* North River dock; *Scene 4* On tour; *Scene 5* Salon in the Fifth Avenue Hotel; *Scene 6* Walhalla Hall (The Policemen's Ball); *Scene 7* Castle garden; *Scene 8* Finale. *Act I*: Overture (Orchestra), "Extra! Extra!" (Newsboys & Newspaper Readers), "What Do I Have to Do to Get My Picture Took?" ("I'd Like My Picture Took") (Maisie, Horace, Dancers) [this replaced "What Do I Have to Do to Get My Picture in the Paper?," which was dropped early on in the production], "The Most Expensive Statue in the World" (Pulitzer, Bennett, Mayor, Singers), "A Little Fish in a Big Pond" (Horace, Maisie, Bill Bradley, Allen Knowles, Kaz Kokic, Bob Pagent), "Let's Take an Old-Fashioned Walk" (Horace, Monique, Singers, Dancers) [the hit], "Homework" (Maisie), "Paris Wakes up and Smiles" (A Lamplighter, Monique, Ensemble), "Only for Americans" (Countess, Horace, Singers, Dancers), "Just One Way to Say I Love You" (Horace & Monique). *Act II*: "Miss Liberty" (Chorus), "The Train" (dance arr: Trude Rittman) (Monique & The Train), "You Can Have Him" (Maisie & Monique), "The Policemen's Ball" (Maisie, Another Lamplighter, Ensemble), "Homework" (reprise) (Maisie), "Follow the Leader Jig" (dance) (Ensemble), "Me an' My Bundle" (dance) (Horace, Monique, Company), "Falling Out of Love Can be Fun" (Maisie), "Give Me Your Tired, Your Poor" (Monique & Ensemble) [these are the words on the base of the Statue of Liberty, part of Emma Lazarus' poem "The New Colossus"].

It had an advance sale of $400,000. Broadway reviews were divided. Given the talent that went into it, the show held out a lot of promise, which it didn't live up to. Joe Lynn, the stage tech, won a Tony.

452. *Miss Saigon*

Kim is a young Vietnamese girl forced to become a prostitute in the days just before the U.S. withdrawal from Saigon in 1975. On her first night in a bar she meets and falls in love with Chris, a Marine guard at the embassy, who returns to the USA, leaving her pregnant. Three years later they meet again in Bangkok, she with the child, and he now married. In order that the child be taken to the safety of the USA, Kim commits suicide. On the fringes of the story is a cynical and sinister Eurasian called the Engineer, owner of the Dreamland bar. The production had a three-quarter size helicopter (weighing 8,700 pounds) landing at the U.S. Embassy.

Before Broadway. Claude-Michel Schoenberg and Alain Boublil saw a news photo of a Vietnamese woman giving up her child to an American GI during the Fall of Saigon, and this gave them the inspiration to update Puccini's opera *Madama Butterfly*. The music. lyrics and book were written in Paris and taken straight to Cameron Mackintosh in London, where the show had its world premiere, at the THEATRE ROYAL, DRURY LANE, on 9/20/89. Alain Boublil and Richard Maltby Jr. translated the French lyrics into English. It was a huge hit, taking in $33 million. Stars Jonathan Pryce and Lea Salonga won Olivier Awards. It closed on 10/30/99, the third-most profitable musical in British stage history up to that time, after *Cats* and *Les Miserables*. The London cast recording was released in 1990. DIRECTOR: Nicholas Hytner. **Cast**: ENGINEER: Jonathan Pryce, *Hilton MacRae, Junix Inosian, Cocoy Laurel, Leo Valdez* (94–95), *Junix Inosian, Leo Valdez* (in the closing months of 99); KIM: Lea Salonga, *Meera Popkin, Monique Wilson, Jenine Desiderio, Joanne Ampill* (by 3/95), *Riva Salazar, Maya Barredo*; ALTERNATE KIM: Monique Wilson, *Jenine Desiderio, Jamie Rivera, Roanne Monte* (by 3/95), *Riva Salazar*; CHRIS: Simon Bowman, *John Barrowman, Jerome Pradon, Simon Bowman, John Barrowman, Graham Bickley* (by 3/95), *Mike Scott* (alternating with *Mark O'Malley*); JOHN: Peter Polycarpou, *Milton Craig Nealy* (by 3/95); THUY: Keith Burns, *Miguel M. Diaz* (by 3/95), MIMI: Monique Wilson; GIGI: Isay Alvarez; ELLEN: Claire Moore, *Ruthie Henshall, Niki Ankara, Jacqui Scott* (by 3/95), *Sarah Jane Hassell*. The U.K. tour did not end until 12/03. The production was so big that the show could play only in eight theatres in the U.K., and each move cost over a million dollars.

Jonathan Pryce was British. In 8/90 the Asian-American theatrical community in the USA objected to him playing an Asian on Broadway. Equity supported them on 8/7/90, and barred Mr. Pryce. But, as he had had to do with *Les Miserables*, Cameron Mackintosh threatened a boycott if they didn't allow Mr. Pryce in, and to return the $25 million Broadway advance box-office sales (this advance would later grow to over $36 million). Equity backed down on 8/16/90, and gave Mr. Pryce six months in the role (after that time, he would be replaced by Francis Ruivivar). On 8/22/90, however, the Asian-American theatre community took a full-page ad in *Variety*, protesting Mr. Pryce's casting. On 9/17/90 Cameron Mackintosh felt safe enough to move ahead with the Broadway production, but on 1/7/91 the same minority community protested the casting of Lea Salonga, who was Filipino, and who had played Kim in London, and was set to play the role on Broadway. Apparently Asian-Americans did not regard the Philippines as part of Asia. This time Mr. Mackintosh won his case, although Kam Cheng would play Kim in matinees.

The Broadway Run. BROADWAY THEATRE, 4/11/91–1/28/01. 19 previews from 3/23/91. 4,097 PERFORMANCES. PRESENTED BY Cameron Mackintosh; MUSIC: Claude-Michel Schoenberg; ORIGINAL FRENCH LYRICS: Alain Boublil; ENGLISH LYRICS: Richard Maltby Jr. & Alain Boublil; BOOK: Alain Boublil & Claude-Michel Schoenberg; ADDITIONAL MATERIAL: Richard Maltby Jr.; DIRECTOR: Nicholas Hytner; CHOREOGRAPHER: Bob Avian; SETS: John Napier; COSTUMES: Andreane Neofitou & Suzy Benzinger; LIGHTING: David Hersey; SOUND: Andrew Bruce; MUSICAL SUPERVISOR: David Caddick & Robert Billig; MUSICAL DIRECTOR: Robert Billig (91), *Dale Rieling* (91–94), *Edward G. Robinson* (94–98), *Paul Raiman* (from 98–99); ORCHESTRATIONS: William David Brohn; LONDON CAST RECORDING on Geffen; PRESS: The Fred Nathan Company; CASTING: Johnson — Liff & Zerman; ASSOCIATE PRODUCER: Martin McCallum; GENERAL MANAGER: Alan Wasser; COMPANY MANAGER: Martin Cohen, *Susan Bell*; PRODUCTION STAGE MANAGER: Fred Hanson (91–93), *Karl Lengel & Mahlon Kruse* (93–94), *Beverly Jenkins* (94–98); STAGE MANAGER: Sherry Cohen (91–98), *Mark Dobrow* (from 98–99); ASSISTANT STAGE MANAGER: Tom Capps (91–98), *Peter Wolf* (from 98–99). **Cast:** SAIGON: 1975: THE ENGINEER: Jonathan Pryce (1) ☆, *Francis Ruivivar* (from 8/19/91), *Jonathan Pryce* (from 9/30/91), *Francis Ruivivar* (12/16/91–3/93), *Herman Sebek* (from 3/93), *Raul Aranas* (from 93–94), *Alan Muraoka* (by 94–95), *Raul Aranas* (from 94–95), *Luoyong Wang* (from 10/2/95), *Joseph Anthony Foronda* (from 11/11/96), *Luoyong Wang* (from 12/11/97), *Joseph Anthony Foronda* (from 8/7/00), *Luoyong Wang* (from 8/21/00), *Joseph Anthony Foronda* (from 1/14/01), *Luoyong Wang* (from 1/24/01); KIM: Lea Salonga (until 3/92) (2) ☆, *Leila Florentino* (from 3/16/92), *Rona Figueroa* (8/93–7/95), *Joan Almedilla* (7/95–7/97), *Deedee Lynn Magno* (from 7/21/97), *Lea Salonga* (1/18/99–5/15/99), *Deedee Lynn Magno* (from 6/14/99), *Melinda Chua* (5/22/00–6/17/00), *Deedee Lynn Magno* (from 6/19/00), *Melinda Chua* (7/17/00–12/30/00), *Lea Salonga* (from 1/2/01); KIM (ALTERNATE): Kam Cheng (Wednesday evenings & Saturday matinees) (7) ☆, *Annette Calud* (from 91–92), *Kam Cheng, Rona Figueroa, Emy Baysic* (9/93–7/95), *Roxanne Taga* (7/95–96), *Emy Baysic, Elizabeth Paw* (from 5/97), *Roxanne Taga* (from 6/97), *Chloe Stewart* (from 9/97), *Alex Lee Tano* (by 98–99), *Kristine Remigio* (from 6/14/99), *Liz Paw* (11/22/99–12/30/00), *Melinda Chua* (from 1/2/01); GIGI: Marina Chapa, *Sharon Leal* (by 93–94), *Imelda de los Reyes* (by 94–95), *Emily Hsu* (by 96–97), *Charlene Carabeo* (by 98–99); MIMI: Sala Iwamatsu, *Zoie Lam* (from 92–93), *Susan Ancheta* (by 98–99); YVETTE: Imelda de los Reyes, *Chloe Stewart* (by 94–95), *Ai Goeku* (by 96–97), *Chloe Stewart, Franne Calma* (by 98–99); YVONNE: JoAnn M. Hunter, *Lyd-Lyd Gaston* (from 91–92), *Mirla Criste* (by 93–94), *Johanna Tacadena* (by 96–97), *Emy Cologado* (by 98–99), *Moon Hi Hanson*; BAR GIRLS: Raquel C. Brown (gone by 92–93), Annette Calud (*Emy Baysic* by 92–93 & *gone by 94–95*), Mirla Criste (gone by 93–94), Jade Stice (gone by 93–94), Melanie Mariko Tojio (gone by 94–95), Cheri Nakamura (added by 91–92 & gone by 94–95), Sharon Leal (by 92–93 & gone by 93–94), Margaret Ann Gates (by 93–94 & gone by 96–97), Christine Langner (by 93–94 & gone by 94–95), Ai Goeku (by 94–95 & gone by 96–97), Emily Hsu (by 94–95), Elizabeth Paw (by 94–95 & gone by 96–97, but back by 98–99), Michelle Nigalan (new by 96–97), Frances Calma (new by 96–97), Sekiya Billman (new by 96–97), Lisa Yuen (new by 96–97), Luzviminda Lor (new by 98–99), Jenni Padula (new by 98–99), Johanna

Tacadena (new by 98–99); CHRIS: Willy Falk (4) ☆, *Sean McDermott* (from 12/16/91), *Jarrod Emick* (from 92–93), *Christopher Pecaro* (from 92–93), *Jarrod Emick* (from 93–94), *Eric Kunze* (from 93–94), *Sean McDermott, Peter Lockyer* (by 94–95), *Jay Douglas* (during Mr. Lockyer's vacation, 94–95), *Eric Kunze* (by 95–96), *Tony Capone, Pat McRoberts, Eric Kunze, Tyley Ross* (from 95–96), *Matt Bogart* (12/20/96–7/98), *Will Chase* (from 7/20/98), *Michael Flanigan* (7/3/00–12/30/00), *Will Chase* (from 1/2/01); JOHN: Hinton Battle (3) ☆, *Alton F. White* (from 91–92), *Timothy Robert Blevins* (from 92–93), *Keith Byron Kirk* (from 93–94), *Norm Lewis* (from 94–95), *Milton Craig Nealy* (by 7/97), *Leonard Joseph* (by 6/98), *Matthew Dickens* (from 8/98), *Leonard Joseph* (until 5/99), *W. Ellis "Billy" Porter* (5/17/99–1/1/00), *C.C. Brown* (1/3/00–12/30/00), *Charles E. Wallace* (from 1/2/01); MARINES: Paul Dobie (gone by 93–94), Michael Gruber (gone by 92–93, but back by 93–94 & gone again by 94–95), Leonard Joseph (*Frank Wright II* by 96–97, *Thos Shipley* by 98–99), Paul Matsumoto (gone by 94–95), Sean McDermott (*Jarrod Emick* from 91–92, *Reed Armstrong* by 92–93 & gone by 93–94), Thomas James O'Leary (gone by 93–94), Gordon Owens (*General McArthur Hambrick* from 91–92, *Jamie* by 92–93, *Donnell Aarone* by 94–95), Christopher Pecaro (gone by 92–93), Matthew Pedersen (*Andrew Driscoll* by 96–97, *Buddy Casimano* by 98–99, *Frankie Braxton* by 99–00), Kris Phillips (gone by 92–93), W. Ellis "Billy" Porter (gone by 92–93), Alton F. White (*Kingsley Leggs* from 91–92, *Michael McElroy* by 92–93 & gone by 93–94), Bruce Winant (*Howard Kaye* by 94–95, *Stephen Tewksbury* by 96–97). 91–92 additions: *Sean Grant* (gone by 92–93), *Herman Sebek* (gone by 92–93). 92–93 replacements: *Robert Bartley* (gone by 96–97), *Craig Bennett* (gone by 94–95), *Alvin Crawford* (*C.C. Brown* by 94–95, *Tony Capone* by 96–97, *Kurt Andrew Hansen* by 98–99), *Matthew Dickens* (gone by 94–95), *Jim Harrison* (gone by 93–94), *Kevin Neil McCready* (*Ronald Cadet Bastine* by 96–97, *Roger Seyer* from 96–97), *Grant Norman* (gone by 93–94), *Jeff Reid*. 93–94 replacements: *Yancey Arias* (gone by 94–95), *Randy Bettis* (gone by 94–95), *Tony Capone* (*Erik Bates* by 94–95, *Jay Douglas* [sic] by 98–99), *Jay Douglas* (*Frank Baiocchi* by 96–97 & back by 98–99 but gone by 99–00), *Eric Kunze* (gone by 94–95), *Welly Yang* (gone by 96–97). 94–95 replacements: *Norman Wendell Kauahi, Robert Weber* (gone by 99–00). 96–97 replacement: *Steve Geary* (gone by 99–00). 98–99 replacements: *J. T. Moye, Robert Orosco, Rusty Reynolds, Blake Riley*. 1999–2000 replacement: *Frankie Braxton*; BARMEN: Zar Acayan (stayed with show throughout), Alan Ariano (stayed with show throughout), Jason Ma (*Yancey Arias* by 92–93, *Ming Lee* by 93–94), *Eric Chan* (added by 92–93); VIETNAMESE CUSTOMERS: Tony C. Avanti (gone by 92–93), Eric Chan (gone by 92–93), Francis J. Cruz (stayed with show throughout), Darren Lee (gone by 93–94), Ray Santos (gone by 98–99 but back by 99–00), Nephi Jay Wimmer (gone by 94–95), *Tito Abeleda* (added during 91–92 & gone by 96–97), *Dennis Akiyama* (added by 92–93 & gone by 93–94), *Darrell Autor* (added by 92–93), *Corey Smith* (added by 92–93 & gone by 94–95), *Rob Narita* (added by 92–93; *Juan P. Pineda* by 94–95 & left in 7/97), *Jim Harrison* (added by 95–96 & gone by 96–97), *Thomas C. Kouo* (added by 96–97 & gone by 98–99), *Glenn Sabalza* (added by 96–97 & gone by 98–99), *Devanand N. Janki* (added by 98–99), *Edmund Antonio Nalzaro* (added by 98–99), *Robert Tatad* (added by 99–00); ARMY NURSE: Jane Bodle, Anne Torsiglieri (by 92–93), *Alisa Gyse Dickens* (from 92–93), *Misty Cotton* (from 93–94), *Heidi Meyer* (by 94–95), *Andrea Rivette* (by 96–97), *Lucy Vance* (by 98–99); THUY: Barry K. Bernal (6) ☆, *Jason Ma* (from 92–93), *Yancey Arias* (from 93–94), *Michael K. Lee* (by 96–97), *Welly Yang* (97–7/97), *Juan P. Pineda* (from 7/21/97), *Yancey Arias* (by 1/99), *Edmund Antonio Nalzaro* (1/24/99–2/30/00), *Michael K. Lee* (from 1/2/01); EMBASSY WORKERS/SAIGON INHABITANTS/VENDORS: Company. Ho Chi Minh City (formerly Saigon): April 1978: ELLEN: Liz Callaway (5) ☆, *Jane Bodle* (from 91–92), *Candese Marchese* (from 93–94), *Tami Tappan* (from 93–94), *Misty Cotton* (from 94–95), *Anastasia Barzee* (9/96–10/98), *Margaret Ann Gates* (10/26/98–12/30/00), *Jacquelyn Piro* (from 11/21/00), *Ruthie Henshall* (from 1/2/01); TAM: Brian R. Baldomero, *Philipp Lee Carabuena* (from 91–92), *Jeffrey Chang* (from 92–93), *Nicholas Chang* (from 93–94), *Keith Hong* (from 93–94), *Kailip Boonrai* (by 93–94), *Melanie Carabuena* (by 94–95), *Justin Lee Wong* (by 94–95), *Ambrose Eng* (by 96–97), *Thi Kim Thu Nguyen* (by 96–97), *Victoria Chin* (by 98–99), *Vivian King* (by 98–99), *Skyla Choi, Gail A. Quintos, Albert G. Yalun*; TAM (ALTERNATE): Phillip Lyle Kong (the evenings of Tuesday, Wednesday, Friday & Saturday), *Brandon Paragas Ngai* (from 91–92), *Eric Ordinario* from 92–93), *Adrick Aznar*; GUARDS: Tony C. Avanti (gone by 93–94) & Francis J. Cruz (stayed with show throughout), *Rob Narita* (added by 92–93; *Juan P. Pineda* by 94–95; *Devanand N. Janki* from 7/97); ASSISTANT COMMISSAR: Eric Chan, *Jason Ma* (from 91–92), *Yancey Arias* (from 92–93), *Welly Yang* (from 93–94), *Eric Chan* (by 96–97); DRAGON ACROBATS: Darren Lee, Michael Gruber, Nephi Jay Wimmer. 92–93 line-up: *Darrell Autor, Jim Harrison* (*Michael Gruber* by 93–94; *Jim Harrison* by 94–95; *Steve Geary* by 96–97), *Corey Smith* (*Robert Weber* by 94–95). 98–99 list: *Darrell Autor, J.T. Moye, Blake Riley, Frankie Braxton* (added in 99–00); SOLDIERS: Zar Acayan (gone by 96–97), Alan Ariano (stayed with show throughout), Jason Ma (*Tito Abeleda* by 92–93 & gone by 96–97), Paul Matsumoto (gone by 94–95), Ray Santos (stayed with show throughout), Nephi Jay Wimmer (gone by 94–95), *Darrell Autor* (*Corey Smith* by 93–94 & gone by 94–95, Darrell Autor returned by 98–99), *Norman Wendell Kauahi* (new by 94–95), *Glenn Sabalza* (new by 96–97 & gone by 98–99), *Thomas C. Kouo* (new by 96–97 & gone by 98–99), *Eric Chan* (gone by 98–99). 98–99 replacements: *Francis J. Cruz, Devanand N. Janki, Ming Lee, Edmund Antonio Nalzaro, Robert Tatad*; CITIZENS OF HO CHI MINH CITY/REFUGEES: Company. USA: September 1978: CONFERENCE DELEGATES: Company. Bangkok: October 1978: HUSTLERS: Zar Acayan (gone by 96–97), Jason Ma (gone by 92–93), Paul Matsumoto (gone by 94–95), Ray Santos (stayed with the show throughout), Nephi Jay Wimmer (gone by 94–95), *Alan Ariano* (by 92–93 & gone by 95–96), *Tito Abeleda* (by 92–93 & gone by 94–95), *Yancey Arias* (by 93–94 & gone by 94–95), *Welly Yang* (by 93–94 & gone by 96–97), *Corey Smith* (by 93–94 & gone by 94–95), *Norman Wendell Kauahi* (new by 94–95), *Jim Harrison* (new by 94–95 & gone by 96–97), *Eric Chan* (new by 96–97), *Thomas C. Kouo* (new by 96–97 & gone by 98–99), *Glenn Sabalza* (new by 96–97 & gone by 98–99), *Edmund Antonio Nalzaro* (new by 98–99), *Robert Tatad* (new by 98–99); MOULIN ROUGE OWNER: Francis J. Cruz; INHABITANTS/BAR GIRLS/VENDORS/TOURISTS: Company. Saigon: April 1975: SHULTZ: Thomas James O'Leary, *Craig Bennett* (from 92–93), *Bruce Winant* (from 93–94), *Howard Kaye* (by 94–95), *Stephen Tewksbury* (by 96–97); ANTOINE: Alton F. White [this character was replaced by 91–92 by that of Doc]; DOC: *Kingsley Leggs* (91–92), *Michael McElroy* (by 92–93), *Michael Gruber* (from 92–93), *Eric Kunze* (by 93–94), *Tony Capone* (from 93–94), *Erik Bates* (from 93–94), *Jay Douglas* (by 98–99) [new character by 91–92]; REEVES: Bruce Winant, *Craig Bennett* (by 92–93), *Alvin Crawford* (from 92–93), *C.C. Brown* (by 94–95), *Tony Capone* (by 96–97), *Kurt Andrew Hansen* (by 98–99); GIBBONS: Paul Dobie, *Kevin Neil McCready* (by 93–94), *Ronald Cadet Bastine* (by 96–97), *Roger Seyer* (by 98–99); TROY: Leonard Joseph, *Frank Wright II* (by 96–97), *Thos Shipley* (by 98–99); NOLEN: Gordon Owens, *General McArthur Hambrick* (from 91–92), *Jamie* (by 92–93), *Donnell Aarone* (by 94–95); HUSTON: Matthew Pedersen, *Andrew Driscoll* (by 96–97), *Buddy Casimano* (by 98–99), *Frankie Braxton* (by 99–00); FRYE: Sean McDermott, *Jarrod Emick* (from 91–92), *Reed Armstrong* (by 92–93), *Matthew Dickens* (by 93–94), *Jay Douglas* (by 94–95), *Frank Baiocchi* (by 96–97), *Rusty Reynolds* (by 98–99); MARINES/VIETNAMESE CIVILIANS: Company. Bangkok: October 1978: INHABITANTS/MOULIN ROUGE CUSTOMERS: Company. **Understudies**: Engineer: Tony C. Avanti (91), Paul Matsumoto (91–94), *Ray Santos* (91–01), *Herman Sebek* (91–92), *Dennis Akiyama* (92–93), *Ming* Lee (93–01), *Rob Narita* (93–94), *Norman Wendell Kauahi* (94–01); Kim: Annette Calud (91–92), Imelda de los Reyes (91–96), Melanie Mariko Tojio (91–93), *Emy Baysic* (92–93); *Elizabeth Paw* (93–98), *Roxanne Taga* (93–01), *Chloe Stewart* (94–96), *Michelle Nigalan* (96–98), *Jenny Padula* (98–01); Chris: Sean McDermott (91), Christopher Pecaro (91–92), *Jarrod Emick* (91–92), *Reed Armstrong* (92–93), *Grant Norman* (92–93), *Robert Bartley* (93–96), *Tony Capone* (93–94, 96–98), *Jay Douglas* (93–01), *Erik Bates* (94–98), *Frank Baiocchi* (96–98), *Stephen Tewksbury* (98–01); John: Leonard Joseph (91–96), Alton F. White (91), *Kingsley Leggs* (91–92), *Michael McElroy* (92–93), *Alvin Crawford* (93–94), *Donnell Aarone* (94–01), *C.C. Brown* (94–96), *Frank Wright II* (96–98), *Jeff Reid* (98–01), *Thos Shipley* (98–01); Ellen: Jane Bodle (91–92), *Jade Stice* (91–92), Anne Torsiglieri (92–93), *Heidi Meyer* (94–96), *Ai Goeku* (96–98), *Andrea Rivette* (96–98), *Charlene Carabeo* (98–01), *Lucy Vance* (98–01); Thuy: Zar Acayan (91–92, 95–96), Jason Ma (91–92), Marc Oka (91–92, 94–96), *Yancey Arias* (92–93), *Jim Harrison* (94–96), *Welly Yang* (94–96), *Juan*

P. Pineda (94–7/97), *Thomas C. Kouo* (96–98), *Dev Janki* (98–01), *Edmund A. Nalzaro* (98–01). **Swings**: Sylvia Dohi (stayed with the show throughout), Henry Menendez (91–93, 98–01), Marc Oka (91–93, 94–01), Todd Zamarripa (91–93, 96–98), *Eric Chan* (92–93, 94–96), *Zoie Lam* (92–93), *Kevin Neil McCready* (92–93), *Frank J. Maio* (94–96), *Fay Rusli* (94–96), *Jeff Siebert* (94–01), *Karl Christian* (96–98), *Samuel T. Gerongco* (96–01), *Tina Horii* (96–98), *Leonard Joseph* (96–98), *Howard Kaye* (96–01), *Jason Ma* (96–01), *Blake Riley* (96–98), *Paul Dobie* (98–01), *Moon Hi Hanson* (98–99), *Charles Munn* (98–01), *Cristina Ablaza* (by 98–99), *Emy Cologado* (99–01). **Orchestra**: KEYBOARDS: Jay Alger & Peter Calandra; BASSOON: Braden Toan; CONCERTMASTER: Louann Montesi; VIOLINS: Mineko Yajima, Ming Yeh, Sandra Billingslea; VIOLA: Mitsue Takayama; CELLI: David Bakamjian & Julie Green; BASS: Douglas Romoff; FLUTES: Timothy Malosh & David Weiss; CLARINET: Lino Gomez & Sal Spicola; SAX: Sal Spicola; OBOE: Blair Tindall; FRENCH HORNS: Russell Rizner & Daniel Culpepper; TRUMPETS: Richard Henly & Anthony Gorruso; TROMBONE: Jack Gale; BASS TROMBONE/TUBA: John Hahn; GUITARS: Doug Quinn; PERCUSSION: Michael Hinton & Howard Joines. **Act I**: *Scene 1* Saigon; April 1975: "The Heat is on in Saigon" (Engineer, Girls, Marines, Company), "The Movie in My Mind" (Gigi, Kim, Girls), "The Transaction" (John, Engineer, Chris, Company), "Why, God, Why?" (Chris), "Sun and Moon" (Kim & Chris), "The Telephone" (John, Chris, Engineer), "The Ceremony" (Kim, Chris, Girls), "The Last Night of the World" (Kim & Chris); *Scene 2* Ho Chi Minh City (formerly Saigon); April 1978: "The Morning of the Dragon" (Company, Thuy, Engineer), "I Still Believe" (Kim & Ellen), "Back in Town" (Kim, Engineer, Thuy), "You Will Not Touch Him" (Kim & Thuy), "If You Want to Die in Bed" (Engineer), "I'd Give My Life for You" (Kim & Company). **Act II**: *Scene 1* USA; Sept. 1978: "Bui-Doi" (John & Company); *Scene 2* Bangkok; Oct. 1978: "What a Waste" (Engineer & Company), "Please" (John & Kim); *Scene 3* The Fall of Saigon; April 1975: "The Guilt Inside Your Head" (The Fall of Saigon, 1975) (Thuy, Kim, Chris, John, Company); *Scene 4* Bangkok; Oct. 1978: "Sun and Moon" (reprise) (Kim), "Room 317" (Ellen & Kim), "Now that I've Seen Her" (Ellen), "The Confrontation" (Ellen, Chris, John), "The American Dream" (Engineer & Company), "Little God of My Heart" (Kim & Tam).

Asian-American groups picketed the theatre on opening night, protesting not only the casting but also the fact that Asians were depicted as whores and pimps. However, *Miss Saigon* was a major hit on Broadway. Reviews were divided. It was the first Broadway show to charge $100 for mezzanine seats. It won Tonys for Jonathan Pryce, Lea Salonga and Hinton Battle, and was nominated for musical, score, book, direction of a musical, choreography, sets, lighting, and for Willy Falk. It recovered its $10.9 million capital investment in 39 weeks. It cost $400,000 a week to keep running (96–97 figures). On 9/4/93 Leila Florentino, who was then playing Kim, was married on stage, by Mayor David Dinkins. On 10/13/97 the show passed *My Fair Lady* to become the 10th-longest-running musical in Broadway history. On 2/2/98 it passed the original *Hello, Dolly!* to become 9th-longest. By 9/14/99 it was being rumored that Lea Salonga would return to role of Kim in 1999, and she did. On 4/27/00 Cameron Mackintosh announced that the Broadway run would end on 12/31/00. However, on 11/3/00 he announced it would extend its run another month, until 1/28/01. Several new (and old) cast members came in for this last month. Lea Salonga returned as Kim from a production in the Philippines. By 10/02 it was 6th-longest-running show of all kinds in Broadway history (on 11/2/00 it had become only the 6th Broadway show to run 4,000 performances. In 4/04 it was passed by *Beauty and the Beast*.

After Broadway. IMPERIAL THEATRE, Tokyo. 1992. **Cast:** KIM: Minako Honda; CHRIS: Satoshi Kishida; ELLEN: Honoka Suzuki.

TOUR. Opened on 10/12/92, in Chicago. DIRECTOR: Nicholas Hytner; MUSICAL DIRECTOR: Kevin Stites. **Cast**: ENGINEER: Raul Aranas, *Alan Muraoka, Kevin Gray* (by 1/95), *Joseph Anthony Foronda*; KIM: Jennie Kwan, *Jennifer C. Paz* (by 1/95), *Cristina Paras*; ALTERNATE KIM: Jennifer C. Paz, *Hazel Anne Raymundo, Melanie Mariko Tojio* (by 1/95), *Melinda Chua*; CHRIS: Jarrod Emick, *Eric Kunze, Peter Lockyer* (by 1/95), *Eric Kunze, Peter Lockyer, Pat McRoberts*; JOHN: Keith Byron Kirk; THUY: Allen D. Hong, *Charles Azulay*; ELLEN: Christiane Noll, *Tami Tappan* (by 1/95), *Misty Cotton*. **Understudy**: Kim: Rona Figueroa. ALSO WITH:

Philip Michael Baskerville, Randy Bettis, Steve Geary, General McArthur Hambrick, Donna Pompei, Jade K. Stice. STUTTGART, 12/2/94–12/19/99. *Cast*: KIM: Caselyn Francis, *Aura Deva*; CHRIS: Kurt Kovalenko, *Uwe Kruger* (until 7/18/99).

TOUR. Opened on 3/29/95, at the Paramount Theatre, Seattle. Previews from 3/16/95. TOUR DIRECTOR: Nicholas Hytner; MUSICAL DIRECTOR: Paul Raiman. *Cast*: ENGINEER: Thom Sesma, *Joseph Anthony Foronda* (from 4/22/97); CHRIS: Matt Bogart, *Will Chase* (from 4/16/96), *Steve Pasquale* (from 6/30/97), *Greg Stone* (from 1/19/99), *Will Swenson* (from 12/22/99); KIM: Deedee Lynn Magno, *Elizabeth Paw* (from 6/97), *Cristina Paras, Kristine Remigio, Kim Hoy* (from 1/19/99), *Mika Nishida* (from 7/21/99); KIM AT MATINEES: Cristina Paras, *Alex Lee Tano, Michelle Nigalan*; JOHN: C.C. Brown, *Eugene Barry-Hill* (from 10/22/98); GIGI: Sala Iwamatzu; ELLEN: Anastasia Barzee, *Jacquelyn Piro* (from 4/27/99), *Christine Allocca* (from 1/28/00); THUY: Michael K. Lee, *Johnny Fernandez* (from 7/20/99); ALSO WITH: Devanand N. Janki, Andrea Rivette.

PRINCESS OF WALES THEATRE, Toronto. Closed on 4/30/95. *Cast*: ENGINEER: Kevin Gray, *Alan Muraoka, Herman Sebek*; KIM: Ma-Anne Dionisio; ALTERNATE KIM: Cornilla Luna; CHRIS: H.E. Green, *Kevin McIntyre*; JOHN: Rufus Bonds Jr.; THUY: Charles Azulay; ELLEN: Melissa Thornson. *Understudy*: Kim: Carmen de Jesus.

SYDNEY, 1995. *Cast*: KIM: Joanna Ampill CHRIS: Peter Cousens.

NETHERLANDS. Opened 11/24/96. Dutch version, translated by Seth Gaaikema. PRESENTED BY Joop Van Den Ende, in association with Cameron Mackintosh. *Cast*: DE REGELAAR: Willem Nijholt [i.e. the Engineer role]; KIM: Linda Wagenmakers; CHRIS: Tony Neef.

PAPER MILL PLAYHOUSE, New Jersey, 9/6/02–10/20/02. Previews from 9/4/02. Rehearsals began 8/12/02, in New York City. DIRECTOR: Mark S. Hoebee; CHOREOGRAPHER: Darren Lee; MUSICAL DIRECTOR: Tom Helm. *Cast*: ENGINEER: Kevin Gray; KIM: Dina Morishita; ALTERNATE KIM: Roxanne Taga; CHRIS: Aaron Ramey; JOHN: Alan H. Green; ELLEN: Kate Baldwin; THUY: Stephen Eng.

A new version, smaller, no helicopter, and six times cheaper than the original, opened in PLYMOUTH, ENGLAND, 7/14/04–8/21/04, then toured. DIRECTOR: Mitchell Lemsky; CHOREOGRAPHER: Maggie Goodwin; ADDITIONAL CHOREOGRAPHY: Geoffrey Garratt; SETS: Adrian Vaux; COSTUMES: Andreane Neofitou; LIGHTING: Jenny Kagan; ORCHESTRATIONS: William David Brohn.

The show has performed in 18 countries, in nine languages, and has grossed almost a billion dollars.

453. *Mr. President*

A U.S. president, his family, their last days in the White House, and a retirement into civilian life.

Before Broadway. The numbers "If You Haven't Got an Ear for Music," "I've Got an Ear for Music," "Nepotism," "Poor Joe," "Why Shouldn't I Like Me?" and "Words without Music" were all unused. "Anybody Can Write," an unproduced 1956 Irving Berlin number, was revised for this show, but not used. "Mr. President" (also known as "Prologue") and "Ev'ry Four Years" were both cut before Broadway.

The Broadway Run. ST. JAMES THEATRE, 10/20/62–6/8/63. 4 previews from 10/17/62. 265 PERFORMANCES. PRESENTED BY Leland Hayward; MUSIC/LYRICS: Irving Berlin; BOOK: Howard Lindsay & Russel Crouse; DIRECTOR: Joshua Logan; CHOREOGRAPHER: Peter Gennaro; SETS/LIGHTING: Jo Mielziner; COSTUMES: Theoni V. Aldredge; STAGE TECHNICIAN: Solly Pernick; MUSICAL DIRECTOR/MUSICAL UNDERSCORING: Jay Blackton; ORCHESTRATIONS: Philip J. Lang; DANCE MUSIC ARRANGEMENTS: Jack Elliott; PRESS: Richard Maney & Martin Shwartz; GENERAL MANAGER: Herman Bernstein; COMPANY MANAGER: Warren O'Hara; PRODUCTION STAGE MANAGER: Howard J. Whitfield; STAGE MANAGER: Fred Hearn; ASSISTANT STAGE MANAGER: Beau Tilden & Bob La Crosse. *Cast*: MANAGER: David Brooks; PRESIDENT STEPHEN DECATUR HENDERSON: Robert Ryan (1); NELL HENDERSON: Nanette Fabray (2); WALTER O'CONNOR, A SECRETARY: Jack Rains; DAVID CALDWELL: Warren J. Brown; LESLIE HENDERSON: Anita Gillette (3); LARRY HENDERSON: Jerry Strickler; YOUSSEIN DAVAIR: Jack Washburn; TIPPY

TAYLOR, A SECRETARY: Charlotte Fairchild; PAT GREGORY, OF THE SECRET SERVICE: Jack Haskell; CHARLEY WAYNE, OF THE SECRET SERVICE: Stanley Grover; PRINCESS KYRA: Wisa D'Orso; RUSSIAN SOLDIER: Jack Mette; COL. WILSON: Van Stevens; MRS. LOTTA PENDLETON: Marian Haraldson; GEORGE PERKINS: Beau Tilden; MR. THOMAS: Carl Nicholas; DEBORAH CHAKRONIN: Baayork Lee; ARTHUR BLANCHARD: Jack McMinn; RADIO OPERATOR: John Aman; ALI HASSOUD: Anthony Falco; ABOU: Carlos Bas; COMMENTATORS: Louis Kosman & Jack McMinn; A WORKMAN: Dan Siretta; MISS BARNES: Lispet Nelson; THE DEACON: Carl Nicholas; SGT STONE, OF THE SECRET SERVICE: Beau Tilden; CHESTER KINCAID: John Cecil Holm; BETTY CHANDLER: Carol Lee Jensen; SPIELER: Jack Rains; GOVERNOR HARMON BARDAHL: David Brooks; SINGERS (not mentioned below): John Aman, Kellie Brytt, Marian Haraldson, Carol Lee Jensen, Mary Louise, Jack McMinn, Jack Mette, Donna Monroe, Lispet Nelson, Carl Nicholas, Jack Rains, Ruth Shepard, Van Stevens, Maggie Worth; DANCER (not mentioned below): Bob La Crosse; DANCERS & SINGERS IN THE TRIP: TAHITIANS: Louis Kosman, Carlos Bas, Lynn Gay Lorino; BUTTERFLIES: Anna Marie Moylan, Barbara Newman, Mari Shelton; KABUKI SPIDER: Lowell Purvis; JAPANESE BEATNIKS: Lynn Ross & Bob Bakanic; KABUKI LION: Anthony Falco; SOUTH SEA WARRIOR: LaVerne French; ELEPHANT: Carlos Bas & Louis Kosman; LORD KRISHNA: Connie Burnett; EAST INDIAN MARCHING TEAM: Lynn Bernay, Anna Marie Moylan, Barbara Newman, Mari Shelton, Arline Woods, Don Atkinson, Sterling Clark, Dan Siretta; LEADER: Baayork Lee. *Understudies*: Steve: David Brooks; Nell: Charlotte Fairchild; Leslie: Lynn Bernay; Larry: Don Atkinson; Kyra: Lynn Ross; Youssein: Jack Mette; Walter/Charley/Spieler: Van Stevens; Tippy: Maggie Worth. *Act I*: *Scene 1* Oval Room at the White House: "Let's Go Back to the Waltz" (Nell & Ensemble); *Scene 2* Private sitting room in the White House: "In Our Hide-Away" (Nell & Steve), "The First Lady" (Nell); *Scene 3* A lawn party in Chevy Chase: "Meat and Potatoes" (Pat & Charley), "I've Got to Be Around" (Pat), "The Secret Service" (Leslie); *Scene 4* The President's bedroom: "It Gets Lonely in the White House" (Steve); *Scene 5* The President's office: "Is He the Only Man in the World?" (Nell & Leslie); *Scene 6* The trip: "They Love Me" (Nell); *Scene 7* The President's plane: "Pigtails and Freckles" (Pat & Leslie); *Scene 8* A street in the Middle East; *Scene 9* Youssein's apartment: "Don't Be Afraid of Romance" (Youssein); *Scene 10* The President's plane; *Scene 11* Airfield; *Scene 12* Television studios; *Scene 13* The private sitting room in the White House: "Laugh it Up" (Nell, Steve, Leslie, Larry); *Scene 14* An office in the White House: "Empty Pockets Filled with Love" (Pat & Leslie); *Scene 15* The President's office: "In Our Hide-Away" (reprise) (Nell & Steve). *Act II*: *Scene 1* A street in Mansfield: "Glad to Be Home" (Nell & Ensemble); Scene 2 The living room of the Henderson home: "Laugh it Up" (reprise) (Nell & Steve), "You Need a Hobby" (Nell & Steve); *Scene 3* An anteroom in the White House: "Don't Be Afraid of Romance" (reprise) (Youssein), "The Washington Twist" (Leslie & Dancers); *Scene 4* The judging pavilion of the Tioga County Fair: "Pigtails and Freckles" (reprise) (Pat); *Scene 5* The midway of the fair: "The Only Dance I Know" (Song for Belly Dancer) (Kyra); *Scene 6* Another part of the fair: "Meat and Potatoes" (reprise) (Pat), "Is He the Only Man in the World?" (reprise) (Leslie), "I'm Gonna Get Him" (Nell & Leslie) (written by Irving Berlin in 1956); *Scene 7* The living room of the Henderson home: "This is a Great Country" (Steve), Finale (Entire Company).

The show had an advance sale of over $2,500,000 and reviews were terrible. Solly Pernick won a Tony as best stage tech, and Irving Berlin won a special Tony. The show also received nominations for musical direction, and for Nanette Fabray.

454. *Mr. Strauss Goes to Boston*

Described as a comedy with music, but really it was a musical. It concerned the waltz king's visit to the World Peace Jubilee in Boston in 1872, and his conducting of the event, which had an orchestra of 1,000, a chorus of 20,000, and 150 featured soloists. "Any similarity to actual history is coincidental," it says. The promotions boys tell the world Mr. Strauss is unmarried (a ploy to get the girls to come to the show), but he is, indeed, married to a girl back home—Hetty. In America wealthy Brook Whitney tries to get him. Strauss wires for his wife to come over as soon as possible, and with the help of President Grant, she gets her husband back on course.

Before Broadway. It had out-of-town tryouts.

The Broadway Run. NEW CENTURY THEATRE, 9/6/45–9/16/45. 12 PERFORMANCES. PRESENTED BY Felix Brentano; MUSIC: Johann Strauss Jr. (as adapted by Robert Stolz); LYRICS: Robert Sour; BOOK: Leonard L. Levinson; BASED ON an original story by Alfred Gruenwald & Geza Herczeg; DIRECTOR: Felix Brentano; CHOREOGRAPHER: George Balanchine; SETS: Stewart Chaney; COSTUMES: Walter Florell; MUSICAL DIRECTOR: Robert Stolz; ORCHESTRATIONS: George Lessner; PRESS: James D. Proctor & Frank Goodman; GENERAL MANAGER: Milton Baron; COMPANY MANAGER: Joseph Moss; STAGE MANAGER: R.O. Brooks. *Cast:* DAPPER DAN PEPPER: Ralph Dumke (3); POLICEMAN McGILLICUDDY: Brian O'Mara; INSPECTOR GOGARTY: Don Fiser; 1ST REPORTER: Dennis Dengate; 2ND REPORTER: Larry Gilbert; 3RD REPORTER: Joseph Monte; PEPI: Florence Sundstrom; BELLHOP: Frank Finn; JOHANN STRAUSS: George Rigaud (1); ELMO TILT: Edward J. Lambert; HOTEL MANAGER: Lee Edwards; BROOK WHITNEY: Virginia MacWatters (2); A WAITER: Paul Mario; MRS. DEXTER: Laiyle Tenen; MRS. BLAKELY: Rose Perfect; MRS. WHITNEY: Sydney Grant; MRS. TAYLOR: Arlene Dahl; MRS. HASTINGS: Selma Felton; MRS. IVERSON: Marie Barova; MRS. BYRD: Cecile Sherman; BUTLER: John Oliver; TOM AVERY: Jay Martin; A PHOTOGRAPHER: John Harrold; EARL: Brian O'Mara; HETTY STRAUSS: Ruth Matteson (4); MAN IN OVERALLS: Paul Mario; AIDE TO PRESIDENT: Lee Edwards; PRESIDENT GRANT: Norman Roland; MR. POTTINGER: Don Fiser; SOLO DANCERS: Harold Lang (5), Babs Heath, Margit De Kova; LADIES & GENTLEMEN OF SINGING ENSEMBLE: Nancy Baskerville, Jeanne Beauvais, Arlene Carmen, Dennis Dengate, Lee Edwards, Doris Elliott, Alma Fernandez, Frank Finn, Larry Gilbert, John Harrold, Philip Harrison, Lucy Hillary, Paul Mario, Joseph Monte, John Oliver, Brian O'Mara, Olga Pavlova, Mia Stenn, Mary Lou Wallace; CORPS DE BALLET: Stephen Billings, Mary Burr, Jacqueline Cezanne, Sylvia de Penso, Andrea Downing, Helen Gallagher, Arlene Garver, Mary Grey, Fiala Mraz, Paul Olson, Virginia Poe, William Sarazen, Tilden Shanks, Terry Townes. *Act I*: *Scene 1* The lobby of the Grand Palace Hotel, NYC; June 16, 1872: "Can Anyone See?" (Ensemble); *Scene 2* Corridor in the hotel; immediately after: "Radetzky March-Fantasie" * (Dancing Girls), "For the Sake of Art" (Dapper Dan, Reporters, Girls); *Scene 3* Sitting-room of Strauss's suite: "Laughing-Waltz" * (Brook); *Scene 4* Off to Boston: "Mr. Strauss Goes to Boston" (Dapper Dan, Pepi, Elmo); *Scene 5* Drawing-room of the Whitney home in Boston; two weeks later: "Down with Sin" (Dapper Dan, Elmo, Boston Ladies), "Who Knows" (Brook); *Scene 6* Reception in honor of Johann Strauss: "Midnight Waltz" * (danced by Babs Heath, Harold Lang, Corps de Ballet), "Into the Night" (Tom), "Coloratura Waltz" * (Brook), "The Gossip Polka" * (Ensemble) (danced by Babs Heath, Harold Lang, Corps de Ballet). *Act II*: *Scene 1* Bedroom of Johann Strauss at the Governor Winthrop House; a few hours later: Dream Scene (Ensemble), "Going Back Home" (Hetty); *Scene 2* The balcony of the Governor Winthrop House; the next morning: "You Never Know What Comes Next" (Pepi), "Mr. Strauss Goes to Boston" (reprise) (Johann, Hetty, Dapper Dan), "You Never Know What Comes Next" (reprise) (danced by Harold Lang); *Scene 3* Along the Charles River; evening of the Fourth of July: "Into the Night" (reprise) (Tom & Ensemble) (ballet danced by Harold Lang, Margit De Kova, Corps de Ballet), "What's a Girl Supposed to Do?" (Brook & Tom), "The Grand and Glorious Fourth" (Ensemble) (ballet danced by Harold Lang, Helen Gallagher, Corps de Ballet), "Who Knows?" (reprise) (Brook), "Waltz Finale" * (Entire Company).

Note: asterisked numbers indicate musical arrangements of Strauss melodies by Robert Stolz & George Lessner.

On Broadway it was unanimously panned. Helen Gallagher and Harold Lang got the few good notices. The production lost $180,000.

455. *Mr. Wonderful*

Charlie, an unambitious night club singer, is pushed by his girl friend Ethel, and by Fred, a talentless entertainer.

Before Broadway. The show first played on 2/18/56, at the Shubert Theatre, Philadelphia, as a benefit for the American Jewish Congress. Then it tried out for three weeks at the same theatre, from 2/21/56.

The Broadway Run. BROADWAY THEATRE, 3/22/56–2/23/57. 383 PERFORMANCES. PRESENTED BY Jule Styne & George Gilbert, in association with Lester Osterman Jr.; MUSIC/LYRICS: Jerry Bock, Larry Holofcener, George Weiss; ADDITIONAL MUSIC & LYRICS: Jerry Bock; BOOK: Joseph Stein & Will Glickman; CONCEIVED BY: Jule Styne; DIRECTOR/CHOREOGRAPHER: Jack Donohue; SETS: Oliver Smith; COSTUMES: Robert Mackintosh; ASSISTANT COSTUMES: Florence Klotz; LIGHTING: Peggy Clark; MUSICAL SUPERVISOR/VOCAL ARRANGEMENTS: Oscar Kosarin; MUSICAL DIRECTOR: Morton L. Stevens; ORCHESTRATIONS: Ted Royal & Morton L. Stevens; PRESS: John L. Toohey & Max Gendel, *Ben Kornzweig*; PRODUCTION STAGE MANAGER: John Barry Ryan; STAGE MANAGER: Bernard Gersten; ASSISTANT STAGE MANAGER: Michael Wettach. *Cast:* UNEMPLOYED ACTRESS: Ann Buckles; HAL: Hal Loman (6); SONG PLUGGER: Richard Curry; SOPRANO: Rina Falcone; RITA ROMANO: Chita Rivera (5); TWO COMICS: Bob Leslie & Larry B. Leslie; AUDITION ANNIE: Pat Wilkes; JOHNNIE: John Pelletti; A SINGER: Karen Shepard; DANCERS: Tempy Fletcher, Shirley Graser, Suan Hartman, Sally Neal, Patti Ann Rita, Sylvia Shay, Patti Wharton; SISTERS: Gail Kuhr, Barbara Leigh, Sherry McCutcheon; ACROBAT: Dorothy D'Honau; HOOFERS: Marvin Arnold, Bill Reilly, Jimmie Thompson; TALENT SCOUT: T.J. Halligan (8), *Larry B. Leslie* (from 5/28/56) [early in the run this role shifted position to after the Counterman]; ANNIE'S FRIEND: Charlotte Foley; BOP MUSICIANS: Harold Gordon, Albert Popwell, Claude Thompson; FRED CAMPBELL: Jack Carter (2); LIL CAMPBELL: Pat Marshall (3), *Kay Medford* (from 5/28/56); COUNTERMAN: Herb Fields; MR. FOSTER: Malcolm Lee Beggs, *T. J. Halligan* (from 5/28/56); UNCLE: Will Mastin; DAD: Sammy Davis Sr. (7); CHARLIE WELCH: Sammy Davis Jr. (1); ETHEL PEARSON: Olga James (4); BARTENDER: Bob Leslie [role added early in the run]; STAGE MANAGER: Bob Kole; SCRIPT GIRL: Ginny Perlowin; STAGEHANDS: Frank Marti & Tony Rossi; CIGARETTE GIRL: Jerri Gray; LITTLE GIRL: Marilyn Cooper; SOPHIE'S BOY: Ronnie Lee. *Standbys*: Dad/Uncle: George Watts; Ethel: Louise Woods. *Understudies*: Freddie: Bob Leslie; Lil: Pat Wilkes; Rita: Patti Wharton; Hal: Jimmie Thompson; Foster: T.J. Halligan (for Malcolm Lee Beggs; *Bob Leslie* for T.J. Halligan). *Act I*: *Scene 1* 1617 Broadway, New York City; the present: "1617 Broadway" (Rita, Hal, Ensemble), "Without You, I'm Nothing" (Fred & Lil); *Scene 2* The Bandbox in Union City, New Jersey: "Jacques d'Iraq" (Charlie, Uncle, Dad, Ensemble), "Ethel, Baby" (Ethel & Charlie), "Mr. Wonderful" (Ethel) [a hit], "Charlie Welch" (Fred), "Big Time" [added after opening]; *Scene 3* 1617 Broadway; two weeks later: "Charlie Welch" (reprise) (Fred & Ensemble), "Talk to Him" (Lil & Ethel), "Too Close for Comfort" (Charlie) [a big hit]; *Scene 4* Fred & Lil's apartment; several days later: "Without You, I'm Nothing" (reprise) (Fred & Charlie); *Scene 5* An audition hall: Rita's Audition (Rita) (dance): Dance Improvisation (Rita, Hal, Ensemble); The Audition (dance) (Charlie, Uncle, Dad), "Sing, You Sinners" (m: Sam Coslow; l: W. Frank Harling) [from the movie *Honey*], "Daddy, Uncle and Me" (m/l: Sid Kuller & Lyn Murray), "Because of You" (m: Dudley Wilkinson; l: Arthur Hammerstein), "That Old Black Magic" (m: Harold Arlen; l: Johnny Mercer) [from the movie *Star Spangled Rhythm*], "Birth of the Blues" (m: Ray Henderson; l: B.G. "Buddy" De Sylva & Lew Brown) [from *George White's Scandals of 1926*], "It's All Right with Me" (m/l: Cole Porter) [from *Can-Can*]. *Act II*: *Scene 1* The Bandbox; after hours; several months later: "There" (Charlie); *Scene 2* An arcade in Miami, Fla.; next day: "Miami" (Lil & Ensemble) [early in the run it became by Rita & Tourists], "I've Been Too Busy" (Ethel, Fred, Lil, Charlie); *Scene 3* Backstage at the Palm Club, Miami Beach; *Scene 4* Charlie's dressing room: "Mr. Wonderful" (reprise) (Ethel); *Scene 5* The Palm Club: The Act (all following numbers by Charlie, Uncle, Dad): Dance, "Sing, You Sinners" (reprise), "Daddy, Uncle and Me" (reprise), "Because of You" (reprise), "That Old Black Magic" (reprise), "Birth of the Blues" (reprise), "It's All Right with Me" (reprise), "Dearest (You're the Nearest to My Heart)" (instrumental) (m: Benny Davis; l (lyrics not used here): Harry Akst), "Liza" (instrumental) (m: George Gershwin; l (lyrics not used here): & Ira Gershwin & Gus Kahn) [from *Show Girl*]; *Finale*: "Mr. Wonderful" (reprise) (Entire Company).

Broadway reviews were not good. The program actually said (relating to star billing): "*Mr. Wonderful*, a new musical comedy, with the Will Mastin Trio, starring Sammy Davis Jr." The Will Mastin Trio was Sammy himself, his father (Sammy Davis Sr.) and Will Mastin (young Sammy's uncle). The show was primarily a vehicle to make Sammy Jr. a solo star (or so it seemed).

456. *Molly*

Radio's *The Goldbergs* as a musical. Set in the Bronx in the spring of 1933. Molly's husband, Jake, loses his job as a cutter of ladies' dresses, and plans to move the family to California, but Jake's brother arrives at the end of Act I. Sammy was Molly's son, and Rosalie was her daughter.

Before Broadway. Backers' auditions were conducted in a novel way for this show. In order to raise money, Kaye Ballard, complete with costume and makeup, appeared on Carol Burnett's TV show and sang "Go in the Best of Health." Also, anyone who bought advance tickets at the box-office received a free bottle of Yoo Hoo chocolate drink, in honor of Molly's signature greeting. Lyricist Leonard Adelson died, and was succeeded by Mack David (Hal's brother). It tried out in Boston. Paul Aaron, the director, was fired, and various individuals were asked if they would like to take over — Michael Bennett, Morton Da Costa, and Burt Shevelove, but they all refused. Alan Arkin finally accepted. Bert Michaels was replaced as choreographer by Grover Dale. Patricia Gosling was replaced in the cast by Connie Day. 15th-billed Ellie Smith was demoted to understudy. One of the more bizarre aspects of this show was that Kaye Ballard changed her first name to Kay for this show, to satisfy the advice of a numerologist.

The Broadway Run. ALVIN THEATRE, 11/1/73–12/29/73. 40 previews from 9/27/73. 68 PERFORMANCES. PRESENTED BY Don Saxon, Don Kaufman, and George Daley, in association with Complex IV (Larry Spellman); MUSIC: Jerry Livingston; LYRICS: Leonard Adelson & Mack David; ADDITIONAL MUSIC & LYRICS: Norman L. Martin (uncredited); BOOK: Louis Garfinkle & Leonard Adelson (book doctored by Murray Schisgal); BASED ON the characters from the radio and TV series *The Goldbergs* (1929–1955), by Gertrude Berg; DIRECTOR: Alan Arkin; ASSISTANT DIRECTOR: Ted Chapin; CHOREOGRAPHER: Grover Dale; SETS: Marsha L. Eck; COSTUMES: Carrie F. Robbins; LIGHTING: Jules Fisher; SOUND: Gary Harris; MUSICAL DIRECTOR/VOCAL ARRANGEMENTS: Jerry Goldberg; ORCHESTRATIONS: Eddie Sauter, DANCE MUSIC ARRANGEMENTS: Arnold L. Gross; PRESS: Saul Richman & Sara Altshul; GENERAL MANAGER: Paul B. Berkowsky; COMPANY MANAGER: Malcolm Allen; PRODUCTION STAGE MANAGER: Martin Gold; STAGE MANAGER: Jean Weigel; ASSISTANT STAGE MANAGER: Gerald Teijelo. **Cast:** ANGELINA FRAZINI: Suzanne Walker (15); MRS. SULLIVAN: Camila Ashland (9); MR. SULLIVAN: Eddie Phillips (11); MRS. FRAZINI: Justine Johnston (12); MOLLY GOLDBERG: Kaye Ballard (1) ☆; MRS. KRAMER: Molly Stark (13); BELLE SEIDENSCHNEER: Ruth Manning (7); MRS. BLOOM: Hazel Weber Steck (14); MRS. DUTTON: Toni Darnay; ROSALIE GOLDBERG: Lisa Rochelle (6); JAKE GOLDBERG: Lee Wallace (4); UNCLE DAVID: Eli Mintz (2) ☆; SAMMY GOLDBERG: Daniel Fortus (5); STELLA HAZELCORN: Connie Day (8); MICHAEL STONE: Swen Swenson (3); COUSIN SIMON: Mitchell Jason (10); MAX: Martin Garner; ENSEMBLE: SKEETER: Don Bonnell; RALPH: Rodney Griffin; REGGIE: Bob Heath; HAROLD: Don Percassi; VINNIE: Sal Pernice; SHEALA: Linda Rose; GEORGE: Leland Schwantes; WALTER: Gerald Teijelo; ELLEN: Mimi Wallace; SARAH: Miriam Welch. **Understudies:** Molly: Molly Stark; Jake: Mitchell Jason; David/Simon: Martin Garner; Sammy: Bob Heath; Rosalie: Ellie Smith; Belle/Mrs. Bloom/Mrs. Frazini/Mrs. Kramer/Mrs. Sullivan: Toni Darnay; Michael/Max: Gerald Teijelo; Stella: Miriam Welch; Mr. Sullivan: Don Percassi. **Act I: Scene 1** The Goldberg apartment: "There's a New Deal on the Way" * (Angelina & Company), "If Everyone Got What They Wanted" ☆ (Molly & Company); **Scene 2** The Goldberg apartment: "A Piece of the Rainbow" * (Molly); **Scene 3** The front sidewalk: "Cahoots" * (Michael & Molly); **Scene 4** The rooftop: "Sullivan's Got a Job" (Company), "In Your Eyes" * (Sammy); **Scene 5** The front sidewalk: "Cahoots" (reprise) * (Belle & Molly); **Scene 6** Belle's apartment; **Scene 7** A street; **Scene 8** The Goldberg apartment: "High Class Ladies

and Elegant Gentlemen" * (Michael, Stella, Goldbergs), "So I'll Tell Him" * (Molly); **Scene 9** The Goldberg apartment; the following day: "Appointments" (Uncle David), "There's Gold on the Trees" * (Jake, Molly, Company). **Act II: Scene 1** The Mandarin Palace: "The Mandarin Palace on the Grand Concourse" * (Company), "I Want to Share it with You" * (Michael, Stella, Company); **Scene 2** Outside the Mandarin Palace: "In Your Eyes" (reprise) * (Sammy); **Scene 3** The Goldberg apartment: "I Was There" * (Molly & Jake), "Oak Leaf Memorial Park" (Molly), "If Everyone Got What They Wanted" (reprise) * (Uncle David & Rosalie), "I See a Man" (l: uncredited, but actually by Norman L. Martin) (Molly) [this number was added at the last minute]; **Scene 4** The Goldberg kitchen; **Scene 5** The Goldberg apartment: "The Tremont Avenue Cruisewear Fashion Show" (Company), "I've Got a Molly" (Jake), "Go in the Best of Health" (Molly).

Note: All numbers had lyrics by Leonard Adelson, unless otherwise stated. Those numbers asterisked had lyrics by Mack David.

It was mostly panned by the critics, and lost $600,000 on a $400,000 investment. The main problem with the show was that the character of Molly Goldberg was so identified with Gertrude Berg that Kaye Ballard, as good as she may have been, couldn't live up to it.

457. *The Moony Shapiro Songbook*

This musical is all fiction. Moony Shapiro, a recently deceased pop songwriter, had started off life in Ireland as Michael Moony, of uncertain parentage, emigrated to the USA, changed his name to Moony Shapiro, and been adopted by a comic Lower East Side Jewish family. His life and career are satirically traced in revue style from his "East River Rhapsody" in a 1926 *Follies* show, to talkies, Broadway musicals, to protest songs, rock, and his death at age 69 due to electrocution by his synthesizer. Five actors play about 100 characters, mostly show business types.

Before Broadway. *Songbook* (as it was known in Britain) debuted at the UNIVERSITY OF WARWICK ARTS CENTRE, on 5/2/79. PRESENTED BY the Cambridge Theatre Company & Stoll Productions. Then it toured the English towns of Darlington, Cambridge, Croydon, and Oxford, until 6/9/79. It ran at the GLOBE THEATRE, London, 7/25/79–1/12/80. 208 PERFORMANCES. PRESENTED BY Jack Gill for Stoll Productions, by arrangement with the Cambridge Theatre Company; DIRECTOR: Jonathan Lynn; CHOREOGRAPHER: Gillian Lynne; SETS: Saul Radomsky; MUSICAL DIRECTOR: Ray Cook, *Grant Hossack*; CAST RECORDING on DRG. **Cast:** Anton Rodgers, Gemma Craven, Diane Langton, Andrew C. Wadsworth, Bob Hoskins (*David Healy*). **Understudy:** For Gemma: Zoe Bright.

The Broadway Run. MOROSCO THEATRE, 5/3/81. 15 previews. 1 PERFORMANCE. PRESENTED BY Stuart Ostrow, in association with T.A.T. Communications; MUSIC: Monty Norman; LYRICS: Julian More; BOOK: Monty Norman & Julian More; DIRECTOR: Jonathan Lynn; CHOREOGRAPHER: George Faison; SETS: Saul Radomsky; COSTUMES: Franne Lee; LIGHTING: Tharon Musser; SOUND: Otts Munderloh; MUSICAL SUPERVISOR: Stanley Lebowsky; MUSICAL DIRECTOR: Elman Anderson; ORCHESTRATIONS: Dave Lindup, Roy Moore, Ray Cook, Alec Gould, John Owen Edwards, Grant Hossack; ADDITIONAL ORCHESTRATIONS: Arthur Harris; VOCAL ARRANGEMENTS: Ray Cook; DANCE MUSIC ARRANGEMENTS: Timothy Graphenreed; PRESS: John Springer Associates; CASTING: Johnson — Liff; GENERAL MANAGERS: Joseph Harris & Ira Bernstein; PRODUCTION STAGE MANAGER: Phil Friedman; STAGE MANAGER: Perry Cline; ASSISTANT STAGE MANAGER: Philip Hoffman. **Cast:** JEFF GOLDBLUM, MR. SHAPIRO, ROCCO THE SHOESHINE BOY, LOUIS DA ROSA, FRENCH CROONER, STREET TRUMPETER, MARVIN, LEE PYONG-DO: Jeff Goldblum (1); JUDY KAYE, REVEREND MOTHER, MRS. SHAPIRO, MRS. KLEINBERG, SALVATION ARMY GIRL, TORCH SINGER, ANOTHER TORCH SINGER, BELLA, MARLENE, RUSTY, KIM-SUNG, SHEILA O'TOOLE: Judy Kaye (2); TIMOTHY JEROME, MOONY SHAPIRO, MR. WOO, COP, SENATOR "BEANPOLE" PICKLES: Timothy Jerome (3); ANNIE McGREEVEY, TILLY, MARY CASSIDY, MAE FELDMAN, ASTRID KALMAR, DOLLY RALSTON, FRENCH MUSIC HALL SINGER, BRITISH COMEDIENNE,

BONNIE VAN HEYSEN, KGB OFFICER, LIN-CHI, DEBBIE STELLMAN, JUDE, MAGDA GYOR: Annie McGreevey (4); GARY BEACH, DEAD END KID, RABBI KOTCHINSKY, SAILOR, U.S. IMMIGRATION OFFICER, 1ST NEWSBOY, 2ND NEWSBOY, RUDY VALLEE, BUM, DANCER, BUSBY BERKELEY, TENOR, WAITER, FLOWER SELLER, GESTAPO OFFICER, PRISONER OF WAR GUARD, BONNIE'S SINGING PARTNER, CHUCK, SCHMUEL, JOHNNY BAKUBA, PRESS PHOTOGRAPHER, BRITISH TRADE UNION LEADER, ACADEMY AWARDS SINGER, ALVIN BURNS, BOB DYLAN, BOB DYLAN'S SPOKESMAN, BENEDICT RICKENBACKER: Gary Beach (5); TALKING PICTURE STARS, BIG BAND VOCAL GROUP, ISRAELI DANCERS: Jeff Goldblum (1), Judy Kaye (2), Annie McGreevey (4), Gary Beach (5); BUSBY BERKELEY GIRLS: Judy Kaye (2) & Annie McGreevey (4); FAT GERMANS/USO ENTERTAINERS: Jeff Goldblum (1), Judy Kaye (2), Timothy Jerome (3), Annie McGreevey (4), Gary Beach (5); RUSSIAN SINGERS: Jeff Goldblum (1), Annie McGreevey (4), Gary Beach (5); LIVERPOOL POP GROUP: LEADER: Gary Beach (5); SINGERS: Judy Kaye (2) & Annie McGreevey (4); DRUMMER: Jeff Goldblum (1); MARCH OF TIME ANNOUNCER: Philip Hoffman (7); VOICE-OVER: Harold Prince (6); BACK-UP SINGERS: Philip Hoffman, Audrey Lavine, Brenda Pressley. ***Standbys***: For Jeff: Christopher Chadman; For Judy & Annie: Maureen Moore. ***Understudies***: For Judy: Audrey Lavine; For Annie: For Annie: Brenda Pressley; For Timothy & Gary: Philip Hoffman. **Act I**: "Songbook" [from the movie *Baltimore Ballyhoo*, 1948] (Company), "East River Rhapsody" [from the revue *Feldman Follies of 1926*] (Gary & Company), "Talking Picture Show" [from the movie *Evermore*, 1928] (Jeff, Judy, Annie, Gary), "Meg" [trunk song, 1929] (Timothy), "Mister Destiny" [from the hit recording, 1930] (Judy), "Your Time is Different to Mine" [from the hit recording, 1932] (Judy), "Pretty Face" [from the movie *Pretty Faces of 1934*] (Gary, Annie, Judy), "Je Vous Aime, Milady" [from the hit recording, 1935] (Jeff), "Les Halles" [cabaret song, 1935] (Annie), "Olympics '36" [from the hit recording, 1936] (Company), "Nazi Party Pooper" [trunk song, 1936] (Timothy), "I'm Gonna Take Her Home to Momma" [from the hit recording, 1938] (Annie, Judy, Jeff, Gary), War Songs—1939–1945: "Bumpity-Bump" (Annie), "The Girl in the Window" ("Das Maedchen am Fenster") (Judy), "Victory V" (Company) [end of War Songs sequence], Academy Award–Winning "Hollywood Evergreens"—1945–1948: "April in Wisconsin" [from the movie *A Yank at the Vatican*] (Gary), "It's Only a Show" [from the movie *Let's Do the Show Right Here*] (Gary), "Bring Back Tomorrow" [from the movie *Bring Back Tomorrow*] (Gary) [end of "Hollywood Evergreens" sequence], "Songbook" (reprise) (Company). **Act II**: "Happy Hickory" [title song of the musical, 1954] (Annie), "When a Brother is a Mother to His Sister" (Timothy) [cut during previews], *Happy Hickory* rejects: "Climbin'" (Annie), "Don't Play That Lovesong Anymore" (Timothy), Vocal Gems from *Happy Hickory*: "Happy Hickory" (Company), "Lovely Sunday Mornin'" (Annie & Gary), "Rusty's Dream Ballet" (Judy & Jeff), "A Storm in My Heart" (Gary, Annie, Jeff, Judy) [cut during previews], "The Pokenhatchit Public Protest Committee" (Company), "Happy Hickory" (reprise) (Company) [end of Vocal Gems from "Happy Hickory" sequence], "Happy Hickory" [from the Tel Aviv & Moscow productions, 1956] (Gary, Annie, Judy, Jeff), "I Accuse" [from the musical *Red White and Black*] (Annie & Judy), "Messages I" [trunk song, 1958] (Jeff), "Messages II" [version for Bob Dylan, 1963] (Gary), "I Found Love" [from the hit recording, 1964] (Annie, Judy, Jeff, Gary), "Don't Play That Lovesong Any More" (reprise) (Judy), "Golden Oldie" [trunk song, 1972] (Timothy), "Climbin'" (reprise) [from the hit recording, 1972] (Annie, Gary, Jeff, Judy, Timothy), "Nostalgia" [trunk song, 1977] (Jeff), Finale (Company).

Broadway reviews were terrible. The show received a Tony nomination for book.

458. *The Most Happy Fella*

Tony is an aging Napa Valley vintner who sees a young waitress, Amy (who he calls Rosabella), in a San Francisco restaurant, and falls for her. When he gets back to the valley, he writes to her. They begin a romance by mail, and finally he asks her if she'll come out and be his bride. But he sends a picture of his hand-

some young foreman, Joe, instead of one of himself. She comes, and discovers the truth. She goes through with the wedding, reluctantly, but sleeps with Joe while Tony is recovering from a car crash in which he has broken both legs. She gradually falls in love with Tony and then finds she's pregnant with Joe's child. At first Tony is shocked and ashamed, but then he agrees to raise the child as his own, and at the end declares himself "the most happy fella."

Before Broadway. Playwright Samuel Taylor (who wrote *The Happy Time*) suggested to Frank Loesser that he might want to musicalize Sidney Howard's play *They Knew What They Wanted*, as a follow-up to *Guys and Dolls*. It took him four years to do so, and it opened at the Shubert Theatre, Boston, on 3/13/56, and at the Shubert Theatre, Philadelphia, on 4/10/56. 4th-billed Morley Meredith was replaced by Art Lund, who now got 3rd billing. 3rd-billed Mona Paulee was shunted down to 8th. Out of town tryouts involved cutting down the score because there was so much music. Rosabella's first number, "House and Garden," was one such casualty. On the other hand, "Standing on the Corner," which hadn't made it into *Guys and Dolls*, was retrieved by Mr. Loesser when *The Most Happy Fella* needed a boost during tryouts. As it was, when the show hit Broadway it had a record 33 musical numbers, including arias, duets, trios, quartets and choral pieces, and recitatives.

The Broadway Run. IMPERIAL THEATRE, 5/3/56–10/19/57; BROADWAY THEATRE, 10/21/57–12/14/57. Total of 678 PERFORMANCES. PRESENTED BY Kermit Bloomgarden & Lynn Loesser; MUSIC/LYRICS/BOOK: Frank Loesser; BASED ON the 1924 Pulitzer Prize–winning drama *They Knew What They Wanted*, by Sidney Howard, which in turn was based on the Italian drama *Paolo e Francesca*; DIRECTOR: Joseph Anthony; CHOREOGRAPHER: Dania Krupska; SETS/LIGHTING: Jo Mielziner; ASSISTANT SETS: John Harvey & Ming Cho Lee; COSTUMES: Motley; ORCHESTRA & CHORAL DIRECTOR: Herbert Greene; ORCHESTRATIONS: Don Walker; CAST RECORDING on Columbia; PRESS: Arthur Cantor & Robert Ganshaw; COMPANY MANAGER: Joseph Harris, *Max Allentuck*; PRODUCTION STAGE MANAGER: Henri Caubisens; STAGE MANAGER: Terence Little; ASSISTANT STAGE MANAGER: Arthur Rubin. **Cast:** THE CASHIER: Lee Cass; CLEO: Susan Johnson (4); ROSABELLA: Jo Sullivan (2); THE WAITRESSES: Marlyn Greer (*Marcella Dodge*), Martha Mathes, Myrna Aaron (*Ann Sparkman*), Meri Miller, Beverly Gaines; THE POSTMAN: Lee Cass; TONY ESPOSITO: Robert Weede (1) ✫ (evenings only), Richard Torigi (at matinees); GLADYS: Betsy Bridge [new character written in after opening night]; MARIE: Mona Paulee (6); MAX: Louis Polacek, *Art Arney*; HERMAN: Shorty Long (5); CLEM: Alan Gilbert; JAKE: John Henson, *Richard Hermany*; AL: Roy Lazarus; JOE: Art Lund (3); GIUSEPPE: Arthur Rubin; PASQUALE: Rico Froehlich; CICCIO: John Henson, *Ralph Farnworth, Bob Roman*; COUNTRY GIRL: Meri Miller; CITY BOY: John Sharpe, *Hunter Ross*; THE DOCTOR: Keith Kaldenberg; THE PRIEST: Russell Goodwin; TESSIE: Zina Bethune; GUSSIE: Christopher Snell; NEIGHBORS: Myrna Aaron (*Ann Sparkman*), Helon Blount (*Marsha Reynolds*), Henry Director, Beverly Gaines, Hunter Ross, Bob Daley; NEIGHBOR LADIES: Lillian Shelby, Lois Van Pelt, Marjorie Smith; BRAKEMAN: Norris Greer, *Hal Norman*; BUS DRIVER: Ralph Farnworth, *Tony Rossi*; ALL THE NEIGHBORS & ALL THE NEIGHBORS' NEIGHBORS: Myrna Aaron (*Ann Sparkman*), Art Arney, Ken Ayers (gone by 56–57), Helon Blount, Theodora Brandon, Betsy Bridge, Bob Daley, Thelma Dare (gone by 56–57), Lanier Davis, Henry Director, Ralph Farnworth (*Tony Rossi*), Beverly Gaines, Alan Gilbert, Russell Goodwin, Marlyn Greer (*Marcella Dodge*), Norris Greer (*Hal Norman*), Richard Hermany, Athan Karras, Walter Kelvin, Jerry Kurland (gone by 56–57), Roy Lazarus, Martha Mathes, Carolyn Maye, Meri Miller, Genevieve Owens, Arthur Partington, Louis Polacek (gone by 56–57), Hunter Ross, Patti Schmidt (gone by 56–57), John Sharpe, Lillian Shelby, Marjorie Smith, Toba Sherwood (gone by 56–57), Evans Thornton (gone by 56–57), Lois Van Pelt, *Thelma Scott, Joyce Foss, Nancy Davis, Jack McCann, Tony Gardell, Jack Irwin, James Schlader, Stuart Hodes*. **Understudies:** Tony: Richard Torigi, *Norman Young* (added as 2nd understudy); Rosabella: Carolyn Maye; Marie: Lillian Shelby; Herman: John Henson; Cleo: Helon Blount, *Jane Romano*; Doctor: Ken Ayers; Postman: Lou Polacek, *Walter Kelvin*; Giuseppe: Lou Polacek, *Tony Rossi*; Cashier: Walter

Kelvin; Ciccio: Ralph Farnworth, *Art Arney*; Pasquale: Ted Thurston, *Tony Gardell*; Tessie/Gussie: Barbara Myers, *Joan Terrace*; Joe: *Jack Irwin*. **Act I**: "Prelude, Act I" or "Overture" (Orchestra); **Scene 1** A restaurant in San Francisco; Jan. 1927: "Ooh! My Feet!" (Cleo), "I Know How it Is" (Cleo & Rosabella), "Seven Million Crumbs" (Cleo), "I Don't Know" (The Letter) (Rosabella), "Maybe He's Kind of Crazy" (Cleo), "Somebody Somewhere" (Rosabella); **Scene 2** Main Street, Napa, California; April: "The Most Happy Fella" (Tony & All the Neighbors), "A Long Time Ago" (Marie & Tony), "Standing on the Corner" (Herman, Clem, Jake, Al) [the big hit], "The Letter Theme" (Tony & Marie), "Joey, Joey, Joey" (Joe) [a showstopper], "Soon You Gonna Leave Me, Joe" (Tony), "Rosabella" (Tony); **Scene 3** In Tony's barn; a few weeks later; night: "Abbondanza" (Giuseppe, Pasquale, Ciccio) [a showstopper], "Plenty Bambini" (Tony); **Scene 4** Tony's front yard; immediately following: "Sposalizio" (All the Neighbors), "Special Delivery!" (I Seen Her at the Station) (Postman), "Benvenuta" (Giuseppe, Pasquale, Ciccio, Joe) [a showstopper], "Aren't You Glad?" (Rosabella), "No Home, No Job" (Rosabella), "Don't Cry" (Joe, to Rosabella) [a showstopper], Finale Act I. **Act II**: **Scene 1** A clearing at the edge of Tony's vineyard; one week later — May: Prelude Act II, "Fresno Beauties"/"Cold and Dead" (Workers, Rosabella, Joe), "Love and Kindness" (Doctor), "Happy to Make Your Acquaintance" (Rosabella, Tony, Cleo), "I Don't Like This Dame" (Marie & Cleo), "Big D" (Cleo, Herman, All the Neighbors) [a hit]; **Scene 2** The arbor; later in May: "How Beautiful the Days" (Tony, Rosabella, Marie, Joe); **Scene 3** The clearing at the edge of Tony's vineyard; a month later — June: "Young People" (Marie, Tony, All the Young Neighbors), "Warm All Over" (Rosabella), "Old People (Gotta)" (Tony); **Scene 4** The barn: "I Like Everybody" (Herman & Cleo); **Scene 5** The clearing at the edge of Tony's vineyard; an afternoon in July: "I Love Him" (Rosabella), "I Know How it Is" (reprise) (Cleo), "Like a Woman Loves a Man" (Rosabella, to Tony), "My Heart is So Full of You" (Tony & Rosabella), "Hoedown" (Tony, Rosabella, All the Neighbors), "Mamma, Mamma" (Tony). **Act III**: **Scene 1** The barn; an hour later: Prelude, Act III, "Abbondanza" (reprise) (Pasquale, Giuseppe, Ciccio), "Goodbye, Darlin'" (Cleo & Herman), "I Like Everybody" (reprise) (Cleo & Herman), "Song of a Summer Night" (The Doctor & All the Neighbors), "Please Let Me Tell You" (Rosabella); **Scene 2** Napa Station; a little later: "Tony's Thoughts" ("Tell Tony and Rosabella Goodbye for Me") (Tony), "She's Gonna Come Home Wit' Me" (Tony, Marie, Cleo), "Nobody's Ever Gonna Love You" (Marie, Tony, Cleo), "I Made a Fist!" (Herman & Cleo), Finale (Tony, Rosabella, The Whole Napa Valley).

The show got great reviews, but it confused critics and public alike in that it was really an opera, one continual song, as it were. It had a 36-piece orchestra, including 24 strings, a harp, and no piano. Consequently it didn't really work, but it had a good run. The musical numbers were not listed in the original program, but the three-record album set that came out included all songs and dialogue. It received Tony Nominations for musical, direction, choreography, musical direction, and for Robert Weede and Jo Sullivan. It also won the New York Drama Critics' Circle Award for musical. During the run Frank Loesser separated from his wife Lynn, and married Jo Sullivan, his leading lady.

After Broadway. Tour. Opened on 12/23/57, at the Riviera, Detroit, and closed on 6/28/58, at the Philharmonic Auditorium, Los Angeles. Musical Director: Anton Coppola. *Cast:* Cashier/Postman: Walter Kelvin; Cleo: Helen Blount; Rosabella: Jo Sullivan; Tony: Robert Weede, Richard Torigi (alternate); Marie: Rina Falcone; Joe: Art Lund; Pasquale: Rico Froehlich; Priest: Richard Weede; Chorus included: Henry Director, Maggie Task, Ceil Delli, Bob La Crosse, Jim McArdle.

City Center, NYC, 2/10/59–2/22/59. 16 performances. Presented by the New York City Center Light Opera Company; Director: Dania Krupska; Choreographer: Arthur F. Partington; Art Director: Watson Barratt; Costumes: Ruth Morley; Musical Director: Abba Bogin. *Cast:* Cashier/Postman: Lee Cass; Cleo: Libi Staiger; Rosabella: Paula Stewart; Tony: Norman Atkins; Marie: Muriel Birckhead; Max/Train Conductor: Win Mayo; Herman: Jack De Lon; Clem: James Schlader; Jake: Ken Adams; Al: Roy Lazarus; Joe: Art Lund; Giuseppe: Kenneth Lane; Pasquale: Bruce MacKay; Ciccio: Michael Davis; Doctor: Keith Kaldenberg; Tessie: Bernadette Peters; Chorus included: Maggie Task, Jeanne Schlegel, John Dorrin,

Del Horstmann, Bob La Crosse, Sheldon Ossosky, Mike Scrittorale, Sherry McCutcheon, Sybil Scotford. The show received a 1959 Tony Nomination for stage technician (Edward Flynn).

Coliseum, London, 4/21/60. 288 performances. Director: Jerome Eskow; Choreographer: Ralph Beaumont; Sets/Costumes: Tony Walton; Cast recording on HMV. *Cast:* Cleo: Libi Staiger; Rosabella: Helena Scott; Tony: Inia Te Wiata; Herman: Jack De Lon; Joe: Art Lund; Giuseppe: Ralph Farnworth; Pasquale: Rico Froehlich.

Paper Mill Playhouse, New Jersey, 1965. Director: Stone Widney. *Cast:* Art Lund, Edwin Steffe, Margot Moser.

City Center, NYC, 5/11/66–5/22/66. 15 performances. Part of the spring season of four Frank Loesser revivals (the others were *How to Succeed in Business Without Really Trying*, *Where's Charley?* and *Guys and Dolls*). Presented by the New York City Center Light Opera Company; Director/Choreographer: Ralph Beaumont; Sets: Jo Mielziner; Costumes: Frank Thompson; Lighting: Peggy Clark; Musical Director: Abba Bogin. *Cast:* Cashier/Postman: Lee Cass; Cleo: Karen Morrow; Rosabella: Barbara Meister; Tony: Norman Atkins; Marie: Fran Stevens; Herman: Jack De Lon; Al: John A. Boni; Joe: Art Lund; Ciccio: Ed Becker; Priest: Dick Ensslen; Chorus included: Lillian Bozinoff, Kay Cole, Frank Coppola, Vito Durante, Marvin Goodis, Ina Kurland, Bob La Crosse, Rita Metzger, Rita O'Connor.

459. *The Most Happy Fella (1979 Broadway revival)*

The Broadway Run. Majestic Theatre, 10/11/79–11/25/79. 52 performances. Presented by Sherwin M. Goldman, in association with the Michigan Opera Theatre (David Di Chiera, general director) & Emhan, Inc.; Music/Lyrics/Book: Frank Loesser; Based on the play *They Knew What They Wanted*, by Sidney Howard; Director: Jack O'Brien; Choreographer: Graciela Daniele; Sets: Douglas W. Schmidt; Costumes: Nancy Potts; Lighting: Gilbert V. Hemsley Jr.; Musical Director: Andrew Meltzer; Conductor: Eric Stern; Orchestrations: Don Walker; Press: The Merlin Group; Casting: Johnson — Liff; General Manager: Mario De Maria; Production Stage Manager: Herb Vogler; Stage Manager: Ben Janney; Assistant Stage Manager: Philip Jerry. *Cast:* Cashier: Bill Hastings; Cleo: Louisa Flaningam; Rosabella: Sharon Daniels, Linda Michele (Wednesday & Saturday matinees); Waitresses: Karen Giombetti, Tina Paul, D'Arcy Phifer, Smith Wordes; Busboy: Tim Flavin; Postman: Dan O'Sullivan; Tony: Giorgio Tozzi (1) ☆, Frederick Burchinal (Wednesday & Saturday matinees); Marie: Adrienne Leonetti; Max: Steven Alex-Cole; Herman: Dennis Warning; Clem: Dean Badolato; Jake: David Miles; Al: Kevin Wilson; Sheriff: Stephen Dubov; Joe: Richard Muenz; Giuseppe: Gene Varrone; Pasquale: Darren Nimnicht; Ciccio: Franco Spoto; Doctor: Joe McGrath; Priest: Lawrence Asher; Brakeman: Bill Hastings; Neighbor Ladies: Melanie Helton, Dee Etta Rowe, Jane Warsaw, Sally Williams; Bus Driver: Michael Capes; Neighbors & Neighbors' Neighbors: Steven Alex-Cole, Lawrence Asher, Dean Badolato, Michael Capes, Richard Croft, Stephen Dubov, Tim Flavin, Karen Giombetti, Bill Hastings, D. Michael Heath, Melanie Helton, David Miles, Tina Paul, D'Arcy Phifer, Patrice Pickering, Candace Rogers, Dee Etta Rowe, Bonnie Simmons, Jane Warsaw, Richard White, Carla Wilkins, Sally Williams, Kevin Wilson, Smith Wordes. **Understudies**: Cleo: Dee Etta Rowe; Herman: David Miles; Marie: Carla Wilkins; Pasquale: Dan O'Sullivan; Joe/Cashier/Brakeman: Richard White; Giuseppe/Doctor: Franco Spoto; Ciccio: Richard Croft; Postman: Lawrence Asher; Al: Stephen Dubov; Jake: D. Michael Heath; Clem: Michael Capes. **Swings**: Philip Jerry & Laurie Scandurra. **Act I**: Overture (Orchestra); **Scene 1** A restaurant in San Francisco; January, mid–1930s: "Ooh! My Feet!" (Cleo), ... I know how it is (Cleo & Rosabella), ... Seven million crumbs (Cleo), ... I don't know (Rosabella), ... Maybe he's kind of crazy (Rosabella & Cleo), "Somebody Somewhere" (Rosabella); **Scene 2** Main Street, Napa, Calif.; April: "The Most Happy Fella" (Tony & Neighbors), ... A long time ago (Marie & Tony), "Standing on the Corner" (Herman, Clem, Jake, Al), "Joey, Joey, Joey" (Joe), ... Soon you gonna leave me, Joe (Tony), "Rosabella" (Tony);

Scene 3 Tony's yard; a few weeks later: "Abbondanza" (Giuseppe, Pasquale, Ciccio), ... Plenty bambini (Tony), "Sposalizio" (Neighbors), ... Special delivery! (Postman), "Benvenuta" (Giuseppe, Pasquale, Ciccio, Joe), ... Aren't you glad? (Rosabella), ... No home, no job (Rosabella), ... Eyes like a stranger (Marie), "Don't Cry" (Joe & Rosabella). *Act II*: Prelude; *Scene 1* Near the vineyards; May: "Fresno Beauties" (Workers), ... Cold and dead (Rosabella & Joe), ... Love and kindness (Doctor), "Happy to Make Your Acquaintance" (Rosabella, Tony, Cleo), ... I don't like this dame (Marie & Cleo), "Big D" (Cleo, Herman, Neighbors); *Scene 2* Later in May: "How Beautiful the Days" (Tony, Rosabella, Marie, Joe); *Scene 3* Near the vineyards; June: "Young People" (Marie, Tony, Young Neighbors), "Warm All Over" (Rosabella), ... Old people gotta (Tony); *Scene 4* The barn: "I Like Everybody" (Herman & Cleo); *Scene 5* Near the vineyards; July: ... I love him (Rosabella), ... I know how it is (Cleo), ... Like a woman loves a man (Rosabella), "My Heart is So Full of You" (Tony & Rosabella), "Hoedown" (Tony, Rosabella, Neighbors), "Mamma, Mamma" (Tony); *Scene 6* Out of the yard and into Tony's yard; an hour later: "Abbondanza" (reprise) (Pasquale, Giuseppe, Ciccio), ... Goodbye, darlin' (Cleo & Herman), "I Like Everybody" (reprise) (Herman & Cleo), "Song of a Summer Night" (Doctor & Neighbors), "Please Let Me Tell You" (Rosabella); *Scene 7* Napa Station; a little later: ... Tell Tony and Rosabella goodbye for me (Joe), ... She gonna come home wit' me (Tony), ... Nobody's ever gonna love you (Tony, Marie, Cleo), ... I made a fist! (Herman & Cleo), Finale.

Note: those numbers preceded by three dots are musical introductions, rather than actual song titles.

Reviews were mostly good. Giorgio Tozzi was nominated for a Tony.

After Broadway. NEW YORK STATE THEATRE, 9/4/91–10/18/91. 10 PERFORMANCES IN REPERTORY. The setting was updated to 1953. PRESENTED BY the New York City Opera; DIRECTOR: Arthur Allan Seidelman; CHOREOGRAPHER: Dan Siretta; SETS: Michael Anania; COSTUMES: Beba Shamash; LIGHTING: Mark W. Stanley; SOUND: Abe Jacob; CONDUCTOR: Chris Nance; ORCHESTRATIONS: Don Walker. *Cast:* CASHIER/POSTMAN: William Ledbetter; CLEO: Joanna Glushak & Karen Ziemba; ROSABELLA: Elizabeth Walsh & Michele McBride; TONY: Louis Quilico & John Fiorito; MARIE: Elaine Bonazzi & Susanne Marsee; HERMAN: Lara Teeter & Brian Quinn; JOE: Burke Moses & John Leslie Wolfe; GIUSEPPE: Arthur Rubin; CICCIO: John Lankston; THE PRIEST: Don Yule.

460. *The Most Happy Fella (1992 Broadway revival)*

This was a more intimate production that utilized duo-piano reduction instead of Frank Loesser's ambitious orchestral score. There was now an intermission after Act I.

Before Broadway. This revival originated at the GOODSPEED OPERA HOUSE, Conn., in 1991. It had the same basic cast as for the subsequent Broadway run, except for HERMAN: Guy Stroman. The ENSEMBLE was: Bill Badolato, Molly Brown, Kyle Craig, John Easterline, Mary Helen Fisher, Bob Freschi, Ramon Galindo, T. Doyle Leverett, Ken Nagy, Gail Pennington, Steven Petrillo, Roma Prindle, Ed Romanoff, Jane Smulyan, John Soroka, Laura Streets.

Later in 1991 this production played at the AHMANSON THEATRE, Los Angeles, PRESENTED BY the Center Theatre Group. It had the same crew, except SOUND: Jon Gottlieb; STAGE MANAGER: Michael McEowen. Robert Ashford & Keri Lee were in the chorus then (they were dropped for Broadway). The named cast was the same as for Broadway, except ROSABELLA: Mary Gordon Murray.

The Broadway Run. BOOTH THEATRE, 2/13/92–8/30/92. 23 previews from 1/24/92. 229 PERFORMANCES. The Goodspeed Opera House production, PRESENTED BY Center Theatre Group/Ahmanson Theatre, Lincoln Center Theatre, The Shubert Organization, Japan Satellite Broadcasting/Stagevision, and Suntory International Corporation; MUSIC/LYRICS/BOOK: Frank Loesser; BASED ON the play *They Knew What They Wanted*, by Sidney Howard; DIRECTOR: Gerald Gutierrez; CHOREOGRAPHER: Liza Gennaro; SETS: John Lee Beatty; COSTUMES: Jess Gold-

stein; LIGHTING: Craig Miller; SOUND CONSULTANT: Scott Lehrer; MUSICAL DIRECTOR: Tim Stella; DUO PIANO ARRANGEMENTS: Robert Page; NEW CAST RECORDING on RCA Victor; PRESS: Merle Debuskey & Susan Chicoine; CASTING: Warren Pincus; ARTISTIC ASSOCIATE: Jo Sullivan; GENERAL MANAGER: Steven C. Callahan; COMPANY MANAGERS: Rheba Flegelman & Edward J. Nelson; PRODUCTION STAGE MANAGER: Michael Brunner; STAGE MANAGER: Kate Riddle; ASSISTANT STAGE MANAGER: Christopher C. Wigle. *Cast:* CASHIER: Tad Ingram; CLEO: Liz Larsen; ROSABELLA: Sophie Hayden (2) ☆; POSTMAN: Tad Ingram; TONY: Spiro Malas (1) ☆; HERMAN: Scott Waara; CLEM: Bob Freschi; JAKE: John Soroka; AL: Ed Romanoff; MARIE: Claudia Catania; MAX: Bill Badolato; JOE: Charles Pistone; PASQUALE: Mark Lotito; CICCIO: Buddy Crutchfield; GIUSEPPE: Bill Nabel; PRIEST: Bill Badolato; DOCTOR: Tad Ingram; FOLKS OF SAN FRANCISCO AND NAPA VALLEY: John Aller, Anne Allgood, Bill Badolato, Molly Brown, Kyle Craig, Mary Helen Fisher, Bob Freschi, Ramon Galindo, T. Doyle Leverett, Ken Nagy, Gail Pennington, Ed Romanoff, Jane Smulyan, John Soroka, Laura Streets, Thomas Titone, Melanie Vaughan; PIANISTS: Tim Stella & Michael Rafter. *Standby:* Tony: Jack Dabdoub. *Understudies:* Tony/Al: T. Doyle Leverett; Rosabella: Anne Allgood; Cleo: Melanie Vaughan & Molly Brown; Herman: John Soroka; Joe: Ed Romanoff; Marie: Jane Smulyan; Cashier/Postman/Doctor: Bob Freschi; Pasquale/Ciccio: John Aller; Giuseppe/Clem/Jake: Thomas Titone; *Swings:* Robert Ashford & Keri Lee. *Act I*: *Scene 1* A restaurant in San Francisco; 1927: "Ooh! My Feet!," "Somebody Somewhere;" *Scene 2* Main Street, Napa, Calif.; April: "The Most Happy Fella," "Standin' on the Corner," "Joey, Joey, Joey," "Rosabella;" *Scene 3* Tony's barn; a few weeks later: "Abbondanza," "Sposalizio," "Benvenuta," "Don't Cry;" *Scene 4* The front yard; later that night. *Act II*: *Scene 1* A clearing at the edge of Tony's vineyard; one week later: "Fresno Beauties," "Happy to Make Your Acquaintance," "Big D;" *Scene 2* The arbor; later in May: "How Beautiful the Days;" *Scene 3* The clearing at the edge of Tony's vineyard; a month later: "Young People," "Warm All Over;" *Scene 4* The barn: "I Like Everybody;" *Scene 5* The clearing at the edge of Tony's vineyard; an afternoon in July: "My Heart is So Full of You," "Mamma, Mamma." *Act III*: *Scene 1* The barn; an hour later: "Song of a Summer Night," "Please Let Me Tell You;" *Scene 2* Main Street, Napa, Calif.; a little later: "I Made a Fist!;" Finale.

Broadway reviews were good. Scott Waara won a Tony, and the show was nominated for revival, and for Sophie Hayden and Liz Larsen.

After Broadway. In 1998 a three-CD set was recorded on Jay Records, starring Emily Loesser as Rosabella, and her husband Don Stephenson sang Herman.

461. *Mother Earth*

A rock musical. The musical numbers and sketches centered on mankind's abuse of the environment.

Before Broadway. The world premiere of this show was at the AMERICAN CONSERVATORY THEATRE, San Francisco, in 1971. 103 PERFORMANCES. Its East Coast premiere was at FORD'S THEATRE, Washington, DC, 10/20/71. 40 PERFORMANCES. PRESENTED BY Ford's Theatre Society, in association with Steven L. Parkes; DIRECTOR: Sid Grossfield; CHOREOGRAPHER: Steve Merritt; SETS/LIGHTING: Jim McKie; COSTUMES: Ricky Hansen & Warden Neil; VISUALS: Kenneth Shearer. *Cast:* Patti Austin, Christine Avila, Elaine Blankston, Ron De Salvo, Michael Devin, Joel Kimmel, Peter Jason, Tip Kelley, Carol Kristy, Arlene Parness.

The Broadway Run. BELASCO THEATRE, 10/19/72–10/28/72. 6 previews from 10/13/72. 12 PERFORMANCES. Ray Golden's production, PRESENTED BY Roger Ailes; MUSIC: Tony Shearer; LYRICS/SKETCHES: Ron Thronson; DIRECTOR: Ray Golden; CHOREOGRAPHER: Lynn Morris; SETS: Alan Kimmel; COSTUMES: Mary McKinley; LIGHTING: Paul Sullivan; VISUALS: Kenneth Shearer; MUSICAL SUPERVISOR/MUSICAL DIRECTOR: Larry White; ORCHESTRATIONS: Alf Clausen; DANCE MUSIC ARRANGEMENTS: Sande Campbell; PRESS: Max Eisen & Milly Schoenbaum; PRODUCTION SUPERVISOR: Roger Ailes; CONSULTANT: Kermit Bloomgarden; COMPANY MANAGER: Robert P. Cohen; PRODUCTION STAGE MANAGER: Donald W. Christy; STAGE MANAGER: Lanier Davis.

Cast: Gail Boggs, Frank T. Coombs, Kimberly Farr, Kelly Garrett, Will Jacobs, Carol Kristy, Laura Michaels, John Bennett Perry, Rick Podell, Charlie J. Rodriguez. *Act I*: *Scene 1* Out of Space, "Mother Earth" (Kelly & Company); *Scene 2* The Client, "The Time of Our Life" (Laura & Charlie), "Corn on the Macabre" (m/l: Ron Thronson, Roger Ailes, Ray Golden) (Carol, Rick, Gail); *Scene 3* The Mask Parade, "Too Many Old Ideas" (Kelly); *Scene 4* The Cheerleader (by Jerry Patch, William Black, Ray Golden), Uneasy Rider, Landscape With Figures, "Room to Be Free" (Rick); *Scene 5* Model Wife, "Rent a Robot" (Will); *Scene 6* A Hike in the Woods (by Jerry Patch & William Black), Flash Gordon, "Plow it All Under" (Carol & Company); *Scene 7* Ewe Turn (by Ray Golden), The Offal Truth (Ain't it Offal) (by Jack Marlowe & Ray Golden), The Killathon (by Ron Thronson, Roger Ailes, Ray Golden), "Taking the Easy Way Out" (John, Frank, Charlie); *Scene 8* Joggers, "Ozymandias" (John), "Talons of Time" (Kelly), "Corn on the Macabre" (reprise) (Laura, Kimberly, Frank); *Scene 9* The Nursery, "Save the World for Children" (Gail), "Sail on Sweet Universe" (Kelly & Company). *Act II*: *Scene 1* "Mater Terra" (Company), "Xanadu" (Carol & Company); *Scene 2* Breath-Out, "Ecology Waltz" (l: Ray Golden) (Kimberly & Rick); *Scene 3* Chic Diners, "Corn on the Macabre" (reprise) (Carol, Gail, Charlie); *Scene 4* Women Shoppers (by Ron Thronson & Ray Golden), The Swan, "Good Morning World" (John); *Scene 5* The Last Redwoods, The Animals (by Ray Golden), "Tiger! Tiger!" (Kelly); *Scene 6* Concrete Proposal, "Happy Mother's Day, Mother Earth" (Charlie); *Scene 7* Radioactive Terminate, "Pills" (m/l: Ray Golden) (Kelly, Gail, Carol, Company); *Scene 8* The Billboards (by Jack Marlowe & Ray Golden), "Corn on the Macabre" (reprise) (Kelly, Rick, Frank); *Scene 9* Total Recall (by Ray Golden), Finale.

Note: sketches do not have quotes; songs do.
Reviews were bad.

462. *Movin' Out*

A bookless musical, no dialogue, heavy on dance and music. 95 minutes long, with no intermission. All numbers (pre-existing Billy Joel songs) are performed by singer and Billy Joel-looka-like Michael Cavanaugh, who leads an on-stage band during the show. There is a cast of 27 (all members of Twyla Tharp Dance). The story is about six lifelong friends, told over the course of two turbulent decades. In the 1960s Brenda and Eddie break up. Brenda takes up with Tony. James and Judy are forever sweethearts. The three boys go to Vietnam, where James is killed. Tony can't re-connect with Brenda, and Eddie can't connect with anyone. Tony comes to blame Eddie for the death. All ends happily.

Before Broadway. On 10/8/97 Billy Joel announced that he was considering a Broadway show using his old songs. At first it was called *The Thoel Project* (choreographer Twyla Tharp & Billy Joel). James L. Nederlander produced the workshop, 10/6/01–10/7/01. **Cast**: Michael Cavanaugh, Scott Wise, Elizabeth Parkinson. On 1/31/02 it acquired its new name. The numbers "Miami 2017 (The Night the Lights Went Out on Broadway)," "New York State of Mind" and "Running on Ice" were not used. Rehearsals began on 4/29/02, and on 7/19/02 it opened at the Shubert Theatre, Chicago, for tryouts. Previews from 6/25/02 (a date put back from 6/15/02). Reviews were divided, mostly negative. It closed there on 8/4/02, then went to Broadway. During post-tryout script changes Eddie became no longer partly responsible for James's death, and the role of Judy, a war widow, was increased in importance.

The Broadway Run. RICHARD RODGERS THEATRE, 10/24/02–. 28 previews from 9/30/02. PRESENTED BY James L. Nederlander, Hal Luftig, Scott E. Nederlander, Terry Allen Kramer, Clear Channel Entertainment, and Emanuel Azenberg; MUSIC/LYRICS/ORCHESTRATIONS: Billy Joel; CONCEIVED BY/DIRECTOR/CHOREOGRAPHER: Twyla Tharp; ASSISTANT DIRECTOR/ASSISTANT CHOREOGRAPHER: Scott Wise; DANCE SUPERVISOR: Stacy Caddell; SETS: Santo Loquasto; COSTUMES: Suzy Benzinger; LIGHTING: Donald Holder; SOUND: Brian Ruggles & Peter J. Fitzgerald; MUSICAL SUPERVISOR/ADDITIONAL ORCHESTRATIONS & MUSICAL ARRANGEMENTS/MUSICAL CONTINUITY/PERFORMED CLASSI-CAL PIECES: Stuart Malina; ORCHESTRATIONS: Billy Joel & Stuart Malina; CAST RECORDING on Sony Classical; PRESS: Barlow — Hartman Public Relations/Bill Coyle; CASTING: Jay Binder Casting/Sarah Prosser; GENERAL MANAGER: Abbie M. Strassler; COMPANY MANAGER: Sean Free; PRODUCTION STAGE MANAGER: Tom Bartlett, *Kim Vernace*; STAGE MANAGER: Kim Vernace, *Joshua Halperin*; ASSISTANT STAGE MANAGER: Gregory Victor. **Cast:** EDDIE: John Selya (1); EDDIE ALTERNATE (Wednesday & Saturday matinees): William Marrie (until 11/15/02), *Ron Todorowski, John Selya, Christopher Body, Ted Banfalvi*; BRENDA: Elizabeth Parkinson (2) (until 5/8/04), *Nancy Lemenager (from 5/9/04), Elizabeth Parkinson (from 2/8/05)*; BRENDA ALTERNATE (Wednesday & Saturday matinees): Holly Cruikshank & Karine Plantadit-Bageot, *Oriada*; TONY: Keith Roberts (3), *Christopher Body, Keith Roberts (injured in 6/04), Ian Carney (stood in 6/04–8/04), Desmond Richardson (from 8/21/04, while Mr. Roberts recovered)*; TONY ALTERNATES (Wednesday & Saturday matinees): David Gomez & Ian Carney, *Stuart Capps*; JUDY: Ashley Tuttle (4); JUDY ALTERNATE: Dana Stackpole, *Meg Gurin-Paul, Mabel Modrono, Meg Paul*; JAMES: Benjamin G. Bowman (6), *Kurt Froman*; JAMES ALTERNATE (Wednesday & Saturday matinees): Alex Brady, *Kurt Froman, Christopher Body*; SGT O'LEARY/DRILL SERGEANT: Scott Wise (5); PIANO/LEAD VOCALS: Michael Cavanaugh (7), *Darren Holden (2/9/05–2/20/05, for 10 performances)*; PIANO/LEAD VOCALS ALTERNATE (Wednesday & Saturday matinees): Wade Preston; ENSEMBLE: Mark Arvin, Alexander Brady, Holly Cruikshank, Ron de Jesus, Melissa Downey, Scott Fowler, David Gomez, Rod McCune, Jill Nicklaus, Rika Okamoto, Karine Plantadit-Bageot, *R.J. Durell, Michael Balderrama, Melissa Downey, Pascale Faye, Philip Gardner, Tiger Martina, Christopher Body, Brian Letendre, Shawn Stevens, Matt Loehr*. **Understudies:** Eddie: Andrew Allagree, William Marrie, Lawrence Rabson, *David Gomez, Ron Todorowski, Ted Banfalvi, Brendan King, Chris Body*; Brenda: Karine Plantadit-Bageot & Holly Cruikshank, *Laurie Kanyok, Meg Gurin-Paul, Carolyn Doherty*; James: Alexander Brady, *Chris Body, Stuart Capps, Eric Otto*; Tony: Ron de Jesus & David Gomez, *Ian Carney, Stuart Capps, Corbin Popp, Chris Body*; James: Scott Fowler, *Seth Belliston, Alexander Brady, Kurt Froman, Corbin Popp*; Judy: Meg Gurin-Paul & Dana Stackpole, *Mabel Modrono, Melanie Bergeron*; O'Leary/Drill Sergeant: John J. Todd, *Philip Gardner, Ian Carney, David Gomez, Ted Banfalvi, Stuart Capps*; For Piano/Lead Vocals: Wade Preston, *Darren Holden (from 8/27/03; Henry Haid)*. **Swings**: Dana Stackpole, Andrew Allagree, Aliane Baqucrot, Laurie Kanyok, Meg Gurin-Paul, Lawrence Rabson, John J. Todd, William Marrie, *Philip Gardner, Ron Todorowski, Ian Carney, Kurt Froman, Mabel Modrono, Ted Banfalvi, Seth Belliston, Melanie Bergeron, Stuart Capps, Carolyn N. Doherty, Sean Kelly, Brendan King, Corbin Popp, Timothy W. Bish, Lisa Gajda, Chris Body, Brian Letendre, Lorin Latarro, Eric Otto, Justin Peck*. **Orchestra**: LEADER/GUITAR: Tommy Byrnes; PIANO/LEAD VOCALS: Michael Cavanaugh, *Henry Haid*; KEYBOARD/ALTERNATE PIANO: Wade Preston; TRUMPET: Barry Danielian; SAX: Scott Kreitzer; TROMBONE/WHISTLER/VOCALS: Kevin Osborne; LEAD SAX/PERCUSSION: John Scarpulla; LEAD GUITAR: Dennis Delgaudio; BASS: Greg Smith; DRUMS: Chuck Burgi. **Act I**: Overture ("It's Still Rock and Roll to Me") (Company); *Scene 1* Brenda & Eddie split: "Scenes from an Italian Restaurant" (Brenda, Eddie, Tony, James, Judy, O'Leary, Ensemble); *Scene 2* Tony moves out: "I Go to Extremes" [cut following tryouts], "Movin' Out" ("Anthony's Song") (Tony, Eddie, James, O'Leary); *Scene 3* James and Judy are forever: "Reverie (Villa d'Este)"/"Just the Way You Are" (James, Judy, Ensemble); *Scene 4* Brenda is back: "For the Longest Time"/"Uptown Girl" (Brenda, Eddie, Tony, Ensemble); *Scene 5* Tony and Brenda get together: "This Night" (Tony, Brenda, Ensemble); *Scene 6* Eddie knows: "Summer Highland Falls" (Eddie, Brenda, Tony, Ensemble); *Scene 7* Off to war: "Waltz # 1" ("Nunley's Carousel") (Tony, Eddie, James, Drill Sgt, Ensemble); *Scene 8* The sky falls: "We Didn't Start the Fire" (Judy, Brenda, James, Tony, Eddie, Ensemble); *Scene 9* Two bars: Hicksville/Saigon: "She's Got a Way" (Tony, Brenda, Ensemble); *Scene 10* Coming home: "The Stranger" (Judy & Ensemble), "Elegy" ("The Great Peconic") (Judy, Brenda, Tony, Eddie, Drill Sgt, Ensemble), "2,000 Years" (cut before Broadway). *Act II*: *Scene 1* Vets cast out: "Invention in C Minor" (Eddie & Ensemble); *Scene 2* Eddie rages: "Angry Young Man" (Eddie & Ensemble); *Scene 3* Tony disconnects: "Big Shot" (Tony, Brenda, Ensemble); *Scene 4* A contest of pain: "Big Man on Mulberry Street" (Tony,

Brenda, Ensemble); *Scene 5* Eddie gets high: "Captain Jack" (Eddie & Ensemble); *Scene 6* Eddie reaches out: "Innocent Man" (Eddie & Ensemble); *Scene 7* Eddie's nightmares: "Pressure" (Judy, Eddie, Ensemble); *Scene 8* Eddie's journey back: "Goodnight, Saigon" (Eddie, Judy, James, Tony, Ensemble); *Scene 9* Brenda's lost dreams: "Air (Dublinesque)" (Brenda); *Scene 10* Tony and Brenda reconcile: "Shameless" (Brenda & Tony); *Scene 11* Judy releases Eddie: "James" (Judy & Eddie); *Scene 12* Eddie attains grace: "River of Dreams"/"Keeping the Faith"/"Only the Good Die Young" (Eddie & Ensemble); *Scene 13* The reunion begins: "I've Loved These Days" (Tony, Brenda, Eddie, Ensemble); *Scene 14* Reunion/Finale: "Scenes from an Italian Restaurant" (reprise) (Company).

It got good reviews. On 11/16/02 ensemble dancer William Marrie, who had been playing Eddie at matinees, died in a motor cycle crash. The show won Tonys for choreography and orchestrations, and was nominated for musical, direction of a musical, lighting, and for John Selya, Elizabeth Parkinson, Keith Roberts, Ashley Tuttle, and Michael Cavanaugh. It missed the 8/14/03 performance due to the big power blackout. The show, capitalized at $10 million, had recouped its investment by the middle of Aug. 2004. Elizabeth Parkinson went on maternity leave, and returned in early 2005.

After Broadway. Tour. Began on 1/27/04 (date put back a day), at the Fisher Theatre, Detroit, sponsored by Visa. It had the same producers as for the Broadway run. Musical Supervisor: Stuart Malina. *Cast*: Lead Vocals: Darren Holden (Matt Williams at certain performances), *Michael Cavanaugh* (from 2/8/05); Brenda: Holly Cruikshank & Laurie Kanyok; Tony: David Gomez & Corbin Popp; Eddie: Brendan King & Ron Todorowski; James: Matthew Dibble; Judy: Julieta Gros; Also with: Kristine Bendul, Kim Craven. The Detroit run ended on 2/15/04 and then the show went off on the rest of the tour.

Mr. President see 453

Mr. Strauss Goes to Boston see 454

Mr. Wonderful see 455

463. *Music in My Heart*

A romantic musical play with melodies of Tchaikovsky. It was really an operetta. It tells how Tchaikovsky meets Desiree, French girl opera singer, falls in love with her, and she ditches him for a handsome officer from the Imperial Court, a friend of Tchaikovsky's. So, Tchaikovsky writes "Song without Words" for her.

Before Broadway. It tried out from 8/20/45, at the Philharmonic Auditorium, Los Angeles, as *Song Without Words*. Presented by Theodore Bachenheimer & James A. Doolittle. The rest of the crew was the same as for the later Broadway run. It had the same cast, except Mischa: Herman Moore; Desiree: Florence George, *Marguerite Piazza*. Before Broadway Patsy Ruth Miller replaced Frederick Jackson as the librettist, and in the cast Martha Wright replaced Marguerite Piazza. The numbers "Kiss Me Tonight" and "Night Wind" were cut.

The Broadway Run. Adelphi Theatre, 10/2/47–1/24/48. 124 performances. Presented by Henry Duffy; Music: Franz Steininger (he adapted the music of Tchaikovsky); Lyrics: Forman Brown; Book: Patsy Ruth Miller; Director/Lighting: Hassard Short; Choreographer: Ruth Page; Sets/Costumes: Alvin Colt; Music Adapted by/Musical Director: Franz Steininger; Orchestrations: Hans Spialek; Choral Arrangements: Clay Warnick; Press: Richard Maney & Frank Goodman, *Jean Dalrymple* (for the re-opening); Casting: Maynard Morris & Maurice La Pue; Co-Producer: Julie Winslow; Company Manager: Harry Benson; Stage Manager: Eddie Dimond; Assistant Stage Manager: John Scott. *Cast:* Girl in Ballet: Dorothy Etheridge; Boy in Ballet: Nannon Millis; Stage Manager: Harold Norman; Tatiana Kerskaya: Vivienne Segal (3), *Joan Kibrig* (for the re-opening); Mischa: George Lambrose; Peter Ilych Tchaikovsky: Robert Carroll (5); Stage

Doorman: Allan Lowell; Desiree Artot: Martha Wright (2); Maurice Cabanne: Jan Murray (4); Capt. Nicholas Gregorovitch: Charles Fredericks (1); Ivan Petrofski: James Starbuck (7); Natuscha: Dorothy Etheridge (8); Gypsy: Jean Handzlik (9); Joseph: Robert Hayden; Princess Katherine Dolgoruki: Della Lind (6); Lady in Waiting: Martha Flynn; Olga: Pauline Goddard; Messenger of the Tsar: Edward White; Sonya: Jeanne Shelby; Vera Remisova: Olga Suarez (10); Lord Chamberlain: Ralph Glover; Prima Ballerina (Beauty): Olga Suarez; Premier Danseur (Beast): Nicholas Magallanes (11), *Nicolai Polajenko* (for the re-opening); Ballet Girls: Dorothy Bauer, Iris Burton, Barbara Cole, Francy Falk, Mary Haywood, Ann Hubbell, Clara Knox, Sheila Lawrence, Nannon Millis, Carol Nelson, Nina Popova, Yvonne Tibor, Marjorie Winters; Ballet Boys: James Barron, Robert Cadwallader, Ronald Chetwood, Charles Dickson, Charles L. Grasse, Jack Miller, Nicolai Polajenko; Vocal Girl Ensemble: Dorothea Berthelson, Anne Marie Biggs, Eleanor Burrow, Audrey Dearden, Jane Flynn, Martha Flynn, Joyce Homiere, Joan Kibrig, Barbara Weaver, Kathleen Zaranova; Vocal Boy Ensemble: Jack Cassidy, Peter Hagen, Bernie Koveler, Allan Lowell, Harold Norman, Robert Rippy, Michael Risk, John Vanderhoof, Frank Whitmore; Stagehands/Footmen/Claque, etc: Jack Cassidy, Peter Hagen, Bernie Koveler, Robert Rippy, Michael Risk. **Understudies:** Desiree: Anne Marie Biggs; Kerskaya: Jeanne Shelby; Tchaikovsky: George Lambrose; Nikki: Robert Hayden; Maurice: Ralph Glover; Ivan: Charles L. Grasse; Gypsy: Kathleen Zaranova; Olga: Nannon Millis; Natuscha: Barbara Cole; Premier Danseur: Nicolai Polajenko. *Act I*: *Scene 1a* Ballet rehearsal. Ballet: "Unrequited Love, or The Storm" (this ballet to music by Rossini typifies the Italian style of dancing and the Italian music in vogue in Russia before the success of Tchaikovsky's first ballets). Girl: Dorothy Etheridge; Boy: Nannon Millis; *Scene 1b* Stage of Odeon Theatre, St. Petersburg: "Flower Waltz" (Desiree); *Scene 2* The Café Samovar; a few weeks later: "Natuscha" (Ivan, Natuscha, Ensemble), "Love is a Game for Soldiers" (Nikki), "Stolen Kisses" (Katherine & Nikki), "No! No! No!" (Kerskaya & Maurice), "While There's a Song to Sing" (Desiree & Ensemble), "The Balalaika Serenade" (Gypsy), "Danse Arabe" (dance) (Olga), "Trepak" (Ensemble), Finale: "Am I Enchanted" (Desiree, Nikki, Ensemble). *Act II*: *Scene 1* Nikki's country house; a month later: "Gossip" (Ivan, Natuscha, Ballet), "Once Upon a Time" (Desiree & Nikki), "Three's a Crowd" (Desiree, Katherine, Nikki); *Scene 2* Road to St. Petersburg; that night: "Song of the Troika" (Desiree & Nikki); *Scene 3* Foyer of Imperial Opera House; a few weeks later: "The Ballerina's Story" (Kerskaya), "Song of the Claque" (Maurice); *Scene 4* Stage of Imperial Opera House; a few minutes later; *Scene 4a* Ballet: "Beauty and the Beast" (Beauty & Beast); *Scene 4b* "Love Song" (Desiree); *Scene 5* Backstage of Imperial Opera House: "Love is the Sovereign of My Heart" (Desiree & Nikki), Finale.

On Broadway it was panned by the critics. John Chapman, reviewing it in the *New York Daily* News, did not know that Robert Carroll was actually playing the piano, and this caused interesting reading and retractions in the paper. The run was suspended 1/3/48–1/11/48, and during this time Henry Duffy gave up his production rights to W.L. Richardson, who re-opened with a few changes in cast and crew. It did no good, and the show closed a couple of weeks later, for good.

After Broadway. Franz Steininger tried it again — as *The Lady from Paris*. He produced it, and supervised the whole production, which tried out at the Erlanger Theatre, Philadelphia, 9/26/50–10/7/50. Jose Ruben directed and wrote additional dialogue on top of Patsy Ruth Miller's original book, so new characters were introduced. Forman Brown's lyrics were still used. Choreographer: Anthony Nelle; Sets/Lighting: Furth Ullman. *Cast*: Tchaikovsky: Helmut Dantine; Desiree: Marthe Errolle; Kerskaya: Irene Bordoni; Nikki: Charles Fredericks & William S. Difenderfer (alternating); Katherine: Della Lind & Emily Stephenson (alternating); Maurice Schumann: Sig Arno; Andrew Carnegie: Marvin Goodis; Victor Herbert: John Stamford; Taranova: Patricia Bowman. It was then ditched for ever, never reaching Broadway again.

464. *Music in the Air*

A musical adventure. The story revolved around the creation of an operetta in Europe. In the original 1932 production it was set in Munich, but for the 1951 (post-war) production Oscar Hammerstein II changed the locale to Zurich, and made everyone Swiss. Dr. Lessing is a composer who has a new song, "I've Told Ev'ry Little Star." His daughter and her friend try to help him get it published. Soon they become involved with glamorous star Frieda and her lover, librettist Bruno Mahler, during rehearsals of Bruno's new work "Tingle Tangle."

Before Broadway. The original ran on Broadway at the ALVIN THEATRE, 11/8/32–3/13/33. 146 PERFORMANCES; then moved to the 44TH STREET THEATRE, 3/31/33–9/16/33. 196 PERFORMANCES. PRESENTED BY Peggy Fears; DIRECTOR: Jerome Kern & Oscar Hammerstein II; MUSICAL DIRECTOR: Victor Baravalle; ORCHESTRATIONS: Russell Bennett. *Cast:* BRUNO: Tullio Carminati; SIEGLINDE: Katherine Carrington; LESSING: Al Shean; CORNELIUS: Reinald Werrenrath; KARL: Walter Slezak; ERNST: Nicholas Joy; FRIEDA: Natalie Hall; ANNA: Marjorie Main. It was filmed in 1934. DIRECTOR: Joe May. *Cast:* Gloria Swanson, John Boles, Al Shean, June Lang.

The Broadway Run. ZIEGFELD THEATRE, 10/8/51–11/24/51. 56 PERFORMANCES. PRESENTED BY Reginald Hammerstein (for Billy Rose); MUSIC: Jerome Kern; LYRICS/BOOK/BOOK REVISIONS/DIRECTOR: Oscar Hammerstein II; SETS/COSTUMES: Lemuel Ayers; LIGHTING: Charles Elson; MUSICAL DIRECTOR: Maurice Levine; ORCHESTRATIONS: Russell Bennett; PRESS: Michel Mok & John L. Toohey; COMPANY MANAGER: Rube Bernstein; GENERAL STAGE MANAGER: Paul Shiers; STAGE MANAGERS: Walter Russell & Jim Hammerstein. *Cast:* MRS. PFLUGFELDER: Julie Kelety; TILA: Marybeth Fitzpatrick; HERMAN: Richard Case; KARL REDER, THE SCHOOLMASTER: Mitchell Gregg; BURGOMASTER: Hal Frye; SIEGLINDE LESSING: Lillian Murphy (5); DR. WALTHER LESSING, THE MUSIC TEACHER: Charles Winninger (3); SCHMIDT: Carlo Corelli; PRIEST: Milton Watson; PFLUGFELDER: Walter Born; ERNST WEBER, THE MUSIC PUBLISHER: Conrad Nagel (4); UPPMANN: Guy Spaull; MARTHE: Terry Saunders; FRIEDA HATZFELD: Jane Pickens (2); BRUNO MAHLER: Dennis King (1); WAITER: John Michael King; ZOO ATTENDANT: Waldorf; ANNA: Norah Howard; PORTER: James Beni; KIRSCHNER: Richard Bishop; LILLI: Muriel O'Malley; SOPHIE: Julie Kelety; ASSISTANT STAGE MANAGER: John Michael King; LAWYER BAUM: Gordon Alexander; BARMAID: Biruta Ramoska; WILLI: James Beni; FRAU SCHREIMANN: Jean Ellsperman; FRAU MOELLER: Susan Steell; VARIOUS CHARACTERS OF EDENDORF & ZURICH: Gordon Alexander, Robert Baird, James Beni, Walter Born, Robert Busch, Madelaine Chambers, Carlo Corelli, Charles Dunn, Jean Ellsperman, Warren Galjour, Robert Gilson, Joan Keenan, Julie Kelety, John Michael King, William Krach, Rosemary Kuhlmann, Sheila Mathews, Grace Olsen, Frederick Olsson, Biruta Ramoska, Fred Rivetti, Marjorie Samsel, Helen Stanton, Susan Steell, Donald Thrall; CHILDREN: Richard Case, Georgianna Catal, Marybeth Fitzpatrick, Mary Hoyer, Charles Lee Saari. *Understudies*: Bruno: Milton Watson; Frieda: Terry Saunders; Karl: John Michael King; Sieglinde: Grace Olsen; Lilli: June Kelety; Priest: Warren Galjour; Marthe: Rosemary Kuhlmann. *Act I: Scene 1* Etude. A schoolroom in Edendorf; morning; *Scene 2* Impromptu. Ernst Weber's office in Zurich; three days later. *Act II: Scene 1* Sonata. The zoo; that afternoon; *Scene 1a* Interlude; *Scene 2* Caprice. Sieglinde's hotel room; that night; *Scene 3* Rhapsody. A star dressing room; four weeks later; *Scene 4* Intermezzo. Stage and orchestra pit; about an hour later; *Scene 5* Humoresque. The star dressing room; later the same night; *Scene 6* Rondo. Three weeks later. *Act I:* Dr. Lessing's Chorale: "Melodics of May" (based on the second movement of Beethoven's Piano Sonata No. 3 in C, Opus 2. voc arr: Jerome Kern) (Choral Society), "I've Told Ev'ry Little Star" (Karl, Sieglinde, Choral Society), "Prayer" ("Our Journey May Be Long") (Schoolroom Ensemble), "There's a Hill Beyond a Hill" (Walking Club) [end of chorale], "I've Told Ev'ry Little star" (reprise) (Sieglinde), "And Love was Born" [in the 1932 original, but cut from the 1951 production], Bubble Dance [in the 1932 original, but cut from the 1951 production], Bruno's Play: "I'm Coming Home" (Letter Song) (Bruno), "I'm Alone" (Frieda), "I Am So Eager" (Bruno & Frieda) [end of Bruno's Play], Finaletta (Marthe, Lessing, Ernst). *Act II:* "One More Dance" (Bruno), "Night Flies By" (Frieda), "When the Spring is in the Air" (Sieglinde, Lilli, Lessing), "In Egern on the Tegern See" (Lilli), "The Song is You" (Bruno), "The Song is You" (reprise) (Frieda & Bruno), "We Belong Together" (Edendorf Ensemble).

Despite a rave, Broadway reviews for the 1951 revival were generally unfavorable. The book let it down more than anything.

After Broadway. LAMB'S THEATRE, NYC, 1994. 2 PERFORMANCES. This was a concert version. PRESENTED BY Musicals in Concert & B.T. McNicholl; DIRECTOR: James Hammerstein; MUSICAL DIRECTOR: James Stenborg. *Cast:* Lynne Wintersteller, Jason Workman, John Fiedler, Emily Loesser, Keith Jurosko, Dennis Kelly.

465. *Music Is*

Before Broadway. It was George Abbott's idea. The show premiered at the SEATTLE REPERTORY THEATRE on 10/13/76. 30 PERFORMANCES. It had the same basic crew as for the subsequent Broadway run, and the cast was identical, except CAPTAIN: Seymour Pentzer. "When First I Saw My Lady's Face," "Masquerade," "The Time is Ripe for Loving," "Should I Speak of Loving You," "Big Bottom Betty," "Paeans of Paradise," "Needing No One," "Time Gone By," "Sing Hi," "I Am It," "Tennis Song," "No Matter Where," "The Duel," "Please Be Human," "What You Will." It then ran at the Kennedy Center, Washington, DC, 11/10/76–12/4/76. Don Smith was replaced as musical director by Paul Gemignani before Broadway.

The Broadway Run. ST. JAMES THEATRE, 12/20/76–12/26/76. 14 previews. 8 PERFORMANCES. PRESENTED BY Richard Adler, Roger Berlind & Edward R. Downe Jr.; MUSIC: Richard Adler; LYRICS: Will Holt; BOOK/DIRECTOR: George Abbott; BASED ON the 1601 comedy *Twelfth Night*, by William Shakespeare; ASSISTANT DIRECTOR: Judith Abbott; CHOREOGRAPHER: Patricia Birch; SETS: Eldon Elder; COSTUMES: Lewis D. Rampino; LIGHTING: H.R. Poindexter; MUSICAL DIRECTOR: Paul Gemignani; ORCHESTRATIONS: Hershy Kay; DANCE MUSIC & VOCAL ARRANGEMENTS: William Cox; ADDITIONAL ARRANGEMENTS: Jim Tyler; PRESS: Mary Bryant & Richard Kagey; GENERAL MANAGEMENT: Theatre Now; COMPANY MANAGER: Robert H. Wallner; PRODUCTION STAGE MANAGER: Bob D. Bernard; STAGE MANAGER: Elise Warner. *Cast:* WILLIAM SHAKESPEARE: Daniel Ben-Zali (2); VALENTINE: William McClary (9); DUKE ORSINO: David Holliday (6); CURIO: David Brummel (3); VIOLA: Catherine Cox (4); CAPTAIN: Paul Michael (10); CLOWN: William Shakespeare; MARIA: Laura Waterbury (13); SIR TOBY BELCH: David Sabin (12); MALVOLIO: Christopher Hewett (1); OLIVIA: Sherry Mathis (8); ANTONIO: Marc Jordan (7); SEBASTIAN: Joel Higgins (5); FESTE: Daniel Ben-Zali (2); SIR ANDREW AGUECHEEK: Joe Ponazecki (11); 1ST OFFICER: David Brummel; 2ND OFFICER: Doug Carfrae; CUPIDS: Helena Andreyko & Ann Crowley; MEMBERS OF THE COURT: Helena Andreyko, Doug Carfrae, Jim Corti, Ann Crowley, Dennis Daniels, Dawn Herbert, Dana Kyle, Jason McAuliffe, Wayne Mattson, Carolann Page, Susan Elizabeth Scott, Denny Shearer, Melanie Vaughan, Mimi B. Wallace; COURT MUSICIANS: REEDS: Donald Hettinger; GUITAR: Steve Uscher. *Understudies*: Valentine/Curio: Doug Carfrae; Orsino/Captain/Antonio: David Brummel; Viola/Olivia: Carolann Page; Feste/Malvolio: William McClary; Aguecheek: Denny Shearer; Sebastian: Jason McAuliffe; Sir Toby: Paul Michael; Maria: Susan Elizabeth Scott. *Act I: Prologue* "Music Is" (Shakespeare & Company); *Scene 1* Orsino's garden: "When First I Saw My Lady's Face" (Orsino); *Scene 2* The seacoast: "Lady's Choice" (Viola & Captain); *Scene 3* Orsino's garden: "The Time is Ripe for Loving" (Company), "Should I Speak of Loving You?" (Viola), "Dance for Six" (Miss Andreyko, Miss Crowley, Miss Wallace, Mr. Shearer, Mr. Daniels, Mr. Corti); *Scene 4* The seacoast: "Hate to Say Goodbye to You" (Antonio & Sebastian); *Scene 5* Olivia's garden: "Big Bottom Betty" (Feste), "Twenty-One Chateaux" (Viola, Olivia, Company), "Sudden Lilac" (Olivia); *Scene 6* Olivia's orchard: "Sing Hi" (Sir Toby, Sir Andrew, Feste, Maria); *Scene 7* Orsino's palace: "Blindman's Buff" (dance) (Viola, Orsino, Company). *Act II: Scene 1* Street with a tailor shop: "The Tennis Song" (Orsino, Valentine, Company); *Scene 2* A haystack near Olivia's house: "I Am It" (Malvolio); *Scene 3* Olivia's orchard: "No Matter Where" (Olivia & Viola), "The Duel" (Sir Toby, Sir Andrew, Viola, Feste); *Scene 4* A room in Olivia's house: "Please Be Human" (Olivia & Sebastian); *Scene 5* Corridor — Malvolio's bedroom; *Scene 6* Olivia's bedroom; *Scene 7* Front of Olivia's house: "What You Will" (Shakespeare & Company).

Broadway reviewers roundly panned it; the main reason was that fundamentally it was just *Twelfth Night* without Shakespeare's dialogue, and had little else to recommend it except good score, and choreography (for which Patricia Birch was nominated for a Tony Award). In short, there was no point in putting it on in the first place.

466. *The Music Man*

"Professor" Harold Hill is a charming, small-time con man (Harold Hill is not his right name, it seems; it may be Gregory, but then it may not be that either) who sells musical instruments and band uniforms. He moves about the mid–west, from small town to small town, prevailing upon school bands to buy his stuff on the promise of teaching the band members how to play. He claims to have been a graduate of the Conservatory of Gary, Indiana, in Ought-Five, but the trouble is, Hill can't read a note of music, and always leaves town on a freight train, after collecting his money and breaking a few hearts. The opening sequence is a train (complete with real steam billowing out over the stage) on the Rock Island Railroad full of traveling salesmen, with no opening song, just the patter of the salesmen to the rhythm of the train, as they pull into River City, Iowa, on July 4, 1912. Here Hill runs into an old accomplice, Marcellus. He falls in love with Marian the straitlaced librarian, collects his money, but decides to stay in town to face the music, which is awful as the children perform badly, but to the delight of their parents. Charlie Cowell, an anvil salesman who has been run out of many towns several times on account of the bad reputation left behind by Hill, has the goods on Hill, and is ready to expose him. However, Marian has already learned that he's a fake (the town of Gary, Indiana wasn't there until Ought-Six). The town and Marian forgive him, as the town is now a happier place because of the children. Marian's younger brother, Winthrop, has had a very bad lisp for years and hardly speaks. Hill transforms him. "Pick-a-Little" featured the neighborhood gossips. The Buffalo Bills was a barbershop quartet. Amaryllis was the little girl taking piano lessons from Marian.

Before Broadway. Meredith Willson, author and radio personality, had published a volume of reminiscences about his childhood in Mason City, Iowa and about his experiences playing flute in John Philip Sousa's band in the early 1920s. Frank Loesser, a friend, suggested he do a musical of it. Originally called *The Silver Triangle*, the script was taken by Mr. Willson and his wife Rini to producers' offices and apartments, where they sang all the parts. The producing team of Cy Feuer and Ernest Martin wanted to do it, but were too busy at the moment, and asked Mr. Willson to wait for them, and to fix the book at the same time, which he did — he fixed the book, anyway, but after Feuer and Martin kept him waiting he went to Kermit Bloomgarden. CBS turned down an opportunity to back it, saying it was too corny. Mr. Willson tried using eight songs he had previously written, but eventually he discarded most of them. They included: "Fireworks," "I Found a Horseshoe," "Rasmussin's Law," "You Don't Have to Kiss Me Tonight," "Tomorrow" (this was later tried in *The Unsinkable Molly Brown*, but cut before that show reached Broadway), and "I've A'ready Started in (To Try to Figure Out a Way to Go to Work to Try to Get You)" (although this was later used in *The Unsinkable Molly* Brown). The last to go was three weeks before rehearsals. At that point he wrote a new one, "Lida Rose." The lead was turned down by Danny Kaye, Dan Dailey, Gene Kelly and Phil Harris. Meredith Willson used the innovative device of rhythmic spoken dialogue to bridge the non-musical scenes to the songs. Frank Loesser was, aside from being associate producer, also publisher and licensor of the stock and amateur rights, a deal that didn't do him any harm financially.

The Broadway Run. MAJESTIC THEATRE, 12/19/57–10/15/60; BROADWAY THEATRE, 10/17/60–4/15/61. Total of 1,375 PERFORMANCES. PRESENTED BY Kermit Bloomgarden, with Herbert Greene, in association with Frank Productions (Frank Loesser); MUSIC/LYRICS/BOOK: Meredith Willson; BASED ON a story by Meredith Willson & Franklin

Lacey, which in turn was based on the 1948 memoir *And There I Stood With My Piccolo*, by Meredith Willson; DIRECTOR: Morton Da Costa; CHOREOGRAPHER: Onna White; ASSISTANT CHOREOGRAPHER: Tom Panko; SETS/LIGHTING: Howard Bay; COSTUMES: Raoul Pene du Bois; ASSISTANT COSTUMES: Willa Kim; MUSICAL DIRECTOR/VOCAL ARRANGEMENTS: Herbert Greene; ORCHESTRATIONS: Don Walker; ADDITIONAL ORCHESTRATIONS: Sidney Fine, Irwin Kostal, Seymour Ginzler, Walter Eiger; DANCE MUSIC ARRANGEMENTS: Laurence Rosenthal; CAST RECORDING on Capitol; PRESS: Arthur Cantor; CASTING: Vaughan Bellaver; GENERAL MANAGER: Max Allentuck; COMPANY MANAGER: Milton Pollack, *Albert H. Rosen* (from 58–59); PRODUCTION STAGE MANAGER: Henri Caubisens; STAGE MANAGER: Herman Magidson; ASSISTANT STAGE MANAGER: Arthur Rubin, *Bob Howard* (by 5/58), *Vernon Lusby* (by 59–60). **Cast:** TRAVELING SALESMEN: Russell Goodwin (*Jack McCann* by 59–60), Hal Norman, Robert Howard, James Gannon, Robert Lenn (*Richard Hermany* from 58–59), Vernon Lusby, Robert Evans; CHARLIE COWELL: Paul Reed (8), *Hal Norman* (from 59–60); CONDUCTOR: Carl Nicholas, *Robert Gorman* (from 59–60); HAROLD HILL: Robert Preston (1) ☆, *Norwood Smith* (during Mr. Preston's vacation in 58–59), *Eddie Albert* (from 59–60), *Hal March, Bert Parks, Norwood Smith*; MAYOR GEORGE SHINN: David Burns (3), *Paul Ford* (from 58–59), *Mort Marshall* (from 59–60); THE (FOUR) BUFFALO BILLS (5): EWART DUNLOP: Al Shea; OLIVER HIX: Wayne Ward; JACEY SQUIRES: Vern Reed; OLIN BRITT: Bill Spangenberg; MARCELLUS WASHBURN: Iggie Wolfington (6), *Dean Dittmann* (from 59–60); TOMMY DJILAS: Danny Carroll (10); MARIAN PAROO: Barbara Cook (2), *Arlyne Frank* (from 59–60), *Barbara Williams, Marlys Watters*; MRS. PAROO: Pert Kelton (4), *Leora Thatcher* (from 59–60); AMARYLLIS: Marilyn Siegel, *Laurie Wright* (from 59–60); WINTHROP PAROO: Eddie Hodges (9), *Paul O'Keefe* (from 58–59); EULALIE MacKECKNIE-SHINN: Helen Raymond (7), *Adnia Rice*; ZANEETA SHINN: Dusty Worrall (11), *Lynda Lynch, Joan Bowman*; GRACIE SHINN: Barbara Travis, *Karen Lee* (by 5/58), *Frances Underhill* (from 58–59), *Patti Lee Hilka* (from 59–60); ALMA HIX: Adnia Rice; MAUD DUNLOP: Elaine Swann; ETHEL TOFFELMIER: Peggy Mondo; MRS. SQUIRES: Martha Flynn; CONSTABLE LOCKE: Carl Nicholas, *Robert Gorman* (from 59–60); RIVER CITY TOWNSPEOPLE & KIDS: Pamela Abbott (gone by 59–60), Joan "Pixie" Bowman (she later became Joan Bouley) (gone by 59–60), Elisabeth Buda, Alice Clift (gone by 59–60), Ronn Cummins (gone by 58–59), Nancy Davis (gone by 5/58), Babs Delmore, Robert Evans, Martha Flynn (gone by 59–60), James Gannon (gone by 59–60), Russell Goodwin (gone by 59–60), Penny Ann Green (gone by 59–60), Janet Hayes, Robert Howard, Peter Leeds (gone by 59–60), Robert Lenn (gone by 59–60), Vernon Lusby, Lynda Lynch (gone by 59–60), Jacqueline Maria (gone by 59–60), Bob Mariano, Pat Mariano, Gary Menteer (gone by 5/58), Peggy Mondo, Carl Nicholas (gone by 59–60), Hal Norman, Tom Panko (gone by 59–60), Marilyn Poudrier (gone by 59–60), Art Rubin (gone by 5/58), Marie Santell (gone by 59–60), John Sharpe, Elaine Swann (gone by 59–60), Gerald Teijelo, Babs Warden (gone by 59–60), Marlys Watters (gone by 5/58), Vernon Wendorf, Barbara Williams, Roy Wilson (gone by 59–60). 57–58 replacements: *Ken Ayers, Nancy Dale, Larry Fuller* (gone by 59–60), *Basha Regis, Ronnie Tourso* (gone by 59–60). 58–59 replacements: *Margaret Baxter, Richard Hermany, Peter J. Laird* (gone by 59–60), *Bernard Eastoe* (gone by 59–60). 59–60 replacements: *Fred Albee, Barbara Beck, Carolyn Clark, Robert Gorman, Marion Hunter, Suzie Kaye, Jack McMinn, Eric Paynter, Nana Prudente, Nancy Radcliffe, Glenn Richards, Michael Roberts, George Tregre, Eleanore Treiber, Kip Watson, Lynn Wendell, Carolee Wynne.* **Standbys:** Harold: Larry Douglas, *Norwood Smith* (by 59–60). **Understudies:** Marian: Marlys Watters, *Barbara Williams* (by 5/58); Mayor/Marcellus: Paul Reed, *Hal Norman* (by 59–60); Mrs. Paroo: Adnia Rice; Charlie: Hal Norman, *Bob Howard* (by 59–60); Tommy: John Sharpe; Zaneeta: Lynda Lynch, *Pixie Bowman* (by 59–60); Ewart: Robert Lenn, *Richard Hermany* (by 58–59); Oliver: Russell Goodwin, *Ken Ayers* (by 59–60); Jacey: Art Rubin, *Carl Nicholas* (by 5/58), *Robert Gorman* (by 59–60); Olin: Bob Howard, *James Gannon* (by 59–60); Winthrop: Bob Mariano, *Ronald Tourso* (by 5/58), *Glenn Richards* (by 59–60), *Paul Floyd*; Eulalie: Adnia Rice; Alma/Maud: Martha Flynn; Ethel: Martha Flynn, *Adnia Rice* (by 59–60); Gracie: Pat Mariano; Amaryllis: Barbara Travis, *Karen Lee* (by 5/58), *Frances Underhill* (by 58–59), *Patti Lee Hilka* (by 59–60). **Act I:** Overture (Orchestra); *Scene 1* A railway coach; morning, July 4, 1912: "Rock Island" (Charlie & Traveling Salesmen); *Scene 2* River City, Iowa, center of town; immediately following: "Iowa Stubborn" (Townspeople of River City), "(Ya Got) Trouble" (Harold & Townspeople); *Scene 2a* A street; immediately following; *Scene 3* The Paroos' house; early that evening: "Piano Lesson" (Marian, Mrs. Paroo, Amaryllis), "Goodnight, My Someone" (Marian); *Scene 4* Madison Gymnasium; 30 minutes later: "Seventy-Six Trombones" (Harold, Boys & Girls) [a big hit]; *Scene 4a* A street; immediately following: "Sincere" (Buffalo Bills); *Scene 5* Exterior of Madison Library; immediately following: "The Sadder-but-Wiser Girl (for Me)" (Harold & Marcellus), "Pick-a-Little (Talk-a-Little)" (Eulalie, Maud, Ethel, Alma, Mrs. Squires, Ladies of River City), "Goodnight Ladies" (Buffalo Bills); *Scene 6* Interior of Madison Library; immediately following: "Marian the Librarian" (Harold, Boys & Girls) [a hit]; *Scene 7* A street; the following Saturday afternoon; *Scene 8* The Paroos' porch; that evening: "My White Knight" (Marian) [some say Frank Loesser wrote it and that it was one of the songs cut from *The Most Happy Fella*]; *Scene 9* Center of town; noon, the following Saturday: "The Wells Fargo Wagon" (Winthrop & Townspeople). *Act II*: *Scene 1* Madison Gymnasium; the following Tuesday evening: "It's You" (Buffalo Bills, Eulalie, Maud, Ethel, Alma, Mrs. Squires), "Shipoopi" (Marcellus, Harold, Marian, Tommy, Zaneeta, Kids), "Pickalittle" (reprise) (Eulalie, Maud, Ethel, Alma, Mrs. Squires, Ladies); *Scene 2* The hotel porch; the following Wednesday evening: "Lida Rose" (Buffalo Bills), "Will I Ever Tell You" (Marian); *Scene 3* The Paroos' porch; immediately following: "Gary, Indiana" (Winthrop) [a hit]; *Scene 4* The footbridge; 15 minutes later: "It's You" (reprise) (Townspeople, Boys & Girls), "Till There Was You" (Marian & Harold) [the big hit]; *Scene 5* A street; immediately following: "Seventy-Six Trombones"/"Goodnight My Someone" (reprise) (Harold & Marian); *Scene 6* Madison Park; a few minutes later: "Till There Was You" (reprise) (Harold); *Scene 7* River City High School assembly room; immediately following: Finale (Entire Company).

Broadway critics only raved. The show won 1958 Tony Awards for musical, book, composer, lyrics, musical direction, and for Robert Preston, David Burns, and Barbara Cook. It was also nominated for direction, choreography, and stage technician (Sammy Knapp), and for Iggie Wolfington. It also won a 1959 [sic] Tony for stage technician (Sammy Knapp). The show won the first ever Grammy Award for best cast album. *The Music Man* was the third-longest-running musical of the 1950s.

After Broadway. TOUR. Opened on 8/18/58, at the Philharmonic Auditorium, Los Angeles, and closed on 3/17/62, at the Shubert Theatre, Boston. MUSICAL DIRECTOR: Michel Perriere. *Cast:* CHARLIE: Harry Hickox, *Ed Fuller* (from 61–62); CONDUCTOR/LOCKE: Earl George; HAROLD: Forrest Tucker; MAYOR: Cliff Hall; THE FRISCO FOUR [this group was originally called The Buffalo Bills]; MARCELLUS: Benny Baker; TOMMY: Robert Piper, *James Pompeii* (from 59–60), *Patrick Cummings* (from 60–61); MARIAN: Joan Weldon, *Marian Savage* (from 61–62); MRS. PAROO: Lucie Lancaster; AMARYLLIS: Kay Cole, *Debbie Devine* (from 59–60), *Monique Vermont* (from 60–61), *Jo-Ann Trama* (from 61–62); WINTHROP: Lynn Potter, *Randy Garfield* (from 59–60), *Mike Murphy* (from 61–62); EULALIE: Carol Veazie, *Aileen Poe* (from 59–60), *Jane Lillig* (from 59–60); ZANEETA: Susan Luckey, *Sheila Forbes* (from 59–60), *Jean Lyons* (from 60–61); GRACIE: Jan Tanzy, *Kay Cole* (from 60–61), *Jo-Ann Trama* (from 61–62); ALMA: Jean Bruno, *Kay Cole* (from 59–60), *Arlene Blaha* (from 60–61), *Lillian Curtiss* (from 61–62); MAUD: Mary-Alice Wunderle, *Emily Ruhberg* (from 60–61); ETHEL: Lu Leonard, *Arlene Blaha* (during Miss Leonard's absence in 59–60), *Dawna Shove* (from 61–62); MRS. SQUIRES: Marceline Decker, *Leta Schoellis* (from 59–60), *Shirley Jean Mann* (from 59–60), *Norma Larkin* (by 60–61), *Frances Koll* (by 61–62). *Original tour understudies*: Harold: Harry Hickox & Robert Cosden; Marian: Dianne Barton; Mayor/Marcellus/Charlie: Earl George; Mrs. Paroo: Mary-Alice Wunderle; Tommy: Bert Michaels; Zaneeta: Marissa Mason; Ewart: Robert Cosden; Jaccy: Lewis Bolyard; Oliver: Richard Fredricks; Olin: Walter Kelvin; Winthrop: Jeffrey Allen; Eulalie: Jean Bruno; Alma/Maud/Ethel: Marceline Decker; Amaryllis: Jan Tanzy; Locke: Larry Devon.

ADELPHI THEATRE, London. Opened on 3/16/61. 395 PERFORMANCES. PRESENTED BY Harold Fielding, in association with Kermit Bloomgarden; DIRECTOR: Robert Merriman; CHOREOGRAPHER: James

Barron. *Cast:* HAROLD: Van Johnson; MAYOR: C. Denier Warren; MARCELLUS: Bernard Spear; TOMMY: Ben Stevenson; MARIAN: Patricia Lambert; MRS. PAROO: Ruth Kettlewell; WINTHROP: Dennis Waterman; EULALIE: Nan Munro.

TOUR. Opened on 9/18/61, at the Rajah Theatre, Reading, Pa., and closed on 4/28/62, at the Bushnell Theatre, Hartford, Conn. MUSICAL DIRECTOR: Paul Cianci. *Cast:* CHARLIE: David Huddleston; CONDUCTOR/LOCKE: Joe Kirkland; HAROLD: Harry Hickox; MAYOR: Tom Flatley Reynolds; MARCELLUS: Art Wallace; TOMMY: Bill Stanton; MARIAN: Dianne Barton; MRS. PAROO: Elizabeth Kerr; AMARYLLIS: Mary Lou Metzger; WINTHROP: Scott Bloom; EULALIE: Lidie Murfi; ZANEETA: Mimi Funes.

THE MOVIE. 1962. The film was a very faithful reproduction of the stage musical. "My White Knight" was replaced by another song, "Being in Love" (Marian). Another new song was "If You Don't Mind" (Marian & Mrs. Paroo). DIRECTOR: Morton Da Costa. *Cast:* CHARLIE: Harry Hickox; HAROLD: Robert Preston; MAYOR: Paul Ford; THE (FOUR) BUFFALO BILLS: EWART: Al Shea; OLIVER: Wayne Ward; JACEY: Vern Reed; OLIN: Bill Spangenberg; MARCELLUS: Buddy Hackett; MARIAN: Shirley Jones; MRS. PAROO: Pert Kelton; WINTHROP: Ronny Howard; EULALIE: Hermione Gingold; ZANEETA: Susan Luckey; ETHEL: Peggy Mondo; ALMA: Adnia Rice.

CITY CENTER, NYC, 6/16/65–6/27/65. 15 PERFORMANCES. This was part of a package of four City Center musicals (the others were *Guys and Dolls*, *Kiss Me, Kate*, and *South Pacific*). PRESENTED BY the New York City Center Light Opera Company; DIRECTOR: Gus Schirmer Jr.; CHOREOGRAPHER: Vernon Lusby; SETS/LIGHTING: Howard Bay; COSTUMES: Raoul Pene du Bois; MUSICAL DIRECTOR: Liza Redfield; ORCHESTRATIONS: Don Walker. *Cast:* CHARLIE: Alan Dexter; HAROLD: Bert Parks; MAYOR: Milo Boulton; THE (FOUR) BUFFALO BILLS: EWART: Al Shea; OLIVER: Wayne Ward; JACEY: Vern Reed; OLIN: Dale Jones; MARCELLUS: Art Wallace; TOMMY: William Glassman; MARIAN: Gaylea Byrne; MRS. PAROO: Sibyl Bowan; AMARYLLIS: Garda Hermany; WINTHROP: Dennis Scott; EULALIE: Doro Merande; ZANEETA: Sandy Duncan; GRACIE: Roma Hermany; ALMA: Adnia Rice; MAUD: Jeanne Schlegel; ETHEL: Amelia Varney; MRS. SQUIRES: Paula Trueman; CHORUS INCLUDED: Laurie Franks, Ronn Forella, Jodell Ann Kenting, Carlos Macri, Ron Stratton, Austin Colyer, Jack Davison, Russell Goodwin, John Herbert, Howard Kahl, Ripple Lewis, Dan Resin, Van Stevens. *Understudy:* Marian: Laurie Franks.

PAPER MILL PLAYHOUSE, New Jersey, 1974. DIRECTOR: Larry Forde. *Cast:* Ken Berry, Susan Watson, Louise Kirtland, Gary Gage.

WOLF TRAP FARM PARK, Vienna, Va., 8/29/78. 8 PERFORMANCES. DIRECTOR: Morton Da Costa; CHOREOGRAPHER: Tom Panko; SETS: Peter Wolf; COSTUMES: Brooks Van-Horn. *Cast:* Tony Randall, Linda Michele, Nancy Cushman, Benny Baker, Barney Martin.

JONES BEACH THEATRE, New York. 6/28/79–9/2/79. 67 PERFORMANCES. PRESENTED BY Richard Horner, in association with the Long Island State Parks & Recreation Commission; DIRECTOR: John Fearnley; CHOREOGRAPHER: Frank Wagner; SETS: Lynn Pecktal; COSTUMES: Robert Fletcher; MUSICAL DIRECTOR: Sande Campbell; MANAGING DIRECTOR: Alvin Dorfmann. *Cast:* TRAVELING SALESMEN: Jack Fletcher, Andrew Gale, G. Jan Jones, Bruce Sherman; CHARLIE: Ralph Vucci; HAROLD: Don Stewart; MAYOR: Alan North; OLIN: Clifford F. Fearl; MARCELLUS: Gibby Brand; TOMMY: George Pesaturo; MARIAN: Mary D'Arcy; MRS. PAROO: Toni Darnay; EULALIE: Joan Shea; MAUD: Marcia Brushingham; MRS. SQUIRES: Dixie Stewart; CHORUS INCLUDED: Phyllis Bash, Debra Lyman, Tina Paul, Pat Register, Mark Bove, Tim Flavin, Ramon Galindo, Norb Joerder, Larry Ross.

THE DICK VAN DYKE TOURING REVIVAL. Opened on 10/18/79, at the Sahara, Reno, and closed on 5/25/80, in Chicago. Then it went to City Center, NYC, 6/5/80–6/22/80. 8 previews 5/28/80–6/4/80. Limited run of 21 PERFORMANCES. Reviews were very divided, several raves and a pan among them. PRESENTED BY James M. Nederlander, Raymond Lussa, and Fred Walker; DIRECTOR/CHOREOGRAPHER: Michael Kidd; SETS: Peter Wolf; COSTUMES: Stanley Simmons; LIGHTING: Marcia Madeira; SOUND: Barry Rimler; MUSICAL DIRECTOR: Milton Rosenstock; PRODUCTION STAGE MANAGER: Conwell S. Worthington II; STAGE MANAGER: John M. Galo. *Cast:* TRAVELING SALESMEN: Dennis Holland, Lee Winston, Michael J. Rockne, Randy Morgan, Tom Garrett, Ralph Braun, Andy Hostettler, Dennis Batutis, Larry Cahn; CHAR-

LIE COWELL: Jay Stuart (8); CONDUCTOR: Peter Wandel; HAROLD HILL: Dick Van Dyke (1); MAYOR SHINN: Iggie Wolfington (3); THE QUARTET (11): EWART DUNLOP: Larry Cahn; OLIVER HIX: Randy Morgan; JACEY SQUIRES: Lee Winston; OLIN BRITT: Ralph Braun; MARCELLUS WASHBURN: Richard Warren Pugh (5); TOMMY DJILAS: Calvin McRae (10); MARIAN PAROO: Meg Bussert (2); MRS. PAROO: Carol Arthur (4); AMARYLLIS: Lara Jill Miller; WINTHROP PAROO: Christian Slater (7); EULALIE MACKECHNIE SHINN: Jen Jones (6); ZANEETA SHINN: Christina Saffran (9); ALMA HIX: Marcia Brushingham; MAUD DUNLOP: Mary Gaebler; ETHEL TOFFELMIER: P.J. Nelson; MRS. SQUIRES: Mary Roche; CONSTABLE LOCKE: Dennis Holland; RIVER CITY TOWNSPEOPLE: Victoria Ally, Carol Ann Basch, Dennis Batutis, David Beckett, Mark A. Esposito, Tom Garrett, Liza Gennaro, Dennis Holland, Andy Hostettler, Tony Jaeger, Wendy Kimball, Ara Marx, Darleigh Miller, Gail Pennington, Rosemary Rado, Michael J. Rockne, Coley Sohn, Peter Wandel. *Standby*: Harold: Jay Stuart. *Understudies*: Charlie/Ewart: Dennis Holland; Conductor/Marcellus/Constable: J.J. Jepson; Salesmen: Larry Cahn; Mayor: Ralph Braun; Olin: Michael J. Rockne; Jacey: Randy Morgan; Oliver: Tom Garrett; Tommy: Tony Jaeger; Mrs. Paroo/Eulalie: Mary Gaebler; Marian: Darleigh Miller; Zaneeta: Ara Marx; Amaryllis/Winthrop: Coley Sohn; Alma: Mary Roche; Maud/Ethel/Mrs. Squires: Wendy Kimball. *Swing Dancers*: Alis-Elaine Anderson & J.J. Jepson. The new scene breakdown, with songs (the characters are the same as in the 1957 original, even though the songs may be in a slightly different order) was: *Act I*: *Scene 1* A railway coach; morning, July 4, 1912: "Rock Island;" *Scene 2* River City Iowa, center of town; immediately following: "Iowa Stubborn," "Trouble;" *Scene 3* A street; immediately following; *Scene 4* The Paroos' house; early that evening: "Piano Lesson," "Goodnight My Someone;" *Scene 5* Madison Gymnasium; 30 minutes later: "Seventy-Six Trombones," "Sincere;" *Scene 6* A street; immediately following: "The Sadder-but-Wiser Girl," "Pick-a-Little," "Goodnight Ladies;" *Scene 7* Madison Library; immediately following: "Marian the Librarian;" *Scene 8* A street; the following Saturday afternoon; *Scene 9* The Paroos' porch; immediately following: "My White Knight;" *Scene 10* Center of town; noon, the following Saturday: "Wells Fargo Wagon." *Act II*: *Scene 1* Madison Gymnasium; the following Tuesday evening: "It's You," "Shipoopi," "Pick-a-Little" (reprise); *Scene 2* The hotel porch; the following Wednesday evening: "Lida Rose," "Will I Ever Tell You;" *Scene 3* The Paroos' porch; immediately following: "Gary, Indiana;" *Scene 4* The footbridge; 15 minutes later: "It's You" (reprise), "Till There Was You;" *Scene 5* A street; immediately following: "Seventy-Six Trombones"/"Goodnight My Someone" (reprise); *Scene 6* Madison Park; a few minutes later: "Till There Was You" (reprise); *Scene 7* Madison Gymnasium; immediately following: Finale.

NEW YORK STATE THEATRE, 2/26/88–4/10/88. 51 PERFORMANCES. PRESENTED BY the New York City Opera; DIRECTOR: Arthur Masella; CHOREOGRAPHER: Marcia Milgrom Dodge; COSTUMES: Andrew Marlay; SETS: David Jenkins; LIGHTING: Duane Schuler; CONDUCTOR: Donald Pippin. *Cast*: CHARLIE: Rex Hays; HAROLD: Bob Gunton; MAYOR: Richard McKee; EULALIE: Muriel Costa-Greenspon; ZANEETA: Jill Powell; MAUD: Lee Bellaver; MRS. SQUIRES: Rita Metzger; MARCELLUS: James Billings; OLIVER: Robert Brubaker; OLIN: Don Yule; MARIAN: Leigh Munro; MRS. PAROO: Brooks Almy; WINTHROP: Joel Chaiken; TOMMY: Steven M. Schultz.

467. *The Music Man (Broadway revival)*

Also known as *Meredith Willson's The Music Man*.

Before Broadway. Early rumors had Steve Martin, Matthew Broderick, Alec Baldwin, Scott Bakula, Bill Irwin, and Patrick Swayze cast as Harold Hill. By mid–1999 Scott Bierko was being touted as the lead, and he was confirmed on 10/18/99. On 11/16/99 Ruth Williamson was confirmed as Eulalie. Rebecca Luker was being rumored for Marian by 12/10/99, and she was confirmed on 1/4/00. Max Casella was confirmed on 2/16/00. The show was originally planned for the fall of 1999, but it was put back. This was Susan Stroman's Broadway debut as director. Broadway previews began on 4/5/00 (put back from 4/3/00).

The Broadway Run. NEIL SIMON THEATRE, 4/27/00–12/30/01. 24 previews from 4/5/00. 698 PERFORMANCES. PRESENTED BY Dodger Theatricals, John F. Kennedy Center for the Performing Arts, Elizabeth Williams/Anita Waxman, Kardana — Swinsky Productions, Lorie Cowen Levy/Dede Harris; MUSIC/LYRICS/BOOK: Meredith Willson; BASED ON a story by Meredith Willson & Franklin Lacey; DIRECTOR/CHOREOGRAPHER: Susan Stroman; ASSOCIATE DIRECTOR: Ray Roderick; ASSOCIATE CHOREOGRAPHER: Tara Young; SETS: Thomas Lynch; COSTUMES: William Ivey Long; LIGHTING: Peter Kaczorowski; SOUND: Jonathan Deans; MUSICAL SUPERVISOR/MUSICAL DIRECTOR: David Chase; ORIGINAL ORCHESTRATIONS: Don Walker; ORIGINAL ADDITIONAL ORCHESTRATIONS: Sidney Fine, Irwin Kostal, Seymour Ginzler, Walter Eiger; NEW ORCHESTRATIONS: Doug Besterman; ORIGINAL VOCAL ARRANGEMENTS: Herbert Greene; ORIGINAL DANCE MUSIC ARRANGEMENTS: Laurence Rosenthal; NEW DANCE MUSIC ARRANGEMENTS/INCIDENTAL MUSIC ARRANGEMENTS: David Krane; REHEARSAL PIANISTS: Rob Berman & David Krane; NEW CAST RECORDING on Q Records, made on 5/1/00 and released on 6/13/00; PRESS: Boneau/Bryan-Brown; CASTING: Jay Binder; COMPANY MANAGER: Kimberly Kelley; PRODUCTION STAGE MANAGER: Steven Zweigbaum, *Rolt Smith* (from 10/00); STAGE MANAGER: Rolt Smith, *Kim Vernace* (from 10/00).

ASSISTANT STAGE MANAGER: Kari Thompson. **Cast:** CONDUCTOR: Andre Garner, *Ric Ryder*; CHARLIE COWELL: Ralph Byers (7), *Andrew Boyar*; TRAVELING SALESMEN: Liam Burke (*Mark Moreau*), Kevin Bogue, E. Clayton Cornelious, Michael Duran, Blake Hammond, Michael McGurk, Dan Sharkey, John Sloman, *Tommar Wilson*; HAROLD HILL: Craig Bierko (1) ☆, *Eric McCormack* (5/8/01–8/5/01), *Robert Sean Leonard* (from 8/7/01); OLIN BRITT: Michael-Leon Wooley; AMARYLLIS: Jordan Puryear, *Malika Samuel*; MAUD DUNLOP: Martha Hawley; EWART DUNLOP: Jack Doyle; MAYOR SHINN: Paul Benedict (4), *Kenneth Kimmins* (from 4/10/01); ALMA HIX: Leslie Hendrix; ETHEL TOFFELMIER: Tracy Nicole Chapman, *Christine Toy Johnson* (from 11/21/01); OLIVER HIX: John Sloman; JACEY SQUIRES: Blake Hammond, *Bruce Dow*; MARCELLUS WASHBURN: Max Casella (3), *Joel Blum* (from 1/5/01); TOMMY DJILAS: Clyde Alves, *Manuel Herrera* (from 4/10/01); MARIAN PAROO: Rebecca Luker (2) ☆; MRS. PAROO: Katherine McGrath (6); WINTHROP PAROO: Michael Phelan, *William Ullrich*; EULALIE MACKECKNIE SHINN: Ruth Williamson (5), *Ruth Gottschall* (from 8/17/00); ZANEETA SHinn: Kate Levering, *Cameron Adams* (from 2/20/01); GRACIE SHINN: Ann Whitlow Brown, *Jennie Ford, Tiler Peck*; MRS. SQUIRES: Ann Brown, *Nancy Johnston*; CONSTABLE LOCKE: Kevin Bogue; RIVER CITY RESIDENTS & KIDS: Cameron Adams, Kevin Bogue, Sara Brenner, Chase Brock, Liam Burke (*Mark Moreau*), E. Clayton Cornelious, Michael Duran, Andre Garner, Ellen Harvey, Mary Illes, Joy Lynn Matthews, Michael McGurk, Robbie Nicholson, Ipsita Paul, Pamela Remler, Dan Sharkey, Lauren Ullrich, Travis Wall, *Lesley Jennings, Lindsay Dunn, Tina Ou, Jennifer Tangjerd, Jean Marie, Mitchell Federan, Suzanne Hevner, Alice Rietveld*. **Standbys:** Harold/Marcellus: Jim Walton; Charlie: John Sloman, *Jim Walton*. **Understudies:** Harold: John Sloman; Marian: Mary Illes & Cynthia Leigh Heim; Marcellus: Kevin Bogue, *Liam Burke*; Mayor: Ralph Byers & Jack Doyle; Eulalie: Leslie Hendrix & Ellen Harvey; Mrs. Paroo: Martha Hawley & Ellen Harvey; Winthrop: Travis Wall & Lauren Ullrich; Amaryllis: Lauren Ullrich & Sara Brenner; Charlie: Jeff Williams; Tommy: Chase Brock & Michael McGurk; Zaneeta: Sara Brenner & Jennie Ford; Gracie: Cameron Adams & Sara Brenner; Olin: Dan Sharkey & Kevin Bogue; Ewart: Michael Duran & Jeff Williams; Oliver: Jeff Williams & Dan Sharkey; Jacey: Andre Garner & Michael Duran; Maud: Ellen Harvey & Joy Lynn Matthews; Alma: Cynthia Leigh Heim & Ellen Harvey, *Ipsita Paul & Martha Hawley*; Mrs. Squires: Cynthia Leigh Heim & Joy Lynn Matthews; Ethel: Joy Lynn Matthews & Ipsita Paul. **Swings:** Jennie Ford, Cynthia Leigh Heim, Jason Snow, Jeff Williams, *Lesley Jennings, Liam Burke*. **Orchestra:** TROMBONES: Dick Clark & Kenneth Finn; BASS TROMBONE/TUBA: Matthew Ingman; TRUMPETS: Danny Cahn, John Dent, Wayne J. duMaine; FRENCH HORN: Chris Komer; WOODWINDS: Andrew Sterman, Tony Brackett, Chuck Wilson, Rick Heckman, Mark Thrasher; VIOLIN: Paul Woodiel; CELLO: Sarah Carter; DRUMS: David Ratajczak; PERCUSSION: James Baker; BASS: Richard Sarpola; HARP: Grace Paradise; PIANO: Rob Berman.

Note: The barbershop quartet in this production was known as the

Hawkeye Four. *Act I*: *Scene 1* A railway coach; morning, July 3, 1912: "Rock Island" (Charlie & Traveling Salesmen); *Scene 2* Train depot, River City, Iowa; *Scene 3* The center of town: "Iowa Stubborn" (Townspeople), "(Ya Got) Trouble" (Harold & Townspeople); *Scene 4* A street; *Scene 5* The Paroos' house: "Piano Lesson" (Marian, Mrs. Paroo, Amaryllis), "Goodnight, My Someone" (Marian); *Scene 6* Madison Gymnasium; July 4th: "Seventy-Six Trombones" (Harold & Townspeople); *Scene 7* The center of town: "Sincere" (Olin, Oliver, Ewart, Jacey); *Scene 8* A street just off the center of town: "The Sadder-But-Wiser Girl" (Harold & Marcellus), "Pickalittle (Talkalittle)" (Alma, Ethel, Eulalie, Maud, Mrs. Squires, Ladies of River City), "Goodnight Ladies" (Olin, Oliver, Ewart, Jacey); *Scene 9* Madison Library: "Marian the Librarian" (Harold, Boys & Girls); *Scene 10* A street; the following Saturday, late afternoon; *Scene 11* The Paroos' porch; immediately following: "Gary, Indiana" (Harold & Mrs. Paroo), "My White Knight" (Marian); *Scene 12* The edge of town; noon, the following Saturday: "The Wells Fargo Wagon" (Winthrop & Townspeople). *Act II*: *Scene 1* Madison Gymnasium; the following Tuesday evening: "It's You" (Olin, Oliver, Ewart, Jacey, Harold, Townspeople), "Pickalittle" (reprise) (Eulalie, Maud, Ethel, Alma, Mrs. Squires, Ladies); *Scene 2* The front of the hotel; the following Wednesday evening: "Lida Rose" (Olin, Oliver, Ewart, Jacey), "Will I Ever Tell You?" (Marian); *Scene 3* The Paroos' porch; immediately following: "Gary, Indiana" (reprise) (Winthrop, Mrs. Paroo, Marian); *Scene 4* Madison Park: "Shipoopi" (Marcellus, Harold, Townspeople); *Scene 5* The footbridge: "Till There Was You" (Marian), "Seventy Six Trombones" (reprise) & "Goodnight, My Someone" (reprise) (Harold & Marian), "Till There Was You" (reprise) (Harold); *Scene 6* The center of town; immediately following: Finale (Company).

Broadway reviews were mostly excellent. The show received Tony nominations for revival of a musical, direction of a musical, choreography, sets, costumes, orchestrations, and for Craig Bierko and Rebecca Luker. Ruth Williamson contracted a scalp infection probably caused by the many hat changes she had to make, and was out three times before finally relinquishing the role in 8/00. After the 9/11/01 attack on New York City *The Music Man* and several other shows suffered set-backs at the box-office. On 9/25/01 the show posted a closing notice for 9/30/01, but on 9/27/01 the notice came down as many people and organizations made concessions to enable these shows to keep running.

After Broadway. NON-EQUITY TOUR. Opened on 10/2/01, in Des Moines. This tour caused a stir by virtue of charging Broadway tour prices. PRESENTED BY Dodger Theatricals; DIRECTOR: Ray Roderick; CHOREOGRAPHER: Liam Burke.

HOLLYWOOD BOWL, 8/4/02. Concert version. HOLLYWOOD BOWL ORCHESTRA DIRECTED BY: John Mauceri. *Cast:* CHARLIE: Lyle Kanouse; HAROLD: Eric McCormack; MAYOR: Lenny Wolpe; OLIVER: Gibby Brand; JACEY: Michael DeVries; EWART: Kevin Earley; MARCELLUS: Jason Graae; MARIAN: Kristin Chenoweth; MRS. PAROO: Brooks Almy; EULALIE: Ruth Williamson; ALMA: Marsha Kramer; MRS. SQUIRES: Carol Swarbrick.

TV PRODUCTION. 2/16/03. Part of ABC's *Wonderful World of Disney* series. PRODUCED BY: Craig Zadan & Neil Meron; DIRECTOR: Jeff Bleckner; CHOREOGRAPHER: Kathleen Marshall. *Cast:* HAROLD: Matthew Broderick; MARIAN: Kristin Chenoweth; MAYOR: Victor Garber; MRS. PAROO: Debra Monk; EULALIE: Molly Shannon; MARCELLUS: David Aaron Baker.

468. *Musical Chairs*

The characters on stage are members of an audience watching the opening night of an Off Broadway play.

Before Broadway. This show was originally produced Off Broadway, at the PARK ROYAL.

The Broadway Run. RIALTO THEATRE, 5/14/80–5/25/80. 6 previews from 5/6/80. 15 PERFORMANCES. The Equity Library Theatre production, PRESENTED BY Lesley Savage & Bert Stratford; MUSIC/LYRICS: Tom Savage; BOOK: Barry Berg, Ken Donnelly, Tom Savage; BASED ON an original story concept by Larry P. Pontillo; DIRECTOR/CHOREOGRAPHER: Rudy Tronto; ASSISTANT DIRECTOR/ASSISTANT CHOREOGRAPHER/DANCE CAPTAIN:

Susan Stroman; SETS: Ernest Allen Smith; COSTUMES: Michael J. Cesario; LIGHTING: Peggy Clark; MUSICAL DIRECTOR: Barry H. Gordon; ORCHESTRATIONS/ARRANGEMENTS: Ada Janik & Dick Lieb; PRESS: Jeffrey Richards Associates; CASTING: Mary Jo Slater; GENERAL MANAGER: Leonard A. Mulhern; COMPANY MANAGER: Malcolm Allen; PRODUCTION STAGE MANAGER: Douglas F. Goodman; STAGE MANAGER: Douglas Walker. *Cast:* JOE PRESTON: Ron Holgate (1), *Tom Urich* (from 5/18/80); MATTY: Eileen McCabe; STAGE MANAGER: Douglas Walker; SALLY'S BOYFRIEND: Scott Ellis; MILLIE: Enid Blaymore; ROBERTA: Grace Keagy (7), *Helen Blount* (from 5/20/80); BRAD: Randall Easterbrook; MIRANDA: Leslie-Anne Wolfe; LILLIAN: Patti Karr (4); HAROLD: Brandon Maggart (3); GARY: Jess Richards (5); JANET: Joy Franz (6); BROWN SUIT: Edward Earle; BLUE SUIT: Tom Breslin; TUXEDO: Rick Emery; VALERIE BROOKS: Lee Meredith (2). *Act I*: Overture (Orchestra), "Tonight's the Night" (Company), "My Time" (Joe), "Who's Who" (Company), "If I Could Be Beautiful" (Miranda & Boys), "What I Could Have Done Tonight" (Harold & Janet), "There You Are" (Tuxedo), "Sally" (Sally's Boyfriend & Company), "Other People" (Janet), "My Time" (reprise) (Joe), "Hit the Ladies" (Lillian & Ladies). *Act II*: "Musical Chairs" (Tuxedo, Blue Suit, Brown Suit), "Suddenly Love" (Gary), "Better than Broadway" (Millie & Roberts), "Every Time the Music Starts" (Brad & Company), "There You Are" (reprise) (Tuxedo, Joe, Valerie), "My Time" (reprise) (Joe).

Reviews were generally not good.

469. *A Musical Jubilee*

A "potpourri" claiming to demonstrate the development of the American musical, specifically the Broadway musical. A musical entertainment.

The Broadway Run. ST. JAMES THEATRE, 11/13/75–2/1/76. 2 previews. 92 PERFORMANCES. PRESENTED BY the Theatre Guild & Jonathan Conrow; WRITER: Max Wilk; DEVISED BY: Marilyn Clark & Charles Burr; DIRECTOR: Morton Da Costa; CHOREOGRAPHER: Robert Tucker; SETS: Herbert Senn; COSTUMES: Donald Brooks; LIGHTING: Thomas Skelton; MUSICAL SUPERVISOR: Lehman Engel; MUSICAL DIRECTOR: John Lesko; ORCHESTRATIONS: Philip J. Lang, Hershy Kay, Elman Anderson; DANCE MUSIC ARRANGEMENTS/MUSICAL CONTINUITY: Trude Rittman; PRESS: Joe Wolhandler Associates, Sol Jacobson; GENERAL MANAGER: Victor Samrock; PRODUCTION STAGE MANAGER: William Dodds; STAGE MANAGER: Marnel Sumner; ASSISTANT STAGE MANAGER: James Frasher. *Cast:* John Raitt (1) ☆ (*Igors Gavon*), Patrice Munsel (2) ^, Lillian Gish ☆ (special guest star), Dick Shawn (5) ☆ (*David King*), Tammy Grimes (3) ☆, Larry Kert (6) ☆, Cyril Ritchard (4) ☆; ENSEMBLE: Steven Boockvor, Eric Brotherson, Marcia Brushingham, Igors Gavon, Nana, David King, Jeanne Lehman, Bettye Malone, Estella Munson, Julie Pars, Dennis Perren, Leland Schwantes, Craig Yates. **Understudies**: For John Raitt: Igors Gavon; For Patrice Munsel: Estella Munson; For Tammy Grimes: Jeanne Lehman; For Dick Shawn: David King; For Cyril Ritchard: Eric Brotherson; For Larry Kert: Craig Yates; For Lillian Gish: Marcia Brushingham. *Act I*: OPENING: "Happy Days" (m: Johann Strauss; l: Howard Dietz) (Company); AMERICAN FRONTIER: "Whoa-Haw" (Larry), "Lorena" (m: J.P. Webster; l: Rev. H.D.L. Webster) (John), "Sweet Betsy from Pike" (Tammy), "Skip to My Lou" (Patrice & Larry), "Whoa-Haw" (reprise) (Company); AMERICAN MILITARY: "Hold on Abraham" (m/l: William B. Bradbury) (Ensemble), "Bonnie Blue Flag" (m: Valentine Vousden; l: Harry Macarthy) (Larry, Steve, Igors, David, Dennis, Leland, Craig), "Tipperary" (m/l: Jack Judge & Harry Williams) (Tammy & Male Ensemble), "I Didn't Raise My Boy to Be a Soldier" (m: Al Piantadosi; l: Alfred Bryan) (Lillian), "Mademoiselle from Armentieres" (m/l: Howard Ross) (Cyril & Dick), "Over There" (m/l: Irving Berlin) (Patrice & Male Ensemble), "Battle Hymn of the Republic" (l: Julia Ward Howe) (John & Company); OLD VIENNA: "Wien, Wien, You're Calling Me" (m: Rudolf Sieczynski) (Patrice, John, Ensemble), "I'm in Love with Vienna" (m: Johann Strauss; l: Oscar Hammerstein II) [from the movie *The Great Waltz*] (Patrice, John, Ensemble), "Der Shimmy" (m: Emmerich Kalman) (Tammy), "I've Got Something" (m: Franz Lehar; l: Harry B. & Robert B. Smith) (Cyril, Marcia, Nana, Jeanne, Bettye, Julie, Estella), "Oh, the Women" (m: Franz Lehar) (Larry, Igors, Dennis), "Gypsy Love" (m: Franz

Lehar; l: Harry B. & Robert B. Smith) [from *Gypsy Love*] (Patrice & Ensemble); BRITAIN: "And Her Mother Came Too" (m: Ivor Novello; l: Dion Titheradge) [from *From A to Z*] (Cyril); EARLY BROADWAY: "Song of the Vagabonds" (m: Rudolf Friml; l: Brian Hooker & W.H. Post) [from *The Vagabond King*] (John & Male Ensemble), "Totem Tom Tom" (m: Rudolf Friml; l: Otto Harbach & Oscar Hammerstein II) [from *Rose Marie*] (Tammy & Female Ensemble), "Serenade" (m: Sigmund Romberg; l: Dorothy Donnelly) [from *The Student Prince*] (Larry), "Violetta" (sketch) (Cyril, Larry, Eric, Tammy), "Moonstruck" (m: Ivan Caryll & Lionel Monckton; l: James T. Tanner) [from *Our Miss Gibbs*] (Lillian & Male Ensemble), "You Are Love" (m: Jerome Kern; l: Oscar Hammerstein II) [from *Show Boat*] (Patrice & John), "I've Told Ev'ry Little Star" (m: Jerome Kern; l: Oscar Hammerstein II) [from *Music in the Air*] (Dick & Female Ensemble), "Why Was I Born?" (m: Jerome Kern; l: Oscar Hammerstein II) [from *Sweet Adeline*] (Patrice), "The Best Things in Life Are Free" (m: Ray Henderson; l: Lew Brown & B.G. "Buddy" De Sylva) [from *Good News*] (Larry & Ensemble), "They Didn't Believe Me" (m: Jerome Kern; l: Herbert Reynolds) [from *The Girl from Utah*] (Tammy), "The Song is You" (m: Jerome Kern; l: Oscar Hammerstein II) [from *Music in the Air*] (John), "Something Seems Tingle Ingleing" (m: Rudolf Friml; l: Leo Dietrichstein & Otto Harbach) [from *High Jinks*] (Cyril & Female Ensemble), "(I Want to Hear a) Yankee Doodle Tune" (by George M. Cohan) [from the 1903 production of *Mother Goose*] (Dick & Company). *Act II*: THE SMART SET: "We're Blase" (m: Ord Hamilton; l: Bruce Sevier) [from *Bow Bells*] (John, Cyril, Patrice, Tammy), "Poor Little Rich Girl" (m/l: Noel Coward) [from *Charlot's Revue*] (Tammy), "You Go to My Head" (m: J. Fred Coots; l: Haven Gillespie) (John), "Find Me a Primitive Man" (m/l: Cole Porter) [from *Fifty Million Frenchmen*] (Patrice & Tammy), "I Guess I'll Have to Change My Plans" (m: Arthur Schwartz; l: Howard Dietz) [from *The Little Show*] (Dick), "Sophisticated Lady" (m: Duke Ellington; l: Mitchell Parish & Irving Mills) (Larry), "Love Me or Leave Me" (m: Walter Donaldson; l: Gus Kahn) [from *Whoopee!*] (Patrice), "Gilbert the Filbert" (m: Herman Finck; l: Arthur Wimperis) [from *The Girl from Utah*] (Cyril), "We're Blase" (reprise) (John, Cyril, Dick, Larry, Patrice, Tammy); VAUDEVILLE: "At the Moving Picture Ball" (m: Joseph H. Santly; l: Howard Johnson) (Ensemble), "Miss Annabelle Lee" (m: Lew Pollack; l: Sidney Clare & Harry Richman) (Dick), "I Wanna Be Loved by You" (m: Harry Ruby; l: Bert Kalmar) [from *Good Boy*] (Patrice, Tammy, Lillian), The Green Eye of the Little Yellow God (sketch) (by Reginald Purdell; based on the poem by Milton Hayes) (Cyril, Dick, Eric); JAZZ: "How Jazz Was Born" (m: Fats Waller; l: Andy Razaf & Henry Creamer) (Larry & Ensemble), "Ain't Misbehavin'" (m: Fats Waller & Harry Brooks; l: Andy Razaf) [from *Hot Chocolates*] (Larry), "I'm Just Wild About Harry" (m: Eubie Blake; l: Noble Sissle) [from *Shuffle Along*] (Tammy), "Me and My Shadow" (m: Al Jolson & Dave Dreyer; l: Billy Rose) (Dick), "Sometimes I'm Happy" (m: Vincent Youmans; l: Irving Caesar) [from *Hit the Deck*] (Patrice), "Great Day" (m: Vincent Youmans; l: Billy Rose & Edward Eliscu) [from *Great Day*] (John), "How Jazz Was Born" (reprise) (John, Dick, Larry, Patrice, Tammy, Ensemble); LATE BROADWAY: "Lullaby of Broadway" (m: Harry Warren; l: Al Dubin) [from the movie *Golddiggers of 1935*] (Ensemble), "(This is My) Lucky Day" (m: Ray Henderson; l: B.G. "Buddy" De Sylva & Lew Brown) [from *George White's Scandals of 1926*] (Dick), "If You Knew Susie" (m: Joseph Meyer; l: B.G. "Buddy" De Sylva) [from *Big Boy*] (Cyril), "S'Wonderful" (m: George Gershwin; l: Ira Gershwin) [from *Funny Face*] (Lillian), "Fascinating Rhythm" (m; George Gershwin; l: Ira Gershwin) [from *Lady, Be Good*] (Larry), "Liza" (All the Clouds'll Roll Away) (m: George Gershwin; l: Ira Gershwin & Gus Kahn) [from *Show Girl*] (Tammy), "Where or When" (m: Richard Rodgers; l: Lorenz Hart) [from *Babes in Arms*] (Patrice), "Hallelujah" (m: Vincent Youmans; l: Clifford Grey & Leo Robin) [from *Hit the Deck*] (John & Company).

It got good reviews.

After Broadway. TOUR. Opened on 5/31/76, in Toronto. *Cast*: Howard Keel, Patrice Munsel, Eartha Kitt, Cyril Ritchard, Larry Kert.

470. *My Darlin' Aida*

A heavy adaptation of the opera, with the Nile becoming the American Confederate States, and Memphis, Egypt becoming Memphis, Ten-nessee. Set on and about General Farrow's plantation near Memphis, during the first year of the Civil War (1861). Farrow was Pharaoh in the original *Aida*, and Rumford was Ramfis, high priest. In this show, Aida was Jessica's half-black slave, who is in love with young Captain Demarest (Radames in the opera). However, Demarest is unhappily pledged to Jessica (Amneris in the opera). Aida's stepfather, Adam, returns from the North, via the Underground, to head a slave uprising, and Demarest becomes involved in the plot. The plot is discovered; Brown is shot dead; Aida is wounded; and Demarest is fatally whipped by masked and hooded Knights of the White Cross. The lovers die together in a rickety Negro church, while outside, Jessica prays for the repose of Demarest's soul. The opera's famous Triumphal Scene became a celebration of the Southern victory at Bull Run, near the end of Act I. The original song "Celeste Aida" became "My Darlin' Aida" here.

Before Broadway. Charles Friedman began writing his adaptation in 1947. It cost $300,000, the most lavish show put on on Broadway since *The Great Waltz* in 1934. There were no out-of-town tryouts because of its sheer size; instead there were two weeks of New York previews (this was a first; there had been one or two shows that had a night or two of New York previews, but nothing as long as this). The two ladies who played Aida were white, and this was protested by the Coordinating Council of Negro Performers. However, the producers claimed they couldn't find suitable black performers.

The Broadway Run. WINTER GARDEN THEATRE, 10/27/52–1/11/53. 89 PERFORMANCES. PRESENTED BY Robert L. Joseph; MUSIC: Giuseppe Verdi; LYRICS/BOOK/NEWLY CONCEIVED BY/DIRECTOR: Charles Friedman; BASED ON the 1871 opera *Aida*, by Verdi; CHOREOGRAPHER: Hanya Holm; SETS/COSTUMES: Lemuel Ayers; LIGHTING/PRODUCTION SUPERVISOR: Hassard Short; MUSICAL DIRECTOR: Franz Allers; CHORAL DIRECTOR: Robert Shaw; NEW ORCHESTRAL ARRANGEMENTS: Hans Spialek; PRESS: Karl Bernstein & Harvey Sabinson; COMPANY MANAGER: Clarence Taylor; STAGE MANAGERS: Samuel Liff, Gene Perlowin, Ben Kranz. *Cast*: RUMFORD: William Wilderman; MAYOR BRAD SOURBY: Stanley Carlson; AIDA: Elaine Malbin (2) (evenings), Eileen Schauler (matinees); RAYMOND DEMAREST: William Olvis (3) (evenings), Howard Jarratt (4) (matinees); JASON: Alonzo Bosan; MORNING STAR: Ida Johnson; ZEPORAH: Lavinia Williams; LOLLY: Olive Moorefield; WHEAT: George Fisher; FROG: John Fleming; LIZ: Fredye Marshall; REBECCA: Billie Allen; LUCY: Joyce Sellinger; YANCEY HOYT: William Sutherland; JESSICA FARROW: Dorothy Sarnoff (1) (evenings), Bette Dubro (matinees); GENERAL FARROW: Kenneth Schon; CHOIR SOLOIST: Theresa Green; SIS: Ruth Anne Fleming; DOLLY: Ruth McVayne; BONNIE: Sue Dorris; MAGGIE: Muriel Birkhead; AGGIE: Martha Flynn; LAURIE: Lola Fisher; MARY: Ruth Schumacher; NELLIE: Mary Ann Tomlinson; BETTIE: Jane Copeland; ONNIE: Carol Jones; MAIDS: Billie Allen, Jacqueline Hairston, Lavinia Williams; MAGICIAN: Gordon Hamilton; MRS. SOURBY: Jo Anne Taylor; HOWIE: Walter Kelvin; BULL: Edward Wellman; STEVE: Robert Busch; HUTCH: Thornton Marker; ADAM BROWN: William Dillard; FLOWER: Jacqueline Hairston; SUSIE: Gloria Davy; LILLY: Charlotte Holloman; PORK: Ned Wright; MAJOR STANHOPE: William Sutherland; SINGERS: Robert Baird, Gino Baldi, Muriel Birckhead, Robert Busch, Dorothy Candee, Benjamin Cassidy, Jane Copeland, Jack Dabdoub, Calvin Dash, Gloria Davy, Sue Dorris, George Fisher, Lola Fisher, Ruth Ann Fleming, John Fleming, Martha Flynn, Theresa Green, Arthur Hammond, Charlotte Holloman, Ida Johnson, Carol Jones, Walter Kelvin, Thornton Marker, Fredye Marshall, Ruth McVayne, William Noble, Michael O'Carolan, Charles O'Neill, Robert Price, Michael Roberts, Joyce Sellinger, Ruth Schumacher, William Sutherland, Jo Anne Taylor, Edgar Thompson, Mary Ann Tomlinson, Casper Vecchione, Robert Watts, Edward Wellman, Ned Wright, Robert Yeager; DANCERS: Billie Allen, Betty Buday, Nanci Darken, Paul Gannon, Bettye Griffin, Dody Goodman, Jacqueline Hairston, Gordon Hamilton, Erona Harris, Eddie Heim, Ed Holleman, Louis Johnson, Joan Kruger, Carmelita Lanza, Joe Nash, Walter Nicks, Paul Olson, Frank Seabolt, Claude Thompson, Lavinia Williams, Doris Wright; CHILDREN: Paula Anderson, Denis Bradler, Gail Culberson, Sharyn Kenney, Vincent Yearwood. *Act I: Scene 1* The terrace of the Big House; May 7, 1861, evening: Prelude & Opening, "My Darlin' Aida" (Raymond), "Love is Trouble" (Jessica & Raymond), "Love is Trouble" (reprise) (Aida, Jessica, Raymond), "Me and Lee" (General,

Rumford, Raymond, Aida, Jessica, Company); *Scene 2* The Giant Oak; immediately afterwards: "Me and Lee" (reprise) (Men), "March on for Tennessee" (Aida); *Scene 3* The cemetery by the Negro Church; the following night: "Why Ain't We Free?" (Choir Leader & Women's Choir), "Knights of the White Cross" (Rumford, Raymond, Knights); *Scene 4* Jessica's boudoir in the Big House; three months later: "A Jamboree" (dance number) (Jessica & Girls), Dance (The Maids), "Letter Duet" (dance) (Aida & Jessica), "Me and Lee" (reprise) (Men); *Scene 5* The square at the boat landing; immediately afterwards: "Homecoming" (dance) (Company), "When You Grow Up" (Women & Children), "Soldiers' March" (dance) (Men), Ballet (Dancers), "King Called Cotton" (Company), "Gotta Live Free" (Adam), "Master and Slave" (sextette) (Adam, Aida, Raymond, Jessica,Rumford, General, Company), "Sing! South! Sing!" (Company). *Act II*: *Scene 1* The terrace of the Big House; three weeks later, night: Spiritual (The Choir), "I Want to Pray" (Jessica), "Alone" (Aida), "Three Stones to Stand On" (Aida & Adam), "You're False" (Aida & Adam), "There'll Have to Be Changes Made" (Aida & Raymond), "Away" (Aida & Raymond), "Land of Mine" (Aida, Raymond, Adam); *Scene 2* The path to the quarter; immediately afterwards; *Scene 3* The quarter; immediately afterwards: Ballet (Dancers & Singers); *Scene 4* The hallway in the Big House; toward dawn: "I Don't Want You" (Jessica & Raymond); *Scene 5* The Negro Church and cemetery; immediately afterwards: "The Trial" (dance) (Jessica, Rumford, Knights), "You Are My Darlin' Bride" (Raymond), "Oh, Sky, Goodbye" (Aida), "Why Ain't We Free?" (reprise) (Aida, Raymond, Jessica, Choir).

It was reviewed by both drama and music critics; reviews were divided. Elaine Malbin and Dorothy Sarnoff came in for great praise, as did Lem Ayers' sets and costumes. The show won a Donaldson Award for costumes. Some of the sets and costumes from this show went to later productions, notably a 1955–56 production of *Die Fledermaus*. The story of *Aida* was not attempted again until 2000 (see *Aida*)

471. *My Dear Public*

A "revusical story." Barney, a wealthy zipper manufacturer, is persuaded to back a musical written by Byron, an arty, temperamental young poet from Greenwich Village, and which stars Daphne, his ex-wife, a former actress. Barney is in love with a soubrette, Jean.

Before Broadway. On 1/12/42 the singing group The Revuers, consisting of Betty Comden, Adolph Green, and Judy Tuvim (who later became Judy Holliday) signed the contract to feature in this musical (this was Judy's first musical), which opened for tryouts on 3/3/42, in New Haven, then went on to the Shubert Theatre, Boston, and in early April folded in Philadelphia. DIRECTOR: Joseph Pevney; CHOREOGRAPHERS: Felicia Sorel & Carl Randall. *Cast:* BARNEY: Joe Smith; JEAN: Joy Hodges; WALTERS: Karl Malden; GUS: Charles Dale; ALSO WITH: Rose Brown; ENSEMBLE: The Martins (singing group, included Hugh Martin & Ralph Blane), The Revuers, Smith & Dale (comedy act), Cora Witherspoon, Mitzi Green, Tamara Geva. The show was revised. The numbers "Rain on the Sea" (m: Caesar & Lerner; l: Marks) and "Now that I'm Free" (m: Caesar; l: Hollander) were cut. The show was recast, and went to Broadway.

The Broadway Run. FORTY-SIXTH STREET THEATRE, 9/9/43–10/16/43. 45 PERFORMANCES. PRESENTED BY Irving Caesar; MUSIC/LYRICS: Irving Caesar (assisted by Sammy Lerner, Gerald Marks, Irma Hollander); BOOK: Irving Caesar (assisted by Charles "Chuno" Gottesfeld); DIRECTOR: Edgar MacGregor; CHOREOGRAPHER: Felicia Sorel (assisted by Loretta Jefferson & Henry Le Tang); SETS: Albert Johnson; COSTUMES: Lucinda Ballard; LIGHTING: Albert Alloy; MUSICAL DIRECTOR: Harry Levant; ORCHESTRATIONS: Hans Spialek & Ted Royal; VOCAL ARRANGEMENTS: Buck (i.e. Clay) Warnick; PRESS: Helene Hanff. *Cast:* WALTERS: David Burns (4); TAPPS: Georgie Tapps; JEAN: Nanette Fabray (3); DAPHNE DREW: Ethel Shutta (2); BARNEY SHORT: Willie Howard (1) ☆; RENEE: Renee Russell; LOUISE: Louise Fiske; MITZI: Mitzi Perry; BYRON BURNS: Eric Brotherson; LULU: Sherle North; GORDON: Gordon Gifford; PLAYWRIGHT: William Nunn; GUS WAGNER: Jesse White (5); KELLY: Al Kelly; ROSE BROWN: Rose Brown; ANNOUNCER: Dave Hamilton; RUTH: Janice Wallace; EDITH: Edith Laumer; ALSO

WITH: The Crandall Sisters (Truda, Mickey & Heather), Harmoneers (Dave Hamilton, Louise Rose, Bill Jones, Michael Kozak), Della Lorrie, Harry Day, Lee Varrett, Monica Boyar, Marylou Arden, Helene and her violin; CHORUS GIRLS: Renee Russell, Marylin Johnson, Zynaid Spencer, Ann Middleton, Betty Burns, Virginia Stevens, Janice Wallace, Joan Sommers, Mitzi Perry, Edith Laumer, Louise Fiske, Marjorie Gaye, Betty Leighton, Jean Cooke, Dorothy Thomas, Billie Ferguson, Robin Marlowe, Vivian Newell, Dorothy Hyatt, Lorene Gray, Ginger Lynne; CHORUS BOYS: Jack Lyons, Richard Andre, Paul Vincent, Ernie Di Gennaro, Larry Evers, William Hunter, William Lundy. *Act I*: *Scene 1* Backstage; *Scene 2* Inside Barney Short's office; *Scene 3* Private room in the Crystal Hill Hospital; *Scene 4* Backstage; *Scene 5* Private room in the Crystal Hill Hospital; *Scene 6* Backstage. *Act II*: *Scene 1* Pan American Airport (LaGuardia Field); *Scene 2* Barney Short's Office; *Scene 3* Backstage; *Scene 4* Jean's Dressing Room; *Scene 5* Finale. *Act I*: Opening—"Feet on the Sidewalk (Head in the Sky)" (by Lerner & Marks) (Tapps, Jean, Truda & Mickey Crandall, Monica Boyar, Harmoneers, Boys & Girls), "My Dear Public" (Gordon, Lulu, Gus, Monica Boyar, Lee Varrett, Marylou Arden, Crandall Sisters, Harmoneers), "Last Will and Testament" (Byron), "Little Gamins" (Daphne & Ensemble), "(This is) Our Private Love Song" (m: Caesar; l: Lerner) (Byron, Jean, Helene & her violin), "My Spies Tell Me (You Love Nobody but Me)" (m: Marks; l: Caesar & Lerner) (Walters, Lulu, Crandall Sisters), "(There Ain't No) Color Line (Around the Rainbow)" (m: Caesar; l: Marks & Lerner) (Rose) [the show-stopper], "If You Want a Deal with Russia" (Barney), "May All Our Children Have Rhythm" (Tapps, Jean, Crandall Sisters, Harmoneers, Della Lorrie, Harry Day, Girls & Boys). *Act II*: "Pipes of Pan-Americana" (m: Marks; l: Caesar) (Gordon, Harmoneers, Monica Boyar, Della Lorrie, Harry Day, Boys & Girls), "Rhumba Jake" (Barney & Daphne), "Lulu" (Walters & Lulu), "Love is Such a Cheat" (m/l: Caesar, Marks, Hollander) (Daphne, Harmoneers, Helene & her violin), Enesco's Rumanian Rhapsody No. 1 (ballet) (Marylou Arden, Helene, Boys & Girls), "I Love to Sing the Words" (m: Caesar; l: Marks & Lerner) (Jean, Tapps, Boys & Girls), Finale: "May All Our Children Have Rhythm" (reprise) (Entire Company).

On opening night people streamed out of the theatre in Act II, partly due to the lousy show, and partly to the screwed-up PA system. The reviewers universally panned it. The show lost $180,000. Willie Howard was always at the race track, and couldn't remember his lines without his own form of cue cards—his lines written on a race-meet sheet.

472. *My Fair Lady*

An updating of the ancient myth of Pygmalion the sculptor falling in love with Galatea, the statue he has created. Set in London in 1912. Professor Henry Higgins, an arrogant phonetics expert and confirmed bachelor, comes across Eliza, a Cockney flower girl, at Covent Garden where he is taking notes on English dialects. He tells her that he and his friend Pickering can teach her to speak correctly, so she can be a lady and open up her own florist's shop. Eliza's idle father thinks this is a marvelous idea. But she does show up at Higgins's place (27a Wimpole Street) for instruction, which nearly drives them both mad ("The rain in Spain stays mainly in the plain"). But she succeeds, and Higgins introduces her to society at the Ascot races. Freddy falls for her and finally she is taken to a ball, where she succeeds. She leaves Higgins and rejects Freddy, and her father has become famous through his homespun philosophy. Doolittle has been living with a woman for years, and decides it's time to get married. Eliza has gone to Higgins's mother's house. All ends happily as they get together (in Shaw's play the implication was that she would marry Freddy and open up her flower shop), and this "implication" of a happy ending, while it did not expressly include it in the musical and thus tamper too much with Shaw's ideas, was a vital factor in making it a success with audiences.

Before Broadway. There had been a musical called *My Fair Lady*—a Gershwin one at that — in 1925, but it changed its title to *Tell Me More*. This was not connected to Shaw or Lerner & Loewe. Just a coincidence. As for the Shaw play, *Pygmalion*, Mrs. Patrick Campbell was the first to star in it in New York. In 1926 Lynn Fontanne starred in a Theatre Guild production. Gabriel Pascal, the French film-maker, made it as a movie with Leslie Howard and Wendy Hiller. A Broadway revival opened 12/26/45 (179 performances), at the Barrymore Theatre, starring Gertrude Lawrence and Raymond Massey. Monsieur Pascal had long wanted to do a musical of *Pygmalion*, but Shaw wouldn't allow it as long as he lived. Once Shaw died (late 1950), Pascal set about trying again. He needed someone to write it, but Schwartz & Dietz, Harburg & Saidy, Cole Porter, and Noel Coward all turned him down. On 10/10/51 *Variety* reported that Rodgers & Hammerstein were considering doing it, starring Mary Martin. But R & H were unable to see it through to completion partly because it wasn't a love story, and partly because the action never really leaves Higgins's study. Finally M. Pascal & the Theatre Guild (as producers) hired Lerner & Loewe to do the job. By 8/52 Mary Martin and Rex Harrison were being considered for the leads, but later in the year the project had come to nothing, and the team of Lerner & Loewe broke up temporarily. Mr. Pascal died, and Lerner & Loewe, now back together, acquired the rights to *Pygmalion*, and overcame the difficulties. Mary Martin turned the show down, thinking the score was no good. Over 50 girls were auditioned in New York and London. Rex Harrison couldn't sing, so his role was tailored by the writers to fit his talents. By 2/55 the title was *Lady Liza*, and by 10/55 *My Lady Liza*. By this time Julie Andrews had been cast opposite Rex Harrison. CBS funded it. Rehearsals began on 1/3/56. The numbers "Come to the Ball" and "Say a Prayer" were cut. "Say a Prayer" later showed up in the Lerner & Loewe movie *Gigi*. The ballet "Decorating Liza" was also cut. The writers now went, unenthusiastically, for a new title—*My Fair Lady*. It ran at the Shubert Theatre, New Haven, 2/4/56–2/11/56; then at the Erlanger Theatre, Philadelphia, from 2/15/56; and then it moved on to Broadway.

The Broadway Run. MARK HELLINGER THEATRE, 3/15/56–2/24/62; BROADHURST THEATRE, 2/28/62–4/14/62; BROADWAY THEATRE, 4/18/62–9/29/62. Total of 2,717 PERFORMANCES. PRESENTED BY Herman Levin; MUSIC: Frederick Loewe; LYRICS/BOOK: Alan Jay Lerner; BASED ON the 1914 comedy *Pygmalion*, by George Bernard Shaw; DIRECTOR: Moss Hart; ASSISTANT DIRECTOR: Stone Widney; CHOREOGRAPHER: Hanya Holm; ASSISTANT CHOREOGRAPHER: David Nillo; SETS: Oliver Smith; COSTUMES: Cecil Beaton; LIGHTING: Feder; MUSICAL DIRECTOR: Franz Allers, *Charles Jaffe* (by 60–61); MUSICAL ARRANGEMENTS: Robert Russell Bennett & Phil Lang; DANCE MUSIC ARRANGEMENTS: Trude Rittman; CHORAL ARRANGEMENTS: Gino Smart; CAST RECORDING on Columbia, made on 3/18/56, and took 17 hours to complete. It sold over 8 million copies; PRESS: Richard Maney, Peggy Phillips (gone by 56–57), Robert Hector (gone by 56–57), Martin Shwartz, Lila Glaser; GENERAL MANAGER: Philip Adler; COMPANY MANAGER: *Al Jones* (by 61–62); PRODUCTION STAGE MANAGER: Samuel Liff; STAGE MANAGERS: Jerry Adler & Bernard Hart (gone by 60–61), *Rex Partington* (added by 59–60). **Cast:** 1ST BUSKER: Imelda De Martin, *Maxine Berke* (from 56–57), *Joan Derby* (from 58–59), *Joan Diehl* (from 59–60); 2ND BUSKER: Carl Jeffrey (he later became Carl Jablonski), *Tom Hester* (from 56–57), *Thatcher Clarke* (from 58–59), *Bentley Roton* (from 59–60); 3RD BUSKER: Joe Rocco, *Bob Karl* (from 58–59), *Bill Atkinson* (from 59–60), *Christian Alderson* (from 60–61); MRS. EYNSFORD-HILL: Viola Roache (6), *Regina Wallace* (from 56–57); ELIZA DOOLITTLE: Julie Andrews (2) ☆, *Karen Shepard* (stood in), *Lola Fisher* (during Miss Andrews' vacation, from 8/14/56), *Sally Ann Howes* (from 2/3/58), *Pamela Charles* (from 2/2/59), *Margot Moser* (from 1/30/61), *Rosemary Rainer* (from 61–62); *Margot Moser*; FREDDY EYNSFORD-HILL: John Michael King (8), *Loren Driscoll* (from 59–60), *Dan Resin* (from 61–62); COLONEL PICKERING: Robert Coote (5), *Reginald Denny* (from 57–58), *Melville Cooper* (from 59–60); A BYSTANDER: Christopher Hewett, *Leo Britt, Robin Craven* (from 6/4/56), *Crandall Diehl* (from 56–57), *Glenn Kezer* (from 61–62); PROFESSOR HENRY HIGGINS: Rex Harrison (1) ☆ (his 750th and last performance was 12/23/57), *Tom Helmore* (during Mr. Harrison's vacation, from 8/17/56), *Edward Mulhare* (during Mr. Harrison's vacation, from 11/29/57, and permanently from 12/24/57), *Bramwell Fletcher* (during

Mr. Mulhare's absence, from 8/25/58), *Michael Allinson* (from 2/10/60); SELSEY MAN: Gordon Dilworth, *James Kenny* (from 61–62); HOXTON MAN: David Thomas, *John Dorrin* (from 61–62); ANOTHER BYSTANDER: Rodney McLennan; 1ST COCKNEY: Reid Shelton, *Lindsey Bergen* (from 56–57), *William Krach* (from 58–59), *Robert Price* (from 61–62); 2ND COCKNEY: Glenn Kezer; 3RD COCKNEY: James Morris, *Ray Hyson* (from 56–57), *Bill Diehl* (from 58–59); 4TH COCKNEY: Herb Surface; BARTENDER: David Thomas, *John Dorrin* (from 61–62); HARRY: Gordon Dilworth (11), *James Kenny* (from 61–62); JAMIE: Rodney McLennan (12); ALFRED P. DOOLITTLE: Stanley Holloway (3), *Ronald Radd* (from 12/23/57), *Gordon Dilworth* (from 61–62); MRS. PEARCE: Philippa Bevans (7), *Leta Bonynge* (from late 58), *Joyce Worsley* (from 61–62); MRS. HOPKINS: Olive Reeves-Smith (9), *Maribel Hammer* (stood in); BUTLER: Reid Shelton, *Glenn Kezer* (from 56–57); 1ST SERVANT: Rosemary Gaines, *Jean Maggio* (from 58–59), *Helen Ahola* (from 59–60), *Rosemary Rainer* (by 60–61), *Joan Cory* (from 61–62); 2ND SERVANT: Glenn Kezer, *Herb Surface* (from 56–57); 3RD SERVANT: Colleen O'Connor; 4TH SERVANT: Muriel Shaw, *Linda McNaughton* (from 56–57), *Lynn Barret* (from 59–60), *Susan Fellows* (by 60–61), *Helen Ahola* (from 61–62); 5TH SERVANT: Gloria Van Dorpe, *Karen Shepard* (from 56–57), *Margaret Broderson* (from 59–60); MRS. HIGGINS: Cathleen Nesbitt (4), *Viola Roache* (from 56–57), *Margery Maude* (from 58–59); CHAUFFEUR: Barton Mumaw, *Harry Woolever* (from 61–62); 1ST FOOTMAN: Gordon Ewing, *Paul Brown* (from 56–57), *Lawrence Keith* (from 60–61); 2ND FOOTMAN: William Krach, *Tom Vaughan* (from 61–62); LORD BOXINGTON: Gordon Dilworth (11), *James Kenny* (from 61–62); LADY BOXINGTON: Olive Reeves-Smith (9), *Maribel Hammer* (stood in); CONSTABLE: Barton Mumaw, *Harry Woolever* (from 61–62); FLOWER GIRL: Cathy Conklin, *Barbara Siman* (from 61–62); ZOLTAN KARPATHY: Christopher Hewett (10), *Leo Britt, Robin Craven* (from 6/4/56), *Guy Spaull* (from 61–62); FLUNKEY: Paul Brown, *Lawrence Keith* (from 60–61), *Tom Vaughan* (from 61–62); QUEEN OF TRANSYLVANIA: Maribel Hammer, *Kay Kendall* (unbilled — one night only, 12/23/57, the night of her husband's last performance as Higgins), *Lynn Barret* (from 59–60), *Susan Fellows* (from 60–61), *Lee Dougherty* (from 61–62); AMBASSADOR: Rodney McLennan (12) *Moss Hart* (unbilled, one night only, 12/23/57 — the night of Rex Harrison's last performance as Higgins); BARTENDER: Paul Brown, *John H. Jones* (from 60–61), *Bill Diehl* (from 61–62); MRS. HIGGINS'S MAID: Judith Williams, *Margaret Cuddy* (from 56–57), *Barbara Heath* (from 61–62); SINGING ENSEMBLE: Paul Brown (*Lawrence Keith* from 60–61), Melisande Congdon (gone by 59–60), Gordon Ewing (gone by 58–59), Lola Fisher (gone by 61–62), Rosemary Gaines (*Jean Maggio* by 58–59 & gone by 59–60), Maribel Hammer (gone by 59–60), Glenn Kezer, William Krach (*Tom Vaughan* from 61–62), James Morris (gone by 58–59), Colleen O'Connor, Muriel Shaw (*Linda McNaughton* by 57–58; *Lynn Barret* from 59–60; *Susan Fellows* from 60–61 & gone by 61–62), Reid Shelton (gone by 56–57), Patti Spangler (gone by 58–59), Herb Surface, David Thomas, Gloria Van Dorpe (*Karen Shepard* by 57–58, *Margaret Broderson* from 59–60), *Helen Ahola* (by 58–59 & gone by 59–60, but back by 60–61), *Mary Sue Berry* (by 59–60 and gone by 60–61), *Diana Chase* (by 59–60), *Rosemary Rainer* (by 60–61; *Joan Cory* from 61–62), *Ann Casey* (by 60–61), *Lee Dougherty* (by 60–61), *John H. Jones* (by 58–59), *Don Grilley* (by 58–59 & gone by 59–60), *Bill Diehl* (by 58–59), *Robert Price* (by 61–62); DANCING ENSEMBLE: Estelle Aza (gone by 58–59), Thatcher Clarke (*Bentley Roton* by 59–60), Cathy Conklin, Margaret Cuddy, Imelda De Martin (*Maxine Berke* by 56–57, *Joan Derby* by 57, *Joan Diehl* from 60), Pat Diamond (gone by 58–59), Crandall Diehl, Pat Drylie (gone by 58–59), David Evans (gone by 60–61), Barbara Heath, Carl Jeffrey [he later became Carl Jablonski] (*Tom Hester* from 57 & gone by 58–59), Vera Lee (gone by 58–59), Nancy Lynch (gone by 59–60), Barton Mumaw (gone by 61–62), Gene Nettles (gone by 60–61), Paul Olson (gone by 58–59), Joe Rocco (*Bob Karl* by 58–59, *Bill Atkinson* by 59–60; *Christian Alderson* by 60–61), Fernando Schaffenburg (gone by 59–60), James White (gone by 58–59), Judith Williams (gone by 58–59), *Eddie Roll* (by 56–57 & gone by 58–59), *Betty Buday* (by 56–57 and gone by 58–59), *Katia Geleznova* (by 56–57 & gone by 59–60), *Svetlana McLee* (by 58–59 & gone by 59–60), *Barbara Siman* (by 58–59), *Kiki Minor* (by 58–59 & gone by 61–62), *Marc West* (by 58–59 & gone by 59–60), *Glenn Olson* (by 58–59), *Harry Woolever* (by 58–59), *Robert St. Clair* (by 58–59), *Iva March* (by 59–60 & gone by 61–62), *Rosemary Jourdan* (by 59–60 & gone by 60–61), *Janise Gardner* (by 59–60 & gone by 60–61), *Dieter Klos* (by 59–60 & gone by 61–62), *Christopher Edwards* (by 59–60 and gone by 61–62), *Dorothy Scott* (by 60–61), *Gretl Bauer* (by 60–61), *Ronald Rosanoff* (by 60–61), *Kim Hayward* (by 60–61), *Colleen Corkrey* (by 61–62), *Betty Krasnor* (by 61–62), *Dick Colacino* (by 61–62), *Ronnie Lee* (by 61–62), *Roy Harsh* (by 61–62). **Standby**: Eliza: Constance Brigham. **Understudies**: Eliza: Karen Shepherd, *Lola Fisher* (by 58–59), *Rosemary Rainer* (by 60–61); Doolittle: Gordon Dilworth; Freddy: Reid Shelton, *John H. Jones* (by 58–59); Mrs. Pearce/Mrs. Eynsford-Hill: Olive Reeves-Smith; Karpathy: David Thomas; Jamie: Paul Brown, *Lawrence Keith* (by 60–61), *Tom Vaughan* (by 61–62); Mrs. Higgins: Viola Roache, *Regina Wallace* (by 58–59); Harry: Glenn Kezer; Mrs. Hopkins: Maribel Hammer, *Helen Ahola* (by 59–60); Higgins: Christopher Hewett, *Lawrence Keith* (by 61–62); Pickering: Rod McLennan, *Leo Britt*. **Act I: Scene 1** Outside the Opera House, Covent Garden; a cold March night: Street Entertainers (The Three Buskers), "Why Can't the English?" (Higgins), "Wouldn't it Be Lovely?" (Eliza & Cockneys) [a bit hit]; **Scene 2** A tenement section — Tottenham Court Road; immediately following: "With a Little Bit of Luck" (Doolittle, Harry, Jamie) [a hit]; **Scene 3** Higgins's study; the following morning: "I'm an Ordinary Man" (Higgins); **Scene 4** Tenement section — Tottenham Court Road; three days later: "With a Little Bit of Luck" (reprise) (Doolittle & Ensemble); **Scene 5** Higgins's study; later that day: "Just You Wait" (Eliza), "The Rain in Spain" (Higgins, Eliza, Pickering) [a hit], "I Could Have Danced All Night" (Eliza, Mrs. Pearce, Maids) [a hit]; **Scene 6** Near the race meeting, Ascot; a July afternoon; **Scene 7** Inside a club tent, Ascot; immediately following: "The Ascot Gavotte" (Full Ensemble); **Scene 8** Outside Higgins's house, Wimpole Street; later that afternoon: "On the Street Where You Live" (Freddy) [the big hit]; **Scene 9** Higgins's study; six weeks later; **Scene 10** The promenade of the Embassy; later that night; **Scene 11** The ballroom of the Embassy; immediately following: "The Embassy Waltz" (Higgins, Eliza, Karpathy, Full Ensemble). **Act II: Scene 1** Higgins's study; 3:00 the following morning: "You Did It" (Higgins, Pickering, Mrs. Pearce, Servants), "Just You Wait" (reprise) (Eliza); **Scene 2** Outside Higgins's house, Wimpole Street; immediately following: "On the Street Where You Live" (reprise) (Freddy), "Show Me" (Eliza & Freddy); **Scene 3** Flower Market of Covent Garden; 5:00 that morning: "Wouldn't it Be Lovely?" (reprise) (Eliza & The Cockneys), "Get Me to the Church on Time" (Doolittle, Harry, Jamie, Ensemble) [a bit hit]; **Scene 4** Upstairs hall of Higgins's house: 11:00 that morning: "A Hymn to Him" (Higgins); **Scene 5** The conservatory of Mrs. Higgins's house; later that day: "Without You" (Eliza & Higgins); **Scene 6** Outside Higgins's house, Wimpole Street; immediately following: "I've Grown Accustomed to Her Face" (Higgins); **Scene 7** Higgins's study; immediately following: Finale (Higgins & Eliza).

The reviewers only raved. The show won Tonys for musical, direction, sets, costumes, musical direction, and for Rex Harrison. It was also nominated for choreography, and for Robert Coote, Stanley Holloway and Julie Andrews. It ran six years and broke *Oklahoma!*'s record as the longest-running Broadway musical. It cost over $400,000, and took in $20,257,000, a record for Broadway musicals at the time. Julie Andrews left in 3/58, replaced by Sally Ann Howes. John Michael King, who played Freddy, was the son of Broadway star Dennis King (who had succeeded Raymond Massey as Higgins in the 1940s Gertrude Lawrence *Pygmalion*). By the end of 2002 it was still the 14th-longest running show of any kind in Broadway history, and the 11th-longest running musical.

After Broadway. TOUR. Opened on 3/18/57, at the Auditorium, Rochester, NY, and closed on 12/14/63, at the O'Keefe, Toronto. MUSICAL DIRECTOR: Sylvan Levin, *Anton Coppola* (by 59–60), *Albert L. Fiorillo Jr.* (by 62–63), *Aaron Benar* (by 63–64). **Cast**: HIGGINS: Brian Aherne, *Michael Evans* (from 6/30/58), *Ronald Drake* (from 61–62); ELIZA: Anne Rogers, *Diane Todd* (from 58–59), *Caroline Dixon* (from 61–62), *Gaylea Byrne* (from 11/8/62); DOOLITTLE: Charles Victor; PICKERING: Hugh Dempster, *Eric Brotherson* (from 3/17/63); MRS. PEARCE: Katherine Hynes; MRS. HIGGINS: Margery Maude, *Joan White* (from 58–59), *Margaret Bannerman* (from 59–60); FREDDY: Reid Shelton, *Richard Young* (from 61–62); AMBASSADOR: Eric Brotherson, *Robert M. Driscoll* (from 58–59), *Ted Bloecher* (from 61–62), *Reese*

Burns (from 62–63), *Roland Ireland* (from 63–64); JAMIE: Eric Brotherson, *Robert Hocknell* (from 63–64); 2ND COCKNEY: Robert Hocknell, *David Hartman* (from 62–63), *Roland Ireland* (from 63–64). **Understudies**: Eliza: Gaylea Byrne; Pickering: Eric Brotherson.

THEATRE ROYAL, DRURY LANE, London, 4/30/58–10/19/63. 2,281 PERFORMANCES. PRESENTED BY H.M. Tennent, Ltd; MUSICAL DIRECTOR: Cyril Ornadel. **Cast**: MRS. EYNSFORD-HILL: Linda Gray, *Elaine Garreau*; ELIZA: Julie Andrews, *Anne Rogers* (by 60), *Tonia Lee, Jean Scott*; FREDDY: Leonard Weir, *Peter Gilmore, Alan Thomas*; PICKERING: Robert Coote, *Hugh Paddick, Gavin Gordon, John Huson, Tom Chatto*; HIGGINS: Rex Harrison, *Alec Clunes, Charles Stapley* (by 60), *Max Oldaker*; DOOLITTLE: Stanley Holloway, *James Hayter* (by 60), *John Law*; MRS. PEARCE: Betty Woolfe; MRS. HIGGINS: Zena Dare, *Linda Gray*; LORD BOXINGTON/HARRY: Alan Dudley, *Wally Thomas*; LADY BOXINGTON: Elaine Garreau, *Betty Benfield, Mercia Glossop*; KARPATHY/BYSTANDER: Max Oldaker, *Lennard Pearce, Vernon Joyner*; ENSEMBLE INCLUDED: Jill Martin.

CITY CENTER, NYC, 5/20/64–6/28/64. 47 PERFORMANCES. PRESENTED BY the New York City Center Light Opera Company; DIRECTOR: Samuel Liff; COSTUME SUPERVISOR: Stanley Simmons; MUSICAL DIRECTOR: Anton Coppola. **Cast**: MRS. EYNSFORD-HILL: Claire Waring; ELIZA: Marni Nixon; FREDDY: Russell Nype; PICKERING: Byron Webster; HIGGINS: Myles Eason; SELSEY MAN/LORD BOXINGTON: Charles Penman; DOOLITTLE: Reginald Gardiner; MRS. PEARCE: Dorothy Sands; MRS. HOPKINS/LADY BOXINGTON: Olive Reeves-Smith; MRS. HIGGINS: Margery Maude; KARPATHY: Sandor Szabo; DANCERS INCLUDED: Margaret Cuddy, Katia Geleznova, Kiki Minor, Robert Fitch, Ronn Forella, Jerry Trent, Harry Woolever. SINGERS INCLUDED: Margaret Broderson, Elaine Labour, Terry Marone, Donna Monroe, Jack Eddleman, Stokely Gray, William Krach.

THE MOVIE. 1964. Jack Warner paid a record $5 million for the rights, and wanted Cary Grant and Audrey Hepburn, but Mr. Grant refused. Warner also wanted James Cagney for Doolittle. Marni Nixon (who played Eliza in the 1964 City Center production) supplied the vocals for Miss Hepburn (thus depriving Miss Hepburn of the chance of an Oscar — unfair because Deborah Kerr had been nominated for *The King and I*, and hadn't sung the songs either). Rex Harrison won an Oscar, as did the film. Julie Andrews won one also, but for *Mary Poppins*. DIRECTOR: George Cukor. **Cast**: HIGGINS: Rex Harrison; ELIZA: Audrey Hepburn; DOOLITTLE: Stanley Holloway; PICKERING: Wilfred Hyde-White; FREDDY: Jeremy Brett (singing dubbed by Bill Shirley); MRS. HIGGINS: Gladys Cooper; KARPATHY: Theodore Bikel; MRS. HOPKINS: Olive Reeves-Smith.

TOUR. Corning Summer Theatre, NY (6/25/64–7/5/64), Country Playhouse, Syracuse, NY (7/6/64–7/11/64), Northland Playhouse, Detroit (7/28–8/2/64), Royal Alexandra, Toronto (8/3/64–8/8/64), John Drew Theatre, East Hampton, NY (8/24/64–9/5/64). **Cast**: Allyn Ann McLerie, George Gaynes, Jean Muir.

CITY CENTER, NYC, 6/13/68–6/30/68. 22 PERFORMANCES. PRESENTED BY the New York City Center Light Opera Company, by arrangement with Tams-Witmark Music Library; DIRECTOR: Samuel Liff; CHOREOGRAPHER: Harry Woolever; COSTUME SUPERVISOR: Stanley Simmons; LIGHTING: Feder; MUSICAL DIRECTOR: Anton Coppola. **Cast**: BUSKERS: George Bunt, John Johann, Kiki Minor; MRS. EYNSFORD-HILL: Claire Waring; ELIZA: Inga Swenson; FREDDY: Evan Thomas; PICKERING: Byron Webster; BYSTANDER/JAMIE/BOXINGTON: James Beard; HIGGINS: Fritz Weaver; SELSEY MAN/HARRY/AMBASSADOR: Charles Goff; HOXTON MAN/3RD COCKNEY: Jack Fletcher; 1ST COCKNEY: Laried Montgomery; 2ND COCKNEY: Stokely Gray; 4TH COCKNEY/BUTLER: William James; BARTENDER: Larry Devon; DOOLITTLE: George Rose; MRS. PEARCE: Leta Bonynge; MRS. HOPKINS/LADY BOXINGTON: Blanche Collins; SERVANTS: Jeanne Shea, Hanna Owen, Maggie Worth, Joyce Olson, William James, Stokely Gray; MRS. HIGGINS: Margery Maude; CHAUFFEUR: Todd Butler; FOOTMEN: Darrell Sandeen & Peter Costanza; CONSTABLE: Richard Maxon; FLOWER GIRL: Kiki Minor; KARPATHY: Erik Rhodes; FLUNKEY/BARTENDER: Darrell Sandeen; QUEEN: Maggie Worth; MRS. HIGGINS' MAID: Jeanne Shea; SINGING ENSEMBLE INCLUDED: Marcia Brushingham, Spring Fairbank. DANCING ENSEMBLE INCLUDED: Joyce Maret.

473. *My Fair Lady* (1976 Broadway revival)

This was the 20th Anniversary production.

The Broadway Run. St. James Theatre, 3/25/76–12/5/76; Lunt—Fontanne Theatre, 12/9/76–2/20/77. 7 previews. Total of 377 performances. Presented by Herman Levin; Music: Frederick Loewe; Lyrics/Book: Alan Jay Lerner; Based on the 1914 comedy *Pygmalion*, by George Bernard Shaw; Director: Jerry Adler (based on the original staging by Moss Hart); Choreographer: Crandall Diehl (based on Hanya Holm's original choreography); Sets: Oliver Smith; Costumes: Cecil Beaton; Lighting: John Gleason; Sound: Leonard Will; Musical Director: Theodore Saidenberg; Musical Arrangements: Robert Russell Bennett & Philip J. Lang; Dance Music Arrangements: Trude Rittman; Press: Seymour Krawitz, Ted Goldsmith, Patricia McLean Krawitz; Casting: Geri Windsor & Associates — Vincent Liff & Nancy Robbins; General Manager: Philip Adler; Company Manager: Malcolm Allen; Production Stage Manager: Nicholas Russiyan; Stage Manager: Alisa Jill Adler; Assistant Stage Manager: Robert O'Rourke. **Cast:** Buskers: Debra Lyman, Stan Picus, Ernie Pysher (*Ken Henley*); Mrs. Eynsford-Hill: Eleanor Phelps (11); Freddy Eynsford-Hill: Jerry Lanning (6); Eliza Doolittle: Christine Andreas (2) ✩, *Vickie Patik* (during Miss Andreas's illness); Colonel Pickering: Robert Coote (4) ✩, *Eric Brotherson;* Professor Henry Higgins: Ian Richardson (1) ✩; 1st Cockney: Kevin Marcum; 2nd Cockney: Jack Starkey; 3rd Cockney: William James; 4th Cockney: Stan Page; Bartender: Kevin Lane Dearinger; Harry: John Clarkson; Jamie: Richard Neilson (9), *Eric Brotherson;* Alfred P. Doolittle: George Rose (3) ✩; Mrs. Pearce: Sylvia O'Brien (7); Mrs. Hopkins: Margaretta Warwick (10); Butler: Clifford Fearl; Servants: Kevin Lane Dearinger, Lynn Fitzpatrick, Karen Gibson, Sonja Anderson (*Kris Karlowski*), Vickie Patik; Mrs. Higgins: Brenda Forbes (5); Chauffeur: Jack Karcher; Footmen: Kevin Lane Dearinger & Stan Page; Lord Boxington: John Clarkson; Lady Boxington: Margaretta Warwick; Constable: Timothy Smith, *David Evans;* Flower Girl: Dru Alexandrine; Flunkey: William James; Zoltan Karpathy: John Clarkson (8); Queen of Transylvania: Karen Gibson; Ambassador: Richard Neilson (9), *Eric Brotherson;* Bartender: Clifford Fearl; Mrs. Higgins's Maid: Mari McMinn; Singing Ensemble: Sonja Anderson (*Kris Karlowski*), Alyson Bristol, Kevin Lane Dearinger, Clifford Fearl, Lynn Fitzpatrick, Karen Gibson, William James, Kevin Marcum, Cynthia Meryl, Stan Page, Vickie Patik, Jack Starkey; Dancing Ensemble: Dru Alexandrine, Richard Ammon, Sally Benoit (replaced during run), Marie Berry, Jeremy Blanton, David Evans, Jack Karcher, Debra Lyman, Mari McMinn, Richard Maxon, Stan Picus, Ernie Pysher (*Ken Henley*), Gena Ramsel, Catherine Rice, Rick Schneider, Sonja Stuart, Timothy Smith, Bonnie Walker. Replacements during run: *Jean Busada, Richard Dodd, Jackie Elliott, Mickey Gunnersen, Michael Heather, Nancy Lynch.* **Standbys:** Higgins: Patrick Horgan; Eliza: Vickie Patik. **Understudies:** Doolittle: John Clarkson; Pickering: Richard Neilson, *Eric Brotherson;* Mrs. Higgins: Eleanor Phelps; Freddy: William James; Mrs. Pearce: Margaretta Warwick; Harry/Karpathy: Kevin Marcum; Jamie: Stan Page; Mrs. Hopkins: Cynthia Meryl, *Alyson Bristol;* Mrs. Eynsford-Hill: Karen Gibson.

Reviews were very good, especially Clive Barnes's *New York Times* rave for the show, for Ian Richardson and George Rose. George Rose won a Tony, and Ian Richardson was nominated.

After Broadway. Tour. Opened on 10/10/77, at the American Theatre, St. Louis, and closed on 5/28/78, at Heinz Hall, Pittsburgh. Musical Director: Albert L. Fiorillo Jr. **Cast:** Higgins: Edward Mulhare; Eliza: Anne Rogers; Pickering: Ronald Drake; Freddy: Kevin Lane Dearinger; Mrs. Eynsford-Hill: Enid Rogers; Doolittle: Thomas Bowman; Mrs. Hopkins/Queen: Celia Tackaberry.

474. *My Fair Lady* (1981 Broadway revival)

Before Broadway. This was the touring company come to Broad-way. The tour opened at the Saenger Performing Arts Center, New Orleans, 9/14/80–10/5/80. It had the same crew as in the subsequent Broadway run, except Costume Supervisor: John David Ridge; Press: Seymour Krawitz, Martin Shwartz, Patricia McLean Krawitz, Joel W. Dein. It had the same cast too, except Eliza: Cheryl Kennedy; [Only] Footman: John Caleb; Ambassador: Clifford Fearl. Cheryl Kennedy developed nodes on her larynx; her standby, Kitty Sullivan, left the show; and Miss Kennedy had to be replaced by her standby Nancy Ringham at the Saturday matinee preview just prior to Broadway opening night. Valerie Lee became standby. Nancy Ringham did well; she had also been in the chorus (where Cynthia Sophiea replaced her). Lynne Savage replaced Karen Paskow as a dance alternate.

The Broadway Run. Uris Theatre, 8/18/81–11/29/81. 5 previews. 119 performances. A Dome/Cutler-Herman production, Presented by Don Gregory & Mike Merrick; Music: Frederick Loewe; Lyrics/Book: Alan Jay Lerner; Based on the 1914 comedy *Pygmalion*, by George Bernard Shaw; Director: Patrick Garland re-created Moss Hart's original staging; Choreographer: Crandall Diehl re-created Hanya Holm's original choreography; Sets: Oliver Smith; Costumes: John David Ridge re-created Cecil Beaton's original costumes; Lighting: Ken Billington; Sound: John McClure; Musical Director: Franz Allers; Original Musical Arrangements: Robert Russell Bennett & Phil Lang; Original Dance Music Arrangements: Trude Rittman; Press: Seymour Krawitz, Patricia McLean Krawitz, Janet Tom; Casting: Julie Hughes & Barry Moss; General Manager: Arthur Anagnostou; Company Manager: Martin Cohen; Stage Managers: Jack Welles & William Weaver; Assistant Stage Managers: Paul Schneeberger & Scott Harris. **Cast:** Buskers: Eric Alderfer, Alan Gilbert, Lisa Guignard; Mrs. Eynsford-Hill: Harriet Medin; Eliza Doolittle: Nancy Ringham (2); Freddy Eynsford-Hill: Nicholas Wyman (6); Colonel Pickering: Jack Gwillim (5); Professor Henry Higgins: Rex Harrison (1) ✩; Selsey Man: Ben Wrigley, *Gary Gage* (from 9/22/81); Hoxton Man: Clifford Fearl; A Bystander: Joseph Billone; Another Bystander: Ned Coulter; 1st Cockney: John Caleb; 2nd Cockney: Ned Coulter; 3rd Cockney: Ned Peterson; 4th Cockney: Jeffrey Calder; Bartender: David Cale Johnson; Harry: Ben Wrigley, *Gary Gage* (from 9/22/81); Jamie: Clifford Fearl; Alfred P. Doolittle: Milo O'Shea (3), *Ben Wrigley* (from 9/22/81); Mrs. Pearce: Marian Baer; Mrs. Hopkins: Mary O'Brien; Butler: Frank Bouley; Servants: Jeralyn Glass, David Miles, Ellen McLain, Judith Thiergaard; Mrs. Higgins: Cathleen Nesbitt (4); Chauffeur: Alan Gilbert; Footmen: John Caleb & Ned Peterson; Lord Boxington: Richard Ammon; Lady Boxington: Mary O'Brien; Constable: Alan Gilbert; Flower Girl: Karen Toto; Zoltan Karpathy: Jack Sevier; Major Domo: David Cale Johnson; Queen of Transylvania: Svetlana McLee Grody; Ambassador: Ben Wrigley, *Gary Gage* (from 9/22/81); Bartender: Ned Peterson; Mrs. Higgins's Maid: Elizabeth Worthington; Singing Ensemble: Frank Bouley, Jeffrey Calder, John Caleb, Ned Coulter, Diana Lynne Drew, Julie Ann Fogt, Terri Gervaise, Jeralyn Glass, David Cale Johnson, Michael McGifford, Ellen McLain, David Miles, Mary O'Brien, Ned Peterson, Cynthia Sophiea, Judith Thiergaard; Dancing Ensemble: Eric Alderfer, Richard Ammon, Joseph Billone, Arlene Columbo, Ron Crofoot, Raul Gallyot, Alan Gilbert, Svetlana McLee Grody, Lisa Guignard, Scott Harris, Lynn Keeton, Gail Lohla, James Boyd Parker, Karen Paskow, Karen Toto, Elizabeth Worthington. **Standbys:** Higgins: Michael Allinson; Eliza: Valerie Lee. **Understudies:** Pickering: Clifford Fearl; Doolittle: Ben Wrigley, *Gary Gage;* Mrs. Pearce/Mrs. Eynsford-Hill: Mary O'Brien; Freddy: Jeffrey Calder; Harry: Jack Sevier; Karpathy/Jamie: Frank Bouley; Mrs. Higgins/Mrs. Hopkins: Harriet Medin; **Ensemble Alternates:** Scott Harris & Lynne Savage.

Reviews were quite awful. The production took the great musical too much for granted, and not enough effort went into it. Rex Harrison was mechanical. It closed its Broadway run only to resume its tour. 94-year-old Cathleen Nesbitt couldn't remember the name Boxington, and would introduce all manner of alternate names to Eliza. The musical received a Tony nomination for reproduction of a play or musical.

After Broadway. Touring revival. Opened on 3/10/89, in Providence, Rhode Island, and closed in 6/89, in Tokyo. Presented by AMPAC Enterprises & Robert Young Associates; Director: James Hammerstein; Choreographer: Michael Shawn; Costumes: Michael

Bottari & Ronald Case; LIGHTING: Steve Cochrane; SOUND: Abe Jacob; MUSICAL DIRECTOR: Richard Parrinello. *Cast*: HIGGINS: Noel Harrison (Mr. Harrison was Rex's son); ELIZA: Katharine Buffaloe; PICKERING: Richard Neilson; FREDDY: Michael DeVries; MRS. EYNSFORD-HILL: Marilyn Hudgins; DOOLITTLE: Ben Wrigley; MRS. PEARCE: Darcy Pulliam; KARPATHY: Tom Souhrada; BUSKER: Bill Brassea. The tour reopened on 6/23/89, at Segerstrom Hall, Orange County Performing Arts Center, Costa Mesa, Calif., again with Noel Harrison, and it closed there on 7/2/89. CONDUCTOR: Glen Clugston.

475. *My Fair Lady (1993 Broadway revival)*

Before Broadway. This was a touring company come to Broadway. The tour had opened 4/5/93 (previews from 4/3/93), at the Barbara B. Mann Performing Arts Hall, Fort Myers, Fla. It had the same basic cast and crew as for Broadway. On tour Meg Tolin took over for Melissa Errico during illness; David Bryant played George the bartender.

The Broadway Run. VIRGINIA THEATRE, 12/9/93–5/1/94. 16 previews from 11/26/93. 165 PERFORMANCES. PRESENTED BY Barry & Fran Weissler, Jujamcyn Theatres, in association with PACE Theatrical Group, Tokyo Broadcasting System, and Martin Rabbett; MUSIC: Frederick Loewe; LYRICS/BOOK: Alan Jay Lerner; BASED ON the 1914 comedy *Pygmalion*, by George Bernard Shaw; DIRECTOR: Howard Davies; CHOREOGRAPHER: Donald Saddler; SETS: Ralph Koltai; COSTUMES: Patricia Zipprodt; LIGHTING: Natasha Katz; SOUND: Peter J. Fitzgerald; MUSICAL DIRECTOR/VOCAL DIRECTOR: Jack Lee; ORIGINAL MUSICAL ARRANGEMENTS: Robert Russell Bennett & Phil Lang; ORIGINAL DANCE MUSIC ARRANGEMENTS: Trude Rittman; PRESS: Richard Kornberg & Associates; CASTING: Stuart Howard & Amy Schecter; GENERAL MANAGER: Charlotte W. Wilcox; COMPANY MANAGER: Frank Lott; PRODUCTION STAGE MANAGER: Maureen F. Gibson; STAGE MANAGER: Peter Wolf; ASSISTANT STAGE MANAGER: James Bernardi. *Cast*: ELIZA DOOLITTLE: Melissa Errico (2); FREDDY EYNSFORD-HILL: Robert Sella (6); MRS. EYNSFORD-HILL: Lisa Merrill McCord; COLONEL PICKERING: Paxton Whitehead (4); HENRY HIGGINS: Richard Chamberlain (1) ☆, *Paxton Whitehead, Michael Moriarty* (from 4/8/94); 1ST BYSTANDER: James Young; HOXTON MAN: Bruce Moore; 2ND BYSTANDER: Bill Ullman; THE "LOVERLY" QUARTET: Jeffrey Wilkins, Bruce Moore, Michael Gerhart, Jamie MacKenzie; GEORGE, THE BARTENDER: Bill Ullman; JAMIE: Michael J. Farina; HARRY: James Young; MRS. PEARCE: Glynis Bell (7); BUTLER: Jeffrey Wilkins; ALFRED P. DOOLITTLE: Julian Holloway (3); SERVANTS: Michael Gerhart, Marilyn Kay Huelsman, Edwardyne Cowan, Corinne Melancon, Meg Tolin; CHARLES, THE CHAUFFEUR: Michael Gerhart; MRS. HIGGINS: Dolores Sutton (5); LORD BOXINGTON: Jeffrey Wilkins; LADY BOXINGTON: Marnee Hollis; POLICEMAN: Ron Schwinn; FLOWER GIRL: Corinne Melancon; FOOTMAN: Ben George; PROF. ZOLTAN KARPATHY: James Young; QUEEN OF TRANSYLVANIA: Patti Karr; MRS. HIGGINS' MAID: Sue Delano; ENSEMBLE: Edwardyne Cowan, Laurie Crochet, Alexander de Jong, Sue Delano, Rebecca Downing, Michael J. Farina, Ben George, Michael Gerhart, Marnee Hollis, Marilyn Kay Huelsman, Patti Karr, Tom Kosis, John Vincent Leggio, Jamie MacKenzie, Lisa Merrill McCord, Corinne Melancon, Bruce Moore, Ron Schwinn, Meg Tolin, Bill Ullman, Jeffrey Wilkins, James Young. *Understudies*: Higgins: Paxton Whitehead; Eliza: Meg Tolin & Edwardyne Cowan; Doolittle: James Young; Pickering: Jeffrey Wilkins & Bill Ullman; Mrs. Higgins: Patti Karr; Freddy: Michael Gerhart; Mrs. Pearce: Lisa Merrill McCord. *Swings*: Newton Cole, Wendy Oliver, John Scott. *Orchestra*: TRUMPET 1: Burt Collins; TRUMPET 2: Laurie Frink; TRUMPET 3: Greg Ruvolo; TENOR TROMBONE: Dan Levine; BASS TROMBONE: Alan Raph; FRENCH HORN: Glen Estrin; FLUTE/PICCOLO: Billy Kerr; CLARINET: Mitchell Estrin; ENGLISH HORN/OBOE: Dennis Anderson; BASSOON: Steven Boschi; BASS: Ray Kilday; DRUMS/PERCUSSION: David Tancredi; SYNTHESIZER: John Mulcahy; CONCERTMASTER: Christopher Cardona; VIOLA: Alfred Brown; CELLO: Anne Callahan. *Act I*: Overture (Orchestra); *Scene 1* Outside Covent Garden: "Why Can't the English?" (Higgins), "Wouldn't it Be Loverly" (Eliza & Quartet); *Scene 2* The pub — Tottenham Court Road: "With a Little Bit of Luck" (Doolittle, Harry, Jamie, Company); *Scene 3* Higgins' laboratory: "I'm an Ordinary Man" (Higgins); *Scene 4* Higgins' laboratory; *Scene 5* Higgins' laboratory — the lessons: "Just You Wait" (Eliza), "The Servants' Chorus" (The Servants), "The Rain in Spain" (Higgins, Eliza, Pickering); *Scene 6* The bed: "I Could Have Danced All Night" (Eliza); *Scene 7* Outside Ascot; *Scene 8* Ascot: "Ascot Gavotte" (Company); *Scene 9* Wimpole Street: "On the Street Where You Live" (Freddy); *Scene 10* Higgins' laboratory. *Act II*: Entr'acte (Orchestra); *Scene 1* The ballroom: "The Embassy Waltz" (Company); *Scene 2* Higgins' laboratory: "You Did It" (Higgins, Pickering, Servants), "Just You Wait" (reprise) (Eliza); *Scene 3* Wimpole Street: "On the Street Where You Live" (reprise) (Freddy), "Show Me" (Eliza); *Scene 4* Covent Garden: "Wouldn't it Be Loverly" (reprise) (Company), "Get Me to the Church on Time" (Doolittle & Company); *Scene 5* Higgins' laboratory: "Hymn to Him" (Higgins); *Scene 6* The garden of Mrs. Higgins: "Without You" (Eliza); *Scene 7* Wimpole Street: "I've Grown Accustomed to Her Face" (Higgins); *Scene 8* Higgins' laboratory.

Broadway reviews were divided.

After Broadway. NATIONAL THEATRE, London. Opened in 3/01. This was a major new revival, 3 hours & 15 minutes long. After a sell-out run at the National, it moved to the THEATRE ROYAL, DRURY LANE, 7/21/01–8/30/03. Previews from 7/9/01. It took in 10 million pounds in advance sales. Two days later the cast recording was released on First Night Records. The show broke even in an astonishing 18 weeks. PRESENTED BY Sir Cameron Mackintosh; DIRECTOR: Trevor Nunn; CHOREOGRAPHER: Matthew Bourne; SETS: Anthony Ward; SOUND: Paul Groothuis; MUSICAL DIRECTOR: Nick Davies. Martine McCutcheon, who was starring as Eliza, was ill and rarely on stage, her understudy Alexandra Jay performing more often than not. Miss McCutcheon quit on 12/8/01, to be replaced by Joanna Riding on 12/10/01 (Alexandra Jay would continue, as first alternate, playing Eliza on Monday evenings & Wednesday matinees; second alternate was Kerry Ellis). The show proved so popular that the run was extended by four months to 12/21/02, then again to 12/19/03 (however, it closed early). *Cast*: HIGGINS: Jonathan Pryce, *Alex Jennings* (from 5/20/02), *Anthony Andrews* (from 3/03); ELIZA: Martine McCutcheon, *Alexandra Jay* (see above), *Joanna Riding* (from 12/10/01), *Laura Michelle Kelly* (from 3/03); DOOLITTLE: Dennis Waterman, *Russ Abbott* (from 3/03); PICKERING: Nicholas Le Prevost, *Malcolm Sinclair* (from 5/20/02); MRS. PEARCE: Patsy Rowlands; MRS. EYNSFORD-HILL: Jill Martin; MRS. HIGGINS: Caroline Blakiston; FREDDY: Mark Umbers; QUEEN: Valerie Cutko; KARPATHY: Sevan Stephan. This production did not come to Broadway because of Cameron Mackintosh's too-busy schedule.

CHICAGO CENTER FOR THE PERFORMING ARTS. An irreverent and incredibly intimate two-piano version. It won great acclaim. Previews began 4/18/02; the run ended on 6/16/02. PRESENTED BY the Court Theatre; DIRECTOR: Gary Griffin; MUSICAL DIRECTOR: Tom Murray. *Cast*: ELIZA: Kate Fry; HIGGINS: Kevin Gudahl; PICKERING: John Reeger; DOOLITTLE: Bradley Mott.

HOLLYWOOD BOWL, 8/3/03. A semi-staged concert reading, part of the *Weekend Spectacular* series. DIRECTOR: Gordon Hunt; the Hollywood Bowl Orchestra directed by John Mauceri. *Cast*: HIGGINS: John Lithgow; ELIZA: Melissa Errico; DOOLITTLE: Roger Daltrey; PICKERING: Paxton Whitehead; FREDDY: Kevin Earley; MRS. HIGGINS: Rosemary Harris; MRS. PEARCE: Lauri Johnson.

476. *My Favorite Year*

Set in New York City in 1954. Nostalgia for the days of live TV and the Hit Parade mixed with intensive father-daughter and male-female relationships.

Before Broadway. Lynn Ahrens and Stephen Flaherty were approached by the University of New York system to write a full-fledged musical for their *New Musicals* series. However, by the time that series folded Miss Ahrens, Mr. Flaherty, playwright Joseph Dougherty and director Ron Lagomarsino were well into the musical stage adaptation of the 1982 movie *My Favorite Year*, but it wasn't finished, let alone ready to produce for the series. They carried on with it anyway, and in 10/90 they did their first private read-through. On 5/13/91 the show had its first reading, at PLAYWRIGHTS HORIZONS, NY. *Cast*: ALICE: Faith Prince; SWANN: Victor Garber. This was followed by a workshop at Lincoln Center. CHOREOGRAPHER: Thommie Walsh. The character of Iphey Hopper (based on Imogene Coca) was cut, being too similar to the character of Alice. New songs were written, and old ones re-written in four weeks. Broadway rehearsals began on 9/22/92. This was the first new American musical presented at the Vivian Beaumont. During Broadway previews the Act II opening number "Pop, Fizz, Happy" was cut. "Clarence Duffy" [which was Swann's real name] was replaced by "Exits," which now opened Act II. "It's Only Rehearsal" was replaced by "The Gospel According to King." Also cut during previews was the expensive production number "Monday Monday."

The Broadway Run. VIVIAN BEAUMONT THEATRE, 12/10/92–1/10/93. 44 previews from 10/31/92. Limited run of 37 PERFORMANCES. PRESENTED BY Lincoln Center Theatre, in association with AT&T OnStage; MUSIC/VOCAL ARRANGEMENTS: Stephen Flaherty; LYRICS: Lynn Ahrens; BOOK: Joseph Dougherty; BASED ON the 1982 movie screenplay of the same name, written by Norman Steinberg & Dennis Palumbo, which in turn was based on a story by Dennis Palumbo; DIRECTOR: Ron Lagomarsino; CHOREOGRAPHER: Thommie Walsh; SETS: Thomas Lynch; COSTUMES: Patricia Zipprodt; LIGHTING: Jules Fisher; ASSOCIATE LIGHTING: Peggy Eisenhauer; SOUND: Scott Lehrer; MUSICAL DIRECTOR: Ted Sperling; ORCHESTRATIONS: Michael Starobin (unless otherwise stated); BOW MUSIC ORCHESTRATIONS: Michael Gibson; DANCE MUSIC ARRANGEMENTS: Wally Harper; CAST RECORDING on RCA; PRESS: Merle Debuskey & Susan Chicoine; CASTING: Daniel Swee, Aisha Coley, Erica Tener; GENERAL MANAGER: Steven C. Callahan; COMPANY MANAGER: Edward J. Nelson; PRODUCTION STAGE MANAGER: Robin Rumpf; STAGE MANAGER: Dale Kaufman; ASSISTANT STAGE MANAGER: Jane Seiler. *Cast*: BENJY STONE: Evan Pappas; KING KAISER: Tom Mardirosian; SY BENSON: Josh Mostel; K.C. DOWNING: Lannyl Stephens; ALICE MILLER: Andrea Martin; HERB LEE: Ethan Phillips; BELLE STEINBERG CARROCA: Lainie Kazan; LEO SILVER: Paul Stolarsky; ALAN SWANN: Tim Curry; ROOKIE CARROCA: Thomas Ikeda; TESS: Katie Finneran; UNCLE MORTY: David Lipman; AUNT SADIE: Mary Stout; ENSEMBLE: Leslie Bell, Maria Calabrese, Kevin Chamberlin, Colleen Dunn, Katie Finneran, James Gerth, Michael Gruber, David Lipman, Roxie Lucas, Nora Mae Lyng, Michael McGrath, Alan Muraoka, Jay Poindexter, Russell Ricard, Mary Stout, Thomas Titone, Bruce Winant, Christina Youngman. *Standby*: SWANN: Michael O'Gorman. *Understudies*: Benjy: Michael McGrath & Thomas Titone; King: Michael McGrath & Bruce Winant; Herb: Thomas Titone & Kevin Chamberlin; Sy: Bruce Winant & Kevin Chamberlin; Leo: Bruce Winant & James Gerth; K.C.: Katie Finneran; Alice: Roxie Lucas & Mary Stout; Belle: Nora Mae Lyng & Mary Stout; Swann: James Gerth; Rookie: Alan Muraoka. *Swings*: Robert Ashford & Aimee Turner. *Orchestra*: WOODWINDS: Alva Hunt, Ken Hitchcock, Rick Heckman, Gene Scholtens; TRUMPETS: Lawrence Lunetta, Phil Granger, Darryl Shaw; TROMBONES: Sonny Russo & Jack Schatz; FRENCH HORN: Kaitilin Mahoney; VIOLINS: Belinda Whitney-Barratt, Janine Kam-Lal, Susan Lorentsen; VIOLA: Ruth Siegler; CELLO: Matthias Naegele; BASS: John Babich; KEYBOARDS: Joseph Thalken & Jan Rosenberg; DRUMS: John Redsecker; PERCUSSION: Larry Spivack. *Act I*: *Scene 1* The broadcast studio: "Twenty Million People" (Benjy & Company); *Scene 2* The writers' office; morning: "Larger than Life" (Benjy); *Scene 3* The writers' office; later that day: "The Musketeer Sketch" (Benjy, Sy, King, Alice, K.C., Leo, Herb); *Scene 4* Swann's Waldorf suite: "Waldorf Suite" (Benjy), "Rookie in the Ring" (Belle); *Scene 5* Streets of New York: "Manhattan" ("The Night is Young") (orch: Danny Troob) (Swann, Benjy, Ensemble); *Scene 6* The broadcast studio: "Naked in Bethesda Fountain" (Sy, Alice, Leo, Herb, K.C.), "The Gospel According to King" (King, Swann, Company), "The Musketeer Sketch Rehearsal" (Benjy, Swann, Ensemble); *Scene 7* The ladies' room: "Funny"/"The Duck Joke" (K.C. & Alice); *Scene 8* The broadcast studio: "The Musketeer Sketch Rehearsal (Part II)" (King, Swann, Ensemble); *Scene 9* Belle's apartment: "Welcome to Brooklyn" (Morty, Rookie, Belle, Sadie, Benjy, Swann, Neighbors), "If the World Were Like the Movies" (Swann). *Act II*: Entr'acte (Orchestra); *Scene 1* Central Park: "Exits" (Swann); *Scene 2* The Plaza Hotel; *Scene 3* Swann's Waldorf suite: "Shut up and Dance"

(K.C. & Benjy); *Scene 4* The Broadcast studio: "Professional Showbizness Comedy" (Alice, King, Ensemble); *Scene 5* Swann's dressing room: "The Lights Come Up" (Swann & Benjy); *Scene 6* The Broadcast studio: "Maxford House" (Maxford House Girls), "The Musketeer Sketch Finale" (Company), "My Favorite Year" (Benjy & Company).

Broadway reviews were mostly bad. Andrea Martin won a Tony, and Tim Curry and Lainie Kazan were nominated.

After Broadway. There was a concert reading in New York City, 4/22/03–5/4/03, part of the *Musicals Tonight!* series. *Cast*: SWANN: David Stoller; ROOKIE: Wayne Pretlow.

477. *My One and Only*

Set in 1927. A revised version of *Funny Face*, with, in addition, songs from other Gershwin musicals. Billy Buck, a daredevil aviator who wants to be the first to fly solo across the Atlantic, falls for Edith, an English Channel swimmer, and, thus distracted, is beaten by Charles Lindbergh. They get involved with Montgomery, a bootlegging Harlem minister; Mr. Magix, an enigmatic tap-dancing philosopher; and Achmed, a blackmailing Russian spy. The chorus was composed of white females and black males.

Before Broadway. It all started when 25-year-old director Peter Sellars wanted to re-stage the 1927 Gershwin musical *Funny Face*, with Tommy Tune in the lead. Mr. Tune suggested Twiggy as co-star. Mr. Sellars and playwright Timothy S. Mayer totally re-did *Funny Face*, but it didn't work. The producers fired Mr. Sellars, and Thommie Walsh and Tommy Tune became the new directors. Craig Smith, the musical director, was fired, and replaced with Jack Lee. Mike Nichols and Michael Bennett came in to doctor the show, and Peter Stone re-wrote the libretto. Tony Walton replaced Adrianne Lobel as set designer (even though Miss Lobel's name is on the credits). During the Boston tryouts Tommy Tune apologized nightly to the audience for the rough shape the show was in. In fact, the 1/29/83 first Boston preview had to be canceled. But, by the time it got to Broadway it was ready, and had changed its name from *Funny Face* to *My One and Only*.

The Broadway Run. ST. JAMES THEATRE, 5/1/83–3/3/85. 767 PERFORMANCES. A King Street production (Bernard Garragher, Obie Bailey, Bernard Bailey), PRODUCED BY Lewis Allen, and PRESENTED BY Paramount Theatre Productions, Francine LeFrak, and Kenneth — Mark Productions, in association with Jujamcyn Theatres, and by arrangement with Tams-Witmark Music Library; MUSIC: George Gershwin; LYRICS: Ira Gershwin, Arthur Francis, B.G. "Buddy" De Sylva; BOOK: Peter Stone & Timothy S. Mayer; DIRECTORS/CHOREOGRAPHERS: Thommie Walsh & Tommy Tune; ASSOCIATE DIRECTOR: Philip Oesterman; ASSOCIATE CHOREOGRAPHER: Baayork Lee; SPECIAL CHOREOGRAPHIC MATERIAL: Charles "Honi" Coles; SETS: Adrianne Lobel; COSTUMES: Rita Ryack; LIGHTING: Marcia Madeira; SOUND: Otts Munderloh; MUSICAL DIRECTOR/VOCAL DIRECTOR: Jack Lee; ORCHESTRATIONS: Michael Gibson; MUSICAL CONCEPT: Wally Harper; DANCE MUSIC ARRANGEMENTS: Peter Larson & Wally Harper; PRESS: Jacksina & Freedman; CASTING: Julie Hughes/Barry Moss; GENERAL MANAGEMENT: Joseph P. Harris Associates; PRODUCTION STAGE MANAGER: Peter von Mayrhauser; STAGE MANAGER: Robert Kellogg; ASSISTANT STAGE MANAGER: Betty Lynd. *Cast*: THE NEW RHYTHM BOYS: David Jackson, Ken Leigh Rogers, Ronald Dennis; CAPT. BILLY BUCK CHANDLER: Tommy Tune (2) ☆, *Ronald Young* (during Mr. Tune's vacation, 1/10/84–1/17/84), *Don Correia* (from 11/1/84), *Tommy Tune* (from 2/5/85); MICKEY: Denny Dillon (5), *Georgia Engel* (from 11/1/84); PRINCE NICOLAI ERRACLYOVITCH TCHATCHAVADZE: Bruce McGill (4), *Don Amendolia* (from 11/1/84); (SIX) FISH: FLOUNDER: Nana Visitor, *Jill Cook*; STURGEON: Susan Hartley; MINNOW: Stephanie Eley, *Niki Harris*; PRAWN: Jill Cook, *Stephanie Eley*; KIPPER: Niki Harris, *Sandra Menhart*; ANCHOVY: Karen Tamburelli, *Kerry Casserly*; EDITH HERBERT: Twiggy (1) ☆, *Stephanie Eley* (1/3/84–1/10/84), *Twiggy, Sandy Duncan* (from 11/1/84); RT. REV. J.D. MONTGOMERY: Roscoe Lee Browne (6), *Tiger Haynes* (from 11/1/84); REPORTER: Jill Cook, *Nana Visitor*; MR. MAGIX: Charles "Honi" Coles (3); RITZ QUARTET: Casper Roos (10), Paul David Richards (9) (*Adam Petroski*),

Carl Nicholas (8), Will Blankenship (7); POLICEMAN: Paul David Richards, *Adam Petroski*; STAGE DOORMAN: Paul David Richards, *Adam Petroski*; MRS. O'MALLEY: Ken Leigh Rogers; CONDUCTOR: Adrian Bailey; DANCING GENTLEMEN (ENSEMBLE): Adrian Bailey, Bardell Conner, Ronald Dennis, David Jackson, Alde Lewis Jr. (*Shaun Baker-Jones*), Bernard Manners, Ken Leigh Rogers, *Jan Mickens, Ben Bagby*; ACHMED: Bruce McGill (4). *Standbys*: Nikki: Ron Young, *Walter Hook*; Billy: Ron Young, *Jeff Calhoun*; Edith: Nana Visitor, *Stephanie Eley, Susan Hartley, Niki Harris*; J.D.: Leon Morenzie, *Judd Jones*; Mickey: Jill Cook, *Kerry Casserly, Karen Tamburelli*; Mr. Magix: David Jackson, *David Jackson, Ron Young, Luther Fontaine*. *Swings*: Merilee Magnuson, Melvin Washington, *Patti D'Beck, Luther Fontaine, Walter Hook*. Act I: SCENE 1 Pennsylvania Station; May 1, 1927: "I Can't Be Bothered Now" [from the movie *A Damsel in Distress*] (New Rhythm Boys, Billy, Edith, Nikki, Mickey, Ensemble), "Blah, Blah, Blah" [from the movie *Delicious*] (Billy); *Scene 2* Billy's hangar: "Boy Wanted" [from *A Dangerous Maid*] (l: Arthur Francis) (Edith & Reporter), "Soon" [from *Strike Up the Band*] (Billy); *Scene 3* Mr. Magix's Emporial: "High Hat" [from *Funny Face*]/"Sweet and Low-Down" [from *Tiptoes*] (Magix, Billy, New Rhythm Boys, Ensemble); *Scene 4* Club Havana: "Blah, Blah, Blah" (reprise) (Edith), "Just Another Rumba" [an unused song from the 1938 movie *The Goldwyn Follies*] (J.D. & Ensemble) [cut early in the run]; *Scene 5* Cinema: "He Loves and She Loves" [from *Funny Face*] (Billy & Edith), "He Loves and She Loves" (reprise) (Ritz Quartette); *Scene 6* Central Park; *Scene 7* The hangar: "I Can't Be Bothered Now" (reprise) (New Rhythm Boys); *Scene 8* A deserted beach: "'S Wonderful" [from *Funny Face*] (Billy & Edith), "'S Wonderful" (reprise) (Ritz Quartette), "Strike up the Band" [from the show of the same name] (Billy). Act II: *Scene 1* Aquacade: "In the Swim" [from *Funny Face*]/"What Are We Here For?" [from *Treasure Girl*] (Fish & Nikki), "Nice Work if You Can Get It" [from the movie *A Damsel in Distress*] (Edith); *Scene 2* Mr. Magix's Emporial: "My One and Only" (special material by Charles "Honi" Coles) [from *Funny Face*] (Magix & Billy); *Scene 3* Pennsylvania Station; *Scene 4* The hangar: "Funny Face" (from *Funny Face*] (Mickey & Nikki); *Scene 5* Club Oasis: "My One and Only" (reprise) (Billy); *Scene 6* The Uptown Chapel: "Kickin' the Clouds Away" (l: B.G. De Sylva & Ira Gershwin) [from *Tell Me More*] (dance mus arr: Peter Howard) (J.D. & Ensemble), "How Long Has This Been Goin' On?" [unused in *Funny Face*] (Edith & Billy); SCENE 7 Bows and Finale: "Strike up the Band" (reprise) (Company).

Note: all songs have lyrics by Ira Gershwin unless indicated otherwise.

It was a big hit with the critics and the public. It won Tonys for choreography, and for Tommy Tune and Honi Coles. It was also nominated for musical, book, direction of a musical, costumes, and for Twiggy and Denny Dillon.

After Broadway. TOUR. Opened on 3/8/85, at the Kennedy Center, Washington, DC, (it ran there until 4/14/85), and closed on 3/29/86, at the Forrest Theatre, Philadelphia. *Cast*: BILLY BUCK: Tommy Tune; EDITH: Sandy Duncan, *Lucie Arnaz* (from 8/27/85); MR. MAGIX: Charles "Honi" Coles; MICKEY: Peggy O'Connell; NICOLAI: Don Amendolia; J.D.: Tiger Haynes.

PAPER MILL PLAYHOUSE, New Jersey, 1987. DIRECTOR: Richard Casper; CHOREOGRAPHER: Patti D'Beck; SETS: Adrianne Lobel & Tony Walton; LIGHTING: Marc B. Weiss. *Cast*: George Dvorsky, Donna Kane.

CHICHESTER FESTIVAL THEATRE, England. It was a sell-out, and went to the West End, to the PICCADILLY THEATRE, London. 2/25/02–8/3/02. Previews from 2/9/02. DIRECTOR: Loveday Ingram; CHOREOGRAPHER: Craig Revel Horwood; SETS/COSTUMES: Lez Brotherston; SOUND: Fergus O'Hare; MUSICAL SUPERVISOR: Gareth Valentine. *Cast*: EDITH: Janie Dee; BILLY BUCK: Tim Flavin.

478. *My Romance*

A fantasy operetta. In the prologue Tom, a pure minister of St. Giles' Church, in New York City, warns his grandson against falling in love with an actress. The story then reveals Tom himself, years earlier, falling in love with Rita, an immoral Italian opera star.

Before Broadway. The straight play *Romance*, upon which this musical was based, opened on Broadway at the MAXINE ELLIOTT THEATRE, 2/10/13. 160 PERFORMANCES. It starred the playwright's wife Doris Keane. It was revived at THE PLAYHOUSE, 2/28/21. 106 PERFORMANCES.

The musical opened for a pre–Broadway tryout tour on 2/12/48, at the Shubert Theatre, New Haven, and closed at the Great Northern Theatre, Chicago, on 5/9/48. PRESENTED BY the Messrs Shubert; MUSIC: Denes Agay; ADDITIONAL MUSIC: Philip Redowski; LYRICS: Rowland Leigh, Fred Jay, Irving Reid; CHOREOGRAPHER: Myra Kinch; MUSICAL DIRECTOR: Ving Merlin. The rest of the crew was basically the same as for the later Broadway run. *Cast*: TOM: Charles Fredericks; SUZETTE: Judy Searles; ALICE: Marion Mason; MISS POTHERTON: Hildegarde Halliday; HARRY: William Berrian; CORNELIUS: Melville Ruick; SUSAN: Hazel Dawn Jr.; PERCIVAL: Tom Bate; MRS. VANDERWITT: Barbara Patton (character's name changed for Broadway); VERONICA: Gail Adams; OCTAVIA: Mary Jane Sloan; FRED: Robert Eckles (this character was bumped up a social notch to Sir Frederick for Broadway); MRS. PUTNAM: Jean McBride (this character became Lady Putnam for Broadway); RUPERT: Warde Donovan, *Melton Moore*; VLADIMIR: Nat Burns; MISS JOYCE: Natalie Norman; BERTIE: Charles Graves, *Norval Tormsen*; GEORGIANNA: Verna Epperly; MARGARET JOYCE: Lorraine Carroll (this character became Margaret Fears for Broadway); LAWRENCE: Andy Aprea; THYRA: Florine Moore; DEWITT BODEEN: Lawrence Weber; ROSELLA: Allegra Varron; RITA: Anne Jeffreys; CHARLOTTE: Madeleine Holmes; TOSATTI: Tito Coral; ARLEEN: Florine Moore (role cut for Broadway); LUCILLE: Mona Bradford (role cut for Broadway); CORINNE BREWSTER: June St. Clair (role cut for Broadway); SIEGFRIED HERZIG: William Leonard (role cut for Broadway); JEANNE SALVERT: Ruth Thomas (role cut for Broadway); GERMAN WAITER: Manfred Hecht (role cut for Broadway); 1ST MAID: Edith Lane; 2ND MAID: Patricia Boyer; PAGE BOY: Norval Tormsen; OTHER GUESTS: Martha Burnett, June Reimer, Muriel Birckhead, Harold Ronk, LeRoy Bush.

It was revised, and re-opened on Broadway several months later, with new music by Sig Romberg (his last show). The first number, "Tingle," was cut before Broadway. "Entre Nous" was replaced by "1898" and "Debutante." "Laugh at Life" and "You're Near and Yet So Far" were cut before Broadway, as were "Come Farfalle," "Ev'ry Time I Dance the Polka," "First Bouquet," "Food for Thought," "Romance," "Magic Moment" and "The Vision." In short, it was almost an entirely new score. Rowland Leigh (by himself) provided the new lyrics.

The Broadway Run. SHUBERT THEATRE, 10/19/48–11/29/48; ADELPHI THEATRE, 12/7/48–1/8/49. Total of 95 PERFORMANCES. PRESENTED BY the Shuberts; MUSIC: Sigmund Romberg; LYRICS/BOOK/DIRECTOR: Rowland Leigh; BASED ON the 1913 drama *Romance*, by Edward Brewster Sheldon (1886–1946); CHOREOGRAPHER: Frederic N. Kelly; SETS: Watson Barratt; COSTUMES: Lou Eisele; MUSICAL DIRECTOR: Roland Fiore; ORCHESTRATIONS: Don Walker; PRESS: C.P. Greneker & Joe Conkle; COMPANY MANAGER: John Shubert; STAGE MANAGERS: Edward J. Scanlon, Nat Burns, Charles Wood. *Cast*: BISHOP TOM ARMSTRONG: Lawrence Brooks (2); SUZETTE ARMSTRONG: Joan Shepard; ALICE: Marion Bradley; MISS POTHERTON: Hildegarde Halliday; HARRY ARMSTRONG: William Berrian; CORNELIUS VAN TUYL: Melville Ruick; SUSAN VAN TUYL: Hazel Dawn Jr.; PERCIVAL HAWTHORNE-HILLARY: Tom Bate; MRS. DEWITT: Barbara Patton; VERONICA DEWITT: Gail Adams, *Edith Lane*; OCTAVIA FOTHERINGHAM: Luella Geer (3); SIR FREDERICK PUTNAM: Rex Evans; LADY PUTNAM: Doris Patston; RUPERT CHANDLER: Melton Moore; VLADIMIR LUCCACHEVITCH: Nat Burns; MISS JOYCE: Natalie Norman; BERTIE WESSEL: Lawrence Weber; GEORGIANNA CURTRIGHT: Verna Epperly; MARGARET FEARS: Mary Jane Sloan; LAWRENCE RILEY: Andy Aprea; THYRA WINSLOW: Lou Maddox; DEWITT BODEEN: Donald Crocker; ROSELLA: Allegra Varron; MME MARGUERITA "RITA" CAVALLINI: Anne Jeffreys (1); CHARLOTTE ARMSTRONG: Madeleine Holmes; TOSATTI, THE ORGAN GRINDER: Tito Coral; 1ST MAID: Edith Lane; 2ND MAID: Patricia Boyer; PAGE BOY: Norval Tormsen; OTHER GUESTS: Muriel Birckhead, Martha Burnett, LeRoy Bush, June Reimer, Harold Ronk. *Understudies*: Rita: Muriel Birckhead; Tom: Melton Moore; Octavia: Mary Jane Sloan; Susan: June Reimer; Rosella: Barbara Patton; Suzette: Patricia Boyer; Miss Potherton/Veronica: Lou Maddox; Cornelius: Lawrence Weber; Harry: Norval Tormsen; Tosatti: Andy Aprea; Charlotte: Marion Bradley. ***Prologue***: Bishop Armstrong's library in the rectory of St. Giles' Church; 1948: "Souvenir" (Tom). ***Act I***: Home of Cornelius Van Tuyl, New York City; 1898: "1898" (Ensemble), "Debutante" (Susan & Veronica), "Written in Your Hand" (Susan & Tom), "Millefleurs" (Rita), "Love and Laughter" (Rita & Tom), "From Now Onward" (Rita & Tom), "Little Emmaline" (Octavia), "Aria" (Rita). ***Act II***: The rectory at St. Giles' Church; six weeks later: "Desire" (Tom), "Polka" (dance) (Veronica, Mrs. DeWitt, Ensemble), "If Only" (Rita), "Bella Donna" (Tosatti, Rita, Ensemble), "Paradise Stolen" (Rita & Tom), "In Love with Romance" (Rita & Tom), Finaletto (Tom). ***Act III***: Mme Cavallini's suite at Brevoort House; four hours later: "Waltz Interlude" (dance) (Rosella), "Musical Scene" (Rita & Tom), "Prayer" (Rita). ***Epilogue***: The library; Jan. 1, 1949: Finale (Rita & Tom).

On Broadway the show was panned.

479. *The Mystery of Edwin Drood*

A play-within-a-play adaptation. Charles Dickens died before finishing his novel, so this musical is somewhat unique in that it allows the audience to choose the murderer (there is no clue as to who the murderer is, or, indeed, if there ever was a murder) and also to see how the lovers pair up at the end. The audience is balloted for their choice of solution, and it is then enacted for them. The show is performed as if it were being done by London's Music Hall Royale in 1873, led by an enthusiastic chairman. Following the custom of the day, Drood is played by a woman. Drood disappears and is presumed dead. The chairman then reviews the suspects among several intriguing characters: Rosa, the victim's angelic former fiancee; Princess Puffer, the mysterious owner of a London opium den; Neville, a visitor from Ceylon and his sphinx-like sister Helena; and Jasper, Edwin's uncle and choirmaster of the cathedral in Cloisterham who secretly desires Rosa. Datchery is the mysterious, bearded detective.

Before Broadway. *The Mystery of Edwin Drood* had been filmed in 1935, as a straight drama, but it wasn't until the 1980s that a stage production happened. Gail Merrifield, Joseph Papp's wife, caught Rupert Holmes's musical act at a nightclub, and sent a note backstage asking him if he would like to write a musical for the New York Shakespeare Festival, of which Gail Merrifield was director of play development. It first ran Off Broadway, as a Festival production at the DELACORTE THEATRE, Central Park, 8/4/85–9/1/85, for 3 previews and 24 free (i.e. no charge to audience) performances. It had the same basic crew as for the subsequent Broadway run, except SOUND: Otts Munderloh. At this stage the show was three hours long, with jugglers, magicians and unicyclists playing prior to Act I, in order to get the audience warmed up. In the cast the character Cedric Moncrieffe was then known as Wilfred Barking-Smythe, and was played by Larry Shue (the playwright who wrote *The Foreigner*), who died in a plane crash, and was succeeded for the Broadway run by George N. Martin. Master Nick Cricker was then known as Robert Bascomb, and was played by Don Kehr. Stephen Glavin played Christopher Lyon (playing the Statue), and Herndon Lackey played Alan Eliot (playing Julian — a role that was discontinued). The Brothel Clients were played by Nicholas Gunn, Brad Miskell, Robert Grossman, Herndon Lackey (these four actors played Harry, Montague, James, and Alan respectively). At that point Robert Grossman was playing James Thottle (playing Howard), but Peter McRobbie took over for Broadway. Robert Grossman also understudied the Chairman and Durdles. Brian (played by Charles Goff) also played the Portrait, and understudied Bazzard and Crisparkle. At that point the citizens were played by: Karen Giombetti, Stephen Glavin, Charles Goff, Nicholas Gunn, Robert Grossman, Judy Kuhn, Herndon Lackey, Francine Landes, Brad Miskell, Donna Murphy. Then the show transferred to Broadway.

The Broadway Run. IMPERIAL THEATRE, 12/2/85–5/16/87. 24 previews. 608 PERFORMANCES. PRESENTED BY New York Shakespeare Festival; MUSIC/LYRICS/BOOK/ORCHESTRATIONS: Rupert Holmes; SUGGESTED BY the 1870 unfinished novel of the same name, by Charles Dickens; DIRECTOR: Wilford Leach; CHOREOGRAPHER: Graciela Danieli;

SETS: Bob Shaw; COSTUMES: Lindsay W. Davis; LIGHTING: Paul Gallo; SOUND: Tom Morse; MUSICAL SUPERVISOR: Michael Starobin; MUSICAL DIRECTOR: Edward Strauss; PRESS: Merle Debuskey, Richard Kornberg, Bruce Campbell, Barbara Carroll, William Schelble, Don Anthony Summa; GENERAL MANAGER: Laurel Ann Wilson, *Bob MacDonald* (added by 86–87); COMPANY MANAGER: Bob MacDonald, *David Conte*; PRODUCTION STAGE MANAGER: James Harker; STAGE MANAGER: Robin Herskowitz, *Pamela Singer & Michele Pigliavento*. **Cast** (the Dickens character(s) first, then, in parentheses, and in italics, the 1873 troupe actor playing the role): MAYOR THOMAS SAPSEA (*Your Chairman, William Cartwright*): George Rose; STAGE MANAGER/BARKEEP (*Mr. James Throttle*): Peter McRobbie; JOHN JASPER (*Mr. Clive Paget*): Howard McGillin; REV. MR. SEPTIMUS CRISPARKLE (*Mr. Cedric Moncrieffe*): George N. Martin; EDWIN DROOD (*Miss Alice Nutting*): Betty Buckley, *Donna Murphy* (from 6/16/86), *Paige O'Hara* (during Miss Murphy's vacation, 12/15/86–12/22/86); ROSA BUD (*Miss Deirdre Peregrine*): Patti Cohenour, *Karen Culliver* (from 8/16/86); ALICE (*Miss Isabel Yearsley*): Judy Kuhn, *Lorraine Goodman* [note: this character was later called Wendy]; BEATRICE (*Miss Florence Gill*): Donna Murphy, *Mary Robin Roth*; HELENA LANDLESS (*Miss Janet Conover*): Jana Schneider, *Alison Fraser* (from 8/13/86); NEVILLE LANDLESS (*Mr. Victor Grinstead*): John Herrera; DURDLES (*Mr. Nick Cricker*): Jerome Dempsey, *Tony Azito*; DEPUTY/STATUE (*Master Nick Cricker*): Stephen Glavin, *Brad Miskell, Steve Clemente*; PRINCESS PUFFER (*Miss Angela Prysock*): Cleo Laine, *Loretta Swit* (from 6/9/86), *Karen Morrow* (from 12/8/86); SHADE OF JASPER (*Mr. Harry Sayle*): Nicholas Gunn; SHADE OF DROOD (*Mr. Montague Pruitt*): Brad Miskell; CLIENTS OF PRINCESS PUFFER: *Mr. Alan Eliot*: Herndon Lackey; *Mr. Christopher Lyon*: Rob Marshall, *Robert Radford*; SUCCUBAE: *Miss Gwendolyn Pynn*: Francine Landes, *Catherine Ulissey*: *Miss Sarah Cook*: Karen Giombetti, *Camille de Ganon*; *Miss Florence Gill*: Donna Murphy, *Mary Robin Roth*: *Miss Isabel Yearsley*; Judy Kuhn, *Lorraine Goodman*; SATYR (*Master Nick Cricker*): Stephen Glavin, *Brad Miskell, Steve Clemente*; (THREE) SERVANTS: *Mr. Philip Bax*: Joe Grifasi, *David Cromwell*; *Miss Violet Balfour*: Susan Goodman, *Mary Robin Roth*; *Miss Gwendolyn Pynn*: Francine Landes; HAROLD (*Mr. James Throttle*): Peter McRobbie; HORACE (*Mr. Brian Pankhurst*): Charles Goff; BAZZARD (*Mr. Philip Bax*): Joe Grifasi, *David Cromwell*; DICK DATCHERY: George Spelvin [the name George Spelvin is traditionally used on Broadway to denote an actor who wishes to remain unidentified]; CITIZENS OF CLOISTERHAM: Karen Giombetti, Charles Goff, Susan Goodman, Nicholas Gunn, Judy Kuhn, Herndon Lackey, Francine Landes, Rob Marshall, Peter McRobbie, Brad Miskell, Donna Murphy. ***Understudies***: Drood/Rosa: Judy Kuhn, *Paige O'Hara, Lorraine Goodman*; Alice/Deirdre: Paige O'Hara; Jasper: Herndon Lackey, *Rick Negron*; Neville: Herndon Lackey, *John De Luca*; Chairman: Peter McRobbie, *David Cromwell, Charles Goff*; Crisparkle: Peter McRobbie, *Charles Goff*; Deputy/Statue: Brad Miskell, *Steve Clemente, Robert Radford*; Helena/Puffer: Donna Murphy, *Mary Robin Roth*; Durdles/Horace: Joe Pichette; Satyr: Rick Negron, *Brad Miskell*; Bazzard: Joe Pichette, *Nicholas Gunn*; Stage Manager: Charles Goff; Beatrice/Wendy: Michele Pigliavento. ***Swings***: Laurent Giroux, Michele Pigliavento, *Rick Negron, John De Luca*. ***Orchestra*** (* means "added for Broadway," i.e. they were not in the Delacorte production): VIOLINS: Ronald Oakland *, Alvin E. Rogers *, Katsuko Esaki *, Marshall Coid *, Gayle Dixon *, Sandra Billingslea *; CELLI: Peter Prosser, Laura Blustein, *Jeanne LeBlanc *; REEDS: David Weiss, Richard Heckman, Lester Cantor, Seymour Red Press *; TRUMPETS: Wilmer Wise & Phil Granger; TROMBONE/BARITONE HORN: Santo Russo; BASS TROMBONE/TUBA: Earl P. McIntyre; FRENCH HORN: Russell Rizner; HORN: R. Allen Spanjer *; KEYBOARDS: James Koval, Edward Strauss, Donald Rebic; BASS: Melanie L. Punter; PERCUSSION: Skip Reed; DRUMS: Glenn Rhian. ***Act I***: THE SITUATION: Prologue: The Music Hall Royale: "There You Are" (Chairman & Company); *Scene 1* The home of John Jasper at Minor Canon Corner in the cathedral city of Cloisterham; a morning in late December: "A Man Could Go Quite Mad" (Jasper), "Two Kinsmen" (Drood & Jasper); *Scene 2* The conservatory of the Nuns' House, a seminary for young women in Cloisterham High Street; later that morning: "Moonfall" (Rosa), "Moonfall" (reprise) (Rosa & Helena, Alice & Beatrice); *Scene 3* Cloisterham High Street, outside the residence of Mayor Thomas Sapsea; the following afternoon; *Scene 4* The opium den of Princess Puffer in the East End of London; dawn, the next day: "The Wages of Sin" (Puffer), "Jasper's Vision" (dance) (Shades of Jasper & Drood, Succubae, Satyr); *Scene 5* Cloisterham High Street; that afternoon: "Ceylon" (Drood, Rosa, Helena, Neville, Ensemble), "Both Sides of the Coin" (Jasper, Chairman, Ensemble); *Scene 6* The crypts of Cloisterham Cathedral; late that night; *Scene 7* The ruins of Cloisterham; Christmas Eve: "Perfect Strangers" (Drood & Rosa); *Scene 8* The home of John Jasper; a short time later: "No Good Can Come from Bad" (Neville, Drood, Rosa, Helena, Crisparkle, Jasper, Bazzard); *Scene 9* Minor Canon Corner; Christmas Day & Night: "Never the Luck" (Philip), "The Name of Love"/"Moonfall" (reprise) (Rosa, Jasper, Ensemble). *Act II*: THE SLEUTHS: Prologue: The Music Hall Royale; *Scene 1* Cloisterham Station; six months later: "Settling up the Score" (Datchery, Puffer, Ensemble); *Scene 2* Cloisterham High Street: "Off to the Races" (Chairman, Durdles, Deputy, Ensemble), "Don't Quit While You're Ahead" (Puffer), "Don't Quit While You're Ahead" (reprise) (Puffer & Company); THE VOTING: "Settling up the Score" (reprise) (Chairman & Suspects); The Solution: "The Garden Path to Hell" (Puffer), "Puffer's Confession" (Puffer), "Out on a Limerick" (Datchery), "Jasper's Confession" (Jasper), "Murderer's Confession" [five different versions are available, depending on who the audience votes for], "Perfect Strangers" (reprise) [whichever pair of lovers the audience votes for in the happy ending], FINALE: "The Writing on the Wall" (Drood), "Don't Quit While You're Ahead" (reprise) (Company).

It got very good Broadway reviews. George Rose, as the MC, had to adlib a lot of lines to warm up the audience. The show changed its name (but only for Broadway and the subsequent national tour) to *Drood* on 11/13/86, in order to try to bolster a flagging box office. It won Tonys for musical, score, book, direction of a musical, and for George Rose. This was the first time in the history of the Tonys that one person had won awards for music, lyrics, and book for the same show. It was also nominated for choreography, and for John Herrera, Howard McGillin, Patti Cohenour, Jana Schneider and Cleo Laine.

After Broadway. LONDON, 5/7/87. 68 PERFORMANCES. *Cast*: DROOD: Julia Hills; WILLIAM CARTWRIGHT: Ernie Wise; PUFFER: Lulu; JASPER: David Burt; HELENA: Marilyn Cutts; NEVILLE: Mark Ryan; ROSA: Patti Cohenour.

TOUR (it was called *Drood!*). Opened on 4/5/88, at the Kennedy Center, Washington, DC, and closed on 10/2/88, in Wilmington, Del. DIRECTOR: Edward M. Greenberg; CHOREOGRAPHERS: Rob & Kathleen Marshall; MUSICAL DIRECTOR: Raymond Allen. *Cast*: CARTWRIGHT/CHAIRMAN: George Rose, *Clive Revill*; PUFFER/ANGELA: Jean Stapleton; JASPER/PADGET: Mark Jacoby; DROOD/ALICE: Paige O'Hara; BAZZARD/BAX: Ronn Carroll; IMAGE OF ROSA/GWENDOLEN: Kathleen Marshall; CHRISTOPHER: Troy Myers; DURDLES/NICK: Tony Azito; NEVILLE/VICTOR: John De Luca; ROSA/DEIRDRE: Teresa De Zarn. "There You Are," "Two Kinsmen," "Moonfall," "The Wages of Sin," "Jasper's Vision," "A British Subject," "Both Sides of the Coin," "Never the Luck," "Off to the Races," "A Private Investigation," "The Name of Love," "Don't Quit While You're Ahead," "The Garden Path to Hell," "The Solution."

TOUR. Opened on 9/27/88, at Burruss Hall, Blacksburg, Va. PRESENTED BY the Music Theatre Group; DIRECTOR: Joe Leonardo; CHOREOGRAPHER: Daniel Pelzig; SETS/COSTUMES: Neil Bierbower; MUSICAL DIRECTOR/ORCHESTRATIONS/ARRANGEMENTS: Hampton F. King Jr. *Cast*: DROOD: Kris Montgomery; PUFFER: Karlah Hamilton.

BRIDEWELL THEATRE, London, 8/6/03–8/23/03. DIRECTOR: Rachel Moorhead; CHOREOGRAPHER: Edz Barrett; MUSICAL DIRECTOR: Ryan Weber. *Cast*: DROOD: Melanie Morrissey; PUFFER: Annabelle Williams; CHAIRMAN: John Horwood.

480. *Nellie Bly*

Joseph Pulitzer's New York newspaper, the *World*, assigns young girl reporter Nellie Bly to circle the globe in an attempt to beat Jules Verne's record of 80 days. Frank Jordan, managing editor of James Gordon Bennett's New York *Herald*, engages Fogarty, who has been working as a "stable boy for the Hoboken Ferry," to race Nellie. Jordan goes along too, and falls for the girl reporter. Based on fact. Setting out in Nov. 1889, the real Nellie

(Elizabeth Seaman —1867–1922) made it in 72 days, cabling dispatches to her paper en route.

Before Broadway. The original libretto was written by Morrie Ryskind and Sig Herzig, but they quit during tryouts, refusing to allow their names to appear. Edgar MacGregor replaced Charles Friedman as director, and Robert Sidney was replaced as choreographer by Edward Caton and Lee Sherman. In the cast Joy Hodges replaced Marilyn Maxwell after the Philadelphia tryout.

The Broadway Run. ADELPHI THEATRE, 1/21/46–2/2/46. 16 PERFORMANCES. PRESENTED BY Nat Karson & Eddie Cantor; MUSIC: James Van Heusen; LYRICS: Johnny Burke; BOOK: Joseph Quillan; BASED ON the story by Jack Emmanuel; DIRECTOR: Edgar J. MacGregor; CHOREOGRAPHERS: Edward Caton & Lee Sherman; SETS/COSTUMES/LIGHTING: Nat Karson; MUSICAL SUPERVISOR: Joseph Lilley; MUSICAL DIRECTOR: Charles Drury; ORCHESTRATIONS: Ted Royal & Elliott Jacoby; CHORAL DIRECTOR: Simon Rady; PRESS: Karl Bernstein & Martha Dreiblatt; GENERAL MANAGER: Irving Cooper; GENERAL STAGE DIRECTOR: Milton Stern; COMPANY MANAGER: S.M. Handelsman; STAGE MANAGER: Hal Voeth; ASSISTANT STAGE MANAGER: Joe Hahn. *Cast*: JOSEPH PULITZER: Walter Armin (9); JAMES GORDON BENNETT: Edward H. Robins (8); NEWSBOY: William O'Shay; FRANK JORDAN: William Gaxton (1) ☆; FERRY CAPTAIN: Fred Peters; DECKHAND: Harold Murray; PHINEAS T. FOGARTY: Victor Moore (2) ☆; 1ST REPORTER: Robert Strauss (10); MURPHY: Artells Dickson (11); WARDHEELER: Jack Voeth; 2ND REPORTER: Larry Stuart; 3RD REPORTER: Eddy Di Genova; NELLIE BLY: Joy Hodges (4); BATTLE ANNIE: Benay Venuta (3); STEWARD: Larry Stuart; HONEYMOON COUPLE: Doris Sward & Jack Voeth; FRENCH GIRL: Drucilla Strain; GRISETTE: Lubov Roudenko (6); FRENCH DANDY: Jack Whitney (7); FRENCH MAYOR: Walter Armin; SANTOS-DUMONT: Fred Peters; REPORTERS: The Debonairs (5); CZAR: Walter Armin; RUSSIAN CAPTAIN: Fred Peters; 1ST SHEIK: Robert Strauss (10); 2ND SHEIK: Edward H. Robins (8); 3RD SHEIK: Larry Stuart; OFFICIAL: Harold Murray; COPYGIRL: Suzie Baker; CHOIR GIRLS: Marjorie Anderson, Suzie Baker, Johnsie Bason, Jeannine Burke, Betty de Cormier, Margaret Lide, Betty Spain, Drucilla Strain, Ruth Strickland, Doris Sward, Julie Van Dusen; CHOIR BOYS: Eddy Di Genova, William Golden, Bernard Griffin, Alfred Homan, Karl Newart, Merrill Shea, Larry Stuart; DANCING GIRLS: Rita Barry, Charlotte Bergmeier, Faith Dane, Mimi Gomber, Mary Grey, Sandra Scott, Dorothy Jeffers, Nathalie Kelepovska, Terry Lasky, Michael Neale, Nancy Newton, Mitzi Perry, Ronan York; DANCING BOYS: Ed Dragon, Bob Gari, William O'Shay, Jack Richards, William Segar, Kenny Springer. *Act I*: *Scene 1* Barclay Street ferry slip, New York; *Scene 2* In front of ferry house at Barclay Street; *Scene 3* Battle Annie's saloon; *Scene 4* City Hall Square; *Scene 5* Steamship pier in Hoboken; *Scene 6* The after deck; *Scene 7* Stateroom in the SS *Augusta Victoria*; *Scene 8* At the gates of the Paris Exposition; *Scene 9* Paris Exposition. *Act II*: *Scene 1* City room of the *New York Herald*; *Scene 2* Stratosphere; *Scene 3* Public square, Moscow; *Scene 4* Street in Aden; *Scene 5* The pass; *Scene 6* Street in Aden; *Scene 7* Somewhere in Texas; *Scene 8* In transit; *Scene 9* Barclay Street ferry slip. *Act I*: "There's Nothing Like Travel" (Ensemble & Phineas), "All Around the World" (Frank & Nellie), "Fogarty the Great" (Phineas & Fogarty Boosters), "That's Class" (Battle Annie), "Nellie Bly" (Nellie Bly Social Club), "Nellie Bly"/"Fogarty the Great" (reprise) (Ensemble), "May the Best Man Win" (Entire Cast), "How About a Date?" (Suzie Baker, Johnsie Bason, Sandra Scott, Drucilla Strain, Debonairs), "You Never Saw That Before" (Battle Annie), "L'Exposition Universalle" (dance) (Lubov Roudenko, Jack Whitney, Ensemble), "Sky High" (sung by Frank, Nellie, Ensemble). *Act II*: "No News Today" (dance) (Debonairs & New York *Herald* Employees), "Choral Russe" (dance) (Czar, Officers, Guards, Muscovites), "Just My Luck" (Frank, Nellie, Ensemble), "Aladdin's Daughter" (Battle Annie), "Start Dancin'" (dance) (Frank, Annie, Lobov Roudenko, Jack Whitney, Ensemble), "Harmony" (Frank & Phineas), Finale: "You May Not Love Me" (Entire Company).

It got one rave, but the rest of the Broadway reviews were terrible. The show lost $300,000.

481. *The Nervous Set*

A show about beatniks. The program provided a glossary of beatnik terms so the audience could follow the words.

Before Broadway. Several numbers were not used: "Apples in the Lilac Tree," "Night Remembers," "It's Nice Weather for Ducks," "Pitch for Pot," "Season in the Sun," "Tell Me Lies," "You Can't Go Home Again." "Spring Can Really Hang You up the Most" was cut before Broadway. Tom and Theoni Aldredge were married. This was Larry Hagman's Broadway debut.

The Broadway Run. HENRY MILLER'S THEATRE, 5/12/59–5/30/59. 23 PERFORMANCES. PRESENTED BY Robert Lantz; MUSIC/MUSICAL DIRECTOR/ORCHESTRATIONS: Tommy Wolf; LYRICS: Fran Landesman; BOOK/DIRECTORS: Jay Landesman & Theodore J. Flicker; BASED ON the novel of the same name, by Jay Landesman; SETS/LIGHTING: Paul Morrison; COSTUMES: Theoni Vachlioti Aldredge; PRESS: Dorothy Ross; GENERAL MANAGER: Richard Horner; STAGE MANAGER: Allan Mankoff; ASSISTANT STAGE MANAGER: David Sallade. *Cast:* BUMMY CARWELL: Larry Hagman (3); BRAD: Richard Hayes (1), Don Heller (matinees); DANNY: Thomas Aldredge (6); JAN: Tani Seitz (2); YOGI: Del Close (4); A CUSTOMER: Barry Primus; LANDLADY: Florence Gassner; JOAN: Arlene Corwin; SARI SHAW: Janice Meshkoff; DANNY'S GIRL: Elvira Pallas; MAX THE MILLIONAIRE: Gerald Hiken (5); HENRY CALHOUN: David Sallade; KATHERINE SLOAN-WITTIKER: Florence Gassner; IRVING: Don Heller; TONY: Lee Lindsey; REJECTED BOY: Zale Kessler. *Act I: Scene 1* Washington Square Park, New York City; Sunday afternoon; late summer, now; *Scene 2* Brad & Jan's apartment on Perry Street; the following spring; *Scene 3* Jan's parents' home, Fairfield County, Connecticut; that weekend; *Scene 4* The bottom of an unfilled pool; the same evening; *Scene 5* Inside the house again; later; *Scene 6* Bummy Carwell's apartment on Avenue A; the next weekend. *Act II*: *Scene 1* Brad & Jan's apartment; a few days later; *Scene 2* The Melancholy Pigeon; the same day; *Scene 3* Katherine Sloan-Wittiker's apartment on Sutton Place; that evening; *Scene 4* Brad & Jan's apartment; later. *Act I*: "Man, We're Beat" (Company), "New York" (Brad, Danny, Jan), "What's to Lose" (Jan & Brad), "Stars Have Blown My Way" (Jan & Brad), "Fun Life" (Brad), "How Do You Like Your Love?" (Yogi), "Party Song" (Company), "If I Could Put You in a Song" (Brad), "Night People" (Brad & Jan), "I've Got a Lot to Learn About Life" (Jan), "Rejection" (Danny & Company), "The Ballad of the Sad Young Men" (Jan) [the big number]. *Act II*: "A Country Gentleman" (Brad & Jan), "Max the Millionaire" (Max, Brad, Yogi, Danny), "Laugh, I Thought I'd Die" (Brad), "Travel the Road of Love" (Bummy & Company), "Fun Life" (reprise) (Company).

Reviews were not good.

482. *Never Gonna Dance*

Lucky, a vaudeville hoofer, wants to marry Margaret, daughter of Mr. Chalfont, one of the leading citizens of Punxsatawney, Pa. Chalfont makes him go to New York to earn $25,000 in a month, by any means except dancing. He meets Penny, a dance instructor, and they form a successful act and fall in love. Margaret then arrives. Ricardo, the bandleader, is Penny's admirer. Mabel is Penny's friend. Miss Tattersall is Major Bowes' assistant. Mr. Pangborn is the owner of the dance studio. Set in 1936.

Before Broadway. This show was in development for years before its New York City workshop of 11/29/01–12/1/01. *Cast*: LUCKY: Noah Racey; PENNY: Nancy Lemenager; RICARDO: David Pittu; PANGBORN: Peter Bartlett. It was going to try out at the Ahmanson Theatre, Los Angeles, 1/14/04–3/7/04, but on 5/15/03, when it was found that *Urban Cowboy* was going to leave the Broadhurst, it found a Broadway theatre and canceled L.A. The number "Bojangles of Harlem" was not used.

The Broadway Run. BROADHURST THEATRE, 12/4/03–2/15/04. 44 previews from 10/27/03. 84 PERFORMANCES. PRESENTED BY Weissberger Theatre Group (Jay Harris, producer), Edgar Bronfman Jr., James Walsh, Ted Hartley/RKO Pictures, Harvey Weinstein; MUSIC: Jerome Kern; LYRICS: various writers; BOOK: Jeffrey Hatcher; EXPANDED FROM the 1936 RKO movie *Swing Time* (which originally was going to be called *Never Gonna Dance*) with Fred Astaire & Ginger Rogers, and which had been based on a story by Erwin Gelsey; DIRECTOR: Michael Greif; CHOREOGRAPHER: Jerry Mitchell; SETS: Robin Wagner; COSTUMES: William Ivey Long; LIGHTING: Paul Gallo; SOUND: ACME Sound Partners;

MUSICAL DIRECTOR/VOCAL ARRANGEMENTS: Robert Billig; ORCHESTRATIONS: Harold Wheeler; DANCE MUSIC ARRANGEMENTS: Zane Mark; INCIDENTAL MUSIC & SONG ARRANGEMENTS: James Sampliner; PRESS: Boneau/Bryan-Brown; CASTING: Bernard Telsey; GENERAL MANAGEMENT: Nina Lannan Associates, with Devin Keudell; COMPANY MANAGER: Leslie A. Glassburn; PRODUCTION STAGE MANAGER: Kristen Harris; STAGE MANAGER: Michael John Egan; ASSISTANT STAGE MANAGER: Jason Trubitt. *Cast:* THE CHARMS: Roxane Barlow, Sally Mae Dunn, Jennifer Frankel; JOHN "LUCKY" GARNETT: Noah Racey (1); A STAGE MANAGER: Timothy J. Alex [role dropped shortly after opening]; MR. CHALFONT: Philip LeStrange (8); MARGARET CHALFONT: Deborah Leamy (9); A MINISTER: Kirby Ward; MABEL PRITT: Karen Ziemba (3); PENNY CARROLL: Nancy Lemenager (2); ALFRED J. MORGANTHAL: Peter Gerety (4); MR. PANGBORN: Peter Bartlett (6); MAJOR BOWES: Ron Orbach (5); MISS TATTERSALL: Julie Connors; RICARDO ROMERO: David Pittu (7); THE ROME-TONES: Julio Agustin, Jason Gillman, T. Oliver Reid; SPUD: Eugene Fleming (10); VELMA: Deidre Goodwin (11); DICE RAYMOND: Timothy J. Alex; WAITRESSES: Sally Mae Dunn, Jennifer Frankel, Ipsita Paul; A CONSTRUCTION WORKER: Kirby Ward; VAUDEVILLIANS/WEDDING GUESTS/NEW YORKERS/REPORTERS: Timothy J. Alex, Julio Agustin, Roxane Barlow, Julie Connors, Sally Mae Dunn, Jennifer Frankel, Jason Gillman, Greg Graham, Kenya Unique Massey, Ipsita Paul, T. Oliver Reid, Kirby Ward, Tommar Wilson. *Understudies*: Pangborn: Julio Agustin & Philip LeStrange; Ricardo: Julio Agustin & Timothy J. Alex; Bowes/Chalfont: Timothy J. Alex & Kirby Ward; Penny: Nili Bassman & Deborah Leamy; Margaret: Julie Connors; Mabel: Sally Mae Dunn & Jennifer Frankel; Lucky: Jason Gillman & Greg Graham; Velma: Kenya Unique Massey & Ipsita Paul; Morganthal: Ron Orbach & Kirby Ward; Spud: T. Oliver Reid & Tommar Wilson. *Swings*: Nili Bassman, Ashley Hull, Denis Jones, Tony Yazbeck. *Orchestra*: REEDS: Chuck Wilson, Rick Heckman, Mark Thrasher; TRUMPETS: Don Downs & John Chudoba; TROMBONES: Keith O'Quinn & Michael Boschen; FRENCH HORN: Russell Rizner; VIOLINS: Mineko Yajima (Concertmaster), James Tsao, Jonathan Dinklage, Claire Chan; CELLO: Sarah Carter; KEYBOARDS: James Sampliner & Zane Mark; BASS: Benjamin Franklin Brown; DRUMS: Dean Sharenow; PERCUSSION: Howard Joines. *Act I*: PUNXSATAWNEY, PA: "Dearly Beloved" (Johnny Mercer) (Lucky & His Charms), "Put Me to the Test" (Ira Gershwin) (Lucky); NEW YORK CITY: "I Won't Dance" (Oscar Hammerstein II, Dorothy Fields, Jimmy McHugh, Otto Harbach) (Lucky & Company), "Pick Yourself Up" (Dorothy Fields) (Penny & Lucky), "Pick Yourself Up" (reprise) (Mabel & Morganthal); "Who" (Oscar Hammerstein II & Otto Harbach) (Ricardo & Rome Tones), "I'm Old Fashioned" (Johnny Mercer) (Penny), Spud & Velma's Audition: "She Didn't Say Yes, She Didn't Say No" (Otto Harbach) (Spud & Velma), "The Song is You" (Oscar Hammerstein II) (Mabel, Morganthal, Waitresses), "The Way You Look Tonight" (Dorothy Fields) (Lucky & Penny). *Act II*: "Waltz in Swing Time" (Dorothy Fields) (Company), "Shimmy with Me" (P.G. Wodehouse) (Mabel & Company), "A Fine Romance" (Dorothy Fields) (Penny, Lucky, Mabel, Morganthal), "I'll Be Hard to Handle" (Bernard McDougall) (Spud & Velma), "I Got Love" (Dorothy Fields) (Mabel), "The Most Exciting Night" (Dorothy Fields & Otto Harbach) (Ricardo & Rome Tones), "Remind Me" (Dorothy Fields) (Penny & Lucky), "Never Gonna Dance" (Dorothy Fields) (Lucky & Penny), Finale: "Dearly Beloved" (reprise)/"I Won't Dance" (reprise) (Company).

Note: all music by Jerome Kern. Names in parentheses beside each song indicate the lyricists.

Broadway reviews were mixed, but mostly positive. On 2/2/04 it was announced that the show would close on 2/15/04 due to bad weather and the fact that it couldn't find an audience. It received Tony nominations for choreography and for Karen Ziemba.

After Broadway. Osaka and Tokyo in spring 2005. PRESENTED BY Fuji Television Network; CHOREOGRAPHER: Jerry Mitchell.

483. *New Faces of 1952*

One of the most influential revues, not only of the 1950s, but of all time. It was one of a series that had begun in 1934 and would end in 1968, and the 1952 was the best of the lot.

Before Broadway. The first of Leonard Sillman's *New Faces* shows was first presented in PASADENA as *Low and Behold*, and had to give 137 auditions before being able to raise the $15,000 to put it on Broadway, as *New* Faces, at the FULTON THEATRE, 3/15/34–7/21/34. 149 PERFORMANCES. New faces that year included Henry Fonda and Imogene Coca. *New Faces of 1936* featured, among others: Imogene Coca [sic], Van Johnson, Ralph Blane, Karl Swenson. It ran at the VANDERBILT THEATRE, 5/19/36–11/7/36. 193 PERFORMANCES. *New Faces of 1943*, at the RITZ THEATRE, 12/22/42–3/13/43. 94 PERFORMANCES. WRITER: John Lund; ADDITIONAL LYRICS & SKETCHES: June Carroll & J.B. Rosenberg. *Cast*: Alice Pearce, John Lund, Irwin Corey, Doris Dowling, Marie Lund.

For the 1952 production Paul Lynde auditioned by phone, doing his explorer sketch. Alice Ghostley's material was written with Charlotte Rae in mind, but she went off to do *Three Wishes for Jamie*. John Beal replaced Roger Price as sketch director before the show got to Broadway.

The Broadway Run. ROYALE THEATRE, 5/16/52–3/28/53. 365 PERFORMANCES. PRESENTED BY Walter P. Chrysler Jr.; PRODUCER/COMPILER/ASSEMBLER/PRODUCTION SUPERVISOR: Leonard Sillman; MUSIC/LYRICS/SKETCHES: various writers; DEVISED BY/DIRECTOR: John Murray Anderson; SKETCH DIRECTOR: John Beal; CHOREOGRAPHER: Richard Barstow; SETS: Raoul Pene du Bois; COSTUMES: Thomas Becher & Raoul Pene du Bois; MUSICAL DIRECTOR/SPECIAL ORCHESTRATIONS: Anton Coppola; ORCHESTRAL ARRANGEMENTS: Ted Royal; PRESS: Bill Doll & Company; GENERAL MANAGER: Elias Goldin, *Leon Spachner*; PRODUCTION STAGE MANAGER: Arthur Barkow; STAGE MANAGER: Mortimer Halpern; ASSISTANT STAGE MANAGER: Clark Ranger, *Leonard Auerbach*. **Act I**: Overture (Orchestra); *Scene 1* Opening. (m/l: Ronny Graham; dial: Peter DeVries): READER: Ronny Graham; ALSO WITH: Company; *Scene 2* Crazy, Man! (by Ronny Graham & Roger Price): COUNSELLOR HOLLY: Paul Lynde; SENATOR MARBLE: Joseph Lautner; SENATOR HUTCHINSON: Bill Mullikin; A POLICEMAN: Jimmy Russell; DAZZ ROCCO: Ronny Graham; *Scene 3* "Lucky Pierre" (m/l: Ronny Graham): GIRLS: Virginia de Luce, Patricia Hammerlee, Rosemary O'Reilly; PIERRE: Robert Clary; REPORTER: Bill Mullikin; *Scene 4* "Guess Who I Saw Today" (m: Murray Grand; l: Elisse Boyd) (sung by June Carroll); *Scene 5* "Restoration Piece" (m: Arthur Siegel; l/dial: June Carroll): INTRODUCTION BY: Virginia de Luce; LADY SYLVIA MALPRACTICE: Alice Ghostley; SIMPLE: Patricia Hammerlee; SIR SOLEMNITY SOURPUSS: Paul Lynde; SIR MILITANT MALPRACTICE: Joseph Lautner; *Scene 6* "Love is a Simple Thing" (m: Arthur Siegel; l: June Carroll) (sung by Rosemary O'Reilly, Robert Clary, Eartha Kitt, June Carroll): 1ST COUPLE: Virginia Bosler & Allen Conroy; 2ND COUPLE: Carol Nelson & Jimmy Russell; 3RD COUPLE: Carol Lawrence & Michael Dominico; *Scene 7* "Boston Beguine" (m/l: Sheldon Harnick): INTRODUCED BY: Virginia de Luce; SUNG BY: Alice Ghostley; *Scene 8* "The Bard and the Beard" (m: Arthur Siegel; l: June Carroll; additional lyrics: Sheldon Harnick; dialogue: Ronny Graham): INTRODUCED BY: Virginia de Luce; MISS LEIGH: June Carroll; SIR LAURENCE: Ronny Graham; CALL BOY: Bill Mullikin; MAID: Rosemary O'Reilly; *Scene 9* "Nanty Puts Her Hair Up" (m: Arthur Siegel; l: Herbert Farjeon): INTRODUCED BY: Virginia de Luce; NANTY: Virginia Bosler; FATHER: Joseph Lautner; MOTHER: Alice Ghostley; BROTHER: Bill Mullikin; HIGHLANDER: Allen Conroy; *Scene 10* Oedipus Goes South (by Ronny Graham) [take-off on Truman Capote]: INTRODUCED BY: Virginia de Luce; KAPUT: Ronny Graham; *Scene 11* "Time for Tea" (m: Arthur Siegel; l: June Carroll) (sung by June Carroll & Alice Ghostley): MARCELLA: Alice Ghostley; LAVINIA: June Carroll; LAVINIA, THE GIRL: Virginia Bosler; MARCELLA, THE GIRL: Carol Nelson; MOTHER: Rosemary O'Reilly; FATHER: Joseph Lautner; JOHN: Jimmy Russell; GUESTS: Virginia de Luce, Allen Conroy, Michael Dominico; *Scene 12* "Bal, Petit Bal" (by Francis Lemarque): INTRODUCED BY: Robert Clary; SUNG BY: Eartha Kitt; *Scene 13* Of Fathers and Sons (by Melvin Brooks) (spoof of *Death of a Salesman*; a pickpocket feels betrayed by a son who shuns the family business): MAE: Alice Ghostley; HARRY: Paul Lynde; STANLEY: Ronny Graham; POLICEMEN: Jimmy Russell & Allen Conroy; *Scene 14* Three for the Road (by Ronny Graham): INTRODUCED BY: Virginia de Luce (*Joseph Lautner*). Comprising the following songs: "Raining Memories:" Robert Clary; "Waltzing in Venice:" Rosemary O'Reilly & Joseph Lautner, with Virginia Bosler, June Carroll, Allen Conroy, Michael Dominico, Patricia Hammerlee, Eartha Kitt, Carol Lawrence, Paul Lynde, Bill Mullikin, Carol Nelson (*Virginia De Luce*),

Jimmy Russell; "Take off the Mask:" Alice Ghostley, Ronny Graham, Company; *Entr'acte*: READER: Ronny Graham; "Take off the Mask:" Carol Nelson; "Love is a Simple Thing:" Allen Conroy; "Boston Beguine:" Carol Lawrence; "Monotonous:" Jimmy Russell; "Nanty:" Virginia Bosler; "Miss Logan:" Michael Dominico; *Intermission. Act II*: *Scene 1* "Don't Fall Asleep" (m/l/dial: Ronny Graham): WIFE: Rosemary O'Reilly; HUSBAND: Jimmy Russell; *Scene 2* After Canasta—What?: INTRODUCED BY: Virginia de Luce & Robert Clary; DOROTHY: June Carroll; ELSIE: Alice Ghostley; *Scene 3* "Lizzie Borden" (m/l: Michael Brown; cos: Raoul Pene du Bois): TOWNSPEOPLE: Rosemary O'Reilly, Carol Lawrence, Virginia de Luce, Carol Nelson, Virginia Bosler, Allen Conroy, Jimmy Russell, Michael Dominico; MAN: Bill Mullikin; JUDGE: Paul Lynde; LIZZIE: Patricia Hammerlee; DISTRICT ATTORNEY: Joseph Lautner; *Scene 4* "I'm in Love with Miss Logan" (m/l: Ronny Graham): INTRODUCED BY: Virginia de Luce; BOY: Robert Clary; MISS LOGAN: Rosemary O'Reilly; MAN: Joseph Lautner; *Scene 5* Trip of the Month (by Paul Lynde) (the hero, swathed in bandages, tells of his misadventures on African safari): INTRODUCED BY: Virginia de Luce; MR. CANKER, THE EXPLORER: Paul Lynde; *Scene 6* "Hark, the Extra-Marital Lark." m: Ronny Graham; l/dial: Ronny Graham & Peter DeVries): CHORUS: Bill Mullikin; JOHN JEROME: Ronny Graham; HIS WIFE: Alice Ghostley; A MADEMOISELLE: Carol Nelson; CROUPIER: Robert Clary; A BLONDE: Virginia de Luce; MOROCCAN GIRL: Carol Lawrence; POLYNESIAN GIRL: Eartha Kitt; POLYNESIAN MAN: Allen Conroy; HUNTRESS: Patricia Hammerlee; *Scene 7* "Penny Candy" (m: Arthur Siegel; l: June Carroll; cos: Raoul Pene du Bois) (sung by June Carroll): WOMAN: June Carroll; GUSSIE: Carol Lawrence; POOR KIDS: Virginia Bosler & Jimmy Russell; RICH KIDS: Carol Nelson & Michael Dominico; CANDY VENDOR: Bill Mullikin; *Scene 8* "Convention Bound" (m/l: Ronny Graham) (sung by Ronny Graham, Paul Lynde, Bill Mullikin, Joseph Lautner, Patricia Hammerlee, Allen Conroy, Rosemary O'Reilly); *Scene 9* Whither America? (Another Revival), or The Energy Contained in a Glass of Water Would Drive an Ocean Liner? (by Luther Davis & John Cleveland): SWITCHBOARD OPERATOR: Virginia de Luce; STENOGRAPHER: June Carroll; MAN: Jimmy Russell; *Scene 10* "Monotonous" (m: Arthur Siegel; l: June Carroll; add l: Ronny Graham) (sung by Eartha Kitt); *Scene 11* "The Great American Opera" (by Ronny Graham) a take-off on *The Medium*] (special orch: Anton Coppola): INTRODUCED BY: Virginia de Luce; TOBY: Ronny Graham; MADAME FLORA: Alice Ghostley; EFFIE: Rosemary O'Reilly; SCENE 12 Finale: Entire Company. **Standbys**: Clark Ranger, Dinnie Smith, Jimmie Komack, Dorothy Love, Lance Avant.

Note: As Virginia De Luce introduced her sketches, she would cross the stage trying to complete her song "He Takes Me off His Income Tax" (m: Arthur Siegel; l: June Carroll), but the orchestra kept cutting in on her, and she never finished the number. It was a running gag.

It got great reviews. The order of some of the scenes changed throughout the run.

After Broadway. TOUR. Opened on 4/6/53, at the Shubert Theatre, Boston, and closed on 4/10/54, at the Cass Theatre, Detroit. Most of the Broadway cast was on the tour, except Virginia Bosler, Virginia de Luce (*Lee Perkins* took her place), Michael Dominico, Alice Ghostley (*Jenny Lou Law* took her place). Other new faces on tour were: Johnny Laverty, James Shelton, George Smiley, Polly Ward.

THE MOVIE. 1954. Some songs were taken out, others added, sketches were moved around. Eartha Kitt sang three additional songs: "Uskadara," "C'est Si Bon," and "Santa, Baby," and Robert Clary sang "Alouette." Most of the cast who were on the tour were in the film, except Patricia Hammerlee, Joseph Lautner and James Shelton. Alice Ghostley & Virginia de Luce, who had not been on tour, were back for the film. New faces for the film were: Elizabeth Logan and Faith Burwell. Clark Ranger, who had been a standby in the Broadway production, was also in the film.

New Faces of 1952 was revived Off Broadway by the EQUITY LIBRARY THEATRE, 10/28/82–11/21/82. 30 PERFORMANCES. It had only a few minor changes. DIRECTOR: Joseph Patton; CHOREOGRAPHERS: Joseph Patton & Wende Pollock; SETS: Rob Hamilton; MUSICAL DIRECTOR: Stephen Bates. *Cast*: Randy Brenner, Suzanne Dawson, Jack Doyle, Michael Ehlers, Lillian Graff, Anna Maria Gutierrez, Philip Wm. McKinley, Roxann Parker, Michele Pigliavento, Alan Safier, Denise Schafer (*Eartha Kitt*), Staci Swedeen, Michael Waldron.

It was revived again, again as *New Faces of 1952*, at ST. BART'S PLAY-HOUSE, 5/11/95–5/20/95. 8 PERFORMANCES. PRESENTED BY St. Bart's Players; DIRECTOR: Christopher Catt; CHOREOGRAPHER: Stacey Brown Einhorn; MUSICAL DIRECTOR: Steven Silverstein.

484. *New Faces of 1956*

The next revue in the series. T.C. Jones, female impersonator, did Tallulah Bankhead among other sketches. He was also MC (mistress of ceremonies).

The Broadway Run. ETHEL BARRYMORE THEATRE, 6/14/56–12/22/56. 221 PERFORMANCES. PRESENTED BY Leonard Sillman & John Roberts, in association with Yvette Schumer; MUSIC/LYRICS/SKETCHES: various artists; CONCEIVED BY/SUPERVISOR: Leonard Sillman; SKETCH DIRECTOR: Paul Lynde; CHOREOGRAPHER: David Tihmar; ASSISTANT CHOREOGRAPHER: Peter Conlow; SETS: Peter Larkin; COSTUMES: Thomas Becher; LIGHTING: Peggy Clark; MUSICAL DIRECTOR: Jay Blackton; ORCHESTRATIONS: Ted Royal, Albert Sendry, Joe Glover; PRESS: Bill Doll & Robert Ullman; GENERAL MANAGER: J.H. Del Bondio; PRODUCTION STAGE MANAGER: Morty Halpern; STAGE MANAGER: Leonard Auerbach; ASSISTANT STAGE MANAGER: Bill O'Brien. *Act 1*: *Scene 1* Opening (m/l: Ronny Graham) (Entire Company) (introduction by T.C. Jones & Company); *Scene 2* Madame Interpreter (by Danny & Neil Simon): FRANCE: Maggie Smith; UNITED STATES: Bob Shaver; ITALY: Johnny Haymer; GREAT BRITAIN: Bill McCutcheon; INDIA: Amru Sani; BRAZIL: Virginia Martin; USSR: John Reardon; MME INTERPRETER: Jane Connell; *Scene 3* "What Does That Dream Mean?" (m: Harold Karr; l: Matt Dubey): THE DREAMER: Johnny Haymer; HIS DREAMS: Franca Baldwin, Suzanne Bernard, Dana Sosa, Johnny Laverty, Jimmy Sisco, Rod Strong, Johnny Haymer, Ann Henry, Tiger Haynes, Bill McCutcheon, Virginia Martin, Billie Hayes; *Scene 4* Stars in the Rough (by Paul Lynde): ANNOUNCER: John Reardon; SOPRANO: Inga Swenson; HELEN HUNT: T.C. Jones; PATTY POTTS: Dana Sosa; OLD LADY: Jane Connell; TONY TAPS: Johnny Laverty; *Scene 5* "One Perfect Moment" (m: Dean Fuller; l: Marshall Barer & Leslie Julian-Jones) (sung by Maggie Smith): WOMAN: Maggie Smith; VIOLINIST: Johnny Haymer; LOVER: Bill McCutcheon; *Scene 6* "Tell Her" (m: Arthur Siegel; l: June Carroll) (sung by John Reardon) (danced by Franca Baldwin & Jimmy Sisco); *Scene 7* "The Washingtons Are Doin' Okay" (m/l: Michael Brown) (featuring Tiger Haynes); *Scene 8* A Canful of Trash (by Louis Botto): INTRODUCTION: Maggie Smith; ZELDA: Virginia Martin; MANNY: Bill McCutcheon; MOE: Johnny Haymer; JUNK MAN: Bob Shaver; 1ST SANITATION MAN: Rod Strong; 2ND SANITATION MAN: Johnny Laverty; *Scene 9* "April in Fairbanks" (m/l: Murray Grand) (sung by Jane Connell); *Scene 10* "A Doll's House" (m: Arthur Siegel; l: June Carroll): NURSE: Maggie Smith; TINA: Inga Swenson; URCHIN: Suzanne Bernard; FATHER DOLL: Jimmy Sisco; MOTHER DOLL: Virginia Martin; GIRL DOLL: Dana Sosa; PRINCESS DOLL: Franca Baldwin; PRINCE DOLL: Rod Strong; SWEEPER DOLL: Billie Hayes; *Scene 11* "And He Flipped" (m/l: John Rox; staged by Bob Hamilton) (sung by Ann Henry); *Scene 12* Sketch: "Girls 'n' Girls 'n' Girls" (m/l: Irvin Graham) (sung by John Reardon & Inga Swenson): MOTHER: Inga Swenson; JOHNNY: Johnny Laverty; FATHER: John Reardon; GRACE: Franca Baldwin; AVA: Suzanne Bernard; MARILYN: Virginia Martin; *Scene 13* "I Could Love Him" (m/l: Paul Nassau) (sung by Billie Hayes); *Scene 14* Steady Edna (by Paul Lynde): INTRODUCTION: T.C. Jones, *Virginia Martin;* ERIC: Johnny Haymer; EDNA: Jane Connell; DOC: Bill McCutcheon; STEFFANY: Maggie Smith; FATHER: Johnny Laverty; NATIVE CHIEF: Rod Strong; *Scene 15* "Hurry" (m: Murray Grand; l: Mr. Grand & Elisse Boyd) (sung by Amru Sani; *Scene 16* "Isn't She Lovely?" (m: Dean Fuller; l: Marshall Barer) (sung by T.C. Jones & Company): INTRODUCTION: T.C. Jones; PRODUCTION SINGER: John Reardon; PONIES: Franca Baldwin, Suzanne Bernard, Dana Sosa, Billie Hayes; CHORUS BOYS: Johnny Laverty, Bob Shaver, Jimmy Sisco, Rod Strong; THE BOY FRIEND: Bill McCutcheon; MISS BIRD CAGE: Virginia Martin; MISS BLUE FISH: Inga Swenson; MISS ORANGE: Maggie Smith; MISS HAT: Jane Connell; MOTH OF DESIRE: T.C. Jones. *Act II*: *Entr'acte*: INTRODUCTION: T.C. Jones; "I Could Love Him:" Johnny Laverty; "Girls 'n' Girls 'n' Girls: Dana Sosa, "Blues:" Jimmy Sisco; "Don't Wait:" Franca Baldwin; "Tell Her:" Rod Strong;

Scene 1 Twenty Years in the Blackboard Jungle (by Terry Ryan & Barry Blitzer): INTRODUCTION: T.C. Jones; TEACHER: Billie Hayes; MAHONEY: Jimmy Sisco; LEVINE: Tiger Haynes; KOWALSKI: Bob Shaver; ROGER: Johnny Laverty; HAIRY HILDA: Virginia Martin; GIRL MONITOR: Franca Baldwin; POLICEMAN: Rod Strong; PRINCIPAL: Bill McCutcheon; *Scene 2* "Don't Wait 'til it's Too Late to See Paris" (m: Arthur Siegel; l: June Carroll) (sung by John Reardon & Suzanne Bernard): HUSBAND: John Reardon; WIFE: Inga Swenson; GAMIN: Suzanne Bernard; ICE CREAM VENDOR: Jimmy Sisco; GIRL: Dana Sosa, BOY: Rod Strong; *Scene 3* "Rouge" (by Murray Grand) (sung by Jane Connell); *Scene 4* Darts (by Phil Green & Paul Lynde): GEORGE: Bill McCutcheon; HARRIET: Maggie Smith; MAN: John Reardon; *Scene 5* "Scratch My Back" (m: Dean Fuller; l: Marshall Barer) (sung by Ann Henry & Tiger Haynes); *Scene 6* "Boy Most Likely to Succeed" (m: Arthur Siegel; l: June Carroll) (sung by Inga Swenson): GRADUATING CLASS: Franca Baldwin, Suzanne Bernard, Dana Sosa, Johnny Laverty, Jimmy Sisco, Rod Strong; CLASS VALEDICTORIAN: Bob Shaver; PRINCIPAL: Bill McCutcheon; *Scene 7* "Talent" (m/l: Paul Nassau) (sung by Virginia Martin); *Scene 8* "The Broken Kimona" (m: Robert Stringer; sk/l: Richard Maury) (sung by T.C. Jones & Entire Company): INTRODUCTION: Maggie Smith; MESSENGER: Johnny Laverty; BARTENDER: Jimmy Sisco; BAMBOO BROTHERS: Bill McCutcheon, John Reardon, Rod Strong; DAUGHTER: T.C. Jones; BROKEN KIMONA: Johnny Haymer; WATER COLOR: Tiger Haynes; PURA: Maggie Smith; CALLER: Bob Shaver; TOWNSPEOPLE: Franca Baldwin, Suzanne Bernard, Billie Hayes, Dana Sosa; FILLY: Ann Henry; *Scene 9* La Ronde, with the song "This is Quite a Perfect Night" (m: Dean Fuller; l: Marshall Barer): INTRODUCTION: Rod Strong; ROUE: Johnny Haymer; JEUNE FILLE: Inga Swenson; ADOLESCENT: Bob Shaver; FEMME DU MONDE: Virginia Martin; *Scene 10* "The White Witch of Jamaica" (m: Arthur Siegel; l: June Carroll): TOURISTS: Suzanne Bernard, Maggie Smith, Johnny Laverty, Bob Shaver; NATIVE MAN: John Reardon; NATIVE WOMAN: Dana Sosa; LOLA: Franca Baldwin; OVERSEER: Jimmy Sisco; *Scene 11* "The Greatest Invention" (m/l: Matt Dubey, Harold Karr, Sid Silvers) (sung by Billie Hayes & Johnny Haymer); *Scene 12* "Mustapha Abdullah Abu Ben Al Raajid" (m: Dean Fuller; l: Marshall Barer) (sung by Amru Sani): MRS. MUSTAPHA: Amru Sani; HAREM HOURIS: Maggie Smith, Inga Swenson, Jane Connell, Suzanne Bernard, Dana Sosa, Franca Baldwin; *Scene 13* Powers Below (by Paul Lynde): INTRODUCTION: T.C. Jones; WIFE: Jane Connell; SUPERINTENDENT: Johnny Haymer; MRS. CARRUTHERS: Virginia Martin [Note: during the run this sketch was replaced with the song: "The Pioneer" (m/l: Bob Van Scoyk & Allan Manings) (sung by Johnny Haymer)]; *Scene 14* "She's Got Everything" (m: Dean Fuller; l: Marshall Barer) (sung by T.C. Jones & Company): MC: Johnny Haymer; FOUR ARISTOCRATS: Johnny Laverty, John Reardon, Bob Shaver, Jimmy Sisco; HOPE DIAMOND: T.C. Jones; Scene 15 Finale (Entire Company). *Standbys*: Shellie Farrell, Bill O'Brien, Jack Parker, Tom Roland, Ruth Tarson, Patti Williams.

Broadway reviews were divided. The sets came in for much praise.

485. *New Faces of 1962*

A *New Faces* revue NOT produced by Leonard Sillman.

Before Broadway. Several numbers cut before Broadway: "Ballad of a Bus" (by Jack Holmes), "Althea" ("The Three Faces of Love") (by Elisse Boyd), "Do You Wonder What Became of Romanoff?," "Girls in Their Summer Dresses," "I Was Beautiful" (by Murray Grand), "Wanna Make a Bet."

The Broadway Run. ALVIN THEATRE, 2/1/62–2/24/62. 2 previews on 1/31/62. 28 PERFORMANCES. PRESENTED BY Carroll & Harris Masterson; MUSIC/LYRICS/SKETCHES: various writers; CONCEIVED BY/DIRECTOR: Leonard Sillman; SKETCH CO-DIRECTOR: Richard Maury; CHOREOGRAPHER: James Moore (mostly); SETS/LIGHTING: Marvin Reiss; COSTUMES: Thomas Becher; TECHNICAL CONSULTANT: Mortimer Halpern; MUSICAL DIRECTOR: Abba Bogin; ORCHESTRATIONS: Jay Bower, Mark Bucci, Sy Oliver, Ted Royal, David Terry; DANCE MUSIC ARRANGEMENTS: Jack Holmes; PRESS: Betty Lee Hunt & Diane Judge; GENERAL MANAGER: Richard Horner; COMPANY MANAGER: Leonard Soloway; PRODUCTION STAGE MANAGER: Lo Hardin; STAGE MANAGER:

Robert Calhoun; ASSISTANT STAGE MANAGER: Michael Foley. *Act I*: *Scene 1* "Opening" (m/l: Ronny Graham; dial: Joey Carter; ch: James Moore; introduced by Jim Corbett; gowns from the collection of Luis Estevez) (Entire Company); *Scene 2* Quickies; *Scene 3* The Reds Visit Mount Vernon (by Paul Lynde): INTRODUCED BY: Patti Karr (1); FATHER: R.G. Brown; MOTHER: Marian Mercer (3); GEORGE: Joey Carter (2); *Scene 4* "Moral Rearmament" (m/l: Jack Holmes) (Travis Hudson, James Moore, Tom Arthur); *Scene 5* "Pi in the Sky" (m: Mark Bucci; sketch by Jean Shepherd): INTRODUCED BY: Sylvia; PILOT: Michael Fesco; STEWARDESSES: Maria Nieves & Mickey Wayland; PASSENGERS: Patti Karr, James Moore, Erin Martin, Charles Barlow, Joan Thornton, R.G. Brown, Marian Mercer, Michael Fesco, Helen Kardon, Jim Corbett; *Scene 6* "In the Morning" (m/l: Ronny Graham) (Sylvia Lord); *Scene 7* "Happiness" (m: Marie Gordon; l: David Rogers): MAN: R.G. Brown; HAPPINESS GIRLS: Joan Thornton, Helen Kardon, Sylvia, Marian Mercer, Travis Hudson, Mickey Wayland; *Scene 8* Impressions and Folk Songs (written & performed by Joey Carter); *Scene 9* "Togetherness" (m/l: Mavor Moore) [dropped during the run]: CARDINAL: R.G. Brown; BISHOP: Charles Barlow; PATRIARCH: Michael Fesco; MODERATOR: James Moore; *Scene 10* "(A) Moment of Truth" (m/l: Jack Holmes; suggested by Ronny Graham) (Patti Karr); *Scene 11* "I Want You to Be the First to Know" (m: Arthur Siegel; l: June Carroll) (Mickey Wayland, Charles Barlow, Michael Fesco): 1ST COUPLE: James Moore & Erin Martin; 2ND COUPLE: Juan Carlos Copes & Maria Nieves; 3RD COUPLE: Jim Corbett & Patti Karr; YOUNG MAN: Tom Arthur; *Scene 12* Lemon Coke (by R.G. Brown) [dropped during the run]: BOY: R.G. Brown; GIRL: Marian Mercer (3); *Scene 13* "ABCs" (m: Mark Bucci; l: David Rogers): GIRL: Helen Kardon; CHILDREN: Erin Martin, Maria Nieves, Jim Corbett, Juan Carlos Copes, James Moore; *Scene 14* "(It) Depends on How You Look at Things" (m: Arthur Siegel; l: June Carroll): HUSBAND: R.G. Brown; WIFE: Travis Hudson; THINGS: Helen Kardon, Joan Thornton, Mickey Wayland, Erin Martin, Patti Karr, Maria Nieves, Sylvia; *Scene 15* It Takes a Heap (by Tony Geiss & Paul Lynde): INTRODUCED BY: Patti Karr (1); FOREMAN: Joey Carter (2); WITH: Michael Fesco, Helen Kardon, Jim Corbett, Patti Karr, Mickey Wayland, Maria Nieves, Erin Martin; *Scene 16* "Freedomland" (m/l: Jack Holmes) (Marian Mercer); *Scene 17* "Over the River and Into the Woods" (m/l: Jack Holmes) (gown from the collection of Luis Estevez) (Sylvia Lord); *Scene 18* Nose Cone (by R.G. Brown): REPORTER: Michael Fesco; MR. THURMAN: R.G. Brown; MRS. THURMAN: Marian Mercer (3); *Scene 19* "Johnny Mishuga" (m: Mark Bucci; l: David Rogers & Mark Bucci; sketch: David Rogers): INTRODUCED BY: Tom Arthur; MOMMA: Travis Hudson; HYMIE: Joey Carter (2); WAITER: Jim Corbett; GRINGO: Charles Barlow; JOHNNY: R.G. Brown; YASMIN: Marian Mercer (3); DEPUTY: James Moore; CUSTOMERS: Erin Martin, Patti Karr, Sylvia, Maria Nieves, Helen Kardon, Michael Fesco. *Act II*: *Entr'acte* (ch: James Moore) (Argentinean section choreographed & danced by Maria Nieves): INTRODUCED BY: Joan Thornton & Sylvia; DANCERS: Jim Corbett, Juan Carlos Copes, Michael Fesco, Patti Karr, Erin Martin, James Moore, Maria Nieves; *Scene 1* Quickies; *Scene 2* The Scarsdale Sentence (by David Rogers): INTRODUCED BY: Patti Karr (1); BETTINA: Marian Mercer (3); WARREN: R.G. Brown; *Scene 3* Madison Avenue Executive (by Ronny Graham): EXECUTIVE: James Moore; *Scene 4* "Collective Beauty" (m: William Roy; l: Michael McWhinney): LADY: Travis Hudson; REVLONITES: Helen Kardon, Mickey Wayland, Charles Barlow, Jim Corbett, Maria Nieves, Patti Karr; CUSTOMERS: Erin Martin, Sylvia, Joan Thornton; *Scene 5* Happy Person (by Herbert Hartig): GIRL: Marian Mercer (3); BOY: R.G. Brown; *Scene 6* Untouchables (by Joey Carter): WITH: Erin Martin & Charles Barlow; *Scene 7* "The Other One" (m: Arthur Siegel; l: June Carroll) (gowns by Baba Originals): WOMAN: Marian Mercer (3); MAN: Jim Corbett; DANCERS: Patti Karr, Sylvia, Joan Thornton, Mickey Wayland, Tom Arthur, Charles Barlow, Michael Fesco, Juan Carlos Copes; *Scene 8* Our Models: Joan Thornton & Sylvia; *Scene 9* "The Untalented Relative" (m: Arthur Siegel; l: Joey Carter & Richard Maury): INTRODUCED BY: Patti Karr (1); FOLK SINGER: Joey Carter (2); FOLK: Patti Karr, Juan Carlos Copes, Marian Mercer, Mickey Wayland, James Moore, Michael Fesco, Charles Barlow, Helen Kardon, Erin Martin, Jim Corbett; *Scene 10* It's All in a Day's Work (by Joey Carter): GIRL: Joan Thornton; *Scene 11* "Love is Good for You" (m: Arthur Siegel; l: June Carroll) (Sylvia Lord); *Scene 12* Where Are Our Parents? (by Ronny Graham, Arnie Sul-

tan, Marvin Worth): FATHER: Joey Carter (2); MOTHER: Marian Mercer (3); ROGER: R.G. Brown; MARY: Mickey Wayland; COP: Jim Corbett; *Scene 13* "Wall Street Reel" (m; Arthur Siegel; l: Jim Fuerst; introduction written by Richard Maury) (introduced by Patti Karr); *Scene 14* Finale (Entire Company).

It got bad Broadway reviews.

486. *New Faces of 1968*

Also called *Leonard Sillman's New Faces of 1968*. It was the last of the *New Faces* revues to run on Broadway.

The Broadway Run. BOOTH THEATRE, 5/2/68–6/15/68. 16 previews from 4/18/68. 52 PERFORMANCES. An All-Corduroy production, PRESENTED BY Jack Rollins; MUSIC/LYRICS/SKETCHES: various artists; CONTINUITY/ADDITIONAL DIALOGUE: William F. Brown; CONCEIVED BY/STAGED BY: Leonard Sillman; DIRECTOR/CHOREOGRAPHER: Frank Wagner; SETS/COSTUMES: Winn Morton; LIGHTING: Paul Sullivan; SOUND: John F. Goodson; MUSICAL DIRECTOR: Ted Simons; ORCHESTRATIONS: Lanny Meyers; CAST RECORDING on Warner Bros — 7 Arts; PRESS: Sol Jacobson & Lewis Harmon; GENERAL MANAGER: Richard Osorio; COMPANY MANAGER: Martin Cohen; PRODUCTION STAGE MANAGER: Jack Timmers; STAGE MANAGER: Paul Sullivan; ASSISTANT STAGE MANAGER: Rod Barry. *Act I*: "Illustrated Overture;" *Scene 1* Definitions by Random House: GIRL: Gloria Bleezarde; BOY: Rod Barry; *Scene 2* Welcome: THE PRODUCER: Leonard Sillman; *Scene 3* "Opening" (m/l: Ronny Graham) (performed by the Entire Company); *Scene 4* Audition (by Robert Klein): THE AUDITIONER: Robert Klein; *Scene 5* "By the Sea" (m/l: Clark Gesner) (sung by Brandon Maggart); *Scene 6* "Where is the Waltz?" (m/orch: Alonzo Levister; l: Paul Nassau) (sung by Michael K. Allen). Dance: Dottie Frank, Elaine Giftos, Trudy Carson; *Scene 7* "A New Waltz" (m: Fred Hellerman; l: Fran Minkoff) (sung by Marilyn Child). Dance: Robert Lone & Joe Kyle; *Scene 8* Happy Landings (by Jack Sharkey): AIRLINE STEWARDESS: Madeline Kahn; *Scene 9* "The Girl in the Mirror" (m: Fred Hellerman; l: Fran Minkoff) (sung by Rod Perry). ISOLATION: Joe Kyle & Gloria Bleezarde; *Scene 10* The American Hamburger League (by Norman Kline) [this sketch was dropped after the opening]: INTRODUCTION: Rod Barry; BETH: Madeline Kahn; HELENE: Marilyn Child; REX: Brandon Maggart; DEXTER: George Ormiston; WAYNE: Robert Klein; ISOLATION: Trudy Carson & Rod Barry; *Scene 11* Love Songs. INTRODUCTION: Leonard Sillman. "Something Big" (m: Sam Pottle; l: David Axelrod) (sung by George Ormiston & Elaine Giftos), "Love in a New Tempo" (m/l: Ronny Graham) (sung by Robert Klein), "Hungry" (m/l: Murray Grand) (sung by Suzanne Astor to Rod Barry); *Scene 12* "Luncheon Ballad" (m: Jerry Powell; l: Michael McWhinney) (sung by Suzanne Astor, Marilyn Child, Madeline Kahn, Nancie Phillips); *Scene 13* The Underachiever (by Peter DeVries): INTRODUCTION: Gloria Bleezarde; FRESHMAN: Robert Klein; HIS WIFE: Madeline Kahn; *Scene 14* "You're the One I'm For" (m/l: Clark Gesner) (sung by Brandon Maggart); *Scene 15* "Where is Me?" (m: Arthur Siegel; l: June Carroll) (sung by Marilyn Child). Isolation — "Right About Here" (m/l: Arthur Siegel) (performed by Michael K. Allen); *Scene 16* Gospel According to Jack (by William F. Brown): Performers: Suzanne Astor, Rod Barry, Trudy Carson, Marilyn Child, Dottie Frank, Madeline Kahn, Robert Klein, Robert Lone, Brandon Maggart, Rod Perry. ISOLATION: Robert Klein & Elaine Giftos; *Scene 17* Mama Doll (by Charles Tobias & Nat Simon; conception by George Ormiston & Nancie Phillips): DOLL: Nancie Phillips; LITTLE BOY: George Ormiston. "Toyland" (m/l/dial: Gene P. Bissell): PRODUCTION SINGER: Madeline Kahn; COMPERE: Robert Klein. *Act II*: INTRODUCTION: Leonard Sillman & Gloria Bleezarde; *Scene 1* "Hullabaloo at Thebes" (m/l: Ronny Graham): INTRODUCTION: Leonard Sillman; OEDIPUS: Robert Klein; JOCASTA: Suzanne Astor; ANTIGONE: Trudy Carson; ISMENE: Elaine Giftos; *Scene 2* "#X9RL220" (m: Jerry Powell; l: Michael McWhinney) (sung by Gloria Bleezarde); *Scene 3* "You Are" (m/l: Clark Gesner) (sung by Brandon Maggart); *Scene 4* "Evil" (m/l: Sydney Shaw) (sung by Michael K. Allen); *Scene 5* The Refund (by Peter DeVries): INTRODUCTION & CLARIFICATION: George Ormiston; FRED ABERNATHY: Robert Klein; BEN ABERNATHY: Brandon Maggart; SARAH COBLEIGH: Dottie Frank; *Scene 6* "Prisms" (m: Carl Friberg; l: Hal Hackady) (performed by Marilyn Child); *Scene 7* "Tango" (m: Sam Pottle; l: David Axelrod): INTRODUCTION: Leonard Sillman; PERFORMED BY: The Company. Isolation — "Cymbals and Tambourines" (m/l: Arthur Siegel) (performed by Gloria Bleezarde & Robert Lone); *Scene 8* "Philosophy" (m: Carl Friberg; l: Hal Hackady) (sung by Rod Perry). Dance: Dottie Frank, Joe Kyle, Elaine Giftos; *Scene 9* The Pile-Up (performed by Brandon Maggart); *Scene 10* "Das Chicago Song" (m: Michael Cohen; l: Tony Geiss) (sung by Madeline Kahn); *Scene 11* "Missed America" (m/l/dial: Kenny Solms & Gail Parent; additional dialogue: Ronny Graham): EMCEE: George Ormiston; MISS ALABAMA: Nancie Phillips; MISS MINNESOTA: Dottie Frank; MISS CONNECTICUT: Suzanne Astor; *Scene 12* "Die Zusammenfuegung" (m: Sam Pottle; l: David Axelrod): INTRODUCTION: Gloria Bleezarde; SCHEISS: Brandon Maggart; PFEFFER: Robert Klein; HEIDI: Madeline Kahn; THE CONNECTION: George Ormiston; *Scene 13* "Opening" (reprise): INTRODUCTION: Leonard Sillman; *Scene 14* "The Girl of the Minute" (m: David Shire; l: Richard Maltby Jr.) (performed by the Entire Company). *Standbys*: Kelly Britt (for the ladies), F. David Halpert (for the gentlemen), David Merrick (for Leonard Sillman). *Musicians*: ELECTRIC PIANO: Jack Easton; DRUMS: Jerry Fisher; PERCUSSION: Irv Cooper; BASS: John Beal; HARP: Gene Bianco.

Broadway reviews were divided, but basically unfavorable.

After Broadway. *The American Hamburger League*, originally one of the sketches from *New Faces of 1968*, was later produced as a separate revue, a series of comedy skits about contemporary neuroses, at the NEW THEATRE, 9/16/69. 1 PERFORMANCE. PRESENTED BY Leonard Sillman; DIRECTOR: George Luscombe. *Cast*: Jack Fletcher, Liz Sheridan, Richard B. Shull, Jane Hoffman, Dorothy Lyman, Bill Hinnant.

Not So New Faces of '82, no connection to the previous "official" series by Leonard Sillman, was an Off Broadway spoof musical revue, an evening of wanton mischief and songs. It ran in New York, at the WESTSIDE MAINSTAGE, 12/15/82–12/30/82. 16 PERFORMANCES. PRESENTED BY Actors Producing Company; MUSIC/LYRICS/SKETCHES: several authors (including Ronald Reagan & William Shakespeare); CONCEIVED BY/DIRECTOR: Stuart Ross; CHOREOGRAPHER: Edmond Kresley; MUSICAL DIRECTOR: Jonny Bowden. *Cast*: Nancy Ringham, Scott Robertson, Carole Schweid, Mary Testa, William Thomas Jr., Margery Cohen, George Bohn. "Not-So-New Faces," "Schizophrenia 101A," "Ask the Doctor," "Summer's Breeze," "Nobody Knows that it's Me," "Night of the Living Preppies," "Hollywood Has Got Her," "Mom, I've Got Something to Tell You," "The Boyfriend," "Christmas Tree," "P.M. With Lufa," "Princess Di," "The News," "Edie," "E.T.," "Portman Kick," "Cell of the Well-to-Do," "Rosie," "The Dancer and the Dance," "Amyl," "Your Back," "French Tickler," "Special Guest Spot," "Last Call," "Dueling Neurotics," "Baby, You Give Good Heart," "New Face in Town," "Friends Like You." It had another run, at the CENTURY CAFE, 3/17/83–4/6/83. 16 PERFORMANCES. *Cast*: Barry Preston, Nancy Ringham, Mary Testa, William Thomas Jr.

Not So New Faces of '84 continued the idea. It ran at Upstairs at Greene Street, NYC, 4/5/84–6/28/84. 24 performances. MUSIC/LYRICS/SKETCHES: Michael Feingold, Ellen Fitzhugh, Larry Grossman, Jason McAuliffe, Stuart Ross, Karen Trott, David Zippel, etc; CHOREOGRAPHER: Ed Kresley; MUSICAL DIRECTOR: John Spalla. *Cast*: Nancy Ringham, John Spalla, Mary Testa, William Thomas Jr.

Used Faces of 2004, a parody, a comic revue, ran at DON'T TELL MAMA, 5/3/04–5/31/04. MUSIC/LYRICS: Michael Ogborn; DIRECTOR: Kelly Briggs: *Cast*: Jerry Christakos, Dori Legg, Lorinda Lisitza.

487. New Girl in Town

Anna quits her job in a turn-of-the-century St. Paul, Minnesota, brothel to come east to New York City for a reunion with her father, barge captain Chris, who is ignorant of her profession, as is stoker Mat, who falls for her, until beer-guzzling Marthy tells him. He confronts Anna and gets the truth. He stays away a year before coming back to claim her.

Before Broadway. Bob Merrill came up with the idea of adapting Eugene O'Neill's famous play to an MGM musical movie called *A Saint She Ain't*, in a modern setting. It was never done, but it evolved into the stage musical. Doris Day liked some of the songs from this never-done movie, and in 1956 she was in Hollywood talking about them to George Abbott. Mr. Abbott called Hal Prince and Bobby Griffith in New York, and asked them to get in touch with Bob Merrill about these songs. They all decided to do a stage musical, and Mr. Merrill wrote additional songs. MGM released to them the score and the screen rights to *Anna Christie*. Mr. Abbott also persuaded Eugene O'Neill's widow to sell him the stage rights to the play. George Abbott wrote the libretto in six weeks and kept as close as possible to the original play. He switched the time period from the 1920s to the turn of the 20th century. Bob Merrill's songs, accordingly, seemed now too modern, and he wrote 16 new songs in 11 days, and another three after rehearsals began. Only two of the original songs that he wrote for the never-made movie were used, one of them being "It's Good to Be Alive." "Here We Are Again" and "Pay as You Go" were among those cut, as was "Elegance" (although this was used later in *Hello, Dolly!*). Gwen Verdon won the role after many actresses had been auditioned. The original concept had been to have no dancing, as this was basically a somber story, and the producing team felt dancing would have compromised it. The choice of dancer Gwen Verdon did compromise the show, as more and more space was given to her. Bob Fosse's second-act "Red Light Ballet" was cut after the producers saw the shocked reaction of the tryout audiences in New Haven. The producers also destroyed the $40,000 staircase it involved. The show then went to Boston, with much tension between the Fosse-Verdon side and the Abbott-Prince side. During the Boston tryout Gwen got the flu, and four understudies stood in for her while she recovered. A revised form of the sequence (without the staircase) was put back in for a few months after the Broadway opening, but the relationship between the principals was damaged beyond repair.

The Broadway Run. FORTY-SIXTH STREET THEATRE, 5/14/57–5/24/58. 431 PERFORMANCES. PRESENTED BY Frederick Brisson, Robert E. Griffith, Harold S. Prince; MUSIC/LYRICS: Bob Merrill; BOOK/DIRECTOR: George Abbott; BASED ON the 1921 drama *Anna Christie*, by Eugene O'Neill; CHOREOGRAPHER: Bob Fosse; SETS/COSTUMES: Rouben Ter-Arutunian; MUSICAL DIRECTOR: Hal Hastings; ORCHESTRATIONS: Robert Russell Bennett & Philip J. Lang; DANCE MUSIC DEVISED BY: Roger Adams; CAST RECORDING on RCA; PRESS: Reuben Rabinovitch & Helen Richards; GENERAL MANAGER: Carl Fisher; PRODUCTION STAGE MANAGER: Fred Hebert; ASSISTANT STAGE MANAGERS: Dennis Murray & John Ford. *Cast*: LILY: Lulu Bates; MOLL: Pat Ferrier; KATIE: Mara Lynn; ALDERMAN: Michael Quinn; CHRIS CHRISTOPHERSON: Cameron Prud'homme (4); JOHNSON: Jeff Killion; SEAMAN: H.F. Green; MARTHY OWEN: Thelma Ritter (2) ☆; OSCAR: Del Anderson; PETE: Eddie Phillips; MRS. DOWLING: Ann Williams; SMITH: Stokely Gray; MRS. SMITH: Dorothy Stinnette; BARTENDER: Mark Dawson; IVY: Rita Noble; ROSE: Ginny Perlowin; ANNA CHRISTIE: Gwen Verdon (1) ☆; FLO: Drusilla Davis; PEARL: Mara Landi; MAT BURKE: George Wallace (3); MRS. HAMMACHER: Jean Handzlik; REPORTER: Herb Fields; MASHER: John Aristedes; SVENSON: Ray Mason; VIOLET: Deedy Irwin; WAITER: Louis Polacek; DOWLING: Ripple Lewis; POLITICIAN: H.F. Green; KRIMP: John Ford; HENRY: Edgar Daniels; DANCERS: John Aristedes, Robert Bakanic, Claiborne Cary, Drusilla Davis, Dorothy Dushock, Pat Ferrier, Harvey Hohnecker, Harvey Jung, Marie Kolin, Mara Lynn, Ethel Martin, Dale Moreda, John Nola, Joan Petlak, Eddie Phillips, Alton Ruff; SINGERS: Del Anderson, Edgar Daniels, Herb Fields, John Ford, Stokely Gray, H.F. Green, Jean Handzlik, Deedy Irwin, Jeff Killion, Mara Landi, Ripple Lewis, Ray Mason, Rita Noble, Ginny Perlowin, Louis Polacek, Michael Quinn, Dorothy Stinnette, Ann Williams. **Act I**: Overture (Orchestra); *Scene 1* The waterfront: "Roll Yer Socks Up" (Seaman, Singers, Dancers); *Scene 2* A street with a mesh fence: "Anna Lilla" (Chris); *Scene 3* Johnny-the-Priest's saloon: "Sunshine Girl" (Oscar, Pete, Bartender), "On the Farm" (Anna); *Scene 4* A street in the warehouse district: "Flings" (Marthy, Lily, Pearl); *Scene 5* Chris's barge on a foggy night at sea, off Provincetown: "(It's) Good to Be Alive" (Anna); *Scene 6* A street near the waterfront: "Look at 'er" (Mat); *Scene 7* The waterfront: "(It's) Good to Be Alive" (reprise) (Mat); *Scene 8* The street with the fence: "Yer My Friend, Ain'tcha?" (Marthy & Chris); *Scene 9* Chris's room: "Did You Close Your Eyes?" (Anna & Mat); *Scene 10* A street scene: "At the Check Apron Ball" (Dancers & Singers); *Scene 11* The Check Apron Ball: "There Ain't No Flies on Me" (Anna & Company). *Act II*: *Scene 1* The Check Apron Ball: "Ven I Valse" (Anna, Chris, Dancers, Singers); *Scene 2* In the street, outside the brewery; *Scene 3* A street in the warehouse district: "Sunshine Girl" (reprise) (Dancers & Singers); *Scene 4* Chris's room: "If That Was Love" (Anna), Ballet (Anna, Masher, Dancers); *Scene 5* The waterfront; one year later: "Chess and Checkers" (Marthy, Dancers, Singers), "Look at 'er" (reprise) (Mat).

Broadway prices were $9.20 for orchestra divan seats and $8.60 for regular orchestra seats on weekends. Reviews were divided, nothing special. The show won Tony Awards for Gwen Verdon and Thelma Ritter. It was also nominated for musical, choreography, and for Cameron Prud'homme. On 6/23/57 (Bob Fosse's birthday), during the run, the "Red Light Ballet" was re-introduced, but in a much modified form and without the famous staircase. But it still didn't work. Soon after the show closed, Freddie Brisson returned to live in California, thus breaking up the partnership of Prince-Griffith-Brisson that had been responsible for *The Pajama Game*, *Damn Yankees* and *Redhead*. The production, capitalized at $300,000, made a profit.

After Broadway. EQUITY LIBRARY THEATRE, 1/9/75–1/26/75. 22 PERFORMANCES. The dance numbers were cut. DIRECTOR: Richard Michaels; CHOREOGRAPHER: Lynne Gannaway; SETS: Kenneth Foy. *Cast*: ANNA: Livia Genise; MARTHY: Peggy Pope; CHRIS: John Dorrin; MAT: Scot Stewart; LIL: Maureen Sadusk; PEARL: Rosamond Lynn.

YORK THEATRE COMPANY, 11/15/02–11/17/02. Part of the *Musicals in Mufti* series. DIRECTOR: Michael Montel; MUSICAL DIRECTOR: Jack Lee. *Cast*: ANNA: Kelly Ann Lamb; CHRIS: Pete Gerety; MARTHY: Kathleen Doyle; MAT: Steve Wilson; PEARL: Jane Summerhays.

488. *The News*

A rock musical. It had only 9 minutes of dialogue. Its theme was sensational journalism. Set at present, in the City Room of a large metropolitan newspaper; the bedroom of a 15-year-old girl; a one-room apartment; a city street.

Before Broadway. The show originally ran at BURT REYNOLDS JUPITER THEATRE, Florida, then at WESTPORT COUNTRY PLAYHOUSE, Conn.

The Broadway Run. HELEN HAYES THEATRE, 11/7/85–11/9/85. 20 previews. 4 PERFORMANCES. PRESENTED BY Zev Bufman, Kathleen Lindsey, Nicholas Neubauer, R. Vincent Park, with Martin & Janice Barandes; MUSIC/LYRICS: Paul Schierhorn; BOOK: Paul Schierhorn, David Rotenberg, Vincent Park; DIRECTOR: David Rotenberg; CHOREOGRAPHER: Wesley Fata; SETS: Jane Musky; COSTUMES: Richard Hornung; LIGHTING: Norman Coates; SOUND: Gary Scott Peck/ATI; MUSICAL SUPERVISOR/ORCHESTRATIONS: John Rinehimer; ADDITIONAL ORCHESTRATIONS: Leon Pendarvis, Jefrey Silverman, Paul Schierhorn, Peter Valentine, David Rinehimer; MUSICAL ARRANGEMENTS: John Rinehimer & Paul Schierhorn; CONDUCTOR: John Rinehimer; PRESS: Jeffrey Richards Associates; CASTING: David Tochterman; GENERAL MANAGEMENT: Dorothy Olim Associates (including George Elmer); COMPANY MANAGER: Patricia Berry; PRODUCTION STAGE MANAGER: Robert I. Cohen; STAGE MANAGER: K.R. Williams; ASSISTANT STAGE MANAGER: Jay Adler. *Cast*: REPORTER: Cheryl Alexander; CIRCULATION EDITOR: Frank Baier; EXECUTIVE EDITOR: Jeff Conaway (1) ☆; KILLER: Anthony Crivello (2) ☆; CITY EDITOR: Michael Duff; FEATURE EDITOR: Jonathan S. Gerber; TALK SHOW HOST: Anthony Hoylen; REPORTER: Patrick Jude; GIRL: Lisa Michaelis (3) ☆; REPORTER: Charles Pistone; SPORTS EDITOR: John Rinehimer; STYLE EDITOR: Peter Valentine; MANAGING EDITOR: Billy Ward. **Standbys**: Killer: Patrick Jude; Male Reporters: Anthony Hoylen; Host: Jay Adler; Female Reporter/Girl: Julie Newdow. *Act I*: "I Am the News" (Executive Editor & Company), "They Write the News" (Exec Editor), "Mirror Mirror" (Girl), "Front Page Expose" (Exec Editor & Reporters), "Dad" (Girl), "Hot Flashes (I)" (Reporters), "She's on File" (Exec Editor), "Super Singo" (Exec Editor & Reporters), "Dear Felicia" (Exec Editor & Circulation Editor), "Horoscope" (Cheryl, Patrick, Charles, Band), "Hot Flashes (II)" (Band & Reporters), "Classifieds/Personals" (Band, Reporters, Girl, Killer), "Wonderman" (Girl), "Shooting Stars" (Killer), "What's the Angle?" (Reporters & Exec

Editor), "The Contest" (Exec Editor, Reporters, Feature Editor, Band), "Dear Editor" (Killer), "Editorial" (Exec Editor, Reporters, Killer, Band). *Act II*: "Hot Flashes (Financial)" (Band), "Talk to Me" (Killer & Girl), "Pyramid Lead" (Exec Editor & Reporters), "Beautiful People" (Exec Editor, Cheryl, Killer, Reporters, Band), "Hot Flashes (III)" (Reporters & Band), "Sports" (Reporters & Bands), "Open Letter" (Exec Editor, Killer, Company), "Mirror, Mirror" (reprise) (Girl), "Ordinary Extraordinary Day" (Killer & Girl), "What's the Angle?" (reprise) (Reporters & Band), "Violent Crime" (Exec Editor, Girl, Reporters), "What in the World" (Patrick, Reporters, Band), "Acts of God" (Births, Deaths and the Weather) (Company).

On Broadway the press didn't take kindly to the show, as its story attacked their immorality. Opening Act II, for about seven seconds before the Band came on, the first number played itself by means of a sequencer (a machine that enabled two or more synthesizers to play at the same time). This was a first on Broadway. The show received a Tony nomination for score.

489. *Nick and Nora*

Set in Hollywood in 1937.

Before Broadway. It was in the works for five years. It proved exceptionally difficult to raise the money, despite the big names involved. Josie de Guzman played Maria Valdez during previews, but she was fired. Revisions were drastic. The following numbers were cut: "It's Easy," "Battlecry," "Hollywood," "People Like Us," "Cocktails for One," "A Dangerous Man," "The Road to Guadalajara," "See Me," "Time to Go."

The Broadway Run. MARQUIS THEATRE, 12/8/91–12/15/91. 71 previews from 10/8/91. 9 PERFORMANCES. PRESENTED BY Terry Allen Kramer, Charlene & James M. Nederlander, Daryl Roth, and Elizabeth Ireland McCann, in association with James Pentecost & Charles Suisman; MUSIC/DANCE & INCIDENTAL MUSIC: Charles Strouse; LYRICS: Richard Maltby Jr.; BOOK/DIRECTOR: Arthur Laurents; BASED ON characters created by Dashiell Hammett in his *Thin Man* novels, and in the movies from those novels; CHOREOGRAPHER: Tina Paul; ASSISTANT CHOREOGRAPHER: Luis Perez; SETS: Douglas W. Schmidt; COSTUMES: Theoni V. Aldredge; LIGHTING: Jules Fisher; ASSOCIATE LIGHTING: Peggy Eisenhauer; SOUND: Peter Fitzgerald; MUSICAL DIRECTOR/VOCAL DIRECTOR: Jack Lee; ORCHESTRATIONS: Jonathan Tunick; DANCE & INCIDENTAL MUSIC ARRANGEMENTS: Gordon Lowry Harrell; CAST RECORDING on TER (another, American release, was on Jay); PRESS: Jeffrey Richards Associates; CASTING: Stuart Howard & Amy Schecter; ANIMALS BY: William Berloni Theatrical Animals; GENERAL MANAGER: Ralph Roseman; COMPANY MANAGER: Robb Lady; PRODUCTION STAGE MANAGER: Robert Bennett; STAGE MANAGER: Maureen F. Gibson; ASSISTANT STAGE MANAGERS: Andrew Felgin & Cynthia Thole. **Cast:** ASTA: Riley; NORA CHARLES: Joanna Gleason (2) ☆; NICK CHARLES: Barry Bostwick (1) ☆; TRACY GARDNER: Christine Baranski (3); YUKIDO: Thom Sesma (12); MAVIS: Kathy Morath; DELLI: Kristen Wilson; MAX BERNHEIM: Remak Ramsay (5); VICTOR MOISA: Chris Sarandon (4); SPIDER MALLOY: Jeff Brooks (11); LORRAINE BIXBY: Faith Prince (6); EDWARD J. CONNORS: Kip Niven (10); LT. WOLFE: Michael Lombard (7); MARIA VALDEZ: Yvette Lawrence (9); LILY CONNORS: Debra Monk (8); SELZNICK: Hal Robinson; MONSIGNOR FLAHERTY: John Jellison; MARIACHIS: Tim Connell & Kris Phillips; WAITRESS: Kristen Wilson. **Standbys**: Nora/Tracy: Kay McClelland; Nick/Victor: Richard Muenz. **Understudies**: Max/Wolfe: Hal Robinson; Lorraine/Lily: Kathy Morath; Maria: Kristen Wilson; Spider/Connors: John Jellison; Yukido: Kris Phillips; Asta: B.J. **Swings**: Mark Hoebee & Cynthia Thole. **Orchestra**: WOODWINDS: Les Scott, Seymour Red Press, Charles Millard, Dennis Anderson, Wally Kane; TRUMPETS: Brian O'Flaherty, Burt Collins, Kamau Adilifu; TROMBONES: Bruce Bonvissuto & Earl McIntyre; FRENCH HORN: Roger Wendt; VIOLINS: Elliot Rosoff, Ethel Abelson, Melanie Baker, Katsuko Esaki, Marion Guest, Robert Lawrence; CELLI: Anne Callahan & Jeff Szabo; HARP: Francesca Corsi; SYNTHESIZER: Patrick Brady; BASS: Raymond Kilday; DRUMS/PERCUSSION: Ronald Zito. *Act I*: *Scene 1* Nick and Nora's bungalow, the Garden of Allah: "Is There Anything Better than Dancing?" (Nick, Nora, Tracy); *Scene 2* The studio: "Everybody Wants to Do a Musical" [replaced "Now You See Me, Now You Don't" (Tracy), which was cut during previews]; *Scene 3* Lorraine's (Max's version): "Not Me" (Max, Lorraine, Connors); *Scene 4* The studio: "Swell" [replaced "Quartet in Two Bars" (same performers — Nick, Spider, Nora, Victor), which was cut during previews]; *Scene 5* Nick and Nora's bungalow: "As Long as You're Happy" (Nick & Nora), "People Get Hurt" (Lily); *Scene 6* Lorraine's (Victor's version): "Men" (Lorraine, Victor, Connors, Tracy); *Scene 7* Beverly Hills: "May the Best Man Win" (Nick, Nora, Tracy), "Detectiveland" (Company); *Scene 8* Lorraine's: "Look Who's Alone Now" (Nick). *Act II*: *Scene 1* Victor's villa: "Class" (Victor); *Scene 2* Nick & Nora's bungalow: "Let's Go Home" [replaced "There's More" (Nora) and then "Beyond Words" (Nora), both cut during previews. Originally "Let's Go Home" had been the final number]; *Scene 3* Lorraine's (Maria's version); *Scene 4* Lorraine's: "A Busy Night at Lorraine's" (Nick, Nora, Spider, Suspects); *Scene 5* The Big Tamboo: "Boom Chicka Boom" (Maria & Mariachis); *Scene 6* Tracy's terrace: "Let's Go Home" (reprise) (Nick & Nora) [Originally "Let's Go Home" (not the reprise) had been here. Then during previews it was replaced with "The Second Time We Met" (Tracy & Robert) which was cut during previews, and replaced with this reprise].

Broadway reviews were generally disastrous. Joanna Gleason and Chris Sarandon got married in real life. The show received a Tony nomination for score.

490. *The Night That Made America Famous*

A program of dramatized songs written and sung by recording star Harry Chapin, many of them making social comment, and most of them in the rock or country style. Set during the last 15 years.

The Broadway Run. ETHEL BARRYMORE THEATRE, 2/26/75–4/6/75. 47 PERFORMANCES. PRESENTED BY Edgar Lansbury & Joseph Beruh, in association with The Shubert Organization; MUSIC/LYRICS: Harry Chapin; DIRECTOR: Gene Frankel; CHOREOGRAPHER: Doug Rogers; ASSISTANT CHOREOGRAPHER: Mercedes Ellington; SETS: Kert Lundell; COSTUMES: Randy Barcelo; LIGHTING: Imero Fiorentino; LIGHTING SUPERVISOR: Fred Allison; SOUND: Michael Solomon; MUSICAL DIRECTOR: Stephen Chapin; DANCE MUSIC ARRANGEMENTS: John Morris; PRESS: Gifford/Wallace; CASTING: Geri Windsor & Associates, Vincent G. Liff; GENERAL MANAGEMENT: Marvin A. Krauss Associates; COMPANY MANAGER: Al Isaac; PRODUCTION STAGE MANAGER: Herb Vogler; ASSISTANT STAGE MANAGER: Bonnie Walker. *Cast:* Harry Chapin (1) ✩, Kelly Garrett, Delores Hall, Gilbert Price, Bill Starr, Alexandra Borrie, Mercedes Ellington, Sid Marshall, Ernie Pysher, Lynne Thigpen. *Understudies*: For Harry Chapin: Tom Chapin; For Kelly Garrett: Alexandra Borrie; For Delores Hall: Lynne Thigpen; For Gilbert Price: Sid Marshall; For Bill Starr: Ernie Pysher; For Alexandra Borrie/Lynne Thigpen: Mercedes Ellington. *Orchestra*: KEYBOARDS: Stephen Chapin; GUITAR/BANJO/HARMONICA: Tom Chapin; PERCUSSION: Jim Chapin; DRUMS: Howie Fields; LEAD GUITAR: Doug Walker; BASS: John Wallace; CELLO: Mike Masters; WOODWINDS: Buzz Brauner; VIOLIN: Harry Cyekman. *Act I*: Songs of the 1960s: Prologue (Company), "Six String Orchestra" (Harry & Company), "Give Me a Road" (Company), "Sunday Morning Sunshine" (Harry & Company), "It's My Day" (Kelly), "Give Me a Cause" (Company), "Welfare Rag" (Delores, Bill, Gilbert, Company), "Better Place to Be" (Harry & Company), "Give Me a Wall" (Company), "Peace Teachers" (Kelly), "Pigeon Run" (Gilbert), "Changing of the Guard" (Gilbert), "When I Look Up" (Delores), "Sniper" (Harry & Company). *Act II*: Songs of the 1970s: "Great Divide" (Harry), "Taxi" (Harry & Kelly), "Cockeyed John" (Company), "Mr. Tanner" (Harry & Gilbert), "Maxie" (Kelly), Fugue: "Love Can't" (Bill), "When Maudey Wants a Man" (Delores), "I'm a Wonderfully Wicked Woman" (Kelly) [end of Fugue], "Battleground Bummer" (Gilbert), "Stoopid" (Bill), "Cat's in the Cradle" (Harry & Company), "Cockeyed John, Give Me My Dream" (Company), "Too Much World" (Kelly, Delores, Bill, Gilbert, Harry, Company), "As I Grow Older" (Kelly), "Beginning of the End" (Company), Epilogue ("The Night that Made America Famous") (Harry & Company).

Reviews were divided. The show received Tony nominations for Gilbert Price and Kelly Garrett.

491. *Nine*

Set in a Venetian spa, in the early 1960s. There is little actual plot. Italian movie director Guido has come here to revitalize himself creatively and emotionally. After three flops he can't think of a new idea, and is distracted by real and dreamlike intrusions from the women in his life. He sits alone, in a white-tiled set, then gradually 22 women enter, all dressed in black costumes. In a mock Folies Bergere number a feather boa stretches into infinity. In an extended montage Guido's movie idea becomes a lavish spectacle about Casanova, replete with gondolas, chandeliers and elaborate gowns. This is the Grand Canal number, starring Raul Julia and the Pink Ladies. Luisa is Guido's wife; Liliane was his French producer; Claudia is his leading actress; Carla is his mistress.

Before Broadway. In the 1960s Hal Prince was approached by Federico Fellini's agent to see if he would be interested in doing a musical of the Italian director's movie *Otto e mezzo* (*Eight and a Half*). He refused. Maury Yeston, always fascinated by *8½*, finally created the show *Nine*. By 1973 he was ready to present three songs from it at the BROADCAST MEDIA, INC. (BMI) WORKSHOP. He and Mario Fratti collaborated, with Mr. Fratti doing a libretto. In 1979 the musical was given a staged reading at the EUGENE O'NEILL MEMORIAL THEATRE CENTER in Waterford, Conn., and was well received, and won the first Richard Rodgers Production Award for a new musical developed at the Center. But Fellini was withholding the rights to the film, so they couldn't go ahead with a public musical version of his film. Katherine Hepburn, who had seen the staged reading, intervened on behalf of Yeston and Fratti, and Fellini agreed, on condition that his film not be mentioned in any of the advertising. In 1980 Tommy Tune was hired to direct, and, because of creative differences, Mr. Fratti was replaced as librettist by Arthur Kopit. Tommy Tune came up with the idea of having Guido as the only male character in the cast (aside from some school chums of young Guido). Over 1,000 actresses auditioned for the 22 female roles.

The Broadway Run. FORTY-SIXTH STREET THEATRE, 5/9/82–2/4/84. 7 previews. 732 PERFORMANCES. PRESENTED BY Michel Stuart, Harvey J. Klaris and Roger S. Berlind, James M. Nederlander, Francine LeFrak, and Kenneth D. Greenblatt, in association with Shulamith & Michael N. Appell, Jerry Wexler & Michel Kleinman Productions; MUSIC/LYRICS: Maury Yeston; BOOK: Arthur Kopit; BASED ON the Oscar-winning semi-autobiographical Italian movie *Otto e mezzo* (*8½*), written by Federico Fellini; ADAPTED FROM THE ITALIAN BY: Mario Fratti; DIRECTOR: Tommy Tune; CHOREOGRAPHERS: Tommy Tune & Thommie Walsh; SETS: Lawrence Miller; COSTUMES: William Ivey Long; LIGHTING: Marcia Madeira; ASSISTANT LIGHTING: Natasha Katz; SOUND: Jack Mann; MUSICAL SUPERVISOR/ORCHESTRATIONS: Jonathan Tunick; MUSICAL DIRECTOR: Wally Harper; CHORAL COMPOSITION/MUSICAL CONTINUITY: Maury Yeston; CAST RECORDING on Columbia; PRESS: Jacksina & Freedman; CASTING: Hughes/Moss; ARTISTIC ASSOCIATE: Thommie Walsh; GENERAL MANAGEMENT: Weiler/Miller; PRODUCTION STAGE MANAGER: Charles Blackwell; STAGE MANAGER: Bruce H. Lumpkin; ASSISTANT STAGE MANAGER: Nancy Lynch, *Kenneth Cox.* **Cast:** GUIDO CONTINI: Raul Julia (1) ✩, *Bert Convy* (1/10/83–1/24/83), *Raul Julia, Sergio Franchi* (from 5/9/83); GUIDO AT AN EARLY AGE: Cameron Johann; LUISA CONTINI: Karen Akers, *Maureen McGovern* (from 12/6/82), *Eileen Barnett* (from 11/83); CARLA: Anita Morris, *Beth McVey* (5/2/83–5/16/83), *Anita Morris, Beth McVey* (from 8/15/83), *Wanda Richert* (from 9/12/83); CLAUDIA: Shelly Burch, *Kim Criswell* (from 1/31/83), *Barbara Stock, Beth McVey*; GUIDO'S MOTHER: Taina Elg; LILIANE LA FLEUR: Liliane Montevecchi, *Priscilla Lopez* (11/8/82–11/22/82), *Liliane Montevecchi*; LINA DARLING: Laura Kenyon; STEPHANIE NECROPHORUS: Stephanie Cotsirilos, *Rita Rehn*; OUR LADY OF THE SPA: Kate Dezina; MAMA MADDELENA, CHIEF OF CHAMBERMAIDS: Camille Saviola; SARAGHINA: Kathi Moss, *Jennifer Light*; THE

ITALIANS: MARIA: Jeanie Bowers; FRANCESCA: Kim Criswell, *Beth McVey*; VENETIAN GONDOLIER: Colleen Dodson; GIULIETTA: Louise Edeiken; ANNABELLA: Nancy McCall; DIANA: Cynthia Meryl, *Nancy Callman*; RENATA: Rita Rehn, *Lauren Mitchell, Catherine Campbell*; THE GERMANS: GRETCHEN VON KRUPF: Lulu Downs; HEIDI VON STURM: Linda Kerns; OLGA VON STURM: Dee Etta Rowe; ILSA VON HESSE: Alaina Warren Zachary; YOUNG GUIDO'S SCHOOLMATES: Evans Allen (*Andrew Cassese, Scott Grimes*), Jadrien Steele, Patrick Wilcox; SOLO DANCER: Tina Paul. **Standby**: Guido: Clifford David. **Understudies**: Luisa: Cynthia Meryl, *Colleen Dodson*; Liliane: Cynthia Meryl, *Patrice Pickering*; Claudia: Kim Criswell, *Colleen Dodson*; Carla: Kim Criswell, *Laura Kenyon*; Guido's Mother: Alaina Warren Zachary, *Nancy McCall*; Our Lady of the Spa: Colleen Dodson, *Patrice Pickering*; Stephanie: Rita Rehn, *Laura Kenyon*; Saraghina: Camille Saviola, *Linda Kerns*; Mama Maddelena: Lulu Downs, *Alaina Warren Zachary*; Young Guido: Patrick Wilcox; Germans: Julie J. Hafner, *Leigh Finner*; Italians: Dorothy Kiara, *Patrice Pickering*; Lina: Dorothy Kiara & Patrice Pickering. **Act I**: "Overture delle Donne" (Company): "Spa Music," "Not Since Chaplin" [end of Overture], "Guido's Song" (Guido), "Coda di Guido" [this number is an appendix to "Guido's Song"] (Company), The Germans at the Spa (Mama, Italians, Germans), "My Husband Makes Movies" (Luisa), "A Call from the Vatican" (Carla), "Only With You" (Guido), "Folies Bergere" (Liliane, Stephanie, Company), "Nine" (Guido's Mother & Company), "Ti Voglio Bene"/"Be Italian" (Saraghina, Boys, Company), "The Bells of St. Sebastian" (Guido, Boys, Company). **Act II**: "A Man Like You"/"Unusual Way" (duet) (Claudia & Guido), "Now's the Moment" (Guido) [added for the subsequent national tour], The Grand Canal (Guido & Company): Contini Submits/The Grand Canal/Tarantella/Every Girl in Venice/Marcia di Ragazzi (Pas de Boys)/Recitativo/Amor/Recitativo/Only You/Finale [end of Grand Canal sequence], "Simple" (Carla), "Be on Your Own" (Luisa), "Waltz di Guido" [cut before Broadway], "I Can't Make This Movie" (Guido), "Getting Tall" (Young Guido), "Nine"/"Long Ago"/"Nine" (Guido).

Broadway reviews were divided. The show won Tonys for musical, score, direction of a musical, costumes, and for Liliane Montevecchi, and was also nominated for book, choreography, sets, lighting, and for Raul Julia, Karen Akers, and Anita Morris. Miss Morris's risque number "A Call from the Vatican" was considered too salacious to be broadcast on the Tony awards ceremony on TV.

After Broadway. TOUR. Opened on 3/31/84, at the Kennedy Center, Washington, DC. The set was changed from a spa to a railroad station in order to make transporting the sets easier. CHOREOGRAPHERS: Thommie Walsh & JoAnn Ogawa; MUSICAL SUPERVISOR: Tommy Crasker. **Cast**: GUIDO: Sergio Franchi; LUISA: Diane M. Hurley; LILIANE: Jacqueline Douguet; CARLA: Karen Tamburelli; CLAUDIA: Lauren Mitchell; SARAGHINA: Camille Saviola; GUIDO'S MOTHER: Leigh Beery; ISHI DARLING: Chikae Ishikawa (note change of character name).

PAPER MILL PLAYHOUSE, New Jersey, 1995. DIRECTOR: Robert Johanson; CHOREOGRAPHER: D.J. Salisbury; SETS: Michael Anania; MUSICAL DIRECTOR: Jim Coleman. **Cast**: Judith McCauley, Judy McLane, Glory Crampton, Stephanie Pope, Paul Schoeffler, Lauren Kennedy, Sally Ann Tumas, Paolo Montalban, Valerie Cutko.

FOLIES BERGERE, Paris, 9/16/97–11/15/97. The French adaptation. It failed. FRENCH LYRICS: Eric-Emmanuel Schmitt; DIRECTOR: Saverio Marconi; CHOREOGRAPHER: Fabrizio Angelini; SETS/COSTUMES: David Belugou. **Cast**: GUIDO: Jerome Pradon; CLAUDIA: Lisbet Bongarcon; SARAGHINA: Mimma Lovoi; NOTRE DAME DES LUNES: Alyssa Landry (this was the Our Lady of the Spa character).

492. *Nine* (*Broadway revival*)

Before Broadway. This revival had its origins several years in the past, when a revised form of *Nine* was presented at the DONMAR WAREHOUSE, London, 12/12/96–3/8/97. Previews from 12/6/96. DIRECTOR: David Leveaux; CHOREOGRAPHER: Jonathan Butterell; SETS/COSTUMES: Anthony Ward; LIGHTING: Paul Pyant; SOUND: John A. Leonard; MUSICAL DIRECTOR: Gareth Valentine. **Cast**: GUIDO: Larry Lamb; YOUNG GUIDO: Ian Covington; GUIDO'S MOTHER: Dilys Laye; SARAGHINA: Jenny Galloway; CARLA: Clare Burt; LILIANE: Sara Kestelman; LUISA:

Susannah Fellows; ALSO WITH: Ria Jones, Eleanor David, Stuart Neal, Owen Proctor Jackson, Norma Atallah, Sarah Parish, Kristin Marks, Tessa Pritchard, Emma Dears. Producer Gustavo Levit saw the 1996 London production, and bought the rights, signed Gerardo Romano as Guido for the Argentinean version (called *Nueve*), but then suspended production. Mr. Romano quit, and Juan Darthes came in when it resumed at the METROPOLITAN THEATRE 2, Buenos Aires, 5/7/98–9/6/98. It failed. DIRECTOR: David Leveaux; CHOREOGRAPHER: Jonathan Butterell; SETS/COSTUMES: Anthony Ward; MUSICAL DIRECTOR: Omar Cyrulnik. **Cast**: GUIDO: Juan Darthes; LILIANE: Luz Kerz; LUISA: Andrea Cantoni; CARLA: Sandra Ballesteros.

On 8/2/02 *Variety* reported that this revival would be produced on Broadway. It had an initial staged reading at the Eugene O'Neill Music Theatre Conference, in Waterford, Conn. At first Roundabout was considering putting it into Studio 54, but *Cabaret* was there, and running well. On 8/15/02 Antonio Banderas was confirmed in his role. On 10/23/02 it was announced that Mary Stuart Masterson had been offered the role of Luisa. This was Chita Rivera's first Broadway performance since *Kiss of the Spider Woman*. The show also marked the return to the stage of Laura Benanti who had been injured during *Into the Woods*. This was a smaller production of *Nine*, 16 women instead of 21, and one boy instead of four. Broadway previews were delayed from 3/11/03 to 3/18/03, then to 3/21/03.

The Broadway Run. EUGENE O'NEILL THEATRE, 4/10/03–12/14/03. 23 previews from 3/21/03. 283 PERFORMANCES. PRESENTED BY the Roundabout Theatre Company; MUSIC/LYRICS: Maury Yeston; BOOK: Arthur Kopit; BASED ON Federico Fellini's movie *Otto e mezzo* (8½); ADAPTED FROM THE ITALIAN BY: Mario Fratti; DIRECTOR: David Leveaux; CHOREOGRAPHER: Jonathan Butterell; SETS: Scott Pask; COSTUMES: Vicki Mortimer; LIGHTING: Brian MacDevitt; SOUND: Jon Weston; MUSICAL DIRECTOR: Kevin Stites; ORCHESTRATIONS: Jonathan Tunick; NEW CAST RECORDING on PS Classics, recorded in Manhattan on 4/28/03, and released on 6/17/03; PRESS: Boneau/Bryan-Brown; CASTING: Jim Carnahan & Jeremy Rich; ASSOCIATE ARTISTIC DIRECTOR: Scott Ellis; GENERAL MANAGER: Sydney Davolos; COMPANY MANAGER: Barbara Crompton; PRODUCTION STAGE MANAGER: Arthur Gaffin; STAGE MANAGER: Laurie Goldfeder; ASSISTANT STAGE MANAGER: Bradley McCormick. **Cast**: LITTLE GUIDO: William Ullrich, Anthony Colangelo (Wednesday & Saturday matinees), *Evan Daves & Daniel Manche*; GUIDO CONTINI: Antonio Banderas ☆ (until 10/5/03), *John Stamos* (from 10/7/03), *Paul Schoeffler* (stood in 11/15/03–11/18/03); LUISA CONTINI: Mary Stuart Masterson ☆; CARLA: Jane Krakowski ☆ (until 10/5/03), *Sara Gettelfinger* (from 10/7/03); RENATA, AN ITALIAN: Elena Shaddow, *Nikki Renee Daniels*; GUIDO'S MOTHER: Mary Beth Peil (until 10/5/03), *Marni Nixon* (from 10/7/03); STEPHANIE NECROPHORUS: Saundra Santiago; DIANA, AN ITALIAN: Rachel de Benedet; OLGA VON STURM, A GERMAN: Linda Mugleston, *Farah Alvin*; MARIA, AN ITALIAN: Sara Gettelfinger (until 10/03), *Christine Arand*; LINA DARLING: Nell Campbell; SOFIA: Kathy Voytko, *Jessica Leigh Brown* (stood in); SARAGHINA: Myra Lucretia Taylor; JULIETTE: Rona Figueroa; ANNABELLA, AN ITALIAN: Kristin Marks; CLAUDIA: Laura Benanti ☆ (until 8/31/03), *Rebecca Luker* (from 9/2/03); OUR LADY OF THE SPA: Deidre Goodwin (until 6/22/03), *Jacqueline Hendy* (from 6/24/03); LILIANE LA FLEUR: Chita Rivera ☆ (until 10/5/03), *Eartha Kitt* (from 10/7/03). **Standby**: Guido: Paul Schoeffler. **Understudies**: Annabella/Juliette/Maria/Renata: Stephanie Bast; Liliane: Nell Campbell & *Leslie Becker*; Diana/Olga/Sofia: Jessica Leigh Brown; Lina: Rona Figueroa; Carla: Sara Gettelfinger, *Rona Figueroa*; Stephanie: Sara Gettelfinger, *Leslie Becker*; Luisa: Kristin Marks & Linda Mugleston, *Leslie Becker*; Saraghina: Linda Mugleston, *Farah Alvin, Kristin Marks*; Claudia: Elena Shaddow, *Stephanie Bast, Kathy Voytko*; Our Lady: Kathy Voytko, *Rachel de Benedet*; Guido's Mother: Rachel de Benedet & *Leslie Becker*. **Swing**: Stephanie Bast, Leslie Becker, Jessica Leigh Brown. **Orchestra**: CONCERTMASTER/VIOLIN: Martin Agee; VIOLIN II: Conrad Harris; VIOLA: Liuh-Wen Ting; CELLO: Sarah Seiver; BASS: Brian Cassier; FLUTE: Brian Miller; CLARINET/SAX: Les Scott; BASSOON: Marc Goldberg; FRENCH HORN: Theresa MacDonnell; TRUMPETS: Timothy Schadt & Raymond Riccomini; TROMBONE: Randy Andos; HARP: Barbara Biggers; DRUMS/PERCUSSION: Bill Miller; KEYBOARD: Gregory Dlugos. **Act I**: "Overture delle Donne" (Company): "Spa Music," "Not Since Chaplin" [end of Overture],

"Guido's Song" (Guido); "Coda di Guido" (Company) [this number is an appendix to "Guido's Song"], "My Husband Makes Movies" (Luisa), "A Call from the Vatican" (Carla), "Only With You" (Guido), "The Script" (Guido), "Folies Bergere" (La Fleur, Necrophorus, Company), "Nine" (Guido's Mother & Company), "Ti Voglio Bene"/"Be Italian" (Saraghina, Little Guido, Company), "The Bells of St. Sebastian" (Guido, Little Guido, Company). *Act II*: "A Man Like You"/"Unusual Way" (Duet) (Claudia & Guido), "The Grand Canal" (Guido & Company): Contini Submits/The Grand Canal/Every Girl in Venice/Recitativo/ Amor/Recitativo/Only You/Finale [end of Grand Canal sequence], "Simple" (Carla), "Be on Your Own" (Luisa), "Waltz di Guido" (Guido), "I Can't Make This Movie" (Guido), "Getting Tall" (Little Guido), "My Husband Makes Movies" (reprise)/"Nine" (reprise) (Guido).

It was meant to be a limited run, up to 6/29/03, but a day after the show officially opened (to good reviews) it extended to 8/10/03, and then to 10/03, and finally to 1/4/04 (but it finally closed on 12/14/03). The show won Tonys for revival of a musical, and for Jane Krakowski. It was nominated for direction of a musical, lighting, orchestrations, and for Antonio Banderas, Mary Elizabeth Mastrantonio, Mary Stuart Masterson, and Chita Rivera. It missed a performance due to the 8/14/03 power blackout. Mary Stuart Masterson was going to leave on 10/5/03, but extended her run to the end. Jenna Elfman was going to take over as Carla on 10/7/03, but her start was delayed by the director because he felt she should have more rehearsal time. In the end understudy Sara Gettelfinger got the role.

493. *The 1940s Radio Hour*

Set in WOV Broadcast Studios, in the Algonquin Room, on the ground floor of the Hotel Astor, New York City, on Dec. 21, 1942, about 8 p.m. A simulation of events and personalities of a 1940s live radio broadcast of "The Mutual Manhattan Variety Cavalcade," with hit tunes of the period. There was no intermission.

Before Broadway. In late 1972 Walton Jones presented a one-man radio drama in a Tampa theatre. Songs, and the character of the radio studio, were added, and on 7/18/74 *The 1940s Radio Hour* opened at New Haven's Ensemble Company's Summer Cabaret. It had its world premiere as a special presentation at YALE REPERTORY THEATRE, 12/28/77. 16 PERFORMANCES. At that stage the show was set in the time period 12/28/42–1/14/43. PRESENTED BY Robert Brustein; DIRECTOR: Walton Jones; CHOREOGRAPHERS: Wesley Fata, Joe Grifasi, Rebecca Nelson, Eric Elice, Caris Corfman; SETS: Nancy Thun; LIGHTING: Robert Heller; MUSICAL DIRECTOR: Gary Fagin; VOCAL DIRECTOR: Paul Schierhorn; ARRANGEMENTS: Gary Fagin & Paul Schierhorn. *Cast*: BIFF: John Doolittle; SAMMY BRYANT: Eric Elice; JOHNNY: Stephen Rowe; CLIFTON FEDIMAN: Walt Jones; BUDDY GIBSON: Richard Bey; MIMI LA ROCHE: Rebecca Nelson; CONNIE: Caris Corfman; NATALIA NAVARRO: Shaine Marinson; BABS RITCHIE: Joe Grifasi; EVELYN VAUGHN: Nancy Mayans; SKIP WILLIS: Tom Derrall; POP: James Haverly; GRIP: H. Lloyd Carbaugh; BEST BOY: Richard Houpert. With the Zoot Doubleman Orchestra. In 1978 a tour opened at the Loeb Drama Center, Boston. PRESENTED BY Robert Brustein.

The first time it was produced in its final (i.e. Broadway) form was at the ARENA STAGE THEATRE, Washington, DC, 11/8/78. 64 PERFORMANCES. DIRECTOR: Walton Jones; CHOREOGRAPHER: Thommie Walsh; MUSICAL DIRECTOR: Gary Fagin; VOCAL DIRECTOR: Paul Schierhorn; ARRANGEMENTS: Gary Fagin & Paul Schierhorn. *Cast*: Sherman Lloyd, David Lipman, Timothy Jerome, Jack Hallett, Stephen James, Crissy Wilzak, Franchelle Stewart Dorn. In 12/78 a special version was presented at the White House Christmas Party. In 1979 it went to Broadway.

The Broadway Run. ST. JAMES THEATRE, 10/7/79–1/6/80. 14 previews. 105 PERFORMANCES. PRESENTED BY Jujamcyn Productions, Joseph P. Harris, Ira Bernstein, Roger Berlind; MUSIC/LYRICS/BOOK/DIRECTOR: Walton Jones; BASED ON an idea by Walton Jones & Carol Lees; CHOREOGRAPHER: Thommie Walsh; SETS: David Gropman; COSTUMES: William Ivey Long; LIGHTING: Tharon Musser; SOUND: Otts Munderloh; ASSISTANT SOUND: Tony Meola; MUSICAL SUPERVISOR/MUSICAL

DIRECTOR: Stanley Lebowsky; ASSISTANT CONDUCTOR/VOCAL ARRANGEMENTS: Paul Schierhorn; ORCHESTRATIONS: Gary S. Fagin; PRESS: The Merlin Group; CASTING: Johnson—Liff; GENERAL MANAGER: Frank Scardino; COMPANY MANAGER: Susan Bell; PRODUCTION STAGE MANAGER: Edwin Aldridge; STAGE MANAGER: Craig Jacobs; ASSISTANT STAGE MANAGER: James Lockhart. *Cast*: POPS BAILEY: Arny Freeman; STANLEY: John Sloman; CLIFTON A. FEDDINGTON: Josef Sommer; ZOOT DOUBLEMAN: Stanley Lebowsky; WALLY FERGUSSON: Jack Hallett; LOU COHN: Merwin Goldsmith; JOHNNY CANTONE: Jeff Keller; GINGER BROOKS: Crissy Wilzak; CONNIE MILLER: Kathy Andrini; B.J. GIBSON: Stephen James; NEAL TILDEN: Joe Grifasi; ANN COLLIER: Mary-Cleere Haran; GENEVA LEE BROWNE: Dee Dee Bridgewater; BIFF BAKER: John Doolittle; DARLA—WOV PAGE: Jo Speros; *Orchestra*: ZOOT DOUBLEMAN: Stanley Lebowsky; NEELEY "FLAPS" KOVACS: Maurice Mark; BONNIE CAVANAUGH: Jane Ira Bloom; CUSTIS JONES: Billy Butler; GUS BRACKEN: Ray Shanfield; SCOOPS MILLIKAN: Dennis Elliot; MOE "LOCKJAW" AMBROSE: Josh Edwards; BIFF BAKER: John Doolittle; FRITZ CANIGLIARO: Joe Petrizzo; CHARLIE "KID LIPS" SNYDER: Dennis Anderson; NED "WOOF" BENNETT: J.D. Parran; TOOTS SCHOENFELD: Mel Rodnon; RED BRADFORD: Rick Centalonza [this character was previously called Fess "Snookie" Davenport]; BOB "BOBO" LEWIS: Jon Goldman; BUZZ CRANSHAW: Ron Tooley; PHIL BENTLEY: Bruce Samuels; PIEFACE MINELLI: Lloyd Michaels. *Standbys*: Ann/Ginger: Susan Elizabeth Scott; Geneva: Etta Green; Johnny/Neal: Bob Freschi; Biff/Wally/Stanley: Lynn Stafford; Pops/Lou/Feddington: James Lockhart. *Understudies*: Connie: Jo Speros; B.J.: John Sloman. "Chattanooga Choo Choo" (m: Harry Warren; l: Mack Gordon) [from the movie *Sun Valley Serenade*] (Feddington, Ann, Geneva Lee, Neal, B.J., Connie, Ginger, Wally), "How About You" (m: Burton Lane; l: Ralph Freed) [from the movie *Babes on Broadway*] (B.J. & Connie), "Blue Moon" (m: Richard Rodgers; l: Lorenz Hart) (Neal), "Have Yourself a Merry Little Christmas" (m/l: Ralph Blane & Hugh Martin) [from the movie *Meet Me in St. Louis*] (Ann), "I Got it Bad and That Ain't Good" (m: Duke Ellington; l: Paul Francis Webster) [from *Jump for Joy*], "Little Brown Jug" (the Bill Finegan arrangement used by the Glenn Miller Band), "At Last" (m: Harry Warren; l: Mac Gordon) [from the movie *Orchestra Wives*] (B.J.), "Jingle Bells" (the Bill Finegan, Glenn Miller, Eddie Sauter arrangement) (Biff, Neal, Group), "I'll Be Seeing You" (m: Sammy Fain; l: Irving Kahal) [from *Right This Way*] (Company), "(Our) Love is Here to Stay" (m: George Gershwin; l: Ira Gershwin) [from the movie *The Goldwyn Follies*], "You, You're Driving Me Crazy" (m/l: Matt Dennis), "Boogie Woogie Bugle Boy from Company B" (m/l: Don Raye & Hughie Prince) (B.J., Connie, Ginger), "I'll Never Smile Again" (m/l: Ruth Lowe) [from the movie *Las Vegas Night*] (Neal, B.J., Ann, Ginger, Connie, Johnny), "Rose of the Rio Grande" (m: Harry Warren & Ross Gorman; l: Edgar Leslie) (Geneva Lee, Men, Band), "Ain't She Sweet" (m: Milton Ager; l: Jack Yellen) (Biff, B.J., Ginger, Geneva Lee, All), "Blues in the Night" (m: Harold Arlen; l: Johnny Mercer) [from the movie *Blues in the Night*] (Ginger & Men), "Strike up the Band" (m: George Gershwin; l: Ira Gershwin) [from the movie *Strike Up the Band*] (Company), "Daddy" (m/l: Bobby Troupe) (The Band & Connie), "That Old Black Magic" (m: Harold Arlen; l: Johnny Mercer) [from the movie *Star Spangled Rhythm*] (Ann), "The Mutual Manhattan Variety Cavalcade" (m: Stanley Lebowsky), "Chiquita Banana" (m/l: Len Mackenzie, Garth Montgomery, William Wirges) (All Girls), "Pepsi-Cola Radio Jingle" (Neal, B.J., Connie, Ginger, Feddington).

Reviews were not great, and recommended it only for nostalgia buffs.

After Broadway. THE THEATRE IN THE SQUARE, Marietta, Ga., has been putting it on every Christmas season since 1982.

PAPER MILL PLAYHOUSE, New Jersey, 1995. DIRECTOR/CHOREOGRAPHER: Robert Johanson; SETS: Michael Anania; MUSICAL DIRECTOR: Jim Coleman. *Cast*: Larry Grey, Donna Kane, Melodee Savage, John Scherer, Dorothy Stanley, Lenny Wolpe, Bob Walton.

494. *No, No, Nanette*

Set on a weekend in early summer 1925 in the Smiths' New York City home, and at Chickadee Cottage, Atlantic City. Jimmy, a married bible publisher, and guardian of Nanette, has been giving financial support to three flappers in three different cities. Finally, of course, everyone, including Jimmy's attorney Billy and sarcastic comedy maid Pauline, meets at Chickadee Cottage.

Before Broadway. The original was one of the most popular Broadway musicals of the 1920s, running at the GLOBE THEATRE, 9/16/25–6/19/26. 321 PERFORMANCES. PRESENTED BY/DIRECTOR: H.H. Frazee. **Cast**: JIMMY: Charles Winninger; NANETTE: Louise Groody; ALSO WITH: Eleanor Dawn. Certain numbers from this production were cut for the 1971 revival—"The Boy Next Door," "I Don't Want a Girlie," and "Santa Claus."" It was filmed in 1930. DIRECTOR: Clarence Badger. **Cast**: NANETTE: Bernice Claire. It was filmed again in 1940. PRODUCER/DIRECTOR: Herbert Wilcox. **Cast**: Anna Neagle. This time the music was relegated to the background.

Harry Rigby conceived the idea of a revival, but was bought out by his co-producer Cyma Rubin (actually she erased his name from the billing, but he successfully sued her for $300,000 and got his name reinstated). Burt Shevelove replaced Busby Berkeley as director, even though Mr. Berkeley, then 75, had done very little except lend his name to the show. Mr. Shevelove also provided additional lyrics, replacing Charles Gaynor in that role. Mr. Shevelove also adapted the original book, another job he took over from Mr. Gaynor. Additional music by Mr. Gaynor was deleted during the well-received Boston tryouts. The original choreography for this revival was by Mr. Berkeley, assisted by Ted Cappy, Mary Ann Niles and Bobby Van, but all those were replaced by Donald Saddler. In the cast, first-featured Carole Demas was replaced by Susan Watson; Hiram Sherman was replaced by Frank McHugh, who was, in turn, replaced by Jack Gilford. This was Ruby Keeler's return to Broadway after 41 years.

The Broadway Run. FORTY-SIXTH STREET THEATRE, 1/19/71–2/4/73. 13 previews from 1/6/71. 861 PERFORMANCES. PRESENTED BY Pyxidium Ltd (Cyma Rubin); MUSIC: Vincent Youmans; LYRICS: Irving Caesar, Otto Harbach, Zelda Sears; BOOK: Otto Harbach & Frank Mandel (book adapted by Burt Shevelove); BASED ON the 1919 three-act farce *My Lady Friends*, by Emil Nyitray & Frank Mandel, which, in turn, was based on the story *Oh, James/His Ladyfriends*, by May Edington; DIRECTOR: Burt Shevelove; CHOREOGRAPHER: Donald Saddler; ASSISTANT CHOREOGRAPHER: Mary Ann Niles; TAP CHOREOGRAPHY SUPERVISORS: Mary Ann Niles & Ted Cappy; SETS/COSTUMES: Raoul Pene du Bois; ASSISTANT COSTUMES: David Toser; LIGHTING: Jules Fisher; SOUND: Jack Shearing; MUSICAL DIRECTOR/VOCAL ARRANGEMENTS: Buster Davis; ORCHESTRATIONS: Ralph Burns; DANCE MUSIC ARRANGEMENTS/INCIDENTAL MUSIC: Luther Henderson; AT TWIN PIANOS: Colston & Clements; CAST RECORDING on Columbia; PRESS: Merle Debuskey, M.J. Boyer (*Robert W. Larkin*), Faith Geer; PRODUCTION SUPERVISOR: Busby Berkeley; GENERAL MANAGEMENT: Gatchell & Neufeld; PRODUCTION STAGE MANAGER: *Marnel Sumner* (by 71–72); STAGE MANAGER: Robert Schear, *Michael Turque*; ASSISTANT STAGE MANAGER: John H. Lowe III, *Mary Ann Niles*. **Cast**: PAULINE: Patsy Kelly (6) ✫, *Ruth Donnelly* (during Miss Kelly's illness), *Ruth Donnelly, Lillian Hayman* (10/30/72–11/6/72), *Martha Raye* (from 11/6/72); LUCILLE EARLY: Helen Gallagher (4) ✫; SUE SMITH: Ruby Keeler (1) ✫, *Penny Singleton* (8/16/71–8/31/71), *Ruby Keeler, Ruth Maitland* (3/27/72–4/4/72), *Ruby Keeler, Ruth Maitland* (7/31/72–8/14/72), *Ruby Keeler, Ruth Maitland* (11/6/72–11/13/72), *Joy Hodges* (from 11/13/72); JIMMY SMITH: Jack Gilford (2) ✫, *Ted Tiller* (from 1/3/72), *Benny Baker* (from 1/10/72); BILLY EARLY: Bobby Van (3) ✫, *Larry Ellis, Anthony S. Teague* (from 4/10/72), *Bobby Van* (from 8/1/72); TOM TRAINOR: Roger Rathburn (7); NANETTE: Susan Watson (5) ✫, *Barbara Heuman* (from 12/71); FLORA LATHAM: K.C. Townsend (9), *Sandra O'Neill* (from 3/17/71), *Sally Cooke* (from 8/71); BETTY BROWN: Loni Zoe Ackerman (8), *Jilly Jaress, Linda Rose* (from 1/73); WINNIE WINSLOW: Pat Lysinger (10), *Gwen Miller, Judy Knaiz* (from 5/1/72); NANETTE'S FRIENDS: Bob Becker, John Beecher, Joretta Bohannon (gone by 71–72), Roger Braun (gone by 71–72), Marcia Brushingham, Kenneth Carr, Jennie Chandler, Kathy Conry, Christine Cox (gone by 71–72), Kevin Daly (gone by 71–72), Ed Dixon (gone by 71–72), Ellen Elias, Mercedes Ellington, Jon Engstrom, Marian Haraldson, Gregg Harlan, Jamie Haskins (gone by 71–72), Gwen Hillier (gone by 71–72), Sayra Hummel, Scott Hunter,

Dottie Lester (gone by 71–72), Cheryl Locke (gone by 71–72), Joanne Lotsko (gone by 71–72), Mary Ann Niles (gone by 71–72), Kate O'Brady (gone by 71–72), Sue Ohman (gone by 71–72), Jill Owens, Ken Ploss (gone by 71–72), John Roach (gone by 71–72), Linda Rose, Ron Schwinn, Sonja Stuart (gone by 71–72), Monica Tiller, Pat Trott, Phyllis Wallach. 71–72 replacements: *Douglas Allen, Cindi Bulak, Andrea Duda, Lynne Gannaway, Reggie Israel, Frances Ruth Lea, Christopher Nelson, Frank Newell, Sally O'Donnell, Shelly Rann, James Robinson, Bobbie Rhine, Stefan J. Ross, Kathie Savage, Denny Shearer*. **Standbys**: Sue: Betty Wragge; Jimmy: Ted Tiller; Pauline: Dorothy Claire. **Understudies**: Sue: Ruth Maitland; Pauline: Ruth Donnelly; Billy: Roger Braun, *Denny Shearer*; Lucille: Pat Lysinger, *Judy Knaiz*; Nanette: Kathy Conry; Tom: Kenneth Carr; Betty: Linda Rose; Flora: Dottie Lester, *Cindi Bulak*; Winnie: Gwen Hillier, *Sayra Hummel*.

Note: the girls in the chorus were the Busby Berkeley Girls, and all received joint 11th billing. *Act I*: The home of James Smith, New York City: "Too Many Rings Around Rosie" (l: Caesar) (Lucille, Boys & Girls), "I've Confessed to the Breeze" (l: Harbach) (Nanette & Tom) [song added for this new production], "The Call of the Sea" (l: Harbach) (Billy & Girls), "I Want to Be Happy" (l: Caesar) (Jimmy, Nanette, Sue, Boys & Girls), "No, No, Nanette" (l: Harbach) (Nanette & Tom), Finaletto Act I (Nanette, Boys & Girls). *Act II*: The garden of Chickadee Cottage, Atlantic City: "A Peach on the Beach" (l: Harbach) (Nanette, Boys & Girls) [song added for this new production; it replaced "The Deep Blue Sea," "My Doctor" and "Fight Over Me"], "Tea for Two" (l: Caesar) (Nanette, Tom, Boys & Girls), "You Can Dance With Any Girl (At All)" (l: Caesar) (Lucille & Billy), "Finaletto Act II" (Entire Company). *Act III*: The living room at Chickadee Cottage: "(Hello Hello) Telephone Girlie" (l: Harbach) (Billy, Betty, Flora, Winnie), "Who's the Who?" ("The Where-Has-My-Hubby-Gone Blues") (l: Caesar) (Lucille & Boys), "Waiting for You" (l: Harbach) (Nanette & Tom) [this number replaced the 1925 production's "Pay Day Pauline" (l: Harbach)], "Take a Little One-Step" (l: Sears) (Sue, Billy, Lucille, Pauline, Boys & Girls) [song added for this new production], Finale (Entire Company).

Note: The lyricist is noted in parentheses.

The show got very good Broadway reviews. It won Tonys for choreography, costumes, and for Helen Gallagher and Patsy Kelly. It was also nominated for direction of a musical, and for Bobby Van.

After Broadway. TOUR. Opened on 12/27/71, at the Hanna Theatre, Cleveland. **Cast**: SUE: June Allyson, *Virginia Mayo* (from 10/30/72); JIMMY: Dennis Day, *Elliott Reid*; PAULINE: Judy Canova; NANETTE: Dana Swenson; FLORA: Laura Waterbury; WINNIE: Gwen Hillier; BETTY: Connie Danese; TOM: Bill Biskup; LUCILLE: Sandra Deel, *Arlene Fontanna* (from 1/73); BILLY: Jerry Andes.

TOUR. Opened on 10/6/72, at the Music Hall, Dallas, and closed on 8/4/73, at the Garden State Arts Center, Woodbridge, NJ. **Cast**: SUE: Evelyn Keyes; JIMMY: Don Ameche; PAULINE: Ruth Donnelly, *Ann B. Davis*; BILLY: Swen Swenson; NANETTE: Darlene Anders. It opened again on 9/14/73, at Scranton, Pa., still with Evelyn Keyes, but this time with JIMMY: Benny Baker; PAULINE: Betty Kean, and closed on 3/12/74, after 93 cities.

LONDON. Opened on 5/15/73. 277 PERFORMANCES. **Cast**: SUE: Anna Neagle; JIMMY: Tony Britton; BILLY: Teddy Green; LUCILLE: Anne Rogers; PAULINE: Thora Hird; NANETTE: Susan Maudslay; TOM: Peter Gale; FLORA: Anita Graham; BETTY: Elaine Holland.

PAPER MILL PLAYHOUSE, New Jersey, 9/18/73–11/30/73. DIRECTOR: John Lowe III; MUSICAL DIRECTOR: Glen Clugston. **Cast**: Dennis Day, Barbara Britton, Helen Gallagher, Lillian Hayman, Jerry Andes, Cynthia Parva.

CARNEGIE HALL, 4/2/86–4/6/86. 5 PERFORMANCES. Concert version. DIRECTOR/CONDUCTOR: John McGlinn. **Cast**: PAULINE: Jane Connell; SUE: Leigh Beery; NANETTE: Rebecca Luker; BILLY: Cris Groenendaal; TOM: George Dvorsky; LUCILLE: Judy Kaye; WINNIE: Maureen Brennan. Overture, Opening Act I, "The Call of the Sea," "Too Many Rings Around Rosie," "I've Confessed to the Breeze," "I Want to Be Happy," "Charleston Specialty," "No, No, Nanette," Finale Act I, "A Peach on the Beach," "My Doctor," "Fight Over Me," "Tea for Two," "You Can Dance With Any Girl," Finale Act II, "Hello Hello, Telephone Girlie," "The Where-Has-My-Hubby-Gone Blues," "Take a Little One-Step," "Pay-Day Pauline," Finale Ultimo.

PAPER MILL PLAYHOUSE, New Jersey, 4/9/97–5/25/97. DIRECTOR/CHOREOGRAPHER: Donald Saddler; MUSICAL DIRECTOR: Jim Coleman. *Cast*: PAULINE: Kaye Ballard; JIMMY: Eddie Bracken; SUE: Helen Gallagher; BILLY: Lee Roy Reams; LUCILLE: Virginia Sandifur.

GOODSPEED OPERA HOUSE, Conn., 7/30/99–10/2/99. Previews from 7/9/99. This was the 1971 Broadway version. DIRECTOR: Stephen Terrell; SETS: Howard Jones; COSTUMES: Suzy Benzinger; LIGHTING: Mary Jo Dondlinger; MUSICAL DIRECTOR: Michael O'Flaherty. *Cast*: PAULINE: Marilyn Cooper; NANETTE: Andrea Chamberlain; TOM: Joel Carlton; JIMMY: Gerry Vichi; SUE: Margery Beddow; BILLY: Mark Martino; FLORA: Tanya Perkins; WINNIE: Jessica Wright.

495. *No Strings*

Barbara is an internationally successful model in Paris who falls in love with expatriate American former Pulitzer Prize–winning novelist David, who has lost confidence in his writing abilities and is beginning to lapse into the idle life led by his buddy Mike, who is being supported by Oklahoma heiress, Comfort. Barbara gives up her job and goes away with David to a secluded place where he can write, but they quarrel, and David goes off with Mike and Comfort on a trip. Barbara finally convinces David to return to Maine, to try to resume his career. The couple finally splits, but with options left open — "no strings." No mention is made of racial color.

Before Broadway. Richard Rodgers was watching *The Tonight Show* on TV (while Jack Paar was still host) when he saw Diahann Carroll singing "Goody, Goody," and decided he must write a musical for her. His partner, Oscar Hammerstein II, was now dead, so Rodgers went it alone, music and lyrics. The show had a cast of 41. The orchestra was on stage, not in the pit. There were no strings, only brass and woodwinds. The principals and chorus moved the scenery in full view of the audience. The number "Yankee, Go Home" was cut before Broadway.

The Broadway Run. FIFTY-FOURTH STREET THEATRE, 3/15/62–9/29/62; BROADHURST THEATRE, 10/1/62–8/3/63. 1 preview on 3/14/62. Total of 580 PERFORMANCES. PRESENTED BY Richard Rodgers, in association with Samuel Taylor; MUSIC/LYRICS: Richard Rodgers; BOOK: Samuel Taylor; DIRECTOR/CHOREOGRAPHER: Joe Layton; ASSOCIATE CHOREOGRAPHER: Buddy Schwab; SETS/LIGHTING: David Hays; COSTUMES: Fred Voelpel & Donald Brooks; MUSICAL DIRECTOR/DANCE MUSIC ARRANGEMENTS: Peter Matz; ASSISTANT CONDUCTOR: Milton Greene; ORCHESTRATIONS: Ralph Burns; CAST RECORDING on Capitol; PRESS: Frank Goodman, Ben Washer, Arlene Wolf; CASTING: Edward Blum; PRODUCTION SUPERVISOR: Jerome Whyte; GENERAL MANAGER: Morris Jacobs; COMPANY MANAGER: Maurice Winters; PRODUCTION STAGE MANAGER: Charles Atkin; STAGE MANAGER: Fred Smith; ASSISTANT STAGE MANAGER: Harry Clark. *Cast:* BARBARA WOODRUFF: Diahann Carroll (2), *Barbara McNair* (from 7/15/63); DAVID JORDAN: Richard Kiley (1), *Howard Keel* (from 7/15/63); JEANETTE VALMY, LUC'S ASSISTANT: Noelle Adam (4), *Yvonne Constant*; LUC DELBERT, PHOTOGRAPHER: Alvin Epstein (7); MOLLIE PLUMMER, FASHION WRITER: Polly Rowles (3); MIKE ROBINSON: Don Chastain (6); LOUIS DE POURTAL, BARBARA'S TUTOR: Mitchell Gregg (8); COMFORT O'CONNELL: Bernice Massi (5); GABRIELLE BERTIN: Ann Hodges (9); MARCELLO AGNOLOTTI: Paul Cambeilh (10); DANCERS: Susanne Cansino (gone by 62–63), Julie Drake, Jean Eliot (gone by 62–63), Ginny Gan, Gene GeBauer, Ellen Graff (gone by 62–63), Kay Hudson, Ann Hodges, Diana Hrubetz (gone by 62–63), Scott Hunter, Alan Johnson, Sandy Leeds, Michael Maurer (gone by 62–63), Larry Merritt (gone by 62–63), Anna Marie Moylan (gone by 62–63), David Neuman, Patti Pappathatos, Janet Paxton (gone by 62–63), Wakefield Poole, Dellas Rennie (*Judy Keirn*), Bea Salten, Carol Sherman, Calvin von Reinhold (gone by 62–63), Mary Zahn, *Ellen Fluhr, Ellen Halpin, Paula Tracy [this was Paula Tracy Smuin], Louise Quick, Nancy Lynch, Elinor Coffee, Jere Admire, Walter Stratton, Joe McWherter*. **Standbys**: David/Mike: John Carter; Barbara: Vi Velasco. **Understudies**: Jeanette: Dellas Rennie, *Judy Keirn*; Mollie/Comfort: Ann Hodges; Louis: Paul Cambeilh; Luc: Alan Johnson; Gabrielle:

Diana Hrubetz & Elinor Coffee; Marcello: Calvin von Reinhold, *Gene GeBauer*. **Instrumental Characters**: FLUTE: Walter Wegner; CLARINET: Aaron Sachs; OBOE: Ernest Mauro; TRUMPET: James Sedlar; TROMBONE: James Dahl; DRUMS: Ronnie Bedford, *Archie Freedman*; BASSOON: Walter Kane. *Act I*: *Prolog*; *Scene 1* Paris; an enormous photographic studio; *Scene 2* A Paris street; *Scene 3* Barbara's apartment; *Scene 4* Monte Carlo auto races. *Act II*: *Scene 1* Honfleur — at the edge of the sea on the Normandy coast; *Scene 2* House in Honfleur; *Scene 3* Deauville casino; *Scene 4* A beach near St. Tropez; *Scene 5* Luc's photographic studio in Paris; *Scene 6* A street in Paris. *Act I*: "The Sweetest Sounds" (Barbara & David) [the big song], "How Sad" (David), "The Sweetest Sounds" (reprise) (David) "Loads of Love" (Barbara), "The Man Who Has Everything" (Louis), "Be My Host" (David, Comfort, Mike, Luc, Gabrielle, Dancers), "La La La" (Jeanette & Luc), "You Don't Tell Me" (Barbara), "Love Makes the World Go" (Mollie, Comfort, Dancers), "Nobody Told Me" (David & Barbara). *Act II*: "Look No Further" (David & Barbara), "Maine" (David & Barbara), Casino Ballet (Company), "An Orthodox Fool" (Barbara), "Eager Beaver" (Comfort, Mike, Dancers), "No Strings" (David & Barbara), "Maine" (reprise) (David & Barbara), "The Sweetest Sounds" (reprise) (David & Barbara).

The show opened to very good Broadway reviews. It won Tonys for composer, choreographer, and for Diahann Carroll. Richard Rodgers won a special Tony. It was also nominated for musical, direction of a musical, sets, costumes, musical direction, and for Richard Kiley.

After Broadway. THE MOVIE. Warners planned to do the movie with Nancy Kwan. This was very upsetting to Diahann Carroll. Hollywood audiences were not yet ready for a black-white relationship, but they seemed to be okay with a white–Oriental relationship. There was much controversy about this, and the film was never made.

TOUR. Opened on 8/3/63, at the Shubert Theatre, Boston. MUSICAL DIRECTOR: Jack Lee. *Cast*: BARBARA: Barbara McNair, *Beverly Todd* (from 10/24/63); DAVID: Howard Keel; JEANETTE: Beti Seay; LOUIS: Ferdinand Hilt. **Understudies**: Jeanette: Donna Baccala.

HER MAJESTY'S THEATRE, London. Opened 12/30/63. MUSICAL DIRECTOR: Johnnie Spence; LONDON CAST RECORDING on Decca. *Cast*: Art Lund, Hy Hazell, David Holliday, Beverly Todd, Ferdy Mayne, Erica Rogers, Geoffrey Hutchings, Marti Stevens.

EQUITY LIBRARY THEATRE, NYC, 3/9/72–3/26/72. 22 PERFORMANCES. DIRECTOR: Richard Michaels; CHOREOGRAPHER: Lynne Gannaway; SETS: Billy Puzo; COSTUMES: Sally Krell; LIGHTING: Cammie Caroline Lavine; MUSICAL DIRECTOR/VOCAL ARRANGEMENTS/PIANIST: Don Sturrock. *Cast*: BARBARA: Mary Louise; DAVID: Robert Tananis; JEANETTE: Patti Haine; LUC: Ronn Hansen; COMFORT: Ann Hodges; JACK MONE: Paul Gilbert (Jack Mone was a new character); MARIA MONE: Patricia Garland (Maria Mone was a new character).

CITY CENTER, NYC, 5/8/03–5/11/03. 5 PERFORMANCES. Part of the *Encores!* series. DIRECTOR/CHOREOGRAPHER: Ann Reinking; LIGHTING: Ken Billington; MUSICAL DIRECTOR: Rob Fisher. *Cast*: DAVID: James Naughton; BARBARA: Maya Days; LOUIS: Len Cariou; JEANETTE: Caitlin Carter; MOLLIE: Penny Fuller; MIKE: Marc Kudisch; COMFORT: Emily Skinner; LUC: Casey Biggs; GABRIELLE: Mary Ann Lamb; MARCELLO: Denis Jones. Vanessa Williams had been rumored for an *Encores!* production of *No Strings* in the 2001 season, but she quit to go into the Broadway production of *Into the Woods*. She was also rumored for this production, but never made it.

496. *Nowhere to Go But Up*

Suggested by the exploits of the famous Prohibition agents Izzy and Moe, and their unorthodox methods. Set in a Big City somewhere in the USA.

Before Broadway. The numbers "(We're a) Couple of Clowns," "Gimmie, Gimmie, Gimmie," "Here I Am," and "Ain't it a Joy" were all cut during tryouts. This was Dorothy Loudon's Broadway debut. It was the only Broadway musical directed by Sidney Lumet. And it was the first Broadway show choreographed by Ron Field.

The Broadway Run. WINTER GARDEN THEATRE, 11/10/62–11/17/62. 3 previews from 11/8/62. 9 PERFORMANCES. PRESENTED BY Kermit Bloomgarden & Herbert Greene, in association with Steven H. Scheuer; MUSIC: Sol Berkowitz.; LYRICS/BOOK: James Lipton; DIRECTOR: Sidney Lumet; CHOREOGRAPHER: Ronald Field; ASSISTANT CHOREOGRAPHER: Michael Bennett; SETS: Peter Larkin; COSTUMES: Robert Fletcher; LIGHTING: Tharon Musser; MUSICAL DIRECTOR/VOCAL ARRANGEMENTS: Herbert Greene; ORCHESTRATIONS/MUSICAL ARRANGEMENTS: Robert Ginzler; CAST RECORDING on Columbia; PRESS: James D. Proctor, Leo Stern, Louise Weiner; GENERAL MANAGER: Max Allentuck; COMPANY MANAGER: Milton M. Pollack; PRODUCTION STAGE MANAGER: Kermit Kegley; STAGE MANAGER: Don Doherty; ASSISTANT STAGE MANAGER: Rico Froehlich. *Cast:* IZZY EINSTEIN: Tom Bosley (1) ☆; MOE SMITH: Martin Balsam (2) ☆; ANTHONY BAIELLO: Bruce Gordon (3) ☆; WILMA RISQUE: Dorothy Loudon (4); TOMMY DEE: Bert Convy (7); JEAN MORGAN: Mary Ann Mobley (6); HYMIE: Phil Leeds (5); BEGGAR: Robert Avian; LADY WITH LAUNDRY: Sally Ann Carlson; HOP WONG: Phil Leeds; HOP FAMILY: Sally Lee, Jodi Kim Long (12), Bill Starr, Eleanore Treiber; POLICEMAN: Rico Froehlich; REPORTERS & PHOTOGRAPHERS: H.F. Green (10), Val Avery (9), Art Wallace (11); WOMAN WITH POODLE: Eleanore Treiber; LUPO: Frank Campanella (8); THE GANG: Marty Allen, Robert Avian, Tod Jackson, Larry Merritt, Frank Pietri, Bill Starr, Gerald Teijelo, James Weiss, Blair Hammond, Michael Maurer; STAGE MANAGER: Joel Craig; LA VIE GIRLS: Nicole Barth, Sally Ann Carlson, Diane Coupe, Dorothy D'Honau, Lillian D'Honau, Maureen Hopkins, Jami Landi, Sally Lee, Sandra Roveta, Dean Taliaferro, Barbara Marcon, Eleanore Treiber; SALLY: Sally Lee; GUARD: Don Rehg; POLICEMAN: Val Avery (9). *Standby*: Moe: Don Doherty. *Understudies*: Izzy: H.F. Green; Baiello: Val Avery; Wilma: Dean Taliaferro; Jean: Barbara Marcon; Tommy: Joel Craig; Hop Wong/Hymie: Art Wallace; Lupo: James Weiss. *Act I*: *Scene 1* A cartoon; *Scene 2* A street: "Ain't You Ashamed?" (Izzy & Moe); *Scene 3* Hop Wong Laundry: "The 'We Makin' Cash with Sour Mash; No Rickie-Tickie No Licqie' Rag" [known during tryouts as "The We Makin' Dough, You So and So; No Rickie-Tickie No Washie Rag"] (Hop Wong), "The 'We Makin' Cash'" song (reprise) (Hop Wong, Hop Family, Izzy & Moe); *Scene 4* A speakeasy: "Live a Little" (Wilma, Izzy, Moe, Company); *Scene 5* A street; *Scene 6* Baiello's office: "Yes, Mr. Baiello" (Baiello & Gang), Dance (Gang); *Scene 7* Backstage corridor, Club *La Vie Est Gaie*: "When a Fella Needs a Friend" (Izzy & Moe, Tommy & Jean), Dance (Izzy & Moe, Tommy & Jean); *Scene 8* La Vie Est Gaie: "The Odds and Ends of Love" (Wilma), "Nowhere to Go but Up" (Wilma & La Vie Girls); *Scene 9* Exterior, *La Vie Est Gaie*; *Scene 10* Baiello's office: "Take Me Back" (Baiello & Jean), "Yes, Mr. Baiello" (reprise) (Baiello & Gang); *Scene 11* Backstage corridor: "I Love You for That" (Wilma & Moe); *Scene 12* La Vie Est Gaie: "Nowhere to Go but Up" (reprise) (La Vie Girls). *Act II*: *Scene 1* La Vie Est Gaie: "Baby, Baby" (Moe & Wilma); *Scene 2* The La Vie Girls' dressing room: "Natural Allies" (Izzy & La Vie Girls); *Scene 3* The backstage corridor; *Scene 4* Exterior, *La Vie Est Gaie*: "Out of Sight, Out of Mind" (Tommy); *Scene 5* Baiello's office: "Follow the Leader" (Septet — Baiello, Izzy & Moe, Wilma, Jean, Tommy, Hymie); *Scene 6* The backstage corridor; then the city: "Dear Mom" (Izzy & Moe), Responses: Baiello, Lupo, Gang; *Scene 7* The distillery: Finale: "Nowhere to Go but Up" (reprise) (Izzy & Moe, Company).

Broadway reviews were generally dreadful. When Kermit Bloomgarden announced after a week that the show was closing, a group of investors hired a lawyer to file an injunction preventing such a closure. Investors picketed the theater, but when Mr. Bloomgarden informed them no money was coming in, they went home.

497. *Of Thee I Sing*

Before Broadway. The original 1930s production was the third-longst-running musical of that decade, and the first musical ever awarded the Pulitzer Prize for drama. MUSIC BOX THEATRE. Opened on 12/26/31; 46TH STREET THEATRE, 10/10/32–1/14/33. Total of 441 PERFORMANCES. PRESENTED BY Sam H. Harris; DIRECTOR: George S. Kaufman; CHOREOGRAPHER: George Hale; SETS: Jo Mielziner; MUSICAL DIRECTOR: Charles Previn; ORCHESTRATIONS: Russell Bennett. *Cast:* WINTERGREEN: William Gaxton; THROTTLEBOTTOM: Victor Moore; GILHOO-

LEY: Harold Moffett; SAM: George Murphy; FRENCH AMBASSADOR: Florenz Ames; CHIEF JUSTICE: Ralph Riggs. The show returned to the IMPERIAL THEATRE, 5/15/33–6/10/33. 32 PERFORMANCES. It had the same basic cast and crew, except MUSICAL DIRECTOR: Eugene Fuerst; ADDITIONAL ORCHESTRATIONS: William Daly. A sequel, *Let 'em Eat Cake*, with the same crew, ran at the IMPERIAL THEATRE, 10/21/33–1/6/34. 90 PERFORMANCES. *Cast:* WINTERGREEN: William Gaxton; THROTTLEBOTTOM: Victor Moore. "Wintergreen for President," "Tweedledee for President," "Union Square," "Down with Everyone Who's Up," "Shirts by Millions," "Comes the Revolution," "Mine," "Climb up the Social Ladder" [dropped after the opening], "Cloistered from the Noisy City," "On and On and On," "Let 'em Eat Cake," "Blue, Blue, Blue," "Who's the Greatest," "No Comprenez, No Capish," "When the Judges Doff the Ermine," "That's What He Did," "I Know a Foul Ball," "Throttle Throttlebottom," "A Hell of a Hole," "Hanging Throttlebottom in the Morning." For the 1952 Broadway production Victor Moore turned down the chance to recreate his old role of Throttlebottom. Helen Tamiris was replaced as choreographer by Jack Donohue before Broadway.

The Broadway Run. ZIEGFELD THEATRE, 5/5/52–7/5/52. 72 PERFORMANCES. PRESENTED BY Chandler Cowles & Ben Segal; MUSIC: George Gershwin; LYRICS: Ira Gershwin; BOOK: George S. Kaufman & Morrie Ryskind; DIRECTOR: George S. Kaufman; CHOREOGRAPHER: Jack Donohue; SETS: Albert Johnson; COSTUMES: Irene Sharaff; ASSISTANT COSTUMES: Florence Klotz; LIGHTING: Peggy Clark; MUSICAL SUPERVISOR/VOCAL DIRECTOR: David Craig; MUSICAL DIRECTOR: Maurice Levine; ORCHESTRATIONS: Don Walker; DANCE MUSIC ARRANGEMENTS: David Baker; PRESS: Nat Dorfman & Irvin Dorfman; GENERAL MANAGER: Paul Groll; GENERAL STAGE MANAGER: Joseph Olney; STAGE MANAGER: Jerry Adler; ASSISTANT STAGE MANAGER: Tom Wells. *Cast:* FRANCIS X. GILHOOLEY: J. Pat O'Malley; LOUIS LIPPMAN: Robert F. Simon; CHAMBERMAID: Louise Carlyle; MATTHEW ARNOLD FULTON: Loring Smith; SENATOR CARVER JONES: Howard Freeman; SENATOR ROBERT E. LYONS: Donald Foster; ALEXANDER THROTTLEBOTTOM: Paul Hartman (2); JOHN P. WINTERGREEN: Jack Carson (1); BEAUTY CONTESTANT: Jean Bartel; MARY TURNER: Betty Oakes (5); SAM JENKINS: Jonathan Lucas; DIANA DEVEREAUX: Lenore Lonergan (4); EMILY BENSON: Joan Mann; ANNOUNCER: Mort Marshall; VLADIMIR VIDOVITCH: Abe Stein; YUSSEF YUSSEVITCH: Bob Oran; THE CHIEF JUSTICE: Jack Whiting (3); GUIDE: Jack Whiting (3); A SIGHTSEER: Parker Wilson; THE FRENCH AMBASSADOR: Florenz Ames (6); CHIEF SENATE CLERK: Mort Marshall; SENATOR FROM MASSACHUSETTS: Jack Whiting; ATTACHÉ: Tom Wells; CHIEF FLUNKEY: Al McGranary; FLUNKEYS: William Krach, Michael King, Ken Ayers; SINGERS: Ken Ayers, Claudia Campbell, Louise Carlyle, Norman Clayton, Warren Galjour, Jay Harnick, Keith Kaldenberg, Joe Kerrigan, Michael King, William Krach, James McCracken, Helen Rice, Jeanne Schlegel, Joanne Spiller, Gloria Van Dorpe, Larry Weber; DANCERS: Vicki Barrett, Betty Buday, Georgine Darcy, Crandall Diehl, J. Corkey Geil, Skeet Guenther, Peggy Merber, Frank Seabolt, Pat Stanley, Robert Tucker, Parker Wilson; SHOW GIRLS: Arlene Anderson, Jean Bartel, Gregg Evans, Charlotte Foley, Dorothy Richards, Siri, Jeanne Tyler, Charlotte Van Lein. *Understudies*: Throttlebottom: Mort Marshall; Diana: Jean Bartel; Gilhooley/Clerk: Tom Wells; Sam: J. Corky Geil & Bobby Tucker; Miss Benson: Vicki Barrett; Announcer: Tom Wells & Norman Clayton. *Act I*: *Scene 1* Main Street: "Wintergreen for President" (Ensemble); *Scene 2* A smoke-filled room; *Scene 3* Atlantic City: "Who is the Lucky Girl to Be?" (Diana & Ensemble), "The Dimple on My Knee" (Diana, Sam, Ensemble), "Because (Because)" (Diana, Sam, Ensemble), "Never Was There a Girl So Fair" (Company), "Some Girls Can Bake a Pie" (Wintergreen & Company); *Scene 4* Madison Square Garden: "Love is Sweeping the Country" (Sam, Miss Benson, Ensemble), "Of Thee I Sing" (Wintergreen, Mary, Company); *Scene 5* Election Night; *Scene 6* Washington: Finale: "The Supreme Court Judges" (Justices), "(Here's) a Kiss for Cinderella" (Wintergreen & Ensemble), "I Was the Most Beautiful Blossom" (Diana). *Act II*: *Scene 1* The White House: "Hello, Good Morning" (Sam, Miss Benson, Secretaries), "Mine" (Wintergreen & Mary) [this was not from the 1931 production, but from the 1933 sequel, *Let 'em Eat Cake*], "Who Cares" (Wintergreen, Mary, Reporters), "Garcon, S'il Vous Plait" (French Soldiers), "The Illegitimate Daughter" (French Ambassador & Ensemble); *Scene 2* The Capitol; *Scene 3* The Senate: "The Senate Roll Call"

(Throttlebottom & Ensemble), "Jilted" (Diana & Company), "Who Could Ask for Anything More?" ("I'm About to Be a Mother") (Mary & Company), "Posterity (is Just Around the Corner)" (Wintergreen & Company); *Scene 4* Again the White House; *Scene 5* The Yellow Room: "Trumpeter, Blow Your Horn" (Ensemble), Finale: "On that Matter No One Budges" (Entire Company).

Broadway reviews were divided. The show was now outdated.

After Broadway. NEW ANDERSON THEATRE, NYC, 3/7/69–3/23/69. 21 PERFORMANCES. DIRECTOR: Michael Gordon; CHOREOGRAPHER: Michael C. Penta; SETS: Bob Olson; COSTUMES: James Bidgood; LIGHTING: William Marshall; MUSICAL DIRECTOR: Leslie Harnley. *Cast:* JONES: John Aman; LYONS: Edward Penn; THROTTLEBOTTOM: Lloyd Hubbard; WINTERGREEN: Hal Holden; MARY: Joy Franz; DIANA: Katie Anders; CHIEF JUSTICE: Bob Freschi. Several 1952 songs were deleted. "Mary's Announcement" and "Posterity" were added. "Trumpeter, Blow Your Horn" was now called "Trumpeter, Blow Your Golden Horn." New scene breakdown: The Parade, The Committee, The Contest, The Rally, The Returns, The Inauguration, The New Administration, The Impeachment, The Happy Ending.

CBS-TV PRODUCTION, 10/24/72. DIRECTOR: Dave Powers. *Cast:* Carroll O'Connor, Jack Gilford, Cloris Leachman, Michele Lee.

BROOKLYN ACADEMY OF MUSIC, 1987; KENNEDY CENTER, Washington, DC, 5/27/87–6/14/87. A staged concert version, performed with *Let 'em Eat Cake,* at *Cast:* Jack Gilford, Larry Kert, Maureen McGovern.

SYMPHONY SPACE, 3/29/90–4/15/90. 16 PERFORMANCES. PRESENTED BY the New York Gilbert & Sullivan Players; DIRECTOR: Kristen Garver; CHOREOGRAPHER: Bill Fabris; SETS: Jack Garver. *Cast:* LOUIS: Steven Ungar; LYONS: Michael Collins; THROTTLEBOTTOM: Alan Hill; WINTERGREEN: Keith Jurosko; MARY: Kate Egan; MISS BENSON: Sally Ann Swarm; CHIEF JUSTICE/SENATOR: David Jones.

ARENA STAGE, Washington, DC, 1992. DIRECTOR: Douglas C. Wager; CHOREOGRAPHER: Marcia Milgrom Dodge. *Cast:* THROTTLEBOTTOM: David Marks; WINTERGREEN: Gary Beach; MARY: Lauren Mitchell; JENKINS: Keith Savage; DIANA: Terry Burrell; MISS BENSON: Kyme.

PAPER MILL PLAYHOUSE, New Jersey, 9/12/04–10/17/04. Previews from 9/8/04. DIRECTOR: Tina Landau; CHOREOGRAPHER: Joey Pizzi; MUSICAL DIRECTOR: Tom Helm. *Cast:* WINTERGREEN: Ron Bohmer; THROTTLEBOTTOM: Wally Dunn; DIANA: Sarah Knowlton; MARY: Garrett Long; MISS BENSON: JoAnn M. Hunter; GILHOOLEY: Nick Corley; SENATOR JONES: Herndon Lackey; LYONS: Hal Blankenship.

498. *Oh, Brother!*

A musical with no intermission. Set at the present time, in the Persian Gulf, during a revolution. Lew is searching for a pair of lost sons. His wife had given birth to identical twins in the Middle East, and the couple then adopted another set of identical twins born in the same hospital. One child of each pair got separated when the plane carrying that pair was hijacked to Iraq; the other pair is now helping their father search for the missing pair.

The Broadway Run. ANTA THEATRE, 11/10/81–11/11/81. 13 previews. 3 PERFORMANCES. PRESENTED BY Zev Bufman & The John F. Kennedy Center, in association with the Fisher Theatre Foundation, Joan Cullman, Sidney Shlenker; MUSIC: Michael Valenti; LYRICS/BOOK/DIRECTOR/CHOREOGRAPHER: Donald Driver; SUGGESTED BY the 1591 comedy *The Comedy of Errors,* by William Shakespeare, and the comedies of Plautus; CONSULTANT TO DONALD DRIVER: Rudy Tronto; SETS: Michael J. Hotopp & Paul de Pass; COSTUMES: Ann Emonts; LIGHTING: Richard Nelson; SOUND: Richard Fitzgerald; MUSICAL DIRECTOR/VOCAL & DANCE MUSIC ARRANGEMENTS: Marvin Laird; ORCHESTRATIONS: Jim Tyler; PRESS: Fred Nathan & Associates; CASTING: Julie Hughes & Barry Moss; GENERAL MANAGEMENT: Theatre Now; COMPANY MANAGER: Robb Lady; PRODUCTION STAGE MANAGER: Nicholas Russiyan; STAGE MANAGER: Robert O'Rourke; ASSISTANT STAGE MANAGER: Eric Scheps. *Cast:* REVOLUTIONARY LEADER: Larry Marshall; REVOLUTIONARY: Mark

Martino; REVOLUTIONARY: Thomas Lo Monaco; BUGLER: Sal Provenza; REVOLUTIONARY WOMAN: Alyson Reed; REVOLUTIONARY WOMAN: Pamela Khoury; REVOLUTIONARY WOMAN: Kathy Mahony-Bennett; REVOLUTIONARY WOMAN: Geraldine Hanning; REVOLUTIONARY WOMAN: Suzanne Walker; REVOLUTIONARY WOMAN: Karen Teti; REVOLUTIONARY: Steve Bourneuf; REVOLUTIONARY: Michael-Pierre Dean; LEW: Richard B. Shull; A CAMEL: Steve Sterner & Eric Scheps; WESTERN MOUSADA: Harry Groener; WESTERN HABIM: Alan Weeks; FATATATATATIMA: Alyson Reed; EASTERN HABIM: Joe Morton; EASTERN MOUSADA: David-James Carroll; SAROYANA: Judy Kaye (1); MUSICA: Mary Elizabeth Mastrantonio; REVOLUTIONARY: Steve Sterner; REVOLUTIONARY: Eric Scheps; BALTHAZAR: Bruce Adler; AYATOLLAH: Thomas Lo Monaco; LILLIAN: Geraldine Hanning. **Understudies**: Balthazar: Sal Provenza; Bugler: Steve Bourneuf; Habims: Michael-Pierre Dean; Mousadas/Leader: Mark Martino; Saroyana: Kathy Mahony-Bennett; Musica: Pamela Khoury; Fatatatatatima: Suzanne Walker; Lillian: Karen Teti; Ayatollah: Eric Scheps. **Swings**: Nancy Meadows & David Michael Lang. "We Love an Old Story" (Leader & Revolutionaries), "I to the World" (Mousada Twins & Habim Twins), "How Do You Want Me?" (Saroyana), "That's Him" (Musica & Revolutionaries), "Everybody Calls Me by My Name" (Western Mousada & Revolutionaries), "OPEC Maiden" (Western Mousada & Revolutionaries), "A Man" (Eastern Mousada), "How Do You Want Me?" (reprise) (Saroyana), "Tell Sweet Saroyana" (Eastern Mousada, Western Habim, Arabs), "What Do I Tell People This Time?" (Saroyana), "OPEC Maiden" (reprise) (Musica & Women), "A Loud and Funny Song" (Saroyana, Musica, Fatatatatatima), "The Chase" (dance) (Full Company), "I to the World" (reprise) (Mousada Twins & Habim Twins), "Oh, Brother!" (Full Company).

Despite good word of mouth during Broadway previews, it was roundly panned by the critics on Broadway opening night.

After Broadway. YORK THEATRE COMPANY, spring 1994. This was the first of the *Musicals in Mufti* series. REVISED BY: Dion Driver & Michael Valenti; DIRECTOR: Charles Abbott.

499. *Oh! Calcutta!*

The world's longest-running erotic musical. Full-frontal nudity was one of the orders of the day, wife-swapping, masturbation, fetishes. The title came from a painting by Clovis Trouille, and was a deliberate pun on the French expression "O quel cul t'as" (Oh, what an ass you have !).

Before Broadway. British theatre critic Ken Tynan, who came up with the idea for this entertainment with music, said in *Village Voice*, "it occurred to me that there was no place for a civilized man to take a civilized woman to spend an evening of civilized erotic stimulation. At one end there's burlesque, at the other an expensive nightclub. We're trying to fill the gap with this show." Michael Bennett quit as choreographer before the show opened Off Broadway, at the EDEN THEATRE, where it ran 6/17/69–2/21/71. 704 PERFORMANCES. It had the same basic crew as for the subsequent Broadway run, except: GENERAL MANAGER: Norman Kean; COMPANY MANAGER: Edmonstone F. Thompson Jr.; STAGE MANAGERS: John Actman, Harry Chittendon, Greg Taylor. *Cast:* Raina Barrett, Mark Dempsey (*Mel Auston, Martin Speer*), Katie Drew-Wilkinson (*Lynn Oliver, Patricia Hawkins*), Boni Enten (*Kathrin King*), Bill Macy (*Eddie Phillips Jr.*), Alan Rachins, Leon Russom (*Mitchell McGuire*), Margo Sappington (*Maureen Byrnes*), Nancy Tribush, George Welbes (*Michael S. Riordan, Michael Cavanaugh*), The Open Window (Robert Dennis, Peter Schickele, Stanley Walden). During its run at the Eden, the show was re-classified as "Limited Broadway" when that term came into use. On 2/25/71 the show transferred to Broadway.

The Broadway Run. BELASCO THEATRE, 2/25/71–8/12/72. 610 PERFORMANCES. An E.P.I.C. production, PRESENTED BY Hillard Elkins, in association with Michael White, Gordon Crowe and George Platt; MUSIC/LYRICS: The Open Window (Robert Dennis, Peter Schickele, Stanley Walden); CONCEIVED BY: Jacques Levy; DEVISED BY: Kenneth Tynan; CONTRIBUTORS: Samuel Beckett, Jules Feiffer, Dan Greenburg, John Lennon, Jacques Levy, Leonard Melfi, David Newman & Robert Benton, Sam Shepard, Clovis Trouille, Kenneth Tynan, Sherman Yellen;

DIRECTOR: Jacques Levy; CHOREOGRAPHER: Margo Sappington; SETS: James Tilton; COSTUMES: Fred Voelpel; LIGHTING: David F. Segal; AUDIO DESIGN: Robert Liftin; MUSICAL DIRECTOR: Norman Bergen; PRESS: Samuel J. Friedman, Louise Weiner Ment, Shirley Herz; GENERAL MANAGER: Edmonstone F. Thompson Jr., *Bill Liberman*; STAGE MANAGER: Greg Taylor, *John Actman*; ASSISTANT STAGE MANAGER: Janet Beroza, *Ray Edelstein*. **Cast:** Mel Auston, Raina Barrett, Ray Edelstein (*Jack Shearer* by 3/71; Ray became standby), Samantha Harper, Patricia Hawkins, William Knight, Mitchell McGuire, Pamela Pilkenton, Gary Rethmeier, Nancy Tribush (*Cyndi Howard* by 3/71). Also appeared in 71–72: *Evamarii Johnson, Steven Keats, Ron Osborne, Eddie Phillips, Patricia Post, Richard Quarry, David Rosenbaum, Ellie Smith, Rusty Blitz, Boni Enten, Onni Johnson, Marcia Greene, Mary-Jennifer Mitchell, Richard Ryder, Angelyn Forbes, Marian Ellis, B.J. DeSimone*. **Standby:** For all women roles: Maureen Byrnes. **Part I**: Prologue (Company); Taking off the Robe (Company): "Oh! Calcutta!;" Dick and Jane (Raina & Gary) [Off Broadway it had been Alan & Nancy]; Suite for Five Letters (Mitchell, Samantha, Patricia, William, Patricia) [Off Broadway it had been Mark, Katie, Boni, Nancy, George]: "Dear Editor;" "(Will Answer All) Sincere Replies" (song & sketch) (Nancy, Samantha, Gary, Ray) [Off Broadway it had been Bill, Leon, Margo, Nancy]; "Paintings of Clovis Trouille" (The Open Window) [Clovis Trouille was a famous French surrealist painter of the 20th century]; "Jack & Jill" (song & sketch) (Patricia & Mitchell) [Off Broadway it had been Boni & George]; Delicious Indignities (or, the Deflowering of Helen Axminster) (Samantha & William) [Off Broadway it had been Mark & Katie]; Was it Good for You Too? (Raina, Nancy, William, Pamela, Gary, Ray) [Off Broadway it had been Raina, Mark, Bill, Alan, Boni, Nancy]; "Green Pants," "I Like the Look." **Part II**: "Much Too Soon" (m/l: The Open Window & Jacques Levy) (Company & The Open Window); "Once on One" (Clarence and Mildred) (Mel & Pamela) [Off Broadway it had been Margo & George]; "Rock Garden" (William & Mitchell) [Off Broadway it had been Leon & Bill]; Who: Whom ("Exchanges of Information") (Mark, Katie, Nancy) [It was in this position during the original Off Broadway run, but did not go to Broadway, at least not initially. During the run it was re-inserted to open Act II, before "Much Too Soon," but this time performed by Raina, Cyndi and David]; Four in Hand (Mel, Mitchell, Ray, Gary) [Off Broadway it had been George, Leon, Alan, Bill]; "Coming Together, Going Together" (Company).

After Broadway. 1976 REVIVAL. This was a Middle Broadway (or Limited Broadway) production, put together in time for the nation's bicentennial. This production did not use the Samuel Beckett contribution used in the original, but instead used one by Lenore Kandel. EDISON THEATRE, 9/24/76–8/6/89. 5,959 PERFORMANCES. PRESENTED BY Hillard Elkins, Norman Kean, and Robert S. Fishko. ADDITIONAL MUSIC: Stanley Walden & Jacques Levy; DIRECTOR: Jacques Levy; ASSISTANT TO THE DIRECTOR: Nancy Tribush; CHOREOGRAPHER: Margo Sappington; SETS: James Tilton, *Harry Silverglat Darrow*; COSTUME SUPERVISOR: James Tilton; COSTUMES: Kenneth M. Yount; LIGHTING: Harry Silverglat Darrow; SOUND: Sander Hacker; MUSICAL DIRECTOR: Stanley Walden; PRESS: Les Schecter Associates; CASTING: Feuer & Ritzer; GENERAL MANAGER: Norman Kean; COMPANY MANAGERS: James Fiore & Doris J. Buberl; PRODUCTION STAGE MANAGER: David Rubinstein; STAGE MANAGERS: Maria Di Dia, Ron Nash, Bruce Kagel. **Cast:** Haru Aki (*Cheryl Hartley* from 76–77; Miss Hartley was there until the end in 1989, and held the record for the longest run by a performer in the same show, over ten years, and over 5,000 performances), Jean Andalman (gone by 78–79), Bill Bass (gone by 78–79), Dorothy Chansky (gone by 78–79), Cress Darwin (gone by 78–79), John Hammil (gone by 78–79), William Knight (*William Mesnick* from 78–79), Cy Moore (*Billy Padgett* from 76–77 & gone by 78–79), Coline Morse (gone by 78–79), Pamela Pilkenton (*Katherine Liepe* from 76–77), *Jacqueline Carol* (77–82), *Scott Baker* (77–78, 87–88), *Robert Beau Golden* (77–78), *Mary Hendrickson* (77–79), *September Thorp* (77–80), *Barra Kahn* (78–79), *James K. Reiley* (78–79), *Jerry Clark* (from 78–79), *Tom Lantzy* (78–79, 80–81), *Richard Easley* (80–81), *Gary Meitrott* (80–81), *Ann Neville* (80–82, 87–89), *Lee Ramey* (80–82), *Julie Ridge* (80–82), *Dara Norman* (80–82), *David Heisey* (80–87), *Daryl Adams* (81–82), *Deborah Bauers* (81–87; she became Deborah Robertson by 84–85), *Charles E. Gerber* (81–85), *Nick Mangano* (81–83), *Tom Pieczara* (81–82), *Sean Sullivan* (81–82), *Nannette Bevelander* (82–85), *Michael A. Clarke* (82–86; *William Thomas* from 86–87 until end of run), *Mary Kilpatrick* (82–85), *James E. Mosiej* (from 83–84 & still there 86–87), *Terry Hamilton* (84–85), *Jodi Johnson* (84–87), *Vivian Paxton* (from 85–86; *Danielle P. Connell* from 86–87), *Charles Klausmeyer* (from 85–86), *Louis Silvers* (from 86–87), *Jacqueline Fay* (87–89), *Amy Fortgang* (87–89), *Philip Gibson* (87–88), *Peter J. Lanigan* (87–89), *Katherine Miller* (87–89), *Samuel D. Cohen* (88–89), *Norman Dutweiler* (88–89). **Original Understudies**: Women: Peggy Jean Waller; Men: Bill Bass. **The Band:** KEYBOARDS: Michael Tschudin; GUITARS: Dan Carter; DRUMS: Robin Gould III; PERCUSSION: Jeff Gerson; BASS: Harvey Swartz; VOCALS: Michael Tschudin & Dan Carter. **Act I**: **Scene 1** Taking off the Robe (Company): "Oh! Calcutta!;" **Scene 2** "Will Answer All Sincere Replies" (song & sketch): SUE ELLEN: Dorothy Chansky; DALE: John Hammil; MONTE: William Knight (or Cy Moore); CHERIE: Jean Andalman; **Scene 3** Rock Garden: MAN: William Knight; BOY: Cress Darwin; **Scene 4** Delicious Indignities (or, The Deflowering of Helen Axminster): HELEN: Dorothy Chansky; ALFRED: William Knight (or Cy Moore); **Scene 5** "Paintings of Clovis Trouille," "Much Too Soon" (Cress Darwin), "Dance for George" (danced by Pamela Pilkenton). Dedicated to the memory of the late George Welbes, who had been a performer in the original Off Broadway production; **Scene 6** "Suite for Five Letters" (John Hammil, William Knight, Dorothy Chansky, Pamela Pilkenton); **Scene 7** One on One (Haru Aki & Bill Bass; or Haru Aki & Cress Darwin), "Clarence" (Jean Andalman). **Act II**: **Scene 1** "Jack & Jill" (song & sketch) (Pamela Pilkenton & John Hammil); **Scene 2** Spread Your Love Around (Haru Aki & Pamela Pilkenton): "Spread Your Love Around" (Jean Andalman), Love Lust Poem (Pamela Pilkenton & Haru Aki); **Scene 3** Was it Good for You Too?: PERLMUTTER: Cress Darwin; INTERVIEWER: Haru Aki; DR. BRONSON: Jean Andalman; DR. JASPERS: William Knight; NURSE: Pamela Pilkenton; ATTENDANT: Bill Bass (or Cy Moore); WOMAN: Dorothy Chansky; GYPSIES: John Hammil & Haru Aki; GYPSY DOG: G. Grover Lightstone; "Green Pants," "I Like the Look;" **Scene 4** "Coming Together, Going Together" (Company). Note: The sketches and musical numbers would change order sometimes throughout the long run. Some would be dropped, and others added. This production alternated as a repertory piece with *Me and Bessie* in the Edison, a converted ballroom in the Edison Hotel. *Me and Bessie* closed on 12/5/76, but *Oh! Calcutta!* continued to run alone, from 12/7/76, and run, and run. Under the provisions of a special "middle contract" it often had 10 or 11 performances a week (as opposed to the eight of most shows). Tourists, especially Japanese, were the main ticket-buyers (pubic hair being a great taboo in Japan). The specter of AIDS killed the show more than anything, and Norman Kean killing his wife Gwyda DonHowe and then taking the big jump didn't do much for business either (that was on 1/11/88). By the end of the run, it was estimated that *Oh! Calcutta!* as a show had been seen by 85 million people around the world, and had grossed more than $350 million. If you include this run as Broadway (as opposed to Limited or Middle Broadway), then by the end of 2002 it was still the fifth-longest-running show of any kind ever on Broadway.

500. *Oh Captain!*

Henry, when he's at home in Surrey with his very proper wife Maud, is the very model of the proper Englishman. However, when he sails from London to Paris every week (in the movie it was between Gibraltar and North Africa) on the S.S. *Paradise*, he becomes a Mr. Hyde–type character in Paris, having a wife there too, Bobo, a singer at Le Club Paradis, owned by Mae. He's not so proper with Bobo. One day Maud surprises him in Paris, and all hell breaks loose (in the movie the wives never meet). Manzoni was the first mate.

Before Broadway. The score was announced for Richard Adler & Jerry Ross, then for Sammy Cahn & Jimmy Van Heusen, and finally for Bob Merrill. But Livingston & Evans wound up doing it as their Broadway debut. As leading man, Danny Kaye was first choice, then David

Wayne, Dennis King, George Sanders, and Sid Caesar. For a while Laurence Olivier thought about taking it on. When Jose Ferrer was assigned to direct and to co-write the libretto, he thought about playing the role himself. However, the best choice was made — Tony Randall. Xavier Cugat (Abbe Lane's husband) was scheduled to play the 3rd-billed Manzoni, but he quit before tryouts, and was replaced by Edward Platt (who dropped billing). It got good reviews during the Philadelphia tryouts. The numbers "Anywhere but Here," "The Frenchman's Paree," and "Jubi-lie, Jubi-lo" were all cut before Broadway.

The Broadway Run. ALVIN THEATRE, 2/4/58–7/19/58. 192 PERFORMANCES. PRESENTED BY Howard Merrill & Theatre Corporation of America (Donald H. Coleman); MUSIC: Jay Livingston; LYRICS: Jay Livingston & Ray Evans; BOOK: Al Morgan & Jose Ferrer; BASED ON the 1953 movie *The Captain's Paradise*, written by Alec Coppel, and starring Alec Guinness; DIRECTOR: Jose Ferrer; CHOREOGRAPHER: James Starbuck; SETS/LIGHTING: Jo Mielziner; COSTUMES: Miles White; MUSICAL DIRECTOR/VOCAL & BALLET ARRANGEMENTS: Jay Blackton; ORCHESTRATIONS: Robert Ginzler, Joe Glover, Ray Jaimes, Philip J. Lang, Walter Eiger, Sy Oliver, Cornel Tanassy, Oscar Kosarin; CAST RECORDING on Columbia; PRESS: Harvey B. Sabinson, David Powers, Bernard Simon; GENERAL MANAGER: C. Edwin Knill; PRODUCTION STAGE MANAGER: George Quick; STAGE MANAGER: Doris S. Einstein; ASSISTANT STAGE MANAGER: Raphael Ferrer. *Cast:* CAPTAIN HENRY ST. JAMES: Tony Randall (1); MRS. MAUD ST. JAMES: Jacquelyn McKeever (3); ENRICO MANZONI: Edward Platt (4), *Bruce MacKay*; THE CREW OF S.S. *Paradise*: George Ritner, Bruce MacKay, Louis Polacek, Nolan Van Way; A CLERK: Jack Eddleman; THE NEIGHBORS: Betty McGuire, Dee Harless, Jean Sincere; LISA, THE FLOWER SELLER: Alexandra Danilova (6); BOBO: Abbe Lane (2), *Denise Darcel* (during Miss Lane's vacation), *Dorothy Lamour* (from 7/16/58); THE GUIDE: Stanley Carlson; A SPANIARD: Paul Valentine (7); MAE: Susan Johnson (5); ENSEMBLE (ENGLISH TOWNSPEOPLE, DOCKWORKERS, TOURISTS, PARISIANS): Bill Atkinson, Alvin Beam, Cherie Burgess, Kevin Carlisle, Allen Conroy, Shirley De Burgh, Sally Gura, Brigitta Kiviniemi, David Lober, Gordon Marsh, Asia Mercoolova, Kiki Minor, Mona Pivar, Adriane Rogers, Sybil Scotford, Doug Spingler, Mona Tritsch, Ken Urmston, Eddie Verso, Joyce Carroll, Dee Harless, Sheila Mathews, Betty McGuire, Alice Nunn, Jean Sincere, Helene Whitney, Jack Eddleman, Bruce MacKay, Louis Polacek, George Ritner, Tony Rossi, Charles Rule, James Stevenson, Nolan Van Way. *Understudies:* Captain: Jack Eddleman; Maud: Sheila Mathews; Bobo: Betty McGuire; Enrico: Stanley Carlson; Lisa: Shirley De Burgh; Guide: Bruce MacKay; Spaniard: Tony Rossi; Clerk: Alvin Beam; Mae: Helene Whitney. *Act I:* "A Very Proper Town" (Captain & Company), "Life Does a Man a Favor (When it Gives Him Simple Joys)" (Maud & Captain), "A Very Proper Week" (English Townspeople), "Life Does a Man a Favor (When it Leads Him Down to the Sea)" (Captain, Manzoni, Crew), "Captain Henry St. James" (Crew), The Dock Dance (Dockworkers), "Three Paradises" (Captain), "Surprise" (Maud & Neighbors), "Life Does a Man a Favor (When it Puts Him in Paree)" (Captain), "Hey Madame" (sung & danced by Captain & Lisa), "Femininity" (Bobo), "It's Never Quite the Same" (Manzoni & Crew), "It's Never Quite the Same" (reprise) (Maud, Manzoni, Crew), "We're Not Children" (Maud & Spaniard), "Give it All You Got" (Mae & Tourists), "Love is Hell" (Mae & Ladies of the Ensemble), "Keep it Simple" (Bobo & Her Dancing Companions). *Act II:* "The Morning Music of Montmartre" (Mae & People of Montmartre), "You Don't Know Him" (Bobo & Maud), "I've Been There and I'm Back" (Manzoni & Captain), "Double Standard" (Bobo & Maud), "All the Time" (Captain) [this had been a commercial recording by Johnny Mathis, and was slightly changed for the show. It had the same melody as "Three Paradises"], "You're So Right for Me" (Manzoni & Bobo), "All the Time" (reprise) (Maud), Finale (Entire Company).

The show opened on Broadway to an advance sale of over $2 million, and got very good reviews. Because Abbe Lane was a recording artist with RCA, she was not allowed to participate in the original cast recording — by Columbia (she did later record some of the songs from *Oh Captain!*). Eileen Rodgers took her place on the recording. Jose Ferrer and his wife Rosemary Clooney (whose name is mentioned in the show) later did a complete *Oh Captain!* album of their own. Three nights before the show closed Dorothy Lamour made her Broadway debut,

replacing Abbe Lane. Just after it closed Donald H. Coleman, one of the producers, was sued in two separate suits for misappropriation of funds. The charges were that even though the show ran for six months, it lost almost all its $300,000 investment. The fact that Mr. Coleman had allowed Jose Ferrer to put his (Mr. Ferrer's) lawyer on the payroll, and to hire his (Mr. Ferrer's) brother as assistant stage manager, was used as evidence. The show was nominated for several Tony Awards — musical, sets, costumes, and for Tony Randall, Jacquelyn Mckeever, and Susan Johnson.

After Broadway. ST. PETER'S CHURCH, NYC, 9/27/96–9/29/96. 5 PERFORMANCES. PRESENTED BY the York Theatre Company, as part of their *Musicals in Mufti* series; DIRECTOR: Robert Tolan; MUSICAL DIRECTOR: Kevin Wallace. *Cast:* CAPTAIN: Robin Haynes; BOBO: Gayton Scott; MAUD: Karen Ziemba; MAE: SuEllen Estey; CLERK: Jay Aubrey Jones.

501. *Oh Coward!*

A musical revue, using the words and music of Noel Coward.

Before Broadway. It was first produced Off Broadway, at the NEW THEATRE, 10/4/72–6/17/73. 294 PERFORMANCES. PRESENTED BY Wroderick Productions; DIRECTOR: Roderick Cook; CHOREOGRAPHER: George Bunt; SETS: Helen Pond & Herbert Senn; MUSICAL DIRECTOR/ARRANGEMENTS: Rene Wiegert; ADDITIONAL ARRANGEMENTS: Herbert Helbig & Nicholas Deutsch; PIANISTS: Rene Wiegert & Uel Wade; DRUMS: Bernard Karl. *Cast:* Barbara Cason, Roderick Cook (*Christian Gray* during Mr. Cook's vacation), Jamie Ross.

TOUR. 1/6/75–3/22/75. It played 43 cities. *Cast:* Patricia Morison.

ON STAGE THEATRE, NEW YORK (Off Broadway). 5/24/81–7/5/81. 37 PERFORMANCES. PRESENTED BY Barbara Darwall & John Montagnese, in association with Talent to Amuse; DIRECTOR: Roderick Cook; CHOREOGRAPHER: Clarence Tetters; COSTUMES: Jack McGroder; LIGHTING: F. Mitchell Dana; MUSICAL DIRECTOR: Russell Walden. *Cast:* Terri Klausner, Russ Thacker, Dalton Cathey, Kay Walbye.

Before the 1986 Broadway run, it played at Westport Country Playhouse, Conn.

The Broadway Run. HELEN HAYES THEATRE, 11/17/86–1/3/87. 56 PERFORMANCES. PRESENTED BY Raymond J. Greenwald; MUSIC/LYRICS: Noel Coward; DEVISED BY/DIRECTOR: Roderick Cook; SETS: Helen Pond & Herbert Senn; COSTUMES: David Toser; LIGHTING: F. Mitchell Dana; MUSICAL DIRECTOR: Dennis Buck; MUSICAL ARRANGEMENTS: Rene Wiegert; PRESS: Jeffrey Richards Associates (including Ken Mandelbaum); CASTING: Myers/Techner; GENERAL MANAGEMENT: Sylrich Management; PRODUCTION STAGE MANAGER: J. Andrew Burgreen; STAGE MANAGER: Jim Woolley. *Cast:* Roderick Cook, Catherine Cox, Patrick Quinn. *Standbys:* For Miss Cox: Marianne Tatum; For Mr. Cook/Mr. Quinn: Dalton Cathey. *Musicians:* PIANOS: Dennis Buck & David Evans; BASS: Ray Kilday; DRUMS/PERCUSSION: David Cox. *Act I:* INTRODUCTION: The Boy Actor (Company); OH COWARD! (all songs by Company): "Something to Do with Spring" [from the London production of *Words and Music*], "Bright Young People" [from the London production of *Cochran's 1931 Revue*], "Poor Little Rich Girl" [from the London production of *On with the Dance*], "Zigeuner" [from *Bitter Sweet*], "Let's Say Goodbye" [from the London production of *Words and Music*], "This is a Changing World" [from the London production of *Pacific 1860*], "We Were Dancing" [from *Tonight at 8:30*], "Dance, Little Lady" [from *This Year of Grace*], "Room with a View" [from *This Year of Grace*], "Sail Away" [from the London production of *Ace of Clubs*, and subsequently from the show *Sail Away*]; ENGLAND: "London is a Little Bit of All Right" [from *The Girl Who Came to Supper*] (Mr. Quinn), "The End of the News" [from *Sigh No More*] (Miss Cox & Mr. Cook), "The Stately Homes of England" [from the London production of *Operette*, and subsequently from the show *Set to Music*] (Mr. Quinn & Mr. Cook), "London Pride" (Miss Cox); FAMILY ALBUM: (We Must All Be Very Kind to) Auntie Jessie (Mr. Cook), "Uncle Harry" [from the London production of *Pacific 1860*] (Miss Cox & Mr. Quinn); MUSIC HALL: Introduction (Mr. Cook), "Chase Me, Charlie" [from the London production of *Ace of Clubs*] (Miss Cox), "Saturday Night at the Rose and Crown" [from *The Girl Who Came to Supper*] (Company), "Island of Bolamazoo" [from the London production of *Operette*] (Mr. Quinn), "What Ho, Mrs. Brisket!" [from *The Girl Who Came to Supper*] (Mr. Cook), "Has Anybody Seen Our Ship?" [from *Tonight at 8:30*] (Company), "Men About Town" [from *Tonight at 8:30*] (Mr. Quinn & Mr. Cook); "IF LOVE WERE ALL" [from *Bitter Sweet*] (Miss Cox); TRAVEL: "Too Early or Too Late" (Mr. Cook), "Why Do the Wrong People Travel?" [from *Sail Away*] (Miss Cox & Mr. Quinn), "The Passenger's Always Right" [from *Sail Away*] (Company); "DON'T PUT YOUR DAUGHTER ON THE STAGE, MRS. WORTHINGTON" (Company). *Act II*: "MAD DOGS AND ENGLISHMEN" [from the London production of *Words and Music*] (Company); (I WENT TO A) MARVELOUS PARTY: "The Party's Over Now" [from the London production of *Words and Music*] (Mr. Cook); DESIGN FOR DANCING: "Dance, Little Lady" (reprise) (Company); "YOU WERE THERE" [from *Tonight at 8:30*] (Mr. Quinn); THEATRE: "Three White Feathers" [from the London production of *Words and Music*] (Miss Cox & Mr. Cook). The Star (Mr. Quinn), The Critic (Mr. Cook), The Elderly Actress (Miss Cox); LOVE: Gertie (Mr. Cook), Loving (Mr. Quinn), I Am No Good at Love (Mr. Cook), Sex Talk (Mr. Quinn), A Question of Lighting (Messrs Quinn & Cook), "Mad About the Boy" [from the London production of *Words and Music*] (Miss Cox); WOMEN: Introduction (Mr. Cook), "Nina" [from the London production of *Sigh No More*] (Mr. Quinn), "Mrs. Wentworth-Brewster" (Mr. Cook) [the 1972 Off Broadway production had "A Bar on the Piccola Marina" and "Alice is at it Again" here]; "WORLD WEARY" [from *This Year of Grace*] (Company); "LET'S DO IT" (m: Cole Porter; l: Noel Coward) (Company); FINALE: "Where are the Songs We Sung?" [from the London production of *Operette*] (Mr. Quinn), "Someday I'll Find You" [from *Private Lives*] (Mr. Cook), "I'll Follow My Secret Heart" [from *Conversation Piece*] (Miss Cox), "If Love Were All" (reprise) (Company), "Play, Orchestra, Play" [from *Tonight at 8:30*] (Company), "I'll See You Again" [from *Bitter Sweet*] (Company).

Note: program subject to change.

Reviews were very divided. Roderick Cook and Catherine Cox were nominated for Tony Awards.

502. *Oh, Kay!*

All-black version. Set in 1926 at the home of Jimmy Winter in Harlem (in the original it was Jimmy Winters, and his home was the town of Beachampton, Long Island). He is about to marry, when he discovers he has fallen in love with Kay Jones (Kay Denham in the original).

Before Broadway. The original opened on Broadway at the IMPERIAL THEATRE, 11/8/26. 256 PERFORMANCES. DIRECTOR: John Harwood; CHOREOGRAPHER: Sammy Lee. *Cast*: KAY: Gertrude Lawrence; JIMMY: Oscar Shaw; SHORTY: Victor Moore; MAE: Constance Carpenter; MOLLY: Betty Compton; LARRY: Harland Dixon. It returned to Broadway, to the CENTURY THEATRE, 1/2/28–1/14/28. 16 PERFORMANCES. *Cast*: KAY: Julia Sanderson; MAE: Helen Arden; JIMMY: Frank Crumit; PEGGY: May Wynn.

The next production of any significance was Off Broadway, at the EAST 74TH STREET THEATRE, 4/16/60. 89 PERFORMANCES. DIRECTOR: Bertram Yarborough; CHOREOGRAPHER: Dania Krupska; MUSICAL DIRECTOR: Dorothea Freitag. *Cast*: KAY: Marti Stevens; JIMMY: David Daniels; IZZY: Linda Lavin; POLLY: Penny Fuller; MOLLY: Sybil Scotford; LARRY: Eddie Phillips; REVENUE OFFICER: Mike Mazurki, *Joe Hill*; EARL OF BLANDINGS: Murray Matheson, *Keith Harrington*; McGEE: Bernie West, *George S. Irving*. "The Woman's Touch," "The Twenties Are Here to Stay," "Home," "Stiff Upper Lip," "Maybe," "The Pophams," "Do, Do, Do," "Clap Yo' Hands," "Someone to Watch Over Me," "Fidgety Street," "You'll Still Be There," "Little Jazz Bird," "Oh, Kay, You're Okay."

STUDIO ARENA, Buffalo, 4/27/67. 31 PERFORMANCES. DIRECTOR: Allan Leicht. *Cast*: Michael Bradshaw, John Schuck, Kenneth McMillan, Elaine Kerr, Renee Leicht.

A revised production intended for Broadway opened at the Royal Alexandra Theatre, Toronto, on 7/18/78, and closed at the Kennedy Center, Washington, DC, on 9/23/78. PRESENTED BY Cyma Rubin; BOOK: Thomas Meehan; DIRECTOR/CHOREOGRAPHER: Donald Saddler; ASSOCIATE CHOREOGRAPHER: Mercedes Ellington; SETS/COSTUMES: Raoul Pene du Bois; LIGHTING: Beverly Emmons; SOUND: Richard Fitzgerald; MUSICAL DIRECTOR/DANCE MUSIC ARRANGEMENTS: Wally Harper; ORCHESTRATIONS: Bill Byers, *Michael Gibson*; VOCAL ARRANGEMENTS: William Elliott; ASSOCIATE PRODUCERS: Raoul Pene du Bois, Nathan J. Miller, Keith Davies. *Cast*: SHORTY McGEE: Jack Weston; LADY KAY WELLINGTON: Jane Summerhays; JIMMY WINTER: David-James Carroll, *Jim Weston*; FRED LA RUE: Gene Castle; CONSTANCE WASHBROOK: Marie Cheatham; AGENT BALDWIN: David Cromwell, *Eddie Lawrence*; VELMA DELMAR: Alexandra Korey; SEN. ALBERT G. WASHBROOK: Thomas Ruisinger; RIGHTY: Reno Roop; POLLY: Janet Arters; MOLLY: Louise Arters; LUIGI SPAGNOLI/MINISTER: Joe Palmieri; LUCIA SPAGNOLI: Annette Michelle; THUGS: Jameson Foss & Peter Heuchling; AL FRESCO: Joe Palmieri; CIGARETTE GIRL: Annette Michelle; LADIES: Barbara Hanks, Holly Jones, Jean McLaughlin, Annette Michelle, Diana Lee Mirras, Dana J. Moore, Terry Reiser, Yveline Semeria, Dorothy Stanley, Roxanna White; GENTLEMEN: Stephen Bray, Jon Engstrom, Jameson Foss, Tom Garrett, Peter Heuchling, Timothy R. Kratoville, Michael Lichtefeld, Dirk Lumbard, Bob Morrisey, Danny Robbins, J. Thomas Smith, Thomas J. Stanton. *Understudies*: Shorty: Eddie Lawrence; Velma: Annette Michelle; Fred: Bob Morrisey; Senator: Joe Palmieri. *Swings*: Linda Kinnaman & Bob Heath. *Prologue*: The beach at Southampton: "We've Got to Be There" (Ensemble). *Act I*: *Scene 1* The living-room of Jimmy Winter's Southampton cottage; afternoon: "Heaven on Earth" (Shorty, Kay, Ladies), "I've Got a Crush on You" (Jimmy & Constance), "Dear Little Girl" (Jimmy & Ladies), "Maybe" (Kay & Jimmy), "How Long Has This Been Going On?" (Kay); *Scene 2* The following morning: "Blah, Blah, Blah" (Shorty), "Do, Do, Do" (Kay & Jimmy), "Clap Yo' Hands" (Velma & Ensemble). *Act II*: *Scene 1* The terrace of Jimmy Winter's Southampton cottage; midday: "Stiff Upper Lip" (Shorty, Kay, Baldwin), "Someone to Watch Over Me" (Kay), "Oh, Kay!" (Kay & Gentlemen), "Bride and Groom" (Ensemble), "Maybe" (reprise) (Kay & Ensemble), "Oh, So Nice" (Jimmy); *Scene 2* Star Island Casino; that night: "Fidgety Feet" (Fred & Ensemble), "Don't Ask" (Shorty & Velma), "Oh, Kay!" (reprise) (Company).

The 1990 production, David Merrick's first musical in a decade, was "Inspired by recent productions at the Goodspeed, and at the Birmingham Theatre, Mich.," where the credits were as follows: DIRECTOR: Martin Connor; CHOREOGRAPHER: Dan Siretta; ARTISTIC CONSULTANT: Sheldon Epps; SETS: Kenneth Foy; COSTUMES: Judy Dearing; LIGHTING: Craig Miller; MUSICAL DIRECTOR: David Evans. *Cast*: REV. DuGRASS: Alexander Barton; LARRY: Marion J. Caffey; SHORTY: Helmar Augustus Cooper; KAY JONES/LADY KATIE: Pamela Isaacs; DUKE: Stanley Wayne Mathis; CONSTANCE DuGRASS: Brenda Pressley; JIMMY WINTER: Ron Richardson; JANSON: Mark Kenneth Smaltz; ENSEMBLE: Tracy M. Bass, Keith Robert Bennett, Yvette Curtis, Denise Heard, Lynise Heard, Larry Johnson, Dexter Jones, Sara Beth Lane, Sharon Moore, Ken Leigh Rogers, Lynn Sterling, Horace Turnbull.

The numbers "Somehow it Seldom Comes True" and "Where's the Boy? Here's the Girl" were cut during Broadway previews.

The Broadway Run. RICHARD RODGERS THEATRE, 11/1/90–1/5/91. 19 previews from 10/16/90. 77 PERFORMANCES. PRESENTED BY David Merrick, by arrangement with Tams-Witmark Music Library; MUSIC: George Gershwin; LYRICS: Ira Gershwin; BOOK: Guy Bolton & P.G. Wodehouse; ADAPTED BY: James Racheff; NEWLY CONCEIVED BY/DIRECTOR/CHOREOGRAPHER: Dan Siretta; SETS: Kenneth Foy; COSTUMES: Theoni V. Aldredge; LIGHTING: Craig Miller; SOUND: Jan Nebozenko; MUSICAL DIRECTOR/VOCAL & ADDITIONAL DANCE MUSIC ARRANGEMENTS: Tom Fay; ORCHESTRATIONS: Arnold Goland; DANCE MUSIC ARRANGEMENTS: Donald W. Johnston; DUO PIANISTS: Donald Johnston (*David Evans* for the attempted comeback) & Ronald Colston; PRESS: The Joshua Ellis Office, *Michael Alpert* (for the attempted comeback); CASTING: Leonard Finger; GENERAL MANAGER: Leo K. Cohen; PRODUCTION STAGE MANAGER: Harold Goldfaden; STAGE MANAGER: Tracy Crum, *Ara Marx* (for the attempted comeback); ASSISTANT STAGE MANAGER: Brian A. Kaufman. *Cast*: BILLY LYLES: Gregg Burge (4); DOLLY

GREENE: Kyme (7); DUKE: Stanley Wayne Mathis; NICK: David Preston Sharp; JOE: Fracaswell Hyman; WAITER/JAKE: Frantz Hall; LARRY POTTER: Kevin Ramsey (5); SHORTY: Helmar Augustus Cooper (3); SAM: David Preston Sharp; B.J.: Keith Robert Bennett; FLOYD: Frederick J. Boothe; ZEKE: Ken Roberson; JIMMY WINTER: Brian Mitchell [he became Brian Stokes Mitchell] (2), *Ron Richardson* (for the attempted comeback); CONSTANCE DU GRASSE: Tamara Tunie Bouquett (9), *Natalie Oliver* (for the attempted comeback); CHAUFFEUR: Byron Easley; KAY JONES: Angela Teek (1) ✩, *Rae Dawn Chong* (for the attempted comeback); JANSON: Mark Kenneth Smaltz (6); REV. ALPHONSE DU GRASSE: Alexander Barton (8); ENSEMBLE: Keith Robert Bennett, Jacquelyn Bird, Frederick J. Boothe, Cheryl Burr, Byron Easley, Robert H. Fowler, Karen E. Fraction, Melissa Haizlip, Frantz Hall, Garry Q. Lewis, Greta Martin, Sharon Moore, Elise Neal, Ken Roberson, Ken Leigh Rogers, David Preston Sharp, Allyson Tucker, Mona Wyatt (*Sarah Beth Lane* for the attempted comeback). *Understudies*: Kay: Tamara Tunie Bouquett; Dolly: Sharon Moore; Constance: Karen E. Fraction; Shorty: Fracaswell Hyman, *Mark Kenneth Smaltz* (for the attempted comeback); Reverend: Fracaswell Hyman, *Ken Roberson* (for the attempted comeback); Janson: Fracaswell Hyman, *Ken Leigh Rogers* (for the attempted comeback). *Swings*: Melissa Haizlip (*Sarah Beth Lane* for the attempted comeback) & Ken Leigh Rogers. *Orchestra* (replacements for the attempted comeback in italics): CONCERTMISTRESS/VIOLIN I: Suzanne Ornstein, *Martin Agee* (concertmaster/Violin I); VIOLINS: Peter Dimitriades, Andy Stein, Martin Agee (*Carol Pool*); VIOLAS: Maxine Roach & Crystal Garner (*Juliet Haffner*); CELLI: Garfield Moore & Rachel Steurmann (*Alvin McCall*); HORNS: Anthony Cecere (*Joe DiAngelis*) & Virginia Benz; TRUMPETS: Wilmer Wise, Jeff Kievit (*Jim Hynes*), Danny Cahn (*Bob Millikan*); TROMBONE: Morty Bullman; REEDS: Les Scott, John Moses, Rick Heckman, Gene Scholtens; BASS: Linc Milliman; DRUMS: Tony Tedesco; GUITAR/BANJO: Rick Loewus; PERCUSSION: Marty Grupp. **Act I**: *Scene 1* Onstage at the Paradise Club: "Slap That Bass" [from the movie *Shall We Dance?*] (Billy, Dolly, Ensemble) [for the attempted comeback it was Billy, Dolly, Jay, Ensemble]; *Scene 2* Backstage at the Paradise Club; *Scene 3* Jimmy Winter's townhouse; late that night: "When Our Ship Comes Sailing In" (Duke, Shorty, Male Ensemble) [cut from the original] [for the attempted comeback it was Billy, Shorty, Male Ensemble], "Dear Little Girl" * (Jimmy & Shorty), "Maybe" * (Jimmy & Kay); *Scene 4* Jimmy Winter's townhouse; the next morning: "You've Got What Gets Me" (Billy & Dolly), "Do, Do, Do" * (Jimmy & Kay), "Clap Yo' Hands" * (Potter & Ensemble). **Act II**: *Scene 1* Jimmy's terrace; that afternoon: "Oh, Kay!" * (l: Ira Gershwin & Howard Dietz) (Billy, Kay, Ensemble), "Ask Me Again" (Jimmy) [previously unpublished], "Fidgety Feet" * (Duke & Ensemble) [for the attempted comeback it was Billy & Ensemble], "Ask Me Again" (reprise) (Jimmy), "Someone to Watch Over Me" * (Kay); *Scene 2* Onstage at the Paradise Club: "Heaven on Earth" * (l: Ira Gershwin & Howard Dietz) (Potter, Duke, Billy) [for the attempted comeback it was Potter & Billy]; *Scene 3* Backstage at the Paradise Club; *Scene 4* Onstage at the Paradise Club: "Show Me the Town" [cut from the original])/"Sleepless Nights" (Kay, Billy, Dolly, Potter, Duke, Ensemble) [for the attempted comeback it was Kay, Billy, Dolly, Potter, Ensemble], "Someone to Watch Over Me" (reprise) (Jimmy & Kay).

Note: An asterisk means that that song was in the 1926 original.

Reviews really had to be oh kay, and they were. After it closed on Broadway, David Merrick re-cast certain characters, and the characters of Duke, Sam, Joe, Waiter, Jake, and Floyd were cut. This attempted comeback re-opened for previews at the Lunt—Fontanne Theatre on 4/2/91, but closed (without officially opening) after 16 new previews, on 4/14/91, after another several hundred thousand dollars had been poured into it, canceling its 4/18/91 opening night. The show received Tony nominations for choreography and for Gregg Burge.

After Broadway. In 1998 Joe DiPietro began revising the script of *Oh, Kay!* on commission from the George & Ira Gershwin estate, who wanted to see a modern version of the old hit. He got rid of most of the old libretto, and called it *They All Laughed!* There was a private reading in late 1999, and on 1/18/00 and 1/20/00 it had an industry reading in Manhattan. *Cast*: Dick Latessa, Tovah Feldshuh, Mary Beth Piel, Donna English. It then had a production at the GOODSPEED OPERA HOUSE, Connecticut, 6/29/01–9/22/01. PRESENTED BY Jonathan Pollard,

Dena Hammerstein, Bernie Kukoff; DIRECTOR: Christopher Ashley (he replaced John Rando before opening); CHOREOGRAPHER: Joey McKneely. *Cast*: Marla Schaffel, James Ludwig. After this Christopher Ashley revised the script, cut and added songs using numbers from the Gershwin catalogue, and renamed the show *Heaven on Earth*. This change of name was mostly because the title song "They All Laughed!" was cut, and the title of the finale, "Heaven on Earth" seemed more appropriate. Other numbers added included: "Someone to Watch Over Me," "Let's Call the Whole Thing Off," "Do it Again," "S'Wonderful," "That Certain Feeling," and an expanded version of "I've Got a Crush on You." There was a reading in 6/02. There were Broadway plans, with CHOREOGRAPHER: Randy Skinner; SETS: David Gallo; COSTUMES: David C. Woolard; LIGHTING: Ken Billington; MUSICAL DIRECTOR: Eric Stern. But it too soon after the previous Broadway production, which, moreover, had been a failure, and Broadway never happened.

503. *Oh, What a Lovely War*

An anti-war musical entertainment, a revue based on factual data about World War I—official records, memoirs and commentaries, including those of the Imperial War Museum, Kaiser Wilhelm II, Gen. Erich Ludendorf, Field Marshal Graf von Schlieffen, Marshal Joffre, Field Marshal Earl Haig, Field Marshal Sir John French, Gen. Sir Henry Wilson, Rt Hon David Lloyd George, Philip Noel-Baker, Alan Clark, Engelbracht & Hanighen, Siegfried Sassoon, Sir Philip Gibbs, Edmund Blunden, Leon Wolff, Capt. Liddell Hart, Barbara Tuchman, Herman Kahn, and the London newspapers *Times* & *Daily Express*. An electric sign, hanging upstage, periodically spelled out statistics about World War I.

Before Broadway. Charles Chilton came up with the idea after finding his father's World War I grave in Arras among 35,942 other soldiers, and realized that the holocaust that had taken place there. The show was developed at Joan Littlewood's Stratford Theatre Workshop, in England, by Miss Littlewood and Mr. Chilton, from improvisations and ideas and bits of dialogue from a group of writers. The theme was always the folly of war, and the scenes were all relevant to 1914–18. Ted Allan suggested the title and wrote a treatment. Detailed research was done by Charles Chilton and Gerry Raffles. It opened on 3/19/63, at the Theatre Royal, Stratford East, and moved to the Wyndham's Theatre on 6/29/63. 501 performances. London cast recording on Decca. Several actors in the London production also played on Broadway: Victor Spinetti, George Sewell, Larry Dann, Colin Kemball, Murray Melvin, Brian Murphy, and Bob Stevenson; and Myvanwy Jenn and Fanny Carby. Others who didn't transfer were: Mary Preston, John Gower, Avis Bunnage, Tony Holland, Godfrey James, Barry Bethell, Judy Cornwell, Griffith Davies.

The Broadway Run. BROADHURST THEATRE, 9/30/64–1/16/65. 1 preview on 9/29/64. 125 PERFORMANCES. PRESENTED BY David Merrick & Gerry Raffles (a Theatre Workshop Group production); MUSIC/LYRICS: various songwriters; BOOK: Charles Chilton & the Theatre Workshop Group; DEVISED BY/DIRECTOR: Joan Littlewood; INSPIRED BY the BBC TV program *The Long, Long Road* (about World War I songs); STAGE DIRECTOR: Kevin Palmer; CHOREOGRAPHER: Bob Stevenson; DESIGN SUPERVISOR: Klaus Holm; SETS/LIGHTING: John Bury; COSTUMES: Una Collins; MUSICAL DIRECTOR: Shepard Coleman; MUSICAL ARRANGEMENTS: Alfred Ralston; PRESS: Max Eisen & Maurice Turet; MILITARY ADVISER: Raymond Fletcher; GENERAL MANAGER: Jack Schlissel; COMPANY MANAGER: Richard Highley; STAGE MANAGER: Jerry Adler. *Cast*: The Pierrots & their roles: Victor Spinetti (Master of Ceremonies, General Lanzerac, Drill Sergeant), Murray Melvin (France, French Lieutenant), Brian Murphy (England, Sir John French, Padre), Frank Coda (Russia, English Signaler), Richard Curnock (French Captain, Assassin), Peter Dalton (Gendarme), Larry Dann (Russia, Luxemburg Signaler, Irish Private), Colin Kemball (Moltke, Belgium), Ian Paterson (Sir Henry Wilson, German Officer), George Sewell (Kaiser, Sir

Douglas Haig), Bob Stevenson (Swimmer, Irish Standard Bearer), Barbara Windsor, Fanny Carby, Jack Eddleman, Myvanwy Jenn, Linda Loftis, Reid Shelton, Valerie Walsh. *Act I*: "Row, Row, Row" (m: James V. Monaco; l: William Jerome) (Ensemble), "We Don't Want to Lose You (Your King and Country Want You)" (m/l: Paul Rubens) (Ladies), "Belgium Put the Kibosh on the Kaiser" (m/l: Alf Ellerton) (Miss Walsh), Medley: "Are We Downhearted? No" (m/l: Worton David & Lawrence Wright) (Men), "It's a Long Way to Tipperary" (m/l: Jack Judge & Harry H. Williams) (Men), "Hold Your Hand Out, Naughty Boy" (m/l: Clarence W. Murphy & Worton David) (Men) [end of Medley], "I'll Make a Man of You" (m/l: Arthur Wimperis & Arthur Finck) [from the London production of *The Passing Show of 1914*] (Miss Windsor), "Pack up Your Troubles (in Your Old Kit Bag)" (m: George Powell; l: George Asaf) (Men), "Hitchy Koo" (m: Lewis F. Muir & Maurice Abrahams; l: L. Wolfe Gilbert) (Miss Carby), "Heilige Nacht" ("Silent Night") (Mr. Kemball), "Christmas Day in the Cookhouse" (Mr. Murphy), "Goodbye-ee" (m: Bert Lee; l: R.P. Weston) (Mr. Spinetti). *Act II*: "Oh, What a Lovely War" (Oh, It's a Lovely War) (m/l: J.P. Long & Maurice Scott, and revised by B. Kelsey) (Ensemble), "Gassed Last Night" (Men), "Roses of Picardy" (m: Haydn Wood; l: Frederick F. Weatherley) (Miss Loftis & Mr. Paterson), "Hush, Here Comes a Whizzbang" [soldiers' parody of "Hush, Hear Comes the Dream Man" (m/l: R.P. Weston, Fred J. Barnes, Maurice Scott)] (Men), "There's a Long, Long Trail" (m: Zo Elliott; l: Stoddard King) (Mr. Paterson), "I Don't Want to Be a Soldier" [soldiers' parody of "I'll Make a Man of You" (m/l: Arthur Wimperis & Arthur Finck)] (Men), "Kaiser Bill" (Men), "They Were Only Playing Leapfrog" (mus arr: Alfred Ralston) (Men), "Old Soldiers Never Die" (Mr. Melvin), "If You Want the Old Battalion" (Men), "Far, Far from Wipers" (m/l: Bingham & Greene) (Mr. Kemball), "If the Sergeant Steals Your Rum" (Men), "I Wore a Tunic (When You Wore a Tulip)" [soldiers' parody of "When You Wore a Tulip I Wore a Big Red Rose" (m: Percy Wenrich; l: Jack Mahoney)] (Mr. Paterson), "Forward, Joe Soap's Army" (Men), "Fred Karno's Army" (Men), "When This Lousy War is Over" [parody of "When This Cruel War is Over" (m: Henry Tucker; l: Charles Carroll Sawyer)] (Mr. Kemball), "Wash Me in the Water" (Men), "I Want to Go Home" (mus arr: Alfred Ralston) (Men), "The Bells of Hell" (mus arr: Alfred Ralston) (Men), "Keep the Home Fires Burning" (m: Ivor Novello; l: Lena Guilbert Ford) (Miss Jenn), "Sister Susie's Sewing Shirts (for Soldiers)" (m: Herman Darewski; l: R.P. Weston) (Miss Windsor), Finale (Ensemble): "La Chanson de Craonne" (m/l: Paul Vaillant-Couturier), "I Don't Want to Be a Soldier" (reprise), "And When They Ask Us" (m: Jerome Kern).

On Broadway it got divided reviews, some raves. It was forced out of the Broadhurst, to make way for *Kelly*. Victor Spinetti won a Tony, and the show was also nominated for musical, direction of a musical, and for Barbara Windsor.

After Broadway. STUDIO ARENA, Buffalo, 10/28/65. 16 PERFORMANCES. DIRECTOR: Edward Parone; DESIGNER: Robert Motley designed, using sets, costumes, slides & props from the original London production. *Cast*: Carol Arthur, Jamie Ross. This production also ran at the THEATRE GROUP, UCLA, Los Angeles, 1/19/66. 32 PERFORMANCES. *Cast*: Susan Browning, Lola Fisher, Mitzi Hoag, Christopher Cary, Maria Lennard. It also ran at the ALLEY THEATRE, Houston, 6/2/67. 40 PERFORMANCES. SETS: Robin Wagner. *Cast*: Alexandra Berlin, April Shawhan.

LONG WHARF, New Haven, Conn., 9/30/66. 31 PERFORMANCES. DIRECTOR: Jon Jory; COSTUMES: Rosemary Ingham. *Cast*: Stacy Keach, Jennifer Darling.

CHARLES PLAYHOUSE, Boston, 3/9/67. 47 PERFORMANCES. DIRECTOR: Eric House. *Cast*: Barbara Alleyn, Lee Caldwell, Jill Clayburgh, Jack Gianino.

GOODMAN THEATRE, Chicago, 5/5/67. 23 PERFORMANCES. DIRECTOR: Patrick Henry. *Cast*: Terry Lomax, Susan Breeze, Carrie Snodgress, Dolores Kenan.

THE MOVIE. 1969. DIRECTOR: Richard Attenborough. It had an all-star cast. Several songs were added: "Bonsoir, M'amour," "Comrades," "Here Comes the Dream Man," "I Do Like to Be Beside the Seaside," "Mademoiselle from Armentieres," "When the Moon Shines Bright on Charlie Chaplin," "Never Mind," "The Old Barbed Wire," "The Old Brigade," "Over There," and "Rule Britannia."

504. *Oklahoma!*

Set in Indian Territory in 1907, just as the territory is getting set to become the state of Oklahoma.

Before Broadway. It all began with a straight play *Green Grow the Lilacs*, by Lynn Riggs, which was first produced by the Theatre Guild for a limited run during the 1930–31 season. It starred Franchot Tone and June Walker. Theresa Helburn, of the Theatre Guild, had always felt that *Green Grow the Lilacs* should be a musical, and approached Richard Rodgers, who had become similarly convinced after seeing a stock production at the Westport Country Playhouse, Connecticut. Rodgers' partner, Jerome Kern, was not in any shape to collaborate even if he'd wanted to (which he didn't), so Rodgers suggested Oscar Hammerstein. It was the first in the R & H partnership, even though they had wanted to work together for a long time. Hammerstein had, for two years, been thinking about doing the show anyway, but had not seriously pursued it. The Guild rented studio space in Steinway Hall, and held a series of backers' auditions, at some of which Hammerstein sang some of the songs, backed by Rodgers on piano. Mr. Hammerstein created the character of Will, and built up the characters of Ado Annie and Ali Hakim, but left pretty much everyone else the same as in the original play. The show was capitalized at $83,000 (the 28 original backers were to see a 2,500 per cent increase on their investment). Theresa Helburn originally wanted Shirley Temple to play Laurey and Groucho Marx as Ali Hakim. Mary Martin turned down the lead to do Vinton Freedley's musical *Dancin' in the Streets* (43), which never made Broadway. Until rehearsals this most famous of musicals still had the title *Green Grow the Lilacs*. On 3/11/43 it began rehearsals in New Haven, as *Away We Go!* and played as such in a limited run from 3/15/43 for four days in New Haven (where it impressed theatregoers) and two days in Boston, before changing its name there to match the song "Oklahoma!" (other names had been considered in those few days —*Swing Your Lady*, *Cherokee Strip*, and *Yessirree*). Because the show had no big opening girlie number, and no stars, and no elaborate scenery, and because of the simple and innocent story line, it wasn't given much of a chance to succeed on the Great White Way. Mike Todd (or one of columnist Walter Winchell's informants, or pretty much everyone else) is reputed to have walked out during Act I in New Haven, saying "No girls, no legs, no jokes, no chance." But it did succeed, to become arguably the most famous musical ever. *Oklahoma!* struggled to survive during tryouts, and dropped "When Ah Goes Out Walkin' with Mah Baby" and "Boys and Girls Like You and Me" (but both were used later, in the 1996 production of *State Fair*). In addition, new lyrics were written for "All er Nothin'." In Boston the staging of the title song was changed to make it a rousing number for the whole company.

The Broadway Run. ST. JAMES THEATRE, 3/31/43–5/29/48. 2,248 PERFORMANCES (including 36 half-price Tuesday matinees for servicemen only). PRESENTED BY The Theatre Guild; MUSIC: Richard Rodgers; LYRICS/BOOK: Oscar Hammerstein II; BASED ON the play *Green Grow the Lilacs* by Lynn Riggs; DIRECTOR: Rouben Mamoulian; CHOREOGRAPHER: Agnes de Mille; BALLET SUPERVISOR: Vladimir Kostenko; SETS: Lemuel Ayers; COSTUMES: Miles White; MUSICAL DIRECTOR: Jacob Schwartzdorf, *Arthur Norris, Richard Baravalle (47–48)*; ORCHESTRATIONS: Robert Russell Bennett; CAST RECORDING on Decca. The record album (recorded by the cast in 9/43 and not before, due to the Musicians Union strike), was one of the first original cast albums in the USA (the practice of recording original theatrical casts had been going on a long time in London), and sold over a million copies; PRESS: Alfred Tamarin & Dick Weaver, *Joseph Heidt* & *Peggy Phillips (44–45 to end of run), June Greenwall*; CASTING: Bettina Cerf; PRODUCTION SUPERVISORS: Lawrence Langner & Theresa Helburn (of the Theatre Guild); COMPANY MANAGER: Max A. Meyer; GENERAL STAGE MANAGER: *Reginald Hammerstein (44–45), Jerome Whyte (from 45 to end of run)*; STAGE MANAGER: Ted Hammerstein; ASSISTANT STAGE MANAGER: Herbert Rissman, *Elaine Anderson*. **Cast:** AUNT ELLER MURPHY: Betty Garde (1), *Ruth Weston (by 44), Edith Gresham (from 47–48)*; CURLY MCLAIN: Alfred Drake (2), *Harry Stockwell (by 44), Bob Kennedy (until 9/45), Harold Keel (from 9/24/45 — Mr. Keel later became Howard Keel), Jack Kilty (from 46–47), John Raitt, James Alexander, Wilton Clary*; LAUREY

WILLIAMS: Joan Roberts (4), *Evelyn Wyckoff* (by 44), *Mary Hatcher, Iva Withers* (by 45), *Betty Jane Watson* (from 45 to 46–47), *Ann Crowley* (alternate 46–48), *Mary Hatcher* (from 46–47 to 47–48), *Gloria Hamilton* (2nd alternate in 47–48), *Peggy Engel, Carolyn Tanner*; IKE SKIDMORE: Barry Kelley, *Joseph Meyer* (by 45–46), *John Alda* (by 46–47 & until 47–48), *Owen Martin* (alternate in 47–48), *Tom Spencer*; FRED: Edwin Clay, *Paul Shiers* (by 44), *Allen Sharp* (by 45–46); SLIM: Herbert Rissman; WILL PARKER: Lee Dixon (5), *Paul Crabtree* (by 44), *Tom Avera* (by 45), *James Parnell* (by 45–46), *Guy Smith* (by 47–48), *William Sutherland*; JUD FRY: Howard Da Silva (6), *Richard Rober* (by 44), *Bruce Hamilton* (from 45–46); ADO ANNIE CARNES: Celeste Holm (7), *Shelley Winters* (from 44), *Edna Skinner* (from 44), *Bonita Primrose* (by 45–46), *Dorothea MacFarland* (by 46–47), *Vivienne Allen* (from 46–47), *Shelley Winters* (1st alternate in 47–48), *Celeste Holm* (2nd alternate in 47–48); ALI HAKIM: Joseph Buloff (3), *David Burns* (by 46–47), *Max Willenz* (by 47–48), *Guy Rennie* (from 47–48), *Owen Martin* (alternate in 47–48), *Marek Windheim*; GERTIE CUMMINGS: Jane Lawrence, *Vivienne Allen* (by 44 and until 46–47), *Patricia Allen* (from 46–47), *Patricia Englund* (by 47–48), *Margot Moser* (from 47–48), *Vivienne Allen* (1st alternate in 47–48), *May Muth* (2nd alternate in 47–48), *Pamela Britton, Bonita Atkins*; ELLEN: Katharine Sergava, *Dania Krupska* (by 45–46), *Gemze de Lappe* (by 46–47), *Alicia Krug* (from 46–47); KATE: Ellen Love, *Helen Wagner* (by 44), *May Muth* (by 45–46), *Donna Phillips* (from 47–48), *Sherry Shadburne* (alternate in 47–48), *Marianna Peterson*; SYLVIE: Joan McCracken, *Louise Fornaca* (by 44), *Beatrice Lynn* (by 45–46), *Betty Lynn, Jane Fischer* (from 46–47); ARMINA: Kate Friedlich, *Muriel Gray* (by 44), *Irene Larson* (by 45–46), *Phyllis Gehrig* (from 45–46), *Nancy Hachenberg* (by 46–47), *Ginger Vetrand* (from 46–47), *Jacqueline Dodge* (from 46–47), *Elena Salamatova* (from 47–48), *Joan Hansen*; AGGIE: Bambi Linn, *Ruth Harte* (from 44–45 until 47–48), *Margaret Nelson* (alternate in 46–47), *Tiny Shimp*; ANDREW CARNES: Ralph Riggs, *Florenz Ames* (by 44); CORD ELAM: Owen Martin, *Herbert Rissman* (alternate in 47–48); JESS: George Church, *Vladimir Kostenko* (by 44); CHALMERS: Marc Platt, *David Tihmar, Scott Merrill* (by 44), *John Butler* (by 45–46), *Tom Avera* (from 45–46), *Erik Kristen* (by 46–47), *Boris Runanin* (from 46–47 until 47–48), *Eric Kristen*; MIKE: Paul Shiers [role cut by 44]; JOE: George Irving, *Joseph Cunneff* (by 44), *Harold Gordon, Lloyd Cole* (by 45–46), *Stokely Gray* (from 45–46 until 47–48), *Chris Robinson* (in 47–48), *Kenneth Buffet* (from 47–48), *Joe Landis*; COWBOY: Jack Harwood [role cut by 44]; SAM: Hayes Gordon, *Lloyd Cole* & *Arthur Ulisse, Remi Martel* (by 45–46) [role cut during last season]; DREAM BALLET: LAUREY: Katharine Sergava, *Dania Krupska* (by 45–46); CURLY: Marc Platt, *Scott Merrill* (by 44); CHILD: Bambi Linn, Ruth Harte; JUD: George Church, *Vladimir Kostenko*; JUD'S POSTCARDS: Joan McCracken, Kate Friedlich, Margit De Kova, Louise Fornaca, Beatrice Lynn, Valentina Oumansky, Frances Rainer; LAUREY'S FRIENDS: Rhoda Hoffman, Rosemary Schaefer, Nona Feid, Maria Harriton, Diana Adams (*June Graham*), Billie Zay, *Marian Horosko, Marie Korjinska, Irene Larson, Miriam Pandor*; COWBOYS: Garry Fleming, Erik Kristen, Jack Dunphy, Ray Harrison, Kenneth Le Roy, Eddie Howland, Kenneth Buffet, *Pat Meany, Jack Miller, David Neuman, George Stecher, Bill Sumner, Jack Ward, Buster Burnell*; OTHER POSTCARDS: Bobby Barrentine & Vivian Smith, *Nona Feid, June Graham, Muriel Gray, Irene Larson* [end of Dream Ballet sequence]; DANCING ENSEMBLE: Diana Adams (*June Graham*), Bobby Barrentine, Kenneth Buffett, Margit De Kova, Jack Dunphy, Nona Feid, Garry Fleming, Kate Friedlich, Ray Harrison, Maria Harriton, Rhoda Hoffman, Edmund Howland, Erik Kristen, Bambi Linn, Joan McCracken, Rosemary Schaefer, Vivian Smith, Billie Zay, *Pat Meany, Jack Baker, Buster Burnell, Maxwell Coker, Payne Converse, Louise Fornaca, Muriel Gray, Ruth Harte, Marian Horosko, Marie Korjinska, Irene Larson, Pat Likely, Beatrice Lynn, Remi Martel, Jack Miller, Ann Newland, Remington Olmsted, Valentina Oumansky, Robert Pagent* (replaced a dancer one day after opening night), *Miriam Pandor, Frances Rainer, George Stecher, Bill Sumner, J.T. Ward, Joe Layton* (47–48); SINGING ENSEMBLE: Elsie Arnold, John Baum, Harvey Brown, Edwin Clay, Hayes Gordon, George Irving, Suzanne Lloyd, Ellen Love, Dorothea MacFarland, Virginia Oswald, Robert Penn, Herbert Rissman, Paul Shiers, Vivienne Simon, Faye Smith, Arthur Ulisse, *Remo Arlotta, Tom Bowman, Lloyd Cole, Ann Crowley, Joseph Cunneff, Miriam Day, J. Gould, Harold Gordon, May Muth, Carl Nelson, Susan Pearce, Gary Smith*

Jr., *Jean Strider, Frank Vespia, Helen Wagner, Birgin Haldorson, Rem Olmsted*. Standbys: Curly/Will: Milton Watson. Swings: Kenny Buffett, Jack Dunphy, Garry Fleming, Ray Harrison, Eddie Howland, Erik Kristen, Pat Meany, *Buster Burnell, Jack Miller*. **Act I: Scene 1** The front of Laurey's farm house. Aunt Eller is churning butter as handsome young ranch hand Curly comes by looking for Laurey. Laurey pretends she isn't interested, but he asks her to the box social. Will arrives from Kansas City, telling of amazing things he's seen there. With $50 he won in steer-roping contest, he can now marry Ado Annie. He accuses man-crazy Annie of flirting with other men while he's been away. One of her beaux is Ali Hakim, a Persian peddler, who dodges shotgun weddings and sells questionable merchandise, and who has invited Ado Annie to a hotel room. He sells Laurey a bottle of Egyptian Elixir, which will conjure up dreams of her future. Gertie, with the loud annoying laugh, flirts with Curly, and Laurey agrees to go with Jud, the disreputable farm hand who works for her and Aunt Eller (Jud was named Jeeter in the original play). In the middle of a dance number Joan McCracken pretends to fall down, but gets up again. This was something of a novelty. Laurey begins to regret her date with Jud: "Oh, What a Beautiful Mornin'" (Curly) [the big hit], "The Surrey with the Fringe on Top" (Curly, Laurey, Aunt Eller) [a bit hit], "Kansas City" (Will, Aunt Eller, Boys), "I Cain't Say No" (Annie), "Many a New Day" (Laurey & The Girls). (Danced by the Girl Who Falls Down, Kate Friedlich, Margit De Kova), "It's a Scandal! It's an Outrage!" (Ali Hakim & Boys), "People Will Say (We're in Love)" (Curly & Laurey); **Scene 2** The Smoke House. Jud's living quarters, with wanted posters on the walls. Curly warns Jud to stay away from Laurey, and suggests that Jud hang himself. Curly gets Jud to admit that he killed a man. Jud threatens Curly, and asks Ali Hakim if he would sell him a telescope with a knife that comes out of the end: "Pore Jud (is Daid)" (Curly & Jud), "Lonely Room" (Jud); **Scene 3** A grove on Laurey's farm. Laurey uses the elixir which conjures up a dream of Jud being victorious. She comes out of her dream and goes off to the box social with Jud: "Out of My Dreams" (Laurey & Girls), "Laurey Makes up Her Mind" (the dream ballet) (Laurey, Curly, Jud, Child, Jud's Post Cards, Laurey's Friends, Cowboys). **Act II: Scene 1** The Skidmore ranch. At the box social. The bidding for Laurey's picnic box becomes a personal contest between Jud and Curly. Curly finally puts up everything he owns, and wins. Jud offers the telescope to Curly and almost gets him to look into it. However, Aunt Eller, warned by Ali Hakim, insists that Curly dance with her: "The Farmer and the Cowman" (Carnes, Aunt Eller, Curly, Will, Ike, Annie, Slim, Ensemble) (Danced by Marc Platt), "All er Nothin'" (Will & Annie) (sung in front of curtain during scene change) (Danced by Joan McCracken & Kate Friedlich); **Scene 2** Skidmore's kitchen porch. Jud menaces Laurey and she fires him. During the scene change Will tells Annie how it's going to be after they're married: "People Will Say We're in Love" (reprise) (Curly & Laurey); **Scene 3** Laurey's farm; three weeks later. A meadow in front of Laurey's house. Curly and Laurey are just married. Oklahoma has just become a state. A shivaree is held for the couple. Jud turns up, drunk, and with a knife. He rushes for Curly but in the struggle Jud falls on his own knife and dies. The sheriff wants to take Curly to jail, but Aunt Eller says he can't do that on the wedding night. The trial is held immediately, and Curly is acquitted. The men then bring a surrey with a fringe on top onto the stage, and the young couple are put into it: "Oklahoma!" (Curly, Laurey, Aunt Eller, Ike, Slim, Carnes, Cord, Ensemble), "Oh, What a Beautiful Mornin'" (reprise) (Laurey, Curley, Ensemble), Finale: "Oklahoma!" (reprise) (Ensemble).

Oklahoma! opened in a major snowstorm, and there were empty seats. Top ticket price at the first performance was $4.80. Reviews were terrific, and the show soon sold out. Joan McCracken came in for the sort of raves that Gwen Verdon would get a decade later in *Can-Can*. The show received a special citation from the Pulitzer Prize committee. It was not eligible for the Pulitzer Prize for Drama, being an adaptation. No Pulitzer Prize was given that year. *Oklahoma!* is generally recognized as the first stage musical to integrate song, dance and story, although *Show Boat* 16 years earlier (or *Pal Joey* in 1940) may well claim that honor. More than 4½ million people saw it on Broadway. On 7/1/46 it overtook *Hellzapoppin* (1940) as the longest running Broadway musical, and subsequently beat *Chu Chin Chow* as the world's longest-running. It was beaten in 1961 (by *My Fair Lady*). At the time, also, it was 4th-longest-running Broadway production of any kind (*Life With Father, Tobacco Road,* and *Abie's Irish Rose* all straight plays, had it beat). By the end of 2002 it was the still the 20th-longest-running show of any kind ever on Broadway. On 5/6/53 the state of Oklahoma adopted the title song as its state song. By 1953 Rodgers & Hammerstein had bought out the original producers, The Theatre Guild. In 1993 it would win a special Tony Award for its 50th birthday.

After Broadway. TOUR. Opened on 10/15/43. PRESENTED BY Richard Rodgers & Oscar Hammerstein II; RE-STAGED BY: Jerome Whyte; SETS: Lemuel Ayers; COSTUMES: Miles White. **Cast:** AUNT ELLER: *Mary Marlo* (by 49–50); CURLY: Harry Stockwell, *Ridge Bond* (by 49–50); LAUREY: Evelyn Wyckoff, *Patricia Northrop* (by 49–50); WILL: *Walter Donahue* (by 49–50); JUD: *Henry Clarke* (by 49–50); ADO ANNIE: Pamela Britton, *Sara Dillon* (by 49–50); ALI HAKIM: David Burns, *Jerry Mann* (by 49–50); GERTIE: *Patricia Johnson* (by 49–50); SYLVIE: *Betsy Scott* (by 49–50); KATE: *Carol Austin* (by 49–50); ARMINA: *Christy Peterson* (by 49–50); AGGIE: *Joan Bowman* (by 49–50); ANDREW: *Dave Mallen* (by 49–50); SLIM: *Henry Austin* (by 49–50); CHALMERS: *Roy Milton* (by 49–50); BALLET JUD: *Ray Dorian* (by 49–50). The tour returned to Broadway in 1951.

Oklahoma! also went out on USO tours, and during the war years over 1,500,000 servicemen saw it, and free recordings of the show went out to most military bases.

THEATRE ROYAL, DRURY LANE, London, 4/30/47–5/27/50; STOLL THEATRE, 5/29/50–10/21/50. Total of 1,548 PERFORMANCES. BROADWAY PRODUCTION RE-PRODUCED BY: Jerome Whyte; BALLET MISTRESS: Gemze de Lappe [her choreographic debut]; MUSICAL DIRECTOR: Salvatore Dell'Isola. **Cast:** AUNT ELLER: Mary Marlo, *Jennie Gregson*; CURLY: Harold Keel, *Chris Robinson, Ian Stuart, Jack Kilty, Stokely Gray*; LAUREY: Betty Jane Watson, *Isabel Bigley, Babette Regnier*; JUD: Henry Clarke, *Alfred Cibelli*; ADO ANNIE: Dorothea MacFarland, *Betty Jo Jones, Jacqueline Daniels, Patricia Englund, Billie Love*; GERTIE: Jacqueline Daniels, *Eleanor Drew, Louise Barnhart, Pam Marmont*; ARMINA: Isabel Bigley, *Aileen Kelly*; TERRY: Gemze de Lappe, *Babette Regnier*; ELLEN: Suzanne Lloyd, *Brenda Barker, Laura Hedley*; SINGERS: Suzanne Lloyd, Marjorie Austin, Elise Kilgerman, Marianne Peterson, Louise Barnhart, Margot Moser, Isabel Bigley, Brenda Barker. It broke all attendance and number of performance records.

505. *Oklahoma!* (1951 return to Broadway)

This was the original Broadway tour returned to Broadway.
The Broadway Run. BROADWAY THEATRE, 5/29/51–7/28/51. 72 PERFORMANCES. It had the same basic crew as for the tour, except for: ORCHESTRA DIRECTOR: Peter Laurini; PRESS: Joseph Heidt; COMPANY MANAGER: Peter Davis; PRODUCTION STAGE MANAGER: David Sidney Weinstein; STAGE MANAGERS: Dale Johnson & Philip Cook. **Cast:** AUNT ELLER: Mary Marlo; CURLY: Ridge Bond, Warren Schmoll (alternate); LAUREY: Patricia Northrop, Patricia Johnson (alternate); CORD: Owen Martin; FRED: Warren Schmoll; WILL: Walter Donahue; JUD: Henry Clarke; ADO ANNIE: Jacqueline Sundt; ALI HAKIM: Jerry Mann; GERTIE: Patricia Johnson; SYLVIE: Audree Wilson; KATE: Judy Rawlings; ARMINA: Jeanne Parsons; AGGIE: Patricia Barker; GIRL WHO FALLS DOWN: Audree Wilson; ANDREW: Dave Mallen; SLIM: John Addis; JESS: Robert Early; ELLEN: Claire Pasch; CHALMERS: Philip Cook; JUD IN BALLET: Valentin Froman; MIKE: Charles Scott; DANCERS: Edmund Gasper, Glenn Forbes, Joseph Ribeau, George Stecher, Edmund Howland, Peyton Townes, Harry Asmus, Betty Gour, Carmen Froman, Nancy Milton, Marquita Living, Jeanne Parsons, Audree Wilson, Josephine Andrews, Jean Bledsoe, Muriel Ives, Patricia Brooks, Patricia Barker; SINGERS: Charles Scott, Warren Schmoll, Robert Early, James Fox, Donald Swenson, John Addis, George Cayley, Beth Johnson, Dolores Kempner, Enid Little, Virginia Walker, Judy Rawlings, Eileen Coffman, Sara Jane Wilson, Jeanine B. Cowles. **Understudies**: Aunt Eller: Nancy Milton; Cord/Jud: Dale Johnson; Will/Chalmers: Philip Cook; Ado Annie: Dolores Kempner; Ali Hakim/Andrew: Owen Martin; Gertie: Judy Rawlings; Ellen: Josephine Andrews; Aggie: Jeanne Parsons; Ballet Jud: Don Swenson.

It got rave reviews.

After Broadway. TOUR. After the Broadway run the show went back on tour. The tour re-opened on 9/27/51, at Hershey, Pennsylvania, and closed on 3/15/52, at Rochester, NY. It had the same cast and crew as for the 1951 Broadway return. It re-opened again on 8/29/52, at Hartford, Conn., and closed on 5/9/53, at the Colonial Theatre, Boston. *Hartford cast*: AUNT ELLER: Mary Marlo; CURLY: Ralph Lowe; LAUREY: Florence Henderson; CORD: Charles Hart; FRED: Charles Scott; SLIM: John Addis; WILL: Victor Griffin; JUD: Alfred Cibelli Jr.; ADO ANNIE: Jacqueline Daniels; ALI HAKIM: Harold Gray, *Jerry Mann*; GERTIE: Judy Rawlings; ELLEN: Margery Reilley; KATE: Davis Gladstone; SYLVIE: Jean Bledsoe; ARMINA: Marquita Living; AGGIE: Anita Berman; ANDREW: Owen Martin; CHALMERS: Victor Reilley; MIKE: Bob Lord. After a hiatus, the tour returned to New York, to City Center.

CITY CENTER, NYC, 8/31/53–10/3/53. 40 PERFORMANCES. It had the same basic crew as for the original phase of the tour, except: CHOREOGRAPHER: Betty Gour; ORCHESTRA DIRECTOR: Peter Laurini; PRESS: Michel Mok, George A. Florida, Peggy Phillips; COMPANY MANAGER: Harry Shapiro; STAGE MANAGERS: David Sidney Weinstein, Philip Johnson, Charles Scott. **Cast:** AUNT ELLER: Mary Marlo; CURLY: Ridge Bond; LAUREY: Florence Henderson; CORD: Charles Hart; FRED: Charles Scott; SLIM: Charles Rule; WILL: Harris Hawkins; JUD: Alfred Cibelli Jr.; ADO ANNIE: Barbara Cook; ALI HAKIM: David Le Grant; GERTIE: Judy Rawlings; ELLEN: Maggi Nelson; KATE: Barbara Reisman; SYLVIE: Patti Parsons; ARMINA: Lynne Broadbent; AGGIE: Cathy Conklin; ANDREW: Owen Martin; CHALMERS: George Lawrence; MIKE: Bob Lord; SINGERS: Lenore Arnold, Lois Barrodin, Marylin Hardy, Frances Irby, Heidi Palmer, Barbara Reisman, Jeanne Shea, William Ambler, Dino Dante, James Fox, Christopher Golden, Bob Lord, Charles Rule, Charles Scott; DANCERS: Lynne Broadbent, Bette Burton, Cathy Conklin, Betty Koerber, Gayle Parmelee, Patti Parsons, Cynthia Price, Georganne Shaw, Louellen Sibley, Marguerite Stewart, Payne Converse, Nick Dana, Jack Ketcham, Ronnie Landry, John Pero Jr., Tom Pickler, Joe Ribeau. Reviews were not great. After closing at City Center this production went on to the final phase of the national tour. Frances Irby replaced Barbara Reisman as Kate, but aside from that the cast and crew were the same. The 10-year tour finally closed on 5/1/54, at the Shubert, Philadelphia (a tour record not beaten until the 4th tour of *Cats* in 1999).

THE MOVIE. 1955. The first film in Todd-AO. **Cast:** AUNT ELLER: Charlotte Greenwood; CURLY: Gordon MacRae; LAUREY: Shirley Jones; IKE: Jay C. Flippen; WILL: Gene Nelson; JUD: Rod Steiger; ADO ANNIE: Gloria Grahame; ALI HAKIM: Eddie Albert; GERTIE: Barbara Lawrence; DREAM CURLY: James Mitchell; DREAM LAUREY: Bambi Linn; ANDREW: James Whitmore.

CITY CENTER, NYC, 3/19/58–3/30/58. 16 PERFORMANCES. PRESENTED BY the New York City Center Light Opera Company; DIRECTOR: John Fearnley; CHOREOGRAPHER: Gemze de Lappe; SETS: Lemuel Ayers; COSTUME SUPERVISOR: Florence Klotz; LIGHTING: Peggy Clark; MUSICAL DIRECTOR: Frederick Dvonch. **Cast:** AUNT ELLER: Betty Garde; CURLY: Herbert Banke; LAUREY: Lois O'Brien; WILL: Gene Nelson; JUD: Douglas Fletcher Rodgers; ADO ANNIE: Helen Gallagher; ALI HAKIM: Harvey Lembeck; GERTIE: Patricia Finch; SYLVIE/BALLET LAUREY: Gemze de Lappe; BALLET CURLY: Michael Maule; BALLET JUD: George Church; GIRL WHO FALLS DOWN: Evelyn Taylor; ANDREW: Owen Martin; CORD: Sheppard Kerman; SINGERS INCLUDED: Lois Van Pelt, Ralph Farnworth, Sam Kirkham, Casper Roos, Ralph Vucci; DANCERS INCLUDED: Patricia Birch, Ilona Murai, Toodie Wittmer, Jenny Workman, Eddie Weston.

CITY CENTER, NYC, 2/27/63–3/10/63. 15 PERFORMANCES. Return engagement 5/15/63–5/26/53. 15 PERFORMANCES. PRESENTED BY The New York City Center Light Opera Company; DIRECTOR: John Fearnley; CHOREOGRAPHER: Agnes de Mille; ASSISTANT CHOREOGRAPHER: Gemze de Lappe, *Mavis Ray* (from 5/15/63); SETS: Lem Ayers; COSTUMES: Stanley Simmons; LIGHTING: Peggy Clark; CONDUCTOR: Julius Rudel. **Cast:** AUNT ELLER: Betty Garde; CURLY: Peter Palmer; LAUREY: Louise O'Brien; WILL: Richard France; JUD: Daniel P. Hannafin; ADO ANNIE: Ann Fraser, *Fay De Witt* (from 5/15/63); ALI HAKIM: Gabriel Dell, *Barry Newman* (from 5/15/63); GERTIE: Marilyne Mason; BALLET CURLY: Grover Dale; BALLET LAUREY: Evelyn Taylor; BALLET JUD: George Church; THE GIRL WHO FALLS DOWN: Gemze de Lappe, *Mavis Ray* (from 5/15/63); ANDREW: William Tierney; CORD: John Carver,

Kermit Kegley (from 5/15/63); DANCERS INCLUDED: Virginia Bosler, Lucia Lambert, Dennis Cole, Loren Hightower, Vernon Lusby, Mavis Ray; SINGERS INCLUDED: Julie Sargant, Herb Surface, Ralph Vucci. **Understudies**: Laurey: Jamie Thomas, *Sharon Vaughn* (from 5/15/63); Jud: John Carver, *Robert Carle* (from 5/15/63).

CITY CENTER, NYC, 12/15/65–1/2/66. 24 PERFORMANCES. PRESENTED BY the New York City Center Light Opera Company; DIRECTOR: John Fearnley; CHOREOGRAPHER: Gemze de Lappe; MUSICAL DIRECTOR: Pembroke Davenport; ASSISTANT CONDUCTOR: Abba Bogin. **Cast**: AUNT ELLER: Ruth Kobart; CURLY: John Davidson; LAUREY/BALLET LAUREY: Susan Watson; WILL: Richard France; JUD: Daniel P. Hannafin; ADO ANNIE: Karen Morrow; ALI HAKIM: Jules Munshin; GERTIE/THE GIRL WHO FALLS DOWN: Loi Leabo; BALLET CURLY: Dean Crane; BALLET JUD: James Albright; THE CHILD IN BALLET: Jane Levin; ANDREW: Sammy Smith; CORD: Herb Surface; GIRL DANCERS INCLUDED: Cathy Conklin, Carol Estey, Toodie Wittmer; GIRL SINGERS INCLUDED: Vicki Belmonte, Maggie Worth; BOY SINGERS INCLUDED: Victor Helou. **Understudies**: Laurey: Laurie Franks & Sharon Herr.

NEW YORK STATE THEATRE, 6/23/69–9/6/69. 88 PERFORMANCES. PRESENTED BY the Music Theatre of Lincoln Center; DIRECTOR: John Kennedy; CHOREOGRAPHER: Gemze de Lappe; SETS/LIGHTING: Paul C. McGuire; COSTUMES: Miles White; MUSICAL DIRECTOR: Jay Blackton. **Cast**: AUNT ELLER: Margaret Hamilton; CURLY: Bruce Yarnell; LAUREY: Lee Beery [i.e. Leigh Beery]; IKE: Sam Kirkham; SLIM: Del Horstmann; JOE: Kurt Olson; WILL: Lee Roy Reams; JUD: Spiro Malas; ADO ANNIE: April Shawhan; ALI HAKIM: Ted Beniades; GERTIE: June Helmers; BALLET CURLY: Brynar Mehl; BALLET LAUREY/GIRL WHO FALLS DOWN: Sandra Balesti; BALLET JUD: James Albright; BALLET CHILD: Lee Wilson; DONNA: Donna Monroe; JUDITH: Judith McCauley; ANDREW: William Griffis; CORD: John Gerstad; DANCERS INCLUDED: Graciela Daniele, Sally Ransone, Lana Sloniger, Toodie Wittmer, Jenny Workman, Mary Zahn, Paul Berne, Andy Bew, Bjarne Buchtrup, William Glassman, Ralph Nelson; SINGERS INCLUDED: Dixie Stewart, Maggie Task, Maggie Worth, John Dorrin, Robert Lenn, Alexander Orfaly, Ken Richards.

JONES BEACH THEATRE, New York, 6/27/75–8/31/75. PRESENTED BY Guy Lombardo; DIRECTOR: John Fearnley; CHOREOGRAPHER: Robert Pagent; SETS: John W. Keck; COSTUMES: Winn Morton; LIGHTING: Thomas Skelton; MUSICAL DIRECTOR: Jay Blackton; CHORAL DIRECTOR: Robert Monteil; COMPANY MANAGER: Sam Pagliaro; PRODUCTION STAGE MANAGER: Morty Halpern; ASSISTANT STAGE MANAGERS: Stan Page & Tony Slez. **Cast**: AUNT ELLER: Nancy Andrews; CURLY: Thomas McKinney; LAUREY: Judith McCauley; IKE: Lee Cass; SLIM: Stan Page; WILL: Harvey Evans; JUD: Will Roy; ADO ANNIE: Patricia Masters; ALI HAKIM: Bruce Adler; GERTIE: Sherry Lambert; BALLET CURLY: Jeremy Blanton; BALLET LAUREY: Dru Alexandrine; BALLET JUD: Russell Anderson; ANDREW: John Dorrin; CORD: Bob Pagent; CHORUS: Jean Busada, Doris Galiber, Mickey Gunnersen, Joyce McDonald, Kathleen Robey, Dixie Stewart, Candace Tovar, Ralph Vucci, Tony Slez.

506. *Oklahoma!* (1979 Broadway revival)

Before Broadway. Zev Bufman put on a revival of *Oklahoma!* in Miami in 1/79. **Cast**: AUNT ELLER: Mary Wickes; CURLY: Harve Presnell; LAUREY: Betsy Beard; ADO ANNIE: Maureen Moore; ALI HAKIM: Lewis J. Stadlen. It was such a success that Mr. Bufman recast it, and took it on the road in 6/79. On 8/9/79 it opened at KENNEDY CENTER (40 PERFORMANCES). In December it wound up on Broadway. William Hammerstein was Oscar II's son.

The Broadway Run. PALACE THEATRE, 12/13/79–8/31/80. 9 previews. 301 PERFORMANCES. PRESENTED BY Zev Bufman & James M. Nederlander, in association with Donald C. Carter; MUSIC: Richard Rodgers; LYRICS/BOOK: Oscar Hammerstein II; BASED ON the play *Green Grow the Lilacs*, by Lynn Riggs; DIRECTOR: William Hammerstein; CHOREOGRAPHER: Gemze de Lappe (re-created Agnes de Mille's choreography); TAP CHOREOGRAPHY SEQUENCES: Miriam Nelson; ROPE SEQUENCES: Montie Montana; SETS: Michael J. Hotopp & Paul de Pass; COSTUMES: Bill Hargate; LIGHTING: Thomas Skelton; SOUND: Les Ginsberg; MUSI-

CAL DIRECTOR: Jay Blackton; ORIGINAL ORCHESTRATIONS: Robert Russell Bennett; CAST RECORDING on RCA; PRESS: Fred Nathan & Eric Elice; CASTING: Julie Hughes & Barry Moss; GENERAL MANAGER: Theatre Now; COMPANY MANAGER: James Awe; PRODUCTION STAGE MANAGER: Bob D. Bernard; STAGE MANAGER: Elise Warner; ASSISTANT STAGE MANAGER: Philip Rash. **Cast**: AUNT ELLER: Mary Wickes (3) ✶; CURLY: Laurence Guittard (1) ✶, *Joel Higgins* (from 5/12/80); LAUREY: Christine Andreas (2) ✶; IKE SKIDMORE: Robert Ray; SLIM: Stephen Crane; WILL PARKER: Harry Groener (6); JUD FRY: Martin Vidnovic (4), *David Brummel*; ADO ANNIE CARNES: Christine Ebersole (5), *Susan Bigelow* (from 6/10/80), *Catherine Cox* (from 7/80); ALI HAKIM: Bruce Adler (7); GERTIE CUMMINGS: Martha Traverse; DREAM BALLET: CURLY: David Evans; LAUREY: Louise Hickey; JUD: Anthony Santiago; THE CHILD: Judy Epstein; POSTCARDS: Patti Ross, Ilene Strickler, Susan Whelan; LAUREY'S FRIENDS: Sydney Anderson, Tonda Hannum, Kristina Koebel, Leslie Morris, Martha Traverse; COWBOYS: Eric Aaron, Brian Bullard, Philip Candler, Joel T. Myers, Michael Page, Kevin Ryan, Robert Sullivan [end of Dream Ballet sequence]; ANDREW CARNES: Philip Rash (8); CORD ELAM: Nick Jolley; SINGERS: Sydney Anderson, Stephen Crain, Lorraine Foreman, Nick Jolley, John Kildahl, Jessica Molaskey, Joel T. Myers, Philip Rash, Robert Ray, Martha Traverse, M. Lynne Wieneke; DANCERS: Eric Aaron, Brian Bullard, Phillip Candler, Judy Epstein, David Evans, Tonda Hannum, Louise Hickey, Kristina Koebel, Leslie Morris, Michael Page, Patti Ross, Kevin Ryan, Anthony Santiago, Ilene Strickler, Robert Sullivan, Susan Whelan. **Standby**: Ali Hakim: Robertson Carricart. **Understudies**: Curly: Stephen Crain; Laurey: M. Lynne Wieneke; Aunt Eller: Lorraine Foreman; Jud: John Kildahl; Ado Annie: Sydney Anderson; Will: Eric Aaron; Dancing Laurey: Leslie Morris; Dancing Curly: Robert Sullivan; Dancing Jud: Philip Candler; Andrew: Nick Jolley; **Swing Dancers**: Gina Martin & Jerry Ziaja.

Broadway reviews were very divided. Harry Groener and Christine Andreas were nominated for Tonys. Richard Rodgers died on 12/30/79, aged 77. After Broadway this revival continued with its tour.

After Broadway. After Broadway Zev Bufman's tour of *Oklahoma!* continued, opening on 12/29/80, at the Civic Auditorium, Jacksonville, Fla. Same basic crew, except for CHOREOGRAPHER: David Evans. **Cast**: AUNT ELLER: Mary Boucher; CURLY: William Mallory; LAUREY: Christine Andreas, *Jeannine Taylor* (from 3/17/81); IKE: Dennis D. Driskill; SLIM: Ralph Bard; WILL: Lara Teeter; JUD: Richard Leighton; ADO ANNIE: Paige O'Hara; ALI HAKIM: Bruce Adler; GERTIE: Catherine Campbell; ANDREW: Robertson Carricart; DREAM LAUREY: Louise Hickey, *Bronwyn Thomas*; DREAM CURLY: Michael Ragan, *Jeff Fahey*; DREAM JUD: Michael Howell Deane; THE CHILD: Judy Epstein; JUD'S POSTCARDS: Patti Ross (*Elena Malfitano*), Kristina Koebel (*Jan Ilene Miller*), Susan Whelan.

HAYMARKET THEATRE, Leicester, England, 1/80; then it toured; then it ran at the PALACE THEATRE, London, 9/17/80–9/19/80. PRESENTED BY Cameron Mackintosh & Emile Littler; DIRECTOR: James Hammerstein; RE-STAGED & ADAPTED BY: Gemze de Lappe; SETS/COSTUMES: Tim Goodchild; MUSICAL DIRECTOR: John Owen Edwards. There was a live cast recording. **Cast**: CURLY: John Diedrich; LAUREY: Rosamund Shelley, *Maria Friedman*; WILL: Mark White; JUD: Alfred Molina; ADO ANNIE: Jillian Mack, *Maria Friedman*; ALI HAKIM: Linal Haft; GERTIE: Norma Atallah; ANDREW: Robert Bridges; DORIS: Maria Friedman [her West End debut]. **Understudy**: Laurey/Ado Annie: Maria Friedman.

507. *Oklahoma!* (2002 Broadway revival)

This was the much-vaunted "new" *Oklahoma!*, come from London. It had new, updated, staging by Trevor Nunn, and new choreography by Susan Stroman (i.e this was the first production of *Oklahoma!* to feature choreography that was not the legendary Agnes de Mille choreography of the 1943 production. The actors who played Laurey and Curly also played those roles in the dream sequences, whereas the original choreography had had other actors play those parts.

Before Broadway. OLIVIER THEATRE (part of the Royal National Theatre), 7/15/98–10/3/98. Previews from 7/6/98. Then it transferred to the West End, to the LYCEUM THEATRE, 1/20/99–10/3/01, for a limited run. DIRECTOR: Trevor Nunn; NEW CHOREOGRAPHY BY: Susan Stroman; SETS/COSTUMES: Anthony Ward; LIGHTING: David Hersey; SOUND: Paul Groothuis; MUSICAL SUPERVISOR: David Caddick; MUSICAL DIRECTOR: John Owen Edwards; ORIGINAL ORCHESTRATIONS: Robert Russell Bennett; ADDITIONAL ORCHESTRATIONS: William David Brohn; NEW DANCE MUSIC ARRANGEMENTS: David Krane. *Cast:* AUNT ELLER: Maureen Lipman; CURLY: Hugh Jackman; LAUREY: Josefina Gabrielle; WILL: Jimmy Johnston; JUD: Shuler Hensley; ADO ANNIE: Vicki Simon; ALI HAKIM: Peter Polycarpou; GERTIE: Rebecca Thornhill. The show got raves, and won four Olivier Awards, including best musical and one for Shuler Hensley. The show broke all RNT box-office records, then went to Broadway.

The first attempt to bring over the London revival, with an all–British cast, was nixed by Equity in New York on 2/16/99. Then it was going to play at the Ford Center for the Performing Arts in the fall of 2000, but, again, it never made it, because of the tight schedules of Susan Stroman and Trevor Nunn. On 5/17/01 Cameron Mackintosh first announced that it would finally come to Broadway. On 8/16/01 Shuler Hensley and Patrick Wilson were confirmed in their roles. Josefina Gabrielle, who appeared by permission of Actors Equity, was confirmed in her role on 12/12/01. The rest of the cast was confirmed on 1/3/02.

The Broadway Run. GERSHWIN THEATRE, 3/21/02–2/23/03. 25 previews 2/23/02–3/20/02. 388 PERFORMANCES. The Royal National Theatre production, PRESENTED BY Cameron Mackintosh, by arrangement with The Rodgers & Hammerstein Organization. It had the same basic crew as for the London production, except: MUSICAL DIRECTOR: Kevin Stites; PRESS: The Publicity Office; CASTING: Tara Rubin Casting & Johnson — Liff Associates; EXECUTIVE PRODUCERS: David Caddick, Nicholas Allott, Matthew Dalco; GENERAL MANAGERS: Alan Wasser Associates; COMPANY MANAGER: Susan Bell; PRODUCTION STAGE MANAGER: Mahlon Kruse; STAGE MANAGERS: Steven R. Gruse & Beverly Jenkins. *Cast:* AUNT ELLER MURPHY: Andrea Martin, *Patty Duke* (from 12/14/02), *Audrie Neenan*; CURLY MCLAIN: Patrick Wilson (until 11/17/02), *Stephen R. Buntrock* (from 11/19/02); LAUREY WILLIAMS: Josefina Gabrielle (until 2/17/03), *Amy Bodnar*; IKE SKIDMORE: Ronn Carroll, *John Jellison*; FRED: Greg Stone; SLIM: Kevin Bernard; WILL PARKER: Justin Bohon; JUD FRY: Shuler Hensley (until 1/5/03), *Merwin Foard* (from 1/7/03); ADO ANNIE CARNES: Jessica Boevers; ALI HAKIM: Aasif Mandvi; GERTIE CUMMINGS: Mia Price; ELLEN: Rosena M. Hill; KATE: Elizabeth Loyacano; SYLVIE: Kathy Voytko; ARMINA: Audrie Neenan; AGGIE: Amy Bodnar; ANDREW CARNES: Michael McCarty; CORD ELAM: Michael X. Martin; JESS: Clyde Alves, *Enrique Brown*; CHALMERS: Merwin Foard (until 1/7/03); MIKE: Michael Thomas Holmes; JOE: Stephen R. Buntrock; SAM: Nicholas Dromard; CORKY: Matt Allen; SUSIE: Bradley Benjamin; JAKE: Chris Holly; LIL' TICH: Julianna Rose Mauriello; ROSIE: Rachelle Rak; TOM: Jermaine R. Rembert; TRAVIS: Stephen Scott Scarpulla, *P.J. Verhoest*; VIVIAN: Laura Shoop; EMILY: Sarah Spradlin-Bonomo; DESIREE: Lauren Ullrich; MAVERICK: William Ullrich; LUCY: Catherine Wreford, *Jennifer MacKensie Dunn*. **Understudies:** Laurey: Amy Bodnar & Laura Shoop; Curly: Stephen R. Buntrock & Greg Stone, *Aaron Lazar*; Andrew/Ike: Harvey Evans; Aunt Eller: Audrie Neenan; Jud: Merwin Foard & Michael X. Martin; Ado Annie: Kathy Voytko & Catherine Wreford; Will: Matt Allen & Nicholas Dromard; Ali Hakim: Michael Thomas Holmes & Tony Yazbeck. **Swings:** Dilys Croman, Rommy Sandhu, Jennifer West, Tony Yazbeck, *Tom Flagg, Sarah Jayne Jensen, Tyler Hanes*. **Orchestra:** KEYBOARD: Paul Raiman; CELLI: Charles duChateau & Sarah Carter; CONCERTMASTER: Martin Agee; VIOLINS: Cenovia Cummins, Xin M. Zhao, James Tsao; VIOLA: Ken Burward-Hoy; BASS: Peter Donovan; REEDS: Ed Joffe, Matt Dine, John J. Moses, Steve Kenyon, Thomas Sefcovic; TRUMPETS: Don Downs, Tino Gagliardi; TROMBONE: Keith O'Quinn; FRENCH HORNS: Lawrence DiBello & Peter Schoettler; DRUMS: Perry Cavari; PERCUSSION: James Baker; GUITAR/BANJO: Greg Utzig; HARP: Grace Paradise. Broadway reviews were great, but not as great as in London. The show won a Tony Award for Shuler Hensley, and received nominations for revival of a musical, direction of a musical, choreography, light-

ing, Patrick Wilson and Andrea Martin. PBS aired it on TV on 11/22/03.

After Broadway. ROYAL ALBERT HALL, London, 2002. In concert. BBC ORCHESTRA DIRECTED BY: Kenneth Anderson. *Cast:* AUNT ELLER: Maureen Lipman; CURLY: Brent Barrett; LAUREY: Lisa Vroman; WILL: Tim Flavin; JUD: Karl Daymond; ADO ANNIE: Klea Blackhurst.

NON-EQUITY TOUR. It first played at the Kennedy Center, Washington, DC, 6/30/03–9/6/03, then continued the tour. DIRECTOR: Trevor Nunn; CHOREOGRAPHER: Susan Stroman.

NON-EQUITY TOUR. Opened on 12/16/03, at the Buell Theatre, Denver. The production retained the sets, costumes, and lighting from the West End production of the "new" *Oklahoma!* (upon which it was based). PRESENTED BY Ken Gentry/NETworks; DIRECTOR: Fred Hanson; CHOREOGRAPHER: Ginger Thatcher, The tour closed, but resumed on 9/14/04, at the BJCC Concert Hall, Birmingham, Ala. *Cast:* CURLY: Jeremiah James; LAUREY: Julie Burdick; ADO ANNIE: Carrie Love; ALI HAKIM: Sorab Wadia; AUNT ELLER: Brenda Martindale.

Over 30,000 productions of *Oklahoma!* have been put on worldwide, and that's just those given licenses through the Rodgers and Hammerstein Theatre Library, which controls the show.

508. *Oliver!*

Set in the North of England and in London about 1850. In the workhouse Oliver dares to ask Mr. Bumble for more gruel, and is locked up, while Bumble and widow Corney flirt. Oliver is taken to work for Sowerberry, but is even more badly treated here, and runs away. He is befriended by the Artful Dodger, one of Fagin's gang of pickpockets, which include Bill Sikes and his girlfriend Nancy. Oliver goes out to pick pockets, but is falsely arrested for stealing the handkerchief of a rich old gentleman, Mr. Brownlow, who, however, has Oliver released and taken home with him. Fagin is alarmed that the boy might talk, so Sikes bullies Nancy into getting him back. Mr. Brownlow is struck by Oliver's resemblance to his late daughter, who disappeared many years ago. He adopts Oliver, but Nancy gets Oliver back to Fagin's den. Meanwhile Sally, an old woman on her deathbed in the workhouse, confesses that she stole a brooch from Oliver's mother when she died years ago. Bumble and Widow Corney, who have now married, put it together that Oliver is really Mr. Brownlow's grandson, and Bumble goes to Brownlow, hoping to get a reward for the brooch, but Brownlow threatens to have him imprisoned for mistreating his workhouse charges. Nancy goes to see Brownlow, admits her guilt, and arranges to deliver Oliver to Mr. Brownlow at night on London Bridge, but Bill Sikes kills her, snatches Oliver, and after a chase is killed himself. Oliver is restored to Mr. Brownlow. Fagin considers going straight.

Before Broadway. The very first production of this British tour de force by Lionel Bart was at the WIMBLEDON THEATRE, on the outskirts of London. It opened there on 6/10/60, and almost folded. Then it moved to London's West End, to the NEW THEATRE, 6/30/60–9/10/66. 2,618 PERFORMANCES. PRESENTED BY Donald Albery; DIRECTOR: Peter Coe; CHOREOGRAPHER: Malcolm Clare; SETS/COSTUMES: Sean Kenny; LIGHTING: John Wyckham; MUSICAL DIRECTOR: Ronnie Franklin, *Marcus Dods*; ORCHESTRATIONS: Eric Rogers; LONDON CAST RECORDING on Decca. *Cast:* FAGIN: Ron Moody, *John Bluthal, Aubrey Woods, Johnny Lockwood*; NANCY: Georgia Brown, *Vivienne Martin, Judith Bruce, Nicolette Roeg, Elizabeth Perry, Penny Allen*; SOWERBERRY: Barry Humphries, *Michael Bretton, David Pugh, David Monico*; OLIVER: Keith Hamshere, *Royston Thomas, Martin Stephens, Colin Page, Michael Mennick, Kit Williams, Stevie Walters, Terence Holmes, Kim Goodman, Robert Cook, Peter Bartlett, Raymond Ward, Tommy Mann*; BUMBLE: Paul Whitsun-Jones, *Robert Bridges, Rob Inglis*; THE DODGER: Martin Horsey, *Tony Robinson, Michael Goodman, Chris Andrews, Leonard Whiting, David Jones* [he was later Davy Jones, of the Monkees], *Jimmy Handley, Jimmy Thomas, Stephen Leigh*; SIKES: Danny Sewell, *John Orchard, Harry Goodier, *George Little*; BROWNLOW: George Bishop; MRS. CORNEY: Hope Jackman, *Olwen Griffiths, Brenda Scaife*; MRS. SOWERBERRY: Sonia Fraser, *Julia Nelson, Edna Dore*; SALLY: Betty Turner; NOAH: Trevor Ray, *David Beaumont*; BET: Dian Grey, *Vivien Read, Gillian Hoyle, Deborah Cranston, Winnie Hunt, Carla Challoner, Lynn Bartlett, Sally Handley, Janet Krasowski, Marian Dore, Beryl Corsan, Kathryn Handley, Glenda Sims*; CHARLOTTE: Apple Brook, *Janet Pate, Penny Reid, Irene French.*

It was the longest-running West End musical of the 1960s — indeed, until *Jesus Christ Superstar*. There was a UK tour of this production. One of the assistant stage managers on this tour was a young Cameron Mackintosh.

Then the show came to the USA. There was a newspaper strike (12/8/62–3/31/63), so the show went out on tour before Broadway, playing Los Angeles, San Francisco, Detroit, and Toronto, before coming to Broadway, where its opening date of 12/27/62 had been delayed. David Jones replaced Michael Goodman as the Artful Dodger before Broadway and his billing was raised from 11th to 4th. Bruce Prochnik's billing was raised similarly from 10th to 3rd. Frederic Warriner was replaced by Barry Humphries. Then it went to Broadway. Much radio advertising was done for the Broadway run. Bruce Prochnik's father was fined £5 by the British government for allowing his under-age son to work out of the UK. The sets were magnificent and the complex scene changes were done with seemingly no effort.

The Broadway Run. IMPERIAL THEATRE, 1/6/63–9/12/64; SHUBERT THEATRE, 9/16/64–11/14/64. Total of 774 PERFORMANCES. PRESENTED BY David Merrick & Donald Albery; MUSIC/LYRICS/BOOK: Lionel Bart; FREELY ADAPTED from the 1838 novel *Oliver Twist*, by Charles Dickens; DIRECTOR: Peter Coe; CHOREOGRAPHER: none listed; SETS: Sean Kenny; COSTUMES: M. Berman Ltd.; LIGHTING: John Wyckham; MUSICAL DIRECTOR: Donald Pippin, *Oscar Kosarin*; ORCHESTRATIONS: Eric Rogers; BROADWAY CAST RECORDING on RCA Victor; PRESS: Harvey B. Sabinson, Lee Solters, David Powers, *Lila Glaser* (by 63–64 she had become Lila Glaser King); CASTING: Michael Shurtleff & Alan Shayne; GENERAL MANAGER: Jack Schlissel; COMPANY MANAGER: Richard Highley; PRODUCTION STAGE MANAGER: Ross Bowman; STAGE MANAGER: Edward Hastings; ASSISTANT STAGE MANAGER: Moose Peting. **Cast:** OLIVER TWIST: Bruce Prochnik (3), *Paul O'Keefe, Ronnie Kroll* (from 11/18/63), *Victor Stiles* (from 9/25/64); AT THE WORKHOUSE: MR. BUMBLE, THE BEADLE: Willoughby Goddard (5); MRS. CORNEY, THE MATRON: Hope Jackman (6), *Helena Carroll*; OLD SALLY, A PAUPER: Ruth Maynard; AT THE UNDERTAKER'S: MR. SOWERBERRY, THE UNDERTAKER: Barry Humphries (11), *Robin Ramsey*; MRS. SOWERBERRY, HIS WIFE: Helena Carroll (10), *Ruth Maynard*; CHARLOTTE, THEIR DAUGHTER: Cherry Davis; NOAH CLAYPOLE, THEIR APPRENTICE: Terry Lomax; AT THE THIEVES' KITCHEN: FAGIN: Clive Revill (1) ☆, *Robin Ramsey* (during Mr. Revill's absences, for a short time until 8/19/63, and again 10/14/63–10/21/63, and again from 9/25/63); THE ARTFUL DODGER: David Jones (4), *George Priolo*; NANCY: Georgia Brown (2) ☆, *Maura K. Wedge* (during Miss Brown's vacations, from 7/22/63 and from 9/25/63); BET: Alice Playten, *Joan Lombardo*; BILL SIKES: Danny Sewell (9); AT THE BROWNLOWS': MR. BROWNLOW: Geoffrey Lumb (7); DR. GRIMWIG: John Call (8); MRS. BEDWIN: Dortha Duckworth; WORKHOUSE BOYS/FAGIN'S GANG: Johnny Borden (gone by 63–64), Eugene Endon, Bryant Fraser, Randy Gaynes (gone by 63–64), Bobby Gold (gone by 63–64), Sal Lombardo (gone by 63–64), Christopher Month, Patrick O'Shaughnessy, Alan Paul (gone by 63–64), Barry Pearl (gone by 63–64), George Priolo, Robbie Reed, Christopher Votos. 63–64 replacements: *Bobbie Bradley, Stuart Getz, Paul Kroll, Ronald Kroll, Bart Larsen, Blaise Morton, Jackie Perkuhn, Malcolm Taylor, Victor Stiles*; LONDONERS: Jed Allan (gone by 63–64), Barbara Bossert (gone by 63–64), Jack Davison, James Glenn, Lesley Hunt, John M. Kimbro, Michael Lamont (gone by 63–64), Allan Lokos, Dodie Marshall (gone by 63–64), Richard Miller, Moose Peting, Ruth Ramsey, Nita Reiter (gone by 63–64), Ray Tudor, Maura K. Wedge, *Linda Barrie, Johnny Borden, Lucille Cole, Michael Roberts, Terry Robinson, Ann Tell, Howard Ross*. **Standbys:** Nancy: Maura K. Wedge, Rae Allen; Mrs. Sowerberry: *Rae Allen, Ann Tell*. **Understudies:** Oliver: Eugene Endon, *Randy Gaynes, Blaise Morton, Victor Stiles*; Fagin: Barry Humphries (*Robin Ramsey*) & Richard Miller; Dodger: Johnny Borden (*Malcolm Taylor*) & George Priolo, *Paul Kroll*; Sikes: Jed Allan, *Michael Roberts*; Bumble: John Call; Widow Corney:

Helena Carroll, *Ann Tell*; Brownlow: Allan Lokos; Grimwig: John M. Kimbro; Sowerberry: Ray Tudor; Charlotte/Bet: Lesley Hunt; Noah: Michael Lamont; Sally/Mrs. Bedwin: Ruth Ramsey. **Act I: Scene 1** The workhouse: "Food, Glorious Food" (Oliver & Boys) [a big hit], "Oliver!" (Bumble, Widow Corney, Oliver & Boys); **Scene 2** The workhouse parlor: "I Shall Scream" (Widow Corney & Bumble); **Scene 3** The undertaker's: "Boy for Sale" (Bumble), "That's Your Funeral" (Sowerberry, Bumble, Mrs. Sowerberry), "Where is Love?" (Oliver); **Scene 4** Paddington Green: "Consider Yourself" (Dodger, Oliver & Crowd) [a hit]; **Scene 5** The Thieves' Kitchen: "You've Got to Pick a Pocket or Two" (Fagin, Oliver & Boys) [a hit], "It's a Fine Life" (Nancy, Bet & Boys), "I'd Do Anything" (Dodger, Nancy, Oliver, Bet, Fagin & Boys) [a hit]; **Scene 6** Streets of London: "Be Back Soon" (Fagin, Dodger, Oliver & Boys). **Act II: Scene 1** *The Three Cripples* tavern: "Oom-Pah-Pah" (Nancy & Chorus), "My Name" (Sikes), "As Long as He Needs Me" (Nancy) [a big hit]; **Scene 2** The Brownlows': "Where is Love?" (reprise) (Mrs. Bedwin), "Who Will Buy?" (Oliver & Chorus) [a big hit]; **Scene 3** The Thieves' Kitchen: "It's a Fine Life" (reprise) (Sikes, Nancy, Fagin, Boys), "Reviewing the Situation" (Fagin) [a hit]; **Scene 4** The workhouse: "Oliver" (reprise) (Bumble & Widow Corney); **Scene 5** The Brownlows': "As Long as He Needs Me" (reprise) (Nancy), "Reviewing the Situation" (reprise) (Fagin); **Scene 6** London Bridge: Finale, consisting of: "Food, Glorious Food" (reprise) (Boys), "Consider Yourself" (reprise) (Boys), "I'd Do Anything" (reprise) (Company).

Critics mostly raved. The show won Tony Awards for composer & lyricist, sets, and musical direction, and was nominated for musical, producers of a musical, book, direction of a musical, and for Clive Revill, Georgia Brown, and David Jones. During the Broadway run Bruce Prochnik outgrew the role and was replaced by Paul O'Keefe, who was also appearing on Patty Duke's TV series. *Oliver!* was the longest-running British musical in Broadway history until surpassed by *Evita*.

After Broadway. TOUR. Opened on 9/30/64, at the Community Theatre, Hershey, Pennsylvania, while the Broadway show was still running. PRESENTED BY Henry Guettel & Arthur Cantor; DIRECTOR: Edward Hastings; SETS: James Hamilton; COSTUMES: Patton Campbell; LIGHTING: Peter Hunt; MUSICAL DIRECTOR: William Brohn. **Cast:** OLIVER: Christopher Spooner; BUMBLE: Dale Malone; MRS. CORNEY: Lu Leonard; MRS. SOWERBERRY/SALLY: Patricia Drylie; FAGIN: Jules Munshin; THE ARTFUL DODGER: Chris Andrews; NANCY: Joan Eastman; SIKES: Vincent Beck; HAT VENDOR: Ronn Carroll; MRS. BEDWIN: Christine Thomas.

POST-BROADWAY TOUR. Opened on 11/16/64, at the Shubert Theatre, Cincinnati. MUSICAL DIRECTOR: Robert McNamee. **Cast:** OLIVER: Ronnie Kroll; BUMBLE: Alan Crofoot; MRS. CORNEY: Dawna Shove; MRS. SOWERBERRY/SALLY: Ruth Maynard; FAGIN: Robin Ramsey; THE ARTFUL DODGER: David Jones; NANCY: Judy Bruce, *Maura K. Wedge*; BET: Joan Lombardo; SIKES: Danny Sewell; GRIMWIG: John Call; MRS. BEDWIN: Dortha Duckworth. In 1965 this tour returned to Broadway (see below).

509. *Oliver!* (1965 return to Broadway)

This was the 1964 post–Broadway tour returned to Broadway.

The Broadway Run. MARTIN BECK THEATRE, 8/2/65–9/25/65. Limited run of 64 PERFORMANCES. It had the same basic crew as for the 1963 Broadway production, except: MUSICAL DIRECTOR: Robert McNamee; NEW CAST RECORDING on Decca; PRESS: Lee Solters, Harvey B. Sabinson, Jay Russell; GENERAL MANAGER: Jack Schlissel; PRODUCTION STAGE MANAGER: Ben D. Kranz; STAGE MANAGER: Geoffrey Johnson. **Cast:** OLIVER TWIST: Victor Stiles; AT THE WORKHOUSE: MR. BUMBLE, THE BEADLE: Alan Crofoot; MRS. CORNEY, THE MATRON: Dawna Shove; OLD SALLY, A PAUPER: Sherill Price; AT THE UNDERTAKER'S: MR. SOWERBERRY, THE UNDERTAKER: John Miranda; MRS. SOWERBERRY, HIS WIFE: Sherill Price; CHARLOTTE, THEIR DAUGHTER: Lynda Sturner; NOAH CLAYPOLE, THEIR APPRENTICE: Billy Brandon; AT THE THIEVES' KITCHEN: FAGIN: Robin Ramsey; THE ARTFUL DODGER: Joey Baio; NANCY: Maura K. Wedge; BET: Donnie Smiley; BILL SIKES:

Danny Sewell; AT THE BROWNLOWS': MR. BROWNLOW: Bram Nossen; DR. GRIMWIG: Fred Miller; MRS. BEDWIN: Dodi Protero; WORKHOUSE BOYS/FAGIN'S GANG: Tommy Battreall, Ronnie K. Douglas, Paul Dwyer, Anthony Endon, Eugene Endon, Harry Gold, Lee Koenig, Bart Larsen, Christopher Month, Jackie Perkuhn, Sonny Rocco, Ricky Rosenthal, Brett Smiley; LONDONERS: Walter Blocher, Ted Bloecher, Reese Burns, Dominic Chianese, Sally Cooke, Marise Counsell, Georgia Dell, Walter Hook, Lesley Hunt, Michael McCormick, Richard Miller, Moose Peting, Terry Robinson, Virginia Sandifur, Gretchen Van Aken, Richard Wulf. ***Understudies***: Oliver: Brett Smiley & Ronnie K. Douglas; Fagin: Richard Miller; Nancy: Gretchen Van Aken; Dodger: Harry Gold & Eugene Endon; Sikes: Richard Wulf; Bumble: Fred Miller; Mrs. Corney/Mrs. Bedwin: Georgia Dell; Brownlow: Walter Hook; Grimwig: John Kimbro; Mrs. Sowerberry/Sally: Marise Counsell; Sowerberry: Dominic Chianese; Charlotte/Bet: Lesley Hunt; Noah: Michael McCormick.

PAPER MILL PLAYHOUSE, New Jersey, 1966. DIRECTOR: Stone Widney. **Cast:** Robin Ramsey, Maura K. Wedge, Michael Kermoyan.

PICCADILLY THEATRE, London, 4/26/67–2/3/68. 331 PERFORMANCES. This revival began only 7½ months after the original London production ended. PRESENTED BY Donald Albery; DIRECTOR: David Phethean; SETS/COSTUMES: Sean Kenny; MUSICAL DIRECTOR: Michael Moores, *Michael Reeves*. **Cast:** OLIVER: Paul Bartlett, *Freddie Foot, John Hicks, Stephen Newman*; BUMBLE: Tom de Ville; MRS. CORNEY: Pamela Pitchford; SALLY: Audrey Leybourne; SOWERBERRY: Glyn Worsnip; MRS. SOWERBERRY: Edna Dore; NOAH: Philip Collins; FAGIN: Barry Humphries, *Robin Ramsey*; THE ARTFUL DODGER: Leslie Stone, *Stephen Leigh, Raymond Milross*; NANCY: Marti Webb; BET: Miriam Mann, *Linda Stembridge*; SIKES: Martin Dell; BROWNLOW: Gavin Gordon.

THE MOVIE. 1968. The film won six Oscars, including for best picture. Onna White won a special Oscar for choreography. SCREENPLAY: Vernon Harris; DIRECTOR: Carol Reed. **Cast:** OLIVER: Mark Lester; BUMBLE: Harry Secombe; MRS. CORNEY: Peggy Mount; SOWERBERRY: Leonard Rossiter; MRS. SOWERBERRY: Hylda Baker; FAGIN: Ron Moody; THE ARTFUL DODGER: Jack Wild; NANCY: Shani Wallis; SIKES: Oliver Reed; BROWNLOW: Joseph O'Conor.

TOURING REVIVAL. Opened on 5/3/73, at the Dorothy Chandler Pavilion, Los Angeles, and closed on 8/18/73, at the Curran Theatre, San Francisco. PRESENTED BY Glenn Jordan & The Los Angeles Civic Light Opera Association; DIRECTOR: Jack Donohue; CHOREOGRAPHER: Lee Theodore; SETS/LIGHTING: John Bury; MUSICAL DIRECTOR: Jay Blackton. **Cast:** OLIVER: Colin Duffy; BUMBLE: Dale Malone; FAGIN: Ron Moody; THE ARTFUL DODGER: David Jones; NANCY: Karen Morrow; SIKES: Jon Cypher; BROWNLOW: Hedley Mattingly; GRIMWIG: Mickey Deems.

PAPER MILL PLAYHOUSE, New Jersey, 1976. DIRECTOR: Charles Gray. **Cast:** John Carradine, Michael Kermoyan, Barbara Marineau.

THE FIRST CAMERON MACKINTOSH REVIVAL. Enormously successful British revival. Opened at the HAYMARKET THEATRE, Leicester, England, on 7/21/77, then toured; then moved to London's West End, to the ALBERY THEATRE, 12/21/77–9/20/80. 1,139 PERFORMANCES. PRESENTED BY Cameron Mackintosh; DIRECTORS: Robin Midgley & Robin Oaks; SETS/COSTUMES: Sean Kenny; MUSICAL DIRECTOR: Chris Walker, *Tony Britten*. **Cast:** OLIVER: Marcus D'Amico, *Alan Younger, Graham Hutchins, Gary Bishop, Mark Eager, Roger Fairhead*; BUMBLE: Robert Bridges, *Thick Wilson*; MRS. CORNEY: Joan Turner, *Margaret Burton*; SOWERBERRY: Graham Hamilton, *John Fleming*; FAGIN: Roy Hudd, *George Sewell, Roy Dotrice*; THE ARTFUL DODGER: Stephen Kebell, *Colin Morgan, Paul Ryan, Jonathan Ellis, Steven Milton, Matthew Peters*; NANCY: Gillian Burns, *Helen Shapiro*; SIKES: Michael Attwell, *Linal Haft, Chris Ellison*; BROWNLOW: Jack Allen, *Geoffrey Toone*.

510. *Oliver! (1984 Broadway revival)*

Before Broadway. The second Cameron Mackintosh revival first ran at the ALDWYCH THEATRE, London, 12/14/83–1/14/84. 37 PERFORMANCES. In 2 acts & 10 scenes. PRESENTED BY Cameron Mackintosh; DIRECTOR: Peter Coe; MUSICAL DIRECTOR: Anthony Howard Williams. **Cast:** OLIVER: Anthony Pearson; BUMBLE: Peter Bayliss; MRS. CORNEY:

Meg Johnson; SOWERBERRY: Richard Frost; FAGIN: Ron Moody; THE ARTFUL DODGER: David Garlick; NANCY: Jackie Marks; SIKES: Linal Haft; BROWNLOW: Geoffrey Toone. After London it went to Broadway.

The Broadway Run. MARK HELLINGER THEATRE, 4/29/84–5/13/84. 12 previews from 4/19/84. 17 PERFORMANCES. PRESENTED BY Cameron Mackintosh, Carole J. Shorenstein, and James M. Nederlander, by arrangement with The Southbrook Group; DIRECTOR: Peter Coe; CHOREOGRAPHER: none listed; SETS: Sean Kenny; LIGHTING: Andrew Bridge; SOUND: Jack Mann; MUSICAL DIRECTOR: John Lesko; ORCHESTRATIONS: Eric Rogers; PRESS: Fred Nathan, Anne Abrams, Leslie Anderson, Ted Killmer, Bert Fink; CASTING: Johnson — Liff; GENERAL MANAGERS: Gatchell & Neufeld; COMPANY MANAGER: Steven H. David; PRODUCTION STAGE MANAGER: Sam Stickler; STAGE MANAGER: Bethe Ward; ASSISTANT STAGE MANAGER: Richard Jay-Alexander. **Cast:** OLIVER TWIST: Braden Danner, Cameron Johann (alternate); AT THE WORKHOUSE: MR. BUMBLE, THE BEADLE: Michael McCarty; MRS. BUMBLE, THE MATRON: Elizabeth Larner; OLD SALLY, A PAUPER: Susan Willis; AT THE UNDERTAKER'S: MR. SOWERBERRY, THE UNDERTAKER: Roderick Horn; MRS. SOWERBERRY, HIS WIFE: Frances Cuka; CHARLOTTE, THEIR DAUGHTER: Andi Henig; NOAH CLAYPOLE, THEIR APPRENTICE: Alan Braunstein; AT THE THIEVES' KITCHEN: FAGIN: Ron Moody; THE ARTFUL DODGER: David Garlick; NANCY: Patti LuPone; BET: Sarah E. Litzsinger; BILL SIKES: Graeme Campbell; BULLSEYE: Vito & Buffy (alternating); AT THE BROWNLOWS': MR. BROWNLOW: Michael Allinson; DR. GRIMWIG: Louis Beachner; MRS. BEDWIN: Elizabeth Larner; WORKHOUSE BOYS/FAGIN'S GANG: Robert David Cavanaugh, Samir Chowdhury, Ruben Cuevas, Roshi Handwerger, Cameron Johann, Mark Manasseri, Michael Manasseri, Kipp Marcus, Shawn Morgal, Brian Noodt, Roy Nygaard, R.D. Robb, Dennis Singletary, Zachary A. Stier; LONDONERS: Diane Armistead, Louis Beachner, Alan Braunstein, Frances Cuka, W.P. Dremak, Gregg Edelman, Tony Gilbert, Eleanor Glockner, Beth Giuffre, Andi Henig, Roderick Horn, Jan Horvath, Michael McCarty, William McClary, Marcia Mitzman, Martin Moran, Barbara Moroz, Cheryl Russell, Clark Sayre, Jane Strauss, Susan Willis. **Standby**: Fagin: Stephen Hanan. **Understudies**: Oliver: Cameron Johann & Zachary A. Stier; Nancy: Marcia Mitzman; Sikes: Tony Gilbert; Mrs. Bumble: Eleanor Glockner; Brownlow: Louis Beachner; Dodger: Kipp Marcus & Michael Manasseri; Bet: Andi Henig; Mrs. Bedwin: Diane Armistead; Grimwig: W.P. Dremak; Charlotte: Jane Strauss; Sowerberry: William McClary; Noah: Martin Moran; Mrs. Sowerberry: Susan Willis. SWINGS: Edward Prostak, Carrie Wilder, Joe Anthony Wright.

The critics raved, and Ron Moody was nominated for a Tony.

After Broadway. PAPER MILL PLAYHOUSE, New Jersey, 1994. DIRECTOR: Robert Johanson; CHOREOGRAPHER: Daniel Stewart; SETS: Michael Anania; LIGHTING: F. Mitchell Dana; MUSICAL DIRECTOR: Jim Coleman. **Cast:** OLIVER: David Lloyd Watson; BUMBLE: David Vosburgh; SOWERBERRY: Keith Perry; MRS. SOWERBERRY: Lou Williford; FAGIN: George S. Irving; THE ARTFUL DODGER: Robert Creighton; NANCY: Judy McLanc; BET: Aileen Quinn; SIKES: Christopher Innvar; BROWNLOW: Michael Allinson.

THE THIRD CAMERON MACKINTOSH REVIVAL. London Palladium, 12/8/94. This was the longest running production ever at the London Palladium. Oliver's creator, Lionel Bart, and Sam Mendes, director of the show, went back to the original Dickens novel for additional dialogue, and Mr. Bart added some new music and lyrics. PRESENTED BY Cameron Mackintosh; DIRECTOR: Sam Mendes; CHOREOGRAPHER: Matthew Bourne; SETS: Anthony Ward; NEW ORCHESTRATIONS: William David Brohn. **Cast:** OLIVER: Gregory Bradley; FAGIN: Jonathan Pryce, *Jim Dale, Russ Abbott*; THE ARTFUL DODGER: Adam Searles; NANCY: Sally Dexter, *Ruthie Henshall*; SIKES: Miles Anderson, *Paul McGann*. The show then went on a UK tour. Then it went to Toronto, with plans for Broadway in the spring of 2000. Toronto happened; Broadway didn't because of the sheer cost of the proposition. It opened for previews at the PRINCESS OF WALES THEATRE, Toronto, 11/4/99 (Lionel Bart had died on 4/4/99). The closing date in Toronto was extended to 1/15/00. *Toronto* **Cast:** FAGIN: Russ Abbott; NANCY: Sonia Swaby. This production also played in AUSTRALIA from 5/02.

THE REVISED REVIVAL IN THE USA. Cameron Mackintosh was going to produce an Equity tour of the USA of the 1994 London production, but scaled down and darker in content. However, he couldn't come to an agreement with the union, and instead, on 1/23/02 announced that it would be a non–Equity tour, to open in 6/03. A proposed opening at the Ordway Center, St. Paul, Minn., 7/22/03–8/10/03 never materialized, and instead the 35-week tour opened on 11/11/03, at the Buell Theatre, Denver. There were 82 in the company (40 on-stage). PRESENTED BY Ken Gentry; DIRECTOR: Graham Gill; CHOREOGRAPHER: Geoff Garratt; SETS: Adrian Vaux; COSTUMES: Anthony Ward; LIGHTING: Jenny Kagan; MUSICAL DIRECTOR: Dominick Amendum; ORCHESTRATIONS: William David Brohn. *Cast:* OLIVER: Justin S. Pereira; FAGIN: Mark McCracken; THE ARTFUL DODGER: Andrew Blau; NANCY: Renata Renee Wilson; SIKES: Shane R. Tanner.

511. *On a Clear Day You Can See Forever*

For obvious reasons this musical is generally referred to as *On a Clear Day*. Set in the present, in New York City. Daisy can predict the future. When she is hypnotized by Mark, a handsome psychiatrist, she recalls her life as Melinda in 18th-century London, including a love affair. Mark becomes infatuated with Melinda, and Daisy runs away. However, they are reunited.

Before Broadway. In 1962 Alan Jay Lerner, who was really into ESP, got together with Richard Rodgers to produce and write a musical called *I Picked a Daisy*, about a girl who talks to daisies and convinces them to grow. Robert Horton and Barbara Harris were hired as the stars, and Gower Champion as director/choreographer. The show was scheduled for a 3/63 Broadway opening, but it didn't materialize, so Mr. Lerner got together with Burton Lane, and the show was re-titled. Gower Champion left, and Robert Horton went into *110 in the Shade*. Cy Feuer and Ernie Martin came in as the new producers, and Bob Fosse as choreographer. Rehearsals were set for 1/64, but they were delayed because the book and lyrics were not ready. Feuer & Martin and Bob Fosse left (Mr. Fosse after 14 months on the show), and Robert Lewis was taken on as director. Six actors were announced for the leading man role, but it finally went to Louis Jourdan, who wound up being replaced by John Cullum during the Boston tryouts (whereas Mr. Jourdan had been top-billed, Mr. Cullum was 2nd-billed).

The Broadway Run. MARK HELLINGER THEATRE, 10/17/65–6/11/66. 3 previews from 10/14/65. 272 PERFORMANCES. PRESENTED BY Alan Jay Lerner, in association with Rogo Productions (Norman Rosemont & Robert Goulet); MUSIC: Burton Lane; LYRICS/BOOK: Alan Jay Lerner; DIRECTOR: Robert Lewis; CHOREOGRAPHER: Herbert Ross; SETS: Oliver Smith; COSTUMES: Freddy Wittop; BARBARA HARRIS' MODERN CLOTHES: Donald Brooks; LIGHTING: Feder; MUSICAL DIRECTOR: Theodore Saidenberg; ORCHESTRATIONS: Robert Russell Bennett; MUSICAL CONTINUITY/VOCAL ARRANGEMENTS: Trude Rittman; DANCE MUSIC: Betty Walberg; CAST RECORDING on RCA Victor; PRESS: Mike Merrick Company, Barry Kobrin; PRODUCTION SUPERVISOR: Stone Widney; GENERAL MANAGER: Irving Squires, *Barry Kobrin*; PRODUCTION STAGE MANAGER: Ross Bowman; STAGE MANAGER: Pat Chandler; ASSISTANT STAGE MANAGER: Edward Preston. *Cast:* DR. MARK BRUCKNER: John Cullum (2) ☆; MRS. HATCH: Rae Allen (6), *Evelyn Page*; STUDENT: Gerald M. Teijelo Jr.; DAISY GAMBLE: Barbara Harris (1) ☆; MURIEL BENSON: Barbara Monte; JAMES PRESTON: William Reilly; SAMUEL WELLES: Gordon Dilworth; MRS. WELLES: Blanche Collins; SIR HUBERT INSDALE: Byron Webster (9); DOLLY WAINWHISTLE: Hanne Marie Reiner; BLACKAMOOR: Bernard Johnson; BOB BRODY: Dan Resin; JIMMY DERN: Ken Richards; MILLARD CROSS: Paul Reid Roman, *Gerald M. Teijelo*; WARREN SMITH: William Daniels (4); PRUDENCE CUMMING: Barbara Remington; EDWARD MONCRIEF: Clifford David (5); FLORA: Carol Flemming; DR. PAUL BRUCKNER: Gerry Matthews (8); DR. CONRAD BRUCKNER: Michael Lewis (7); EVANS BOLAGARD: Hamilton Camp, *Dan Resin*; THEMISTOCLES KRIAKOS: Titos Vandis (3); T.A.A. OFFICIAL: David Thomas; MELINDA WELLES: Barbara Harris (1) ☆; SINGING ENSEMBLE: Rudy Challenger, Paul Eichel, Eddie Ericksen, Rita Golden, Stokely Gray, Bennett Hill, Joy Holly, Zona Kennedy, Pat Lysinger, Art Matthews, Caroline Parks, Nancy Reeves, Dan Resin, Ken Richards,

Jeannette Seibert, Dixie Stewart; DANCING ENSEMBLE: Rita Agnese, Sterling Clark, Marion Fels, Carol Flemming, Leslie Franzos, Luigi Gasparinetti, Bettye Jenkins, Bernard Johnson, Kazimir Kokich, Louis Kosman, Charlene Mehl, Barbara Monte, Marco Pogacar, William Reilly, Hanne Marie Reiner, Barbara Remington, Ronald B. Stratton, Gerald M. Teijelo Jr. **Standbys:** Daisy/Melinda: Rita Gardner; Mark/Edward: Hal Linden. **Understudies:** Mrs. Hatch: Pat Lysinger; Mark/Paul/Warren: Dan Resin; Kriakos: Gordon Dilworth; Conrad: Art Matthews; Insdale/Welles: Michael Lewis; Official: Ken Richards; Bolagard: David Thomas; Mrs. Welles: Jeannette Seibert. *Act I: Scene 1* A lecture room at the Bruckner Clinic; late afternoon, spring; *Scene 2* The solarium of the clinic; several days later; *Scene 3* Dr. Mark Bruckner's office; immediately following: "Hurry! It's Lovely up Here" (Daisy), "Ring Out the Bells" (Mr. & Mrs. Welles, Insdale, Servants), "I'll Not Marry" (Melinda), "Tosy and Cosh" (Melinda), "On a Clear Day You Can See Forever" (Mark); *Scene 4* The rooftop of Daisy's apartment; later that night: "On the S.S. *Bernard Cohn*" (Daisy, Muriel, James, Millard); *Scene 5* Dr. Mark Bruckner's office; the following afternoon: At the Hellrakers' (Dance Ensemble), "Don't Tamper with My Sister" (Edward, Insdale, Ensemble), "She Wasn't You" (Edward); *Scene 6* Dr. Mark Bruckner's office; early evening, a week later: "Melinda" (Mark). *Act II: Scene 1* The solarium of the clinic; a week later: "When I'm Being Born Again" (Kriakos) [for the tours that followed, this number was re-titled "When I Come Around Again" (James & Students)]; *Scene 2* Dr. Mark Bruckner's office; immediately following: "What Did I Have (That I Don't Have)" (Daisy); *Scene 3* The rooftop of Daisy's apartment; late that night: "Wait Till We're Sixty-Five" (Warren & Rooftoppers); *Scene 4* Dr. Mark Bruckner's office; afternoon, one week later: "Come Back to Me" (Mark); *Scene 5* The Municipal Airport; later that day: "Come Back to Me" (reprise) (Ensemble), "On a Clear Day You Can See Forever" (reprise) (Mark & Ensemble).

Note: Soon after opening the three opening scenes were condensed into one scene.

Broadway reviews were very divided, mostly unfavorable. The show received Tony Nominations for composer & lyricist, and for John Cullum and Barbara Harris. Although the score was very good, the book was always a problem.

After Broadway. TOUR. Opened on 9/12/66, at the Hanna Theatre, Cleveland, and closed on 10/29/66, at the Shubert Theatre, New Haven. *Cast:* MARK: Van Johnson; MRS. HATCH: Rita Metzger; JAMES: Walter Willison; DAISY: Linda Lavin; WELLES: Sean Walsh; MRS. WELLES: Elaine Johnson; INSDALE: Don Wofford; EDWARD: John Michael King; SOLICITOR: Fred Bennett [a new character]. The number "Ring Out the Bells" was dropped for this tour, and replaced with "Marriage a la Mode" (Solicitor, Insdale, Welles, Mrs. Welles, Ensemble). The dance At the Hellrakers' was also dropped.

TOUR. Opened on 5/22/67, at the O'Keefe, Toronto, and closed on 10/7/67, at the Shubert Theatre, Chicago. PRESENTED BY Zev Bufman, in association with Nederlander — Steinbrenner Productions; DIRECTOR: Milton Katselas; CHOREOGRAPHER: Eddie Roll; SETS: Peter Wexler; COSTUMES: Brooks — Van Horn; LIGHTING: James Riley; MUSICAL DIRECTOR: Richard Parrinello. *Cast:* MARK: Howard Keel; MRS. HATCH: Francine Beers; DAISY/MELINDA: Barbara Lang; WELLES: Leon Benedict; MURIEL: Jodi Perselle; JAMES/INSDALE: William J. Coppola; WARREN: Cy Young; EDWARD: Lester James; SOLICITOR: George Comtois. The number "Marriage a la Mode" was dropped. Added for this tour were "First Regression" (Melinda & Edward), "Solicitor's Song" (Solicitor, Insdale, Welles), and "Spasm Song" (Muriel & Company).

TOUR. Opened on 12/31/67, in Sacramento, and closed on 5/26/68, at the Music Hall, Seattle. It played in 71 cities. PRESENTED BY Robert Cherin Productions, in association with Joseph Weill & Arthur C. Kellman; DIRECTOR: Ross Bowman; CHOREOGRAPHER: Luis de Yberrando; SETS: Herbert Senn & Helen Pond; MUSICAL DIRECTOR: Gordon Munford. *Cast:* MARK: Howard Keel, John Raitt, Bill Hayes, John Ericson (all alternating); MRS. HATCH/MRS. WELLES: Ruth Warshawsky; DAISY/MELINDA: Tammy Grimes, *Linda Michele* & *Carla Alberghetti*; MURIEL: Sandra Nitz; INSDALE: John Rubinstein; CHORUS INCLUDED: Susan Stewart. "First Regression" and "The Spasm" were dropped for this tour, and added were "The Gout" (Daisy, Muriel, Chorus) and "Trelawney No. 1" (Chorus).

THE MOVIE. 1970. It had an altered score, with two new numbers: "Go to Sleep" and "Love with All the Trimmings." DIRECTOR: Vincente Minnelli. *Cast:* Barbra Streisand, Yves Montand.

HAROLD CLURMAN THEATRE, 5/5/93–5/29/93. 26 PERFORMANCES. This was a revised Off Broadway version. PRESENTED BY Opening Doors; DIRECTOR: Tom Klebba; CHOREOGRAPHER: David Lowenstein; MUSICAL DIRECTOR: Robert Berman; ARTISTIC CONSULTANT: Burton Lane. *Cast:* Jennifer Prescott, Jim Madden. "Ring Out the Bells" was replaced by the new "Solicitor's Song;" "Tosy and Cosh" was cut; "When I'm Being Born Again" used the new title "When I Come Around Again."

CITY CENTER, NYC, 2/10/00–2/13/00. 5 PERFORMANCES, in concert. This was part of the City Center's *Encores!* series. ADAPTED BY: David Ives; DIRECTOR: Mark Brokaw; CHOREOGRAPHER: John Carrafa; LIGHTING: Donald Holder. *Cast:* MARK: Peter Friedman; MRS. HATCH: Nancy Opel; DAISY: Kristin Chenoweth; MURIEL: Darcie Roberts; JAMES: Brooks Ashmanskas; WELLES: Dale Hensley; MRS. WELLES: Beth McVey; INSDALE: Ed Dixon; MILLARD: Jim Newman; WARREN: Roger Bart; MONCRIEF: Brent Barrett; FLORA: Rachel Coloff; CONRAD: Gerry Bamman; KRIAKOS: Louis Zorich.

In late 4/02 a new revised version had a reading at the NEW YORK THEATRE WORKSHOP. NEW BOOK: Paul Selig; DIRECTOR: Michael Mayer. The film songs were used.

512. *On the Town*

Three young gobs in training at the Brooklyn Navy Yard — Gabey, Ozzie and Chip, on a 24-hour leave in war-time New York City, their first time in the big city. Gabey falls in love with a subway photo of Ivy, "Miss Turnstiles" for the month of June, and sets out to find her. Ozzie and Chip help out. Chip falls in with Hildy, a lady taxi driver, and Ozzie meets Claire, an anthropologist. The girls join in the search for Ivy. After looking everywhere — Carnegie Hall, Central Park, Times Square, the Museum of Natural History, Coney Island, in subways and night clubs, and after a disastrous blind date with Lucy Schmeeler, Gabey finds Ivy, just as his leave comes to an end.

Before Broadway. *Fancy Free.* On the Town was based on *Fancy Free*, the Ballet Theatre's (later the American Ballet Theatre) production, created by Jerome Robbins (choreographer) and Leonard Bernstein (music); Oliver Smith provided sets and came up with the original idea about three sailors (played by Harold Lang, John Kriza and Jerome Robbins) on shore leave competing with each other to pick up girls in a bar. Muriel Bentley and Janet Reed were the passersby. Shirley Eckl was the walk-on at the end of the ballet. The show ran about half an hour, and premiered at the MET on 4/18/44. It opened with "Big Stuff," heard on a recording on the bar's jukebox. Billie Holiday was to have sung this number, but her sister, Shirley, did it instead, and was the soloist recorded. The ballet received 25 curtain calls. The show would be extended to become *On the Town. Fancy Free* ran at COVENT GARDEN, London, in 1946, with Jerome Robbins, Michael Kidd and John Kriza as the sailors, and Donald Saddler as the bartender. Gemze de Lappe was in a 1953 London revival of *Fancy Free* at COVENT GARDEN, and Harold Lang was in another revival there, in 1956. *Fancy Free* is still revived by the American Ballet Theatre. Nothing of the *Fancy Free* music, choreography or design was kept in *On the Town*.

On the Town was a Broadway first for Jerome Robbins, Betty Comden & Adolph Green, and Leonard Bernstein. It was also a first for the new production company of Oliver Smith & Paul Feigay. Also a first was that the show had four black singers and four black dancers. Sono Osato was half–Japanese. Oliver Smith had wanted John Latouche to do the lyrics, but Leonard Bernstein brought in his friends Comden & Green, who also wrote the book and played main characters in the show. Mr. Bernstein also wrote some of the lyrics. Although Mr. Bernstein & Hershy Kay are credited with the orchestrations, this is the way the show's music was actually arranged: Don Walker did the Chip & Hildy numbers, as well as "I Get Carried Away;" Ted Royal did "Lucky to Be Me;" Elliott Jacoby did most of the nightclub sequence; and Hershy Kay did

the rest. It is not clear what Mr. Bernstein did in the way of orchestrations. Part of the show was written in a hospital room shared by Mr. Bernstein & Adolph Green (they had agreed to have their operations done at the same time, so they could collaborate while recuperating — a deviated septum for Bernstein and tonsils for Green). The producers had a problem coming up with the money to start with, until MGM paid $250,000 for the movie rights (it was the first Broadway musical to sell the movie rights prior to opening night). Although this freed them up artistically, they couldn't get a better theatre than the Adelphi, because all Broadway was booked solid. Kirk Douglas was the first choice for Gabey, but he couldn't sing. "The Intermission's Great," a choral number to open Act II, was dropped. After the tryout in Boston (where the songwriters wrote "Some Other Time"), it went to Broadway.

The Broadway Run. ADELPHI THEATRE, 12/28/44–6/2/45; FORTY-FOURTH STREET THEATRE, 6/5/45–7/28/45; MARTIN BECK THEATRE, 7/30/45–2/2/46. Total of 462 PERFORMANCES. PRESENTED BY Oliver Smith & Paul Feigay; MUSIC/ADDITIONAL LYRICS: Leonard Bernstein; LYRICS/BOOK: Betty Comden & Adolph Green; BASED ON the 1944 ballet *Fancy Free*, by Jerome Robbins & Leonard Bernstein, which in turn was based on an idea by Oliver Smith; DIRECTOR: George Abbott; CHOREOGRAPHER: Jerome Robbins; SETS: Oliver Smith; SET PAINTERS: Eugene Dunkel & Marcel Lestarquit; COSTUMES: Alvin Colt; TECHNICAL DIRECTOR/STAGE MANAGER: Peggy Clark; LIGHTING: Sam Amdurs; MUSICAL DIRECTOR: Max Goberman, *Frank Nowicki*; ORCHESTRATIONS: Leonard Bernstein & Hershy Kay; CAST RECORDING on Decca (actually, the show was unrecorded, but soon afterwards a studio recording was made, with John Reardon singing Gabey); PRESS: Karl Bernstein & Martha Dreiblatt; GENERAL MANAGER: Charles Harris; COMPANY MANAGER: Sidney Harris; GENERAL STAGE MANAGER: Larry Bolton. *Cast:* WORKMAN: Marten Sameth; 2ND WORKMAN: Frank Milton; 3RD WORKMAN: Herbert Greene; GIRL IN YELLOW: Lavina Nielsen, *Helen Franklin*; OZZIE: Adolph Green (4); CHIP: Cris Alexander (7); SAILOR: Lyle Clark; GABEY: John Battles (5), *Marten Sameth*; ANDY: Frank Westbrook, *Ben Piazza, Bill Weaver*; TOM: Richard D'Arcy; STREET SWEEPER: Carl Erbele; GIRL IN GREEN: Cyprienne Gabelman; SAILOR: Don Weissmuller; FLOSSIE: Florence MacMichael, *Marion Kohler*; FLOSSIE'S FRIEND: Marion Kohler, *Lila King*; BILL POSTER: Larry Bolton, *Stuart Allen, Charles Rhyner*; LITTLE OLD LADY: Maxine Arnold; POLICEMAN: Lonny Jackson; S. UPERMAN: Milton Taubman, *Johnny Stearns*; BRUNHILDE "HILDY" ESTERHAZY: Nancy Walker (2); POLICEMAN: Roger Treat; WALDO FIGMENT: Remo Bufano, *Henry Sherwood*; CLAIRE DE LOONE: Betty Comden (3); HIGH SCHOOL GIRL: Nelle Fisher; SAILOR IN BLUE: Richard D'Arcy; ANNOUNCER: Frank Milton; VOICE: Frances Cassard; SINGER: Dorothy Johnson; ACTOR: Marten Sameth; MUSICIANS: Sam Adams & Herbert Greene; PASSERBY: Carl Erbele; 1ST BALLET GIRL: Cyprienne Gabelman; BOY: Ben Piazza, *Bill Weaver*; 2ND BALLET GIRL: Allyn Ann McLerie; BOY: Frank Westbrook; 3RD BALLET GIRL: Barbara Gaye; MADAME MAUDE P. DILLY: Susan Steell, *Zamah Cunningham*; IVY SMITH: Sono Osato (1), *Allyn Ann McLerie*; LUCY SCHMEELER: Alice Pearce; LADY IN RED: Malka Farber; JUDGE PITKIN W. BRIDGEWORK: Robert Chisholm (6); MC: Frank Milton; NIGHTCLUB SINGER: Frances Cassard; NIGHT CLUB PATRON: Nelle Fisher; DOLL GIRL: Allyn Ann McLerie; WAITER: Herbert Greene; SPANISH SINGER: Jeanne Gordon, *Regina Owens*; SHAWL GIRL: Lavina Nielsen, *Helen Franklin*; THE GREAT LOVER: Ray Harrison; CONDUCTOR: Herbert Greene; RAJAH BIMMY: Robert Lorenz, *Sam Adams*; SINGERS: Van Atkins, Shirley Ann Burton, Frances Cassard, Jeanne Gordon, Herbert Greene, Melvin Howard, Lonny Jackson, Dorothy Johnson, Lila King, Marion Kohler, Frances Lager, Robert Lorenz (*Sam Adams*), Frank Milton, Regina Owens, Marten Sameth, Kathleen Stanley, Milton Taubman (*Johnny Stearns*), Roger Treat, Benjamin Trottman, *Tom Morgan*; DANCERS: Aza Bard, John Butler, Lyle Clark, Clara Cordery, Richard D'Arcy, Carl Erbele, Malka Farber, Nelle Fisher, Cyprienne Gabelman, Barbara Gaye, Jean Handy, Ray Harrison, Jean Houloose, Welland Lathrop, Allyn Ann McLerie, Dorothy McNichols, Douglas Matheson, Virginia Miller, Frank Neal, Lavina Nielsen (*Helen Franklin*), Duncan Noble, Ben Piazza (*Bill Weaver*), James Flashe Riley, Atty Vandenberg, Royce Wallace, Don Weissmuller, Frank Westbrook, Parker Wilson, *Lee Morrison*. **Act I**: Overture (Orchestra); **Scene 1** The Brooklyn Navy Yard: "I Feel Like I'm Not Out of Bed Yet" (Workmen), "New York, New York" (Chip, Ozzie,

Gabey, Chorus) [the hit]; **Scene 2** A subway train in motion; **Scene 3** A New York street: "Gabey's Comin'" (Ozzie, Chip, Gabey, Mannequins) [cut by George Abbott before Broadway]; **Scene 4** Presentation of Miss Turnstiles: "(Presentation of) Miss Turnstiles" (ballet) (Contestants, Ivy, Manhattanites); **Scene 5** A taxicab: "Come Up to My Place" (Hildy & Chip); **Scene 6** Museum of Natural History: "(I Get) Carried Away" (Claire, Ozzie, Primitive Man & Woman); **Scene 7** A busy New York street (Outside the park): "Lonely Town" (Gabey & New Yorkers) (danced by Nelle Fisher, Richard D'Arcy, Ballet) [originally called "Lonely Me"]; **Scene 8** Carnegie Hall — a corridor; **Scene 9** Mme Dilly's studio (Carnegie Hall): "Do-Do-Re-Do" ("Carnegie Hall Pavane") (Ivy, Maude, Teachers, Students); **Scene 10** Claire's apartment; **Scene 11** Hildy's apartment: "I Can Cook Too" (Hildy & Chip); **Scene 12** Times Square: "Lucky to Be Me" (Gabey & New Yorkers), "Sailors on the Town" (Times Square Ballet) (Entire Company); PENNY ARCADE BOY: Don Weissmuller. **Act II**: **Scene 1a** Diamond Eddie's Club: "So Long (Baby)" (dance) (Diamond Eddie's Girls); **Scene 1b** Congacabana Club: "I Wish I Was Dead" (also called "I'm Blue," and usually referred to as "The Nightclub Song") (Nightclub Singer & Spanish Singer) [this number replaced "Ain't Got No Tears Left," a torch song for the nightclub sequence]; **Scene 1c** Slam-Bang Club: "Ya Got Me" (Hildy, Claire, Ozzie, Chip); **Scene 2** The subway train to Coney Island [this scene and its musical number were added during the run]: "Subway Ride" ("Subway to Coney Island") (Gabey & The People of New York) (dance); **Scene 3** The dream Coney Island (Gabey in the Playground of the Rich) [originally Scene 2]: "Imaginary Coney Island–The Great Lover Displays Himself— Pas de Deux" (ballet — also known as "I Understand") (Ivy, The Great Lover, High Society Dancers); **Scene 4** Subway platform [this scene was originally Scene 3]: "Some Other Time" (Claire, Hildy, Ozzie, Ozzie) [this number replaced "Dream with Me"]; **Scene 5** The real Coney Island [originally Scene 4]: "The Real Coney Island" (dance) (Bimmy); **Scene 6** The Brooklyn Navy Yard [originally Scene 5]: Finale: reprises of: "I Feel Like I'm Not Out of Bed Yet" (workmen), "New York, New York" (Ensemble).

Reviews were mostly raves or favorable, but John Chapman of the *Daily News* panned it.

After Broadway. THE MOVIE. 1949. DIRECTORS: Gene Kelly & Stanley Donen; CHOREOGRAPHER: Gene Kelly. Most of the Broadway score was replaced by a new one by Roger Edens. Still, it is a phenomenal movie. New songs included: "Prehistoric Man," "Main Street," "You're Awful," "On the Town," "Count on Me." **Cast**: GABEY: Gene Kelly; CHIP: Frank Sinatra; OZZIE: Jules Munshin; HILDY: Betty Garrett; CLAIRE: Ann Miller; IVY: Vera-Ellen; LUCY: Alice Pearce; MADAME DILYOVSKA: Florence Bates.

CARNEGIE HALL PLAYHOUSE, 1/15/59–3/15/59. 70 PERFORMANCES. PRESENTED BY Nancy Elliott Nugent, in association with Ulysses Productions; DIRECTOR: Gerald Freedman; CHOREOGRAPHER: Joe Layton. **Cast**: GABEY: Harold Lang; IVY: Wisa D'Orso; HILDY: Pat Carroll; CHIP: Joe Bova; OZZIE: Bill Hickey; CLAIRE: Evelyn Russell.

In 1960 Leonard Bernstein conducted a recording starring four of the original leads and himself (billed anagrammatically as Randel Striboneen, playing the role of Coney Island's Rajah Bimmy).

PRINCE OF WALES THEATRE, London, 5/30/63. 63 PERFORMANCES. PRESENTED BY H.M. Tennent, with Roger L. Stevens & Oliver Smith; DIRECTOR/CHOREOGRAPHER: Joe Layton. **Cast**: OZZIE: Elliott Gould; GABEY: Don McKay; CHIP: Franklin Kiser; IVY: Andrea Jaffe; HILDY: Carol Arthur; CLAIRE: Gillian Lewis; MME DILLY: Elspeth March; LUCY: Rosamund Greenwood; SOLDIER: Harry Naughton.

513. *On the Town* (1971 Broadway revival)

Set in New York City, in June 1944. The musical numbers were as for the 1944 production, except that "So Long Baby" was now an ice revue danced by Gina & Skaters. "Nightclub Song" was still there (as sung by Nightclub Singer, who was given a name — Diana Dream), followed by "The Nightclub Song" (in Spanish) by

the Spanish singer, who was also given a name — Senorita Dolores. The dance "The Real Coney Island" was replaced by "Coney Island Hep Cats" a singing number, sung by Flossie, Flossie's Friend, Zoot Suit Dancers. It had the same plot as in the 1944 production, but with a few changes, including some new characters, notably Gina Henie, the ice skater. Several smaller characters were cut.

Before Broadway. Second-featured Kurt Peterson was replaced by Ron Husmann (who was elevated to star billing). Bill Gerber was replaced by Remak Ramsay, and Charles Goeddertz by John Mineo.

The Broadway Run. IMPERIAL THEATRE, 10/31/71–1/1/72. 4 previews from 10/27/71. 65 PERFORMANCES. The Ron Field production, PRESENTED BY Jerry Schlossberg & Vista Productions; MUSIC: Leonard Bernstein; LYRICS/BOOK: Betty Comden & Adolph Green; ADDITIONAL LYRICS: Leonard Bernstein; BASED ON the 1944 ballet *Fancy Free*, by Jerome Robbins & Leonard Bernstein; DIRECTOR/CHOREOGRAPHER: Ron Field; ASSISTANT CHOREOGRAPHER: Michael Shawn; SETS: James Trittipo; COSTUMES: Ray Aghayan & Bob Mackie; LIGHTING: Tharon Musser; MUSICAL DIRECTOR: Milton Rosenstock; ORCHESTRATIONS: Leonard Bernstein & Hershy Kay; PRESS: Betty Lee Hunt Associates; GENERAL MANAGERS: George Thorn & Leonard A. Mulhern; PRODUCTION STAGE MANAGER: Lee Murray; STAGE MANAGER: Robert Corpora; ASSISTANT STAGE MANAGER: Martin De Martino. **Cast**: WORKMAN: David Wilder; CHIP: Jess Richards (5); OZZIE: Remak Ramsay (6); GABEY: Ron Husmann (3) ✮; FLOSSIE: Carol Petri; FLOSSIE'S FRIEND: Marybeth Kurdock; BILL POSTER: Don Croll; LITTLE OLD LADY: Zoya Leporska (10); ANNOUNCER: Orrin Reiley; IVY SMITH: Donna McKechnie (4); HILDY ESTERHAZY: Bernadette Peters (2) ✮; S. UPERMAN: David Wilder; WALDO FIGMENT: Orrin Reiley; CLAIRE DE LOONE: Phyllis Newman (1) ✮; MAUDE P. DILLY: Fran Stevens (8); JUDGE PITKIN W. BRIDGEWORK: Tom Avera (9); LUCY SCHMEELER: Marilyn Cooper (7); GINA HENIE: Gina Paglia; MC AT DIAMOND EDDIE'S: Dennis Roth; DIANA DREAM: Sandra Dorsey; MC AT CONGACABANA: Don Croll; SENORITA DOLORES: Laura Kenyon; RAJAH BIMMY: Larry Merritt; CONEY ISLAND ZOOT SUIT DANCERS: John Mineo & Tony Stevens; SINGERS: Don Croll, Martha Danielle, Sandra Dorsey, Bobbi Franklin, Laura Kenyon, Richard Marr, Gail Nelson, Orrin Reiley, Dennis Roth, Marie Santell, Luke Stover, David Wilder, Craig Yates; DANCERS: Andy Bew, Carole Bishop, Eileen Casey, Paul Charles, Jill Cook, Nancy Dalton, Marybeth Kurdock, Bruce Lea, Nancy Lynch, Larry Merritt, John Mineo, Gina Paglia, Pamela Peadon, Carol Petri, Jeff Phillips, Kenn Scalice, Doug Spingler, Tony Stevens, Chester Walker. **Understudies**: Claire/Lucy: Laura Kenyon; Ivy: Marilyn Cooper & Pamela Peadon; Gabey/Ozzie: Orrin Reiley; Chip: Andy Bew; Pitkin: Richard Marr; Maude: Bobbi Franklin; Little Old Lady: Nancy Lynch. **Act I**: **Scene 1** Brooklyn Navy Yard; **Scene 2** Subway train; **Scene 3** New York street; **Scene 4** Miss Turnstiles; **Scene 5** Taxi cab; **Scene 6** Museum of Natural History; **Scene 7** New York street; **Scene 8** Carnegie Hall; **Scene 9** Claire's apartment; **Scene 10** Hildy's apartment; **Scene 11** Times Square. **Act II**: **Scene 1** Night clubs; **Scene 1a** Diamond Eddie's Manhattan Roof; **Scene 1b** Congacabana; **Scene 1c** Slam-Bang; **Scene 2** Subway train; **Scene 3** Imaginary Coney Island; **Scene 4** Coney Island Express; **Scene 5** Coney Island; **Scene 6** Brooklyn Navy Yard.

Broadway reviews were only just favorable. Bernadette Peters was nominated for a Tony.

After Broadway. In 1987 a revue was being planned for Nancy Walker, called *Back on the Town*, but it was never made.

GOODSPEED OPERA HOUSE, Conn. Part of the 1993–94 season. DIRECTOR/CHOREOGRAPHER: Marcia Milgrom Dodge; MUSICAL DIRECTOR: Michael O'Flaherty. **Cast**: GABEY: Keith Bernardo; IVY: Charlotte d'Amboise; OZZIE: Frank Di Pasquale; CLAIRE: Donna English; CHIP: Michael O'Steen; HILDY: Amelia Prentice; MME DILLY: Maureen Sadusk; PITKIN: Gordon Stanley.

514. *On the Town* (1998 Broadway revival)

Before Broadway. This Broadway revival began at the New York Shakespeare Festival's DELACORTE THEATRE IN CENTRAL PARK, 8/17/97–

8/31/97. 14 previews from 7/31/97. 12 PERFORMANCES. It was the Delacorte's first musical since *The Mystery of Edwin Drood* in 1985. The number "Gabey's Comin" was re-instated. George Wolfe created a stir when he announced that the choreography was going to be new, i.e. not Jerome Robbins'. As early as 7/21/97 Betty Comden was expressing the hope for a Broadway transfer. Enhancement money for this Delacorte production was added by Roger Berlind, Margo Lion, Scott Rudin, and Jujamcyn, but the Public Theatre would remain sole producer throughout. It had the same basic crew as for the subsequent Broadway run, except CHOREOGRAPHER: Eliot Feld; STAGE MANAGER: Lisa Buxbaum. *Cast*: WORKMAN/ANNOUNCER: Luis-Ottavio Faria; OZZIE: Robert Montano; CHIP: Jesse Tyler Ferguson; GABEY: Jose Llana; FLOSSIE: Linda Mugleston; FLOSSIE'S FRIEND: Chandra Wilson; BILL POSTER/RAJAH: Glenn Turner; LITTLE OLD LADY/MME DILLY: Mary Testa; ANNOUNCER/DIANA/DOLORES: Nora Cole; IVY: Sophie Salguero; POLICEMAN: Jesse Means II; UPERMAN/MC: Blake Hammond; HILDY: Lea De Laria; FIGMENT: Leslie Feagan; CLAIRE: Kate Suber; PRIMITIVES: Nickemil Concepcion & Margaux Zadikian; PAS DE DEUX DANCERS: Patricia Tuthill & Jassen Virolas; PITKIN: Jonathan Freeman; LUCY: Annie Golden; ENSEMBLE: Rachel Alvarado, Andy Blankenbuehler, Nickemil Concepcion, Karl duHoffmann, Ivy Fox, Darren Gibson, Clay Harper Jackson, Keri Lee, Joanne McHugh, Patricia Tuthill, Jassen Virolas, Margaux Zadikian. *Swings*: Byron Easley, Carol Bentley. It was reviewed at the Delacorte, and although reviews were generally very good, and Lea De Laria came in for raves (notably from Ben Brantley of the *New York Times*), Mr. Brantley panned Eliot Feld's choreography, so much so that Mr. Feld offered to resign if the show went on to Broadway. In fact it did, and by early 1/98 Mr. Feld had been replaced by Christopher d'Amboise. There had been major problems with condensation on the Delacorte's outdoor stage, and several times the dance sequences had to be abandoned mid–performance. The show (with its huge set) was re-designed in preparation for Broadway, which was going to be spring 1998, at the St. James Theatre, with rehearsals to start on 2/24/98, and Broadway previews from 4/7/98. Then, after rumors that the transfer was being canceled, it postponed to late September or early October 1998, with rehearsals to start in August. Reasons for the postponement were partly director George Wolfe's kidney failure and his subsequent transplant, and partly the disagreement between him and choreographer Christopher d'Amboise. Mr. d'Amboise it was who left. By 1/6/98 Lea De Laria had been confirmed as reprising her role for Broadway. The show was budgeted at between $5 million and $5.7 million. On 6/12/98 various announcements were made: Keith Young was the new choreographer (his Broadway debut), and the Gershwin Theatre (Broadway's biggest house) was now the new destination. On 8/3/98 it was announced that 11/19/98 would be the official opening night (put back from 11/15/98), and that rehearsals would begin 9/8/98. There was a sneak press preview of rehearsals on 10/1/98. During rehearsals Ivan Thomas was replaced in the cast by Gregory Emanuel Rahming. The Broadway previews of 11/10/98 and 11/12/98 were canceled, and the Broadway opening date was delayed until 11/22/98, so that Mr. Young's new choreography could be doctored by Joey McKneely.

The Broadway Run. GERSHWIN THEATRE, 11/22/98–1/17/99. 37 previews from 10/20/98. 65 PERFORMANCES. PRESENTED BY The Joseph Papp Public Theatre/New York Shakespeare Festival; MUSIC: Leonard Bernstein; LYRICS/BOOK: Betty Comden & Adolph Green; BASED ON the 1944 ballet *Fancy Free*, by Jerome Robbins & Leonard Bernstein; DIRECTOR: George C. Wolfe; CHOREOGRAPHER: Keith Young; ADDITIONAL CHOREOGRAPHY: Joey McKneely (unbilled); SETS: Adrianne Lobel; COSTUMES: Paul Tazewell; LIGHTING: Paul Gallo; SOUND: Jon Weston; MUSICAL DIRECTOR: Kevin Stites; ORCHESTRATIONS: Bruce Coughlin; PRESS: Carol R. Fineman, Thomas V. Naro, Bill Coyle; CASTING: Jordan Thaler & Heidi Griffiths; GENERAL MANAGEMENT: 101 Productions; COMPANY MANAGER: Julie Crosby; PRODUCTION STAGE MANAGER: Karen Armstrong; STAGE MANAGER: Kenneth J. McGee; ASSISTANT STAGE MANAGER: Donna A. Drake. *Cast*: WORKMAN: Gregory Emanuel Rahming; QUARTET: Tom Aulino, Christopher F. Davis, Blake Hammond, John Jellison (*Don Mayo*); OZZIE: Robert Montano; CHIP: Jesse Tyler Ferguson; GABEY: Perry Laylon Ojeda; FLOSSIE: Linda Mugleston; FLOSSIE'S FRIEND: Chandra Wilson; SUBWAY BILL POSTER: John Jellison, *Don Mayo*; LITTLE OLD LADY: Mary Testa; MANNEQUINS: Dottie Earle,

Jennifer Frankel, Amy Heggins, Judine Richard; MISS TURNSTILES ANNOUNCERS: Nora Cole & Gregory Emanuel Rahming; IVY SMITH: Tai Jiminez; POLICEMAN: Christopher F. Davis; MR. S UPERMAN: Blake Hammond; HILDY ESTERHAZY: Lea De Laria; WALDO FIGMENT: Tom Aulino; CLAIRE DE LOONE: Sarah Knowlton; PRIMITIVE MAN & WOMAN: Stephen Campanella & Judine Richard; PAS DE DEUX DANCERS: Kristine Bendul & Darren Gibson; MME MAUDE P. DILLY: Mary Testa; WOMEN OF CARNEGIE HALL: Nora Cole, Linda Mugleston, Chandra Wilson; PITKIN W. BRIDGEWORK: Jonathan Freeman; LUCY SCHMEELER: Annie Golden; DIAMOND EDDIE'S GIRLS: Kristine Bendul, Jennifer Frankel, Amy Heggins, Keenah Reid, Judine Richard; MC: Blake Hammond; DIANA DREAM/DOLORES DOLORES: Nora Cole; RAJAH BIMMY: John Jellison, *Don Mayo*; NEW SAILORS IN TOWN: Brad Aspel, Stephen Campanella, Christopher F. Davis; THE PEOPLE OF NEW YORK: Tom Aulino, Blake Hammond, John Jellison (*Don Mayo*), Linda Mugleston, Gregory Emanuel Rahming, Chandra Wilson; DANCE ENSEMBLE: Brad Aspel, Tom Aulino, Kristine Bendul, Stephen Campanella, R.J. Durell, Dottie Earle, Jennifer Frankel, Edgard Gallardo, Darren Gibson, Amy Heggins, John Jellison, Darren Lee, Keenah Reid, Judine Richard. *Juliet Fischer*. **Standbys**: For Messrs Rahming, Jellison, Hammond, Aulino: David Lowenstein; For Miss Jiminez: Dana Stackpole. **Understudies**: Ozzie: Brad Aspel; Chip: Brad Aspel & Darren Lee; Gabey: Stephen Campanella & Darren Lee; Hildy/Maude: Linda Mugleston; Pitkin/Workman: John Jellison; Lucy: Chandra Wilson; Diana: Judine Richard; Flossie: Jennifer Frankel; Flossie's Friend: Keenah Reid; Policemen/Sailors: Wes Pope, Rommy Sandhu, Scott Spahr; Primitive Woman: Kim Craven & Sloan Just; Pas de Deux: Kim Craven, R.J. Durell, Dana Stackpole; Men: David Lowenstein; Ivy: Dana Stackpole. **Swings**: Kim Craven, Sloan Just, Wes Pope, Rommy Sandhu, Scott Spahr.

There was an advance sale of $2.5 million at the box office as the show opened. Broadway reviews were not good, it being considered a pale imitation of the original. There were rumors that the show had a limited run until 2/7/99, but in fact it was an open-ended run. It didn't matter, because on 1/12/99 it was announced that it would close on 1/17/99, simply because audiences weren't coming. It lost $6 million. Mary Testa was nominated for a Tony. Adolph Green died on 10/23/02, and Broadway dimmed its lights.

After Broadway. ENGLISH NATIONAL OPERA, 3/5/05–4/19/05. DIRECTOR: Jude Kelly; CHOREOGRAPHER: Stephen Mear. *Cast*: GABEY: Aaron Lazar; CHIP: Adam Garcia; OZZIE: Timothy Howar; IVY: Helen Anker; CLAIRE: Lucy Schaufer; MME DILLY: Sylvia Syms; LUCY: Janine Duvitski; WORKMAN: Willard W. White; HILDY: Caroline O'Connor.

515. *On the Twentieth Century*

A battle of the sexes on a cross-country trip on the famous train, the *Twentieth Century Limited*, as it speeds from Chicago to New York in 16 hours in the early 1930s. Producer-director Oscar Jaffe, the High Priest of Broadway, now desperately broke, makes a final effort to succeed again by signing his ex-lover and student, tempestuous movie star Lily Garland (original name Mildred Plotka) to star in his next epic, *The Passion of Mary Magdalene*. However, Lily now has a new boyfriend, actor Bruce Granit (a character created for this musical), and there is a rival producer Max Jacobs. When Lily is tricked into signing a contract by Oscar, she signs as Peter Rabbit. Jaffee was modeled after David Belasco and Jed Harris, but John Cullum, in this musical, played him as John Barrymore had played Jaffee in the classic movie (even though Columbia Pictures had not allowed this musical to adapt anything from the movie). Mrs. Primrose is the heir to the Restoria Pills fortune.

Before Broadway. In the mid–1970s Cy Coleman and Comden & Green decided to do a musical together. With difficulty they obtained the rights to the play *Twentieth Century*, then re-wrote it, first as *The Twentieth Century, Ltd.* It took over a year before it made it to Broadway. In that time Cy Coleman wrote the musical *I Love My Wife*, and Comden & Green did their own Broadway *Party*. Cy Feuer & Ernest

Martin, the producers, asked Hal Prince to direct. Danny Kaye was considered for Jaffe, but Madeline Kahn strenuously objected. Hal Prince insisted on John Cullum for the lead, whereas Feuer & Martin wanted Alfred Drake. Feuer & Martin left. The show tried out at the Colonial Theatre, Boston, from 1/7/78, to basically good reviews (some pans, some raves, some in between). Robin Wagner's sets were praised.

The Broadway Run. ST. JAMES THEATRE, 2/19/78–3/18/79. 7 previews. 453 PERFORMANCES. PRESENTED BY The Producers Circle 2 (Robert Fryer, Mary Lea Johnson, James Cresson, Martin Richards), in association with Joseph Harris & Ira Bernstein; MUSIC: Cy Coleman; LYRICS/BOOK: Betty Comden & Adolph Green; BASED ON the 1932 farce *20th Century*, by Ben Hecht & Charles MacArthur, from the unproduced play *The Napoleon of Broadway*, by Charles Bruce Millholland [Note: it was not based on the famous 1934 movie, with John Barrymore & Carole Lombard, because those rights were not available]; DIRECTOR: Harold Prince; ASSISTANT DIRECTOR: Ruth Mitchell; CHOREOGRAPHER: Larry Fuller; SETS: Robin Wagner; COSTUMES: Florence Klotz; LIGHTING: Ken Billington; SOUND: Jack Mann; MUSICAL DIRECTOR: Paul Gemignani; ORCHESTRATIONS: Hershy Kay; CAST RECORDING on Columbia; PRESS: Bill Evans, Mary Bryant, Mark Hunter, Philip Rinaldi; CASTING: Joanna Merlin; GENERAL MANAGERS: Joseph Harris & Ira Bernstein; PRODUCTION STAGE MANAGER: George Martin; STAGE MANAGER: E. Bronson Platt; ASSISTANT STAGE MANAGERS: Gerald R. Teijelo & Andrew Cadiff. *Cast:* In the new Scene 1, which was added after the opening: PRIEST: Ken Hilliard; BISHOP: Charles Rule; STAGE MANAGER: Ray Gill; JOAN: Maris Clement; WARDROBE MISTRESS: Carol Lurie; ACTOR: Hal Norman; FANNY: Peggy Cooper [end of new Scene 1]; PORTERS: Keith Davis (12), Quitman D. Fludd III (12), Ray Stephens (12), Joseph Wise (12); CONDUCTOR FLANAGAN: Tom Batten (9); TRAIN SECRETARY ROGERS: Stanley Simmonds; LETITIA PEABODY PRIMROSE: Imogene Coca (3) ✩, *Betty Comden* (1/16/79–1/22/79), *Imogene Coca*; OWEN O'MALLEY: George Coe (4); OLIVER WEBB: Dean Dittmann (5); REDCAP: Mel Johnson Jr. (13); CONGRESSMAN LOCKWOOD: Rufus Smith (7); ANITA: Carol Lugenbeal; OSCAR JAFFEE: John Cullum (2) ✩; MAX JACOBS: George Lee Andrews (8), *Jeff Keller*; IMELDA: Willi Burke (11); MAXWELL FINCH: David Horwitz; MILDRED PLOTKA/LILY GARLAND: Madeline Kahn (1) ✩, *Judy Kaye* (stood in for Miss Kahn, then took over permanently from 4/25/78), *Christine Ebersole* (stood in for Miss Kaye); OTTO VON BISMARK: Sal Mistretta; BRUCE GRANIT: Kevin Kline (6), *Nicholas Wyman* (from 1/16/79); AGNES: Judy Kaye (10), *Melanie Vaughan* (from 4/25/78), *Christine Ebersole*; HOSPITAL ATTENDANTS: Sal Mistretta & Carol Lurie; DR. JOHNSON: Willi Burke (11); FEMALE SINGERS: Susan Cella, Maris Clement, Peggy Cooper, Karen Gibson, Carol Lugenbeal, Carol Lurie, Melanie Vaughan; MALE SINGERS: Ray Gill, Ken Hilliard, David Horwitz, Craig Lucas, Sal Mistretta, Hal Norman, Charles Rule, David Vogel. **Standby**: Oscar: George Lee Andrews. **Understudies**: Lily: Judy Kaye (until 4/25/78), *Christine Ebersole*; Letitia: Peggy Cooper; Owen: David Vogel; Webb/Lockwood: Hal Norman; Bruce: Ray Gill; Max: Craig Lucas; Flanagan: Stanley Simmonds; Agnes: Melanie Vaughan; Imelda/Dr. Johnson: Karen Gibson; Porters: Mel Johnson Jr. **Swing Singers**: Linda Poser & Gerald Teijelo. **Act I**: Overture (Orchestra); **Scene 1** Stranded again [this scene was added during the run. It is set on stage during a play]: "Stranded Again" (Bishop, Actors, Singers) [this number was added during the run]; **Scene 1** Chicago; La Salle Station platform [this was the original Scene 1]: "On the *Twentieth Century*" (Porters, Letitia, Flanagan, Rogers, Passengers); **Scene 2** The observation car and Drawing Room "A:" "I Rise Again" (Oscar, Owen, Oliver); **Scene 3** Flashback to the bare stage of a theatre: "Indian Maiden's Lament" (Imelda & Mildred), "Veronique" (Lily & Male Singers); **Scene 4** Drawing Room "A:" "I Have Written a Play" (Flanagan); **Scene 5** The observation car and corridor: "Together" (Porters, Passengers, Oscar); **Scene 6** Drawing Room "B:" "Never" (Lily, Owen, Oliver), "Our Private World" (Lily & Oscar); **Scene 7** The observation car: "Repent" (Letitia); **Scene 8** Triple scene of the observation car, Drawing Room "A" and Drawing Room "B:" "Mine" (Oscar & Bruce); **Scene 9** Drawing Rooms "A" and "B:" "I've Got it All" (Lily & Oscar); **Scene 10** Drawing Room "A:" "On the *Twentieth Century*" (reprise) (Company). **Act II**: **Entr'acte** ("Life is Like a Train") (Porters); **Scene 1** Drawing Room "A:" "Five Zeros" (Owen, Oliver, Letitia, Oscar); **Scene 2** Drawing Room "B:" "Sextet" ("Sign, Lily, Sign") (Owen, Oliver, Oscar, Letitia, Lily,

Bruce); **Scene 3** The observation car: "She's a Nut" (Company), "Max Jacobs" (Max); **Scene 4** Drawing Room "B" in the middle of the night: "Babbette" (Lily); **Scene 5** The observation car: "The Legacy" (Oscar), "Lily, Oscar" (Lily & Oscar).

First night reviews were very divided—a couple of raves, a couple of pans, and some in between. Madeline Kahn (a trained opera singer) missed 10 of the first 74 performances (her understudy Judy Kaye going on for her); apparently she was having trouble with the singing range. Miss Kahn suggested that she be allowed to do only seven performances a week, as Liza Minnelli was doing in *The Act*. Instead, Hal Prince replaced her with Judy Kaye, and Miss Kahn apparently got a $100,000 settlement of her contract. This was the show that made Judy Kaye famous. Hal Prince tried to persuade the Tony Awards committee to make Judy Kaye eligible, but they wouldn't go for it. Madeline Kahn was nominated, but Liza Minnelli won for *The Act*. The set of the train cost $196,500, and was a sensation. The whole production was capitalized at $1,064,000. The show won Tonys for score, book, set, and for John Cullum and Kevin Kline. Other nominations (aside from Madeline Kahn) were musical, direction of a musical, and for Imogene Coca.

After Broadway. TOUR. Opened on 6/8/79, at the Fisher Theatre, Detroit, and closed on 11/24/79, at the Orpheum Theatre, San Francisco. MUSICAL DIRECTOR: Jonathan Anderson. *Cast*: JAFFE: Rock Hudson; LETITIA: Imogene Coca; LILY: Judy Kaye; BRUCE: Patrick Quinn; TRAIN SECRETARY: Stanley Simmonds; PORTER: Quitman Fludd III; PRIEST: Ken Hilliard.

TOUR. Opened on 10/10/86, at the Coconut Grove Playhouse, Miami, and closed on 3/5/87, in Scranton, Pa. PRESENTED BY Jerry Kravat Entertainment; DIRECTOR: Jeffrey B. Moss; CHOREOGRAPHER: Barbara Siman; LIGHTING: Richard Winkler; MUSICAL DIRECTOR: Kay Cameron. *Cast*: OWEN: King Donovan; LETITIA: Imogene Coca; JAFFE: Frank Gorshin; MAX: Mark Basile; LILY: Judy Kaye; NURSE: Wysandria Woolsey.

LONDON, 3/19/80. 165 PERFORMANCES. Julia McKenzie got phenomenal reviews, which is more than the show got. *Cast*: JAFFE: Keith Michell; LILY: Julia McKenzie; LETITIA: Ann Beach; BRUCE: Mark Wynter.

YORK THEATRE COMPANY, NYC, 10/25/85–11/17/85. 20 PERFORMANCES. DIRECTOR/CHOREOGRAPHER: Dennis Rosa; LIGHTING: Mary Jo Dondlinger; MUSICAL DIRECTOR: Lawrence W. Hill. *Cast*: JAFFE: Jeff McCarthy; LILY: Victoria Brasser; BRUCE: Tom Galantich; OWEN: Leonard John Crofoot; IMELDA: Barbara McCulloh; AGNES: Mimi Bessette; FINCH/CYRIL: Steve Fickinger.

GOODSPEED OPERA HOUSE, Conn., 4/30/99–7/3/99. Previews from 4/9/99. DIRECTOR: Ted Pappas; CHOREOGRAPHER: Peggy Hickey; SETS: James Noone; LIGHTING: David F. Segal; MUSICAL DIRECTOR: Michael O'Flaherty; ORCHESTRATIONS: Christopher Jahnke. *Cast*: JAFFE: Mark Jacoby; LILY: Donna English; BRUCE: Tony Lawson (Marc Kudisch was going to play role but dropped out due to a family emergency); OWEN: Michael McCormick; OLIVER: Peter Van Wagner; LETITIA: Jan Neuberger. This acclaimed revival had tour hopes for the fall of 2000 which never happened.

FREUD PLAYHOUSE, UCLA, Los Angeles, 1/21/03–2/2/03. This production was part of the *Reprise!* series. DIRECTOR: David Lee; CHOREOGRAPHER: Kay Cole. *Cast*: JAFFE: Bob Gunton (he replaced Douglas Sills before opening); LILY: Carolee Carmello (she replaced Kristin Chenoweth, who left before opening); LETITIA: Mimi Hines; BRUCE: Damon Kirsche; OLIVER: Robert Picardo; OWEN: Dan Butler.

AMERICAN MUSICAL THEATRE OF SAN JOSE, Calif., 10/31/03–11/16/03. DIRECTOR: Marc Jacobs; CHOREOGRAPHER: Patti Colombo; MUSICAL DIRECTOR: Craig Bohmler. *Cast*: Jo Anne Worley, Mark Jacoby, Judith Blazer, Jamie Torcellini, Craig Mason.

516. *On Your Toes*

The first two scenes take place 15 years ago, and thereafter the action is contemporary. Junior Dolan, son of vaudeville performers, becomes a music teacher. One of his pupils has written a jazz ballet, and he persuades the visiting Russian Ballet to perform it.

Before Broadway. Originally written by Rodgers & Hart as a movie vehicle for Fred Astaire, but he turned it down, so the songwriters turned it into a Broadway musical. It first opened on Broadway, at the IMPERIAL THEATRE, on 4/11/36. It moved to the MAJESTIC THEATRE, 11/9/36–1/23/37. Total of 315 PERFORMANCES. It was initially directed by George Abbott, and was his first Broadway musical. However, Mr. Abbott withdrew, and Worthington Miller, who replaced him, got the credit. After a disastrous Boston tryout, Mr. Abbott acted as play doctor. This was the first musical to use serious ballet in its choreography, with the two famous Balanchine ballets "Slaughter on Tenth Avenue" and "Princess Zenobia." SETS: Jo Mielziner; COSTUMES: Irene Sharaff. This show made Ray Bolger a star. **Cast**: VERA: Tamara Geva; SERGEI: Monty Woolley; PEGGY: Luella Geer; JUNIOR: Ray Bolger; FRANKIE: Doris Carson. **Act I**: **Scene 1** A vaudeville stage, 16 years ago: "Two a Day for Keith;" **Scene 2** The vaudeville dressing room; **Scene 3** A classroom of Knickerbocker University, WPA Extension: "The Three Bs," "It's Got to Be Love;" **Scene 4** Vera's apartment; the next morning: "Too Good for the Average Man;" **Scene 5** Central Park; night: "There's a Small Hotel;" **Scene 6** A Green Room, Cosmopolitan Opera House; next evening: "The Heart is Quicker than the Eye;" **Scene 7** A dressing room, Cosmopolitan Opera House; **Scene 8** "La Princesse Zenobia" ballet, Cosmopolitan Opera House. **Act II**: **Scene 1** A Planetarium roof garden: "Quiet Night," "Glad to Be Unhappy;" **Scene 2** The stage of the Cosmopolitan Opera House: "On Your Toes;" **Scene 3** The Green Room; a week later; **Scene 4** "Slaughter on Tenth Avenue" ballet; **Scene 5** The stage of the Cosmopolitan Opera House: Finale.

PALACE THEATRE, London, 2/5/37. **Cast**: Jack Whiting, Vera Zorina, Gina Malo, Olive Blakeney.

THE MOVIE. 1939. DIRECTOR: Ray Enright. It used music only for background and for the ballets. **Cast**: Vera Zorina, Eddie Albert, Alan Hale, Frank McHugh, James Gleason, Donald O'Connor.

The Broadway Run. FORTY-SIXTH STREET THEATRE, 10/11/54–12/4/54. 64 PERFORMANCES. PRESENTED BY George Abbott; MUSIC: Richard Rodgers; LYRICS: Lorenz Hart; BOOK: Richard Rodgers, Lorenz Hart, George Abbott; DIRECTOR: George Abbott; CHOREOGRAPHER: George Balanchine (recreated his own original choreography); SETS: Oliver Smith; COSTUMES: Irene Sharaff; LIGHTING: Peggy Clark; MUSICAL DIRECTOR: Salvatore Dell'Isola; ORIGINAL ORCHESTRATIONS: Hans Spialek; NEW ORCHESTRATIONS: Don Walker; PRESS: Reuben Rabinovitch & Abner Klipstein; COMPANY MANAGER: Richard Horner; PRODUCTION STAGE MANAGER: Robert E. Griffith; STAGE MANAGERS: James Hammerstein & Bertram Wood. **Cast**: PHIL DOLAN II: Jack Williams; LIL DOLAN: Eleanor Williams; PHIL DOLAN III (JUNIOR): David Winters; STAGE MANAGER: George Church; LOLA: Dorene Kilmer; JUNIOR (15 YEARS LATER): Bobby Van (2); FRANKIE FRAYNE: Kay Coulter (5); SIDNEY COHN: Joshua Shelley (6); VERA BARONOVA: Vera Zorina (1); ANUSHKA: Patricia Wilkes; PEGGY PORTERFIELD: Elaine Stritch (3); SERGEI ALEXANDROVITCH: Ben Astar (4); KONSTANTINE MORROSINE: Nicolas Orloff; SNOOPY: John Robb; THUG: Nathaniel Frey; MISHKA: Patrick Welch; IVAN: John Nola; VASSILI: Edward Pfeiffer; DMITRI: Ted Adkins; LEO: Robert Lindgren; BALLET STAGE MANAGER: Bertram Wood; COP: Arthur Grahl; CHORUS GIRLS: Phyllis Campbell, Lillian D'Honau, Patricia Drylie, Katia Geleznova, Carolyn George, Marilyn Hale, Dorene Kilmer, Helen Kramer, Sonja Lindgren, Paula Lloyd, Barbara Michaels, Lois Platt, Nina Popova, Sigyn, Ruth Sobotka, Mary Stanton, Carol Stevens, Wendy Winn; CHORUS BOYS: Ted Adkins, Marvin Arnold, Johnny Bowen, Timmy Everett, Arthur Grahl, Edward Kerrigan, Jack Leigh, Robert Lindgren, John Nola, Edward Pfeiffer. **Act I**: **Scene 1** Vaudeville stage: "Two a Day for Keith" (Phil II, Phil III, Lil) [dropped after opening]; **Scene 2** Dressing-room; **Scene 3** Vaudeville stage; **Scene 4** Broadcasting studio; **Scene 5** Sergei's bedroom; **Scene 6** Classroom of Knickerbocker University, WPA Extension: "The 3 B's" (Junior & Chorus), "It's Got to Be Love" (Junior & Frankie); **Scene 7** Vera's apartment: "Too Good for the Average Man" (Peggy & Sergei); **Scene 8** Central Park; **Scene 9** Green Room, Cosmopolitan Opera House: "There's a Small Hotel" (Junior & Frankie); **Scene 10** Dressing-room: "The Heart is Quicker than the Eye" (Peggy & Junior); **Scene 11** La Princesse Zenobia Ballet: "Princess Zenobia Ballet" (danced by Vera, Junior, Konstantine, Stage Manager, Chorus); **Scene 12** In front of curtain; **Scene 13** Backstage. **Act II**: **Scene 1** Planetarium Roof Garden:

"Quiet Night" (Sidney & Chorus); **Scene 2** Opera House stage: "Glad to Be Unhappy" (Frankie & Sidney); **Scene 3** Green Room: "On Your Toes" (Frankie, Junior, Sidney, Chorus); **Scene 4** In front of curtain: "Jitterbug Couple" (dance) (Dorene Kilmer & Timmy Everett), "Adagio Couple" (dance) [Katia Geleznova (*Paula Lloyd*) & Edward Pfeiffer (*Robert Lindgren*)], "You Took Advantage of Me" (Peggy) [taken from *Present Arms!* (1928)]; **Scene 5** Ballet of "Slaughter on Tenth Avenue:" "Slaughter on Tenth Avenue" (ballet) (Vera, Junior, Stage Manager, Chorus); **Scene 6** Opera House stage: Finale (reprise of "On Your Toes") (Entire Company).

The 1954 production was the first Broadway revival of the 1936 hit, but it was by now hopelessly outdated, and flopped. Reviews were very bad. Elaine Stritch's performance in this show led to her being cast in *Goldilocks*.

517. *On Your Toes (Broadway revival)*

Before Broadway. George Balanchine was set to choreograph, but fell ill, and his steps for the ballets "Slaughter on Tenth Avenue" and "Princess Zenobia" were realized by his protégé Peter Martins, while Donald Saddler choreographed the remaining dance numbers. Valentina Kozlova was married to Leonid Kozlov. In 12/82 Natalia Makarova was hit by a pipe during tryouts at the Kennedy Center, Washington, DC, (12/9/82–1/16/83). It broke her shoulder blade and cut her head. The show also played in Seattle before going to Broadway.

The Broadway Run. VIRGINIA THEATRE, 3/6/83–5/20/84. 7 previews. 505 PERFORMANCES. The ANTA — Kennedy Center production, PRESENTED BY Alfred de Liagre Jr., Roger L. Stevens, John Mauceri, Donald R. Seawell, Andre Pastoria; MUSIC: Richard Rodgers; LYRICS: Lorenz Hart; BOOK: Richard Rodgers, Lorenz Hart, George Abbott; DIRECTOR: George Abbott; CHOREOGRAPHER: Donald Saddler; ADDITIONAL BALLET CHOREOGRAPHY: Peter Martins; SETS/COSTUMES: Zack Brown; LIGHTING: John McLain; SOUND: Jan Nebozenko; MUSICAL DIRECTOR: John Mauceri; ORIGINAL ORCHESTRATIONS: Hans Spialek; CAST RECORDING on Polydor; PRESS: Jeffrey Richards Associates; CASTING: Hughes/Moss; GENERAL MANAGERS: Charlene Harrington & C. Edwin Knill; COMPANY MANAGER: Edwin Blacker; PRODUCTION STAGE MANAGER: William Dodds; STAGE MANAGER: Amy Pell; ASSISTANT STAGE MANAGER: Sarah Whitham, *Donnis Honeycutt*. **Cast**: PHIL DOLAN II: Eugene J. Anthony; LIL DOLAN: Betty Ann Grove; PHIL DOLAN III, JUNIOR: Philip Arthur Ross; STAGE MANAGER: Dirk Lumbard, *Robert Meadows*; LOLA: Mary C. Robare; JUNIOR DOLAN (15 YEARS LATER): Lara Teeter (6); MISS PINKERTON: Michaela K. Hughes; SIDNEY COHN: Peter Slutsker; FRANKIE FRAYNE: Christine Andreas (5); JOE McCALL: Jerry Mitchell; VERA BARONOVA: Natalia Makarova (1) ☆, *Galina Panova* (from 6/14/83), *Valentina Kozlova* (1/17/84–1/31/84), *Galina Panova*, Starr Danias (Saturday matinees); ANUSHKA: Tamara Mark, *Leslie Woodies*; PEGGY PORTERFIELD: Dina Merrill (3), *Kitty Carlisle Hart* (6/14/83–7/26/83), *Dina Merrill, Kitty Carlisle* Hart (from 12/20/83); SERGEI ALEXANDROVITCH: George S. Irving (2), *David Gold* (8/30/83–9/6/83), *George S. Irving*; KONSTANTINE MORROSINE: George de la Pena (4), *Leonid Kozlov* (1/17/83–1/31/83), *George de la Pena, Sandor Nemethy* (from 3/6/84), *Leonid Kozlov* (from 3/13/84), *Terry Edelfsen* (from 3/27/84); OSCAR: Eugene J. Anthony; STAGE DOORMAN: David Gold; A WOMAN REPORTER: Betty Ann Grove; DMITRI: Chris Peterson; IVAN: Don Steffy; LOUIE: George Kmeck; "PRINCESS ZENOBIA BALLET:" PRINCESS ZENOBIA: Natalia Makarova ☆; BEGGAR: George de la Pena; KRINGA KHAN: George Kmeck; ALI SHAR: Eugene J. Anthony; AHMUD BEN B'DU: David Gold [end of ballet sequence]; HANK JAY SMITH: Michael Vita; "ON YOUR TOES" BALLET: BALLET LEADERS: Alexander Filipov (*Malcolm Grant*) & Starr Danias; TAP LEADERS: Dirk Lumbard & Dana Moore [end of ballet sequence]; COP: Michael Vita; A MESSENGER BOY: Dean Badolato; "SLAUGHTER ON TENTH AVENUE" BALLET: HOOFER: Lara Teeter; STRIP TEASE GIRL: Natalia Makarova ☆, *Galina Panova* (from 6/14/83), *Valentina Kozlova* (1/17/84–1/31/84), *Galina Panova*, Starr Danias (Saturday matinees); BIG BOSS: Michael Vita [end of ballet sequence]; COP: Jerry Mitchell; ENSEMBLE: Dean Badolato, Melody A. Dye, Alexander Filipov (*Malcolm Grant*), David Gold, Michaela K. Hughes, George Kmeck, Wade Laboissonniere, Dirk Lumbard, Tamara

Mark, Robert Meadows, Jerry Mitchell, Dana Moore, Chris Peterson, Mary C. Robare, Don Steffy, Kirby Tepper, Marcia Lynn Watkins, Leslie Woodies, Sandra Zigars, *Teresa DeRose, Marguerite Hickey, Jane Lanier, James Walski*. **Understudies**: Lil: Dana Moore; Junior/Phil II: Dirk Lumbard; Frankie: Marcia Lynn Watkins; Sidney: Kirby Tepper; Vera: Starr Danias; Peggy: Michaela K. Hughes, *Leslie Woodies*; Sergei: David Gold; Konstantine: Alexander Filipov, *Don Steffy*; Louie: Jerry Mitchell; Phil III: Steven Ross. **Act I**: **Scene 1** A vaudeville stage; about 1920: "Two a Day for Keith" (Phil II, Lil, Phil III); **Scene 2** The vaudeville dressing room; **Scene 3** A classroom at Knickerbocker University — WPA extension: "Questions and Answers" ("The Three Bs") (Junior & Students), "It's Got to Be Love" (Frankie, Junior, Students); **Scene 4** Vera's apartment; the next morning: "Too Good for the Average Man" (Sergei & Peggy), "The Seduction" (Vera & Junior); **Scene 5** The schoolroom: "There's a Small Hotel" (Frankie & Junior); **Scene 6** The bare stage, Cosmopolitan Opera House; the next morning; **Scene 7** Cosmopolitan Opera House: "Princess Zenobia Ballet." **Act II**: **Scene 1** The bare stage, Cosmopolitan Opera House: "The Heart is Quicker than the Eye" (Peggy & Junior), "Glad to Be Unhappy" (Frankie); **Scene 2** The classroom: "Quiet Night" (Hank & Students), "On Your Toes" (Frankie & Students); **Scene 3** The bare stage, Cosmopolitan Opera House; **Scene 4** The stage door, Cosmopolitan Opera House: "Quiet Night" (reprise) (Sergei); **Scene 5** Stage of the Cosmopolitan Opera House: "Slaughter on Tenth Avenue" Ballet.

By now the show was considered a vintage piece, rather than merely outdated (as it had been in 1954 when last revived on Broadway), and it received generally excellent reviews. This was the first speaking role for Natalia Makarova, premiere danseuse with the American Ballet Theatre. She was a big hit. The show won Tonys for reproduction of a play or musical, and for Natalia Makarova. It was also nominated for choreography, and for Lara Teeter and Christine Andreas. George Abbott was 95 when he directed this, his 120th Broadway production, and was still not his last Broadway show!.

After Broadway. Tour. Opened on 3/21/84, at the Theatre of the Performing Arts, Miami, and closed on 4/28/84, at the Majestic Theatre, Dallas. Presented by Zev Bufman, Sidney Shlenker, Allen J. Becker, Barry Lewis, Miles Wilkin, and the Nederlander Producing Company. **Cast**: Vera: Leslie Caron (Natalia Makarova alternate); Junior: Michael Kubala; Sergei: Stephen Pearlman; Peggy: Frances Bergen; Morrosine: Alexander Filipov. In April Leslie Caron tore a hip muscle, and had to alternate with Natalia Makarova, but eventually she was hospitalized, and the tour ended prematurely. In 10/84 $1.4 million was paid by Lloyds of London in insurance to the producers, for the loss of revenue caused by Miss Caron's injury — a record payoff in theatre history.

Palace Theatre, London, 6/12/84. **Cast**: Peggy: Honor Blackman; Junior: Tim Flavin; Vera: Natalia Makarova, *Galina Panova* (from 10/1/84), *Doreen Wells*; Frankie: Siobhan McCarthy; Sergei: John Bennett; Morrosine: Nicholas Johnson.

Los Angeles, 7/25/86. **Cast**: Vera: Natalia Makarova; Junior: Lara Teeter; Sergei: Michael Kermoyan; Peggy: Dina Merrill; Frankie: Kathleen Rowe McAllen; Morrosine: George de la Pena.

Royal Festival Hall, London, 8/7/03–9/6/03. This was the first London revival since 1984. The production tried out at the Haymarket Theatre, Leicester. Director: Paul Kerryson; Choreographer: Adam Cooper; Sets/Costumes: Paul Farnsworth; Musical Director: Julian Kelly. **Cast**: Peggy: Kathryn Evans; Vera: Sarah Wildor; Junior: Adam Cooper.

518. *Once on This Island*

Set on an island in the French Antilles, in the Caribbean, during a stormy night. It is a fable told to a young girl to calm her during the storm. The story goes that Ti Moune is plucked from such a storm by the gods and placed in a tree for shelter. She grows into a beautiful peasant girl who rescues Daniel, the mulatto son of a wealthy landowner after he has been hurt in a car crash. Ti Moune makes a pact with the gods — her life for

Daniel's — for she is convinced that her love is so strong it can conquer death. He is finally healed, but rejects her. The gods give her eternal life by turning her into a tree. In the novel, Ti Moune is trampled to death by the crowd as they rush to witness the wedding between Daniel and Andrea. Lynn Ahrens and Stephen Flaherty wrote a happier ending. There was no intermission.

Before Broadway. In 6/88 Lynn Ahrens was in a bookstore, and for $1.50 bought a novel, *My Love, My Love*, by Trinidadian author Rosa Guy, which she liked and took to Stephen Flaherty. They began work on it, turning it into a musical. They approached Rosa Guy with an outline and four songs. At that time the project was called *Ti Moune*. They acquired the rights from Miss Guy. It had a four-week workshop at Playwrights Horizons, followed by 3 performances, directed by Graciela Daniele, with 11 actors. Then it ran at Playwrights Horizons, in association with AT & T: Onstage, 5/6/90–5/27/90. 36 previews. 24 performances. It had the same cast, crew and musicians as for the subsequent Broadway run. However, at that stage understudies were: Mama/Asaka/Ti Moune/Andrea: Fuschia Walker; Erzulie: Nikki Rene; Daniel/Armand/Julian: Keith Tyrone; Agwe/Papa Ge: Gerry McIntyre. The numbers "Come Down from the Tree" and "When Daniel Marries" were cut before Broadway.

The Broadway Run. Booth Theatre, 10/18/90–12/1/91. 19 previews from 10/2/90. 469 performances. Presented by The Shubert Organization, Capital Cities/ABC, Suntory International Corporation, and James Walsh, in association with Playwrights Horizons; Music/Vocal & Dance Music Arrangements: Stephen Flaherty; Lyrics/Book: Lynn Ahrens; Based on the novel *My Love, My Love*, by Rosa Guy; Director/Choreographer: Graciela Daniele; Associate Choreographer: Willie Rosario; Sets: Loy Arcenas; Costumes: Judy Dearing; Lighting: Allen Lee Hughes; Sound: Scott Lehrer; Musical Director: Steve Marzullo; Orchestrations: Michael Starobin; Cast Recording on RCA; Press: Philip Rinaldi & Tim Ray; Casting: Alan Filderman & Daniel Swee; General Manager: James Walsh; Company Manager: Florie Seery; Production Stage Manager: Leslie Loeb; Stage Manager: Fred Tyson. **Cast**: Daniel: Jerry Dixon; Erzulie, Goddess of Love: Andrea Frierson, *Rozz Morehead*; Mama Euralie: Sheila Gibbs; Ti Moune: La Chanze; Asaka, Mother of the Earth: Kecia Lewis-Evans, *Lillias White* (from 1/8/91); Little Ti Moune: Afi McClendon, *Desiree Scott* (stood in), *Ibijoke Akinola*; Armand: Gerry McIntyre; Agwe, God of Water: Milton Craig Nealy; Andrea: Nikki Rene; Papa Ge, Demon of Death: Eric Riley; Tonton Julian: Ellis E. Williams. **Standbys**: Mama/Asaka/Erzulie: Fuschia Walker; Ti Moune/Andrea: PaSean Wilson; Little Ti Moune: Desiree Scott; Daniel/Armand/Tonton/Agwe: Keith Tyrone. **Understudy**: Papa Ge: Gerry McIntyre. "We Dance" (Storytellers), "One Small Girl" (Mama Euralie, Tonton Julian, Little Ti Moune, Storytellers), "Waiting for Life" (Ti Moune & Storytellers), "And the Gods Heard Her Prayer" (Asaka, Agwe, Papa Ge, Erzulie), "Rain" (Agwe & Storytellers), "Pray" (Ti Moune, Tonton Julian, Mama Euralie, Guard, Storytellers), "Forever Yours" (Ti Moune, Daniel, Papa Ge), "The Sad Tale of the Beauxhommes" (Armand & Storytellers), "Ti Moune" (Mama Euralie, Tonton Julian, Ti Moune), "Mama Will Provide" (Asaka & Storytellers), "Waiting for Life" (reprise) (Ti Moune), "Some Say" (Storytellers), "The Human Heart" (Erzulie & Storytellers), "Pray" (reprise) (Storytellers), "Some Girls" (Daniel), "The Ball" (Andrea, Daniel, Ti Moune, Storytellers), "Forever Yours" (reprise) (Papa Ge, Ti Moune, Erzulie, Storytellers), "A Part of Us" (Mama Euralie, Little Ti Moune, Tonton Julian, Storytellers), "Why We Tell the Story" (Storytellers).

Reviews were divided. The production closed on Broadway at the 12/1/91 matinee. The show received Tony nominations for musical, score, book, direction of a musical, choreography, costumes, lighting, and for La Chanze.

After Broadway. Tour. Opened on 4/2/92, at the Shubert Theatre, Chicago. Co-produced by the Kennedy Center; Musical Director: Mark Lipman. Ran at the Kennedy Center, Washington, DC, 5/22/92–7/19/92. **Cast**: Mama Euralie: Sheila Gibbs; Papa Ge: Gerry McIntyre; Erzulie: Natalie Venetia Belcon; Ti Moune: Vanita Harbour; Agwe: James Stovall; Armand: Keith Tyrone; Julian: Miles Watson; Young Ti Moune: Nilyne Fields; Asaka: Carol Dennis, *Alvaleta Guess*; Andrea: Monique Cintron; Daniel: Darius de Haas.

STUDIO ARENA, Buffalo. Part of the 1993–94 season. DIRECTOR: Bob Baker. **Cast**: MAMA: Salome Bey; AGWE: Timothy Robert Blevins; ARMAND: Tyrone Gabriel; TI MOUNE: Vanita Harbour.

REPERTORY THEATRE OF ST. LOUIS. 1993–94 season. DIRECTOR/CHOREOGRAPHER: Eric Riley. **Cast**: DANIEL: Donnell Aarone; MAMA: Lynette DuPre; ERZULIE: Fredi Walker.

BIRMINGHAM REPERTORY THEATRE, England, 7/94; ROYALTY THEATRE (re-named the Island Theatre for this run only), London, 9/28/94. 145 PERFORMANCES. It won an Olivier Award for best musical. **Cast**: MAMA EURALIE: Shezwae Powell; AGWE: Trevor Michael Georges; TI MOUNE: Lorna Brown; ERZULIE: P.P. Arnold; DANIEL: Anthony Corriette; PAPA GE: Clive Rowe; ARMAND: Mark Vincent; LITTLE TI MOUNE: Elizabeth Kerr (replaced at Birmingham Rep by *Monique Mason*, who took it to the West End); TONTON: Johnny Worthy; ANDREA: Suzanne Packer; ASAKA: Sharon D. Clarke.

VIRGINIA STAGE COMPANY. Part of the 1995–96 season. DIRECTOR: Gerry McIntyre. **Cast**: TI MOUNE: Vanita Harbour.

A version for children, nicknamed *Once Upon This Island* Jr. [note that the word "Jr." is not part of the title], first showed at Rahway, New Jersey, on 12/3/98.

A new treatment was performed at BAY STREET THEATRE, Sag Harbor, Long Island, 8/10/04–9/5/04. DIRECTOR: Marcia Milgrom Dodge. **Cast**: TI MOUNE: Kenita Miller; ANDREA: Carey Brown; ERZULIE: Monique Midgette; DANIEL: Josh Tower; TONTON: Dathan Williams; AGWE: Alan Greene; PAPA GE: Kevyn Morrow; ASAKA: Soara Joye Ross; MAMA: Kena Dorsey.

519. *Once Upon a Mattress*

The Minstrel tells us this true story happened many moons ago (i.e. in the spring of 1428). The kingdom is in a sorry state. The King has been struck dumb, and will never talk again "until the Mouse devours the Hawk." The court tries several unsuccessful experiments with large mice and small hawks. Queen Aggravain takes over, and decrees that no one may marry until her son, Dauntless, has married a "true princess of royal blood." But the Queen is determined that he shall remain single, and he is dominated by her. 11 girls have failed tests given by the Queen and the Wizard. With Sir Harry and Lady Larken in love, not married, but about to become parents, it becomes imperative to find a princess of the royal blood for Dauntless. Sir Harry goes to the swamps (the only place left unsearched) to undertake the Perilous Labor of finding a princess. In Wallows-on-the-Mire he finds Princess Winnifred of Farfelot, who has no royal graces, but Dauntless is taken with her. The Queen plans a sensitivity test for her — will she feel the pea under 20 mattresses? With the aid of the Minstrel and the Jester she passes the test. Dauntless defies the Queen, in other words the Mouse has devoured the Hawk, the Queen is struck dumb, and the King regains control. We find that the Minstrel has placed — under the top mattress — his lute, a helmet, and a large spiked ball, a couple of lobsters and some old jousting equipment.

Before Broadway. Originally created as a one-act musical by Mary Rodgers (Richard Rodgers' daughter) and Marshall Barer at an adult summer camp. With Jay Thompson and Dean Fuller they expanded the work into a full musical. Mary Rodgers had comedienne Nancy Walker in mind when she created the character, but director George Abbott wanted an unknown (Carol Burnett — this was the show that made her a star). Before moving to Broadway, it ran Off Broadway, at the PHOENIX THEATRE, 5/11/59–11/15/59. 216 PERFORMANCES. It had the same crew, except PRESS: Ben Kornzweig, Robert Feinberg, Karl Bernstein; COMPANY MANAGER: Nathan Parnes; STAGE MANAGERS: John Allen & George Quick. **Cast**: MINSTREL: Harry Snow; PRINCE: Jim Maher; PRINCESS: Chris Karner; QUEEN: Gloria Stevens; WIZARD: Robert Weil; PRINCESS NUMBER TWELVE: Mary Stanton; LADY ROWENA: Dorothy Aull; LADY MERRILL: Patsi King; PRINCE DAUNTLESS: Joe Bova; THE QUEEN: Jane

White; LADY LUCILLE: Luce Ennis; LADY LARKEN: Anne Jones; SIR STUDLEY: Jerry Newby; THE KING: Jack Gilford; JESTER: Matt Mattox; SIR HARRY: Allen Case; PRINCESS WINNIFRED: Carol Burnett; SIR HAROLD: David Neuman; LADY BEATRICE: Gloria Stevens; SIR LUCE: Tom Mixon; LADY MABELLE: Chris Karner; THE NIGHTINGALE OF SAMARKAND: Ginny Perlowin; LADY DOROTHY: Dorothy D'Honau; SIR CHRISTOPHER: Christopher Edwards [became Sir Nicholas on Broadway]; LORD HOWARD: Howard Parker; LADY DORA: Dorothy Frank [became Lady Jerane on Broadway]; SIR DANIEL: Dan Resin [became Lord Casper on Broadway]; SIR STEVEN: Jim Stevenson; LORD PATRICK: Julian Patrick [became Sir Paul on Broadway]. **Understudies**: Dorothy Aull, Jim Stevenson, Jerry Newby, Dan Resin, Mary Stanton, Patsi King, Tom Mixon, Will Lee.

The Broadway Run. ALVIN THEATRE, 11/25/59–2/22/60; WINTER GARDEN THEATRE, 2/24/60–4/23/60; CORT THEATRE, 4/25/60–5/7/60; ST. JAMES THEATRE, 5/9/60–7/2/60. Total of 244 PERFORMANCES. PRESENTED BY The Phoenix Theatre (T. Edward Hambleton & Norris Houghton) & William & Jean Eckart; MUSIC: Mary Rodgers; LYRICS: Marshall Barer; BOOK: Jay Thompson, Marshall Barer, Dean Fuller; BASED ON the fairy tale *The Princess and the Pea*, by Hans Christian Andersen; DIRECTOR: George Abbott; CHOREOGRAPHER: Joe Layton; SETS/COSTUMES: William & Jean Eckart; LIGHTING: Tharon Musser; MUSICAL DIRECTOR: Hal Hastings; CONDUCTOR: Clay Warnick; ORCHESTRATIONS: Hershy Kay, Arthur Beck, Carroll Huxley; DANCE MUSIC ARRANGEMENTS: Roger Adams; PRESS: Ben Kornzweig, Karl Bernstein, Robert Ganshaw, Lawrence Witchel; CASTING: Judith Abbott; GENERAL MANAGER: Carl Fisher; COMPANY MANAGER: Harry Essex; PRODUCTION STAGE MANAGER: John Allen; STAGE MANAGER: Jack Sydow; ASSISTANT STAGE MANAGER: George Quick. **Cast**: MINSTREL: Harry Snow; PRINCE: Gene Kelton; PRINCESS: Chris Karner, *Marjorie Pragon*; QUEEN: Dorothy Frank; WIZARD: Robert Weil; PRINCESS NUMBER TWELVE: Mary Stanton, *Cheryl Kilgren*; LADY ROWENA: Patti Karr; LADY MERRILL: Cheryl Kilgren, *Anne Fielding, Carla Huston*; PRINCE DAUNTLESS THE DRAB: Joseph Bova (2); QUEEN AGGRAVAIN: Jane White (4); LADY LUCILLE: Dorothy Aull, *Ellie Zalon*; LADY LARKEN: Anne Jones; SIR STUDLEY: Tom Mixon, *Stuart Hodes*; KING SEXTIMUS: Will Lee (3); JESTER: Jerry Newby; SIR HARRY: Dan Resin; PRINCESS WINNIFRED: Carol Burnett (1); SIR HAROLD: David Neuman; LADY BEATRICE: Dorothy Frank; SIR LUCE: Stuart Hodes, *John Baylis*; LADY MABELLE: Marjorie Pragon; THE NIGHTINGALE OF SAMARKAND: Gina Viglione; LADY DOROTHY: Dorothy D'Honau; SIR NICHOLAS: Peter Holmes [this role had been Sir Christopher before Broadway]; SIR EDMUND: Edmund Balin, *Gene Kelton* [this role was added for Broadway]; SIR JOSEPH: Joseph Carow [this role was added for Broadway]; LORD HOWARD: Gene Kelton; LADY BETH: Beth Howland [this role was added for Broadway]; LADY JERANE: Jerane Michel [this role had been Lady Dora before Broadway]; LORD CASPER: Casper Roos [this role had been Sir Daniel before Broadway]; SIR STEVEN: Jack Schwartz; SIR PAUL: Paul Richards [this role had been Lord Patrick before Broadway]; LADY ELIZABETH: Betty Hyatt Linton [a new character in the last few months of the run]. **Understudies**: Winnifred: Dorothy Aull; Minstrel: Paul Richards; Jester: Stuart Hodes; Harry: Casper Roos; Larken: Carla Huston; Queen: Gina Viglione; Dauntless: John Baylis; King/Wizard: Jack Sydow. **Act I**: **Prologue** "Many Moons Ago" (Minstrel & Court); **Scene 1** Throne room: "An Opening for a Princess" (Dauntless, Larken, Knights, Ladies), "In a Little While" (Larken & Harry); **Scene 2** The Yellow Gallery: "In a Little While" (reprise) (Larken & Harry); **Scene 3** Courtyard: "Shy" (Winnifred, Sir Studley, Knights, Ladies), "The Minstrel, The Jester and I" (King, Minstrel, Jester); **Scene 4** A corridor: "Sensitivity" (Queen & Wizard); **Scene 5** Winnifred's dressing chamber: Fanfare, "Swamps of Home" (Winnifred, Dauntless, Ladies); **Scene 6** The Grey Gallery; **Scene 7** On the greensward: Tents, "Normandy" (Minstrel, Jester, King, Larken); **Scene 8** The Yellow Gallery; **Scene 9** Great Hall: "Spanish Panic" (Jester, Jerane, Beatrice, Queen, Winnifred, Dauntless, Knights, Ladies), "Song of Love" (Dauntless, Winnifred, Knights, Ladies). **Act II**: **Entr'acte** Opening — Act II (Company); **Scene 1** Castle: "Quiet" (Jester, Queen, Knights, Ladies); **Scene 2** Winnifred's dressing chamber: "Happily Ever After" (Winnifred); **Scene 3** A corridor: "Man to Man Talk" (King & Dauntless); **Scene 4** Wizard's chamber; **Scene 5** The Grey Gallery: "Very Soft Shoes" (Jester, Knights, Ladies); **Scene 6** The bed chamber: "Yesterday I Loved You" (Harry & Larken); *Scene 7* A corridor: "(Nightingale) Lullaby" (The Nightingale of Samarkand); *Scene 8* Breakfast hall: Finale (Entire Court).

The show received Tony nominations for musical, and for Carol Burnett.

After Broadway. TOUR. Opened on 9/1/60, at the Erlanger Theatre, Chicago, and closed on 3/18/61, at the Colonial Theatre, Boston. PRESENTED BY Sol Hurok; MUSICAL DIRECTOR: Carmen Coppola. *Cast*: WINNIFRED: Dody Goodman; DAUNTLESS: Cy Young; QUEEN: Fritzi Burr; KING: Buster Keaton; JESTER: Harold Lang; LADY MABELLE: Mrs. Buster Keaton.

ADELPHI THEATRE, London, 9/20/60. 38 PERFORMANCES. PRESENTED BY Williamson Music; DIRECTOR: Jerome Whyte; MUSICAL DIRECTOR: Robert Lowe. *Cast*: WINNIFRED: Jane Connell; WIZARD: Bill Kerr; DAUNTLESS: Robin Hunter; SIR HARRY: Bill Newman; QUEEN: Valerie Holmann; KING: Milo O'Shea.

TOUR. Opened at the Veterans' Memorial Hospital, Providence, Rhode Island, and closed on 5/27/61, at the National Theatre, Washington, DC. PRESENTED BY Michael Dewell & Frances Ann Hersey; MUSICAL DIRECTOR: Cee Davidson. *Cast*: WINNIFRED: Imogene Coca; KING: Edward Everett Horton; DAUNTLESS: King Donovan; SIR STUDLEY: Joe Sutherin; NIGHTINGALE: Maura K. Wedge.

TV. There were two CBS productions, both with Carol Burnett and Jane White reprising their Broadway roles. The first was aired on 6/3/64. Joe Bova reprised his Broadway role. A new number — "Under a Spell" — was inserted. DIRECTOR: Joe Layton. The second, aired on 12/12/72. *Cast*: DAUNTLESS: Ken Berry; KING: Jack Gilford; LARKEN: Bernadette Peters.

520. *Once Upon a Mattress (Broadway revival)*

Before Broadway. Bea Arthur and Dorothy Loudon were both rumored to be playing the Queen, but Mary Lou Rosato wound up in the role. Rehearsals began on 10/7/96. On 11/1/96 it was announced that Michael McGrath, who was to play the Jester, had been replaced by David Hibbard. During Broadway previews, Sarah Jessica Parker developed a bronchial infection. The performance on 12/6/96 was canceled, and her understudy, Janet Metz, went on for her for the two performances of 12/7/96. The 12/9/96 preview was canceled as well. There was a fight between Gerald Gutierrez and Marshall Barer. Mr. Barer was, apparently, coaching Miss Parker on how to play the role, so Mr. Gutierrez, the director, banned him from the set. "Gerry has directed it as if it were *Medea*," Mr. Barer was reported as saying.

The Broadway Run. BROADHURST THEATRE, 12/19/96–5/31/97. 33 previews from 11/18/96. 187 PERFORMANCES. PRESENTED BY Dodger Productions & Joop Van Den Ende; MUSIC: Mary Rodgers; LYRICS: Marshall Barer; BOOK: Jay Thompson, Marshall Barer, Dean Fuller; DIRECTOR: Gerald Gutierrez; CHOREOGRAPHER: Liza Gennaro; SETS: John Lee Beatty; COSTUMES: Jane Greenwood; LIGHTING: Pat Collins; SOUND: Tom Morse; MUSICAL DIRECTOR: Eric Stern, *Todd Ellison* (from 3/97); ORCHESTRATIONS: Bruce Coughlin; VOCAL ARRANGEMENTS/INCIDENTAL MUSIC ARRANGEMENTS: Eric Stern; DANCE MUSIC ARRANGEMENTS: Tom Fay; NEW CAST RECORDING on RCA Victor. made on 1/6/97, at New York's Hit Factory, and released on 3/27/97; PRESS: Boneau/Bryan-Brown; CASTING: Jay Binder; GENERAL MANAGEMENT: David Strong Warner; COMPANY MANAGER: Marcia Goldberg; PRODUCTION STAGE MANAGER: Steven Beckler; STAGE MANAGER: Brian Meister; ASSISTANT STAGE MANAGER: Tracy Burns. *Cast*: KING SEXTIMUS: Heath Lamberts (2); QUEEN AGGRAVAIN: Mary Lou Rosato (4); PRINCE DAUNTLESS, THEIR SON: David Aaron Baker (9); WINNIFRED, PRINCESS OF FARFELOT: Sarah Jessica Parker (1) ☆; SIR HARRY, KNIGHT OF THE HERALD: Lewis Cleale (5); LADY LARKEN, A LADY-IN-WAITING: Jane Krakowski (3), *Ann Brown* (during Miss Krakowski's vacation, 4/97), *Lannyl Stephens* (by 5/97); JESTER: David Hibbard (8), *Thom Christopher Warren*; MASTER MERTON, CONFIDANT TO THE QUEEN: Tom Alan Robbins (7); THE NIGHTINGALE OF SAMARKAND, A ROYAL PET: Ann Brown; THE ROYAL CELLIST: Laura Bontrager; THE ROYAL BALLET: Arte Phillips & Pascale

Faye; MINSTREL, A TRAVELING PLAYER: Lawrence Clayton (6); PLAYER QUEEN: David Jennings; PLAYER PRINCE: David Elder; PLAYER PRINCESS: Bob Walton; OTHER PLAYERS: Arte Phillips, Nick Cokas, Stephen Reed; KNIGHTS & LORDS ATTENDING THE QUEEN: Nick Cokas, David Elder, David Jennings, Sebastian La Cause, Jason Opsahl, Arte Phillips, Stephen Reed, Bob Walton, *Thom Christopher Warren*; LADIES ATTENDING THE QUEEN: Ann Brown, Maria Calabrese, Thursday Farrar, Pascale Faye, Janet Metz, Tina Ou, Aixa M. Rosario Medina, Jennifer Smith. *Understudies*: Winnifred: Janet Metz; King: Tom Alan Robbins; Queen: Jennifer Smith; Dauntless/Jester: Bob Walton; Harry: David Elder; Larken: Ann Brown; Merton: Stephen Reed; Minstrel: Jason Opsahl. *Swings*: Pamela Gold & Thomas Titone. *Orchestra*: WOODWINDS: Edward Joffe, Rick Heckman, Roger Rosenberg; TRUMPETS: Joe Mosello & Glenn Drewes; TROMBONE: Keith O'Quinn; CONCERTMASTER: Michael Roth; VIOLA: Liuh-Wen Ting; CELLI: Daniel D. Miller & Laura Bontrager; BASS: Richard Sarpola; DRUMS/PERCUSSION: John Meyers; KEYBOARDS: Todd Ellison & Adam Ben-David. *Act I*: Overture, "Many Moons Ago" (Minstrel & Players), "An Opening for a Princess" (Dauntless, Larken, Knights, Ladies), "In a Little While" (Larken & Harry), "Shy" (Winnifred & Knights), "The Minstrel, the Jester and I" (King, Minstrel, Jester), "Sensitivity" (Queen), "Swamps of Home" (Winnifred, Dauntless, Ladies), "Normandy" (Minstrel, Jester, King, Larken), "Spanish Panic" (Queen, Winnifred, Dauntless, Knights, Ladies), "Song of Love" (Dauntless, Winnifred, Knights, Ladies). *Act II*: Entr'acte; "Quiet" (Entire Court), "Goodnight, Sweet Princess" (Dauntless) [a new number], "Happily Ever After" (Winnifred), "Man to Man Talk" (King & Dauntless), "Very Soft Shoes" (Jester), "Yesterday I Loved You" (Harry & Larken), "Lullaby" (Nightingale), Finale (Entire Court).

Broadway reviews were divided, mostly negative. On 4/27/97 Carol Burnett attended the matinee. On 5/15/97 its closing was announced for 5/31/97. The cast gave its final performance as part of the 6/1/97 Tony awards ceremony. The show was nominated for revival of a musical.

After Broadway. SAN FRANCISCO, 12/8/04–1/2/05. PRESENTED BY 42nd Street Moon. *Cast*: WINNIFRED: Lea De Laria.

ABC-TV SPECIAL, 2004. DIRECTOR: Kathleen Marshall. *Cast*: WINNIFRED: Tracey Ullman [Marissa Jaret Winokur had previously been announced for this role]; QUEEN AGGRAVAIN: Carol Burnett; WIZARD: Edward Hibbert; DAUNTLESS; Denis O'Hare; SIR HARRY: Matthew Morrison; LADY LARKEN: Zooey Deschanel; KING: Tommy Smothers.

521. *110 in the Shade*

Set in the drought-stricken Western town of Three Point, on a hot summer day from dawn to midnight. Starbuck appears, claiming to be a rainmaker. A brash con man, he brings hope to everyone except Lizzie, a plain and shy farmgirl, who calls him a fake. However, they make love while the town is at its annual picnic. Starbuck wants her to run away with him, but she is no big dreamer, and chooses to remain with her suitor, File. Then the rain comes.

Before Broadway. This show was originally called *Rainbow*. Robert Horton replaced Hal Holbrook in the lead two weeks before rehearsals began (Mr. Horton had been the first to be offered the role of Starbuck, but instead had chosen to do *I Picked a Daisy* which, when it was canceled, left him free to change his mind). 7th-billed Fred Miller and 9th-billed Adriane Rogers were both dropped before Broadway. Rumor has it that 100 songs were written for this show. Those cut included: "110 in the Shade," "Why Can't They Leave Me Alone?," "Come on Along," "Pretty Is," "Too Many People Alone," "Whole Hog or Nothin'," "I Can Dance," "I Live by Myself (and I Like It)," "Dance Hall Saturday Night," "Evening Star" (had the same music as "Another Hot Day"), "Fliberty Jibits," "Inside My Head," "Just Fine," "Sweet River."

The Broadway Run. BROADHURST THEATRE, 10/24/63–8/8/64. 2 previews on 10/23/63. 330 PERFORMANCES. PRESENTED BY David Merrick, with the co-operation of Rainbow Ventures; MUSIC: Harvey Schmidt; LYRICS: Tom Jones; BOOK: N. Richard Nash (based on his 1954 comedy *The Rainmaker*); DIRECTOR: Joseph Anthony; CHOREOGRAPHER: Agnes de Mille; SETS: Oliver Smith; ASSISTANT SETS: Robin

Wagner; COSTUMES: Motley; LIGHTING: John Harvey; MUSICAL DIRECTOR: Donald Pippin; ORCHESTRATIONS: Hershy Kay; DANCE MUSIC ARRANGEMENTS: William Goldenberg; VOCAL ARRANGEMENTS: Robert De Cormier; CAST RECORDING on Victor; PRESS: Harvey B. Sabinson, Lee Solters, David Powers; GENERAL MANAGER: Jack Schlissel; COMPANY MANAGER: Ethel Davis; PRODUCTION STAGE MANAGER: Bill Ross; STAGE MANAGERS: Charles Blackwell & May Muth; ASSISTANT STAGE MANAGER: Seth Riggs. **Cast:** TOBY: George Church; SHERIFF FILE: Stephen Douglass (3); H.C. CURRY: Will Geer (4); NOAH CURRY: Steve Roland (5); JIMMIE CURRY: Scooter Teague (6); LIZZIE CURRY: Inga Swenson (2), *Joan Fagan* (from 4/23/64); SNOOKIE: Lesley Warren (who became Lesley Ann Warren); MRS. JENSEN: Diane Deering; PHIL MACKEY: Seth Riggs; TOMMY: Christopher Votos; BELINDA: Renee Dudley; GESHY TOOPS: Don Crabtree; GIL DEMBY: Jerry Dodge, *Arthur Whitfield*; OLIVE BARROW: Leslie Franzos; WALLY SKACKS III: Loren Hightower, *Bob Bishop*; MAURINE TOOPS: Evelyn Taylor; BO DOLLIVAN: Vernon Lusby; MR. CURTIS: Robert Shepard, *Robert Spelvin*; BILL STARBUCK: Robert Horton (1); WALLY SKACKS: Carl Nicholas; HANNAH: Dori Davis; TOWNSPEOPLE: Don Atkinson, Lynne Broadbent, Frank Derbas, Jerry Dodge, Leslie Franzos, Ben Gillespie, Loren Hightower, Lucia Lambert, Paula Lloyd, Vernon Lusby, Evelyn Taylor, Esther Villavicencio, Arthur Whitfield, Florence Willson, *Barbara Bossert, Gretchen Cryer, Dori Davis, Diane Deering, Clifford Fearl, Carolyn Kemp, Urylee Leonardos, David London, Carl Nicholas, Stan Page, Donna Sanders*. **Standby:** Lizzie: Joan Fagan. **Understudies:** Starbuck: Seth Riggs; File: Stan Page; H.C.: Robert Shepard; Jimmie: Jerry Dodge; Noah: Don Crabtree; Snookie: Florence Willson; Toby: Vernon Lusby & Carl Nicholas. **Act I:** Overture (Orchestra); *Scene 1* The depot: "(Gonna Be) Another Hot Day" (File & Townspeople); *Scene 2* File's office on Main Street: "Lizzie's Comin' Home" (H.C., Noah, Jimmy), "Love, Don't Turn Away" (Lizzie); *Scene 3* A picnic area near the bandstand: "Poker Polka" (File, H.C., Noah); *Scene 4* The Rainwagon (Starbuck's truck): "Hungry Men" (Townspeople), "The Rain Song" (Starbuck & Townspeople); *Scene 5* Another picnic area: "You're Not Foolin' Me" (Lizzie & Starbuck), "Raunchy" (Lizzie & H.C.); *Scene 6* The edge of the woods: "A Man and a Woman" (Lizzie & File), "Old Maid" (Lizzie). **Act II:** *Scene 1* The park: "Everything Beautiful Happens at Night" (Toby, Jimmie, Snookie, Townspeople); *Scene 2* The Rainwagon: "Melisande" (Starbuck); *Scene 3* A picnic area: "Simple Little Things" (Lizzie), "Little Red Hat" (Snookie & Jimmie); *Scene 4* The Rainwagon: "Is it Really Me?" (Lizzie & Starbuck), "Wonderful Music" (File, Starbuck, Lizzie); *Scene 5* Near the bandstand: Finale: "The Rain Song" (reprise) (Full Company).

Broadway reviews were divided, mostly good. The score got raves, as did Inga Swenson. The show received Tony nominations for composer & lyricist, direction of a musical, and for Will Geer and Inga Swenson.

After Broadway. TOUR. Opened on 8/10/64, at the Curran Theatre, San Francisco. MUSICAL DIRECTOR: Pembroke Davenport. **Cast:** TOBY: George Church; FILE: Stephen Douglass, *John Carter* (from 12/23/64); H.C.: Will Geer; NOAH: John Carter (until 12/64); JIMMY: Scooter Teague; LIZZIE: Inga Swenson, *Jeannie Carson* (from 12/23/64); SNOOKIE: Lesley Warren, *Leslie Daniel*; MRS. JENSEN: Addi Negri; GIL: Arthur Whitfield; MAURINE: Cathy Conklin; BO: Vernon Lusby; CURTIS: Joe E. Hill; STARBUCK: Ray Danton, *Biff McGuire* (from 12/23/64); WALLY: Joe Kirkland.

PALACE THEATRE, London. Opened on 2/8/67. The number "110 in the Shade" (cut for Broadway), was re-instated here.

NEW YORK STATE THEATRE, 7/18/92–11/15/92. 12 PERFORMANCES in repertory with *Regina*. PRESENTED BY the New York City Opera; DIRECTOR: Scott Ellis; CHOREOGRAPHER: Susan Stroman; SETS: Michael Anania; COSTUMES: Lindsay W. Davis; LIGHTING: Jeff Davis; SOUND: Abe Jacob; MUSICAL DIRECTOR: Paul Gemignani; ORCHESTRATIONS: Hershy Kay; ADDITIONAL ORCHESTRATIONS: William D. Brohn; ADDITIONAL DANCE MUSIC ARRANGEMENTS: Peter Howard. **Cast:** TOMMY: Robert Mann Kayser; DANCE COUPLE: Jennifer Paulson Lee & K. Craig Innes (*John Scott*); FILE: Richard Muenz; JIMMY: David Aaron Baker; NOAH: Walter Charles; H.C.: Henderson Forsythe; LIZZIE: Karen Ziemba; SNOOKIE UPDEGRAFF: Crista Moore; STARBUCK: Brian Sutherland. **Act I:** "(Gonna Be) Another Hot Day" (File & Townspeople), "Lizzie's Comin' Home" (Jimmy, Noah, H.C.), "Love, Don't Turn Away" (Lizzie), "Overheard" (Townspeople) [newly written for this produc-

tion], "Poker Polka" (Jimmy, Noah, H.C., File), "Why Can't They Leave Me Alone?" (File) [this was a new song, cut from the original], "Come on Along" (Townspeople) [this number was unused in the original], "Cinderella" (Children) [newly written for this production], "Raunchy" (Lizzie), "A Man and a Woman" (File & Lizzie), "Old Maid" (Lizzie). **Act II:** "Come on Along" (reprise) (Townspeople), "Everything Beautiful Happens at Night" (Townspeople), "Shooting Star" (Starbuck) [newly written for this production], "Melisande" (Starbuck), "Simple Little Things" (Lizzie), "Little Red Hat" (Jimmy & Snookie), "Is it Really Me?" (Lizzie & Starbuck), "Wonderful Music" (Starbuck, File, Lizzie), Finale: "Rain Song" (reprise) (Company).

PASADENA PLAYHOUSE, 6/18/04–7/25/04. DIRECTOR: David Lee. **Cast:** Marin Mazzie, Jason Danieley.

522. *One Touch of Venus*

Rodney, a barber from Ozone Heights (the book and original musical libretto were set in Victorian London), in order to prove that fiancee Gloria's hand is more delicate, places the wedding ring he has just bought her on the finger of a priceless, historic statue of Venus recently imported and unveiled in Savory's New York museum, and the statue comes to life. Rodney's action has broken the spell that had turned her into stone, and she is now in love with Rodney. Venus makes Gloria disappear, and Rodney is accused of murdering her, and is sent to The Tombs. Venus helps him escape, and spends a night with him in a hotel room. Venus restores Gloria, who then stalks out of Rodney's life. But Venus considers a life in Ozone Heights, and returns to being a statue. Rodney meets a girl who looks just like Mary Martin, and they fall in love and go back to Ozone Heights. Molly is Savory's secretary. Taxi Black is a private detective.

Before Broadway. Designer Aline Bernstein had the idea of turning *The Tinted Venus* into a musical, and approached Cheryl Crawford, who agreed. She thought of Marlene Dietrich for Venus. Bella Spewack's book (now called *One Man's Venus*— it would later go through other title changes: *La Belle Venus*, and *Who Loves Who?*) was to Miss Dietrich's satisfaction, but not to Miss Crawford's, and so it was ditched (at which point Bella Spewack fainted. She never spoke to Cheryl Crawford again). A new libretto was written by S.J. Perelman and Ogden Nash, but Marlene Dietrich didn't like it, saying it was "too racy and profane." After Gertrude Lawrence, Vera Zorina and Leonora Corbett all turned down the role, Mary Martin accepted it as her return to Broadway after five years in Hollywood (last time she was on Broadway she had sung "My Heart Belongs to Daddy" in Cole Porter's *Leave it to Me!*). This was Elia Kazan's first musical, and dress designer Mainbocher's debut on the stage. The gowns cost $20,000, a record up to that time. Venus had 14 costume changes. The numbers "Simply Paranoia," "Love in a Mist" and "Who Am I?" were all cut before Broadway.

The Broadway Run. IMPERIAL THEATRE, 10/7/43–1/24/44; FORTY-SIXTH STREET THEATRE, 1/26/44–2/10/45. Total of 567 PERFORMANCES. PRESENTED BY Cheryl Crawford, in association with John Wildberg; MUSIC/ORCHESTRATIONS/ARRANGEMENTS: Kurt Weill; LYRICS: Ogden Nash; BOOK: S.J. Perelman & Ogden Nash; SUGGESTED BY the 1884 novella *The Tinted Venus*, by F. Anstey, which in turn was based on the Pygmalion myth; DIRECTOR: Elia Kazan; CHOREOGRAPHER: Agnes de Mille; SETS: Howard Bay; COSTUMES: Paul du Pont (unless otherwise stated); MARY MARTIN'S WARDROBE: Mainbocher; SOUND: Saki Oura; MUSICAL DIRECTOR: Maurice Abravanel; CAST RECORDING on Decca; PRESS: Jean Dalrymple & Anthony Buttitta; GENERAL MANAGER: Nick Holde; STAGE MANAGER: Frank Coletti; ASSISTANT STAGE MANAGERS: Paul Morrison & Jimmie Gelb. **Cast:** WHITELAW SAVORY: John Boles (3) ☆; MOLLY GRANT: Paula Laurence (4); TAXI BLACK: Teddy Hart (5), *Jack Mann*; STANLEY: Harry Clark, *Edward Ubell*; RODNEY HATCH: Kenny Baker (2) ☆; VENUS: Mary Martin (1) ☆; MRS. MOATS: Florence Dunlap; STORE MANAGER: Sam Bonnell; BUS STARTER: Lou Wills Jr.; SAM: Zachary A. Charles, *Philip Gordon*; MRS. FLORA BELL KRAMER: Helen Raymond; GLORIA KRAMER: Ruth Bond; POLICE LIEUTENANT:

Bert Freed, *Arthur Davies*; ROSE: Jane Hoffman; ZUVETLI: Harold J. Stone; DR. ROOK: Johnny Stearns; ANATOLIANS: Sam Bonnell & Matthew Farrar; PREMIERE DANSEUSE: Sono Osato (6), *Anita Alvarez*; SINGERS: Lynn Alden, Arthur Davies, Jane Davies, Rose Marie Elliott, Matthew Farrar, Beatrice Hudson, Julie Jefferson, Willa Rollins, Betty Spain, Jeffrey Warren, *Diana Gray, Marion Kohler, Lester Wolf*; DANCERS: Carl Erbele, Nelle Fisher, William Garrett, Ruth Harte, Jinx Heffelfinger, Jean Houloose, Ann Hutchinson, Pearl Lang, Ralph Linn, Allyn Ann McLerie, Lavina Nielsen, Duncan Noble, Ginee Richardson, Patricia Schaeffer, Kevin Smith, Kirsten Valbor, William Weber, Lou Wills Jr., Parker Wilson, *Diana Adams, Peter Birch, Dolores Goodman, Ray Harrison, Welland Lathrop, Regis Powers, Mack Shanks, Frank West-brook.* **Act I**: Overture (Orchestra); *Scene 1* Main Gallery of the Whitelaw Savory Foundation of Modern Art: "New Art is True Art" (Savory & Chorus), "One Touch of Venus" (Molly & Girls); *Scene 2* Rodney's Room: "(That's) How Much I Love You" (Rodney), "I'm a Stranger Here, Myself" (Venus); *Scene 3* Arcade of NBC Building, Radio City: "Forty Minutes for Lunch" (ballet) (played by Orchestra) (danced by Sono Osato, Peter Birch, dancers), "West Wind" (Savory); *Scene 4* Waiting-Room of the Mid-City Bus Terminal: "Way Out West in Jersey" (Mrs. Kramer, Gloria, Rodney) (danced by Gloria & Bus Starter), "That's How I Am Sick of Love" (Rodney) [in the 1996 revival, but not in this 1943 production]; *Scene 5* The Roof of the Museum: "(Poor) Foolish Heart" (Venus) (danced by Sono Osato & Robert Pagent); *Scene 6* Rodney's Barber Shop: "The Trouble with Women" (Rodney, Savory, Taxi-Black, Stanley), "Speak Low (When You Speak Love)" (Venus & Rodney) the hit); *Scene 7* The Roof of the Museum: "(Here's to) Doctor Crippen" (cos: Kermit Love) (Savory & Dancers). **Act II**: Entr'acte; *Scene 1* Savory's bedroom: "Very, Very, Very" (Molly); *Scene 2* The Tombs: "Speak Low (When You Speak Love)" (reprise) (Rodney & Venus), "Catch Hatch" (Savory, Molly, Mrs. Kramer, Chorus); *Scene 3* A Hotel Room: "That's Him" (Venus), "(Waiting for Our) Wooden Wedding" (Rodney), "(Venus in) Ozone Heights" (ballet) (cos: Kermit Love): VENUS: Mary Martin; CHILDREN: Ruth Harte, Jean Houloose, Ralph Linn, Lou Wills Jr.; SHY GIRLS: Diana Adams, Allyn Ann McLerie; THE HEAD NYMPH: Sono Osato; THE JUMPING NYMPHS: Nelle Fisher, Kirsten Valbor, Pearl Lang; THE AVIATOR AND HIS GIRL: Kevin Smith & Patricia Schaeffer; GODS: Robert Pagent & Peter Birch; FAUNS, NYMPHS, SATYRS, GODS; *Scene 4* Main Gallery of the Foundation: "Finaletto" (reprise of "Speak Low") (Venus, Rodney, Chorus).

There was a record advance sale of $100,000 at the Broadway box-office. Reviews were great. In 8/44 Miss Martin suffered from heat stroke, and was out of the production for nine days. The show won Donaldson Awards for choreography, and for Mary Martin, Kenny Baker, and Sono Osato (as female dancer). This was Kurt Weill's longest-running Broadway show.

After Broadway. TOUR. The successful post–Broadway tour closed in Chicago when Mary Martin had a miscarriage.

THE MOVIE. 1948. DIRECTOR: William A. Seiter. Only five of the stage songs were retained, and some new ones added by other writers. *Cast*: VENUS: Ava Gardner (singing dubbed by Eileen Wilson); EDDIE HATCH: Robert Walker; MOLLY: Eve Arden; JOE GRANT: Dick Haymes; GLORIA: Olga San Juan; WHITFIELD SAVORY II: Tom Conway.

ABC TV VERSION. 8/28/55. DIRECTOR: George Schaefer. *Cast*: VENUS: Janet Blair; RODNEY: Russell Nype; SAVORY: George Gaynes; GLORIA: Laurel Shelby.

BARBICAN CINEMA 1, London, 8/16/92–9/6/92. This stage production was part of the *Lost Musicals* series. DIRECTOR: Ian Marshall-Fisher; MUSICAL DIRECTOR: Kevin Amos. *Cast*: VENUS: Louise Gold; RODNEY: Teddy Kempner; SAVORY: Peter Gale; MOLLY: Mandy More; GLORIA: Ashleigh Sendin; MRS. KRAMER: Myra Sands.

CITY CENTER, NYC, 3/28/96–3/30/96. 4 PERFORMANCES. Part of the *Encores!* series. ADAPTED/DIRECTOR: Leonard Foglia; CHOREOGRAPHER: Hope Clarke; SETS: John Lee Beatty; COSTUMES: David C. Woolard; MUSICAL DIRECTOR: Rob Fisher. *Cast*: SAVORY: David Alan Grier; MOLLY: Carol Woods; TAXI BLACK: Danny Rutigliano; STANLEY: Kevin Chamberlin; RODNEY: Andy Taylor; VENUS: Melissa Errico; MRS. MOATS: Sheryl McCallum; BUS STARTER: Peter Flynn; MRS. KRAMER: Marilyn Cooper; GLORIA: Jane Krakowski; LIEUTENANT: Timothy Robert Blevins; ROOK: Keith Byron Kirk; MATRON: Melinda Klump.

LINDBURY STUDIO THEATRE, Royal Opera House, London, 12/9/00 –12/17/00. DIRECTOR: Ian Marshall-Fisher; CHOREOGRAPHERS: Antonio Castilla & Tim Almass; MUSICAL DIRECTOR: Kevin Amos. *Cast*: VENUS: Louise Gold; RODNEY: Michael Cantwell; SAVORY: Ethan Freeman; MRS. KRAMER: Myra Sands; MOLLY: Jessica Martin; GLORIA: Lori Haley Fox.

523. *Onward Victoria*

Set in New York City and Washington, DC, in 1871. Victoria Woodhull made a fortune as a stockbroker, then ran for the office president of the United States in 1872 as a proponent of equality for the sexes and free love. She has an affair with Henry Ward Beecher (which never happened in real life), and the show traces her life.

Before Broadway. In 1972 it was announced by producer Albert Selden that Carol Channing would play Victoria Woodhull in a musical called *Vicky for President*, with music by Arthur Schwartz, lyrics by E.Y. Harburg, and a libretto by Burt Shevelove and Herb Sargent. It was announced for the spring, as the opening attraction at Mr. Selden's Astor Place Theatre. But it never happened.

In 1976 Patricia Morison and Janet Blair starred in a musical about Victoria and her sister Tennessee Claflin, called *Winner Take All*, but it never reached Broadway.

Onward Victoria started Off Off Broadway, in 1979, with a reading at the MANHATTAN THEATRE CLUB, and then, in 2/79, it started a 3-week run at the GREENWICH MEWS THEATRE. PRESENTED BY Joseph Jefferson Theatre Company. *Cast*: Susan Bigelow, Michael Zaslow. Producer John Hart had great difficulty raising the money for the Broadway run. Before Broadway Pamela Blair was replaced by Beth Austin, and Arthur Faria was replaced as choreographer by Michael Shawn. This was the scene-by-scene breakdown during Broadway previews (same performers as for the Broadway run, unless noted differently): **Act I:** *Scene 1* Opening — New York City; 1871: "The Only Sin is Being Timid" [this number was replaced by "The Age of Brass" during previews, with the same performers as for the Broadway run]; *Scene 2* Commodore Cornelius Vanderbilt's office: "Magnetic Healing;" *Scene 3* Victoria's salon; six months later: "Curiosity;" *Scene 4* Plymouth Church, Brooklyn Heights: "Beecher's Processional;" *Scene 5* Woodhull & Claflin's Brokerage: "I Depend on You;" *Scene 6* Washington DC, Congress; May 24, 1871; *Scene 7* Victoria's campaign tour: "Onward Victoria" [this number changed to "Victoria's Banner" during previews, with the same performers as for the Broadway run]; "Changes;" *Scene 8* Beecher's study; the next day: "A Taste of Forever;" *Scene 9* Victoria's brokerage/Beecher's study; three months later; *Scene 10* Delmonico's restaurant; two hours later: "Unescorted Women." **Act II:** *Scene 1* Victoria's brokerage; the next day: "Love and Joy;" *Scene 2* Beecher's study; two months later: "Every Day I Do a Little Something for the Lord," "It's Easy for Her;" *Scene 3* Victoria's brokerage; early evening; *Scene 4* Steinway Hall: "You Cannot Drown the Dreamer;" *Scene 5* Victoria's brokerage; two days later: "Respectable," "Another Life" (Victoria); *Scene 6* Brokerage/street/jail: "Read it in the Weekly;" *Scene 7* Exterior and interior of courtroom; six months later: "A Valentine for Beecher," "Beecher's Defense," "Another Life" (reprise) (Victoria & Henry Beecher), "You Cannot Drown the Dreamer" (reprise).

The Broadway Run. MARTIN BECK THEATRE, 12/14/80. 23 previews. 1 PERFORMANCE. PRESENTED BY John N. Hart Jr., in association with Hugh J. Hubbard & Robert M. Browne; MUSIC: Keith Herrmann; LYRICS/BOOK: Charlotte Anker & Irene Rosenberg; BASED ON events in the life of suffragette Victoria Woodhull (1838–1927); DIRECTOR: Julianne Boyd; CHOREOGRAPHER: Michael Shawn; SETS: William Ritman; COSTUMES: Theoni V. Aldredge; LIGHTING: Richard Nelson; SOUND: Lewis Mead; MUSICAL DIRECTOR: Larry Blank; ORCHESTRATIONS: Michael Gibson; DANCE MUSIC ARRANGEMENTS: Donald Johnston; VOCAL ARRANGEMENTS: Keith Herrmann & Larry Blank; PRESS: Shirley Herz Associates; CASTING: TNI Casting (Julie Hughes & Barry Moss); GENERAL MANAGERS: Joseph Harris & Ira Bernstein; PRODUCTION STAGE MANAGER: Ed Aldridge; STAGE MANAGER: Joseph Corby; ASSISTANT STAGE MANAGER: Renee F. Lutz. *Cast:* LITTLE GIRL: Lora

Jeanne Martens; VICTORIA WOODHULL: Jill Eikenberry (1); TENNIE CLAFLIN: Beth Austin (3); TELEGRAPH BOY: Marty McDonough; JIM: Dan Cronin; CORNELIUS VANDERBILT: Ted Thurston (5); MRS. FLEMING: Carrie Wilder; MRS. BAXTER: Karen Gibson; MRS. RANDOLPH: Lora Jeanne Martens; FLEMING: Gordon Stanley; RANDOLPH: Marty McDonough; BAXTER: John Kildahl; WOMAN INVESTOR # 1: Carol Lurie; JOHNSON: Scott Fless; PERKINS: Ian Michael Towers; WILLIAM EVARTS: Rex Hays (10); WOMAN INVESTOR # 2: Dru Alexandrine; BETH TILTON: Martha Jean Sterner (9); THEODORE TILTON: Edmond Genest (4); ELIZABETH CADY STANTON: Laura Waterbury (6); JIM'S GIRLFRIEND: Lauren Goler; CONGRESSMAN BUTLER: Kenneth H. Waller; HENRY WARD BEECHER: Michael Zaslow (2); SUSAN B. ANTHONY: Dorothy Holland; GRANT SPEAKER: Kenneth H. Waller; EUNICE BEECHER: Linda Poser; CHARLIE DELMONICO: Lenny Wolpe (8); MAGINNES: Kenneth H. Waller; ANTHONY COMSTOCK: Jim Jansen (7); JUDGE: Kenneth H. Waller; FULLERTON: Lenny Wolpe. ***Understudies***: Victoria: Dorothy Holland; Tennie: Lora Jeanne Martens; Beecher/Tilton: Rex Hays; Delmonico/Vanderbilt: Ken Waller; Evarts: Gordon Stanley; ***Swing Dancers***: Douglas Bentz, Joan Bell. ***Act I***: ***Scene 1*** New York City; 1871: "The Age of Brass" (Victoria, Tennie, Henry Beecher, Comstock, the Tiltons, Elizabeth, Susan, Ensemble); ***Scene 2*** Commodore Cornelius Vanderbilt's office: "Magnetic Healing" (Cornelia, Tennie, Vanderbilt); ***Scene 3*** Victoria's salon; six months later: "Curiosity" (Evarts, the Tiltons, Elizabeth, Vanderbilt, Ensemble); ***Scene 4*** Plymouth Church, Brooklyn Heights: "Beecher's Processional" (Henry Beecher & Congregation); ***Scene 5*** Woodhull & Claflin's Brokerage: "I Depend on You" (Victoria & Tennie); ***Scene 6*** Washington, DC; May 24, 1872; ***Scene 7*** Victoria's campaign tour: "Victoria's Banner" (Victoria, Tennie, Elizabeth, Susan, Ensemble), "Changes" (Victoria); ***Scene 8*** Beecher's study; the next day; ***Scene 9*** Victoria's brokerage/Beecher's study; three months later: "A Taste of Forever" (Victoria & Theodore Tilton); ***Scene 10*** Delmonico's Restaurant; two hours later: "Unescorted Women" (Delmonico, Tennie, Victoria, Ensemble). ***Act II***: ***Scene 1*** Victoria's brokerage; the next day: "Love and Joy" (Victoria & Henry Beecher); ***Scene 2*** Beecher's study; two months later: "Every Day I Do a Little Something for the Lord" (Comstock), "It's Easy for Her" (Henry Beecher); ***Scene 3*** Steinway Hall: "You Cannot Drown the Dreamer" (Victoria & Elizabeth); ***Scene 4*** Victoria's brokerage; two days later: "Respectable" (Tennie); ***Scene 5*** Brokerage/street/jail: "Read it in the Weekly" (Victoria, Henry Beecher, Theodore Tilton, Tennie, Comstock, Newsboys, Readers); ***Scene 6*** Exterior and interior of courtroom; six months later: "A Valentine for Beecher" (Ensemble), "Beecher's Defense" (Victoria), "Another Life" (Victoria & Henry Beecher), "You Cannot Drown the Dreamer" (reprise) (Victoria & Tennie).

On Broadway it was roundly panned by the critics.

After Broadway. YORK THEATRE COMPANY, Spring 1995. Part of the *Musicals in Mufti* series. DIRECTOR: Adele Aronheim; MUSICAL DIRECTOR: David Kirshenbaum.

524. *Out of This World*

A version of the Amphitryon legend. The action takes place Then and Now, in Heaven and on Earth. Jupiter assumes the form of the mortal general Amphitryon, so he can come to earth and sleep with Amphitryon's wife. The Arcadia Inn is the earthly setting. Art and Helen are the American couple. Niki is a gangster. Juno, the main role, is Jupiter's jealous wife. There wasn't much attire worn by the male dancers.

Before Broadway. The show's first libretto was by Dwight Taylor. Several titles were considered: *Laughter in the Sky; Heaven on Earth; Day Dream; Stolen Fruit; Just Imagine; Summer Lightning;* and *Made in Heaven*, before settling for *Out of This World*. Cole Porter was not happy with the script, and asked Betty Comden & Adolph Green to do another one. They did, but it was never used. Reginald Lawrence revised Dwight Taylor's book, and in the end it was Mr. Taylor & Reginald Lawrence who got librettist credit. Charlotte Greenwood, who hadn't been on Broadway since 1927, got the main part only after it had been turned down by Carol Channing (she chose *Gentlemen Prefer Blondes* instead),

Judy Holliday, Hermione Gingold, and Martha Raye. During the first tryout, at the Shubert Theatre, Philadelphia from 11/4/50, Agnes de Mille was fired as director, and George Abbott was brought in. Miss de Mille retained credit, and Mr. Abbott only got an acknowledgement in the back of the playbill. Mr. Abbott brought in F. Hugh Herbert to do further work on the libretto. The number "From This Moment On," was cut. It was a song for the character of Art, but William Eythe was not a singer. The Shubert Theatre, Boston, was the next stop, from 11/28/50, and here the censor found problems with some of the risqué material (for example, the character of Mercury sings "Pandora, who let me open her box"). The following numbers were also cut: "We're on the Road to Athens," "Hush, Hush, Hush," "Away from it All," "Midsummer Night," "Oh, It Must Be Fun," "To Hell with Everyone but Us," "Tonight I Love You More," and "Why Do You Want to Hurt Me So?." Then, just before the opening in New York, William Eythe was arrested in the mens' room of a subway having sex with another man, and it was only bribes to the right authorities that enabled him to open in the show.

The Broadway Run. NEW CENTURY THEATRE, 12/21/50–5/5/51. 157 PERFORMANCES. PRESENTED BY Saint Subber & Lemuel Ayers; MUSIC/LYRICS: Cole Porter; BOOK: Dwight Taylor & Reginald Lawrence; BASED ON the Amphitryon legend, and on the play *Amphitryon '38*, by Jean Giraudoux, as adapted by S.N. Behrman (and which starred Lunt & Fontanne); DIRECTOR: Agnes de Mille; CHOREOGRAPHER: Hanya Holm; SETS/COSTUMES: Lemuel Ayers; MUSICAL DIRECTOR: Pembroke Davenport; ORCHESTRATIONS: Robert Russell Bennett; DANCE MUSIC ARRANGEMENTS: Genevieve Pitot; INCIDENTAL MUSIC ARRANGEMENTS: Trude Rittman; CAST RECORDING on Columbia; PRESS: George & Dorothy Ross and Madelin Blitzstein; GENERAL MANAGER: C. Edwin Knill; PRODUCTION STAGE MANAGER: Ward Bishop; STAGE MANAGERS: John Mayo & Frank Milton. **Cast:** MERCURY: William Redfield (4); JUPITER: George Jongeyans (6) [this was the actor George Gaynes]; HELEN: Priscilla Gillette (3); WAITER: Frank Milton; ART O'MALLEY: William Eythe (2); "NIGHT:" Janet Collins; VULCANIA: Peggy Rea; JUNO: Charlotte Greenwood (1) ☆; CHLOE: Barbara Ashley; NIKI SKOLIANOS: David Burns (5); STREPHON: Ray Harrison; SINGING ENSEMBLE: Ken Ayers, Robert Baird, Richard Curry, Nola Fairbanks, Enid Hall, Joe Hill, Orrin Hill, Leo Kayworth, B.J. Keating, Michael Kingsley, Lois Monroe, Shirley Ann Prior, John Schickling, John Schmidt, Barbara Weaver; DANCING ENSEMBLE: Doria Avila, Virginia Bosler, Joan Engel, Eleanor Fairchild, Jan Kovac, Eric Kristen, Joan Kruger, Paul Lyday, Barton Mumaw, David Nillo, Jacqueline Sager, Stanley Simmons, Gisella Svetlik, Glen Tetley. ***Act I***: Overture (Orchestra); Prologue (Mercury); Curtain; ***Scene 1*** Jupiter's portico, Mount Olympus: "I Jupiter, I Rex" (Jupiter & Male Ensemble); ***Scene 2*** New York bar and Mount Olympus: "Use Your Imagination" (Mercury & Helen); ***Scene 3*** Curtain of Night; ***Scene 4*** Great Hall, Olympus: "Hail, Hail, Hail" (Vulcania, Mercury, Ensemble), "Juno's Ride" (Ensemble) [not in this production, but it was in the 1989 Off Broadway revival and in the 1995 concert version], "I Got Beauty" (Juno & Ensemble); ***Scene 5*** Road to Athens; ***Scene 6*** Arcadia Inn: "Maiden Fair" (Chloe & Female Ensemble), "Where, Oh Where?" (Chloe) (danced by Boys & Girls), "I Am Loved" (Helen) [this was at the end of Act I in the 1995 concert version]; ***Scene 7*** Colonnade: "They Couldn't Compare to You" (Mercury, Singing Girls, Dancing Boys), "From This Moment On" (Art & Helen) [cut during out of town tryouts, but restored for the 1995 concert version, for which orchestrations were by Jonathan Tunick]; ***Scene 8*** Inn tavern: "What Do You Think About Men?" (Helen, Chloe, Juno); ***Scene 9*** Arcadia Inn: "Dance of the Long Night" ("Night Ballet") (Night & Attendants), "You Don't Remind Me" (Jupiter) [cut before Broadway, but restored for the 1995 concert version], "I Sleep Easier Now" (Juno). ***Act II***: Entr'acte (Orchestra); ***Scene 1*** Mount Olympus: "Climb up the Mountain" (Juno, Niki, Company); ***Scene 2*** Curtain of Night: "Dance of the Dawn" (Night & Attendants) [not in this production, but it was in the 1995 concert version]; ***Scene 3*** Arcadia Inn: "No Lover (for Me)" (Helen); ***Scene 4*** Colonnade: "Cherry Pies Ought to Be You" (Mercury & Chloe; Juno & Niki); ***Scene 5*** Bedroom: "I Am Loved" (reprise) (Helen); ***Scene 6*** Curtain of Night: "Hark to the Song of the Night" (Jupiter); ***Scene 7*** Mountain Shrine: Dance (Strephon, Chloe, Ensemble); ***Scene 8*** Another part of the forest: "Nobody's Chasing Me" (Juno), Dance (Ensemble); ***Scene 9*** Arcadia Inn and Heaven: Finale: "Use Your

Imagination" (reprise) (Entire Company) [in the 1995 concert version this was a reprise of "From This Moment On"].

Reviews were divided. It was the book that was the problem. The score is one of Cole Porter's best, the sets were wonderful, and the cast recording (without being encumbered by the book) shows the musical off to best advantage.

After Broadway. The first revival, reasonably successful, was Off Broadway, at the ACTORS' PLAYHOUSE, 1955, and re-written by Rick Besoyan. CAST: JUNO: Jane Romano.

THE EQUITY LIBRARY THEATRE mounted a production on 11/30/62. 9 PERFORMANCES.

It was re-done in 1971 as *Use Your Imagination*, and the gods were anti-war hippies, and Apollo was overtly gay.

THE EQUITY LIBRARY THEATRE did it again, 3/8/73–3/25/73. 19 PERFORMANCES. NEW BOOK: George Oppenheimer; DIRECTOR: Richard Michaels; CHOREOGRAPHER: Carole Schweid. **Cast**: VENUS/NIGHT: Barbara Monte-Britton; JUNO: Joy Franz; CERES/CHLOE: Gail Johnston; MARS/MR. WARD: Michael Serrecchia; MINERVA/LEDA: Lana Caradimas; MERCURY: Joel Craig; JUPITER: Kenneth Cory; APOLLO/JEFF: Ward Smith; DIANA/HELEN: Marsha Kramer; BACCHUS/STREPHON: Paul Latchaw. "High Flyin' Wings on My Shoes," "I Jupiter, I Rex," "A Woman's Career," "Time-Passage," "Cherry Pies Ought to Be You," "From This Moment On," "Where, Oh Where," "They Couldn't Compare to You," "No Lover," "You're the Prize Guy of Guys," "When Your Troubles Have Started," "I Could Kick Myself," "Night Ballet," "Nobody's Chasing Me," "I Am Loved," "Climb up the Mountain," "You Don't Remind Me," "Use Your Imagination," Finale.

LAS PALMAS THEATRE, Calif., 1978. Re-written again, this time as *Heaven Sent*. NEW BOOK/DIRECTOR: Lawrence Kasha. **Cast**: Charlotte Rae, *Jo Anne Worley*. It was aiming for, but never got to, Broadway.

ALL SOULS CHURCH, NYC, 4/20/89–5/14/89. 19 PERFORMANCES. PRESENTED BY the All Souls Players; DIRECTOR/CHOREOGRAPHER: Jeffrey K. Neill; SETS: Robert Edmonds; MUSICAL DIRECTOR: Wendell Kindberg. **Cast**: JUNO: Lynn Alice Webster; JUPITER: Andrew Hammond; HELEN: Teri Bibb; NIKI: Regis Bowman; NIGHT: Mirla Criste Agnir; APOLLO: Steve Correia; DIANA: Roxanne Fay; MINERVA: Patty Noonan. The score used most of the numbers that had been cut from the original. "I Jupiter, I Rex," "Use Your Imagination," "Hail, Hail, Hail," "Juno's Ride," "I Got Beauty," "We're on the Road to Athens," "Maiden Fair," "Where, Oh Where," "From This Moment On," "They Couldn't Compare to You," "What Do You Think About Men?," "You Don't Remind Me," "I Sleep Easier Now," "I Am Loved," "Hush, Hush, Hush," "Midsummer Night," "Climb up the Mountain," "Oh, It Must Be Fun," "No Lover for Me," "Cherry Pies," "Hark to the Song of the Night," "Nobody's Chasing Me," Finale.

CITY CENTER, NYC, 3/30/95–4/1/95. 4 PERFORMANCES. In concert form, part of the *Encores!* series. ADAPTED BY: David Ives; DIRECTOR: Mark Brokaw; CHOREOGRAPHER: John Carrafa; SETS: John Lee Beatty; LIGHTING: Marc B. Weiss; SOUND: Scott Lehrer; MUSICAL DIRECTOR: Rob Fisher. **Cast**: JUNO: Andrea Martin; MERCURY: Peter Scolari; JUPITER: Ken Page; CHLOE: La Chanze; NIKI: Ernie Sabella; ART: Gregg Edelman; HELEN: Marin Mazzie; ENSEMBLE: Dale Hensley, David Masenheimer, Chris Monteleone, Christiane Noll, Francis Ruivivar, John Scherer, Elizabeth Walsh.

In 1982 it had been announced that Howard Ashman was writing yet another libretto, but it wasn't seen until 18 years later, when 42nd Street Moon presented a new version of *Out of This World*, which was a combination of the original, the 1955 revival, and the (now) late Mr. Ashman's book (in which Act I was set in Hollywood). EUREKA THEATRE, San Francisco, 7/14/00–7/30/00. Previews from 7/12/00. Art is now a Hollywood screenwriter, married to movie queen Helen. Apollo is now obviously gay. Isadora is a gossip columnist. The Cole Porter Trust not only okayed these changes, but after the success of the production they made it the standard version to be used in all future productions. ADAPTED BY/DIRECTOR: Greg MacKellan; CHOREOGRAPHER: Jayne Zaban; MUSICAL DIRECTOR: John Florencio. **Cast**: JUPITER: John-Elliott Kirk; HELEN VANCE: Stephanie Rhoads; JUNO: Darlene Popvic; MERCURY: Steven Rhyne; ART: Kurt Kroesche; ISADORA ST. JOHN: Lisa Peers; CHLOE: Caroline Altman; APOLLO: Matt Riutta. By popular demand it was brought back, 10/19/00–10/29/00, with the same cast and crew, except MUSICAL DIRECTOR: Dave Dobrusky.

525. *Over Here!*

"America's Big Band Musical." About wartime entertainers. Nostalgic reminiscences of the home front in World War II — training and entertaining troops.

Before Broadway. Laverne, the third member of the Andrews Sisters, died six years prior to the show's opening.

The Broadway Run. SHUBERT THEATRE, 3/6/74–1/4/75. 13 previews from 2/21/74. 341 PERFORMANCES. PRESENTED BY Kenneth Waissman & Maxine Fox; MUSIC/LYRICS: Richard M. Sherman & Robert B. Sherman; BOOK: Will Holt; DIRECTOR: Tom Moore; CHOREOGRAPHER: Patricia Birch; SETS: Douglas W. Schmidt; COSTUMES: Carrie F. Robbins; LIGHTING: John Gleason; SOUND: Jack Shearing; MEDIA DESIGN: Stan J. Goldberg & Jeanne H. Livingston; MUSICAL DIRECTOR: Joseph Klein; ORCHESTRATIONS: Michael Gibson & Jim Tyler; VOCAL ARRANGEMENTS/SPECIAL DANCE MUSIC: Louis St. Louis; PRESS: Betty Lee Hunt Associates; CASTING: Otto & Windsor Casting; GENERAL MANAGER: Edward H. Davis; COMPANY MANAGER: Leo K. Cohen; PRODUCTION STAGE MANAGER: T. Schuyler Smith; STAGE MANAGER: Martha Knight; ASSISTANT STAGE MANAGERS: John Fennesy & John Scoullar. **Cast:** NORWIN SPOKESMAN: Douglass Watson (4); MAKE-OUT: Jim Weston (13); FATHER: MacIntyre Dixon (6); MOTHER: Bette Henritze (8); RANKIN: William Griffis (7); DONNA: Marilu Henner (14); WILMA: Phyllis Somerville (17); MAGGIE: Ann Reinking (16); MITZI: Janie Sell (3); MISFIT: John Travolta (11); UTAH: Treat Williams (18); LUCKY: John Mineo (15); SARGE: William Newman (12); SAM: Samuel E. Wright (10); JUNE: April Shawhan (5); BILL: John Driver (9); PAULINE DE PAUL: Maxene Andrews (1) ☆; PAULETTE DE PAUL: Patty Andrews (1) ☆. **Standbys:** Pauline/Paulette/Mitzi/Mother: Chevi Colton; Father/Spokesman: Jack Naughton; Rankin/Sarge: Jack Naughton; June/Maggie: Chris Callan; Donna/Wilma: Chris Callan; Bill/Utah/Make-Out: John Fennesy; Lucky/Misfit: John Fennesy; Sam: Edmond Wesley. *The Big Band Soloists:* LEADER: Joseph Klein; LEAD TRUMPET: Jimmy Sedlar; LEAD SAX: Bernie Berger; LEAD CLARINET: Mike Cavin; LEAD TROMBONE: Harry Di Vito; DRUMS: Ted Sommer; PIANO/ACCORDION: Clay Fullum; BASS: Doc Solomon; SAXOPHONES: Harvey Estrin, Michael Schuster, Sol Schlinger; TROMBONES: Merv Gold, Jack Gale, Vincent Forchetti; TRUMPETS: Bob Millikan, Jay Brower, Charles Sullivan; CELLO: Ruben Rivera; PIANO: Hal Schaefer; PERCUSSION: Warren Hard; GUITAR/BANJO: Carmen Mastren; BAND CHICK: Patricia Birch; BAND BOY: Louis St. Louis. *Act I*: "The Beat Begins" (Overture) (Big Band & Company), "Since You're Not Around" (Make-Out & Company), "Over Here!" (Paulette & Pauline), "Buy a Victory Bond" (Company), "My Dream for Tomorrow" (June & Soldiers), "Charlie's Place" (Pauline, Maggie, Lucky, Big Band, Company), "Hey, Yvette"/"The Grass Grows Green" (Spokesman, Rankin, Father), "My Dream for Tomorrow" (reprise) (June & Bill), "The Good-Time Girl" (Paulette & Company), "Wait for Me, Marlena" (Mitzi & Company), "We Got It" (Paulette, Pauline, Mitzi, Company). *Act II*: Entr'acte: "The Beat Continues" (Big Band & Company), "Wartime Wedding" (Paulette, Pauline, Company), "Don't Shoot the Hooey to Me, Louie" (Sam), "Where Did the Good Times Go?" (Paulette), "Dream Drummin'"/"Soft Music" (Misfit, Big Band, Company), "The Big Beat" (Paulette, Pauline, Mitzi), "No Goodbyes" (Paulette, Pauline, Company).

Note: Messrs Sherman and St. Louis wish to acknowledge the creative contribution of Walter Wechsler on "Over Here!," "We Got It," and "The Big Beat."

The show got very good Broadway reviews. Ann Reinking suffered a cracked vertebra while doing a flip during a jitterbug number. Janie Sell won a Tony, and the show was also nominated for musical, direction of a musical, choreography, and costumes.

526. *Pacific Overtures*

This bold musical covered 120 years of Japan's history from its isolated days when Commodore Perry arrived in July 1853 on a trade mission (and caused such a shock in Japan that it brought it into the 19th century), through changes in society, dress and customs to the present day and how modern Japan has become. Presented as Kabuki theatre and from a Japanese point of view. The score was a very faithful reproduction of the real Japanese sound.

Before Broadway. When John Weidman was a student at Yale Law School he wrote the outline for a play about Commodore Perry's 1853 expedition to Japan. Being the son of Jerome Weidman (author of Hal Prince's musical *Fiorello!*) he had an in with Mr. Prince, who liked the Perry script and optioned it. After many re-writes, it was read in the basement of the Shubert Theatre, with George S. Irving as Perry. At this point Mr. Prince decided to do it as a musical, and Steve Sondheim was brought on board to do the score. Mr. Sondheim referred to the show as a "documentary vaudeville." Finding enough Asian actors to play all the Asian roles was difficult. Most were Asian-Americans, but Isao Sato was actually from Japan. 19 actors finally played the 61 solo roles in the show. There were 140 costumes. The show opened for tryouts on 11/11/75, in Boston. It got terrible reviews and played to empty houses. It needed work. Soon-Teck Oh was demoted from 2nd-star billing during tryouts to leading featured player. Hal Prince invested his own money in order to bring it further, and lost it all. The show then ran at the Kennedy Center, 12/4/75–12/27/75, to good reviews, before going on to Broadway previews.

The Broadway Run. WINTER GARDEN THEATRE, 1/11/76–6/27/76. 13 previews. 193 PERFORMANCES. PRESENTED BY Harold Prince, in association with Ruth Mitchell; MUSIC/LYRICS: Stephen Sondheim; BOOK: John Weidman; ADDITIONAL MATERIAL: Hugh Wheeler; SUGGESTED BY U.S. Commodore Matthew Perry's 1853 visit to Japan, and his "pacific overtures" (his term) to the Japanese; DIRECTOR: Harold Prince; CHOREOGRAPHER: Patricia Birch; SETS: Boris Aronson; COSTUMES: Florence Klotz; MASKS/DOLLS: E.J. Taylor; LIGHTING: Tharon Musser; SOUND: Jack Mann; MUSICAL DIRECTOR: Paul Gemignani; ORCHESTRATIONS: Jonathan Tunick; DANCE MUSIC ARRANGEMENTS: Daniel Troob; CAST RECORDING on RCA; PRESS: Mary Bryant & Randy Kaplan; CASTING: Joanna Merlin; KABUKI CONSULTANT: Haruki Fujimoto; GENERAL MANAGER: Howard Haines; COMPANY MANAGER: Leo K. Cohen; PRODUCTION STAGE MANAGER: George Martin; STAGE MANAGER: John Grigas; ASSISTANT STAGE MANAGER: Carlos Gorbea. **Cast:** RECITER: Mako (1) ☆; LORD ABE, 1ST COUNCILLOR: Yuki Shimoda (3); MANJIRO: Sab Shimono (4); 2ND COUNCILLOR: James Dybas (8); SHOGUN'S MOTHER: Alvin Ing (6); 3RD COUNCILLOR: Freddy Mao; KAYAMA: Isao Sato (5); TAMATE (KAYAMA'S WIFE): Soon-Teck Oh (2); SAMURAI: Soon-Teck Oh (2); STORYTELLER: Soon-Teck Oh (2); SWORDSMAN: Soon-Teck Oh (2); SAMURAIS: Ernest Abuba & Mark Hsu Syers (9); SERVANT: Haruki Fujimoto; OBSERVERS: Alvin Ing (6) & Ricardo Tobia; FISHERMAN: Jae Woo Lee; MERCHANT: Alvin Ing (6); SON: Timm Fujii; GRANDMOTHER: Conrad Yama; THIEF: Mark Hsu Syers (9); ADAMS: Ernest Abuba; WILLIAMS: Larry Hama; COMMODORE PERRY: Haruki Fujimoto; SHOGUN'S WIFE: Freda Foh Shen; PHYSICIAN: Ernest Harada (7); PRIESTS: Timm Fujii & Gedde Watanabe; SOOTHSAYER: Mark Hsu Syers (9); SUMO WRESTLERS: Conrad Yama & Jae Woo Lee; SHOGUN'S COMPANION: Patrick Kinser-Lau (10); SHOGUN: Mako (1) ☆; MADAM: Ernest Harada (7); GIRLS: Timm Fujii, Patrick Kinser-Lau (10), Gedde Watanabe, Leslie Watanabe; OLD MAN: James Dybas (8); BOY: Gedde Watanabe; WARRIOR: Mark Hsu Syers (9); IMPERIAL PRIEST: Tom Matsusaka; NOBLES: Ernest Abuba & Timm Fujii; AMERICAN ADMIRAL: Alvin Ing (6); BRITISH ADMIRAL: Ernest Harada (7); DUTCH ADMIRAL: Patrick Kinser-Lau (10); RUSSIAN ADMIRAL: Mark Hsu Syers (9); FRENCH ADMIRAL: James Dybas (8); LORDS OF THE SOUTH: Larry Hama & Jae Woo Lee; JONATHAN GOBLE: Mako (1) ☆; JAPANESE MERCHANT: Conrad Yama; SAMURAI'S DAUGHTER: Freddy Mao; BRITISH SAILORS: Timm Fujii, Patrick Kinser-Lau (10), Mark Hsu-Syers (9); PROSCENIUM SERVANTS/SAILORS/TOWNSPEOPLE: Susan Kikuchi, Diane Lam, Kim Miyori, Freda Foh Shen, Kenneth S. Eiland, Timm Fujii, Joey Ginza, Patrick Kinser-Lau, Tony Marino, Kavin Maung, Dingo Secretario, Mark Hsu Syers, Ricardo Tobia, Gedde Watanabe, Leslie Watanabe; **Musicians:** SHAMISEN: Fusako Yoshida; PERCUSSION: Genji Ito. UNDERSTUDIES: Reciter: Jae Woo Lee; Tamate: Gedde Watanabe; Samurai/Storyteller: Freddy Mao; Swordsman/Abe: Ernest Abuba; Manjiro: Patrick Kinser-Lau; Kayama: Tom Matsusaka; 2nd Councillor: Ricardo Tobia; 3rd Councillor: Tony Marino.

Act I: July 1853: **Scene 1** Japan in July 1853; Shogun's court: "The Advantages of Floating in the Middle of the Sea" (Reciter & Company); **Scene 2** A small Japanese house in Uraga: "There is No Other Way" (Tamate & Observers); **Scene 3** The Japanese shore: "Four Black Dragons" (Fisherman, Thief, Reciter, Townspeople); **Scene 4** The deck of the U.S.S. *Powhatan*; **Scene 5** The Shogun's chamber: "Chrysanthemum Tea" (Shogun [Reciter], Shogun's Mother, Soothsayer, Shogun's Wife, Priests, Shogun's Companion, Physician, Sumo Wrestlers); **Scene 6** The Shogun's chamber; en route to Uraga; the house at Uraga: "Poems" (Kayama & Manjiro); **Scene 7** The village of Kanagawa: "Welcome to Kanagawa" (Madam & Girls); **Scene 8** Exchange of gifts; **Scene 9** Kanagawa; **Scene 10** The Treaty House at Kanagawa: "Someone in a Tree" (Old Man, Reciter, Boy, Warrior); **Scene 11** Lion dance: "Lion Dance" (Perry). *Act II*: From then on: **Scene 1** The imperial court at Kyoto; **Scene 2** The Admirals' visit: "Please Hello" (Abe, Reciter, Admirals); **Scene 3** The imperial court; **Scene 4** The houses of Kayama and Manjiro: "A Bowler Hat" (Kayama & Manjiro); **Scene 5** Ten years later; **Scene 6** A private garden: "Pretty Lady" (British Sailors); **Scene 7** Japan 1863–1975: "Next" (Reciter & Company).

Broadway reviews were extremely divided. The show won Tony Awards for sets and costumes, and was nominated for musical, score, book, direction of a musical, choreography, lighting and for Isao Sato and Mako. The show lost its entire $650,000 investment. One of the performances was videotaped and shown on Japanese TV (a first).

After Broadway. TOUR. Opened on 8/31/76, at the Dorothy Chandler Pavilion, Los Angeles, and closed on 12/18/76, at the Curran Theatre, San Francisco. PRESENTED BY Harold Prince, in association with Ruth Mitchell & the Los Angeles Civic Light Opera Company. It had the Broadway cast.

In 1982 Hal Prince failed to mount a production at the Mermaid Theatre, London. There was a scaled down Off Broadway revival at the CHURCH OF HEAVENLY REST, 3/27/84–4/14/84. Previews from 3/20/84. 20 PERFORMANCES. PRESENTED BY the York Theatre Company; DIRECTOR: Fran Soeder; CHOREOGRAPHER: Janet Watson; SETS: James Morgan; COSTUMES: Mark Passarell; LIGHTING: Mary Jo Dondlinger; MUSICAL DIRECTOR: James Stenborg. **Cast:** Ernest Abuba, Tony Marino, Kevin Gray, Henry Ravelo, Thomas Ikeda, Tom Matsusaka, Ronald Yamamoto, Eric Miji, Lester J.N. Mau, Allan Tung, John Bantay, Tim Ewing, John Baray, Francis Jue, Khin-Kyaw Maung. It moved to the PROMENADE THEATRE, 10/25/84–1/27/85. 109 PERFORMANCES. PRESENTED BY The Shubert Organization and McCann & Nugent. It had the same basic crew except MUSICAL DIRECTOR: Eric Stern. **Cast:** RECITER: Ernest Abuba; LORD ABE: Tony Marino; SHOGUN'S MOTHER/BRITISH ADMIRAL: Chuck Brown; KAYAMA YESAEMON: Kevin Gray; TAMATE: Timm Fujii; JOHN MANJIRO/FISHERMAN/FRENCH ADMIRAL: John Caleb; MERCHANT: Ronald Yamamoto; THIEF: Tim Ewing; PERRY: John Bantay; MADAM/RUSSIAN ADMIRAL: Thomas Ikeda; OLD MAN/AMERICAN ADMIRAL: John Baray; BOY/DUTCH ADMIRAL: Francis Jue; WARRIOR: Ray Contreras; BRITISH SAILORS: Timm Fujii, Francis Jue, Ray Contreras; IMPERIAL PRIEST: Tom Matsusaka; FENCING MASTER'S DAUGHTER: Allan Tung; PROSCENIUM SERVANTS: Gerri Igarashi, Galyn Kong, Diane Lam, Christine Toy. **Understudy**: John Aller. **Orchestra**: WOODWINDS: David Weiss; HARP: Ray Poole; PERCUSSION: Bruce Doctor; SYNTHESIZER: David Loud; PIANO: Eric Stern. This production lost all its almost half million dollar investment. Hal Prince had nothing to do with this production, and didn't see it.

THE BRITISH PRODUCTION. Opened at THE FORUM, WYTHENSHAWE, on 4/30/86. **Cast**: Simon Clark, Paul Hegarty, Paul Baden, Christopher Brown, Mick Sebastian, Thom Booker. Then it went to the COLISEUM, London, 9/10/87–11/26/87, in repertory. PRESENTED BY The English National Opera; PRODUCER: Keith Warner; SETS: Ralph Koltai; CONDUCTOR: James Holmes; CAST RECORDING on TER.

THE JAPANESE PRODUCTION. Ran at THE PIT, Tokyo, 10/2/00–10/21/00. 25 PERFORMANCES. PRESENTED BY New National, Tokyo. This was the Japanese version, translated by Kunihoko Hashimoto. DIRECTOR/CHOREOGRAPHER: Amon Miyamoto. **Cast:** RECITER/SHOGUN/EMPEROR: Takeharu Kunimoto. This production ran at AVERY FISHER HALL, Lincoln Center, 7/9/02–7/13/02; and at the KENNEDY CENTER, Washington, DC, 9/3/02–9/8/02. In addition, it was the production that went on to play on Broadway in 2004.

NAVY PIER, Chicago, 10/10/01–1/6/02. This revival was the first hit production of this musical in the USA. There was talk of a New York transfer, but it never happened. PRESENTED BY The Chicago Shakespeare Theatre; DIRECTOR: Gary Griffin; SETS: Dan Ostling; COSTUMES: Mara Blumenfeld; MUSICAL DIRECTOR: Tom Murray. *Cast:* RECITER: Joseph Anthony Foronda; KAYAMA: Kevin Gudahl; SHOGUN'S MOTHER: Blake Hammond; MANJIRO: Christopher Mark Peterson; THIEF: Richard Manera. It moved to the DONMAR WAREHOUSE, London, 6/30/03–9/6/03. Previews from 6/20/03. It had the same basic crew in London as in Chicago, except LIGHTING: Hugh Vanstone; MUSICAL DIRECTOR: Thomas Murray; ORCHESTRATIONS: James Stenborg. *Cast:* Joseph Anthony Foronda, Kevin Gudahl, Richard Manera, Richard Henders, Togo Igawa, Cornell John, Teddy Kempner, Ian McLarnon, Jerome Pradon, Mo Zainal.

527. *Pacific Overtures (Broadway revival)*

Before Broadway. On 9/12/03 it was announced that the Roundabout Theatre Company and Gorgeous Entertainment were going to revive the show on Broadway in the fall of 2004, in the form of the 2000 Tokyo version, in English, with Asian-American actors, with new staging by Amon Miyamoto, and with women in the cast. This was the first time a Japanese had directed a Broadway musical. Just prior to the first preview Francis Jue injured his knee and had to be replaced temporarily by his understudy and a swing.

The Broadway Run. STUDIO 54, 12/2/04–1/30/05. 24 previews from 11/12/04. Limited run of 69 PERFORMANCES. PRESENTED BY the Roundabout Theatre Company, in association with Gorgeous Entertainment; MUSIC/LYRICS: Stephen Sondheim; BOOK: John Weidman; ADDITIONAL MATERIAL: Hugh Wheeler; DIRECTOR: Amon Miyamoto; SETS/MASKS: Rumi Matsui; COSTUMES: Junko Koshino (Emi Wada had been announced earlier); LIGHTING: Brian MacDevitt; SOUND: Dan Moses Schreier; MUSICAL DIRECTOR: Paul Gemignani; ORCHESTRATIONS: Jonathan Tunick; NEW CAST RECORDING made on 2/1/05, and released in 5/05, on PS Classics; PRESS: Boneau/Bryan-Brown; CASTING: Jim Carnahan; GENERAL MANAGER: Sydney Beers; COMPANY MANAGER: Nicole Larson; PRODUCTION STAGE MANAGER: Arthur Gaffin; STAGE MANAGER: Kenneth J. McGee. *Cast:* RECITER: B.D. Wong; LORD ABE, 1ST COUNCILLOR: Sab Shimono; OFFICERS: Darren Lee & Evan D'Angeles; MANJIRO: Paolo Montalban; 2ND COUNCILLOR: Ming Lee; SHOGUN'S MOTHER; Alvin Y.F. Ing; 3RD COUNCILLOR: Alan Muraoka; KAYAMA: Michael K. Lee; TAMATE: Yoko Fumoto; SAMURAI: Joseph Anthony Foronda; STORYTELLER: Joseph Anthony Foronda; OLDER SWORDSMAN: Scott Watanabe; SAMURAI BODYGUARD: Scott Watanabe; SHOGUN'S WIFE'S SERVANT: Yuka Takara; OBSERVERS: Evan D'Angeles & Telly Leung; FISHERMAN: Scott Watanabe; MERCHANT: Hoon Lee; SON: Yuka Takara; GRANDMOTHER: Alan Muraoka; THIEF: Joseph Anthony Foronda; COMMODORE PERRY: Hoon Lee; SHOGUN'S WIFE: Hazel Anne Raymundo; PHYSICIAN: Scott Watanabe; PRIESTS: Ming Lee & Daniel Jay Park; MADAM: Francis Jue; SOOTHSAYER: Joseph Anthony Foronda; SHOGUN'S COMPANION: Telly Leung; MADAM: Francis Jue; KANAGAWA GIRLS: Mayumi Omagari, Yuka Takara, Daniel Jay Park, Hazel Anne Raymundo; OLD MAN: Alvin Y.F. Ing; BOY: Telly Leung; WARRIOR: Evan D'Angeles; NOBLES: Fred Isozaki & Telly Leung; AMERICAN ADMIRAL: Darren Lee; BRITISH ADMIRAL: Evan D'Angeles; DUTCH ADMIRAL: Francis Jue; RUSSIAN ADMIRAL: Scott Watanabe; FRENCH ADMIRAL: DANIEL JAY PARK; LORD OF THE SOUTH: Hoon Lee; SAMURAI'S DAUGHTER: Mayumi Omagari; SAILORS: Darren Lee, Hoon Lee, Telly Leung; EMPEROR: Ming Lee. *Swings:* Eric Bondoc, Rick Edinger, Kim Varhola, *Michael J. Bulatao, Orville Mendoza*. **Orchestra:** FLUTE/CLARINET: Kenneth J. Anderson; CELLO: Deborah Assael; SYNTHESIZER # 1: Paul Ford; SYNTHESIZER # 2: Mark Mitchell; VIOLIN/VIOLA: Suzanne Ornstein; DRUMS: Paul Pizzuti; PERCUSSION: Thad Wheeler.

Hoon Lee was not in the cast opening night, having sustained shoulder and neck injuries during previews. His understudy and a swing stood in for his roles. There were other replacements too, that night.

Francis Jue played only some of his role — not all. Reviews were divided, erring on the side of respectfully bad. The show quit Studio 54 for a revival of *A Streetcar Named Desire.*

528. *Paint Your Wagon*

It is the time of the Gold Rush in Northern California, and Ben Rumson is a grizzled old prospector. His daughter Jennifer discovers gold near their camp. Word quickly spreads and soon there are 4,000 inhabitants of new town of Rumson. Jennifer falls in love with Julio, Mexican prospector; she goes east to school, returning to Julio when the gold strike peters out. Ben is now left alone with his hopes and dreams.

Before Broadway. It tried out at the Shubert Theatre, Philadelphia, from 9/17/51, for three weeks. Before Broadway John Sheehan was replaced by Bert Matthews; Ann Crowley by Olga San Juan; Angus Cairns by Richard Aherne; and Newton Sullivan by Jared Reed. Newt Sullivan was relegated to the chorus. The characters of Sing Yuy, Elsie, and Joe were added just before Broadway, and the character of Jack (played by Del Anderson) was cut, and Mr. Anderson replaced Feodore Tedick as Sam. The roles of Ed (played by Edgar Thompson) and Johansen (played by John Anderson) were also cut. In the dancing chorus Lorraine Havercroft, Kenneth Le Roy, Martha Mathes, Evelyn Taylor, Duncan Noble, Naomi Boneck, and Guy Stanbaugh were replaced by Mary Burr, Robert Morrow, Dick Price, Charlotte Ray, Mavis Ray, Frederick Schaeffen, John Smolko, and Gisella Svetlik. Broadway opening night was put off twice and the tryout period extended by seven weeks.

The Broadway Run. SHUBERT THEATRE, 11/12/51–7/19/52. 289 PERFORMANCES. PRESENTED BY Cheryl Crawford; MUSIC: Frederick Loewe; LYRICS/BOOK: Alan Jay Lerner; DIRECTOR: Daniel Mann; CHOREOGRAPHER: Agnes de Mille; SETS: Oliver Smith; COSTUMES: Motley; LIGHTING: Peggy Clark; MUSICAL DIRECTOR/CHORAL DIRECTOR: Franz Allers; ORCHESTRATIONS: Ted Royal; DANCE MUSIC ARRANGEMENTS: Trude Rittman; PRESS: Wolfe Kaufman & Merle Debuskey; GENERAL MANAGER: John Yorke; PRODUCTION STAGE MANAGER: Ward Bishop; STAGE MANAGER: Stone Widney; ASSISTANT STAGE MANAGER: John Schmidt. *Cast:* WALT: Bert Matthews; JENNIFER RUMSON: Olga San Juan (2), *Nola Fairbanks, Ann Crowley*; SALEM TRUMBULL: Ralph Bunker; JASPER: Ted Thurston; BEN RUMSON: James Barton (1), *Burl Ives, Eddie Dowling*; STEVE BULLNACK: Rufus Smith; PETE BILLINGS: James Mitchell (4), *Scott Merrill*; CHERRY: Kay Medford; JAKE WHIPPANY: Robert Penn; MIKE MOONEY: John Randolph; DR. NEWCOMB: David Thomas; SING YUY: Tom Ai; LEE ZEN: Chun-Tao Cheng (also known as Stephen Cheng); EDGAR CROCKER: Richard Aherne; SANDY TWIST: Jared Reed; REUBEN SLOANE: Gordon Dilworth; JULIO VALVERAS: Tony Bavaar (3); JACOB WOODLING: Josh Wheeler; ELIZABETH WOODLING: Marijane Maricle; SARAH WOODLING: Jan Sherwood; DUTCHIE: Bert Matthews; CARMELITA: Lorraine Havercroft; YVONNE SOREL: Gemze de Lappe; SUZANNE DUVAL: Mary Burr; ELSIE: Gisella Svetlik; RAYMOND JANNEY: Gordon Dilworth; ROCKY: James Tarbutton; JOE: Norman Weise; SAM: Delbert Anderson; SINGERS: Delbert Anderson, John Anderson, Gino Baldi, Edward Becker, Jack Dabdoub, John Faulkner, Robert Flavelle, John Schickling, John Schmidt, John Spach, Newton Sullivan, Feodore Tedick, David Thomas, Edgar Thompson, Ted Thurston, Norman Weise; DANCERS: Mary Burr, Tamara Chapman, Gemze de Lappe, Joan Djorup, Katia Geleznova, Dorothy Hill, Stuart Hodes, Jean Houloose, Carmelita Lanza, Robert Morrow, Ilona Murai, Paul Olson, Dick Price, Charlotte Ray, Mavis Ray, Frederick Schaeffen, John Smolko, Gisella Svetlik, James Tarbutton. **Understudies**: Ben: Bert Matthews; Jennifer: Nola Fairbanks; Salem/Reuben/Janney: David Thomas; Steve: John Anderson; Pete: Stuart Hodes; Jake/Crocker: Ted Thurston; Cherry/Carmelita: Carmelita Lanza; Mike: John Schmidt; Doc/Dutchie: Norman Weise; Sandy: Newton Sullivan; Julio: Gino Baldi; Jacob: Jack Dabdoub; Sarah/Elizabeth: Lorraine Havercroft; Yvonne: Mavis Ray; Suzanne: Ilona Murai; Rocky: John Smolko. *Act I:* Overture (Orchestra); *Scene 1* A hilltop in Northern California; a spring evening, 1853: "I'm on My Way" (Steve, Jake, Mooney, Zen, Sing Yuy, Sandy, Crocker,

Sloane, Miners); *Scene 2* Outside Salem's store, Rumson Town; evening; four months later: "Rumson (Town)" (Jake), "What's Goin' on Here?" (Jennifer), "I Talk to the Trees" (sung & danced by Julio & Jennifer) [a hit], "They Call the Wind Maria" (Steve & Miners) [a big hit]; *Scene 3* Outside Rumson's cabin; evening, two months later; *Scene 4* Rumson's cabin; immediately following: "I Still See Elisa" (Ben), "How Can I Wait?" (Jennifer); *Scene 5* A hillside near Rumson Town; two months later: "Trio" (Elizabeth, Sarah, Jacon); *Scene 6* At Dutchie's Saloon; the following Sunday: "Rumson (Town)" (reprise) (Jake), "In Between" (Ben), "Whoop-Ti-Ay!" (sung & danced by Ben, Elizabeth, Miners); *Scene 7* Outside Rumson's cabin; later that night; *Scene 8* Julio's cabin; later that night: "How Can I Wait?" (reprise) (Jennifer & Julio), "Carino Mio" (Julio & Jennifer); *Scene 9* The diggin's; the next morning: "There's a Coach Comin' In" (Miners); *Scene 10* Rumson Square; immediately following: Finaletto (danced by the Fandangos & Miners). *Act II*: Entr'acte (Orchestra); *Scene 1* In Jake's Palace; Oct. 1855: "Hand Me Down That Can o' Beans" (Jake & Miners), Rope Dance (Fandangos, Ben, Yvonne), Can-Can (danced by Mary Burr, James Tarbutton, Fandangos, Miners), "Another Autumn" (Julio) (danced by Yvonne & Ben); *Scene 2* The diggin's; two months later: "Movin'" (Sandy, Joe, Sam, Jasper, Zen, Miners), "I'm on My Way" (reprise) (Miners); *Scene 3* Rumson's cabin; two days later: "All for Him" (Jennifer), "(I Was Born Under a) Wand'rin' Star" (Ben) [the big hit]; *Scene 4* A street in Rumson Town; evening, next day: "I Talk to the Trees" (reprise) (Jennifer); *Scene 5* Jake's Palace; that night: "Strike!" (Steve, Jasper, Jake); *Scene 6* A hillside near Rumson Town; the following dawn: "Wand'rin' Star" (reprise) (Jake, Steve, Sandy, Miners); *Scene 7* Rumson Square; the following spring: Finale.

Reviews were generally good. The show won Donaldson Awards for Tony Bavaar, and for female debut (Olga San Juan), and female dancer (Gemze de Lappe).

After Broadway. TOUR. Opened on 10/2/52, at the Hartman Theatre, Columbus, Ohio, and closed on 1/31/53, at the Blackstone Theatre, Chicago. PRESENTED BY John Yorke; DIRECTOR OF ORCHESTRA & CHORUS: Arthur Norris. *Cast*: BEN: Burl Ives; JENNIFER: Nola Fairbanks; SALEM: Joseph Cusanelli; MIKE: Andrew Duggan; JACK: Jared Reed; DUTCHIE: James Schlader; JULIO: Edward Chappel; REUBEN: Gordon Dilworth; SUZANNE: Ilona Murai; YVONNE: Elizabeth Logue. The show was revised into 2 acts and 15 scenes. "Wand'rin' Star," which had proved to be the big hit on Broadway, now opened the show, and a new song—"Take the Wheels off the Wagon" (Ben)—replaced it in its old place in Act II.

HER MAJESTY'S THEATRE, London, 2/11/53–4/3/54. 478 PERFORMANCES. PRESENTED BY Jack Hylton; DIRECTOR: Richard Bird; CHOREOGRAPHER: Mavis Ray; MUSICAL DIRECTOR: Harry Rabinowitz; CAST RECORDING on Columbia. *Cast*: JENNIFER: Sally Ann Howes; BEN: Bobby Howes; SALEM: Colin Cunningham; JULIO: Ken Cantril; JAKE: Laurie Payne; ED: Terence Cooper; STEVE: Joe Leader; JACK: John Hughes. A performance for TV only was given on 1/25/54.

NAVE THEATRE, NYC, 11/8/68–11/14/68. 7 PERFORMANCES. CONCEIVED BY/DIRECTOR: Charles Willard; CHOREOGRAPHER: Jane McLaughlin; SETS: Jeffrey B. Moss; LIGHTING: Edward Greenberg; MUSICAL CONCEPTION: John De Main; MUSICAL DIRECTOR: Byron Grant; ARRANGEMENTS: Jim Turner, John De Main, Bill Schustik; PRODUCTION ADVISER: Margot Moser. *Cast*: BEN: Robert Dagny; JENNIFER: Carolyn Mignini; SUSAN: Susan Kraemer; JULIO: Herb Downer.

THE MOVIE. 1969. It had the same title, some of the same songs, but a different story. WRITER: Paddy Chayefsky; DIRECTOR: Joshua Logan. *Cast*: BEN: Lee Marvin; PARDNER: Clint Eastwood; ELIZABETH: Jean Seberg; ROTTEN LUCK WILLIE: Harve Presnell; MAD DOG DUNCAN: Ray Walston. There were five new songs by Alan Jay Lerner & Andre Previn: "Gold Fever," "A Million Miles Away Behind the Door," "The Gospel of No Name City," "The Best Things (in Life Are Dirty)," "The First Thing You Know." A 45-rpm record was released with Lee Marvin singing (on the A side) "Wand'rin' Star" and Clint Eastwood singing (on the B side) "I Talk to the Trees," both extraordinarily well done, and the record was a huge hit.

GOODSPEED OPERA HOUSE, Conn., 1993. DIRECTOR: Andre Ernotte; CHOREOGRAPHER: Tony Stevens; SETS: James Noone; MUSICAL DIRECTOR: Michael O'Flaherty. *Cast*: BEN: George Ball; JENNIFER:

Marla Schaffel; BULLNACK: Luke Lynch; WHIPPANY: Mark C. Reis; DUTCHIE: Anthony S. Bernard; JULIO: David Bedella; WOODLING: Stephen Lee Anderson; ELIZABETH: Liz McCartney; SARAH: Leigh-Anne Wencker.

PLANNED BROADWAY REVIVAL. A new production in 2003, aiming for Broadway, and due to begin as a six-month tour, with David Hasselhoff as Ben, did not happen.

BRENTWOOD THEATRE, Calif., 12/1/04–1/9/05. Previews from 11/23/04. PRESENTED BY the Geffen Playhouse; NEW ADAPTATION by David Rambo; DIRECTOR: Gilbert Cates; CHOREOGRAPHER: Kay Cole; SETS/LIGHTING: Daniel Ionazzi; MUSICAL DIRECTOR/ORCHESTRATIONS: Steve Orich. *Cast*: Sharon Lawrence, Andy Umberger, David Jennings.

529. *The Pajama Game*

Set during the present. The love story of Babe, a union organizer in Cedar Rapids, Iowa, and Sid, her new plant superintendent at the Sleep-Tite Pajama Factory, is set during a strike, when the workers go for a raise of 7½ cents an hour. When their request is not met, they stage a slow down. Babe wrecks a machine and Sid is forced to suspend her. Sid gets Gladys (the president's secretary) drunk at the dive known as Hernando's Hideaway, and gets the keys to the private ledgers, which prove to the president that Sid now knows the factory is making a profit, that the prez had been hiding these figures from the directors, and that the workers can have their raise. Gladys and Hines, an insanely jealous time-study man, also have an affair.

Before Broadway. Bobby Griffith read a review of Richard Bissell's novel *7½ Cents*, and asked Hal Prince to read the book, which he did, and then obtained the rights. They had to sell the idea to a reluctant George Abbott as director and mentor. Mr. Abbott came up with the title for the musical while walking along Fifth Avenue. He also agreed to write the libretto with Richard Bissell. It took Mr. Bissell only four days to pack up his family and house and move to Connecticut to begin work. The producers set about raising a crew, but the theme of the musical scared off lyricists and composers such as Rodgers & Hammerstein, Frank Loesser, Cole Porter, Irving Berlin, Harold Arlen, and others; and writers, including Abe Burrows. Frank Loesser did, however, recommend the songwriting team of Adler & Ross. This would be their first complete score. It's more than likely, too, that Mr. Loesser contributed the main musical strain of "Hey There" and "A New Town is a Blue Town," and may well have written two others. The producers' first choice for choreographer was Jerome Robbins, but he was unavailable and recommended Bob Fosse (in his choreographic debut on Broadway). However, Mr. Robbins did come on board. This was his first credit as director, even though he didn't really direct — he was there only to oversee Bob Fosse (Robbins did wind up staging two numbers — "There Once was a Man" and "7½ cents"). Because Griffith & Prince were a new producing team, they were low on funds, and Mr. Abbott allowed them to work out of his office for no rent. There were 11 backers' auditions altogether, but the idea scared off the usual angels. In later backers' auditions, held in Edie Adams' living room, the industrial strike angle in the story was played down and the love story played up. Finally, there were 164 small backers, including members of the chorus, backstage employees, family and friends. Not quite enough capital was raised, so George Abbott loaned the $28,000 shortfall. Freddie Brisson (who had become the third producer) raised the money to pay back Mr. Abbott. The show was capitalized at $250,000 (but actually cost under $170,000). Finally, a year after they had obtained the rights to the novel, they began rehearsals at the Winter Garden on Broadway. The budget was so tight that Prince & Griffith worked as their own stage managers. Mr. Abbott wanted to cut "Steam Heat" and "Hey There" because they slowed the progress of the story — which shows that even the great man was wrong sometimes. Before tryouts Ralph Meeker was replaced by John Raitt. The show opened at the Shubert Theatre, New Haven, on 4/10/54, got great reviews, and ran there for eight days. It also opened in Boston to similar reviews, and scalpers here were selling tickets at $60. 4th-billed Charlotte Rae had her part eliminated, and 10th-billed Clarence Nordstrom was dropped. The Act II number "The World Around Us" (between "Steam Heat" and "Think of the Time I Save"), was cut before Broadway.

The Broadway Run. St. James Theatre, 5/13/54–11/10/56; Shubert Theatre, 11/12/56–11/24/56. Total of 1,063 performances. Presented by Frederick Brisson, Robert E. Griffith, Harold S. Prince; Music/Lyrics: Richard Adler & Jerry Ross; Book: George Abbott & Richard Bissell; Based on the 1953 Book-of-the-Month Club novel *7½ Cents*, by Richard Bissell, about the author's pajama factory in Dubuque, Iowa; Directors: George Abbott & Jerome Robbins; Choreographer: Bob Fosse; Assistant Choreographer: Zoya Leporska; Sets/Costumes: Lemuel Ayers; Musical Director: Hal Hastings, *Philip Ingalls (by 54–55)*; Orchestrations: Don Walker; Dance Music Arrangements: Roger Adams; Press: Reuben Rabinovitch, *Howard Newman*; Casting: Judith Abbott & Mary Wharton; General Manager: Richard Horner, *Carl Fisher (by 54–55)*, Stage Managers: Bobby Griffith, Hal Prince, Jean Barrere, *Fred Hebert, Dennis Murray*. **Cast:** Vernon Hines: Eddie Foy Jr. (3) ☆, *Buster West (from 55–56)*; Prez: Stanley Prager (7); Joe: Ralph Farnworth, *Gordon Woodburn (from 54–55)*; Hasler: Ralph Dunn (6); Gladys: Carol Haney (4), *Helen Gallagher (from 54–55)*, *Neile Adams (from 55–56)*; Sid Sorokin: John Raitt (1) ☆; Mabel: Reta Shaw (5), *Ruth Gillette (from 54–55)*; 1st Helper: Jack Drummond, *John Ford (from 54–55)*; 2nd Helper: Buzz Miller, *Jim Hutchison (from 54–55)*, *Frank Derbas (from 55–56)*; Charlie: Ralph Chambers; Babe Williams: Janis Paige (2) ☆, *Pat Marshall (from 54–55)*, *Julie Wilson (from 55–56)*; Mae: Thelma Pelish (11); Brenda: Marion Colby (9), *Patricia Marand (from 54–55)*, *Mary Stanton (from 55–56)*; Poopsie: Rae Allen, *Carmen Alvarez (from 54–55)*, *Michele Burke (from 55–56)*; Salesman: Jack Waldron (8); Eddie: Jim Hutchison; Pop: William David; Worker: Peter Gennaro, *Frank Derbas (from 54–55)*, *Kenneth Le Roy (from 55–56)*; Dancers: Carmen Alvarez (gone by 55–56), Robert Evans (gone by 54–55), Marilyn Gennaro (gone by 54–55), Jim Hutchison (gone by 54–55), Lida Koehring (gone by 54–55), Eric Kristen, Shirley MacLaine (*Sandra Devlin* by 54–55 & gone by 55–56), Dale Moreda, Marsha Reynolds (gone by 54–55), Augustin Rodriguez (gone by 54–55), Ben Vargas (gone by 54–55), Anne Wallace. 54–55 replacements: *Betty Buday* (gone by 55–56), *Doris Lorenz, Lynda Lynch, Charlene Hargrove, Jack Konzal, Kenneth Le Roy* (gone by 55–56), *Phil Gerard* (gone by 55–56), *Alton Ruff, Keith Willis* (gone by 55–56). 55–56 replacements: *Nancy Hachenberg, Cordelia Ware, Chele Graham, Billy Sumner, Gardiner Meade, Vito Durante*; Singers: Rudy Adamo (gone by 55–56), Rae Allen (gone by 54–55), Sara Dillon (gone by 55–56), Bob Dixon (gone by 54–55), Jack Drummond (gone by 54–55), Ralph Farnworth (gone by 54–55), John Ford, Mara Landi, Virginia Martin (gone by 54–55), Mary Roche, Mary Stanton (gone by 54–55), Gordon Woodburn. 54–55 replacements: *Peggy Kinard* (gone by 55–56), *Michele Burke, Colleen O'Connor* (gone by 55–56), *Del Anderson, Art Carroll, Jack Matthew*. 55–56 replacements: *Deedy Irwin, Marion Lauer, Ramona Robinson, Leo Kayworth*. **Understudies:** Sid: Art Carroll (by 54–55); Babe: Patricia Marand (by 54–55), *Mary Stanton* (only after Pat Marshall left); Hines: Jack Waldron (by 54–55), *Stanley Prager* (only after Eddie Foy left); Gladys: Shirley MacLaine, *Sandra Devlin* (by 54–55), *Lynda Lynch* (by 54–55); Prez: Del Anderson (by 54–55); Hasler/Pop: Ralph Chambers (by 54–55); Mabel: Colleen O'Connor (by 54–55), *Deedy Irwin* (by 55–56); Worker: Kenneth Le Roy (only after Pete Gennaro left), *Eric Kristen* (by 55–56); Eddie/2nd Helper: Eric Kristen (by 54–55); Charlie: Gordon Woodburn (by 54–55); Mae: Mara Landi (by 54–55); Salesman: John Ford (by 54–55); Brenda: Sara Dillon (only after Marion Colby left), *Mary Roche* (only after Pat Marand left); Poopsie: Deedy Irwin (only after Carmen Alvarez left). **Act I: *Scene 1*** Sewing room of the Sleep-Tite Pajama Factory: "The Pajama Game" (Hines); ***Scene 2*** The Sleep-Tite Pajama Factory shop floor: "Racing with the Clock" (Girls), "A New Town is a Blue Town" (Sid), "Racing with the Clock" (reprise) (Girls); ***Scene 3*** A hallway in the factory: "I'm Not at All in Love" (Babe & the Girls); ***Scene 4*** The factory office: "I'll Never Be Jealous Again" (Hines & Mabel), "Hey There" (Sid) [the big hit]; ***Scene 5*** A wooded path on the way to the Union picnic: "Her Is" (Prez & Gladys); ***Scene 6*** The picnic grounds: "Sleep-Tite" (Babe & Boys and Girls) [cut from the album], "Once a Year Day" (Sung by Sid, Babe,

Company. Danced by Gladys, 2nd Helper, Worker); ***Scene 7*** The wooded path; twilight: "Her Is" (reprise) (Prez & Mae); ***Scene 8*** The kitchen of Babe's house: "Small Talk" (Sid & Babe); ***Scene 9*** A hallway in the factory: "There Once Was a Man" (Sid & Babe); ***Scene 10*** The factory shop: "Hey There" (reprise) (Sid). **Act II: *Scene 1*** Eagle Hall: "Steam Heat" (Gladys, 2nd Helper, Worker) [a hit]; ***Scene 2*** The kitchen of Babe's house: "Hey There" (reprise) (Babe); ***Scene 3*** A hallway in the factory: "Think of the Time I Save" (Hines & Girls); ***Scene 4*** The factory office; ***Scene 5*** Hernando's Hideaway: "Hernando's Hideaway" (Sid, Gladys, & Co) [a big hit]; ***Scene 6*** Morning in the office: "Jealousy Ballet" (Hines, Gladys, Mabel, Boys); ***Scene 7*** A street near the park: "7½ Cents" (Babe, Prez, Girls and Boys), "There Once Was a Man" (reprise) (Sid & Babe), "The Pajama Game — Finale" (Company).

Advance sales at the Broadway box-office were over $40,000, and it opened to raves. The classic showbiz fairy tale happened. Carol Haney hurt her leg and couldn't go on for a Wednesday matinee early in the run; her understudy Shirley MacLaine went on for her, and was spotted by Hollywood producers Hal Wallis & Bob Goldstein, who had come specifically to see Miss Haney. The production ran into the black after 14 weeks, and wound up earning $1,365,941 on its investment. It won Tony Awards for musical, choreography, and for Carol Haney; and Donaldson Awards for musical, composers, lyrics, book, direction, choreography, and for Carol Haney (supporting actress & best female dancer). It was only the eighth Broadway musical to have a run over 1,000 performances.

After Broadway. Tour. Opened on 1/29/55, at the Shubert Theatre, New Haven, and closed on 2/16/57, at the Civic Theatre, New Orleans. Musical Director: George Hirst. **Cast:** Sid: Larry Douglas; Babe: Fran Warren, *Betty O'Neil*; Gladys: Pat Stanley, *Barbara Bostock*; Chorus included: Mickey Gunnersen, Dana Sosa.

London. Opened on 10/13/55. 584 performances. Director: Robert E. Griffith; Choreographer: Zoya Leporska; Musical Director: Robert Lowe; London cast recording on EMI. **Cast:** Gladys: Elizabeth Seal, *Barbara Ferris*; Hines: Max Wall; Babe: Joy Nichols; Sid: Edmund Hockridge, *Nevil Whiting*; Prez: Frank Lawless; Hasler: Felix Felton; Salesman: Arthur Lowe; Dancer: Teddy Green; Brenda: Olga Lowe; Poopsie: Susan Irvin; Singers: Terry Donovan & Myra de Groot.

City Center, NYC, 5/15/57–6/2/57. 23 performances. This revival opened less than 6 months after the long Broadway run ended. Presented by the New York City Center Light Opera Company; Director: Jean Barrere; Choreographer: Eric Kristen; Sets/Costumes: Lemuel Ayers; Costume Supervisor: Ruth Morley; Lighting: Peggy Clark; Musical Director: Frederick Dvonch. **Cast:** Hines: Paul Hartman; Prez: Stanley Prager; Joe: Sam Kirkham; Hasler: Ralph W. Chambers; Gladys: Pat Stanley; Sid: Larry Douglas; Mabel: Marguerite Shaw; Helpers: Richard France & Cy Young; Charlie: Eugene Wood; Babe: Jane Kean; Mae: Thelma Pelish; Brenda: Ann Buckles; Poopsie: Chele Graham; Salesman: Jack Waldron; Pop: William David; Dancers included: Dorothy Etheridge, Mickey Gunnersen. Singers included: Julia Gerace, Vince McMahon, Mildred Slavin, Ralph Vucci, Miriam Gulager.

The movie. 1957. Directors: George Abbott & Stanley Donen. This was a virtual copy of the play. During filming Carol Haney collapsed several times from exhaustion, and was diagnosed as a diabetic. From then on in her career she concentrated on choreography, rather than dancing. **Cast:** Babe: Doris Day; Sid: John Raitt; Gladys: Carol Haney; Hines: Eddie Foy Jr.; Mabel: Reta Shaw; Mae: Thelma Pelish; Hasler: Ralph Dunn; Charlie: Ralph Chambers; Poopsie: Barbara Nichols; Prez: Jack Straw; Featured Dancers: Buzz Miller & Kenneth Le Roy.

Richard Bissell subsequently wrote *Say, Darling*, an account of his experiences during the making of *The Pajama Game*, and this was turned into a musical in 1958.

530. *The Pajama Game (Broadway revival)*

The element of inter-racial relations came in with the casting of Barbara McNair and Cab Calloway. Musical numbers were slightly different from the original. The reprise of "Racing with Clock" in Act I, Scene 1, was cut. In Act II, Scene 2, in place of the reprise of "Hey There" (a reprise which Richard Adler never liked, but was obliged to put there by George Abbott, who was trying to promote the song in 1954) was now a new number written by Mr. Adler, "Watch Your Heart" (Babe), actually a re-working of "What's Wrong with Me?" (from *Kwamina*). Act II, Scene 7, now had a third number—a reprise of "There Once Was a Man" (Sid & Babe), placed between "7½ Cents" and "Pajama Game." "Jealousy Ballet" was dropped. Jerome Robbins staged the new version of "7½ Cents." "Watch Your Heart" was subsequently re-worked as "If You Win, You Lose," with new melody and lyrics, and as such featured in several regional productions of *The Pajama Game*, taking the place of a reprise of "Hey There."

Before Broadway. Marilyn Nell was replaced by Mary Jo Catlett.

The Broadway Run. LUNT—FONTANNE THEATRE, 12/9/73–2/3/74. 5 previews from 12/5/73. 65 PERFORMANCES. PRESENTED BY Richard Adler & Bert Wood, in association with Nelson Peltz; MUSIC/LYRICS: Richard Adler & Jerry Ross; BOOK: George Abbott & Richard Bissell; BASED ON the 1953 novel *7½ Cents*, by Richard Bissell; DIRECTOR: George Abbott; CHOREOGRAPHER: Zoya Leporska re-staged Bob Fosse's original choreography; SETS: David Guthrie; COSTUMES: Ben Benson; LIGHTING: John Gleason; MUSICAL DIRECTOR: Joyce Brown; ORCHESTRATIONS: Don Walker; PRESS: Jay Bernstein Public Relations; CASTING: Martin Gage & Janice Nevins; GENERAL MANAGER: Helen Richards; ASSISTANT GENERAL MANAGER: Steve Suskin; COMPANY MANAGER: William Stewart; STAGE MANAGERS: Bert Wood, Bob Bernard, Stan Page. *Cast:* VERNON HINES: Cab Calloway (2) ☆; PREZ: Marc Jordan (7); JOE: Gerrit de Beer; HASLER: Willard Waterman (5); GLADYS: Sharron Miller (4); SID SOROKIN: Hal Linden (3) ☆, *Jay Stuart*; MABEL: Mary Jo Catlett (6); 1ST HELPER: David Brummel; 2ND HELPER: Jon Engstrom; CHARLIE: Tiger Haynes (9); BABE WILLIAMS: Barbara McNair (1) ☆; MAE: Margret Coleman (10); BRENDA: Chris Calloway (8); POOPSIE: Wyetta Turner (11); SALESMAN: Hal Norman; POP: Baron Wilson (12); DANCERS: Dru Alexandrine, P.J. Benjamin, Hank Brunjes, Eileen Casey, Jon Engstrom, Vicki Frederick, Mickey Gunnersen, Ben Harney, Randal Harris, David Kresser Jr., Cameron Mason, Sally Neal, JoAnn Ogawa, Chester Walker; SINGERS: Gerrit de Beer, Chalyce Brown, David Brummel, Doug Carfrae, Susan Dyas, Rebecca Hoodwin, Patricia Moline, Stan Page, Marie Santell, Ward Smith, Cynthia White, Teddy Williams. *Standby*: Hines: Tiger Haynes. *Understudies*: Babe: Chris Calloway; Sid: David Brummel; Gladys: Wyetta Turner; Hasler: Hal Norman; Mabel: Chalyce Brown; Prez: Gerrit de Beer; Brenda: Cynthia White; Mae: Rebecca Hoodwin; Poopsie: Sally Neal; Salesman: Stan Page; Joe/Charlie: Teddy Williams; Helpers: Hank Brunjes.

This revival got mostly very good reviews. The production cost only $300,000.

After Broadway. NEW YORK STATE THEATRE, 3/3/89–4/16/89. 51 PERFORMANCES. The action was now set in June 1957. PRESENTED BY the New York City Opera; DIRECTOR/CHOREOGRAPHER: Theodore Pappas; SETS: Michael Anania; COSTUMES: Marjorie McCown; LIGHTING: Ken Tabachnick; CONDUCTOR: Peter Howard. *Cast:* HINES: Avery Saltzman; PREZ: David Green; JOE: Jim Borstelmann; HASLER: Steve Pudenz; GLADYS: Lenora Nemetz; MAE: Susan Nicely; BRENDA: Joyce Campana; POOPSIE: Lillian Graff; SID: Richard Muenz; CHARLIE: Louis Perry; MABEL: Brooks Almy; BABE: Judy Kaye; MAX: Don Yule; PAT: Paula Hostetter; POP: William Ledbetter. *Understudy*: Gladys: Karen Ziemba.

GOODSPEED OPERA HOUSE, Conn., 4/2/98–6/26/98. Preview on 4/1/98. The production got great reviews. DIRECTOR/CHOREOGRAPHER: Greg Ganakas; MUSICAL DIRECTOR: Michael O'Flaherty. *Cast:* SID: Sean McDermott; BABE: Colleen Fitzpatrick; GLADYS: Valerie Wright; PREZ: Casey Nicholaw; HINES: Bob Walton.

FREUD PLAYHOUSE, UCLA, Los Angeles, 5/6/98–5/17/98. 15 PERFORMANCES. Part of the *Reprise! Broadway's Best in Concert* series. DIRECTOR: Will MacKenzie; CHOREOGRAPHER: Patti Colombo. On 5/6/98 a gala celebration was held, with John Raitt & Janis Paige (stars of the original 1954 Broadway run). *Cast:* Dorian Harewood, Christine Ebersole, Jane Lanier.

BRITISH REVIVAL. BIRMINGHAM REPERTORY THEATRE, 4/23/99 (5 weeks). DIRECTOR: Simon Callow; CHOREOGRAPHER: David Bintley; SETS: Frank Stella; MUSICAL SUPERVISOR: John Harle; MUSICAL DIRECTOR: Nick Barnard. *Cast:* MABEL ELLIS: Anita Dobson; VERNON J. HINES: John Hegley; PREZ: Jonathan D. Ellis; CATHERINE "BABE" WILLIAMS: Ulrika Jonsson; SID: Graham Bickley; GLADYS HOTCHKISS: Alison Therese Limerick. PRINCESS OF WALES THEATRE, Toronto, 6/17/99–7/24/99. PRESENTED BY Ed & David Mirvish. Most of the Birmingham cast remained, but Camilla Scott took over as Babe. VICTORIA PALACE THEATRE, London, 10/4/99–12/18/99. Leslie Ash took over as Babe. Alison Therese Limerick injured her foot, and understudy Jenny-Ann Topham went on opening night. Composer Richard Adler hated this production.

CITY CENTER, NYC, 5/2/02–5/5/02. 5 PERFORMANCES. Concert revival. Part of the *Encores!* series. Richard Adler offered his new number "If You Win, You Lose" to the show, but they turned him down, preferring to go with the original score. DIRECTOR: John Rando; CHOREOGRAPHER: John Carrafa. *Cast:* BABE: Karen Ziemba; SID: Brent Barrett; PREZ: Daniel Jenkins; HINES: Mark Linn-Baker (Jason Alexander had been rumored for this role); ALSO WITH: Ken Page, Deidre Goodwin, Gina Ferrall, Jennifer Cody, Edgar Godineaux, Tony Capone, Joy Hermalyn, Caitlin Carter, April Nixon, Marc Oka, Tina Ou, Josh Prince.

NEW BROADWAY ATTEMPT. On 5/1/02 a new Broadway production (not connected to the *Encores!* production) was announced by none other than Richard Adler, as "definite" for the fall of 2002, but it didn't happen. It was to have featured Mr. Adler's post–1973 new song "If You Win, You Lose." By mid–2003 it was on again, for late spring or early summer 2004, with a revised book (based on the original, of course) by Peter Ackerman; and to be produced by Jeffrey Richards & James Fuld; Kathleen Marshall was to be director/choreographer (it would have been her directorial debut). There were two new songs. The production was capitalized at $8 million. It was postponed again, to the 2004–05 season, but again, never happened. Thought to be shelved, it was therefore a surprise when on 1/8/05 it was announced that Harry Connick Jr. would play Sid in the production due on Broadway in 11/05.

531. *Pal Joey*

Set in the late 1930s, in Chicago. Joey is an amoral, ambitious night club entertainer and mc who would do anything to get his name in lights. He gets a job at Mike's Club, where he meets Linda, then dumps her for Vera, a tough, rich older lady who sets him up in his own bistro, Chez Joey. Lowell and Gladys are blackmailers. Vera soon gets bored with Joey, and turns him out onto the street at the final curtain.

Before Broadway. John O'Hara wrote to Richard Rodgers suggesting a musical. It ran on Broadway at the ETHEL BARRYMORE THEATRE, 12/25/40–8/16/41. 270 PERFORMANCES. This was the vehicle that made Gene Kelly a star, and was the only Broadway musical in which he played a major role. PRESENTED & DIRECTED BY George Abbott; CHOREOGRAPHER: Robert Alton; SETS/LIGHTING: Jo Mielziner. *Cast:* JOEY: Gene Kelly; VERA: Vivienne Segal; GLADYS: June Havoc; LINDA: Leila Ernst; VICTOR: Van Johnson; ALBERT DOANE: Stanley Donen; LUDLOW LOWELL: Jack Durant; ALSO WITH: Jerome Whyte. Along with *Show Boat* (1927) and *Oklahoma!* (1943), the 1940 production of *Pal Joey* is now considered a breakthrough in the development of musicals—integration of plot, dance and song to further the story. Moreover, it told a seamy story, and, although it got very good reviews, 1940 audiences weren't ready for it (as George Abbott had predicted. By 1952 they had become accustomed to such things, and that's when *Pal Joey* was revived). The 1940 production returned to the SHUBERT THEATRE, Broadway, on 9/1/41, and moved to the ST. JAMES THEATRE, 10/21/41–11/29/41. Total of 104 PERFORMANCES at the last two theatres. *Cast:* JOEY: Gene Kelly; VERA: Vivienne Segal; GLADYS: Vivienne Allen; LINDA: Anne Blair; VICTOR: Van Johnson; ALBERT DOANE: Phil King; LUDLOW LOWELL: David Burns.

Columbia bought the rights, with a view to starring Gene Kelly in a movie, but MGM, to whom Mr. Kelly was under contract, wanted too much money for his services, and the project was dropped. The unaccountable yet palpable belated success in the late 1940s of one number in particular — "Bewitched" — created an awareness of the entire score of *Pal Joey* that had never before existed, and in 1950 Columbia released an edited version of the score on LP, with Vivienne Segal and Harold Lang in the main roles. Jule Styne caught a summer stock run in East Hampton, NY, in 1951, with Bob Fosse as Joey, and Carol Bruce as Vera. Mr. Styne determined to revive the original 1940 show on Broadway. There were some lyric changes (some had aged too much since 1940), and some of the numbers were re-assigned to different characters (not hard to understand if one has heard Lionel Stander sing). During New Haven tryouts Elaine Stritch was also understudying Ethel Merman on Broadway in *Call Me Madam*.

The Broadway Run. BROADHURST THEATRE, 1/2/52–4/18/53. 542 PERFORMANCES. PRESENTED BY Jule Styne & Leonard Key, in association with Anthony Brady Farrell; MUSIC: Richard Rodgers; LYRICS: Lorenz Hart; BOOK: John O'Hara (helped by uncredited George Abbott); BASED ON the 1939 series of John O'Hara short stories in the *New Yorker*, written as if they were letters sent by "pal Joey" to "pal Ted," a famous bandleader; DIRECTOR/CHOREOGRAPHER/PRODUCTION SUPERVISOR: Robert Alton; BOOK DIRECTOR: David Alexander; SETS: Oliver Smith; COSTUMES: Miles White; ASSISTANT COSTUMES: Florence Klotz; TECHNICAL SUPERVISOR/LIGHTING: Peggy Clark; MUSICAL DIRECTOR: Max Meth; ORIGINAL ORCHESTRATIONS: Hans Spialek; SPECIAL ORCHESTRATIONS: Don Walker; BALLET MUSIC ARRANGEMENTS: Oscar Kosarin; CAST RECORDING on Columbia (recorded before the show opened); PRESS: John L. Toohey; CASTING: Howard Hoyt; COMPANY MANAGER: Mike Goldreyer; PRODUCTION STAGE MANAGER: Neil Hartley; STAGE MANAGER: Barry Ryan; ASSISTANT STAGE MANAGER: Reed Allyn. **Cast:** MIKE SPEARS: Jack Waldron; JOEY EVANS: Harold Lang; KID: Helen Wood; GLADYS BUMPS: Helen Gallagher (2), *Nancy Walker*; AGNES: Janyce Ann Wagner; MICKEY: Phyllis Dorne; DIANE: Frances Krell; DOTTIE: Lynn Joelson; SANDRA: Eleanor Boleyn; ADELE: Rita Tanno; FRANCINE: Gloria O'Malley; LINDA ENGLISH: Patricia Northrop; VERA SIMPSON: Vivienne Segal (1); VALERIE: Barbara Nichols; JANET: Ina Learner [role added — or rather, specified, during the run]; FRASER: Ethel Martin [role added — or rather, specified, during the run]; WAITER: George Martin; AMARILLA: Thelma Tadlock; ERNEST: Gordon Peters; VICTOR: Robert Fortier; DELIVERY BOY: Barry Ryan; STAGE MANAGER: Clarke Gordon; LOUIS THE TENOR: Lewis Bolyard; MELBA SNYDER: Elaine Stritch (4); LUDLOW LOWELL: Lionel Stander (3); COMMISSIONER O'BRIEN: T.J. Halligan; DANCERS: Harry Asmus, Eleanor Boleyn, Bonnie Brae, Hank Brunjes, Phyllis Dorne, Eleanor Fairchild, Jean Goodall, Peter Holmes, Patty Ann Jackson, Lynn Joelson, Helene Keller, Frances Krell, Ray Kyle, Ina Learner, Ethel Martin, George Martin, June McCain, Buzz Miller, David Neuman, Gloria O'Malley, Stanley Simmons, Thelma Tadlock, Rita Tanno, Norma Thornton, George Vosburgh, Janyce Ann Wagner, *Aleen Buchanan*. **Standby:** Joey: Bob Fosse. **Act I: Scene 1** Mike's South Side nightclub; a September afternoon: "You Mustn't Kick it Around" (Joey, Gladys, Boys & Girls); **Scene 2** The Pet Shop; that evening: "I Could Write a Book" (Joey & Linda); **Scene 3** Mike's night club; an evening a month later: "Chicago" (Girls), "That Terrific Rainbow" (Gladys, Victor, Boys & Girls); **Scene 4a** A phone booth; next afternoon; **Scene 4b** Vera's boudoir; same time: "What is a Man?" (Vera) [shortly after the opening of the 1940 original production this number replaced "Love is My Friend"]; **Scene 5** Mike's night club; after closing time, that evening: "Happy Hunting Horn" (Joey, Kid, Victor, George Martin, Buzz Miller, Boys & Girls); **Scene 6** The tailor shop; a few days later: "Bewitched, Bothered and Bewildered" (Vera) [the big hit], "Pal Joey" ("What Do I Care for a Dame") (Joey); **Scene 7** "Joey Looks into the Future" (ballet) (Joey, Agnes, Company). **Act II: Scene 1** Chez Joey; a few weeks later: "The Flower Garden of My Heart" (Louis, Gladys, George Martin, Boys & Girls), "Zip" (Melba), "Plant You Now, Dig You Later" (Gladys, Victor, Boys & Girls); **Scene 2** Joey's apartment; next morning: "In Our Little Den (of Iniquity)" (Vera & Joey); **Scene 3** Chez Joey; that afternoon: "Morocco" (a Dance Rehearsal) (set to the tune of "Chicago") (Boys & Girls); **Scene 4** Joey's apartment; later that afternoon: "Do it the Hard Way" (Joey) [in the 1940 original this number was in Scene 3], "Take Him" (Linda & Vera), "Bewitched, Bothered and Bewildered" (reprise) (Vera) [this reprise was in the 1940 original,

but cut for this 1952 production]; **Scene 5** The Pet Shop; later that evening: "I Could Write a Book" (reprise) (Joey) [this reprise was in the 1940 original, but was cut for this 1952 production].

This revival of *Pal Joey* got raves, and was far more successful than the original. This was the opening night at which *New York Times* critic Brooks Atkinson, who had disliked the original, now publicly ate crow. The show won Tonys for choreography, musical direction, and for Helen Gallagher. It also won a New York Critics' Circle Award for best musical, even though this contravened the NYDCC's own policy of not giving such an award to a revival. It also won Donaldson Awards for musical, composer, lyrics, book, direction, choreography, sets, costumes, and for Vivienne Segal, Helen Gallagher, and Harold Lang (best male dancer). Helen Gallagher left to star in *Hazel Flagg*.

After Broadway. TOUR. Opened on 4/20/53, at the Shubert Theatre, Washington, DC, and closed on 11/28/53, at the Nixon Theatre, Pittsburgh. MUSICAL DIRECTOR: Jacques Rabiroff. Harold Lang, Lionel Stander, Jack Waldron, Lewis Bolyard, Gordon Peters, T.J. Halligan, and Barbara Nichols all reprised their Broadway roles. DANCERS INCLUDED: Dick Korthaze. **Understudy:** Joey: Ward Ellis. In 8/53, Lionel Stander, the Equity representative on the show, was fired after a backstage argument with company manager Joe Grossman, with whom he had been feuding.

PRINCE'S THEATRE, London, 3/31/54–10/30/54. 245 PERFORMANCES. PRESENTED BY Jack Hylton; DIRECTOR: Neil Hartley; CHOREOGRAPHER: George Martin; MUSICAL DIRECTOR: Cyril Ornadel. **Cast:** JOEY: Harold Lang, *Richard France*; VERA: Carol Bruce; LINDA: Sally Bazely; MIKE: Arthur Lowe; LUDLOW: Lou Jacobi; SANDRA: Babs Warden; VALERIE: Vera Day; MELBA: Olga Lowe; DELIVERY BOY: Lionel Blair.

THE MOVIE. It was finally filmed by Columbia in 1957, with a nicer Joey (i.e. a heel, but not such a heel). The setting was changed from Chicago to San Francisco. **Cast:** JOEY: Frank Sinatra; VERA: Rita Hayworth (singing dubbed by Jo Ann Greer); LINDA: Kim Novak (singing dubbed by Trudy Erwin); GLADYS: Barbara Nichols (she had played Valerie on Broadway). The movie had a shortened musical score, and other Rodgers & Hart songs were put in — "My Funny Valentine" and "The Lady is a Tramp" [both from *Babes in Arms*], "There's a Small Hotel" [from *On Your Toes*], "I Didn't Know What Time it Was" [from *Too Many Girls*]. Robert Alton, choreographer of the 1952 Broadway revival, died during filming, and was replaced by Hermes Pan.

CITY CENTER, NYC, 5/31/61–6/25/61. 31 PERFORMANCES. It got rave reviews, and Bob Fosse won unanimous acclaim as the best Joey ever. "Joey's Tango" was added to Act II Scene 4, between "Take Him" and the reprise of "Bewitched" (which had been re-instated). PRESENTED BY the New York City Center Light Opera Company; DIRECTOR: Gus Schirmer Jr.; CHOREOGRAPHER: Ralph Beaumont; COSTUMES: Frank Thompson; MUSICAL DIRECTOR: Jay Blackton. **Cast:** MIKE: Jack Waldron; JOEY: Bob Fosse; GLADYS: Sheila Bond; IRIS: Lillian D'Honau (this character had been named Agnes in the original); MICKEY: Aura Vainio; DIANE: Dorothy Dushock; ADELE: Barbara Monte; FRANCINE: Ellen Halpin; LINDA: Christine Mathews; VERA: Carol Bruce; VALERIE: Betty Hyatt Linton; ERNEST: Emory Bass; VICTOR: Joe Milan; SCHOLTZ: Gene Gavin; LOUIS: John Lankston; MELBA: Eileen Heckart; LUDLOW: Harvey Stone; CHORUS INCLUDED: Marilyn D'Honau, Richard E. Korthaze, Vernon Lusby, Mitchell Nutick.

CITY CENTER, NYC, 5/29/63–6/9/63. 15 PERFORMANCES. "What is a Man" succeeded "Love is My Friend" in Act I Scene 4. "Joey's Tango" (from the 1961 City Center production) became "Joey's Class Act." PRESENTED BY the New York City Center Light Opera Company; DIRECTOR: Gus Schirmer Jr.; CHOREOGRAPHERS: George & Ethel Martin; SETS: Howard Bay; COSTUMES: Frank Thompson; LIGHTING: Peggy Clark; MUSICAL DIRECTOR: Pembroke Davenport. **Cast:** MIKE: Art Barnett; JOEY: Bob Fosse; KID: Pat Turner; GLADYS: Elaine Dunn; IRIS: Dorothy D'Honau; DIANE: Dorothy Dushock; DOTTIE: Shellie Farrell; SANDRA: Mercedes Ellington; FRANCINE: Marilyn D'Honau; LINDA: Rita Gardner; VERA: Viveca Lindfors; VALERIE: Betty Hyatt Linton; ERNEST: Emory Bass; LOUIS: John Lankston; MELBA: Kay Medford; LUDLOW: Jack Durant; DANCERS INCLUDED: Sigyn Lund, Carmen Morales, Barbara Richman, Babs Warden, Gerard Brentte, Danny Jasinski, David M. Lober, Paul Reid Roman. Bob Fosse was nominated for a Tony.

532. *Pal Joey (Broadway revival)*

Before Broadway. Eleanor Parker was replaced by Joan Copeland, and Edward Villella by Christopher Chadman. Both replacements were the original understudies.

The Broadway Run. CIRCLE IN THE SQUARE UPTOWN, 6/27/76–8/29/76. 33 previews. 73 PERFORMANCES. PRESENTED BY Circle in the Square; MUSIC: Richard Rodgers; LYRICS: Lorenz Hart; BOOK: John O'Hara (with George Abbott); BASED ON the 1939 series of John O'Hara short stories in the *New Yorker*; DIRECTOR: Theodore Mann; CHOREOGRAPHER: Margo Sappington; SETS: John J. Moore; COSTUMES: Arthur Boccia; LIGHTING: Ron Wallace; MUSICAL DIRECTOR/ADDITIONAL DANCE MUSIC ARRANGEMENTS: Scott Oakley; PRINCIPAL ORCHESTRATOR: Michael Gibson; PRESS: Merle Debuskey & Susan L. Schulman; CASTING: Roger Sturtevant; COMPANY MANAGER: William Conn; PRODUCTION STAGE MANAGER: Randall Brooks; STAGE MANAGER: James Bernardi. *Cast:* MIKE: Harold Gary (6); JOEY EVANS: Christopher Chadman (5) ☆; KID: Terri Treas (16); GLADYS BUMP: Janie Sell (2) ☆; GAIL: Gail Benedict (11); MURPHY: Murphy Cross (12); ROSAMOND: Rosamond Lynn (15); MARILU: Marilu Henner (14); DEBBIE: Deborah Geffner (13); LINDA ENGLISH: Boni Enten (7); VERA SIMPSON: Joan Copeland (1) ☆; GENT: David Hodo (18); ERNEST: Austin Colyer (8); WALDO THE WAITER: Denny Martin Flinn (17); VICTOR: Michael Leeds (19); DELIVERY BOY: Kenn Scalice (20); LOUIS, THE TENOR: Adam Petroski (9); MELBA SNYDER: Dixie Carter (4) ☆; LUDLOW LOWELL: Joe Sirola (3) ☆; O'BRIEN: Ralph Farnworth (10); BOYS & GIRLS: Gail Benedict, Murphy Cross, Denny Martin Flinn, Deborah Geffner, Marilu Henner, David Hodo, Michael Leeds, Rosamond Lynn, Kenn Scalice, Terri Treas. *Understudies*: Ludlow/Mike: Ralph Farnworth; Gladys: Marilu Henner; Linda: Gail Benedict; O'Brien/Louis: Austin Colyer; Melba: Rosamond Lynn. *Swing Girl*: Lisa Brown. *Swing Boy*: Richard Dodd. *Act I: Scene 1* Mike's Southside night club; a September afternoon: "You Mustn't Kick it Around" (Joey, Gladys, Girls); *Scene 2* The pet shop; that evening: "I Could Write a Book" (Joey & Linda); *Scene 3* Mike's night club; an evening a month later: "Chicago" (Girls), "That Terrific Rainbow" (Gladys & Girls); *Scene 4a* Mike's night club; the next afternoon; *Scene 4b* Vera's boudoir; same time: "What is a Man?" (Vera); *Scene 5* Mike's night club; after closing time that evening: "Happy Hunting Horn" (Joey, Boys & Girls); *Scene 6* The tailor shop; a few days later: "Bewitched, Bothered and Bewildered" (Vera), "Pal Joey" (Joey); *Scene 7* "Joey Looks into the Future" (Joey, Gail, Company). *Act II: Scene 1* Chez Joey; a few weeks later: "The Flower Garden of My Heart" (Tenor, Gladys, Boys & Girls); SHOW GIRLS: HEATHER: Rosamond Lynn; VIOLET: Deborah Geffner; SUNFLOWER: Murphy Cross; LILAC: Gail Benedict; LILY: Marilu Henner; AMERICAN BEAUTY: Terri Treas; "Zip" (Melba), "Plant You Now, Dig You Later" (Gladys & Ludlow, Boys & Girls); *Scene 2* Joey's apartment; next morning: "In Our Little Den" (Vera & Joey); *Scene 3* Chez Joey; that afternoon: "Do it the Hard Way" (Ludlow & Gladys); *Scene 4* Joey's apartment; later that afternoon: "Take Him" (Linda & Vera), "Bewitched, Bothered and Bewildered" (reprise) (Vera); *Scene 5* On a street; later that evening.

The show opened at the 6/27/76 matinee. Reviews were decidedly divided. Christopher Chadman was panned and Joan Copeland was highly praised.

After Broadway. A lavish production known as *Pal Joey '78* opened at the AHMANSON THEATRE, Los Angeles, on 4/21/78. 136 PERFORMANCES. PRESENTED BY: Center Theatre Group; PRODUCER: Robert Fryer; ADAPTED BY: Jerome Chodorov & Mark Bramble; DIRECTOR: Michel Kidd (he had replaced Gower Champion); CHOREOGRAPHER: Claude Thompson (he had also replaced Gower Champion); SETS: Robert Randolph; COSTUMES: Robert Fletcher; MUSICAL DIRECTOR: John Myles. *Cast:* JOEY: Clifton Davis; VERA: Lena Horne; ALSO WITH: Josephine Premice, Louisa Flaningam, Norman Matlock, Marjorie Barnes, John La Motta.

HALF MOON THEATRE, London; then it transferred to the West End, to the ALBERY THEATRE, 9/25/80 (succeeding the revival of *Oliver!*). *Cast:* Sian Phillips, Denis Lawson, Danielle Carson.

GOODSPEED OPERA HOUSE, Conn., 1990. DIRECTOR/CHOREOGRAPHER: Dan Siretta; SETS: Kenneth Foy; MUSICAL DIRECTOR: Tim Stella; ADDITIONAL ORCHESTRATIONS: Tim Stella & Tom Fay. *Cast:* JOEY: Peter Reardon; VERA: Florence Lacey; LINDA: Anne Allgood; LOUIS/O'BRIEN: Michael Hayward-Jones; GLADYS: Kari Nicolaisen; ALSO WITH: Maria Calabrese, Pam Klinger. "A Great Big Town," "You Mustn't Kick it Around," "I Could Write a Book," "That Terrific Rainbow," "Do it the Hard Way," "What is a Man?," "Happy Hunting Horn," "Bewitched, Bothered and Bewildered," "What Do I Care for a Dame?," Ballet, "Flower Garden of My Heart," "Zip," "Plant you Now, Dig You Later," "Den of Iniquity," "He Was Too Good to Me," "I'm Talking to My Pal," Finale.

HUNTINGTON THEATRE COMPANY, Boston, 1992. DIRECTOR: David Warren; CHOREOGRAPHER: Thommie Walsh. *Cast:* JOEY: Robert Knepper; VERA: Donna Murphy; LINDA: Judy Blazer; GLADYS: Linda Hart; VAL: Carolee Carmello; TILDA: Nora Brennan; ERNEST/TED: John Deyle; LUDLOW: David Thome; DIANE: Valerie Wright; COOKIE: Aimee Turner.

CITY CENTER, NYC, 5/4/95–5/6/95. 4 PERFORMANCES. This was part of the *Encores!* series. ADAPTED for concert version by: Terrence McNally; DIRECTOR: Lonny Price; CHOREOGRAPHER: Joey McKneely; SETS: John Lee Beatty; LIGHTING: Richard Pilbrow & Dawn Chiang; SOUND: Scott Lehrer; MUSICAL DIRECTOR: Rob Fisher; ORIGINAL ORCHESTRATIONS: Hans Spialek; NEW CAST RECORDING on DRG. *Cast:* JOEY: Peter Gallagher; VERA: Patti LuPone; LINDA: Daisy Prince; MELBA: Bebe Neuwirth; LUDLOW: Ned Eisenberg; VALERIE: Mamie Duncan-Gibbs; MIKE: Ron Orbach; GLADYS: Vicki Lewis; TERRY: Mary Ann Lamb; TILDA: Dana Moore; LOUIS: Arthur Rubin; JANET: Lynn Sterling. *Act I*: Overture, "A Great Big Town," "You Mustn't Kick it Around," "I Could Write a Book," "That Terrific Rainbow," "What is a Man?," "Happy Hunting Horn," "Bewitched," "Pal Joey," Ballet. *Act II*: Entr'acte; "Flower Garden of My Heart," "Zip," "Plant You Now, Dig You Later," "Den of Iniquity," "Do it the Hard Way," "Take Him," Finale.

FAILED BROADWAY PLANS. Livent had acquired the rights to the entire Rodgers & Hart songbook, and were going to interpolate other songs by that duo into this new revival of *Pal Joey*. Frank Galati was going to direct; Ann Reinking was going to choreograph. There was a reading in the summer of 1998, at the Festival of New Musicals, at York University, Toronto (Terrence McNally had just finished a working draft of the revised book—he had also adapted the book for the 1995 *Encores!* production). There was another, small private, reading in the fall of 1998, with Glenn Close, Liz Larsen, and Harry Connick Jr. At that stage, out-of-town tryouts were being planned for the end of 1999, then on to Broadway in 2000. However, by 2/27/99 it was still in the script stage, and Livent was in trouble. The proposed revival died with Livent. By 2003 Barry & Fran Weissler had acquired an option on *Pal Joey* and were looking at the possibility of a Broadway revival to be directed by Robert Altman.

533. *Parade*

At 4 a.m., Sunday, April 27, 1913, the night watchman of the National Pencil Company factory (re-named Scripto for the musical), in the Atlanta suburb of Marietta, Georgia, discovered the raped and strangled body of 13-year-old Mary Phagan, a pretty worker at the factory, who had been employed attaching metal eraser clasps to pencil ends. The day before, a Saturday and Confederate Memorial Day (there was a parade), she'd come to pick up $1.80 back pay from Leo Frank, the factory manager, a workaholic, tense, bespectacled Jew married only a few years to Atlanta girl Lucille. He had come down from Brooklyn to take over the job. Conley, the illiterate black sweeper at the factory, was the only witness against Leo, and the jury believed him. The case became world-famous, and the governor commuted the sentence from death to life imprisonment after listening to Mrs. Frank's pleas. At midnight on Aug. 16, 1915, Leo was dragged from his bed in the state penitentiary at Milledgeville, by 25 armed men calling themselves Knights of Mary Phagan, and hanged from an oak tree in Marietta. This was a very pleasing turn of events to many folk in Georgia. Leo's widow stayed in Atlanta, working in a clothing store. Governor Slaton's career was finished. 12 years later Conley was shot while engineering a burglary. Those are the facts.

Before Broadway. In 1996 Hal Prince's daughter, Daisy Prince, directed Jason Robert Brown's *Songs for a New World*. When Alfred Uhry brought the Leo Frank idea to Mr. Prince, Mr. Prince immediately knew it was for him, and that Brent Carver must play Leo. Hal Prince announced on 3/27/97 that he would direct. Stephen Sondheim was asked to write the score, but turned it down. Later in 1997 a six-week workshop was done in Toronto, with several actors who would go to Broadway: Evan Pappas, Brent Carver, Jeff Edgerton, Herndon Lackey, Don Chastain, Rufus Bonds Jr., Carolee Carmello, and Jessica Molaskey. A reading took place in 6/97, in New York, with Matthew Broderick, Evan Pappas, and Carolee Carmello. There was another workshop in New York, on 9/8/97; and on 10/15/97, 10/16/97, and 10/17/97 three private performances were given in Toronto. A 1998 tour was planned, followed by a fall 1998 Broadway opening, but that didn't happen. It was then scheduled for 1/99. Broadway rehearsals began on 9/14/98. It was due to be a limited run only, through 2/28/99.

The Broadway Run. VIVIAN BEAUMONT THEATRE, 12/17/98–2/28/99. 39 previews from 11/12/98. 85 PERFORMANCES. PRESENTED BY Lincoln Center Theatre, in association with Livent (U.S.); MUSIC/LYRICS/ADDITIONAL ORCHESTRATIONS: Jason Robert Brown; BOOK: Alfred Uhry; CONCEIVED BY: Alfred Uhry & Harold Prince; DIRECTOR: Harold Prince; CHOREOGRAPHER: Patricia Birch; SETS: Riccardo Hernandez; COSTUMES: Judith Dolan; LIGHTING: Howell Binkley; SOUND: Jonathan Deans; MUSICAL SUPERVISOR/MUSICAL DIRECTOR: Eric Stern; ORCHESTRATIONS: Don Sebesky; CAST RECORDING on RCA Victor, made on 3/1/99 and released on 4/27/99; PRESS: Philip Rinaldi; CASTING: Beth Russell & Mark Simon, Daniel Swee; GENERAL MANAGER: Steven C. Callahan; COMPANY MANAGER: Mala Yee Mosher; STAGE MANAGER: Clayton Phillips; ASSISTANT STAGE MANAGERS: Lisa Dawn Cave & Joshua Halperin. *Cast:* YOUNG SOLDIER: Jeff Edgerton; AIDE: Don Stephenson; ASSISTANT: Melanie Vaughan; OLD SOLDIER: Don Chastain; LUCILLE SELIG FRANK: Carolee Carmello; LEO FRANK: Brent Carver; HUGH DORSEY: Herndon Lackey; GOVERNOR JOHN M. SLATON: John Hickok; SALLY SLATON: Anne Torsiglieri; FRANKIE EPPS: Kirk McDonald; MARY PHAGAN: Christy Carlson Romano; IOLA STOVER: Brooke Sunny Moriber; JIM CONLEY: Rufus Bonds Jr.; J.N. STARNES: Peter Samuel; OFFICER IVEY: Tad Ingram; NEWT LEE: Ray Aranha; PRISON GUARD: Randy Redd; MRS. PHAGAN: Jessica Molaskey; LIZZIE PHAGAN: Robin Skye; FLOYD MacDANIEL: J.B. Adams; BRITT CRAIG: Evan Pappas; TOM WATSON: John Leslie Wolfe; ANGELA: Angela Lockett; RILEY: J.C. Montgomery; LUTHER ROSSER: J.B. Adams; FIDDLIN' JOHN: Jeff Edgerton; JUDGE ROAN: Don Chastain; NURSE: Adinah Alexander; MONTEEN: Abbi Hutcherson; ESSIE: Emily Klein; MR. PEAVY: Don Stephenson; ENSEMBLE: Adinah Alexander, Duane Boutte, Diana Brownstone, Thursday Farrar, Will Gartshore, Abbi Hutcherson, Tad Ingram, Emily Klein, Angela Lockett, Megan McGinnis, J.C. Montgomery, Brooke Sunny Moriber, Randy Redd, Joel Robertson, Peter Samuel, Robin Skye, Don Stephenson, Bill Szobody, Anne Torsiglieri, Melanie Vaughan, Wysandria Woolsey. *Understudies:* Leo: Jeff Edgerton & Don Stephenson; Lucille: Jessica Molaskey & Anne Torsiglieri; Sally: Robin Skye & Diana Brownstone; Mary: Brooke Sunny Moriber & Abbi Hutcherson; Craig: Jeff Edgerton & Randy Redd; Mrs. Phagan: Adinah Alexander & Melanie Vaughan; Angela: Thursday Farrar; Young Soldier/Epps: Will Gartshore & Randy Redd; Guard: Will Gartshore; Peavey: Will Gartshore & Joel Robertson; Old Soldier/Judge: Peter Samuel & Tad Ingram; Dorsey/Watson/Governor: Peter Samuel & Don Stephenson; Rosser: Tad Ingram & Joel Robertson; Ivey/Starnes: Joel Robertson; Conley/Lee: J.C. Montgomery & Duane Boutte; Iola/Monteen/Essie: Megan McGinnis; Nurse/Lizzy/Assistant: Megan McGinnis & Wysandria Woolsey; Riley: Duane Boutte; Aide: Joel Robertson & Will Gartshore. *Swings:* Rob Ashford, Joel Robertson, Will Gartshore, Megan McGinnis, Wysandria Woolsey. *Orchestra:* CONCERTMASTER: Rick Dolan; VIOLINS/VIOLAS: Karen Milne & Mia Wu; CELLI: Sarah Carter & Chungsun Kim; WOODWINDS: Chuck Wilson, Rick Heckman, Ed Matthew, Mark Thrasher; TRUMPETS: Terry Szor & Alec Holten;

TENOR TROMBONE: Vernon Post; STRING BASS/TUBA: Ron Raffio; FRENCH HORNS: John David Smith & Jill Williamson; GUITAR: Jack Cavari; DRUMS: Tom Partington; PERCUSSION: Dean Thomas; KEYBOARDS: Henry Aronson. *Act I*: *Scene 1* By an oak tree in a field near Marietta, Georgia; April 26, 1863, during the Civil War; immediate flash forward to April 26, 1913 and a Confederate memorial Day Parade; PROLOGUE: "The Old Red Hills of Home" (Young Soldier, Old Soldier, Ensemble), ANTHEM: "Dream of Atlanta" (Ensemble); *Scene 2* Leo & Lucille's bedroom; *Scene 3* The parade: "How Can I Call This Home?" (Leo & Ensemble), "The Picture Show" (Epps & Mary); *Scene 4* Leo's office and Leo's home (split scene): "Leo at Work" (Leo)/"What Am I Waiting For?" (Lucille); *Scene 5* The Frank home; early next morning; *Scene 6* Police station; factory basement: Interrogation: "I am trying to remember..." (Newt); *Scene 7* Outside McDaniel's Saloon in Atlanta; garbage alley: "Big News!" (Craig); *Scene 8* Solicitor Dorsey's office; *Scene 9* Prison; *Scene 10* Mary Phagan's funeral: "There is a Fountain" (traditional hymn by William Cowper, melody by Lowell Mason, 1772)/"It Don't Make Sense" (Epps & Ensemble), "Watson's Lullaby" (Watson); *Scene 11* Dorsey settles on Leo as the suspect: "Somethin' Ain't Right" (Dorsey); *Scene 12* Dorsey cooks up evidence against Leo: "Real Big News" (Craig, Reporters, Ensemble); *Scene 13* Lucille hounded by reporters; *Scene 14* The Frank home: "You Don't Know This Man" (Lucille); *Scene 15* Prison; *Scene 16* Prison visitation room; *The Trial* (Finale Act I): PART I: "It is Time Now" (Fiddlin' John, Watson, Ensemble); PART II: "Twenty Miles from Marietta" (Dorsey); PART III: Frankie's Testimony (Epps, Mary, Watson, Ensemble); PART IV: "The Factory Girls"/"Come up to My Office" (Iola, Essie, Monteen, Leo); PART V: Newt Lee's Testimony (Newt & Ensemble); PART VI: "My Child Will Forgive Me" (Mrs. Phagan); PART VII: "That's What He Said" (Conley & Ensemble); PART VIII: Leo's Statement: "It's hard to speak my heart" (Leo); PART IX: Closing Statements & Verdict (Ensemble). *Act II*: *Scene 1* Leo is condemned: "It Goes On and On" (Craig), "A Rumblin' and a Rollin'" (Riley, Angela, Newt, Conley); *Scene 2* Prison: "Do it Alone" (Lucille); *Scene 3* A tea-dance at Governor Slaton's mansion: "Pretty Music" (Governor); *Scene 4* Judge Roan writes a letter: "Letter to the Governor" (Judge); *Scene 5* Prison; late at night: "This is Not Over Yet" (Leo, Lucille, Factory Girls, Newt); *Scene 6* Interviews with Factory Girls and Newt Lee; *Scene 7* Chain gang: Blues: "Feel the Rain Fall" (Conley & Ensemble); *Scene 8* Crowd scene: "Where Will You Stand When the Flood Comes?" (Watson, Dorsey, Ensemble); *Scene 9* New minimum-security prison: "All the Wasted Time" (Leo & Lucille); *Scene 10* Prison; that night; *Scene 11* Early next morning, Marietta: "Sh'ma" (Leo); Finale: Confederate Memorial Day parade, Atlanta: "The Old Red Hills of Home" (Ensemble).

Broadway reviews were divided, but most were favorable. The limited run was changed to an open-ended run (it still ended on 2/28/99, as it happened). The production lost $5.5 million. The show won Tonys for score and book, and was nominated for musical, direction of a musical, choreography, sets, orchestrations, and for Carolee Carmello and Brent Carver.

After Broadway. TOUR. Opened at the Fox Theatre, Atlanta, 6/13/00–6/19/00. PRESENTED BY Chris Manos; DIRECTOR: Harold Prince; CHOREOGRAPHER: Patricia Birch; SETS: Riccardo Hernandez; COSTUMES: Judith Dolan; LIGHTING: Howell Binkley; MUSICAL DIRECTOR: Jason Robert Brown. *Cast:* LEO: David Pittu; LUCILLE: Andrea Burns; MRS. PHAGAN: Adinah Alexander; NEWT: Ray Aranha; MARY: Kristen Cullen; YOUNG SOLDIER/FIDDLIN' JOHN: Jeff Edgerton; OLD SOLDIER/ROAN: Donald Grody; GOVERNOR: Rick Hilsabeck; FRANKIE: Daniel Frank Kelly; JIM: Keith Byron Kirk; BRITT: Randy Redd; HUGH: Peter Samuel; LUTHER/FLOYD: David Vosburgh; WATSON: John Leslie Wolfe; ESSIE: Emily Klein; ENSEMBLE: Mimi Bessette, Diana Brownstone, David Dannehl, Raissa Katona.

534. *Pardon Our French*

Before Broadway. It started in 1949 as a small revue in California called *A la Carte*, starring Gale Robbins and Bill Shirley. This mutated into an Olsen & Johnson musical revue, *Tsk, Tsk, Tsk, Paree*, with most of the actors from *A la Carte* (but not Gale Robbins), as well as the musical numbers. A problem was that Ole & Chic were by now outdated. It opened in San Diego 4/17/50, sans Ole Olsen (who had broken his leg four days before in a car crash), and finally got to Broadway as *Pardon Our French*.

The Broadway Run. BROADWAY THEATRE, 10/5/50–1/6/51. 100 PERFORMANCES. PRESENTED BY Olsen & Johnson; MUSIC: Victor Young; ADDITIONAL MUSIC/MUSICAL DIRECTOR: Harry Sukman; LYRICS: Edward Heyman; ADDITIONAL LYRICS/SKETCHES: Olsen & Johnson; DIRECTOR: unbilled; CHOREOGRAPHERS: Ernst & Maria Matray; SETS: Albert Johnson; COSTUMES: Jack Mosser; ORCHESTRAL & CHORAL ARRANGEMENTS: Al Woodbury, Ruby Raskin, Fran Frey; PRESS: Samuel J. Friedman & Ted Isaacs; COMPANY MANAGER: John J. Garrity; STAGE MANAGERS: Dennis Murray, Howard Joslin, Walter Russell. *Act I: Scene 1* "Pardon Our French" (m: Harry Sukman; l: Olsen & Johnson): THE STAGE HAND: Phil Terry; THE NEWSBOY: Fred Curt; THE DANDIES: Robert Rossellat & Richard Wyatt; LADIES IN RED: Christine Petersen & Joy Walker; THE POST CARD VENDOR: Phil Gerard; THE TOURISTS: Richard Cahill, Carolyn Wells, Pepper Cole; THE APACHES: Gloria Stone & Brahm Van Den Berg; THE WAITERS: Jack Monts & George Tomal; THE SHADOW DANCER: George Zoritch (9); DANCERS & SINGERS; *Scene 2* Street Scene: THEMSELVES: Olsen & Johnson (1) ☆; THE QUIZZER: June Johnson (4); THE QUIZZED: Bill Shirley (5); THE LITTLE MOTHER: Chickie Johnson; THE PLEADER: Phil Terry; THE MODEL: Sandra Insel; THE WINNER: Millicent Roy; THE VENDOR: Bill Kay; THE PENN-STATERS: Marjorie Milliard & Charles Young; THE SHADY CHARACTERS: Ivor Boden & Jack Zlik; THE WHIZ: George Day; THE CHASERS: Iris Burton, Christine Petersen, Gloria Braun; *Scene 3* No. 96 rue Blondel (a man is about to score with a girl in a bawdy house on rue Blondel; a cop bursts in on them; the girl explains that the client is her brother, and she has given him a gift of suspenders): THE BOY: Leo Anthony; THE GIRL: Denise Darcel (2); THE MAID: June Johnson (4); THE FRIEND: Chickie Johnson; ANOTHER FRIEND: Robert Rossellat; THE PATRONS: Olsen & Johnson (1) ☆; THE WATCHERS: David Collyer, Nina Varela (12), J.C. Olsen (8); *Scene 4* "There's No Man Like a Snowman." Sung & danced by Helene Stanley (6). SCHOOLGIRLS: Gloria Braun, Pepper Cole, Christine Petersen, Salli Sorvo, Gloria Stone, Joy Walker, Carolyn Wells; SNOWMEN: Richard Cahill, Fred Curt, Robert Rossellat, George Tomal, Brahm Van den Berg, Richard Wyatt, Steve Kochanski, Charles Young; *Scene 5* Life of a Salesman: SALESMEN: Marty May (3), Bill Shirley (5), Phil Terry; CLICK, CLICK: Chickie Johnson; MAN IN HIDING: George Day; *Scene 6* "I Ought to Know More About You." Sung by Fay De Witt (11), Bill Shirley (5), and Les Huit Chanteuses (13). THE COLUMNISTS: Carolyn Wells & Richard Clayton; THE WIFE: Nina Varela (12); THE HUSBAND: Bill Kay; THE MAN IN RED: Fred Curt; THE MAN FROM HOME: George Tomal; THE CHASTE: Marion Konyot; THE REPORTER: Robert Konyot; *Scene 7* An Evening with Marie Antoinette (set in her bedroom): MAID: Helene Stanley (6); MARIE: June Johnson (4); GENTLEMAN CALLERS: Leo Anthony, Richard Wyatt, Bill Shirley (5); PAGES: Bill Kay & Leo Anthony; TRUMPETERS: Sandra Insel & Millicent Roy; LOUIS XVI: Chic Johnson (1) ☆; HIS OTHER SELF: Phil Terry; HIS SHADOW: Charles Young; LORD CALVERT: Walter Russell; SOLDIERS: The Six Mighty Atoms (George Day, Ivor Boden, Charles Young, Steve Kochanski, Teddy Kiss, Jack Zlik); THE VICTOR: Marty May (3); LADIES OF THE COURT: Chickie Johnson, Millicent Roy, Marjorie Milliard; *Scene 8* The Konyots (Robert & Marion): THE MODELS: Cynthia Cavanaugh, Felice Ingersoll, Jackson Jourdan, Diana Laye, June St. Clair, Helen L. Thompson; THE VOICE: Stacey Scott; *Scene 9* "Venezia and Her Three Lovers" (a ballet by Ernst Matray): PROLOGUE: THE LOVERS: George Zoritch (9), Richard Cahill, Brahm Van den Berg; THE GONDOLIER: Chic Johnson (1) ☆; BALLET: VENEZIA: Patricia Denise (7); THE TAILOR: Robert Rossellat; THE FIRST LOVER: George Zoritch (9); THE SECOND LOVER: Richard Cahill; THE THIRD LOVER: Brahm Van den Berg; THE DRUNKARD: Phil Terry; *Scene 10* Marty May (3); *Scene 11* "A Face in the Crowd." Sung by Bill Shirley (5). 1ST POLICEMAN: George Zoritch (9); THE SEEKER: Bill Shirley (5); ALSO SEEKING: June Johnson (4); THE FACE: Patricia Denise (7); THE APACHE CHIEF: Leo Anthony; 2ND POLICEMAN: David Collyer; THE STROLLERS: Joan Bonomo, Margot Carmen, Bunny Lane; OTHER APACHES: Richard Cahill, Robert Rossellat, Phil Gerard, Richard Wyatt, Phil Terry; THE HUNTERS: Chic Johnson (1) ☆ & Marty May (3); THE WHISTLER: J.C. Olsen (8); THE

WHIZ: George Day; THE SINISTER ONE: Leo Anthony; THE SHAKER: Phil Terry; THE STREET CLEANER: Robert Rossellat; THE LOSER: June Johnson (4); THE PAGES: Ivor Boden, Charles Young, Teddy Kiss, Steve Kochanski; THE BALLERINA: Patricia Denise (7); CORPS DE BALLET: Joan Bonomo, Gloria Braun, Pepper Cole, Chris Petersen, Salli Sorvo, Gloria Stone, Joy Walker, Carolyn Wells. *Act II: Scene 1* "I'm Gonna Make a Fool Out of April." Sung by Bill Shirley (5) & Helene Stanley (6)]. THE GIRLS WITH UMBRELLAS: Gloria Stone, Pepper Cole, Joy Walker, Carolyn Wells; THE GENDARMES: Robert Rossellat, Brahm Van den Berg, Richard Wyatt, Richard Cahill; BOY: Bill Shirley (5); GIRL: Helene Stanley (6); PARISIENNES: Chickie Johnson, Fay De Witt (12), Cecile Descant, Margot Carmen, Bunny Lane, Joan Rodgers, Stacey Scott, Salli Sorvo, Gloria Braun, Joan Bonomo, Iris Burton, Felice Ingersoll, Sandra Insel, Diana Laye, Millicent Roy, June St. Clair, Helen L. Thompson; PARISIANS: Phil Gerard, Edward Andrews, Robert Arnold, David Collyer, Walter Russell, Harry Snow, Leo Anthony, George Tomal, Phil Terry, Jack Monts; *Scene 2* "The Flower Song" [Chic Johnson (1) ☆ & Marty May (3)]; *Scene 3* Tourist Service: THE VISITING ROTARIANS: Chic Johnson (1) ☆ & Marty May (3); MISS INFORMATION: June Johnson (4); THE COUNTERMAN: David Collyer; BEAUTY ON A BINGE: Marjorie Milliard; THE PETITE GIRL: Chickie Johnson; BIG JOHN: Robert Arnold; LITTLE JOHN: Ivor Boden; ALONG CAME LAUGHING WATER: J.C. Olsen (8); MR. POP-UP: Phil Terry; MR. LACK-LUSTRE: Bill Kay; MR. MYSTERY: John Ciampa; *Scene 4* "Dolly from the Folies Bergere" (m: Harry Sukman; l: Olsen & Johnson). Sung by Denise Darcel (2)]. THE BLUEBEARDS: Fred Curt, George Tomal, Brahm Van den Berg; THE MIDINETTES: Margot Carmen, Chickie Johnson, Bunny Lane; *Scene 5* A Night on the *Ile de France* (on an ocean liner during a heavy passage, and the consequent seasickness): THE PASSENGER: Chic Johnson (1) ☆; THE PURSER: Leo Anthony; MRS. TACIT: June Johnson (4); THE TOURISTS: Phil Terry, Bill Kay, J.C. Olsen (8), Marjorie Milliard, Ivor Boden, George Day, Steve Kochanski, Charles Young; *Scene 6* "The Poker-Polka:" THE GENTLEMAN: Bill Shirley (5); THE PAGES: Ivor Boden & Steve Kochanski; THE GAMBLERS: Edward Andrews, Richard Cahill, Fred Curt, Jack Monts, Robert Rossellat, George Tomal, Brahm Van den Berg, Richard Wyatt; LADIES OF THE CASINO: Joan Bonomo, Gloria Braun, Pepper Cole, Christine Petersen, Gloria Stone, Salli Sorvo, Joy Walker, Carolyn Wells; THE POLKA DANCERS: Lubov Roudenko (10) & George Zoritch (9); THE LADY IN RICKSHA: June Johnson (4); Les Huit Chanteuses (13) & Showgirls; *Scene 7* Olsen & Johnson (1) ☆ and Nina Varela (12); *Scene 8* Finale (Entire Company).

ALSO WITH: Howard Joslin; SHOWGIRLS: Orlando Merdene, Helene Perry, Cynthia Cavanaugh, Felice Ingersoll, Sandra Insel, Jackson Jourdan, Diana Laye, Millicent Roy, June St. Clair, Helen L. Thompson; DANCERS: Edward Andrews, Joan Bonomo, Iris Burton, Gloria Braun, Richard Cahill, Pepper Cole, Fred Curt, Phil Gerard, Jack Monts, Christine Petersen, Salli Sorvo, Gloria Stone, George Tomal, Brahm Van den Berg, Joy Walker, Carolyn Wells, Richard Wyatt; SINGERS: Robert Arnold, Margot Carmen, Cecile Descant, Bunny Lane, Joan Rodgers, Walter Russell, Stacey Scott, Harry Snow.

Reviews were mixed, but, on the whole, not good. The production vacationed 12/17/50–12/24/50.

535. *Park*

Described as a play with music, it is really a genuine musical. Set in the present, in spring, in a park. Four members of a family come together as strangers in a park, and discover in each other their common human and emotional needs.

Before Broadway. *Park* had its world premiere at CENTER STAGE, BALTIMORE, on 2/25/70. 32 PERFORMANCES. It was aided by a grant from the National Endowment for the Arts. It had the same basic crew as for the subsequent Broadway run, except SETS: Jason Phillips; COSTUMES: Ritchie M. Spencer; LIGHTING: C. Mitch Rogers. It had the same cast, except YOUNG MAN: Ted Leplat.

The Broadway Run. JOHN GOLDEN THEATRE, 4/22/70–4/25/70. 5 previews. 5 PERFORMANCES. PRESENTED BY Edward Padula, a division of Eddie Bracken Ventures; MUSIC: Lance Mulcahy; LYRICS/BOOK: Paul

Cherry; DIRECTOR: John Stix; CHOREOGRAPHER: Lee Theodore; SETS/COSTUMES: Peter Harvey; LIGHTING: Martin Aronstein; SOUND: John Goodson; MUSICAL DIRECTOR/ARRANGEMENTS: Oscar Kosarin; PRESS: Marc Olden; GENERAL MANAGER: Helen Richards; COMPANY MANAGER: Peter Neufeld; PRODUCTION STAGE MANAGER: Henry Garrard; ASSISTANT STAGE MANAGER: Robert Tucker. **Cast:** YOUNG MAN: Don Scardino (4) ☆; YOUNG WOMAN: Joan Hackett (1) ☆; MAN: David Brooks (3) ☆; WOMAN: Julie Wilson (2) ☆. **Park Band:** BANDLEADER/ELECTRIC PIANO: Oscar Kosarin; FLUTE: Richard Cooper; PERCUSSION: Bernie Karl; GUITAR: Rick Loewus; BASS: Bruce Scott; FRENCH HORN: Gregory Squires. **Act I:** "All the Little Things in the World Are Waiting" (Young Man), "Hello is the Way Things Begin" (Young Woman), "Bein' a Kid" (Young Man & Young Woman), "Elizabeth" (Man), "He Talks to Me" (Woman & Man), "Tomorrow Will Be the Same" (Quartet), "One Man" (Woman), "Park" ("A Park is for People") (Young Man). **Act II:** "I Want it Just to Happen" (Young Woman), "I Can See" (Woman), "Compromise" (Young Man), "Jamie" (Young Man & Man), "Tomorrow Will Be the Same" (reprise) (Ensemble), "I'd Marry You Again" (Woman & Man), "Bein' a Kid" (reprise) (Quartet), "Park" ("A Park is for People") (reprise) (Quartet).

Reviewers were not unkind, but if you read them you stayed away from *Park*, and people did.

After Broadway. EQUITY LIBRARY THEATRE, NYC, 11/11/71–11/28/71. 22 PERFORMANCES. DIRECTOR: Bick Goss; SETS: Billy Puzo; COSTUMES: Paulette Olson; LIGHTING: Art Grand; MUSICAL DIRECTOR/ARRANGEMENTS: John L. De Main; PIANIST: John R. Williams. The characters now had names: JAMIE: Don Amendolia; ELIZABETH: Lynn Archer; AUSTIN: John High; SARA: Louise Shaffer.

536. *Park Avenue*

A musical satire. Madge is a wealthy young Park Avenue sophisticate about to marry young and charming Charleston, SC, boy Ned at the Long Island summer home of Madge's mother, Sybil and her fourth husband Ogden. Guests include all of Sybil's ex-husbands (Charles, Reggie and Richard) and their current spouses, all of which appalls Ned. Then partners begin swapping, until one ex-husband selects his own daughter (this scenario was changed, but only during the run, to an 18-year-old unrelated person). Fortunately the whole thing ends happily.

Before Broadway. This was Ira Gershwin's last original Broadway show. It opened on 9/23/46, at the Colonial Theatre, Boston, where it ran for two weeks. After this Eugene Loring was replaced by Helen Tamiris as choreographer (assisted by Daniel Nagrin). In the cast a new character, Mr. Meachem, a divorce lawyer, was created, played by Jed Prouty, but Mr. Prouty was replaced by Ralph Riggs, then J. Pat O'Malley, and finally by David Wayne prior to the Broadway opening.

The Broadway Run. SHUBERT THEATRE, 11/4/46–1/4/47. 72 PERFORMANCES. PRESENTED BY Max Gordon; MUSIC: Arthur Schwartz; LYRICS: Ira Gershwin; BOOK: Nunnally Johnson & George S. Kaufman; BASED ON Nunnally Johnson's short story "Holy Matrimony," published in the *Saturday Evening Post* in 1933; BOOK DIRECTOR: George S. Kaufman; CHOREOGRAPHER: Helen Tamiris; ASSISTANT CHOREOGRAPHER: Daniel Nagrin; SETS/LIGHTING: Donald Oenslager; COSTUMES: Tina Leser; LEONORA CORBETT'S GOWNS: Mainbocher; MUSICAL DIRECTOR: Charles Sanford; ORCHESTRATIONS: Don Walker; VOCAL DIRECTOR/MUSICAL ADAPTATION FOR DANCES: Clay Warnick; PRESS: Nat Dorfman & Martha Dreiblatt; PRODUCTION SUPERVISOR: Arnold Saint Subber; GENERAL MANAGER: Ben A. Boyar; COMPANY MANAGER: Michael Goldreyer; STAGE MANAGERS: Barbara Adams & Randell Henderson. **Cast:** CARLTON: Byron Russell; NED SCOTT: Ray McDonald (7); MADGE BENNETT: Martha Stewart (6); OGDEN BENNETT: Arthur Margetson (2) ☆; MRS. SYBIL BENNETT: Leonora Corbett (1) ☆; CHARLES CROWELL: Robert Chisholm (10); MRS. ELSA CROWELL: Marthe Errolle; REGGIE FOX: Charles Purcell (9); MRS. MYRA FOX: Ruth Matteson (8); RICHARD NELSON: Raymond Walburn (3); MRS. BETTY NELSON: Mary Wickes (4); TED WOODS: Harold Mattox; MRS. LAURA WOODS: Dorothy Bird; JAMES MEREDITH: William Skipper; MRS. BEVERLY

MEREDITH: Joan Mann; MR. MEACHEM: David Wayne (5), *George Keane*; FREDDIE COLEMAN: Wilson Smith, *Gilbert O. Herman*; CAROLE BENSWANGER: Virginia Gordon; BRENDA STOKES: Adelle Rasey; BRENDA FOLLANSBEE: Sherry Shadburne; BRENDA FOLLANSBEE-STOKES: Carol Chandler; BRENDA FOLLANSBEE-STOKES-FOLLANSBEE: Betty Ann Lynn; BRENDA CADWALLADER: Kyle MacDonnell; BRENDA STUYVESANT: Eileen Coffman; BRENDA CATHCART: June Graham; BRENDA CATHCART-CATHCART: Betty Low; BRENDA KERR: Virginia Morris; BRENDA KERR-KERR-KERR: Judi Blacque; BRENDA QUINCY ADAMS: Gloria Anderson; BRENDA WRIGHT JR., SR., III: Margaret Gibson. **Act I:** The terrace of the Bennett home; lunchtime: "Tomorrow is the Time" (Laura & Bridesmaids), "For the Life of Me" (Ned & Madge), Dance (Ned, Madge, James, Ted, Bridesmaids), "The Dew Was on the Rose" (Sybil, Ogden, Reggie, Richard, Charles), "Don't Be a Woman if You Can" (Betty, Elsa, Myra), "Sweet Nevada" (Sybil & Meachem), In the Courtroom (dance): PLAINTIFFS: Dorothy Bird, Joan Mann, Betty Low; JUDGE: David Wayne; COURT ATTENDANTS: William Skipper & Harold Mattox; OTHER PLAINTIFFS: All Brendas; "There's No Holding Me" (Madge & Ned), "The Dew Was on the Rose" (reprise) (Sybil & Ogden), "There's Nothing Like Marriage for People" (Entire Company). **Act II:** The drawing-room; dinner time: "Hope for the Best" (Bridesmaids, Ted, James), "My Son-in-Law" (Sybil, Madge, Richard), "Land of Opportunities" (Ogden, Richard, Reggie, Charles), Dance (Laura, Beverly, All Brendas), "Goodbye to All That" (Madge & Ned) [the hit], "Echo" (dance) (Ted, Laura, James, Beverly, Bridesmaids), Finale (Entire Company).

Broadway reviews were not good. The show failed primarily because of its content — divorce — which wasn't a very popular subject back then.

After Broadway. THEATRE TEN TEN (99-seat theatre at 1010 Park Avenue, NYC, also known as Theatre 1010), 5/7/99–6/6/99. 1 preview on 5/6/99. 19 PERFORMANCES. This was the first professional revival of *Park Avenue*. A script had been recovered from George Kaufman's family. Using the original producers' papers (now in the Max Gordon Collection at Princeton University), and with the approval of the Gershwin Trust, the creative team re-worked the script. Allan Greene, who was musical director/arranger, recreated the score from piano-vocal selections. PRESENTED BY Judith Jarosz & David Fuller; DIRECTOR: David Fuller; CHOREOGRAPHER: Barbra Brandt. **Cast:** SYBIL: Judith Jarosz; NED: Luke Walrath; MADGE: Jennifer Stafford.

537. *Passion*

A 1 hour 50 minute chamber opera, without intermission. Set in 1863. It opens in Milan, with army officer Giorgio in bed with his mistress Clara, a beautiful married woman. Later he is transferred to a remote army outpost where he meets Fosca, his captain's sickly, unattractive cousin, who relentlessly pursues him, offering him "love without reason." This terrifies Giorgio, and he writes to Clara, asking her to marry him. But she can't leave her child, and so Giorgio surrenders to Fosca.

The Broadway Run. PLYMOUTH THEATRE, 5/9/94–1/7/95. 52 previews from 3/24/94. 280 PERFORMANCES. PRESENTED BY The Shubert Organization, Capital Cities/ABC, Roger Berlind, and Scott Rudin, by arrangement with Lincoln Center Theatre; MUSIC/LYRICS: Stephen Sondheim; BOOK/DIRECTOR: James Lapine; BASED ON the 1981 movie *Passione d'amore*, directed by Ettore Scola, which was based on the 1869 novel *Fosca*, by Igino Tarchetti; SETS: Adrianne Lobel; COSTUMES: Jane Greenwood; LIGHTING: Beverly Emmons; SOUND: Otts Munderloh; MUSICAL DIRECTOR: Paul Gemignani; ORCHESTRATIONS: Jonathan Tunick; CAST RECORDING on Broadway Angel; PRESS: Philip Rinaldi, James L.L. Morrison, William Schelble, Dennis Crowley, Kathy Haberthur; CASTING: Wendy Ettinger; GENERAL MANAGEMENT: Marvin A. Krauss Associates; COMPANY MANAGER: Nina Skriloff; PRODUCTION STAGE MANAGER: Beverley Randolph; STAGE MANAGER: Mireya Hepner; ASSISTANT STAGE MANAGER: Frank Lombardi. **Cast:** CLARA: Marin Mazzie (3); GIORGIO BACHETTI: Jere Shea (2) ☆; COL. RICCI: Gregg Edelman (4); DR. TAMBOURRI: Tom Aldredge (5) [William Duff-Griffin played this role during Broadway previews]; LT. TORASSO: Francis Ruivivar; SGT. LOMBARDI, THE COOK: Marcus Olson; LT. BARRI, VETERINARIAN: William Parry; MAJ. RIZZOLI: Cris Groenendaal, *T.J. Meyers*; PVT. AUGENTI: George Dvorsky, *John Antony*; FOSCA: Donna Murphy (1) ☆, *Linda Balgord* (during Miss Murphy's absences, about 18 performances); FOSCA'S MOTHER: Linda Balgord; FOSCA'S FATHER: John Leslie Wolfe, *Andy Umberger*, LUDOVIC: Matthew Porretta, *Gregg Edelman*; MISTRESS: Juliet Lambert, *Colleen Fitzpatrick*. **Understudies:** Giorgio: Matthew Porretta & George Dvorsky; Ludovic: George Dvorsky; Fosca: Linda Balgord & Colleen Fitzpatrick; Clara: Juliet Lambert & Colleen Fitzpatrick; Mother/Mistress: Colleen Fitzpatrick; Tambourri/Father: Gibby Brand; Augenti: Frank Lombardi & Gibby Brand; Ricci: William Parry; Torasso/Rizzolli/Barri/Lombardi: John Leslie Wolfe. **Orchestra:** CONCERTMISTRESS: Suzanne Ornstein; VIOLIN: Xin Zhao; VIOLA: Sally Shumway; CELLO: Scott Ballantyne; BASS: Judith Sugarman; WOODWINDS: Dennis Anderson, John Campo, Al Regni, Les Scott; TRUMPET: Stu Satalof; HORNS: Ron Sell & Michael Ishii; KEYBOARDS: Nick Archer & Paul Ford; PERCUSSION: Thad Wheeler. *Scene 1* In bed: "Happiness" (Clara & Giorgio); *Scene 2* In the officers' mess: "First Letter" (Clara & Giorgio), "Second Letter" (Clara & Giorgio), "Third Letter" (Clara & Giorgio), "I Read" (Fosca); *Scene 3* In the garden: "Fourth Letter" (Clara & Giorgio), "Garden Sequence" (Clara); *Scene 4* The mess hall; *Scene 5* On the way to the train; Fosca's drawing room; Giorgio and Clara's bedroom: "Trio" (Giorgio, Clara, Fosca); *Scene 6* At Fosca's: "This Godforsaken Place" (Soldiers); *Scene 7* Fosca's sickroom: "I Wish I Could Forget You" (Fosca & Giorgio); *Scene 8* The poolroom: "Soldiers' Gossip" (Soldiers), "Flashback" (Mistress, Fosca, Ludovic, Colonel, Father); *Scene 9* Outdoors, far from camp: "Sunrise Letter" (Clara), "Is This What You Call Love?" (Giorgio); *Scene 10* Giorgio's bedroom; *Scene 11* In the train; at the post: "Forty Days" (Clara), "Loving You" (Fosca); *Scene 12* In Milan; *Scene 13* A Christmas party: "Farewell Letter" (Giorgio & Clara); *Scene 14* Fosca's room; a dueling ground: "No One Has Ever Loved Me" (Giorgio); *Scene 15* At a desk: Finale (Giorgio, Fosca, Company).

Broadway reviews were very divided. The show won Tonys for musical, score, book, and for Donna Murphy, and was also nominated for direction of a musical, costumes, lighting, and for Tom Aldredge, Jere Shea, and Marin Mazzie. PBS showed it on 9/8/96.

After Broadway. QUEEN'S THEATRE, London, 3/26/96–9/28/96. Previews from 3/13/96. 232 PERFORMANCES. It got divided reviews. Maria Friedman won an Olivier Award. PRESENTED BY Bill Kenwright & the Theatre Royal, Plymouth; DIRECTOR: Jeremy Sams; CHOREOGRAPHER: Jonathan Butterell. **Cast:** FOSCA: Maria Friedman; GIORGIO: Michael Ball; CLARA: Helen Hobson; TAMBOURRI: Hugh Ross; TORASSO: Simon Green; LOMBARDI: Michael Cantwell.

KENNEDY CENTER, Washington, DC, 7/20/02–8/23/02. 1 preview on 7/19/02. Press night was on 7/21/02. This production was part of the *Stephen Sondheim Celebration* series, which included *Company, Merrily We Roll Along, Sunday in the Park with George, A Little Night Music,* and *Sweeney Todd.* DIRECTOR: Eric Schaeffer. **Cast:** GIORGIO: Michael Cerveris; FOSCA: Judy Kuhn; CLARA: Rebecca Luker; TAMBOURRI: Philip Goodwin; RICCI: John Leslie Wolfe; LOMBARDI: Bob McDonald; TORASSO: Daniel Felton; BARRI: Lawrence Redmond.

RAVINIA FESTIVAL, Highland Park, Ill., 8/22/03–8/23/03. Concert. Steve Sondheim took part in the pre-concert discussion on the first night. DIRECTOR: Lonny Price. **Cast:** GIORGIO: Michael Cerveris; FOSCA: Patti LuPone; CLARA: Audra McDonald.

AMSTERDAM THEATRE, Broadway, 10/20/04 (one night only). This was a 10th-anniversary revival, in concert form, to benefit Friends in Deed. DIRECTOR: James Lapine; MUSICAL DIRECTOR: Paul Gemignani. **Cast:** CLARA: Marin Mazzie; GIORGIO: Michael Cerveris; RICCI: Malcolm Gets; TAMBOURRI: John McMartin; LOMBARDI: Timothy Gulan; BARRI: William Parry; RICCIOLI: John Jellison; AUGENTI: Alexander Gemignani; FOSCA: Donna Murphy; FOSCA'S MOTHER: Colleen Fitzpatrick; FOSCA'S FATHER: John Leslie Wolfe; LUDOVIC: Matthew Porretta; MISTRESS: Juliet Lambert.

There were plans for a 2005 concert version at Lincoln Center, part of their *American Songbook* series. **Cast:** CLARA: Audra McDonald.

Peep Show see 447
Peep Show see 447

538. *Perfectly Frank*

A revue of Frank Loesser songs, subtitled: *Frank Loesser Revived.* Jo Sullivan, Mr. Loesser's widow, narrated reminiscences of Mr. Loesser (1910–69), and the songs were entwined with this narration.

Before Broadway. It first ran at the WESTWOOD PLAYHOUSE, Los Angeles. **Cast:** Kelly Bishop, Pamela Myers.

Before Broadway Fritz Holt was replaced as director by Ron Field, but got to keep credit. A. Robert Altschuler was replaced as production stage manager by Lani Ball.

The Broadway Run. HELEN HAYES THEATRE, 11/30/80–12/13/80. 24 previews. 17 PERFORMANCES. PRESENTED BY Gladys Rackmil & Fred Levinson, in association with Emhan, Inc. (Jo Sullivan Loesser); MUSIC/LYRICS: Frank Loesser (unless otherwise stated); WRITER/CONCEPT: Kenny Solms (billing removed); DIRECTOR: Fritz Holt; CHOREOGRAPHER: Tony Stevens (with uncredited Ron Field); ASSISTANT CHOREOGRAPHER: John Calvert (uncredited); SETS/COSTUMES: John Falabella; LIGHTING: Ken Billington; SOUND: Larry Spurgeon; MUSICAL DIRECTOR: Yolanda Segovia; ORCHESTRATIONS: Bill Byers; DANCE MUSIC ARRANGEMENTS: Ronald Melrose; MUSIC CONSULTANT: Larry Grossman; PRESS: Shirley Herz Associates; CASTING: Amos Abrams & Joan Welles; GENERAL MANAGER: Leonard Soloway & Allan Francis; COMPANY MANAGER: Michael O'Rand; PRODUCTION STAGE MANAGER: Lani Ball; STAGE MANAGER: T.L. Boston; ASSISTANT STAGE MANAGER: Michael Byers. **Cast:** Andra Akers, Wayne Cilento, Jill Cook, Don Correia, David Holliday, David Ruprecht, Virginia Sandifur, Debbie Shapiro, Jo Sullivan, Jim Walton. **Standbys:** For Mr. Cilento/Mr. Correia: Bob Brubach; For Mr. Holliday/Mr. Ruprecht/Mr. Walton: Michael Byers; For Misses Akers/Shapiro/Sullivan: Emily Greenspan; For Misses Cook/Sandifur: Barbara Hanks. **Act I:** PROLOGUE (Company): "Three Cornered Tune" [from *Guys and Dolls*], "I Hear Music" (m: Burton Lane) [from the movie *Dancing on a Dime*]; SCREEN TEST—1941 (Miss Sandifur): "Kiss the Boys Goodbye" (m: Victor Schertzinger) [from the movie of the same name], "Snug as a Bug in a Rug" (m: Matt Malneck) [from the movie *The Gracie Allen Murder Case*], "The Moon of Manakoora" (m: Alfred Newman) [from the movie *The Hurricane*], "The Boys in the Backroom" (m: Frederick Hollander) [from the movie *Destry Rides Again*]; USO SHOW: "Murder, He Says" (m: Jimmy McHugh) [from the movie *Happy Go Lucky*] (Miss Cook & Mr. Cilento), "Some Like it Hot" (m: Gene Krupa & Remo Biondi) [from the movie *Some Like it Hot*], "I Don't Want to Walk without You" (m: Jule Styne) [from the movie *Sweater Girl*] (Miss Shapiro), "Roseanna" [from the movie *Roseanna McCoy*] (Mr. Walton), "I Wish I Didn't Love You So" [from the movie *The Perils of Pauline*] (Mr. Holliday), "Where Are You Now (That I Need You)?" [from the movie *Red, Hot and Blue*] (Mr. Holliday), "They're Either Too Young or Too Old" (m: Arthur Schwartz) [from the movie *Thank Your Lucky Stars*] (Miss Akers), "What Do You Do in the Infantry?" (Miss Akers & Men), "Praise the Lord and Pass the Ammunition" (Mr. Holliday), "Spring Will Be a Little Late This Year" (Miss Sullivan); DRESSING ROOM: "I Believe in You" [from *How to Succeed in Business Without Really Trying*] (Mr. Ruprecht & Men); UNDERSTUDY REHEARSAL—1948 (Mr. Correia & Miss Cook): "Make a Miracle" [from *Where's Charley?*], "My Darling, My Darling" [from *Where's Charley?*]; MANHATTAN: "My Time of Day" [from *Guys and Dolls*] (Mr. Holliday), "Two Sleepy People" (m: Hoagy Carmichael) [from the movie *Thanks for the Memory*] (Miss Akers & Mr. Ruprecht), "No Two People" [from the movie *Hans Christian Andersen*] (Mr. Correia & Miss Cook), "Baby, It's Cold Outside" [from the movie *Neptune's Daughter*] (Miss Sandifur & Mr. Walton), "Luck Be a Lady" [from *Guys and Dolls*] (Mr. Holliday), "Fugue for Tinhorns" [from *Guys and Dolls*] (Miss Shapiro, Mr. Cilento, Mr. Holliday), "Take Back Your Mink" [from *Guys and Dolls*] (Miss Sandifur), "Howd'ja Like to Love Me?" (m: Burton Lane) [from the movie *College Swing*] (Miss Cook), "The Lady's in Love with You" (m: Burton Lane) [from the movie *Some Like it Hot*] (Miss Shapiro), "Guys and Dolls" [from *Guys and Dolls*] (Company), "I've Never Been in Love Before" [from *Guys and Dolls*] (Mr. Holliday & Company). **Act II:** ENTR'ACTE: medley from the movie *Hans Christian Andersen*; RUMBLE, RUMBLE: "Rumble, Rumble, Rumble" [from the movie *The Perils of Pauline*] (Miss Shapiro, Mr. Walton, Miss Cook); MARRIAGE: "Standing on the Corner" [from *The Most Happy Fella*] (Mr. Ruprecht, Mr. Cilento, Mr. Walton), "Once in Love with Amy" [from *Where's Charley?*] (Mr. Cilento), "Marry the Man Today" [from *Guys and Dolls*] (Miss Sandifur, Miss Akers, Miss Cook), "Happy to Keep His Dinner Warm" [from *How to Succeed in Business Without Really Trying*] (Miss Sandifur), "Never Will I Marry" [from *Greenwillow*] (Mr. Walton), "Adelaide's Lament" [from *Guys and Dolls*] (Miss Akers); CASTING OFFICE—1956 [this scene was cut during previews]; ROSABELLA (FROM *The Most Happy Fella*): "Ooh, My Feet!," "I Don't Know Nothing About You" (The Letter) (Miss Sullivan & Mr. Holliday), "Somebody, Somewhere" (Miss Sullivan), "Rosabella" (Mr. Holliday), "Warm All Over" (Miss Sullivan), "Like a Woman Loves a Man" (Miss Sullivan), "My Heart is So Full of You" (Mr. Holliday); DRESSING ROOM: Central Park Duck (Miss Sullivan); BLUES: "Can't Get Out of This Mood" (m: Jimmy McHugh) [from the movie *Seven Days Leave*] (Miss Sandifur), "Luck Be a Lady" (dance) [from *Guys and Dolls*] (Miss Shapiro & Mr. Correia), "Junk Man" (m: Joseph Meyer) (Miss Shapiro); FINALE: "More I Cannot Wish You" [from *Guys and Dolls*] (Company), "If I Were a Bell" [from *Guys and Dolls*] (Miss Sandifur & Mr. Holliday), "Hoop-Dee-Do" (m: Milton Delugg) (Mr. Cilento, Miss Sandifur, Mr. Correia, Miss Cook), "Just Another Polka" (m: Milton Delugg) (Company), "The New Ashmolean Marching Society and Students' Conservatory Band" [from *Where's Charley?*] (Company), "Bubbles in the Wine" (m: Lawrence Welk) (Mr. Ruprecht), "What Are You Doing New Year's Eve?" (Mr. Holliday & Miss Shapiro), "Sposalizio" [from *The Most Happy Fella*] (Company), "Jingle, Jangle, Jingle" (m: Joseph J. Lilley) [from the movie *The Forest Rangers*] (Mr. Cilento & Mr. Correia), "Big D" [from *The Most Happy Fella*] (Miss Cook, Mr. Cilento, Mr. Correia, Miss Shapiro), "Anywhere I Wander" [from the movie *Hans Christian Andersen*] (Miss Sullivan), "Sand in My Shoes" (m: Victor Schertzinger) [from the movie *Kiss the Boys Goodbye*], "Sing a Tropical Song" (m: Jimmy McHugh) [from the movie *Happy Go Lucky*] (Mr. Ruprecht & Miss Akers), "Dolores" (m: Louis Alter) [from the movie *Las Vegas Nights*] (Mr. Holliday & Men), "Sit Down, You're Rockin' the Boat" [from *Guys and Dolls*] (Company), "Brotherhood of Man" [from *How to Succeed in Business Without Really Trying*] (Company), "On a Slow Boat to China" (Miss Sandifur), "Small Fry" (m: Hoagy Carmichael) [from the movie *Sing You Sinners*] (Miss Cook), "A Bushel and a Peck" [from *Guys and Dolls*] (Miss Akers), "Heart and Soul" (m: Hoagy Carmichael) [from the movie short *A Song is Born*] (Company).

Note: Excerpts only from each number.

Reviews were very divided, but Debbie Shapiro got raves. The TV version aired in 1/82 on Showtime, starring Cloris Leachman and David Ruprecht.

539. *Peter Pan*

Peter Pan, a flying elfin boy spirit, refuses to grow up. He lives in Never Neverland. Peter is always played by a girl. The pirate ship is the *Jolly Roger*. This 1954 production had an effete Hook.

Before Broadway. None of the previous productions (and there had been many) were musicals. The straight play first ran in LONDON, in 1904, starring Nina Boucicault. It debuted on Broadway, at the EMPIRE THEATRE, 11/6/05. 223 PERFORMANCES. *Cast:* PETER: Maude Adams; DARLING/HOOK: Ernest Lawford. Miss Adams toured with it for years, and the role became thoroughly identified with her. On 11/6/24, Charles Dillingham revived it at the KNICKERBOCKER THEATRE. 96 PERFORMANCES. *Cast:* Marilyn Miller, Leslie Banks. It had the songs "Peter Pan, I Love You" (by Robert King & Ray Henderson) and "The Sweetest Thing in Life" (m: Jerome Kern; l: B.G. "Buddy" De Sylva). Eva Le Gallienne was the next actress to become identified with the role, including it in her repertory.

THE JEAN ARTHUR PRODUCTION. IMPERIAL THEATRE, Broadway, 4/24/50–1/27/51; ST. JAMES THEATRE, 10/3/50. Total of 320 PERFORMANCES. PRESENTED BY Peter Lawrence & Roger L. Stevens; DIRECTOR: John Burrell; ASSOCIATE DIRECTOR: Wendy Toye; FLYING: Peter Foy;

SETS/LIGHTING: Ralph Alswang; COSTUMES: Motley; MUSICAL DIRECTOR: Ben Steinberg; ORCHESTRATIONS: Hershy Kay; MUSICAL CO-ORDINATOR & ARRANGER: Trude Rittman. It did have song songs in it (written by Leonard Bernstein), and incidental music by Alec Wilder. The songs were: "Who Am I?" (Wendy), "The Pirate Song" (Hook & Pirates), "Never-Land" (Mermaids), "My House" (Wendy), "Peter, Peter" (Wendy), "The Plank" (Hook & Pirates). "Captain Hook's Soliloquy" was cut before Broadway. *Cast:* PETER: Jean Arthur; HOOK/DARLING: Boris Karloff; CECCO: Nehemiah Persoff; SMEE: Joe E. Marks; INDIAN: Loren Hightower.

The 1954 musical is the most famous of all the Peter Pans. Jerome Robbins came up with idea of a play starring Mary Martin as Peter, and some incidental songs by Moose Charlap & Carolyn Leigh. Edwin Lester produced it on the West Coast, as part of his Los Angeles & San Francisco Light Opera series. But the play had problems, so Mr. Robbins, the director/choreographer (his first outing at both roles), hired Jule Styne to compose, and Betty Comden and Adolph Green to do the lyrics for six additional songs. Comden & Green also revised J.M. Barrie's original dialogue to some extent. By now, as it arrived on Broadway it was a full-fledged musical.

The Broadway Run. WINTER GARDEN THEATRE, 10/20/54–2/26/55. 149 PERFORMANCES. The Edwin Lester production, PRESENTED BY Richard Halliday; MUSIC: Mark "Moose" Charlap; ADDITIONAL MUSIC: Jule Styne; LYRICS: Carolyn Leigh; ADDITIONAL LYRICS: Betty Comden & Adolph Green; BOOK: uncredited; CONCEIVED BY/DIRECTOR/CHOREOGRAPHER: Jerome Robbins; BASED ON the 1904 London fantasy of the same name, by J.M. Barrie, which was based on his character who first appeared in the 1902 novel *The Little White Bird*; FLYING EFFECT: Joseph Kirby; FLYING SUPERVISOR: Peter Foy; SETS: Peter Larkin; COSTUMES: Motley; TECHNICAL DIRECTOR: Richard Rodda; LIGHTING: Peggy Clark; MUSICAL DIRECTOR: Louis Adrian; ORCHESTRAL ARRANGEMENTS: Albert Sendry; INCIDENTAL MUSIC: Elmer Bernstein & Trude Rittman; PRESS: Michel Mok & Peggy Phillips; GENERAL MANAGER: Herman Bernstein; COMPANY MANAGER: Abe Cohen; EXECUTIVE STAGE MANAGER: Robert Linden; STAGE MANAGER: Walter Neal; ASSISTANT STAGE MANAGER: Frank Roberts. *Cast:* WENDY DARLING: Kathy Nolan (3); JOHN DARLING: Robert Harrington; LIZA: Heller Halliday; MICHAEL DARLING: Joseph Stafford; NANA: Norman Shelly; MRS. DARLING: Margalo Gillmore (4); MR. DARLING: Cyril Ritchard (2); PETER PAN: Mary Martin (1) ☆; LION: Richard Wyatt; KANGAROO: Don Lurio, *Robert Banas*; OSTRICH: Joan Tewkesbury; SLIGHTLY: David Bean; TOOTLES: Ian Tucker; CURLY: Stanley Stenner; NIBS: Paris Theodore; CROCODILE: Norman Shelly; 1ST TWIN: Alan Sutherland, *Jackie Scholle*; 2ND TWIN: Darryl Duran; CAPTAIN HOOK: Cyril Ritchard (2); MR. SMEE, HOOK'S FIRST MATE: Joe E. Marks; TIGER LILY: Sondra Lee; CECCO: Robert Tucker, *Richard Winter*; NOODLER: Frank Lindsay; JUKES: William Burke, *Frank Bouley*; GENTLEMAN STARKEY: Robert Vanselow; MULLINS: James White; WENDY GROWN-UP: Sallie Brophy, *Ann Connolly*; JANE: Kathy Nolan; VOICE OF TINKERBELL: Jayne Rubanoff; PIRATES: William Burke (*Frank Bouley*), Chester Fisher, Frank Lindsay, Frank Marasco, John Newton, Arthur Tookoian, Robert Tucker, Robert Vanselow, James White, Richard Winter, *Lucky Kargo, Albert Linville*; INDIANS: Robert Banas, Linda Dangcil, Lisa Lang, Suzanne Luckey, Don Lurio, Robert Piper, William Sumner, Joan Tewkesbury, Richard Wyatt, *George Lake*. **Standby**: Hook/Darling: John Holland. **Understudies**: Wendy/Jane: Heller Halliday; Liza: Suzanne Luckey; Smee: Robert Piper, *Carl Erbele*; Indian: Robert Piper, *Carl Erbele*; 2nd Indian: Ronnie Lee; Lost Boy: John Smith; Tinkerbell: John Morris; Pirate: Robert Tucker. *Act I: Scene 1* The Nursery of the Darling Residence: "Tender Shepherd" (Mrs. Darling, Wendy, John, Michael), "I've Got to Crow" (Peter), "Never Neverland" (Styne; Comden & Green) (Peter) ["Neverland" was what J.M. Barrie called it; "Never Neverland" was a term coined for this production], "I'm Flying" (Peter, Wendy, John, Michael); *Scene 2* Flight to Neverland. *Act II: Scene 1* Neverland: "Pirate Song" (Hook & Pirates), "A Princely Scheme" (Hook & Pirates), "Indians!" (Tiger Lily & Indians), "Wendy" (Styne; Comden & Green) (Peter & Boys), "Another Princely Scheme" (tarantella) (Hook & Pirates), "Neverland Waltz" (Styne; Comden & Green) (Liza); *Scene 2* Path through the Woods: "I Won't Grow Up" (Peter & Boys), "Mysterious Lady" (Styne; Comden & Green)(Peter & Hook); *Scene 3* Neverland Home

Underground: "Ugg-a-Wugg" (Styne; Comden & Green) (Peter, Tiger Lily, Children, Indians), "The Pow-Wow Polka" (Styne; Comden & Green) (Peter, Tiger Lily, Children, Indians), "Distant Melody" (Styne; Comden & Green)(Peter). ***Act III**: **Scene 1** The Pirate Ship: "To the Ship" (Peter & Company), "(Captain) Hook's Waltz" (Styne; Comden & Green)(Hook & Pirates), "The Battle" (Peter, Hook, Company); **Scene 2** Path through the Woods: "I've Got to Crow" (reprise) (Peter, Liza, Company); **Scene 3** The Nursery of the Darling Residence: "Tender Shepherd" (reprise) (Wendy, John, Michael), "I Won't Grow Up" (reprise) (The Darling Family & Lost Boys); **Scene 4** The Nursery Many Years Later: "Never Never Land" (reprise) (Peter).

Note: all numbers have music by Mark Charlap, and lyrics by Carolyn Leigh, unless marked "(Styne; Comden & Green)," which means music by Jule Styne, and lyrics by Betty Comden & Adolph Green.

It got great reviews (the famous one being Walter Kerr's, in the *Herald—Tribune*; "I don't know what all the fuss is about. I always knew Mary Martin could fly"). It had a limited Broadway run because of the producer's exclusive agreement with NBC (they paid the show's producer $225,000), which was to broadcast a two-hour special performance live (with the original Broadway cast) from its Brooklyn studios. The network didn't want any stage performances to detract from the viewership of their TV show. It showed on 3/7/55, and was watched by 70 million people. The TV show was so popular that it was re-done (and re-staged), live, and aired, in color, for NBC, on 1/9/56, with only a few changes in the cast. Again it was re-staged, and videotaped in color, on NBC, and aired on 12/8/60, with the two stars and most of the original Broadway cast intact. It took Mary Martin finally to supplant Maude Adams as Peter in the minds of American theatregoers. Heller Halliday, who played Liza, was Mary Martin's 12-year-old daughter. The show won Tony Awards for stage technician (Richard Rodda), and for Mary Martin and Cyril Ritchard. It also won a Donaldson Award for Mary Martin, and two for Mr. Ritchard — best actor and supporting actor!.

After Broadway. PAPER MILL PLAYHOUSE, New Jersey, 1966. DIRECTOR: Jacques D'Amboise. **Cast**: PETER: Betsy Palmer; WENDY: Sandy Duncan; MRS. DARLING: Constance Carpenter.

540. *Peter Pan (1979 Broadway revival)*

Also called *The Boy Who Wouldn't Grow Up*.

Before Broadway. Zev Bufman was impressed with Sandy Duncan in her nightclub act, and he proposed starring her in a Broadway show of her choice. But she couldn't think of one she wanted to do. Mr. Bufman suggested *Peter Pan*, but the rights were owned by Michael Bennett, who was planning a production of his own. Mr. Bennett was persuaded to release the rights, and the show was on with Miss Duncan. It tried out in Dallas, then Atlanta, then at the Kennedy Center, Washington, DC (7/18/79–8/79). Rob Iscove, the director of Miss Duncan's nightclub act, was replaced as director and choreographer by Ron Field (who was uncredited). Camille Ranson was replaced as company manager by Robb Lady.

The Broadway Run. LUNT—FONTANNE THEATRE, 9/6/79–1/4/81. 28 previews. 551 PERFORMANCES. PRESENTED BY Zev Bufman & James M. Nederlander, in association with Jack Molthen, Spencer Tandy, J. Ronald Horowitz; MUSIC: Mark "Moose" Charlap; ADDITIONAL MUSIC: Jule Styne; LYRICS: Carolyn Leigh; ADDITIONAL LYRICS: Betty Comden & Adolph Green; BOOK: uncredited (doctored by Ron Field); BASED ON the 1904 British play by J.M. Barrie; DIRECTOR/CHOREOGRAPHER: Rob Iscove; FLYING SUPERVISOR: Foy (i.e. Garry Foy); FLYING TECHNICIAN: Julian Williams; SETS: Peter Wolf; COSTUMES: Bill Hargate; LIGHTING: Thomas Skelton; SOUND: Richard Fitzgerald; MUSICAL DIRECTOR/VOCAL DIRECTOR: Jack Lee; ORCHESTRATIONS: Ralph Burns; DANCE MUSIC ARRANGEMENTS: Wally Harper; ADDITIONAL DANCE MUSIC ARRANGEMENTS: David Krane; PRESS: Solters & Roskin; CASTING: TNI Casting (Julie Hughes & Barry Moss); PRODUCTION SUPERVISOR: Ron Field; GENERAL MANAGEMENT: Theatre Now; COMPANY MANAGER: Robb Lady; PRODUCTION STAGE MANAGER: Barbara-Mae Phillips; STAGE MANAGER: David Rubinstein; ASSISTANT STAGE MANAGER: Nelson K. Wilson. **Cast:** MICHAEL DARLING: Jonathan Ward (8); NANA:

James Cook (9); LIZA: Maggy Gorrill (10), *Spence Ford*; WENDY DARLING: Marsha Kramer (3); JOHN DARLING: Alexander Winter (7); MRS. DARLING: Beth Fowler (5); MR. DARLING: George Rose (2), *Christopher Hewett* (from 10/17/79); PETER PAN: Sandy Duncan (1) ✰; LION: Jim Wolfe; TURTLE: Cleve Asbury, *Richard Loreto*; KANGAROO: Reed Jones, *Robert Brubach*; OSTRICH: Maggy Gorrill (10), *Spence Ford*; SLIGHTLY: Chris Farr, *Matthew McGrath*; CURLY: Michael Estes; 1ST TWIN: Rusty Jacobs, *Robert McGuire*; 2ND TWIN: Joey Abbott, *Johnny Morgal*; TOOTLES: Carl Tramon, *Demetrius Pena*; NIBS: Dennis Courtney; CAPTAIN HOOK: George Rose (2) ✰, *Christopher Hewett* (from 10/17/79); NOODLER: Guy Stroman; SMEE: Arnold Soboloff (6), *Ronn Carroll*; CROCODILE: Kevin McCready; TIGER LILY: Maria Pogee (4), *Marybeth Kurdock*; STARKEY: Jon Vandertholen; CECCO: Trey Wilson (12), *Gibby Brand*; MULLINS: Steven Yuhasz; JUKES: Gary Daniel, *Anthony Hoylen*; WENDY, GROWN UP: Neva Rae Powers (11); JANE: Marsha Kramer; TINKERBELL: created by Laser Media, Inc.; TREES: C.J. McCaffrey, Kevin McCready, David Storey, *Roger Preston Smith*; PIRATES: William Carmichael, James Cook, Gary Daniel (*Anthony Hoylen*), Dianna Hughes, Guy Stroman, Jon Vandertholen, Trey Wilson, Steven Yuhasz; INDIANS: Cleve Asbury (*Richard Loreto*), Maggy Gorrill (*Spence Ford*), Sharon-Ann Hill (*Lee Heinz*), Reed Jones (*Robert Brubach*), C.J. McCaffrey, Kevin McCready, David Storey, Jim Wolfe, *Roger Preston Smith*. **Understudies**: Peter: Maggy Gorrill; Tiger Lily: Maggy Gorrill, *Lee Heinz*; Hook/Darling: Arnold Soboloff, *Ronn Carroll*; Smee: Trey Wilson, *Gibby Brand*; Wendy/Jane: Dianna Hughes, *Janie Gleason*; Mrs. Darling: Neva Rae Powers; John: Chris Farr, *Matthew McGrath*; Michael: Carl Tramon, *Robert McGuire*; Liza/Grown-up Wendy: Penny Peters McGuire; Nana: Nelson K. Wilson. **Swing Dancers:** Penny Peters McGuire, Jack Magradey, *Janie Gleason, Greg Minahan*. **Act I: Scene 1** Nursery of the Darling home: "Tender Shepherd" (Mrs. Darling, Wendy, John, Michael), "I've Got to Crow" (Peter), "Neverland" * (Peter), "I'm Flying" * (Peter, Wendy, John, Michael). **Act II: Scene 1** Neverland: "Morning in Neverland" * (Never Animals & Lost Boys), "Pirate Song" (Pirates), "A Princely Scheme" (Hook & Pirates), "Indians!" (dance arr: Dorothea Freitag) (Tiger Lily & Indians), "Wendy" * (Peter & Lost Boys), "Another Princely Scheme" (Hook & Pirates); **Scene 2** Path to Lagoon: "I Won't Grow Up" (Peter & Lost Boys); **Scene 3** Neverland Forest: "Mysterious Lady" * (Peter, Hook, Never Trees); **Scene 4** Home Underground: "Ugg-a-Wugg" * (Peter, Tiger Lily, Indians, Lost Boys, Darling Children), "Distant Melody" * (Wendy). **Act III: Scene 1** The *Jolly Roger*: "Hook's Waltz" * (Hook & Pirates), "The Battle" (Peter & Hook); **Scene 2** Neverland: "I've Got to Crow" (reprise) (Peter, Darling Children, Tiger Lily, Lost Boys); **Scene 3** Nursery of the Darling home: "Tender Shepherd" (reprise) (Mrs. Darling, Wendy, John, Michael), "I Won't Grow Up" (reprise) (Darling Family & Lost Boys); **Scene 4** The nursery; many years later: "Neverland" * (reprise) (Peter).

Note: Those numbers asterisked are by Styne, Comden & Green.

Broadway reviews were somewhat divided. Sandy Duncan played Peter as a boy, and not as a boy/woman as Mary Martin had done. On 10/28/79 Arnold Soboloff, playing Smee, finished a number in Act II, exited to the wings, and collapsed with a fatal heart attack. He was 48. The show received Tony nominations for reproduction of a play or musical, and for Sandy Duncan.

After Broadway. POST-BROADWAY TOUR. Opened on 4/15/81, at the Municipal Opera House, Boston. **Cast**: PETER: Sandy Duncan; DARLING/HOOK: Christopher Hewett; WENDY: Marsha Kramer; STARKEY: Jon Vandertholen; LION: Jim Wolfe; CURLY: Michael Estes; NIBBS: Dennis Courtney; MRS. DARLING: Adrienne Angel; JOHN: Matt McGrath; MICHAEL: Johnny Morgal; NANA: James Cook; LIZA: Anne McVey; MULLINS: Bill Mullikin; OSTRICH: C.J. McCaffrey; TOOTLES: Michael Emery Jr.; NOODLER: J.C. Sheets.

TOUR. Opened on 6/15/82, in Providence, Rhode Island, and closed on 7/17/83, in San Antonio. PRESENTED BY Kolmar—Luth Entertainment; DIRECTOR/CHOREOGRAPHER: Ron Field; SETS: Michael Hotopp & Paul de Pass; MUSICAL SUPERVISOR: Jack Lee; MUSICAL DIRECTOR: Glen Clugston. **Cast**: PETER: Karyn Cole; LIZA/SHADOW: Anne McVey; DARLING/HOOK: Rip Taylor; CROCODILE: Jim Wolfe; OSTRICH: C.J. McCaffrey; WENDY GROWN-UP: Missy Whitchurch; MICHAEL: Ann Marie Lee; JOHN: Christopher Wooten; MICHAEL: Johnny Morgal; NANA/SMEE: Andy Hostettler; MRS. DARLING: Lola Fisher; SLIGHTLY:

Michael Emery Jr.; TOOTLES: Dodd Wooten; NOODLER: J.C. Sheets. **Understudy**: Peter: Missy Whitchurch.

LONDON, 1982. This was a new production, but of the same musical (i.e. it was not a rival musical in any way). There were some new tunes by Stephen Oliver — "Peter's First Tune," "Peter's Second Tune," "Mrs. Darling's Lullaby." PRESENTED BY the Royal Shakespeare Company; MUSICAL DIRECTOR: Nigel Hess.

ALDWYCH THEATRE, London, 12/20/85. 73 PERFORMANCES. This was the classic 1954 Broadway musical. **Cast**: PETER: Bonnie Langford (many say she was the best Peter ever); DARLING/HOOK: Joss Ackland.

In *Jerome Robbins' Broadway* (qv), 1989, a segment was devoted to *Peter Pan*, and Charlotte d'Amboise played Peter.

541. *Peter Pan (1990 Broadway revival)*

Before Broadway. Cathy Rigby, the star, was the famous former Olympic gymnast. Thomas P. McCoy, the producer, was her husband. This production was part of a tour, handled by Marvin A. Krauss & Irving Siders, that had begun at the Colonial Theatre, Boston, on 12/19/89. It had the same crew as for the subsequent Broadway run, except PRESS: Patt Dale Associates. It had the same cast too, except MICHAEL: Jeremy Cooper; NEVER BEAR/2ND TWIN: Courtney Wyn.

The Broadway Run. LUNT—FONTANNE THEATRE, 12/13/90–1/20/91. 3 previews from 12/11/90. Limited run of 45 PERFORMANCES. The Thomas P. McCoy — Keith Stava production, PRESENTED BY James M. Nederlander, Arthur Rubin, in association with P.P. Investments, Inc. & Jon B. Platt; MUSIC: Mark "Moose" Charlap; ADDITIONAL MUSIC: Jule Styne; LYRICS: Carolyn Leigh; ADDITIONAL LYRICS: Betty Comden & Adolph Green; BASED ON the play by J.M. Barrie; DIRECTOR: Fran Soeder; CHOREOGRAPHER: Marilyn Magness; FLYING: Foy; NEVERLAND SETS: James Leonard Joy; COSTUMES: Mariann Verheyen; LIGHTING: Natasha Katz; SOUND: Peter J. Fitzgerald; MUSICAL SUPERVISOR/MUSICAL DIRECTOR: Kevin Farrell; NEW ORCHESTRATIONS: Brian W. Tidwell; ADDITIONAL MUSICAL ARRANGEMENTS: M. Michael Fauss & Kevin Farrell; PRESS: Shirley Herz Associates; GENERAL MANAGEMENT: Lonn Entertainment; COMPANY MANAGER: Stephen Arnold; PRODUCTION STAGE MANAGER: John M. Galo; STAGE MANAGER: Eric Insko. **Cast:** WENDY DARLING: Cindy Robinson; JOHN DARLING: Britt West; MICHAEL DARLING: Chad Hutchison; LIZA/INDIAN: Anne McVey; NANA: Bill Bateman; MRS. DARLING: Lauren Thompson; MR. DARLING: Stephen Hanan; PETER PAN: Cathy Rigby (1); THE NEVER BEAR: Adam Ehrenworth; CURLY: Alon Williams; 1ST TWIN: Janet Kay Higgins; 2ND TWIN: Courtney Wyn; SLIGHTLY: Christopher Ayers; TOOTLES: Julian Brightman; MR. SMEE: Don Potter; CECCO: Calvin Smith; GENTLEMAN STARKEY: Carl Packard; NOODLER: Barry Ramsey; BILL JUKES: Andy Ferrara; CAPTAIN HOOK: Stephen Hanan; CROCODILE: Barry Ramsey; TIGER LILY: Holly Irwin; PIRATES/INDIANS: Bill Bateman, Andy Ferrara, Anne McVey, Christian Monte, Carl Packard, Barry Ramsey, Joseph Savant, Calvin Smith, Timothy Talman, David Thome, John Wilkerson; WENDY GROWN-UP: Lauren Thompson; JANE: Cindy Robinson. **Understudies**: Peter: Cindy Robinson; Darling/Hook: Carl Packard; Mrs. Darling: Anne McVey; Smee: Bill Bateman; Wendy/Tiger Lily: Courtney Wyn; John: Christopher Ayers; Michael/Twins/Curly: Adam Ehrenworth; Tootles/Slightly: Janet Kay Higgins. **Swing**: Jim Alexander. **Musicians**: PIANO/SYNTHESIZER: Brian Tidwell; KEYBOARDS/TINKERBELL: Craig Barna; DRUMS: Steve Bartosik; HARP: Sally Foster; PERCUSSION: James Saporito; GUITAR: Bruce Uchitel; CONCERTMASTER: Diana Halprin; VIOLINS: Maura Giannini, Cecelia Hobbs Gardner, Lisa Brooke; CELLI: Roger Shell & Eliana Mendoza; ACOUSTIC BASS: Joe Bongiorno; ELECTRIC BASS: Jaime Austria; FLUTES: Dan Gerhart & David Weiss; PICCOLO: Dan Gerhart; BARITONE SAX: David Weiss; CLARINETS: Alva Hunt & John Winder; TENOR SAX: Alva Hunt; BASS CLARINET/BASSOON: John Winder; OBOE/ENGLISH HORN: David Kosoff; TRUMPETS: Chris Jaudes, John Frosk, Larry Lunetta; TROMBONE: Dan Cloutier; FRENCH HORN: Ron Sell. **Act I**: The nursery of the Darling residence: "Tender Shepherd," "I've Got to Crow," "Neverland," "I'm Flying." **Act II**: **Scene 1** Neverland: "Pirate March" (Hook & Pirates), "A Princely Scheme" (Hook's Tango) (m: Trude Rittman; l: Carolyn Leigh) (Hook & Pirates), "Indians!" (Tiger Lily & Indians),

"Wendy" (Peter & Lost Boys), "Another Princely Scheme" (tarantella) (Hook & Pirates); **Scene 2** Cavern (Marooner's Rock): "I Won't Grow Up" (Peter, Wendy, Lost Boys); **Scene 3** The home underground: "Ugg-a-Wugg" (Peter, Tiger Lily, Wendy, Lost Boys, Indians), "Distant Melody" (Peter). **Act III**: **Scene 1** The pirate ship: "Hook's Waltz" (Hook & Pirates), "I've Got to Crow" (reprise) (Peter & Company); **Scene 2** The nursery of the Darling residence: "Tender Shepherd" (reprise) (Wendy, John, Michael), "I Won't Grow Up" (reprise) (The Darling Family & Lost Boys); **Scene 3** The nursery; many years later: "Neverland" (reprise) (Peter).

This revival got mostly good reviews, although there was a noticeable dose of sniping. The production received Tony nominations for revival, and for Cathy Rigby. After Broadway it went on tour again.

542. *Peter Pan (1991 return to Broadway)*

This was the 1990–1991 Broadway production returned to Broadway after touring.

The Broadway Run. MINSKOFF THEATRE, 11/27/91–1/5/92. 48 PERFORMANCES. PRESENTED BY Thomas P. McCoy, Keith Stava, P.P. Investments, Jon B. Platt. It had the same basic crew as before, except RESTAGED BY: Bill Bateman; SETS: Michael J. Hotopp, Paul de Pass; NEVERLAND SETS: James Leonard Joy; MUSICAL DIRECTOR: Brian W. Tidwell; STAGE MANAGER: Frank Hartenstein & Eric Insko. It had the same cast, except JOHN: David Burdick; MICHAEL: Joey Cee; DARLING/HOOK: J.K. Simmons; TIGER LILY: Michelle Schumacher. The characters of Never Bear and Jukes were cut. Other Pirates & Indians were played by Charlie Marcus, Joseph Savant, David Thome, John Wilkerson. All understudies were the same, except Michael: David Burdick; Twins: Julian Brightman; Tootles/Slightly/Curly: Janet Kay Higgins.

543. *Peter Pan (1998 Broadway revival)*

Sub-titled *The Boy Who Wouldn't Grow Up*. The lyrics and book were brought up to date, with no more mentions of "redskins."

Before Broadway. This revival arrived on Broadway as part of a tour that had opened on 11/7/97, in La Mirada, Calif. (It had then played at Seattle, from 11/28/97). The plan was to bring the tour to Broadway in the fall of 1998 (which it achieved). Eli Simon was going to direct, but was replaced by Glenn Casale. It had the same basic crew as for the later Broadway run. **Pre-Broadway tour cast**: MRS. DARLING: Helen Hobson, *Barbara McCulloh* (by 6/98); WENDY: Elisa Sagardia; JOHN: Michael La Volpe, *Chase Kniffen* (from 4/20/98); MICHAEL: Paul Tiesler, *Drake English* (from 2/2/98); TIGER LILY: Susan Lamontagne, *Dana Solimando* (by 6/98); NANA/CROCODILE: Buck Mason; DARLING/HOOK: Paul Schoeffler; PETER: Cathy Rigby; CURLY: Alon Williams; 1ST TWIN: Janet Kay Higgins; 2ND TWIN: Doreen Chila; SLIGHTLY: K.W. Miller, *Scott Bridges* (by 6/98); TOOTLES: Aileen Quinn; SMEE: Michael Nostrand; STARKEY: Sam Zeller; GROWN-UP WENDY/NARRATOR: Jenny Agutter; NEVER BIRD: Danny Schmittler; ALSO WITH: Kim Arnett, William Alan Coats, Casey Miles Good, Randy A. Davis, Jeffrey Elass, Ray Garcia (*Roger Preston Smith* by 6/98), Jose Restrepo (*Tony Spinosa* by 6/98), Brian Shepard. On 6/26/98 the Broadway preview, as well as the opening and closing dates were announced. On 9/14/98 the Marquis was announced as the Broadway house.

The Broadway Run. MARQUIS THEATRE, 11/23/98–1/3/99; GERSHWIN THEATRE, 4/7/99–8/29/99. 5 previews from 11/20/98. Total of 214 PERFORMANCES (48 at the Marquis; 166 at the Gershwin). PRESENTED BY McCoy Rigby Entertainment, The Nederlander Organization, and La Mirada Theatre for the Performing Arts (Cathy Rigby & Thomas P. McCoy), in association with Albert Nocciolino, Larry Payton, and J. Lynn Singleton; MUSIC: Mark "Moose" Charlap; ADDITIONAL MUSIC: Jule Styne; LYRICS: Carolyn Leigh; ADDITIONAL LYRICS: Betty Comden

& Adolph Green; BOOK: uncredited; BASED ON the play by J.M. Barrie; DIRECTOR: Glenn Casale; CHOREOGRAPHER: Patti Colombo; SETS: John Iacovelli; COSTUMES: Shigeru Yaji; LIGHTING: Martin Aronstein; SOUND: Francois Bergeron; MUSICAL DIRECTOR/VOCAL ARRANGEMENTS: Craig Barna; NEW ORCHESTRATIONS: Craig Barna, Kevin Farrell, M. Michael Fauss, Brian Tidwell, Steve Bartosik; NEW CAST RECORDING on Jay Records, released on 2/1/98, during the pre–Broadway tour, and distributed by Allegro; PRESS: The Pete Sanders Group; CASTING: Julia Flores; EXCLUSIVE TOUR DIRECTORS: Dodger Touring; GENERAL MANAGEMENT: 101 Productions; COMPANY MANAGER: Robert Tevyaw; PRODUCTION STAGE MANAGER: Micheal McEowen; STAGE MANAGER: Nevin Hedley; ASSISTANT STAGE MANAGER: Gina Farina. *Cast:* MRS. DARLING: Barbara McCulloh; WENDY DARLING: Elisa Sagardia; JOHN DARLING: Chase Kniffen, *Barry Cavanagh* (from 4/7/99), *Doreen Chila*; MICHAEL DARLING: Drake English; LIZA: Dana Solimando; NANA: Buck Mason; MR. DARLING: Paul Schoeffler (2); PETER PAN: Cathy Rigby (1) ☆; CURLY: Alon Williams; 1ST TWIN: Janet Kay Higgins; 2ND TWIN: Doreen Chila; SLIGHTLY: Scott Bridges; TOOTLES: Aileen Quinn, *Michelle Berti* (stood in for Miss Quinn), *Hally McGehean* (from 4/7/99); MR. SMEE: Michael Nostrand; CECCO: Tony Spinosa; GENTLEMAN STARKEY: Sam Zeller; NOODLER: Randy A. Davis; BILL JUKES: Buck Mason; CAPTAIN HOOK: Paul Schoeffler (2); CROCODILE: Buck Mason; TIGER LILY: Dana Solimando; MERMAID: Barbara McCulloh; PIRATES & INDIANS: Kim Arnett, Randy A. Davis, Jeffrey Elass, Casey Miles Good, Buck Mason, Brian Shepard, Roger Preston Smith, Tony Spinosa, Sam Zeller; WENDY GROWN-UP: Barbara McCulloh; JANE: Aileen Quinn, *Michelle Berti* (stood in for Miss Quinn), *Hally McGehean* (from 4/7/99). *Understudies*: Peter: Janet Higgins; Darling/Hook: Sam Zeller & Roger Preston Smith; Liza: Kim Arnett & Doreen Chila; Mrs. Darling/Mermaid/Wendy Grown-Up/Tiger Lily: Kim Arnett; Smee: Roger Preston Smith & William Alan Coats; Nana/Crocodile: William Alan Coats; Wendy: Aileen Quinn & Elisa Sagardia, *Hally McGehean*; Jane: Aileen Quinn, *Hally McGehean*; John/Slightly: Doreen Chila; Michael: Michael Kirsch, *Austin Colaluca* (from 4/7/99); Twins: Michelle Berti; Curly: Michelle Berti & Randy Davis; Tootles: Randy Davis, *Hally McGehean*; Starkey: Jeffrey Elass. *General Understudy*: Michelle Berti. *Swing*: William Alan Coats. *Orchestra:* KEYBOARD I: Bruce Barnes; KEYBOARD II: Michael Rice; VIOLINS: Sylvia D'Avanzo, Margaret Jones, Heidi Stubner, Maura Giannini; CELLI: Roger Shell & Deborah Assael; HARP: Laura Sherman; REEDS: David Wechsler, Phil Chester, Tuck Lee, Tom Christensen, Mike Migliore; TRUMPETS: Larry Pyatt, Jon Owens, Joe Reardon; TROMBONES: Jason Ingram & Bill Whitaker; FRENCH HORN: Richard Tremarello; BASS: Tom Mendel; PERCUSSION: Ed Shea; DRUMS: Todd Barnard & Steve Bartosik. *Act I: Scene 1* The nursery of the Darling residence: "Tender Shepherd" (Mrs. Darling, Wendy, John, Michael), "I Gotta Crow" (Peter), "Neverland" (Peter), "I'm Flying" (Peter, Wendy, John, Michael). *Act II: Scene 1* Neverland: "Pirate March" (Hook & Pirates), "A Princely Scheme" (Hook & Pirates), "Indians!" (Tiger Lily & Indians), "Wendy" (Peter & Boys), "I Won't Grow Up" (Peter, Wendy, Boys), "Another Princely Scheme" (Hook & Pirates); *Scene 2* Marooner's Rock; *Scene 3* The home underground: "Ugg-a-Wugg" (orch: Craig Barna & Steve Bartosik) (Peter, Tiger Lily, Wendy, Boys, Indians) [certain racially offensive lyrics were omitted from this number which, aside from that, was totally re-choreographed to much acclaim], "Distant Melody" (Wendy & Peter). *Act III: Scene 1* The Pirate Ship: "Hook's Waltz" (Hook & Pirates), "I Gotta Crow" (reprise) (Peter & Company); *Scene 2* The nursery of the Darling residence: "Tender Shepherd" (reprise) (Wendy, John, Michael), "I Won't Grow Up" (reprise) (The Darling Family & Lost Boys); *Scene 3* The nursery; many years later: "Neverland" (reprise) (Peter).

Broadway reviews were not good, but it was so popular that it was planned to bring it back to the Neil Simon Theatre, for another limited run, from the matinee of 4/7/99 to 8/29/99, but in fact it moved to the Gershwin. The show received a 1999 Tony nomination for revival of a musical. After Broadway it continued to tour, 11/2/99–2/20/00.

After Broadway. NEW TOUR. Opened at La Mirada, California, 9/24/04–10/10/04, then on with the tour until the summer of 2005, and aiming for Broadway in late 2005. This was Cathy Rigby's farewell to the role. DIRECTOR: Glenn Casale; CHOREOGRAPHER: Patti Colombo; SETS/COSTUMES: John Iacovelli; MUSICAL DIRECTOR/VOCAL ARRANGE-

MENTS: Craig Barna. *Cast*: PETER: Cathy Rigby; MR. DARLING/HOOK: Howard McGillin; WENDY: Elisa Sagardia; TIGER LILY: Dana Solimando.

RIVAL VERSIONS. There have been several other *Peter Pan* musicals, and spin-offs and parodies, with different scores, written by different people. Piers Chater-Robinson, for example, wrote the "British" *Peter Pan* musical (which was also produced in Spain in 1998, with Raquel Grijalbo as Peter). In 1998 Michael Jackson & Larry Hart (who had been involved together on *Sisterella*) began collaboration on a new musical, based loosely on *Peter Pan*, called *PanJam*. Mr. Hart provided most of the songs. Another was *Peter Pan: a Musical Adventure*, set in post–World War II London, and with 15 new songs. MUSIC: George Stiles; LYRICS: Anthony Drewe; BOOK: Willis Hall. After premiering in COPENHAGEN in 1999 it made its London bow at the ROYAL FESTIVAL HALL, 4/26/01. DIRECTOR: Julia McKenzie. *Cast*: John Thaw, Sheila Hancock. It re-ran, same venue, 12/19/02–1/12/03. 32 PERFORMANCES. DIRECTOR: Ian Talbot; SETS: Will Bowen; with the Royal Philharmonic Orchestra. *Cast*: HOOK: Richard Wilson; PETER: James Gillan; WENDY: Lottie Mayor; SMEE: David Bamber; MRS. DARLING: Claire Moore; NARRATOR: Susannah York. It made its US debut as *Peter Pan and Wendy*, at the PRINCE MUSIC THEATRE, Philadelphia, 12/18/02–12/29/02. Previews from 12/11/02). SETS: Fred Kinney; COSTUMES: Loyce Arthur; LIGHTING: Howell Binkley; SOUND: Nick Courtides; MUSICAL DIRECTOR: Louis F. Goldberg; ORCHESTRATIONS: John Cameron; PUPPETS: Kim Meyer. *Cast*: STORYTELLER: Rita Gardner; HOOK/DARLING: Christopher Innvar; MRS. DARLING: Joanna Glushak; SMEE: Romain Fruge; PETER: Michael Longoria.

544. *The Phantom of the Opera*

For obvious reasons this musical is generally referred to as *Phantom*. The Phantom (real name Erik, but this is not mentioned in the musical) is one of the architects of the Paris Opera House (in reality the house was built 1861–75 by architect Charles Garnier). He has been horribly disfigured since birth. During the construction Erik had built a secret hideaway for himself far beneath the massive seven-story theatre, where he could be by himself, away from people, and write music. Erik falls obsessively in love with soprano Christine (in the book she was a dancer in the corps de ballet). Christine is in love with handsome Raoul. Erik kills people who thwart Christine's career. Eventually Christine must choose between the two men. The set includes a slow boat ride through the Opera's underground lake, and a crashing half-ton chandelier (the cost for theatres to modify their stage to take its fall was anywhere between $50,000 to $100,000). It was a huge production. Mme Giry (known as Giry) was the ballet mistress, and Meg was her daughter, a promising dancer. Lefevre is retiring as manager of the Opera House, and two new managers, Andre and Firmin, are coming in. Ubaldo Piangi is the principal tenor. Carlotta is the leading soprano, who the Phantom arranges to have replaced by Christine. M. Reyer is the chief repetiteur (a sort of stage director). Buquet is the aging chief of the stage flies (he is killed by the Phantom).

Before Broadway. There was a UK stage version of the straight play in 1975, and an American version in 1978. In the late 1970s there was a Mexican musical with music/lyrics/book by Raul Astor, and starring Julio Aleman.

An earlier, unrelated *Phantom of the Opera*, ran at the THEATRE ROYAL STRATFORD EAST, London, 5/9/84–6/7/84. PRESENTED BY Joan Littlewood. It used public domain operas by Verdi, Gounod and Offenbach. BOOK/DIRECTOR: Ken Hill. The first choice for Christine was Sarah Brightman, but she was unavailable. "Welcome Sir, I'm so delighted," "Accursed, all base pursuit of earthly pleasures," "How dare she?," "Late last night," "Love has gone never returning," "While floating high above," "She says she's got the nodules," "What do I see?," "To pain my heart selfishly dooms me," "Ah! Do I hear my lover's voice?," "No sign! I see no sign," "The lake," "Somewhere above the sun shines bright," "Born with a monstrous countenance," "A sharp whipping," "What an awful way to perish," "Ne'er forsake me, here remain," "He will not go without a friend," "Play out," "While floating high above" (reprise). In 1990 this version was touring in the USA. A London revival opened at the SHAFTESBURY THEATRE, on 10/12/91. ***Cast:*** Steven Pacey, Toni Palmer, Peter Straker, Christina Collier, Michael McLean, Richard Tate, Reginald Marsh.

Another earlier, unrelated *Phantom of the Opera* opened on 4/19/86, at the CAPITAL REPERTORY THEATRE, Albany, NY. MUSIC: David Bishop; LYRICS: Kathleen Masterson; DIRECTOR: Peter H. Clough; MUSICAL DIRECTOR: Hank Levy. ***Cast:*** RAOUL: Joseph Kolinski; MEG: Tracy Daniels; CHRISTINE: Yvette de Botton; MME GIRY: Jan Buttram; PHANTOM: Al DeCristo; USBEK: Patti Perkins; ARMAND: Robert Ousley.

LONDON PRODUCTION. Andrew Lloyd Webber saw the 1984 Ken Hill production, and decided to do his own version. Cameron Mackintosh became the producer. Mr. Lloyd Webber wrote the role of Christine for his wife, Sarah Brightman. Originally Mr. Lloyd Webber was going to use established and recognized classical pieces for the score, with himself writing only incidental music to connect the pieces, but Jim Sharman, the Australian director, persuaded him to write his own score, which he did. Richard Stilgoe wrote the lyrics and Andrew Lloyd Webber and Mr. Stilgoe wrote the book. In June 1985 Hal Prince came on board as director. In July 1985 Sarah Brightman played Christine in a tryout production of Act I put on by Andrew Lloyd Webber as part of a summer festival at his home in Sydmonton. Colm Wilkinson played the Phantom. Maria Bjornson designed the sets (falling chandelier and all). The reception was very good, and the production aimed for the West End. Rehearsals began 8/18/86. The authors asked Alan Jay Lerner if he would write the new lyrics and book, but Mr. Lerner was (literally) dying in London. So Tim Rice was approached, but he was working on *Chess* at that time. So Charles Hart came on board as the new lyricist. The famous Andrew Lloyd Webber version of *The Phantom of the Opera* opened on 10/9/86, at HER MAJESTY'S THEATRE, London. CAST RECORDING on Polydor. ***Cast:*** RAOUL: Steve Barton, *Matthew Camelle* (by 8/01), *Robert Finlayson* (from 3/11/02), *Matthew Camelle* (from 12/2/02), *Ramin Karimloo* (from 10/6/03), *Oliver Thornton* (from 9/6/04); CARLOTTA: Rosemary Ashe, *An Lauwereins* (by 8/01), *Nan Christie* (by 7/02), *Judith Gardner* (from 10/6/03), *Sally Harrison* (from 9/6/04); PIANGI: John Aron, *Jeremy Secomb* (by 8/01), *Rohan Tickell* (from 9/6/04); MEG: Janet Devenish, *Lucy Middleton* (by 8/01), *Hayley Driscoll, Claire Tilling* (from 9/6/04); CHRISTINE: Sarah Brightman, *Deborah Dutcher* (by 8/01), *Celia Graham* (from 3/11/02), *Katrina Murphy* (at certain performances), *Katie Knight* (from 10/6/03), *Rachel Barrell* (from 9/6/04); MME GIRY: Mary Millar (for 4 years), *Janet Murphy* (by 8/01), *Liz Robertson* (from 3/11/02), *Heather Jackson*; REYER: Philip Griffiths; LEFEVRE: David Jackson, *Tim Morgan* (by 8/01); ANDRE: David Firth, *Charles Shirvell* (by 8/01), *Robert Irons*; FIRMIN: John Savident, *Bruce Montague* (by 8/01); BUQUET: Janos Kurucz, *Donald Francke* (by 8/01); PHANTOM: Michael Crawford, *Peter Karrie* (for 18 months), *John Owen Jones* (by 8/01); MME FIRMIN: Patricia Richards, *Davina Adshead* (by 8/01). On 8/12/03 the show played its 7,000th performance.

On 6/10/87 Sarah Brightman was denied entry to perform the role of Christine on Broadway, American Equity insisting that this major role be taken by an American actress. The only exception, at that time, was if the actor was an "international star," and Miss Brightman did not qualify. According to Equity, Michael Crawford did. Andrew Lloyd Webber objected, and a deal was struck on 6/30/87, whereby an American actress would, at some stage shortly thereafter, be given the lead in a London production as a quid pro quo. This would happen when Ann Crumb starred in the British production of Mr. Lloyd Webber's next musical, *Aspects of Love.* The Broadway *Phantom* had 40 stagehands. It had a record $16 million in advance ticket sales. On its first night of Broadway previews, it took in $920,272 at a $50 top ticket price, smashing the record of a first day's take by *Les Miserables* by more than double.

The Broadway Run. MAJESTIC THEATRE, 1/26/88–. 16 previews from 1/9/88. PRESENTED BY Cameron Mackintosh & The Really Useful Theatre Company; MUSIC: Andrew Lloyd Webber; LYRICS: Charles Hart; ADDITIONAL LYRICS: Richard Stilgoe; BOOK: Richard Stilgoe & Andrew Lloyd Webber; Based on the 1911 novel of the same name (*Le*

fantome de l'opera) by Gaston Leroux; DIRECTOR: Harold Prince; ASSISTANT DIRECTOR: Ruth Mitchell; CHOREOGRAPHER: Gillian Lynne; SETS/COSTUMES: Maria Bjornson; LIGHTING: Andrew Bridge; SOUND: Martin Levan; MUSICAL SUPERVISOR/MUSICAL DIRECTOR: David Caddick; ORCHESTRATIONS: David Cullen & Andrew Lloyd Webber; LONDON CAST RECORDING on PolyGram/Polydor; PRESS: The Fred Nathan Company, *Merle Frimark, Marc Thibodeau*; CASTING: Johnson — Liff & Zerman; GENERAL MANAGER: Alan Wasser; COMPANY MANAGER: Michael Gill; PRODUCTION STAGE MANAGER: Mitchell Lemsky, *Frank Marino* (by 88–89); STAGE MANAGERS: Fred Hanson (88–91), Bethe Ward (from 88), *Mark Rubinsky* (88–89), *Franklin Keysar* (91), *Steve McCorkle* (from 91), *Richard Hester* (from 93), *Barbara-Mae Phillips* (from 93). ***Cast:*** AUCTIONEER: Richard Warren Pugh, *Peter Atherton* (stood in while Mr. Pugh was playing Firmin 5/94–7/94), *Richard Warren Pugh* (from 7/94), *David P. Cleveland* (by 12/94), *Richard Warren Pugh* (by 3/95), *John Kuether* (by 6/01), *James Romick* (by 3/02), *John Kuether* (by 4/02), *James Romick* (by 12/02), *John Kuether* (by 1/03), *Carrington Vilmont* (by 6/03); 1ST PORTER: William Scott Brown, *Maurizio Corbino* (by 7/90), *David Cleveland* (stood in in 10/91), *Maurizio Corbino* (from 10/91), *Scott Mikita* (from 3/99), *Maurizio Corbino* (by 5/99), *Torrance Blaisdell* (by 9/99), *John Wasiniak* (by 6/01), *Scott Mikita* (from 1/04), *John Wasiniak* (from 2/04) in 2/96, when the role of the 2nd Porter was cut, the 1st Porter became merely The Porter]; 2ND PORTER: Jeff Keller, *David Cleveland* (by 5/89), *Gary Lindemann* (by 1/90) [role cut by 2/96]; FLUNKY: Barry McNabb, *Jeff Siebert* (from 10/89), *Wesley Robinson* (by 1/92), *Jeff Siebert* (by 4/92), *Thomas Terry* (from 6/92), *Wesley Robinson* (7/92–9/92), *Thomas Terry* (by 5/93), *Jack Hayes* (by 6/93), *Thomas Terry* (by 9/93), *Gary Giffune* (by 5/95), *Thomas Terry* (by 7/95) [role cut in 6/97]; RAOUL, VICOMTE DE CHAGNY: Steve Barton (4), *Kevin Gray* (by 9/89), *Davis Gaines* (from 3/12/90), *Kevin Gray* (by 7/90), *Hugh Panaro* (from 12/90), *Keith Buterbaugh* (by 6/93), *Ciaran Sheehan* (by 11/93), *Brad Little* (by 1/95), *Gary Mauer* (by 10/96), *John Schroeder* (by 4/98), *Gary Mauer* (by 5/98), *Ciaran Sheehan* (from 10/13/98), *Gary Mauer* (from 4/19/99), *Jim Weitzer* (from 4/23/01), *Gary Mauer* (by 6/01), *Jim Weitzer* (by 8/01), *Michael Shawn Lewis* (by 11/2/01), *Jim Weitzer* (by 10/01), *Michael Shawn Lewis* (by 1/02), *John Cudia* (by 10/02), *Michael Shawn Lewis* (by 11/02), *John Cudia* (by 12/02), *Jim Weitzer* (stood in late 3/03–early 4/03), *John Cudia* (from 4/03), *Jim Weitzer* (from 11/03), *John Cudia* (from 11/03), *Jim Weitzer* (from 12/03), *John Cudia* (from 1/04); CAST OF *Hannibal*: HANNIBAL: played by Piangi; ELISSA: played by Carlotta; PRINCESS: Rebecca Luker, *Mary D'Arcy* (by 3/89), *Raissa Katona* (by 5/89), *Virginia Croskery* (by 5/94), *Kimilee Bryant* (from 5/31/94), *Melissa Dye* (by 8/95), *Megan Starr-Levitt* (by 9/95), *Rebecca Pitcher* (by 2/98), *Susan Owen* (from 3/99), *Elizabeth Southard* (by 7/99), *Marie Danvers* (by 11/99), *Susan Facer* (by 7/00), *Elizabeth Southard* (by 12/00), *Susan Facer* (by 4/02), *Elizabeth Southard* (by 6/02), *Susan Facer* (by 8/02), *Elizabeth Southard* (by 9/02), *Julie Hanson* (from 6/23/03), *Susan Owen* (by 9/03); SLAVE GIRLS: played by Meg & Christine; SLAVE MASTER: Luis Perez, *David Loring* (by 10/88), *Wesley Robinson* (by 4/92), *David Loring* (7/92–9/92), *Wesley Robinson* (by 10/92), *Thomas Terry* (by 6/93), *Paul B. Sadler Jr.* (by 9/93), *Daniel Rychlec* (by 8/97), *William Patrick Dunne* (from 4/98), *Daniel Rychlec* (by 6/98), *David Scamardo* (from 5/99), *Daniel Rychlec* (by 7/99), *Paul B. Sadler Jr.* (by 9/99), *Daniel Rychlec* (by 1/00), *John J. Todd* (by 11/01), *Daniel Rychlec* (by 2/02), *John J. Todd* (from 3/02), *Eric Otte* (by 6/02), *David Scamardo* (from 8/03), *Eric Otte* (by 9/03) [end of Hannibal sequence], *Jack Hayes* (from 10/04); CARLOTTA GIUDICELLI: Judy Kaye (3), *Marilyn Caskey* (from 1/2/89), *Elena Jeanne Batman* (by 5/93), *Marilyn Caskey* (by 8/97), *Geena Jeffries* (by 11/97), *Patricia Hurd* (by 2/98), *Kelly Ellenwood* (by 4/98), *Leigh Munro* (by 7/98), *Liz McCartney* (by 5/99), *Elena Jeanne Batman* (stood in in 7/00, then played it permanently by 12/00), *Rebecca Eichenberger* (by 1/01), *Liz McCartney* (from 4/01), *Elena Jeanne Batman* (by 10/01), *Rebecca Eichenberger* (by 1/02), *Wren Marie Harrington* (by 3/02), *Rebecca Eichenberger* (by 4/02), *Wren Marie Harrington & Patty Goble* (stood in in 1/03), *Rebecca Eichenberger* (by 2/03), *Patricia Phillips* (by 7/03), *Julie Schmidt* (stood in in mid 4/04), *Patricia Phillips* (from 4/19/04), *Julie Schmidt* (by 6/04 and until 11/13/04); *Anne Runolfsson* (from 11/16/04) UBALDO PIANGI: David Romano (8), *John Horton Murray* (by 5/90), Nicholas F. Saverine (by 10/90), Gary Rideout (by 8/91), *Frederic Heringes* (by 9/93), *Donn Cook* (by 12/94), *Frederic Heringes* (by 3/95), *Patrick Jones* (by 9/95), *Frederic Heringes* (from 4/96), *Patrick Jones* (by 7/96), *Nicholas F. Saverine* (by 10/96), *Frederic Heringes* (by 1/97), *John McMaster* (by 4/97), *Frederic Heringes* (by 10/97), *Erick Buckley* (from 4/98), *Nicholas F. Saverine* (from 6/98), *Larry Wayne Morbitt* (by 12/98), *David Gaschen* (by 7/01), *Larry Wayne Morbitt* (by 8/01), *David Gaschen* & *John Wasiniak* (stood in in 3/03), *Larry Wayne Morbitt* (from 3/03), *John Wasiniak* (by 1/04), *Larry Wayne Morbitt* (by 2/04), *David Gaschen* & *John Wasiniak* (stood in during Mr. Morbitt's vacation, 4/04), *Larry Wayne Morbitt* (from 4/04); MEG GIRY: Elisa Heinsohn (9), *Catherine Ulissey* (by 7/90), *Tener Brown* (by 2/93), *Geralyn Del Corso* (by 8/97), *Kate Wray* (stood in in 5/99), *Geralyn Del Corso* (from 5/99), *Joella Gates* (by 10/99 & until 8/4/03), *Heather McFadden* (by 8/03); CHRISTINE DAAE: Sarah Brightman (2), *Patti Cohenour* (from 6/7/88), *Rebecca Luker* (from 6/5/89), *Karen Culliver* (by 2/91), *Mary D'Arcy* (by 6/93), *Tracy Shayne* (by 11/93 & until 1/26/98), *Sandra Joseph* (from 1/27/98), *Adrienne McEwen* (from 8/2/99), *Sarah Pfisterer* (from 1/17/00), *Sandra Joseph* (from 10/30/00), *Sarah Pfisterer* (from 8/6/01), *Elizabeth Southard* (from 3/25/02), *Lisa Vroman* (from 4/22/02), *Elizabeth Southard* (by 8/02), *Lisa Vroman* (by 9/02), *Rebecca Pitcher* (from 2/5/03 for a week), *Lisa Vroman* (from 2/03), *Adrienne McEwan* (for a few days in 3/03), *Lisa Vroman* (from 3/03), *Sandra Joseph* (from 6/10/03); CHRISTINE (ALTERNATE): Patti Cohenour (Thurs evenings & Sat Matinees), *Dale Kristien* (Mon & Weds evenings from 7/88), *Rebecca Luker* (Mon & Weds evenings from 3/89), *Katharine Buffaloe* (Mon & Weds evenings from 6/5/89), *Luann Aronson* (Mon & Weds evenings from 6/92), *Laurie Gayle Stephenson* (by 5/94), *Teri Bibb* (4/96–4/97), *Adrienne McEwan* (filled in for Miss Bibb during a week's vacation in 4/97, then took over permanently 4/21/97–4/12/98), *Kimilee Bryant* (4/98–10/21/98), *Adrienne McEwen* (from 10/26/98), *Sarah Pfisterer* (from 8/2/99), *Adrienne McEwan* (from 1/17/00), *Lisa Vroman* (from 10/30/00), *Adrienne McEwan* (from 7/9/01), *Elizabeth Southard* (for a few days in 3/03), *Adrienne McEwan* (from 3/03), *Julie Hanson* (from 6/23/03), *Adrienne McEwan* (by 7/03), *Julie Hanson* (by 9/03); MADAME GIRY: Leila Martin (7), *Kristina Maria Guiguet* (by 2/94), *Leila Martin* (by 3/94), *Sally Williams* (by 8/98), *Leila Martin* (by 5/99), *Sally Williams* (by 6/00), *Leila Martin* (by 7/00 and left 4/21/01), *Marilyn Caskey* (from 4/01), *Sally Williams* (by 3/02), *Marilyn Caskey* (by 4/02), *Sally Williams* (by 9/02), *Marilyn Caskey* (by 10/02); WARDROBE MISTRESS: Mary Leigh Stahl, *Elena Jeanne Batman* (from 5/92), *Diana Ketchie* (by 5/93) [role cut 9/93–11/95], *Mary Leigh Stahl* (by 11/95), *Leslie Giammanco* (by 6/97), *Mary Leigh Stahl* (by 8/97), *Leslie Giammanco* (stood in in 8/99), *Mary Leigh Stahl* (by 9/99); MONSIEUR REYER: Peter Kevoian, *Frank Mastrone* (by 1/89), *Peter Kevoian* (by 8/89), *Gary Barker* (by 5/90), *Ted Keegan* (by 7/95), *Jim Weitzer* (by 8/98), *Ted Keegan* (from 8/98), *Richard Poole* (by 3/99), *Ted Keegan* (by 7/99), *Michael Gerhart* (by 8/99), *Richard Poole* (by 9/99), *D.C. Anderson* (by 1/01), *Richard Poole* (from 5/01), *Scott Mikita* (by 6/01), *Richard Poole* (by 7/01), *Michael Babin* (by 6/03), *Richard Poole* (from 8/03); MONSIEUR LEFEVRE: Kenneth H. Waller, *David Cleveland* (by 6/98), *Paul Harman* (from 6/98), *Kenneth H. Waller* (by 8/98), *Chip Huddleston* (stood in in 3/00), *Kenneth H. Waller* (from 3/00), *Kenneth Kantor* (from 6/21/04); MONSIEUR GILLES ANDRE: Cris Groenendaal (5), *Jeff Keller* (by 5/89), *George Lee Andrews* (stood in 5/94–7/94 while Jeff Keller was playing the Phantom), *Jeff Keller* (from 7/94), *George Lee Andrews* (by 12/94), *Jeff Keller* (by 3/95), *George Lee Andrews* (by 10/99), *Jeff Keller* (by 11/99), *George Lee Andrews* (from 4/01), *Scott Mikita* (until 3/10/04), *Richard Poole* (3/11/04–3/13/04), *George Lee Andrews* (from 3/15/04); MONSIEUR RICHARD FIRMIN: Nicholas Wyman (6), *George Lee Andrews* (by 5/90), *Richard Warren Pugh* (stood in 5/94–7/94 while George Lee Andrews was playing Andre), *George Lee Andrews* (from 7/94), *Richard Warren Pugh* (by 12/94), *George Lee Andrews* (by 3/95), *Jeff Keller* (by 10/99), *George Lee Andrews* (by 11/99), *Jeff Keller* (from 4/01), *John Kuether* (by 12/02), *Jeff Keller* (by 1/03), *David Hunergayer* (5/17/04–5/29/04), *Jeff Keller;* JOSEPH BUQUET: Philip Steele, *Joe Gustern* (by 5/94), *Chip Huddleston* (from 6/99), *Joe Gustern* (by 8/99), *Chip Huddleston* (by 5/00), *Joe Gustern* (by 6/00), *Chip Huddleston* (by 7/00), *Brian Noonan* (by 7/01), *Richard Warren Pugh* (by 8/01); THE PHANTOM OF THE OPERA: Michael Crawford (1), *Timothy Nolen* (from 12/10/88), *Cris Groenendaal* (from 3/20/89), *Steve Barton* (3/19/90–12/1/90), *Kevin Gray* (from 12/3/90), *Mark Jacoby* (from 2/21/91), *Marcus Lovett* (from 5/24/93), *Jeff Keller* (by

5/94), *Davis Gaines* (7/4/94–10/5/96), *Thomas James O'Leary* (from 10/11/96–1/30/99), *Hugh Panaro* (from 2/1/99–8/21/99), *Ted Keegan* (stood in for Mr. Panaro in 8/99), *Howard McGillin* (from 8/23/99), *Brad Little* (stood in 9/16/02–10/5/02), *Howard McGillin* (10/02–4/12/03), *Hugh Panaro* (from 4/14/03), *Howard McGillin* (12/22/03–1/4/04 while Mr. Panaro was on vacation), *Hugh Panaro* (from 1/5/04); *Howard McGillin* (from the matinee of 6/26/04 to the evening performance of 7/3/04, during Mr. Panaro's vacation), *Hugh Panaro* (from 7/5/04); MADAME FIRMIN: Beth McVey, *Dawn Leigh Stone* (by 5/89), *Melody Johnson* (by 9/93 — she became Melody Rubie in 9/00), *Patty Goble* (by 7/02), *Melody Rubie* (by 8/02), *Patty Goble* (by 9/02), *Melody Rubie* (by 7/03); CAST OF *Il Muto*: COUNTESS: played by Carlotta; SERAFIMO, THE PAGE BOY: played by Christine; HAIRDRESSER: Gary Lindemann (by 2/96), *Fred Rose* (by 8/97), *Gary Lindemann* (by 11/97), *John Schroeder* (from 7/98), *Richard Poole* (by 1/99), *Michael Lackley* (from 3/99), *Richard Poole* (by 7/99), *David Gaschen* (by 9/99), *D.C. Anderson* (by 1/01), *Richard Poole* (by 5/01), *Scott Mikita* (by 6/01), *Richard Poole* (by 7/01), *Richard Poole* (by 3/03), *Michael Babin* (by 6/03), *Richard Poole* (from 8/03) [new role by 2/96]; JEWELER: Ted Keegan (by 11/95), *David Gaschen* (by 7/96), *Ted Keegan* (by 1/97), *David Gaschen* (by 5/97), *Ted Keegan* (by 6/97), *Jim Weitzer* (by 8/98), *Ted Keegan* (from 8/98), *Richard Poole* (by 3/99), *Michael Lackley* (by 5/99), *Ted Keegan* (by 7/99), *David Gaschen* (by 7/99) [role not billed between 8/99 & 1/01], *David Gaschen* (by 1/01), *Michael Babin* (by 7/01), *David Gaschen* (by 8/01), *Stephen Alexander Horst* (from 7/03), *David Gaschen* (by 9/03) [new role by 11/95]; COUNTESS'S CONFIDANTE: Mary Leigh Stahl, *Elena Jeanne Batman* (from 5/92), *Diana Ketchie* (by 5/93) [role cut 9/93–11/95], *Mary Leigh Stahl* (from 11/95), *Leslie Giammanco* (by 6/97), *Mary Leigh Stahl* (by 8/97); DON ATTILIO: George Lee Andrews, *Thomas Sandri* (from 89–90), *Peter Atherton* (by 2/93), *Thomas Sandri* (by 3/94), *Philip Steele* (by 5/94), *Craig A. Benham* (by 8/97), *John Kuether* (by 2/98), *James Romick* (by 10/99), *John Kuether* (by 11/99), *D.C. Anderson* (by 3/01), *Scott Mikita* (in 3/01), *John Kuether* (by 4/01), *James Romick* (by 3/02), *John Kuether* (by 4/02), *James Romick* (by 12/02), *John Kuether* (by 1/03), *Gregory Emanuel Rahming* (by 5/03), *Matthew R. Jones* (by 10/04 he was sharing the role with Mr. Rahming) [end of *Il Muto* sequence]; SOLO DANCER: Thomas Terry [role not billed 8/89–6/92], *Thomas Terry* (by 6/92), *Jack Hayes* (by 6/93), *Thomas Terry* (by 9/93) [role not billed 1/94–7/96], *Thomas Terry* (by 7/96) [role not billed 8/96–6/97], *Thomas Terry* (by 6/97), *Paul B. Sadler Jr.* (by 8/97) *Richard Toda* (by 7/98), *Paul B. Sadler Jr.* (from 7/98), *David Scamardo* (by 1/00), *Paul B. Sadler Jr.* (by 9/00), *Shaun R. Parry* (stood in in 9/00), *Paul B. Sadler Jr.* (by 9/00), *Richard Toda* (by 2/02), *Paul B. Sadler Jr.* (from 3/02), *Richard Toda* (by 4/02), *David Scamardo* (from 12/02), *Richard Toda* (by 1/03), *Cornell Crabtree* (from 8/03), *Richard Toda* (from 9/03), *Daniel Rychlec* (from 12/03. From 11/04 he played the role Mondays through Wednesdays), Jack Hayes (from 11/04, Thursdays through Saturdays); STAGE HAND: Barry McNabb, *Jeff Siebert* (from 10/89), *Wesley Robinson* (by 1/92), *Jeff Siebert* (by 4/92), *Thomas Terry* (from 6/92), *Wesley Robinson* (7/92–9/92), [role cut 9/92–2/94], *Thomas Terry* (by 2/94), *Gary Giffune* (by 5/95), *Thomas Terry* (by 7/95) [role cut permanently from 6/97]; POLICEMAN: Charles Rule, *Stacey Robinson* (by 2/93), *Paul Laureano* (by 6/93), *Thomas Sandri* (by 11/93), *Scott Watanabe* (by 7/94), *Thomas Sandri* (by 9/94) [role cut in 3/96]; FIRECHIEF: Kenneth H. Waller, *Chip Huddleston* (stood in in 3/00), *Kenneth H. Waller* (from 3/00), *Kenneth Kantor* (from 6/21/04); FIREMAN: William Scott Brown, *Maurizio Corbino* (by 7/90), *David Cleveland* (stood in in 10/91), *Maurizio Corbino* (from 10/91), *Scott Mikita* (from 3/99), *Maurizio Corbino* (by 5/99), *Torrance Blaisdell* (by 9/99), *John Wasiniak* (by 6/01), *Scott Mikita* (from 1/04), *John Wasiniak* (from 2/04); 2ND FIREMAN: Richard Warren Pugh (from 6/01), *Brian Noonan* (by 8/01), *Aaron Lazar* (by 3/02), *Jim Weitzer* (by 12/02), *Michael Babin* (by 2/03), *Jim Weitzer* (by 3/03)[new role by 6/01, and cut by 8/03]; MARKSMAN: Jeff Keller, *David Cleveland* (by 5/89), *Gary Lindemann* (by 1/90), *Fred Rose* (by 8/97), *Gary Lindemann* (by 11/97), *John Schroeder* (from 7/98), *Gary Lindemann* (by 1/00), *John Schroeder* (from 1/00), *Carrington Vilmont* (from 1/01), *Michael Babin* (from 12/03), *Carrington Vilmont* (by 1/04), *Michael Shawn Lewis* (by 2/04); CAST OF *Don Juan Triumphant*: PASSARINO: George Lee Andrews, *Thomas Sandri* (by 6/92), *Peter Atherton* (by 2/93), *Thomas Sandri* (by 3/94), *Scott Watanabe* (by 7/94), *Thomas Sandri* (by 9/94),

Matthew R. Jones (by 8/97), *Craig A. Benham* (by 4/98), *Richard Poole* (by 6/98), *John Kuether* (by 1/99), *James Romick* (by 10/99), *John Kuether* (by 11/99), *D.C. Anderson* (by 3/01), *Scott Mikita* (in 3/01), *John Kuether* (by 4/01), *James Romick* (by 3/02), *John Kuether* (by 4/02), *James Romick* (by 12/02), *John Kuether* (by 1/03), *Gary Mauer* (by 6/03), *Jim Weitzer* (from 11/03), *Carrington Vilmont* (from 12/03), *Michael Shawn Lewis* (from 12/03), *Carrington Vilmont* (by 2/04); 1ST PAGE: Candace Rogers-Adler, *Rhonda Dillon* (by 1/89), *Elena Jeanne Batman* (by 4/90) [role cut in 5/92 but re-instated in 9/93], *Dawn Leigh Stone* (from 9/93), *Marcy de Gonge-Manfredi* (by 11/93), *Alba Quezada* (by 2/94), *Marcy de Gonge-Manfredi* (by 3/94), *Wren Marie Harrington* (by 8/95), *Jennifer Little* (by 1/97), *Wren Marie Harrington* (by 8/97), *Diane Jennings* (by 4/98) [role not billed between 1/99 & 7/99], *Wren Marie Harrington* (in 7/99) [role not billed between 8/99 & 12/99], *Diane Jennings* (by 12/99), *Sally Williams* (by 7/00), *Kris Koop* (by 1/01) [role cut by 6/01]; 2ND PAGE: Olga Talyn, *Patrice Pickering* (by 5/90), *Leslie Giammanco* (stood in in 9/99), *Patrice Pickering* (from 9/99), *Patty Davidson-Gorbea* (by 12/00), *Leslie Giammanco* (in 1/01 & 2/01), *Sharon Wheatley* (by 3/01), *Kris Koop* (by 6/01); DON JUAN: played by Piangi; GYPSY DANCER: played by Meg; AMINTA: played by Christine; INNKEEPER'S WIFE: Jan Horvath, *Wysandria Woolsey* (by 8/89), *Lorian Stein* (by 1/90), *Rebecca Eichenberger* (from 7/90), *Alba Quezada* (by 7/92), *Rebecca Eichenberger* (by 9/92), *Teresa Eldh* (by 12/92), *Suzanne Ishee* (by 8/98), *Teresa Eldh* (from 8/98), *Johanna Wiseman* (by 9/99), *Wren Marie Harrington* (by 12/99), *Erin Stewart* (from 8/04); SPANISH LADY: Diane Ketchie (by 5/93), *Marci De Gonge-Manfredi* (by 11/93), *Alba Quezada* (by 2/94), *Marcy de Gonge-Manfredi* (by 3/94), *Wren Marie Harrington* (by 8/95), *Jennifer Little* (by 1/97), *Wren Marie Harrington* (by 8/97), *Diane Jennings* (by 4/98), *Liz McCartney* (by 3/99), *Sally Williams* (by 5/99), *Wren Marie Harrington* (by 6/99), *Diane Jennings* (by 12/99), *Sally Williams* (by 7/00), *Kris Koop* by 1/01), *Sally Williams* (by 3/03) [new role by 5/93] [end of the *Don Juan Triumphant* sequence]; BALLET CHORUS OF THE OPERA POPULAIRE: Irene Cho (gone by 10/88), Nicole Fosse (gone by 8/89; back by 11/89 & gone by 1/90), Lisa Lockwood (gone by 9/89; back by 5/91 & gone by 8/91), Lori MacPherson (gone by 4/89; back by 8/89 & gone by 11/92; back by 5/93 & gone by 1/95; back by 3/95 & gone by 5/97; back by 8/97 & gone by 2/99; back by 3/99 & gone by 5/99; back by 9/99 & gone by 7/00; back by 8/00 & gone by 5/03), Dodie Pettit (gone by 8/89; back by 9/89 & gone by 2/91), Catherine Ulissey (gone by 5/90; back by 6/90 & gone by 11/90), *Charlene Gehm* by 10/88 & gone by 3/89), *Alina Hernandez* by 3/89 & gone by 4/92; back by 5/92 & gone by 1/97), *Tener Brown* by 4/89 & gone by 2/91; back by 4/92 & gone by 2/93), *Tania Philip* (by 8/89 & gone by 3/95), *Teresa DeRose* (by 1/90 & gone by 5/90; back by 2/94 & gone by 3/94; back by 5/94 & gone by 5/95; back by 4/96 & gone by 5/96; back by 8/96 & gone by 9/96; back by 12/96 & gone by 2/97; back by 4/97 & gone by 6/97; back by 8/97 & gone by 4/98; back by 6/98 & gone by 8/98; back by 1/99 & gone by 10/99; back by 5/00 & gone by 7/01; back by 9/01 & gone by 1/02), *Natasha McAller* (by 5/90 & gone by 7/90), *Cherylyn Jones* (from 7/90 & gone by 5/94; back by 5/95 & gone by 5/97), *Christine Spizzo* (by 8/90 & gone by 9/90; back by 11/90 & gone by 12/90; back by 2/91 & gone by 5/92; back by 6/92 & gone by 8/00), *Kate Solmssen* (by 2/91 & gone by 9/92; back by 6/93 & gone by 2/94; back by 5/94 & gone by 5/95), *Alexia Hess* (by 9/92 & gone by 5/93), *Joan Tsao* (by 9/92 & gone by 5/93), *Harriet M. Clark* (by 12/92 & gone by 2/94), *Deanne Albert* (by 12/93 & gone by 2/94; back by 5/94 & gone by 10/94; back by 12/94), *Annemarie Lucania* (by 9/94 & gone by 1/95), *Wendi Lees Smart* (by 9/94 & gone by 1/95), *Nina Goldman* (by 3/95 & gone by 2/96; back by 8/96 & gone by 8/96; back by 2/97 & gone by 4/97; back by 8/97 & gone by 10/97; back by 1/98 & gone by 2/98; back by 8/98 & gone by 9/98; back by 3/99 & gone by 6/99; back by 7/99 & gone by 9/99), *Geralyn Del Corso* (by 5/95 & gone by 8/97), *Laurie LeBlanc* (by 8/95 & gone by 11/95), *Careen Hobart* (by 2/96 & gone by 10/97), *Emily Addona* (by 8/97 & gone by 1/01; back by 5/03 & gone by 7/03; back by 8/03 & gone by 9/03; back by 11/03; gone by 2/04; back by 3/04), *Marisa Cerveris* (from 4/97 & gone by 7/99; back by 9/99 & gone by 12/00), *Heather McFadden* (by 10/97 & gone by 2/99; back by 3/99 & gone by 8/99; back by 1/00 & gone by 8/01; back by 3/03 & gone by 7/03), *Elizabeth Nackley* (by 5/97 & gone by 8/03; back by 10/03 & gone by 11/03; back by 1/04), *Kitty Skillman Hilsabeck* (by 8/98 & gone by

9/98), *Diana Gonzalez* (by 8/98 & gone by 9/98; back by 11/98 & gone by 2/99), *Susannah Israel* (by 9/98 & gone by 11/98), *Kate Wray* (by 10/98 & left in 2/01; back by 8/01 & gone by 3/03), *Susan Gladstone* (by 3/99 & gone by 3/99), *Dana Stackpole* (by 6/99 & gone by 8/99), *Erin Brooke Reiter* (by 8/99 & gone by 9/99), *Leslie Judge* (by 10/99 & gone by 3/00), *Christina Lombardozzi* (by 7/00 & gone by 1/01), *Laura Martin* (by 8/00 & gone by 8/01; back by 9/01 & gone by 8/02), *Victoria Born* (by 12/00 & gone by 3/02; back by 4/02 & gone by 8/03), *Gianna Russillo* (by 1/01; she became Gianna Loungway in 10/01), *Anita Intrieri* (by 2/01 & gone by 5/01; back by 7/01 & gone by 1/02 back by 6/02 & gone by 12/02) 3/03), *Jessica Rudetsky* (by 3/03), *Carly Blake Sebouhian* (by 6/03), *Dianna Warren* (by 6/03), *Polly Baird* (by 7/03), *Sabra Lewis* (by 8/03). **Understudies**: Phantom: Jeff Keller (88–00), *Gary Barker* (91–93), *Hugh Panaro* (92–93), *Ciaran Sheehan* (93–94), *James Romick* (99–00); Christine: Rebecca Luker (88), *Jan Horvath* (88–89), *Raissa Katona* (89–99), *Laurie Gayle Stephenson* (93–99), *Elizabeth Southard* (99–00); Raoul: Cris Groenendaal (88), *Keith Buterbaugh* (88–89), *David Cleveland* (88–89), *James Romick* (89–00), *Gary Lindemann* (89–99), *John Schroeder* (99–00), *Jim Weitzer* (99–00); Carlotta: Beth McVey (88), Jan Horvath (88–89), *Suzanne Ishee* (89–93), *Dawn Leigh Stone* (89–93), *Elena Jeanne Batman* (91–93), *Rebecca Eichenberger* (91–93), *Diane Ketchie* (92–93), *Marci de Gonge-Manfredi* (93–99), *Teresa Eldh* (93–99), *Melody Johnson* (93–00), *Wren Marie Harrington* (99–00), *Johanna Wiseman* (99–00); Firmin: Peter Kevoian (88), George Lee Andrews (88–89), *Paul Laureano* (88–99), *Richard Warren Pugh* (89–00), *Peter Atherton* (92–99), *James Romick* (99–00), *John Kuether* (99–00); Andre: Peter Kevoian (88), George Lee Andrews (88–89, 99–00), *Frank Mastrone* (88–89), *Gary Barker* (89–93), *Nicholas F. Saverine* (91), *James Romick* (91–99), *James Thomas O'Leary* (92–99), *Richard Poole* (99–00); Piangi: Richard Warren Pugh (88–00), William Scott Brown (88–90), *Maurizio Corbino* (91–00); Mme Giry: Olga Talyn (88), Mary Leigh Stahl (88–00), *Suzanne Ishee* (89–93), *Patrice Pickering* (89–00), *Susan Russell* (99–00); Meg: Catherine Ulissey (88–90), Dodie Pettit (88–90), *Tener Brown* (91–93), *Cherylyn Jones* (91–99), *Kate Solmssen* (91–99), *Lori MacPherson* (91–99), *Kate Wray* (99–00), *Teresa DeRose* (99–00); Slave Master: Barry McNabb (88–89), *Jeff Siebert* (91), *Thomas Terry* (98–99), *Paul B. Sadler Jr.* (99–00); Solo Dancer: Barry McNabb, *Jeff Siebert* (91), *Wesley Robinson* (92–93), *Paul Sadler Jr.* (93–99), *Daniel Rychlec* (99–00). **Ballet Swings**: Denny Berry (gone by 4/89; back by 8/89 & gone by 5/90; back by 6/90 & gone by 2/94), *Lori MacPherson* (by 4/89 & gone by 8/89; back by 5/90 & gone by 6/90; added by 11/92 & gone by 5/93; back by 6/97 & gone by 6/97), *Harriet M. Clark* (by 2/94 & gone by 1/97; back by 4/98 & gone by 6/99; back by 8/00), *Laurie LeBlanc* (added by 8/95 & gone by 9/95), *Teresa DeRose* (added 4/96–7/96 & again in 6/97 & gone in 6/97; back by 6/99 7 gone by 6/99), *Susan Gladstone* (from 6/99 & gone by 8/00). **Swings:** Frank Mastrone (gone by 4/89), Alba Quezada (gone by 8/88; back by 6/89 & gone by 1/90; back by 5/92 & gone by 6/92; back by 12/92 & gone by 2/93), Keith Buterbaugh (gone by 1/90), *Suzanne Ishee* (by 8/88 & gone by 6/89; back by 1/90 & gone by 5/93; back by 4/96 & gone by 7/96), *Dodie Pettit* (by 8/89 & gone by 8/89), *James Romick* (from 1/90 & gone by 10/99; back by 11/99), *Paul Laureano* (by 4/89 & gone by 6/93), *Lawrence Anderson* (by 5/92 & gone by 7/92; back by 9/94 & left in 7/95), *John Dewar* (by 11/92 & gone by 5/93), *Laurie Gayle Stephenson* (by 5/93 & gone by 5/94), *Grant Norman* (by 6/93 & gone by 3/94), *Amick Byram* (by 6/93 & gone by 12/93), *Louise Edeiken* (by 5/94 & gone by 1/95), *Brad Little* (by 5/94 & gone by 1/95), *David P. Cleveland* (by 7/94 & gone by 10/94; back by 1/95 & gone by 1/95; back by 3/95 & gone by 5/95; back by 9/95 & gone by 11/95; back by 9/96 & gone by 12/96; back by 10/97 & gone by 4/98; back by 5/98 & left in 7/98), *Linda Poser* (by 7/94 & gone by 10/94; back by 1/95 & left in 7/98; back by 8/98 & gone by 5/99), *Virginia Croskery* (by 9/94 & gone by 3/95; back by 8/95 & gone by 11/95), *Gary Mauer* (by 7/95 & gone by 5/96; back by 3/03 & gone by 5/03), *Matthew R. Jones* (by 7/96 & gone by 4/98; back by 7/03), *Fred Rose* (by 4/96 & gone by 9/96), *Leslie Giammanco* (by 10/97 & gone by 12/97; back by 6/98 & gone by 2/99; back by 3/99 & gone by 7/99; back by 8/00 & gone by 5/01), *John Schroeder* (by 4/98 & left in 7/98), *Jim Weitzer* (by 7/98 & gone by 5/99; back by 6/99 & left 11/29/99; back by 12/00 & gone by 12/00), *D.C. Anderson* (by 8/98 & gone by 9/98), *Scott Mikita* (by 3/99 & gone by 4/99; back by 5/99 & gone by 6/99;

back by 6/00 & gone by 9/00; back by 2/01), *Sally Williams* (by 5/99 & gone by 7/99; back by 1/00 & gone by 6/00), *Susan Russell* (by 7/99 & gone by 5/00; back by 6/00 & gone by 8/02), *Michael Gerhart* (by 9/99 & gone by 11/99), *Ray Gabbard* (from 11/29/99 & gone by 9/00), *Michael Lackley* (by 8/00 & gone by 8/00), *Brian Noonan* (by 12/00 & gone by 7/01), *Sharon Wheatley* (by 8/01 & gone by 11/01; back by 10/01 & gone by 1/02; back by 10/04 & gone by 11/04), *Michael Babin* (by 9/01 & gone by 11/01; back by 8/02 & gone by 12/02; back by 1/03 & gone by 3/03; back by 7/03 & gone by 7/03), *Janet Saia* (by 8/02), *D.B. Bonds* (from 10/04). **Orchestra:** CONCERTMASTER: Louann Montesi, *Joyce Hammann*; VIOLINS: Louann Montesi (*Joyce Hammann*), Fred Buldrini, Alvin E. Rogers, Gayle Dixon, David Davis, Abraham Appleman, Leonard Rivlin, Jan Mullen; VIOLAS: Stephanie Fricker & Veronica Salas; CELLI: Bonnie Hartman (*Ted Ackerman*) & Jeanne LeBlanc; BASS: John Beal; HARP: Henry Fanelli; FLUTE: Sheryl Henze & Ralph Olsen; CLARINETS: Ralph Olsen & Matthew Goodman; OBOE: Robert Botti; BASSOON: Atsuko Sato; TRUMPETS: Lowell Hershey & Francis Bonny; BASS TROMBONE: Garfield Fobbs; FRENCH HORNS: Gary Johnson, R. Allen Spanjer (*David Smith*), Peter Reit; PERCUSSION: Eric Cohen & Jan Hagiwara; KEY-BOARDS: Jeffrey Huard (*Gregory J. Dlugos*) & Kristen Blodgette. **Prologue** The Stage of the Paris Opera House, 1911: Overture (Orchestra); **Act I:** Paris; 1881: **Scene 1** The dress rehearsal of *Hannibal*: "Think of Me" (Carlotta, Christine, Raoul); **Scene 2** After the gala: "Angel of Music" (Christine & Meg); **Scene 3** Christine's dressing room: "Little Lotte"/"The Mirror" (Angel of Music) (Raoul, Christine, Phantom); **Scene 4** The Labyrinth underground: "The Phantom of the Opera" (l: Mike Batt & Richard Stilgoe) (Phantom & Christine); **Scene 5** Beyond the lake: "The Music of the Night" (Phantom); **Scene 6** Beyond the lake; the next morning: "I Remember"/"Stranger than You Dreamt It" (Christine & Phantom); **Scene 7** Backstage: "Magical Lasso" (Buquet, Meg, Mme Giry, Ballet Girls); **Scene 8** The manager's office: "Notes/Prima Donna" (Firmin, Andre, Raoul, Carlotta, Mme Giry, Meg, Piangi, Phantom); **Scene 9** A performance of *Il Muto*: "Poor Fool, He Makes Me Laugh" (Carlotta & Company); **Scene 10** The roof of the Opera House: "Why Have You Brought Me Here?"/"Raoul, I've Been There" (Raoul & Christine), "All I Ask of You" (Raoul & Christine), "All I Ask of You" (reprise) (Phantom). **Act II:** Six months later: Entr'acte; **Scene 1** The staircase of the Opera House; New Year's Eve: "Masquerade"/"Why So Silent" (Full Company); **Scene 2** Backstage; **Scene 3** The manager's office: "Notes/Twisted Every Way" (Andre, Firmin, Carlotta, Piangi, Raoul, Christine, Mme Giry, Phantom); **Scene 4** A rehearsal of *Don Juan Triumphant*; **Scene 5** A graveyard in Peros: "Wishing You Were Somehow Here Again" (Christine), "Wandering Child"/"Bravo, Bravo" (Phantom, Christine, Raoul); **Scene 6** The Opera House stage before the premiere; **Scene 7** *Don Juan Triumphant*: "The Point of No Return" (Phantom & Christine); **Scene 8** The labyrinth underground: "Down Once More"/"Track Down This Murderer" (Full Company); **Scene 9** Beyond the lake.

Note: All music by Andrew Lloyd Webber. All lyrics by Charles Hart and Richard Stilgoe, unless otherwise indicated.

Broadway critics raved. The show recovered its $8 million capital investment in 60 weeks. It won Tonys for musical, direction of a musical, sets, costumes, and lighting, and for Michael Crawford, Judy Kaye, and was nominated for score, book, and choreography. In 1990 Andrew Lloyd Webber was sued by a relatively unknown Baltimore songwriter named Ray Repp, who claimed that Mr. Lloyd Webber had stolen his (Mr. Repp's) 1978 song "Till You," and that he had turned it into the title theme of *Phantom*. Mr. Lloyd Webber claimed never to have heard "Till You," but after it was brought to his attention, he countersued, saying that Mr. Repp had stolen "Till You" from "Close Every Door" (from the show *Joseph and the Amazing Technicolor Dreamcoat*). In 1994 the Repp suit was dismissed, but the Lloyd Webber countersuit continued until 1996, when it, too, was thrown out. However, in 1997 Mr. Repp got his decision reversed, and opened the case again. Mr. Lloyd Webber finally won on 12/15/98. In late 10/96 twelve actors were fired to relieve long-run-itis. This caused a stir with Equity and picketing actors. Like all Broadway shows it suffered from the 9/11/01 attack, and crew and cast agreed to a 25 per cent pay cut for a couple of weeks, to enable the show to go on. On 5/9/02 it became Broadway's 4th-longest-running musical of all time with 5,960 performances (*Oh! Calcutta!* had 5,959; *A*

Chorus Line had 6,137). By that date over 9 million people had seen the show on Broadway (and over 100 million worldwide) and it had taken in over $3 billion worldwide, making it the most successful stage musical of all time. At the 10/12/02 matinee it became the 3rd-longest-running Broadway show of all time, beating *A Chorus Line*. Cameron Mackintosh had now produced the three longest-running shows in Broadway history—*Cats*, *Les Miserables*, and *The Phantom of the Opera* (his *Miss Saigon* was then at No. 6). With the closing of *Les Miz* on 5/18/03, *Phantom* looked likely to storm ahead. The performance of 2/17/03 was canceled due to snow, and the 3/10/03 performance was canceled due to the musicians' strike. Howard McGillin was going to leave the role on 2/16/03, but carried on until 4/12/03 (he did 1,278 performances). It missed a performance during the 8/14/03 power blackout. On 8/28/03 it played its 6,500th performance, and on 2/2/04, with its 6,681th performance, it passed *Les Miserables* to become the second-longest running show of any kind ever in Broadway history (after *Cats*). At the 11/10/04 matinee *Phantom* played its 7,000th performance, and was now only 485 performances behind *Cats*. By that time 10 million people had seen it on Broadway, and it had taken in over $550 million.

After Broadway. JAPANESE TOUR. Opened on 4/29/88, in Tokyo. Previews from 4/15/88. It then played all around Japan, closing on 4/3/92, in Tokyo.

THEATER AN DER WIEN, Vienna, 12/21/88–4/8/90. Previews from 12/2/88. It then went to the RAIMUND THEATER, 6/10/90–6/30/93.

TOUR. Company No. 1, which became known as the Christine Company, Opened on 5/31/89, at the Ahmanson Theatre, Los Angeles. Previews from 5/18/89. It closed on 8/29/93, then went to the Curran Theatre, San Francisco, 12/12/93–1/3/98 (closing date extended from 12/13/97). Previews from 12/2/93. It played more than 2,100 performances at the Curran, and was San Francisco's most successful musical; three million people saw it there, and it took in over $150 million. MUSICAL DIRECTOR: Roger Cantrell. **Cast:** PORTERS: Maurizio Corbino (*Sean Smith*) & William Scott Brown; RAOUL: Reece Holland, *Michael Piontek, Ray Saar, Aloysius Gigl* (from 5/2/95), *Christopher Carl* (from 7/2/96); CARLOTTA: Leigh Munro, *Geena Jeffries* (in 6/96); PIANGI: Gualtiero Negrini; MEG: Elisabeth Stringer; CHRISTINE: Dale Kristien, *Lisa Vroman* (for the entire San Francisco stint); CHRISTINE (ALTERNATE): Mary D'Arcy, *Cristin Mortenson, Karen Culliver* (from 6/3/97); MME GIRY: Barbara Lang; ANDRE: Norman Large; FIRMIN: Calvin Remsberg; PHANTOM: Michael Crawford, *Robert Guillaume* (alternate, and then permanently from 5/1/90), *Michael Crawford, Davis Gaines, Franc D'Ambrosio* (from 3/28/94); PAGES: Patrice Pickering, Rhonda Dillon, Candace Rogers-Adler. **Swing:** Irene Cho.

TORONTO PRODUCTION. This production was actually a tour that only ever played in one venue. PANTAGES THEATRE, 9/20/89–10/31/99. Previews from 9/13/89. 4,226 PERFORMANCES. PRESENTED BY Garth Drabinsky, in association with Tina Vander Heyden & The Really Useful Theatre Company of Canada. This was the first major show produced by Garth Drabinsky (via his Cineplex Odeon—he resigned from Cineplex and founded Livent on 12/1/89, at which point, as he owned the rights to *Phantom*, the Toronto production became a Livent show). DIRECTOR: Hal Prince; MUSICAL DIRECTOR: Jeffrey Hubbard. **Cast:** PORTER/MARKSMAN: Laird Mackintosh (until 8/95); RAOUL: Byron Nease, *David Rogers* (by 2/94), *Christopher Shyer* (by 4/95), *Laird Mackintosh* (by 8/95), *David Rogers*; PRINCESS: *Melissa Dye* (in 94); SLAVE MASTER: Mark Dovey; CARLOTTA: Lyse Guerin, *Leigh Munro* (by 2/94), *Lyse Guerin* (by 4/95), *Sandra Mergolea* (in 4/95), *Kim Stengel* (by 4/96); PIANGI: Peter Cormican; MEG: Donna Rubin; CHRISTINE: Rebecca Caine, *Mary D'Arcy, Patti Cohenour, Teresa De Zarn* (by 2/94), *Glenda Balkan* (by 4/95), *Gay Willis, Glenda Balkan* (from 8/95), *Teresa De Zarn* (by 2/1/97), *Sylvia Rhyne* (by 4/97), *Margaret Ann Gates* (in 8/97), *Elizabeth De Grazia* (in 4/99), *Melissa Dye*; MME GIRY: Kristina Maria Guiguet (for the entire run); ANDRE: Paul Massell; FIRMIN: Gregory Cross, *Terry Hodges* (he closed the show); PHANTOM: Colm Wilkinson (for 4 years), *Jeff Hyslop* (from 94), *Cris Groenendaal* (from 94), *Ciaran Sheehan* (by 4/95), *Ethan Freeman* (from 96–97), *Peter Karrie* (for 2 years), *Rene Simard* (4/2/99–5/23/99), *Paul Stanley* (5/25/99–8/1/99), *Jeff Hyslop* (8/3/99–9/26/99), *Paul Stanley* (from 9/28/99). **Standby:** Phantom: Cris Groenendaal. **Male Swing:** Devin Dalton (for the entire run). It extended its closing date of 9/26/99. The *Fosse* tour came in to the Pantages on 12/8/99 to replace it. Many of the physical properties of this production went down to Mexico in 1999 (see below).

OSCARSTEATERN, Stockholm, 10/27/89–6/18/95. *Cast:* CHRISTINE: Elisabeth Berg, *Inger Olsson Moberg*; PHANTOM: Mikael Samuelson (for the entire run).

RIVAL VERSION. As used here, the term rival version means another musical which came out after Andrew Lloyd Webber's famous *Phantom of the Opera*, and which also using Gaston Leroux's story. The first of these rival versions was a serio-comical musical, *The Phantom of the Opera*, in 2 acts &12 scenes. It opened at the AL HIRSCHFELD THEATRE, Miami Beach on 2/5/90. A Karen Poindexter production, PRESENTED BY Abraham Hirschfeld; MUSIC/LYRICS: Lawrence Rosen & Paul Schierhorn; ADAPTED FROM the novel by Bruce Falstein; DIRECTOR/CHOREOGRAPHER: Darwin Knight; SETS: Ken Kurtz; COSTUMES: Susan Tsu; LIGHTING: Norman Coates; SOUND: Jeff Curtis; MUSICAL DIRECTOR: Sand Lawn; ORCHESTRATIONS: Curtis J. McKinly & Joe Gianono. *Cast:* RAOUL: Grant Norman; CARLOTTA: Beth McVey; CHRISTINE: Elizabeth Walsh; MME GIRY: Kim Ostrenko; BUQUET: James Baldwin; PHANTOM: David Staller. "Spirit of Music," "Shadows in the House," "Running the Show," "Jewel Song" (from *Faust*), "Light and Darkness," "An Able Woman," "Perfect Music, Perfect Love," "Danse Macabre," "Oh, Hellish Wrath," "Something Out There," "Excerpt from *Otello*," "Back into the Darkness."

TOUR. Company No. 2, which became known as the Raoul Company, opened on 6/2/90, at the Auditorium, Chicago. Previews from 5/24/90. It closed there on 2/6/91. Then it continued with the tour in various cities, including three stints at the Kennedy Center, Washington, DC — 6/6/91–9/28/91, 6/30/93–10/2/93, and 6/14/97–10/4/97. It also took in Chicago again, 12/18/93–6/25/94, and the Pantages Theatre, Los Angeles, 10/15/97–1/31/98 and again 8/30/98–11/15/98, where the tour ended. MUSICAL DIRECTOR: Jack Gaughan. *Cast:* RAOUL: Keith Buterbaugh, *Nat Chandler* (from 8/92), *Lawrence Anderson, Jason Pebworth* (from 1/13/98), *Lawrence Anderson* (from 7/98); PRINCESS: Sarah Pfisterer, *Dodie Pettit*; CARLOTTA: Patricia Hurd; PIANGI: Donn Cook; MEG: Patricia Ward; CHRISTINE: Karen Culliver, *Teri Bibb, Laurie Stephenson* (by 93–94), *Sandra Joseph* (3/26/96–1/98), *Marie Danvers* (from 1/13/98), *Teri Bibb* (from 4/98), *Marie Danvers* (from 6/98); CHRISTINE (ALTERNATE): Teri Bibb, *Sarah Pfisterer, Sandra Joseph* (from 2/27/96), *Susan Owen* (from 9/24/96), *Rita Harvey* (from 3/98), *Susan Facer* (from 6/98); MME GIRY: Olga Talyn; ANDRE: Rick Hilsabeck; FIRMIN: David Hunergayer; PHANTOM: Mark Jacoby, *Kevin Gray, Rick Hilsabeck* (93), *Craig Schulman* (1/30/97–9/97), *Ron Bohmer* (from 9/97), *Davis Gaines* (from 8/28/98).

NEUE FLORA THEATER, Hamburg, 6/29/90–6/30/01. Previews from 6/19/90.

AUSTRALIAN TOUR. Ran first in Melbourne, 12/8/90–6/5/93. Previews from 11/29/90. It ended in Perth, 9/13/98. *Cast*: PHANTOM: Anthony Warlow.

CANADIAN TOUR. Opened on 4/26/91, at the Ottawa National Arts Centre. It took in Singapore and Hong Kong in 1995.

TOUR. Company No. 3, which became known as the Music Box Company, opened on 12/13/92, at the Fifth Avenue Theatre, Seattle. Previews from 12/3/93. It closed there on 3/6/93, and continued with the tour. It was still running in 2003. MUSICAL DIRECTOR: Glenn Langdon. *Cast:* RAOUL: Ciaran Sheehan, *John Schroeder, Jason Pebworth* (from 1/29/97), *Jim Weitzer, Jason Pebworth* (from 7/22/98), *Richard Todd Adams* (from 3/31/99), *Jim Weitzer* (from 1/12/00), *John Cudia, Tim Martin Gleason*; CARLOTTA: Geena L. Jeffries, *Kelly Cae Hogan, Marilyn Caskey*; CHRISTINE: Tracy Shayne, *Adrienne McKewan* (from 9/20/95), *Diane Fratantoni* (from 3/12/96), *Adrienne McKewan* (from 7/30/96), *Kimilee Bryant* (from 11/1/96), *Kate Suber* (from 3/26/96), *Marie Danvers* (until 1/98), *Amy Jo Arrington, Rebecca Pitcher* (from 3/31/99), *Kathy Voytko, Julie Hanson, Rebecca Pitcher, Lisa Vroman*; CHRISTINE (AT MATINEES): Lisa Vroman, *Sylvia Rhyne, Susan Facer, Kimilee Bryant* (from 8/28/96), *Tamra Hayden* (from 11/1/96), *Marie Danvers, Megan Starr-Levitt* (from 1/21/98), *Marni Raab, Kathy Voytko*; ANDRE: Roger E. DeWitt; FIRMIN: David Cryer; PHANTOM: Franc D'Ambrosio, *Grant Norman, Thomas James O'Leary* (from 6/20/95), *Brad Little* (from 9/28/96), *Ted Keegan* (from 3/31/99), *Brad Little* (from 6/28/99), *Ted Keegan* (from 2/28/00), *Brad Little*; OTHERS: Mark Agnes & Gloria Hodes.

RIVAL VERSION. This was the second rival version, and was an entirely new version called, simply *Phantom*, with a more complex plot. PAPER MILL PLAYHOUSE, New Jersey, 1992–93 season. MUSIC/LYRICS: Maury Yeston; BOOK: Arthur Kopit; DIRECTOR: Robert Johanson; CHOREOGRAPHER: Sharon Halley; SETS: Michael Anania; LIGHTING: F. Mitchell Dana; MUSICAL DIRECTOR: Tom Helm. *Cast:* CHRISTINE: Marie-Laurence Danvers; COUNT: Paul Schoeffler; LA CARLOTTA: Patti Allison; JOSEPH BUQUET: J. Courtney Pollard; ERIK, THE PHANTOM: Richard White; GERARD: Jack Dabdoub; CHOLET: Vince Trani; CULTURE MINISTER: John Wilkerson; BALLET MASTER: John Wiltberger; JEAN-CLAUDE: Michael Hayward-Jones; FLORENCE: Alicia Richardson; FLORA: Conny Lee Sasfai; FLEURE: Ginger Thatcher; DESIGNER: Kevin Bogue; MUSIC DIRECTOR/BARITONE: William Paul Michals; INSPECTOR: Larry Grey; POLICEMEN: Kevin Bogue & Jeremy Koch; WAITERS: Kevin Bogue, Jeremy Koch, Dillon McCartney; OBERON: John Wasiniak; DIVAS: Joy C. Hermalyn & Mary C. Sheehan; DANCING BELLADOVA: Christiane Farr; YOUNG CARRIERE: Kirk Ryder; YOUNG ERIK: Matt Fasano. "Home," "Melodie de Paris," "My True Love," "This Place is Mine," "You Are Music," "You Are My Own." It had several regional tryouts.

VSB CIRCUSTHEATER, Scheveningen, Netherlands, 8/15/93–8/1/96. Previews from 8/1/93. 1,094 PERFORMANCES. This was the Dutch-language premiere. Hans Peter Janssens played both the Phantom & Raoul during the run. It was the longest-running theatre show in Netherlands history. 1,863,082 people saw it there. The cast recording (in Dutch) was the best-selling ever in Netherlands history.

UK TOUR. Opened on 10/19/93, at the Opera House, Manchester. Previews from 10/9/93. It closed on 1/7/95.

MUSICAL THEATER MESSE, Basel, Switzerland, 10/12/95–7/27/97.

CANADIAN TOUR. Opened on 4/30/97, at the Ford Center for the Performing Arts, Vancouver. Previews from 4/24/97. It closed there in 1998, without actually touring. *Cast:* PHANTOM: Peter Karrie; CHRISTINE: Teresa De Zarn.

UK TOUR. Opened on 6/30/98, at the Hippodrome, Birmingham. Previews from 6/24/98. It closed on 11/11/00, at the Opera House, Manchester.

Phantom II. By 1998 Andrew Lloyd Webber had written part of a libretto for a sequel to his famous musical *Phantom of the Opera*, and called it *Phantom II.* He also wrote one song for it — "The Heart is Slow to Learn" (which Kiri Te Kanawa sang at the composer's 50th birthday party). Frederick Forsyth's novel *The Phantom in Manhattan* was thought to be a prelude to this sequel, but it wasn't, apparently, and the sequel was shelved.

STADSSCHOUWBURG, Antwerp, 10/24/99–7/2/00. This was the Belgian premiere, in Dutch (the Dutch-language premiere, however, was in 1993 — see above). PRESENTED BY Music Hall; TRANSLATOR: Seth Gaaikema; DIRECTOR: Arthur Masella (re-produced Hal Prince's direction). *Cast:* RAOUL: Michael Lewis; CHRISTINE: Susanne Duwe; PHANTOM: Hans Peter Janssens.

TEATRO ALAMEDA I, Mexico City, 12/99–1/14/01. 400 PERFORMANCES. This was the Mexican premiere of *El Fantasma de la Opera*. PRESENTED BY OCESA & Morris Gilbert; DIRECTOR: Hal Prince. *Cast:* PHANTOM: Saulo Vasconcelos; CHRISTINE: Irasema Terrazas; RAOUL: Jose Joel. The sets, lighting, props, wigs and many of the costumes came from recently-closed Toronto production. The first Spanish-language recording was made from this production and released in 1/01.

SHANGHAI, China, 12/18/04–3/5/05. 97 PERFORMANCES.

THE MOVIE. In 1925 Lon Chaney made the character a household name in his remarkable (straight) movie portrayal. It has been made many times since, but always as a straight film (i.e. not a musical), including the famous 1943 version with Claude Rains. A movie of the musical had been rumored since 1997, when John Travolta was the main choice for the lead. By the late 1990s Antonio Banderas was front-runner, and he remained that way into 2003, along with Hugh Jackman. By this time Andrew Lloyd Webber had bought back the film rights from Warner Brothers, and things were beginning to move. It opened in London on 12/6/04, and in the USA on 12/22/04. DIRECTOR: Joel Schumacher. *Cast:* PHANTOM: Gerard Butler; CHRISTINE: Emmy Rossum; RAOUL: Patrick Wilson; CARLOTTA: Minnie Driver; ALSO WITH: Miranda Richardson, Ciaran Hinds, Simon Callow. There was one new song, written by Andrew Lloyd Webber (music) and Charles Hart (lyrics)—"Learn to Be Lonely" (Carlotta).

545. *Pickwick*

A musical "designed for the introduction of diverting characters and incidents attempting no ingenuity of plot" (Dickens' own words in the preface to his novel). Set in 1827, in and around London and Rochester.

Before Broadway. Originally called *Mr. Pickwick*, this British show opened for tryouts at the Palace Theatre, Manchester, on 6/3/63, then moved to London's West End, to the SAVILLE THEATRE, 7/4/63–2/27/65. 694 PERFORMANCES. DIRECTOR: Peter Coe; CHOREOGRAPHER: Leo Kharibian; SETS: Sean Kenny; COSTUMES: Roger Furse; MUSICAL DIRECTOR: Michael Reeves; ORCHESTRATIONS: Eric Rogers; LONDON CAST RECORDING on Philips. *Cast:* PICKWICK: Harry Secombe; HOT TODDY SELLER: Norman Warwick; SNODGRASS: Julian Orchard; JINGLE: Anton Rodgers, *Barrie Ingham*; MRS. BARDELL: Jessie Evans, *Hope Jackman*; COLD TODDY SELLER: Ian Burford; SLAMMER: Brendan Barry; BUZFUZ: Peter Bull; DODSON: Michael Darbyshire; TUPMAN: Gerald James, *Roderick Jones*; WINKLE: Oscar Quitak; FOGG: Tony Sympson; MARY: Dilys Watling; TONY WELLER: Robin Wentworth; RACHEL: Hilda Braid; ROKER: Reg Grey, *Terence Rigby*; SAM WELLER: Teddy Green.

After coming from England, and before Broadway, it opened at the Curran Theatre, San Francisco, on 4/19/65, and ran there for seven weeks; then it toured, very profitably. Broadway tryouts were at the Fisher Theatre, Detroit, 8/9/65–9/4/65. Roy Castle replaced David Jones (who later became Davy Jones, of the Monkees); Peter Bull replaced Brendan Barry; Edmond Varrato replaced Stanley Simmonds; and Brian Chapin replaced Sheldon Golomb. At that stage Sean Kenny was doing the lighting as well as the sets. Aside from that, it was the same basic crew as for the subsequent Broadway run (the stage managers were different, however). The musical numbers then were: "Business is Booming," "Debtors Lament," "That's What I'd Like for Christmas," "The Pickwickians," "A Bit of a Character," "Learn a Little Something," "There's Something About You," "You Never Met a Feller Like Me," "I'll Never Be Lonely Again," "More of Everything," "A Hell of an Election," "Very," "If I Ruled the World," "Talk," "That's the Law," "Do as You Would Be Done By." Certain numbers that had been in the British production never made it into the San Francisco (or Broadway) production — "British Justice," "Good Old Pickwick," "Learn a Little Something," "(That's) The Trouble with Women." For Broadway one of the San Francisco scenes was cut, and the order of appearance of some of the characters was changed.

The Broadway Run. FORTY-SIXTH STREET THEATRE, 10/4/65–11/20/65. 5 previews from 9/29/65. 56 PERFORMANCES. PRESENTED BY David Merrick, in association with Bernard Delfont; MUSIC: Cyril Ornadel; LYRICS: Leslie Bricusse; BOOK: Wolf Mankowitz; BOOK DOCTORED BY: Sidney Michaels; BASED ON the 1837 novel *The Posthumous Papers of the Pickwick Club* (better known as *The Pickwick Papers*), by Charles Dickens; ADAPTED BY: Keith Waterhouse & Willis Hall (billing removed); DIRECTOR: Peter Coe; CHOREOGRAPHER: Gillian Lynne; SETS: Sean Kenny; COSTUMES: Roger Furse & Peter Rice; LIGHTING: Jules Fisher; MUSICAL DIRECTOR/VOCAL ARRANGEMENTS: Ian Fraser; ORCHESTRATIONS: Eric Rogers; PRESS: Harvey B. Sabinson, Lee Solters, Lila King, David Powers; GENERAL MANAGER: Jack Schlissel; COMPANY MANAGER: Richard Highley; PRODUCTION STAGE MANAGER: William Dodds; STAGE MANAGERS: Peter Stern & Stanley Simmonds. *Cast:* HOT TODDY SELLER: Jim Connor; COLD DRINKS SELLER: Edmond Varrato; BIRD SELLER: Roger Le Page; HOT POTATO MAN: Gerrit de Beer; TURNKEY: Allan Lokos; ROKER: Peter Costanza; PICKWICK: Harry Secombe (1) ✩, *Taylor Reed*; AUGUSTUS SNODGRASS: Julian Orchard (6); TRACY TUPMAN: John Call; NATHANIEL WINKLE: Oscar Quitak; SAM WELLER: Roy Castle (2); MR. WARDLE: Michael Logan; RACHEL: Helena Carroll; ISABELLA: Nancy Haywood; EMILY: Sybil Scotford; FAT BOY: Joe Richards; MRS. BARDELL: Charlotte Rae (3); BARDELL JR.: Brian Chapin; MARY: Nancy Barrett; MR. JINGLE: Anton Rodgers (4); MAJOR DOMO: Jim Connor; DR. SLAMMER: Peter Costanza; 1ST OFFICER: Richard Neil-

son; 2ND OFFICER: Haydon Smith; LANDLORD: Edmond Varrato; MRS. LEO HUNTER: Elizabeth Parrish; MR. LEO HUNTER: Gerrit de Beer; DODSON: Michael Darbyshire; FOGG: Tony Sympson; WICKS: Haydon Smith; JACKSON: Keith Perry; USHER: Taylor Reed; BAILIFF: Stanley Simmonds; SGT BUZFUZ: Peter Bull (5); JUDGE: Richard Neilson; SGT SNUBBINS: Allan Lokos; JURY FOREMAN: Roger Le Page; ENSEMBLE (PASSERS-BY, OSTLERS, DEBTORS, MAIDS, DRINKERS, POTBOYS): Jyll Alexander, Michael Amber, Bruce Becker, Bill Black, Susan Cartt, William Coppola, Ann Davies, Gerrit de Beer, Jo Freilich, Mary Keller, Clyde Laurents, Don Lawrence, Roger Le Page, Selma Marcus, Ginia Mason, Lani Michaels, Ross Miles, Bill Nuss, Keith Perry, Taylor Reed, Haydon Smith, Nancy Stevens, Don Strong, Ann Tell, Edmond Varrato, Larry Whiteley; CHILDREN: Michael Easton, Richard Easton, Tracy Evans, Leslie Ann Mapes, Bonnie Turner. ***Understudies:*** Pickwick/Tupman: Taylor Reed; Sam: Roger Le Page; Snodgrass/Dodson: Keith Perry; Winkle: Larry Whiteley; Mrs. Bardell: Ann Tell; Wardle: Bill Coppola; Mary: Mary Keller; Fogg: Gerrit de Beer; Buzfuz: Peter Costanza; Jingle: Richard Neilson; Rachel: Elizabeth Parrish; Emily: Ann Davies; Isabella: Jill Alexander; Mrs. Leo Hunter: Selma Marcus; Bardell Jr.: Michael Easton; Judge/1st Officer: Clyde Laurents; Slammer/Roker: Stanley Simmonds. **Act I:** *Scene 1* The Pickwickians; *Scene 2* Introduces Mr. Pickwick to a new and not uninteresting scene in the great drama of life; *Scene 3* The first day's adventures; *Scene 4* Strongly illustrative of the position that the course of true love is not a railway; *Scene 5* Descriptive of a very important proceeding on the part of Mr. Pickwick; no less an epoch in his life than in his history; *Scene 6* Too full of adventure to be briefly described. **Act II:** *Scene 1* Some account of Eatanswill; the state of parties therein; and of the election of a member to serve in Parliament for that ancient, loyal and patriotic borough; *Scene 2* How the Pickwickians, when Mr. Pickwick stepped out of the frying-pan, walked gently and comfortably into the fire; *Scene 3* Showing how Dodson and Fogg were men of business; and how an affecting interview took place between Mr. Weller and his employer; *Scene 4* Is wholly devoted to a full and faithful report of the memorable trial of Bardell against Pickwick; *Scene 5* What befell Mr. Pickwick when he got into the Fleet; what prisoners he saw there; and how he passed the night; *Scene 6* In which the Pickwick Club is finally dissolved and everything concluded to the satisfaction of everybody. **Act I:** "I Like the Company of Men" (Pickwick, Snodgrass, Tupman, Winkle), "That's What I'd Like for Christmas" (Pickwick & Company), "The Pickwickians" (Pickwick, Snodgrass, Tupman, Winkle), "A Bit of a Character" (Jingle, Snodgrass, Winkle, Tupman), "There's Something About You" (Jingle, Rachel, Company), "A Gentleman's Gentleman" (Sam & Mary), "You Never Met a Feller Like Me" (Pickwick & Sam), "I'll Never Be Lonely Again" (Pickwick & Mrs. Bardell) [written specially for Broadway]. **Act II:** "Fizkin & Pickwick" (Company), "Very" (Jingle, Pickwick, Wardle), "If I Ruled the World" (Pickwick & Company) [the big hit], "I'll Never Be Lonely Again" (reprise) (The Pickwickians), "Talk" (Sam & Company), "That's the Law" (Pickwick, Dodson, Fogg, Company), "Damages" (Pickwick & Mrs. Bardell), "If I Ruled the World" (reprise) (Pickwick & Company).

Broadway reviews were totally divided. Harry Secombe, Roy Castle, and Charlotte Rae all received Tony nominations. David Merrick closed the show prematurely, while Harry Secombe was out with the mumps.

After Broadway. CHICHESTER, England, 1993. *Cast:* Harry Secombe, Roy Castle, Alexandra Bastedo, Glyn Houston, Ruth Madoc, Michael Howe, Peter Land.

546. *Pipe Dream*

Set in Cannery Row, Monterey County, California. Doc experiments in his biological lab without having an MD's certificate. He is attracted to tough girl drifter Suzy. Fauna is the owner of the local whorehouse, the Bear Flag Cafe.

Before Broadway. Cy Feuer and Ernest Martin bought the musical rights to John Steinbeck's 1945 novel *Cannery Row*, and hired Mr. Steinbeck to write the libretto. Frank Loesser was engaged to write the music and lyrics, and Henry Fonda and Julie Andrews were sought as stars. While Steinbeck was working on the libretto, he was also working on a new novel, *Sweet Thursday*, a re-working of *Cannery Row*, using the same setting and characters. Feuer & Martin decided to go with *Sweet Thursday* instead, but after a year they gave up, and handed the project to Rodgers & Hammerstein, who were now interested in doing their own musical of *Sweet Thursday*. The show cost $250,000, all funded by Rodgers & Hammerstein, with 20 percent of profits to go to Feuer & Martin (there were no profits, as it turned out). Russell Nype was announced for the role of Doc, and then David Wayne was. The part finally went to Bill Johnson, who was then on Broadway in *Kismet*. Richard Rodgers had a cancer operation while working on the show. Reviews of the Boston tryouts were favorable, and two songs—"The Happiest House on the Block" and "How Long?"—were both written on the road. Harold Clurman had never directed a Broadway musical before, and wasn't up to it. Mr. Hammerstein took over direction, and Josh Logan came in to help. "Sitting on the Back Porch" was cut before Broadway.

The Broadway Run. SHUBERT THEATRE, 11/30/55–6/30/56. 246 PERFORMANCES. PRESENTED BY Richard Rodgers & Oscar Hammerstein II; MUSIC: Richard Rodgers; LYRICS/BOOK: Oscar Hammerstein II; BASED ON the 1954 novel *Sweet Thursday*, by John Steinbeck; DIRECTOR: Harold Clurman; CHOREOGRAPHER: Boris Runanin; BALLET MASTER: Kazimir Kokich; SETS/LIGHTING: Jo Mielziner; COSTUMES: Alvin Colt; ASSISTANT COSTUMES: Florence Klotz & Frank Spencer; MUSICAL DIRECTOR: Salvatore Dell'Isola; ORCHESTRATIONS: Robert Russell Bennett; DANCE MUSIC ARRANGEMENTS: John Morris; PRESS: Michel Mok & Howard Atlee; CASTING: John Fearnley & Barbara Wolferman; PRODUCTION SUPERVISOR: Jerome Whyte; SECRETARY: Word Baker; GENERAL MANAGER: Morris Jacobs; COMPANY MANAGER: Maurice Winters; GENERAL STAGE MANAGER: Charles Atkin; STAGE MANAGER: Ruth Mitchell; ASSISTANT STAGE MANAGER: Beau Tilden. **Cast:** DOC: William Johnson (2); HAZEL: Mike Kellin (4); MILLICENT HENDERSON: Jayne Heller, *Mildred Slavin*; MAC: G.D. Wallace; SUZY: Judy Tyler (3); FAUNA: Helen Traubel (1), *Nancy Andrews*; JIM BLAIKEY: Rufus Smith, *Stokely Gray*; RAY BUSCH: John Call; GEORGE HERMAN: Gus Raymond; BILL: Steve Roland; RED: Keith Kaldenberg, *Don Blackey*; WHITEY: Hobe Streiford; DIZZY: Nicholas Orloff; EDDIE: Warren Kemmerling; ALEC: Warren Brown; JOE, THE MEXICAN: Kenneth Harvey; PANCHO, A WETBACK: Ruby Braff; AGNES: Temple Texas, *Sally Crane*; MABLE: Jackie McElroy; EMMA: Marilynn Bradley; BEULAH: Mildred Slavin; MARJORIE: Louise Troy; CHO CHO SEN: Pat Creighton; SUMI: Sandra Devlin; SONNY BOY: Joseph Leon; ESTEBAN, A WETBACK: Jerry La Zarre; A WAITER: Kazimir Kokich; HARRIET: Patricia Wilson; HILDA: Ruth Kobart; FRED: Marvin Krauter; SLICK: Gene Kevin; SLIM: Don Weissmuller; BASHA: Sigyn; BUBBLES: Marsha Reynolds, *Frances Martin*; SONYA: Annabelle Gold; KITTY: Jenny Workman; WEIRDE: Patti Karkalits, *Sally Crane*; JOHNNY GARRIAGRA: Scotty Engel; PEDRO: Rodolfo Cornejo; DR. ORMONDY: Calvin Thomas. **Understudies:** Fauna: Ruth Kobart; Doc/Jim: Warren Kemmerling; Suzy: Patricia Wilson; Mac/George: Warren Brown; Hazel: Guy Raymond; Ray: Keith Kaldenberg; Joe: Jerry La Zarre; Sonny Boy: Kaz Kokich; Millicent: Millie Slavin; Johnny/Pedro: Richard Mercado. Overture (Orchestra). **Act I: Scene 1** The Western Biological Laboratory: "All Kinds of People" (Doc & Hazel), "The Tide Pool" (Doc, Hazel, Mac, to Suzy), "All Kinds of People" (reprise) (Jim), "Everybody's Got a Home (But Me)" (Suzy); **Scene 2** Cannery Row; a few weeks later; **Scene 3** The Palace Flophouse; immediately following: "(On) A Lopsided Bus" (Mac, Hazel, Kitty, Sonya, The Flophouse Gang), "Bums' Opera" ("You Can't Get Away with a Dumb Tomato") (Fauna's Song) (Fauna, Joe, Pancho, The Flophouse Gang) [this version differs from the one heard on the cast recording]; **Scene 4** Cannery Row; a few days later, on a Sweet Thursday; **Scene 5** The Western Biological Laboratory: "The Man I Used to Be" (Doc) (danced by Slim), "Sweet Thursday" (Fauna); **Scene 6** Cannery Row; **Scene 7** A Room in the Bear Flag Cafe: "Suzy is a Good Thing" (Fauna & Suzy); **Scene 8** Cannery Row; Scene 9 Sonny Boy's Pier Restaurant: "All at Once You Love Her" (Doc, Suzy, Esteban). **Act II:** Entr'acte; **Scene 1** A Room in the Bear Flag Cafe; the following morning: "The Happiest House on the Block" (Fauna & The Girls); **Scene 2** Cannery Row: "The Party that We're Gonna Have Tomorrow Night"

(Mac & The People of Cannery Row); **Scene 3** The Palace Flophouse; the following night: Masquerade Brawl at the Flophouse (dance): a/ "The Party Gets Going" (Company); b/ "I Am a Witch" (published in the vocal score as "We Are a Gang of Witches") (Fauna, Agnes, Marjorie, Beulah, Mable); c/ "Will You Marry Me?" (Suzy, Fauna, Doc); **Scene 4** Cannery Row; next day: "Thinkin'" (Hazel); **Scene 5** The Bear Flag Cafe; a few weeks later: Serenade: "All at Once You Love Her" (reprise) (Fauna); **Scene 6** Cannery Row; next evening: "How Long?" (Fauna, Doc, Flophouse Boys, Bear Flag Girls); **Scene 7** Inside "The Pipe:" "The Next Time it Happens" (Suzy & Doc); **Scene 8** Cannery Row; the next morning; **Scene 9** The Western Biological Laboratory: Finale: "Sweet Thursday" (reprise) (Company).

The show had advance sales of $1.2 million, the largest in Broadway history to that time. For this show Rodgers & Hammerstein lifted their ban (in place since 1946) on theatre parties, and *Pipe Dream* opened with more than 70 performances sold to groups. Broadway reviews were so-so and divided, and Steinbeck himself predicted that the show would be a Rodgers & Hammerstein two-year flop. It won a Tony Award for costumes, and was also nominated for musical, direction, choreography, sets, musical direction, and for Bill Johnson, Mike Kellin, and Judy Tyler. In late 3/56 the show was revised, and several numbers were moved around. Helen Traubel began missing performances, and when her contract came up three weeks before the end of the run, she quit, and was replaced by Nancy Andrews. It lost a small amount of its investment. The reason for its failure may be that it was sanitized, the characters cleaned up. Helen Traubel was another reason. But the show was without suspense or conflict.

After Broadway. There was no tour. It was scheduled for an autumn 1956 opening in London's Theatre Royal, Drury Lane, but it never happened. Again, a movie never happened, even though it was proposed years later, using the Muppets as the stars.

547. *Pippin*

Pippin (a variant spelling of Pepin), son of Frankish ruler Charles, searches for himself as warrior, lover, king, and family man. He finally settles down with Catherine. The action takes place in and around the year 780, in and around the Holy Roman Empire. No intermission.

Before Broadway. Stephen Schwartz (using the name Lawrence Stephens) wrote *Pippin, Pippin* (as he called it then) while he was a student at Carnegie-Mellon University, Pittsburgh, where it was first produced on 5/1/67. After the success of Mr. Schwartz's *Godspell* on Broadway, *Pippin* (it had been renamed) was optioned for Broadway by Stuart Ostrow. Motown invested $135,000 in exchange for the rights to record the original cast album, but the producer could only come up with another $365,000 of the additional $565,000 necessary. But with cuts (mostly in the sets) it worked. Stuart Ostrow put up $120,000, and Bob Fosse put up $3,500 as a trust fund for his daughter Nicole. Roger O. Hirson re-wrote the story, and Mr. Fosse also contributed. There was a lot of tension between Stephen Schwartz and Bob Fosse, the young Mr. Schwartz claiming that Mr. Fosse was perverting his work. Mr. Fosse finally banned him from all rehearsals. Rehearsals took place in New York, then the show went to the Kennedy Center, Washington, DC, for tryouts, 9/20/72–10/4/72. Roger Stevens, director of the Kennedy Center's Opera House, put in another $120,000, and guaranteed a $50,000 a week gross during its run there. At this point Bob Fosse's friend Paddy Chayefsky recommended cutting the intermission.

The Broadway Run. IMPERIAL THEATRE, 10/23/72–3/13/77; MINSKOFF THEATRE, 3/15/77–6/12/77. 5 previews from 10/17/72. 1,944 PERFORMANCES. PRESENTED BY Stuart Ostrow; MUSIC/LYRICS: Stephen Schwartz; BOOK: Roger O. Hirson; DIRECTOR/CHOREOGRAPHER: Bob Fosse; ASSISTANT DIRECTORS/ASSISTANT CHOREOGRAPHERS: Louise Quick & Kathryn Doby; SETS: Tony Walton; COSTUMES: Patricia Zipprodt; LIGHTING: Jules Fisher; SOUND: Abe Jacob; MUSICAL DIRECTOR: Stanley Lebowsky (gone by 75–76), *Rene Wiegert* (added by 74–75), *Milton Setzer* (added by 76–77); ORCHESTRATIONS: Ralph Burns; DANCE MUSIC ARRANGEMENTS: John Berkman; CAST RECORDING on Motown;

PRESS: Solters/Sabinson/Roskin; CASTING: Michael Shurtleff; GENERAL MANAGERS: Joseph Harris & Ira Bernstein; COMPANY MANAGER: *Nancy Simmons* (by 75–76); PRODUCTION STAGE MANAGER: Phil Friedman; STAGE MANAGERS: Lola Shumlin & Paul Phillips (Mr. Phillips gone by 75–76), *Roger A. Bigelow* (by 73–74 & gone by 75–76), *Herman Magidson* (by 74–75), *Edward Preston* (by 74–75 & gone by 75–76), *John H. Lowe III* (by 75–76), *Andy Keyser* (by 75–76), *Paul Bowen* (by 76–77). **Cast**: LEADING PLAYER: Ben Vereen (5) ☆, *Northern J. Calloway* (from 2/18/74), *Ben Vereen* (from 5/7/74), *Samuel E. Wright* (from 12/74), *Irving Lee* (from 6/75), *Ben Harney* (from 1/12/76), *Northern J. Calloway* (from 5/24/76); PIPPIN: John Rubinstein (6) ☆, *Dean Pitchford* (on Mondays), *Michael Rupert* (from 11/74), *Dean Pitchford* (12/1/75–12/8/75), *Michael Rupert*; CHARLES: Eric Berry (1) ☆; LEWIS: Christopher Chadman, *Justin Ross* (by 74–75), *Jerry Colker* (by 75–76); FASTRADA: Leland Palmer (3) ☆, *Priscilla Lopez* (from 1/6/74), *Patti Karr* (from 8/5/74), *Antonia Ellis* (from 1/5/76); MUSICIAN: John Mineo, *Ken Urmston* (by 74–75) [this character later became the Sword Bearer]; THE HEAD: Roger Hamilton; BERTHE: Irene Ryan (4) ☆, *Lucie Lancaster* (from 4/73), *Dorothy Stickney* (from 6/11/73), *Lucie Lancaster* (from 7/74), *Fay Sappington* (during Miss Lancaster's vacation, 8/18/75–9/1/75), *Fay Sappington* (from 12/75); BEGGAR: Richard Korthaze, *Larry Merritt* (by 74–75), *Roger A. Bigelow* (by 75–76), *Ken Miller* (from 75–76); PEASANT: Paul Solen, *Chet Walker* (by 74–75), *John Windsor* (by 76–77); NOBLE: Gene Foote, *Larry Giroux* (from 73–74), *Bryan Nicholas* (by 75–76); FIELD MARSHAL: Roger Hamilton; CATHERINE: Jill Clayburgh (2) ☆, *Betty Buckley* (from 6/11/73), *Joy Franz* (from 2/10/76); THEO: Shane Nickerson, *Douglas Grober* (by 75–76), *Shamus Barnes* (by 76–77); PLAYERS: Kathryn Doby, Jennifer Nairn-Smith, Candy Brown, Ann Reinking, Pamela Sousa, *Sandahl Bergman, Patti D'Beck, Vicki Frederick, Kathrynann Wright*. **Standbys**: Leading Player: Northern J. Calloway, *Irving Lee* (by 73–74), *P.J. Benjamin*; Pippin: Walter Willison; Berthe: Lucie Lancaster; Theo: Will McMillan, *Mathew Anton* (by 73–74). **Understudies**: Leading Player: Gene Foote, *Quitman Fludd III* (by 75–76); Pippin: Dean Pitchford (73–74), *John Windsor*; Berthe: Fay Sappington (by 74–75), *Dortha Duckworth* (by 75–76); Theo: George Parry (by 74–75), *Evan Turtz* (by 75–76), *Sparky Shapiro*; Charles: Roger Hamilton; Catherine: Ann Reinking, *Louise Quick* (by 73–74), *Joy Franz* (by 74–75), *Verna Pierce* (by 75–76), *Carol Fox Prescott*; Fastrada: Candy Brown, *Mitzi Hamilton* (by 74–75), *Patti D'Beck* (by 75–76), *Virginia McColl*. **Dance Alternates**: Cheryl Clark (gone by 75–76), Roger A. Bigelow, *Andy Keyser* (by 74–75 and gone by 75–76)), *Jill Owens* (by 74–75), *Eileen Casey* (by 75–76). **Orchestra**: KEYBOARDS: Edward Strauss & Michael Alterman; WOODWINDS: Daniel Trimboli, Seymour Red Press, Samson Giat, John Campo; BRASS: Irving Berger, Eddie Bert, Kenny Rupp, Tony Salvatori, Arthur Goldstein, Doug Norris; STRINGS: Marvin Morgenstern, Fred Manzella, Al Fishman, Maurice Bialkin, Ronald Lipscomb; GUITARS: Don Thomas, Charles Macey, Michael Fleming; PERCUSSION: Maurice Mark, Stanley Koor, Bernie Karl; HARP: Nancy Brennand. *Scene 1* The opening: "Magic to Do" (Players), "Corner of the Sky" (Pippin); *Scene 2* Home: "Welcome Home" (Charles & Pippin); *Scene 3* War: "War is a Science" (Charles & Pippin), "Glory" (Leading Player); *Scene 4* The flesh: "Simple Joys" (Leading Player), "No Time at All" (Berthe & Boys, "With You" (Pippin & Girls); *Scene 5* Revolution: "Spread a Little Sunshine" (Fastrada), "Morning Glow" (Pippin); *Scene 6* Encouragement: "On the Right Track" (Leading Player & Pippin); *Scene 7* The hearth: "Kind of Woman" (Catherine & Girls), "Extraordinary" (Pippin), "Love Song" (Pippin & Catherine); *Scene 8* The finale: Finale (Players).

The advance at the Broadway box-office was only $350,000. Reviews were mostly excellent, but after an initial rush at the gate, receipts dropped off alarmingly. It was decided to do 30-second TV commercial, showing extracts from the war sequence, with Ben Vereen, Pamela Sousa and Candy Brown. And it worked. It was the first Broadway musical to do this. It was the fourth-longest running musical of the 1970s, returning a net profit of $3,318,415. It won Tonys for direction of a musical, choreography, sets, lighting, and for Ben Vereen, and was also nominated for musical, score, book, costumes, and for Irene Ryan and Leland Palmer. In 1999 Ben Vereen's Tony was stolen and held to ransom — by his daughter's ex-boyfriend.

After Broadway. LONDON, 10/30/73. 85 PERFORMANCES. It got bad reviews. *Cast*: LEADING PLAYER: Northern J. Calloway; PIPPIN: Paul Jones; CHARLES: John Turner; CATHERINE: Patricia Hodge; FASTRADA: Diane Langton; BERTHE: Elisabeth Welch.

TOUR. Opened on 9/20/74, at the Masonic Temple, Scranton, Pa., and closed on 4/5/75, in Wilmington, Del., after 91 cities. MUSICAL DIRECTOR: Milton Setzer. *Cast*: LEADING PLAYER: Irving Lee; PIPPIN: Barry Williams; LEWIS: Adam Grammis; FASTRADA: Louisa Flaningam; BERTHE: Dortha Duckworth; FIELD MARSHAL: Loyd Sannes.

POST-BROADWAY TOUR. Opened on 8/3/77, in Washington, DC. It ran at the Kennedy Center, Washington, DC, from 9/7/77. MUSICAL DIRECTOR: Roland Gagnon. *Cast*: PIPPIN: Michael Rupert; LEADING PLAYER: Larry Riley; CHARLES: Eric Berry; LEWIS: Jerry Colker; FASTRADA: Antonia Ellis, *Carole Schweid*; SWORDBEARER: Ken Urmston; HEAD/FIELD MARSHAL: David Pursley; BERTHE: Thelma Carpenter; BEGGAR: Lee Mathis; PEASANT: Clayton Strange; NOBLE: Andy Hostettler; CATHERINE: Alexandra Borrie; THEO: Shamus Barnes. **Standbys**: Berthe: Lynn Archer; Theo: Jo Jo Barnes.

PAPER MILL PLAYHOUSE, New Jersey, 1978. DIRECTOR: Gene Foote. *Cast*: Northern J. Calloway.

TOUR. Opened on 7/8/86, in Dallas, and closed on 11/9/86, at the Van Wezel Theatre, Sarasota, Fla. PRESENTED BY Tom Mallow & James Janek; DIRECTOR: Ben Vereen; CHOREOGRAPHER: Kathryn Doby; SETS: Tony Walton; COSTUMES: Patricia Zipprodt; LIGHTING: Ken Billington; SOUND: Abe Jacob; MUSICAL DIRECTOR: David Loeb. *Cast*: LEADING PLAYER: Ben Vereen; CHARLES: Ed Dixon; LEWIS: Michael Kubala (2); FASTRADA: Ginger Prince; NOBLE: Greg Schanuel; BERTHE: Betty Ann Grove; PIPPIN: Sam Scalamoni.

Enabled by a court ruling, Stephen Schwartz restored the script to his original concept for unsuccessful productions in Mexico and Australia. Thus there are really two different versions of *Pippin*, the well-known one being Bob Fosse's, and the other being Stephen Schwartz's.

PAPER MILL PLAYHOUSE, New Jersey, 6/16/00–7/23/00. 11 previews from 6/7/00. 45 PERFORMANCES. This version was slightly revised by Stephen Schwartz & Roger O. Hirson. There was a sneak press preview on 6/1/00, at the Lawrence A. Wein Dance Center, Manhattan. DIRECTOR: Robert Johanson; NEW CHOREOGRAPHY: Rob Ashford (Bob Fosse's choreography did not appear); SETS: Michael Anania; COSTUMES: Gregg Barnes; OPENING NUMBER COSTUMES: Gene Meyer; LIGHTING: Kirk Bookman; SOUND: David B. Smith; MUSICAL DIRECTOR: Danny Kosarin; NEW ORCHESTRATIONS: David Siegel; DANCE MUSIC ARRANGEMENTS: David Chase; MAGIC CONSULTANT: Charles Reynolds. *Cast*: PIPPIN: Jack Noseworthy; LEADING PLAYER: Jim Newman; BERTHE: Charlotte Rae; ALSO WITH: Sara Gettelfinger, Ed Dixon, Natascia A. Diaz; ENSEMBLE: Timothy J. Alex, Roxane Barlow, Amy Heggins, Matt Lashey, Aixa M. Rosario Medina. At 10.25, 6/7/00, on the first night of previews, pyrotechnics caused a fire alarm to go off, the show was stopped and 838 people had to be evacuated. There was no fire [Note: On 1/14/80 an arsonist had torched the original Paper Mill Playhouse, and it burned to the ground. A new one was built in 1982, after a huge subscription drive].

GRAND BALLROOM, Manhattan Center, 11/29/04. One-night all-star concert, to benefit the National AIDS fund, and the non-profit Storm Theatre. It raised $93,000 before expenses. PRESENTED BY Kate Shindle & Jamie McGonnigal; DIRECTOR: Gabriel Barre (Jamie McGonnigal was to have directed); CHOREOGRAPHER: Andy Blankenbuehler; MUSICAL DIRECTOR: Mark Hartman. *Cast*: LEADING PLAYER: Darius de Haas, Billy Porter, Kate Shindle, Rosie O'Donnell; PIPPIN: Michael Arden; CHARLES: Terrence Mann; LEWIS: Cameron Mathison; FASTRADA: Julia Murney; BERTHE: Charles Busch; CATHERINE: Laura Benanti; THEO: Harrison Chad; ALSO WITH: Kristoffer Cusick, Barrett Foa, Cheyenne Jackson, Jordan Gelber, Robb Sapp.

FREUD PLAYHOUSE, UCLA, Calif., 1/25/05–2/6/05. Part of the *Reprise!* series.

548. *The Pirates of Penzance*

Frederic is accidentally apprenticed to a Pirate King, and falls in love with Mabel, one of Maj.-Gen. Stanley's 20 daughters. The score was radically re-orchestrated to include synthesizers and to bring Gilbert and Sullivan's story up to date.

Before Broadway. The original 12/31/1879 [sic] production premiered at the FIFTH AVENUE THEATRE, NY — the only Gilbert and Sullivan operetta to premiere in the USA. Being a Gilbert and Sullivan it has been performed many times, of course, over the years. The New York Shakespeare Festival production (Joseph Papp, producer) ran Off Broadway at the DELACORTE THEATRE, 7/15/80–8/31/80. 10 previews. 42 PERFORMANCES. Pop stars Linda Ronstadt and Rex Smith were brought in to appeal to younger audiences. It had the same basic credits as for the subsequent Broadway run, except COMPANY MANAGERS: Roger Gindi & Rheba Flegelman. It had the same cast too, except RUTH: Patricia Routledge (replaced by Estelle Parsons before Broadway); EDITH: Alice Playten (replaced before Broadway by Alexandra Korey); ANOTHER DAUGHTER: Audrey Lavine (also replaced before Broadway). Scott Burkholder, Ray Gill, George Kmeck, Daniel Marcus, and Ellis Skeeter Williams were not in the cast, whereas Keith David and Barry Tarallo were. *Understudies*: Pirate King: Keith David; Frederic: Barry Tarallo; Sergeant: Tim Flavin; Stanley: Walter Niehenke; Mabel: Nancy Heikin; Edith/Kate/Isabel: Maria Guida. *Swing*: Audrey Lavine. Then the show went to Broadway.

The Broadway Run. URIS THEATRE, 1/8/81–8/8/81; MINSKOFF THEATRE, 8/12/81–11/28/82. 15 previews. Total of 772 PERFORMANCES. The New York Shakespeare Festival production, PRESENTED BY Joseph Papp; MUSIC: Arthur S. Sullivan; LYRICS/BOOK: W.S. (William Schwenk) Gilbert; a new production of the 1879 British Comic Operetta, ADAPTED BY William Elliott; DIRECTOR: Wilford Leach; CHOREOGRAPHER: Graciela Daniele; SETS: Bob Shaw & Wilford Leach; SET SUPERVISOR: Paul Eads; PIRATE BOAT DESIGNER: Jack Chandler; COSTUMES: Patricia McGourty; LIGHTING: Jennifer Tipton; SOUND: Don Ketteler; MUSICAL DIRECTOR/ORCHESTRATIONS/VOCAL PREPARATION: William Elliott; CAST RECORDING on Elektra/Asylum Records; PRESS: Merle Debuskey; CASTING: Rosemarie Tichler, Stanley Soble, Ellyn Long Marshall, Sarah Ream; GENERAL MANAGER: Robert Kamlot; COMPANY MANAGER: Charles Willard; PRODUCTION STAGE MANAGER: Zane Weiner; STAGE MANAGER: Frank Di Filia; ASSISTANT STAGE MANAGER: Roy Alan, *Bonnie Panson*. **Cast:** THE PIRATE KING: Kevin Kline (1) ☆, *Treat Williams* (from 8/25/81), *Walter Niehenke* (1/12/82–1/26/82), *Treat Williams*, *Gary Sandy* (from 3/23/82), *James Belushi* (from 8/27/82), *Wally Kurth* (from 9/14/82); SAMUEL, HIS LIEUTENANT: Stephen Hanan, *Walter Niehenke, Louis Valenzi*; FREDERIC, THE PIRATE APPRENTICE: Rex Smith (5) ☆, *Mark Beudert* (stood in during Mr. Smith's illness, 6/81), *Robby Benson* (from 7/28/81), *Patrick Cassidy* (from 1/5/82), *Rex Smith* (during Mr. Cassidy's vacation, 4/13/82–4/27/82), *Peter Noone* (from 7/27/82); RUTH, A PIRATE MAID-OF-ALL-WORK: Estelle Parsons (2) ☆, *Kaye Ballard* (from 9/15/81), *Marsha Bagwell* (from 9/28/82); MAJ-GEN. STANLEY'S DAUGHTERS: EDITH: Alexandra Korey, *Nancy Heikin*; KATE: Marcie Shaw, *Bonnie Simmons, Valerie Piacenti*; ISABEL: Wendy Wolfe, *Maria Guida*; MABEL: Linda Ronstadt (3) ☆ (until 5/81), *Karla De Vito* (during Miss Ronstadt's illness, from 1/9/81, then took over permanently from 6/2/81), *Maureen McGovern* (from 9/8/81), *Kathryn Morath* (during Miss McGovern's vacation, 2/16/82–3/2/82), *Pam Dawber* (6/29/82–7/20/82), *Maureen McGovern*; AND: Robin Boudreau, Maria Guida, Nancy Heikin, Bonnie Simmons, *Cheryl Hodges, Janene Lovullo, Donna Lee Marshall, Kathy Morath*; MAJOR GENERAL STANLEY: George Rose (4) ☆, *George S. Irving* (from 12/8/81), *Joseph Pichette* (from 3/9/82), *George Rose* (from 3/16/82); THE SERGEANT OF POLICE: Tony Azito, *David Garrison* (from 12/8/81), *Tony Azito* (from 3/16/82); PIRATES AND POLICEMEN: Dean Badolato, Mark Beudert, Brian Bullard (gone by 81–82), Scott Burkholder, Walter Caldwell, Tim Flavin, Ray Gill (gone by 81–82), George Kmeck, Daniel Marcus (*Wally Kurth*), G. Eugene Moose (*Nick Jolley*), Joseph Neal, Walter Niehenke, Joe Pichette, Ellis Skeeter Williams, Michael Edwin Willson (gone by 81–82), *Phil La Duca, Jeff McCarthy, James Caddell, Don Goodspeed, Morgan MacKay, Robert Polenz, Michael Scott, Martin Walsh, Mark Watson, Thom Fielder, Gary T. Raglan, Dean Regan*; ENSEMBLE: *Spring Fairbank, Larry French, Susan Goodman, Phil La Duca*. **Understudies**: Pirate King: Ray Gill, *Walter Niehenke* (81–82), *Jeff McCarthy* (81–82), *Wally Kurth, Michael Scott*; Samuel: G. Eugene Moose, *Nick Jolley*; Ruth: Wendy Wolfe, *Spring Fairbank*; Frederic: Scott Burkholder (81–82), *Marc Beudert* (81–82), *Robert Polenz, Louis Valenzi*; Edith: Nancy Heikin, *Donna Lee Marshall*; Stanley: Joe Pichette, *Martin Walsh*; Sergeant: Daniel Marcus, *Wally Kurth*; Mabel: Karla De Vito,

Kathy Morath (81–82), *Janene Lovullo*; Kate: Bonnie Simmons, *Susan Goodman*; Isabel: Maria Guida, *Cheryl Hodges*. **Swings**: Laurie Beechman, Roy Alan, *Robert Polenz* (81–82), *Donna Lee Marshall* (81–82), *Valerie Piacenti* (81–82), *Iris Revson*. **Orchestra:** WINDS: Richard Cohen & Simeon Westbrooke; FLUTES: Keith Underwood & Sheryl Henze; TRUMPETS: Lauren Draper & Ron Stinson; TROMBONES: Keith Greene; KEYBOARDS: Dan Berlinghoff, Allen Shawn, Susan Anderson, Ada Janik; PERCUSSION: William Moersch, William Ruyle, Larry Spivack; BASS: Dennis Masuzzo & Michael Tomasulo; CLARINET: Steven Hartman. **Act I**: "Pour, O Pour the Pirate Sherry" (Pirate King, Samuel, Frederic, Pirates), "When Frederic Was a Little Lad" (Ruth), "Oh, Better Far to Live and Die" (Pirate King & Pirates), "O False One, You Have Deceived Me!" (Ruth & Frederic), "Climbing Over Rocky Mountain" (Edith, Kate, Daughters), "Stop, Ladies, Pray!" (Frederic & Daughters), "Oh, Is There Not One Maiden Breast?" (Frederic & Daughters), "Poor Wandering One" (Mabel & Daughters), "What Ought We to Do?" (Edith, Kate, Daughters), "How Beautifully Blue the Sky" (Mabel, Frederic, Daughters), "(Stay), We Must Not Lose Our Senses" (Frederic, Daughters, Pirates), "Hold Monsters!" (Mabel, Samuel, Major-General, Daughters, Pirates), "I Am the Very Model of a Modern Major-General" (Major-General & Ensemble), "O Men of Dark and Dismal Fate" (Ensemble). **Act II**: "Oh, Dry the Glistening Tear" (Mabel & Daughters), "Then Frederic" (Major-General & Frederic), "When the Foeman Bares His Steel" (Sergeant, Mabel, Police, Daughters), "Now for the Pirates' Lair!" (Frederic, Pirate King, Ruth), "When You Had Left Our Pirate Fold" (Ruth, Frederic, Pirate King), "My Eyes Are Fully Open" [from *Ruddigore*] (Frederic, Ruth, Pirate King), "Away! Away! My Heart's on Fire" (Ruth, Pirate King, Frederic), "All is Prepared" (Mabel & Frederic), "Stay, Frederic, Stay!" (Mabel & Frederic), "Sorry Her Lot" [from *HMS Pinafore*] (Mabel), "No, I Am Brave" (Mabel, Sergeant, Police), "When a Felon's Not Engaged in His Employment" (Sergeant & Police), "A Rollicking Band of Pirates We" (Pirates, Sergeant, Police), "With Cat-Like Tread (Upon Our Prey We Steal)" (Pirates, Police, Samuel), "Hush, Hush! Not a Word!" (Frederic, Pirates, Police, Major-General), "Sighing Softly to the River" (Major-General & Ensemble), Finale (restoration of part of the 1879 New York finale by Richard Traubner) (Ensemble).

This was the only Gilbert and Sullivan comic opera to have a commercial run on Broadway. Reviews were tremendous. The show won Tonys for reproduction of play or musical, direction of a musical, and for Kevin Kline. It was also nominated for choreography, and for Tony Azito, George Rose, and Linda Ronstadt. On the second night Miss Ronstadt became ill, and after only one rehearsal Karla De Vito stood in for her. In 6/81 Rex Smith fell ill, and his understudy was on vacation. Chorus member Mark Beudert persuaded the stage manager that he knew the role, and went on, bringing the house down. Joe Papp was in the audience that night, and Mr. Beudert was advanced to co-understudy for the role.

After Broadway. TOUR. Opened on 6/10/81, at the Ahmanson Theatre, Los Angeles. CONDUCTOR: Vincent Fanuele. **Cast**: PIRATE KING: Barry Bostwick, *James Belushi* (from 9/23/81); STANLEY: Clive Revill, *Leo Leyden* (from 12/1/81); FREDERIC: Andy Gibb, *Patrick Cassidy* (from 9/23/81), *Peter Noone* (from 12/1/81); RUTH: Jo Anne Worley, *Marsha Bagwell* (from 12/1/81); MABEL: Pam Dawber, *Caroline Peyton* (from 9/23/81); ISABEL: Patti Cohenour, *Janene Lovullo*; SERGEANT: Paxton Whitehead, *Paul Ainsley* (from 12/1/81), *Wally Kurth* (during Mr. Ainsley's absence, 2/13/82–3/18/82).

LONDON. Opened on 5/26/82. **Cast**: PIRATE KING: Tim Curry; RUTH: Annie Ross; MABEL: Pamela Stephenson; STANLEY: George Cole; FREDERIC: Michael Praed; SERGEANT: Chris Langham.

THE MOVIE. 1983. DIRECTOR: Wilford Leach. The cast had Angela Lansbury instead of Estelle Parsons, but most of the other original Broadway cast appeared in the film.

549. *Plain and Fancy*

Set in the present. Don, a sophisticated New Yorker, owns a farm in Bird-in-Hand, an Amish community in Pennsylvania where cars, phones, indoor plumbing and buttons are some of the things eschewed as a modern evil. He comes to Bird-in-Hand with his wise-cracking girlfriend Ruth, to sell the farm to strict Amish farmer Yoder, who has arranged a marriage for his less devout daughter Katie, to Ezra Reber. Katie, however, is in love with Ezra's brother, Peter, her childhood sweetheart, who has been "shunned" (exiled) from the community for being too independent. Yoder's farm burns down when lightning strikes it, and the community blames Peter for putting a hex on it. Peter rescues his brother from a carnival brawl and is re-instated into the good graces of the fickle sect.

Before Broadway. It first ran at the SHUBERT THEATRE, New Haven, 12/11/54–12/18/54.

The Broadway Run. MARK HELLINGER THEATRE, 1/27/55–2/26/55; WINTER GARDEN THEATRE, 2/28/55–11/7/55; MARK HELLINGER THEATRE, 11/9/55–3/3/56. Total of 461 PERFORMANCES. PRESENTED BY Richard Kollmar & James W. Gardiner, in association with Yvette Schumer; MUSIC: Albert Hague; LYRICS: Arnold B. Horwitt; BOOK: Joseph Stein & Will Glickman; DIRECTOR: Morton Da Costa; CHOREOGRAPHER: Helen Tamiris; ASSISTANT CHOREOGRAPHER: Daniel Nagrin; SETS/COSTUMES: Raoul Pene du Bois; LIGHTING: Peggy Clark; MUSICAL DIRECTOR/CHORAL DIRECTOR: Franz Allers; ORCHESTRATIONS: Philip J. Lang; VOCAL ARRANGEMENTS: Crane Calder; PRESS: Bill Doll, Robert Ullman, Merle Debuskey, Seymour Krawitz; GENERAL MANAGER: Al Green, *Al Jones*; PRODUCTION STAGE MANAGER: John Cornell; STAGE MANAGER: Edward Strum; ASSISTANT STAGE MANAGER: Alan North. **Cast:** RUTH WINTERS: Shirl Conway (4); DAN KING: Richard Derr (1), *Eric Fleming* (from 1/56); A MAN: John Dennis, *James Schlader*; ANOTHER MAN: Chris Robinson; KATIE YODER: Gloria Marlowe (8); PAPA YODER: Stefan Schnabel (7); ISAAC MILLER: Sammy Smith; EMMA MILLER: Nancy Andrews (5); EZRA REBER: Douglas Fletcher Rodgers (9); HILDA MILLER: Barbara Cook (2); A YOUNG MILLER: Scotty Engel; ANOTHER YOUNG MILLER: Elaine Lynn; PETER REBER: David Daniels (3); RACHEL: Ethel May Cody; SAMUEL ZOOK: Daniel Nagrin (6); LEVI STOLZFUSS: William Weslow; JACOB YODER: Will Able; SAMUEL LAPP: Chris Robinson; ABNER ZOOK: Edgar Thompson; IKE PILERSHEIM: James S. Moore; MOSES ZOOK: John Dennis, *James Schlader*; ABNER ZOOK [sic]: Tim Worthington; AN AMISHMAN: Robert Lindgren; ANOTHER AMISHMAN: Herbert Surface; BESSIE: Faith Daltry; SARAH: Renee Orin; ESTHER: Sybil Lamb; REBECCA: Betty McGuire; MARY: Muriel Shaw; STATE TROOPER: Ray Hyson; DANCERS: Sara Aman, Saint Amant, Joan Darby, Imelda De Martin, Crandall Diehl, Ina Hahn, Marcia Howard, Lucia Lambert, Ronnie Lee, Bob Lindgren, James S. Moore, Philip Nasta, Ann Needham, Robert St. Clair, Tao Strong, Beryl Towbin, William Weslow, David Wood, *Cathy Conklin, Jeff Duncan, Diana Hunter*; SINGERS: Marilynn Bradley, Paul Brown, John Dennis, Faith Daltry, Janet Hayes, Ray Hyson, Jack Irwin, Bob Kole, Sybil Lamb, Betty McGuire, Renee Orin, Chris Robinson, Jim Schlader, Muriel Shaw, Herb Surface, Edgar F. Thompson, Tim Worthington, Betty Zollinger, *Suzanne Easter, Martha* Flynn. **Standbys:** Papa: Richard Sharretts; Emma/Ruth: Jo Hurt. **Understudies:** Dan: Chris Robinson; Katie: Renee Orin; Jacob: Bob St. Clair; Ezra: Edgar F. Thompson; Samuel Lapp: Crandall Diehl; Peter Reber: Ray Hyson; Hilda: Sybil Lamb; Isaac: Alan North; State Trooper: James Schlader. **Act I:** *Scene 1* A section of road, outside Lancaster, Pa.: "You Can't Miss It" (Dan, Ruth, Ensemble), "It Wonders Me" (Katie) [intended as the big number]; *Scene 2* Another part of the road; *Scene 3* The Yoder barnyard: "Plenty of Pennsylvania" (Emma, Ezra, Another Young Miller, Ensemble), "Young and Foolish" (Peter) [the big hit]; *Scene 4* The Yoder parlor: "Why Not Katie?" (Ezra & the Men); *Scene 5* Side porch of the Yoder house; *Scene 6* Barnyard on the River Farm: "Young and Foolish" (reprise) (Katie & Peter), "By Lantern Light" (danced by Daniel Nagrin, Ann Needham, with Sara Aman, Lucia Lambert, Tao Strong, Saint Amant, Crandall Diehl, Bob St. Clair); *Scene 7* A bedroom in the Yoder home: "It's a Helluva Way to Run a Love Affair" (Ruth), "This is All Very New to Me" (sung & danced by Hilda, Another Amishman, Levi, Ensemble); *Scene 8* The Yoder barnyard: "Plain We Live" (Papa & Ensemble); *Scene 9* In the Yoder barn: The Shunning (Company). **Act II:** *Scene 1* The River Farm: "How Do You Raise a Barn?" (Papa, Ezra, Emma, Samuel, Ensem-

ble), "Follow Your Heart" (Peter, Katie, Hilda); *Scene 2* Kitchen of the Yoder home: "City Mouse, Country Mouse" (Emma, with Sarah, Esther, Mary, Rachel, Rebecca); *Scene 3* Back porch of the Yoder home; *Scene 4* Bedroom of the Yoder home: "I'll Show Him!" (Hilda); *Scene 5* A section of the road: "Young and Foolish" (reprise) (Katie); *Scene 6* A carnival grounds: Carnival Ballet (Hilda, Ezra, Company): On the Midway: MAMBO JOE: Daniel Nagrin; SCRANTON SAL: Sara Aman; SWAMI: Robert Lindgren; SAILOR: Will Able; BARKERS: Philip Nasta, Chris Robinson, Edgar F. Thompson [end of Midway sequence]; Dance Hall (Company); *Scene 7* Side porch of the Yoder house; *Scene 8* The Yoder barnyard: "Take Your Time and Take Your Pick" (Hilda, Dan, Ruth), Finale: "Plenty of Pennsylvania" (reprise) (Entire Company).

Broadway reviews were great. It had to vacate the Mark Hellinger to make way for another incoming musical—*Ankles Aweigh*. It went to the Winter Garden, then got kicked out of there, for a similar reason (*The Vamp* was coming in), and went back to the Hellinger, where it continued to do good business. By mid–1956 it closed because *My Fair Lady* was coming in.

After Broadway. THEATRE ROYAL, Drury Lane, London, 1/25/56–10/27/56. 315 PERFORMANCES. CHOREOGRAPHER: Philip Nasta; MUSICAL DIRECTOR: Reginald Burston. **Cast:** RUTH: Shirl Conway, *Roberta Huby*; DAN: Richard Derr, *Bruce Trent*; ABNER: Terence Donovan; ANOTHER MAN/TROOPER: Ivor Emmanuel, *Edwin Hill*; ISAAC: Bernard Spear; EZRA: Reed de Rouen; PETER: Jack Drummond, *Ivor Emmanuel*; HILDA: Joan Hovis.

TOUR. Opened on 3/6/56, at the Forrest Theatre, Philadelphia, and closed on 5/5/56, at the Nixon Theatre, Pittsburgh. MUSICAL DIRECTOR: Jay Chernis. **Cast:** PAPA YODER: Stefan Schnabel; ISAAC: Sammy Smith; PETER: David Daniels; SAMUEL: Daniel Nagrin; JACOB: Will Able; ABNER: Edgar Thompson; IKE: James S. Moore; TROOPER: Ray Hyson; EMMA: Nancy Andrews; RACHEL: Ethel May Cody; REBECCA: Betty McGuire; RUTH: Evelyn Page; DAN: James Nichols; KATIE: Faye Winfield; EZRA: Harry Fleer; HILDA: Dran Seitz; LEVI: Robert Piper; SAMUEL/ANOTHER MAN: George Ritner; ESTHER: Lu Leonard; DANCING CHORUS INCLUDED: Bob St. Clair.

For a few years it was produced all over the country by amateur groups, but then it began to look very out of date.

EQUITY LIBRARY THEATRE, NYC, 3/6/80–3/30/80. 31 PERFORMANCES. DIRECTOR: Bill Herndon; CHOREOGRAPHER: Diana Baffa-Brill; MUSICAL DIRECTOR: Kristen Blodgette. **Cast:** DAN: David Greenan; HILDA: Beverly Lambert; EMMA: Mary Stout; KATIE: Donna Bullock.

550. *Platinum*

A musical with a flip side. Lila is a 1940s movie musical star, now reduced to touring companies of *Hello, Dolly!* and *Mame*. In the opening number, "Nothing But," she is in Hollywood's newest environmental recording studio trying to record where her old soundstage used to be, and reminiscing about what it took to be a movie star back then. She tries a comeback, and in a recording studio meets fading rock star Dan Danger, who writes her a hit song, and with whom she starts a relationship. Act II is six weeks later. The *Wings of Destiny* sequence was conceived and directed by Joe Layton.

Before Broadway. It started out as *Sunset*, a staged reading at the MANHATTAN THEATRE CLUB in 1976. DIRECTOR: James Coco. It was Mr. Coco's idea to expand it into a full-sized musical, and as such it premiered at the STUDIO ARENA, Buffalo, in the fall of 1977, with Alexis Smith in the lead, and Lisa Mordente in the cast. BOOK: Louis La Russo II; DIRECTOR: Tommy Tune. Before it tried out at the Kennedy Center, in Washington, DC, the name was changed to *Platinum*, Joe Layton replaced Tommy Tune as director, and a new book was written by Will Holt and Bruce Vilanch. Paramount Pictures partly funded it, and allowed the show to rehearse on one of its old soundstages.

The Broadway Run. MARK HELLINGER THEATRE, 11/12/78–12/10/78. 12 previews. 33 PERFORMANCES. The Joe Layton production, PRESENTED BY Gladys Rackmil, Fritz Holt, Barry M. Brown; MUSIC:

Gary William Friedman; LYRICS: Will Holt; BOOK: Will Holt & Bruce Vilanch; BASED ON an original idea by Will Holt; DIRECTOR/CHOREOGRAPHER: Joe Layton; ADDITIONAL CHOREOGRAPHY/ASSISTANT CHOREOGRAPHER: Damita Jo Freeman; SETS: David Hays; COSTUMES: Bob Mackie; LIGHTING: John Gleason; SOUND: Charles Bugbee Jr., Paramount Sound, Steve Wooley; SOUND CONSULTANT: Abe Jacob; MULTIMEDIA DESIGN: Sheppard Kerman; MUSICAL DIRECTOR: Fred Thaler; ORCHESTRATIONS: Fred Thaler & Jimmie Haskell; MUSICAL ARRANGEMENTS: Fred Thaler, Jimmie Haskell, Gary William Friedman; PRESS: Shirley Herz & Jan Greenberg; CASTING: Amos Abrams; GENERAL MANAGER: Marvin A. Krauss; COMPANY MANAGER: Sam Pagliaro; PRODUCTION STAGE MANAGER: Frank Hartenstein; STAGE MANAGER: Charles Collins; ASSISTANT STAGE MANAGER: Bonnie Walker. *Cast:* SHULTZ: Tony Shultz (8); LILA HALLIDAY: Alexis Smith (1) ✩; SNAKE: Ronnie B. Baker; MINKY: Jonathan Freeman; BORIS: John Hammil; DAMITA: Damita Jo Freeman (4); ROBIN: Robin Grean (5); AVERY: Avery Sommers (6); JEFF LEFF: Stanley Kamel (7); CRYSTAL MASON: Lisa Mordente (3); DAN DANGER: Richard Cox (2) ✩; CHRISTINE: Christine Faith; WENNDY: Wenndy Leigh MacKenzie; ALAN FAIRMONT: Jonathan Freeman; THE SIDEMEN: FRED (PIANO): Fred Thaler; GREG (VIOLIN): Gregory Bloch; DICK (GUITAR): Dick Frank; STEVE (BASS): Steve Mack; ROY (DRUMS): Roy Markowitz; *Wings of Destiny Film Sequence Cast*: WAR BRIDE: Lila Halliday (Alexis Smith); MACK: Alan Fairmont (Jonathan Freeman). *Understudies*: Dan: Tony Shultz; Crystal, Damita, Robin, Avery: Wenndy Leigh MacKenzie; Shultz: Jonathan Freeman; Jeff: Ronnie B. Baker. *Side I:* "Back with a Beat"/"Nothing But"(Lila), "Sunset" (Crystal, Avery, Damita, Robin), "Ride, Baby, Ride" (Dan, Damita, Robin, Avery), "Destiny" (War Bride), "Disco Destiny" (orch: Harold Wheeler) (Crystal & Company), "I Am the Light" (Dan), "Movie Star Mansion" (Dan & Lila). *Flip Side*: "Platinum Dreams" (Avery, Damita, Robin), "Trials and Tribulations"/"I Like You" (Crystal & Lila), "1945" (Dan & Lila), "Too Many Mirrors" (Lila), "Old Times, Good Times" (orch: Harold Wheeler) (Lila & Company).

Broadway reviews were mostly awful, although Alexis Smith got raves. The production closed losing $1,743,000 on an intended investment of $1,125,000. Alexis Smith and Richard Cox were both nominated for Tonys.

After Broadway. The revised version, with the original title (*Sunset*), presented in a Hollywood cafe setting, about the lives of four entertainers, opened Off Broadway, at the VILLAGE GATE DOWNSTAIRS, 11/7/83. 13 previews. 1 performance. MUSIC/ORCHESTRATIONS: Gary William Friedman; WORDS: Will Holt; DIRECTOR: Andre Ernotte; CHOREOGRAPHER: Buzz Miller; SETS: Kate Edmunds; COSTUMES: Patricia Zipprodt; MUSICAL DIRECTOR: Donald York. *Cast:* Tammy Grimes, Ronee Blakley, Kim Milford, Walt Hunter. "Sunset City," "La Bamba," "Nothing But," "Funky," "Destiny," "Back with a Beat," "Standing in Need," "Rock is My Way of Life," "Sunset Dreams," "Rap," "Cheap Chablis," "Stuck on the Windshield of Life," "1945," "Retreat," "I Am the Light," "Moments," "Old Times, Good Times," "This One's for Me."

551. *Play Me a Country Song*

A bundle of country songs packaged as an all-night party in a favorite truck-stop saloon that is about to close.

The Broadway Run. VIRGINIA THEATRE, 6/27/82. 14 previews. 1 PERFORMANCE. PRESENTED BY Frederick R. Selch; MUSIC/LYRICS: John R. Briggs & Harry Manfredini; BOOK: Jay Broad; DIRECTOR: Jerry Adler; CHOREOGRAPHER: Margo Sappington; SETS: David Chapman; COSTUMES: Carol Oditz; LIGHTING: Marc B. Weiss; SOUND: Robert Kerzman; MUSICAL DIRECTOR/VOCAL ARRANGEMENTS: Phil Hall; PRESS: Alpert/LeVine Public Relations; CASTING: Cheryl Raab; GENERAL MANAGER: Robert S. Fishko; PRODUCTION STAGE MANAGERS: Alisa Adler & Jonathan Weiss. *Cast:* NORM: Reed Jones; ELLEN: Mary Gordon Murray; TONY: Stephen Crain; FRED: Jay Huguely; HOWARD: Ronn Carroll; LIZZIE: Louisa Flaningam; FRANCES: Karen Mason; PENNY: Mary Jo Catlett; BUSTER: Kenneth Ames; MEG: Candace Tovar; JEROME: Rene Clemente; HANK: Rick Thomas. *Understudies*: Fred/Howard/Tony/

Hank: Kevin Scannell; Norm/Buster/Jerome: Brad Miskell; Lizzie/Penny/Frances: Brooks Almy; Ellen/Meg: Susan Powers. *The Band*: PIANO: Phil Hall; BASS: Harvey Auger; ELECTRIC GUITAR: John Cariddi; DRUMS: Perry Cavari; ELECTRIC KEYBOARDS: Ronald Delseni; PEDAL STEEL GUITAR/BANJO: Marc Horowitz; FIDDLE/ACOUSTIC GUITAR: Kenny Kosek; BACKUP SINGERS: Brooks Almy, Brad Miskell, Susan Powers. *Act I*: "Sail Away" (Ellen), "Rodeo Dreams" (Norm), "Why Does a Woman Leave Her Man?" (Fred), "Eighteen-Wheelin' Baby" (Meg, Lizzie, Penny, Ellen), "Waitin' Tables" (Lizzie & Company), "Playing for Position" (Jerome & Buster), "Just Thought I'd Call" (Hank), "Sing-a-Long" (Frances, Howard, Company), "Sail Away" (reprise)/"If You Don't Mind" (Ellen & Tony), "Play Me a Country Song" (Company). *Act II*: "Coffee, Beer and Whiskey" (Fred & Company), "Only a Fool" (Meg & Hank), "You Can't Get Ahead" (Penny), "You Have to Get it Out to Get Away" (Ellen), "Big City" (Buster), "My Sweet Woman" (Fred & Men), "All of My Dreams" (Lizzie & Women), "Rodeo Rider" (Tony & Company).

Reviews were awful.

552. *Play On!*

Set in the Magic Kingdom of Harlem during the Swingin' 40s. Vy comes up from the south to be a songwriter, but discovers that it's a man's world. With the help of her cousin, Jester, she dresses as a man, and is introduced to the world's greatest bandleader, Duke, who is in a slump after a breakup with his girlfriend, Lady Liv, the best and most beautiful singer in the world. Duke sends Vy (dressed as a man) to Liv with one of Vy's songs, but Liv falls in love with Vy. Rev, uptight club manager, is in love with Liv. Sweets is the conductor. C.C. is Jester's girl.

Before Broadway. Originally produced by the OLD GLOBE THEATRE, San Diego, 9/14/96, with the same crew and cast as for the subsequent Broadway run, except DENIZENS OF HARLEM: Crystal Allen, Wendee Lee Curtis, Frantz G. Hall, Bryan Haynes, Kimberly Hester, Derrick Demetrius Parker, Stacie Precia, Lisa Scialabba, William Wesley, Darius Keith Williams.

The Broadway Run. BROOKS ATKINSON THEATRE, 3/20/97–5/11/97. 19 previews from 3/7/97. 61 PERFORMANCES. PRESENTED BY Mitchell Maxwell, Eric Nederlander, Thomas Hall, Hal Luftig, Bruce Lucker, Mike Skipper, and Victoria Maxwell, in association with Kery Davis & Alan J. Schuster; MUSIC/LYRICS: Duke Ellington (unless otherwise noted); BOOK: Cheryl L. West; BASED LOOSELY ON *Twelfth Night*, by William Shakespeare; CONCEIVED BY/DIRECTOR: Sheldon Epps; CHOREOGRAPHER: Mercedes Ellington; SETS: James Leonard Joy; COSTUMES: Marianna Elliott; LIGHTING: Jeff Davis; SOUND: Jeff Ladman; MUSICAL SUPERVISOR/ORCHESTRATIONS: Luther Henderson; MUSICAL DIRECTOR: J. Leonard Oxley; CAST RECORDING on Varese Sarabande; PRESS: Richard Kornberg, Jim Byk, Rick Miramontez, Don Summa; GENERAL MANAGER: Charlotte W. Wilcox; COMPANY MANAGER: Susan Sampliner; STAGE MANAGERS: Robert Mark Kalfin, Lurie Horns Pfeffer, Jimmie Lee Smith, Matthew Aaron Stern. *Cast:* VY: Cheryl Freeman; JESTER: Andre De Shields; SWEETS: Larry Marshall; MISS MARY: Yvette Cason; CC: Crystal Allen; DUKE: Carl Anderson; REV: Lawrence Hamilton; LADY LIV: Tonya Pinkins; DENIZENS OF HARLEM: Ronald Cadet Bastine, Jacquelyn Bird, Wendee Lee Curtis, Byron Easley, Alan H. Green, Frantz G. Hall, Gil P., Lacy Darryl Phillips, Lisa Scialabba, Erika Vaughn, Karen Callaway Williams. *Understudies*: Liv: Angela Robinson; Vy/Mary: Stacie Precia & Angela Robinson; Duke: William Wesley & Alan H. Green; Rev: Frantz G. Hall & Alan H. Green; Sweets: Gil P. & Alan H. Green; Jester: Bryan S. Haynes & Lacy Darryl Phillips; CC: Wendee Lee Curtis. *Swings*: Germaine Goodson, Bryan S. Haynes, Stacie Precia, William Wesley. *Musicians*: PIANO: George Caldwell; REEDS: Jerome Richardson, William Easley, Jimmy Cosier; TRUMPETS: Earl Gardner, Virgil Jones, Stanton Davis; TROMBONE: Britt Woodman; BASS: Ben Brown; PERCUSSION: Brian Grice. *Act I*: *Scene 1* Grand Central Station: "Take the A Train" (m/l: Billy Strayhorn) (Vy & Ensemble); *Scene 2* 125th Street: "Drop Me off in Harlem" (l: Nick Kenny) (Vy &

Denizens of Harlem), "Jester's Snake Song" (m: Luther Henderson) [number cut before Broadway], "I've Got to Be a Rug Cutter" (Jester, Vy, Cotton Club Dancers); *Scene 3* The Duke's apartment: "I Let a Song Go Out of My Heart" (m/l: Duke Ellington, Irving Mills, Henry Nemo, John Redmond) (Duke); *Scene 4* The Cotton Club: "C Jam Blues" (Cotton Club Dancers), "Mood Indigo" (m/l: Duke Ellington, Irving Mills, Albany Bigard) (Lady Liv); *Scene 5* Lady Liv's dressing room: "Don't Get Around Much Any More" (l: Bob Russell) (Vy & Lady Liv), "Don't You Know I Care?" (l: Mack David) (Rev); *Scene 6* The Cotton Club: "It Don't Mean a Thing (If It Ain't Got That Swing)" (l: Irving Mills) (Jester, Miss Mary, Sweets, Rev); *Scene 7* The Duke's studio: "I Got it Bad and That Ain't Good" (l: Paul Francis Webster) (Duke & Vy), "Hit Me with a Hot Note and Watch Me Bounce" (l: Don George) (Vy, Duke, Duke's Band); *Scene 8* The Cotton Club; *Scene 9* Alley outside of the Cotton Club: "I'm Just a Lucky So and So" (l: Mack David) (Jester & Cotton Club Dancers); *Scene 10* The Cotton Club: "Everything but You" (m/l: Duke Ellington, Don George, Harry James) (Lady Liv & Vy), "Solitude" (m/l: Duke Ellington, Eddie DeLange, Irving Mills) (Vy, Duke, Lady Liv, Rev). *Act II*: *Scene 1* The Cotton Club: "Perdido" (m/l: Juan Tizol, H.J. Lengsfelder, Ervin Drake) [number cut before Broadway], "Black Butterfly" (m/l: Duke Ellington, Ben Carruthers, Irving Mills) (Lady Liv's Escorts), "I Ain't Got Nothin' but the Blues" (l: Don George) (Lady Liv); *Scene 2* Lady Liv's dressing room; *Scene 3* The Cotton Club: "I'm Beginning to See the Light" (m: Duke Ellington, Don George, Harry James, Don Hodges) (Rev & Cotton Club Dancers), "I Got it Bad and That Ain't God" (reprise) (Rev); *Scene 4* Outside of the Cotton Club: "I Didn't Know About You" (l: Bob Russell) (Vy) [number added for Broadway after San Diego tryouts]; *Scene 5* The Cotton Club: "Rocks in My Bed" (Sweets & Jester); *Scene 6* Lady Liv's apartment: "Something to Live For" (l: Billy Strayhorn) (Rev & Lady Liv); *Scene 7* Outside of the Cotton Club: "Love You Madly" (Miss Mary & Sweets); *Scene 8* The Duke's apartment: "Prelude to a Kiss" (m/l: Duke Ellington, Irving Gordon, Irving Mills) (Vy & Duke); *Scene 9* 125th Street: "In a Mellow Tone" (l: Milt Gabler) (Vy, Duke, Lady Liv, Rev, Denizens of Harlem).

Broadway reviews were divided. The show received Tony nominations for orchestrations, and for Andree de Shields and Tonya Pinkins.

After Broadway. It was re-worked slightly and re-presented in several regional theatres, for example the PASADENA PLAYHOUSE, where it was filmed by PBS in 8/99, and shown by them on TV on 6/21/00, as part of their *Great Performances* series.

553. *La Plume de Ma Tante*

A satirical revue on all things French — cuisine, air travel, entertainment, lovers. It was a sort of French *Hellzapoppin*, with its speed and precision timing. There were some words, but most of it was panto. Farce reigned throughout. The production numbers varied from lengthy pantomimes and ballet sequences to short blackouts, such as "Take-Off." Robert Dhery was narrator between many of the scenes. The title refers to a basic sentence in the first French lessons — "the pen of my aunt."

Before Broadway. It originally played in Paris to great acclaim. Then it went to England: the KING'S THEATRE, Southsea, from 10/24/55; then to the West End, to the GARRICK THEATRE, London, 11/3/55–6/29/57. 694 PERFORMANCES. PRESENTED BY Jack Hylton; DIRECTOR: Alec Shanks; CHOREOGRAPHER: Colette Brosset; MUSICAL DIRECTOR: Robert Probst. *Cast*: Robert Dhery, Jacques Legras, Christian Duvaleix, Frank Daubray, Pierre Olaf, Laurence Soupault, Roger Caccia, Colette Brosset, Nicole Parent. DANCERS: Patricia Barratt, Charmian Buchel, Patricia Ellis, Ann Hardie, Maureen Hill, Jill Hougham, Gillian Low, Mary Reynolds.

The Broadway Run. ROYALE THEATRE, 11/11/58–12/17/60. 835 PERFORMANCES. The Jack Hylton production, PRESENTED BY David Merrick & Joseph Kipness; MUSIC/MUSICAL ARRANGEMENTS: Gerard Calvi; WRITER/DEVISED BY/DIRECTOR: Robert Dhery; FRENCH LYRICS: Francis Blanche; ENGLISH LYRICS: Ross Parker; DIRECTOR: Alec Shanks; CHOREOGRAPHER: Colette Brosset; BALLET MISTRESS: Rita Charisse; SET

SUPERVISOR/LIGHTING: Charles Elson; SETS/COSTUMES: see individual sketches below; CURTAIN DESIGN: Vertes; MUSICAL DIRECTOR: Gershon Kingsley; ORCHESTRATIONS: Gerard Calvi, Billy Ternent, Ronnie Monro; PRESS: Frank Goodman, Seymour Krawitz, Ruth Cage (only Seymour Krawitz by 59–60); GENERAL MANAGER: Jack Schlissel; COMPANY MANAGER: Ben Boyar; PRODUCTION STAGE MANAGER: Neil Hartley; STAGE MANAGER: Howard Stone; ASSISTANT STAGE MANAGER: Hal Halvorsen, *Edmond Varrato* & *C.K. Alexander* (both added by 59–60). *Act I*: *Scene 1* The Company is introduced by Robert Dhery; *Scene 2* Speakerine [Colette Brosset (2)]; *Scene 3* Amsterdam (Jean Lefevre); *Scene 4* Mobile Squad (Bicycles): THE PRIDE OF THE FORCE: Jacques Legras, Pierre Olaf, Michel Modo, Henri Pennec; *Scene 5* "Rider to the Sea" (Michael Kent); *Scene 6* "Le Bal Chez Madame de Mortemouille" (designed by Dignimont): MADAME DE MORTEMOUILLE: Pamela Austin, *Joan Fagan*; THE MAJOR-DOMO: Michael Kent; GENERAL GROSFUT: Ross Parker; THE ATTACHÉ: Henri Pennec; THE MAITRE D'HOTEL: Roger Caccia; THE SPAHI: Michel Modo; JOHNNY WALKER: Jean Lefevre; MASTER PERCY SMITH: Pierre Olaf (3); MR. SPRATTS: Jacques Legras; MISS INNOCENT: Mary Reynolds; MADEMOISELLE COLETTE: Colette Brosset (2); MONSIEUR ROBERT: Robert Dhery (1); *Scene 7* Husbands Beware!: THE WIFE: Yvonne Constant; THE LOVER: Pierre Olaf (3); THE ELEVATOR ATTENDANT: Henri Pennec; THE HUSBAND: Ross Parker. "Dance of the Wardrobes;" *Scene 8* Light Soprano ("The Song of the Balloon") (designed by Erte) [performed by Pamela Austin (*Joan Fagan*)] (the soprano with the tiered skirt which gets taller and taller with every high note she hits, until she is 20 feet tall); *Scene 9* In a Small Café (designed by Lilla De Nobili): THE WAITER: Robert Dhery (1); THE LATER DINER: Ross Parker; *Scene 10* "Ballet Classique" (designed by Erte) (with the Entire Corps de Ballet): THE SPIRIT OF THE NIGHT: Coka Brossecola; THE PRINCE: Pierre Olaf (3); THE PRINCESS: Genevieve Coulombel; THE WITCH GIRL: Nicole Parent, *Evee Lynn*; Note: for fun, there was no Scene 11; *Scene 12* "Song of the Swing" (designed by Alec Shanks): VERONIQUE: Pamela Austin, *Joan Fagan*; FLORESTAN: Michael Kent; *Scene 13* "Precision" (Kickline routine) (Colette Brosset dancing out of step with the Royal Croquettes); *Scene 14* Courting Time (designed by Erte): THE FATHER: Ross Parker; THE MOTHER: Roger Caccia; THEIR DAUGHTER: Brigitte Peynaud; HER LOVER: Pierre Olaf; THE EXPLORER: Michel Modo; THE GENDARME: Jacques Legras; *Scene 15* Femmes Fatales" (dance) (dresses designed by Jacques Esterel): LES FEMMES: Nicole Parent (*Evee Lynn*), Jill Hougham, Yvonne Constant, Mary Reynolds, Brigitte Peynaud, Colette Brosset; *Scene 16* On the Beach [Roger Caccia, Jacques Legras, Jean Lefevre, Ross Parker, Genevieve Zanetti (*Deirdre Ottewill*), Anna Stroppini (*Ruth Ann Ullom*)] (beach bathhouse sequence; the men try to open the women's doors); *Scene 17* Queen of the Strip-Tease ("Ne Comptez Pas Sur Moi...Pour Me Montrer Toute Nue" [Colette Brosset(2)] (a stripper has a stuck zipper): "La Plume de Ma Tante" (Girls); *Scene 18* Freres Jacques (performed by Pierre Olaf, Jacques Legras, Roger Caccia, Michel Modo, Ross Parker) (four tired monks pulling long bell ropes; this becomes a crazy, confused rock 'n roll maypole, very frenzied, then the head monk enters and gradually they all reverse their steps until they are sedate again). *Act II*: *Scene 1* "Hommage Musicale" (designed by Henri Pennec) (performed by Robert Dhery & His Festival Ensemble): GUEST ARTISTES: The Ladies Athenian Choir; *Scene 2* Domingo Blazes and His Latin American Orchestra; *Scene 3* In an Indian Temple (dance): TEMPLE GIRLS: The Dugudu Dancers; THE HIGH PRIESTESS: Yvonne Constant; *Scene 4* This Other Eden: EVE: Colette Brosset (2); ADAM: Robert Dhery (1); THE SERPENT: Jacques Legras. "Like a Little Pussy Cat;" *Scene 5* Men at Work: THE WORKMEN: Jean Lefevre & Henri Pennec; *Scene 6* "Administration" (designed by Lilla De Nobili): FILING CLERKS: Roger Caccia & Jacques Legras; THE SECRETARY: Yvonne Constant; THE BOSS: Ross Parker; *Scene 7* In the Tuileries Gardens (designed by Dignimont): THE TIE VENDOR: Jean Lefevre; THE CURE: Henri Pennec; THE BYSTANDER: Michel Modo; THE LOVERS: Nadine Gorbatcheff & Yvonne Constant; THE BIRD LOVER: Mary Reynolds; AGENT DE POLICE: Michael Kent; THE SCHOOLMISTRESS: Pamela Austin, *Joan Fagan*; HER PUPILS: Genevieve Coulombel, Anna Stroppini (*Ruth Ann Ullom*), Francoise Dally, Jill Hougham, Brigitte Peynaud, Claude Perrin; PICKPOCKETS: Roger Caccia & Jacques Legras; CLOWNS: Pierre Olaf & Colette Brosset; *Scene 8* Take-Off (the famous scene in which a man climbs the stairs leading to an airplane, finds that the trip has been canceled, stands at the stairs staring into space, suddenly spins his bow tie as if it were a propeller, and flies off into the air as the lights black out): AIR HOSTESS: Yvonne Constant; THE PASSENGER: Roger Caccia; *Scene 9* "Ballet Moderne:" THE DANCERS: Genevieve Coulombel, Francoise Dally, Nicole Parent (*Evee Lynn*), Mary Reynolds; THE MUSICIANS: DRUMS: Stan Krell; CLARINET: Ernie Mauro; PIANO: Milt Kraus; BASS: Aaron Juvelier; *Scene 10* The Ventriloquist [Jean Lefevre (*Pierre Olaf*)]; Note: for fun, just as in Act I, there was no Scene 11; *Scene 12* Trapped (Pissotiere) (designed by Dignimont) (three visitors trying to get out of a public bathroom in Paris): THE VICTIMS: Jacques Legras & Robert Dhery; A BUTCHER: Ross Parker; A POLICEMAN: Henri Pennec; A PASSER-BY: Mary Reynolds; *Scene 13* Acrobatie [Colette Brosset (2)]; *Scene 14* Le Finale de Paris (designed by Erte) (performed by the Entire Company & The Entire Corps de Ballet), Paris is the End!, "La Plume de Ma Tante"/Striptease/Monks (reprise).

Note: Nadine Gorbatcheff, Françoise Dally, and Claude Perrin were all gone by 59–60.

Note: The order of sketches and numbers in Act II was changed for the second season.

During the Broadway run a sign was hung outside on the marquee saying "English Spoken Inside." The show opened to mostly raves. Robert Dhery and Colette Brosset were married. The show vacationed 7/4/59–8/3/59. It won a special 1959 Tony for the entire cast. It was also nominated for musical, direction, and musical direction.

After Broadway. TOUR. Opened on 7/26/61, at the Alcazar Theatre, San Francisco, and closed on 6/2/62, at the McVickers Theatre, Chicago. MUSICAL DIRECTOR: Murray Kellner. *Cast*: Maurice Bacquet, Robert Clary, Françoise Dally, Jacques Legras, Donna Monroe, Liliane Montevecchi, Frederick O'Brady, Henri Pennec, Corinne Reichel, Roger Saget, Judy Thelen, Pierre Tornade, Edmond Varrato, Richard Winter. *Understudies*: John Dorman, Charles Floyd, Jacqueline Maria, Corinne Reichel, Edmond Varrato.

554. *Polonaise*

The Polish uprising set to Chopin's music. Thaddeus Kosciusko (1746–1817), after helping the Americans with their revolution, returned to Poland for another one, and a girl, Marisha.

Before Broadway. The original director was Edward Duryea Dowling, but he was replaced by Stella Adler. Rose Inghram was pulled out of *Up in Central Park* a few days before that show's opening date of 1/27/45, to begin rehearsals for *Polonaise*.

The Broadway Run. ALVIN THEATRE, 10/6/45–12/45; ADELPHI THEATRE, 12/3/45–1/12/46. Total of 113 PERFORMANCES. PRESENTED BY W. Horace Schmidlapp, in association with Harry Bloomfield; MUSIC: Frederic Chopin; ORIGINAL NUMBERS: Bronislaw Kaper; LYRICS: John Latouche; BOOK: Gottfried Reinhardt & Anthony Veiller; ADAPTED BY Bronislaw Kaper from Chopin's compositions; DIRECTOR: Stella Adler; CHOREOGRAPHER: David Lichine; SETS: Howard Bay; COSTUMES: Mary Grant; MUSICAL DIRECTOR: Max Goberman; ORCHESTRATIONS: Don Walker; CHORAL DIRECTOR: Irving Landau; PRESS: Karl Bernstein & Martha Dreiblatt; GENERAL MANAGER: Ralph R. Kravatte; GENERAL STAGE MANAGER: Murray Queen; STAGE MANAGER: Walter E. Munroe. *Cast:* CAPTAIN ADAMS: John V. Schmidt; GENERAL WASHINGTON: Josef Draper, *Walter Munroe*; COLONEL HALE: Martin Lewis; GENERAL THADDEUS KOSCIUSKO: Jan Kiepura (1) ☆; SERGEANT WACEK ZAPOLSKI: Curt Bois (3); PRIVATE TOMPKINS: Sidney Lawson; PRIVATE SKINNER: Arthur Lincoln; PRIVATE MOTHERWELL: Martin Cooke; MARISHA: Marta Eggerth (2) ☆; WLADEK: Rem Olmsted; TECLA: Tania Riabouchinska (6), *Jean Harris*; GENERAL BORIS VOLKOFF: Harry Bannister (5); COUNT CASIMIR ZALESKI: Josef Draper, *Graham Velsey*; PENIATOWSKI: Lewis Appleton; KOLLONTAJ: Andrew Thurston; POTOCKI: Gary Green; COUNTESS LUDWIKA ZALESKI: Rose Inghram (4); OLD NOBLEMAN: Victor Savidge; BLACKSMITH: Martin Cooke, *George Spelvin*; BUTCHER: Larry Beck; PRIEST: Larry O'Dell; PIANIST: Zadel Skolovsky; KING STANISLAUS AUGUSTUS: James MacColl; COUNT GRONSKI: Walter

Appler, *Martin Cooke*; COURTIER: Jay Dowd; PRINCESS MARGARITA: Candy Jones, *Mary McQuade*; PRINCESS LYDIA: Leta Mauree, *Ann Dennis*; PRINCESS LANIA: Sherry Shadburne; PRINCESS ANNA: Martha Emma Watson; PEASANT GIRL: Bettye Durrence, *Alicia Krug*; SINGERS: Lewis Appleton, Eileen Ayers, Oakley Bailey, Joan Bartels, Larry Beck, Oliver Boersma, Marjorie Chandler, Martin Cooke, Jean Cumming, Ann Dennis, Gary Green, Leigh Hoffman, Raynor C. Howell, Sidney Lawson, Arthur Lincoln, Mary McQuade, Larry O'Dell, John Schmidt, Otto Simanek, Andrew Thurston, Michael Vertzilous, Mary Woodley, *Barbara Barlow, Tony Montell, Jeanette Weiss*; DANCERS: Virginia Barnes, Hubert Bland, May Block, Adele Bodroghy, Joan Collenette, Jay Dowd, Bettye Durrence, Jerry Florio, Jean Harris, Sergei Ismaeloff, Pamela Kastner, Martin Kraft, Alicia Krug, Dorothy Love, Ruthanna Mitchell [she later became Ruth Mitchell], Tangi Nicelli, Shaun O'Brien, Ruth Riekman, Martin Schneider, Dorothy Scott, Amalia Velez, Marc West.

Note: George Spelvin is a nom de guerre, a Broadway tradition, to denote an actor in more than one role. So we don't know who he is. *Act I*: Overture (Chopin Melodies); *Scene 1* The Ramparts, West Point; 1783; *Scene 2* The waterfront, New York; *Scene 3* A hayfield near Cracow, Poland; some time later: "Autumn Songs" (Marisha, Wladek, Peasants), "Laughing Bells" (m: Bronislaw Kaper) (Tecla & Zapolski), "O Heart of My Country" [from Chopin's "Nocturne in E Flat"] (Kosciusko), "Stranger" (m: Bronislaw Kaper) (Marisha); *Scene 4* The road to the Manor House, near Cracow; *Scene 5* The Manor House: "Au Revoir, Soldier" (m: Bronislaw Kaper) (Ludwika), "Meadowlark" [from Chopin's "Mazurka in B Flat"] (Kosciusko & Peasants), "Mazurka" [from various themes of Chopin] (Tecla, Wladek, Peasants), "Hay, Hay, Hay" (Zapolski); *Scene 6* The road to the hayfield; *Scene 7* The hayfield; that night: "Just for Tonight" [from Chopin's "Etude in E"] (Kosciusko & Marisha) [the main song], "Moonlight Soliloquy" [Chopin's "Nocturne in F Sharp Major"] (Tecla), Finale [from "Polonaise in A Flat" & "Revolutionary Etude," by Chopin]. *Act II*: *Scene 1* The Royal Palace, Warsaw; a few weeks later: "Gavotte" [from Chopin's "Variations on a French Air"] (Courtiers), "Exchange of Lovers" ("An Imperial Conference") [from various themes of Chopin) (Corps de Ballet]: "The Marquis's Snuff Box" or "Exchange of Lovers:" THE PRINCESS: Ruth Riekman; THE PRINCE: Shawn O'Brien; THE HIGHWAYMAN: Sergei Ismaeloff; THE PAGE: Amalia Velez; THE BALLERINAS: Jean Harris, Virginia Barnes, Adele Bodroghy, Joan Collenette [end of the "Exchange of Lovers" sequence], "Polonaise" [Chopin's "Polonaise in A Flat"] (Zadel Skolovsky — pianist); *Scene 2* A balcony of the Royal Palace: "Now I Know Your Face by Heart" [from Chopin's "Waltz in D Flat"] (Kosciusko & Marisha), "The Next Time I Care" (m: Bronislaw Kaper) (Ludwika) [the show stopper]; *Scene 3* The Royal Palace, Warsaw: "Tecla's Mood" [various themes of Chopin] (Tecla & Girls), "Motherhood" (m: Bronislaw Kaper) (Zapolski & the Four Princesses), "Wait for Tomorrow" (Kosciusko); *Scene 4* A street in Warsaw: "I Wonder as I Wander" [from "Waltz in A Minor" and "Fantasie Impromptu," by Chopin] (Marisha); *Scene 5* The Battle of Macijowice: "Battle Ballet" (Chopin's Four Etudes): SPIRIT OF THE FLAG: Tania Riabouchinska; SPIRIT OF THE SOLDIER: Rem Olmsted; BUGLER: Sergei Ismaeloff; DRUMMER: Hubert Bland; And Corps de Ballet; *Scene 6* Volkoff's headquarters; after the battle: "Just for Tonight" (reprise) (Kosciusko & Marisha); *Scene 7* The waterfront, Philadelphia; some time later: "Wait for Tomorrow" (reprise) [various themes of Chopin] (Kosciusko), Finale.

The show was universally panned. In 11/45 Horace Schmidlapp relinquished his managerial rights, leaving Harry Bloomfield the sole producer thereafter.

555. *Porgy and Bess*

Before Broadway. The original straight play (with 11 spiritual songs) was produced on Broadway by the Theatre Guild, 10/10/27. 231 PERFORMANCES. *Cast*: PORGY: Frank Wilson; BESS: Evelyn Ellis; SPORTIN' LIFE: Percy Verwayne; CROWN: Jack Carter.

The famous opera *Porgy and Bess* came about after George Gershwin was offered a free hand by the Metropolitan Opera to produce a grand opera for them. He chose *Porgy*, but couldn't do it because blacks were not allowed at the Met, and Mr. Gershwin didn't want to have it done in black face. While he was considering how to overcome this problem, Jerome Kern & Oscar Hammerstein II made a good offer to author DuBose Heyward for the musical rights to *Porgy*. They had Al Jolson in mind to play Porgy. This prompted George Gershwin to commit to a Broadway run for his own *Porgy and Bess*. Mr. Heyward began sending the libretto to Mr. Gershwin in late 1933, scene by scene, and Mr. Gershwin wrote the score between Feb. 1934 and Jan. 1935, then spent the next ten months orchestrating it. The first production tried out at the Colonial Theatre, Boston, got a standing ovation, but was too long, and was cut. It ran on Broadway at the ALVIN THEATRE, 10/10/35–1/25/36. 124 PERFORMANCES. It was one of the events of the year, reviews were divided, and it wasn't a financial success. PRESENTED BY the Theatre Guild; DIRECTOR: Rouben Mamoulian. **Cast**: PORGY: Todd Duncan; BESS: Anne Wiggins Brown; CROWN: Warren Coleman; MINGO: Ford L. Buck; SPORTIN' LIFE: John W. Bubbles (George Gershwin had Cab Calloway in mind for this role, but Mr. Calloway was too busy, and making too much money with his band); CLARA: Abbie Mitchell; JAKE: Edward Matthews; SERENA: Ruby Elzy; MARIA: Georgette Harvey; CHORUS: THE EVA JESSYE CHOIR, which included: Catherine Jackson Ayres, Harriett Jackson, Rosalie King, Assotta Marshall, Annabelle Ross, Musa Williams, Reginald Beane, John Diggs. It then went on a tour for three months, and in 1938 had a brief run on the West Coast (Gershwin had died by this time).

It had a very successful Broadway revival at the MAJESTIC THEATRE, 1/22/42–9/26/42. 286 PERFORMANCES. It had a $2.75 top ticket price. There were several changes — the orchestra (down from 42 to 27 members) and cast had been severely reduced in size. The musical director had cut all the recitatives (and returned to spoken libretto), thus reducing the running time of the show by 45 minutes. It was received rapturously. It had the same crew as for the 1943 Broadway run. **Cast**: MARIA: Georgette Harvey; LILY: Helen Dowdy; ANNIE: Catherine Ayers; CLARA: Harriett Jackson; JAKE: Edward Matthews; SPORTIN' LIFE: Avon Long; MINGO: Jimmy Waters; ROBBINS: Henry Davis; SERENA: Ruby Elzy, *Alma Hubbard* (when Miss Elzy died); JIM: Jack Carr; PETER: Robert Ecton; PORGY: Todd Duncan; CROWN: Warren Coleman; BESS: Anne Brown (Miss Brown was formerly known as Anne Wiggins Brown — she left in 5/42), *Etta Moten* (from 6/42; Miss Moten refused to say the word "nigger," so the offending word was cut); 1ST POLICEMAN: John Demmigar, *William Richardson*; 2ND POLICEMAN: Paul du Pont; DETECTIVE: Gibbs Penrose; UNDERTAKER: John Garth; FRAZIER: J. Rosamund Johnson; NELSON: William Bowers; STRAWBERRY WOMAN: Helen Dowdy; CRAB MAN: William Woolfolk; CORONER: Al West; CHORUS: THE EVA JESSYE CHOIR. The production then went on tour for 17 months, and then returned to Broadway (as the subject of this entry). After this brief Broadway visit, it went on the road again. It returned to New York, to CITY CENTER, where it ran 2/7/44–2/19/44. 16 PERFORMANCES. It had the same crew and cast as for the 1943 Broadway run, except PORGY: William Franklin; CRAB MAN: Leslie Gray. Virginia Girvin was replaced in the Eva Jessye Choir by Frances Brock and Olive Ball, and Edward Tyler had gone. It came back to CITY CENTER for a further run, 2/28/44–4/8/44. 48 PERFORMANCES.

There was a production in COPENHAGEN, 3/23/43. PRESENTED BY the Royal Danish Opera. An all-white cast (!) ran for several performances in the face of Nazi opposition.

The Broadway Run. FORTY-FOURTH STREET THEATRE, 9/13/43–10/2/43. Limited run of 24 PERFORMANCES. PRESENTED BY Cheryl Crawford, in association with John J. Wildberg; MUSIC: George Gershwin; LYRICS: DuBose Heyward & Ira Gershwin; BOOK: DuBose Heyward; FOUNDED ON the 1927 drama *Porgy*, by Dorothy & DuBose Heyward, which they in turn adapted from DuBose Heyward's 1925 novel *Porgy*; DIRECTOR: Robert Ross; SETS: Herbert Andrews; COSTUMES: Paul du Pont; MUSICAL DIRECTOR: Alexander Smallens; CHORAL DIRECTOR: Eva Jessye; PRESS: Jean Dalrymple; GENERAL MANAGER: Charles Stewart; COMPANY MANAGER: Clarence Jacobson; STAGE MANAGER: Don Darcy; ASSISTANT STAGE MANAGER: Kenneth Konopka. **Cast**: MARIA: Georgette Harvey; LILY: Catherine Ayers; ANNIE: Musa Williams; CLARA: Harriet Jackson; JAKE: Edward Matthews; SPORTIN' LIFE: Avon Long (3); MINGO: Jerry Laws; ROBBINS: Henry Davis; SERENA: Alma Hubbard; JIM: William C. Smith; PETER: George Randol; PORGY: Todd Duncan (1); CROWN: Warren Coleman; BESS: Etta Moten (2); POLICEMAN: Ken-

neth Konopka; DETECTIVE: Richard Bowler; UNDERTAKER: Coyal McMahan; LAWYER FRAZIER: Charles Welch; NELSON: Charles Colman; STRAWBERRY WOMAN: Catherine Ayers; CRAB MAN: Edward Tyler; CORONER: Don Darcy; RESIDENTS OF CATFISH ROW/FISHERMEN/CHILDREN/STEVEDORES, ETC: THE EVA JESSYE CHOIR: Virginia Girvin, Gladys Goode, Eulabel Riley, Louise Howard, Assotta Marshall, Sadie McGill, Annabelle Ross, Zelda Shelton, Eloise Uggams, Musa Williams, John Diggs, Leslie Gray, Jerry Laws, William C. Smith, Harold Desverney, Roger Arford, Charles Colman, Coyal McMahan, Edward Tyler, William O'Neal; CHILDREN: Robert Tucker, Ruthetta Anderson, Kenneth Tucker, Thomas Tucker, Douglas Rice, Patricia Rice. **Understudy**: Porgy: Edward Matthews. **Act I**: *Scene 1* Catfish Row, Charleston, SC; a summer evening. Clara sings a lullaby to her baby. Robbins enters a crap game while his wife begs him not to play. The crippled beggar, Porgy, comes on, and also joins the game. He is accused of being soft on Crown's Bess. the burly and menacing stevedore Crown and the seductive Bess enter. The crap game culminates in a drunken fight between Crown and Robbins, in which Crown kills Robbins with a cotton hook. Crown flees, while Bess seeks sanctuary in Porgy's room: Lullaby: "Summer Time" (Clara), "A Woman is a Sometime Thing" (Jake & Ensemble), Entrance of Porgy: "They Pass by Singing" (Porgy), Crap Game Fugue ("Roll Them Bones") (Porgy, Sportin' Life, Crown, Men) [restored after being dropped from the 1935 original]; *Scene 2* Serena's Room; the following night. The "saucer burial" of Robbins, who has died penniless. Friends contribute to the funeral expenses. A detective enters and, to secure a witness to the Robbins murder, arrests Peter. Serena is told that unless the body of her husband is buried the following day it will be given to medical students. The undertaker enters, and agrees to bury the body the following morning: "Gone, Gone, Gone!" (Ensemble), "Overflow" (Ensemble), Arioso: "My Man's Gone Now" (Serena & Ensemble), Train Song: "Leavin' fo' de Promis' Lan'" (Bess & Ensemble). *Intermission*—10 minutes. **Act II**: *Scene 1* Catfish Row; a month later. Porgy and Bess are at their window. Sportin' Life, the slinky dope peddler, enters. Lawyer Frazier comes to sell Bess a divorce from Crown. Sportin' Life offers Bess dope, and is threatened by Porgy. The Negro community leaves for a picnic on Kittiwah Island. Bess goes, leaving Porgy alone in Catfish Row (he can't go because of his infirmity): Rowing Song: "It Takes a Long Pull to Get There" (Jake & Fishermen), "I Got Plenty o' Nuttin'" (Porgy), Divorce Scene: "Woman to Lady" (Porgy, Bess, Frazier, Ensemble), Duet: "Bess, You is My Woman Now" (Porgy & Bess), Picnic Song: "Oh, I Can't Sit Down" (Orphan Band & Ensemble); *Scene 2* A palmetto jungle; evening of the same day. The picnic party pauses for a final celebration on the way back to the excursion steamer. Crown, who has been hiding on the island, persuades Bess to remain with him for the night: "It Ain't Necessarily So" (Sportin' Life & Ensemble), Duet: "What You Want with Bess?" (Crown & Bess); *Scene 3* Catfish Row; before dawn, a week later. Bess has returned, delirious, to Catfish Row, begging forgiveness from Porgy, who swears vengeance on Crown. Serena leads a prayer for Bess's recovery. Street vendors enter, crying their wares. Bess joins Porgy on the doorstep. They confess their love for each other and Porgy promises to protect her from Crown. A bell sounds the hurricane alarm and Clara, whose husband Jake, is out with the fishing fleet, falls in a faint. The storm descends on Catfish Row: "Time and Time Again" (Serena & Ensemble), Street cries: Strawberry Woman, Crab Man, Duet: "I Loves You, Porgy" (Porgy & Bess); *Scene 4* Serena's Room; dawn of the following day. The storm is raging while the frightened negroes sing and pray. A knock is heard at the door which they believe to be the summons of death. Crown enters. He ridicules Porgy. From the window Clara sees that Jake's boat has been wrecked. Clara gives her baby to Bess to keep until she returns and rushes out. Crown laughs at the frightened negroes, defies the storm and leaves to help Clara. He warns Bess that he will return for her: "Oh, de Lawd Shake de Heaven" (Ensemble), "A Red-Headed Woman" (Crown & Ensemble), "Oh, Doctor Jesus" (Principals & Ensemble). **Act III**: *Scene 1* Catfish Row; the next night. In one of the rooms a group of women is mourning for the dead of the storm. Sportin' Life enters and intimates to Maria that Crown is still alive. In Porgy's room Bess can be heard singing to the baby, Crown enters and approaches Porgy's door. He is seized by Porgy who, in the ensuing fight, strangles Crown: "Clara, Don't You Be Downhearted" (Ensemble); *Scene 2* Catfish Row; early morning. The detective and coroner enter, determined to discover Crown's murderer. They interrogate the residents of the court, but are unsuccessful. The coroner insists that Porgy go with him to identify the body of Crown at the inquest. Filled with superstitious terror at the thought of looking at the victim's face, Porgy refuses, and is dragged away. Bess is approached by Sportin' Life, who tries to persuade her to go to New York with him. She refuses. Sportin' Life leaves a small packet containing "happy dust" upon her doorstep and departs. In despair at losing Porgy forever, she picks up the "happy dust:" "There's a Boat That's Leavin' Soon for New York" (Sportin' Life & Bess); *Scene 3* Catfish Row; five days later. Catfish Row awakens and starts its day. Porgy is brought home by the police patrol. He has played craps in jail and with the proceeds has bought a dress as a present for Bess. Knowing that Bess has left with Sportin' Life and overcome with sympathy for Porgy, his friends withdraw. Porgy now calls Bess, who does not answer. He learns that Bess has gone to New York. Calling for his goat and cart, he sets off to find her: "Where's My Bess?" (Porgy) [in the 1935 original this was a trio: Porgy, Lily, Serena], "I'm on My Way" (Porgy & Ensemble).

After Broadway. In 1945 the film *Rhapsody in Blue* featured a segment with Anne Brown doing her Bess part.

556. *Porgy and Bess (1953 Broadway revival)*

Before Broadway. This production of *Porgy and Bess* began as a tour of Berlin, Vienna, London, and Paris, and it was acclaimed as the best of all the productions of this American opera so far. It restored a lot of the music that had been cut from the 1942 production, and used some music never before heard. Before it set off on its European tour it was going to play at the Met, in New York City, but that institution was still racially intolerant. It ran in London, at the Stoll Theatre, from 10/9/52. 142 performances. It had the same cast as for the Broadway run, except that William Warfield (who had been recommended to the producers by Cheryl Crawford) alternated with Le Vern Hutcherson as Porgy (later during the tour Leslie Scott alternated with Irving Barnes), and Leslie Scott (replaced on tour by Hugh Dilworth and then Uriel Porter) played Jim. In the chorus Hugh Dilworth played the role Irving Barnes would play on Broadway, and Osborne E. Smith and Sherman Sneed (he was also understudy for Jim) were dropped when the show came to Broadway, and replaced by Miriam Burton and Joy McLean. Joseph Crawford replaced Merritt Smith, and Barbara Ann Webb replaced Eva Taylor in the chorus. Leslie Scott was understudy for Frazier, and Irving Barnes for Porgy/Jake. Charles Colman (who would understudy for Jake on Broadway) understudied for Robbins. After the tour it came to Broadway.

The Broadway Run. ZIEGFELD THEATRE, 3/10/53–11/28/53. 305 PERFORMANCES. PRESENTED BY Blevins Davis & Robert Breen; MUSIC: George Gershwin; LYRICS: DuBose Heyward & Ira Gershwin; BOOK: DuBose Heyward; FOUNDED ON the 1927 drama *Porgy*, by Dorothy & DuBose Heyward, which in turn they adapted from DuBose Heyward's 1925 novel *Porgy*; DIRECTOR: Robert Breen; SETS: Wolfgang Roth; COSTUMES: Jed Mace; MUSICAL DIRECTOR: Alexander Smallens; CHORAL DIRECTOR: Eva Jessye; PRESS: Bill Doll & Company, Robert Ullman, Seymour Krawitz, Bill Watters; GENERAL MANAGER: Ben Boyar, *Leonard Field*; COMPANY MANAGER: Zelda Dorfman; STAGE MANAGER: George Quick, *Ella Gerber*; ASSISTANT STAGE MANAGERS: Walter Riemer, Willis Daily, Jerry Laws, *Sam Kasakoff, Cecil Rutherford, J.C. Hodgin*. **Cast:** CLARA: Helen Colbert; MINGO: Jerry Laws; SPORTIN' LIFE: Cab Calloway (2) ✩; SERENA ROBBINS: Helen Thigpen; JAKE: Joseph James; ROBBINS: Howard Roberts; JIM: Hugh Dilworth, Sherman Sneed (alternate); PETER (THE HONEY MAN): Joseph Crawford; LILY (THE STRAWBERRY WOMAN): Helen Dowdy; MARIA: Georgia Burke; PORGY: Le Vern Hutcherson (3) ✩, Leslie Scott (alternate), Irving Barnes (alternate); CROWN: John McCurry; ANNIE: Catherine Ayers; BESS: Leontyne Price (1) ✩, Urylee Leonardos (alternate); POLICEMAN: Sam Kasakoff; DETECTIVE: Walter Riemer; UNDERTAKER: William Veasey; FRAZIER: Moses LaMarr; DANCIN' RUBY: Elizabeth Foster; CRAB MAN: Ray Yeates; CORONER: Sam Kasakoff; POLICEMAN: Willis Daily; PORGY'S GOAT:

Jebob VI; RESIDENTS OF CATFISH ROW: Joseph Attles, Irving Barnes, Lawson Bates, James Hawthorne Bey, Rhoda Boggs, Walter P. Brown, Miriam Burton, Sibol Cain, Elsie Clark, Charles Colman, Clarisse Crawford, Helen Ferguson, Doris Galiber, Ruby Greene, Kenneth Hibbert, George A. Hill, Joy McLean, Pauline Phelps, Edna Ricks, Annabelle Ross, George A. Royston, Dolores Swan, Clyde Turner, Eloise C. Uggams, Barbara Ann Webb, *John Garth*; CHILDREN: Jacqueline Barnes & George Royston Jr. **Understudies:** Porgy: Irving Barnes; Bess: Helen Colbert & Elizabeth Foster; Maria: Helen Dowdy; Serena: Barbara Ann Webb & Miriam Burton; Crown: Walter P. Brown; Clara: Dolores Swan; Jake: Charles Colman; Lily: Rhoda Boggs; Mingo: James Hawthorne Bey; Peter: George A. Royston; Crab Man: Joseph Attles; Undertaker: Kenneth Hibbert; Sportin' Life: Kenneth Hibbert & Joseph Attles; Annie: Helen Ferguson; Detective: Willis Daily. **General Understudies:** Hugh Dilworth & Elizabeth Foster. *Act I:* *Scene 1* Lullaby: "Summertime" (Clara), "A Woman is a Sometime Thing" (Jim, Jake, Sportin' Life, Ensemble), Entrance of Porgy: "They Pass by Singing" (Porgy), Crap Game Fugue ("Roll Them Bones") (Porgy, Sportin' Life, Crown, Men); *Scene 2* "Gone, Gone, Gone!" (Ensemble), "Overflow" (Ensemble), Arioso: "My Man's Gone Now" (Serena & Ensemble), Train Song: "Leavin' fo' de Promis' Lan'" (Bess & Ensemble); *Scene 3* Rowing Song: "It Takes a Long Pull" (Jim, Jake, Ensemble), "I Got Plenty of Nuttin'" (Porgy), Divorce Scene: "Woman to Lady" (Porgy, Bess, Frazier, Ensemble), Duet: "Bess, You is My Woman Now" (Porgy & Bess), Picnic Song: "Oh, I Can't Sit Down" (Ensemble). *Act II:* *Scene 1* "I Ain't Got No Shame" (Sportin' Life & Ensemble) [new song], "It Ain't Necessarily So" (Sportin' Life & Ensemble), Duet: "What You Want with Bess?" (Crown & Bess); *Scene 2* "Time and Time Again" (Serena & Ensemble), "Street Cries" (Strawberry Woman & Crab Man), Duet: "I Loves You, Porgy" (Porgy & Bess); *Scene 3* "Oh, de Lawd Shake de Heaven" (Ensemble), "A Redheaded Woman" (Crown & Ensemble), "Oh, Doctor Jesus" (Principals & Ensemble) [this number was dropped during the run]. *Act III* [from the summer of 1953 Acts II & 3 were combined into a second act of 6 scenes]: *Scene 1* "Clara, Don't You Be Downhearted" (Ensemble); *Scene 2* "There's a Boat That's Leavin' Soon for New York" (Sportin' Life & Bess); *Scene 3* "Buzzard (Song)" (Porgy) [new song], "Where's My Bess?" (Porgy), "I'm on My Way" (Porgy & Ensemble).

On Broadway it got rave reviews, but scathing ones from the black press. Stage tech Larry Bland was nominated for a Tony.

After Broadway. TOUR. After closing on Broadway, it went out on tour, opening at the Forrest Theatre, Philadelphia, on 12/2/53. It played 23 cities in the USA and Canada, and (with the help of the State Department) a four-year tour in 28 countries in Europe, the Middle East and Latin America, including much publicized stints at Leningrad and Moscow. In the cast: Leontyne Price, Irene Williams and Elizabeth Foster now all alternated as Bess. Maya Angelou played Ruby. Merritt Smith replaced Joseph Crawford as The Honey Man. Cecil Rutherford replaced Willis Daily as the Policeman. In the chorus Paul Harris and Lillian Hayman replaced Walter P. Brown and Miriam Burton, and Fredye Marshall replaced Pauline Phelps. Eva Taylor replaced Catherine Van Buren, and three new chorus members were brought in: Barbara Ann Webb, Millard Williams, and Ned Wright. This was the first American production seen in Russia since the 1917 Revolution. Truman Capote joined the company as observer, and wrote about it in *The Muses Are Heard.*

THE MOVIE. 1959. It was Sam Goldwyn's last film, and an extremely expensive one. WRITER: N. Richard Nash. If the originally-contracted Rouben Mamoulian had directed, it might have been a more successful movie, but Otto Preminger was too heavy-handed. Harry Belafonte turned down the role of Porgy. **Cast:** PORGY: Sidney Poitier (singing dubbed by Robert McFerrin); BESS: Dorothy Dandridge (singing dubbed by Adele Addison); SPORTIN' LIFE: Sammy Davis Jr.; CROWN: Brock Peters; CLARA: Diahann Carroll (singing dubbed by Loulie Jean Norman); MARIA: Pearl Bailey; SERENA: Ruth Attaway (singing dubbed by Inez Matthews); JIM: Ivan Dixon.

CITY CENTER, NYC, 5/17/61–5/28/61. 16 PERFORMANCES. PRESENTED BY the New York City Center Light Opera Company; DIRECTOR: William Ball; SETS: Stephen O. Saxe; COSTUMES: Stanley Simmons; LIGHTING: Paul Morrison; MUSICAL DIRECTOR: Julius Rudel. **Cast:** CLARA: Billy Lynn Daniel; MINGO: Jerry Laws; SPORTIN' LIFE:

Rawn Spearman; JAKE: Irving Barnes & Leonard Parker; SERENA: Barbara Webb; ROBBINS: Ned Wright; MARIA: Carol Brice; PORGY: William Warfield & Irving Barnes; CROWN: James Randolph; BESS: Leesa Foster & Martha Flowers; DETECTIVE: Bill Coppola; ANNIE: Alyce Webb; CRAB MAN: Clyde Turner; CHILDREN INCLUDED: Donna Mills; CHORUS INCLUDED: Garrett Morris, Robert Guillaume, Phyllis Bash, Lillian Hayman, Eloise C. Uggams, Glory Van Scott, Elijah Hodges.

CITY CENTER, NYC, 3/31/62–4/7/62. 6 PERFORMANCES IN REPERTORY. PRESENTED BY the New York City Opera; DIRECTOR: William Ball; SETS: Stephen O. Saxe; COSTUMES: Stanley Simmons; CONDUCTOR: Julius Rudel. *Cast*: CLARA: Gwendolyn Walters; MINGO: Harold Pierson; SPORTIN' LIFE: Rawn Spearman; JAKE: Irving Barnes; SERENA: Barbara Webb; ROBBINS: Ned Wright; MARIA: Carol Brice; PORGY: Lawrence Winters; CROWN: James Randolph; BESS: Leesa Foster; UNDERTAKER: Wanza King; ANNIE: Alyce Webb; FRAZIER: Eugene Brice; DETECTIVE: Richard Fredricks; CRAB MAN: Clyde Turner.

CITY CENTER, NYC, 5/6/64–5/17/64. 15 PERFORMANCES. PRESENTED BY the New York City Center Light Opera Company; DIRECTOR: John Fearnley; SETS: Stephen O. Saxe; COSTUMES: Stanley Simmons; LIGHTING: Nananne Porcher; MUSICAL DIRECTOR: Julius Rudel. *Cast*: CLARA: Marie Young; MINGO: Tony Middleton; SPORTIN' LIFE: Robert Guillaume; JAKE: Irving Barnes; SERENA: Gwendolyn Walters; PETER: Garrett Morris; MARIA: Carol Brice; PORGY: William Warfield & Irving Barnes; CROWN: William Dillard; BESS: Veronica Tyler & Barbara Smith Conrad; DETECTIVE: Walter Riemer; UNDERTAKER: Wanza King; ANNIE: Alyce Elizabeth Webb; CRAB MAN: Clyde Turner; PEARL: Lillian Hayman; CHORUS INCLUDED: Ruby Greene Aspinall, Kay Barnes, Phyllis Bash, Elijah Bennett, Marceline Decker, Claretta Freeman, Helen Guile, Caryl Paige, Garwood Perkins, John Richardson, Eloise C. Uggams, James Wamen, Laurence Watson.

CITY CENTER, NYC, 3/5/65–3/14/65. 6 PERFORMANCES IN REPERTORY. There was no second intermission in this production. PRESENTED BY the New York City Opera; DIRECTOR: Ella Gerber; SETS: Roger Sullivan; COSTUMES: Stanley Simmons; CONDUCTOR: Dean Ryan. *Cast*: CLARA: Claudia Lindsay; MINGO: Jerry Laws; SPORTIN' LIFE: Avon Long; JAKE: Edward Pierson; SERENA: Phyllis Bash; PETER: Carrington Lewis; MARIA: Carol Brice; PORGY: Andrew Frierson; CROWN: James Randolph; BESS: Joyce Bryant; ANNIE: Alyce Webb; FRAZIER: Eugene Brice; DETECTIVE: Jack Bittner; CRAB MAN: Joseph Attles.

BUS-TRUCK TOUR. Opened on 12/26/66, and closed on 3/20/67, after 52 cities. *Cast*: PORGY: Le Vern Hutcherson; SPORTIN' LIFE: Avon Long; ALSO WITH: Joyce Bryant, Val Pringle.

557. *Porgy and Bess* (1976 Broadway revival)

This was a fully restored version, the closest ever to what the composer had in mind when he wrote it in the 1930s.

Before Broadway. This Broadway run was a stint in a hugely successful tour by the Houston Grand Opera Company.

The Broadway Run. URIS THEATRE, 9/25/76–12/5/76; MARK HELLINGER THEATRE, 12/7/76–1/9/77. 7 previews. Total of 122 PERFORMANCES. PRESENTED BY Sherwin M. Goldman & the Houston Grand Opera, by arrangement with Tams-Witmark Music Library; MUSIC: George Gershwin; LYRICS: DuBose Heyward & Ira Gershwin; BOOK: DuBose Heyward; FOUNDED ON the 1927 drama *Porgy*, by Dorothy & DuBose Heyward, which they in turn adapted from DuBose Heyward's 1925 novel *Porgy*; DIRECTOR: Jack O'Brien; CHOREOGRAPHER: Mabel Robinson; SETS: Robert Randolph; DESIGNER OF ADDITIONAL SCENIC ELEMENTS FOR KITTIWAH ISLAND: John Rothgeb; COSTUMES: Nancy Potts; LIGHTING: Gilbert V. Hemsley Jr.; MUSICAL DIRECTOR/CHORUS MASTER: John De Main; ASSOCIATE CONDUCTOR: Clay Fullum; CAST RECORDING on RCA Victor; PRESS: Michael Alpert, Marilynn LeVine, Warren Knowlton; GENERAL MANAGER: Robert A. Buckley; COMPANY MANAGER: Bill Liberman; PRODUCTION STAGE MANAGER: Helaine Head; STAGE MANAGER: Sally McCravey; ASSISTANT STAGE MANAGER: William Gammon. *Cast*: JASBO BROWN: Ross Reimueller, *Clay Fullum*; CLARA (Tuesdays; Wednesday evenings; Thursdays; Fridays; Saturdays):

Betty D. Lane (14) ☆, *Elizabeth Graham*; CLARA (Sunday matinees): Alma Johnson; CLARA: (Wednesday matinees): Myra Merritt; MINGO (Tuesdays; Thursdays; Saturday evenings): Bernard Thacker; MINGO (Wednesdays; Fridays; Saturday matinees; Sunday matinees): Wardell Woodard; JAKE (Tuesdays; Wednesday evenings; Fridays; Saturday evenings; Sunday matinees): Curtis Dickson (13) ☆, *Alexander Smalls*; JAKE (Wednesday matinees; Thursdays; Saturday matinees): Bruce A. Hubbard; SPORTIN' LIFE: Larry Marshall (10) ☆, Bernard Thacker (stood in for Mr. Marshall, 12/20/76–1/3/77); SPORTIN' LIFE: (Wednesday matinees): Bernard Thacker; ROBBINS: Glover Parham; SERENA ROBBINS (Wednesday evenings; Thursdays; Saturday matinees; Sunday matinees): Delores Ivory-Davis (6) ☆; SERENA ROBBINS (Tuesdays; Fridays; Saturday evenings): Wilma Shakesnider (3) ☆; SERENA ROBBINS (Wednesday matinees): Shirley Baines; JIM: Hartwell Mace; PETER: Mervin Wallace; LILY: Myra Merritt; LILY (Wednesday matinees): Barbara Buck; MARIA (Wednesday matinees; Thursdays; Saturday matinees, Sunday matinees): Carol Brice (9) ☆, *Barbara Ann Webb*; MARIA (Tuesdays; Wednesday evenings; Fridays; Saturday evenings): Queen Yahna; SCIPIO: Alex Carrington; PORGY (Tuesdays; Thursdays; Saturday evenings): Donnie Ray Albert (1) ☆; PORGY (Wednesday matinees; Fridays; Sunday matinees): Abraham Lind-Oquendo (4) ☆; PORGY (Wednesday evenings; Saturday matinees): Robert Mosley (7) ☆; CROWN (Tuesdays; Wednesday evenings; Fridays; Saturday evenings): George Robert Merritt (12) ☆; CROWN (Wednesday matinees; Thursdays; Saturday matinees; Sunday matinees): Andrew Smith (11) ☆; CROWN (Wednesday matinees; Thursdays; Saturday matinees; Sunday matinees): John D. Anthony, *Andrew Smith* (from 10/76); BESS (Tuesdays; Thursdays; Saturday evenings): Clamma Dale (2) ☆; BESS (Wednesday matinees; Fridays; Sunday matinees): Esther Hinds (5) ☆; BESS (Wednesday evenings; Saturday matinees): Irene Oliver (8) ☆, *Phyllis Bash*; DETECTIVE: Hansford Rowe; POLICEMAN: William Gammon; UNDERTAKER: Cornel Richie, *Earl Grandison*; ANNIE: Shirley Baines; ANNIE (Wednesday matinees): Barbara L. Young; FRAZIER: Raymond Bazemore, *Earl Grandison*; MR. ARCHDALE: Kenneth Barry; STRAWBERRY WOMAN: Phyllis Bash; STRAWBERRY WOMAN (Wednesday matinees): *Barbara Buck;* CRAB MAN: Steven Alex-Cole; CORONER: John B. Ross; ENSEMBLE: John D. Anthony, Shirley Baines, Earl Baker, Phyllis Bash, Kenneth Bates, Raymond Bazemore (dropped during run), Barbara Buck, Steven Alex-Cole, Ella Eure, Wilhelmenia Fernandez, Elizabeth Graham, Earl Grandison, Kenneth Hamilton (dropped during run), Betty Harris (dropped during run), Loretta Holkmann, Alma Johnson, Cora Johnson (*Christal Lockley*), Roberta Long, Hartwell Mace, Patricia McDermott, Myra Merritt, Naomi Moody, Glover Parham, William Penn, Dwight Ransom, Cornel Richie, Rodrick Ross, Alexander B. Smalls (promoted to main cast during run), Bernard Thacker, Mervin Wallace, Barbara Ann Webb (promoted to main cast during run), Wardell Woodard, Denice Woods, Barbara L. Young. *Christopher Deane, Bruce A. Hubbard, James Pickens*. **Understudies**: Clara: Elizabeth Graham, Myra Merritt, Alma Johnson; Jake: Kenneth Hamilton & Alexander B. Smalls; Sportin' Life: Bernard Thacker, *Steven Alex-Cole*; Serena: Shirley Baines; Maria: Barbara Ann Webb; Porgy: Hartwell Mace; Bess: Phyllis Bash, *Wilhelmenia Fernandez*; Detective: John B. Ross, *William Gammon*; Archdale/Coroner: William Gammon; Crown: John D. Anthony, *Andrew Smith*; Lily/Strawberry Woman: Barbara Buck, *Denice Woods*; Annie: Barbara L. Young, *Naomi Moody*; Peter: Kenneth Bates; Nelson/Crab Man: Dwight Ransom; Mingo: Wardell Woodard, *Dwight Ransom*; Frazier: Earl Grandison; Undertaker: Earl Grandison & James Pickens; Robbins: Rodrick Ross; Jim: William Penn. *Act I: Scene 1* Catfish Row; a summer evening: Introduction (Piano), "Jasbo Brown Blues" (Piano) [from the original 1935 production], "Summertime" (Clara), "A Woman is a Sometime Thing" (Jake & Men), "Here Come de Honey Man" (Peter), "They Pass by Singin'" (Porgy), "Oh Little Stars" (Porgy); *Scene 2* Serena's Room; the following night: "Gone, Gone, Gone!" (Ensemble), "Overflow" (Ensemble), "My Man's Gone Now" (Serena), "Leavin' for the Promis' Lan'" (Bess & Ensemble); *Scene 3* Catfish Row; a month later: "It Takes a Long Pull to Get There" (Jake & Men), "I Got Plenty o' Nuttin'" (Porgy & Ensemble), "Buzzard Song" (Porgy & Ensemble), "Bess, you is My Woman (Now)" (Porgy & Bess), "Oh, I Can't Sit Down" (Ensemble); *Scene 4* Kittiwah Island; late afternoon: "I Ain't Got No Shame" (Ensemble), "It Ain't Necessarily So" (Sportin' Life & Ensemble), "(So,) What You Want wid Bess?" (Bess &

Crown). ***Act II***: ***Scene 1*** Catfish Row; before dawn, a week later: "Oh, Doctor Jesus" (Serena, Maria, Peter, Lily, Porgy), "I Loves You, Porgy" (Porgy & Bess); ***Scene 2*** Serena's Room; dawn of the following day: "Oh, Hev'nly Father" (Ensemble), "Oh De Lawd Shake de Heavens" (Ensemble), "Oh, Dere's Somebody Knockin' at de Do'" (Ensemble), "A Red Headed Woman" (Crown & Ensemble); ***Scene 3*** Catfish Row; the next night: "Clara, Clara" (Ensemble), "There's a Boat Dat's Leavin' Soon for New York" (Sportin' Life & Bess), "Good Mornin', Sistuh!" (Porgy); ***Scene 4*** Catfish Row; the next afternoon; ***Scene 5*** Catfish Row; a week later: "Oh, Bess, Oh, Where's My Bess?" (Porgy, Maria, Serena), "Oh, Lawd, I'm on My Way" (Porgy & Ensemble).

It got rave reviews on Broadway, and won a Tony for the most innovative production of a revival (the first year for revivals). It was also nominated for direction of a musical, sets, costumes, and for Clamma Dale and Larry Marshall.

After Broadway. After Broadway it continued its tour on 3/15/77, in Boston. It ran at the Kennedy Center, Washington, DC, 7/13/77–7/31/77. *Cast*: PORGY ALTERNATES: Robert Mosley, Bruce A. Hubbard, Donnie Ray Albert; BESS ALTERNATES: Wilhelmenia Fernandez, Gail Nelson, Naomi Moody, Clamma Dale; SPORTIN' LIFE: Larry Marshall; CROWN ALTERNATES: George Robert Merritt & Andrew Smith.

RADIO CITY MUSIC HALL, 4/7/83–5/15/83. 22 previews. 45 PERFORMANCES. 2 acts; 9 scenes. DIRECTOR: Jack O'Brien; CHOREOGRAPHER: George Faison; SETS: Douglas W. Schmidt; COSTUMES: Nancy Potts; LIGHTING: Gilbert V. Hemsley Jr.; MUSICAL DIRECTOR: C. William Harwood. *Cast*: JASBO: Edward Strauss; CLARA: Priscilla Baskerville & Luvenia Garner; MINGO: Timothy Allen; JAKE: Alexander Smalls & James Tyeska; SPORTIN' LIFE: Larry Marshall; ROBBINS: Tyrone Jolivet; SERENA ALTERNATES: Shirley Baines, Regina McConnell, Wilma A. Shakesnider, Veronica Tyler; JIM: Donald Walter Kase; PETER: Mervin Bertel Wallace; LILY: Y. Yvonne Matthews; MARIA: Loretta Holkmann & Gwendolyn Shepherd; SCIPIO: Akili Prince; PORGY ALTERNATES: Robert Mosley Jr., Michael V. Smartt, Jonathan Sprague, James Tyeska; CROWN: Gregg Baker & George Robert Merritt; BESS ALTERNATES: Priscilla Baskerville, Henrietta Elizabeth Davis, Naomi Moody, Daisy Newman; DETECTIVE: Larry Storch; POLICEMAN: William Moize; UNDERTAKER: Joseph S. Eubanks; ANNIE: Lou Ann Pickett; FRAZIER: Raymond H. Bazemore; STRAWBERRY WOMAN: Denice Woods; CRAB MAN: Thomas J. Young; NELSON: Everett McCorvey; CORONER: Richard Easley; ENSEMBLE: Loretta Abbott, Timothy Allen, Earl L. Baker, Emerson Battles, Raymond H. Bazemore, Shirley Black-Brown, Roslyn Burrough, Vertrelle Cameron, Seraiah Carol, Duane Clenton Carter, Dabriah Chapman, Louise Coleman, Janice D. Dixon, Diallobe Dorsey, Cisco Xavier Drayton, Alberta M. Driver, Joseph S. Eubanks, Karen E. Eubanks, Lori Eubanks, Beno Foster, Jerry Godfrey, Earl Grandison, Milton B. Grayson Jr., Elvira Green, Lawrence Hamilton, Gurcell Henry, Angela Holcomb, Lisa D. Holkmann, Janice T. Hutson, David-Michael Johnson, Leavata Johnson, Tyrone Jolivet, Dorothy L. Jones, Donald Walter Kase, Robert Kryser, Roberta Alexandra Laws, Eugene Little, Jason Little, Ann Marie Mackey, Barbara Mahajan, Amelia Marshall, Richard Mason, Y. Yvonne Matthews, Everett McCorvey, John McDaniels, William Moize, Byron Onque, H. William Penn, Marenda Perry, Lou Ann Pickett, Herbert Lee Rawlings Jr., Roumel Reaux, Noelle Richards, David Robertson, Lattilia Ronrico, Renee L. Rose, Myles Gregory Savage, Sheryl Shell, Kiki Shepard, Kevin L. Stroman, Charee Adia Thorpes, Chuck Thorpes, Mervin Bertel Wallace, Pamela Warrick-Smith, Cornelius White, Rodney Wing, Tarik Winston, Denice Woods, Thomas J. Young. ***Understudies***: Porgy/Crown: Duane Clenton Carter; Clara: Gurcell Henry; Maria: Elvira Green; Jake: Donald Walter Kase & Rodney Wing; Sportin' Life: Herbert Lee Rawlings Jr.; Mingo: David-Michael Johnson; Robbins: John McDaniels; Peter: Beno Foster; Annie: Leavata Johnson; Frazier: Earl Grandison; Lily: Sheryl Shell; Strawberry Woman: Y. Yvonne Matthews; Jim: Byron Onque; Crab Man: Myles Gregory Savage; Detective: Richard Easley; Nelson: William Moize. Musical numbers were the same as for the 1976 production, except that "Struttin' Style" (Maria) was inserted between "I Got Plenty of Nuttin'" & "Buzzard Song." The show received 1983 Tony nominations for choreography, and for Michael V. Smartt [this was a rare example of a non–Broadway show being eligible for Tony Awards].

ROYAL THEATRE, Madrid, 12/19/97–1/3/98. 8 PERFORMANCES.

MUSICAL DIRECTOR: Chris Nance. *Cast*: PORGY: Willard White; BESS: Cynthia Haymon.

NEW YORK STATE THEATRE, 3/7/00–3/25/00. 10 PERFORMANCES IN REPERTORY. PRESENTED BY the New York City Opera; DIRECTOR: Tazewell Thompson; CHOREOGRAPHER: Julie Arenal; SETS: Douglas W. Schmidt; COSTUMES: Nancy Potts; CONDUCTOR: John De Main. *Cast*: CLARA: Anita Johnson; SPORTIN' LIFE: Dwayne Clark; SERENA: Angela Simpson & Monique McDonald; MARIA: Sabrina Elayne Carten; PORGY: Alvy Powell and Richard Hobson; CROWN: Timothy Robert Blevins and Lester Lynch; BESS: Marquita Lister and Kishna Davis; CORONER: John Henry Thomas.

558. *Portofino*

A cynical car-racing Italian duke falls for Kitty, a rival driver from Texas. The Duke has a young granddaughter, a witch. Guido, the Devil's emissary, is in danger of being fired by his boss.

Before Broadway. It opened in Philadelphia, where it was poorly received. John Larson was replaced as director by Karl Genus. Richard Ney (an actor who had once been married to Greer Garson) posted the closing notice, but left it up to the cast to decide if the show should go on to Broadway. They voted for it. Several songs were cut before Broadway (all with lyrics by Richard Ney)—"Beware of Love," "Come to Portofino," "Little Boy Blue," and "The Padre's Theme" (all with music by Louis Bellson), and "Drink the Wine," "I Don't Care," and "You'll Never Make Heaven That Way" (all with music by Will Irwin). Also cut was "The Madrigal" (music by Mr. Ney).

The Broadway Run. ADELPHI THEATRE, 2/21/58–2/22/58. 3 PERFORMANCES. PRESENTED BY Richard Ney; MUSIC: Louis Bellson & Will Irwin; LYRICS/BOOK: Richard Ney; ADDITIONAL LYRICS: Sheldon Harnick; DIRECTOR: Karl Genus; CHOREOGRAPHERS: Charles Weidman & Ray Harrison; SETS: Wolfgang Roth; COSTUMES: Michael Travis; LIGHTING: Lee Watson; MUSICAL DIRECTOR/UNDERSCORING: Will Irwin; ORCHESTRATIONS: Philip J. Lang; VOCAL ARRANGEMENTS: Joseph Moon; PRESS: David Lipsky; GENERAL MANAGER: Paul Vroom; COMPANY MANAGER: Lee Martinec; PRODUCTION STAGE MANAGER: Jerry Leider; STAGE MANAGER: Morgan James; ASSISTANT STAGE MANAGER: Webb Tilton. *Cast*: NIKI, THE DUKE: Georges Guetary (1); KITTY: Helen Gallagher (2); PADRE: Robert Strauss (3); GUIDO, THE DEVIL'S EMISSARY: Robert Strauss (3); ANGELA: Jan Chaney; SANDRO: Wallace Eley; TULLIO: Darryl Richard; TAVERN KEEPER: Webb Tilton; SINGERS: Charles Aschmann, Jim Fullerton, Marvin Goodis, Patricia Greenwood, Joy Marlene, Mitchell May, Louise Pearl, Bill Ryan, Joy Lynne Sica, Lynne Stuart, Pat Tolson; DANCERS: Sari Clymas, Stuart Fleming, John Foster, Kenley Hammond, Tom Hester, Harvey Jung, Jimmy Kirby, Diki Lerner, Roy Palmer, Hilbert Rapp, Barbara Richman, Karen Sargent, Leslie Snow, Gerrie Still, Patricia Ann White, Sally Wile. ***Understudies***: Nicky: Webb Tilton; Kitty: Patricia Ann White; Tullio: Michael Smela. ***Act I***: A piazza in Portofino, a lovely Italian resort town; early evening; today: ***Prologue*** (m: Irwin) (l: Harnick) (Padre); ***Scene 1*** Early evening: Opening—"Come Along" (m: Irwin) (Company), "No Wedding Bells for Me" (m: Irwin) (Nicky), Festa—"Come Along" (reprise) (Company), "Red-Collar Job" (m: Bellson & Irwin; l: Harnick) (Guido), "Here I Come" (m: Bellson& Irwin; l: Harnick) (Kitty), "New Dreams for Old" (m: Bellson) (Nicky), "A Dream for Angela" (m: Bellson) (Angela), "Isn't it Wonderful" (m: Bellson) (Kitty, Nicky, Company), "Dance of the Whirling Wimpus" (Angela), "Under a Spell" (m: Bellson; l: Ney & Harnick) (Nicky & Girls). ***Act II***: ***Scene 1*** Immediately following: "Under a Spell" (reprise) (Nicky & Girls), "That's Love" (m: Ney) (Nicky & Company), "Too Little Time for Love" (m: Irwin) (Tavern Keeper) [before Broadway this version, with music by Irwin, replaced the one with music by Bellson), "Guido's Tango" (Guido & Kitty), "It Might Be Love" (m: Bellson) (Nicky), "Here I Come" (reprise) (Kitty), "Bacchanale" (Company); ***Scene 2*** The next morning: "Morning Prayer" (m: Irwin) (Company), "Kitty Car Ballet" (Kitty & Boys), "The Grand Prix of Portofino" (m: Irwin) (Company), "Portofino" (m: Bellson; l: Ney) (Nicky), "I'm in League with the Devil" (m: Irwin) (Kitty),

"Why Not for Marriage" (m: Bellson) (Nicky), "Portofino" (reprise) (Company).

Note: all lyrics by Richard Ney, unless otherwise stated.

On Broadway it was universally panned. Again, Walter Kerr provided the classic line in his *Herald-Tribune* review: "Nor will I say that *Portofino* is the worst musical *ever* produced, because I've only been seeing musicals since 1919."

559. *Pousse Cafe*

The original locale was Berlin. In order that leading actress Lilo be acceptable in her role, it was shifted to New Orleans in the early 1920s. A stern Latin professor at a military school confronts club performer/prostitute Solange who has been corrupting his best student. Bewitched by the lady, he winds up marrying her and performing a humiliating clown number in her show. He tries to return to his profession, but is ultimately destroyed by his passion. Havana is the club singer and madam.

Before Broadway. Previously called *Sugar City* and then *Red Petticoats*. Henry Ford II and Mrs. Barry Goldwater were two of the investors. During tryouts in Detroit Jose Quintero (in his only Broadway musical as director) replaced Richard Altman on 2/14/66. Jerome Weidman and Malvin Isaacson replaced Don Appell as librettists on the same day, and re-wrote the book in 48 hours, but Mr. Isaacson's billing was removed. Valerie Bettis replaced Marvin Gordon as choreographer. However Mr. Gordon retained credit. Originally Will Steven Armstrong was going to do both sets and lighting, but V.C. Fuqua took over the lighting. Albert Wolsky joined Patricia Zipprodt on costumes. In the cast Walter Slezak was the first choice for the Professor, but the part went to Theo Bikel. Travis Hudson replaced 3rd-billed Beatrice Kay. Lilo was married to the producer, the Marquis de la Passardiere, and it was her first Broadway outing since *Can-Can* in 1953.

The Broadway Run. Forty-Sixth Street Theatre, 3/18/66–3/19/66. 5 previews from 3/10/66. 3 performances. Presented by Guy de la Passardiere; Music: Duke Ellington; Lyrics: Marshall Barer & Fred Tobias; Book: Jerome Weidman; Based on the 1930 movie *Der Blaue Engel* (*The Blue Angel*), written by Carl Zuckmayer, Karl Vollmoller, Robert Liebman, from the 1905 novel *Professor Unrath*, by Heinrich Mann (although neither book nor film was mentioned in the program); Director: Jose Quintero; Choreographer: Valerie Bettis; Musical Numbers & Dances Staged by: Marvin Gordon; Sets: Will Steven Armstrong; Costumes: Patricia Zipprodt & Albert Wolsky; Lighting: V.C. Fuqua; Musical Director: Sherman Frank; Orchestrations: Larry Wilcox; Press: Bill Doll & Company, Midori Tsuji, Robert Ganshaw, Dick Spittel; General Manager: Monty Shaff; Production Stage Manager: Henri Caubisens; Stage Manager: Herman Magidson. **Cast:** Ellis: Ellis Larkins; Havana: Travis Hudson (5); Duchess: Madge Cameron; Monty: Al Nesor (6); Harry: Tommy Karaty; Sourball: Robert Rovin; Bill: Ben Bryant; Arthur Owen Jr.: Jeff Siggins; John Harmon: Gary Krawford (3); Professor George Ritter: Theodore Bikel (1) ☆; Solange: Lilo (2) ☆; Sailor: Dom Angelo; Policeman: Hal Norman; Paul: Don Crabtree; Maurice: Charles Durning; Artie: Coley Worth (7); Tourist Lady: Fran Stevens; Louise: Marlena Lustik; Dean Stewart: Charles Durning; Danny: Richard Tone (4); Ensemble: Dom Angelo, Kay Cole, Joel Conrad, Mervin Crook, Elaine Giftos, Altovise Gore, Peter Hamparian, Jo Anna Lehmann, Marlena Lustik, Iva March, Simon McQueen, Rita O'Connor, Martin Ross, Barbara Saatan, Scotty Salmon. **Standby:** Professor: Peter Johl. **Understudies:** Solange: Simon McQueen; Havana: Madge Cameron; Danny: Dom Angelo; Harmon: Tommy Karaty; Sourball/Bill/Monty: Marty Ross; Harry: Joel Conrad; Arthur: Scotty Salmon; Artie: Charles Durning; Maurice/Paul: Hal Norman; Duchess: Fran Stevens. **Act I: Prologue;** *Scene 1* Schoolroom; *Scene 2* Cafe and bar; *Scene 3* Solange's dressing room; *Scene 4* Cafe and bar; *Scene 5* Dormitory; *Scene 6* Solange's dressing room; *Scene 7* Solange's dressing room; the next morning; *Scene 8* Professor's quarters; *Scene 9* Professor's quarters and Solange's dressing room; *Scene 10* Cafe and bar. **Act**

II: *Scene 1* Cafe and bar; *Scene 2* Solange's dressing room; *Scene 3* Cafe and bar; *Scene 4* Professor's quarters; *Scene 5* Cafe and bar; *Scene 6* Solange's dressing room; *Scene 7* Schoolroom. **Act I:** "The Spider and the Fly" (Havana & Dance Ensemble), "Rules and Regulations" (Professor, Harmon, Sourball, Bill, Arthur, Harry), "Follow Me up the Stairs" (Solange), "Goodbye Charlie" (Havana & Ensemble), "C'est Comme Ca" (Solange), "Thank You Ma'am" (Professor & Solange), "The Eleventh Commandment" (Monty, Sourball, Arthur, Harry), "Someone to Care For" (Professor), "The Wedding" (Ensemble). **Act II:** Entr'acte (Orchestra); "Let's" (rehearsal scene) (Danny, Louise, Dance Ensemble), "The Good Old Days" (Solange, Paul, Monty, Artie, Maurice), "Easy to Take" (Danny & Solange), "C'est Comme Ca" (reprise) (Professor), "C'est Comme Ca" (reprise) (Solange), "Let's" (reprise) (Solange & Male Dancers), "Old World Charm" (Professor), "The Spider and the Fly" (reprise) (Havana).

Broadway reviews were absolutely terrible, but Travis Hudson got good ones. Lilo was visibly too old, and the score and book were weak. The show lost $450,000. Following the closing of the show the French nobleman/producer was charged with violating financing regulations and temporarily banned from Broadway.

560. *Prince of Central Park*

Margie, the middle-aged heroine, befriends a 12-year-old, Jay-Jay, who escapes his abusive mother by hiding in a tree house in Central Park. This is a Central Park with a friendly park ranger, a gang of teens, a quaint bag lady, and a couple of well-dressed men emerging from the bushes.

Before Broadway. Originally done as a 1976 TV movie, with T.J. Hargrave, Lisa Richards and Ruth Gordon. As a stage musical, Jan McArt, owner of a chain of dinner playhouses in Florida, presented it at her cabaret theatre in Key West, starring Nanette Fabray. Then real-estate man Abe Hirschfeld presented it at his theatre, the Al Hirschfeld Theatre [sic], in Miami Beach. Miss McArt and Mr. Hirschfeld then took the show to New York, minus Miss Fabray, but with Gloria De Haven. However, Miss De Haven was fired, and Jo Anne Worley stepped in. There were changes during Broadway previews: the Street People were added; the Construction Worker (played by T.J. Meyers) was cut; and the character of Twitchy was added. Mr. Meyers was replaced as the Carpenter, the Maitre d', and in the Chorus by Terry Eno. The songs were tinkered with.

The Broadway Run. Belasco Theatre, 11/9/89–11/11/89. 19 previews. 4 performances. Presented by Abe Hirschfeld & Jan McArt; Music/Musical Supervisor/Orchestrations Supervisor: Don Sebesky; Lyrics: Gloria Nissenson; Book: Evan H. Rhodes (based on his 1974 novel of the same name); Director/Choreographer: Tony Tanner; Sets/Costumes: Michael Bottari & Ronald Case; Lighting: Norman Coates; Sound: Daryl Bornstein; Musical Director/Vocal Arrangements: Joel Silberman; Additional Orchestrations: Larry Hochman; Additional Vocal Arrangements: John McMahon; Dance Music Arrangements: Henry Aronson; Press: Shirley Herz Associates; Casting: Elissa Myers; General Management: George Elmer Productions; Company Manager: Richard Berg; Production Stage Manager: Steven Ehrenberg; Stage Manager: Susan Whelan; Assistant Stage Manager: Michael A. Clarke. **Cast:** Jay-Jay: Richard H. Blake (2) ☆; School Guard: Sel Vitella; Street People: John Hoshko & Adrian Bailey; Agnes: Bonnie Perlman; Officer Washinski: Ruth Gottschall; Bag Lady: Marilyn Hudgins; Anna Squagliatoria: Bonnie Perlman; May Berg: Anne-Marie Gerard; Aerobics Instructor: Stephen Bourneuf; Margie Miller: Jo Anne Worley (1) ☆; Sally: Chris Callan (4); Officer Simpson: Adrian Bailey; Stock Broker: John Hoshko; Fist: Sean Grant; Bird Brain: Jason Ma; Feather: Alice Yearsley; Elmo: Anthony Galde (3); Park Ranger Rupp: Sel Vitella; Carpenter: Terry Eno; Young Richard: John Hoshko; Young Margie: Ruth Gottschall; Ballet Dancer: Alice Yearsley; Floor Walker: Marilyn Hudgins; Maitre D': Terry Eno; Waiter: Sel Vitella; Twitchy: Anne-Marie Gerard; Aerobics Students: Adrian Bailey, Ruth Gottschall, Anne-Marie Gerard, Terry Eno, John Hoshko,

Sel Vitella; TAP DANCERS: Adrian Bailey, Stephen Bourneuf, Ruth Gottschall, John Hoshko, Bonnie Perlman; MANNEQUINS/TANGO DANCERS: Adrian Bailey, Stephen Bourneuf, Ruth Gottschall, John Hoshko, Jason Ma, Bonnie Perlman, Alice Yearsley. *Standbys*: Margie: Jan McArt; Jay-Jay: David Burdick. *Understudies*: Elmo: Sean Grant; Feather/Ballet Dancer: Anne-Marie Gerard; Sally/Bag Lady/Agnes: Terry Iten. SWINGS: Terry Iten & Jody Keith Barrie. *Musicians:* KEYBOARDS: Joel Silberman; SYNTHESIZER: Henry Aronson & Ron Delsini; DRUMS: Jim Young; FENDER BASS: Vince Fay; GUITAR: Ken Sebesky; TRUMPETS: Tony Kadleck & Jeff Parke; TROMBONE: Keith O'Quinn; WOODWINDS: John Purcell & Lawrence Feldman. *Act I*: "Here's Where I Belong" (Jay-Jay & Ensemble), "All I've Got is Me" (Jay-Jay), "New Leaf" (Margie & Aerobics Club), "Follow the Leader" (Elmo, Gang, Jay-Jay), "Hey, Pal" (Jay-Jay) [cut during previews], Montage: "Here's Where I Belong" (Ensemble), "We Were Dancing" (Margie, Young Richard, Young Margie), "One of a Kind" (Margie & Jay-Jay) [newly inserted for opening night], "I Fly by Night" (Elmo & Gang) [newly inserted here for opening night], "Can't Believe My Eyes" [during previews this was here instead of the above two numbers], "Zap" (Margie, Jay-Jay, Ensemble). *Act II*: "Good Evening" (Ensemble), "All I've Got is Me" (reprise) (Margie & Jay-Jay), "They Don't Give You Life at Sixteen" (Elmo & Gang), "Red" (Margie & Ensemble), "I Fly by Night" (reprise) (Elmo, Gang, Jay-Jay) [this was here during previews, but not as a reprise], "The Prince of Central Park" (Jay-Jay), "One of a Kind" (reprise) (Margie) [this was here during previews, but not as a reprise].

Tavern on the Green, which was unashamedly plugged throughout the show, hosted the opening night celebration. Broadway reviews were about as bad as they can get.

The Prince of Liederkranz see 665

561. *The Producers*

Set in New York in 1959. Max Bialystock, once the toast of Broadway, but now a down-at-heels and overbearing New York theatrical producer, teams up with meek accountant Leopold Bloom to perpetrate a scam. Their intention is to produce a deliberate Broadway flop, take the investors' money, and head to Rio. The musical they produce is called *Springtime for Hitler*, and is designed to offend. However, the audiences love it, and it becomes a hit. Franz is the crazy Nazi songwriter living in a Brooklyn tenement. Ulla is the boys' vampish secretary. Roger is the camp director with his "common-law assistant," the even more camp Carmen. LSD, a rock singer brought in to play Hitler, and his song "Love Power," were cut before rehearsals began.

Before Broadway. As early as 5/97 Mel Brooks and David Geffen were talking about *The Producers* as a Broadway musical. Nathan Lane was everybody's logical choice to play Max, but Mr. Brooks initially wanted Martin Short as Leo. By 7/97 Mr. Geffen had dropped out. The original director was going to be Mike Ockrent, but he died in 12/99, and by 1/00 Mr. Brooks had replaced him with his widow, Susan Stroman (who had always been the choreographer of choice). In 5/00 Miss Stroman directed a staged reading with Nathan Lane as Max and Evan Pappas as Leo. On 3/2/00 Nathan Lane was standing in for Dave Letterman on late night TV, and Mel Brooks was a guest. Mr. Brooks whipped out a contract and asked Mr. Lane to sign as star of *The Producers*. On 11/16/00 Roger Bart, Gary Beach, Cady Huffman, and Ron Orbach were all confirmed in their roles for the tryouts, rehearsals for which began on 12/11/00, and it ran at the Cadillac Palace, Chicago, 2/1/01–2/25/01. It was sold out before it opened. A parody of *Gypsy* was objected to by Arthur Laurents & Steve Sondheim, and was dropped. Ron Orbach, who was playing Franz, injured his knee during rehearsals, and missed tryout previews and opening night. He was replaced by Brad Oscar. Mr. Orbach came back, but had to relinquish the role again, and Mr. Oscar took it to Broadway. During Broadway previews Matthew Broderick had to miss 3/22/01–3/25/01 because of vocal strain. His

understudy, Jamie La Verdiere went on. For one of the April previews Gene Wilder (who had played Leo in the movie) was in the audience.

The Broadway Run. ST. JAMES THEATRE, 4/19/01–. 33 previews from 3/21/01. PRESENTED BY Rocco Landesman, SFX Theatrical Group, the Frankel — Baruch — Viertel — Routh Group, Bob & Harvey Weinstein, Rick Steiner, Robert F.X. Sillerman, and Mel Brooks, in association with James D. Stern & Douglas Meyer; MUSIC/LYRICS: Mel Brooks; BOOK: Mel Brooks & Thomas Meehan; BY SPECIAL ARRANGEMENT WITH StudioCanal; BASED ON the 1967 movie of the same name, written by Mel Brooks (for which he won an Oscar); DIRECTOR/CHOREOGRAPHER: Susan Stroman; SETS: Robin Wagner; COSTUMES: William Ivey Long; LIGHTING: Peter Kaczorowski; SOUND: Steve Canyon Kennedy; MUSICAL SUPERVISOR/MUSICAL ARRANGEMENTS: Glen Kelly; MUSICAL DIRECTOR/VOCAL ARRANGEMENTS: Patrick S. Brady; ORCHESTRATIONS: Doug Besterman and (uncredited) Larry Blank; CAST RECORDING ON Sony Classical, made on 3/11/01, and released on 4/23/01; PRESS: Barlow—Hartman Public Relations; CASTING: Johnson — Liff Associates; GENERAL MANAGEMENT: Richard Frankel Productions; COMPANY MANAGER: Kathy Lowe; PRODUCTION STAGE MANAGER: Steven Zweigbaum; STAGE MANAGER: Ira Mont; ASSISTANT STAGE MANAGER: Casey Eileen Rafter. *Cast:* USHERETTES: Bryn Dowling & Jennifer Smith, *Courtney Young* (stood in); MAX BIALYSTOCK: Nathan Lane (1) ☆ (until 3/17/02), *Ray Wills* (during Mr. Lane's absences, a mid–May Sunday matinee, then 5/29/01–5/30/01), *Henry Goodman* (3/19/02–4/14/02), *Brad Oscar* (4/16/02–4/27/03. Mr. Oscar had stood in for Mr. Lane 6/29/01–7/4/01, then during Mr. Lane's vacation, 9/17/01–9/23/01, and then during his illnesses, 11/2/01–11/3/01, and 2/2/02–2/3/02, and 2/9/02–2/10/02), *Lewis J. Stadlen* (4/29/03–9/24/03), *John Treacy Egan* (stood in), *Fred Applegate* (10/7/03–12/28/03), *Nathan Lane* (12/30/03–4/4/04; 112 performances), *Brad Oscar* (4/6/04–12/12/04), *John Treacy Egan*, *Richard Kind* (from 12/21/04; Mr. Kind had originally been scheduled to come in on 1/11/05); LEO BLOOM: Matthew Broderick (2) ☆ (until 3/17/02), *Jamie La Verdiere* (during Mr. Broderick's vacations, 9/4/01 –9/9/01, and again 1/8/02–1/13/02), *Steven Weber* (3/19/02–12/15/02), *Roger Bart* (12/17/02–5/18/03), *Don Stephenson* (from 5/20/03), *Matthew Broderick* (12/30/03–4/4/04; 112 performances), *Roger Bart* (4/6/04–6/13/04), *Hunter Foster* (from 6/15/04), *Alan Ruck* (from 1/11/05); HOLD-ME TOUCH-ME: Madeleine Doherty; MR. MARKS: Ray Wills, *Mark Lotito, Brad Oscar* (from 12/30/03); FRANZ LIEBKIND: Brad Oscar ☆, *Jim Borstelmann* (4/16/02–5/2/02), *John Treacy Egan* (5/4/02–4/24/03), *Peter Samuel* (from 4/25/03), *John Treacy Egan* (from 10/7/03); CARMEN GHIA: Roger Bart ☆ (until 6/30/02), *Sam Harris* (7/2/02–12/15/02), *Brad Musgrove* (from 12/17/02), *Roger Bart* (12/30/03–4/4/04), *Brad Musgrove* (4/6/04–8/29/04), *Brooks Ashmanskas* (from 8/31/04); ROGER DE BRIS: Gary Beach ☆ (until 4/24/03), *John Treacy Egan* (4/25/03–10/5/03), *Gary Beach* (10/7/03–8/29/04), *Jonathan Freeman* (from 8/31/04); BLIND VIOLINIST: Jeffry Denman (until 6/9/02), *Jim Borstelmann* (from 6/18/02); BRYAN: Peter Marinos; KEVIN: Ray Wills, *Mark Lotito, Brad Oscar* (from 12/30/03); SCOTT: Jeffry Denman (until 6/9/02), *Jim Borstelmann* (from 6/18/02); SHIRLEY: Kathy Fitzgerald; ULLA: Cady Huffman ☆ (until 8/3/03), *Sarah Cornell* (8/5/03–11/2/03), *Angie L. Schworer* (from 11/4/03); LICK-ME BITE-ME: Jennifer Smith; KISS-ME FEEL-ME: Kathy Fitzgerald; JACK LEPIDUS: Peter Marinos; DONALD DINSMORE: Jeffry Denman (until 6/9/02), *Jim Borstelmann* (from 6/18/02); JASON GREEN: Ray Wills, *Mark Lotito, Brad Oscar* (from 12/30/03); LEAD TENOR: Eric Gunhus; SERGEANT: Ray Wills, *Mark Lotito, Brad Oscar* (from 12/30/03); O'ROURKE: Abe Sylvia, *Mike McGowan, Jason Patrick Sands*; O'RILEY: Matt Loehr, *Justin Bohon*; O'HOULLIHAN: Robert H. Fowler; GUARD: Jeffry Denman (until 6/9/02), *Jim Borstelmann* (from 6/18/02); BAILIFF: Abe Sylvia, *Mike McGowan, Jason Patrick Sands*; JUDGE: Peter Marinos, *Mel Brooks* (12/31/03; one night only); FOREMAN OF JURY: Kathy Fitzgerald; TRUSTEE: Ray Wills, *Mark Lotito, Brad Oscar* (from 12/30/03); ENSEMBLE: Jeffry Denman (*Jim Borstelmann*), Madeleine Doherty, Bryn Dowling, Kathy Fitzgerald, Robert H. Fowler, Ida Gilliams, Eric Gunhus, Kimberly Hester, Naomi Kakuk, Matt Loehr, Peter Marinos, Angie L. Schworer, Jennifer Smith, Abe Sylvia, Tracy Terstriep, Ray Wills, *Wendy Waring, Courtney Young, Jenny-Lynn Suckling, Charley Izabella King, Mike McGowan, Kimberly Jones, Jennifer Paige Chambers, Ida Leigh Curtis*. **Understudies**: Max: Ray Wills & Brad Oscar, *John Treacy Egan, Mark Lotito, Brad Oscar* (12/30/03–1/11/04); Roger: Brad Oscar, Jim

Borstelmann, Brad Musgrove, *John Treacy Eagan, Mark Lotito, Brad Oscar* (from 12/30/03); Ulla: Ida Gilliams & Angie L. Schworer, *Charley Izabella King, Ida Leigh Curtis, Jennifer Paige Chambers*; Leo: Jamie La Verdiere & Jeffry Denman, *Stacey Todd Holt* (from 6/18/02), *Larry Raben, Matt Loehr, Roger Bart*; Carmen: Jamie La Verdiere & Brad Musgrove, *Stacey Todd Holt, Larry Raben*; Franz: Jim Borstelmann & Jeffry Denman, *Ray Wills, John Treacy Egan, Mark Lotito, Brad Oscar* (from 12/30/03). **Swings**: Jim Borstelmann, Adrienne Gibbons, Jamie La Verdiere, Brad Musgrove, Christina Marie Norrup, *Angie C. Creighton, Jason Patrick Sands, Courtney Young, Larry Raben*. **Orchestra:** CONCERTMASTER: Rick Dolan; VIOLINS: Ashley D. Horne, Louise Owen, Karen M. Karlsrud, Helen Kim; WOODWINDS: Vincent Della Rocca, Steven J. Greenfield, Jay Hassler, Alva F. Hunt, Frank Santagata; TRUMPETS: David Rogers, Nich Marchione, Frank Greene; TENOR TROMBONES: Dan Levine & Tim Sessions; BASS TROMBONE: Chris Olness; FRENCH HORN: Jill Williamson; CELLO: Laura Bontrager; HARP: Anna Reinersman; STRING BASS: Robert Renino; DRUMS: Cubby O'Brien; PERCUSSION: Benjamin Herman; KEYBOARD: Phil Reno. *Act I*: *Scene 1* Shubert Alley: "Opening Night" (Ensemble), "The King of Broadway" (Max & Ensemble); *Scene 2* Max's office; June 16, 1959: "We Can Do It" (Max & Leo); *Scene 3* The Chambers Street offices of Whitehall & Marks: "I Wanna Be a Producer" ("Unhappy") (Leo & Accountants); *Scene 4* Max's office: "We Can Do It" (reprise) (Max & Leo); *Scene 5* The rooftop of a Greenwich Village apartment building: "In Old Bavaria" (Franz), "Der Guten Tag Hop Clop" (Franz, Max, Leo); *Scene 6* The living-room of renowned theatrical director Roger de Bris' elegant Upper East Side townhouse on a sunny Tuesday afternoon in June: "Keep it Gay" (Roger, Bryan, Carmen, Kevin, Scott, Shirley, Max, Leo); *Scene 7* Max's office: "When You Got It, Flaunt It" (Ulla); *Scene 8* Little Old Lady Land: "Along Came Bialy" (Max & Little Old Ladies), "Act I Finale" (Max, Leo, Franz, Ulla, Roger, Carmen, Bryan, Kevin, Scott, Shirley, Ensemble). *Act II*: *Scene 1* Max's office; late morning, a few weeks later: "That Face" (Leo, Ulla, Max); *Scene 2* The bare stage of a Broadway theatre: "Haben Sie Gehoert Das Deutsche Band?" (Jason & Franz); *Scene 3* Shubert Alley: "Opening Night" (reprise) (Usherettes), "You Never Say 'Good Luck' on Opening Night" (Roger, Max, Carmen, Franz, Leo); *Scene 4* The stage of the Shubert Theatre: "Springtime for Hitler" (Lead Tenor, Roger, Ulla, Ensemble) [in this number an actor mouths the lines "Don't be stupid, Be a smartic, Come and join the Nazi party" while Mel Brooks's voice is heard from offstage as a cameo. Mr. Brooks had spoken these lines in the movie]; *Scene 5* Max's office; later that night: "Where Did We Go Right?" (Max & Leo); *Scene 6* The holding-cell of a NY courthouse; 10 days later: "Betrayed" (Max); *Scene 7* A New York courtroom: "'til Him" (Leo & Max); *Scene 8* Sing Sing: "Prisoners of Love" (The Convicts); *Scene 9* The stage of the Shubert Theatre: "Prisoners of Love" (continued) (Roger, Ulla, Ensemble); *Scene 10* Shubert Alley: "Leo and Max" (Leo & Max); **Curtain Call**: "Goodbye!" (Company).

The show was capitalized at $10.5 million, and had advance sales of over $12 million. It opened to great reviews. On 4/22/01 Nathan Lane sprained his ankle on stage. By May Mr. Lane was having major problems with his vocal cords, and began missing performances. Brad Oscar, his understudy (he was also playing Franz), stood in for him over 70 times. The show won the unprecedented number of 12 Tonys: musical, score, book, director of a musical, choreography, sets, costumes, lighting, orchestrations, and for Cady Huffman, Gary Beach, and Nathan Lane. It was also nominated for Matthew Broderick, Brad Oscar, and Roger Bart. *The Producers*, like all the Broadway shows running at that time, was suspended 9/11/01 and 9/12/01, for 3 performances, following the attack on New York City. By 10/01 the management were selling 50 tickets a night for $480, in order to forestall scalpers (so they said). By 12/01 Nathan Lane was doing six performances a week instead of eight (Brad Oscar went on for the other two). Mr. Lane & Mr. Broderick's contracts were up on 3/17/02. On 2/5/02 it was announced that Henry Goodman, the British comic, would replace Nathan Lane as Max, and on 2/7/02 that Steven Weber would replace Matthew Broderick as Leo. After the 4/14/02 matinee Mr. Goodman, then playing the lead, was fired because he wasn't funny enough. The way he was notified of his dismissal (his agent called him from London on the day) caused some consternation on Broadway. He was paid the remaining eight months of his contract, at $15,000 a week. Critics re-visited the show on 5/1/02–5/2/02, and gave it raves all over again. At that point Jim Borstelmann was playing Franz. Jeffry Denman, who played Scott, wrote the book *A Year with The Producers*. After Lane and Broderick left, the box-office receipts fell off, and on 8/6/03 it was announced that there was a strong possibility of them returning for the last three months of 2003. Then it was announced that they would come back on New Year's Eve, 2003, and finally on 12/30/03 (at $100,000 a week each). The show missed the 8/14/03 performance due to power blackout. Lewis J. Stadlen left in 10/03 due to a hip injury. Who were to play Max and Leo after Lane and Broderick left in 4/04? Perhaps Lane and Broderick themselves. By mid–Jan. 2004 they were in discussions to extend to 4/25/04. However, Kelsey Grammer was also in talks by 1/04 to play Max (he never did play Max).

After Broadway. TOUR. This was the First National Tour, later known as the Max Company. It opened on 9/18/02 (rehearsals from late 7/02; previews from 9/10/02), at the Benedum Center, Pittsburgh, and closed 1/30/05, in Pittsburgh. Mel Brooks made some minor changes to the lyrics and book, and Susan Stroman made some of her own choreographic changes. Although everyone knew who would star in it, confirmation of the cast came on 7/2/02. A major stop along the tour's way was an 8-month stint at the Pantages Theatre, Los Angeles, where it opened on 5/29/03 (previews from 4/21/03—this date was brought forward from 5/2/03). The L.A. advance sale was over $11 million. During this stint Mel Brooks did a cameo as the judge. After the L.A. run ended on 1/4/04, the tour continued, beginning at Denver 1/6/04–1/31/04. It ran at the Kennedy Center, Washington, DC, 6/23/04–8/22/04. *Cast*: MAX: Lewis J. Stadlen (until 4/20/03), *Jason Alexander* (from 4/21/03), *Lewis J. Stadlen* (from 1/6/04); LEO: Don Stephenson (until 4/20/03), *Martin Short* (from 4/21/03), *Alan Ruck* (1/6/04–12/19/04), *Hunter Foster* (from 1/14/05); FRANZ: Fred Applegate, *Michael McCormick*; CARMEN: Jeff Hyslop (until 11/12/02), *Alan Bennett, Michael Paternostro* (from 11/22/02), *Josh Prince* (from 1/6/04), *Harry Bouvy*; ROGER: Lee Roy Reams, *Gary Beach* (until 9/28/03), *Lee Roy Reams* (from 9/30/03); ULLA: Angie L. Schworer (until 11/2/03), *Ida Leigh Curtis* (from 11/4/03), *Charley Izabella King* (from 1/6/04); CHORUS: Alan Bennett, Meg Gillentine, Nancy Johnston, Kimberly Jones, Kevin Ligon, Melissa Rae Mahon, Patrick Wetzel.

TOUR. This was the Second National Tour, later known as the Leo Company. It opened in 7/03 (previews from 6/17/03), at the Colonial Theatre, Boston, and closed 6/19/05, at the fair Park, Dallas. Then it went to Japan for three weeks. *Cast*: MAX: Lewis J. Stadlen, *Brad Oscar* (until 11/30/03), *Bob Amaral* (from 11/25/03—for the last week in Chicago); LEO: Don Stephenson, *Andy Taylor*; CARMEN: Rich Affannato; ULLA: Ida Leigh Curtis (until 11/2/03), *Renee Klapmeyer* (from 11/4/03); FRANZ: Bill Nolte; ROGER: Lee Roy Reams (until 9/28/03), *Stuart Marland* (from 10/1/03). After 13 weeks in Boston it continued with the tour, beginning in Chicago.

TORONTO PRODUCTION. Opened on 12/11/03, at the CANON THEATRE (renovated and re-named the Pantages). Previews from 11/21/03. PRESENTED BY David & Ed Mirvish; DIRECTOR: Susan Stroman; SOUND: Steve Canyon Kennedy; MUSICAL DIRECTOR: Rick Fox. *Cast*: LEO: Sean Cullen; MAX: Michael Therriault; ROGER: Juan Chioran; FRANZ: Paul O'Sullivan; ULLA: Sarah Cornell; CARMEN: Brandon McGibbon. It closed early at Toronto, on 7/4/04, after 258 PERFORMANCES.

PRINCESS THEATRE, Melbourne. Opened 4/18/04. Previews from 4/2/04. *Cast*: MAX: Reg Livermore; LEO: Tom Burlinson; ULLA: Chloe Dallimore; ROGER: Tony Sheldon; ALSO WITH: Bert Newton.

LONDON. The London premiere was not until 11/9/04. Previews from 10/22/04. At first it was going to play at the Prince Edward Theatre, shunting out *Mamma Mia*. But, instead, it opened at the THEATRE ROYAL, DRURY LANE. Originally Nathan Lane and Matthew Broderick were being touted as the leads, but by mid–2003, with those two stars booked for a Broadway return, attention shifted to Robert Lindsay and Lee Evans. Finally Richard Dreyfuss landed the role of Max. It had the same basic crew as for Broadway. DIRECTOR: Susan Stroman. *Cast*: MAX: Nathan Lane (Richard Dreyfuss pulled out, or was pulled out; Mr. Lane made 38,000 pounds a week, a record in the West End); *Brad Oscar* (from 1/10/05); LEO: Lee Evans; ULLA: Leigh Zimmerman; CARMEN:

James Dreyfus; ROGER: Conleth Hill; FRANZ: Nicolas Colicos. Nathan Lane was going to leave the production in 12/04, but extended to 1/8/05. The 12/16/04 evening performance had Prince Charles in the audience, but no Nathan Lane on stage. He was out with two slipped discs, and would bow out of the role early, Cory English, his understudy, standing in until Brad Oscar took over on 1/10/05.

THE MOVIE. Due out in late 2005. Filmed in Brooklyn. DIRECTOR: Susan Stroman. *Cast*: MAX: Nathan Lane; LEO: Matthew Broderick; ULLA: Uma Thurman (Nicole Kidman was originally going to play this role, but bowed out in 12/04); CARMEN: Roger Bart; ROGER: Gary Beach; FRANZ: Will Ferrell; ALSO WITH: Debra Monk, Andrea Martin.

562. *Promises, Promises*

Set in New York City at the present time. Chuck curries favor with higher-up executives in his company, Consolidated Life, by lending them the key to his apartment so they can take their mistresses there. J.D.'s mistress, Fran, attempts suicide in the apartment when J.D. decides to go back to his wife, and this blows open the whole secret. Chuck looks after her, quits his job, and the two begin a relationship. In the Broadway production Chuck would often step out of character to address the audience directly. Scenes would be replayed the way he wanted them to come out, rather than the way they happened in reality. Each member of the chorus was given a distinct personality, and the scene changes were made into numbers. Back-up vocalists were placed in the orchestra pit, a novelty at the time. This was the only Broadway musical from the phenomenally successful pop song writers of the 1960s, Bacharach & David (until *The Look of Love*).

Before Broadway. Six months before rehearsals began, Bob Fosse went off to direct the movie version of *Sweet Charity* and was replaced as director of *Promises, Promises* by Robert Moore and as choreographer by Michael Bennett (Hal Prince had turned down the offer to direct). The show tried out in Boston, where Arthur Rubinstein, the musical director, left, and was replaced by Harold Wheeler. The numbers "Let's Pretend We're Grown Up," "What Am I Doing Here?," "You've Got it All Wrong," and "Tick, Tock, Goes the Clock" were all cut.

The Broadway Run. SHUBERT THEATRE, 12/1/68–1/1/72. 7 previews. 1,281 PERFORMANCES. PRESENTED BY David Merrick; MUSIC: Burt Bacharach; LYRICS: Hal David; BOOK: Neil Simon; BASED ON the 1960 movie *The Apartment*, written by Billy Wilder & I.A.L. Diamond; DIRECTOR: Robert Moore; CHOREOGRAPHER: Michael Bennett; ASSISTANT CHOREOGRAPHER: Bob Avian; DANCE CAPTAIN: Margo Sappington, *Baayork Lee*; SETS: Robin Wagner; COSTUMES: Donald Brooks; LIGHTING: Martin Aronstein; SOUND: Thomas R. Hardcastle; MUSICAL DIRECTOR: Harold Wheeler, *Arthur Azenzer* (by 69–70); ORCHESTRATIONS: Jonathan Tunick; DANCE MUSIC ARRANGEMENTS: Harold Wheeler; CAST RECORDING on United Artists; PRESS: Harvey B. Sabinson, Lee Solters, David Powers, *Marilynn LeVine* (by 69–70); CASTING: Alan Shayne Associates; GENERAL MANAGER: Jack Schlissel; COMPANY MANAGER: Richard Highley, *Vince McKnight* (by 69–70); PRODUCTION STAGE MANAGER: Charles Blackwell, *Alan Hall*; STAGE MANAGER: Henry Velez, *May Muth* (by 69–70), *Henry Velez* (by 70–71); STAGE MANAGER: Andie Wilson Kingwill; ASSISTANT STAGE MANAGER: Robert St. Clair, *Peter Lombard*. *Cast*: CHUCK BAXTER: Jerry Orbach (1) ✩, *Gene Rupert* (8/3/70–8/17/70), *Jerry Orbach, Anthony Roberts* (from 10/26/70), *Gene Rupert* (from 4/12/71), *Bill Gerber* (from 11/8/71); J.D. SHELDRAKE: Edward Winter (3) ✩, *James Congdon* (from 12/7/70); FRAN KUBELIK: Jill O'Hara (2) ✩, *Patti Davis* (8/17/70–8/31/70), *Jill O'Hara, Jenny O'Hara* (from 12/7/70), *Lorna Luft* (from 10/18/71); BARTENDER EDDIE: Ken Howard, *Dick Sabol* (from 68–69); MR. DOBITCH: Paul Reed (5), *Dick O'Neill*; SYLVIA GILHOOLEY: Adrienne Angel (11); MR. KIRKEBY: Norman Shelly (7), *Ronn Carroll* (from 69–70), *Dick Korthaze*; MR. EICHELBERGER: Vince O'Brien (8), *Henry Sutton* (from 69–70); VIVIEN DELLA HOYA: Donna McKechnie (12), *Baayork Lee* (from 69–70); DR. DREY-

FUSS: A. Larry Haines (4), *Norman Shelly* (from 11/69); JESSE VANDERHOF: Dick O'Neill (6), *Don Fellows*; DENTIST'S NURSE: Rita O'Connor, *Carolyn Kirsch* (from 69–70), *Sandra West* (relieved Miss Kirsch during 69–70, and took over role in 70–71); COMPANY NURSE: Carole Bishop, *Eileen Taylor* (from 70–71); COMPANY DOCTOR: Gerry O'Hara, *Joe Nelson* (from 69–70), *Andy Bew* (from 70–71), *Spencer Henderson III*; PEGGY OLSON: Millie Slavin (10); LUM DING HOSTESS: Baayork Lee (13), *Barbara Monte-Britton* (from 69–70); WAITER: Scott Pearson, *Gene Cooper* (from 69–70), *Scott Salmon*; MADISON SQUARE GARDEN ATTENDANT: Michael Vita, *Frank Pietri* (from 69–70); DINING ROOM HOSTESS: Betsy Haug, *Peggy Haug* (from 70–71), *Debra Lyman*; MISS POLANSKY: Margo Sappington, *Julane Stites* (from 69–70), *Barbara Alston* (relieved Miss Stites in 69–70, and took over the role in 70–71), *Sandra West*; MISS WONG: Baayork Lee (13), *Barbara Monte-Britton* (from 69–70); BARTENDER EUGENE: Michael Vita, *Frank Pietri* (from 69–70); MARGE MACDOUGALL: Marian Mercer (9), *Pam Zarit* (from 12/1/69), *Mary Louise Wilson* (from 7/20/70), *Marilyn Child* (from 5/71); CLANCY'S LOUNGE PATRONS: Rod Barry (gone by 70–71), Carole Bishop (*Eileen Taylor* by 70–71), Gene Cooper (*Scott Salmon* by 70–71), Bob Fitch (gone by 70–71), Neil F. Jones (gone by 70–71), Rita O'Connor (*Carolyn Kirsch* by 69–70, *Sandra West* from 69–70), Scott Pearson, Michael Shawn (*Joe Nelson* by 69–70 & gone by 70–71), Julane Stites (gone by 70–71), Melissa Stoneburn (gone by 70–71). New by 69–70: *Pam Blair, Dick Korthaze* (gone by 70–71), *Fred Benjamin* (gone by 70–71), *Ralph Nelson* (gone by 70–71). New by 70–71: *Jacki Garland, Oscar Antony, John Medeiros*. Later replacements: *Karen Burke, Rodney Griffin, Tod Miller, Terry Violino*; CLANCY'S EMPLOYEES: Graciela Daniele (*Carol Hanzel* by 69–70), Betsy Haug (*Peggy Haug* by 70–71, *Debra Lyman*), Margo Sappington (*Eileen Casey* by 69–70); HELEN SHELDRAKE: Kay Oslin, *Marylou Sirinek* (from 70–71), *Lynne Taylor*; KARL KUBELIK: Ken Howard, *Dick Sabol* (from 68–69); NEW YOUNG EXECUTIVE: Rod Barry, *Frank Newell* (from 69–70), *Terry Violino*; INTERNS: Gerry O'Hara (*Ronn Forella* by 69–70 & gone by 70–71), Michael Shawn (*Joe Nelson* by 69–70), *Bob Fitch* (by 70–71), *John Medeiros* (by 70–71), *Scott Salmon*; INTERNS' DATES: Barbara Alston, Graciela Daniele (*Carol Hanzel* by 69–70), *Karen Burke, Rita Rudner*; ORCHESTRA VOICES: Kelly Britt (*Patti Davis* by 69–70, *Ilene Graff* by 70–71), Margot Hanson (*Marylou Sirinek* by 69–70, *Rei Golenor* by 70–71), Bettye McCormick, Ilona Simon, *Sandra Thornton*. **Standby**: Chuck/J.D.: Peter Lombard. **Understudies**: Fran: Margo Sappington, *Patti Davis* (by 69–70), *Ilene Graff* (by 70–71); Dreyfuss: Norman Shelly; Dobitch: Dick O'Neill; Vanderhof: Henry Sutton; Eichelberger: Henry Sutton, *Ronn Carroll, Bob Fitch*; Marge: Kelly Britt, *Kay Oslin* (by 69–70), *Rei Golenor* (by 70–71); Kirkeby: *Dick Korthaze* (by 69–70); Peggy: Carole Bishop, *Kay Oslin* (by 69–70), *Carol Hanzel* (by 70–71), *Lynne Taylor*; Vivien: *Betsy Haug* (by 69–70), *Barbara Monte-Britton* (by 70–71); Karl: *Frank Pietri* (by 69–70); Sylvia: *Carol Hanzel* (by 69–70), *Lynne Taylor*. **Swing Dancers**: Debra Lyman (by 69–70, *Miranda Fellows*), Don Lopez (by 69–70, *Andy Bew* by 70–71, *Spence Henderson*). **Act I**: *Scene 1* The offices of Consolidated Life; Second Avenue bar: "Half as Big as Life" (Chuck), "Grapes of Roth" (dance) (Dancers); *Scene 2* Chuck's apartment house: "Upstairs" (Chuck); *Scene 3* Medical office: "You'll Think of Someone" (Fran & Chuck); *Scene 4* Mr. Sheldrake's office: "(It's) Our Little Secret" (Chuck & Sheldrake); *Scene 5* Lobby: "She Likes Basketball" (Chuck); *Scene 6* Lum Ding's Restaurant and Madison Square Garden: "Knowing When to Leave" (Fran); *Scene 7* Lobby: Executive dining-room; Executive sun-deck: "Where Can You Take a Girl?" (Dobitch, Kirkeby, Eichelberger, Vanderhof), "Wanting Things" (Sheldrake); *Scene 8* At the elevator; *Scene 9* 19th Floor Christmas party: "Turkey Lurkey Time" (Vivien, Miss Polansky, Miss Wong). **Act II**: *Scene 1* Clancy's Lounge: "A Fact Can Be a Beautiful Thing" (Chuck, Marge, Bar Patrons); *Scene 2* Chuck's apartment: "Whoever You Are (I Love You)" (Fran), "A Young Pretty Girl Like You" (Chuck & Dreyfuss), "I'll Never Fall in Love Again" (Fran & Chuck) [the big hit]; *Scene 3* The offices of Consolidated Life; *Scene 4* Lum Ding's Restaurant and Street: "Promises, Promises" (Chuck); *Scene 5* Chuck's apartment.

The show opened on Broadway to great reviews. It won Tonys for Jerry Orbach and Marian Mercer, and was also nominated for musical, choreography, and for Larry Haines, Edward Winter, and Jill O'Hara. During the run Jenny O'Hara took over from her sister Jill as Fran. Jerry

Orbach got a salary of $2,500 a week. On 9/13/71 David Merrick decided to open his show at 8 p.m., rather than the traditional 7.30. He claimed that this was to help diners enjoy a more relaxed meal before the show, but, in fact, the show was dying and he was merely trying another Merrick gimmick.

After Broadway. PRINCE OF WALES THEATRE, London, 10/2/69. 560 PERFORMANCES. *Cast:* CHUCK: Tony Roberts, *Bob Sherman* (from 4/70); FRAN: Betty Buckley; J.D.: James Congdon; DREYFUSS: Jack Kruschen, *Bernard Spear* (from 4/70); MARGE: Kelly Britt, *Julia McKenzie* (from 4/70).

TOUR. Opened on 5/11/70, at the Civic Auditorium, San Diego. It ran 14 months. MUSICAL DIRECTOR: Don Jennings. *Cast:* CHUCK: Tony Roberts, *Anthony Teague* (from 10/70); FRAN: Melissa Hart; SYLVIA: Susan Luckey; KIRKEBY: Larry Douglas; DREYFUSS: Jack Kruschen; J.D.: Bob Holiday; MARGE: Kelly Britt.

TOUR. Opened on 9/16/71, at the Mosque Auditorium, Scranton, Pa., and closed on 5/14/72, at the Comerford Theatre, Wilkes-Barre, Pa., after 119 cities. *Cast:* CHUCK: Will MacKenzie; FRAN: Syndee Balaber; J.D.: Mace Barrett; DREYFUSS: Alan North.

EQUITY LIBRARY THEATRE, 5/12/83–6/5/83. 30 PERFORMANCES. It had a song that wasn't in the original—"Christmas Day" (Act II, Scene 2, 2nd song). DIRECTOR: Alan Fox; CHOREOGRAPHER: Derek Wolshonak; MUSICAL DIRECTOR: Bob Goldstone. *Cast:* CHUCK: Gordon Lockwood; FRAN: Beth Leavel; DREYFUSS: Larry Hirschhorn; J.D.: Lew Resseguie; KIRKEBY: Ron Wisniski; CHORUS INCLUDED: Elyssa Paternoster, Lorena Palacios, Mimi Quillin.

CITY CENTER, NYC, 3/20/97–3/23/97. 5 PERFORMANCES. This was a concert version, part of the *Encores!* series. Neil Simon revised it for this production. It was wildly received by critics and public, and there was talk of it going to Broadway, but that never happened. DIRECTOR: Rob Marshall; CHOREOGRAPHER: Kathleen Marshall; MUSICAL DIRECTOR: Rob Fisher. *Cast:* CHUCK: Martin Short; J.D.: Terrence Mann; FRAN: Kerry O'Malley; EDDIE: Sean Martin Hingston; DOBITCH: Eugene Levy; SYLVIA: Mary Ann Lamb; KIRKEBY: Samuel E. Wright; GINGER WONG: Cynthia Onrubia; EICHELBERGER: Joe Grifasi; VIVIEN: Carol Lee Meadows; DREYFUSS: Dick Latessa; VANDERHOF: Ralph Byers; COMPANY NURSE: Jill Matson; PEGGY: Jenifer Lewis; WAITER: Harrison Beal; MADISON SQUARE GARDEN ATTENDANT: Vince Pesce; EUGENE: Sergio Trujillo; MARGE: Christine Baranski; KARL: Mike O'Malley. *Act I:* Overture (Orchestra & Company); *Scene 1* The offices of Consolidated Life: "Half as Big as Life" (Chuck); *Scene 2* First Avenue Bar: "Grapes of Roth" (Ensemble); *Scene 3* Outside Chuck's apartment: "Upstairs" (Chuck); *Scene 4* Medical office: "You'll Think of Someone" (Fran & Chuck); *Scene 5* Mr. Sheldrake's office: "Our Little Secret" (Chuck & J.D.); *Scene 6* Lobby: "She Likes Basketball" (Chuck); *Scene 7* Lum Ding's Chinese restaurant and Madison Square Garden: "Knowing When to Leave" (Fran); *Scene 8* Executive dining room and sun deck of Consolidated Life: "Where Can You Take a Girl?" (Dobitch, Kirkeby, Eichelberger, Vanderhof), "Wanting Things" (J.D.); *Scene 9* At the elevator: "You've Got it All Wrong" (Peggy & Fran); *Scene 10* Nineteenth-Floor Christmas party: "Turkey Lurkey Time" (Sylvia, Vivien, Ginger, Ensemble). *Act II:* Entr'acte (Orchestra); *Scene 1* Clancy's Lounge: "A Fact Can Be a Beautiful Thing" (Chuck, Marge, Ensemble); *Scene 2* Chuck's apartment: "Whoever You Are" (Fran), "Christmas Day" (Orchestra Voices), "A Young Pretty Girl Like You" (Chuck & Dreyfuss), "I'll Never Fall in Love Again" (Fran & Chuck); *Scene 3* Mr. Sheldrake's office; *Scene 4* Outside Lum Ding's Chinese Restaurant: "Promises, Promises" (Chuck); *Scene 5* Chuck's apartment.

LOS ANGELES, 5/14/97–5/18/97. This was a concert version, part of the *Reprise!* series. DIRECTOR: Stuart Ross. *Cast:* CHUCK: Jason Alexander; J.D.: Alan Thicke; FRAN: Karen Fineman. By popular demand it was brought back, 8/14/97–8/24/97.

A brief & limited touring revival of the revised 1997 *Encores!* version ran 2/23/01–3/4/01, at the Playhouse Theatre, Wilmington, Del., then 3/6/01–3/11/01, at the Bushnell Theatre, Hartford, Conn. DIRECTOR/CHOREOGRAPHER: Tony Stevens; MUSICAL DIRECTOR: Lawrence Goldberg. *Cast:* CHUCK: Evan Pappas; FRAN: Kelli Rabke; J.D.: Paul Schoeffler; MARGE: Beth Glover; PEGGY: Brenda Braxton; DREYFUSS: Gordon Stanley; ALSO WITH: Jennifer West, Rod Weber, Michael Hayward-Jones, Michele Ragusa.

563. *Pump Boys and Dinettes*

An intimate and simple revue. Set in the Double Cupp Diner, across Highway 57 from the gas station, between Frog Level and Smyrna, SC. It was basically an extended cabaret act. The songs were sung and played by four gas station attendants across the street and two waitresses, Rhetta and Prudie Cupp (the Dinettes). The thin libretto serves to introduce the songs.

Before Broadway. Jim Wann and Mark Hardwick were playing at the Cattleman Restaurant one summer when they started appearing in gas station pump boys' outfits, and came up with the idea for a show. At the same time Cass Morgan (then Jim Wann's wife) and Debra Monk were writing their own cabaret act about two waitresses — the Cupp Sisters, Prudie and Rhetta, or the Dinettes. Wann and Hardwick were joined by John Foley and John Schimmel, and the four lads took the pump boys show on the road. Finally the pump boys and the dinettes coalesced. The 90-minute late-night show opened Off Off Broadway, at WESTSIDE ARTS THEATRE, 7/10/81. 20 PERFORMANCES. It moved to the COLONNADES, 10/13/81–1/17/82. Previews from 10/1/81. 112 PERFORMANCES. Then to Broadway.

The Broadway Run. PRINCESS THEATRE, 2/4/82–6/19/83. 573 PERFORMANCES. PRESENTED BY Dodger Productions, Louis Busch Hager, Marilyn Strauss, Kate Studley, Warner Theatre Productions, Max Weitzenhoffer; MUSIC/LYRICS: Jim Wann (unless otherwise stated); ADDITIONAL MUSIC & LYRICS: other members of the original cast; BOOK: the Company; CONCEIVED & WRITTEN BY: Pump Boys & Dinettes (i.e. the original Broadway cast); SETS: Doug Johnson & Christopher Nowak; COSTUMES: Patricia McGourty; LIGHTING: Fred Buchholz; SOUND: Bill Dreisbach; CAST RECORDING on CBS; PRESS: Hunt/Pucci; GENERAL MANAGEMENT: Dodger Productions; STAGE MANAGER: Mo Donley; ASSISTANT STAGE MANAGER: Lucia Schliessmann. *Cast:* JACKSON: John Foley, *Jimmy Ryan, Malcolm Ruhl*; L.M.: Mark Hardwick, *John Lenehan, Mark Hardwick, Malcolm Ruhl*; PRUDIE CUPP: Debra Monk, *Rhonda Coullet, Debra Monk*; RHETTA CUPP: Cass Morgan, *Ronee Blakley* (from 9/29/82), *Cass Morgan* (from 1/3/83), *Margaret LaMee* (from 2/9/83), *Rhonda Coullet*; EDDIE: John Schimmel, *Bruce Samuels, John Schimmel, Malcolm Ruhl*; JIM: Jim Wann, *Loudon Wainwright III* (from 8/25/82), *Tom Chapin* (from 1/5/83), *John Foley, Malcolm Ruhl.* **Understudies:** If Prudie or Rhetta Cupp aren't around to take your order, Rhonda Coullet serves the food at the Double Cupp Diner. If Jackson, L.M., Eddie, or Jim can't make it to the station on time, Malcolm Ruhl (*Erik Frandsen; Michael Sansonia*) will help pump gas. *Act I:* "Highway 57" (Company), "Taking it Slow" (by Messrs Foley, Hardwick, Schimmel, Wann) (Pump Boys) [this replaced the Pump Boys' number "Takin' My Time" by Spider John Koerner, with additional lyrics by John Foley], "Serve Yourself" (L.M.) [this replaced L.M.'s number "Who Will the Next Fool Be?," written by Charlie Rich], "Menu Song" (m/l: Miss Morgan & Miss Monk) (Dinettes), "The Best Man" (Prudie), "Fisherman's Prayer" (Pump Boys), "Caution: Men Cooking" (m/l: Miss Monk, Miss Morgan, Mr. Wann, Mr. Foley) (Pump Boys) [this replaced the Pump Boys' number "Catfish" (m/l: Jim Wann & Bland Simpson)], "Mamaw" (Jim), "Be Good or Be Gone" (Rhetta), "Drinkin' Shoes" (m/l: Mr. Hardwick, Miss Morgan, Miss Monk) (Company). *Act II:* "Pump Boys" (Pump Boys), "Mona" (Jackson), "T.N.D.P.W.A.M." ("The Night Dolly Parton Was Almost Mine") (L.M.), "Tips" (m/l: Miss Monk & Miss Morgan) (Dinettes), "Sisters" (m/l: Miss Morgan) (Dinettes), "Vacation" (Company), "No Holds Barred" (m/l: Mr. Wann & Miss Morgan) (Company), "Farmer Tan" (L.M. & Dinettes), "Highway 57" (reprise) (Company), "Closing Time" (Company).

Broadway reviews were great. During the run there was a nightly raffle, with the winner chosen from the audience. The prize was a car air-freshener. The show received a Tony nomination for musical.

After Broadway. TOUR. Opened on 10/29/82, at the Fisher Theatre, Detroit, and closed there on 12/5/82. *Cast:* RHETTA: Maria Muldaur; PRUDIE: Shawn Colvin; EDDIE: Gary Bristol; JIM: Tom Chapin; JACKSON: Richard Perrin; L.M.: George Clinton.

LONDON PRODUCTION. Ran as *Straight from the Heart*, at RICHMOND THEATRE-ON-THE-GREEN, 6/26/84–6/30/84. Then to other venues; returned to Richmond as *Pump Boys and Dinettes*, 7/30/84–8/4/84. Then to the West End, to the PICCADILLY THEATRE, 9/20/84–1/85. Previews from 8/6/84. Then it moved to the ALBERY THEATRE. DIRECTOR: David Taylor; CHOREOGRAPHER: Dominic Winter; SETS: Tim Goodchild; SOUND: Jonathan Deans; MUSICAL SUPERVISOR: Roger Ward. *Cast*: JIM: Paul Jones; RHETTA: Kiki Dee; PRUDIE: Carlene Carter; JACKSON: Julian Littman; EDDIE: Gary Holton; L.M.: Brian Protheroe.

CHARLOTTE REPERTORY THEATRE, NC, 9/11/03–10/5/03. Previews from 9/6/03. This was the 20th-anniversary production, and was newly-staged. Jim Wann wrote a new number—"Wild About Honey." DIRECTOR: Michael Bush; CHOREOGRAPHER: Janet Watson; SETS: Jim Gloster; COSTUMES: Bob Croghan; LIGHTING: Tracy Klainer; SOUND: Rossi Craft; MUSICAL SUPERVISOR: Joel Silberman. *Cast*: PRUDIE: Emily Skinner; RHETTA: Lynne Wintersteller; JIM: Jim Wann; JACKSON: Miles Aubrey; L.M.: Randy Redd; EDDIE: Louis Tucci. Broadway plans were discussed, but were vague.

564. *Purlie*

Set in South Georgia, not too long ago. Purlie, a black preacher, returns to his small Southern home town to start his own church. Attempts to buy Big Bethel Church run him up against segregationist plantation owner Ol' Cap'n, who wants the church for himself. Purlie eventually gets the church, and Ol' Cap'n dies of a heart attack. Purlie marries Lutiebelle. In the musical the story begins with Ol' Cap'n's funeral & story is told in flashback, i.e. the action of Acts I & II takes place chronologically before that of the Prologue & Epilogue.

Before Broadway. *Purlie Victorious*, the straight comedy written by Ossie Davis, opened on Broadway at the CORT THEATRE, on 9/28/61. PRESENTED BY Philip Rose; DIRECTOR: Howard Da Silva. On 11/20/61 it moved to the LONGACRE THEATRE, where it closed on 5/13/62 after a TOTAL OF 261 PERFORMANCES. *Cast*: PURLIE: Ossie Davis; LUTIEBELLE: Ruby Dee (Mrs. Ossie Davis in real life); GITLOW: Godfrey M. Cambridge; OL' CAP'N: Sorrell Boooke; CHARLEY: Alan Alda.

Producer Philip Rose asked author Ossie Davis to collaborate on the libretto of the musical. The number "I Got Love" was added just before the opening.

The Broadway Run. BROADWAY THEATRE, 3/15/70–12/14/70; WINTER GARDEN THEATRE, 12/16/70–3/13/71; ANTA THEATRE, 3/15/71–11/6/71. 28 previews. Total of 688 PERFORMANCES. PRESENTED BY Philip Rose; MUSIC: Gary Geld; LYRICS: Peter Udell; BOOK: Ossie Davis, Philip Rose, Peter Udell; BASED ON the 1961 satirical Broadway play *Purlie Victorious*, by Ossie Davis; DIRECTOR: Philip Rose; CHOREOGRAPHER: Louis Johnson; SETS: Ben Edwards; COSTUMES: Ann Roth; LIGHTING: Thomas Skelton; SOUND: Jack Tolbutt; AUDIO DESIGN: Robert Liftin; MUSICAL SUPERVISOR: Garry Sherman; CONDUCTOR: Joyce Brown; ORCHESTRATIONS/CHORAL ARRANGEMENTS: Garry Sherman & Luther Henderson; ADDITIONAL MUSICAL ARRANGEMENTS: Ray Wright; DANCE MUSIC ARRANGEMENTS: Luther Henderson; CAST RECORDING on AMPEX; PRESS: Merle Debuskey & Faith Geer; CASTING: Lynda Watson; GENERAL MANAGER: Helen Stern Richards; PRODUCTION STAGE MANAGER: Leonard Auerbach; STAGE MANAGER: Mortimer Halpern, *Jerry Laws*; ASSISTANT STAGE MANAGER: Charles Briggs, *Bert Wood*. *Cast*: PURLIE VICTORIOUS JUDSON: Cleavon Little (1) *, *Robert Guillaume* (from 10/4/71); CHURCH SOLOIST: Linda Hopkins (8); LUTIEBELLE GUSSIE MAE JENKINS: Melba Moore (2) *, *Patti Jo* (from 3/30/71); MISSY JUDSON: Novella Nelson (5), *Carol Jean Lewis* (from 3/30/71); GITLOW JUDSON: Sherman Hemsley (4); CHARLIE COTCHIPEE: C. David Colson (6); IDELLA LANDY: Helen Martin (7); OL' CAP'N COTCHIPEE: John Heffernan (3) *, *Art Wallace* (from 10/20/71); DANCERS: Loretta Abbott, Hope Clarke, Judy Gibson (*Patti Harris*), Morris Donaldson, George Faison, Lavinia Hamilton, Al Perryman, Harold Pierson (*Michael Peters*), Arlene Rowlant, William Taylor, Ella Thompson, Larry Vickers (*Andy Torres*), Myrna White; SINGERS: Carolyn Byrd, Barbara Christopher (*Vera Moore*), Peter Colly, Denise Elliott,

Milt Grayson, Synthia Jackson, Mildred Lane, Tony Middleton, Ray Pollard, Mildred Pratcher, Alyce Webb. *Ted Ross*. **Standbys**: Purlie: Robert Jackson, *Morgan Freeman*; Cap'n/Charlie: Curt Williams. **Understudies**: Lutiebelle: Synthia Jackson; Gitlow: Ted Ross; Missy/Idella: Alyce Webb; Soloist: Mildred Lane, *Alyce Webb*. **Swing Dancer**: Ted Goodridge. **Act I: Prologue** Big Bethel, a country church: "Walk Him up the Stairs" (Entire Company); **Scene 1** A shack on the plantation: "New Fangled Preacher Man" (Purlie), "Skinnin' a Cat" (Gitlow & Field Hands), "Purlie" (Lutiebelle), "The Harder They Fall" (Purlie & Lutiebelle); **Scene 2** Outside Ol' Cap'n Commissary: Charlie's Songs (Charlie): "The Barrels of War," "The Unborn Love" [end of Charlie's Songs sequence], "Big Fish, Little Fish" (Ol' Cap'n & Charlie); **Scene 3** Outside Ol' Cap'n Commissary: "I Got Love" (Lutiebelle) [the show stopper], "Great White Father" (Cotton Pickers), "Skinnin' a Cat" (reprise) (Gitlow & Charlie); **Scene 4** The shack: "Down Home" (Purlie & Missy). **Act II: Scene 1** On the plantation; 4 a.m.: "First Thing Monday Mornin'" (Cotton Pickers); **Scene 2** The shack; just before dawn: "He Can Do It" (Missy & Lutiebelle), "The Harder They Fall" (reprise) (Gitlow, Lutiebelle, Missy), "The World is Comin' to a Start" (Charlie & Company); **Epilogue** Time & place as in prologue: "Walk Him up the Stairs" (reprise) (Entire Company).

Broadway reviews were very divided (including a couple of raves) but people didn't come. Philip Rose then hired publicist Sylvester Leaks, who brought in blacks from church groups and the like. This was the first Broadway musical written by a black author to run over 500 performances since *Shuffle Along* in 1921. It won Tony Awards for Cleavon Little (it was this musical that made him a star) and Melba Moore, and was nominated for musical, direction of a musical, and choreography.

After Broadway. TOUR. Opened on 11/20/71, at the Shubert Theatre, Philadelphia. *Cast*: PURLIE: Robert Guillaume; LUTIEBELLE: Patti Jo; MISSY: Carol Jean Lewis; OL' CAP'N: Art Wallace; GITLOW: Sherman Hemsley; CHARLIE: Tommy Breslin; FIELD HANDS: Andy Torres, Lonnie McNeil, Ted Ross. This touring company returned to Broadway.

565. *Purlie (1972 return to Broadway)*

This was the tour of the original 1970 Broadway production returned to New York.

The Broadway Run. BILLY ROSE THEATRE, 12/27/72–1/7/73. 2 previews. 14 PERFORMANCES. It had the same crew as for the original 1970 run, except CONDUCTOR: Charles Austin; PRESS: Merle Debuskey & Maurice Turet; GENERAL MANAGER/COMPANY MANAGER: Helen Richards; PRODUCTION STAGE MANAGER: Steven Zweigbaum; STAGE MANAGER: Lou Rodgers III; ASSISTANT STAGE MANAGER: Ra Joe Darby. *Cast*: PURLIE: Robert Guillaume; CHURCH SOLOIST: Shirley Monroe; LUTIEBELLE: Patti Jo; MISSY: Laura Cooper; GITLOW: Sherman Hemsley; FIELD HANDS: Every Hayes, Lonnie McNeil, Ted Ross; CHARLIE: Douglas Norwick; IDELLA: Helen Martin & Louise Stubbs (alternating); OL' CAP'N: Art Wallace; DANCERS: Darlene Blackburn, Deborah Bridges, Raphael Gilbert, Linda Griffin, Every Hayes, Reggie Jackson, Alton Lathrop, Robert Martin, Karen E. McDonald, Lonnie McNeil, Debbie Palmer, Andre Peck, Zelda Pulliam; SINGERS: DeMarest Grey, Barbara Joy, Ursuline Kairson, Shirley Monroe, Alfred Rage, Beverly G. Robnett, Ted Ross, Frances Salisbury, Vanessa Shaw, David Weatherspoon, Joe Williams Jr. **Understudies**: Purlie: Ra Joe Darby; Lutiebelle: DeMarest Grey & Ursuline Kairson; Ol' Cap'n: Bill Nunnery; Charlie: John Hammil; Gitlow: Ted Ross & Alfred Rage; Missy: Beverly G. Robnett & Barbara Joy; Idella: Frances Salisbury. **Swing Dancer**: Reggie Jackson.

After this Broadway run, the show returned to its national tour. The number "The Harder They Fall" (reprise) was replaced by "Easy Goin' Man" (Gitlow).

After Broadway. KENNEDY CENTER, Washington, DC, 7/30/98–8/2/98. This was a concert version, part of the *Words and Music* series. DIRECTOR/CHOREOGRAPHER: George Faison. *Cast*: Stephanie Mills, Reginald VelJohnson, Dorian Harewood, Larry Storch.

CITY CENTER, NYC, 3/31/05–4/3/05. Part of the *Encores!* series of staged readings. DIRECTOR: Sheldon Epps. *Cast*: PURLIE: Blair Underwood; ALSO WITH: John Cullum, Lillias White, Anika Noni Rose. Then it went on to a full presentation at the PASADENA PLAYHOUSE, Calif., 6/24/05–7/31/05, Mr. Epps directing again, and then the plans were for Broadway in the 2005–06 season. Ossie Davis died on 2/3/05, aged 87.

566. *Putting It Together*

Called "a musical review" [sic]. A party is the setting for this revue of Sondheim songs from some of his well-known earlier shows, as well as from *The Frogs* and the movie *Dick Tracy*. The title came from a number in Sondheim's earlier show *Sunday in the Park with George*.

Before Broadway. It was first PRESENTED BY Cameron Mackintosh at the OLD FIRE STATION, Oxford, England, on 1/27/92. Back then it was a loosely-plotted revue of Sondheim songs from earlier shows, plus several from the movie *Dick Tracy*. DIRECTOR: Julia McKenzie; CAST RECORDING on RCA. *Cast*: Diana Rigg.

In the USA it ran at STAGE I of the Manhattan Theatre Club, (Off Broadway) at City Center, 4/1/93–5/23/93. Previews from 3/2/93. 96 PERFORMANCES. PRESENTED BY Cameron Mackintosh, in association with the Manhattan Theatre Club; DIRECTOR: Julia McKenzie; CHOREOGRAPHER: Bob Avian; SETS: Robin Wagner; COSTUMES: Theoni V. Aldredge; LIGHTING: Tharon Musser; SOUND: Scott Lehrer; MUSICAL DIRECTOR: Scott Frankel; MUSICAL ARRANGEMENTS: Chris Walker; STAGE MANAGER: Franklin Keysar. *Cast*: Julie Andrews (her first New York show in ages), Michael Rupert (*Patrick Quinn*), Christopher Durang, Rachel York, Stephen Collins. *Standbys*: For Miss Andrews: Jeanne Lehman; For Mr. Collins: Dennis Parlato; For Mr. Rupert/Mr. Durang: Patrick Quinn; For Miss York: Juliet Lambert. Musical Numbers (the show each song was taken from is only included here if the song is not in the Broadway run list below): *Act I*: "Invocations and Instructions to the Audience," "Putting it Together," "Rich and Happy," "Merrily We Roll Along," "Lovely," "Everybody Ought to Have a Maid" (Wife), "Sooner or Later," "I'm Calm" [from *A Funny Thing Happened on the Way to the Forum*], "Impossible" [from *A Funny Thing Happened on the Way to the Forum*], "Ah, But Underneath…!" [from the London production of *Follies*], "Hello, Little Girl," "My Husband the Pig"/"Every Day a Little Death," "Have I Got a Girl for You," "Pretty Women," "Now" [from *A Little Night Music*], "Bang!," "Country House," "Could I Leave You" [from *Follies*], Entr'acte/"Back in Business." *Act II*: "Rich and Happy" (reprise), "Night Waltzes," "Gun Song" [from *Assassins*], "The Miller's Son" [from *A Little Night Music*], "Live Alone and Like It," "Sorry-Grateful" [from *Company*], "Sweet Polly Plunkett" [from *Sweeney Todd*], "I Could Drive a Person Crazy" [from *Company*], "Marry Me a Little," "Getting Married Today," "Being Alive," "Like it Was," "Old Friends," "Putting it Together" (reprise).

The West Coast premiere was at the 99-seat COLONY STUDIO THEATRE, Los Angeles, 1/24/97–4/13/97. Previews from 1/16/97.

By 7/98 *Variety* was reporting that *Putting it Together* was bound for Broadway. Steve Sondheim had re-written it for Carol Burnett, and the show now included some previously unheard Sondheim songs. First it played at the MARK TAPER FORUM, Los Angeles, 10/22/98–12/6/98. Previews from 10/4/98. The closing date was extended from 11/29/98. DIRECTOR: Eric D. Schaeffer; CHOREOGRAPHER: Bob Avian. *Cast*: AMY (THE WIFE): Carol Burnett; CHARLES (THE HUSBAND): John McCook; JULIE (THE YOUNGER WOMAN): Susan Egan; BARRY (THE YOUNGER MAN): John Barrowman; THE OBSERVER: Bronson Pinchot. *Understudies*: David Engel, George McDaniel, Christina Marie Norrup, Teri Ralston. By 12/98 it was officially announced that the show would go to Broadway in the spring or fall of 1999, with Carol Burnett. During the weekend of 11/12/99 Carol Burnett was out of Broadway previews with flu, and her standby, Ronnie Farer, went on that weekend.

The Broadway Run. ETHEL BARRYMORE THEATRE, 11/21/99–2/20/00. 22 previews from 10/30/99. 101 PERFORMANCES. PRESENTED BY Cameron Mackintosh, in association with the Mark Taper Forum; MUSIC/LYRICS: Stephen Sondheim; DEVISED BY Stephen Sondheim & Julia McKenzie; DIRECTOR: Eric D. Schaeffer; CHOREOGRAPHER: Bob Avian; SETS: Bob Crowley; CAROL BURNETT'S COSTUMES DESIGNED BY: Bob Mackie; LIGHTING: Howard Harrison; SOUND: Andrew Bruce/Mark Menard; MUSICAL DIRECTOR: Paul Raiman; ORCHESTRATIONS: Jonathan Tunick; 1993 OFF BROADWAY CAST RECORDING on RCA; PRESS: The Publicity Office; CASTING: Johnson — Liff; EXECUTIVE PRODUCERS: David Caddick & Martin McCallum; GENERAL MANAGER: Alan Wasser; COMPANY MANAGER: Gillian Roth; PRODUCTION STAGE MANAGER: Peter von Mayrhauser; STAGE MANAGER: Robert Witherow; ASSISTANT STAGE MANAGER: Susie Walsh. *Cast*: THE WIFE: Carol Burnett (1), *Kathie Lee Gifford* (6) (Tuesday evenings from 12/7/99, but not those of 12/21/99 or 12/28/99, when Miss Burnett played the role); THE HUSBAND: George Hearn (2); THE YOUNGER MAN: John Barrowman (3); THE YOUNGER WOMAN: Ruthie Henshall (4); THE OBSERVER: Bronson Pinchot (5), *David Engel, Evan Pappas* (during Mr. Pinchot's injury, 1/4/00–1/9/00; Mr. Pinchot was back 1/11/00). *Standby*: Wife: Ronnie Farer. *Understudies*: Husband: John Jellison; Man: David Engel; Observer: David Engel & Evan Pappas; Woman: Christina Marie Norrup. *Orchestra*: SYNTHESIZER: Nicholas Archer; KEYBOARDS: Matthew Sklar; BASS: Louis Bruno; DRUMS/PERCUSSION: David Silliman; OBOE/ENGLISH HORN: Elizabeth Kieronski; CLARINET: Les Scott; BASSOON: John Campo; TRUMPET: Stu Satalof. *Act I*: "Invocation and Instructions to the Audience" [from *The Frogs*] (Observer), "Putting it Together" [from *Sunday in the Park with George*] (Company), "Rich and Happy" [from *Merrily We Roll Along*] (Company), "Do I Hear a Waltz?" [from *Do I Hear a Waltz?*] (Wife & Husband), "Merrily We Roll Along # 1" [from *Merrily We Roll Along*] (Observer), "Lovely" [from *A Funny Thing Happened on the Way to the Forum*] (Company), "Hello, Little Girl" [from *Into the Woods*] (Husband & Younger Woman), "My Husband the Pig" [an unused number from *A Little Night Music*] (Wife), "Every Day a Little Death" [from *A Little Night Music*] (Wife & Younger Woman), "Everybody Ought to Have a Maid" [from *A Funny Thing Happened on the Way to the Forum*] (Observer & Wife) [During Broadway previews this number replaced "Come Play Wiz Me," from *Anyone Can Whistle*], "Have I Got a Girl for You" [from *Company*] (Younger Man & Husband), "Pretty Women" [from *Sweeney Todd*] (Younger Man & Husband), "Sooner or Later" [from the movie *Dick Tracy*] (Younger Woman), "Bang!" [an unused number from *A Little Night Music*] (Younger Man, Observer, Younger Woman), "Country House" [from the London production of *Follies*] (Wife & Husband), "Unworthy of Your Love" [from *Assassins*] (Younger Man & Younger Woman), "Merrily We Roll Along # 2" [from *Merrily We Roll Along*] (Observer), "Could I Leave You?" [from *Follies*] (Wife), "Rich and Happy" (reprise) (Company). *Act II*: Entr'acte (Orchestra); "Back in Business" [from the movie *Dick Tracy*] (Company), "It's Hot up Here" [from *Sunday in the Park with George*] (Company), "The Ladies Who Lunch" [from *Company*] (Wife), "The Road You Didn't Take" [from *Follies*] (Husband), "Live Alone and Like It" [from the movie *Dick Tracy*] (Younger Man), "More" [from the movie *Dick Tracy*] (Younger Woman), "There's Always a Woman" [an unused number from *Anyone Can Whistle*] (Wife & Younger Woman), "Buddy's Blues" [from *Follies*] (Observer), "Good Thing Going" [from *Merrily We Roll Along*] (Husband), "Marry Me a Little" [from *Company*] (Younger Man), "Getting Married Today" [from *Company*] (Wife), "Merrily We Roll Along # 3" [from *Merrily We Roll Along*] (Company), "Being Alive" [from *Company*] (Company), "Like it Was" [from *Merrily We Roll Along*] (Wife), Finale: "Old Friends" [from *Merrily We Roll Along*] (Company).

Broadway reviews were not good. Kathie Lee Gifford, a devout Christian, objected to the line "wait a goddamn minute" in the number "Could I Leave You," and for her performances it was changed. On 12/12/99 Bronson Pinchot slipped, and tore a calf muscle, and was out for a few days. Carol Burnett was not interested in renewing her contract (it was only for three months), and Cameron Mackintosh, unable to find the right replacement, posted closing notices on 1/7/00. George Hearn was nominated for a Tony. HBO taped a performance, and showed it on TV on 1/4/03.

After Broadway. INTERNATIONAL CITY THEATRE, Los Angeles, 11/8/02–12/9/02. DIRECTOR: Michael Michetti. *Cast*: WIFE: Colleen Fitzpatrick; HUSBAND: Hank Adams; YOUNGER MAN: Tom Schmid; YOUNGER WOMAN: Brittany Page.

567. *Raggedy Ann*

Set on a New York riverfront, sometime earlier in the 20th century. The show's story was the delirious dream of a sick child,

Marcella. Her father is an alcoholic, and her mother has deserted them. The father gives Marcella a doll, Raggedy Ann, which comes to life. Raggedy Ann and her friends save Marcella from General Doom, and bring her to the Doll Doctor in Los Angeles. The Doll Doctor is Marcella's father, and Raggedy Ann gives her heart to Marcella so she may live. Marcella wakes up from her dream, and finds that her doll's heart has gone.

Before Broadway. Joe Raposo had already written songs for the animated film *Raggedy Ann and Andy*, and recycled some of these for this stage musical. The musical first ran in ALBANY, NY, as *Raggedy Ann and Andy*. Then on 12/7/84 it opened at the EMPIRE STATE INSTITUTE FOR THE PERFORMING ARTS, Albany, again as *Raggedy Ann and Andy*. DIRECTOR: Patricia Birch. On 10/25/85 it opened again at the EMPIRE STATE INSTITUTE FOR THE PERFORMING ARTS, Albany, this time as *Rag Dolly*. It had the same basic crew as for the subsequent Broadway run, except MUSICAL DIRECTOR: Gregg A. Barnes. **Cast:** DOCTORS: Neal Ben-Ari, Joe Barrett, Gary O. Aldrich; POPPA: Gibby Brand; MARCELLA: Tricia Brooks; RAGGEDY ANN: Ivy Austin; RAGGEDY ANDY: Scott Schafer; BABY DOLL: Carolyn Marble Valentis; PANDA: Jeanne Vigliante; GENERAL D: David Schramm; BAT: Pamela Sousa; WOLF: Tom Pletto; CAMEL WITH WRINKLED KNEES: Joel Aroeste; WITCH: Elizabeth Austin; COMPANY: Michaela Hughes, Nina Hennessey, Laura Carusone, Scott Evans, Helena Binder, John Thomas Maguire III, Betsy Normile. In the fall of 1985 it was sent to Moscow as part of a cultural exchange, with CBS footing the bill. It was very popular with the Russians (who saw it as *Rag Dolly*), and later that year the show emerged on Broadway.

The Broadway Run. NEDERLANDER THEATRE, 10/16/86–10/19/86. 15 previews. 5 PERFORMANCES. PRESENTED BY Jon Silverman Associates, The John F. Kennedy Center for the Performing Arts, The Empire State Institute for the Performing Arts, and Donald K. Donald, in association with CBS; MUSIC/LYRICS: Joseph Raposo; BOOK: William Gibson; BASED ON stories written by Johnny Gruelle for his ill daughter, Marcella; DIRECTOR/CHOREOGRAPHER: Patricia Birch; FLYING BY: Foy; SETS: Gerry Hariton & Vicki Baral; COSTUMES: Carrie F. Robbins; LIGHTING: Marc B. Weiss; SOUND: Abe Jacob; MUSICAL SUPERVISOR/DANCE MUSIC ARRANGEMENTS: Louis St. Louis; MUSICAL DIRECTOR: Ross Allen & Roy Rogosin; ORCHESTRATIONS: Stan Applebaum; PRESS: Shirley Herz Associates; CASTING: Johnson — Liff Associates; GENERAL MANAGER: Ralph Roseman; COMPANY MANAGER: Marion Finkler; PRODUCTION STAGE MANAGER: Peggy Peterson; STAGE MANAGERS: Franklin Keysar & Amy Pell. **Cast:** DOCTORS: Dick Decareau, Joe Barrett, Richard Ryder (all equal 12th billing); POPPA: Bob Morrisey (6); MARCELLA: Lisa Rieffel (7); RAGGEDY ANN: Ivy Austin (1); RAGGEDY ANDY: Scott Schafer (4); BABY DOLL: Carolyn Marble (11); PANDA: Michelan Sisti (10); GENERAL D: Leo Burmester (2); BAT: Gail Benedict (5); WOLF: Gordon Weiss (8); CAMEL WITH THE WRINKLED KNEES: Joe Aroeste (9); MOMMY: Elizabeth Austin (3); COMPANY: Melinda Buckley, Gregory Butler, Anny De Gange, Susann Fletcher, Michaela Hughes, Steve Owsley, Andrea Wright. *Understudies:* Wolf: Joe Barrett; Raggedy Andy/Panda: Kenneth Boys; Bat: Melinda Buckley; Marcella: Sara Carbone; Poppa: Dick Decareau; Mommy: Anny De Gange; Raggedy Ann: Susann Fletcher; Doctors: Steve Owsley; Camel: Ric Ryder; General: Gordon Weiss; Baby Doll: Andrea Wright. *Swings:* Helena Andreyko & Kenneth Boys. **Act I:** Overture (Orchestra), "Gingham and Yarn" (Company), "Carry On" (Poppa), "Diagnosis" (Doctors), "The Light" (Dolls & Marcella), "Make Believe" (Raggedy Ann & General D), "Blue" (Camel & Raggedy Ann), "Make Believe" (reprise) (Raggedy Ann, Marcella, Dolls, Company), "Make Believe" (reprise) (Raggedy Ann & Marcella), "Something in the Air" (Company): "Delighted" (Clouds), "So Beautiful" (Raggedy Ann, Marcella, Clouds), "A Heavenly Chorus" (Yellow Yum Yum), "The Shooting Star" (Mommy, Poppa, The Rat in the Rolls Royce), "The Wedding" (Company) [end of "Something in the Air" sequence], "Rag Dolly" (Raggedy Ann). **Act II:** "Gingham and Yarn" (reprise) (Company), "You'll Love It" (Bat, Raggedy Ann, The Batettes), "A Little Music" (Marcella, Camel, Raggedy Ann, Dolls), "Gone" (Dolls & Company), "Why Not" (Mommy), "What Did I Lose" (Mommy), "Somewhere" (Raggedy Ann), "Welcome to L.A." (Nurses), "Diagnosis" (reprise) (Doctors), "I Come Riding" (General D), "Gingham and Yarn" (reprise) (Company), Finale: "Rag Dolly" (reprise) (Company).

Reviews were devastatingly bad.

568. *Rags*

Set in New York City's Lower East Side. In 1910 Rebecca and her son David arrive at Ellis Island from the Russian pogroms. Rebecca is looking for her husband Nathan who arrived in the USA a few years before and who is meant to meet them in New York. The couple are befriended by another immigrant, Bella, who takes them in. Rebecca gets a job in a sweatshop, where she runs afoul of Saul, the union organizer, because she won't join the union. Saul, however, takes to Rebecca, and teaches her and David English, and takes them to the Yiddish Theatre. They soon fall in love. David is beaten up by a villain, and at that point Nathan arrives, now calling himself Nat Harris, a small-time politician. Bella is killed in a fire at the shop, and Rebecca leads a workers' revolt.

Before Broadway. This show was first seen in 1984 as a workshop production at Theatre 890. DIRECTOR: Stephen Schwartz. There were no stars in it, and no central character. In 1986, about three weeks into rehearsal of the actual Broadway show, Joan Micklin Silver was dismissed as director and Stephen Schwartz and Charles Strouse took over. However, when it opened in Boston no director was listed. Teresa Stratas failed to appear on opening night in Boston and for a week afterwards, and her place as Rebecca was taken by her understudy, Christine Andreas. But, Miss Stratas came back, and performed brilliantly. Toward the end of the Boston tryout, Gene Saks took over as director, and Ken Rinker was replaced as choreographer by Ron Field. All this time Jay Presson Allen was doing uncredited book re-writes. Then it went into Broadway previews, during which there were several changes to the score and book. This was the scene-by-scene breakdown during previews: *Act I: Scene 1* Ellis Island, April 1910: HOMESICK IMMIGRANT: Andy Gale; REBECCA HERSHKOWITZ: Teresa Stratas; DAVID HERSHKOWITZ: Josh Blake; GUARDS: John Aller & Peter Samuel. "I Remember" (Homesick Immigrant); *Scene 2* Battery Park, immediately following: THE AMERICANS: Michael Cone & Michael Davis; BELLA COHEN: Judy Kuhn; AVRAM COHEN: Dick Latessa. "Greenhorns" (1st American & New Immigrants); *Scene 3* East Side streets and Blumberg tenement apartment; that afternoon: ANNA BLUMBERG: Evalyn Baron; JACK BLUMBERG: Mordecai Lawner. "Brand New World" (Rebecca & David); *Scene 4* East Broadway and offices of the Lower East Side: BEN: Lonny Price; RECRUITERS: Andy Gale & Stan Rubin; NATHAN'S LANDLADY: Irma Rogers; MILLIE, HER NEIGHBOR: Bonnie Schon; EDITOR OF NEWSPAPER: Stan Rubin; SOCIAL WORKER: Joanna Glushak. "Children of the Wind" (Rebecca, Avram, David); *Scene 5* A street and sweatshops a few days later: KLEZMORIM: TUBA: Teddy Bragin; TROMBONE: Sean Mahony; TRUMPET: Bruce Engel; CLARINET: Harold Seletsky; VIOLIN: Marshall Coid; MR. BRONSTEIN: Sam Rubin; (THREE) SWEATSHOP WORKERS: ROSA: Audrey Lavine; ESTHER: Joan Finkelstein; SAM: Gabriel Barre; SAUL, A UNION ORGANIZER: Terrence Mann; CIGAR BOSS: Peter Samuel; RACHEL HALPERN: Marcia Lewis; AN AVID SHOPPER: Joanna Glushak; MR. ROSEN: John Aller. "Penny a Tune" (Rachel, Klezmorim, Peddlers, Workers); *Scene 6* Outside Bronstein's sweatshop; later that day and weeks following; *Scene 7* A Yiddish theatre; a few weeks later: HAMLET: Peter Samuel; OPHELIA: Joanna Glushak; GERTRUDE: Irma Rogers; ROSENKRANTZ: Michael Cone; LAERTES: Gabriel Barre. "Hard to Be a Prince" (Hamlet & Company); *Scene 8* Suffolk Street and under the Brooklyn Bridge; later that night: "Blame it on a Summer Night" (Rebecca & Clarinetist); *Scene 9* McCarthy's Bar: FRANKIE: Michael Cone; MIKE: Michael Davis; "BIG TIM" SULLIVAN: Rex Everhart; NATHAN HERSHKOWITZ: Larry Kert. "What's Wrong with That?" (Frankie, Mike, Tim, Nathan); *Scene 10* The Blumberg apartment; evening; July 3: IRISH TENOR ON RECORDING: Michael Cone. "For My Mary" (Irish Tenor & Ben); *Scene 11* Suffolk Street and above Fourteenth Street; immediately following: RAGMAN: Gabriel Barre; WEALTHY NEW YORKERS: Bill Hastings, John Aller, Michael Davis, Joan Finkelstein, Joanna Glushak, Wendy Kimball, Robert Radford, Peter Samuel, Catherine Ulissey. "Rags" (Bella & Avram); *Scene 12* The street market; July 4: MAN ON STILTS: Gabriel Barre; THUGS: Andy Gale & Peter Samuel. "On the Fourth of July" (Picknickers & Company); *Scene 13* The Blumberg apartment; immediately following: "To America" (Rebecca & Mr. Harris). *Act II*: *Scene 1* The rooftop; evening, July 4: "Yankee Boy" (Mr. Harris & Neighbors); *Scene 2* The rooftop; later that night: "Uptown" (Mr. Harris & Rebecca), "Wanting" (Rebecca & Saul); *Scene 3* The street market; the next day: "Three Sunny Rooms" (Rachel & Avram); *Scene 4* A few days later: A PASSERBY: Stan Rubin; MORRIS, A LITTLE BOY: Devon Michaels; HIS MOTHER: Bonnie Schon; VIOLINIST: Marshall Coid; HIS MOTHER: Irma Rogers; IRISH GIRL: Wendy Kimball; HER MOTHER: Audrey Lavine; ITALIAN TENOR: Andy Gale; HIS MOTHER: Joanna Glushak. "The Sound of Love" (Ben, David, Shoppers), "For My Mary" (reprise) (Bella & Ben); *Scene 5* The Lower East Side Democratic Club; a week later: MRS. SULLIVAN: Bonnie Schon. "Democratic Club Dance" (Rebecca, Tim, Mr. Harris, Mrs. Sullivan, Democrats); *Scene 6* The Blumberg apartment; some time later; *Scene 7* Bronstein's sweatshop: "Bread and Freedom" (Rosa, Rebecca, Esther, Sam); *Scene 8* Union Square; a protest demonstration; later that day: "Dancing with the Fools" (Rebecca, Mr. Harris, Strikers); *Scene 9* Suffolk Street and Battery Park ; a few weeks later: HERSCHEL COHEN: John Aller. FINALE (Rebecca, David, The Americans, New Immigrants).

The Broadway Run. MARK HELLINGER THEATRE, 8/21/86–8/23/86. 18 previews. 4 PERFORMANCES. PRESENTED BY Lee Guber, Martin Heinfling, Marvin A. Krauss; MUSIC: Charles Strouse; LYRICS: Stephen Schwartz; BOOK: Joseph Stein; DIRECTOR: Gene Saks; CHOREOGRAPHER: Ron Field; SETS: Beni Montresor; COSTUMES: Florence Klotz; LIGHTING: Jules Fisher; ASSOCIATE LIGHTING: Peggy Eisenhauer; SOUND: Peter Fitzgerald; MUSICAL DIRECTOR/ADDITIONAL ARRANGEMENTS: Eric Stern; ORCHESTRATIONS: Michael Starobin; PRESS: Solters/Roskin/Friedman; CASTING: Meg Simon & Fran Kumin; GENERAL MANAGEMENT: Marvin A. Krauss Associates; COMPANY MANAGER: Allan Williams; STAGE MANAGERS: Joel Tropper & John Actman. *Cast* (scenes are those in which a particular character is introduced; he/she may well appear in later scenes as well; the relevant musical numbers are included): *Act I*: *Scene 1* Ellis Island; April: HOMESICK IMMIGRANT: Andy Gale; REBECCA HERSHKOWITZ: Teresa Stratas (1) ☆; DAVID HERSHKOWITZ: Josh Blake (8); GUARDS: John Aller & Peter Samuel. "I Remember" (Homesick Immigrant); *Scene 2* Battery Park; immediately following: AMERICANS: Michael Cone & Michael Davis; BELLA COHEN: Judy Kuhn (6); AVRAM COHEN: Dick Latessa (3); BEN: Lonny Price (5); RECRUITERS: Andy Gale & Stan Rubin. "Greenhorns" (Americans & New Immigrants); *Scene 3* East Side streets, and Cohen tenement apartment; that afternoon: ANNA COHEN: Evalyn Baron (10); JACK COHEN: Mordecai Lawner (9). "Brand New World" (Rebecca & David); *Scene 4* East Broadway, and offices on the Lower East Side; the next few days: NATHAN'S LANDLADY: Irma Rogers; MILLIE, HER NEIGHBOR: Bonnie Schon; EDITOR OF NEWSPAPER: Stan Rubin; SOCIAL WORKER: Joanna Glushak. "Children of the Wind" (Rebecca, Avram, David); *Scene 5* A street and sweatshops; a few days later: KLEZMORIM: TUBA: Teddy Bragin; TROMBONE: Sean Mahony; TRUMPET: Bruce Engel; CLARINET: Harold Seletsky; VIOLIN: Marshall Coid; RACHEL HALPERN: Marcia Lewis (7); MR. BRONSTEIN: Stan Rubin; (THREE) SWEATSHOP WORKERS: ROSA: Audrey Lavine; ESTHER: Joan Finkelstein; SAM: Gabriel Barre; SAUL, A UNION ORGANIZER: Terrence Mann (4); CIGAR BOSS: Peter Samuel; AN AVID SHOPPER: Joanna Glushak; MR. ROSEN: John Aller. "Penny a Tune" (Rachel, Klezmorim, Peddlers, Workers); *Scene 6* Outside Bronstein's sweatshop; later that day and weeks following: "Easy for You" (Saul, Rebecca, David); *Scene 7* A Yiddish theatre; a few weeks later: HAMLET: Peter Samuel; OPHELIA: Joanna Glushak; GERTRUDE: Irma Rogers; ROSENCRANTZ: Michael Cone; LAERTES: Gabriel Barre. "Hard to Be a Prince" (Hamlet & Company); *Scene 8* Suffolk Street, and under the Brooklyn Bridge; later that night: "(Blame it on the) Summer Night" (Rebecca & Clarinetist); *Scene 9* The Cohen apartment; evening, July 3: IRISH TENOR ON RECORDING: Michael Cone. "For My Mary" (Irish Tenor & Ben); *Scene 10* Suffolk Street, and above 14th Street; immediately following: RAGMAN: Gabriel Barre; WEALTHY NEW YORKERS: Bill Hastings, John Aller, Michael Davis, Joan Finkelstein, Joanna Glushak, Wendy Kimball, Robert Radford, Peter Samuel, Catherine Ulissey. "Rags" (Bella & Avram); *Scene 11* Pat's Tavern: FRANKIE: Michael Cone; MIKE: Michael Davis; "BIG TIM" SULLIVAN: Rex Everhart (11); NATHAN HERSHKOWITZ (MR. HARRIS): Larry Kert (2) ☆. "What's Wrong with That?" (Frankie, Mike, "Big Tim," Nathan); *Scene 12* The street

market; July 4: MAN ON STILTS: Gabriel Barre; THUGS: Andy Gale & Peter Samuel. "On the Fourth Day of July" (Picknickers & Band); *Scene 13* Suffolk Street; immediately following: "In America" (Rebecca & Nathan). *Act II*: *Scene 1* The rooftop; evening, July 4: "Yankee Boy" (Nathan & Neighbors); *Scene 2* The rooftop; later that night: "Uptown" (Nathan & Rebecca), "Wanting" (Rebecca & Saul); *Scene 3* The street market; the next day: "Three Sunny Rooms" (Rachel & Avram); *Scene 4* A few days later: A PASSERBY: Stan Rubin; MORRIS, A LITTLE BOY: Devon Michaels; HIS MOTHER: Bonnie Schon; VIOLINIST: Marshall Coid; HIS MOTHER: Irma Rogers; IRISH GIRL: Wendy Kimball; HER MOTHER: Audrey Lavine; ITALIAN TENOR: Andy Gale; HIS MOTHER: Joanna Glushak. "The Sound of Love" (Ben, David, Shoppers), "For My Mary" (reprise) (Bella & Ben); *Scene 5* The Lower East Side Democratic Club; a week later: MRS. SULLIVAN: Bonnie Schon. "Democratic Club Dance" (Rebecca, "Big Tim," Nathan, Mike, Mrs. Sullivan, Democrats, Band); *Scene 6* "Prayer" (Avram, Rebecca, Men); *Scene 7* The Cohen apartment; some time later; *Scene 8* Bronstein's sweatshop: "Bread and Freedom" (Rosa, Rebecca, Esther, Sam]; *Scene 9* Union Square, a protest demonstration; later that day: "Dancing with the Fools" (Rebecca, Nathan, Strikers); *Scene 10* Suffolk Street and Battery Park; a few weeks later: HERSCHEL COHEN: John Aller. FINALE (Rebecca, David, Americans, New Immigrants). *Understudies*: Rebecca: Audrey Lavine; Mr. Harris/Saul: Peter Samuel; David: Devon Michaels; Bella: Joanna Glushak; Jack/Avram: Stan Rubin; Ben: John Aller; Anna: Irma Rogers. *Swings*: Patti Mariano, Cissy Rebich, Mark Fotopoulos.

Broadway reviews were terrible. There was much concern as to whether the fragile Teresa Stratas could sing every night. After the third Broadway performance (a Saturday matinee), the cast marched down Broadway from the theatre to Duffy Square in an attempt to stop the show from being closed, but in fact, that evening's show was the last. Closing announcements said that the show would re-open in a few weeks. It never did. It received Tony Nominations for musical, score, book, choreography, and for Teresa Stratas. It lost $5.5 million. Martin Heinfling, of Sergio Valente Jeans, had $2 million invested.

After Broadway. It has since been produced many times, somewhat revised, but not on Broadway. THE AMERICAN JEWISH THEATRE did one of these revised versions, 11/2/91–12/29/91. 59 PERFORMANCES. "If We Never Meet Again" was a new song, and the song order was changed from that seen on Broadway. DIRECTOR/CHOREOGRAPHER: Richard Sabellico. *Cast*: Ann Crumb, Rachel Black, Jonathan Kaplan, Crista Moore, David Pevsner, Alec Timmerman.

569. *Ragtime*

Set in 1906. Three intertwining stories: a prosperous family in New Rochelle; Coalhouse, a ragtime pianist in Harlem; Tateh, an immigrant widower from Latvia and his daughter, the Little Girl. The rich family take in Coalhouse's abandoned girlfriend, Sarah and her baby, which leads them into contact with his world. Tateh finds only disillusionment in New York, and moves to Boston, where he is overworked in a sweatshop which finally goes on strike, helped by anarchist Emma. Younger Brother has to have a cause and becomes involved with Evelyn, whose husband, Thaw, has killed her lover, Stanford White, the architect, in what has become known as The Crime of the Century. He then becomes involved in the strike and in Coalhouse's finally fatal struggle against the white authorities. Father dies in the Lusitania in 1915, and Mother marries Tateh, now a pioneer in the movies, and they go to California. Younger Brother goes to Mexico to join Zapata.

Before Broadway. After the novel came the movie, in 1981, a straight film (which E.L. Doctorow, the author, did not like). DIRECTOR: Milos Forman. *Cast*: RHEINLANDER WALDO: James Cagney; YOUNGER BROTHER: Brad Dourif; BOOKER T: Moses Gunn; EVELYN: Elizabeth McGovern; CONKLIN: Kenneth McMillan; DELMAS: Pat O'Brien; EVELYN'S DANCING INSTRUCTOR: Donald O'Connor; FATHER: James Olson; TATEH: Mandy Patinkin; COALHOUSE: Howard E. Rollins

Jr.; MOTHER: Mary Steenburgen; SARAH: Debbie Allen; HOUDINI: Jeffrey De Munn; WHITE: Norman Mailer; THAW: Robert Joy; GRANDFATHER: Edwin Cooper; MORGAN: Donal Bissett. The Police Commissioner Waldo role was not carried on into the stage musicals, nor was Delmas and certain other roles.

In 1/94 Livent acquired the theatrical rights to the novel. Lynn Ahrens & Stephen Flaherty began writing the musical in 1995. They first wrote four songs — the opener "Ragtime," the Act I finale "Till We Reach That Day," "Gliding," and another song for Evelyn after she has gone to bed with Younger Brother. The last song was dropped as Evelyn's character was changed during re-writes. In 8/95 there was a reading at YORK UNIVERSITY, Toronto. *Cast*: COALHOUSE: Brian Mitchell (in 1996 Mr. Mitchell would become Brian Stokes Mitchell); MOTHER: Donna Murphy; TATEH: Peter Friedman; EMMA: Tovah Feldshuh. On 12/16/95 & 12/17/95 a second reading was held, also at YORK. The characters of Thaw and White were absent from this second reading. *Cast*: COALHOUSE: Brian Mitchell; MOTHER: Ann Crumb; TATEH: Peter Friedman; EMMA: Tovah Feldshuh. In 5/96 a six-week workshop production began at the JOEY AND TOBY TANNENBAUM OPERA CENTRE, Toronto, under the auspices of Livent. *Cast*: MOTHER: Marin Mazzie; SARAH: La Chanze; TATEH: Peter Friedman; LITTLE GIRL: Afton Eddy; EMMA: Judy Kaye; FATHER: Timothy Jerome; LITTLE BOY: Nicholas Rose; YOUNGER BROTHER: Steven Sutcliffe; EVELYN: Lynnette Perry; HOUDINI: Gabriel Barre; FORD: Michael Fletcher; GRANDFATHER: Conrad McLaren; MORGAN: Michael McCarty; WILLIE: David Mucci; BOOKER T: Michael Lofton; ENSEMBLE: Kevin Bogue, Anne Kanengeiser, Jeffrey Kuhn, Joe Langworth, Michael McElroy, William Paul Michals, Darlene Bel Grayson, Maria Calabrese, Jamie Chandler-Torns, Allyson Tucker, Bruce Winant. A concept album, "Songs from *Ragtime*, the Musical," recorded in the studio by RCA, with many of the Toronto cast, was released on 11/12/96.

The world premiere of the musical was at the FORD CENTER FOR THE PERFORMING ARTS, Toronto, on 12/8/96 (date brought forward from 2/97, then from 12/9/96), replacing *Sunset Boulevard* at that theatre. Previews from 11/19/96. "Show Biz" (Houdini & Evelyn) was a number heard on the concept album, but replaced in Toronto by "I Have a Feeling." A third song was written for Houdini & Evelyn by Lynn Ahrens & Stephen Flaherty — "Welcome to Vaudeville," but this one never made it to the Toronto previews (all three songs were cut for Broadway). Brent Carver had been rumored for a role in this production, but it never happened. The plan was to play only 16 weeks in Toronto, then move to Broadway. By 7/12/96 the casting was confirmed of Brian Mitchell, Marin Mazzie, Peter Friedman, Audra McDonald, and Steven Sutcliffe, as was the new opening date of 12/8/96. By 7/17/96 Camille Saviola was being rumored as the new Emma. PRESENTED BY Garth Drabinsky. Reviews were tremendous. The show cost $11 million. *Cast*: COALHOUSE: Brian Stokes Mitchell, *Alton Fitzgerald White*; MOTHER: Marin Mazzie; TATEH: Peter Friedman; SARAH: Audra McDonald; YOUNGER BROTHER: Steven Sutcliffe; EMMA: Camille Saviola; FATHER: Mark Jacoby; HOUDINI: Jim Corti; BOOKER T: Richard Allen; FORD: Larry Daggett; SARAH'S FRIEND: Vanessa Townsell-Crisp; GRANDFATHER: Paul Soles; MORGAN: Mike O'Carroll; WILLIE: David Mucci; LITTLE GIRL: Lea Michele; EDGAR: Paul Franklin Dano; ENSEMBLE: Anne Kanengeiser, Joe Langworth, Bruce Winant. Minor changes were made to the production in 2/97 and 3/97, the most notable being that the finale was changed from a reprise of "Ragtime" to a reprise of "Wheels of a Dream." The run was only going to be until 3/9/97, but the show got an extension until 4/27/97, then on 2/19/97 the run extended again to 6/29/97. The Toronto production closed on 8/31/97, to get ready for the move to Broadway.

On 6/15/97 came the Los Angeles premiere, at the SHUBERT THEATRE, Century City. Previews from 5/29/97. This second company (not a tour) had been announced as early as 12/18/96, and the leading cast members by 2/18/97. Brian Stokes Mitchell was a surprise, as it was thought that the Toronto company, which he was leading, would go intact to Broadway. As it happens, he was able to do both — leave Toronto for L.A., then go from L.A. to Broadway in time for previews there. The L.A. production moved to Vancouver, then to Chicago. *Cast:* COALHOUSE: Brian Stokes Mitchell, *Kingsley Leggs* (from 11/97), *Hinton Battle* (in Chicago), *James Stovall* (closed the show in Chicago); TATEH:

John Rubinstein, *Peter Kevoian* (closed the show in Chicago); MOTHER: Marcia Mitzman Gaven, *Donna Bullock* (5/98–12/98), *Barbara Walsh* (closed the show in Chicago); SARAH: La Chanze (until 12/98), *Stephanie Mills* (from early 5/99 and she closed the show in Chicago); FATHER: John Dossett, *Joseph Dellger* (from 5/98), *John Davidson* (from early 5/99 and closed the show in Chicago); EMMA: Judy Kaye, *Mary Gutzi* (from 11/97 and she closed the show in Chicago); YOUNGER BROTHER: Scott Carollo (until 12/98), *Tom Daugherty* (from 5/98), *John Frenzer* (closed the show in Chicago); HOUDINI: Jason Graae, *William Akey* (from 5/98), *David Bonanno* (closed the show in Chicago); BOOKER T: Allan Louis; EVELYN: Susan Wood, *Jamie Chandler-Torns, Michelle Dason* (closed the show in Chicago); FORD: Bill Carmichael, *Rick Hilsabeck* (closed the show in Chicago); CONKLIN: Wade Williams, *Michael McCarty, Fred Zimmerman* (closed the show in Chicago); GRANDFATHER: Robert Nichols; SARAH'S FRIEND: Jewel Tompkins; LITTLE BOY: Blake McIver Ewing, *Andrew Keenan-Bolger* (closed the show in Chicago); LITTLE GIRL: Danielle Wiener. On 6/20/97, during previews, the show was halted for 28 minutes after a piece of scenery fell on to the stage, injuring two actors during the opening number. On 12/27/97 it was announced that the L.A. run would end on 3/8/98, but on 1/23/98 it was announced that there had been an extension to 4/11/98, and that the show would then go on to Vancouver. On 3/16/98 it was announced that after Vancouver it would open on 11/8/98 (previews from 10/27/98), at Chicago's newly-reconstructed Oriental Theatre, now to be known as the Ford Center for the Performing Arts, Oriental Theatre. It closed in Vancouver on 7/26/98 (date brought forward from 8/30/98). Then indeed, it went to Chicago, where it was meant to run until 2/14/99. On 2/4/99 it was announced that the production had an extension, to 6/13/99, but then had to make way for the incoming *Fosse*. However, after another two-week extension, it finally closed on 6/27/99.

The scheduled Broadway opening date had always been for sometime in the 97–98 season. As for a Broadway house in which to run *Ragtime*, Livent bought two neighboring 42nd Street theatres, the Lyric (built in 1903, and demolished in the fall of 1996), and the Apollo (built in 1910), and made one 1,839-seat theatre out of it, at a cost of $22.5 million, and tentatively called it the Lyric — Apollo. On 1/28/97 it was announced that the new theatre would be called the Ford Center for the Performing Arts. A certain (undisclosed) sum of money was paid by the Ford Motor Company to Livent for the use of the name and the logo on the theatre's marquee (after all, Henry Ford was a character in the show). On 9/12/97 it was announced that Camille Saviola had turned down the Broadway role of Emma, and that Judy Kaye was going to fill this role. The only other leading players not to transfer from Toronto to Broadway were Paul Soles and Paul Franklin Dano. Broadway previews began on 12/26/97 (date brought forward from 1/98). The cost of the Broadway production was about $10 million.

The Broadway Run. FORD CENTER FOR THE PERFORMING ARTS, 1/18/98–1/16/00. 26 previews from 12/26/97. 861 PERFORMANCES. PRESENTED BY Livent (U.S.) (Garth H. Drabinsky, chairman) [Livent became SFX Entertainment in 9/99]; MUSIC/VOCAL ARRANGEMENTS: Stephen Flaherty; LYRICS: Lynn Ahrens; BOOK: Terrence McNally; BASED ON the best-selling 1975 novel of the same name by E.L. Doctorow; DIRECTOR: Frank Galati; CHOREOGRAPHER: Graciela Daniele; SETS: Eugene Lee; COSTUMES: Santo Loquasto; LIGHTING: Jules Fisher & Peggy Eisenhauer; SOUND: Jonathan Deans; MUSICAL SUPERVISOR: Jeffrey Huard; MUSICAL DIRECTOR: David Loud; ORCHESTRATIONS: William David Brohn; DANCE MUSIC ARRANGEMENTS: David Krane; CAST RECORDING on RCA, released on a special two-disk set on 4/28/98 (date put back from 4/2/98); PRESS: Mary Bryant, Wayne Wolfe, Ian Rand; MAGIC ILLUSIONS: Franz Haray; CASTING & CREATIVE DEVELOPMENT: Arnold J. Mugioli & Beth Russell; GENERAL MANAGER: Frank P. Scardino; COMPANY MANAGER: Jim Brandeberry; STAGE MANAGERS: Randall Whitescarver & Dean Greer. *Cast:* THE LITTLE BOY: Alex Strange (until 12/27/98), *Anthony Blair Hall* (from 12/29/98), *Pierce Cravens* (Wednesday & Saturday matinees instead of Mr. Hall, from 12/29/98); FATHER: Mark Jacoby, *John Dossett* (from 4/99), *Joseph Dellger* (from 9/99); MOTHER: Marin Mazzie (until 12/20/98), *Donna Bullock* (from 12/22/98); MOTHER'S YOUNGER BROTHER: Steven Sutcliffe (until 12/27/98), *Scott Carollo* (from 12/29/98); GRANDFATHER: Conrad McLaren (until 12/20/98), *Tom Toner* (from 12/22/98); COALHOUSE

WALKER JR.: Brian Stokes Mitchell (until 12/27/98), *Alton Fitzgerald White* (from 12/29/98); SARAH: Audra McDonald (until 12/27/98), *La Chanze* (from 12/29/98), *Darlesia Cearcy* (from 9/99); BOOKER T. WASHINGTON: Tommy Hollis; TATEH/BARON ASHKENAZY: Peter Friedman (until 12/20/98), *John Rubinstein* (12/22/98–8/1/99), *Michael Rupert* (from 8/3/99); THE LITTLE GIRL: Lea Michele (until 12/20/98), *Elizabeth Lundberg* (from 12/22/98), *Dara Paige Bloomfield* (Wednesday & Saturday matinees from 12/22/98); HARRY HOUDINI: Jim Corti, *Bernie Yvon*; HOUDINI'S MOTHER: Anne L. Nathan; J.P. MORGAN: Mike O'Carroll, *Erick Devine, Ray Friedeck*; HENRY FORD: Larry Daggett, *David Masenheimer* (from 9/98), *Larry Daggett* (from 3/99); EMMA GOLDMAN: Judy Kaye; EVELYN NESBITT: Lynnette Perry, *Janine LaManna* (from 8/98), *Michelle Dawson*; STANFORD WHITE: Kevin Bogue; HARRY K. THAW: Colton Green; ADMIRAL PEARY: Rod Campbell; MATTHEW HENSON: Duane Martin Foster; JUDGE: Mike O'Carroll, *Erick Devine, Ray Friedeck*; FOREMAN: Conrad McLaren (until 12/20/98), *Tom Toner* (from 12/22/98); REPORTER: Jeffrey Kuhn; KATHLEEN: Anne Kanengeiser (until 1/20/99), *Ann Van Cleave*; POLICEMAN: Larry Daggett, *David Masenheimer* (from 9/98), *Larry Daggett* (from 3/99); DOCTOR: Bruce Winant (until 1/20/99), *Paul Harman, Ron Trenouth*; EVIL MAN: Bruce Winant (until 1/20/99), *Paul Harman, Ron Trenouth* [this role was also known as the Dirty Old Man]; POLICEMAN: Colton Green; SARAH'S FRIEND: Vanessa Townsell-Crisp, *Tina Fabrique*; TROLLEY CONDUCTOR: Gordon Stanley; WILLIE CONKLIN: David Mucci; FIREMAN: Jeffrey Kuhn; BRIGIT: Anne L. Nathan; CONDUCTOR: Joe Locarro; TOWN HALL BUREAUCRAT: Larry Daggett, *David Masenheimer* (from 9/98), *Larry Daggett* (from 3/99); 2ND BUREAUCRAT: Anne Kanengeiser (until 1/20/99), *Ann Van Cleave*; CLERK: Jeffrey Kuhn; WHITE LAWYER: Bruce Winant (until 1/20/99), *Paul Harman, Ron Trenouth*; BLACK LAWYER: Duane Martin Foster; NEWSBOYS: Joe Langworth, Colton Green, Jeffrey Kuhn; REPORTERS: Rod Campbell & Gordon Stanley; WELFARE OFFICIAL: Anne Kanengeiser (until 1/20/99), *Ann Van Cleave*; BARON'S ASSISTANT: Anne L. Nathan; GANG MEMBER: Duane Martin Foster; HARLEM PAS DE DEUX: Monica L. Richards & Keith La Melle Thomas (*Bernard Dotson*); CHARLES S. WHITMAN: Gordon Stanley; LITTLE COALHOUSE: Michael Redd & Shane Rogers (*Landel Thorman & Isiah S. Henderson*); ENSEMBLE: Shaun Amyot, Darlene Bel Grayson, Kevin Bogue, Sondra M. Bonitto, Jamie Chandler-Torns, Ralph Deaton, Rodrick Dixon, Bernard Dotson, Donna Dunmire, Adam Dyer, Duane Martin Foster, Patty Goble, Colton Green, Elisa Heinsohn (*Amy Bodnar*), Anne Kanengeiser (until 1/20/99; *Ann Van Cleave*), Jeffrey Kuhn, Joe Langworth (until 1/20/99), Joe Locarro, Anne L. Nathan, Panchali Null, Mimi Quillin, Monica L. Richards, Orgena Rose, Gordon Stanley, Angela Teek, Keith La Melle Thomas, Allyson Tucker, Leon Williams, Bruce Winant (until 1/20/99; *Paul Harman; Ron Trenouth*), James D. Beeks, Rod Campbell, Sean Grant, Jeff Hairston, Rosena M. Hill, Adam Hunter, Kimberly JaJuan, Rusty Mowery, Zoie Quinde, Laurie Williamson, Leslie Bell, Albert Christmas, Tonya Dixon, Kimberly Dawn Neumann, Art Palmer, Mindy Franzese Wild. **Understudies**: Coalhouse: Duane Martin Foster; Booker: Duane Martin Foster & Leon Williams; Mother: Patty Goble & Anne Kanengeiser; Tateh: Jim Corti & Bruce Winant; Father: Rod Campbell & Todd Thurston; Sarah: Monica L. Richards, Orgena Rose, Angela Teek; Brother: Joe Locarro, Jeffrey Kuhn, Joe Langworth; Houdini: Jeffrey Kuhn, Joe Langworth, Colton Green; Evelyn: Jamie Chandler-Torns & Elisa Heinsohn, *Amy Bodnar*; Whitman: Colton Green; Emma: Valerie Hawkins & Anne L. Nathan; Boy: Pierce Cravens; Girl: Nicole Dos Santos; Ford: Todd Thurston & Bruce Winant; Grandfather/Peary: Todd Thurston; Sarah's Friend: Darlene Bel Grayson & Sondra M. Bonitto; Henson: Mark Cassius. **Swings**: Karen Andrew, John D. Baker, Albert Christmas, Dioni Michelle Collins, Mary Sharon Dziedzic, Valerie Hawkins, Kennl Hobson, Todd Thurston, *Sherry Boone, Robert Barry Fleming, Jaquelyn Hodges, Susan Burk, Keith La Melle Thomas*. **Act I**: *Prologue* "Ragtime" (Company); *Scene 1* Dock in New York Harbor/At sea: "Goodbye, My Love" (Mother), "Journey On" (Father, Tateh, Mother); *Scene 2* A vaudeville theatre, New York City: "The Crime of the Century" (Evelyn, Younger Brother, Ensemble); *Scene 3* Mother's garden, New Rochelle: "What Kind of Woman" (Mother); *Scene 4* Ellis Island/Lower East Side: "A Shtetl iz Amereke" (Tateh, Little Girl, Immigrants), "Success" (Tateh, Morgan, Houdini, Ensemble); *Scene 5* The Tempo Club/Harlem/Ford's assembly line: "Gettin' Ready Rag" (Coal-

house & Ensemble), "Henry Ford" (Ford, Coalhouse, Ensemble); *Scene 6* Railroad station, New Rochelle: "Nothing Like the City" (Tateh, Mother, Little Boy, Little Girl); *Scene 7* Emerald Isle Firehouse; *Scene 8* Mother's house, New Rochelle: "Your Daddy's Son" (Sarah), "New Music" (Father, Mother, Younger Brother, Coalhouse, Sarah, Ensemble); *Scene 9* A hillside above New Rochelle: "Wheels of a Dream" (Coalhouse & Sarah); *Scene 10* A union hall in New York City/Lawrence, Mass./A train: "The Night that Goldman Spoke at Union Square" (Younger Brother, Emma, Ensemble), "Lawrence, Massachusetts" (Ensemble), "Gliding" (Tateh); *Scene 11* New Rochelle and New York City: "Justice" (Coalhouse, Ensemble), "President" (Sarah), "Till We Reach That Day" (Sarah's Friend, Coalhouse, Emma, Younger Brother, Mother, Tateh, Ensemble). **Act II**: *Entr'acte* "Harry Houdini, Master Escapist" (Little Boy, Houdini); *Scene 1* The streets of New Rochelle/Mother's house: "Coalhouse's Soliloquy" (Coalhouse), "Coalhouse Demands" (Company); *Scene 2* The Polo Grounds: "What a Game" (Father, Little Boy, Ensemble); *Scene 3* Mother's house; "Atlantic City" (Evelyn & Houdini): "New Music" (reprise) (Father); *Scene 4* Atlantic City/Million Dollar Pier/Boardwalk: "Atlantic City, Part II" (Ensemble), "The Crime of the Century"/"Harry Houdini, Master Escapist" (reprise) (Evelyn & Houdini), "Buffalo Nickel Photoplay, Inc." (Ashkenazy), "Our Children" (Mother & Ashkenazy); *Scene 5* Harlem/Coalhouse's hideout: "Sarah Brown Eyes" (Coalhouse & Sarah), "He Wanted to Say" (Emma, Younger Brother, Coalhouse, Coalhouse's Men); *Scene 6* The beach, Atlantic City: "Back to Before" (Mother); *Scene 7* The Morgan Library, New York City: "Look What You've Done" (Booker, Coalhouse, Coalhouse's Men), "Make Them Hear You" (Coalhouse); *Epilogue* "Ragtime"/"Wheels of a Dream" (reprise) (Company).

Reviews were mostly excellent (except for Ben Brantley in the *New York Times*). Tickets sold from $31 to $125 (the latter price being for VIP tickets, a new trend, and the price was to go up to $135). The show won Tonys for score, book, orchestrations, and for Audra McDonald. It was also nominated for musical, direction of a musical, choreography, sets, costumes, lighting, and for Brian Stokes Mitchell, Marin Mazzie and Peter Friedman. On 7/16/99 Alton White was wrongly arrested in New York just hours before the Friday night performance. He missed the performance, and the subsequent ones over that weekend. He later brought an action against the police. By 10/25/99 rumors had begun of a closing of the show, it being too costly to maintain, and on 10/28/99 a closing date was set—1/16/00.

After Broadway. TOUR. On 3/16/98 it was announced that the national tour would open at the National Theatre, Washington, DC, on 4/29/98. Previews from 4/14/98. Bill & Hillary Clinton, and Al Gore, went to the matinee of 4/26/98. A change had been made on this tour—the Act II opener, a magic act featuring Houdini, was called back to make it less costly, and Act II now began with "Coalhouse's Soliloquy." *Cast*: COALHOUSE: Alton Fitzgerald White, *Lawrence Hamilton* (from 12/28/98 in Seattle); TATEH: Michael Rupert; FATHER: Cris Groenendaal; MOTHER: Rebecca Eichenberger; SARAH: Darlesia Cearcy, *Lovena Fox* (from 7/31/99); HOUDINI: Bernie Yvon; BOOKER T: Allan Louis; EVELYN: Melissa Dye; YOUNGER BROTHER: Aloysius Gigl; EMMA: Teresa Tova; FORD: Larry Cahn. On 11/18/98 Livent went bankrupt while the tour was at the Orpheum, Minneapolis. The stunned cast had been told the day before that the tour would be closing, and that they would all be out of work from 11/21/98, as the show went into a state of "suspension." However, on 11/19/98 PACE Theatrical Group, who handled tours, picked it up by arrangement with Equity and the bankruptcy courts, and saved the day, taking the show on to Seattle by 12/3/98, then to Boston, where it closed on 3/28/99, to be trimmed and made ready for a new tour. The new tour was re-conceived and re-mounted by the original creative crew, and again produced by PACE. It had been trimmed down from 55 players to 43 in order to make it more cost-effective. On 2/4/99 PACE & Livent had announced that the new tour would cover 50 cities between summer 1999 & 2001. Rehearsals began on 6/28/99, in New York City. It opened on 8/3/99, at Jones Hall, Houston. Previews from 7/31/99. DIRECTOR: Frank Galati; CHOREOGRAPHER: Graciela Daniele. Michael Rupert was scheduled to play Tateh on this tour, but instead went to the Broadway production to replace John Rubinstein. The tour closed on 6/10/01, at the Wang Theatre, Boston. *Cast*: COALHOUSE: Lawrence Hamilton; MOTHER: Cathy Wydner, *Victoria Strong* (from

2/20/00); FATHER: Stephen Zinnato, *Joseph Dellger* (from 10/31/00); SARAH: Lovena Fox; YOUNGER BROTHER: Aloysius Gigl, *Adam Hunter* (from 2/00), *John Frenzer* (from 2/8/00), *Sam Samuelson* (from 8/8/00); TATEH: Jim Corti; EVELYN: Michele Ragusa, *Jacqueline Bayne* (from 11/9/99); BOOKER T: *Leon Williams* (from 2/00); GRANDFATHER: Austin Colyer; HOUDINI: Eric Olson; FORD: Jay Bodin; MORGAN: Jeff Cyronek; EMMA: Cyndi Neal, *Mary Gutzi* (from 8/8/00); WILLIE: Al Bundonis; SARAH'S FRIEND: Inga Ballard.

A Noise in the Silence. An unrelated one-woman, non-musical portrait, *Emma Goldman: a Noise in the Silence*, ran Off Broadway, at MINT SPACE, 2/4/98–2/15/98, just after *Ragtime* opened on Broadway. WRITERS: Claudia Traub, Tamara Ellis Smith, Deborah Heimann; DIRECTOR: Deborah Heimann. *Cast*: Claudia Traub.

Ragtime IN LONDON. On 2/10/98 it was announced that a production of *Ragtime* would be opening in the spring of 1999, at the Prince Edward Theatre, London. In early 7/98 it was confirmed to be opening on 3/9/99, but that date was prematurely given out, and the show never happened. *Ragtime*'s UK debut was not until 10/26/02, when it opened at the INTERNATIONAL FESTIVAL OF MUSICAL THEATRE, CARDIFF, Wales, in concert form. DIRECTOR: Stafford Arima; MUSICAL DIRECTOR: David Loud. It was filmed by the BBC. *Cast*: TATEH: Graham Bickley; MOTHER: Maria Friedman; COALHOUSE: Lawrence Hamilton; FATHER: Dave Willetts; YOUNGER BROTHER: Matthew White; SARAH: Kenita Miller. This became a regular production, although a much-scaled-down version, freshly conceived and designed, with an orchestra of 20 and a cast of 30. It opened at the PICCADILLY THEATRE, London, on 3/19/03. Previews from 3/8/03. PRESENTED BY Sonia Friedman Productions (Sonia Friedman was Maria Friedman's sister), Waxman Williams Entertainment, Clear Channel Entertainment, and TEG Productions; DIRECTOR: Stafford Arima; CHOREOGRAPHER: Candace Jennings; SETS/COSTUMES: Robert Jones; LIGHTING: Howard Harrison; SOUND: Autograph/Peter Hylenski; MUSICAL SUPERVISOR: Chris Walker; MUSICAL DIRECTOR: Sheila Walker. *Cast*: MOTHER: Maria Friedman; COALHOUSE: Kevyn Morrow; FATHER: Dave Willetts; TATEH: Graham Bickley; SARAH: Rosalind James; YOUNGER BROTHER: Matthew White. It got divided reviews. On 3/27/03 it extended its closing date to 9/6/03, but closed early, on 6/14/03.

570. *Rainbow Jones*

Set in the present. Rainbow is a shy young lady, with major psychological problems, who can't hold down a job, and lives under the thumb of her domineering maiden aunt. She consoles herself with a large book of *Aesop's Fables*, from which animal characters, her only friends, jump out and accompany her on lonely walks through Central Park. One day she meets a jogger, Joey, who helps her confront her past and return to normality.

Before Broadway. It was originally called *R.J.*

The Broadway Run. MUSIC BOX THEATRE, 2/13/74. 3 previews from 2/9/74. 1 PERFORMANCE. PRESENTED BY Rubykate, Inc. (Gene & Ruby Persson), in association with Phil Gillin & Gene Bambic; MUSIC/LYRICS/BOOK: Jill Williams; DIRECTOR: Gene Persson; CHOREOGRAPHER: Sammy Bayes; SETS: Richard Ferrer; COSTUMES: James Berton Harris; LIGHTING: Spencer Mosse; MUSICAL DIRECTOR/VOCAL ARRANGEMENTS: Danny Holgate; ORCHESTRATIONS: Preston Sandiford; PRESS: Michael Alpert, Marilynn LeVine, Ellen Levene; GENERAL MANAGER: James Walsh; COMPANY MANAGER: Max Allentuck; PRODUCTION STAGE MANAGER: Kate Pollock; STAGE MANAGER: Ferne Bork; ASSISTANT STAGE MANAGER: Harris Shore. *Cast:* RAINBOW JONES: Ruby Persson (1); LEONA: Peggy Hagen Lamprey (4); BONES: Andy Rohrer (6); C.A. FOX: Gil Robbins (5); CARDIGAN: Stephanie Silver (7); JOEY MILLER: Peter Kastner (2); AUNT FELICITY: Kay St. Germain (8); UNCLE ITHACA: Daniel Keyes (3). **Standbys**: Female Roles: Fay Reed. Male Roles: Harris Shore. ***Act I: Prologue*** "A Little Bit of Me in You" (Leona, Bones, Fox, Cardigan); *Scene 1* Noon; Central Park, New York City: "Free and Easy" (Rainbow); *Scene 2* Later; Aunt Felicity's apartment: "Do Unto Others" (Rainbow, Leona, Bones, Fox, Cardigan); *Scene 3* A few hours later; Joey Miller's office: "I'd Like to Know You Better" (Joey);

Scene 4 Minutes later; Central Park: "Bad Breath" (Leona, Cardigan, Bones, Fox), "I'd Like to Know You Better" (reprise) (Joey, Rainbow, Leona, Fox, Cardigan, Bones); *Scene 5* That evening; Aunt Felicity's apartment: "Alone, at Last, Alone" (Felicity); *Scene 6* The next day at noon; Central Park: "Free and Easy" (reprise) (Rainbow), "Her Name is Leona" (Rainbow, Bones, Cardigan, Fox, Leona), "We All Need Love" (Cardigan, Bones, Fox, Leona). **Act II**: *Scene 1* A few minutes later; Central Park: "We All Need Love" (reprise) (Cardigan, Fox, Bones, Leona), "The Only Man for the Job" (Bones); *Scene 2* A week later; Uncle Ithaca's farm: "It's So Nice" (Felicity & Ithaca); *Scene 3* A moment later; Central Park: "Wait a Little While" (Leona); *Scene 4* A week later; the parlor car of the Ohio Express/Felicity's apartment: "It's So Nice" (reprise) (Rainbow, Felicity, Ithaca, Joey), "One Big Happy Family" (Joey, Fox, Bones, Cardigan, Leona); *Scene 5* A few hours later; Central Park: "Who Needs the Love of a Woman" (Joey & Rainbow), "We All Need Love"/"A Little Bit of Me in You" (reprise) (Joey, Rainbow, Cardigan, Bones, Fox, Leona).

The show got terrible Broadway reviews.

571. *Raisin*

A poor black Chicago South Side tenement family in the 1950s comes into an insurance check from Mama's late husband. Mama wants to buy a house in the white neighborhood of Clybourne Park, but her son Walter Lee wants to buy a liquor store. Mama gives him part of the money but his partner swindles him out of it. However, they finally move into their new home, despite opposition. The title is from the Langston Hughes poem: "What happens to a dream deferred?/Does it dry up/Like a raisin in the sun?"

Before Broadway. The lyricist for this musical, Bob Brittan, had, coincidentally, been developing a score for Lorraine Hansberry's play *Raisin in the Sun* since 1966 as a class project in Lehman Engel's BMI Workshop. Except that he didn't have the rights to the play. Miss Hansberry had been married to Bob Nemiroff, but had died of cancer on 1/12/65, aged 34. Finally Mr. Nemiroff decided to produce a musical version, for which he also co-wrote the libretto. While trying to find financing, it was called *Didn't You Hear That Thunder?* After the name change, it played to favorable reviews at the ARENA STAGE THEATRE, Washington, DC, before going to Broadway. It had the same crew as for the subsequent Broadway run, except MUSICAL DIRECTOR: Joyce Brown; ORCHESTRATIONS: Al Cohn; DANCE MUSIC: Dorothea Freitag. The Washington cast was also the same, except BENEATHA: Shezwae Powell; AFRICAN DRUMMER: Aristide Pereira; WILLIE/PASTOR: Norman Matlock; COBRA/ORATOR/GEORGE: Herb Downer; MOVING MEN: Al Perryman & Chuck Thorpes; TRAVIS'S FRIEND: Kofi Burbridge.

The Broadway Run. FORTY-SIXTH STREET THEATRE, 10/18/73–12/28/74; LUNT—FONTANNE THEATRE, 1/14/75–12/7/75. 9 previews from 10/10/73. Total of 847 PERFORMANCES. PRESENTED BY Robert Nemiroff; MUSIC/DANCE MUSIC ARRANGEMENTS: Judd Woldin; LYRICS: Robert Brittan; BOOK: Robert Nemiroff & Charlotte Zaltzberg (Joseph Stein was uncredited); BASED ON the 1959 drama *A Raisin in the Sun*, by Lorraine Hansberry; DIRECTOR/CHOREOGRAPHER: Donald McKayle; SETS: Robert U. Taylor; COSTUMES: Bernard Johnson; LIGHTING: William Mintzer; SOUND: James Travers; MUSICAL DIRECTOR: Howard A. Roberts, *Margaret Harris* (added by 74–75); ORCHESTRATIONS: Al Cohn & Robert Freedman; VOCAL ARRANGEMENTS: Joyce Brown & Howard A. Roberts; INCIDENTAL MUSIC ARRANGEMENTS: Dorothea Freitag; CAST RECORDING on CBS; PRESS: Max Eisen, Maurice Turet, Barbara Eisen, *Barbara Glenn, Judy Jacksina*; GENERAL MANAGER/COMPANY MANAGER: Helen Richards, *John Corkill* (added by 74–75); PRODUCTION STAGE MANAGER: Helaine Head; STAGE MANAGER: Nate Barnett; ASSISTANT STAGE MANAGER: Anthony Neely, *Autris Paige* (added by 74–75). *Cast*: PERSONS OF THE SOUTHSIDE: Elaine Beener, Glenn Brooks (*Talbert Stanislaus, Glenn Brooks*), Karen Burke, Paul Carrington, Marilyn Hamilton, Don Jay, Eugene Little, Marenda Perry (*Alyce Elizabeth Webb*), Zelda Pulliam, Renee Rose, Keith Simmons, Chuck Thorpes, Gloria Turner (*Vanessa Shaw*), *Edward M. Love Jr., Eric Townsley, Clinton Keen*; PUSHER:

Al Perryman (11), *Chuck Thorpes*; VICTIM: Loretta Abbott (8); RUTH YOUNGER: Ernestine Jackson (3) ☆, *Mary Seymour* (from 11/11/75); TRAVIS YOUNGER: Ralph Carter (7), *Paul Carrington* (during Mr. Carter's absence, 73–74, and then again from 9/3/74), *Darren Green* (from 11/74); MRS. JOHNSON: Helen Martin (6); WALTER LEE YOUNGER: Joe Morton (2) ☆, *Autris Paige* (from 11/11/75); BENEATHA YOUNGER: Deborah Allen (5); LENA YOUNGER (MAMA): Virginia Capers (1) ☆; BAR GIRL: Elaine Beener; BOBO JONES: Ted Ross (12), *Irving D. Barnes* (from 10/1/74); WILLIE HARRIS: Walter P. Brown (9); JOSEPH ASAGAI: Robert Jackson (4), *Herb Downer*; AFRICAN DRUMMER: Chief Bey; PASTOR: Herb Downer (10), *Milt Grayson*; PASTOR'S WIFE: Marenda Perry, *Alyce Elizabeth Webb*; KARL LINDNER: Richard Sanders (13), *Will Mott* (during Mr. Sanders' absence in 73–74). **Standby**: Mama: Barbara Montgomery (73–74). **Understudies**: Mama/Mrs. Johnson: Marenda Perry, *Alyce Elizabeth Webb*; Ruth: Gloria Turner, *Vanessa Shaw*; Walter/Asagai: Herb Downer, *Autris Paige* (added by 74–75); Beneatha: Renee Rose; Karl: Will Mott; Willie/Bobo: Don Jay; Pastor: Don Jay, *Autris Paige* (added by 74–75); Travis: Paul Carrington, *Eric Townsley*; Bar Girl: Zelda Pulliam. **Act I**: *Prologue* Night; the block; Southside, Chicago: Prologue (jazz ballet) (Company); *Scene 1* The Younger family living room/kitchenette; early morning: "Man Say" (Walter Lee), "Whose Little Angry Man" (Ruth); *Scene 2* The Southside and the Loop; morning rush hour: "Runnin' to Meet the Man" (Walter Lee & Company); *Scene 3* The apartment; late afternoon: "A Whole Lotta Sunlight" (Mama); *Scene 4* A Southside bar; that night: "Booze" (Bar Girl, Bobo, Walter Lee, Willie, Company); *Scene 5* The apartment; next morning: "Alaiyo" (Asagai & Beneatha); *Scene 6* The apartment; that night: "Same Old Color Scheme" (recording, sung by Elaine Beener), "African Dance" (Beneatha, Walter, Company), "Sweet Time" (Ruth & Walter Lee), "You Done Right" (Walter Lee). **Act II**: *Scene 1* A Southside church; Sunday morning: "He Come Down This Mornin'" (Pastor, Pastor's Wife, Mama, Mrs. Johnson, Ruth, Travis, Company); *Scene 2* The bar; *Scene 3* The block and the apartment; that night: "It's a Deal" (Walter Lee); *Scene 4* The apartment; moving day, some weeks later: "Sweet Time" (reprise) (Ruth & Walter Lee); *Scene 5* The block; immediately following: "Sidewalk Tree" (Travis); *Scene 6* The apartment; shortly later: "Not Anymore" (Walter Lee, Ruth, Beneatha); *Scene 7* The front stoop; immediately following: "Alaiyo" (reprise) (Asagai); *Scene 8* The apartment; immediately following: "It's a Deal" (reprise) (Walter Lee), "Measure the Valleys" (Mama), "He Come Down this Mornin'" (reprise).

On Broadway it got divided reviews. Virginia Capers stayed for the entire run, and then headed the national tour. Charlotte Zaltzberg died of cancer shortly after the opening. The show won Tonys for musical, and for Virginia Capers, and was nominated for score, book, direction of a musical, choreography, and for Joe Morton, Ralph Carter, and Ernestine Jackson.

After Broadway. TOUR. Opened on 12/9/75, at the Playhouse, Wilmington, Del. MUSICAL DIRECTOR: Margaret Harris, *Jack Holmes*. *Cast*: MAMA: Virginia Capers, *Sandra Phillips* (from 3/30/77); WALTER LEE: Autris Paige, *Gregg Baker*; WILLIE: Walter P. Brown, *Gregg Baker, Roderick Sibert*; ASAGAI: Milton Grayson; BOBO: Irving D. Barnes; BENEATHA: Arnetia Walker; RUTH: Mary Seymour; TRAVIS: Darren Green.

EQUITY LIBRARY THEATRE, 5/14/81–6/7/81. 36 PERFORMANCES. DIRECTOR: Helaine Head; CHOREOGRAPHER: Al Perryman; MUSICAL SUPERVISOR: Chapman Roberts. *Cast*: WALTER LEE: Nate Barnett; RUTH: Rhetta Hughes; MRS. JOHNSON: Saundra McClain; MAMA: Claudia McNeil; WILLIE: Ronald E. Richardson; BENEATHA: Deborah Lynn Sharpe.

INTERNATIONAL CITY THEATRE, Long Beach, Calif., 2/7/03–3/9/03. Previews from 2/4/03. This was the 30th-anniversary production. Nell Carter, due to play Mama, died on 1/23/03, aged 54. Carol Dennis played the role.

JOHN HOUSEMAN THEATRE, 10/25/04. In concert, one performance only, the second of the *Blast from the Past* benefits. This Off Broadway production was the first New York revival since the original Broadway run. PRESENTED BY AMAS Musical Theatre; DIRECTOR: Kevin Ramsey; CHOREOGRAPHER: Maria Torres. *Cast*: LENA: Tina Fabrique; WILLIE: Chuck Cooper; RUTH: Tamara Tunie; WALTER LEE: Norm Lewis; ALSO WITH: Kenita Miller, Venida Evans, Curtis I'Cook, Patrick Jude. Lillias White was going to be in it at one time.

572. *The Rape of Lucretia*

Billed as a musical drama, it was really an opera. Set in Rome, in 509 BC, and told by the Chorus. Lucretia, the chaste wife of Roman general Collatinus, is raped by Etruscan prince Tarquinius, is remorseful, and commits suicide. The cast was dressed in Roman clothing.

Before Broadway. It was first produced as an opera in GLYNDEBOURNE, ENGLAND, on 7/12/46. *Cast*: Kathleen Ferrier, Owen Brannigan, Peter Pears. It had its first London run with the SADLERS WELLS company, 8/28/46–9/21/46. 26 PERFORMANCES. DIRECTOR: Rudolf Bing. *Cast*: Nancy Evans (*Kathleen Ferrier*). It made its U.S. debut in Chicago, in the spring of 1947.

The Broadway Run. ZIEGFELD THEATRE, 12/29/48–1/16/49. 23 PERFORMANCES. PRESENTED BY Marjorie & Sherman Ewing and Giovanni Cardelli; MUSIC: Benjamin Britten; BOOK: Ronald Duncan; OPERATIC CONCEPT SUGGESTED BY Rudolf Bing; BASED ON the 1931 play *Le Viol de Lucrece*, by Andre Obey (uncredited), which in turn was based on a story first found in Livy, and then in other writers, such as Ovid & Shakespeare; DIRECTOR: Agnes de Mille; SETS/COSTUMES: John Piper, courtesy of the English Opera Group; COSTUME SUPERVISOR: Frank Thompson; LIGHTING: Peggy Clark; MUSICAL DIRECTOR: Paul Breisach; VOCAL DIRECTOR: John Daggett Howell; PRESS: Leo Freedman & June Greenwall; GENERAL MANAGER: Warren P. Munsell Jr.; STAGE MANAGER: Arthur Marlowe & Peter Brysac. *Cast*: THE MALE CHORUS: Edward Kane & Donald Clarke; THE FEMALE CHORUS: Brenda Lewis & Patricia Neway; COLLATINUS: Holger Sorensen & Edwin Steffe; JUNIUS, A ROMAN GENERAL: Emile Renan; TARQUINIUS: George Tozzi & Andrew Gainey; LUCRETIA: Kitty Carlisle (all evening performances), Belva Kibler (Saturday & Sunday matinees); BIANCA, LUCRETIA'S NURSE: Vivian Bauer & Eunice Alberts; LUCIA, LUCRETIA'S MAID: Marguerite Piazza & Adelaide Bishop; ROMAN WOMAN: Lidija Franklin; TWO ETRUSCAN SOLDIERS: Kazimir Kokic & Lucas Hoving; ROMAN MAN: Robert Pagent; ROMAN YOUTH: Stanley Simmons; A PROSTITUTE: Bunty Kelley.

Note: where there are two performers per role, the first is always Wednesday, Friday, Sunday evenings, and Saturday matinees, unless otherwise noted; and the second performer is always Tuesday, Thursday, Saturday evenings, and Sunday matinees, unless otherwise noted. *Act I*: *Scene 1* The General's tent in the camp outside Rome: "Rome is now ruled by the Roman upstart" (Male Chorus), "Here the thirsty evening has drunk the wine of light" (Male Chorus), "Who reaches Heaven first is the best philosopher" (Collatinus), "Good night, Tarquinius!" (Junius); *Interlude*: "Tarquinius does not wait for his servant to wake" (Male Chorus); *Scene 2* Lucretia's house in Rome; the same evening: "Lucretia!" (Junius), "Listen! I heard a knock. Somebody is at the gate" (Lucretia), "Time turns upon the hands of women" (Female Chorus), "None of the women move. It is too late for a messenger" (Female Chorus). *Act II*: *Scene 1* Lucretia's bedroom; that night: "The prosperity of the Etruscans was due to the richness" (Female Chorus), "She sleeps as a rose upon the night" (Female Chorus), "When Tarquinius desires, then Tarquinius will dare" (Tarquinius), "Within this frail crucible of light" (Tarquinius), "Lucretia!" (Tarquinius); *Interlude*: "Here in this scene you see virtue assailed by sin" (Female & Male Chorus); *Scene 2* Lucretia's house; the next morning: "O what a lovely day" (Lucia), "Hush! Here she comes!" (Bianca), "Flowers bring to ev'ry year the same perfection" (Lucretia), "Lucretia! Lucretia! O never again must we two dare to part" (Collatinus), "This dead hand lets fall all that my heart held when full" (Collatinus), "Is it all? Is all this suffering and pain, is this all in vain?" (Female Chorus).

Broadway reviews were mostly bad.

After Broadway. It was produced as an opera in many European capitals.

573. *Razzle Dazzle*

This was basically a re-hashing of the 1950 Off Broadway revue *Come What May*, which had been written by Michael Stewart in his

New York debut. After *The Medium & The Telephone*, *Razzle Dazzle* was the first musical to be shown in an arena (or theatre-in-the-round) type of theatre. The Arena Theatre was in the Edison Hotel.

The Broadway Run. ARENA THEATRE, 2/19/51–2/24/51. 8 PERFORMANCES. PRESENTED BY David Heilweil & Derrick Lynn-Thomas, in association with Madeline Capp & Greer Johnson; MUSIC: Bernice Kroll; LYRICS/SKETCHES: Mike Stewart; DIRECTOR: Edward Reveaux; CHOREOGRAPHER: Nelle Fisher; ASSOCIATE CHOREOGRAPHER: Jerry Ross; SETS/COSTUMES: William Riva; MUSICAL DIRECTOR/DANCE MUSIC ARRANGEMENTS: James Reed Lawlor; MUSICAL ARRANGEMENTS: Herbert Schutz; AT THE TWO PIANOS: James Reed Lawlor & Herbert Schutz; PERCUSSION: Irwin Cooper; PRESS: Reginald Denenholz; STAGE MANAGER: Leonard Soloway. *Act* I: *Scene 1* "What's a Show" (m: Shelley Mowell): RINGMASTER: James Jewell; ACROBAT: Kate Friedlich; CLOWN: Dorothy Greener (1); EQUESTRIENNE: Flori Waren; ROMEO: Frank Reynolds; JULIET: Jet MacDonald (2); GIRL WITH ROSES: Jean Sincere; SWEETHEARTS: Christine Karner & Bob Herget; GIRL WITH HAT: Barbara Hamilton; RIVETER: James Harwood; TEXAN: Lee Goodman; KIT: Cris Goodyear; KEYSTONE COP: Peter Conlow; GIRL WITH SHOULDERS: Jane White (3); *Scene 2* "MGM" (a lead-in to the recurring Bambi sketch): THE GIRL: Dorothy Greener (1); *Scene 3* "Sign Here" (m: Leo Schumer): WIFE: Jean Sincere; HUSBAND: James Harwood; OWNER: Lee Goodman; RUFUS MCBAIN: Frank Reynolds; MCBAIN SISTERS: Kate Friedlich & Christine Karner; BOYFRIENDS: Peter Conlow & Bob Herget; BETH: Flori Waren; *Scene 4* "Then I'm Yours" (m: Leo Schumer) [sung by Jet MacDonald (2) and James Jewell]; *Scene 5* All About Bambi — Part 1 (the main sketch, a running parody of *All About Eve*, with Barbara Hamilton as the star, and Dorothy Greener as the would-be star): a/ Dressing Room: BAMBI: Barbara Hamilton; GIRL: Dorothy Greener (1); b/ *The Wages of Sin*—1925 (m: James Reed Lawlor): WAITER: Robert H. Baron; BOY: Frank Reynolds; BUNNY GIRL: Christine Karner; NELL'S DATE: Bob Herget; LITTLE NELL: Kate Friedlich; NELL'S FATHER: James Harwood; NELL'S MOTHER: Flori Waren; BAMBI: Barbara Hamilton; *Scene 6* "N.Y.C." (m: Leo Schumer): GIRL: Jean Sincere; SCARECROW: Peter Conlow; *Scene 7* "Magic in the Woods:" THE AUTHOR: Lee Goodman; *Scene 8* "Haven't We Met Before?" (m: Irma Jurist): THE PRODUCER: James Harwood; FIRST LADY: Jane White (3); SECOND LADY: Jean Sincere; VISITOR: Barbara Hamilton; *Scene 9* "What a Way to Make a Living" (m: Leo Schumer) [sung by Jet MacDonald (2) & Lee Goodman]; *Scene 10* All About Bambi — Part 2: a/ Dressing Room: BAMBI: Barbara Hamilton; GIRL: Dorothy Greener (1); b/ *Frivolity Frolics*—1930 (m: Leo Schumer): SINGER: James Harwood; GIRLS: Kate Friedlich, Christine Karner, Flori Waren, Jet MacDonald (2), Jean Sincere; STRIPPER: Jane White (3); BAMBI: Barbara Hamilton. *Act II*: *Scene 1* "Catch Me if You Can" (m: Shelley Mowell): THE GIRL: Jet MacDonald (2); THE MEN: Peter Conlow, Bob Herget, Frank Reynolds; *Scene 2* "You're Only Young Once or Twice" (m: Bernice Kroll): GIRL: Christine Karner; BOY: James Jewell; *Scene 3* All About Bambi — Part 3: a/ The Stage: BAMBI: Barbara Hamilton; GIRL: Dorothy Greener (1); STAGE MANAGER: Bob Herget; ACTOR: Lee Goodman; b/ *Love on Shrove Tuesday*—1939: DIANTHA: Barbara Hamilton; MAID: Dorothy Greener (1); GREGORY: Lee Goodman; BUTLER: James Harwood; *Scene 4* "The Light Fantastic" (m: James Reed Lawlor): THE WITCH: Flori Waren; NARRATOR: James Harwood; *Scene 5* Grace Fogarty: GIRL: Dorothy Greener (1); *Scene 6* "Someone" (m: Shelley Mowell) [sung by Jane White (3)] (danced by Kate Friedlich & Bob Herget); *Scene 7* All About Bambi — Part 4: a/ Dressing Room; b/ *Two Hearts in Gypsy Time*—1951 (m: Shelley Mowell): DANCER: Peter Conlow; FLOWERGIRL: Kate Friedlich; INNKEEPER: James Harwood; GIRLS: Jean Sincere, Jane White (3), Christine Karner, Flori Waren; WAITERS & STUDENTS: Cris Goodyear, Bill Newey, James Jewell, Robert H. Baron; RUPERT: Frank Reynolds; PRINCE STANISLAUS: Lee Goodman; ZAZA: Dorothy Greener (1); GYPSY: Barbara Hamilton; *Scene 8* Finale (Entire Company).

It got divided Broadway reviews.

574. *The Red Mill*

Set in about 1900. Two American tourists, Con and Kid, are stuck without funds in the mythical Dutch town of Katwyk-ann-Zee; to avoid paying their bill at the inn called "The Sign of the Red Mill" they climb out of the window, but are caught by the burgomaster, and jailed. The innkeeper agrees that they can work off their bill, so Con becomes an interpreter and Kid a waiter. They become entangled in the love life of the innkeeper's daughter Gretchen, who is being forced to marry a much older man, the Governor of Zeeland. Gretchen is really in love with the handsome Van Damm. The boys help her escape out of the window on the sails of a windmill. All is set for the wedding, but the bride is missing. The innkeeper offers a reward, and even sends for Sherlock Holmes and Dr. Watson, who do show up (Con and Kid disguised). The innkeeper withdraws his objections to Van Damm when he realizes the officer is about to inherit a large fortune. The Governor plans to marry another girl. All ends happily.

Before Broadway. The original of this Victor Herbert farcical operetta opened on Broadway at the KNICKERBOCKER THEATRE, on 9/24/06. 274 PERFORMANCES. PRESENTED BY Charles Dillingham. It was written as a showcase for the comedy team of Dave Montgomery & Fred Stone. The character of Hendrik was then known as Doris, and in the 1919 London production Doris was changed to Boris. In 1944 the PAPER MILL PLAYHOUSE, in New Jersey, put it on, with Billie Worth and Nils Landin.

The 1945 Broadway revival started life at the LOS ANGELES CIVIC LIGHT OPERA, as their opening production for the 1945 spring season. It had a revised book and additional lyrics, and several other changes were made to the original. Fred Stone's two daughters were very involved with this new 1945 production. DIRECTOR: Billy Gilbert. *Cast*: Eddie Foy Jr., Lee Dixon, Nancy Kenyon, Charles Collins, Dorothy Stone (i.e. Mrs. Charles Collins), Morton Bowe. It was such a success that it went to Broadway for a limited run of six weeks. The numbers "Good-a-Bye, John," "A Widow Has Ways" (Bertha) and "You Never Can Tell About a Woman" were cut before Broadway.

The Broadway Run. ZIEGFELD THEATRE, 10/16/45–12/22/45; FORTY-SIXTH STREET THEATRE, 12/24/45–1/4/47; SHUBERT THEATRE, 1/6/47–1/18/47. Total of 531 PERFORMANCES. PRESENTED BY Paula Stone & Hunt Stromberg Jr., by arrangement with the Tams-Witmark Music Library; MUSIC: Victor Herbert; LYRICS/BOOK: Henry Blossom; ADDITIONAL LYRICS: Forman Brown; NEW DIALOGUE: Milton Lazarus; DIRECTOR: Billy Gilbert; CHOREOGRAPHER: Aida Broadbent; SETS: Arthur Lonergan; COSTUMES: Walter Israel; TECHNICAL SUPERVISOR/LIGHTING: Adrian Awan; MUSICAL DIRECTOR/NEW ORCHESTRATIONS/NEW DANCE MUSIC ARRANGEMENTS: Edward Ward; CHORAL DIRECTOR: William Tryoler; DIRECTOR OF VOCAL NUMBERS: George Cunningham; PRESS: Bernard Simon; GENERAL MANAGER: Irving Cooper; COMPANY MANAGER: John Tuerk; GENERAL STAGE MANAGER: Leslie Thomas; STAGE MANAGER: Marvin Kline; ASSISTANT STAGE MANAGER: Erle Waltman. *Cast*: TOWN CRIER: Billy Griffith, *Erle Waltman, P.J. Kelly*; WILLEM: Hal Price; FRANZ: George Meader; TINA: Dorothy Stone (4); BILL POSTER: Tom Halligan, *Leland Ledford, Gordon Boelzner*; FLORA: Hope O'Brady; LENA: Lois Potter; DORA: Mardi Bayne, *Gloria Sullivan, Betty Galavan*; THE BURGOMASTER: Frank Jaquet; A SAILOR: Thomas Spengler, *Calvin Lowell*; JULIANA: Lorna Byron, *Marthe Errolle*; CON KIDDER: Michael O'Shea (2), *Jack Whiting*; KID CONNER: Eddie Foy Jr. (1), *Jack Albertson*; GRETCHEN: Ann Andre; CAPT. HENDRIK VAN DAMM: Robert Hughes; GASTON: Charles Collins (5); PENNYFEATHER: Billy Griffith, *Erle Waltman, P.J. Kelly*; MADAME LA FLEUR: Odette Myrtil (3); GEORGETTE: Phyllis Bateman, *Roslynd Lowe, Jean Walburn*; SUZETTE: Nony Franklin, *Betty Galavan*; FLEURETTE: Kathleen Ellis, *Betty Fadden*; NANETTE: Jacqueline Ellis; LUCETTE: Patricia Gardner, *Charlotte Christman, Rosemary O'Shea*; YVETTE: Joan Johnston; THE GOVERNOR: Edward Dew; BALLET SOLOISTS: Mildred Ann Mauldin, Dorothy Bauer, Patricia Sims, Tom Halligan (*Wally Mohr*), Elton Howard; GIRLS OF THE BALLET: Dorothy Bauer, Donna Biroc, Elaine Corbett, Gloria DeWerd, June Fitzpatrick, Shirley Glickman, Barbara Hallstone, Joan Hansen, Jackie Lindberg, Mildred Ann Mauldin, Barbara Penland, Georgia Reed, Pat Sims; GIRLS OF THE SINGING ENSEMBLE: Phyllis Bateman (*Roslynd Lowe; Jean Walburn*), Mardi Bayne (*Gloria Sullivan*), Jane Bender, Betty Brusher, Charlotte Christman (*Rosemary*

O'Shea), Kathleen Ellis (*Betty Fadden*), Jacqueline Ellis, Nony Franklin, Betty Galavan, Patricia Gardner, Carol Johnston, Joan Johnston, Hope O'Brady, Lois Potter, Patsy Tongstrom, *Lynn Alden, Eleanor Winter*; BOYS OF THE SINGING ENSEMBLE: Lloyd R. Bell, Gordon Boelzner, Pete Civello, Kenneth Davies, Tom Decker, Jack Garland, Elton Howard, Michael King, Leland Ledford, Wally Mohr, Thomas Spengler, Calvin Swihart, *David Lee, Jack Cassidy*. **Act I**: The Inn at the Red Mill (scenic sketches by Arthur Lonergan): Opening Chorus (Village Girls, Boys, Artists), "Mignonette" (Tina, Boys, Dancing Girls), "Whistle It" (Con, Kid, Tina), "Isle of Our Dreams" (Gretchen & Hendrik), a/ "The Dancing Lesson" (Gaston & Ballet), b/ "In Old New York" (Con, Kid, Dancers), "When You're Pretty and the World is Fair" (Madame, Pennyfeather, Ensemble), "Moonbeams" and Finale (Gretchen, Hendrik, Ballet, Tina, Gaston, Burgomaster, Ensemble). **Act II** (scenic sketches by Richard Jackson): *Scene 1* A neighborhood street: Opening, a/ "Why the Silence?" (Boys & Girls), b/ "Legend of the Mill" (Juliana, Ensemble, Ballet): PRINCESS: Dorothy Bauer; SAILOR: Elton Howard; KING: Tom Halligan; "Every Day is Ladies' Day (with Me)" (Governor, Male Chorus, Madame's Daughters), "I Want You to Marry Me" (Gretchen & Hendrik), "Al Fresco" (Tina & Gaston) [new to the show, it came from *It Happened in Nordland*], a/ "Because You're You" (Governor, Juliana, Dancing Boys & Girls), b/ Romanza? (Kid & Madame La Fleur); *Scene 2* Home of the Burgomaster: "Wedding Bells" (Guests, Bridesmaids, Governor, Madame, Juliana, Burgomaster, Gretchen, Hendrik), Finale (Entire Company).

Despite divided reviews, it sold out, and extended its limited six-week Broadway run to an open commercial run. Mr. and Mrs. Fred Stone attended the opening, and sat in the third row. It was Victor Herbert's most successful of his 41 operettas. This production beat *Rosalinda* (1942) as the longest-running Broadway musical revival.

After Broadway. PALACE THEATRE, London. 5/1/47–5/17/47. 22 PERFORMANCES. The book was revised by Harold Purcell for British audiences. DIRECTOR: Charles Hickman; CHOREOGRAPHER: Phyllis Blakston. *Cast*: KID: Jimmy Jewell; CON: Ben Warris; TINA: Doreen Duke; MME LA FLEUR: Maudie Edwards.

EASTSIDE THEATRE, NYC, 10/28/81–11/29/81. 35 PERFORMANCES. PRESENTED by the Light Opera of Manhattan; DIRECTOR/MUSICAL DIRECTOR: William Mount-Burke; CHOREOGRAPHER: Jerry Gotham; COSTUMES: James Nadeaux; LIGHTING: Peggy Clark. *Cast*: KID: Kevin Usher; CON: James Nadeaux; TINA: Joyce Bolton; CAPT. DORIC VAN DAMM: Anthony Michalik. **Act I**: "By the Side of the Mill" (Ensemble), "Mignonette" (Tina & Girls), "You Never Can Tell About a Woman" (Burgomaster & Willem), "If You Love but Me" (Gretchen & Van Damm), "Go While the Goin' is Good" (Con, Kid, Gretchen, Tina), "The Accident" (Ensemble), "When You're Pretty and the World is Fair" (Bertha, Governor, Ensemble), "A Widow Has Ways" (Bertha), "Moonbeams" (Gretchen, Van Damm, Burghers), Finale (Ensemble). **Act II**: Entr'acte (Orchestra); "Gossips Corner" (Ensemble), "The Legend of the Mill" (Burgomaster & Ensemble), "I Want You to Marry Me" (Franz & Tina), "Every Day is Ladies' Day with Me" (Governor & Gentlemen), "Because You're You" (Bertha & Governor), "In Old New York" (Con & Kid), "The Isle of Our Dreams" (Gretchen & Van Damm), "Entrance of the Wedding Guests" (Ensemble), Finale (Ensemble).

575. *The Red Shoes*

Set in the world of the Ballet Lermontov, in London, Paris, and Monte Carlo, 1921–22.

Before Broadway. Broadway previews were troubled. Roger Rees starred as Boris at that stage. Rene Ceballos and Tim Jerome were replaced. Stanley Donen took over direction from Susan H. Schulman (it was Mr. Donen's first Broadway musical). Margaret Illmann got co-star status before the show opened. This was the musical line-up then: *Act I*: *Scene 1* Covent Garden Opera House, London: Swan Lake (Irina, Ivan, Grisha, Company), "I Make the Rules" (Lermontov & Grisha) [cut, and replaced with "Impresario" (Lermontov), which was also cut]; *Scene 2* Covent Garden Opera House — Lermontov's office; *Scene 3* Lady Neston's town house, Mayfair, London; *Scene 4* Covent Garden

Rehearsal Hall: "The Audition" (Vicky), "Corps de Ballet" (Grisha & Company); *Scene 5* Julian's hotel room, Paris: "When it Happens to You" (Julian); *Scene 6* Paris Opera House — Lermontov's office; *Scene 7* Paris Opera House — on stage: "Top of the Sky" (Lermontov & Vicky); *Scene 8* Paris Opera House — rehearsal hall and on stage: Ballet montage (Vicky & Company); *Scene 9* Monte Carlo Opera House — Vicky's dressing room; *Scene 10* Lermontov's villa — Monte Carlo: "It's a Fairy Tale" (Lermontov, Julian, Grisha, Sergei, Dmitri); *Scene 11* Monte Carlo Opera House — on stage; *Scene 12* A restaurant — Monte Carlo: "The Rag" (Grisha & Company); *Scene 13* A promenade — Monte Carlo: "Be Somewhere" (Julian); *Scene 14* Monte Carlo Opera House — on stage: "Am I to Wish Her Love?" (Lermontov & Vicky). *Act II*: *Scene 1* Monte Carlo Opera House — Vicky's dressing room; *Scene 2* Monte Carlo Opera House: "The Ballet of the Red Shoes;" *Scene 3* Monte Carlo Opera House — on stage, Lermontov's office, backstage: "Do Svedanya" (Grisha, Sergei, Company), "Miss Page" (Lermontov); *Scene 4* Vicky and Julian's flat in London: "Alone in the Night;" *Scene 5* Monte Carlo Opera House — Lermontov's office: "Come Home" (Lermontov); *Scene 6* Vicky and Julian's flat in London/Monte Carlo Opera House — Lermontov's office: "When You Dance for a King" (Lermontov & Vicky); *Scene 7* Monte Carlo Opera House — backstage; *Scene 8* Monte Carlo Opera House — Vicky's dressing room; SCENE 9 Monte Carlo Opera House — on stage.

The Broadway Run. GERSHWIN THEATRE, 12/16/93–12/19/93. 51 previews from 11/2/93. 5 PERFORMANCES. PRESENTED BY Martin Starger, in association with MCA/Universal & James M. Nederlander; MUSIC: Jule Styne; LYRICS: Marsha Norman & Paul Stryker (Paul Stryker was really Bob Merrill); BOOK: Marsha Norman; BASED ON the British 1947 Rank movie; DIRECTOR: Stanley Donen; CHOREOGRAPHER: Lar Lubovitch; FLYING: Foy; SETS: Heidi Landesman; COSTUMES: Catherine Zuber; LIGHTING: Ken Billington; SOUND: Tony Meola; MUSICAL DIRECTOR/VOCAL ARRANGEMENTS: Donald Pippin; ORCHESTRATIONS: Sid Ramin & William D. Brohn; BALLET & DANCE MUSIC ARRANGEMENTS: Gordon Lowry Harrell; PRESS: Frimark & Thibodeau Associates; CASTING: Julie Hughes & Barry Moss; GENERAL MANAGER: Robert Kamlot; COMPANY MANAGER: Bruce Klinger; PRODUCTION STAGE MANAGER: Martin Gold; STAGE MANAGER: Frank Lombardi; ASSISTANT STAGE MANAGER: Richard Hester. *Cast*: GRISHA LJUBOV: George de la Pena (4); IRINA BORONSKAYA: Leslie Brown (5); IVAN BOLESLAVSKY: Jon Marshall Sharp; LIVY: Robert Jensen; SERGEI RATOV: Tad Ingram (6); DMITRI: Charles Goff; BORIS LERMONTOV: Steve Barton (1) ☆; JULIAN CRASTER: Hugh Panaro (3); LADY OTTOLINE NESTON: Pamela Burrell; VICTORIA PAGE: Margaret Illmann (2) ☆, Amy Wilder (Wednesday & Saturday matinees); MISS HARDIMAN: Lydia Gaston [i.e. Lyd-Lyd Gaston]; MISS LOVAT: Laurie Gamache; DR. COPELIAS: Daniel Wright; JAMES (*Les Sylphides*): Scott Fowler, Don Bellamy (Wednesday & Saturday matinees); MARGUERITE: Jamie Chandler-Torns; THE PRIEST: Robert Jensen; JEAN LOUIS: Scott Fowler, Don Bellamy (Wednesday & Saturday matinees); THE ANGEL: Jeff Lander; COMPANY OF THE BALLET LERMONTOV: Jennifer Alexander, Don Bellamy, Mucuy Bolles, Jamie Chandler-Torns, Geralyn Del Corso, Scott Fowler, Antonia Franceschi, Laurie Gamache, Lydia Gaston, Nina Goldman, Anita Intrieri, Robert Jensen, Christina Johnson, Jeff Lander, Christina Marie Norrup, Oscar Ruge, Marie Barbara Santella (dropped during previews), Keith L. Thomas (replaced Jonathan Riseling during previews), Joan Tsao, James Weatherstone, Daniel Wright. *Understudies*: Lermontov: Robert Jensen; Dmitri: Robert Jensen & James Weatherstone; Vicky: Christina Johnson; Lady Neston: Laurie Gamache; Irina: Nina Goldman & Laurie Gamache; Grisha: Alexies Sanchez; Julian: James Weatherstone; Sergei: Charles Goff; Ivan: Scott Fowler & Alexies Sanchez; Marguerite: Christina Marie Norrup; Livy: Oscar Ruge & James Weatherstone. *Swings*: Kellye Gordon, James Hadley, Alexies Sanchez, Catherine Ulissey, Aliceann Wilson. *Orchestra*: WOODWINDS: Katherine Fink, Joshua Siegel, Virgil Blackwell, Eugene Scholtens, Lawrence Feldman, Kenneth Dybisz; TRUMPETS: John Frosk & Richard Raffio; TROMBONES: Santo Russo & David Bargeron; FRENCH HORNS: John Clark, Paul Riggio, Janet Lantz; VIOLINS: Elliot Rosoff, Yuri Vodovoz, Paul Woodiel, Blair Lawhead, Maura Giannini; VIOLAS: John Dexter & Richard Spencer; CELLI: Beverly Lauridsen & Eileen Folson; BASS: Ronald Raffio; HARP: Francesca Corsi; KEYBOARDS: Bryan Louiselle & Sande Campbell; PER-

CUSSION: Raymond Marchica & Henry Jaramillo. *Act I*: *Scene 1* Covent Garden Opera House, London: Swan Lake (Irina, Ivan, Grisha, Company); *Scene 2* Lady Neston's town house, Mayfair, London; *Scene 3* Covent Garden Rehearsal Hall: "The Audition" (Vicky), "Corps de Ballet" (Grisha & Company); *Scene 4* Julian's hotel room, Paris: "When it Happens to You" (Julian); *Scene 5* Paris Opera House — Lermontov's office; *Scene 6* Paris Opera House — on stage: "Top of the Sky" (Lermontov & Vicky); *Scene 7* Paris Opera House — rehearsal hall and on stage: Ballet Montage (*Swan Lake, Coppelia, Sleeping Beauty, Les Sylphides, Swan Lake*) (Vicky & Company); *Scene 8* Monte Carlo Opera House — Vicky's dressing room; *Scene 9* Lermontov's villa — Monte Carlo: "It's a Fairy Tale" (Lermontov, Julian, Grisha, Sergei, Dmitri); *Scene 10* Monte Carlo Opera House — on stage; *Scene 11* A promenade — Monte Carlo: "Be Somewhere" (Julian); *Scene 12* A restaurant — Monte Carlo: "The Rag" (Grisha & Company); *Scene 13* Monte Carlo Opera House — on stage: "Am I to Wish Her Love?" (Lermontov & Vicky). *Act II*: *Scene 1* Monte Carlo Opera House — rehearsal hall: "Do Svedanya" (Grisha, Sergei, Company); *Scene 2* Monte Carlo Opera House–Lermontov's office: "Come Home" (Lermontov); *Scene 3* Vicky and Julian's flat in London/Monte Carlo Opera House — Lermontov's office: "When You Dance for a King" (Lermontov & Vicky); *Scene 4* Monte Carlo Opera House, backstage; *Scene 5* Monte Carlo Opera House, Vicky's dressing room; *Scene 6* Monte Carlo Opera House: "The Ballet of the Red Shoes." THE GIRL: Victoria Page; THE SHOEMAKER: Grisha Ljubov; THE YOUNG MAN: Jean-Louis.

Broadway reviews were generally not good.

After Broadway. The ballet from the Broadway show, complete with sets and orchestrations, was resurrected by the American Ballet Theatre in their production at the Metropolitan Opera House, NYC, 5/2/94, with Kathleen Moore and Keith Roberts.

576. *Red, White and Maddox*

"A thing with music;" a vicious satire on former governor Lester Maddox of Georgia.

Before Broadway. The premiere was in Atlanta.

The Broadway Run. CORT THEATRE, 1/26/69–3/2/69. 15 previews. 41 PERFORMANCES. Theatre Atlanta's production, PRESENTED BY Edward Padula; MUSIC/LYRICS: Don Tucker; BOOK/DIRECTORS/CHOREOGRAPHERS: Don Tucker & Jay Broad; SETS/COSTUMES: David Chapman; DESIGN SUPERVISOR/LIGHTING: Richard Casler; ASSISTANT MUSICAL DIRECTOR: Michael Cohen; CAST RECORDING on Metromedia Records; PRESS: Sol Jacobson & Lewis Harmon; GENERAL MANAGER: George Thorn & Leonard A. Mulhern; PRODUCTION STAGE MANAGER: Peter J. Perry; ASSISTANT STAGE MANAGERS: Harry Chittendon & Terry Newlon. *Cast:* THE KIDS: LESTER MADDOX: Jay Garner (1); ALBERTA: Georgia Allen; STUDENT LEADER: Fran Brill; CYNICAL CAMPAIGNER: Lois Broad; THE SENATOR: Ronald Bush; AIR FORCE GENERAL: Fred Chappell; GOVERNOR OF INDIANA: Mitchell Edmonds; STANDARD BEARER: Karl Emery; INTERLOCUTOR: Clarence Felder; GENERAL OF THE ARMIES: Gary Gage; RADIO COMMENTATOR: William Gammon; STUDENT DELEGATE: Elaine Harris; BUTTERCUP BOY: Ted Harris; BOMBARDIER: Christopher Lloyd; ROCK SINGER: Bettye Malone; BOY FROM THE NEW LEFT: Ted Martin; THE REDNECK: Sandy McCallum; VIRGINIA MADDOX: Muriel Moore; GIRL FROM THE NEW LEFT: Arlene Nadel; POLITICAL COMMENTATOR: Steve Renfroe; LITTLE MARY SUE: Judy Schoen; PROTESTOR: Susan Shaloub; CIA CHIEF: William Trotman; ROCK SINGER: James Weston. *Act I*: Set 100 years later, as we see Maddox start as owner of the ultra-conservative segregationist Picrick Restaurant in Atlanta, and become surprise governor of Georgia in 1966: "What America Means to Me" (Entire Company), "Givers and Getters" (Company), "Jubilee Joe" (Company), "Ballad of a Redneck" (Men), "First Campaign Song" (Salvation Army Band/Company), "Hoe Down" (Entire Company), "Phooey" (Maddox), "Second Campaign Song" (Salvation Army Band/Company), "God is an American" (Entire Company). *Act II*: is set 100 years too late. What would have happened if Governor Maddox had become president of the USA. His uncanny ability to turn a non-sequitur into a comic routine, or consistently to say the wrong

thing at the right time created the term "Lesterism," and this musical is full of them: "Hip-Hooray for Washington" (Maddox), "City Life" (Company), "Song of the Malcontents" (Company), "The General's Song" (Company), "Little Mary Sue" (Company), "Billie Joe Ju" (Company), "The Impeachment Waltz" (Company), "Red, White and Maddox Kazoo March" (The Entire Company).

Broadway reviews were divided. Jay Garner got raves. The concept was too regional to succeed, Mr. Maddox being only a vague figure to most Americans.

577. *Redhead*

A Jack the Ripper mystery musical whodunit, set in London in the early 1900s. Essie, an English spinster, makes all the models at Simpson Sisters' Waxworks where she is an apprentice. One model is that of a recently murdered young woman. Essie and Tom (her boyfriend) join forces to solve the murder, committed by a killer with a red beard, who creeps through waxworks strangling girls with a purple scarf. We don't know if Tom is the killer.

Before Broadway. Originally called *The Works*, it was begun in 1950 by Herbert & Dorothy Fields, with Beatrice Lillie in mind in the starring role. But they couldn't find a producer. They tried to interest various stars in the hope that a big name would attract a producer, but it was turned down by Ethel Merman, Mary Martin, Celeste Holm, and Gisele MacKenzie. Irving Berlin was going to write the music and lyrics, but backed out, and Albert Hague came on board. Six years later they re-wrote it with Sidney Sheldon, and with Gwen Verdon in mind. However, Miss Verdon was contracted to star in a musical produced by Robert Fryer and Lawrence Carr and written by David Shaw. However, that project was abandoned and the writer and producers joined this new production. This show was Bob Fosse's first effort as director/choreographer (he had been recommended — indeed, insisted upon — by Gwen Verdon). Herbert Fields died on 3/24/58, leaving his sister Dorothy somewhat distracted. Sidney Sheldon and David Shaw were brought in to assist her. It tried out in New Haven, where the number "It Doesn't Take a Minute" was cut, and then in Philadelphia, where a jail-cell set crashed to the stage during a performance, pinning Gwen Verdon's foot to the stage. Five doctors in the house rushed to the stage, but Miss Verdon carried on. The show's very existence was threatened by technical problems, and by Miss Verdon's illnesses. By the time it hit Broadway it had undergone a fantastic number of revisions. The numbers "What Has She Got?," "You Love I," "My Gal's a Mule," and "You Might Be Next" had all been cut.

The Broadway Run. FORTY-SIXTH STREET THEATRE, 2/5/59– 3/19/60. 452 PERFORMANCES. PRESENTED BY Robert Fryer & Lawrence Carr; MUSIC: Albert Hague; LYRICS: Dorothy Fields; BOOK: Herbert Fields, Dorothy Fields, David Shaw, Sidney Sheldon; DIRECTOR/CHOREOGRAPHER: Bob Fosse; ASSOCIATE CHOREOGRAPHER: Donald McKayle; SETS/COSTUMES: Rouben Ter-Arutunian; ASSISTANT COSTUMES: Patton Campbell; LIGHTING: Jean Rosenthal; MUSICAL DIRECTOR/VOCAL ARRANGEMENTS: Jay Blackton; ORCHESTRATIONS: Philip J. Lang & Robert Russell Bennett; DANCE MUSIC ARRANGEMENTS: Roger Adams; PRESS: Arthur Cantor, Gertrude Kirschner, Tony Geiss; GENERAL MANAGER: Ben F. Stein; STAGE MANAGER: Ross Bowman; ASSISTANT STAGE MANAGER: Walter Rinner. *Cast:* RUTH LA RUE: Pat Ferrier; MAUDE SIMPSON: Cynthia Latham; SARAH SIMPSON: Doris Rich; MAY: Joy Nichols, *Iva Withers*; TILLY: Pat Ferrier; ESSIE WHIMPLE: Gwen Verdon (1) ☆; INSPECTOR WHITE: Ralph Sumpter; HOWARD CAVANAUGH: William Le Massena; GEORGE POPPETT: Leonard Stone; TOM BAXTER: Richard Kiley (2) ☆; ALFY, STAGE DOORMAN: Lee Krieger; SIR CHARLES WILLINGHAM: Patrick Horgan, *Michael McAloney*; THE TENOR: Bob Dixon; INEZ, THE BLONDE: Bette Graham; JAILER: Buzz Miller; SINGERS: Mame Dennis, Bob Dixon, Joan Fagan, Clifford Fearl, Lydia Fredericks, Bette Graham, Dee Harless, Janie Janvier, John Lankston, Larry Mitchell, Stan Page, Shev Rodgers, Kelley Stephens, *Pat McEnnis, Donna Monroe, Connie Sharman, Amelia Haas, Marianne Gale, Burt Bier*; DANCERS: John Aristedes, Margery Beddow, Kevin Carlisle, Shirley de Burgh, Pat Ferrier, David Gold, Harvey Hohnecker, Reby Howells, Patti

Karr, Elaine King, Kazimir Kokich, Dale Moreda, Noel Parenti, Liane Plane, Alton Ruff, Dean Taliaferro, *William Guske, Mary Burr, Dorothy Dushock, Curtis Hood, Ken Urmston, Gayle Young*. **Standby**: Essie: Allyn McLerie. **Understudies**: George: Lee Krieger; Ruth: Margery Beddow; Sarah/Maude: Elizabeth Kerr; Howard: John Lankston; Inspector: Shev Rodgers; Sir Charles: David Gold; Jailer: Kevin Carlisle; May: Dee Harless; Tilly: Liane Plane; Alfy: Bob Dixon; Inez: Joan Fagan, *Elaine King*. **Act I**: *Prologue* A theatre dressing room: Overture (Orchestra); *Scene 1* Outside the Simpson Sisters' Waxworks: "The Simpson Sisters" (Singers & Dancers); *Scene 2* The interior of the Waxworks: "The Right Finger of My Left Hand" (Essie); *Scene 3* Essie's workshop: "Just for Once" (Essie, Tom, George), "(I Feel) Merely Marvelous" (Essie); *Scene 4* A street; *Scene 5* On the stage of the Odeon Theatre: "The Uncle Sam Rag" (George, Singers, Dancers), "Erbie Fitch's Twitch" (Essie), "She's Not Enough Woman for Me" (Tom & George); *Scene 6* Corridor, backstage: "Behave Yourself" (Essie, Maude, Sarah, Tom); *Scene 7* Tom's apartment: "Look Who's in Love" (Essie & Tom); *Scene 8* Outside the museum: "My Girl is Just Enough Woman for Me" (Tom & Passers-by); *Scene 9* Backstage of the Odeon Theatre: "Essie's Vision" ("Dream Dance") (Essie & Her Dream People); *Scene 10* On the stage of the Odeon Theatre: "Two Faces in the Dark" (Essie, The Tenor, Singers, Dancers). **Act II**: *Scene 1* Tom's apartment: "I'm Back in Circulation" (Tom); *Scene 2* A street; *Scene 3* The *Green Dragon* Pub: "We Loves Ya, Jimey" (Essie, May, Tilly, Clientele of the *Green Dragon*); *Scene 4* The jail cell: "Pick-Pocket Tango" (Essie & Jailer); *Scene 5* Corridor, backstage: "Look Who's in Love" (reprise) (Tom); *Scene 6* The museum: "I'll Try" (Essie & Tom) [dropped during the run], Finale: The Chase (Essie, Tom, Company).

Redhead was the first Broadway musical to charge $9.20 for orchestra seats (it was capitalized at $300,000). It had built up a one million dollar box-office advance, and opened to raves, especially for Gwen Verdon and Bob Fosse. Brooks Atkinson, in the *New York Times*, gave it a mixed review, one which contained the immortal line "Perhaps in the future all musical comedies should be written by choreographers." It won Tonys for musical, book, choreography, costumes, and for Gwen Verdon and Richard Kiley. The show also received nominations for musical direction, and for Leonard Stone. United Artists talked about a movie, starring Gwen Verdon, but it was never made.

After Broadway. TOUR. Opened on 3/23/60, at the Shubert Theatre, Chicago. MUSICAL DIRECTOR: Sherman Frank. It had the original Broadway cast, except ALFY: Matthew Tobin; SIR CHARLES: Michael Sinclair; JAILER: Bill Guske. A new character was introduced—the STREET CUSTOMER: Elizabeth Kerr. Of the singing chorus only Mame Dennis, Bette Graham, Bob Dixon and Shev Rodgers reprised. Several members of the dancing chorus reprised. The number "I'll Try," which had been dropped during the Broadway run, was still dropped. During the Chicago run Gwen Verdon and Bob Fosse were secretly married in Evanston.

GOODSPEED OPERA HOUSE, Conn., 9/23/98–12/13/98. DIRECTOR: Christopher Ashley. **Cast:** ESSIE: Valerie Wright (until 11/8/98), *Cindy Robinson* (from 11/11/98); TOM: Timothy Warmen; MAUDE: Marilyn Cooper; SARAH: Carol Morley; ALSO WITH: Eddie Korbich. Valerie Wright got raves, but left to play Dolly in Broadway's *Annie Get Your Gun*. Her standby took over.

578. *Reggae*

A musical revelation. Set in one day in Jamaica. About rastas and rude boys. Reggae and Rastafarianism blended in a Broadway musical.

Before Broadway. It was originally being produced by Leon Gluckman, but he died in 1978 (the program has a dedication—"In memory, for contribution and inspiration, Leon Gluckman, 1923–1978"), and it was taken on by others.

The Broadway Run. BILTMORE THEATRE, 3/27/80–4/13/80. 11 previews from 3/11/80. 21 PERFORMANCES. The Michael Butler production, PRESENTED BY Michael Butler & Eric Nezhad, with David Cogan; MUSIC/LYRICS: various writers; BOOK: Melvin Van Peebles, Kendrew Lascelles, Stafford Harrison; BASED ON a story by Kendrew Lascelles;

CONCEIVED BY: Michael Butler; DIRECTOR: Glenda Dickerson; ADDITIONAL DIRECTION: Gui Andrisano; CHOREOGRAPHER: Mike Malone; SETS: Ed Burbridge; COSTUMES: Raoul Pene du Bois; LIGHTING: Beverly Emmons; SOUND: Lou Gonzalez; MUSICAL DIRECTOR: Michael Kamen; BAND LEADER: Jackie Mittoo; PRESS: The Merlin Group; CASTING: Mae Washington; GENERAL MANAGER: Ken Myers; COMPANY MANAGER: Dennis Purcell; PRODUCTION STAGE MANAGER: Robert D. Currie; STAGE MANAGER: Lee Murray; ASSISTANT STAGE MANAGER: Breena Clarke. **Cast:** ANANCY, THE SPIDER: Alvin McDuffie; FAITH: Sheryl Lee Ralph (2) ☆; ESAU: Philip Michael Thomas (1) ☆; ROCKETS: Obba Babatunde (4); MRS. BROWN: Fran Salisbury (6); LOUISE: Louise Robinson; RAS JOSEPH: Calvin Lockhart (3) ☆; NATTY: Ras Karbi (5); GORSON: Charles Wisnet (7); BINGHI MAYTAL: Sam Harkness; ENSEMBLE: Loretta Abbott, Breena Clarke, Ralph Glenmore, Jeffrey Anderson Gunter, Thomas Pinnock, Louise Robinson, Kiki Shepard, Beth Shorter, Paul Cook'Tartt, Bruce Taylor, Ras-jarawa Tesfa, Avon Testamark, Constance Thomas, Juanita Grace Tyler, Byron Utley, Lewis Whitlock. **Understudies**: Esau: Obba Babatunde; Faith: Constance Thomas; Ras Joseph: Thomas Pinnock; Rockets/Binghi: Paul Cook'Tartt; Natty: Ras-jarawa Tesfa; Mrs. Brown: Louise Robinson; Anancy: Ralph Glenmore. **Alternates**: Brenda Braxton & Andy Torres (Alternates). **The Band**: KEYBOARDS: Jackie Mittoo; BASS: Norbert Sloley; RHYTHM GUITAR: Vision; LEAD GUITAR: Bryant Montiro; PERCUSSION: Larry McDonald & Bradley Simmons; TROMBONE/FLUTE: Art Baron; TRUMPET: Joe Wilder; DRUMS: Ronald Murphy. **Act I**: Junkanoo (Masquerade Parade): "Junkanoo" (m: Michael Kamen) (Masquerade Parade); *Scene 1* Jamaican airport: "Jamaica is Waiting" (m/l: Ras Karbi, Max Romeo, Michael Kamen) (Ensemble); *Scene 2* A mountain village: "Rise Tafari" (m/l: Ras Karbi) (Natty & The Rastas); *Scene 3* A deserted greathouse on the road to Kingston: "Farmer" (m/l: Max Romeo) (Esau), "Hey Man" (m/l: Ras Karbi & Michael Kamen) (Faith & Esau), "Mash 'em Up" (m/l: Kendrew Lascelles, Ras Karbi, Jackie Mittoo, Michael Kamen) (Rockets & Rude Boys); *Scene 4* Mrs. Brown's yard: "Mrs. Brown" (m/l: Stafford Harrison & Max Romeo) (Mrs. Brown, Louise, Ensemble), "Everything that Touches You" (m/l: Michael Kamen) (Mr. & Mrs. Brown); *Scene 5* A road through a forest: "Mash Ethiopia" (m/l: Kendrew Lascelles, Stafford Harrison, Ras Karbi, Jackie Mittoo, Michael Kamen) (Rockets & Rude Boys), "Star of Zion" (m/l: Michael Kamen) (Natty); *Scene 6* A Kingston rehearsal hall: "Reggae Music Got Soul" (m/l: Jackie Mittoo) (Binghi Maytal & Ensemble), "Talkin' 'bout Reggae" (m/l: Kendrew Lascelles, Stafford Harrison, Michael Kamen, Jackie Mittoo) (Binghi Maytal & Ensemble), "Everything that Touches You" (reprise) (Faith). **Act II**: *Scene 1* Ras Joseph's yard: "Rise up Jah-Jah Children" (m/l: Ras Karbi) (The Rastas & Ras Joseph), "No Sinners in Jah Yard" (m/l: Max Romeo & Ras Karbi) (Ras Joseph & The Rastas); *Scene 2* A Kingston market: "Banana, Banana, Banana" (m/l: Ras Karbi & Michael Kamen) (Ensemble), "Promised Land" (m/l: Ras Karbi) (Natty); *Scene 3* On the edge of the ghetto: "Rasta Roll Call" (m/l: Ras Karbi) (Ras Joseph & The Rastas), "Ethiopian Pageant" (instrumental, by Michael Kamen), "Rastafari" (m/l: Michael Kamen) (Ensemble), "Roots of the Tree" (m/l: Kendrew Lascelles & Ras Karbi) (Ras Joseph & The Rastas), "I and I" (m/l: Kendrew Lascelles & Max Romeo) (Faith & Esau); *Scene 4* The ghetto: "Gotta Take a Chance" (m/l: Max Romeo & Michael Kamen) (Rockets & Rude Boys), "Star of Zion" (reprise) (Natty & Faith), "Chase the Devil" (m/l: Max Romeo) (Esau), "Now I See It" (m/l: Kendrew Lascelles & Randy Bishop) (Faith); *Scene 5* The benefit concert: "Now I See It" (reprise) (Reggae) (Faith & Ensemble), "Everything that Touches You" (reprise) (Faith & Esau), "Reggae Music Got Soul" (reprise) (Faith, Esau, Ensemble), "Jamaica is Waiting" (reprise) (Faith, Esau, Ensemble).

It was roundly panned. It closed at the 4/13/80 matinee.

579. *Regina*

The story of the despicable Hubbard family.

Before Broadway. Commissioned in 5/46 by Serge Koussevitsky and the Koussevitsky Music Foundation, it took Marc Blitzstein three intensive and painful years to write. He came under attack from Lillian Hellman, and finally dropped an act and made it into 2 acts for Broadway. It opened for tryouts at New Haven, on 10/6/49.

The Broadway Run. FORTY-SIXTH STREET THEATRE, 10/31/49–12/17/49. 56 PERFORMANCES. PRESENTED BY Cheryl Crawford, in association with Clinton Wilder; MUSIC/TEXT/ORCHESTRATIONS: Marc Blitzstein; LIBRETTO based on the 1939 drama *The Little Foxes*, by Lillian Hellman; DIRECTOR: Robert Lewis; CHOREOGRAPHER: Anna Sokolow; SETS: Horace Armistead; COSTUMES: Aline Bernstein; LIGHTING: Charles Elson; MUSICAL DIRECTOR: Maurice Abravanel; PRESS: Wolfe Kaufman, Bob Hector, Merle Debuskey; GENERAL MANAGER: John Yorke; STAGE MANAGERS: Jules Racine, Earl McDonald, Walter Stane. *Cast*: ADDIE, THE COOK: Lillyn Brown; CAL, THE BUTLER: William Warfield; ALEXANDRA (ZAN) GIDDENS, REGINA'S DAUGHTER: Priscilla Gillette (3); CHINKYPIN: Philip Hepburn; JAZZ ANGEL BAND: TRUMPET: William Dillard; BANJO: Bernard Addison; CLARINET: Buster Bailey; TRAPS: Rudy Nichols; TROMBONE: Benny Morton; REGINA GIDDENS: Jane Pickens (1); BIRDIE HUBBARD, OSCAR'S WIFE: Brenda Lewis (2); OSCAR HUBBARD, REGINA'S BROTHER: David Thomas; LEO HUBBARD, OSCAR'S SON: Russell Nype; WILLIAM MARSHALL: Donald Clarke; BEN HUBBARD, REGINA'S BROTHER: George Lipton; BELLE, THE MAID: Clarisse Crawford; PIANIST: Marion Carley; VIOLINIST: Alfred Bruning; HORACE GIDDENS, REGINA'S HUSBAND: William Wilderman (4); MANDERS: Lee Sweetland; ETHELINDA: Peggy Turnley; TOWNSPEOPLE: Robert Anderson, Kay Borron, Karl Brock, Ellen Carleen, Sara Carter, Keith Davis, Isabelle Felder, Derek MacDermot, Earl McDonald, Barbara Moser, Kayton Nesbitt; DANCERS: Wana Allison, Joan Engel, Barbara Ferguson, Kate Friedlich, Leo Guerard, Robert Hanlin, Regis Powers, Boris Runanin, Walter Stane, John Ward, Gisella Weidner, Onna White. *Understudies*: Addie: Clarisse Crawford; Zan: Barbara Moser; Birdie: Sara Carter; Ben/Oscar: Lee Sweetland; Leo: Keith Davis; Horace: Robert Anderson; Marshall: Kayton Nesbitt. *Prologue*: Late morning in spring, 1900, the Alabama town of Bowden, veranda of the Giddens home: "Naught's a Naught" (Addie, Cal, Trumpet, Zan). *Act I*: *Scene 1* Living-room of the Giddens home; the same evening: Introduction and Birdie (Birdie), Small Talk (Regina, Marshall, Leo, Oscar, Zan, Ben), Goodbyes (Oscar, Regina, Marshall, Birdie), Big Rich (Oscar, Ben, Regina, Birdie), I Don't Know (Regina, Ben, Oscar), My, My (Oscar, Ben, Regina), Away! (Regina & Ben), "The Best Thing of All" (Regina & Ben), "What Will it Be?" (Zan), Birdie and Zan (Birdie & Zan); *Scene 2* The same; a week later, evening: Oh, Addie, where are you? (Regina), "Deedle-doodle" (Leo), These ceegars what you lookin' for, Son? (Oscar, Leo, Regina), Horace's entrance (Horace, Addie, Zan), Greetings (Horace, Addie, Regina, Oscar, Leo, Ben), Horace and Regina (Horace & Regina): "Summer Day;" Business (Horace, Leo, Regina, Ben, Zan, Oscar); *Scene 3* Ballroom and veranda of the Giddens home; later the same night: Sing Hubbard (Chorus), "Chinkypin" (Trumpet), "Blues" (Addie & Birdie) [this number was cut, but restored for the 1953 City Center revival, but sung by Addie & Regina], Waltz (Regina), Introduction and Gallop (Regina, Ben, Chorus). *Act II*: Living-room of the Giddens home; the next afternoon: Rain Quartet (Birdie, Zan, Horace, Addie, Trumpet): "Make a Quiet Day," "Consider the Rain," "Certainly, Lord" [end of Rain Quartet sequence], "Lionnet" (Birdie's Aria) (Birdie), Horace and Regina (Horace & Regina), Regina's Aria (Regina & Horace), Melodrama (Ben, Oscar, Leo, Regina), "Greedy Girl" (Regina & Ben), Horace's Death; Ben's Last (Regina, Ben, Oscar, Zan), Finale (Regina, Zan, Trumpet, Chorus): "Certainly, Lord" (reprise).

Reviewed by both drama and music critics (although Marc Blitzstein insisted this was a musical drama, some critics claimed it was a dramatic opera). Reviews were completely divided. The music critics seemed to view it more highly than the drama critics did. It won Tonys for costumes and musical direction.

After Broadway. CITY CENTER, NYC, 4/2/53–4/29/53. 3 PERFORMANCES IN REPERTORY. It was restored to 3 acts, an intermission now coming between Act I Scene 1 and Act I Scene 2. PRESENTED BY the New York City Opera; DIRECTOR: Robert Lewis; CHOREOGRAPHER: John Butler; SETS: Horace Armistead; COSTUMES: Aline Bernstein; LIGHTING: Jean Rosenthal; MUSICAL DIRECTOR: Julius Rudel. *Cast*: ADDIE: Lucretia West; CAL: Lawrence Winters; ZAN: Priscilla Gillette; JAZZ: William Dillard; REGINA: Brenda Lewis; BIRDIE: Eileen Faull; OSCAR: Emile Renan; LEO: Michael Pollock; MARSHALL: Lloyd Thomas Leech; BEN: Leon Lishner; BELLE: Margaret Tynes; HORACE: William Wilderman; MANDERS: Charles Kuestner.

CITY CENTER, NYC, 10/9/53–10/15/53. 2 PERFORMANCES IN REPERTORY. The crew and cast were the same as for the earlier 1953 City Center production, except ZAN: Dorothy McNeil; BIRDIE: Willabelle Underwood; COOK: Lucretia West; BELLE: Margaret Tynes.

CITY CENTER, NYC, 4/17/58–5/2/58. 3 PERFORMANCES IN REPERTORY. This production contained the intermission between Act I Scene 1 and Act I Scene 2. The Jazz band in the cast was cut. PRESENTED BY the New York City Opera Company; DIRECTOR: Herbert Shumlin; CHOREOGRAPHER: Robert Joffrey; SETS: Howard Bay; COSTUMES: Aline Bernstein; CONDUCTOR: Samuel Krachmalnick. *Cast*: ADDIE: Carol Brice; CAL: Andrew Frierson; ZAN: Helen Strine; BIRDIE: Elisabeth Carron; OSCAR: Emile Renan; LEO: Loren Driscoll; REGINA: Brenda Lewis; MARSHALL: Ernest McChesney; BEN: George S. Irving; HORACE: Joshua Hecht.

CITY CENTER, NYC, 4/19/1959–5/1/59. 2 PERFORMANCES IN REPERTORY. This was return of the 1958 production. The crew and cast were as before, except for ZAN: Margot Moser.

NEW YORK STATE THEATRE, 10/9/92–10/24/92. 4 PERFORMANCES, in repertory with *110 in the Shade*. PRESENTED BY the New York City Opera; DIRECTOR: Rosalind Elias; SETS: James Leonard Joy; LIGHTING: Jeff Davis; CONDUCTOR: Laurie Ann Hunter. *Cast*: ADDIE: Denise Woods; CAL: Michael Lofton; ZAN: Elizabeth Futral; BIRDIE: Sheryl Woods; OSCAR: Ron Baker; LEO: John Daniecki; REGINA: Leigh Munro; MARSHALL: Paul Austin Kelly; BENJAMIN: Andrew Wentzel; HORACE: LeRoy Lehr. *Prologue*: morning. *Act I*: evening the same day; *Act II*: *Scene 1* one week later, early evening; *Scene 2* later that night. *Act III*: following day.

YORK THEATRE COMPANY, NYC, 10/19/01–10/21/01. A staged reading, part of the York's *Musicals in Mufti* series. DIRECTOR: Harold Scott; MUSICAL DIRECTOR: Jack Lee. *Cast*: REGINA: Tracey Moore (Anne Bobby at matinees); ZAN: Susan Derry; BENJAMIN: Guy Stroman; LEO: Keith Crowningshield; HORACE: Steve Bedila; ADDIE: Brenda Pressley; MARSHALL: J. Mark McVey; BIRDIE: Connie Coit; JABEZ (JAZZ): Glenn Turner; OSCAR: Harry Danner.

KENNEDY CENTER, Washington, DC, 3/10/05–3/12/05. Semi-staged concert. DIRECTOR: Gerald Freedman (replaced Lonny Price); SETS: Jim Noone; COSTUMES: Tracey Christensen; LIGHTING: Kevin Adams; SOUND: Scott Lehrer; CONDUCTOR: Steven Mercurio. *Cast*: ADDIE: Marietta Simpson; CAL: Elmore James; REGINA: Patti LuPone; BIRDIE: Sheryl Woods; OSCAR: Timothy Nolen; LEO: Mark Ledbetter (replaced Neil Patrick Harris); BEN: Tim Noble; HORACE: Shuler Hensley (replaced George Hearn); WILLIAM MARSHALL: Eugene Galvin; ALEXANDRA: Leena Chopra.

580. *Rent*

A musical revue, set in the lower East Side of Manhattan. The story revolves around characters such as Roger, a struggling musician dying of AIDS who wants to make a contribution; Mark, a film maker and narrator; Mimi, a drug-addicted dancer working in an S & M club; Angel, a drag queen and his lover, Collins. This is their world, the world of drugs, AIDS, poverty, struggle, artistry and integrity. They are renting not only their dwellings but also, with no guarantee of a future, their lives.

Before Broadway. In the late 1980s Billy Anderson, a playwright, wanted to write a musical update of Puccini's opera *La Boheme*. In 1989 he got together with Jonathan Larson, another playwright, who came up with the title *Rent*. In 1991 Larson decided to do the project alone, and in the spring of 1993 the New York Theatre Workshop (NYTW) put on a reading. Upon the advice of his mentor, Stephen Sondheim, Larson applied for and received a Richard Rodgers Foundation grant for $45,000 to bring the musical to a workshop production. Jim Nicola, artistic director of the NYTW brought on board director Michael Greif in 1/94, and 10/29/94–11/6/94 they held the very successful seven-performance workshop. It had the same basic crew as for the later Broadway run, except SETS/COSTUMES: Angela Wendt; SOUND: S.R. White. During this run producers Seller, McCollum and Gordon became involved. *Cast*: MIMI: Daphne Rubin-Vega; MARK: Anthony Rapp; JOANNE: Shelley Dickinson; ANGEL DUMOTT SCHUNARD: Mark Setlock; ROGER: Tony Hoylen;

MAUREEN: Sarah Knowlton; TOM: Pat Briggs; BENNY: Michael Potts; BLOCKBUSTER REP: Erin Hill; ALSO WITH: Gilles Chiasson, Deirdre Boddie-Henderson, Sheila Kay Davis, John Lathan, Jessie Sinclair Lenat. This was the musical number line-up then: "Message # 1," "Rent," "Cool"/"Fool," "Today for You"/"Business," "Female to Female," "He Says," "Right Brain," "Light My Candle," "Christmas Bells," "Message # 2," "Another Day," "Santa Fe," "I'll Cover You," "Will I?," "Over It," "Over the Moon," "La Vie Boheme," "I Should Tell You," "Message # 3," "Seasons of Love," "Out Tonight," "Message # 4," "Without You," "Message # 5," "Contact," "Goodbye Love," "Real Estate," "Open Road," "Message # 6," Finale. Jonathan Larson died of an aortic aneurysm the night of the final dress rehearsal, 1/25/96, and the show opened for 19 previews on 1/26/96, and officially on 2/13/96, at the 150-seat NEW YORK THEATRE WORKSHOP, for a six-week run, budgeted at $250,000, and immediately sold out. By this time the musical numbers were pretty much in place: "Door"/"Wall" (Mark & Roger) was still in at that time, immediately after "Another Day," and "Will I?" was still placed after "I'll Cover You." The crew was basically the same as it would be for Broadway, except SOUND: Darron L. West; STAGE MANAGER: Crystal Huntington. The cast was the same as for Broadway opening night. This last workshop closed 3/31/96, after 49 PERFORMANCES. It got rave reviews. The show was immeasurably boosted by a fantastic four-page spread in the Sunday edition of the *New York Times* on 3/17/96, and on 4/9/96 the show won the Pulitzer Prize for Drama.

The Broadway Run. NEDERLANDER THEATRE, 4/29/96. 16 previews from 4/16/96. PRESENTED BY Jeffrey Seller, Kevin McCollum, Allan S. Gordon, New York Theatre Workshop; MUSIC/LYRICS/BOOK: Jonathan Larson; ORIGINAL CONCEPT/ADDITIONAL LYRICS/ORIGINAL CHOREOGRAPHIC CONCEPT: Billy Aronson; DIRECTOR: Michael Greif; CHOREOGRAPHER: Marlies Yearby; SETS: Paul Clay; COSTUMES: Angela Wendt; LIGHTING: Blake Burba; SOUND: Kurt Fischer; FILM MAKER: Tony Gerber; MUSICAL SUPERVISOR/ADDITIONAL ARRANGEMENTS: Tim Weil; MUSICAL DIRECTOR: *Boko Suzuki*; ASSOCIATE CONDUCTOR: Daniel A. Weiss; ARRANGEMENTS: Steve Skinner; CAST RECORDING on Dreamworks; PRESS: Richard Kornberg & Associates; CASTING: Bernard Telsey; DRAMATURGE: Lynn M. Thomson; GENERAL MANAGERS: Emanuel Azenberg & John Corker; COMPANY MANAGER: Brig Berney; PRODUCTION STAGE MANAGER: John Vivian; STAGE MANAGER: Crystal Huntington; ASSISTANT STAGE MANAGER: Catherine J. Haley. **Cast:** ROGER DAVIS: Adam Pascal (until 11/2/97), *Norbert Leo Butz* (played Sunday evenings when Mr. Pascal cut from eight to seven performances a week to preserve his vocal cords. Mr. Butz took over permanently from 11/97), *Richard H. Blake* (alternate, by 97–98), *Luther Creek* (7/10/98–9/2/98), *Manley Pope* (from 9/5/98), *Norbert Leo Butz* (6/29/00–8/6/00), *Manley Pope* (8/8/00–12/29/02), *Sebastian Arcelus* (12/30/02–6/8/03), *Cary Shields* (until 8/30/03), *Ryan Link* (9/8/03–11/10/03), *Jeremy Kushnier* (from 11/14/03, while Mr. Link rested his vocal cords), *Ryan Link* (1/4/04–2/1/04), *Jeremy Kushnier*. Stand-ins have included: Dean Balkwill, Christian Mena, Tony Vincent, Chad Richardson, Peter Matthew Smith, Josh Kobak, Dean Armstrong, Matt Caplan, Owen Johnston II; MARK COHEN: Anthony Rapp, *Gilles Chiasson* (stood in 1997–8/15/97), *Anthony Rapp* (for a few days), *Gilles Chiasson* (while Mr. Rapp was sick), *Anthony Rapp* (until 1/4/98), *Jim Poulos* (for one evening in 1/98), *Gilles Chiasson* (stood in), *Christian Anderson* (from 1/98 for a month), *Jim Poulos* (2/98–5/21/00), *Trey Ellett* (from 5/23/00), *Jim Poulos* (from 7/6/00), *Trey Ellett* (7/20/00–5/19/02), *Matt Caplan* (from 5/20/02), *Joey Fatone* (8/5/02–12/22/02), *Matt Caplan* (from 12/23/02), *Drew Lachey* (from 9/10/04). Stand-ins have included: Matt Murphy, Chad Richardson, Dean Balkwill, Tony Vincent, Peter Matthew Smith, Scott Hunt, Josh Kobak, Colin Hanlon; TOM COLLINS: Jesse L. Martin (until 7/13/97), *Mark Leroy Jackson* (during Mr. Martin's absence for 2½ weeks in 3/97), *Michael McElroy* (7/97–9/99), *Rufus Bonds Jr.* (from 9/7/99), *Alan Mingo Jr.* (from 4/10/00), *Michael McElroy, Mark Leroy Jackson* (from 1/15/01), *Mark Richard Ford* (from 2/4/02). Stand-ins have included: Byron Utley, Calvin Grant, Dwayne Clarke, Horace V. Rogers, Stu James, David St. Louis, John Eric Parker, Todd Pettiford, Philip Dorian McAdoo; BENJAMIN "BENNY" COFFIN III: Taye Diggs (until 8/31/97), *Jacques C. Smith* (from 9/12/97), *Stu James* (from 3/13/00), *D'Monroe* (from 3/01, during Mr. James's vacation; again on 3/13/01, and again from 3/18/01), *Stu James* (from 3/25/01), *D'Monroe* (from 4/7/01), *Stu James* (from 4/29/01), *D'Monroe* (from 02). Stand-ins have included: Darryl Ordell, Calvin Grant, Carl Thornton, Brent Davin Vance, Andy Senor, John Eric Parker, Todd Pettiford, Philip Dorian McAdoo; JOANNE JEFFERSON: Fredi Walker (until 11/2/97), *Gwen Stewart* (from 11/97), *Shelley Dickinson* (by 97–98), *Gwen Stewart* (from 97–98 & until 11/1/98), *Alia Leon* (from 11/98), *Shayna Steele* (from 1/3/99), *Kenna J. Ramsey* (from 6/30/99), *Danielle Lee Greaves* (from 10/8/99), *Robin Walker* (from 10/3/00), *Natalie Venetia Belcon* (10/13/00–10/28/01), *Myiia Watson-Davis* (10/29/01–10/27/02), *Merle Dandridge* (from 10/28/02), *Kenna J. Ramsey* (from 3/3/03), *Merle Dandridge* (11/24/03–2/1/04), *Danielle Lee Greaves* (from 2/3/04), *Merle Dandridge*. Stand-ins have included: Shayna Steele, Kamilah Martin, Aisha de Haas, Maia Nkenge Wilson, Catrice Joseph, Frenchie Davis. ANGEL SCHUNARD: Wilson Jermaine Heredia (until 11/30/97), *Wilson Cruz* (12/2/97–4/98), *Shaun Earl* (stood in 4/98–7/98), *Wilson Cruz* (7/28/98–12/98), *Jai Rodriguez* (from 1/99), *Jose Llana* (until 8/1/99), *Jai Rodriguez, Wilson Jermaine Heredia* (8/6/99–1/30/00), *Andy Senor* (from 1/31/00), *Jai Rodriguez* (3/11/02–2/26/03), *Andy Senor* (from 2/17/03), *Justin Johnston* (from 1/6/04), *Jai Rodriguez* (7/5/04–8/14/04). Stand-ins have included: Pierre Angelo Bayuga, Juan Carlos Gonzalez, Jai Rodriguez, Owen Johnston II, Enrico Rodriguez; MIMI MARQUEZ: Daphne Rubin-Vega (until 4/5/97), *Marcy Harriell* (4/5/97–6/6/99), *Krysten Cummings* (6/8/99–9/5/99), *Maya Days* (from 9/23/99), *Loraine Velez* (from 4/29/00), *Karmine Alers* (from 1/12/02), *Krystal L. Washington* (from 5/16/03), *Scary Spice* (i.e. Melanie Brown) (4/19/04–8/21/04). Stand-ins have included: Laura Dias, Sharon Leal, Julia Santana, Yassmin Alers, Shayna Steele, Saycon Sengbloh, Jackie Walrath, Karen Olivo, Dominique Roy, Dana Dawson, Caren Lyn Manuel, Antonique Smith; MAUREEN JOHNSON: Idina Menzel (until 7/1/97), *Sherie Scott* (from 7/97), *Kristen Lee Kelly* (by 3/98), *Carla Bianco* (until 12/6/98), *Tamara Podemski* (by 1/1/99), *Carly Thomas* (from 1/3/99), *Tamara Podemski* (from 6/30/99), *Cristina Fadale* (10/8/99–10/28/01), *Maggie Benjamin* (10/29/01–10/27/02), *Cristina Fadale* (from 10/28/02), *Maggie Benjamin* (7/14/03–8/30/03, during Miss Fadale's vacation), *Cristina Fadale* (from 9/2/03), *Maggie Benjamin* (from 1/19/04). Stand-ins have included: Jessica Boevers, Yassmin Alers, Carly Thomas, Kendra Kassebaum, Michelle Smith, Karmine Alers, Karen Olivo, Jodi Carmeli, Antonique Smith, Amy Ehrlich, Caren Lyn Manuel; MARK'S MOM: Kristen Lee Kelly, *Jessica Boevers* (by 97–98), *Tamara Podemski* (from 7/98), *Carly Thomas* (by 99), *Maggie Benjamin* (from 12/30/99), *Kendra Kassebaum* (from 9/5/00), *Anika Larsen* (from 8/18/01), *Jodi Carmeli* (from 8/27/01), *Amy Ehrlich* (4/28/02–12/6/02), *Kendra Kassebaum* (12/7/02–2/8/04), *Kristen Lee Kelly* (from 2/8/04). Stand-ins have included: Yassmin Alers, Erica Munoz, Hallie Bulleit, Karen Olivo, Haven Burton, Kamilah Martin, Robin Walker, Shayna Steele, Dana Dawson, Dominique Roy, Karmine Alers, Antonique Smith, Catrice Joseph, Caren Lyn Manuel; CHRISTMAS CAROLER: As for Mr. Jefferson; MRS. JEFFERSON: Gwen Stewart (until 11/2/97), *Shelley Dickinson* (from 11/97), *Sharon Leal* (from 7/98), *Shelley Dickinson, Schele Williams* (from 1/3/99), *Aisha de Haas* (from 10/25/99), *Maia Nkenge Wilson* (from 2/2/01), *Aisha de Haas* (from 2/12/01), *Myiia Watson-Davis* (from 4/10/01), *Maia Nkenge Wilson* (from 10/27/01), *Aisha de Haas* (from 3/11/03), *Frenchie Davis* (5/16/03–11/14/03), *Gwen Stewart* (11/15/03–2/1/04), *Catrice Joseph* (from 2/1/04), *Frenchie Davis* (from 6/1/04; she was out 8/10/04–8/22/04). Stand-ins have included: Shayna Steele, Yassmin Alers, Erica Munoz, Wichasta Reese, Karen Olivo, Yassmin Ennis, Robin Walker, Dana Dawson, Catrice Joseph, Antonique Smith, Cicily Daniels; GORDON: Timothy Britten Parker, *Mark Setlock* (during Mr. Parkers' absence, 10/97–11/97), *Juan Carlos Gonzalez, Robert Glean* (until 8/30/98), *Mark Setlock* (by 99), *Chad Richardson* (from 8/24/99), *Matt Murphy* (from 1/17/00), *Chad Richardson* (from 2/20/00), *Peter Matthew Smith* (from 6/9/00), *Scott Hunt* (from 7/20/00), *Chad Richardson* (from 8/6/00), *Darryl Ordell* (from 10/8/00), *Chad Richardson* (from 11/26/00), *Curtis Cregan* (3/14/02–3/26/02, during Mr. Richardson's vacation; and again, 7/29/02–8/5/02), *Chad Richardson* (until 6/8/03), *Colin Hanlon* (by 12/03), *Josh Kobak* (stood in, 3/4/04–4/10/04). Stand-ins have included: Tony Vincent, Josh Greene, Jai Rodriguez, Enrico Rodriguez, Dean Balkwill, John Eric Parker, Philip Dorian McAdoo, Owen Johnston II, Sebastian Arcelus; STEVE: Gilles Chiasson, *Jim Poulos* (from early 1/98 for a month), *Will Chase* (2/98–7/98), *Matthew Murphy* (by 99), *Chad Richardson* (from 6/30/99), *Owen Johnston II* (from 8/24/99), *Jai*

Rodriguez (from 10/3/00), Owen Johnston II (from 12/3/00), Jai Rodriguez (from 6/24/01 for 6 weeks during Mr. Johnston's vacation), Justin H. Johnston (from 5/2/02), Enrico Rodriguez (from 1/6/04). Stand-ins have included: Calvin Grant, Dean Balkwill, Tony Vincent, Peter Matthew Smith, Scott Hunt, Enrico Rodriguez, Scott Hunt, Thom Allison, Jake Manabat, Matt Caplan, John Eric Parker, Sebastian Arcelus, Josh Kobak; MAN WITH SQUEEGEE: As for Steve; PAUL: Rodney Hicks (until 10/97), *Darryl Ordell (from 10/97), Robert Glean (from 1/17/00), Darryl Ordell (from 2/20/00), Robert Glean (from 6/4/00), Darryl Ordell (from 7/6/00), Jai Rodriguez (from 10/8/00), Darryl Ordell (from 11/22/00), D'Monroe (from 3/3/01), Darryl Ordell (from 3/17/01; he was sick, 2/12/03–4/4/03), Shaun Earl (from 03).* Stand-ins have included: Leslie Odom Jr., Brent Davin Vance, Owen Johnston II, Enrico Rodriguez, Peter Matthew Smith, Scott Hunt, John Eric Parker, Philip Dorian McAdoo, Matt Caplan, Sebastian Arcelas; ALEXI DARLING: Aiko Nakasone, *Julie P. Danao (from 2/98), Tina Ou (by 99), Kim Varhola (from 10/8/99), Sala Iwamatsu (from 8/6/01), Kim Varhola (from 1/7/02), Mayami Ando (from 8/10/02).* Stand-ins have included: Hallie Bulleit, Tricia Young, Karen Olivo, Yassmin Alers, Dana Dawson, Karmine Alers, Dominique Roy, Antonique Smith; ALISON: As for Mark's Mom; COP: As for Paul; ROGERS'S MOM: As for Alexi Darling; THE MAN: As for Gordon; MR. JEFFERSON: Byron Utley (until 10/97), *Mario Burrell (from 10/97), Byron Utley (by 99), John Eric Parker (from 6/9/00), Byron Utley (from 11/22/00), David St. Louis (from 3/12/01), Todd Pettiford (10/27/01–2/1/04), Destan Owens (from 2/1/04).* Stand-ins have included: Calvin Grant, Richard H. Blake, Peter Matthew Smith, Robert Glean, Dan Robbins, Jai Rodriguez, Horace Rogers, Marcus Mitchell, Owen Johnston II, Darryl Ordell, Sebastian Arcelus, Philip Dorian McAdoo; PASTOR: As for Mr. Jefferson; MR. GRAY: As for Gordon; WOMAN WITH BAGS: As for Mrs. Jefferson; WAITER: As for Steve: OTHERS: As for Mr. Jefferson, Mrs. Jefferson, Gordon, Steve Paul, Mark's Mom, Alexi Darling. ***Understudies:*** Roger/Mark: Gilles Chiasson (96–98), David Driver (96–97), *Richard H. Blake (97–00), Will Chase (99–00), Dean Balkwill (98–00), Owen Johnston II (99–02),* Chad *Richardson (99–00), Peter Matthew Smith (99–00), Norbert Leo Butz, Sebastian Arcelus (from 5/20/02), Matt Caplan (from 8/5/02–02), Josh Kobak (1/4/03–7/3/03), Sebastian Arcelus (from 03), Colin Hanlon (from 03), Owen Johnston II (from 03);* Mimi: Yassmin Alers (96–97, 99–00), Simone (96–97), *Shayna Steele (97–02), Sharon Leal (97–00), Julie P. Danao (97–00), Karen Olivo (99–01; Dominique Roy from 8/4/01), Antonique Smith (from 2/7/02), Karmine Alers (by 02); Dana Dawson (from 02), Caren Lyn Manuel (from 02), Karmine Alers (from 6/2/03);* Joanne: Shelley Dickinson (96–00), Simone (96–97), *Shayna Steele (97–02), Sharon Leal (97–00), Aisha de Haas (99–00), Yassmin Alers, Maia Nkenge Wilson (by 02), Dana Dawson (from 02), Catrice Joseph (from 02; Haneefah Wood from 04);* Maureen: Yassmin Alers (96–97), Kristen Lee Kelly (96–00), *Julie P. Danao (97–99), Jessica Boevers (97–00), Maggie Benjamin (99–00), Antonique Smith (from 2/7/02), Karmine Alers (by 02), Jodi Carmeli (by 02), Kendra Kassebaum (from 02), Karmine Alers (from 6/2/03), Kristen Lee Kelly (from 2/8/04 for 6 months);* Collins: Mark Leroy Johnson (96–97), Darius de Haas (96–97), Byron Utley (96–00), *Calvin Grant (97–00), Robert Glean (99–00), Todd Pettiford (by 02), John Eric Parker (by 02; Philip Dorian McAdoo from 02), Destan Owens (from 04);* Benny: Darius de Haas (96–97), Rodney Hicks (96–97), *Calvin Grant (97–00), Darryl Ordell (97–02), John Eric Parker (by 02; Philip Dorian McAdoo from 02), Destan Owens (from 04);* Angel: Darius de Haas (96–97), Mark Setlock (96–00), Juan Carlos Gonzalez (97–00), *Jai Rodriguez (99–04; Justin H. Johnston from 02), Owen Johnston II (99–04), Shaun Earl (from 04).* ***Other Understudies:*** Hallie Bulleit, Ray Garcia (97, 99), Enrico Rodriguez (from 5/30/00), John Eric Parker. ***Swings:*** Yassmin Alers (96–97, 99–01), Darius de Haas (96–97), Shelley Dickinson (96–97), Dave Driver (96–97), Mark Setlock (96–97), Simone (96–97), *Richard H. Blake (97–00), Julie P. Danao (97–00), Juan Carlos Gonzalez (97–00), Calvin Grant (97–00), Sharon Leal (97–00), Shayna Steele (97–00, 02), Dean Balkwill (by 99), Erica Munoz (by 99), Jai Rodriguez (98–02), Tony Vincent (by 99), Robert Glean (99–01), Kamilah Martin (99–01), Karen Olivo (99–01; Dominique Roy from 8/4/01), Peter Matthew Smith (99–01), Scott Hunt (00–01), Anika Larsen (00–01), Dean Armstrong (by 01 & until 10/28/01), Matt Caplan from 10/29/01), John Eric Parker (by 01; David St. Louis from 3/01; Calvin Grant from*

3/01; John Eric Parker by 02), Enrico Rodriguez (from 6/24/01), Dana Dawson (01–03), Antonique Smith (2/7/02–11/24/02; Caren Lyn Manuel, Karmine Alers (02, 03, 04), Owen Johnston II (from 5/2/02); Sebastian Arcelus (from 5/20/02), Curtis Cregan (7/15/02–7/22/02), Catrice Joseph (from 02; Haneefah Wood from 2/1/04), Philip Dorian McAdoo (from 02), Josh Kobak (1/4/03–7/3/03), Cicily Daniels (from 03), Karen Olivo (from 03). **Vacation Swings:** *Dan Robbins (Danny Rockett) (12/98), Matthew Murphy (from 03).* **The Band:** KEYBOARDS: Tim Weil; BASS: Steve Mack; GUITAR: Kenny Brescia; DRUMS: Jeff Potter; KEYBOARDS 2/GUITAR 2: Daniel A. Weiss. **Act I:** "Intro" (Company), "Tune Up # 1"/"Voice Mail # 1"/"Tune Up # 2" (Mark, Roger, Mrs. Cohen, Collins, Benny), "Rent" (Company), "You Okay Honey?" (the street) (Angel & Collins), "Tune Up # 3" (the loft) (Mark, Roger, Mrs. Cohen, Collins, Benny), "One Song Glory" (Roger), "Light My Candle" (Roger & Mimi), "Voice Mail # 2" (Mr. & Mrs. Jefferson), "Today 4 U" (the loft) (Angel), "You'll See" (Benny, Mark, Collins, Roger, Angel), "Tango: Maureen" (Mark & Joanne), "Life Support" (Paul, Gordon, Company), "Out Tonight" (Mimi's apartment) (Mimi), "Another Day" (Roger, Mimi, Company), "Will I?" (Company), "On the Street" (Company), "Santa Fe" (add l: Billy Aronson) (Collins & Company), "We're Okay" (Joanne), "I'll Cover You" (Angel & Collins), "Christmas Bells" (various locations; St. Mark's Place) (Company), "Over the Moon" (the lot) (Maureen), "La Vie Boheme" (Life Cafe)/"I Should Tell You"/"La Vie Boheme B" (add l: Billy Aronson) (Company). **Act II:** "Seasons of Love" (Company; The actress who played Mrs. Jefferson sang the solo), "Happy New Year" (the street)/"Voice Mail # 3"/"Happy New Year B" (Mimi, Roger, Mark, Maureen, Joanne, Collins, Angel, Mrs. Cohen, Alexi Darling, Benny), "Take Me or Leave Me" (Joanne's loft) (Maureen & Joanne), "Seasons of Love B" (Company), "Without You" (Mimi's apartment) (Roger & Mimi), "Voice Mail # 4" (Alexi Darling), "Contact" (various fantasy bed locales) (Company), "I'll Cover You" (reprise) (Angel's memorial) (Collins & Company), "Halloween" (outside the church) (Mark), "Goodbye Love" (Mark, Mimi, Roger, Maureen, Joanne, Collins, Benny), "What You Own" (Pastor, Mark, Collins, Benny, Roger), "Voice Mail # 5" (Roger's Mom, Mimi's Mom, Mrs. Jefferson, Mrs. Cohen), Finale (the lot & the loft)/"Your Eyes"/"Finale B" (Roger & Company).

On Broadway it was hailed as the first rock musical since *Hair* to deal with generation issues. It cost $3 million, but had $6 million in advance sales. By the first week in 8/96 it had recouped its investment (after only 4 months). The cast album cost $1,000,000 to record. The show won Tonys for musical, score, book, and for Wilson Jermaine Heredia, and was also nominated for direction of a musical, choreography, lighting, and for Adam Pascal, Idina Menzel, and Daphne Rubin-Vega. Robert De Niro and Miramax bought the rights to the film in 8/96. In 1996 Lynn Thomson, a dramaturge who, for a fee, had worked on re-writes of the show before Broadway, now claimed to have written a third of the book and re-written many of the lyrics, and thus had been underpaid. She sued. On 7/23/97 her suit was dismissed after a three-day trial. She appealed, and lost again. Of the original cast Daphne Rubin-Vega was first to leave, in 4/97. At that time it was also rumored that Jesse Martin was going to leave (he did, too, not long afterwards). On 8/4/98, with 807 performances, it became the Nederlander Theatre's longest-running show of all time, beating *Inherit the Wind* (1955). Like all other Broadway shows it suffered from the 9/11/01 attack on New York City, and the cast and crew agreed to a 25 per cent pay cut for a couple of weeks, in order that the show could continue. On 1/7/02 it overtook *Annie* to become Broadway's 15th-longest-running musical ever, with 2,378 performances. In its last week in 12/01 it grossed $701,772.50, making that its most successful week ever. There was a new press opening on 8/28/02, to review rock star Joey Fatone as the new Mark. It was hoped that Mr. Fatone (who began rehearsals on 7/8/02) would bring in the 14-year olds. *Rent* has been called the most innovative and influential musical since *A Chorus Line.* Due to the musicians' strike it canceled its 3/10/03 performance. On 7/11/03 it celebrated its 3,000th performance. Ryan Link was meant to stay on as Roger until 2/1/04 but left early. On 2/10/04 *Rent* became the 10th-longest-running show in Broadway history with its 3,243th performance, overtaking the original run of *Fiddler on the Roof.* In 6/04 it beat *Grease* to become the 9th-longest-running. Scary Spice was meant to come in on 4/16/04 but she had inflamed vocal cords, and was three days late.

After Broadway. THE "ANGEL TOUR." This was the first tour, known as the "A Tour," or more popularly the "Angel Tour." Opened on 11/18/96, at the Shubert Theatre, Boston. Previews from 11/5/96. This was the first production of _Rent_ outside New York. Being a Monday night, the entire Broadway cast was in the audience opening night. It had $4 million in advance sales, and extended its Boston run to 4/27/97, then to 5/25/97. It then went intact to the Ordway, St. Paul, Minn., 6/8/97–8/17/97. Previews from 6/5/97. Then to Washington, DC, for 11 weeks, from 8/20/97, then it continued on tour, ending in San Francisco on 9/5/99 (after 6 months there). MUSICAL DIRECTOR: Jim Abbott. **Cast:** ROGER: Sean Keller, _Manley Pope_ (3/14/97–4/98), _Christian Anderson_ (from 4/98), _Dean Balkwill_ (from 1/99); MARK: Luther Creek (until 10/18/97), _Christian Anderson & Daniel J. Robbins_ (shared the role, 10/97–11/97), _Christian Anderson_ (from 11/5/97), _Anthony Rapp_ (for a month in 1/98), _Christian Anderson, Trey Ellett_ (from 4/98); COLLINS: C.C. Brown (until 6/17/98), _Alan Mingo Jr. & John Eric Parker_ (alternated in role, 6/98–7/98), _Rufus Bonds Jr._ (7/10/98–9/98), _Dwayne Clark_ (from 9/98), _Mark Leroy Jackson_ (from 1/99); BENNY: James Rich, _Dwayne Clark_ (from 11/97), _D'Monroe_ (from 9/30/98), _Brian M. Love_ (from 12/98); JOANNE: Sylvia MacCalla (until 4/98), _Kamilah Martin_ (from 4/98); ANGEL: Stephan Alexander, _Shaun Earl_ (during Mr. Alexander's absence to rest his vocal cords — 6/5/97–8/17/97; then he replaced him permanently from 11/97), _Evan D'Angeles_ (4/8/98–6/98), _Kristoffer Cusick_ (from 6/98), _Shaun Earl_ (from 7/10/98); MIMI: Simone (until 4/98), _Laura Dias_ (4/98–11/6/98), _Daphne Rubin-Vega_ (1/20/99–4/11/99), _Karen Olivo, Sharon Seal_; MAUREEN: Carrie Hamilton [she was Carol Burnett's daughter], _Amy Spanger_ (6/5/97–4/5/98), _Erin Keaney_ (from 4/8/98); MRS. JEFFERSON: Queen Esther, _Terita Redd_ (from 6/97), _Danielle Lee Greaves_ (from 11/4/98), _Robin S. Walker_ (from 3/99); MR. JEFFERSON: John Eric Parker, _Alan Mingo Jr._ (from 6/98), _John Eric Parker_ (from 7/98), _Marcus Chaney_ (from 11/4/98), _Danny Blanco_ (from 12/6/98), _Marcus Chaney_ (by 12/98), _Alan Mingo Jr._; STEVE: Lambert Moss; MARK'S MOM: Amy Spanger, _Alicia Westelman_ (6/97–8/22/99); ALEXI: Julie P. (Relova) Danao (until 2/98), _Cristina Ablaza_ (2/98–9/98), _Cheri Smith_ (from 9/30/98); GORDON: Christian Anderson, _Daniel J. Robbins_ (11/5/97–9/98), _Josh Greene_ (from 9/30/98), _Christian Anderson_ (from 3/99); PAUL: D'Monroe, _Daniel J. Robbins_ (until 11/97), _Kristoffer Cusick_ (from 11/5/97), _Evan D'Angeles_ (4/8/98–6/98), _Christopher Freeman_ (6/98–7/98), _Evan D'Angeles_ (from 7/98); ALSO WITH: Ray Garcia, Lambert Moss, Schele Williams (until 7/97).

THE "BENNY TOUR." This was the second tour, known as the "B Tour," or more popularly the "Benny Tour." Previews began at the La Jolla Playhouse, Calif., on 7/1/97. Even before it opened it extended its La Jolla run to 9/14/97 (it actually finished on 9/13/97). All the design team recreated their roles. Then it moved in toto to the Ahmanson Theatre, Los Angeles, on 9/28/97. Previews from 9/16/97. It continued on tour from there, and finally closed on 7/15/01. DIRECTOR: Michael Greif. **Cast:** MARK: Neil Patrick Harris, _Kirk McDonald, Neil Patrick Harris_ (12/1/98–12/6/98), _Kirk McDonald, Scott Hunt, Matt Caplan_ (from 2/1/00); ROGER: Christian Mena, _Cary Shields, Christian Mena, Cary Shields_ from (11/30/99), _Jeremy Kushnier_ (from 3/8/01); MIMI: Julia Santana, _Saycon Sengbloh_ (from 11/30/99), _Dominique Roy_ (from 12/5/00); ANGEL: Wilson Cruz (until 11/16/97), _Andy Senor_ (from 11/26/97), _Pierre Angelo Bayuga, Shaun Earl_ (from 11/23/99); COLLINS: Mark Leroy Jackson, _Dwayne Clark, Horace V. Rogers, Mark Richard Ford_ (from 6/13/99); BENNY: D'Monroe (until 9/98), _Brian Love, Carl Thornton, Stu James_ (from 8/31/99), _Brian Love_ (from 2/29/00); JOANNE: Kenna J. Ramsey, _Monique Daniels, Danielle Lee Greaves, Jacqueline B. Arnold_; MAUREEN: Leigh Hetherington, _Carla Bianco, Leigh Hetherington, Cristina Fadale, Michelle Joan Smith_ (from 9/28/99), _Erin Keaney_ (from 4/7/00), _Maggie Benjamin_ (from 9/12/00); MARK'S MOM: Carla Bianco, _Anika Larsen, Haven Burton_; MR. JEFFERSON: Kevyn "Kye" Brackett, _Marcus Chaney_; MRS. JEFFERSON: Sharon Brown, _Maia Nkenge Wilson, Cicily Daniels_; GORDON: Curt Skinner, _Trey Ellett, Curtis Cregan_; STEVE: Andy Senor, _Pierre Angelo Bayuga, Jake Manabat_; PAUL/WAITER: Brent Davin Vance, _Justin Johnston_; ALEXI: Sala Iwamatsu, _Tricia Young, Sala Iwamatsu_. **Original Swings:** Hallie Bulleit, Veronique Daniels, Laura Dias, Owen Johnston II, Ron Christopher Patric, Paul Oakley Stovall.

CANADIAN PRODUCTION. Garth Drabinsky and his company Livent wanted the Canadian rights to _Rent_, but were beaten to it by rival David Mirvish, who acquired them on 4/26/96. Mr. Mirvish planned for a fall 1996 opening in a Toronto theatre, followed by a Canadian tour, then on to London. But, there wasn't a Toronto theatre available, so the tour and the London gig evaporated too. Then they booked in at the Elgin Theatre, but then Livent sued the theatre over another issue, thus prohibiting _Rent_ from moving in. Livent won the suit. It then re-scheduled for the Royal Alexandra Theatre, for 11/97, for a 20-week run. It finally opened at the ROYAL ALEXANDRA THEATRE on 12/7/97. Previews from 11/25/97. It closed there on 7/26/98. It cost $CAN3,000,0000. DIRECTOR: Michael Greif. **Cast:** MARK: Chad Richardson; COLLINS: Danny Blanco; MAUREEN: Jenifer Aubry; JOANNE: Karen Leblanc; ROGER: Luther Creek; ANGEL: Jai Rodriguez; BENNY: Damian Perkins; MIMI: Krysten Cummings, _Saskia Garel_ (her understudy; from 3/11/98). The national tour began in Ottawa in 8/98. In 9/98 it went to Vancouver.

SHAFTESBURY THEATRE, London, 5/12/98–10/30/99. Previews from 4/21/98. This was the first time the show was seen outside North America. DIRECTOR: Michael Greif. **Cast:** ANGEL: Wilson Jermaine Heredia (until 10/3/98), _Andy Senor_; COLLINS: Jesse L. Martin (until 9/12/98), _Mark Leroy Jackson_ (from 9/14/98 for a couple of weeks), _Mark Vincent_; ROGER: Adam Pascal (until 9/12/98), _Adrian Lewis Morgan_ (9/14/98–12/18/98), _Peter Eldridge_ (from 12/31/98); MARK: Anthony Rapp (until 10/7/98), _Josh Cohen_ (for 10 days), _Joe McFadden_ (from 10/98); BENNY: Bonny Lockhart (until 5/22/99), _Desune Coleman_ (from 6/7/99); MIMI: Krysten Cummings (until 11/14/98), _Laura Dias_ (11/16/98–2/11/99), _Krysten Cummings_ (from 2/12/99), _Loraine Velez_ (from 5/17/99); JOANNE: Jaqui Dubois, _Sharon D. Clarke_ (from 9/12/98), _Jaqui Dubois_ (as of 5/99); MAUREEN: Jessica Tezier (until 8/19/98), _Jocelyn Hughes_.

THEATRE ROYAL, Sydney, 11/4/98. Previews from 10/20. Melbourne, 3/26/99. DIRECTOR: Michael Greif. **Cast:** ROGER: Roger Corser; MAUREEN: Michelle Smith; JOANNE: Genevieve Davis; MIMI: Christine Anu; MARK: Justin Smith; ANGEL: Opell Ross.

NORWAY and DENMARK both had productions opening in 3/99.

Heinz Rudolf Kunze translated into German. Promoter Marek Lieberberg premiered it in DUSSELDORF, 2/25/99. **Cast:** MARK: Alex Melcher; ANGEL: Sean Ghazi.

TEATRO ALAMEDA 2, Mexico City. 6/7/99–2/27/00. Previews from 6/4/99. This was the first Spanish-language production (it kept the title _Rent_). DIRECTOR: Abby Epstein; CHOREOGRAPHER: Christine Bandelow.

TEATRO SMERALDO, Milan, 2/4/00. It ran eight weeks; then to Bologna. DIRECTORS: Fabrizio Angelini & Michael Greif; ITALIAN LYRICS: Michele Centonzi; MUSICAL DIRECTOR: Lorenzo Sebastiani. **Cast:** ROGER: Michele Carfora; MIMI: Karima Machehour; MARK: Gabriele Foschi.

AMSTERDAM, 10/3/00. This was the first time it was performed in Dutch. TRANSLATOR: Daniel Cohen; DIRECTOR: Ivo Van Hove. **Cast:** ROGER: Jim de Groot; MARK: Tom Van Landuyt.

UK TOUR. Opened on 2/17/01, at the Haymarket Theatre, Leicester. It closed with a brief West End stint at the PRINCE OF WALES THEATRE, London, 12/4/01–1/26/02, in order to fill that theatre between runs of _The Witches of Eastwick_ and _The Full Monty._ DIRECTOR: Paul Kerryson; CHOREOGRAPHER: Mykal Rand. **Cast:** MARK: Adam Rickett; COLLINS: Mykal Rand; ROGER: Damian Flood; MIMI: Debbi Kurup; ANGEL: Neil Couperthwaite; JOANNE: Wendy Mae Brown; MAUREEN: Lucy Williamson; BENNY: Jason Pennycooke. This production was revived for a limited run at the PRINCE OF WALES THEATRE, 12/6/02–3/8/03. It had the same basic crew and cast, except: MAUREEN: Caprice; MARK: Dougal Irvine; MIMI: Krysten Cummings (at certain performances).

THE "COLLINS TOUR." This was the third U.S. tour, and was non–Equity. It opened in 2001. **Cast:** ROGER: Kevin Spencer; MARK: Dominic Bogart, _Ashton Holmes_; COLLINS: Bruce Wilson Jr.; BENNY: Matthew Morgan; JOANNE: Bridget Anne Mohammed; ANGEL: Justin Rodriguez; MIMI: Krystal Washington (until 5/03); MAUREEN: Sara Schatz, _Cassie Levy_; MARK'S MOM: Clark Mims; MR. JEFFERSON: Rick Younger; MRS. JEFFERSON: Haneefah Wood; GORDON: Jay Wilkison, _Brian Ashton Miller_; STEVE: Cole McClendon, _D.J. Gregory_; PAUL: Damien DeShaun Smith; ALEXI: Jackie Maraya, _Veronica Arriola_.

THE MOVIE. At one time there was talk of Spike Lee directing a movie of *Rent*, but the project never got off the ground. But by 2004 it was up again, as a $40 million project, this time with Chris Columbus writing and directing, and to be released in Nov. 2005. *Cast*: BENNIE: Taye Diggs; ANGEL: Wilson Jermaine Heredia; COLLINS: Jesse L. Martin; MAUREEN: Idina Menzel; MARK: Anthony Rapp; ROGER: Adam Pascal; MIMI: Rosario Dawson; JOANNE: Tracie Thoms.

581. *Rex*

A musical biography of Henry VIII, as husband and father.

Before Broadway. Richard Adler came up with the idea. The book was meant to have been written by Jerome Lawrence and Robert E. Lee, but Sherman Yellen did it instead. Michael Bennett was set to direct, but when he demanded ten per cent of the net profits he was fired (he went into *A Chorus Line*, which turned out to be a better deal!). Richard Adler went to England to see if he could attract the biggest stars for the role of Henry, and he got Nicol Williamson. It tried out first in Wilmington, Delaware, and then went to the Kennedy Center, Washington, DC, 3/3/76–3/20/76. Nicol Williamson released this gem of positiveness to the press at this point: "I feel as though I'm dying. Every single moment is like being taken away in an ambulance." Mr. Williamson terrified the crew and cast with his mood swings. Edwin Sherin said, "I was under fire in Korea, and that was simple compared to this." The beheading of Anne Boleyn was cut, but other heads rolled. During the show's third tryout, in Boston, Hal Prince took over direction, but Edwin Sherin stayed on and Mr. Prince is not credited. Before Broadway the numbers "Dear Jane," "I'll Miss You," "Tell Me" and "Eternal Stars" were cut. Melanie Vaughan was replaced as the Nurse(maid) by Lillian Shelby.

The Broadway Run. LUNT—FONTANNE THEATRE, 4/25/76–6/5/76. 14 previews. 49 PERFORMANCES. PRESENTED BY Richard Adler, in association with Roger Berlind & Edward R. Downe Jr.; MUSIC: Richard Rodgers; LYRICS: Sheldon Harnick; BOOK: Sherman Yellen; BASED ON an idea by Richard Adler; DIRECTOR: Edwin Sherin; CHOREOGRAPHER: Dania Krupska; SETS/COSTUMES: John Conklin; LIGHTING: Jennifer Tipton; SOUND: James Travis; MUSICAL DIRECTOR: Jay Blackton; ORCHESTRATIONS: Irwin Kostal; DANCE MUSIC ARRANGEMENTS: David Baker; CAST RECORDING on RCA; PRESS: Jeffrey Richards, James Storrow, Barbara Shelley; CASTING: Judy Abbott; WRESTLING ADVISER: John Androsca; GENERAL MANAGEMENT: Theatre Now; COMPANY MANAGER: Leo K. Cohen; PRODUCTION STAGE MANAGER: Bob Bernard; STAGE MANAGER: Jack Timmers; ASSISTANT STAGE MANAGER: Elise Warner. *Cast:* NORFOLK: Charles Rule; CARDINAL WOLSEY: William Griffis; WILL SOMERS: Tom Aldredge (3); HENRY VIII, KING OF ENGLAND: Nicol Williamson (1) ✩; MARK SMEATON: Ed Evanko; PRINCESS MARY: Glenn Close; QUEEN CATHERINE OF ENGLAND: Barbara Andres; LADY JANE SEYMOUR: April Shawhan; FRANCIS, KING OF FRANCE: Stephen D. Newman; ENGLISH HERALD ("TE DEUM"): Danny Ruvolo; FRENCH HERALD: Jeff Phillips; QUEEN CLAUDE OF FRANCE: Martha Danielle; ANNE BOLEYN: Penny Fuller (2) ✩; DAUPHIN: Keith Koppmeier; COMUS: Merwin Goldsmith; 1ST GUARD: Ken Henley; LADY MARGARET: Martha Danielle; LADY IN WAITING: Melanie Vaughan; YOUNG PRINCESS ELIZABETH: Sparky Shapiro; NURSE: Lillian Shelby; 2ND GUARD: Dennis Daniels; THOMAS CROMWELL: Gerald R. Teijelo Jr.; CATHERINE HOWARD: Valerie Mahaffey; PRINCE EDWARD: Michael John; PRINCESS ELIZABETH: Penny Fuller (2) ✩; QUEEN KATHERINE PARR OF ENGLAND: Martha Danielle; LADIES & GENTLEMEN OF THE COURTS: Dennis Daniels, Harry Fawcett, Paul Forrest, Pat Gideon, Ken Henley, Dawn Herbert, Robin Hoff, Don Johanson, Jim Litten, Craig Lucas, Carol Jo Lugenbeal, Valerie Mahaffey, G. Eugene Moose, Jeff Phillips, Charles Rule, Danny Ruvolo, Lillian Shelby, Jo Speros, Gerald R. Teijelo Jr., Candace Tovar, John Ulrickson, Melanie Vaughan; SWORD & MORRIS DANCERS: Dennis Daniels, Ken Henley, Don Johanson, Jim Litten, Jeff Phillips, Danny Ruvolo. *Understudies*: Henry: Stephen D. Newman; Anne: Martha Danielle; Somers: Jeff Phillips; Elizabeth/Jane: Carol Jo Lugenbeal; Catherine: Lillian Shelby; Mary/Margaret: Pat Gideon; Claude: Valerie Mahaffey; Katherine Parr: Candace Tovar; Smeaton: Craig Lucas; Comus/Francis: Gerald R. Teijelo Jr.; Wolsey: Charles Rule; Edward: Keith Koppmeier; Dauphin: Michael John. *Act*

I: *Scene 1* Greenwich Palace: "Te Deum" (Company); *Scene 2* Henry's Tent: "No Song More Pleasing" (Smeaton); *Scene 3* Field of Cloth of Gold: "Where is My Son?" (Henry & Company), "The Field of Cloth of Gold" (Company); *Scene 4* French Pavilion: Basse Dance (Company); *Scene 5* Comus's Chambers; *Scene 6* Hever Castle: "The Chase" (Comus, Will, Smeaton, Gentlemen); *Scene 7* Hampton Court Palace: "Away from You" (Henry); *Scene 8* Chapel: "As Once I Loved You" (Catherine) [Before Broadway Scene 9 was the Palace hallway, with no songs. Scene 10 was The Throne Room, Scene 11 was Hampton Court corridor, and so on]; *Scene 9* The Throne Room: "Away from You" (reprise) (Anne & Henry) [before Broadway this reprise was shifted to a later scene]; *Scene 10* Hampton Court Corridor; *Scene 11* Queen Anne's Bedroom: "Elizabeth" (lullaby) (Smeaton, Lady Margaret, Lady in Waiting); *Scene 12* Comus's Laboratory: "What Now?" (Henry) [this number was replaced after the opening with "Why" (Henry)]; *Scene 13* The Palace: "No Song More Pleasing" (reprise) (Jane & Henry), "So Much You Loved Me" (Anne) [dropped before Broadway], "So Much You Loved Me" (reprise) (Anne) (dropped before Broadway], "Away from You" (reprise) (Anne); *Scene 14* The Tower of London; *Scene 15* The Coronation; *Scene 16* The City of London: "Te Deum" (reprise) (Company) [before Broadway this was the first time this number was heard, i.e. it was not a reprise]. *Act II*: ten years later: *Scene 1* Hampton Court Palace: "Christmas at Hampton Court" (Elizabeth, Edward, Mary); *Scene 2* The Great Hall at Hampton Court Palace: "The Wee Golden Warrior" (Will, Edward, Elizabeth, Mary, Ladies, Gentlemen), Sword Dance (Sword Dancers) and Morris Dance (Morris Dancers), "The Masque" (Will, Edward, Elizabeth, Mary, Ladies & Gentlemen); *Scene 3* The Throne Room: "From Afar" (Henry); *Scene 4* Hampton Court Corridor: "In Time" (Elizabeth & Will); *Scene 5* Comus's Laboratory; *Scene 6* Henry's Bedroom; *Scene 7* The Throne Room: "In Time" (reprise) (Elizabeth & Edward), "Te Deum" (reprise) (Company).

Broadway reviews were terrible. Top weekend ticket prices were $17.50. On 5/13/76 the unfortunate incident happened that is so well remembered. Nicol Williamson, who was, of course, very unpopular with cast and crew, slapped Jim Litten during a curtain call. The audience was shocked. Litten had said "That's a wrap" during bows, and Williamson thought he said "That's crap."

After Broadway. YORK THEATRE COMPANY, 10/13/00–10/15/00. This was the first revival of Rex, and was part of the *Musicals in Mufti* series. The script was revised by Sheldon Harnick and Sherman Yellen. Two songs cut from the Broadway production were added here. DIRECTOR: Jay Binder; MUSICAL DIRECTOR: Kevin Stites. *Cast:* NORFOLK/KING OF FRANCE: Paul Schoeffler; WOLSEY/CROMWELL: William Parry; WILL: B.D. Wong; HENRY: Patrick Page; CATHERINE: Rebecca Eichenberger; JANE SEYMOUR: Amanda Watkins; ANNE/ELIZABETH: Melissa Errico; COMUS: Richard Easton.

582. *Rhapsody*

An operetta set in 17th-century Vienna during the reign of the Empress Maria Theresa, from noon to midnight on the Emperor's birthday. Madame Pompadour, Casanova, and Madame Boticini are plotting to overthrow the empress.

The Broadway Run. NEW CENTURY THEATRE, 11/22/44–12/2/44. 13 PERFORMANCES. PRESENTED BY Blevins Davis, in association with Lorraine Manville Dresselhuys; MUSIC: Fritz Kreisler; MUSIC ADAPTED BY: Russell Bennett; LYRICS: John Latouche; ADDITIONAL LYRICS: Russell Bennett & Blevins Davis; BOOK: Leonard Louis Levinson & Arnold Sundgaard; BASED ON an original story by A.N. Nagler; DIRECTOR/CHOREOGRAPHER: David Lichine; SETS: Oliver Smith; COSTUMES: Frank Bevan; LIGHTING: Stanley McCandless; MUSICAL DIRECTOR: Fritz Mahler; ORCHESTRATIONS: Russell Bennett; MUSICAL ENSEMBLE TRAINED BY Fritz Mahler, assisted by Herbert Winkler; PRESS: Karl Bernstein & Martha Dreiblatt; COMPANY MANAGER: Allan Attwater; PRODUCTION STAGE MANAGER: Arthur Mayberry; STAGE MANAGERS: Stuart Allen & Dan Sattler. *Cast:* LOTZI HUGENHAUGEN: John Cherry; LILI HUGENHAUGEN: Gloria Story; CHARLES ECKERT: John Hamill; FRAU TINA HUGENHAUGEN: Bertha Belmore; ILSE BONEN: Patricia Bowman;

GRETA, A MAID: Mildred Jocelyn; CASANOVA: Eddie Mayehoff (3); MADAME BOTICINI: Rosemarie Brancato; DÉMI-TASSE: Mister Johnson; IVAN: George Zoritch; SONYA: Alexandra Denisova; EMPEROR FRANCIS I: George Young (2); EMPRESS MARIA THERESA: Annamary Dickey (1); CAPTAIN OF THE PALACE GUARD: Randolph Symonette; RICKSHAW MAN: Nicholas Beriozoff; THE DANDY (SPECIALTY DANCER): Jerry Ross; JAILER: Robert W. Kirland, *Gar Moore*; COURT OCTETTE: Carl Anders, Gordon Gaines, William Hearne, Barbara Jevne, Muriel O'Malley, Lucille Shea, Camille Fischelli, Gar Moore; MAYWINE OCTETTE: Nina Allen, Angela Carabella, John Henson, Mildred Jocelyn, Evelyn Keller, Thomas Lo Monaco, Rudy Rudisill, Harry Ward; RHAPSODY DOUBLE QUINTETTE: Betty Baker, Bette Van, Stephanie Turash, Ella Mayer, Maxine Dorelle, Lewis Rose, Robert Marco, Tony Coffaro, Robert W. Kirland, Rudolph Bain; CORPS DE BALLET: Adele Bodroghy, Leslie Cater, Joan Collenette, Joan Hansen, Betty Jayne, Jane Kiser, Irene Larson, Kirra Lehachova, Marina Lvova, Cecile Mann, Anna Mauldin, Dorothy Scott, Pat Sims, Salli Sorvo, Yvonne Tibor, Janie Ward, Betty Yeager, Charles Bockman, Jack Donald Claus, Walter Roberts, Igor Storojeff. *Act I: Scene 1* Music room of the Hugenhaugen home: "They're All the Same" (Casanova, Ilse, Misses Allen, Carabella, Fischelli, Lvova, Mayer, Tibor, Turash, Ward), "My Rhapsody" (Lili & Charles), "Scherzo" (Mme Boticini), "Heaven Bless Our Home" (Francis); *Scene 2* Gardens at Schoenbrunn Palace: "The World is Young Again" (Maria Theresa & Ladies of the Court), Presentation (Maria Theresa, Francis, Mme Boticini, Captain of the Guard, Ensemble), Chinese Porcelain Ballet (Ilse, Ivan, Rickshaw Man, Ladies of the Corps de Ballet); *Scene 3* Maywine Pavilion, outside Vienna: "To Horse" (Mme Boticini, Casanova, Tina, Lotzi), The Dandy's Polka (Jerry Ross), May Wine Polka (Corps de Ballet & Ensemble), "Take Love" (Lili, Charles, Ensemble), The Hunt (Ilse, Corps de Ballet, Ensemble), The Roulette Game (Sonya, assisted by Nicholas Beriozoff, Corps de Ballet, Ensemble), "Song of Defiance" (Charles & Ensemble). *Act II: Scene 1* The jail: "Because You're Mine" (Charles), "When Men are Free" (Charles & Ensemble); *Scene 2* Apartment of Casanova in the palace: "Happy Ending" (Maria Theresa), "Rosemarin" (Mme Boticini); *Scene 3* The ballroom of Schoenbrunn Palace: "Caprice Viennois" (Maria Theresa & Francis), Midnight Ballet (Ilse, Ivan, Sonya, Corps de Ballet), Finale (Entire Company).

Many people walked out opening night, it was roundly panned by the critics, and the producers lost $365,000.

583. *The Rink*

Set in an abandoned roller rink, on a crime-ridden boardwalk, somewhere on the Eastern Seaboard during the 1970s. Angel, after years in hippy communes and on protest marches in the 1960s, returns home after seven years, and is horrified to find that her mother, Anna, has just sold the rink, the wreckers are about to move in, and Anna is getting ready to go back to Italy. Angel wants to re-open it. The story is heavy with symbolism. The action covers only a few hours, but flashbacks cover over 30 years. Anna's husband Dino has deserted them. Anna, now pretty loose, is raped by local hoods. Angel has a reunion with her father, who she believed was dead. Finally the granddaughter Anna didn't know she had arrived. Anna and Angel patch up their differences, and Angel can let go of the rink. Fausto is Angel's uncle, a nasty character.

Before Broadway. Kander & Ebb came up with the idea as a starring vehicle for Chita Rivera, and they wrote the first treatment with Albert Innaurato, who was then writing a book about a roller-skating palace on New York City's Lower East Side that was about to be converted into a roller disco. Arthur Laurents was approached to direct, but turned them down, suggesting instead Terrence McNally as librettist. A.J. Antoon was brought on board to direct his first musical. After a workshop production in New York, it was planned as an Off Broadway production, then as Broadway. During Broadway previews an intermission was added.

The Broadway Run. MARTIN BECK THEATRE, 2/9/84–8/4/84. 29 previews. 204 PERFORMANCES. PRESENTED BY Jules Fisher, Roger Berlind, Joan Cullman, Milbro Productions, and Kenneth — John Productions, in association with Jonathan Farkas & Jujamcyn Theatres; MUSIC: John Kander; LYRICS: Fred Ebb; BOOK: Terrence McNally; DIRECTOR: A.J. Antoon; CHOREOGRAPHER: Graciela Daniele; SETS: Peter Larkin; COSTUMES: Theoni V. Aldredge; LIGHTING: Marc B. Weiss; SOUND: Otts Munderloh; MUSICAL DIRECTOR: Paul Gemignani; ORCHESTRATIONS: Michael Gibson; DANCE MUSIC ARRANGEMENTS: Tom Fay; PRESS: Merle Debuskey & William Schelble; CASTING: Johnson — Liff; GENERAL MANAGER: Marvin A. Krauss; COMPANY MANAGER: Sue Frost; PRODUCTION STAGE MANAGER: Ed Aldridge; STAGE MANAGER: Craig Jacobs. *Cast:* ANGEL: Liza Minnelli, *Lenora Nemetz* (during Miss Minnelli's absence), *Mary Testa* (from 7/3/84), *Stockard Channing* (from 7/14/84); LITTLE GIRL: Kim Hauser, *Kimi Parks*; THE (SIX) WRECKERS: LINO: Jason Alexander; BUDDY: Mel Johnson Jr.; GUY: Scott Holmes; LUCKY: Scott Ellis; TONY: Frank Mastrocola; BEN: Ronn Carroll; ANNA ANTONELLI: Chita Rivera; DINO: Scott Holmes; DINO'S FATHER: Ronn Carroll; LENNY: Jason Alexander; HIRAM: Mel Johnson Jr.; TOM: Frank Mastrocola; SUGAR: Scott Ellis; PUNKS: Jason Alexander, Scott Ellis, Frank Mastrocola; MRS. SILVERMAN: Ronn Carroll; MRS. JACKSON: Mel Johnson Jr.; ARNIE: Scott Ellis; CHARLIE: Mel Johnson Jr.; UNCLE FAUSTO: Jason Alexander; SUITORS: Mel Johnson Jr., Frank Mastrocola, Scott Ellis; FATHER ROCCO: Scott Holmes; BOBBY PERRILLO: Scott Ellis; SISTER PHILOMENA: Ronn Carroll; PETER REILLY: Frank Mastrocola; JUNIOR MILLER: Mel Johnson Jr.; DEBBIE DUBERMAN: Scott Holmes; DANNY: Scott Ellis. *Standbys:* Anna: Patti Karr; Angel: Lenora Nemetz & Mary Testa. *Understudies:* Lino/Lucky/Tony: Rob Marshall; Guy: Frank Mastrocola; Ben/Buddy: Jim Tushar; Little Girl: Kimi Parks, *Barclay de Veau*. *Act I:* "Colored Lights" (Angel), "Chief Cook and Bottle Washer" (Anna), "Don't 'Ah Ma' Me" (Anna & Angel), "Blue Crystal" (Dino), "Under the Roller Coaster" (Angel), "Not Enough Magic" (Dino, Angel, Anna, Sugar, Hiram, Tom, Lenny, Dino's Father), "We Can Make It" (Anna), "After All These Years" (Wreckers), "Angel's Rink and Social Center" (Angel & Wreckers), "What Happened to the Old Days?" (Anna, Mrs. Silverman, Mrs. Jackson), Finale Act I — "Colored Lights" (reprise) (Angel). *Act II:* "The Apple Doesn't Fall" (Anna & Angel), "Marry Me" (Lenny), "We Can Make It" (reprise) (Anna), "Mrs. A" (Anna, Angel, Lenny, Suitors), "The Rink" (Suitors), "Wallflower" (Anna & Angel), "All the Children in a Row" (Angel & Danny), Coda (Anna & Angel).

By and large the Broadway reviews were terrible. On 4/9/84 Liza Minnelli was away in Hollywood for the Oscars ceremony. Lenora Nemetz went on in her place. The producers knew about her Oscars deal well in advance but didn't put it in that day's newspaper. Three days before she was due to leave the show, Miss Minnelli, then heavily into drug and alcohol problems, was forced to go the Betty Ford Clinic for treatment, and Stockard Channing took over. Chita Rivera won a Tony, and the show also received nominations for score, choreography, sets, and for Liza Minnelli.

After Broadway. WYTHENSHAWE, Manchester, England, 1987. DIRECTOR: Paul Kerryson; MUSICAL DIRECTOR: David Beer. *Cast:* ANNA: Josephine Blake; ANGEL: Diane Langton; GUY/DINO: Gareth Snook; BUDDY: Richard Bodkin. Then it went to the West End, to the CAMBRIDGE THEATRE, London, 1988. 38 PERFORMANCES. It failed because it had no big starring names.

584. *The Roar of the Greasepaint — The Smell of the Crowd*

For obvious reasons this musical is generally referred to as *Roar of the Greasepaint*, or even just *Greasepaint*. Set in a rocky place, in the present. The set resembled a huge gaming table. The show is an allegory about playing the game — religion, hunger, work, love, success, death, rebellion. Sir represents the establishment, authority. Cocky represents the masses who play the game according to the rules. Emboldened by the Negro, Cocky challenges Sir's dominance at the end and they come to realize that power must be shared between them.

Before Broadway. The original British production opened at the THEATRE ROYAL, NOTTINGHAM, England, on 8/3/64, then toured through the Northern towns. It never had a London run. DIRECTOR: Anthony Newley; CHOREOGRAPHER: Gillian Lynne; SETS: Sean Kenny; COSTUMES: Leslie Hurry; MUSICAL DIRECTOR: Peter Knight. *Cast:* COCKY: Norman Wisdom; SIR: Willoughby Goddard; KID: Sally Smith; NEGRO: Cy Grant; GIRL: Dilys Watling; STRANGER: Ross Hutchinson [this role was discarded when the show went to Broadway]; BULLY: Bruce Wells; CHORUS INCLUDED: Wendy Padbury, Ann Holloway, Elaine Paige.

David Merrick bought the U.S. rights, and gave it a 13½ week tour before taking it to Broadway.

The Broadway Run. SHUBERT THEATRE, 5/16/65–12/4/65. 7 previews from 5/11/65. 232 PERFORMANCES. PRESENTED BY David Merrick, in association with Bernard Delfont; MUSIC/LYRICS/BOOK: Leslie Bricusse & Anthony Newley; DIRECTOR: Anthony Newley; CHOREOGRAPHER: Gillian Lynne; SETS/LIGHTING: Sean Kenny; COSTUMES: Freddy Wittop; SOUND: Robert Maybaum; MUSICAL DIRECTOR: Herbert Grossman; ORCHESTRATIONS: Philip J. Lang; VOCAL & DANCE MUSIC ARRANGEMENTS: Peter Howard; PRESS: Harvey B. Sabinson, Lee Solters, David Powers; GENERAL MANAGER: Jack Schlissel; COMPANY MANAGER: Vince McKnight; PRODUCTION STAGE MANAGER: Gene Perlowin; STAGE MANAGER: Bob Broadway; ASSISTANT STAGE MANAGER: Linda Rae Hager. *Cast:* COCKY: Anthony Newley (1) ☆, *Orson Bean* (from 11/22/65); SIR: Cyril Ritchard (2) ☆; THE KID: Sally Smith (3); THE GIRL: Joyce Jillson (5); THE NEGRO: Gilbert Price (4); THE BULLY: Murray Tannenbaum; THE URCHINS: Rawley Bates, Lori Browne, Lori Cesar, Jill Choder, Gloria Chu, Kay Cole, Marlene Dell, Boni Enten, Mitzi Feinn, Pamela Gruen, Linda Rae Hager, Cyndi Howard, Laura Michaels, Debbie Palmer, Heather Taylor. *Standbys:* Cocky: Edward Earle; Sir: Rod McLennan; Negro: Bob Broadway. *Understudies:* Kid: Jill Choder; Girl: Kay Cole. *Act I:* "The Beautiful Land" (Urchins), "A Wonderful Day Like Today" (Sir, Cocky, Urchins), "It isn't Enough" (Cocky & Urchins), "Things to Remember" (Sir, Kid, Urchins), "Put it in the Book" (Kid & Urchins), "With All Due Respect" (Cocky) [in the original British production, but dropped for Broadway], "This Dream" (Cocky), "Where Would You Be without Me?" (Sir, Cocky, Kid), "Look at That Face" (Sir, Kid, Urchins), "My First Love Song" (Cocky & Girl), "The Joker" (Cocky), "Put 'im in the Box" (Urchins), "Who Can I Turn to (When Nobody Needs Me)?" (Cocky) [a big hit]. *Act II:* "A Funny Funeral" (Urchins), "That's What it is to Be Young" (Urchins), "What a Man!" (Cocky, Sir, Kid, Urchins), "Feeling Good" (Negro & Urchins), "Nothing Can Stop Me Now!" (Cocky & Urchins), "Things to Remember" (reprise) (Sir), "My Way" (Cocky & Sir), "Who Can I Turn to (When Nobody Needs Me)?" (reprise) (Sir), "The Beautiful Land" (reprise) (Urchins), "Sweet Beginning" (Cocky & Sir).

Broadway reviews were totally divided. Walter Kerr's was devastatingly bad in the *Herald Tribune.* The show received Tony nominations for producer of a musical, composer & lyricist, direction of a musical, sets, costumes, and for Cyril Ritchard. Tony Bennett's recording of "Who Can I Turn to?" helped the show succeed.

After Broadway. PAPER MILL PLAYHOUSE, New Jersey, 1966. DIRECTOR: Buff Shurr. *Cast:* Kenneth Nelson, Christopher Hewett, Jill Choder.

TOUR. Opened on 9/21/67, at the Rajah Theatre, Reading, Pennsylvania, and closed on 4/6/68, at the Hershey Community Theatre, Pennsylvania, after 106 cities. PRESENTED BY Barry C. Tuttle & William A. Carrozo; DIRECTOR/CHOREOGRAPHER: Edward Earle; SETS/LIGHTING: Barry C. Tuttle; MUSICAL DIRECTOR: Suzanne Wigg. *Cast:* COCKY: Edward Earle; SIR: David C. Jones; KID: Sherry Lynn Diamant, Edie Andrews; GIRL: Lisa Damon, Luise White; NEGRO: Henry Baker; BULLY: Harold Norbut.

PAPER MILL PLAYHOUSE, New Jersey, 1990. DIRECTORS: Robert Johanson & Larry Grey; CHOREOGRAPHER: Susan Stroman; SETS: Michael Anania. *Cast:* COCKY: Robert Johanson; SIR: George S. Irving; KID: Denise Nolin; GIRL: Mia Malm; STRANGER: Ron Richardson [this role was formerly the Negro, not the original Stranger role]; ALSO WITH: Bill Brassea, Mirla Criste, Matt Zarley.

COCONUT GROVE PLAYHOUSE, Miami, 1990. DIRECTOR: Arnold Mittelman; CHOREOGRAPHER: Wayne Cilento; MUSICAL DIRECTOR/REVISED ORCHESTRATIONS: Donald Chan. *Cast:* Larry Kert, Obba Babatunde, Vivian Reed, Melinda Cartwright, Robert Weber.

14TH STREET Y, NYC, 12/4/02–12/22/02. Part of the *Musicals Tonight!* series. DIRECTOR: Thomas Mills; MUSICAL DIRECTOR: Barbara Anselmi. *Cast:* COCKY: David Edwards; SIR: George S. Irving; GIRL: Mamie Paris; KID: Leslie Ann Hendricks; BULLY: Drake Andrew; NEGRO: Jimmy Rivers; URCHINS: Amy Estein, Lauren Lebowitz, Andrienne Pisoni, Sandie Rosa, Jennifer Rose, Margie Stokley, Heather Stone.

585. *The Robber Bridegroom*

A country folk musical. Set in & around Rodney, in the old legendary Mississippi Territory, in 1795. A bridegroom searches for his bride. Musgrove was a tobacco grower fooled by dashing thief Jamie into believing that Jamie saved his life; Rosamund falls in love with Jamie when he is disguised as the "Bandit of the Woods," but who hates him when he is himself; Salome is Rosamund's jealous stepmother who attempts to kill her; Little Harp & Big Harp are brothers, the latter a talking head without a body. No intermission.

Before Broadway. THE MUSICAL THEATRE LAB PRODUCTION. It was first produced Off Broadway at ST. CLEMENT'S CHURCH, NYC, 11/4/74–11/9/74. Limited run of 6 PERFORMANCES. PRESENTED BY Musical Theatre Lab (a joint project of Stuart Ostrow Foundation & St. Clement's Church). This was a smaller production than the later Middle Broadway and Broadway ones. It had the same basic crew as for the Broadway run, except CHOREOGRAPHER: Don Redlich; LIGHTING: Gary Porto; PRESS: Alan Eichler; STAGE MANAGER: Mary Burns. *Cast:* SALOME: Susan Berger; 1ST LANDLORD: Bill Hunnery; 2ND LANDLORD: Carolyn McCurry; 3RD LANDLORD: William Brenner; ROSAMUND: Rhonda Coullet; MIKE FINK: John Getz; AIRIE/RAVEN: Cynthia Herman; JAMIE: Raul Julia; GOAT: Trip Plymale; GOAT'S MOTHER: Carolyn McCurry; ROBBERS/INDIANS: Thomas Oglesby, David Summers, William Brenner, Dana Kyle; BIG HARP: Bill Hunnery; LITTLE HARP: Ernie Sabella; CLEMMENT: Steve Vinovich.

John Houseman saw this production, and The Acting Company (of which Mr. Houseman was artistic director) opened very successfully with it at the Saratoga Festival, then toured with it.

THE MIDDLE BROADWAY run. The Acting Company then ran it at the HARKNESS THEATRE (a Middle Broadway theatre), 10/7/75–10/18/75. 1 preview. Limited run of 15 PERFORMANCES, as part of its repertory season. Due to a musicians' strike it was the only musical appearing on "Broadway" that month. It was a surprise hit. It had the same basic crew as for the Broadway production that followed, except COMPANY MANAGER: Mannie Kladitis. *Cast:* JAMIE LOCKHART, A ROBBER: Kevin Kline; MIKE FINK, A FLATBOATMAN: Norman Snow; CLEMMENT MUSGROVE, A RICH PLANTER: David Schramm; GOAT, A SIMPLETON: Robert Bacigalupi; LITTLE HARP, A ROBBER: J.W. Harper; BIG HARP, THE HEAD OF A ROBBER: Anderson Matthews; (SIX) NEIGHBORS: KYLE NUNNERY: Brooks Baldwin; TOM PLYMALE: Richard Ooms; BILLY BRENNER: Nicholas Surovy; JOHN OGLESBY: Roy K. Stevens; ERNIE SUMMERS: Peter Dvorsky; HERMAN MCLAUGHLIN: Michael Tolaydo; SALOME, MUSGROVE'S SECOND WIFE: Mary Lou Rosato; ROSAMUND, MUSGROVE'S DAUGHTER: Patti LuPone; GOAT'S MOTHER: Glynis Bell; AIRIE, GOAT'S SISTER: Sandra Halperin; RAVEN: Elaine Hausman; QUEENIE SUE STEVENS: Cynthia Dickason; THE FIDDLER: Alan Kaufman. *Music performed by*: The Wretched Refuse: Bob Jones, Alan Kaufman, David Markowitz, Richard Shulberg, Steve Tannenbaum. "With Style" (Jamie & Company), "The Real Mike Fink" (Jamie, Musgrove, Fink) [this number was not in the later Biltmore Theatre production because the character of Mike Fink was cut], "The Pricklepear Bloom" (Salome), "Nothin' Up" (Rosamund), "Deeper in the Woods" (Company), "Riches" (Musgrove, Jamie, Salome, Rosamund). "Love Stolen" (Jamie), "Poor Tied Up Darlin'" (Litle Harp & Goat), "Goodbye Salome" (Company), "Sleepy Man" (Rosamund). This production received 1976 Tony nominations for book, and for Patti LuPone.

MAINSTAGE OF THE MARK TAPER FORUM, Los Angeles. Opened on 7/15/76. 54 PERFORMANCES. PRESENTED BY the Center Theatre Group. It had the same cast and crew as for the subsequent Broadway production. A few changes had been made to the music, book and lyrics.

During a Broadway dress rehearsal at the Biltmore Barry Bostwick fell 12 feet to the floor and broke his elbow, when the rope he was swinging on snapped. He opened the show with a cast on his arm.

The Broadway Run. BILTMORE THEATRE, 10/9/76–2/13/77. 12 previews. 145 PERFORMANCES. PRESENTED BY John Houseman, Margot Harley, Michael B. Kapon, by arrangement with The Acting Company; MUSIC: Robert Waldman; LYRICS/BOOK: Alfred Uhry; BASED ON the 1942 novella of the same name, by Eudora Welty, which, in turn, had been inspired by a Grimm fairy tale; DIRECTOR: Gerald Freedman; CHOREOGRAPHER: Donald Saddler; SETS: Douglas W. Schmidt; COSTUMES: Jeanne Button; LIGHTING: David F. Segal; MUSICAL ARRANGEMENTS: Robert Waldman; PRESS: The Merlin Group; CASTING: Johnson — Liff Associates; GENERAL MANAGEMENT: McCann & Nugent; PRODUCTION STAGE MANAGER: Mary Porter Hall; STAGE MANAGER: Bethe Ward. *Cast:* JAMIE LOCKHART, A GENTLEMAN ROBBER: Barry Bostwick (1) ✩; CLEMMENT MUSGROVE, A RICH PLANTER: Stephen Vinovich (5); ROSAMUND, HIS DAUGHTER: Rhonda Coullet (2) ✩; SALOME, HIS SECOND WIFE: Barbara Lang (3) ✩; LITTLE HARP, A ROBBER: Lawrence John Moss (4); BIG HARP, THE HEAD OF A ROBBER: Ernie Sabella (9); GOAT, A SIMPLETON: Trip Plymale (8); GOAT'S MOTHER: Susan Berger; AIRIE, GOAT'S SISTER: Jana Schneider (10); RAVEN: Carolyn McCurry; RESIDENTS OF RODNEY: KYLE NUNNERY: George DeLoy; HARMON HARPER: Gary Epp; NORMAN OGELSBY: B.J. Hardin (6); QUEENIE BRENNER: Mary Murray (7); ROSE OTTO: Melinda Tanner; GERRY G. SUMMERS: Dennis Warning (11); K.K. PONE: Tom Westerman; *McVoutie River Volunteers:* LEADER: Tony Trischka; GUITARS: Bob Jones & Steve Mandell; FIDDLES: Bob Jones, Alan Kaufman, Evan Stover; MANDOLIN: Alan Kaufman; BANJOES: Steve Mandell & Tony Trischka; ACOUSTIC/ELECTRIC BASS: Roger Mason. *Understudies:* Jamie: George DeLoy; Musgrove: B.J. Hardin; Rosamund: Mary Murray; Salome: Carolyn McCurry; Little Harp: Ernie Sabella; Big Harp/Kyle/Norman/Gerry/K.K.: Gary Epp; Goat: Tom Westerman; Goat's Mother/Airie/Raven/Queenie: Melinda Tanner. "Once Upon the Natchez Trace" (Company), "Two Heads" (Big Harp & Little Harp), "Steal with Style" (Jamie), "Rosamund's Dream" (Rosamund), "The Pricklepear Bloom" (Salome), "Nothin' Up" (Rosamund), "Deeper in the Woods" (Company), "Riches" (Musgrove, Jamie, Salome, Rosamund), "Love Stolen" (Jamie). This is where the intermission was during the subsequent national tour. "Poor Tied Up Darlin'" (Little Harp & Goat), "Goodbye Salome" (Company), "Sleepy Man" (Rosamund), "Where Oh Where (is My Baby Darlin')?" (Jamie, Musgrove, Rosamund).

The show got good reviews. During each performance Rhonda Coullet appeared naked for a while. Barry Bostwick won a Tony.

After Broadway. FORD'S THEATRE, Washington, DC. Opened on 5/14/78. 14 PERFORMANCES. DIRECTOR: Mary Porter Hall; CHOREOGRAPHER: Norman Snow. *Cast:* Tom Wopat, Rhonda Coullet, Glynis Bell, Trip Plymale, Ernie Sabella.

586. *Rock 'n' Roll! The First 5,000 Years*

A musical revue about the origins and growth of rock 'n' roll, 1955–1982.

The Broadway Run. ST. JAMES THEATRE, 10/24/82–10/31/82. 23 previews. 9 PERFORMANCES. PRESENTED BY Jules Fisher & Annie Fargue, in association with Dick Clark, Inc. & Fred Disipio; CONCEIVED BY/MEDIA: Bob Gill & Robert Rabinowitz; DIRECTOR: Joe Layton; CHOREOGRAPHERS: Joe Layton & Jerry Grimes; SETS: Mark Ravitz; COSTUMES: Franne Lee; LIGHTING: Jules Fisher; SOUND: Bran Ferren; MUSICAL SUPERVISOR/ORCHESTRATIONS/MUSICAL CONTINUITY/DANCE MUSIC ARRANGEMENTS/VOCAL ARRANGEMENTS: John Simon; MUSICAL DIRECTOR: Andrew Dorfman; ASSOCIATE ORCHESTRATOR: Steven Wexler; ADDITIONAL ORCHESTRATIONS: Joseph Daley, Joseph Gianono Jr., Jay Dryer; SPECIAL CONSULTANT: Dick Clark; CAST RECORDING on CBS; PRESS: The Merlin Group; CASTING: Johnson — Liff; GENERAL MANAGER: Marvin A. Krauss; PRODUCTION STAGE MANAGER: Peter Lawrence; STAGE MANAGER: Jim Woolley; ASSISTANT STAGE MANAGER: Sarah Whitham. *Cast:* Carl E. Weaver, Jim Riddle, William "Gregg Hunter," Russell Velasquez, Tom Teeley, Patrick Weathers, Rob Barnes, Shaun Solomon, Raymond Patterson, Dave MacDonald, Marion Ramsey, Wenndy Leigh MacKenzie, Ka-Ron Brown, Jenifer Lewis, Lillias White, Karen Mankes, Michael Pace, Rich Hebert, Barbara Walsh, Sandy Dillon, Joyce Leigh Bowden, Andrew Dorfman, Lon Hoyt, Bill Jones, Bob Miller. *Act I:* "Love is a Many-Splendored Thing" (m: Sammy Fain; l: Paul Francis Webster) (Frank Sinatra recording), "Tutti Frutti" (m/l: Dorothy La Bostrie, "Little Richard" Penniman, Joe Lubin) (Carl), "Rock Around the Clock" (m/l: Max Friedman & Jimmy DeKnight) (Jim), "Blueberry Hill" (m/l: Al Lewis, Larry Stock, Vincent Rose) (William), "Wake up Little Susie" (m/l: Felice & Boudleaux Bryant) (Russell & Tom), "Great Balls of Fire" (m/l: Otis Blackwell & Jack Hammer) (Tom), "Johnny B. Goode" (m/l: Chuck Berry) (Carl), "Heartbreak Hotel" (m/l: Mae Boren Axton, Tommy Durden, Elvis Presley) (Patrick), "Hound Dog" (m/l: Jerry Leiber & Mike Stoller) (Patrick), "Love Me Tender" (m/l: Vera Matson & Elvis Presley) (Patrick), "Why Do Fools Fall in Love?" (m/l: Frankie Lymon & Morris Levy) (Carl, Rob, Shaun, William, Raymond), "Sh-Boom" ("Life Could Be a Dream") (m/l: James Edwards, Carl Feaster, James Keyes, Floyd F. McRae) (Dave), "Will You Still Love Me Tomorrow?" (m/l: Gerry Goffin & Carole King) (Marion), "Da Doo Ron Ron" (m/l: Jeff Barry, Ellie Greenwich, Phil Spector) (Wenndy), "The Twist" (m/l: Hank Ballard) (Raymond) [Ka-Ron featured dancer], "Land of a Thousand Dances" (m/l: Chris Kenner & Antoine "Fats" Domino) (William) [Ka-Ron featured dancer], "Reach Out, I'll Be There" (m/l: Hal Davis, Berry Gordy, Bob West, Willie Hutch) (Rob), "You Keep Me Hangin' On" (m/l: Eddie Holland, Lamont Dozier, Brian Holland) (Jenifer, Lillias, Marion), "Proud Mary" (m/l: John C. Fogerty) (Marion), "A Hard Day's Night" (m/l: John Lennon & Paul McCartney) (Jim, Russell, Tom, Bob), "I Got You, Babe" (m/l: Sonny Bono) (Karen & Michael), "Good Vibrations" (m/l: Brian Wilson & Mike Love) (Rich, Carl, Jim), "Here Comes the Sun" (m/l: George Harrison) (Tom), "The Sunshine of Your Love" (m/l: Jack Bruce, Eric Clapton, Peter Brown) (Tom & Russell), "Blowin' in the Wind" (m/l: Bob Dylan) (Patrick), "Like a Rolling Stone" (m/l: Bob Dylan) (Patrick), "A Whiter Shade of Pale" (m/l: Keith Reed & Gary Brooker) (Dave) [Ka-Ron featured dancer], "Mrs. Robinson" (m/l: Paul Simon) (Russell & Tom) [Ka-Ron featured dancer], "White Rabbit" (m/l: Grace Slick) (Barbara, Karen, Wenndy), "Respect" (m/l: Otis Redding) (Lillias), "The Night They Drove Old Dixie Down" (m/l: J. Robbie Robertson) (Patrick), "People Got to Be Free" (m/l: Edward Brigate & Felix Cavaliere) (Russell), "Cry Baby" (m/l: Burt Russell & Norman Meade) (Sandy), "Forever Young" (m/l: Bob Dylan) (Barbara), "Everybody's Talking" (m/l: Fred Neil) (Michael), "Joy to the World" (m/l: Hoyt Axton) (Russell), "Both Sides Now" (m/l: Joni Mitchell) (Wenndy), "Higher and Higher" (m/l: Renard Miner, Gary Jackson, Carl Smith) (Raymond). *Act II:* "Tubular Bells" (m: Mike Oldfield) (Bob) [instrumental], "I Feel the Earth Move" (m/l: Carole King) (Joyce), "Satisfaction" (m/l: Mick Jagger & Keith Richards) (Dave), "When Will I Be Loved" (m/l: Phil Everly) (Joyce), "My Generation" (m/l: Pete Townsend) (Jim), "You've Got a Friend" (m/l: Carole King) (Michael), "Nothing from Nothing" (m/l: Billy Preston & Bruce Fisher) (William) [Ka-Ron featured dancer], "Say it Loud, I'm Black and Proud" (m/l: James Brown) (Rob), "Summer in the City" (m/l: John Sebastian, Steve Boone, Mark Sebastian) (Jim) [Ka-Ron featured dancer], "Whole Lotta Love" (m/l: John Baldwin, John Bonham, James Patrick "Jimmy" Page, Robert A. Plant) (Russell & Jim), "Star Spangled Banner" (instrumental: arr: Jimi Hendrix) (Tom), "Boogie Woogie Bugle Boy" (m/l: Don Raye & Hughie Prince) (Joyce), "I-Feel-Like-I'm-Gonna-Die Rag" (m/l: Joe McDonald) (Dave), "American Pie" (m/l: Don McLean) (Rich), "Imagine" (m/l: John Lennon) (Tom), "School's Out" (m/l: Alice Cooper & Michael Bruce) (Dave), "Rock and Roll All Night" (m/l: Paul Stanley & Gene Simmons) (Jim), "Benny and the Jets" (m/l: Elton John & Bernie Taupin) (Lon), "Space Oddity" (m/l: David Bowie) (Michael & Russell), "Take a Walk on the Wild Side" (m/l: Lou Reed) (Patrick), "Everybody is a Star" (m/l: Sylvester Stewart) (Carl, Lillias, Raymond, William) [Ka-Ron featured dancer], "Stayin' Alive" (m/l: Barry Gibb, Robin Gibb, Maurice Gibb) [from the movie *Saturday Night Fever*] (Lon, Michael, Rich), "Love to Love You, Baby" (m/l: Pete Bellote, Giorgio Moroder, Donna Summer) (Jenifer), "I Will Survive" (m/l: Dino Fekaris & Frederick J. Perren) (Lillias), "On the Run" (m: Roger Waters, David Gilmour, Rick Wright; l: Roger Waters) (Andrew & Russell) (instrumental), "Jocko Homo" (m/l: Mark Mothersbaugh) (Dave), "Message in a Bottle" (m/l: Sting Sumner) (Lon), "Our Lips are Sealed" (m/l: Jane Weidlin & Terry Hall) (Karen), "Concrete Shoes" (m: Chosei Funahara; l: Rod Swenson) (Sandy & Shaun), "Rock and Roll Music" (m/l: Chuck Berry) (Company).

Note: the Company formed part of every song, behind featured performer(s), except in on "Love is a Many Splendored Thing," "A Hard Day's Night," "Star Spangled Banner" and "On the Run."

Reviews were divided, but generally not great.

587. *Rockabye Hamlet*

A massively produced, almost all-sung (in opera form), and very free rock version adaptation of Shakespeare, with black Hamlet, Gertrude and Claudius. Ophelia commits suicide by strangling herself with microphone cord. The entire action takes place at a rock concert.

Before Broadway. Originally entitled *Kronberg: 1582*. It was commissioned by the Canadian Broadcasting Company's Radio Variety department. It was created by Cliff Jones, a Canadian musician and TV music director, and performed on radio and stage at CHARLOTTETOWN FESTIVAL, Prince Edward Island, Canada. Colleen Dewhurst, who was from Charlottetown, saw the production, and recommended to Lester Osterman that he bring it to New York.

The Broadway Run. MINSKOFF THEATRE, 2/17/76–2/21/76. 21 previews. 7 PERFORMANCES. PRESENTED BY Lester Osterman Productions (Lester Osterman & Richard Horner) & Joseph Kipness, in association with Martin Richards, Victor D'Arc, and Marilyn Strauss, and by arrangement with Champlain Productions; MUSIC/LYRICS/BOOK: Cliff Jones; BASED ON the 1602 tragedy *Hamlet*, by William Shakespeare (uncredited); DIRECTOR: Gower Champion; CHOREOGRAPHERS: Gower Champion & Tony Stevens; SWORDPLAY: Larry Carpenter; SETS: Kert F. Lundell; COSTUMES: Joseph G. Aulisi; LIGHTING: Jules Fisher; SOUND: Abe Jacob; MUSICAL DIRECTOR/VOCAL ARRANGEMENTS: Gordon Lowry Harrell; DANCE MUSIC ARRANGEMENTS: Douglas Katsaros; BAND ARRANGEMENTS: Alan Raph, Tom Pierson, Horace Ott, Bill Brohn, Jim Tyler; PRESS: Betty Lee Hunt Associates; CASTING: Feuer & Ritzer; GENERAL MANAGER: Leonard Soloway; PRODUCTION STAGE MANAGER: David Taylor; STAGE MANAGER: Bethe Ward; ASSISTANT STAGE MANAGER: Tony Manzi. *Cast:* HORATIO: Rory Dodd (11); HAMLET: Larry Marshall (1) ☆; CLAUDIUS: Alan Weeks (2) ☆; GERTRUDE: Leata Galloway (4); PRIEST: Meat Loaf (7); POLONIUS: Randal Wilson (5); OPHELIA: Beverly D'Angelo (3); LAERTES: Kim Milford (6); ROSENCRANTZ: Christopher Chadman (9); GUILDENSTERN: Winston DeWitt Hemsley (10); PLAYER: Irving Lee (8); PLAYERESS/HONEYBELLE HUCKSTER: Judy Gibson (12); POCKER ROCKER: Bruce Paine [role cut during previews]; GRAVEDIGGER: William Parry [role cut during previews]; ACOLYTES/SWORDSMEN/NOBLES/COURTESANS: Tommy Aguilar, Steve Anthony, Terry Calloway, Prudence Darby, George Giraldo, Larry Hyman, Kurt Johnson, Clinton Keen, Paula Lynn, JoAnn Ogawa, Sandi Orcutt, Merel Poloway, Joseph Pugliese, Yolanda Raven, Michelle Stubbs, Dennis Williams; SINGERS: James Braet, Judy De Angelis, B.G. Gibson, Judy Gibson, Pat Gorman, Suzanne Lukather, Bruce Paine, Bill Parry; ROADIES: Chet D'Elia, David Fredericks, David Lawson, Jeff Spielman; *Rockabye Hamlet Band:* Gordon Lowry Harrell, Allen Herman, Michael Levinson, Peter Phillips, Phil Davis, Billy Schwartz, Richie Resnicoff, Erik Frandsen, Ron McClure, Lowell Hershey, Peter Yellin, Bruce Shaffel, Gene Lowinger, Marc Horowitz. *Standby:* Hamlet/Laertes: Philip Casnoff. *Swing Dancer:* Chuck Thorpes. *Act I: Prologue* "Why Did He Have to Die?" (Horatio & Chorus); *Scene 1* The chapel: "The Wedding" (Hamlet, Claudius, Gertrude, Priest, Chorus), "That it Should Come to This" (Hamlet); *Scene 2* The throne room: "Set it Right" (Claudius, Hamlet, Gertrude, Chorus), "Hello-Hello" (Ophelia & Hamlet), "Don't Unmask Your Beauty to the Moon" (Hamlet & Laertes), "If Not to You" (Ophelia & Chorus), "Have I Got a Girl for You" (Rosencrantz, Guildenstern, Hamlet, Chorus), "Mad Waltz" (Claudius, Gertrude, Rosencrantz, Guildenstern) [cut during previews], "Tis Pity, Tis True" (Polonius, Claudius, Gertrude); *Scene 3* The Queen's bedchamber: "Shall We Dance" (Hamlet & Gertrude), "All My Life" (Gertrude); *Scene 4* The disco: "Something's Rotten in Denmark" (Hamlet, Player, Playeress, Chorus), "Denmark is Still" (Hamlet, Ophelia, Chorus), "Twist Her

Mind" (Horatio, Hamlet, Ophelia, Chorus), "Get Thee to a Nunnery" (Hamlet, Ophelia, Priest, Chorus) [cut during previews], "Gentle Lover" (Ophelia), "Where is the Reason" (Hamlet); *Scene 5* The Great Hall: "The Wart Song" (Players & Chorus) [added during previews], "Pass the Biscuits, Mama" (Players & Chorus) [cut during previews], "He Got it in the Ear" (Honeybelle), "It is Done" (Hamlet & Horatio). *Act II: Scene 1* The chapel: "Midnight—Hot Blood" (Hamlet), "I Cannot Turn to Love" (Claudius, Hamlet) [cut during previews], "Midnight Mass" (Hamlet, Gertrude, Claudius, Priest, Choir), "Hey…!" (Rosencrantz, Guildenstern, Claudius), "Sing Alone" (Hamlet); *Scene 2* Limbo: "Your Daddy's Gone Away" (Horatio), "Rockabye Hamlet" (Ophelia), "Off Her Rocker and Roll" (Pocker Rocker) [cut during previews], "All by Yourself" (Laertes), "The Rosencrantz & Guildenstern Boogie" (Claudius & Chorus Girls), "Laertes Coercion" (Claudius, Laertes, Gertrude, Chorus Girls), "The Last Blues" (Gertrude); *Scene 3* The graveyard: "With a Pick and a Shovel" (Gravediggers) [cut during previews], "Didn't She Do it for Love" (Priest, Claudius, Hamlet, Laertes, Chorus), "If My Morning Begins" (Hamlet); *Scene 4* The Great Hall: "Swordfight" (Claudius, Hamlet, Laertes, Gertrude, Horatio, Chorus).

On Broadway it was universally panned. Then a very bitter Cliff Jones recorded his own original cast album, and embarked on an anti–New York critics campaign. Three weeks after it closed CBC did an eight-hour broadcast post mortem of the show's beginnings and (especially) its failure.

588. *The Rocky Horror Show*

A transvestite musical from outer space that made fun of old horror movies. The time: Then and now. The place: Here and there. Brad and Janet are an innocent young couple, all–American high-school sweethearts. On a stormy night in the forest their car breaks down and they see a castle with lights on. Here they hope to find help. They knock on the castle door, and enter, and stumble into the annual convention of transvestite aliens from the "far-out" planet Transsexual, in the galaxy of Transylvania. Frank is a pouting, sex-mad transvestite; Rocky is Frank's pet toy boy; Riff is the dastardly butler; Magenta is Riff's sister. It was presented in two acts, but with no intermission.

Before Broadway. It began at the ROYAL COURT THEATRE UPSTAIRS, London, 6/19/73. PRESENTED BY Michael White; DIRECTOR: Jim Sharman. *Cast:* FRANK: Tim Curry; NARRATOR: Jonathan Adams; ROCKY: Rayner Bourton; COLUMBIA: Little Nell; RIFF RAFF: Richard O'Brien; MAGENTA: Patricia Quinn; EDDIE/SCOTT: Paddy O'Hagan; JANET: Julie Covington; BRAD: Christopher Malcolm. On 8/14/73 it opened at the CLASSIC THEATRE, Chelsea, then on 11/3/73 moved to the ESSOLDO THEATRE, King's Road, Chelsea. It ran at the COMEDY THEATRE, in the West End, 4/6/79–9/13/80. It had a total run, in and out of the West End, of 2,960 PERFORMANCES. Tracey Ullman was one of the actresses who played Janet during the run.

AUSTRALIA, 1974. *Cast:* FRANK: Reg Livermore; NARRATOR: Arthur Dignam; MAGENTA: Kate Fitzpatrick. There was a cast recording of this production.

U.S. PREMIERE. ROXY THEATRE, Los Angeles, 3/22/74. PRESENTED BY Lou Adler. Abigale Haness took over as Janet from Susan Morse just before performances began. The cast went intact to Broadway, except that Bruce Scott was replaced by Richard O'Brien for Broadway, and Graham Jarvis by William Newman. On Broadway the Belasco was converted into a cabaret theatre for this show.

The Broadway Run. BELASCO THEATRE, 3/10/75–4/6/75. 4 previews. 32 PERFORMANCES. The Michael White production, PRESENTED BY Lou Adler; MUSIC/LYRICS/BOOK: Richard O'Brien; DIRECTOR: Jim Sharman; SETS: Brian Thomson; COSTUMES: Sue Blane; LIGHTING: Chipmonck; SOUND: Abe Jacob; SPECIAL EFFECTS: Robert E. McCarthy; MUSICAL DIRECTOR: D'Vaughn Pershing; MUSICAL ARRANGEMENTS: Richard Hartley; PRESS: Michael Alpert Public Relations Associates, Ellen Levene, Marilynn LeVine, Anne Weinberg, Warren Knowlton, Paul Wasserman, Jim Mahoney & Associates; CASTING: Geri Windsor & Associates; GEN-

ERAL MANAGERS: Brian Avnet & Marvin A. Krauss; COMPANY MANAGER: Brian Avnet; PRODUCTION STAGE MANAGER: David H. Banks; STAGE MANAGER: August Amarino; ASSISTANT STAGE MANAGER: Judy Burns. **Cast:** BELASCO POPCORN GIRL (TRIXIE): Jamie Donnelly (3); JANET WEISS: Abigale Haness (5); BRAD MAJORS: Bill Miller (8); NARRATOR: William Newman (2); RIFF RAFF: Ritz O'Brien (i.e. Richard O'Brien) (9); COLUMBIA: Boni Enten (4); MAGENTA: Jamie Donnelly (3); DR. FRANK 'N' FURTER: Tim Curry (1) ☆; ROCKY HORROR: Kim Milford (7); EDDIE: Meat Loaf (6); DR. SCOTT: Meat Loaf (6). **Standbys:** Eddie/Scott: David P. Kelly; Janet/Magenta: Pamela Palluzzi; Brad/Rocky: Robert Rhys. **Act I: Prologue** Movie theatre: "Science Fiction Double Feature" (Trixie); **Scene 1** In a car outside Denton Episcopal Church: "Damn it, Janet" ("Wedding Song") (Brad & Janet); **Scene 2** In a car, on the wrong fork, outside Frank 'n Furter's Castle: "Over at the Frankenstein Place" ("There's a Light") (Brad & Janet); **Scene 3** Inside a big hall-type room, the foyer of the castle: "Sweet Transvestite" (Frank), "Time Warp" (Magenta, Columbia, Riff Raff, Narrator); **Scene 4** In the lab: "The Sword of Damocles" (Rocky), "I Can Make You a Man" ("Charles Atlas Song Part 1)" (Frank), "Hot Patootie, Bless My Soul" ("Whatever Happened to Saturday Night?") (Eddie), "I Can Make You a Man" (reprise) ("Charles Atlas Song Part 2") (Frank). **Act II: Scene 5** Janet's room; **Scene 6** Brad's room; **Scene 7** In the lab: "Touch-a, Touch-a, Touch-a, Touch Me" (Janet, Magenta, Columbia); **Scene 8** Dining room, the theatre of the castle: "Once in a While" (Brad); **Scene 9** Same: "Eddie's Teddy" (Dr. Scott, Columbia, Company), "Planet Shmanet Janet" ("Wise Up Janet Weiss") (Frank); **Scene 10** Same: "Rose Tint My World" ("It Was Great When it All Began") ("Don't Dream It") (Columbia, Rocky, Brad, Janet), "We're a Wild and Untamed Thing" (Company), "I'm Going Home" (Brad); **Scene 11** Movie theatre: "Super Heroes" (Trixie), "Science Fiction Double Feature" (reprise) (Trixie), "Sweet Transvestite" (reprise) (Company), "Time Warp" (reprise) (Company), Finale: Epilogue.

As was expected it was roundly panned by the Broadway critics. The show received a Tony nomination for lighting.

After Broadway. TOUR. Opened on 2/3/76, at the Montgomery Playhouse, San Francisco. PRESENTED BY D.J. Enterprises; DIRECTOR: Michael Amarino; SETS: George Barcos; COSTUMES: Mary Piering; LIGHTING: Fred Kopp; MUSICAL DIRECTOR: Steven Applegate. **Cast:** FRANK: David James; ROCKY: Bill Tackey; JANET: Sharon Widman; BRAD: Robert Reynolds; RIFF RAFF: Buddy King; MAGENTA/TRIXIE: Vikki D'Orazzi; COLUMBIA: Kelli Whitehill; EDDIE/SCOTT: Emil Borelli; NARRATOR: Richard Gee; BACK-UP SINGER: Kelly St. John.

THE MOVIE. 1976. Adapted for the screen by Richard O'Brien, and retitled *The Rocky Horror Picture Show*. DIRECTOR: Jim Sharman. **Cast:** FRANK: Tim Curry; JANET: Susan Sarandon; BRAD: Barry Bostwick; RIFF RAFF: Richard O'Brien; SCOTT: Jonathan Adams; COLUMBIA: Nell Campbell (alias Little Nell); ROCKY: Peter Hinwood; NARRATOR: Charles Gray; MAGENTA: Patricia Quinn; EDDIE: Meatloaf.

PICCADILLY THEATRE, London, 7/16/90. This revival was PRESENTED BY Christopher Malcolm & Howard Panter; DIRECTOR: Robin Lefevre. **Cast:** NARRATOR: Jonathan Adams; ROCKY: Adam Caine; BRAD: Adrian Edmondson; FRANK: Tim McInnerney, *Anthony Head*; RIFF: Edward Tudor-Poll; JANET: Gina Bellman; MAGENTA: Mary Maddox; COLUMBIA: Linda Davidson; EDDIE/SCOTT: Gordon Kennedy.

In 2/96 Sandra Bernhard was being rumored to play Frank [sic] in a soon-to-be-made Broadway production. It never happened.

TIFFANY THEATRE, Los Angeles, 1/29/99–4/25/99. It was a hit. PRESENTED BY Paula Holt; DIRECTOR: Dennis Erdmann. **Cast:** ROCKY: James Capinello; FRANK: David Arquette, *Bob Simon*; NARRATOR: Paxton Whitehead; COLUMBIA: Hynden Walch; MAGENTA: Kirsten Benton; BRAD: Tim Fitz-Gerald; SCOTT: Eric Leviton; JANET: Lacey Kohl; RIFF: Donnie Kehr; EDDIE: Erik Garcia.

589. *The Rocky Horror Show (Broadway revival)*

Before Broadway. Early auditions included Sandra Bernhard, Lea De Laria, and Alice Ripley. Miss Bernhard was offered the role of Magenta, at $2,000 a week, but it was too little money. By 7/00 Daphne

Rubin-Vega was being heavily touted as the new Magenta. The 8/22/00 edition of *Variety* was the first to name the cast. There was no out-of-town tryout. It went straight to Broadway. Broadway previews began on 10/20/00 (date put back from 10/3/00). The originally scheduled opening date of Halloween (10/31/00) was put back to 11/15/00.

The Broadway Run. CIRCLE IN THE SQUARE UPTOWN, 11/15/00– 1/6/02. 30 previews from 10/20/00. 437 PERFORMANCES. PRESENTED BY Jordan Roth, by arrangement with Christopher Malcolm, Howard Panter, and Richard O'Brien, for the Rocky Horror Company; MUSIC/LYRICS/BOOK: Richard O'Brien; DIRECTOR: Christopher Ashley; CHOREOGRAPHER: Jerry Mitchell; SETS: David Rockwell; COSTUMES: David C. Woolard; LIGHTING: Paul Gallo; SOUND: T. Richard Fitzgerald & Domonic Sack; MUSICAL DIRECTOR/VOCAL ARRANGEMENTS: Henry Aronson; ORIGINAL ORCHESTRATIONS: Richard Hartley; NEW ORCHESTRATIONS: Doug Katsaros; NEW CAST RECORDING on RCA, made in Manhattan on 3/12/01, and released on 5/15/01; Kristen Lee Kelly stood in for Joan Jett; PRESS: The Jacksina Company; CASTING: Bernard Telsey; GENERAL MANAGEMENT: Richard Frankel Productions; COMPANY MANAGER: Eric Muratalla; PRODUCTION STAGE MANAGER: Brian Meister; STAGE MANAGERS: Brendan Smith & Marisha Ploski. **Cast:** USHERETTES: Daphne Rubin-Vega, Joan Jett (*Kristen Lee Kelly from 5/22/01, Ana Gasteyer 6/12/01–8/19/01, Kristen Lee Kelly 8/21/01–9/23/01, Liz Larsen from 10/30/01*); JANET WEISS: Alice Ripley, *Kristen Lee Kelly (from 10/30/01*); BRAD MAJORS: Jarrod Emick, *Luke Perry (during Mr. Emick's vacation, 6/26/01–8/5/01), John Jeffrey Martin, Jarrod Emick (from 8/7/01*); NARRATOR: Dick Cavett, *Kate Clinton (during Mr. Cavett's vacation, 7/2/01–7/8/01), Dick Cavett 7/23/01; from 10/30/01, for a week), Robin Leach (11/6/01–11/11/01), Gilbert Gottfried (11/13/01–11/18/01), Dave Holmes (11/20/01–11/25/01), Jerry Springer (11/27/01–12/2/01), Cindy Adams (12/4/01–12/9/01), Sally Jesse Raphael (12/11/01–12/16/01), Penn & Teller (12/18/01–12/23/01), Dick Cavett (12/25/01–1/6/02*); RIFF RAFF: Raul Esparza (until 5/13/01), *Mark Price, Jason Wooten (9/4/01–9/23/01), Sebastian Bach (from 10/30/01*); MAGENTA: Daphne Rubin-Vega; COLUMBIA: Joan Jett (until 5/22/01), *Kristen Lee Kelly (from 5/22/01), Ana Gasteyer (6/12/01–8/19/01), Kristen Lee Kelly (8/21/01–9/23/01), Liz Larsen (from 10/30/01*); FRANK 'N' FURTER: Tom Hewitt (until 8/19/01), *Terrence Mann (from 8/30/01*); ROCKY: Sebastian La Cause, *Jonathan Sharp (from 10/30/01*); EDDIE: Lea De Laria, *Jason Wooten (from 10/30/01*); DR. SCOTT: Lea DeLaria, *Jason Wooten (from 10/30/01*); PHANTOMS: Kevin Cahoon, Deirdre Goodwin, Aiko Nakasone, Mark Price, Jonathan Sharp, James Stovall, *Rosa Curry, Jim Osorno, Asa Somers, Jason Wooten, Matthew Morrison*. **Understudies:** Brad: John Jeffrey Martin & Jonathan Sharp; Janet: Kristen Lee Kelly & Aiko Nakasone; Frank: Kevin Cahoon & James Stovall; Magenta: Deidre Goodwin & Aiko Nakasone; Columbia: Kristen Lee Kelly & Aiko Nakasone; Riff Raff: Mark Price & John Jeffrey Martin; Rocky: Jonathan Sharp & John Jeffrey Martin; Eddie/Scott: James Stovall & Mark Price; Narrator: James Stovall, Kevin Cahoon, Asa Somers. **Swings:** John Jeffrey Martin & Kristen Lee Kelly. **Musicians:** KEYBOARD: Henry Aronson; SYNTHESIZER: John Korba; DRUMS: Clint de Ganon; ELECTRIC BASS: Irio O'Farrill; GUITAR: John Benthal. **Act I: Prologue** "Science Fiction Double Feature" (Usherettes & Phantoms); **Scene 1** In car outside church: "Damn it, Janet" (Brad, Janet, Phantoms); **Scene 2** In car outside castle: "Over at the Frankenstein Place" ("There's a Light") (Brad, Janet, Riff Raff, Phantoms); **Scene 3** Inside big hall-type room: "The Time Warp" (Brad, Magenta, Columbia, Narrator, Company), "Sweet Transvestite" (Frank, Brad, Riff Raff, Magenta, Columbia, Phantoms); **Scene 4** In the lab: "The Sword of Damocles" (Rocky, Narrator, Company), "I Can Make You a Man" ("Charles Atlas Part 1") (Frank & Company), "Hot Patootie (Bless My Soul)" (Eddie & Company), "I Can Make You a Man" (reprise) ("Charles Atlas Part 2") (Frank & Company). **Act II: Scene 5** Janet's room; **Scene 6** Brad's room: **Scene 7** In the lab: "Touch-a-Touch-a-Touch Me" (Janet, Magenta, Columbia, Phantoms), "Once in a While" (Brad & Phantoms); **Scene 8** Dining room: "Eddie's Teddy" (Scott, Narrator, Columbia, Frank, Company), "Planet Schmanet — Wise Up, Janet Weiss" (Frank & Company), "Floor Show/Rose Tint My World" (Columbia, Rocky, Brad, Janet, Frank, Riff Raff, Company), "I'm Going Home" (Frank & Company), "Super Heroes" (Brad, Janet, Narrator, Phantoms), "Science Fiction Double Feature" (reprise) (Usherettes & Phantoms).

Broadway reviews were divided. In 5/01 Flea (a musician) was being rumored as the next Riff-Raff, but it never happened. On 5/22/01 it was announced by the production that Joan Jett was going to leave on 6/10/01. This announcement so angered Miss Jett that she stormed out that evening (5/22/01) never to return. Jarrod Emick's return, scheduled for 7/29/01, was put back to 8/7/01, and Luke Perry's last performance was put back from 7/29/01 to 8/5/01. The show received Tony nominations for revival of a musical, direction of a musical, costumes, and for Tom Hewitt. In early 8/01 it was announced that Tom Hewitt was leaving the show, and he left on 8/19/01. His understudy filled in until Terrence Mann arrived. Then 9/11/01 hit New York City, and the show was obliged to close on 9/23/01, after 356 performances. However, it re-opened on 10/30/01, and continued to run until 1/6/02.

After Broadway. A 30th-anniversary U.K. touring revival, called *The Rocky Horror Big 30 Show*, opened at the Churchill Theatre, Bromley, England, on 10/4/02. Previews from 9/30/02. It closed at Milton Keynes, on 11/22/03. It took in a two-week stint at the QUEEN'S THEATRE, in the West End of London, 6/23/03–7/5/03. DIRECTOR: Christopher Malcolm. *Cast*: FRANK: Jonathan Wilkes; RIFF RAFF: Neil Couperthwaite; ROCKY: Graham Tudor; EDDIE: Drew Jaymson; COLUMBIA: Sally Hunt; BRAD: Jon Boydon; MAGENTA: Andrea Stevens; JANET: Katie Rowley-Jones; NARRATOR: Nick Bateman, *Rhona Cameron, John Stalker, Christine Hamilton, Kevin Kennedy, Lionel Blair.*

590. *Rollin' on the T.O.B.A.*

A musical revue, sub-titled *A Tribute to the Last Days of Black Vaudeville*. Segments were devoted to Bojangles, Bert Williams, and Butterbeans & Suzie. The songs, tap dances and comic sketches were drawn from the heyday of the "Chitlin Circuit," the old black vaudeville empire whose proper name was the Theatre Owners' Booking Association (which the performers tended to nickname "Tough on Black Asses"). Set in 1931.

Before Broadway. It first ran at the AMAS MUSICAL THEATRE, 7/23/98. 16 PERFORMANCES. It had the same basic crew as for the subsequent Broadway run, except COSTUMES: Joey Hooks; LIGHTING: Melody Beal. It had the same cast. Then it had an Off Broadway run, at the 47TH STREET THEATRE, 1/28/99–3/7/99. 9 previews from 1/20/99. 46 PERFORMANCES. At that stage it had only pianist David Alan Bunn as accompaniment. It had the same cast and crew as for the subsequent Broadway run, except STAGE MANAGER: Juliana Hannett. It then moved to the Kit Kat Klub, in the Henry Miller's Theatre (where the 1998 revival of *Cabaret* had played before moving to Studio 54, and which in 2001 would be subtly re-named the Henry Miller Theatre). Because the Kit Kat Klub had qualified as a Broadway theatre (one seat over the necessary 499) *Rollin' on the T.O.B.A.* qualifies as a Broadway musical revue. Besides, the production was on a Broadway contract. Previews were put back from 3/17/99. An orchestra was now brought in. The production cost $200,000, with an additional $250,000 to cover the move to the Kit Kat Klub.

The Broadway Run. THE KIT KAT CLUB AT HENRY MILLER'S THEATRE, 3/24/99–4/4/99. 6 previews from 3/19/99. 14 PERFORMANCES. PRESENTED BY John Grimaldi, Ashton Springer, and Frenchmen Productions; FEATURING several excerpts taken from Langston Hughes's "The Simple Stories;" ADDITIONAL MATERIAL: Irvin S. Bauer; CONCEIVED BY: Ronald "Smokey" Stevens & Jaye Stewart; DIRECTORS: Ronald "Smokey" Stevens & Leslie Dockery; CHOREOGRAPHER: Leslie Dockery; SETS: Larry W. Brown; COSTUMES: Michele Reisch; LIGHTING: Jon Kusner; SOUND: Shabach Audio; MUSICAL DIRECTOR/ARRANGEMENTS: David Alan Bunn; PRESS: The Jacksina Company; GENERAL MANAGEMENT: Theatre Management Associates; STAGE MANAGER: Femi S. Heggie. *Cast:* SMOKEY STEVENS: Ronald "Smokey" Stevens; JAYE STEWART: Rudy Roberson; BERTHA MAE LITTLE: Sandra Reaves-Phillips. **Standbys**: Jaye/Smokey: Jackie Jay Patterson; Bertha Mae: Alyson Williams. *Act I: Overture* "Rollin' on the T.O.B.A." (m/l: Mr. Stevens, Miss Reaves-Phillips, Chapman Roberts, Benny Key, David Alan Bunn) (Smokey, Jaye, Bertha Mae); *Scene 1* On the train: Toast to Harlem (by Langston Hughes) (Jaye & Smokey); *Scene 2* Monogram Theatre: "Bill

Robinson Walk" (m/: Bill "Bojangles" Robinson) (Smokey), Evolution (by Flournoy Miller & Aubrey Lyles)/"Ugly Chile" (m: Clarence Williams; l: Johnny Mercer) (Jaye & Smokey); *Scene 3* Bertha's phone call: "Travelin' Blues" (m/l: Mr. Stevens & Miss Reaves-Phillips) (Bertha Mae); *Scene 4* Dressing room: Lincoln West (by Gwendolyn Brooks)/The Liar (Staggolee) (by Terrence Cooper) (Jaye & Smokey); *Scene 5* Royal Theatre: "(Saturday Night) Fish Fry" (m/l: Ellis Walsh & Louis Jordan) (Jaye & Smokey); *Scene 6* Bertha's letter/On the train: "St. Louis Blues" (m/l: W.C. Handy) (Bertha Mae); *Scene 7* Booker T. Theatre: "The Poker Game" [sketch by Bert Williams, set to the song "Black and Tan Fantasy" (m: Duke Ellington) (Smokey)], "Nobody" (m/l: Bert Williams) (Smokey), "Huggin' and Chalkin'" (m/l: Kermit Goell & Clancy Hayes) (Jaye), "Sexy Blues"/"You've Taken My Blues and Gone" (m/l: Miss Reaves-Phillips, Chapman Roberts and Mr. Stevens. Sketch by Langston Hughes) (Bertha Mae), The Car Crash and Broken Dialog (by Flournoy Miller & Aubrey Lyles) (Jaye & Smokey), Conversationalization (by Flournoy Miller & Aubrey Lyles) (Jaye & Smokey), "Let the Good Times Roll" (m/l: Sam Theard & Fleecie Moore) (Smokey, Jaye, Bertha Mae). *Act II: Entr'acte* Piano Interlude (David Alan Bunn); *Scene 1* Regal Theatre: "(New Orleans) Hop Scop Blues" (m: Clarence Williams) (Smokey), The Chess Game [sketch set to "Funeral March of the Marionettes" m: Charles Gounod)] (Jaye & Smokey); *Scene 2* Bertha's show/The Regal Theatre: "Take Me as I Am" (by Miss Reaves-Phillips) (Bertha Mae), "One Hour Mama" (m/l: Porter Grainger) (Bertha Mae), "Million Dollar Secret" (m/l: Helen Humes & Jules Bihari) (Bertha Mae), Freddie and Flo (by Butterbeans & Suzie) (Bertha Mae & Jaye), "A Good Man is Hard to Find" (m/l: Eddie Green) (Bertha Mae), "Take Me as I Am" (reprise) (Bertha Mae); *Scene 3* On the train: Simple on Integration (by Langston Hughes) (Jaye & Smokey), Soul Food (by Langston Hughes) (Jaye, Smokey, Bertha Mae); *Scene 4* On the train: Banquet in Honor (by Langston Hughes) (Jaye & Smokey), I'm Still Here (by Langston Hughes)/Trouble in Mind (by Richard Jones) (Jaye, Smokey, Bertha Mae), "Rollin' on the T.O.B.A." (reprise) (Smokey, Jaye, Bertha Mae).

Broadway reviews were not good.

After Broadway. EL PORTAL CENTER FOR THE ARTS, Los Angeles, 3/17/00. This was the show's West Coast premiere. *Cast*: BERTHA MAE: Sandra Reaves-Phillips; STEVENS: Ronald "Smokey" Stevens; STEWART: Ted Levy.

591. *Romance/Romance*

Also known as *Romance Romance*, and *Romance-Romance*. Billed as "two new musicals." An evening of two musical one-act meditations on love.

Before Broadway. It opened Off Broadway at the ACTORS OUTLET, 10/30/87. 19 previews. 37 PERFORMANCES. Then it went to Broadway.

The Broadway Run. HELEN HAYES THEATRE, 5/1/88–1/15/89. 10 previews from 4/20/88. 297 PERFORMANCES. PRESENTED BY Dasha Epstein, Harve Brosten, and Jay S. Bulmash, in association with George Krynicki & Marvin A. Krauss; MUSIC: Keith Herrmann; LYRICS/BOOK/DIRECTOR: Barry Harman; BASED ON: 1/ the short story *The Little Comedy*, by Arthur Schnitzler, as translated by George Edward Reynolds, and 2/ the play *Summer Share*, translated by Max Gulack from the original play *Pain de menage*, by Jules Renard; CHOREOGRAPHER: Pamela Sousa; SETS: Steven Rubin; COSTUMES: Steven Jones; LIGHTING: Craig Miller; SOUND: Peter Fitzgerald; MUSICAL DIRECTOR: Kathy Sommer; ORCHESTRATIONS: Michael Starobin; ADDITIONAL ORCHESTRATIONS: Daniel Troob & Joe Gianono; VOCAL & DANCE MUSIC ARRANGEMENTS: Keith Herrmann & Kathy Sommer; CAST RECORDING on MCA Classics; PRESS: Henry M. Luhrman Associates; CASTING: Leonard Finger Associates; GENERAL MANAGERS: Marvin A. Krauss, Gary Gunas, Joey Parnes; COMPANY MANAGER: Steven Suskin; PRODUCTION STAGE MANAGER: James A. Pentecost; STAGE MANAGER: Joseph Onorato. *Act I: The Little Comedy*: Set in Vienna, at the turn of the 20th century. A bored woman and man about town pretend to belong to the working class in order to seek romance there. They meet and are fooled by each other's disguises. *Cast*: ALFRED VON WILMERS: Scott Bakula (1) ☆, *Sal Viviano, Barry Williams* (from 10/4/88); JOSEFINE WENINGER: Alison Fraser (2) ☆; "HIM:" Robert Hoshour (4); "HER:" Deborah Graham (3). "The Little Comedy" (Alfred & Josefine), "Goodbye, Emil" (Josefine), "It's Not Too Late" (Alfred & Josefine), "Great News" (Alfred & Josefine), "Oh, What a Performance!" (Alfred & Josefine), "I'll Always Remember the Song" (Alfred & Josefine), "Happy, Happy, Happy" (Alfred), "Women of Vienna" (Alfred), "Yes, It's Love" (Josefine), "A Rustic Country Inn" (Alfred & Josefine), "The Night it Had to End" (Josefine), Finale: "The Little Comedy" (reprise) (Alfred & Josefine). *Act II*: *Summer Share*: Set in the Hamptons during August of the current year. Two married couples share a summer cottage and move toward cross-marital sex, despite resolutions to avoid this. *Cast*: LENNY: Robert Hoshour (4); BARB: Deborah Graham (3); SAM: Scott Bakula (1) ☆, *Sal Viviano, Barry Williams* (from 10/4/88); MONICA: Alison Fraser (2) ☆. "Summer Share" (Company), "Think of the Odds" (Barb & Lenny), "It's Not Too Late" (reprise) (Sam & Monica), "Plans A & B" (Monica & Lenny), "Let's Not Talk About It" (Sam & Barb), "So Glad I Married Her" (Company), "Small Craft Warnings" (Barb & Lenny), "How Did I End up Here?" (Monica), "Words He Doesn't Say" (Sam), "My Love for You" (Lenny & Barb), "Moonlight Passing Through a Window" (Sam), "Now" (Monica), "Romantic Notions" (Sam, Barb, Lenny, Monica), "Romance! Romance!" (Company). *Standbys*: Jana Robbins & Sal Viviano. *Musicians*: KEYBOARDS: Kathy Sommer; BASS: Tony Coniff; DRUMS/PERCUSSION: Ron Tierno; ALTO SAX/SOPRANO SAX/PICCOLO: Scott Schachter; CLARINET/FLUTE: Scott Schachter & Rick Heckman; TENOR SAX/OBOE/ENGLISH HORN: Rick Heckman; TRUMPET/PICCOLO TRUMPET: Hollis Burridge; SYNTHESIZER: Neal Kirkwood.

Reviews were divided, and mixed. This show made a star out of Alison Fraser. It received Tony nominations for musical, score, book, and for Alison Fraser and Scott Bakula.

After Broadway. GIELGUD THEATRE, London, 3/4/97–4/19/97. Previews from 2/27/97. PRESENTED BY Pat Gilgallon & Roger Lawrence; DIRECTOR: Steven Dexter. *Cast:* JOSEPHINE/MONICA: Caroline O'Connor; ALFRED/SAM: Mark Adams; HER/BARB: Linzi Hateley; HIM/LENNY: Michael Cantwell.

592. *The Rothschilds*

About some of the Rothschild family, between 1772 and 1818. Act I is about Mayer raising his five boys to become rich businessmen. Meyer is kept alive longer than he was alive in real life. Act II revolves around the romance of Nathan and Hannah.

Before Broadway. In 1963 producer Hilly Elkins hired Wolf Mankowitz to adapt Frederic Morton's best selling book about the great European banking family, and offered the score to Jerry Bock and Sheldon Harnick, who were then working on *Fiddler on the Roof*. Mr. Mankowitz's libretto was discarded, then four other writers had a go over the years (Sidney Michaels being one of them), and finally it was a combination of Sherman Yellen's libretto and Bock & Harnick's eventual availability that brought the show together. It tried out in Detroit, where Michael Kidd replaced Derek Goldby as director and Eliot Feld as choreographer. Mr. Feld had already replaced Grover Dale as choreographer. Leila Martin replaced Joan Hackett in the cast. This was Bock & Harnick's seventh and last musical together (they quarreled during this production).

The Broadway Run. LUNT—FONTANNE THEATRE, 10/19/70–1/2/72. 13 previews from 10/7/70. 507 PERFORMANCES. The Hillard Elkins production, PRESENTED BY Lester Osterman; MUSIC: Jerry Bock; LYRICS: Sheldon Harnick; BOOK: Sherman Yellen (book doctored by William Gibson & Joseph Stein); BASED ON the 1962 biography of the same name by Frederic Morton; DIRECTOR/CHOREOGRAPHER: Michael Kidd; SETS/COSTUMES: John Bury; SET & COSTUME SUPERVISOR: Fred Voelpel; LIGHTING: Richard Pilbrow; SOUND: Ray Yowell; MUSICAL DIRECTOR/VOCAL ARRANGEMENTS: Milton Greene; ORCHESTRATIONS: Don Walker; DANCE MUSIC ARRANGEMENTS: Clay Fullum; CAST RECORDING on Columbia; PRESS: Samuel J. Friedman, Rod Jacobsen, Louise Weiner Ment; CASTING: Linda Otto; PRODUCTION ASSISTANTS:

Theodore Chapin & Nicholas Gill; GENERAL MANAGER: Emanuel Azenberg; COMPANY MANAGER: Edmonstone Thompson Jr.; PRODUCTION STAGE MANAGER: Charles Gray; STAGE MANAGER: John Actman; ASSISTANT STAGE MANAGER: F. Mitchell Dana. *Cast:* PRINCE WILLIAM OF HESSE: Keene Curtis, *Reid Shelton* (from 7/12/71); GUARD: Roger Hamilton; MAYER ROTHSCHILD: Hal Linden (5) ☆, *Howard Honig* (during Mr. Linden's absence, 8/17/71); 1ST URCHIN: Michael Maitland; 2ND URCHIN: Kim Michels; 3RD URCHIN: Robby Benson; GUTELE (MAMA) ROTHSCHILD: Leila Martin (2) ☆; 1ST VENDOR: Thomas Trelfa; 2ND VENDOR: Kenneth Bridges; 3RD VENDOR: Jon Peck; GENERAL: Paul Tracey; BUDURUS: Leo Leyden (6); 1ST BANKER: Elliott Savage; 2ND BANKER: Carl Nicholas; YOUNG AMSHEL ROTHSCHILD: Lee Franklin; YOUNG SOLOMON ROTHSCHILD: Robby Benson; YOUNG NATHAN ROTHSCHILD: Michael Maitland; YOUNG JACOB ROTHSCHILD: Mitchell Spera, *Paris Themmen*; BLUM: Howard Honig; MRS. KAUFMAN: Nina Dova; MRS. SEGAL: Peggy Cooper; PEASANT: Christopher Chadman; AMSHEL ROTHSCHILD: Timothy Jerome (8), *Sidney Ben-Ali* (from 4/20/71); SOLOMON ROTHSCHILD: David Garfield (9); JACOB ROTHSCHILD: Chris Sarandon (7), *David Rounds*; NATHAN ROTHSCHILD: Paul Hecht (1) ☆, *Timothy Jerome* (from 6/7/71); KALMAN ROTHSCHILD: Allan Gruet (10); JOSEPH FOUCHE: Keene Curtis (3) ☆, *Reid Shelton* (from 7/12/71); HERRIES: Keene Curtis (3) ☆, *Reid Shelton* (from 7/12/71); SKEPTIC: Paul Tracey; BANKER: Roger Hamilton; HANNAH COHEN: Jill Clayburgh (4) ☆, *Caroline McWilliams* (from 2/28/71), *Prairie Dern* (8/71–10/18/71), *Caroline McWilliams*; PRINCE METTERNICH: Keene Curtis (3) ☆, *Reid Shelton* (from 7/12/71); MEMBERS OF THE HESSIAN COURT/PEOPLE OF THE FRANKFURT GHETTO/MEMBERS OF AUSTRIAN COURT/GRENADIERS/COURIERS/CROWNED HEADS OF EUROPE/BANKER-BROKERS: Rick Atwell, Steve Boockvor, Kenneth Bridges, Henry Brunjes, Christopher Chadman, Peggy Cooper, Patrick Cummings, Nina Dova, Vicki Frederick, Penny Guerard, Roger Hamilton, Ann Hodges, Howard Honig, Del Lewis, John Mineo, Carl Nicholas, Jon Peck, Ted Pejovich, Denise Pence, Jean Richards, Elliott Savage, Wilfred Schuman, Lani Sundsten, Paul Tracey, Thomas Trelfa. *Understudies*: Mayer: Howard Honig; Nathan: Chris Sarandon; Gutele: Nina Dova; Fouche/Herries/Metternich: Roger Hamilton; Hannah: Jean Richards; Budurus: Elliott Savage; Solomon/Amshel: Del Lewis; Jacob: Ted Pejovich; Kalman: John Mineo; Young Rothschilds: Kim Michels; Urchins: Lee Franklin. *Act I*: *Prologue*: 1772; Hesse: "Pleasure and Privilege" (Prince William & Ensemble); *Scene 1* 1772; The gate of the Frankfurt ghetto; *Scene 2* 1772; The Rothschild shop, Frankfurt ghetto: "One Room" (Mayer & Mama); *Scene 3* 1773; The Frankfurt Fair: "He Tossed a Coin" (Mayer, Vendors, Ensemble); *Scene 4* 1773; The study of Prince William of Hesse; *Scene 5* 1788; The Rothschild shop: "Sons" (Mayer, Mama, Young Amshel, Young Solomon, Young Nathan, Young Jacob); *Scene 6* 1788; The Rothschild shop; *Scene 7* 1804; The Rothschild shop: "Everything" (Nathan, Mama, Solomon, Kalman, Amshel, Jacob); *Scene 8* 1804; Prince William's study: "Rothschild and Sons" (Mayer, Nathan, Solomon, Kalman, Amshel, Jacob); *Scene 9* 1804; The Rothschild shop: "Allons" (Fouche & Male Ensemble), "Rothschild and Sons" (reprise) (Mayer, Nathan, Solomon, Kalman, Amshel, Jacob), Finale Act I: "Sons" (reprise) (Mama & Mayer). *Act II*: *Scene 1* 1805; The London Royal Stock Exchange: Hymn: "Give England Strength" ("The British Free Enterprise Auction") (Herries & Male Ensemble), "This Amazing London Town" (Nathan); *Scene 2* 1806; The London Royal Stock Exchange: "They Say" (Skeptic & Male Ensemble), "I'm in Love! I'm in Love!" (Nathan); *Scene 3* 1806–1811; The garden of Hannah Cohen, London: "I'm in Love! I'm in Love! (reprise) (Hannah); *Scene 4* 1812; The Rothschild home: "In My Own Lifetime" (Mayer); *Scene 5* 1818; the Ballroom at Aix-la-Chapelle: "Have You Ever Seen a Prettier Little Congress?" (Metternich), "Stability" (Metternich & Ensemble); *Scene 6* 1818; The Rothschild home; *Scene 7* 1818; Various European capitals: "Bonds" (Nathan, Solomon, Kalman, Amshel, Jacob, Metternich, Ensemble); *Scene 8* 1818; The Rothschild home; *Scene 9* Finale: Finale "The Will" (Mayer).

Broadway reviews were generally not good. The show returned only 25 percent of its original investment. Hal Linden won a Tony, and the show was also nominated for musical, score, lyrics, book, direction of a musical, choreography, sets, and for Keene Curtis.

After Broadway. TOUR. Opened on 5/9/72, at the Curran Theatre,

San Francisco. *Cast*: MAYER: Hal Linden; NATHAN: C. David Colson; GUTELE: Carol Fox Prescott; PRINCE/FOUCHE/HERRIES/METTERNICH: Reid Shelton; HANNAH: Sandra Thornton.

AMERICAN JEWISH THEATRE, 2/25/90–4/8/90. Previews from 2/10/90. 56 PERFORMANCES. This production got better reviews than the original; it moved to CIRCLE IN THE SQUARE DOWNTOWN, for a commercial Off Broadway run, 4/27/90–3/24/91. 379 PERFORMANCES—making a total of 435 PERFORMANCES. PRESENTED BY Jeffrey Ash & Susan Quint Gallin, in association with Tommy Valando & the American Jewish Theatre. Lonny Price, one of the children in the original tour, directed and scaled the show down. The cast was reduced from 40 to 16, with all actors doubling and tripling roles. ASSISTANT DIRECTOR: Daisy Prince; CHOREOGRAPHER: Michael Arnold; MUSICAL DIRECTOR: Grant Sturiale; GENERAL MANAGEMENT after transfer: George Elmer Productions. *Cast*: MAYER: Mike Burstyn; KALMAN: Joel Malina; NATHAN: Bob Cuccioli, *John Loprieno* (from 12/19/90); BUDURUS: Ted Forlow, *David Wasson* (upon transfer), *Christopher Coucill*; JACOB: Nick Corley; MRS. SEGAL: Judith Thiergaard. **Understudy**: Budurus: David Wasson (until the transfer).

593. *Roza*

Roza is an aging, Polish-Jewish former prostitute and concentration camp survivor, who earns her living raising the children of her colleagues in the Parisian immigrant quarter of Belville in 1970. Belleville then was still poor and relatively "undiscovered" by the French. In the 1980s it began to be gentrified. The story revolves around her close relationship with one of the boys, a young Arab named Momo, who is looking for his real parents. Lola is a transsexual.

Before Broadway. Gilbert Becaud, the French singer, after seeing the movie *Madame Rosa*, wanted to do a musical of it. The problem about securing the rights was that Romain Gary had used a pseudonym (the name of a real person, as it turned out) to write the book, and that involved legal problems. Eventually these problems were resolved, and M. Becaud wrote his musical and approached Hal Prince to direct. Paris was selected as the place to premiere it. When that fell through in 1981, a London theatre, the Adelphi, was chosen, and the show was to open there on 6/26/84. Then financing fell through just days before rehearsals were to begin, and London was canceled. Hal Prince then selected Baltimore, where it duly ran, at the CENTER STAGE THEATRE, 12/12/86–1/87. It was well-received by critics and audiences, and set a new Center Stage box-office record. It had the same basic credits as for the subsequent Broadway run, except SOUND: Lawrence R. Smith. *Cast*: HAMIL: Neal Ben-Ari; MME BOUAFFA: Michelle Mais; JASMINE: Yamil Borges; DR. KATZ: Jerry Matz; MME KATZ: Mary Lou Rosato; N'DA AMADEE: Ira Hawkins; SALIMA: Monique Cintron; MICHEL: Max Barabas; BANANIA: Mandla Msomi; YOUNG MOMO: Brian Noodt; MAX: Al DeCristo; MADAME ROZA: Georgia Brown; LOLA: Bob Gunton; YOUNG MOISE: Stephen Rosenberg; MOMO: Alex Paez; MOISE: Manny Jacobs; YUSSEF KADIR: Neal Ben-Ari. From there it went to the Mark Taper Forum, Los Angeles, where Hal Prince added a new opening number, some new scenes, and some new lyrics. It was, again, well-received, and extended its run. At this point the Producers Circle persuaded the Shubert Organization to come on board as co-producers, and Broadway's Royale Theatre was booked for 8/27/87. At this very moment Mr. Prince was just getting another show ready for Broadway—*Phantom of the Opera*, as well as rehearsing the revival of *Cabaret*. Opening date for *Roza* was put back.

The Broadway Run. ROYALE THEATRE, 10/1/87–10/11/87. 20 previews from 9/14/87. 12 PERFORMANCES. PRESENTED BY The Producer Circle Company (Mary Lea Johnson, Martin Richards, Sam Crothers) & The Shubert Organization, by arrangement with Les Editions Musicales et Artistiques (EMA); MUSIC: Gilbert Becaud; LYRICS/BOOK: Julian More; BASED ON the 1974 novel *La vie devant soi*, by Romain Gary, and on the Oscar-winning movie made from it, *Madame Rosa* (1977), starring Simone Signoret; DIRECTOR: Harold Prince; CHOREOGRAPHER: Patricia Birch; SETS: Alexander Okun; COSTUMES: Florence Klotz; LIGHTING: Ken Billington; SOUND: Otts Munderloh; MUSICAL DIREC-

TOR/VOCAL & DANCE MUSIC ARRANGEMENTS: Louis St. Louis; ORCHESTRATIONS: Michael Gibson; PRESS: Mary Bryant & David Musselman; EXECUTIVE PRODUCER: Ruth Mitchell; GENERAL MANAGEMENT: Gatchell & Neufeld; COMPANY MANAGER: Michael Gill; PRODUCTION STAGE MANAGER: Beverley Randolph; STAGE MANAGER: Michael J. Frank; ASSISTANT STAGE MANAGER: Anny De Gange. *Cast*: MADAME ROZA: Georgia Brown (1) ☆; MAX: Al DeCristo; RAOUL: Ira Hawkins; MADAME BOUAFFA: Michelle Mais; JASMINE: Yamil Borges; HAMIL: Neal Ben-Ari; DOCTOR KATZ: Jerry Matz; MADAME KATZ: Marcia Lewis; MICHEL: David Shoichi Chan; BANANIA: Mandla Msomi; SALIMA: Monique Cintron; YOUNG MOMO: Max Loving; LOLA: Bob Gunton (2); YOUNG MOISE: Stephen Rosenberg; WOMAN: Thuli Dumakude; MAN: Richard Frisch; MOISE: Joey McKneely; MOMO: Alex Paez; YUSSEF KADIR: Neal Ben-Ari. **Standbys**: Roza: Chevi Colton; Lola: Bob Frisch. **Understudies**: Bouaffa: Thuli Dumakude; Max/Katz: Richard Frisch; Hamil/Yussef: Richard Frisch; Young Momo/Young Moise: Francisco Paler-Large; Michel/Banania: Francisco Paler-Large; Woman/Salima/Jasmine: Anny De Gange; Momo/Moise: Raymond del Barrio. **Orchestra**: KEYBOARDS: Louis St. Louis; SYNTHESIZERS: Lawrence Yurman & Ted Sperling; ACCORDION: Lawrence Yurman; DRUMS/ELECTRIC PERCUSSION: Luther Rix; BASS: Stu Woods; GUITARS/BANJO: Chuck D'Aloia; PERCUSSION: Jamey Haddad & Joe Passaro; HADGINI DRUMS/DRUM MACHINE/SEQUENCING: Jamey Haddad; MALLETS: Joe Passaro; REEDS: Bill Drewes & Ted Nash; TROMBONE: Earl McIntyre. *Act I*: 1970: "Happiness" (Roza), "Max's Visit" (Max & Roza), "Different" (Lola, Roza, Mme Katz, Bouaffa, Jasmine), "Is Me" (Young Momo, Young Moise, Salima, Michel, Banania, Mme Bouaffa, Jasmine), "Get the Lady Dressed" (Roza, Lola, Young Momo, Young Moise, Salima, Michel, Banania), "Hamil's Birthday" (Company), "Bravo, Bravo" (Roza), "Moon Like a Silver Window" (Young Momo, Momo, Company). *Act II*: 1974: "Merci" (Momo & Moise), "House in Algiers" (Roza), "Yussef's Visit" (Yussef, Roza, Momo, Moise, Lola), "Life is Ahead of Me" (Momo), "Sweet 17" (Bouaffa, Jasmine, Momo, Moise), "Lola's Ceremony" (Lola & Company), "Don't Make Me Laugh" (Roza & Lola), "Live a Little" (Roza), Finale (Company).

Although preview audiences enjoyed the show, Broadway critics didn't. Georgia Brown got raves, however. This was the only Broadway musical directed by Hal Prince that was not recorded.

594. *Rugantino*

An imported "Roman musical spectacle," set in Rome in 1830, during the reign of Pope Pius VIII. A likable rogue makes a wager that he can seduce the wife of one of Rome's leading citizens; he succeeds but he is guillotined for it. Sung in Italian, with English sub-titles projected onto a screen.

The Broadway Run. MARK HELLINGER THEATRE, 2/6/64–2/29/64. 1 preview on 2/5/64. 28 PERFORMANCES. PRESENTED BY Alexander H. Cohen & Jack Hylton; MUSIC: Armando Trovaioli; LYRICS/DIRECTORS: Pietro Garinei & Sandro Giovannini; ENGLISH LYRICS: Edward Eager; BOOK: Garinei & Giovannini [as this writing partnership was known], in collaboration with Festa Campanile & Massimo Franciosa; SUBTITLES (i.e. the English version of the book): Alfred Drake; TITLE CONSULTANT: Herman G. Weinberg; TITLE CO-ORDINATOR: Jack Harrold; CHOREOGRAPHER: Dania Krupska; SET SUPERVISOR: Eldon Elder; SETS/COSTUMES: Giulio Coltellacci; TECHNICAL DIRECTOR: Ralph Alswang; LIGHTING: Vannio Vanni; MUSICAL DIRECTOR: Anton Coppola; CAST RECORDING on Warner Brothers; PRESS: David P. Rothenberg, Michael Alpert, Romano Camilli; GENERAL MANAGER: Roy A. Somlyo; COMPANY MANAGER: Gino Giglio & Carlo Saviotti; STAGE MANAGERS: Harry Young & Jack Harrold, Gian Pace & Carlo Maresti. *Cast*: RUGANTINO: Nino Manfredi (1); MARIOTTO: Goffredo Spinedi; RUBASTRACCI: Giuseppe Pennese; STRAPPALENZOLA: Fernando Martino; BROTHER TAPPETTO: Lino Benedetti; BELLACHIOMA: Toni Ventura; THE BRIGADIER: Willy Colombini; CHIEF BANDIT: Armando Silverini; ROSETTA: Ornella Vanoni (2); GNECCO, ROSETTA'S HUSBAND: Renzo Palmer; MASTRO TITTA: Aldo Fabrizi (3); BOJETTO, HIS SON: Carlo Delle Piane; DONNA MARTA PARITELLI: Franca Tamantini; DON NICOLO

PARITELLI: Toni Ucci; EUSEBIA: Bice Valori; THE BARBER: Giorgio Zaffaroni; THORWALDSEN, THE SCULPTOR: Cesare Gelli; DON FULGENZIO: Giorgio Fabretti; THE TROUBADOUR/THE SERENADER/CALLASCIONE: Nunzio Gallo; THE LOVER: Marcello Serrallonga; THE GOAT KEEPER: Luciano Bonanni; OLD LADY OF THE CATS: Simona Sorlisi; CARDINAL SEVERINI: Gino Mucci; A GENTLEMAN: Angelo Pericet; TWO GENDARMES: Renato Ghigi & Angelo Michelotti; DANCERS & SINGERS: Lino Benedetti, Luciano Bernardi, Maurizia Camilli, Willy Colombini, Yvonne De Vintar, Franco Di Toro, Angelo Infanti, Brigitte Kirfel, Fernando Martino, Gabriella Panenti, Giuseppe Pennese, Carla Russo, Gina Sampieri, Barbara Schaub, Marcello Serrallonga, Goffredo Spinedi, Josephine Spinedi, Toni Ventura, Lida Vianello, Gabriele Villa, Giorgio Zaffaroni, Letti Zaffaroni, Renata Zamengo, Gianna Zorini; CHORUS OF NORA ORLANDI: Margherita Brancucci, Raffaella Caratelli, Armando Silverini, Ercole Vulpiani. *Understudies*: Rugantino: Toni Ucci; Rosetta: Franca Tamantini; Titta: Renzo Palmer; Eusebia: Angela Luce; Gnecco: Goffredo Spinedi; Paritelli: Cesare Gelli; Thorwaldsen: Gino Mucci; Marta: Simona Sorlisi; Mariotto: Angelo Infanti; Troubadour: Giorgio Zaffaroni. *Act I*: *Scene 1* The square before Mastro Titta's tavern; *Scene 2* Rosetta's bedroom; *Scene 3* A room in the Paritelli Palace; *Scene 4* The square; *Scene 5* Rosetta's bedroom; *Scene 6* The square; *Scene 7* Outside the Paritelli Palace; *Scene 8* The docks; *Scene 9* The dining hall of the Paritelli Palace; *Scene 10* The street-barber's; *Scene 11* The studio of the sculptor Thorwaldsen; *Scene 12* The parish church; *Scene 13* The square; *Scene 14* San Michele Prison; *Scene 15* The square on Lantern Night; *Scene 16* Rosetta's bedroom. *Act II*: *Scene 1* A corner of Campo Vaccino; *Scene 2* The square before the Church of San Pasquale; *Scene 3* A corner of the forum frequented by the hungry stray cats of Rome; *Scene 4* The square; *Scene 5* The churchyard; *Scene 6* Mastro Titta's cellar; *Scene 7* San Michele Prison; *Scene 8* A square in Rome at dawn. *Act I*: "The Game of Morra" (La morra) (The Men), "Rugantino in the Stocks" (La berlina) (Rugantino's "Friends"), "A House is Not the Same without a Woman" (E bello ave'na donna dentro casa) (Mastro Titta), "Nothing to Do" (Ballata di Rugantino) (Rugantino & The Romans), "Just Look!" (Anvedi si che paciocca) (Rosetta, Callascione, The Boys), "The Saltarello" (Eusebia, Mastro Titta, Ensemble), "Tirrallallera" (The Serenader), "The Headsman and I" (Eusebia), "Nothing to Do" (reprise) (Rugantino), "Ciumachella" (Ciumachella de Trastevere) (The Serenader), "Lantern Night" (Lantern Vendor & Ensemble), "(The Lights of) Roma" (Roma nun fa la stupida stasera) (Rugantino, Rosetta, Eusebia, Mastro Titta, Ensemble). *Act II*: "Ciumachella" (reprise) (Ensemble), "I'm Happy" (Tira a Campa) (Rugantino), "Just Stay Alive" (Sempre boia e) (Mastro Titta & Ensemble), "San Pasquale" (Eusebia & Spinsters), "Passatella" (The Drinking Game) (Callascione, Agnolotto, Mariotto, Rugantino, The Boys), "It's Quick and Easy" ('na botta e via) (Rosetta & The Boys), "Dance of the Candle Killers" (Ensemble), "Boy and Man" (E l'omo mio) (Rosetta), Finale (Eusebia, Rosetta, Mastro Titta, Rugantino).

Broadway reviews were generally bad.

After Broadway. In the mid–1970s a very successful revival made an international tour.

TEATRO SISTINA, Rome, 12/22/98–4/23/99. Returned 12/21/99–3/00. DIRECTOR: Pietro Garinei; CHOREOGRAPHER: Gino Landi. There was a cast recording. There was also talk of a Broadway transfer (Mr. Garinei was talking to Alex Cohen). *Cast*: ROSETTA: Sabrina Ferilli; RUGANTINO: Valerio Mastandrea.

595. *Rumple*

The creator of an immensely popular American comic strip can no longer draw after a plane crash. His leading characters, Rumple and Anna, come to life to get him to revive his career, otherwise they will be sent to Oblivia, the place for obsolete comic strip characters.

Before Broadway. This was Elliott Gould's Broadway debut. The show tried out in Boston, where the number "General Consensus of Opinion" was cut.

The Broadway Run. ALVIN THEATRE, 11/6/57–12/14/57. 45 PER-FORMANCES. PRESENTED BY Paula Stone & Mike Sloan; MUSIC: Ernest G. Schweikert; LYRICS: Frank Reardon; BOOK: Irving Phillips; BASED ON the play *Caricature*; CREATOR OF ORIGINAL CARICATURES OF RUMPLE: Mort Drucker; DIRECTOR: Jack Donohue; CHOREOGRAPHER: Bob Hamilton; SETS/LIGHTING: George Jenkins; COSTUMES: Alvin Colt; MUSICAL DIRECTOR: Frederick Dvonch; ORCHESTRATIONS: Ted Royal; DANCE MUSIC ARRANGEMENTS: Robert Atwood; PRESS: Bill Doll, Samuel J. Friedman, Maurice J. Turet, Shirley Herz; GENERAL MANAGER: Robert Rapport; PRODUCTION STAGE MANAGER: Edward Padula; STAGE MANAGERS: Chet O'Brien & Clayton Coots. *Cast:* THE CHIEF OF OBLIVIA: Clayton Coots; JUDY MARLOWE: Lois O'Brien; GINNY: Ginny Perlowin; JUDY MARLOWE'S FRIENDS: Bonnie West, Janyce Wagner, Sally Wile, Sari Clymas; NELSON CRANDAL: Stephen Douglass (3); KATE DREW, THE WRITER: Gretchen Wyler (2); RUMPLE: Eddie Foy, Jr. (1); ANNA: Barbara Perry (4); J.B. CONWAY: Milo Boulton; THE PHOTOGRAPHERS: Elliott Gould & Larry Stevens; BRANNIGAN: Ken Harvey; BARNEY: Jackie Warner; DR. WELLINGTON WINSLOW: Jerome Cowan; NURSE: Sari Clymas; THE WEIRD ONES: Elliott Gould, Doris Lorenz, Pat White, Lila Popper, Gail Kuhr, William Milie; THE DISSENTER: George Martin; THE MATCH BOX: Claire Gunderman; HE WHO GETS SLAPPED: Elliott Gould; REPORTER: Eddie Weston; THE POWDER ROOM: Pat White; THE UNRAVELED: Bonnie West; GIRLS ON A BENCH: Doris Lorenz & Lila Popper; LT MALLORY: Ken Harvey; THE VOICE OF OBLIVIA: Ken Harvey; ENSEMBLE: Bill Carter, Sari Clymas, Elliott Gould, Claire Gunderman, Larry Howard, Gail Kuhr, Doris Lorenz, George Martin, William Milie, Roy Palmer, Lila Popper, Larry Stevens, Janyce Wagner, Bonnie West, Eddie Weston, Pat White, Sally Wile. *Understudies*: Rumple: Jackie Warner; Kate: Bonnie West; Nelson/Winslow: Ken Harvey; Judy: Ginny Perlowin; Anna: Sally Wile. *Act I*: *Prologue* Somewhere in Oblivia; *Scene 1* Nelson Crandal's New York studio apartment; evening: "It's You for Me" (Nelson & Judy), "In Times Like These" (Rumple & Anna); *Scene 2* Barney's Bar; later that night: "Red Letter Day" (Kate, Ensemble, Barney), "The First Time I Spoke of You" (Nelson & Judy); *Scene 3* Nelson's apartment; next morning: "Oblivia" (Rumple, Anna, Cartoon Characters, Holiday Girls), "Peculiar State of Affairs" (Rumple & Kate); *Scene 4* Central Park; later that morning: "How Do You Say Goodbye?" (Judy); *Scene 5* Nelson's apartment; that night: "Gentlemen of the Press" (Nelson, Cartoon Characters, Holiday Girls). *Act II*: *Scene 1* Office of Dr. Winslow, psychiatrist; afternoon: "To Adjust is a Must" (Winslow & Weird Ones), "Coax Me" (Kate); *Scene 2* Barney's Bar; later that afternoon: "How Do You Say Goodbye?" (reprise) (Nelson), "All Dressed Up" (Kate & Ensemble); *Scene 3* Nelson's apartment; early evening: "In Times Like These" (reprise) (Kate & Winslow), "Peculiar State of Affairs" (reprise) (Anna); *Scene 4* Central Park; that night: "Wish" (Rumple); *Scene 5* Nelson's apartment; later that night: Finale (Entire Company).

Reviews were divided. There was a rave, a pan, and several in between. Eddie Foy was nominated for a Tony.

596. *Runaways*

A loosely-structured musical, a musical theatre piece. Or, in the words of Elizabeth Swados, "a collage around the profound effects of deteriorating families." Set in the present, on a playground. Extensively researched and partially improvised, with several actual runaways in the cast, aged 11–25. Only 5 of the 19 actors had professional acting experience.

Before Broadway. In 5/77 Elizabeth Swados approached Joe Papp, head of the New York Shakespeare Festival, with an idea about runaway children. With his financial support she researched the subject, and wrote the script. Originally produced by the Festival, at the Public's CABARET THEATRE, 3/9/78–4/29/78. 14 previews from 2/21/78. 62 PACKED PERFORMANCES.

The Broadway Run. PLYMOUTH THEATRE, 5/13/78–12/31/78. 191 PERFORMANCES. The New York Shakespeare Festival production, PRESENTED BY Joseph Papp; MUSIC/LYRICS/BOOK/DIRECTOR: Elizabeth Swados; SETS: Douglas W. Schmidt & Woods Mackintosh; COSTUMES: Hilary Rosenfeld; LIGHTING: Jennifer Tipton; SOUND: Bill Dreisbach; ARRANGE-

MENTS: improvised by the musicians; HORN ARRANGEMENTS: Larry Morton; CAST RECORDING on Columbia; PRESS: Merle Debuskey & Richard Kornberg; ENGLISH—SPANISH TRANSLATIONS: Josie de Guzman; GENERAL MANAGER: Robert Kamlot; COMPANY MANAGERS: Bob MacDonald & Roger Gindi; PRODUCTION STAGE MANAGER: Gregory Meeh; STAGE MANAGER: Peter Glazer; ASSISTANT STAGE MANAGER: Patricia Morinelli. *Cast:* HUBBELL: Bruce Hlibok [a deaf boy in real life]; INTERPRETER FOR HUBBELL: Lorie Robinson; A.J.: Carlo Imperato [before Broadway he was Anthony Imperato]; JACKIE: Rachael Kelly; LUIS: Ray Contreras; NIKKI KAY KANE: Nan-Lynn Nelson; LIDIA: Josie de Guzman; MANNY: Randy Ruiz; EDDIE: Jon Matthews; SUNDAR: Bernie Allison; ROBY: Venustra K. Robinson; LAZAR: David Schechter; ERIC: Evan H. Miranda; IGGY: Jonathan Feig; JANE: Kate Schellenbach; EZ: Leonard "Duke" Brown; MEX-MONGO: Mark Anthony Butler; MELINDA: Trini Alvarado; DEIDRE: Karen Evans; MOCHA: Sheila Gibbs; CHORUS: Paula Anderson, Kenya Brome, Jerome Dekie, Karin Dekie, Lisa Dekie, John Gallogly, Timmy Michaels, Toby Parker. Note: Sheila Gibbs & Toby Parker were the chorus in the pre–Broadway production at the Public. *Understudies* ("new" means they weren't understudies at the prior production at the Public Theatre): Carey Bond (new), Michele Dagarvarian, Jerome Dekie (new), Katherine Diamond, Sheila Gibbs (new), C.S. Hayward, Michael Laylor, Timmy Michaels, Toby Parker, Rachael Kelly (dropped for Broadway). *Musicians:* PIANO/TOY PIANO: Judith Fleisher; STRING BASS: John Schimmel; TRAP SET/TRIANGLE/GLASS/RATCHET: David Sawyer; CONGAS/TIMBALES/BONGOS/BELLS/DIREN/OTHERS: Leopoldo F. Fleming; SAXES/FLUTES: Patience Higgins; GUITAR: Elizabeth Swados; SAX: Jeffrey Hest [added for Broadway]; TRUMPETS: Mark Green & Austin Hall [added for Broadway]. *Act I:* "You Don't Understand" (Hubbell & Lorie) (with improvisation by Bruce Hlibok), "I Had to Go" (A.J. & John Schimmel), "Parent/Kid Dance" (Company), "Appendectomy" (Jackie), "Where Do People Go?" (Company), "Footstep" (Nikki, Schimmel, Lidia, Manny) (Spanish argument improvised by Josie de Guzman & Randy Ruiz), "Once Upon a Time" (Lidia & Company), "Current Events" (Eddie), "Every Now and Then" (A.J., Sundar, Company) [in the pre–Broadway production at the Public, A.J. was not part of this number], "Out on the Street" (Hubbell & Interpreter) (with improvisation by Bruce Hlibok), "Minnesota Strip" (Roby), "Song of a Child Prostitute" (Jackie, Lidia, Manny, Luis), "Christmas Puppies" (Nikki), "Lazar's Heroes" (Lazar) (with improvisation by David Schechter), "Find Me a Hero" (Lazar & Company), "Scrynatchkielooaw" (Nikki), "The Undiscovered Son" (Eric, Judith Fleisher, Schimmel), "I Went Back Home" (Iggy & Jane) [in the pre–Broadway production at the Public, this was a number for Iggy & Jackie], "This is What I Do When I'm Angry" (A.J. & Nikki) [in the pre–Broadway production at the Public this was Deidre's number], "The Basketball Song" (EZ & Company) (Danced by Luis & Mex-Mongo), "Spoons" (Manny), "Lullaby for Luis" (Lidia, Luis, Patience Higgins, Company), "We Are Not Strangers" (Eric & Company). *Act II:* "In the Sleeping Line" (Company) [the actors in this number are the original improvisers of the scenes. They are also the actors who played in the scenes, except Diane Lane, who was replaced for Broadway by Rachael Kelly]: A.J.'S DREAM: Carlo Imperato; ROBY'S DREAM: Venustra K. Robinson; JACKIE'S DREAM: Diane Lane; LAZAR'S DREAM: David Schechter; EDDIE'S DREAM: Vincent Stewart; NIGHTMARES IN SPANISH: Josie de Guzman, Randy Ruiz, Ray Contreras; "Lullaby from Baby to Baby" (Melinda, Hubbell, Deidre), "Tra Gog Vo in Dein Whole" ("I Will Not Tell a Soul") (Lazar & Hubbell), "Revenge Song" (Company), "Enterprise" (Deidre, Nikki, Mex-Mongo, Company), "Mr. Graffiti" (Mex-Mongo) [this number shifted position for Broadway; see below], "Sometimes" (Roby, Lazar, Company), "Clothes" (Iggy), "We Are Not Strangers" (reprise) (Mocha, EZ, Company) [new for Broadway], "Mr. Graffiti" (Mex-Mongo) [new position; see above], "Where Are Those People Who Did *Hair*?" [this number shifted position for Broadway; see below], "The Untrue Pigeon" (Nikki), "Senoras de la Noche" (Lidia, Manny, Nikki), "We Have to Die?" (Deidre), "Where Are Those People Who Did *Hair*?" (Lazar, Deidre, Company) [new position; see above], "Appendectomy II" (Jackie & Melinda), "Let Me Be a Kid" (Company), "To the Dead of Family Wars" (Deidre), "Problem After Problem" (Hubbell & Interpreter), "Lonesome of the Road" (Luis, Sundar, Company).

Reviews were good. The show received Tony nominations for musical, score, book, direction of a musical, and choreography.

597. *Sadie Thompson*

Described as "a play with music." However, it is a real musical. A hypocritical preacher tries to reform prostitute Sadie. Impressive jungle sets included real rain effects. It followed the play closely, although the role of Dr. McPhail, the understanding missionary, was cut.

Before Broadway. This show was written for Ethel Merman, but on 9/29/44, less than two weeks into rehearsals, she quit, not happy with the lyrics, and was replaced by June Havoc. The show was then still called *Sadie*. William Linn was replaced by Walter Burke. In the program, producer A.P. Waxman thanked Mary Pickford for her co-operation which enabled him to produce the show.

The Broadway Run. ALVIN THEATRE, 11/16/44–1/6/45. 60 PERFORMANCES. A Rouben Mamoulian production, PRESENTED BY A.P. Waxman; MUSIC: Vernon Duke; LYRICS: Howard Dietz; BOOK: Howard Dietz & Rouben Mamoulian; BASED ON the 1922 drama *Rain*, by John Colton & Clemence Randolph (and starring Jeanne Eagels), which itself was based on the short story *Miss Thompson,* by Somerset Maugham; DIRECTOR: Rouben Mamoulian; CHOREOGRAPHER: Edward Caton; SETS: Boris Aronson; COSTUMES: Motley; JUNE HAVOC'S COSTUMES from studies by Azadia Newman (Mrs. Rouben Mamoulian) from her painting of *Sadie Thompson;* MUSICAL DIRECTOR: Charles G. Sanford; MUSICAL ARRANGEMENTS: Charles Cooke, Walter Eiger, John Klein, Joseph Glover, Irving Landau, Julian Work, Vernon Duke; VOCAL ARRANGEMENTS: Vernon Duke; CHORAL ENSEMBLES trained by: Millard Gibson; CAST RECORDING: none, because the musicians' union was on strike; PRESS: Jean Dalrymple & Anthony Buttitta; COMPANY MANAGER: John H. Potter; STAGE MANAGER: Don Darcy. *Cast:* JOE HORN: Ralph Dumke (4); CORPORAL HODGSON: Daniel Cobb; PRIVATE GRIGGS: Norman Lawrence (7); SERGEANT TIM O'HARA: James Newill (3); AMEENA, HORN'S WIFE: Grazia Narciso (11); HONEYPIE: Beatrice Kraft (10); MRS. ALFRED DAVIDSON: Zolya Talma (5); CICELY ST. CLAIR: Doris Patston (6); LAO LAO: Remington Olmsted; SADIE THOMPSON: June Havoc (1); QUARTERMASTER BATES: Walter Burke; REV. ALFRED DAVIDSON: Lansing Hatfield (2); POLYNESIAN GIRL: Milada Mladova (8); POLYNESIAN BOY: Chris Volkoff (9); SINGERS: Jimmy Allison, Anthony Amato, Adolph Anderson, Harold Bayne (*Neil Chirico*), Ann Browning (dropped during run), Arlene Carmen, Paula Carpino, John "Jack" Cassidy, Mollie Causley, Ethel Greene, Delmar Horstmann, Robert Lawrence, Marilyn Merkt, Dorris Moore, Alan Noel, Linda White; DANCERS: Fred Bernaski, Vivian Cherry, Toni Darnay, Andrea Downing, Bob Gari, Mary Grey, T.C. Jones, Lil Liandre, William Lundy, Virginia Meyer, Mischa Pompianov, Theodora Roosevelt, Anna Scarpova, Alla Shishkina, Ruth Sobotka, William Vaux, John Ward, Vanessi (featured female dancer), *William Hunter, Faith Dane, Joan Dubois, Igor Tamarin, Natalie Wynn*; POLYNESIAN MUSICIANS: Wasantha Singh & His Group (Minakshi, S.R. Mandel, Frank De Silva, Karla Margot Pries). *Act I*: *Scene 1* Trader Joe Horn's hotel-store in Pago Pago, on the island of Tutuila, in the South Seas. Polynesian scene: "Barrel of Beads" (Griggs & Honeypie), "Fisherman's Wharf" (Sadie) [replaced "If You Can't Get the Love You Want" (Sadie)], "When You Live on an Island" (O'Hara & Choral Ensemble), "Poor as a Churchmouse" (Sadie); *Scene 2* The jungle: Jungle Dance: a/ Beatrice Kraft & Natives; b/ Milada Mladova, Chris Volkoff, Natives; "The Love I Long For (I've No Right to Demand)" (Sadie & O'Hara); Dance to the Sun God (Rem Olmsted, Vanessi, Natives); "Garden in the Sky" (Davidson). *Act II*: Same as Act I, Scene 1: "Dancing Lesson" (Cicely & Native Girls), "Siren of the Tropics" (Honeypie, Bates, Griggs, Hodgson), "Life's a Funny Present (from Someone)" (Sadie), "Born All Over Again" (Davidson), "Sailing at Midnight" (O'Hara & Sadie), Montage: Sadie's Conversion: a/ The Inner Voices (O'Hara & Davidson); b/ Hot Spot (Sadie & O'Hara); c/ Sunflowers: YOUNG SADIE: Milada Mladova; THE BOY: Chris Volkoff; THAT MAN: Remington Olmsted; d/ The Lamplit Street (Sadie, Mischa Pompianov, William Vaux, William Lundy); e/ Kangaroo Farm (Sadie & O'Hara); f/ Prison & Conversion (Sadie, Davidson, O'Hara). The Living Curtain (Choral Group & Dancers); Ballet: The Mountains of Nebraska: Davidson; Davidson's Other Self (Chris Volkoff); Sadie

Thompsons (Milada Mladova & Dancers), "Fisherman's Wharf" (reprise) (Sadie), Finale: "When You Live on an Island" (reprise) (Company & Ensemble).

Broadway reviews were divided. There were several raves, though, especially for June Havoc. The show lost $180,000.

After Broadway. To compensate for the lack of an original cast recording, in 2002 a studio recording was made by Original Cast Records. ARRANGEMENTS/ORCHESTRATIONS: Joshua Pearl. *Sung by:* Davis Gaines Melissa Errico, Ron Morehead, Ron Raines. The musical numbers were: "When You Live on an Island," "Join the Marines," "Fisherman's Wharf" (Sadie), "Weeping Sky," "Cradle to the Grave," "Back in Circulation" (Sadie), "Where the Sun God Walks," "The Love I Long For (I've No Right to Demand)," "You USA," "Hurdy Gurdy," "Below the Equator," "Sailing at Midnight," "Key to the Gates," "The Love I Long For (I've No Right to Demand)" (reprise), "Garden in the Sky," "I Lived in a Home with a Piano"/"Circles Under Your Eyes" (Sadie), "Sailing at Midnight" (reprise), "Life's a Funny Present (from Someone)."

598. *Sail Away*

A satire on cruise travel, as seen through the eyes of Mimi, hostess on the Cunard ship *Coronia* (with mostly American passengers) as it sails from New York to Europe.

Before Broadway. Noel Coward came up with the concept, as an extension of his song "A Bar on the Piccola Marina." It was to be about a newly-widowed Englishwoman who visits Capri with her children, and is swept up in the Bohemian atmosphere. But this idea was discarded. Mr. Coward re-developed it, as *Later Than Spring*, with Rosalind Russell in mind, but she turned it down, and Mr. Coward considered tailoring it to the talents of Irene Dunne, Judy Holliday or Kay Thompson. There were two tryouts in Boston (the first from 8/9/61, at the Colonial Theatre; the second ending on 9/2/61, where reviews were good; and one in Philadelphia, where reviews were divided. During the Philly run an entire sub-plot was cut. This involved Verity Craig (played by Jean Fenn), an unhappy, confused wife taking a cruise while contemplating divorcing husband Lawford (played by William Hutt). She has an on-board romance with Johnny, attempts suicide, and is finally reconciled with her husband. However, this sub-plot was forcing the show to have two leading ladies, and was thus slowing down the action. Aside from that it was clear from audience reaction that they wanted more of Elaine Stritch. The cut eliminated William Hutt and Jean Fenn. Miss Fenn received two months salary. Elaine Stritch's part was built up, and it was now she who had the romance with Johnny. Child actor Karen Lynn Reed's role was also cut, as was the role of Clara (played by Wish Mary Hunt). The music and lyrics were also changed considerably. Elaine Stritch inherited one of Jean Fenn's numbers, "Something Very Strange;" several songs were cut: "This is a Changing World," "This is a Night for Lovers," and "I Never Knew" (all of which were originally in Noel Coward's 1946 flop London musical *Pacific 1860*), "Bronxville Darby and Joan" (later added for the London production of *Sail Away*), "Somethin' You Gotta Find Out Yourself," "Don't Let Father See the Frescoes," "Patterson, Pennsylvania," and "You and I" (originally written for the unfinished *Later Than* Spring). James Hurst got two new songs to go with the new love plot, and the score was much better than before.

The Broadway Run. BROADHURST THEATRE, 10/3/61–2/24/62. 1 preview on 10/2/61. 167 PERFORMANCES. PRESENTED BY Bonard Productions (Helen Bonfils & Haila Stoddard), in association with Charles Russell; MUSIC/LYRICS/BOOK/DIRECTOR/POSTER ART: Noel Coward; CHOREOGRAPHER: Joe Layton; SETS: Oliver Smith; COSTUMES: Oliver Smith & Helene Pons; LIGHTING: Peggy Clark; MUSICAL DIRECTOR/DANCE MUSIC ARRANGEMENTS: Peter Matz; ORCHESTRATIONS: Irwin Kostal; VOCAL ARRANGEMENTS: Fred Werner; CAST RECORDING on Capitol; PRESS: Frank Goodman, Ben Washer, Walter Alford, Fred Weterich; GENERAL MANAGER: Morton Gottlieb; COMPANY MANAGER: Richard Seader; STAGE MANAGER: Joe Dooley; ASSISTANT STAGE MANAGER: Warren Crane & James Frasher. *Cast:* JOE, THE SHIP'S PURSER: Charles Braswell; SHUTTLEWORTH, A STEWARD: Keith Prentice; RAWLINGS, A PASSENGER WHO DRINKS: James Pritchett; SIR GERARD NUTFIELD: C. Stafford Dickens; LADY NUTFIELD: Margaret Mower; BARN-

ABY SLADE: Grover Dale (5); ELMER CANDIJACK: Henry Lawrence; MAIMIE CANDIJACK, HIS WIFE: Betty Jane Watson; GLEN CANDIJACK, THEIR SON: Alan Helms; SHIRLEY CANDIJACK, THEIR DAUGHTER: Patti Mariano; MR. SWEENEY: Jon Richards; MRS. SWEENEY: Paula Bauersmith; ELINOR SPENCER-BOLLARD: Alice Pearce (4); NANCY FOYLE, HER NIECE: Patricia Harty; ALVIN LUSH: Paul O'Keefe; MRS. LUSH, HIS MOTHER: Evelyn Russell; JOHNNY VAN MIER: James Hurst (2); MRS. VAN MIER, HIS MOTHER: Margalo Gillmore (3); MIMI PARAGON: Elaine Stritch (1); ALI, AN ARAB GUIDE: Charles Braswell; MAN FROM AMERICAN EXPRESS: Richard Woods; VOICE OF CAPT. WILBERFORCE: Noel Coward; CARRINGTON: David Evans [role added during the run]; DECK STEWARD: James Frasher [role added during the run]; GIRL PASSENGER: Ann Fraser [role added during the run]; ARABS/ITALIANS/PASSENGERS/STEWARDS/CHILDREN: Jere Admire, Bobby Allen, Don Atkinson, Gary Crabbe, David Evans, Pat Ferrier, Dorothy Frank, Ann Fraser, James Frasher, Gene Gavin, Paul Gross, S. Curtis Hood, Wish Mary Hunt, Cheryl Kilgren, Bridget Knapp, Nancy Lynch, Patti Mariano, Mary Ellen O'Keefe, Alan Peterson, Dennis Scott, Alice Shanahan, Dan Siretta, Gloria Stevens, Christopher Votos. *Understudies:* Mimi: Betty Jane Watson; John: Keith Prentice; Elinor: Evelyn Russell; Mrs. Van Mier: Paula Bauersmith; Joe/Ali: James Pritchett; Nancy: Ann Fraser; Barnaby: David Evans; Alvin: Bobby Allen; Elmer/Sir Gerard/Mr. Sweeney: Richard Woods; Glen: Don Atkinson. **Act I:** *Scene 1* The main hall of the Cunard steamship *Coronia*: "Come to Me" (Mimi & Stewards); *Scene 2* John Van Mier's cabin: "Sail Away" (Johnny) [originally written for *Ace of Clubs*]; *Scene 3* The sundeck; New York Harbor: "Come to Me" (reprise) (Mimi), "Sail Away" (reprise) (Johnny & Company); *Scene 4* Elinor Spencer-Bollard's cabin: "Where Shall I Find Him?" (Nancy); *Scene 5* The sundeck, at sea; several days later: "Beatnik Love Affair" (Barnaby, Nancy, The Passengers), "Later than Spring" (Johnny) [originally written for the unfinished show *Later Than Spring*], "The Passenger's Always Right" (Joe & Stewards) [originally written for *Later Than Spring*]; *Scene 6* Mimi Paragon's cabin: "(Useless) Useful Phrases" (Mimi); *Scene 7* The sundeck; moonlight: "Where Shall I Find Her?" (Barnaby); *Scene 8* The promenade deck; later that night: "Go Slow, Johnny" (Johnny); *Scene 9* The sundeck; Gibraltar: "You're a Long, Long Way from America" (Mimi & Company). **Act II:** *Scene 1* Tangier: "The Customer's Always Right" (Ali & Arabs), "Something Very Strange" (Mimi); *Scene 2* "Italian Interlude" (ballet) (Company); *Scene 3* The ship's nursery: "The Little Ones' ABC" (Mimi, Alvin, The Children); *Scene 4* The sundeck at night, Bay of Naples: "Don't Turn Away from Love" (Johnny); *Scene 5* The boat deck; Villefranche; *Scene 6* The Parthenon: "When You Want Me" (Barnaby & Nancy); *Scene 7* The sundeck; moonlight: "Later than Spring" (reprise) (Mimi); *Scene 8* The promenade deck: "Why Do the Wrong People Travel?" (Mimi) [originally written for *Later Than Spring*]; *Scene 9* The main hall: "When You Want Me" (reprise) (Company), Finale.

Broadway reviews were favorable, though mild; it was considered too old-fashioned. Noel Coward wrote in his diary that it had a poor Broadway run "owing to an almost sensational lack of enthusiasm from the New York public." Elaine Stritch was nominated for a Tony, as were producers of a musical. The show was replaced by *My Fair Lady*, which had moved from the Mark Hellinger.

After Broadway. BRISTOL HIPPODROME, England, 5/31/62–6/15/62; SAVOY THEATRE, London, 6/21/62–1/26/63. 252 PERFORMANCES. Although Elaine Stritch won raves, and the show ran longer than on Broadway, reviews were very bad. PRESENTED BY Harold Fielding; DIRECTOR: Noel Coward; CHOREOGRAPHER: Joe Layton; SETS/COSTUMES: Loudon Sainthill; LIGHTING: Michael Northen; MUSICAL DIRECTOR: Gareth Davies. *Cast:* MIMI: Elaine Stritch; NANCY: Sheila Forbes; BARNABY: Grover Dale; JOE/ALI: John Hewer; GLEN: Nicholas Chagrin; ELINOR: Dorothy Reynolds; JOHNNY: David Holliday; MRS. VAN MIER: Mavis Villiers; MRS. LUSH: Margaret Christensen; MAIMIE: Stella Moray. There was an Australian production not long after the London one. The London cast album was re-released 7/22/03, on Fynsworth Alley, and included "Bronxville Darby and Joan."

To mark the centenary of Noel Coward's birth a concert was given at the 260-seat WEILL RECITAL HALL (attached to Carnegie Hall), 11/3/99–11/13/99. 10 PERFORMANCES. DIRECTOR: Gerald Gutierrez; MUSICAL DIRECTOR: Ben Whitely; ORCHESTRATIONS: Rowland Lee.

Cast: MIMI: Elaine Stritch; NANCY: Andrea Burns; MR. SWEENEY: Gordon Connell; MRS. SWEENEY: Jane Connell; MRS. LUSH: Alison Fraser; JOE: Jonathan Freeman; JOHNNY: Jerry Lanning; BARNABY: James Patterson; ELINOR: Marian Seldes; ALVIN: Paul Iacono; MRS. VAN MIER: Jane White; ELMER: Bill Nolte; MAIMIE: Anne Allgood; SIR GERARD: Herb Foster. Act I Scene 8 was now the ship's nursery, with the number "The Little Ones' ABC." Stewart Nicholls restored the number "Bronxville Darby and Joan" as the song in Act II Scene 4 (now The promenade deck at night).

Claudia Shear re-worked it; it had a reading in late 10/02 at the NEW YORK THEATRE WORKSHOP. DIRECTOR: Christopher Ashley. Its appearance at this time was pertinent, because Miss Stritch was enjoying a remarkable success with her one-woman Broadway show *Elaine Stritch at Liberty* (in which she sang "Why do the Wrong People Travel," from *Sail Away*).

599. *St. Louis Woman*

This musical had an all-black cast. It is set in St. Louis, in 1898. Della, a tough saloon owner, is Biglow's woman, but she falls for Augie, a jockey with an incredible winning streak. Biglow beats her up and Augie sets out to get Biglow, but is beaten to it by a bullet from one of Biglow's ex-girlfriends. As Biglow dies he puts a curse on Augie, causing the jockey to lose his winning streak. The fickle Della leaves Augie.

Before Broadway. Sam Katz and Arthur Freed of MGM supplied all the money and the star—Lena Horne as Della. However, before rehearsals began Miss Horne bowed out, agreeing with the NAACP that the musical was demeaning to black people. Ruby Hill replaced her. Two days before rehearsals librettist Countee Cullen, well-known Harlem poet, died. During Boston tryouts director Lemuel Ayers was replaced by Rouben Mamoulian, and choreographer Anthony Tudor was replaced by Charles Walters. Fayard Nicholas and Rex Ingram came into the cast during tryouts. After tryouts Ruby Hill was fired in favor of the more experienced Muriel Rahn. After three New York previews (that is, previews in New York, not Broadway previews as such, not as we know them today) Pearl Bailey led a deputation of actors in protest against the firing of Ruby Hill, and demanded her re-instatement, otherwise no show. Miss Hill came back. Several numbers written for the show were not used: "High, Low, Jack and the Game," "A Man's Gotta Fight," "Somethin' You Gotta Find Out Yourself," "Sow the Seed and Reap the Harvest," "Lim'ricks," and "Talkin' Glory."

The Broadway Run. MARTIN BECK THEATRE, 3/30/46–7/6/46. 113 PERFORMANCES. PRESENTED BY Edward Gross; MUSIC: Harold Arlen; LYRICS: Johnny Mercer; BOOK: Arna Bontemps & Countee Cullen (based on their 1933 drama *God Sends Sunday*, which in turn was based on Mr. Cullen's 1931 novel of that name); DIRECTOR: Rouben Mamoulian; CHOREOGRAPHER: Charles Walters; SETS/COSTUMES: Lemuel Ayers; MUSICAL DIRECTOR/CHORAL ARRANGEMENTS: Leon Leonardi; ORCHESTRATIONS: Ted Royal, Allan Small, Menotti Salta, Walter Paul; CAST RECORDING on Capitol; PRESS: Phyllis Perlman; MANAGER: Rube Bernstein; GENERAL STAGE MANAGER: Frank Hall; STAGE MANAGERS: William McFadden & Ed Brinkmann. *Cast:* BADFOOT: Robert Pope (7); LI'L AUGIE: Harold Nicholas (1); BARNEY: Fayard Nicholas (1); LILA: June Hawkins (5); SLIM: Louis Sharp; BUTTERFLY: Pearl Bailey (2); DELLA GREEN: Ruby Hill (4); BIGLOW BROWN: Rex Ingram (3); RAGSDALE: Elwood Smith; PEMBROKE: Merritt Smith; JASPER: Charles Welch; THE HOSTESS: Maude Russell; DRUM MAJOR: J. Mardo Brown; MISSISSIPPI SLIM: Milton J. Williams; CAKE WALK: DRUM MAJOR: J. Mardo Brown; QUARTET: Rhoda Boggs, Rosalie King, Robert Pope, Milton J. Williams; COMPETING COUPLES: Betty Nichols & Smalls Boykins, Rita Garrett & Theodore Allen, Dorothea Green & Milton Wood, Royce Wallace & Lonny Reed, Gwendolyn Hale & Norman DeJoie, Enid Williams & George Thomas, Pearl Bailey & Fayard Nicholas, Ruby Hill & Harold Nicholas [end of Cake Walk sequence]; DANDY DAVE: Frank Green; LEAH: Juanita Hall (6); JACKIE: Joseph Eady; CELESTINE: Yvonne Coleman; PIGGIE: Herbert Coleman; JOSHUA: Lorenzo Fuller; MR. HOPKINS: Milton Wood; PREACHER: Creighton Thompson; WAITER: Carrington

Lewis; CHORAL GROUP: Olive Ball, Rhoda Boggs, J. Mardo Brown, Miriam Burton, John Diggs, Leon Edwards, Lorenzo Fuller, Theodore Hines, Rosalie King, Jerry Laws, Arthur Lawson, Maude Russell, Zelda Shelton, Merritt Smith, Charles Welch, Lori Wilson; GIRL DANCERS: Rita Garrett, Dorothea Green, Gwendolyn Hale, Betty Nichols, Marguerite Roan, Royce Wallace, Enid Williams; BOY DANCERS: Theodore Allen, Smalls Boykins, Norma DeJoie, Frank Green, Lonny Reed, Arthur Smith, George Thomas. *Act I*: Overture (Orchestra); *Scene 1* A stable; early afternoon of a day in August: "Li'l Augie is a Natural Man" (Badfoot); *Scene 2* Biglow's bar; late afternoon, same day: "Sweeten Water" (Barney, Badfoot, Slim, Della, Ensemble) [this number was here only in the 1998 revival], "Any Place I Hang My Hat is Home" (Della), "I Feel My Luck Comin' Down" (Augie), "(I Had Myself a) True Love" (Lila); *Scene 3* Outside Barney's room; at twilight: "Legalize My Name" (Butterfly, to Barney); *Scene 4* A ballroom; evening of same day: "Cakewalk Your Lady" (dance) (Company). *Act II*: *Scene 1* Augie's & Della's home; late afternoon, following week: "Come Rain or Come Shine" (Della & Augie) [the big hit], "Sweeten Water" (reprise) (Della) [only in the 1998 revival], "Chinquapin Bush" (Children), "We Shall Meet to Part, No Never" (Piggie) [cut from 1998 revival], "Lullaby" (Della), "Sleep Peaceful (Mr. Used-to-Be);" [This was the beginning of Act II in the 1998 revival]; *Scene 2* The alley; *Scene 3* The funeral parlor: Funeral Prelude, "Leavin' Time" (Choral Group). *Act III*: *Scene 1* Augie's & Della's home; early evening: "Come Rain or Come Shine" (reprise) (Della) [replaced during the run with a new number, "I Wonder What Became of Me" (Della)], "Come Rain or Come Shine" (reprise) (Augie) [only in the 1998 revival]; *Scene 2* The alley: "(It's) a Woman's Prerogative" (Butterfly); *Scene 3* The bar: "Ridin' on the Moon" (Augie & Ensemble), "I Wonder What Became of Me" (Lila) [this song was placed here only in the 1998 revival]; *Scene 4* The stable: "Least, That's My Opinion" (Badfoot); *Scene 5* Street corner close to the race track: "Racin' Form" (Leah), "Come On, Li'l Augie" (Ensemble), Finale: "Come Rain or Come Shine" (reprise) (Entire Company).

Reviews were divided. The Nicholas Brothers were very popular then, but Pearl Bailey stole the show, and won a Donaldson Award for female debut. The original orchestrations have been lost over the years.

After Broadway. A revised version, *Free and Easy* (those words were in the first line of the number "Any Place I Hang My Hat is Home") ran in 1959, in Amsterdam and Paris, with other Harold Arlen songs added.

CITY CENTER, NYC, 4/30/98–5/3/98. 5 PERFORMANCES. In concert, in 2 acts, part of the *Encores!* series. ADAPTED/DIRECTOR: Jack O'Brien; CHOREOGRAPHER: George Faison; LIGHTING: Peter Kaczorowski; APPAREL: Theoni V. Aldredge; MUSICAL DIRECTOR: Rob Fisher; NEW ORCHESTRATIONS: Ralph Burns; DANCE MUSIC ARRANGEMENTS: Luther Henderson. *Cast*: BADFOOT: Chuck Cooper; BARNEY: Victor Trent Cook; LILA: Helen Goldsby; SLIM: Wendell Pierce; DELLA: Vanessa L. Williams; BIGLOW: Charles S. "Roc" Dutton; RAGSDALE: Roger Robinson; BUTTERFLY: Yvette Cason; AUGIE: Stanley Wayne Mathis; JOSHUA: Jesse Means II.

PRINCE MUSIC THEATRE, Philadelphia, 2000. Concert performance. DIRECTOR: Ben Levit. *Cast*: DELLA: Sondra M. Bonitto; AUGIE: Vernel Bagneris; BADFOOT: Johnnie Hobbs Jr.

7/8/03–7/13/03. Dance Theatre of Harlem produced *St. Louis Woman–a Blues Ballet*, at NEW YORK STATE THEATRE, in repertory, as part of the Lincoln Center Festival. BALLET CONCEPT/NEW BOOK: Jack Wrangler; CHOREOGRAPHER: Michael Smuin; SETS: Tony Walton; COSTUMES: Willa Kim; LIGHTING: Jules Fisher; CONDUCTOR: Jonathan Tunick.

600. *The Saint of Bleecker Street*

Opera about murder and incest. It had a cast of 100. Set in the Italian community of Bleecker Street, New York, in the 1950s. Annina is a sickly young woman who, every Good Friday, experiences stigmata. Her neighbors want her to perform miracles. She cures Maria Corona's mute son. Annina and her friend Carmela pray to become nuns, but Carmela backs out, having become engaged to Salvatore. Annina's brother Michele, who loves her obsessively, objects to handing her over to anyone else, including God, and comes up against the priest, Don Marco. When Michele's girlfriend Desideria accuses him of loving his sister too much, he stabs Desideria to death. Annina takes the veil and dies as her brother looks on.

The Broadway Run. BROADWAY THEATRE, 12/27/54–4/2/55. 92 PERFORMANCES. PRESENTED BY Chandler Cowles; MUSIC/BOOK: Gian-Carlo Menotti; DIRECTOR: Gian-Carlo Menotti; SETS: Robert Randolph (after the paintings by George Tooker); COSTUMES: Robert Randolph; LIGHTING: Jean Rosenthal; MUSICAL DIRECTOR: Thomas Schippers; ASSOCIATE MUSICAL DIRECTOR: Samuel Krachmalnick; CAST RECORDING on RCA (it featured Gabrielle Ruggiero & David Poleri and basically the rest of the cast); PRESS: Bill Doll, Robert Ullman, Merle Debuskey; CASTING: Gian-Carlo Menotti; COMPANY MANAGER: H.H. Light; PRODUCTION STAGE MANAGER: James Vincent Russo; STAGE MANAGER: Roger Perry. *Cast:* ASSUNTA: Catherine Akos; CARMELA: Maria Di Gerlando; MARIA CORONA: Maria Marlo; HER DUMB SON: Ernesto Gonzalez; DON MARCO: Leon Lishner; ANNINA: Virginia Copeland (2) & Gabrielle Ruggiero (alternating) (Miss Copeland sang on opening night); MICHELE: David Poleri (1) & Davis Cunningham (3) (alternating) (Mr. Poleri sang on opening night); DESIDERIA: Gloria Lane (4); SALVATORE: David Aiken; CONCETTINA: Lucy Becque; A YOUNG MAN: Richard Cassilly; AN OLD WOMAN: Elisabeth Carron; BARTENDER: Russell Goodwin; 1ST GUEST: Keith Kaldenberg; 2ND GUEST: John Reardon; A NUN: Dorothy Krebill; A YOUNG PRIEST: Robert Barry; NEIGHBORS/FRIENDS/POLICEMEN, ETC: Robert Barry, Theodora Brandon, Betsy Bridge, Lorraine Bridges, Michael Bulzomi, Elisabeth Carron, Richard Cassilly, Doris Davis, Mignon Dunn, Elizabeth Dunning, Joyce Duskin, Rico Froehlich, Elaine Galante, Russell Goodwin, Gary Gordon, Jeanne Grant, Don Grobe, Mary Hensley, Carol Jones, Fred Jones, Keith Kaldenberg, Dorothy Krebill, Chester Ludgin, William McCully, Leslie MacLennan, Michael MacLennan, Dan Merriman, Bessie Mijanovich, Doris Okerson, John Reardon, Francesca Roberto, Donna Sanders, Reid Shelton, Alan Smith, Robert Watts. *Understudies:* Michele: Richard Cassilly; Maria Corona: Elisabeth Carron; Desideria/Assunta: Mignon Dunn; Don Marco: William McCully; Carmela: Theodora Brandon; Salvatore: Chester Ludgin. **Act I:** INTRODUCTION; *Scene 1* A coldwater flat on Bleecker Street; Good Friday afternoon: "Rosa Mystica" (Assunta), "Well...I'm tired of waiting" (Assunta), "The vision has begun" (Ensemble), "Ah, Sweet Jesus, spare me this agony" (Annina), "Look, the Stigmata!" (Ensemble), "Stop it!" (Ensemble), "Ah, poor Michele, it is not I your rival" (Don Marco); *Interlude* (Orchestra); *Scene 2* A vacant lot on Mulberry Street; SAN GENNARO DAY: "Canta Ninna, Canta Nanna, al mio bambino" (Assunta), "Annina, I've something to confess to you" (Assunta), "Annina, Annina!" (Assunta), "Michele, Michele!" (Annina), "Sister, I shall hide you and take you away" (Annina), "Veglia su di noi, santo del sangue" (Annina). **Act II:** An Italian restaurant; the following May: INTRODUCTION; "Hai l'occhio nero, nero della quaglia" (Annina), "Where is Michele?" (Desideria), "Eh, gia, giovinotti, voglion stare attorno a te" (Desideria), "Ah, Michele, don't you know that love can turn to hate" (Desideria), "You will regret it" (Annina), "I know that you all hate me" (Michele), "You are wrong, Michele" (Annina), "Yes, Michele, go home, go, go..." (Desideria). **Act III:** INTRODUCTION; *Scene 1* A subway station; a few months later: "There she is" (Annina), "Weeping, these, for him, are days of weeping" (Annina); Interlude (Orchestra); *Scene 2* The coldwater flat; several days later: "Agnus Dei, qui tollis peccata mundi" (Assunta), "Annina, Annina, prepare yourself for a great day" (Annina), "Oh, my love, at last the hour has come" (Annina), "Maria, Salvatore!" (Assunta), "Gloria tibi domine in saeculum et in saeculum saeculi" (Annina), "Annina, Annina!" (Assunta).

It got great reviews. It was televised on 1/16/55, on *The Ed Sullivan Show*, as a 20-minute performance of Act II, with the original Broadway cast. After 3/19/55 only 4 performances a week were given — on weekends. The show won a Pulitzer Prize for Music, and a Tony Award for musical direction. The production lost about $125,000.

After Broadway. NBC TV. It was televised again, this time in a slightly abridged form, on NBC, as an *Opera Theatre* presentation, on 5/15/55. PRODUCER: Samuel Chotzinoff; DIRECTOR: Kirk Browning. *Cast:* ASSUNTA: Mignon Dunn; CARMELA: Maria Di Gerlando; MARIA

CORONA: Elisabeth Carron; DON MARCO: Leon Lishner; ANNINA: Virginia Copeland; MICHELE: Richard Cassilly; DESIDERIA: Rosemary Kuhlmann; SALVATORE: David Aiken.

BBC TV. 10/4/56. DIRECTOR: Rudolph Cartier. *Cast:* CARMELA: June Bronhill; ANNINA: Virginia Copeland.

CITY CENTER, NYC, 3/18/65–3/18/65. 2 PERFORMANCES IN REPERTORY; 9/29/65–10/9/65. 2 PERFORMANCES IN REPERTORY. The second run had the same crew as the first run, but a partially different cast. The actor who played a role in the second run is in italics below.

PRESENTED BY the New York City Opera; DIRECTOR: Francis Rizzo; SETS/COSTUMES: Robert Randolph; CONDUCTOR: Vincent La Selva; PRODUCTION SUPERVISOR: Gian-Carlo Menotti. *Cast:* ASSUNTA: Muriel Greenspon; CARMELA: Mary Jennings; MARIA CORONA: Anita Darian; HER SON: Clyde Ventura; DON MARCO: Thomas Paul, *Malcolm Smith*; ANNINA: Joan Sena, *Julia Migenes*; MICHELE: Enrico Di Giuseppe, *Harry Theyard*; DESIDERIA: Beverly Wolff; SALVATORE: David Smith, *William Beck*; CONCETTINA: Wendy Morris; A YOUNG MAN: Anthony Safina; A YOUNG WOMAN: Charlotte Povia, *Jodell Kenting*; WOMAN: Anthea DeForest [role cut for the second run]; BARTENDER: Don Henderson; FIRST GUEST: Richard Krause; SECOND GUEST: William Ledbetter.

NEW YORK STATE THEATRE, 11/5/76–11/10/76. 3 PERFORMANCES IN REPERTORY. Return engagement 4/13/78–4/23/78. 3 PERFORMANCES IN REPERTORY. PRESENTED BY the New York City Opera; DIRECTOR: Francis Rizzo; CHOREOGRAPHER: Thomas Andrew; SETS: Beeb Salzer; COSTUMES: Carol Luiken; LIGHTING: Hans Sondheimer; CONDUCTOR: Cal Stewart Kellogg. *Cast:* ASSUNTA: Jane Shaulis; MARIA CORONA: Judith De Rosa; CARMELA: Diana Soviero; DON MARCO: Irwin Densen; ANNINA: Catherine Malfitano; MICHELE: Enrico Di Giuseppe; CONCETTINA: Danielle Brisebois, *Lila Herbert* (for the return engagement); DESIDERIA: Jeanne Piland, *Sandra Walker* (for the return engagement); SALVATORE: William Ledbetter. This production was televised.

SPOLETO FESTIVAL, 1986. DIRECTOR: Gian-Carlo Menotti. *Cast:* ANNINA: Adriana Morelli; MICHELE: Richard Burke; DESIDERIA: Adriana Cigogna; DON MARCO: Gabriele Monici; CARMELA: Antonia Brown; SALVATORE: Giorgio Gatti; ASSUNTA: Graziella Biondini; MARIA CORONA: Margaret Haggart.

SPOLETO FESTIVAL, 2001. MUSICAL DIRECTOR: Richard Hickox; CAST RECORDING on Chandos. *Cast:* ANNINA: Julia Melinek; ASSUNTA: Yvonne Howard; DESIDERIA: Pamela Helen Stephen; MARIA CORONA: Amelia Farrugia; MICHELE: Timothy Richards; CARMELA: Sandra Zeltzer; DON MARCO: John Marcus Bindel.

601. *Sally*

Set in the early 1920s. An orphan, Sally of the Alley, becomes a Ziegfeld dancing star.

Before Broadway. The original Broadway production was a reworking of the unfinished musical *The Little Thing*, by Jerome Kern, P.G. Wodehouse and Guy Bolton. It ran at the NEW AMSTERDAM THEATRE, 12/21/20–4/22/22. 561 PERFORMANCES. PRESENTED BY Florenz Ziegfeld; DIRECTOR/CHOREOGRAPHER: Edward Royce. *Cast:* SALLY: Marilyn Miller; CONNIE: Leon Errol; OTIS: Walter Catlett; BLAIR FARQUAR: Irving Fisher; ROSALIND RAFFERTY: Mary Hay; JIMMIE HOOPER: Stanley Ridges. It ran again, at the NEW AMSTERDAM THEATRE, 9/17/23–10/6/23. 24 PERFORMANCES. PRESENTED BY Florenz Ziegfeld Jr.; DIRECTOR: Edward Royce. *Cast:* SALLY: Marilyn Miller; OTIS: Water Catlett; CONNIE: Leon Errol. It was filmed in 1929. DIRECTOR: John Francis Dillon. Marilyn Miller, in her movie debut, reprised her Broadway role. Pert Kelton made her movie debut.

The 1948 revival was outdated before it started. It had a totally different score to the 1920 original. Willie Howard incorporated some of his established routines into Act II.

The Broadway Run. MARTIN BECK THEATRE, 5/6/48–6/5/48. 36 PERFORMANCES. PRESENTED BY Hunt Stromberg Jr. & William Berney; MUSIC: Jerome Kern; LYRICS: Clifford Grey, P.G. Wodehouse, B.G. "Buddy" De Sylva, Anne Caldwell; BOOK: Guy Bolton; DIRECTOR: Billy Gilbert; CHOREOGRAPHER: Richard Barstow; SETS/LIGHTING: Stewart Chaney; COSTUMES: Henry Mulle; MUSICAL SUPERVISOR: Pembroke Davenport; MUSICAL DIRECTOR: David Mordecai; ORCHESTRATIONS:

Robert Russell Bennett; ADDITIONAL ORCHESTRATIONS: Philip J. Lang; PRESS: Dick Weaver; GENERAL MANAGER: Irving Cooper; COMPANY MANAGER: Sam Schwartz; STAGE MANAGERS: Milton Stern & Stratton Walling. The producers wished to express their appreciation for assistance to Miss Catherine Littlefield and Morey Amsterdam. *Cast:* NADINA: Gloria Sullivan; THE YOUNG WAITER: Charles Wood; THE OLD WAITER: Holger Sorensen; OTIS HOOPER: Jack Goode; ROSIE: Kay Buckley; LILI BEDLINGTON: Bibi Osterwald; SHENDORF: Henry Calvin; MICKEY SINCLAIR: Robert Shackleton (3); SALLY GREEN: Bambi Linn (2); THE GRAND DUKE CONSTANTINE OF CZECHOGOVINIA: Willie Howard (1) ✩; MRS. VISCHER VAN ALSTYN: Kathryn Cameron; TOTO: Lucy Hillary; OLGA: Andrea Mann; SINGERS: Lucy Hillary, Ruth Johnston, Andrea Mann, Audrey Guard, Jean Olds, Eila Brynn, Gloria Hayden, Gloria Sullivan, Charles Wood, John George, Lynn Alden, Richard Oneto, Holger Sorensen, Steve Coleman, Hank Roberts, Brian Otis; DANCERS: Aura Vainio, Marcella Dodge, Mary Alice Bingham, Carmina Cansino, Gretchen Houser, Karlyn DeBoer, Carol Lee, Marcia Maier, Dolores Nevins, Jo McCann, Tommy Randall, Lee Lindsey, Dusty McCaffrey, Joe Vilane, Frank Reynolds, Garry Fleming, Jack Miller, Jimmy Russell. *Act I*: *Scene 1* Shendorf's Café in Greenwich Village; *Scene 2* The Long Island garden of Mrs. Van Alstyn. *Act II*: *Scene 1* The Church Around the Corner; *Scene 2* Kitchen of Shendorf's Cafe; *Scene 3* "The Follies;" *Scene 4* Backstage; *Scene 5* The Church Around the Corner. *Act I*: "Down Here in Greenwich Village" (Ensemble), "Bungalow in Quogue" (Rosie & Otis), "Look for the Silver Lining" (Sally & Mickey), "Looking All Over for You" (Principals & Ensemble), "Tulip Time in Sing Sing" (Constantine & Waiters), "The Whippoorwill Waltz" (dance) (Ensemble): WALTZERS: Jimmy Russell & Aura Vainio; "The Siren Song" [from the score of Jerome Kern's *Leave it to Jane*] (Sally, Mickey, Ensemble), "Cleopatra" [from score of Jerome Kern's *Leave it to Jane*] (Lili), "(A Wild) Wild Rose" (Sally, Mickey, Male Ensemble). *Act II*: "The Church Around the Corner" (sung by Rosie & Otis): SAILORS: Tommy Randall & Dusty McCaffrey; SAILORS' GIRL FRIEND: Carmina Cansino; OLD MAN: Joe Vilane; HIS BRIDE: Gretchen Houser; GUEST: Frank Reynolds; LOVESICK COUPLE: Mary Alice Brigham & Jack Miller; "Dear Little Girl" (Mickey & Sally), "Look for the Silver Lining" (reprise) (Sally & Constantine), "Reaching for Stars" (Sally & Ensemble), Finale (Entire Company).

Broadway reviews were generally not good.

After Broadway. *Sally (in Concert).* THE ACADEMY, 1/20/88–1/24/88. 5 PERFORMANCES. PRESENTED BY the New Amsterdam Theatre Company; DIRECTOR/CHOREOGRAPHER: James Brennan; SETS: Roger LaVoie; MUSICAL DIRECTOR: Jack Lee. *Cast:* SALLY: Christina Saffran; OTIS: Alan Sues; ROSALINE RAFFERTY: Louisa Flaningam; CONNIE: Jack Dabdoub; BLAIR FARQUAR: Don Correia; MRS. TEN BROCK: Jen Jones; CUSTARD: Sandy; RICHARD FARQUAR: Edwin Bordo; POPS: Gabor Morea; CHORUS: K. Craig Innes & Carolyn Kirsch. "In the Night Time," "On with the Dance," "Joan of Arc," "Look for the Silver Lining," "Sally," "The Social Game," "A Wild Wild Rose," "The Schnitza Komiski," "Whip-Poor-Will," "The Lorelei," "The Church Around the Corner," "The Nockerova Ballet," Finale.

602. *Sarafina!*

Set in Morris Isaacson High School near Soweto, in apartheid-riven South Africa, the site of the real-life 1976 student uprising protesting the use of Afrikaans in schools, and during which several hundred dissident students were killed by police. The plot involves the efforts of the students to mount a show in honor of imprisoned leader Nelson Mandela. The students are led by a brave girl, Sarafina, who had once been arrested and tortured. Despite government repression, their teacher, Mistress It's a Pity, teaches them about their heroes, such as Mandela and Steve Biko. The set is surrounded by barbed wire, and the musicians are dressed in khaki, as a reminder of the presence of the Army. The show climaxes with the students discarding their drab school uniforms in favor of colorful African clothes.

Before Broadway. In 1986 composer/director Mbongeni Ngema created this piece to commemorate the students. The show used Mbaqanga, the popular music of the South African townships. With the sponsorship of the Committed Artists Company of the Market Theatre of Johannesburg, Mr. Ngema recruited 23 South African performers, many of them teenagers and amateurs. The show premiered at the MARKET THEATRE in 6/87. On 10/25/87 Gregory Mosher, artistic director of Lincoln Center Theatre, presented it Off Broadway for 81 PERFORMANCES at the MITZI E. NEWHOUSE THEATRE, to good audience reaction. It closed on 1/3/88, and moved to Broadway.

The Broadway Run. CORT THEATRE, 1/28/88–7/2/89. 11 previews. 597 PERFORMANCES. The Committed Artists production, PRESENTED BY Lincoln Center Theatre, in association with Lucille Lortel & The Shubert Organization; MUSIC/MUSICAL ARRANGEMENTS: Mbongeni Ngema & Hugh Masekela; WRITER/CONCEIVED BY/DIRECTOR/CHOREOGRAPHER: Mbongeni Ngema; ADDITIONAL CHOREOGRAPHY/MUSICAL CONDUCTOR: Ndaba Mhlongo; SETS/COSTUMES: Sarah Roberts; LIGHTING: Mannie Manim; SOUND: Tom Sorce; PRESS: Merle Debuskey; GENERAL MANAGER: Steven C. Callahan; COMPANY MANAGERS: Lynn Landis, Helen V. Meier, Mali Hlatshwayo; PRODUCTION STAGE MANAGER: Bruce A. Hoover; STAGE MANAGER: Jerry Cleveland; ASSISTANT STAGE MANAGER: Monique Martin. *Cast:* MAGUNDANE (STUDENT): Ntomb'khona Dlamini; SCABHA (STUDENT): Khumbuzile Dlamini; COLGATE: Pat Mlaba; TEASPOON: Lindiwe Dlamini; CROCODILE: Dumisani Dlamini; SILENCE: Congo Hadebe; STIMELA SASE-ZOLA: Nhlanhla Ngema; S'GINCI, POLICE SERGEANT: Mhlathi Khuzwayo; SARAFINA: Leleti Khumalo; MISTRESS IT'S A PITY: Baby Cele; DUMADU (STUDENT): Nonhlanhla Mbambo; CHINA (STUDENT): Linda Mchunu; LINDIWE (STUDENT): Lindiwe Hlengwa; ZANDILE (STUDENT): Zandile Hlengwa; SIBONISO (STUDENT): Siboniso Khumalo; TIMBA (POLICEMAN): Cosmas Sithole; PRIEST: Thandani Mavimbela; CHARNELE: Charnele Dozier Brown; MUBI (STUDENT): Mubi Mofokeng; NANDI (STUDENT): Nandi Ndlovu; THANDEKILE (STUDENT): Thandekile Nhlanhla; POLICE LIEUTENANT: Pumi Shelembe; KIPZANE (STUDENT): Kipzane Skweyiya; REGINA: Regina Taylor; THANDI (STUDENT): Thandi Zulu. *Musicians:* KEYBOARDS: Master "Amos" Mathibe & Eddie Mathibe; TRUMPETS: Makate Peter Mofolo & Ray Molefe; LEAD GUITAR: Douglas Mnisi; DRUMS: Bruce Mwandla; BASS: S'Manga Nhlebela. *Act I*: 1. Overture (by Mr. Ngema) (Band); 2. Zibuyile Emasisweni ("It's Finally Happening") (m/l: Mr. Ngema) (Company); 3. "Niyayibona Lento Engiyibonayo" ("Do You See What I See?") (traditional) (Company); 4. "Sarafina" (m/l: Mr. Masekela) (Mhlathi Khuzwayo & Nhlanhla Ngema); 5. "The Lord's Prayer" (traditional) (Baby Cele & Company); 6. "Yes! Mistress It's a Pity" (m/l: Mr. Masekela & Mr. Ngema) (Baby Cele & Company); 7. "Give Us Power" (m/l: Mbongeni Ngema) (Thandi Zulu, Ntomb'khona Dlamini, Baby Cele, Company); 8. "Afunani Amaphoyisa eSoweto?" ("What is the Army Doing in Soweto?") (m/l: Mr. Ngema) (Company); 9. "Nkosi Sikeleli'Afrika" (traditional) (Company); 10. "Freedom is Coming Tomorrow" (m/l: Mr. Ngema) (Company). *Act II*: ENTR'ACTE: Excuse Me Baby, Please If You Don't Mind Baby, Thank You (m/l: Mr. Masekela) (Band); 1. "Talking About Love" (m/l: Mr. Masekela & Mr. Ngema) (Ntomb'khona Dlamini, Kipizane Skweyiya, Baby Cele, Lindiwe Hlengwa, Company); 2. "Meeting Tonight" (m/l: Mr. Masekela) (Thandekile Nhlanhla & Company); 3. "We Are Guerrillas" (traditional) (Thandekile Nhlanhla & Company); 4. "Uyamemeza Ungoma" (m/l: Mr. Ngema) (Thandi Zulu); 5. "We Will Fight for Our Land" (m/l: Mr. Ngema) (Thandani Mavimbela, Thandi Zulu, Dumisani Dlamini, Company); 6. "Mama" (by Mr. Ngema) (Ntomb'khona Dlamini, Thandekile Nhlanhla, Baby Cele, Company); 7. "Sechaba" (m/l: Mr. Masekela) (Company); 8. "Isizwe" ("The Nation is Dying") (m/l: Mr. Ngema) (Thandekile Nhlanhla); 9. "Kilimanjaro" (m/l: Mr. Ngema) (Company); 10. "Africa Burning in the Sun" (m/l: Mr. Masekela) (Company); 11. "Stimela Sase-Zola" (m/l: Mr. Ngema) (Nhlanhla Ngema & Company); 12. "Olayithi" ("It's All Right") (m/l: Mr. Ngema) (Company); 13. "Bring Back Nelson Mandela" (m/l: Mr. Masekela) (Leleti Khumalo & Company); 14. "Wololo!" (traditional) (Company).

Broadway reviews were guardedly and politely good. The show received Tony nominations for musical, score, direction of a musical, choreography, and for Leleti Khumalo.

After Broadway. TOUR. Opened on 3/19/90, at the Shubert Theatre, New Haven. It ran at the Kennedy Center, Washington, DC, 4/24/90–5/27/90, and also at the Ahmanson Theatre, Los Angeles. Except for a few minor roles, the tour cast was the same as for Broadway.

THE MOVIE. 1992, with Whoopi Goldberg, Miriam Makeba, Leleti Khumalo, and Mbongeni Ngema.

Sarafina! 2. In 1996 a sequel, *Sarafina! 2,* also written by Mbongeni Ngema, and focusing on AIDS rather than apartheid, was closed by the South African government (there was a question of misappropriation of funds, however). The show cost 14.2 million rand ($US 3.26 million).

603. *Saratoga*

Set in 1880. Clio, an illegitimate Creole gold-digger, returns to New Orleans to be respectable, and to revenge herself on the Dulaine family who exiled her mother from town. Posing as an American countess raised in France, she meets Montana cowboy Clint, who is out for revenge on the railroad barons who took his family's property. Clint induces Clio to accompany him to Saratoga, where she can seduce Van Steed, one of the railroad barons. Clint becomes rich helping Van Steed, and Clio marries Clint.

Before Broadway. Edna Ferber had long wanted to make a musical out of her novel. She asked Moss Hart (that didn't work) and then in the mid–50s Rodgers & Hammerstein, but they did *Pipe Dream* instead. Lerner & Loewe agreed to do it, but they backed out after *My Fair Lady* opened in 1956. Morton Da Costa then took it on, but when Miss Ferber read his libretto she wrote one of her own (it was ignored, and she bowed out). Rock Hudson and Jeanmaire were originally planned as the leads. The show tried out at the Shubert Theatre, Philadelphia, 10/26/59–11/28/59, and Harold Arlen became discouraged and sick (this was his last score), so Johnny Mercer wrote music and lyrics for three songs. Several numbers were cut: "Al Fresco," "Bon Appetit," "I'm Headed for Big Things," "Here Goes Nothing," "Lessons in Love," "Parks of Paris," "Reading the News," "Work Songs," "You for Me." Edith King replaced Jane Darwell, who quit after Philadelphia.

The Broadway Run. WINTER GARDEN THEATRE, 12/7/59–2/13/60. 80 PERFORMANCES. PRESENTED BY Robert Fryer; MUSIC: Harold Arlen (with Johnny Mercer); LYRICS: Johnny Mercer; CO-PRODUCER/BOOK/DIRECTOR: Morton Da Costa; BASED ON the 1941 novel *Saratoga Trunk,* by Edna Ferber, and on the 1942 movie, with Gary Cooper; CHOREOGRAPHER: Ralph Beaumont; SETS/COSTUMES: Cecil Beaton; LIGHTING: Jean Rosenthal; MUSICAL DIRECTOR: Jerry Arlen; ORCHESTRATIONS: Philip J. Lang; VOCAL ARRANGEMENTS: Herbert Greene; DANCE MUSIC ARRANGEMENTS: Genevieve Pitot; CAST RECORDING on RCA Victor; PRESS: Arthur Cantor; GENERAL MANAGER: Benjamin F. Stein; COMPANY MANAGER: David Lawlor; PRODUCTION STAGE MANAGER: Edward Padula; STAGE MANAGER: Duane Camp; ASSISTANT STAGE MANAGERS: Lanier Davis & Louis Kosman. *Cast:* CUPIDE, THE DWARF: Tun Tun (7); CLIO DULAINE: Carol Lawrence (2) ☆; KAKOU: Carol Brice (5); BELLE PIQUERY: Odette Myrtil (3); THE DRAPERY MAN: Mark Zeller; THE CARPENTER: Albert Popwell; SHORTY: Augie Rios; MAUDEY: Brenda Long; THE CHARWOMAN: Virginia Capers; MRS. LECLERC: Martha King; M. AUGUSTIN HAUSSY: Richard Graham (9); CLINT MAROON: Howard Keel (1) ☆; M. BEGUE: Truman Gaige (10); GRANDMOTHER DULAINE: Natalie Core; MADAME DULAINE: Beatrice Bushkin; CHARLOTTE THERESE: Jeannine Masterson; LEON, A WAITER: Mark Zeller; EDITOR: Truman Gaige; HABERDASHERY CLERK: Frank Green; FABRIC SALESMAN: Barney Johnston; M. LAFOSSE: Lanier Davis; MRS. SOPHIE BELLOP: Edith King (4); MRS. PORCELAIN: Natalie Core; MR. GOULD: Truman Gaige; BART VAN STEED: Warde Donovan (6); MR. BEAN: James Milhollin (8); DAISY PORCELAIN: Gerrianne Raphael; CLARISSA VAN STEED: Isabella Hoopes; MISS DIGGS: Janyce Wagner; ENSEMBLE (MARKET VENDORS, TOWNSPEOPLE, WAITERS, BUSBOYS, GAMBLERS, CROUPIERS, HOTEL GUESTS, OTHERS): Socrates Birsky, John Blanchard, Betsy Bridge, Beatrice Bushkin, Virginia Capers, Joseph Crawford, Lanier Davis, Paul Dixon, Vito Durante, Jose Falcion, Julius Fields, John Ford, Jerry Fries, Gene Gavin, Frank Green, Nathaniel Horne, Barney Johnston, Martha King, Louis Kosman, Ina Kurland, Jeannine Masterson, Jack Matthew, Oran Osburn, John Pero, Harold Pierson, Albert Popwell, Charles Queenan, Gerrianne Raphael, Carol Taylor, Merritt Thompson, Lois Van Pelt, Janyce Wagner, Beverley Jane Welch, Mark Zeller; CHILDREN: Brenda Long, Augie Rios, Wayne Robertson, Linda Wright. *Act I*: *Scene 1* The Rampart Street house, New Orleans, 1880: "I'll Be Respectable" (Clio), "One Step — Two Step" (Clio, Shorty, Maudey, Ensemble), "Gettin' a Man" (m: Johnny Mercer) (Belle & Kakou); *Scene 2* Exterior of the Rampart Street house; *Scene 3* The waterfront market: "Petticoat High" (Charwoman, Clio, Belle, Cupide, Ensemble); *Scene 4* The museum; *Scene 5* Begue's restaurant: "Why Fight This?" (m: Johnny Mercer) (Clio & Clint), "Game of Poker" (Clint & Clio); *Scene 6* The garden of the Rampart Street house: "Love Held Lightly" (Belle), "Game of Poker" (reprise) (Clio, Clint, Belle); *Scene 7* The Casino: "The Gamblers" (dance) (Clio, Gamblers, Croupiers), "Saratoga" (Clint & Clio); *Scene 8* The United States Hotel, Saratoga: "Saratoga" (reprise) (Ensemble), "The Gossip Song" (Mrs. Bellop & Ensemble); *Scene 9* Clint and Clio's rooms in the United States Hotel: "Countin' Our Chickens" (Clio & Clint), "You or No One" (Clint). *Act II*: *Scene 1* The Springs, Saratoga: "The Cure" (Ensemble), "The Men Who Run the Country" (m: Johnny Mercer) (Robber Barons); *Scene 2* Corridor of the United States Hotel; *Scene 3* Clint and Clio's rooms: "The Man in My Life" (Clio & Clint); *Scene 4* The verandah: "The Polka" (Clio, Bart, Ensemble), "Love Held Lightly" (reprise) (Clio); *Scene 5* The corridor: "Goose Never Be a Peacock" (Kakou); *Scene 6* On a flatcar and at the railroad station, Binghampton, New York: "Dog Eat Dog" (Clint & His Men), "The Railroad Fight" (Clint, Cupide, The Men); *Scene 7* The corridor; *Scene 8* The ballroom of the United States Hotel: "Petticoat High" (reprise) (Clio & Ensemble).

The show had over $1.5 million advance sales for Broadway (it cost $400,000 to make, a sum provided mostly by NBC and RCA). Reviews were unfavorable. The show won a Tony for costumes, and was nominated for sets (musical).

604. *Sarava*

The new hot musical. Sarava (with the stress on the last syllable) means "ciao," or "shalom." Set in Bahia, Brazil, from carnival to carnival. Flor's husband Vadinho is killed while helping a philandering friend defend himself against an angry husband. Through voodoo Vadinho comes back, but appears only to Flor, and sets out to ruin her new marriage to Teo, a quiet pharmacist.

Before Broadway. This was the only Mitch Leigh musical not directed by Albie Marre. Betty Walker replaced Grace Keagy during tryouts. Before Broadway Scott Matthews was understudy for Vadinho/Antonio. There was a TV saturation campaign to sell the Broadway previews to customers, and it was successful if a little risque (and risky). Because the ads were effective, the official Broadway opening night was postponed twice (1/30/79 and 2/9/79) before the press, led by *New York Times* critic Richard Eder, Clive Barnes (then of the *Post*) and Douglas Watt of the *Daily News*, got tired of that and reviewed it anyway, on 2/12/79 (*Variety* reviewed it on 2/14/79). Despite producer Eugene Wolsk publicly wishing evil upon Richard Eder, that particular critic, strangely, gave it a favorable review, but all the others hated it (this review, along with his equally at-odds reviews for *They're Playing Our Song* and *Ballroom,* demonstrated to the *New York Times* that Mr. Eder wasn't seeing the same shows other critics were seeing, and in 6/79 he was relegated to another department of the paper). However, the TV ads kept running, and the show never did have an official opening night. However, because the majority of the press reviewed it on 2/23/79 that has been the date arbitrarily selected as the official opening night.

The Broadway Run. MARK HELLINGER THEATRE, 2/23/79–3/4/79; BROADWAY THEATRE, 3/6/79–6/17/79. 37 previews from 1/11/79. Total of 140 PERFORMANCES. The Mitch Leigh production, PRESENTED BY Eugene V. Wolsk; MUSIC: Mitch Leigh; LYRICS/BOOK: N. Richard Nash; BASED ON the 1966 Brazilian novel *Dona Flor and Her Two Hus-*

bands, by Jorge Amado, and on the subsequent Brazilian film; DIRECTOR/CHOREOGRAPHER: Rick Atwell; SETS/COSTUMES: Santo Loquasto; LIGHTING: David F. Segal; SOUND: Robert Kerzman; MUSICAL DIRECTOR/VOCAL ARRANGEMENTS: David Friedman; ORCHESTRATIONS: Daniel Troob; DANCE MUSIC ARRANGEMENTS: Dom Salvador; PRESS: John A. Prescott & M.J. Boyer; CASTING: Mary Jo Slater; GENERAL MANAGEMENT: GRQ Productions & Manny Kladitis; STAGE MANAGER: Douglas F. Goodman; ASSISTANT STAGE MANAGER: John Brigleb. **Cast:** VADINHO: P.J. Benjamin (2); FLOR: Tovah Feldshuh (1) ☆; ARIGOF: Roderick Spencer Sibert (7), *Reginald Cannon-Jackson;* COSTAS: Doncharles Manning; MANUEL: Wilfredo Suarez; CARD GAME DEALER: Jack Neubeck; CASINO OWNER: Ken Waller [role added during previews]; DIONISIA: Carol Jean Lewis (5); POLICEMEN: Loyd Sannes (*Daniel Lorenzo*) & Gaetan Young; DONA PAIVA: Betty Walker (4); ROSALIA: Randy Graff (6); ANTONIO: Alan Abrams (8); PRIEST: Ken Waller; TEO: Michael Ingram (3); SENHOR BALDEZ: Jack Neubeck; PINHO: David Kottke; PEOPLE OF BAHIA: Steve J. Ace, Frank Cruz, Donna Cyrus, Marlene Danielle, Adrienne Frimet, Brenda Garratt, Trudie Green, Jane Judge, David Kottke, Daniel Lorenzo, Doncharles Manning, Jack Neubeck, Thelma Anne Nevitt, Ivson Polk, Wynonna Smith, Michelle Stubbs, Wilfredo Suarez, Ken Waller, Freida Ann Williams, John Leslie Wolfe, Gaetan Young. **Understudies**: Flor/Rosalia: Donna Cyrus; Vadinho/Antonio: Jack Neubeck; Teo: Ken Waller; Dona Paiva: Jane Judge; Dionisia: Freida Ann Williams; Arigof: Doncharles Manning & Gaetan Young; Costas: Gaetan Young; Priest: Daniel Lorenzo, *John Leslie Wolfe*; Policeman/Manuel: Frank Cruz; Dealer/Baldez/Pinho: John Brigleb. **Act I**: A STREET: "Sarava" (Vadinho, Flor, Others); BARRABAS CASINO: "Makulele" (Manuel, Costas, Vadinho, Arigof), "Vadinho is Gone" (Flor); KITCHEN IN FLOR'S HOUSE; A CEMETERY: "Hosanna" (Flor & Others); TEO'S PHARMACY: "Nothing's Missing" (Teo & Flor); BEDROOM IN FLOR'S HOUSE: "Nothing's Missing" (reprise) (Flor); DIONISIA'S CANDOMBLE: "I'm Looking for a Man" (Dionisia & Others); TEO'S PHARMACY: "A Simple Man" (Teo); KITCHEN IN FLOR'S HOUSE; A CHURCH: "Viva a Vida" (All). **Act II**: A HOTEL TERRACE: "Muito Bom" (Flor, Teo, Others); FLOR'S HOUSE: "Nothing's Missing" (reprise) (Flor & Teo); BARRABAS CASINO: "Play the Queen" (Flor, Vadinho, Arigof, Others); BEDROOM IN FLOR'S HOUSE: "Which Way Do I Go?" (Flor), "Remember" (Vadinho), "A Simple Man" (reprise) (Teo); DIONISIA'S: "You Do" (Dionisia & Others); A STREET: "A Single Life" (Vadinho), "Vadinho is Gone" (reprise) (Flor); FINALE: "Sarava" (reprise) (All).

It was panned by the critics. After a week it had to get out of the Mark Hellinger, to make way for *Home Again, Home Again* (which, as it happens, never made it to Broadway). Tovah Feldshuh was nominated for a Tony.

605. *Saturday Night Fever*

Also known as *Saturday Night Fever: The Musical*. Set in 1976, or whenever you were 19. The place is New York City (Brooklyn and Manhattan). The show had a cast of 43.

Before Broadway. LONDON PALLADIUM, 5/5/98–2/26/00. Previews from 4/21/98. PRESENTED BY Robert Stigwood, Paul Nicholas, David Ian; DIRECTOR/CHOREOGRAPHER: Arlene Phillips. **Cast**: TONY: Adam Garcia.

COLOGNE, Germany, 9/11/99. Previews from 7/26/99. DIRECTOR: Peter Weck; CHOREOGRAPHER: Arlene Phillips.

Final Broadway auditions were held on 5/7/99, when James Carpinello was picked for the role of Tony, and Paige Price for Stephanie. Writer Norman Wexler died 8/23/99.

The Broadway Run. MINSKOFF THEATRE, 10/21/99–12/31/00. 35 previews from 9/28/99. 502 PERFORMANCES. PRESENTED BY Robert Stigwood; MUSIC/LYRICS (unless otherwise stated): B.R. Gibb & M. Gibb (i.e. Barry & Maurice Gibb, of the Bee Gees); BASED ON the Paramount/RSO movie of the same name written by Norman Wexler, which in turn was based on a story, "The Tribal Rites of the New Saturday Night," by Nik Cohn; ADAPTED FOR THE STAGE BY Nan Knighton, in collaboration with Paul Nicholas, Arlene Phillips, and Robert Stigwood; DIRECTOR/CHOREOGRAPHER: Arlene Phillips; SETS: Robin Wagner; COSTUMES: Andy Edwards; BROADWAY COSTUMES: Suzy Benzinger;

LIGHTING: Andrew Bridge; SOUND: Mick Potter; MUSICAL SUPERVISOR/DANCE MUSIC & VOCAL ARRANGEMENTS: Phil Edwards; MUSICAL DIRECTOR: Martyn Axe; ORCHESTRATIONS: Nigel Wright; PRESS: Bill Evans & Associates; CASTING: Bernard Telsey; GENERAL MANAGEMENT: Niko Associates; COMPANY MANAGERS: Dan Swartz & James Lawson; PRODUCTION STAGE MANAGER: Perry Cline; STAGE MANAGER: Maximo Torres; ASSISTANT STAGE MANAGER: Rebecca C. Monroe. **Cast:** TONY MANERO: James Carpinello (1), *Sean Palmer* (from 7/7/00); STEPHANIE MANGANO: Paige Price (2); ANNETTE: Orfeh (3); BOBBY C: Paul Castree; JOEY: Sean Palmer; DOUBLE J: Andy Blankenbuehler, *Todd Stuart;* GUS: Richard H. Blake; MONTY: Bryan Batt, *David Coburn, Michael Paternostro;* FRANK MANERO: Casey Nicholaw; FLO MANERO/LUCILLE: Suzanne Costallos; FRANK JUNIOR: Jerry Tellier; FUSCO/AL: Frank Mastrone; JAY LANGHART/BECKER: David Coburn; CHESTER: Andre Ward; CESAR: Michael Balderrama; VINNIE: Chris Ghelfi; SAL: Danial Jerod Brown; DINO: Brian J. Marcum, *Matt Wall* (from 7/5/00); LOU: Rick Spaans; DOM: Miles Alden; ROBERTO: Ottavio; ANTONIO: Drisco Fernandez; IKE: David Robertson, *Jody Reynard* (6/00–10/00); SHIRLEY: Karine Plantadit-Bageot; MARIA: Natalie Willes; CONNIE: Jeanine Meyers; DOREEN: Angela Pupello; LINDA MANERO/PATTI: Aliane Baquerot; GINA: Rebecca Sherman; SOPHIA: Paula Wise; DONNA: Shannon Beach; ROSALIE: Deanna Dys, *Suzanne Harrer;* LOLA: Jennifer Newman; INEZ: Danielle Jolie; LORELLE: Stacey Martin; KENNY: Kristoffer Cusick; NICK: Karl duHoffmann; ROCKER: Roger Lee Israel; NATALIE: Anne Nicole Biancofiore; ANN MARIE: Marcia Urani; ANGELA: Gina Philistine. **Standby**: Tony: Sean Palmer. **Understudies**: Tony: Richard H. Blake; Stephanie: Jeanine Meyers & Angela Pupello; Annette: Jeanine Meyers & Gina Philistine; Bobby C: Miles Alden & Rick Spaans, *Josh Prince;* Joey: Chris Ghelfi & Rick Spaans; Double J: Danial Jerod Brown & Chris Ghelfi; Gus: Miles Alden, Danial Jerod Brown, Kristoffer Cusick; Monty: David Coburn & Jerry Tellier; Frank: David Coburn & Frank Mastrone; Flo/Lucille: Deanna Dys & Angela Pupello; Frank Jr.: Karl duHoffmann & Brian J. Marcum; Fusco/Al: David Coburn, David Eggers, Brian J. Marcum; Jay/Becker: Karl duHoffmann & David Eggers. **Swings**: Anne Nicole Biancofiore, Kristoffer Cusick, Karl duHoffmann, David Eggers, Roger Lee Israel, Gina Philistine, Amanda Plesa, Marcia Urani, *Rod Weber.* **Orchestra:** REEDS: Lawrence Feldman & William Meade; TRUMPETS: David Stahl & Earl Gardner; TROMBONES: Larry Farrell & Randall Andos; FRENCH HORN: Will Parker; BASS: Ian Stewart; GUITARS: Johan Nilson & Jeff Lee Campbell; KEYBOARDS: Henry Aronson, Philip Fortenberry, Eddie Rabin, John Samorian; PIANO/VOCALS: Farah Alvin, Scott Beck, Julie Danao, Solomon, Alan Souza, Donna Vivino; PERCUSSION: John Berger & James Musto; DRUMS: Chris Parker. **Act I**: **Scene 1** The Neighborhood — Bay Ridge, Brooklyn: "Stayin' Alive" (Tony & Company); **Scene 2** The Manero house; **Scene 3** Outside *2001 Odyssey*; Saturday night: "Boogie Shoes" (m/l: Harry Casey & Richard Finch) (Tony & The Faces); **Scene 4** Inside *2001 Odyssey*; Saturday night: "Disco Inferno" (m/l: Leroy Green & Ron Kersey) (Monty & Company), "Night Fever" (Tony & Company); **Scene 5** The Neighborhood paint store; **Scene 6** The Manero house; **Scene 7** Dale Dance Studios: "Disco Duck" (m/l: Rick Dees) (Monty), "More than a Woman" (Tony & Stephanie); **Scene 8** The Neighborhood: "If I Can't Have You" (Annette); **Scene 9** Inside *2001 Odyssey*; Saturday night: "It's My Neighborhood" (newly written by the Bee Gees) (Company), "You Should Be Dancing" (Tony & Company). **Act II**: **Scene 1** The Verrazano Narrows Bridge; Saturday night: "Jive Talkin'" (Tony, Annette, The Faces, Company); **Scene 2** Dale Dance Studios: "First and Last" / "Tragedy" (Bobby C); **Scene 3** The Neighborhood; **Scene 4** Stephanie's apartment, Manhattan: "What Kind of Fool" (m/l: Barry Gibb & Albhy Galuten) (Stephanie); **Scene 5** Park bench near the Bridge; **Scene 6** The Neighborhood; **Scene 7** Inside *2001 Odyssey*; Saturday night: "Nights on Broadway" (Annette, Stephanie, Company), The Dance Competition: "Night Fever" (reprise) (Company), "Open Sesame" [m/l: Robert Bell, Ronald Bell, George Brown, Charles Smith, Dennis Thomas (Kool & the Gang)] (Chester & Shirley), "More than a Woman" (reprise) (Tony & Stephanie), "Salsation" (m: David Shire) (Cesar & Maria) [end of the Dance Competition sequence]; **Scene 8** Exterior *2001 Odyssey*; Saturday night: "Immortality" (Tony); **Scene 9** Verrazano Narrows Bridge; Saturday night; **Scene 10** Park bench near the Bridge: "How Deep is Your Love" (Tony & Stephanie).

Other music credits for Act I: "A Fifth of Beethoven" (m: Walter Murphy), "Also Sprach Zarathustra" (m: Richard Strauss), "Night on Disco Mountain" (m: David Shire).

The Broadway opening night audience included Ben Vereen and Frank Wildhorn. Against all odds (including terrible reviews) it ran over 500 performances, but lost money.

After Broadway. TOUR. Opened on 3/6/01, at the Ford Center for the Performing Arts, Chicago. Previews from 3/3/01. It had originally been scheduled to start on 1/30/01, at the Orpheum Theatre, Minneapolis. *Cast*: TONY: Richard H. Blake; STEPHANIE: Jeanine Meyers; ANNETTE: Aileen Quinn; BOBBY C: Jim Ambler; JOEY: Andy Karl; DOUBLE J: Joey Calveri; GUS: Danial Jerod Brown; MONTY: Joseph Ricci.

TOUR. Opened on 11/1/02, in Saginaw, Mich. PRESENTED BY Robert Stigwood & Jon B. Platt; DIRECTOR/CHOREOGRAPHER: Arlene Phillips. *Cast*: TONY: Ryan Ashley, *Joey Calveri*; STEPHANIE: Jennifer Mrozik, *Jennie Marshall*; ANNETTE: Dena Di Giacinto; BOBBY C: Cameron Stevens; JOEY: Michael D. Jablonski; DOUBLE J: Ven Daniel; GUS: Jose Restrepo; MONTY: Darren Lorenzo; GINA: Melissa Cohen.

APOLLO VICTORIA THEATRE, London, 7/6/04. It followed a sell-out tour of the U.K. It replaced *Bombay Dreams* at the Apollo Victoria. PRESENTED BY Robert Stigwood, in association with Adam Spiegel; DIRECTOR/CHOREOGRAPHER: Arlene Phillips; SETS: Eamon D'Arcy; SOUND: Mick Potter; ORCHESTRATIONS: Nigel Wright. *Cast*: ANNETTE: Kim Marsh; MONTY: Shaun Williamson; TONY: Stephane Anelli.

606. *Say, Darling*

About an author whose book becomes a Broadway musical. It was based on Richard Bissell's adventures while making the 1954 Broadway musical *The Pajama Game*. Ted was supposedly based on Hal Prince, which didn't amuse the latter, apparently. Hackett was based on Bobby Griffith, Rudy on Richard Adler, and Jack on Richard Bissell himself.

Before Broadway. The numbers "And a Host of Others Too Numerous to Mention" and "My Little Yellow Dress" were cut before opening night. This was Matt Mattox's first solo choreographic credit on Broadway.

The Broadway Run. ANTA THEATRE, 4/3/58–12/6/58; MARTIN BECK THEATRE, 12/8/58–1/17/59. Total of 332 PERFORMANCES. PRESENTED BY Jule Styne & Lester Osterman; MUSIC: Jule Styne; LYRICS: Betty Comden & Adolph Green; BOOK: Richard Bissell, Abe Burrows, Marian Bissell; BASED ON the 1957 satirical novel of the same name by Richard Bissell; DIRECTOR: Abe Burrows; CHOREOGRAPHER: Matt Mattox; SETS: Oliver Smith; COSTUMES: Alvin Colt; LIGHTING: Peggy Clark; AT PIANOS: Colin Romoff & Peter Howard; PRESS: John L. Toohey; GENERAL MANAGER: Sylvia Herscher; PRODUCTION STAGE MANAGER: Robert Downing; STAGE MANAGER: Daniel S. Broun; ASSISTANT STAGE MANAGER: Michael Wettach. *Cast*: MR. SCHNEIDER: Gordon B. Clarke; FRANKIE JORDAN: Constance Ford; JACK JORDAN: David Wayne (1); PHOTOGRAPHER: Jack Naughton, *Hal England*; PILOT ROY PETERS: Jack Manning; TED SNOW: Robert Morse (4); JUNE, THE SECRETARY: Eileen Letchworth, *Kelly Leigh*; SCHATZIE HARRIS: Horace McMahon; RICHARD HACKETT: Jerome Cowan; IRENE LOVELLE: Vivian Blaine (2); RUDY LORRAINE: Johnny Desmond (3); SIDEMEN: Wendell Marshall & Peter Howard (*Lou Stein*); CHARLIE WILLIAMS: Robert Downing; MAURICE, A PIANIST: Colin Romoff; ARLENE MCKEE: Wana Allison; JENNIFER STEVENSON: Jean Mattox; EARL JORGESON: Elliott Gould; CHERYL MERRILL: Virginia Martin, *Paula Wayne*; ACCOMPANIST: Peter Howard; SAMMY MILES: Steve Condos; REX DEXTER: Mitchell Gregg; BORIS RESCHEVSKY: Matt Mattox (5); WAITER: Jack Naughton; MORTY KREBS: Walter Klavun; TATIANA: Jean Mattox, *Marcella Dodge*; JOYCE: Kelly Leigh, *Wana Allison*; KIDS IN THE SHOW: Wana Allison, Marcella Dodge, Barbara Hoyt, Kelly Leigh, Julie Marlowe, Jean Mattox, Carolyn Morris, Elliott Gould, Charles Morrell, Richard Tone, Calvin von Reinhold. *Understudies*: Jack: Jack Manning; Irene: Virginia Martin; Rudy: Bill Heyer; Richard: Walter Klavun; Frankie: Eileen Letchworth; Schatzie: Morty Krebs; Ted: Jack Naughton; Boris: Richard Tone. *Act I*: *Scene 1* An airport in the Corn Country; time is the present; *Scene 2* Hackett

& Snow's office in the Big City: "Chief of Love" (recording); *Scene 3* Stamford, the house that Jack took; *Scene 4* The office: "Try to Love Me (As I Am)" (Irene), "It's Doom" (Rudy), "The Husking Bee" (Rudy & Jack). *Act II*: *Scene 1* The auditions: "It's the Second Time You Meet that Matters" (Rudy), "Let the Lower Lights Be Burning" (Jack & Hackett), "Chief of Love" (reprise) (Irene); *Scene 2* Stamford; *Scene 3* Rehearsals: "Say, Darling" (Rudy), "The Carnival Song" (Jack, Irene, Sammy), Boris' Dance (Boris); *Scene 4* Stamford; *Scene 5* Irene Lovelle's apartment; *Scene 6* Stamford [this scene was dropped after the opening]. *Act III*: *Scene 1* That hotel room in New Haven; *Scene 2* Stamford; *Scene 3* Back to that hotel room in New Haven: "Try to Love Me (As I Am)" (reprise) (Rudy), "Dance Only with Me" (Irene & Rex), "Something's Always Happening on the River" (Jack, Rudy, Irene, Rex, others); *Scene 4* Idlewild Airport in New York.

Reviews were divided, but mostly good. Robert Morse was nominated for a Tony Award.

After Broadway. CITY CENTER, NYC, 2/25/59–3/8/59. 16 PERFORMANCES. "My Little Yellow Dress" was added to the end of Act II. Act II, which on Broadway had comprised 4 scenes, now had only one scene, set in That hotel room in New Haven. PRESENTED BY the New York City Center Light Opera Company; DIRECTOR: David Clive; CHOREOGRAPHER: Matt Mattox; LIGHTING: Peggy Clark; MUSICAL DIRECTOR: Colin Romoff. *Cast*: SCHNEIDER: Gordon B. Clarke; FRANKIE: Betsy von Furstenburg; JACK: Orson Bean; TED: Robert Morse; JUNE: Kelly Leigh; SCHATZIE: Jack Waldron; HACKETT: Alexander Clark; IRENE: Mindy Carson; RUDY: David Atkinson; MAURICE: Brooks Morton; ARLENE: Janyce Wagner; JENNIFER/TATIANA: Jean Mattox; EARL: Elliott Gould; CHERYL: Paula Wayne; REX: Mitchell Gregg; BORIS: Matt Mattox; KIDS INCLUDED: Marcella Dodge, Calvin von Reinhold, Elliott Gould, George Martin, Jean Mattox, Eddie Weston.

WEST END THEATRE, NYC, 5/24/96–6/17/96. 16 PERFORMANCES. This was a revised revival. DIRECTOR: Robert Armin; CHOREOGRAPHER: Sven Toorvald; MUSICAL DIRECTOR: Michael Lavine. *Cast*: JACK: Bill Tatum; IRENE: Lynn Bowman; SAMMY: Max Perlman; RUDY: Paul Amodeo; BORIS: Charles Black; MORTY: Donald Brennan; REX: John Canary; TED: Steve Gibbons; SCHATZIE: Bonnie Perlman. This production used songs based on the original 1958 production, as well as from the show *Two on the Aisle*. "Chief of Love," "Try to Love Me," "It's Doom," "The Husking Bee," "It's the Second Time You Meet that Matters," "Let the Lower Lights Be Burning," "If You Hadn't But You Did" (from *Two on the Aisle*), "Say, Darling," "Carnival Song," "Hold Me," "Give a Little, Get a Little" (from *Two on the Aisle*), "Dance Only with Me," "Something Always Happening on the River."

607. *The Scarlet Pimpernel*

A musical adventure, set in England and France, from May into July 1794. Sir Percy Blakeney poses as an effeminate dandy, but in reality is the Scarlet Pimpernel, rescuing aristocrats from the guillotine in Paris. A pimpernel is a small English flower, and it was the crest of the Blakeney family. Sir Percy used it on his signet ring. By the end of Broadway run there had been so many versions, that the cast and crew jokingly referred to them as Versions 1.0, 2.0, 3.0, and 4.0.

Before Broadway. This show began in 1992 as a concept album on Angel Records, featuring Linda Eder, Chuck Wagner, and Dave Clemmons. This was while the show was being developed by the Nederlander Organization in New York. The musical numbers on the album were: "Madame Guillotine," "Into the Fire," "The Riddle," "The Creation of Man," "Home Again," "I'll Forget You," "Marguerite," "Now when the Rain Falls," "Our Separate Ways," "The Scarlet Pimpernel," "Story Book," "There Never was a Time," "They Seek Him Here," "When I Look at You," "You Are My Home," and "The Pimpernel Fanfare." It was much re-worked over the next few years by Nan Knighton & Frank Wildhorn. There was a reading of the revised show in 1997. Eight of the songs had been dropped by then, and there was a completely new title song. *Cast at the reading*: PERCY: Greg Zerkle; MARGUERITE: Carolee Carmello.

Version 1.0 (as it later became known as) was first announced to be opening on Broadway on 10/2/97 (a date put back to 11/2/97, then to 11/9/97, and finally to 11/11/97). Rehearsals began in 9/97 (put back from mid–July). On 2/19/97 it was announced that the Minskoff would be the theatre. On 8/21/97 it was announced that Walter Painter, the choreographer, had quit. On 9/3/97 the rest of the main cast was confirmed (Douglas Sills, Terrence Mann and Christine Andreas having already been announced). There was a press preview on 9/4/97. "Madame Guillotine" was now the opening number.

The Broadway Run. Version 1.0 ran at the MINSKOFF THEATRE, 11/11/97–10/1/98; Version 2.0 also ran at the MINSKOFF THEATRE, 11/4/98–5/30/99; Version 3.0 ran at the NEIL SIMON THEATRE, 9/10/99–1/2/00. 39 previews from 10/7/97. Total of 772 PERFORMANCES (640 at the Minskoff; 132 at the Neil Simon). PRESENTED BY Pierre Cossette, Bill Haber, Kathleen Raitt, Hallmark Entertainment, Radio City Entertainment & Theodore J. Forstmann (these later two took over on 7/23/98); MUSIC: Frank Wildhorn; LYRICS/BOOK: Nan Knighton; BASED ON Baroness Orczy's 1905 novel of the same name; DIRECTOR: Peter Hunt, *Robert Longbottom* (from 9/98); CHOREOGRAPHER: Adam Pelty (his Broadway debut), *Robert Longbottom* (from 9/10/99); SETS: Andrew Jackness; COSTUMES: Jane Greenwood; LIGHTING: Natasha Katz; SOUND: Karl Richardson; MUSICAL SUPERVISOR: Jason Howland; MUSICAL DIRECTOR/VOCAL ARRANGEMENTS: Ron Melrose; ORCHESTRATIONS: Kim Scharnberg; DANCE MUSIC ARRANGEMENTS: David Chase; CAST RECORDING on Atlantic, released on 2/3/98 [this is not to be confused with the original concept album]; PRESS: Boneau/Bryan-Brown, *Barlow—Hartman* (from 9/10/99); CASTING: Julie Hughes & Barry Moss; GENERAL MANAGEMENT: 101 Productions; COMPANY MANAGER: Ron Gubin, *Charles Underhill* (from 9/10/99); PRODUCTION STAGE MANAGER: Steven Beckler, *Kenneth J. Davis* (from 9/10/99); STAGE MANAGER: Bonnie L. Becker; ASSISTANT STAGE MANAGER: Marcos Dinnerstein, *Jack Gianino*. **Version 1.0 cast**: MADAME ST. CYR: Marine Jahan; ST. CYR: Tim Shew, *Mark McGrath*; MARIE: Elizabeth Ward [later Elizabeth Ward Land]; TUSSAUD: Philip Hoffman; DEWHURST: James Judy; CHAUVELIN: Terrence Mann (2) ☆; SIR PERCY BLAKENEY/THE SCARLET PIMPERNEL: Douglas Sills (3) ☆; MARGUERITE ST. JUST: Christine Andreas (1) ☆ (until 10/4/98) [sic], *Lauri Landry* (stood in many times); LADY DIGBY: Sandy Rosenberg; LADY LLEWELLYN: Pamela Burrell; ARMAND ST. JUST: Gilles Chiasson (4), *James Bohanek* (from 8/9/98); OZZY: Ed Dixon; LORD FARLEIGH: Allen Fitzpatrick; LEGGETT: Bill Bowers; ELTON: Adam Pelty, *Russell Garrett* (from 8/20/98); HAL: Ron Sharpe, *Michael Hance* (from 7/26/98); HASTINGS: William Thomas Evans; BEN: Dave Clemmons (until 4/8/98), *Ken Land* (from 4/9/98); NEVILLE: R.F. Daley, *Darrin Baker, Casey Nicholaw*; ROBESPIERRE: David Cromwell; GRAPPIN: Ken Labey; COUPEAU, THE FRENCH JAILER: Eric Bennyhoff [on 7/26/98 Mr. Bennyhoff changed his name to Timothy Eric Hart]; MERCIER: Jeff Gardner; JESSUP/EXECUTIONER: James Dybas; PRINCE OF WALES: David Cromwell; HELENE: Melissa Hart; MANON ROLAND: Lauri Landry; CHLOE: Alison Lory; SOUS-CHEF: Sutton Foster (until 2/22/98), *Kay Story*; JAILER: Don Mayo (T. Doyle Leverett from 7/15/98); FISHERMAN: David Cromwell; FRENCH MOB/SOLDIERS/GUESTS: Stephanie Bast, Nick Cavarra, Sutton Foster (*Kay Story*), Melissa Hart, Lauri Landry, Alison Lory, Don Mayo (*T. Doyle Leverett*), Kevyn Morrow, Katie Nutt, Terry Richmond, Craig Rubano, Charles West. **Standby**: Percy: George Dvorsky. **Understudies**: Percy: Bryan Batt; Marguerite: Lauri Landry; Chauvelin: Eric Bennyhoff; Armand: Craig Rubano; Robespierre/Prince: James Dybas; Ozzy: Ed Sala; Dewhurst: Adam Pelty, *Russell Garrett*. **Swings**: Paul Castree (*Richard Roland* from 5/25/98), Sarah Knapp, Catherine LaValle, Ed Sala, Stacia Fernandez (*Natalie Blalock* from 6/20/98), *Drew Geraci*. **Orchestra:** CONCERTMASTER: Michael Roth; VIOLINS: Joan Kwuon, Britt Swenson, Lisa Matricardi, Laura Oatts, Ashley Horne; VIOLAS: Liuh-Wen Ting & Leslie Tomkins; CELLI: Daniel D. Miller & Sarah Hewitt; BASSOON/CONTRABASSOON: Gilbert DeJean; BASS: Richard Sarpola; WOODWINDS: Edward Joffe, James Roe, Andrew Sterman; TRUMPET: Chris Gekker; TROMBONE: Mike Christianson; FRENCH HORNS: Chris Komer & Kelly Dent; KEYBOARDS: Wendy Bobbitt, Robert Gustafson, Andrew Wilder; PERCUSSION: John Meyers & Benjamin Herman.

VERSION 1.0 MUSICAL NUMBERS: *Act I:* Overture ("The Pimpernel Fanfare") (Orchestra), "Madame Guillotine" (French Chorus), "Believe" (Percy, Marguerite, British Chorus) [new number since 1992], "Vivez!" (Marguerite, Lady Digby, Lady Llewellyn, Percy, et al [new number since 1992], "Prayer" (Percy), "Into the Fire" (Percy & His Men), "Falcon in the Dive" (Chauvelin), "When I Look at You" (Marguerite), "The Scarlet Pimpernel" (Percy, Marguerite, Marie, Armand, Lady Digby, Lady Llewellyn, Servants) [same title as in 1992, but a new song], "Where's the Girl" (Chauvelin) [new number since 1992], "When I Look at You" (reprise) (Percy), "The Creation of Man" (Percy, Prince of Wales, Percy's Men), "The Riddle" (Chauvelin, Marguerite, Percy, et al). *Act II:* "They Seek Him Here" (Percy, Prince, Lady Digby, Lady Llewellyn, et al), "Only Love" (Marguerite) [new number since 1992], "She Was There" (Percy), "Storybook" (Leontine & French Chorus), "Lullaby" (Helene & Chloe), "You Are My Home" (Marguerite, Armand, French Prisoners) [new number since 1992], "Believe" (reprise) (Company).

Broadway reviews were terrible, and the show never really found its audience. It received Tony nominations for musical, book, and for Douglas Sills. By the summer of 1998 the production was reported to have already lost $10 million, and to be losing $100,000 a week. On 7/23/98 it was announced that the producers, Pierre Cossette, Bill Haber and Kathleen Raitt (John Raitt's ex-wife) had sold the show to Cablevision Systems Corporation and entrepreneur Ted Forstmann (both new parties to be 50-50). This was a unique move in Broadway history — existing producers selling a show to a corporation during the course of the run. The show had long been in trouble, of course, and it was now decided to do something about it. On 8/13/98 it was announced that Bobby Longbottom was coming in as the new director, to re-stage, and that he, Frank Wildhorn and Nan Knighton would collaborate on a new version. There was rumor that Terrence Mann would leave, and that David Hasselhoff might take over as Chauvelin, but that never happened. On 8/26/98 it was announced that Christine Andreas would bow out on 10/4/98, and on 8/31/98 that Douglas Sills would stay on as Percy, and Terrence Mann would definitely leave. It was also rumored that Rachel York and Rex Smith were the replacements (they were confirmed by 9/22/98). During 9/98 the cast rehearsed the new show and performed the old one, and on 10/1/98 the show closed while the new show was loaded into place.

VERSION 2.0. There were several changes. Aside from the changes in music and lyrics, the choreography had been added to (and changed in) the Wedding Dance sequence, to the "Creation of Man," and to the gavotte at the Prince of Wales' dress-up ball. Percy was even more effeminate. 10/13/98 was the date scheduled for the new opening at the same theatre (the Minskoff), but this date was put forward to the 10/10/98 matinee, which became the first date for a new set of previews. Douglas Sills missed the 10/11/98 and three subsequent performances due to laryngitis. His standby went on for him. The new official opening date became 11/4/98. The new show was so changed that the producers hoped it might be considered for Tonys all over again. It opened to better reviews and box-office receipts. On 1/24/99 it was announced that Douglas Sills would be leaving the show on 3/7 (he didn't, as it happens), and Ron Bohmer was rumored to be his replacement. On 4/13/99 Rex Smith was mugged (but not hurt) in his apartment complex in New York City, and missed the week's performances (his understudy went on for him). On 5/30/99 the show left the Minskoff to make way for the incoming *Saturday Night Fever*. **Cast of Version 2.0 and tour**: MARGUERITE ST. JUST: Rachel York (until 5/30/99), *Carolee Carmello* (from 7/27/99); CHAUVELIN: Rex Smith, *Tom Zemon* (stood in for a week from 4/13/99, after Mr. Smith was mugged. Mr. Smith was back by 4/20/99. He finally left the show on 5/30/99), *Marc Kudisch* (from 7/27/99); PERCY: Douglas Sills (until 5/30/99), *Nat Chandler* (during Mr. Sills' illness, 10/11/98–10/14/98, during previews of Version 2.0), *Ron Bohmer* (from 7/27/99); MARIE: Elizabeth Ward [later Elizabeth Ward Land], *Mary Illes* (from 1/2/99); ARMAND: James Bohanek (until 5/30/99), *Kirk McDonald* (from 7/27/99); TUSSAUD: Philip Hoffman (until 5/30/99), *David Masenheimer* (from 7/27/99); COUPEAU: Timothy Eric Hart, *Stephonne Smith* (from 7/27/99); MERCIER: Jeff Gardner (until 5/30/99), *David St. Louis* (from 7/27/99); OZZY: Ed Dixon (until 5/30/99), *Harvey Evans* (from 7/27/99); ELTON: Russell Garrett, *Adam Pelty* (until 5/30/99), *Russell Garrett* (from 7/27/99); FARLEIGH: Tom Zemon, *Matthew Shepard* (from 9/10/99); DEWHURST: James Judy (until 5/30/99), *Ken Land* (from 7/27/99); JESSUP/EXECUTIONER: James Dybas (until 5/30/99), *Charles*

West (from 7/27/99); BEN: Ken Land, *James Hindman* (from 1/2/99), *Dave Clemmons* (until 5/30/99), *James Hindman* (from 7/27/99); HASTINGS: William Thomas Evans; NEVILLE: Stephen Hope; LEGGETT: Douglas Storm; HAL: Michael Hance, *Danny Gurwin* (from 7/27/99); ROBESPIERRE: David Cromwell; LADY DIGBY: Sandy Rosenberg; LADY LLEWELLYN: Pamela Burrell; PRINCE OF WALES: David Cromwell; JAILER: T. Doyle Leverett: FRENCH MOB/SOLDIERS/DANCERS/BRITISH GUESTS/SERVANTS: Stephanie Bast, Nick Cavarra, Michael Halling, Marine Jahan, John Lathan, Alison Lory, Mark McGrath, Katie Nutt, Jessica Phillips, Terry Richmond, Craig Rubano, Cynthia Sophiea, Charles West. TOUR ENSEMBLE (from 7/27/99): Charles West, Alicia Irving, Jessica Phillips, Jennifer Smith, Stephonne Smith, David Masenheimer, Emily Hsu, Robb McKindles, Katie Nutt, Elizabeth O'Neill, Terry Richmond, Laura Schuter. *Standby*: Percy: Nat Chandler, *Bryan Batt* (from 2/10/99). *Understudies*: Percy: William Thomas Evans; Marguerite: Jessica Phillips & Elizabeth Ward; Chauvelin: Timothy Eric Hart, Mark McGrath, Tom Zemon; Armand: Nick Cavarra & Craig Rubano; Robespierre/Prince: James Dybas, James Van Treuren; Ozzy/Dewhurst/Farleigh: James Van Treuren, Stephen Hope, Ken Land; Marie: Jessica Phillips & Terry Richmond; Lady Digby/Lady Llewellyn: Sarah Knapp, Cynthia Sophiea. *Swings* (by 7/27/99): Peter Flynn, Drew Geraci, Cynthia Leigh Helm, Jennifer Smith, James Van Treuren.

VERSION 2.0 MUSICAL NUMBERS: *Act I*: *Scene 1* Onstage; Comedie Francaise: "Storybook" (Marguerite & French Ensemble); *Scene 2* Backstage: Comedie Francaise & Place de la Bastille; *Scene 3* The prison; *Scene 4* Place de la Bastille: "Madame Guillotine" (Chauvelin); *Scene 5* England, the Blakeney estate, the wedding of Percy & Marguerite: "You Are My Home" (Percy & Marguerite), Wedding Dance (Ensemble); *Scene 6* England, the Blakeney estate; then limbo, as the scene is transformed to Percy's schooner: "Prayer" (Percy); *Scene 7* Percy's schooner: "Into the Fire" (Percy & The League); *Scene 8* Place de la Bastille: The Rescue Ballet (Ensemble), "Falcon in the Dive" (Chauvelin), "The Scarlet Pimpernel" (transition); *Scene 9* Blakeney estate; the drawing room: "When I Look at You" (Marguerite), "When I Look at You" (reprise) (Marguerite & Percy); *Scene 10* Blakeney estate; the drawing room: "Where's the Girl?" (Chauvelin), "You Are My Home" (reprise) (Marguerite); *Scene 11* Blakeney estate; the library: "The Creation of Man" (Percy & The League); *Scene 12* England; the Royal Palace: "The Riddle" (Chauvelin, Marguerite, Percy, Company). *Act II*: *Scene 1* England; the Royal Palace; ballroom: "The Scarlet Pimpernel" (Percy, Marguerite, Ball Guests), "They Seek Him Here" (Percy & Company), The Gavotte (Ensemble); *Scene 2* A footbridge in the garden: "She Was There" (Percy); *Scene 3* France; the cafe (the bistro): "Storybook" (reprise) (Marguerite & French Girls), "Where's the Girl?" (reprise) (Chauvelin); *Scene 4* The prison & a Paris street: *Scene 5* The Hideaway (the Batcave): "Into the Fire" (reprise) (The League); *Scene 6* The prison: "I'll Forget You" (Marguerite); *Scene 7* Outside the prison; *Scene 8* Interior of a rumbling carriage; *Scene 9* A remote spot on the French seacoast: The Duel (Percy, Chauvelin, Marguerite); *Scene 10* The English Channel; aboard Percy's schooner: Finale: "When I Look at You" (reprise) (Percy & Marguerite) & "Into the Fire" (reprise) (Company).

VERSION 3.0. After the show vacated the Minskoff Theatre on 5/30/99, the plan was to take a new, revised again version (Version 3.0) on a mini-tour before going back to Broadway, at the Neil Simon Theatre, on 9/10/99. There were some minor staging and set changes, but no changes in the music and lyrics (except that the Act II reprises were cut) or other major changes. DIRECTOR/CHOREOGRAPHER: Robert Longbottom. On 6/4/99 the touring cast was announced. The number of cast members was cut, following a complicated deal with Equity, from 41 to 20 and then 9 new members were added, so it was a more intimate show. The tour opened at the Music Hall, Dallas, 7/27/99–8/8/99. Then to Houston's Wortham Center, 8/10/99–8/22/99, then to the Fox Theatre, Atlanta, 8/25/99–8/30/99. Then back to Broadway. Officially it was "resuming performances" when it re-opened at the Neil Simon, rather than starting fresh, as it had done earlier at the Minskoff. And this time there was no new preview period. It had the same basic crew as for Version 2.0, except for PRESS: Barlow — Hartman; STAGE MANAGER: Kenneth J. Davis. *Version 3.0 cast*: MARGUERITE: Carolee Carmello; CHAUVELIN: Marc Kudisch; PERCY: Ron Bohmer; MARIE: Elizabeth Ward Land; ARMAND: Kirk McDonald; TUSSAUD: David Masenheimer;

COUPEAU: Stephonne Smith; MERCIER: David St. Louis; OZZY: Harvey Evans; ELTON: Russell Garrett; DEWHURST: Ken Land; JESSUP: Charles West; BEN: James Hindman; FARLEIGH: Matthew Shepard; HAL: Danny Gurwin; ROBESPIERRE/PRINCE OF WALES: David Cromwell; OPERA DANCERS/SOLDIERS/PRISONERS/BRITISH GUESTS/SERVANTS: Emily Hsu, Alicia Irving, David Masenheimer, Robb McKindles, Katie Nutt, Elizabeth O'Neill, Terry Richmond, Laura Schuter, Charles West, Debra Wiseman. *Understudies*: Percy: Peter Flynn & Matthew Shepard; Marguerite: Elizabeth Ward Land & Debra Wiseman; Chauvelin: David Masenheimer & Matthew Shepard; Armand: Danny Gurwin & Robb McKindles; Robespierre/Prince of Wales: David Masenheimer & James Van Treuren; Ozzy: James Hindman & James Van Treuren; Dewhurst: Peter Flynn, James Hindman, James Van Treuren; Marie: Terry Richmond & Debra Wiseman; Elton: Peter Flynn & Drew Geraci; Ben/Hal: Drew Geraci & Robb McKindles. *Swings*: Peter Flynn, Drew Geraci, Cynthia Leigh Heim, Jennifer Smith, James Van Treuren. *Orchestra*: KEYBOARDS: Wendy Bobbitt Cavett, Andrew Wilder, Robert Gustafson; CONCERTMASTER: Laura Oatts; VIOLINS: Britt Swenson & Ashley Horne; VIOLA: Liuh-Wen Ting; CELLI: Daniel D. Miller & Sarah Hewitt; BASS: Richard Sarpola; WOODWINDS: Steven Greenfield & James Roe; TRUMPET: Roger Lee; TROMBONE: Mike Christianson; FRENCH HORNS: Jill Williamson & Kelly Dent; PERCUSSION: John Meyers & Benjamin Herman.

On 10/29/99 it was announced that the show would close in 1/00 to go on a national tour, and on 11/11/99 the closing date was set at 1/4/00.

After Broadway. VERSION 4.0. This was the post–Broadway national tour, with revised sets but no change to the music and Lyrics. On 12/22/99 Douglas Sills had been announced to play Percy again, for 17 weeks only. The tour opened on 2/20/00, at the Shubert Theatre, New Haven, and was to have run through mid–summer 2001, but it finally closed on 4/1/01, in Grand Rapids, Mich. Part of the tour was at the Ahmanson Theatre, Los Angeles, 5/3/00–6/18/00. DIRECTOR/CHOREOGRAPHER: Robert Longbottom. *Cast*: PERCY: Douglas Sills, *Robert Patteri* (from 6/27/00), *Ron Bohmer* (from 12/12/00 in Denver, when Mr. Patteri suffered a vocal injury); MARGUERITE: Amy Bodnar; CHAUVELIN: William Paul Michals.

608. *The Secret Garden*

Set in 1906. Mary Lennox is a lonely and ill-tempered orphan whose parents have died in a cholera epidemic in India, and she has come to live with her cold uncle Archibald Craven in the Yorkshire moors, at his gloomy and mysterious estate, Misselthwaite Manor. Craven has ceaselessly mourned the loss of his wife Lily ten years before in childbirth, and is grief-stricken for his bedridden son, ten-year-old Colin. Mary discovers Lily's secret garden on the estate, and with the aid of Colin, she cultivates the garden. In doing so she, Colin and Craven are all brought back to health and vigor. A new character, Neville, was written in to the musical. He had been secretly in love with Lily.

Before Broadway. Frances Hodgson Burnett's story had been filmed — straight — in 1949. *Cast*: MARY: Margaret O'Brien; ARCHIBALD: Herbert Marshall; COLIN: Dean Stockwell; MRS. MEDLOCK: Gladys Cooper. Another straight version would be released in 1993.

Heidi Landesman was sent a record of the 1982 British musical *The Secret Garden* (see appendix). She didn't like it, but she re-read the book, and determined to do her own musical version of the Burnett story. She contacted her friend, Pulitzer Prize–winning dramatist Marsha Norman, to do the lyrics and book. Lucy Simon, sister of Carly Simon, was hired to do the music, and the show was first presented at SKIDMORE COLLEGE, then at the VIRGINIA STAGE COMPANY, Norfolk, Va., from 2/6/90. DIRECTOR: R.J. Cutler; SETS: Heidi Landesman; COSTUMES: Martin Pakledinaz; LIGHTING: Roger Morgan; MUSICAL DIRECTOR: David Loud. *Cast*: Victoria Clark, Jedediah Cohen, Christopher Davis, Suzanne Dowaliby, Walter Hudson, Bonny Hughes, Michael McCormick, Stacey

Moseley, Louis Padilla, Wade Raley, Molly Regan, Sharon Scruggs, Melanie Vaughan, William Youmans, Aaron Boone, Jonathan Frank, Jessica Greene, Joshua Ivey, Mark Molineaux, Greg Moore. R.J. Cutler was fired, and Susan H. Schulman was brought in. In 10/90 there was a staged reading at the Michael Bennett studio.

The Broadway Run. St. James Theatre, 4/25/91–1/3/93. 22 previews from 4/5/91. 706 performances. Presented by Heidi Landesman, Rick Steiner, Frederic H. Mayerson, Elizabeth Williams, Jujamcyn Theatres/TV ASAHI, and Dodger Productions; Music: Lucy Simon; Lyrics/Book: Marsha Norman; Based on the classic 1911 children's novel of the same name, by Frances Hodgson Burnett; Director: Susan H. Schulman; Choreographer: Michael Lichtefeld; Sets: Heidi Landesman; Costumes: Theoni V. Aldredge; Lighting: Tharon Musser; Sound: Otts Munderloh; Musical Director/Vocal Arrangements: Michael Kosarin; Orchestrations: William David Brohn; Dance Music Arrangements: Jeanine Levenson; Cast recording on Columbia/Sony; Press: Adrian Bryan-Brown; Casting: Wendy Ettinger; General Management: David Strong Warner; Company Manager: Sandy Carlson; Production Stage Manager: Perry Cline; Stage Managers: Francis Lombardi & Maximo Torres, *Elisabeth Farwell* (added by 91–92). *Cast:* Lily: Rebecca Luker; Mary Lennox: Daisy Eagan, *Lydia Ooghe* (from 3/12/92); Mary Lennox (Wednesday matinees & Thursday evenings): Kimberly Mahon, *Lee Alison Marino*. In Colonial India; 1906: Fakir: Peter Marinos; Ayah: Patricia Phillips, *Elizabeth Acosta*; Rose, Mary's mother: Kay Walbye; Capt. Albert Lennox, Mary's father: Michael DeVries, *David Elledge*; Lt. Peter Wright: Drew Taylor; Lt. Ian Shaw: Paul Jackel; Maj. Holmes: Peter Samuel; Claire, his wife: Rebecca Judd; Alice (Rose's friend): Nancy Johnston. At Misselthwaite Manor, North Yorkshire, England: Archibald Craven (Mary's uncle): Mandy Patinkin, *Howard McGillin* (from 8/22/91); Dr. Neville Craven, his brother: Robert Westenberg; Mrs. Medlock, the housekeeper: Barbara Rosenblat; Martha, a chambermaid: Alison Fraser; Dickon, her brother: John Cameron Mitchell, *Jedediah Cohen*; Ben, the gardener: Tom Toner; Colin: John Babcock, *Diedrich Stelljes*; Jane: Teresa De Zarn, *Laurie Gayle Stephenson*; William: Frank Di Pasquale; Betsy: Betsy Friday; Timothy: Alec Timmerman, *Brian Quinn*; Mrs. Winthrop, the headmistress: Nancy Johnston; Others: Ensemble. *Standby*: Archibald: Greg Zerkle. *Understudies*: Archibald: Michael DeVries & Peter Samuel; Lily: Teresa De Zarn & Nancy Johnston, *Laurie Gayle Stephenson*; Mary: Melody Kay, *Cammie McCardell-Fossel & Lee Alison Marino*; Neville: Michael DeVries & Paul Jackel; Mrs. Medlock: Rebecca Judd & Jane Seaman, *Priscilla Quinby*; Martha: Betsy Friday & Jennifer Smith; Alice: Betsy Friday & Jennifer Smith, *Patricia Quinby*; Dickon/Shaw: Kevin Ligon & Alec Timmerman, *Brian Quinn*; Fakir: Kevin Ligon & Alec Timmerman, *Frank Di Pasquale*; Ben: Bill Nolte & Drew Taylor; Colin: Joel E. Chaiken, *Parker Conrad & Lance Robinson*; Rose: Teresa De Zarn & Betsy Friday; Lennox: Paul Jackel & Greg Zerkle, *Frank Di Pasquale & Michael Brien Watson*; Ayah/Mrs. Winthrop: Rebecca Judd & Jennifer Smith; Wright/Holmes: Frank Di Pasquale & Bill Nolte; Claire: Betsy Friday & Jane Seaman, *Priscilla Quinby*. *Swings*: Kevin Ligon, Bill Nolte, Jane Seaman, Jennifer Smith. *Orchestra:* Keyboard: Jeanine Levenson; Basses: Jeff Carney; Guitar: Kevin Kuhn; Hammered Dulcimer: Steve Schneider; Harp: Susan Jolles; Percussion: James Saporito; Trumpet: Neil Balm; Trombone: Matt Finders; French Horns: Kaitilin Mahoney, Katharine Dennis, Leise Anscheutz; Woodwinds: Keith Underwood, Andrew Sterman, Vicki Bodner, Don McGeen; Concertmaster: Dale Stuckenbruck; Violins: Cecelia Hobbs Gardner, Ann Labin, Rudy Perrault, Evan Johnson, Yong Tae Kim; Viola: Julien Barber; Celli: Mark Shuman & Maria Kitsopoulos. *Act I*: *Opening:* "Opening Dream" ("Clusters of Crocus") (Lily, Fakir, Mary, Company); India: "There's a Girl" (Company); The Library at Misselthwaite Manor; a train platform in Yorkshire; the door to Misselthwaite Manor: "The House Upon the Hill" (Company); Mary's room; the gallery: "I Heard Someone Crying" (Mary, Archibald, Lily, Company); *Scene 1* Mary's sitting room: "(If I Had) A Fine White Horse" (Martha); *Scene 2* The ballroom: "A Girl in the Valley" (Lily, Archibald, Dancers); *Scene 3* In the maze; the greenhouse: "It's a Maze" (Ben, Mary, Martha, Dickon); The edge of the moor: "Winter's on the Wing" (Dickon), "Show Me the Key" (Mary & Dickon); *Scene 4* Archibald's library: "A Bit of Earth"

(Archibald); *Scene 5* The gallery: "Storm I" (Company), "Lily's Eyes" (Archibald & Neville); *Scene 6* The hallway: "I Heard someone Crying" (reprise) (Mary) [this reprise was added for the subsequent national tour], "Storm II" (Mary & Company); *Scene 7* Colin's room: "Round-Shouldered Man" (Colin & Mary); *Scene 8* On the grounds; the door to the garden: "Final Storm" (Company). *Act II*: *Scene 1* The tea party dream; the other side of the door: "The Girl I Mean to Be" (Mary & Company); *Scene 2* Archibald's dressing room: "Quartet" (Archibald, Neville, Rose, Lily); *Scene 3* Colin's room: "Race You to the Top of the Morning" (Archibald); *Scene 4* The greenhouse: "Wick" (Dickon & Mary); *Scene 5* Colin's room: "Come to My Garden" (Lily & Colin); *Scene 6* In the maze; the garden: "Come Spirit, Come Charm" (Mary, Martha, Dickon, Fakir, Ayah, Lily, Company), "A Bit of Earth" (reprise) (Lily, Rose, Albert); *Scene 7* The library: "Disappear" (Neville); *Scene 8* Mary's room; Paris: "Hold On" (Martha), "Letter Song" (Mary & Martha); *Scene 9* Archibald's rooms in Paris: "Where in the World" (Archibald), "How Could I Ever Know?" (Lily & Archibald); *Scene 10* The garden: Finale (Company).

Reviews were divided. The show won Tony Awards for book, sets, and for Daisy Eagan who, at 11 years old, was the youngest Tony winner to that date. It was also nominated for musical, score, costumes, and for Alison Fraser. The production cost $6 million. Most of the crew were women, a rarity on Broadway.

After Broadway. Tour. Opened on 4/28/92, at the Palace Theatre, Cleveland, and closed on 5/22/94. During the tour it ran at the Kennedy Center, Washington, DC, 12/26/92–1/31/93. Presented by George MacPherson; Musical Director: Constantine Kitsopoulos. *Cast:* Mary: Melody Kay, *Kimberly Mahon, Demaree Alexander, Lydia Ooghe*; Lily: Anne Runolfsson, *Jacquelyn Piro*; Archibald: Kevin McGuire; Neville: Douglas Sills, *Peter Samuel*; Mrs. Medlock: Mary Fogarty; Rose: Jacquelyn Piro, *Jill Patton*; Lennox: Kevin Dearinger; Dickon: Roger Bart, *Romain Fruge*; Colin: Sean Considine & Luke Hogan, *Walter Dreyer Binger & Andy Bowser*.

A revised revival (it had some new songs, and the ghosts had now gone), Presented by the Royal Shakespeare Company, at their theatre in Stratford-upon-Avon, was the RSC's first musical in over a decade. It opened on 11/28/00, and broke all the theatre's box-office records. It moved to the West End's Aldwych Theatre, 2/27/01–6/2/01. Previews from 2/17/01. Director: Adrian Noble; Choreographer: Gillian Lynne; Sets: Anthony Ward; Lighting: Chris Parry; Sound: Andrew Bruce & Terry Jardine; Musical Supervisor: Chris Walker; Orchestrations: William David Brohn. *Cast*: Archibald: Philip Quast; Neville: Peter Polycarpou; Martha: Linzi Hateley; Dickon: Craig Purnell; Lily: Meredith Braun; Ben: Freddy Davies; Mrs. Medlock: Dilys Laye; Albert: Alistair Robbins; Rose: Carmen Cusack; Mary: Natalie Morgan, Tamsin Egerton Dick, Eliza Caird; Colin: Luke Newberry, Eddie Brown, Adam Clarke.

609. *Seesaw*

Set in New York City in the present. The love affair of a young Nebraska attorney with a would-be dancer from the Bronx.

Before Broadway. Bill Gibson's straight play *Two for the Seesaw* was first produced on Broadway on 1/16/58. 750 performances. Director: Arthur Penn. Cast: Henry Fonda, Anne Bancroft. *Seesaw*, which was based on *Two for the Seesaw*, was Dorothy Fields' last musical. It tried out 1/16/73–2/10/73, at the Fisher Theatre, Detroit, where Michele Lee replaced $3,000-a-week star Lainie Kazan; Tommy Tune replaced 4th-billed Bill Starr; Cecelia Norfleet replaced 3rd-billed Joshie Jo Armstead; 5th-billed Richard Ryder was dropped; 6th-billed Crissy Wilzak was dropped to the chorus; and as director, Michael Bennett replaced Edwin Sherin, and dance music arranger Hugh Forrester was replaced by Cy Coleman. As for the book, it was written by Michael Stewart, then tampered with during tryouts by Neil Simon (Jerry's phone call scenes and the Japanese restaurant scene are his), Michael Bennett, and several other people. However, it remains basically Mike Stewart's libretto, even though he, Dorothy Fields, and Neil Simon did not want their names on the credits (ironically Michael Bennett put his name on the libretto, and was nominated for a Tony).

The Broadway Run. Uris Theatre, 3/18/73–7/21/73; Mark Hellinger Theatre, 8/1/73–12/8/73. 25 previews from 2/19/73. Total of 296 performances. Presented by Joseph Kipness & Lawrence Kasha, James Nederlander, George M. Steinbrenner III, Lorin E. Price; Music/Dance Music Arrangements Supervisor: Cy Coleman; Lyrics: Dorothy Fields; Book: Michael Bennett (with Neil Simon); Based on the 1958 comedy *Two for the Seesaw*, by William Gibson; Director: Michael Bennett; Choreographers: Michael Bennett & Grover Dale; Associate Choreographers: Bob Avian & Tommy Tune; Assistant to Grover Dale: Anita Morris; Sets: Robin Wagner; Costumes: Ann Roth; Lighting: Jules Fisher; Sound: Dick Maitland, Bob Ring, Lou Gonzalez, *Jack Shearing*; Musical Director/Vocal Arrangements: Donald Pippin; Orchestrations: Larry Fallon; Dance Music Arrangements: Elman Anderson, Cy Coleman, Marvin Hamlisch, David Spangler; Press: Bill Doll & Company; General Manager: Phil Adler; Company Manager: Max Allentuck; Production Stage Manager: Robert L. Borod; Stage Managers: Tony Manzi & Nicholas Russiyan, *Marc B. Weiss*; Assistant Stage Managers: Gerry O'Hara, *Gregory Christopher Fauss*. **Cast:** Jerry Ryan: Ken Howard (2) ✫, *John Gavin (from 8/1/73)*; Gittel Mosca: Michele Lee (1) ✫; David: Tommy Tune (3); Sophie: Cecelia Norfleet (4); Julio Gonzales: Giancarlo Esposito (5), *David Craig Miskin (from 8/1/73)*; Armando Gonzales: Felix Greco; Loida Gonzales: Loida Iglesias [individually billed only from 8/1/73]; Sparkle: LaMonte Peterson (6) [she became LaMonte DesFontaines during the run]; Tess: Amanda McBroom [individually billed only from 8/1/73]; Oscar: Gerry O'Hara, *Kenneth Carr (from 8/1/73)* [individually billed only from 8/1/73]; Nurse: Judy McCauley, *Frolic Taylor (from 8/1/73)*; Ethel: Cathy Brewer-Moore; Dentist: Tom Urich [individually billed only from 8/1/73]; Baby Ballerina: Baayork Lee (7) [individually billed only from 8/1/73]; Citizens of New York City: John Almberg, Steve Anthony, Cathy Brewer-Moore, Eileen Casey, Wayne Cilento, Patti D'Beck, Terry Deck, Judy Gibson, Felix Greco, Mitzi Hamilton, Loida Iglesias, Bobby Johnson, Baayork Lee, Amanda McBroom, Judy McCauley, Anita Morris (8), Gerry O'Hara, Michon Peacock, Frank Pietri, Yolanda Raven, T. Michael Reed, Orrin Reiley, Don Swanson, William Swiggard, Tom Urich, Dona D. Vaughn, Clyde Walker, Thomas J. Walsh, Crissy Wilzak, *Richard Cooper Bayne, Chuck Beard, Pam Blair, Kenneth Carr, Richard Christopher, Marcelo Gamboa, Marilyn Hamilton, Lee Hooper, Debra Lyman, Barbara Monte-Britton, Frank H. Newell, Jimmy Roddy, Michael Serrecchia, Keith Simmons, Allan Sobek, Scott Stevensen, Frolic Taylor*. **Standbys**: Gittel: Patti Karr; Jerry: *Nicholas Coster*. **Understudies**: Sophie: Judy Gibson; David: *Frank H. Newell*. **Swings**: Jerry Yoder & Merel Poloway.

Note: all replacements from 8/1/73. **Act I**: *Scene 1* Prologue: "Seesaw" (Company); *Scene 2* Times Square area: "My City" (Jerry & Neighborhood Girls) [on 3/23/73 New York City's mayor, John Lindsay, replaced Mr. Howard for 7 minutes on this number. Everyone had been startled by Mr. Howard's resemblance to the mayor]; *Scene 3* Dance studio on West 54th Street: "Nobody Does it Like Me" (Gittel); *Scene 4* Japanese restaurant on 46th Street and Lincoln Center: "In Tune" (Gittel & Jerry); *Scene 5* East 116th Street: "Spanglish" (Julio, Gittel, Jerry, Sophie, Company); *Scene 6* Gittel's apartment in the East Village: "Welcome to Holiday Inn!" (Gittel); *Scene 7* Jerry's apartment: "You're a Lovable Lunatic" (Jerry); *Scene 8* Gittel's apartment, then the street: "He's Good for Me" (Gittel); *Scene 9* The Banana Club: "Ride Out the Storm" (Sparkle, Sophie, Company); *Scene 10* Gittel's apartment. **Act II**: *Scene 1* St. Vincent's Hospital: "We've Got It" (Jerry), "Poor Everybody Else" (Gittel) [this number had been cut from *Sweet Charity*]; *Scene 2* Dance studio: "Chapter 54, Number 1909 (The Late Great State of New York)" (ch: Tommy Tune) (David, Jerry, Gittel, Dance Company); *Scene 3* Jerry's apartment: "The Concert" (Gittel & Dance Company), "It's Not Where You Start" (ch: Tommy Tune) (David & Company); *Scene 4* Backstage at the theatre; *Scene 5* Central Park; later that night; *Scene 6* Gittel's apartment; phone booth at Kennedy Airport; *Scene 7* Gittel's apartment; 2 a.m.: "I'm Way Ahead" (Gittel), "Seesaw" (reprise) (Gittel); *Scene 8* Gittel's apartment; Jerry's apartment; a few days later.

The show got very good Broadway reviews, but lost its $750,000

capitalization, and an additional $525,000 to boot. It won Tony Awards for choreography (Michael Bennett), and for Tommy Tune, and was nominated for musical, direction of a musical, score, book, and for Michele Lee.

After Broadway. Tour. Opened on 9/28/74, and closed on 2/15/75, after 68 cities. **Cast:** Jerry: John Raitt; Gittel: Lucie Arnaz. The number "The Party's on Me" (Gittel) was added in place of "Ride Out the Storm."

610. *The Selling of the President*

An "electronic vaudeville" about elections. A group of media experts and young people turn a senator (Mason) into a hot presidential candidate by means of product-advertising techniques, virtually confining the whole campaign (and the only set) to a TV studio. Although time and place are unspecified, it is 1976, and the president will be the 39th (but it reflects the selling of the 37th president Richard Nixon to the American people in 1968).

Before Broadway. It first tried out at the Geary Theatre, San Francisco, 3/30/71. 24 performances. Presented by the American Conservatory Theatre; Stage Script: Stuart Hample; Director: Ellis Rabb; Costumes: Elizabeth Covey; Lighting/Still Projections: James Tilton; Film Director: Michael Jackson; Sound: Charles Richmond; Musical Director: Vaughn Aubrey; Orchestrations/Choral Arrangements: Bob James. The cast of characters and actors was different to the Broadway production: The American Flag: Megan: Carolyn Blakey; Lotus: Nancy Blossom; Beige: Light Brown; Randymann: Michael Cavanaugh; Cochise: Jeff Chandler; King George: John Hancock; Roxie Rideout: Lee McCain; Chunky Berman: Deborah Sussel; Canibus Sativa: Ann Weldon; Steven Tudd: Mark Wheeler; George Smith: G. Wood [end of American Flag sequence]; Irene Jantzen: Michael Learned; Ted Bacon: Josef Sommer; Ward Nichols: Scott Thomas; Walter: Joseph Bird; George Mason: Peter Donat; Gracie Mason: Joy Carlin; Norman Bille Emerson: William Patterson; Mart "Smiles" Faranghetti: Martin Berman.

Jack O'Brien, who started as composer only, soon became co-librettist as well, and then, during tryouts in Philadelphia, he replaced Robert H. Livingston as director (Mr. Livingston had replaced Ellis Rabb). As choreographer Ethel Martin replaced Talley Beatty. In the cast Mr. Fitzsimmons replaced Howard St. John. The character of Ward Nichols (played by 6th-billed John Glover) was dropped. Jay Gerber had been standby for this role. Delores Hall was replaced by Tasha Thomas. Then there was a different song line-up for Act I: "Something Holy," "If You Like People," "Sunset," "If You Like People" (reprise), "Little Moon," "Come-on-a-Good Life," "I've Got to Trust You," "If You Like People" (another reprise), "Mason Cares," "On the Winning Side," "Captain Terror," "He's a Man." Act II was the same, except that "Minority Ticket" was not in yet. It was the first musical in which the three top-billed players had non-singing roles (Hingle, Morrow, Barrie).

The Broadway Run. Shubert Theatre, 3/22/72–3/25/72. 6 previews from 3/16/72. 5 performances. Presented by John Flaxman, in association with Harold Hastings & Franklin Roberts; Music: Bob James; Lyrics: Jack O'Brien; Book: Jack O'Brien & Stuart Hample (book doctored by Kenny Solms & Gail Parent); Based on the 1969 book of the same name by Joe McGinniss (actually it only used the title. There is little resemblance between the musical and the original book); Director: Jack O'Brien (uncredited); Choreographer: Ethel Martin; Sets: Tom John; Costumes: Nancy Potts; Lighting: Thomas Skelton; Sound: Jack Mann; Musical Director: Harold Hastings; Orchestrations: Jonathan Tunick; Press: Gifford/Wallace; Production Supervisor/Casting: Arlene Caruso; Company Manager: John Caruso; Production Stage Manager: Martha Knight; Stage Manager: Jason Travis; Assistant Stage Manager: Larry Ziegler. **Cast:** Senator George W. Mason: Pat Hingle (1) ✫; Grace Mason: Barbara Barrie (3); Senator Hiram Robinson: Richard Goode; Sydney Wales: Robert Fitzsimmons (6); Irene Jantzen: Karen Morrow (2); Ted Bacon: Robert Darnell (5); Johnny Olson: Johnny Olson (4); Arthur Hayes: John Bentley; Minister: Tim Noble; Captain Terror:

Steve Schochet; TIMMY: Sheilah Rae; CREEPY: Philip M. Thomas; GHOULIE: Pi Douglass; (TWELVE) TV STUDIO DANCERS & SINGERS: DAVEY: Tim Noble; VAN DENISOVICH: Rick Atwell; CASEY STEELE: Jamie Carr; FRANKLIN DOUGLASS PIERCE: Pi Douglass; BONNIE SUE TAYLOR: SuEllen Estey; GLORIA MILLER: Tasha Thomas; LINDA ALLINGTON: Pamela Myers; RALPH REEDER: Tim Noble; BURGUNDY MOORE: Trina Parks; MOLLY KILGALLEN: Sheilah Rae; INGA BRAND: Deborah St. Darr; BARNEY ZAWICKI: Steve Schochet; DR. LLOYD BLENHEIM: Bill Rienecke; MRS. PEARLINE GIBBONS: Lurlu Lindsay; MR. WARREN STEVENSON: Peter Grounds; RANDALL PHILLIPS: Philip M. Thomas; FLEETWING HORN: Vilma Vaccaro; JULIA MILANO: Pam Zarit; ALSO WITH: George Andrew Robinson & Michael Serrecchia. *Standbys*: Mason: Leon B. Stevens; Ted: Jay Gerber; Grace/Irene: Christine Pickles. *Understudy*: Olson: John Bentley. *Act I*: "Something Holy" (Gloria & Ensemble), "If You Like People:" Duet (Bonnie Sue & Ralph), Quintet (Burgundy, Randall, Gloria, Isaac, Julie), Soloists (Casey, Franklin, Linda), Sextette (Inga, Van, Barney, Fleetwing, 2 unspecifieds) [end of the "If You Like People" sequence], "Sunset" (Van, Ralph, Franklin, Barney), "Mason Cares" (Julie, Molly, Bonnie Sue), "Little Moon" (Casey & Fleetwing), "Come-on-a-Good-Life" (Franklin), "Acupressure" (Ensemble), "On the Winning Side" (Linda), "Captain Terror" (Terror, Creepie, Ghoulie), "Gap Game" (Casey), "He's a Man" (Burgundy, Julia, Gloria). *Act II*: "Stars of Glory" (Ralph), "Terminix" (Barney, Bonnie Sue, Linda, Inga), "Take My Hand" (Casey, Gloria, Ralph, Fleetwing), "A Passacaglia" (Ensemble), "We're Gonna Live It Together" (Ensemble), "Minority Ticket" (Randall), "America" (Ensemble).

It was panned on Broadway. The show cost half a million. A tenth of that had been invested by Terminix, an exterminating company, and another 10 percent by Stax, the record company that was going to produce the cast album but never did.

611. *Seussical*

Listed on the logos as *Seussical: The Musical*, it was, nevertheless called just *Seussical*. A musical recycling of several Dr. Seuss stories. Set in and around Horton the elephant's home — the Jungle of Nool. Horton hears the cries of the people on a tiny planet called Who, which is the size of a speck of dust. The Cat in the Hat is the narrator, our guide through the jungle. JoJo is a boy from Who who thinks too many thinks and is sent off to the Army. Gertrude, Horton's next-door-neighbor, is a bird with a tiny tail. She wants to be more exotic so that Horton will notice her. Mayzie is a diva with voluptuous plumage who finds herself caring for an egg she never expected to have. So she asks Horton to hatch it while she goes off to feather nests elsewhere.

Before Broadway. Garth Drabinsky came up with the idea, and on 8/16/97 he announced that his company Livent had bought the rights to musicalize Dr. Seuss's works, and he was going to produce, as *The Seussical* (this name was to change). Ken Ludwig was commissioned to write the libretto. However, by 6/97 Eric Idle had replaced Mr. Ludwig. But Livent got into trouble and folded. SFX, Barry & Fran Weissler, and Universal Studios bought Livent in 1999 (SFX also owned PACE Theatricals) [Sequel: Mr. Drabinsky, unable to return to the USA after 1999, or he would be arrested for fraud, was arrested for fraud in Canada, on 10/22/02. Not everyone cheered, by any means]. On 5/3/99, in NEW YORK, rehearsals for two staged first-draft readings began. The readings took place on 5/14/99. *Cast*: CAT: Eric Idle; GERTRUDE: Janine LaManna; HORTON: Kevin Chamberlin; MAYZIE: Michele Pawk; SCHMITZ: Erick Devine; MAYOR: Stuart Zagnit; SOUR KANGAROO: Sharon Wilkins; MARSHAL: Ann Harada; MRS. MAYOR: Alice Playten; ALSO WITH: Ruth Williamson, Victor Trent Cook, Madeleine Doherty, Lovette George, Leon Williams, David Garrison, Jason Fuchs, Eric Jordan Young, David Lowenstein, Joy Hermalyn [note: Tracy Nicole Chapman was going to read, but didn't]. Rehearsals for a workshop in TORONTO began on 7/26/99, and ran in performance 8/19/99–8/21/99, and they got raves. Dr. Seuss's widow, Audrey Geisel, was present at the workshops. DIRECTOR: Frank Galati; CHOREOGRAPHER: Kathleen Marshall; MUSICAL

DIRECTOR: David Holcenberg; DANCE MUSIC ARRANGEMENTS: David Chase; STAGE MANAGER: Jeff Markowitz. *Cast*: CAT: Andrea Martin; HORTON: Kevin Chamberlin; JOJO ALTERNATE: Andrew Keenan-Bolger; MAYZIE: Michele Pawk; MAYOR: Stuart Zagnit; GRANDPA WHO: Eddie Korbich; GERTRUDE: Janine LaManna; SCHMITZ: Erick Devine; MARSHAL: Ann Harada; SOUR KANGAROO: Sharon Wilkins; MRS. MAYOR: Alice Playten; CAT'S HELPERS: Joyce Chittick & Justin Greer; ALSO WITH: Jeffrey Broadhurst, Jason Fuchs, Jeffrey Hankinson, Amy Heggins, Catrice Joseph, David Lowenstein, Michelle O'Steen, Cynthia Sophiea, Eric Jordan Young, Troy Adams, Diane Coatsworth, Heidi Ford, Susan Henley, Taborah Johnson, Denis Lupien, Avery Saltzman, Jay Turvey. For Broadway Andrea Martin turned down the lead role she had played in workshops. After the producers unsuccessfully sought Elayne Boosler, Roger Bart, B.D. Wong, and others, on 6/16/00 the casting of David Shiner was confirmed. Rehearsals began in Manhattan on 7/10/00. The out of town tryout was at the Colonial Theatre, Boston. On the day the tryout opened for previews (8/27/00), costume designer Catherine Zuber was fired, and replaced by William Ivey Long, who was confirmed in his new role on 9/5/00 (Miss Zuber's costumes were the ones used). The show opened in Boston officially on 9/6/00, and got bad reviews, especially from Ed Siegel in the *Boston Globe*. The show never recovered from that review. Certain characters seen in the Boston run were dropped for Broadway: THE ONCE-LER: Eddie Korbich; EVERY-THINGABLE: Mary Ann Lamb; HUMMINGFISH: Casey Nicholaw; THE LORAX: Alice Playten. Scheduled originally to run in Boston until 9/17/00, the show got a two-week extension, but after Mr. Siegel killed it, the shows of 9/19/00 and 9/20/00 were canceled, and they packed up on 9/24/00, and fled to a Manhattan rehearsal studio on 9/26/00. In 9/00 Tony Walton was called in to help on the sets. In 10/00 Rob Marshall was called in to replace Frank Galati as director, and also to improve the choreography of his own sister, Kathleen Marshall. Originally the first Broadway preview had been planned for 9/00, then as the production neared Broadway it was put back to 10/15/00, 10/18/00, 10/29/00, 10/30/00, and finally 11/1/00). After three weeks of Broadway previews both act-openers—"Our Story Begins" and "Our Story Resumes"—were cut. Added during previews was a rousing new curtain call—"Green Eggs and Ham," a dance number which is on the cast album. The official opening date, originally scheduled for 11/9/00, was put back to 11/30/00. Anthony Blair Hall's voice was changing, and he became the alternate for Broadway (it had been Andrew Keenan-Bolger who had been alternate in Boston).

The Broadway Run. RICHARD RODGERS THEATRE, 11/30/00-5/20/01. 34 previews from 11/1/00. 197 PERFORMANCES. PRESENTED BY SFX Theatrical Group, Barry & Fran Weissler, and Universal Studios, in association with Kardana/Swinksy Productions, Hal Luftig, and Michael Watt; MUSIC/VOCAL ARRANGEMENTS: Stephen Flaherty; LYRICS: Lynn Ahrens; BOOK: Lynn Ahrens & Stephen Flaherty; CONCEIVED BY: Lynn Ahrens, Stephen Flaherty, Eric Idle; BASED ON stories for children written & illustrated by Theodor S. "Ted" Geisel (known as Dr. Seuss); DIRECTOR: Rob Marshall; CHOREOGRAPHER: Kathleen Marshall; FLYING EFFECTS: Flying by Foy; SETS: Eugene Lee; COSTUMES: William Ivey Long; LIGHTING: Natasha Katz; SOUND: Jonathan Deans; MUSICAL DIRECTOR: David Holcenberg; ORCHESTRATIONS: Doug Besterman; DANCE MUSIC ARRANGEMENTS: David Chase; CAST RECORDING on Decca Broadway, released on 2/6/01; PRESS: Barlow—Hartman Public Relations; CASTING: Jay Binder; GENERAL MANAGEMENT: Alan Wasser Associates; COMPANY MANAGER: Lizbeth Cone; STAGE MANAGERS: Andrew Fenton & Joshua Halperin, *Kenneth J. McGee*. *Cast*: THE CAT IN THE HAT: David Shiner, *Rosie O'Donnell* (during Mr. Shiner's vacation, 1/16/01–2/10/01), *Bryan Batt* (stood in for Mr. Shiner during vacation), *David Shiner* (from 2/14/01), *Cathy Rigby* ☆ (from 3/15/01); HORTON THE ELEPHANT: Kevin Chamberlin; GERTRUDE McFUZZ: Janine LaManna; MAYZIE LA BIRD: Michele Pawk; JOJO: Anthony Blair Hall (6 performances a week), Andrew Keenan-Bolger (Wednesday evenings & Saturday matinees), *Aaron Carter* (alone, 3/30/01–5/13/01); THE SOUR KANGAROO: Sharon Wilkins; THE MAYOR OF WHOVILLE: Stuart Zagnit; MRS. MAYOR: Alice Playten; CAT'S HELPERS: Joyce Chittick, Jennifer Cody, Justin Greer, Mary Ann Lamb, Darren Lee, Jerome Vivona; GENERAL GENGHIS KHAN SCHMITZ: Erick Devine; BIRD GIRLS: Natascia Diaz, Sara Gettelfinger, Catrice Joseph;

WICKERSHAM BROTHERS: David Engel, Tom Plotkin, Eric Jordan Young; THE GRINCH: William Ryall; VLAD VLADIKOFF: Darren Lee; JUDGE YERTLE THE TURTLE: Devin Richards; MARSHALL OF THE COURT: Ann Harada; GRANDPA WHO: Eddie Korbich; JOJO'S TEACHER: Monique L. Midgette; JOJO'S PRINCIPAL: Casey Nicholaw; CITIZENS OF THE JUNGLE OF NOOL/WHOS/MAYOR'S AIDES/FISH/CADETS/HUNTERS/CIRCUS MCGURKUS ANIMALS & PERFORMERS: Joyce Chittick, Jennifer Cody, Erick Devine, Natascia Diaz, David Engel, Sara Gettelfinger, Justin Greer, Ann Harada, Catrice Joseph, Eddie Korbich, Mary Ann Lamb, Darren Lee, Monique L. Midgette, Casey Nicholaw, Tom Plotkin, Devin Richards, William Ryall, Jerome Vivona, Sharon Wilkins, Eric Jordan Young. *Standby*: Cat: Bryan Batt. *Understudies*: Cat: Eric Jordan Young; Horton/Mayor: Casey Nicholaw; Gertrude: Jenny Hill; Vlad: Shaun Amyot; Wickersham Brothers: Shaun Amyot & David Lowenstein; Cat's Helpers: Shaun Amyot, Jenny Hill, Michelle Kittrell, David Lowenstein; Grinch/Yertle: David Lowenstein; Mayzie: Sara Gettelfinger; Mrs. Mayor: Ann Harada; Bird Girls: Jenny Hill & Michelle Kittrell; Gertrude/Marshal/Teacher: Jenny Hill; Sour Kangaroo: Catrice Joseph & Monique L. Midgette; Schmitz: William Ryall. *Swings*: Shaun Amyot, Jenny Hill, Michelle Kittrell, David Lowenstein. *Orchestra*: CONCERTMISTRESS: Naomi Katz; VIOLIN: Karl Kawahara; VIOLA: Maxine Roach; CELLO: Stephanie Cummins; WOODWINDS: Paul Sundfor, Dan Willis, John Winder; TRUMPETS: Brian O'Flaherty & John Reid; TROMBONE: Larry Farrell; GUITARS: Jeffrey Lee Campbell & Jack Cavari; ELECTRIC BASS: Francisco Centeno; DRUMS: Warren Odze; PERCUSSION: Charles Descarfino; KEYBOARDS: Steve Marzullo & Philip Fortenberry. *Act I*: Overture (Orchestra), "Oh, the Thinks You Can Think!" (Cat & Company), "Our Story Begins" (Cat) [cut during previews], "Horton Hears a Who" (Bird Girls, Horton, Citizens), "Biggest Blame Fool" (Kangaroo, Horton, Wickershams, Bird Girls, Gertrude, Mayzie, Citizens, Cat), "Here on Who" (Mayor, Mrs. Mayor, Grinch, Whos, Horton), "A Day for the Cat in the Hat" (Cat, JoJo, Cat's Helpers), "It's Possible (in McElligot's Pool)" (JoJo, Cat, Fish), "How to Raise a Child" (Mayor & Mrs. Mayor), "The Military" (General, Mayor, Mrs. Mayor, JoJo, Cadets), "Alone in the Universe" (Horton & JoJo), "The One Feather Tail of Miss Gertrude McFuzz" (Gertrude), "Amayzing Mayzie" (Mayzie, Gertrude, Bird Girls), "Amayzing Gertrude" (Gertrude, Cat, Bird Girls), "Monkey Around" (Wickershams), "Chasing the Whos" (Horton, Kangaroo, Bird Girls, Wickershams, Cat, Vlad, Whos), "How Lucky You Are" (Cat), "Notice Me, Horton" (Gertrude & Horton), "How Lucky You Are" (reprise) (Mayzie, Horton, Cat), "Horton Sits on the Egg"/Act I Finale (Full Company). *Act II*: "How Lucky You Are" (reprise) (Cat), "Our Story Resumes" (Cat, Horton, Mayor, Mrs. Mayor, JoJo, General, Cadets, Gertrude, Bird Girls) [cut during previews], "Egg, Nest and Tree" (Kangaroo, Bird Girls, Wickershams, Cat, Cat's Helpers, Hunters), "The Circus McGurkus" (Cat, Horton, Circus Animals & Performers), "The Circus on Tour" (Horton), "Mayzie in Palm Beach" (Mayzie, Cat, Horton), "Solla Sollew" (Horton, Animals & Performers, Mayor, Mrs. Mayor, JoJo), "The Whos' Christmas Pageant" (Grinch & Whos), "A Message from the Front" (General, Mayor, Mrs. Mayor, Cadets), "Alone in the Universe" (reprise) (JoJo & Horton), "Havin' a Hunch" (Cat, JoJo, Cat's Helpers), "All for You" (Gertrude & Bird Girls), "The People Versus Horton the Elephant" (Horton, Kangaroo, Wickershams, Marshal, Judge, Bird Girls, Gertrude, Mayor, Mrs. Mayor, JoJo, Whos, Cat), Finale/"Oh, the Thinks You Can Think!" (Full Company), "Green Eggs and Ham" (curtain call).

Broadway reviews were mostly negative. TV star Rosie O'Donnell volunteered to come on to the show temporarily, to replace David Shiner, who went on a month's vacation. She did it in an attempt to boost flagging box-office sales, and she succeeded, doing six shows a week for four weeks, and giving her salary to charity. Donny Osmond, who had recorded two of the show's songs on an album, was touted as the replacement for Rosie O'Donnell, but it never happened. David Shiner came back. Cathy Rigby began secret rehearsals on 2/28/01, and was confirmed as the new Cat on 3/6/01. Kevin Chamberlin received a Tony nomination.

After Broadway. TOUR. Opened on 9/17/02, at Clowes Memorial Hall, Indianapolis. PRESENTED BY McCoy Rigby Entertainment & NETworks. This was a version re-worked by Steven Flaherty & Lynn Ahrens. 20 percent of the music and lyrics was new. Much dance music had been cut. JoJo became much more the focal point of the story. The number "A Day for the Cat in the Hat" was cut. The opening number, "Oh, the Thinks You Can Think!" was now performed by Cat & JoJo. Rehearsals began on 8/13/02, in Manhattan. DIRECTOR: Christopher Ashley; CHOREOGRAPHER: Patti Colombo; SETS: James Kronzer; COSTUMES: David Woolard; LIGHTING: Howell Binkley; SOUND: Brian Ronan; MUSICAL DIRECTOR: John Mezzio. *Cast* (announced on 7/2/02): CAT: Cathy Rigby; GERTRUDE: Garrett Long; HORTON: Eric Leviton; MAYZIE: Gaeleen Gilliland; JOJO: Richard Miron & Drake English; MAYOR: Don Stitt; MRS. MAYOR: Amy Griffin; KANGAROO: NaTasha Williams; SCHMITZ: Stuart Marland; BIRD GIRLS: Liz Pearce, Danielle Garner, Dioni Collins; WICKERSHAM BROTHERS: Luis Villabon, Venny Carranza, Brian-Thomas Williams; VLAD: Brian Shepard; JUDGE YERTLE: Brian Mathis; GRINCH: Richard Raven.

THE NON-EQUITY TOUR of *Seussical: the Musical* opened 10/10/03, Yakima, Washington. 2 previews, 10/4/03 & 10/5/03, at Alto, NM. PRESENTED BY NETworks; DIRECTOR: Stafford Arima; CHOREOGRAPHER: Patti Wilcox; SETS: James Kronzer; COSTUMES: William Ivey Long; LIGHTING: Kirk Bookman; SOUND: Brian Ronan.

612. *Seven Brides for Seven Brothers*

For obvious reasons this musical is generally referred to as *Seven Brides*. Set in the Pacific Northwest in the 1850s. The seven Pontipee brothers find wives, and are gradually tamed.

Before Broadway. THE 1954 MOVIE. CHOREOGRAPHER: Michael Kidd. *Cast*: ADAM: Howard Keel; MILLY: Jane Powell; GIDEON: Russ Tamblyn; CALEB: Matt Mattox; DORCAS: Julie Newmayer (this was Julie Newmar); FRANK: Tommy Rall.

The 1982 Broadway production was a new musical in that four of the movie's songs were deleted and seven new ones written by Al Kasha & Joel Hirschhorn. It began touring in the 1978–79 season, starring Howard Keel and Jane Powell. A new tour opened at the Fox Theatre, San Diego, on 12/21/81, and after touring, went to Broadway. The tour had the same crew as for Broadway, except LIGHT: Robert Randolph; COMPANY MANAGER: Drew Murphy; STAGE MANAGERS: Larry Dean, Polly Wood, Jack Ritschel. It had the same cast too, except ADAM: Laurence Guittard, *David-James Carroll* (he took over on the road); MRS. McCLANE/PREACHER'S WIFE: Jeanne Bates; ZEKE: Kurtis Woodruff (he also understudied Frank). The characters of The Indian, Townboy and Dorcas's sister were not yet elevated to individual billing, the actors of each being listed under Townspeople, who were: Jeanne Bates, Cheryl Crandall, Fred Curt, Gino Gaudio, Russell Giesenschlag, James Horvath, Marylou Hume, Gary Moss, David Pavlovsky, Jack Ritschel, Conley Schnaterbeck, Sam Singhaus, Katherine Somers (this is how Marykatherine Somers was then being billed), Don Steffy, Clark Sterling, Stephanie Stromer, Kurtis Woodruff. Fred Curt understudied for The Preacher, and Katherine Somers understudied for Mrs. McClane.

The Broadway Run. ALVIN THEATRE, 7/8/82–7/11/82. 15 previews. 5 PERFORMANCES. PRESENTED BY Kaslan Productions (Lawrence N. Kasha & David S. Landay); MUSIC: Gene de Paul; LYRICS: Johnny Mercer; BOOK: Lawrence N. Kasha & David S. Landay; NEW SONGS: Al Kasha & Joel Hirschhorn; BASED ON the 1954 MGM movie of the same name, which in turn had been based on the 1928 short story *The Sobbin' Women*, by Stephen Vincent Benet; DIRECTOR: Lawrence N. Kasha; CHOREOGRAPHER: Jerry Jackson; SETS: Robert Randolph; COSTUMES: Robert Fletcher; LIGHTING: Thomas Skelton; SOUND: Abe Jacob; MUSICAL DIRECTOR: Richard Parrinello; ORCHESTRATIONS: Irwin Kostal; DANCE MUSIC ARRANGEMENTS: Robert Webb; PRESS: David A. Powers & Barbara Carroll; GENERAL MANAGERS: Marvin A. Krauss, Gary Gunas, Eric Angelson, Steven C. Callahan; STAGE MANAGERS: Polly Wood & Jack Ritschel. *Cast*: THE PONTIPEE BROTHERS: ADAM: David-James Carroll; BENJAMIN: D. Scot Davidge; EPHRAIM: Jeffrey Reynolds; CALEB: Lara Teeter; DANIEL: Jeff Calhoun; FRANK: Michael Ragan; GIDEON: Craig Peralta; MR. BIXBY: Fred Curt; MRS. BIXBY: Jeanne Bates; PREACHER: Jack Ritschel; MR. PERKINS: Gino Gaudio; LUMBERMEN: James Horvath, Russell Giesenschlag, Don Steffy, Gary Moss, Clark Sterling, Kevin McCready; INDIAN: Conley Schnaterbeck; THE SEVEN BRIDES: MILLY:

Debby Boone; RUTH: Sha Newman; MARTHA: Laurel Van der Linde; SARAH: Linda Hoxit; LIZA: Jan Mussetter; ALICE: Nancy Fox; DORCAS: Manette La Chance; JEB: Russell Giesenschlag; ZEKE: Kevin McCready; CARL: Don Steffy; MATT: Gary Moss; LUKE: James Horvath; JOEL: Clark Sterling; DORCAS' SISTER: Marylou Hume; MRS. PERKINS: Marykatherine Somers; TOWNBOY: David Pavlovsky; TOWNSPEOPLE: Jeanne Bates, Cheryl Crandall, Fred Curt, Gino Gaudio, Russell Giesenschlag, James Horvath, Marylou Hume, Kevin McCready, Gary Moss, David Pavlovsky, Jack Ritschel, Conley Schnaterbeck, Sam Singhaus, Marykatherine Somers, Don Steffy, Clark Sterling, Stephanie Stromer. *Standby*: Milly: Cheryl Crandall. *Understudies*: Adam/Preacher: Gino Gaudio; Gideon: Russell Giesenschlag; Daniel: Gary Moss; Benjamin: Don Steffy; Frank: Kevin McCready; Ephraim: Clark Sterling; Caleb: James Horvath; Alice/Sarah: Marylou Hume; Dorcas/Ruth/Mrs. Bixby: Marykatherine Somers; Liza/Martha: Stephanie Stromer; Luke/Zeke: David Pavlovksy; Carl/Matt: Conley Schnaterbeck; Jeb/Joel: Sam Singhaus; Bixby/Perkins: Jack Ritschel; Mrs. Perkins: Jeanne Bates. *Alternates*: Stephanie Stromer & Sam Singhaus. *Act I*: *Scene 1* On the road: "Bless Your Beautiful Hide" (Adam) ["Get a Wife" was the opening number on the pre–Broadway tour, but was cut]; *Scene 2* The town square; *Scene 3* The restaurant: "Wonderful, Wonderful Day" (Milly & Brides); *Scene 4* The Pontipee house: "One Man" * (Milly) ["I Married Seven Brothers" was in this position during the tour, but was replaced for Broadway]; *Scene 5* The Pontipee house; later the same evening; *Scene 6* The Pontipee house; the next morning: "Goin' Courting" (Milly & Brothers); *Scene 7* Churchyard: "Social Dance" (Milly, Adam, Bride, Brothers, Suitors, Townspeople); *Scene 8* The road home; *Scene 9* The Pontipee house: "Love Never Goes Away" * (Adam, Milly, Gideon); *Scene 10* The barn: "Sobbin' Women" (Adam & Brothers). *Act II*: *Scene 1* The town; *Scene 2* Echo Pass: "The Townsfolk's Lament" * (Suitors & Townspeople) [not on the tour]; *Scene 3* The Pontipee yard: "A Woman Ought to Know Her Place" * (Adam); *Scene 4* The barn: "We Gotta Make it Through the Winter" * (Brothers), "You Gotta Make it Through the Winter" * (Milly & Brides) [during the tour "It's up to Us" was in this position]; *Scene 5* The Pontipee yard: "Spring Dance" * (Brides & Brothers); *Scene 6* The trapping cabin: "A Woman Ought to Know Her Place" * (reprise) (Adam & Gideon); *Scene 7* The Pontipee house: "Glad that You Were Born" * (Milly, Brides, Brothers); *Scene 8* The woods; *Scene 9* Churchyard: "Wedding Dance" (Milly, Adam, Brides, Brothers, Townspeople).

An asterisk means new songs written for this production.

The Broadway cast (sans Debby Boone) picketed the offices of the *New York Times* for two days in protest against Frank Rich's bad review (most of the Broadway reviewers felt the same way, if not as intensely as Mr. Rich). The show received a Tony nomination for score.

After Broadway. GOODSPEED OPERA HOUSE, Conn., 4/22/05–7/3/05. This production had a revised score and book. PRESENTED BY Michael P. Price, of Goodspeed; DIRECTOR: Greg Ganakas; CHOREOGRAPHER: Patti Colombo. A fall 2005 tour going into 2006 was planned.

613. *The Seven Lively Arts*

A musical revue. Seven players each represent a different art. The surrealist paintings of the Seven Lively Arts were painted by Salvador Dali especially for exhibition in the downstairs lounge of the theatre.

Before Broadway. It opened for tryouts at the Forrest Theatre, Philadelphia, on 11/24/44, The number "Pretty Little Missus Bell" (Beatrice Lillie) was dropped before the New York opening. The following songs were unused: "Dainty Quainty Me" (intended for Bert Lahr), "I Wrote a Play" (probably intended for Bill Tabbert), "If I Hadn't a Husband" (the music was later used for "Should I Tell You I Love You" in *Around the World*), "Where Do We Go from Here?" (intended for Bea Lillie & Bert Lahr), "Cafe Society Still Carries On" (intended for Bert Lahr). Then it went to Broadway.

The Broadway Run. ZIEGFELD THEATRE, 12/7/44–5/12/45. 183 PERFORMANCES. PRESENTED BY Billy Rose; MUSIC/LYRICS: Cole Porter; SKETCHES: various authors, with contributions also from Robert Pirosh

& Joseph Schrank; DOC ROCKWELL'S COMMENTS WRITTEN BY Ben Hecht; DIRECTOR/LIGHTING: Hassard Short; SKETCH DIRECTOR: Philip Loeb; CHOREOGRAPHER: Jack Donohue; SETS: Norman Bel Geddes; COSTUMES: Mary Grant; MODERN GOWNS: Valentina; MUSICAL DIRECTOR: Maurice Abravanel; ORCHESTRAL ARRANGEMENTS: Russell Bennett, Ted Royal, Hans Spialek; CHORAL GROUP TRAINED BY Robert Shaw; PRESS: Wolfe Kaufman & Tom Van Dyke; GENERAL MANAGER: Robert Milford; COMPANY MANAGER: John Tuerk; GENERAL STAGE MANAGER: Frank Hall; STAGE MANAGER: R.O. Brooks; ASSISTANT STAGE MANAGER: George Hunter. Overture—"Frahngee-Pahnee" (by Cole Porter). *Act I*: *Scene 1* Song: "Big Town." MR. AUDIENCE: Doc Rockwell (6); AND THE YOUNG HOPEFULS: PAINTER: Nan Wynn; TAP DANCER: Jere McMahon; RADIO SINGER: Paula Bane; BALLET DANCER: Billie Worth; PLAYWRIGHT: Bill Tabbert; MOVIE ACTRESS: Dolores Gray; STAGE ACTRESS: Mary Roche; Ensemble; *Scene 2* Song: "Is it the Girl (or is it the Gown?)" (sung by Dolores Gray) with The Ladies of Fashion (selected with the assistance of Harry Conover): Savona King, Jean Colleran, Alma Holt, Cissy Smith, Truly Barbara, Viki Maulsby, Gwen Shirey, Susan Blanchard, Adrian Storms, Paddy Ellerton, Gayle Mellott, Temple Texas; *Scene 3* Sketch: "Local Boy Makes Good" (written by George S. Kaufman). Scene: A theatrical producer's office. About the lofty independence of stagehands, and a stagehand who hates scenery. THE SECRETARY: Billie Worth; THE PRODUCER: Albert Carroll; THE AGENT: Michael Barrett; THE STAGEHAND: Bert Lahr (2) ☆; *Scene 4* Song: "Ev'ry Time We Say Goodbye" [a hit]. THE GIRL: Nan Wynn; THE BOY: Jere McMahon; ENSEMBLE; *Scene 5* Sketch: "There'll Always Be an England" (written by Moss Hart). Scene: An English garden which has been turned into an outdoor canteen. English titled lady tries to be hip with some American doughboys based over there. LADY CARLETON: Dennie Moore; LADY AGATHA PENDLETON: Beatrice Lillie (1) ☆; 1ST SOLDIER: Thomas Kenny; 2ND SOLDIER: Edward Hackett; COLONEL CHARTERIS: Albert Carroll; 3RD SOLDIER: Michael Barrett; *Scene 6* Song: "Only Another Boy and Girl." THE GIRL: Mary Roche; THE BOY: Bill Tabbert; "FRAGONARD IN PINK:" Beatrice Lillie (1) ☆ & Bert Lahr (2) ☆; ENSEMBLE; *Scene 7* Song: "Wow-Ooh-Wolf!" (sung by Nan Wynn, Dolores Gray, Mary Roche); *Scene 8* Sketch: "Ticket for the Ballet" (written by Moss Hart). Scene: The lobby of a theatre. Customer standing in line, anxious to get in but not knowing the name of the ballet (she thought it might be *S. Hurok*), and enacting the "Dying Swan" in front of the box-office to indicate her choice. THE CUSTOMER: Beatrice Lillie (1) ☆; THE BOX OFFICE MAN: Michael Barrett; THE MANAGER: Albert Carroll; A MAN IN THE LINE: King Ross; *Scene 9* Song: "Drink" [sung by Bert Lahr (2) ☆ & Male Ensemble] (Bert Lahr as an English admiral on the deck of old battleship singing a drinking song until he got drunk on the lyrics alone); *Scene 10* Song: "When I Was a Little Cuckoo" [sung by Beatrice Lillie (1) ☆]; *Scene 11* Sketch: "Billy Rose Buys the Metropolitan Opera House!." What might happen to that institution if Mr. Rose got hold of it; *Aida* with a silver Jumbo; all-black version of *Carmen* (Jere McMahon did the Toreador dance); aquacade version of *Rheingold*). Benny Goodman (3) ☆ (and his combo—Teddy Wilson, Red Norvo, Morey Feld, Sid Weiss, Cozy Cole for a short while), led a jam session to a number called "Metropolitan Opera Pipe Dream." *Act II*: *Scene 1* "Scene de Ballet" (excerpts). Specially-commissioned music: Igor Stravinsky (ch: Anton Dolin). Danced by Alicia Markova (4) ☆, Anton Dolin (5) ☆, and the Corps de Ballet [Franca Baldwin, Virginia Barnes, John Begg, Phyllis Brown, Angelina Buttignol, Evangeline Collis, Margaretta de Valera, Bettye Durrence, Adriana Favaloro, Louise Ferrand, Jerry Florio, Nina Frenkin (*Bettina Rosay*), Helen Gallagher, Arlene Garver, Mimi Gomber, Edward Hackett, Jean Harris, Ray Johnson, Harriet Katzman, Thomas Kenny, Lee Lauterbur, Constance Love, Richard Martini, Paul Olson, Michael Pober, Lester Russon]; *Scene 2* Song: sung by Beatrice Lillie (1) ☆; *Scene 3* Sketch: "The Great Man Speaks" (written by Charles Sherman). Scene: A doctor's office. Dealing with the vanity of actor Orson Welles. This sketch bombed. THE NURSE: Billie Worth; THE DOCTOR: Albert Carroll; THE PATIENT: Bert Lahr (2) ☆; *Scene 4* Weber's Concertina for Clarinet (solo played by Benny Goodman (3) ☆); *Scene 5* a/ Song: "Frahngee-Pahnee" (sung by Bill Tabbert & Ensemble); b/ Song: "Dancin' to a Jungle Drum (Let's End the Beguine)" [sung by Beatrice Lillie (1) ☆]; *Scene 6* Song: "Hence It Don't Make Sense" (sung by Nan Wynn, Mary Roche, Dolores Gray, Billie

Worth. Danced by Jere McMahon & Billie Worth); *Scene 7* Sketch: "Heaven on Angel Street" (written by Moss Hart). Scene: The living-room in *Angel Street*. MR. MANNINGHAM: Anton Dolin (5) ☆; MRS. MANNINGHAM: Beatrice Lillie (1) ☆ (her line "Please, can't I have just One Meat Ball?" became a classic); MR. CLARENCE DAY: Bert Lahr (2) ☆ (from *Life with Father*); MRS. DAY: Dennie Moore; DUDE LESTER: Michael Barrett (from *Tobacco Road*); JEETER LESTER: Albert Carroll; GEORGE JEAN NATHAN: Robert Austin; MAID: Billie Worth [Note: this scene was replaced during the run with "The Band Started Swinging a Song" (sung by Nan Wynn)]; *Scene 8* Song: "Is it the Girl (or is it the Gown?)" (reprise) [sung by Mary Roche. Lecture by Doc Rockwell (6)]; *Scene 9* Pas de Deux. Concert version of Cole Porter's "Easy to Love." Danced by Alicia Markova (4) ☆ & Anton Dolin (5) ☆; *Scene 10* "They All Made Good" [Doc Rockwell (6) & Young Hopefuls]; *Scene 11* Finale: Song: "Yours for a Song" [Mr. Audience (6) & Entire Company]. Replaced during the run with "The Big Parade" [Mr. Audience (6) & Entire Company].

SINGERS: Robert Austin, Johnsie Bason, Charlotte Bruce, Irene Carroll, Nina Dean, Rose Marie Elliott, Paul Fairleagh, Vincent Henry, Bob Herring, Raynor Howell, Stella Hughes, Jimmy Kane, Robert Kimberly, Mary Ann Krejci, Ethel Madson, John Mathews, Helen Molveau, Louise Newton, Richmond Page, Allen Sharp, Gordon Taylor, William Utely, Martha Emma Watson; PAGE BOYS: Charles Franklin Beck (*Marty Miller*), Sonny Cavell, Alan Grossman, Barry Laffin, Buddy Millard, Dickie Millard, Donald Rose (*Jimmy Dutton*).

Opening night seats cost $24, but champagne during intermission was free. Reviews were divided. This was Billy Rose's first production as the new owner of the Ziegfeld Theatre (he had bought the movie house for $700,000, and renovated it). There was much tension between Cole Porter, Bea Lillie, Bert Lahr and Billy Rose. This show was Helen Gallagher's Broadway debut (she was also an understudy). Despite a $500,000 box office advance the show lost its hefty investment of $350,000. Bea Lillie won a Donaldson award. The number "Ev'ry Time We Say Goodbye" backed with "Only Another Boy and Girl" was a hit in the charts for the Benny Goodman Quintet in 1945 (Peggy Mann sang on the A-side and Jane Harvey on the B-side).

614. *Seventeen*

The turbulence caused in an Indianapolis neighborhood in the summer of 1907 by the arrival at May's house of Lola, a flirtatious young woman who speaks in baby-talk and carries her dog Floppit wherever she goes. Willie falls for her, and George is a rival. She dumps Willie and leaves town. Willie gets her in the end (not in the novel, however). Jane is Willie's sister, and Genesis is the Baxters' black servant.

Before Broadway. Booth Tarkington's novel was made into a Broadway musical called *Hello Lola!* which opened at the ELTINGE THEATRE, 1/12/26, and moved to the MAXINE ELLIOTT'S THEATRE, 2/8/26–2/20/26. Total of 47 PERFORMANCES. MUSIC: William B. Kernell; LYRICS/BOOK: Dorothy Donnelly. **Cast**: LOLA: Edythe Baker; JOE BULLITT: Elisha Cook Jr.

The Broadway Run. BROADHURST THEATRE, 6/21/51–11/24/51. 182 PERFORMANCES. PRESENTED BY Milton Berle, Sammy Lambert, and Bernie Foyer; MUSIC: Walter Kent; LYRICS: Kim Gannon; BOOK: Sally Benson; BASED ON the 1916 novel of the same name, by Booth Tarkington; DIRECTOR/LIGHTING: Hassard Short; BOOK DIRECTOR: Richard Whorf; CHOREOGRAPHER: Dania Krupska; SETS: Stewart Chaney; COSTUMES: David ffolkes; MUSICAL DIRECTOR: Vincent Travers; ORCHESTRATIONS: Ted Royal; CHORAL ARRANGEMENTS: Crane Calder; DANCE MUSIC ARRANGEMENTS: Jess Meeker; PRESS: Richard Maney & Frank Goodman; GENERAL MANAGER: Nick Hode; STAGE MANAGERS: Robert Downing & Jerry Adler. **Cast:** GENESIS: Maurice Ellis; JOHNNIE WATSON: John Sharpe; WILLIE BAXTER: Kenneth Nelson (1); JANE BAXTER: Betty Jane Seagle [she later became Bettijane Sills]; BERT: Greg O'Brien; CHARLIE: Jim Moore; DAVE: Bill Reilly; JOE BULLITT: Dick Kallman (5); LESTER: Richard France; DARRELL: Darrell Notara; DON: Bob Bakanic; LOLA PRATT: Ann Crowley (2); MRS. BAXTER: Doris Dalton;

MAY PARCHER: Ellen McCown (4); EMMIE: Helen Wood (3); IDA: Carol Cole; MADGE: Bonnie Brae; SUE: Elizabeth Pacetti; JENNY: Sherry McCutcheon; NAN: Joan Bowman; MR. BAXTER: Frank Albertson; MR. PARCHER: King Calder; MRS. PARCHER: Penny Bancroft; GEORGE CROOPER: Harrison Muller; MR. GENESIS: Alonzo Bosan; PORTER: Joseph James; SINGERS WITH ORCHESTRA: Margaret Baxter, Stan Grover, Henry Lawrence, Dorothy Manko, Bill Nuss, Jeanne Shea, Paula Stewart, Ray Thomas. *Understudies*: Willie: Dick Kallman; Lola/May: Paula Stewart; Mrs. Baxter: Penny Bancroft; Joe: Richard France; Johnny: Jim Moore; Jane: Rochelle Enker; George: Bill Reilly; Emmie: Carol Cole; Mr. Baxter/Mr. Parcher: Al McGranary; Genesis/Mr. Genesis: Joseph James. *Act I*: *Scene 1* The Baxter's house, Indianapolis, 1907: "Weatherbee's Drug Store" (Joe, Don, Lester, Charlie, Darrell, Dave, Johnnie), "This Was Just Another Day" (Lola & Willie); *Scene 2* On a path: "Things Are Gonna Hum This Summer" (Lola, May, Emmie, Joe, Johnnie, Charlie, Madge, Lester); *Scene 3* In Willie's room: "How Do You Do, Miss Pratt?" (Willie); *Scene 4* At the Parcher house: "Summertime is Summertime" (Emmie, Lester, May, Joe, Friends), "Reciprocity" (Lola, Don, Charlie, Lester, Dave, Darrell, Johnnie); *Scene 5* On a path: "Ode to Lola" (May, Emmie, Nan, Madge, Ida, Jenny, Sue); *Scene 6* The Baxters' house: "A Headache and a Heartache" (Mrs. Baxter & Mr. Baxter), "OO-OOO-OOO, What You Do to Me!" (George). *Act II*: *Scene 1* In the woods: "The Hoosier Way" (George, Emmie, Lester, Charlie, Ida, Friends), "I Could Get Married Today" (Willie, Genesis, Mr. Genesis), "After All, It's Spring" (May, Joe, Friends); *Scene 2* On Harper Road; *Scene 3* In Willie's room; *Scene 4* On the Parchers' lawn: "If We Only Could Stop the Old Town Clock" (Lola, Willie, George, Joe, May, Emmie, Friends); *Scene 5* At the railroad station: "After All, It's Spring" (reprise) (Company).

Broadway reviews were divided, but mostly unfavorable. The original writers of this 1951 production — John Cecil Holm, Stella Unger, and Alec Templeton — received royalties, even though they were not credited.

After Broadway. The tour lasted a week. Bettijane Sills played Jane.

615. *1776*

A historically accurate musical about the signing of the Declaration of Independence, although some events were condensed for the sake of pacing. The Founding Fathers were portrayed as flawed humans, rather than god-like characters. It takes place in May, June and July 1776 in a single setting representing the Chamber and Anteroom of the Continental Congress, in Philadelphia; and certain reaches of John Adams's mind. No intermission.

Before Broadway. Sherman Edwards originally wrote the music, lyrics and book, and took ten years to do so. The producer, Stuart Ostrow, then brought Peter Stone on board to do a new book, while Sherman Edwards concentrated on the music and lyrics. The production cost half a million dollars, with Columbia Records investing 20 percent, and Edgar M. Bronfman, of Seagram's, putting in $250,000. The show tried out in Washington, DC. Predictions about its success were gloomy, some of the reasons being that there was no singing and dancing chorus, it was mostly a male cast, and had no stars. During tryouts Rhoda Levine was replaced as choreographer by Onna White. In the cast Pamela Burrell was replaced by Betty Buckley.

The Broadway Run. FORTY-SIXTH STREET THEATRE, 3/16/69–12/27/70; ST. JAMES THEATRE, 12/28/70–4/24/71; MAJESTIC THEATRE, 4/26/71–2/13/72. 5 previews. Total of 1,217 PERFORMANCES. PRESENTED BY Stuart Ostrow; MUSIC/LYRICS: Sherman Edwards (based on his conception); BOOK: Peter Stone; DIRECTOR: Peter H. Hunt; CHOREOGRAPHER: Onna White; SETS/LIGHTING: Jo Mielziner; COSTUMES: Patricia Zipprodt; MUSICAL DIRECTOR/DANCE MUSIC ARRANGEMENTS: Peter Howard; ORCHESTRATIONS: Eddie Sauter; VOCAL ARRANGEMENTS: Elise Bretton; CAST RECORDING on Columbia (Franklin is sung by Rex Everhart, because Howard Da Silva was sick); PRESS: Lee Solters, Harvey B. Sabinson, Harry Nigro (*Cheryl Sue Dolby* by 69–70), Sandra Manley; CASTING: Michael Shurtleff; GENERAL MANAGERS: Joseph Harris & Ira Bernstein; PRODUCTION STAGE MANAGER: Peter Stern; STAGE MAN-

AGER: Lee Murray; ASSISTANT STAGE MANAGER: Herman Magidson, *Hal Norman.* **Cast:** MEMBERS OF THE CONTINENTAL CONGRESS: PRESIDENT: JOHN HANCOCK: David Ford (6), *Charles Cioffi* (from 69–70), *Roy Cooper* (from 71), *James Noble* (from 71); NEW HAMPSHIRE: DR. JOSIAH BARTLETT: Paul David "Dal" Richards; MASSACHUSETTS: JOHN ADAMS: William Daniels (1) ☆, *John Cunningham* (from 5/4/71); RHODE ISLAND: STEPHEN HOPKINS: Roy Poole (4) ☆, *Edmund Lyndeck* (from 1/70), *Truman Gaige* (from 9/6/71); CONNECTICUT: ROGER SHERMAN: David Vosburgh, *Dan Entriken*; NEW YORK: LEWIS MORRIS: Ronald Kross, *Stanley Simmonds* (from 70–71), *John Ferrante*; ROBERT LIVINGSTON: Henry LeClair; NEW JERSEY: REV. JONATHAN WITHERSPOON: Edmund Lyndeck, *Arthur Anderson* (from 69–70), *Charles Rule* (by 70–71), *Philip Polito* (from 70–71); PENNSYLVANIA: BENJAMIN FRANKLIN: Howard Da Silva (5) ☆, *Rex Everhart* (during Mr. Da Silva's illness), *Jay Garner* (from 7/12/71); JOHN DICKINSON: Paul Hecht (2) ☆, *David Ford* (from 7/70), *George Hearn* (from 8/30/71); JAMES WILSON: Emory Bass (15), *Philip Polito*; DELAWARE: CAESAR RODNEY: Robert Gaus (14); COL. THOMAS McKEAN: Bruce MacKay (11); GEORGE READ: Duane Bodin, *Edward Roll*; MARYLAND: SAMUEL CHASE: Philip Polito, *Charles Rule* (from 70–71), *Haskell Gordon*; VIRGINIA: RICHARD HENRY LEE: Ronald Holgate (9), *Gary Oakes* (from 2/9/71), *Ronald Holgate* (from 5/11/71), *Jon Peck* (from 8/30/71); THOMAS JEFFERSON: Ken Howard (7), *David Cryer*, *John Fink* (from 5/30/69), *Jon Cypher* (from 9/16/69), *Peter Lombard* (from 11/24/69), *Brian Foley* (from 1/15/71); NORTH CAROLINA: JOSEPH HEWES: Charles Rule, *William Stenson* (from 69–70), *Karl Thomas*; SOUTH CAROLINA: EDWARD RUTLEDGE: Clifford David (3) ☆, *John Fink*, *David Cryer* (from 5/30/69), *John Cullum* (from 5/19/70), *Paul David "Dal" Richards* (from 9/13/71), *Gary Beach* (from 71–72); GEORGIA: DR. LYMAN HALL: Jonathan Moore (12), *Edmund Lyndeck* (from 69–70), *Ronald Kross* (from 70–71); CONGRESSIONAL SECRETARY: CHARLES THOMSON: Ralston Hill (13), *John Eames*; CONGRESSIONAL CUSTODIAN: ANDREW McNAIR: William Duell (16), *Stuart Germain*; A LEATHER APRON: B.J. Slater, *Allin Leslie*; COURIER: Scott Jarvis (17); ABIGAIL ADAMS: Virginia Vestoff (8), *Ellen Hanley* (stood in for Miss Vestoff, 12/69–2/16/70), *Rita Gardner* (from 10/19/71); MARTHA JEFFERSON: Betty Buckley (10), *Mary Bracken Phillips* (from 8/28/69), *Betty Buckley* (from 10/5/70), *Pamela Hall* (from 4/13/71), *Chris Callan* (from 7/4/71). **Standby:** Franklin: Rex Everhart (69–70). **Understudies:** Franklin: Bruce MacKay (69–71), *Charles Rule* (70–71); Abigail/Martha: Gretchen Cryer, *Janet McCall, Jamie Thomas* (69–70), *Chris Callan* (70–71); Rutledge: Dal Richards (69–71), *Gary Beach*; Sherman: Dan Entriken; Adams: Jonathan Moore (69), *John Cullum* (69–70), *Dal Richards* (69–71), *Ronald Kross* (69–70); Hancock: Ronald Kross, *William Stenson* (69–70), *Charles Rule* (70–71); Dickinson: Bruce MacKay (69–70), *Ronald Kross, James Noble* (70–71), *Roy Cooper*; Wilson: Ronald Kross (69–71); Hopkins: Ronald Kross (69–71), *Ed Lyndeck* (69–70); McKean: Charles Rule (68–71), *Evan Thompson, William Stenson* (69–70); Thomson: Evan Thompson, *Ed Lyndeck* (70–71); Jefferson: B.J. Slater, *Evan Thompson* (69–71), *Ed Lyndeck* (69–70); Lee: Evan Thompson (69–71), *Hal Norman* (69–70); McNair: Eddie Roll (69–70), *Duane Bodin* (70–71); Courier: B.J. Slater (69–71), *Allin Leslie* (69–70); Hall: Ed Lyndeck (69–70), *Stanley Simmonds* (70–71), *John Ferrante*; Rodney: David Vosburgh (69–71). **General Understudies:** Hal Norman (69–70), Arthur Anderson (69–71), Evan Thompson (70–71), Stanley Simmonds. *Scene 1* The Chamber of the Continental Congress: "Sit Down, John" (Adams & Congress), "Piddle, Twiddle and Resolve" (Adams), "Till Then" (John & Abigail Adams); *Scene 2* The Mall: "The Lees of Old Virginia" (Lee, Franklin, Adams); *Scene 3* The Chamber: "But, Mr. Adams" (Adams, Franklin, Jefferson, Sherman, Livingston); *Scene 4* Jefferson's Room above High Street: "Yours, Yours, Yours" (John & Abigail Adams), "He Plays the Violin" (Martha Jefferson, Franklin, Adams); *Scene 5* The Chamber: "Cool, Cool, Considerate Men" (Dickinson & Conservatives), "Momma Look Sharp" (Courier, McNair, Leather Apron) [This is where an Act II would begin if there was one]; *Scene 6* The Congressional anteroom: "The Egg" (Franklin, Adams, Jefferson); *Scene 7* The Chamber: "Molasses to Rum" (Rutledge), "Yours, Yours, Yours" (reprise) (Abigail), "Is Anybody There?" (Adams), Finale (Congress).

Its advance at the Broadway box-office was only $60,000. It got mostly raves from the critics. On George Washington's birthday in 1970 the Broadway cast, at the command of President Nixon, did a special per-

formance at the White House, the first Broadway musical ever to play a complete performance at that venue. It won Tony Awards for musical, direction, and for Ron Holgate. William Daniels was nominated for a Tony for best featured actor in a musical (as his name was below the title), but he refused the nomination, saying that his role was a leading one. The award, instead, went to Ron Holgate (leading actor went to Jerry Orbach, in *Promises, Promises*). Virginia Vestoff was also nominated, as were the sets.

After Broadway. TOUR. Opened on 4/23/70, at the Curran Theatre, San Francisco, and ran 2 years and 2 months. PRESENTED BY Stuart Ostrow; MUSICAL DIRECTOR: Jonathan Anderson, *Gordon Lowry Harrell, Glen Clugston.* **Cast:** ADAMS: Patrick Bedford; FRANKLIN: Rex Everhart; DICKINSON: George Hearn, *Edmund Lyndeck*; JEFFERSON: Jon Cypher, *Robert Elston, George Blackman* (from 11/16/70), *Robert Elston, Michael Beirne*; HOPKINS: Truman Gaige, *William Griffis*; SHERMAN: Stanley Simmonds, *Donald Norris*; McKEAN: Gordon Dilworth; ABIGAIL: Barbara Lang; MARTHA: Pamela Hall, *Kristen Banfield* (from 4/71), *Chris Callan*; COURIER: Ty McConnell, *Michael Glenn-Smith, James Ferrier*; RUTLEDGE: Jack Blackton, *Michael Davis* (from 11/16/70); LEE: Gary Oakes, *Virgil Curry* (from 12/7/70).

TOUR. Opened on 9/18/70, at the Masonic Auditorium, Scranton, Pa., and closed on 5/14/71, at the Palace Theatre, Albany, NY, after 217 performances in 128 cities. DIRECTOR: Gordon Hunt; MUSICAL DIRECTOR: Glen Clugston. **Cast:** ADAMS: Don Perkins; FRANKLIN: Paul Tripp, *Sam Kressen*; JEFFERSON: William Jennings; ABIGAIL: Ann Clements, *Mara Worth*; MARTHA: Pat Gorman; BARTLETT: Gary Beach, *John Almberg*; SHERMAN: Dan Entriken; RUTLEDGE: Jerry Lanning, *Gary Beach*; LEE: Reid Shelton.

LONDON, 1970. It ran for only 168 PERFORMANCES, despite great reviews. **Cast:** FRANKLIN: Ronald Radd; ADAMS: Lewis Fiander; MARTHA: Cheryl Kennedy; RUTLEDGE: David Kernan.

PAPER MILL PLAYHOUSE, New Jersey, 1972. DIRECTOR: Larry Forde. **Cast:** Robert Horton, Jay Gardener.

THE MOVIE. 1972. WRITER: Peter Stone (from his original Broadway libretto); DIRECTOR: Peter H. Hunt; CHOREOGRAPHER: Onna White. William Daniels, Howard Silva, Ken Howard, and Ron Holgate all reprised their Broadway roles. Jack Warner cut out the number "Cool, Cool, Considerate Men" because he thought it was too anti–Conservative. The soundtrack was on Columbia.

BUS-TRUCK TOUR. Opened on 9/13/75, and closed on 5/23/76. This tour included a special Bicentennial summer run in Philadelphia. **Cast:** ADAMS: Don Perkins.

616. *1776 (Broadway revival)*

Only very minor cuts to the original were made, and a line or two from the movie were added for clarification. There were now 2 acts (Act II beginning with Scene 6). The Act II reprise of "Yours, Yours, Yours" was replaced by a new song — "Compliments" (Abigail).

Before Broadway. By 4/97 Tom Aldredge was the only cast member to be confirmed. Actress Cass Morgan was obliged to leave during rehearsals due to a broken foot. 7/2/97 was an open rehearsal.

The Broadway Run. CRITERION CENTER STAGE RIGHT, 8/14/97–11/16/97; 34 previews from 7/16/97. 109 performances; GERSHWIN THEATRE, 12/3/97–6/14/98. 224 performances. Total of 333 PERFORMANCES. PRESENTED BY the Roundabout Theatre Company, joined on transfer to the Gershwin by the Gershwin Theatre Producers, James M. Nederlander, Stewart F. Lane, Rodger Hess, Bill Haber, Robert Halmi Jr., Dodger Endemol Theatricals, and Hallmark Entertainment; MUSIC/LYRICS: Sherman Edwards (based on his conception); BOOK: Peter Stone; DIRECTOR: Scott Ellis; CHOREOGRAPHER: Kathleen Marshall; SETS: Tony Walton; COSTUMES: William Ivey Long; LIGHTING: Brian Nason; SOUND: Brian Ronan; MUSICAL DIRECTOR: Paul Gemignani; ORIGINAL ORCHESTRATIONS: Eddie Sauter; ADDITIONAL ORCHESTRATIONS: Brian Besterman; DANCE MUSIC ARRANGEMENTS: Peter Howard; CONDUCTOR: Mark Mitchell; NEW CAST RECORDING on TVT Records, recorded on 11/11/97 & 11/13/97, at Edison Studios, NY, and released on 12/16/97 (for this recording they added the reprises to all the songs — which were not in the original); PRESS: Boneau/Bryan-Brown; CASTING: Jim Carnahan; COMPANY MANAGERS: Denys Baker & Jeff Dyksterhouse; PRODUCTION STAGE MANAGER: Lori M. Doyle; STAGE MANAGER: David Sugarman. *Cast:* PRESIDENT: JOHN HANCOCK: Richard Poe; NEW HAMPSHIRE: DR. JOSIAH BARTLETT: Michael X. Martin; MASSACHUSETTS: JOHN ADAMS: Brent Spiner (until 3/1/98), *Michael McCormick* (from 3/4/98); RHODE ISLAND: STEPHEN HOPKINS: Tom Aldredge; CONNECTICUT: ROGER SHERMAN: John Herrera; NEW YORK: LEWIS MORRIS: Tom Riis Farrell, *John Ellison Conlee*; ROBERT LIVINGSTON: Daniel Marcus; NEW JERSEY: REV. JOHN WITHERSPOON: Jerry Lanning; PENNSYLVANIA: BENJAMIN FRANKLIN: Pat Hingle (until 3/1/98), *David Huddleston* (from 3/4/98); JOHN DICKINSON: Michael Cumpsty; JAMES WILSON: Michael Winther; DELAWARE: CAESAR RODNEY: Michael McCormick, *William Duell*; COL. THOMAS MCKEAN: Bill Nolte; GEORGE READ: Kevin Ligon; MARYLAND: SAMUEL CHASE: Ric Stoneback; VIRGINIA: RICHARD HENRY LEE: Merwin Foard; THOMAS JEFFERSON: Paul Michael Valley; NORTH CAROLINA: JOSEPH HEWES: David Lowenstein; SOUTH CAROLINA: EDWARD RUTLEDGE: Gregg Edelman; GEORGIA: DR. LYMAN HALL: Robert Westenberg (until 8/23/97), *Brian Sutherland* (from 8/25/97); CONGRESSIONAL SECRETARY: CHARLES THOMSON: Guy Paul; CONGRESSIONAL CUSTODIAN: ANDREW MCNAIR: MacIntyre Dixon; A LEATHER APRON: Joseph Cassidy; COURIER: Dashiell Eaves, *Erik J. McCormack*; ABIGAIL ADAMS: Linda Edmond (until 3/1/98), *Carolee Carmello* [she was Mrs. Gregg Edelman in real life] (from 3/4/98); MARTHA JEFFERSON: Lauren Ward; PAINTER: Ben Sheaffer, *Ryan Shively*. *Standbys:* Franklin: Rex Everhart; Abigail/Martha: Diane Fratantoni. *Understudies:* Hancock: Michael McCormick & John Herrera; Adams: Michael McCormick, John Herrera, Jim Hindman, Richard Poe; Bartlett: Rob Donohoe, Richard Thomsen, Ryan Shively; Hopkins/McNair/Rodney: Rob Donohoe & Richard Thomsen; Sherman: Joe Cassidy & Michael X. Martin; Lee: Joe Cassidy & Brian Sutherland; Painter: Joe Cassidy & Erik J. McCormack; Rutledge: Joe Cassidy & Kevin Ligon; Morris: Tim Fauvell; Hewes: Tim Fauvell & Ryan Shively; Livingston: Tim Fauvell & Kevin Ligon; Witherspoon: Jim Hindman & Richard Thomsen; McKean/Thomson: Jim Hindman; Hall/Dickinson: Jim Hindman & Michael X. Martin; Wilson: David Lowenstein & Kevin Ligon; Thomson: David Lowenstein; Read: Ben Sheaffer, *Rob Donohoe*; Apron/Courier: Ben Sheaffer, *Rob Donohoe* & *Ryan Shively*; Jefferson: Ben Sheaffer, Brian Sutherland, Ryan Shively; Abigail/Martha: Rebecca Eichenberger; Franklin: Bill Nolte & Tom Roland; Chase: Tim Fauvell & John Ellison Conlee.

Note: the replacements occurred when the show transferred. *Orchestra:* VIOLIN: Brenda Vincent; CELLO: Tatyana Margulis; WOODWINDS: Eric Weidman; TRUMPETS: Dominic Derasse; BASS TROMBONE/TUBA: Dean Plank; BASS: Anthony Morris; PERCUSSION: Thad Wheeler; KEYBOARD: Mark Mitchell.

Reviews were mostly positive. On 9/3/97 it was announced that the production would be looking for a larger Broadway house — the Gershwin, perhaps. The Gershwin had 1,933 seats as opposed to the Criterion's 499. However, the producers had to raise $3 million for the move, and on 10/10/97 they said that unless a miracle happened there wouldn't be a move. But Hallmark Entertainment came to the rescue, and on 10/29/97 the Gershwin was officially announced as the next destination for *1776*. It closed after 109 performances at the Criterion (it had been a limited run, first through 10/19/97, a date that was brought forward to 10/12/97, then back to 11/9/97, then finally to 11/16/97). On 12/3/97 (date put back from 11/27/97) it moved to the Gershwin. The set was expanded slightly on transfer. Reviews were great. Rumors that the show would close were rife for weeks, as it was a reported $3 million in the red, and on 6/13/98 it was announced it would close the following day, after 224 performances at the Gershwin. The show received Tony nominations for revival of a musical, direction of a musical, and for Gregg Edelman.

After Broadway. FORD'S THEATRE, Washington, DC, 3/17/03–6/1/03. Previews from 3/12/03. DIRECTOR: David H. Bell; SETS: James Joy. *Cast:* ADAMS: Lewis Cleale; FRANKLIN: David Huddleston; JEFFERSON: James Ludwig; ABIGAIL: Anne Kanengeiser; MARTHA: Kate Baldwin; HANCOCK: John Leslie Wolfe; RUTLEDGE: Trent Blanton; DICKINSON: Michael Forrest; LEE: Graham Rowat.

In 2003 producers Craig Zadan & Neil Meron were planning a TV version as part of the *Wonderful World of Disney* series on ABC.

617. *Seventh Heaven*

Set in and around Paris, 1914–18. Diane is a prostitute. Boule is the rascally taxi driver who narrates the show. Chico is the "King of the Paris Sewers." He lives in a seventh-floor garret, and that's where he and Diane finally get together. He has a dream that he will marry Diane, then he goes off to fight in World War I.

Before Broadway. The original, which was not a musical, ran on Broadway at the BOOTH THEATRE, from 10/30/22. 704 PERFORMANCES. PRODUCER/DIRECTOR: John Golden. *Cast:* DIANE: Helen Menken; CHICO: George Gaul; NANA: Marion Kirby; BRISSAC: Frank Morgan. It was filmed in 1927, with Janet Gaynor. The 1955 musical was originally planned for Edith Piaf and her husband Jacques Pills, but instead Gloria De Haven and Ricardo Montalban made their Broadway debuts. Paul Hartman was replaced by Kurt Kasznar in New Haven, during the first tryouts. The show then went to Philadelphia, then to Boston, where Fifi D'Orsay, as the madam, was replaced by Bea Arthur. This was Pete Gennaro's Broadway debut as choreographer, although Jerome Robbins doctored the choreography.

The Broadway Run. ANTA THEATRE, 5/26/55–7/2/55. 44 PERFORMANCES. PRESENTED BY Gant Gaither & William Bacher; MUSIC: Victor Young; LYRICS: Stella Unger; BOOK: Victor Wolfson & Stella Unger; BASED ON the 1937 movie of the same name, starring Jimmy Stewart & Simone Simon, which in turn was based on the 1927 movie, which, in turn, was based on the 1922 melodrama written by Austin Strong and produced by John Golden; DIRECTOR: John C. Wilson; CHOREOGRAPHER: Peter Gennaro; ASSISTANT CHOREOGRAPHER: Lee Becker; SETS/COSTUMES: Marcel Vertes; LIGHTING: Feder; MUSICAL DIRECTOR: Max Meth; ORCHESTRAL ARRANGEMENTS: David Terry; CHORAL DIRECTOR: Crane Calder; PRESS: David Lipsky & Jay Russell; GENERAL MANAGER: Robert Willey; PRODUCTION STAGE MANAGER: Ward Bishop; STAGE MANAGERS: Earl J. Brisgal & Ernestine Perrie. *Cast:* BOULE: Kurt Kasznar (3) ☆; CAMILLE: Gerrianne Raphael (8); COLLETTE: Patricia Hammerlee (6); FIFI: Chita Rivera (7); MME SUZE: Beatrice Arthur (5); FATHER CHEVILLON: Malcolm Lee Beggs; DIANE: Gloria De Haven (1) ☆; 1ST SAILOR: Philip Cook; 2ND SAILOR: Leo Kayworth; POLICEMAN: Walter Brandin; 1ST NUN: Nanette Vezina; 2ND NUN: Joy Marlene; STREET CLEANER: Ralph Quist; ORGAN GRINDER: William Carson; 1ST SENEGALESE: Ray Saint Jacques; 2ND SENEGALESE: James E. Wall; DANDY: John Carter; BAKER BOY: Joseph Flynn; HOUSEWIFE: Jeanne Schlegel; ARTIST: Jimmy White; STREETWALKERS: Lee Becker, Bonnie Evans, Helena Seroy; MIDINETTE: Nancy Lynch; FLEEGLE (THE RAT): Robert Clary (4); INSPECTOR: Scott Merrill; GOBIN: David Collyer; VULMIR: Ferdi Hoffman; CHICO: Ricardo Montalban (2) ☆; CHILDREN: Betty Jane Seagle (she later became Bettijane Sills), Barbara Stabile, Barclay Hodges; FRENCH OFFICIAL: George Burles; FLOWER VENDOR: Winifred Ainslee; 1ST FRENCH SOLDIER: Ray Saint Jacques; 2ND FRENCH SOLDIER: James E. Wall; 1ST AMERICAN SOLDIER: Ralph Quist; 2ND AMERICAN SOLDIER: Joseph Flynn; APACHES: Edmund Hall & Ralph Wayne; ACCORDIONIST: Dominic Cortese; DANCERS: Lee Becker, Bonnie Evans, Nancy Lynch, Helena Seroy, Rebecca Vorno, Philip Cook, Victor Duntiere, William Guske, Philip Salem, Jimmy White; SINGERS: Winifred Ainslee, Gwen Harmon, Joy Marlene, Alexandra Moss, Jeanne Schlegel, Nanette Vezina, Walter Brandin, George Burles, William Carson, John Carter, Joseph Flynn, Edmund Hall, Leo Kayworth, Ralph Quist, Ray Saint Jacques, James E. Wall, Ralph Wayne. *Understudies:* Diane: Gerrianne Raphael; Chico: Scott Merrill; Boule: David Collyer; Rat: Joe Flynn; Suze: Winifred Ainslee; Collette: Bonnie Evans; Fifi: Lee Becker; Camille: Helena Seroy; Inspector: Philip Cook; Chevillon/Gobin: Walter Brandin; Vulmir: Leo Kayworth. *Act I:* Scene 1 A cul-de-sac; *Scene 2* A street in Paris; *Scene 3* Chico's sewer; *Scene 4* Rue Notre Dame de Lorette; *Scene 5* Chico's attic; *Scene 6* The street; *Scene 7* "Heaven," four days later; *Scene 8* Rue Notre Dame de Lorette; *Scene 9* Fete Montmartre. *Act II:* Scene 1 Railroad station; *Scene 2* The street; *Scene 3* In the trenches; *Scene 4* No man's land;

Scene 5 Behind the lines, a canteen; **Scene 6** The search; **Scene 7** The cul de-sac. **Act I**: "C'est la Vie" (Fleegle, Boule, Suze, Company), "Where is That Someone for Me" (Diane), "Camille, Collette, Fifi" (Fifi, Collette, Camille), "Man with a Dream" (Chico & Company), "Remarkable Fellow" (Chico, Fifi, Inspector, Company), "If it's a Dream" (Diane), "Happy Little Crook" (Fleegle), "Sun at My Window, Love at My Door" (Diane, Chico, Company), "Where is That Someone for Me?" (reprise) (Diane), Glove Dance (Bonnie Evans, Nancy Lynch, Helena Seroy, Rebecca Vorno, Philip Cook, Victor Duntiere, Philip Salem, Jimmy White). **Act II**: "A 'Miss You' Kiss" (Chico & Company), "Camille, Collette, Fifi" (reprise) (Fifi, Collette, Camille), "Chico's Reverie" (White and Gold Ballet) (ballet) (Company), "Love, Love, Love" (Camille, Collette, Fifi, Jimmy White), "If it's a Dream" (reprise) (Diane), "Love Sneaks up on You" (Fleegle & Collette), Finale (Entire Company).

Reviews were divided, but Chita Rivera (as one of the three prostitutes) got raves.

618. *70, Girls, 70*

Set in New York City. A group of elderly adventurers in a West Side old folks home, the Sussex Arms Hotel, organize themselves into a gang of thieves to steal from the haves, refurbish the hotel, and invite in the elderly have-nots, after Ida, a frumpy old lady who has gone off to die, returns with the discovery that no one notices when old people steal something. Finally they get scared after a job, and decide on one final heist that will enable them to buy their hotel. At the International Fur Show at the Coliseum, the gang is caught. Ida remains behind to take the rap, and dies. Eunice and Walter get married, and Ida returns on a crescent moon to tell all those assembled there to say "yes" to life.

Before Broadway. It was Kander & Ebb's idea to make a stage musical of the British movie *Make Mine Mink*, but originally they planned to do it Off Broadway. However, their then director/choreographer, Ron Field, felt that Broadway would be better. The Broadway idea stayed, but Ron Field didn't, and was replaced before rehearsals by Paul Aaron as director, and Onna White as choreographer. Joe Masteroff left the project at an early stage, and was replaced as librettist by Norman Martin. Eddie Foy, the leading man, was not in good shape, and was replaced by 68-year-old David Burns. The show tried out to good reviews at the Forrest Theatre, Philadelphia, 2/27/71–3/20/71. During the Saturday, 3/12/71 matinee in Philadelphia, David Burns was performing to the number "Go Visit Your Grandmother." He got a big laugh, then went to the wings, keeled over and died just after the matinee ended. Co-star Lillian Roth took Mr. Burns's lines for the evening performance. The tryouts came to an end, and Paul Aaron was fired and replaced by Stanley Prager (although Mr. Aaron retained credit). David F. Segal left as lighting designer, and Robert Randolph took that on as well as set design. The show then returned to New York for re-casting and more rehearsals. David Burns was replaced by Hans Conried, and the role was altered. Mr. Burns had played an ex-vaudevillian who was now the hotel's desk clerk. Mr. Conried played just another resident. Others in the cast to go before the show got to Broadway were: Sammy Smith, Violet Carlson, Beatrice Kay, Renie Riano.

The Broadway Run. BROADHURST THEATRE, 4/15/71–5/15/71. 9 previews from 4/7/71. 36 PERFORMANCES. PRESENTED BY Arthur Whitelaw, in association with Seth Harrison; MUSIC: John Kander; LYRICS: Fred Ebb; BOOK: Fred Ebb & Norman L. Martin; BASED ON the 1958 British comedy *Breath of Spring*, by Peter Coke (actually it was based on the movie *Make Mine Mink*, but legal problems prevented this musical from mentioning that film, which was also based on Peter Coke's play); ADAPTED BY Joe Masteroff; DIRECTOR: Paul Aaron; CHOREOGRAPHER: Onna White; SETS/LIGHTING: Robert Randolph; COSTUMES: Jane Greenwood; MUSICAL DIRECTOR/VOCAL ARRANGEMENTS: Oscar Kosarin; ASSISTANT MUSICAL DIRECTOR: Karen Gustafson; ORCHESTRATIONS: Don Walker; DANCE MUSIC: Dorothea Freitag; CAST RECORDING on Columbia; PRESS: Max Eisen, Warren Pincus, Milly Schoenbaum; CASTING: Shirley Rich; PRODUCTION SUPERVISOR: Stan-

ley Prager; GENERAL MANAGER: Marvin A. Krauss; COMPANY MANAGER: David Wyler; PRODUCTION STAGE MANAGER: Edwin P. Aldridge; STAGE MANAGER: Edwin P. Aldridge & Victor Straus; ASSISTANT STAGE MANAGER: John Johann. *Cast:* IDA: Mildred Natwick (1) ✰; HARRY: Hans Conried (2) ✰; GERT: Lillian Roth (3) ✰; WALTER: Gil Lamb (4); MELBA: Lillian Hayman (5); EUNICE: Lucie Lancaster (6); FRITZI: Goldye Shaw (7); LORRAINE: Dorothea Freitag (8); DETECTIVE CALAHAN: Joey Faye (9); GRANDMOTHER: Henrietta Jacobson (10); OFFICER KOWALSKI: Coley Worth (11); EDDIE: Tommy Breslin (13); ENSEMBLE: Thomas Anderson (17), Robert G. Dare (18), Sally De May (19), Ruth Gillette (12), Lloyd Harris (20), Marjorie Leach (21), Abby Lewis (16), Steve Mills (14), Naomi Price (22), Beau Tilden (23), Bobbi Tremain (15), Jay Velie (24). **Standbys**: Lorraine: Karen Gustafson; Ida/Gert: Nancy Andrews. **Understudies**: Harry: Coley Worth; Walter: Joey Faye; Melba: Naomi Price; Eunice: Abby Lewis; Fritzi: Henrietta Jacobson; Calahan/Kowalski/for Mr. Mills: Robert G. Dare; Grandmother: Ruth Gillette; Eddie: John Johann; For Miss Lewis/Miss Leach: Sally De May; for Mr. Dare: Beau Tilden. **Act I**: **Prologue**: "Old Folks" (Company); **Scene 1** The Cornucopia Tea Room: "Home" (Ida, Gert, Eunice, Walter, Harry, Melba, Fritzi); **Scene 2** The Broadhurst Theatre: "Broadway, My Street" (Melba, Fritzi, Mr. Anderson, Calahan, Mr. Harris, Grandmother, Mr. Tilden, Miss Tremaine, Mr. Velie, Kowalski); **Scene 3** Ida's room; **Scene 4** The Broadhurst Theatre: "The Caper" (Harry); **Scene 5** Sadie's Fur Salon; **Scene 6** The Broadhurst Theatre: "Coffee (in a Cardboard Cup)" (Melba & Fritzi); **Scene 7** Lobby of the Sussex Arms: "You and I, Love" (Mr. Mills, Miss Lewis, Mr. Anderson, Mr. Harris, Mr. Velie, Kowalski, Miss Gillette, Miss Tremain), "Do We?" (Eunice & Walter), "Hit it, Lorraine" (Ida, Gert, Eunice, Lorraine, Harry); **Scene 8** The Broadhurst Theatre; **Scene 9** Bloomingdale's: "See the Light" (Gert, Calahan, Kowalski, Mr. Anderson, Mr. Velie); **Scene 10** Lobby of the Sussex Arms. **Act II**: Entr'acte (Miss Gillette, Calahan, Mr. Harris, Mr. Velie); **Scene 1** The Broadhurst Theatre: "Boom Ditty Boom" (Ida, Gert, Melba, Eunice, Fritzi, Harry, Walter); **Scene 2** Arctic Cold Storage Company: "Believe" (Melba, Ida, Gert, Eunice, Fritzi, Harry, Walter); **Scene 3** The Broadhurst Theatre: "Go Visit (Your Grandmother)" (Eddie & Grandmother); **Scene 4** Lobby of the Sussex Arms: "70, Girls, 70" (Company); **Scene 5** The Broadhurst Theatre: "The Elephant Song" (Ida, Melba, Fritzi); **Scene 6** The Coliseum; **Scene 7** The Broadhurst Theatre; **Scene 8** A chapel: "Yes" (Ida & Company); Finale. Broadway reviews were very divided. The production lost $600,000. Mildred Natwick was nominated for a Tony.

After Broadway. A revised revival had an initial run at CHICHESTER FESTIVAL THEATRE, England. Then it toured; then it had a West End run at the VAUDEVILLE THEATRE, London, from 6/17/91. PRESENTED BY Newpalm (John Newman & Daphne Palmer); MUSICAL DIRECTOR: Wendy Gadian; NEW CAST RECORDING on Jay. *Cast:* IDA: Dora Bryan; GERT: Joan Savage; EDDIE: Stuart Morrison; MELBA: Shezwae Powell; ALSO WITH: Pip Hinton, Jan Hunt, James Gavin, Brian Greene, Buster Skeggs, Len Howe, Stephanie Voss. "Old Folks" (opening), "Home," "Well-Laid Plans," "Coffee in a Cardboard Cup," "Hit it, Lorraine," "Do We?," "Emma Finch," "Broadway, My Street," "Boom Ditty Boom," "Believe," "Go Visit Your Grandmother," "I Can't Do That Anymore," "70, Girls, 70," "Yes," "Old Folks Finale."

YORK THEATRE COMPANY, 1/28/00–1/30/00. 5 PERFORMANCES. Part of the *Musicals in Mufti* series (staged readings, with piano as accompaniment). REVISED BOOK: David Thompson; DIRECTOR: Michael Leeds; LIGHTING: Patrick Vaccariello. *Cast:* IDA: Jane Powell; EUNICE: Jane Connell; WALTER: George S. Irving; FRITZI: Mimi Hines; SADIE: Marilyn Cooper; HARRY: Robert Fitch; JOE: Don Percassi; PETE: Danny Carroll; MELBA: Charlotte Rae; GERT: Helen Gallagher. **Act I**: **Scene 1** Limbo: "Old Folks" (Ida, Eunice, Walter, Harry, Gert, Melba, Fritzi); **Scene 2** The Sussex Arms: "Home" (Ida, Eunice, Walter, Harry, Gert, Melba, Fritzi); **Scene 3** Ida's room: "The Caper" (Harry); **Scene 4** Sadie's Fur Salon; **Scene 5** Limbo: "Coffee in a Cardboard Cup" (Melba & Fritzi); **Scene 6** The Sussex Arms: "Hit it, Lorraine" (Ida, Eunice, Gert, Harry, Lorraine), "Do We?" (Walter & Eunice); **Scene 7** Bloomingdale's: "Emma Finch" (Gert, Pete, Joe); **Scene 8** The Sussex Arms: "Broadway, My Street" (Fritzi, Melba, Ida, Eunice, Walter, Harry, Gert). **Act II**: **Scene 1** Cold storage vault: "Believe" (Fritzi, Melba, Ida, Eunice, Walter, Harry, Gert); **Scene 2** Limbo: "Go Visit Your Grandmother" (Eddie

& Sadie); *Scene 3* The Sussex Arms: "I Can't Do That Anymore" (Harry & Walter); *Scene 4* Limbo: "Where Does an Elephant Go?" (Ida & Company); *Scene 5* Fur show: "70, Girls, 70" (Ida, Eunice, Gert, Harry, Walter, Melba, Fritzi); *Scene 6* The Sussex Arms: "Yes" (Company).

619. *Shakespeare's Cabaret*

A musical cabaret. No intermission. A revue with lyrics, from Shakespeare's works, particularly the songs and poems.

Before Broadway. The show originally ran, in 2 parts, at the COLONNADES THEATRE LAB, 2/1/80–3/16/80. 40 PERFORMANCES. DIRECTOR: Michael Lessac; MUSICAL DIRECTOR: Don Jones; PRESS: Philip Rinaldi; STAGE MANAGER: R.T. Schwartz. **Cast**: Alan Brasington, Maureen Brennan, Mel Johnson Jr., Patti Perkins, Roxanne Reese, Keith R. Rice, Peter Van Norden. **Orchestra**: KEYBOARDS: Don Jones; LEAD GUITARS/LEAD GUITAR ARRANGEMENTS: Steve Postel; DRUMS/PERCUSSION: Bud Clark; BASS: Richie Bremem. Musical numbers were different then; several transferred to Broadway, but may not have been in the same order. Others were dropped for Broadway and replaced by new ones. To avoid redundancy, only the non–Broadway ones have their sources given here: *Part I*: "If Music and Sweet Poetry Agree" (Ensemble), "How Should I Your True Love Know?" [from *Hamlet*] (Alan), "Come Live with Me and Be My Love" (Mel), "If I Profane" [from *Romeo and Juliet*] (Peter & Maureen), "Tell Me, Where is Fancy Bred?" (Ensemble), "The *Venus and Adonis* Suite" (Patti & Mel), "What Thou See'st When Thou Dost Awake" (Ensemble), "Come Away Death" [from *Twelfth Night*] (Keith), "All that Glisters (is Not Gold)" (Maureen, Patti, Roxanne), "Crabbed Age and Youth" (Alan). *Part II*: "If Music Be the Food of Love" (Alan), "Fathers that Wear Rags" (Roxanne), "Epitaph for Marina" (Keith & Patti), "Will You Buy Any Tape?" [from *The Winter's Tale*] (Maureen), "The Willow Song" (Patti), "Pyramus, Arise" [from *A Midsummer Night's Dream*] (Alan), "Shepherd's Song" [from *The Passionate Pilgrim*] (Peter), "Shall I Compare Thee to a Summer's Day?" (Mel), "Come Unto These Yellow Sands" (Ensemble), "Lawn as White as Driven Snow" (Ensemble), "I Am St. Jacques' Pilgrim" [from *All's Well That Ends Well*] (Ensemble), "The Phoenix and the Turtle" (Ensemble), "Tomorrow is St. Valentine's Day" (Patti), "Rosalynde" (Alan, Keith, Peter), "Then Let Me the Canakin Clink" (Ensemble), "Shakespeare's Epitaph and Celebration" (Ensemble).

The Broadway Run. BIJOU THEATRE, 1/21/81–3/8/81. 12 previews. 54 PERFORMANCES. PRESENTED BY Arthur Shafman; MUSIC: Lance Mulcahy; WRITER: William Shakespeare; BASED ON a concept by Lance Mulcahy; DEVELOPED BY: Michael Lessac; DIRECTOR: John Driver; CHOREOGRAPHER: Lynne Taylor-Corbett; SETS/COSTUMES: Frank J. Boros; LIGHTING: Marc B. Weiss; MUSICAL DIRECTOR/ORCHESTRATIONS/VOCAL ARRANGEMENTS: Donald G. Jones; PRESS: Jeffrey Richards, Robert Ganshaw, C. George Willard, Ben Morse, Ted Killmer, Helen Stern; GENERAL MANAGER: Sherman Gross; PRODUCTION STAGE MANAGER: Kitzi Becker; STAGE MANAGER: John Handy. **Cast**: Alan Brasington, Catherine Cox (as Catherine; replaced by *Dee Hoty* as Dee), Pauletta Pearson, Patti Perkins, Larry Riley, Michael Rupert. **Understudies**: *Weyman Thompson*; *Maureen McNamara* (for Dee). "If Music and Sweet Poetry Agree" [from *The Passionate Pilgrim*] (Ensemble), "What Thou See'st When Thou Dost Awake" [from *A Midsummer Night's Dream*] (Ensemble), "All that Glisters (is Not Gold)" [from *The Merchant of Venice*] (Catherine, Patti, Pauletta), "Why Should This a Desert Be?" [from *As You Like It*] (Michael), "Crabbed Age and Youth" [from *The Passionate Pilgrim*] (Alan & Patti), "Orpheus with His Lute" [from *Henry VIII*] (Pauletta), "Music with Her Silver Sound" [from *Romeo and Juliet*] (Catherine, Michael, Patti, Alan), "Come Live with Me and Be My Love" [from *The Passionate Pilgrim*, but attributed to Christopher Marlowe] (Larry), "Have More than Thou Showest" [from *King Lear*] (Michael & Alan), "The *Venus and Adonis* Suite" (Ensemble), "Tell Me, Where is Fancy Bred?" [from *The Merchant of Venice*] (Ensemble), "If Music Be the Food of Love" [from *Twelfth Night*] (Alan & Pauletta), "Epitaph for Marina" [from *Pericles*] (Michael & Catherine), "The Phoenix and the Turtle" (Alan, Patti, Pauletta, Catherine, Michael), "Now" [from *A Midsummer Night's Dream*] (Larry), "The Willow Song"

& Sadie); "Immortal Gods" [from *Timon of Athens*] (Alan), "Tomorrow is St. Valentine's Day" [from *Hamlet*] (Patti), "Fathers that Wear Rags" [from *King Lear*] (Pauletta), "The Grave Digger's Song" [from *Hamlet*] (Larry), "Now" (reprise) (Larry, Patti, Pauletta, Catherine, Alan), "Come Unto These Yellow Sands" [from *The Tempest*] (Ensemble), "Shall I Compare Thee to a Summer's Day?" [from Sonnet 18] (Catherine & Alan), "Lawn as White as Driven Snow" [from *The Winter's Tale*] (Ensemble), "Rosalynde" [from *As You Like It*] (Larry & Alan), "Let Me the Canakin Clink" [from *Othello*] (Ensemble), "Shakespeare's Epitaph" [from *Cymbeline*] (Ensemble), "Fear No More the Heat of the Sun" [from *Cymbeline*] (Ensemble), "Shakespeare's Epitaph" (reprise) (Ensemble).

Reviews were divided, mixed, but mostly kind. The Broadway Run closed at the 3/8/81 matinee. The score was nominated for a Tony.

After Broadway. A sequel, *Sweet Will*, ran Off Broadway, at DON'T TELL MAMA, 2/2/85–3/3/85. 20 PERFORMANCES. PRESENTED BY David K. Drummond; MUSIC: Lance Mulcahy; LYRICS: William Shakespeare; DIRECTOR: John Olon; CHOREOGRAPHER: Dennis Dennehy; LIGHTING: John Michael Deegan; MUSICAL DIRECTOR: Michael Ward. **Cast**: Keith Amos, Stephanie Cotsirilos, Roslyn Burrough, Stephen Lehew. "Hark, Hark the Lark," "Where the Bee Sucks," "Sigh No More, Ladies," "Who is Sylvia?," "All that Glisters," "Venus and Adonis," "Shall I Compare Thee," "O Mistress Mine," "Over Hill, Over Dale," "Under the Greenwood Tree," "Farewell Dear Love." It ran again, at JOANN'S NEW SILVER LINING CABARET THEATRE, 1/5/86–1/11/86. 13 previews from 12/26/85. 9 PERFORMANCES.

620. *Shangri-La*

A group of westerners, led by Conway, are transported from a patrol station on the Tibetan border into a Himalayan community called Shangri-La, run by the High Lama (originally a French priest named Perrault, who discovered the valley, and set up the Lamasery), where no one ages. Conway returns to civilization. Miss Brinklow was a comic missionary. Robert and Rita were a pair of USO hoofers. The sets were made of Lucite, and had a translucent, tilted floor with colored lights beneath.

Before Broadway. Although James Hilton got co-librettist billing, he had died in 1954, during the very early stages of the first (abortive) production. The producers wanted to use unpublished Vincent Youmans songs, and wanted Walter Kerr to direct. That all fell through, and Robert Fryer & Lawrence Carr picked up the project. After the opening of the Boston tryout, Marshall Jamison, much to his surprise, was replaced as director by Albie Marre. In the cast Lew Ayres quit, and was replaced by Jack Cassidy (who already had a smaller role in the show) until main star Dennis King was ready; and Susan Cabot was replaced by Shirley Yamaguchi. The show closed in Boston in order to get a couple of weeks of extra rehearsal.

The Broadway Run. WINTER GARDEN THEATRE, 6/13/56–6/30/56. 21 PERFORMANCES. PRESENTED BY Robert Fryer & Lawrence Carr; MUSIC: Harry Warren; LYRICS: Jerome Lawrence & Robert E. Lee; ADDITIONAL LYRICS: Sheldon Harnick; BOOK: James Hilton, Jerome Lawrence, Robert E. Lee, and (unbilled) Luther Davis; BASED ON the 1933 novel *Lost Horizon*, by James Hilton, and upon the 1937 movie based on it, starring Ronald Colman; DIRECTOR: Albert Marre; CHOREOGRAPHER: Donald Saddler; SETS: Peter Larkin; COSTUMES: Irene Sharaff; MUSICAL DIRECTOR/CHORAL ARRANGEMENTS/MUSICAL CONTINUITY: Lehman Engel; ORCHESTRATIONS: Philip J. Lang; BALLET MUSIC COMPOSED & ARRANGED BY: Genevieve Pitot; ADDITIONAL DANCE MUSIC ARRANGEMENTS: John Morris; PRESS: Arthur Cantor, Robert Ganshaw, Gertrude Kirschner; GENERAL MANAGER: Ben F. Stein; STAGE MANAGER: Ross Bowman; ASSISTANT STAGE MANAGER: Duane Camp. **Cast**: HUGH CONWAY: Dennis King (1); CHAO-LI: Kaie Deei [he later became Khigh Dhiegh] (4); ROBERT HENDERSON: Harold Lang (4); RITA HENDERSON: Joan Holloway; CHARLES MALLINSON: Jack Cassidy (5); MISS BRINKLOW: Alice Ghostley (6); CHANG: Martyn Green (3); ARANA: Carol Lawrence (7); TI: Edwin Kim Ying; THE LITTLE ONE: Leland Mayforth; LO-TSEN: Shirley Yamaguchi (2); RIMSHI: Ed Kenney; HIGH LAMA: Berry Kroeger; THE DANCER PERRAULT: Robert Cohan;

THE PEOPLE OF SHANGRI LA: SINGERS: Jay Bacon, Edward Becker, Sara Bettis, Elizabeth Burgess, Joan Cherof, Sylvia Fabry, Walter Farrell, George Lenz, Bob McClure, David McDaniel, Teresa Montes, Eileen Moran, Jack Rains, Ed Stroll, Ted Wills, Maggie Worth, Marvin Zeller; DANCERS: Ralph Beaumont, Michael De Marco, Ray Dorian, Eddie Heim, Dorothy Hill, Greb Lober, Ellen Matthews, Ilona Murai, Mary Ann Niles, Rico Riedl, Ed Stinnett, Doris Wright. **Standby**: Chang/ Lama: G. Wood. **Understudies**: Conway: Jack Cassidy; Henderson: Ralph Beaumont; Mallinson: Ed Stroll; Lo-Tsen: Carol Lawrence; Miss Brinklow: Elizabeth Burgess; Rita: Mary Ann Niles; Arana: Eileen Moran. **Act I**: **Scene 1** A patrol station on the Tibetan border; **Scene 2** Night on the mountain: "Om Mani Padme Hum" (Male Singers); **Scene 3** The mountain pass; **Scene 4** The terrace of the lamasery: "Lost Horizon" (Entire Company), "Dance of Welcome" (dance) (Dancer Perrault & Ti): POLE BOYS: Ray Dorian, Eddie Heim, Rico Riedl; LOTUS GIRL: Ilona Murai; TIGERS: Ed Stinnett & Michael De Marco; TIGER TAMER: Ralph Beaumont; "The Man I Never Met" (Lo-Tsen); **Scene 5** A bedchamber in the lamasery: "Every Time You Danced with Me" (Robert & Rita); **Scene 6** A music room: Dance of Moderate Chastity (Miss Brinklow & Dancers); **Scene 7** The rope bridge: "The World Outside" (Lo-Tsen & Charles); **Scene 8** The terrace: "Requiem" (Singers & Dancers); **Scene 9** A corridor: "I'm Just a (Little) Bit Confused" (Miss Brinklow); **Scene 10** The terrace: "The Beetle Race" (Chang & Ensemble); **Scene 11** Outside Conway's room: "Somewhere" (Charles); **Scene 12** Chamber of the High Lama: The Story of Shangri-La (dance) (Dancer Perrault & Dancers). **Act II**: **Scene 1** A prison camp; **Scene 2** Chang's library: "What Every Old Girl Should Know" (Miss Brinklow & Chang); **Scene 3** A bedchamber in the lamasery: "Second Time in Love" (Robert & Rita), "Talkin' with Your Feet" (Robert & Rita); **Scene 4** A corridor: "Walk Sweet" (Lo-Tsen); **Scene 5** Chamber of the High Lama; **Scene 6** A corridor: "Love is What I Never Knew" (Lo-Tsen & Charles); **Scene 7** A terrace: "We've Decided to Stay" (Miss Brinklow, Robert, Rita); **Scene 8** A glacier: Dance of Time (Lo-Tsen & Dancers); **Scene 9** A prison camp; **Scene 10** The terrace: "Shangri-La" (Conway).

Broadway reviews were generally awful, but the sets and costumes got a lot of praise. At the opening night party Jack Cassidy introduced his friend Jerry Bock to Sheldon Harnick, and thus began one of the great songwriting teams of the Broadway musical theatre. The show received a Tony nomination for costumes.

After Broadway. NBC TV re-made the stage musical *Shangri-La*, and it was shown on 10/24/60, on *Hallmark Hall of Fame*. **Cast:** Richard Basehart, Marisa Pavan, Claude Rains, Gene Nelson, Helen Gallagher, Alice Ghostley (in her Broadway role). In the movies a (hopeless) musical version of *Lost Horizon* was released in 1973, with Peter Finch & Liv Ullmann (in contrast, the original 1937 — straight — movie was a classic).

621. *She Loves Me*

Set in "a city in Europe" (it has to be Budapest), in the 1930s, the show is in 2 acts & 10 scenes. It tells the story of the people who work in Maraczek's Parfumerie, primarily Amalia, the sales clerk and Georg, the manager, who are always fighting. It is soon revealed that they are anonymous pen pals who agree to meet one night at the Café Imperiale, though neither knows the other's identity. Georg realizes who his pen pal has been when he sees Amalia waiting in the café, but he doesn't tell her. After her pen pal doesn't show up, she gets so depressed she calls in sick to work, and Georg brings her ice cream. Finally he quotes to her from one of his letters, and they fall in love. The orchestra consisted mainly of strings, as opposed to brass.

Before Broadway. Aside from the 1940 Lubitsch film, MGM also remade the story into the 1949 musical movie *In the Good Old Summertime*, starring Judy Garland and Van Johnson. It was Lawrence Kasha's idea to do a stage musical of *The Shop Around the Corner*. Joe Masteroff wrote the libretto as a straight play, and then he and the songwriters worked out where the songs should go. Bock & Harnick wrote 30 songs,

of which 24 were used. The six not used were: "Christmas Eve," "Hello, Love," "Merry Christmas Bells," "My Drugstore," "Seasonal Pleasure" and "Tell Me I Look Nice." The producers' first choice as director was Gower Champion, but he was about to start another project, and asked them to wait for him. Instead, they went with Hal Prince, then a relative novice. Later, Mr. Champion's project fell through, and he declared his availability. Hal Prince volunteered to step aside, but the producers now wanted him. Lawrence Kasha had obtained the rights to the story from MGM, or at least thought he had. There was some confusion until Hal Prince came on board and took care of it. This was the first time Mr. Prince had both producer and director of a Broadway musical. Julie Andrews was to have been the star, but she was tied up with a film (*The Americanization of Emily*). She asked them to wait until the fall of 1963, but that would have been 6 months too late, so Mr. Prince went with Barbara Cook. The casting of Georg took ages, but they finally settled on Daniel Massey. There were out-of-town tryouts at the Forrest Theatre, Philadelphia, and at the Shubert Theatre, New Haven (where it opened on 3/18/63). It got good reviews. Sig Arno was replaced by Nathaniel Frey. During the making of the show Sheldon Harnick married Elaine May. Hal Prince decided against using the Ziegfeld Theatre because it was too big, and instead settled for the Eugene O'Neill.

The Broadway Run. EUGENE O'NEILL THEATRE, 4/23/63–1/11/64. 1 preview on 4/22/63. 302 PERFORMANCES. PRESENTED BY Harold S. Prince, in association with Lawrence N. Kasha & Philip C. McKenna; MUSIC: Jerry Bock; LYRICS: Sheldon Harnick; BOOK: Joe Masteroff; BASED ON the 1937 Hungarian comedy *Parfumerie*, by Miklos Laszlo, and on the 1940 Ernst Lubitsch film made from it, *The Shop Around the Corner*, starring Jimmy Stewart & Margaret Sullavan; DIRECTOR: Harold S. Prince; CHOREOGRAPHER: Carol Haney; SETS/LIGHTING: William & Jean Eckart; COSTUMES: Patricia Zipprodt; MUSICAL DIRECTOR: Hal Hastings; ORCHESTRATIONS: Don Walker; INCIDENTAL MUSIC ARRANGEMENTS: Jack Elliott; CAST RECORDING on MGM, made on 4/28/63 as a double-album, with every note of the production on it, and released in 5/63; PRESS: Sol Jacobson, Lewis Harmon, Mary Bryant, Warren Pincus; GENERAL MANAGER: Carl Fisher; PRODUCTION STAGE MANAGER: Ruth Mitchell; STAGE MANAGER: Tom Stone; ASSISTANT STAGE MANAGER: Jack Leigh. **Cast:** ARPAD LASZLO: Ralph Williams (7); LADISLAV SIPOS: Nathaniel Frey (5); ILONA RITTER: Barbara Baxley (3) ☆, *Marion Brash* (11/2/63–12/2/63), *Barbara Baxley*; STEVEN KODALY: Jack Cassidy (4); GEORG NOWACK: Daniel Massey (2) ☆; MR. MARACZEK: Ludwig Donath (6); WINDOW SHOPPERS: Jety Herlick & Judy West; 1ST CUSTOMER: Marion Delano; 2ND CUSTOMER: Peg Murray; 3RD CUSTOMER: Trude Adams; AMALIA BALASH: Barbara Cook (1) ☆, *Trude Adams* (11/12/63–11/18/63), *Barbara Cook*; 4TH CUSTOMER: Judy West; 5TH CUSTOMER: Jety Herlick; 6TH CUSTOMER: Vicki Mansfield; MR. KELLER: Gino Conforti (10); WAITER: Wood Romoff (9); BUSBOY: Al DeSio; VIOLINIST: Gino Conforti; VIKTOR: Pepe de Chazza; STEFANIE: Vicki Mansfield; MAGDA: Judy West; FERENCZ: Bob Bishop; COUPLE: Peg Murray & Joe Ross; NURSE: Jety Herlick; CAROLERS: Jo Wilder (8), Joe Ross, Gino Conforti; PAUL: Les Martin. **Understudies**: Amalia: Jo Wilder; Miss Ritter: Marion Delano; Georg/Kodaly: Les Martin; Maraczek: Wood Romoff; Arpad: Al DeSio; Sipos/Waiter: Joe Ross. **Act I**: In and around Maraczek's Parfumerie — a morning in June through an evening in early December; and Cafe Imperiale — later that evening: Overture (Orchestra), "Good Morning, Good Day" (Arpad, Sipos, Ilona, Kodaly, Georg), "Sounds While Selling" (Georg, Sipos, Kodaly, Customers), "Thank You, Madam" (Sipos, Georg, Kodaly, Ilona, Customers), "Days Gone By" (Maraczek), "No More Candy" (Amalia), "Three Letters" (Amalia & Georg), "Tonight at Eight" (Georg), "I Don't Know His Name" (Amalia & Ilona), "Perspective" (Sipos), "Goodbye, Georg" (Georg, Ilona, Sipos, Kodaly, Arpad, Customers), "Will He Like Me?" (Amalia), "Ilona" (Kodaly, Sipos, Arpad), "I Resolve" (Ilona), "A Romantic Atmosphere" (Waiter, Busboy, Violinist, Couple, Stefanie, Viktor, Magda, Ferencz), "Tango Tragique" (Georg), "Dear Friend" (Amalia). Entr'acte (Orchestra). **Act II**: Hospital — the next day; Amalia's apartment — later the same day; in and around Maraczek's Parfumerie–later that evening to Dec. 24: "Try Me" (Arpad), "Days Gone By" (reprise) (Maraczek), "Where's My Shoe?" (Amalia & Georg), "(Vanilla) Ice Cream" (Amalia), "She Loves Me" (Georg), "A Trip to the Library" (Ilona), "Grand Knowing You" (Kodaly), "Twelve Days to

Christmas" (Carolers & Company), Finale: "(Vanilla) Ice Cream" (reprise) (Amalia & Georg).

Broadway reviews were great, with the exception of Walter Kerr (then of the *Herald Tribune*), and the show was appreciated everywhere but at the box-office. It was capitalized at $300,000, and made back only $50,000—losing a quarter of a million. Jack Cassidy won a Tony Award, and the show was also nominated for musical, producer of a musical, book, and direction of a musical.

After Broadway. LYRIC THEATRE, London, 4/29/64. 189 PERFORMANCES. DIRECTOR: Harold Prince; Carol Haney was choreographing the show but caught pneumonia (she died soon afterwards in New York). Nyree Dawn Porter was announced for the lead, but illness forced her to be replaced by Rita Moreno. The number "Heads I Win" was added for this production. LONDON CAST RECORDING was made on 5/10/64 and 5/11/64. CAST: ILONA: Rita Moreno, *Amanda Barrie*; AMALIA: Anne Rogers; GEORG: Gary Raymond; KODALY: Gary Miller; ZOLTAN MARACZEK: Karel Stepanek; SIPOS: Peter Sallis; HEAD WAITER: Carl Jaffe; ARPAD: Gregory Phillips.

CHARLES PLAYHOUSE, Boston, 12/23/64. 48 PERFORMANCES. DIRECTOR: Ben Shaktman; CHOREOGRAPHER: David M. Figg; MUSICAL DIRECTOR: Joseph Raposo. **Cast**: Mimi Turque, James Rado, Beryl Towbin, Muni Seroff.

TOWN HALL, NYC, 3/29/77. 24 PERFORMANCES. Advertised as "Broadway in Concert at Town Hall." PRESENTED BY Richard Grayson & John Bowab; DIRECTOR: John Bowab; GOWNS: Donald Brooks; LIGHTING: Ken Billington; MUSICAL DIRECTOR: Wally Harper. **Cast**: SIPOS: Tom Batten; ARPAD: George David Connolly; ILONA: Rita Moreno; KODALY: Laurence Guittard; GEORG: Barry Bostwick; MARACZEK: George Rose; CUSTOMERS: Bette Glenn, Marti Bucklew, Janet McCall; AMALIA: Madeline Kahn; KELLER: Michael Hayward-Jones; WAITER: John La Motta; CHORALER: William James. **Understudies**: Ilona/Amalia: Bette Glenn; Georg/Kodaly/Arpad/Keller: William James; Maraczek: Tom Batten; Sipos/Waiter: Michael Hayward-Jones.

OPERA ENSEMBLE OF NEW YORK, 5/3/89–5/21/89. 9 PERFORMANCES. DIRECTOR: John J.D. Sheehan; CHOREOGRAPHER: Lavinia Plonka; MUSICAL DIRECTOR: Jonathan Tunick. **Cast**: ILONA: Annie McGreevey; KODALY: Davis Gaines; GEORG: Gregg Edelman; AMALIA: Elizabeth Walsh.

622. *She Loves Me (Broadway revival)*

This 30th-anniversary revival specifies that the story is set in Budapest, in 1934. The number "Thank You, Madam" was abbreviated and tacked onto the end of "Sounds While Selling." "Tango Tragique," newly orchestrated by David Krane, was reduced to an instrumental insert during the number "A Romantic Atmosphere." The Act II reprise of "Days Gone By" was not in this production.

The Broadway Run. CRITERION CENTER STAGE RIGHT, 6/10/93–8/1/93. 31 previews from 5/15/93. 61 PERFORMANCES; BROOKS ATKINSON THEATRE, 10/7/93–6/19/94. 11 previews from 9/28/93. 294 PERFORMANCES. Total of 355 PERFORMANCES. The Roundabout Theatre Company production, PRESENTED BY James M. Nederlander & Elliot Martin, with Herbert Wasserman, Freddy Bienstock, and Roger L. Stevens; MUSIC: Jerry Bock; LYRICS: Sheldon Harnick; BOOK: Joe Masteroff; BASED ON the 1937 Hungarian comedy *Parfumerie*, by Miklos Laszlo, and on the 1940 film made from it, *The Shop Around the Corner*; DIRECTOR: Scott Ellis; CHOREOGRAPHER: Rob Marshall; ASSISTANT CHOREOGRAPHER: Kathleen Marshall; SETS: Tony Walton; COSTUMES: David Charles & Jane Greenwood; LIGHTING: Peter Kaczorowski; SOUND: Tony Meola; MUSICAL DIRECTOR/ADDITIONAL VOCAL ARRANGEMENTS/DANCE MUSIC: David Loud; ORCHESTRATIONS: Frank Matosich Jr. & David Krane adapted Don Walker's original orchestrations; NEW CAST RECORDING on Varese Sarabande; PRESS: Boneau/Bryan-Brown; CASTING: Pat McCorkle, Rich Cole, Tim Sutton; GENERAL MANAGEMENT: Niko Associates; COMPANY MANAGER: Erich Hamner; PRODUCTION STAGE MANAGER: Kathy J. Faul; STAGE MANAGER: Matthew T. Mundinger; ASSIS-

TANT STAGE MANAGER: Michael A. Clarke. **Cast**: LADISLAV SIPOS: Lee Wilkof (6) ✩; ARPAD LASZLO: Brad Kane (5) ✩, *Danny Cistone* (from 3/1/94); ILONA RITTER: Sally Mayes (3) ✩; STEVEN KODALY: Howard McGillin (8) ✩, *Dennis Parlato* (from 5/31/94); GEORG NOWACK: Boyd Gaines (1) ✩; MR. MARACZEK: Louis Zorich (7) ✩; 1ST CUSTOMER: Tina Johnson; 2ND CUSTOMER: Kristi Lynes; 3RD CUSTOMER: Trisha M. Gorman; 4TH CUSTOMER: Cynthia Sophiea; 5TH CUSTOMER: Laura Waterbury; AMALIA BALASH: Judy Kuhn (until 8/27/93), Diane Fratantoni (2) ✩ (from 9/28/93); KELLER: Nick Corley; HEAD WAITER: Jonathan Freeman (4) ✩; BUSBOY: Joey McKneely; TANGO COUPLE: Bill Badolato & Kristi Lynes; ENSEMBLE: Bill Badolato, Peter Boynton, Nick Corley, Trisha Gorman, Tina Johnson, Kristi Lynes, Joey McKneely, Cynthia Sophiea, Laura Waterbury. **Standbys**: Amalia: Teri Bibb; Georg: James Clow; Maraczek: Peter Johl. **Understudies**: Head Waiter: Bill Badolato & Nick Corley; Kodaly/Georg: Peter Boynton; Sipos: Nick Corley; Amalia: Mary Illes; Ilona: Kristi Lynes; Arpad: Joey McKneely. **Swings**: Mary Illes & Mason Roberts. **Orchestra**: PERCUSSION: Bruce Doctor; TRUMPET: Phil Granger; WOODWINDS: Rick Prior & Frank Basille; VIOLIN: Elliot Rosoff; BASS: Bob Renino; SYNTHESIZERS: David Loud & Todd Ellison; CELLO: Diane Barere.

This production was the first musical presented by the Roundabout after it had taken a 20-year lease on the fairly new 499-seat Criterion Center Stage Right. It ran 61 performances, then moved to the larger Brooks Atkinson. There was a second set of previews from 9/28/93, and then it ran an additional 294 performances. Reviews were very good. Boyd Gaines won a Tony, and the show was also nominated for revival of a musical, direction of a musical, choreography, sets, costumes, and for Jonathan Freeman, Sally Mayes, and Judy Kuhn.

After Broadway. RONACHER THEATER, Vienna, 9/19/96. This was the first German-language version. Jerry Bock & Sheldon Harnick were there. Scott Ellis (listed as director) supervised the previews but before the premiere had to go back to the USA because his mother was ill. **Cast**: Rene Rumpold, Christine Rothacker.

FREUD PLAYHOUSE, UCLA, Los Angeles, 3/18/03–3/30/03. Part of the *Reprise!* series. DIRECTOR: Gordon Hunt; CHOREOGRAPHER: Dan Mojica; MUSICAL DIRECTOR: Gerald Sternbach. **Cast**: KODALY: Damon Kirsche (Patrick Cassidy had been scheduled); AMALIA: Rebecca Luker; ALSO WITH: Kaitlin Hughes, Scott Waara.

PAPER MILL PLAYHOUSE, New Jersey, 10/27/04–12/5/04. DIRECTOR: James Brennan; SETS: Michael Anania; COSTUMES: Gail Baldoni; LIGHTING: F. Mitchell Dana; SOUND: Robert Edwards & Randy Hansen; MUSICAL DIRECTOR: Tom Helm. **Cast**: GEORG: George Dvorsky; AMALIA: Michele Ragusa; ILONA: Nancy Anderson; KODALY: David Hess; MARACZEK: George S. Irving; HEAD WAITER: Paul Schoeffler (replaced Ed Dixon before opening); SIPOS: Bill Bateman; ARPAD: Bradford Anderson.

623. *Shelter*

The first Broadway musical to be written entirely by women. A musical fantasy, set at the present time, in a TV studio set. It concerns a writer of TV commercials, and the women in his life. He lives in a TV studio with a talking computer named Arthur.

Before Broadway. The world premiere was at the PLAYHOUSE IN THE PARK, Cincinnati, 6/1/72. 22 PERFORMANCES. DIRECTOR: Word Baker; SETS: Ed Wittstein; COSTUMES: Caley Summers; LIGHTING: David F. Segal; MUSICAL DIRECTORS: George Broderick & Worth Gardner. **Cast**: PENELOPE/MAUD: Marcia Rodd; MICHAEL: Keith Charles; WEDNESDAY NOVEMBER: Susan Browning; GLORIA: Anne Murray; TV CREW: Mark Brown, Maureen Flanigan, David Holbrook, Richard Jaffe, Richard Michaelson, Richard Loder, Linda Nolan, Charlotte Patton, Nancy Scanlon, Connie Shutt, Margo Bourgeois, Marja Scheeres; VOICE OF ARTHUR: Charles Collins; VOICE OF THE DIRECTOR: Philip Kraus.

The Broadway Run. JOHN GOLDEN THEATRE, 2/6/73–3/3/73. 16 previews from 1/22/73. 31 PERFORMANCES. PRESENTED BY Richard Fields & Peter Flood; MUSIC: Nancy Ford; LYRICS/BOOK: Gretchen Cryer; DIRECTOR: Austin Pendleton; CHOREOGRAPHER: Sammy Bayes; SETS/COSTUMES: Tony Walton; LIGHTING: Richard Pilbrow; MUSICAL DIREC-

TOR/VOCAL ARRANGEMENTS: Kirk Nurock; ORCHESTRATIONS/ELEC-TRONIC ARRANGEMENTS: Thomas Pierson; CAST RECORDING on Columbia (never released); PRESS: Solters/Sabinson/Roskin; GENERAL MANAGERS: NR Productions; STAGE MANAGER: John Andrews; ASSISTANT STAGE MANAGER: Charles Collins. *Cast:* MAUD: Marcia Rodd (1) ☆; MICHAEL: Terry Kiser (2) ☆; WEDNESDAY NOVEMBER: Susan Browning (3) ☆; GLORIA: Joanna Merlin (4) ☆; TELEVISION CREW: Charles Collins (7) & Britt Swanson (8); VOICE OF ARTHUR: Tony Wells (5); VOICE OF THE DIRECTOR: Philip Kraus (6). *Standbys:* Michael: David Snell; Maud/Gloria: Lucy Martin; Wednesday: Britt Swanson; Arthur: Charles Collins. *Shelter Orchestra:* Ben Aronov, John Beal, Sam Brown, Burt Collins, Harold Feldman, Hank Jaramillo, David Jolley, David Sella. *Act I:* Overture (Arthur), "Changing" (Maud & Arthur), "Welcome to a New World" (Michael & Arthur), "It's Hard to Care" (Michael, Arthur, Maud), "Woke up Today" (Maud & Arthur), "Mary Margaret's House in the Country" (Maud & Arthur), "Woman on the Run" (Arthur), "Don't Tell Me it's Forever" (Maud, Michael, Arthur). *Act II:* "Sunrise" (Arthur), "I Bring Him Seashells" (Wednesday), "She's My Girl" (Michael, Maud, Arthur), "Welcome to a New World" (reprise) (Maud, Michael, Arthur, Wednesday), "He's a Fool" (Wednesday & Maud), "Goin' Home with My Children" (Maud & Arthur), "Sleep, My Baby, Sleep" (Arthur).

The show got terrible Broadway reviews. Marcia Rodd was nominated for a Tony.

After Broadway. *The Last Sweet Days of Isaac.* The songwriters who wrote *Shelter* (Nancy Ford & Gretchen Cryer) also wrote a big hit Off Broadway rock musical called *The Last Sweet Days of Isaac,* which ran at the EASTSIDE PLAYHOUSE, 1/26/70–5/2/71. 485 PERFORMANCES. It comprised two one-act musicals: *The Elevator* and *I Want to Walk to San Francisco. The Elevator* had a boy and girl trapped in limbo on an elevator; *I Want to Walk to San Francisco* had them in jail as protestors. DIRECTOR: Word Baker; SETS: Ed Wittstein; MUSICAL DIRECTOR: Clay Fullum. *Cast:* Austin Pendleton, Fredricka Weber, *Alice Playten* (from 5/26/70). Musical numbers from *The Elevator:* "The Last Sweet Days of Isaac," "A Transparent Crystal Moment," "My Most Important Moments Go By," "Love, You Came to Me." Musical numbers from *I Want to Walk to San Francisco:* "I Want to Walk to San Francisco," "Touching Your Hand is Like Touching Your Mind," "Yes, I Know that I'm Alive."

The Last Sweet Days. These two musicals—*Shelter* and *The Last Sweet Days of Isaac*—were combined to form one new musical called *The Last Sweet Days,* which ran Off Broadway at ST. PETER'S CHURCH, 3/26/97–5/4/97. 12 previews. 29 PERFORMANCES. PRESENTED by the York Theatre Company; DIRECTOR: Worth Gardner; SETS: James Morgan; COSTUMES: Jonathan C. Bixby; NEW CAST RECORDING, called "Shelter," on Original Cast Records. *Cast:* ISAAC/MICHAEL: Willy Falk; INGRID: Ellen Foley; VOICE OF ARTHUR: Romain Fruge; WEDNESDAY: Ellen Sowney. "The Last Sweet Days of Isaac," "A Transparent Crystal Moment," "My Most Important Moments," "Liebestod," "Woman on the Run," "Changing," "It's Hard to Care," "Mary Margaret's House in the Country," "Sleep, My Baby, Sleep," "I Bring Him Sea Shells," "She's My Girl," "Like a River," "Goodbye Plastic Flowers," Finale.

624. *Shenandoah*

Set in the Shenandoah Valley, in Virginia, during the Civil War. Widowed prosperous farmer Charlie wants no part of the war. He is determined that the only way his six sons are going to fight is in defense of their land. But this attitude has to change. First, his youngest son is kidnapped by Union soldiers, and Charlie and several family members go off in search of him. While they are away, Charlie's eldest son, daughter-in-law and grandchild are killed.

Before Broadway. The first choice for Charlie was Robert Ryan, then Jack Palance. Finally John Cullum was acquired. Unable to obtain Broadway funding Philip Rose arranged a tryout at the Goodspeed Opera House, in Connecticut, as part of their 1974 summer season. This production got raves from Walter Kerr in the *New York Times* and Kevin Kelly in the *Boston Globe.* Boston tryouts had divided

reviews. The show was known during tryouts as *Shenandoah, the Only Home I Know.*

The Broadway Run. ALVIN THEATRE, 1/7/75–3/27/77; MARK HELLINGER THEATRE, 3/29/77–8/7/77. Total of 1,050 PERFORMANCES. PRESENTED BY Philip Rose, Gloria Sher, Louis K. Sher; MUSIC: Gary Geld; LYRICS: Peter Udell; BOOK: James Lee Barrett, with Peter Udell & Philip Rose; BASED ON the 1965 movie of the same title, written by James Lee Barrett, and starring James Stewart; DIRECTOR: Philip Rose; CHOREOGRAPHER: Robert Tucker; SETS: C. Murawski; COSTUMES: Pearl Somner & Winn Morton; LIGHTING: Thomas Skelton; SOUND: Grayson Wideman; MUSICAL DIRECTOR: Lynn Crigler, *Richard Parrinello* (by 75–76); ORCHESTRATIONS: Don Walker; DANCE MUSIC ARRANGEMENTS: Russell Warner; CAST RECORDING on RCA; PRESS: Merle Debuskey, Leo Stern, *William Schelble* (added by 76–77); CASTING: Lynda Watson; GENERAL MANAGER: Helen Richards; ASSISTANT GENERAL MANAGER: Steven Suskin (gone by 75–76); PRODUCTION STAGE MANAGER: Steve Zweigbaum; STAGE MANAGER: Arturo E. Porazzi; ASSISTANT STAGE MANAGER: Sherry Lambert. *Cast:* CHARLIE ANDERSON: John Cullum (1) ☆, *William Chapman* (during Mr. Cullum's vacation, 75–76; Mr. Cullum's last performance was on 11/1/76, then Mr. Chapman took over permanently from 11/2/76; he ran until 6/6/77), *John Cullum* (from 6/7/77); JACOB: Ted Agress (5), *Roger Berdahl* (from 7/29/76); JAMES: Joel Higgins (4), *Wayne Hudgins* (from 2/17/76), *Paul Myrvold* (from 2/4/77); NATHAN: Jordan Suffin (11), *Craig Lucas* (from 9/26/76), *Kevin Wilson* (from 5/31/77); JOHN: David Russell (10); JENNY: Penelope Milford (3), *Maureen Silliman* (from 9/8/75), *Emily Bindiger* (from 5/17/77); HENRY: Robert Rosen (9); ROBERT (THE BOY): Joseph Shapiro (8), *Mark Perman* (from 4/26/76), *Steve Grober* (from 8/16/76); ANNE: Donna Theodore (2), *Leslie Denniston* (from 10/12/76); GABRIEL: Chip Ford (7), *Brent Carter* (from 10/20/75), *David Vann* (from 3/29/76), *Donny Cooper* (from 6/9/76), *Tony Holmes* (from 10/5/76); REVEREND BYRD: Charles Welch (12), *P.L. Carling* (by 76–77); SAM: Gordon Halliday (6); SERGEANT JOHNSON: Edward Penn (13); LIEUTENANT: Marshall Thomas (19); TINKHAM: Charles Welch (12), *Richard Flanders* (by 76–77); CAROL: Casper Roos (18); CORPORAL: Gary Harger (15); MARAUDER: Gene Masoner (17), *Joe Howard* (by 76–77); ENGINEER: Ed Preble (14), *E. Allan Stevens* (by 75–76); CONFEDERATE SNIPER: Craig Lucas (16), *Dennis Cooley* (by 75–76), *Robert Johanson* (by 76–77); ENSEMBLE: Tedd Carrere, Stephen Dubov, Gary Harger, Brian James, Robert Johanson, Sherry Lambert, Craig Lucas, Gene Masoner, Paul Myrvold, Dan Ormond, Casper Roos, J. Kevin Scannnell, Jack Starkey (gone by 75–76), E. Allan Stevens, Marshall Thomas. 75–76 replacements: *Dennis Cooley, Richard Flanders, Kathleen Gordon, David Cale Johnson, Emily Bindiger.* 76–77 replacements: *James Ferrier, Joe Howard, Timothy Wallace, Martin Walsh, Kevin Wilson, Suzy Brabeau.* **Understudies:** Charlie: Edward Penn (75–76), *Casper Roos* (75–77); Jacob: Gene Masoner; James: Marshall Thomas (75), *Paul Myrvold* (75–76), *James Ferrier* (76–77); Nathan: Craig Lucas (75), *Matt Gavin* (75), *Paul Myrvold* (75–76), *Kevin Wilson* (76–77); John: Matt Gavin (75–77), *Robert Johanson* (75); Henry: Robert Johanson (75–77), *Craig Lucas* (75), *Dennis Cooley* (75–76); Robert: Jeffrey Rea (75), *Steve Grober* (75–76), *Gibby Gibson* (76–77); Gabriel: Brent Carter (75), *Donny Cooper* (75–76), *Christopher Blount* (76–77); Jenny: Betsy Beard (75), *Emily Bindiger* (75–76), *Suzy Brabeau* (76–77); Anne: Kay Coleman (75), *Kathleen Gordon* (75–76); Sam: Robert Rosen (75–76), *Richard Flanders* (75–77); Byrd: Ed Preble (75), *Casper Roos* (75–77); Johnson: Casper Roos, *Marshall Thomas* (75–76); Carol: J. Kevin Scannell (75–76); Tinkham: Ed Preble (75), *E. Allan Stevens* (75–77); Marauder: E. Allan Stevens (75–76), Robert Johanson (75), *Dan Ormond* (76–77); Engineer: E. Allan Stevens, *Dan Ormond* (75–77); Lieutenant: Ted Carrere (75–76). **Ensemble Swing:** Matt Gavin (75). **Orchestra:** CONCERT MEISTER: Herbert Sorkin; HARMONICAS: Richard Hayman; STRINGS: Herbert Sorkin, Diana Halprin, Paul Cianci, Richard Dickler, Carolyn Halik, Russ Savakus; FRENCH HORNS: Tony Miranda & Clarence Cooper; TRUMPETS: Joe Wilder & John Bova; TROMBONE: Sonny Russo; WOODWINDS: Jacqueline Giat, Albert Regni, Ronald Jannelli; PERCUSSION: Douglas Allen; FRETTED INSTRUMENTS: Scott Kuney; KEYBOARDS: Donald Pippin; HARP: Kathryn Easter. *Act I:* The spring: *Prologue:* Outside the Anderson house: "Raise the Flag (of Dixie)" (Confederate & Union Soldiers); *Scene 1* Inside the Anderson house; on Sunday morning: "I've Heard It All Before" (Charlie); *Scene 2* A country road; *Scene 3* Inside the church: "Pass the Cross to Me" (Congregation); *Scene 4* A country road; moments later: "Why Am I Me?" (Boy & Gabriel); *Scene 5* The Anderson farmyard: "Next to Lovin' (I Like Fightin')" (The Anderson Sons: Jacob, James, Nathan, John, Henry); *Scene 6* The Anderson porch: "Over the Hill" (Jenny), "The Pickers are Comin'" (Charlie), "Next to Lovin' (I Like Fightin')" (reprise) (The Anderson Sons & Jenny); *Scene 7* Martha's grave: "Meditation" (Charlie); *Scene 8* Inside the Anderson parlor; *Scene 9* Anne's bedroom; minutes before the wedding: "We Make a Beautiful Pair" (Anne & Jenny); *Scene 10* Sam and Jenny's wedding in the farmyard: "Violets and Silverbells" (Jenny, Sam, The Family); *Scene 11* Inside the Anderson parlor; moments later: "It's a Boy" (Charlie). *Act II*: The autumn: *Scene 1* The Anderson farmyard: "Freedom" (Anne & Gabriel), "Violets and Silverbells" (reprise) (James & Anne); *Scene 2* A wooded area near a railroad track; night: "Papa's Gonna Make It All Right" (Charlie); *Scene 3* A clearing in the woods; later that evening: "The Only Home I Know" (Corporal & Soldiers); *Scene 4* Anne's bedroom: "Papa's Gonna Make It All Right" (reprise) (Jenny); *Scene 5* Martha's grave: "Meditation" (reprise) (Charlie); *Scene 6* Inside the church: "Pass the Cross to Me" (reprise) (Congregation).

Broadway reviews were very divided. The run was helped by TV commercials. It won Tonys for book (at the ceremonies, the authors thanked Kevin Kelly and Walter Kerr) and for John Cullum. It was also nominated for musical, score, choreography, and for Donna Theodore.

After Broadway. WOLF TRAP FARM PARK, Vienna, Va., 6/14/76. Special 5-PERFORMANCE production. CHOREOGRAPHER: Ted Agress. The cast included several members of the Broadway company while the show was still running in New York: John Cullum, Leslie Denniston, Penelope Milford, Joel Higgins, Roger Berdahl, Richard Flanders, Tony Holmes, Paul Corey.

BUS-TRUCK TOUR. 10/1/76–3/20/77. *Cast*: John Raitt.

TOUR. Opened on 10/5/77, at the Ariel Crown Theatre, Chicago. MUSICAL DIRECTOR: Richard Laughlin. *Cast*: CHARLIE: John Cullum, *John Raitt* (from 10/25/77); JENNY: Suzy Brabeau; ANNE: Jana Schneider, *Lola-Belle Smith*; JAMES: Paul Myrvold; JACOB: Dean Russell; GABRIEL: Tony Holmes; ROBERT: Steve Grober; SAM: Gordon Halliday.

PAPER MILL PLAYHOUSE, New Jersey, 1977. DIRECTOR: Philip Rose. *Cast*: Ed Ames, Christine Ebersole, Deborah Combs.

PAPER MILL PLAYHOUSE, New Jersey, 1979. DIRECTOR/CHOREOGRAPHER: Robert Johanson. *Cast*: John Raitt.

PAPER MILL PLAYHOUSE, New Jersey, 1988. DIRECTOR: Robert Johanson; CHOREOGRAPHER: Susan Stroman; SETS: Michael Anania; MUSICAL DIRECTOR: Kay Cameron. *Cast*: CHARLIE: Timothy Nolen; SAM: Brent Barrett; JAMES: George Dvorsky; JENNY: Patricia Ben Peterson; NATHAN: Malcolm Gets; ANNE: Tricia Witham, *Jacquey Maltby*; JOHNSON: Kenneth Kantor; CORPORAL: Sean McDermott.

625. *Shenandoah (Broadway revival)*

Before Broadway. This production was previously presented in 1989 at the QUEEN ELIZABETH THEATRE, Toronto. *Cast*: Hal Linden.

The Broadway Run. VIRGINIA THEATRE, 8/8/89–9/2/89. 17 previews. Limited run of 31 PERFORMANCES. PRESENTED BY Howard Hurst, Sophie Hurst, Peter Ingster; MUSIC: Gary Geld; LYRICS: Peter Udell; BOOK: James Lee Barrett, with Peter Udell & Philip Rose; BASED ON the 1965 movie of the same name, written by James Lee Barrett; ADAPTED BY Reginald Brunskill; DIRECTOR: Philip Rose; CHOREOGRAPHER: Robert Tucker; SETS: Reginald Brunskill adapted Kert Lundell's original sets; COSTUMES: Guy Geoly; LIGHTING: Stephen Ross; MUSICAL DIRECTOR: David Warrack; PRESS: The Joshua Ellis Office; CASTING: Karen Hazzard; GENERAL MANAGER: Charlotte W. Wilcox; COMPANY MANAGER: Leo K. Cohen; PRODUCTION STAGE MANAGER: Mortimer Halpern; STAGE MANAGER: Jim Roe; ASSISTANT STAGE MANAGER: Amelia Linden. *Cast*: CHARLIE ANDERSON: John Cullum (1) ✫; JACOB: Burke Lawrence (6); JAMES: Christopher Martin (4); NATHAN: Nigel Hamer (1); JOHN: Stephen McIntyre (8); JENNY: Tracey Moore (2); HENRY: Robin Blake (7); ROBERT (THE BOY): Jason Zimbler (10); ANNE: Camilla Scott (3); GABRIEL: Roy McKay (11); REV. BYRD: Donald Saun-

ders (12); SAM: Thomas Cavanagh (9); SERGEANT JOHNSON: Jim Selman; LIEUTENANT: Casper Roos; TINKHAM: Richard Liss; CAROL: Jim Bearden; CORPORAL: Stephen Simms; MARAUDER: Sam Mancuso; ENGINEER: Donald Saunders; CONFEDERATE SNIPERS: David Connolly & Gerhard Kruschke; ENSEMBLE: Henry Alessan, Jim Bearden, Mark Bernkoff, David Connolly, Lesley Corne, Mark Ferguson, Brian Gow, Jennifer Griffin, Gerhard Kruschke, Richard Liss, Robert Longo, Sam Mancuso, Casper Roos, Fernando Santos, Jim Selman, Stephen Simms. **Understudies**: Charlie: Casper Roos; Anne: Lesley Corne; Jenny: Jennifer Griffin; Jacob/Nathan: Fernando Santos; John/Henry: Mark Bernkoff; James: Brian Gow; Robert: David Connolly, *Michael Maronna*; Corporal: David Connolly; Gabriel: Z Wright; Sam: Robert Longo; Byrd: Richard Liss. **Swing**: Paul Mulloy. **Orchestra**: Barbara Ackerman, Robert Bonfiglia, John Bova, Lester Cantor, Lynn Crigler, William Ellison, Phil Granger, Charles Homewood, Susan Jolles, Janet Lantz, Martin Morrell, Porter Poindexter, Robert Steen, Gregory Utzig, David Warrack, Roger Wendt.

Broadway reviews were awful.

After Broadway. GOODSPEED OPERA HOUSE, Conn., 1994. DIRECTOR/CHOREOGRAPHER: J. Randall Hugill; SETS: James Morgan; LIGHTING: Mary Jo Dondlinger; MUSICAL DIRECTOR: Michael O'Flaherty. *Cast*: CHARLIE: Walter Charles; JACOB: Marc Kudisch; JAMES: Michael Park; NATHAN: James Ludwig; JENNY: Stephanie Douglas; JOHNSON/ENGINEER: Jon Vandertholen; LIEUTENANT: Alex Sharp.

626. *Sherry!*

Set between Dec. 10 and Christmas Day, 1938, in Mesalia, Ohio. An "intoxicating musical" about Sheridan Whiteside, famous acerbic critic and literary figure, who is forced to billet with the Stanley family after he suffers an accident on their property during a publicity tour. He terrorizes the family. Seductive actress Lorraine (who enters after 45 minutes and belts out "Sherry!") wants to turn playwright Bert's play into a musical. Bert protests, saying, "But, it's a play," to which Lorraine answers "Of course. So was every musical—once." Bert says that his play is a tragedy, and Lorraine tells him that that's just what Broadway needs, "a really tragic musical comedy." Banjo was a Harpo Marx–type character. Maggie was Whiteside's secretary.

Before Broadway. This show was previously entitled *Dinner with Sherry*. George Sanders, not liked by the Boston critics, left the cast in Boston after his wife fell ill, to be replaced by Clive Revill. Morton Da Costa (director) and Ron Field (choreographer) were both replaced by Joe Layton.

The Broadway Run. ALVIN THEATRE, 3/28/67–5/27/67. 14 previews from 3/8/67. 72 PERFORMANCES. PRESENTED BY Lee Guber, Frank Ford, and Shelly Gross; MUSIC: Laurence Rosenthal; LYRICS/BOOK: James Lipton; BASED ON the Broadway play *The Man Who Came to Dinner*, by George S. Kaufman & Moss Hart, which starred Monty Woolley, and which opened on 10/16/39 and ran for 739 performances; DIRECTOR/CHOREOGRAPHER: Joe Layton; SETS/LIGHTING: Robert Randolph; COSTUMES: Robert Mackintosh; MUSICAL DIRECTOR/VOCAL ARRANGEMENTS: Jay Blackton; ORCHESTRATIONS: Philip J. Lang; DANCE MUSIC ARRANGEMENTS: John Morris; CAST RECORDING on RCA Victor; PRESS: Saul Richman & Eleanor McCann; GENERAL MANAGER: Philip Adler; PRODUCTION STAGE MANAGER: Michael Thoma; STAGE MANAGERS: John Actman, Lee Welling, Haydon Smith. *Cast*: DAISY STANLEY: Mary Loane (11); MISS PREEN: Janet Fox (6); JOHN: Merritt Smith; SARAH: Barbara Webb (7); MAGGIE CUTLER: Elizabeth Allen (3) ✫; ERNEST W. STANLEY: Donald Burr (10); DR. BRADLEY: Cliff Hall (8); SHERIDAN WHITESIDE: Clive Revill (1) ✫; HARRIET STANLEY: Paula Trueman (9); BERT JEFFERSON: Jon Cypher (4); LORRAINE SHELDON: Dolores Gray (2) ✫; COSETTE: June Lynn Compton; BEVERLY CARLTON: Byron Webster (5); WESTCOTT: Haydon Smith; BILLY: Del Hinkley; BANJO: Eddie Lawrence (7); GINGER: Leslie Franzos; ENSEMBLE: Diane Arnold, Lucille Blackton, June Lynn Compton, Edie Cowan, Peter de Nicola, Frank De Sal, Glenn Dufford, Carol Estey, Herb Fields, Robert Fitch, Leslie Franzos, Luigi

Gasparinetti, Altovise Gore, Carol Hanzel, Del Hinkley, Joe Kirkland, Rita Metzger, Duane Morris, Denise Nickerson, Carol Perea, Roger Allan Raby, Jeannette Seibert, Haydon Smith, Doug Spingler, Ted Sprague, Trudy Wallace, Clyde Williams. **Standbys:** Whiteside: Byron Webster; Lorraine/Maggie: Roberta MacDonald. **Understudies:** Bert: Del Hinkley; Beverly: Duane Morris; Bradley/Stanley: Joe Kirkland; Miss Preen: June Lynn Compton; Harriet: Jeannette Seibert; Daisy: Rita Metzger; Sarah: Altovise Gore; John: Clyde Williams; Banjo: Herb Fields. **Act I: Scene 1** The Stanley living room: "Turn on Your Radio" (Maggie, Daisy, John, Sarah, Ensemble) [during previews this number replaced "In the Very Next Moment" (same singers)], "Why Does the Whole Damn World Adore Me?" (Whiteside); **Scene 2** The township of Mesalia: "Meet Mesalia" (Maggie, Bert, Ensemble) [during previews this number replaced "Maggie's Date" (same singers)]; **Scene 3** Exterior of the Stanley residence: "Maybe it's Time for Me" (Maggie); **Scene 4** The Stanley residence [during previews this scene was The Stanley library]: "How Can You Kiss Those Good Times Goodbye?" (Whiteside & Maggie); **Scene 5** A jewelry shop: "With This Ring" (Maggie, Bert, Whiteside, Bradley); **Scene 6** The Stanley living room: "Sherry!" (Lorraine & Whiteside), "Alas, Lorraine" (Beverly) [this number was added during previews], "Au Revoir" (Beverly); **Scene 7** Mansion House Hotel in Mesalia: "Proposal Duet" (Lorraine & Beverly), "Listen Cosette" (Lorraine & Cosette); **Scene 8** The Stanley living room: "Christmas Eve Broadcast" (Whiteside, Lorraine, Ensemble). **Act II: Scene 1** Billy's tavern: "Putty in Your Hands" (Lorraine & Ensemble); **Scene 2** The Stanley solarium: "Harriet's Pavan" (Harriet) [this number was added during previews], "Imagine That" (Maggie & Whiteside); **Scene 3** The Stanley library: "Marry the Girl Myself" (Whiteside & Banjo) [during previews this number was performed by Whiteside, Maggie, Banjo, Ginger, Ensemble], "The Fred Astaire Affair" (Whiteside, Banjo, Ginger) [this number was added during previews], "How Can You Kiss Those Good Times Goodbye?" (reprise) (Maggie) [this reprise was added during previews]; **Scene 4** The Stanley living room: "Putty in Your Hands" (reprise) (Lorraine, Whiteside, Banjo), "Harriet Sedley" (Whiteside, Banjo, Mr. Stanley), "Sherry!" (reprise) (Company) [this reprise was cut during previews].

Broadway reviews were mostly good.

After Broadway. STUDIO RECORDING. Made in 2003 and released on Angel Records in 2/04. *Cast:* MAGGIE: Bernadette Peters; WHITESIDE: Nathan Lane; LORRAINE: Carol Burnett; BEVERLY: Tommy Tune; BANJO: Mike Myers; ALSO WITH: Lillias White, Phyllis Newman, Siobhan Fallon, Tom Wopat, Keith David, Marian Hampton, The Manhattan Rhythm Kings.

627. *Shinbone Alley*

archy is a thoughtful cockroach with a penchant for free verse, the reincarnation of a poet who writes on an old typewriter belonging to a newspaper columnist, but he can't manage to get to the key that provides the capital letters. He attempts to reform mehitabel, a cat with a penchant for free love who believes her soul once belonged to Cleopatra. The entire action takes place in Shinbone Alley and its environs. It was one of the first musicals to feature an entirely racially integrated cast.

Before Broadway. First it was an LP, *archy and mehitabel*, recorded in 1954, with Carol Channing, Eddie Bracken, and David Wayne. Later that year it was performed as a 45-minute concert piece at TOWN HALL, by the Little Orchestra Society. "archy and mehitabel," "Cheerio, My Deario," "Cheerio, My Deario" (reprise), "Dance of the Cockroach," "I Am Only a Poor Humble Cockroach," "Lightning Bug Song," "Look at the Pretty Kittens," "mehitabel, the Way She Used to Be," "mehitabel and bill Duet," "mehitabel's Return," "There's a Dance or Two in the Old Girls Yet," "archy and mehitabel — finale." This was expanded into the Broadway production. There were no out-of-town tryouts. Before Broadway Norman Lloyd was replaced as director by Sawyer Falk, but neither received billing (not as director, anyway; Mr. Falk was billed as "production supervisor").

The Broadway Run. BROADWAY THEATRE, 4/13/57–5/25/57. 49 PERFORMANCES. PRESENTED BY Peter Lawrence; MUSIC/ORCHESTRA-TIONS: George Kleinsinger; LYRICS: Joe Darion; BOOK: Joe Darion & Mel Brooks; BASED ON the 1954 back-alley opera *archy and mehitabel*, written by George Kleinsinger & Joe Darion, from the stories by Don Marquis (which he introduced in 1916); DIRECTOR: unbilled; CHOREOGRAPHER: Rod Alexander; ADDED CHOREOGRAPHY: Arthur Mitchell (for revisions during the run); SETS: Eldon Elder; COSTUMES: Motley; LIGHTING: Tharon Musser; MUSICAL & CHORAL DIRECTOR: Maurice Levine; ADDITIONAL ORCHESTRATIONS: Irwin Kostal; ADDITIONAL MUSICAL ROUTINES: John Morris; MUSICAL MATERIALS UNDER THE SUPERVISION OF: Arnold Arnstein; PRESS: George Ross & Madi Blitzstein; PRODUCTION SUPERVISOR: Sawyer Falk; GENERAL MANAGER: Elias Goldin; PRODUCTION STAGE MANAGER: Morty Halpern; STAGE MANAGERS: Julian Barry & Gil Cates. *Cast:* VOICE OF NEWSPAPERMAN: Julian Barry; ARCHY, THE COCKROACH: Eddie Bracken (2) ✩; MEHITABEL, THE CAT: Eartha Kitt (1) ✩; PHYLLIS: Reri Grist; MOTHER: Lillian Hayman; RICKY: Dorothy Aull; JAIL CRONIES: Buzz Halliday, Elmarie Wendel, Cathryn Damon, Elizabeth Taylor, Carmen Gutierrez, Nora Reho, Gwen Harmon; "COPPER:" James Marley; BUZZ: Howard Roberts; BUTCH: Moses LaMarr; RUSTY: Cathryn Damon; BIG BILL: George S. Irving (4); BROADWAY: Ross Martin; EDIE: Gwen Harmon (7); BLACKIE: Larry Montaigne; GLADYS: Carmen Gutierrez; FRANKIE: Jacques D'Amboise (5); FIGHTING DOGS: Don Farnworth, Gene Gavin, Harold E. Gordon, Claude Thompson; TYRONE T. TATTERSAL: Erik Rhodes (3); SHORTY: David Winters; HARRY: Jack Eddleman; LADY BUGS: Dorothy Aull, Gwen Harmon, Buzz Halliday; BARTENDER: Bruce MacKay; PENNY: Allegra Kent (6); TALL CATS: Albert Popwell & James Tarbutton; DANCERS: Jacques D'Amboise, Cathryn Damon, Don Farnworth, Gene Gavin, Carolyn George, Harold E. Gordon, Carmen Gutierrez, Allegra Kent, Albert Popwell, Nora Reho, Dorothy Scott, James Tarbutton, Elizabeth Taylor, Claude Thompson, Myrna White, David Winters; SINGERS: Dorothy Aull, Jack Eddleman, Reri Grist, Buzz Halliday, Gwen Harmon, Lillian Hayman, Moses LaMarr, James Marley, Bruce MacKay, Jack Rains, Howard Roberts, Elmarie Wendel. **Standbys**: mehitabel: Chita Rivera; archy: Tom Poston. **General Understudy**: Lawrence Montaigne. **Act I**: **Scene 1** A newspaper office; **Scene 2** Shinbone Alley: "What Do We Care?" (mehitabel, Singing & Dancing Ensemble), "Toujours Gai" (mehitabel); **Scene 3** The ASPCA lock-up: "Queer Little Insect" (mehitabel), "Queer Little Insect" (reprise) (archy); **Scene 4** Shinbone Alley: "big bill" (big bill & Ladies of the Dancing Ensemble), "True Romance" (sung by mehitabel & Big Bill; danced by mehitabel); **Scene 5** A street: "The Lightning Bug Song" (archy), "I Gotta Be" (Broadway & archy); **Scene 6** Shinbone Alley: "Dog and Cat Ballet" (danced by Frankie & Ensemble), "Flotsam and Jetsam" (archy & mehitabel), "Come to Mee-ow" (tyrone), "Suicide Song" (archy); **Scene 7** A street; **Scene 8** Tyrone's trunk apartment, in Greenwich Village; **Scene 9** Shinbone Alley: "Shinbone Alley" (big bill & Denizens of Shinbone Alley). **Act II**: **Scene 1** A street: "The Moth Song" (archy); **Scene 2** Shinbone Alley: "A Woman Wouldn't Be a Woman" (sung & danced by mehitabel & Ensemble); **Scene 3** A street corner; **Scene 4** Shinbone Alley: "The Lullaby" (mehitabel & Singing Girls); **Scene 5** Another street; **Scene 6** mehitabel's new home: "What the Hell" (mehitabel), "Pretty Kitty" (sung by Singing Girls; danced by mehitabel); **Scene 7** A bar beneath the street: "Way Down Blues" (mehitabel), "The Lady Bug Song" (sung by The Lady Bugs); **Scene 8** A vacant lot: "Vacant Lot Ballet" (danced by Frankie, Penny, Rusty, Shorty, The Dancing Ensemble); **Scene 9** mehitabel's new home: "Be a Pussycat" (sung by mehitabel); **Scene 10** A quiet street: "Quiet Street" (archy); **Scene 11** Shinbone Alley: Finale: "Toujours Gai" (reprise) (archy, mehitabel, Ensemble).

In late April 1957 Act I was shortened, and Act II was heavily revised. This was the new scene by scene breakdown: **Act I: Scene 1** A newspaper office; **Scene 2** Shinbone Alley: "What Do We Care?" (mehitabel, Singing & Dancing Ensembles); **Scene 3** The ASPCA lock-up: "Cheerio My Deerio" (mehitabel), "Queer Little Insect" (mehitabel), "Queer Little Insect" (reprise) (archy); **Scene 4** Shinbone Alley: "big bill" (big bill & Ladies of the Dancing Ensemble), "True Romance" (sung by mehitabel & big bill; danced by mehitabel); **Scene 5** A street: "The Lightning Bug Song" (archy), "I Gotta Be" (Broadway & archy); **Scene 6** Shinbone Alley: "Dog and Cat Ballet" (danced by Frankie & Ensemble), "Flotsam and Jetsam" (archy & mehitabel), "Come to Mee-ow" (tyrone), "Suicide Song" (archy), "Shinbone Alley" (big bill & Denizens of Shinbone Alley). **Act**

II: *Scene 1* A street: "The Moth Song" (archy); *Scene 2* A vacant lot: "Vacant Lot Ballet" (danced by Frankie, Penny, Rusty, Shorty, Dancing Ensemble); *Scene 3* Tyrone's trunk apartment in Greenwich Village; *Scene 4* Shinbone Alley: "A Woman Wouldn't Be a Woman" (mehitabel & Ensemble); *Scene 5* Another street; *Scene 6* Shinbone Alley: "The Lullaby" (mehitabel & Singing Girls); *Scene 7* Another street: *Scene 8* mehitabel's new home: "mehitabel's a House Cat" (archy, big bill, Ensemble) [dropped before the end of the run], "Pretty Kitty" (Singing Girls; danced by mehitabel), "Be a Pussycat" (mehitabel); *Scene 9* A bar beneath the street: "The Lady Bug Song" (sung by the Lady Bugs); *Scene 10* Shinbone Alley: "Flotsam and Jetsam" (reprise) (archy & mehitabel), Finale: "Shinbone Alley" (reprise) (archy, mehitabel, Ensemble).

Broadway reviews were generally kind but not all that good. Brooks Atkinson, in his review for the *New York Times*, made an eerily prophetic statement, "The world of cats is ideal for ballet." There was no original cast recording, but the show was taped through the theatre's sound system and then recorded.

After Broadway. There have been other, unrelated, productions of Don Marquis's famous characters (see appendix entries # 865 and # 866).

archy and mehitabel was televised on 5/16/60. **Cast**: Eddie Bracken, Tammy Grimes.

1971. Animated feature film, *Shinbone Alley*. WRITERS: Mel Brooks & Joe Darion. Eddie Bracken and Carol Channing provided the voices of the two main characters.

628. *Shogun*

Also known as *James Clavell's Shogun: The Musical* and also as *Shogun: The Musical*. Set between April and July, 1600, in feudal Japan. Blackthorne, a shipwrecked English sea captain, becomes involved in a Japanese political power struggle while having an affair with a Japanese noblewoman. The show began with the wreck of his ship, complete with green laser-beam lighting. There was also an earthquake, and a battle on horseback in the snow.

Before Broadway. James Clavell's book had already been a successful 12-hour TV mini-series, and in 1982 he decided to musicalize it. However, it took eight years to get it off the ground. The main problem was that the story was too complex to present as a 2½ hour musical. It had a cast of 38, and over 300 costumes; by the time it was presented it seemed to be a blatant attempt to be another *Les Miserables* or *Phantom of the Opera*. During tryouts in Washington, DC much of the music was cut (e.g. "Crucified" and "Torment"), and a lot of dialogue was added (up to that point, it had been almost entirely sung). Paul Chihara, the composer, objected to this, and was fired, as was leading man Peter Karrie (replaced by Philip Casnoff). On 11/13/90, while singing "Death Walk" during a press preview, Philip Casnoff was knocked unconscious by large screen that fell on him. He made it back for Broadway opening night.

The Broadway Run. MARQUIS THEATRE, 11/29/90–1/20/91. 19 previews from 11/1/90. 72 PERFORMANCES. PRESENTED BY James Clavell, Joseph Harris, Haruki Kadokawa; MUSIC: Paul Chihara; LYRICS/BOOK: John Driver; BASED ON the 1976 novel *Shogun*, by James Clavell; DIRECTOR: Michael Smuin; CHOREOGRAPHERS: Michael Smuin & Kirk Peterson; SETS: Loren Sherman; COSTUMES: Patricia Zipprodt; LIGHTING: Natasha Katz; SOUND: Tony Meola; MUSICAL DIRECTOR: Edward G. Robinson; ORCHESTRATIONS: David Cullen; ADDITIONAL ORCHESTRATIONS: Steven Margoshes; PRESS: Shirley Herz Associates; CASTING: Julie Hughes & Barry Moss; GENERAL MANAGER: Jeremiah Harris; COMPANY MANAGER: Robb Lady; PRODUCTION STAGE MANAGER: S. Randolph Post; STAGE MANAGERS: Deborah Clelland, Michael Pule, Donna A. Drake. **Cast:** JOHN BLACKTHORNE, ENGLISH SEA CAPTAIN OF THE *Erasmus*: Philip Casnoff; CREW OF THE *Erasmus*: ROPER: Ron NaVarre; PIETERZOON: Lee Lobenhofer; SONK: Terry Lehmkuhl; FATHER ALVITO, A PORTUGUESE PRIEST: John Herrera; LORD BUNTARO, DAIMYO OF ANJIRO PROVINCE, MARRIED TO LADY MARIKO: Joseph Foronda; OMI, A SAMURAI IN LOVE WITH KIKU: Eric Chan; A CAPTURED SAMURAI: Tito Abeleda; GYOKO, MADAM OF THE TEA HOUSE, OWNER OF KIKU'S CON-

TRACT: Freda Foh Shen; KIKU, COURTESAN OF THE FIRST CLASS: JoAnn M. Hunter; 1ST SAMURAI GUARD: Darren Lee; 2ND SAMURAI GUARD: Marc Oka; 3RD SAMURAI GUARD: Owen Johnston; LORD TORANAGA, OVERLORD OF CENTRAL PROVINCE, SECOND MOST POWERFUL DAIMYO IN JAPAN, MEMBER OF THE COUNCIL OF REGENTS: Francis Ruivivar; SAZUKO, TORANAGA'S YOUNGEST CONSORT: Jenny Woo; OSAGI, SON OF LORD TORANAGA: Jason Ma; LADY MARIKO, EDUCATED BY THE JESUITS, MARRIED TO LORD BUNTARO: June Angela; CAPT. GEN. FERRIERA, PORTUGUESE CAPTAIN OF THE BLACK SHIP: Lee Lobenhofer; THE COURTIER OF OSAKA: Darren Lee; CATHOLIC DAIMYOS: Cholsu Kim, Marc Oka, Kenji Nakao; LORD ISHIDO, THE MOST POWERFUL DAIMYO IN JAPAN: Alan Muraoka; A NINJA: Andrew Pacho; FUJIKO, WIDOW OF OSAGI, CONSORT TO BLACKTHORNE: Leslie Ishii; ISHIDO'S HEAD SAMURAI: Tito Abeleda; OSAKA GUARDS: Kenji Nakao & Andrew Pacho; ISHIDO'S GENERAL, CHALLENGER TO OMI AT THE RIVER CROSSING: Jason Ma; CHIMMOKO, MAID TO LADY MARIKO: Kiki Moritsugu; AN ACOLYTE: Jason Ma; SLATTERNS OF THE HOVEL: Tina Horii, Linda Igarashi, Chi-En Telemaque; THE RED GUARDS OF OSAKA CASTLE: Marc Oka & Alan Ariano; NINJA ATTACKERS: Ron NaVarre, Terry Lehmkuhl, Tito Abeleda, Andrew Pacho, Darren Lee, Owen Johnston, Jason Ma, Cholsu Kim, Cheri Nakamura; TAIKO DRUMMERS: Lee Lobenhofer, Marc Oka, Jason Ma, Leslie Ishii. **Swings & Other Dancers**: Ted Hewlett, Herman W. Sebek, Victoria Lee, Lyd-Lyd Gaston, Kathy Wilhelm, Betsy Chang, Deborah Geneviere. **Act I**: "Karma" (Orchestra) (DANCERS IN STORM SCENE: JoAnn M. Hunter, Kiki Moritsugu, Kathy Wilhelm, Darren Lee, Cholsu Kim, Andrew Pacho), "Night of Screams" (Sailors, Blackthorne, Ensemble), "This is Samurai" (Samurai), "How Nice to See You" (Toranaga, Buntaro, Alvito, Mariko) (DANCERS IN TORANAGA'S ENTRANCE: 1ST GUARD: Darren Lee; 2ND GUARD: Marc Oka; 3RD GUARD: Owen Johnston; ALSO WITH: Tito Abeleda, Cholsu Kim, Andrew Pacho), "Impossible Eyes" (Mariko & Blackthorne), "He Let Me Live" (Mariko), "Honto" (Blackthorne), "Assassination" (Alvito & Ferriera), "Shogun" (Hostages), "Royal Blood" (Ishido & Toranaga), "An Island" (Toranaga) (DANCER: THE KUROKO FALCON HANDLER: Lee Lobenhofer), "No Word for Love" (Mariko), "Mad Rum Below"/ "Escape" (Blackthorne & Ensemble), "Karma" (reprise) (Toranaga) (DANCERS: Tito Abeleda, Betsy Chang, Deborah Geneviere, Tina Horii, JoAnn M. Hunter, Linda Igarashi, Jason Ma, Kiki Moritsugu, Cheri Nakamura, Kenji Nakao, Chi-en Telemaque, Kathy Wilhelm, Jenny Woo), "Born to Be Together" (Mariko & Blackthorne). **Act II**: "Fireflies" (Ensemble, Mariko, Blackthorne) (DANCERS: JoAnn M. Hunter, Eric Chan, Betsy Chang, Deborah Geneviere, Linda Igarashi, Kiki Moritsugu, Kathy Wilhel, Jenny Woo, Tito Abeleda, Owen Johnston, Darren Lee, Jason Ma, Marc Oka, Cholsu Kim. KUROKO "FIREFLIES:" Alan Ariano, Tina Horii, Andrew Pacho, Cheri Nakamura, Kenji Nakao, Ron NaVarre), "Sail Home" (Blackthorne), "Mad Rum Below" (reprise) (Blackthorne, Toranaga, Ensemble) (DANCERS: Betsy Chang, Tina Horii, Linda Igarashi, Kiki Moritsugu, Kathy Wilhelm, Jenny Woo, Cholsu Kim, Owen Johnston, Darren Lee, Jason Ma, Marc Oka, Andrew Pacho), "Pillowing" (Gyoko, Kiku, Ladies), "Born to Be Together" (reprise) (Mariko & Blackthorne), "No Man" (Blackthorne), "Cha-No-Yu" (Mariko & Buntaro), "Absolution" (Alvito, Acolyte, Ensemble, Mariko), "Poetry Competition" (Ishido, Sazuko, Mariko), "Death Walk" (Ensemble & Blackthorne), "One Candle" (Mariko & Blackthorne) (DANCERS: JoAnn M. Hunter & Kiki Moritsugu), "Ninja Raid" (Orchestra), "One Candle" (reprise) (Mariko & Blackthorne), "Winter Battle" (Orchestra), "Resolutions" (Toranaga & Ensemble), "Trio" (Toranaga, Blackthorne, Mariko), Finale (Ensemble).

Reviews were terrible. The show relied to some extent on Japanese tourists, and when the Gulf War happened, and these tourists didn't come any more, the show closed. The production lost about $7 million, much of it James Clavell's. The show received Tony nominations for costumes, and for June Angela.

629. *Show Boat*

Also seen as *Showboat*. The story of *Show Boat* spans 40 years, from the mid–1880s to 1927 (when the musical first appeared on Broadway) and focuses on Magnolia, the daughter of Cap'n Andy and Parthy Ann (real name Parthenia), owners of the paddlewheel-driven riverboat *Cotton Blossom*, which is also a traveling music hall. Magnolia meets gambler Gaylord on the levee and they fall in love. They become actors on the show boat, then marry and move to Chicago, but the marriage is not happy, Gaylord loses his money, and they separate. Magnolia goes on to become a musical comedy star, as does her daughter Kim. Years later she and Gaylord are re-united on the *Cotton Blossom*. Subplots involve Julie, a half-caste singer, and her marriage to Steve, and her alcoholism. Joe gives voice to the anguish of black stevedores in "Ol' Man River." It dealt with adult themes, such as miscegenation and unhappy marriage, a first for stage musicals.

Before Broadway. THE ORIGINAL 1927 BROADWAY PRODUCTION OF *Show Boat*. It ran at the ZIEGFELD THEATRE, 12/27/27–5/4/29. 572 PERFORMANCES. PRESENTED BY Florenz Ziegfeld; DIRECTORS: Zeke Colvan & (uncredited) Oscar Hammerstein II; CHOREOGRAPHER: Sammy Lee; SETS: Joseph Urban; MUSICAL DIRECTOR: Victor Baravalle; ORCHESTRATIONS: Robert Russell Bennett. *Cast:* CAP'N ANDY: Charles Winninger; JOE: Jules Bledsoe [this role was written with Paul Robeson in mind]; QUEENIE: Aunt Jemima (i.e. Tess Gardella); FRANK: Sammy White; PARTHY ANN: Edna May Oliver; JULIE: Helen Morgan; GAYLORD RAVENAL: Howard Marsh; MAGNOLIA: Norma Terris.

LONDON PRODUCTION. THEATRE ROYAL, DRURY LANE. Opened on 5/3/28. 350 PERFORMANCES. *Cast:* Edith Day, Paul Robeson (he sang a new song — "I Still Suits Me").

THE ORIGINAL MOVIE. 1929. Originally a silent film, with the advent of sound it finally emerged as a part-talkie. DIRECTOR: Harry Pollard. *Cast:* CAP'N ANDY: Otis Harlan; JULIE: Alma Rubens; GAYLORD: Joseph Schildkraut; MAGNOLIA: Laura LaPlante [singing dubbed by Eva Olivetti].

1932 BROADWAY REVIVAL. It ran at the CASINO, 5/19/32–10/22/32. 180 PERFORMANCES. It had the same basic cast as the original Broadway production, except GAYLORD: Dennis King; MAGNOLIA: Irene Dunne; JOE: Paul Robeson.

THE 1936 MOVIE RE-MAKE. This was THE movie version. Added were three new Kern-Hammerstein songs: "I Have the Room Above Her" (Gaylord & Magnolia), "Ah Still Suits Me" (Joe & Queenie), "Gallivantin' Around" (Magnolia). "Why Do I Love You?" was almost totally cut out. DIRECTOR: James Whale. *Cast:* STEVE: Donald Cook; QUEENIE: Hattie McDaniel; CAP'N ANDY: Charles Winninger; JULIE: Helen Morgan; GAYLORD: Allan Jones; MAGNOLIA: Irene Dunne; JOE: Paul Robeson.

Even though Oscar Hammerstein wanted the 1946 production to be known as a new production, not as a revival (as it was somewhat altered and updated since 1927), one "front scene" and three minor songs from the 1927 production were dropped, a new number "Nobody Else but Me" was added, but aside from that it was pretty much the 1927 show re-presented. Jerry Kern had died on 11/11/45, before rehearsals began, so it wasn't really his production at all (despite the 1946 credits). Rodgers & Hammerstein persuaded Jan Clayton to leave their own hit *Carousel* to play Magnolia.

The Broadway Run. ZIEGFELD THEATRE, 1/5/46–1/4/47. 418 PERFORMANCES. PRESENTED BY (the late) Jerome Kern & Oscar Hammerstein II (for MGM); MUSIC: Jerome Kern; LYRICS/BOOK: Oscar Hammerstein II; BASED ON the novel of the same name, by Edna Ferber; DIRECTOR: Hassard Short; BOOK DIRECTOR: Oscar Hammerstein II; GENERAL STAGE DIRECTOR: Reginald Hammerstein; CHOREOGRAPHER: Helen Tamiris; ASSISTANT CHOREOGRAPHER: Daniel Nagrin; SETS: Howard Bay; COSTUMES: Lucinda Ballard; MUSICAL DIRECTOR: Edwin McArthur; ORCHESTRATIONS: Robert Russell Bennett; CHORAL DIRECTOR: Pembroke Davenport; CAST RECORDING on Columbia; PRESS: Michel Mok & Mary Ward; GENERAL MANAGER: Robert Milford; STAGE MANAGER: William Hammerstein; ASSISTANT STAGE MANAGERS: William Torpey & Paul Shiers. *Cast:* WINDY McLAIN: Scott Moore; STEVE BAKER: Robert Allen; PETE GAVIN: Seldon Bennett; QUEENIE: Helen Dowdy; PARTHY ANN HAWKS: Ethel Owen; CAP'N ANDY HAWKS: Ralph Dumke (2); ELLIE MAY CHIPLEY: Collette Lyons; FRANK SCHULTZ: Buddy Ebsen (6); RUBBERFACE: Francis X. Mahoney; JULIE LA VERNE:

Carol Bruce (3); GAYLORD RAVENAL: Charles Fredericks (4); SHERIFF IKE VALLON: Ralph Chambers; MAGNOLIA HAWKS: Jan Clayton (1), *Nancy Kenyon*; JOE: Kenneth Spencer (5); BACKWOODSMAN: Howard Frank; JEB: Duncan Scott; SAL: Pearl Primus; SAM: LaVerne French; BARKER: Hayes Gordon; LA BELLE FATIMA: Jean Reeves; OLD SPORT: Willie Torpey; STRONG WOMAN: Paula Kaye; CONGRESS OF BEAUTIES (EIGHT OF THEM): SPANISH: Andrea Downing; ITALIAN: Vivian Cherry; FRENCH: Janice Bodenhoff; SCOTCH: Elana Keller; GREEK: Audrey Keane; ENGLISH: Marta Becket; RUSSIAN: Olga Lunick; INDIAN: Eleanor Boleyn; DAHOMEY QUEEN: Pearl Primus; ATA: Alma Sutton; MALA: Claude Marchant; BORA: Talley Beatty; LANDLADY: Sara Floyd; ETHEL: Assotta Marshall; SISTER: Sheila Hogan; MOTHER SUPERIOR: Iris Manley; KIM (AS A CHILD): Alyce Mace; JAKE: Max Showalter; JIM: Jack Daley; MAN WITH GUITAR: Thomas Bowman; DOORMAN AT TROCADERO: William C. Smith; DRUNK: Paul Shiers; LOTTIE: Nancy Kenyon, *Evelyn Wick*; DOLLY: Lydia Fredericks; SALLY: Bettina Thayer; KIM IN HER 20S: Jan Clayton, *Nancy Kenyon*; OLD LADY ON THE LEVEE: Frederica Slemons; JIMMY CRAIG: Charles Tate; CHILDREN: Betty Barker, Billy De Forest, Dolores Gamble, Roland Gamble, Edward Hayes, Carol Lewis, Billy O'Connor, Miriam Quinn, Eugene Steiner, Sybil Stocking; SINGERS: Jerome Addison, Gilbert Adkins, Carmine Alexandria, William Bender, Thomas Bowman, Grace Brenton, Robert Bulger, Glenn Burris, Edward Chappel, William Cole, Clarisse Crawford, Erno Czako, Richard Di Silvera, Lydia Fredericks, Adah Friley, John Garth III, Hayes Gordon, Marion Hairston, George H. Hall, Katie Hall, Marion Holvas, Jean Jones, Thomas Jordan, Frances Joslyn, Charlotte Junius, Robert Kimberly, James Lapsley, Albert McCary, William McDaniel, Bowling H. Mansfield, Assotta Marshall, Linda Mason, Walter Mosby, Clarence Redd, Eulabel Riley, Paul Shiers, William C. Smith, William Sol, Agnes Sundgren, Bettina Thayer, Rodester Timmons, David Trimble, Fannie Turner, Ethel Brown White, Evelyn Wick, *Ivory Bass, Glenn Burris, Thomas Jordan*; DANCERS: Talley Beatty, Marta Becket, Elmira Jones Bey, Janice Bodenhoff, Eleanor Boleyn, Vivian Cherry, Terry Dawson, Andrea Downing, LaVerne French, Betty Jane Geiskopf, Carol Harriton, Vickie Henderson, Eddie Howland, Paula Kaye (dance captain), Audrey Keane, Elana Keller, Ora Leak, Gerard Leavitt, Olga Lunick, Claude Marchant, William Miller, Nick Nadeau, Joseph Nash, Jean Reeves, Stanley Simmons, Alma Sutton, Viola Taylor, Yvonne Tibor, William Weber, Henry Wessel, Francisco Xavier. *Act I: Scene 1* The levee at Natchez on the Mississippi; in the '80s: "Cotton Blossom" (Stevedores & Townspeople), Show Boat Parade and Ballyhoo (dance) (Cap'n Andy, Show Boat Troupe, Townspeople), "Where's the Mate for Me" (Gaylord) [in the original 1927 production, but dropped for this 1946 production], "(Only) Make Believe" (Gaylord & Magnolia), "Ol' Man River" (Joe & Stevedores); *Scene 2* Kitchen pantry of the *Cotton Blossom*; five minutes later: "Can't Help Lovin' Dat Man (o' Mine)" (Julie, Queenie, Magnolia, Joe, Ensemble); *Scene 3* Auditorium and stage of the *Cotton Blossom*; one hour later; *Scene 4* Box-office on foredeck; three weeks later: "Life Upon the Wicked Stage" (Ellie & Ensemble): "No Gems, No Roses, No Gentlemen" (dance) (Ellie & Stage Door Admirers) [end of "Life Upon the Wicked Stage" sequence], "Till Good Luck Comes My Way" (Gaylord & Men) [in the 1927 original, but dropped for this 1946 production]; *Scene 5* Auditorium and stage during the 3rd act of *The Parson's Bride*; that night: "I Might Fall Back on You" (Ellie, Frank, Girls) [in the 1927 original, but dropped for this 1946 production], Ballyhoo (Queenie & Ensemble): "No Shoes" (dance) [Sal & Sam (two late comers), Theatregoers] [end of Ballyhoo sequence]; *Scene 6* The top deck; later that night: "You are Love" (Magnolia & Gaylord); *Scene 7* The levee at Greenville; next morning: Finale (Entire Ensemble): "Levee Dance" (Claude Marchant, Talley Beatty, LaVerne French, Levee Dancers). *Act II: Scene 1* The Midway Plaisance — Chicago World's Fair; 1893: "At the Fair" (Sightseers, Barkers, Ushers): "Congress of Beauties" (dance) (Beauties & Ushers) [end of "At the Fair" sequence], "Why Do I Love You?" (Magnolia, Gaylord, Cap'n Andy, Parthy Ann, Ensemble): Waltz (Audrey Keane, Charles Tate, Couples) [end of "Why Do I Love You?" sequence], "In Dahomey" (Dahomey Village): "Dance of the Dahomeys" (Dahomey Queen, Villagers, The Bewitched — Ata, Mala, Bora), "Avenue A Release" (Dahomey Queen, Villagers, The Bewitched–Ata, Mala, Bora) [end of "In Dahomey" sequence]; *Scene 2* A room on Ontario Street; 1904; *Scene 3* Rehearsal room — Trocadero Music Hall; a few days later: "Bill" (m: Jerome Kern; l: P.G. Wodehouse & Oscar Hammerstein II) (Julie) [originally a number with music by Kern, and lyrics by Wodehouse, and featured in the 1918 production of *Oh Lady! Lady!* The lyrics were revised by Buddy De Sylva for the 1919 show *Zip, Goes a Million*, but it wasn't used. The music & lyrics were revised again, by Kern and Hammerstein, for the 1927 production of *Show Boat*], "Can't Help Lovin' Dat Man" (reprise) (Magnolia); *Scene 4* St. Agatha's Convent; about the same time: St. Agatha's Convent Service Music; *Scene 5* Trocadero Music Hall; just before midnight, New Year's Eve, 1905: "Only Make Believe" (reprise) (Ravenal), "Goodbye, My Lady Love" (Cake Walk) (Frank & Ellie), Magnolia's debut in Trocadero Music Hall: "After the Ball" (by Charles K. Harris) (Magnolia); *Scene 6* Stern of the Show Boat; 1927: "Ol' Man River" (reprise) (Joe), "You Are Love" (reprise) (Gaylord); *Scene 7* Top deck of the *Cotton Blossom*; that night; *Scene 8* Levee at Greenville; the next night: "Nobody Else but Me" (Kim) [an unpublished 1935 Jerome Kern instrumental called "Dream of a Ladies' Cloakroom Attendant," which had lyrics added to it by Hammerstein, and was re-titled. It took the place of what had been in this spot in the 1927 production of *Show Boat*—a series of imitations of 1920s stars by the original Magnolia, Norma Terris], "Dance 1927" (Kim, Jimmy, Flappers, Cake Eaters, Levee Dancers, Finale (Entire Company).

The show got almost unanimously great reviews. The rather contrary critic for the *Post*, Wilella Waldorf, not a Hammerstein fan, collapsed just after handing in her unfavorable review of *Show Boat*. She died on 3/12/46. The show, despite the reviews, still lost money, due to the great production expense.

After Broadway. TOUR. After the 1946 Broadway run the production went on tour, returning to New York, to CITY CENTER, 9/7/48–9/18/48. 15 PERFORMANCES. MUSICAL DIRECTOR: David Mordecai. *Cast:* WINDY: George Spellman; PETE/JEB: Gerald Prosk; STEVE: Fred Brookins; QUEENIE: Helen Dowdy; PARTHY ANN: Ruth Gates; CAP'N ANDY: Billy House; ELLIE: Claire Alden; FRANK: Sammy White; RUBBERFACE: Gordon Alexander; JULIE: Carol Bruce; GAYLORD: Norwood Smith; VALLON: Fred Ardath; MAGNOLIA: Pamela Caveness; JOE: William C. Smith; BACKWOODSMAN: Howard Frank; SAM/DAHOMEY KING: LaVerne French [the Dahomey King was a role new to this production]; BARKER/DRUNK: Walter Russell; FATIMA: Sylvia Myers; OLD SPORT: Robert Fleming; LANDLADY: Sara Floyd; ETHEL: Assotta Marshall; MOTHER SUPERIOR: Lorraine Waldman; KIM AS A CHILD: Danice Dodson; JAKE: King Brill; JIM: Seldon Bennett; MAN WITH GUITAR: Albert McCary; DOORMAN: Walter Mosby; LOTTIE: Sara Dillon; DOLLY: Elaine Hume; SALLY: Janet Van Derveer; OLD LADY ON LEVEE: Ann Lloyd. There were several changes for this City Center production: Act I Scene 4: "Life Upon the Wicked Stage" was replaced with "I Might Fall Back on You" (Frank & Ellie), and immediately after it came Olio Dance (Frank). "Congress of Beauties" was dropped from Act II, as were the "Why Do I Love You" waltz, the St. Agatha Convent Music, "Nobody Else but Me," and "Dance 1927."

THE 1951 MOVIE RE-MAKE. Judy Garland, who had been set to play Julie, quarreled with the studio and was replaced. Marge & Gower Champion danced "I Might Fall Back on You," "Life Upon the Wicked Stage" and "Buck and Wing Dance." *Cast:* CAP'N ANDY: Joe E. Brown; JULIE: Ava Gardner [singing dubbed by Eileen Wilson]; GAYLORD: Howard Keel; MAGNOLIA: Kathryn Grayson; JOE: William Warfield.

CITY CENTER, NYC, 4/8/54–5/2/54. 3 PERFORMANCES IN REPERTORY. Return engagement 5/5/54–5/16/54. 15 PERFORMANCES. This was the 1946 production, but Act I Scene 2 and Act I Scene 3 were combined; and Act II Scene 8 was re-set in the Auditorium and Stage of the *Cotton Blossom*. The first 3 performances (in repertory) were not reviewed by the *New York Times*, which did review the 5/5/54 re-opening night. PRESENTED BY the New York City Opera Company; DIRECTOR: William Hammerstein; SETS: Howard Bay; COSTUMES: John Boyt; LIGHTING: Jean Rosenthal; CONDUCTOR: Julius Rudel; PRESS: John L. Toohey; COMPANY MANAGER: Gilman Haskell; PRODUCTION STAGE MANAGER: Lucia Victor; STAGE MANAGERS: Hans Sondheimer & Lee Williams. *Cast:* WINDY/BACKWOODSMAN: Arthur Newman; STEVE: Robert Gallagher; PETE/JIM: Boris Aplon; QUEENIE: Helen Phillips; PARTHY ANN: Marjorie Gateson; CAP'N ANDY: Stanley Carlson, *Burl Ives* (from 5/5/54); ELLIE: Diana Drake; FRANK: Jack Albertson, *Donn Driver* (from 5/5/54); RUBBERFACE: Thomas R. Powell; JULIE: Helena Bliss; GAYLORD: Robert

Rounseville; VALLON/JEB: Lawrence Haynes; MAGNOLIA: Laurel Hurley; JOE: William C. Smith, *Lawrence Winters* (from 5/5/54); FATIMA: Ann Barry; BARKERS: Thomas R. Powell & Charles Kuestner; MAN WITH GUITAR/DRUNK: Charles Kuestner; SPORT: Roland Miles; STRONG WOMAN: Meri Miller; LANDLADY/OLD LADY: Sara Floyd; ETHEL: Gloria Wynder; JAKE: Milton Lyon; DOORMAN: Bill Smith; MOTHER SUPERIOR: Ellen Gleason; NUN: Barbara Ford; KIM AS A CHILD: Adele Newton; LOTTIE: Marilyn Bladd; DOLLY: Dorothy Mirr; SALLY: Gloria Sacks; KIM IN HER 20s: Greta Thormsen; CONGRESS OF BEAUTIES: Joanne Budill, DeAnn Mears, Peg Shirley, Barbara Sohmers; CHILDREN: Ginger Brooks, Georgianna Catal, Claudia Crawford, Dale Dennard, Leonard Grinnage, Joan Nickel, Bonnie Sawyer; SINGING ENSEMBLE: Benjamin Bajorek, Marilyn Bladd, Adelaide Boatner, Eugene S. Brice, Doryce Brown, Walter P. Brown, Joseph E. Crawford, Dawin Emanuel, Rina Falcone, John Fleming, Barbara Ford, Mareda Gaither, Ellen Gleason, Russell Goodwin, Louise Hawthorne, Ida Frances Johnson, Charles Kuestner, William McDaniel, Sheila Mathews, James Martindale, Roland Miles, Dorothy Mirr, John Neilsen, Benjamin Plotkin, Madeline Porter, William W. Reynolds, Gloria Sacks, Christine Spencer, William Starling, Joseph Tanner, Frederick L. Thomas, Greta Thormsen, DeLoyd Tibbs, Rodester Timmons, Clyde S. Turner, Rose Virga, Gloria Wynder. *Understudies:* Julie: Rina Falcone; Fatima/Ellie: Meri Miller; Windy/Vallon: Russell Goodwin; Pete/Barker/Jim: Roland Miles; Rubberface/Backwoodsman/Jeb: Benjamin Plotkin; Magnolia: Sheila Mathews; Ethel: Louise Hawthorne; Man with Guitar/Drunk: Ben Bajorek.

CITY CENTER, NYC. 10/28/54–10/31/54. 2 PERFORMANCES. This was the 1954 City Center production returned to City Center again. It had the same crew. It was reviewed again by the *New York Times*. *Cast:* WINDY/BACKWOODSMAN: Arthur Newman; STEVE: Robert Gallagher; PETE/JIM: Michael Pollock; QUEENIE: Betty Allen; PARTHY ANN: Jean Handzlik; CAP'N ANDY: Richard Wentworth; ELLIE: Marian Niles (Ellie) [Marian Niles was Mary Ann Niles, Bob Fosse's wife]; FRANK: Jack Blair; JULIE: Helena Bliss; GAYLORD: Robert Rounseville; VALLON/BACKWOODSMAN: Roy Urhausen; MAGNOLIA: Laurel Hurley; JOE: Lawrence Winters; MAN WITH GUITAR: Charles Kuestner; PIANO PLAYER: Milton Lyon; LANDLADY/OLD LADY: Sara Floyd; ETHEL: Gloria Wynder; DOORMAN: Walter Brown; KIM AS A CHILD: Adele Newton.

WEST COAST REVIVAL. Opened on 8/15/60, at the Philharmonic Auditorium, Los Angeles, and closed on 11/5/60, at the Curran Theatre, San Francisco. PRESENTED BY Edwin Lester & the Los Angeles Civic Light Opera Association; DIRECTOR: Edward Greenberg; CHOREOGRAPHER: Ernest Flatt; SETS/LIGHTING: Howard Bay; MUSICAL DIRECTOR: Louis Adrian. *Cast:* QUEENIE: Virginia Capers; CAP'N ANDY: Joe E. Brown, *Andy Devine*; PARTHY ANN: Helen Raymond; FRANK: Eddie Foy Jr.; JULIE: Julie Wilson; STEVE: Thomas Gleason; GAYLORD: Richard Banke; MAGNOLIA: Jacquelyn McKeever; JOE: Lawrence Winters; DANCING CHORUS INCLUDED: Thelma Oliver, Carlton Johnson.

CITY CENTER, NYC, 4/12/61–4/23/61. 13 PERFORMANCES. For this production Act II Scene 8 was re-set on the Levee at Natchez. PRESENTED BY the New York City Center Light Opera Company; DIRECTOR: Dania Krupska; CHOREOGRAPHER: Arthur Partington; SETS/LIGHTING: Howard Bay; COSTUMES: Stanley Simmons; MUSICAL DIRECTOR: Julius Rudel. *Cast:* PETE/JAKE: Bill Coppola; WINDY: Scott Moore; QUEENIE: Carol Brice; CAP'N ANDY: Joe E. Brown; PARTHY ANN: Isabella Hoopes; ELLIE: Jane Kean; FRANK: Richard France; JULIE: Anita Darian; STEVE: Herbert Fields; GAYLORD: Robert Rounseville; IKE VALLON: John Martin; MAGNOLIA/KIM IN HER 20s: Jo Sullivan; JOE: Andrew Frierson; RUBBERFACE/MAN WITH GUITAR: J. Patrick Carter; BACKWOODSMAN: Norman A. Grogan; JEB/HEADWAITER: Feodore Tedick; MISS PARKINGTON: Carmen Lindsay; BARKER/JIM: Henry Lawrence; OLD SPORT: Jack Rains; ETHEL: Alyce Elizabeth Webb; LANDLADY: Claire Waring; AL: John J. Smith; MAZIE: Sherry McCutcheon; PIANIST: John Cooke; CHARLEY: Ned Wright; MOTHER SUPERIOR: Miriam Lawrence; KIM AS A CHILD: Bridget Knapp; DOTTIE: Helen Guile; DOLLY: Mara Wirt; OLD LADY ON LEVEE: Sara Floyd; DANCERS INCLUDED: Eric Kristen, Ellen Halpin, Barbara Monte, Garold Gardner, Leu Comacho, Julius Fields, Lavinia Hamilton, Nat Horne, Glory Van Scott.

NEW YORK STATE THEATRE, 7/19/66–9/10/66. 5 previews. 64 PERFORMANCES. This production came closer to the original than any other previous revival. It had a few minor changes, such as the reversing of positions of the Act I numbers "Queenie's Ballyhoo" and "Life Upon the Wicked Stage," and the Act II reprises of "You Are Love" and "Ol' Man River." Another change: "I Might Fall Back on You" was cut during rehearsals (but added for the subsequent tour). "Can't Help Lovin' Dat Man" and "Ol' Man River" were re-written to be politically correct. There were now 8 scenes in Act I, the new Scene 6 being The stage door. Scenes 7 & 8 were the old Scenes 6 & 7. Act II now had only 6 scenes: the old Scenes 6 & 7 were cut, and the last scene was now Scene 6 (on the levee at Greenville). PRESENTED BY Music Theatre of Lincoln Center; DIRECTOR: Lawrence Kasha; CHOREOGRAPHER: Ron Field; SETS: Oliver Smith; COSTUMES: Stanley Simmons; LIGHTING: Jean Rosenthal; MUSICAL DIRECTOR: Franz Allers; ASSOCIATE CONDUCTOR: Bill Brohn; NEW ORCHESTRATIONS: Robert Russell Bennett. *Cast:* RUBBERFACE: Bob La Crosse; CAP'N ANDY: David Wayne; WINDY: David Thomas; JOE: William Warfield; QUEENIE: Rosetta Le Noire; ELLIE: Allyn Ann McLerie; FRANK: Eddie Phillips; PARTHY ANN: Margaret Hamilton; PETE: Bob Monroe; JULIE: Constance Towers; STEVE: William Traylor; GAYLORD: Stephen Douglass; VALLON: Barton Stone; MAGNOLIA: Barbara Cook; BACKWOODSMAN: Neil McNelis; JEB: Jess Green; 1ST BARKER: George McWhorter; 2ND BARKER: Garrett Morris; 3RD BARKER: Neil McNelis; FATIMA: Sally Neal; LANDLADY/OLD LADY: Helen Noyes; MOTHER SUPERIOR: Mary Manchester; KIM: Maureen McNab; MAN WITH GUITAR: Paul Adams; SINGERS INCLUDED: Phyllis Bash, Frances Buffalino, Ernestine Jackson, Estella Munson; DANCERS INCLUDED: Rita O'Connor. The show got mostly rave reviews, especially for Constance Towers. The show then went on a tour that opened on 9/12/66, at the Fisher Theatre, Detroit, and closed on 11/19/66, at the Shubert Theatre, Philadelphia. The only cast changes were: FRANK: Lou Wills; JOE: Irving Barnes.

ADELPHI THEATRE, London, 1971. 909 PERFORMANCES. This was a major revival, the longest run ever of *Show Boat*. It had new orchestrations, and added was the number "How d'ya Like to Spoon with Me?." DIRECTOR: Wendy Toye. *Cast:* JOE: Thomas Carey; FRANK: Kenneth Nelson; JULIE: Cleo Laine; GAYLORD: Andre Jobin; MAGNOLIA: Lorna Dallas.

JONES BEACH THEATRE, New York, 7/1/76–9/5/76. 67 PERFORMANCES. PRESENTED BY Guy Lombardo; DIRECTOR: John Fearnley; CHOREOGRAPHER: Robert Pagent; SETS: John W. Keck; COSTUMES: Winn Morton; MUSICAL DIRECTOR: Jay Blackton. *Cast:* CAP'N ANDY: Max Showalter; WINDY: Robert Pagent; JOE: Edward Pierson; QUEENIE: Alyce Elizabeth Webb; ELLIE: Connie Day; FRANK: Lee Roy Reams; PARTHY ANN: Lizabeth Pritchett; PETE: Ralph Vucci; JULIE: Beth Fowler; GAYLORD: Robert Peterson; VALLON: John Dorrin; MAGNOLIA: Barbara Meister; BACKWOODSMAN/JIM: Lee Cass; JEB: Dale Muchmore; CHORUS INCLUDED: Doris Galiber, Mickey Gunnersen, Sherry Lambert, Janette Moody.

630. *Show Boat (1983 Broadway revival)*

Before Broadway. After playing at the Kennedy Center, in Washington, DC, 1/6/83–2/20/83, the production moved to Broadway. Lonette McKee was the first black actress ever to play Julie.

The Broadway Run. URIS THEATRE, 4/24/83–6/26/83. 5 previews. 73 PERFORMANCES. The Houston Grand Opera production, PRESENTED BY James M. Nederlander, the John F. Kennedy Center, and the Denver Center; MUSIC: Jerome Kern; LYRICS/BOOK: Oscar Hammerstein II; BASED ON the novel of the same name, by Edna Ferber; DIRECTOR: Michael Kahn; CHOREOGRAPHER: Dorothy Danner; SETS: Hebert Senn & Helen Pond; COSTUMES: Molly Maginnis; LIGHTING: Thomas Skelton; SOUND: Richard Fitzgerald; MUSICAL DIRECTOR: John De Main; PRESS: Marilynn LeVine Public Relations; CASTING: Hughes/Moss; GENERAL MANAGERS: Robert A. Buckley & Douglas Urbanski; COMPANY MANAGER: Martin Cohen; PRODUCTION STAGE MANAGER: Warren Crane; STAGE MANAGER: Amy Pell; ASSISTANT STAGE MANAGER: Fred Tyson. *Cast:* WINDY McLAIN: Richard Dix; STEVE: Wayne Turnage; PETE: Glenn Martin; QUEENIE: Karla Burns; PARTHY ANN HAWKS: Avril Gentles; CAP'N ANDY HAWKS: Donald O'Connor (1) ☆; ELLIE: Paige

O'Hara; FRANK: Paul Keith; MAHONEY: Randy Hansen; JULIE LA VERNE: Lonette McKee (2) ☆; GAYLORD RAVENAL: Ron Raines (3) ☆; VALLON: Jacob Mark Hopkin; MAGNOLIA HAWKS: Sheryl Woods (4) ☆; JOE: Bruce Hubbard; BACKWOODSMAN: Lewis White; JEB: James Gedge; BARKERS: Lewis White, Randy Hansen, James Gedge; LA BELLE FATIMA: Lynda Karen; OLD SPORT: Larry Hansen; LANDLADY: Mary Rocco; JIM: Jacob Mark Hopkin; JAKE: Randy Hansen; YOUNG MAN WITH GUITAR: Larry Hansen; CHARLIE: P.L. Brown; MOTHER SUPERIOR: Linda Milani; YOUNG KIM: Tracy Paul; LOTTIE: Gloria Parker; DOLLY: Dale Kristien; OLD LADY ON LEVEE: Mary Rocco; OLDER KIM: Karen Culliver; RADIO ANNOUNCER'S VOICE: Hal Douglas; FEMALE CHORUS: Vanessa Ayers, Joanna Beck, Karen Culliver, Olivia Detante, Kim Fairchild, Cheryl Freeman, Lynda Karen, Dale Kristien, Linda Milani, Gloria Parker, Veronica Rhodes, Mary Rocco, Molly Wassermann, Carrie Wilder; MALE CHORUS: P.L. Brown, Michael-Pierre Dean, Merwin Foard, Joe Garcia, James Gedge, Michael Gray, Larry Hansen, Randy Hansen, Jacob Mark Hopkin, Glenn Martin, Randy Morgan, Dennis Perren, Leonard Piggee, Alton Spencer, Robert Vincent, Lewis White, Wardell Woodard. *Standby:* Parthy Ann: Lizabeth Pritchett. *Understudies:* Cap'n Andy: Richard Dix; Julie: Gloria Parker; Gaylord: Wayne Turnage; Magnolia: Dale Kristien; Queenie: Vanessa Ayers; Frank/Mahoney: Larry Hansen; Ellie: Carrie Wilder; Joe: P.L. Brown; Vallon/Windy/Jim: Lewis White; Steve/Pete: Robert Vincent; Backwoodsman/Jake: James Gedge; Landlady/Old Lady: Linda Milani; Charlie: Dennis Perren; Mother Superior: Kim Fairchild; Jeb/Barkers/Guitarist/Old Sport: Tom Garrett; Lottie/Older Kim: Suzanne Ishee; Dolly: Joanna Beck; Fatima: Jeane July; Young Kim: Karen Culliver. *Swings:* Jeane July, Suzanne Ishee, Tom Garrett, Ed Battle. Overture (Orchestra). **Act I: Scene 1** The levee at Natchez on the Mississippi; in the 1880s: "Cotton Blossom" (Stevedores & Townspeople), "Show Boat Parade and Ballyhoo" (Cap'n Andy, Show Boat Troupe, Townspeople), "Only Make Believe" (Gaylord & Magnolia), "Ol' Man River" (Joe & Stevedores); **Scene 2** Kitchen pantry of the *Cotton Blossom*; five minutes later: "Can't Help Lovin' Dat Man" (Julie, Queenie, Magnolia, Joe, Ensemble); **Scene 3** Outside a riverfront gambling saloon; simultaneously; **Scene 4** Auditorium and stage of the *Cotton Blossom*; one hour later: "Life Upon the Wicked Stage" (Ellie & Ensemble), "I Might Fall Back on You" (Frank & Ellie); **Scene 5** Box-office, on foredeck; three weeks later: "Queenie's Ballyhoo" (Queenie, Cap'n Andy, Ensemble); **Scene 6** Auditorium and stage during the 3rd act of *The Parson's Bride* that night; **Scene 7** The top deck; later that night: "You Are Love" (Magnolia & Gaylord); **Scene 8** The levee at Greenville; next morning: Finale (Entire Ensemble). **Act II: Scene 1** The Midway Plaisance, Chicago World's Fair; 1893: "At the Fair" (Sightseers & Barkers); **Scene 2** A room on Ontario Street; 1904: "Why Do I Love You?" (Magnolia, Gaylord, Cap'n Andy, Parthy Ann, Ensemble); **Scene 3** Rehearsal room, Trocadero Music Hall; a few days later: "Bill" (Julie), "Can't Help Lovin' Dat Man" (reprise) (Magnolia); **Scene 4** St. Agatha's Convent; about the same time: Service & Scene Music, St. Agatha's Convent, "Only Make Believe" (reprise) (Gaylord); **Scene 5** Trocadero Music Hall; New Year's Eve, ringing in the year 1905: "Goodbye My Lady Love" (Cake Walk) (Frank & Ellie), Magnolia's debut at the Trocadero Music Hall: "After the Ball" (Magnolia & Ensemble); **Scene 6** Top deck of the *Cotton Blossom*; 1927: "Ol' Man River" (reprise) (Joe), "You Are Love" (reprise) (Gaylord), "Hey, Feller" (Queenie & Ensemble); **Scene 7** The levee at Greenville; the next night: Finale (Entire Ensemble).

The show received mostly raves from the Broadway critics, and it garnered Tony Nominations for direction of a musical, and for Lonette McKee and Karla Burns.

After Broadway. PAPER MILL PLAYHOUSE, New Jersey, 1984. DIRECTOR: Robert Johanson.

MUSICAL DIRECTOR: Jim Coleman. *Cast:* Leigh Beery, Eddie Bracken, Judith McCauley, Richard White.

PAPER MILL PLAYHOUSE, New Jersey, 1988. This production featured material cut from the original Broadway production. DIRECTOR: Robert Johanson; CHOREOGRAPHER: Sharon Halley; SETS: Michael Anania; LIGHTING: Ken Billington; MUSICAL DIRECTOR: Peter Howard; CAST RECORDING, made by John McGlinn, featured Teresa Stratas, Frederica Van Stade, and Jerry Hadley. *Cast:* CAP'N ANDY: Eddie Bracken; STEPHEN BAKER: Robert Jensen; PARTHY ANN: Marsha Bagwell; QUEENIE: Ellia English; FRANK SCHULTZ: Lee Roy Reams; ELLIE MAY: Lenora

Nemetz; JULIE: Shelly Burch; GAYLORD: Richard White; MAGNOLIA: Rebecca Baxter; JOE: P.L. Brown. This production was later broadcast on PBS.

U.K. NATIONAL TOUR AND LONDON RUNS. The West End runs were part of the tour that opened in 12/89. LONDON PALLADIUM, 8/1/90–9/22/90. Previews from 7/25/90. Return engagement, 3/13/91–5/18/91. DIRECTOR: Ian Judge; CHOREOGRAPHER: Lindsay Dolan; SETS: Russell Claig; COSTUMES: Alexander Reid; MUSICAL DIRECTOR: Wyn Davies. *Cast:* CAP'N ANDY: Geoffrey Hutchings; PARTHY ANN: Margaret Courtenay; QUEENIE: Karla Burns; JOE: Bruce Hubbard; ELLIE MAY: Janie Dee; JULIE: Sally Burgess; GAYLORD: Peter Savidge; MAGNOLIA: Janis Kelly.

631. *Show Boat* (1994 Broadway revival)

Before Broadway. This Hal Prince revival used material from the 1927 original, the 1928 London script, the 1946 Broadway revival, and the 1936 film. The Chicago World's Fair scene, which always opened Act II, was substituted with a series of cinematic montages which covers the period World War I and most of the 1920s. Hal Prince began work on the revival in 1992. Rather surprisingly, he kept in the word "nigger." It opened in the fall of 1993 at NORTH YORK PERFORMING ARTS CENTRE, near Toronto (Lonette McKee played Julie). Then it moved to Broadway, where it set the record for the largest Broadway box-office advance sale for a musical revival.

The Broadway Run. GERSHWIN THEATRE, 10/2/94–1/5/97. 12 previews from 9/22/94. 951 PERFORMANCES. PRESENTED BY Livent (U.S.); MUSIC: Jerome Kern; LYRICS/BOOK: Oscar Hammerstein II; BASED ON the novel of the same name, by Edna Ferber; DIRECTOR: Harold Prince; ASSISTANT DIRECTOR: Ruth Mitchell; CHOREOGRAPHER: Susan Stroman; SETS: Eugene Lee; COSTUMES: Florence Klotz; LIGHTING: Richard Pilbrow; SOUND: Martin Levan; MUSICAL SUPERVISOR: Jeffrey Huard; ORIGINAL ORCHESTRATIONS: Robert Russell Bennett; NEW ORCHESTRATIONS: William David Brohn; DANCE MUSIC ARRANGEMENTS: David Krane; CAST RECORDING on Capitol (although the original Toronto cast was recorded on Quality Music); PRESS: Mary Bryant; GENERAL MANAGER: Frank P. Scardino; COMPANY MANAGER: Jim Brandeberry; PRODUCTION STAGE MANAGER: Randall Buck; STAGE MANAGER: Betsy Nicholson, *Peter Wolf*; ASSISTANT STAGE MANAGERS: Andrew Fenton & Lisa Dawn Cave. *Cast:* STEVE: Doug LaBrecque (10), *Fred Love* (from 9/26/95); QUEENIE: Gretha Boston (9); PETE: David Bryant; PARTHY ANN HAWKS: Elaine Stritch (2) ☆, *Carole Shelley* (from 9/12/95); WINDY: Ralph Williams; CAP'N ANDY HAWKS: John McMartin (1) ☆, *John Cullum* (1/30/96–11/3/96), *John McMartin* (from 11/5/96); ELLIE: Dorothy Stanley (8), *Beth Leavel* (from 11/95), *Clare Leach*; FRANK: Joel Blum (7); JULIE LaVERNE: Lonette McKee (5) ☆, *Marilyn McCoo* (from 9/26/95), *Lonette McKee* (from 2/13/96); GAYLORD RAVENAL: Mark Jacoby (4) ☆, *Hugh Panaro* (from 11/95); VALLON: Jack Dabdoub; MAGNOLIA HAWKS: Rebecca Luker (3) ☆, *Sarah Pfisterer* (from 2/96); JOE: Michel Bell (6), *Andre Solomon-Glover* (from 2/13/96); DEALER: Bob Walton; BALCONY SOLOIST: Lorna Hampson [role specified only later in run]; JEB: David Earl Hart; BACKWOODSMAN: Mike O'Carroll; YOUNG KIM: Larissa Auble; ETHEL: Danielle Greaves; LANDLADY: Lorraine Foreman, *Panchali Null* (from early 2/96); MOTHER SUPERIOR: Sheila Smith; JIM: Mike O'Carroll; JAKE: Bob Walton; CHARLIE: Michael Scott; LOTTIE: Louise-Marie Mennier; DOTTIE: Karen Curlee; DRUNK: David Bryant; RADIO ANNOUNCER: Michael Scott; FAN (ON THE LEVEE): Kim Lindsay [role specified only later in run]; KIM: Tammy Anderson; OLD LADY (ON THE LEVEE): Sheila Smith; CHILDREN: Larissa Auble, Kimberly Jean Brown, Joran Corneal, Edwin Hodge, Imani Parks; ENSEMBLE: Van Abrahams, Timothy Albrecht, Derin Altay, Kevin Bagby, Hal Beasley, Timothy Robert Blevins, David Bryant, Joseph Cassidy, Roosevelt Andre Credit, Karen Curlee, Jack Dabdoub, Debbie de Coudreaux, Lorraine Foreman, Jose Garcia, Ron Gibbs, Steve Girardi, Danielle Greaves, Jeff Hairston, Lorna Hampson, Linda Hardwick, Pamela Harley, David Earl Hart, Richard L. Hobson, Michel La Fleche, Karen Lifshey, Kim Lindsay, Jesse Means II, Louise-Marie Mennier, Kiri-Lyn Muir, Panchali Null, Mike

O'Carroll, Amy Jo Phillips, Catherine Pollard, Jimmy Rivers, Michael Scott, Jill Slyter, Bob Walton, Laurie Walton, Cheryl Warfield, Jo Ann Hawkins White, Dathan B. Williams, Gay Willis, Lonel Woods, Darlene B. Young, *Renee Bergeron, Julia Gregory, Roberta Gumbel, Kimberley Michaels, Darcy Pulliam, Dominic Rambaran, Mark Santoro, Alonzo Saunders, Alex Sharp, Sheila Smith, Joseph Webster*; BAND ON THE *Cotton Blossom*: CYMBALS: Derin Altay, *Jeanette Palmer*; GLOCKENSPIEL: Bob Walton; CLARINET: Paul Gallo; TROMBONE: Dan Levine; BASS DRUM: Michael Scott; TUBA: Nathan Durham; FLUTE: Brian Miller. **Standbys**: Cap'n Andy: Ralph Williams; Parthy Ann: Sheila Smith; Joe: Andre-Solomon Glover. **Understudies**: Parthy Ann: Lorraine Foreman, *Darcy Pulliam*; Cap'n Andy: Mike O'Carroll; Mother Superior/Old Lady: Lorraine Foreman & Panchali Null, *Darcy Pulliam*; Magnolia: Kim Lindsay & Gay Willis, *Michelle Dawson*; Gaylord: Doug LaBrecque & Joseph Cassidy, *Fred Love*; Julie: Derin Altay & Debbie de Coudreaux, *Roberta Gumbel, Kimberley Michaels*; Queenie: Pamela Harley & Jo Ann Hawkins White, *Amy Jo Phillips*; Joe: Richard L. Hobson & Jose Garcia; Steve: Michael Scott & David Earl Hart; Vallon/Backwoodsman/Jim: Michael Scott & David Dannehl; Pete/Windy/Drunk: David Earl Hart & David Dannehl; Frank: Bob Walton, Steve Girardi, Ron Gibbs; Ellie: Karen Curlee & Tari Kelly; Kim: Kiri-Lyn Muir & Karen Lifshey, *Renee Bergeron*; Young Kim: Kimberly Jean Brown; Jake/Jeb/Dealer/Charlie: David Dannehl & Dennis Daniels; Ethel/Balcony Soloist: Kimberley Michaels & Louise St. Cyr; Landlady: Panchali Null, *Darcy Pulliam*; Lottie/Dottie: Laurie Walton & Tari Kelly; Fan on Levee: Conny Sasfai. **Swings**: Dennis Daniels, David Dannehl, Tari Kelly, Richie McCall, Kimberley Michaels, Louise St. Cyr, *Jeffrey Ferguson, Peggy Taphorn, Conny Sasfai*. **Orchestra:** CONCERTMASTER: Yuval Waldman; VIOLINS: Yuval Waldman, Joel Pitchon, Mara Milkis, Lesa Terry, Christopher Cardona, Nina Simon, Byung Kwak, Christine Sunnerstam; VIOLAS: Susan Follari, Katherine Sinsabaugh; CELLI: David Calhoun & Ellen Hassman; BASS: Jeffrey Levine; FLUTES: Brian Miller & Vincent Della Rocca; PICCOLO: Brian Miller; CLARINETS: Vincent Della Rocca, Paul Gallo, Dale Kleps; SOPRANO SAX: Vincent Della Rocca; BASS CLARINET/ALTO SAX: Dale Kleps; BASSOON/TENOR SAX: George Morera; OBOE/ENGLISH HORN: Marsha Heller; TRUMPETS: Robert Millikan & Richard Kelly; TENOR TROMBONE: Dan Levine; TUBA/BASS TROMBONE: Nathan Durham; FRENCH HORNS: Katie Dennis & Jeffrey Scott; DRUMS: Hank Jaramillo; PERCUSSION: Richard Fitz; HARP: Pattee Cohen; BANJO/GUITAR: Scott Kuney; PIANO: David Holcenberg. **Act I:** Overture (Orchestra). *Scene 1* The levee at Natchez, on the Mississippi River; 1887: "Cotton Blossom" (Stevedores, Gals, Townspeople), "Cap'n Andy's Ballyhoo" (Cap'n Andy, Parthy Ann, Showboat Troupe, Stevedores, Gals, Townspeople), "Where's the Mate for Me?" (Ravenal), "(Only) Make Believe" (Ravenal & Magnolia), "Ol' Man River" (Joe & Stevedores); *Scene 2* Kitchen pantry of the *Cotton Blossom*, five minutes later: "Can't Help Lovin' Dat Man" (Julie, Queenie, Joe, Magnolia, Ensemble); *Scene 3* Natchez. Outside a riverfront gambling saloon: "Till Good Luck Comes My Way" * (Ravenal, Pete, Frank, Townsmen); *Scene 4* Auditorium of the *Cotton Blossom*: "Mis'ry's Comin' Aroun'" * (Queenie, Stevedores, Gals); *Scene 5* The windows of Magnolia's cabin and Ravenal's room: "I Have the Room Above Her" * (Ravenal & Magnolia); *Scene 6* Fort Adams. Box office on the foredeck of the *Cotton Blossom*: "Life Upon the Wicked Stage" (Ellie & Townswomen), "Queenie's Ballyhoo" (Queenie, Stevedores, Gals); *Scene 7* Auditorium and stage of the *Cotton Blossom*: *Scene 8* Upper deck of the *Cotton Blossom*: "You Are Love" (Ravenal & Magnolia); *Scene 9* The levee in Natchez: Act I Finale: "The Wedding Celebration" * (Company). *Act II:* Entr'acte; *Scene 1* The levee in Natchez. Exterior of the *Cotton Blossom*; 1889; *Scene 2* Magnolia's room on the *Cotton Blossom*: "Why Do I Love You?" (Parthy Ann & Company); *Scene 3* Montage I: Chicago; 1889: "Dandies on Parade" * (City Folk); On the dock at Natchez; 1899; Outside the Palmer House Hotel, Chicago, 1899; *Scene 4* Chicago. A room in a boarding house; *Scene 5* Chicago. St. Agatha's Convent: "Alma Redemptoris Mater" (Choir), "Ol' Man River" (reprise) (Joe); *Scene 6* Chicago. Rehearsal at the Trocadero Nightclub: "Bill" (m: Jerome Kern; l: P.G. Wodehouse; lyr revised by Oscar Hammerstein II) (Julie), "Can't Help Lovin' Dat Man" (reprise) (Magnolia); *Scene 7* Entrance to the Palmer House Hotel; New Year's Eve, 1899; *Scene 8* Trocadero Nightclub: "Goodbye My Lady Love" (by Joseph E. Howard) (Frank & Ellie), "After the Ball" (by Charles K. Harris) (Magnolia & Ensemble); *Scene 9* Montage II (1900–1921): The levee at Natchez: "Ol' Man River" (reprise) (Joe); The streets of Chicago; The revolving door of the Palmer House Hotel; *Scene 10* The levee at Natchez; 1927: "Dance Away the Night" * (Magnolia); *Scene 11* Later on the levee: "Kim's Charleston" (Kim, Parthy Ann, Company), Act II Finale (Joe & Company).

Note: Those songs asterisked were cut from the 1927 original production, and restored for the first time in this 1994 revival.

Broadway reviews were great. Top ticket prices were $75 (a new Broadway record). The show won Tony Awards for revival of a musical, direction of a musical, choreography, costumes, and for Gretha Boston; and was nominated for John McMartin, Mark Jacoby, Michel Bell, Joel Blum, and Rebecca Luker. The show cost more than $600,000 a week to run, and paid back its entire initial investment by the fall of 1995. Garth Drabinsky announced as early as 6/96 that the production would be closing. This was the most successful version so far.

After Broadway. TOUR. The first tour of the Broadway production opened on 3/24/96, at the Auditorium, Chicago, and closed in early 1998. *Cast:* STEVE: Todd Noel; QUEENIE: Anita Berry, *Jo Ann Hawkins White*; PARTHY ANN: Dorothy Loudon, *Joyce Van Patten* (from 2/97), *Anita Gillette* (from 6/97), *Dorothy Loudon* (until 12/17/97); CAP'N ANDY: John McMartin, *Dick Van Patten* (from 12/96), *Pat Harrington* (from 5/12/97); ELLIE: Clare Leach, *Ann Van Cleave* (from 5/12/97); FRANK: Eddie Korbich; JULIE: Marilyn McCoo, *Terry Burrell* (from 2/97); GAYLORD: Mark Jacoby, *Kevin Gray* (from 9/96), *Doug LaBrecque* (from 2/97), *Keith Buterbaugh* (from 5/12/97); MAGNOLIA: Gay Willis; JOE: Michel Bell, *Kenneth Nichols* (from 2/97).

TOUR. The second tour opened on 11/17/96, at the Ahmanson Theatre, Los Angeles. Previews from 11/12/96. It ran there for 21 weeks, then began the proper tour in 4/97, finally closing in 1998. MUSICAL DIRECTOR: Derek Bate, *Roger Cantrell*. *Cast:* STEVE: Todd Noel, *Kip Wilborn* (from 3/29/97), *Ross Neil* (from 5/97); QUEENIE: Anita Berry, *Jo Ann Hawkins White*; PARTHY ANN: Cloris Leachman, *Karen Morrow* (from 2/97), *Cloris Leachman* (from 4/97); CAP'N ANDY: George Grizzard, *Ned Beatty* (from 1/22/97), *Len Cariou* (from 5/96), *Tom Bosley* (from 2/97), *Len Cariou* (from 4/97), *Dean Jones* (from 9/30/97); ELLIE: Jacquey Maltby, *Kerri Clarke* (by 11/97), *Tari Kelly*; FRANK: Keith Savage; JULIE: Valarie Pettiford, *Karen-Angela Bishop* (from 5/97); GAYLORD: J. Mark McVey, *Hugh Panaro* (from 4/97), *Stephen Bogardus* (from 6/22/97), *Keith Buterbaugh* (from 1/13/98), *Kevin Gray*; MAGNOLIA: Teri Hansen, *Gay Willis* (from 1/13/98); JOE: Dan Tullis Jr., *Michel Bell*. **Understudy:** Gaylord: Kip Wilborn. During the run Teri Hansen & Kip Wilborn were married.

POST-BROADWAY TOUR. Opened on 3/11/97, in Detroit, and closed on 12/6/98, as the production company Livent was imploding. *Cast:* STEVE: Greg Zerkle, *John Clonts, Craig Ashton* (from 3/6/98); QUEENIE: Gretha Boston, *Janelle Robinson* (from 2/23/98); PARTHY ANN: Carole Shelley, *Karen Morrow* (from 4/97); CAP'N ANDY: John McMartin, *Tom Bosley* (from 4/97); ELLIE: Beverly Ward; FRANK: Kirby Ward; JULIE: Debbie de Coudreaux; GAYLORD: John Ruess, *Alex Sharp*; VALLON/BACKWOODSMAN: David Earl Hart; MAGNOLIA: Sarah Pfisterer; JOE: Andre-Solomon Glover; LANDLADY/OLD LADY: Darcy Pulliam; JIM: Michael Scott; KIM: Elizabeth Mary O'Neil.

LYRIC THEATRE, Sydney. Opened on 4/7/98. Previews from 3/26/98. Budgeted at $A10 million, it pulled in $A8 million in advance sales alone. PRESENTED BY Livent & Marriner Theatres of Melbourne. *Cast:* PARTHY ANN: Nancye Hayes; CAP'N ANDY: Barry Otto; GAYLORD: Peter Cousens; MAGNOLIA: Marina Prior; JOE: Dan Tullis Jr. *It got great reviews.* Gough Whitlam and Paul Keating were there opening night; Garth Drabinsky was not—he had a back problem which made long-distance flying difficult.

PRINCE EDWARD THEATRE, London, 4/28/98–9/19/98. Previews from 4/20/98. Top price tickets were 35 pounds (a new West End record). It had the same basic crew as for the Broadway production. PRESENTED BY Livent. *Cast:* QUEENIE: Gretha Boston; PARTHY ANN: Carole Shelley; CAP'N ANDY: George Grizzard; ELLIE: Clare Leach; FRANK: Joel Blum; JULIE: Terry Burrell; GAYLORD: Hugh Panaro; MAGNOLIA: Teri Hansen; JOE: Michel Bell.

632. *Show Girl*

A small, intimate musical revue.

Before Broadway. Carol Channing was married to co-producer Charles Lowe. Before Broadway the number "Mr. Wally Griffin Spot" was cut, as was the sketch "Under the Influence."

The Broadway Run. EUGENE O'NEILL THEATRE, 1/12/61–4/8/61. 2 previews on 1/11/61. 100 PERFORMANCES. PRESENTED BY Oliver Smith, James A. Doolittle, and Charles Lowe; MUSIC/LYRICS/SKETCHES/SKETCH DIRECTOR: Charles Gaynor; ADDITIONAL SKETCHES: Ernest Chambers; CHOREOGRAPHER: Richard D'Arcy; SETS/PRODUCTION SUPERVISOR: Oliver Smith; COSTUMES: Miles White; CAROL CHANNING'S GOWNS: Orry-Kelly; LIGHTING: Peggy Clark; MUSICAL DIRECTOR/ORCHESTRATIONS: Robert Hunter; ADDITIONAL ORCHESTRATIONS: Clare Grundman; MUSIC CONSULTANT: Milton Rosenstock; PRESS: Richard Maney & Martin Shwartz; GENERAL MANAGER: Michael Goldreyer; COMPANY MANAGER: Paul Groll; PRODUCTION STAGE MANAGER: Frank Coletti; STAGE MANAGER: Ed Loessin. *Act I: Scene 1* Opening—"The Girl in the Show" [Carol Channing (1) *]; *Scene 2* Report from Las Vegas [Carol Channing (1) *]; *Scene 3* Theatre Piece: LYNN: Carol Channing (1) *; ALFRED: Jules Munshin (2); *Scene 4* "Calypso Pete" [Carol Channing (1) *]; *Scene 5* Report from Paris ["Mamba Java" (m/l: Noel Guyves)] [Les Quat' Jeudis (3)]; *Scene 6* Keeping up with the Noahs (by Ernest Chambers): NAOMI: Carol Channing (1) *; ELIJAH: Jules Munshin (2); *Scene 7* "The Girl Who Lived in Montparnasse" [Jules Munshin (2) & Les Quat' Jeudis (3)]; *Scene 8* Carol's Musical Theatre [Carol Channing (1) *]: The Opening Choruses: a/ "Join Us in a Little Cup of Tea, Boys" [originally in *Lend an Ear*]; b/ "This is a Darned Fine Funeral;" The Love Songs: a/ "In Our Teeny Little Weeny Nest for Two" [originally in *Lend an Ear*]; b/ "Love is a Sickness;" The Dance Numbers: a/ "The Old Yahoo Step" [originally in *Lend an Ear*]; b/ "Switchblade Bess." *Act II: Scene 1* "The Story of Marie" [Carol Channing (1) * & Les Quat' Jeudis (3)]; *Scene 2* S. Eureka Presents… (sk: Ernest Chambers; m: Charles Gaynor) [Jules Munshin (2)]; *Scene 3* "My Kind of Love" [Carol Channing (1) * & Jules Munshin (2)]; *Scene 4* The Inside Story (Cecilia Sisson sketch) [Carol Channing (1) *]; *Scene 5* The Foreign Star (Marlene Dietrich sketch) [Carol Channing (1) *]; *Scene 6* Les Quat' Jeudis (3); *Scene 7* The Palace Theatre [Carol Channing (1) *]: "You Haven't Lived Until You've Played the Palace"/"Somewhere There's a Little Bluebird;" *Scene 8* Finale [Carol Channing (1) * & Company].

The show opened on Broadway to terrific reviews, and Carol Channing got raves. She was nominated for a Tony.

633. *Shuffle Along*

Before Broadway. The original ran on Broadway at DALY'S 63RD STREET MUSIC HALL, 5/23/21–7/15/22. 484 PERFORMANCES. *Cast:* AT THE PIANO: Eubie Blake; TOM SHARPER, POLITICAL BOSS: Noble Sissle; ALSO WITH: Adelaide Hall. A sequel, *Shuffle Along of 1933*, ran at the MANSFIELD THEATRE, 12/26/32–1/7/33. 17 PERFORMANCES. The story concerned the financing of a molasses factory. It had the same creative crew. *Cast:* AT THE PIANO: Eubie Blake; TOM SHARP [sic]: Noble Sissle; CAESAR JONES: Mantan Moreland; SAM JENKINS: Flournoy Miller. "Labor Day Parade," "Sing and Dance Your Troubles Away," "Chickens Come Home to Roost," "Bandana Ways," "Breakin' 'em In," "In the Land of Sunny Sunflowers," "Sugar Babe," "Joshua Fit de Battle," "Sore Foot Blues," "Glory," "Saturday Afternoon," "Here 'tis," "Falling in Love," "Dusting Around," "If it's Any News to You," "Harlem Moon," "You Gotta Have Koo Wah."

The Broadway Run. BROADWAY THEATRE, 5/8/52–5/10/52. 4 PERFORMANCES. PRESENTED BY Irving Gaumont, in association with Grace Rosenfield; MUSIC: Eubie Blake; LYRICS: Noble Sissle; ADDITIONAL MUSIC & LYRICS: Joseph Meyer & Floyd Huddleston; BOOK: Flournoy Miller & Paul Gerard Smith; DEVISED BY: George Hale; DIRECTORS: George Hale & Paul Gerard Smith; CHOREOGRAPHER: Henry Le Tang; SETS: Albert Johnson; COSTUMES: Waldo Angelo; ORCHESTRATIONS: Charles L. Cooke; VOCAL ARRANGEMENTS: Claude Garreau; PRESS: Karl Bernstein, Harvey Sabinson, Merle Debuskey; GENERAL MANAGER: John

Yorke; STAGE MANAGERS: Lawrence Seymour, James E. Wall, Henry Pierre. *Cast:* BUGLER: William Dillard; MASTER SGT ROCKY MASON: James E. Wall; CPL. BETTY LEE: Thelma Carpenter; LT. JIM CROCKER: Avon Long; COL. ALEXANDER POPHAM: Earl Sydnor; MAJ. JOSEPH GANTT: William McDaniel; CAPT. FREDERICK GRAHAM: T.S. Krlgarin; SGT. LUCY DUKE: Delores Martin; CPL. LOUIE BAUCHE: Leslie Scott; CAPT. HARRY GAILLARD: Napoleon Reed; PVT. CYPHUS BROWN: Flournoy Miller; PVT. LONGITUDE LANE: Hamtree Harrington; CHAPLAIN: Laurence Watson; MABLE: Mable Lee; FIFETO: Henry Sherwood; ROSA PASINI: Louise Woods; SS TROOPER: Harro Meller; LAURA POPHAM: Urylee Leonardos; SGT. MABEL POWERS: Marie Young; MARGIE: Sara Lou Harris; NOBLE SISSLE: Himself; EUBIE BLAKE: Himself; PRINCIPAL DANCERS: Mable Lee & Arleigh Peterson; FEATURED DANCER: Eddie Rector; DANCING GROUP: Wini Benson, Sterling Bough, Smalls Boykins, Mildred Clemons, Katherine Davidson, Bill Del Campo, Tempy Fletcher, Harold Gordon, Dolores Harper, Erona Harris, Robert Harris, Marie Kenney, Celise King, James McMillan, Stefhan Maroud, Sophie Miller, Carson Moore, Ruth Mosley, Joel Noble, Leigh Parham, Jackie Petty, Estelle Price, Conrad Pringle, Lew Smith, James A. Smith; MODELS: Sara Lou Harris, Lois Kibler, Courteney Olden; SINGING GROUP: William Dillard, George Fisher, Barbara Jai, T.S. Krlgarin, William McDaniel, Fredye Marshall, Rosalie Maxwell, Henry Pierre, Leslie Scott, Rodester Timmons, Audrey Vanterpool, Louise Woods, Marie Young. *Act I*: Northern Italy; spring, 1945: *Scene 1* The Castle Del Vezzio; *Scene 2* An Alpine pass; *Scene 3* The Clutterhorn; *Scene 4* A street in Genoa; *Scene 5* The Cafe Fifeto. *Act II*: New York; the following spring: *Scene 1* Le Salon de Madame Lucy, New York City; the following spring: *Scene 2* A street in New York; *Scene 3* Popham's office; *Scene 4* Pier 17. *Act I*: "Jive Drill" (Bugler, Rocky, Ensemble), "Bitten by Love" (m: Joseph Meyer; l: Floyd Huddleston) (Betty, Jim, Ensemble), "Falling" (Lucy & Harry), "I'm Just Wild About Harry" (Lucy, Harry, Ensemble), "City Called Heaven–Juba-lee" (Chaplain & Ensemble), "Bongo-Boola" (Mable, Bugler, Drummer, Ensemble), "Swanee Moon" (Betty & Singers) (danced by Eddie Rector), "Love Will Find a Way" (Lucy, Jim, Louie, Rosa, Singers), "Rhythm of America" (Lucy & Entire Company). *Act II*: "It's the Gown that Makes the Gal that Makes the Guy" (l: Joan Javits) (Ensemble), "You Can't Overdo a Good Thing" (m: Joseph Meyer; l: Floyd Huddleston) (Lucy & Models), "My Day" (m: Joseph Meyer; l: Floyd Huddleston) (Jim & GIs), "Give it Love" (m: Joseph Meyer; l: Floyd Huddleston) (Betty & WACS), "Farewell with Love" (Lucy), "Here 'tis" (Mable), "Reminiscing" (Sissle & Blake), Finale (Entire Company).

634. *Side By Side By Sondheim*

A "musical entertainment." An anthology revue of 29 Sondheim songs and some medleys. It had a bare stage except for four stools for actors, and two pianos.

Before Broadway. In the beginning David Kernan, in London, decided to produce a Sunday concert of Sondheim songs. Ned Sherrin put the show together. Millicent Martin and Julia McKenzie also took part. This concert led to a 6,000-pound stage production, which opened at the MERMAID THEATRE, London, on 5/4/76, and became phenomenally successful. It moved to the WYNDHAMS THEATRE on 7/7/76, and again on 10/3/77 to the GARRICK THEATRE. PRESENTED BY H.M. Tennent & The InComes Company (Theatre) Ltd (Cameron Mackintosh); DIRECTOR: Ned Sherrin; CHOREOGRAPHER: Bob Howe; SETS: Peter Docherty; COSTUMES: Gina Fratini; LIGHTING: John Wood; MUSICAL SUPERVISOR: Ray Cook; CAST RECORDING on RCA. There were two casts. The first was: Millicent Martin, Julia McKenzie, David Kernan, and Ned Sherrin (narrator). The second was: Maggie Fitzgibbon, Gay Soper, David Firth, and Robin Ray.

Hal Prince brought it to Broadway, and capitalized it at $250,000. There was an Equity fuss over bringing in the four British actors, but Mr. Prince did a deal with the union.

The Broadway Run. MUSIC BOX THEATRE, 4/18/77–2/19/78; MOROSCO THEATRE, 2/22/78–3/19/78. 6 previews. Total of 384 PERFORMANCES. PRESENTED BY Harold Prince, in association with Ruth

Mitchell, by arrangement with The InComes Company; MUSIC: Stephen Sondheim; LYRICS: Stephen Sondheim (unless otherwise stated); ADDITIONAL MUSIC: Leonard Bernstein, Mary Rodgers, Richard Rodgers, Jule Styne; DIRECTOR/CONTINUITY: Ned Sherrin; CHOREOGRAPHER: Bob Howe; SETS: Peter Docherty; SET SUPERVISOR: Jay Moore; COSTUMES: Florence Klotz; LIGHTING: Ken Billington; SOUND: Jack Mann; MUSICAL SUPERVISOR: Paul Gemignani; MUSICAL DIRECTOR: Ray Cook; PIANISTS: Daniel Troob & Albin Konopka; PRESS: Mary Bryant & Bruce Cohen; CASTING: Joanna Merlin; GENERAL MANAGER: Howard Haines; STAGE MANAGER: John Grigas; ASSISTANT STAGE MANAGER: Artie Masella. *Cast:* Millicent Martin (1) (*Nancy Dussault* from 9/19/77), Julia McKenzie (2) (*Bonnie Schon* from 9/12/77; *Georgia Brown* from 10/17/77; *Carol Swarbrick* from 2/17/78) [see note below on Miss McKenzie's name], David Kernan (3) (*Larry Kert* from 8/1/77; *Jack Blackton* from 2/17/78), Ned Sherrin (narrator) (4) (*Fernanda Maschwitz* — alternate; *Hermione Gingold* from 10/17/77; *Burr Tilstrom, Kukla & Ollie* from 2/27/78). Standbys: For Miss Martin: Carol Swarbrick; For Miss McKenzie: Bonnie Schon, *Barbara Heuman*; For Mr. Kernan: Jack Blackton.

Note: in the USA Julia McKenzie was known as Julie N. McKenzie, because another actress already had the name Julia McKenzie. *Act I*: "Comedy Tonight" [from *A Funny Thing Happened on the Way to the Forum*], "Love is in the Air" [cut from *A Funny Thing Happened on the Way to the Forum*], "If Momma Was Married" [from *Gypsy*] (m: Jule Styne), "You Must Meet My Wife" [from *A Little Night Music*], "The Little Things You Do Together" [from *Company*], "Getting Married Today" [from *Company*], "I Remember" [from the 1966 TV show *Evening Primrose*] [dropped during the run], "Can That Boy Foxtrot!" [cut from *Follies*], "Company" [from *Company*], "Another Hundred People" [from *Company*] [dropped during the run], "Barcelona" [from *Company*], "Marry Me a Little" [cut from *Company*], "I Never Do Anything Twice" [from the movie *The Seven Per Cent Solution*], "Bring on the Girls" [this was "Beautiful Girls" re-named] [from *Follies*]/"Ah, Paris!" [from *Follies*]/"Buddy's Blues" [from *Follies*], "Broadway Baby" [from *Follies*], "You Could Drive a Person Crazy" [from *Company*]. *Act II*: "Everybody Says Don't" [from *Anyone Can Whistle*], "Anyone Can Whistle" [from *Anyone Can Whistle*] [dropped during the run], "Send in the Clowns" [from *A Little Night Music*], "We're Gonna Be All Right" [from *Do I Hear a Waltz* — lyrics restored] (m: Richard Rodgers), "A Boy Like That"/"I Have a Love" [from *West Side Story*] (m: Leonard Bernstein) [dropped during the run], "The Boy from…" [from *The Mad Show*] (m: Mary Rodgers), "Pretty Lady" [from *Pacific Overtures*], "You Gotta Get a Gimmick" [from *Gypsy*] (m: Jule Styne), "Losing My Mind" [from *Follies*], "Could I Leave You?" [from *Follies*] [dropped during the run], "I'm Still Here" [from *Follies*], "Conversation Piece" (medley) [arr: Caryl Brahms & Stuart Pedlar], "Side by Side by Side" [from *Company*].

In the London and other versions, and even on Broadway, various numbers were added or dropped, or moved around. The list of numbers above is the original Broadway one. Others added during the Broadway run were: (in Act I): "Being Alive" [from *Company*], "The Ladies Who Lunch" [from *Company*], "The Two of You" [written in 1952 for the *Kukla, Fran and Ollie* TV show, but not used], "Little Lamb" [from *Gypsy*], and (in Act II): "Waiting for the Girl Upstairs" [from *Follies*], "The Miller's Son" [from *A Little Night Music*], "I Feel Pretty" [from *West Side Story*]. Others used have been: "Too Many Mornings" [from *Follies*], "There Won't Be Trumpets" [cut from *Anyone Can Whistle*], "Sorry-Grateful" [from *Company*], "Everybody Ought to Have a Maid" [from *A Funny Thing Happened on the Way to the Forum*].

Broadway reviews were very divided, but mostly good. It received Tony nominations for musical and for the four actors.

After Broadway. TOUR. Opened at Drury Lane Theatre, Chicago, on 10/30/77. Previews from 10/27/77. CHOREOGRAPHER: John Grigas. *Cast*: Carol Swarbrick (*Marina MacNeal* during Miss Swarbrick's absence, 11/11/77–12/1/77), Bonnie Schon (*Marina MacNeal* during Miss Schon's absence, 12/2/77–12/15/77), David Chaney (*J.T. Cromwell* during Mr. Chaney's absence, 12/2/77–12/10/77), Cyril Ritchard (narrator; Mr. Ritchard was felled by a heart attack on 11/25/77, and replaced that day by *Brenda Forbes*, and by *Burr Tilstrom, Kukla & Ollie* on 12/14/77; *Arlene Francis* from 7/1/78; *Elliott Reid* from 7/8/78). The number "Don't Laugh" (m: Mary Rodgers) [from *Hot Spot*] was added for this tour.

DUBLIN, 1977. *Cast*: Gemma Craven, Gay Byrne, Tony Kenny, Loreto O'Connor.

TOUR. Opened on 3/6/78, at the Parker Playhouse, Fort Lauderdale. On 4/7/78 it opened in Hollywood. PIANISTS: John Berkman & Terry Trotter. *Cast*: Millicent Martin, Barbara Heuman, Larry Kert, Hermione Gingold (narrator).

AUSTRALIA, 1977–78 season. Played most of the major cities. DIRECTOR: Ray Cook; CHOREOGRAPHER: Robina Beard. *Cast*: Jill Perryman, Geraldene Morrow, Bartholomew John, John Laws (special guest).

PAPER MILL PLAYHOUSE, New Jersey, 1984. DIRECTOR: Robert Johanson; MUSICAL DIRECTOR: Jim Coleman. *Cast*: Helen Gallagher, Judy Kaye, Larry Kert, George Rose.

635. *Side Show*

About real-life mid–1920s British musical act The Hilton Sisters (born 1908), who were Siamese twins. They were in Todd Browning's exploitative movie *Freaks*, and also did one called *Chained for Life*. The two actresses come onto the stage from opposite sides, join in the middle, and get on with the show. Only at the end do they leave each other's side and go back to their respective corners. Daisy was extroverted — liked men, wanted limelight. Violet was introverted — read books, wanted the simple life. Terry is the press agent who brings them out of side shows into vaudeville. Buddy is his friend and partner, who performs with the girls.

Before Broadway. Rehearsals began in 7/97. There was no out-of-town tryout. Aside from the cut numbers mentioned in the song list, also eliminated during Broadway previews were "Stuck with You" and "Ready to Play."

The Broadway Run. RICHARD RODGERS THEATRE, 10/16/97–1/3/98. 31 previews from 9/19/97. 91 PERFORMANCES. PRESENTED BY Emanuel Azenberg, Joseph Nederlander, Herschel Waxman, Janice McKenna, Scott Nederlander; MUSIC: Henry Krieger; LYRICS/BOOK: Bill Russell; DIRECTOR/CHOREOGRAPHER: Robert Longbottom; SETS: Robin Wagner; COSTUMES: Gregg Barnes; LIGHTING: Brian MacDevitt; SOUND: Tom Clark; MUSICAL DIRECTOR/VOCAL & DANCE MUSIC ARRANGEMENTS: David Chase; ORCHESTRATIONS: Harold Wheeler; CAST RECORDING on Sony, made on 11/3/97, and released on 12/9/97; PRESS: Bill Evans; CASTING: Johnson — Liff; GENERAL MANAGERS: Abbie M. Strassler & John S. Corker; PRODUCTION STAGE MANAGER: Perry Cline; STAGE MANAGER: Maximo Torres; ASSISTANT STAGE MANAGER: Rebecca C. Monroe. *Cast* (in alphabetical actor order): REPTILE MAN: Barry Finkel; BEARDED LADY: Andy Gale; ROUSTABOUT # 1: Billy Hartung; SNAKE GIRL: Emily Hsu; FORTUNE TELLER: Alicia Irving; FAKIR: Devanand N. Janki; THE BOSS: Ken Jennings (6); JAKE: Norm Lewis (5); TERRY CONNOR: Jeff McCarthy (3); ROUSTABOUT # 3: David McDonald; 6TH EXHIBIT: Judy Malloy; SHEIK: David Masenheimer; GEEK: Phillip Officer; BUDDY FOSTER: Hugh Panaro (4); DOLLY DIMPLES: Verna Pierce; VIOLET HILTON: Alice Ripley (1), *Kristen Behrendt* (during Miss Ripley's absence); ROUSTABOUT # 2: Jim T. Ruttman; DAISY HILTON: Emily Skinner (2), *Lauren Kennedy* (during Miss Skinner's illness, 10/29/97); HAREM GIRL # 2: Jenny-Lynn Suckling; HAREM GIRL # 1: Susan Taylor; ROUSTABOUT # 4: Timothy Warmen; HAREM GIRL # 3: Darlene Wilson; REPORTERS/VAUDEVILLIANS/THE FOLLIES COMPANY/PARTY GUESTS/RADIO SHOW SINGERS/THE MOVIE CREW/HAWKERS: The Company. *Standbys*: Violet: Kristen Behrendt; Daisy: Lauren Kennedy; Jake: Todd Hunter. *Understudies*: Terry: David McDonald & David Masenheimer; Buddy: John Frenzer; Boss: David Masenheimer; *Swings*: John Paul Almon, Kelly Cole, John Frenzer, Michelle Millerick, J. Robert Spencer. *Orchestra*: WOODWINDS: Lawrence Feldman, Edward Salkin, Dennis Anderson, Roger Rosenberg; TRUMPETS: Robert Millikan, Glenn Drewes, Earl Gardner; TROMBONES: Larry Farrell & Jack Schatz; FRENCH HORN: Roger Wendt; VIOLINS: Mary Rowell, Paul Woodiel, Jonathan Kass, Nancy Reed; CELLI: Clay Ruede & Eileen Folson; BASS: Robert Renino; KEYBOARDS: Philip Fortenberry & Lawrence Yurman; HARP: Susan Jolles; GUITAR: Gregory Utzig; DRUMS:

Raymond Grappone; PERCUSSION: Eric Kivnick. *Act I*: THE MIDWAY: "Come Look at the Freaks" (Boss & Company), "Like Everyone Else" (Daisy & Violet), "You Deserve a Better Life" (Terry), "Crazy, Deaf and Blind" (Boss), "The Devil You Know" (Jake & Attractions), "More than We Bargained For" (Terry & Buddy), "Feelings You've Got to Hide" (Daisy & Violet), "When I'm by Your Side" (Daisy & Violet), "Say Goodbye to the Freak Show" (Company); VAUDEVILLE: "Overnight Sensation" (Terry & Reporters), "Leave Me Alone" (Daisy & Violet), "We Share Everything" (Daisy, Violet, Vaudevillians), "The Interview" (Daisy, Violet, Reporters), "Who Will Love Me as I Am?" (Daisy & Violet). *Act II*: THE FOLLIES: "Rare Songbirds on Display" (Company), "New Years Day" (Terry, Buddy, Jake, Daisy, Violet, Company), "Private Conversation" (Terry); ON THE ROAD: "One Plus One Equals Three" (Buddy, Daisy, Violet), "You Should Be Loved" (Jake), "They Hardly Know I'm Around" (Violet, Buddy, Daisy) [cut during previews]; THE TEXAS CENTENNIAL: "Tunnel of Love" (Terry, Buddy, Daisy, Violet), "Beautiful Day for a Wedding" (Boss & Hawkers), "She's Gone" [cut during previews], "Marry Me, Terry" (Daisy), "I Will Never Leave You" (Daisy & Violet), Finale: "Come Look at the Freaks" (reprise) (Company).

Broadway reviews were divided, mostly good. From the start, the show struggled at the box-office. The 10/28/97 performance was canceled when Emily Skinner couldn't go on because of a sore throat. Lauren Kennedy stood in for her the next day. Closing notices were posted on 12/21/97. Despite a campaign led by cast members to save the show over Christmas 1997, it failed, and lost $7 million. Audiences stayed away, thinking it was a mere freak show, and this misconception couldn't be overcome by the limited advertising available to the budget. The producers considered re-opening in 4/98 or 5/98, to take advantage of box-office sales that might result from possible Tony nominations, but investors, who had lost a lot of money, were scared away from re-investing. Keeping the cast together was another problem, as was the lack of the right amount of advertising. Ira Pettelman, a long-time friend of the composer Henry Krieger, volunteered to put up the money via his company. The question of whether *Side Show* would re-open or not was finally answered on 1/23/98 — in the negative. Aside from all that, Bobby Longbottom had quit. However, the load-out (removal of sets, costumes, etc) from the Richard Rodgers hadn't happened by 2/9/98, fueling rumors of a re-opening (which never happened). The show received Tony nominations for musical, score, and book, and for Alice Ripley and Emily Skinner (together).

After Broadway. On 10/30/97 the probability of a North American tour was announced, to open in Toronto in the summer of 1998, but due to the poor showing of the Broadway production, it never happened.

A 1998 London production was announced as a possibility on 10/30/97, but, again, never happened, also due to the poor showing on Broadway.

THEATREWORKS, Palo Alto, Calif., 10/24/99–11/8/99. Previews from 10/21/99. DIRECTOR: Robert Kelley; CHOREOGRAPHER: Bick Goss. *Cast*: VIOLET: Kristen Behrendt; DAISY: Debra Wiseman.

NORTH LIGHT THEATRE, Skokie, Ill., 5/24/00–7/9/00. Previews from 5/17/00. The closing date was extended twice — from 6/18/00, and again from 7/2/00. This production broke box-office records. DIRECTOR: Joe Leonardo; CHOREOGRAPHER: Marc Robin; MUSICAL DIRECTOR: Jeff Lewis. *Cast*: VIOLET: Kristen Behrendt; DAISY: Susie McGonagle; BUDDY: Sam Samuelson; TERRY: James Moye; THE BOSS: Jonathan Weir, *David Girolmo* (during the second extension).

PARK SQUARE THEATRE, St. Paul, Minn., 1/12/02–2/16/02. Previews from 1/9/02. Bill Russell himself directed, and re-inserted "She's Gone" (Violet), which had been cut from the Broadway production.

636. *Silk Stockings*

Set in 1955, in Paris and Moscow. Steve, a fast-talking talent agent, is trying to convince Boroff, a Soviet composer, to write the score for a gaudy Hollywood movie version of *War and Peace*. He meets and wins Ninotchka, the Communist sent from Moscow to check up on the three Russian emissaries sent to get the composer back from Paris.

Before Broadway. The following numbers were cut: "Art," "There's a Hollywood That's Good," "Give Me the Land," "If Ever We Get Out of Jail," "Let's Make it a Night," "The Perfume of Love," "Under the Dress," "What a Ball," "Why Should I Trust You?," "Bebe of Gay Paree," "Keep Your Chin Up," "I'm the Queen Thamar."

The show was originally going to be a production by Frank Loesser, George S. Kaufman and Jerome Robbins. That was in 1954, and it was due for a Broadway opening of 11/54. Mr. Loesser decided instead to do *The Most Happy Fella*, and Mr. Robbins had to leave to attend to his show *Peter Pan*, which was about to go to Broadway. Finally, with the new team, *Silk Stockings* began rehearsals in 10/54, and tried out at the Shubert Theatre, Philadelphia, from 11/26/54. Yvonne Adair was due to play Janice, but left before the Philly opening. Marilyn Ross took over. The show looked so bad here that producer Cy Feuer fired director George S. Kaufman and took over that role himself. Abe Burrows was hurriedly brought in to replace Mr. Kaufman and his wife Leueen McGrath on libretto (even though the final credits gave credit to all three). Marilyn Ross was replaced by Sherry O'Neill. It went on to further tryouts at the Shubert Theatre, Boston, from 1/4/55 (with Yvonne Adair re-hired and Sherry O'Neill now gone), and at the Shubert Theatre, Detroit, from 2/1/55 (with Gretchen Wyler having taken over as Janice). By this time Jerry Robbins had come back as choreographer, replacing Eugene Loring. Then finally it made it to Broadway (two more projected openings, one at Christmas 1954 and the other at New Year's 1955, had had to be deferred). This was Cole Porter's last musical.

The Broadway Run. IMPERIAL THEATRE, 2/24/55–4/14/56. 476 PERFORMANCES. PRESENTED BY Cy Feuer & Ernest H. Martin; MUSIC/LYRICS: Cole Porter; BOOK: George S. Kaufman, Leueen McGrath, Abe Burrows; BASED ON the 1939 movie *Ninotchka*, starring Greta Garbo & Melvyn Douglas, which had been taken from the satire of that year with the same name, by Melchior Lengyel; DIRECTOR: Cy Feuer; CHOREOGRAPHER: Eugene Loring; DANCE SUPERVISOR: Merritt Thompson; SETS/LIGHTING: Jo Mielziner; COSTUMES: Lucinda Ballard; ADDITIONAL COSTUMES: Robert Mackintosh; MUSICAL DIRECTOR: Herbert Greene, *Anton Coppola*; VOCAL ARRANGEMENTS: Herbert Greene; ORCHESTRATIONS: Don Walker; DANCE MUSIC ARRANGEMENTS: Tommy Goodman; PRESS: Karl Bernstein, Harvey B. Sabinson, Robert Ganshaw; COMPANY MANAGER: Joseph Harris; PRODUCTION STAGE MANAGER: Henri Caubisens, *Herman Magidson*; STAGE MANAGERS: Terence Little & Lawrence Kasha; ASSISTANT STAGE MANAGER: Arthur Rubin. **Cast:** PETER ILYITCH BOROFF: Philip Sterling; HOTEL DOORMAN: Walter Kelvin, *Ben Raisen*; HOTEL MANAGER: Stanley Simmonds; FLOWER GIRL: Geraldine Delaney, *Greb Lober*; IVANOV: Henry Lascoe; BRANKOV: Leon Belasco; BIBINSKI: David Opatoshu; STEVE CANFIELD: Don Ameche (2), *Lawrence Brooks, Norwood Smith*; FIRST COMMISSAR: Edward Becker; GUARDS: Lee Barry & Dick Humphrey, *Marvin Goodis*; VERA: Julie Newmar; COMMISSAR VASSILY MARKOVITCH: George Tobias (4); CHOREOGRAPHER: Kenneth Chertok, *Win Mayo*; NINA "NINOTCHKA" YOSHENKA: Hildegarde Neff (1); REPORTERS: Edward Becker, Tony Gardell, Arthur Rubin, *David Collyer, Marvin Goodis*; JANICE DAYTON: Gretchen Wyler (3); PIERRE BOUCHARD: Marcel Hillaire, *Arthur Ulisse*; CHIEF COMMISSAR: Forrest Green; MINISTER: Tony Gardell, *David Collyer*; PRESIDENT OF POLITBURO: Walter Kelvin, *Marvin Goodis*; SALESLADY: Ludie Claire, *Jan Sherwood*; M. FABOUR: Paul Best; BOOKSTALL MAN: Louis Polacek, *Win Mayo*; FRENCH COMRADES: Win Mayo & Arthur Ulisse (*Charles Aschmann & Adam Petroski*); MOVIE DIRECTOR: Paul Best; ASSISTANT DIRECTOR: Lee Barry; SONIA: Devra Kline, *Pat McBride*; GRISHA: Forrest Green; ANNA: Alexandra Moss, *Christiane Felsmann, Christina Rush*; MUSICIANS: Maurice Kogan, Leon Merian, Mervin Gold; GUARD: Edward Becker; DANCERS: Martin Allen, Tommy Andrew, Estelle Aza, Barbara Bostock, Verna Cain, Geraldine Delaney, George Foster, Bruce Hoy, Devra Kline, Pat McBride, John Ray, Carol Risser, Carol Stevens, Onna White, *Dorothy Dushock, Lynne Broadbent, Jane Hennessy, Greb Lober, Tom O'Steen, Ann Sparkman, Ken Urmston*. **Standby:** Steve: Lawrence Brooks. **Understudies:** Ninotchka: Ludie Claire, *Jan Sherwood*; Janice: Carol Risser, *Dee Harless, Greb Lober*; Markovitch: Forrest Green, *David Collyer*; Brankov: Forrest Green, *Ben Raisen*; Fabour: Ben Raisen; Ivanov: Forrest Green; Bibinski: Stanley Simmonds; Boroff: Kenneth Chertok; Pierre: David Collyer; Anna: Verna Cain; Vera: Devra Kline; Sonia/Saleslady: Pat McBride; Movie Director: Win Mayo. **Act I**: "Too Bad" (Ivanov, Brankov, Bibinski, Hotel Staff), "Paris Loves Lovers" (Steve & Ninotchka), "Stereophonic Sound" (Janice), "It's a Chemical Reaction, That's All" (Ninotchka), "All of You" (Steve), "Satin and Silk" (Janice), "Without Love" (Ninotchka), "All of You" (reprise) (Steve). **Act II:** "Hail Bibinski" (Ivanov, Brankov, Bibinski, French Comrades), "As on Through the Seasons We Sail" (Steve & Ninotchka), "Josephine" (Janice & Chorus): JOSEPHINE: Gretchen Wyler; NAPOLEON: Stanley Simmonds; "Siberia" (Ivanov, Brankov, Bibinski), "Silk Stockings" (Steve), "The Red Blues" (The Russians), Finale (Entire Company).

Reviews were divided, but mostly favorable.

After Broadway. TOUR. Opened on 4/23/56, at the Curran Theatre, San Francisco. MUSICAL DIRECTOR: Irving Schlein. **Cast**: STEVE: Don Ameche; BOROFF: Philip Sterling; HOTEL MANAGER: Stanley Simmonds; BRANKOV: Leon Belasco; JANICE: Gretchen Wyler; BIBINSKI: David Opatoshu; GUARD: Lee Barry; MARKOVITCH: George Tobias; REPORTER: Tony Gardell; MUSICIAN: Leon Merian; NINOTCHKA: Jan Sherwood; FLOWER GIRL: Ann Sparkman; IVANOV: Leon Janney; VERA: Karen Shepard; DANCING CHORUS: Claiborne Cary, Ethelyne Dunfee, Betty Koerber.

THE MOVIE. 1957. DIRECTOR: Rouben Mamoulian. Two new musical numbers were written—"Fated to Be Mated" and "The Ritz Roll and Rock." **Cast**: STEVE: Fred Astaire; NINOTCHKA: Cyd Charisse (singing dubbed by Carole Richards); PEGGY DAYTON: Janis Paige; MARKOVITCH: George Tobias; BRANKOV: Peter Lorre.

EQUITY LIBRARY THEATRE, NYC, 5/5/77–5/22/77. 22 PERFORMANCES. DIRECTOR: Richard Michaels; CHOREOGRAPHER: Karin Baker; MUSICAL DIRECTOR: Robert Plowman. **Cast**: STEVE: Mark Zimmerman; NINA: Carolyn Kirsch; JANICE: Carole Schweid; CHORUS INCLUDED: Debra Pigliavento.

ALL SOULS CHURCH, NYC, 2/14/86–3/2/86. 16 PERFORMANCES. Two songs that had been deleted before the original Broadway opening were re-instated for this production—"Art" (the second number in Act I) and "Give Me the Land" (the last number in Act II before the finale). PRESENTED BY The All Souls Players; PRODUCERS: Tran William Rhodes & Howard Van Der Meulen; DIRECTOR: Jeffrey K. Neill; SETS: Robert Edmonds; MUSICAL DIRECTOR: Wendell Kindberg. **Cast**: NINOTCHKA: Jean McClelland; STEVE: Joe Gram; JANICE: Trudi Anne Posey; MARKOVITCH: William Walters.

The big revival planned for 1998 by producers Michael Kessler & Melinda Jackson didn't happen. They revised it with Ken Friedman, but the Cole Porter Trust didn't like the revisions. Tony Stevens was to have directed and choreographed.

637. *Simply Heavenly*

A black musical, about Jess Simple, a poor but likeable factory worker in Harlem, torn between two loves and his dreams. Nothing ever goes right for him. He loves Joyce, who is very conservative. He learns that his wife in Buffalo now has a boyfriend and that boyfriend is willing to pay for two-thirds of the divorce. After trials and tribulations, he gets his divorce, and marries Joyce. Zarita is the fast next-door neighbor. Paddy's Bar is the local hangout.

Before Broadway. It had a successful run Off Broadway, at the 86TH STREET PLAYHOUSE, 5/21/57. 44 PERFORMANCES. PRESENTED BY Stella Holt; DIRECTOR: Josh Shelley; SETS: Charles Brandon; LIGHTING: Norman Blumenfeld; VOCAL ARRANGEMENTS: Bill Heyer. It had the same cast as for the subsequent Broadway run, except MADAME BUTLER: Alma Hubbard; MRS. CADDY/NURSE/PARTY GUEST: Javotte Sutton Greene; HOPKINS: Lawson Bates; GITFIDDLE: Ray Thompson; ZARITA: Ethel Ayler; BIG BOY/COP: Pierre Rayon. It got great reviews (it was reviewed by the *New York Times*), but the theatre was condemned as a fire hazard, and the show moved to Broadway, with new producers, new sets, some cast changes, and orchestrations instead of twin pianos. Other songs cut for Broadway (in addition to the ones mentioned in the Broadway song list) were: "Gatekeeper of My Castle," "Calypso (Beat it Out, Mon)," "The Hunter and the Hunted," "I Want Somebody to Come

Home To," "He's a Great Big Bundle of Joy," "A Sweet Worriation," "Deep in Love with You," "Yankee-Dixie March."

The Broadway Run. PLAYHOUSE THEATRE, 8/20/57–10/12/57. 62 PERFORMANCES. PRESENTED BY the Playhouse Heavenly Company (Vincent Cerow & Abel Enklewitz); MUSIC/ORCHESTRATIONS: David Martin; LYRICS/BOOK: Langston Hughes (based on his novel *Simple Takes a Wife*); DIRECTOR: Joshua Shelley; SETS/LIGHTING: Raymond Sovey; MUSICAL DIRECTOR: Sticks Evans; PRESS: David Lipsky & Philip Bloom; PRODUCTION STAGE MANAGER: Larry Parker; COMPANY MANAGER: Nat Parnes; STAGE MANAGER: Larry Parker & Laurence Olvin. **Cast:** JESSE B. SIMPLE (A HARLEMITE): Melvin Stewart; MADAME BUTLER (SIMPLE'S LANDLADY): Wilhelmina Gray; ANANIAS BOYD (SIMPLE'S NEIGHBOR): Stanley Greene; MRS. CADDY (JOYCE'S LANDLADY): Dagmar Craig; JOYCE LANE (SIMPLE'S GIRL): Marilyn Berry; HOPKINS (A BARTENDER): Duke Williams; BAR PIANIST (A BARFLY): Willie Pritchett; MISS MAMIE (A PLUMP DOMESTIC): Claudia McNeil; BODIDDLY (A DOCK WORKER): Charles A. McRae; CHARACTER (A SNOB): Allegro Kane; MELON (A FRUIT VENDOR): John Bouie; GITFIDDLE (A GUITAR PLAYER): Brownie McGhee; ZARITA (A GLAMOROUS GOODTIMER): Anna English; ARCIE (BODIDDLY'S WIFE): Josephine Woods; JOHN JASPER (HER SON): Charles Harrigan; BIG BOY/COP: Maxwell Glanville; NURSE/PARTY GUEST: Dagmar Craig. **Act I: Scene 1** Simple's room; an early spring evening; **Scene 2** Joyce's room; same evening: "(Love Is) Simply Heavenly" (Joyce); **Scene 3** Paddy's bar; just before midnight: "Let Me Take You for a Ride" (Zarita & Simple), "Broken String Blues" (Gitfiddle) [not in the prior Off Broadway run]; **Scene 4** Hospital room; next day; **Scene 5** Paddy's bar; Saturday night: "Did You Ever Hear the Blues?" (Mamie, Melon, Bar Characters); **Scene 6** Joyce's room; Sunday evening; **Scene 7** Simple's room; a month later: "(I'm Gonna Be) John Henry" (Simple). **Act II: Scene 1** Paddy's bar; an evening a week later: "When I'm in a Quiet Mood" (Mamie & Melon) [not in the prior Off Broadway run], "Look for the Morning Star" (Zarita) [this replaced "Shade and Shadows" (Zarita), which had been here during the Off Broadway run]; **Scene 2** Joyce's room; an evening two weeks later; **Scene 3** Simple's room; an evening, a week later: "Let's Ball Awhile" (Zarita & Ensemble); **Scene 4** Paddy's bar; next morning: "The Men in My Life" (Zarita); **Scene 5** Lenox Avenue; that evening; **Scene 6** Joyce's room; same evening; **Scene 7** Simple's room; same evening; **Scene 8** Paddys' bar; a winter evening: "(I'm a) Good Old Girl" (Mamie); **Scene 9** A phone booth; Christmas Eve; **Scene 10** Simple's room; same evening: "Look for the Morning Star" (reprise) (Ensemble).

Broadway reviews were mixed, and it failed. It went back Off Broadway for a couple of months, to the RENATA THEATRE, 11/8/57–12/31/57. 63 PERFORMANCES. In 1959 it was shown on TV, with the original leads.

After Broadway. ADELPHI THEATRE, London, 5/20/58–6/7/58. 23 PERFORMANCES. PRESENTED BY Jack Hylton & Laurence Harvey; DIRECTOR: Laurence Harvey; CHOREOGRAPHER: Malcolm Clare; MUSICAL DIRECTOR: Leslie Hutchinson. **Cast:** SIMPLE: Melvin Stewart; JOYCE: Marpessa Dawn; ZARITA: Ilene Day; MAMIE: Bertice Reading; MME BUTLER: Rita Stevens; BOYD: Earl Cameron; MRS. CADDY: Evelyn Dove; HOPKINS: Chris Gill; BODIDDLY: Charles A. McRae; GITFIDDLE: Don Johnson; ARCIE: Richardena Jackson; MELON: John Bouie; JOHN JASPER: Conrad Pringle; BAR PIANIST: David Wu; CHARACTER: Bari Johnson; NURSE: Isabelle Lucas; DANCERS: Dorothy Hall, Jacqueline Chan, Yolanda.

YOUNG VIC, London, 2004. Re-opened at the TRAFALGAR STUDIOS (formerly the Whitehall Theatre), London, on 10/25/04 (after 10 days of previews). PRESENTED BY Josette Bushell-Mingo; SETS/COSTUMES: Rob Howell. **Cast:** WATERMELON JOE: Clive Rowe; MAMIE: Ruby Turner; SIMPLE: Rhashan Stone.

638. *Sing Out, Sweet Land!*

An American folk-music pageant, a salute to American folk and popular music over the centuries, as seen through the eyes of the ageless hero Barnaby. He is constantly pursued by his non-singing nemesis, Parson Killjoy. Bibi Osterwald played Barnaby's romantic link in various episodes.

Before Broadway. It was first produced in 12/27 (102 PERFOR-

MANCES), by the Catholic University of Washington, DC (where Walter Kerr was drama teacher until he came to Broadway for good in 1949).

The Broadway Run. INTERNATIONAL THEATRE, 12/27/44–3/24/45. 102 PERFORMANCES. PRESENTED BY the Theatre Guild; SPECIAL MUSIC: Elie Siegmeister & Edward Eager; BOOK: Walter Kerr; DIRECTOR: Leon Leonidoff; BOOK DIRECTOR: Walter Kerr (Elia Kazan doctored it, without credit); CHOREOGRAPHERS: Doris Humphrey & Charles Weidman; SETS/LIGHTING: Albert Johnson; COSTUMES: Lucinda Ballard; MUSICAL DIRECTOR/ORCHESTRATIONS: Elie Siegmeister; VERSE CHORUS DIRECTOR: Arthur Lessac; CAST RECORDING on Decca; PRESS: Alfred H. Tamarin & Lorella Val-Mery; CASTING: Bettina Cerf; PRODUCTION SUPERVISORS: Lawrence Langner & Theresa Helburn; COMPANY MANAGER: Harry Essex; STAGE MANAGER: Peter Lawrence; ASSISTANT STAGE MANAGERS: Morty Halpern & Jules Racine. **Cast:** BARNABY GOODCHILD: Alfred Drake (1). **Act I: Scene 1** Puritan New England: PARSON KILLJOY: Philip Coolidge (5); CHARITY WOULDLOVE: Ellen Love; PRISCILLA: Alma Kaye (4); PURITAN: Robert Penn (7). "Who is the Man (That Life Doth Will)?" (Puritan hymn) (sung by Vocal Ensemble), "As I Was Going Along" (m: Elie Siegmeister; l: Edward Eager; based on folk music) (sung by Barnaby); **Scene 2** A New England town: THE PATRIOT: Jack McCauley (6); HIS DAUGHTER: Alma Kaye (4). "Way Down the Ohio" (folk song; author unknown) (sung by Barnaby); **Scene 3** Illinois Wilderness: FIDDLER: Burl Ives (2); BEAR: Jules Racine; BILL: Ted Tiller; MARY JANE: Irene Jordan; MARY JANE'S FATHER: Philip Coolidge (5); FARM GIRL: Adrienne Gray; FARM WOMAN: Bibi Osterwald (3); MOHEE: Alma Kaye (4). "Mountain Whippoorwill" (by Stephen Vincent Benet) (recited by Barnaby), Country Dance (staged by Charles Weidman) (danced by Dancing Ensemble), "When I Was Single" (folk song; author unknown) (sung by Farm Woman) [the show stopper], "Foggy, Foggy Dew" (folk song; author unknown) (sung by Fiddler), "Hardly Think I Will" (folk song; author unknown) (sung by Farm Girl & Bill), "The Devil and the Farmer's Wife" (folk song; author unknown) (sung by Barnaby & Ensemble), "Little Mohee" (Kentucky mountain ballad; author unknown) (sung by Barnaby & Mohee); **Scene 4** The Oregon Trail: 1ST MAN: Robert Penn (7); 2ND MAN: Charles Hart; 3RD MAN: Jules Racine; TOUGH WOMAN: Ellen Love; BIG BEAR OF A MAN: James Westerfield (8). "The Oregon Trail" (by James Marshall) (recited by Tough Woman & Verse Chorus), "Oh, Susannah" (by Stephen Foster) (sung by Vocal Ensemble), "Springfield Mountain" (author unknown) (sung by Barnaby); **Scene 5** The South: WATERMELON WOMAN: Juanita Hall. "Hammer Ring" (work chant; author unknown) (sung by Spiritual Ensemble), "Watermelon Cry" (author unknown) (sung by Watermelon Woman), "You Better Mind" (spiritual; author unknown) (sung by Spiritual Ensemble), "Didn't My Lord Deliver Daniel" (spiritual; author unknown) (sung by Spiritual Ensemble); **Scene 6** The Mississippi boat: JOHNNY: Jack McCauley (6); FRANKIE: Alma Kaye (4); FRANKIE'S MOTHER: Ellen Love; TRASKER: Robert Penn (7); BONAFORTE: Burl Ives (2); BARTENDER: Ted Tiller; CAPTAIN: Charles Hart; SHERIFF: Philip Coolidge (5); NELLIE BLY: Christine Karner; SPECIALTY DANCERS: Peter Hamilton & Irene Hawthorne (10). "The Roving Gambler" (ballad; author unknown) (sung by Johnny, Frankie, Frankie's Mother), "Louisiana Gals" (minstrel song; by Cool White) (sung by Vocal Ensemble), "Camptown Races" (by Stephen Foster) (staged by Charles Weidman) (danced by Peter Hamilton, Irene Hawthorne, Dancing Ensemble), "Frankie and Johnny" (folk song; author unknown) (staged by Walter Kerr) (sung by Bonaforte, Frankie, Johnny, Sheriff, Nellie, Bartender), "Polly Wolly Doodle" (folk song; author unknown) (staged by Doris Humphrey) (sung by Company). **Act II: Scene 1** Civil War campfire: 1ST SOLDIER: Burl Ives (2); LIEUTENANT: Philip Coolidge (5); CORPORAL: Ted Tiller. "Cap'n Jinks" (Civil War song; author unknown) (sung by Male Ensemble), "Blue Tail Fly" (Civil War song; author unknown) (sung by 1st Soldier), "Marching Down This Road" (folk song; author unknown) (sung by Barnaby & 1st Soldier); **Scene 2** Railroad station, Texas: YARD BOSS: James Westerfield (8); MRS. CASEY JONES: Bibi Osterwald (3); HER DAUGHTERS: Pat Newman, Peggy Campbell, Dorothy Baxter; OLD TIMER: Morty Halpern; JOLLY TRAMP: Burl Ives (2); GENTLEMAN TRAMP: Jack McCauley (6); SAD TRAMP: Robert Penn (7); FAT TRAMP: Charles Hart. "Casey Jones" (m: Eddie Newton; l: T. Lawrence Seibert) (sung by Mrs. Casey Jones, Yard Boss, Old Timer), "Big Rock Candy Mountain" (hobo song; author unknown) (sung by Jolly Tramp), "I Have Been a Good Boy" (folk song; author unknown) (sung by Gentleman Tramp), "Wanderin'" (hobo song; author unknown) (sung by Barnaby), "Hallelujah, I'm a Bum" (hobo song; words by Joe Hill) (sung by Barnaby), "Jesse James" (by William Rose Benet) (recited by Old Timer & Verse Chorus) (dance staged by Charles Weidman; danced by Peter Hamilton); *Scene 3* City park: DAISY: Alma Kaye (4); JACK: Ted Tiller; VILLAIN: Philip Coolidge (5); POLICEMAN: Burl Ives (2). "While Strolling Through the Park" (by Ed Haley) (sung by Vocal Ensemble), "Bicycle Built for Two" (by Harry Dacre) (sung by Daisy & Jack), "Heaven Will Protect the Working Girl" (m: A. Baldwin Sloane; l: Edgar Smith) (sung by Daisy & Jack), "(A) Hot Time in the Old Town (Tonight)" (m: Theodore H. Metz; l: Joe Hayden) (sung by Barnaby, Policeman, Daisy, Jack); *Scene 4* Five o'clock whistle (ch: Doris Humphrey): BLUES SINGER: Ruth Tyler; BLUECOAT: Jules Racine; BLUEJEANS: Peter Hamilton; BLUENOSE: Philip Coolidge (5); RED LIGHT GIRL: Ethel Mann (11). "Trouble, Trouble" (blues; author unknown) (sung by Blues Singer). Ragtime songs (all danced by Dancing Ensemble): a/ "By the (Beautiful) Sea" (m: Harry Carroll; l: Harold R. Atteridge); b/ "Come Josephine (in My Flying Machine)" (m: Fred Fisher; l: Alfred Bryan); c/ "Maxixe" (m/l: Dave Ringle, William Tracy, Ray Walker) (dance); "Funny Bunny Hug" (m/l: Dave Ringle, William Tracy, Ray Walker) (sung by Barnaby); d/ "Temptation Rag" (by Louis Weslyn & Henry Lodge); "Hey! Mr. Bossman" (jail song; by Elie Siegmeister) (sung by Blues Singer), "Basement Blues" (early blues by W.C. Handy) (sung by Blues Singer & Spiritual Ensemble; danced by Dancing Ensemble), "Some of These Men" (blues; author unknown) (sung by Blues Singer & Ensemble); *Scene 5* Speakeasy Night Club: Speakeasy dance numbers staged by Charles Weidman, and danced by Peter Hamilton, Irene Hawthorne, Dancing Ensemble: TYCOON: Jack McCauley (6); MAXIE: Bibi Osterwald (3); BARTENDER: Charles Hart; TRIGGER: James Westerfield (8); BABY: Alma Kaye (4); DRUNK: Jules Racine; POLICE CHIEF: William Sharon; SPECIALTY DANCERS: Peter Hamilton & Irene Hawthorne (10). "I Got Rhythm" (by George Gershwin) [from *Girl Crazy*] (danced by Dancing Ensemble), "At Sundown" (by Walter Donaldson) (sung by Barnaby), "My Blue Heaven" (m: Walter Donaldson; l: Richard Whiting) [from *Ziegfeld Follies of 1927*] (sung by Barnaby), "Yes Sir, That's My Baby" (m: Walter Donaldson; l: Gus Kahn) (sung by Maxie), "The Charleston" (m/l: Cecil Mack & James P. Johnson) [from *Runnin' Wild*]; *Scene 6* Aircraft Carrier: BOATSWAIN: Burl Ives (2); TOM: Ted Tiller; DICK: Lawrence Gilbert; HARRY: George Cassidy; GEORGE: Sam Green; MURPH: Robert Penn (7); AIDE: Calvin Harris; COMMANDER: Philip Coolidge (5). "Sea Chanty" (author unknown) (sung by Boatswain), "Where" (m: James Mundy; l: Edward Eager) (sung by Barnaby); *Scene 7* Finale (staged by Doris Humphrey): Barnaby: Alfred Drake (1). "More than These" (m: James Mundy; l: Edward Eager) (sung by Barnaby & Entire Company).

VOCAL ENSEMBLE: Dorothy Baxter, George Cassidy, Cathleen Chambers, Marjorie Chandler, Charles Ford, Lawrence Gilbert, Sam Green, Carol Hall, Calvin Harris, Irene Jordan, Fred Kohler, Edwin Marsh, Fred Rivetti, Selma Rogoff, Ludlow White, Phyllis Wilcox, Maria Wilde; DANCERS: Peggy Campbell, Roberta Cassell, Kendrick Coy, Margaret Cuddy, Joseph Gifford, Ann S. Halprin, Christine Karner, Joseph Landis, Ethel Mann (11), Robert Mayo, Pat Newman, Miriam Pandor, Joseph Precker, Frances Rainer, Harriett Roeder, Sam Steen, Bill Summer, Helen Waggoner, Bill Weaver, Ann Williams; VERSE CHORUS: Morty Halpern, Ellen Love, Dorothy Baxter, George Cassidy, Joseph Gifford, Sam Green, Carol Hall, Irene Jordan, Christine Karner, Ethel Mann (11), Robert Mayo, Patricia Newman, Frances Rainer, Fred Rivetti, Ludlow White; SPIRITUAL ENSEMBLE (coached by Juanita Hall): Hercules Armstrong, Harry Bolden, Oscar Brooks, James Gordon, Juanita Hall, Rhoda Boggs, Claretta Freeman, Massie Patterson, Virtes Reese, Wilson Woodbeck, William Sol.

Broadway reviews were divided. Lead dancer Peter Hamilton was injured, and the number of his dances became limited, so Charles Weidman danced for him in Act I, Scene 6. Burl Ives won a Donaldson Award.

639. *Singin' in the Rain*

Set in Hollywood in the 1920s, during the transition from silents to talkies.

Before Broadway. It began at the LONDON PALLADIUM, 6/30/83. 894 PERFORMANCES.

The Broadway production was Twyla Tharp's Broadway debut as choreographer. During Broadway previews there were several changes made in the cast, and in the character line-up, and characters were shifted in their order. The Warner Brother character was added during previews, and four other characters were dropped—Phil (played by Ray Benson), Bert (played by Raymond Kurshals), Conductor (played by Gene Sager), and Stage Manager (played by Austin Colyer). John Carrafa, who played Sid in previews, was replaced with Martin Van Treuren. This was the scene-by-scene breakdown during previews (where the performers or songwriters are the same as for the Broadway run, they are omitted here): *Act I: Part I* The premiere of *The Royal Rascal*: *Scene 1* Grauman's Chinese Theatre at the premiere, September 1927; *Scene 2* Altoona, Pa.—a vaudeville theatre; ten years earlier: "Fit as a Fiddle;" *Scene 3* Studios of Monumental Pictures; five years later, filming a western; *Scene 4* Grauman's Chinese Theatre, onstage and backstage, at the premiere; *Scene 5* Hollywood Boulevard; later that evening: "You Stepped Out of a Dream" (l: Gus Kahn) (Don); *Scene 6* The Coconut Grove party after the premiere: "I've Got a Feelin' You're Foolin'" (Kathy & Ensemble). *Part II* The studios of Monumental Pictures: *Scene 7* Silent stage, Oct. 7, 1927: "Make 'em Laugh," "Hub Bub;" *Scene 8* Shooting *The Dueling Cavalier*; *Scene 9* Filming musical shorts: "Wedding of the Painted Doll," "Rag Doll," "Temptation," "Takin' Miss Mary to the Ball" (singers: Mr. Benson & Miss D'Arcy; Dancing Horse: John Carrafa & Tom Rawe), "Love is Where You Find It;" *Scene 10* An empty soundstage: "You Are My Lucky Star;" *Scene 11* Diction lessons: "Moses Supposes." *Act II: Scene 1* The Glendale Theatre, sneak preview of *The Dueling Cavalier*, Jan. 1928; *Scene 2* Don's house; later that evening: "Good Mornin';" *Scene 3* A street near Kathy's house: "Singin' in the Rain;" *Scene 4* Monumental Pictures recording studio: (a) The next day; (b) Later that week; "Would You?;" *Scene 5* Title production number in *The Dancing Cavalier*: "Broadway Rhythm," "Blue Prelude." Cast was the same as in the Broadway run; *Scene 6* Grauman's Chinese Theatre: "Would You" (reprise), "You Are My Lucky Star" (reprise), "Singin' in the Rain" (reprise).

The Broadway Run. GERSHWIN THEATRE, 7/2/85–5/18/86. 38 previews. 367 PERFORMANCES. PRESENTED BY Maurice Rosenfield, Lois F. Rosenfield, Cindy Pritzker, Inc.; MUSIC: Nacio Herb Brown (unless otherwise noted); LYRICS: Arthur Freed (unless otherwise noted); BASED ON the 1952 MGM film of the same name (with screenplay by Betty Comden & Adolph Green, and choreography by Gene Kelly & Stanley Donen), starring Gene Kelly, Donald O'Connor & Debbie Reynolds; ADAPTED BY Betty Comden & Adolph Green; DIRECTOR/CHOREOGRAPHER: Twyla Tharp; SETS: Santo Loquasto; COSTUMES: Ann Roth; LIGHTING: Jennifer Tipton; SOUND: Sound Associates; FILM SEQUENCES: Gordon Willis; MUSICAL SUPERVISOR/DANCE & VOCAL ARRANGEMENTS: Stanley Lebowsky; MUSICAL DIRECTOR: Robert Billig; ORCHESTRATIONS: Larry Wilcox; PRESS: Shirley Herz Associates; CASTING: Slater/MLC; COMPANY MANAGER: Steven Suskin; PRODUCTION STAGE MANAGER: Steven Zweigbaum; STAGE MANAGER: Arturo E. Porazzi; ASSISTANT STAGE MANAGER: Amy Pell. **Cast:** DORA BAILEY: Melinda Gilb; COSMO BROWN: Peter Slutsker [he was later, in the late 1990s, known as Peter Marx] (3); LINA LAMONT: Faye Grant (4); DON LOCKWOOD: Don Correia (1), *Ray Benson* (stood in for several weeks during Mr. Correia's illness & vacation); R.F. SIMPSON: Hansford Rowe (5); ROSCOE DEXTER: Richard Fancy (6); ROD: Robert Radford (4); KATHY SELDEN: Mary D'Arcy (2); SID PHILLIPS: Martin Van Treuren; PHOEBE DINSMORE: Jacque Dean; DICTION COACH: Austin Colyer; SOUND ENGINEER: John Spalla; TICKET TAKER: Martin Van Treuren; A WARNER BROTHER: Austin Colyer; ZELDA ZANDERS: Mary Ann Kellogg; ENSEMBLE: Ray Benson, John Carrafa (*Mark Frawley*), Richard Colton, Austin Colyer, Jacque Dean, Diane Duncan, Yvonne Dutton, Craig Frawley, Melinda Gilb, Katie Glasner, Barbara Hoon, David-Michael Johnson, Mary Ann Kellogg, Raymond Kurshals, Alison Mann, Barbara Moroz, Kevin O'Day, Robert Radford, Tom Rawe, Gene Sager, John Spalla, Amy Spencer, Cynthia Thole, Martin Van Treuren, Shelley Washington, Laurie Williamson; *Cast in film sequences*: *The Royal Rascal*: PHILIPPE: Don Lockwood (Don Correia), *Ray Benson* (stood in for several weeks during Mr. Correia's illness & vacation); JEANETTE: Lina Lamont (Faye

Grant); ENEMIES OF THE KING: Ray Benson, Craig Frawley, Gene Sager, Martin Van Treuren; TALKING PICTURE DEMONSTRATION: MAN ON SCREEN: John Spalla; *The Dueling Cavalier* AND *The Dancing Cavalier*: YVONNE: Lina Lamont (Faye Grant); LADY-IN-WAITING: Cynthia Thole; LADIES OF THE COURT: Diane Duncan, Alison Mann, Barbara Moroz; PIERRE: Don Lockwood (Don Correia); MANSERVANT: Gene Sager; VILLAIN: Martin Van Treuren. **Understudies**: Don: Donn Simione, *Ray Benson*; Kathy: Cynthia Thole, *Christina Saffran* (added during the run); Cosmo: Brad Moranz; Lina: Barbara Moroz; Simpson: Austin Colyer; Roscoe: John Spalla. **Swings**: David Askler, Cheri Butcher, Brad Moranz, *Christina Saffran* (added during the run). **Act I: Part I**: The premiere of *The Royal Rascal*: **Scene 1** Grauman's Chinese Theatre at the premiere; September 1927; **Scene 2** Altoona, Pa.—A vaudeville theatre; ten years earlier: "Fit as a Fiddle" * (Don & Cosmo); **Scene 3** Grauman's Chinese Theatre, onstage & backstage, at the premiere; **Scene 4** Hollywood Boulevard; later that evening: "Beautiful Girl" [from the movie *Going Hollywood*] (Don & Fans); **Scene 5** The Coconut Grove party after the premiere: "I've Got a Feelin' You're Foolin'" [originally from the movie *Broadway Melody of 1936*] (Kathy & the Coconut Grove Coquettes). **Part II**: The studios of Monumental Pictures: **Scene 6** Silent stage; Oct. 7, 1927: "Make 'em Laugh" (Cosmo), "Hub Bub" (m: Stanley Lebowsky) (Cosmo & The Studio Stage Hands — Messrs Carrafa (*Mark Frawley*), Colton, Kurshals, O'Day, Radford, Rawe) [not from the movie *Singin' in the Rain*]; **Scene 7** Shooting *The Dueling Cavalier*, a silent film; **Scene 8** An empty soundstage: "You Are My Lucky Star" (Don & Kathy); **Scene 9** Diction lessons: "Moses Supposes" * (m: Roger Edens; l: Betty Comden & Adolph Green) (Don & Cosmo); **Scene 10** Shooting of *The Dueling Cavalier* as a talking picture. **Part III**: Conversion of *The Dueling Cavalier* to a musical. **Scene 11** The Glendale Theatre, sneak preview of *The Dueling Cavalier* as a talking picture; January 1928; **Scene 12** Don's house; later that evening: "Good Mornin'" * [originally from the movie *Babes in Arms*] (Don, Kathy, Cosmo); **Scene 13** A street near Kathy's house: "Singin' in the Rain" * [originally from the movie *Hollywood Revue of 1929*] (Don). **Act II**: **Scene 1** Filming musical numbers at Warner Brothers studio: "Wedding of the Painted Doll" (Miss Duncan, Miss Dutton, Miss Glasner, Mr. O'Day, Miss Spencer, Miss Thole), "Rag Doll" (Mr. Colton, Miss Hoon, Mr. Kurshals) [not from the movie *Singin' in the Rain*], "Temptation" (singer–Miss Gilb; dancers–Miss Kellogg, Mr. Radford, Miss Washington) [not from the movie *Singin' in the Rain*], "Takin' Miss Mary to the Ball" (l: Edward Heymann) (singers — Mr. Benson & Miss Mann; dancing horse–Mr. Carrafa [*Mark Frawley*] & Mr. Rawe) [not from the movie *Singin' in the Rain*], "Love is Where You Find It" (l: Gus Kahn) (Ensemble) [not from the movie *Singin' in the Rain*]; **Scene 2** Monumental Pictures recording studio: (a) The next day; (b) Later that week; "Would You?" (Kathy); **Scene 3** Title production number in *The Dancing Cavalier*: "Broadway Rhythm" (Company), "Blue Prelude" (m: Al Bishop; l: Gordon Jenkins) (Company) [not from the movie *Singin' in the Rain*]. COURT AT FROLIC: Mr. Benson, Mr. Carrafa (*Mark Frawley*), Mr. Colton, Miss Hoon, Miss Kellogg, Mr. Kurshals, Mr. Radford, Mr. Rawe, Miss Spencer, Miss Thole, Miss Washington. PIERRE: Don Lockwood (Don Correia); MANSERVANT: Gene Sager; VILLAIN: Martin Van Treuren; LADIES OF THE COURT: Misses Duncan, Mann, Moroz; APACHE DANCERS: Mr. Carrafa (dropped during the run and not replaced), Mr. Colton, Miss Dutton, Miss Glasner, Miss Hoon, Miss Kellogg, Mr. Kurshals, Mr. O'Day, Mr. Rawe, Miss Spencer; CHANTEUSE: Miss Williamson; DANSEUSE: Miss Washington; SAVATE FIGHTERS: Mr. Benson & Mr. Kurshals; PEASANTS: Mr. Colyer, Miss Dean, Craig Frawley, Miss Gilb, Mr. Johnson, Mr. Spalla; **Scene 4** Grauman's Chinese Theatre, the premiere of *The Dancing Cavalier*: "Would You?" (reprise) (Kathy), "You Are My Lucky Star" (reprise) (Don, Kathy, Company), "Singin' in the Rain" (Company).

Note: an asterisk means as choreographed by Gene Kelly & Stanley Donen in the film.

The production got terrible reviews from the Broadway critics. It received Tony nominations for book, and for Don Correia.

After Broadway. TOUR. Opened on 6/10/86, at the Dallas Music Hall, and closed on 6/7/87, at the Tennessee Performing Arts Center, Nashville. This was a very different production from the one on Broadway. PRESENTED BY Marvin A. Krauss, Irving Siders, and Pace Theatri-

cal Group, by arrangement with the original Broadway producers; DIRECTOR: Lawrence Kasha; CHOREOGRAPHER: Peter Gennaro; SETS: Peter Wolf; CONCEPTS/COSTUMES: Robert Fletcher; LIGHTING: Thomas Skelton; SOUND: Sound Associates; MUSICAL DIRECTOR: Raymond Allen; ORCHESTRATIONS: Larry Wilcox; Stanley Lebowsky's original dance & vocal arrangements were used, but with additional arrangements by Wally Harper; and all the rest of the crew was different. The cast was not only new but the roles were re-arranged. The musical numbers were re-arranged, and some omitted and some new ones added, and others taken away. "What's Wrong with Me?" (m: Nacio Herb Brown; l: Edward Heyman) (Lina) was added to Act II, Scene 3. **Cast**: DORA BAILEY: Lou Williford; ZELDA ZANDERS: Valerie Dowd; OLGA MARA: Jennifer Hammond; MARY MARGARET: Deborah Bartlett; R.F. SIMPSON: Elek Hartman; ROSCOE DEXTER: Alan Sues; COSMO BROWN: Brad Moranz; LINA LAMONT: Jennifer Smith; DON LOCKWOOD: Donn Simione; YOUNG DON/ASSISTANT DIRECTOR: Frank Kosik; YOUNG COSMO: Rick Conant; VILLAIN/DIRECTION TEACHER: Gerry Burkhardt; LADY IN WAITING IN FILM/MISS DINSMORE: Holly K. Watts; ROD: Steve Goodwillie; KATHY SELDEN: Cynthia Ferrer; POLICEMAN/SID PHILLIPS: Darryl Ferrera; BUTLER: Jim Kirby; 1ST ASSISTANT DIRECTOR: George Giatrakis; PRODUCTION SINGER: Campbell Martin; ENSEMBLE: Kelli Barclay-Boelsterli, Beverly Ann Britton, Newton Cole, Andrea Hopkins, Dana Lewis, Ann Neiman, Mark T. Owens, Erin Robbins, James Van Treuren.

PAPER MILL PLAYHOUSE, New Jersey, 1994. DIRECTOR: James Rocco; CHOREOGRAPHER: Linda Goodrich; SETS: Michael Anania. **Cast**: DON: Michael Gruber; STRIPPER: Candy Cook; KATHY: Christina Saffran.

WEST YORKSHIRE PLAYHOUSE, England, 12/99–2/00; OLIVIER THEATRE, London, 6/22/00–7/20/00. Previews from 6/19/00); re-ran at the OLIVIER THEATRE, 12/18/00–1/27/01. DIRECTOR: Jude Kelly; CHOREOGRAPHER: Stephen Mear; SETS/COSTUMES: Huntley Muir; LIGHTING: Andrew Ridge; SOUND: Simon Whitehorn. **Cast**: DON LOCKWOOD: Paul Robinson; LINA LAMONT: Rebecca Thornhill; DORA BAILEY/MISS DINSMORE: Annette McLaughlin; ALSO WITH: Saskia Butler, Ben Garner, Zoe Hart.

HOBBY CENTER FOR THE PERFORMING ARTS, Houston, 12/2/04–12/19/04. PRESENTED BY Theatre Under the Stars (TUTS). Then it played at the 5TH AVENUE THEATRE, Seattle, 2/12/05–3/5/05. DIRECTOR/CHOREOGRAPHER: Jamie Rocco; SETS: Michael Anania; COSTUMES: Gregg Barnes; LIGHTING: David Neville, *Tom Sturge* (in Seattle); SOUND: Christopher "Kit" Bond; MUSICAL DIRECTOR: Jeff Rizzo. **Cast:** DON: Michael Gruber; COSMO: Randy Rogel, *Michael Arnold* (in Seattle); KATHY: Danette Holden, *Christina Saffran Ashford* (in Seattle); ROSCOE: Charles Bailey; LINA: Rachel de Benedet, *Lisa Estridge* (in Seattle); SIMPSON: William McCauley; DORA/MRS. DINSMORE: Chesley Santoro; ROD/DICTION TEACHER: Stewart Gregory; ENSEMBLE INCLUDED: Robert M. Armitage, Shane Dickson, Kristy Richmond, Robin Levine.

640. *1600 Pennsylvania Avenue*

Subtitled: *A Musical About the Problems of Housekeeping*, i.e. at the White House, in Washington, DC. In a series of episodes, Ken Howard played all the presidents from George Washington to Teddy Roosevelt, and Patricia Routledge all the first ladies. The show was set against the characters of the two main servants, Jefferson's daughter Seena, and Lud, who get married.

Before Broadway. Alan Jay Lerner started work on this project in 1972. This was going to be THE big Bicentennial musical. Coca-Cola backed it to the tune of $1.2 million. The original producer, Saint Subber, quit when Mr. Lerner couldn't come up with a script. Frank Corsaro was the director and Donald McKayle the choreographer. When it arrived for tryouts in Philadelphia it was 3 hours 45 minutes long, and got very bad reviews. The number with the ironical title, "They Should Have Stayed Another Week in Philadelphia," was cut. The director and choreographer were replaced by George Faison and Gilbert Moses, who shared both those chores. Coca-Cola removed its name from the program. Leonard Bernstein wanted to cancel the show after the Philly tryouts, but Alan Jay Lerner objected, and it went on to Washington, DC, where it played at the National Theatre, 3/17/76–4/17/76. Tony Walton, who had been doing sets and costumes, insisted his name be removed from the program, and in the end he got "design supervisor" credit.

The Broadway Run. MARK HELLINGER THEATRE, 5/4/76–5/8/76. 13 previews. 7 PERFORMANCES. PRESENTED BY Roger L. Stevens & Robert Whitehead, in association with the Coca-Cola Company (this last was removed from the billing during tryouts), and by arrangement with Saint Subber; MUSIC: Leonard Bernstein; LYRICS/BOOK: Alan Jay Lerner; DIRECTORS/CHOREOGRAPHERS: Gilbert Moses & George Faison; SETS: Kert Lundell; SET SUPERVISOR: Tony Walton; COSTUMES: Whitney Blausen & Dona Granata; LIGHTING: Tharon Musser; SOUND: John McClure; MUSICAL DIRECTOR: Roland Gagnon; ORCHESTRATIONS: Sid Ramin & Hershy Kay; PRESS: Seymour Krawitz, Patricia McLean Krawitz, Ted Goldsmith; GENERAL MANAGER: Oscar E. Olesen; COMPANY MANAGER: James Walsh; PRODUCTION STAGE MANAGER: William Dodds; STAGE MANAGERS: Marnel Sumner & Michael Turque. *Cast:* THE PRESIDENT: Ken Howard (1) ☆; THE PRESIDENT'S WIFE: Patricia Routledge (2) ☆; LUD: Gilbert Price (3) ☆; SEENA: Emily Yancy (4); LITTLE LUD: Guy Costley (13); STAGE MANAGER: David E. Thomas (12); THE THIRTEEN DELEGATES: MASSACHUSETTS: Howard Ross (11); NEW YORK: Reid Shelton (5); PENNSYLVANIA: Ralph Farnworth (8); NEW HAMPSHIRE: J.T. Cromwell; RHODE ISLAND: Lee Winston; CONNECTICUT: Richard Chappell; NEW JERSEY: Walter Charles; VIRGINIA: Edwin Steffe (6); NORTH CAROLINA: John Witham (7); SOUTH CAROLINA: Richard Muenz; DELAWARE: Alexander Orfaly; MARYLAND: Raymond Cox; GEORGIA: Randolph Riscol; THE STAFF: HENRY: Raymond Bazemore; RACHEL: Urylee Leonardos; COLEY: Carl Hall (10); JOBY: Janette Moody; BROOM: Howard Ross (11); JIM: Cornel J. Richie; SALLY: Louise Heath; THE (NINE) BRITISH: ORDWAY: Walter Charles; PIMMS: John Witham (7); BARKER: Lee Winston; GLEIG: Raymond Cox; MAITLAND: Alexander Orfaly; ROSS: Edwin Steffe (6); PRATT: Richard Chappell; SCOTT: J.T. Cromwell; BUDGEN: Richard Muenz; COCKBURN: Reid Shelton (5); REV. BUSHROD: Bruce A. Hubbard; AUCTIONEER: Lee Winston; JAMES HOBAN: Edwin Steffe (6); ROYAL VISITOR: Randolph Riscol; SECRETARY OF THE SENATE: Howard Ross (11); MR. HENRY: Lee Winston; SENATOR ROSCOE CONKLING: Reid Shelton (5); BABCOCK: Lee Winston; JUDGE: Edwin Steffe (6); SINGERS: Raymond Bazemore, Elaine Bunse, Nancy Callman, Richard Chappell, Walter Charles, Raymond Cox, J.T. Cromwell, Beth Fowler, Carl Hall, Louise Heath, Bruce A. Hubbard, Kris Karlowski, Urylee Leonardos, Joyce McDonald, Janette Moody, Richard Muenz, Sharon Powers, Cornel J. Richie, Randolph Riscol, Martha Thigpen, Lee Winston; DANCERS: Jo-Ann Baldo, Clyde-Jacques Barrett, Joella Breedlove, Allyne De Chalus, Linda Griffin, Bob Heath, Michael Lichtefeld, Diana Mirras, Hector Jaime Mercado (9), Cleveland Pennington, Al Perryman, Renee Rose, Juliet Seignious, Thomas J. Stanton, Clayton Strange, Mimi B. Wallace. *Understudies:* President: Richard Chappell; First Lady: Beth Fowler; Lud: J. Edwards Adams; Seena: Louise Heath; Little Lud: Karl M. Horton. *Swings:* Leah Randolph & Martial Roumain. *Act I:* Overture, "Rehearse! (It's Gonna Be Great)" (President, First Lady, Lud, Seena, Company), "If I Was a Dove" (Little Lud), "(On) Ten Square Miles by the Potomac River" (President Washington & Delegates), "Welcome Home, Miz Adams" (Henry, Rachel, Staff), "Take Care of This House" (Mrs. Adams, Little Lud, President Adams, Staff), "The President Jefferson Sunday Luncheon Party March" (President Jefferson, Little Lud, Guests), "Seena" (Lud), "Sonatina (The British)" (Cockburn, Officers, Citizens): Allegro con brio, Tempo di menuetto (including an authentic harmonization of "To Anacreon in Heav'n," 1740, later known as "The Star Spangled Banner," Rondo [end of Sonatina], Lud's Wedding (Lud, Seena, Staff) [added just before Broadway], "I Love My Wife" (Lud, Seena, Staff) [added just before Broadway], "Auctions" (Auctioneer & Buyers) [added just before Broadway], "The Little White Lie" (President & Eliza Monroe) [before Broadway this number replaced "Monroviad" (President & Mrs. Monroe)], "We Must Have a Ball" (President Buchanan), The Ball (Company), "Take Care of This House" (reprise) (Company) [this reprise was cut before Broadway]. *Act II:* Entr'acte; "Forty Acres and a Mule" (Lud, Seena, Staff), "Bright and Black" (Seena & Staff), "Duet for One (The First Lady of the Land)" (Julia Grant, Lucy Hayes, Company), "American Dreaming" (Lud & Seena) [cut before Broadway], "When We Were

Proud" (Lud, Seena, Little Lud) [cut before Broadway], "The Robber-Baron Minstrel Parade" (Conkling & Minstrels), "Pity the Poor" (Minstrels), "The Mark of a Man" (President Arthur) [cut before Broadway], "The Red, White and Blue" (Minstrels), "I Love This Land" (President), "Rehearse! (It's Gonna Be Great)" (reprise) (Company).

It was roundly panned on Broadway. Leonard Bernstein refused to allow the score to be recorded.

After Broadway. KENNEDY CENTER, Washington, DC, 1992. PRESENTED BY Indiana University Opera Theatre; DIRECTOR: Erik Haagensen; CHOREOGRAPHERS: Robert Sullivan & Sean Watters; MUSICAL DIRECTORS: Robert E. Stoll & Michael Butterman. *Cast:* PRESIDENT: William Schumacher; PRESIDENT'S WIFE: Kathryn Foss-Pittman; LUD: Alfred Bailey; SEENA: Angela Brown. Prelude, "Me," "On Ten Square Miles by the Potomac River," "If I Was a Dove," "The Nation that Wasn't There," "Welcome Home, Miz Adams," "Take Care of This House," "President Jefferson Sunday Luncheon Party March," "Seena," "Sonatina," "What Happened?," "Lud's Wedding" ("I Love My Wife"), "Auctions," "Monroviad," "This Time," "We Must Have a Ball," "Philadelphia," "Uncle Tom's Funeral"/"Bright and Black," "Duet for One," "First Lady of the Land," "Hail," "Money Lovin' Minstrel Show," "Pity the Poor," "Grand Ol' Party," "The Red White and Blues," "American Dreaming," "Voices that Live in the Walls," "To Make Us Proud."

641. *Skyscraper*

The action took place yesterday in New York City, and in and around a large skyscraper and a very small brownstone. Georgina daydreams about all the men she meets. She is reluctant to sell her brownstone and antique shop to a developer who wants to put up a skyscraper in its place.

Before Broadway. Originally Nanette Fabray was to have starred. Then Rodgers and Hammerstein became interested in the property; then producers Cy Feuer and Ernest Martin announced that Cy Coleman and Carolyn Leigh would write the score for Carol Channing. However, Peter Stone eventually wrote the libretto, with a score by Jimmy Van Heusen and Sammy Cahn. Peter Stone combined two properties that Feuer and Martin owned and wanted to produce as musicals—Dream Girl, and an idea that Feuer and Martin had about a woman who owned a house and wouldn't sell to developers. In Detroit, where it tried out, the show was heavily re-written, and began to resemble Elmer Rice's play (Dream Girl) less and less. Victor Spinetti was replaced by Charles Nelson Reilly in the lead. It postponed its Broadway opening in favor of 22 previews in New York. Dorothy Kilgallen, the *Journal American* columnist, wrote a bad review of it on 10/22/65—after seeing a preview, a practice that has never been acceptable. On 11/8/65 Miss Kilgallen died under mysterious circumstances. This was Julie Harris's only Broadway musical.

The Broadway Run. LUNT—FONTANNE THEATRE, 11/13/65–6/11/66. 22 previews from 10/20/65. 241 PERFORMANCES. PRESENTED BY Cy Feuer & Ernest Martin; MUSIC: James Van Heusen; LYRICS: Sammy Cahn; BOOK: Peter Stone; BASED partly on the 1945 comedy *Dream Girl*, by Elmer Rice, and partly on an idea by Cy Feuer & Ernest Martin; DIRECTOR: Cy Feuer; CHOREOGRAPHER: Michael Kidd; SETS/LIGHTING: Robert Randolph; COSTUMES: Theoni V. Aldredge; MUSICAL DIRECTOR: John Lesko; ORCHESTRATIONS: Fred Werner; DANCE MUSIC ARRANGEMENTS: Marvin Laird; CAST RECORDING on Capitol, made on 8/14/65; PRESS: Merle Debuskey, Lawrence Belling, Violet Welles; COMPANY MANAGER: Milton M. Pollack; PRODUCTION STAGE MANAGER: Phil Friedman; STAGE MANAGERS: Jack Leigh, Merritt Thompson, Gene Gavin. *Cast:* GEORGINA ALLERTON: Julie Harris (1) ☆; MRS. ALLERTON: Nancy Cushman (4); MR. ALLERTON: Donald Burr (6); CHARLOTTE: Lesley Stewart (8); MAYOR: Burt Bier; DOCTOR: Richard Korthaze; HERBERT BUSHMAN: Dick O'Neill (5); STANLEY: Rex Everhart (7); TIMOTHY BUSHMAN: Peter L. Marshall (2) ☆; ROGER SUMMERHILL: Charles Nelson Reilly (3) ☆; WOMAN CUSTOMER: Georgia Creighton; AUCTIONEER: Burt Bier; HARRY THE WAITER: John Anania; CAB DRIVER: Ken Ayers; JAZZ MUSICIAN: Walter P. Brown; PHOTOGRAPHER: Christian Gray; APPEARING IN THE FILM SEQUENCE: PAOLA: Pola Chapelle; FRANCESCO:

Paul Sorvino [end of Film sequence]; SINGERS: John Anania, Ken Ayers, Eleanor Bergquist, Burt Bier, Walter P. Brown, Georgia Creighton, Ceil Delli, Christian Gray, Maryann Kerrick, Randy Phillips, Casper Roos; DANCERS: Barbara Beck, Trudy Carson, Ray Chabeau, Marilyn Charles, Suzanne France, Gene Gavin, Ellen Graff, Curtis Hood, Lauren Jones, Gene Kelton, Ray Kirchner, Richard Korthaze, Darrell Notara, Renata Powers, Bill Starr, Kent Thomas. *Standby*: Georgina: Lesley Stewart. *Understudies*: Roger: Christian Gray; Tim: Randy Phillips; Mrs. Allerton: Georgia Creighton; Herbert: Burt Bier; Mr. Allerton: Casper Roos; Stanley: John Anania; Charlotte: Maryann Merrick. *Act I*: *Scene 1* Georgina's bedroom: "Occasional Flight of Fancy" (Georgina & Officials); *Scene 2* The construction site; *Scene 3* The Bushman Building; construction shack: "Run for Your Life" (Timothy & Herbert); *Scene 4* The construction site: "Local 403" ("Socially Conscious Iron Workers") (Stanley, Construction Workers, Girls); *Scene 5* Skyscraper — ground level; *Scene 6* The construction site; *Scene 7* The construction shack: "Opposites" (Georgina & Timothy), "Run for Your Life" (reprise) (Timothy); *Scene 8* The construction site; *Scene 9* The Litter Bug (antique shop); *Scene 10* The construction site: "Just the Crust" (Roger & Herbert); *Scene 11* The Litter Bug: "Everybody Has a Right to Be Wrong" (Georgina & Timothy), "Everybody Has a Right to be Wrong" (reprise) (Georgina), "Wrong!" (Georgina, Mrs. Allerton, Charlotte, Customers); *Scene 12* The construction site; *Scene 13* Two phones; *Scene 14* Knickerbocker Auction Galleries: "The Auction" (ballet) (Customers); *Scene 15* Two phones; *Scene 16* Georgina's bedroom at night: "Occasional Flight of Fancy" (reprise) (Georgina). *Act II*: *Scene 1* The Gaiety Delicatessen: "The Gaiety" (Customers); *Scene 2* Limbo; *Scene 3* The film festival; *Scene 4* The construction site; *Scene 5* Atop the unfinished skyscraper: "More than One Way" (Timothy & Construction Workers); *Scene 6* The construction site: "Haute Couture" (Stanley, Models, Construction Workers); *Scene 7* The Litter Bug: "Don't Worry" (Roger & Herbert), "Don't Worry" (reprise) (Georgina & Roger), "I'll Only Miss Her When I Think of Her" (Timothy); *Scene 8* The skyscraper — a dream: "Spare That Building" (Georgina, Timothy, Roger, Company); *Scene 9* The Allerton bedroom.

Finally it opened to pretty good reviews. Michael Kidd's choreography gained plaudits, as did Julie Harris. The show received Tony Nominations for musical, direction of a musical, choreography, sets (actually for Robert Randolph's entire year), and for Julie Harris.

642. *Sleepy Hollow*

Set in the autumn of 1795 in the village of Sleepy Hollow up by the Tappan Zee on the east bank of the Hudson River, near Tarrytown, New York. Timid, lanky schoolmaster Ichabod is the victim of a Headless Horseman practical joke perpetrated by Katrina, who, in a fit of pique at her true love, Bones, had agreed to marry Ichabod, and now wants to drive him (Ichabod) out of town.

The Broadway Run. ST. JAMES THEATRE, 6/3/48–6/12/48. 12 PERFORMANCES. PRESENTED BY Lorraine Lester; MUSIC: George Lessner; LYRICS/BOOK: Russell Maloney & Miriam Battista; ADDITIONAL LYRICS: Ruth Hughes Aarons; SUGGESTED BY Nicholas Bela, "with the assistance of Marc Connelly;" BASED ON the 1819 story *The Legend of Sleepy Hollow*, by Washington Irving; DIRECTORS: John O'Shaughnessy & Marc Connelly; CHOREOGRAPHER: Anna Sokolow; SETS/LIGHTING: Jo Mielziner; COSTUMES: David ffolkes; CONDUCTOR: Irving Actman; ORCHESTRATIONS: Hans Spialek, Ted Royal, George Lessner; CHORAL ARRANGEMENTS: Elie Siegmeister; PRESS: Karl Bernstein & John L. Toohey; COMPANY MANAGER: Joe Moss; STAGE MANAGER: Ed Brinkmann. *Cast:* IKE: William Ferguson; ROELF: Larry Robbins; MRS. VAN BRUNT: Laura Pierpont; MRS. VAN TASSEL: Ruth McDevitt; MRS. VAN RIPPER: Jean Handzlik; WILHELMINA: Ellen Repp; MR. VAN BRUNT: Bert Wilcox; MR. VAN TASSEL: Tom Hoier; MR. VAN RIPPER: Morley Evans; JACOB VAN TASSEL: Bobby White; WILLIE VAN TWILLER: Walter Butterworth; HANS VAN RIPPER: Alan Shay; MARTIN VAN HORSEN: Richard Rhoades; STUYVELING VAN DOORN: Lewis Francis Scholle; TEENA: Doreen Lane; HILDA: Robin Sloane; GRETA: Sylvia Lane; BROM

"BONES" VAN BRUNT: Hayes Gordon (3); KATRINA VAN TASSEL: Betty Jane Watson (2); HENDRICK: Ward Garner; EVA: Mary McCarty (4); LUTHER: Russell George; ICHABOD CRANE: Gil Lamb; ANNIE: Margery Oldroyd; LENA: Peggy Ferris; NICK: Franklin Wagner; PIET: Shaun O'Brien; BALT: Ray Drakeley; WALT: James Starbuck; CHRIS: John Ward; BERTHA: Margaret Ritter; MARGARET: Jo Sullivan; ELIZABETH: Kaja Sumdsten; JENNY: Ann Dunbar; MR. VAN HOOTEN: Ken Foley; JOOST: John Russel; CONSCIENCE: Ty Kearney; INDIAN: Kenneth Remo; COTTON MATHER: William Mende; LADY FROM NEW HAVEN: Dorothy Bird; VILLAGE GIRLS WHO DANCE: Aza Bard, Clara Courdery, Ann Dunbar, Kate Friedlich, Saida Gerrard, Carmella Gutierrez, Margaret McCallion, Kaja Sumdsten; VILLAGE BOYS WHO DANCE: Alex Dunaeff, Don Farnworth, Jay Lloyd, Remi Martel, Joseph Milan, Shaun O'Brien, Franklin Wagner, John Ward; VILLAGE GIRLS WHO SING: Ilona Albok, Joan Barrett, Peggy Ferris, Deda La Petina, Margery Oldroyd, Margaret Ritter, Janice Sprei, Jo Sullivan; VILLAGE BOYS WHO SING: Ray Drakeley, William Ferguson, Ken Foley, Russell George, Vincent Lubrano, William Mende, Larry Robbins, John Russel; VILLAGE CHILDREN: Walter Butterworth, Doreen Lane, Sylvia Lane, Richard Rhoades, Lewis Francis Scholle, Alan Shay, Robin Sloane. *Standbys*: Lady from New Haven: Kate Friedlich; Walt: Alex Dunaeff. *Understudies*: Katrina: Margaret Ritter; Eva: Peggy Ferris; Bones: Russell George; Hendrick: Kenneth Remo; Ichabod: Ty Kearney; Conscience: John Russel; Indian: Larry Robbins. *Act I*: *Scene 1* The churchyard at the crossroads of the village; noontime: "Time Stands Still" (Villagers), "I Still Have Plenty to Learn" (Bones), "Ask Me Again" (Katrina), "I Still Have Plenty to Learn" (reprise) (Bones & Katrina), "Never Let Her Go" (Villagers), "There's History to Be Made" (l: Russell Maloney, Miriam Battista, Ruth Hughes Aarons) (Ichabod); *Scene 2* The river bank; the following morning: "Here and Now" (Bones & Katrina), Dance (Lady from New Haven & Walt); *Scene 3* The schoolroom in a clearing; later that morning: "Why Was I Born on a Farm?" (l: Ruth Hughes Aarons) (Eva), "If" (Ichabod); *Scene 4* Kitchen of the Van Tassel house; the following morning: "My Lucky Lover" (Katrina, Wilhelmina, Eva, Sleepy Hollow Girls), "A Musical Lesson" (Ichabod); *Scene 5* The river bank; several days later: "You've Got That Kind of a Face" (Hendrick & Eva), Couple Dance: 1ST COUPLE: Clara Courdery & Jay Lloyd; 2ND COUPLE: Aza Bard & Joseph Milan; 3RD COUPLE: Kate Friedlich & Alex Dunaeff; GIRL WITH A FLOWER: Kaja Sumdsten; *Scene 6* The churchyard; Sunday evening: "I'm Lost" (l: Ruth Hughes Aarons) (Bones), "Goodnight" (Villagers), "The Englishman's Head" (Wilhelmina, Bones, Villagers). *Act II*: *Scene 1* The Van Tassel barn: "Pedro, Ichabod" (Bones, Walt, Village Boys), "Poor Man" (l: Russell Maloney, Miriam Battista, Ruth Hughes Aarons) (Ichabod), "The Things that Lovers Say" (Katrina), "I'm Lost" (reprise) (Bones); *Scene 2* The attic room in Eva's house; that night: "Ichabod" (Conscience, Indian, Mather), Dance (Lady from New Haven); *Scene 3* The kitchen of the Van Tassel house; the following night: "Bouree" (dance) (Village Dancers); *Scene 4* The churchyard; that night: "Headless Horseman Ballet" (Ichabod & Village Dancers); *Scene 5* The churchyard; the following morning: "The Gray Goose" (Jacob & Ensemble).

Broadway reviews were terrible. This show succeeded *Oklahoma!* at the St. James. Jo Mielziner won a Tony for sets (really it was for his entire season, which also included *South Pacific* and *Death of a Salesman*). Miriam Battista was married to Russell Maloney.

643. *Small Wonder*

An intimate musical revue in which, among other things, Mary McCarty satirized Lana Turner, Lauren Bacall, Lizabeth Scott and Dorothy Lamour.

The Broadway Run. CORONET THEATRE, 9/15/48–1/8/49. 134 PERFORMANCES. PRESENTED BY George Nichols III; MUSIC: Baldwin Bergersen & Albert Selden; LYRICS: Phyllis McGinley & Billings Brown (who was really Burt Shevelove); SKETCHES: Charles Spalding, Max Wilk, George Axelrod, Louis Laun; DIRECTOR: Burt Shevelove; CHOREOGRAPHER: Gower Champion; SETS/LIGHTING: Ralph Alswang; COSTUMES: John Derro; MUSICAL DIRECTOR: William Parson; ORCHESTRATIONS: Ted Royal; VOCAL ARRANGEMENTS: Herbert Greene; PRESS: Philip

Bloom & David Lipsky; GENERAL MANAGER: Samuel H. Schwartz; COMPANY MANAGER: Phil Adler; STAGE MANAGERS: John E. Sola, Tony Albert, Mort Marshall. *Act I: Scene 1* "Count Your Blessings" (m: Bergersen; l: McGinley) (Entire Company); *Scene 2* The Normal Neurotic [Tom Ewell (1) in a recurring sketch]; *Scene 3* "The Commuters' Song" ("Between the 5:08 and the 8:01") (m: Bergersen; l: McGinley) (Marilyn Day & Alan Ross); *Scene 4* "A Ballad for Billionaires" (m: Selden; l: Brown) (about rich southwesterners): JUNIOR: Chandler Cowles, *Jim Kirkwood*; POP: Mort Marshall; LOUISE VAN STEELE: Mary McCarty (3); CLINT LARUE: Hayes Gordon; *Scene 5* "No Time" (m: Bergersen; l: McGinley) (musical development for dance: Richard Priborsky). FIRST VARIATION: Jonathan Lucas & Kate Friedlich; SECOND VARIATION: Tommy Rall & Evelyn Taylor; THIRD VARIATION: J.C. McCord & Joan Mann; *Scene 6* The Human Body [Tom Ewell (1)]; *Scene 7* "Flaming Youth" (m: Selden; l: Brown) [Mary McCarty (3), in a Clara Bow routine) [the showstopper]; *Scene 8* D-e-m-ocracy (Alice Pearce as a European peasant responding to lessons in democracy as presented by Tom Ewell in radio soap operas): THE NORMAL NEUROTIC: Tom Ewell (1); THE WIFE: Alice Pearce (2); THE HUSBAND: Mort Marshall; *Scene 9* "Show Off" (m: Selden; l: Brown) (musical development for dance: Richard Priborsky) (a young man performs before a shaving mirror and his younger sister) (danced by Tommy Rall) (also with Marilyn Day); *Scene 10* I Could Write a Book (satire on best-sellers): THE NORMAL NEUROTIC: Tom Ewell (1); 1/ MOM: Alice Pearce (2); JOEY: Jonathan Lucas; GABBY: Joan Mann; 2/ EDDIE: Chandler Cowles, *Jim Kirkwood*; DOLORES: Marilyn Day; 3/ JOY POLLOI: Mary McCarty (3); CZAR NICHOLAS: Mort Marshall; *Scene 11* "Badaroma" (m: Selden; l: Brown) (J.C. McCord & Entire Company). *Act II: Scene 1* "Nobody Told Me" (m: Bergersen; l: McGinley): THE BRIDE: Joan Diener (4); THE GROOM: Hayes Gordon; THE MAID OF HONOR: Devida Stewart, *Sue Benjamin*; THE BEST MAN: Alan Ross; THE MOTHER: Alice Pearce (2); THE BRIDESMAIDS: Mary McCarty (3), Marilyn Day, Virginia Oswald; THE USHERS: Jonathan Lucas, Jack Cassidy, Bill Ferguson (*Scott Merrill*); *Scene 2* The Civilized Thing (by Richard F. Maury) [Tom Ewell (1)]; *Scene 3* "Pistachio" (m/l: Mark Lawrence) (about ice-cream flavors) [Alice Pearce (2) & Mort Marshall]; *Scene 4* "When I Fall in Love" (m/l: Selden) (musical development for dance: Richard Priborsky) (danced by Jonathan Lucas & Kate Friedlich; assisted by Joan Mann, Evelyn Taylor, Tommy Rall, J.C. McCord); *Scene 5* (This is an Adv.) (satire on the ads in the *Saturday Evening Post*): THE NORMAL NEUROTIC: Tom Ewell (1); *Scene 6* "Saturday's Child" (m: Bergersen; l: McGinley) [Mary McCarty (3)]; *Scene 7* "William McKinley High" (m: Selden; l: Brown) [Marilyn Day, Jonathan Lucas, Tommy Rall, Jack Cassidy, Chandler Cowles (*Jim Kirkwood*), Mort Marshall, Alan Ross]; *Scene 8* The Happy Ending: 1/ SMALL BOY: Tom Ewell (1); NINA: Joan Mann; 2/ MAURICE: Tom Ewell (1); BERYL: Alice Pearce; ELVIRA: Kate Friedlich; 3/ NICK: Tom Ewell (1); THE KID: Mary McCarty (3); HER BROTHER: Tommy Rall; TONY AKIMBO: Jack Cassidy; "From A to Z" (m: Selden; l: Brown)] [Mary McCarty (3), Jack Cassidy, the Megalo-Golden-Mania Girls]; *Scene 9* "Just an Ordinary Guy" (m: Selden; l: McGinley & Brown) (Virginia Oswald & Entire Company).

This was Gower Champion's Broadway debut as a choreographer. Broadway reviews were middle-of-the-road and divided. The top ticket prices were $6.

644. *Smile*

A musical satire. Contestants for the state finals of the *Young American Miss* pageant are put through their paces. Robin, smart and out of place, rooms with Doria, a devout believer in beauty pageants who comes from a broken home, a perpetual loser. Brenda is a former YAM winner; her husband is Big Bob, who is also one of the judges. Doria loses in the preliminaries, and decides to teach Robin how to win, urging her to use her fatherlessness to win points with the judges. Another girl finds the opportunity she's been looking for to humiliate Maria, a fellow contestant who won the talent competition, when she finds Brenda's son taking pictures of the girls showering. Brenda, under

consideration for the position of national pageant spokeswoman, saves the day after Maria's humiliation, and gets the job; Robin, following Doria's advice, loses; Doria is runner-up; Brenda and Big Bob go home to work on their family problems; Robin, goes home with her mother; Doria goes on to the next pageant, still hoping to win.

Before Broadway. Carolyn Leigh wrote the original lyrics to *Smile*, and Marvin Hamlisch wrote the music to them (he also wrote the music for the movie). Howard Ashman was turned down as librettist, and Thomas Meehan got the job. Jack Heifner then wrote a new book, and this was the version that played at a 1983 workshop. DIRECTOR/CHOREOGRAPHER: Graciela Daniele. *Cast*: Maureen McGovern, Trini Alvarado, Grover Dale, Jane Krakowski, Saundra Santiago. Carolyn Leigh died shortly thereafter. Jack Heifner's book was considered too unsympathetic, and Neil Simon came close to writing a new libretto. Howard Ashman finally did write a new libretto, and lyrics, and also directed (his Broadway debut). Marvin Hamlisch decided to write an entirely new musical score, keeping only the melody from the title number. In late 1985 a new workshop was produced, after which the Shuberts and David Geffen withdrew as producers. With new producers it tried out in Baltimore. Incidentally, the TV program *60 Minutes* was following every move the show made, from workshop to tryouts to Broadway.

The Broadway Run. LUNT—FONTANNE THEATRE, 11/24/86–1/3/87. 11 previews. 48 PERFORMANCES. PRESENTED BY Lawrence Gordon, Richard M. Kagan, Sidney L. Shlenker; MUSIC: Marvin Hamlisch; LYRICS/BOOK: Howard Ashman; BASED ON the 1975 movie *Smile*, written by Jerry Belson; DIRECTOR: Howard Ashman; CHOREOGRAPHER: Mary Kyte; SETS: Douglas W. Schmidt; COSTUMES: William Ivey Long; LIGHTING: Paul Gallo; SOUND: Otts Munderloh; MUSICAL DIRECTOR: Paul Gemignani; ORCHESTRATIONS: Sid Ramin, Bill Byers, Dick Hazard, Torrie Zito; VOCAL ARRANGEMENTS: Buster Davis; PRESS: The Fred Nathan Company; CASTING: Albert Tavares; GENERAL MANAGEMENT: Gatchell & Neufeld; COMPANY MANAGER: Roger Gindi; PRODUCTION STAGE MANAGER: Alan Hall; STAGE MANAGER: Ruth E. Rinklin; ASSISTANT STAGE MANAGERS: Paul Mills Holmes & Betsy Nicholson. *Cast*: CONTESTANTS: ROBIN GIBSON, ANTELOPE VALLEY: Anne Marie Bobby (3); DORIA HUDSON, YUBA CITY: Jodi Benson (4); SANDRA-KAY MACAFFEE, BAKERSFIELD: Veanne Cox (7); MARIA GONZALES, SALINAS: Cheryl-Ann Rossi (5); SHAWN CHRISTIANSON, LA JOLLA: Tia Riebling (6); VALERIE SHERMAN, SACRAMENTO: Lauren Goler (8); HEIDI ANDERSON, ANAHEIM: Deanna D. Wells; PATTI-LYNN BIRD, EL CENTRO: Mana Allen; DEBRALEE DAVIS, EUREKA: Andrea Leigh-Smith; KATE GARDNER, FRESNO: Mia Malm; LINDA LEE, SAN FRANCISCO: Valerie Lau-Kee; KIMBERLY LYONS, PALO ALTO: Julie Tussey; GINA MINELLI, SAN LUIS OBISPO: Donna Marie Elio; DANA SIMPSON, SAUSALITO: Renee Veneziale; CONNIE-SUE WHIPPLE, VISALIA: Cindy Oakes; COOKIE WILSON, CARSON: Nikki Rene; ... AND LAST YEAR'S WINNER, JOANNE MARSHAL: Mia Malm; ADULTS: BRENDA DiCARLO FREELANDER: Marsha Waterbury (1); BIG BOB FREELANDER: Jeff McCarthy (2); TOMMY FRENCH, THE PAGEANT CHOREOGRAPHER: Michael O'Gorman (9); DALE WILSON-SHEARS, CHAIRMAN OF THE *Young American Miss* FOUNDATION: Richard Woods (10); TED FARLEY, AN MC: Dick Patterson (11); CAROL, BRENDA'S ASSISTANT: Ruth Williamson; TONY, A VOLUNTEER: Jeffrey Wilkins; OTHER VOLUNTEERS: Laura Gardner & KC Wilson; ROBIN'S MOM: Laura Gardner; PHOTOGRAPHER: KC Wilson; KIDS: LITTLE BOB FREELANDER: Tommy Daggett; FREDDY: Andrew Cassese; JUDGES: Laura Gardner & KC Wilson. *Understudies*: Brenda: Joyce Nolen; Big Bob: Jeffrey Wilkins; Robin: Mana Allen & Susan Dow; Doria: Donna Marie Elio & Deanna D. Wells; Ted/Dale: KC Wilson; Maria: Donna Marie Elio & Nikki Rene; Shawn: Lauren Goler & Deanna D. Wells; Sandra-Kay: Susan Dow & Cindy Oakes; Valerie: Andrea Leigh-Smith & Mia Malm; Tommy: Michael Bologna. *Swings*: Michael Bologna, Susan Dow, Linda Hess, Woody Howard, Joyce Nolen. *Orchestra*: John Beal, Michael Berkowitz, Francis Bonny, Anthony Cecere, Nick Cerrato, Andy Drelles, Dennis Elliot, Eileen M. Folson, Jack Gale, Clarissa Howell, Al Hunt, Stephen Marzullo, Ronald Melrose, John J. Moses, Brian O'Flaherty, Caryl Paisner, Dean Plank, Marilyn Reynolds, Gene Scholtens, Les Scott, Ron Sell, Steve Uscher, Lorraine Wolf, Ann Yarbrough. *Act I* Santa Rosa Junior College; three days last summer: Prologue (Contestants), "Orientation/Postcard # 1" (Brenda, Robin, Contestants), "Disneyland" (Doria), "Shine" (Contestants, Tommy, Brenda), "Postcard # 2" (Robin), "Nerves" (Contestants), "Young and American" (Preliminary Night) (Contestants), "Until Tomorrow Night" (Contestants, Brenda, Big Bob). *Act II* Santa Rosa Junior College; Saturday night: "Postcard # 3/Dressing Room Scene" (Robin, Doria, Ted, Contestants), "Smile" (Ted & Contestants), "In Our Hands" (Contestants), "Pretty as a Picture" (Ted, Big Bob, Robin, Contestants).

The show got bad reviews. The book was nominated for a Tony.

645. *Smokey Joe's Cafe*

Also called: *Smokey Joe's Cafe: the Songs of Leiber and Stoller.* A musical revue that showcased the award-winning songs of Leiber & Stoller.

Before Broadway. Jack and Tom Viertel went to see a review of Leiber & Stoller songs, called *Smokey Joe's Cafe: a New Rhythm 'n' Blues Revue,* written and directed by M. Burke Walter, at EMPTY SPACE THEATRE, in Seattle, didn't care for it too much, but did see the potential in doing a show featuring the songs of those legendary tunesmiths. It began as a workshop in New York, directed by Australian Stephen Helper. Its first full production was at the ROYAL GEORGE THEATRE, Chicago, where it opened in 7/94 as *Baby, That's Rock 'n' Roll.* DIRECTOR: Otis Sallid. Then, after revisions and a name change, it moved to the AHMANSON/DOOLITTLE THEATRES, Los Angeles, in 11/94. PRESENTED BY the Center Theatre Group. At this stage Jerry Zaks came in as director, and Joey McKneely as choreographer. It had the same crew as for the subsequent Broadway run; it had the same cast too, except Robert Torti (replaced for Broadway by Michael Park).

The Broadway Run. VIRGINIA THEATRE, 3/2/95–1/16/00. 24 previews from 2/8/95. 2,036 PERFORMANCES. The Center Theatre Group production, PRESENTED BY Richard Frankel, Thomas Viertel, Steven Baruch, Jujamcyn Theatres/Jack Viertel, Rick Steiner, Frederic H. Mayerson, Center Theatre Group/Ahmanson Theatre/Gordon Davidson; MUSIC/LYRICS: Jerry Leiber & Mike Stoller; ORIGINAL CONCEPT: Stephen Helper, Jack Viertel, Otis Sallid; DIRECTOR: Jerry Zaks; CHOREOGRAPHER: Joey McKneely; ADDITIONAL CHOREOGRAPHY: Otis Sallid; SETS: Heidi Landesman; COSTUMES: William Ivey Long; LIGHTING: Timothy Hunter; SOUND: Tony Meola; CONDUCTOR/ARRANGEMENTS: Louis St. Louis; ORCHESTRATIONS: Steve Margoshes; CAST RECORDING on Atlantic; PRESS: Boneau/Bryan-Brown; CASTING: Peter Wise & Associates; GENERAL MANAGEMENT: Richard Frankel Productions; COMPANY MANAGER: Laura Green, *Jessica R. Jenen*; PRODUCTION STAGE MANAGER: Kenneth Hanson; STAGE MANAGER: Maximo Torres; ASSISTANT STAGE MANAGER: Mary MacLeod, *Ira Mont & Lisa Dawn Cave.* **Cast:** Ken Ard, Adrian Bailey, Brenda Braxton, Victor Trent Cook (gone by 96–97; *James Beeks* from 9/8/97; *Victor Trent Cook* from 10/6/98), B.J. Crosby (*D'Atra Hicks* during Miss Crosby's vacation, 9/97, and permanently from 1/3/98; *B.J. Crosby* from 10/6/98), Pattie Darcy Jones (*Terri Dixon; Deb Lyons* by 9/99), DeLee Lively (*Natasha Rennalls* by 96–97, when Miss Lively went to open the London production; *Paige Price* from 96–97; *DeLee Lively* from 6/97), Frederick B. Owens, Michael Park (*Jerry Tellier* from 9/9/97; *Matt Bogart* by 9/99), *Billy Porter* (added by 12/96; *Bobby Daye* from 6/97), *Robert Neary* (added by 12/96), *Bobby Daye* (added by 12/96), *Devin Richards.* **Celebrity Guests:** Ben E. King (6/23/98–6/28/98; 12/15/98–12/27/98), Lou Rawls (4/6/99–4/18/99), Gladys Knight (5/11/99–5/22/99), Tony Orlando (6/8/99–6/20/99), Lesley Gore (7/13/99–7/25/99), Gloria Gaynor (8/3/99–8/15/99), Gladys Knight (8/17/99–8/29/99), Rick Springfield (10/19/99–10/31/99). **Standbys:** For Mr. Cook/Mr. Park: Bobby Daye (95–99); For Mr. Ard/Mr. Bailey/Mr. Owens: Kevyn Morrow (95–96), For Miss Braxton/Miss Lively: *April Nixon* (95–96); For Miss Crosby/Miss Jones: *Monica Page* (95–96); *David Bedella* (96–98); For Miss Lively: *Natasha Rennalls* (from 6/97); *J.C. Montgomery* (by 96–99); *Ramona Keller* (98–99); *Paige Price, Charles E. Wallace, Devin Richards* (98–99); *Rick Springfield, Jerry Tellier, D'Atra Hicks, Michael Demby-Cain* (98–99); *Virginia Woodruff* (98–99); *Marlayna Sims* (98–99); *Colleen Hawks* (98–99). **Understudies:** Felicia Finley (by 96–99), *Stacy Francis* (by 96–98), *Cee-Cee Harshaw* (96–98). **The Band**— The

Night Managers: PIANO: Louis St. Louis; SYNTHESIZER: David Keyes; BASS: Frank Canino; DRUMS: Brian Brake; GUITARS: Drew Zingg; SAXOPHONES: Chris Eminizer; PERCUSSION: Frank Pagano. *Act I:* "Neighborhood" (m/l: L/S & Ralph Dino, 1974) (Company), "Young Blood" (m/l: L/S & Doc Pomus, 1957) (Adrian, with Fred, Ken, Victor), "Falling" (1957) (DeLee), "Ruby Baby" (1955) (Michael, with Adrian, Fred, Ken, Victor), "Dance with Me" (m/l: L/S & Louis Lebish, George Treadwell, Irv Nathan, 1959) (Ken & B.J., with Adrian, Fred, Victor), "Neighborhood" (reprise) (B.J., Brenda, DeLee, Pattie), "Keep on Rollin'" (1961) (Victor, Adrian, Ken, Fred), "Searchin'" (1957) (Victor, with Adrian, Ken, Fred), "Kansas City" (1952) (B.J., Pattie, Michael), "Trouble" (1958) (DeLee & Brenda), "Love Me" (1954)/ "Don't" (Adrian & Pattie), "Fools Fall in Love" (1957) (B.J.), "Poison Ivy" (1959) (Ken, with Adrian, Fred, Victor), "Don Juan" (1961) (Brenda), "Shoppin' for Clothes" (m/l: L/S & Kent Harris, 1960) (Victor & Fred, with Adrian, Ken, Michael), "I Keep Forgettin'" (1962) (Pattie), "On Broadway" (m/l: L/S & Barry Mann & Cynthia Weil, 1962) (Adrian, Fred, Ken, Victor), "D.W. Washburn" (1968) (Victor & Company), "Saved" (1961) (B.J. & Company). *Act II:* "That is Rock 'n Roll" (1959) (Company), "Yakety Yak" (1958) (Company), "Charlie Brown" (1959) (Company), "Stay a While" (1959) (Louis, with Dave on synthesizer), "Pearl's a Singer" (m/l: L/S & Ralph Dino, John Sembello, 1974) (Pattie), "Teach Me How to Shimmy" (1961) (Michael & DeLee, with Adrian & Victor), "You're the Boss" (1961) (Fred & Brenda), "Smokey Joe's Cafe" (1955) (Fred & Company), "Loving You" (1957) (Ken & Company), "Treat Me Nice" (1957) (Victor), "Hound Dog" (1956) (B.J.), "Little Egypt" (1961) (Fred, with Adrian, Ken, Michael, Victor), "I'm a Woman" (1961) (B.J., Brenda, DeLee, Pattie), "There Goes My Baby" (m/l: L/S & Benjamin Nelson, Lover Patterson, George Treadwell, 1962) (Adrian, with Fred, Ken, Michael, Victor), "Love Potion # 9" (1959) (Adrian, with Fred, Ken, Michael, Victor), "Some Cats Know" (1966) (Brenda), "Jailhouse Rock" (1957) (Michael & Company), "Fools Fall in Love" (reprise) (B.J.), "Spanish Harlem" (m/l: Phil Spector & Jerry Leiber, 1960) (Ken & Brenda), "I (Who Have Nothing)" (m/l: L/S & Mogol & Carlo Donida) (Victor), "Neighborhood" (reprise) (Pattie), "Stand by Me" (m/l: L/S & Ben E. King, 1961) (Adrian & Company), "That is Rock & Roll" (reprise) (Company).

Note: The musical numbers were subject to change.

Note: All songs have music and lyrics by Jerry Leiber & Mike Stoller (L/S) alone, unless otherwise stated.

Broadway reviews were divided, mostly favorable. After a shaky start, it was helped by Tony nominations for musical, direction of a musical, choreography, and for Victor Trent Cook, Brenda Braxton, B.J. Crosby, DeLee Lively. It was also helped by having new money pumped in (it cost $5.5 million). It became the surprise hit of the 94–95 Broadway year. On 6/2/99 it became the longest-running musical revue in Broadway history, with 1,775 performances (beating *Dancin's* 1,774). In 1998 Ben E. King was the first of a string of guest celebrities drafted to boost box-office sales. Aside from those guests mentioned above in the cast, Joan Jett was going to be one of them, but backed out. On 9/24/99 closing announcements were made for 1/16/00. By the end of 2002 it was still the 22nd-longest show of any kind in Broadway history. HBO taped a performance during the run, and showed it in early 2003.

After Broadway. TOUR. Opened on 8/16/96, in Minneapolis, and ran for a year. *Cast:* Eugene Fleming, Darrian C. Ford, Trent Kendall (*Dwayne Clark* from 4/14/97), Reva Rice, Alltrinna Grayson, Kim Cea, Mary Ann Hermansen, Jerry Tellier, Ashley Howard Wilkinson.

PRINCE OF WALES THEATRE, London, 10/23/96. It got good reviews. *Cast:* DeLee Lively, Victor Trent Cook.

SPHERE THEATRE, Tokyo, 4/18/98–4/29/98.

LUCILLE LORTEL THEATRE, Off Broadway, Spring 2003. PRESENTED BY Inside Broadway. A special 50-minute edition, weekends only.

646. *Something More!*

Carol is the wife of best-selling novelist Bill who becomes discontented with the Long Island suburb of Mineola, and takes the family off to Italy to look for something more. They're tempted by jet-setters, but eventually return to Long Island. The Marchesa is a sculptress who attempts to seduce Bill.

Before Broadway. This was one of the three 1964 musicals produced by Lester Osterman and Jule Styne and financed by ABC — Paramount (see *High Spirits* for more details). It was almost going to be called by the novel's title (*Portofino, P.T.A.*), but someone remembered a flop musical called *Portofino*, and the name was changed. Florence Henderson was the first choice for the role Barbara Cook finally took. The show tried out at the Shubert Theatre, Philadelphia, 9/28/64–10/24/64. It was here that Joe Layton replaced Jule Styne as director (but took no credit). Joan Copeland replaced Viveca Lindfors.

The Broadway Run. EUGENE O'NEILL THEATRE, 11/10/64–11/21/64. 14 previews from 10/28/64. 15 PERFORMANCES. PRESENTED by Lester Osterman (and Jule Styne, with ABC — Paramount); MUSIC: Sammy Fain (helped by Jule Styne); LYRICS: Marilyn & Alan Bergman; BOOK: Nate Monaster; BASED ON the 1962 novel *Portofino P.T.A.*, by Gerald Green; DIRECTOR: Jule Styne; CHOREOGRAPHER: Bob Herget; SETS/LIGHTING: Robert Randolph; COSTUMES: Alvin Colt; MUSICAL DIRECTOR: Oscar Kosarin; ORCHESTRATIONS: Ralph Burns; VOCAL DIRECTOR/VOCAL ARRANGEMENTS: Buster Davis; DANCE MUSIC ARRANGEMENTS: Robert Prince; CAST RECORDING on ABC — Paramount; PRESS: Harvey B. Sabinson, Lee Solters, Leo Stern; GENERAL MANAGER: Richard Horner; COMPANY MANAGER: Nicholas A.B. Gray; PRODUCTION STAGE MANAGER: Jose Vega; STAGE MANAGERS: Max Evans & Richard Lyle. *Cast:* BILL DEEMS: Arthur Hill (1) ✩; CAROL DEEMS: Barbara Cook (2) ✩; SUZY DEEMS: Neva Small; FREDDY DEEMS: Kenny Kealy; ADAM DEEMS: Eric White; JULIE: Katey O'Brady; DICK: Hal Linden; GLADYS: Marilyn Murphy; JOE SANTINI: Rico Froehlich (8); TONY SANTINI: Victor R. Helou (7); POLICEMAN: Rico Froehlich; MRS. FERENZI: Peg Murray (5); MONTE CHECKOVITCH: Ronny Graham (4); LUIGI: Victor R. Helou (7); LEPESCU: Michael Kermoyan (6); MARCHESA VALENTINA CRESPI: Joan Copeland (3); TONY: Chris Man; MARIA: Katey O'Brady; THE KING: Taylor Reed; THE KING'S COMPANION: Connie Sanchez; MR. VELOZ: Jo Jo Smith (9); MRS. VELOZ: Paula Kelly; COMMANDATORE VERMELLI: James Lavery; CLUBWOMAN: Laurie Franks; DANCERS: Joan Bell, Bob Bishop, Shari Greene, Steve Jacobs, Lynn Kollenberg, Richard Lyle, Barry Preston, Connie Sanchez, Bill Starr, Mimi Wallace; SINGERS: Natalie Di Silvio, Laurie Franks, Bobbi Lange, James Lavery, Marilyn Murphy, Taylor Reed, Ed Varrato. *Understudies:* Bill/Monte: Hal Linden; Carol/Marchesa: Laurie Franks; Lepescu: Rico Froehlich; Mrs. Ferenzi: Bobbi Lange; Joe/Policeman: James Lavery; Tony/Luigi: Ed Varrato; Mr. Veloz: Bill Starr; Mrs. Veloz: Connie Sanchez; Freddy/Adam: Christopher Man; Suzy: Katey O'Brady. *Act I: Scene 1* The Deems' living room, Mineola, New York; *Scene 2* Same; a few days later; *Scene 3* Mineola, New York to Portofino, Italy; *Scene 4* The villa, Portofino; *Scene 5* Portofino Square; *Scene 6* The road to the monastery; *Scene 7* The old monastery; *Scene 8* The villa. *Act II: Scene 1* "Bill Remembers;" later that night; *Scene 2* In front of the marchesa's studio; *Scene 3* The marchesa's studio; *Scene 4* In front of the marchesa's studio; *Scene 5* The villa; *Scene 6* The road to the beach; *Scene 7* The beach; dawn; *Scene 8* The road to the villa; *Scene 9* The villa. *Act I:* "Something More!" (Bill), "Who Fills the Bill? (Carol, Suzy, Freddy, Adam, Dick, Committee Members), "The Straw that Broke the Camel's Back" (Bill), "Better All the Time" (Carol), "Don't Make a Move" (Santini Brothers), "Don't Make a Move" (reprise) (Santini Brothers, Portofino Branch), "No Questions" (Carol), "Church of My Choice" (Checkovitch), "Jaded, Degraded Am I!" (Checkovitch), "I've Got Nothin' to Do" (Carol, Mrs. Ferenzi, Suzy, Freddy, Adam), "I've Got Nothin' to Do" (reprise) (Mrs. Ferenzi), "Party Talk" (Guests), "In No Time at All" (Marchesa), "The Master of the Greatest Art of All" (Lepescu), "Grazie per Niente" (Checkovitch, Carol, Mr. & Mrs. Veloz, Guests), "I Feel Like New Year's Eve" (Carol), "One Long Last Look" (Carol). *Act II:* "Ode to a Key" (Bill), "Bravo, Bravo, Novelisto" (Bill, Policeman, Luigi), "Life is Too Short" (Checkovitch & Mrs. Ferenzi), "Il Lago de' Innamorati" (beach dance composed/arr by Robert Prince) (Mr. & Mrs. Veloz, Ensemble), "Mineola" (Carol), "Come Sta?" (Mrs. Ferenzi, Suzy, Freddy, Adam, Maria, Tony), Finaletto (Bill & Carol).

Broadway reviews were divided, mostly unfavorable. Barbara Cook's scene in the bikini is (justly) memorable, but still the show lost $350,000. The show was not recorded (the only one of Barbara Cook's that wasn't).

647. *Something's Afoot*

A musical murder mystery spoof. Set in late spring of 1935. Ten house guests and servants marooned on an island estate, Rancour's Retreat, in the English Lake District, threatened with murder, one by one, in the manner of Agatha Christie's *Ten Little Niggers*.

Before Broadway. First produced at the GOODSPEED OPERA HOUSE, Connecticut. Then at the AMERICAN THEATRE, Washington, DC, 11/13/73. 64 PERFORMANCES. PRESENTED by Chelsea Projects, in association with Arch Lustberg & Jerry Schlossberg; DIRECTOR: Tony Tanner; SETS: Raymond T. Kurdt; ADAPTED BY/SET SUPERVISOR: Richard Talcott; LIGHTING: Alice O'Leary. *Cast:* LETTIE: Patti Perkins; FLINT: Pierre Epstein; CLIVE: Henry Victor; HOPE: Barbara Heuman; GRAYBURN: Boris Aplon; NIGEL: Gary Beach; LADY GRACE: Liz Sheridan; GILLWEATHER: Gary Gage; MISS TWEED: Lu Leonard; GEOFFREY: Steve Scott. Then it had a run at the AMERICAN CONSERVATORY THEATRE, San Francisco, in 1974. DIRECTOR: Tony Tanner; SETS: Richard Seger; COSTUMES: Walter Watson; LIGHTING: Fred Kopp; MUSICAL DIRECTOR: John Price. *Cast:* LETTIE: Pamela Myers; FLINT: Darryl Ferrera; CLIVE: Douglas Broyles; HOPE: Barbara Heuman; GRAYBURN: Jack Schmidt; NIGEL: Gary Beach; LADY GRACE: Liz Sheridan; GILLWEATHER: Gary Gage; MISS TWEED: Lu Leonard; GEOFFREY: Willard Beckham.

There was a run at the PAPER MILL PLAYHOUSE, New Jersey, in 1975. DIRECTOR: Tony Tanner. *Cast:* Pat Carroll.

The Broadway Run. LYCEUM THEATRE, 5/27/76–7/18/76. 13 previews. 61 PERFORMANCES. PRESENTED by Emanuel Azenberg, Dasha Epstein, John Mason Kirby; MUSIC/LYRICS/BOOK: James McDonald, David Vos, Robert Gerlach; ADDITIONAL MUSIC: Ed Linderman; ADAPTED FROM Agatha Christie's play *Ten Little Niggers*; DIRECTOR/CHOREOGRAPHER: Tony Tanner; SETS: Richard Seger; COSTUMES: Walter Watson & Clifford Capone; LIGHTING: Richard Winkler; SOUND: Robert Weeden; MUSICAL DIRECTOR: Buster Davis; ORCHESTRATIONS: Peter M. Larson; PRESS: The Merlin Group; GENERAL MANAGER: Marvin A. Krauss; COMPANY MANAGER: Robert Frissell; PRODUCTION STAGE MANAGER: Robert V. Straus; STAGE MANAGER: Marilyn Wilt; ASSISTANT STAGE MANAGER: Sal Mistretta. *Cast:* LETTIE: Neva Small (9); FLINT: Marc Jordan (6); CLIVE: Sel Vitella (10); HOPE LANGDON: Barbara Heuman (5); DR. GRAYBURN: Jack Schmidt (7); NIGEL RANCOUR: Gary Beach (2); LADY GRACE MANLEY-PROWE: Liz Sheridan (8); COLONEL GILLWEATHER: Gary Gage (4); MISS TWEED: Tessie O'Shea (1) ✩; GEOFFREY: Willard Beckham (3). *Standbys:* Miss Tweed/Lady Grace: Lu Leonard; Gillweather/Grayburn/Flint/Clive: Bryan Hull; Hope/Lettie: Meg Bussert; Nigel/Geoffrey: Sal Mistretta. *Act I:* The entrance hall of Rancour's Retreat: "A Marvelous Weekend" (Company, except Geoffrey), "Something's Afoot" (Company, except Geoffrey), "Carry On" (Miss Tweed & Ladies), "I Don't Know Why I Trust You (But I Do)" (Hope & Geoffrey), "The Man with the Ginger Moustache" (Lady Grace), "Suspicious" (Company). *Act II:* The same; immediately following: "The Legal Heir" (Nigel), "You Fell Out of the Sky" (Hope), "Dinghy" (Lettie & Flint), "I Owe It All (to Agatha Christie)" (Miss Tweed, Hope, Geoffrey), "New Day" (Hope & Geoffrey).

The show got divided reviews, mostly very bad.

After Broadway. THEATRE ROYAL, Norwich, England, 6/77. PRESENTED by Danny O'Donovan & Alan Cluer; MUSICAL DIRECTOR: Ian MacPherson. *Cast:* LETTIE: Ruth Madoc; FLINT: Peter Rutherford; CLIVE: Michael Bevis; HOPE: Sally Smith; GRAYBURN: Robert Dorning; NIGEL: Dudley Stevens; GRACE: Joyce Grant; GILLWEATHER: Peter Bayliss; MISS TWEED: Sheila Bernette; GEOFFREY: Martin Smith. It moved to the AMBASSADORS THEATRE, London, in the summer of 1977. There was no London cast recording.

648. *Song and Dance*

A two-part "theatrical concert." Set at the present time in New York and Los Angeles. Act I (*Tell Me on a Sunday*), which is all singing, is about Emma, a lonely but high-spirited British hat designer wearing a man's suit and tie, and her four romantic adventures in New York. There is no dialog. Act II (*Variations*), which is all dancing, with music adapted from various classical and modern sources, shows one of the men (Joe) expressing himself in dance. The two halves are joined when Emma and Joe are united.

Before Broadway. The dance piece, *Variations*, composed by Andrew Lloyd Webber as a set of variations on Paganini's "A-Minor *Caprice* (No. 24)," which he had written for his cellist brother Julian, was recorded in 1978. Before he became involved in *Cats* Wayne Sleep had suggested the idea of using *Variations* as the score for an hour-long ballet to form the second half of his own dance show with his group "Dash," but the idea came to nothing. Incidentally, in 1980, it was also suggested joining *Variations* to the early *Cats* songs to make a full evening's entertainment, but, again, nothing had come of it (except *Cats,* of course). The first version of Act I of what would become *Song and Dance* was written by Andrew Lloyd Webber and Don Black in 1979, and tried out as a concert piece, or "song-cycle," called *Tell Me on a Sunday: An English Girl in America*, at Mr. Lloyd Webbers's festival at SYDMONTON, with Marti Webb (for whom it had been written). Following this it was recorded as a hit album by Marti Webb (this is what made her a star in Britain), then played at an invited concert at the Royalty Theatre, London, in 1/80, staring Marti Webb, and on 2/12/80 this was televised by the BBC. At that point it consisted of 13 musical pieces of varying sizes as well as several linking reprises. The recording sold well, and the title song became very popular. The complete musical, now called *Song and Dance — A Concert for the Theatre*, comprising the two pieces (*Tell Me on a Sunday* and *Variations*), had its first West End run at the PALACE THEATRE, 4/7/82–3/31/84. 13 previews from 3/26/82. 781 PERFORMANCES. PRESENTED BY Cameron Mackintosh & The Really Useful Company. John Caird directed the first half and Anthony Van Laast choreographed the second. SETS/LIGHTING: David Hersey; MUSICAL DIRECTOR: Ian MacPherson. The original form of *Tell Me on a Sunday* was expanded by the addition of three new songs — "The Last Man in My Life," "I Love New York," and "Married Man," and the sequence of songs and joining sections was re-arranged. A recording was done on Polydor. The score was quite different from the Broadway one: Overture, "Let Me Finish," "It's Not the End of the World," "Letter Home to England," "Sheldon Bloom," "Capped Teeth and Caesar Salad," "You Made Me Think You Were in Love," "Second Letter Home," "The Last Man in My Life," "Come Back with the Same Look in Your Eyes," "Take That Look off Your Face," "Tell Me on a Sunday," "I Love New York," "Married Man," "I'm Very You, You're Very Me," "Let Me Finish (reprise)/"Let's Talk About You," "Nothing Like You've Ever Known," "Let Me Finish" (reprise). As each actress succeeded Marti Webb, the lyrics were adjusted, and the order of songs changed to fit the performer. *Tell Me on a Sunday* was sung by: Marti Webb, *Gemma Craven, Carol Nielsson, Lulu, Liz Robertson*. Standby: For Marti Webb: Verity Ann Meldrum. *Variations* was danced by: Sandy Strallen (*Stewart Avon-Arnold*), Claude Paul Henry (*Robert B.J. Ryan*), Paul Tomkinson, Andy Norman, Wayne Sleep (*Stephen Jefferies, Graham Fletcher, John Meehan*), Linda Gibbs (*Lizzie Saunderson*), Jane Darling (*Jo Telford*), Linda Mae Brewer (*Angela Robinson*). It was broadcast on BBC-TV, on 8/27/84. MUSICAL DIRECTOR: David Caddick. Sung by Sarah Brightman, and danced by Stewart Avon-Arnold, Claude Paul Henry, Paul Tomkinson, Andy Norman, Jane Darling, Lizzie Saunderson, Angela Robinson, and Cherida Langford. It toured the U.K. and Australia. It was recorded anew on RCA.

The show was revised heavily for Broadway. Richard Maltby Jr. helped Don Black with many of the lyric changes.

The Broadway Run. ROYALE THEATRE, 9/18/85–11/8/86. 15 previews. 474 PERFORMANCES. A Cameron Mackintosh/Shubert Organization production, PRESENTED BY Cameron Mackintosh, Inc., The Shubert Organization, F.W.M. Producing Group, by arrangement with The Really Useful Company; MUSIC: Andrew Lloyd Webber; LYRICS: Don Black; AMERICAN ADAPTATION/ADDITIONAL LYRICS/DIRECTOR: Richard Maltby Jr.; ENTIRE PRODUCTION SUPERVISED BY Richard Maltby Jr. & Peter Martins; CHOREOGRAPHER: Peter Martins; ASSOCIATE TAP CHOREOGRAPHER: Gregg Burge; SETS: Robin Wagner; COSTUMES: Willa Kim; LIGHTING: Jules Fisher; SOUND: Martin Levan; MUSICAL SUPERVI-

SOR/MUSICAL DIRECTOR: John Mauceri; ORCHESTRATIONS: Andrew Lloyd Webber & David Cullen; PRODUCTION MUSIC ADVISER: David Caddick; PRESS: The Fred Nathan Company; CASTING: Johnson — Liff; GENERAL MANAGER: Gatchell & Neufeld; COMPANY MANAGER: Roger Gindi; PRODUCTION STAGE MANAGER: Sam Stickler; STAGE MANAGER: Richard Jay-Alexander; ASSISTANT STAGE MANAGER: Mitchell Lemsky. *Act I*: EMMA: Bernadette Peters (1) ✫, *Betty Buckley* (from 10/6/86). Overture, "Take That Look off Your Face" (Maltby), "Let Me Finish" (Maltby), "So Much to Do in New York" (Maltby), "First Letter Home" (Maltby), "English Girls" (Maltby), "Capped Teeth and Caesar Salad," "You Made Me Think You Were in Love," "Capped Teeth and Caesar Salad" (reprise), "So Much to Do in New York (II)," "Second Letter Home" (Maltby), "Unexpected Song," "Come Back with the Same Look (in Your Eyes)," "Take That Look off Your Face" (reprise), "Tell Me on a Sunday," "I Love New York" (Maltby)/"So Much to Do in New York (III)," "Married Man," "Third Letter Home" (Maltby), "Nothing Like You've Ever Known" (Maltby), "Let Me Finish" (reprise), "What Have I Done?" (Maltby), Finale: "Take That Look off Your Face" (reprise). *Act II*: New York City: JOE: Christopher d'Amboise (2), *Victor Barbee* (from 1/6/86), *Christopher d'Amboise* (3/31/86), *Victor Barbee* (from 6/23/86), *John Meehan*. *Scene 1* A New York subway station; *Scene 2* The City; *Scene 3* A street outside a disco: WOMAN IN GOLD: Mary Ellen Stuart; HER ESCORTS: Scott Wise & Gregory Mitchell; *Scene 4* Billboards; *Scene 5* A bar: WOMAN IN BLUE: Charlotte d'Amboise; TOURIST CUSTOMER: Gen Horiuchi, *Buddy* Balou'; HIS TWO PICKUPS: Cynthia Onrubia & Denise Faye; *Scene 6* A city street: MAN FROM THE STREETS: Gregg Burge (3); *Scene 7* Wall Street: WOMAN IN GRAY FLANNEL: Cynthia Onrubia; *Scene 8* A park; *Scene 9* Fifth Avenue; *Scene 10* A department store fashion show; *Scene 11* New York; "Unexpected Song" (Emma & Joe). *Standby*: Emma: Maureen Moore. *Understudies*: Joe: Bruce Falco & Scott Wise; For Misses Stuart/Faye/d'Amboise: Valerie Wright & Mary Ann Lamb; For Miss Onrubia: Mary Ann Lamb & Denise Faye; For Mr. Burge: Bruce Anthony Davis; For Mr. Wise/Mr. Mitchell: Kenneth Ard; For Mr. Horiuchi: Ramon Galindo.

Note: all music is by Andrew Lloyd Webber; all lyrics are by Don Black, unless Richard Maltby Jr. was co-lyricist, in which case "Maltby" is added in parentheses.

Broadway reviews were not very good. Bernadette Peters won a Tony. The show was also nominated for musical, score, direction of a musical, choreography, costumes, lighting, and for Christopher d'Amboise.

After Broadway. TOUR. Opened on 6/23/87. PRESENTED BY Tom Mallow, James B. Freydberg, Max Weitzenhoffer; CHOREOGRAPHER: Cynthia Onrubia; MUSICAL DIRECTOR: Jerry Sternbach. *Cast:* EMMA: Melissa Manchester; JOE: Bruce Falco, *Victor Barbee, Christopher d'Amboise, John Meehan*; THE WOMEN: Mindy Cooper, Cynthia Onrubia, Deborah Roshe, Valerie C. Wright; THE MEN: Eugene Fleming, Danny Herman, Herman Sebek, Scott Wise.

Tell Me on a Sunday was re-done at the KENNEDY CENTER, Washington, DC, 12/17/02–1/12/03. DIRECTOR: Marcia Milgrom Dodge; MUSICAL DIRECTOR: Steve Marzullo; ORCHESTRATIONS: Daryl Waters. *Cast*: Alice Ripley. *Standby*: Leslie Kritzer.

Tell Me on a Sunday was revised by Andrew Lloyd Webber and Don Black in London, with additional material by Jackie Clune, so that it could run on its own. It starred Denise Van Outen, for whom they fashioned the new production. She was most famous as the star of morning TV's *The Big Breakfast*. The new show opened at the GIELGUD THEATRE, London, 4/23/03. Previews from 4/8/03. It had a limited run of 8 weeks, but extended to 1/10/04). An album was released at the same time. PRESENTED BY Bill Kenwright & the Really Useful Company; DIRECTOR: Matthew Warchus; MUSICAL DIRECTOR: Simon Lee. "Take That Look off Your Face," "Let Me Finish # 1," "It's Not the End of the World," "Goodbye Mum, Goodbye Girls," "Haven in the Sky," "First Letter Home," "Speed Dating," "Second Letter Home," "Tyler King," "Capped Teeth and Caesar Salad," "You Made Me Think You Were in Love," "Capped Teeth and Caesar Salad" (reprise), "It's Not the End of the World (If He's Younger)," "Third Letter Home," "Unexpected Song," "Come Back with the Same Look (in Your Eyes)," "Let's Talk About You," "Take That Look off Your Face" (reprise), "Tell Me on a Sunday," "It's Not the End of the World (If He's Married)," "Fourth Letter Home,"

"Ready Made Life"/"I'm Very You," "Let Me Finish # 2," "Nothing Like You've Ever Known," "Fifth Letter Home," "Somewhere, Someplace, Sometime." Denise Van Outen left on 8/23/03; there were no performances 8/25/03–8/30/03; then Julie-Alanah Brighten played the role 9/1/03–9/20/03; then Denise Van Outen returned on 9/25/03 (with Miss Brighten playing the role in the newly-instituted matinees). The run was extended again, and on 1/13/04 Marti Webb took over the role.

649. *Song of Norway*

A costume operetta, a romanticized story of three years (1860–63) in the life of Norwegian composer Edvard Grieg, son of a fish merchant, telling of how he is torn between his girl-friend Nina and his native Norway on the one hand, and the glamour of the wider world and the more worldly opera singer Louisa on the other. While in Rome with the diva, as her accompanist, Grieg learns of the death of his dear friend, the poet Nordraak (who is also his rival for Nina), and rushes home to be with Nina. After reading the last, patriotic, poem by Nordraak, Grieg is inspired to write his famous Concerto in A Minor.

Before Broadway. Movie producer Sam Goldwyn approached operetta producer Edwin Lester with the idea of doing a movie about Hans Christian Andersen. Lester suggested a stage musical, using the music of Andersen's fellow Norwegian, Edvard Grieg. The Andersen idea was dropped, and Lester set out on his own to do the Grieg story. Homer Curran, his partner, wrote an outline, and Milton Lazarus wrote the final book. It was first produced in 7/44 by the Los Angeles and San Francisco Civic Light Opera Association (of which Mr. Lester was the producer). Reviews were good, and eight Broadway producers bid on it. Lee Shubert bought 50 per cent of the rights.

The Broadway Run. IMPERIAL THEATRE, 8/21/44–4/13/46; BROADWAY THEATRE, 4/15/46–9/7/46. Total of 859 PERFORMANCES. PRESENTED BY Edwin Lester; MUSIC: based on that of Edvard Grieg; MUSICAL ADAPTATIONS/LYRICS: Robert Wright & George Forrest; BOOK: Milton Lazarus (based on an outline play by Homer Curran); DIRECTOR: Charles K. Freeman; CHOREOGRAPHER/SINGING ENSEMBLES STAGED BY: George Balanchine; SETS: Lemuel Ayers; SET SUPERVISOR: Carl Kent; COSTUMES: Robert Davison; LIGHTING: Howard Bay; MUSICAL DIRECTOR/ORCHESTRAL & CHORAL ARRANGEMENTS: Arthur Kay; PIANO SOLOIST: Louis Teicher; CAST RECORDING on Decca; PRESS: C.P. Greneker, *Ben Kornzweig*; COMPANY MANAGER: Gerald O'Connell, *R. Victor Leighton*; STAGE MANAGER: Peter Bronte, *Dan Brennan*. **Cast:** RIKARD NORDRAAK: Robert Shafer (4); SIGRID: Janet Hamer; EINAR: Kent Edwards, *John Henson*; ERIC: Robert Antoine, *William Carroll, Michael Guerard*; GUNNAR: William Carroll, *Gerald Matthews, Alexander Goudovitch*; GRIMA: Patti Brady, *Grace Carroll, Sharon Randall*; HELGA: Jackie Lee, *Diane Woods, Gloria Stone*; NINA HAGERUP: Helena Bliss (2), *Kirsten Kenyon*; EDVARD GRIEG: Lawrence Brooks (3); FATHER GRIEG: Walter Kingsford; FATHER NORDRAAK: Philip White; MOTHER GRIEG: Ivy Scott; FREDDY: Frederic Franklin (7), *James Starbuck, Richard Reed*; COUNT PEPPI LE LOUP: Sig Arno (5); COUNTESS LOUISA GIOVANNI: Irra Petina (1); MEMBERS OF THE FACULTY: Ewing Mitchell, Audrey *Guard, Paul De Poyster*; INNKEEPER: Lewis Bolyard; FRAU PROFESSOR NORDEN: Doreen Wilson, *Margaret Ritter*; ELVERA: Sharon Randall; HEDWIG: Karen Lund; GRETA: Gwen Jones; MARGARETA: Ann Andre, *Kaye Connor*; HILDA: Elizabeth Bockoven; MISS ANDERS: Sonia Orlova; HENRIK IBSEN: Dudley Clements; TITO: Frederic Franklin, *Sviatoslav Toumine, Richard Reed*; WAITRESSES AT TITO'S: Gloria Stone & Jeanne Jones; MAESTRO PISONI: Robert Bernard; BUTLER: Cameron Grant; ADELINA: Alexandra Danilova (6), *Dorothie Littlefield*; THE MAIDEN NORWAY: Nora White, *Olga Suarez*; SIGNORA ELEANORA: Barbara Boudwin; CHILDREN: Sylvia Allen, Grace Carroll, Pat O'Rourke, Shannon Randolph, *Sharon Randall, Michael Guerard*; THE MINSTREL: Roland Guerard [role added during the run]; DANCING PEASANTS/EMPLOYEES AT TITO'S/THE BALLET OF THE TEATRO REALE/CHARACTERS OF THE FANTASY: Artist Personnel of the Ballet Russe de Monte Carlo (Sergei J. Denham, director) (the Ballet Russe got 8th billing): Alexandra Danilova, Frederic Franklin, Nathalie Krassovska, Leon Danielian, Maria Tallchief, Ruthanna Boris, Alexander Goudovitch, Mary Ellen Moylan, Sergei Ismaeloff, Anna Istomina, Nicholas Magallanes, Michael Katcharoff, Julia Horvath, Peter Deign, Alan Banks, Herbert Bliss, Vida Brown, Alfredo Corvino, Pauline Goddard, Elena Kramarr, Karel Shook, Gertruda Swobodina, Nikita Talin, Nora White (*Olga Suarez*), Roland Guerard, James Starbuck, Dorothie Littlefield, Sonia Orlova, Sviatoslav Toumine, Betty Burge, Adda Pourmel, Rosine Sedova, Jeanne Jones, Carlyle Ramey, Jean Faust, Anna Wiman, Marjorie Castle, Toni Stuart, Gloria Stone, Harold Haskin, Milton Feher, Yura Radine, Nat Stoudenmire, Francis Kiernan, Robert Bernoff, Erik Kristen; SINGING PEASANTS/GUESTS & FACULTY AT COPENHAGEN/GUESTS AT THE VILLA PINCIO: The Singing Ensemble of the Los Angeles & San Francisco Civic Light Opera: GIRLS: Ann Andre, Elizabeth Bockoven, Barbara Boudwin, Mary Bradley, Shirley Conklin, Kaye Connor, Audrey Dearden, Audrey Guard, Leonne Hall, Gwen Jones, Karen Lund, Sharon Randall, Margaret Ritter, Mary Walker, Doreen Wilson; BOYS: Robert Bailes, Lewis E. Bolyard, Frank Brenneman, John Chaloupka, Paul De Poyster, Cameron Grant, Larry Haynes, Hal Horton, Raymond Keast, Hal McMurrin, Arthur Waters, Maurice Winthrop, Stanley Wolfe, Walter Young. **Act I:** *Scene 1* Troldhaugen (Hill of the Trolls) — just outside the town of Bergen, Norway; Midsummer's Eve, in the 1860s: Prelude (Orchestra), "The Legend" (Rikard) [adapted from the A Minor Concerto], "Hill of Dreams" (Nina, Edvard, Rikard) [also from the A Minor Concerto]; *Scene 2* A square on the outskirts of Bergen: "In the Holiday Spirit" (Dancing Peasants), "Freddy and His Fiddle" (Einar, Sigrid, Freddy, Singing Townspeople) [from "Norwegian Dance"], "Now!" (Louisa & Townspeople) [from Waltz Op. 12, No. 2, and the Violin Sonata in G Major], "Strange Music" (Edvard & Nina) [from "Nocturne" and "Wedding in Troldhaugen"] [the hit], "Midsummer's Eve" (Rikard & Louisa) [from "'twas on a Lovely Eve in June" and "Scherzo"], "March of the Trollgers" (The Cake Lottery) (Entire Ensemble) [from "Mountaineers' Song," "Halling" in G Minor, and "March of the Dwarfs"], Finale of Act I: a/ "Hymn of Betrothal" (Mother Grieg & Villagers) ("To Spring"); b/ "Strange Music" (reprise) (Edvard, Nina, Chorus); c/ "Midsummer's Eve" (reprise) (Rikard, Nina, Chorus). **Act II:** *Scene 1* Copenhagen — Reception room of the Royal Conservatory; one year later: Introduction: "Papillon," "Bon Vivant" — Part I (Edvard & Girls) [from "Water Lily"], "Bon Vivant" – Part II (Peppi, Edvard, Miss Anders, Girls) [from "The Brook" of Haugtussa Cycle], "Three Loves" (Louisa & Edvard) [from "Albumblatt" and "Poem Erotique"], Finaletto: a/ "Down Your Tea" (Louisa, Faculty, Guests); b/ "Nordraak's Farewell" (Rikard) ("Springtide"); c/ "Three Loves" (reprise) (Louisa, Nina, Ensemble); *Scene 2* Rome — Tito's chocolate shop; one year later: "Chocolat Pas de Trois" (Tito & His Employees) [from "From Monte Pincio" and "Rigaudon"]; *Scene 3* Rome — ballroom of Villa Pincio: "Waltz Eternal" (Ladies & Gentlemen) [from "Waltz Caprice"], "Peer Gynt" (Ballet of the Italian Opera): a/ Solvejg's Melody; b/ Hall of the Dovre King; c/ Anitra's Dance; "I Love You" (Nina) ("Ich Liebe Dich"); *Scene 4* Troldhaugen — interior of the Grieg home; some time later: "At Christmastime" (Father Grieg, Mother Grieg, Nina) [from "Woodland Wanderings"], "Midsummer's Eve" (reprise) (Edvard & Nina), "Strange Music" (reprise) (Edvard & Nina); *Scene 5* The Song of Norway: "The Song of Norway" [from the A-Minor Piano Concerto] (Edvard).

Broadway reviews were terrific. The cast recording, on Decca, featured Kitty Carlisle as Louisa. Irra Petina made her own album of the show for Columbia, with Robert Weede co-starring. At the end of the Broadway run the show, with most of its original cast still intact, went on a national tour.

After Broadway. PALACE THEATRE, London, 3/7/46–4/26/47. 526 PERFORMANCES. DIRECTOR: Charles Hickman; CHOREOGRAPHERS: Robert Helpmann & Pauline Grant. **Cast:** GRIEG: John Hargreaves, *Paul Gavert*; LOUISA: Janet Hamilton-Smith, *Gladys Walthoe*; NINA: Halina Victoria, *Brenda Stanley*; NORDRAAK: Arthur Servent, *David Young*; FATHER GRIEG: Colin Cunningham, MOTHER GRIEG: Olive Sturgess; PEPPI: Bernard Ansell; ADELINA: Moyra Fraser. It re-ran at the PALACE THEATRE, 7/11/49–9/10/49. 72 PERFORMANCES. **Cast:** GRIEG: Ivor Evans; LOUISA: Peggy Rowan; NINA: Brenda Stanley; NORDRAAK: Arthur Servent; FATHER GRIEG: Dale Williams; MOTHER GRIEG: Olive Sturgess; PEPPI: Frank Rydon; IBSEN: Ian Ainsley; ADELINA: Shelagh Day.

JONES BEACH THEATRE, NY, 1958. PRESENTED BY Guy Lombardo & Leonard Ruskin. Over 400,000 people saw it during its 10-week run. It was repeated in 1959.

WEST COAST REVIVAL. Opened on 4/23/62, at the Philharmonic Auditorium, Los Angeles, and closed on 7/28/62, at the Curran Theatre, San Francisco. There were several amendments to the musical numbers. PRESENTED BY Edwin Lester, Robert Schuler, and the Los Angeles Civic Light Opera Association; DIRECTOR: Edward Greenberg; CHOREOGRAPHER: Aida Broadbent; SETS: George Jenkins; COSTUMES: Miles White; TECHNICAL DIRECTOR: Richard Rodda; LIGHTING: Peggy Clark; MUSICAL DIRECTOR: Louis Adrian. *Cast*: GRIEG: John Reardon; LOUISA: Patrice Munsel; NORDRAAK: Frank Porretta; SIGRID: April Shawhan; CHRISTA/MISS ANDERS: Susan Luckey; FATHER GRIEG: Jerome Cowan; MOTHER GRIEG: Muriel O'Malley, *Roberta Maxwell*; PEPPI: Sig Arno. *Understudy*: Mother Grieg: Roberta Maxwell.

THE MOVIE. 1970. CHOREOGRAPHER: Lee Becker Theodore. The score was somewhat revised, and the movie was punishingly dull. *Cast*: GRIEG: Toralv Maurstad; NINA: Florence Henderson; ALSO WITH: Edward G. Robinson.

NEW YORK STATE THEATRE, 9/3/81–9/13/81. 14 PERFORMANCES. PRESENTED BY the New York City Opera; DIRECTOR: Gerald Freedman; CHOREOGRAPHER: Eliot Feld; SETS: David Jenkins; COSTUMES: Ann Roth; LIGHTING: Gilbert V. Hemsley Jr.; CONDUCTOR/ADDITIONAL ORCHESTRATIONS: Scott Bergeson; SPECIAL DANCE ORCHESTRATIONS: Sol Berkowitz. *Cast*: NORDRAAK: David Eisler; GUNNAR: Jamie Cohen; CHRISTA: Catherine Ulissey; NINA: Sheryl Woods; GRIEG: Stephen Dickson; FREDDY: Jeff Satinoff; MOTHER GRIEG: Muriel Costa-Greenspon; FATHER GRIEG: Dan Sullivan; FATHER NORDRAAK: Ralph Bassett; PEPPI: David Rae Smith; LOUISA: Susanne Marsee; MISS NORDEN: Rita Metzger; GRETA: Lee Bellaver; IBSEN: James Billings; PISONI: Joaquin Romaguera.

650. *Sophie*

Based on the early years (up to 1922) of the professional life of legendary American entertainer Sophie Tucker (1884–1966). Set in Hartford, Conn., New York, and London, in the early 1900s.

Before Broadway. The show tried out in Columbus, Detroit, and Philadelphia, in all of which towns it got bad reviews. In Detroit Gene Frankel was replaced as director by Jack Sydow. 7th-billed Gloria Smith left the cast before Broadway. The numbers "Fight for the Man," "You'd Know It," "One Little Thing" and "They Led Me to Believe" were cut.

The Broadway Run. WINTER GARDEN THEATRE, 4/15/63–4/20/63. 8 PERFORMANCES. PRESENTED BY Len Bedsow & Hal Grossman, in association with Michael Pollock & Max Fialkov; MUSIC/LYRICS: Steve Allen; BOOK: Phillip Pruneau; DIRECTOR: Jack Sydow; CHOREOGRAPHER: Donald Saddler; SETS/LIGHTING: Robert Randolph; COSTUMES: Fred Voelpel; MUSICAL DIRECTOR/VOCAL ARRANGEMENTS: Liza Redfield; ORCHESTRATIONS/MUSICAL ARRANGEMENTS: Sid Ramin & Arthur Beck; DANCE MUSIC ARRANGEMENTS: Genevieve Pitot; PRESS: Marvin Kohn; COMPANY MANAGER: Boris Bernardi; PRODUCTION STAGE MANAGER: Mortimer Halpern; STAGE MANAGER: Julian Barry. *Cast*: SOPHIE TUCKER: Libi Staiger (1); MOE: Douglas Clarke; MAMA: Berta Gersten (5); WILLIAM MORRIS: Phil Leeds (4); THEONA: Diana Hunter; MRS. QUIVE: Urylee Leonardos; SCHMIDT: Don Crabtree; POLICEMEN: Nat Horne & Ralph McWilliams; CHRIS BROWN: Ted Thurston (9); STAGE MANAGER: John Drew; GIRL: Bella Shalom; MOTHER: Janet Gaylord; ACROBAT: Tim Harum; SYLVAIN KROUSE: Patsi King (8); STAGEHAND: Jordan Bowers; JUGGLER: Stuart Hodes; MOLLIE: Rosetta Le Noire (3); MARCUS LOEW: David Thomas (10); MICKEY MULDOON: Eddie Roll (6); HARRY EMERSON: David Thomas; FRANK WESTPHAL: Art Lund (2); QUEENIE: Maralyn Thoma; JULIAN MITCHELL: Ted Thurston; SANDY: Richard Hermany; NORA BAYES: Betty Colby; STELLA: Diana Hunter; MR. KILBY: David Thomas; REPORTERS: Don Crabtree, John Drew, Richard Hermany; THEATRE MANAGER: Ted Thurston; TED: Michael Nestor; METROPOLE MANAGER: David Thomas; ENSEMBLE: Jordan Bowers, Carol Carlin, Douglas Clarke, Betty Colby, John Drew,

Louise Ferrand, Janet Gaylord, Ellen Graff, Tim Harum, Florence Hayle, Richard Hermany, Stuart Hodes, Nat Horne, Diana Hunter, Urylee Leonardos, Ralph McWilliams, Michael Nestor, Kelli Scott, Beti Seay, Bella Shalom, Maralyn Thoma, Elizabeth Wullen. *Understudies*: Sophie: Florence Hayle; Frank: Don Crabtree; Molly: Urylee Leonardos; William Morris: Ted Thurston; Mama: Betty Colby. *Act I*: *Scene 1* Sophie Tucker Tonight; *Scene 2* The family restaurant in Hartford; *Scene 3* Sophie in New York; *Scene 4* Backstage, 125th Street Theatre; *Scene 5* Theatre alley; *Scene 6* Third Avenue "El;" *Scene 7* A street; *Scene 8* Gaiety Burlesque Theatre; *Scene 9* Sophie trouping; *Scene 10* Backstage Ziegfeld Follies. *Act II*: *Scene 1* Roof of a theatrical hotel; *Scene 2* Frank's dressing room; *Scene 3* Sophie's dressing room; *Scene 4* Freeport Variety Club; *Scene 5* Hartford Railroad Station; *Scene 6* Dressing rooms and on stage; *Scene 7* Freeport Variety Club; *Scene 8* Dockside; *Scene 9* Dressing room in London; *Scene 10* Cafe Metropole, London. *Act I*: "(I'm a) Red Hot Mama" (Sophie), "Sunshine Face" (Sophie), "Mr. Henry Jones" (Sophie), "Sophie in New York" (Sophie & Company), "Patsy" (Mollie), "I'll Show Them All" (Sophie), "I'll Show Them All" (reprise) (Sophie), "Hold on to Your Hats" (Morris & Mollie), "Fast Cars and Fightin' Women" (Frank), "Queen of the Burlesque Wheel" (Sylvain & Ensemble), "When You Carry Your Own Suitcase" (Sophie, Mickey, Ensemble), "When You Carry Your Own Suitcase" (reprise) (Frank), "When I'm in Love" (Sophie & Mollie), "Hold on to Your Hats" (reprise) (Sophie, Frank, Mollie, Morris), "Sailors of the Sea" (Ensemble), "I Want the Kind of a Fella" (Sophie), "I'll Show Them All" (reprise) (Sophie). *Act II*: "Who Are We Kidding" (Mickey & Sylvain), "Don't Look Back" (Entire Company), "I'd Know It" (Frank), "You've Got to Be a Lady" (Mollie), "Ragtime" (Ensemble), "Waltz" (Sophie, Frank, Ensemble), "When I'm in Love" (reprise) (Frank), "I Love You Today" (Sophie & Frank), "With You" (Sophie), "(I'm a) Red Hot Mama" (reprise) (Sophie), "I've Got 'em Standin' in Line" (Sophie), "They've Got a Lot to Learn" (Frank), "(I'm a) Red Hot Mama" (reprise) (Sophie).

The trouble with this show was that Sophie Tucker herself was not the star. However, she was in the audience on opening night, and took a bow at the beginning of the performance. Reviews were not good. Although there was no original cast recording, Judy Garland did sing three songs from *Sophie* on her CBS TV show.

651. *Sophisticated Ladies*

Also called: *Duke Ellington's Sophisticated Ladies*. A musical revue. A reproduction of the Cotton Club in Harlem, the old nightclub, complete with full 21-piece orchestra led by Duke Ellington's son, Mercer, and a large cast of singers and dancers, including Duke's granddaughter, Mercedes. Essentially it was a volatile string of Ellington numbers, each preceded by a lead-in (written by Donny McKayle). Judith Jamison was the leading dancer with the Alvin Ailey Dance Theatre.

Before Broadway. When this show opened for tryouts in Philadelphia on 12/9/80, the neon lighting, so necessary for the show, arrived broken. The show was too long, and reviews were very bad. Several playwrights tried coming up with a workable libretto that would tie the songs together. Samm-Art Williams was one of them, brought in to revise the show for its next, Washington, DC, run (where reviews again were terrible). Gregory Hines was fired, and his understudy, Gregg Burge, was ordered to replace him. But Mr. Burge had not kept pace with all the changes, and only knew the Philadelphia version, which was much different from the Washington version. So, the producers, cap in hand, got ready to ask Mr. Hines back, but Mr. Hines had disappeared. So, the producers canceled that day's matinee, they reverted to the Philadelphia version, and Mr. Burge got ready. However, the cast refused to work with Donny McKayle, who they blamed for the firing of Gregory Hines. Fortunately, they finally found Mr. Hines in a Washington restaurant, about to leave town, and he came back, and they played that night's performance in the Philadelphia style. Michael Smuin of the San Francisco Ballet took over as director from Donny McKayle during the unsuccessful Washington tryouts, and he cut all the dialogue, re-staged the show, and added his own choreography and that of tap dancer Henry Le

Tang, as well as re-arranging the order of the songs and adding nine new ones. In fact, he cut the number of songs from 53 to 36. This was the program at that stage (only those songs not described in the Broadway musical number list have details beside them here): ***Act I***: Overture; ***Scene 1*** Prologue; ***Scene 2*** The Kentucky Club: "East St. Louis Toodle-oo" (m: DE & Bob Miley; 1927) (Mr. Benjamin & Miss Klausner), "Just a Closer Walk with Thee" (traditional) (Miss Baskerville); ***Scene 3*** The Cotton Club: "The Mooche," "I've Got to Be a Rug Cutter," "Black Beauty" (m: DE; 1928) (Miss Jamison & Mr. Hines), "It Don't Mean a Thing;" ***Scene 4*** Le Jazz Hot/Anywhere, U.S.A.: "Take the 'A' Train," "Bli-Blip," "Cotton Tail," "Take the 'A' Train" (reprise); ***Scene 5*** Long Distance: "Solitude," "Don't Get Around Much Anymore," "I Let a Song Go Out of My Heart;" ***Scene 6*** Abroad: "Caravan," "King of the Magi" (m: DE; l: Nick Kenny; 1974) [from the film *Les Rois Noirs*] (Mr. Battle, Miss Klausner, Miss Jamison, Mr. Benjamin); ***Scene 7*** Back Home: "Drop Me off in Harlem," "Rockin' in Rhythm." ***Act II***: ***Scene 1*** Duke's Place: "Duke's Place;" ***Scene 2*** Woman: "Warm Valley" (m: DE; l: Bob Russell; 1941) (Mr. Hines & Band), "In a Sentimental Mood," "Woman" (music: DE; 1968) (Mr. Hines), "Prelude to a Kiss" (m: DE; l: Irving Mills & Irving Gordon; 1933) (Miss Hyman), "The Black and Tan Fantasy" (m: DE & Bob Miley; 1957) (Miss Jamison), "Satin Doll," "Just Squeeze Me," "Sophisticated Lady;" ***Scene 3*** Night Life: "Dancers in Love," "Echoes of Harlem," "I'm Just a Lucky So-and-So," "Rhythm Pum-te-Dum" (m: DE & Billy Strayhorn; 1956) (Miss Jamison, Mr. Hines, Mr. Battle, Mr. Burge, Miss Baskerville, Ensemble), "Hey Baby," "Imagine My Frustration;" ***Scene 4*** La Joint/Games of Love: "Kinda Dukish," "Ko-Ko," "I'm Checking Out Goombye," "Do Nothing 'til You Hear from Me," "I Got it Bad and That Ain't Good," "Mood Indigo;" ***Scene 5*** The Party's Over: "I'm Beginning to See the Light" (by DE, Don George, Johnny Hodges, Harry James; 1944) (Miss Jamison & Mr. Hines); ***Scene 6*** Sacred Works: "Heaven" (by DE; 1968) (Mr. Battle & Miss Baskerville), "Tell Me it's the Truth" (by DE; 1966) (Miss Hyman); Epilogue: "It Don't Mean a Thing" (reprise).

The Broadway Run. LUNT—FONTANNE THEATRE, 3/1/81–1/2/83. 15 previews from 2/16/81. 767 PERFORMANCES. PRESENTED BY Roger S. Berlind, Manheim Fox, Sondra Gilman, Burton L. Litwin & Louise Westergaard, in association with Belwin Mills Publishing & NorZar Productions (Jacques Nordman & Sidney Lazard); MUSIC: Duke Ellington; LYRICS: various writers; CONCEIVED BY: Donald McKayle; DIRECTOR: Michael Smuin; CHOREOGRAPHERS: Donald McKayle & Michael Smuin; SPECIAL TAP CHOREOGRAPHY: Henry Le Tang; ASSISTANT CHOREOGRAPHER: Mercedes Ellington; SETS: Tony Walton; COSTUMES: Willa Kim; LIGHTING: Jennifer Tipton; SOUND: Otts Munderloh; MUSICAL DIRECTOR: Mercer Ellington; MUSICAL ARRANGEMENTS/DANCE MUSIC ARRANGEMENTS: Lloyd Mayers; ORCHESTRATIONS: Al Cohn; VOCAL ARRANGEMENTS: Malcolm Dodds & Lloyd Mayers; MUSIC CONSULTANT/ADDITIONAL ARRANGEMENTS: Paul Chihara; CAST RECORDING on RCA; PRESS: Fred Nathan; CASTING: TNI Casting (Julie Hughes & Barry Moss); GENERAL MANAGERS: Joseph P. Harris & Ira Bernstein; PRODUCTION STAGE MANAGER: Martin Gold; STAGE MANAGER: Carlos Gorbea; ASSISTANT STAGE MANAGER: Kenneth Hanson. ***Cast:*** Gregory Hines (1) ☆ (*Maurice Hines* from 1/5/82), Judith Jamison (2) ☆, Phyllis Hyman (3) ☆, Gregg Burge (7) (*Michael Scott Gregory* from 1/5/82), Mercedes Ellington (8), Hinton Battle (6) (*Gary Chapman* from 1/5/82, *T.A. Stephens* from 10/82), Terri Klausner (5) (*Donna Drake* from 1/5/82), P.J. Benjamin (4) (*Don Correia* from 3/29/82), Priscilla Baskerville (9). SOPHISTICATED LADIES: Claudia Asbury (gone by 81–82), Mercedes Ellington, Paula Lynn (gone by 81–82), Wynonna Smith (gone by 81–82), *Leslie Dockery, D'Arcy Phifer, Christina Saffran*; SOPHISTICATED GENTLEMEN: Adrian Bailey, Michael Lichtefeld (gone by 81–82), Michael Scott Gregory (gone by 81–82), T.A. Stephens, *Calvin McRae, Richard Pessagno*. **Standbys**: For Miss Hyman: Anita Moore; For Miss Baskerville: Naomi Moody. **Understudies**: For Gregory Hines: Hinton Battle & Gregg Burge; For Maurice Hines: Alan Weeks, Adrian Bailey, Jeff Veazey; For Mr. Chapman: Lloyd Culbreath; For Mr. Gregory: Lloyd Culbreath & Richard Pessagno; For Miss Jamison: Wynonna Smith & Valarie Pettiford, *Mercedes Ellington*; For Mr. Burge: Michael Scott Gregory & Faruma S. Williams; For Mr. Battle: T.A. Stephens & Faruma S. Williams; For Miss Klausner: Paula Lynn; For Mr. Benjamin: Michael Lichtefeld, *Calvin McRae & Richard Pessagno*; For Miss Hyman: Naomi

Moody; For Miss Drake: Christina Saffran & Denise DiRenzo; Ladies: Valarie Pettiford, *Denise DiRenzo*; Gentlemen: Faruma S. Williams & Jeff Veazey, *Lloyd Culbreath*. ***Musicians:*** REEDS: Bill Easley, Harold Minerve, Joe Temperle, Norris Torney, David Young; PERCUSSION: Charles Simon, Quentin White, Johnny Longo; DRUMS: Richard Pratt (soloist); TROMBONES: Art Baron; BASS TROMBONE: Charles Connors; TRUMPETS: Kamau Adilifu, Barry Lee Hall (soloist), Lloyd Michels, Johnny Longo (soloist); FLUGELHORNS: Kamau Adilifu, Barry Lee Hall, Lloyd Michels; BASS: Dominic Fiore; FRENCH HORN: Al Richmond; PIANO: Lloyd Mayers (soloist); GUITAR/BANJO: Rudy Stevenson. ***Act I***: Overture (Mercer Ellington & Band), "I've Got to Be a Rug Cutter" (m/l: DE; 1937) (Messrs Battle, Burge, Gregory, Lichtefeld), "Music is a Woman" (based on "Jubilee Stomp," 1928) (m: DE; l: John Guare) (Mr. Hines & Miss Jamison), "The Mooche" (m: DE & Irving Mills; 1929) (Mr. Burge with Miss Asbury, Miss Ellington, Miss Lynn, Miss Smith), "Hit Me with a Hot Note (and Watch Me Bounce)" (m: DE; l: Don George; 1945) (Miss Klausner), "(I) Love You Madly" (m/l: DE; 1950)/"Perdido" (1971) (m/l: Juan Tizol, Ervin Drake, Hans Lengsfelder) (Miss Jamison, Mr. Burge, Mr. Battle), "Fat and Forte" (m/l: Al Hibbler & DE) (Mr. Benjamin) [this number was replaced during the run, and for the subsequent tour, by "Everything but You" (m: DE & Harry James; l: Don George), 1945], "It Don't Mean a Thing (if it Ain't Got That Swing)" (m: DE; l: Irving Mills; 1929) (Miss Hyman, Mr. Burge, Mr. Hines, with Messrs Bailey, Lichtefeld, Gregory, Stephens), "Bli-Blip" (m: DE; l: DE & Sid Kuller; 1941) (Mr. Benjamin & Miss Klausner), "Cotton Tail" (m: DE; 1940) (Mr. Benjamin, Miss Klausner, Ensemble), "Take the 'A' Train" (m: Billy Strayhorn; 1941) (Miss Hyman & Mr. Hines), "Solitude" (m: DE; l: Eddie DeLange & Irving Mills, 1934) (Miss Jamison & Miss Baskerville), "Don't Get Around Much Anymore" (m: DE; l: Bob Russell; 1942) (Mr. Hines), "I Let a Song Go Out of My Heart" (m: DE; l: Irving Mills & John Redmond; 1938) [from *Cotton Club Parade*] (Miss Jamison), "Caravan" (m: DE & Juan Tizol; l: Irving Mills; 1937) (Mr. Burge, Miss Ellington, Ensemble), "Something to Live For" (m/l: DE & Billy Strayhorn; 1939) (Mr. Hines), "Old Man Blues" (m/l: DE & Irving Mills; 1930) (Miss Jamison & Mr. Battle), "Prelude to a Kiss" (m: DE; l: Irving Gordon & Irving Mills) [this number was added only for the subsequent tour, and sung by Paula Kelly], "Drop Me off in Harlem" (m: DE; l: Nick Kenny; 1933) (Mr. Battle, Mr. Benjamin, Mr. Burge, Mr. Hines, Miss Baskerville, Ensemble), "Rockin' in Rhythm" (m: DE, Irving Mills, Harry Carney; 1933) [from *Earl Carroll's Vanities of 1932*] (Company). ***Act II***: "Duke's Place" (m: DE; l: Bill Katz & Robert Thiele; 1957) (Mr. Hines), "Diminuendo in Blue" (m: DE; 1942) (Mr. Hines), "In a Sentimental Mood" (m: DE; l: Manny Kurtz & Irving Mills; 1935) (Miss Hyman), "I'm Beginning to See the Light" (m/l: DE, Don George, Johnny Hodges, Harry James; 1944) (Miss Jamison & Mr. Hines), "Satin Doll" (m: DE; l: Billy Strayhorn & Johnny Mercer; 1958) (Mr. Benjamin), "Just Squeeze Me" (m: DE; l: Lee Gaines; 1946) (Miss Klausner), "Dancers in Love" (m: DE; 1945) (Mr. Burge, Mr. Battle, Miss Ellington), "Echoes of Harlem" (m: DE; 1936) (Mr. Burge, Mr. Battle, Ladies), "I'm Just a Lucky So-and-So" (m: DE; l: Mack David; 1945) (Mr. Hines & Gentlemen), "Hey Baby" (m/l: DE; 1946) (Mr. Benjamin & Miss Ellington), "Imagine My Frustration" (m/l: DE, Billy Strayhorn, Gerald Wilson; 1966) (Miss Klausner, Mr. Burge, Company), "Kinda Dukish" (m: DE; 1955) (Mr. Hines), "Ko-Ko" (m: DE; 1939) (Mr. Hines, and Messrs Bailey, Lichtefeld, Gregory, Stephens), "I'm Checking Out Goombye" (m/l: DE & Billy Strayhorn; 1939) (Miss Hyman), "Do Nothing 'til You Hear from Me" (m: DE; l: Bob Russell; 1943) (Mr. Hines), "I Got it Bad (and That Ain't Good)" (m: DE; l: Paul Francis Webster; 1941) [from *Jump for Joy*] (Miss Hyman), "Mood Indigo" (m: DE, Irving Mills, Albany "Barney" Bigard; 1931) (Miss Hyman & Miss Klausner), "Sophisticated Lady" (m: DE; l: Mitchell Parish & Irving Mills; 1933) (sung by Mr. Hines; danced by Miss Jamison; Company), Finale: "It Don't Mean a Thing (if it Ain't Got That Swing)" (reprise) (Mr. Hines & Company).

DE means Duke Ellington.

The success of the show on Broadway came as a surprise (reviews were generally outstanding). It won Tonys for costumes, and for Hinton Battle. It was also nominated for musical, direction of a musical, choreography, costumes, lighting, and for Gregory Hines and Phyllis Hyman.

After Broadway. TOUR. Opened on 1/27/82, at the Shubert Theatre, Los Angeles. This was the first ever Broadway show to be broadcast live on pay-per-view TV (on 11/5/83), a special performance made up mostly of touring cast members. *Cast*: Gregory Hines, Paula Kelly, Dee Dee Bridgewater, Hinton Battle, Gregg Burge, Terri Klausner, Mark Fotopoulos, Leata Galloway, Wynonna Smith, Sheri Cowart.

TOUR. Opened on 12/28/82, in Las Vegas. *Cast*: Harold Nicholas, Paula Kelly, Freda Payne (she took the Broadway roles played by Phyllis Hyman & Priscilla Baskerville), Eugene Fleming, George Ratliff, Beth Bowles, Garry Q. Lewis.

TOUR. Opened on 5/24/83, in Pittsburgh. *Cast*: Gregg Burge (dancer) & Ira Hawkins (singer) (both in the role taken by Gregory Hines on Broadway), Janet Hubert, Dee Dee Bridgewater (took the roles played by Phyllis Hyman & Priscilla Baskerville on Broadway), Bruce Anthony Davis, Jamie Rocco, Christina Saffran.

TOUR. Opened on 10/1/88, in Moscow, Russia. PRESENTED BY Jarvis Theatre Projects & Irving Schwartz, in association with the USSR Cultural Fund, Theatre Workers' Union & Soyuzteatr, under the auspices of the original producers; DIRECTOR/CHOREOGRAPHER: Claudia Asbury; SETS: Yuri Kuper; COSTUMES: Slava Zaitsev & Willa Kim; LIGHTING: Richard Winkler; MUSICAL SUPERVISOR: Paul Chihara; CONDUCTOR: Boris Frumkin. *Cast*: Cleve Asbury, Bryant Baldwin, Hinton Battle, Gregg Burge, Tim Connell, T. Michael Dalton, Lauren Goler, Mary Lilygren, Mary Frances McCatty, Lonette McKee, Kevyn Morrow, Elise D. Neal, Alan Onickel, Jackie Patterson, Christina Saffran, Gayle Samuels, David Washington, Crystal Williams, Donna Wood.

652. *The Sound of Music*

Set in Salzburg, in the Austrian Tyrol, in 1938. The true story of Maria, a postulant at Nonnberg Abbey, who alarms her superiors by taking off into the mountains and listening to the sound of music. Deemed unready to become a nun, she is placed as governess to the seven lonely children of Captain Trapp, a gruff ex-naval widower, who is engaged to socially prominent Elsa. Maria teaches music to the children, and falls in love with the Captain. Trapp's daughter Liesl, aged 16, is in love with Rolf, aged 17, an incipient Nazi. Maria and Trapp marry, the family becomes a singing ensemble, and with the aid of the nuns from her old convent, the family escapes the invading Nazis over the mountains to Switzerland. Max is Trapp's friend, and he becomes a Nazi too. In real life Georg von Trapp died in 1947, and Maria came to the USA, eventually becoming a US citizen. The producers of the original Broadway hit cut Maria in on the profits. She died in 1987. Her youngest child, Johannes runs the Trapp Family Lodge in Vermont.

Before Broadway. Maria Trapp's autobiographical novel *The Trapp Family Singers* was published in 1949, and shortly thereafter Hollywood approached her to see if she would consent to sell the title only. But she wanted them to make the book, or nothing. In 1956 she was conned by German film maker Wolfgang Reinhardt (Max's son) into selling her rights to him for $9,000. He then made the German movie *Die Trapp-Familie*. Paramount optioned the U.S. rights, and Vincent Donehue, recently hired by Paramount, saw the film, and realized its potential as a stage musical, with Mary Martin in the lead. Mr. Donehue tried to find Mrs. Trapp, unaware she had no legal rights to the property, but she was in New Guinea. Until she saw Mary Martin in *Annie Get Your Gun*, she had no interest in the story becoming a musical. Richard Halliday was Mary Martin's husband, and he and Leland Hayward came up with the original concept, which was to do it as a straight play by Lindsay & Crouse, with some authentic Tyrolean music by the Trapp family, and perhaps a song by Rodgers and Hammerstein. R & H did not like that idea, so they became co-producers and wrote the whole score. Mary Martin invested $200,000; Rodgers & Hammerstein $100,000; Lindsay & Crouse $80,000; and NBC $20,000. This was the last Broadway musical from Rodgers & Hammerstein as a team. "Edelweiss" was Oscar Hammerstein's final lyric.

The Broadway Run. LUNT—FONTANNE THEATRE, 11/16/59–11/3/62; MARK HELLINGER THEATRE, 11/6/62–6/15/63. 5 previews. Total of 1,143 PERFORMANCES. PRESENTED BY Leland Hayward, Richard Halliday, Richard Rodgers, and Oscar Hammerstein II; MUSIC: Richard Rodgers; LYRICS: Oscar Hammerstein II; BOOK: Howard Lindsay & Russel Crouse; SUGGESTED BY the 1949 autobiography *The Trapp Family Singers*, by Maria Augusta Trapp; DIRECTOR: Vincent J. Donehue; CHOREOGRAPHER: Joe Layton; CHORUS CAPTAIN: Zoya Leporska; SETS: Oliver Smith; COSTUMES: Lucinda Ballard; ASSISTANT COSTUMES: Florence Klotz; MARY MARTIN'S CLOTHES: Mainbocher (except the postulant costume, and the last two costumes, which were designed by Lucinda Ballard); LIGHTING: Jean Rosenthal; MUSICAL DIRECTOR: Frederick Dvonch; ORCHESTRATIONS: Robert Russell Bennett; CHORAL ARRANGEMENTS: Trude Rittman; PRESS: Frank Goodman & Ben Washer; CASTING: Edward Blum; GENERAL MANAGER: Herman Bernstein; COMPANY MANAGER: Warren O'Hara, *Tom Kilpatrick* (by 62–63); PRODUCTION STAGE MANAGER: Peter Zeisler; STAGE MANAGER: Randall Brooks, *Richard Via* (by 61–62); ASSISTANT STAGE MANAGERS: Steven Meyer & Tom Millott, *Cliff Cothren* (by 61–62). *Cast*: MARIA RAINER: Mary Martin (1) ☆, *Martha Wright* (from 10/61), *Jeannie Carson* (from 7/2/62), *Nancy Dussault* (from 9/4/62); SISTER BERTHE, MISTRESS OF NOVICES: Elizabeth Howell (12), *Lizabeth Pritchett* (from 61–62); SISTER MARGARETTA, MISTRESS OF POSTULANTS: Muriel O'Malley (11), *Nadine Lewis* (from 61–62); THE MOTHER ABBESS: Patricia Neway (3), *Elizabeth Howell* (from 61–62); SISTER SOPHIA: Karen Shepard (13); CAPTAIN GEORG VON TRAPP: Theodore Bikel (2), *Donald Scott* (from 61–62); FRANZ, THE BUTLER: John Randolph (6), *Jay Barney* (from 62–63); FRAU SCHMIDT, THE HOUSEKEEPER: Nan McFarland (7); CHILDREN OF CAPTAIN VON TRAPP: LIESL: Lauri Peters (8), *Marissa Mason* [she later became known as Mary Burke] (from 62–63); KURT: Joseph Stewart, *Tommy Leap* (from 61–62); LOUISA: Kathy Dunn; FRIEDRICH: Billy Snowden, *Ronnie Tourso* (from 60–61), *Royston Thomas* (from 62–63); BRIGITTA: Marilyn Rogers (10), *Mary Susan Locke* (from 60–61), *Nita Novy* (from 62–63); MARTA: Mary Susan Locke, *Evanna Lien* (from 60–61), *Christopher Norris* (from 62–63); GRETL: Evanna Lien, *Valerie Lee* (from 60–61), *Laura Michaels* (from 61–62), *Leslie Smith* (from 62–63); ROLF GRUBER: Brian Davies (9), *Jon Voight* (from late 61), *Peter Van Hattum* (from 62–63); ELSA SCHRAEDER: Marion Marlowe (5), *Lois Hunt* (from 61–62), *Jen Nelson* (from 62–63); URSULA, A MAID: Luce Ennis, *Bernice Saunders* (from 61–62); MAX DETWEILER: Kurt Kasznar (4), *Paul Lipson* (from 62–63); HERR ZELLER: Stefan Gierasch, *Milton Luchan* (from 60–61); BARON ELBERFELD: Kirby Smith, *Webb Tilton* (by 61–62); A NEW POSTULANT: Sue Yaeger, *Sara Letton* (from 61–62); ADMIRAL VON SCHREIBER: Michael Gorrin, *Jay Velie* (from 62–63); NEIGHBORS OF CAPTAIN VON TRAPP/NUNS/NOVICES/POSTULANTS/CONTESTANTS IN THE FESTIVAL CONCERT: Joanne Birks, Patricia Brooks (gone by 60–61), June Card (gone by 60–61), Dorothy Dallas (gone by 60–61), Ceil Delli (gone by 60–61), Luce Ennis (gone by 61–62), Cleo Fry, Barbara George (gone by 60–61 but back by 61–62), Joey Heatherton (gone by 60–61), Lucas Hoving (gone by 60–61), Patricia Kelly (gone by 60–61), Maria Kova (gone by 61–62), Shirley Mendonca (gone by 62–63), Kathy Miller (gone by 62–63), Lorna Nash (gone by 61–62), Keith Prentice (gone by 61–62), Nancy Reeves, Bernice Saunders, Connie Sharman (gone by 61–62), Gloria Stevens (gone by 60–61 but back by 61–62), Tatiana Troyanos (gone by 62–63), Mimi Vondra (gone by 61–62). 60–61 replacements: *Catherine Gale* (gone by 61–62 but back by 62–63), *Helen Feit* (gone by 62–63), *Maureen Bailey* (gone by 61–62), *Lu Ann Ragle* (gone by 62–63), *Sarah Hageman, Connie Webber* (gone by 61–62). 61–62 replacements: *Sara Letton, Barbara Gregory* (gone by 62–63), *Dan Ferrone* (gone by 62–63), *Estelle Tyner, Ann Gardner* (gone by 62–63), *Mitzi Wilson, Kenny Dore* (gone by 62–63), *Barbara Meister, Laura Michaels* (gone by 62–63), *Webb Tilton* (gone by 62–63). 62–63 replacements: *Lois Van Pelt, Harry Packwood, Ellen Berse, Anne Nunnally, Betty Christianson, Imelda De Martin.* **Standbys**: Maria: Renee Guerin; Trapp: Kenneth Harvey. **Understudies**: Maria: *Marlys Watters* (by 62–63); Trapp: *Webb Tilton* (by 62–63); Max: Sheppard Kerman; Mother Abbess: Elizabeth Howell, *Lizabeth Pritchett* (by 61–62); Frau Schmidt: Elizabeth Howell, *Sarah Hageman* (by 61–62); Elsa: Karen Shepard; Liesl: Joey Heatherton, *Maureen Bailey* (by 60–61), *Sara Letton* (by 61–62), *Imelda De Martin*; Louisa: Joey Heatherton, *Patty Michaels* (by 60–61), *Imelda De Martin*;

Friedrich/Kurt: David Gress, *Kenny Dore* (by 60–61), *Scott Kennedy* (by 62–63), *Wayne Sullivan*; Gretl: Frances Underhill, *Laura Michaels* (by 60–61), *Valerie Lee*; Marta: Frances Underhill, *Laura Michaels* (by 60–61), *Evanna Lien*; Brigitta: Mary Susan Locke, *Evanna Lien* (by 60–61); Berthe: Dorothy Dallas, *Cleo Fry*; Margaretta: Nancy Reeves; Sophia: Maria Kova, *Shirley Mendonca, Bernice Saunders* (by 62–63); Rolf: Keith Prentice, *Dan Ferrone, Harvey Packwood* (by 62–63), *Philip Proctor*; Zeller: Lucas Hoving, *Steven Meyer* (by 60–61), *Webb Tilton* (by 61–62); Franz/Admiral: Kirby Smith, *Webb Tilton* (by 61–62). *Act I: Scene 1* The Nonnberg Abbey: "Praeludium" (The Nuns of Nonnberg Abbey); *Scene 2* A mountainside near the abbey: "The Sound of Music" (Maria) [a big hit]; *Scene 3* The office of the Mother Abbess; the next morning: "Maria" (Mother Abbess, Sisters Margaretta, Berthe, Sophia), "My Favorite Things" (Maria & Mother Abbess) [a big hit]; *Scene 4* A corridor in the Abbey: "My Favorite Things" (reprise) (Maria & Sister Margaretta); *Scene 5* The living room of the Trapp villa; that afternoon: "Do Re Mi" (Maria & Children) [a hit]; *Scene 6* Outside the Trapp villa; that evening: "(You Are) Sixteen, Going on Seventeen" (Liesl & Rolf); *Scene 7* Maria's bedroom; late that evening: "The Lonely Goatherd" (Maria & Children) [a big hit]; *Scene 7a* A hallway in the Trapp villa; *Scene 8* The terrace of the Trapp villa; six weeks later: "How Can Love Survive?" (Elsa, Max, Captain), "The Sound of Music" (reprise) (Maria, Captain, Children); *Scene 9* A hallway in the Trapp villa; one week later; *Scene 10* The living room; the same evening: Party Waltz (Party Ensemble), Laendler Waltz (Captain & Maria), "So Long, Farewell" (Children); *Scene 11* A corridor in the Abbey: "Morning Hymn" ("Rex Admirabilis") (Nuns); *Scene 12* The office of the Mother Abbess; three days later: "Climb Ev'ry Mountain" (Mother Abbess) [a big hit]. *Act II: Scene 1* The terrace; the same day: Opening Act II (Orchestra), "No Way to Stop It" (Captain, Max, Elsa), "(An) Ordinary Couple" (Maria & Captain); *Scene 2* A corridor in the Abbey; two weeks later; *Scene 3* The office of the Mother Abbess; immediately following; *Scene 4* A cloister overlooking the chapel: "Gaudeamus Domino" ["(Wedding) Processional"] (Ensemble), "Maria" (reprise) (Nuns), "Confitemini Domino" (Nuns); *Scene 5* The living room; one month later: "(You Are) Sixteen, Going on Seventeen" (reprise) (Maria & Liesl), "Do Re Mi" (reprise) (Maria, Captain, Children); *Scene 6* The concert hall; three days later: "Edelweiss" (Captain, Maria, Children), "So Long, Farewell" (reprise) (Maria, Captain, Children); *Scene 7* The garden of Nonnberg Abbey; that night. Finale Ultimo: "Climb Ev'ry Mountain" (reprise) (Company).

Advance sales were well over $2 million, and perhaps over $3 million. Reviews were great. The show won Tony Awards for musical, sets of a musical, musical direction, and for Mary Martin and Patricia Neway. It was also nominated for direction of a musical, and for Theo Bikel, Kurt Kasznar, Lauri Peters and the Children. When Mary Martin beat Ethel Merman (in *Gypsy*) for the best actress Tony, la Merman said, "How do you buck a nun?." Mr. Hammerstein died on 8/23/60, nine months after the opening. Broadway totally blacked out on 8/31/60, for a full minute. The show vacationed 7/2/61–7/16/61. *Sound of Music* was the second-longest-running musical of the 1950s, and the fourth-longest-running of all time to that date.

After Broadway. TOUR. Opened on 2/27/61, at the Riviera, Detroit. It ran for 2 years 9 months. MUSICAL DIRECTOR: Salvatore Dell'Isola. *Cast:* MARIA: Florence Henderson, *Barbara Meister*; ABBESS: Beatrice Krebs [she played it more than 800 times]; SOPHIA: Grace Olsen, *Jeanne Shea*; CAPTAIN: John Myhers; FRANZ: Shev Rodgers; LIESL: Imelda De Martin, *Jane Zachary*; BRIGITTA: Nita Novy, *Ilona Podsada*; MARTA: Linda Ross, *Maryanne Kohler*; GRETL: Christopher Norris, *Bunny Nash*; ELSA: Lynn Brinker, *Marthe Errolle*; ELBERFELD: Kenneth Mars, *Grant Gordon*.

PALACE THEATRE, London. Opened on 5/18/61. 2,385 PERFORMANCES. It was the longest-running American musical in the West End to that time. PRESENTED BY Williamson Music; DIRECTOR: Jerome Whyte; CHOREOGRAPHER: Joe Layton; LONDON CAST RECORDING on EMI. *Cast:* MARIA: Jean Bayless; BERTHE: Sylvia Beamish; MARGARETTA: Olive Gilbert; ABBESS: Constance Shacklock; SOPHIA: Lynn Kennington; CAPTAIN: Roger Dann; FRANZ: Jay Denyer; FRAU SCHMIDT: Diana Beaumont; ELSA: Eunice Hayson; MAX: Harold Kasket; HERR ZELLER: Peter Swanwick.

TOUR. Opened on 9/17/62. PRESENTED BY Henry Guettel. *Cast:*

MARIA: Jeannie Carson; BERTHE: Jessica Quinn; CAPTAIN: John Van Dreelen; LIESL: Ethelyne Dunfee; FRIEDRICH: Tommy Long; ELSA: Marijane Maricle.

PAPER MILL PLAYHOUSE, New Jersey, 1964. *Cast:* MARIA: Barbara Meister; CAPTAIN: Webb Tilton.

THE MOVIE. 1965. This was the most successful movie musical in history. "An Ordinary Couple," "How Can Love Survive?" and "No Way to Stop It" were dropped, and "I Have Confidence" and "Something Good" (both with music and lyrics by Richard Rodgers) were added. These two new songs have been in most of the post–1965 stage productions. Other changes to the score were made: "My Favorite Things," formerly a Maria—Mother Abbess duet, now became a Maria solo, and took the place of "The Lonely Goatherd" in the storm scene, while "The Lonely Goatherd" became part of the puppet scene. RCA recorded the soundtrack. PRODUCER/DIRECTOR: Robert Wise. *Cast:* MARIA: Julie Andrews; ABBESS: Peggy Wood; SOPHIA: Marni Nixon; CAPTAIN: Christopher Plummer (singing dubbed by Bill Lee); BARONESS: Eleanor Parker; MAX: Richard Haydn.

CITY CENTER, NYC, 4/26/67–5/14/67. 23 PERFORMANCES. This production was part of City Center's spring season of three musical revivals (the others were *Finian's Rainbow* and *Wonderful Town*). PRESENTED BY the New York City Center Light Opera Company; DIRECTOR: John Fearnley; CHOREOGRAPHER: Reid Klein; SETS: Oliver Smith; COSTUMES: Stanley Simmons; LIGHTING: Peggy Clark; MUSICAL DIRECTOR: Frederick Rudolph Dvonch; ORCHESTRATIONS: Robert Russell Bennett; CHORAL ARRANGEMENTS: Trude Rittman. *Cast:* MARIA: Constance Towers; ABBESS: Eleanor Steber; CAPTAIN: Bob Wright; LIESL: Sandy Duncan; ROLF: Reid Klein; ELSA: M'el Dowd; MAX: Christopher Hewett; ADMIRAL: Jay Velie. *Standby:* Captain: Webb Tilton. *Understudy:* Maria: Estella Munson. This production opened Act II with a reprise of "My Favorite Things," and, as per the movie "An Ordinary Couple" was replaced with "Something Good" (and this run at City Center was the first major stage production of *The Sound of Music* since the movie came out in 1965).

PAPER MILL PLAYHOUSE, New Jersey, 1970. DIRECTOR: Christopher Hewett. *Cast:* MARIA: Barbara Meister; CAPTAIN: Erik Silju.

JONES BEACH THEATRE, New York, 7/1/70–9/6/70. Return engagement 7/8/71–9/5/71. PRESENTED BY Guy Lombardo; DIRECTOR: John Fearnley; CHOREOGRAPHER: Vincent Alexander; SETS: Peter Wolf; COSTUMES: Winn Morton; LIGHTING: Peggy Clark; MUSICAL DIRECTOR: Oscar Kosarin. *Cast:* MARIA: Constance Towers; ABBESS: Beatrice Krebs, *Maggie Task* (for the return engagement); SOPHIA: Lorna Dallas, *Jeanne Shea* (for the return engagement); CAPTAIN: John Michael King; ROLF: Vincent Alexander; MAX: Christopher Hewett; ELBERFELD: Lee Cass; ADMIRAL: Jay Velie.

TOURING REVIVAL. Opened on 6/21/77, in Dallas, and closed on 9/4/77, at the Arie Crown Theatre, Chicago. PRESENTED BY James M. Nederlander; PRODUCED BY: Tom Hughes; DIRECTOR: Forrest Carter; CHOREOGRAPHER: Eivie McGehee; SETS: Peter Wolf; COSTUMES: Arthur Boccia; MUSICAL DIRECTOR: Gordon Browne. *Cast:* MARIA: Shirley Jones; CAPTAIN: H.M. Wynant; BRIGITTA: Sarah Jessica Parker; MAX: William Le Massena.

PAPER MILL PLAYHOUSE, New Jersey, 1979. DIRECTOR/CHOREOGRAPHER: Robert Johanson. *Cast:* MARIA: Barbara Meister; CAPTAIN: Jean-Pierre Aumont.

JONES BEACH THEATRE, New York, 6/26/80–8/31/80. PRESENTED BY Richard Horner; DIRECTOR: John Fearnley; CHOREOGRAPHER: Frank Wagner; SETS/COSTUMES: Robert Fletcher; MUSICAL DIRECTOR: Jack Gaughan; MANAGING DIRECTOR: Alvin Dorfmann. *Cast:* MARIA: Constance Towers; SOPHIA: Dixie Stewart; CAPTAIN: Earl Wrightson.

AUSTRALIA, 1983. Julie Anthony starred as Maria in this famous Australian production.

NEW YORK STATE THEATRE, 3/8/90–4/22/90. 6 previews. 54 PERFORMANCES. This version had the original 1959 score. PRESENTED BY the New York City Opera, in association with James M. Nederlander; DIRECTOR: James Hammerstein; CHOREOGRAPHER: Joel Bishoff; SETS/LIGHTING: Neil Peter Jampolis; COSTUMES: Suzanne Mess; SOUND: Abe Jacob; CONDUCTOR: Richard Parrinello. *Cast:* MARIA: Debby Boone; BERTHE: Jill Bosworth; MARGARETTA: Michele McBride; ABBESS: Claudia Cummings; SOPHIA: Robin Tabachnik; CAPTAIN: Laurence Guittard; FRANZ: David Rae Smith; FRAU SCHMIDT: Ellen Tovatt; LIESL: Emily Loesser [Miss Loesser was Frank's daughter]; FRIEDRICH: Richard H. Blake; LOUISA: Kelly Karbacz; KURT: Ted Huffman; BRIGITTA: Kia Graves; MARTA: Lauren Gaffney; GRETL: Mary Mazzello; ROLF: Marc Heller; ELSA: Marianne Tatum; URSULA: Bridget Ramos; MAX: Werner Klemperer; ZELLER: Louis Perry; ELBERFELD: William Ledbetter; POS-TULANT: Barbara Shirvis; ADMIRAL: Glenn Rowen. This production went on tour, opening on 11/30/93, at Baltimore's Lyric Opera House. Previews from 11/27/93. It had the same crew as for New York. *Cast:* MARIA: Marie Osmond; ABBESS: Claudia Cummings; CAPTAIN: Keir Dullea, *Garrett Stakes, Laurence Guittard, Neal Ben-Ari*; LIESL: Vanessa Dorman; FRIEDRICH: Eric McCormack, *James J. Kee*; ROLF: Richard H. Blake; ELSA: Jane Seaman, *Lauren Thompson*; MAX: John Tillotson, *Terry Runnels*; ELBERFELD: Jim Oyster.

653. *The Sound of Music (Broadway revival)*

Before Broadway. The idea for this revival came to the producers after Melissa Errico scored so well in the *Encores!* revival of *One Touch of Venus*. Miss Errico then wanted to do a revival of *The Sound of Music*, but instead went into the Broadway production of *High Society*. The producers still wanted to do *The Sound of Music*, and wanted Rebecca Luker as Maria. Miss Luker announced her role, and Jan Maxwell's and Patti Cohenour's, on 10/1/97. On 1/7/98 there was a special press presentation.

The Broadway Run. MARTIN BECK THEATRE, 3/12/98–6/20/99. 38 previews from 2/6/98. 533 PERFORMANCES. PRESENTED BY Hallmark, Thomas Viertel, Steven Baruch, Richard Frankel, and Jujamcyn Theatres, in association with The Rodgers & Hammerstein Organization, Charles Kelman Productions, Simone Genatt Haft, Marc Routh, Jay Binder, and Robert Halmi Jr.; MUSIC: Richard Rodgers; LYRICS: Oscar Hammerstein II; BOOK: Howard Lindsay & Russel Crouse; SUGGESTED BY the 1949 autobiography *The Trapp Family Singers*, by Maria Augusta Trapp; DIRECTOR: Susan H. Schulman; CHOREOGRAPHER: Michael Lichtefeld; SETS: Heidi Ettinger; COSTUMES: Catherine Zuber; LIGHTING: Paul Gallo; SOUND: Tony Meola; MUSICAL DIRECTOR/CONDUCTOR: Michael Rafter; ORIGINAL ORCHESTRATIONS: Robert Russell Bennett; NEW ORCHESTRATIONS: Bruce Coughlin; ORIGINAL CHORAL AND DANCE MUSIC ARRANGEMENTS: Trude Rittman; NEW DANCE MUSIC ARRANGEMENTS/INCIDENTAL MUSIC: Jeanine Tesori; NEW CAST RECORDING on RCA Victor, recorded on 3/16/98, and released on 5/19/98; PRESS: Peter Cromarty; CASTING: Jay Binder; GENERAL MANAGERS: Richard Frankel & Laura Green; COMPANY MANAGER: Kathy Lowe; STAGE MANAGER: Ira Mont. *Cast:* SISTER MARGARETTA, MISTRESS OF POSTULANTS: Jeanne Lehman, *Roxann Parker* (from 2/2/99); SISTER BERTHE, MISTRESS OF NOVICES: Gina Ferrall; THE MOTHER ABBESS: Patti Cohenour, *Jeanne Lehman* (from 2/2/99); SISTER SOPHIA: Ann Brown; MARIA RAINER: Rebecca Luker, *Laura Benanti* (from 3/10/99), *Meg Tolin* (alternate); CAPTAIN GEORG VON TRAPP: Michael Siberry, *Dennis Parlato* (from 11/4/98), *Richard Chamberlain* (from 3/10/99); FRANZ, THE BUTLER: John Curless; FRAU SCHMIDT, THE HOUSEKEEPER: Patricia Conolly; LIESL VON TRAPP: Sara Zelle; FRIEDRICH VON TRAPP: Ryan Hopkins (until 8/6/98), *Lou Taylor Pucci, Christopher Trousdale*; LOUISA VON TRAPP: Natalie Hall (until 8/2/98), *Nora Blackall* (from 8/4/98), *Rachel Beth Levenson*; KURT VON TRAPP: Matthew Ballinger (until 8/6/98), *Marshall Pailet, Christopher Cordell*; BRIGITTA VON TRAPP: Tracy Allison Walsh; MARTA VON TRAPP: Andrea Bowen; GRETL VON TRAPP: Ashley Rose Orr, *Christiana Anbri, Ashlee Keating*; ROLF GRUBER: Dashiell Eaves, *Ben Sheaffer*; URSULA, A MAID: Lynn C. Pinto; ELSA SCHRAEDER: Jan Maxwell, *Kay McClelland* (7/28–9/20/98), *Jan Maxwell* (from 9/23/98); MAX DETWEILER: Fred Applegate, *Patrick Quinn, Lenny Wolpe* (from 3/10/99); THE TRIO OF THE SAENGERBUND OF HERWEGAN: Ann Brown, Gina Ferrall, Joan Barber (*Mary Kate Law*); HERR ZELLER: Timothy Landfield, *Brian Sutherland*; BARON ELBERFELD: Gannon McHale; FRAU ZELLER: Kelly Cae Hogan; BARONESS ELBERFELD: Martha Hawley; A NEW POSTULANT: Laura Benanti; ADMIRAL VON SCHREIBER: Reno Roop; A NAZI LIEUTENANT: Matt Loney; ENSEMBLE: Anne Allgood, Joan

Barber, Nora Blackall, Patricia Conolly, Rachel de Benedet, Kelly Cae Hogan, Siri Howard, Patricia Phillips, Lynn C. Pinto, Julie Prosser, Sylvia Rhyne, Michelle Rios, Kristie Dale Sanders, Ben Sheaffer, Erik Sorensen. *Understudies:* Maria: Laura Benanti, Meg Tolin, Betsi Morrison; Captain: Timothy Landfield, Brian Sutherland, Matt Loney; Abbess: Jeanne Lehman, Joan Barber, Roxann Parker, Sylvia Rhyne; Elsa: Kelly Cae Hogan, Kristie Dale Sanders, Rachel de Benedet, Sylvia Rhyne; Berthe: Joan Barber, Julie Prosser, Mary Kate Law; Margaretta: Julie Prosser, Margaret Shafer, Elsa de Benedet; Sophia: Betsi Morrison & Lynn C. Pinto; Rolf: Ben Sheaffer & Erik Sorensen; Liesl: Siri Howard; Marta/Gretl: Morgan Billings; Friedrich/Kurt: Christopher Trousdale & Eric Jarboe; Louisa/Brigitta: Rachel Beth Levenson; Ursula: Betsi Morrison; Franz: Craig Mason & Reno Roop; Baroness/New Postulant: Betsi Morrison & Margaret Shafer; Zeller: Matt Loney & Craig Mason; Max: Gannon McHale & Craig Mason; Baron/Admiral/Nazi: Craig Mason; Frau Schmidt: Martha Hawley. *Swings:* Craig Mason, Tad Ingram, Betsi Morrison, Margaret Shafer. **Act I:** "Praeludium: Dixit Dominus/Morning Hymn/Alleluia" (Nuns), "The Sound of Music" (Maria), "Maria" (Mother Abbess & Nuns), "I Have Confidence" (Maria) [from the movie], "Do Re Mi" (Maria & Children), "Sixteen, Going on Seventeen" (Rolf & Liesl), "My Favorite Things" (Maria & Children), "How Can Love Survive?" (Elsa, Max, Captain), "The Sound of Music" (reprise) (Maria), "Laendler Waltz" (Captain & Maria), "So Long, Farewell" (Children), "Climb Ev'ry Mountain" (Mother Abbess). **Act II:** Opening Act II (Max & Children), "No Way to Stop It" (Captain, Max, Elsa), "Something Good" (Maria & Captain) [this replaced "An Ordinary Couple"], "Wedding Processional/Canticle" (Ensemble), "Sixteen, Going on Seventeen" (reprise) (Maria & Liesl), "The Lonely Goatherd" (Maria & Children), "Edelweiss" (Captain), "So Long, Farewell" (reprise) (Maria, Captain, Children), Finale Ultimo (Company).

Broadway reviews were evenly divided. The show received a Tony Nomination for revival of a musical. On 12/22/98 it was announced that Richard Chamberlain would take over the role of the Captain on 3/9/99 (on 2/4/99 this date was put back to 3/10/99), for 17 weeks, and then take the show on a national tour. On 2/4/99 it was also announced that Laura Benanti and Lenny Wolpe would take over the roles of Maria and Max respectively. On 6/8/99 it was announced that the show would close on 6/27/99 (it actually closed early, on 6/20/99).

After Broadway. TOUR. First announced on 11/4/98, it opened on 8/23/99, at the Orpheum Theatre, Minneapolis, and closed on 5/14/00, in San Francisco. DIRECTOR: Susan H. Schulman. *Cast:* MARIA: Meg Tolin; BERTHE: Linda Strasser; MARGARETTA: Sylvia Rhyne; ABBESS: Jeanne Lehman; SOPHIA: Betsi Morrison; CAPTAIN: Richard Chamberlain, *Robert Stoeckle*; FRANZ: Tad Ingram; FRAU SCHMIDT: Joy Franz; LIESL: Megan McGinnis; FRIEDRICH: Greg Sullo; LOUISA: Diana Rice; KURT: Alex Bowen; BRIGITTA: Carissa Farina; MARTA: Andrea Bowen; GRETL: Ashley Keating; ROLF: Ben Sheaffer; ELSA: Rachel de Benedet; MAX: Drew Eshelman; ZELLER: Robert Stoeckle; ELBERFELD: Michael Hayward-Jones; BARONESS: Lenora Eve; SCHREIBER: Steve Pudenz; NEW POSTULANT: Aimee Pilgermeyer; NAZI LIEUTENANT: Luke Walrath.

NON-EQUITY TOUR. PRESENTED BY Troika. It was due to open in Toronto on 9/19/00, but ran into some problems. Corbin Bernsen was announced as the Captain, but when he found out it was non-Equity (i.e. a show that paid considerably less than a Union show) he quit (this was announced on 8/15/00). The Toronto opening gig was canceled. Barry Williams, another Equity member, replaced him, but on 9/21/00 it was announced that Mr. Williams, too, had quit. But he hadn't. He diminished his financial core status within Equity, thus placing him outside the jurisdiction of the union, and then went ahead with the tour, which finally opened in Fort Myers, Florida, 10/27/00. Equity felt that Mr. Williams was still subject to their control, and fined him $52,000 on 1/17/01. Aside from that, Equity members picketed the show wherever it went on tour.

TOUR. Opened on 7/6/03, at the Miller Outdoor Theatre, Houston. DIRECTOR: Drew Scott Harris; CHOREOGRAPHER: Norb Joerder. *Cast:* MARIA: Marla Schaffel; MOTHER ABBESS: Jeanne Lehman; CAPTAIN: Burke Moses; ELSA: Colleen Fitzpatrick; MAX: Ed Dixon.

PAPER MILL PLAYHOUSE, New Jersey, 10/31/03–12/14/03. Previews from 10/29/03. DIRECTOR/CHOREOGRAPHER: James Brennan; MUSICAL DIRECTOR: Tom Helm. *Cast:* MARIA: Amanda Watkins; MOTHER ABBESS:

Meg Bussert; CAPTAIN: Robert Cuccioli; FRANZ: William Solo; ELSA: Donna English; MAX: Ed Dixon.

654. *South Pacific*

This was the fourth "Rodgers and Hammerstein musical" (after *Oklahoma!*, *Carousel*, and *Allegro*).

Before Broadway. There had been a short-lived, unconnected, 1943 straight Broadway play of the same name, written by Howard Rigbsy and Dorothy Heyward, about a black American from Georgia and his shipmates who are torpedoed and land on a Japanese-held South Pacific island; with Canada Lee, Ruby Dee and — in a walk on part — Ossie Davis.

MGM looked at the possibility of filming James Michener's collection of short stories about the South Sea Islands during World War II, but decided not to. Kenneth MacKenna, head of the story department there, recommended it as a stage production to Josh Logan, who read it and decided to do it. The story *Fo' Dolla*, with naval lieutenant Joe Cable falling in love with beautiful 17-year-old Tonkinese girl Liat, was his starting point, and the character of shrewd and avaricious Bloody Mary (a local trader who was also Liat's mother), added color. In 1948 he took the idea to producer Leland Hayward, who warned him not to mention this to anyone until they had acquired the rights. However, Logan did mention it — to Richard Rodgers at a party. Rodgers and Hammerstein bought 51 per cent of the rights, leaving the other 49 to Logan & Hayward. Originally Oscar Hammerstein was to have written the libretto, but as Josh Logan had been in the South Pacific during the War, it was judged best that he write it. In the end, Logan wrote at least half the book, but received no credit. Once work had begun on the project, it became clear that *Fo' Dolla* was too similar to the Madame Butterfly story, so they focused on *Our Heroine*, another story in the Michener collection. This involved Nellie, a nurse from Little Rock, Arkansas, and Emile, a middle-aged French planter who has two children by a now-deceased island woman. Nellie has problems with his interracial marriage, and leaves him. Some of the elements of *Fo' Dolla* came back in, as the subplot involves Cable, and his affair with Liat. Cable realizes his family back home would never accept an Asian girl as their daughter-in-law. Emile and Cable go on a dangerous mission behind Japanese lines. The lieutenant dies, but Emile is re-united with Nellie. The action takes place on two Pacific islands, and the time is a lull during the fighting with Japan. There is a lapse of time between the two acts. The song "Suddenly Lucky," that Josh Logan judged as wrong for the setting of the relationship between Cable and Liat, was dropped, and wound up becoming "Getting to Know You," in *The King and I* two years later. "My Girl Back Home," a song for Cable and Nellie, was also cut (but it was used again for the movie). "Now is the Time" (Emile) was cut too, but re-appeared in various later productions. Mary Martin washing her hair on stage was a novelty. The show tried out in New Haven and Boston, *to raves*. Emlyn Williams cut ten minutes from the running time (he is uncredited). In Boston, where top prices were $5.40, all tickets were sold in advance. There was a lot of fighting between Logan and the Rodgers & Hammerstein team, over billing and royalties, and when the two producers offered Logan *The King and I* to direct, he turned them down. Although Josh Logan is credited with the choreography in *South Pacific*, there really wasn't any. Archie Savage did a soft-shoe number, and the nurses did some dancing in the number "Honey Bun," but that was about it.

The Broadway Run. MAJESTIC THEATRE, 4/7/49–5/16/53; BROADWAY THEATRE, 6/29/53–1/16/54. Total of 1,925 PERFORMANCES. PRESENTED BY Richard Rodgers & Oscar Hammerstein II, in association with Leland Hayward & Joshua Logan; MUSIC: Richard Rodgers; LYRICS: Oscar Hammerstein II; BOOK: Oscar Hammerstein II & Joshua Logan; BASED ON James A. Michener's 1948 Pulitzer Prize–winning collection of stories *Tales of the South Pacific*; DIRECTOR/CHOREOGRAPHER: Joshua Logan; SETS/LIGHTING: Jo Mielziner; COSTUMES: Motley; MUSICAL DIRECTOR: Salvatore Dell'Isola, *L. Frank Nowicki* (by 52–53); ORCHESTRATIONS: Robert Russell Bennett; DANCE & INCIDENTAL MUSIC ARRANGEMENTS/ASSISTANT TO RICHARD RODGERS: Trude Rittman; PRESS: Michel Mok & Helen Hoerle, *John L. Toohey, Peggy Phillips*,

Frank Goodman; CASTING: John Fearnley; GENERAL MANAGER: Morris Jacobs; COMPANY MANAGER: Maurice Winters, *Rube Bernstein* (by 52–53); PRODUCTION STAGE MANAGER: Charles Atkin; GENERAL STAGE MANAGER: Jean Barrere, *Philip Mathias*; ASSISTANT STAGE MANAGER: Beau Tilden, *James Hammerstein*. **Cast:** NGANA: Barbara Luna, *Dolores Decin* (from 50–51), *Bunny Warner* (alternate by 49–50), *Rosalina Davila* (from 50–51), *Maria Suarez* (from 52–53), *Cristanta Cornejo*; JEROME: Michael De Leon (*Jose Perez* from 50–51, *Thomas Griffen* from 52–53) & Noel De Leon (*Robert Cortazal* from 49–50, *George Armand* from 50–51). Fabian Acosta was an alternate; HENRY: Richard Silvera; ENSIGN NELLIE FORBUSH: Mary Martin (1), *Martha Wright* (from 6/51), *Cloris Leachman* (for 3 weeks in 52–53, during Miss Wright's absence); EMILE DE BECQUE: Ezio Pinza (2) (until 5/31/50), *Richard Eastham* (during Mr. Pinza's absences), *Ray Middleton* (from 6/50), *Roger Rico* (from 51–52), *George Britton* (from 51–52); BLOODY MARY: Juanita Hall (4), *Diosa Costello* (from 51–52), *Odette Myrtil* (from 51–52), *Juanita Hall* (from 52–53), *Musa Williams* (from 52–53); BLOODY MARY'S ASSISTANT: Musa Williams, *Katherine Graves* (from 52–53); ABNER: Archie Savage, *Albert Popwell* (from 50–51); STEWPOT: Henry Slate, *Dort Clark* (from 50–51), *Jack Weston* (from 52–53); LUTHER BILLIS: Myron McCormick (3); PROFESSOR: Fred Sadoff, *Gene Saks* (from 50–51); LT. JOSEPH CABLE, USMC: William Tabbert (5); CAPT. GEORGE BRACKETT, USN: Martin Wolfson; CDR. WILLIAM HARBISON, USN: Harvey Stephens, *Bartlett Robinson* (from 52–53); YEOMAN HERBERT QUALE: Alan Gilbert, *William McGraw* (from 50–51); SGT. KENNETH JOHNSON: Thomas Gleason; SEABEE RICHARD WEST: Richard Eastham (sometimes credited as Dickinson Eastham — his real name), *Webb Tilton* (from 49–50), *Don Fellows* (from 52–53); SEABEE MORTON WISE: Henry Michel; SEAMAN TOM O'BRIEN: Bill Dwyer, *William McGraw* (from 49–50), *Peter Kelley* (from 50–51), *Steve Roland* (from 52–53), *Peter Smith*; RADIO OPERATOR BOB McCAFFREY: Biff McGuire, *Jack Fontan* (from 49–50), *Bill Thunhurst* (from 50–51), *Steve Holland* (from 52–53), *Kermit Kegley* (from 52–53); MARINE CPL. HAMILTON STEEVES: Jim Hawthorne, *Robert Rippy* (from 50–51); STAFF SGT. THOMAS HASSINGER: Jack Fontan, *Eugene Smith* (from 49–50); SEAMAN JAMES HAYES: Beau Tilden [this role was cut by 52–53, and replaced by the roles of Moulton & Schulz]; PVT VICTOR MOULTON: Arthur Hammond [this role and that of Schulz were created for the 52–53 season, to replace that of Hayes]; SEAMAN GUSTL SCHULZ: William Diehl [this role and that of Moulton were created for the 52–53 season, to replace that of Hayes]; LT. GENEVIEVE MARSHALL: Jacqueline Fisher, *Betty Gillett* (from 50–51), *Patricia Marand* (from 51–52), *Dorothy Richards* (from 52–53); ENSIGN DINAH MURPHY: Roslynd Lowe, *Mimi Kelly* (from 51–52), *Betty Early* (from 52–53); ENSIGN JANET MacGREGOR: Sandra Deel, *Billie Worth* (from 49–50), *Mimi Kelly* (from 50–51), *Leigh Allen* (from 51–52), *Merle Muskal* (from 52–53); ENSIGN CORA MACRAE: Bernice Saunders, *Betty Gillett* (from 51–52); ENSIGN SUE YAEGER: Pat Northrop, *Melle Matthews* (from 49–50), *Betty O'Neil* (from 50–51), *Roberta MacDonald* (from 51–52); ENSIGN LISA MINELLI: Gloria Meli, *Leigh Allen* (from 50–51), *Pat Finch* (from 51–52); ENSIGN CONNIE WALEWSKA: Mardi Bayne, *Karen Lewis* (from 49–50), *Merle Muskal* (from 51–52), *Helen Clayton* (from 52–53), *Jean Shore* (from 52–53); ENSIGN PAMELA WHITMORE: Evelyn Colby, *Mardi Bayne* (from 49–50), *Elizabeth Early* (from 51–52), *Joan Kavanagh* (from 52–53); ENSIGN BESSIE NOONAN: Helena Schurgot, *Virginia Martin* (from 52–53); LIAT: Betta St. John (6), *Irma Sandre* (from 51–52); MARCEL, HENRY'S ASSISTANT: Richard Loo; LT. BUZZ ADAMS: Don Fellows, *Bill Dwyer* (from 49–50); ISLANDERS/SAILORS/MARINES/OFFICERS: Mary Ann Reeve, Chin Yu (gone by 50–51), Alex Nicol (*Don Leslie* from 49–50 & gone by 50–51), Eugene Smith (gone by 50–51), Richard Loo, William Ferguson (gone by 50–51), *Dorothy Maruki* (new in 50–51), *Donald Covert* (new in 50–51 and gone by 51–52), *William McGraw*. **Understudies**: Nellie: Sandra Deel, *Billie Worth, Mimi Kelly* (by 50–51), *Betty Early* (by 52–53); Emile: Dick Eastham, *Webb Tilton, Henry Michel* (by 51–52); Bloody Mary: Musa Williams, *Katherine Graves* (by 52–53); Billis: Henry Slate, *Dort Clark* (by 50–51), *Jack Weston* (by 52–53); Cable: Alan Gilbert, *Bill Thunhurst* (by 50–51), *Peter Kelley* (by 51–52), *William Diehl* (by 52–53); Brackett: Thomas Gleason; Harbison: Henry Michel; Henry: Richard Loo; Professor: *Gene Smith* (by 49–50); Adams: *William McGraw* (by 49–50); Liat: *Dorothy Maruki* (from 50–51); Stewpot: *Steve Holland* (by 51–52), *Kermit Kegley* (by 52–53); Quale/

McCaffrey: *Arthur Hammond* (by 52–53); Ngana: Rosalina Davila; Jerome: George Finn. Overture (Orchestra). ***Act I: Scene 1*** The terrace of Emile de Becque's plantation home: "Dites-Moi (Pourquoi)" (Ngana & Jerome), "A Cockeyed Optimist" (Nellie), "Twin Soliloquies" ("Wonder How it Feels") (Nellie & Emile), "Some Enchanted Evening" (Emile) [the big hit], "Dites-Moi (Pourquoi)" (reprise) (Ngana, Jerome, Emile); ***Scene 2*** A camp on the beach in another part of the island: "Bloody Mary (is the Girl I Love)" (Sailors, Seabees, Marines, Bloody Mary); ***Scene 3*** Edge of a palm grove near the beach: "There is Nothin' Like a Dame" (Billis, Sailors, Seabees, Marines) [a bit hit], "Bali Ha'i" (Bloody Mary) [a hit], "Bali Ha'i" (reprise) (Cable); ***Scene 4*** The Company street; ***Scene 5*** Inside the Island Commander's office; ***Scene 6*** The Company street; ***Scene 7*** Another part of the beach: "I'm Gonna Wash That Man Right Outa My Hair" (Nellie, Dinah, Janet, Girls' Chorus) [a big hit], "Some Enchanted Evening" (reprise) (Emile & Nellie), "(I'm in Love With) A Wonderful Guy" (Nellie & Nurses); ***Scene 8*** Inside the Island Commander's office; ***Scene 9*** On the island of Bali Ha'i: "Bali Ha'i" (reprise) (French & Native girls); ***Scene 10*** Inside Liat's hut on Bali Ha'i: "Younger than Springtime" (Cable) [a big hit] [a re-working of "My Wife," which had been cut from Rogers & Hammerstein's previous musical, *Allegro*]; ***Scene 11*** Near the beach on the island of Bali Ha'i: "Bali Ha'i" (reprise) (French & Native Girls); ***Scene 12*** Emile's terrace: "(I'm in Love With) A Wonderful Guy" (reprise) (Nellie & Emile), "This is How it Feels" (Emile & Nellie), Act I Finale: "I'm Gonna Wash That Man Right Outa My Hair" (reprise) (Nellie & Emile). ***Act II: Scene 1*** The stage during the Company show *The Thanksgiving Follies*: Soft Shoe Dance ("Thanksgiving Follies") (Nellie, Nurses, GIs); ***Scene 2*** Backstage at The Follies: "Happy Talk" (Bloody Mary, Liat & Cable), "Younger than Springtime" (reprise) (Cable); ***Scene 3*** The stage of The Follies; the performance resumes: "Honey Bun" (Nellie, Billis, Girls); ***Scene 4*** Backstage at The Follies: "(You've Got to Be) Carefully Taught" (Cable), "This Nearly Was Mine" (Emile); ***Scene 5*** The Communications Office; ***Scene 6*** Another part of the island; ***Scene 7*** The Communications Office; ***Scene 8*** The Company street; ***Scene 9*** Another part of the beach: "Some Enchanted Evening" (reprise) (Nellie) [before Broadway this reprise replaced "Bright Canary Yellow" (Emile), which was not published until 1951, but only then as an instrumental called "Loneliness of Evening." However, it was used finally in the 1993 production of *Cinderella*—see appendix]; ***Scene 10*** Company Street: "Honey Bun" (reprise) (Sailors, Seabees, Marines); ***Scene 11*** Emile's terrace: Finale: "Dites-Moi (Pourquoi)" (reprise) (Nellie, Emile, Ngana).

By the time it arrived on Broadway it had taken in over half a million dollars in advance sales, a huge record at the time. At the opening the future team of Hal Prince and Steve Sondheim met for the first time. Critics did nothing but rave. The show won a Pulitzer Prize for Drama. It also won a 1949 Tony Award for sets (actually for Jo Mielziner's entire year), and 1950 Tony Awards for musical, producers of a musical, composer, book, direction, and for Ezio Pinza, Mary Martin, Myron McCormick, and Juanita Hall. By its second year it was still playing to Standing Room Only audiences. Ezio Pinza was absent for more than 50 performances, and suffered $25,000 penalties. The show vacationed 12/17/50–12/25/50. George Sanders was about to take over from Ray Middleton as Emile, but reneged (Roger Rico took role instead). The show closed on 5/16/53 for a 6-week tour in Boston, then re-opened at the Broadway Theatre on 6/29/53. Shirley Jones played one of the nurses in the 53–54 season. By the time it closed, 3,500,000 people had seen it. *South Pacific* was the second-longest running musical of the 1940s (after *Oklahoma!*).

After Broadway. Tour. 1949–50. Re-opened on 11/14/50, at the Shubert Theatre, Chicago. Altogether, the tour ran over 5 years, and visited 118 cities. MUSICAL DIRECTOR: Will Irwin, *Robert Stanley* (by 54–55). **Cast:** NGANA: Maria Migenes & Julia Migenes; NELLIE: Janet Blair, *Martha Wright* (from 3 weeks during Miss Blair's absence), *Jeanne Bal* (from 53–54), *Iva Withers* (from 54–55); EMILE: Richard Eastham, *Webb Tilton* (from 51–52), *Allen Gerard* (from 54–55); BLOODY MARY: Diosa Costello, *Irene Bordoni* (from 11/14/50), *Dorothy Franklin* (from 52–53); BLOODY MARY'S ASSISTANT: Jeanette Migenes; STEWPOT: Lee Krieger, *Ted Beniades* (from 11/14/50), *John Ferry* (from 52–53); BILLIS: Ray Walston, *David Burns* (from 11/14/50), *Benny Baker* (from 52–53); PROFESSOR: Bill Mullikin, *Don Wortman* (from 11/14/50), *Earl Drebing* (from

52–53); CABLE: Robert Whitlow, *Stanley Grover* (from 52–53), *Jack Ringstad* (from 54–55); BRACKETT: Robert Emmett Keane, *Russ Brown* (from 53–54); HARBISON: Alan Baxter, *Robert De Cost* (from 54–55); QUALE: Patrick Tolson, *Vincent McMahon* (from 53–54); WISE: Sam Kirkham; O'BRIEN: Bill Bloxsom, *David Daniels* (from 52–53), *David Ferris* (from 53–54); MCCAFFREY: Leroy Busch, *John Ferry* (from 51–52); PVT SVEN LARSEN: Lanier Davis, *Don Swenson* (from 52–53), *Sam Kirkham* (from 53–54) [role created in 52–53]; HASSINGER: John Ferry, *Gordon Ewing* (from 52–53) [role cut by 53–54]; DINAH: Dody Heath, *Edith Lane* (from 50–51), *Joan Tansgrud* (from 51–52); JANET: Laurel Shelby, *Joan Tansgrud* (from 52–53), *Bernice Massi* (from 52–53), *Priscilla Mullins* (from 53–54), *Millie Slavin* (from 54–55); LISA: Trudy De Luz, *Millie Slavin* (from 52–53), *Christy Palmer* [she was Mrs. Alan Baxter] (from 53–54); MARCEL: Perry Lopez; LIAT: Norma Calderon, *Marie Young* (from 53–54).

THEATRE ROYAL, Drury Lane, London, 11/1/51–9/26/53. 802 PERFORMANCES. DIRECTOR/CHOREOGRAPHER: Jerome Whyte; MUSICAL DIRECTOR: Reginald Burston. **Cast:** NELLIE: Mary Martin, *Julie Wilson, Patricia Hartley*; EMILE: Wilbur Evans; BLOODY MARY: Muriel Smith; ABNER: Archie Savage; STEWPOT: Bill Nagy; BILLIS: Ray Walston, *Colin Croft, Fredd Wayne*; CABLE: Peter Grant, *David Williams*; BRACKETT: Hartley Power, *John McLaren*; QUALE: Larry Hagman, *Nevil Whiting*; JOHNSON: Ivor Emmanuel; JANET: Deirdre de Payer, *Millicent Martin*; SUE: June Whitfield, *Carol Leslie, Margaret Miles*; LISA: Joyce Blair, *Louie Ramsay*; LIAT: Betta St. John, *Chin Yu*.

CITY CENTER, NYC, 5/4/55–5/15/55. 15 PERFORMANCES. PRESENTED BY the New York City Center Light Opera Company; DIRECTOR: Charles Atkin; SETS: Jo Mielziner; COSTUMES: Motley; COSTUME SUPERVISOR: Frank Spencer; MUSICAL DIRECTOR: Frederick Dvonch. **Cast:** NGANA: Margaret Sokal; JEROME: Antonio Obregon; HENRY: Richard Silvera; NELLIE: Sandra Deel; EMILE: Richard Collett; BLOODY MARY: Sylvia Syms; BLOODY MARY'S ASSISTANT: Julie Winston; ABNER: J.J. Riley; STEWPOT: Frank Maxwell; BILLIS: Henry Slate; PROFESSOR: Gene Saks; CABLE: Herb Banke; BRACKETT: Martin Wolfson; HARBISON: Warren J. Brown; QUALE: Seth Riggs; JOHNSON: Howard Lear; WEST: Evans Thornton; WISE: Murray Vines; O'BRIEN: Dick Armbruster; MCCAFFREY: Clifford Fearl; HASSINGER: Ralph Vucci; GENEVIEVE: Eileen Moran; DINAH: Edith Lane; JANET: Janice Samarie; CORA: Louise Pearl; BESSIE: Michelle Reiner; CONNIE: Helen Baisley; PAMELA: Elaine Spaulding; SUE: Theresa Mari; LIAT: Carol Lawrence; BUZZ: Don Fellows; SHORE PATROL: Bob Rippy. **Understudy**: Bloody Mary: Rosetta Le Noire.

CITY CENTER, NYC, 4/24/57–5/12/57. 23 PERFORMANCES. PRESENTED BY the New York City Center Light Opera Company; DIRECTOR: John Fearnley; SETS: Jo Mielziner; COSTUMES: Motley; COSTUME SUPERVISOR: Florence Klotz; LIGHTING: Peggy Clark; MUSICAL DIRECTOR: Frederick Dvonch. **Cast:** NGANA: Lynn Kikuchi; NELLIE: Mindy Carson; EMILE: Robert Wright; BLOODY MARY: Juanita Hall; BLOODY MARY'S ASSISTANT: Julia Gerace; ABNER: Jim McMillan; STEWPOT: Lou Wills Jr.; BILLIS: Harvey Lembeck; PROFESSOR: Bill Mullikin; CABLE: Allen Case; BRACKETT: Martin Wolfson; HARBISON: Alan Baxter; QUALE: Ray Weaver; JOHNSON: Van Stevens; WEST: Daniel Hannafin; WISE: Evans Thornton; SGT. JUAN CORTEZ: Quinto Biagioni [Cortez was a new character]; O'BRIEN: Jack McMinn; MCCAFFREY: Sam Kirkham; STEEVES: Lee Warren; HASSINGER: Charles Aschmann; HAYES: Ralph Vucci; GENEVIEVE: Miriam Gulager; DINAH: Christy Palmer; JANET: Mildred Slavin; CORA: Pat Finch; BESSIE: Barbara Saxby; PAMELA: Betty Graeber; SUE: Peggy Hadley; LISA: Betty McNamara; LIAT: Imelda De Martin; BUZZ: Dick Button; SHORE PATROL: Peter Held.

THE MOVIE. 1958. **Cast:** NELLIE: Mitzi Gaynor; EMILE: Rossano Brazzi (singing dubbed by Giorgio Tozzi); BLOODY MARY: Juanita Hall (singing dubbed by Muriel Smith); BILLIS: Ray Walston; CABLE: John Kerr (singing dubbed by Bill Lee); LIAT: France Nuyen; NATIVE CHIEF: Archie Savage; CO-PILOT: Ron Ely.

CITY CENTER, NYC, 4/26/61–5/14/61. 23 PERFORMANCES. This was a stop in a national tour. PRESENTED BY the New York City Center Light Opera Company; DIRECTOR: John Fearnley; SETS: Paul Morrison (adapted Jo Mielziner's original design); COSTUMES: Stanley Simmons; MUSICAL DIRECTOR: Julius Rudel. **Cast:** JEROME: Delfino de Arco; NELLIE: Allyn Ann McLerie; EMILE: William Chapman; BLOODY MARY:

Rosetta Le Noire; BLOODY MARY'S ASSISTANT: Musa Williams; ABNER: Jim McMillan; STEWPOT: Jeff Harris; BILLIS: Dort Clark; CABLE: Stanley Grover; BRACKETT: Edmund Baylies; HARBISON: Wesley Addy; QUALE: Kenny Adams; JOHNSON: Daniel P. Hannafin; WEST: Don Becker; MCCAFFREY: John Aman; STAFF SGT GIULIO FASCINATO: Richard Nieves [Fascinato was a new character]; HAYES: Ralph Vucci; JANET: Betty Jane Schwering; CORA: Penny Fuller; SUE: Sybil Scotford; LIAT: Coco Ramirez; BUZZ: Don Corby; SHORE PATROL: Casper Roos. *Understudy*: Nellie: Penny Fuller.

PAPER MILL PLAYHOUSE, New Jersey, 1962. DIRECTOR: James Hammerstein. *Cast:* NELLIE: Betsy Palmer; EMILE: William Chapman; ALSO WITH: Gabriel Dell.

CITY CENTER, NYC, 6/2/65–6/13/65. 15 PERFORMANCES. Part of a City Center four-musical package (the others were: *Guys and Dolls, Kiss Me, Kate* and *The Music Man*). PRESENTED BY the New York City Center Light Opera Company; DIRECTOR: James Hammerstein; CHOREOGRAPHER: Albert Popwell; SETS: Jo Mielziner; COSTUMES: Stanley Simmons; LIGHTING: Peggy Clark; MUSICAL DIRECTOR: Anton Coppola. *Cast:* NGANA: Dana Shimizu; JEROME: Keenan Shimizu, HENRY: Sab Shimono; NELLIE: Betsy Palmer; EMILE: Ray Middleton; BLOODY MARY: Honey Sanders; BLOODY MARY'S ASSISTANT: Maureen Tiongco; ABNER: Victor Duntiere; STEWPOT: Tom Pedi; BILLIS: Alan North; PROFESSOR: Mickey Karm; CABLE: Richard Armbruster; BRACKETT: Murvyn Vye; HARBISON: Sam Kirkham; QUALE: Walter P. Brown; JOHNSON: William Wendt; WEST: Ken Ayers; WISE: Scott Blanchard; HASSINGER: Philip Lucas; SUE: Jody Lane; SEAMAN JOHN CLARK: Don Yule [Clark was a new character]; LIAT: Eleanor A. Calbes.

NEW YORK STATE THEATRE, 6/12/67–9/9/6. 104 PERFORMANCES. PRESENTED BY Music Theatre of Lincoln Center; DIRECTOR: Joe Layton; SETS/COSTUMES: Fred Voelpel; LIGHTING: Jules Fisher; MUSICAL DIRECTOR: Jonathan Anderson; NEW CAST RECORDING on Columbia. *Cast:* NGANA: Dana Shimizu; JEROME: Keenan Shimizu; HENRY: Robert Ito; NELLIE: Florence Henderson; EMILE: Giorgio Tozzi; BLOODY MARY: Irene Byatt; ABNER: Judd Jones; STEWPOT: Brad Sullivan; BILLIS: David Doyle; PROFESSOR: Mickey Karm; CABLE: Justin McDonough; BRACKETT: Lyle Talbot; HARBISON: Bob Monroe; QUALE: Ted Story; JOHNSON: William Lutz; WEST: Frank Scannelli, *Mark East*; WISE: Alexander Orfaly, *Gordon Cook*; O'BRIEN: James O'Sullivan; MCCAFFREY: Roger Brown; STEEVES: Dick Ensslen; HASSINGER: Phil Lucas; SEABEE JAMES JEROME: Joseph Della Sorte; PVT SVEN LARSEN: Don Dolan; PVT JACK WALTERS: Bob Barbieri; PVT DICK SEDERHOLM: Jess E. Richards; SEABEE ROGER PITT: Marvin Camillo; SEABEE JOHN NATHAN: David Jarratt [role added during the run]; SEABEE KEITH MOORE: Laried Montgomery, *Dale Westerman*; GENEVIEVE: Jane Coleman; LISA: Lisa Damon; CONNIE: Martha Danielle; JANET: Susan Campbell; BESSIE: Joyce Maret; PAMELA: Patti Davis [role dropped during the run]; ENSIGN RITA ADAMS: Anne Nathan; SUE: Judy Case, *Joyce McDonald*; CORA: Lynn Dovel; DINAH: Bobbi Baird; LIAT: Eleanor Calbes; BUZZ: Jack Knight. *Standby*: Emile: Gene Hollman. *Understudies*: Nellie: Bobbi Baird; Cable: David Jarratt; Brackett: Howard Fischer; Ngana: Nancy Asai.

JONES BEACH THEATRE, NY, 6/27/68–9/2/68. 61 PERFORMANCES. PRESENTED BY Guy Lombardo; DIRECTOR: William Hammerstein; CHOREOGRAPHER: Jane McLaughlin; SETS: Fred Voelpel; COSTUMES: Winn Morton; LIGHTING: Peggy Clark; MUSICAL DIRECTOR: John Lesko. *Cast:* NELLIE: Kathleen Nolan; EMILE: Jerome Hines; BLOODY MARY: Martha Larrimore.

JONES BEACH THEATRE, NY, 7/3/69–9/1/69. A repeat of the 1968 run. MUSICAL DIRECTOR: Frederick Dvonch. *Cast:* NELLIE: Nancy Dussault; EMILE: Jerome Hines; BLOODY MARY: Martha Larimmore; BILLIS: Jerry Lester; PROFESSOR: James Woods. *Understudy*: Emile: Webb Tilton.

PAPER MILL PLAYHOUSE, New Jersey, 1974. DIRECTOR: Larry Forde. *Cast:* NELLIE: Betsy Palmer; EMILE: Jerome Hines; BLOODY MARY: Sylvia Syms; ALSO WITH: John Stewart, Barney Martin.

WOLF TRAP FARM PARK, Vienna, Va. 8/22/77. 7 PERFORMANCES. DIRECTOR: Donald Driver; CHOREOGRAPHER: Arthur Faria; SETS: Peter Wolf; COSTUMES: Brooks Van-Horn; MUSICAL DIRECTOR: Herbert Hecht. *Cast:* NELLIE: Jane Powell; EMILE: Howard Keel; ALSO WITH: Brandon Maggart, Queen Yahna, Joanna Pang, James Ferrier.

TOURING REVIVAL. Opened on 5/14/85, at the Dorothy Chandler

Pavilion, Los Angeles, and closed there on 7/6/85. PRESENTED BY Don Gregory, Jon Cutler, and Irving Mansfield, in association with Kenneth F. Martel & Martel Media Productions; DIRECTOR: A.J. Antoon; CHOREOGRAPHER: Richard Levi; SETS: Andrew Jackness; COSTUMES: Linda Fisher. *Cast:* NELLIE: Meg Bussert; EMILE: Richard Kiley; BILLIS: Al Mancini. *Understudy*: Liat: Jacquey Maltby.

NEW YORK STATE THEATRE, 2/27/87–4/26/87. 68 PERFORMANCES. PRESENTED BY the New York City Opera; DIRECTOR: Gerald Freedman; CHOREOGRAPHER: Janet Watson; SETS/COSTUMES: Desmond Heeley; LIGHTING: Duane Schuler; SOUND: Thomas Maher; CONDUCTOR: Paul Gemignani. *Cast:* NELLIE: Susan Bigelow & Marcia Mitzman; EMILE: Justino Diaz & Stanley Wexler; BLOODY MARY: Muriel Costa-Greenspon & Camille Saviola; BILLIS: Tony Roberts; CABLE: Richard White & Cris Groenendaal; BRACKETT: James Billings; HARBISON: Daren Kelly & Joseph Culliton; PROFESSOR: Jeff Blumenkrantz; WEST: Robert Brubaker; CONNIE: Deborah Darr; LISA: Ivy Austin; RITA: Deanna Wells; LIAT: Ann Yen & Adrienne Telemaque.

TOUR. 1987–88. This tour broke several records. PRESENTED BY PACE Theatricals; DIRECTOR: Ron Field. *Cast:* EMILE: Robert Goulet.

LONDON, 1988. This revival also toured Japan. MUSICAL DIRECTOR: Alan Bence; CAST RECORDING on First Night. *Cast:* NELLIE: Gemma Craven; EMILE: Emile Belcourt; BLOODY MARY: Bertice Reading; CABLE: Andrew C. Wadsworth.

PAPER MILL PLAYHOUSE, New Jersey, 1993. DIRECTOR: Robert Johanson; SETS: Michael Anania; LIGHTING: F. Mitchell Dana. *Cast:* NELLIE: Marguerite MacIntyre; EMILE: Ron Raines; BILLIS: Gary Marachek; CABLE: J. Mark McVey; QUALE: John Cudia; O'BRIEN: John Bolton; MORTON: Bill E. Dietrich [Morton was a new character]; JANET: M. Kathryn Quinlan; LIAT: Marilyn Villamar.

DALLAS THEATRE CENTER, 4/13/99–5/16/99. Previews from 4/7/99. The run closed after a two-week extension. Exact 50th birthday celebration production, to mark the opening of the original 1949 production. DIRECTOR: Richard Hamburger; CHOREOGRAPHER: Willie Rosario; MUSICAL DIRECTOR: Andrew Gerle. *Cast:* NELLIE: Michele Ragusa; EMILE: John Wilkerson; BILLIS: Kevin Ligon; CABLE: Sean McDermott; BRACKETT: Charles Hyman; LIAT: Sara Hugh-Harper.

PASADENA CIVIC AUDITORIUM, 7/6/99–7/11/99. 8 PERFORMANCES. 50th-anniversary production. DIRECTOR: Norb Joerder. *Cast:* NELLIE: Jodi Benson; EMILE: John Cullum; BLOODY MARY: Armelia McQueen; ALSO WITH: Michael Gerhart.

ABC TV PRODUCTION. 3/26/01. DIRECTOR: Richard Pearce. *Cast:* NELLIE: Glenn Close; EMILE: Rade Sherbedgia; CABLE: Harry Connick Jr.

TOUR. Opened at the Ordway Center, St. Paul, Minn., 7/25/01–8/12/01. 1 preview on 7/24/01. It was then taken on a 50-week tour, first running at the Auditorium Theatre, Indiana University, Bloomington, 9/21/01–9/22/01, after two days of previews; then it opened on 9/25/01 at the Palace, Columbus, Ohio. PRESENTED BY Barry & Fran Weissler, in association with Clear Channel Entertainment; DIRECTOR: Scott Faris; CHOREOGRAPHER: Gary Chryst; SETS: Derek McLane; COSTUMES: Gregg Barnes; LIGHTING: Ken Billington; SOUND: Jonathan Deans; PRODUCTION SUPERVISOR: Jerry Zaks. *Cast:* NGANA: Joreen Baquilod (for the Ordway run only), *Angie Ha*; JEROME: Jocef Baquilod (for the Ordway run only), *Jeff Yalun*; NELLIE: Erin Dilly (until 3/17/02), *Amanda Watkins* (from 3/19/02); EMILE: Robert Stilwell (for the Ordway run only), *Michael Nouri* (until 3/17/02), *Robert Goulet* (from 3/19/02); BLOODY MARY: Armelia McQueen (until 2/3/02), *Gretha Boston* (from 2/5/02); BILLIS: David Warshofsky; CABLE: *Lewis Cleale* (from 2/5/02); BRACKETT: John Wilkerson; HARBISON: James Judy; LIAT: Kisha Howard.

OLIVIER THEATRE, London (part of the National Theatre), 12/12/01–4/27/02. Strictly limited run. Previews from 12/3/01. Produced in order to celebrate Richard Rodgers' birthday. DIRECTOR: Trevor Nunn; CHOREOGRAPHER: Matthew Bourne; SETS: John Napier; COSTUMES: Elise Napier & John Napier; SOUND: Paul Groothuis; MUSICAL SUPERVISOR: Derek White; ADDITIONAL ORCHESTRATIONS: William David Brohn. *Cast:* NELLIE: Lauren Kennedy; EMILE: Philip Quast; BLOODY MARY: Sheila Francisco; BILLIS: Nick Holder; CABLE: Edward Baker Duly; BRACKETT: John Shrapnel; LIAT: Elaine Tan.

ARENA STAGE, Washington, DC, 12/13/02–2/2/03. Rehearsals from 11/5/02. Previews from 12/6/02. A new song, cut from the original, but in the 1958 movie, was "My Girl Back Home." DIRECTOR: Molly Smith [her first large-scale musical]; CHOREOGRAPHER: Baayork Lee; SETS: Kate Edmunds; COSTUMES: Robert Perdziola; MUSICAL DIRECTOR: George Fulginiti-Shakar. *Cast:* EMILE: Richard White; NELLIE: Kate Baldwin; BLOODY MARY: Lori Tan Chinn; STEWPOT: Max Perlman; BILLIS: Lawrence Redmond; CABLE: Brad Anderson; LIAT: Liz Paw.

ISAAC STERN AUDITORIUM, CARNEGIE HALL, 6/9/05. One night only, in concert. DIRECTOR: Walter Bobbie; ADAPTED BY Walter Bobbie & David Ives; SET CONSULTANT: John Lee Beatty; COSTUME CONSULTANT: Catherine Zuber; CONDUCTOR OF THE ORCHESTRA OF ST. LUKE's: Paul Gemignani (replacing Patrick Summers before the event). *Cast:* EMILE: Brian Stokes Mitchell; NELLIE: Reba McEntire; BLOODY MARY: Lillias White; CABLE: Jason Danieley; BRACKETT: Conrad John Schuck.

655. *Star Time*

Also known as *Startime*. A variety, or vaudeville, show.

The Broadway Run. MAJESTIC THEATRE, 9/12/44–12/9/44. 120 PERFORMANCES. PRESENTED BY Paul Small; PRODUCED BY: Richard Maney & Maurice Turet; DIRECTOR: Macklin Megley; MUSICAL DIRECTOR: Waldemar Guiterson; GENERAL MANAGER: Emmett Callahan. *Act I*: Lou Holtz (1) ✰. Master of Ceremonies: He told his favorite Sam Lapidus stories, "O Sole Mio," "Me and My Gal;" The Whitson Brothers (four comic acrobats); The Mulcays (Jimmy & Mildred Mulcay—harmonica players); Shirley Dennis (*Dorothy Donegan*). Miss Dennis was described as "une chaude chanteuse," and sang a selection of songs from *Showboat*, including: "Ol' Man River;" "Napoleon and Josephine" (French drama performed by Armand Cortez, Francine Bordeau, and George Prospery); The De Marcos (Tony & Sally De Marco) (ballroom dancing); Lou Holtz (1) ✰ (ended the first half). Intermission (just as in *Othello*). *Act II*: Lou Holtz (1) ✰ (introduced the second half); The Berry Brothers (black hoofers. Bud was one of them). They did a Pogo dance. Singer *Connee Boswell* replaced them during the run; Benny Fields (2): "Over There," "Lullaby of Broadway;" The Paul Small Art Players; Finale.

The show cost $13,500 a week to operate. Tickets sold at $2.50 a head. Lou Holtz, the MC, made $3,000 a week. The De Marcos made $750. Reviews were generally good, and Lou Holtz got raves.

656. *Stardust*

The Mitchell Parish musical. A revue, subtitled *A Musical Romance,* showcasing some of the 700 songs of Mr. Parish.

Before Broadway. Originally produced Off Off Broadway, at THEATRE OFF PARK, 11/11/86–1/4/87. 9 previews from 10/29/86. 50 PERFORMANCES. It had the same crew as for the subsequent Broadway run, except GENERAL MANAGEMENT: Whitbell Productions; STAGE MANAGERS: William Hare & Susie Mara. It had the same cast. It then went to Broadway.

The Broadway Run. BILTMORE THEATRE, 2/19/87–5/17/87. 16 previews. 102 PERFORMANCES. The Theatre Off Park production, PRESENTED BY Burton L. Litwin, Howard Rose, Martin I. Rein, and Louise Westergaard, in association with Paula Hutter Gilliam; MUSIC: various songwriters; LYRICS: Mitchell Parish; BASED ON an idea by Burton L. Litwin & Albert Harris; CONCEIVED BY/DIRECTOR: Albert Harris; CHOREOGRAPHER: Patrice Soriero; TAP CHOREOGRAPHER: Henry Le Tang; SETS: David Jenkins; COSTUMES: Mardi Philips; LIGHTING: Ken Billington; SOUND: Gary Harris; MUSICAL SUPERVISOR/MUSICAL DIRECTOR/ORCHESTRATIONS/DANCE MUSIC & VOCAL ARRANGEMENTS: James Raitt; PRESS: Henry Luhrman Associates; CASTING: Warren Pincus; GENERAL MANAGEMENT: Weiler/Miller Associates; PRODUCTION STAGE MANAGER: Wm. Hare; STAGE MANAGER: Rachel S. Levine. *Cast:* Michele Bautier, Maureen Brennan, Kim Criswell, Andre De Shields, Jason Graae, Jim Walton. *Standbys:* Female Roles: Leata Galloway & Deborah Graham; Male Roles: Joel Blum & Vondie Curtis-Hall. *Musicians:* PIANO: James Raitt; PERCUSSION: Clint de Ganon; GUITAR/

BANJO: Bill Cadieux; BASS/TUBA: Greg Maker; REED I: Bill Meade; REED II: Al Hunt; TRUMPET: Ed Kalney; TROMBONE: Wayne Andre; HARP: Kathryn Easter. *Act I*: "Carolina Rolling Stone" (1921; m: Eleanor Young & Harry D. Squires) (Jason & Company), "Riverboat Shuffle" (1924; m: Hoagy Carmichael, Dick Voynow, Irving Mills) (Andre & Company), "One Morning in May" (1933; m: Hoagy Carmichael) (Maureen) [dropped late in the run], "Sweet Lorraine" (1928; m: Cliff Burwell) (Jim), "Sentimental Gentleman from Georgia" (1932; m: Frank Perkins) (Women), "Sophisticated Lady" (1933; m: Duke Ellington; l: Mr. Parish & Irving Mills) (Michele), "Dixie After Dark" (1934; m: Ben Oakland & Irving Mills) (Andre & Jim), "Stairway to the Stars" (1935; m: Matty Malnick & Frank Signorelli) (Kim), "Wealthy, Shmelthy, as Long as You're Healthy" (1935; m: Sammy Fain) (Jason), "The 1930s Unrequited Love Montage: "Hands Across the Table" (1934; m: Jean Delettre) [from *Continental Varieties*] (Michele), "You're So Indiff'rent" (1935; m: Sammy Fain) (Jason), "It Happens to the Best of Friends" (1934; m: Rube Bloom) (Kim), "I Would if I Could, But I Can't" (1933; m: Bing Crosby & Alan Grey) (Jim), "The Scat Song" (1932; m: Frank Perkins & Cab Calloway) (Andre & Maureen), "Sidewalks of Cuba" (1934; m: Ben Oakland & Irving Mills) [from *Cotton Club Parade of 1934*] (Kim & Jason), "Evenin'" (1934; m: Harry White) (Michele) [this number was replaced late in the run with "The Lamp is Low" (1939; m: Peter de Rose & Bert Shefter, adapted from Ravel's "Pavanne pour une Infante Defunte")], "Deep Purple" (1934; m: Peter de Rose) (Andre & Company) [end of montage]. *Act II*: Entr'acte (Orchestra); "Sophisticated Swing" (1936; m: Will Hudson) (Kim, Maureen, Jim), "Midnight at the Onyx" (1937; m: Will Hudson) (Andre, Maureen, Jim), "Tell Me Why" (1945; m: Michael Edwards & Sigmund Spaeth) (Jason), "Does Your Heart Beat for Me?" (1936; m: Russ Morgan & Arnold Johnson) (Jason), "Stars Fell on Alabama" (1934; m: Frank Perkins) (Jim & Maureen), "Don't Be That Way" (1935; m: Benny Goodman & Edgar Sampson) (Andre & Michele), "Organ Grinder's Swing" (1936; m: Will Hudson; l: Mr. Parish & Irving Mills) (Men), "Moonlight Serenade" (1939; m: Glenn Miller) (Company), "Star Dust" (1929; m: Hoagy Carmichael) (Michele), Your Cavalcade of Hits: HOST: Andre De Shields. "Belle of the Ball" (1951; m: Leroy Anderson) (Jason & Maureen), "The Syncopated Clock" (1946; m: Leroy Anderson) (Maureen, Jason, Kim, Jim), "Take Me in Your Arms" (1932; m: Fred Markush) (Maureen), "Ciao, Ciao Bambino" (1959; m: Domenico Modugno) (Kim), "Sleigh Ride" (1949; m: Leroy Anderson) (Maureen, Jason, Kim, Jim), "Volare" (1958; m: Domenico Modugno) (Jim & Company), "Your Cavalcade of Hits" Theme (m: James Raitt; l: Jay Jeffries), "Happy Cigarettes" Theme (m: James Raitt; l: Peter Jablonski) [end of Cavalcade of Hits], "Ruby" (1953; m: Heinz Roemheld) (from the movie *Ruby Gentry*) (Andre), "Forgotten Dreams" (1954; m: Leroy Anderson) (Company), "Star Dust" (reprise) (Company).

Note: All lyrics by Mitchell Parish (except the two themes mentioned above, in which case the composer & lyricist are both given). Music by various composers (in parentheses after the year of the song).

Broadway reviews were divided. The production fell victim to financial problems, despite William H. Kessler coming in as a new co-producer late in the run.

After Broadway. It was re-staged and given a lavish production at the KENNEDY CENTER, Washington, DC, 2/20/90–3/25/90, with the intention of going for Broadway again (it failed). NEW CHOREOGRAPHY BY: Donald McKayle; NEW SETS & COSTUMES: Erte; SOUND: Charles Bugbee; MUSICAL DIRECTOR: Peter Howard; NEW ORCHESTRATIONS: Harold Wheeler; NEW DANCE MUSIC ARRANGEMENTS: Marvin Laird. *Cast:* Betty Buckley, Christine Andreas, Michael Scott Gregory, Kevin Ligon, Karen Ziemba, Hinton Battle.

657. *Starlight Express*

The personification and glorification of railroad trains. A huge, spectacular musical on roller skates, with actors portraying various trains. A little boy dreams of a Championship race, with a lineup of international locomotives vying for the big prize. Rusty is a little steam engine with a big heart who enters the race against Greaseball, a muscular diesel-driven engine, and Electra, an androgynous electric train. Rusty hopes to impress Pearl, a svelte sidecar. The set included a huge, revolving suspension bridge. The 24-member orchestra played live in a specially-designed acoustical "orchestra room" off-stage.

    Before Broadway. In 1973 Andrew Lloyd Webber, who had always loved trains, was asked to compose the music for a series of TV cartoons based on the *Thomas the Tank Engine* children's stories, but the TV show was never made. In the summer of 1982 his son Nicholas was struck with wonder when he saw his first steam train. This inspired Mr. Lloyd Webber to write a new piece, as a concert for schools, and later that year it was performed at his Sydmonton Festival. Trevor Nunn heard it here, and it was planned that the piece should open the new Barbican Centre in London, as a concert sung by all the schools of the City of London, but Mr. Nunn suggested a stage musical with roller skates (it became the first musical to be performed solely on roller skates). PRESENTED BY Andrew Lloyd Webber's Really Useful Theatre Company, as a monstrous show at the APOLLO VICTORIA THEATRE, London (it cost 2.25 million pounds to put on), opening on 3/27/84. Previews from 3/19/84. The theatre was augmented with tracks and ramps that allowed the singing trains to zoom up into the balconies and around the orchestra. DIRECTOR: Trevor Nunn; CHOREOGRAPHER: Arlene Phillips; SETS: John Napier; MUSICAL DIRECTOR: Tony Stenson; CAST RECORDING on Polydor. **Cast:** FLAT TOP: Paul Reeves, *Mark Davis* (by 85–86), *Eddie Kemp* (by 86–87), *Jeff Baptista* (by 90–91), *Michael Cahill* (by 91–92), *Gary Noakes* (by 92), *Richard Mylan* (by 92–93), *Darryl Paul* (by 94–95), *Ian Stanley* (by 96–97), *Ian Meeson* (by 97–98), *Andrew Spillett* (by 98–99), *Jamie Golding* (by 99–00), *Ross Dawes* from 7/00); WELTSCHAFT: Mark Davis, *Simon Caine* (by 85–86), *Nils Saibaek* (by 86–87), *Eamon Geoghegan* (by 87–88), *Scott Pattison* (by 92), *Kevyn Waby* (by 92–93), *Dale Branston* (by 94–95), *Dennis Silkwood* (by 96–97), *Mark Pollard* (by 98–99), *Matt Raynor* (by 99–00), *Jamie Capewell* (by 00–01), *Craig Scott* (by 01–02) [in 1992 the name of this train changed to Ruhrgold]; BOBO: Tom Jobe, *Nick Lloyd* (by 85–86), *Norman Warren* (by 86–87), *Greg Ellis* (by 87–88), *Robert Yeal* (by 88–89), *Michael Gyngell* (by 92), *Stuart Scott* (by 92–93), *Mathew Cutts* (by 93–94), *Stuart Cross* (by 94), *Scott Pattison* (by 11/94), *David Hulston* (by 95–96), *Nicholas Bonner* (by 96–97), *Nigel Thomas* (by 97–98), *Stuart Sweeting* (by 98–99), *Barry McNeill* (by 99–00), *Richard Woodford* (by 01–02); GREASEBALL: Jeff Shankley, *Drue Williams* (by 86–87), *Nigel Casey* (by 91–92), *John Francis Davies* (by 92), *Mark Walker* (by 92), *Maynard Williams* (from 10/92), *Nigel Casey* (by 93–94), *Tony Rouse* (by 94–95), *Simon Marlow* (by 96–97), *Nigel Casey* (by 97–98), *Tony Rouse* (by 98–99), *Lez Dwight* (by 99–00), *Dustin Dubreuil* (by 01–02); RUSTY: Ray Shell, *Kofi Missah* (by 86–87), *Bobby Collins* (by 89–90), *Gary Cordice* (by 90–91), *Michael Cahill* (by 92), *Greg Ellis* (by 92–93), *Paul Baker* (by 94–95), *James Gillan* (by 97–98), *Neil Couperthwaite* (by 98–99), *Adrian Hansel* (by 99–00), *Mark McGee* (by 01–02); ASHLEY: Chrissy Wickham, *Voyd* (by 85–86), *C Jay Ranger* (by 88–89), *Erin Lordan* (by 89–90), *Nikki Belsher* (by 90–91), *Victoria Maxwell* (by 91–92), *Anna Louise Mountford* (by 92), *Samantha Lane* (by 92–93), *Lisa Pearce* (by 93), *Claudia Bradley* (by 2/94), *Deborah Spellman* (by 94–95), *Dawn Buckland* (by 95–96), *Samantha Lane* (by 96–97), *Francesca Newitt* (by 98–99), *Danni Kearsley-Wooller* (by 99–00), *Amanda Valentine* (by 00–01), *Lucie Fentum* (by 01–02); BUFFY: Nancy Wood, *Robin Cleaver* (by 85–86), *Caron Cardelle* (by 86–87), *Nola Haynes* (by 90–91), *Michelle Ballentyne* (by 91–92), *Voyd* (by 92–93), *Natalie Powers* (by 93–94), *Anna Jane Casey* (by 95–96), *Gael Johnson* (by 96–97), *Rebekka Gibbs* (by 97–98), *Sharon Mudie* (by 98–99), *Roni Bruno* (by 99–00), *Chellie Michaels* (by 00–01), *Amy Field* (by 01–02); DINAH: Frances Ruffelle, *Beverley Kay* (by 85–86), *Debbie Wake* (by 86–87), *Beverley Kay* (by 87–88), *Debbie Wake* (by 89–90), *Beverley Braybon* (by 90–91), *Sally Taylor* (by 91–92), *Caron Cardelle* (by 92–93), *Deborah Spellman* (by 95–96), *Anna Jane Casey* (by 96–97), *Natalie Powers* (by 97–98), *Gail Easdale* (by 98–99), *Irene Warren* (by 99–00), *Leyla Pellegrini* (by 00–01), *Helen Latham* (by 01–02); PEARL: Stephanie Lawrence, *Kim Leeson* (by 85–86), *Maria Hyde* (by 86–87), *Kim Leeson* (by 87–88), *Beverley Braybon* (by 89–90), *Kim Leeson* (by 90–91), *Reva Rice* (by 92), *Samantha Lane* (by 93–94), *Shelley Meredith* (by 6/94), *Claudia Bradley* (by 94–95) [Miss Bradley became Claudia Bradley-Rouse], *Amanda Salmon* (by 96–97), *Cheryl McAvoy* (by 98–99), *Marissa*

Dunlop (by 99–00), *Jo Gibb* (by 01–02); JOULE: Debbie Wake, *Becky Norman* (by 86–87), *Annabel Daniels* (by 87–88), *Stephanie Alimbau* (from 89), *Rebecca Price* (by 92), *Rebecca Holland* (by 92–93), *Casey-Lee Jolleys* (by 93–94), *C Jay Ranger* (by 94–95), *Sasha Kane* (by 96–97), *Simone White* (by 97–98), *Lisa Beckwith* (by 98–99), *Emma Dodd* (by 00–01); VOLTA: Voyd, *Caron Cardelle* (by 85–86), *C Jay Ranger* (by 86–87), *Ruth Welby* (by 88–89), *Nicky Lawson* (by 92), *C Jay Ranger* (by 92–93), *Lyndi Oliver* (by 93–94), *Marissa Dunlop* (by 95–96), *Rebekka Gibbs* (by 96–97), *Stephanie Spellman* (by 97–98), *Danielle Harley* (by 98–99), *Amanda Valentine* (by 99–00), *Gabrielle Noble* (by 00–01), *Louise Jones* (by 01–02); ROCKY I: Danny John-Jules, *Attlee Baptiste* (by 85–86), *Sebastian Craig* (by 86–87), *Attlee Baptiste* (by 87–88), *Rory Williams* (by 88–89), *Anthony Garfield* (by 89–90), *Mykal Rand* (by 90–91), *Kevin F.T. Duala* (by 91–92), *Rory Williams* (by 96–97), *Kevin F.T. Duala* (by 97–98), *David Obinyan* (by 98–99), *Michael Skyers* (by 99–00), *Martin Booth* (by 00–01), *Michael Skyers* (from 6/00), *Scott Murtaugh* (by 01–02); ROCKY II: Attlee Baptiste, *Ruel George Campbell* (by 85–86), *Tristan Rafuel* (by 87–88), *Mykal Rand* (by 88–89), *Kevin F.T. Duala* (by 89–90), *Algernon Williams* (by 91–92), *David Obinyan* (by 97–98), *Tim Noble* (by 98–99), *Rob Grose* (by 99–00), *Leo Bidwell* (by 01–02); ROCKY III: Richard Bodkin, *Sebastian Craig* (by 85–86), *Winston Pitt* (by 86–87), *Rory Williams* (by 87–88), *Trevor Hodge* (by 88–89), *Rory Williams* (by 89–90), *Jason Pennycooke* (by 96–97), *Rory Williams* (by 97–98), *Algernon Williams* (by 98–99); DUSTIN: Gary Love, *Drue Williams* (by 85–86), *Geoffrey Stevens* (by 86–87), *Nick Lloyd* (by 87–88), *Greg Ellis* (by 88–89), *Danny Metcalfe* (by 89–90), *Gary Noakes* (by 90–91), *George Canning* (by 91–92), *Mark Davis* (by 92), *Graham Martin* (by 92–93), *Jason Capewell* (by 95–96), *Carl Sanderson* (by 97–98), *Graham Martin* (by 98–99), *Dale Branston* (by 00–01); RED CABOOSE: Michael Staniforth, *Paul Reeves* (by 86–87), *Robin Wright* (by 87–88), *Eddie Kemp* (by 90–91), *William Adams* (by 91–92) [this character became CB in 85/86, and was cut in 1992]; ESPRESSO: Ruel George Campbell, *Maynard Williams* (by 85–86), *Bob Lee Dysinger* (by 86–87), *Cy Newton* (by 87–88), *Robert Northwood* (by 88–89), *Craig Cameron* (by 92–93), *Michael Aaron Peth* (by 94–95), *Robert Northwood* (from 95), *Andrew Spillett* (by 96–97), *Richard Twyman* (by 97–98), *Todd Talbot* (by 98–99), *Craig Scott* (by 00–01), *Jamie Capewell* (by 01–02); TURNOV: Bobby Collins, *Marek Kurpiel* (by 85–86), *Stephen Le'Roche* (by 86–87), *Robert Northwood* (by 87–88), *Erick Rainey* (by 88–89), *Paul Whitaker* (by 92), *Craig Cameron* (by 94–95), *Dennis Silkwood* (by 95–96), *Simon David Trout* (by 96–97), *Adrian Smith* (by 97–98), *Chris Bennett* (by 98–99), *Dustin Dubreuil* (by 99–00), *Mark Hedges* (by 00–01), *Mark Oxtoby* (by 01–02); CITY OF MILTON KEYNES: Ray Hatfield, *Geoffrey Abbott* (by 86–87), *Kevyn Waby* (by 88–89), *Sean O'Sullivan* (by 92), *Mathew Cutts* (by 92–93), *Jason Capewell* (by 93–94), *Marvin Giles* (by 95–96), *Neil Dale* (by 98–99), *Adrian Smith* (by 99–00), *Ben Clare* (by 00–01), *Martin Neely* (by 01–02) [in 1992 this train became The Prince of Wales]; HASHAMOTO: Drue Williams, *Eamon Geoghegan* (by 85–86), *Trevor Hodge* (by 87–88), *Gary Forbes* (by 88–89), *Simon Harrison-Scott* (by 92), *Scott Pattison* (by 92–93), *Grant Anthony* (by 94–95), *Adam Floyd* (by 95–96), *Andrew Spillett* (by 97–98), *Richard Twyman* (by 98–99), *Adam Floyd* (by 99–00), *Leo Bidwell* (by 00–01), *Paul Ramsey* (by 01–02) [in 1992 this train became known as Nintendo]; KRUPP: Eddie Kemp, *Gary Noakes* (by 85–86), *George Canning* (by 86–87), *Michael Skyers* (by 92), *Julian Cannonier* (by 93–94), *Paul Aloysius* (from 95), *Michael Skyers* (by 98–99), *Richard Ray-Allen* (by 99–00); WRENCH: Carole Amphlett, *Michelle-Ann Musty* (by 92), *Samantha Biddulph* (by 92–93), *Sophie Hamilton* (by 93–94), *Tara Wilkinson* (by 94–95), *Jane Housely* (by 95–96), *Sharon Mudie* (by 96–97), *Pippa Gebette* (by 98–99), *Amy Field* (99–00), *Kate Alexander* (by 00–01); PURSE: Kofi Missah, *Robin Wright* (by 86–87), *Gary Cordice* (by 87–88), *Robert Yeal* (by 92), *Marco Ferraro* (by 92–93), *Sandy Rass* (by 94–95), *Stuart Sweeting* (by 95–96), *Sharon Mudie* (by 96–97), *David Hulston* (by 97–98), *Sebastian Craig* (by 98–99), *Martin Matthias* (by 99–00), *Todd Talbot* (by 01–02); ELECTRA: Jeffrey Daniels, *Tom Jobe* (by 85–86), *Maynard Williams* (by 86–87), *Kofi Missah* (by 90–91), *Christian Hughes* (by 91–92), *Greg Ellis* (by 92), *John Partridge* (by 92–93), *Richard Mylan* (by 94–95), *Chris Lennon* (by 96–97), *Spencer Stafford* (by 97–98), *Grant Anthony* (by 98–99), *Chris Copeland* (by 99–00); BELLE: P.P. Arnold, *Shezwae Powell* (by 85–86), *Erin Lordan* (by 90–91), *Samantha Lane* (by 91–92) [this character was cut in 1992); POPPA: Lon Sattin, *Ray Shell* (by 96–97), *Trevor Michael Georges* (by 98–99); GOOK: Gary Noakes (by 85–86), *Sebastian Craig* (by 86–87), *Gary Forbes* (by 87–88), [this character was introduced in 85–86, and was cut by 92]; TANK: Mark Davis (by 85–86), *Nils Saibaek* (by 86–87), [this character was introduced in 85–86 and cut by 92]; LUBE: Nick Lloyd (by 85–86), *Eamon Geoghegan* (by 86–87), *Robert Northwood* (by 87–88), [this character was introduced in 85–86 and cut by 92]; STARLIGHT EXPRESS: Lon Sattin (by 85–86) [this character was introduced in 85–86 and cut by 92]. **Act I**: Overture, "Rolling Stock," "Call Me Rusty," "A Lotta Locomotion," "Pumping Iron," "Freight," "AC/DC," "He Whistled at Me," "The Race," "There's Me," "Poppa's Blues," "Belle the Sleeping Car," "Starlight Express." **Act II**: "The Rap," "U.N.C.O.U.P.L.E.D.," "Rolling Stock" (reprise), "CB," "Right Time, Right Place," "I Am the Starlight," "He Whistled at Me" (reprise), "Race: The Final," "No Comeback," "One Rock 'n Roll Too Many," "Only He," "Only You," "Light at the End of the Tunnel." The press was not impressed, but audiences were dazzled. It was a hit, both popular and financial. On 11/23/92 the show was re-vamped: "Crazy" (a new number for Rusty, Pearl, Buffy, Ashley, Dinah) and "Laughing Stock" were added in Act I, and two new numbers — "Next Time You Fall in Love" (Rusty & Pearl) and "Starlight Megamix" — were added in Act II. There was some shuffling around of the other, existing, songs, as well. The London run finally ended after almost 18 years, on 1/12/02, after 7,406 PERFORMANCES, making it the second-longest West End musical run after *Cats*. 8 million people saw it there.

The Broadway Run. GERSHWIN THEATRE, 3/15/87–1/8/89. 22 previews. 761 PERFORMANCES. PRESENTED BY Martin Starger & Lord Grade (i.e. Lew Grade), in association with MCA Music Entertainment Group, Stage Promotions (Four) Strada Holdings, and the Weintraub Entertainment Group; MUSIC: Andrew Lloyd Webber; LYRICS: Richard Stilgoe; DIRECTOR: Trevor Nunn; CHOREOGRAPHER: Arlene Phillips; STUNT CO-ORDINATOR: J.P. Romano; SKATING COACH & CONSULTANT: Michal Fraley; SETS/COSTUMES: John Napier; SCENIC & BRIDGE ENGINEER: William M. Mensching; LIGHTING: David Hersey; SOUND: Martin Levan; MUSICAL SUPERVISOR: David Caddick; MUSICAL DIRECTOR: Paul Bogaev & David Caddick; ORCHESTRATIONS: David Cullen & Andrew Lloyd Webber; CONCEPT ALBUM on MCA Compact Discs, HiQ Cassettes & Records; PRESS: Bill Evans & Associates; CASTING: Johnson — Liff; GENERAL MANAGEMENT: Gatchell & Neufeld; COMPANY MANAGER: Roger Gindi, *Tom Domenici* (added by 87–88); PRODUCTION STAGE MANAGER: Frank Hartenstein; STAGE MANAGER: Perry Cline; ASSISTANT STAGE MANAGERS: Randall Whitescarver, Janet Friedman, Michael J. Passaro, *Bonnie Panson, Clayton Phillips*. **Cast:** BOBO: A.C. Ciulla, *Brian Carmack*; ESPRESSO: Philip Clayton [the name of this train is sometimes — wrongly — seen as Expresso]; WELTSCHAFT: Michael Berglund; TURNOV: William Frey, *Ron De Vito*; HASHAMOTO: D. Michael Heath, *Ken Rose*; PRINCE OF WALES: Sean McDermott; GREASEBALL: Robert Torti, *John Schiappa*; GREASEBALL'S GANG: Todd Lester (*Marc Villa*), Sean Grant, Ronald Garza, Angel Vargas, Joey McKneely (*Roger Kachel*), Gordon Owens; RUSTY: Greg Mowry; PEARL: Reva Rice; DINAH: Jane Krakowski; ASHLEY: Andrea McArdle, *Stacia Goad*; BUFFY: Jamie Beth Chandler, *Lola Knox*; ROCKY I: Frank Mastrocola, *Bryan Batt*; ROCKY II: Sean Grant; ROCKY III: Ronald Garza; ROCKY IV: Angel Vargas; DUSTIN: Michael Scott Gregory, *Keith Allen*; FLAT-TOP: Todd Lester, *Marc Villa*; RED CABOOSE: Berry K. Bernal, *Todd Lester*; KRUPP, ELECTRA'S ARMAMENTS TRUCK: Joey McKneely, *Roger Kachel*; WRENCH, ELECTRA'S REPAIR TRUCK: Christina Youngman; JOULE, ELECTRA'S DYNAMITE TRUCK: Nicole Picard, *Kimberly Blake*; VOLTA, ELECTRA'S FREEZER TRUCK: Mary Ann Lamb, *Dorie Herndon*; PURSE, ELECTRA'S MONEY TRUCK: Gordon Owens; ELECTRA: Ken Ard; POPPA: Steve Fowler; BELLE, THE SLEEPING CAR: Janet Williams Adderley; VOICE OF THE BOY: Braden Danner; VOICE OF THE MOTHER: Melanie Vaughan; *Starlight* CHORUS: Paul Binotto (*Willy Falk*), Lon Hoyt, Melanie Vaughan, Mary Windholtz. **Understudies**: Ashley: Jamie Beth Chandler, Amelia Prentice, Christina Youngman; Belle: Lola Knox & Amelia Prentice, *Janice Lorraine*; Bobo: Mark Frawley, Anthony Galde, Ron Morgan, Dwight Toppin, *D. Michael Heath*; Buffy: Lola Knox, Mary Ann Lamb, Christine Langner, *Janice Lorraine, Jennifer Prescott*; Dinah: Christine Langner, Nicole Picard, *Kimberly Blake, Dorie Herndon, Amelia Prentice, Jennifer Prescott*; Dustin: Anthony Galde, D. Michael Heath, Sean McDermott,

Ron Morgan; Electra: Michael Demby-Cain, Philip Clayton, Gordon Owens, Broderick Wilson; Espresso: Mark Frawley, Ron Morgan, Broderick Wilson, *Anthony Galde, D. Michael Heath*; Flat Top: Mark Frawley, Anthony Galde, Joey McKneely, *D. Michael Heath*; Greaseball: Mark Frawley, William Frey, Frank Mastrocola, *Bryan Batt, Ron De Vito*; Hashamoto: Mark Frawley, Ron Morgan, Dwight Toppin; Joule: Lola Knox, Christine Langner, Amelia Prentice, *Janice Lorraine, Jennifer Prescott*; Krupp: Mark Frawley, Anthony Galde, Ron Morgan, Dwight Toppin, Broderick Wilson; Pearl: Lola Knox, Christine Langner, *Janice Lorraine, Jennifer Prescott*; Poppa: Danny Strayhorn & Broderick Wilson; Prince of Wales: Mark Frawley, Ron Morgan, Broderick Wilson; Purse: Michael Demby-Cain, Dwight Toppin, Broderick Wilson, *Ron Morgan*; Red Caboose: Mark Frawley, Anthony Galde, Todd Lester, *Ron Morgan*; Rocky I: Michael Demby-Cain, William Frey, Broderick Wilson, *Ron Morgan, Dwight Toppin*; Rocky II: Michael Demby-Cain, Dwight Toppin, Broderick Wilson, *Ron Morgan, Dwight Toppin*; Rocky III: Michael Demby-Cain, A.C. Ciulla, Dwight Toppin, *Ron Morgan*; Rocky IV: Michael Demby-Cain, Sean Grant, Dwight Toppin, Broderick Wilson; Rusty: Michael Demby-Cain, Sean Grant, Sean McDermott; Turnov: Mark Frawley, Ron Morgan, Dwight Toppin; Volta: Lola Knox, Christine Langner, Christina Youngman, *Janice Lorraine, Amelia Prentice, Jennifer Prescott*; Weltschaft: Mark Frawley, Anthony Galde, Ron Morgan, *D. Michael Heath, Ron Morgan*; Wrench: Lola Knox, Christine Langner, Amelia Prentice, *Janice Lorraine, Jennifer Prescott*. **Swings**: Michael Demby-Cain, Anthony Galde, D. Michael Heath, Ron Morgan, Janice Lorraine, Amelia Prentice, Jennifer Prescott, Dwight Toppin, Broderick Wilson. **Orchestra:** TRUMPETS: Joe Mosello, Brian O'Flaherty, James Hynes, Greg Ruvolo; TROMBONES: Ed Neumeister & Keith O'Quinn; BASS TROMBONES: Joe Randazzo & George Moran; FRENCH HORN: Kaitilin Mahoney; REEDS: Mort Silver, Bob Mintzer, Ralph Olsen, Robert Eldridge; PERCUSSION: Nicholas Cerrato; KEYBOARDS: Lee Musiker, Brett Sommer, Gary Dienstadt, Jan Rosenberg; GUITARS: Steve Bargonetti & Robbie Kirshoff; BASS: Jeff Ganz; DRUMS: Ray Marchica. **Act I**: Overture (Orchestra), "Rolling Stock" (Greaseball & Gang), "Engine of Love" (derived from an original lyric by Peter Reeves) (Rusty, Pearl, Dinah, Ashley, Buffy), "Taunting Rusty" (Greaseball & Gang) [added for the subsequent national tour], "Lotta Locomotion" (Dinah, Ashley, Buffy, Rusty), "Freight" (Company), "AC/DC" (Electra, Krupp, Wrench, Joule, Volta, Purse, Company), "Pumping Iron" (Greaseball, Pearl, Ashley, Dinah, Buffy, Joule, Volta, Wrench), "Coda of "Freight" (a reprise of "Freight") (Company), "Make up My Heart" (Pearl), "Race One" (Greaseball & Dinah, Weltschaft & Joule, Turnov & Red Caboose, Electra & Pearl), "There's Me" (Red Caboose & Dinah), "Poppa's Blues" (Poppa, Rocky I, II, III, and IV, Rusty), "Belle (the Sleeping Car)" (Belle, Poppa, Rocky I, II, III and IV, Rusty, Dustin, Flat-Top), "Race Two" (Bobo & Buffy, Hashamoto & Volta, Espresso & Ashley, Poppa & Dustin), "Laughing Stock" (Company), "Starlight Express" (Rusty). **Act II**: "Silver Dollar" (Company) [replaced with "The Rap" for the subsequent national tour], "U.N.C.O.U.P.L.E.D." (Dinah, Ashley, Buffy), "Rolling Stock" (reprise) (Dinah, Ashley, Buffy), "Wide Smile, High Style, That's Me" (Red Caboose, Electra, Krupp, Wrench, Joule, Volta, Purse), "First Final" (Greaseball & Pearl, Electra & Dinah, Hashamoto & Volta, Rusty & Red Caboose), "Right Place, Right Time" (Rocky I, II, III, and IV), "I Am the Starlight" (Rusty & Poppa), "Final Selection" (Rusty, Dustin, Dinah, Electra, Pearl, Greaseball, Red Caboose), "One Rock and Roll Too Many" [added during the run], "Only You" (Pearl & Rusty), "Chase" (Company) [dropped during the run], "One Rock and Roll Too Many" (Greaseball, Electra, Red Caboose), "Light at the End of the Tunnel" (Company).

The show was toned down for Broadway, the action being confined to the stage. It cost over $8 million (MCA invested $5 million, partly to secure the motion picture rights), the most expensive show to that date, with $2 million alone going on the set. Reaching speeds of 40 mph, the cast whizzed around the stage of the Gershwin Theatre, and suffered numerous injuries. Reviews were generally not good, except, of course, for the fantastic technique exhibited by the production. Broadway expenses being greater than in London, the New York show, despite a long run, was not a success financially. It won a Tony for costumes, and was nominated for musical, score, direction of a musical, choreography, lighting, and for Robert Torti.

After Broadway. JAPANESE/AUSTRALIAN TOUR. Opened in Tokyo, on 11/15/87, and closed in Adelaide, on 5/8/88.

STARLIGHT-EXPRESS-THEATER, Bochum, Germany. 6/12/88. Still running in 2003.

POST-BROADWAY TOUR, sub-titled *Tracking Across America*. Opened on 11/7/89. PRESENTED BY James M. Nederlander, Columbia Artists Management, Concert Productions International, PACE Theatrical Group; DIRECTOR/CHOREOGRAPHER: Arlene Phillips; LIGHTING: Rick Belzer & Ted Mather; MUSICAL DIRECTOR: Paul Bogaev. *Cast*: GREASE-BALL: Ron De Vito; RUSTY: Sean McDermott; DINAH: Dawn Marie Church; ROCKY I: Ronald Garza; ROCKY II: Dwight Toppin; ROCKY III: Angel Vargas; RED CABOOSE: Todd Lester; WELTSCHAFT: Fred Tallaksen; PURSE: Michael Demby-Cain; CHORUS: Paul Binotto.

HILTON HOTEL, Las Vegas, 9/14/93–96. No intermission. The songs were basically those of the post–1992 London production. The number "Right Place, Right Time" was cut during the run. PRESENTED BY Troika. The million-dollar costumes were retained for the 2003 tour.

Starlight on Ice. A ice tour, with famous skaters from all over the world skating to pre-recorded music. Opened at Lakeland Center, Florida, 8/29/97. PRESENTED BY Kenneth Feld.

REVISED VERSION. Grand Hotel & Casino, Biloxi, Miss., 4/1/03–4/27/03. It then went on a national non–Equity tour, opening at the Hobby Center, Houston, 5/2/03–5/25/03. This version was a combination of the original, the 1992–1996 Vegas production, and the German script. Andrew Lloyd Webber worked on new songs, and it had new lyrics by David Yazbek, and new 3-D film sequences by Julian Napier, son of this production's set designer, John Napier. PRESENTED BY Troika Entertainment; DIRECTOR/CHOREOGRAPHER: Arlene Phillips. Rehearsals began 1/03.

658. *Starmites*

A rock musical that takes place now, on Earth and in Innerspace. A teenager, Eleanor, battles forces that threaten the Solar System.

Before Broadway. It was first produced by the ARK THEATRE COMPANY, then Off Broadway, by Musical Theatre Works at CSC THEATRE, 4/24/87–5/9/87. 16 PERFORMANCES. DIRECTOR: Mark Herko; CHOREOGRAPHER: Ed Kresley; SETS: Evelyn Sakash; COSTUMES: Amanda J. Klein; LIGHTING: Clarke W. Thornton; MUSICAL DIRECTOR/ARRANGEMENTS: Dianne Adams; STAGE MANAGER: Sheila Bam. *Cast*: ELEANOR/BIZARBARA: Liz Larsen; MOTHER/DIVA: Sharon McKnight; ACK ACK: Bennett Cale; HERBIE: Victor Trent Cook; TRINKULUS: Gabriel Barre; SPACE PUNK: Steve Watkins; DISMO DITTERSDORF: Keith Crowningshield (this character became Dazzle Razzledorf on Broadway); SHAK GRAA: George Spelvin (George Spelvin is a nom de guerre, traditionally used on Broadway to denote an actor in more than one role. So we don't know who this is); CANIBELLE: Norma Jean Sitton; MALIGNA: Sarah Knapp; BALBRAKA: Kristine Nevins. "Superhero Girl," "Starmites," "Trink's Narration," "Afraid of the Dark," "Lullaby," "Cry of the Banshee," "Hard to Be a Diva," "Love Song," "Festival Dance of Pleasure and Pulchritude," "Bizarbara's Wedding," "Milady," "Beauty Within," "The Cruelty Stomp," "Reach Right Down," "Immolation," Finale. It was subsequently developed and produced at the AMERICAN STAGE FESTIVAL, Milford, New Hampshire.

The Broadway Run. CRITERION CENTER STAGE RIGHT, 4/27/89–6/18/89. 35 previews. 60 PERFORMANCES. PRESENTED BY Hinks Shimberg, Mary Keil, Steven Warnick; MUSIC/LYRICS: Barry Keating; BOOK: Stuart Ross & Barry Keating; DIRECTOR: Larry Carpenter; CHOREOGRAPHER: Michele Assaf; SETS: Lowell Detweiler; COSTUMES: Susan Hirschfeld; LIGHTING: Jason Kantrowitz; SOUND: John Kilgore; MUSICAL DIRECTOR/DANCE MUSIC ARRANGEMENTS: Henry Aronson; ASSOCIATE MUSICAL DIRECTOR/VOCAL ARRANGEMENTS: Dianne Adams; ORCHESTRATIONS: James McElwaine; PRESS: Shirley Herz Associates; CASTING: Julie Hughes & Barry Moss; GENERAL MANAGER: Albert Poland; COMPANY MANAGER: Mitchell A. Weiss; PRODUCTION STAGE MANAGER: Zoya Wyeth; STAGE MANAGER: Mary Ellen Allison; ASSIS-TANT STAGE MANAGER: John-Michael Flate. *Cast*: ON EARTH: ELEANOR FAIRCHILD: Liz Larsen; HER MOTHER: Sharon McNight; INNERSPACE: SHAK GRAA: Ariel Grabber; SPACEPUNK: Brian Lane Green; TRINKULUS: Gabriel Barre; (THREE) STARMITES: ACK ACK ACKERMAN: Bennett Cale; HERBIE HARRISON: Victor Trent Cook; DAZZLE RAZZLEDORF: Christopher Zelno; DIVA: Sharon McNight; BIZARBARA, HER DAUGHTER: Liz Larsen; BANSHEES: SHOTZI: Mary Kate Law [character newly created for Broadway, i.e. not in the pre–Broadway production]; CANIBELLE: Gwen Stewart; BALBRAKA: Freida Williams; MALIGNA: Janet Aldrich; DROIDS: John-Michael Flate & Ric Ryder. *Standby*: Eleanor/Bizarbara/Banshees/Droid: Wendy-Jo Vaughn. *Understudies*: Mother/Diva: Janet Aldrich; Shak Graa/Spacepunk/Trinkulus: John-Michael Flate; Starmites: Ric Ryder. *Musicians*: KEYBOARDS: Henry Aronson & Dianne Adams; GUITARS: Robert Kirshof; BASS GUITAR: Brian Hamm; PERCUSSION: Jeffrey Potter. *Prelude*: *Prologue*: Eleanor's bedroom, Planet Earth: "Superhero Girl" (Eleanor). *Act I*: *Scene 1* A sacrificial lab in Innerspace: "Starmites" (Starmites & Spacepunk), "Trink's Narration" (Trinkulus & Starmites), "Afraid of the Dark" (Spacepunk, Starmites, Eleanor, Trinkulus); *Scene 2* Shriekwood Forest: "Little Hero" (Eleanor), "Attack of the Banshees" (Banshees); *Scene 3* Castle Nemesis: the Great Hall: "Hard to Be a Diva" (Diva & Banshees); *Scene 4* The castle mortuary: "Love Duet" (Spacepunk & Eleanor); *Scene 5* Castle Nemesis: the Great Hall: "The Dance of Spousal Arousal" (additional lyr/melody by Freida Williams) (percussion arr: Jeffrey Potter) (Banshees & Bizarbara); *Finaletto* (Company). *Act II*: Entr'acte (Band); *Scene 1* Castle Nemesis: the Great Hall: "Bizarbara's Wedding" (Bizarbara & Banshees), "Milady" (Spacepunk & Starmites); *Scene 2* The Chamber of Psychosorcery: "Beauty Within" (Diva & Bizarbara); *Scene 3* Castle Nemesis: the Great Hall: "The Cruelty Stomp" (Trinkulus & Company), "Reach Right Down" (Starmites, Diva, Banshees); *Scene 4* A sacrificial lab in Innerspace: "Immolation" (Eleanor, Shak Graa, Spacepunk), "Starmites"/"Diva" (reprise) (Diva, Starmites, Banshees); *Epilogue*: Eleanor's bedroom, Planet Earth: Finale (Company).

Note: eight musical numbers were recorded, but not released until 12/8/99, on Original Cast Records, an album that also included six other numbers recorded in 1998.

It was the first show of any kind to play at the Criterion Center Stage Right, the latest Broadway theatre (499 seats). Aside from the usual, and not unexpected mixed reviews, it received a favorable one from Mel Gussow in the *New York Times*, and became a cult show. It received Tony nominations for musical, direction of a musical, choreography, and for Gabriel Barre, Brian Lane Green, and Sharon McNight.

After Broadway. HARTLEY HOUSE, NYC, 12/14/90–1/18/91. 20 PERFORMANCES. PRESENTED BY On Stage Productions; DIRECTOR: Gabriel Barre; CHOREOGRAPHER: Denise Webb; MUSICAL DIRECTOR: Wayne Blood. *Cast*: ELEANOR/BIZARBARA: Susan Levine; MOTHER/DIVA: Michele Floor; BALBRAKA: Jozie Hill; SHOTZI: Carol Cornicelli; HERBIE: Hollis Lewis; CANIBELLE: Sue Lynn Yu; TRINKULUS: Randall E. Lake; SPACE PUNK: Ryan Bonn; DAZZLE: Benjamin Bedenbaugh; ACK ACK: Robert Belfry; SHAK GRAA: Allan Larkeed; MALIGNA: Sheryl McCallum.

Starmites 2001. This was the revised revival, although the musical numbers were the same. Eleanor is mysteriously thrust into her favorite comic book. She awakes in Innerspace to find that she is the legendary Milady, a teenage superhero who has to team with the Starmites in order to save the Universe from the forces of Evil. The flamboyant Diva is the Queen of Innerspace, with her Banshee Warriors, and Spacepunk is a boyish heartthrob. A mixture of live action and puppetry. Theatre 3, NYC, 3/22/01–4/8/01. 7 previews from 3/14/01. 17 performances. PRESENTED BY AMAS Musical Theatre, in association with Jim Steinman & Mary Keil; MUSIC/LYRICS/DIRECTOR: Barry Keating; BOOK: Barry Keating & Stuart Ross; SETS: Beowulf Boritt; COSTUMES: John Russell; LIGHTING: Aaron Spivey; MUSICAL DIRECTOR: Wendy Bobbitt-Cavett; PUPPET DESIGNERS: Richard Druther, Michael Duffy, Jeffrey Wallach. *Cast*: ELEANOR/BIZARBARA: Nicole Leach; MOTHER/DIVA: Gwen Stewart; TRINKULUS: Larry Purifory; SPACE PUNK: Craig Bonacorsi; DISMO RAZZLE DAZZLE: Jason Wooten; ACK ACK HACKERAXE: Adam Fleming; S'UP S'UP SENSABOI: Eric Millegan; SHOTZI/ORAGALA: Pegg Winter; MALIGNA: Darlene Bel Grayson; BALBRAKA: Valerie A. Hawkins; CANIBELLE: Kim Cea.

659. *State Fair*

Set on the Frake farm in Brunswick, Iowa, and at the Iowa State Fair, in Des Moines, over five days in late August of 1946. This new stage adaptation used music and lyrics of the 1945 movie *State Fair*, the 1962 movie remake, and songs (some previously unused) from other Rodgers & Hammerstein shows.

Before Broadway. The show tried out at the Stevens Center (named for Roger L. Stevens), Winston-Salem, NC, as part of the Broadway Preview series instigated by Ron Kumin. It had the same basic crew as for the later Broadway run, except DIRECTOR: Randy Skinner; SOUND: Jonathan Deans; MUSICAL DIRECTOR: John McDaniel; STAGE MANAGER: John M. Galo. *Cast*: ABEL: Michael McCarty, *Lenny Wolpe*; GUS: Eric Gunhus; MELISSA: Jan Pessano; WAYNE: Michael Hayden, *Lewis Cleale*; DAVE/JUDGE: Charles Goff; ELEANOR: Karen Lifshey; MARGY: Susan Egan; HARRY: Philip Lehl; PAT: Michael Halpin; CHARLIE: Robert Loftin; HOOP-LA BARKER: Tina Johnson; EMILY: Lisa Akey; STRALENKO/LEM: Tom Hafner; COOCH DANCERS: Kelli Barclay & Tina Johnson; CLAY: Edward Badrak; CHORUS: Han Masters, Stafeanie Morse, Cori Lanting McCormick, Jacquiline Rohrbacker, Michael Lee Scott. "Our State Fair," "It Might as Well Be Spring," "That's for Me," "Isn't it Kinda Fun?," "More than Just a Friend," "You Never Had it So Good," "When I Go Walking with My Baby," "This isn't Heaven," "It's a Grand Night for Singing," "Marriage-Type Love," "The Man I Used to Be," "All I Owe Ioway," "That's the Way it Happens," "I Haven't Got a Worry in the World," "There's a Music in You," "Boys and Girls Like You and Me," "The Next Time it Happens," Finale.

En route to Broadway it had a pre–Broadway tour, produced by Sonny Everett, Bonnie Nelson Schwartz, Matt Garfield, and Ron Kumin, which played at, among other venues, the Kennedy Center, Washington, DC, 1/2/96–1/28/96. David Merrick invested $1 million just before Broadway previews began, and so became a producer of the show. It was his 88th production.

The Broadway Run. MUSIC BOX THEATRE, 3/27/96–6/30/96. 8 previews from 3/20/96. 110 PERFORMANCES. The Theatre Guild production, PRESENTED BY David Merrick; PRODUCED BY: Philip Langner, Robert Franz, Natalie Lloyd, Jonathan C. Herzog, Meredith Blair, Gordon Smith, in association with Mark N. Sirangelo & the PGI Entertainment Company; MUSIC: Richard Rodgers; LYRICS: Oscar Hammerstein II; BOOK: Tom Briggs & Louis Mattioli; BASED ON the 1945 and 1962 movies of the same name, written by Oscar Hammerstein II, which in turn were based on the novel by Phil Stong; DIRECTORS: James Hammerstein [Oscar's son] & Randy Skinner; CHOREOGRAPHER: Randy Skinner; SETS: James Leonard Joy; COSTUMES: Michael Bottari & Ronald Case; LIGHTING: Natasha Katz; SOUND: Brian Ronan; MUSICAL DIRECTOR/VOCAL ARRANGEMENTS: Kay Cameron; ORCHESTRATIONS: Bruce Pomahac; DANCE MUSIC ARRANGEMENTS: Scot Woolley; CAST RECORDING on DRG; PRESS: Susan L. Schulman; CASTING: Caro Jones & Pat McCorkle; GENERAL MANAGER: Ralph Roseman; COMPANY MANAGER: Tom Domenici; PRODUCTION STAGE MANAGER: Warren Crane; STAGE MANAGERS: Donald Christy & Anita Ross. *Cast:* ABEL FRAKE: John Davidson (1) ☆; GUS, THE FRAKES' HIRED MAN: James Patterson; MELISSA FRAKE, ABEL'S WIFE: Kathryn Crosby (2) ☆; WAYNE FRAKE, THEIR SON: Ben Wright (6) ☆; DAVE MILLER, THE LOCAL STOREKEEPER: Charles Goff; ELEANOR, WAYNE'S GIRLFRIEND: Susan Haefner; MARGY FRAKE, WAYNE'S SISTER: Andrea McArdle (3) ☆, *Susan Haefner, Susan Egan*; HARRY, MARGY'S BOYFRIEND: Peter Benson; UNCLE SAM: Michael Lee Scott; FAIR ANNOUNCER: J. Lee Flynn; MIDWAY COW: Kelli Barclay; MIDWAY PIG: Jackie Angelescu; THE HOOP-LA BARKER: Tim Fauvell; EMILY ARDEN: Donna McKechnie (4) ☆; THE ASTOUNDING STRALENKO: Steve Steiner; VIVIAN, A COOCH DANCER: Tina Johnson; JEANNE, A COOCH DANCER: Leslie Bell; MRS. EDWIN METCALF OF POTTSVILLE: Jacquiline Rohrbacker; PAT GILBERT, A NEWSPAPER REPORTER: Scott Wise (5) ☆; CHARLIE, A NEWSPAPER PHOTOGRAPHER: Darrian C. Ford; LEM, A FARMER: John Wilkerson; CLAY, A FARMER: J. Lee Flynn; HANK MUNSON, A FARMER: Newton R. Gilchrist; THE CHIEF OF POLICE: Steve Steiner; VIOLET, HIS DAUGHTER: Jackie Angelescu; THE FAIRTONES: Ian Knauer, James Patterson, Michael Lee Scott, Scott Willis; JUDGE HEPPENSTAHL: Charles Goff; BARKERS/JUDGES/VENDORS/FAIRGOERS: Kelli

Barclay, Leslie Bell, Linnea Dakin, SuEllen Estey, Tim Fauvell, Amy Gage, Susan Haefner, Tina Johnson, Ian Knauer, James Patterson, Michael Lee Scott, Mary C. Sheehan, Steve Steiner, Scott Willis; ROUSTABOUTS: Michael Lee Scott & Scott Willis. *Understudies*: Melissa: SuEllen Estey; Abel: J. Lee Flynn; Wayne: Ian Knauer; Margy: Susan Haefner; Emily: Leslie Bell; Violet/Eleanor: Linnea Dakin; Mrs. Metcalf: Mary C. Sheehan; Harry: James Patterson; Hoop-La Barker: Tina Johnson; Vivian/Jeanne: Kelli Barclay; Hank/Lem/Dave/Judge: Tim Fauvell; Clay: Steve Steiner; Pat/Stralenko/Police Chief: Scott Willis; Charlie/Gus/Uncle Sam/Fairtones/Roustabouts: John Scott; Cow/Pig: Julie Lira. *Swings*: Julie Lira & John Scott. *Orchestra:* KEYBOARDS: Robert Berman & Pam Sumner; DRUMS: Richard Rosenzweig; BASS: Leon Maleson; PERCUSSION: Lou Oddo; TRUMPETS: Peter Olstad, Gregory Gisbert, Phil Granger; TROMBONES: Larry Ferrell & Rock Ciccarone; TUBA: Marcus Rojas; FRENCH HORNS: David Wakefield & Leisa A. Paer; WOODWINDS: Steve Kenyon, Charles Pillow, Scott Schachter, Don McGeen; VIOLINS: Rob Shaw & Cecelia Hobbs Gardner; VIOLA: Debra Shufelt; CELLO: Daniel D. Miller; HARP: Park Stickney. *Act I*: Overture (Orchestra); *Scene 1* The Frake farm; a Tuesday afternoon in August: Opening ("Our State Fair") [from the 1945 movie] (Abel, Melissa, Wayne), "It Might as Well Be Spring" (Margy) [from the 1945 movie]; *Scene 2* On the road to Des Moines; Wednesday morning before sawn: "Driving at Night" [new unused music from *Allegro*] (The Frakes); *Scene 3* The midway at the Hoop-La Booth; later that morning: "Our State Fair" (reprise) (Ensemble); *Scene 4* The midway at the Temple of Wonder; later that morning: "That's for Me" [from the 1945 movie] (Wayne); *Scene 5* The beer tent; that afternoon: "More than Just a Friend" ("Sweet Hog of Mine") (l: Richard Rodgers) [from the 1962 movie re-make] (Abel, Lem, Hank, Clay); *Scene 6* Outside the Dairy Pavilion; later that afternoon: "Isn't it Kinda Fun?" [from the 1945 movie] (Pat & Margy); *Scene 7* The Starlight Dance Meadow; that night: "You Never Had it So Good" [cut from *Me and Juliet*] (Emily & Fairtones); *Scene 8* Camper's Hill; Thursday morning: "It Might as Well Be Spring" (reprise) (Margy), "When I Go Out Walking with My Baby" [cut from *Oklahoma!*] (Abel & Melissa); *Scene 9* Exhibition hall; that afternoon; *Scene 10* A nearby hillside; early that night: "So Far" [from *Allegro*] (Wayne & Emily); *Scene 11* The Starlight Dance Meadow; later that night: "It's a Grand Night for Singing" [from the 1945 movie] (Company). *Act II*: Entr'acte; *Scene 1* Outside the Livestock Pavilion; Friday afternoon: "The Man I Used to Be" [from *Pipe Dream*] (Pat, Vivian, Jeanne), "All I Owe Ioway" [from the 1945 movie] (Abel & Company); *Scene 2* Outside the Dairy Pavilion; early that night: "The Man I Used to Be" (reprise) (Pat), "Isn't it Kinda Fun?" (reprise) (Margy); *Scene 3* The Starlight Dance Meadow; immediately following: "That's the Way it Happens" [from *Me and Juliet*] (Emily & Fairtones); *Scene 4* The hillside; later that night; *Scene 5* Camper's Hill; later that night: "Boys and Girls Like You and Me" [cut from *Oklahoma!*] (Abel & Melissa); *Scene 6* On the midway; immediately following: "The Next Time it Happens" [from *Pipe Dream*] (Margy); *Scene 7* The Frake farm; Saturday night after supper: Finale (Company).

Broadway reviews were very divided, and it failed partly because it was such an expensive show to run, even though it cost only $2.5 million. David Merrick (who was then 84) had to spend an enormous amount of money to promote it and to cover operational cost debts. The Tony committee said that only four songs were eligible — and Mr. Merrick sued them (the case was dismissed). The show received Tony nominations for score, and for Scott Wise. On 6/5/96 Andrea McArdle broke her ankle during a performance, and had to be replaced by Susan Egan.

After Broadway. TOUR. This was a scaled-down version of the Broadway show. There was a tussle with Equity before the tour began, as it was intended to be non–Equity, despite the presence of John Davidson. It was settled, and the tour proceeded. It opened on 9/7/97, at the Eisenhower Auditorium, University Park, Pa. PRESENTED BY NETworks. *Cast*: ABEL: John Davidson; MELISSA: Carol Swarbrick, *SuEllen Estey* (stood in 10/21/97–11/17/97).

660. *Steel Pier*

An American fable, a dance-marathon musical set on Atlantic City's Steel Pier in August 1933. Rita is secretly married to Mick, the opportunistic MC. Bill is a daredevil pilot. Shelby began as a logging-camp cook, until a forest fire put her out of work. Then she became cook for the marathon dancers, until she saw how much money could be made dancing. Becker, wiry and obsessed with winning, came up through vaudeville.

Before Broadway. There was an eight-week workshop at 890 Broadway in June and July 1996, with the same basic cast and crew as for the subsequent Broadway run. Broadway rehearsals began on 1/13/97.

The Broadway Run. RICHARD RODGERS THEATRE, 4/24/97–6/28/97. 33 previews from 3/27/97. 76 PERFORMANCES. PRESENTED BY Roger Berlind; MUSIC: John Kander; LYRICS: Fred Ebb; BOOK: David Thompson; CONCEIVED BY: Scott Ellis, Susan Stroman, David Thompson; DIRECTOR: Scott Ellis; CHOREOGRAPHER: Susan Stroman; SETS: Tony Walton; COSTUMES: William Ivey Long; LIGHTING: Peter Kaczorowski; SOUND: Tony Meola; MUSICAL DIRECTOR/VOCAL ARRANGEMENTS: David Loud; ORCHESTRATIONS: Michael Gibson; DANCE & INCIDENTAL MUSIC ARRANGEMENTS: Glen Kelly; CAST RECORDING on RCA Victor, released on 7/29/97; PRESS: Boneau/Bryan-Brown; CASTING: Johnson—Liff; GENERAL MANAGER: Marvin A. Krauss; COMPANY MANAGER: Carl Pasbjerg; PRODUCTION STAGE MANAGER: Beverley Randolph; STAGE MANAGER: Frank Lombardi; ASSISTANT STAGE MANAGER: James Marr. *Cast:* BILL KELLY: Daniel McDonald (3) ✩, *Brian Sutherland* (during Mr. McDonald's absence from 5/7/97, due to injuring his leg during the Wednesday matinee); RITA RACINE: Karen Ziemba (2) ✩; SHELBY STEVENS: Debra Monk (4) ✩; MICK HAMILTON: Gregory Harrison (3) ✩; MR. WALKER: Ronn Carroll; BUDDY BECKER: Joel Blum; BETTE BECKER: Valerie Wright; JOHNNY ADEL: Timothy Warmen; DORA FOSTER: Alison Bevan; HAPPY MCGUIRE: Jim Newman; PRECIOUS MCGUIRE: Kristin Chenoweth; LUKE ADAMS: John C. Havens; MICK'S PICKS: Mary Illes, Rosa Curry, Sarah Solie Shannon; CORKY: Casey Nicholaw; DR. JOHNSON: John MacInnis, *Brian O'Brien*; SONNY: Gregory Mitchell; PREACHER: Adam Pelty; THE FLYING DUNLAPS: Leigh-Ann Wencker, Jack Hayes, JoAnn M. Hunter, Robert Fowler, John MacInnis (*Brian O'Brien*); STEEL PIER MARATHON COUPLES: COUPLE # 39: Karen Ziemba & Daniel McDonald; COUPLE # 32: Debra Monk & John C. Havens; COUPLE # 17: Valerie Wright & Joel Blum; COUPLE # 4: Kristin Chenoweth & Jim Newman; COUPLE # 26: Alison Bevan & Timothy Warmen; COUPLE # 46: JoAnn M. Hunter & Gregory Mitchell; COUPLE # 8: Dana Lynn Mauro & Andy Blankenbuehler; COUPLE # 50: Elizabeth Mills & Jack Hayes; COUPLE # 56: Leigh-Anne Wencker & Robert Fowler; COUPLE # 44: Ida Gilliams & Adam Pelty; COUPLE # 51: Sarah Solie Shannon & Casey Nicholaw; COUPLE # 54: Mary Illes & Brad Bradley; COUPLE # 3: Rosa Curry & John MacInnis (*Brian O'Brien*); COUPLE # 18: Leigh-Anne Wencker & Jack Hayes; COUPLE # 41: Ida Gilliams & John MacInnis; COUPLE # 11: Rosa Curry & Robert Fowler; COUPLE # 30: Elizabeth Mills & Adam Pelty; COUPLE # 25: Kristin Chenoweth & Gregory Mitchell; COUPLE # 19: Mary Illes & Casey Nicholaw; COUPLE # 14: Leigh-Anne Wencker & Brad Bradley; COUPLE # 40: Ida Gilliams & Robert Fowler; COUPLE # 55: Sarah Solie Shannon & Brad Bradley; COUPLE # 34: Rosa Curry & Jack Hayes; COUPLE # 29: Mary Illes & Timothy Warmen [during previews this was Couple # 62]. *Standbys*: Mick/Bill: Brian Sutherland; Rita/Shelby: Cady Huffman. *Understudies*: Mick: Timothy Warmen; Bill: Jim Newman; Shelby: Alison Bevan; Buddy: Brad Bradley & Adam Pelty; Walker: Brad Bradley & Casey Nicholaw; Luke: Adam Pelty & Casey Nicholaw; Johnny: Gregory Mitchell & Julio Agustin; Happy: John MacInnis (*Brian O'Brien*) & Scott Taylor; Rita: Valerie Wright; Precious: Mary Illes & Sarah Solie Shannon; Dora: Angelique Ilo & Leigh-Ann Wencker; Bette: Leslie Bell & JoAnn M. Hunter. *Swings*: Julio Augustin, Leslie Bell, Angelique Ilo, Scott Taylor. *Orchestra*: TRUMPETS: Jim Kievit, Christian Jaudes, Richard Kelly; TENOR TROMBONE: Charles Gordon; BASS TROMBONE/TUBA: Earl McIntyre; FRENCH HORNS: Roger Wendt & Anita Miller; BASS: Robert Renino; GUITAR/BANJO: Greg Utzig; KEYBOARDS: Antony Geralis & James Moore; DRUMS: Bruce Doctor; PERCUSSION: Mark Sherman; CONCERTMASTER: Alexander Vselensky; VIOLINS: Alexander Vselensky, Christopher Cardona, Paul Woodiel; VIOLAS: Susan Follari & Jill Jaffe; CELLO: Jennifer Langham; WOODWINDS: Lawrence Feldman, William Shadel, Andy Drelles, Ken Berger. *Act I*: *Prelude*; *Scene 1* The beach/the boardwalk: "Willing to Ride" (Rita)

[during previews this number was titled "Waiting to Ride"]; *Scene 2* The Steel Pier Ballroom: "Everybody Dance" (Mick, Mick's Picks, Company), "Second Chance" (Bill); *Scene 3* Mick Hamilton's office; *Scene 4* The rest stations: "In Here" (Shelby, Buddy, Happy, Bette, Luke, Rita, Johnny, Precious, Dora, Bill) [cut during previews]; *Scene 5* The Steel Pier Ballroom: Montage I: "The Shag" (Company); *Scene 6* Behind the bandstand: "A Powerful Thing" (Mick & Company) [during previews this number replaced "Winning" (Mick & Company)]; *Scene 7* The Steel Pier Ballroom: "Dance with Me"/"The Last Girl" (Mick, Rita, Bill, Company), Montage II: "Harmonica Specialty" (Company); *Scene 8* Mick Hamilton's office; *Scene 9* The Steel Pier Ballroom: "Everybody's Girl" (Shelby); *Scene 10* The diving horse tank: "Wet" (Rita & Bill); *Scene 11* The Steel Pier Ballroom/the Trenton Air Show: "Lovebird" (Rita), "Everybody Dance" (reprise) (Mick & Company). *Act II*: *Entr'acte*; *Scene 1* The rest stations: "Leave the World Behind" (Bill, Rita, Company); *Scene 2* A corridor near the dance floor; *Scene 3* The Steel Pier Ballroom: Montage III: "The Sprints Two-Step" (Company); *Scene 4* Outside the Steel Pier Ballroom: "Somebody Older" (Shelby); *Scene 5* The rooftop of the Ballroom: "Running in Place" (Rita); *Scene 6* The Steel Pier Ballroom: "Looking for Love" (Mick) [cut during previews], "Two Little Worlds" (Precious, Mick's Picks, Company), "First You Dream" (Bill & Rita); *Scene 7* The women's rest station; *Scene 8* The Steel Pier Ballroom: "Steel Pier" (Mick, Rita, Mick's Picks); *Scene 9* The women's rest station/outside the Steel Pier: "Steel Pier" (reprise) (Company).

Note: musical numbers are subject to change.

Broadway reviews were divided. The show received Tony nominations for musical, score, book, direction of a musical, choreography, sets, orchestrations, and for Daniel McDonald, Joel Blum, Debra Monk, and Karen Ziemba.

661. *Stop the World—I Want to Get Off*

A "new-style musical." Set in the interior of a circus tent. Littlechap is a Chaplinesque clown. We see him go through birth, school, marriage, business, politics, and death. The more he conforms to convention, the more successful he becomes. There are four women in his life: Evie (British), Anya (Russian), Ilse (German), and Ginny (American). Cast members dressed in loose-fitting tights and looked a bit like circus clowns. They were seated on side benches. As the play begins Littlechap enters through a tunnel, the symbol of life. He twists himself into position of a child about to be born. He plays a newborn infant, then a child who does not speak but conveys ideas through body movements. Then he is a young lad working his way up the executive ladder, he marries the boss's daughter, who is pregnant with his child, until he becomes a top executive. He advances in social prestige, becomes a Member of Parliament, reaches the exalted position of being dubbed "Master of Doubletalk," is knighted, and receives a medal for his ability to talk a lot and say nothing. During his phenomenal rise to power he has affairs with Anya, Ilse and Ginny. His daughter becomes pregnant out of wedlock, has to marry, and Littlechap attends the wedding out of social responsibility. However, when his next daughter is married he is too busy to attend. He is so engrossed in his own affairs that he doesn't know his wife is critically ill until she dies, and then he sings "What Kind of Fool Am I?," which depicts his empty and self-centered life. Finally he dies, by exiting through the same tunnel he originally came out of. Much was done symbolically. For example, when Littlechap first approached the boss's office he had to reach high for the door knob, but the higher he got in the firm, the more accessible the knob became. In many ways it resembled Marcel Marceau's pantomime *The Seven Ages of Man*. Sometimes

Mr. Newley would step to the front of the stage and yell "Stop the World!," and then tell an irrelevant joke.

Before Broadway. In 1961 British songwriter Leslie Bricusse went to New York to write a new revue for Beatrice Lillie. Tony Newley accompanied him, and they came up with the idea for a show of their own, *Stop the World—I Want to Get Off*. Most of the script was written in Bea Lillie's New York apartment. It was first PRESENTED BY Bernard Delfont at the OPERA HOUSE, Manchester, England, 6/20/61, for 3 weeks, then on 7/15/61 it opened at NOTTINGHAM, which is where David Merrick saw it and immediately acquired the rights for a U.S. production. It then ran in London, at the QUEEN'S THEATRE, 7/20/61–11/17/62. 478 PERFORMANCES. It had the same basic crew as for the subsequent Broadway run, except PRESENTED BY Bernard Delfont, in association with H.M. Tennent & Marigold Music; COSTUMES: Kiki Byrnes; MUSICAL DIRECTOR: Ian Fraser, *Michael Reeves*; CAST RECORDING on Decca. *Cast*: Anthony Newley (*Tony Tanner*), Anna Quayle (*Thelma Ruby*), Baker Twins (*the Allman Twins*, i.e. Janet & Jennifer Allman). CHORUS: Marti Webb, Julia Sutton, Jenny Wren.

The Broadway Run. SHUBERT THEATRE, 10/3/62–9/7/63; AMBASSADOR THEATRE, 9/9/63–2/1/64. 1 preview on 10/2/62. Total of 555 PERFORMANCES. PRESENTED BY David Merrick, in association with Bernard Delfont; MUSIC/LYRICS/BOOK: Anthony Newley & Leslie Bricusse; DIRECTOR: Anthony Newley; CHOREOGRAPHER: Virginia Mason re-staged John Broome's London choreography; SETS/LIGHTING: Sean Kenny; MUSICAL SUPERVISOR: Ian Fraser; MUSICAL DIRECTOR: Milton Rosenstock; ORCHESTRATIONS: Ian Fraser, with David Lindup, Gordon Longford, Burt Rhodes; PRESS: Harvey B. Sabinson, Lee Solters, David Powers; GENERAL MANAGER: Jack Schlissel; COMPANY MANAGER: Eugene Wolsk; STAGE MANAGER: Ben Strobach. *Cast*: LITTLECHAP: Anthony Newley (1), *Kenneth Nelson* (during Mr. Newley's absence, 7/22/63–8/5/63), *Joel Grey* (from 11/4/63); EVIE/ANYA/ILSE/GINNIE: Anna Quayle (2), *Joan Eastman* (during Miss Quayle's absence, 7/22/63–8/5/63, and then permanently from 11/4/63); JANE: Jennifer Baker; SUSAN: Susan Baker [Jennifer's twin]; CHORUS: Rawley Bates, Ronnie Brody, Diana Corto, Mark Hunter, Jo-Anne Leeds, Karen Lynn Reed, Paul Rufo, Sylvia Tysick, Stephanie Winters. *Understudies*: For Mr. Newley: Ken Nelson; For Miss Quayle: Joan Eastman; For Mr. Hunter: Paul Rufo. ALTERNATE GIRL: Patience Jarvis. *Act I*: Overture, "The A.B.C. Song" (Chorus), "I Wanna Be Rich" (Littlechap & Chorus), "Typically English" (Evie & Littlechap), "A Special Announcement" (Chorus), "Lumbered" (Littlechap), Susan's Birth & "Lumbered" (reprise) (Littlechap), "Welcome to Sludgepool" (Chorus), "Gonna Build a Mountain" (Littlechap & Chorus) [a hit], Jane's Birth (Littlechap), Moscow Music & "Glorious Russian" (Anya), "Meilinki Meilchick" (Littlechap, Anya, Chorus), "Family Fugue" (Littlechap, Evie, Susan, Jane), "Typische Deutsche" (Ilse & Chorus), "Family Fugue" (reprise) & "Nag! Nag! Nag!" (Littlechap, Evie, Susan, Jane, Chorus), "Typische Deutsche" (reprise) & "Nag! Nag! Nag!" (reprise). *Act II*: Entr'acte; New York Music & "All-American (Music)" (Ginnie), "Once in a Lifetime" (Littlechap & Girl) [a hit], "Mumbo Jumbo" (Littlechap & Chorus), "Once in a Lifetime" (reprise), "Welcome to Sunvale" (Chorus), "Someone Nice Like You" (Littlechap & Evie), "What Kind of Fool Am I?" (Littlechap) [the big hit], March Out Music.

The Broadway production cost only $75,000 to produce, and advance sales were good. Broadway reviews were divided. Anna Quayle won a Tony, and the show was also nominated for musical, composer & lyricist, musical director, book, and for Anthony Newley.

After Broadway. TOUR. Opened on 3/25/63, at the Pabst Theatre, Milwaukee, and closed on 4/18/64, at the Forrest Theatre, Philadelphia. MUSICAL DIRECTOR: Oscar Kosarin. *Cast*: Joel Grey (*Kenneth Nelson*), Julie Newmar (*Joan Eastman*), Janet & Jennifer Allman.

PAPER MILL PLAYHOUSE, New Jersey, 1965. DIRECTOR: Kenneth Nelson. *Cast:* Kenneth Nelson, Joan Eastman.

THE MOVIE. 1966. DIRECTOR: Philip Saville. The album is on Warners. There were some new numbers: "I Believed it All," "New York Scene" (instrumental) (both songs by Al Ham), and "Typically Japanese." *Cast*: LITTLECHAP: Tony Tanner; EVIE/ANYA/ARA/GINNIE: Millicent Martin; SUSAN: Leila Croft; JANE: Valerie Croft.

BUS-TRUCK TOUR. 9/2/67–11/30/67. Re-ran 1/23–3/31/68. Played a total of 104 cities. *Cast*: Jackie Warner.

NEW YORK STATE THEATRE, 8/3/78–8/27/78. 1 preview. 29 PERFORMANCES. This run was part of a year-long tour of the USA. A Hillard Elins production, PRESENTED BY James & Joseph Nederlander, in association with City Center of Music and Drama; DIRECTOR: Mel Shapiro; CHOREOGRAPHER: Billy Wilson; SETS/COSTUMES: Santo Loquasto; LIGHTING: Pat Collins; MUSICAL SUPERVISOR/ARRANGEMENTS: Ian Fraser; MUSICAL DIRECTOR: George Rhodes; ORCHESTRATIONS: Billy Byers & Joseph Lippman; CAST RECORDING on Warner/Curb Records. The number "Nag! Nag! Nag!" was replaced with "Life is a Woman." "Welcome to Sludgepool" was re-titled "Welcome to Sludgeville." "The A.B.C. Song" and "Special Announcement" were dropped. Reviews were generally terrible. Sammy Davis got paid $60,000 a week. *Cast*: LITTLECHAP: Sammy Davis Jr.; BATON TWIRLER/DEATH/SNOBBS COUNTRY CLUB MC: Dennis Daniels; SCHOOLGIRL/ELECTION NEWSCASTER: Donna Lowe; EVIE/ANYA/ILSE/LORENE: Marian Mercer; 1ST GIRL IN CROW'S NEST: Deborah Masterson; 2ND GIRL IN CROW'S NEST/HADASSAH MC/SOLO SINGER IN SUNVALE: Joyce Nolen; SUSAN: Wendy Edmead; GUITAR PLAYER/MC SPANISH GROUP: Patrick Kinser-Lau; JANE: Shelly Burch; THE BOY: Charles Willis Jr.; MC BLACK GROUP/SPEAKER OF THE HOUSE: Edwetta Little; ENSEMBLE: Marcus B.F. Brown, Karen Giombetti, Linda Griffin, Billy Newton-Davis, Robert Yori-Tanner. This version was filmed in 1979 as *Sammy Stops the World*.

TOUR. Opened on 9/23/86, at Houston Music Hall, and closed on 2/18/87, at the Embassy Theatre, Fort Wayne, Ind. PRESENTED BY Barry & Fran Weissler and the PACE Theatrical Group; CHOREOGRAPHER: Philip Burton & Lynne Taylor-Corbett; SETS: David Chapman; MUSICAL DIRECTOR: Tom Fay. *Cast*: LITTLECHAP: Anthony Newley; EVIE/ANYA/ILSE: Suzie Plaskin; JANE: Diana Georger; ALSO WITH: Jill Powell, Karyn Quackenbush, Joey Rigol, Beth Blatt, Danette Cuming, Madeleine Doherty, Kathy Leonardo, Stacey Logan, Janet Metz, Chikae Ishikawa, Teresa Tracy.

662. *La Strada*

Set in and around cities and villages of Southern Italy in the early 1950s. It followed the film. Zampano travels with his strongman act. He buys simple-minded Gelsomina as his concubine/assistant. Her clowning makes her the star of the act, and she falls in love with Zampano despite the brutal way he treats her. When the two join a circus, Gelsomina finds a confidant in acrobat-clown Mario, but the jealous Zampano kills him. Zampano finally leaves the inconsolable Gelsomina to die on the road (la strada) and goes on.

Before Broadway. The first manifestation of this show was a studio cast recording, with all the songs by Lionel Bart. Tryouts were in Detroit, and Vincent Beck was replaced in the cast by Stephen Pearlman; and Miriam Phillips by Anne Hegira. 4th-billed Patricia Marand was written out of the script; Alvin Ailey replaced Joyce Trisler as choreographer. Lionel Bart's score was gradually removed until, on Broadway opening night only three of his songs remained. Martin Charnin and Elliot Lawrence, although they had written almost an entirely new score, did not take credit. Only Elliot Lawrence was credited on the back of the program, as "orchestra personnel supervisor." This was Bernadette Peters' first Broadway lead.

The Broadway Run. LUNT—FONTANNE THEATRE, 12/14/69. 12 previews. 1 PERFORMANCE. PRESENTED BY Charles K. Peck Jr. & Canyon Productions (B.G. Cantor); MUSIC/LYRICS: Lionel Bart; ADDITIONAL MUSIC: Elliot Lawrence; ADDITIONAL LYRICS: Martin Charnin; BOOK: Charles K. Peck Jr.; BASED ON the 1954 Italian movie of the same name, written by Federico Fellini, Tullio Pinelli & Ennio Flaiano, directed by Fellini, and starring Anthony Quinn; DIRECTOR: Alan Schneider; CHOREOGRAPHER: Alvin Ailey; SETS: Ming Cho Lee; COSTUMES: Nancy Potts; LIGHTING: Martin Aronstein; MUSICAL DIRECTOR: Hal Hastings; ORCHESTRATIONS: Eddie Sauter; DANCE MUSIC ARRANGEMENTS: Peter Howard; PRESS: Frank Goodman, Les Schecter, Barbara Schwei; CIRCUS CONSULTANT: Hovey Burgess; GENERAL MANAGERS: Joseph Harris & Ira Bernstein; COMPANY MANAGER: Sam Pagliaro; PRODUCTION STAGE

MANAGER: Terence Little; STAGE MANAGER: William Callan; ASSISTANT STAGE MANAGERS: Stan Page & Lola Shumlin. **Cast:** THE OLD MAN: John Coe (7); GELSOMINA: Bernadette Peters (1) ☆; MOTHER: Anne Hegira (4); ELSA: Lisa Bellaran; EVA: Mary Ann Robbins; SOPHIA: Susan Goeppinger; ZAMPANO: Stephen Pearlman (3) ☆; CASTRA: Lucille Patton (5); ACROBATS: Paul Charles & Harry Endicott; MARIO, THE FOOL: Larry Kert (2) ☆; MAMA LAMBRINI: Peggy Cooper (6); ALBERTI: John Coe (7); SISTER CLAUDIA: Susan Goeppinger; COMPANY: Loretta Abbott, Glenn Brooks, Henry Brunjes, Connie Burnett, Robert Carle, Paul Charles, Barbara Christopher, Peggy Cooper, Betsy Dickerson, Harry Endicott, Anna Maria Fanizzi, Jack Fletcher, Nino Galanti, Susan Goeppinger, Rodney Griffin, Mickey Gunnersen, Kenneth Kreel, Don Lopez, Joyce Maret, Stan Page, Odette Panaccione, Mary Ann Robbins, Steven Ross, Larry Small, Eileen Taylor. **Standby:** Gelsomina: Lynn Lipton. **Understudies:** Mario: Hank Brunjes; Mother/Castra: Peggy Cooper. **Act I: Scene 1** A desolate beach near Gelsomina's house: "Seagull, Starfish, Pebble" (Gelsomina); **Scene 2** Along the road (la strada): "The Great Zampano" (m/l: Lionel Bart) (Gelsomina & Zampano), "What's Going on Inside?" (Zampano); **Scene 3** The outskirts of a village: "Belonging" (m/l: Lionel Bart) (Gelsomina); **Scene 4** A farmhouse yard: Wedding Dance (Entire Company); **Scene 5** The farm stable: "I Don't Like You" (Gelsomina); **Scene 6** Along the road: Encounters (dance) (Gelsomina & Entire Company), "There's a Circus in Town" (m/l: Lionel Bart) (Mario); **Scene 7** The Alberti Circus grounds: "You're Musical" (Mario & Gelsomina); **Scene 8** A performance of the Alberti Circus: "Only More!" (Gelsomina). **Act II: Scene 1** The circus grounds: "What a Man" (Gelsomina & Mama Lambrini), "Everything Needs Something" (Gelsomina); **Scene 2** A village square: "Sooner or Later" (Mario), "Sooner or Later" (reprise) (Gelsomina); **Scene 3** A convent: "Belonging" (reprise) (Gelsomina); **Scene 4** Along the road; **Scene 5** A camp site in the mountains; **Scene 6** The end of the road: "The End of the Road" (Entire Company).

Note: in reality all numbers were by Elliot Lawrence (music) and Martin Charnin (lyrics), unless Lionel Bart's name is beside them.

The show was panned by the critics, and lost $650,000.

663. *Street Corner Symphony*

A retro musical revue, which featured pop and soul music of the 1960s and 1970s.

Before Broadway. It first tried out at West Palm Beach's new Burt Reynolds Theatre Institute. Kenneth Waissman saw it there, and came in as producer. There were a lot of changes during Broadway previews. Opening night was postponed from 11/18/97 to 11/24/97.

The Broadway Run. BROOKS ATKINSON THEATRE, 11/24/97–2/1/98. 25 previews from 10/28/97. 79 PERFORMANCES. PRESENTED BY Kenneth Waissman & Brian Bantry; CONCEIVED BY/DIRECTOR/CHOREOGRAPHER: Marion J. Caffey; SETS: Neil Peter Jampolis; COSTUMES: Jonathan Bixby; LIGHTING: Jules Fisher & Peggy Eisenhauer; SOUND: Jonathan Deans; MUSICAL SUPERVISOR/ORCHESTRATIONS/DANCE MUSIC ARRANGEMENTS: Daryl Waters; MUSICAL DIRECTOR: Lon Hoyt; VOCAL ARRANGEMENTS: Michael McElroy; PRESS: The Pete Sanders Group; CASTING: Peter Wise; GENERAL MANAGER: Charlotte Wilcox; COMPANY MANAGER: Dave Harris; PRODUCTION STAGE MANAGER: Robert Mark Kalfin; STAGE MANAGER: Jimmie Lee Smith; ASSISTANT STAGE MANAGER: CJay Hardy. **Cast:** CLARENCE: Eugene Fleming (8); NARRATOR/MRS. CYNTHIA: Carol Dennis (1); JESSIE-LEE: Jose Llana (4); SUKKI: Catherine Morin (5); C.J.: C.E. Smith (6); DEBBIE: Debra Walton (7); CHIP: Victor Trent Cook (2); SUSAN: Stacy Francis (3). **Understudies:** For Miss Dennis: Toni SeaWright; For Misses Francis/Morin/Walton: Cjay Hardy; for Men: Jamie. **Orchestra:** SYNTHESIZERS: Lon Hoyt & Ronald Metcalfe; BASS: Konrad "Cheesecake" Adderley; PERCUSSION: Annette Aguilar; GUITAR: Steve Bargonetti; WOODWINDS: Jimmy Cozier; DRUMS: Clint de Ganon; TRUMPET: Craig Johnson.

NEIGHBORHOOD MEMORIES—THE 1960s [during previews this was called Act I]: "Dancin' in the Street" (m/l: Marvin Gaye, William Stevenson, Ivy Hunter) (The Guys), "Dance to the Music" (m/l: Sylvester Stewart) (Company), "Try to Remember" (m: Harvey Schmidt; l: Tom Jones) [from *The Fantasticks*]/"The Way We Were" (m/l: Marvin Hamlisch,

Marilyn Bergman, Alan Bergman) (Mrs. Cynthia) [these two numbers were dropped during previews], "The Way You Do the Things You Do" (m/l: William "Smokey" Robinson Jr. & Robert Rogers) (Chip & Clarence with the Guys) [during previews it was performed by Clarence, with the Guys), "Good Old Acapella" (by Les & Susan Carter) (C.J. with the Company) [this number was dropped during previews], "I Wanna Know Your Name" (m/l: Kenneth Gamble & Leon Huff) (Chip with the Guys), "Good Old Acapella" (reprise) (C.J. with the Guys) [this reprise was dropped during previews], "My Girl"/"My Guy" (by William "Smokey" Robinson Jr. & R. White) (Susan, Chip, Company) [this number was dropped during previews], "My Boyfriend's Back" (m/l: Robert Feldman, Gerald Goldstein, Richard Gottehrer) (Sukki, Debbie, Susan), "It's in His Kiss" ("Shoop Shoop Song") (m/l: Rudy Clark) (Susan with Sukki & Debbie), "Hot Fun in the Summertime" (m/l: Sylvester Stewart) (Company) [this number was dropped during previews], "Try a Little Tenderness" (m/l: Harry M. Woods, James Campbell, Reginald Connolly) (Clarence), "R-E-S-P-E-C-T" (m/l: Otis Redding) (Mrs. Cynthia & Girls), "Baby Workout" (m/l: Alonzo Tucker & Jackie Wilson) (Jessie-Lee & Debbie, with the Company) [during previews it was performed by Jessie-Lee & Company], "Dance Chant" (based on an idea of and inspired by Andre De Shields) (Company), "Baby Workout" (reprise) (Jessie-Lee & Debbie with the Company) [during previews this reprise was performed by Jessie-Lee & Company], "Grandma's Hands" (by Bill Withers) (Mrs. Cynthia with C.J. & Debbie) [this number was dropped during previews], "Dancin' in the Street" (reprise) (Clarence with the Company) [this reprise was dropped during previews], "(Love is Like a) Heat Wave" (by Brian Holland, Lamont Dozier, Edward Holland Jr.) (Sukki with Debbie & Susan) [this number was dropped during previews], "Please, Please, Please" (by James Brown & Johnny Terry) (C.J. with the Company) [this number was dropped during previews], "Unchained Melody" (m: Alex North; l: Hy Zaret) (C.J.), "Good Old Acapella" (reprise) (C.J. with the Guys) [this reprise was dropped during previews], "A Prayer for C.J." (traditional spiritual prayer) (Mrs. Cynthia) [this prayer was dropped during previews], "Grandma's Hands" (reprise) (Mrs. Cynthia) [this reprise was dropped during previews], "What's Going On?" (Clarence) [this number was dropped during previews], "Psychedelic Shack" (m/l: Norman J. Whitfield & Barrett Strong) (Company), "Cloud Nine" (m/l: Norman J. Whitfield & Barrett Strong) (Company), "I Want to Take You Higher" (m/l: Sylvester Stewart) (Company), "I Want to Take You Higher" (reprise) (Company) [this reprise was cut during previews], "Ohio" (m/l: Neil Young)/"Machine Gun" (m/l: Jimi Hendrix) (Jessie-Lee with the Company), "American Pie" (m/l: Don McLean) (Mrs. Cynthia), "Love's in Need of Love Today" (m/l: Stevie Wonder) (Mrs. Cynthia), "Love's in Need of Love Today"/"American Pie" (reprise) (Company) [these reprises were dropped during previews]. CONCERT FANTASIES—THE 1970s [during previews this was called Act II]: "Get Ready" (m/l: William "Smokey" Robinson Jr.) (Chip with the Company), "Best of My Love" (Mrs. Cynthia, with Sukki, Debbie, Susan) [this number was dropped during previews], "Jimmy Mack" (Debbie, Sukki, Susan) [this number was dropped during previews], "Want Ads" (m/l: J. Perry, B. Perkins, G. Johnson) (Susan with Sukki & Debbie), "Love Train" (m/l: Kenneth Gamble & Leon Huff) (Clarence with the Guys), "Oh, Girl" (m/l: Eugene Record) (Jessie-Lee with the Guys), "Betcha, by Golly, Wow!" (m/l: Thomas Bell & Linda Creed) (Chip with the Guys), "Heaven Must Be Missing an Angel" (m/l: Frederick J. Perren & Kenneth St. Lewis) (The Guys), "The Tracks of My Tears" (by Marvin Tarplin, Warren Moore, William "Smokey" Robinson Jr.) (Susan), "Can I?" (m/l: Herman Griffith & Hal Davis) (Chip), "Midnight Train to Georgia" (m/l: James D. Weatherly) (Mrs. Cynthia with Clarence, Jessie-Lee, C.J.), "Me and Mrs. Jones" (m/l: Kenneth Gamble, Leon Huff, Cary Gilbert) (The Guys), "Proud Mary" (m/l: John Fogerty) (Debbie with Sukki & Susan), "Hold On, I'm Coming" (m/l: Isaac Hayes Jr. & David Porter) (C.J. & Clarence), "Soul Man" (m/l: Isaac Hayes Jr. & David Porter) (C.J. & Clarence), "End of the Road" (m/l: Antonio Reid, Daryl Simmons, Kenneth Edmonds) (Mrs. Cynthia with the Company), "Love Train" (reprise) (Company) [during previews this replaced a reprise of "Dance to the Music" (Company)].

Reviews were terrible. Kenneth Waissman withdrew as producer after the opening. The show posted closing notices on 1/15/98.

664. *Street Scene*

A dramatic musical. Set on a sidewalk in front of a sandstone tenement house, in New York City. The play is a look at the inhabitants of the tenement on a hot summer's day. Anna's loveless marriage to bullying, drunken Frank drives her to an affair which ends tragically. Their frustrated daughter Rose can't give herself to either smooth-talking sharpie Harry or earnest neighbor Sam. Henry was a black janitor.

Before Broadway. It tried out, to sparse audiences, at the Shubert Theatre, Philadelphia, from 12/16/46. During tryouts Brian Sullivan replaced Richard Manning, and the number "Italy in Technicolor" was dropped.

The Broadway Run. ADELPHI THEATRE, 1/9/47–5/17/47. 148 PERFORMANCES. PRESENTED BY Dwight Deere Wiman & The Playwrights' Company (including Elmer Rice); MUSIC: Kurt Weill; LYRICS: Langston Hughes, with Elmer Rice; BOOK: Elmer Rice; BASED ON Elmer Rice's Pulitzer Prize-winning Broadway drama of the same name, directed by Mr. Rice, and starring Erin O'Brien Moore, and which ran at the Playhouse 1/10/29 (601 performances). It was filmed (straight) in 1931 by King Vidor, with Sylvia Sydney (Rose) and William Collier Jr. (Sam); DIRECTOR: Charles Friedman; CHOREOGRAPHER: Anna Sokolow; SETS/LIGHTING: Jo Mielziner; COSTUMES: Lucinda Ballard; MUSICAL DIRECTOR: Maurice Abravanel; MUSICAL ARRANGEMENTS/ORCHESTRATIONS: Kurt Weill; CAST RECORDING on Columbia; PRESS: William Fields & John L. Toohey; CASTING: Lina Abarbanell; GENERAL STAGE MANAGER: John E. Sola; STAGE MANAGER: Ambrose Costello; ASSISTANT STAGE MANAGER: George Nichols. *Cast:* ABRAHAM KAPLAN: Irving Kaufman; GRETA FIORENTINO: Helen Arden; CARL OLSEN: Wilson Smith; EMMA JONES: Hope Emerson (6); OLGA OLSEN: Ellen Repp; SHIRLEY KAPLAN: Norma Chambers; HENRY DAVIS: Creighton Thompson; WILLIE MAURRANT: Peter Griffith; ANNA MAURRANT: Polyna Stoska (3), Bette Van (alternate); SAM KAPLAN: Brian Sullivan (4); DANIEL BUCHANAN: Remo Lota; FRANK MAURRANT: Norman Cordon (1); GEORGE JONES: David E. Thomas; STEVE SANKEY: Lauren Gilbert; LIPPO FIORENTINO: Sydney Rayner (5); JENNIE HILDEBRAND: Beverly Janis; 2ND GRADUATE: Zosia Gruchala; 3RD GRADUATE: Marion Covey; MARY HILDEBRAND: Juliana Gallagher; CHARLIE HILDEBRAND: Bennett Burrill; MRS. LAURA HILDEBRAND: Elen Lane; GRACE DAVIS: Helen Ferguson; 1ST POLICEMAN: Ernest Taylor; ROSE MAURRANT: Anne Jeffreys (2); HARRY EASTER: Don Saxon; MAE JONES: Sheila Bond; DICK McGANN: Danny Daniels; VINCENT JONES: Robert Pierson; DR. JOHN WILSON: Edwin G. O'Connor, *John Sweet*; OFFICER HARRY MURPHY: Norman Thomson; A MILKMAN: Russell George; A MUSIC PUPIL: Joyce Carroll; CITY MARSHAL JAMES HENRY: Randolph Symonette, *Joseph E. Scandur*; FRED CULLEN: Paul Lilly; AN OLD CLOTHES MAN: Edward Reichert; AN INTERNE: Roy Munsell; AN AMBULANCE DRIVER: John Sweet; 1ST NURSEMAID: Peggy Turnley; 2ND NURSEMAID: Ellen Carleen; A MARRIED COUPLE: Bette Van & Joseph E. Scandur (*Russell George*); PASSERS-BY/NEIGHBORS/CHILDREN, ETC: Larry Baker, Aza Bard, Tom Barragan, Mel Bartell, Ellen Carleen, Joyce Carroll, Victor Clarke, Marion Covey, Diana Donne, Bessie Franklin, Russell George, Zosia Gruchala, Juanita Hall, Bobby Horn, Beverly Janis, Bernard Kovler, Elen Lane, Marie Leidal, Roy Munsell, Edwin G. O'Connor, Sasha Pressman, Biruta Ramoska, Edward Reichert, Joseph E. Scandur, John Sweet, Ernest Taylor, Peggy Turnley, Bette Van, Wilson Woodbeck, *Marcella Uhl*. **Act I**: An evening in June: "Ain't it Awful, the Heat?" (Mrs. Fiorentino, Mrs. Jones, Mrs. Olsen, Kaplan, Olsen, Neighbors), "(I Got a) Marble and a Star" (Henry), "Get a Load of That" (Mrs. Jones, Mrs. Fiorentino, Mrs. Olsen)), "When a Woman Has a Baby" (Buchanan, Mrs. Fiorentino, Mrs. Jones, Mrs. Maurrant), "Somehow I Never Could Believe" (Mrs. Maurrant), "Get a Load of That" (reprise) (Mrs. Jones, Mrs. Fiorentino, Jones, Olsen), "(I'm Nuts About) Ice Cream" (Sextet) (Lippo, Mrs. Jones, Mrs. Fiorentino, Henry, Jones, Olsen, Mrs. Olsen), "Let Things Be Like They Always Was" (Maurrant), "Wrapped in a Ribbon and Tied in a Bow" (Jennie & Neighbors), "Lonely House" (Sam), "Wouldn't You Like to Be on Broadway?" (Easter), "What Good Would the Moon Be?" (Rose), "Moon-Faced, Starry-Eyed" (dance) (Dick & Mae), "Remember that I Care" (Sam & Rose). **Act II**: **Scene 1** The following morning: "Catch Me

if You Can" (Charlie, Mary, Willie, Children), "There'll Be Trouble" (Maurrant, Mrs. Maurrant, Rose), "A Boy Like You" (Mrs. Maurrant), "We'll Go Away Together" (Sam & Rose), "The Woman Who Lived up There" (Ensemble); **Scene 2** Afternoon of the same day: "Lullaby" (Nursemaids), "I Loved Her, Too" (Maurrant, Rose, Ensemble), "Don't Forget the Lilac Bush" (Sam & Rose), "Ain't it Awful, the Heat?" (reprise) (Mrs. Fiorentino, Mrs. Jones, Mrs. Olsen, Kaplan).

The poem *When Lilacs Last in the Dooryard Bloomed*, referred to in "Remember that I Care" and "Don't Forget the Lilac Bush," was written by Walt Whitman.

Broadway reviews were of the 1/11/47 matinee, and were very good. The show won 1947 Tony Awards for costumes (actually for Lucinda Ballard's entire season of work), and a Special Tony for Kurt Weill. It also won a Donaldson Award for Polyna Stoska. The show cost $160,000.

After Broadway. CITY CENTER, 4/2/59–4/29/59. 7 PERFORMANCES IN REPERTORY. Return engagement 9/27/59–10/15/59. 2 PERFORMANCES IN REPERTORY. Another return engagement 2/13/60–2/19/60. 3 PERFORMANCES. PRESENTED BY the New York City Opera; DIRECTOR/CHOREOGRAPHER: Herbert Machiz; SUPERVISOR OF THE CHILDREN'S NUMBER: Robert Joffrey; SETS/COSTUMES: Paul Sylbert; CONDUCTOR: Samuel Krachmalnick. *Cast:* ABRAHAM: Howard Fried, *Grant Williams* (from 9/27/59); GRETA: Dolores Mari & Jacquelynne Moody (alternating) [Miss Mari alone by 9/27/59]; CARL: Arnold Voketaitis; EMMA: Ruth Kobart; OLGA: Beatrice Krebs; SHIRLEY: Florence Anglin; MRS. DAVIS: Marie Louise; HENRY: Andrew Frierson; WILLIE: Michael Mann; ANNA: Wilma Spence & Elisabeth Carron (alternating) [Miss Carron only by 9/27/59]; SAM: David Poleri & Frank Porretta (alternating) [Mr. Poretta alone by 9/27/59]; DANIEL: Keith Kaldenberg; FRANK: William Chapman; GEORGE: Arthur Newman, *Chester Ludgin* (from 9/27/59); STEVE: Arthur Storch & David Frank (alternating) [Mr. Storch alone by 9/27/59]; LIPPO: Jack De Lon, *Jack Harrold* (by 9/27/59); JENNIE: Nancy Dussault; 2ND GRADUATE: Fiddle Viracola, *Sylvia De Van* (from 9/27/59); 3RD GRADUATE: Jennie Andrea; MRS. HILDEBRAND: Elizabeth Mannion, *Sophia Steffan* (by 9/27/59); CHARLIE: Richard Clemence; MARY: Lynn Taussig; GRACE: Sharon Williams; ROSE: Helena Scott & Joy Clements (alternating); HARRY: Scott Merrill, *Seth Riggs* (from 9/27/59); MAE: Sondra Lee; DICK: Richard Tone; VINCENT: Albert Lewis; DR. WILSON: John Macurdy; MURPHY: Dan Merriman; CITY MARSHAL: George Del Monte; FRED: William Zachariasen & William Saxon (alternating); 1ST NURSEMAID: Mary Le Sawyer; 2ND NURSEMAID: Greta Wolff, *Rita Metzger* (by 9/27/59).

CITY CENTER, 4/26/63–5/10/63. 3 PERFORMANCES IN REPERTORY. PRESENTED BY the New York City Opera; DIRECTOR: Herbert Machiz; CHOREOGRAPHERS: Sondra Lee & Richard Tone; CONDUCTOR: Skitch Henderson. *Cast:* ABRAHAM: Howard Fried; GRETA: Dolores Mari; CARL: Arnold Voketaitis; EMMA: Ruth Kobart; OLGA: Muriel Greenspon; SHIRLEY: Florence Anglin; HENRY: Andrew Frierson; WILLIE: Robert Buckley; ANNA: Elisabeth Carron; SAM: William DuPree; DANIEL: L.D. Clements; FRANK: Robert Trehy; GEORGE: Richard Wentworth; STEVE: Richard Armbruster; LIPPO: Jack Harrold; JENNIE: Barbara Maier; 2ND GRADUATE: Anthea DeForest; 3RD GRADUATE: Marilyne Mason; MRS. HILDEBRAND: Anita Lynch; CHARLIE: Charles Cash; MARY: Neva Small; GRACE: Andrea Frierson; ROSE: Joy Clements; HARRY: John Reardon; MAE: Sondra Lee; DICK: Richard Tone; VINCENT: Albert Lewis; DR. WILSON: Glenn Dowlen; MURPHY: David Smith; CITY MARSHAL: Arthur Graham; FRED: Don Yule; 1ST NURSEMAID: Helen Guile; 2ND NURSEMAID: Lou Ann Wyckoff.

NEW YORK STATE THEATRE OF LINCOLN CENTER, 2/24/66–3/19/66. 6 PERFORMANCES IN REPERTORY. PRESENTED BY the New York City Opera; DIRECTOR: Herbert Machiz; CHOREOGRAPHER: Richard Tone; SETS/COSTUMES: Paul Sylbert; CONDUCTOR: Charles Wilson. *Cast:* ABRAHAM: Nico Castel; GRETA: Dolores Mari; CARL: George S. Irving; EMMA: Ruth Kobart; OLGA: Muriel Greenspon; SHIRLEY: Florence Anglin; MRS. DAVIS: Alyce Elizabeth Webb [role added during the run]; HENRY: Edward Pierson, *Robert Mosley*; WILLIE: Bruce Papa; ANNA: Eileen Schauler, *Elisabeth Carron*; SAM: William DuPree, *William Lewis*; DANIEL: L.D. Clements; FRANK: William Chapman; GEORGE: Jack Bittner; STEVE: Richard Armbruster; LIPPO: Jack De Lon; JENNIE: Betsy Hepburn; 2ND GRADUATE: Janet Morris; 3RD GRADUATE: Lila Herbert; MRS. HILDEBRAND: Beverly Evans, *Kay Creed*; CHARLIE: Tom Brooke;

MARY: Jeanne Tanzy; GRACE: Donna Babbs; ROSE: Anne Elgar, *Catherine Christensen*; HARRY: Seth Riggs; MAE: Sondra Lee; DICK: Alan Peterson; VINCENT: Barney Martin; DR. WILSON: Don Carlo; MURPHY: David Smith; CITY MARSHAL: Don Yule; FRED: Paul Corder; 1ST NURSEMAID: Charlotte Povia, *Joan August*; 2ND NURSEMAID: Marie Wyckoff, *Jodell Kenting*; JOAN: Leslie Morris [role added during the run]; SALVATION ARMY GIRLS: Harriet Greene & Anne Pretzat [roles added during the run]; VIOLIN GIRL: Wendy Morris [role added during the run]; MYRTLE: Debbie Thomas [role added during the run].

NEW YORK STATE THEATRE, 10/28/78–11/12/78. 4 PERFORMANCES IN REPERTORY. Return engagement 10/13/79–11/10/79. 5 PERFORMANCES IN REPERTORY. PRESENTED BY the New York City Opera; DIRECTOR: Jack O'Brien; CHOREOGRAPHER: Patricia Birch; SETS: Paul Sylbert; COSTUMES: Nancy Potts; LIGHTING: Gilbert V. Hemsley Jr.; CONDUCTOR: John Mauceri. *Cast:* GRETA: Martha Thigpen; EMMA: Diane Curry; ABRAHAM: Nico Castel, *Leo Postrel* (for the return engagement); ANNA: Eileen Schauler; SAM: Alan Kays; MRS. BUCHANAN: Lila Herbert; FRANK: William Chapman; LIPPO: Jonathan Green; ROSE: Catherine Malfitano; HARRY: Alan Titus, *Harlan Foss* (for the return engagement).

EQUITY LIBRARY THEATRE, NYC, 1//82–1/31/82. 32 PERFORMANCES. DIRECTOR: Robert Brink. *Cast:* GRETA: Mimi Sherwin; ANNA: Jane Seaman; FRANK: Casper Roos; ROSE: Sue Anne Gershenson; MAE: Katherine Meloche.

NEW YORK STATE THEATRE, 9/7/90–9/29/90. 6 PERFORMANCES IN REPERTORY. A New York City Opera production, PRESENTED BY Jack O'Brien; DIRECTOR: Jay Lesenger; CHOREOGRAPHER: Patricia Birch; SETS: Paul Sylbert; COSTUMES: Lindsay W. Davis; LIGHTING: Gilbert V. Hemsley Jr.; CONDUCTOR: Chris Nance. *Cast:* EMMA: Joyce Castle; OLGA: Susanne Marsee; CARL: Robert Ferrier; ABRAHAM: David Rae Smith; ANNA: Margaret Cusack; SAM: Kevin P. Anderson; MRS. BUCHANAN: Lila Herbert; FRANK: William Parcher; GEORGE: William Ledbetter; LIPPO: Jonathan Green; ROSE: Sheryl Woods; HARRY: Harlan Foss; DICK: John MacInnis; MURPHY: David Frye.

665. *The Student Gypsy*

Also called *The Prince of Liederkranz.* Set in the late 19th century, in the kingdom of Singspielia. A parody of musicals such as *The Student Prince* and *Naughty Marietta.* Years ago Zampa, the gypsy queen, stole the heir of Liederkranz, and put her son in his place. There is now a war between Singspielia and Liederkranz.

Before Broadway. Edward Padula was the original producer, but he couldn't raise the money, so one of his investors, insurance man Sandy Farber, took over, with Rick Besoyan as co-producer (he is not credited). There was not enough money for an out-of-town tryout, so the show went straight into Broadway previews for 2 weeks.

The Broadway Run. FIFTY-FOURTH STREET THEATRE, 9/30/63–10/12/63. 16 PERFORMANCES. PRESENTED BY Sandy Farber; MUSIC/LYRICS/BOOK/DIRECTOR: Rick Besoyan; CHOREOGRAPHER: Ray Harrison; SETS/COSTUMES: Raoul Pene du Bois; LIGHTING: Paul Morrison; MUSICAL DIRECTOR: Shepard Coleman; ORCHESTRATIONS/MUSICAL ARRANGEMENTS: Arnold Goland; PRESS: Robert Larkin; GENERAL MANAGER/COMPANY MANAGER: David Lawlor; PRODUCTION STAGE MANAGER: Duane Camp; STAGE MANAGER: Tony Manzi; ASSISTANT STAGE MANAGER: Richard Marshall. *Cast:* "PAPA" JOHANN SEBASTIAN GLOCKENSPIEL, PROPRIETOR OF THE *Round Robin* TAVERN: Allen Swift; HIS THREE ADOPTED DAUGHTERS: GINGER GLOCKENSPIEL: Mitzie Welch; EDELWEISS GLOCKENSPIEL: Joleen Fodor; MERRY MAY GLOCKENSPIEL: Eileen Brennan; RUDOLPH VON SCHLUMP, A GRENADIER: Don Stewart; MUFFIN D. RAGAMUFFIN, D.D. (RET), A VAGABOND: Dom De Luise; GRYPHON ALLESCU, THE GYPSY PRINCE: Bill Fletcher; ZAMPA ALLESCU, THE GYPSY QUEEN: Shannon Bolin; COL. HELMUT BLUNDERBUSS, ANOTHER GRENADIER: Dick Hoh; PFC WOLFGANG HUMPERDINCK, ANOTHER GRENADIER: Edward Miller; OSGOOD THE GOOD, KING OF LIEDERKRANZ: Donald Babcock; ELSIE UMLAUT, HIS WARD: Linda Segal; THE GLOCKENSPIEL GIRLS: BRUNHILDE: Rosemary McNamara; PUPPCHEN: Mary Jay; DRESDEN: Jean Palmerton; ERMINTROUT: Maria Graziano; SHOENHEIT: Jacque Dean; ROSALINDE: Ann Collins; ZUCKER:

Jean Middlebrooks; SCHMETTERLING: Katherine Sutter; PAMPELMUSE: Jamie Simmons; PRIVATES IN THE ROYAL GRENADIERS: OFFENBACH: Ralph Vucci; ROMBERG: Doug Robinson; KORNGOLD: Robert Edsel; STRAUSS II: Marc Destin; VON WEBER: Richard Marshall; MOZART: William Wheless; LEHAR: Nino Galanti; VON FLOTOW: Tony Marlowe; SULLIVAN: Arnold Whyler. **Standby**: Papa/Blunderbuss/Osgood: Walter Kattwinkel. **Understudy**: Merry May: Joleen Fodor. **Swing Couple**: Anne Nunnally & Edward Royce. *Act I:* *Scene 1* The border of Singspielia; a summer afternoon; *Scene 2* In front of the *Round Robin* tavern; *Scene 3* A forest path; *Scene 4* In front of Muffin's wagon; *Scene 5* In front of the tavern; *Scene 6* Inside the tavern; *Scene 7* Muffin's wagon; *Scene 8* In front of the tavern. *Act II:* *Scene 1* The grenadiers' campsite; *Scene 2* The wine cellar; *Scene 3* The path; *Scene 4* Muffin's wagon; *Scene 5* In front of the tavern; *Scene 6* The border of Singspielia. *Act I:* "Welcome Home (Anthem)" (Glockenspiel Girls), "Singspielia" (Glockenspiel Girls), "Romance" (Merry May & Glockenspiel Girls), "Somewhere" (Rudolph), "It's a Wonderful Day to Do Nothing" (Muffin), "The Gypsy Life" (Zampa, Muffin, Merry May), "The Grenadiers' Marching Song" (Blunderbuss & Grenadiers), "Welcome Home (Anthem)" (reprise) (Glockenspiel Girls), "Greetings" (Grenadiers), "Kiss Me" (Glockenspiel Girls & Grenadiers), "Ting-a-Ling Dearie" (Ginger & Blunderbuss), "Merry May" (Muffin & Merry May), "Seventh Heaven Waltz" (Merry May & Rudolph), "A Gypsy Dance" (Zampa, Muffin, Gryphon), "Walk-on" (Zampa), Finale Act I: "You're a Man" (Ensemble). *Act II:* "A Whistle Works" (Humperdinck), "Gypsy of Love" (Rudolph), "Our Love Has Flown Away" (Merry May), "A Woman is a Woman is a Woman" (Blunderbuss, Rudolph, Muffin), "Romance" (reprise) (Glockenspiel Girls), "Very Much in Love" (Ginger & Glockenspiel Girls), "My Love is Yours" (Rudolph & Merry May), "There's Life in the Old Folks Yet" ("Papa" Johann, Zampa, Osgood), "The Drinking Song" (Merry May, Muffin, Ginger, Blunderbuss), Finale Act II: (Entire Company).

It got bad reviews. The show received a Tony nomination for costumes.

666. *The Student Prince*

An operetta set in the 1830s (in the 1976 Off Broadway revival it was set in the spring of 1860), it tells how a prince, studying at Heidelberg University, falls for Kathie, a charming waitress. The romance is cut short when the old king dies and the prince returns to take up his new role and to marry Princess Margaret.

Before Broadway. There were several productions of the straight play *Old Heidelberg* done from 1902 onwards. The early productions of the musical were called *The Student Prince of Heidelberg.* As such it opened at JOLSON'S 59TH STREET THEATRE, 12/2/24; moved to the AMBASSADOR THEATRE, 12/14/25; moved to the CENTURY THEATRE, 2/1/26–3/29/26; moved back to JOLSON'S 59TH STREET THEATRE, 4/5/26, and closed there on 5/26/26. Total of 608 PERFORMANCES. PRESENTED BY Messrs Shubert; DIRECTOR: J.C. Huffman; CHOREOGRAPHER: Max Scheck; SETS: Watson Barratt. It had a company of 150. *Cast:* PRINCE: Howard Marsh; GRETCHEN: Violet Carlson; KATHIE: Ilse Marvenga. Then it toured continuously for 25 years.

THE MOVIE. 1927. DIRECTOR: Ernst Lubitsch. *Cast:* Ramon Navarro, Norma Shearer.

It ran again at the MAJESTIC THEATRE, 1/29/31–3/7/31. 42 PERFORMANCES. DIRECTOR: Edward Scanlon; MUSICAL DIRECTOR: Pierre de Reeder. *Cast:* KARL FRANZ: Edward Nell Jr.; KATHIE: Eliz Gergely.

The Broadway Run. BROADWAY THEATRE, 6/8/43–10/2/43. 153 PERFORMANCES. PRESENTED BY The Messrs Shubert; MUSIC: Sigmund Romberg; LYRICS/BOOK: Dorothy Donnelly; BASED ON *Old Heidelberg,* Richard Mansfield's adaptation of *Alt Heidelberg,* by Wilhelm Meyer-Foerster; DIRECTOR: J.J. Shubert; CHOREOGRAPHERS: Ruthanna Boris & Alexis Dolinoff (by permission of the Metropolitan Opera Association); SETS: Watson Barratt; COSTUMES: Stage Costumes, Inc.; MUSICAL DIRECTOR: Pierre de Reeder & Fred Hoff; PRESS: C.P. Greneker; COMPANY MANAGER: Edward J. Scanlon; STAGE MANAGER: Walter Johnson.

Cast: 1ST LACKEY: Howard Roland [Colin Harvey during tryouts]; 2ND LACKEY: Dennis Dengate [Larry O'Dell during tryouts]; 3RD LACKEY: Fred Lane [Jonathan Reed during tryouts]; 4TH LACKEY: Ken Harlan [John McCarthy during tryouts]; PRIME MINISTER VON MARK: William Pringle; DR. ENGEL (THE PRINCE'S TUTOR): Everett Marshall (1) ✫; PRINCE KARL FRANZ: Frank Hornaday (3); RUDER (LANDLORD OF *Inn of Three Golden Apples*): Walter Johnson; GRETCHEN (MAID AT THE INN): Ann Pennington (6); TONI (A WAITER): Nathaniel Sack; DETLEF (A STUDENT LEADER): Roy Barnes; VON ASTERBERG (ANOTHER STUDENT LEADER): Lyndon Crews; LUCAS (ANOTHER STUDENT LEADER): Daniel De Paolo; KATHIE (NIECE OF RUDER): Barbara Scully (2); LUTZ (VALET TO THE PRINCE): Detmar Poppen (4); HUBERT (THE VALET'S VALET): Jesse M. Cimberg; GRAND DUCHESS ANASTASIA: Nina Varela; PRINCESS MARGARET (THE PRINCE'S FIANCEE): Helene Arthur (5); CAPTAIN TARNITZ: Charles Chesney [Ray Jacquemont during tryouts]; COUNTESS LEYDON (LADY-IN-WAITING TO THE PRINCESS): Helene Le Berthon; RUDOLPH (COUSIN OF KATHIE): Herman Magidson; POSTILLION: Jimmy Russell [during tryouts this character was the Captain of the Guard, played by Jack Richards]; LADIES OF THE ENSEMBLE: Judy Turnbull, Phyllis Manning, Gloria Hope, Marilyn Merkt, Harriet Williams, Elaine Haslett, Page Morton, Shirley Gordon, Carol Hunter, Jacqueline Max, Helene Le Berthon, Gale Sterling (dropped during tryouts), Marvel Conheeny (dropped during tryouts); GENTLEMEN OF THE ENSEMBLE: Colin Harvey, Eden Burrows, Ernst Nibbe, George Tallone, Kent Williams, Elliott Robertson, Gurney Bowman, Jimmy Russell, Herman Magidson, Howard Roland, Don Powell, Fred Lane, Dennis Dengate, Ken Harlan, Robert LaMarr, George Lombroso, Anthony Coffaro, Dale Spangler, Fred Catania, Andrew Thurston, Stanton Barrett. During tryouts this was the male ensemble: Lewis Pierce, Fred Catania, Jack Richards, Eugene Gadol, Roland Power, Colin Harvey, Stanton Barrett, Paul Campbell, Steve Wilson, Dale Spangler, Andrew Thurston, George T. Miller, Jonathan Reed, Warren Dunning, Robert Lauren, John McCarthy, James Growner, Merrill Moorman, Stanley Turner, Eden Burrows, Herman Magidson, Larry O'Dell, Charles M. Perry. *Prologue*: "By Our Bearing So Sedate" (Lackeys), "Golden Days" (Prince & Engel). *Act I*: *Scene 1* Ante-chamber in the Palace at Karlsburg; *Scene 2* Garden of the *Inn of Three Golden Apples*, at the University of Heidelberg: "To the Inn We're Marching" (Detlef, Von Asterberg, Lucas, Kathie, Students), "Drink, Drink, Drink" ("The Drinking Song") (Detlef, Von Asterberg, Lucas, Students) [a big hit], "You're in Heidelberg" (Prince & Engel), "Welcome to Prince" (Kathie, Ruder, Gretchen, Girls), Duet: "Deep in My Heart (Dear)" (Prince & Kathie), "Serenade" ("Overhead the Moon is Beaming") (Prince, Engel, Detlef, Von Asterberg, Lucas, Students) [the big hit], Finale Act I (Come Sir, Will You Join Our Noble Saxon Corps) (Prince, Kathie, Detlef, Von Asterberg, Lucas, Ruder, Lutz, Engel, Gretchen, Hubert, Students, Girls). *Act II*: Sitting-room of Prince Karl Franz at the Inn; three months later: "I've Never Heard About Love" (Engel & Students) [new to this production; "Farmer Jacob" was here in the original 1924 production], "Student Life" (Prince, Kathie, Engel, Detlef, Gretchen, Von Asterberg, Lucas, Students), "Golden Days" (reprise) (Engel) [this replaced "Farewell, Dear" which was here in the 1924 production], Duet: "Deep in My Heart" (reprise) (Prince & Kathie), Finale Act II (Prince, Kathie, Von Mark, Engel). *Act III*: A room of state in the Royal Palace at Karlsburg; two years later: "Waltz Ensemble" (ch: Miss Boris & Mr. Dolinoff) (Ambassadors, Officers, Countess, Baron Arnheim, Ladies of Court), "Just We Two" (Princess, Tarnitz, Officers), "Gavotte" (Prince, Princess, Countess, Tarnitz), "What Memories" (Prince), Finale Act III (Prince, Kathie, Von Mark, Engel). *Act IV*: Garden of the *Inn of Three Apples*; the next day: Opening: "Sing a Little Song" (Students & Girls): "To the Inn We're Marching" (Detlef, Von Asterberg, Students): (a) "Serenade" (reprise) (Detlef, Von Asterberg, Students, King); (b) "Let's All Be Gay, Boys" (Detlef, Von Asterberg, Students), Finale: "Deep in My Heart (Dear)" (reprise) (King, Princess, Kathie, Rudolph, Gretchen, Hubert, Lutz, Duchess, Detlef, Von Asterberg, Entire Ensemble).

The show had a top ticket price of $2.75. It good good Broadway reviews, as much out of sentiment for a grand old operetta as anything else.

After Broadway. TOURING REVIVAL. Opened on 12/25/51, at the Boston Opera House, and closed on 4/5/52, at the Auditorium, Rochester,

NY. PRESENTED BY The Messrs Shubert. *Cast:* Glenn Burris, Grace Aurelia.

THE MOVIE RE-MAKE. 1954. *Cast:* KARL: Edmund Purdom (singing dubbed by Mario Lanza); KATHIE: Ann Blyth.

A production aiming at Broadway opened as a pre–Broadway tour on 6/5/73, at the Academy of Music, Philadelphia. The Lehman Engel production, PRESENTED BY Moe Septee, in association with Jack L. Wolgin & Victor H. Potamkin. It was in 2 acts, with a prologue. DIRECTOR: George Schaefer; CHOREOGRAPHER: David Nillo; SETS/LIGHTING: Clarke Dunham; COSTUMES: Winn Morton & Sara Brook; MUSICAL DIRECTOR: John Lesko (although at the premiere Lehman Engel conducted). *Cast:* PRINCE: Harry Danner & Jon Garrison; ENGEL: Richard Torigi; TONI: Warren Galjour; LUTZ: George Rose, *Ray Walston*; TARNITZ: William Covington, *Robert Rounseville*; LUCAS: Don Estes; COUNT HUGO: Ed Dixon [new role]; ANASTASIA: Fran Stevens; COUNTESS: Mary Roche. It then played the Mechanic Theatre, Baltimore; the Opera House, Washington, DC; the Shubert Theatre, Chicago; The Royal Alexandra Theatre, Toronto; and The Clowes Theatre, Indianapolis, and closed on 10/21/73, at the State Fair, Dallas, without making Broadway.

EASTSIDE PLAYHOUSE (Off Broadway), 5/11/76–8/1/76. 54 PERFORMANCES. PRESENTED BY the Light Opera of Manhattan; CHOREOGRAPHER: Jerry Gotham; LIGHTING: Peggy Clark. *Cast:* PRINCE: Dennis Britten; KATHIE: Georgia McEver; MARGARET: Elizabeth Tanner. It was now set in the spring of 1860. *Act I*: *Prologue* (Lackeys), "Golden Days" (Prince & Engel); *Scene 1* Ante-chamber in the palace at Karlsburg; *Scene 2* Garden of the *Inn of the Three Apples*, at the University of Heidelberg: "To the Inn We're Marching" (Students), "Drinking Song" (Students), "Come Boys" (Kathie & Students), "Heidelberg" (Prince & Engel), "Gaudeamus Igitur" (Students), "Golden Days" (reprise) (Engel), "Deep in My Heart, Dear" (Kathie & Prince), Finale Act I ("Serenade"). *Act II*: *Scene 1* Sitting room of Prince Karl Franz at the inn; four months later: "Student Life" (Students), "Thoughts Will Come to Me" (Prince); *Scene 2* A room of state in the Royal Palace at Karlsburg: Gavotte (Ensemble), "Just We Two" (Prince & Tarnitz), "The Flag that Flies Above Us" (Ensemble), "Just We Two" (reprise) (Ensemble), "What Memories" (Prince); *Scene 3* Garden of the *Inn of the Three Apples*; the next day: "Drinking Song" (reprise) (Students), "Gaudeamus Igitur" (reprise) (Students), "Deep in My Heart, Dear" (reprise) (Prince & Kathie).

LOOM produced it again, 10/18/78–11/26/78. 42 PERFORMANCES. DIRECTOR/MUSICAL DIRECTOR: William Mount-Burke; CHOREOGRAPHER: Jerry Gotham. *Cast:* PRINCE: Dennis Britten; KATHIE: Georgia McEver; ANASTASIA: Jeanne Beauvais; MARGARET: Cheryl Savitt.

PAPER MILL PLAYHOUSE, New Jersey, 1979. DIRECTOR/CHOREOGRAPHER: Robert Johanson. *Cast:* Allan Jones, Harry Danner, Judith McCauley.

NEW YORK STATE THEATRE, 8/29/80–9/7/80. 13 PERFORMANCES. Return engagement 8/27/81–8/30/81. 6 PERFORMANCES. PRESENTED BY the New York City Opera; BOOK ADAPTED BY Hugh Wheeler; DIRECTOR: Jack Hofsis; STAGE DIRECTOR: Christian Smith; CHOREOGRAPHER: Donald Saddler, *Jessica Redel* (re-staged Mr. Saddler's choreography for the return engagement); SETS: David Jenkins; COSTUMES: Patton Campbell; LIGHTING: Gilbert V. Hemsley Jr.; CONDUCTOR: Andrew Meltzer, *Brian Salesky* (for the return engagement). *Cast* (if the players were different for the return engagement they are in *italics*): DR. ENGEL: Dominic Cossa; COUNT VON MARK: David Rae Smith; PRINCE KARL FRANZ: Jacque Trussel, *Henry Price*; LUTZ: James Billings, *Jack Harrold*; GRETCHEN: Martha Thigpen, *Penny Orloff*; RUDER: Dan Sullivan; NICHOLAS: Robert La Fosse, *Taras Kalba*; TONI: Jack Harrold, *James Billings*; HUBERT: Harlan Foss, *William Ledbetter*; DETLEF: John Lankston; VON ASTERBERG: Thomas Jamerson; LUCAS: Ralph Bassett; FRESHMAN: Louis Perry; KATHIE: Leigh Munro, *Elizabeth Hynes*; ANASTASIA: Muriel Costa-Greenspon; PRINCESS MARGARET: Kathryn Bouleyn, *Nadia Pelle*; TARNITZ: Joseph Evans, *William Eichorn*; COUNTESS LEYDON: Jane Shaulis, *Rita Metzger*. It was now set in Set in Karlsberg, Germany, in the Golden Years. *Prologue*: Garden of the palace at Karlsberg: "By Our Bearing So Sedate" (Lackeys), "Golden Days" (von Mark & Prince). *Act I*: Garden of the Inn of the Three Golden Apples, in Heidelberg: "Garlands Bright with Glowing Flowers" (Gretchen, Ruder,

Girls), "To the Inn We're Marching" (Students' Marching Song) (Detlef, Lucas, von Asterberg, Students), "Drink, Drink, Drink" (Drinking Song) (Detlef, Lucas, von Asterberg, Students), "Come Boys, Let's All Be Gay, Boys" (Kathie, Detlef, Lucas, von Asterberg, Students), "Drink, Drink, Drink"/"To the Inn We're Marching" (reprise) (Detlef, Lucas, von Asterberg, Students), "Heidelberg, Beloved Vision of My Heart" (Engel, Prince, Kathie, Ruder, Gretchen, Girls), "Gaudeamus Igitur" (Students), "Golden Days" (reprise) (Engel), "Deep in My Heart, Dear" (Kathie & Prince), "Come Sir, Will You Join Our Noble Saxon Corps" (Students), "Overhead the Moon is Beaming" (Serenade) (Prince & Students), "When the Spring Wakens Everything" (Carnival of Springtime) (Company). **Act II**: Prince Karl Franz's rooms at the inn; four months later: "Farmer Jacob Lay a-Snoring" (Students), "Student Life" (Company), "Golden Days" (reprise) (Prince & Engel), "Thoughts Will Come to Me" (Prince & Engel), Finale (Kathie & Prince). ACT III: **Scene 1** The Royal Palace at Karlsberg: Ballet (Orchestra), "Just We Two" (Margaret, Tarnitz, Men), "What Memories, Sweet Rose" (Company); **Scene 2** Garden of the Inn of the three Golden Apples; the next day: "Let Us Sing a Song" (Students), "If He Knew" (Kathie & Margaret), Finale (Company).

NEW YORK STATE THEATRE, 7/5/85–7/21/85. 9 PERFORMANCES IN REPERTORY. PRESENTED BY the New York City Opera; BOOK ADAPTED BY Hugh Wheeler; DIRECTOR: Jack Hofsis; STAGE DIRECTOR: Christian Smith; CHOREOGRAPHER: Donald Saddler; SETS: David Jenkins; COSTUMES: Patton Campbell; LIGHTING: Gilbert V. Hemsley Jr.; CONDUCTOR: Paul Gemignani. *Cast:* ENGEL: Adib Fazah; VON MARK: David Rae Smith; PRINCE: Jerry Hadley; LUTZ: Jack Harrold; GRETCHEN: Carol Sparrow; RUDER: Joseph McKee; NICHOLAS: Douglas Hamilton; TONI: James Billings; HUBERT: William Ledbetter; DETLEF: Stephen O'Mara; VON ASTERBERG: Robert Brubaker; LUCAS: Wilbur Pauley; FRESHMAN: Louis Perry; KATHIE: Elizabeth Hynes; ANASTASIA: Muriel Costa-Greenspon; MARGARET: Cynthia Rose; TARNITZ: Cris Groenendaal; COUNTESS LEYDON: Jane Shaulis.

NEW YORK STATE THEATRE, 7/11/87–11/8/87. 14 PERFORMANCES IN REPERTORY. PRESENTED BY the New York City Opera; BOOK ADAPTED BY Hugh Wheeler; DIRECTOR: Jack Hofsis; STAGE DIRECTOR: Christian Smith; CHOREOGRAPHER: Jessica Redel; SETS: David Jenkins; COSTUMES: Patton Campbell; LIGHTING: Gilbert V. Hemsley Jr.; CONDUCTOR: Jim Coleman. *Cast:* ENGEL: Brian Steele & Chester Ludgin; VON MARK: David Rae Smith; PRINCE KARL FRANZ: John Stewart & Jon Garrison; LUTZ: James Billings & Jack Harrold; GRETCHEN: Susanne Marsee; RUDER: Joseph McKee; NICHOLAS: Douglas Hamilton; TONI: Jack Harrold & James Billings; HUBERT: William Ledbetter; DETLEF: Stanley Cornett; VON ASTERBERG: Robert Brubaker; LUCAS: Robert Ferrier; FRESHMAN: Louis Perry; KATHIE: Claudette Peterson & Leigh Munro; ANASTASIA: Muriel Costa-Greenspon; PRINCESS MARGARET: Lisbeth Lloyd & Cynthia Rose; TARNITZ: Cris Groenendaal; COUNTESS LEYDON: Rebecca Russell.

NEW YORK STATE THEATRE, 8/17/93–8/28/93. 13 PERFORMANCES. PRESENTED BY the New York City Opera; BOOK ADAPTED BY Hugh Wheeler; DIRECTOR: Christian Smith; CHOREOGRAPHER: Jessica Redel; SETS: David Jenkins; COSTUMES: Patton Campbell; LIGHTING: Gilbert V. Hemsley; CONDUCTOR: Scott Bergeson. *Cast:* ENGEL: Louis Otey; VON MARK: David Rae Smith; PRINCE KARL FRANZ: Michael Rees Davis; LUTZ: James Billings; GRETCHEN: Sandra Ruggles; RUDER: Joseph McKee; NICHOLAS: Gunnar Waldman; TONI: Jonathan Green; HUBERT: William Ledbetter; DETLEF: Gordon Gietz; VON ASTERBERG: Ron Baker; LUCAS: David Langan; FRESHMAN: Steven Raiford; KATHIE: Michele Patzakis; ANASTASIA: Muriel Costa-Greenspon; MARGARET: Michele McBride; TARNITZ: Jeff Matsey; COUNTESS LEYDON: Dulcy Reyes.

PAPER MILL PLAYHOUSE, New Jersey, 4/12/00–5/27/00. This was the ninth time the Paper Mill had produced it, but this time Robert Johanson and Jerome Chodorov revised the script, and Albert Evans revised the lyrics. DIRECTOR/CHOREOGRAPHER: Robert Johanson; SETS: Michael Anania; MUSICAL DIRECTOR: Tom Helm. *Cast:* ENGEL: Jerome Hines; PRINCE KARL FRANZ: Brandon Jovanovich; GRETCHEN: Susan Spiedel; KATHIE: Christiane Noll; OLD JOSEF: Eddie Bracken [a new character]; ANASTASIA: Jane Connell; PRINCESS MARGARET: Glory Crampton.

667. *Subways Are for Sleeping*

Two love affairs in New York. Angie is a staff writer for *Madame* magazine, working on a feature story about the well-dressed bums of Manhattan. Tom is a dropout who helps people find jobs and places to sleep. Angie pretends to be a newcomer to town and in need of some help. When Tom finds out the truth he is angry. Tom and Angie are re-united and he decides to write a book about his life as a drifter, calling it *Subways are for Sleeping*. Martha is a former beauty contestant stranded in her hotel room (dressed in a towel) because she can't pay her bill. Charlie, Tom's friend, comes to her assistance.

Before Broadway. Jule Styne bought the rights to Edmund G. Love's stories which were based on real experiences, but they were essentially plotless and unconnected. Mr. Styne approached Betty Comden & Adolph Green to do the lyrics and libretto, but they only wanted to do the libretto. After Ketti Frings, Arthur Laurents, and Abe Burrows all turned down the offer of doing the libretto, Comden & Green agreed to do it. David Merrick came in as producer at this stage, and he hired Michael Kidd direct and choreograph. Rosalind Russell was mentioned as a possible star, as were Phil Silvers, Ray Bolger, and Comden & Green themselves, but Syd Chaplin was cast, with Carol Lawrence as his leading lady. The supporting comic pair were Phyllis Newman and Orson Bean. It tried out first in Philadelphia, where it was drastically re-written. Several songs were cut before Broadway: "Getting Married," "I Walk a Little Dog," "Life's Not That Simple," "A Man of Vision," "Now I Have Someone," "Hey, Fellas," "(Hey, Charlie) Let's Talk," and "A Man with a Plan." Just before the show came to New York, David Merrick placed 2,800 posters with just the title in all the subway stations and trains. Bums took this as permission to sleep there, and the Transit authorities forced him to take them down.

The Broadway Run. ST. JAMES THEATRE, 12/27/61–6/23/62. 2 previews from 12/25/61. 205 PERFORMANCES. PRESENTED BY David Merrick; MUSIC: Jule Styne; LYRICS/BOOK: Betty Comden & Adolph Green; BASED ON a 1957 collection of 10 stories by Edmund G. Love; DIRECTOR/CHOREOGRAPHER: Michael Kidd; ASSOCIATE CHOREOGRAPHER: Marc Breaux; SETS/LIGHTING: Will Steven Armstrong; COSTUMES: Freddy Wittop; MUSICAL DIRECTOR: Milton Rosenstock; ORCHESTRATIONS: Philip J. Lang; DANCE MUSIC ARRANGEMENTS: Peter Howard; PRESS: Harvey B. Sabinson, David Powers, Lila Glaser; CASTING: Michael Shurtleff & Alan Shayne; GENERAL MANAGER: Jack Schlissel; COMPANY MANAGER: Vince McKnight, *Richard Highley*; PRODUCTION STAGE MANAGER: Howard Whitfield, *Joe Calvan*; STAGE MANAGER: Joe Calvan, *Warren Brown*; ASSISTANT STAGE MANAGER: Lawrence Pool. *Cast:* THE SLEEPERS: Gene Varrone (*Anthony Saverino*), Cy Young, Bob Gorman, John Sharpe; MYRA BLAKE: Grayson Hall; ANGELA MCKAY: Carol Lawrence (2); TOM BAILEY: Sydney Chaplin (1); STATION GUARD: Robert Howard; J. EDWARD SYKES: Joe Hill; BILL: Anthony Saverino; HARRY SHELBY: Eugene R. Wood; GUS HOLT: Cy Young; CHARLIE SMITH: Orson Bean (3); JACK: Gene Varrone, *Anthony Saverino*; A DRUNK: Jim Weiss; MAX HILLMAN: Gene Varrone, *Anthony Saverino*; MARTHA VAIL: Phyllis Newman (4); MR. PITMAN: Gordon Connell; A DELIVERY BOY: Michael Bennett; LANCELOT ZUCKERMAN: Horase; FREDDIE: Bob Gorman; MAC, A CARETAKER: John Sharpe; SOCIAL WORKER: Joe Hill; PHOTOGRAPHER: John Sharpe; THE MODELS: Sari Clymas & Diane Ball; TEENAGERS: John Sharpe & Michael Bennett; ZACK FLINT: Lawrence Pool; LT PILSUDSKI: Robert Howard; MARY TOMPKINS: Dean Taliaferro; JOE, THE MUSEUM GUARD: Anthony Saverino; RELIEF DOORMAN: Robert Howard; MR. BARNEY: Joe Hill; SINGERS: Helen Baisley, Vicki Belmonte, Bob Gorman, Stokely Gray, Joe Hill, Robert Howard, Jeannine Michael, Bruce Payton, Anthony Saverino, Joan Sheller, Ruth Shepard, *Betty Munro*; DANCERS: Diane Ball, Carlos Bas, Michael Bennett, Pepe de Chazza, Sari Clymas, Joel Craig, Robert Evans, Ted Forlow, Valerie Harper, Reby Howells, Gene Kelton, Victoria Mansfield, Wendy Nickerson, Larry Roquemore, Sandra Roveta, Ron Stratton, Dean Taliaferro, Jim Weiss. **Standby**: Tom: Hal Linden. **Understudy**: Max: *Robert Howard*. **Act I**: **Scene 1** A street in New York; present time: "Subways Are for Sleeping" (The Sleepers); **Scene 2** Executive office of *Madame* magazine: "Girls Like Me" (Angie); *Scene 3* Grand Central Station: "Station Rush" (People Who Are Going Places), "I'm Just Taking My Time" (Tom); *Scene 4* A subway platform: "Subway Directions" (Tom, Angie, Subway Riders), "Ride Through the Night" (Tom, Angie, Subway Riders); *Scene 5* A corridor in the Brunswick Arms; *Scene 6* Martha's room: "I Was a Shoo-In" (Martha); *Scene 7* A street: "Who Knows What Might Have Been?" (Angie & Tom); *Scene 8* The Egyptian wing of the Metropolitan Museum: "Swing Your Projects" (Tom); *Scene 9* A telephone booth: "Strange Duet" (Martha & Charlie); *Scene 10* A street near Madison Square Park: "I Said it and I'm Glad" (Angie) [dropped during the run]; *Scene 11* Times Square: "Be a Santa" (Tom, Angie, Shoppers, Santas); *Scene 12* Rockefeller Plaza. *Act II*: *Scene 1* The subway: "Subway Incident" (Angie & Teenagers); *Scene 2* A street: "How Can You Describe a Face?" (Tom) [dropped during the run]; *Scene 3* Martha's room: "I Just Can't Wait" (Charlie); *Scene 4* The French wing of the metropolitan Museum: "Comes Once in a Lifetime" (Angie & Tom); *Scene 5* A street; *Scene 6* A parking lot: "What is This Feeling in the Air?" (Tom, Angie, Charlie, Entire Company).

This was the show for which David Merrick, after seeing the disappointing Broadway reviews, invented his own by gathering seven men with the same names as the famous critics and getting them to agree to his rave quotes, which were published in the *Herald Tribune* on 1/4/62. Within a few weeks of opening night two songs were dropped (they can still be heard on the cast recording, however). Carol Lawrence and Syd Chaplin made little effort on stage to conceal their animosity for each other. The show returned 85 per cent of its investment thanks to David Merrick's stunts, and to theatre parties, and to the fact that Broadway economics were different then. Phyllis Newman won a Tony, and Orson Bean was nominated, as was the choreographer.

668. *Sugar*

Set in 1931 in Chicago and Miami, and in between. Two musicians, Jerry and Joe, witness the St. Valentine's Day Massacre in Chicago and flee from Spats' mob disguised as members of an all-girl band, Sweet Sue and Her Society Syncopaters. The band winds up in Miami, where there are complications when the lads are mistaken for girls. Osgood is the Miami millionaire who falls for Daphne (Jerry in drag). Joe (Josie) has his eye on Sugar.

Before Broadway. Robert Fryer, Lawrence Carr and Joseph P. Harris were the first group to option the rights to the original German screenplay *Fanfaren der Liebe*, but they also really needed the rights to the Billy Wilder movie *Some Like it Hot*, which they couldn't get (MGM wouldn't allow them to use the title, either), and so they dropped the project. David Merrick was the next to try, and he came across the same stumbling block. In the meantime he got Mike Stewart to fashion a libretto out of the German movie, and it was called *Fanfare*, then *Nobody's Perfect*, and finally *One of the Girls*. It was about two GIs returning from World War II, and joining Dixie Trotter's All-Girl Orchestra in order to escape from black market mafioso Antonio "Gumdrops" De Luca. However, the *Some Like it Hot* rights became available, and David Merrick decided to start again, with that familiar movie story. Mike Stewart and Jerry Herman (who had started to write a score) felt that the show would be unfavorably compared to the movie, which was generally regarded as a perfect film. They wanted to stick with the 1945 era, swing-music, and all that jazz. But Mr. Merrick was insistent that they go with 1931 and the St. Valentine's Day Massacre, as in the movie. So Merrick brought in Jule Styne and Bob Merrill to write music and lyrics respectively. They wrote 75 songs for the show (only some of which were used, of course). Among those cut were "Nice Ways," "The People in My Life," and "All You Gotta Do is Tell Me." George Axelrod replaced Mike Stewart as librettist. However, Mr. Axelrod was replaced by Peter Stone just before rehearsals began (and Neil Simon would, reportedly, contribute material that was seen at the show's opening). None of Jerry Herman's songs made it in to the eventual show, although "Hundreds of Girls" and "Big Time" later made into *Mack and Mabel*. By 8/71 the show was known as *All for Sugar*, then, still later, as *Doing it for Sugar*. Ann-Margret was the first choice as leading lady, but other commitments prohib-

ited her from taking it on. Relations between several of the key crew members were tense. The show tried out in Washington (where Johnny Desmond was replaced by Steve Condos as Spats, and set designer Jo Mielziner and his sets were replaced by Robin Wagner and his sets), Toronto, Philadelphia (where it opened on 2/22/72, now finally known as *Sugar*) and Boston. Business was good in all of these towns, despite bad reviews. Choreographer Gower Champion allowed Steve Condos to choreograph the gangster tap sequences (Mr. Condos, playing Spats, was a tap dancer), and Donald Saddler to choreograph two other numbers. Sugar's three numbers were cut and then put back in. A rumor went around that Jerry Herman was called back to doctor the Jule Styne score. The Broadway opening date was postponed from 2/29/72 to 3/14/72, and then again to 4/9/72.

The Broadway Run. MAJESTIC THEATRE, 4/9/72–6/23/73. 14 previews from 3/29/72. 505 PERFORMANCES. PRESENTED BY David Merrick; MUSIC: Jule Styne; LYRICS: Bob Merrill; BOOK: Peter Stone; BASED ON the 1959 movie *Some Like it Hot* (starring Marilyn Monroe, Tony Curtis and Jack Lemmon), written by Billy Wilder & I.A.L. Diamond, which in turn was based on the 1935 German movie *Fanfaren der Liebe*, written by Robert Thoeren; DIRECTOR/CHOREOGRAPHER: Gower Champion; ADDITIONAL CHOREOGRAPHY: Donald Saddler & Steve Condos; SETS: Robin Wagner; COSTUMES: Alvin Colt; LIGHTING: Martin Aronstein; SOUND: Otts Munderloh; MUSICAL DIRECTOR/VOCAL ARRANGEMENTS: Elliot Lawrence; ORCHESTRATIONS: Philip J. Lang; DANCE MUSIC ARRANGEMENTS: John Berkman (with Jule Styne); CAST RECORDING on United Artists; PRESS: Harvey B. Sabinson, Sandra Manley, Edie Kean; CASTING: Geri Windsor; GENERAL MANAGER: Jack Schlissel; COMPANY MANAGER: Vince McKnight; PRODUCTION STAGE MANAGER: Charles Blackwell; STAGE MANAGER: Henry Velez; ASSISTANT STAGE MANAGER: Bob St. Clair, *Robert L. Hultman* (added by 72–73). **Cast:** SWEET SUE: Sheila Smith (5); SOCIETY SYNCOPATERS: PIANO: Harriett Conrad; DRUMS: Linda Gandell, *Pam Blair*, BASS: Nicole Barth, *Karen Kristin*; TRUMPETS: Leslie Latham (*Lauren Draper*) & Marylou Sirinek (*Lana Sloniger*); TROMBONES: Terry Cullen & Kathleen Witmer; SAXOPHONES: Pam Blair, Eileen Casey (*Lynne Gannaway*), Debra Lyman, Sally Neal (*Marianne Selbert*), Mary Zahn; BIENSTOCK: Alan Kass (7); JOE: Tony Roberts (2) ☆; JERRY: Robert Morse (1) ☆; UNION CONTRACTOR: Gene Cooper; SPATS PALAZZO: Steve Condos (6); DUDE: Gerard Brentte; SPATS' GANG: Andy Bew, Roger Bigelow, Gene Cooper, Arthur Faria, Gene GeBauer, John Mineo (*Richard Maxon*), Don Percassi; KNUCKLES NORTON: Dick Bonelle, *Dale Muchmore*; 1ST POKER PLAYER: Igors Gavon; KNUCKLES' GANG: Ken Ayers (*George Blackwell*), Richard Maxon, Dale Muchmore, Alexander Orfaly (*Robert L. Hultman*); SUGAR KANE: Elaine Joyce (4); CAB DRIVER: Ken Ayers, *Don Percassi*; OLGA: Eileen Casey, *Lana Sloniger*; DOLORES: Mary Zahn; ROSELLA: Pam Blair; MARYLOU: Debra Lyman; SUNBATHERS: Nicole Barth, Pam Blair, Eileen Casey, Robin Hoctor, Debra Lyman, Peggy Lyman, Sally Neal, Pamela Sousa; TRAIN CONDUCTOR: George Blackwell; BELLBOY: Andy Bew; OSGOOD FIELDING JR.: Cyril Ritchard (3) ☆; "CHICAGO" SINGERS: Ken Ayers, George Blackwell, Dick Bonelle, Igors Gavon, Hal Norman. *Robert L. Hultman*. **Standby**: Jerry: Scott Jarvis. **Understudies**: Joe: Igors Gavon; Fielding/Bienstock: George Blackwell; Sugar: Pam Blair; Sweet Sue: Harriett Conrad; Spats: Gerard Brentte. **Swing Dancers**: Sandra Brewer & Denny Martin Flinn. *Act I*: *Scene 1* Chicago theatre; *Scene 2* Backstage Chicago theatre; *Scene 3* Chicago street; *Scene 4* Clark Street garage; *Scene 5* Dearborn Street Railroad Station; *Scene 6* The Dixie Flyer; *Scene 7* The Seminole-Ritz Hotel veranda; *Scene 8* Josephine & Daphne's hotel room. *Act II*: *Scene 1* The beach; *Scene 2* The hotel veranda; *Scene 3* The New Caledonia yacht; *Scene 4* Josephine & Daphne's hotel room; *Scene 5* The hotel night club; *Scene 6* The hotel service corridor; *Scene 7* The New Caledonia yacht. *Act I*: Overture (Orchestra), "Windy City Marmalade" (Sweet Sue & All-Girl Band), "Penniless Bums" (Jerry, Joe, Unemployed Musicians), "Tear the Town Apart" (dance) (Spats & Gang), "The Beauty that Drives Men Mad" (Jerry & Joe), "We Could Be Close" (Jerry & Sugar), "Sun on My Face" (Jerry, Joe, Sugar, Sweet Sue, Bienstock, Ensemble), "November Song" (Osgood & Millionaires), "(Doing it for) Sugar" (Jerry & Joe). *Act II*: Entr'acte (Orchestra); "Hey, Why Not!" (ch: Donald Saddler) (Sugar & Ensemble), "Beautiful Through and Through" (ch: Donald Saddler) (Osgood & Jerry), "What Do You Give to a Man Who's Had Everything?" (Joe & Sugar), "Magic Nights" (Jerry), "It's Always Love" (Joe), "When You Meet a Man in Chicago" (Jerry, Joe, Sugar, Sweet Sue, All-Girl Band, Chorus Line).

It got pretty bad Broadway reviews, but Bobby Morse received raves. It won a Tony for direction of a musical, and received nominations for musical, choreography, and for Robert Morse.

After Broadway. TOUR. Opened on 9/3/74, at the Dorothy Chandler Pavilion, Los Angeles. Cyril Ritchard had been set to star as Fielding, but on 8/25/74, during a preview performance in L.A., he collapsed with a heart attack and had to be hospitalized. *Cast*: JERRY: Robert Morse; JOE: Larry Kert; FIELDING: Gale Gordon; SUGAR: Leland Palmer. The number "See You Around" (Sugar) was added for this tour [it was now the fourth song in Act I, between "The Beauty that Drives Men Mad" and "We Could Be Close"]. "Sun on My Face" was replaced with "Nice Ways" (Sugar), and "What Do You Give to a Man Who's Had Everything?" was replaced with "Don't Be Afraid" (Joe & Sugar). "It's Always Love" was replaced by two songs—"I'm Engaged" (Jerry) and "People in My Life" (Joe).

PRINCE EDWARD THEATRE, London, 1992. This revival was now called *Some Like it Hot*. Bob Merrill did not like this production. It got bad reviews, and ran 3 months. CAST RECORDING on First Night Records. *Cast*: JOE: Tommy Steele; JERRY: Billy Boyle; ALSO WITH: Mandy Perryment, Royce Mills. Overture: "Some Like it Hot," "Maple Leaf Rag," "Penniless Bums," "Meet a Man in Chicago," "The Beauty that Drives Men Mad," "With the Sun on My Face," "Dirty Old Men," "Doing it for Sugar," "Dirty Old Men (reprise), "What Do You Give to a Man Who's Had Everything?," "I'm Naive," "Beautiful Through and Through," "Magic Nights," "It's Always Love," Finale: "Some Like it Hot" (reprise).

A revised version, also called *Some Like it Hot*, with a new book by Peter Stone, was PRESENTED BY Diane Masters & Jeffrey Spolan. The songs all came from the 75 that were written originally by Jule Styne & Bob Merrill for *Sugar*. The producers had acquired the rights to use the title for the life of their staging. It began rehearsals in Manhattan the week of 5/6/02, and then went on a 50-city tour on 6/4/02, opening in the Hobby Center, Houston (it opened the Theatre Under the Stars 2002 season there). The press date was 6/8/02. Broadway was the ultimate aim. DIRECTOR/CHOREOGRAPHER: Dan Siretta; SETS: James Leonard Joy; COSTUMES: Suzy Benzinger; LIGHTING: Ken Billington; MUSICAL DIRECTOR: Lynn Crigler. *Cast*: JOE: Timothy Gulan; JERRY: Arthur Hanket; OSGOOD FIELDING III: Tony Curtis (his Broadway debut, aged 77); SUGAR: Jodi Carmeli; SWEET SUE: Lenora Nemetz; BIENSTOCK: Gerry Vichi, *Larry Storch*; SPATS: William Ryall; SPATS' THUGS: Scott Burrell, Bobby Clark, Timothy Joe Falter, Mark Adams; SOCIETY SYNCOPATERS: Sarah Anderson, Jacqueline Bayne, Ashlee Fife, Brenda Hamilton, Pamela Jordan, Elise Molinelli, Heather Parcells, Elizabeth Polito, Marisa Rozek, Karen Sieber; TOOTHPICK CHARLIE: David Monzione; TOOTHPICK'S GANG: Derek Isetti & Ryan Migge; MECHANIC: Gair Morris. *Swings*: Todd Bradley Smith & Shannon Hudson. "Some Like it Hot," "Penniless Bums," "Doin' it for Sugar," "When You Meet a Man in Chicago," "November Song," "Shell Oil"/"Hey, Why Not!," "The Beauty that Drives Men Mad," "Sun on My Face," "It's Always Love," "We Could Be Close," "Magic Nights," "Runnin' Wild," "We Play in the Band," "Tear the Town Apart," "I Fall in Love Too Easily" (Osgood) [from the film *Anchors Aweigh*], "People in My Life" (Sugar).

669. *Sugar Babies*

A "burlesque musical," inspired by the burlesque shows of 1905–1930. Nearly all the Columbia Wheel Burlesque shows had quartets to support the principal comedian in his specialty turn.

Before Broadway. Ralph G. Allen, professor of theatre at the University of Tennessee and artistic director of the Clarence Brown Theatre in Knoxville, had collected about 5,000 burlesque sketches, and he wrote a scholarly paper on the subject which he delivered to a conference of theatre historians at Lincoln Center, NY, in 11/77. In the audience was Harry Rigby, the producer of nostalgic musicals. He and Mr. Allen decided to put on the show. Six unpublished Jimmy McHugh songs

went into the show with new lyrics by Arthur Malvin, who, himself, wrote four new songs for the show. The production went on a pre–Broadway tour that opened on 5/8/79, at the Curran Theatre, San Francisco.

The Broadway Run. MARK HELLINGER THEATRE, 10/8/79–8/28/82. 8 previews. 1,208 PERFORMANCES. PRESENTED BY Terry Allen Kramer & Harry Rigby, in association with Columbia Pictures; MUSIC/LYRICS: various writers; SKETCHES: Ralph G. Allen (based on traditional burlesque material); CONCEIVED BY: Ralph G. Allen & Harry Rigby; DIRECTOR/CHOREOGRAPHER/PRODUCTION SUPERVISOR: Ernest O. Flatt; SKETCH DIRECTOR: Rudy Tronto; SETS/COSTUMES: Raoul Pene du Bois; LIGHTING: Gilbert V. Hemsley Jr.; SOUND: Herbert Syers; MUSICAL DIRECTOR: Glen Roven, *Larry Blank*; ORCHESTRATIONS: Dick Hyman; ASSOCIATE ORCHESTRATORS: Dick Lieb, Stan Freeman, Arnold Gross, Joseph Lippman, Sy Johnson; DANCE MUSIC ARRANGEMENTS: Arnold Gross; VOCAL ARRANGEMENTS: Arthur Malvin; ADDITIONAL VOCAL ARRANGEMENTS: Hugh Martin & Ralph Blane; PRESS: Henry Luhrman Associates; CASTING: Elizabeth R. Woodman; GENERAL MANAGERS: Jack Schlissel & Jay Kingwill; COMPANY MANAGER: Alan Wasser; PRODUCTION STAGE MANAGER: Thomas Kelly, *Kay Vance* (by 80–81); STAGE MANAGER: Bob Burland; ASSISTANT STAGE MANAGERS: Jay B. Jacobson & David Campbell. *Cast*: MICKEY: Mickey Rooney (1) ☆, *Joey Bishop* (during Mr. Rooney's vacation, 2/2/81–3/2/81. He played Joey), *Rip Taylor* (during Mr. Rooney's vacation, 6/29/81–7/8/81, and again 12/17/81–12/26/81. He played Rip), *Eddie Bracken* (during Mr. Rooney's vacation, 5/31/82–6/13/82. He played Eddie. Mr. Rooney was back 6/14/82; SCOT: Scot Stewart (9); JILLIAN: Ann Jillian (4), *Anita Morris* (from 3/8/80, as Anita), *Jane Summerhays* (from 11/80, as Jane); TOM: Tom Boyd (10); PETER: Peter Leeds (7); JACK: Jack Fletcher (5), *Maxie Furman* (by 80–81, as Maxie), *Sammy Smith* (during Mr. Furman's vacation, 81–82); JIMMY: Jimmy Mathews (8); ANN: Ann Miller (2) ☆, *Jane Summerhays* (during Miss Miller's illness, 1/81), *Helen Gallagher* (during Miss Miller's vacation, 9/21/81–10/12/81); SID: Sid Stone (3), *Maxie Furman* (by 81–82); BOB WILLIAMS: Bob Williams (6) [dog trainer]; MICHAEL: *Michael Allen Davis* (a juggling act, who replaced Bob Williams on 3/2/81), *Ronn Lucas* (during Mr. Davis's vacation, 81–82) [Mr. Lucas was a ventriloquist]; GAIETY QUARTET: Jonathan Aronson (*Henry Brunjes* by 80–81), Eddie Pruett, Michael Radigan, Jeff Veazey; SUGAR BABIES: Laura Booth (*Kaylyn Dillchay* from 79–80), Christine Busini (gone by 81–82), Diane Duncan (gone by 80–81), Chris Elia, Debbie Gornay (*Leslie Kingsley* from 79–80 & gone by 81–82), Barbara Hanks (*Clare Leach* from 79–80 & gone by 81–82), Jeri Kansas (*Dana Moore* from 79–80 & gone by 80–81. Miss Kansas was back by 81–82), Barbara Mandra (*Dorothy Stanley* from 79–80. Miss Mandra was back by 80–81 but gone again the same season), Robin Manus, Faye Fujisaki Mar, Linda Ravinsky (also known as Linda Ravin), Michele Rogers, Rose Scudder, Patti Watson (gone by 80–81). 80–81 replacements: *Carol Ann Basch, Melanie Montana, Regina Newsome*. 81–82 replacements: *Carole Cotter, Kimberly Dean, Candy Durkin*. **Note**: Chaz Chase (who ate light bulbs) was added by 80–81 & Ronn Lucas played his role during vacation, 81–82. The Agostinos & Elizabeth Hermines were added by 80–81, but gone by 81–82. Richard Galuppi added by 81–82. **Standby**: Mickey: Rudy Tronto (79–80). **Understudies**: Mickey: Tom Boyd (79–80), *Maxie Furman*; Ann: Rose Scudder (79–82) & Toni Kaye (79–80), *Jane Summerhays* (81–82); Jillian: Diane Duncan & Michele Rogers (both 79–80); Jack: Tom Boyd (79–80); Peter: Tom Boyd (79–80), *Richard Galuppi* (81–82); Sid/Jimmy: Tom Boyd (79–81), *Maxie Furman* (80–81); Jane: Michele Rogers (80–82), *Chris Elia* (81–82); Scot: Michael Radigan (79–82); Tom: Hank Brunjes (79–82); Maxie: *Tom Boyd* (by 80–81); Gaiety Quartet: Hank Brunjes (79–80), *Edward Pfeiffer* (80–81), *Ken Mitchell* (81–82). **Alternates**: Laurie Sloan (79–81), Terpsie Toon (*Carole Cotter* from 79–80; *Laurie Jaeger* by 81–82). **Act I**: Overture (Orchestra); **Scene 1** A Memory of Burlesque: "A Good Old Burlesque Show" (m: Jimmy McHugh; l: Arthur Malvin) (Mickey & Friends); **Scene 2** Welcome to the Gaiety: "Let Me Be Your Sugar Baby" (m/l: Arthur Malvin) (Peter, Jack, Sugar Babies); **Scene 3** Meet Me 'round the Corner (Jimmy, Scot, Peter, Mickey, Rose Scudder, Chris Elia, Michele Rogers, Jillian) [this was one of the most famous of all burlesque scenes, originally based on the Homestead Quartet, a minstrel show afterpiece] [replaced during the run by "I Want a Girl (Just Like the Girl that Married Dear Old Dad)" (m: Harry von Tilzer; l: William Dillon) (same performers)]; *Scene 4* Travelin': "In Lou'siana" (m: Jimmy McHugh; l: Arthur Malvin) (Ann, Sugar Babies, Gaiety Quartet), "I Feel a Song Comin' On" (m: Jimmy McHugh; l: Dorothy Fields & George Oppenheimer) [from the movie *Every Night at Eight*] (Ann, Sugar Babies, Gaiety Quartet), "(Goin') Back to New Orleans" (m/l: Arthur Malvin) (Ann, Sugar Babies, Gaiety Quartet) [for the post–Broadway tour this number was revised as "(Goin') Back to Cucamonga"]; *Scene 5* The Broken Arms Hotel (Jack, Tom, Mickey, Jimmy, Rose Scudder); *Scene 6* Feathered Fantasy (Salute to Sally Rand) (Scot, Barbara Hanks, Sugar Babies), "Sally" (m: Jimmy McHugh; l: Arthur Malvin) (Scot, Barbara Hanks, Sugar Babies); *Scene 7* The Pitchman — with Sid Stone [replaced during the run with Bon Appetit (Chaz Chase & Chris Elia)]; *Scene 8* Ellis Island Lament [named changed during run to Ellis Island Love Story], "Immigration Rose" (m: Jimmy McHugh; l: Eugene West & Irwin Dash) (Mickey & Gaiety Quartet) [dropped for the tour]; *Scene 9* Scene from Domestic Life (Jillian, Jimmy, Jack, Peter, Tom, Scot, Robin Manus, Laura Booth, Debbie Gornay); *Scene 10* Torch Song (after Bobby Clark) [changed during the run to A Very Moving Love Song — a Salute to Ed Wynn], "Don't Blame Me" (m: Jimmy McHugh; l: Dorothy Fields) [from the Chicago production of *Clowns in the Clover*] (Ann & Eddie Pruett); *Scene 11* Orientale (Christine Busini — introduced by Jack) [in remembrance of Little Egypt, the sensation of the 1893 Columbian Exposition, and many imitators on the variety stages, including La Sylphe, a "Salome" dancer who caused a big stir in burlesque in 1908]; *Scene 12* The Little Red Schoolhouse (Ann, Rose Scudder, Diane Duncan, Jimmy, Mickey) [Mickey played the naughty little boy]; *Scene 13* The New Candy-Coated Craze [There were many sister acts in burlesque, although not many were actual sisters in real life] [changed during the run to Presenting the Springboard Sisters (Who Sing in All The Dives): "The Sugar Baby Bounce" (m/l: Jay Livingston & Ray Evans) (Jillian, Chris Elia, Linda Ravinsky) [on tour this was sometimes replaced with "Monkey Business"]; *Scene 14* Special Added Attraction: Madame Rentz and Her All-Female Minstrels Featuring the Countess Francine [one of the earliest of all burlesque shows was the Rentz Troupe, owned by M.B. Leavitt]: INTRODUCTION: Jack Fletcher; COUNTESS FRANCINE: Mickey Rooney. "Down at the Gaiety Burlesque" (m/l: Arthur Malvin) (Ann, Mickey, Jeff Veazey, Sugar Babies), "Mr. Banjo Man" (m/l: Arthur Malvin) (Ann, Mickey, Jeff Veazey, Sugar Babies). *Act II*: *Scene 1* Candy Butcher (Sid & Gaiety Quartet); *Scene 2* Girls and Garters [the first girl to throw garters at a burlesque audience appears to have been Millie de Leon, "The Girl in Blue." Her act was a hot number on the circuits during the first decade of the 20th century. As a result of her generosity she spent several nights in jail]: "I'm Keeping Myself Available for You" (m: Jimmy McHugh; l: Arthur Malvin) (Jillian & Sugar Babies), "Exactly Like You" (m: Jimmy McHugh; l: Dorothy Fields) (Jillian & Sugar Babies); *Scene 3* Justice Will Out (Tom, Peter, Mickey, Ann) [Mickey played a lascivious judge in the manic courtroom scene] [name changed to Court of Last Resort and later Court of Last Retort during the run]; *Scene 4* In a Greek Garden (Salute to Rosita Royce): "Warm and Willing" (m: Jimmy McHugh; l: Jay Livingston & Ray Evans) (Jillian) [replaced on tour with "I'm in the Mood for Love"]; *Scene 5* Presenting Madame Alla Gazaza (Peter, Sid, Ann, Jeff Veazey, Mickey, Jimmy, Jack, Eddie Pruett, Jillian, Jonathan Aronson, Chris Elia); *Scene 6* Tropical Madness: "Cuban Love Song" (m: Jimmy McHugh & Herbert Stothart; l: Dorothy Fields) (Scot & Michele Rogers); *Scene 7* Cautionary Tales (Rose Scudder, Jimmy, Eddie Pruett, Michael Radigan, Jeri Kansas, Jack, Peter, Tom, Sid); *Scene 8* McHugh Medley (Mickey & Ann): "Every Day Another Tune" (m/l: Arthur Malvin) (Mickey & Ann) [dropped on tour], "I Can't Give You Anything but Love, Baby" (m: Jimmy McHugh; l: Dorothy Fields) (Mickey & Ann), "I'm Shooting High" (m: Jimmy McHugh; l: Ted Koehler) (Mickey & Ann), "When You and I Were Young, Maggie Blues" (m: Jimmy McHugh; l: Jack Frost) (Mickey & Ann), "On the Sunny Side of the Street" (m: Jimmy McHugh; l: Dorothy Fields) (Mickey & Ann). Note: for the post–Broadway tour this medley was augmented with one called Early Sophie (a tribute to the great Sophie Tucker), with Carol Channing performing: "(I'm the) Last of the Red Hot Mamas (m: Milton Ager; l: Jack Yellen), "Papa, Don't Go Out Tonight" (m: Milton Ager; l: Jack Yellen), "Some of These Days" (m/l: Shelton Brooks); *Scene 9* Presenting Bob Williams [replaced during the run with Michael Allen

Davis]; *Scene 10* Old Glory [this finale commemorates a famous act, Madame Hilda Case & the Red Raven Cadets, who were headliners on the Empire Circuit in 1905]: "You Can't Blame Your Uncle Sammy" (m: Jimmy McHugh; l: Al Dubin & Irwin Dash) (Company).

On Broadway it got very divided reviews. Mickey Rooney was making his legitimate stage debut. The show received Tony nominations for musical, score, book, direction of a musical, choreography, costumes, and for Mickey Rooney and Ann Miller.

After Broadway. TOUR. Opened on 8/12/80, in Dallas, and closed on 11/1/80, at the Colonial Theatre, Boston (this last engagement had opened on 9/25/80). MUSICAL DIRECTOR: Patrick Holland. *Cast*: Carol Channing, Robert Morse, Jay Stuart, William Linton, Sally Benoit, Chaz Chase, Maxie Furman. SUGAR BABIES: Carol Ann Basch, Candy Durkin, Melanie Montana, Regina Newsome.

TOUR. Opened on 9/15/81, at the Macauley Center, Louisville, and closed on 5/2/82, at the Palace Theatre, Cincinnati. PRESENTED BY Gingerbread Productions; MUSICAL DIRECTOR: Kay Cameron. *Cast*: Eddie Bracken, Jaye P. Morgan (*Mimi Hines*), Jay Stuart, Phil Ford, Toni Kaye, Sam Kressen. SUGAR BABY: Mary Anne Fiordallisi.

POST-BROADWAY TOUR. Opened on 11/8/82, at the Arie Crown Theatre, Chicago, and closed on 4/20/86, at the Spartanburg Memorial Auditorium, SC. MUSICAL DIRECTOR: Sherman Frank. *Cast*: Ann Miller (*Toni Kaye* from 2/10/83; *Carol Lawrence* 3/14/83–5/15/83, after Miss Miller had injured her foot; *Jane Summerhays* 4/2/85–5/3/85, after Miss Miller had injured her knee; Mickey Rooney, Mickey Deems, Maxie Furman, Milton Frome, Jay Stuart, Michael Allen Davis (*James Marcel, Frank Olivier, Daniel Rosen*), Lori Street (*Gail Dahms, Julie Miller, Lucianne Buchanan*), Phil Ford (*Rudy Tronto, William Linton, Jack Fletcher*), Ronn Lucas (*Senor Wences* during Mr. Lucas's absence in 82–83; *Senor Wences* was added to the cast in 1986). SUGAR BABIES: Carol Ann Basch (*Carole Cotter*), Candy Durkin (*Robin Manus*), Yvonne Dutton, Chris Elia, Faye Fujisaki Mar (*Kris Mooney*), Rose Scudder (*Sarah Grove, Kimberly Campbell*). **Understudies**: For Ann Miller: Jane Summerhays.

SAVOY THEATRE, London, 9/20/88–1/7/89. *Cast*: Mickey Rooney, Ann Miller.

670. *Sunday in the Park with George*

Although suggested by the life of French painter Georges Seurat (1859–1891), and by his 1884–1886 pointillist painting *Sunday Afternoon on the Island of La Grande Jatte* (a depiction of strolling Parisians rendered in thousands of colored dots), all the characters in this musical are products of the author's imagination; set and costume designs were adapted from the painting. George, a painter, paints the Parisians as they stroll through a park. Dot, a model, is his girlfriend. We follow the creation of the painting, and get to know the people. As George becomes obsessed with the painting, Dot, who is pregnant, leaves him for a baker, whose work is immediately appreciated (Seurat never sold a painting during his life time). She then goes, with the child, to America. Act II has Seurat's great grandson George presenting his kinetic laser sculpture at the Museum of Modern Art. Like his ancestor, George is going through an emotional and creative crisis after creating his seventh chromolume. In the final scene George returns to the island of La Grande Jatte and is met by the ghost of Dot who again serves as his inspiration.

Before Broadway. It was first presented Off Broadway, as a workshop at PLAYWRIGHTS HORIZONS, 7/6/83–7/30/83. Limited run of 26 PERFORMANCES. PRESENTED in association with the Herrick Theatre Foundation. It had the same crew as in the subsequent Broadway run, except SOUND: Scott Lehrer. Charles Blackwell was not yet production stage manager. It had the same basic cast, except OLD LADY: Carmen Mathews; CELESTE # 2: Mary Elizabeth Mastrantonio; LOUIS/PHOTOGRAPHER: Kevin Marcum; BOY: Bradley Kane; YOUNG MAN/SOLDIER/ALEX: Kelsey Grammer; JULES: Ralph Byers; CLARISSA: Christine Baranski. Kurt Knudson's character's name changed from Mr. Robert Blackmun to Lee Randolph. The workshop production told the story in one act, and it was what to do with Act II that caused the writers problems. What came closest, perhaps, but still failed, was a history of the Seurat painting from its first exhibition in France until it was acquired by the Art Institute of Chicago. Finally, however, the authors set Act II in 1984. Re-writing continued into the period when Broadway previews were being held at the Booth. Less than two weeks before the official opening, two ballads were added—"Children and Art" and "Lesson # 8."

The Broadway Run. BOOTH THEATRE, 5/2/84–10/13/85. 35 previews. 604 PERFORMANCES. PRESENTED BY The Shubert Organization & Emanuel Azenberg, by arrangement with Playwrights Horizons; MUSIC/LYRICS: Stephen Sondheim; BOOK/DIRECTOR: James Lapine; MOVEMENT: Randolyn Zinn; SETS: Tony Straiges; COSTUMES: Patricia Zipprodt & Ann Hould-Ward; LIGHTING: Richard Nelson; SOUND: Tom Morse; MUSICAL DIRECTOR: Paul Gemignani; ORCHESTRATIONS/PROGRAMMED CHROMOLUME MUSIC: Michael Starobin; PRESS: Fred Nathan & Associates; CASTING: John S. Lyons; GENERAL MANAGER: Robert Kamlot; COMPANY MANAGER: Richard Berg; PRODUCTION STAGE MANAGER: Charles Blackwell; STAGE MANAGER: Fredric H. Orner; ASSISTANT STAGE MANAGER: Loretta Robertson, *Steven Shaw*. **Cast: Act I:** GEORGE, AN ARTIST: Mandy Patinkin (1), *Robert Westenberg (from 9/18/84), Cris Groenendaal (during Mr. Westenberg's vacation, 1/15/85–1/22/85), Harry Groener (from 4/23/85), Mandy Patinkin (from 8/5/85)*; DOT, HIS MISTRESS: Bernadette Peters (2) (until 2/24/85), *Joanna Glushak (during Miss Peters' vacation, 8/27/85–9/10/84), Betsy Joslyn (from 2/26/85), Maryann Plunkett (from 3/12/85)*; OLD LADY: Barbara Byrne; HER NURSE: Judith Moore; FRANZ, A SERVANT: Brent Spiner; BOY BATHING IN THE RIVER: Danielle Ferland; YOUNG MAN SITTING ON THE BANK: Nancy Opel; MAN LYING ON THE BANK: Cris Groenendaal, *T.J. Meyers (1/15/85–1/22/85, during time Mr. Groenendaal was lead)*; JULES, ANOTHER ARTIST: Charles Kimbrough; YVONNE, HIS WIFE: Dana Ivey; BOATMAN: William Parry; CELESTE # 1: Melanie Vaughan; CELESTE # 2: Mary D'Arcy; LOUISE, DAUGHTER OF JULES AND YVONNE: Danielle Ferland; FRIEDA, A COOK: Nancy Opel; LOUIS, A BAKER: Cris Groenendaal, *T.J. Meyers (1/15/85–1/22/85, during time Mr. Groenendaal was lead)*; SOLDIER: Robert Westenberg; MAN WITH BICYCLE: John Jellison; LITTLE GIRL: Michele Rigan [role dropped for second season]; WOMAN WITH BABY CARRIAGE: Sue Anne Gershenson [role dropped for second season]; MR.: Kurt Knudson; MRS.: Judith Moore. **Act II:** GEORGE, AN ARTIST: Mandy Patinkin (1), *Robert Westenberg (from 9/18/84), Cris Groenendaal (during Mr. Westenberg's vacation, 1/15/85–1/22/85), Harry Groener (from 4/23/85), Mandy Patinkin (from 8/5/85)*; MARIE, HIS GRANDMOTHER: Bernadette Peters (2) (until 2/24/85), *Joanna Glushak (during Miss Peters' vacation, 8/27/84–9/10/84), Betsy Joslyn (from 2/26/85), Maryann Plunkett (from 3/12/85)*; DENNIS, A TECHNICIAN: Brent Spiner; BOB GREENBERG, MUSEUM DIRECTOR: Charles Kimbrough; NAOMI EISEN, COMPOSER: Dana Ivey; HARRIET PAWLING, PATRON OF THE ARTS: Judith Moore; BILLY WEBSTER, HER FRIEND: Cris Groenendaal, *T.J. Meyers (1/15/85–1/22/85, during time Mr. Groenendaal was lead)*; PHOTOGRAPHER: Sue Anne Gershenson; MUSEUM ASSISTANT: John Jellison; CHARLES REDMOND, VISITING CURATOR: William Parry; ALEX, AN ARTIST: Robert Westenberg; BETTY, AN ARTIST: Nancy Opel; LEE RANDOLPH, PUBLICIST: Kurt Knudson; BLAIR DANIELS, ART CRITIC: Barbara Byrne; WAITRESS: Melanie Vaughan; ELAINE: Mary D'Arcy. **Understudies:** George: Robert Westenberg, *Cris Groenendaal*; Dot/Marie: Joanna Glushak; Old Lady/Blair/Nurse: Sara Woods; Mrs./Harriet: Sara Woods; Franz/Dennis: Cris Groenendaal & Ray Gill; Soldier/Alex: Cris Groenendaal & Ray Gill; Randolph: Ray Gill, *T.J. Meyers*; Man/Louis/Billy: Ray Gill & John Jellison, *T.J. Meyers*; Boy/Louise: Michele Rigan; Young Man/Frieda/Betty: Sue Anne Gershenson; Celeste # 2/Elaine: Sue Anne Gershenson, *Joanna Glushak*; Jules/Greenberg: John Jellison; Boatman/Redmond: John Jellison, *T.J. Meyers*; Celeste # 1: Joanna Glushak & Sue Anne Gershenson; Yvonne/Naomi: Sara Woods; Waitress: Joanna Glushak, *Sue Anne Gershenson*; Museum Assistant/Mr.: *T.J. Meyers*. **Musicians:** CONCERTMISTRESS: Marilyn Reynolds; VIOLIN: Cecelia Hobbs; VIOLA: Karl Bargen; CELLO: Eileen M. Folson; PIANO: Paul Ford; SYNTHESIZERS: Paul Ford & Ted Sperling; HARP: Beth Schwartz Robinson; FRENCH HORN: Ronald Sell; WOODWINDS: Les Scott & Al Hunt; PERCUSSION: Robert Ayers. **Act I:** takes place on a series of Sundays, 1884–1886, and alternates between a park on an island in the Seine, just outside Paris, and George's studio. George is breaking new impressionist ground: "Sunday in the Park with George" (Dot), "No Life" (Jules & Yvonne), "Color and Light" (Dot & George), "Gossip" (Celeste # 1, Celeste # 2, Boatman, Nurse, Old Lady, Jules, Yvonne), "The Day Off" (George, Nurse, Franz, Frieda, Boatman, Soldier, Celeste # 1, Celeste # 2, Yvonne, Louise, Jules, Louise), "Everybody Loves Louis" (Dot), "Finishing the Hat" (George), "We Do Not Belong Together" (Dot & George), "Beautiful" (Old Lady & George), "Sunday" (Company). **Act II:** takes place in 1984 at an American art museum, and on the island in the Seine: "It's Hot up Here" (Company), "Chromolume # 7" (George & Marie), "Putting It Together" (George & Company), "Children and Art" (Marie), "Lesson # 8" (George), "Move On" (George & Dot), "Sunday" (reprise) (Company).

Broadway reviews were divided. The show won a Pulitzer Prize for Drama; and Tony Awards for sets and lighting. It was also Tony nominated for musical, score, book, direction of a musical, costumes, and for Mandy Patinkin, Bernadette Peters, and Dana Ivey. The production lost half a million dollars. A videotape of the Broadway production was made, which had most of the original cast, and was shown on TV on Showtime (2/18/86) and on PBS. The song "Putting it Together" was made famous by a recording by Barbra Streisand.

After Broadway. LYTTLETON THEATRE, London, 3/15/90–6/16/90. 117 PERFORMANCES IN REPERTORY. PRESENTED BY the Royal National Theatre; DIRECTOR: Scott Pimlott; CHOREOGRAPHER: Aletta Collins; SETS/COSTUMES: Tom Cairns; LIGHTING: Wolfgang Gobble; MUSICAL DIRECTOR: Jeremy Sams. **Cast:** GEORGE: Philip Quast; DOT/MARIE: Maria Friedman; JULES/BOB: Gary Raymond; YVONNE/NAOMI: Nyree Dawn Porter; SOLDIER/ALEX: Nicolas Colicos; MR./CHARLES: Matt Zimmerman; MRS./BILLIE: Vivienne Martin.

ST. JAMES THEATRE, Broadway, 5/15/94. 1 night only. This was a 10th-anniversary reunion concert. PRESENTED BY Friends in Deed; PRODUCED BY: B.T. McNicholl; SOUND: Lucas Rico Corrubia; MUSICAL DIRECTOR: Paul Gemignani. It had the same cast as for the original Broadway production, except FRANZ/DENNIS: Bruce Adler; LOUIS/BILLY: Jeff Keller; SOLDIER/ALEX: Howard McGillin. The Sue Ann Gershenson and Michele Rigan roles were cut (as they had been during the run of the original production).

ARENA STAGE, Washington, DC, 4/20/97–6/15/97. Previews from 4/11/97. This slightly revised version was first announced on 3/22/96. In Act II George is now a visual artist in TV design. The old laser show is now state-of-the-art projections. There was talk of inserting a Sondheim song dropped from the original Broadway production, but it didn't happen. However, "Putting it Together" got some new lyrics. DIRECTOR: Eric D. Schaeffer; SETS: Zack Brown; COSTUMES: Patricia Zipprodt; LIGHTING: Allen Lee Hughes; SOUND: Timothy Thompson; MUSICAL DIRECTOR: Jon Kalbfleisch. **Cast:** GEORGE: Sal Viviano; DOT: Liz Larsen; JULES/BOB: Robert Du Sold; YVONNE/NAOMI: SuEllen Estey; FRIEDA/BETTY: Carter Calvert; SOLDIER/ALEX: Christopher Monteleone.

KENNEDY CENTER, Washington, DC. Previews from 5/31/02. This production was part of the *Sondheim Celebration* series. **Cast:** GEORGE: Raul Esparza; DOT: Melissa Errico; YVONNE: Florence Lacey; JULES: Cris Groenendaal; NURSE/MRS.: Donna Migliaccio; FRANZ: Jason Gilbert; CELESTE # 1: Tracy Lynn Olivera; CELESTE # 2: Sherri Edelen; BOATMAN: Michael L. Forrest; LOUIS: Bob McDonald; FRIEDA: Amy McWilliams; SOLDIER: Matthew Shepard; HORN PLAYER: Daniel Felton; WOMAN WITH BABY CARRIAGE: Mary Jane Raleigh; MR.: Harry Winter; OLD LADY: Linda Stephens; BOY BATHING IN RIVER/JULES & YVONNE'S DAUGHTER: Annie Simon.

RAVINIA FESTIVAL, Chicago, 9/3/04–9/5/04. DIRECTOR: Lonny Price; CONDUCTOR: Paul Gemignani. **Cast:** DOT: Audra McDonald; GEORGE: Michael Cerveris; YVONNE: Patti LuPone; OLD LADY: Sharon Carlson.

671. *Sunset Boulevard*

Set in Los Angeles, 1949–50. Norma Desmond is a former silent screen star desperate for a comeback as Salome, in a script to be written by her and her younger lover, Joe, who is eventually found floating in Miss Desmond's pool. The Broadway production was dedicated to the memory of R. Tyler Gatchell, Jr.

Before Broadway. It began at the ADELPHI THEATRE, London, 7/12/93–4/5/97. 1,529 PERFORMANCES. Patti LuPone had won the role over Meryl Streep (it had been touch and go between the two actresses for a long time but by 2/93 we knew Miss LuPone had it). Billy Wilder was in the audience on opening night. Patti LuPone recorded on the original London cast album (on Polydor). The show closed because, as on Broadway, the producers couldn't find a replacement star big enough to play the lead, and audiences were dropping off. DIRECTOR: Trevor Nunn; CHOREOGRAPHER: Bob Avian. *Cast*: NORMA: Patti LuPone, *Betty Buckley, Elaine Paige* (during Miss Buckley's emergency appendectomy operation in 11/94), *Petula Clark*; ALSO WITH: Kevin Anderson, Nicolas Colicos, Michael Bauer, Gareth Snook, Meredith Braun.

In the USA, in 4/93, Andrew Lloyd Webber announced that Glenn Close would play Norma in the pre–Broadway tryout at the Shubert Theatre, Los Angeles, although Patti LuPone had it in her contract that she was to star in the Broadway production, whenever it opened. By 10/93, however, rumors were starting to go around that Glenn Close would, indeed, play it on Broadway, not Patti LuPone. These rumors intensified after the L.A. opening of 12/9/93, when Glenn Close got unanimous raves. It became one of the big Broadway guessing games of the decade. On 2/3/94 Andrew Lloyd Webber announced that Betty Buckley was taking over from Patti LuPone in London, and she did, and even as late as that date Mr. Lloyd Webber was still insisting that Miss LuPone was going to play it on Broadway. However, on 2/14/94 the story broke that Miss LuPone was not going to play it on Broadway, and this was confirmed by Mr. Lloyd Webber on 2/17/94. It was a definite breach of contract. Patti LuPone had been making $25,000 a week in her London role. By 5/16/94 she and the producers had reached a settlement of a reported million dollars. Meanwhile, back in the States, Faye Dunaway was due to replace Glenn Close in L.A. on 7/12/94, but instead Andrew Lloyd Webber fired her on 6/22/94 and closed the show, saying her voice wasn't up to it. Miss Dunaway sued for $6 million on 8/25/94. *L.A. cast*: Glenn Close, Judy Kuhn, George Hearn, Alan Campbell, Sal Mistretta, Alan Oppenheimer, Rick Podell, Vincent Tumeo.

The Broadway Run. MINSKOFF THEATRE, 11/17/94–3/22/97. 17 previews from 11/1/94. 977 PERFORMANCES. PRESENTED BY The Really Useful Company; MUSIC: Andrew Lloyd Webber; LYRICS/BOOK: Don Black & Christopher Hampton; BASED ON the 1950 movie of the same name, written by Billy Wilder (and starring Gloria Swanson, William Holden & Erich von Stroheim), which was based on the book by Billy Wilder, Charles Brackett, D.M. Marsham Jr.; DIRECTOR: Trevor Nunn; CHOREOGRAPHER: Bob Avian; SETS: John Napier; COSTUMES: Anthony Powell; LIGHTING: Andrew Bridge; SOUND: Martin Levan; MUSICAL SUPERVISOR: David Caddick; MUSICAL DIRECTORS: David Caddick & Paul Bogaev; ORCHESTRATIONS: David Cullen & Andrew Lloyd Webber; CAST RECORDING on Polydor; PRESS: Boneau/Bryan-Brown; CASTING: Johnson — Liff; GENERAL MANAGEMENT: The Really Useful Management Company (Nina Lannan); COMPANY MANAGER: Abbie M. Strassler; PRODUCTION STAGE MANAGER: Peter Lawrence; STAGE MANAGERS: John Brigleb, Jim Woolley, Lynda J. Fox. *Cast*: NORMA DESMOND: Glenn Close (1) ✩, *Karen Mason* (during vacation & illness, 3/7/95–3/19/95), *Betty Buckley* (from 7/4/95), *Elaine Paige* (from 8/26/96); JOE GILLIS: Alan Campbell (2) ✩, *John Barrowman*; MAX VON MAYERLING: George Hearn (4) ✩; BETTY SCHAEFER: Alice Ripley (3) ✩; CECIL B. DE MILLE: Alan Oppenheimer, *Rod Loomis*; ARTIE GREEN: Vincent Tumeo, *Jordan Leeds*; HAREM GIRLS: Sandra Allen & Lada Boder; YOUNG WRITER: Bryan Batt, *John Scherer, Bruce Alan Johnson*; HEATHER: Susan Dawn Carson, *Alisa Endsley*; CLIFF: Matthew Dickens, *Jim Newman, Matthew Dickens*; JEAN (3RD HAREM GIRL): Colleen Dunn, *Angie L. Schworer, Lisa Mandel*; MORINO: Steven Stein-Grainger; LISA: Kim Huber, *Jane Bodle, Kristen Behrendt*; FINANCEMEN: Rich Hebert (*Larry Small*) & Tom Alan Robbins (*Stephen Breithaupt*); KATHERINE: Alicia Irving, *Danielle Lee Greaves*; MARY: Lauren Kennedy, *Jennifer West*; SHELDRAKE: Sal Mistretta; JOHN: Mark Morales; MYRON: Rick Podell, *Dale Hensley*; JONESY: David Eric, *James Dybas*; CHOREOGRAPHER: Rick Sparks, *Dan O'Grady*; BEAUTICIANS: Sandra Allen, Lada Boder, Colleen

Dunn (*Angie L. Schworer, Lisa Mandel*); FILM ACTOR: Rich Hebert, *Larry Small*; DOCTOR: Kim Huber, *Jane Bodle, Kristen Behrendt*; PSYCHIATRIST: Alicia Irving, *Danielle Lee Greaves*; JOANNA: Wendy Walter; SAMMY: David Eric, *James Dybas*; MANFRED: Rick Podell, *Dale Hensley*; SALESMEN: Bryan Batt (*John Scherer, Bruce Alan Johnson*), Matthew Dickens (*Jim Newman, Matthew Dickens*), Steven Stein-Grainger, Rich Hebert (*Larry Small*), Mark Morales, Tom Alan Robbins (*Stephen Breithaupt*), David Eric (*James Dybas*), Rick Sparks (*Dan O'Grady*); 1ST MASSEUSE: Lauren Kennedy, *Jennifer West*; 2ND MASSEUSE: Susan Dawn Carson, *Alisa Endsley*; DE MILLE'S ASSISTANT: Bryan Batt, *John Scherer, Bruce Alan Johnson*; POLICE CHIEF: Sal Mistretta; YOUNG GUARD: Matthew Dickens, *Jim Newman, Matthew Dickens*; PARTY GUEST: Tom Alan Robbins, *Stephen Breithaupt*; HOG EYE: Steven Stein-Grainger; ASTROLOGER: Wendy Walter; HEDY LAMARR: Colleen Dunn, *Angie L. Schworer, Lisa Mandel*; VICTOR MATURE: Mark Morales. **Standby**: Norma: Karen Mason, *Maureen Moore*. **Understudies**: Norma: Susan Dawn Carson, *Alisa Endsley, Alicia Irving*; Joe: Bryan Batt & Matthew Dickens, *John Scherer, Jim Newman, Bruce Alan Johnson, Jordan Leeds*; Betty: Kim Huber & Lauren Kennedy, *Jane Bodle, Jennifer West, Kristen Behrendt*; De Mille: Steven Stein-Granger & David Eric, *James Dybas*; Sheldrake: David Eric, *James Dybas, Peter Kapetan*; Writer/Salesmen/Assistant: *Matthew Dickens, Darrin Baker, Harvey Evans*; Cliff/Morino/Hog Eye: *Matthew Dickens, Darrin Baker, Harvey Evans*; Financemen/Film Actor/Police/John: *Matthew Dickens, Darrin Baker, Harvey Evans*; Sammy/Jonesy/Choreographer: *Matthew Dickens, Darrin Baker, Harvey Evans*; Artie: Matthew Dickens & Darrin Baker, *Jim Newman*; Max: Rich Hebert & Steven Stein-Grainger; Manfred: *Peter Kapetan*; Harem Girls/Beautician: Rosemary Loar, *Darlene Wilson*; Lisa/Doctor: Rosemary Loar, *Darlene Wilson*; Heather/Masseuses: Rosemary Loar, *Darlene Wilson*; Hedy/Joanna: Rosemary Loar, *Darlene Wilson*; Astrologer/Katherine: Rosemary Loar, *Darlene Wilson*; Psychiatrist/Mary: Rosemary Loar, *Darlene Wilson*; Male Roles: John Hoshko; Female Roles: *Jennifer Stetor, Colleen Sudduth, Darlene Wilson*. **Orchestra:** CONCERTMASTER: Sanford Allen; VIOLINS: Sylvia D'Avanzo, Myra Segal, Paul Woodiel, Kurt Coble, Avril Brown, Kurt Briggs; VIOLAS: Richard Brice & Henry Kao; CELLO: Francesca Vanasco; BASS/ELECTRIC BASS: Douglas Romoff; FLUTE: M. Bernard Phillips & Edward Salkin; PICCOLO/ALTO FLUTE: M. Bernard Phillips; ALTO SAX/BASS CLARINET: Andrew Sterman; CLARINETS: Edward Salkin & Andrew Sterman; TENOR SAX: Edward Salkin; FRENCH HORNS: Theresa MacDonnell-Hardison & Steve Zimmerman; TRUMPET/PICCOLO TRUMPET: Christian Jaudes; BASS TROMBONE: Jeffrey Nelson; DRUMS/PERCUSSION: James Saporito; GUITAR: David Boguslaw; KEYBOARDS: Robert Gustafson, Maggie Torre, James May. *Act I*: Overture; *Scene 1* Exterior/dawn; the house on Sunset: Prologue (Joe); *Scene 2* Ext/day; Paramount Studios: "Let's Have Lunch" (Joe & Ensemble); *Scene 3* Ext/day; on the road; *Scene 4* Ext/day; the garage on Sunset; *Scene 5* Interior/day & evening; the house on Sunset: "Surrender" (Norma), "With One Look" (Norma), "Salome" (Norma & Joe); *Scene 6* Int/night; Norma's guest house: "The Greatest Star of All" (Max); *Scene 7* Int/evening; Schwab's Drugstore: "Every Movie's a Circus" (Joe, Betty, Artie, Ensemble), "Girl Meets Boy" (Joe & Betty); *Scene 8* Ext/night; the terrace on Sunset; *Scene 9* Int/evening; the house on Sunset: "New Ways to Dream" (Norma); *Scene 10* Int/day; the house on Sunset: "The Lady's Paying" (Manfred, Norma, Joe, Salesmen); *Scene 11* Int/night; the house on Sunset: "The Perfect Year" (Norma & Joe); *Scene 12* Int/night; Artie Green's apartment: "This Time Next Year" (Joe, Betty, Artie, Ensemble); *Scene 13* Int/night; the house on Sunset. *Act II*: Entr'acte; *Scene 1* Ext/day; Norma's swimming pool: "Sunset Boulevard" (Joe), "The Perfect Year" (reprise) (Norma); *Scene 2* Ext/day; Paramount Studio: "As if We Never Said Goodbye" (Norma), "Surrender" (reprise) (de Mille); *Scene 3* Int/night; Betty's office at Paramount: "Girl Meets Boy" (reprise) (Betty & Joe); *Scene 4* Int/day; the house on Sunset: "Eternal Youth is Worth a Litle Suffering" (Norma's Consultants); *Scene 5* Int/ext/night; Betty's office/Paramount backlot: "Too Much in Love to Care" (Betty & Joe); *Scene 6* Ext/night; the house on Sunset: "New Ways to Dream" (reprise) (Max); *Scene 7* Ext/int/night; the house on Sunset: "Sunset Boulevard" (reprise) (Joe & Betty); *Scene 8* Ext/int/dawn; the house on Sunset: "The Greatest Star of All" (reprise) (Max & Norma), "Surrender" (reprise) (Norma).

The Broadway production had advance sales of $37 million. Broadway reviews were very divided. On the first day it broke the record for one-day ticket sales ($1,491,110), beating the record previously held by *Beauty and the Beast*. It won Tonys for musical, score, book, sets, and lighting, and for Glenn Close and George Hearn. It was also nominated for direction of a musical, choreography, costumes, and for Alan Campbell. On 12/8/95 the sprinkler system failed, putting the orchestra pit under four inches of water. It was the third time a performance of this show had had to be canceled for technical reasons. *Sunset Boulevard* cost $730,000 a week just to keep running, and it finally closed just short of its break-even point. Glenn Close's Broadway earnings were $30,000 a week plus 10 per cent of gross over $600,000. It later came out that TV interviewer Barbara Walters had invested $100,000 in the show. As one of her interviews (on the TV show *20/20*) was Andrew Lloyd Webber, she had kept quiet about her investment.

After Broadway. GERMANY. The first German-language version ran from 1995 to 5/3/98. 992 PERFORMANCES. This was the first time The Really Useful Group (R.U.G.) had been primary producers in a German production (previously they had been merely associated with the German company Stella Musical Management, on such shows as *Cats, Phantom,* and *Starlight Express*, but now Stella was in financial trouble). From the start, despite great reviews, the production suffered from marketing difficulties, and R.U.G. lost money when only 830,000 people came. *Cast*: Uwe Kruger, Helen Schneider, Michael Bauer, Kenn Darby.

TORONTO, 10/15/95. This was a short run. *Cast*: NORMA: Diahann Carroll; MAX: Walter Charles; JOE: Rex Smith; BETTY: Anita Louise Combe; ALSO WITH: Marilyn Caskey, John Hoshko, Lisa Mandel, Marianne McCord.

TOUR. Opened on 6/28/96, at the Denver Center for the Performing Arts. This tour was planned to run for six years, but, in fact, ran less than one. Because of the fantastic sets, it cost a million every time it moved to another city (it needed a minimum stay of five weeks in each city, with big audiences, to cover the costs). *Cast*: NORMA: Linda Balgord; JOE: Ron Bohmer; MAX: Ed Dixon; BETTY: Lauren Kennedy; DE MILLE: William Chapman; ARTIE: James Clow; ALSO WITH: Philip Michael Baskerville, Harvey Evans, Kenny Morris, William Solo, Jillana Urbina.

SYDNEY, 10/26/96–6/97. Previews from 10/12/96. This was the Australian premiere. During previews Debra Byrne fell, and two previews were canceled. Brian Stacey, the conductor, was killed on a motorcycle. Rumors of Glenn Close replacing Miss Byrne during the run were unfounded. *Cast*: NORMA: Debra Byrne; JOE: Hugh Jackman; MAX: Norbert Lamla; BETTY: Catherine Porter.

TOURING REVIVAL. It opened on 12/1/98, at the Benedum Center, Pittsburgh, and played 47 cities in 60 weeks. It had the same script, score and costumes as for the Broadway production, but the 1996 tour had taught the producers a lesson about the size of the sets. Derek McLane came in as the new set designer. PRESENTED BY PACE Theatrical Group & Columbia Artists; DIRECTOR: Susan Schulman; CHOREOGRAPHER: Kathleen Marshall; LIGHTING: Peter Kaczorowski; SOUND: Tony Meola. *Cast*: NORMA: Petula Clark; JOE: Lewis Cleale; MAX: Allen Fitzgerald; BETTY: Sarah Uriarte Berry; DE MILLE: George Merner; ARTIE: Michael Berry.

In early 2003 rumors started going around that Liza Minnelli would star in a movie version of the musical.

672. *Sweeney Todd*

Also called: *Sweeney Todd, the Demon Barber of Fleet Street*. A black comedy musical thriller. Insane barber Sweeney Todd returns to grim and grimy Victorian London. 15 years earlier he had been unjustly sentenced to imprisonment in Australia by evil Judge Turpin who had wanted Todd out of the way so he could have the barber's wife. Todd's wife is now dead. In addition, Todd's daughter Johanna, now 16 years old, has become Turpin's ward, and is about to be forced into an unwanted marriage with her lecherous benefactor. Anthony, a young sailor, who saved Todd's life on the trip back from Australia, falls in love with Johanna. Todd turns his vengeance on all of London, and uses his razor to slit the throats of customers. Todd's helper, Mrs. Lovett, in the pie store below the barber shop, receives the bodies as they tumble through a trap door, and then cooks them and makes them into meat pies which she sells to the general public. A jarring factory whistle was frequently used to remind the audience that this was a statement against the dehumanizing effects of the Industrial Revolution. It also featured a pipe organ to highlight its gothic nature. Set in and around Fleet Street in the 19th century.

Before Broadway. The history of this Broadway production really begins in England, on 4/17/72, when Christopher G. Bond's new (straight) treatment of the Todd story, depicting Todd as the victim of a corrupt class system, opened at the VICTORIA THEATRE, Stoke-on-Trent, England. Todd is driven to his crimes by injustices dealt him by the lascivious judge with designs on Todd's wife and daughter. INCIDENTAL MUSIC: Trevor T. Smith. *Cast*: TODD: Brian Murphy; MRS. LOVETT: Avis Bunnage; RAGG: Christopher Bond. In 1973 the play had a run at Joan Littlewood's THEATRE WORKSHOP, Stratford East, London, which is where Steve Sondheim saw it in 1974 while he was helping to prepare the West End production of *Gypsy*. He thought it would be a great opera, and bought up all existing published versions of the story, not that he intended to use them, but to protect himself. Mr. Sondheim contacted Richard Barr and Charles Woodward, the producers who were then bidding on U.S. rights to Christopher Bond's production of *Sweeney Todd*. Barr & Woodward did not have a musical in mind. Steve Sondheim convinced them to do a musical, but it was the summer of 1977 before he was able to get to work on it. Hal Prince was brought in as director, and Hugh Wheeler as librettist, and the show moved away from opera to musical thriller. It was first read in 5/78, and by this stage Mr. Sondheim had completed seven songs, and Hugh Wheeler had a first draft of Act I. There was another reading in the summer of 1978, and a third one in the fall. Len Cariou and Angela Lansbury were cast very early on. Rehearsals took place at ANTA, in New York. Because the set, fashioned after a deliberately skyless Victorian foundry, was so complex, the show was not taken out of town for tryouts. It was capitalized at $900,000 (it wound up costing $1.3 million), with 271 investors. $100,000 came from RCA.

The Broadway Run. URIS THEATRE, 3/1/79–6/29/80. 19 previews from 2/6/79. 557 PERFORMANCES. PRESENTED BY Richard Barr, Charles Woodward, Robert Fryer, Mary Lea Johnson, Martin Richards, in association with Dean & Judy Manos; MUSIC/LYRICS: Stephen Sondheim; BOOK: Hugh Wheeler; BASED ON the 1973 British drama *Sweeney Todd*, by Christopher Bond, which in turn had been adapted from the 1847 melodrama *The String of Pearls, or the Fiend of Fleet Street*, by George Dibdin Pitt, from the 1846 serialized novel *The String of Pearls, A Romance*, by Thomas Peckett Prest, from the 1825 *Tell-Tale Magazine* article *A Terrible Story of the Rue de la Harpe*, from an earlier account in the French *Archives de Police*, by Joseph Fouche; DIRECTOR: Harold Prince; ASSISTANT DIRECTOR: Ruth Mitchell; CHOREOGRAPHER: Larry Fuller; SETS: Eugene Lee; COSTUMES: Franne Lee; LIGHTING: Ken Billington; SOUND: Jack Mann; MUSICAL DIRECTOR: Paul Gemignani; ORCHESTRATIONS: Jonathan Tunick; CAST RECORDING on RCA; PRESS: Mary Bryant; CASTING: Joanna Merlin; GENERAL MANAGEMENT: Gatchell & Neufeld; COMPANY MANAGER: Drew Murphy, *James G. Mennen* (added by 79–80); PRODUCTION STAGE MANAGER: Alan Hall; STAGE MANAGER: Ruth E. Rinklin; ASSISTANT STAGE MANAGER: Arthur Masella, *Larry Mengden*. *Cast*: ANTHONY HOPE: Victor Garber (3), *Cris Groenendaal* (from 8/79); SWEENEY TODD: Len Cariou (2) ☆, *George Hearn* (from 3/4/80); BEGGAR WOMAN: Merle Louise (5); MRS. LOVETT: Angela Lansbury (1) ☆, *Marge Redmond* (9/3/79–9/12/79), *Angela Lansbury, Dorothy Loudon* (from 3/4/80); JUDGE TURPIN: Edmund Lyndeck (6); BEADLE BAMFORD: Jack Eric Williams (9); JOHANNA: Sarah Rice (7), *Betsy Joslyn* (from 1/22/80); TOBIAS RAGG: Ken Jennings (4); PIRELLI: Joaquin Romaguera (8); JONAS FOGG: Robert Ousley; ENSEMBLE: Duane Bodin, Walter Charles, Carole Doscher, Nancy Eaton (*Nancy Callman*), Mary-Pat Green, Cris Groenendaal (*Kevin Marcum* from 8/79), Skip Harris, Marthe Ihde, Betsy Joslyn (*Candace Rogers* from 1/22/80), Nancy

Killmer, Frank Kopyc, Spain Logue, Craig Lucas, Pamela McLernon, Duane Morris, Robert Ousley, Richard Warren Pugh (*Michael Kalinyen*), Maggie Task. **Standby**: Mrs. Lovett: Marge Redmond. **Understudies**: Mrs. Lovett: Maggie Task; Todd: Walter Charles; Anthony: Cris Groenendaal, *Robert Henderson*; Johanna: Betsy Joslyn, *Candace Rogers*; Beadle: Richard Warren Pugh, *Michael Kalinyen*; Judge: Robert Ousley; Tobias: Skip Harris; Pirelli: Frank Kopyc; Beggar Woman: Pamela McLernon. **Swings**: Heather B. Withers & Robert Henderson. **Act I**: "The Ballad of Sweeney Todd" (Company), "No Place Like London" (Anthony, Todd, Beggar Woman), "The Barber and His Wife" (Todd) [cut from the 1989 revival], "The Worst Pies in London" (Mrs. Lovett), "Poor Thing" (Mrs. Lovett & Company), "My Friends" (Todd & Mrs. Lovett), "Green Finch and Linnet Bird" (Johanna), "Ah, Miss" (Anthony, Johanna, Beggar Woman), "Johanna" ("Judge's Song") (Anthony) [this number (and its reprises), was cut during Broadway previews, but was recorded on the cast album, and restored for the 1989 revival), "Pirelli's Miracle Elixir" (Tobias, Todd, Mrs. Lovett, Company), "The Contest" (Pirelli), "Johanna" (reprise) (Anthony) [cut during Broadway previews], "Wait" (Mrs. Lovett & Beggar Woman), "Kiss Me" (Johanna & Anthony) [cut from the 1989 revival), "Ladies in Their Sensitivities" (Beadle & Judge) [cut from the 1989 revival), "Quartet" (Johanna, Anthony, Beadle, Judge) [cut from the 1989 revival], "Pretty Women" (Judge & Todd), "Epiphany" (Todd), "A Little Priest" (Mrs. Lovett & Todd). **Act II**: "God, That's Good!" (Tobias, Mrs. Lovett, Todd, Beggar Woman, Customers), "Johanna" (reprise) (Anthony, Todd, Johanna, Beggar Woman) [cut during Broadway previews], "By the Sea" (Mrs. Lovett), "Wigmaker Sequence" (Todd, Anthony, Quintet) [only in the 1989 revival], "Not While I'm Around" (Tobias & Mrs. Lovett), "Parlor Songs" (Beadle & Mrs. Lovett), "City on Fire!" (Lunatics, Johanna, Anthony), "The Judge's Return" (Todd & Judge) [only in the 1989 revival], Final Sequence (Anthony, Beggar Woman, Todd, Judge, Mrs. Lovett, Johanna, Tobias), "The Ballad of Sweeney Todd" (reprise) (Company).

The show opened to generally excellent Broadway reviews, but still lost money. It won Tonys for musical, book, director of a musical, score, set, costumes, and for Angela Lansbury and Len Cariou. It was nominated for lighting.

After Broadway. THEATRE ROYAL, Drury Lane, London, 7/2/80–11/15/80. 157 PERFORMANCES. The number "Parlor Songs" was dropped, and a new number, "Beggar Woman's Lullaby" was added. MUSICAL DIRECTOR: Ray Cook. **Cast**: TODD: Denis Quilley; MRS. LOVETT: Sheila Hancock; HOPE: Andrew C. Wadsworth; JOHANNA: Mandy Moore; TURPIN: Austin Kent; BAMFORD: David Wheldon-Williams; BEGGAR WOMAN: Dilys Watling; RAGG: Michael Staniforth.

TOUR. Opened on 10/25/80, at the Kennedy Center, Washington, DC, and closed on 9/20/81. MUSICAL DIRECTOR: Jim Coleman. **Cast**: TODD: George Hearn; MRS. LOVETT: Angela Lansbury, Denise Lor (at matinees); HOPE: Cris Groenendaal; TURPIN: Edmund Lyndeck; JOHANNA: Betsy Joslyn; RAGG: Ken Jennings; PIRELLI: Sal Mistretta; FOGG: Michael Kalinyen; BAMFORD: Calvin Remsberg; BEGGAR WOMAN: Angelina Reaux. This production was aired on TV by The Entertainment Channel, 9/12/82. George Hearn won an Emmy.

TOUR. Opened on 2/22/82, at the Playhouse, Wilmington, Del., and closed on 7/17/82, at the Royal Alexandra Theatre, Toronto. PRESENTED BY Tom Mallow in association with James Janek; MUSICAL DIRECTOR: Randy Booth. **Cast**: TODD: Ross Petty; MRS. LOVETT: June Havoc; TURPIN: Robert Ousley; BAMFORD: Calvin Remsberg; RAGG: Steven Jacob; PIRELLI: Richard Warren Pugh; FOGG: Michael Kalinyen; JOHANNA: Betsy Joslyn, *Melanie Vaughan*; BEGGAR WOMAN: Carolyn Marlow.

Hal Prince re-staged it in an operatic version, with the number of chorus singers doubled to 32, and the orchestra expanded from 25 to 50 pieces. This became part of the repertoire of the New York City Opera. It ran at the NEW YORK STATE THEATRE, 10/11/84–11/16/84. 13 PERFORMANCES IN REPERTORY. PRESENTED BY the New York City Opera; DIRECTOR: Hal Prince; CHOREOGRAPHER: Larry Fuller; SETS: Eugene Lee; COSTUMES: Franne Lee; LIGHTING: Ken Billington; CONDUCTOR: Paul Gemignani. **Cast**: HOPE: Cris Groenendaal; TODD: Timothy Nolen; BEGGAR WOMAN: Adair Lewis; MRS. LOVETT: Rosalind Elias; TURPIN: William Dansby; BEADLE: John Lankston; JOHANNA: Leigh Munro; RAGG: Paul Binotto; PIRELLI: Jerold Siena; FOGG: William Ledbetter.

It was successfully produced again at the NEW YORK STATE THEATRE, 7/29/87–10/4/87. 11 PERFORMANCES IN REPERTORY. PRESENTED BY the New York City Opera; DIRECTOR: Hal Prince; CHOREOGRAPHER: William Kirk; CONDUCTOR: Paul Gemignani. **Cast**: HOPE: Cris Groenendaal; TODD: Stanley Wexler & Timothy Nolen; BEGGAR WOMAN: Brooks Almy & Ivy Austin; MRS. LOVETT: Marcia Mitzman & Joyce Castle; TURPIN: Joseph McKee & Will Roy; BAMFORD: John Lankston; JOHANNA: Susan Powell & Leigh Munro; RAGG: Robert Johanson; PIRELLI: Jerold Siena; FOGG: William Ledbetter.

673. *Sweeney Todd (Broadway revival)*

This production was scaled down and shortened. There were some changes to the score (for details, see the list of musical numbers in the original Broadway production).

Before Broadway. This revival was originally presented Off Broadway by the YORK THEATRE COMPANY, 3/31/89–4/29/89. 24 PERFORMANCES. It had the same cast and crew as for the subsequent Broadway run, except DORA: Dawn Leigh Stone; BEADLE: Calvin Remsberg. It was successfully received, then moved to Broadway.

The Broadway Run. CIRCLE IN THE SQUARE UPTOWN, 9/14/89–2/25/90. 46 previews from 8/5/89. 189 PERFORMANCES. A York Theatre Company production, PRESENTED BY Circle in the Square; MUSIC/LYRICS: Stephen Sondheim; BOOK: Hugh Wheeler; ADAPTED by Christopher Bond; DIRECTOR: Susan H. Schulman; CHOREOGRAPHER: Michael Lichtefeld; SETS: James Morgan; COSTUMES: Beba Shamash; LIGHTING: Mary Jo Dondlinger; MUSICAL DIRECTOR: David Krane; PRESS: Merle Debuskey & Leo Stern; CASTING: Julie Hughes & Barry Moss; COMPANY MANAGER: Susan Elrod; PRODUCTION STAGE MANAGER: Perry Cline; STAGE MANAGER: Trey Hunt. **Cast**: JONAS FOGG: Tony Gilbert; POLICEMAN: David E. Mallard; BIRD SELLER: Ted Keegan; DORA: Sylvia Rhyne; MRS. MOONEY: Mary Phillips; ANTHONY HOPE: Jim Walton; SWEENEY TODD: Bob Gunton; BEGGAR WOMAN: SuEllen Estey; MRS. LOVETT: Beth Fowler; JUDGE TURPIN: David Barron; THE BEADLE: Michael McCarty; JOHANNA: Gretchen Kingsley; TOBIAS RAGG: Eddie Korbich; PIRELLI: Bill Nabel. **Understudies**: Todd: David Chaney & R.F. Daley; Jonas/Bird Seller: R.F. Daley; Mrs. Lovett: Annie McGreevey; Beggar Woman: Annie McGreevey, Rebecca Judd, Sylvia Rhyne; Judge: Tony Gilbert; Johanna: Carol Logan & Sylvia Rhyne; Tobias: Franc D'Ambrosio & David E. Mallard; Beadle: Bill Nabel & David Vosburgh; Pirelli: Franc D'Ambrosio & David Vosburgh; Anthony: Franc D'Ambrosio & Ted Keegan; Dora: Carol Logan.

Broadway reviews were very good, and the production received Tony nominations for revival, direction of a musical, and for Bob Gunton and Beth Fowler.

After Broadway. PAPER MILL PLAYHOUSE, New Jersey, 1992. DIRECTOR: Michael Montel; CHOREOGRAPHER: Sharon Halley; SETS: Eugene Lee; LIGHTING: Ken Billington; MUSICAL DIRECTOR: Jeff Saver. **Cast**: TODD: George Hearn; MRS. LOVETT: Judy Kaye; HOPE: Jay Montgomery; JOHANNA: Rebecca Baxter; TURPIN: Nick Wyman; TOBIAS: Robert Johanson; BEADLE: Steven Harrison; BEGGAR WOMAN: Mary Beth Piel; PIRELLI: Stephen Hanan.

COTTESLOE THEATRE, London, 6/2/93–10/19/93. PRESENTED BY the Royal National Theatre; DIRECTOR: Declan Donnellan; SETS/COSTUMES: Nick Ormerod; MUSICAL DIRECTOR: Paddy Cunneen. **Cast**: ANTHONY: Adrian Lester; TODD: Alun Armstrong; MRS. LOVETT: Julia McKenzie; TURPIN: Denis Quilley; BEADLE: Barry James; JOHANNA: Carol Starks; PIRELLI: Nick Holder; BEGGAR WOMAN: Sheila Reid; RAGG: Adrian Lewis Morgan. Musical numbers were the same as in the original 1979 Broadway production, except that "Johanna" was restored. It re-ran, in repertory, at the LYTTELTON THEATRE, London, 12/16/93–6/1/94.

GOODSPEED OPERA HOUSE, Conn., 4/10/96–6/21/96. DIRECTOR: Gabriel Barre; MUSICAL DIRECTOR: Michael O'Flaherty. **Cast**: TODD: Timothy Nolen; BEGGAR WOMAN: Rebecca Judd.

AHMANSON THEATRE, Los Angeles, 3/12/99–3/14/99. This was the 20th-anniversary production, in concert form, part of the *Reprise!* series. **Cast**: Kelsey Grammer, Christine Baranski, Davis Gaines, Dale Kristien, Melissa Manchester.

AVERY FISHER HALL, Lincoln Center, 5/4/00–5/6/00. 3 PERFOR-MANCES. This was a New York Philharmonic concert performance. DIRECTOR: Lonny Price; CONDUCTOR: Andrew Litton. *Cast*: TODD: George Hearn; MRS. LOVETT: Patti LuPone; BEGGAR WOMAN: Audra McDonald; HOPE: Davis Gaines; RAGG: Neil Patrick Harris; JOHANNA: Heidi Grant Murphy; JUDGE: Paul Plishka; BEADLE: John Aller.

KENNEDY CENTER, Washington, DC, 5/10/02. This was the first in the *Sondheim Celebration* series, and ran in repertory with *Company* and *Sunday in the Park with George*. DIRECTOR: Christopher Ashley; CHORE-OGRAPHER: Daniel Pelzig; SETS: Derek McLane; COSTUMES: David C. Woolard; LIGHTING: Howell Binkley; SOUND: Tom Morse; MUSICAL DIRECTOR: Larry Blank. *Cast*: TODD: Brian Stokes Mitchell; MRS. LOVETT: Christine Baranski; HOPE: Hugh Panaro; BEGGAR WOMAN: Mary Beth Peil; TURPIN: Walter Charles; BEADLE: Ray Friedeck; JOHANNA: Celia Keenan-Bolger; TOBIAS: Mark Price; PIRELLI: Kevin Ligon; JONAS: Cupo.

BRITISH REVIVAL. Began at the 216-seat WATERMILL THEATRE (the West Berkshire Playhouse), in Newbury, England, 2/4/04–3/27/04; then, after a limited tour, it moved to the new 400-seat London performing space called TRAFALGAR STUDIOS, 7/27/04–9/9/04. Previews from 7/22/04. Then it moved again, 10/13/04–2/5/05, to the NEW AMBAS-SADORS THEATRE. PRESENTED BY Adam Kenwright, The Ambassador Theatre Group, and Ted Tulchin; DIRECTOR/SETS: John Doyle; LIGHT-ING: Richard G. Jones; MUSICAL DIRECTOR/ARRANGEMENTS: Sarah Travis. There were nine actors and no ensemble. *Cast*: TODD: Paul Hegarty; MRS. LOVETT: Karen Mann; BEADLE: Michael Howcroft; TOBIAS: Sam Kenyon; PIRELLI: Stephanie Jacob; JOHANNA: Rebecca Jenk-ins; ANTHONY: David Ricardo-Pearce; JUDGE: Colin Wakefield; BEGGAR WOMAN: Rebecca Jackson. The run extended to 2/5/05. By late 12/04 there were talks of it going to Broadway for an opening in 10/05 (pre-views from 9/05), John Doyle to direct.

NEW YORK STATE THEATRE, at Lincoln Center, 3/5/04–3/28/04 (in repertory). This was the 25th-Anniversary production. PRESENTED BY the New York City Opera; Hal Prince's staging was used; DIRECTOR: Arthur Masella; CHOREOGRAPHER: Larry Fuller; SETS: Eugene Lee; COSTUMES: Franne Lee; LIGHTING: Ken Billington; SOUND: Abe Jacob; CONDUC-TOR: George Manahan. *Cast*: TODD: Mark Delavan & Timothy Nolen; MRS. LOVETT: Elaine Paige, Myrna Paris (at the 3/6/04 and 3/13/04 matinees); JOHANNA: Sarah Coburn & Tonna Miller; RAGG: Keith Jame-son; PIRELLI: Andrew Drost; HOPE: Keith Phares & Scott Hogshed; JUDGE: Walter Charles; BEGGAR WOMAN: Judith Blazer; FOGG: William Ledbetter; BEADLE: Roland Rusinek.

THE MOVIE. There had been a British film in 1939, of the straight play. The musical was filmed in 2004. DIRECTOR: Sam Mendes.

674. *Sweet Charity*

Set in and around New York City in the mid–1960s. Char-ity is a soft-hearted dance-hall hostess at the Fan-Dango Ball-room, in the Times Square area, where dance palaces would charge a man $6.50 a half-hour to talk, dance or grope a little with one of the hostesses. Charity is a girl who wants to be loved. She has a tattoo on her arm with the name "Charlie" on it. In the opening scene she is in the park with a man who takes her money and pushes her into the lake. A crowd gathers, but no one helps her, even though she appears to be drowning. She finally saves herself and returns to the Fan-Dango, where she vows never to throw herself at another man. But, she soon becomes innocently involved with Italian movie star, Vittorio, who has just had a row with his latest amour, and he takes her to his apartment. How-ever, his girlfriend returns to make up and Charity has to hide in a closet for hours. Then it's back to the Fan-Dango, but she knows there's gotta be something better, so, in order to improve herself, she goes to the 92nd Street "Y" to attend a lecture, and becomes trapped between floors in the elevator with straitlaced accountant and claustrophobe Oscar. They begin a relationship.

He takes her on a parachute ride in Coney Island, and they again become stuck in mid–air. This time it's Oscar who calms Char-ity. Up till now she has told Oscar she works in a bank, but he knows the truth and wants to marry her anyway. However, he finally can't get over her past, and they split up. At the end, Char-ity is on her own again, still hoping to fall in love with Mr. Right. It should have had a happy ending, because Gwen Verdon won so much audience sympathy with her performance. She wore basically one costume throughout, a short black dress with splits in the sides.

Before Broadway. It was Bob Fosse's idea to convert Fellini's film into a musical set in New York in the 1960s as a comeback vehicle for Gwen Verdon. He enlisted the producers, and they paid $25,000 to Fellini for the stage rights. Fosse flew to Italy and talked with Fellini, who wished Fosse well but expressed no desire to become involved. Gwen Ver-don actually worked in such a place as the Fan-Dango for two nights as part of her research into the role, and went to most of them as an observer. Mr. Fosse's research was more extensive. While the project was still called *The Small World of Charity*, Mr. Fosse (using the name Bert Lewis) also wrote the first libretto, but it didn't quite work. It was orig-inally going to be Act I of a double bill of one-acters (Elaine May's *Rob-bers and Cops* was going to be Act II). After Neil Simon was called in to re-write it (in 10/65), it was fleshed out to two acts (besides that, Elaine May's play too closely resembled *Drat! The Cat!*). In 11/65 Neil Simon demanded and got sole credit (he had been "contributing writer"). Dyan Cannon auditioned for the role of Ursula, but bowed out in order to marry Cary Grant. Rehearsals began in 12/65. The show tried out at the Shubert Theatre, Philadelphia, 12/6/65–12/18/65. Several numbers were cut: "So, What Now?," "Poor Everybody Else," "Pink Taffeta, Sample Size 10," "Did You Ever Look at You?," "Free Thought in Action Class Song," "Gimme a Raincheck," "A Good Impression," "I Can't Let You Down," "I'll Take Any Man," "I'm Way Ahead," "I've Tried Everything," "Keep it in the Family," "When Did You Know?," "You Can't Lose 'em All," "You Wanna Bet." Word soon spread that it was a hit, and some of the songs began to be recorded. Peggy Lee introduced "Big Spender" at the Copacabana before the show opened on Broadway. The next tryout was at the Fisher Theatre, Detroit, at Christmas 1965. The Palace, on Broadway, had formerly been for vaudeville acts and one-person shows, and had most recently been a movie theater. It had just been bought by the Nederlanders. *Sweet Charity* restored the Palace as a legit theater. The original Broadway opening date of 12/28/65 was postponed due to exten-sive renovations on the theatre. Capitol Records, even though they didn't record the original company album, were the biggest investor of the show, which cost $400,000.

The Broadway Run. PALACE THEATRE, 1/29/66–7/15/67. 10 pre-views from 1/18/66. 608 PERFORMANCES. PRESENTED BY Robert Fryer, Lawrence Carr, Sylvia Harris, Joseph Harris; MUSIC: Cy Coleman; LYRICS: Dorothy Fields; BOOK: Neil Simon; BASED ON the 1957 Italian movie *Le Notti di Cabiria* (*Nights of Cabiria*), directed by Federico Fellini, and written by Mr. Fellini, Tullio Pinelli, and Ennio Flaiano; CON-CEIVED BY: Bob Fosse; DIRECTOR/CHOREOGRAPHER: Bob Fosse; SETS/LIGHTING: Robert Randolph; COSTUMES: Irene Sharaff; MUSICAL DIREC-TOR/DANCE MUSIC ARRANGEMENTS: Fred Werner; ORCHESTRATIONS: Ralph Burns; CAST RECORDING on Columbia; PRESS: Betty Lee Hunt, Fred Weterick, Henry Luhrman; GENERAL MANAGER: Joseph P. Harris; COMPANY MANAGER: Sam Pagliaro; STAGE MANAGERS: Paul J. Phillips, Michael Sinclair, Nick Malekos, *Vincent Lynne* (added by 66–67). *Cast*: CHARITY HOPE VALENTINE: Gwen Verdon (1) ☆, *Helen Gallagher* (dur-ing Miss Verdon's vacation, 7/11/66–7/25/66, and from 7/1/67, for the last two weeks); DARK GLASSES: Michael Davis; BYSTANDER: John Strat-ton; MARRIED COUPLE: Bud Vest (*Michael Vita*) & Elaine Cancilla; WOMAN WITH HAT: Ruth Buzzi (7); FOOTBALL PLAYER: John Sharpe, *Ray Chabeau*; ICE CREAM VENDOR: Gene Foote; BALLPLAYERS: Harold Pier-son & Eddie Gasper (*Bick Goss*); CAREER GIRL: Barbara Sharma (10), *Lynn Gay Lorino*; YOUNG SPANISH MAN: Lee Roy Reams, *Dennis Nahat*; 1ST COP: John Wheeler; 2ND COP: David Gold; HELENE: Thelma Oliver (4); CARMEN: Carmen Morales [role cut during run]; NICKIE: Helen Gallagher (3), *Elaine Cancilla* (7/11/66–7/25/66, while Miss Gallagher was playing Charity); HERMAN: John Wheeler (9); DOORMAN: I.W. Klein; URSULA: Sharon Ritchie (8), *Marie Wallace* (from 2/14/66); VITTORIO VIDAL: James Luisi (5); WAITER: John Stratton; MANFRED: Bud Vest, *Michael Vita*; RECEPTIONIST: Ruth Buzzi (7); OLD MAID: Elaine Cancilla; POETRY LOVER: Alice Evans [new role by 66–67]; OSCAR LINDQUIST: John McMartin (2), *Peter Lombard* (during Mr. McMartin's vacation); DADDY JOHANN SEBASTIAN BRUBECK: Arnold Soboloff (6); BROTHER HAROLD: Harold Pierson; BROTHER EDDIE: Eddie Gasper, *Ray Chabeau*; POLICEMAN: Harold Pierson; ROSIE: Barbara Sharma (10), *Carolyn Kirsch*; BARNEY: David Gold; MIKE: Michael Davis; GOOD FAIRY: Ruth Buzzi; THE SINGERS & DANCERS OF TIMES SQUARE: Elaine Cancilla (gone by 66–67), Suzanne Charney (*Louise Quick*), Michael Davis, Betsy Dickerson (gone by 66–67), Kathryn Doby, Alice Evans, Gene Foote, Eddie Gasper (*Bick Goss*), David Gold, Patrick Heim, I.W. Klein, Mary Louise (gone by 66–67), Carmen Morales (gone by 66–67), Darrell Notara, Harold Pierson, Lee Roy Reams (*Dennis Nahat*), Charlene Ryan, John Sharpe (*Ray Chabeau*), Christine Stewart, Bud Vest (*Michael Vita*), Mickey Gunnersen, Carolyn Kirsch, Lynn Gay Lorino, Janet Moody-Morris, Annie McGreevey. **Understudies:** Charity: Helen Gallagher; Oscar: John Stratton; Vittorio: Michael Davis, *Michael Vita* (added by 66–67); Nickie: Elaine Cancilla; Helene: Barbara Sharma, *Charlene Ryan, Lynn Gay Lorino*; Ursula: Charlene Ryan; Career Girl/Rosie: Suzanne Charney; Brubeck: David Gold. *Act I:* **Prologue** "Charity's Wish" (Charity's Theme) (dance) (Charity & Orchestra); *Scene 1* The park: "You Should See Yourself" (Charity & Dark Glasses) [dropped soon after opening], "To the Lake" (Orchestra), "The Rescue" (Passers-by); *Scene 2* Hostess Room; *Scene 3* Fan-Dango Ballroom: "(Hey), Big Spender" (Nickie, Helene, Fan-Dango Girls) [the big hit], "Charity's Soliloquy" ("And She Lived Hopefully Ever After") (Charity); *Scene 4* A New York street: "Stroke of Luck" (Orchestra); *Scene 5* Pompeii Club: "Rich Man's Frug" (Miss Sharma, Messrs Gasper & Sharpe, Patrons), "Who is It?" (Orchestra), "Words of Love" (Orchestra); *Scene 6* Vittorio's apartment: "This Scene" (Orchestra), "If My Friends Could See Me Now!" (Charity) [a big hit], "Too Many Tomorrows" (Vittorio), "If My Friends Could See Me Now!" (reprise) (Charity), "Morning Music" (Orchestra), "Ciao, Baby" (Charity); *Scene 7* Hostess Room: "There's Gotta Be Something Better than This" (Charity, Nickie, Helene), "Charity's Wish" (reprise) (Orchestra), "Big Decision" (Orchestra); *Scene 8* YMHA — 92nd Street "Y:" "Elevator Sting # 1" (Orchestra), "I'm the Bravest Individual" (Charity & Oscar). *Act II:* **Entr'acte;** *Scene 1* YMHA — 92nd Street "Y:" "Elevator Sting # 2" (Orchestra); *Scene 2* Rhythm of Life Church: "Rhythm of Life" (Brubeck, Brother Harold, Brother Eddie, Worshipers), "Rhythm of Life Sermon" (Chorus); *Scene 3* Going cross-town: "Subway" (Orchestra); *Scene 4* Charity's apartment: "Baby, Dream Your Dream" (Nickie & Helene); *Scene 5* Coney Island: "Coney Island Waltz" (Orchestra), "Sweet Charity" (Oscar); *Scene 6* Fan-Dango Ballroom: "(Hey), Big Spender" (reprise) (Helene & Girls), "Re-Vamp" (Orchestra), "Where Am I Going?" (Charity) [dropped soon after opening]; *Scene 7* Times Square; *Scene 8* Barney's Chile Hacienda; *Scene 9* "I'm a Brass Band:" "I'm a Brass Band" (Charity & Her Brass Band); *Scene 10* Fan-Dango Ballroom: "I Love to Cry at Weddings" (Mr. Wheeler, Mr. Davis, Charity, Helene, Girls, Patrons); *Scene 11* The park: Finale, Bows: "If My Friends Could See Me Now" (reprise).

It opened to generally excellent reviews. The show won a Tony for choreography, and was nominated for musical, composer & lyricist, direction of a musical, sets, costumes (actually for Robert Randolph's entire year), and for John McMartin, Gwen Verdon, and Helen Gallagher. When Gwen Verdon fell ill (from exhaustion), attendance dropped off markedly, and when she finally quit in summer 1967, the show closed. It was her show, she was on stage most of the time.

After Broadway. CAESAR'S PALACE, Las Vegas. Opened on 12/29/66. MUSICAL DIRECTOR: Nat Brandywynne. *Cast:* CHARITY: Juliet Prowse, Elaine Dunn (on alternate Mondays); HELENE: Paula Kelly; NICKIE: Elaine Dunn; VITTORIO: Ronald Holgate; OSCAR: Peter Lombard; BRUBECK: Jack Eddleman; BROTHER BEN: Ben Vereen; CHORUS INCLUDED: Lillian D'Honau, Ann McGreevey.

PRINCE OF WALES THEATRE, London. 12/29/66. 484 PERFORMANCES. LONDON CAST RECORDING on CBS ("Charity's Soliloquy" was cut). *Cast:* CHARITY: Juliet Prowse. Miss Prowse got raves.

TOUR. Opened on 9/11/67, at the Shubert Theatre, Boston, and

closed on 1/20/68, at the O'Keefe, Toronto. "Charity's Soliloquy" was cut, as it had been in London. CHOREOGRAPHERS: Robert Linden & Paul Glover (re-staged Bob Fosse's choreography); MUSICAL DIRECTOR: Jack Lee. *Cast:* CHARITY: Chita Rivera; HELENE: Thelma Oliver, *Elaine Cancilla*; NICKIE: Helen Gallagher; VITTORIO: James Luisi; BRUBECK: Ben Vereen; OSCAR: Lee Goodman.

THE MOVIE. 1969. Joseph E. Levine had bought the film rights for $2 million just after the 1966 stage premiere. Gwen Verdon was not a movie star, so she didn't do the film (she coached Shirley MacLaine). Two new numbers replaced two stage numbers: "My Personal Property" replaced "You Should See Yourself," and "It's a Nice Face" replaced "I'm the Bravest Individual," and a couple of other stage songs were dropped too. DIRECTOR: Bob Fosse. *Cast:* CHARITY: Shirley MacLaine; HELENE: Paula Kelly; NICKIE: Chita Rivera; VITTORIO: Ricardo Montalban; OSCAR: John McMartin; BIG DADDY: Sammy Davis Jr.; RHYTHM OF LIFE DANCER: John Wheeler.

675. *Sweet Charity (Broadway revival)*

Before Broadway. In 1984 Joseph Harris, one of the producers of the 1966 production of Sweet Charity, asked Bob Fosse if he would like to direct a revival, but Mr. Fosse was working on *Big Deal* at the time. He finally came in as production supervisor. They tried to be as faithful as possible to the original, but it was extremely difficult to reconstruct the dances from memory, from the few videos that existed, and from the 1969 movie. "Charity's Soliloquy" was dropped. "You Should See Yourself" was re-instated, and new music was added for "I'm the Bravest Individual" and "Sweet Charity." Rehearsals began in late spring 1985. Although during the early stages of production, and when the revival opened in Los Angeles and San Francisco in the fall of 1985, John Bowab was credited as director, Gwen Verdon was probably the main guider of this production. However, by the time it opened on Broadway Bob Fosse was fully credited as director/choreographer. The show got raves on the West Coast, but there was long gap between there and Broadway because Fosse was still involved on *Big Deal*.

The Broadway Run. MINSKOFF THEATRE, 4/27/86–3/15/87. 368 PERFORMANCES. PRESENTED BY Jerome Minskoff, James M. Nederlander, Arthur Rubin, Joseph Harris; MUSIC: Cy Coleman; LYRICS: Dorothy Fields; BOOK: Neil Simon; BASED ON the 1957 Italian movie *Le Notti di Cabiria*, directed by Federico Fellini, and written by Mr. Fellini, Tullio Pinelli and Ennio Flaiano; DIRECTOR/CHOREOGRAPHER: Bob Fosse; ASSISTANTS TO BOB FOSSE: Gwen Verdon & Christopher Chadman; SETS/LIGHTING: Robert Randolph; COSTUMES: Patricia Zipprodt; SOUND: Otts Munderloh; MUSICAL DIRECTOR: Fred Werner; ORCHESTRATIONS: Ralph Burns; CAST RECORDING on EMI America; PRESS: Jeffrey Richards Associates; CASTING: Howard Feuer; GENERAL MANAGERS: Joseph Harris Associates; PRODUCTION STAGE MANAGER: Craig Jacobs; STAGE MANAGER: Lani Ball; ASSISTANT STAGE MANAGER: David Blackwell. *Cast:* CHARITY HOPE VALENTINE: Debbie Allen (1) ☆, *Ann Reinking* (from 10/28/86); DARK GLASSES: David Warren Gibson; MARRIED COUPLE: Quin Baird & Jan Horvath; 1ST YOUNG MAN: Jeff Shade; WOMAN WITH HAT: Celia Tackaberry (9); ICE CREAM VENDOR: Kelly Patterson; YOUNG SPANISH MAN: Adrian Rosario; COP: Tanis Michaels; HELENE: Allison Williams (5); NICKIE: Bebe Neuwirth (4); MIMI: Mimi Quillin; HERMAN: Lee Wilkof (7); PANHANDLER: Celia Tackaberry (9); DOORMAN: Tom Wierney; URSULA: Carrie Nygren (8); VITTORIO VIDAL: Mark Jacoby (6); WAITER: Tom Wierney; MANFRED: Fred C. Mann III; RECEPTIONIST: Celia Tackaberry (9); OLD MAID: Jan Horvath; OSCAR: Michael Rupert (2); DADDY JOHANN SEBASTIAN BRUBECK: Irving Allen Lee (3); BROTHER HAROLD: Tanis Michaels; BROTHER RAY: Stanley Wesley Perryman; ROSIE: Dana Moore; GOOD FAIRY: Celia Tackaberry (9); SINGERS & DANCERS OF TIMES SQUARE: Quin Baird, Christine Colby, Alice Everett Cox, David Warren Gibson, Kim Morgan Greene, Jan Horvath, Jane Lanier, Fred C. Mann III, Allison Renee Manson, Tanis Michaels, Dana Moore, Michelle O'Steen, Kelly Patterson, Stanley Wesley Perryman, Mimi Quillin, Adrian Rosario, Jeff Shade, Tom Wierney. **Alternates:** Michelle O'Steen, Chet Walker. **Standby:** Charity: Bebe Neuwirth. **Understudies:** Charity: Kim Morgan Greene; Oscar: David Warren Gibson & Michael Licata; Vittorio: Michael Licata & Kelly Patterson; Nickie: Dana Moore; Helene: Kirsten Childs; Herman: Tom Wierney; Brubeck: Tanis Michaels; Ursula: Christine Colby; For Celia Tackaberry: Jan Horvath. *Orchestra:* VIOLINS: Abraham Appleman, Richard Henrickson, Sidney Kaufman, Sang Kim, Deborah Wong; VIOLA: Avron Coleman; CELLO: Eileen M. Folson; TRUMPETS: Glenn Drewes, Frank Fighera, David Rogers; TROMBONES: Sy Berger, Garfield Fobbs, Bob Hankle; REEDS: John Campo, Jerry Dodgion, Ken Hitchcock, Alva Hunt, Eddie Salkin; BASS: David Finck; PERCUSSION: Joseph Passaro; KEYBOARDS: Don Rebic; GUITARS: Craig Snyder; DRUMS: Jim Young.

Reviews were not great. Debbie Allen being black was never raised as an issue. She left after her six-month contract expired. In 12/86 a stage hand sterilized a prop beer bottle from which Ann Reinking took a drink on stage, and inadvertently left hydrogen peroxide in it. Miss Reinking fled the stage but came back on after a long intermission, but she had to go to hospital with mouth blisters. There was a rumor of sabotage. The show won Tony Awards for reproduction of a play or musical, costumes, and for Michael Rupert and Bebe Neuwirth. Debbie Allen was also nominated.

After Broadway. TOUR. Opened on 7/5/87, at the Royal Alexandra Theatre, Toronto, and closed on 11/7/87, in Boston. During this tour, 23 minutes after the curtain went up on the Washington, DC, opening night, Bob Fosse had a heart attack and died. CONDUCTOR: Wayne Green. *Cast:* CHARITY: Donna McKechnie; HELENE: Stephanie Pope; NICKIE: Lenora Nemetz; VITTORIO: Mark Jacoby; HAROLD: Lloyd Culbreath; GOOD FAIRY: Celia Tackaberry; MIMI: Mimi Quillin; CHORUS INCLUDED: Quin Baird, Bill Hastings, Jan Horvath, Lynn Sterling.

CHURCHILL THEATRE, Bromley, UK, 3/98; VICTORIA PALACE THEATRE, London, 5/19/98–8/15/98. Previews from 5/9/98. PRESENTED BY Back Street Productions. *Cast:* CHARITY: Bonnie Langford; VITTORIO: Mark Wynter; OSCAR: Cornell John [unusual casting for a black actor].

THE TOURING REVIVAL THAT NEVER HAPPENED. There had been talk of a national touring revival (revised by Neil Simon), bound for Broadway, starring and choreographed by Paula Abdul, with Wayne Cilento as director, but it never happened. It was to have opened on 7/13/99 in Green Bay, Wisc., followed by 40 weeks in 20 to 25 cities. It was postponed until the 2001–02 season, but those plans were also canceled.

HIRSCHFELD THEATRE, Broadway, 4/21/05. Previews from 4/4/05. In June 2002 Barry and Fran Weissler confirmed their plans for a Broadway revival for the spring of 2003 (to be co-produced with Clear Channel Entertainment), following out-of-town tryouts, to be directed by Walter Bobbie. It had a revised libretto by Neil Simon, a somewhat new conception of *Sweet Charity.* There was one new number (for Oscar, whose role had been expanded). It was a trunk song from Cy Coleman and Dorothy Fields). Jenna Elfman was the first choice for Charity, in what would be her Broadway debut, but on 9/19/02 it was announced that she had backed out. Marisa Tomei replaced her (Fran Weissler confirmed the new casting on 10/20/02). Bob Cuccioli would play Vittorio. On 12/6/02 it was announced that the Broadway opening date would be 8/17/03, and that the show would try out at the Canon Theatre, Toronto, 5/20/03–6/29/03, and after Toronto on to the Shubert Theatre, Chicago, 7/1/03–7/20/03. However, the Canon gig was canceled, and other dates became subject to change. On 2/12/03 it was announced that Walter Bobbie had quit as director, and that the Broadway run was now scheduled to begin in Jan. 2004. There was a new workshop, 6/23/03–7/15/03. DIRECTOR: Timothy Sheader; CHOREOGRAPHER: Mark Dendy. *Cast:* CHARITY: Jane Krakowski; ALSO WITH: Rob Bartlett. By 9/03 Melanie Griffith was being mentioned as Charity, but by 10/03 no one really knew who the star would be. By 10/8/03 Walter Bobbie was back in talks to direct, and on 10/16/03 he was confirmed. By that stage the producers were trying to get Marisa Tomei back as Charity. On 1/12/04 it was announced that Christina Applegate had been offered the role of Charity. By the middle of March 2004, the new Broadway opening night had been set as 4/21/05. Cy Coleman died in Nov. 2004, and this revival was dedicated to him. Rehearsals began in New York City on 12/27/04, and by the first week in 1/05 the Hirschfeld had been confirmed as the Broadway venue. There was a sneak preview in New York City on 1/19/05, then the show tried out at the Orpheum Theatre, Minneapolis, 2/8/05–2/20/05 (where reviews were mixed);

Palace, Chicago (2/23/05–3/13/05); and the Colonial Theatre, Boston (3/18/05–3/27/95). There were two new numbers, both Coleman—Fields trunk songs: "A Good Impression" (Oscar) came after "Rhythm of Life," and "If There Were More People" (Herman) replaced "I Love to Cry at Weddings" (which director Walter Bobbie found lyrically insufficient for his purposes). "If There Were More People" had originally been written for a show called *Eleanor* (about Mrs. Roosevelt). The drama continued: on 3/11/05, in Chicago, just a couple of days before the show was due to wrap up there, Christina Applegate broke her foot, and was replaced by understudy Dilys Croman (3/11/05–3/13/05). Standby Charlotte d'Amboise opened in Boston as Charity. As of this writing it was not known who would open on Broadway. Between Chicago and Boston Kyra DaCosta replaced Solange Sandy as Helen and Janine Lamanna replaced Natascia Diaz as Nickie. PRESENTED BY Barry & Fran Weissler, and Clear Channel Entertainment; REVISED BOOK: Neil Simon; DIRECTOR: Walter Bobbie; CHOREOGRAPHER: Wayne Cilento; SETS: Scott Pask; COSTUMES: William Ivey Long. *Cast:* CHARITY: Christina Applegate; HERMAN: Ernie Sabella; BIG DADDY: Rhett George; OSCAR: Denis O'Hare.

676. *Sweet Smell of Success*

Set in Manhattan in 1952. J.J. is the most powerful newspaper columnist in America (based on the real life Walter Winchell). Sidney Falcone is a grasping press agent who comes under J.J.'s wing. J.J. changes his name to Sidney Falco. Susan is J.J.'s sister. Rita is Sidney's girlfriend. Dallas is Susan's jazz-musician boyfriend. Madge is J.J.'s secretary.

Before Broadway. After the initial workshops, the word was good, and it became, to many, the hope of Broadway. It tried out at the Shubert Theatre, Chicago, 12/23/01–1/27/02, to unfavorable reviews. Several changes were made between Chicago and New York, including a new ending.

The Broadway Run. MARTIN BECK THEATRE, 3/14/02 –6/15/02. 18 previews 2/23/02–3/13/02. 109 PERFORMANCES. PRESENTED BY Clear Channel Entertainment, David Brown, Ernest Lehman, Marty Bell, Martin Richards, Roy Furman, Joan Cullman, Bob Boyett, East of Doheny, Bob & Harvey Weinstein, in association with The Producer Circle Company, Allen Spivak, Larry Magid; MUSIC: Marvin Hamlisch; LYRICS: Craig Carnelia; BOOK: John Guare; BASED ON the 1957 MGM movie of the same name, written by Clifford Odets & Ernest Lehman, directed by Alexander Mackendrick, and starring Burt Lancaster and Tony Curtis, which in turn was based on a novella by Ernest Lehman; DIRECTOR: Nicholas Hytner; CHOREOGRAPHER: Christopher Wheeldon; SETS/COSTUMES: Bob Crowley; LIGHTING: Natasha Katz; SOUND: Tony Meola; MUSICAL DIRECTOR: Jeffrey Huard; ORCHESTRATIONS: William David Brohn; DANCE MUSIC ARRANGEMENTS: Ron Melrose; CAST RECORDING on Sony Classical Cast, made on 4/23/02; PRESS: Barlow—Hartman Public Relations; CASTING: Mark Simon; GENERAL MANAGEMENT: Alan Wasser Associates/Allan Williams; COMPANY MANAGER: Lane Marsh; STAGE MANAGER: Richard Hester; ASSISTANT STAGE MANAGERS: Michael J. Passaro & Michelle Bosch. *Cast:* J.J. HUNSECKER: John Lithgow (1) ☆; SIDNEY FALCO: Brian d'Arcy James (2); SUSAN HUNSECKER: Kelli O'Hara (3); DALLAS COCHRAN: Jack Noseworthy (4); RITA O'ROURKE: Stacey Logan (5); MADGE: Joanna Glushak; ABIGAIL BARCLAY: Elena L. Shaddow; TONY: Frank Vlastnik; BILLY VAN CLEVE: Michael Paternostro; PREGNANT WOMAN: Jamie Chandler-Torns; PEPPER WHITE'S ESCORT: Eric Sciotto; CHARLOTTE VON HABSBURG: Michelle Kittrell; OTIS ELWELL: Eric Michael Gillett; LESTER: Steven Ochoa; KELLO: David Brummel; CLUB ZANZIBAR SINGER: Bernard Dotson; CATHEDRAL SOLOIST: Kate Coffman-Lloyd; SENATOR: Allen Fitzpatrick; SENATOR'S GIRLFRIEND: Jill Nicklaus; J.J.'S VAUDEVILLE PARTNER: Jennie Ford; PRESS AGENT: Timothy J. Alex; OTHER PARTS PLAYED BY members of the Company. *Understudies:* J.J.: Allen Fitzpatrick; Rita: Jill Nicklaus; Dallas: Eric Sciotto; Susan: Elena L. Shaddow; Sidney: Frank Vlastnik. *Swings:* Josh Rhodes (Mark Arvin in previews), Lisa Gajda, Laura Griffith, Drew Taylor. *Orchestra:* PIANO: Ron Melrose; KEYBOARD: Joel Fram; DRUMS: Steve Bartosik; REEDS: Ted Nash, Dennis Anderson, Charles Pillow, Ken Dybisz, Ron Jannelli; TRUMPETS: Bob Millikan & Larry Lunetta; TROMBONES: Michael Dais & Randy Andos; BASS TROMBONE: Douglas Purviance; FRENCH HORN: Roger Wendt; CELLO: Clay Ruede; BASS: John Beal; PERCUSSION: Bill Hayes. *Act I*: "The Column" (J.J., Sidney, Ensemble), "I Could Get You In, J.J." (Sidney), "I Cannot Hear the City" (Dallas), "Welcome to the Night" (J.J., Sidney, Ensemble), "Laughin' All the Way to the Bank" (Club Zanzibar Singer), "At the Fountain" (Sidney), "Psalm 151" (J.J. & Sidney) [cut during previews], "Don't Know Where You Leave Off" (Dallas & Susan), "What If" (Susan & Ensemble), "For Susan" (J.J.), "One Track Mind" (Dallas), "I Cannot Hear the City" (Dallas) [this reprise was cut during previews], End of Act I (Ensemble). *Act II*: "Break it Up" (J.J., Sidney, Ensemble), "Rita's Tune" (Rita), "Dirt" (Ensemble), "I Could Get You In, J.J." (reprise) [this reprise was placed here during previews, but cut for Broadway], "I Cannot Hear the City" (reprise) (Susan & Dallas), "Don't Look Now" (dance) (J.J. & Ensemble), "At the Fountain" (reprise) (Sidney & Ensemble), Finale (J.J., Susan, Sidney, Ensemble).

Broadway reviews were generally not good, but John Lithgow and Brian d'Arcy James got raves. Closing notices were posted on 6/3/02. John Lithgow was absent on 6/7/02 and 6/8/02. The production lost its entire $10 million initial investment. John Lithgow won a Tony, and the show was also nominated for musical, score, book, lighting, orchestrations, and for Brian d'Arcy James.

677. *Sweethearts*

An operetta. Prince Franz loves Sylvia, a laundry maid who turns out to be a princess.

Before Broadway. The original opened on Broadway, at the NEW AMSTERDAM THEATRE, on 9/8/13. It moved to the LIBERTY THEATRE, 11/10/13, and closed there on 1/3/14. Total of 136 PERFORMANCES. DIRECTOR: Frederick Latham; CHOREOGRAPHER: Charles S. Morgan. *Cast*: SYLVIA: Christie MacDonald. It ran again, at JOLSON'S 59TH STREET THEATRE, 9/21/29–10/5/29. 17 PERFORMANCES. DIRECTOR: Milton Aborn; MUSICAL DIRECTOR: Louis Kroll. *Cast*: SYLVIA: Gladys Baxter; FRANZ: Charles Massinger; VAN TROMP: Detmar Poppen. It was filmed in 1938. DIRECTOR: W.S. Van Dyke II. The movie had a different plot from the stage musical. Cast: Nelson Eddy, Jeanette MacDonald.

During tryouts for the 1947 production Gloria Story was replaced by June Knight as Liane, while Miss Story replaced Margaret Spencer as Sylvia (a role Miss Spencer took later in the Broadway run, when she, in turn, replaced Miss Story).

The Broadway Run. SHUBERT THEATRE, 1/21/47–9/27/47. 288 PERFORMANCES. PRESENTED BY Paula Stone & Michael Sloane; MUSIC: Victor Herbert; LYRICS: Robert B. Smith (unless otherwise stated); BOOK: Harry B. Smith (book revised by Fred De Gresac; later revised, for this production, by John Cecil Holm); DIRECTOR: John Kennedy; CHOREOGRAPHER: Theodore Adolphus; ENSEMBLES BY Catherine Littlefield; SETS: Peter Wolf; COSTUMES: Michael Lucyk; MUSICAL DIRECTOR: Edwin McArthur; MUSICAL ARRANGEMENTS: Robert Russell Bennett; VOCAL DIRECTOR: Pembroke Davenport; PRESS: Zac Freedman; GENERAL MANAGER: Ben F. Stein; COMPANY MANAGER: Samuel C. Brin; GENERAL STAGE MANAGER: Mortimer O'Brien; STAGE MANAGER: Fred Hebert. *Cast:* (SIX) DAUGHTERS: DOREEN: Marcia James; CORINNE: Nony Franklin; EILEEN: Janet Medlin; PAULINE: Betty Ann Busch; KATHLEEN: Martha Emma Watson; NADINE: Gloria Lind, *Rosemary O'Shea*; GRETCHEN: Eva Soltesz; HILDA: Muriel Bruenig; LT. KARL: Robert Shackleton (6); DAME LUCY: Marjorie Gateson (2); PEASANTS: Robert Reeves & Raynor Howell; LIANE: June Knight (3), *Gloria Lind*; MIKEL MIKELOVIZ: Bobby Clark (1) ☆; SYLVIA: Gloria Story (4), *Margaret Spencer*; PRINCE FRANZ: Mark Dawson (5); PETER: Richard Benson; HANS: Ken Arnold, *Phil Crosbie*; BARON PETRUS VON TROMP: Paul Best (7); HON. BUTTERFIELD A. SLINGSBY: Anthony Kemble-Cooper (8); PRIMA BALLERINA: Janice Cioffi; FOOTMEN: ADOLPHUS: John Anania; HOMBERG: Cornell MacNeil; AMBASSADORS: Robert Feyti & Louis de Mangus; CAPTAIN LAURENT: Tom Perkins; SINGING GIRLS: Ella Mayer, Florence Gault, Peggy Gavan, Gertrude Hild, Nora Neal, Lillian Shelley, LaVernn Yotti, Alice Arnold, Marjorie Wellock; SINGING BOYS:

Richard Benson, Phil Crosbie, Louis de Mangus, Arnold Knippenburg, Wilbur Nelson, Robert Reeves, Charles Wood, Raynor Howell, Robert Feyti, Tom Perkins, Frank Whitmore; DANCING GIRLS: Jeanette Tannan, Aura Vainio, Bernice Brady, Ingrid Secretan, Connie Wege, Marie Louise Forsythe, Olivia Cardone, Jeanne Lewis, Dorothea Weidner, Alma Lee, Salli Sorvo; DANCING BOYS: James Russell, Bruce Cartwright, Peter Holmes, John Ward. *Act I*: In the village square in the mythical town of Zilania: Opening: (a) "Iron, Iron" (The Daughters); (b) On Parade (Karl, Singing Ensemble, Ballet); "Sweethearts" (Sylvia, Daughters, Singing Ensemble), "For Every Lover Must Meet His Fate" (Franz, Daughters, Singing Ensemble), "Game of Love" (Karl, Daughters, Ballet Ensemble): Pas de deux danced by: COQUETTE: Eva Soltesz; CAVALIER: Bruce Cartwright; STRONG-MINDED GIRL: Aura Vainio; IMPETUOUS FELLOW: James Russell; THE ROMANTIC GIRL: Janice Cioffi; THE POET: Peter Holmes; THE MARTIAL MAID: Olivia Cardone; THE SOLDIER: John Ward [Note: "Game of Love" was replaced with "Lorelei" (Karl & Liane)], "The Angelus" (Sylvia & Singing Ensemble), "Jeanette and Her Little Wooden Shoes" (Mikel, Liane, Slingsby, von Tromp, Ballet), Finale Act I (Franz, Sylvia, Mikel, Liane, Karl, von Tromp, Dame Lucy, Daughters, Singing Ensemble). *Act II*: In the palace: Opening (Prima Ballerina), "Pretty as a Picture" (Mikel, Male Chorus, Ballet), "Land of My Own Romance" (Sylvia & Franz), "I Might Be Your Once-in-a-While" (Liane & Karl): the dance suitors: LT. KARL: James Russell; VON TROMP: Bruce Cartwright; SLINGSBY: Peter Holmes; "Pilgrims of Love" (Mikel, Karl, von Tromp, Slingsby, Adolphus, Homberg), Finale (Entire Company).

Broadway reviews were divided. There were several pans.

After Broadway. It was revived, Off Broadway, at the EASTSIDE PLAYHOUSE and CHERRY LANE THEATRE, 5/7/86–6/29/86. 56 PERFORMANCES. This was closer to the 1913 original. PRESENTED by the Light Opera of Manhattan; DIRECTORS: Raymond Allen & Jerry Gotham; CHOREOGRAPHER: Jerry Gotham; MUSICAL DIRECTOR: Todd Ellison. *Cast*: SYLVIA: Susan Davis Holmes; FRANZ: Jon Bothers; LIANE: Mary Setrakian; MIKEL: Tom Boyd; PAULA: Ann J. Kirschner; LT KARL: Mark Henderson; HON. PERCIVAL SLINGSBY: George H. Croom; VAN TROMP: David Green; ARISTIDE CANICHE: Donavan Armbruster; CAPT. LAURENT: Bill Partlow; JEANETTE: Sally Jo Ries; CLAIRETTE: Eileen Merle; BABETTE: Ruth Alison; LIZETTE: Cindy Lee Fairfield; TOINETTE: Andrea Calarco; NANETTE: Theresa Hudson. *Act I*: Courtyard of the laundry of the White Geese, Bruges, Belgium: "Iron! Iron! Iron!" (Laundresses), "On Parade" (Soldiers & Laundresses), "There is Magic in a Smile" (Liane & Laundresses), "Sweethearts" (Sylvia & Chorus), "(For) Every Lover Must Meet His Fate" (Prince & Chorus), "Mother Goose" (Sylvia & Laundresses), "Talk About This — Talk About That" (Karl & Liane), "The Angelus" (Sylvia & Prince), "Jeanette and Her Little Wooden Shoes" (Liane, Slingsby, Van Tromp, Caniche), Finale (Company). *Act II*: The Royal Hunting Lodge, Zilania; a year later: "Waiting for the Bride" (Men), "Pretty as a Picture" (Van Tromp & Chorus), "What She Wanted — and What She Got" (Paula & Daughters), "In the Convent They Never Taught Me That" (Sylvia & Chorus), "(To the) Land of My Own Romance" (l: Harry B. Smith) [new song] (Sylvia & Prince), "The Game of Love" (Karl & Chorus), "The Cricket on the Hearth" (Sylvia & Prince), "Pilgrims of Love" (Karl & Chorus), "When You're Away" (Sylvia), Finale (Company).

678. *Swing!*

A revue in two hours. Swing music from different eras. Ann Hampton Callaway, in her Broadway debut, was the centerpiece vocalist.

Before Broadway. It was announced on 5/27/99 that it would have Broadway previews from 10/1/99 (this date was put back to 11/2/99).

The Broadway Run. ST. JAMES THEATRE, 12/9/99–1/14/01. 43 previews from 11/2/99. 461 PERFORMANCES. PRESENTED BY Marc Routh/Richard Frankel/Steven Baruch/Tom Viertel, Lorie Cowen Levy/Stanley Shopkorn, and Jujamcyn Theatres, in association with BB Promotion, Dede Harris/Jeslo Productions, PACE Theatrical Group/SFX Entertainment, Libby Adler Mages/Mari Glick, Douglas L. Meyer/James D. Stern, TV Asahi/Hankyu, MARS Theatrical Productions, and Judith

Marinoff; ORIGINAL CONCEPT BY: Paul Kelly; DIRECTOR/CHOREOGRAPHER: Lynne Taylor-Corbett; SETS: Thomas Lynch; COSTUMES: William Ivey Long; LIGHTING: Kenneth Posner; SOUND: Peter Fitzgerald; MUSICAL SUPERVISOR: Michael Rafter; MUSICAL DIRECTOR: Jonathan Smith; ORCHESTRATIONS: Harold Wheeler; MUSICAL ARRANGEMENTS: Jonathan Smith (unless noted otherwise); CAST RECORDING on Sony, released on 1/25/00; PRESS: Helene Davis Publicity; CASTING: Johnson — Liff Associates & Carol Hanzel & Associates; PRODUCTION SUPERVISOR: Jerry Zaks; GENERAL MANAGEMENT: Richard Frankel Productions; PRODUCTION STAGE MANAGER: Karen Armstrong; STAGE MANAGER: Tripp Phillips; ASSISTANT STAGE MANAGER: Donna A. Drake. **Cast:** Ann Hampton Callaway (1) (absent 5/3/00–5/7/00), Everett Bradley (2), Laura Benanti (3) (until 11/5/00; *Jennifer Schrader*), Michael Gruber, Laureen Baldovi, Kristine Bendul, Carol Bentley, Caitlin Carter, Geralyn Del Corso, Desiree Duarte, Beverly Durand, Erin East, Scott Fowler, Ryan Francois, Kevin Michael Gaudin, Edgar Godineaux, Aldrin Gonzales, Robert Royston, Carlos Sierra-Lopez, Jenny Thomas, Keith Lamelle Thomas, Maria Torres. **Standbys:** For Miss Benanti & Miss Callaway: Janine LaManna; For Mr. Bradley/Mr. Gruber/Mr. MacGill: J.C. Montgomery; For Mr. Francois: Arte Phillips. **Swings:** Kristine Bendul, Desiree Duarte, Erin East, Kevin Michael Gaudin, Rod McCune. **Casey MacGill & the Gotham City Gates:** PIANO/KEYBOARD: Jonathan Smith; GUITARS: Dan Hovey; BASS: Conrad Korsch; DRUMS/PERCUSSION: Scott Neumann; WOODWINDS: Matt Hong & Lance Bryant; TRUMPET: Douglas Oberhamer; TROMBONE: Steve Armour. *Act I:* "It Don't Mean a Thing (If It Ain't Go That Swing)" (1932) (m: Duke Ellington; l: Irving Mills) (mus arr: Jonathan Smith & Steve Armour) (Mr. MacGill & Band), "Air Mail Special" (1941) (m: Benny Goodman, James R. Mundy, Charlie Christian) (dance arr: Ian Herman) (Company)/"Jersey Bounce" (1942) (m: B. Plater, T. Bradshaw, E. Johnson, B. Feyhe, Duke Ellington) (dance arr: Ian Herman) (Company)/"Opus One" (1945) (m: Don George, Johnny Hodges, Harry James) (dance arr: Ian Herman) (Company), "Jumpin' at the Woodside" (1938) (m: William "Count" Basie) (Ryan Francois, Jenny Thomas, Company) (Mr. Francois & Miss Thomas performed their own choreography), "Bounce Me Brother (With a Solid Four)" (1941) (m/l: Don Raye & Hughie Prince) (Miss Callaway, Mr. Oberhamer, Company), "Two and Four" (1999) (m: Ann Hampton Callaway) (vocal arr: Miss Callaway) (Miss Benanti, Mr. MacGill, Band)/"Hit Me with a Hot Note and Watch Me Bounce" (1945) (m: Duke Ellington; l: Don George) (vocal arr: Michael Rafter) (Miss Benanti, Mr. MacGill, Band), "Rhythm" (1998) (m: Casey MacGill) (Mr. MacGill, Mr. Gruber, Company), "Throw That Girl Around" (1999) (m: Everett Bradley, Ilene Reid, Michael Heitzman) (dance arr: Jonathan Smith, Mr. Bradley, Lynne Taylor-Corbett) (Mr. Bradley & Company) (West Coast Swing Couple: Miss Durand & Mr. Gonzales; Latin Swing Couple: Mr. Sierra-Lopez & Miss Torres)/"Show Me What You Got" (1999) (by Everett Bradley & Jonathan Smith) (dance arr: Mr. Smith, Mr. Bradley, Lynne Taylor-Corbett) (Mr. Bradley & Company) (West Coast Swing Couple: Miss Durand & Mr. Gonzales; Latin Swing Couple: Mr. Lopez & Miss Torres), "Bli-Blip" (1941) (by Duke Ellington & Sid Kuller) (add l: Ann Hampton Callaway) (vocal arr: Everett Bradley & Miss Callaway) (Miss Callaway & Mr. Bradley), "Billy-a-Dick" (m: Hoagy Carmichael; l: Paul Francis Webster) (add l: Sean Martin Hingston) (dance arr: Ian Herman) (Mr. Gruber & Company), "Harlem Nocturne" (1940) (m: Earl M. Hagen & Dick Rogers) (mus arr: Jon C. Cowherd) (Miss Carter & Mr. Korsch), "Kitchen Mechanics' Night Out" (1999) (m/l: Casey MacGill, Jonathan Smith, Lynne Taylor-Corbett, Paul Kelly) (Mr. MacGill, Mr. Francois, Miss Thomas, Company), "Shout and Feel It" (m: William "Count" Basie) (Mr. Francois & Miss Thomas performed their own ch), "Boogie Woogie Bugle Boy" (1941) (m/l: Don Raye & Hughie Prince) (arr: Everett Bradley) (Mr. Bradley, Mr. Thomas, Mr. Godineaux, with Mr. Oberhamer, and Mr. Bryant & Mr. Hong), The USO: "GI Give" (1943) (m/l: Johnny Mercer) (arr: Jonathan Smith & Michael Rafter) (Miss Benanti, Miss Del Corso, Miss Carter), "A String of Pearls" (1941) (m: Jerry Gray; l: Edgar DeLange) (Messrs Gonzales, Thomas, Gruber, Company)/"I've Got a Gal in Kalamazoo" (1942) (m: Harry Warren; l: Mack Gordon) (Messrs Gonzales, Thomas, Gruber, Company)/"Candy" (1944) (m/l: Mack David, Joan Whitney, Alex C. Kramer) (Messrs Gonzales, Thomas, Gruber, Company), "I'm Gonna Love You Tonight" (1998) (m: Casey MacGill; l: Jack Murphy) (add l: Lynne Taylor-Corbett) (vocal arr: Michael Rafter) (Miss Benanti, Mr. Gruber, Company), "I'll Be Seeing You" (1938) (m: Sammy Fain; l: Irving Kahal) (dance arr: Ian Herman) (voc arr: Ann Hampton Callaway) (Miss Callaway, Mr. Fowler, Miss Bentley), "In the Mood" (1939) (m: Joe Garland; l: Andy Razaf) (dance arr: Jeanine Tesori; vocal arr: Yaron Gershovsky) (Company)/"Don't Sit Under the Apple Tree" (m/l: Lew Brown, Sam H. Stept, Charlie Tobias) (Company) [end of the USO sequence]. *Act II:* "Swing, Brother, Swing" (m/l: Walter Bishop, Lewis Raymond, Clarence Williams) (arr/vocal arr: Casey MacGill) (Miss Callaway, Miss Benanti, Mr. Bradley, Mr. Gruber, Mr. MacGill, Company) (Mr. Fowler performed his own choreography), "Caravan" (m: Duke Ellington & Juan Tizol; l: Irving Mills) (arr: Jonathan Smith & Steve Armour; orch: Mr. Armour) (The Gotham City Gates), "Dancers in Love" (1945) (m: Duke Ellington (Miss Del Corso & Mr. Thomas), "Cry Me a River" (m/l: Arthur Hamilton) (trombone arr: Steve Armour) (Miss Benanti & Mr. Armour), "Blues in the Night" (1941) (m: Harold Arlen; l: Johnny Mercer) (Miss Callaway, Miss Carter, Mr. Godineaux), "Take Me Back to Tulsa" (1941)/"Stay a Little Longer" (1947) (both with music by Bob Wills & Tommy Duncan) (Messrs Bradley, Gruber, MacGill, Company), "Boogie Woogie Country" (1999) (m: Jack Murphy & Jonathan Smith) (Michael Gruber, Mr. Royston, Miss Baldovi, Company) (Mr. Royston & Miss Baldovi performed their own ch), "All of Me" (1931) (m: Gerald Marks; l: Seymour Simons) (add l: Ann Hampton Callaway) (mus arr: Miss Callaway & Jon C. Cowherd; vocal arr: Miss Callaway) (Mr. Bradley & Miss Callaway)/"I Won't Dance" (1934) (m: Jerome Kern; l: Dorothy Fields, Otto A. Harbach, Jimmy McHugh, Oscar Hammerstein II) (add l: Ann Hampton Callaway) (mus arr: Miss Callaway & Jon C. Cowherd; vocal arr: Miss Callaway) (Mr. Bradley & Miss Callaway), "Bill's Bounce" (1994) (m: Bill Elliott) (mus arr: Ann Hampton Callaway & Jon C. Cowherd; vocal arr: Miss Callaway) (Mr. Gonzalez, Mr. Fowler, Miss Durand, Miss Bentley), "Stompin' at the Savoy" (1934) (m: Benny Goodman, Edgar M. Sampson, Chick Webb; l: Andy Razaf) (add l: Ann Hampton Callaway) (vocal arr: Miss Callaway & Yaron Gershovsky) (Miss Callaway), Finale (Company); comprising: "Swing, Brother, Swing" (reprise) (arr: Ryan Francois & Jonathan Smith; vocal arr: Yaron Gershovsky), "Sing, Sing, Sing" (m/l: Louis Prima, Andy Razaf, Leon Berry) (arr: Ryan Francois & Jonathan Smith; vocal arr: Yaron Gershovsky)/"Christopher Columbus" (by Andy Razaf & Leon Berry), "It Don't Mean a Thing" (reprise) (mus arr: Ryan Francois & Jonathan Smith; vocal arr: Yaron Gershovsky).

Broadway reviews were good. The show was fine-tuned at various points during the run. The number "Skylark" (m: Hoagy Carmichael; l: Johnny Mercer) was inserted as a new number on 3/10/00, for Miss Benanti (and was in the subsequent tour as sung by Ann Crumb). Miss Callaway took a break 5/3/00–5/7/00 to appear in City Center's *Encores!* series production of *Wonderful Town*. On 9/29/00 it was announced the show would close on 1/14/01. It received Tony nominations for musical, direction of a musical, choreography, orchestrations, and for Laura Benanti and Ann Hampton Callaway.

After Broadway. TOUR. It was to have opened in New Haven, but in fact opened at the Ahmanson Theatre, Los Angeles, on 11/29/00. Previews from 11/20/00. It ran there until 1/14/01 then the tour pressed on elsewhere, closing on 6/17/01, at Columbus, Ohio. **Cast:** Ann Crumb, Jessica Dillan, Alan H. Green, Charlie Marcus, Scott Fowler (*Jeb Bounds* from 12/20/00), Matt Rivera, Dana Solimando, Kim Craven, Jeb Bounds, Desiree Duarte, Kevin Michael Gaudin, Jermaine R. Rembert.

679. *Swinging on a Star: The Johnny Burke Musical*

A musical revue.

Before Broadway. This show was originally produced by the GEORGE STREET PLAYHOUSE, New Brunswick, NJ, from 4/16/94. It was, at that point in time, subtitled *A Musical Celebration of Johnny Burke*. It had the same basic crew as for the subsequent Broadway run, except SETS: Deborah Jasien. **Cast:** Lisa Akey, Clare Bathe, Terry Burrell, Lewis

Cleale, Kathy Fitzgerald, Michael McGrath, Alton F. White. In 1994 it ran at the GOODSPEED OPERA HOUSE, Connecticut. It had the same cast as the Broadway run, except that Gregg Burge and Valerie Wright were in it, and Denise Faye and Eugene Fleming were not. It ran again at the GOODSPEED, in 1995; same crew and cast as for Broadway, except that Lori Hart was in the role that Denise Faye would finally take on Broadway.

The Broadway Run. MUSIC BOX THEATRE, 10/22/95–1/14/96. 19 previews from 10/6/95. 97 PERFORMANCES. PRESENTED BY Richard Seader, Mary Burke Kramer, Paul B. Berkowsky, and Angels of the Arts, in association with Sally Sears, Corey Goldstein, Howard A. Tullman, and Herbert Goldsmith Productions; MUSIC: Johnny Burke, Joe Bushkin, Erroll Garner, Bob Haggart, Arthur Johnston, James Monaco, Harold Spina, Jimmy Van Heusen; LYRICS: Johnny Burke; CONCEIVED BY/BOOK/DIRECTOR: Michael Leeds; CHOREOGRAPHER: Kathleen Marshall; SETS: James Youmans; COSTUMES: Judy Dearing; LIGHTING: Richard Nelson; SOUND: T. Richard Fitzgerald; MUSICAL DIRECTOR/ORCHESTRATIONS/VOCAL ARRANGEMENTS: Barry Levitt; ASSISTANT MUSICAL DIRECTOR/ADDITIONAL MUSICAL ARRANGEMENTS: Ron Drotos; DANCE MUSIC ARRANGEMENTS: Peter Howard; PRESS: Keith Sherman & Associates; CASTING: Pat McCorkle & Tim Sutton; GENERAL MANAGER: Paul B. Berkowsky; COMPANY MANAGER: Peter Bogyo; PRODUCTION STAGE MANAGER: Mary Porter Hall; STAGE MANAGER: R. Wade Jackson; ASSISTANT STAGE MANAGER: Daniel S. Rosokoff. *Act I*: *Section 1* Speakeasy — Chicago: THE WAITER: Michael McGrath; MAME: Terry Burrell; REGINALD: Lewis Cleale; CLEO: Alvaleta Guess; JEANNIE: Denise Faye; FLORA: Kathy Fitzgerald; BEN: Eugene Fleming. "You're Not the Only Oyster in the Stew" (Spina) (Cleo, Jeannie, Flora), "Chicago Style" (Van Heusen) [from the movie *Road to Bali*] (Ben, Jeannie, Flora, Waiter), "Ain't it a Shame About Mame" (Monaco) [from the movie *Rhythm on the River*] (Ben & Mame), "What's New?" (Haggart) (Jeannie), "Doctor Rhythm" (Monaco) [cut from the movie of the same name] (ch: Kathleen Marshall & Eugene Fleming) (Cleo & Ben); *Section 2* Depression — The Bowery: THE HOMELESS MAN: Lewis Cleale; THE STREET PEOPLE: Alvaleta Guess, Denise Faye, Eugene Fleming, Terry Burrell; THE POLISH GENTLEMAN: Michael McGrath; THE HOUSEWIFE: Kathy Fitzgerald; THE SUITORS: Lewis Cleale, Michael McGrath, Eugene Fleming. "Pennies from Heaven" (Johnston) [from the movie of the same name] (Homeless Man), "When Stanislaus Got Married" (Van Heusen) [from the movie *And the Angels Sing*] (Polish Gentleman & Street People), "His Rocking Horse Ran Away" (Van Heusen) [from the movie *And the Angels Sing*] (Housewife), "Annie Doesn't Live Here Anymore" (m: Spina; l: Young & Burke) (Suitors); *Section 3* Radio Show — New York City: THE BURKETTES: Eugene Fleming, Alvaleta Guess, Terry Burrell; THE ANNOUNCER: Lewis Cleale; BUDDY: Michael McGrath; BETTY: Denise Faye; VICKY VOYAY: Kathy Fitzgerald. "Annie Doesn't Live Here Anymore" (reprise) (Buddy, Betty, Announcer, Burkettes), "Scatterbrain" (Keene Bean & Frankie Masters) [from the movie of the same name] (Buddy), "One, Two, Button Your Shoe" (Johnston) [from the movie *Pennies from Heaven*] (Betty & Buddy), "Whoopsie Daisy Day" (Burke by himself) (Announcer/Burkettes), "What Does it Take to Make You Take to Me?" (Van Heusen) (Vicky), "Irresistible" (Spina) (Announcer/Vicky/Burkettes), "An Apple for the Teacher" (Johnston) [from the movie *The Star Maker*] (All); *Section 4* USO Show — The Pacific Islands: EMCEE: Michael McGrath [the emcee was known as Don Carter in previews]; BUZZ ALBRIGHT: Eugene Fleming; MISS SOUTH DAKOTA: Kathy Fitzgerald; MISS NORTH CAROLINA: Denise Faye; MISS RHEINGOLD: Terry Burrell; LENA GEORGE: Alvaleta Guess; EDDIE: Lewis Cleale. "Thank Your Lucky Stars and Stripes" (Van Heusen) [from the movie *Playmates*] (Emcee & Buzz), "Personality" (Van Heusen) [from the movie *Road to Utopia*] (Miss South Dakota, Miss North Carolina, Miss Rheingold), "There's Always the Blues" (Bushkin) (Lena), "Polka Dots and Moonbeams" (Van Heusen) (Eddie), "Swinging on a Star" (Van Heusen) [from the movie *Going My Way*] (All), "Thank Your Lucky Stars and Stripes" (reprise) (All). *Act II*: *Section 5* Ballroom — Hotel Roosevelt, Akron, Ohio: THE MANAGER: Lewis Cleale; THE COAT CHECK GIRL: Denise Faye; THE WAITER: Eugene Fleming; THE VOCALIST: Terry Burrell; THE MAN: Michael McGrath; THE DATE: Kathy Fitzgerald; THE WOMAN ALONE: Alvaleta Guess. "Don't Let That Moon Get Away" (Monaco) [from the movie *Sing You Sinners*] (Waiter), "All You Want to

Do is Dance" (Johnston) [from the movie *Double or Nothing*]/"You Danced with Dynamite" (Van Heusen) (Date & Man), "Imagination" (Van Heusen) (Vocalist, Waiter, Coat Check Girl), "It Could Happen to You" (Van Heusen) [from the movie *And the Angels Sing*] (Woman Alone); *Section 6* Road to — Paramount Studios, Hollywood: ASSISTANT DIRECTOR: Eugene Fleming [role cut during previews]; BING: Lewis Cleale; BOB: Michael McGrath; DOROTHY: Kathy Fitzgerald; THE SHEIK: Eugene Fleming [role added during previews]; GIRLS: Denise Faye & Terry Burrell; SOUTHERN WOMAN: Alvaleta Guess; SPECIAL ADVISER: Dorothy Lamour. "Road to Morocco" (Van Heusen) (from the movie *Road to Morocco*) (Bing & Bob) [added during previews], "Apalachicola, Fla" (Van Heusen) [from the movie *Road to Rio*] (Bing, Bob, Dorothy), "Ain't Got a Dime to My Name" (Van Heusen) (Bing & Bob) [added during previews], "You Don't Have to Know the Language" (Van Heusen) [from the movie *Road to Rio*] (Bing, Bob, Girls), "Going My Way" (Van Heusen) [from the movie *Going My Way*] (Bing), "Shadows on the Swanee" (m: Spina; l: Young & Burke) (Southern Woman, Bing, Bob, Dorothy), "Pakistan" (Van Heusen) (Sheik, Dorothy, Bing, Bob) [during previews this number replaced "Rhythm on the River" (Monaco) (from the movie of the same name) (All)], "Road to Morocco" (reprise) (Bing, Bob, Dorothy) [during previews this was not a reprise]; *Section 7* Starlight Supper Club — Manhattan, the present: THE LOVERS: Denise Faye & Lewis Cleale; Alvaleta Guess & Michael McGrath; Terry Burrell & Eugene Fleming; Kathy Fitzgerald. ORIGINAL GOWNS CREATED BY: Oscar de la Renta. "But Beautiful" (Van Heusen) [from the movie *Road to Rio*] (Miss Burrell), "Like Someone in Love" (Van Heusen) (Miss Faye) [this number was added during previews], "Moonlight Becomes You" (Van Heusen) [from the movie *Road to Morocco*] (Mr. Cleale), "If Love Ain't There (it Ain't There)" (Burke by himself) (Mr. McGrath) [this number was added during previews], "Sunday, Monday or Always" (Van Heusen) [from the movie *Dixie*] (Mr. Guess), "Misty" (Garner) (Mr. Fleming), "Here's That Rainy Day" (Van Heusen) [from *Carnival in Flanders*] (Miss Fitzgerald), "Pennies from Heaven" (reprise) (All), "Swinging on a Star" (reprise) (All).

Note: all lyrics by Johnny Burke. The composers are listed in parentheses after the name of the song.

Understudies: Mame/Cleo/Vocalist/Lena: Deborah Burrell-Cleveland; Vicky/Dorothy/Jeannie/Betty/others: Naomi Naughton; Eddie/Bing/Buddy/Bob/others: Joe Joyce; Ben/Sheik/others: Frantz Hall. ***Orchestra:*** PIANO: Barry Levitt; SYNTHESIZER: Ron Drotos; BASS: Mark Minkler; SAX: Bill Easley; TRUMPET: Gary Guzio; DRUMS/PERCUSSION: Brian Grice.

Broadway reviews were very divided. The show received a Tony nomination for musical.

680. *Taboo*

Set in an abandoned London warehouse, which was formerly the location of the hottest club of the 1980s — *Taboo*. It tells of the rise and fall of pop cult figure Boy George of the group Culture Club. The show had 16 new songs, in addition to several Boy George hits. Charles Busch wrote a new book for the American stage. In London the protagonist had been Billy, a fictional character, with Boy George as a supporting character. Mr. Busch did away with Billy and his mother, and made Boy George the star. Philip is a night club impresario; Big Sue is Leigh's closest friend; Marcus is a sexually confused young photographer in Boy George's life (a character new for Broadway); Nicola is Leigh's young muse (also new for Broadway). Marilyn is a drugged drag artist with an attitude.

Before Broadway. *Taboo* began at THE VENUE, London (a new 300-seat West End theatre, in Leicester Square), 1/29/02–4/26/03. Previews from 1/12/02. Michael Winner was at the first night of previews. PRESENTED BY Adam Kenwright; DIRECTOR: Christopher Renshaw; LONDON CAST RECORDING released on 10/14/02. ***Cast:*** BOY GEORGE: Euan Morton (until 11/16/02), *Stephen Ashfield* (11/18/02–2/1/03), *Euan Morton* (from 2/3/03); LEIGH BOWERY: Matt Lucas (until 4/27/02), *Boy*

George (5/6/02–6/15/02), *Mark Little* (6/17/02–8/3/02), *Julian Clary* (from 9/9/02), *Boy George* (from 11/18/02 with some missed performances); PHILIP SALLON: Paul Baker (until 11/16/02), *Phil Nichol* (from 11/18/02); STEVE STRANGE: Drew Jaymson (until 8/02), *Ryan Molloy* (8/02–2/1/03), *Nathan Taylor* (from 2/3/03); JOSIE: Gemma Craven (until 4/27/02), *Lyn Paul* (5/6/02–11/16/02), *Mari Wilson* (11/18/02–2/1/03), *Jackie Clune* (from 2/3/03); KIM: Dianne Pilkington (until 8/17/02), *Lucy Newton* (from 8/19/02); BIG SUE: Gail McKinnon (until 3/12/03), *Jody Butterworth* (from 3/14/03); BILLY: Luke Evans (until 9/7/02), *Declan Bennett* (from 9/9/02). "Ode to Attention Seekers" (Philip & Freaks), "Safe in the City" (Billy), "Freak" (Philip & Freaks), "Stranger in This World" (Boy George), "Genocide Peroxide" (Marilyn), "I'll Have You All" (Leigh, Billy, Philip), "(Love is a) Question Mark" (Billy & Kim), "Shelter" (Petal & Tarts), "Pretty Lies" (Kim), "Guttersnipe" (George & Marilyn), "Talk Amongst Yourselves" (Josie), "Do You Really Want to Hurt Me?" (Boy George), "Touched by the Hand of Cool" (Leigh, Billy, Slaves), "Everything Taboo" (Leigh & Full Company), "Petrified" (Philip), "I See Through You" (Billy), "Independent Woman" (Josie, Kim, Philip), "Ich bin Kunst" (Leigh), "Out of Fashion" (Steve), "Il Adore" (Big Sue), "Pie in the Sky" (Boy George). Mark Little starred as Leigh in the U.K. tour.

In 2002 Rosie O'Donnell was making plans to bring it to Broadway by 5/03, but that was delayed until the fall. There was a reading in 1/03, in New York City, PRESENTED BY Rosie O'Donnell, Adam Kenwright, and Michael Fuchs; NEW AMERICAN BOOK: Charles Busch; DIRECTOR: Christopher Renshaw; CHOREOGRAPHER: Mark Dendy. Then it proceeded toward Broadway. On 6/26/03 Raul Esparza was announced in his role. On 7/1/03 Sarah Uriarte Berry and Cary Shields were confirmed in their roles. Broadway previews were delayed from 10/21/03 to 10/24/03 because rehearsals were late in starting, and then again to 10/28/03. Mark Davies, the original writer, was not happy with the very re-vamped Broadway production. In 10/03 Jeff Calhoun was brought on board as choreographic consultant. Raul Esparza missed some Broadway previews due to a throat ailment, and Donnie Keshawarz went on for him.

The Broadway Run. PLYMOUTH THEATRE, 11/13/03–2/8/04. 16 previews from 10/28/03. 100 PERFORMANCES. PRESENTED BY Rosie O'Donnell & Adam Kenwright, in association with Daniel MacDonald, Lori E. Seid, and Michael Fuchs; MUSIC: George O'Dowd (i.e. Boy George), Kevan Frost, John Themis, Richie Stevens; LYRICS: Boy George; ORIGINAL BOOK: Mark Davies; NEW AMERICAN BOOK: Charles Busch; CONCEIVED BY: George O'Dowd (i.e. Boy George) & Christopher Renshaw; DIRECTOR: Christopher Renshaw; CHOREOGRAPHER: Mark Dendy; CHOREOGRAPHIC CONSULTANT: Jeff Calhoun; SETS: Tim Goodchild; COSTUMES: Mike Nicholls & Bobby Pearce; LIGHTING: Natasha Katz; SOUND: Jonathan Deans; MUSICAL SUPERVISOR/VOCAL, DANCE & INCIDENTAL MUSIC ARRANGEMENTS: John McDaniel; MUSICAL DIRECTOR: Jason Howland; ORCHESTRATIONS: Steve Margoshes; AMERICAN CAST RECORDING made on 2/2/04; PRESS: Barlow—Hartman Public Relations; CASTING: Bernard Telsey Casting; GENERAL MANAGEMENT: The Charlotte Wilcox Company; COMPANY MANAGER: Rob Wallner; PRODUCTION STAGE MANAGER: Peter Wolf; STAGE MANAGER: Karen Moore; ASSISTANT STAGE MANAGER: Andrea O. Saraffian. **Cast:** PHILIP SALLON: Raul Esparza; BIG SUE: Liz McCartney (until 12/1/03, when she went on maternity leave), *Brooke Elliott* (12/3/03–1/4/04), *Liz McCartney* (from 1/6/04); BOY GEORGE (GEORGE O'DOWD): Euan Morton; NICOLA: Sarah Uriarte Berry; MARILYN: Jeffrey Carlson; MARCUS: Cary Shields; LEIGH BOWERY: George Alan O'Dowd (AKA Boy George); ENSEMBLE: Jennifer Cody, Dioni Michelle Collins, Brooke Elliott, Felice B. Gajda, William Robert Gaynor, Curtis Holbrook, Jennifer K. Mrozik, Nathan Peck, Alexander Quiroga, Asa Somers, Denise Summerford, Gregory Treco, *Kimberly Rehfuss*. **Standbys:** Leigh/Philip: Donnie R. Keshawarz; Big Sue: Brooke Elliott. **Understudies:** George: Asa Somers & Gregory Treco; Big Sue: Dioni Michelle Collins, *Kimberly Rehfuss*; Marcus: Bob Gaynor & Curtis Holbrook; Leigh: Bob Gaynor; Philip: Asa Somers; Nicola: Lori Holmes, Jennifer K. Mrozik, Denise Summerford; Marilyn: Alexander Quiroga & Gregory Treco. **Swings:** Lori Holmes, Jody Reynard, James Tabeek. TABOO **Orchestra:** KEYBOARD # 1: Jason Howland; KEYBOARD # 2: Daniel A. Weiss; GUITARS: Daniel A. Weiss & Kevan Frost; DRUMS: Chris Jago; BASS: David Kuhn; REEDS:

Charles Pillow; VIOLIN: Sean Carney; VIOLA: Arthur Dibble; CELLO: Ted Mook. *Act I*: "Freak"/"Ode to Attention Seekers" (Philip & Ensemble), "Stranger in This World" (George, Big Sue, Philip, Ensemble), "Safe in the City" (Nicola & Ensemble), "Dress to Kill" (Ensemble), "Genocide Peroxide" (written by Boy George & John Themis) (Marilyn & Ensemble), "I'll Have You All" (Leigh & Men), "Sexual Confusion" (Big Sue, Philip, George, Marcus), "Pretty Lies" (George), "Guttersnipe" (George, Marilyn, Ensemble), "(Love is a) Question Mark" (Marcus, George, Leigh, Nicola), "Do You Really Want to Hurt Me?" (written by Boy George, Jon Moss, Michael Craig, Roy Hay) (George & Ensemble), "Church of the Poison Mind" (written by Boy George, Jon Moss, Michael Craig, Roy Hay)/"Karma Chameleons" (written by Boy George, Jon Moss, Michael Craig, Roy Hay, Phil Pickett) (George & Ensemble). *Act II*: "Everything Taboo" (Leigh & Ensemble), "Talk Amongst Yourselves" (Big Sue), "The Fame Game" (George & Ensemble), "I See Through You" (Marcus), "Ich bin Kunst" (Leigh), "Petrified" (Philip), "Out of Fashion" (George, Marilyn, Philip, Marcus, Leigh), "Il Adore" (written by Boy George & John Themis) (Nicola & Ensemble) [footage taken from the documentary *The Legend of Leigh Bowery*, by film maker Charles Atlas], "Come on in from the Outside" (Company).

Broadway reviews were not good. When Liz McCartney went on maternity leave there were rumors that Rosie O'Donnell herself would stand in for her as Big Sue. This did not happen. On 1/13/04 closing notices were posted. Despite a big TV ad campaign it failed because it was too esoteric. It received Tony nominations for original score written for the theatre, costumes, and for Euan Morton and Raul Esparza. Rosie O'Donnell lost $10 million.

681. *Take a Bow*

A variety show, or "vaudeville revue," originally called *Slap Happy*.

The Broadway Run. BROADHURST THEATRE, 6/15/44–6/24/44. 12 PERFORMANCES. PRESENTED BY Lou Walters; MUSIC/LYRICS: various writers; DIRECTOR: Wally Wanger; CHOREOGRAPHER: Marjery Fielding; SETS: Kaj Velden; COSTUMES: Ben Wallace; MUSICAL DIRECTOR: Ray Kavanaugh; PRESS: Dorothy Ross; GENERAL MANAGER: Ralph Kravatte; STAGE MANAGER: Jerry Phillips. *Act I*: *Scene 1* "Take a Bow" (m: Ted Murray; l: Benny Davis). Sung by Chorus Girls. Danced by Marjery Fielding's Dancers—Gloria Riley, Helen Simpson, Dede Barrington, Amita Artega, Kathryn Reed, Rae Hardin. MASTER OF CEREMONIES: Jay C. Flippen (1); MAN IN THE BOX: Chico Marx (2); *Scene 2* The Whitson Brothers (four acrobats); *Scene 3* Banjo & pantomime act. Gene Sheldon (3), assisted by Loretta Fischer; *Interlude* Jokes (Jay C. Flippen); *Scene 4* Tap Dancing (Johnny Mack, backed by Show Girls); *Scene 5* "Don't Play with Strangers" (poker game routine from the Marx Brothers movie *The Cocoanuts* [Chico Marx (2) & Gene Sheldon (3)]; *Interlude* Jokes (Jay C. Flippen); *Scene 6* Cross & Dunn (Alan Cross & Henry Dunn) (Song Stylists). Newman Fear at the piano; *Interlude* Jokes (Jay C. Flippen); *Scene 7* Let's Reminisce. Jitterbugging to "The Daughter of Rosie O'Grady" (m: Walter Donaldson; l: Monty C. Brice) [Pat Rooney (4) with one of the chorus girls]; *Interlude* Jokes (Mr. Flippen); *Scene 8* "Think-a-Drink" Hoffman, a mime (introduced by Jay C. Flippen); Intermission (introduced by Jay C. Flippen). *Act II*: *Scene 1* "The Hollywood Jump" (Marjery Fielding's Dancers); *Interlude* Jokes (Mr. Flippen); *Scene 2* Interlude with Gene Sheldon. Burlesque of a classical dance; *Scene 3* "A Study in Black and White" (Marjery Fielding's Dancers); *Scene 4* "Poetry in Motion" (ballroom dance) Raye & Naldi (i.e. Mary Raye & Mario Naldi); *Scene 5* The Murtah Sisters in a cycle of their inimitable songs (Kate-Ellen, Jean, Onriett); *Interlude* Jokes (Mr. Flippen); *Scene 6* Chico Marx and his piano; *Scene 7* Finale (The Whitson Brothers, J.C. Flippen, Company).

LADIES OF THE ENSEMBLE: Elaine Singer, Bee Farnum, Kay Popp, Doris Call, Rosemary Ryan, June Powers, Betty Francys, Marion Kay, Darlene Zito, Betty Baussher, Charlotte Lorraine, Elaine Meredith.

Reviews were divided, mostly unfavorable.

682. *Take Me Along*

Set in Centerville, Conn., July 4 & 5, 1910. The story traces the growing pains of Richard, son of Nat the newspaper editor. Richard ardently woos Muriel by quoting literary morsels that Muriel's father finds so offensive that he withdraws his ads from the newspaper. Muriel is forbidden to see Richard, who goes on a binge. They are reconciled, and Richard gets ready to go to Yale. A sub-plot involves Sid's efforts to get off the booze, get a job, and settle down and marry Lily, Nat's spinster sister.

Before Broadway. It was originally going to be called *Connecticut Summer*. It tried out in Philadelphia. Ruth Warrick was replaced by Una Merkel. Peter Glenville was fired as director (he is still credited as director on the program). The numbers "That Man's Wife," "Thinkin' Things," and "Patience of a Saint" were cut before Broadway.

The Broadway Run. SHUBERT THEATRE, 10/22/59–12/17/60. 448 PERFORMANCES. PRESENTED BY David Merrick; MUSIC/LYRICS: Bob Merrill; BOOK: Joseph Stein & Robert Russell; ADAPTED FROM Eugene O'Neill's 1933 comedy *Ah, Wilderness!*; DIRECTOR: Peter Glenville; CHOREOGRAPHER: Onna White (with Herbert Ross); SETS: Oliver Smith; COSTUMES: Miles White; LIGHTING: Jean Rosenthal; MUSICAL DIRECTOR/VOCAL ARRANGEMENTS: Lehman Engel; ORCHESTRATIONS: Philip J. Lang; BALLET & INCIDENTAL MUSIC: Laurence Rosenthal; PRESS: Harvey B. Sabinson, David Powers, Ted Goldsmith; CASTING: Michael Shurtleff; GENERAL MANAGER: Jack Schlissel; COMPANY MANAGER: Vince McKnight, *Richard Horner*; PRODUCTION STAGE MANAGER: Lucia Victor; STAGE MANAGER: Charles Blackwell, *Frank Dudley*. **Cast:** NAT MILLER: Walter Pidgeon (2), *Sidney Blackmer*; MILDRED MILLER, ARTHUR'S SISTER: Zeme North, *Patricia Mount*; ART MILLER, OLDER SON: James Cresson; TOMMY MILLER: Luke Halpin, *Rusty Parker*; ESSIE MILLER, HIS WIFE: Una Merkel (4), *Doris Dalton*; LILY MILLER, NAT'S SISTER: Eileen Herlie (3); RICHARD MILLER, YOUNGER SON: Robert Morse (5); MURIEL MACOMBER, DAVID'S DAUGHTER: Susan Luckey; DAVE MACOMBER, STORE OWNER: Fred Miller; SID DAVIS, ESSIE'S BROTHER: Jackie Gleason (1), *William Bendix*; WINT, ARTHUR'S FRIEND: Peter Conlow; LADY ENTERTAINERS: Valerie Harper, Diana Hunter, Rae McLean, *Nicole Barth*; BARTENDER: Jack Collins, *Bill Richards*; BELLE, ARTIST FOR HIRE: Arlene Golonka; THE DRUNK: Gene Varrone; PATRONS OF THE BAR: Elna Laun, Paula Lloyd, Janice Painchaud, Jack Konzal, Pat Tolson, Lee Howard, *Diana Hunter*; SALESMAN: Bill McDonald; THE BEARDSLEY DWARF: Charles Bolender; SALOME: Rae McLean; TOWNSWOMEN: Nicole Barth, Renee Byrns, Lyn Connorty, Barbara Doherty, Katia Geleznova, Valerie Harper, Diana Hunter, Elna Laun, Paula Lloyd, Nancy Lynch, Rae McLean, Janice Painchaud, *Julie Marlowe*; TOWNSMEN: Alvin Beam, Frank Borgman, John Carter, Lee Howard, Jack Konzal, Bill McDonald, Henry Michel, Jack Murray, John Nola, Rusty Parker (*Michael O'Shaughnessy*), Bill Richards, Harry Lee Rogers, Walter Strauss, Jimmy Tarbutton, Pat Tolson, Gene Varrone, Marc West, Chad Block, Bill Starr. **Standby:** Lily/Essie: Ruth Warrick. **Understudies:** Sid: Jack Collins; Nat: Henry Michel; Richard: Bill Starr; Muriel: Zeme North, *Patricia Mount*; Macomber: Gene Varrone; Art: John Carter; Belle: Renee Byrns; Tommy: Rusty Parker, *Michael O'Shaughnessy*; Mildred: Barbara Doherty; Wint: Bill McDonald; Bartender: Frank Borgman. **Act I: Scene 1** The Miller home; early morning of July 4: "The Parade" (Marvelous Fire Machine) (Nat & Townspeople), "Oh, Please" (Nat, Essie, Lily, Family); **Scene 2** The Macomber home; the same morning: "I Would Die" (Muriel & Richard); **Scene 3** The Car Barn; later that morning: "Sid, Ol' Kid" (Sid & Townspeople); **Scene 4** The Miller home; a little later: "(I'm) Staying Young" (Nat), "I Get Embarrassed" (Sid & Lily), "We're Home" (Lily); **Scene 5** A street: "Take Me Along" (Sid & Nat); **Scene 6** The picnic grounds; that afternoon: "For Sweet Charity" (Volunteer Firemen Picnic) (Sid, Nat, Lady Entertainers, Townspeople); **Scene 7** The Miller home; that evening: "Pleasant Beach House" (Wint's Song) (Wint), "That's How it Starts" (Richard). **Act II: Scene 1** Bar room of the Pleasant Beach House; the same night: "The Beardsley Ballet" (Richard, Muriel, The Dwarf, Salome, Ensemble); **Scene 2** The Miller home; later that night: "Oh, Please" (reprise) (Nat & Essie), "Promise Me a Rose" (A Slight Detail)

(Lily & Sid), "(I'm) Staying Young" (reprise) (Nat); **Scene 3** Richard's bedroom; afternoon of the following day: "(Little) Green Snake" (Sid); **Scene 4** The beach; that evening: "Nine O'clock" (Richard); **Scene 5** The Miller home; a little later: "But Yours" (Sid & Lily); **Scene 6** The Car Barn; later that evening: "Take Me Along" (reprise) (Lily, Sid, Townspeople).

Reviews were divided, but mostly favorable. Jackie Gleason won a Tony. The show was also nominated for musical, direction of a musical, choreography, costumes, musical director, stage technician (Al Alloy), and for Robert Morse, Walter Pidgeon, and Eileen Hurley. There was a well-publicized feud between David Merrick and Jackie Gleason. The show vacationed 7/9/60–8/1/60.

After Broadway. PAPER MILL PLAYHOUSE, New Jersey, 1966. DIRECTOR: Robert Ennis Turoff. **Cast:** Tom Bosley, Tommy Sands, Lanny Ross, Louise Kirtland.

MANHATTAN COMMUNITY COLLEGE PERFORMING ARTS CENTER, 3/15/84–3/28/84. 4 previews. 12 PERFORMANCES. DIRECTORS/CHOREOGRAPHERS: Geraldine Fitzgerald & Mike Malone; ADDITIONAL CHOREOGRAPHY: Dianne McIntyre; SETS: James Wolk; COSTUMES: Myrna Colley-Lee; LIGHTING: Toshiro Ogawa; MUSICAL DIRECTORS: Coleridge-Taylor Perkinson & Frederick Gripper; ADDITIONAL MUSIC/ARRANGEMENTS: Coleridge-Taylor Perkinson; STAGE MANAGER: Otis White. **Cast:** NAT: Duane Jones; ESSIE: Mary Alice; LILY: Rhetta Hughes; ARTHUR: Mario Van Peebles; MILDRED: Marchand Odette; SID: Jeffrey V. Thompson; RICHARD: Mark Wade; DAVE: Robert Kya-Hill; WINT: Michael Darden; BELLE: Vanessa Bell; BARTENDER: Kirk Taylor; MURIEL: Sandy Williams; MRS. MACOMBER: Olivia Ward.

683. *Take Me Along (Broadway revival)*

Set in 1906.

Before Broadway. This unsuccessful Broadway revival began at the Goodspeed Opera house, Connecticut, on 9/12/84. It had the same basic crew then as for the subsequent Broadway run. It had the same cast too, except that Maggy Gorrill, Sarah Navin and Amy O'Brien did not make it to New York, whereas Alyson Kirk, Nikki Sahagen, Kathy Andrini, Michael Kelly Boone, Mercedes Perez and Keith Savage, none of whom played at Goodspeed, did make it.

The Broadway Run. MARTIN BECK THEATRE, 4/14/85. 7 previews. 1 PERFORMANCE. The Goodspeed Opera House production, PRESENTED BY the John F. Kennedy Center for the Performing Arts, by arrangement with the Shubert Performing Arts Center, New Haven; MUSIC/LYRICS: Bob Merrill; BOOK: Joseph Stein & Robert Russell; BASED ON the 1933 comedy *Ah, Wilderness!*, by Eugene O'Neill; DIRECTOR: Thomas Gruenewald; CHOREOGRAPHER: Dan Siretta; SETS: James Leonard Joy; COSTUMES: David Toser; LIGHTING: Craig Miller; SOUND: Jan Nebozenko; MUSICAL DIRECTOR: Lynn Crigler; ORCHESTRATIONS: Philip J. Lang; ADDITIONAL ORCHESTRATIONS: Lynn Crigler & Allen Cohen; DANCE MUSIC ARRANGEMENTS: Allen Cohen; PRESS: David Powers; CASTING: Warren Pincus; GENERAL MANAGER: Alan C. Wasser; PRODUCTION STAGE MANAGER: John J. Bonanni; STAGE MANAGER: Bryan Harris; ASSISTANT STAGE MANAGER: Andy Hostettler. **Cast:** NAT MILLER (EDITOR OF *The Centerville Globe*): Robert Nichols; ESSIE MILLER (NAT'S WIFE): Betty Johnson; ARTHUR MILLER (RICHARD'S OLDER BROTHER, AT YALE): Stephen McDonough; MILDRED MILLER (THE YOUNGEST MILLER): Alyson Kirk; LILY MILLER (NAT'S SISTER): Beth Fowler; MURIEL MACOMBER (MACOMBER'S DAUGHTER, AND FRIEND TO RICHARD): Taryn Grimes; RICHARD MILLER (NAT'S YOUNGER SON): Gary Landon Wright; DAVID MACOMBER (DRY GOODS STORE OWNER): Richard Korthaze; SID DAVIS (ESSIE'S BROTHER): Kurt Knudson; BELLE (A TRAVELING ARTISTE FOR HIRE): Nikki Sahagen; WINT (ARTHUR'S FRIEND): Joel Whittaker; BARTENDER: David Vosburgh; THE SALESMAN: John Witham; TROLLEY CONDUCTORS/FIREMEN/TOWNSFOLK/BAR PATRONS/LADIES OF THE EVENING: Kathy Andrini, Blake Atherton, Michael Kelly Boone, Ed Brazo, Richard Dodd, Andy Hostettler, Richard Korthaze, Patrick S. Murphy, Mercedes Perez, Keith Savage, David Vosburgh, Joel Whittaker, Betty Winsett, John Witham. **Understudies:** Nat: David Vosburgh; Essie/Lily: Betty Winsett; Arthur: Joel Whittaker; Mildred/Muriel: Kathy Andrini;

Richard: Patrick S. Murphy & Michael Kelly Boone; Wint: Michael Kelly Boone; David/Bartender/Salesman: Keith Savage; Sid: John Witham; Belle: Mercedes Perez. *Swing Dancers*: Kimberly Campbell & Erik Geier. *Act I*: Overture (Orchestra); *Scene 1* The Miller home: "Marvelous Fire Machine" (The Parade) (Nat & Ensemble), "Oh, Please" (Essie & Nat), "Oh, Please" (reprise) (Essie, Nat, Lily, Arthur, Mildred); *Scene 2* The Macomber yard: "I Would Die" (Richard & Muriel); *Scene 3* The Centerville Car Barn: "Sid, Ol' Kid" (Sid, Belle, Townspeople); *Scene 4* The Miller home: "(I'm) Staying Young" (Nat), "I Get Embarrassed" (Sid & Lily), "We're Home" (Lily), "Take Me Along" (Nat & Sid); *Scene 5* The picnic grounds: "Take Me Along" (reprise) (Company), "The Only Pair I've Got" (Belle & Ensemble), "(In) the Company of Men" (Sid, Nat, Male Ensemble); *Scene 6* The Miller home: "Knights on White Horses" (Lily & Essie); *Scene 7* The Miller home: "That's How it Starts" (Richard). *Act II*: Entr'acte (Orchestra); *Scene 1* The Pleasant Beach House: "If Jesus Don't Love Ya" (Richard, Belle, Ensemble); *Scene 2* The Miller home: "Oh, Please" (reprise) (Nat & Essie); *Scene 3* The Miller home: "Promise Me a Rose" (Lily), "(I'm) Staying Young" (reprise) (Nat); *Scene 4* Richard's bedroom: "(Little) Green Snake" (Sid); *Scene 5* The dock: "Nine O'clock" (Richard), "Nine O'clock" (reprise) (Richard & Muriel); *Scene 6* The Miller home: "But Yours" (Sid & Lily); *Scene 7* The Miller home: *Scene 8* The Centerville Car Barn: Finale (Sid & Lily).

Reviews were middle-of-the-road, as if critics didn't wish to hurt a venerable old musical. Kurt Knudson was nominated for a Tony.

684. *Tango Argentino*

A dance revue in Spanish. The tango interpreted in song, story and dance by Argentinean artists.

Before Broadway. This show was originally commissioned by the FESTIVAL D'AUTOMNE, Paris. It also ran in BUENOS AIRES. In New York it first ran at CITY CENTER, 6/25/85–6/30/85. 7 PERFORMANCES IN REPERTORY. PRODUCED in association with the 55th Street Dance Theatre Foundation. Singers Roberto Goyeneche and Maria Grana were dropped for Broadway, as were their musical numbers: "Cancion desesperada" (m/l: E.S. Discepolo) (Miss Grana), "Caseron de Tejas" (m/l: S. Piana & C. Castillo), "Sin palabras" (m/l: M. Mores & E.S. Discepolo) (Miss Grana), "Malena" (m/l: L. Demare & C. Castillo) (Mr. Goyeneche), "El motivo" (m/l: J.C. Cobian & P. Contursi) (Mr. Goyeneche). Singer Alba Solis was added.

The Broadway Run. MARK HELLINGER THEATRE, 10/9/85–3/30/86. 1 preview. 198 PERFORMANCES. PRESENTED BY Mel Howard & Donald K. Donald; CONCEIVED BY/DIRECTORS/SETS/COSTUMES: Claudio Segovia & Hector Orezzoli; CHOREOGRAPHER: Juan Carlos Copes; LIGHTING: Eugene Lowery; MUSICAL DIRECTORS: Jose Libertella, Luis Stazo, Osvaldo Berlingieri; CAST RECORDING on Atlantic; PRESS: Marilynn LeVine — PR Partners; GENERAL MANAGEMENT: McCann & Nugent; COMPANY MANAGER: Daniel Kearns; STAGE MANAGER: Otto von Breuning. *Cast:* SINGERS: Raul Lavie, Jovita Luna, Elba Beron, Alba Solis; DANCERS: Naanim Timoyko (soloist), Juan Carlos Copes & Maria Nieves, Nelida & Nelson, Gloria & Eduardo, Mayoral & Elsa Maria (i.e. Hector & Elsa Maria Mayoral), Virulazo & Elvira, The Dinzels (Gloria & Rodolfo), Maria & Carlos Rivarola. *Musicians:* SEXTETO MAYOR: BANDONEONS: Jose Libertella & Luis Stazo; VIOLINS: Mario Abramovich & Eduardo Walczak; PIANO: Oscar Palermo; BASS: Osvaldo Aulicino. AND: PIANO: Osvaldo Berlingieri; BANDONEON/FLUTE: Ruben Oscar Gonzalez; VIOLINS: Rodolfo Fernandez & Juan Schiaffino; VIOLONCELLO: Dino Carlos Quarleri; BANDONEON: Lisandro Adrover. *Program*: Part I: "Quejas de bandoneon" (m: J. de Dios Filiberto) (Orchestra), "El apache argentino" (m: M. Aroztegui & A. Mathon) (Ballet) (two thugs entwine and dance the tango), "El esquinazo" (m: A. Villoldo) (Ballet) (Couples of "outsiders" dance the "milonga"), "Milonga del tiempo heroico" (by F. Canaro) (Mr. Copes & Miss Nieves), "La punalada" (m: P. Castellanos & E.C. Flores) (Mr. Berlingieri & Orchestra), "La morocha" (m: E. Saborido & A. Villoldo) (Gloria & Maria Rivarola) (two young girls dance the tango "discreetly"), "El choclo" (m/l: A. Villoldo & E.S. Discepolo) (Miss Beron) ("with this tango, the tango was

born and, weeping, fled the mud, searching for the sky..."), "La Cumparsita" (m: G.H. Matos Rodriguez) (Maria & Carlos Rivarola) (European dance hall), "Mi noche triste" (m/l: S. Castriotta & P. Contursi) (Mr. Lavie) (For me there is no consolation and that's why I get drunk, to forget our love), "Orgullo criollo" (m: J. de Caro & P. Laurenz) (Virulazo & Elvira; ch by Virulazo), "De mi barrio" (m/l: Roberto Goyeneche) (Miss Luna), "Bandoneones" (Messrs Libertella, Stazo, Adrover, Gonzalez), Milonguita (the story of a young girl of the barrio who, seduced by a ruffian, follows the road of her ruin). Comprising: "Milonguita" (m: E. Delfino & S. Linning), "Divina" (m: J. Mora & J. de la Calle), "Melenita de oro" (m: E. Delfino & S. Linning), "Re-Fa-Si" (m: E. Delfino). MILONGUITA: Miss Timoyko; RUFFIAN: Mr. Copes; RUFFIAN'S ACCOMPLICE: Nelida; BRIDEGROOM: Nelson; CABARET'S CUSTOMERS: Eduardo, Mayoral, Mr. Rivarola; PROSTITUTES: Gloria, Elsa Maria, Miss Dinzel, Miss Rivarola [end of Milonguita sequence], "Nostalgias" (m: J.C. Cobian & E. Cadicamo) (Sexteto Mayor) (Bandoneon, groan your gray tando, perhaps you also suffer from love), "Cuesta abajo" (by Gardel & Le Pera) (Mr. Lavie) (I carry my shame everywhere, shame to have been and pain of being no more), "El entrreriano" (m: R. Mendizabal) (The Dinzels; ch: Rodolfo Dinzel), "Canaro en Paris" (m: A. Scarpino & J. Caldarella) (Mr. Belingieri & Orchestra), "Taquito militar" (m: M. Mores) (Mr. Copes, Miss Nieves, Nelida & Nelson, Gloria & Eduardo). *Part II*: "Milongueando en el '40" (m: Armando Pontier) (Gloria & Eduardo; ch by Eduardo), "Uno" (m/l: E.S. Discepolo & M. Mores) (Miss Solis) (One is so alone with her pain, one is so blind in her sorrow), "La ultima curda" (m/l: A. Troilo & C. Castillo) (Miss Solis) (Life is an absurd wound), "La yumba" (by O. Pugliese) (Mayoral & Elsa Maria; ch by Mayoral), "Nunca tuve novio" (m/l: E. Cadicamo & A. Bardi) (Mr. Lavie, Mr. Berlingieri & Orchestra) (Poor and alone, you are without illusion, without faith), "Jealousy" (Jacob Gade) (Nelida & Nelson; ch by Nelida & Nelson), "Desencuentro" (m/l: A. Troilo & C. Castillo) (Miss Beron) (Your luck is so bad that when you want to put the last bullet in your pistol into your head — it won't fire), "Tanguera" (m: M. Mores) (Orchestra), "Verano porteno" (by Astor Piazzolla) (Mr. Copes & Miss Nieves), "Balada para mi muerte" (m: Astor Piazzolla; l: H. Ferrei) (Miss Luna) (I'll toss the cloak of dawn around my shoulders, my next to last whiskey will age in its glass, my death, in love, will arrive on a tango step, and I will die precisely at six o'clock), "Adios Nonino" (m: Astor Piazzolla) (Sexteto Mayor), "Danzarin" (m: J. Plaza)/"Quejas de bandoneon" (by J. de Dios Filiberto) (Ballet) (The dance floor fills with the sound of the orchestra, and under the spotlights, the marionettes embrace).

Note: program subject to change.

When it came to Broadway it was a surprise hit. Reviews were generally good. It received Tony nominations for musical, direction of a musical, and choreography.

After Broadway. TOUR. Opened on 3/5/87, at the Sundome, Phoenix, and closed on 7/18/87, at the Kennedy Center, Washington, DC. It had essentially the same cast as for Broadway.

ALDWYCH THEATRE, London, 5/3/91. Princess Diana attended the opening night. The show won an Olivier Award.

Tango x 2. CITY CENTER, NYC. *Tango x 2*, a theatrical evening of dance. 11/7/96–11/17/96. 11 performances. Created, choreographed and performed by Miguel Angel Zotto & Milena Plebs, current stars of *Tango Argentino*.

685. *Tango Argentino (Broadway revival)*

Before Broadway. This revival began in Buenos Aires on 11/3/99. The Mayorals taught Bill Clinton a few tango steps while he was in town. Then the show came to Broadway.

The Broadway Run. GERSHWIN THEATRE, 11/17/99–1/9/00. 8 previews from 11/11/99. 63 PERFORMANCES. PRESENTED BY DG Produccions (Daniel Grinbank); CONCEIVED BY/DIRECTORS/SETS/COSTUMES/LIGHTING: Claudio Segovia & Hector Orezzoli; CHOREOGRAPHERS: the dancers; LIGHTING CONSULTANT: Marcelo Cuervo; SOUND: Gaston Brisky; MUSICAL DIRECTORS: Osvaldo Berlingieri, Julio Oscar Pane,

Roberto Pansera; PRESS: Boneau/Bryan-Brown; GENERAL MANAGEMENT: Nina Lannan Associates; COMPANY MANAGER: Roberto Antier; TOUR MANAGER: Carlos Rivadulla. *Cast:* SINGERS: Raul Lavie, Maria Grana, Jovita Luna, Alba Solis; DANCERS: Nelida & Nelson, Hector & Elsa Maria Mayoral, Carlos & Ines Borquez, Norma & Luis Pereyra, Carlos Copello & Alicia Monti, Roberto & Lorena (i.e. Roberto Herrera & Lorena Yacono), Guillermina Quiroga, Vanina Bilous, Antonio Cervila Jr., Johana Copes; GUEST ARTISTS: Juan Carlos Copes & Maria Nieves, Pablo Veron. *Musicians:* PIANO: Osvaldo Berlingieri & Christian Zarate; BANDONEONS: Roberto Pansera, Horacio Romo, Ruben Oscar Gonzalez; PERCUSSION/FLUTE: Ruben Oscar Gonzalez; VIOLINS: Pablo Agri, Pablo Aznarez, Raul Di Renzo, Gustavo Roberto Mule, Walter Sebastian Prusac, Leonardo Suarez Paz; VIOLONCELLO: Dino Carlos Quarleri; CONTRABASS: Enrique Guerra. *Program: Act I:* "Quejas de bandoneon" (m: J. de Dios Filiberto) (Orchestra), "El apache argentino" (m: M. Aroztegui & A. Mathon) (Messrs Cervila, Veron, Pereyra, Copes, Borquez, Copello), "El portenito" (m: A. Villoldo) (Miss Quiroga, Miss Pereyra, Miss Monti, Miss Copes, Miss Borquez), "El esquinazo" (m: A. Villoldo) (Mr. Veron & Miss Quiroga), "La punalada" (m: P. Castellanos & E. C. Flores) (Orchestra), "El choclo" (m: A. Villoldo & E.S. Discepolo) (Orchestra), "La Cumparsita" (m: G. H. Matos Rodriguez) (Mr. Veron & Miss Quiroga), "Mi noche triste" (m: S. Castriotta & P. Contursi) (Mr. Lavie), "El entrerriano" (m: R. Mendizabal) (by Mr. & Miss Pereyra), "De mi barrio" (m/l: Roberto Goyeneche) (Miss Luna), "Chique" (Mr. & Miss Copes), "Bandoneones" (Messrs Pansera, Romo, Gonzalez, Zarate), Milonguita (comprising): "Milonguita" (m: E. Delfino & S. Linning), "Divina" (m: J. Mora & J. de la Calle), "Melenita de oro" (m: E. Delfino & S. Linning), "Re-Fa-Si" (m: E. Delfino). Cast: Miss Bilous, Nelida & Nelson, Mr. Cervila, Miss Mayoral, Miss Pereyra, Miss Borquez, Miss Monti, Miss Quiroga, Miss Copes, and Messrs Mayoral, Pereyra, Borquez, Veron, Copello [end of Milonguita sequence], "Nostalgias" (m: J.C. Cobian & E. Cadicamo) (Orchestra), "La Yumba" (m: O. Pugliese) (Mr. & Miss Borquez), "Cautivo" (Miss Grana), "Recuerdo" (m: O. Pugliese) (Mr. Copello & Miss Monti), "Canaro en Paris" (m: A. Scarpino & J. Caldarella) (Orchestra), "Nocturna" (m: J. Plaza) (Miss & Mr. Pereyra, Miss & Mr. Borquez, Mr. Copello & Miss Monti, Mr. Cervila & Miss Copes, Mr. Herrera & Miss Yacono). *Act II:* "Milongueando en el '40" (m: Armando Pontier) (Mr. Herrera & Miss Yacono), "Uno" (m/l: E.S. Discepolo & M. Mores) (Miss Solis), "La ultima curda" (m: A. Troilo & C. Castillo) (Miss Solis), "Milonguero viejo" (Mr. & Miss Mayoral), "Celos" ("Jealousy") (m: Jacob Gade) (Nelida & Nelson), "Naranjo en Flor" (m/l: H.Y.V. Esposito) (Mr. Lavie), "Tanguera" (m: M. Mores) (Mr. Veron & Miss Quiroga), "La mariposa" (Orchestra), "Patetico" (Mr. Copes & Miss Nieves), "Cancion desesperada" (Miss Grana), "Verano porteno" (m: Astor Piazzolla) (Miss Bilous & Mr. Cervila), "Balada para mi muerte" (m/l: H. Ferrer & Astor Piazzolla) (Orchestra), "Danzarin" (m: J. Plaza) & "Quejas de Bandoneon" (reprise) (Mr. Copes & Miss Nieves, Nelida & Nelson, Mr. & Miss Mayoral, Mr. Veron & Miss Quiroga, Mr. Cervila, Miss & Mr. Borquez, Miss & Mr. Pereyra, Mr. Copello & Miss Monti, Mr. Herrera & Miss Yacono).

Reviews were generally very good. The show received a Tony nomination for revival of a musical.

686. *Tango Pasion*

A dance musical, set in a Buenos Aires barroom.

Before Broadway. The show began in Buenos Aires. Its U.S. premiere was at the COCONUT GROVE PLAYHOUSE, Miami, in 11/92. It had the same cast and crew as for the subsequent Broadway run, except that Anibal Arias was replaced by Tomas Giannini on bandoneon, and Delfor Perlata, one of the company, died before the transition to Broadway.

The Broadway Run. LONGACRE THEATRE, 4/28/93–5/2/93. 6 previews from 4/23/93). 5 PERFORMANCES. PRESENTED BY Mel Howard, Donald K. Donald Productions (Donald Tarlton & Debra Rathweil), Irving Schwartz; CONCEIVED BY/PRODUCTION SUPERVISOR: Mel Howard; CHOREOGRAPHER: Hector Zaraspe (although many of the tango duets are based on the original choreography of the dancers); SETS/COSTUMES: John Falabella; SETS BASED ON paintings by Ricardo Carpani; LIGHTING: Richard Pilbrow & Dawn Chiang; SOUND: Jan Nebozenko; MUSICAL

DIRECTORS/ORCHESTRATIONS/ARRANGEMENTS: Jose Libertella & Luis Stazo; CAST RECORDING on Broadway Angel; PRESS: Boneau/Bryan-Brown; GENERAL MANAGEMENT: Norman Rothstein & Associates; COMPANY MANAGER: Julie Crosby; PRODUCTION STAGE MANAGER: Joe Lorden; STAGE MANAGER: Jack Gianino. *Cast:* RICARDO, THE ARTIST: Alberto del Solar; PEDRO MONTERO: Jorge Torres; LILA QUINTANA: Pilar Alvarez; LUCAS, THE MAITRE D': Osvaldo S. Ciliento; JUAN LAROSSA: Gustavo Marcelo Russo; SENORITA VIRGINIA: Veronica Gardella; CARMELA, THE WAITRESS: Alejandra Mantinan; JULIO CAMARGO: Marcelo Bernadaz; DR. BERTOLINI: Luis Castro; SENORA ROSALINDA BERTOLINI: Claudia Patricia Mendoza; CARLOS BRONCO: Armando Orzuza; SENORA DORA BRONCO: Daniela Arcuri; GRISEL, CARLOS'S MISTRESS: Graciela A. Garcia; ROMERO BRANDAN, THE SPOILER: Jorge Romano; ROSENDO FRIAS, POOL PLAYER: Fernando Jimenez; ANGELA, ROSENDO'S GIRLFRIEND: Judit Aberastain; RODOLFO, THE CLUB SINGER: Daniel Bouchet; FLORA ROSA, THE CLUB SINGER: Yeni Patino; ZULLY, THE LIEUTENANT'S DATE: Viviana M. Laguzzi; THE LIEUTENANT: Juan O. Corvalan; LUDMILLA ORLINSKAYA (THE EUROPEAN MOVIE STAR): Gunilla Wingquist. *The Sexteto Mayor Tango Orchestra:* BANDONEONS: Jose Libertella, Luis Stazo; VIOLINS: Mario Abramovich & Eduardo Walczak; PIANO: Oscar Palermo; BASS: Osvaldo Aulicino. OTHER MUSICIANS: BANDONEON: Tomas Giannini; KEYBOARDS/SYNTHESIZER: Juan Zunini; PERCUSSION: Jorge Orlando. *Prologue to Act I:* Time: the Present. *Act I:* Time: the late 1940s. *How could I forget you, my Cafetin of Buenos Aires?* Mi Buenos Aires querido (by Gardel) (Orchestra), Payadora (by J. Plaza) (Company), "Cafetin de Buenos Aires" (by M. Mores & E.S. Discepolo) (singer: Alberto del Solar). *Sitting at your tables which ask no questions, I wept the bitter tears of my first heartbreak.* El internado (by F. Canaro) (dancers: Armando & Daniela), El moleston (by Jose Libertella & Luis Stazo) (dancer: Romano), Taquito Militar (by M. Mores) (dancers: Romano & Graciela), "Nostalgias" (by E. Cadicamo & J.C. Cobian) (singer: Daniel Bouchet). *I lift my glass and make a toast to the cruel misfortunes of love.* Chique (by Brignolo) (dancers: Luis & Claudia), "Uno" (by M. Mores) (singer: Yeni Patino). *One crawls and slithers between thorns simply trying to feel love.* La Cumparsita (by G.H. Matos Rodriguez) (Orchestra), "Recitado" (Alberto del Solar). *I wasted my life shuffling empty dreams.* "Canto" (Daniel Bouchet). *If you only knew how much I still love you.* Danza (Juan & Viviana), Copete (anonymous) (dancers: Fernando & Judit), Milonga del 900 (by Piana) (dancers: Gustavo, Fernando, Marcelo, Osvaldo, Armando, Juan), La tablada (by Canaro) (dancers: Osvaldo & Graciela), Ojos negros (anonymous) (Gunilla, Osvaldo, Alberto), Hotel Victoria (by Latasa) (dancers: Yeni, Juan, Osvaldo, Romano, Armando, Gustavo), El moleston (reprise) (dancers: Romano & Daniela), El Firulete (by M. Mores) (dancers: Armando, Daniela, Gustavo, Alejandra, Luis, Claudia, Juan, Viviana), Ojos negros (reprise) (dancers: Luis, Gunilla, Juan), Orgullo criollo (by J. de Caro & P. Laurenz) (dancers: Gustavo & Alejandra), Preludio a Francini (by Mario Abramovich & Luis Stazo) (dancers: Luis & Claudia), "El dia que me quieras" (by Gardel & Le Pera) (singers: Daniel Bouchet & Yeni Patino). *The soft sound of your breathing caresses my daydreams.* Milonga de mis amores (by P. Laurenz) (dancers: Fernando & Judit), Responso (by A. Troilo) (dancers: Romano & Claudia), Re-fa-si (by E. Delfino) (Company), Canaro en Paris (by A. Scarpino) (Orchestra), Orchestra Solo (Sexteto Mayor), Finale (Company). *Act II:* Time: the Present. *I am because you have dreamed me.* Rapsodia de Arrabal (by Jose Libertella) (Orchestra), "Balada para un loco" (by Astor Piazzolla & H. Ferrer) (singer: Alberto del Solar; dancers: Jorge & Pilar), Bailonga (by M. Mores) (Company), Melancolico (by J. Plaza) (dancers: Armando, Daniela, Osvaldo, Graciela), "A media luz" (by Donato) (singers: Yeni Patino & Daniel Bouchet). *When the lights are low, love casts a magic spell.* Seleccion de Milongas (by P. Castellanos, A. Villoldo, P. Laurenz) (dancers: Juan, Gustavo, Fernando, Romano), "Asi se baila el tango" (by Marvil) (singer: Alberto del Solar). *This is how you tango; the arm, like a serpent, coils around the waist.* Quejas de bandoneon (by J. de Dios Filiberto) (dancers: Jorge & Pilar), Celos (by Jacob Gade) (Sexteto Mayor), "Balada para mi vida" (by Jose Libertella & H. Ferrer) (singers: Alberto del Solar, Yeni Patino, Daniel Bouchet). *We will be lovers forever, passionate for eternity, two fires of God.* Melancolico Buenos Aires (by Astor Piazzolla) (dancers: Marcelo & Veronica), Libertango (by Astor Piazzolla) (dancers: Graciela, Viviana, Alejandra, Judit, Osvaldo, Juan, Gustavo,

Fernando), Verano porteno (by Astor Piazzolla) (dancers: Juan & Jorge), Fuga y misterio (by Astor Piazzolla) (dancers: Marcelo, Luis, Gustavo, Viviana), "Balada para un loco" (reprise) (dancers: Luis, Pilar, Gunilla; singer: Alberto del Solar). *Love me just as I am; loco, loco, loco!* Adios Nonino (by Astor Piazzolla) (Sexteto Mayor), Provocacion: (dancers: Jorge, Pilar, Company), Paris otonal (by Libertella), Rapsodia de Arrabal (reprise), Primavera portena (by Astor Piazzolla) [end of Provocacion sequence], Onda 9 (by Astor Piazzolla) (Company).

Broadway reviews were mostly bad.

After Broadway. LYRIC THEATRE, London, 5/26/99–7/17/99. Previews from 5/24/99; DOMINION THEATRE, 3/21/00–3/23/00.

687. *The Tap Dance Kid*

Willie is a ten-year-old black lad who dreams of being a tap dancer on the New York stage. His lawyer father, William, is against such a move, fearing that this would be a move backwards into racial stereotyping. However, with the aid of Willie's uncle, Dipsey, a professional dancer, the boy is able to realize his dream. Set in New York City's Roosevelt Island and Manhattan.

Before Broadway. Evelyn Barron discovered the Louise Fitzhugh book in 1977 and turned it into a straight (i.e. not a musical) afternoon TV show called *The Tap Dance Kid*, which won three Emmys. Miss Barron then hired Charles Blackwell, who had played the father on TV, to write the libretto. A national audition for Willie produced over 1,000 applicants, but Alfonso Ribeiro, who couldn't tap dance at all, was picked by director Vivian Matalon and taught to tap dance by Danny Daniels, the choreographer. This was the scene-by-scene breakdown during Broadway previews: *Prologue. Act I: Scene 1* Dining room: "Another Day" (Ginnie, Emma, Dulcie); *Scene 2* Little Rio Club; *Scene 3* William's study: "Four Strikes Against Me" (Emma), "Class Act" (Ginny, Dipsey, Daddy Bates); *Scene 4* Playground: "They Never Hear What I Say" (Emma & Willie), "Dancing is Everything" (Willie); *Scene 5* Manhattan: "Crosstown" (Willie & New Yorkers); *Scene 6* The Westway Hotel ballroom: "Fabulous Feet" (Dipsey, Carole, Dancers), "I Could Get Used to Him" (Carole & Dancers); *Scene 7* William's study; *Scene 8* Terrace: "Man in the Moon" (Dipsey). *Act II: Scene 1* Dining room: "Like Him" (Ginnie & Emma); *Scene 2* Dipsey's loft: "My Luck is Changing" (Dipsey), "I Remember How it Was" (Ginnie); *Scene 3* Willie's bedroom: "Someday" (Emma & Willie}, "Lullabye" (Ginnie), "Tap Tap" (Daddy Bates, Willie, Dipsey); *Scene 4* Manhattan Tram station: "Dance if it Makes You Happy" (Willie, Dipsey, Daddy Bates, Carole, Dancers); *Scene 5* William's study; *Scene 6* Dipsey's loft: "William's Song" (William); *Scene 7* Outside Dipsey's loft: Finale: "Class Act" (reprise) (The Family).

The Broadway Run. BROADHURST THEATRE, 12/21/83–3/11/84; MINSKOFF THEATRE, 3/27/84–8/11/85. 38 previews. Total of 669 PERFORMANCES. PRESENTED BY Stanley White, Evelyn Barron, Harvey J. Klaris, and Michel Stuart, in association with Michel Kleinman Productions; MUSIC: Henry Krieger; LYRICS: Robert Lorick; BOOK: Charles Blackwell; BASED ON the novel *Nobody's Family is Going to Change*, by Louise Fitzhugh; DIRECTOR: Vivian Matalon; CHOREOGRAPHER: Danny Daniels; ASSOCIATE CHOREOGRAPHER: D.J. Giagni (Danny Daniels' son); SETS: Michael J. Hotopp & Paul de Pass; COSTUMES: William Ivcy Long; LIGHTING: Richard Nelson; SOUND: Jack Mann; MUSICAL SUPERVISOR/ORCHESTRATIONS/VOCAL ARRANGEMENTS: Harold Wheeler; MUSICAL DIRECTOR/VOCAL DIRECTOR: Don Jones; DANCE MUSIC ARRANGEMENTS: Peter Howard; PRESS: Jacksina & Freedman; CASTING: Julie Hughes & Barry Moss; GENERAL MANAGEMENT: Theatre Now; COMPANY MANAGER: Mark A. Schweppe; PRODUCTION STAGE MANAGER: Joe Lorden; STAGE MANAGER: Jack Gianino; ASSISTANT STAGE MANAGER: Ed Fitzgerald. **Cast:** WILLIE SHERIDAN: Alfonso Ribeiro (6), *Jimmy Tate* (from 6/26/84), *Savion Glover* (from 11/84); GINNIE SHERIDAN: Hattie Winston (1) ☆, *Gail Nelson* (from 6/84); DULCIE: Barbara Montgomery (8); EMMA SHERIDAN: Martine Allard (5); WILLIAM SHERIDAN: Samuel E. Wright (1) ☆, *Ira Hawkins* (from 2/5/85); DIPSEY BATES: Hinton Battle (1) ☆, *Eugene Fleming* (from 7/8/85); MONA: Karen Paskow; CAROLE: Jackie Lowe (7); DADDY BATES: Alan Weeks (4); WINSLOW: Michael

Blevins, *Tony Jaeger*; JOE: Jackie Patterson, *Byron Easley* [this role was added during previews]; OFFSTAGE VOICE: Lloyd Culbreath [this role was added during previews]; LITTLE RIO DANCERS & NEW YORKERS: Leah Bass, Kevin Berdini, Michael Blevins, Karen Curlee, Suzzanne Douglas, Rick Emery, Karen E. Fraction, D.J. Giagni, J.J. Jepson, Rodney Alan McGuire, Karen Paskow, Jackie Patterson, Mayme Paul, Jamie M. Pisano, Ken Prescott, Oliver Woodall (added during previews), James Young. *Tony Jaeger, Kimberly Meyers, Gary Sullivan.* **Standby**: William: Donny Burks. **Understudies**: Dipsey/Daddy: Jackie Patterson, *Lloyd Culbreath*; Ginnie: Suzzanne Douglas, *Vanessa Shaw*; Emma: Tracey Mitchem, *Michelle Weeks*; Willie: David Calloway & Jimmy Tate, *Hassoun Tatum*; Carole/Dulcie: Leah Bass; Winslow: D.J. Giagni, *Kevin Berdini, J.J. Jepson*; Mona: Jamie M. Pisano; Joe: Lloyd Culbreath. **Swings**: Lloyd Culbreath, Linda von Germer. **Act I: Scene 1** Dining room: "Another Day" (Ginnie, Emma, Willie) [this number was replaced for the subsequent national tour by "Dipsey's Comin' Over" (Willie)]; **Scene 2** Dipsey's loft [for the national tour this scene was set in a Rehearsal studio]: "High Heels" (Dipsey, Carole, Dancers) [this number was only in the national tour], "Something Better, Something More" (Dipsey) [this number was only in the national tour]; **Scene 3** William's study: "Four Strikes Against Me" (Emma), "Class Act" (Ginnie, Dipsey, Daddy); **Scene 4** Playground: "They Never Hear What I Say" (Emma & Willie), "Dancing is Everything" (Willie); **Scene 5** Manhattan: "Crosstown" (Willie & New Yorkers); **Scene 6** The Westway Hotel ballroom: "Fabulous Feet" (Dipsey, Carole, Dancers), "I Could Get Used to Him" (Carole & Dancers); **Scene 7** William's study; Scene 8 Terrace: "Man in the Moon" (Dipsey). **Act II: Scene 1** Dining room: "Like Him" (Emma & Ginnie); **Scene 2** Playground: "Someday" (Emma & Willie); **Scene 3** Dipsey's loft [for the national tour this scene became Scene 4, and was set in a Rehearsal studio]: "My Luck is Changing" (Dipsey), "Dipsey's Vaudeville" (Dancers, Dipsey, Carole) [this number was only in the national tour, in the new Scene 4], "I Remember How it Was" (Ginnie); **Scene 4** Willie's bedroom [this became Scene 5 in the national tour]: "Lullabye" (Ginnie): "Tap Tap" (Daddy, Willie, Dipsey); **Scene 5** Manhattan tram station [this scene was dropped for the national tour]: "Dance if it Makes You Happy" (Willie, Dipsey, Daddy, Carole, Dancers); **Scene 6** Dipsey's loft [for the national tour, Scene 6 was set in a Theatre]: "William's Song" (William); **Scene 7** Street: Finale: "Class Act" (reprise) (The Family).

Reviews were divided. The show won Tony Awards for choreography and for Hinton Battle, and was nominated for musical, book, direction of a musical, and for Samuel E. Wright and Martine Allard. The book let it down, but the dancing (and TV advertising) kept it on Broadway for 18 months.

After Broadway. TOUR. Opened on 8/4/85, in San Francisco, closed, then re-opened on 10/4/86, at Purdue, Lafayette, Indiana, and finally closed on 1/4/87, at the Mechanic Theatre, Baltimore. The book and score were drastically revised. DIRECTOR: Jerry Zaks. **Cast:** WILLIE: Dule Hill; GINNIE: Monica Page; EMMA: Martine Allard; WILLIAM: Ben Harney, *Chuck Cooper*; DIPSEY: Hinton Battle, *Eugene Fleming*; CAROLE: Theresa Hayes; DADDY BATES: Harold Nicholas; WINSLOW: Mark Santoro; CHORUS INCLUDED: J.J. Jepson, Maryellen Scilla.

688. *Teddy and Alice*

Theodore Roosevelt's first White House term, with the stress on family ties — especially Teddy's boisterously patriotic attitudes and his daughter Alice's escapades. Edith is T.R.'s second wife. Nick is Alice's suitor.

Before Broadway. When Stone Widney was doing research for Alan Jay Lerner's musical *1600 Pennsylvania Avenue*, he had enough unused material left over for a musical about Teddy Roosevelt and his flamboyant daughter Alice Longworth. Mr. Lerner was adviser, and even though the show was produced after his death, he got credit as artistic consultant. The show took seven years to get off the ground, during which time Robert Preston was the first choice for the lead; a backers audition was held on TV. Incidentally, Jerome Alden had already written a play about Teddy called *Bully*. After spending a long time on *Teddy and Alice*, Stone Widney was replaced as director by John Driver during tryouts at Tampa Bay Performing Arts Center.

The Broadway Run. MINSKOFF THEATRE, 11/12/87–1/17/88. 11 previews. 77 PERFORMANCES. PRESENTED BY Hinks Shimberg, in association with Jon Cutler; MUSIC: John Philip Sousa; LYRICS: Hal Hackady; BOOK: Jerome Alden; ADAPTATIONS & FOUR ORIGINAL SONGS: Richard Knapp; DIRECTOR: John Driver; CHOREOGRAPHER: Donald Saddler; ADDITIONAL CHOREOGRAPHY: D.J. Giagni; SETS: Robin Wagner; COSTUMES: Theoni V. Aldredge; LIGHTING: Tharon Musser; SOUND: Peter Fitzgerald; MUSICAL SUPERVISOR/VOCAL ARRANGEMENTS: Donald Pippin; MUSICAL DIRECTOR: Larry Blank; ORCHESTRATIONS: Jim Tyler; DANCE MUSIC ARRANGEMENTS: Gordon Lowry Harrell; PRESS: Jeffrey Richards Associates; CASTING: Myers/Teschner; ARTISTIC CONSULTANT: Alan Jay Lerner; GENERAL MANAGEMENT: Sylrich Management; COMPANY MANAGER: G. Warren McClane; PRODUCTION STAGE MANAGER: Mary Porter Hall; STAGE MANAGER: Marc Schlackman; ASSISTANT STAGE MANAGER: John C. McNamara. *Cast:* JAMES AMOS: Tony Floyd (13); BELLE HAGNER: Karen Ziemba (15); J.P. MORGAN: David Green (10); HARRIMAN: John Witham (11); HENRY CABOT LODGE: Raymond Thorne (6); ELIHU ROOT: Gordon Stanley (7); WILLIAM HOWARD TAFT: Michael McCarty (5); THEODORE "TEDDY" ROOSEVELT: Len Cariou (1) ☆; EDITH ROOSEVELT: Beth Fowler (3); TED ROOSEVELT JR.: Robert D. Cavanaugh (17); KERMIT ROOSEVELT: Seth Granger (19); ETHEL ROOSEVELT: Sarah Reynolds (20); ARCHIE ROOSEVELT: Richard H. Blake (16); QUENTIN ROOSEVELT: John Daman (18); IDA TARBELL: Mary Jay (12); WHEELER: John Remme (9); OFFICER O'MALLEY: Christopher Wells (14); ALICE ROOSEVELT: Nancy Hume (4); ELEANOR ROOSEVELT: Nancy Opel (8); NICK LONGWORTH: Ron Raines (2); FRANKLIN ROOSEVELT: Alex Kramarevsky; ADMIRAL MURPHY: David Green (10); SAMUEL GOMPERS: John Witham (11); ELLIOTT ROOSEVELT: Ken Hilliard; GHOST: Pamela McLernon; SERVANTS/REPORTERS/TEA PARTY LADIES/MARINES/AMBASSADORS: Ellyn Arons, Ruth Bormann, Kathleen Gray, Ken Hilliard, Alex Kramarevsky, Mark Lazore, Keith Locke, Pamela McLernon, Elizabeth Mozer, Keith Savage, Jeff Shade. *Understudies:* Teddy: Gordon Stanley; Edith: Mary Jay; Alice: Karen Ziemba; Nick: Christopher Wells; Morgan/Harriman/Lodge: Tom Boyd; Root/Taft/Murphy/Gompers: Tom Boyd; Ida: Ellyn Arons; Ethel: Diana Stadlen; Ted Jr.: Seth Granger; Kermit/Quentin/Archie: Andrew Harrison Leeds; Belle: Kathleen Gray; Eleanor: Ruth Bormann; Amos: Travis Layne Wright; Wheeler/O'Malley: Keith Locke. *Swings:* Kaylyn Dillehay, Travis Layne Wright. *Musicians:* REEDS: George Berg & Ken Dybisz; VIOLINS: Abe Appleman, Sandra Billingslea, A. Ceroni, Katsuko Esaki; TRUMPETS: Neil Balm & John Bova; GUITAR: A. Cesarano; HARP: Katherine Easter; BASS: William Ellison; CELLO: S. Figne; PERCUSSION: David Carey. *Act I: Prelude* "The Thunderer" (Orchestra); *Scene 1* Interior of White House; fall, 1901, shortly after President McKinley's assassination: "This House" (Teddy, Family, Friends, Staff, Reporters); *Scene 2* White House yard: "But Not Right Now" (Alice); *Scene 3* The President's office: "She's Got to Go" (Taft, Root, Lodge); *Scene 4* Alice's dressing room; different day: "The Fourth of July" (Alice & Eleanor); *Scene 5* Presidential bedroom suite: "Charge" (Teddy, Edith, Ted Jr., Kermit, Ethel, Archie, Quentin), "Battle Lines" (Edith); *Scene 6* Rose Garden of the White House; later that evening: "The Coming-Out Party Dance" (Teddy, Alice, Nick, Edith, Guests), "Leg o' Mutton" (Alice, Nick, Guests), "Not Love" (Nick, Taft, Root, Lodge); *Scene 7* Public area in the White House; several months later: "Her Father's Daughter" (Teddy), "Perfect for Each Other" (Nick); *Scene 8* North Portico of the White House; three weeks later: "He's Got to Go" (Taft, Root, Lodge, Nick); *Scene 9* Republican National Convention; summer, 1904: "Wave the Flag" (Teddy, Edith, Eleanor, Roosevelt Children, Harriman, Morgan, Hecklers, Supporters). *Act II: Entr'acte* (Orchestra); *Scene 1* Main Entrance Hall, White House; summer, 1904: "Fourth of July" (reprise) (Teddy), "Fourth of July" (reprise) (Alice, Eleanor, Edith, Ladies); *Scene 2* Area of birch trees, near the White House; same day: "(You've) Nothing to Lose" (Nick & Alice); *Scene 3* Election day: "Election Eve" (Taft, Root, Lodge, Gompers, Morgan, Reporters); *Scene 4* The President's office: "Perfect for Each Other" (reprise) (Alice); *Scene 5* Campsite near the White House, in the woods: "Can I Let Her Go?" (Teddy); Scene 6 East Room of the White House: "Private Thoughts" (Taft, Root, Lodge, Edith, Ted, Ethel, Kermit, Archie, Quentin, Servants, Staff, Reporters), "This House" (reprise) (Teddy, Edith, Guests).

Broadway reviews were not good.

After Broadway. SEVEN ANGELS THEATRE, Waterbury, Conn., 10/19/96. This was a revised version. DIRECTOR: Richard Sabellico; CHOREOGRAPHERS: Richard Sabellico & Don Johanson; SETS: Robert John Andrusko; COSTUMES: Theoni V. Aldredge; LIGHTING: Peter Petrino; SOUND: Eric Talorico; MUSICAL DIRECTOR: Richard DeRosa. *Cast:* TEDDY: John Davidson; ALICE: Jennifer Lee Andrews; EDITH: Roxann Parker; NICK: Dan Sharkey; LODGE: Richard Bell; TAFT: Stephen Carter-Hicks; ROOT: Bob Freschi; WHEELER: Tom Cochrane; ROSE SCHNEIDERMAN: Andrea Drobish; ELEANOR: Stephanie Fredricks; MURPHY/REPORTER: Scott Kealy; TARBELL: Robin Manning; MAME: Pamela Peach; FDR/REPORTER: Shannon Stoeke; ETHEL: Ashleigh Davidson; ARCHIE: Regan Flynn; AGNES O'DAVIS: Marisa Follo; QUENTIN: Richard Giusti Jr.; TED: Matthew Johnson; KERMIT: Bryan Rosengrant. *Act I:* "This House," "But Not Right Now," "She's Got to Go," "A Girl Made of Lace," "Battle Lines," "Leg o' Mutton," "Cronies Conspiracy," "She's Got to Go" (reprise), "Fourth of July," "He's Got to Go," "Perfect for Each Other," "Her Father's Daughter," "Can I Let Her Go?." *Act II:* "Fourth of July" (two reprises), "(You've) Nothing to Lose," "I Told You So," "You Must Let Her Go," "Private Thoughts," "Wave the Flag."

689. *Tenderloin*

Set in the Tenderloin district of Manhattan in the 1890s. Brock is a crusading minister out to close down the Tenderloin, the downtown vice district supported by corrupt cops and politicians. It begins with a hymn in a Park Avenue church. Tommy is an ambitious young reporter with the *Tatler*, and becomes friendly with Brock, only to warn the cops when Brock is about to raid a brothel. Tommy helps frame Brock, but at the trial (done in an all-sung sequence) he finally tells the truth. The Tenderloin is closed down, but the church, offended by the scandal, asks for Brock's resignation. Tommy flees town to avoid the cops who are out to get him, and Brock moves to Detroit to continue his campaign there.

Before Broadway. James and Bill Goldman had received a Ford Foundation grant to follow the show from the beginning, as observers, and they actually did some work on the libretto. Certain numbers written for the show were not used: "Lovely Laurie," "Not Peace but a Sword," "The Orgy Burlesque," "Sea Shell Song," and "Tis Thy Beauty." And others — "First Things First," "Finally," "I Wonder What it's Like," "Lord of All Creation" and "Nobody Cares" were all cut before Broadway. Jeri Archer was in the pre–Broadway cast.

The Broadway Run. FORTY-SIXTH STREET THEATRE, 10/17/60–4/23/61. 6 previews from 10/12/60. 216 PERFORMANCES. PRESENTED BY Robert E. Griffith & Harold S. Prince; MUSIC: Jerry Bock; LYRICS: Sheldon Harnick; BOOK: George Abbott & Jerome Weidman; BASED ON the 1959 novel of the same name by Samuel Hopkins Adams, which fictionalized the life of the Rev. Dr. Charles H. Parkhurst, pastor of Madison Square Presbyterian Church; DIRECTOR: George Abbott; CHOREOGRAPHER: Joe Layton; SETS/COSTUMES: Cecil Beaton; ASSISTANT SETS: Robert Randolph; ASSISTANT COSTUMES: Patton Campbell; MUSICAL DIRECTOR: Hal Hastings; ORCHESTRATIONS: Irwin Kostal; DANCE MUSIC ARRANGEMENTS: Jack Elliott; PRESS: Sol Jacobson, Lewis Harmon, Mary Bryant; CASTING: Judith Abbott; GENERAL MANAGER: Carl Fisher; PRODUCTION STAGE MANAGER: Ruth Mitchell; STAGE MANAGER: John Allen; ASSISTANT STAGE MANAGER: Jack Leigh. *Cast:* TOMMY: Ron Husmann (2); NITA: Eileen Rodgers (4); LT SCHMIDT (THE PANTATA): Ralph Dunn; REV. DR. BROCK: Maurice Evans (1); GERTIE: Lee Becker; MARGIE: Margery Gray; DOROTHY: Dorothy Frank; GIRL: Patsy Peterson, *Margaret Gathright, Maria Graziano*; YOUNG MAN: Dargan Montgomery; JESSICA: Irene Kane; LAURA: Wynne Miller (3); ELLINGTON: Gordon Cook; JOE: Rex Everhart; PURDY: Raymond Bramley; MARTIN: Lanier Davis; DEACON: Roy Fant; FRYE: Eddie Phillips; ROONEY: Jordon Howard; NELLIE: Marguerite Shaw; BECKER: Michael Roberts; CALLAHAN: Jack McCann; PROSTITUTES: Erin Martin & Margery Gray; DRUNK: Bob Fitch; MAGGIE: Pat Turner; LIZ: Christine

Norden, *Anne Francine*; MRS. BARKER: Elaine Rogers; CHAIRMAN: Joe Hill; DANCERS: Jere Admire, David Evans, Bob Fitch, Dorothy Frank, Margery Gray, Mickey Gunnersen, Sandy Leeds, Jack Leigh, Erin Martin, Marjorie Pragon, Wakefield Poole, Ronald B. Stratton, Jayne Turner, Pat Turner, *Jack Konzal, Kenneth Urmston*; SINGERS: Charles Aschmann, Carvel Carter, Nancy Emes, John Ford, Stokely Gray, Maria Graziano, Joe Hill, Jordon Howard, Gail Johnston, Jack McCann, Dargan Montgomery, Patsy Peterson (*Margaret Gathright*), Claire Richard, Michael Roberts, Elaine Rogers, *Mary Rocks*. **Understudies**: Brock/Purdy: Joe Hill; Tommy: Gordon Cook; Nita: Nancy Emes; Laura: Gail Johnston; Schmidt: Michael Roberts; Joe/Deacon: Jordon Howard; Frye: Bob Fitch; Jessica: Margery Gray; Gertie: Erin Martin; Martin: Stokely Gray; Ellington: David Evans; Liz: Marguerite Shaw. **Act I**: Overture (Orchestra) [written specially by Billy May]; **Scene 1** *Prologue*; Limbo; Rev. Brock's church, New York City; 1890s: "Bless This Land!" (The Choir), "Little Old New York" (Nita, Gertie, Company); **Scene 2** A street outside the church; **Scene 3** A parish house: "Dr. Brock" (Brock), "Artificial Flowers" (Tommy), "What's in it for You?" (Brock & Tommy); **Scene 4** A street in front of the 19th Police Precinct station house; **Scene 5** The 19th Police Precinct station house; **Scene 6** Precinct street: "Reform" (Gertie, Nancy Emes, Carvel Carter); **Scene 7** The living room of Laura Crosbie's Fifth Avenue house: "Tommy, Tommy" (Laura); **Scene 8** A street in front of Clark's; **Scene 9** Clark's, a popular Tenderloin haunt: "Artificial Flowers" (reprise) (Margie), "The Picture of Happiness" (Tommy), Dance (Gertie, Frye, Company); **Scene 10** A street in front of Clark's; **Scene 11** The beach at Coney Island: "Dear Friend" (Brock, Laura, Jessica, Jayne Turner), "The Army of the Just" (Brock, Lanier Davis, Jack Leigh, Charles Aschmann, Stokely Gray); **Scene 12** A street in front of Clark's; **Scene 13** Clark's; 11:00 p.m.: "How the Money Changes Hands" (Brock, Nita, Liz, Frye, Gertie, Company). **Act II**: Entr'acte (Orchestra); **Scene 1** Central Park: "Good Clean Fun" (Brock & Company), "My Miss Mary" (Tommy, Laura, Singers); **Scene 2** A street; **Scene 3** Clark's: "My Gentle Young Johnny" (Nita), "The Picture of Happiness" (reprise) (Gertie, Margie, Ensemble); **Scene 4** The trial: "The Trial" (Company); **Scene 5** Clark's: "The Tenderloin Celebration" (Frye, Gertie, Company); **Scene 6** The parish house at night; **Scene 7** Precinct street; **Scene 8** The courtroom; **Scene 9** A street: "Reform" (reprise) (Gertie, Margie, Liz, Company); **Scene 10** The parish house: "Tommy, Tommy" (reprise) (Laura); **Epilogue** Detroit: "Little Old New York" (reprise) (Company).

Broadway reviews were mostly unfavorable. The show received Tony nominations for costumes in a musical, and for Maurice Evans and Ron Husmann. The production lost about half its $350,000 investment. Bobby Darin had a chart success with "Artificial Flowers."

After Broadway. LAS VEGAS. In 1961, immediately after closing on Broadway, the show moved to the Dunes Hotel, Las Vegas, and ran six weeks in an 80-minute tab version with the original cast minus Maurice Evans and Eileen Rodgers.

EQUITY LIBRARY THEATRE, NYC, 11/6/75–11/23/75. 22 PERFORMANCES. DIRECTOR: Robert Brink; CHOREOGRAPHER: Rick Atwell; MUSICAL DIRECTOR: Bill Grossman. **Cast**: BROCK: Stan Page; TOMMY: Brad Blaisdell; LAURA: Pamela McLernon; JAKE: Jerry Colker; NITA: Sherry Rooney. The numbers "I Wonder What it's Like" (immediately before "Tommy Tommy") and "Lovely Laurie" (immediately after "Tommy Tommy"), both cut from the original, were back in.

CITY CENTER, NYC, 3/24/00–3/27/00. 5 PERFORMANCES. This production was in concert form, part of the *Encores!* series. ADAPTED BY: John Weidman & Walter Bobbie; DIRECTOR: Walter Bobbie; CHOREOGRAPHER: Rob Ashford; CAST RECORDING on DRG Records, made on 4/18/00, and released on 7/25/00. **Cast**: NITA: Debbie Gravitte; BROCK: David Ogden Stiers; TOMMY: Patrick Wilson; LAURA: Sarah Uriarte Berry; GERTIE: Yvette Cason; JESSICA: Melissa Rain Anderson; JOE: Tom Alan Robbins; LIZ: Sara Gettelfinger; MARGIE: Jessica Stone; SCHMIDT: Kevin Conway; FRYE: Bruce MacVittie; MARTIN: Stanley Bojarski; PURDY: Guy Paul; CHORUS: Mindy Cooper, Tina Ou, Angie L. Schworer, Dale Hensley, Sean Grant, Denis Jones, Timothy Shew, Angelo Fraboni, Gregory Emanuel Rahming, Mark Price, Derric Harris, Greg W. Goodbrod, Julie Connors, Margaret Ann Gates, Shannon Lewis, Ann Kittredge.

690. *Texas, Li'l Darlin'*

A musical spoof about Texas politics and a magazine empire. The time is 1949, and the scenes are laid in the office of Harvey Small in New York City, and in Hominy Smith's political domain in Texas. Hominy is a Texas grassroots political candidate for state senate who keeps getting elected by employing singing cowboys and a homespun philosophy and appearance. He is opposed by Easy Jones, a young war veteran. Dallas is Easy's girlfriend, back from a failed theatrical career in Chicago. She also happens to be Hominy's daughter. Harvey, a New York picture magazine publisher, becomes interested in Hominy as possible presidential material.

Before Broadway. It tried out in 7/49 in Westport (Connecticut) summer stock, with Elaine Stritch as Dallas.

The Broadway Run. MARK HELLINGER THEATRE, 11/25/49–9/9/50. 293 PERFORMANCES. PRESENTED BY Studio Productions, Inc. & Anthony Brady Farrell Productions; MUSIC: Robert Emmett Dolan; LYRICS: Johnny Mercer; BOOK: John Whedon & Sam Moore; DIRECTOR: Paul Crabtree; CHOREOGRAPHER: Al White Jr.; SETS/LIGHTING: Theodore Cooper; COSTUMES: Eleanor Goldsmith; MUSICAL DIRECTOR: Will Irwin; ORCHESTRATIONS: Robert Russell Bennett; PRESS: Nat Dorfman, Reginald Denenholz, Irvin Dorfman; COMPANY MANAGER: Hugo Schaap; STAGE MANAGERS: John Larson, Alden Aldrich, Ned Wertimer. **Cast**: HARVEY SMALL: Loring Smith; JOHN BAXTER TRUMBULL: Charles Bang; PARKER STUART ELIOT: Alden Aldrich; WILLIAM DEAN BENSON JR.: Edward Platt; FROTHINGHAM FRY: Ned Wertimer; BREWSTER AMES II: Fredd Wayne; THE THREE COYOTES (played by the Texas Rhythm Boys): BUNKHOUSE: Eddy Smith; MULESHOES: Bill Horan; FRED: Joel McConkey; HOMINY SMITH: Kenny Delmar; DOGIE SMITH: Betty Lou Keim; AMOS HALL: Dante Di Paolo; SHERM: Cameron Andrews; DUANE FAWCETT: William Ambler; BRANCH PEDLEY: Ray Long; DELIA PRATT: Ronnie Hartmann; RED: Merrill Hilton; JO ANN WOODS: Elyse Weber; CALICO MUNSON: Dorothy Love; REBECCA BASS: Carol Lee; SALLY TUCKET: Ruth Ostrander; SUE CROCKETT: Doris Schmitt; SARAH BOONE: Arleen Ethane; BELLE COOPER: Yvonne Tibor; DALLAS SMITH: Mary Hatcher; EASY JONES: Danny Scholl; SAM: Jared Reed; MELISSA TATUM: Kate Murtah; THREE LITTLE MAIDS: Elyse Weber, Carol Lee, Dorothy Love; THREE PROSPECTORS: Elliott Martin, Edmund Hall, Carl Conway; STAN: Edmund Hall; HERB: Ralph Patterson; JACK PROW: Bob Bernard; HARRY STERN: Joey Thomas; COWBOYS: Ray Long, Dante Di Paolo, Merrill Hilton; OIL WORKERS: Jack Purcell, Carol Lee, Tommy Maier; DRUM MAJORETTE: Jacqueline James; CHEER LEADER: Elyse Weber; FOOTBALL PLAYER: Edmund Hall; TEXAS RANGERS: Charles Bang, Ralph Patterson, Edward Platt, William Ambler; VOICE OF "TREND:" Edward Platt; "TREND" SECRETARIES: Jacqueline James, Ronnie Hartmann, Elyse Weber, Dorothy May Richards, Marion Lauer, B.J. Keating; GUARD: Ray Long; RADIO ANNOUNCER: Charles Bang; ENGINEER: Alden Aldrich; JOE RAKER: Cameron Andrews; NEIGHBORS: Elliott Martin, Patricia Jennings, Carl Conway, Lloyd Knight, Jo Gibson, Muriel Bullis. **Understudies**: Dallas: Elyse Weber; Easy: Edmund Hall; Melissa: Jacqueline James; Small: Ed Platt; Brewster: Ned Wertimer; Raker/Fry: Alden Aldrich; Dogie: Susan Harris. **Prelude**: The office of Harvey Small, in New York City. **Act I**: **Scene 1** Hominy Smith's mansion: "Whoopin' and a-Hollerin'" (Dogie, Hominy, The Three Coyotes), "Texas, Li'l Darlin'" (Hominy & Chorus), "They Talk a Different Language" (The Yodel Blues) (Dallas, Hominy, The Three Coyotes), "A Month of Sundays" (Dallas & Easy); **Scene 2** Down the road a piece: "Down in the Valley" (Three Little Maids & Three Prospectors); **Scene 3** Hominy's back yard: "Hootin' Owl Trail" (Easy, Dogie, Chorus), "They Talk a Different Language" (reprise) (Dallas & Chorus), "The Big Movie Show in the Sky" (Easy & Chorus) [the big number], "Horseshoes Are Lucky" (Easy), "The Big Movie Show in the Sky" (reprise) (Sam, Easy, Chorus); **Scene 4** God's Country: "Love Me, Love My Dog" (Hominy, Easy, Chorus). **Act II**: **Scene 1** "The Trend of the Times:" "Take a Crank Letter" (Secretaries); **Scene 2** Hominy's headquarters at the fair: "Politics" (Hominy & Harvey); **Scene 3** Another part of the fair: "Ride 'em, Cowboy" (Dallas, to

Dogie); *Scene 4* On the midway: "Square Dance" (Branch, Hominy, Dallas, Chorus), "Take a Crank Letter" (reprise) (Brewster & Secretaries); *Scene 5* Dallas's dressing tent: "Affable, Balding Me" (Dallas & Brewster), "A Month of Sundays" (reprise) (Dallas & Easy), "Whichaway'd They Go?" (Dallas, Sam, Dogie, Friends); *Scene 6* The ballroom of the Hotel Pioneer: "It's Great to be Alive" (Easy & Chorus).

Kenny Delmar was famous as radio's voice of Senator Claghorn, on the Fred Allen Show. Broadway reviews were divided and mixed. The show vacationed 7/15/50–8/21/50.

691. *They're Playing Our Song*

Inspired by, but not really based on, the tempestuous real-life romance between songwriters Marvin Hamlisch and Carole Bayer Sager. This is basically a two-hander, but with other actors representing their three different inner selves, a sort of chorus. Vernon is a neurotic, wise-cracking composer who tells his troubles to a tape recorder. Sonia is a neurotic, wise-cracking lyricist whose wardrobe is made up of used theatre costumes. They try to have a relationship, which is hard when she is being interrupted all the time by phone calls from her ex-lover who she's still very fond of. At the end they commit only to continue writing songs and seeing each other, but not living together or marrying.

Before Broadway. Neil Simon wrote the comedy-drama *The Gingerbread Lady* in 1970, and later in the 1970s asked Marvin Hamlisch & Carole Bayer Sager to write the music and lyrics for a proposed musical of it. The musical never got made, but it inspired Mr. Simon to write sketch about the songwriters themselves. First choices Gilda Radner and John Rubinstein were unavailable. It was produced by Center Theatre Group, at the AHMANSON THEATRE, Los Angeles, 12/1/78. 66 PERFORMANCES. It had the same cast and crew as for the subsequent Broadway run. There were a few minor alterations made to the show before Broadway. In L.A. there were two additional scenes that didn't make it to Broadway. At that point Scene 5 was Aboard American Airlines Flight # 7, two months later; and Scene 6 was the Baggage Claim area, L.A. So, Scene 7 became Scene 5 for Broadway, and so on.

The Broadway Run. IMPERIAL THEATRE, 2/11/79–9/6/81. 11 previews. 1,082 PERFORMANCES. PRESENTED BY Emanuel Azenberg; MUSIC: Marvin Hamlisch; LYRICS: Carole Bayer Sager; BOOK: Neil Simon; DIRECTOR: Robert Moore; CHOREOGRAPHER: Patricia Birch; SETS: Douglas W. Schmidt; COSTUMES: Ann Roth; LIGHTING: Tharon Musser; SOUND: Tom Morse; MUSICAL DIRECTOR: Larry Blank; ORCHESTRATIONS: Ralph Burns, Richard Hazard, Gene Page; CAST RECORDING on Casablanca Records; PRESS: Bill Evans, Howard Atlee, Claudia McAllister; CASTING: TNI Casting (Julie Hughes & Barry Moss); GENERAL MANAGER: Jose Vega; COMPANY MANAGER: Susan Bell (gone by 80–81), *Maurice Schaded*; PRODUCTION STAGE MANAGER: Robert D. Currie, *Craig Jacobs*; STAGE MANAGER: Philip Cusack, *David Taylor*; ASSISTANT STAGE MANAGER: Bernard Pollock, *Pat Trott*. **Cast:** VERNON GERSCH: Robert Klein (1) ☆, *John Hammil* (from 11/27/79), *Tony Roberts* (from 12/17/79), *John Hammil, Ted Wass* (from 4/7/81), *Victor Garber* (from 8/4/81); SONIA WALSK: Lucie Arnaz (2) ☆, *Stockard Channing* (from 3/6/80), *Rhonda Farer* (from 6/2/80), *Anita Gillette* (from 9/23/80), *Diana Canova* (from 4/7/81), *Marsha Skaggs* (from 8/4/81); VOICES OF VERNON GERSCH: Wayne Mattson (5), Andy Roth (6) (*D. Michael Heath*), Greg Zadikov (8) (*John Hillner*); VOICES OF SONIA WALSK: Helen Castillo (3), Celia Celnik Matthau (4), Debbie Shapiro (7) (*Donna Murphy; Dorothy Kiara*); VOICE OF PHIL THE ENGINEER: Philip Cusack (9), *Hal Shane*. **Standby:** Vernon: John Getz, *Ray Gill*. **Understudies:** Sonia: Debbie Shapiro, *Rhonda Farer, Pat Gorman*; Vernon: Philip Cusack, *John Hammil, Hal Shane, John Hillner*; Phil: Wayne Mattson, *Michael William Schaefer*. **Swing Singers & Dancers:** Rhonda Farer, Philip Cusack, Donna Murphy, Max Stone, Lani Sundsten, *Andy Roth, Hal Shane, Dorothy Kiara, Pat Gorman, Connie Gould*. **Act I:** *Scene 1* Vernon's apartment, Central Park West, New York City: "Fallin'" (Vernon); *Scene 2* Vernon's studio; five days later: "Workin' it Out" (Vernon, Sonia, Voices), "If He Really Knew Me" (Sonia & Vernon); *Scene 3* Le Club: "They're Playing Our Song" (Vernon & Sonia); *Scene 4* Sonia's apartment; an

hour and a half later: "If He Really Knew Me" (reprise) (Vernon & Sonia), "Right" (Sonia, Voices, Vernon); *Scene 5* On the street; *Scene 6* On the road; *Scene 7* A beach house in Quogue, Long Island: "Just for Tonight" (Sonia) [this number replaced "If We Give it Time," which had been positioned here during the pre–Broadway run in L.A.]. *Act II:* *Scene 1* Vernon's apartment; a few days later: "When You're In My Arms" (Vernon, Sonia, Voices); *Scene 2* Vernon's bedroom; three weeks later; *Scene 3* Vernon's bedroom; the middle of the night; *Scene 4* A recording studio; 11 o'clock the next morning: "I Still Believe in Love" (Sonia); *Scene 5* A hospital room, Los Angeles; a few months later: "Fill In the Words" (Vernon); *Scene 6* Sonia's apartment; a few months later: Finale (Vernon, Sonia, Voices).

Broadway reviews were quite divided (a couple of pans, a rave and some favorables). The show received Tony nominations for musical, book, direction of a musical, and for Robert Klein.

After Broadway. TOUR. Opened on 12/1/79, Shubert Theatre, Chicago. It was on the road for two years. MUSICAL DIRECTOR: Al Cavaliere, *Jack Everly*. **Cast:** VERNON: Victor Garber; SONIA: Ellen Greene (*Marsha Skaggs* from 8/80).

LONDON. Opened on 9/20/80. **Cast:** VERNON: Tom Conti, *Martin Shaw* (from 7/27/81), *Tom Conti* (from 3/82); *Martin Shaw* (from 6/82); SONIA: Gemma Craven, *Sheila Brand* (from 12/28/81).

TOUR. Opened on 1/19/81, at the Playhouse, Wilmington, Del., and toured for 15 months. PRESENTED BY Tom Mallow; MUSICAL DIRECTOR: Albert L. Fiorillo Jr., *Roger Neill*. **Cast:** VERNON: John Hammil, *Richard Ryder*; SONIA: Lorna Luft, *June Gable, Dawn Wells* (from 11/29/81).

692. *13 Daughters*

A Hawaiian musical, about a Chinese family in Hawaii in the late 19th century. As the curtain opens Emmy, a Hawaiian, defies her gods and marries Chun, a foreigner. It is prophesied that they will have 13 daughters who will not marry until 13 trees blossom. The show then flashes forward 30 years. Chun is attempting to arrange a marriage between his eldest daughter Isabel to a local prince, because Isabel must marry before the other daughters. However, Isabel is a missionary, and is secretly in love with her colleague, Dr. Willoughby. But, after she is dismissed from the mission after using the hula to teach the alphabet to her students, she agrees to marry the prince, who himself is secretly in love with one of Isabel's sisters, Malia. Emmy blames herself for the misfortunes of her daughters, and attempts to sacrifice herself in a storm. Finally, Chun saves the precarious finances of Hawaii and is made an honorary Hawaiian. The curse is lifted and the daughters marry.

Before Broadway. Bob Magoon was a wealthy Hawaiian real-estate broker and songwriter. The show was first produced in Hawaii in 1956. MUSICAL DIRECTOR: Alvina Kaulili; CAST RECORDING on Mahalo. **Cast:** Tamara Long, Kam Fong Chun, James Kaina, Lord Kaulili, Richard Kuga, Robin Rankin, Napua Stevens. The financing for the Broadway production came mostly from Hawaiians, the balance provided by ABC–Paramount in exchange for the recording rights. John Fearnley, casting director for Rodgers & Hammerstein, was the original director but was replaced on the road by Rod Alexander (the Broadway playbill listed no director, but it did list Billy Matthews as "book stager"). Certain songs used in the 1956 production were not repeated for Broadway: "Calabash Cousins," "Daughter or Dowry," "Goodbye is Hard to Say," "Lei of Memories," and "Wedding Processional." Others were cut before Broadway: "Father and Son," "Listen for the Rooster," "Never without Your Love," "Violets and Violins," and a song by Cy Coleman (mus) & Carolyn Leigh (lyr), called "You Fascinate Me So."

The Broadway Run. FIFTY-FOURTH STREET THEATRE, 3/2/61–3/25/61. 1 preview on 3/1/61. 28 PERFORMANCES. PRESENTED BY Jack H. Silverman; MUSIC/LYRICS/BOOK: Eaton "Bob" Magoon Jr.; ADDITIONAL BOOK MATERIAL: Leon Tokatyan; DIRECTOR: Billy Matthews; CHOREOGRAPHER: Rod Alexander; ASSISTANT CHOREOGRAPHER/HAWAIIAN

CONSULTANT: Noan Beamer; SETS/LIGHTING: George Jenkins; COS-TUMES: Alvin Colt; MUSICAL DIRECTOR/VOCAL ARRANGEMENTS: Pembroke Davenport; ORCHESTRATIONS: Joe Glover; ADDITIONAL ORCHESTRATIONS: Robert Russell Bennett; DANCE MUSIC ARRANGEMENTS: Bob Atwood; PRESS: Philip Bloom & Fred Weterick; COMPANY MANAGER: Morton Zolotow; STAGE MANAGER: Joseph Dooley; ASSISTANT STAGE MANAGER: Warren Crane. *Cast:* KAHUNA: Paul Michael; YOUNG KAHUNA & CHANTER: Keola Beamer; BOYS: Miki Lamont, Augie Rios, Delfino de Arco, Ado Sato, Steve Curry; KINAU: Sylvia Syms (4); CHUN: Don Ameche (1) ✩; EMMALOA (EMMY): Monica Boyar (2); MANA, PRINCE OF HAWAII: Ed Kenney (3); MALIA: Diana Corto; KAMAKIA: Honey Sanders; WILLIAM, CHUN'S SECRETARY: John Battles; JACQUES: Richard Tone; ISABEL: Gina Viglione; SUSIE: Constance Di Giovanni; SALLY: Vivian Hernandez; DR. WILLOUGHBY: Stanley Grover; JANE: Diana Baffa; MAUDE: Karen Lynn Reed; DESDEMONA: Shirley De Burgh; CORA: Jo-Anne Leeds; MARY: Nikki Sowinski; MAY: Connie Burnett; MILLIE LEE: Gloria Gabriel; MINNIE LOU: Jeanne Armin; CECILIA: Isabelle Farrell; GOVERNORS: Paul Michael, Jack Murray, Jack Mathers, Irving Barnes; PRIME MINISTER: George Hirose; KEOKI, KING OF HAWAII: George Lipton; DAVID SCOTT, ATTORNEY-GENERAL: Konrad Matthaei; GUARDS: Bill Jason & Jose Ahumada; GOVERNORS' WIVES: Kelli Scott, Doris Galiber, Lynn Barret, Veronica McCormick; SIR CYRIL: Peter Pagan; ASSISTANT CONSUL: Nathaniel White; SERVANTS, ETC.: Jose Ahumada, Kalani Cockett, Bill Jason; CHILDREN: Steve Curry, Delfino de Arco, Constance Di Giovanni, Vivian Hernandez, Miki Lamont, Karen Lynn Reed, Augie Rios, Ado Sato; SINGERS: Irving Barnes, Lynn Barret, Doris Galiber, Jack Mathers, Paul Michael, Jack Murray, Veronica McCormick, Kelli Scott; DANCERS: Jeanne Armin, Diana Baffa, Carlos Bas, Keola Beamer, Connie Burnett, Shirley De Burgh, Humberto D'Elia, Antony De Vecchi, Gloria Gabriel, Blair Hammond, Jo-Anne Leeds, Roger Le Page, Carlos Macri, Michael Maurer, Jerome Michael, Mitchell Nutick, Candy Recla, Nikki Sowinski, Mary Zahn. *Understudies*: Chun: John Battles; Emmy: Lynn Barret; Mana: Blair Hammond; Malia: Kelli Scott; Kinau: Honey Sanders; Jacques: Roger Le Page; Kahuna/William/Sir Cyril: Nathaniel White; Willoughby: Konrad Matthaei; Isabel: Veronica McCormick; Cecilia: Jo-Anne Leeds. *Act I*: *Prologue* The valley: "Kuli Kuli" (Kinau & Company), "House on the Hill" (Chun); *Scene 1* Chun's house; 26 years later: "13 Daughters" (Chun & Daughters), "Paper of Gold" (dance) (Jacques & Daughters); *Scene 2* King's pavilion; *Scene 3* By a stream: "Let-a-Go Your Heart" (Mana & Malia); *Scene 4* Mission school: "Alphabet Song" (m: Nona Beamer) (Children); *Scene 5* By a stream: "Throw a Petal (in the Stream)" (Malia), "When You Hear the Wind" (Mana); *Scene 6* The valley: "Ka Wahine Akamai" ("Smart Woman") (Kinau, Kamakia, Emmaloa, Daughters, Suitors); *Scene 7* Emmaloa's bedroom: "You Set My Heart to Music" (Emmaloa, Chun, Isabel); *Scene 8* The Gold Pavilion of the Waikiki Hotel: "13 Daughters" (reprise) (Chun, Daughters, Suitors), "The Cotillion" (Company). *Act II*: *Scene 1* Chun's house: "13 Old Maids" (Daughters); *Scene 2* Chun's shop: "Oriental Plan" (m/l: Sherman Edwards & Sid Wayne) (Chun) [replaced during the run by "Nothing Man Cannot Do" (Chun)]; *Scene 3* Chun's house: "Hoomalimali" (Baiting the Hook) (Kinau), "My Pleasure" (Willoughby & Isabel), "Puka Puka Pants" (Cecilia & Jacques); *Scene 4* A beach near Honolulu Harbor: "My Hawaii" (Mana); *Scene 5* King's pavilion; *Scene 6* The valley: Hiiaka Ritual Dance (Dancers), "Hiiaka" (Emmaloa), "House on the Hill" (reprise) (Chun), "My Hawaii" (reprise) (Company).

Broadway reviews were divided, but mostly terrible. As it happens, ABC—Paramount did not do the cast recording after all. As for Tony Awards, it was nominated for sets (musical) and musical direction.

693. *Thoroughly Modern Millie*

In 1922 Millie leaves Kansas for New York City, determined to become thoroughly modern. She takes up residence at the Hotel Priscilla, run by a sort of Japanese lady named Mrs. Meers, who is really a failed diva turned white slaver, assisted by her laundrymen Ching Ho and Bun Foo. Millie, a top stenographer, soon gets a job at the Sincere Trust Insurance Company, working for the very handsome, but very square Trevor. She is also attracted to the first man she met in New York, Jimmy, whose friends include the rather prim Dorothy and the black singer Muzzy.

Before Broadway. It was the idea of Dick Scanlan, who, in the late 1980s was watching the 1967 movie on TV, and decided to do a Broadway musical of it. In 1991 he approached Richard Morris, the writer of the original movie screenplay, and was flatly rejected at first. However, the two got together, and produced a first draft by 2/96. Michael Mayer was brought in as director, and in the fall of 1996 the show had a staged reading in Manhattan. Fox Theatricals came in as a producer, but wanted the score changed. Jeanine Tesori was brought on board, and she and Dick Scanlan wrote 50 new songs (only a few of which were finally used). Richard Morris died in 1997. At this point they were planning a spring 1999 Broadway opening, but it didn't happen. It did have a workshop in New York, 5/17/99–6/26/99. CHOREOGRAPHER: David Marques. Kristin Chenoweth was first choice for Millie, then Lisa Datz. From 10/10/00 it had a tryout in LA JOLLA PLAYHOUSE, Calif., to rave reviews. A week before previews Erin Dilly, the actress playing Millie, went sick and Sutton Foster stepped in. The producers were in town, caught the act, and Miss Foster was in, and Miss Dilly was out. It had the same basic crew as for the subsequent Broadway run, except COSTUMES: Robert Perdziola; SOUND: Otts Munderloh. *Cast*: MILLIE: Sutton Foster; MISS DOROTHY: Sarah Uriarte Berry; CHING HO: Stephen Sable; BUN FOO: Francis Jue; JIMMY: Jim Stanek; MRS. MEERS: Pat Carroll; TAXI DRIVER: Randl Ask; MISS FLANNERY: Anne L. Nathan; TREVOR: Marc Kudisch; MUZZY: Tonya Pinkins; DOROTHY PARKER: Julie Connors; MAITRE D': Yusef Miller; ANNIVERSARY COUPLE: Chane't Johnson & Randl Ask; LADIES' LOUNGE ATTENDANT: Zina Camblin; MODERNS: Randl Ask, Kate Baldwin, Joshua Bergasse, Zina Camblin, Julie Connors, David Eggers, Nicole Foret, Matthew Gasper, Greg Goodbrod, Susan Haefner, Chane't Johnson, Matt Lashey, Michael Malone, Yusef Miller, Anne L. Nathan, Tina Ou, Noah Racey, Megan Sikora, Leigh-Anne Wencker. On 9/10/01 rehearsals for Broadway began. At the 3/23/02 preview Gavin Creel injured his knee and was out until 4/9/02. Brandon Wardell, his understudy, played the role in previews from 3/25/02–4/7/02. The 4/8/02 preview was canceled to allow Sutton Foster's understudy, Catherine Brunell, to get into the role.

The Broadway Run. MARQUIS THEATRE, 4/18/02–6/20/04. 32 previews from 3/19/02. 903 PERFORMANCES. PRESENTED BY Michael Leavitt, Fox Theatricals, Hal Luftig, with Stewart F. Lane, James L. Nederlander, Independent Presenters Network, John York Noble, Libby Adler Mages & Mari Glick Stuart, Dramatic Forces, Whoopi Goldberg; NEW MUSIC/VOCAL ARRANGEMENTS/INCIDENTAL MUSIC: Jeanine Tesori; NEW LYRICS: Dick Scanlan; BOOK: Richard Morris & Dick Scanlan; BASED ON the 1967 Universal movie of the same name, starring Julie Andrews, Mary Tyler Moore, John Gavin, Carol Channing, and written by Richard Morris; DIRECTOR: Michael Mayer; CHOREOGRAPHER: Rob Ashford; SETS: David Gallo; COSTUMES: Martin Pakledinaz; LIGHTING: Donald Holder; SOUND: Jon Weston; MUSICAL DIRECTOR: Michael Rafter; ORCHESTRATIONS: Ralph Burns & Doug Besterman, and (uncredited) Larry Blank; DANCE MUSIC ARRANGEMENTS: David Chase; CAST RECORDING on RCA, made on 4/22/02; GENERAL MANAGER: Nina Lannan Associates; COMPANY MANAGER: Ken Davenport, *Jim Brandeberry*; PRODUCTION STAGE MANAGER: Bonnie L. Becker; STAGE MANAGER: Pat Sosnow; ASSISTANT STAGE MANAGER: Charles Underhill. *Cast:* MILLIE DILLMOUNT: Sutton Foster (until 2/15/04), *Catherine Brunell* (for 3 performances, 1/22/02–1/23/02, during Miss Foster's illness; Miss Foster returned 1/25/02; *Catherine Brunell* & *Susan Haefner* stood in during Miss Foster's absences of 2/2/03, 2/17/03–2/23/03, and 2/26/03–2/28/03; during Miss Foster's vacation, 8/5/03–8/10/03 the role was handled by *Megan Campbell* in the evenings and *Emily Rozek* at matinees), *Susan Egan* (from 2/16/04—she replaced Sutton Foster), *Emily Rozek* (6/11/04–6/13/04), *Jessica Grove* (6/14/04–6/20/04); MUZZY VAN HOSSMERE: Sheryl Lee Ralph (until 4/12/03), *Terry Burrell* (4/14/03–4/21/03), *Leslie Uggams* (from 4/22/03); MRS. MEERS: Harriet Harris (until 8/3/03), *Terry Burrell* (8/5/03–9/4/03), *Candy Buckley* (from 9/5/03), *Delta Burke* (9/26/03–2/15/04), *Terry Burrell* (2/16/04–

2/23/04), *Dixie Carter* (2/24/04–6/6/04), Harriet Harris (6/7/04–6/20/04); MR. TREVOR GRAYDON III: Marc Kudisch (until 1/26/03), *Christopher Sieber* (1/28/03–4/28/03), *Marc Kudisch* (5/13/03–7/20/03), *Ben Davis* (7/22/03–12/14/03), *Kevin Earley* (from 12/16/03); JIMMY SMITH: Gavin Creel (until 4/27/03), *Christian Borle* (from 4/29/03), *Richard Roland* (from 2/16/04), *Christian Borle*; MISS DOROTHY BROWN: Angela Christian (until 6/9/04), *Jessica Grove* (from 6/1/04–6/13/04), *Emily Rozek* (6/13/04–6/20/04); CHING HO: Ken Leung (until 3/30/03), *Davis Rhee* (from 4/1/03); BUN FOO: Francis Jue, *Peter Kim*; MISS FLANNERY: Anne L. Nathan (until 2/29/04), *Liz McCartney* (from 3/1/04); LUCILLE: Kate Baldwin (until 8/25/02), *Megan McGinnis*; DAPHNE: Kate Baldwin, *Roxane Barlow*; CORA: Catherine Brunell; MATHILDE: Catherine Brunell; RITA: Jessica Grove; GLORIA: JoAnn M. Hunter, *Kim Varhola*; ALICE: Alisa Klein; ETHEL PEAS: Joyce Chittick, *Jessica Dillan*; RUTH: Megan Sikora; KENNETH: Brandon Wardell (until 7/21/02); DOROTHY PARKER: Julie Connors, *Linda Romoff*; DISHWASHERS: Aldrin Gonzales, Aaron Ramey (*Darren Ritchie*), Brandon Wardell (until 7/21/02), *Meredith Vieira* (on 4/2/03 only): THE LETCH: Noah Racey; OFFICER: Casey Nicholaw; DEXTER: Casey Nicholaw; RODNEY: Aaron Ramey (until 8/11/02), *Darren Ritchie* (from 8/23/02); SPEED TAPPISTS: Casey Nicholaw & Noah Racey, *Meredith Vieira* (on 4/2/03 only); THE PEARL LADY: Roxane Barlow; GEORGE GERSHWIN: Noah Racey; MUZZY'S BOYS: Greg Goodbrod, Darren Lee (*Richard Feng Zhu*), Dan LoBuono, John MacInnis, Noah Racey, T. Oliver Reid, *Jason Gillman* (from 10/22/02); ENSEMBLE: Kate Baldwin (*Megan McGinnis*), Roxane Barlow, Catherine Brunell (*Megan Campbell*), Joyce Chittick (*Jessica Dillan*), Julie Connors (*Linda Romoff*), David Eggers, Aldrin Gonzales, Greg Goodbrod, Jessica Grove, Amy Heggins, JoAnn M. Hunter (*Kim Varhola*), Alisa Klein, Darren Lee (*Richard Feng Zhu*), Dan LoBuono (until 10/20/02), John MacInnis, Casey Nicholaw, Noah Racey, Aaron Ramey (until 8/11/02; *Darren Ritchie*), T. Oliver Reid, Megan Sikora, Brandon Wardell (until 7/21/02), *Matt Farnsworth, Jason Gillman* (from 10/22/02), *Tripp Hanson, Cheyenne Jackson* (7/23/03–9/03), *Alisa Klein, Emily Rozek, Matt Wall, Shannon Hammons*. **Standby**: Mrs. Meers/Muzzy: Sharon Scruggs, *Terry Burrell*. **Understudies**: Millie: Catherine Brunell & Susan Haefner, *Megan Campbell* & *Emily Rozek*; Miss Flannery: Susan Haefner, *Linda Romoff*; Miss Dorothy: Kate Baldwin & Jessica Grove, *Megan McGinnis*; Jimmy: Brandon Wardell, *Darren Ritchie*; Jimmy/Trevor: Aaron Ramey, *Cheyenne Jackson* & *Matt Farnsworth*; Trevor: Greg Goodbrod, Ben Davis (until 7/20/03); Bun Foo: JoAnn M. Hunter, *Kim Varhola*; Bun Foo/Ching Ho: Darren Lee, *Richard Feng Zhu*; Mrs. Meers: *Anne L. Nathan*), Ethel: *Jessica Dillan*. **Swings**: Melissa Bell Chait, J.P. Christensen, Susan Haefner, Matt Lashey (until 6/30/02; *David Spangenthal* from 7/2/02), *Leah Horowitz, Michelle O'Steen-Vivona, Kevin Bernard, Paul Canaan*. **Orchestra:** PIANO: Lawrence Goldberg; PERCUSSION: Charles Descarfino; WOODWINDS: Lawrence Feldman, Walt Weiskopf, Dan Willis, Allen Won; TRUMPETS: Craig Johnson, Brian O'Flaherty, Glenn Drewes; TROMBONES: Larry Farrell & Jeff Nelson; FRENCH HORN: Brad Gemeinhardt; VIOLINS: Belinda Whitney, Eric DeGioia, Laura Oatts, Karl Kawahara, Mary Whitaker; CELLI: Stephanie Cummins & Anik Oulianine; HARP: Emily Mitchell; BASS: Ray Kilday; GUITAR; Jack Cavari; DRUMS: Warren Odze. **Act I**: Overture (Orchestra); *Scene 1* A New York City street: "Not for the Life of Me" (Millie), "Thoroughly Modern Millie" (m: James Van Heusen; l: Sammy Cahn) (Millie & Ensemble); *Scene 2* The Hotel Priscilla lobby: "Not for the Life of Me" (reprise) (Ruth, Gloria, Rita, Alice, Cora, Lucille), "How the Other Half Lives" (Miss Dorothy & Millie); *Scene 3* The laundry room of the Priscilla: "Not for the Life of Me" (reprise) (Ching Ho & Bun Foo); *Scene 4* The Sincere Trust Insurance Company: "The Speed Test" (m: Sir Arthur Sullivan; l: W.S. Gilbert; add l: Dick Scanlan) (Mr. Graydon, Millie, Miss Flannery, Office Workers); *Scene 5* The 12th floor of the Priscilla: "They Don't Know" (Mrs. Meers); *Scene 6* A New York City street; *Scene 7* The Tie-One-On Club: "The Nuttycracker Suite" (dance) (by Jeanine Tesori; based on the mus by Peter Ilych Tchaikovsky) (Millie, Miss Dorothy, Jimmy, Gloria, Alice, Ruth, Speakeasy Patrons); *Scene 8* A jail: "What Do I Need with Love?" (Jimmy); *Scene 9* The 12th floor of the Priscilla: *Scene 10* Muzzy's penthouse: "Only in New York" (by Jay Thompson; add m: Jeanine Tesori; add l: Dick Scanlan) (Muzzy, Jimmy, Millie); *Scene 11* The penthouse terrace: "Jimmy" (Millie) (added during previews); *Scene 12* The 12th

floor of the Priscilla. **Act II**: Entr'acte (Chorus); *Scene 1* The Sincere Trust Insurance Company: "Forget About the Boy" (Millie, Miss Flannery, Typists), "I'm Falling in Love with Someone" (m: Victor Herbert; l: Rida Johnson Young) (Mr. Graydon & Miss Dorothy); *Scene 2* The window ledge: "I Turned the Corner" (Jimmy & Millie), "I'm Falling in Love with Someone" (quartet) (Jimmy, Millie, Mr. Graydon, Miss Dorothy); *Scene 3* The 12th floor of the Priscilla: "Muqin" (by Walter Donaldson, Sam M. Lewis, Joe Young; add l: Dick Scanlan) (Mrs. Meers, Ching Ho, Bun Foo); *Scene 4* The floor show & kitchen at Cafe Society: "Long as I'm Here with You" (Muzzy, Millie, Ensemble) [during previews this number replaced "Ain't No Prohibition on Romance" (Muzzy & Ensemble)]; *Scene 5* Muzzy's dressing-room at Cafe Society: "Gimme, Gimme" (Millie) [during previews this number replaced a reprise of "Not for the Life of Me" (Millie)]; *Scene 6* The dining-room at Cafe Society: *Scene 7* The Hotel Priscilla lobby; *Scene 8* The laundry room at the Priscilla: "The Speed Test" (reprise) (Millie, Mr. Graydon, Jimmy, Muzzy), "They Don't Know" (reprise) (Mrs. Meers, Miss Dorothy, Ching Ho) (cut during previews), Finale: "Thoroughly Modern Millie" (reprise) (Jimmy, Miss Dorothy, The Moderns).

It opened to good reviews. The show won Tonys for musical, choreography, costumes, orchestrations, and for Sutton Foster and Harriet Harris. It was also nominated for: score, book, direction of a musical, Gavin Creel, and Marc Kudisch. This was the show that made a star of Sutton Foster. Marc Kudisch was expected to return on 5/28/03, then 5/29/03, but was late (5/13/03). The show missed the 8/14/03 performance due to the New York power blackout. Delta Burke came in four days early as Mrs. Meers (she had been scheduled for 9/30/03). On 12/15/03 it was announced that Sutton Foster and Delta Burke would be leaving the production on 2/15/04, and by late 12/03 Susan Egan was in talks to replace her, which she did, at a special Presidents Day matinee on 2/16/04. She then did the evening performance as well. Dixie Carter was scheduled to come in as Mrs. Meers on 2/23/04 but came in a day later, with Terry Burrell standing in for 2/23/04. The production recouped about 80 percent of its investment.

After Broadway. TOUR. Rehearsals began on 6/9/03. The tour opened on 7/15/03, at the Starlight, Kansas City. The sets were sparer than on Broadway. DIRECTOR: Michael Mayer; CHOREOGRAPHER: Rob Ashford; COSTUMES: Martin Pakledinaz; MUSICAL DIRECTOR: Michael Rafter. **Cast**: MILLIE: Darcie Roberts; JIMMY: Matt Cavenaugh, *Brian McElroy* (he was injured and forced out), *Richard Roland* (from 7/29/04), *Brian McElroy* (from late 8/04); MISS DOROTHY: Diana Kaarina, *Anne Warren*; MRS. MEERS/MISS FLANNERY: Hollis Resnik, *Pamela Hamill* (from 8/10/04); TREVOR: Sean Krill, *John Ganun*; MUZZY: Pamela Isaacs, *Stephanie Pope*; BUN FOO: Darren Lee; CHIN HO: Andrew Pang.

SHAFTESBURY THEATRE, London, 10/21/03–6/26/04. Previews from 10/11/03. It had the same basic crew as for Broadway, except PRODUCERS: Paul Elliott & Duncan Weldon. **Cast**: MILLIE: Amanda Holden; MRS. MEERS: Maureen Lipman (for 6 performances a week; Marti Webb played 2 performances a week), *Anita Dobson* (from 3/04); MUZZY: Sheila Ferguson; TREVOR: Craig Urbani; JIMMY: Mark McGee; DOROTHY PARKER: Helen Baker; MISS FLANNERY: Rachel Izen; BUN FOO: Unku; CHING HO: Yo Santhaveesuk. A 2005 U.K. tour is planned.

NORTH SHORE MUSIC THEATRE, Beverly, Mass., 4/26/05–5/15/05. DIRECTOR: Barry Ivan; MUSICAL DIRECTOR: Dale Rieling. **Cast**: MILLIE: Milena Govich; TREVOR: Richard Roland; JIMMY: Ryan Silverman; MUZZY: Terry Burrell; DOROTHY BROWN: Amanda Serkesevich; BUN FOO: Telly Leung; CHING HO: Davis Rhee; MISS FLANNERY: Becky Barta; MRS. MEERS: Beth McVey.

694. *Thou Shalt Not*

A grisly tale of murderous adultery, set in and around the Ninth Ward of New Orleans, 1946–47. A young married woman's life is changed by the return of a jazz musician following World War II.

Before Broadway. On 9/18/00 a workshop was held at LINCOLN CENTER THEATRE, with Debra Monk in the cast. On 4/18/01 Craig Bierko was rumored to be taking the role of Laurent. On 5/1/01 Kate Levering was announced, and Norbert Leo Butz was announced on 5/4/01. It replaced *Bells Are Ringing*, which closed at the Plymouth on 6/10/01. Broadway previews began on 9/27/01 (postponed from 9/20/01 because of the 9/11/01 crisis).

The Broadway Run. PLYMOUTH THEATRE, 10/25/01–1/6/02. 33 previews from 9/27/01. 85 PERFORMANCES. PRESENTED BY Lincoln Center Theatre; MUSIC/LYRICS: Harry Connick Jr.; BOOK: David Thompson; BASED ON the 1867 novel *Therese Raquin*, by Emile Zola, which had first appeared earlier in the year in serial form as "Un mariage d'amour;" DIRECTOR/CHOREOGRAPHER: Susan Stroman; SETS: Thomas Lynch; COSTUMES: William Ivey Long; LIGHTING: Peter Kaczorowski; SOUND: Scott Lehrer; MUSICAL DIRECTOR: Phil Reno; ORCHESTRATIONS/ARRANGEMENTS: Harry Connick Jr.; CAST RECORDING finally released on 6/18/02; CASTING: Tara Rubin Casting, Kristin McTigue; COMPANY MANAGER: L.A. Glassburn; PRODUCTION STAGE MANAGER: Peter Wolf; ASSISTANT STAGE MANAGERS: Lisa Buxbaum & Mark Dobrow. **Cast:** FLIM FLAM: J.C. Montgomery; PAPA JACK: Ted L. Levy; MONSIGNOR: Patrick Wetzel; SASS: Rachelle Rak; SUGAR HIPS: Davis Kirby; LAURENT LE CLAIRE: Craig Bierko, *David New* (during Mr. Bierko's injury, from 10/26/01), *Craig Bierko* (from 11/13/01); THERESE RAQUIN: Kate Levering; MADAME RAQUIN: Debra Monk; CAMILLE RAQUIN: Norbert Leo Butz; OFFICER MICHAUD: Leo Burmester; OLIVER: Brad Bradley; SUZANNE: JoAnn M. Hunter; ANTOINE: Patrick Wetzel; BUSKER: Ted L. Levy; SANCTIFY SAM: Ted L. Levy; ENSEMBLE: Timothy J. Alex, Brad Bradley, Dylis Croman, Michael Goddard, Amy Hall, Ellen Harvey, Amy Heggins, JoAnn M. Hunter, Cornelius Jones Jr., Davis Kirby, Ted L. Levy, J.C. Montgomery, Rachelle Rak, Kelli Severson, Patrick Wetzel. **Standby:** Laurent/Camille: David New. **Understudies:** Laurent: Timothy J. Alex; Camille: Timothy J. Alex & Brad Bradley; Therese: Dylis Croman & Kelli Severson; Suzanne: Dylis Croman & Emily Hsu; Michaud: J.C. Montgomery & David New; Papa Jack: Timothy J. Alex & Kent Zimmerman; Mme Raquin: Pam Bradley & Ellen Harvey; Sam: J.C. Montgomery; Oliver: James Hadley & Patrick Wetzel. **Swings:** Pam Bradley, James Hadley, Emily Hsu, Kent Zimmerman. **Orchestra:** CONCERTMASTER: Martin Agee; REEDS: Jonathan Levine, Jerry Weldon, Charles "Ned" Goold, Dave Schumacher; TRUMPETS: Roger Ingram, Joe Magnarelli, Derrick Gardner; TROMBONES: John Allred & Joe Barati; KEYBOARDS: Philip Fortenberry & Gregory J. Dlugos; BASS: Benjamin Franklin Brown; DRUMS: Brian Grice; PERCUSSION: Walter "Wally" Usiatynski; VIOLIN II: Cenovia Cummins; VIOLA: Maxine Roach; CELLO: Roger Shell. **Act I:** *Scene 1* French Quarter Jazz Club: "It's Good to Be Home" (Flim Flam, Papa Jack, Ensemble); *Scene 2* The backyard of *The Broken Tea Cup*: "I Need to Be in Love" (ballet) (Therese); *Scene 3* The *Broken Tea Cup*: "My Little World" (Madame Raquin), "While You're Young" (Laurent), "I Need to be in Love" (reprise) (Therese); *Scene 4* *The Broken Tea Cup*: "The Other Hours" (Laurent); *Scene 5* The bedroom: "The Other Hours" (reprise) (ballet) (Laurent & Therese); *Scene 6* The bedroom: "All Things" (Camille); *Scene 7* The French Quarter: "Sovereign Lover" (Therese, Laurent, Busker, Ensemble); *Scene 8* The parlor: "I've Got My Eye on You" (Madame Raquin & Camille); *Scene 9* The alley; *Scene 10* The backyard of *The Broken Tea Cup*; *Scene 11* Mardi Gras: "Light the Way" (Ensemble), "Take Her to the Mardi Gras" (Laurent, Camille, Therese, Ensemble); *Scene 12* Lake Pontchartrain: "Tug Boat" (Camille & Therese). **Act II:** *Scene 1* French Quarter Jazz Club; *Scene 2* The morgue: "Tug Boat" (reprise) (Laurent); *Scene 3* Madame's sitting room: "My Little World" (reprise) (Madame Raquin); *Scene 4* The funeral: "Won't You Sanctify?" (Sanctify Sam & Ensemble), "Time Passing" (Therese, Laurent, Madame Raquin, Ensemble); *Scene 5* The Broken Tea Cup: "Take Advantage" (Michaud); *Scene 6* The bedroom; *Scene 7* The Ninth Ward: "Oh! Ain't That Sweet" (Camille); *Scene 8* The bedroom; *Scene 9* The wharf: "Thou Shalt Not" (ballet) (Therese, Laurent, Ensemble); *Scene 10* The parlor; 4 a.m.; *Scene 11* The parlor; 8 a.m.; *Scene 12* French Quarter Jazz Club: "It's Good to Be Home" (reprise) (Camille).

Reviews were bad (Norbert Leo Butz got the best of them). On opening night Craig Bierko got hit in the larynx during a fight scene and damaged a vocal cord. He finished the show, went to the opening night party afterwards, but the following day began hemorrhaging and had to be taken to hospital. After a limited run the show closed. The show received Tony nominations for score, and for Norbert Leo Butz.

695. *Three for Tonight*

A diversion in song and dance. It was really a showcase for the Champions (Gower and Marge), and for Harry Belafonte. Guests included vocalist Betty Benson and the voices of Walter Schumann.

The Broadway Run. PLYMOUTH THEATRE, 4/6/55–6/18/55. 85 PERFORMANCES. The Paul Gregory & Charles Laughton production, PRESENTED BY Paul Gregory; ORIGINAL MUSIC: Walter Schumann; LYRICS/SPECIAL MATERIAL: Robert Wells; DIRECTOR/CHOREOGRAPHER: Gower Champion; SETS: R.L. Grosh & Sons; COSTUMES: Jack's of Hollywood; MUSICAL DIRECTOR: Richard Pribor; ARRANGEMENTS: Nathan Scott; PRESS: Karl Bernstein, Harvey Sabinson, Robert Ganshaw; COMPANY MANAGER: Emmett Callahan; STAGE MANAGER: Irving Sudrow; ASSISTANT STAGE MANAGER: Thomas Wright. *Part I:* We begin with our Story Teller, Hiram Sherman (5) (mc); The sounds you will hear are Impressions, the Voices of Walter Schumann (4), and they will also sing "All You Need is a Song;" And now Marge & Gower Champion (1) (dancers): "Dance, Dance, Dance" (dance), "The Clock" (dance), "By-Play for Drums" (dance); Back to our Story Teller, who introduces Harry Belafonte (2) (singer), with Millard Thomas and his guitar: "Jerry" (traditional), "Sylvie" (m/l: Harry Belafonte), "Mark Twain" (m/l: Harry Belafonte), "When the Saints Go Marching In" (m/l: Huddie Ledbetter & C.C. Carter); On with our Story Teller to Marge & Gower Champion (1) (dancers): At the Sunday Picnic Social, featuring: "Summer in Fairview Falls," "It Couldn't Be a Better Day," "Here I Stand," "The Auction;" Finale. *Part II:* Our Story Teller, Hiram Sherman (5) introduces Betty Benson (3) and The Voices of Walter Schumann (4): "Fly Bird;" We continue with Harry Belafonte (2) & Millard Thomas (singer & guitarist): "Noah" (traditional; arr: Harry Belafonte & Bill Attaway), "Take My Mother Home" (traditional; arr: Hall Johnson), "In that Great Gettin' Up Mornin'" (written by Jester Hairston); And now we get very formal: Hiram Sherman (5), our Story Teller reads "The Lecture," Demonstrated by Marge & Gower Champion (1); We join Harry Belafonte (2) (singer): "Matilda" [m/l: Harry Thomas (i.e. Harry Belafonte)], "Scarlet Ribbons" (m: Evelyn Danzig; l: Jack Segal); Our Story Teller takes us to Yesterday, with Marge & Gower Champion (1) (dancers): "By the Light of the Silvery Moon" (m: Gus Edwards; l: Edward Madden) [from *Follies of* 1909], "Shine On, Harvest Moon" (m/l: Jack Norworth & Nora Bayes) [from *Follies of* 1909]; "Troubles" (m/l: Harry Belafonte) [sung by Harry Belafonte (2)]; Finale (Entire Company).

CHORUS: John Bennett, Robert Brink, Andrew Case, Gina Christen, Diane Doxee, Elaine Drew, Joyce L. Foss, Dorothy Gill, Nancy Harp, Jimmy Harris, Mark Karl, Jerry Madison, Robert Miller, Ned Romero, Jack Steele, Brad Thomas, Robert Trevis, Karen Vonne, Richard Wessler.

GUITARIST FOR HARRY BELAFONTE: Millard Thomas; WOODWINDS: Sherwin Lichtenfeld; PERCUSSION: Bob Morrison; BASS: Milton Nadel; PIANIST: John Williams.

It got great Broadway reviews.

After Broadway. There was a CBS TV presentation of this show on 6/22/55.

696. *The Three Musketeers*

Before Broadway. There have been several different stage musical versions of *The Three Musketeers* over the years, including *The Four Musketeers*, and other titles. The 1928 production, while it wasn't the first on Broadway, was, and remains, the definitive one. It first ran at the LYRIC THEATRE, 3/13/28–12/15/28. 318 PERFORMANCES. PRESENTED BY Florenz Ziegfeld; DIRECTORS: William Anthony McGuire & Richard Boleslawsky; CHOREOGRAPHER: Albertina Rasch. **Cast:** D'ARTAGNAN: Dennis King; CONSTANCE: Vivienne Segal; PORTHOS: Detmar Poppen; ATHOS: Douglas R. Dumbrille; ARAMIS: Joseph Macaulay; RICHELIEU: Reginald Owen.

This version was revived by the EQUITY LIBRARY THEATRE, NYC,, 5/8/75–5/25/75. 22 PERFORMANCES. DIRECTOR/CHOREOGRAPHER:

Charles Abbott; ASSISTANT DIRECTOR: Alan Rust; MUSICAL DIRECTOR: Jim Coleman. **Cast**: D'ARTAGNAN: Jason McAuliffe; ATHOS: Michael A. Maurice; PORTHOS: David Pursley; ARAMIS: Ray Cox; MILADY: Jane Altman. "Summertime," "All for One and One for All," "The He for Me," "Gascony," "My Sword and I," "Vesper Bells," "Dreams," "March of the Musketeers," "The Colonel and the Major," "Love is the Sun," "Your Eyes," "Welcome to the Queen," "Red Wine," "Ma Belle," "One Kiss from You," "Queen of My Heart," "Each Little While," "The Court Dance," Finale.

The 1984 Broadway revival was a revised version of the 1928 production, originally produced in regional theatre in Stamford, Conn.

The Broadway Run. BROADWAY THEATRE, 11/11/84–11/18/84. 14 previews from 11/4/84. 9 PERFORMANCES. PRESENTED BY Irvin Feld, Kenneth Feld, Ina Lea Meibach, Jerome Minskoff; MUSIC: Rudolf Friml; LYRICS: P.G. Wodehouse & Clifford Grey; ORIGINAL BOOK: William Anthony McGuire; NEW BOOK: Mark Bramble; BASED ON the novel of the same name by Alexandre Dumas; in French it was *Les Trois Mousquetaires*, and had first appeared as a serial in *Le Siecle*, in Paris, in 1843 (the novel was originally going to be called *Athos, Porthos et Aramis*); DIRECTOR: Joe Layton; CHOREOGRAPHER: Lester Wilson; SETS: Nancy Winters; COSTUMES: Freddy Wittop; LIGHTING: Ken Billington; SOUND: Jan Nebozenko; MUSICAL SUPERVISOR/ARRANGEMENTS/MUSIC ADAPTED BY: Kirk Nurock; CONDUCTOR: Gordon Lowry Harrell; ORCHESTRATIONS: Larry Wilcox; VOCAL ARRANGEMENTS/FIGHT MUSIC ARRANGEMENTS: Kirk Nurock; DANCE MUSIC ARRANGEMENTS: Wally Harper & Mark Hummel; PRESS: Jacksina & Freedman; CASTING: Slater — Wilson; GENERAL MANAGEMENT: Joseph Harris Associates; COMPANY MANAGER: Steven H. David; PRODUCTION STAGE MANAGER: Steven Zweigbaum; STAGE MANAGER: Arturo E. Porazzi; ASSISTANT STAGE MANAGER: Amy Pell; SECOND ASSISTANT STAGE MANAGER: Kirsti Carnahan (Todd Lester during previews). **Cast:** QUEEN ANNE OF FRANCE: Darlene Anders; LADY CONSTANCE BONACIEUX: Liz Callaway (4) ☆; CARDINAL RICHELIEU: Ed Dixon (5) ☆; SERGEANT JUSSAC: Raymond Patterson; INNKEEPER: J.P. Dougherty; THE DUKE OF BUCKINGHAM: Joseph Kolinski; THE COMTE DE LA ROCHEFORT: Michael Dantuono; MILADY DE WINTER: Marianne Tatum (6) ☆; D'ARTAGNAN: Michael Praed (7) ☆; ATHOS: Chuck Wagner (1) ☆; ARAMIS: Brent Spiner (3) ☆; PORTHOS: Ron Taylor (2) ☆; SELENUS: J.P. Dougherty; LAUNDRESS: Susan Goodman; DE BEAUVERAIS: Steve Dunnington; CAPTAIN TREVILLE: Peter Samuel; KING LOUIS XIII: Roy Brocksmith; TAVERN WENCH: Susan Goodman; CHAMBERMAID: Elisa Fiorillo; PATRICK: Perry Arthur; MAJOR DOMO: J.P. Dougherty; THE CARDINAL'S GUARDS: Bill Badolato, Steve Dunnington, Craig Heath Nim, Steve Marder, Mark McGrath, Sal Viviano, Faruma Williams; CITIZENS OF POISSY, PARIS, AND CALAIS/THE KING'S MUSKETEERS, ETC: Janet Aldrich, Perry Arthur, Bill Badolato, Tina Belis, Steven Blanchard, Steve Dunnington, Elisa Fiorillo, Terri Garcia, Susan Goodman, Patty Holley, Jeff Johnson, Steve Marder, Mark McGrath, Craig Heath Nim, Suzan Postel, Wynonna Smith, Sal Viviano, Faruma Williams, Sandra Zigars. **Understudies**: D'Artagnan: Jeff Johnson; Athos/Innkeeper: Mark McGrath; Porthos/Cardinal: Peter Samuel; Aramis: Steven Blanchard; Constance: Elisa Fiorillo & Janet Aldrich; Queen: Suzan Postel; Rochefort/Treville: Craig Heath Nim; Buckingham: Sal Viviano; Jussac: Faruma Williams; Richelieu: Peter Samuel; King: J.P. Dougherty; Laundress: Patty Holley; Milady: Janet Aldrich. **Swings**: De Wright Baxter, Kirsti Carnahan (Todd Lester during previews), Craig Frawley, Jacqueline Smith-Lee. **Act I: Scene 1** France; April, 1626: Prologue (Three Musketeers, King, Treville, Queen, Constance, Jussac, Innkeeper, Buckingham, Rochefort, Milady, D'Artagnan); **Scene 2** Poissy, a market town outside Paris: "Gascony Bred" * (D'Artagnan, Innkeeper, Company), "All for One (and One for All)" * (Three Musketeers), "Only a Rose" (D'Artagnan & Constance), "My Sword and I" * (D'Artagnan & Company); **Scene 3** Paris; the night of All Fools Eve: "Carnival of Fools" (Company); **Scene 4** Garden at the Convent of Carmier: "L'Amour, Toujours L'Amour" (Buckingham & Queen); **Scene 5** Streets of Paris: "Come to Us" (Milady & Jussac); **Scene 6** The laundry at No. 7, rue de Colombier: "March of the Musketeers" * (Three Musketeers, D'Artagnan, Company); **Scene 7** The Cardinal's chamber in the Louvre: "Bless My Soul" (Cardinal, Milady, Rochefort); **Scene 8** Gardens of the Tuileries: "Only a Rose" (reprise) (Constance, D'Artagnan, Company); **Scene 9** Palace corridor into the great hall; Scene 10 On the road to

Calais: Act I Finale (D'Artagnan, Three Musketeers, Company). **Act II: Scene 1** The *Golden Lily Tavern*, Calais: "Vive la France" (King & Company), "The Actor's Life" (Three Musketeers & D'Artagnan), "Ma Belle" * (D'Artagnan & Constance); **Scene 2** Streets of Calais, and the ship to England: "The Chase" (Company), "Ma Belle" (reprise) (D'Artagnan & Three Musketeers); **Scene 3** The Duke of Buckingham's castle in England: "Dreams" * (Buckingham); **Scene 4** Milady's bedroom at the *Golden Lily Tavern*, Calais: "L'Amour, Toujours L'Amour" (reprise) (Milady); **Scene 5** The road to Paris: "All for One" (reprise) (Three Musketeers & D'Artagnan); **Scene 6** All over Paris: "Gossip" * (Three Musketeers, D'Artagnan, Milady, Jussac, Cardinal, Constance, Treville, King, Queen, Company); **Scene 7** The Hotel de Ville: Finale (Company).

Note: an asterisk means those numbers were in the original 1928 Broadway production.

Broadway reviews were divided, but generally not good.

697. *Three to Make Ready*

A musical revue, a sequel to *One for the Money* (1939) and *Two for the Show* (1940), both Broadway revues by Morgan Lewis and Nancy Hamilton, and both with Alfred Drake in the cast. Mr. Drake wasn't in the third.

The Broadway Run. ADELPHI THEATRE, 3/7/46–5/18/46; BROADHURST THEATRE, 5/20/46–10/26/46; ADELPHI THEATRE, 10/28/46–12/14/46. Total of 327 PERFORMANCES. PRESENTED BY Stanley Gilkey & Barbara Payne; MUSIC: Morgan Lewis; LYRICS/SKETCHES: Nancy Hamilton; DEVISED BY/DIRECTOR: John Murray Anderson; SKETCH DIRECTOR: Margaret Webster; CHOREOGRAPHER: Robert Sidney; SETS: Donald Oenslager; COSTUMES: Audre; MUSICAL DIRECTOR: Ray M. Kavanaugh; ORCHESTRATIONS: Russell Bennett, Charles L. Cooke, Elliott Jacoby, Ted Royal, Hans Spialek, Walter Paul; VOCAL ARRANGEMENTS: Joe Moon; MUSICAL CONTINUITY: Melvin Pahl; PRESS: Sol Jacobson; GENERAL STAGE MANAGER: Francis Spencer; COMPANY MANAGER: Warren P. Munsell Jr. **Act I: Scene 1** "It's a Nice Night for It." Sung by Gordon MacRae (3). WARDROBE MISTRESS: Bibi Osterwald (5), *Jutta Wolf*; STAGE MANAGER: Garry Davis; STAGEHAND: Carleton Carpenter; BALLERINA: Jane Deering; BALLET DANCER: Harold Lang (4); ENSEMBLE: Mary Alice Bingham, Irwin Charles, Althea Elder, Joe Jonson, Martin Kraft, Mary McDonnell, Candace Montgomery, Meg Mundy (dropped during the run), Jack Purcell, Edythia Turnell, Jimmy Venable; **Scene 2** Post Mortem: HE: Ray Bolger (1); SHE: Rose Inghram; ALEXANDRE BERNIER: Garry Davis; BELLBOY: Carleton Carpenter; **Scene 3** Arthur Godfrey (6) (dropped out during the run), *Garry Davis*; **Scene 4** "There's Something on My Program" (dance): JULIET: Jane Deering; ROMEO: Harold Lang (4); THE NURSE: Meg Mundy, *Candace Montgomery*; CAPULETS: Mary Alice Bingham, Althea Elder, Mary McDonnell, Edythia Turnell; MONTAGUES: Joe Jonson, Martin Kraft, Jack Purcell, Jimmy Venable; **Scene 5** "The Shoe on the Other Foot" (a lady tries on innumerable pairs of shoes in a store and drives the clerk mad; then she leaves and says she was just passing the time before a date): LADY: Brenda Forbes (2); SALESMAN: Ray Bolger (1); **Scene 6** "Tell Me the Story." Sung by Rose Inghram & Gordon MacRae (3); **Scene 7** "The Old Soft Shoe." Sung & danced by Ray Bolger (1). JITTERBUGS: Mary McDonnell & Jack Purcell; SAMBA DANCERS: Mary Alice Bingham & Joe Jonson; **Scene 8** The Russian Lesson (suburban ladies take a Russian lesson): MRS. BUDGE: Rose Inghram; MRS. WATTROUS: Bibi Osterwald (5), *Jutta Wolf*; MRS. PELLOBIE: Meg Mundy; MISS UMSTEDDER: Brenda Forbes (2); **Scene 9** "Barnaby Beach." Sung by Gordon MacRae (3) & Althea Elder. Danced by Jane Deering & Harold Lang (4) (young people on vacation); **Scene 10** Arthur Godfrey (6) (left during the run), *Garry Davis*; **Scene 11** Cold Water Flat (Housing Shortage): JO: Ray Bolger (1); MARY: Rose Inghram; **Scene 12** Arthur Godfrey (6) (dropped out during the run), *Garry Davis*; **Scene 13** "Wisconsin" or "Kenosha Canoe" (a take-off on *An American Tragedy*, done in the style of *Oklahoma!*, with a bow to Richard Rodgers & Oscar Hammerstein II): AUNTIE PLUM: Bibi Osterwald (5), *Jutta Wolf*; CLYDE GRIFFITHS: Ray Bolger (1); ROBERTA: Rose Inghram; JUNE ALDEN: Jane Deering; IDO WANNY: Brenda Forbes (2); MR. SNOW: Gordon MacRae (3); YELLOW BELLY: Garry Davis; JUDGE: Irwin Charles; DANCER: Harold

Lang (4); *Scene 14* "Kenosha Canoe Ballet" [danced by Harold Lang (4), Cowboys, Children, Strumpets]. *Act II*: *Scene 1* "If it's Love" (parody of ballroom dancers). Sung by Rose Inghram & Gordon MacRae (3). Danced by Ray Bolger (1), Althea Elder, Mary McDonnell, Mary Alice Bingham, Edythia Turnell, Jane Deering; *Scene 2* The Story of the Opera [from *One for the Money*] (the confused recital of a Wagner opera) [this sketch was put in only three days before Broadway opening night]: MARILYN: Brenda Forbes (2); LUCY: Bibi Osterwald (5), *Jutta Wolf*; WAITER: Martin Kraft; *Scene 3* "A Lovely, Lazy Kind of Day." Sung by Gordon MacRae (3). SCARECROW: Ray Bolger (1); MILKMAID: Bibi Osterwald (5), *Jutta Wolf*; *Scene 4* "And Why Not I?." Sung by Brenda Forbes (2); *Scene 5* "The Sad Sack" (based on the cartoon character created by Sgt. George Baker — and not by Bill Mauldin, as is often stated): THE SACK: Ray Bolger (1); SERGEANT: Garry Davis; JOE: Joe Jonson; GOLD-BRICKS: Irwin Charles; SLUG: Carleton Carpenter; LIEUTENANT: Harold Lang (4); MP: Martin Kraft; CAPTAIN/COLONEL/GENERAL: Arthur Godfrey, *Garry Davis*; SLEEPER: Jimmy Venable; GREELEY: Jack Purcell; *Scene 6* Solo Act: Ray Bolger (1); *Scene 7* Finale (Entire Company).

OTHER PRINCIPALS: James Elsegood, Iris Linde. *Understudy*: Julie Wilson.

Reviews were not good. During the run Arthur Godfrey (in his Broadway debut) was forced to leave due to complete physical exhaustion. To replace lost time in the program due to his leaving, a new number, "Hot December," sung by Bibi Osterwald (5) (*Jutta Wolf*), was added in Act I, after The Russian Lesson.

698. *Three Wishes for Jamie*

Set in 1896. Jamie is granted three wishes by Una the fairy princess — travel, a beautiful wife, and a son who speaks Gaelic. However, matchmaker Tavish has arranged a marriage for him with Tirsa. There is an altercation with Tirsa's brothers, which culminates in Jamie and Tavish seeming to be washed away in a torrent. They find this convenient, and leave the west coast of Ireland for Georgia, in the USA, to fulfill the three wishes. Jamie marries Maeve at the end of Act I. He finds she can't have children. They adopt Kevin, a mute boy. Tavish dies, leaving Kevin a legacy, and the boy's real father shows up, knowing he can recognize Kevin by his inability to speak. At the end, miraculously, Kevin utters his first words — in Gaelic (taught to him by Tavish).

Before Broadway. Charles O'Neal (father of actor Ryan O'Neal) and Charles Lederer wrote the libretto of the show that was first produced by Edwin Lester, at the LOS ANGELES AND SAN FRANCISCO CIVIC LIGHT OPERAS in the summer of 1951. CO-PRODUCER/DIRECTOR: Albert Lewis; PRODUCTION SUPERVISOR: Edwin Lester. It was in 3 acts then. *Cast*: John Raitt, Marion Bell, Cecil Kellaway, Matt Mattox. Abe Burrows became the director for Broadway, and re-wrote the book, as well as replacing most of the West Coast cast (Marion Bell was replaced by Anne Jeffreys, and Cecil Kellaway by Bert Wheeler). Eugene Loring was replaced as co-choreographer by Herb Ross.

The Broadway Run. MARK HELLINGER THEATRE, 3/21/52–5/24/52; PLYMOUTH THEATRE, 5/26/52–6/7/52. Total of 91 PERFORMANCES. PRESENTED BY Albert Lewis & Arthur Lewis; MUSIC/LYRICS: Ralph Blane; BOOK: Charles O'Neal & Abe Burrows; BASED ON the 1949 novel *The Three Wishes of Jamie McRuin*, by Charles O'Neal; DIRECTOR: Abe Burrows; CHOREOGRAPHER: Ted Cappy, with Herbert Ross; SETS: George Jenkins; COSTUMES: Miles White; LIGHTING: Feder; MUSICAL DIRECTOR: Joseph Littau; ORCHESTRATIONS: Robert Russell Bennett; CHORAL ARRANGEMENTS: William Ellfeldt; PRESS: Karl Bernstein & Harvey B. Sabinson; GENERAL MANAGER: Robert Rapport; STAGE MANAGER: Phil Friedman; ASSISTANT STAGE MANAGER: Robert Radnitz. *Cast*: TIM SHANAHAN: Robert Halliday; NORA: Michele Burke; MCCAFFREY: Wilton Clary; BRIDGIE QUINN: Marie Gibson; TIRSA SHANAHAN: Charlotte Rae (4); OWEN ROE TAVISH: Bert Wheeler (3); JAMIE MCRUIN: John Raitt (2); POWER O'MALLEY: Walter Burke; MAEVE HARRIGAN: Anne Jeffreys (1); RANDAL DEVLIN: Jeff Morrow; AUNT BID: Grania O'Malley; JESS PRODDY: Royal Dano; BIG PATRICK: Wilton

Clary; SHIEL HARRIGAN: Malcolm Keen; DENNIS O'RYAN: Peter Conlow; FATHER KERRIGAN: Ralph Morgan; KEVIN: Billy Chapin; SHERIFF HAINES: Dick Foote; PRINCIPAL DANCERS: Sandra Zell & George Foster; DANCERS: Doris Atkinson, Estelle Aza, Buddy Bryan, James Capp, Ann Deasy, Donn Driver, Mary Haywood, Elizabeth Logue, Mildred Ann Mauldin, Jerry Newby, Greg O'Brien, Robert St. Clair, Janet Sayers, Joe Stember; SINGERS: Leigh Allen, Marion Baird, Robert Baird, Michele Burke, Jerry Cardoni, Clifford Fearl, Marie Gibson, Joan Kibrig, Robert Lamont, Nancy Price, June Reimer, Ann Richards, Richard Scott, Donald Thrall, Tafi Towers, Richard Vine; CHILDREN: KENNETH FRANCIS: Pud Flanagan; JOHNNY FINLEY: Jackie Scholle; SORLEY BOY DONNER: Alfred Catal; LITTLE PATRICK: Martin Walker. *Understudies*: Maeve: Leigh Allen; Jamie/Randal: Wilton Clary; Owen Roe/Tim: Walter Burke; Father Kerrigan/Shiel/Sheriff: Richard Vine; Jess: Dick Foote; Dennis: Greg O'Brien; Tirsa: Michele Burke; Power/McCaffrey: Clifford Fearl; Kevin: Jackie Scholle; Aunt Bid/Nora: Marie Gibson. *Act I*: *Scene 1* The McRuin cottage in the province of Connaught, the west coast of Ireland; 1896; *Scene 2* A road; immediately following; *Scene 3* The camp of Shiel Harrigan's horse traders, in the state of Georgia; *Scene 4* A lane in the forest; *Scene 5* Outside Power O'Malley's shop in Atlanta; *Scene 6* A lane near Harrigan's camp; *Scene 7* Maeve Harrigan's tent; *Scene 8* A lane; the next morning; *Scene 9* The ritual tent. *Act II*: *Scene 1* Harrigan's camp; two years later; *Scene 2* Tirsa's tent; *Scene 3* A lane; *Scene 4* The cook tent; *Scene 5* A lane; *Scene 6* Maeve's tent; *Scene 7* A lane; that evening; *Scene 8* The deep forest; *Scene 9* A lane; a few days later; *Scene 10* The camp; immediately following. *Act I*: "The Wake" (Old Tim, Tirsa, Tavish, Mourners), "The Girl that I Court In My Mind" (Jamie), "Women's Work" (Women of the Camp) [added during the run], "My Home's a Highway" (Maeve & Horse Traders), "We're for Love" (Tavish, Horse Traders, Women of the Camp), "My Heart's Darlin'" (Jamie), "Goin' on a Hayride" (Jamie, Maeve, Boys & Girls), "Love Has Nothing to Do with Looks" (l: Charles Lederer) (Tirsa, Tim, Tavish), "My Heart's Darlin'" (reprise) (Maeve & Jamie), "I'll Sing You a Song" (Tirsa, Tim, Dennis, Tavish, Dennis' Brothers), "It Must Be Spring" (Maeve, Brides, Bridesmaids), Finale: "Wedding March" (Entire Company). *Act II*: "The Army Mule Song" (Jamie, Men & Women of the Camp), "What Do I Know?" (Maeve), "Expectant Father" (ch: Herbert Ross) (special mus: Lee J. Pockriss) (danced by Dennis), "It's a Wishing World" (Maeve & Jamie), "Trottin' to the Fair" (ch: Eugene Loring) (Jamie, Old Tim, Dennis, Men & Women of the Camp), "Love Has Nothing to Do with Looks" (Tirsa & Dennis), "April Face" (Tavish, Maeve, Jamie), Finale: "It's a Wishing World" (reprise) (Entire Company).

Broadway reviews were middle-of-the-road and divided. It failed because it was seen as a weak imitation of *Brigadoon* and *Finian's Rainbow*.

699. *The Threepenny Opera*

The Threepenny Opera is an updated spin off from John Gay's 1728 satirical British play *The Beggar's Opera*, which depicted judges and policemen as being as corrupt as the thieves and prostitutes they chased (see the appendix for more information on various productions of *The Beggar's Opera*). In fact, *The Threepenny Opera* has become even more famous than its parent. Elisabeth Hauptmann wrote *The Threepenny Opera* in German, as *Die Dreigroschenoper* (*The Three Groats Opera*), and it was then adapted by Bertolt Brecht and Kurt Weill and updated to Victorian London. Both plays used the same characters — Macheath the highwayman and his cronies. There have been other spin-offs from the Gay play, notably *Beggar's Holiday* (see under that title in the main part of this book).

Before Broadway. THE FIRST PRODUCTION OF *Die Dreigroschenoper*. THEATER AM SCHIFFBAUERDAMM, Berlin. Opened on 8/31/28. *Cast*: MACHEATH: Harald Paulsen; JENNY: Lotte Lenya [Miss Lenya was Mr. Weill's wife]. It soon became a hit throughout Europe.

It was first filmed in 1931, as *Die Dreigroschenoper*. DIRECTOR: G.W. Pabst. *Cast*: Lotte Lenya, Rudolf Forster.

THE FIRST BROADWAY PRODUCTION OF **The Threepenny Opera**. EMPIRE THEATRE, 4/13/33–4/22/33. 12 PERFORMANCES. NEWLY ADAPTED/NEW LYRICS: Gifford Cochran & Jerrold Krimsky; DIRECTOR: Francesco von Mendelssohn. *Cast:* CAPT. MACHEATH, ALIAS MACKIE MESSER: Robert Chisholm; PIRATE JENNY DIVER: Lotte Lenya; CROOKED FINGER JACK: Burgess Meredith; FILCH: Herbert Rudley; WALTER: Harry Bellaver; LUCY BROWN: Josephine Huston; PEACHUM: Rex Weber.

THE FAMOUS 1950S OFF BROADWAY RUN. Marc Blitzstein wrote a new translation in the late 1940s, and with Kurt Weill's blessing went ahead with it. Weill died before he could see it, but it premiered at an arts festival at BRANDEIS COLLEGE, Waltham, Mass., on 6/14/52. NARRATOR: Marc Blitzstein; CONDUCTOR: Leonard Bernstein; SINGER: Lotte Lenya. Marc Blitzstein coined the name Mack the Knife (Macheath's nickname). Bert Brecht had called his character Mackie Messer, which does mean Mack the Knife in German. This Brandeis production led to the famous Off Broadway production at the THEATRE DE LYS, where the run opened on 3/10/54. 95 PERFORMANCES. PRESENTED BY Carmen Capalbo & Stanley Chase; DIRECTOR: Carmen Capalbo. *Cast:* STREETSINGER: Gerald Price; J.J. PEACHUM: Leon Lishner; MRS. PEACHUM: Charlotte Rae, *Marcella Markham*; POLLY: Jo Sullivan; MACHEATH: Scott Merrill; JENNY: Lotte Lenya; TIGER BROWN: George Tyne; LUCY: Bea Arthur; MATT: John Astin; JAKE: Joseph Beruh; BOB: Bernard Bogin; WALT: Paul Dooley; FILCH: William Duell; MOLLY: Marion Selee.

The Threepenny Opera succeeded Gayle Stine's production of *Bullfight*, which in turn succeeded the original run of *End as a Man*. *The Threepenny Opera* had, in turn, to make way for another incoming show (*I Feel Wonderful*, by Jerry Herman). However, due to public demand and the demand of critics (notably Brooks Atkinson) it was brought back. It was quite a season for the Theatre de Lys.

THEATRE DE LYS. Re-opened on 9/20/55. 2,611 PERFORMANCES. This was the return engagement. It had the same crew, except MUSICAL DIRECTOR: Kelly Wyatt, *Mordecai Sheinkman* (from 58–59). **Return Cast:** STREETSINGER: Tige Andrews, *Jerry Orbach, Len Ross, Chuck Smith*; J.J. PEACHUM: Frederic Downs, *Ed Asner, Emile Renan, Mitchell Jason*; MRS. PEACHUM: Jane Connell, *Nina Dova, Jane Connell, Madeline Lee, Rosemary O'Reilly, Lu Leonard, Jo Hurt, Pert Kelton, Nancy Andrew Slater*; POLLY: Jo Sullivan, *Jo Wilder* (from 55–56), *Judith Paige* (by 58–59), *Cynthia Price* (from 58–59), *Gail Johnston* (from 59–60), *Cherry Davis* (from 60–61); MACHEATH: Scott Merrill, *James Mitchell* (from 56–57), *Gerald Price* (from 56–57), *Scott Merrill* (from 57–58), *Jerry Orbach* (from 57–58), *Gerald Price* (from 58–59), *Charles Rydell* (from 60–61); JENNY: Lotte Lenya, *Grete Mosheim* (from 4/17/56), *Katharine Sergava* (from 6/12/56), *Christiane Felsmann* (from 57–58), *Marion Brash* (from 59–60), *Carole Cook, Valerie Bettis, Dolly Haas*; TIGER BROWN: George Tyne; LUCY: Bea Arthur, *Jean Arnold* (from 55–56), *Ann Mitchell* (from 57–58), *Nadyne Turney* (from 59–60), *Georgia Brown*; MATT: John Astin, *Mitchell Lear* (from 56–57), *Stan Schneider* (from 57–58), *John Astin* (from 59–60), *Malachi Throne* (from 60–61); JAKE: Eddie Lawrence, *Maurice Shrog, Sidney Kay*; FILCH: William Duell; MOLLY: Marion Selee; MRS. COAXER: *Estelle Parsons* (in 1960).

Louis Armstrong and Bobby Darin had big hits with the main number "Mack the Knife." The songs (m: Weill; l: Brecht & Blitzstein) were: "Ballad of Mack the Knife" (Street Singer), "Morning Anthem" (Mr. Peachum), "Instead-Of Song" (Mr. & Mrs. Peachum), "Wedding Song" (Matt, Jake, Bob, Walt), "Pirate Jenny" (Polly), "Army Song" (Mack, Tiger, Gang), "Wedding Song" (reprise) (Matt, Jake, Bob, Walt), "Love Song" (Mack & Polly), "Ballad of Dependency" (Mrs. Peachum), "The World is Mean" (Polly, Mr. & Mrs. Peachum), "Polly's Song" (Mack & Polly), "Ballad of Dependency" (reprise) (Mrs. Peachum), "Tango Ballad" (Mack & Jenny), "Ballad of the Easy Life" (Mack), "Barbara Song" (Lucy), "Jealousy Duet" (Lucy & Polly), "How to Survive" (Mack, Mrs. Peachum, Ensemble), "Useless Song" (Mr. Peachum & Beggars), "Solomon Song" (Jenny), "Call from the Grave" (Mack), "Death Message" (Mack), "The Mounted Messenger" (Ensemble), "The Ballad of Mack the Knife" (reprise) (Street Singer).

The cast recording had the original cast, except Martin Wolfson as The Streetsinger. In 1956 the show won a Tony Award for Lotte Lenya, and a Special Tony for best Off-Broadway production. Scott Merrill was also nominated. This is a rare (but, by no means unheard of) case where Tonys were considered for Off Broadway productions. This became the first-ever long-running Off-Broadway production, and the longest-running Off-Broadway musical until *The Fantasticks*.

THE LONDON PRODUCTION. ROYAL COURT THEATRE, 2/9/56–3/17/56; ALDWYCH THEATRE, 3/21/56–6/9/56; COMEDY THEATRE, 6/19/56–7/14/56. Total of 167 PERFORMANCES. PRESENTED BY Oscar Lewenstein, Wolf Mankowitz, and Helen Arnold; DIRECTOR: Sam Wanamaker; CHOREOGRAPHER: Tutte Lemkow; MUSICAL DIRECTOR: Berthold Goldschmidt. *Cast:* MATT: George Murcell; JAKE: Warren Mitchell; PEACHUM: Eric Pohlmann; TIGER: George A. Cooper; MACHEATH: Bill Owen; POLLY: Daphne Anderson; LUCY: Georgia Brown; JENNY: Maria Remusat.

CANADIAN TOUR. Opened at the Royal Alexandra Theatre, Toronto, and closed there, on 9/30/61. MUSICAL DIRECTOR: Stanley Matlovsky. *Cast:* MACHEATH: Scott Merrill; JENNY: Gypsy Rose Lee; MRS. PEACHUM: Jane Connell; WALT: Herb Edelman; LUCY: Buzz Halliday.

It was filmed again in 1964, as *The Threepenny Opera*. DIRECTOR: Wolfgang Staudte. *Cast:* BALLAD SINGER: Sammy Davis Jr.; MACHEATH: Curt Jurgens; POLLY: June Ritchie; PIRATE JENNY: Hildegarde Neff; LUCY: Marlene Warrlich; TIGER: Lino Ventura; J.J.: Gert Frobe.

Die Dreigroschenoper. CITY CENTER, NYC, 3/11/65–3/27/65. 6 PERFORMANCES IN REPERTORY. In German. PRESENTED BY the New York City Opera; DIRECTOR: Adolf Rott; SETS: Wolfgang Roth; COSTUMES: Ruth Morley; CONDUCTOR: Julius Rudel. *Cast:* ANSAGER (NARRATOR): George S. Irving; PEACHUM: Stefan Schnabel; MRS. PEACHUM: Lilia Skala; POLLY: Anita Hoefer; MACHEATH: Kurt Kasznar; BROWN: Ralph Herbert; LUCY: Marion Brash; FILCH: Mathew Anden; (THE SIX MEMBERS OF) DIE PLATTE (THE GANG): HAKENFINGERJAKOB: Sol Frieder; MUENZMATTHIAS: John Garson; TRAUERWEIDENWALTER: Paul Andor; EDE: Michael Haeusserman; SAEGEROBERT: Claus Jurgens; JIMMY: Curt Lowens; DIE SPELUNKEN-JENNY: Martha Schlamme; HUREN (LADIES OF ILL-REPUTE): Constance Conrad, Carla Huston, Erna Rossman, Ruth Sobotka, Ludmilla Tchor; SMITH: David Smith; PASTOR KIMBALL: Henry Cordy. *Act I*: *Scene 1* A fair in Soho: "Die Moritat von Mackie Messer" (Ansager); *Scene 2* The shop of Jonathan Jeremiah Peachum, outfitter of Beggars: "Der Morgenchorale des Peachum" (Peachum), "Der Anstatt-Das-Song" (Peachum & Mrs. Peachum); *Scene 3* The stable: "Das Hochzeitslied fur aermere Leute" (Ensemble), "Die Seeraeuber-Jenny" (Polly), "Der Kanonen-Song" (Macheath), "Siehst du den Mond ueber Soho" ("Liebeslied") (Polly & Macheath); *Scene 4* Peachum's shop: "Der Song vom Nein und Ja" ("Barbara-Song") (Polly), Erstes Dreigroschen-Finale (Ueber die Unsicherheit menschlicher Verhaeltnisse). *Act II*: *Scene 1* The stable: "Die Ballade von der sexuellen Hoerigkeit" (Mrs. Peachum); *Scene 2* A bordello in Tunbridge: "Die Zuhaelterballade" (Macheath & Jenny); *Scene 3* A cell in the Old Bailey prison: "Die Ballade vom Angenehmen Leben" (Macheath), "Das Eifersuchts-Duett" (Lucy & Polly), Zweites Dreigroschen-Finale (Denn wovon lebt der Mensch?). *Act III*: *Scene 1* The street outside Peachum's shop: "Die Ballade vom der sexuellen Hoerigkeit" (reprise) (Mrs. Peachum), "Das Lied von der Unzulaenglichkeit menschlichen Strebens" (Peachum), "Salomon-Song" (Jenny); *Scene 2* The death cell in the Old Bailey prison; *Scene 3* The gallows: "Ballade, in der Macheath jedermann Abbitte leistet" (Macheath), Drittes Dreigroschen-Finale (Auftauchen des Reitenden-Boten), "Die Moritat von Mackie Messer" (reprise) (Ansager).

THE 1966 BROADWAY PRODUCTION WITH MARIONETTES. BILLY ROSE THEATRE, 10/27/66–11/6/66. Limited run of 13 PERFORMANCES. PRESENTED BY The Stockholm Marionette Theatre of Fantasy (Michael Meschke founder/artistic dir); PRODUCED BY: Jay K. Hoffman; DIRECTOR: Michael Meschke; CHOREOGRAPHER: Holger Rosenquist; SETS/PUPPETS/MASKS: Franciszka Themerson; LIGHTING: Jules Fisher; PRESS: Artie Solomon & Deborah Steinfirst. They weren't really marionettes, but actors behind cut-out figures, or costumed three-dimensionally. One actor supplied the voice of the marionette, and the marionette was played by another actor. The music used was the cast recording of the famous 1954 Off Broadway run (however some songs were deleted, and others cut short), with some of the songs in different order from the original. *Cast* (the names of the actors who played the marionettes are given in parentheses): A STREET SINGER/FILCH: Hakan Serner (Arne Hogsander); MR. J.J. PEACHUM: Ingvar Kjelsson (Ulf

Hakan Jansson); MRS. PEACHUM: Ulla Sjoblom (Zanza Lidums); POLLY PEACHUM: Helena Brodin (Ellika Linden); MACHEATH: Goran Graffman (Per Nielsen); JENNY: Ulla Sjoblom (Ellika Linden); TIGER BROWN: Jan Blomberg (Arne Hogsander); LUCY BROWN: Meta Velander (Ludis De Lind Van Wijngaarden); MACK'S GANG: MATT: Jan Blomberg; JAKE: Heinz Spira; BOB: Folke Tragradh; WALT: Michael Meschke; REST OF CAST: The Company.

HARTFORD, CONN. Opened on 5/24/68. 34 PERFORMANCES. PRESENTED BY the Hartford Stage Company; DIRECTOR: Peter Hunt; MUSICAL DIRECTOR: Arthur Rubinstein. *Cast:* Rue McClanahan, Judith McCauley, Tom Urich, Katherine Helmond.

REPERTORY THEATRE OF NEW ORLEANS. Opened on 3/20/70. 28 PERFORMANCES. DIRECTOR: June Havoc. *Cast:* June Havoc, Shev Rodgers.

AVON THEATRE, STRATFORD FESTIVAL, CANADA. Opened on 6/30/72. 30 PERFORMANCES. DIRECTOR: Jean Gascon. *Cast:* Jack Creley, Lila Kedrova, Anton Rodgers.

The 1976 Broadway production started to take off in 1974. It was the third American translation of the German play. Manheim and Willett's more accurate translation was more like the rough, anti-social original than the smoothed-out Marc Blitzstein adaptation used in the 1954 Theatre de Lys production. It stuck very close to the German original. Joe Papp (head of the New York Shakespeare Festival) wanted Michael Bennett to direct, but Mr. Bennett was not interested in revivals, and, in addition, was planning *A Chorus Line*.

The Broadway Run. VIVIAN BEAUMONT THEATRE, 5/1/76–1/23/77. 307 PERFORMANCES. The New York Shakespeare Festival production, (PRESENTED BY Joseph Papp; MUSIC/ORIGINAL ORCHESTRATIONS: Kurt Weill; LYRICS/BOOK: Bertolt Brecht; NEW TRANSLATION: Ralph Manheim & John Willett; BASED ON Elisabeth Hauptmann's German version of John Gay's 1728 English play *The Beggar's Opera*; DIRECTOR: Richard Foreman; CHOREOGRAPHER: none; SETS: Douglas W. Schmidt; COSTUMES: Theoni V. Aldredge; LIGHTING: Pat Collins; SOUND: Joseph Dungan, *Roger Jay*; MUSICAL DIRECTOR: Stanley Silverman; PRESS: Merle Debuskey & Faith Geer; GENERAL MANAGER: Robert Kamlot; PRODUCTION STAGE MANAGER: D.W. Koehler; STAGE MANAGER: Michael Chambers; ASSISTANT STAGE MANAGER: Frank Di Filia. *Cast:* THE BALLAD SINGER: Roy Brocksmith; MAC THE KNIFE: Raul Julia, *Philip Bosco, Roy Brocksmith*; LOW-DIVE JENNY TOWLER: Ellen Greene; JONATHAN PEACHUM: C.K. Alexander; SAMUEL (PEACHUM'S ASSISTANT): Tony Azito [a new character]; CHARLES FILCH: Ed Zang; MRS. CELIA PEACHUM: Elizabeth Wilson; MATT: Ralph Drischell; POLLY PEACHUM: Caroline Kava, *Blair Brown*; JAKE: William Duell; BOB: KC Wilson; NED: Rik Colitti, *Paul Ukena Jr.* [this role is seen as Ed in certain other productions]; JIMMY: Robert Schlee; WALT: Max Gulack; TIGER BROWN: David Sabin, *Jerome Dempsey*; SMITH: Glenn Kezer; LUCY BROWN: Blair Brown, *Penelope Bodry*; A CONSTABLE: John Ridge, *Lawrence Weber*; MESSENGER: Jack Eric Williams; BEGGARS/POLICEMEN: Pendleton Brown, M. Patrick Hughes, George McGrath, Rick Petrucelli, Craig Rupp, Armin Shimerman, Jack Eric Williams, Ray Xifo; WHORES: Penelope Bodry (*Lisa Kirchner*), Nancy Campbell, Gretel Cummings, Brenda Currin, Mimi Turque. *Standby:* Mac: Keith Charles. *Understudies:* Polly/Lucy: Penelope Bodry; Walt: Pendleton Brown; Mrs. Peachum: Gretel Cummings; Jonathan: Ralph Drischell; Tiger: Glenn Kezer; Bob/Samuel: George McGrath; Matt: John Ridge; Jimmy/Smith: Craig Rupp; Filch/Ned: Armin Shimerman; Jenny: Mimi Turque; Ballad Singer: Tony Azito & Jack Eric Williams; Jake: Ray Xifo. *Ensemble Swings:* Ralph Di Filia & Lisa Kirchner.

Set in London, at the time of Queen Victoria's coronation. Macheath, a highwayman known as Mac the Knife (this translation spells it Mac — most of the others use Mack, which was the spelling used by Marc Blitzstein for his earlier translation) marries Polly, daughter of the leader of Soho's underworld. However, he is betrayed by his in-laws and sent to Newgate Prison. Freed by Lucy, the police chief's daughter, he is betrayed again, this time by Jenny, a whore, and sentenced to hang, but granted a royal reprieve at last moment. ***Act I:*** Overture; ***Prologue:*** A market street in Soho: "Ballad of Mac the Knife" (Ballad Singer, Samuel, Jimmy, Messenger) ("Die Moritat von Mackie Messer"); ***Scene 1*** Peachum's beggars' outfit shop: "Peachum's Morning Hymn" (Peachum) ("Der Morgenchorale des Peachum"), "The 'No They Can't' Song"

(Peachum & Mrs. Peachum) ("Anstatt-Das-Song"); ***Scene 2*** An empty stable: "Wedding Song for the Less Well-Off" (Gang, Beggars, Mac, Polly) ("Das Hochzeitslied fur aermere Leute"), "The Cannon Song" (Mac & Tiger) ("Der Kanonen-Song"), "Liebeslied" (Mac & Polly) ("Liebeslied"); ***Scene 3*** Peachum's house: "Barbara Song" (Polly, Peachum, Mrs. Peachum) ("Barbara-Song"), First Threepenny Finale: "Concerning the Insecurity of the Human State" (Polly, Peachum, Mrs. Peachum) ("Erstes Dreigroschen-Finale"). ***Act II:*** ***Scene 1*** Stable: "Polly's Lied" (Polly) ("Pollys Lied"); ***Interlude*** A street: "Ballad of Sexual Obsession" (Mrs. Peachum) ("Die Ballade von der sexuellen Hoerigkeit"); ***Scene 2*** A brothel in Wapping: "Pirate Jenny" (Jenny), "Ballad of Immoral Earnings" (Mac & Jenny) ("Die Zuhaelterballade"); ***Scene 3*** Newgate Prison: "Ballad of Gracious Living" ("Ballad of Good Living") (Mac) ("Die Ballade vom Angenehmen Leben"), "Jealousy Duet" (Lucy & Polly) ("Das Eifersuchts-Duett"), Second Threepenny Finale: "What Keeps Mankind Alive?" (Mac, Offstage Voice, Jenny, Mrs. Peachum, Chorus) ("Zweites Dreigroschen-Finale"). ***Act III:*** ***Scene 1*** Peachum's house: "Ballad of Sexual Obsession" (last stanza) (Mrs. Peachum), "Song of the Insufficiency of Human Endeavor" (Peachum & Tiger) ("Lied von der Unzulaenglichkeit menschlichen Strebens"); ***Interlude*** A street: "Solomon Song" (Jenny) ("Salomon-Song"); Scene 2 Lucy's home; ***Scene 3*** Newgate Prison — the death cell: "Call from the Grave" (Mac) ("Rauf aus der Grab"), "Epitaph" (Ballad in which Macheath begs all men for forgiveness) (Mac) ("Grabschrift"), Third Threepenny Finale (Chorus, Brown, Mac, Polly, Peachum, Mrs. Peachum) ("Drittes Dreigroschen-Finale"), Ballad of Mac the Knife" (reprise) (Ballad Singer).

Note: The names of the original German musical numbers are in parentheses.

It got good reviews. It received Tony Nominations for revival, costumes, lighting, and for Raul Julia and Ellen Greene.

After Broadway. The Broadway production ran again Off Broadway, at the DELACORTE THEATRE, Central Park, 7/6/77–7/24/77. Previews from 6/28/77. 27 PERFORMANCES. It still starred Ellen Greene, and still had Penelope Bodry (at least) in the cast, but this time with Philip Bosco as well.

700. *3 Penny Opera*

Note the subtle change in spelling.

Before Broadway. This production previously ran at the National Theatre, Washington, DC. There were two intermissions.

The Broadway Run. LUNT-FONTANNE THEATRE, 11/5/89–12/31/89. 20 previews. 65 PERFORMANCES. PRESENTED BY Jerome Hellman, in association with Haruki Kadokawa & James M. Nederlander; MUSIC: Kurt Weill; LYRICS/BOOK: Bertolt Brecht; TRANSLATED FROM THE ORIGINAL GERMAN BY: Michael Feingold; DIRECTOR: John Dexter; CHOREOGRAPHER: Peter Gennaro; SETS/COSTUMES: Jocelyn Herbert; LIGHTING: Andy Phillips & Brian Nason; SOUND: Peter Fitzgerald; MUSICAL DIRECTOR/ADDITIONAL ORCHESTRATIONS/MUSICAL CONTINUITY: Julius Rudel; PRESS: Shirley Herz Associates; CASTING: Johnson — Liff & Zerman; GENERAL MANAGERS: Joseph Harris & Peter T. Kulok; COMPANY MANAGER: Kathleen Lowe; PRODUCTION STAGE MANAGER: Bob Borod; STAGE MANAGERS: Joe Cappelli & Artie Gaffin. *Cast:* A BALLAD SINGER: Ethyl Eichelberger (5); JENNY DIVER, A WHORE: Suzzanne Douglas; JONATHAN JEREMIAH PEACHUM, HEAD OF A GANG OF BEGGARS: Alvin Epstein (3) ☆; FILCH, A BEGGAR: Jeff Blumenkrantz; MRS. PEACHUM: Georgia Brown (4) ☆; POLLY PEACHUM, THEIR DAUGHTER: Maureen McGovern (2) ☆, *Nancy Ringham*; MACHEATH, HEAD OF A GANG OF CROOKS: Sting (1) ☆; MACHEATH'S GANG (SIX MEMBERS): MATT OF THE MINT: Josh Mostel; CROOK-FINGER JACK: Mitchell Greenberg; SAWTOOTH BOB: David Schechter; ED: Philip Carroll; WALTER (CALLED "WALT DREARY"): Tom Robbins; JIMMY: Alex Santoriello; TIGER BROWN, CHIEF OF LONDON POLICE: Larry Marshall; (SIX) WHORES: DOLLY: Anne Kerry Ford; BETTY: Jan Horvath; VIXEN: Teresa De Zarn; MOLLY: Nancy Ringham, *Leslie Castay*; SUKY TAWDRY: KT Sullivan; OLD WHORE: Fiddle Viracola; SMITH, A POLICE CONSTABLE: David Pursley; POLICEMEN: MacIntyre Dixon & Michael Piontek; LUCY, TIGER BROWN'S DAUGHTER: Kim Criswell; BEGGARS/BYSTANDERS: Philip Carroll, MacIntyre Dixon, Michael Piontek, David Schechter, Steven Major

West. *Understudies:* Macheath: Alex Santoriello; Mrs. Peachum: Fiddle Viracola; Matt/Ballad Singer/Smith/Ed/Walter/Jimmy/Bob/Policeman: Robert Ousley; Polly: Nancy Ringham; Mr. Peachum: David Pursley; Lucy: Teresa De Zarn; Jenny: Jan Horvath; Tiger: Steven Major West; Molly/Dolly/Betty/Vixen/Suky: Leslie Castay. *Orchestra:* TRUMPETS: Chris Gekker & Carl Albach; CLARINET: William Blount; TROMBONE: Michael Powell; ACCORDION: William Schimmel; FLUTE: Elizabeth Mann; GUITAR/BANJO: Scott Kuney; ALTO SAX: Ted Nash; TYMPANI: Maya Gungi; CELLO: Myron Lutske; PERCUSSION: Paul Pizzuti; TENOR SAX: Roger Rosenberg; PIANO: Stephen Hinnenkamp; KEYBOARD: Robert Wolinsky; BASS: John Kulowitsch. *Act I: Prologue* Street fair in Soho: Overture (Orchestra), "Ballad of Mack the Knife" ("Moritat") (Ballad Singer); *Scene 1* Peachum's shop; Wednesday morning: "Peachum's Morning Hymn" (Mr. Peachum), "The Why-Can't They Song" (Mr. & Mrs. Peachum); *Scene 2* A deserted stable; 5 p.m.: "Wedding Song" (Gang), "Pirate Jenny" (Polly), "Soldiers' Song" (Macheath & Brown), "Wedding Song" (reprise) (Gang), "Love Song" (Macheath & Polly); *Scene 3* Peachum's shop; Thursday morning: "Barbara Song" (Polly), First 3 Penny Finale (Polly, Mr. & Mrs. Peachum). *Act II: Scene 1* The stable; Thursday afternoon: "Melodrama and Polly's Song" (Macheath & Polly); *Interlude*; "Ballad of the Prisoner of Sex" (Mrs. Peachum); *Scene 2* A whorehouse in Tunbridge; later that afternoon: "Pimp's Ballad" (Tango) (Macheath & Jenny); *Scene 3* Old Bailey jail; immediately afterward: "Ballad of Living in Style" (Macheath), "Jealousy Duet" (Lucy & Polly), Second 3 Penny Finale (Macheath, Mrs. Peachum, Chorus). *Act III: Scene 1* Peachum's shop; late that night: "Ballad of the Prisoner of Sex" (reprise) (Mrs. Peachum), "Song of Futility" (Mr. Peachum); *Scene 2* Lucy's room in the Old Bailey: "Lucy's Aria" (Lucy); *Interlude*; "Solomon's Song" (Jenny); *Scene 3* Macheath's cell in the Old Bailey; 6 a.m., Friday: "Call from the Grave" (Macheath), "Epitaph" (Macheath), "March to the Gallows" (Orchestra), Third 3 Penny Finale (Entire Company).

Reviews were divided, mostly negative. Georgia Brown was nominated for a Tony.

After Broadway. CITY CENTER, NYC, 10/26/95–10/28/95. 3 PERFORMANCES. PRESENTED BY Sir Andrew Lloyd Webber & The National Youth Music Theatre; DIRECTOR: Mark Pattenden; CHOREOGRAPHER: Wendy Cook; MUSICAL DIRECTOR: Alison Berry. *Cast:* MACHEATH: Laurence Taylor; POLLY: Jessica Watson; JENNY: Tiffany Gore.

FREUD PLAYHOUSE, UCLA, Los Angeles, 9/9/98–9/20/98. 14 PERFORMANCES. Part of the *Reprise!* series. DIRECTOR: Glenn Casale; CHOREOGRAPHER: Kay Cole; MUSICAL DIRECTOR: Peter Martz. Greg Jbara and Rachel York were scheduled to star, but both had to leave before the production began. *Cast:* MACHEATH: Patrick Cassidy; PAPA PEACHUM: Theodore Bikel; ALSO WITH: Ken Page, Jonelle Allen, Carrie Hamilton, Marilynn Lovell.

GEARY THEATRE, San Francisco, 9/8/99–10/3/99. Previews: 9/2/99–9/7/99. PRESENTED BY the American Conservatory Theatre; DIRECTOR: Carey Perloff; CHOREOGRAPHER: Luis Perez; MUSICAL DIRECTOR: Peter Maleitzke. *Cast:* JENNY: Bebe Neuwirth; MACHEATH: Philip Casnoff; LUCY: Lisa Vroman; MRS. PEACHUM: Nancy Dussault; MR. PEACHUM: Steven Anthony Jones; POLLY: Anika Noni Rose.

LUCILLE LORTEL THEATRE, 12/18/00. This was a benefit reunion concert for the actors who had been in the famous 1950s Off Broadway production. The Lucille Lortel was the old Theatre De Lys, where the 1950s show had been performed. DIRECTOR/CHOREOGRAPHER: Donald Saddler; MUSICAL DIRECTOR: Glen Clugston. *Cast:* PEACHUM: George S. Irving [Mr. Irving was not an original]; MRS. PEACHUM: Charlotte Rae; POLLY: Jo Sullivan; MACHEATH: Robert Cuccioli [Mr. Cuccioli was not an original]; FILCH: William Duell; JENNY: Bea Arthur [this was the old Lotte Lenya part].

WILLIAMSTOWN THEATRE FESTIVAL, 6/25/03–7/6/03. DIRECTOR: Peter Hunt. *Cast:* STREETSINGER: Laurent Giroux; J.J.: David Schramm; MRS. PEACHUM: Randy Graff; POLLY: Melissa Errico; MACHEATH: Jesse L. Martin; TIGER: Jack Wills; LUCY: Karen Ziemba; FILCH: William Duell; JAKE: Jack Noseworthy; WALT: John Ellison Conlee; MATT: Jim Stanek; BOB THE SAW: Julio Monge; COAXER: Kelly Brady; BETTY: Kathy McCafferty; MOLLY: Rachel Siegel; DOLLY: Sarah Knowlton; JENNY: Betty Buckley; SMITH: Kenneth Garner; REV. KIMBALL: Stephen Gabis.

By June 2003 there was talk of a new Broadway revival for the 2004–2005 season, newly translated and adapted by Wallace Shawn. It had a workshop in 2004. PRESENTED BY the Roundabout Theatre Company; DIRECTOR: Scott Elliott. *Cast:* Edie Falco, Christine Baranski, Wallace Shawn. However, it was canceled. By Jan. 2005 it was brought forward a burner, this time with vague plans for a Jan. 2006 Broadway opening. By Feb. 2005 it was on for a spring 2006 opening on Broadway, at STUDIO 54. DIRECTOR: Scott Elliott. *Cast:* MACK: Alan Cumming; JENNY: Edie Falco; MOLLY: Nellie McKay.

701. *Tickets, Please!*

An intimate musical revue.

Before Broadway. It ran into trouble during the Boston tryouts, and the director, Mervyn Nelson, was fired. George Abbott was brought in, bringing Hal Prince with him as 1st assistant stage manager. There was no chorus line. This was Larry Kert's Broadway debut.

The Broadway Run. CORONET THEATRE, 4/27/50–10/30/50; MARK HELLINGER THEATRE, 11/6/50–11/25/50. Total of 245 PERFORMANCES. PRESENTED BY Arthur Klein; MUSIC/LYRICS: Joan Edwards & Lyn Duddy, Mel Tolkin, Lucille Kallen, Clay Warnick; SKETCHES: Harry Herrmann, Edmund Rice, Jack Roche, Ted Luce; DIRECTOR: Mervyn Nelson; CHOREOGRAPHER: Joan Mann; SETS/LIGHTING: Ralph Alswang; COSTUMES: Peggy Morrison; MUSICAL DIRECTOR: Phil Ingalls; ORCHESTRATIONS: Ted Royal; INCIDENTAL MUSIC: Phil Ingalls & Hal Hastings; PRESS: Karl Bernstein & Harvey B. Sabinson; GENERAL MANAGER: Charles Harris; STAGE MANAGER: Ted Luce; ASSISTANT STAGE MANAGER: H. Smith Prince (this is Hal Prince). *Act I: Prologue* (Grace & Paul Hartman (1) ☆, Mildred Hughes). In this witty prologue the Hartmans told us that the title of the revue came from hearing "Tickets, Please!" continually demanded of audiences in line for *South Pacific*; *Scene 1* "Tickets, Please!" (m: Warnick; l: Tolkin & Kallen) [Bill Norvas & the Upstarts (Dee Arlen, Larry Kert, Ronnie Edwards, Phyllis Cameron) (7); *Scene 2* Roller Derby [Jack Albertson (2), Grace & Paul Hartman (1) ☆, with Grace as an aggressive spectator annoying the commentator]; *Scene 3* "Washington Square" (m: Warnick; l: Tolkin & Kallen) [ch & danced by Dorothy Jarnac (3)]. ARTIST: Jack Albertson (2); *Scene 4* "Darn it, Baby, That's Love" (m: Edwards; l: Duddy) [Jack Albertson (2) & Patricia Bright (4)]; *Scene 5* Roger Price (6) (a comic from West Virginia, who wrote his own monologues. He told of his Confederate uncle Parker who fought with the famous Retreating Forty-Ninth, strategically installed in a position surrounding a still. Mr. Price left during the run, and was replaced by *Gabriel Dell* & *Norman Abbott*, who performed two untitled monologues written by Len Stern); *Scene 6* "The Ballet isn't Ballet Any More" (m/l: Jack Weinstock, Willie Gilbert, Herb Hecht) [Patricia Bright (4)]; *Scene 7* Les Ballets (Grace & Paul Hartman (1) ☆, Roger Price (6), Bill Norvas & the Upstarts) (7); *Scene 8* "Restless" (m: Edwards; l: Duddy) (sung by Midge Parker) [danced by Tommy Wonder (5)]; *Scene 9* A Senate Investigation (Mr. Hartman as an atomic scientist who scares senate investigators by bouncing an A-bomb up and down on the floor like a ball) [Roger Price (6), Jack Albertson (2), Patricia Bright (4), Grace & Paul Hartman (1) ☆]; *Scene 10* "You Can't Take it with You" (m: Edwards; l: Duddy) [sung by Patricia Bright (4), Jack Albertson (2), Grace Hartman (1) ☆]; *Scene 11* Drama — the Plot is Always the Same (sketch about a cookbook author unable to cook dumplings): THE AUTHOR: Roger Price (6); THE THESPIANS: Grace & Paul Hartman (1) ☆, Jack Albertson (2), Patricia Bright (4), Dorothy Jarnac (3), Tommy Wonder (5), Mildred Hughes, Bill Norvas and the Upstarts (7), Midge Parker, Stuart Wade. *Act II: Scene 1* "Back at the Palace" (m: Warnick; l: Tolkin & Kallen; add l: Jack Fox) [Paul Hartman (1) ☆ & Jack Albertson (2)]; *Scene 2* "Symbol of Fire" (m: Warnick; l: Tolkin & Kallen) (sung by Stuart Wade) [danced by Grace & Paul Hartman (1) ☆, Tommy Wonder (5), Bill Norvas, Larry Kert, Ronnie Edwards]; *Scene 3* "(Television's) Tough on Love" (m: Edwards; l: Duddy) [sung by singer-comedienne Patricia Bright (4)]; *Scene 4* Mr. Proggle [Grace & Paul Hartman (1) ☆]; *Scene 5* "The Moment I Looked in Your Eyes" (m: Edwards; l: Duddy) (sung by Stuart Wade & Mildred Hughes); *Scene 6* "Spring Has Come" (m: Mel Tolkin & Max Liebman) [danced by eccentric dancer Dorothy Jarnac (3), hoofer Tommy Wonder (5), comic dancer-singer Jack Albertson (2),

Patricia Bright (4), and Bill Norvas and the Upstarts); *Scene 7* Roger Price (6). He told of his cousin Sally who went to a party naked, and had all the men neglecting the other girls. Sally was once approached by a tall, dark, handsome stranger, who pressed a note into her hand reading, "You are the one and only woman I ever loved. Come to my room, 417, at the Eddison Hotel at midnight." She didn't go, as she wasn't sure he was sincere — the note was mimeographed. Mr. Price left during the run. *Gabe Dell* & *Norm Abbott* replaced him (see Act I Scene 5)]; *Scene 8* "Maha Roger" (m: Warnick; l: Tolkin & Kallen) [Bill Norvas and the Upstarts (7)]; *Scene 9* Maha the Great [Grace & Paul Hartman (1) ☆, Bill Norvas and the Upstarts (7)].

It got good reviews on Broadway.

702. *Tidbits of 1946*

An intimate musical entertainment, or vaudeville show.

Before Broadway. Originally performed by a group of amateurs (the Youth Theatre) during the week of 5/20/46 at the Barbizon-Plaza Hotel. It was then taken over by Arthur Klein and Henry Schumer and professionalized for Broadway. The Mack Triplets (a harmonizing sister trio), and Sherry Simmons were dropped for Broadway.

The Broadway Run. PLYMOUTH THEATRE, 7/8/46–7/13/46. 8 PERFORMANCES. PRESENTED BY Arthur Klein, in association with Henry Schumer; SKETCHES: Sam Locke, credited to the Youth Theatre Group; DIRECTOR: Arthur Klein; SKETCH DIRECTOR: Sam Locke; MUSICAL DIRECTOR: Phil Romano; PRESS: Karl Bernstein; COMPANY MANAGER: Sam Handelsman; STAGE MANAGER: Robert Sharron. *Act I*: Apologia [Lee Trent (3), the master of ceremonies]; Harmonica Days [Eddy Manson (6), harmonica player]; "Hi Havana!" [danced by Carmen & Rolando (5), a South American couple in samba & rumba dances. BONGO BOY: Candido (i.e. Candido Vicenty); On the Veld (South African folk songs) [Josef Marais & Miranda (4), South African folk singers]; Psychiatry in Technicolor (in a psychiatrist's office): DR. SERUTAN PIMENTO: Joey Faye (1); MISS FORTESCUE WIMPY: Josephine Boyer (9); THE OEDIPUS REX: Jack Diamond (10); MR. PICKLING: Joshua Shelley (8); So It Goes at the Met (opera burlesque) [Robert Marshall (7), tenor]; In a Jeep [Joey Faye (1) & Jack Diamond (10)]; "I'm the Belle of the Ballet" [a travesty of ballet] (sung by Josephine Boyer (9)]; "Step This Way" (black tap-dance quintet) [The Debonairs (11)]. *Act II*: "On the Way to Sloppy Joe's" [danced by Carmen & Rolando (5). BONGO BOY: Candido]; A Few Moments with Lee Trent (1), comedian; The Man Who Came to Heaven (a congressman tries to get into Heaven): THE ANGEL: Joey Faye (1); THE CONGRESSMAN: Joshua Shelley (8); Cape Town Capers (South African folk songs) [Josef Marais & Miranda (4)]; Never Kill Your Mother on Mother's Day (m/l: Mel Tolkin) [Lee Trent (1) & Josh Shelley (8), comedians]; The Lass with the Delicate Air [Muriel Gaines (2), black singer-dancer]; Meet Me on Flugle Street [Joey Faye (1) & Jack Diamond (10), burlesque comedian and straight man]; Finale (Company).

Broadway reviews were disastrous.

703. *Timbuktu!*

A musical fable. It was a revised and all-black version of *Kismet.* Set in the ancient West African empire of Mali (the country where Timbuktu is located), in 1361 (752 in the Islam calendar). The songs are basically those in *Kismet.* Sahleem-La-Lume is the wife of wives to the wazir.

Before Broadway. It tried out at the Kennedy Center, Washington, DC, 1/5/78–2/5/78. 1st-billed William Marshall was replaced by Ira Hawkins (who was not 1st-billed).

The Broadway Run. MARK HELLINGER THEATRE, 3/1/78–9/10/78. 22 previews. 221 PERFORMANCES. PRESENTED BY Luther Davis, in association with Sarnoff International Enterprises, William D. Cunningham, and the John F. Kennedy Center for the Performing Arts; MUSIC/LYRICS: Robert Wright & George Forrest (based on the music of Alexander Borodin, and on African folk music); BOOK: Luther Davis (based on the musical *Kismet,* by Charles Lederer & Luther Davis); STORY BASED ON

the 1911 play *Kismet,* by Edward Knoblock; DIRECTOR/CHOREOGRAPHER/COSTUMES: Geoffrey Holder; SETS: Tony Straiges; LIGHTING: Ian Calderon; SOUND: Abe Jacob; MUSICAL SUPERVISOR/MUSICAL DIRECTOR/ARRANGEMENTS/INCIDENTAL MUSIC: Charles H. Coleman; ADDITIONAL ORCHESTRATIONS: Bill Brohn; PRESS: Solters & Roskin; GENERAL MANAGEMENT: Gatchell & Neufeld; COMPANY MANAGER: Drew Murphy; PRODUCTION STAGE MANAGER: Donald Christy; STAGE MANAGERS: Jeanna Belkin & Pat Trott. **Cast:** THE CHAKABA (STILTWALKER): Obba Babatunde; BEGGARS: Harold Pierson, Shezwae Powell, Louis Tucker; HADJI: Ira Hawkins (4); MARSINAH, HIS DAUGHTER: Melba Moore (2) ☆, *Vanessa Shaw* (from 7/14/78); WITCHDOCTOR: Harold Pierson; CHILD: Deborah Waller; M'BALLAH OF THE RIVER: Daniel Barton (9); NAJUA, SERVANT TO SAHLEEM-LA-LUME: Eleanor McCoy (8); THE WAZIR: George Bell (6); CHIEF POLICEMAN: Bruce A. Hubbard (7); SAHLEEM LA-LUME: Eartha Kitt (1) ☆; THREE PRINCESSES OF BAGUEZANE: Deborah K. Brown, Sharon Cuff, Patricia Lumpkin; MUNSHI, BODYSERVANT TO THE MANSA: Miguel Godreau (5); THE MANSA OF MALI: Gilbert Price (3) ☆; ORANGE MERCHANT: Obba Babatunde; BIRDS IN PARADISE: Miguel Godreau & Eleanor McCoy; ANTELOPES: Obba Babatunde & Luther Fontaine; WOMAN IN THE GARDEN: Shezwae Powell; ZUBBEDIYA: Vanessa Shaw; CITIZENS OF TIMBUKTU: Obba Babatunde, Gregg Baker, Daniel Barton, Joella Breedlove, Deborah K. Brown, Tony Carroll, Sharon Cuff, Cheryl Cummings, Luther Fontaine, Michael F. Harrison, Dyane Harvey, Marzetta Jones, Jimmy Justice, Eugene Little, Patricia Lumpkin, Joe Lynn, Tony Ndogo, Harold Pierson, Ray Pollard, Shezwae Powell, Ronald Richardson, Vanessa Shaw, Louis Tucker, Deborah Waller, Renee Warren. **Understudies**: Hadji: Gregg Baker; Sahleem-La-Lume: Shezwae Powell; Marsinah: Vanessa Shaw; Mansa: Bruce A. Hubbard; Wazir: Louis Tucker; Munshi: Eugene Little; Chief of Police: Ron Richardson; Najua: Dyanc Harvey; M'Ballah: Jimmy Justice; Birds: Eugene Little & Dyane Harvey; Princesses: Joella Breedlove; Antelopes: Tony Ndogo. **Swing Dancers**: Rodney Green & Jan Hazell. *Act I*: From dawn to dusk: *Scene 1* The city square of Timbuktu; dawn: "Rhymes Have I" (Hadji, Marsinah, Beggars), "Fate" (Hadji); *Scene 2* The gates of the city: "In the Beginning, Woman" * (Sahleem La-Lume); *Scene 3* The city square at market time: "Baubles, Bangles and Beads" (Marsinah & Merchants); *Scene 4* A garden of a house near the palace: "Birds in Paradise Garden" * (dance), "Stranger in Paradise" (Mansa & Marsinah); *Scene 5* A courtyard of the palace: "Gesticulate" (Hadji & Council); *Scene 6* An attiring pavilion in the palace: "Night of My Nights" (Mansa & Courtiers). *Act II*: From dusk to dawn: *Scene 1* En route to the garden: "Nuptial Celebration" * (dance) (People of Mali); *Scene 2* The garden: "My Magic Lamp" * (Marsinah), "Stranger in Paradise" (reprise) (Marsinah); *Scene 3* A corridor in the palace; *Scene 4* The Wazir's harem: "Rahadlakum" (Sahleem La-Lume & Ladies of the Harem); *Scene 5* Another part of the palace: "And This is My Beloved" (Hadji, Marsinah, Mansa, Wazir); *Scene 6* Palace court: "Golden Land, Golden Life" * (Chief Policeman & Nobles of the Court), "Zubbediya" and dances (Zubbediya, Princesses, Other Marriage Candidates, Court Acrobat), "Night of My Nights" (reprise) (Mansa, Marsinah, Hadji, Nobles of the Court), "Sands of Time" (Hadji & Sahleem La-Lume).

Note: those numbers asterisked were newly written for this production by Wright & Forrest.

The show was panned by the critics. It received Tony nominations for revival, costumes, and for Gilbert Price and Eartha Kitt.

After Broadway. TOUR. Opened on 9/20/78, at the Fisher Theatre, Detroit, and closed on 2/4/79, at the Pantages Theatre, Los Angeles. **Cast:** SAHLEEM-LA-LUME: Eartha Kitt; MARSINAH: Vanessa Shaw; CHILD: Deborah Waller; M'BALLAH: Daniel Barton; WAZIR: George Bell; STRONGMAN: Tony Carroll; SHAKABA: Luther Fontaine; HADJI: Gregg Baker; NAJUA: Dyane Harvey; CHIEF POLICEMAN: Ronald A. Richardson; MUNSHI: Homer Bryant; ANTELOPE: William McPherson; ZUBBEDIYA: Priscilla Baskerville; MANSA: Bruce A. Hubbard; ENSEMBLE: Deborah K. Brown, Patricia Lumpkin, Joe Lynn, Tony Ndogo.

704. *A Time for Singing*

Set about 1900, in the memory of David, flowing freely in time in the Valley, the Town, and the Morgan home in South

Wales. The family life, romances, union agitation against the mine owners, and involvement in a tragic mine accident of the large Morgan family, as remembered fondly and sentimentally by their friend, the Protestant village minister. It was centered around the Morgan family, and involved the formation of a miners' union, and the romance between Angharad and David, who advises her to marry the wealthy son of the mine owner. When a strike is called Angharad finds herself married to her family's enemy. The strikers flood the mines, two men are killed, and Angharad is finally reunited with David.

Before Broadway. The show tried out in Boston. Gower Champion came in to re-stage some of Don McKayle's numbers. Before Broadway the numbers "I'd Be a Fine One to Marry," "Of the 53 Men" and "I'm Not Afraid" were cut. During Broadway previews the first 100 ticket-buyers would get a free folding chair and picnic lunch catered by the Brasserie.

The Broadway Run. BROADWAY THEATRE, 5/21/66–6/25/66. 10 previews from 5/12/66. 41 PERFORMANCES. PRESENTED BY Alexander H. Cohen, in association with Joseph Wishy; MUSIC: John Morris; LYRICS/BOOK: Gerald Freedman & John Morris; BASED ON the 1940 novel *How Green Was My Valley*, by Richard Llewellyn, and the John Ford-directed, Oscar-winning 1941 movie of the same name made from it; DIRECTOR: Gerald Freedman; CHOREOGRAPHER: Donald McKayle (choreography doctored by Gower Champion); SETS: Ming Cho Lee; COSTUMES: Theoni V. Aldredge; LIGHTING: Jean Rosenthal; MUSICAL DIRECTOR: Jay Blackton; ORCHESTRATIONS: Don Walker; CAST RECORDING on Warner Bros; PRESS: James D. Proctor, Robert W. Larkin, Sally Zeitlin; PRODUCTION ASSOCIATES: Hildy Parks & Milton Chwasky; GENERAL MANAGER: Roy A. Somlyo; PRODUCTION STAGE MANAGERS: Jake Hamilton & George Thorn; STAGE MANAGER: Tom Porter. *Cast:* DAVID GRIFFITH: Ivor Emmanuel (1) ☆; PAYMASTER: Jay Gregory; DAI BANDO: John Call; CYFARTHA LEWIS: George Mathews; GWILLYM MORGAN (DADA): Laurence Naismith (4) ☆; DAVEY MORGAN: Gene Rupert (7); IVOR MORGAN: Brian Avery; IANTO MORGAN: George Hearn (8); OWEN MORGAN: Harry Theyard; EVAN MORGAN: Philip Proctor; HUW MORGAN: Frank Griso (5); BETH MORGAN: Tessie O'Shea (2) ☆; ANGHARAD MORGAN: Shani Wallis (3) ☆; BRONWEN JENKINS: Elizabeth Hubbard (6); MR. EVANS: John Malcolm; IESTYN EVANS: David O'Brien; SCHOOL TEACHER: David Thomas; SINGERS: Robert Carle, Ed Ericksen, Jay Gregory, Marian Haraldson, Zona Kennedy, Reid Klein, Henry LeClair, Constance Moffit, Jack Murray, Mari Nettum, Joyce O'Neil, Michael Quinn, Maggie Task, Ann Tell, David Thomas, Maggie Worth; DANCERS: Patty Mount (*Sue Babel*), Bruce Becker, Steven Boockvor, Sandra Brewer, Roger Briant, Sterling Clark, Carolyn Dyer, Mary Ehara, Rodney Griffin, Mimi Wallace; CHILDREN: Paul Dwyer, Peter Falzone, Dewey Golkin, Laura Michaels, Jancie Notaro. *Standbys:* Beth: Travis Hudson; Angharad/Bronwen: Mari Nettum. *Understudies:* David: George Hearn; Dada: George Mathews; Davey/Ivor: Harry Theyard; Owen: Reid Klein; Evan: Sterling Clark; Huw: Peter Falzone & Dewey Golkin; Mr. Evans/Cyfartha: Mike Quinn; Iestyn: Jay Gregory; Dai Bando: David Thomas. *Act I:* "Come You Men" (Male Singing Chorus), "How Green Was My Valley" (David & Chorus), "Old Long John" (Male Singing Chorus), "Here Come Your Men" (Male Singing Chorus), "What a Good Day is Saturday" (Beth, Dada, Angharad, Brothers, Company), "Peace Come to Every Heart" (Company), "Someone Must Try" (David), "Oh, How I Adore Your Name" (Angharad), "That's What Young Ladies Do" (David), "When He Looks at Me" (Angharad), "Far from Home" (Beth, Angharad, Dada, Brothers), "I Wonder If" (Brothers), "What a Party" (Dada, David, Cyfartha, Dai Bando, Brothers), "Let Me Love You" (Angharad), "Why Would Anyone Want to Get Married?" (Huw, Brothers, Beth, Dada), "A Time for Singing" (Beth & Company). *Act II:* "When the Baby Comes" (Company), "I'm Always Wrong" (Angharad), "There is Beautiful You Are" (David), "Three Ships" (Ivor, Bronwen, Beth, Company), "Tell Her" (Dada & Huw), "There is Beautiful You Are" (reprise) (David), "Let Me Love You" (reprise) (Angharad & David), "And the Mountains Sing Back" (David), "Gone in Sorrow" (Company), "How Green Was My Valley" (reprise) (Company).

Broadway reviewers panned the show.

705. *Tintypes*

A cavalcade of old-time songs, spanning the period 1876–1920.

Before Broadway. It began as a cabaret production at ARENA STAGE, Washington, DC, on 2/28/79. Sub-titled *A Ragtime Revue*. It had the same basic crew as for the subsequent Broadway run, except DESIGN CONSULTANT: Hugh Lester; LIGHTING: Roger Milliken. *Cast:* Nedra Dixon, Timothy Jerome, Carolyn Mignini, Mary Catherine Wright, Jerry Zaks, Robert Fisher (at piano). Then it played the ASOLO THEATRE, Sarasota, 1979. Then the THEATRE OF ST. PETER'S CHURCH (Off Off Broadway), 4/17/80–8/10/80. 3 previews. 134 PERFORMANCES. Under the auspices of ANTA. It had the same crew as for the subsequent Broadway run, except COSTUMES: Karyl Ann Leigh; GENERAL MANAGER: Scott Steele; COMPANY MANAGER: John Parsons; STAGE MANAGERS: Bonnie Panson & Pauletta Pearson. It had the same cast, but Wayne Bryan was in the cast, not Jerry Zaks. *Understudies:* Pauletta Pearson, S. Epatha Merkerson, Jeff Brooks (*Wayne Bryan*), Marie King. Then to Broadway.

The Broadway Run. JOHN GOLDEN THEATRE, 10/23/80–1/11/81. 11 previews. 93 PERFORMANCES. The American National Theatre & Academy production, PRESENTED BY Richmond Crinkley & Royal Pardon Productions, Ivan Bloch, Larry J. Silva, and Eve Skina, in association with Joan F. Tobin; TRADITIONAL MUSIC & LYRICS ARRANGED BY: Mel Marvin; CONCEIVED BY: Mary Kyte, with Mel Marvin & Gary Pearle; DIRECTOR: Gary Pearle; CHOREOGRAPHER: Mary Kyte; SETS: Tom Lynch; ASSISTANT SETS: Adrianne Lobel; COSTUMES: Jess Goldstein; LIGHTING: Paul Gallo; SOUND: Jack Mann; MUSICAL DIRECTOR: Mel Marvin; ORCHESTRATIONS: John McKinney; VOCAL ARRANGEMENTS: Mel Marvin & John McKinney; PRESS: Hunt/Pucci; CASTING: Deborah Brown; GENERAL MANAGERS: Elizabeth I. McCann & Nelle Nugent; COMPANY MANAGER: James A. Gerald; PRODUCTION STAGE MANAGER: Steve Beckler; STAGE MANAGER: Bonnie Panson; ASSISTANT STAGE MANAGER: Marie King. *Cast:* Carolyn Mignini, Lynne Thigpen, Trey Wilson, Mary Catherine Wright, Jerry Zaks, Mel Marvin (conducting at the piano). *Standbys:* For Miss Mignini/Miss Wright: Marie King; For Mr. Wilson/Mr. Zaks: Wayne Bryan; For Miss Thigpen: S. Epatha Merkerson. *Production Musicians:* VIOLIN: Jill Jaffe; CELLO: Daryl Goldberg; PERCUSSION: Bruce Doctor; REED: Leslie Scott; TROMBONE: Dean Plank. *Act I:* ARRIVALS: "Ragtime Nightingale" (m/l: Joseph F. Lamb, 1915), "The Yankee Doodle Boy" (m/l: George M. Cohan, 1904) [from *Little Johnny Jones*], "Ta-Ra-Ra-Boom-De-Ay!" (m/l: Henry J. Sayers, 1891), "I Don't Care" (m: Harry O. Sutton; l: Jean Lenox, 1905), "Shine On, Harvest Moon" (by Nora Bayes & Jack Norworth) [deleted before Broadway], "Come Take a Trip in My Air Ship" (m/l: George Evans & Ren Shields, 1904), "Kentucky Babe" (m/l: Richard H. Buck & Adam Geibel, 1896), "(A) Hot Time in the Old Town (Tonight)" (m: Theo H. Metz; l: Joe Hayden, 1896), "Stars and Stripes Forever" (m: John Philip Sousa, 1897); INGENUITY AND INVENTIONS: "Electricity" (m: Karl Hoschna; l: Harry B. Smith, 1905); T.R.: "El Capitan" (m: John Philip Sousa, 1896) [from the show of the same name]; WHEELS: "Pastime Rag" (m: Artie Matthews, 1920), "Meet Me in St. Louis" (m: Kerry Mills; l: Andrew B. Sterling, 1904), "Solace" (m: Scott Joplin, 1909) [before Broadway "Daisy Bell" was here, written by Harry Dacre], "Waltz Me Around Again, Willie" (m: Ren Shields; l: Will D. Cobb, 1906) [from *His Honor the Mayor*], "Wabash Cannonball" (traditional), "In My Merry Oldsmobile" (m: Gus Edwards; l: Vincent P. Bryan, 1905) [before Broadway "The Soldiers in the Park" was here, written by Aubrey Hapwood, Harry Greenbank, Lionel Monckton]; THE FACTORY: "Wayfaring Stranger" (traditional), "Sometimes I Feel Like a Motherless Child" (traditional), "Aye Lye, Lyu Lye" (traditional), "I'll Take You Home Again, Kathleen" (m/l: Thomas P. Westendorf, 1876), "America the Beautiful" (m/l: Katherine Lee Bates & Samuel Ward, 1910), "Wait for the Wagon" (traditional), "What it Takes to Make Me Love You — You've Got It" (m/l: J.W. Johnson & James Reese Europe, 1914); ANNA HELD: "The Maiden with the Dreamy Eyes" (m: Bob Cole; l: J.W. Johnson, 1901) [from *The Little Duchess*], "If I Were on the Stage (Kiss Me Again)" (m: Victor Herbert; l: Henry Blossom, 1905) [from *Mademoiselle Modiste*]; OUTSIDE LOOKING IN: "Shortnin' Bread" (traditional), "Nobody" (m: Alex Rogers; l: Bert Williams, 1905); FITTING IN: "Elite Syncopations" (m: Scott Joplin, 1902), "I'm Goin' to Live Anyhow, 'til I Die" (m/l: Shepard N. Edmonds, 1900). **Act II**: "The Ragtime Dance" (m: Scott Joplin, 1902); PANAMA: "I Want What I Want When I Want It" (m: Victor Herbert; l: Henry Blossom & Victor Herbert, 1905) [from *Mademoiselle Modiste*]; THE LADIES: "It's Delightful to Be Married!" (m: Vincent Scotto; l: Anna Held, 1907) [from *A Parisian Model*], "Fifty-Fifty" (m/l: Jim Burris & Chris Smith, 1914), "American Beauty" (m/l: Joseph F. Lamb, 1913) [before Broadway "Eugenia" was here, written by Scott Joplin]; RICH AND POOR: "Then I'd Be Satisfied with Life" (m/l: George M. Cohan, 1902) [from *Running for Office*, 1903], "Narcissus" (m: Ethelbert Nevin, 1891), "Jonah Man" (m/l: Alex Rogers, 1903), "When it's All Goin' Out and Nothin' Comin' In" (m/l: Bert Williams & George Walker, 1902) [from *Sally in Our Alley*], "We Shall Not Be Moved" (traditional); VAUDEVILLE: "Hello, Ma Baby" (m: Joseph E. Howard; l: Ida Emerson, 1899), "Teddy Da Roose" (m/l: Ed Moran & J. Fred Helf, 1910), "A Bird in a Gilded Cage" (m: Arthur J. Lamb & Harry von Tilzer, 1900), "Bill Bailey, Won't You Please Come Home" (m/l: Hughie Cannon, 1902), "She's Gettin' More Like the White Folks Every Day" (m/l: Bert Williams & George Walker, 1901), "You're a Grand Old Flag" (m/l: George M. Cohan, 1906) [from *George Washington Jr.*], "The Yankee Doodle Boy" (reprise); FINALE: "Toyland" (m: Victor Herbert; l: Glen MacDonough, 1903) [from *Babes in Toyland*], "Bethena" (by Scott Joplin) [dropped before Broadway], "Smiles" (m: Lee S. Roberts; l: J. Will Callahan, 1918) [from *The Passing Show of 1918*].

The day it opened on Broadway (10/23/80) marked the 30th anniversary of the Arena Stage in Washington. Reviews were mixed, and middle-of-the-road, but mostly favorable. The show closed after the 1/11/81 matinee. It received Tony nominations for musical, book, and for Lynne Thigpen.

After Broadway. TOUR. Opened on 9/29/82, at Page Auditorium, Durham, NC, and closed on 3/16/83, at Dixie Hall, New Orleans. PRESENTED BY Gordon Crowe; TOUR DIRECTORS: Bruce Michael/Neil Fleckman Associates; DIRECTOR: Jerry Zaks; CHOREOGRAPHER: Derek Wolshonak; SETS: David Weller; COSTUMES: Carl Heastand; LIGHTING: Robert Strohmeier. **Cast**: CHARLIE: Stuart Zagnit; T.R.: Ronald A. Wisniski; SUSANNAH: Janet Powell; ANNA HELD: Patrice Munsel; EMMA GOLDMAN: Robin Taylor. **Standbys**: Anna: Mimi Wyatt & Deborah Moldow; Emma: Mimi Wyatt; T.R./Charlie: Mark Madama.

MELTING POT THEATRE. 11/20/01–12/16/01 (it closed earlier than its scheduled closing date of 12/30/01). Previews from 11/13/01. This was the first New York revival. DIRECTOR: Nick Corley; CHOREOGRAPHER: Jennifer Paulson Lee; SETS: Michael Brown; COSTUMES: Daryl Stone; LIGHTING: Jeff Croiter; MUSICAL DIRECTOR: Greg Pliska. **Cast**: Mark Lotito, Christine Rea, Michele Ragusa, Josh Alexander, Johmaalya Adelekan.

RUBICON THEATRE, Los Angeles, 9/21/02–10/20/02. DIRECTOR: Bonnie Hellman; CHOREOGRAPHERS: Jim Alexander & Cindy Robinson; MUSICAL DIRECTOR: David Potter. **Cast**: THEODORE ROOSEVELT: Greg Zerkle; SUSANNAH: Darlesia Cearcy; ANNA HELD: Heather Lee; CHARLIE: Eric Olson; EMMA GOLDMAN: Lisa Fishman.

706. *Titanic*

This musical recreates the first and last voyage of the great ship. Set in Southampton, England, and on board the *Titanic*, April 10–15, 1912.

Before Broadway. One of the producers, Michael Braun, died on 1/26/97. Broadway previews began on 3/29/97 (they had originally been scheduled to begin on 3/12/97). The numbers "I Give You My Hand" and "Behind Every Fortune" were cut during previews. Opening night was put back from 4/10/97 to 4/23/97.

The Broadway Run. LUNT–FONTANNE THEATRE, 4/23/97–3/28/99. 28 previews. 804 PERFORMANCES. PRESENTED BY Dodger Endemol Theatricals, Richard S. Pechter, and the John F. Kennedy Center for the Performing Arts; MUSIC/LYRICS: Maury Yeston; BOOK/STORY: Peter Stone; DIRECTOR: Richard Jones; CHOREOGRAPHER: Lynne Taylor-Corbett; ADDITIONAL CHOREOGRAPHY: Mindy Cooper; SETS/COSTUMES: Stewart Laing; LIGHTING: Paul Gallo; SOUND: Steve Canyon Kennedy;

MUSICAL SUPERVISOR/MUSICAL DIRECTOR: Kevin Stites; ORCHESTRATIONS: Jonathan Tunick; CAST RECORDING on RCA; PRESS: Boneau/Bryan-Brown; CASTING: Julie Hughes & Barry Moss; GENERAL MANAGEMENT: Dodger Management Group; COMPANY MANAGER: Steven H. David; PRODUCTION STAGE MANAGER: Susan Green; STAGE MANAGER: Richard Hester; ASSISTANT STAGE MANAGERS: Leigh Catlett & Heather Cousens, *Rick Steiger*. **Cast**: OFFICERS AND CREW OF R.M.S. *Titanic*: CAPT. E.J. SMITH: John Cunningham; 1ST OFFICER WILLIAM MURDOCH: David Costabile, *Danny Burstein*; 2ND OFFICER CHARLES LIGHTOLLER: John Bolton; 3RD OFFICER HERBERT J. PITMAN: Matthew Bennett; FREDERICK BARRETT, STOKER: Brian d'Arcy James (until 8/15/98), *Clarke Thorell, Stephen R. Buntrock*; HAROLD BRIDE, RADIOMAN: Martin Moran, *Don Stephenson*; HENRY ETCHES, 1ST CLASS STEWARD: Allan Corduner, *Henry Stram*; FREDERICK FLEET, LOOKOUT: David Elder; QUARTERMASTER ROBERT HICHENS: Adam Alexi-Malle; 4TH OFFICER JOSEPH BOXHALL: Andy Taylor, *Sean McCourt*; CHIEF ENGINEER JOSEPH BELL: Ted Sperling (until 5/98), *Matthew R. Jones*; WALLACE HARTLEY, ORCHESTRA LEADER/ON STAGE VIOLIN: Ted Sperling (until 5/98), *Matthew R. Jones*; BANDSMAN BRICOUX/ON-STAGE VIOLIN: Adam Alexi-Malle; BANDSMAN TAYLOR/ON-STAGE CELLO/DOUBLE BASS: Andy Taylor, *Sean McCourt*; STEWARDESS ROBINSON: Michele Ragusa; STEWARDESS HUTCHINSON: Stephanie Park; BELLBOY: Mara Stephens; PASSENGERS ABOARD R.M.S. *Titanic*: 1ST CLASS: J. BRUCE ISMAY, *Titanic's* OWNER: David Garrison, *Paul Kandel*; THOMAS ANDREWS, *Titanic's* BUILDER: Michael Cerveris (until 7/4/98), *Matthew Bennett* (from 7/6/98), *Joseph Kolinski*; ISIDOR STRAUSS: Larry Keith; IDA STRAUSS: Alma Cuervo; J.J. ASTOR: William Youmans; MADELINE ASTOR: Lisa Datz, *Christine Long*; BENJAMIN GUGGENHEIM: Joseph Kolinski; MME AUBERT: Kimberly Hester; JOHN B. THAYER: Michael Mulheren; MARION THAYER: Robin Irwin; GEORGE WIDENER: Henry Stram; ELEANOR WIDENER: Jody Gelb; CHARLOTTE CARDOZA: Becky Ann Baker, *Caitlin Clarke* (from 7/97); J.H. ROGERS: Andy Taylor; THE MAJOR: Matthew Bennett; EDITH CORSE EVANS: Mindy Cooper; OTHER 1ST-CLASS PASSENGERS: David Elder, Erin Hill, Charles McAteer, Theresa McCarthy, Jennifer Piech, Clarke Thorell; 2ND CLASS: CHARLES CLARKE: Don Stephenson, *Andy Taylor* (from 8/15/98), *John Bolton*; CAROLINE NEVILLE: Judith Blazer, *Marla Schaffel* (from 4/98); EDGAR BEANE: Bill Buell, *Hal Davis*; ALICE BEANE: Victoria Clark; OTHER 2ND-CLASS PASSENGERS: John Bolton, Mindy Cooper, David Costabile, David Elder; 3RD CLASS: KATE MCGOWEN: Jennifer Piech; KATE MURPHEY: Theresa McCarthy; KATE MULLINS: Erin Hill, *Emily Loesser*; JIM FARRELL: Clarke Thorell (until 8/15/98), *Christopher Wells*; OTHER 3RD-CLASS PASSENGERS: Adam Alexi-Malle, Becky Ann Baker, Matthew Bennett, Mindy Cooper, Alma Cuervo, Lisa Datz, Jody Gelb, Kimberly Hester, Robin Irwin, Larry Keith, Joseph Kolinski, Charles McAteer, Michael Mulheren, Ted Sperling, Mara Stephens, Henry Stram, Andy Taylor, William Youmans; ON SHORE: FRANK CARLSON: Henry Stram. **Understudies**: Barrett: Drew McVety & Andy Taylor; Bride: Drew McVety & John Bolton; Hichens/Farrell: Drew McVety & Jonathan Brody; Boxhall/Rogers: Drew McVety & John Jellison; Lightoller: Andy Taylor & Jonathan Brody; Clarke: Andy Taylor; Murdoch: John Bolton & Peter Kapetan; Fleet: Jonathan Brody; Bell/Hartley: Jonathan Brody & Peter Kapetan; Thayer/Guggenheim: Jonathan Brody, Peter Kapetan, John Jellison; Ismay: Peter Kapetan, Matthew Bennett, David Costabile; Beane/Astor: Peter Kapetan & John Jellison; Pitman/Major/Strauss: John Jellison; Smith: John Jellison & Joseph Kolinski; Andrews: Joseph Kolinski & Matthew Bennett; Etches: Henry Stram & David Costabile; Kate McGowen/Caroline: Lisa Datz & Theresa McCarthy; Kate Mullins/Mme Aubert/Mrs. Astor: Melissa Bell; Mrs. Widener/Mrs. Thayer/Mrs. Cardoza: Kay Walbye; Mr. Widener: John Jellison & Jonathan Brody; Mrs. Strauss/Mrs. Beane: Kay Walbye & Jody Gelb. **Swings**: Melissa Bell, Kay Walbye, Jonathan Brody, John Jellison, Drew McVety, Christopher Wells (*Romain Fruge* from 8/97). **Orchestra:** WOODWINDS: Les Scott, David Kosoff, Steve Kenyon, John J. Moses, John Campo; TRUMPETS: Brian O'Flaherty & Wayne J. duMaine; FRENCH HORNS: Theresa MacDonnell & Michael Ishii; TROMBONES: Keith O'Quinn & Jeff Nelson; PERCUSSION: Charles Descarfino & Dave Ratajczak; CONCERTMASTER: Joel Pitchon; VIOLINS: Carol Zeavin, Naomi Katz, Xiz Zhou, Andrea Schultz, Avril Brown; VIOLAS: Kenneth Burward-Hoy & Sally Shumway; CELLI: Eugene Briskin & Sarah Seiver; BASS: Gregg August;

KEYBOARDS: Matthew Sklar & Nicholas Archer. *Prologue*: Harland & Wolff, shipbuilders, Aberdeen, Scotland: "In Every Age" (Andrews). THE LAUNCHING (SCENES 1–3): *Act I*: *Scene 1* Southampton: the Ocean Dock: "How Did They Build Titanic?" (Barrett), "There She Is" (Barrett, Bride, Fleet), "Loading Inventory" (Smith, Stevedores, Ship's Personnel), "The Largest Moving Object (in the World)" (Ismay, Smith, Andrews), "I Must Get on That Ship" (Pitman, 2nd & 3rd Class Passengers), "The First-Class Roster" (Pitman & Mrs. Beane); *Scene 2* Aboard R.M.S. Titanic; the stern: "Godspeed Titanic" (Company); *Scene 3* The dock; *Scene 4* The Bridge & Boiler Room # 6: "Barrett's Song" (Barrett); *Scene 5* The Saloon ("D") Deck; *Scene 6* The 1st-Class Dining Saloon: "What a Remarkable Age This Is!" (Etches Staff & 1st Class Diners); *Scene 7* The Bridge: "To Be a Captain" (Murdoch); *Scene 8* The Middle ("F") Deck; the 3rd-Class Commissary: "Lady's Maid" (The Kates & Steerage); *Scene 9* The Bridge; *Scene 10* The Radio Room: "The Proposal" (Barrett), "The Night Was Alive" (Bride); *Scene 11* The Boat Deck: 1st-Class Promenade: "Hymn" (Company), "Doing the Latest Rag" (Hartley, Bricoux, Taylor, Company); *Scene 12* ("A") Deck: "I Have Danced" (Alice & Edgar Beane); *Scene 13* The Bridge; then the Promenade ("B") Deck, the Saloon ("D") Deck, the Middle ("F") Deck; the 1st-Class Smoke Room; and the Crow's Nest: "No Moon" (Fleet & Company), "Autumn" (Hartley). *Act II*: *Scene 1* 1st-, 2nd-, 3rd-Class Corridors & the Bridge: "Wake Up, Wake Up!" (Etches, Stewards, Company); *Scene 2* The 1st-Class Grand Salon: "Dressed in Your Pyjamas in the Grand Salon" (Company); *Scene 3* ("E") Deck; a Stairwell: "The Staircase" (The Kates & Farrell); *Scene 4* The Boat Deck. TO THE LIFEBOATS (SCENES 5 & 6): *Scene 5* The Radio Room: "The Blame" (Ismay, Andrews, Smith); *Scene 6* At the Lifeboats: "Getting in the Lifeboat" (Mr. & Mrs. Thayer), "I Must Get on That Ship" (reprise) (Murdoch, Lightoller, Steward, Bellboy, Passengers), "Lady's Maid" (reprise) (Farrell), "Canons" (Company), "The Proposal" (reprise) (Barrett), "The Night Was Alive" (reprise) (Bride), "We'll Meet Tomorrow" (Barrett, Bride, Charles Clarke, Company); *Scene 7* Portholes: "To Be a Captain" (reprise) (Etches); *Scene 8* The Upper Promenade ("A") Deck: "Still" (Isidor & Ida Straus); *Scene 9* The 1st-Class Smoke Room & the deck above: "Mr. Andrews' Vision" (Andrews); *Scene 10* Aftermath: "In Every Age" (reprise) (Company), Finale (Company). *The Decks*: BOAT DECK: Bridge, Radio Room, Life Boats; UPPER PROMENADE ("A") DECK: 1st-Class Promenade; 1st-Class Reading & Writing Room; 1st-Class Smoke Room; PROMENADE ("B") DECK: 1st Class Promenade; UPPER ("C") DECK: 2nd-Class Promenade; SALOON ("D") DECK: 1st-Class Dining Saloon; 2nd-Class Promenade; MAIN ("E") DECK: 2nd-Class Cabins; MIDDLE ("F") DECK: 3rd-Class Dining Saloon; 3rd-Class Promenade; LOWER ("G") DECK: 3rd-Class Steerage Dormitories; ORLOP ("H") DECK: Boiler Room # 6.

Broadway reviews were not good, and the future didn't look rosy, except for one factor that turned the tide in its favor—Rosie O'Donnell's support for the show on her TV program. *Titanic* won Tonys for musical, score, book, sets, and orchestrations. On 4/28/98 the performance stopped midway because of electrical problems. From 5/98, for the summer, the show stopped Sunday matinees, going instead for Monday evenings until 8/31/98 (the normal schedule resumed on 9/13/98). It closed after the 3/28/99 matinee, after making back just over half its initial investment.

After Broadway. TOUR. Opened on 1/10/99, at the Ahmanson Theatre, Los Angeles. Previews from 1/5/99. It left L.A. on 2/28/99, and went on across the country. *Cast*: BARRETT: Brian d'Arcy James (L.A. only), *Marcus Chait*; CAPTAIN: William Parry; ANDREWS: Kevin Gray, *Thom Sesma*; ISMAY: Adam Heller; KATE MURPHEY: Kate Suber; LIGHTOLLER: John Leone; KATE McGOWEN: Melissa Bell; STRAUSS: S. Marc Jordan; MRS. STRAUSS: Taina Elg, *Kay Walbye*; CHARLOTTE: Margot Skinner; EDGAR: David Beditz; ALICE: Liz McConahay, *Sarah Solie Shannon*; CAROLINE: Christianne Tisdale; KATE MULLINS: Jodi Jinks; FARRELL: Richard Roland; BRIDE: Dale Sandish; FLEET: Timothy J. Alex; MURDOCH: David Pittu, *Joe Farrell*; PITMAN/MAJOR: Raymond Sage; EDITH: Sarah Solie Shannon; GUGGENHEIM: Ken Krugman; ELEANOR: Laura Kenyon; ETCHES: Edward Conery.

Tommy see 746

707. *Top Banana*

Jerry, an egomaniacal TV comedian, is ordered by his sponsors, Blendo, to introduce some love interest into the show. He hires a pair of actors who play lovers on the TV. But as they fall in love, Jerry is dismayed because he has fallen in love with the girl himself.

The Broadway Run. WINTER GARDEN THEATRE, 11/1/51–10/4/52. 356 PERFORMANCES. PRESENTED BY Paula Stone & Mike Sloane; MUSIC/LYRICS: Johnny Mercer; BOOK: Hy Kraft; DIRECTOR: Jack Donohue; CHOREOGRAPHER: Ron Fletcher; SETS/LIGHTING: Jo Mielziner; COSTUMES: Alvin Colt; MUSICAL DIRECTOR: Harold Hastings; ORCHESTRATIONS: Don Walker; DANCE MUSIC ARRANGEMENTS: Lee Pockriss; VOCAL DIRECTOR/VOCAL ARRANGEMENTS: Hugh Martin; PRESS: Bill Doll; COMPANY MANAGER: Joe Roth; PRODUCTION STAGE MANAGER: Fred Hebert; STAGE MANAGERS: Danny Brennan & Louis de Mangus. *Cast*: DANNY: Eddie Hanley; SCRIPT GIRL: Eve Hebert; BUBBLE GIRLS: Beverly Weston & Sara Dillon; VIC DAVIS: Jack Albertson (3); TOMMY: Bob Scheerer (4), *Bill Callahan*; WALTER: Walter Dare Wahl; JERRY BIFFLE: Phil Silvers (1) (until 8/3/52), *Jack Carter* (from 8/31/52); CLIFF LANE: Lindy Doherty, *Danny Scholl*; MOE: Herbie Faye; PINKY: Joey Faye (5); BETTY DILLON: Rose Marie (2), *Audrey Meadows* (12/12/51–1/7/52), *Rose Marie*; SALLY PETERS: Judy Lynn; A MAN: Johnny Trama; ELEVATOR OPERATOR: Sara Dillon; MODELS: Marian Burke & Basha Regis; SALES GIRLS: Joy Skylar, Polly Ward, Florence Baum, Eve Hebert; CUSTOMERS: B.J. Keating, Joan Fields, Laurel Shelby, Doug Luther, Betsy Holland; RUSS WISWELL: Zachary A. Charles; MR. PARKER: Bradford Hatton; ANNOUNCER: Dean Campbell; FEATURED DANCERS: Hal Loman & Joan Fields; TV TECHNICIAN: Ken Harvey; MISS PILLSBURY: Betsy Holland; DR. LEROY: Doug Luther; STAGE HAND: Don Covert; TED (SPORT) MORGAN: Himself (he was a dog); DANCE TEAM: Bob Scheerer (*Bill Callahan*) & Polly Ward; JUGGLER: Claude Heater; PHOTOGRAPHERS: Don Covert, Ken Harvey, Herb Fields, Don McKay; A PASSING GIRL: Mary Harmon; THE WIDOW: Judy Sinclair; THE MAGICIAN'S ASSISTANT: Basha Regis; "BUBBLES:" Gloria Smith; DANCERS: Florence Baum, Nikki Cellini, Eve Hebert, Bill Joyce, John Laverty, George Marci, Joy Skylar, Gloria Smith, Vivian Smith, Walter Stane, Bill Sumner, Thelma Tadlock, Ken Urmston, Polly Ward; SINGERS: Marian Burke, Dean Campbell, Don Covert, Sara Dillon, Herb Fields, Mary Harmon, Ken Harvey, Claude Heater, Betsy Holland, B.J. Keating, Bob Kole, Doug Luther, Don McKay, Laurel Shelby, Judy Sinclair, Beverly Weston. *Standby*: Betty: Hope Zee. *Understudies*: Jerry: Jack Albertson; Vic: Ken Harvey; Pinky/Moe: Eddie Hanley; Tommy: Hal Loman; Walter: Don Covert; Russ: Louis de Mangus; Cliff: Dean Campbell; Sally: Sara Dillon; Danny: Danny Brennan; *Featured Dancers*: George Marci & Gloria Smith. *Act I*: *Scene 1* TV studio; *Scene 2* Dressing room; early next morning; *Scene 3* The Gown Shop of MacCracken's Store; *Scene 4* In front of an elevator; *Scene 5* In the book department; *Scene 6* The interior of an elevator; *Scene 7* The fitting room; *Scene 8* TV studio. *Act II*: *Scene 1* TV studio; *Scene 2* 40 West 82nd Street; *Scene 3* Vignettes; *Scene 4* Dressing room; *Scene 5* Top Banana; *Scene 6* Dressing room; *Scene 7* TV studio. *Act I*: "The Man of the Year This Week" (Ensemble), "You're So Beautiful That—" (Cliff), "(If You Want to Be a) Top Banana" (Jerry, Vic, Cliff, Pinky, Moe), "Elevator Song" (Ensemble), "Hail to MacCracken's" (Ensemble), "Only if You're in Love" (Cliff & Sally), "My Home is In My Shoes" (Tommy & Ensemble), "I Fought Every Step of the Way" (orch: Bill Finnigan) (Betty), "OK for TV" (Jerry, Vic, Sally, Pinky, Moe, Danny, Russ), "Slogan Song" (Jerry, Betty, Vic, Sally, Cliff, Tommy, Pinky, Moe, Danny, Russ, Mr. Parker), "Meet Miss Blendo" (Entire Company). *Act II*: "Sans Souci" (orch: Bill Finnigan) (Betty, Featured Dancers, Ensemble), "A Dog is a Man's Best Friend" (Jerry, Sport, Grenadiers), "That's for Sure" (Cliff, Sally, Ensemble) [replaced during the run by "Be My Guest" (same performers)], "A Word a Day" (Jerry & Betty), "Top Banana Ballet" (Jerry & Ensemble), Finale (Entire Company).

Broadway reviewers mostly raved. By the time Phil Silvers left for a vacation, the show was in the black, and the show itself went on vacation, 8/3/52–8/31/52. Audiences did not want to see Jack Carter, Phil's replacement, and the show lost so much money, so quickly, it rapidly closed. Phil Silvers won a Tony Award and a Donaldson Award.

After Broadway. TOUR. Opened on 10/6/52, at the Shubert Theatre, Los Angeles, and closed on 6/27/53, at the Biltmore Theatre, Los Angeles. MUSICAL DIRECTOR: George Reiser. *Cast*: DANNY: Dick Dana; VIC: Jack Albertson; WALTER: Walter Dare Wahl; JERRY: Phil Silvers; CLIFF: Danny Scholl; BETTY: Kaye Ballard; MOE: Herbie Faye; PINKY: Joey Faye; SALLY: Judy Lynn; LITTLE MAN: Johnny Trama; LEROY: Doug Luther; FLASH HOGAN: Himself (a dog).

THE MOVIE. 1954. Shot at the Winter Garden Theatre, with most of the cast intact. TOMMY PHELPS: Johnny Coy; DANNY: Dick Dana.

708. *Toplitzky of Notre Dame*

Toplitzky is a Jewish tavern keeper in New York, and a Notre Dame fan. The angels in Heaven are Notre Dame fans too, so Angelo, an ex-football player angel, comes back to Earth on leave to help Notre Dame beat Army. Toplitzky adopts Angelo, and they win the game. However, Angelo falls in love with Toplitzky's daughter, and is allowed to stay on Earth for a while.

Before Broadway. During tryouts Vivienne Segal was replaced by Doris Patston; Alma Kaye by Marion Colby; and Margaret Phelan by Betty Jane Watson. The show cost $230,000.

The Broadway Run. NEW CENTURY THEATRE, 12/26/46–2/15/47. 60 PERFORMANCES. PRESENTED BY William Cahn; MUSIC: Sammy Fain; LYRICS/BOOK: George Marion Jr.; ADDITIONAL DIALOGUE & LYRICS: Jack Barnett; DIRECTOR: Jose Ruben; CHOREOGRAPHER: Robert Sidney; SETS: Edward Gilbert; COSTUMES: Kenn Barr; MUSICAL DIRECTOR: Leon Leonardi; ORCHESTRAL ARRANGEMENTS: Allan Small, Lewis Raymond, Menotti Salta; VOCAL & CHORAL ARRANGEMENTS: Leon Leonardi; PRESS: Ivan Black & Harry Koenigsberg; COMPANY MANAGER: Harold C. Jacoby; STAGE MANAGERS: John Effrat, Steven Gethers, Charles Conway. *Cast*: ARMY ANGEL: Phyllis Lynne; RECORDING ANGEL: Candace Montgomery; LIONEL: Harry Fleer; ANGELO: Warde Donovan; MRS. STRUTT: Doris Patston; BETTY: Marion Colby; DODO: Estelle Sloan; McCORMACK: Gus Van; ROGER: Walter Long; TOPLITZKY: J. Edward Bromberg; A GIRL: Betty Jane Watson; MAILMAN: Robert Bay; LEARY: Frank Marlowe; PATTI: Phyllis Lynne; MALE QUARTET: Oliver Boersma, John Frederick, Eugene Kingsley, Chris Overson; DANCING GIRLS: Priscilla Callan, Ann Collins, Helen Devlin, Cece Eames, Jessie Fullum, Joan Kavanagh, Pat Marlowe, Mollie Pearson, Frances Wyman; DANCING BOYS: George Andrew, Gene Banks, Charles Dickson, Casse Jaeger, Thomas Kenny, Anthony Starman, Rodney Strong, Joe Wagner, John Wilkins. *Act I*: *Prologue*— Heaven; *Scene 1* Toplitzky's tavern, New York City; a September day; *Scene 2* A field on the Jersey shore; late afternoon; *Scene 3* Toplitzky's tavern; later that day; *Scene 4* Toplitzky's terrace; a late afternoon in October. *Act II*: *Scene 1* Toplitzky's tavern; the day before the big game; *Scene 2* Toplitzky's terrace; evening, same day; *Scene 3* Going to the big game; *Scene 4* Yankee Stadium; Army — Notre Dame game. *Act I*: "Let Us Gather at the Goal Line" (Angelo & Company), "Baby, Let's Face It" (Roger) (danced by Roger, Dodo, Boys & Girls), "Let Us Gather at the Goal Line" (reprise) (Toplitzky & McCormack), "I Wanna Go to City College" (Leary, Betty, Boys & Girls), "Love is a Random Thing" (A Girl), "Common Sense" (Toplitzky), "Love is a Random Thing" (reprise) (Angelo), "A Slight Case of Ecstasy" (Roger, Dodo, Leary, Patti) (danced by Roger, Girls & Boys), Finale (A Girl & Company). *Act II*: "Wolf Time" (Betty & Patti), "McInerney's Farm" (McCormack), "You Are My Downfall" (Angelo & A Girl) (danced by Boys & Girls, Roger, Dodo), "All-American Man" (Patti, Dodo, Betty, Leary, McCormack) (danced by Mailman, Boys & Girls), "The Notre Dame Victory March" (m: Rev. Michael J. Shea; l: John F. Shea), "The Notre Dame Hike Song" (by Joseph Casastana & Vincent F. Fagan), Finale (Entire Company).

Reviews were mostly bad. There was one rave (an error in judgment).

709. *Touch and Go*

An intimate revue.

Before Broadway. George Abbott found this show playing at the

Catholic University, in Washington, DC, where Walter Kerr had been teaching drama (even though he had made a few contributions to Broadway over the years). At that time it was called *Thank You, Just Looking*. Mr. Abbott decided to take it to Broadway. Ray Walston was fired during out-of-town tryouts.

The Broadway Run. BROADHURST THEATRE, 10/13/49–2/25/50; BROADWAY THEATRE, 2/27/50–3/18/50. Total of 176 PERFORMANCES. PRESENTED BY George Abbott; MUSIC: Jay Gorney; LYRICS/SKETCHES: Jean & Walter Kerr; DIRECTOR: Walter Kerr; CHOREOGRAPHER: Helen Tamiris; ASSISTANT CHOREOGRAPHER: Daniel Nagrin; SETS: John Robert Lloyd; LIGHTING: Peggy Clark; MUSICAL DIRECTOR/VOCAL ARRANGEMENTS: Antonio Morelli; ORCHESTRATIONS: Don Walker; BALLET MUSIC: Genevieve Pitot; COMPANY MANAGER: Joe Harris; STAGE MANAGER: Robert E. Griffith; ASSISTANT STAGE MANAGER: Harold S. Prince. *Act I*: *Scene 1* "An Opening for Everybody:" THEATREGOERS: George Hall, Helen Gallagher, Jonathan Lucas, Company; *Scene 2* "This Had Better Be Love" (Nancy Andrews & Dick Sykes); *Scene 3* Gorilla Girl. Set on a movie location. A monkey is smarter than the beautiful, blonde, singing leading lady (Kyle MacDonnell): DIRECTOR: George Hall; ASSISTANT DIRECTOR: Art Carroll; MISS HILTON: Kyle MacDonnell; SKEETS: Jonathan Lucas; TRAINER: Louis Nye; CAMERAMAN: Nathaniel Frey; *Scene 4* "American Primitive" (Funny Little Old World) (inspired by the paintings of Grandma Moses) (sung by Muriel O'Malley) (danced by Pearl Lang, Daniel Nagrin, Greb Lober, David Lober, Richard Reed, William Sumner, Beverly Tassoni, Merritt Thompson, Dorothy Scott, Parker Wilson). FATHER: Art Carroll; DAUGHTER: Helen Gallagher; *Scene 5* "Highbrow, Lowbrow" (Dick Sykes, Jonathan Lucas, Larry Robbins); *Scene 6* Disenchantment: MUFFINS: George Hall; OLD GENT (PIPPY): Dick Sykes; MOONBEAM: Peggy Cass; NEWSBOY: William Sumner; PAPA: Louis Nye; PILGRIM: Larry Robbins; *Scene 7* "Easy Does It:" THE GIRL: Helen Gallagher; THE MAN: Daniel Nagrin; THE OTHER MAN: David Lober; THE GIRL FRIENDS: Eleanor Boleyn & Greb Lober; THE COMPANY; *Scene 8* "Be a Mess." How to look like a mess, make a comeback, and win an Oscar. OLIVIA: Peggy Cass (based on Olivia de Havilland in the movie *The Snake Pit*); BARBARA: Nancy Andrews (based on Barbara Stanwyck in the movie *Sorry, Wrong Number*); JANE: Kyle MacDonnell (based on Jane Wyman in the movie *Johnny Belinda*); *Scene 9* "Broadway Love Song" (Pearl Lang & Jonathan Lucas); *Scene 10* "It'll Be All Right (in a Hundred Years):" BOY: Art Carroll; GIRL: Kyle MacDonnell; *Scene 11* Great Dane a-Comin' (*Hamlet* as it might be done as a musical): KING: Ray Page; QUEEN: Nancy Andrews; HAMLET: Dick Sykes; LAERTES: Daniel Nagrin; OPHELIA: Kyle MacDonnell; POLONIUS: George Hall (as if it might be played by Bobby Clark); THE COMPANY. "This is a Real Nice Castle," "You're a Queer One, Dear Ophelia." *Act II*: *Scene 1* "Wish Me Luck" (sung by Miss Andrews) (danced by Company). About a girl's failed marriage prospects. CROUPIER: David Lober; *Scene 2* "What it Really was Like:" FIRST AIDE: Nat Frey; SECOND AIDE: Louis Nye; GENERAL: Dick Sykes; MALLOY: Larry Robbins; C.O.: George Hall; KERRIGAN: Jonathan Lucas; *Scene 3* "Under the Sleeping Volcano:" THE SINGERS: Pearl Hacker, Lydia Fredericks, Arlyne Frank, Beverly Purvin; CARITA'S SISTER: Ilona Murai; CARITA: Pearl Lang; FELIPE: Daniel Nagrin; FRANCESCO: David Lober; VILLAGERS: Dorothy Scott, Eleanor Boleyn, Beverly Tassoni, Greb Lober, Willy Sumner, Parker Wilson, Merritt Thompson, Richard Reed, George Reich; *Scene 4* "Men of the Water-Mark" (set on a World War II battlefront. Soldiers writing memoirs, one called *The Bloody and the Sweaty*) (Art Carroll, Nat Frey, George Hall, Carl Nicholas, Louis Nye, Larry Robbins); *Scene 5* "Mr. Brown, Miss Dupree" (danced by Mary Anthony, Ilona Murai, Beverly Tassoni, Dorothy Scott, David Lober, Richard Reed, George Reich, Merritt Thompson). MISS DUPREE: Kyle MacDonnell; MAMA: Muriel O'Malley; MR. BROWN: Jonathan Lucas; *Scene 6* "Miss Platt Selects Mate" (sung by Nancy Andrews) [the hit]; *Scene 7* "Cinderella." How Elia Kazan would direct *Cinderella* (when the prince comes looking for the heroine she's in the bathroom): STEPMOTHER: Muriel O'Malley; NEIGHBOR: Helen Gallagher; FIRST SISTER: Nancy Andrews; SECOND SISTER: Peggy Cass; CINDERELLA: Kyle MacDonnell; NEWSBOY: Jonathan Lucas; PRINCE: Louis Nye; PAGE: Larry Robbins; *Scene 8* Finale (Company).

ENSEMBLE: Mary Anthony, Eleanor Boleyn, Art Carroll, Arlyne Frank, Lydia Fredericks, Nathaniel Frey, Pearl Hacker, David Lober,

Greb Lober, Mara Lynn, Ilona Murai, Carl Nicholas, Ray Page, Beverly Purvin, Richard Reed, George Reich, Larry Robbins, Dorothy Scott, William Sumner, Beverly Tassoni, Merritt Thompson, Bobby Trelease, Parker Wilson. *Understudies*: For Kyle MacDonnell: Pearl Hacker; For Nancy Andrews: Beverly Purvin; For George Hall: Larry Robbins; For Dick Sykes: Art Carroll; For Muriel O'Malley: Lydia Fredericks; For Peggy Cass: Arlyne Frank; For Jonathan Lucas/Daniel Nagrin: Richard Reed; For Helen Gallagher: Eleanor Boleyn; For Pearl Lang: Helen Gallagher & Beverly Tassoni.

Broadway reviews were divided, mostly bad. The show won a Tony Award for choreography.

After Broadway. PRINCE OF WALES THEATRE, London, 5/19/50–12/16/50. 353 PERFORMANCES. It was a hit. ADDITIONAL MATERIAL: Joseph Stein, Will Glickman, Arnold B. Horwitt, Happy Felton, Mack Perrin, John Tore; DIRECTORS: Robert E. Griffith & Dick Hurran; CHOREOGRAPHER: Mary Anthony; MUSICAL DIRECTOR: Paul Feneoulhet. *Cast*: Kaye Ballard, Helen Gallagher, Carole Lynne, Beryl Stevens, Bill Fraser, Desmond Walter-Ellis, Sid James, Mary Anthony, David Lober, Eleanor Fazan.

710. *Tovarich*

Tatiana and Mikhail, a former Russian imperial couple, are serving as butler and chambermaid in a wealthy American household in Paris, and at the same time being pursued by a Soviet commissar.

Before Broadway. *Tovarich* first ran on Broadway as a straight play, at the PLYMOUTH THEATRE, 10/15/36. 356 PERFORMANCES. *Cast*: John Halliday, Marta Abba. It was revived at CITY CENTER, NYC, 5/14/52–5/25/52. 16 PERFORMANCES. DIRECTOR/SETS: Harry Horner; STAGE MANAGER: Bernard Gersten. *Cast*: Uta Hagen, Herbert Berghof, Romney Brent, Pat Crowley, Luther Adler, Julia Adler, Bill Hickey, Sudie Bond.

The 1963 production was Vivien Leigh's only musical. In 1/63 the show tried out in Philadelphia. Audiences liked it, but critics said it was old-hat. Vivien Leigh already hated it, and didn't want to do it. Delbert Mann was replaced as director by Peter Glenville. It was well-received in Boston, but Vivien Leigh was headed rapidly toward a nervous breakdown. The numbers "Lullaby for a Princess" and "Opportunity" were cut before Broadway.

The Broadway Run. BROADWAY THEATRE, 3/18/63–6/8/63; MAJESTIC THEATRE, 6/10/63–9/28/63; WINTER GARDEN THEATRE, 10/7/63–11/9/63. Total of 264 PERFORMANCES. PRESENTED BY Abel Farbman & Sylvia Harris, in association with Joseph P. Harris; MUSIC/DANCE MUSIC: Lee Pockriss; LYRICS: Anne Croswell; BOOK: David Shaw; From Robert E. Sherwood's 1936 adaptation of the 1933 comedy by Jacques Deval; DIRECTOR: Peter Glenville; CHOREOGRAPHER: Herbert Ross; SETS: Rolf Gerard; COSTUMES: Motley; LIGHTING: John Harvey; MUSICAL DIRECTOR/VOCAL ARRANGEMENTS: Stanley Lebowsky; ORCHESTRATIONS: Philip J. Lang; ADDITIONAL DANCE MUSIC: Dorothea Freitag; PRESS: Richard Maney & Martin Shwartz; GENERAL MANAGER: Monty Shaff; COMPANY MANAGER: Richard Grayson; STAGE MANAGER: Harry Young; ASSISTANT STAGE MANAGER: Tom Abbott. *Cast*: GOROTCHENKO: Alexander Scourby (3), *Roger DeKoven* (from 5/27/63); VASSILY: Paul Michael (11); PRINCE MIKHAIL: Jean-Pierre Aumont (2) ☆; ADMIRAL BORIS SOUKHOMINE: Michael Kermoyan (9); COUNT IVAN SHAMFOROFF: Gene Varrone (10); BARONESS ROUMEL: Katia Geleznova; MARINA: Rita Metzger; M. CHAUFFOURIER-DUBIEFF: Don McHenry; GRAND DUCHESS TATIANA PETROVNA: Vivien Leigh (1) ☆ (until 9/30/63), *Joan Copeland* (from 10/7/63), *Eva Gabor* (from 10/21/63); NATALIA MAYOVSKAYA: Louise Troy (4); HELEN DAVIS: Margery Gray; GEORGE DAVIS: Byron Mitchell (7); CHARLES DAVIS: George S. Irving (5); GRACE DAVIS: Louise Kirtland (6); LOUISE: Maggie Task, *Patricia Kelly*; BALLET MASTER: Tom Abbott; NADIA: Barbara Monte; MME VAN HEMERT: Patricia Kelly; MME VAN STEUBEN: Eleanore Treiber; THE FOOTMAN AT THE DAVIS HOME: Harald Horn; NIGHT CLUB SINGER: Dale Malone; KUKLA KATUSHA: Bettye Jenkins; IVAN: William Reilly; SERGEI: Larry Roquemore; KUKLA'S FRIENDS: Lorenzo Bianco, Antony

De Vecchi, William Glassman; A FOOTMAN AT THE GRAND BALL: Elliott Savage; BARON GENERAL RASUMOV: Harald Horn; BARONESS RASUMOV: Michele Franchi; PRINCE DOBRYNIN: Antony De Vecchi; PRINCESS DOBRYNIN: Marion Fels; GENERAL BORUVSKY: Dale Malone; MME BORUVSKY: Eleanore Treiber; COUNT YURIEV NEGLINSKY: Tom Abbott; LADY SOUKHOMINE: Joan Trona; MARIA SOUKHOMINE: Bettye Jenkins; COUNT ROSTOFF: Will Parkins; MME MURATOVA: Carol Flemming; ESSAUL OF COSSACKS VOLININ: Lorenzo Bianco; KATRINA VOLININ: Barbara Monte; ELENA VOLININ: Charlene Mehl; PRINCESS MONDOVSKA: Patricia Kelly; IGOR MONDOVSKY OF THE IMPERIAL CORPS OF CADETS: William Glassman; PRINCE OSSIPOVSKY: Larry Roquemore; COLONEL YAROV: William Reilly; SINGERS: Alice Evans, Del Horstmann, Barney Johnston, Pat Kelly, Jeff Killion, Dale Malone, Rita Metzger, Elliott Savage, Maggie Task, Joan Trona; DANCERS: Tom Abbott, Lorenzo Bianco, Antony De Vecchi, Marion Fels, Carol Flemming, Michele Franchi, Katia Geleznova, William Glassman, Harald Horn, Bettye Jenkins, Charlene Mehl, Barbara Monte, Will Parkins, William Reilly, Barbara Richman, Larry Roquemore, Eleanore Treiber. *Standby*: Tatiana: Joan Copeland. *Understudies*: Mikhail: Michael Kermoyan; Gorotchenko/Charles: Del Horstmann; Chaufourrier: Del Horstmann & Jeff Killion; Grace/Louisa: Pat Kelly; George: Larry Roquemore; Helen: Carol Flemming; Vassily: Elliott Savage; Shamforoff: Barney Johnston. *Act I*: *Prologue* Russia; *Scene 1* Tsar Nicholas II's room at the Palace of Tsarkoe Selo; *Scene 2* A garret in Paris; the late 1920s; *Scene 3* A corridor in the house of Mr. and Mrs. Davis, Paris; *Scene 4* The drawing room of the Davis house; *Scene 5* The rehearsal room in the basement of the Kasbek Cafe, Paris; *Scene 6* The wintergarden in the Davis house; *Scene 7* The drawing room. *Act II*: *Scene 1* A street outside the Kasbek Cafe; *Scene 2* The club room of the Kasbek Cafe; *Scene 3* A street outside the Kasbek Cafe; *Scene 4* The drawing room of the Davis house; *Scene 5* A street in Paris; *Scene 6* The kitchen of the Davis house; *Scene 7* A ballroom. *Act I*: "Nitchevo!" (Mikhail, Soukhomine, Shamforoff, Marina, Singers, Dancers), "I Go to Bed" (Mikhail), "You'll Make an Elegant Butler (I'll Make an Elegant Maid)" (m/l: Joan Javits & Philip Springer) (Tatiana), "Stuck with Each Other" (Helen & George), "Say You'll Stay" (Grace & Charles), "You Love Me" (Tatiana & Mikhail), "Introduction Tango" (Tatiana, Helen, Mikhail, George), "That Face" (Natalia), "Wilkes-Barre, Pa." (Tatiana & George), "No! No! No!" (Helen & Mikhail), "A Small Cartel" (Grace, George, Singers). *Act II*: "It Used to Be" (Soukhomine, Shamforoff, Natalia, Vassily), "Kukla Katusha" (Dancers), "Make a Friend" (Tatiana, Helen, Natalia, Mikhail, George, Soukhomine, Shamforoff, Sergei, Ivan), "The Only One" (Tatiana), "Uh-Oh!" (Helen & George), "Managed" (Mikhail), "I Know the Feeling" (Tatiana), "All for You" (Tatiana & Mikhail), "Grande Polonaise" (Helen, Grace, George, Charles, Dancers).

It opened on Broadway during a newspaper strike; reviews, when they came out, were divided, middle-of-the-road. By summer Vivien Leigh was missing performances. She took a week off to return to England for medical attention. She came back, but finally cracked up, right on stage. She won a Tony Award, and Louise Troy was nominated.

After Broadway. TOUR. 1964. It ran for 5 months. *Cast*: TATIANA: Ginger Rogers; MIKHAIL: John Vivyan.

711. *A Tree Grows in Brooklyn*

Only part of Betty Smith's novel was used. A working-class Brooklyn family, the Nolans, at the turn of the 20th Century. Charming but weak Johnny is a boozer; his hard working, devoted wife Katie; their daughter Francie, who idolizes her father; and Katie's sister Cissy, whose affairs with a string of unwed husbands help lighten the basically tragic story.

Before Broadway. The story was filmed (straight) in 1945. *Cast*: CISSY: Joan Blondell; KATIE: Dorothy McGuire; JOHNNY: James Dunn (won an Oscar).

For the Broadway musical Irving Berlin was originally going to do music and lyrics. Jerome Robbins doctored the choreography. The numbers "Tuscaloosa," "Oysters in July," and "The Bride Wore Something Old" were all cut before Broadway.

The Broadway Run. ALVIN THEATRE, 4/19/51–12/8/51. 267 PERFORMANCES. PRESENTED BY George Abbott, in association with Robert Fryer; MUSIC: Arthur Schwartz; LYRICS: Dorothy Fields; BOOK: Betty Smith & George Abbott; BASED ON the 1943 autobiographical novel of the same name, by Betty Smith, which in turn was based on her play; DIRECTOR: George Abbott; CHOREOGRAPHER: Herbert Ross; SETS/LIGHTING: Jo Mielziner; COSTUMES: Irene Sharaff; ASSISTANT COSTUMES: Florence Klotz; MUSICAL SUPERVISOR: Jay Blackton; MUSICAL DIRECTOR: Max Goberman; ARRANGEMENTS: Joe Glover & Robert Russell Bennett; DANCE MUSIC ARRANGEMENTS: Oscar Kosarin; PRESS: Richard Maney, Frank Goodman, Sol Jacobson; CASTING: Judith Abbott; GENERAL MANAGER: Charles Harris; COMPANY MANAGER: Joseph Harris; GENERAL STAGE MANAGER: Robert E. Griffith; STAGE MANAGER: Terence Little; ASSISTANT STAGE MANAGERS: Kenneth Utt & John Mooney. *Cast:* WILLIE: Billy Parsons; ALLIE: Joe Calvan; HILDY: Dody Heath; DELLA: Beverly Purvin; PETEY: Lou Wills Jr. (6); KATIE NOLAN: Marcia Van Dyke (3); ALOYSIUS: Jordan Bentley; JOHNNY NOLAN: Johnny Johnston (2) ☆; CISSY: Shirley Booth (1) ☆; HARRY: Nathaniel Frey (4); MAX: Bruno Wick; MAE: Ruth Amos, *Isabel Price*; MORIARTY: Roland Wood; ANNIE: Claudia Campbell, *Joan Kibrig*; OLD CLOTHES MAN: Harland Dixon; FLORENCE: Janet Parker, *Patti Milligan*; EDGIE: Donald Duerr; FRANCIE: Nomi Mitty (5); JUNIOR: Howard Martin; SWANSWINE: Albert Linville; HICK: Alan Gilbert; JUDGE: Harland Dixon; SALESMAN: Art Carroll; GIRLS IN MAE'S PLACE: Beverly Purvin, Claudia Campbell (*Joan Kibrig*), Jane Copeland, Marta Becket, Mary Statz, Dorothy Hill (*Iona McKenzie*); MAUDIE: Celine Flanagan; DANCERS: Marta Becket, Donn Driver, Dorothy Hill (*Iona McKenzie*), Dick Price (*David Newman*), Mary Statz, Doris Wright, *Olga Briansky, Val Buttignol, Frank Seabolt, Marc West*; SINGERS: Elaine Barrow, Claudia Campbell, Art Carroll, William Carson, Terry Castagna, Jane Copeland, Johnny Ford, Jeanne Grant, James McCracken, John Mooney, Beverly Purvin, Kenneth Utt, Eleanor Williams, *Delbert Anderson, William Carson, Terry Castagna, Feodore Tedick, Beverley Jane Welch*; CHILDREN: John Connoughton, Donald Duerr, Celine Flanagan, Buzzie Martin, Howard Martin, Patti Milligan, Janet Parker. **Understudies:** Johnny: Alan Gilbert; Katie: Elaine Barrow; Cissy: Claudia Campbell, *Marie Foster*; Harry/Moriarty: Kenneth Utt; Allie/Petey/Judge: Donn Driver; Hildy: Beverly Purvin; Aloysius: Art Carroll; Mae: Joan Copeland; Francie: Patti Milligan. *Act I: Scene 1* A street in Brooklyn on a Saturday, nearly 50 years ago: "Payday" (Company), "Mine 'til Monday" (Johnny, Hildy, Company); *Scene 2* Around the corner; a few minutes later: "Mine 'til Monday" (reprise) (Aloysius, Hildy, Petey, Allie, Willie); *Scene 3* Cissy's house; a few weeks later: "Make the Man Love Me" (Katie & Johnny), "I'm Like a New Broom" (Johnny & Friends); *Scene 4* On the corner; early next morning: "I'm Like a New Broom" (reprise) (Johnny & Friends); *Scene 5* Max's furniture store; the same morning: "Look Who's Dancing" [Katie, Cissy, Johnny, Allie, Willie (added during the run), Petey, Mary Statz, Doris Wright, Marta Becket, Dorothy Hill (*Iona MacKenzie*)]; *Scene 6* On the way to Katie's; a year later: "Look Who's Dancing" (reprise) (Friends); *Scene 7* The Nolan kitchen; a year later: "Make the Man Love Me" (reprise) (Katie); *Scene 8* On the street: "Love is the Reason" (Cissy & Annie, Hildy, Della, Eleanor Williams), "Mine Next Monday" (Aloysius & Hildy); *Scene 9* Cissy's house; *Scene 10* A sidewalk: "If You Haven't Got a Sweetheart" [Del Anderson (*James McCracken*) & Company) [Katie & Johnny sang this is in the 2003 revival]; *Scene 11* Up on the roof: "I'll Buy You a Star" (Johnny & Company). *Act II: Scene 1* The courtyard; 12 years later: "That's How it Goes" (Old Clothes Man, Maudie, Florence, Company), "He Had Refinement" (Cissy); *Scene 2* The Nolan kitchen: "Growing Pains" (Johnny & Francie), "Is That My Prince?" (Cissy & Swanswine); *Scene 3* A street corner; *Scene 4* Mae's place; *Scene 5* A dark and deserted street: "Hallowe'en" (ballet) (Johnny, with Petey, Allie, Willie, Dancers, Children); *Scene 6* The Nolan kitchen: "Don't Be Afraid" (Johnny) [in the 2003 revival this was a song for Katie in Act I], "I'm Like a New Broom" (reprise) (Johnny); *Scene 7* An empty street fronting a vacant lot: "Love is the Reason" (reprise) (Cissy & Harry); *Scene 8* The Nolan kitchen; a somber autumn day; *Scene 9* In the street; late June: "Look Who's Dancing" (reprise) (Harry); *Scene 10* The courtyard: "If You Haven't Got a Sweetheart" (reprise) (Company).

The show opened to generally terrific reviews. Shirley Booth won a Donaldson Award.

After Broadway. TOUR. Opened on 10/10/52, at the Klein Auditorium, Bridgeport, Conn., and closed on 11/29/52, at the Shubert Theatre, Chicago. This was a new production. The Hallowe'en Ballet was replaced with the Raffle Ballet for the tour. PRESENTED BY Lee Shubert; DIRECTOR: Gus Schirmer Jr.; CHOREOGRAPHER: Edmund Balin; MUSICAL DIRECTOR: Joseph Littau; DANCE MUSIC ARRANGEMENTS: Dean Fuller. *Cast:* CISSY: Joan Blondell; JOHNNY: Johnny Johnston, *Robert Shackleton*; KATIE: Evelyn Ward; HARRY: John Vivyan; PETEY: Bill Beckham; FRANCINE: Anne Mary Tallon; EDGIE: Bob St. Clair; SWANSWINE: Le Roi Operti.

GOODSPEED OPERA HOUSE, Conn., 11/12/03–12/14/03. Previews from 10/10/03. REVISED BOOK/DIRECTOR: Elinor Renfield; CHOREOGRAPHER: Jennifer Paulson Lee; SETS: James Noone; COSTUMES: Pamela Scofield; LIGHTING: Jeff Croiter; MUSICAL DIRECTOR: Michael O'Flaherty; ORCHESTRATIONS: Dan DeLange. *Cast:* HARRY: Adam Heller; JOHNNY: Deven May; KATIE: Kerry O'Malley; MAX/SWANSON: Steve Routman; ALOYSIUS: Tom Souhrada; CISSY: Sari Wagner; HILDY: Megan Walker; FRANCIE: Remy Zaken. The number "Tuscaloosa," which was cut from the original before Broadway, was here re-instated. "I'm Proud of You" (m: Arthur Schwartz; l: Dorothy Fields), which was not written for this show, was also included. The new libretto tells the same story, but explores it more deeply.

CITY CENTER, NYC, 2/10/05–2/13/05. Part of the Encores! series of staged readings. *Cast:* JOHNNY: Jason Danieley; Katie: Sally Murphy; Cissy: Emily Skinner; ALSO WITH: John Ellison Conlee, Nancy Anderson, Sean Palmer, Beth McVey, Caitlin Carter, Joseph Dellger, James Clow, Lorin Latarro.

712. *Treemonisha*

Also called *Scott Joplin's Treemonisha.* An opera, set in 1866 on a plantation run by Free Blacks in Arkansas, northeast of Texarkana, and three or four miles from the Red River. The legend of Treemonisha, an orphan girl found under a tree and adopted by Monisha and Ned, who works through education to improve the lot of the people of her black community. Being the only educated person of her race, and thus defying superstition, she is kidnapped by the conjurors Zodzetrick and Luddud and their accomplices, who intend to throw her into a wasps' nest, but she is saved by Remus disguised as a scarecrow. The conjurors are captured and Treemonisha and Remus pardon them, and Treemonisha becomes the leader of the community.

Before Broadway. Written by Scott Joplin at the piano, between 1908 and 1911 (the score was published in 1911). Between 1913 and 1917 he worked on the orchestrations with his friend Sam Patterson. It had a single, rehearsal hall run-through at the Lincoln Theatre, Harlem, in May 1915, with singers accompanied by Scott Joplin, in order to attract backers for the show, but there was no interest. Mr. Joplin did not annotate his piano score, and it is rumored that his orchestrations with Sam Patterson were thrown out in the trash in the 1920s. However, the show was discovered in 1970, and, with new orchestrations by Thomas J. Anderson, it had its premiere at MOREHOUSE COLLEGE, Atlanta, 1/27/72. Performed by Atlanta Symphony & Morehouse College Music Department; CONDUCTOR: Robert Shaw; *Cast:* Alpha Floyd, Louise Parker, Seth McCoy, Simon Estes. Using orchestrations by William Bolcom, it ran at WOLF TRAP FARM PARK, Vienna, Va., in 8/72. It played at CARNEGIE HALL, NYC, in 7/73.

In 6/75 the HOUSTON GRAND OPERA did the first professional production — free and outdoors. ORCHESTRATIONS: Gunther Schuller; CAST RECORDING on Deutsches Grammophon, made in 1976. This production ran at the KENNEDY CENTER, Washington, DC, in 9/75, and then went to Broadway.

The Broadway Run. URIS THEATRE, 10/21/75–11/2/75; PALACE THEATRE, 11/3/75–12/14/75. 6 previews. Total of 64 PERFORMANCES (limited engagement). The Houston Grand Opera Association production, PRESENTED BY Adela Holzer, James Nederlander, and Victor Lurie, by arrangement with the Dramatic Publishing Company; MUSIC/

LYRICS/BOOK: Scott Joplin; CONCEIVED BY/DIRECTOR: Frank Corsaro; CHOREOGRAPHER: Louis Johnson; SETS/COSTUMES: Franco Colavecchia; LIGHTING: Nananne Porcher; MUSICAL SUPERVISOR/MUSICAL DIRECTOR/ORCHESTRATIONS: Gunther Schuller; PRESS: Michael Alpert, Marilynn LeVine, Joshua Ellis, Warren Knowlton; GENERAL MANAGER: Nelle Nugent; COMPANY MANAGER: John Scott; PRODUCTION STAGE MANAGER: Ben Janney; STAGE MANAGER: Elizabeth Caldwell; ASSISTANT STAGE MANAGER: Clinton Davis. *Cast:* ZODZETRICK: Ben Harney (6); NED: Willard White (4) *; MONISHA, NED'S WIFE: Betty Allen (2) *, Lorna Myers (matinees); TREEMONISHA: Carmen Balthrop (1) *, Kathleen Battle (matinees); REMUS: Curtis Rayam (3) *; ANDY: Kenneth Hicks (8); LUCY: Cora Johnson (7); PARSON ALLTALK: Edward Pierson (5); SIMON: Raymond Bazemore (11); CEPHUS: Dwight Ransom (10); LUDDUD: Dorceal Duckens (9); CHORUS: Earl L. Baker, Kenneth Bates, Barbara Christopher, Steven Cole, Ella Eure, Gregory Gardner, Melvin Jordan, Patricia McDermott, Janette Moody, Marion Moore, Vera Moore, Lorna Myers, Glover Parham, Patricia Pates, William Penn, Dwight Ransom, Cornel Richie, Patricia Rogers, Christine Spencer, Walter Turnbull, Gloria Turner, Peter Whitehead, Arthur Williams, Barbara Young; DANCERS: Louis Johnson Dance Theatre (12) (Clyde-Jacques Barrett, Thea Barnes, Dwight Baxter, Renee Brailsford, Karen Burke, Veda Jackson, Reggie Jackson, Julia Lema, Anita Littleman, Rick Odums, Dwayne Phelps, Ivson Polk, Mabel Robinson, Martial Roumain, Katherine Singleton, James Thurston, Bobby Walker, Pamela Wilson). *Act I: Scene 1* Morning: Overture (Orchestra, Zodzetrick, Dancers), "The Bag of Luck" (Treemonisha, Monisha, Ned, Zodzetrick), "The Corn-Huskers" (Treemonisha & Chorus), "We're Goin' Around" (Treemonisha, Monisha, Lucy, Remus, Ned, Chorus, Dancers), "The Wreath" (Treemonisha, Monisha, Lucy), "The Sacred Tree" (Monisha), "Surprise" (Treemonisha), "Treemonisha's Bringing Up" (Treemonisha & Monisha), "Good Advice" (Alltalk & Chorus), "Confusion" (Monisha, Lucy, Remus, Ned); *Scene 2* Afternoon of the same day: "Superstition" (Simon & Cephus), "Treemonisha in Peril" (Zodzetrick, Simon, Luddud, Cephus), "The Frolic of the Bears" (Dancers), "The Wasp Nest" (Simon & Cephus), "The Rescue" (Treemonisha & Remus), "We Will Rest Awhile" (Quartet), "Going Home" (Treemonisha, Remus, Foreman), "Aunt Dinah Has Blowed de Horn" (Chorus & Dancers). *Act II: Scene 1* That evening: Prelude (Orchestra), "I Want to See My Child" (Monisha & Ned), "Treemonisha's Return" (Treemonisha, Monisha, Remus, Ned, Andy), "Wrong is Never Right" (Remus & Chorus), "Abuse" (Treemonisha & Andy), "When Villains Ramble Far and Near" (Ned), "Conjuror's Forgiven" (Treemonisha & Andy), "We Will Trust You as Our Leader" (Treemonisha, Monisha, Lucy, Ned), "A Real Slow Drag" (Company), "Aunt Dinah Has Blowed de Horn" (reprise) (Company).

Broadway reviews were divided. Scott Joplin won a special (and, of course, posthumous) Pulitzer Prize. The show received a Tony nomination for score.

After Broadway. LOS ANGELES CIVIC LIGHT OPERA, 1978; HOUSTON GRAND OPERA, 5/81 & 3/82 (on 2/2/86 the Houston Grand Opera production was televised as one of PBS's *Great Performances*); BROOKLYN OPERA SOCIETY, 7/83; TEATRO GHIONE, Rome, 9/85; Part of the CINCINNATI MAY FESTIVAL, 1988; In concert, in the VIRGIN ISLANDS, 1988; BROMLEY FESTIVAL THEATRE, England, 8/90; BIRMINGHAM OPERA THEATRE, Alabama, 3/96.

713. *Tricks*

Set in and around Venice. Octave is Argante's son, and is in love with Hyacinthe; Sylvestre is Octave's servant; Scapin is Leandre's servant; Hyacinthe is the daughter of Geronte, and is in love with Octave; Leandre is the son of Geronte, and is in love with Zerbinetta the Gypsy Queen.

Before Broadway. The world premiere was at the ACTORS THEATRE OF LOUISVILLE, in 1971. DIRECTOR: Jon Jory; SETS: Paul Owen; COSTUMES: Kurt Wilhelm; LIGHTING: Geoffrey T. Cunningham; MUSICAL DIRECTOR: Richard Berg. *Cast:* OCTAVE: Ted Pejovich; SYLVESTRE: Christopher Murney; SCAPIN: Eric Tavaris; HYACINTHE: Carolyn Connors; ARGANTE: Sandy McCallum; GERONTE: Max Wright; LEANDRE:

Stephen Keep; PROPERTY MISTRESS: Adale O'Brien; ZERBINETTA: Donna Curtis; THE COMMEDIA: ARLECCHINO: Richard Berg; PEDROLINO: Karl Kirchner; PANTALONE: Stuart Paine; SCARAMUCCIA: Larry Holt; CAPITANO: Tom Owen.

ARENA STAGE THEATRE, Washington, DC, 5/19/72. 47 PERFORMANCES. It had the same basic crew as for the Louisville run, except LIGHTING: Vance Sorrells; MUSICAL DIRECTOR: Tom Owen. *Cast:* Richard Bauer, Howard Witt, Gary Dontzig, Carolyn Connors, Max Wright, Adale O'Brien. Don Saddler replaced John Sharpe as choreographer before Broadway. Miles White came out of retirement to do the costumes.

The Broadway Run. ALVIN THEATRE, 1/8/73–1/13/73. 5 previews from 1/3/73. 8 PERFORMANCES. PRESENTED BY Herman Levin; MUSIC: Jerry Blatt; LYRICS: Lonnie Burstein; BOOK/DIRECTOR: Jon Jory; BASED ON the 1671 farce *Les Fourberies de Scapin*, by Moliere; CHOREOGRAPHER: Donald Saddler; SETS: Oliver Smith; COSTUMES: Miles White; LIGHTING: Martin Aronstein; SOUND: Jack Shearing; ORCHESTRATIONS: Bert De Coteau; CONDUCTOR: David Frank; DANCE & INCIDENTAL MUSIC ARRANGEMENTS: Peter Howard; PRESS: Frank Goodman, Arlene Wolf, Margaret Wade; GENERAL MANAGER: Philip Adler; COMPANY MANAGER: Milton M. Pollack; STAGE MANAGER: Mitchell Erickson; ASSISTANT STAGE MANAGERS: John Handy & Joe Hill. *Cast:* PROPERTY MISTRESS: Adale O'Brien; OCTAVE: Walter Bobbie (2); SYLVESTRE: Christopher Murney (9); SCAPIN: Rene Auberjonois (1); HYACINTHE: Carolyn Mignini (7); ARGANTE: Mitchell Jason (6); GERONTE: Tom Toner (13); LEANDRE: Randy Herron; ZERBINETTA: June Helmers (4); PANTANELLA: Suzanne Walker; ISABELLA: JoAnn Ogawa (10); CARMELLA: Lani Sundsten (12); GONDOLIER: John Handy (3); THE COMMEDIA: ARLECCHINO/LEAD SINGER: Joe Morton (8); CHARLOTTA: Charlotte Crossley; ERNESTINA: Ernestine Jackson (5); SHEZWAE: Shezwae Powell (11). *Standbys*: Scapin/Sylvestre: Eric Tavares; Argante/Geronte: Joe Hill; Hyacinthe/Property Mistress: Susan Dyas; Pantanella/Carmella/Isabella: Vicki Frederick. *Understudies*: Zerbinetta: Adale O'Brien; Octave: Randy Herron; Leandre: John Handy. *Musicians:* KEYBOARD: David Frank; GUITARS: Tom Owen & Jack Cavari; PERCUSSION: Chuck Spies; REED: William Morimando; TRUMPET: James Bossy; BASS: Art Koenig; VIOLINS: Andrew Gottesman, Stanley Karpienia, Myron Roman, Avram Weiss. *Act I:* PROLOGUE: "Love or Money" (Commedia), "Who Was I?" (Octave & Commedia), "Trouble's a Ruler" (Scapin, Sylvestre, Octave), "Enter Hyacinthe" (Octave & Commedia), "Believe Me" (Octave, Hyacinthe, Commedia), "Tricks" (Scapin & Sylvestre), "A Man of Spirit" (Commedia), "Where is Respect" (Argante & Geronte), "Somebody's Doin' Somebody All the Time" (Scapin & Commedia), "A Sporting Man" (Scapin & Commedia). *Act II:* "Scapin" (Arlecchino), "Anything is Possible" (Scapin & Sylvestre), "How Sweetly Simple" (Hyacinthe & Zerbinetta), "Gypsy Girl" (Zerbinetta & Commedia), EPILOGUE: "Life Can be Funny" (Company).

Broadway reviews were terrible. It received a Tony nomination for costumes.

714. *Triumph of Love*

Set in the garden retreat of Hermocrates (Hesione's brother), an 18th-century Greco-French topiary labyrinth.

Before Broadway. The straight play was first done in the USA at the McCarter Theatre, from 3/24/92. ADAPTED BY/DIRECTOR: Stephen Wadsworth; COSTUMES: Martin Pakledinaz. *Cast:* LEONIDE: Katherine Borowitz; DIMAS: Tom Brennan; HERMOCRATES: Robin Chadwick. On 8/6/93 it opened at the GUTHRIE THEATRE, Minneapolis, and on 10/8/93 at CENTER STAGE, Baltimore.

Susan Birkenhead and James Magruder began work on the musical version in 1994. It premiered at CENTER STAGE, Baltimore, 11/26/96–12/21/96. Previews from 11/21/96. PRESENTED BY Margo Lion, in association with the Yale Repertory Theatre. Then it played at YALE REP, New Haven, 1/16/97–2/8/97. The crew for the Baltimore/New Haven production was the same as for the subsequent Broadway run, except SETS: Heidi Landesman; LIGHTING: Brian MacDevitt; MUSICAL DIRECTOR: Bradley Vieth. *Cast*: LEONIDE: Susan Egan; CORINE: Denny Dillon;

AGIS: Christopher Sieber; HERMOCRATES: Robert LuPone; HESIONE: Mary Beth Piel; HARLEQUIN: Kenny Raskin; DIMAS: Daniel Marcus. *Act I*: "Anything," "The Bond that Can't Be Broken," "You May Call Me Phocion," "The Mysteries of Criticism," "Us," "The Ballad of Cecile," "Serenity," "Issue in Question," "Teach Me Not to Love You." *Act II*: "Three Great Minds," "The Tree," "What Have I Done?," "Henchmen Are Forgotten," "Love Won't Take No for an Answer," Finale. It was planned to bring the Baltimore/Yale Rep production to Broadway in either spring 1997 or (more realistically, given the timing) in the 1997–98 season. On 6/13/97, in an unexpected breach of secrecy, Betty Buckley told the *New York Times* that she was going to star with F. Murray Abraham and Susan Egan. The producers, while not denying this, did not confirm it for another week. Rehearsals began on 7/22/97. In 8/97 Elayne Boosler left the production due to "creative differences," and was replaced by Nancy Opel. There was a press preview on 9/16/97. Broadway previews began on 9/27/97 (date put back from 9/2/97). The number "If I Cannot Love" was cut during previews. Opening night was put back from 9/25/97 to 10/23/97, and the proposed theatre, the Walter Kerr, was switched to the Royale. Michele Pawk went on for Betty Buckley for the previews of 10/1/97, 10/11/97, 10/25/97, 10/28/97, 11/7/97, 11/15/97, and 11/18/97.

The Broadway Run. ROYALE THEATRE, 10/23/97–1/4/98. 31 previews from 9/27/97. 84 PERFORMANCES. PRESENTED BY Margo Lion, Metropolitan Entertainment Group, and Jujamcyn Theatres, in association with PACE Theatrical Group, the Baruch—Frankel—Viertel Group, Alex Hitz, Center Stage, and Yale Repertory Theatre; MUSIC: Jeffrey Stock; LYRICS: Susan Birkenhead; BOOK: James Magruder; BASED ON the 18th century play by Pierre Carlet de Marivaux; DIRECTOR: Michael Mayer; CHOREOGRAPHER: Doug Varone; SETS: Heidi Ettinger; COSTUMES: Catherine Zuber; LIGHTING: Paul Gallo; SOUND: Brian Ronan; MUSICAL SUPERVISOR/MUSICAL ARRANGEMENTS: Michael Kosarin; MUSICAL DIRECTOR: Patrick S. Brady; ORCHESTRATIONS: Bruce Coughlin; CAST RECORDING on Jay (the release date was delayed until 10/7/98); PRESS: Boneau/Bryan-Brown; CASTING: Jay Binder; GENERAL MANAGEMENT: 101 Productions; COMPANY MANAGER: David Auster; PRODUCTION STAGE MANAGER: Arturo E. Porazzi; STAGE MANAGER: Gary Mickelson; ASSISTANT STAGE MANAGER: Cori Gardner. *Cast*: AGIS, A STUDENT OF REASON: Christopher Sieber (4); HESIONE, HIS AUNT, A PHILOSOPHER: Betty Buckley (3) ☆, *Alix Korey* (during Miss Buckley's vacation), *Michele Pawk*; DIMAS, A GARDENER: Kevin Chamberlin (5); HARLEQUIN, THE VALET: Roger Bart (6); HERMOCRATES, A PHILOSOPHER: F. Murray Abraham (2) ☆; PRINCESS LEONIDE: Susan Egan (1) ☆; CORINE, HER MAID SERVANT: Nancy Opel (7). *Understudies*: Leonide: Christianne Tisdale; Corine: Christianne Tisdale, *Alix Korey*; Hermocrates: Paul Harman; Dimas: Paul Harman & Tom Plotkin; Hesione: Alix Korey, *Michele Pawk*; Agis: Tom Plotkin; Harlequin: Paul Harman & Tom Plotkin. *Orchestra*: CONCERTMASTER: Rick Dolan; VIOLA: Richard Brice; CELLO: Chungsun Kim; BASS: William Sloat; WOODWINDS: Chuck Wilson, Rick Heckman, Frank Santagata; HORN: Katie Dennis; TRUMPET: Terry Szor; PERCUSSION: Larry Spivack. *Act I*: "This Day of Days" (Hesione, Harlequin, Dimas, Agis, Hermocrates), "Anything" (Leonide), "The Bond that Can't Be Broken" (Leonide & Agis), "Mr. Right" (m: Van Dyke Parks) (Corine & Harlequin), "You May Call Me Phocion" (Leonide & Hesione), "Mr. Right" (reprise) (Corine & Dimas), "Emotions" (Hermocrates & Leonide), "The Sad and Sordid Saga of Cecile" (Leonide, Agis, Corine, Harlequin, Dimas), "Serenity" (Hesione), "Issue in Question" (Agis), "Teach Me Not to Love You" (Company). *Act II*: "Have a Little Faith" (m: Michael Kosarin) (Corine, Leonide, Harlequin, Dimas), "The Tree" (Hesione & Hermocrates), "What Have I Done?" (Leonide), "Henchmen Are Forgotten" (Harlequin, Dimas, Corine), "Love Won't Take No for an Answer" (Hermocrates, Hesione, Agis), "This Day of Days" (reprise) (Leonide, Agis, Corine, Harlequin, Dimas).

Broadway reviews were very divided, but Betty Buckley was universally praised. She was nominated for a Tony. The production posted provisional closing notices on 12/16/97, and continued on a week-to-week basis. Despite a fan-letter campaign to get people in to see it so it could move to the Eugene O'Neill (it had to leave the Royale to make way for another show), it closed on 1/4/98.

715. *A Tropical Revue*

A dance revue, featuring black dancing from many different parts of the world. The show also featured dance styles including a real Martinique beguine, the black bottom, Charleston, mooch, and the Creole mazurka called the "mazouk." Dixieland jazz musicians were added to boost the show's commercial appeal. This may be the first Broadway musical directed by a woman.

The Broadway Run. MARTIN BECK THEATRE, 9/19/43–11/15/43; FORREST THEATRE, 11/16/43–12/4/43. Total of 87 PERFORMANCES. PRESENTED BY Sol Hurok; CONCEIVED BY/DIRECTOR/CHOREOGRAPHER: Katherine Dunham; SETS/COSTUMES: mostly by John Pratt; LIGHTING: Dale Wasserman; MUSICAL DIRECTOR: Albert Arkuss; MUSICAL ARRANGEMENTS: Luther Henderson; CHORAL DIRECTOR: Helen Dowdy; SUGGESTED MINSTREL TUNES & DANCES: Lawrence Deas & Clarence Muse. *Cast*: Katherine Dunham; The Leonard Ware Trio; THE DUNHAM DANCERS: Rajah (Roger) Ohardieno, Lucille Ellis, Thomas W. "Tommy" Gomez, Lavinia Williams, LaVerne French, Syvilla Fort, Claude Marchant, Lawaune Ingram, Lenwood Morris, Maria Mentiero, Vanoye Aikens, Ramona Erwin, Andre Drew; *Bobby Capo* (Puerto Rican singer—added during the run); DRUMS: Gaucho Vanderhans & Candido Vicenty; 1ST PIANO: Albert Arkuss; 2ND PIANO: Raul Barragan. *Act I*: *Scene 1* Primitive Rhythms: 1/ Rara Tonga (m: Paquita Anderson) (based on a Melanesian folk tale. A god takes a woman and the husband is turned into a snake). NARRATOR: Katherine Dunham; THE CHOSEN WOMAN: Lavinia Williams; THE GOD: Rajah Ohardieno; THE JEALOUS HUSBAND: Tommy Gomez; 2/ Tempo-Son: POSSESSED DANCER: Lucille Ellis [during the run this number was re-named Cuban Slave Lament, and Bobby Capo was added as the singer]; 3/ Tempo-Bolero (m: Paquita Anderson) (Miss Williams, Mr. Gomez, Group) [during the run this number was re-named Moorish Bolero]; *Scene 2* Rumba Suite: 1/ Concert Rumba (m: Morejon) (Miss Dunham, Miss Fort, Miss Williams, Mr. Marchant, Mr. Gomez). This number was replaced during the run by Choro (m: Vadico Gogliano) (a 19th-century Brazilian quadrille) (Miss Dunham, Miss Fort, Mr. Marchant, Mr. Gomez); 2/ Rumba with a Little Jive Mixed In (m: Andre) (Miss Ellis, Mr. French, Mr. Marchant); 3/ Brazilian Carnival Macumba (Miss Dunham & Messrs Morris, Drew, French, Gomez). This number was replaced during the run by "Para Que tu Ver" (Mr. Capo) (Miss Fort & Mr. Ohardieno); 4/ Santos Ritual (dance) (Miss Fort & Mr. Ohardieno); 5/ Mexican Rumba (m: Harl MacDonald) (from "The Rhumba Symphony") (Miss Dunham, Mr. Gomez, Group). *Act II*: *Scene 1* Rites de Passage (tribal rites danced by Tommy Gomez to music adapted from a Haitian theme by Paquita Anderson) (percussion by Gaucho Vanderhans): 1/ The Fertility Ritual—here associated with marriage or mating: MAIDEN IN THE COMMUNITY: Lavinia Williams; MAN IN THE COMMUNITY: LaVerne French; 2/ Male Puberty Ritual: The first section portrays the boy's isolation and his vision of becoming a warrior. In the second, masked men of the community, led by the warrior who has appeared in the boy's vision, come to take him to the formal initiation: BOY INITIATE: Tommy Gomez; WARRIOR: Roger Ohardieno; 3/ Death Ritual: The wives of a chief mourn his death. Through the intervention of the matriarch the defeat of death is accomplished, and the life cycle continued in the ceremonial ritual of fecundation: MATRIARCH: Katherine Dunham; 4/ Rhythm Interlude (Miss Ellis & Drummers) [during the run this number was re-named Street Scene—Port au Prince]; *Scene 2* "Bahiana" (m: Don Alfonso) (a Brazilian song) (Miss Dunham & Messrs Ohardieno, Marchant, Gomez, Morris); *Scene 3* Tropics—"Shore Excursion" (m: Paquita Anderson. PERCUSSION: Gaucho Vanderhans; WOMAN WITH A CIGAR: Katherine Dunham; DOCKHAND: Roger Ohardieno. *Act III*: *Scene 1* 1/ Plantation dances from "Bre'r Rabbit an' de Tah Baby;" 2/ Strutters' Ball (Helen Dowdy & Singers); 3/ Square Dance, Juba, Jennie Cooler, Palmer House, Pas Mala, Ballin' de Jack, Strut, Cakewalk: INTERLOCUTOR: Katherine Dunham; FIELD HANDS: Claude Marchant, Tommy Gomez, Roger Ohardieno, Lenwood Morris, Vanoye Aikens; COUPLE FROM MEMPHIS: Syvilla Fort & LaVerne French; Corps de Ballet; *Scene 2* Leonard Ware Trio; *Scene 3* Le Jazz Hot: 1/ Variations on the theme Boogie Woogie (m: Meade Lux Lewis, Albert Ammons, Smith) (Miss Ellis & Group), 2/ Barrel House (Florida Swamp

Shimmy) (m: Meade Lux Lewis & Albert Ammons) (Miss Dunham & Mr. Ohardieno), 3/ Honky-Tonk Train (m: Meade Lux Lewis): "Cokey" BRAKEMAN: LaVerne French; LADY PASSENGER: Lucille Ellis.

Producer Sol Hurok had Katherine Dunham's legs insured for a quarter of a million dollars. The show was originally due to play only two weeks. The *New York Times* did not review it. During the run some numbers were dropped, others added, and there was a constant re-arrangement of the order of the numbers.

After Broadway. After the Broadway run Katherine Dunham took the show on a tour of the USA and Canada. Added to the tour were the singing group the Helen Dowdy Quartet and two new numbers: "Callate" ("Sh-be Quiet") (m: Candido Vicenty) (Miss Dunham, Mr. Ohardieno, Mr. Morris, Mr. Aikens) and Promenade — Havana 1910 (m: Mercedes Navarro) (Miss Dunham, Company, Mr. Capo, Helen Dowdy Quartet). The show then returned to Broadway.

716. *A Tropical Revue (Return to Broadway)*

NEW CENTURY THEATRE, 12/26/44–1/13/45. 24 PERFORMANCES. PRESENTED BY Sol Hurok; CONCEIVED BY/DIRECTOR/CHOREOGRAPHER: Katherine Dunham; SETS/COSTUMES: mostly by John Pratt; LIGHTING: Dale Wasserman; MUSICAL DIRECTOR/ORCHESTRATIONS/MUSICAL ARRANGEMENTS/PIANIST: Martin Gabowitz; CAST RECORDING on Bat-acuda. **Cast:** Same as in 1943, except that The Leonard Ware Trio were gone, as was Dunham dancer Maria Mentiero. New Dunham dancers were: Talley Beatty, Eddy Clay, Ora Lee, Richardena Jackson, Dolores Harper, Gloria Mitchell. Bobby Capo was still with the show, as was the Dowdy Quartet (Helen Dowdy, Rosalie King, Howard Carlos, Oliver Busch). On drums Gaucho Vanderhans was replaced with Mendez & Estrada (i.e. Julio Mendez & La Rosa Estrada).

Below are the new scenes and numbers (if the information is the same as for the 1943 run then just the title will be given. Otherwise the new information will be put in). **Act I:** *Scene 1* "Rara Tonga:" NARRA-TOR: Katherine Dunham; THE CHOSEN WOMAN: Ramona Erwin; THE GOD: Roger Ohardieno; THE JEALOUS HUSBAND: Tommy Gomez; *Scene 2* "Cuban Slave Lament;" *Scene 3* "Moorish Bolero;" *Scene 4* "Choro" (Miss Dunham, Miss Fort, Mr. Morris, Mr. Beatty) (Lawaune Ingram was alternate for Katherine Dunham); *Scene 5* "Rumba with a Little Jive Mixed In" (Miss Ellis, Mr. Aikens, Mr. Marchant); *Scene 6* "Bahiana" (Miss Dunham & Messrs Ohardieno, Aikens, Beatty, Gomez); *Scene 7* "Tropics" (no drummers listed); *Scene 8* "Para Que tu Veas" (Mr. Capo); *Scene 9* "Promenade — Havana 1910" (a period piece set in Cuba). **Act II:** *Scene 1* "L'Ag'Ya" (m: Robert Sanders; orch: Martin Gabowitz) (from an original story by Katherine Dunham). A long piece. Set in Vauclin, a tiny 18th-century village in Martinique. Loulouse and Alcide are in love. The failed suitor, Julot, seeks the help of the king of the zombies. He obtains the cambois (a powerful love charm) from Roi Zombie. The following evening, during the dance festivities of the Mazouk and the Beguine, Julot arrives, and they go into the Majumba, a love dance of Ancient Africa. Alcide manages to break free of the spell of the cambois, and challenges Julot to the Ag'Ya, a lethal style of wrestling native to Mar-tinique: LOULOUSE: Katherine Dunham; ALCIDE: Vanoye Aikens; JULOT: Claude Marchant, Tommy Gomez (alternate); ROI ZOMBIE: Roger Ohar-dieno; PORTERESSES/VENDORS/FISHERMEN: Dunham Company; ZOM-BIES/TOWNSPEOPLE OF VAUCLIN: Dunham Company; *Scene 2* Street Scene — Port au Prince (Miss Ellis, Mr. Estrada, Mr. Mendez); *Scene 3* "Strutters' Ball" (Dowdy Quartet); *Scene 4* "Cake Walk" (Miss Fort, Mr. Aikens, Ensemble); *Scene 5* "Barrel House;" *Scene 6* 1/ "Flaming Youth, 1927" (m: Brad Gowans) (a lazily rambling satire on the speakeasy days of the roaring 20s): BLUES SINGER: Helen Dowdy; KANSAS CITY WOMAN: Lucille Ellis; SNAKEHIPS TUCKER: Tommy Gomez; 2/ Black Bottom, Charleston, Mooch, Fishtail (Miss Ingram, Mr. Marchant, Ensemble); *Scene 7* Finale (Dunham Dancers).

Roger Ohardieno was dropped during the run.

After Broadway. After Broadway they continued to tour, 1945–46. The re-vamped version, *New Tropical Revue*, toured but did not play Broadway.

717. *Truly Blessed: A Musical Celebration of Mahalia Jackson*

A presentation of the life and songs of the great gospel singer, with occasional excursions into new blues, pop and jazz numbers.

Before Broadway. It was first presented by Frankie Hewitt, as *Don't Let This Dream Go*, at Ford's Theatre, Washington, DC.

The Broadway Run. LONGACRE THEATRE, 4/22/90–5/20/90. 12 previews. 33 PERFORMANCES. PRESENTED BY Howard Hurst, Philip Rose, and Sophie Hurst, in association with Frankie Hewitt; ORIGINAL MUSIC & LYRICS/BOOK/CONCEIVED BY: Queen Esther Marrow; ADDITIONAL MUSIC & LYRICS: Reginald Royal; DIRECTOR: Robert Kalfin; CHOREO-GRAPHER: Larry Vickers; SETS/LIGHTING: Fred Kolo; COSTUMES: Andrew B. Marlay; SOUND: Peter Fitzgerald; MUSICAL SUPERVISOR/ORCHES-TRATIONS: Joseph Joubert; CONDUCTOR: Aaron Graves; PRESS: The Joshua Ellis Office; GENERAL MANAGER: Charlotte Wilcox; PRODUCTION STAGE MANAGER: Kenneth Hanson; STAGE MANAGER: Janice C. Lane; ASSISTANT STAGE MANAGER: Tina Fabrique. **Cast:** MAHALIA JACKSON: Queen Esther Marrow (1) ☆; ENSEMBLE: Carl Hall (2), Doug Eskew (3), Lynette G. DuPre (2), Gwen Stewart (4). **Understudies**: Mahalia: Tina Fabrique & Lynette G. DuPre; For Miss DuPre/Miss Stewart: Tina Fab-rique. **Musicians:** BASS: Konrad "Cheesecake" Adderly (Eluriel Barfield, understudy); DRUMS: Brian Grice (Brian Brake, understudy); ORGAN: Willard Meeks; KEYBOARD UNDERSTUDIES: JoAnn Richardson-Joubert & Fred Gripper. **Act I:** *Scene 1* Opening; *Scene 2* New Orleans; *Scene 3* Going to Chicago; *Scene 4* The church; *Scene 5* Touring; *Scene 6* On the backsteps; *Scene 7* Mayor Daley and the rally; *Scene 8* Mr. Sigmond Galloway; *Scene 9* On top of the world. **Act II:** *Scene 1* Carnegie Hall; *Scene 2* The march on Washington; *Scene 3* Mahalia in the Berkshires; *Scene 4* In the Holy Land; *Scene 5* Epilogue & celebration. **Act I:** "I Found the Answer" (m/l: Johnny Lange), "St. Louis Blues" (m/l: W.C. Handy), "It's Amazing What God Can Do" (m/l: Reginald Royal): Med-ley: "On the Battlefield for My Lord," "Glory Hallelujah" [end of "It's Amazing what God Can Do" sequence], "He May Not Come When You Want Him," "Lord, I'm Determined" (m/l: Queen Esther Marrow), "Happy Days Are Here Again" (m: Milton Ager; l: Jack Yellen) [from the movie *Chasing Rainbows*], "Precious Lord" (m/l: Thomas A. Dorsey), "Jesus Remembers When Others Forget" (m: Joseph Joubert; l: Thomas A. Dorsey), "Thank You for the Change in My Life" (m/l: Queen Esther Marrow), "Come On, Children, Let's Sing." **Act II:** "Even Me" (arranged by Roberta Martin), "Didn't it Rain," Spiritual Medley: "Wade in the Water," "Old Ship of Zion," "Battle Hymn of the Republic," "I've Been 'buked," "Soon I Will Be Done" [end of medley], "His Gift to Me" (m/l: Reginald Royal), "Move on up a Little Higher" (m/l: Mahalia Jackson), "Rusty Bell," "Truly Blessed" (m/l: Reginald Royal), "He's Got the Whole World in His Hands" (traditional; adapted by Geoff Love).

You could sense that several Broadway critics didn't want to say anything that might cast Mahalia Jackson in a bad light, so reviews were mixed, and divided.

718. *Two by Two*

A chamber musical. Set before, during and after the Great Flood. About a nice Jewish family.

Before Broadway. The idea was Martin Charnin's. This was Danny Kaye's first Broadway show since *Let's Face It* (1941). The role of Esther was written for Nancy Andrews, but Danny Kaye didn't want her; Arthur Miller's sister, Joan Copeland, was hired instead. The show opened for out-of-town tryouts at the Shubert Theatre, New Haven, on 9/26/70. It was here that the number "40 Days and 40 Nights" was cut.

The Broadway Run. IMPERIAL THEATRE, 11/10/70–9/11/71. 8 pre-views from 10/28/70. 343 PERFORMANCES. PRESENTED BY Richard Rodgers; MUSIC: Richard Rodgers; LYRICS: Martin Charnin; BOOK: Peter Stone; BASED ON the 1954 comedy *The Flowering Peach*, by Clifford Odets; CONCEIVED BY/DIRECTOR/CHOREOGRAPHER: Joe Layton; SETS: David Hays; COSTUMES: Fred Voelpel; LIGHTING: John Gleason; SOUND: Jim Limberg; MUSICAL DIRECTOR: Jay Blackton; ORCHESTRATIONS:

Eddie Sauter; DANCE MUSIC & VOCAL ARRANGEMENTS: Trude Rittman; CAST RECORDING on Columbia; PRESS: Frank Goodman & Les Schecter; PRODUCTION SUPERVISOR: Jerome Whyte; GENERAL MANAGER: Morris Jacobs; COMPANY MANAGER: Maurice Winters; PRODUCTION STAGE MANAGER: Harry Young; STAGE MANAGER: Phil King; ASSISTANT STAGE MANAGER: Jess Richards. **Cast**: NOAH: Danny Kaye (1) ☆, *Harry Goz* (during Mr. Kaye's incapacity, 2/5/71–2/17/71); ESTHER: Joan Copeland (3); JAPHETH: Walter Willison (6), *John Stewart* (from 8/16/71); SHEM: Harry Goz (2), *Stephen Pearlman* (while Mr. Goz was standing in for Mr. Kaye, 2/5/71–2/17/71), *Jack Davison* (from 9/5/71); LEAH: Marilyn Cooper (8); HAM: Michael Karm (5); RACHEL: Tricia O'Neil (7); GOLDIE: Madeline Kahn (4), *Caryl Jeanne Tenney* (from 8/16/71). **Standbys**: Ham/Japheth: Jess Richards; Shem: Stephen Pearlman; Esther/Leah: Janet McCall; Goldie/Rachel: Caryl Jeanne Tenney. **Understudy**: Noah: Harry Goz. **Act I**: In and around Noah's home: "Why Me?" (Noah), "Put Him Away" (Shem, Ham, Leah), "The Gitka's Song" (The Gitka), "Something, Somewhere" (Japheth & Family), "You Have Got to Have a Rudder on the Ark" (Noah, Shem, Ham, Japheth), "Something Doesn't Happen" (Rachel & Esther), "An Old Man" (Esther), "Ninety Again!" (Noah), "Two by Two" (Noah & Family), "I Do Not Know a Day I Did Not Love You" (Japheth), "Something, Somewhere" (reprise) (Noah). **Act II**: An ark, and atop Mt. Ararat; 40 days and 40 nights later: "When it Dries" (Noah & Family), "Two by Two" (reprise) (Noah & Esther), "You" (Noah), "(Forty Days and) Forty Nights" (Ham) [this number was not in this production, but it was in the 1989 Off Broadway revival], "The Golden Ram" (Goldie), "Poppa Knows Best" (Noah & Japheth), "I Do Not Know a Day I Did Not Love You" (reprise) (Rachel & Japheth), "As Far as I'm Concerned" (Shem & Leah), "Hey Girlie" (Noah), "The Covenant" (Noah).

Broadway reviews were very divided. On 2/5/71 Danny Kaye slipped on a prop and tore a ligament in his ankle. He returned on 2/18/71 in a plaster case and in a green wheelchair, from which he made one expedition onto his feet (but on crutches) during the course of that performance. The musical sported the word "shit" (it was only the second big, family Broadway musical to do this — after *Coco*). If the reminiscences of Walter Willison and others are to be trusted, Danny Kaye was a monster to work with. Mr. Willison was nominated for a Tony.

After Broadway. TOUR. Opened on 9/15/72, at the Dupont Theatre, Wilmington, Del., and closed on 3/11/73, at Memorial Hall, Dayton, Ohio, after 75 cities. PRESENTED BY Tom Mallow; DIRECTOR: Richard Michaels; CHOREOGRAPHER: Rick Atwell; LIGHTING: John Harvey; MUSICAL DIRECTOR: Albert L. Fiorillo Jr. **Cast**: NOAH: Shelley Berman; ESTHER: Taina Elg; JAPHETH: Michel Priaulx; SHEM: William Countryman; LEAH: Mary Jo Gillis; HAM: Roger Brown; RACHEL: Leslie Miller; GOLDIE: Marcia King.

1989 OFF BROADWAY REVIVAL. HARTLEY HOUSE, 4/7/89–4/23/89. 12 PERFORMANCES. PRESENTED BY On Stage Productions; DIRECTOR: Monica M. Hayes; CHOREOGRAPHER: Carol Cornicelli; MUSICAL DIRECTOR: Wayne Blood. **Cast**: NOAH: Robert J. Gardner.

HOLY TRINITY, NYC, 10/4/90–10/28/90. 20 PERFORMANCES. PRESENTED BY the Triangle Theatre Company; DIRECTOR: Michael Ramach; SETS: Bob Phillips; LIGHTING: Nancy Collings; MUSICAL DIRECTOR: Lawrence W. Hill. **Cast**: NOAH: Kip Niven; HAM: Bryan Batt; ESTHER: Meredyth Rawlins.

JEWISH REPERTORY THEATRE, 11/1/99. 1 PERFORMANCE. Concert reading. DIRECTOR: Walter Willison; MUSICAL DIRECTOR: Fred Barton. **Cast**: NOAH: Walter Willison; ESTHER: Rene Ceballos; JAPHETH: Barrett Foa; SHEM: Philip Hernandez; LEAH: Loni Ackerman; HAM: Gregory Zabagoza; RACHEL: June Angela; GOLDIE: Hallie Brown; NARRATOR: Douglas Holmes.

CUMBERLAND PLAYHOUSE, Crossville, Tennessee, 11/12/04–12/18/04. This was a partial–Equity revival, aimed at a pre–Broadway tour, which NETworks was interested in presenting. It was revised by Martin Charnin and Peter Stone, and finished only two months before Mr. Stone died. The number "(Forty Days and) Forty Nights" was used in Act II. DIRECTOR: Martin Charnin; CHOREOGRAPHER: Michele Colvin; MUSICAL DIRECTOR: Ron Murphy. **Cast**: NOAH: Alan Baker; ESTHER: Angela Angel; SHEM: Frank Calamaro; RACHEL: Ellen Domingos; JAPHETH: Andrew Ross; GOLDIE: Holly O'Brien; HAM: Teren Carter; LEAH: Ruthie Ann Miles.

719. *Two Gentlemen of Verona*

Set in Verona, Milan, and the forest. The story mixes Shakespeare's original text with hard-driving rock rhythms, and revolves around the romantic rivalry between friends Valentine and Proteus, and the ladies Silvia and Julia.

Before Broadway. This was the first of several New York Shakespeare Festival presentations to transfer from Off Broadway (in this case the DELACORTE THEATRE, as part of their 1971 summer season in Central Park) to Broadway. Originally it was not intended as a musical. At the suggestion of director Mel Shapiro a rock score was added to bring it up to date. The cast was ethnically mixed, with black performers Clifton Davis and Jonelle Allen and Latin-Americans Raul Julia and Carla Pinza. A week before the Delacorte opening, Joe Papp attended a rehearsal and declared the show a disaster. He did drastic things with it, and a week later it received raves from the non-paying public at its debut on 7/22/71. It ran 14 PERFORMANCES, and closed on 8/8/71. The Off Broadway title was *The Two Gentlemen of Verona*, but for Broadway they dropped the definite article. For Broadway Diana Davila replaced Carla Pinza as Julia, and John Bottoms replaced Jerry Stiller as the servant Launce. Jean Erdman was replaced as choreographer by Dennis Nahat, but the only billing Mr. Nahat got in the Broadway programs was "additional musical staging." He did, however, get choreographer billing on the post-Broadway tour.

The Broadway Run. ST. JAMES THEATRE, 12/1/71–5/20/73. 20 previews from 11/13/71. 613 PERFORMANCES. PRESENTED BY The New York Shakespeare Festival (Joseph Papp, producer); MUSIC: Galt MacDermot; LYRICS: John Guare; BOOK: John Guare & Mel Shapiro; BASED ON the 1592 comedy of the same name by William Shakespeare; DIRECTOR: Mel Shapiro; CHOREOGRAPHER: Jean Erdman; ADDITIONAL MUSICAL STAGING: Dennis Nahat; SETS: Ming Cho Lee; COSTUMES: Theoni V. Aldredge; LIGHTING: Lawrence Metzler; SOUND: Jack Shearing; MUSICAL SUPERVISOR: Harold Wheeler; MUSICAL DIRECTOR: Richard Kaufman; ORCHESTRATIONS: Galt MacDermot & Harold Wheeler; CAST RECORDING on ABC/Dunhill; PRESS: Merle Debuskey & Faith Greer; GENERAL MANAGERS: Eugene Wolsk & Emanuel Azenberg; COMPANY MANAGER: Michael Brandman; PRODUCTION STAGE MANAGER: R. Derek Swire; STAGE MANAGER: D.W. Koehler; ASSISTANT STAGE MANAGER: Anthony Neely. **Cast**: THURIO: Frank O'Brien (7), *Chesley Uxbridge*; SPEED: Jose Perez (8); VALENTINE: Clifton Davis (3) ☆, *Samuel E. Wright* (from 11/28/72), *Joe Morton* (from 3/20/73), *Larry Marshall* (from 4/10/73); PROTEUS: Raul Julia (4) ☆, *Carlos Cestero* (from 10/23/72), *Chris Sarandon* (from 11/28/72); JULIA: Diana Davila (2) ☆; LUCETTA: Alix Elias (6), *Sheila Gibbs*; LAUNCE: John Bottoms (11); ANTONIO: Frederic Warriner (9); CRAB: PHINEAS; DUKE OF MILAN: Norman Matlock (5), *Ellwoodson Williams* (from 4/4/72); SILVIA: Jonelle Allen (1) ☆, *Hattie Winston* (from 11/28/72); TAVERN HOST: Frederic Warriner; EGLAMOUR: Alvin Lum (10); VISSI D'AMORE: Frank O'Brien & Georgyn Geetlein; MILKMAID: Sheila Gibbs; QUARTET (BLACK PASSION): Sheila Gibbs, Signa Joy, Kenneth Lowry, Sakinah Mahammud; CITIZENS OF VERONA AND MILAN: Loretta Abbott, Christopher Alden, Roger Briant, Douglas Brickhouse, Stockard Channing, Paul DeJohn, Nancy Denning, Richard De Russo, Arthur Erickson, Georgyn Geetlein, Sheila Gibbs, Jeff Goldblum, Edward Henkel, Albert Insinnia, Jane Jaffe, Signa Joy, Kenneth Lowry, Sakinah Mahammud, Otis Sallid, Madeleine Swift, *Christopher Cox, Stanton Edghill, Robbee Fian, Larry Giroux, Gregory V. Karliss, Larry Marshall, Craig Richard Nelson, Arnetia Walker*. **Standbys**: Julia: Taro Meyer; Proteus/Speed: Rafael de Guzman; Thurio: Charles Abbott; Eglamour: Jeff Goldblum, *Ed Linderman*; Duke: Don Jay, *Tiger Haynes*. **Understudies**: Valentine: Dorian Harewood; Silvia: Signa Joy & Hattie Winston; Lucetta: Stockard Channing, *Carol Jean Lewis, Taro Meyer*. **Swing Dancers**: Wendy Mansfield & Morton Winston. **Swing Singers**: Dorian Harewood & Jacqueline Britt. **Act I**: "Summer, Summer" (Ensemble), "I Love My Father" (Ensemble), "That's a Very Interesting Question" (Proteus & Valentine), "I'd Like to Be a Rose" (Proteus & Valentine), "Thou, Julia, Thou Hast Metamorphosed Me" (Proteus), "Symphony" (Proteus & Ensemble), "I Am Not Interested in Love" (Julia), "Love, Is That You?" (Vissi d'Amore), "Thou, Proteus, Thou Hast Metamorphosed Me" (Julia), "What Does a Lover Pack?" (Julia,

Proteus, Ensemble), "Pearls" (Launce), "I Love My Father" (reprise) (Proteus), "Two Gentlemen of Verona" (Julia, Lucetta, Ensemble), "Follow the Rainbow" (Valentine, Speed, Proteus, Launce, Julia, Lucetta), "Where's North?" (Valentine, Speed, Duke, Silvia, Thurio, Ensemble), "Bring All the Boys Back Home" (Duke, Thurio, Ensemble), "Love's Revenge" (Valentine), "To Whom it May Concern Me" (Silvia & Valentine), "Night Letter" (Silvia & Valentine), "Love's Revenge" (reprise) (Valentine, Proteus, Speed, Launce), "Calla Lily Lady" (Proteus). *Act II:* "Land of Betrayal" (Lucetta), "Thurio's Samba" (Thurio, Duke, Ensemble), "Hot Lover" (Launce & Speed), "What a Nice Idea" (Julia), "Who is Silvia" (Proteus, Host, Ensemble), "Love Me" (Silvia & Ensemble), "Eglamour" (Eglamour & Silvia), "Kidnapped" (Julia, Duke, Proteus, Thurio, Ensemble), "Mansion" (Valentine), "Eglamour" (reprise) (Silvia & Eglamour), "What's a Nice Girl Like Her" (Proteus), "Dragon Flight" (Dragon, Eglamour, Proteus, Valentine), "Don't Have the Baby" (Julia, Lucetta, Speed, Launce), "Love, Is That You?" (reprise) (Thurio & Lucetta), "Milkmaid" (Launce & Milkmaid), Finale: "I Love My Father" (reprise) (Full Company) & "Love Has Driven Me Sane" (Full Company).

The show got only raves from the critics, but was slow to take off, but it did. It won Tonys for musical and book, and was nominated for score, direction of a musical, choreography, costumes, and for Clifton Davis, Raul Julia, and Jonelle Allen.

After Broadway. TOUR. Opened on 1/22/73, at the O'Keefe, Toronto, and closed on 10/27/73, at the Mechanic Theatre, Baltimore. *Cast:* PROTEUS: Larry Kert; VALENTINE: Clifton Davis; JULIA: Edith Diaz, *Stockard Channing;* SILVIA: Jonelle Allen; THURIO: Frank O'Brien; SPEED: Charlie J. Rodriguez; LAUNCE: Phil Leeds; DUKE: John McCurry; ANTONIO/TAVERN HOST: David Thomas; EGLAMOUR: Alvin Ing; LUCETTA: Jacque Lynn Colton; CHORUS: Edloe, Damita Jo Freeman, Sherrill Harper.

TOUR. Opened on 9/20/73, in Princeton, NJ, and closed on 4/27/74, in Wilmington, Del., after 102 cities. MUSICAL DIRECTOR: Margaret Harris. *Cast:* VALENTINE: Carl Scott; SPEED: Jose Fernandez, *Charlie J. Rodriguez;* JULIA: Louise Shaffer, *Carla Manning;* PROTEUS: Carlos Cestero, *Larry Kert, Jose Fernandez;* THURIO: Roy Brocksmith; EGLAMOUR: Alvin Lum; SILVIA: Rozaa Wortham; ANTONIO/TAVERN HOST: William McClary.

LONDON, 4/26/73. 237 PERFORMANCES. *Cast:* SILVIA: B.J. Arnau; JULIA: Jean Gilbert; VALENTINE: Samuel E. Wright; PROTEUS: Ray C. Davis.

THE NEW YORK SHAKESPEARE FESTIVAL mounted a Mobile Theatre production that toured the parks and playgrounds of New York City, 7/31/73–8/26/73. 23 PERFORMANCES.

TRINITY SQUARE REPERTORY THEATRE, Providence, Rhode Island, 12/30/75. 46 PERFORMANCES. This was a revised version, with additional music & lyrics by Robert Black, William Damkoehler, Vern Graham, Richard Cumming, and Queen Elizabeth I [sic]. DIRECTOR/CHOREOGRAPHER: Word Baker; SETS: Eugene Lee. *Cast:* Robert Black, William Damkoehler, Melanie Jones.

SWAN THEATRE, Stratford-upon-Avon, England, 4/6/93. This was a brand new musical with the same name, but not related to the previous musical. PRESENTED BY the Royal Shakespeare Company; MUSIC/LYRICS: various writers; BOOK: David Thacker. *Cast:* Henry Webster. "Love is the Sweetest Thing," "Somebody Loves Me," "My Heart Stood Still," "Love in Bloom," "Blue Moon," "What'll I Do," "Nice Work if You Can Get It," "More than You Know," "Who is Sylvia?," "Night and Day," "The Glory of Love," "I Only Have Eyes for You," "I'm in the Mood for Love," "Launce Theme," "Love Walked In," "Heartaches," "True," "Riptide," "In the Still of the Night."

GUGGENHEIM MUSEUM, 11/21/04–11/22/04. 2 PERFORMANCES. This was in concert, one of the Museum's "Work & Process" presentations. There was a discussion afterwards, with Galt MacDermot, Mel Shapiro, and John Guare, moderated by Howard Stokar. CONDUCTOR: Galt MacDermot. *Cast:* Luther Creek, Suzanne Griffin, David Damane, Catrice Joseph Hart, Larry Marshall, Chris Monteleone, Melanie Po. *Musicians:* SAX: Allen Won; BARITONE SAX: Patience Higgins; TRUMPET: John Frosk; TROMBONE: Vince MacDermot; BASS: Wilbur Bascomb; DRUMS: Bernard Purdie; PIANO: Galt MacDermot.

720. *Two on the Aisle*

A musical revue.

The Broadway Run. MARK HELLINGER THEATRE, 7/19/51–3/15/52. 276 PERFORMANCES. PRESENTED BY Arthur Lesser; MUSIC: Jule Styne; LYRICS/SKETCHES: Betty Comden & Adolph Green; ADDITIONAL SKETCH: Nat Hiken & William Friedberg; DIRECTOR: Abe Burrows; CHOREOGRAPHER: Ted Cappy; ADDITIONAL CHOREOGRAPHY: Ruthanna Boris; SETS/LIGHTING: Howard Bay; COSTUMES: Joan Personette; ASSISTANT COSTUMES: Florence Klotz; MUSICAL DIRECTOR/VOCAL ARRANGEMENTS: Herbert Greene; ORCHESTRATIONS: Philip J. Lang; DANCE MUSIC ARRANGEMENTS: Genevieve Pitot; PRESS: Nat Dorfman & Irvin Dorfman; COMPANY MANAGER: Joseph Harris; GENERAL STAGE MANAGER: John Sola; STAGE MANAGER: Perry Bruskin; ASSISTANT STAGE MANAGER: Richard Gray, *John Ford*. *Act I: Scene 1* "Show Train:" CONDUCTORS: Stanley Prager, Robert Gallagher, Larry Laurence (*Arthur Arney*), Arthur Rubin (*Dean Michener*), Walter Kelvin; ALSO WITH: Ladies & Gentlemen of the Ensemble; *Scene 2* "Hold Me Tight." Song: "Hold Me — Hold Me — Hold Me." Sung by Dolores Gray (2) ☆. 1ST SUITOR: Frank Reynolds; 2ND SUITOR: John Kelly, *Phil Gerard*; 3RD SUITOR: Bob Emmett; MAID: Jeanett Aquilina; THE GIRL: Dolores Gray (2) ☆; *Scene 3* Highlights from the World of Sports: PRODUCER: Alan LeRoy, *Loney Lewis*; ANNOUNCER: Elliott Reid (3); CAMERAMEN: Richard Gray (*John Ford*) & Robert Gallagher; LEFTY HOGAN: Bert Lahr (1) ☆; *Scene 4* "East River Hoe-Down" ("Here She Comes Now") (Ensemble). Danced by J.C. McCord & Vera Lee (*Betty Buday*); *Scene 5* "There Never Was a Baby Like My Baby." Sung by Dolores Gray (2) ☆. WIFEY: Dolores Gray (2) ☆; HUBBY: Elliott Reid (3); DANCED BY: J.C. McCord; ASSISTED BY: Gloria Danyl, Margery Beddow, Jane Mason, John Kelly, Frank Reynolds; *Scene 6* Space Brigade: HODGKINS: Richard Gray, *John Ford*; HOTCHKISS: Larry Laurence, *Bob Emmett*; HITCHCOCK: Robert Gallagher; CAPTAIN UNIVERSE: Bert Lahr (1) ☆; HIGGINS: Stanley Prager; RADIO VOICE: Walter Kelvin; QUEEN CHLOROPHYL: Kathryne Mylroie [she later became movie actress Kate Manx], *Gloria Danyl*; DENIZENS OF VENUS: Frank Reynolds, John Kelly, Arthur Arney, John Raye, Victor Reilley, *Roscoe French, Buford Jasper, Dean Michener*; *Scene 7* "If You Hadn't, But You Did." Sung by Dolores Gray (2) ☆ [this song was later used in the 1996 Off Broadway revival of *Say, Darling*]: THE GIRL: Dolores Gray (2) ☆; THE OTHER WOMAN: Gloria Danyl, *Betty Buday*; THE MAN: Bob Emmett, *John Allen*; *Scene 8* "The Clown:" THE CLOWN: Bert Lahr (1) ☆; CLOWN'S ASSISTANTS: Gloria Danyl, Vera Lee, Del Parker, Mira Stefan (*Jeanne Tyler*); *Scene 9* The Guide Book: THREE URCHINS: Frank Reynolds, Victor Reilley, John Kelly, *Phil Gerard*; THE GIRL: Colette Marchand (4), *Kathryn Lee*; THE LOVERS: Paul Lyday (*Roscoe French*) & Betty Buday; TRAVELER: Bob Emmett; THE AMERICAN: J.C. McCord; ASSISTED BY: Jane Mason, Jeanett Aquilina, Margery Beddow, Jerry Fries; *Scene 10* Here's What You Said [Elliott Reid (3)]; *Scene 11* "Catch Our Act" (Vaudeville Ain't Dead): TWO VAUDEVILLIANS: Bert Lahr (1) ☆ & Dolores Gray (2) ☆; *Scene 12* "At the Met:" SIEGFRIED: Bert Lahr (1) ☆; BRUNNHILDE: Dolores Gray (2) ☆; THE DRAGON: Stanley Prager; RHINE MAIDENS: Gloria Danyl, Margery Beddow, Vera Lee; DANCED BY: Colette Marchand (4), *Kathryn Lee*. *Act II: Scene 1* "Everlasting." Sung by: Katie Mylroie (*Leila Martin*) & Fred Bryan. Danced by Dorothy Etheridge & Jerry Fries. Assisted by Ladies & Gentlemen of the Ensemble; *Scene 2* Schneider's Miracle (by Nat Hiken & William Friedberg): *Schneider:* Bert Lahr (1) ☆; MRS. HIGGLESTON: Patricia Tobin, *Doris Goodwin*; PIPER: Stanley Prager; MISS FLAHERTY: Kathryne Mylroie, *Gloria Danyl*; INSPECTOR: Robert Gallagher; MAN ON BENCH: Alan LeRoy, *Loney Lewis*; LITTLE GIRL: Jeanett Aquilina; POLICEMAN: Richard Gray, *John Ford*; PASSERS-BY: John Allen, Leila Martin, Frank Reynolds, Walter Kelvin; *Scene 3* "Give a Little — Get a Little Love." Performed by Dolores Gray (2) ☆ & Ladies & Gentlemen of the Ensemble [this number was later used in the 1996 Off Broadway revival of *Say, Darling*]; *Scene 4* Didy Dolls. Performed by Bert Lahr (1) ☆ & Showgirls. VOICE: Arthur Rubin, *James McCracken*; *Scene 5* Triangle. 1. HUBBY: Elliott Reid (3); WIFEY: Dolores Gray (2) ☆; LOVEY: Bert Lahr (1) ☆. 2. HUSBAND: Elliott Reid (3); WIFE: Dolores Gray (2) ☆; CLOSE FRIEND: Bert Lahr (1) ☆. 3. HE: Elliott Reid (3); SHE: Dolores Gray (2) ☆; HIM: Bert Lahr (1) ☆; *Scene 6* Dog Show (ch:

Ruthanna Boris): JUDGE: Bob Emmett, *Phil Gerard*; RUSSIAN WOLF-HOUNDS: Gregg Evans, Rosemary Kittleton, Del Parker, Mira Stefan, Jeanne Tyler, Charlotte Van Lein, *Slats McKinney*; THEIR TRAINER: Jerry Fries; PEKINESE: Dorothy Etheridge, *Jeanett Aquilina*; HER TRAINER: Paul Lyday, *Roscoe French*; COCKER SPANIELS: Gloria Danyl & Jane Mason; THEIR TRAINER: Victor Reilley; DALMATIANS: Betty Buday & Doris Goodwin; THEIR TRAINER: John Kelly, *Frank Reynolds*; FRENCH POODLE: Colette Marchand (4), *Kathryn Lee*; HER MANAGER: Gordon Hamilton; *Scene 7* "How Will He Know?." Sung by Dolores Gray (2) ✰. MR. MURDOCK: Bert Lahr (1) ✰; MISS TRAVERS: Dolores Gray (2) ✰; *Scene 8* Finale [Bert Lahr (1) ✰, Dolores Gray (2) ✰, Colette Marchand (4), Entire Company].

SINGING ENSEMBLE: John Allen, Arthur Arney, Fred Bryan, Buford Jasper, Walter Kelvin, Marion Lauer, Beverly McFadden, Leila Martin, Leslie Parry, John Raye, Peggy Reiss, Arthur Rubin, Carol Sawyer, Joanne Spiller, Julia Williams, *James McCracken, Dean Michener*; DANCING ENSEMBLE: Jeanett Aquilina, Margery Beddow, Betty Buday, Gloria Danyl, Bob Emmett (*Phil Gerard*), Dorothy Etheridge, Jerry Fries, Doris Goodwin, John Kelly, Vera Lee, Paul Lyday, Jane Mason, Victor Reilley, Frank Reynolds, *Roscoe French, Pat Poole*; SHOWGIRLS: Gregg Evans, Rosemary Kittleton, Del Parker, Mira Stefan, Jeanne Tyler, Charlotte Van Lein. **Understudies**: For Mr. Lahr: Loney Lewis; For Miss Gray: Betty O'Neil; For Miss Marchand: Vera Lee; For Mr. Gallagher: Bob Emmett; For Mr. Reid: Robert Gallagher; For Mr. Prager: Perry Bruskin; For Miss Aquilina: Jane Mason; For Mr. Bryan: John Allen; For Mr. LeRoy: Walter Kelvin.

Broadway reviews were mostly raves, especially for Dolores Gray. Ron Fletcher (the famous *Ice-Capades* choreographer) had choreographed a dance piece which became incorporated into this production. The show was famous as well for the feud between Dolores Gray and Bert Lahr.

721. *Two's Company*

A musical revue.

Before Broadway. Bette Davis requested that Jerome Robbins bring in Josh Logan to help on this show, which he did. John Murray Anderson came in to steer the production when Charles Sherman and Jerry Robbins relinquished that role. David Burns replaced Nathaniel Frey. It opened for tryouts in Detroit on 10/19/52, and on that very night Bette Davis fainted on stage. When she came to, she insisted on going on with the show. "You can't say I didn't fall for you," she said to the audience. The Sheldon Harnick number "Merry Little Minuet" was cut before Broadway (but later used in *John Murray Anderson's Almanac*).

The Broadway Run. ALVIN THEATRE, 12/15/52–3/10/53. 90 PERFORMANCES. PRESENTED BY James Russo & Michael Ellis; MUSIC/LYRICS/SKETCHES: various authors; SKETCH DIRECTOR: Jules Dassin; CHOREOGRAPHER: Jerome Robbins; SETS/LIGHTING: Ralph Alswang; COSTUMES: Miles White; MUSICAL SUPERVISOR/CONDUCTOR/VOCAL ARRANGEMENTS: Milton Rosenstock; ORCHESTRATIONS: various composers; BALLET MUSIC: Genevieve Pitot & David Baker; PRESS: Samuel J. Friedman & Lenny L. Traube; PRODUCTION SUPERVISOR: John Murray Anderson; ASSOCIATE MANAGER/GENERAL MANAGER: Clifford Hayman; STAGE MANAGERS: Bill Ross, Perry Bruskin, Howard Graham. **Act I: Opening** "Theatre is a Lady" (m: Vernon Duke; l: Ogden Nash; orch: Don Walker). Introduced by Hiram Sherman (2). Sung & danced by Bill Callahan, with the Boys & Girls; *Scene 1* "Turn Me Loose on Broadway" (m: Vernon Duke; l: Ogden Nash; orch: Clare Grundman). Sung & danced by Bette Davis (1) ✰, Buzz Miller, Robert Pagent, Job Sanders, Stanley Simmons; *Scene 2* And a Little Child (by Arnold Horwitt & Lee Rogow): PRODUCER: George Irving; SECRETARY: Tina Louise; DUDLEY DAWSON: David Burns (3); ROLLO: Michael Mann; BUTLER: Franklin Neil; MRS. WILKINS: May Muth; *Scene 3* "It Just Occurred to Me" (m: Vernon Duke; l: Sammy Cahn; orch: Clare Grundman). Sung by Peter Kelley, Deborah Remsen, and the Singing Ensemble. Danced by Florence Baum, Barbara Heath, Helen Murielle, Ralph Linn, Robert Pagent, Job Sanders; *Scene 4* Jealousy (by Nat Hiken & Billy Friedberg): HELEN: Bette Davis (1) ✰; STANLEY: David Burns (3); *Scene 5* "Baby Couldn't Dance" (m: Vernon Duke; l: Ogden Nash; orch: Clare Grundman): GIRL: Nora Kaye (4); BOY: Bill Callahan; PROFESSOR: Stanley Simmons;

PUPILS: Barbara Heath & Florence Baum; *Scene 6* "A Man's Home" (m/l: Sheldon Harnick; orch: Don Walker). Sung by Hiram Sherman (2); *Scene 7* One's a Crowd (by Mort Green & George Foster): THAT ONE: Bette Davis (1) ✰; REGGIE: Hiram Sherman (2); J.C.: George Irving; HARASSED GENTLEMAN: Stanley Prager; AUDIENCE: Teddy Tavenner, Earl Renard, Tina Louise, Basha Regis, Clifford Fearl, Dorothy Hill, May Muth, Eleanor Boleyn, Sue Hight, Robert Neukum; *Scene 8* "Roundabout" (m: Vernon Duke; l: Ogden Nash; scenario: Horton Foote & Jerome Robbins; orch: Don Walker). Sung by Ellen Hanley. Danced by Nora Kaye (4) with Ralph Linn, Robert Pagent, William Inglis, Eleanor Boleyn, Barbara Heath, and the Dancing Ensemble; *Scene 9* The Voice of Inexperience (by & featuring Oliver Wakefield); *Scene 10* "Roll Along, Sadie" (m: Vernon Duke; l: Ogden Nash; orch: Phil Lang). Sung & danced by Bette Davis (1) ✰, Hiram Sherman (2), Buzz Miller, Ralph Linn, Company. **Act II: Scene 1** "(It Came Out of a) Clear Blue Sky" (m: Vernon Duke; l: Ogden Nash; orch: Don Walker). Sung by Peter Kelley & Sue Hight. Danced by Maria Karnilova & Bob Pagent. Accompanied by the Singers & Dancers; *Scene 2* Street Scenes (by Charles Sherman, with Peter DeVries). Featuring Bette Davis (1) ✰ & Hiram Sherman (2); *Scene 3* "Esther" (m: Vernon Duke; l: Sammy Cahn; orch: Don Walker). Sung by David Burns (3): MELVIN: David Burns (3); ESTHER: Maria Karnilova; NATIVE: Buzz Miller; *Scene 4* When in Rome (by Arnold B. Horwitt & Lee Rogow): STROMBOLINI: David Burns (3); NINA: Helen Murielle; THOMASO: Stanley Prager; PORTER: Earl Renard; JEZEBELA: Bette Davis (1) ✰; MUSICIAN: George Irving; SCENE 5 "Haunted Hot Spot" (m: Vernon Duke; l: Ogden Nash; orch: Don Walker): SUNG BY: Ellen Hanley; DANCED BY: THE STRIPPER: Nora Kaye (4); THE DRUMMER: Bill Callahan; THE PIANIST: Buzz Miller; *Scene 6* "Purple Rose" (m: Vernon Duke; l: Ogden Nash; orch: Phil Lang; sketch: Charles Sherman, with Peter DeVries): SYBILL: Bette Davis (1) ✰; PETER: Hiram Sherman (2); HORATIO: Earl Renard; TERRANCE: George Irving; HILARY: Clifford Fearl; HORTENSE: May Muth; GINGER: Deborah Remsen; CAMERA MAN: Maurice Brenner; BUTLER: Franklin Neil; MAID: Basha Regis; VIRGIL: Robert Neukum; CICERO: Bill Krach; *Scene 7* "Just Like a Man" (m: Vernon Duke; l: Ogden Nash; orch: Phil Lang). Sung by Bette Davis (1) ✰; *Finale* (m: Vernon Duke; l: Ogden Nash; orch: Clare Grundman) (Company).

ALSO WITH: Robert Orton's Teen Aces: Robert Orton (leader), Francis Edwards, Henry Mallory, Gilbert Shipley, Armstead Shobey, Norman Shobey; SINGERS: Art Carroll, Clifford Fearl, Sue Hight, Leonore Korman, Bill Krach, Tina Louise, May Muth, Franklin Neil, Robert Neukum, Basha Regis, Deborah Remsen, Teddy Tavenner, Doris Wolin; DANCERS: Florence Baum, Jeanna Belkin, Eleanor Boleyn, Barbara Heath, Dorothy Hill, William Inglis, John Kelly, Ralph Linn, Julie Marlowe, Helen Murielle, Robert Pagent, Job Sanders, Stanley Simmons. **Understudies**: For Bette Davis: May Muth; For Hiram Sherman: George S. Irving; For David Burns: Stanley Prager; For Ellen Hanley: Sue Hight; For Peter Kelley: Art Carroll; For Sue Hight: Teddy Tavenner.

Broadway reviews were generally not good, and after three sold-out months Bette Davis left with a mysterious bone disease (Josh Logan and others did not believe it to be authentic). Hiram Sherman won a Tony; Donaldson Awards were won for choreography and for best female dancer (Nora Kaye).

722. *The Unsinkable Molly Brown*

For obvious reasons this musical is often referred to as *Molly Brown*. Molly Tobin (1860–1924 in real life) begins life in illiterate poverty in Hannibal, Missouri, but is determined to better herself. She goes to Colorado, works in a saloon, and meets and marries "Leadville" Johnny Brown, a prospector who strikes it rich during the Colorado Silver Strike at the turn of the 20th century. They become extremely wealthy. Her one ambition is to be accepted into upper-class society. Snubbed by Denver, the Browns travel to Europe, and become the toast of the continent, especially in Monte Carlo. Molly returns to the USA, now able to speak several languages, and to play piano and paint. She has an entourage of royalty in tow, but still finds herself ostracized.

The couple separate as Molly returns to Europe over her husband's objections. She gets Johnny back after nearly drowning (and becoming a heroine) on the *Titanic* in 1912 (true!), and ultimately wins acceptance in Denver. Mrs. McGlone was Denver's social leader. Prince de Long wanted to marry Molly.

Before Broadway. In 1955 there was a TV play about Irish girl Molly Tobin Brown, one of the survivors of the *Titanic*, starring Cloris Leachman. Dore Schary and Richard Morris wanted to do a stage musical about Molly. Meredith Willson was hired to write the score of the musical which was then called *The Unsinkable Mrs. Brown*. Vincent J. Donehue was replaced as director by Dore Schary. Tammy Grimes missed four Philadelphia tryout performances due to laryngitis. Miss Grimes had 16 costume changes that required three dressers. She got splinters during a barefoot dance number. Choreographer Pete Gennaro would wait backstage with pair of tweezers. Several numbers were cut before the opening: "The Ambassador's Polka," "Another Big Strike," "Extra! Extra!," "One Day at a Time," "Read the Label" ("Don't Take My Word for It, Neighbor"), and "Up Where the Joke's Goin' On." Another cut number, "Tomorrow," had also been cut from Meredith Willson's previous musical, *The Music* Man.

The Broadway Run. WINTER GARDEN THEATRE, 11/3/60–2/10/62. 1 preview. 532 PERFORMANCES. PRESENTED BY The Theatre Guild & Dore Schary; MUSIC/LYRICS: Meredith Willson; BOOK: Richard Morris; DIRECTOR: Dore Schary; CHOREOGRAPHER: Peter Gennaro; SETS: Oliver Smith; COSTUMES: Miles White; LIGHTING: Peggy Clark; MUSICAL DIRECTOR: Herbert Greene, Max Meth; VOCAL ARRANGEMENTS: Herbert Greene; ORCHESTRATIONS: Don Walker; BALLET MUSIC ARRANGEMENTS: Sol Berkowitz; PRESS: Nat Dorfman, Irvin Dorfman, Jane Randall; GENERAL MANAGER: Peter Davis; PRODUCTION STAGE MANAGER: Jean Barrere; STAGE MANAGER: Elliot Martin; ASSISTANT STAGE MANAGERS: Beau Tilden & Jeb Schary (Tom Larson). *Cast:* MOLLY TOBIN: Tammy Grimes (1) ☆; MICHAEL TOBIN: Sterling Clark, Don Emmons; ALOYSIUS TOBIN: Bill Starr; PATRICK TOBIN: Bob Daley; FATHER FLYNN: Norman Fredericks; SHAMUS TOBIN: Cameron Prud'homme (3); BRAWLING MINERS: Alex Stevens & Joe Pronto; CHARLIE: Woody Hurst; CHRISTMAS MORGAN: Joseph Sirola (7); BURT: Tom Larson; BANJO: Billy Faier [role cut during the run]; PROSTITUTES: Rae McLean (Mary Burr), Anna Marie Moylan, Lynn Gay Lorino [during the run these characters became known as Saloon Girls]; JOHNNY "LEADVILLE" BROWN: Harve Presnell (2), James Hurst (matinees); GITTER: Joe Pronto; A BOY: Paul Floyd [role cut during the run]; SHERIFF: Terry Violino; DENVER POLICEMEN: Wakefield Poole, Terry Violino, Don Emmons; MRS. MCGLONE: Edith Meiser (4); MONSIGNOR RYAN: Jack Harrold (6); ROBERTS: Christopher Hewett (9), Vernon Kidd, Barney Johnston (stood in); PROFESSOR GARDELLA: Dale Malone, Anthony Saverino; GERMAINE: June Card, Lynn Gay Lorino; PRINCESS DE LONG: Mony Dalmes (8), Patricia Finch; PRINCE DE LONG: Mitchell Gregg (5), Vernon Kidd (stood in); COUNTESS ETHANOTOUS: Wanda Saxon, Dell Brownlee; JENAB-ASHROS: Marvin Goodis; GRAND DUCHESS MARIE NICHOLAIOVNA: Patricia Kelly (10); COUNT FERANTI: Michael Davis, Ralph Farnworth; DUCHESS OF BURLINGAME: Barbara Newman; DUKE OF BURLINGAME: Ted Adkins, Danny Joel; THE BARON OF AULD: Bob Daley; MALCOLM BRODERICK: Barney Johnston; MRS. WADLINGTON: Lynne Osborne; MR. WADLINGTON: Norman Fredericks; YOUNG WAITER: Michael Davis, Van Stevens; MAITRE D': Dale Malone, Ralph Farnworth; PAGE: Bobby Brownell [role cut during the run]; MALE PASSENGER: Marvin Goodis; MOTHER: Nada Rowand; WOUNDED SAILOR: Bill Starr; SINGERS: June Card (gone by 8/61), Michael Davis (Van Stevens), Ceil Delli (gone by 8/61), Pat Finch (gone by 8/61), Norman Fredericks, Marvin Goodis, Marian Haraldson, Woody Hurst, Barney Johnston, Patricia Kelly, Tom Larson, Dale Malone (Anthony Saverino), Lynne Osborne, Louis Polacek (Ralph Farnworth), Nada Rowand, Wanda Saxon (Dell Brownlee), Ann Marisse, Caroline Parks, Mimi Vondra; DANCERS: Ted Adkins (gone by 8/61), Sterling Clark (gone by 8/61), Bob Daley, Vito Durante, Don Emmons, Barbara Gine, Diana Hunter, Lynn Gay Lorino, Rae McLean (Mary Burr), Susan May (Sandy Roveta), Anna Marie Moylan, Barbara Newman, Joe Pronto, Nanette Rosen, Mark Ross, Bill Starr, Alex Stevens, Terry Violino. Wakefield Poole, Vernon Wendorf. *Standbys:* Molly: Iva Withers; Johnny: James Hurst; Shamus: Beau Tilden; Mrs. McGlone: Pat Kelly; Princess: Marian Haraldson;

Prince/Ryan: Vernon Kidd; Roberts: Barney Johnston; Morgan: Don Emmons. *Act I*: *Scene 1* Exterior of the Tobin shack, Hannibal, Mo; turn of the century: "I Ain't Down Yet" (Molly & Her Brothers); *Scene 2* The road by the Tobin shack; sun-up the next morning; *Scene 3* The Saddle Rock Saloon, Leadville, Colo.; weeks later: "Belly Up to the Bar, Boys" (Molly, Christmas, Miners); *Scene 4* The street in front of the Saddle Rock; Sunday night, three weeks later: "I've A'ready Started In (To Try to Figure Out a Way to Go to Work to Try to Get You" (Johnny, Christmas, Charlie, Burt, Gitter) [a reject from *The Music Man*]; *Scene 5* Johnny's log cabin; a month later: "I'll Never Say No (to You)" (Johnny), "My Own Brass Bed" (Molly); *Scene 6* The same; three weeks later; *Scene 7* Pennsylvania Avenue, Denver; six months later: "The Denver Police" (Three Policemen); *Scene 8* The terrace of Mrs. McGlone's Denver mansion; later that evening: "(The) Bea-u-ti-ful People of Denver" (Molly), "Are You Sure?" (Molly, Monsignor, Guests); *Scene 9* Pennsylvania Avenue; immediately following: *Scene 10* The Red Parlor of the Browns' Denver mansion; the evening of their housewarming: "I Ain't Down Yet" (reprise) (Molly & Johnny). *Act II*: *Scene 1* The Browns' Paris salon; a spring afternoon, years later: "Happy Birthday, Mrs. J.J. Brown" (Princess, Prince, International Set), "Bon Jour" (The Language Song) (Molly, Prince, International Set), "If I Knew" (Johnny); *Scene 2* Upper hallway of the Browns' Denver mansion; an evening, months later: "Chick-a-Pen" (Molly & Johnny); *Scene 3* The Red Parlor; 8 o'clock, that evening; *Scene 4* The Red Parlor; next morning; *Scene 5* The street in front of the Saddle Rock; months later: "Keep-a-Hoppin'" (Johnny & His Leadville Friends), "Leadville Johnny Brown" (Soliloquy) (Johnny); *Scene 6* Monte Carlo, a club off the Casino; early spring, 1912: "Up Where the People Are" (Monte Carlo Guests), "Dolce Far Niente" (Prince & Molly); *Scene 7* Outside the club; a moment later; *Scene 8* The mid–Atlantic; shortly after 2.30 a.m., April 15, 1912; *Scene 9* Upper hallway of the Brown home; two weeks later; *Scene 10* The Rockies: "Colorado, My Home" (Johnny, Molly, Leadville Friends) [cut after the opening and replaced with a reprise of "I Ain't Down Yet" (Johnny, Molly, Leadville Friends)].

Broadway reviews were middle-of-the-road and divided. Tammy Grimes got raves, and a Tony Award.

After Broadway. TOUR. Opened on 2/13/62, at the Bushnell Theatre, Hartford. MUSICAL DIRECTOR: Max Meth. *Cast:* MOLLY: Tammy Grimes; JOHNNY: Harve Presnell; GITTER: Joe Pronto; RYAN: Jack Harrold. *Understudies:* Molly: Karen Morrow; Johnny: Don Crabtree.

DALLAS. Opened on 6/10/63. DIRECTOR: Lawrence Kasha. *Cast:* MOLLY: Ginger Rogers; JOHNNY: George Wallace.

THE MOVIE. MGM announced plans to do their own version of the story, much to the objection of the stage producers. It didn't happen. In 1964, instead, 20th-Century Fox brought the stage musical to the screen. A song and dance number "He's My Friend" was added, as choreographed by Pete Gennaro, and "Colorado, My Home" (cut during the original Broadway run) was also included. DIRECTOR: Charles Walters. *Cast:* MOLLY: Debbie Reynolds; JOHNNY: Harve Presnell; SHAMUS: Ed Begley; JAM: Grover Dale; DANCEHALL GIRL: Mary Ann Niles; JOE: Gus Trikonis; DAPHNE: Maria Karnilova.

LA MIRADA, CALIF. Opened ON 3/31/00. THIS REVIVAL RAN FOR THREE WEEKS. DIRECTOR: Glenn Casale; CHOREOGRAPHER: Patti Colombo. *Cast:* MOLLY: Cathy Rigby; JOHNNY: Christopher Carl.

SACRAMENTO MUSIC CIRCUS, 7/22/02–7/28/02. DIRECTOR: Marcia Milgrom Dodge; CHOREOGRAPHER: Bob Richard; MUSICAL DIRECTOR: Valerie Gebert. *Cast:* MOLLY: Susan Egan; JOHNNY: Christopher Carl.

723. *Up in Central Park*

Operetta set in the period 1870–72, during the construction of Central Park, in New York City. As a subplot to the Boss Tweed outrages, a *New York Times* reporter, John Matthews (in real life a composite of Lewis Jennings, the original reporter, and other men), who is out to expose the ring's plans to line their pockets with funds designated for the building of the new Central Park, also falls in love with Rosie, an aspiring singer and daughter of

Tweed man Timothy. There is a notable ice-skating ballet sequence in the Currier & Ives snow. George Jones was the real-life owner/publisher of the *New York Times*. Historical fact: Before Tweed built Central Park it was a city dump. Peter Sweeney was the park commissioner. Richard Connolly was comptroller of New York City.

Before Broadway. Some say Mike Todd thought up the idea for this story when he first saw Boston Commons. What seems more likely, however, is that he came up with it while reading the book *Boss Tweed and His Gang*, a history of graft and corruption that went on under New York City Mayor William Marcey Tweed during the construction of Central Park, and about the press outcry, including Thomas Nast's cartoons in *Harper's Weekly*. Either way (or both), Mr. Todd suggested the idea of a musical to the brother and sister team Herbert and Dorothy Fields. The show tried out as *Central Park*. Howard Bay designed a series of backdrops based on nostalgic prints of Currier & Ives. Each scene would begin with the cast frozen in place before the set. Maureen Cannon stepped into the role of Rosie just before opening night.

The Broadway Run. NEW CENTURY THEATRE, 1/27/45–9/45; BROADWAY THEATRE, 9/11/45–4/13/46. 504 PERFORMANCES. PRESENTED BY Michael Todd; MUSIC: Sigmund Romberg; LYRICS: Dorothy Fields; BOOK: Herbert & Dorothy Fields; BASED ON the book *Boss Tweed and His Gang*, by Denis Lynch; DIRECTOR: John Kennedy; CHOREOGRAPHER: Helen Tamiris; ASSISTANT CHOREOGRAPHER: Daniel Nagrin; SETS/LIGHTING: Howard Bay; COSTUMES: Grace Houston & Ernest Schraps; MUSICAL DIRECTOR: Max Meth; ORCHESTRATIONS: Don Walker; CAST RECORDING: none; PRESS: Morton Nathanson & Mary March; CASTING: Arnold Hoskwith; CHORUS CASTING: Margaret Sande; GENERAL MANAGER: James Colligan; COMPANY MANAGER: William G. Norton; GENERAL STAGE MANAGER: Sammy Lambert; STAGE MANAGER: Tony Jochim; ASSISTANT STAGE MANAGER: Herman Glazer. **Cast:** A LABORER: Bruce Lord; DANNY O'CAHANE: Walter Burke (7); TIMOTHY MOORE: Charles Irwin (4); BESSIE O'CAHANE: Betty Bruce (2); ROSIE MOORE: Maureen Cannon (5); JOHN MATTHEWS: Wilbur Evans (1); THOMAS NAST: Maurice Burke (8); WILLIAM DUTTON: John Quigg; ANDREW MUNROE: Robert Field; VINCENT PETERS: Paul Reed (9); MAYOR A. OAKLEY HALL: Rowan Tudor; RICHARD CONNOLLY: George Lane; PETER SWEENEY: Harry Meehan; BOSS WILLIAM MARCEY TWEED: Noah Beery Sr. (3); BUTLER: Herman Glazer; MAIDS: Louise Holden & Eve Harvey [roles added after opening night]; MILDRED WINCOR: Lydia Fredericks; JOE STEWART: Fred Barry; PORTER: Harry Matlock; LOTTA STEVENS: Delma Byron; FANNY MORRIS: Kay Griffith; CLARA MANNING: Martha Burnett; JAMES FISK JR.: Watson White; DANIEL: Daniel Nagrin; GOVERNESS: Louise Holden; 1ST CHILD: Ann Hermann; 2ND CHILD: Joan Lally; 3RD CHILD: Janet Lally; 4TH CHILD: Mary Alice Evans; HEADWAITER: John Quigg; PAGE BOY: Henry Capri; ARTHUR FINCH: Wally Coyle; ELLEN LAWRENCE: Elaine Barry (6); BICYCLE RIDER: Stanley Schimmel; GEORGE JONES: Guy Standing Jr.; BAGPIPE PLAYERS: Isobel Glasgow, James McFadden, Thomas Lorimer; NEWSBOYS: Kenneth Casey & Teddy Casey; ORGAN GRINDERS: William Nuss & Charles Wood; SINGING MEN: Phil Lowry, Charles W. Wood, Jerome Cardinale, Kenneth Renner, Leonard Daye, Stanley Turner, Bruce Lord, Bob Woodward, James Caputo, William Nuss, Rudy Rudisill, Harry Matlock, Sidney Paul, William Sydenstricker; DANCERS: Daniel Nagrin, Saul Bolasni, George Bockman, Henry Capri, Wally Coyle, Payne Converse, Gregor Taksa; SINGING GIRLS: Martha Burnett, Beatrice Lind, Mildred Jocelyn, Elyse Jahoda, Lillian Horn, Claire Saunders, Rose Marie Patane, Donna Hughes, Lydia Fredericks, Joan Gladding; DANCERS: Wana Allison, Joan Dubois, Margaret Gibson, Miriam Kornfield, Rebecca Lee, Ruth Lowe, Peggy Ann Nilsson, Hazel Roy, Evelyn Shaw, Gloria Stevens, Natalie Wynn. **Act I: Scene 1** A site in Central Park; June 1870: "Up from the Gutter" (Bessie), "Up from the Gutter" (reprise) (Bessie, Rosie, Danny, Timothy), "Up from the Gutter" (dance) (Bessie, Rosie, Danny, Timothy, Singers, Dancers), "Carousel in the Park" (ch: Helen Tamiris) (Rosie), "It Doesn't Cost You Anything to Dream" (Rosie & John), "It Doesn't Cost You Anything to Dream" (reprise) (Rosie, Bessie, John); **Scene 2** The Park Commissioner's temporary office in Central Park; July 1870: "Boss Tweed" (Tweed, Mayor, Connolly, Sweeney, Monroe, Peters, Timothy, Men); **Scene 3** The lounge of the Stetson Hotel (formerly

McGowan's Pass Tavern); Christmas Eve, 1870: Opening (Singing Girls & Boys), "When She Walks in the Room" (John), "(Let Me Show You My) Currier and Ives" (Bessie & Joe), "Currier and Ives" (dance) (Bessie, Joe, Daniel, Dancers), "Close as Pages in a Book" (Rosie & John), "Rip Van Winkle" (Rosie, Bessie, Tweed, Joe, Peters, Singers, Dancers), "Rip Van Winkle" (dance) (ch: Helen Tamiris) (Daniel & Dancers); **Scene 4** The bird house in the Central Park Zoo; next day: "Close as Pages in a Book" (reprise) (John); **Scene 5** The Central Park Gardens; February, 1871: Opening (Dancers), "The Fireman's Bride" (ch: Helen Tamiris) (Rosie, Bessie, Joe, Daniel, Can-Can Girls), "The Fireman's Bride" (reprise) (Principals, Singing Girls & Boys). **Act II: Scene 1** The annual Tammany Hall outing; July 1871: "When the Party Gives a Party (for the Party)" (Singing Girls & Boys, Peters, Mayor, Monroe, Sweeney, Timothy, Danny), Maypole Dance (Dancers), Specialty (Joe & Ellen), "The Big Back Yard" (John, Singing Girls & Boys), "April Snow" (Rosie & John), Finaletto: "April Snow" (reprise) (ch: Helen Tamiris) (Dancers, Singing Girls & Boys); **Scene 2** Office of George Jones (owner of *The New York Times*); later that day; **Scene 3** Central Park West; next day at noon; **Scene 4** The Stetson Hotel; the same afternoon: "The Birds and the Bees" (Rosie, Bessie, Timothy, Danny); **Scene 5** The Mall in Central Park; July 4, 1872: Specialty (Bessie); **Scene 6** The bandstand in the Mall; that evening: "The Big Back Yard" (reprise) (ch: Helen Tamiris) (Orchestra), "Close as Pages in a Book" (reprise) (Rosie & John), Finale (Entire Company).

Note: all principals' and singing ensemble numbers were staged by Lew Kesler, except when marked "ch: Helen Tamiris."

On opening night producer Mike Todd brought in the reviewers in horse and carriage from their restaurants to the theater. Afterwards he invited 700 people, including all the reviewers, to a $10,000 midnight supper party for the company at Tavern-on-the-Green. Reviews were divided, but mostly favorable. The show won a Donaldson Award for sets.

After Broadway. CITY CENTER, NYC, 5/19/47–5/31/47. 19 PERFORMANCES. After a profitable but tiring tour the Broadway company of 1945 came back to New York. It had the same basic crew as for Broadway, except DIRECTORS: John Kennedy & Sammy Lambert; MUSICAL DIRECTOR: William Parson. It had largely the same cast, but with some major differences: TWEED: Malcolm Lee Beggs; MATTHEWS: Earle MacVeigh; NAST: Guy Standing Jr.; TIMOTHY: Russ Brown; MILDRED: Lillian Withington; JOE: Jack Stanton; MAYOR HALL/GEORGE JONES: Rowan Tudor.

THE MOVIE. 1948. DIRECTOR: William A. Seiter. There were several songs missing. **Cast:** TWEED: Vincent Price; ALSO WITH: Deanna Durbin, Dick Haymes, Albert Sharpe, Tom Pedi, Nelle Fisher, Tudor Owen.

EQUITY LIBRARY THEATRE, NYC, 3/8/84–4/1/84. 30 PERFORMANCES. DIRECTOR: John Sharpe; CHOREOGRAPHER: Gerald Teijelo; MUSICAL DIRECTOR: Jerald B. Stone. **Cast:** BESSIE: Meredith Murray; ROSIE: Barbara McCulloh; TWEED: Nick Jolley.

724. *Uptown ... It's Hot!*

A musical revue of popular American music from the 1930s to the 1980s.

Before Broadway. The show first ran in Atlantic City and Washington, DC. The numbers "Take the 'A' Train," "Only You," "What'd I Say," and "Theme from *Shaft*" were not used on Broadway.

The Broadway Run. LUNT—FONTANNE THEATRE, 1/28/86–2/16/86. 13 previews from 1/16/86. 24 PERFORMANCES. PRESENTED BY Allen Spivak & Larry Magid; MUSIC/LYRICS: various writers; CONCEIVED BY/DIRECTOR/CHOREOGRAPHER: Maurice Hines; NARRATIONS WRITTEN BY: Jeffrey V. Thompson & Marion Ramsey; ASSISTANT CHOREOGRAPHER: Mercedes Ellington; SETS: Tom McPhillips; COSTUMES: Ellen Lee; LIGHTING: Marc B. Weiss; SOUND: Otts Munderloh; MUSICAL SUPERVISOR/MUSICAL DIRECTOR: Frank Owens; ADDITIONAL ORCHESTRATIONS: Charles Green, Chris White, Fred Norman; DANCE MUSIC ARRANGEMENTS: Frank Owens & Thom Bridwell; PRESS: Michael Alpert & Ruth Jaffe; GENERAL MANAGER: Roy A. Somlyo; COMPANY MAN-

AGER: Jodi Moss; PRODUCTION STAGE MANAGER: Gwendolyn M. Gilliam; STAGE MANAGER: Jerry Cleveland. *Cast:* Alisa Gyse (6), Lawrence Hamilton (4), Maurice Hines (1) ☆, Tommi Johnson (5), Marion Ramsey (2), Jeffery V. Thompson (3); ENSEMBLE: Sheila D. Barker, Toni-Maria Chalmers, Leon Evans, Michael Franks, Robert H. Fowler, Lovette George, Ruthanna Graves, Yolanda Graves, Emera Hunt, Leslie Williams-Jenkins, Gerry McIntyre, Lisa Ann Mallory, Delphine T. Mantz, Christopher T. Moore, Elise Neal, Leesa M. Osborn, Marishka Shanice Phillips, R. La Chanze Sapp, Cheryl Ann Scott, Darius Keith Williams. *Understudies*: For Marion Ramsey/Alisa Gyse: Yolanda Graves; For Jeffery V. Thompson: Gerry McIntyre; For Lawrence Hamilton: Robert H. Fowler & Michael Franks; For Tommi Johnson: Leon Evans. *Act I*: Overture (Uptown Orchestra); PROLOGUE (Mr. Thompson, Miss Gyse, Mr. Hamilton, Mr. Johnson, Miss Ramsey, Mr. Hines, Men's Ensemble); 1930S: "Swing that Music" (m/l: Louis Armstrong & Horace Gerlach) (Miss Ramsey), "Cotton Club Stomp" (m: Duke Ellington & Johnny Hodges) (Miss Ramsey & Ensemble); Three Gents (Messrs Hamilton, Moore, Fowler): "Daybreak Express" (m: Duke Ellington), "Tap Along with Me" (m: Frank Owens), "Dinah" (m: Harry Akst; l: Samuel Muir & Joe Young) [end of the Three Gents sequence], That Shot Got 'em! (Mr. Thompson, Miss Ramsey, Mr. Johnson, Mr. Fowler) (adaptation by: Miss Ramsey & Mr. Thompson), Stormy Weather Medley (Mr. Hines & Miss Gyse): "When Your Lover Has Gone" (m/l: Einar Aaron Swan), "Ill Wind" (m: Harold Arlen; l: Ted Koehler) [from *Cotton Club Parade*, 1934], "Body and Soul" (m: Johnny Green; l: Edward Heyman, Robert Sour, Frank Eyton), "Stormy Weather" (m: Harold Arlen; l: Ted Koehler) [end of medley], "Diga Diga Doo" (m: Jimmy McHugh; l: Dorothy Fields) [from *Blackbirds of 1928*] (Miss Ramsey, Mr. McIntyre, Miss Mantz, Ensemble), "(Oh), Lady Be Good" (m: George Gershwin) (Mr. Hines), Cab Calloway & The Nicholas Brothers (Messrs Johnson, Evans, Williams): "Jim Jam Jumpin'" (m: Cab Calloway); 1940S: Big Band Tribute: Chick Webb Theme Song—"Let's Get Together" (m: Chick Webb) (Orchestra), "A-Tisket A-Tasket" (m/l: Ella Fitzgerald & Van Alexander) (Miss Gyse) [end of Big Band Tribute], Jitterbuggin'!—"Jumpin' at the Woodside" (m: Count Basie) (Mr. Hines, Miss Ramsey, Mr. Thompson, Mr. Hamilton, Miss Mantz, Miss Barker, Ensemble). *Act II*: 1950S & 1960S: Doo Woppers (Miss Gyse, Mr. Hamilton, Mr. Johnson): "Why Do Fools Fall in Love" (m/l: Frankie Lymon & Morris Levy) [end of Doo Woppers sequence], The Apollo: MASTER OF CEREMONIES: Jeffery V. Thompson [end of the Apollo sequence], The Gospel Caravan: "His Eye is on the Sparrow" (traditional) (Mr. Hamilton), "Amazing Grace" (traditional) (Miss Gyse), "Just a Closer Walk with Thee" (traditional) (Mr. Johnson), "Old Landmark" (m/l: M.A. Brunner) (Mr. Hamilton, Miss Gyse, Mr. Johnson, Miss Sapp, Ensemble) [end of Gospel Caravan sequence], Good Mornin' Judge (adaptation by: Mr. Thompson): JUDGE PIGMEAT: Jeffery V. Thompson; DE DISTRICT ATTORNEY: Marion Ramsey; THE DEFENDANT: Alisa Gyse; SONNY RAYBURN: Maurice Hines; Rock & Roll Medley: "You Send Me" (m/l: Sam Cooke) (Mr. Johnson), "Blueberry Hill" (m/l: Al Lewis, Larry Stock, Vincent Rose) (Mr. Thompson), "Tutti Frutti" (m/l: Richard Penniman, i.e. Little Richard, Dorothy La Bostrie, Joe Lubin) (Mr. McIntyre), "Johnny B. Goode" (m/l: Chuck Berry) (Mr. Hamilton & Ensemble Men) [end of medley]; Battle of the Groups: "Will You Still Love Me Tomorrow?" (m/l: Carole King & Gerald Goffin) (Misses Chalmers, Williams-Jenkins, Mantz, Scott), "Be My Baby" (m/l: Phil Spector, Ellie Greenwich, Jeff Barry) (Misses Gyse, Barker, Neal), "Don't Mess with Bill" (m/l: William "Smokey" Robinson) (Misses Sapp, Mallory, Osborn), "Dancin' in the Street" (m/l: Marvin Gaye, Ivy Hunter, William Stevenson) (Yolanda Graves, Miss George, Miss Hunt), "Stop! In the Name of Love" (m/l: Brian Holland, Lamont Dozier, Eddie Holland) (Miss Ramsey, Ruthanna Graves, Miss Phillips), "Ain't Too Proud to Beg" (m/l: Eddie Holland & Norman J. Whitfield) (Messrs Hamilton, Williams, Evans, Johnson, McIntyre), "Proud Mary" (m/l: John C. Fogerty) (Miss Ramsey, Ruthanna Graves, Miss Phillips, Miss Scott); 1970S: Station WHOT (Mr. Thompson), Stevie Wonder Medley (all m/l: Stevie Wonder): STEVIE WONDER: Leon Evans. "Superstition" (Ensemble Dancers), "Keep on Running" (Maurice Hines as the Devil), "Higher Ground" (Alisa Gyse as the Victim), "Do I Do" (Lawrence Hamilton as the Angel); 1980S: Radio Playoffs (Miss Ramsey, Mr. Hamilton, Miss Sapp, Mr. Evans, Mr. McIntyre, Mr. Hines), "Express" (m/l:

B.T. Express) (Miss Ramsey, Mr. Thompson, Ensemble Dancers), Rappers (Mr. Hamilton & Mr. Thompson), "1999" (m/l: Prince) (Full Company).

Reviews were terrible. Maurice Hines was nominated for a Tony.

725. *Urban Cowboy*

Also called *Urban Cowboy: the Musical*. Set during the oil boom of the 1970s, in Gilley's Bar (named for singer Mickey Gilley, who owned it in the movie), a honky tonk club frequented by newly-prosperous oil workers. Jesse [sic] is the owner of Gilley's (she is a new character created for this musical). Wes is the villain. The musical had a five-piece band on stage.

Before Broadway. In 1978 Aaron Latham, journalist, wrote a piece in *Esquire* about young love in Texas, and called it "The Ballad of the Urban Cowboy." In 1980 it became a (straight) movie, written by Mr. Latham. DIRECTOR: James Bridges. *Cast*: BUD: John Travolta; SISSY: Debra Winger; WES: Scott Glenn. Then it became a novel. In 7/97 Mr. Latham received a letter from Phil Oesterman proposing a stage musical. Mr. Oesterman saw it as a country-style *Cabaret*. Mr. Latham wrote the libretto for the new musical. Mr. Oesterman was to direct. In 12/98 there was a reading. James Carpinello was one of the readers. There was another reading, at LINCOLN CENTER, in early 2000. *Cast*: BUD: Jeremy Kushnier; SISSY: Natasha Diaz. There was a workshop in GLOUCESTER, MASS., in the summer of 2000. *Cast*: BUD: David Elder; SISSY: Angela Pupello. In mid–2001 the producers announced plans for a Broadway opening in 3/02, but most observers felt that this was too early, as the show wasn't anywhere near ready at that point. There was a workshop at WESTBETH THEATRE CENTER, NYC, 12/6/01–12/7/01 (dates put back from 10/22/01–11/11/01 due to Phil Oesterman's open-heart surgery on 10/12/01). *Cast*: BUD: Raul Esparza; SISSY: Caroline McMahon; WES: Tom Zemon; JESSE: B.J. Crosby; AUNT CORENE: Sandy Duncan; UNCLE BOB: Reathel Bean. The rather vague Broadway date was still being proposed, with rehearsals to begin around 2/15/02. By 12/6/01 it was being rumored that the Ambassador would be the Broadway house, but by 2/1/02 it had become evident that Broadway wasn't going to happen—not yet anyway. On 4/11/02 it was announced that the show would have a pre-Broadway tryout at the COCONUT GROVE PLAYHOUSE, Florida. Phil Oesterman died on 7/30/02, and on 8/29/02 Lonny Price was announced as the new director. Jason Robert Brown replaced Louis St. Louis as musical director/arranger, and also wrote three new songs (Jeff Blumenkrantz also wrote two). The show ran at Coconut Grove, 11/16/02–12/1/02. Previews were meant to have begun on 11/5/02, but the date was put back to 11/7/02 due to set difficulties. Opening night was also put back from 11/15/02 to 11/16/02. It got great Florida reviews. CHOREOGRAPHERS: Melinda Roy & Robert Royston; SETS: Douglas W. Schmidt; COSTUMES: Gregory Gale; LIGHTING: David F. Segal; GENERAL MANAGER: Victoria Stevenson. *Cast*: BUD: Matt Cavenaugh; SISSY: Jenn Colella (it was going to be Caroline McMahon); AUNT CORENE: Sally Mayes; UNCLE BOB: Leo Burmester; JESSE: Rozz Morehead; PAM: Jodi Stevens. Broadway rehearsals began on 1/03/03, in Manhattan. There was a press-only open rehearsal on 2/13/03. Broadway previews were delayed by one day to 2/28/03. There had been substantial changes since Florida; 30 per cent of the show was new, three songs had been added and several had been cut. The Monday 3/10/03 Broadway preview was canceled because of the Musicians' Union strike.

The Broadway Run. BROADHURST THEATRE, 3/27/03–5/18/03. 26 previews from 2/28/03. 60 PERFORMANCES. PRESENTED BY Chase Mishkin & Leonard Soloway, in association with Barbara & Peter Fodor; MUSIC/LYRICS: a combination of previously recorded music, and original material written expressly for this production; BOOK: Aaron Latham & Philip Oesterman; BASED ON the 1980 Paramount movie of the same name; DIRECTOR: Lonny Price; CHOREOGRAPHER: Melinda Roy; SETS: James Noone; COSTUMES: Ellis Tillman; LIGHTING: Natasha Katz; SOUND: Peter J. Fitzgerald; MUSICAL DIRECTOR: Jason Robert Brown, *Tom Kitt*; ORCHESTRATIONS/ARRANGEMENTS: Jason Robert Brown; PRESS: Pete Sanders Group; CASTING: (Jay) Binder Casting (Jack Bowdan); GENERAL MANAGER: Leonard Soloway; COMPANY MANAGER: Sammy

Ledbetter; STAGE MANAGER: Heather Fields; ASSISTANT STAGE MAN-AGERS: Neil Krasnow & Ron Kidd. *Cast:* JESSE: Rozz Morehead; TRAVIS "TROUBLE" WILLIAMS: Michael Balderrama; BUBBA: Mark Bove; ROAD-KILL: Gerrard Carter; J.D. LETTERLAW: Justin Greer; BABY BOY: Brian Letendre; TRENT WILLIAMS: Barrett Martin; LUKE "GATOR" DANIELS: Chad L. Schiro; "TUFF" LOVE LEVY: Nicole Foret; BEBE "BUBBLES" BAKER: Michelle Kittrell; BARBIE MCQUEEN: Kimberly Dawn Neumann, *Jennie Ford* (stood in); CANDI CANE: Tera-Lee Pollin; BILLIE "VERUKA" WYNETTE: Kelleia Sheerin; BUD: Matt Cavenaugh; UNCLE BOB: Leo Burmester; MARSHALL: Mark Bove; AUNT CORENE: Sally Mayes; SISSY: Jenn Colella; PAM: Jodi Stevens; WES: Marcus Chait; BAMBI JO: Lisa Gajda [role added during previews]. *Standbys:* Aunt Corene/Jesse: Adinah Alexander; Bud/Wes: Greg Stone. *Understudies:* Bob: Mark Bove; Pam: Nicole Foret & Kimberly Dawn Neumann; Sissy: Nicole Foret & Michelle Kittrell; Aunt Corene: Kimberly Dawn Neumann. SWINGS: Tyler Hanes, Josh Rhodes, Cara Cooper, Jennie Ford. *Musicians:* KEY-BOARDS: Jason Robert Brown & Dave Keyes; DRUMS: Brian Brake; GUI-TAR: Gary Sieger; BASS: Kermit Driscoll; FIDDLE: Antoine Silverman; PEDAL STEEL GUITAR/BANJO/ELECTRIC & ACOUSTIC GUITARS: Gordon Titcomb. *Act I:* "Leavin' Home" (Bud) [new for Broadway], "Long, Hard Day" (m/l: Bob Stillman) (Jesse & Ensemble), "Long Hard Day" (reprise) [this reprise was dropped before Broadway], "I'm Gonna Like it Here" (m/l: Jeff Blumenkrantz) (Bud) [dropped before Broadway], "All Because of You" (m/l: Jeff Blumenkrantz) (Corene), "Another Guy" (m/l: Jeff Blumenkrantz) (Sissy), "Boot Scootin' Boogie" (m/l: Ronnie Dunn) (Hard-hats, Bud, Sissy, All), "It Don't Get Better than This" (m/l: Jason Robert Brown) (Bud), "Dancin' the Slow Ones with You" (m/l: Danny Arena & Sara Light) (Pam), "Cowboy, Take Me Away" (m/l: Marcus Hummon & Martie Maguire) (Sissy), "Could I Have This Dance (for the Rest of My Life)?" (m/l: Wayland D. Holyfield & Bob Lee House) (Bud & Ensemble) [from the movie], "My Back's up Against the Wall" (m/l: Carl L. Byrd & Pevin Byrd-Munoz) (Wes & Cowboys), "If You Mess with the Bull" (m/l: Luke Reed & Roger Brown) (Jesse & Ensemble), "I Used to Like it Here" (a reprise of "I'm Gonna Like it Here") Bud) [this reprise was dropped before Broadway], "Honey, I'm Home" (m/l: Shania Twain & R.J. "Mutt" Lange) [dropped before Broadway], "That's How She Rides" (m/l: Jason Robert Brown) (Wes), "I Wish I Didn't Love You" (Bud) [before Broadway this number replaced "I Take it Back" (m/l: Jason Robert Brown) (Bud)]. *Act II:* "That's How Texas Was Born" (m/l: Jason Robert Brown) (Band), "Take You for a Ride" (m/l: Danny Arena, Sara Light, Lauren Lucas) (Pam & Wes), "My Hopalong Heartbreak" (m/l: Jason Robert Brown) (Sissy), "T-R-O-U-B-L-E" (m/l: Jerry Chestnut) (Marshall), "Dances Turn into Dreams" (m/l: Jerry Silverstein) (Jesse), "The Hard Way" (m/l: Clint Black & James Hayden Nicholas) (Sissy & Bud), "Dancin' the Slow Ones with You" (reprise) (Pam) [this reprise was cut before Broadway], "Git It" (m/l: Tommy Conners & Roger Brown) (Jesse & Ensemble), "Something that We Do" (m/l: Clint Black & Skip Ewing) (Corene, Bob, All), "Better Days" (m/l: Rebekka Bremlette, Dorsey Burnette III, Annie L. Roboff) [cut before Broadway], "The Devil Went Down to Georgia" (m/l: Charlie Daniels, Tom Crain, Fred Edwards, Taz DiGregorio, Jim Marshall, Charlie Hayward) (Marshall & Ensemble) [from the movie] [new for Broadway], "It Don't Get Better than This" (reprise) (Bud, Sissy, All) [this reprise was new for Broadway], "Looking for Love" (m/l: Wanda Millette, Patti Ryan, Bob Morrison) (Bud, Sissy, All) [from the movie].

Broadway reviews were shockingly bad, with the exception of Clive Barnes, who gave it a near-rave in the *New York Post*. The day the papers came out notices were announced that the show would close on 3/29/03, after 4 performances. However, it kept going. It finally closed, after a matinee. On 5/24/03 it was ruled ineligible for the best score Tony nomination, but on 5/8/03 this decision was reversed. It was also nominated for choreography. The show cost $4.5 million.

After Broadway. There was a tour planned for the fall of 2004. PRE-SENTED BY Ken Gentry.

726. *Urinetown*

Also known as: *Urinetown, the Musical.* A satirical comedy musical, in a futuristic, Gothamesque setting. Set in a time when

you have to pay to pee because the world has been crippled by a water shortage, and all private toilets have been outlawed. A corporation, headed by the dapper Caldwell, controls Urinetown. Hope is his naive daughter. Bobby is the earnest, fresh-faced urinal attendant. Little Sally is a post-pubescent orphan waif. Lockstock is the corrupt narrator, and his partner is Barrel.

Before Broadway. OFF OFF BROADWAY. The writers took the worst concept they could think of, and gave it full expression. It started Off Off Broadway, on 8/18/99, at the PRESENT COMPANY THEATORIUM, on the Lower East Side, as part of the NEW YORK INTERNATIONAL FRINGE FESTIVAL. It played to standing room only, and was so popular that it extended beyond the festival, to 9/4/99. It won the Festival's FringeX-ellence Award in the category "Overall Excellence — Musical." PRE-SENTED BY Theatre of the Apes (Greg Kotis & Mark Hollmann); DIREC-TOR: Joseph P. McDonnell; SETS: Jane Charlotte Jones & Michael Stuart; COSTUMES: Karen Flood; LIGHT: Peggotty Roecker; STAGE MANAGER: Michael Stuart. *Cast:* JOSEPHINE/MRS. O'HENRY: Kristen Anderson; OLD MAN STRONG/HARRY: Nick Balaban; FIPP: Terry Cosentino; CLAD-WELL: Adam Grant; BOBBY: Wilson Hall; BECKY/SECRETARY: Raquel Hecker; PENELOPE: Carol Hickey; SALLY: Spencer Kayden; BARREL: Victor Khodadad; TOM/BILLEAUX: Zachary Lasher; MCQUEEN: Rob Maitner; SUE/MRS. MILLENNIUM: Bellavia Mauro; LOCKSTOCK: Jay Roderick; HOPE: Louise Rozett; HIDALGO JANE: Allison Schubert; EXECS: Victor Khodadad & Allison Schubert; POOR PERSONS: Terry Cosentino, Victor Khodadad, Rob Maitner.

Off Broadway. Despite the dangers of the title, the producers looked forward to a move to an Off Broadway house, for a more commercial run. The Araca Group then sponsored two readings (the script had minor adjustments), on 1/25/00 and 1/27/00, at NEW DRAMATISTS, in Manhattan. DIRECTOR: John Rando. *Cast:* James Barbour, Nancy Opel, Michael McCormack, Jennifer Laura Thompson, Marcus Lovett, Daniel Marcus, Brooks Ashmanskas, Christopher Murney, Tom Gualtieri, Jessica Frankel, Dale Hensley, Duane Martin Foster, Spencer Kayden, Nanci Bradshaw, Raquel Hecker, Debra Wiseman, Michael St. John. By this time Broadway was definitely the ultimate goal. On 12/11/00 it was announced that it would play Off Broadway, with the Araca Group & Dodger Theatricals producing in association with TheaterDreams, Inc., and Lauren Mitchell; and John Rando directing. Rehearsals began on 2/19/01. On 3/1/01 John Cullum was announced as the surprise lead, and the venue was to be the little-known AMERICAN THEATRE OF ACTORS. 40 previews from 4/1/01. It opened on 5/3/01, for a limited run through 5/14/01. It had the same basic cast and crew as for the later Broadway run, except SOUND: Jeff Curtis (by himself); STAGE MANAGER: Martha Donaldson. The number "Rio" was cut. "Mr. Cladwell" and "Snuff That Girl" were written especially for this Off Broadway production by Greg Kotis and Mark Hollmann. The production was nominated for nine Drama Desk Award awards, and got good reviews. The show was so popular that the closing date was extended to 6/30/01 (and, along with this extension, ticket prices doubled, from $25 to $50), then to 7/1/01, but it finally closed on 6/25/01, after 58 PERFORMANCES. On 5/17/01 it was announced that rather than move to a larger Off Broadway house, which had been expected, it would go straight to the Henry Miller's (now to be called the Henry Miller), which had recently been accorded Broadway status. The new theatre was booked with the understanding that come 3/02 *Urinetown* would vacate to make way for another show. It would open in late 7/01, thus becoming the first musical of the 2001–02 Broadway season. On 5/31/01 it was announced that John Cullum, who had been ready to leave to play in *King Lear* on the West Coast, would, in fact, remain with the show as it went to Broadway. By the end of 5/01 it became apparent that delays in renovating the Henry Miller would force a postponement of the beginning of previews from late July to late August, or even September. On 6/11/01 Hunter Foster and Megan Lawrence (who were married in real life) left, to be replaced by Marcus Lovett and Jennifer Cody. Hunter Foster was expected to return for the Broadway production (which he did), and Megan Lawrence, who had been pregnant throughout the entire Off Broadway run, was also expected to rejoin the Broadway cast in 10/01, after her maternity leave (which she did, but not until 2002). After the show closed Off Broadway it was announced that Broadway previews would begin on 8/6/01, with the official opening date of 9/10/01. However, on 7/5/01 previews were put back to 8/20/01. On 7/24/01 it was announced that previews would be put back again to 8/27/01 (which is, indeed, when they began), and that the new opening date was 9/13/01. They were putting new seats and a new air-conditioning system into the Henry Miller, as well as expanding the box-office. The first number in the Off Broadway production—"Too Much Exposition"—was cut for Broadway; and the reprise of "It's a Privilege to Pee" was new for Broadway. When the attack on New York came on 9/11/01 *Urinetown* was in Broadway previews. The following day it was announced that the 9/13/01 opening date would now be postponed to 9/20/01. About this time there was a serious move to change the name of the show to *U-Town*, but it never happened.

The Broadway Run. HENRY MILLER THEATRE, 9/20/01–1/18/04. 25 previews from 8/27/01. 965 PERFORMANCES. PRESENTED BY The Araca Group (Matthew Rego, Michael Rego, Hank Unger) & Dodger Theatricals, in association with TheaterDreams & Lauren Mitchell; MUSIC: Mark Hollmann; LYRICS: Greg Kotis & Mark Hollmann; BOOK: Greg Kotis; DIRECTOR: John Rando; CHOREOGRAPHER: John Carrafa; SETS: Scott Pask; COSTUMES: Jonathan Bixby & Gregory A. Gale; LIGHTING: Brian MacDevitt; SOUND: Jeff Curtis & Lew Mead; MUSICAL DIRECTOR: Edward Strauss; ORCHESTRATIONS: Bruce Coughlin; OFF BROADWAY CAST RECORDING on RCA Victor, made on 5/15/01, and scheduled for release on 7/10/01 (it actually came out on 8/7/01); PRESS: Boneau/Bryan-Brown; CASTING: Jay Binder; GENERAL MANAGEMENT: Dodger Management Group; COMPANY MANAGER: Marc Borsak, *J. Anthony Magner*; PRODUCTION STAGE MANAGER: Julia P. Jones; STAGE MANAGER: Matthew Lacey; ASSISTANT STAGE MANAGER: Joseph R. Bowerman, *Peggy Taphorn*. **Cast:** OFFICER LOCKSTOCK: Jeff McCarthy, *James Barbour* (6/13/03–7/6/03), *Jeff McCarthy* (from 7/8/03); LITTLE SALLY: Spencer Kayden, *Megan Lawrence* (from 8/27/02), *Spencer Kayden* (from 3/25/03); PENELOPE PENNYWISE: Nancy Opel (left for 3 months on 1/26/03), *Victoria Clark* (1/28/03–4/27/03), *Carolee Carmello* (from 4/29/03); BOBBY STRONG: Hunter Foster (until 20/03), *Charlie Pollock* (from 3/21/03), *Tom Cavanagh* (5/20/03–7/6/03), *Hunter Foster* (7/8/03–7/27/03), *Luther Creek* (from 7/29/03); HOPE CLADWELL: Jennifer Laura Thompson (out from 12/29/02 for a 10-week leave), *Anastasia Barzee* (12/30/02–3/16/03), *Jennifer Laura Thompson* (3/18/03–7/6/03), *Amy Spanger* (from 7/8/03); MR. MCQUEEN: David Beach, *Danny Gurwin* (9/23/03–10/12/03), *David Beach* (from 10/14/03); SENATOR FIPP: John Deyle; OLD MAN STRONG: Ken Jennings; TINY TOM: Rick Crom; DR. BILLEAUX: Rick Crom; SOUPY SUE: Rachel Coloff (until 1/28/02), *Jennifer Cody* (from 1/29/02), *Rachel Coloff*; CLADWELL'S SECRETARY: Rachel Coloff (until 1/28/02), *Jennifer Cody* (from 1/29/02), *Rachel Coloff*; CALDWELL B. CLADWELL: John Cullum (until 8/17/03), *Don Richard, Charles Shaughnessy* (from 9/9/03); ROBBIE THE STOCKFISH: Victor W. Hawks; HOT BLADES HARRY: Ken Jennings; LITTLE BECKY TWO SHOES: Jennifer Cody (until 1/13/02), *Megan Lawrence* (from 1/14/02), *Kirsten Wyatt*; MRS. MILLENNIUM: Jennifer Cody (until 1/13/02), *Megan Lawrence* (from 1/14/02), *Kirsten Wyatt*; OFFICER BARREL: Daniel Marcus, *Bill Buell* (12/6/01–2/17/02), *Daniel Marcus* (from 2/18/02); BILLY BOY BILL: Lawrence E. Street; JOSEPHINE STRONG: Kay Walbye; BUSINESSMAN # 1: Victor W. Hawks; BUSINESSMAN # 2: Lawrence E. Street; OLD WOMAN: Kay Walbye. **Understudies:** Lockstock: Don Richard & Peter Reardon; Sally: Jennifer Cody & Erin Hill; Bobby: Peter Reardon & Victor Hawks; Hope: Erin Hill & Rachel Coloff; Cladwell: Don Richard & Daniel Marcus; Becky/Mrs. Millennium/Sue/Secretary: Erin Hill, *Kirsten Wyatt*; Penelope: Kay Walbye & Rachel Coloff, *Stacie Morgain Lewis & Michele Ragusa*; McQueen: Rick Crom & Lawrence E. Street; Barrel: Victor Hawks & Don Richard; Fipp: Rick Crom & Don Richard; Old Woman/Josephine/Nurse: Rachel Coloff & Erin Hill; Tom/Billeaux: Peter Reardon & Lawrence E. Street; Robbie: Lawrence E. Street & Peter Reardon; Bill: Peter Reardon. **Swing:** Kirsten Wyatt. **The Urinetown Band:** PIANO: Ed Goldschneider; CLARINET/BASS CLARINET/ALTO SAX/SOPRANO SAX: Paul Garment; TENOR TROMBONE/EUPHONIUM: Ben Herrington; DRUMS/PERCUSSION: Tim McLafferty; BASS: Dick Sarpola. **Act I: Scene 1** Amenity # 9, the poorest, filthiest urinal in town: Overture (Orchestra), "Urinetown" (Lockstock & Company), "It's a Privilege to Pee" (Penny & The Poor), "It's a Privilege to Pee" (reprise) (Lockstock & The Poor); **Scene 2** The good

offices of Urine Good Company: "Mr. Cladwell" (Cladwell, McQueen, Hope, UGC Staff); **Scene 3** A street corner: "Cop Song" (Lockstock, Barrel, The Cops), "Follow Your Heart" (Hope & Bobby); **Scene 4** Amenity # 9; "Look to the Sky" (Bobby & The Poor); **Scene 5** The goof offices of UGC: "Don't Be the Bunny" (Cladwell & UGC Staff); **Scene 6** Amenity # 9: "Act I Finale" (Ensemble). **Act II: Scene 1** A secret hideout: "What is Urinetown?" (Ensemble); **Scene 2** A secret hideout: "Snuff That Girl" (Harry, Becky, The Rebel Poor), "Run Freedom Run" (Bobby & The Poor), "Follow Your Heart" (reprise) (Hope); **Scene 3** The good offices of UGC: "Why Did I Listen to That Man?" (Penny, Fipp, Lockstock, Barrel, Hope, Bobby); **Scene 4** A secret hideout: "Tell Her I Love Her" (Sally & Bobby); **Scene 5** Various: "We're Not Sorry" (The Rich & The Poor), "We're Not Sorry" (reprise) (Cladwell & Penny), "I See a River" (Hope & Ensemble).

Most of the reviews were good. In 12/01 Daniel Marcus broke his ankle while leaving the stage after a performance, and was replaced by Bill Buell. On 1/28/02 Rachel Coloff sprained her ankle, and Jennifer Cody stepped in for her. She learned her lines in a couple of hours, and went on that evening. The 6/18/02 evening performance and the 6/19/02 matinee were canceled because of a leak following rain. The show resumed the evening of 6/19/02. *Urinetown* won Tonys for score, book, and direction of a musical, and was nominated for musical, choreography, orchestrations, and for John Cullum, Spencer Kayden, Nancy Opel, and Jennifer Laura Thompson. By 2003 there were movie plans. The show missed a performance in the 8/14/03 power blackout. Alvin Epstein was going to be Cladwell from 8/29/03 but it never happened. On 10/27/03 the production recouped its investment of $3.7 million, but it was also ordered to leave the Henry Miller by 2/15/04 as the theatre (except for the facade) was going to be demolished to make way for a 57-story skyscraper (this was not a surprise). On 11/3/03 it was announced that the show would close on 1/18/04.

After Broadway. TOUR. The year-long national tour was announced on 1/13/02, and opened at the Geary Theatre, San Francisco, on 7/1/03. Previews from 6/24/03. This was the West Coast premiere. It had the same basic crew as for the Broadway run, except that the American Conservatory Theatre (ACT) was an additional producer. **Cast:** CLADWELL: Ron Holgate; LOCKSTOCK: Tom Hewitt; HOPE: Christiane Noll; PENELOPE: Beth McVey; LITTLE SALLY: Meghan Strange; OLD MAN STRONG/HARRY: Jim Corti; BARREL: Richard Ruiz; LITTLE BECKY/MISS MILLENNIUM: Sheri Sanders; BOBBY: Charlie Pollock. The Geary run was not officially part of the tour (although in reality it was); it then went on to an official opening at the Buell Theatre, Denver, on 9/9/03.

BLUMA APPEL THEATRE, Toronto, 5/27/04–7/11/04. Previews from 5/19/04. This was the Canadian premiere. PRESENTED BY CanStage and Dancap Private Equity, Inc.; DIRECTOR: John Rando; CHOREOGRAPHER: John Carrafa; SETS: Scott Pask; COSTUMES: Gregory Gale & Jonathan Bixby; LIGHTING: Brian MacDevitt; MUSICAL DIRECTOR: Stephen Woodjets; ORCHESTRATIONS: Bruce Coughlin. **Cast:** BARREL: Sheldon Davis; LOCKSTOCK: David Keeley; HOPE: Cara Leslie; STRONG/HARRY: Lee MacDougall; PENELOPE: Mary Ann McDonald; BOBBY: Stephen Patterson; SUE/CLADWELL'S SECRETARY: Sophie Schottlander; LITTLE SALLY: Jennifer Waiser; BECKY/MRS. MILLENNIUM: Patricia Zentilli; CLADWELL: Frank Moore.

PREQUEL AND SEQUEL. In early 2004 it was announced that Greg Kotis and Mark Hollmann were working on a prequel, which might have a reading in 4/04, and that they were also planning a sequel, thus making it all a trilogy.

727. *The Utter Glory of Morrissey Hall*

Set in Morrissey Hall School for Girls, in England, at the present time; their pranks and rivalries; hyperactive girls; long-suffering staff.

Before Broadway. It was originally produced as a Broadway tryout at the MCCARTER THEATRE, Princeton, NJ, on 11/3/77. 17 PERFORMANCES. It had the same basic crew as for the subsequent Broadway run, except CHOREOGRAPHER: Michael Maurer (he would be replaced after this tryout by Arthur Faria). *Cast*: Patricia Falkenhain (replacing Eileen Heckart, who walked out only days before the opening), Jane Rose, Margaret Hilton, Lois deBanzie, Jeffrey Jones, Robert Henderson, Daniel Arden. Before it opened on Broadway Patricia Falkenhain was replaced in the lead by Celeste Holm, and Miss Falkenhain assumed a supporting role. Buddy Schwab replaced Arthur Faria as choreographer.

The Broadway Run. MARK HELLINGER THEATRE, 5/13/79. 7 previews from 5/3/79. 1 PERFORMANCE. PRESENTED BY Arthur Whitelaw, Albert W. Selden, and H. Ridgely Bullock, in association with Marc Howard; MUSIC/LYRICS: Clark Gesner; BOOK: Clark Gesner & Nagle Jackson; DIRECTOR: Nagle Jackson; CHOREOGRAPHER: Buddy Schwab; SETS/LIGHTING: Howard Bay; COSTUMES: David Graden; ASSISTANT COSTUMES: Muffie Bullock; SOUND: Charles Bellin; MUSICAL DIRECTOR: John Lesko; ORCHESTRATIONS: Jay Blackton & Russell Warner; DANCE MUSIC ARRANGEMENTS: Allen Cohen; PRESS: Betty Lee Hunt & Maria Cristina Pucci; CASTING: Elizabeth R. Woodman; GENERAL MANAGERS: Jack Schlissel & Jay Kingwill; PRODUCTION STAGE MANAGER: Mark S. Krause; STAGE MANAGER: Bryan Young; ASSISTANT STAGE MANAGER: Gail Pearson. *Cast*: ADMINISTRATION: JULIA FAYSLE, HEADMISTRESS: Celeste Holm (1) ✮; ELIZABETH WILKINS, SECRETARY: Marilyn Caskey (5); STAFF: FORESTA STUDLEY: Patricia Falkenhain (3); TERESA WINKLE: Laurie Franks (4); MRS. DELMONDE: Taina Elg (2); MISS NEWTON: Karen Gibson (7); MR. WEYBURN, GROUNDSKEEPER: John Wardwell (8); SIXTH FORM STUDENTS: CARSWELL: Mary Saunders (12); VICKERS: Gina Franz; BOODY: Adrienne Alexander; DALE: Jill P. Rose; DICKERSON: Kate Kelly; HAVERFIELD: Polly Pen; FIFTH FORM STUDENTS: ALICE: Cynthia Parva; HELEN: Becky McSpadden (11); FRANCES: Dawn Jeffory; ANGELA: Bonnie Hellman; MARJORIE: Anne Kay; MARY: Lauren Shub; VISITORS: RICHARD TIDEWELL: Willard Beckham (6); CHARLES HILL: John Gallogly (10); MR. OSGOOD: Robert Lanchester (9). *Standby*: Studley/Newton: Willi Burke. *Understudies*: Headmistress: Patricia Falkenhain; 5th Form Students: Mary Garripoli; 6th Form Students: Polly Pen; Richard/Charles/Weyburn/Osgood: Jonathan Arterton; Mary: Lauren Shub; Winkle/Delmonde/Elizabeth: Karen Gibson. *Act I*: Overture (Orchestra) ["At the Fair" from "Country Suite," by Desmond Gorss (1885–1958); arr/conducted for the Morrissey Hall Concert Orchestra by Evelyn Potts, Director of Music], "Promenade" (Company), "Proud, Erstwhile, Upright, Fair" (Headmistress, Studley, Elizabeth), "Elizabeth's Song" (Elizabeth), "Way Back When" (Headmistress & Studley) [added during previews], "Lost" (6th Form), "Morning" (Mrs. Delmonde & Dancing Class), "The Letter" (Helen, Charles, Company), "Oh, Sun" (Marjorie as St. George, Angela as the Dragon, Helen, Frances & Mary as the Dryads, Mrs. Delmonde), "Give Me That Key" (Headmistress, Helen, Elizabeth), "Duet" (Elizabeth, Richard, Company). *Act II*: "Interlude and Gallop" (Orchestra & Students), "You Will Know When the Time Has Arrived" (Winkle, Carswell, 5th & 6th Forms), "You Would Say" (Helen, Charles, 5th Form), "See the Blue" (Headmistress & Flowers), "Dance of Resignation" (Mrs. Delmonde), "Reflection" (Headmistress), "The War" (Company) [*Les Preludes*, by Franz Liszt], "Oh, Sun (reprise), "The Ending" (Company).

It was panned by the reviewers.

728. *The Vagabond King*

One of the great operettas. Louis XI makes vagabond poet Villon king for a day. In return Villon must woo the disdainful Katherine and help Louis against the treacherous Duke of Burgundy. If he fails, he will be executed. He succeeds, of course.

Before Broadway. It was filmed straight (i.e. not a musical) in 1920 as *If I Were King*. *Cast*: William Farnum, Betty Ross Clarke.

The original stage musical version opened on Broadway, at the CASINO, 9/21/25; then moved to the CENTURY THEATRE, 11/15/26–12/4/26. Total of 511 PERFORMANCES. PRESENTED BY Russell Janney; DIRECTOR: Max Figman. *Cast*: VILLON: Dennis King.

There was another straight film version, *The Beloved Rogue*, 1928. *Cast*: John Barrymore.

The first filming of the 1925 stage musical version was in 1930. DIRECTOR: Ludwig Berger. *Cast*: VILLON: Dennis King; KATHERINE: Jeanette MacDonald.

There was a straight movie re-make in 1938, *If I Were King*. DIRECTOR: Frank Lloyd. *Cast*: VILLON: Ronald Colman; LOUIS: Basil Rathbone.

The Broadway Run. SHUBERT THEATRE, 6/29/43–8/14/43. 56 PERFORMANCES. PRESENTED BY Russell Janney; MUSIC: Rudolf Friml; LYRICS: Brian Hooker & Russell Janney; BOOK: Brian Hooker & W.H. Post (revised by Russell Janney); ADAPTED BY Brian Hooker & W.H. Post from the 1901 play *If I Were King*, by Justin Huntly McCarthy, which in turn had been adapted from R.H. Russell's novel; DIRECTOR: George Ermoloff; CHOREOGRAPHER: Igor Schwezoff; SETS: Raymond Sovey; COSTUMES: James Reynolds; MUSICAL DIRECTOR/ORCHESTRATIONS: Joseph Majer; CHORUS MASTER: Rubin Kosikoff; STAGE MANAGER: Royal Cutter; ASSISTANT STAGE MANAGER: Zac Caully. *Cast*: RENE DE MONTIGNY: Artells Dickson; CASIN CHOLET: Bert Stanley; JEHAN LE LOUP: George Karle; MARGOT: Jann Moore; ISABEAU: Evelyn Wick; JEHANNETON: Rosalind Madison; HUGUETTE DU HAMEL: Arline Thomson; GUY TABARIE: Will H. Philbrick; TRISTAN L'HERMITE: Douglas Gilmore; LOUIS XI: Jose Ruben (3); FRANCOIS VILLON: John Brownlee (1); KATHERINE DE VAUCELLES: Frances McCann (2); THIBAUT D'AUSSIGNY: Ben Roberts; CAPTAIN OF SCOTCH ARCHERS: Charles Henderson; AN ASTROLOGER: Franz Bendtsen; LADY MARY: Teri Keane; NOEL OF ANJOU: Dan Gallagher; OLIVER LE DAIN: Curtis Cooksey; HERALD OF BURGUNDY: Earl Ashcroft; THE QUEEN: Betty Berry; THE HANGMAN: Craig Newton; THE CARDINAL: Vincent Henry; PREMIER DANCERS: Julia Horvath, Dorothie Littlefield, Peter Birch; THE TWO DICE PLAYERS: Kenneth Sonnenberg & Birger Hallderson; CORPS DE BALLET: Franca Baldwin, Sally Sheppard, Carlyle Ramey, Patricia Leith, Muriel Bruenig, Anna Jacqueline, Ginee Richardson, Davide Daniel; LADIES OF THE ENSEMBLE: Ruth Barber, Muriel Blane, Zola Palmer, Helen Carlson, Claire Wells, Ann Garland, Betty Berry, Doris Blake, Linda Kay, Katrina Van Oss, Rosalind Madison, Iris Howard, Helen George, Evelyn Wick, Mary David, Shirley Conklin, Mary Burns, Bernice Hoffman, Joan Barrie, Mary Ellen Bright; GENTLEMEN OF THE ENSEMBLE: Frederick Langford, Vincent Henry, Charles Arnold, Robert Kimberly, Kenneth Sonnenberg, Chris Gerard, Earl Ashcroft, Al Bartolet, William Gephart, Jay Patrick, Birger Hallderson, George Walker, Norvel Campbell, Max Plagmann, Ernest Pavano, George Beach, Otto Simetti, Jerry Madden, Graham Alexander, Jerry Clayton, Harry Nordin, Charles Trott. *Part I*: The Fir Cone Tavern, Old Paris: Overture, Opening Chorus, "Love for Sale" (Huguette, Peter Birch, Dorothie Littlefield, Chorus), "Drinking Song" (A Flagon of Wine) (Tabarie & Male Chorus), "Song of the Vagabonds" (Villon & Chorus), "Some Day" (Katherine) [a big hit], "Only a Rose" (Katherine & Villon), Fight Music & Finaletto (Entire Company). *Part II*: a/ The court that night: Hunting Number (Noel & Ensemble). DIANA: Julia Horvath; COUNT ETIENNE: Peter Birch. Ballet, "Tomorrow" (Katherine, Villon, Women Chorus); b/ The court, next morning; Finale (Entire Company). *Part III*: The court garden; the masque: "Nocturne (in the Night)" (Ensemble, Obligato, Helen George & Fred Langford), "Tarantella" (Miss Littlefield, Miss Horvath, Mr. Birch, Ballet), "Serenade" (Tabarie, Oliver, Lady Mary), "Waltz Huguette" (Huguette, Noel, Miss Littlefield, Miss Horvath, Ballet), "Love Me Tonight" (Katherine & Villon), Finale (Entire Company). *Part IV*: a/ A Gate of Old Paris: "Te Deum" (Ensemble); b/ The Place de Greve: "Victory March" (Ensemble); Finale Ultimo (Entire Company).

Reviews were divided.

After Broadway. The most famous musical version was in 1956, the only film Hanya Holm choreographed. *Cast*: VILLON: Oreste Kirkop; KATHERINE: Kathryn Grayson; HUGUETTE: Rita Moreno; FERREBOUC: Jack Lord.

OFF BROADWAY REVIVAL. EASTSIDE PLAYHOUSE, 12/3/75. 42 PERFORMANCES. PRESENTED BY The Light Opera of Manhattan; CHOREOGRAPHER: Jerry Gotham. *Cast*: HUGUETTE: Lyn Greene; TABARIE: Julio Rosario; LOUIS: Raymond Allen; VILLON: Gary Ridley; KATHERINE: Georgia McEver; LADY MARY: Diane Armistead. *Act I: Scene 1* The tavern: "Gaudeo" (Ensemble), "Love for Sale" (Huguette), "Drinking Song" (Tabarie), "Song of the Vagabonds" (Villon & Ensemble), "Some Day" (Katherine), "Only a Rose" (Katherine & Villon), Finaletto Scene 1 (Ensemble); *Scene 2* A corridor: "Scotch Guardsmen's Song" (Captain & Guardsmen), "Only a Rose" (reprise) (Katherine), "Tomorrow" (Katherine & Villon); *Scene 3* The court; next morning: Finale Act I

(Ensemble). *Act II*: *Scene 1* The masque: "Nocturne (in the Night)" (Ensemble), Ballet (Tarantella) (Dance Ensemble), "Serenade" (Tabarie, Oliver, Lady Mary), "Huguette Waltz" (Huguette), "Love Me Tonight" (Katherine & Villon); *Scene 2* The procession: "Song of the Vagabonds" (reprise) (Ensemble), "Te Deum Laudamus!" (Ensemble), "The Victory March" (Ensemble); *Scene 3* The gibbet: Finale (Ensemble).

The LOOM did it again, from 1/12/77, this time with Jeanne Beauvais as Huguette, and Joan Lader as Lady Mary.

729. *The Vamp*

Flora, a simple country girl, allows herself to be transformed into a Theda Bara-type silent screen siren so she may win the hand of movie cowboy Dick Hicks, the Yucca Kid. She is presented to the public at Grand Central Station. Bessie was the gossip columnist. Elsie was the Honeybunny Girl. The show began with projected credits, as if in a movie.

Before Broadway. The original star, Danny Scholl, left during rehearsals and was replaced by his understudy, Bob Rippy. The show tried out with the title *Delilah*. Producer Alexander Carson was married to Carol Channing.

The Broadway Run. WINTER GARDEN THEATRE, 11/10/55–12/31/55. 60 PERFORMANCES. PRESENTED BY Oscar S. Lerman, Martin B. Cohen, Alexander F. Carson; MUSIC/ORCHESTRATIONS: James Mundy; LYRICS: John Latouche; BOOK: John Latouche & Sam Locke; BASED ON a story by John Latouche; DIRECTOR: David Alexander; CHOREOGRAPHER/PRODUCTION SUPERVISOR: Robert Alton; SETS/COSTUMES: Raoul Pene du Bois; MUSICAL DIRECTOR/VOCAL ARRANGEMENTS: Milton Rosenstock; INCIDENTAL MUSIC: Jack Pfeiffer; PRESS: Frank Goodman; COMPANY MANAGER: Emmett Callahan; STAGE MANAGER: Charles Millang; ASSISTANT STAGE MANAGER: Clarke Gordon. *Cast:* MYRON H. HUBBARD: Jack Waldron; BESSIE BISCO: Bibi Osterwald (3); MUSCLEMAN: Steve Reeves; BARNEY OSTERTAG: Paul Lipson; OLIVER J. OXHEART: David Atkinson (2); TICKET GIRL: Phyllis Dorne; DICK HICKS (NE STANLEY HUBERMYER): Bob Rippy; STARK CLAYTON: Malcolm Lee Beggs; ELSIE CHELSEA: Patricia Hammerlee; BLUESTONE: Jack Harrold; FLORA WEEMS/DELILAH MODO: Carol Channing (1) ☆; UNCLE GARVEY: Will Geer; AUNT HESTER: Sandyl Cordell; FIRE COMMISSIONER: Roger Franklin; SNAKE CHARMER: David Neuman; SAMSON: Steve Reeves; WHIP MAN: David Kashner; HIGH PRIEST: David Neuman; CHARLIE: Matt Mattox (4); 2ND CAMERAMAN: Dick Eskeli; TYROLEAN COUPLES: Cathryn Damon & Hugh Lambert, Helen Silver & Ron Cecill; DANCERS: Mark Aldon, Chad Block, Ron Cecill, Robert Daley, Cathryn Damon, Pepe de Chazza, Rudy Del Campo, Burnell Dietsch, Mary Jane Doerr, Phyllis Dorne, Suan Hartman, Barbara Heath, Betty Koerber, Hugh Lambert, Lucia Lambert, Barbara Leigh, Robert Norris, Lila Popper, Dom Salinaro, Helen Silver, Mike Stevens, Pat Wharton; SINGERS: Charleen Clark, Dick Eskeli, Roger Franklin, Joyce Gladmon, Stokely Gray, William Krach, Vincent McMahon, Bernice Massi, Donna Sanders, Kelley Stephens, Kay Turner, Ralph Wayne. *Standby*: Flora: Jacqueline James. *Understudies*: Bessie: Phyllis Dorne; Elsie: Bernice Massi; Dick: Stokely Gray; Charlie: Chad Block; Barney/Myron/Stark: Jack Harrold; Garvey: Roger Franklin; Aunt Hester: Kelley Stephens. *Act I*: *Scene 1* Hubbard's Coliseum, Fourteenth Street: "The Spiel" (Hubbard, Bessie, Coliseum Patrons), "The Flickers" (Ticket Girl & Patrons); *Scene 2* A farm in the Bronx; the following morning: "Keep Your Nose to the Grindstone" (Flora, Garvey, Hester), "That's Where a Man Fits In" (Flora), "I've Always Loved You" (Flora & Farm Folk) [this number was dropped during the run]; *Scene 3* Hubbard's Movie House; a few weeks later: "You're Colossal" (Elsie & Dick), "Fan Club Chant" (Movie Fans); *Scene 4* Grand Central Station; three months later: "Have You Met Delilah?" (Oxheart), "Yeemy Yeemy" (Flora & Oriental Entourage), "The Vamps" (Charlie, Babs Heath, Cathryn Damon, Fans); *Scene 5* A rooftop studio in Manhattan; sometime later: "Delilah's Dilemma" (Flora & Movie Fans). *Act II*: *Scene 1a* The northeast corner of Hollywood & Vine: "Four Little Misfits" (Elsie, Bessie, Dick, Charlie); *Scene 1b* OHO Film Company; one year later; *Scene 2* Interior of OHO Studios: "Samson and Delilah" (Flora as Delilah, Char-

lie, Samson, Whip Man, High Priest, Cathryn Damon, Movie Company), "Why Does it Have to Be You?" (Oxheart), "Ragtime Romeo" (Bessie, Charlie, Boys); *Scene 3* Flora's dressing room: "I'm Everybody's Baby" (Flora) [the showstopper]; *Scene 4* Executive office, OHO Film Company; the next day: "I'm Everybody's Baby" (reprise) (Flora, Ostertag, Dick, Hubbard, Clayton), "The Impossible She" (Oxheart & OHO Boys) [this number was dropped during the run]; *Scene 5* Hubbard's Movie Cathedral, Hollywood: Finale (Company).

Broadway reviews were dire (except for Carol Channing, who could do no wrong). The show cost $315,000 and lost more than $350,000. It received Tony nominations for choreography, musical direction, and for Carol Channing.

730. *Very Good Eddie*

The Hudson River dayliner *Catskill* is carrying two honeymooning couples in June 1913. Eddie Kettle is short and timid. Georgina his wife is tall and domineering. The other couple is the other way around—Percy Darling and his new wife Elsie.

Before Broadway. The original opened on Broadway, at the 299-seat PRINCESS THEATRE, on 12/23/15. It moved to the CASINO, on 5/29/15, then again, to the 39TH STREET THEATRE, on 9/11/16, and back for a final run at the PRINCESS THEATRE, 10/2/16–10/14/16. Total of 341 PERFORMANCES. *Cast*: EDDIE: Ernest Truex; ELSIE: Alice Dovey.

The revival was originally performed in 7/75, and again in 10/75, by the Goodspeed Opera House, in Connecticut (Michael P. Price had been executive director there since 1968, and had instituted the policy of one new production and two musical revivals a year). There were some changes in the music and lyrics, and in the final scene (set at the renamed Honeymoon Inn—it had been the Rip Van Winkle Inn in the original). The following songs were in the 1915 original, but not in this revival: "The Same Old Game," "On the Shore at Le Lei Wi," "If I Find the Girl," "The Fashion Show," and "I Wish I Had a Million." Before Broadway James Harder replaced Eddie Phillips in the cast.

The Broadway Run. BOOTH THEATRE, 12/21/75–9/5/76. 19 previews. 288 PERFORMANCES. The Goodspeed Opera House production, PRESENTED BY David Merrick, Max Brown, Byron Goldman; MUSIC: Jerome Kern; LYRICS: various authors; BOOK: Guy Bolton; BASED ON the 1911 farce *Over Night*, by Philip Bartholomae; DIRECTOR: Bill Gile; CHOREOGRAPHER: Dan Siretta; SETS/LIGHTING: Fred Voelpel; COSTUMES: David Toser; MUSICAL DIRECTOR: Russell Warner, *Lawrence Blank*; ARRANGEMENTS: Russell Warner; PRESS: Max Eisen, Warren Pincus, Judy Jacksina; SPECIAL CONSULTANT: Alfred Simon; GENERAL MANAGER: Helen L. Nickerson; COMPANY MANAGER: G. Warren McClane; PRODUCTION STAGE MANAGER: Don Judge; STAGE MANAGER: Mark Potter; ASSISTANT STAGE MANAGER: Pat Trott. *Cast*: STEWARD: James Harder; MR. DICK RIVERS: David Christmas (1); MADAME MATROPPO: Travis Hudson (5); MISS ELSIE LILLY: Cynthia Wells (8); MONSIEUR DE ROUGEMONT: Joel Craig (2); MRS. GEORGINA KETTLE: Spring Fairbank (3); MR. EDDIE KETTLE: Charles Repole (6); MR. PERCY DARLING: Nicholas Wyman (9); MRS. ELSIE DARLING: Virginia Seidel (7); AL CLEVELAND: James Harder (4); MISS LILY POND: Wendy Young; MISS CHRYSTAL POOL: Karen Crossley; MISS CARRIE CLOSEWELL: Gillian Scalici, *Jo-Ann Cifala*; MISS ALWYS INNIT: Robin Herbert; MR. TAYLEURS DUMME: Russ Beasley; MR. DAYR THURST: Jon Engstrom; MR. DUSTIN STACKS: Larry McMillian; MR. ROLLO MUNN: Hal Shane, *James Stein*. *Understudies*: Eddie: Jon Engstrom; Elsie Darling: Robin Herbert; Al/Steward: Joel Craig; Mme Matroppo: Helon Blount; Dick/de Rougemont: Russ Beasley; Percy: David Christmas; Georgina: Jo-Ann Cifala; Elsie Lilly: Wendy Young. *Swing Ensemble*: Candy Darling & Tony Juliano. *Act 1*: A Hudson River Dayliner: "We're on Our Way" (l: Schuyler Greene) (Company), "Some Sort of Somebody (All the Time)" (l: Elsie Janis) (Elsie Lilly & Dick), "(When You Wear a) 13 Collar" (l: Schuyler Greene) (Eddie), "Bungalow in Quogue" * (l: P.G. Wodehouse) [from *The Riviera Girl*] (Elsie Darling & Percy), "Isn't it Great to Be Married" (l: Schuyler Greene) (Elsie Darling, Georgina, Eddie, Percy), "Good Night Boat" * (l: Anne Caldwell & Frank Craven) [from *The Night Boat*] (Company), "Left-All-Alone-Again Blues" * (l: Anne Caldwell) [from

The Night Boat] (Elsie Darling), "Hot Dog!" * (l: Anne Caldwell) [from *The Bunch and Judy*] (Company), "If You're a Friend of Mine" * (l: Harry Graham) [from *Lady Mary*] (Elsie Darling & Eddie), "Wedding Bells Are Calling Me" (l: Harry B. Smith) (Company). *Act II*: *Scene 1* Lobby of Honeymoon Inn, in the Catskills; that evening: "Honeymoon Inn" * (l: P.G. Wodehouse) [from *Have a Heart*] (Elsie Lilly & Company), "I've Got to Dance" * (l: Schuyler Greene) [dropped from the original production of *Very Good Eddie*] (de Rougemont & Company), "Moon of Love" * (l: Anne Caldwell) [from *The Beauty Prize*] (Mme Matroppo & Company), "Old Boy Neutral" (l: Schuyler Greene) (Elsie Lilly & Dick), "Babes in the Wood" (l: Schuyler Greene) (Elsie Darling & Eddie); *Scene 2* The same; the next morning: "Katy-Did" * (l: Harry B. Smith) [from *Oh, I Say!*] (Mme Matroppo), "Nodding Roses" (l: Schuyler Greene & Herbert Reynolds) (Elsie Lilly & Dick), Finale (l: John E. Hazard & Herbert Reynolds) (Company).

Note: an asterisk means that those songs were not in the 1915 original.

Broadway reviews were excellent. The show received Tony nominations for direction of a musical, and for Virginia Seidel and Charles Repole.

After Broadway. PICCADILLY THEATRE, London, 3/23/76. **Cast:** ELSIE DARLING: Prue Clarke; EDDIE: Richard Freeman; GEORGINA: Cookie Weymouth; PERCY: Nigel Williams; MME MATROPPO: Gita Denise; DICK: Robert Swan; ELSIE LILLY: Mary Barrett; AL DALLAS: John Blythe (the character's last name was changed for the London run); DE ROUGEMONT: Teddy Green.

TOUR. Opened on 10/4/76, at the Hanna Theatre, Cleveland, and closed on 1/8/77, at the Shubert Theatre, Boston. **Cast:** AL/STEWARD: Benny Baker; ELSIE: Virginia Seidel; GEORGINA: Spring Fairbank; MME MATROPPO: Travis Hudson; LILY: Candy Darling; CRYSTAL: Kim Carter; EDDIE: J.J. Jepson. **Understudy:** Eddie: Jon Engstrom.

GOODSPEED OPERA HOUSE, Conn., 8/13/03–10/5/03. Previews from 7/11/03. DIRECTOR: B.T. McNicholl; CHOREOGRAPHER: Dan Siretta; SETS: John Coyne; COSTUMES: Suzy Benzinger; LIGHTING: Richard Pilbrow; MUSICAL DIRECTOR: Michael O'Flaherty; ORCHESTRATIONS: Dan DeLange. **Cast:** Perry Ojeda, Donna Lynne Champlin, Jay Douglas, Gerry Vichi, Ann Kittredge, Christianne Tisdale. The production avoided the power blackout of 8/14/03 when the theatre's own generator kicked in; real power went back on for Act II.

731. *Via Galactica*

An all-music musical, in 2 acts and 7 parts. The dialogue was sung in opera style. A bunch of non-conformists on an asteroid 1,000 years in the future (2972). Life has become homogenized and controlled. Everyone wears a permanent spinning hat to control their emotions. Gabriel is a conditioned Earthman. But, on the forgotten asteroid Ithaca, a group of hardy individualists, led by Dr. Isaacs, with his beautiful wife Omaha, plans to take his people out of Earth's orbit, to the stars for a fresh start. Earth, however, objects. Six trampolines were used to suggest weightlessness.

Before Broadway. Originally titled *Up!*, this was the first musical to play in the new Uris Theatre. Broadway previews began on 11/6/72 (delayed from 10/30/72) and the official opening was delayed from 11/19 to 11/21, then to 11/28. Edloe (who had been playing one of the Blue People) replaced Louise Heath as April (Edloe had been understudy) before Broadway, and Chuck Cissel replaced Bill Starr.

The Broadway Run. URIS THEATRE, 11/28/72–12/2/72. 15 previews from 11/6/72. 7 PERFORMANCES. PRESENTED BY George W. George & Barnard S. Straus, in association with Nat Shapiro; MUSIC: Galt MacDermot; LYRICS: Christopher Gore; BOOK: Christopher Gore (story) & Judith Ross (musical dialogue); CONCEIVED BY/DIRECTOR: Peter Hall; CHOREOGRAPHER: George Faison; SETS/COSTUMES: John Bury; LIGHTING: Lloyd Burlingame; SOUND: Jack Shearing; MUSICAL DIRECTOR: Thomas Pierson; ORCHESTRATIONS: Bhen Lanzaroni, Horace Ott, Danny Hurd; VOCAL ARRANGEMENTS: Joyce Brown; PRESS: Solters/

Sabinson/Roskin; CASTING: Shirley Rich & Ellie Heller; GENERAL MANAGERS: George Thorn & Leonard A. Mulhern; PRODUCTION STAGE MANAGER: William Dodds; STAGE MANAGER: Marnell Sumner; ASSISTANT STAGE MANAGER: Haig Shepherd. **Cast:** THE STORYTELLER: Irene Cara (6); GABRIEL FINN: Raul Julia (1) ☆; HELS MIKELLI: Damon Evans (4); APRIL WHITNEY: Edloe (5); OMAHA: Virginia Vestoff (2) ☆; DR. ISAACS: Keene Curtis (3) ☆; PROVO: Bill Starr; ON EARTH: SPOKESMAN: James Dybas; OLD MAN: Chuck Cissel; THE BLUE PEOPLE: Mark Baker, Jacqueline Britt, Melanie Chartoff, Richard De Russo, Sylvia Di Giorgio, Livia Genise, Marion Killinger, Toni Lund, Bob Spencer, Bonnie Walker; ON ITHACA: DIANE: Livia Genise; NICKLAS: Peter Nissen; THE ROUSTABOUT: Alex Ander; THE COOK: Mark Baker; THE MUTE'S FRIEND: Robert Blankshine; THE GYPSY: Jacqueline Britt; THE BOY: Ralph Carter (7); THE GEOLOGIST: Melanie Chartoff; THE STUDENT: Chuck Cissel; THE MUTE: Lily Cockerille; THE LADY: Lorrie Davis; THE MECHANIC: Richard De Russo; THE TEACHER: Sylvia Di Giorgio; THE ENTERTAINER: James Dybas; THE ARTIST: Edloe [role cut before Broadway] [end of Ithaca sequence]; THE WRITER: Livia Genise; THE POLITICIAN: Marion Killinger; THE CHILD: Toni Lund; THE CRIPPLE: Veronica Redd; THE TAILOR: James Rivers; THE CARPENTER: Richard Ryder; THE DOCTOR: Stan Shaw; THE GAMBLER: Leon Spelman; THE JANITOR: Bob Spencer; THE NURSE: Bonnie Walker; THE GRANDMOTHER: J.H. Washington. **Understudies:** Gabriel: Richard De Russo; Omaha: Veronica Redd; Isaacs: James Dybas; Hels: Stan Shaw. **Swing Dancer:** Jorge Diaz. *Act I*: "Via Galactica" (Storyteller), "We Are Alone" (Blue People), "Helen of Troy" (Gabriel), "Oysters" (Hels & April), "The Other Side of the Sky" (Hels), "Children of the Sun" (Omaha), "Different" (April & Company), "Take Your Hat Off" (Omaha & Company), "Ilmar's Tomb" (Omaha), "Shall We Friend?" (Gabriel), "The Lady isn't Looking" (Omaha), "Hush" (Gabriel), "Cross on Over" (Isaacs, Omaha, Company), "The Gospel of Gabriel Finn" (Gabriel). *Act II*: "Terre Haute High" (April), "Life Wins" (Omaha), "The Great Forever Wagon" [cut before Broadway], "The Worm Germ" (Provo), "Isaacs' Equation" (Isaacs), "Dance the Dark Away!" (Storyteller & Company), "Four Hundred Girls Ago" (Gabriel), "All My Good Mornings" (Omaha), "Isaacs' Equation" (reprise) (Isaacs), "Children of the Sun" (reprise) (Omaha & Gabriel), "New Jerusalem" (Company).

The critics absolutely panned it.

732. *Victor/Victoria*

Set in Paris in the 1930s. Toddy is an aging drag-queen, whose idea it is to transform Victoria into Victor, a Polish count and female impersonator who finds fame and love with King, a Chicago gangster (who is somewhat confused).

Before Broadway. Dedicated by the producers to the memory of Henry Mancini, following whose death Frank Wildhorn was brought in to add numbers during the pre–Broadway tour. This show was in development for over 10 years. On 5/7/84 *Variety* announced an upcoming meeting between Blake Edwards, Henry Mancini and Leslie Bricusse to discuss the musical, to star Julie Andrews and Robert Preston. In 7/84 plans were shelved because Mr. Edwards had mononucleosis. Finally it got off the ground. Tryouts took place in Minneapolis. The Act II opener "Attitude" was replaced by "Louis Says." Hillett Gitter understudied the Balloon Man during Broadway previews; and Paul Schoeffler played the Choreographer and understudied King. The numbers "This is Not Going to Change My Life," "The Victoria Variations" ("I've No Idea Where I'm Going"), "Someone Else," "I Guess it's Time," "I Know Were I'm Going" were all cut during previews.

The Broadway Run. MARQUIS THEATRE, 10/25/95–7/27/97. 25 previews from 10/3/95. 738 PERFORMANCES. PRESENTED BY Edwards — Adams Theatrical (Blake Edwards & Tony Adams), Metropolitan Theatrical Entertainment (John Scher), Endemol Theatre Productions (Joop Van Den Ende & Robin De Levita), PolyGram Broadway Ventures (John Scher); MUSIC: Henry Mancini; LYRICS: Leslie Bricusse; BOOK/DIRECTOR: Blake Edwards; ADDITIONAL MUSICAL MATERIAL: Frank Wildhorn; BASED ON the 1982 Blake Edwards film of the same name, starring Julie Andrews, James Garner & Robert Preston, which in turn had been based on the 1933 German film *Viktor und Viktoria*, conceived by Hans Hoemburg and written by Rheinhold Schuenzer; CHOREOGRAPHER: Rob Marshall; CREATIVE ASSOCIATE CHOREOGRAPHER: Kathleen Marshall; SETS: Robin Wagner; COSTUMES: Willa Kim; LIGHTING: Jules Fisher & Peggy Eisenhauer; SOUND: Peter Fitzgerald; MUSICAL DIRECTOR/VOCAL ARRANGEMENTS: Ian Fraser; ORCHESTRATIONS: Billy Byers; DANCE & INCIDENTAL MUSIC: David Krane; CAST RECORDING on Philips; PRESS: Cromarty & Company; CASTING: Johnson — Liff; GENERAL MANAGEMENT: Niko Associates; COMPANY MANAGERS: Erich Hamner & Alex Holt; PRODUCTION STAGE MANAGER: Arturo E. Porazzi; STAGE MANAGER: Bonnie L. Becker; ASSISTANT STAGE MANAGERS: Kimberly Russell & Mireya Hepner. **Cast:** CARROLL TODD ("TODDY"): Tony Roberts (2) ☆; LES BOYS: Michael Demby-Cain, Angelo Fraboni, Darren Lee, Michael O'Donnell, Vince Pesce, Arte Phillips, Rocker Verastique (gone by 96–97), *Bill Burns* (added by 96–97), *Peter Lentz* (added by 96–97), *Gregory Mitchell* (added by 96–97); SIMONE KALISTO: Leslie Stevens [new role added by 96–97]; RICHARD DI NARDO: Michael Cripe (8); COSMETIC PRESIDENT: Cynthia Sophiea [new role added by 96–97]; DEVIANT HUSBAND: Ken Land [new role added by 96–97]; HENRI LABISSE: Adam Heller (6); GREGOR: Casey Nicholaw, *Mason Roberts*; MADAME ROGET: Jennifer Smith, *Linda Gabler Romoff*; VICTORIA GRANT: Julie Andrews (1) ☆, *Anne Runolfsson* (during Miss Andrews' illness for a week beginning 1/13/95; Miss Runolfsson would go on over 100 times in place of Miss Andrews & Miss Minnelli, and also play matinees from 1996), *Liza Minnelli* (1/7/97–2/97, during Miss Andrews' vacation), *Julie Andrews* (2/2/97–6/8/97), *Raquel Welch* (from 6/10/97); CHOREOGRAPHER: Christopher Innvar, *Neal Benari*; MISS SELMER: Cynthia Sophiea; ANDRE CASSELL: Richard B. Shull (5); JAZZ SINGER: Devin Richards, *Todd Hunter*; JAZZ HOT MUSICIANS: Michael Demby-Cain, Arte Phillips, Rocker Verastique (gone by 96–97), *Bill Burns* (added by 96–97), *Gregory Mitchell* (added by 96–97); JAZZ HOT ENSEMBLE: Roxane Barlow, Caitlin Carter, Pascale Faye, Angelo Fraboni, Amy Heggins, Darren Lee, Aixa M. Rosario Medina, Casey Nicholaw, Michael O'Donnell, Cynthia Onrubia, Vince Pesce, *Scott Wise* (1997–6/97); NORMA CASSIDY: Rachel York (4) (until 4/27/97), *Tara O'Brien*; KING MARCHAN: Michael Nouri (3) ☆, *Brian Sutherland* (a few weeks before the end of the run); SQUASH (MR. BERNSTEIN): Gregory Jbara (8), *Tom Sardinia* (stood in for Mr. Jbara when he joined the cast of *Chicago* for 9 weeks); LOUIS SAYS ENSEMBLE: Roxane Barlow, Michael Demby-Cain, Caitlin Carter, Pascale Faye, Angelo Fraboni, Amy Heggins, Darren Lee, Aixa M. Rosario Medina, Michael O'Donnell, Cynthia Onrubia, Vince Pesce, Arte Phillips, Devin Richards, Jennifer Smith, Cynthia Sophiea, Rocker Verastique (gone by 96–97), *Bill Burns* (added by 96–97), *Gregory Mitchell* (added by 96–97); CHAMBERMAID: Jennifer Smith [role cut by 96–97]; APACHE DANCERS: Angelo Fraboni, Darren Lee, Michael O'Donnell, Vince Pesce, Arte Phillips, Rocker Verastique (gone by 96–97), *Bill Burns* (added by 96–97), *Gregory Mitchell* (added by 96–97); STREET SINGER: Tara O'Brien, *Sally Ann Tumas*; NORMA'S GIRLS: Roxane Barlow, Caitlin Carter, Pascale Faye, Amy Heggins, Aixa M. Rosario Medina, Cynthia Onrubia; SAL ANDRETTI: Ken Land; HILLELLA, THE BALLOON BUFFOON: Linda Gabler Romoff [new role by 96–97]; CLAM: Mark Lotito, *Tom Sardinia, George Dudley*; JUKE: Casey Nicholaw, *Mason Roberts*; VICTOR/VICTORIA ENSEMBLE: Roxane Barlow, Michael Demby-Cain, Caitlin Carter, Pascale Faye, Angelo Fraboni, Amy Heggins, Darren Lee, Aixa M. Rosario Medina, Tara O'Brien, Michael O'Donnell, Cynthia Onrubia, Vince Pesce, Arte Phillips, Devin Richards, Jennifer Smith, Rocker Verastique. **Standbys:** Victoria: Anne Runolfsson; Todd: Alex Wipf. **Understudies:** Victoria: Tara O'Brien; Todd: Ken Land; King: Christopher Innvar, *Neal Benari*; Norma: Roxane Barlow & Caitlin Carter, *Kimberly Lyon*; Squash: Mark Lotito, *Tom Sardinia, George Dudley*; Sal: Mark Lotito, *Neal Benari*; Henri: Casey Nicholaw, *Mason Roberts*; Richard: Angelo Fraboni, *Michael O'Donnell*; Jazz Singer: Michael Demby-Cain; Street Singer: Jennifer Smith, *Linda Gabler Romoff*; Cassell: *Tom Sardinia* & *George Dudley* (2nd season only). **Swings:** Mark S. Hoebee, Elizabeth Mozer, Scott Taylor, *Joanne Manning, Robert M. Armitage, Robert Ashford*. **Orchestra:** CONCERTMASTER: Dale Stuckenbruck; VIOLINS: Rebekah Johnson, Karl Kawahara, Karen Karlsrud; VIOLAS: Richard Spencer & Anne-Marie Bedney; CELLO: Diane Barer; BASS: Richard Sarpola; WOODWINDS: Edward Joffe, Albert Regni, Dan Wieloszynski, Kenneth Dybisz, John Campo; TRUMPETS:

John Frosk, Danny Cahn, Bud Burridge; TROMBONES: Jim Pugh & George Flynn; GUITAR: Bob Rose; DRUMS: Perry Cavari; PERCUSSION: Benjamin Herman; ACCORDION: Charlie Giordano; KEYBOARD: Joseph Thalken. **Act I**: Overture (Orchestra); *Scene 1* Small Square/Chez Lui: "Paris by Night" (Toddy & Les Boys); *Scene 2* Small Square/Toddy's flat: "If I Were a Man" (Victoria) [dropped during the run], "Trust Me" (m: Frank Wildhorn) (Toddy & Victoria); *Scene 3* Backstage at Cassell's; *Scene 4* Cassell's Nightclub: "Le Jazz Hot" (Victor & Ensemble); *Scene 5* Backstage at Cassell's; *Scene 6* Left Bank Cafe: "The Tango" (Victor & Norma); *Scene 7* Paris hotel suites: "Paris Makes Me Horny" (Norma), "Crazy World" (Victoria) [when Raquel Welch replaced Miss Andrews in 6/97 this number was replaced with "Who Can I Tell?" (m/l: Leslie Bricusse)]. **Act II**: *Scene 1* Cassell's Nightclub: "Louis Says" (m: Frank Wildhorn) (Victor & Ensemble) [this scene and this number were cut for several performances in mid–April 1996 after Miss Andrews bruised an ankle performing it]; *Scene 2* Victoria's dressing-room; *Scene 3* Paris Hotel Suites: "King's Dilemma" (King); *Scene 4* Chez Lui: "Apache" (Les Boys), "You and Me" (Toddy & Victor); *Scene 5* Small Square: "Paris by Night" (reprise) (Street Singer); *Scene 6* Paris Hotel Suites: "Almost a Love Song" (King & Victoria); *Scene 7* Chicago Speakeasy: "Chicago, Illinois" (Norma & The Girls); *Scene 8* Paris Hotel Suites: "Living in the Shadows" (m: Frank Wildhorn) (Victoria); *Scene 9* Cassell's Nightclub: "Victor/Victoria" (Victoria, Toddy, Company).

Broadway reviews were divided; Julie Andrews got raves. On 1/13/96 Anne Runolfsson, the understudy, replaced Julie when she got the flu (Miss Runolfsson would play matinees from now on). Miss Andrews was off for a week, and attendance dropped drastically. On 2/28/96 Miss Andrews had her gall bladder removed, and was out for two weeks. On 5/8/96 she refused her 1996 Tony nomination because no one else in the show was also nominated. In 1/97 Liza Minnelli stood in for Julie Andrews who was on vacation. At the same time Tony Roberts came down with the flu on 1/26/97. On 2/2/97 Liza finished her month-long replacement gig by missing her third performance in a week with a throat condition. Julie Andrews finally left the show on 6/8/97 (a week later than planned), and Raquel Welch took over on 6/10/97 (she was due to have taken over on 6/3/97). Miss Welch missed only one performance, and Anne Runolfsson stood in (she played Victoria as an American; up to then she had always played her as a British girl). The show, which cost $8.5 million, lost half its investment. There was a long legal wrangle with the insurance company, who claimed that Julie Andrews did not state pre-existing conditions that would disable her from the show. So they failed to compensate the production.

After Broadway. TOUR. The first national tour was fraught with problems stemming from Julie Andrews' vocal problems. This tour was originally going to open in Houston, with Miss Andrews (although Raquel Welch was the first to be considered), in a re-worked version, to be directed by Blake Edwards, at the Theatre Under the Stars (TUTS) on 5/16/97, and to go on to a two-year tour from there. Then it was re-scheduled for previews to begin on 8/26/97. That was changed to 10/14/97, the new venue being Seattle. Miss Andrews' throat surgery pushed that date back to 11/25/97, and Houston became the venue again. Then it was pushed back to the spring of 1998. Then Miss Andrews dropped out, and it was re-scheduled for 5/98, to open in Houston, with Anne Runolfsson as Victoria. In 4/98 Anthony Newley, Michael Nouri and Tara O'Brien all signed up. However, cancer forced Mr. Newley to abandon the Toddy role. Mark S. Hoebee became the new director, and Dan Mojica the choreographer. There were only two weeks of rehearsals. It finally opened on 5/14/98, in HOUSTON. **Cast:** VICTORIA: Anne Runolfsson; KING: Michael Nouri; NORMA: Tara O'Brien. The number "Paris Makes Me Horny" was dropped.

TOUR. Opened on 9/8/98, in Portland, Oregon, and closed on 6/27/99, at the Palace Theatre, Cleveland. PRESENTED BY NETworks/Jeriko; DIRECTOR: Mark S. Hoebee; CHOREOGRAPHER: Dan Mojica. **Cast:** VICKIE: Toni Tennille [of Captain & Tennille fame]; KING: Dennis Cole; TODDIE: Jamie Ross.

PAPER MILL PLAYHOUSE, New Jersey, 2000. DIRECTOR: Mark S. Hoebee; CHOREOGRAPHER: Arte Phillips; SETS: Robin Wagner; COSTUMES: Willa Kim; MUSICAL DIRECTOR: Tom Helm. **Cast:** Lee Roy Reams, Judy McLane, Tara O'Brien, Davis Hall, Robert Cuccioli, Jody Ashworth, Dale Hensley.

Vienna Life see 748

733. *Wait a Minim!*

A South African musical revue. A performance of folk songs from Africa, Europe and Asia, played on a great variety of instruments, with occasional dances and comedy pantomimes satirizing political and social eccentricities, particularly the South African policy of apartheid.

Before Broadway. It ran in South Africa, Rhodesia, and London.
The Broadway Run. JOHN GOLDEN THEATRE, 3/7/66–4/15/67. 9 previews from 2/28/66. 456 PERFORMANCES. PRESENTED BY Frank Productions (Frank Loesser); MUSIC/LYRICS: various writers; Developed by: Leon Gluckman; DIRECTOR: Leon Gluckman; CHOREOGRAPHER: Frank Staff & Kendrew Lascelles; DECOR/LIGHTING: Frank Rembach & Leon Gluckman; DESIGN & LIGHTING SUPERVISOR: Klaus Holm; COSTUMES: Heather Macdonald-Rouse; COSTUME SUPERVISOR: Patton Campbell; MUSICAL DIRECTOR/ARRANGEMENTS: Andrew Tracey; CAST RECORDING on London Records; PRODUCTION SUPERVISOR: Lanier Davis; PRESS: Reuben Rabinovitch & John Springer Associates; GENERAL MANAGER: Ira Bernstein; STAGE MANAGER: Frank Rembach. *Cast:* Andrew Tracey, Paul Tracey, Dana Valery, Kendrew Lascelles, Michel Martel, Nigel Pegram, April Olrich, Sarah Atkinson. *Musical Accompaniments:* Andrew Tracey: GUITAR, GUITAR-LUTE, BAMBOO PIPE, PORTUGUESE GUITAR, MANDOLIN, TREBLE & SOPRANO RECORDERS, RHODESIAN MBIRA, CHOPI TIMBILA, LOZI DRUMS, TUBA, BAGPIPES, INDIAN TABLA DRUMS, CLARINET, TRINIDADIAN STEEL DRUM, SOUSAPHONE, INDIAN GONG; Paul Tracey: GUITAR, H.M. BULL FIDDLE, FLUTE, CHOPI TIMBILA, LOZI DRUMS, PICCOLO, MELODICA, SQUEEZEBOX, BAGPIPES, KALIMBA, TUBA, SOUSAPHONE, INDIAN GONG; Nigel Pegram: GUITAR, H.M. BULL FIDDLE, DOUBLE RESPIRATORY LINGUAPHONE, LOZI DRUMS, BAGPIPES, JAPANESE KOTO ZITHER, TROMBONE, CHOPI TIMBILA, PENNY WHISTLE, INDIAN TANPURA DRONE; Kendrew Lascelles: TRUMPET; The Company: OTHER PERCUSSION INSTRUMENTS. THEMES, Sketches and "Musical Numbers." *Part I:* THIS IS THE LAND: "Ndinosara Nani?" (Karanga folk song, Southern Rhodesia) (Andrew, Michel, Nigel, Dana, Paul), "Hoe Ry Die Boere" (Afrikaans folk song) (Nigel, Paul, Andrew), "This is Worth Fighting For" (Sarah) [this number was replaced during the run by "Home Sweet Home"], "Subuhi Sana" (Swahili) (Andrew), "Jikel' Emaweni" (Xhosa fighting song, Transkei) (arr: Miriam Makeba) (Dana); DINGERE DINGALE: "Ajade Papa" (Tamil lullaby) (Michel), "Dingere Dingale" (Tamil song) (Company), Tuba Man (Kendrew); OVER THE HILLS: "I Know Where I'm Going" (Irish folk song) (Paul, Sarah, Andrew), "Over the Hills" (April & Andrew), "I Gave My Love a Cherry" (English folk song) (Paul, Dana, Michel, Nigel, Andrew) [end of theme]; "Black White Calypso" (m/l: Jeremy Taylor) (Nigel); DIE MEISTERTRINKER: "Deutsches Weinlied" (Company), "Gretl's Cow" (April), "Eine kleine Bombardonmusik" (by Mozart) (Nigel, Paul, Andrew, Kendrew), "Watschplattlanz" (Company) [end of theme]; "Butter Milk Hill" (Irish-American) (Dana) [this number was replaced after opening by "Johnny Soldier" (Irish-American) (Dana)], "Aria" (Paul); OUT OF FOCUS: Snap Happy (April & Kendrew), "Hoshoryu" (Japanese folk song) (Michel & Sarah), The Gentle Art (Kendrew, Michel, Paul) [end of theme]; "Dirty Old Town" (m/l: Ewan MacColl) (Andrew, Paul, Nigel, Dana), "Last Summer" (Andrew, Paul, Nigel, Kendrew); VIVE LA DIFFERENCE: "Lalirette" (Paul, Andrew, Michel, Nigel), "Le roi a fait battre tambour" (medieval ballad) (Michel, Nigel, Paul, Andrew), Tour de France (Kendrew, April, Andrew, Paul, Michel) [end of theme]; "A Piece of Ground" (m/l: Jeremy Taylor) (Nigel), "Ayama" (Andrew, Paul, Michel); NORTH OF THE 'POPO: Professor Piercing: Paul; The Chairman: Nigel. "Mgeniso waMgodo waShambini" (Chopi timbila) (Andrew, Paul, Nigel), "Kupura Kupika" (pounding song, Nyasaland) (Sarah, Dana, April), "The Izicatulo Gumboot Dance" (Company). Part II: TUNES OF GLORY: "The Wee Cooper o' Fife" (Doric diddling) (Paul, Andrew, Nigel), "Red, Red Rose" (Robert Burns) (Paul) [end of theme]; "Hammer Song" (m/l: Pete Seeger & Lee Hayes) (Andrew, Nigel, Michel, Paul), "London Talking Blues" (m/l: Jeremy Taylor) (Nigel), "The Love Life of a Gondolier" (Kendrew, Michel, April), "Foyo" (Hait-

ian patois lullaby) (Paul, Andrew, Nigel), "Cool" (m/l: Andrew & Paul Tracey) (Dana, Paul, Nigel, Andrew), On Guard (Kendrew & April); SIR OSWALD SODDE: Opening Night (Company), "Sir Oswald Sodde" (m/l: Jeffrey Smith) (Andrew, Sarah, Nigel, Paul, Michel), "Table Bay" (Cape Malay) (arr/adapted by Stanley Glasser & Adolf Wood) (Dana); THIS IS SOUTH AFRICA: "Chuzi Mama Gwabi Gwabi" (Marabi dance song) (Dana & Michel), "Celeste Aida" (Michel), "Cingoma Chakabaruka" (Tumbuka or Henga party song, Nyasaland) (Company), "Skalo-Zwi" (m: Stanley Glasser; l: Gwigwi Mrwebe) (Pedi pipe dance specially arranged by Andrew Tracey) (Dana & Company), "Samandoza-we!" (Ndau, Southern Rhodesia) (Company), "Amasalela" (Baca fighting song, Transkei) (Company).

Due to creative staging, among other things (including very good Broadway reviews), it ran on Broadway for over a year.

After Broadway. For the subsequent U.S. tour the replacement number "Home Sweet Home" was kept in (and "This is Worth Fighting For" was cut), and "Jikel' Emaweni" was also cut. "Johnny Soldier" was also kept in (it had replaced "Butter Milk Hill" during the Broadway run).

734. *Walking Happy*

Set in the industrial town of Salford, Lancashire, in 1880. Hobson is a bootmaker. He has three daughters, and is determined to hang on to the eldest, Maggie, an intelligent and fiercely capable girl, who runs his life and manages his business. However, Maggie wants to marry Will, her father's illiterate but skilled employee (in the play he was the crippled apprentice). Will is engaged to another woman, and is not interested in the domineering Maggie, but Maggie is a great saleswoman, and she sees great business possibilities.

Before Broadway. After the straight play *Hobson's Choice* was revived very successfully in London in 1964, it was finally taken up as a musical by Feuer & Martin in 1965 (it was their last, and they produced it at same time as Skyscraper). The musical was originally called *The Bespoke Lover*. Mary Martin was going to star, and the producers were going to shift the story from Lancashire to a Pennsylvania coal-mining town. However, Miss Martin's touring commitments in *Hello, Dolly!* got in the way, and Louise Troy got the role. Roger Hirson replaced Ketti Frings, but she retained co-librettist billing. Tryout reviews were quite good. The numbers "Circle This Day on the Calendar," "Love Will Find a Way—They Say" and "Very Close to Wonderful" were not used.

The Broadway Run. LUNT—FONTANNE THEATRE, 11/26/66–4/16/67. 3 previews from 11/24/66. 161 PERFORMANCES. PRESENTED BY Cy Feuer & Ernest Martin, by arrangement with Lester Linsk; MUSIC: James Van Heusen; LYRICS: Sammy Cahn; BOOK: Roger O. Hirson & Ketti Frings; BASED ON the 1915 British comedy Hobson's Choice, by Harold Brighouse; DIRECTOR: Cy Feuer; CHOREOGRAPHER: Danny Daniels; SETS/LIGHTING: Robert Randolph; COSTUMES: Robert Fletcher; MUSICAL DIRECTOR/VOCAL ARRANGEMENTS: Herbert Grossman; ORCHESTRATIONS: Larry Wilcox; DANCE MUSIC ARRANGEMENTS: Ed Scott; PRESS: Merle Debuskey, Violet Welles, Lawrence Belling; COMPANY MANAGER: Milton M. Pollack; PRODUCTION STAGE MANAGER: Phil Friedman; STAGE MANAGER: Jack Leigh; ASSISTANT STAGE MANAGER: Merritt Thompson. **Cast:** HENRY HORATIO HOBSON: George Rose (3) ✩; GEORGE BEENSTOCK: Ed Bakey (4), Leonard Drum; MINNS: Thomas Boyd; DENTON: Casper Roos; TUDSBURY: Carl Nicholas; HEELER: Michael Quinn; MAGGIE HOBSON: Louise Troy (2) ✩, Anne Rogers (from 4/4/67); ALICE HOBSON: Sharon Dierking; VICKIE HOBSON: Gretchen Van Aken; ALBERT BEENSTOCK: James B. Spann; FREDDIE BEENSTOCK: Michael Berkson; MRS. HEPWORTH: Emma Trekman (6); FOOTMAN: Steven Jacobs; TUBBY WADLOW: Gordon Dilworth (5); WILL MOSSOP: Norman Wisdom (1) ✩; ADA FIGGINS: Jane Laughlin; MRS. FIGGINS: Lucille Benson; THE FIGGINS BROTHERS: Ian Garry & Al Lanti; CUSTOMER: Eleanor Bergquist; HANDBILL BOY: Richard Sederholm; THIEF: Burt Bier; POLICEMAN: Chad Block; BEGGAR: Richard Korthaze; TOWNSMEN: Burt Bier, Chad Block, Thomas Boyd, Ian Garry, Gene Gavin, Steven Jacobs, Richard Korthaze, Al Lanti, Carl Nicholas,

Don Percassi, Michael Quinn, Casper Roos, Richard Sederholm, Dan Siretta; TOWNSWOMEN: Eleanor Bergquist, Diane L. Blair, Sandra Brewer, Ellen Graff, Marian Haraldson, Jane Laughlin, Marie Patrice O'Neill, Nada Rowand, Anne Wallace. *Standby:* Will: Byron Mitchell. *Understudies:* Maggie: Eleanor Bergquist; Hobson: Michael Quinn; George: Casper Roos; Tubby: Burt Bier; Mrs. Hepworth: Nada Rowand; Alice: Sandra Brewer; Vickie: Jane Laughlin; Freddie: Richard Sederholm; Albert: Dan Siretta. *Act I: Scene 1* The Moonrakers pub; night: "Think of Something Else" (Hobson, Beenstock, Townsmen); *Scene 2* Hobson's bootery: "Where Was I?" (Maggie); *Scene 3* The cellar of the bootery: "How D'Ya Talk to a Girl?" (Will & Tubby); *Scene 4* The Moonrakers pub: "Clog and Grog" (Townsmen); *Scene 5* The park: "If I Be Your Best Chance" (Will); *Scene 6* A street in the poor section of Salford: "A Joyful Thing" (dance) (Will, Mrs. Figgins, Ada, Townspeople); *Scene 7* An alley lit by gaslight: "What Makes it Happen?" (Will); *Scene 8* The bootery: "Use Your Noggin" (Maggie, Vickie, Alice). *Act II: Scene 1* Mrs. Hepworth's sitting room: "You're Right, You're Right" (Maggie) [dropped during the run], "I'll Make a Man of the Man" (Maggie); *Scene 2* A cellar: "Walking Happy" (Will, Maggie, Townspeople) [this number was originally cut from the movie Papa's Delicate Condition]; *Scene 3* Flat Iron Market: "Walking Happy" (concluded); *Scene 4* Will and Maggie's cellar: "I Don't Think I'm in Love" (Will & Maggie); *Scene 5* Outside the Moonrakers pub; three weeks later: "Such a Sociable Sort" (Hobson & Friends); *Scene 6* Outside Beenstock's corn-warehouse: "Such a Sociable Sort" (concluded) (Hobson & Friends); *Scene 7* Hobson's bootery: "It Might as Well Be Her" (Will & Tubby); *Scene 8* Inside Beenstock's corn warehouse: "People Who Are Nice" (Hobson) [dropped during the run]; *Scene 9* The Mossop Bootery: "You're Right, You're Right" (reprise) (Will, Maggie, Hobson), "I Don't Think I'm in Love" (reprise) (Will).

It got generally favorable reviews. Norman Wisdom, the British comic, as big as he was in his home country, wasn't appreciated in the USA, and the show lasted five months, despite the reviews. It received Tony Nominations for musical, composer & lyricist, choreography, and for Norman Widsom, Gordon Dilworth, and Louise Troy.

After Broadway. Norman Wisdom and Anne Rogers starred in the tour which opened on 4/25/67, and played the San Francisco and Los Angeles Civic Light Operas for 14 weeks. It was meant to have gone on to London, but it didn't.

735. *Welcome to the Club*

Set in minimum-security alimony prison in New York. Four husbands, two of whom are divorced and two separated. Their wives appear in a series of flashbacks, real visits, dream sequences, and as backup singers.

Before Broadway. It began as *Let 'em Rot*, and was read at the Actors Studio, New York. Then it had a run at the White Barn Theatre, Westport, Conn. DIRECTOR: Morton Da Costa. Then it had played at the Coconut Grove Playhouse, Miami, from 2/16/88. DIRECTOR: Frank Corsaro; CHOREOGRAPHER: Baayork Lee; SETS: David Jenkins; COSTUMES: Richard Schurkamp; LIGHTING: Fred Kolo; MUSICAL DIRECTOR: David Pogue; ORCHESTRATIONS: Joe Gianono. *Cast:* MILTON: Ron Orbach; BRUCE: William Parry; AARON: Martin Vidnovic; GUS/JUDGE LIVERIGHT: Charles Goff; CALVIN DORSET: Jackie J. Patterson; ARLENE: Marilyn Sokol; EVE: Karen Culliver; BETTY/LOIS DORSET: Cady Huffman; CAROL/MRS. VANDERALL: Patricia Ben Peterson; KEVIN: Dirk Lumbard; WINONA: Leilani Mickey. Then it moved to Broadway, with the new title and several characters cut. During Broadway previews Frank Corsaro was called in to help direct, and Larry Gelbart came in to doctor the show. At this point, in the cast Sharon Scruggs was replaced by Eve/Winona standby Sally Mayes. Some musical numbers were shifted around. The production cost $1.5 million.

The Broadway Run. MUSIC BOX THEATRE, 4/13/89–4/22/89. 20 previews. 12 PERFORMANCES. PRESENTED BY Cy Coleman, A.E. Hotchner, William H. Kessler Jr., and Michael M. Weatherly, in association with Raymond J. Greenwald; MUSIC: Cy Coleman; LYRICS: Cy Coleman & A.E. Hotchner; BOOK: A.E. Hotchner (based on his unproduced

play); DIRECTOR: Peter Mark Schifter; CHOREOGRAPHER: Patricia Birch; SETS: David Jenkins; COSTUMES: William Ivey Long; LIGHTING: Tharon Musser; SOUND: Otts Munderloh; MUSICAL DIRECTOR: David Pogue; ORCHESTRATIONS: Doug Katsaros; VOCAL ARRANGEMENTS: Cy Coleman & David Pogue; PRESS: Jeffrey Richards Associates; CASTING: Deborah Aquila & Don Pemrick; GENERAL MANAGEMENT: Richard Seader & Sylrich Management; COMPANY MANAGER: Paul B. Berkowsky; PRODUCTION STAGE MANAGER: Mary Porter Hall; STAGE MANAGER: John C. McNamara; ASSISTANT STAGE MANAGER: Victor Lukas. *Cast:* ARLENE MELTZER: Marilyn Sokol (2) ☆; MILTON MELTZER: Avery Schreiber (1) ☆; GUS BOTTOMLY: Bill Buell (9); AARON BATES: Scott Wentworth (5); BRUCE AIKEN: Samuel E. Wright (4); KEVIN BURSTETER: Scott Waara (7); BETTY BURSTETER: Jodi Benson (8); CAROL BATES: Marcia Mitzman (10); EVE AIKEN: Terri White (3); WINONA SHOOK: Sally Mayes (6). *Standbys:* Arlene/Betty/Carol: Joanna Glushak; Gus/Bruce: Sal Mistretta; Aaron/Kevin: Walter Hudson. *Orchestra:* KEYBOARDS: David Pogue, Donald Sosin, Lee Musiker; REEDS: Ken Hitchcock; GUITAR: Bob Rose; BASS: David Finck; CELLI: Marisol Espada & Astrid Schween; PERCUSSION: David Ratajczak. *Act I:* Overture, "A Place Called Alimony Jail" (Husbands & Wives), "Pay the Lawyer" (Husbands), "Mrs. Meltzer Wants the Money Now!" (Arlene & Husbands), "That's a Woman" (Bates, Carol, Wives), "Piece of Cake" (Eve & Aiken), "Rio" (Meltzer, Wives, Gus), "Holidays" (Arlene), "Meyer Chickerman" (Meltzer) [cut during previews], "The Trouble with You" (Bates, Carol, Husbands, Wives), "Mother-in-Law" (Husbands), "At My Side" (Aiken & Bursteter). *Act II:* "Southern Comfort" (Winona, Bates, Wives, Husbands), "The Two of Us" (Aiken & Meltzer), "It's Love! It's Love!" (Gus & Husbands), "(In) the Name of Love" (Carol), "Miami Beach" (Arlene & Husbands) [during previews it was by Arlene, Aiken, Bursteter, Bates, Gus], "Guilty" (Winona), "Love Behind Bars" (Winona, Bates, Wives), "At My Side" (reprise) (Bursteter & Betty), "It Wouldn't Be You" (Husbands & Wives).

Reviews were awful. It received Tony nominations for direction of a musical, and for Scott Wentworth.

After Broadway. GOODSPEED OPERA HOUSE, Conn., 5/7/98–5/31/98. This was a revised version, known as *Exactly Like You*. Set in and around a courtroom. After Goodspeed it had an Off Broadway run in New York, 4/14/99–5/9/99. Previews from 3/31/99. 31 PERFORMANCES. PRESENTED BY the York Theatre Company; DIRECTOR/CHOREOGRAPHER: Patricia Birch; SETS: James Morgan; COSTUMES: Richard Schurkamp; LIGHTING: Kirk Bookman; SOUND: Peter Hylenski; MUSICAL DIRECTOR/ORCHESTRATIONS: Doug Katsaros. *Cast:* TV COMMENTATOR: Tony Hastings; JUDGE MAXIMILIAN MELTZER: Doug Katsaros; KEVIN BURSTETER: Edward Staudenmayer; PRISCILLA VANDERHOSEN: Susan Mansur; EVE BURSTETER: Kate Levering; ARLENE MURPHY: Lauren Ward; MARTIN MURPHY: Michael McGrath; WINONA SHOOK: Blair Ross; AARON BATES: Robert Bartley; STENOGRAPHER: Donya Lane; LAMARR: Frank Gravis; JUROR: Donna Kelly. Overture, "Courtroom Cantata," "Southern Comfort," "Thanks to Mom," "Why Did You Have to Be a Lawyer?," "I Get Tired," "That's a Woman," "Cottage by the Sea," "In the Name of Love," "I Want the Best for Him," "Don't Mess Around with Your Mother-in-Law," "Good Day," "She Makes Me Laugh," "Rio," "At My Side," "No Further Questions, Please," "You're Good for Me," "Guilty," "Ain't He Cute?," "Ain't She Cute?," "Exactly Like You."

It was later revised as *Lawyers, Lovers and Lunatics*, and played at Metuchen, NJ, 2003. It began as a small tour, then went to Florida. *Cast:* Fred Barton, J. Brandon Savage, Thomas Cannizzaro, Stuart Ambrose, Susan Mansur, Barbara Walsh, Michael McGrath, Stacia Fernandez, Becky Gulsvig.

736. *West Side Story*

Set in the streets of the West Side of New York City, during the last days of summer, 1957. Two gangs, one American — the Jets, and one Puerto Rican — the Sharks, fight it out for control of a small patch of Manhattan turf. Tony is the Polish-American former leader of the Jets, who has decided to quit and go straight. Maria is the Puerto Rican dressmaker he meets at the high school dance. Tony kills Maria's brother Bernardo, leader of the Sharks, while trying to break up a rumble, and this sets off a deadly confrontation between the two gangs. Maria's best friend, Anita, urges Maria to stay away from Tony. Tony is killed by one of the Sharks, and Maria is left alone. There is no chorus. Each gang member has an identity and a history. The show used dance more adventurously than had ever been attempted before, and blended song, dance & book together more than ever.

Before Broadway. In 1949 Jerome Robbins was asked by an actor how *Romeo and Juliet* could be shown in a relevant way today. So, Mr. Robbins created the idea of two gangs on the Lower East Side of Manhattan, with a Jewish girl from Allen Street falling for an Italian boy from Mulberry Street. On 1/6/49 he called Leonard Bernstein about doing the music and lyrics, and on 1/10/49 the two met with Arthur Laurents, who would write the libretto, and they agreed to go for it. They developed this idea, and called it *East Side Story*. By April 1949 a draft of the first four scenes was ready. The title was changed to *Gangway!* However, all three men got involved in the musicalization of James M. Cain's book *Serenade*, which never got done. By 1954, when Arthur Laurents and Leonard Bernstein were talking in Hollywood, the New York gangs had changed nationalities, and Puerto Rican was now big, as reflected in the headlines of a newspaper they were looking at. They contacted Jerry Robbins, and the project was started again, on 9/6/55. The title changed to *West Side Story*. The musical demands on Leonard Bernstein became so great that he had to look for a collaborator, but Betty Comden & Adolph Green, who were the first choices, were busy in Hollywood. Stephen Sondheim had auditioned his songs for *Serenade*, and was approached to do the lyrics. But, he wanted to compose, and almost turned down the offer. However, his mentor, Oscar Hammerstein II, told him, "I think you ought to do this." He was hired. In the end he was given sole credit for the lyrics, even though Bernstein was his collaborator (some say the only reason Bernstein yielded his lyricist credits is that Sondheim actually helped him out by writing some of the music). The show took two years to complete, with Leonard Bernstein taking six months off to finish his score for *Candide*. Also, several producers turned it down, until Cheryl Crawford and Roger Stevens took an option on it. Miss Crawford was already in production when she opted out, and Hal Prince & Bobby Griffith took it over the day after *New Girl in Town* opened on Broadway. Within a week they had raised the necessary $300,000. Casting took six months, and rehearsals began on 7/8/57. The show had its world premiere at the National Theatre, Washington, DC, 8/19/57–9/7/57. It got raves. The number "Kids Ain't" (Anybodys, A-Rab, Baby John) was written in Washington, and rejected. Other numbers cut before Broadway were: "Mix!," "My Greatest Day!," "Once in Your Life," "This Turf is Ours," and "Up to the Moon." When it went to Philadelphia reviews were not so good. Not many changes were made on the road.

The Broadway Run. Winter Garden Theatre, 9/26/57–2/28/59; Broadway Theatre, 3/2/59–5/10/59; Winter Garden Theatre, 5/11/59–6/27/59. Total of 732 performances. Presented by Robert E. Griffith & Harold S. Prince, by arrangement with Roger L. Stevens; Music: Leonard Bernstein; Lyrics: Stephen Sondheim; Book: Arthur Laurents; Based on a 1949 conception by Jerome Robbins, which was based on the 1595 tragedy *Romeo and Juliet*, by William Shakespeare (unbilled); Director: Jerome Robbins; Assistant Director: Gerald Freedman; Choreographers: Jerome Robbins & Peter Gennaro; Assistant Choreographer: Grover Dale; Sets: Oliver Smith; Costumes: Irene Sharaff; Lighting: Jean Rosenthal; Sound: Sound Associates; Musical Director: Max Goberman; Orchestrations: Leonard Bernstein, with Sid Ramin & Irwin Kostal; Cast recording on Columbia; Press: Reuben Rabinovitch, Helen Richards, Howard Newman; Casting: Judith Abbott & Betty Wharton; General Manager: Carl Fisher; Company Manager: Clarence Jacobson; Production Stage Manager: Ruth Mitchell; Stage Manager: Harry Howell, *Lo Hurdin*; Assistant Stage Manager: George Lake. **Cast:** The Jets: Riff, the leader: Mickey Calin (5) (he later became movie star Michael Callan), *Tucker Smith*; Tony, his friend: Larry Kert (2); Action: Eddie Roll (8), *Gus Trikonis*; A-Rab: Tony Mordente (10), *Al DeSio*; Baby John: David Winters (9), *Eliot Feld*; Snowboy: Grover Dale (12); Big Deal: Martin

Charnin; Diesel: Hank Brunjes, *Bill Guske*; Gee-Tar: Tommy Abbott, *Harvey Hohnecker*; Mouthpiece: Frank Green; Tiger: Lowell Harris; Their Girls: Graziella: Wilma Curley, *Ethelyne Dunfee*; Velma: Carole D'Andrea; Minnie: Nanette Rosen, *Gina Trikonis*; Clarice: Marilyn D'Honau, *Beatrice Salten*; Pauline: Julie Oser; Anybodys: Lee Becker (7); The Sharks: Bernardo, the leader: Ken Le Roy (6), *George Marcy*; Maria, his sister: Carol Lawrence (1); Anita, his girl: Chita Rivera (3), *Muriel Bentley, Carmen Alvarez*; Chino, his friend: Jaime Sanchez; Pepe: George Marcy, *Jay Norman*; Indio: Noel Schwartz; Luis: Al DeSio, *Ed Kresley*; Anxious: Gene Gavin, *Gus Trikonis*; Nibbles: Ronnie Lee, *Alan Johnson*; Juano: Jay Norman, *Julius Fields*; Toro: Erne Castaldo; Moose: Jack Murray, *Don Zema*; Their Girls: Rosalia: Marilyn Cooper; Consuelo: Reri Grist, *Ann Marisse*; Teresita: Carmen Gutierrez, *Carmen Morales*; Francisca: Elizabeth Taylor, *Myrna White*; Estella: Lynn Ross, *Genii Prior*; Marguerita: Liane Plane, *Sandy Leeds*; The Adults: Doc: Art Smith (4), *Albert M. Ottenheimer*; Schrank: Arch Johnson (11); Krupke: William Bramley; Glad Hand: John Harkins, *Jerome Dempsey*. **Understudies**: Maria: Carmen Austin; Tony: Frank Green; Anita: Liane Plane, *Carmen Morales*; Riff: Hank Brunjes, *Tom Hasson*; A-Rab: Al DeSio, *Tommy Abbott*; Action: Noel Schwartz, Tommy *Abbott*; Baby John: Al DeSio; Anybodys: Carole D'Andrea; Bernardo: George Marcy, *Noel Schwartz & Jay Norman*; Chino: Erne Castaldo; Doc/Schrank: John Harkins, *Jerome Dempsey*; Krupke: Jack Murray, *Lowell Harris*; Snowboy: Martin Charnin; Big Deal: Grover Dale; Rosalia: Reri Grist, *Genii Prior*; Consuelo: Marilyn Cooper & Lynn Ross; Shark: Alan Johnson; Singer/Dancer: *Bill Guske*. **Act I**: *Scene 1* The Prologue: the Months Before; the street; 5:00 pm: Instrumental (danced by Jets & Sharks), "Jet Song" (danced by Riff, Baby John, Snowboy, Jets); *Scene 2* 5:30 pm; a back yard: "Something's Coming" (Tony); *Scene 3* 6:00 pm; the bridal shop; *Scene 4* 10:00 pm; the gym: The Dance at the Gym (Mambo instrumental) (danced by Jets & Sharks), "Maria" (Tony) [the big hit]; *Scene 5* 11:00 pm; a back alley: "Tonight" (Tony & Maria) [a big hit], "A-me-ri-ca" (Anita, Rosalia, Shark Girls) [a big hit]; *Scene 6* Midnight; Doc's drugstore: "Cool" (Riff & Jets); *Scene 7* The next day: 5:30 pm, the bridal shop: "One Hand, One Heart" (Tony & Maria); *Scene 8* 6:00 pm to 9:00 pm; the neighborhood: "Tonight" (quintet & chorus) (Company); *Scene 9* 9:00 pm; under the highway: "The Rumble" (instrumental—danced by Riff, Bernardo, Jets, Sharks). **Act II**: *Scene 1* 9:15 pm; the bedroom: "I Feel Pretty" (Maria, Rosalia, Teresita, Francisca), "Somewhere" (dream ballet danced by company & sung by Consuelo) [a big hit]; *Scene 2* 10:00 pm; another alley: "Gee, Officer Krupke" (Action, Snowboy, Jets) [a hit] [melody originally written for *Candide*]; *Scene 3* 11:30 pm; the bedroom: "A Boy Like That"/"I Have a Love" (Anita & Maria); *Scene 4* 11:40 pm; the drugstore: "Taunting" (danced by Anita & The Jets); *Scene 5* 11:50 pm; Doc's cellar; *Scene 6* Midnight; the street: Finale (Company).

It was somewhat unappreciated during its initial run, even though critics mostly raved. It won Tonys for choreography and sets, and was nominated for musical, costumes, musical direction, and for Carol Lawrence. It had to leave the Winter Garden to make way for *Juno*, but after a short stint at the Broadway, it moved back into the Winter Garden after *Juno* had folded. It ran 2 years on Broadway, but the run was cut short so that the show could go on tour. The Broadway production made a small profit, but it was recording sales that made up for it, and the movie that made it the world-famous score that it became. Since then *West Side Story* has become one of the all-time major musicals.

After Broadway. Her Majesty's Theatre, London, 12/12/58–6/10/61. 1,039 performances. Presented by H.M. Tennent, Robert E. Griffith, Harold S. Prince. **Cast:** Anita: Chita Rivera, *Mary Preston*; Tony: Don McKay, *David Holliday*; Maria: Marlys Watters, *Roberta D'Esti*; Riff: George Chakiris; Velma: Susan Watson, *Maureen Sims, Christine Haughton*; Juano: Billy Wilson, *Rikki Septimus*; Teresita: Yvonne Othon, *Coral Ellahi, Patsy Porter*; Rosalia: Francesca Bell, *Jill Martin*; Francisca: Gloria Higdon, *Carole Grey*; Estella: Roberta Keith, *Valerie Lloyd*; Marguerita: Lina Soriano; Doc: David Bauer; Schrank: Ted Gunther, *Ed Devereaux*; Krupke: Hal Galili, *Neville Becker*; Glad Hand: David Holliday, *Matt Zimmerman*; Action: Eddie Roll; A-Rab: Tony Mordente, *Jeff L'Cise, Riggs O'Hara*; Baby John: Ed Verso, *Tony Manning*; Snowboy: Riggs O'Hara, *Tony Adams*; Big Deal: David Bean, *Patrick McIntyre*; Diesel: Gary Cockrell, *Franklin Fox*;

GEE-TAR: Michael Kleinman, *Lindsey Dolan*; MOUTHPIECE: Joe Donovan, *Tom Merrifield, Raymond Dalziel, Vincent Logan*; GRAZIELLA: Leslie Franzos, *Leander Fedden*; MINNIE: Inge Roll, *Derina House*; CLARICE: Maureen Gillick, *Caroline Symonds, Leander Fedden, Sarah Hardenberg*; ANYBODYS: Sylvia Tysick; CHINO: Ben Gerard; BERNARDO: Ken Le Roy; PEPE: Marc Scott, *Peter Gordeno*; INDIO: Bud Fleming, *Gordon Wales*; LUIS: Don Percassi; ANXIOUS: Leo Kharibian; NIBBLES: Keith Stewart.

TOUR. The original New York touring company opened at the Erlanger Theatre, Chicago, on 10/8/59, but did not do well there. However, it was a hit on the West Coast, and the tour closed on 4/23/60, at the Shubert Theatre, Boston. It had the same basic credits as for the 1957 Broadway run, except MUSICAL DIRECTOR: Joseph Lewis; PRESS: Sol Jacobson, Lewis Harmon, Mary Bryant; COMPANY MANAGER: Emmett R. Callahan; PRODUCTION STAGE MANAGER: Joe Calvan; STAGE MANAGER: Ross Hertz; ASSISTANT STAGE MANAGER: Larry Pool. *Cast*: RIFF: Thomas Hasson; TONY: Larry Kert; ACTION: Gus Trikonis; A-RAB: Alan Johnson; BABY JOHN: Eliot Feld; SNOWBOY: Vince Baggetta; BIG DEAL: Tucker Smith; DIESEL: Eddie Miller; GEE-TAR: Jerry Norman; MOUTHPIECE: Robert Kole; TIGER: Richard Corrigan; SHORTY: Gary Scharff [this character was not repeated for Broadway]; GRAZIELLA: Lynn Bowin; VELMA: Audrey Hays; MINNIE: Sue Ostrowsky; PAULINE: Judy Aldene; CLARICE: Lee Lewis; ANYBODYS: Sandy Leeds; BERNARDO: Carmine Terra; MARIA: Leila Martin; ANITA: Devra Korwin; CHINO: Erne Castaldo; PEPE: Barry Burns; INDIO: Ed Kresley; LUIS: Ben Vargas; NIBBLES: Ed Dutton; JUANO: Miguel de Vega [this character was not repeated for the 1960 Broadway return run]; TORO: Kent Thomas; ANXIOUS: Danii Prior [this character was not repeated for the 1960 Broadway return run]; ROSALIA: Gloria Lambert; CONSUELO: Ann Marisse; TERESITA: Ella Thompson; FRANCISCA: Anna Marie Moylan; ESTELLA: Genii Prior; MARGUERITA: Barbara Richman; DOC: Albert M. Ottenheimer; SCHRANK: Arch Johnson; KRUPKE: Roger Franklin; GLAD HAND: Ross Hertz. *Understudies*: Tony: Bob Kole; Maria: Jan Canada & Ann Marisse; Anita/Rosalia: Genii Prior; Riff: Tucker Smith; A-Rab/Baby John: Barry Burns; Action: Ed Kresley; Anybodys: Sue Ostrowsky; Bernardo: Ben Vargas; Chino: Miguel de Vega; Doc/Schrank: Ross Hertz; Krupke/Glad Hand: Larry Pool; Big Deal: Vince Baggetta; Snowboy: Tucker Smith.

PAPER MILL PLAYHOUSE, New Jersey, 1960. DIRECTOR: Byrne Piven. *Cast*: Byrne Piven, Gerrianne Raphael.

737. *West Side Story (1960 return to Broadway)*

This was the touring company of the original 1957 run returned to Broadway.

The Broadway Run. WINTER GARDEN THEATRE, 4/27/60–10/22/60; ALVIN THEATRE, 10/24/60–12/10/60. Total of 249 PERFORMANCES. Leonard Bernstein conducted the orchestra on this new Broadway opening night, but the musical director was actually Joseph Lewis (as on the 1959–60 tour). This Broadway re-run had the same crew as for the 1959–60 tour, except ASSISTANT STAGE MANAGER: Arthur Rubin. *Cast*: RIFF: Thomas Hasson; TONY: Larry Kert; ACTION: George Liker; A-RAB: Alan Johnson; BABY JOHN: Barry Burns; SNOWBOY: Eddie Gasper; BIG DEAL: Martin Charnin; DIESEL: Donald Corby; GEE-TAR: Glenn Gibson; MOUTHPIECE: Eddie Miller; TIGER: Richard Corrigan; GRAZIELLA: Sandy Leeds; VELMA: Audrey Hays; MINNIE: Barbara Monte; PAULINE: Judy Aldene; CLARICE: Lee Lewis; ANYBODYS: Patricia Birch; BERNARDO: George Marcy; MARIA: Carol Lawrence; ANITA: Allyn Ann McLerie; CHINO: Miguel de Vega; PEPE: Ben Vargas, *Keith Stewart*; INDIO: Bob Avian; LUIS: Sterling Clark; BURRO: Vince Baggetta [Burro was a new character]; NIBBLES: Ed Dutton; TORO: Kent Thomas; MOOSE: Marc Scott [this character had not been on the 1959–60 tour]; ROSALIA: Gloria Lambert; CONSUELO: Genii Prior; TERESITA: Hope Clarke; FRANCISCA: Anna Marie Moylan; ESTELLA: Danii Prior; MARGUERITA: Poligena Rogers; DOC: Albert M. Ottenheimer; SCHRANK: Ted Gunther; KRUPKE: Roger Franklin; GLAD HAND: Ross Hertz. *Understudies*: Tony/Big Deal: Eddie Miller; Maria: Judy Aldene; Anita/Rosalia: Genii Prior; Riff: Glenn Gibson; A-Rab: Barry Burns; Bernardo:

Ben Vargas, *Keith Stewart*; Baby John: Sterling Clark; Action: Vince Baggetta; Anybodys: Sandy Leeds; Chino: Marc Scott; Doc/Schrank: Ross Hertz; Krupke/Glad Hand: Arthur Rubin.

The critics reviewed it again, more favorably this time. While at the Alvin, Hal Prince wanted to move to the Broadway (the Alvin was expecting another show to come in), but it would have meant several days layoff for the musicians while making the transition, and the musicians' union wouldn't accept that. So Mr. Prince closed the show.

After Broadway. THE MOVIE. 1961. United Artists paid $315,000 plus percentage of profits for the movie rights. DIRECTORS: Jerome Robbins & Robert Wise; CHOREOGRAPHER: Jerome Robbins; ASSISTANT CHOREOGRAPHER: Tommy Abbott. The movie won 11 Oscars, including best picture. The number "A-me-ri-ca" had revised lyrics. *Cast*: MARIA: Natalie Wood (singing dubbed by Marni Nixon); TONY: Richard Beymer (singing dubbed by Jim Bryant); RIFF: Russ Tamblyn; ANITA: Rita Moreno (singing dubbed by Betty Wand); BERNARDO: George Chakiris; BABY JOHN: Eliot Feld; INDIO: Gus Trikonis; VELMA: Carole D'Andrea; ACTION: Tony Mordente; A-RAB: David Winters; GEE-TAR: Tommy Abbott; MOUTHPIECE: Harvey Hohnecker; CHINO: Jose de Vega; PEPE: Jay Norman; GRAZIELLA: Gina Trikonis; GLAD HAND: John Astin; DOC: Ned Glass; KRUPKE: Bill Bramley; SCHRANK: Simon Oakland; JUANO: Eddie Verso; CONSUELO: Yvonne Othon; ICE: Tucker Smith; SNOWBOY: Bert Michaels; JOYBOY: Robert Banas; BIG DEAL: Scooter Teague; TIGER: David Bean; ANYBODYS: Sue Oakes; LOCO: Jaime Rogers; LUIS: Robert Thompson.

CITY CENTER, NYC, 4/8/64–5/3/64. 31 PERFORMANCES. PRESENTED BY the New York City Center Light Opera Company; DIRECTOR: Gerald Freedman; CHOREOGRAPHER: Tommy Abbott; SETS: Peter Wolf; COSTUME SUPERVISOR: Stanley Simmons; MUSICAL DIRECTOR: Charles Jaffe. *Cast*: RIFF: James Moore; TONY: Don McKay; MARIA: Julia Migenes; ANITA: Luba Lisa; BERNARDO: Jay Norman; ROSALIA: Marilyn Cooper; CONSUELO: Carmen Morales; KRUPKE: Frank Downing; MOOSE: Eliot Feld; GLAD HAND: Brooks Morton. This Off Broadway production received 1964 Tony nominations for producers of a musical, and musical direction.

NEW YORK STATE THEATRE, 6/24/68–9/7/68. 89 PERFORMANCES. A Lincoln Center Festival '68 production, PRESENTED BY the Musical Theatre of Lincoln Center & Richard Rodgers; DIRECTOR/CHOREOGRAPHER: Lee Theodore; SETS: Oliver Smith; COSTUMES: Winn Morton; LIGHTING: Peter Hunt; MUSICAL DIRECTOR: Maurice Peress. *Cast*: RIFF: Avind Harum; TONY: Kurt Peterson; ACTION: Ian Tucker; A-RAB: Robert LuPone; BABY JOHN: Stephen Reinhardt; SNOWBOY: George Ramos; BIG DEAL: Roger Briant; DIESEL: Victor Mohica; GEE-TAR: Chuck Beard; MOUTHPIECE: Joseph Pichette; TIGER: Kenneth Carr; GRAZIELLA: Garet De Troia; VELMA: Nancy Dalton; MINNIE: Rachel Lampert; CLARICE: Sherry Lynn Diamant; PAULINE: Carol Hanzel; PUCKY: Jeanne Frey; ANYBODYS: Lee Lund; BERNARDO: Alan Castner; MARIA: Victoria Mallory; ANITA: Barbara Luna; CHINO: Bobby Capo Jr.; PEPE: Edgar Coronado; INDIO: Peter de Nicola; LUIS: Pat Matera; ANXIOUS: Steven Gelfer; NIBBLES: Ramon Caballero; JUANO: Pernett Robinson; TORO: Byron Wheeler; MOOSE: George Comtois; ROSALIA: Kay Oslin; CONSUELO: Lee Hooper; TERESITA: Connie Burnett; FRANCISCA: Eileen Barbaris; ESTELLA: Judith Lerner; MARGUERITA: Carol Lynn Vasquez; FELICIA: Diane McAfee; DOC: Martin Wolfson; SCHRANK: Joseph Mascolo; KRUPKE: Josip Elic; GLAD HAND: Bill McCutcheon.

LONDON, 1975. This was the show that re-opened the Shaftesbury Theatre, as it was going to be demolished by developers. *Cast*: Christina Matthews, Lionel Morton, Petra Siniawski, Nicki Adrian.

738. *West Side Story (1980 Broadway revival)*

The musical numbers were the same, except that in "I Feel Pretty" Teresita is now replaced by Consuelo; and "Somewhere" is now sung by Francisca, rather than Consuelo.

Before Broadway. There were 32 previews at the Kennedy Center, Washington, DC, 1/9/80–2/3/80.

The Broadway Run. MINSKOFF THEATRE, 2/14/80–11/30/80. 8

previews. 333 PERFORMANCES. PRESENTED BY Gladys Rackmil, the John F. Kennedy Center, and James M. Nederlander, in association with Zev Bufman; MUSIC: Leonard Bernstein; LYRICS: Stephen Sondheim; BOOK: Arthur Laurents; BASED ON a 1949 idea by Jerome Robbins; DIRECTOR: Jerome Robbins; BOOK CO-DIRECTOR: Gerald Freedman; CHOREOG-RAPHERS: Jerome Robbins & Peter Gennaro's original choreography reproduced with the assistance of Tom Abbott & Lee Becker Theodore; SETS: Oliver Smith; COSTUMES: Irene Sharaff; LIGHTING: Jean Rosenthal; SOUND: Jack Mann; MUSICAL DIRECTORS: John De Main & Donald Jennings; ORCHESTRATIONS: Leonard Bernstein, with Sid Ramin & Irwin Kostal; MUSICAL CONTRACTOR: Paul Gemignani; PRESS: Hunt/Pucci; CASTING: TNI Casting (Julie Hughes & Barry Moss); EXECUTIVE PRODUCER: Ruth Mitchell; GENERAL MANAGEMENT: Theatre Now; COMPANY MANAGER: Michael Lonergan; PRODUCTION STAGE MANAGER: Patrick Horrigan; STAGE MANAGER: Brenna Krupa; ASSISTANT STAGE MANAGER: Arlene Grayson. *Cast:* THE JETS: RIFF, THE LEADER: James J. Mellon (5); TONY, HIS FRIEND: Ken Marshall (2) *; ACTION: Mark Bove; A-RAB: Todd Lester; BABY JOHN: Brian Kaman; SNOWBOY: Cleve Asbury; BIG DEAL: Reed Jones, *Jeffrey Reynolds*; DIESEL: Brent Barrett; GEE-TAR: G. Russell Weilandich; MOUTHPIECE: Stephen Bogardus, *Brent Barrett*; TIGER: Mark Fotopoulos; THEIR GIRLS (FIVE): GRAZIELLA: Georganna Mills; VELMA: Heather Lee Gerdes; MINNIE: Frankie Wade; CLARICE: Charlene Gehm; PAULINE: Nancy Louise Chismar; ANYBODYS: Missy Whitchurch; THE SHARKS: BERNARDO, THE LEADER: Hector Jaime Mercado (4); MARIA, HIS SISTER: Josie de Guzman (1) *; ANITA, HIS GIRL: Debbie Allen (3) *; CHINO, HIS FRIEND: Ray Contreras(7); PEPE: Michael Rivera; INDIO: Darryl Tribble; LUIS: Adrian Rosario; ANXIOUS: Michael De Lorenzo; NIBBLES: Willie Rosario, *Herman W. Sebek*; JUANO: Michael Franks, *Tony Constantine*; TORO: Mark Morales; MOOSE: Gary-Michael Davies; THEIR GIRLS: ROSALIA: Yamil Borges; CONSUELO: Nancy Ticotin; FRANCISCA: Harolyn Blackwell; TERESITA: Stephanie E. Williams; ESTELLA: Marlene Danielle; MARGUERITA: Amy Lester; THE ADULTS: DOC: Sammy Smith (6); SCHRANK: Arch Johnson (9); KRUPKE: John Bentley; GLAD HAND: Jake Turner (8); *Musicians*: TRUMPET: Gino Bozzacco; PERCUSSION: Richard Brown; DRUMS: Nick Cerrato; GUITAR: Scott Kuney. *Standbys*: Maria: Chris Wheeler & Harolyn Blackwell, *Mary Elizabeth Mastrantonio*; Riff/Action: Will Mead. *Understudies*: Tony: Stephen Bogardus; Anita/Rosalia: Marlene Danielle; Bernardo: Michael Rivera; Riff/Big Deal: Cleve Asbury; Doc/Schrank: John Bentley; Chino: Mark Morales; Glad Hand/Action: Reed Jones; A-Rab: Mark Fotopoulos; Baby John/Mouthpiece: Tim O'Keefe; Krupke: Jake Turner; Anybodys: Nancy Louise Chismar; Graziella: Frankie Wade; Snowboy: Tim O'Keefe & Richard Caceres. *Swing Girl*: Nancy Butchko, *Pamela Khoury*. *Swing Boys*: Richard Caceres & Tim O'Keefe.

Broadway reviews were very divided. This is the show that made Debbie Allen a star. The show received Tony nominations for reproduction of a play or musical, and for Josie de Guzman and Debbie Allen.

After Broadway. KENNEDY CENTER, Washington, DC, 8/31/85–9/3/85. PRESENTED BY Diana Corto & Francine LeFrak, in association with LeFrak Entertainment; DIRECTOR: Ruth Mitchell; CHOREOGRAPHER: Tommy Abbott; SETS: Peter Wolf; COSTUMES: Stanley Simmons; LIGHTING: Marc B. Weiss; SOUND: Jack Mann; MUSICAL DIRECTOR: Milton Rosenstock. *Cast*: BERNARDO: Luis Perez; MARIA: Katharine Buffaloe; TONY: Rex Smith; ANITA: Leilani Jones; KRUPKE: Ron Orbach; RIFF: Kevin Neil McCready.

TOURING REVIVAL. Opened on 8/4/87, at the O'Keefe, Toronto, and closed on 9/13/87, at the Kennedy Center, Washington, DC. PRESENTED BY Lee Guber, Shelly Gross, Robert L. Young Jr.; DIRECTOR/CHOREOGRAPHER: Alan Johnson; SETS: Alan Kimmel; COSTUMES: Gail Cooper-Hecht; LIGHTING: Marc B. Weiss; SOUND: Abe Jacob; MUSICAL DIRECTOR: Milton Rosenstock. *Cast*: TONY: Jack Wagner; MARIA: Lauri Landry; ANITA: Valarie Pettiford; RIFF: John Schiappa; ACTION: Mark Bove; GRAZIELLA: Donna Di Meo; MINNIE: Barbara Hoon; ANYBODYS: Lisa Leguillou; BERNARDO: Rick Negron; DOC: Carl Don; SCHRANK: Daniel P. Hannafin.

WORLD TOUR. Opened on 9/5/95, in Detroit. PRESENTED BY Barry Brown, Marvin A. Krauss, Irving Siders, and The Booking Office; DIRECTOR/CHOREOGRAPHER: Alan Johnson; SETS: Campbell Baird; COSTUMES: Irene Sharaff; LIGHTING: Natasha Katz; SOUND: Otts

Munderloh; MUSICAL DIRECTOR: Donald Chan. *Cast*: TONY: H.E. Geer, *Scott Carollo* (from 11/95), *Jeremy Koch* (from 9/96); MARIA: Marcy Harriell, *Sharen Camille* (from 9/96); ANITA: Natascia A. Diaz, *Michelle DeJean* (from 4/97); RIFF: Jamie Gustis, *Christian Borle* (from 9/96); BERNARDO: Vincent Zamora, *Kevin Bernardo* (from 9/96).

MEXICO. *Amor sin barreras* tried out for 2 performances on 12/21/97, at TEATRO GALERIAS, Guadalajara, before opening in MEXICO CITY in 1/98. PRESENTED BY Cesar Balcazar; DIRECTOR: Cesar Balcazar; CHOREOGRAPHER: Juan Gonzalez; SETS: Luis Fernando Payan; COSTUMES: Gabriela Sanchez; LIGHTING: Carlos Trejo; MUSICAL DIRECTOR: Jesus Carodozo. *Cast*: MARIA: Mariana Garza.

PRINCE EDWARD THEATRE, London, 10/6/98–1/9/99. Previews from 10/1/98; PRINCE OF WALES THEATRE, 1/22/99–1/8/00. *Cast*: TONY: David Habbin, *Paul Manuel*; MARIA: Katie Knight-Adams; ANITA: Anna Jane Casey; RIFF: Edward Baker Duly; BERNARDO: Graham McDuff.

In 2003 it was announced that Kevin McCollum and Jeffrey Seller planned to bring it back to Broadway by spring 2005 at the earliest. Jerry Mitchell was set to direct and choreograph. It didn't happen (not then, anyway).

739. *What Makes Sammy Run?*

Set in a time a generation ago. It traces the story of ruthless movie producer Sammy, his rise from being a copy boy on a New York paper, through being a scriptwriter at World-Wide Pictures, to being the head of a large movie studio. On the way up he crushes his opponents, steals ideas, betrays friends, and drives one of his benefactors to suicide. Al is a newspaper reporter. Sammy passes over Kit, an attractive writer who has fallen in love with him, for Laurette, daughter of a big banker, only to discover at the final curtain that Laurette has been even more ruthless than him.

Before Broadway. There had been a 1959 straight TV play, starring Larry Blyden. The 1964 Broadway musical was adapted by Budd Schulberg and his brother Stuart. Abe Burrows replaced Arthur Storch as director.

The Broadway Run. FIFTY-FOURTH STREET THEATRE, 2/27/64–6/12/65. 3 previews from 2/25/64. 540 PERFORMANCES. A Cates Brothers production, in association with Beresford Productions, PRESENTED by Joseph Cates; MUSIC/LYRICS: Ervin Drake; BOOK: Budd & Stuart Schulberg (helped by Abe Burrows); BASED ON the 1941 novel of the same name, by Budd Schulberg; DIRECTOR: Abe Burrows; CHOREOGRAPHER: Matt Mattox; SETS/LIGHTING: Herbert Senn & Helen Pond; COSTUMES: Noel Taylor; MUSICAL DIRECTOR/VOCAL ARRANGEMENTS: Lehman Engel; ORCHESTRATIONS: Don Walker; DANCE MUSIC ARRANGEMENTS: Arnold Goland; CAST RECORDING on Columbia; PRESS: Gertrude Kirschner & Violet Welles, *Max Eisen, Jeanne Gibson Merrick, William Greenblatt*; GENERAL MANAGER: Marshall Young; STAGE MANAGERS: George Thorn & Bob Maxwell, *Tom Porter* (added during the run). *Cast*: AL MANHEIM: Robert Alda (3); SAMMY GLICK: Steve Lawrence (1), *Paul Anka* (7/13/64–7/20/64), *Steve Lawrence*; O'BRIEN: Ralph Stantley, *Leslie Litomy*; OSBORN: John Dorrin, *Warren Galjour*; BARTENDER: Ralph Vucci, *George Blackwell*; JULIAN BLUMBERG: George Coe, *Stuart Unger*; RITA RIO: Graciela Daniele, *Diann Ainslie, Barbara Andrews*; TRACY CLARK: Richard France; LUCKY DUGAN: Edward McNally; SHIEK ORSINI: Barry Newman; TECHNICAL ADVISER: Robert E. "Bob" Maxwell Jr.; SIDNEY FINEMAN: Arny Freeman; KIT SARGEANT: Sally Ann Howes (2), *Bernice Massi* (from 3/22/65); H.L. HARRINGTON: Walter Klavun, *Ralph Stantley*; LAURETTE HARRINGTON: Bernice Massi (4), *Paula Stewart* (from 3/22/65); SEYMOUR GLICK: Mace Barrett; SINGERS: Darrell J. Askcy, Lillian Bozinoff, Natalie Costa, John Dorrin, Judith Hastings, Jamie Simmons, Richard Terry, Ralph Vucci; DANCERS: Diann Ainslie, Jean Blanchard, Nancy Carnegie, Barbara Gine, Marco Gomez, Lavinia Hamilton, Buck Heller, Nat Horne, Jack Kresy, Bella Shalom, Maralyn Thoma, *Natasha Grishin*; SWING COUPLE: Lynn Gremmler & Doug Spingler, *Juanita Boyle* & *Grant Lashley*. *Understudies*: Sammy: Richard France, *Hal Linden*; Kit: Judy Hastings; Al: Mace Barrett; Laurette: Natalie

Costa; Tracy: Buck Heller, *Grant Lashley*; Rita: Diann Ainslie; O'Brien/Lucky/Fineman/Harrington: John Dorrin. *Act I*: *Scene 1* The city room of the *New York Record*: "A New Pair of Shoes" (Sammy, Al, Ensemble); *Scene 2* Joe's Bar: "You Help Me" (Sammy & Al); *Scene 3* The *New York Record*; *Scene 4* World-Wide Pictures sound stage: "A Tender Spot" (Kit); *Scene 5* The studio street: "Lites-Camera-Platitude" (Sammy, Kit, Al); *Scene 6* The sound stage: "My Home Town" (Sammy) [a hit], "Monsoon" (ballet) (Rita, Tracy, Ensemble); *Scene 7* The patio of Fineman's mansion: "I See Something" (Laurette & Sammy); *Scene 8* Kit's house: "Maybe Some Other Time" (Kit & Al), "You Can Trust Me" (Sammy), "A Room without Windows" (Kit & Sammy) [a hit], "Kiss Me No Kisses" (Kit & Sammy). *Act II*: *Scene 1* The court of Grauman's Chinese Theatre: "I Feel Humble" (Sammy, Shiek, Ensemble); *Scene 2* Joe's Bar; *Scene 3* Kit's terrace: "Something to Live For" (Kit); *Scene 4* The World-Wide penthouse in New York: "Paint a Rainbow" (Rita, Tracy, Ensemble), "You're No Good" (Laurette & Sammy); *Scene 5* Kit's terrace: "Something to Live For" (reprise) (Al); *Scene 6* Sammy's office: "My Home Town" (reprise) (Sammy) [dropped during the run], "The Friendliest Thing" (Laurette); *Scene 7* Sammy's mansion: "Wedding of the Year" (Ensemble); *Scene 8* Kit's house: "Some Days Everything Goes Wrong" (Sammy).

Note: "Bachelor Gal" (Kit) was added when Bernice Massi took over.

Reviews were mixed. The show closed after Steve Lawrence's attendance became somewhat erratic and his ad-libbing grew more noticeable. He even cut one of the songs, but re-instated it after the producers threatened to sue him. He missed seven out of eight performances one week, and there was no understudy. During one four-month period he missed 24 performances, including Winter Festival week (Christmas and New Year's, 1964–65). Then Sally Ann Howes left, and Bernice Massi took over the role of Kit, which didn't work. Several critics covered the show again, giving it bad reviews. It lost about $285,000 of its original $400,000 investment. Steve Lawrence won the New York Drama Critics' Circle Award. The show received Tony nominations for musical direction, and for Steve Lawrence.

After Broadway. TORONTO, 1965. This was a brief run, following Broadway, with the original sets and costumes. *Cast*: Sal Mineo.

VALLEY MUSIC THEATRE, Woodland Hills, Calif., 1966. *Cast*: Frank Gorshin. Robert Armin saw this production; it inspired him to re-write the story 30 years later.

REVISED VERSION. In 2/00 Robert Armin contacted Budd Schulberg and Ervin Drake, and suggested a collaboration on a revised version. Armin and Schulberg re-wrote the book. Some secondary characters were cut, as was the entire dancing ensemble. Two characters from the novel were put back in — Rosalie & Billie, and the whole project was tougher, closer to the 1941 novel. Several ballets were cut, as was "I Feel Humble." Ervin Drake wrote four new songs — "Two-Cent Encyclopedia," "I Can Trust Him," "Don't Bite the Hand that Feeds You," and "Mother of All the Blues." He also revised the lyrics of "A Tender Spot" and "My Hometown." "Bachelor Girl" was also included in the song line-up (this had been added during the run of the original production). It ran as a concert revival in HEMPSTEAD, Long Island, NY, 3/26/03–3/29/03. PRESENTED BY Hofstra Cultural Center & Hofstra USA Productions; DIRECTOR: Bob Spiotto; MUSICAL DIRECTOR: Frank De Monaco. *Cast*: SAMMY: Warren Schein; AL: John Gabriel; KIT: Susan Bigelow; LAURETTE: Barbara Fasano; SIDNEY/BEN: Stuart Zagnit; JULIAN: Jerry Maggio; ROSALIE GOLDBAUM/BILLIE RAND: Cristina Doikos.

740. *What's Up?*

The Rawa of Tanglinia, an East Indian potentate, has become, through an important mineral discovered in his land, vital to the USA in their war effort, and is being brought to the States for a conference with the State Department by an American Air Force crew, accompanied by his interpreter, Virginia, who is in love with Dick, one of the air crew. The plane crashes near Miss Langley's School for Girls, in Crestville, Virginia. The Rawa and crew, taking refuge in the school while awaiting help, are quarantined in the Laurel House of the school for eight days following a measles outbreak. They pass the time singing, dancing and making love, which amuses the Rawa. The entire action takes place in the present.

Before Broadway. This was the first Lerner & Loewe collaboration to make it to Broadway (their 1942 show — *Life of the Party* — with Margaret Dumont and Charlie Ruggles, had died in Detroit). *What's Up?* tried out at the Playhouse, Wilmington, Del., 10/22/43–10/23/43. 3 PERFORMANCES, and at the Walnut Street Theatre, Philadelphia, 10/23/43 (2 weeks). The cast order was slightly different during tryouts. Lois Lee was in it at this point. This was the scene by scene breakdown then: *Act I*: *Scene 1* The living-room. Afternoon: "Miss Langley's School for Girls" (Girls), "From the Chimney to the Cellar" (Jayne & Girls), "My Last Love" (sung by Margaret & Willie, before the curtain); *Scene 2* The men's bedroom. That night: "A Girl is Like a Book" (Lindsay); *Scene 3* The girls' bedroom: "Joshua" (sung by Margaret; danced by Flyers & Girls); *Scene 4* The Rawa's bedroom; *Scene 5* The rumpus room; following morning: "You Wash and I'll Dry" (sung by Margaret, Willie, Susan, Wagner, Ed, Murray. Dance solos by Louise, Jimmy, Pamela, Judy, Eleanor), "How Fly Times" (Willie, Dick, Flyers, Girls), "Just Then" (Virginia). *Act II*: *Scene 1* The boys' & girls' rooms: "Natural Life" (sung by Flyers & Girls before the curtain. Danced by Don Weissmuller); *Scene 2* The living-room: "Just Then" (reprise) (Virginia & May), "Three Girls in a Boat" (sung by Margaret; danced by Jayne & Susan), "You've Got a Hold on Me" (Virginia, Dick, Flyers, Girls), "The Ill-Tempered Clavichord" (Jayne, Susan, Girls, Flyers), "Love is a Step Ahead of Me" (Virginia); *Scene 3* The linen closet: "My Last Love" (reprise) (Moroney); IN FRONT OF CURTAIN: Jimmy Savo; *Scene 4* The living-room: Finale (Entire Company).

The Broadway Run. NATIONAL THEATRE, 11/11/43–1/4/44. 63 PERFORMANCES. PRESENTED BY Mark Warnow; MUSIC: Frederick Loewe; LYRICS: Alan Jay Lerner; BOOK: Arthur Pierson & Alan Jay Lerner; DIRECTOR/CHOREOGRAPHER: George Balanchine; BOOK DIRECTOR: Robert H. Gordon; SETS: Boris Aronson; COSTUMES: Grace Houston; LIGHTING: Albert Alloy; MUSICAL DIRECTOR: Will Irwin; ORCHESTRATIONS: Van Cleeve; VOCAL ARRANGEMENTS: Bobby Tucker; PRESS: Nat Dorfman; STAGE MANAGER: Edward Mendelsohn; ASSISTANT STAGE MANAGERS: Elwell Cobb & Frank Kreig. *Cast:* JAYNE: Mary Roche; SUSAN: Patricia Marshall (4); ELEANOR: Mitzi Perry; MARGARET: Lynn Gardner; HARRIETT SPINNER: Claire Meade; PAMELA: Honey Murray; LOUISE: Sondra Barrett; MARTHA: Sara Macon [role added after tryouts]; MAY: Marjorie Beecher; JENNIFER: Phyllis Hill; DOCTOR: Frank Kreig; SGT. WILLIE KLINK: Larry Douglas; CAPT. ROBERT LINDSAY: Rodney McLennan; SGT. HENRY WAGNER: Jack Baker; 2ND LT. MURRAY BACCHUS: Robert Bay; 1ST LT. ED ANDERSON: Don Weissmuller; SGT. MORONEY: Johnny Morgan (3); JUDY: Helen Wenzel; SGT. DICK BENHAM: William Tabbert; VIRGINIA MILLER: Gloria Warren (1); THE RAWA OF TANGLINIA: Jimmy Savo (2); SGT. JIMMY STEVENSON: Kenneth Buffett. *Act* I: *Scene 1* The living-room; afternoon: "Miss Langley's School for Girls" (Jayne & Girls), "From the Chimney to the Cellar" (Jayne & Girls), "You've Got a Hold on Me" (Virginia, Margaret, Willie); *Scene 2* The men's bedroom; that night: "A Girl is Like a Book" (Lindsay); *Scene 3* The girls' bedroom: "Joshua" (sung by Margaret; danced by Girls & Flyers); *Scene 4* The living-room: "Three Girls in a Boat" (sung by Margaret; danced by Jayne & Susan), Ballet (danced by Rawa & Jennifer), "How Fly Times" (sung by Willie, Dick, Flyers; danced by Ed), "My Last Love" (sung by Jayne, Willie, Margaret, Moroney, Dick, Virginia); BEFORE THE CURTAIN FOR ACT II, dance by Don Weissmuller. *Act II*: *Scene 1* The rumpus room; the following morning: "You Wash and I'll Dry" (sung by Margaret, Willie, Susan, Murray. Danced by Louise, Jimmy, Pamela. Duo by May & Lindsay), "You Wash and I'll Dry" (reprise) (Virginia); *Scene 2* The Rawa's bedroom; *Scene 3* The living-room: "The Ill-Tempered Clavichord" (sung by Jayne, Susan, Virginia. Danced by Flyers, Girls. Dance specialty by Mr. Bay), "You've Got a Hold on Me" (reprise) (sung by Virginia, Dick, Flyers, Girls. Danced by Jennifer & Wagner); IN FRONT OF THE CURTAIN, Jimmy Savo; *Scene 4* The linen closet; *Scene 5* The living-room: Finale (Entire Company).

Broadway reviews were divided. The production lost a lot of money.

741. *Where's Charley?*

Set in Oxford, England, in the summer of 1892. Two undergraduates, Jack and Charles, need a chaperone so they can have a rendezvous with girlfriends Kitty and Amy. Charley disguises himself as his aunt, Donna Lucia, from Brazil ("where the nuts come from"). Then the real Donna Lucia arrives, not an old lady as Charley is portraying, but an attractive woman. The aunt is pursued by the money-hungry guardian of the girls.

Before Broadway. Brandon Thomas's immensely popular play *Charley's Aunt* opened in New York in 1893. It has been revived many times on Broadway (Jose Ferrer was memorable in 1940 and again at City Center in 1953) and filmed several times (notably with Jack Benny). Stock companies and amateur groups have performed it countless times all over the world. John Mills starred in two London revivals, one in 1930 and another in 1955. Ray Bolger (whose wife was Gwen Rickard), had turned down the opportunity of reviving the play in 1939, but the idea of the musical appealed to him. The show tried out in Philadelphia. Mr. Bolger had 11 costume changes during each performance. This was Frank Loesser's Broadway debut, and his first book musical.

The Broadway Run. ST. JAMES THEATRE, 10/11/48–9/9/50. 792 PERFORMANCES. PRESENTED BY Cy Feuer & Ernest H. Martin, in association with Gwen Rickard; MUSIC/LYRICS: Frank Loesser; BOOK: George Abbott; BASED ON the 1892 farce Charley's Aunt, by Brandon Thomas; DIRECTOR: George Abbott; CHOREOGRAPHER: George Balanchine, with Fred Danielli; SETS/COSTUMES: David ffolkes; MUSICAL DIRECTOR: Max Goberman, Edward Simons; VOCAL DIRECTOR/VOCAL ARRANGEMENTS: Gerry Dolin; ORCHESTRATIONS: Ted Royal, Hans Spialek, Phil Lang; CAST RECORDING: none, due to the musicians' strike; PRESS: Karl Bernstein, Lorella Val-Mery, Mary Marsh, Harvey Sabinson; COMPANY MANAGER: Leo Rose, Otto Hartman; PRODUCTION STAGE MANAGER: Robert E. Griffith; STAGE MANAGER: Dan Sattler, Marge Ellis; ASSISTANT STAGE MANAGER: John Friend, George Enke. *Cast:* BRASSETT: John Lynds; JACK CHESNEY: Byron Palmer (3), Larry Douglas; CHARLEY WYKEHAM: Ray Bolger (1) ☆; KITTY VERDUN: Doretta Morrow (4), Hazel Willer; AMY SPETTIGUE: Allyn McLerie (2), Joan Chandler, Beverlee Bozeman; WILKINSON: Edgar Kent; SIR FRANCIS CHESNEY: Paul England; MR. SPETTIGUE: Horace Cooper; A PROFESSOR: Jack Friend [role deleted by 49–50]; DONNA LUCIA D'ALVADOREZ: Jane Lawrence, Rose Inghram; PHOTOGRAPHER: James Lane; PATRICIA: Marie Foster; REGGIE: Douglas Deane; DANCERS: Vicki Barrett, Mary Alice Bingham, Douglas Deane, Geraldine Delancy, Marge Ellis, George Enke, Marie Foster, Jack Friend (gone by 49–50), Bobby Harrell, Marcia Maier, Dusty McCaffrey (gone by 49–50), Walter Rinner, Nina Starkey (gone by 49–50), Susan Stewart, Toni Stuart (gone by 49–50), Bill Weber (gone by 49–50), Gordon West (gone by 49–50), Ken Whelan, Madeleine Detry, Hazel Patterson, Alex Dunaeff, John Martin, Grehan Pearce, Merritt Thompson, Ray Kyle; SINGERS: Rae Abruzzo (gone by 49–50), Robert Baird, James Bird, John Dunsmure (William Scully), Dan Gallagher (Thomas Rieder), Bob Held (gone by 49–50), Jane Judge, Cornell MacNeil (Charles Irwin), Ruth McVayne (gone by 49–50), Betty Oakes (gone by 49–50), Eleanore Parker, Stowe Phelps, Katharine Reeve (Grace Varik), Gloria Sullivan (gone by 49–50), Ernest Taylor, Irene Weston, John Allen, Marion Baird, Jane Carlyle, Marcia James, Don Russell. **Understudies:** Brassett: Stowe Phelps; Jack: Cornell MacNeil, Charles Irwin, Douglas Deane; Charley: Douglas Deane; Kitty: Betty Oakes, Jane Judge; Amy: Marie Foster; Wilkinson: Ernest Taylor; Sir Francis: Dan Gallagher, Tom Rieder; Mr. Spettigue: James Lane; Donna Lucia: Katharine Reeve, Grace Varik; Photographer/Reggie: James Bird.

Act I: Scene 1 A room at Oxford University: "The Years Before Us" (Students) (choral arrangement), "Better Get Out of Here" (Charley, Amy, Kitty, Jack); *Scene 2* A street: "The New Ashmolean Marching Society and Students' Conservatory Band" (Jack, Amy, Kitty, Bobby Harrell, Young Ladies); *Scene 3* The garden: "My Darling, My Darling" (Jack & Kitty) [a hit], "Make a Miracle" (Charley & Amy), "Serenade with Asides" (Mr. Spettigue); *Scene 4* Where the nuts come from: "Lovelier than Ever" (Donna Lucia, Sir Francis, Students, Young Ladies), "The Woman in His Room" (Amy), "Pernambuco" (Charley, Amy, the "Pernambucans"). *Act II: Scene 1* The garden: "Where's Charley?" (Jack, Cornell MacNeil, Stowe Phelps, Students, Young Ladies); *Scene 2* A street: "Once in Love with Amy" (Charley & The Students) [the show-stopping big hit]; *Scene 3* Where the ladies go (i.e. the powder room): "The Gossips" [Young Ladies–Jane Judge, Marie Foster, Rae Abruzzo, Betty Oakes, Katharine Reeve (Grace Varik), Gloria Sullivan, Eleanore Parker, Mary Alice Bingham, Irene Weston, Ruth McVayne, Geraldine Delaney]; *Scene 4* A garden path: *Scene 5* The ballroom: "At the Red Rose Cotillion" (Jack, Kitty, Guests), Dance (Charley & Amy), Finale (Entire Company).

Advance Broadway box-office sales were $250,000. The critics loved the stars, but reviews for the actual show were divided. Ray Bolger would stand at the curtain and lead a willing audience in the singing of "Once in Love with Amy." He won a Tony and a Donaldson Award (as best male dancer). The song "My Darling, My Darling" got another boost when it was hummed by Bea Lillie during one of the sketches in the revue *Inside U.S.A.* Finally Mr. Bolger was exhausted, and, rather than try to find a replacement, the producers closed the show.

742. *Where's Charley?*
(1951 return to Broadway)

Before Broadway. After a suitable rest for Ray Bolger after the original Broadway run ended in 1950 he led the original touring company, which opened in Boston, then went to Broadway again.

The Broadway Run. BROADWAY THEATRE, 1/29/51–3/10/51. Limited run of 4 weeks (extended to 48 PERFORMANCES). There were some crew changes from the 1948 production: MUSICAL DIRECTOR: Edward Scott; ORCHESTRATIONS: Ted Royal & Hans Spialek; VOCAL DIRECTOR/ARRANGEMENTS: Herbert Greene; PRESS: Karl Bernstein & Harvey B. Sabinson; STAGE MANAGERS: Dan Sattler, Howard Lenters, John Martin. *Cast:* BRASSETT: John Lynds; JACK: Bob Shackleton; CHARLEY: Ray Bolger; KITTY: Betty Oakes; AMY: Allyn McLerie; WILKINSON: James Lane; SIR FRANCIS: Paul England; SPETTIGUE: Horace Cooper; DONNA LUCIA: Rose Inghram; PHOTOGRAPHER: James Lane; PATRICIA: Irene Weston; REGGIE: Ralph Lowe; DANCERS: Donna Beaumont, Arun Evans, Ann Lee Hudson, Virginia McClamroch, Nancy Pearson, Gretchen Winnecke, James Capp, Ray Johnson, Jack Konzal, Maurice Phillips, Reggie Powers, Victor Reilley; SINGERS: Michele Burke, Dorothy Juden, Helen Moore, Ann Richards, Lita Terris, Irene Weston, Pat Wilkes, Jennifer Woods, Forrest Carter, John Decker, John Fortna, Ralph Lowe, Gerald Lynch, Gene Scott, Ernest Taylor, Paul Wolff.

After Broadway. THE MOVIE. *Charley's Aunt* was filmed straight many times. The movie musical, Where's Charley? was filmed in 1952. CHOREOGRAPHER: Michael Kidd. *Cast:* CHARLEY: Ray Bolger; AMY: Allyn Ann McLerie; JACK: Robert Shackleton; STEPHEN SPETTIGUE: Horace Cooper; DONNA LUCIA: Margaretta Scott; SIR FRANCIS: Howard Marion Crawford; KITTY: Mary Germaine.

PALACE THEATRE, London, 2/20/58–2/21/59. 379 PERFORMANCES. Frank Loesser had met Norman Wisdom in 1951 in New York, and agreed then that the British comedian would be a perfect Charley. DIRECTOR: William Chappell; CHOREOGRAPHER: Hanya Holm; MUSICAL DIRECTOR: Michael Collins. *Cast:* BRASSETT: John Moore; JACK: Terence Cooper; CHARLEY: Norman Wisdom; KITTY: Pamela Gale; AMY: Pip Hinton; SIR FRANCIS: Jerry Desmonde; SPETTIGUE: Felix Felton; DONNA LUCIA: Marion Grimaldi; PHOTOGRAPHER: Peter Mander; REGGIE: Barry Kent; AGATHA: Jill Martin; SINGER: David Kernan.

CITY CENTER, NYC, 5/25/66–6/5/66. 15 PERFORMANCES. This was part of City Center's spring season of four Frank Loesser revivals (the others were *How to Succeed in Business Without Really Trying, The Most Happy Fella* and *Guys and Dolls*). PRESENTED BY the New York City Center Light Opera Company; DIRECTOR: Christopher Hewett; CHOREOGRAPHER: John Sharpe; ORIGINAL SETS: David ffolkes; COSTUMES: Frank Thompson; LIGHTING/ADDITIONAL SETS: Peggy Clark; MUSICAL DIRECTOR: Pembroke Davenport; BALLET MUSIC ADAPTED BY: Marvin Laird. *Cast:* BRASSETT: Tom Bate; PROFESSOR FORTESQUE: Donald Barton; JACK: David Smith; CHARLEY: Darryl Hickman; KITTY: Karen Shepard; AMY: Susan Watson; WILKINSON: Emory Bass; SIR FRANCIS: Ferdinand

Hilt; SPETTIGUE: Mort Marshall; DONNA LUCIA: Eleanor Steber; REGGIE: Austin Colyer; DANCERS INCLUDED: Rodd Barry, Dennis Cole, Cathy Conklin, Jack Fletcher, Mickey Gunnersen, Beth Howland, Toodie Witmer; SINGERS INCLUDED: Hal Norman, Nina Hirschfeld.

743. *Where's Charley?* (1974 Broadway revival)

The Broadway Run. CIRCLE IN THE SQUARE UPTOWN, 12/19/74–2/23/75. 20 previews from 11/29/74. 78 PERFORMANCES. PRESENTED BY Circle in the Square; MUSIC/LYRICS: Frank Loesser: BOOK: George Abbott; BASED ON the farce Charley's Aunt; DIRECTOR: Theodore Mann; CHOREOGRAPHER: Margo Sappington; SETS: Marjorie Kellogg; COSTUMES: Arthur Boccia; LIGHTING: Thomas Skelton; MUSICAL DIRECTOR/NEW ARRANGEMENTS: Tom Pierson; ORIGINAL ORCHESTRATIONS: Ted Royal, Hans Spialek, Phil Lang; ORIGINAL VOCAL ARRANGEMENTS: Gerry Dolin; PRESS: Merle Debuskey & Susan L. Schulman; CASTING: Roger Sturtevant; COMPANY MANAGER: William Conn; PRODUCTION STAGE MANAGER: Randall Brooks; STAGE MANAGER: James Bernardi. *Cast:* BRASSETT: Louis Beachner (3); JACK CHESNEY: Jerry Lanning (5); CHARLEY WYKEHAM: Raul Julia (1) ✲; KITTY VERDUN: Carol Jo Lugenbeal (6); AMY SPETTIGUE: Marcia McClain (7); SIR FRANCIS CHESNEY: Peter Walker (8); MR. SPETTIGUE: Tom Aldredge (2); DONNA LUCIA D'ALVADOREZ: Taina Elg (4); REGGIE: Dennis Cooley; STUDENTS & YOUNG LADIES: Pamela Burrell, Jacqueline Clark, Dennis Cooley, Karen Jablons, Jack Neubeck, Craig Sandquist, Leland Schwantes, Miriam Welch. *The Sextet:* VIOLINS: Ann Barak & Vladimir Weisman; CELLO: David Everhart; VIOLA: Hugh Loughran; BASS: Donald Palma; HARPSICHORD & PIANO: Tom Pierson. *Understudies:* Charley: Dennis Cooley; Amy: Miriam Welch; Jack: Jack Neubeck; Kitty: Karen Jablons; Donna Lucia: Pam Burrell; Spettigue: Leland Schwantes; Sir Francis: Craig Sandquist; Brassett/Male Chorus: David-James Carroll; Female Chorus: Martha Deering. *Act I: Scene 1* A room at Oxford University: "Where's Charley?" (Students & Young Ladies), "The Years Before Us" (Students), "Better Get Out of Here" (Amy, Kitty, Charley, Jack), "The New Ashmolean Marching Society and Students' Conservatory Band" (Ensemble); *Scene 2* The garden: "My Darling, My Darling" (Kitty & Jack), "Make a Miracle" (Charley & Amy), "Serenade with Asides" (Mr. Spettigue), "Lovelier than Ever" (Donna Lucia, Sir Francis, Students, Young Ladies), "The Woman in His Room" (Amy), "Pernambuco" (Charley & Company). *Act II: Scene 1* The garden: "Where's Charley?" (reprise) (Amy), "Once in Love with Amy" (Charley & The Students); *Scene 2* Where the ladies go: "The Gossips" (Young Ladies — Miss Burrell, Miss Clark, Miss Jablons, Miss Welch); *Scene 3* The ballroom: "At the Red Rose Cotillion" (Jack, Kitty, Ensemble), Finale (Ensemble).

Broadway reviews were divided. The show received Tony Nominations for choreography, costumes, and for Raul Julia, Tom Aldredge, and Taina Elg.

After Broadway. EQUITY LIBRARY THEATRE, NYC, 3/10/83–4/3/83. 30 PERFORMANCES. DIRECTOR: Dennis Grimaldi; CHOREOGRAPHERS: Donald Mark & Dennis Grimaldi. *Cast:* CHARLEY: Charles Abbott; KITTY: Marin Mazzie; AMY: Virginia Seidel; SPETTIGUE: Austin Colyer; DONNA LUCIA: Annette Hunt.

THE KENNEDY CENTER, Washington, DC, 8/13/98–8/16/98. A special concert version. Part of the Words and Music series. ADAPTED BY: Ken Ludwig; DIRECTOR: Charles Repole; CHOREOGRAPHER: Dan Siretta. *Cast:* Emily Loesser, Dick Van Patten, Don Stephenson, Judith Blazer.

OPEN AIR THEATRE, Regents Park, London, 7/26/01–8/16/01. Previews from 7/24/01. DIRECTOR: Ian Talbot; CHOREOGRAPHER: Gillian Gregory; SETS/COSTUMES: Terry Parsons; MUSICAL DIRECTOR: Catherine Jayes. *Cast:* CHARLEY: Cameron Blakely; AMY: Lottie Mayor.

GOODSPEED OPERA HOUSE, 8/11/04–9/25/04. Previews from 7/9/04. This revival had a slightly revised script (with permission from George Abbott's widow, Joy) and score, with six more Frank Loesser songs added: "I Wish I Didn't Love You So" [from the 1947 movie *The Perils of Pauline*], "The Hyacinth" and "Why Fight the Feeling?" [both from the 1950 movie *Let's Dance*], "He Can Waltz" [from the 1947 movie *Variety Girl*], "A Tune for Humming" [an original 1947 song], "Don't

Introduce Me to That Angel" [unused from the original run of *Where's Charley*]. Certain numbers, such as "Pernambuco," were shifted to different positions. Mr. Loesser's widow Jo Sullivan was right behind this project. DIRECTOR: Tony Walton; CHOREOGRAPHER: Lisa Shriver; SETS: Tony Walton & Kelly Hanson; COSTUMES: Tony Walton & Martha Bromelmeier; LIGHTING: Richard Pilbrow; MUSICAL DIRECTOR: Michael O'Flaherty; ORCHESTRATIONS: Larry Moore. *Cast:* CHARLEY: Noah Racey; AMY: Nili Bassman; SIR FRANCIS: Paul Carlin; KITTY: Kristin Huxhold; DONA LUCIA: Mary Illes.

Who to Love see 160

744. *Whoopee!*

Shy guy elopes and goes west.

Before Broadway. *The Nervous Wreck*, upon which the musical was based, opened as a straight comedy in 11/23. *Cast:* Otto Kruger, June Walker. It was filmed in 1926.

The original musical version, re-titled *Whoopee!*, was a Florenz Ziegfeld hit, and ran on Broadway at the NEW AMSTERDAM THEATRE, 12/4/28–7/13/29. 255 PERFORMANCES; it re-ran, same venue, 8/5/29–11/23/29. 157 PERFORMANCES. DIRECTORS: William Anthony McGuire & Seymour Felix; CHOREOGRAPHER: Seymour Felix; MUSICAL DIRECTOR: Gus Salzer. Paul Whiteman's Orchestra replaced George Olsen's for two months during the run. *Cast:* HENRY: Eddie Cantor; SALLY: Frances Upton; MARY: Ethel Shutta; WANENIS: Paul Gregory (character created for the musical); LESLIE: Ruth Etting (character created for the musical); HARRIET: Mary Jane (Ruby Keeler was first choice, but she backed out); ALSO WITH: Buddy Ebsen.

The 1930 movie made stars of Eddie Cantor and choreographer Busby Berkeley. *Cast:* HENRY: Eddie Cantor; MARY: Ethel Shutta; SALLY: Eleanor Hunt; WANENIS: Paul Gregory; BIT PART: Betty Grable. In 1944 Elliott Nugent directed a re-make called *Up in Arms.* *Cast:* Danny Kaye (movie debut), Dinah Shore, Dana Andrews.

The 1979 revival was a Goodspeed production first, before going to Broadway. It was the first professional New York production of this show since the original run in 1928, and aside from a St. Louis Municipal Opera revival in the 1940s, the first major revival anywhere. It wisely omitted several songs from the original — "It's a Beautiful Day Today," "Here's to the Girl of My Heart," "Gypsy Joe," "Come West, Little Girl, Come West," "Where the Sunset Meets the Sea," "Stetson," "My Blackbirds are Bluebirds Now," "I'm Wild About Horns on Automobiles that Go Ta-Ta-Ta-Ta" (Eddie Cantor's Automobile Horn Song), "I Faw Down an' Go Boom," "Big-Hearted Baby," "If I Give up the Saxophone (Will You Come Back to Me?)," "The Song of the Setting Sun," "Love is the Mountain," "Red Mama," "We'll Keep on Caring," "Hallowe'en Tonight."

The Broadway Run. ANTA THEATRE, 2/14/79–8/12/79. 8 previews. 204 PERFORMANCES. The Goodspeed Opera Company production, PRESENTED BY Ashton Springer, Frank C. Pierson, and Michael P. Price, by arrangement with Tams Witmark Music Library; MUSIC: Walter Donaldson; LYRICS: Gus Kahn; BOOK: William Anthony McGuire; BASED ON the 1923 comedy *The Nervous Wreck*, by Owen Davis, which had been based on the short story *The Wreck*, by E.J. Rath; DIRECTOR: Frank Corsaro; CHOREOGRAPHER: Dan Siretta; SETS: John Lee Beatty; COSTUMES: David Toser; LIGHTING: Peter M. Ehrhardt; SOUND: Warren E. Jenkins; MUSICAL DIRECTOR: Lynn Crigler; ORCHESTRATIONS/DANCE MUSIC ARRANGEMENTS: Russell Warner; MUSIC RESEARCH CONSULTANT: Alfred Simon; PRESS: Max Eisen, Irene Gandy, Francine L. Trevens; CASTING: Warren Pincus; GENERAL MANAGEMENT: Theatre Management Associate; COMPANY MANAGER: Alexander Holt; PRODUCTION STAGE MANAGER: John J. Bonanni; STAGE MANAGER: John Beven; ASSISTANT STAGE MANAGER: Jo-Ann Cifala. *Cast:* SHERIFF BOB: J. Kevin Scannell, *Nicholas Wyman*; MARY CUSTER: Carol Swarbrick, *Bonnie Leaders*; JUDSON MORGAN: Bob Allen; SALLY MORGAN: Beth Austin; HENRY WILLIAMS: Charles Repole (1) ✲; WANENIS: Franc Luz; BLACK EAGLE: Leonard Drum; CHESTER UNDERWOOD: Garrett M. Brown, *John Sloman*; HARRIET UNDERWOOD: Catherine Cox; JEROME

UNDERWOOD: Peter Boyden; MORT: Vic Polizos, *John Ahlin*; ANDY McNAB: Bill Rowley; JIM: Al Micacchion; SLIM: Steven Gelfer; JACK: Rick Pessagno; PETE: Paul M. Elkin; RED BUFFALO: Brent Saunders; MATAPE: Candy Darling; LESLIE DAW: Susan Stroman; BECKY: Robin Black; TILLY: Diane Epstein; OLIVE: Teri Corcoran. *Ensemble Alternates*: Jo-Ann Cifala & Jonathan Aronson. *Standby*: Henry: Steven Gelfer. *Understudies*: Bob: Al Micacchion; Mary: Candy Darling; Sally: Robin Black; Wanenis: Paul M. Elkin; Black Eagle/Mort: Brent Saunders; Chester/Andy: Rick Pessagno; Harriet: Susan Stroman; Judson/Jerome: Bill Rowley. *Orchestra*: TRUMPET: Nancy Brown; PERCUSSION: Randall Lombardi. *Act I: Scene 1* Mission Rest, Arizona: "Let's All Make Whoopee Tonight" (Ensemble) [not in the original 1928 production], "Makin' Whoopee!" (Henry & Bridesmaids) [big hit in the original 1928 production], "I'm Bringing a Red, Red Rose" (Wanenis); *Scene 2* En route to Black Top Canyon: "Go Get 'im" (Sheriff & Ensemble); *Scene 3* Black Top Canyon: "Until You Get Somebody Else" (Henry & Sally); *Scene 4* En route to the Bar "M" Ranch: "Go Get 'im" (reprise) (Sheriff & Ensemble); *Scene 5* The Bar "M" Ranch: "Love Me or Leave Me" (Mary & Henry) [this number was a big Ruth Etting hit in the original 1928 production]; *Scene 6* Near the reservation: "I'm Bringing a Red, Red Rose" (reprise) (Wanenis & Sally); *Scene 7* Outside the Bar "M" Ranch: "My Baby Just Cares for Me" (Henry & Ensemble) [not in the original 1928 production], Finaletto: "Go Get 'im" (reprise) (Sheriff & Ensemble). *Act II: Scene 1* Outside the reservation; *Scene 2* Back at the reservation: "Out of the Dawn" (Wanenis & Sally) [not in the original 1928 production], "The Tapahoe Tap" (Indian Ensemble); *Scene 3* In the wilderness: "Reaching for Someone" (Sheriff) [not in the original 1928 production], "You" (m: Walter Donaldson; l: Harold Adamson) (Harriet) [not in the original 1928 production]; *Scene 4* Outside the Bar "M" Ranch: "Yes Sir, That's My Baby" (Henry & Ensemble) [not in the original 1928 production]; *Scene 5* In the desert: "Makin' Whoopee" (reprise) (Ensemble).

Broadway reviews were not good. The show received a Tony nomination for choreography.

After Broadway. TOUR. Heavily revised, and now called *Makin' Whoopee!* The number "I'm Bringing a Red, Red Rose" was replaced in Act I Scene 1 with "Come West, Little Girl, Come West" (Mary & Cowboys). "My Heart is Just a Gypsy" (Harriet) was added as the second song in Act I Scene 3. "Harriet's Ecdysiastical Delight" (specialty dance) was added to Act II Scene 3. *Cast*: MARY: Mamie Van Doren; HARRIET: Imogene Coca.

745. *Whoop-Up*

Joe is a half-Indian rodeo star; Glenda is his on-again, off-again girlfriend whose saloon is half on and half off a U.S. Indian reservation in northern Montana. Set in the present.

Before Broadway. Originally Richard Adler and Jerry Ross were to have written the score, but in the end it was done by Frank Loesser's protégés Moose Charlap and Norman Gimbel. Announced for acting roles at one stage or another were Bob Fosse, Ernie Kovacs, and Edie Adams, but none of them materialized. Paul Ford had a non-singing role. The show tried out in Philadelphia, 11/10/58–12/13/58. The number "I'm on My Way" was cut before Broadway.

The Broadway Run. SHUBERT THEATRE, 12/22/58–2/7/59. 56 PERFORMANCES. PRESENTED BY Cy Feuer & Ernest H. Martin; MUSIC: Moose Charlap; LYRICS: Norman Gimbel; BOOK: Cy Feuer, Ernest H. Martin, Dan Cushman; BASED ON the 1953 novel *Stay Away, Joe*, by Dan Cushman; DIRECTOR: Cy Feuer; CHOREOGRAPHER: Onna White; SETS/LIGHTING: Jo Mielziner; COSTUMES: Anna Hill Johnstone; MUSICAL DIRECTOR/VOCAL DIRECTOR: Stanley Lebowsky; ORCHESTRATIONS: Philip J. Lang; DANCE MUSIC ARRANGEMENTS: Peter Matz; PRESS: Karl Bernstein, Ben Kornzweig, Robert E. Feinberg; GENERAL MANAGER: Ira Bernstein; PRODUCTION STAGE MANAGER: Phil Friedman; STAGE MANAGERS: Lawrence N. Kasha, Michael Kasdan, Paul Michael. *Cast*: GLENDA SWENSON: Susan Johnson (1); JIGGS ROCK MEDICINE: Michael Kermoyan; WALT STEPHENPIERRE: Thomas Raskin; DUB WINTER OWL: Jackie Warner; BIX WINTER OWL: Bobby Shields; LOUIS CHAMPLAIN:

Romo Vincent (4); ANNIE "MAMA" CHAMPLAIN: Sylvia Syms (5); MARY CHAMPLAIN: Julienne Marie (7); MATTHEW BEARCHASER: Tony Gardell; KARL KELLENBACH: Paul Ford (2); CLYDE WALSCHMIDT: Wallace Rooney; GEORGE POTTER: Danny Meehan (6); MEDICINE MAN: Tony Gardell; JOE CHAMPLAIN: Ralph Young (3); MARLENE STANDING RATTLE: Ann Barry; GRAN'PERE: P.J. Kelly (8); BILLIE MAE LITTLEHORSE: Asia (i.e. Asia Mercoolova); JUKE BOX VOICE: Bobby Shields; MRS. KELLENBACH: Vera Walton; BAPTISTE THREE BIRD: Paul Michael; HOTEL PROPRIETOR: Robert Lenn; TEENAGER: Robert Karl; STATE TROOPER: Steve Wiland; JUSTICE OF THE PEACE: Earl Lippy; 1ST STRANGER: Edward Becker; 2ND STRANGER: Socrates Birksy; RESERVATION RESIDENTS: Mari Arnell, Ann Barry, Edward Becker, Jeanna Belkin, Socrates Birksy, Tim Brown, Sandra Devlin, Eleanor Dian, Tina Faye, Tony Gardell, Martha Granese, H.F. Green, Salvador Juarez, Robert Karl, Robert Lenn, Earl Lippy, Rae McLean, Michelle Newton, Estelle Parsons, Yolanda Poropat, Thomas Raskin, Tony Rosa, Marla Stevens, Ben Vargas, Barbara Webb, Steve Wiland. *Understudies*: Mrs. Kellenbach/Glenda: Estelle Parsons; Joe: Michael Kermoyan; Baptiste/Louis: H.F. Green; Mama: Barbara Webb; George: Jackie Warner; Mary: Mari Arnell; Billie Mae: Sandra Devlin; Dub/Bix: Robert Karl; Gran'pere/Walschmidt: Earl Lippy; Rock Medicine: Tom Raskin. *Act I*: "Glenda's Place" (Glenda & Indians), "When the Tall Man Talks" (Glenda), "Nobody Throw Those Bull" (Louis & Indians), "Rocky Boy Ceremonial" (also called "Chief Rocky Boy") (Medicine Man & Members of the Tribe), "Love Eyes" (Joe), "Men" (Glenda), "Never Before" (Mary), "Caress Me, Possess Me Perfume" (Juke Box Voice), "Flattery" (Joe & Glenda), "The Girl in His Arms" (Juke Box), "The Best of What This Country's Got" (George). *Act II*: "I Wash My Hands" (Joe, Mary, Rock Medicine, Stephenpierre), "Quarrel-tet" (Glenda, Joe, Proprietor, Stephenpierre), "Sorry for Myself" (Annie), "Till the Big Fat Moon Falls Down" (Mary, Billie Mae, Friends), "What I Mean to Say" (George), "Montana" (Glenda), "She or Her" (Joe).

Broadway reviews were divided, mostly bad. The show received Tony nominations for choreography, and for Julienne Marie.

After Broadway. THE MOVIE. 1968. Called *Stay Away, Joe*. DIRECTOR: Peter Tewksbury. *Cast*: JOE LIGHTCLOUD: Elvis Presley; CHARLIE LIGHTCLOUD: Burgess Meredith; GLENDA CALLAHAN: Joan Blondell; ANNIE LIGHTCLOUD: Katy Jurado; MAMIE CALLAHAN: Quentin Dean.

746. *The Who's Tommy*

Also called *Tommy*. Set mostly in London, 1941–1963. Tommy is a teenager who, at the age of four, was struck deaf, dumb and blind through the trauma of seeing his father kill his mother's lover. Since then he has been abused by his family and the town bullies, but somehow becomes a pinball wizard, able to communicate through pinball machines. Eventually he recovers his senses, and becomes a messianic superstar. Finally, he returns to his family. For Broadway the story was greatly toned down.

Before Broadway. In 1969 the British rock group The Who issued the double album "Tommy," a rock opera, on Decca, and it was immensely successful world-wide. Its main song, "Pinball Wizard," became a standard. The group performed the opera on stage around the world, even at New York's Metropolitan Opera House ("The Met"), in 1970.

CITY CENTER, NYC, 5/3/72–5/28/72. 31 PERFORMANCES. Les Grands Ballets Canadiens (of Montreal) presented the first production of *Tommy* adapted for ballet, in one act. It was danced to the Decca recording. (Incidentally) it was preceded by two ballets, *Ceremony* and *Hip and Straight*. CHOREOGRAPHER: Fernand Nault; SETS: David Jenkins; COSTUMES: Francois Barbeau. "It's a Boy," "You Didn't Hear It," "Amazing Journey', "Sparks," "Eyesight to the Blind" (m/l: Sonny Boy Williamson), "Christmas," "Cousin Kevin" (m/l: John Entwhistle), "The Acid Queen," Underture, "Do You Think it's Alright?," "Fiddle About" (m/l: John Entwhistle), "Pinball Wizard," "There's a Doctor I've Found," "Go to the Mirror, Boy," "Tommy, Can You Hear Me?," "Smash the Mirror," "Sensation," "Miracle Cure," "Sally Simpson," "I'm Free," "Welcome," "Tommy's Holiday Camp" (m/l: Keith Moon), "We're Not Gonna Take It."

Two concert performances were produced by Lou Reizner at the RAINBOW THEATRE, Finsbury Park, London, on 12/9/72. *Cast*: Sandy Denny, John Entwhistle, Keith Moon, Maggie Bell, Roger Daltrey, Richie Havens, Peter Sellers, Rod Stewart, Stevie Winwood, Pete Townshend, Graham Bell, Merry Clayton.

U.S. TOUR. 1973. *Cast*: Teddy Neeley. It never made New York (at least, as a stage musical) until 1993.

DERBY PLAYHOUSE, England, 5/15/75–5/31/75. This was the first production of the stage musical in the form that would later play on Broadway. DIRECTOR: Jeffrey Dowson; CHOREOGRAPHER: Michael Vernon; MUSICAL DIRECTOR: Paul Herbert. *Cast*: REPORTER/ACID QUEEN: Diana Rowan; EX-PINBALL KING/KEVIN: Jeff Teare; LOVER/ERNIE: John North; MOTHER: Helen Watson; FATHER: Robert French; NARRATOR: Marilyn Cutts; TOMMY: Charles Wegener; HAWKER/DOCTOR: Kean Heanes.

THE MOVIE: 1975. PRODUCED BY: Ken Russell & Robert Stigwood; WRITER/DIRECTOR: Ken Russell. *Cast*: ACID QUEEN: Tina Turner; PINBALL WIZARD: Elton John; UNCLE ERNIE: Keith Moon; FRANK HOBBS: Oliver Reed; NORA WALKER HOBBS: Ann-Margret; GROUP CAPTAIN WALKER: Robert Powell; TOMMY: Roger Daltrey; A. QUACKSON, MENTAL HEALTH SPECIALIST: Jack Nicholson; PREACHER: Eric Clapton; THEMSELVES: John Entwistle & Pete Townshend.

QUEEN'S THEATRE, Hornchurch, Essex, England, 5/2/78–5/20/78. Previews from 4/26/78. DIRECTORS: Paul Tomlinson & John Hole; CHOREOGRAPHER: Lorelei Lynn; SETS: David Knapman; COSTUMES: Jill Pennington; MUSICAL DIRECTOR: Paul Herbert. *Cast*: ACID QUEEN/MOTHER: Dana Gillespie; PINBALL WIZARD/FATHER: David Burt; LOVER: Richard Barnes; NARRATOR: Paul Da Vinci; NURSE: Francesca Lucy; ERNIE/DOCTOR: John Muirhead; KEVIN: Kevin Williams; TOMMY: Allan Love; SALLY: Claire Lewis; MRS. SIMPSON: Vivien Stokes; YOUNG TOMMY Alternates: Daniel Dobson, Philip Carvoso. It ran again, at the QUEEN'S THEATRE, Hornchurch, 6/13/78–6/30/78, with an essentially new cast. Then in the West End of London, at the QUEEN'S THEATRE, 2/6/79–5/19/79. 118 PERFORMANCES. DIRECTORS: Paul Tomlinson & John Hole; CHOREOGRAPHER: Tudor Davies; SETS: David Knapman; COSTUMES: Harry Waistnage; MUSICAL DIRECTOR: Simon Webb. *Cast*: ACID QUEEN/MOTHER: Anna Nicholas; KEVIN: Kevin Williams; PINBALL WIZARD/FATHER: Colin Copperfield; ERNIE/DOCTOR: Bob Grant; LOVER: Steve Devereaux; NARRATOR: Peter Straker; TOMMY: Allan Love; NURSE: Sue Bond; LITTLE TOMMY: Daniel Dobson & John Fowley; LITTLE KEVIN: Philip Carvoso; SALLY: Lorelei Lynn; MRS. SIMPSON: Vivien Stokes.

The Broadway production was originally presented at LA JOLLA PLAYHOUSE, Calif. (Des McAnuff, artistic dir), in the summer of 1992.

The Broadway Run. ST. JAMES THEATRE, 4/22/93–6/17/95. 28 previews from 3/29/93. 899 PERFORMANCES. PRESENTED BY PACE Theatrical Group & Dodger Productions, with Kardana Productions (Andrew Krivine, Victoria Hansen, Tom Carouso), in association with the John F. Kennedy Center for the Performing Arts; MUSIC/LYRICS: Pete Townshend; ADDITIONAL MUSIC & LYRICS: John Entwhistle & Keith Moon; BOOK: Pete Townshend & Des McAnuff; DIRECTOR: Des McAnuff; CHOREOGRAPHER: Wayne Cilento; FLYING: Foy; SETS: John Arnone; COSTUMES: David C. Woolard; LIGHTING: Chris Parry; SOUND: Steve Canyon Kennedy; MUSICAL SUPERVISOR/MUSICAL DIRECTOR: Joseph Church; ORCHESTRATIONS: Steve Margoshes; CAST RECORDING on RCA; PRESS: Boneau/Bryan-Brown; CASTING: Mary Margiotta & Brian Chavanne (L.A.), Hughes Moss Casting (NY); GENERAL MANAGEMENT: David Strong Warner; COMPANY MANAGER: Sandy Carlson; PRODUCTION STAGE MANAGER: Frank Hartenstein, *Dan Hild*; STAGE MANAGER: Karen Armstrong; ASSISTANT STAGE MANAGERS: Kelly Martindale & Jill Larmett. *Cast*: MRS. WALKER: Marcia Mitzman, *Laura Dean, Jessica Molaskey, Christy Tarr*; CAPTAIN WALKER: Jonathan Dokuchitz, *J. Mark McVey*; UNCLE ERNIE: Paul Kandel; MINISTER: Bill Buell; MINISTER'S WIFE: Jody Gelb, *Jeanine Morick*; NURSE: Lisa Leguillou; OFFICER # 1: Michael McElroy, *Adrian Bailey, Alton Fitzgerald White*; OFFICER # 2: Timothy Warmen, *Matthew Farnsworth, Jim Newman*; ALLIED SOLDIER # 1: Donnie Kehr, *Matt Zarley*; ALLIED SOLDIER # 2: Michael Arnold, *Aaron Ellis*; LOVER: Lee Morgan; TOMMY, AGED 4: Carly Jane Steinborn (Monday & Wednesday matinees; Thursdays; Saturday matinees) & Crysta Macalush (Tuesdays; Wednesday evenings; Fridays;

Saturday evenings), *Kimberly Hannon & Nicole Zeidman, Emily Hart & Kimberly Hannon, Nicole Zeidman & Crysta Macalush* (last season). Later alternates for the last season were: *Kelly Maidy, Caitlin Newman, Rachel Beth Levenson*; TOMMY WALKER: Michael Cerveris, *Peter C. Ermides*; JUDGE: Tom Flynn, *Tom Rocco*; TOMMY, AGED 10: Buddy Smith, *Travis Jordan Greisler, Michael Zeidman*; COUSIN KEVIN: Anthony Barrile; KEVIN'S MOTHER: Maria Calabrese, *Sara Miles, Jolie Jenkins*; KEVIN'S FATHER: Tom Flynn, *Tom Rocco*; LOCAL LADS, LATER SECURITY GUARDS: Michael Arnold (*Aaron Ellis*), Paul Dobie (*Kevin Cahoon*), Christian Hoff (*Clarke Thorell*), Donnie Kehr (*Matt Zarley*), Michael McElroy (*Adrian Bailey, Alton White*), Timothy Warmen (*Matthew Farnsworth, Jim Newman*); LOCAL LASSES: Maria Calabrese (*Sara Miles, Jolie Jenkins*), Tracy Nicole Chapman (*April Nixon*), Pam Klinger, Lisa Leguillou, Alice Ripley (*Angela Garrison*), Sherie Scott (*Lacey Hornkohl*); HAWKER: Michael McElroy, *Adrian Bailey, Alton Fitzgerald White*; HARMONICA PLAYER: Lee Morgan, *Lon Hoyt*; THE GYSPY: Cheryl Freeman; 1ST PINBALL LAD: Donnie Kehr, *Matthew Zarley*; 2ND PINBALL LAD: Christian Hoff, *Clarke Thorell*; THE SPECIALIST: Norm Lewis, *Steven Cates*; THE SPECIALIST'S ASSISTANT: Alice Ripley, *Angela Garrison*; NEWS VENDOR: Tom Flynn, *Tom Rocco*; SALLY SIMPSON: Sherie Scott, *Lacey Hornkohl*; MRS. SIMPSON: Pam Klinger; MR. SIMPSON: Bill Buell; DJ: Tom Flynn, *Tom Rocco*; ENSEMBLE: Michael Arnold (*Aaron Ellis*), Bill Buell, Maria Calabrese (*Sara Miles, Jolie Jenkins*), Tracy Nicole Chapman (*April Nixon*), Paul Dobie (*Kevin Cahoon*), Tom Flynn (*Tom Rocco*), Jody Gelb (*Jeanine Morick*), Christian Hoff (*Clarke Thorell*), Donnie Kehr (*Matt Zarley*), Pam Klinger, Lisa Leguillou, Norm Lewis (*Steven Cates*), Michael McElroy (*Adrian Bailey, Alton Fitzgerald White*), Lee Morgan, Alice Ripley (*Angela Garrison*), Sherie Scott (*Lacey Hornkohl*), Timothy Warmen (*Matthew Farnsworth, Jim Newman*). **Understudies**: Tommy: Donnie Kehr & Romain Fruge, *Matt Zarley, Peter Ermides*; Kevin: Donnie Kehr & Romain Fruge, *Aaron Ellis*; Tommy, aged 10: Ari Vernon; Mrs. Walker: Alice Ripley & Jody Gelb, *Angela Garrison, Pam Klinger*; Capt. Walker: Paul Dobie, Timothy Warmen, Todd Hunter, *Matthew Farnsworth, Jim Newman*; Ernie: Bill Buell & Tom Flynn, *Tom Rocco*; Gypsy: Tracey Langran & Tracy Nicole Chapman, *April Nixon*. **Swings**: Victoria Lecta Cave, Romain Fruge, Todd Hunter, Tracey Langran, *Joyce Chittick, Peter Ermides, Doug Friedman, Troy Myers, Steve Dahlem*. **Orchestra**: GUITARS: Kevin Kuhn & John Putnam; DRUMS: Luther Rix; BASS: David Kuhn; KEYBOARDS: Ted Baker, Henry Aronson, Jeanine Levenson; PERCUSSION: Charles Descarfino & John Meyers; FRENCH HORNS: Kaitilin Mahoney & Alexandra Cook; VIOLINS: Dale Stuckenbruck & Cecelia Hobbs Gardner; VIOLA: Crystal Garner; CELLO: Maria Kitsopoulos. *Act I: Overture*: 1941 (Company); *Scene 1* 22 Heathfield Gardens, London, England/POW camp, Germany; 1941: "Captain Walker" (Officers); *Scene 2* Hospital/POW camp; 1945: "It's a Boy" (Nurses & Mrs. Walker), "We've Won" (Captain Walker & Allied Soldiers); *Scene 3* 22 Heathfield Gardens: "Twenty-One" (Mrs. Walker, Lover, Captain Walker), "Amazing Journey" (Tommy); *Scene 4* English courtroom; *Scene 5* Hospital: "Sparks" (instrumental), "Amazing Journey" (reprise) (Tommy); *Scene 6* Church/The home of the relatives; 1950: "Christmas" (Mr. & Mrs. Walker, Minister, Minister's Wife, Ensemble), "See Me, Feel Me" (Tommy); *Scene 7* 22 Heathfield Gardens: "Do You Think it's Alright?" (Mr. & Mrs. Walker), "Fiddle About" (m/l: John Entwhistle) (Uncle Ernie & Ensemble), "See Me, Feel Me" (reprise) (Tommy); *Scene 8* 22 Heathfield Gardens/A youth club: "Cousin Kevin" (m/L; John Entwhistle) (Kevin & Ensemble), "Sensation" (Tommy & Ensemble); *Scene 9* Psychiatric clinic: "Sparks" (reprise); *Scene 10* 22 Heathfield Gardens: "Eyesight to the Blind" (m/l: Sonny Boy Williamson) (Hawker, Harmonica Player, Ensemble); *Scene 11* The Isle of Dogs: "Acid Queen" (The Gypsy); *Scene 12* Amusement arcade: "Pinball Wizard" (Local Lads, Kevin, Ensemble). *Act II: Underture* (i.e. Entr'acte); 1960; *Scene 1* The Sunlight Laundry: "There's a Doctor" (Mr. & Mrs. Walker); *Scene 2* Research laboratory: "Go to the Mirror" (Specialist, Specialist's Assistant, Mr. & Mrs. Walker), "Listening to You" (Tommy, Tommy aged 10, Tommy aged 4); *Scene 3* The street/22 Heathfield Gardens: "Tommy, Can You Hear Me?" (Local Lads); *Scene 4* 22 Heathfield Gardens: "I Believe My Own Eyes" [new song — not on the original album] (Mr. & Mrs. Walker), "Smash the Mirror" (Mrs. Walker), "I'm Free" (Tommy); *Scene 5* The streets of London; 1961–1963: "Miracle Cure" (News Vendor & Local Lads), "Sensation" (reprise) (Tommy & Ensemble), "I'm

Free"/"Pinball Wizard" (reprise) (Tommy & Company); *Scene 6* Holiday Camp: "Tommy's Holiday Camp" (m/l: Keith Moon) (Ernie); *Scene 7* The Simpsons': "Sally Simpson" (Kevin, Security Guards, Sally, Mr. & Mrs. Simpson); *Scene 8* Heathfield Gardens: "Welcome" (Tommy & Ensemble); *Scene 9* Heathfield Gardens: "We're Not Going to Take It" (Tommy & Ensemble); *Scene 10* Heathfield Gardens: "See Me, Feel Me"/"Listening to Me" (reprise)/Finale (Tommy & Company).

Broadway reviews were mostly great. The show won Tonys for direction of a musical, choreography, sets, and lighting, and was nominated for musical, score, book, costumes, and for Michael Cerveris, Paul Kandel, and Marcia Mitzman.

After Broadway. BROADWAY TOUR. Opened on 10/12/93, at the Music Hall, Dallas. MUSICAL DIRECTOR: Wendy Bobbitt. **Cast:** MRS. WALKER: Jessica Molaskey, *Christy Tarr*; MR. WALKER: Jason Workman, *Jordan Leeds*; NURSE: Aiko Nakasone; TOMMY, AGED 4: Kelly Maidy, Caitlin Newman, Rachel Beth Levenson; TOMMY: Steve Isaacs; ERNIE: William Youmans, *Stephen Lee Anderson*; SALLY: Hilary Morse; JUDGE/KEVIN'S FATHER: Tom Rocco; TOMMY, AGED 10: Robert Mann Kayser, *Brett Levenson*; KEVIN: Roger Bart, *Michael Arnold*; GYPSY: Kenna Ramsey; ASSISTANT: Valerie de Pena; CHORUS: Carla Renata Williams, Clarke Thorell, Steve Dahlem.

30TH-ANNIVERSARY TOUR (30 years since the first Tommy album came out). Opened on 3/19/99, at the Playhouse, Wilmington, Del. DIRECTOR: Worth Gardner; MUSICAL DIRECTOR: Scot Woolley. **Cast:** TOMMY: Michael Seelbach; CAPT. WALKER: Christopher Monteleone; MRS. WALKER: Lisa Capps; KEVIN: Michael Gruber; ACID QUEEN/GYPSY: Virginia Woodruff; ERNIE: Paul Dobie.

747. *Wicked*

Set in the Land of Oz. The untold story of the witches of Oz. It tells the story of many of the characters before Dorothy got there. In other words, a sort of prequel to *The Wizard of Oz*. Elphaba and Galinda meet at Shiz, a school where both intend to study sorcery. Galinda is incredibly popular, and Elphaba is very envious. They wind up as room-mates. Madame Morrible is the headmistress. Galinda changes her name to Glinda before her trip to the Emerald City.

Before Broadway. Norbert Leo Butz and Carole Shelley were announced in their roles on 12/11/02 (Kristin Chenoweth and Idina Menzel had been announced previously). The show tried out 5/28/03–6/29/03, at the Curran Theatre, San Francisco. **Cast:** GLINDA: Kristin Chenoweth; DILLAMOND: John Horton; NESSAROSE: Michelle Federer; BOQ: Kirk McDonald; WIZARD: Robert Morse; MME MORRIBLE: Carole Shelley. On 1/31/03 the Gershwin was announced as the Broadway house. Rehearsals began on 3/31/03. Kristin Chenoweth missed the 6/4/03 performance due to a slight neck injury, but was back on 6/5/03. Melissa Bell Chait, her understudy, went on. The first day of Broadway previews was put back from 10/7/03 to 10/8/03, and the official opening date was moved up a day from 10/31/03. It had advance box-office sales of $9.6 million.

The Broadway Run. GERSHWIN THEATRE, 10/30/03–. 25 previews from 10/8/03. PRESENTED BY Marc Platt, Universal Pictures, The Araca Group, Jon B. Platt, and David Stone; MUSIC/LYRICS: Stephen Schwartz; BOOK: Winnie Holzman; BASED ON the novel *Wicked: The Life and Times of the Wicked Witch of the West*, by Gregory Maguire; DIRECTOR: Joe Mantello; CHOREOGRAPHER: Wayne Cilento; SETS: Eugene Lee; COSTUMES: Susan Hilferty; LIGHTING: Kenneth Posner; SOUND: Tony Meola; MUSICAL DIRECTOR: Stephen Oremus; ORCHESTRATIONS: William David Brohn; MUSIC ARRANGEMENTS: Alex Lacamoire & Stephen Oremus; DANCE MUSIC ARRANGEMENTS: James Lynn Abbott; CAST RECORDING on Decca Broadway, made in 11/03, and released on 12/16/03; it was one of the best selling albums of 2004, and won a Grammy; PRESS: The Publicity Office; CASTING: Bernard Telsey; GENERAL MANAGEMENT: EGS; COMPANY MANAGER: Susan Sampliner; STAGE MANAGER: Erica Schwartz; ASSISTANT STAGE MANAGERS: Chris Jamros & Bess Marie Glorioso. **Cast:** GLINDA, THE GOOD WITCH: Kristin Chenoweth (1) ☆, *Melissa Bell Chait* (stood in 11/18/03 and 11/19/03, and again for the

11/22/03 matinee, during Miss Chenoweth's cold; Miss Chenoweth was back for the 11/22/03 evening performance. She left 7/18/04), *Jennifer Laura Thompson* (7/20/04–5/29/05), *Megan Hilty* (from 5/31/05); WITCH'S FATHER: Sean McCourt, *Eddie Korbich* (stood in); WITCH'S MOTHER: Cristy Candler; MIDWIFE: Adinah Alexander, *Jan Neuberger*; ELPHABA: Idina Menzel (1) ☆ (out 6/15/04–7/2/04; she left the show on 1/9/05, but see notes below), *Shoshana Bean* (from 1/11/05); NESSAROSE: Michelle Federer; BOQ: Christopher Fitzgerald, *Randy Harrison* (6/22/04–7/25/04), *Christopher Fitzgerald* (7/26/04–1/2/05), *Robb Sapp* (from 1/4/05), *Jeffrey Kuhn* (from 1/11/05); MADAME MORRIBLE: Carole Shelley (4) (until 5/29/05), *Rue McClanahan* (from 5/31/05); DR. DILLAMOND: William Youmans; FIYERO: Norbert Leo Butz (5) (until 11/23/03), *Kristoffer Cusick* (11/24/03–12/21/03), *Taye Diggs* (12/22/03–1/15/04), *Norbert Leo Butz* (1/16/04 evening performance, and matinee of 1/17/04), *Taye Diggs* (1/17/04 evening and 1/18/04), *Norbert Leo Butz* (back permanently, 1/20/04–7/18/04), *Joey McIntyre* (7/20/04–1/9/05), *David Ayers* (from 1/11/05) OZIAN OFFICIAL: Sean McCourt, *Eddie Korbich* (stood in); THE WONDERFUL WIZARD OF OZ: Joel Grey (3) (left in late 6/04, with bronchitis), *Sean McCourt, George Hearn* (7/20/04–5/29/05), *Ben Vereen* (from 5/31/05); CHISTERY, THE FLYING MONKEY: Manuel Herrera; MONKEYS/STUDENTS/DENIZENS OF THE EMERALD CITY/PALACE GUARDS/OTHER CITIZENS OF OZ: Ioana Alfonso, Stephanie J. Block (replaced during previews), Ben Cameron, Cristy Candler, Kristy Cates (added during previews), Melissa Bell Chait, Marcus Choi, Kristoffer Cusick, Kathy Deitch, Eden Espinosa (added during previews), Melissa Fahn, Rhett G. George, Kristen Leigh Gorski (left during run), Manuel Herrera, Kisha Howard, L.J. Jellison, Sean McCourt, Corinne McFadden, Mark Myars (*Marty Thomas*), Jan Neuberger, Walter Winston O'Neil, Andrew Palermo, Andy Pellick (added during previews), Peter Samuel (replaced during previews), Michael Seelbach, Lorna Ventura (added during previews), Derrick Williams (added during previews), *Adinah Alexander, Stacie Morgain Lewis* (from 4/04). **Standbys:** Glinda: *Laura Bell Bundy, Megan Hilty*; Elphaba: *Eden Espinosa, Shoshana Bean*. **Understudies:** Glinda: Melissa Bell Chait, *Melissa Fahn*; Elphaba: Kristy Cates; Fiyero: Kristoffer Cusick & Derrick Williams (added during previews); Dillamond/Wizard: *Eddie Korbich, Anthony Galde, Sean McCourt*; Morrible: *Adinah Alexander, Jan Neuberger, Lorna Ventura*; Ozian Official/Witch's Father: Ben Cameron; Boq: *Mark Myars, Walter Winston O'Neil, Andrew Palermo*; Nessarose: Cristy Candler & Eden Espinosa; Chistery: Mark Myars (when Mr. Myars left no one replaced him as understudy for Chistery). **Swings:** *Eddie Korbich, Charlie Sutton, Angela Brydon, Kristen Leigh Gorski, Anthony Galde, Mark Myars, Adinah Alexander, Lorna Ventura, Derrick Williams*. **Orchestra:** CONCERTMASTER: Christian Hebel; VIOLIN: Victor Schultz; VIOLA: Kevin Roy; CELLO: Dan Miller; HARP: Laura Sherman; LEAD TRUMPET: Jon Owens; TRUMPET: Tom Hoyt; TROMBONES: Dale Kirkland & Douglas Purviance; FLUTE: Helen Campo; OBOE: Tuck Lee; CLARINETS: John Moses & John Campo; SOPRANO SAX: John Moses; BASSOON/BARITONE SAX: John Campo; FRENCH HORNS: Theo Primis & Kelly Dent; DRUMS: Gary Seligson; BASS: Konrad Adderley; PIANO/SYNTHESIZER: Alex Lacamoire; KEYBOARDS: Paul Loesel & David Evans; GUITARS: Ric Molina & Greg Skaff; PERCUSSION: Andy Jones. *Act I*: "No One Mourns the Wicked" (Glinda & Citizens of Oz), "Dear Old Shiz" (Students), "The Wizard and I" (Morrible & Elphaba), "What is This Feeling" (Galinda, Elphaba, Students), "Something Bad" (Dillamond & Elphaba), "Dancing Through Life" (Fiyero, Galinda, Boq, Nessarose, Elphaba, Students), "Popular" (Galinda), "I'm Not That Girl" (Elphaba), "One Short Day" (Elphaba, Glinda, Denizens of the Emerald City), "A Sentimental Man" (Wizard), "Defying Gravity" (Elphaba, Glinda, Guards, Citizens of Oz). *Act II*: "No One Mourns the Wicked" (reprise) (Citizens of Oz), "Thank Goodness" (Glinda, Morrible, Citizens of Oz), "The Wicked Witch of the East" (Elphaba, Nessarose, Boq), "Wonderful" (Wizard & Elphaba) [this number was slightly revised by Stephen Schwartz when George Hearn came in as the Wizard], "I'm Not That Girl" (reprise) (Glinda), "As Long as You're Mine" (Elphaba & Fiyero), "No Good Deed" (Elphaba), "March of the Witch Hunters" (Boq & Citizens of Oz), "For Good" (Glinda & Elphaba), Finale (All).

Broadway reviews were divided. Kristin Chenoweth got raves. The score let it down. In 11/03 Norbert Leo Butz came down with a back injury. Melissa Bell Chait suffered a mild stroke at 3 a.m. on 3/8/04, was hospitalized, and released in good condition on 3/11/04. The show won Tonys for sets, costumes, and for Idina Menzel, and was nominated for musical, book of a musical, original score written for the theatre, choreography, lighting, orchestrations, and for Kristin Chenoweth. Idina Menzel was going to leave on 1/2/05, but delayed it a week. The production, capitalized at $14 million, recouped its initial investment by 12/04, after 14 months of the run. By late 11/04 Ben Vereen was being talked about as the Wizard. 1/9/05 was scheduled to be Idina Menzel's last performance as Elphaba, and Shoshana Bean, her understudy, was going to replace her permanently on 1/11/05. However, during the matinee performance of 1/8/05 Miss Menzel stepped through a trapdoor on stage, as planned, but the platform under the stage that would have received her was lower than it should have been, and she fell, cracking a rib. Miss Bean played the performance of 1/0/05, at the end of which Miss Menzel came on for a few minutes in a red tracksuit to finish the performance, and to take a bow at curtain call.

After Broadway. TOUR. Opened at the Canon Theatre, Toronto, 3/9/05, one day later than scheduled because Stephanie Block was injured during dress rehearsal, and Kristy Cates stepped in. It closed in Toronto on 4/24/05, then carried on with the tour, first at the Ford Center for the Performing Arts, Chicago, 4/29/05–6/12/05. PRESENTED BY David Stone; DIRECTOR: Joe Mantello; CHOREOGRAPHER: Wayne Cilento. *Cast:* GLINDA: Kendra Kassebaum; ELPHABA: Kristy Cates, *Stephanie J. Block* (from 3/25/05); WIZARD: David Garrison; MME MORRIBLE: Carol Kane; FIYERO: Derrick Williams; NESSAROSE: Jenna Leigh Green; BOQ: Logan Lipton; DILLAMOND: Timothy Britten Parker; CHORUS INCLUDED: Lori Holmes, Emily Rozek, James Tabeek.

748. *Wiener Blut*

Also known as *Vienna Life*. Austrian operetta set during the Congress of Vienna, in 1815. The mistress of ceremonies translated some of it into English, but essentially the musical was sung in German.

Before Broadway. This show first appeared, on Broadway, as *Vienna Life* (in English), at the BROADWAY THEATRE, 1/23/1901–2/23/1901. 35 PERFORMANCES. It had a run at the STOLL THEATRE, London, 8/16/54–9/4/54. 8 PERFORMANCES. PRESENTED BY Peter Daubeny; DIRECTOR: Tony Niessner; CHOREOGRAPHER: Dia Lucca; MUSICAL DIRECTOR: Paul Walter. *Cast:* BALDUIN: Karl Terkal; JOSEF: Tony Niessner.

The 1964 production was the first U.S. revival of note since 1901. The Johann Strauss numbers "The Blue Danube Waltz" & "Acceleration Waltz" were added for it.

The Broadway Run. LUNT–FONTANNE THEATRE, 9/11/64–10/3/64. 27 PERFORMANCES. PRESENTED BY The Greek Theatre Association (James A. Doolittle & Felix G. Gerstman); PRODUCED BY Harold A. Hoeller; MUSIC: Johann Strauss; LYRICS/BOOK: Victor Leon & Leo Stein; ADAPTED/DIRECTOR: Tony Niessner; CHOREOGRAPHER: Fred Meister; SETS: Ferry Windberger; COSTUMES: Hill Rheis-Gromes; LIGHTING/AMERICAN PRODUCTION SUPERVISOR: Thomas Skelton; MUSICAL DIRECTOR: Oswald Unterhauser; MUSICAL ARRANGER: Hans Hagen; PRESS: Max Eisen, Bob Feinberg, Jeanne Gibson Merrick, Maurice Turet; COMPANY MANAGER: Alfred Fischer; PRODUCTION STAGE MANAGER: Pat Chandler; STAGE MANAGER: Sally Cook. *Cast:* MISTRESS OF CEREMONIES: Gita Rena; POLICEMAN: Andreij Halasz; COUNT BALDUIN ZEDLAU, AMBASSADOR FROM REUSS–SCHLEIZ–GREIZ: Erwin von Gross (1); COUNTESS ZEDLAU, HIS WIFE: Maria Kowa (2); FRANZISKA CAGLIARI, DANCER AT THE KARNTNERTOR THEATRE: Clementine Mayer; PEPI PLEININGER, A MODEL: Dagmar Koller; JOSEF, COUNT ZEDLAU'S VALET: Helmut Wallner; PRINCE YPSHEIM-GINDELBACH, PRIME MINISTER OF REUSS–SHLEIZ–GREIZ: Wilhelm Popp; KAGLER, CAGLIARI'S FATHER: Hugo Lindinger; ANNA, CAGLIARI'S MAID: Friederike Mann; A COACHMAN: Werner Karman; COUNT BITOWSKI: Emmerich Godin; COUNTESS BITOWSKI: Else Petry; THE FRENCH AMBASSADOR: Erich Herg; THE ITALIAN AMBASSADOR: Martino Stamos; THE ENGLISH AMBASSADOR: Wolfgang Hackenberg; THE PRUSSIAN AMBASSADOR: Gerhard Kurz; THE RUSSIAN AMBASSADOR: Werner Karman; LAUNDRY MAIDS: LISI: Friederike Mann; LORI: Silvia Holzmayer; A GRENADIER:

Erich Herg; A WATCHMAN (DEUTSCHMEISTER): Wolfgang Hackenberg; A BOY WAITER: Eveline Kohlhammer; PROPRIETOR OF HIETZING CASINO: Werner Karman; SINGING ENSEMBLE: Maria Holoubeck, Silvia Holzmayer, Elfriede Knapp, Angelike Lignu, Friederike Mann, Katherine Stellaki, Wolfgang Hackenberg, Erich Herg, Werner Karman, Gerhard Kurz, Martino Stamos, Achilles Talos; DANCING SOLOISTS: Iwa Slatewa, Flora Lojekova, Andreij Halasz, Kurt Schenker; DANCING ENSEMBLE: Hulda Fuchs, Katja Dooren, Eveline Kohlhammer, Edda Kreen, Katja Pogacnik, Nora Zechner, Ingrid Nedbal. *Understudies*: Count Zedlau: Gerhard Kurz; Countess Zedlau: Elfriede Knapp; Franziska: Silvia Holzmayer; Pepi: Friederike Mann; Josef: Wolfgang Hackenberg; Kagler: Werner Karman. *Act I: Scene 1* A street in Vienna; summer morning: Introduction (Mistress of Ceremonies & Ensemble), "Ich such' jetzt da, ich such jetzt dort" ("I am looking here now, I am looking there now") (Josef); *Scene 2* Cagliari's villa; the same morning: "Pepi! Er?" ("Pepi! He?") (Cagliari & Josef), (Na, also schreib', und tu' nicht schmieren" ("Go on, write and do not scribble") (Count Zedlau & Josef), Polka (Pepi & The Mannequins), "Wunsch' guten Morgen, Herr von Pepi" ("Good Morning, Mr. von Pepi" (Pepi & Josef), Finale I (Cagliari, Josef, Kagler, Prince, Count Zedlau). *Act II*: The palace of Count Bitowksi: "Polonaise" (mc & Ensemble), Pas de Deux (Miss Lojekova & Mr. Halasz), "Wiener Blut" ("Vienna Life") (Countess & Count Zedlau), "Wiener Frauen singen gern" ("Viennese women love to sing") (Cagliari, Bitowski, Ministers), "So, nimm, mein susser Schatz" ("Take it, my sweet darling") (Count Zedlau, Pepi, Josef), Mazurka (Solo Dancers), "Bohmische Polka" ("Bohemian Polka") (Pepi & Kagler), Czardas (Solo Dancers), "Lagunenwalzer" ("Lagoon Waltz") (Italian Ambassador & Ensemble), Finale II (Ensemble), "An der schoenen blau Donau" ("The Blue Danube Waltz") (Iwa Slatewa, Kurt Schenker, Dancing Ensemble). *Act III*: The garden of the Casino at Hietzing: "Geht's und verkauft's mei G'wand" ("Go on and sell my suit") (Lisi & Lori), "A'Walzer von Strauss" ("A Waltz by Strauss") (Kagler, Watchman, Singing Ensemble), Polka (Soloists & Dancing Ensemble), "Accelerationenwalzer" ("Acceleration Waltz") (Ensemble), Finale III (mc & Ensemble).

Reviews were completely divided.

749. *Wild and Wonderful*

Subtitled *A "Big City" Fable*. Set in the present, in the big city. Charlie, an ex–West Pointer, is assigned by the CIA to infiltrate the metropolis's youth movement.

Before Broadway. Laura McDuffie replaced Julie Budd.

The Broadway Run. LYCEUM THEATRE, 12/7/71. 9 previews from 11/29/71. 1 PERFORMANCE. PRESENTED BY Rick Hobard, in association with Raymonde Weil; MUSIC/LYRICS: Bob Goodman; BOOK: Phil Phillips; BASED ON an original work by Bob Brotherton & Bob Miller; DIRECTOR: Burry Fredrik; CHOREOGRAPHER: Ronn Forella; SETS: Stephen Hendrickson; COSTUMES: Frank Thompson; LIGHTING: Neil Peter Jampolis; ASSISTANT LIGHTING: F. Mitchell Dana; MUSICAL DIRECTOR/VOCAL ARRANGEMENTS/DANCE MUSIC COMPOSER & ARRANGER: Thom Janusz; ORCHESTRATIONS: Luther Henderson; PRESS: Max Eisen, Jeanne Gibson Merrick, Milly Schoenbaum; GENERAL MANAGER: William Craver; COMPANY MANAGER: Stanley Brody; PRODUCTION STAGE MANAGER: Robert Keegan; STAGE MANAGER: Louis Pulvino; ASSISTANT STAGE MANAGER: Philip Killian. *Cast:* JENNY: Laura McDuffie (2) ☆; CHARLIE: Walter Willison (1) ☆; LIONEL MASTERS: Robert Burr (3) ☆; BROTHER JOHN: Larry Small (5) ☆; JIMMY: Jimmy Roddy; FATHER DESMOND: Ted Thurston (4) ☆; YVELINE: Yveline Baudez; PAM: Pam Blair; MARY ANN: Mary Ann Bruning; CAROL: Carol Conte; BOB: Bob Daley; ANNA MARIA: Anna Maria Fanizzi; MARCELO: Marcelo Gamboa; ADAM: Adam Grammis; PATTI: Patti Haine; ANN: Ann Reinking; STEVEN: Steven Vincent; EDDIE: Eddie Wright Jr. *Act I*: "Wild and Wonderful" (dance) (Company), "My First Moment" (Jenny), "I Spy" (Charlie), "Desmond's Dilemma" (Desmond & Brother John), "The Moment is Now" (Charlie & Ensemble), "Something Wonderful (Can Happen)" (Jenny), "Chances" (Jenny, Lionel, Ann, Mary Ann, Carol, Anna Maria), "She Should Have Me" (Lionel) [cut during previews],

"Jenny" (Charlie), "Fallen Angels" (Brother John & Dropouts), Dance (Pam, Jimmy, Dropouts). *Act II*: "Petty Crime" (Jenny, Judge, Company), "Come a Little Closer" (Jenny & Charlie), "Little Bits and Pieces" (Lionel & Models) [cut during previews], "Is This My Town" (Jenny), "You Can Reach the Sun" (Brother John & Dropouts), "A Different Kind of World" (Desmond), "Wait for Me" (Charlie), "Wild and Wonderful" (reprise) (Company).

Broadway reviews were terrible.

750. *The Wild Party*

Queenie and her brutal lover, Burrs, throw a debauched Hollywood-style party in 1928 New York City, with seedy showbiz types, gangsters and playboys. No intermission.

There were three different versions of *The Wild Party*, only one of which made it to Broadway, and that was Michael John La Chiusa's version, called here "The Broadway version." The other two, Andrew Lippa's version, and the Studio Theatre version, are treated separately, at the end of this entry.

Before Broadway. The Broadway version had a workshop at the PUBLIC THEATRE, 2/15/99–2/26/99. Previews from 2/4/99. It was still developing at this stage. PRESENTED BY George Wolfe; CHOREOGRAPHER: Joey McKneely. *Cast*: QUEENIE: Vanessa Williams; BURRS: Mandy Patinkin; DOLORES: Eartha Kitt; ALSO WITH: Keith David, Debbie Shapiro Gravitte, Jane Summerhays. It was going to be a full-fledged production at the Public, but on 8/12/99 it was announced that instead of the proposed Off Broadway run, it would go to Broadway. Toni Collette, Mandy Patinkin, and Eartha Kitt were all confirmed in their Broadway roles on 10/14/99. Vanessa Williams couldn't make it due to other commitments. There was a press preview on 2/16/00. Broadway previews began on 3/10/00 (date put back from 3/7/00). The 3/16/00 performance was canceled so Mandy Patinkin's standby, David Masenheimer, could adequately rehearse for taking over while Mr. Patinkin's strained vocal cords healed. Mr. Masenheimer took over on 3/17/00, and Mr. Patinkin was back on 3/28/00. Toni Collette was out with a cold for a week at the end of March 2000, and she was also out on 4/3/00, 4/4/00 and 4/5/00. The 4/5/00 matinee had to be canceled, supposedly to give more rehearsal time for the full cast. Toni Collette was back on 4/6/00. The opening date was put back from 4/6/00 to 4/13/00.

The Broadway Run. VIRGINIA THEATRE, 4/13/00–6/11/00. 36 previews from 3/10/00. 68 PERFORMANCES. PRESENTED BY the Joseph Papp Public Theatre/New York Shakespeare Festival (George C. Wolfe, producer; Rosemarie Tichler, artistic producer) and Scott Rudin/Paramount Pictures, Roger Berlind, Williams/Waxman (Elizabeth Williams & Anita Waxman); MUSIC/LYRICS: Michael John La Chiusa; BOOK: Michael John La Chiusa & George C. Wolfe; BASED ON the 1928 narrative poem by Joseph Moncure March; DIRECTOR: George C. Wolfe; CHOREOGRAPHER: Joey McKneely; SETS: Robin Wagner; COSTUMES: Toni-Leslie James; LIGHTING: Jules Fisher & Peggy Eisenhauer; SOUND: Tony Meola; MUSICAL DIRECTOR: Todd Ellison; ORCHESTRATIONS: Bruce Coughlin; CAST RECORDING on Decca Broadway, made on 4/17/00, and released on 5/23/00; PRESS: Barlow—Hartman Public Relations; CASTING: Jordan Thaler & Heidi Griffiths; GENERAL MANAGEMENT: 101 Productions; COMPANY MANAGER: Charles Underhill; PRODUCTION STAGE MANAGER: Gwendolyn M. Gilliam; STAGE MANAGER: Rick Steiger; ASSISTANT STAGE MANAGER: Lisa Dawn Cave. *Cast*: QUEENIE: Toni Collette, *Nicole Van Giesen* (during Miss Collette's illness); BURRS: Mandy Patinkin, *David Masenheimer* (during Mr. Patinkin's illness); JACKIE: Marc Kudisch; MISS MADELAINE TRUE: Jane Summerhays; SALLY: Sally Murphy; EDDIE MACKREL: Norm Lewis; MAE: Leah Hocking; NADINE: Brooke Sunny Moriber; PHIL D'ARMANO: Nathan Lee Graham; OSCAR D'ARMANO: Michael McElroy; DOLORES: Eartha Kitt; GOLD: Adam Grupper; GOLDBERG: Stuart Zagnit; BLACK: Yancey Arias; KATE: Tonya Pinkins. *Standbys*: Burrs: David Masenheimer & Jeff Gardner; Queenie: Nicole Van Giesen & Dominique Plaisant; Kate: Dominique Plaisant & Jennifer Frankel; Dolores: Ching Valdes-Aran; Black/Jackie: Rene Millan; Mae/Madelaine: Jennifer Frankel; Eddie/Oscar/Phil: Adrian Bailey; Gold/Goldberg: Jeff Gardner; Nadine/Sally: Jennifer Hall. *Orches-*

tra: PIANO: Linda Twine; WOODWINDS: William Easley, Jimmy Cozier, Steven Kenyon, Roger Rosenberg; TRUMPETS: Brian O'Flaherty, Kamau Adilifu; TROMBONE: Tim Sessions; VIOLINS: Lesa Terry, Ashley Horne, Julien Barber; BASS: Benjamin Brown; DRUMS: Brian Grice; PERCUSSION: Bruce Doctor; GUITAR: Steve Bargonetti.

THE VAUDEVILLE: "Queenie Was a Blonde/Marie is Tricky/Wild Party" (Queenie, Burrs, Company); PROMENADE OF GUESTS: "Dry" (Burrs, Jackie, Madelaine, Sally, Eddie, Mae, Nadine, Brothers D'Armano, Dolores), "Welcome to My Party" (Queenie), "Like Sally" (Madelaine), "Breezin' Through Another Day" (Jackie), "Uptown" (Brothers D'Armano), "Eddie & Mae" (Eddie & Mae), "Gold & Goldberg" (Gold & Goldberg), "Movin' Uptown" (Dolores); THE PARTY: "Black Bottom" (Queenie & Company), "Best Friend" (Queenie & Kate), "A Little M-M-M" (Brothers D'Armano), "Tabu/Taking Care of the Ladies" (Oscar, Black, Company), "Wouldn't it Be Nice?" (Burrs), "Lowdown-Down" (Queenie), "Gin" (Burrs & Company), "Wild" (Company), "Need" (Madelaine & Company), "Black is a Moocher" (Kate), "People Like Us" (Queenie & Black); AFTER MIDNIGHT DIES: "After Midnight Dies" (Sally), "Golden Boy" (Eddie & Brothers D'Armano), "The Movin' Uptown Blues" (Gold & Goldberg), "The Lights of Broadway" (Nadine), "More" (Jackie), "Love Ain't Nothin'/Welcome to Her Party/What I Need" (Kate, Burrs, Queenie), "How Many Women in the World?" (Burrs), "When it Ends" (Dolores); FINALE: "This is What it Is" (Queenie), Finale (Queenie, Burrs, Company).

Broadway reviews were divided, but mostly good. Closing notices were posted on 6/6/00 for 6/11/00. The show received Tony nominations for musical, score, book, lighting, and for Mandy Patinkin, Eartha Kitt, and Toni Collette.

After Broadway. Its first revival was at YALE UNIVERSITY, 10/2/03–10/4/03. DIRECTOR: Benjamin Morse.

ANDREW LIPPA'S VERSION OF *The Wild Party*. Andrew Lippa picked up the March poem in Barnes and Noble, and decided to write a musical. He was, at that time, unaware of the straight James Ivory film of 1975, starring Raquel Welch and James Coco. Act I of his musical had a reading by the MANHATTAN THEATRE CLUB (MTC) in 8/96, and there was another reading in 8/97 at the EUGENE O'NEILL THEATRE CONFERENCE, Waterford, Conn., this time of the full piece. There was a six-week fully-staged workshop at the MTC, 4/99–5/99. DIRECTOR: Gabriel Barre; CHOREOGRAPHER: Mark Dendy. *Cast*: BURRS: James Barbour; QUEENIE: Marin Mazzie (Kristin Chenoweth was going to do it but left the cast before the workshop); PHIL: Luther Creek; MADELAINE: Alix Korey; MAY: Jessica Stone; DOLORES: Kevin-Anthony; EDDIE: Bill Nolte; OSCAR: Jayson Page; KATE: Sara Ramirez; JACKIE: Lawrence Keigwin; NADINE: Allison Munn; ALSO WITH: Michael McElroy; ENSEMBLE: Jillian, Steve Ochoa, Robin Irwin, Bill Kocis, Elizabeth Parkinson, William Ryall, Dennis Stowe. As for the full production, Taye Diggs, Julia K. Murney, and Idina Menzel had been confirmed in their roles as early as 9/99. It opened for 34 previews at the MTC's STAGE 1, on 1/25/00, and it opened there officially on 2/24/00 (date put back from 2/22/00). Reviews were mixed, but the house was packed, night after night, and the closing date was extended to 4/9/00 (it ran 54 PERFORMANCES). PRESENTED BY Jeffrey Seller & Kevin McCollum; DIRECTOR: Gabriel Barre; CHOREOGRAPHER: Mark Dendy; SETS: David Gallo; COSTUMES: Martin Pakledinaz; LIGHTING: Kenneth Posner; SOUND: Brian Ronan; MUSICAL DIRECTOR: Stephen Oremus; ORCHESTRATIONS: Michael Gibson; CAST RECORDING on RCA, made on 4/11/00 (most of the numbers were on it), and released on 7/11/00. *Cast*: QUEENIE: Julia K. Murney; BURRS: Brian d'Arcy James; RENO: Todd Anderson; KEGS: Ron J. Todorowski; MADELAINE TRUE: Alix Korey; EDDIE: Raymond Jaramillo McLeod; PEGGY: Megan Sikora; MAX: James Delisco Beeks; ROSE HIMMELSTEEN: Felicity Finley; SAM HIMMELSTEEN: Peter Kapetan; ELLIE: Amanda Watkins; JACKIE: Lawrence Keigwin; OSCAR D'ARMANO: Charles Dillon; PHIL D'ARMANO: Kevin Cahoon; DOLORES: Kena Tangi Dorsey; MAE: Jennifer Cody; NADINE: Kristin McDonald; KATE: Idina Menzel; BLACK: Taye Diggs; NEIGHBOR: Charlie Marcus; COP: Steven Pasquale. *Act I*: "Queenie Was a Blonde" (the first line of the poem, and the same opening number title as for the Broadway version), "The Apartment (Sunday Noon)," "Out of the Blue," "What a Party," "Raise the Roof," "Look at Me Now," "Poor Child," "An Old-Fashioned Love Story," "By Now the Room Was Moving," "The Juggernaut," "A Wild, Wild Party,"

"Two of a Kind," "Maybe I Like it This Way," "What is it About Her?." **Act II**: "The Life of the Party," "Who is This Man?," "The Gal for Me," "I'll Be Here," "Listen to Me," "Let Me Drown," "The Fight," "Tell Me Something," "Come with Me," "Jackie's Last Dance," "Make Me Happy," "How Did We Come to This?/Queenie Was a Blonde (reprise)." This version had its first revival at the UNIVERSITY OF BUFFALO, 11/14/02–11/24/02, and another at the FITZGERALD THEATRE, St. Paul, Minn, 3/16/05–4/3/05 (limited run) (date put back from 2004), Previews from 3/11/05. **Cast**: QUEENIE: Jen Burleigh-Bentz; BURRS: David Anderson; KATE: Jodi Carmeli; MADELAINE TRUE: Nancy Marvy; MAE: Linda Talcott Lee.

THE STUDIO THEATRE VERSION OF *The Wild Party*. This was Joseph Moncure March's poem combined with period song, dance & vaudeville routines. It ran at the 3rd-floor, 50-seat STUDIO THEATRE SECONDSTAGE, in Washington, DC, on 7/18/99–8/9/99. Previews from 7/15/99. DIRECTOR: Keith Alan Baker; CHOREOGRAPHER: Robert Biedermann.

751. *Wildcat*

Set in the Southwestern oil-country border town of Centavo City, in 1912. Wildy is determined to strike oil, and to help her lame sister Janie find a husband.

Before Broadway. Jimmy Van Heusen and Sammy Cahn were set to do the music and lyrics, but Cy Coleman and Carolyn Leigh did them instead. This was Cy Coleman's first Broadway book musical. During Philadelphia tryouts the character of Wildcat in effect became I Love Lucy. Several numbers were cut before Broadway: "Thinkability," "Ain't it Sad," "Angelina," "Foller it Through," "I Like the Ladies," "I Got My Man," "Joe Dynamite's Dentistry Song," "Little What-if, Little Could-be," "We Have So Much in Common," "Bouncing Back for More," "You're Far Away from Home," and "The Day I Do."

The Broadway Run. ALVIN THEATRE, 12/16/60–6/3/61. 2 previews from 12/14/60. 172 PERFORMANCES. PRESENTED BY Michael Kidd & N. Richard Nash (for Desilu Productions); MUSIC: Cy Coleman; LYRICS: Carolyn Leigh; BOOK: N. Richard Nash; DIRECTOR/CHOREOGRAPHER: Michael Kidd; SETS: Peter Larkin; COSTUMES: Alvin Colt; LIGHTING: Charles Elson; MUSICAL DIRECTOR/DANCE MUSIC & VOCAL ARRANGEMENTS: John Morris; ORCHESTRATIONS/ARRANGEMENTS: Robert Ginzler & Sid Ramin; PRESS: Harvey B. Sabinson, David Powers, Ted Goldsmith, Lila Glaser; GENERAL MANAGER: Joseph Harris; PRODUCTION STAGE MANAGER: Terence Little; STAGE MANAGER: Arthur Rubin; ASSISTANT STAGE MANAGER: Ralph Linn. **Cast**: JANE JACKSON: Paula Stewart (4); WILDCAT "WILDY" JACKSON: Lucille Ball (1) ☆, *Betty Jane Watson*; SHERIFF SAM GORE: Howard Fischer (7); BARNEY: Ken Ayers; LUKE: Anthony Saverino; COUNTESS EMILY O'BRIEN: Edith King (3); JOE DYNAMITE: Keith Andes (2) ☆; HANK: Clifford David (5); MIGUEL: H.F. Green; SOOKIE: Don Tomkins (6); MATT: Charles Braswell, *Hal Linden*; CORKY: Bill Linton; ONEY: Swen Swenson (8); SANDY: Ray Mason; TATTOO: Bill Walker; CISCO: Al Lanti; POSTMAN: Bill Richards; INEZ: Marsha Wagner; BLONDE: Wendy Nickerson; SINGERS: Ken Ayers, Lee Green, Jan Leighton, Urylee Leonardos, Virginia Oswald, Anthony Saverino, Jeanne Steel, Gene Varrone; DANCERS: Robert Bakanic, Barbara Beck, Mel Davidson, Penny Ann Green, Valerie Harper, Lucia Lambert, Ronald Lee, Jacqueline Maria, Wendy Nickerson, Frank Pietri, Bill Richards, Adriane Rogers, John Sharpe, Gerald Teijelo, Marsha Wagner. **Standby**: Wildy: Shelah Hackett. **Understudies**: Joe: Charles Braswell; Barney: Hal Linden; Countess: Virginia Oswald; Jane: Jeanne Steel; Sookie/Hank: Bill Linton; Sheriff: H.F. Green; Oney/Corky: Ralph Linn; Matt/Tattoo: Ray Mason; Cisco: John Sharpe; Sandy: Jan Leighton; Miguel: Anthony Saverino. **Act I**: **Scene 1** A street in Centavo City; morning: "I Hear" (People of Centavo City); **Scene 2** A prairie; sunset, a few days later: "Hey, Look Me Over" (Wildy & Jane) [the showstopper & big hit]; **Scene 3** The street; following morning: "Wildcat" (Wildy & Townspeople) [cut after opening]; **Scene 4** The plaza in the Mexican part of town; sunset, same day: "You've Come Home" (Joe); **Scene 5** The Countess' sitting room; the following morning: "That's What I Want for Janie" (Wildy) [cut after opening]; **Scene 6** Sookie's house; an hour later: "What Takes My Fancy" (Wildy & Sookie); **Scene**

7 Prairie; same evening: "You're a Liar" (Wildy & Joe); **Scene 8** The street; an hour later: "One Day We Dance" (Hank & Jane); **Scene 9** Plaza; late afternoon, the following day: "Give a Little Whistle (and I'll Be There)" (Wildy, Joe, Crew, Townspeople); **Scene 10** The jail; a half hour later; **Scene 11** Sookie's hill; early evening, the same day: "Tall Hope" (Tattoo, Oney, Sandy, Matt, Crew). **Act II**: **Scene 1** The Countess' sitting room; two days later: "Tippy Tippy Toes" (Wildy & Countess); **Scene 2** On the way to the fiesta; the following afternoon; **Scene 3** The plaza; immediately following: "El Sombrero" (Wildy, Cisco, Oney, Crew, Townspeople); **Scene 4** The street; a few days later; **Scene 5** Sookie's house; Derrick Day (the following day); **Scene 6** Sookie's hill; immediately following: "Corduroy Road" (Joe, Crew, Townspeople); **Scene 7** Outside Miguel's Cantina; evening, two days later: "You've Come Home" (reprise) (Joe); **Scene 8** Sookie's hill; the following day: Finale (Entire Company).

The show opened on Broadway to praise for Michael Kidd, Peter Larkin's sets and Lucille Ball (in her Broadway debut; she was only doing it to get away from California — her marriage to Desi Arnaz was falling apart). But reviews for the show itself were divided. Miss Ball had added a third act at the curtain call, where she spoke to the audience, danced, and did a reprise of "Hey Look Me Over." On 2/7/61 Miss Ball suspended the show, and flew to Miami Beach suffering from exhaustion. By the time she got back she'd lost interest in the show and wanted to go home. In the next weeks she fractured a finger and injured her back. In early May her divorce from Desi Arnaz became final, and she collapsed on stage during a performance. It was announced that the show (which was still selling well) would suspend again, 6/5/61–8/7/61, so that she could recuperate, then it would re-open. Betty Jane Watson played Wildcat for the remainder of the week after Miss Ball withdrew under doctor's orders and left for the West Coast. The show never re-opened, even though Miss Ball had signed on for 18 months. The official reason was that the musicians wanted full pay during the lay-off period. The production cost $300,000, all money supplied by Desilu (Lucy's company). She met Gary Morton during the run, and he became her next husband.

752. *The Will Rogers Follies*

Also known as: *The Will Rogers Follies: a Life in Revue*. Set in the present, at the Palace Theatre. The story of humorist Will Rogers. Trouble is, there wasn't much of a story, except that Will died in 1935 in a plane crash over Alaska with pilot Wiley Post. So the writers linked his life into the Ziegfeld Follies, with which Mr. Rogers had had a connection. Will returns from Heaven to put on one more Follies production. Ziegfeld's Favorite occasionally crosses the stage holding up cards to identify the scene. The disembodied voice of Ziegfeld comes from the rafters.

Before Broadway. Producer Pierre Cossette hired James Lee Burnett to write a musical treatment of Will Rogers' life with the aim of getting John Denver to play the lead. However, Mr. Denver's asking price was far too high, and Mr. Burnett's multi-set script was far too costly to bring to life. Mr. Cossette then acquired Tommy Tune to direct, Cy Coleman and Comden & Green to write the songs, and Peter Stone for the libretto. Keith Carradine was hired for the lead role. There was almost enough money, and the final funding came from Japan Satellite Broadcasting, in exchange for which they could televise it in Japan. Tommy Tune was simultaneously getting ready to star in a touring revival of *Bye, Bye, Birdie*, with Ann Reinking, and so time was precious. Instead of doing out-of-town tryouts, they went straight into Broadway previews.

The Broadway Run. PALACE THEATRE, 5/1/91–9/5/93. 34 previews from 4/1/91. 983 PERFORMANCES. PRESENTED BY Pierre Cossette, Martin Richards, Sam Crothers, James M. Nederlander, Stewart F. Lane, and Max Weitzenhoffer, in association with Japan Satellite Broadcasting; MUSIC: Cy Coleman; LYRICS: Betty Comden & Adolph Green; BOOK: Peter Stone; INSPIRED BY the words of Will Rogers & Betty Rogers; DIRECTOR/CHOREOGRAPHER: Tommy Tune; ASSOCIATE DIRECTOR: Phillip Oesterman; ASSOCIATE CHOREOGRAPHER: Jeff Calhoun; SETS: Tony Walton; COSTUMES: Willa Kim; LIGHTING: Jules Fisher; SOUND: Peter J. Fitzgerald; MUSICAL DIRECTOR: Eric Stern; ORCHES-

TRATIONS: Billy Byers; MUSICAL ARRANGEMENTS: Cy Coleman; CAST RECORDING on Columbia; PRESS: The Jacksina Company, *Richard Kornberg & Associates* (by 91–92); CASTING: Julie Hughes & Barry Moss; GENERAL MANAGEMENT: Marvin A. Krauss Associates; COMPANY MANAGER: Nina Skriloff; PRODUCTION STAGE MANAGER: Peter von Mayrhauser; STAGE MANAGER: Patrick Ballard, *Peter Wolf*; ASSISTANT STAGE MANAGER: Michael J. Passaro, *Kimberly Russell*. **Cast:** ZIEGFELD'S FAVORITE: Cady Huffman (4), *Susan Anton* (from 12/9/91), *Cady Huffman* (from 1/27/92), *Marla Maples* (from 8/3/92), *Kimberly Hester* (from 5/4/93), *Lisa Niemi* (from 5/27/93), *Dana Leigh Jackson, Jeanne Jones*; INDIAN OF THE DAWN: Jerry Mitchell; INDIAN SUN GODDESS: Jillana Urbina; INDIAN SOLOIST: Jeanne Jones [role added by 92–93]; WILL ROGERS: Keith Carradine (1), *Mac Davis* (from 5/18/92), *Larry Gatlin* (from 2/16/93), *Ron Kidd*; UNICYCLIST: Vince Bruce (6); WILEY POST: Paul Ukena Jr. (7), *David M. Lutken, Tom Flagg*; CLEM ROGERS: Dick Latessa (3), *Robert Fitch, Mickey Rooney* (from 7/6/93); WILL'S SISTERS: Roxane Barlow (gone in 91–92), Maria Calabrese, Colleen Dunn (gone in 91–92), Dana Moore (gone in 91–92), Wendy Waring (gone in 91–92), Leigh Zimmerman (gone in 91–92), *Amy Heggins* (gone by 92–93), *Kimberly Hester, Lynn Michele, Rebecca Downing, Lu Ann Leonard, Kathy Tregeser, Ganine Giorgione, Dana Leigh Jackson, Tara T. Murphy*; MR. ZIEGFELD'S STAGE MANAGER: Tom Flagg [role added by 91–92], *David M. Lutken*; BETTY BLAKE: Dee Hoty (2), *Nancy Ringham* (from 5/18/92); THE WILD WEST SHOW: TRAINERS: Tom & Bonnie Brackney; MADCAP MUTTS: B.A., Cocoa, Gigi, Rusty, Trixie, Zee; BETTY'S SISTERS: Roxane Barlow (gone in 91–92), Maria Calabrese, Colleen Dunne (gone in 91–92), Dana Moore (gone in 91–92), Wendy Waring (gone in 91–92), Leigh Zimmerman (gone in 91–92), *Amy Heggins* (gone by 92–93), *Kimberly Hester, Lynn Michele, Rebecca Downing, Lu Ann Leonard, Kathy Tregeser, Ganine Giorgione, Dana Leigh Jackson, Tara T. Murphy*; WILL ROGERS JR.: Rick Faugno, *James Zimmerman, Robert Mann Kayser*; MARY ROGERS: Tammy Minoff, *Candace N. Walters, Amy Braverman*; JAMES ROGERS: Lance Robinson, *Buddy Smith*; FREDDY ROGERS: Gregory Scott Carter, *Jeffrey Stern*; VAUDEVILLE ANNOUNCER: Jason Opsahl [role added by 91–92]; THE ROPER: Vince Bruce; 2ND ROPER: Thomas Gracilazo [role added by 91–92 & cut by 92–93]; RADIO ENGINEER: John Ganun [role added by 91–92], *Troy Britton Johnson*; THE WILL ROGERS WRANGLERS: John Ganun, Troy Britton-Johnson, Jerry Mitchell, Jason Opsahl, *A.J. Vincent*; THE NEW ZIEGFELD GIRLS: Roxane Barlow (gone in 91–92), Maria Calabrese, Ganine Derleth (she became Ganine Giorgione in 91–92), Rebecca Downing, Colleen Dunn (gone in 91–92), Sally Mae Dunn, Toni Georgiana (gone in 91–92), Eileen Grace, Luba Gregus (gone in 91–92), Tonia Lynn (gone in 91–92), Dana Moore (gone in 91–92), Aimee Turner (gone in 91–92), Jillana Urbina, Wendy Waring (gone in 91–92), Christina Youngman, Leigh Zimmerman (*Kimberly Hester*), *Heather Douglas, Amy Heggins, Lynn Michele, Carole Denise Smith, Susan Trainor*. 92–93 replacements: *Marla Maples, Lu Ann Leonard, Kathy Tregeser. Tara T. Murphy, Jennifer Krater, Kristi Cooke, Heather Douglas*; THE VOICE OF MR. ZIEGFELD: Gregory Peck (5). **Standbys**: Clem: Tom Flagg; Mary/James/Freddy: Erica Dutko, *Eden Riegel*. **Understudies**: Will: Paul Ukena Jr., *David M. Lutken*; Favorite: Dana Moore, *Luba Gregus, Leigh Zimmerman, Kimberly Hester, Mary Lee DeWitt*; Will Jr.: Lance Robinson, *Buddy Smith*; Betty: Luba Gregus, *Belle Calaway*; Wiley: *Jack Doyle, Tom Flagg*; Stage Manager: *Jack Doyle*. **Swings**: Mary Lee DeWitt, Jack Doyle, Angie L. Schworer, *Allyson Tucker*. **Orchestra:** KEYBOARDS: Karl Jurman & Patrick Brady; PERCUSSION: Joe Passaro; DRUMS: Ray Marchica; BASS: Richard Sarpola; GUITARS: Scott Kuney & Larry Campbell; HARMONICA: Robert Paparozzi; TRUMPETS: John Frosk, Joe Mosello, Danny Cahn; TROMBONES: Jim Pugh, Larry Farrell, Paul Faulise; FRENCH HORN: Anthony Cecere; REEDS: Chuck Wilson, Dale Kleps, Alva Hunt, Vincent Della Rocca, Frank Santagata; CONCERTMISTRESS: Amy Hiraga Wyrick; VIOLINS: Heidi Carney & Rob Shaw; VIOLA: Crystal Garner; CELLO: Joe Kimura. **Act I:** *Prelude* "Let's Go Flying" (Ensemble); *Scene 1* The *Follies*: "Will-a-Mania" (Ziegfeld's Favorite & Company), "Give a Man Enough Rope" (Will & Will Rogers Wranglers); *Scene 2* The ranch: "It's a Boy!" (Clem & Will's Sisters), "So Long, Pa" (Will); *Scene 3* The moon: "My Unknown Someone" (Betty); *Scene 4* The *Follies*; *Scene 5* The St. Louis Exposition: "We're Heading for a Wedding" (Will & Betty) [the music for this number had been used in "Thinkability," which had been cut

from *Wildcat*]; *Scene 6* Vaudeville: "The Big Time" (Will, Betty, Children), "My Big Mistake" (Betty); *Scene 7* The *Follies*: "The Powder Puff Ballet" ("My Big Mistake") (New Ziegfeld Girls), "Marry Me Now" (Will)/"I Got You" (Betty); *Act I Wedding Finale*. **Act II:** Entr'acte; *Scene 1* The *Follies*: "Give a Man Enough Rope" (reprise) (Will & Will Rogers Wranglers), "Look Around" (Will); *Scene 2* The convention: "(Our) Favorite Son" (Will & Chorus); *Scene 3* The Hollywood ranch: "No Man Left for Me" (Betty), "Presents for Mrs. Rogers" (Will, Will Rogers Wranglers, New Ziegfeld Girls); *Scene 4* The bare stage: "Will-a-Mania" (reprise) (Will & Clem), "Without You" (reprise of "I Got You") (Betty); *Scene 5* The finale: "Never Met a Man I Didn't Like" (Will & Company).

Broadway reviews were divided. Minority groups protested that there were no blacks in the cast, indeed no non-whites at all. American Indian groups protested over the treatment of Indians in the show, and women's groups protested against some of the seemingly anti-female advertising posters. In 7/91 Equity charged the show with discrimination. Three black dancers were added to the cast and the advertising was changed. The show won Tony Awards for musical, score, direction of a musical, choreography, costumes, and lighting, and was nominated for book, sets, and for Keith Carradine, Cady Huffman, and Dee Hoty. Tommy Tune's staging was one of the major reasons this show ran more than two years on Broadway. Mid-way through the run Marla Maples (Donald Trump's girlfriend) replaced Cady Huffman.

After Broadway. BARN THEATRE, Augusta, Michigan. Tom Wopat, who began his career at the Barn as an apprentice (as Marin Mazzie also did) played Will every summer for 6 years from 1992.

TOUR. Opened on 8/25/92, in San Francisco. MUSICAL DIRECTOR: Kay Cameron. **Cast:** WILL: Keith Carradine, *Mac Davis, Larry Gatlin, Mac Davis, Larry Gatlin*; BETTY: Dee Hoty, *Danette Cuming*; CLEM: George Riddle; FAVORITE: Leigh Zimmerman, *Dana Leigh Jackson*; VOICE OF ZIEGFELD: Gregory Peck.

PAPER MILL PLAYHOUSE, New Jersey, 6/12/98–7/26/98. Previews from 6/10/98. DIRECTOR: Mark S. Hoebee; CHOREOGRAPHER: D.J. Salisbury; SETS: Tony Walton; COSTUMES: Willa Kim; LIGHTING: Marcia Madeira; MUSICAL DIRECTOR: Michael Biagi. **Cast:** WILL: John Davidson; BETTY: Ann Crumb; CLEM: Robert Fitch (Dennis Kelly was to have played this role); FAVORITE: Pamela Jordan.

TOUR. Opened 6/23/03, Starlight, Kansas City. Rehearsals were in New York City. DIRECTOR/CHOREOGRAPHER: Jeff Calhoun; COSTUMES: Roger Kirk; LIGHTING: Marcia Madeira; SOUND: Abe Jacob; MUSICAL DIRECTOR: Ray Allen. **Cast:** WILL: Larry Gatlin; MRS. ROGERS: Jane Bodle; PA: William Riddle; FAVORITE: Nicolette Hart; WILEY: Jason Edwards; VOICE OF ZIEGFELD: George Bush Sr. [Larry Gatlin & the former president were good friends]. **Understudy:** Will: Jason Edwards.

753. *Wind in the Willows*

The adventures of Mole, Rat and Badger (Mole was now a female, and had a romance with Rat).

Before Broadway. Kenneth Grahame's story had been adapted for the stage by A.A. Milne as *Toad of Toad Hall*, which was frequently produced in England as a Christmas pantomime. There were other musicals with this name that never played on Broadway, and one called *The Adventures of Mr. Toad* (see appendix for all of these). The 1985 Broadway production was first produced at the Folger Theatre, Washington, DC. Director Edward Berkeley was replaced by Tony Stevens during Broadway previews.

The Broadway Run. NEDERLANDER THEATRE, 12/19/85–12/22/85. 27 previews. 4 PERFORMANCES. PRESENTED BY RLM Productions & Liniva Productions; MUSIC: William Perry; LYRICS: Roger McGough & William Perry; BOOK: Jane Iredale; ADAPTED FROM Kenneth Grahame's classic 1908 book of the same name; DIRECTOR: Tony Stevens; CHOREOGRAPHER: Margery Beddow; SETS: Sam Kirkpatrick; COSTUMES: Freddy Wittop; LIGHTING: Craig Miller; SOUND: Jack Mann; MUSICAL SUPERVISOR: Jonathan Tunick; MUSICAL DIRECTOR/VOCAL ARRANGEMENTS: Robert Rogers; ORCHESTRATIONS: William D. Brohn; DANCE & INCIDENTAL MUSIC: David Krane; PRESS: The Fred Nathan Company; CASTING: Johnson—Liff; GENERAL MANAGEMENT: Weiler/Miller; PRODUC-

TION STAGE MANAGER: Jim Woolley; STAGE MANAGER: Ellen Raphael; ASSISTANT STAGE MANAGER: Scott Waara. *Cast:* MOLE: Vicki Lewis ☆; MOTHER RABBIT: Nora Mae Lyng; FATHER RABBIT: John Jellison; RAT: David Carroll ☆; TOAD: Nathan Lane ☆; CHIEF STOAT: Donna Drake ☆; BADGER: Irving Barnes ☆; CHIEF WEASEL: P.J. Benjamin ☆; WAYFARER RAT: Jackie Lowe; POLICE SERGEANT: Scott Waara; COURT CLERK: Kenston Ames; JUDGE: John Jellison; PROSECUTOR: Michael Byers; JAILER'S DAUGHTER: Nora Mae Lyng; JAILER: Michael Byers; ENSEMBLE: Kenston Ames, Shell M. Benjamin, Michael Byers, Jackie Lowe, Marguerite Lowell, Nora Mae Lyng, Mary C. Robare, Jamie Rocco, Ray Roderick, Scott Waara. *Understudies*: Mole: Donna Drake; Rat: Scott Waara; Toad: Michael Byers; Badger: John Jellison; Chief Stoat: Shell M. Benjamin; Chief Weasel: Jamie Rocco. *Swings*: Teresa Payne-Rohan & Kevin Winkler. *Act I: Scene 1* A meadow in spring: "The World is Waiting for Me" (Mole); *Scene 2* The River: "When Springtime Comes to My River" (Rat), "Messing About in Boats" (Rat & Mole); *Scene 3* The Wild Wood: "Evil Weasel" (Chief Weasel, Chief Stoat, Weasels, Stoats); *Scene 4* The lawns of Toad Hall: "That's What Friends Are For" (Toad, Rat, Mole, Rabbits); *Scene 5* Rat's Dock in summer; *Scene 6* The Wild Wood: "Follow Your Instinct" (Mole, Rabbits, Weasels, Stoats); *Scene 7* The car park at the Red Lion Inn: "The Gasoline Can-Can" (Toad & The Rabbits), "You'll Love it in Jail" (Chief Weasel, Chief Stoat, Toad, Policemen); *Scene 8* A meadow in autumn: "Mediterranean" (Wayfarer Rat), "The Day You Came into My Life" (Mole). *Act II: Scene 1* The courtroom: "S-S-Something Comes Over Me" (Toad); *Scene 2* Rat's Dock in autumn: "I'd Be Attracted" (Mole & Rat), "When Springtime Comes to My River" (reprise) (Rat), "The Day You Came into My Life" (reprise) (Mole); *Scene 3* Toad Hall: "Moving up in the World" (Chief Weasel, Chief Stoat, Weasels, Stoats); *Scene 4* A jail cell: "Brief Encounter" (Toad & Jailer's Daughter); *Scene 5* The woods: "Where Am I Now?" (Toad), "The Wind in the Willows" (Company); *Scene 6* Rat's Dock: "That's What Friends Are For" (reprise) (Toad, Rat, Badger, Rabbits); *Scene 7* The Grand Dining Room at Toad Hall: "Come What May" (Company).

Reviews were awful. The show received Tony nominations for score and book.

754. *Wish You Were Here*

Camp Karefree is a summer camp for adults, where attractive single New Yorkers look for partners during the course of a two-week vacation, and "where friendships are formed to last a whole lifetime through." Located in the heart of Vacationland; it could be the Berkshires, Adirondacks, Poconos, White Mountains — or even the Catskills. Teddy, a young secretary from Brooklyn engaged to Herman, an older man, comes to the camp, is almost compromised by Pinky, and falls in love with Chick, a law student who is working as a waiter by day, and as a dance partner by night, and who saved her from Pinky. Teddy breaks off her engagement to Herman. Teddy's friend is Fay, who is given to malapropisms and is involved with several men, such as Itchy, the camp social director, and Muscles, the camp jock. Phyllis Newman's only line was "I don't want to be Miss Flushing — I want to be Miss Perth Amboy." Arthur Kober re-worked his play to make all the characters under 30.

Before Broadway. Pat Marand and Jack Cassidy were virtual unknowns when they got the leads. Naturally, with such props as the $28,000 onstage swimming pool that had to be dug into the stage, there could be no out-of-town tryouts, so there were paid previews instead. Today previews are the order of the day, but back then it was unusual. During previews Ray Walston was replaced as Itchy, and the number "Glimpse of Love" was cut.

The Broadway Run. IMPERIAL THEATRE, 6/25/52–11/28/53. Previews (see below). 598 PERFORMANCES. PRESENTED BY Leland Hayward & Joshua Logan; MUSIC/LYRICS: Harold Rome; BOOK: Arthur Kober & Joshua Logan; BASED ON the 1937 comedy *Having Wonderful Time*, by Arthur Kober, which starred John Garfield; DIRECTOR/CHOREOGRA-

PHER: Joshua Logan; SWIMMERS TRAINED BY Eleanor Holm Rose; SETS/LIGHTING: Jo Mielziner; COSTUMES: Robert Mackintosh; ASSISTANT COSTUMES: Florence Klotz; STAGE TECHNICIAN: Abe Kurnit; MUSICAL DIRECTOR: Jay Blackton; ORCHESTRATIONS: Don Walker; MUSICAL CONTINUITY: Trude Rittman; CAST RECORDING on RCA Victor; PRESS: Leo Freedman, Abner Klipstein, Betty Lee Hunt; CASTING: Marshall Jamison; GENERAL MANAGER: Herman Bernstein; COMPANY MANAGER: Carl Fisher; PRODUCTION STAGE MANAGER: Robert E. Griffith; STAGE MANAGER: Dan W. Sattler; ASSISTANT STAGE MANAGER: Joe Calvan. *Cast:* TESSIE "TEDDY" STERN: Patricia Marand (3); CHICK MILLER: Jack Cassidy (2); FAY FROMKIN: Sheila Bond (1); ITCHY FLEXNER: Sidney Armus (4); PINKY HARRIS: Paul Valentine (5); HARRY "MUSCLES" GREEN: John Perkins; LOU KANDEL: Sammy Smith; HERMAN FABRICANT: Harry Clark; MUSIC LOVERS: MARVIN: Fred Sadoff; SONJA: Elaine Gordon; ITCHY'S ASSISTANTS: SCHMUTZ: Larry Blyden; ELI: Frank Aletter; WAITER FRIENDS OF CHICK'S: BARNEY: Ray Hyson; SID: Robert Dixon; FAY'S (THREE) DANCING PARTNERS: LENNY: Richard France; SAM: Joe Milan; MONTY: Tom Ayre; (SIX) WALLFLOWERS: HENRIETTA: Mardi Bayne; GUSSIE: Leila Martin; IRMA: Roslynd Lowe; SHIRLEY: Sybil Lamb; LENA: Denise Griffin; JUDY: Shirley Anne Prior; MIRIAM, WHO HAS HAY FEVER: Nancy Franklin; THE NEW GIRL: Florence Henderson; THE GIRL DIVER: Beverly Weston; THE ACROBAT: Steve Wiland; ECCENTRIC DIVER: Joseph Thomas; WAITERS: MEL: Gus Giordano; FRED: Stan Grover; MORRIE: Bill Hogue; BILL: Leo Kayworth; BUTCH: George Lenz; JOE: Reid Shelton; HARRY: Harry Snow; PHIL: Ray Steele; ALEX: Tom Tryon; MAC: Don Wayne; BATHING BEAUTIES: BILLIE: Sue Brin; KITTY: Norma Doggett; MILDRED: Joan Johnston; SARAH: Phyllis Newman; FELICE: Gloria Van Deweel; ANNA: Jan Stuart; WILMA: Rain Winslow; ATHLETES/GUESTS/STAFF MEMBERS: Nancy Baker, Joan Berke, Elliot Feder, Al Lawrence, Toni Parker, Candy Parsons, Don Paterson, Inga Rode, Wally Strauss. *Understudies*: Fay: Phyllis Newman; Chick: Stan Grover; Teddy: Mardi Bayne; Itchy: Larry Blyden; Pinky: Richard France; Herman/Lou/Schmutz: Frank Aletter; Harry: Tom Tryon; Sonja: Nancy Franklin. *Act I: Scene 1* Outside Teddy's cabin: "Camp Karefree" (Kandel, Waiters, Ensemble), "Goodbye Love" (Teddy, Fay, Girls) [replaced soon after opening night by "(There's) Nothing Nicer than People" (Teddy, Fay, Girls)], "(Ballad of a) Social Director" (Itchy & Ensemble), "Shopping Around" (Fay); *Scene 2* Locker room: "Bright College Days" ("Waiters Song") (Waiters), "Mix and Mingle" (Chick & Waiters); *Scene 3* Porch of the Social Hall: "Could Be" (Girls & Teddy); *Scene 4* Social Hall: "Tripping the Light Fantastic" (Ensemble); *Scene 5* A path through the woods: "Wish You Were Here" (Chick & Teddy) [the big hit], "Where Did the Night Go?" (Chick, Teddy, Ensemble); *Scene 6* Athletic field: "Certain Individuals" (Fay & Ensemble); *Scene 7* A path through the woods; *Scene 8* Eagle Rock (They won't know me): "They Won't Know Me" (Chick); *Scene 9* The boat house: "Summer Afternoon" (Pinky & Ensemble); *Scene 10* The lake front. *Act II: Scene 1* The campfire: "Where Did the Night Go?" (reprise) (Eli & Ensemble), "Don Jose (of Far Rockaway)" (Itchy & Ensemble), "Everybody Love Everybody" (Fay & Ensemble), "Wish You Were Here" (reprise) (Chick & Waiters); *Scene 2* A path through the woods; *Scene 3* Pinky's cabin: "Relax" (Pinky & Teddy); *Scene 4* Porch of the Social Hall: "Where Did the Night Go?" (be-bop version) (Fay & Ensemble), "Flattery" (Teddy, Fay, Itchy); *Scene 5* Basketball court: Finale (Entire Company).

The show opened in a phenomenal heat wave; this was before air-conditioning in theatres. Reviews were bad, Leland Hayward wanted to close, but Josh Logan persuaded him otherwise, and the show was reworked constantly over the next few months, including some new dance numbers choreographed by Jerome Robbins (uncredited in playbills). Eight scenes were re-written to make the heroine more sympathetic, the plot was given more suspense, and two new songs were written. Walter Winchell got behind it in the press, the title song was a monster hit in the charts by Eddie Fisher, and then the show worked, and it had an 18-month run, and was called the "musical miracle of the decade." It won Tonys for stage technician (Abe Kurnit), and for Sheila Bond. Incidentally, the 1941 Broadway musical *Viva O'Brien* had a swimming pool built into the Majestic Theatre.

After Broadway. CASINO, London. Opened on 10/10/53. 282 PERFORMANCES. It didn't do particularly well in Britain, partly because

Britain doesn't have summer camps (they set it in a Butlins holiday camp instead). The British censor had a field day with some of the American character names, which were either too Jewish or would have brought forth gales of ribald laughter from London audiences. PRESENTED BY Jack Hylton; DIRECTOR: Richard Bird; MUSICAL DIRECTOR: Cyril Ornadel. *Cast*: CHICK: Bruce Trent; TEDDY: Elizabeth Larner; PINKY: Christopher Hewett; MUSCLES: Joe "Tiger" Robinson; LOU: Mark Baker; HERMAN: Glen Burns; DICKIE FLETCHER: Dickie Henderson (this was the Itchy Flexner role on Broadway); FAY TOMPKIN: Shani Wallis; SPUD: Milo Lewis (this was the Schmutz role on Broadway); EDDIE: Malcolm McDonald (this was the Eli role on Broadway); DANCER: Jill Ireland.

SHUBERT THEATRE, Chicago. 12/8/53–2/13/54. It had pool and all, and did well. *Cast*: TEDDY: Patricia Marand; FAY: Sheila Bond; MUSCLES: John Perkins; ITCHY: Frank Aletter; ELI: Frank Green; LOU: Sammy Smith; MONTY: Tom Ayre; JOE: Reid Shelton; ECCENTRIC DIVER: Steve Wiland; CHICK: Peter Kelley.

EQUITY LIBRARY THEATRE, NYC, 5/14/87–6/7/87. 2 previews; 30 PERFORMANCES. No pool. DIRECTOR: Don Price; CHOREOGRAPHER: Bob Rizzo; MUSICAL DIRECTOR: Randell Kramer. *Cast*: FAY: Kari Nicolaisen; CHICK: Doug Tompos; PINKY: Sean Hopkins; MUSCLES: Charles Mandracchia; ELI: Carlos Lopez; GUSSIE: Wendy Waring; TEDDY: Tia Riebling; ITCHY: Larry Francer.

YORK THEATRE COMPANY, 1/21/00–1/23/00. 5 PERFORMANCES. Part of the *Musicals in Mufti* series. DIRECTOR: Michael Montel. *Cast*: FAY: Melissa Rain Anderson; CHICK: Perry Laylon Ojeda; TEDDY: Sara Schmidt; PINKY: Matt Bogart; HERMAN: Robert Ari; LOU: David Green; HENRIETTA: Carla Woods.

755. *The Wiz*

Soft-rock musical version of *The Wonderful Wizard of Oz*, with an all-black cast (this is not a simple version of the famous movie). Dorothy, a little girl from Kansas, is blown by a tornado into Munchkinland in the Land of Oz, and meets Scarecrow, Tinman, and Lion, on the Yellow Brick Road. They defeat the evil witch and have an audience with the supposedly all-powerful Wizard of Oz, but who is really a phoney, but who does convince Dorothy that she can do anything she wants if she just believes in herself.

Before Broadway. *The Wiz*, as a musical, was new. However, as a straight production, *The Wizard of Oz* had first appeared on Broadway in 1903, adapted by creator Frank Baum himself. There were 13 later books about Oz written by Mr. Baum, and three silent movies, and, of course, the famous 1939 Judy Garland film made by MGM.

Ken Harper, a radio man, came up with the idea of a musical in 1972. By 1974, when he persuaded 20th-Century Fox to invest $650,000 in exchange for the film rights, he already had music, lyrics and libretto in place. The show played on the road for seven weeks before opening on Broadway, but it was a fraught time. Mr. Harper was advised to close after a disastrous technical rehearsal the day before opening in Baltimore, but kept going. Director Gilbert Moses was fired during the later Detroit tryouts, to be replaced by Geoffrey Holder, who was at that stage the costume designer. Mr. Holder made several changes, including restoring the Tornado Ballet (where a dancer twirls around the stage trailing a long piece of gauzy fabric which grows longer and longer as the tornado whisks Dorothy to Oz). Hinton Battle was taken out of the chorus to replace the sick Stu Gilliam as the Scarecrow. Dorothy's costume was changed from jeans to frilly white dress. The Queen of the Mice, played by Butterfly McQueen, was cut. Philadelphia tryouts were next, and by now the show was getting more and more successful reviews. It was also getting more expensive, and 20th-Century Fox put even more money into it. During Broadway previews finances were tight, as there had been no advance box-office sales to speak of.

The Broadway Run. MAJESTIC THEATRE, 1/5/75–5/25/77; BROADWAY THEATRE, 5/25/77–1/28/79. 6 previews. Total of 1,666 PERFORMANCES. PRESENTED BY Ken Harper; MUSIC/LYRICS: Charlie Smalls; BOOK: William F. Brown; BASED ON the 1900 fairy tale *The Wonderful Wizard of Oz*, by L. Frank Baum; DIRECTOR/COSTUMES: Geoffrey Holder; CHOREOGRAPHER: George Faison; SETS: Tom H. John; LIGHTING: Tharon Musser; SOUND: Richard J.C. Miller; MUSICAL DIRECTOR: Charles H. Coleman, *Tom Pierson (by 76–77)*; ORCHESTRATIONS: Harold Wheeler; VOCAL ARRANGEMENTS: Charles H. Coleman; DANCE MUSIC ARRANGEMENTS: Timothy Graphenreed; CAST RECORDING on Atlantic; PRESS: The Merlin Group; CASTING: Mikki Powell; MAGIC CONSULTANT: Steve Rodman; GENERAL MANAGERS: Emanuel Azenberg & Eugene V. Wolsk; COMPANY MANAGER: Susan Bell; PRODUCTION STAGE MANAGER: Charles Blackwell; STAGE MANAGER: Henry Velez & Jerry Laws, *Christopher Kelly, Robert Burland, Steven Shaw, Donald Christy, Clint Jakeman, Robert D. Currie, Lee Murray, Michael William Schaefer*.

Cast: AUNT EM: Tasha Thomas (8), *Esther Marrow (by 75–76)*; TOTO: Nancy, Westy *(from 76–77)*, *Nancy (from 77–78)*; DOROTHY: Stephanie Mills (4) ✭; UNCLE HENRY: Ralph Wilcox, *Albert Fann (from 75)*, *Toney Watkins (by 75–76)*, *Michael Leslie (by 77–78)*, *James Wigfall*; TORNADO: Evelyn Thomas, *Wendy Edmead (by 75–76)*, *Allison Williams (by 77–78)*; MUNCHKINS: Phylicia Ayers-Allen *(Dyane Harvey from 75–76)*, Pi Douglass *(Leslie Butler from 75–76)*, Joni Palmer *(Lois Hayes from 75–76)*, Andy Torres *(Kwame Johnson from 75–76)*, Carl Weaver, *Howard Porter*; ADDAPERLE: Clarice Taylor (5), *Jozella Reed (during Miss Taylor's absence, 76–77)*, *Marie Bryant*; YELLOW BRICK ROAD: Ronald Dunham *(gone by 77–78)*, Eugene Little *(gone by 77–78)*, John Parks *(Rodney Green from 75–76 & gone by 77–78)*, Kenneth Scott *(gone by 77–78)*. 77–78 replacements: *Alvin Davis, Robert Pittman, Aaron Leavy, Stanley Dalton*. Later replacements: *Paul Hoskins, Kevin Jeff, Chuck Thorpes*; SCARECROW: Hinton Battle (3) ✭, *Gregg Burge (from 12/76)*, *Charles Lavont Williams (during Mr. Burge's illness, 77–78)*; CROWS: Wendy Edmead *(gone by 77–78)*, Frances Morgan *(gone by 77–78)*, Ralph Wilcox *(Albert Fann from 74–75, Thea Nerissa Barnes from 75–76 and gone by 77–78)*. 77–78 replacements: *Renee Rose, Eartha Robinson, Claudia Lewis*; TINMAN: Tiger Haynes (1) ✭, *Ben Harney*; LION: Ted Ross (2) ✭, *James Wigfall (from 5/11/76)*, *Ken Page (from 6/6/77)*, *James Wigfall (from 10/31/77)*, *L. Michael Gray (from 2/7/78)*; KALIDAHS: Philip Bond *(Gregg Burge from 75–76)*, Pi Douglass *(Keith Harris from 75–76)*, Rodney Green *(Alvin McDuffie from 75–76)*, Evelyn Thomas *(Claudia Lewis from 75–76)*, Andy Torres *(Alwin Taylor from 75–76)*, *John Parks, Alma Robinson, Wendy Edmead, Kwame Johnson, Bruce Taylor, Gayle Turner*; POPPIES: Lettie Battle *(Thea Nerissa Barnes from 75–76)*, Leslie Butler, Eleanor McCoy *(Pat Estwick from 75–76)*, Frances Morgan, Joni Palmer *(Lois Hayes from 75–76)*, *Renee Rose*; FIELD MICE: Phylicia Ayers-Allen, Pi Douglass, Carl Weaver, Ralph Wilcox *(Albert Fann)*, *Sam Harkness, Howard Porter*; GATEKEEPER: Danny Beard, *Toney Watkins (from 76–77)*, *Howard Porter (by 77–78)*, *James Wigfall*; EMERALD CITY CITIZENS: Lettie Battle *(Thea Nerissa Barnes from 75–76 & gone by 77–78)*, Philip Bond *(gone by 75–76)*, Leslie Butler, Ronald Dunham *(gone by 77–78)*, Wendy Edmead *(gone by 77–78)*, Rodney Green *(Alvin McDuffie from 76–77 & gone by 77–78)*, Eleanor McCoy *(Pat Estwick from 75–76 & gone by 77–78)*, Eugene Little *(gone by 75–76)*, Frances Morgan *(gone by 77–78)*, Joni Palmer *(Lois Hayes from 75–76)*, John Parks *(gone by 75–76)*, Kenneth Scott *(gone by 77–78)*, Evelyn Thomas *(Claudia Lewis from 75–76)*, Andy Torres *(gone by 75–76)*. 75–76 replacements: *Keith Harris (gone by 77–78)*, *Alwin Taylor (gone by 77–78)*. 76–77 replacements: *Phylicia Ayers-Allen (gone by 77–78)*, *Paul Hoskins (gone by 77–78)*, *Kevin Jeff, Kwame Johnson (gone by 77–78)*, *Alma Robinson (gone by 77–78)*, *Renee Rose, Bruce Taylor (gone by 77–78)*. 77–78 replacements: *Deborah Lynn Bridges, Stanley Dalton, Alvin Davis, Debbie Fitts, Anthony Lawrence, Aaron Leavey, Dwight Leon, Robert Pittman, Howard Porter, Eartha Robinson, Siri Sat Nam Singh, Gayle Turner, Allison Williams, Charles Lavont Williams*; THE WIZ: Andre De Shields (7), *Alan Weeks (5/4/76–1/24/77)*, *Andre De Shields (from 1/25/77)*, *Carl Hall (from 7/17/77)*; EVILLENE: Mabel King (6), *Irene Reid, Edye Byrde (by 75–76)*, *Theresa Merritt (from 4/12/76)*, *Ruth Brisbane (from 9/76)*, *Ella Mitchell (from 7/77)*; LORD HIGH UNDERLING: Ralph Wilcox, *Al Fann (from 74–75)*, *Toney Watkins (by 75–76)*, *Michael Leslie (by 77–78)*, *James Wigfall*; SOLDIER MESSENGER: Carl Weaver, *Charles Lavont Williams (by 77–78)*; WINGED MONKEY: Andy Torres, *Keith Harris (by 75–76)*, *Kevin Jeff (by 77–78)*, *Miguel Godreau*; GLINDA: Dee Dee Bridgewater (9), *Deborah Burrell (from 4/12/76)*; PIT SINGERS: Frank Floyd *(Robert Benjamin from 75–76 and gone by 77–78)*, Sam Harkness *(gone by 77–78)*, Jozella Reed, Tasha Thomas *(DeMarest Grey from*

75–76), *Janyse M. Singleton* (by 75–76), *Sylvester Rickey Powell* (by 77–78), *Esther Marrow* (by 77–78), *Ronald Dorsey*. **Standbys**: Dorothy: Arnetia Walker (75), *Renee Harris* (75–76), *Gayle Turner* (76–78); Addaperle: Butterfly McQueen (75). **Understudies**: Dorothy: Pat Estwick (75–77); Tinman: Ralph Wilcox (75), *Kwame Johnson* (75–76), *Howard Porter* (76–78), *Victor Willis* (76–77), *Siri Sat Nam Singh* (77–78), *Anthony Lawrence* (77–78); Lion: *Toney Watkins* (75–77), *Victor Willis* (76–77), *Michael Leslie* (77–78), *James Wigfall*; Wiz: Kenneth Scott (75–76), *Victor Willis* (76–77), *Toney Watkins* (76–77); *Kwame Johnson* (76–77), *Anthony Lawrence* (77–78), *Sylvester Rickey Powell* (77–78); Scarecrow: Pi Douglass (75), *Carl Weaver* (75–77), *Alvin McDuffie* (76–77), *Charles Lavont Williams* (77–78), *Stanley Dalton* (77–78); Addaperle: Jozella Reed (75–78), *Ruth Brisbane* (75–78); Glinda: Phylicia Ayers-Allen (75–77), *Janyse M. Singleton* (75–78); Aunt Em: Dee Dee Bridgewater (75), *Deborah Burrell* (75–78), *Wendy Edmead* (76–77); Evillene: Tasha Thomas (75), *Ruth Brisbane* (75–78), *Edye Byrde*. **Swing Dancers/Singers**: Cynthia Ashby (75), Otis Sallid (75), *Al Perryman* (76–77), *Carl Hardy* (76–78), *DeMarest Grey* (76–77), *Dyane Harvey, Christian Kimball* (76–77), *Pat Estwick, Deborah Burrell, John Parks, Neisha Folkes* (77–78). **Act I**: **Prologue**: Kansas: "The Feeling We Once Had" (Aunt Em), "Tornado Ballet" (Company); **Scene 1** Munchkin Land: "He's the Wizard" (Addaperle & Munchkins); **Scene 2** Oz Countryside: "Soon as I Get Home" (Dorothy), "I Was Born on the Day Before Yesterday" (Scarecrow & Crows), "Ease on Down the Road" (Dorothy, Scarecrow, Yellow Brick Road) [the big song]; **Scene 3** Woods: "Slide Some Oil to Me" (Tinman, Dorothy, Scarecrow); **Scene 4** Jungle: "(I'm a) Mean Ole Lion" (Lion); **Scene 5** Kalidah Country: "Kalidah Battle" (Friends, Kalidahs, Yellow Brick Road); **Scene 6** Poppy Field: "Be a Lion" (Dorothy & Lion), "Lion's Dream" (Lion & Poppies); **Scene 7** Emerald City: "Emerald City Ballet (Psst)" (m: Timothy Graphenreed & George Faison) (Friends & Company); **Scene 8** Throne Room: "So You Wanted to Meet the Wizard" (Wiz), "What Would I Do if I Could Feel" ("To Be Able to Feel") (Tinman). **Act II**: **Scene 1** West Witch Castle: "(Don't Nobody Bring Me) No Bad News" (Evillene); **Scene 2** Forest: "Funky Monkeys" (Monkeys); **Scene 3** Courtyard: "Everybody Rejoice" (m/l: Luther Vandross) (Friends & Winkies); **Scene 4** Emerald City gate: **Scene 5** Throne Room: "(Who), Who Do You Think You Are?" (Friends), "If You Believe" ("Believe in Yourself") (Wiz); **Scene 6** Fairgrounds: "Y'All Got It!" (Wiz); **Scene 7** The outskirts; **Scene 8** Quadling Country: "A Rested Body is a Rested Mind" (Glinda), "If You Believe" ("Believe in Yourself") (reprise) (Glinda), "Home" (Dorothy).

Note: Friends here indicates Dorothy, Tinman, Lion and Scarecrow.

Press agent Sandy Manley gave free tickets to everyone of influence who could come to opening night, but Broadway reviews were divided, mostly bad, and the production team wanted to close after the first night. Ken Harper persuaded 20th-Century Fox to spend on advertising, especially TV (like *Pippin* had done), and to pull in black audiences. Much to everybody's amazement it ran four years. It won Tonys for musical, direction of a musical, score, choreography, costumes, and for Ted Ross and Dee Dee Bridgewater. It was also nominated for book.

After Broadway. Tour. Opened on 6/16/76, at the Ahmanson Theatre, Los Angeles. MUSICAL DIRECTOR: Larry Ball. **Cast**: DOROTHY: Renn Woods, *Renee Harris* (from 10/76); SCARECROW: Charles "Valentino" Harris; TINMAN: Ben Harney; LION: Ted Ross, *Ken Prymus*; ADDAPERLE: Vivian Bonnell; WIZ: Andre de Shields, *Kamal* [i.e. Kenneth Scott] (from 1/25/77); EVILLENE: Ella Mitchell, *Carolyn Miller*; AUNT EM/GLINDA: Dee Dee Bridgewater, *Roz Clark* (from 10/76), *Peggy Blue*; GATEKEEPER/LORD HIGH UNDERLING: George Bell, *Clent Bowers*.

Tour. Opened on 6/12/78, Washington, DC, then on to Wilmington, Del., 6/23/78, and the tour closed on 7/1/79, at Portland, Ore. PRESENTED BY Tom Mallow, in association with James Janek; MUSICAL DIRECTOR: Joel Alan Levine. **Cast**: DOROTHY: Deborah Malone, *Lillias D. White*; TINMAN: Jai Oscar St. John; WIZ: Charles Douglass; AUNT EM/GLINDA: Juanita Fleming; SCARECROW: Garry Q. Lewis; LION: Bobby Hill.

THE MOVIE. 20th-Century Fox sold the film rights. *The Wiz*, as a musical, was filmed in 1978, on location in New York City, and replacing Kansas with Harlem, and the Emerald City with Midtown Manhattan. DIRECTOR: Sidney Lumet. **Cast**: DOROTHY: Diana Ross; SCARE-

CROW: Michael Jackson; TINMAN: Nipsey Russell; WIZ: Richard Pryor; LION: Ted Ross; GLINDA: Lena Horne (Sidney Lumet's mother-in-law).

756. *The Wiz (Broadway revival)*

The musical numbers were the same as for the 1975 Broadway production, except that a new song, "Wonder Why" was inserted between "Funky Monkeys" and "Everybody Rejoice." Also, Act II Scene 4 was dropped (it had no musical numbers in it).

Before Broadway. This revival was a tour come to Broadway. The tour had opened on 9/16/83, at the Shubert Theatre, Boston. It had the same basic cast and crew as the 1984 Broadway run, except AUNT EM: Juanita Fleming; ADDAPERLE: Jo-Ann Washington.

The Broadway Run. LUNT—FONTANNE THEATRE, 5/24/84–6/3/84. 7 previews. 13 PERFORMANCES. PRESENTED BY Tom Mallow, James Janek, and The Shubert Organization; MUSIC/LYRICS: Charlie Smalls; BOOK: William F. Brown; BASED ON L. Frank Baum's *The Wonderful Wizard of Oz*; DIRECTOR/COSTUMES: Geoffrey Holder; CHOREOGRAPHER: George Faison; SETS: Peter Wolf; LIGHTING: Paul Sullivan; SOUND: Gary M. Stocker; MUSICAL DIRECTOR/VOCAL ARRANGEMENTS: Charles H. Coleman; ORCHESTRATIONS: Harold Wheeler; DANCE MUSIC ARRANGEMENTS: Timothy Graphenreed; PRESS: Max Eisen, Barbara Glenn, Maria Somma, Madelon Rosen; GENERAL MANAGEMENT: American Theatre Productions; COMPANY MANAGER: Daryl T. Dodson; PRODUCTION STAGE MANAGER: Jack Welles; STAGE MANAGER: Luis Montero; ASSISTANT STAGE MANAGER: Nate Barnett. **Cast**: AUNT EM: Peggie Blue; TOTO: Toto; DOROTHY: Stephanie Mills; UNCLE HENRY: David Weatherspoon; TORNADO: Daryl Richardson; MUNCHKINS: Carol Dennis, Ada Dyer, Lawrence Hamilton, Sam Harkness, David Weatherspoon; ADDAPERLE: Juanita Fleming; YELLOW BRICK ROAD: Alfred L. Dove, Germaine Edwards, Dwight Leon, David Robertson; SCARECROW: Charles Valentino; SUNFLOWERS: Carol Dennis, Ada Dyer, Sam Harkness, David Weatherspoon; CROWS: Paula Anita Brown, Marvin Engran, Jasmine Guy; TINMAN: Howard Porter; LION: Gregg Baker; STRANGERS: Carol Dennis, Sam Harkness, David Weatherspoon; KALIDAHS: Marvin Engran, Jasmine Guy, Lawrence Hamilton, Raymond C. Harris, Gigi Hunter, Martial Roumain; POPPIES: Sharon Brooks, Paula Anita Brown, Carla Earle, Tanya Gibson, Gigi Hunter, Daryl Richardson; CHIEF OF FIELD MICE: Ada Dyer; FIELD MICE: Lawrence Hamilton & David Weatherspoon; ROYAL GATEKEEPER: Sam Harkness; HEAD OF SOCIETY OF EMERALD CITY: Sharon Brooks; EMERALD CITY CITIZENS: Paula Anita Brown, Roslyn Burrough, Carol Dennis, Alfred L. Dove, Ada Dyer, Carla Earle, Germaine Edwards, Marvin Engran, Tanya Gibson, Jasmine Guy, Lawrence Hamilton, Sam Harkness, Raymond C. Harris, Gigi Hunter, Dwight Leon, Daryl Richardson, David Robertson, Martial Roumain, David Weatherspoon; THE WIZ: Carl Hall; EVILLENE: Ella Mitchell; LORD HIGH UNDERLING: Lawrence Hamilton; SOLDIER MESSENGER: Marvin Engran; WINGED MONKEY: Germaine Edwards; GLINDA: Ann Duquesnay. **Understudies**: Dorothy: Ada Dyer; Aunt Em: Ann Duquesnay; Glinda/Tornado: Sharon Brooks; Addaperle: Carol Dennis; Evillene: Juanita Fleming; Scarecrow: Germaine Edwards; Lion: Sam Harkness; Wiz: David Weatherspoon; Tinman: Lawrence Hamilton; Winged Monkey: Alfred L. Dove. SWING DANCERS & SINGERS: Sheri Moore & Eugene Little.

Reviews were terrible.

After Broadway. TOUR. It took in, among other places, the BEACON THEATRE, NYC, 3/16/93–4/11/93. 28 PERFORMANCES. PRESENTED BY Atlanta's Theatre of the Stars and Robert L. Young & Associates, in association with the National Black Arts Festival; DIRECTOR/CHOREOGRAPHER: George Faison; SETS: Randel Wright; COSTUMES: Jonathan Bixby; LIGHTING: John McLain; SOUND: Abe Jacob; MUSICAL DIRECTOR: Timothy Graphenreed. **Cast**: AUNT EM/GLINDA: Toni SeaWright; TOTO: Mischief; DOROTHY: Stephanie Mills; HENRY/LORD HIGH UNDERLING: Maurice Lautner; TORNADO: Evelyn Thomas; ADDAPERLE: Ebony Jo-Ann; SCARECROW: Garry Q. Lewis; TINMAN: Eugene Fleming; LION: H. Clent Bowers; GATEKEEPER: Bobby Daye; WIZ: Andre De Shields; EVILLENE: Ella Mitchell. Reprises of "Ease on Down the Road" and "Yellow Brick Road" were added.

PLANNED BROADWAY REVIVAL. In 5/03 a Broadway revival was
announced, scheduled to open in spring 2004. PRESENTED BY Dodger
Theatricals; HIS OWN BOOK UPDATED BY: William F. Brown; DIREC-
TOR: Des McAnuff; SETS: Robert Brill. It was postponed until 4/05.

757. *Woman of the Year*

The 1942 movie, on which this musical was based, starred
Katherine Hepburn as Tess Harding, a political columnist squar-
ing off against earthy sportswriter Sam Craig (played by Spencer
Tracy). This was their first of eight films together. In the musical
adaptation, told in flashback, Tess is now a Barbara Walters type
of TV morning show interviewer, and Sam is a Gary Trudeau type
of cartoonist. Tess makes some cracks about the "funnies," and
Sam strikes back by putting her in his daily strip as a character
called "Tessie Cat." They meet, fall in love, marry, and have problems, split up, reunite, and work out their differences. An animated cartoon cat danced with Lauren Bacall. Alexi was a defect-
ing Russian ballet dancer. Helga was a German maid. Jan was the
frumpy current wife of Tess's ex-husband Larry.

Before Broadway. Tommy Tune doctored the choreography in
Boston for $25,000 plus one percent of gross. The show was capitalized
at $2 million, but it actually cost $2.7 million. The two leading actors
did not sing. In tryouts there was an Asian child that Tess adopts, but
this idea was dropped.

The Broadway Run. PALACE THEATRE, 3/29/81–3/13/83. 11 previews from 3/19/81. 770 PERFORMANCES. PRESENTED BY Lawrence Kasha,
David S. Landay, James M. Nederlander, Warner Theatre Prods/Claire
Nichtern, Carole J. Shorenstein, and Stewart F. Lane; MUSIC: John Kan-
der; LYRICS: Fred Ebb; BOOK: Peter Stone; BASED ON the 1942 MGM
film of the same name, written by Ring Lardner Jr. & Michael Kanin;
DIRECTOR: Robert Moore; CHOREOGRAPHER: Tony Charmoli (chore-
ography doctored by Tommy Tune); SETS/"KATZ" CHARACTERS
DESIGNED BY: Tony Walton; COSTUMES: Theoni V. Aldredge; LIGHTING:
Marilyn Rennagel; SOUND: Abe Jacob; ANIMATIONS: Michael Sporn;
MUSICAL DIRECTOR/VOCAL ARRANGEMENTS: Donald Pippin; ORCHES-
TRATIONS: Michael Gibson; DANCE MUSIC ARRANGEMENTS: Ronald
Melrose; CAST RECORDING on Arista; PRESS: Merle Debuskey Company;
CASTING: Julie Hughes & Barry Moss; GENERAL MANAGEMENT: Mar-
vin A. Krauss Associates; COMPANY MANAGER: G. Warren McClane;
PRODUCTION STAGE MANAGER: David Taylor, *Robert V. Straus*; STAGE
MANAGER: Robert Lo Bianco, *Joel V. Tropper*; ASSISTANT STAGE MAN-
AGER: T.L. Boston, *Pat Trott*. **Cast:** CHAIRPERSON: Helon Blount; TESS
HARDING: Lauren Bacall (1) ✩, *Raquel Welch (12/1/81–12/15/81), Lauren
Bacall, Raquel Welch (6/29/82–1/2/83), Debbie Reynolds (from 2/11/83),
Louise Troy (3/5/83–3/8/83), Debbie Reynolds*; FLOOR MANAGER: Michael
O'Gorman; CHIP SALISBURY: Daren Kelly (6), *John Hammil (during Mr.
Kelly's vacation)*; GERALD: Roderick Cook (3); THE CARTOONISTS: PINKY
PETERS: Gerry Vichi (10); PHIL WITAKER: Tom Avera (7), *Mace Barrett*;
SAM CRAIG: Harry Guardino (2) ✩, *Jamie Ross (12/1/82–12/15/82), Harry
Guardino, Jamie Ross (from 6/29/83)*; ELLIS MCMASTER: Rex Hays (8);
ABBOTT CANFIELD: Lawrence Raiken (9), *John Hillner*; VOICE OF KATZ:
Fred Ebb; MAURY: Rex Everhart (12); HELGA: Grace Keagy (5); ALEXI
PETRIKOV: Eivind Harum (4), *George de la Pena, Victor Barbee*; CLEAN-
ING WOMEN: Helon Blount & Marian Haraldson; JAN DONOVAN: Mar-
ilyn Cooper (11), *Carol Arthur (during Miss Cooper's vacation, 10/13/81–
10/20/81)*; LARRY DONOVAN: Jamie Ross (13), *Ralston Hill, Timothy Jecko*;
CHORUS: De Wright Baxter, Joan Bell, Helon Blount, Sergio Cal, Donna
Drake, Richard Glendon-Larson, Marian Haraldson, Michael Kubala,
Paige Massman, Gene Montoya, Michael O'Gorman, Susan Powers,
Daniel Quinn, Robert Warners (*Mark Bove*), *James Fatta, Nina Hen-
nessey, Elyssa Paternoster, Bubba Dean Rambo, Thomas Anthony, Joanna
Noble, Michele Pigliavento (from 11/82)*. **Standby:** Sam: Jamie Ross, *Tim-
othy Jecko*. **Understudies:** Helga: Marian Haraldson; Alexi: Robert Warn-
ers, *Mark Bove, Daniel Quinn*; Chip: Richard Glendon-Larson; Phil/
Ellis/Larry: Ralston Hill; Abbott/Pinky/Maury: Michael Davis; Jan:
Paige Massman, *Barbara Gilbert*; Gerald: Michael Davis. **Swings:** Ed

Nolfi, Karen Giombetti, *Dennis Batutis, Deborah Roshe, Gene Montoya.*
Act I: Scene 1 Backstage at a hotel ballroom: "Woman of the Year" (Tess
& Women); **Scene 2** A TV studio and Sam's studio: "A Poker Game"
(Sam & Cartoonists), "See You in the Funny Papers" (Sam); **Scene 3**
Tess's office: "When You're Right, You're Right" (Tess & Gerald); **Scene
4** Sam's studio: "Shut Up, Gerald" (Tess, Sam, Gerald), "So, What Else
is New?" (Sam & voice of Katz); **Scene 5** The Inkpot: "One of the Boys"
(Tess, Cartoonists, Maury, Men), "Table Talk" (Tess & Sam); **Scene 6**
Tess's apartment: "The Two of Us" (Tess & Sam); **Scene 7** Around New
York: "It isn't Working" (Cartoonists, Chip, Helga, Gerald, New York-
ers); **Scene 8** Tess's apartment: "I Told You So" (Gerald & Helga); **Scene
9** Tess's apartment and a hotel ballroom: "Woman of the Year" (reprise)
(Tess). **Act II: Scene 1** The street: "So What Else is New?" (reprise) (Sam
& voice of Katz); **Scene 2** The Inkpot: "I Wrote the Book" (Tess &
Cleaning Women); **Scene 3** A ballet rehearsal room: "Happy in the
Morning" (Alexi, Tess, Dancers); **Scene 4** Sam's studio: "Sometimes a
Day Goes By" (Sam); **Scene 5** Larry's house: "The Grass is Always
Greener" (Tess & Jan) [the showstopper]; **Scene 6** The TV studio: "We're
Gonna Work it Out" (Tess & Sam).

The show went over very well, despite very divided reviews. It won
Tonys for book, score, and for Lauren Bacall and Marilyn Cooper, and
was also nominated for musical, and direction of a musical. Harry
Guardino and Lauren Bacall apparently got on very, very well. The show
suspended performances 1/2/83–2/11/83. On 3/5/83, Debbie Reynolds
collapsed, and spent several days in the hospital with transient global
amnesia.

After Broadway. TOUR. Opened on 6/9/83, in Los Angeles. The
last number on tour was "Open the Window, Sam" instead of "We're
Gonna Work it Out," and a new title song (but with the same name)
was written for this tour. The tour was re-choreographed by Joe Layton.
Cast: CHAIRPERSON: Helon Blount; TESS: Lauren Bacall; CHIP: John
Hammil; GERALD: Emory Bass; SAM: Harry Guardino; ELLIS: Ted Agress;
CANFIELD: Dennis Parlato; HELGA: Kathleen Freeman; BALLET MIS-
TRESS: Sybil Scotford; JAN: Marilyn Cooper; LARRY: Del Hinkley; TONY:
Gene Castle.

758. *Wonderful Town*

Two sisters from Columbus, Ohio come to 1935 New York
to seek their fortunes as writer (Ruth) and actress (Eileen). Ruth
is an attractive, self-possessed, witty brunette; Eileen is a baby-
faced blonde. They set up in Greenwich Village, and are talked
into renting an apartment where workers are blasting to make
way for a new subway. There are no curtains on their street-level
windows, and strange characters keep dropping by looking for
Violet, the former tenant, who used to dispose of her favors in
order to make a living. Wreck is the ex-football star. However,
their New York ambitions are not so easily fulfilled. Eileen has
problems fending off suitors, and Ruth has problems getting her
stories accepted by *The Manhatter*. On a freelance newspaper
assignment, Ruth gets to interview seven over-amorous, conga-
dancing Brazilian naval cadets, who cause a near-riot. This lands
Ruth in jail. Just as things look bad for the girls, Eileen lands a
night club spot at the Village Vortex, and Ruth gets a good job
on a newspaper, as well as Baker, the handsome editor.

Before Broadway. *My Sister Eileen*, on which *Wonderful Town* was
based, was a straight comedy (i.e. not a musical), and opened on Broad-
way at the Biltmore Theatre, on 12/26/40. 866 PERFORMANCES. PRE-
SENTED BY Max Gordon; DIRECTOR: George S. Kaufman; SETS: Donald
Oenslager. **Cast:** RUTH: Shirley Booth; EILEEN: Jo Ann Sayers; ROBERT
BAKER: Wiliam Post Jr.; MR. APPOPOULOS: Morris Carnovsky; FRANK
LIPPENCOTT: Richard Quine; THE WRECK: Gordon Jones; VIOLET SHEL-
TON: Effie Afton.

The first idea of doing a musical adaptation of the successful play
and the 1942 movie *My Sister Eileen* was producer Max Gordon's. He
tried to get Dorothy & Herbert Fields to do the lyrics and book, Bur-

ton Lane to do the music, and George S. Kaufman to direct. But that fell through. Next came producer Leland Hayward, who tried to get Dorothy, Herbert and Joseph Fields to do the book, and Cole Porter or Irving Berlin to do the music & lyrics. But that failed too. A third attempt had Ella Logan in the lead. However, Harry Cohn, head of Columbia studios, who owned the film rights, refused to play ball. Finally, Robert Fryer acquired the rights. Leroy Anderson and Arnold Horwitt were hired to do music & lyrics, but five weeks before rehearsals they were fired over a disagreement with the librettists, and Comden & Green were called in, and they in turn called in Leonard Bernstein. A whole new score had to be written in just a short while, so they could keep Rosalind Russell in the show. La Russell, who had not been on stage since 1930, and who had little or no singing voice, was rather afraid to reproduce her film role in a stage musical (her only Broadway musical). Comden & Green were making the lyrics too sharp-edged and cynical for the liking of the librettists, and there was a lot of tension. George Abbott sided with the lyricists and that was that. Jerome Robbins was called in to tighten up the dance numbers during otherwise sensational New Haven tryouts. Also in New Haven Miss Russell was having problems with losing her voice, until Edie Adams showed her how to conserve it. During the Boston tryouts a chorus boy dropped Miss Russell during the "Conga" number and she sprained her back.

The Broadway Run. WINTER GARDEN THEATRE, 2/25/53–7/3/54. 559 PERFORMANCES. PRESENTED BY Robert Fryer; MUSIC: Leonard Bernstein; LYRICS: Betty Comden & Adolph Green; BOOK: Joseph A. Fields & Jerome Chodorov; BASED ON the 1940 comedy *My Sister Eileen*, by Joseph A. Fields & Jerome Chodorov, which in turn was based on the series of sketches in the *New Yorker* by Ruth McKenney; DIRECTOR: George Abbott; CHOREOGRAPHER: Donald Saddler; SETS/COSTUMES: Raoul Pene du Bois; ROSALIND RUSSELL'S CLOTHES BY: Mainbocher; LIGHTING: Peggy Clark; MUSICAL DIRECTOR/VOCAL ARRANGEMENTS: Lehman Engel; ORCHESTRATIONS: Don Walker; PRESS: Phyllis Perlman, Marian Byram, David Powers; GENERAL MANAGER: Charles Harris; STAGE MANAGERS: Robert E. Griffith, Harold Prince, Edmund Balin, *John Effrat, Walter Rinner.* **Cast:** HERMIT: Don Barton; GUIDE: Warren Galjour; APPOPOULOS: Henry Lascoe (4); LONIGAN: Walter Kelvin; HELEN: Michele Burke, *Diana Herbert;* WRECK: Jordan Bentley; VIOLET: Dody Goodman; SPEEDY VALENTI: Ted Beniades; EILEEN SHERWOOD: Edith Adams (3); RUTH SHERWOOD: Rosalind Russell (1) ☆, *Carol Channing* (from 5/6/54); A STRANGE MAN: Nathaniel Frey; DRUNKS: Lee Papell & Delbert Anderson; ROBERT BAKER: George Gaynes (2); ASSOCIATE EDITORS: Warren Galjour & Albert Linville; MRS. WADE: Isabella Hoopes; FRANK LIPPENCOTT: Cris Alexander; CHEF: Nathaniel Frey; WAITER: Delbert Anderson; DELIVERY BOY: Alvin Beam; CHICK CLARK: Dort Clark; SHORE PATROLMAN: Lee Papell; 1ST CADET: David Lober; 2ND CADET: Ray Dorian; POLICEMEN: Lee Papell, Albert Linville, Delbert Anderson, Chris Robinson, Nathaniel Frey, Warren Galjour, Robert Kole (*Michael Mason*); RUTH'S ESCORT: Chris Robinson; GREENWICH VILLAGERS: Delbert Anderson, Ed Balin (gone by 53–54), Alvin Beam, Marta Becket, Maxine Berke, Carol Cole, Margaret Cuddy (gone by 53–54), Geraldine Delaney, Ray Dorian, Jean Eliot, Warren Galjour, Dody Goodman, Edward J. Heim, Pat Johnson (gone by 53–54), Robert Kole (*Michael Mason*), Joe Layton (gone by 53–54), David Lober, Victor Moreno (gone by 53–54), Evelyn Page, Lee Papell, Helen Rice, Chris Robinson, Helena Seroy (gone by 53–54), Libi Staiger (gone by 53–54), William Weslow (gone by 53–54), Patricia Wilkes, *Don Barton, Betty Gillett, Babs Heath, Hugh Lambert, Marion Lauer, Paul Lyday, David Neuman, Virginia Poe, Walter Rinner, Doris Wright.* **Understudies:** Ruth: Patty Wilkes; Eileen: Pat Johnson, *Betty Gillett;* Appopoulos: Lee Papell; Baker: Chris Robinson; Wreck: Joe Layton, *Michael Mason;* Lippencott: Hal Prince; Mrs. Wade: Helen Rice; Helen: Geraldine Delaney; Chick: Del Anderson; Valenti: Warren Galjour. **Act I:** Overture (Orchestra); *Scene 1* Christopher Street, Greenwich Village: "Christopher Street" (Guide, Tourists, Villagers Chorus); *Scene 2* The studio (Ruth & Eileen's studio apartment): "Ohio" (Ruth & Eileen); *Scene 2a* All around New York: "Conquering New York" (dance) (Ruth, Eileen, 1st Cadet, Violet, Villagers; *Scene 3* Christopher Street: "One Hundred Easy Ways (to Lose a Man)" (Ruth); *Scene 4* Baker's office: "What a Waste" (Baker & Associate Editors), Ruth's Story Vignettes (w: Comden & Green) [not on the cast album): REXFORD: Chris Robinson; MR. MALLORY: Delbert

Anderson; DANNY: Nathaniel Frey; TRENT: Lee Papell; **Scene 5** Christopher Street: "A Little Bit in Love (Never Felt This Way Before)" (Eileen); **Scene 6** The back yard, Christopher Street: "Pass the Football" (Wreck & Villagers Chorus), "Conversation Piece" ("Nice People, Nice Talk") (written by Comden & Green) (Ruth, Eileen, Frank, Baker, Chick), "A Quiet Girl" (Baker), "A Quiet Girl" (reprise) (Ruth); **Scene 7** The Navy Yard: "Conga!" (Sung by Ruth. Danced by The Cadets); **Scene 7a** The back yard, Christopher Street: "Conga!" (reprise) (Company). **Act II:** Entr'acte (Orchestra); **Scene 1** The Christopher Street station house (jail): "My Darlin' Eileen" (Eileen, Waiter, Policemen); **Scene 2** Christopher Street: "Swing!" (Ruth & Villagers Chorus); **Scene 3** The studio: "Ohio" (reprise) (Ruth & Eileen) (not on cast album); **Scene 4** The street in front of the Vortex: "It's Love" (Eileen, Baker, Villagers Chorus); **Scene 5** The Vortex: "Ballet at the Village Vortex" (also known as "The Village Vortex Blues," and "Let it Come Down") (Villagers), "Wrong Note Rag" (Ruth, Eileen, Villagers Chorus), Finale: "It's Love" (reprise) (Company).

It opened on Broadway with an advance sale of $400,000. It got only raves from the critics. The show won Tonys for musical, choreography, sets, musical director, and for Rosalind Russell. It also won Donaldson Awards for musical, music, lyrics, book, director, costumes, actress (Rosalind Russell), supporting actress (Edie Adams), female debut (Edie Adams again). During the run Allyn Ann McLerie divorced Adolph Green and married George Gaynes. Reviewers covered the show again in 1954, when Carol Channing took over at the end of Miss Russell's contract, but it couldn't survive without Rosalind Russell. Edie Adams was paid 175 a week; Miss Russell $12,500.

After Broadway. TOUR. Opened on 7/7/54, at the Shubert Theatre, Chicago. **Cast:** RUTH: Carol Channing; EILEEN: Betty Gillett; ROBERT: George Gaynes; STRANGE MAN: Howard Caine; DRUNK/WAITER: Joe Flynn; FRANK: Cris Alexander, *Bob Shaver, Don Barton;* WRECK: Warde Donovan, *Jordan Bentley;* VALENTI: Ted Beniades; CHICK: Dort Clark; HERMIT: Don Barton; 2ND CADET: Ray Dorian; CHORUS INCLUDED: Carol Cole & Marion Lauer.

PRINCES THEATRE, London, 2/23/55–8/20/55. 205 PERFORMANCES. PRESENTED BY Jack Hylton; DIRECTOR: Richard Bird; MUSICAL DIRECTOR: Cyril Ornadel. There was a London cast recording. **Cast:** EILEEN: Shani Wallis; RUTH: Pat Kirkwood; WRECK: Sid James; APPOPOULOS: David Hurst, *Bernard Spear;* LONIGAN: Frank Wilson; HELEN: Shirley Douglas; STRANGE MAN: Ray Browne; CHICK: Colin Croft; ROBERT: Dennis Bowen.

THE MOVIE. 1955. Because of contract disputes, Columbia produced its own movie musical, *My Sister Eileen*, with a different score. **Cast:** EILEEN: Janet Leigh; RUTH: Betty Garrett (Judy Holliday had been scheduled to play this role); BOB: Jack Lemmon; FRANK: Bob Fosse; WRECK: Richard York; CHICK: Tommy Rall.

CITY CENTER, NYC, 3/5/58–3/16/58. 16 PERFORMANCES. PRESENTED BY the New York City Center Light Opera company; DIRECTOR: Jerome Chodorov; CHOREOGRAPHER: Ralph Beaumont; SETS/COSTUMES: Raoul Pene du Bois; COSTUME SUPERVISOR: Ruth Morley; LIGHTING: Peggy Clark; PRODUCTION SUPERVISOR: Herbert Ross; MUSICAL DIRECTOR/VOCAL ARRANGEMENTS: Lehman Engel; ORCHESTRATIONS: Don Walker. **Cast:** APPOPOULOS: George Givot; LONIGAN: Jack Rains; HELEN: Betsy von Furstenburg; WRECK: Jordan Bentley; VIOLET: Paula Wayne; VALENTI: Ted Beniades; EILEEN: Jo Sullivan; RUTH: Nancy Walker; DRUNKS: Daniel P. Hannafin & Jack Fletcher; ROBERT: Peter Cookson; MRS. WADE: Isabella Hoopes; FRANK: Cris Alexander; SINGERS INCLUDED: Joan Fagan, Jane A. Johnston, Elmarie Wendel; DANCERS INCLUDED: Svetlana McLee, Gina Trikonis. **Understudy:** Ruth: Betsy Bartley.

TV SPECIAL EDITION. Aired by CBS, 11/30/58. **Cast:** RUTH: Rosalind Russell; EILEEN: Jacquelyn McKeever; ROBERT: Syd Chaplin; CHICK: Dort Clark; WRECK: Jordan Bentley; HELEN: Michele Burke; FRANK: Cris Alexander.

CITY CENTER, NYC, 2/13/63–2/24/63. 16 PERFORMANCES. PRESENTED BY the New York City Center Light Opera Company; DIRECTOR: Gus Schirmer Jr.; CHOREOGRAPHER: Ralph Beaumont; SETS: Raoul Pene du Bois; COSTUMES: Ruth Morley; LIGHTING: Peggy Clark; CONDUCTOR: Lehman Engel. **Cast:** GUIDE: Warren Galjour; APPOPOULOS: Phil Leeds; LONIGAN: Walter Kelvin; HELEN: Pat Turner; WRECK: Stewart Rose; VIOLET: Betty Hyatt Linton; VALENTI: Ted Beniades; EILEEN: Jacquelyn McKeever; RUTH: Kaye Ballard; ROBERT: Robert Kaye; MRS. WADE: Paula Trueman; FRANK: Jim Kirkwood; CHICK: Gabriel Dell; RUTH'S ESCORT: Reid Shelton; DANCERS INCLUDED: Gerard Brentte, Vito Durante, Mercedes Ellington, Shellie Farrell, Babs Heath, Svetlana McLee, Dom Salinaro, Aura Vainio; SINGERS INCLUDED: Eric Barnes, Steve Elmore, Lynne Ephron, Maria Graziano, Larry Mitchell.

CITY CENTER, NYC, 5/17/67–6/4/67. 23 PERFORMANCES. Part of City Center's spring season of three musical revivals (the others were *Finian's Rainbow* and *The Sound of Music*). PRESENTED BY the New York City Center Light Opera Company; DIRECTOR: Gus Schirmer; CHOREOGRAPHER: Ralph Beaumont; SETS: Raoul Pene du Bois; COSTUMES: Frank Thompson; LIGHTING: Peggy Clark; MUSICAL DIRECTOR: Irving Actman. *Cast*: GUIDE: Austin Colyer; APPOPOULOS: Ted Thurston; LONIGAN: Ronn Carroll; HELEN: Betsy von Furstenburg; WRECK: Jack Knight; VIOLET: Betty Hyatt Linton; VALENTI: George Marcy; EILEEN: Linda Bennett; RUTH: Elaine Stritch; A STRANGE MAN/ROBERT: Nolan Van Way; DRUNKS: Ben Laney & Henry Lawrence; ASSOCIATE EDITORS: Paul Adams & Michael Harrison; MRS. WADE: Claire Waring; FRANK: Jack Fletcher; CHEF: Marvin Goodis; WAITER: Henry LeClair; DELIVERY BOY: Ronny Hedrick; CHICK: Richard France; SHORE PATROLMAN: Edward Taylor; 1ST CADET: Tim Ramirez; 2ND CADET: Vito Durante; BUTCH: Mary Ann Niles; RUTH'S ESCORT: Stokely Gray; CHORUS: Alyce Elizabeth Webb, Maggie Worth, Ina Kurland, Kuniko Narai, Rodd Barry, Vito Durante, George Bunt, Tony Stevens, Mary Ann Niles. *Understudy*: Violet: Mary Ann Niles.

LONDON, 1986. West End revival. *Cast*: Maureen Lipman, Emily Morgan, Nicolas Colicos, Robert Dallas, Lesley Joseph, Ben Stevens, Ray Lonnen. Miss Lipman won an Olivier.

NEW YORK STATE THEATRE, 11/8/94–11/20/94. 14 PERFORMANCES. PRESENTED BY the New York City Opera; DIRECTOR: Richard Sabellico; CHOREOGRAPHER: Tina Paul; SETS: Michael Anania; COSTUMES: Gail Baldoni; LIGHTING: Jeff Davis; SOUND: Abe Jacob; CONDUCTOR: Eric Stern. Reviews were divided. *Cast*: TOUR GUIDE/CHEF: William Ledbetter; APPOPOULOS: Larry Block; LONIGAN: Don Yule; HELEN: Meghan Strange; WRECK: Timothy Warmen; VIOLET: Amanda Green; VALENTI: Carlos Lopez; EILEEN: Crista Moore; RUTH: Kay McClelland; FLETCHER/REXFORD/RUTH'S ESCORT: Gary Jackson; DRUNKS: Mason Roberts & Louis Perry; ESKIMO PIE MAN/2ND CADET: Mason Roberts; ROBERT: Richard Muenz; ASSOCIATE EDITORS: John Lankston & William Ledbetter; MR. MALLORY: Louis Perry; DANNY: Jeffrey Weber; PARTY GUEST: Marilyn Armstrong; TRENT/WAITER: Daniel Shigo; MRS. WADE: Susan Browning; FRANK: Don Stephenson; DELIVERY BOY/1ST CADET: Larry Sousa; CHICK: Stephen Berger; SHORE PATROLMAN: Ron Hilley; BRAZILIAN AMBASSADOR/SOLO POLICEMAN: John Lankston; POLICEMEN: Ron Hilley, Louis Perry, William Ledbetter, Jeffrey Weber; FLOWER SELLERS: Paula Hostetter & Melissa Maravell; CUSTOMER: Beth Pensiero. The number "Conquering New York" was dropped.

LOS ANGELES, 11/19/97–11/23/97. 6 PERFORMANCES. Part of the *Reprise!* series. DIRECTOR: Don Amendolia; CHOREOGRAPHER: Kevin Carlisle; MUSICAL DIRECTOR: Peter Matz. *Cast*: Lucie Arnaz (replaced Tyne Daly who quit before the run, to fulfill a movie contract), Stephanie Zimbalist.

759. *Wonderful Town* *(Broadway revival)*

Before Broadway. The origin of this revival was a staged concert reading at CITY CENTER, 5/4/00–5/7/00, part of the *Encores!* series. BOOK ADAPTED BY: David Ives; DIRECTOR/CHOREOGRAPHER: Kathleen Marshall; MUSICAL DIRECTOR: Rob Fisher. *Cast*: EILEEN: Laura Benanti; RUTH: Donna Murphy; APPOPOULOS: Lewis J. Stadlen; FRANK: David Aaron Baker; ROBERT: Richard Muenz; CHICK: Gregory Jbara; VIOLET: Alix Korey; GUIDE: Patrick Quinn; WRECK: Raymond Jaramillo McLeod; VALENTI: Stephen DeRosa; ALSO WITH: Cynthia Onrubia, Ian Knauer, Joyce Chittick, Vince Pesce, Tina Ou. There was great praise, especially for Donna Murphy, and there was immediate talk by Elizabeth Williams & Anita Waxman of bringing the production to Broadway. By 9/00

Barry & Fran Weissler were the new producers, and the Ford Center for the Performing Arts was being rumored as the Broadway venue. But it never happened. Donna Murphy couldn't wait any longer, and went into a TV show, then she got pregnant. However, by 2003 it was back on track, with Barry & Fran Weissler as producers, for the 2003–04 season, and with Donna Murphy to star. By mid–August 2003 it had found a theatre — the Hirschfeld (the old Martin Beck), for the fall of 2003. Broadway previews were put back a day from 11/4/03. By 9/22/03 the complete cast was confirmed in their roles. Lisa Mayer dropped out of the chorus before Broadway. The 11/6/03–11/9/03 previews were canceled due to Donna Murphy's health (some sort of flu), and from 11/11/03 Linda Mugleston went on for her. Miss Murphy was back on 11/18/03.

The Broadway Run. AL HIRSCHFELD THEATRE, 11/23/03–1/30/05. 16 previews from 11/5/03. 507 PERFORMANCES. PRESENTED BY Roger Berlind, Fran & Barry Weissler, in association with Edwin W. Schloss, Allen Spivak, Clear Channel Entertainment, Harvey Weinstein; MUSIC: Leonard Bernstein; LYRICS: Betty Comden & Adolph Green; BOOK: Joseph Fields & Jerome Chodorov; BASED ON the comedy *My Sister Eileen*, by Joseph Fields and Jerome Chodorov; SCRIPT ADAPTED BY: David Ives; DIRECTOR/CHOREOGRAPHER: Kathleen Marshall; ASSOCIATE CHOREOGRAPHER: Vince Pesce; SETS: John Lee Beatty; COSTUMES: Martin Pakledinaz; LIGHTING: Peter Kaczorowski; SOUND: Lew Mead; SUPERVISING MUSICAL DIRECTOR/VOCAL ARRANGEMENTS: Rob Fisher; ORIGINAL ORCHESTRATIONS: Don Walker; NEW CAST RECORDING on DRG, recorded on 1/12/04 and released 3/6/04; PRESS: The Pete Sanders Group; CASTING: Jay Binder/Laura Stanczyk; GENERAL MANAGER: B.J. Holt; COMPANY MANAGER: Hilary Hamilton, *Penelope Daulton, Bobby Driggers*; PRODUCTION STAGE MANAGER: Peter Hanson; STAGE MANAGERS: Kimberly Russell & Maximo Torres, *Karen Moore & Michael Wilhoite*. *Cast*: TOUR GUIDE: Ken Barnett, *James Clow*; APPOPOULOS: David Margulies (4); OFFICER LONIGAN: Timothy Shew; WRECK: Raymond Jaramillo McLeod (6), *Matthew Shepard* (stood in); HELEN: Nancy Anderson, *Joyce Chittick* (stood in); VIOLET: Linda Mugleston, *Stephanie Fredricks* (stood in); SPEEDY VALENTI: Stanley Wayne Mathis; EILEEN SHERWOOD: Jennifer Westfeldt (2) (until 8/29/04), *Nancy Anderson & Susan Derry* (alternated as stand-ins), *Jennifer Hope Wills* (from 9/28/04); RUTH SHERWOOD: Donna Murphy (1) ☆ (until 9/5/04), *Linda Mugleston* (stood in until 9/26/04), *Brooke Shields* (9/28/04–1/30/05); ITALIAN CHEF: Vince Pesce, *Michael O'Donnell*; ITALIAN WAITER: Rick Faugno, *Alex Sanchez*; DRUNKS: David Eggers & Devin Richards; A STRANGE MAN: Ray Wills, *Darrin Baker*; ESKIMO PIE MAN: J.D. Webster; FRANK LIPPENCOTT: Peter Benson (7); ROBERT BAKER: Gregg Edelman (3); ASSOCIATE EDITORS: Ken Barnett (*James Clow*) & Ray Wills (*Darrin Baker*); MRS. WADE: Randy Danson, *Toni DiBuono*; KID: Mark Price, *Jeffrey Schecter*; CHICK CLARK: Michael McGrath (5); SHORE PATROLMAN/MAN WITH THE SIGN: Ray Wills, *Darrin Baker*; CADETS: David Eggers, Rick Faugno (*Alex Sanchez*), Vince Pesce (*Michael O'Donnell*), Mark Price (*Jeffrey Schecter*), Devin Richards, J.D. Webster; POLICEMEN: Ken Barnett, David Eggers, Vince Pesce (*Michael O'Donnell*), Devin Richards, J.D. Webster, Ray Wills (*Darrin Baker*); GREENWICH VILLAGERS: Ken Barnett, Joyce Chittick, Susan Derry, David Eggers, Rick Faugno (*Alex Sanchez*), Lorin Latarro, Linda Mugleston, Tina Ou, Vince Pesce (*Michael O'Donnell*), Mark Price (*Jeffrey Schecter*), Devin Richards, Angela Robinson, Megan Sikora, J.D. Webster, Ray Wills (*Darrin Baker*), *Laurie Williamson*. **Understudies**: Ruth/Mrs. Wade: Linda Mugleston; Eileen: Nancy Anderson & Susan Derry; Helen: Joyce Chittick; Valenti: Randy Donaldson; Frank: David Eggers; Lonigan/Wreck: Matthew Shepard; Baker: Matthew Shepard & Ken Barnett; Appopoulos/Chick: Ray Wills, *Darrin Baker*; Speedy: J.D. Webster. **Swings**: Randy Donaldson (*Lisa Mayer*), Stephanie Fredricks, Matthew Shepard, *Lee A. Wilkins* (added during the run). **Orchestra**: PIANO: Josh Rosenblum; VIOLINS: Masako Yanagita, Christoph Franzgrote, Lisa Matricardi; VIOLA: Jill Jaffe; CELLO: Diane Barere; BASS: Lou Bruno; WOODWINDS: Steven Kenyon, Lino Gomez, Fred DeChristofaro, Edward Salkin, John Winder; TRUMPETS: Stu Satalof, David Trigg, David Gale, Ron Tooley; TROMBONES: Jack Gale, Jason Jackson, Jack Schatz; DRUMS/PERCUSSION: David Ratajczak.

The show got good reviews, but the public didn't come. Donna Murphy was out again in 12/03, after opening night. The show won a Tony for choreography, and was also nominated for revival of a musical, director of a musical, and for Donna Murphy and Jennifer Westfeldt. On 8/20/04 it was announced that Brooke Shields would take over from Donna Murphy as Ruth. Miss Murphy had been absent from 9/5/04, and it seemed as if she would come back at any time. It was announced that she would be back 9/21/04–9/26/04, but she never came back. Jennifer Westfeldt left the cast due to a "medical condition." On 9/12/04 Jerome Chodorov died, aged 93. The well-received Brooke Shields extended her stay from 1/3/05 to 1/30/05, and the producers decided to end the run on that latter date.

After Broadway. Tour. By 5/04 the news was that the tour would kick off at the Hobby Center, Houston, 9/28/04–10/10/04, but as of 7/04 the tour was canceled.

760. *Working*

A series of character portraits of working people in songs and sketches. Takes place in the present time, in numerous places of employment. The characters are non-fictional; names have been changed, but their words have not. Even in the case of song lyrics, the writers tried to remain as faithful as possible to the characters' original words.

Before Broadway. The show tried out at the GOODMAN THEATRE, Chicago, 12/30/77. 44 PERFORMANCES. *Cast*: MIKE LEFEVRE, STEEL-WORKER: Brad Sullivan; AL CALINDA, PARKING LOT ATTENDANT: Jay Flash Riley; NORA WATSON, EDITOR: Robin Lamont; JOHN FORTUNE, ADVERTISING COPY CHIEF: Steven Boockvor; DIANE WILSON, PROCESS CLERK: Lynne Thigpen; FRED RINGLEY, PRINTING SALESMAN: Joe Ponazecki; KATE RINGLEY, HOUSEWIFE: Jo Henderson; HERB ROSEN, RING-LEY'S BOSS: Rex Everhart; JOHN RINGLEY, NEWSBOY: Jay Footlik; MRS. RINGLEY, FRED'S MOTHER: Bobo Lewis; ROSE HOFFMAN, TEACHER: Bobo Lewis; BABE SECOLI, SUPERMARKET CHECKER: Bobo Lewis; PETE KEE-LEY, EX-BOSS: Jay Flash Riley; LOIS KEELEY, HIS DAUGHTER: Lynne Thig-pen; BARBARA HERRICK, WRITER-PRODUCER: Robin Lamont; JEROME KOSLO, PRIEST: Steven Boockvor; HENRY KOSLO, STEELWORKER: Rex Everhart; HENRIETTA KOSLO, HENRY'S WIFE: Anne De Salvo; HENRY KOSLO'S SON: Steven Boockvor; ANN BOGEN, EXECUTIVE SECRETARY: Bobo Lewis; BRETT MYLETT, BOXBOY: David Patrick Kelly; EMILIO HER-NANDEZ, MIGRANT WORKER: Joe Mantegna; JUAN ORTEGA, BASEBALL PITCHER: Joe Mantegna; JACK HUNTER, PROFESSOR OF COMMUNICA-TIONS: Joe Mantegna; JACK CURRIER, SON OF CORPORATE EXECUTIVE: Joe Mantegna; CONRAD SWIBEL, GAS METER READER: Matt Landers; JILL TORRENCE, MODEL: Terri Treas; ROBERTA VICTOR, CALL GIRL: Anne De Salvo; GRACE CLEMENTS, FELTING MILLWORKER: Anne De Salvo; BUD ROLFING, FOOTBALL COACH: Brad Sullivan; MARCO CAMERONE, HOCKEY PLAYER: Steven Boockvor; JOE ZUTTY, EX-SHIPPING CLERK: Rex Ever-hart; TOM PATRICK, FIREMAN: Matt Landers; BENNY BLUE, BAR PIANIST: Stephen Reinhardt; DELORES DANTE, WAITRESS: Anne De Salvo; HEATHER LAMB, TELEPHONE OPERATOR: Lynne Thigpen; FRAN SWEN-SON, HOTEL SWITCHBOARD OPERATOR: Bobo Lewis; RECEPTIONIST: Robin Lamont; BOOKER PAGE, SEAMAN: Rex Everhart; MRS. WILL ROBINSON, BUS DRIVER'S WIFE: Lynne Thigpen; TIM DEVLIN, SALESMAN: David Patrick Kelly; RALPH WERNER, DEPARTMENT STORE SALESMAN: Matt Landers; CATHLEEN MORAN, HOSPITAL AIDE: Robin Lamont; CHARLIE BLOSSOM, COPY BOY: David Patrick Kelly; CARLA JONAS, PHO-TOGRAPHER: Terri Treas. *Act I*: "All the Livelong Day," "American Dreaming," "Lovin' Al," "Neat to Be a Newsboy," "Nobody Tells Me How," "Treasure Island Trio," "Un Mejor Dia Vendra," "Just a House-wife," "Millwork," "Nightskate," "Joe," "If I Could've Been." *Act II*: "Nobody Goes Out Anymore," "Brother Trucker," "The Working Girl's Apache," "It's an Art," "Fathers and Sons," "Something to Point To."

Between Chicago and the Broadway opening Onna White replaced Graciela Daniele as choreographer, and Ken Billington replaced Pat Collins as lighting designer. In the cast D'Jamin Bartlett replaced Jo Henderson as the housewife, and Miss Bartlett was, in turn, replaced by Susan Bigelow.

The Broadway Run. FORTY-SIXTH STREET THEATRE, 5/14/78–6/4/78. 11 previews. 25 PERFORMANCES. PRESENTED BY Stephen R. Fried-man & Irwin Meyer, in association with Joseph Harris; MUSIC: Stephen

Schwartz, James Taylor, Mary Rodgers, Micki Grant, Craig Carnelia; LYRICS: Stephen Schwartz, James Taylor, Micki Grant, Craig Carnelia, Graciela Daniele, Matt Landers, Susan Birkenhead, Walt Whitman; BASED ON the 1974 oral history *Working: People Talk About What They Do All Day and How They Feel About What They Do*, by Studs Terkel; ADAPTED BY Stephen Schwartz (with Nina Faso); DIRECTOR: Stephen Schwartz; ASSOCIATE DIRECTOR: Nina Faso; CHOREOGRAPHER: Onna White; SETS: David Mitchell; COSTUMES: Marjorie Slaiman; LIGHTING: Ken Billington; SOUND: Jack Mann; MUSICAL DIRECTOR/VOCAL ARRANGEMENTS: Stephen Reinhardt; ORCHESTRATIONS: Kirk Nurock; DANCE & INCIDENTAL MUSIC: Michele Brourman; CAST RECORDING on Columbia; PRESS: Hunt/Pucci Associates; CASTING: Scott Rudin; GENERAL MANAGEMENT: Gatchell & Neufeld; COMPANY MANAGER: Douglas C. Baker; PRODUCTION STAGE MANAGER: Alan Hall; STAGE MANAGER: Ruth E. Rinklin; ASSISTANT STAGE MANAGER: Richard Elkow. *Cast: Act I*: MIKE LEFEVRE, STEELWORKER: Brad Sullivan; AL CALINDA, PARKING LOT ATTENDANT: David Langston Smyrl; NORA WATSON, EDITOR: Patti LuPone (7); JOHN FORTUNE, ADVERTISING COPY CHIEF: Steven Boockvor; DIANE WILSON, SECRETARY: Lynne Thigpen (10); HERB ROSEN, CORPORATE EXECUTIVE: Rex Everhart (2); ANTHONY PALAZZO, STONEMASON: Arny Freeman (3); JOHN RUSHTON, NEWSBOY: Matthew McGrath; ROSE HOFFMAN, TEACHER: Bobo Lewis (6); BABE SECOLI, SUPERMARKET CHECKER: Lenora Nemetz (9); BRETT MEYER, BOXBOY: David Patrick Kelly (5); EMILIO HERNANDEZ, MIGRANT WORKER: Joe Mantegna (8); CONRAD SWIBEL, GAS METER READER: Matt Landers; KATE RUSHTON, HOUSEWIFE: Susan Bigelow (1); BARBARA HER-RICK, AGENCY VICE-PRESIDENT: Robin Lamont; TERRY MASON, STEW-ARDESS: Lenora Nemetz (9); JILL TORRENCE, MODEL: Terri Treas; ROBERTA VICTOR, CALL GIRL: Patti LuPone (7); GRACE CLEMENTS, MILL-WORKER: Bobo Lewis (6); BUD JONAS, FOOTBALL COACH: Bob Gunton (4); MARCO CAMERONE, HOCKEY PLAYER: Steven Boockvor; JOE ZUTTY, RETIRED SHIPPING CLERK: Arny Freeman (3); TOM PATRICK, FIREMAN: Matt Landers. *Act II*: BENNY BLUE, BAR PIANIST: David Patrick Kelly (5); DELORES DANTE, WAITRESS: Lenora Nemetz (9); HEATHER LAMB, TELE-PHONE OPERATOR: Lynne Thigpen (10); FRAN SWENSON, HOTEL SWITCH-BOARD OPERATOR: Bobo Lewis (6); SHARON ATKINS, RECEPTIONIST: Robin Lamont; FRANK DECKER, INTERSTATE TRUCKER: Bob Gunton (4); DAVE McCORMICK, INTERSTATE TRUCKER: Joe Mategna (8); BOOKER PAGE, SEAMAN: Rex Everhart (2); LUCILLE PAGE, SEAMAN'S WIFE: Bobo Lewis (6); WILL ROBINSON, BUS DRIVER: David Langston Smyrl; JoANNE ROBINSON, BUS DRIVER'S WIFE: Lynne Thigpen (10); TIM DEVLIN, SALES-MAN: Matt Landers; CARLA DEVLIN, SALESMAN'S WIFE: Terri Treas; RALPH WERNER, TIE SALESMAN: Matt Landers; CATHLEEN MORAN, HOSPITAL AIDE: Robin Lamont; CHARLIE BLOSSOM, COPY BOY: David Patrick Kelly (5); MAGGIE HOLMES, CLEANING WOMAN: Lynne Thigpen (10); MIKE LEFEVRE, STEELWORKER: Brad Sullivan. *Standbys*: Hank Brunjes, James Congdon, Marilyn Cooper. *Act I*: "All the Livelong Day" (Walt Whit-man's poem "I Hear America Singing," with mus/add lyr by Stephen Schwartz) (Company), "Lovin' Al" (m/l: Micki Grant) (Al & Ensemble) [Al has parked cars for 32 years], "The Mason" (m/l: Craig Carnelia) (Anthony), "Neat to Be a Newsboy" (m/l: Stephen Schwartz) (John & Newsboys), "Nobody Tells Me How" (m: Mary Rodgers; l: Susan Birken-head) (Rose) [a teacher of 42 years regrets the changes in her students], Treasure Island Trio (m: Michele Brourman) (danced by Miss Treas, Miss Nemetz, Miss Thigpen), "Un Mejor Dia Vendra" (m: James Tay-lor; Spanish lyrics: Graciela Daniele & Matt Landers) (Emilio, Mr. Lan-ders, Migrant Workers), "Just a Housewife" (m/l: Craig Carnelia) (Kate & Housewives), "Millwork" (m: Michele Brourman & Stephen Schwartz) (Miss Lamont, Mr. Kelly, Mr. Landers; danced by Miss Treas), Nightskate (m: Michele Brourman & Stephen Schwartz), "Joe" (m/l: Craig Carnelia) (Joe), "If I Could've Been" (m/l: Micki Grant) (Com-pany). *Act II*: "It's an Art" (m/l: Stephen Schwartz) (Delores & Cus-tomers), "Brother Trucker" (m/l: James Taylor) (Dave, Frank, Mr. Kelly, Mr. Landers), Husbands and Wives (m: Michele Brourman) (danced by the Pages, the Robinsons, and the Devlins), "Fathers and Sons" (m/l: Stephen Schwartz) (Mr. Gunton), "Cleanin' Women" (m/l: Micki Grant) (Maggie), "Something to Point To" (m/l: Craig Carnelia) (Company).

Broadway reviews were terrible. The show received Tony nomina-tions for score, book, sets, lighting, and for Steven Boockvor and Rex Everhart.

After Broadway. For some time there had been interest in reviving the show Off Broadway. In 1996 Stephen Schwartz & Eric D. Schaeffer (artistic director of the Signature Theatre, Arlington, Va.) began working on a revised and updated version. Studs Terkel, then 85, agreed to the changes to his original book, and all the songwriters agreed to lyric updates (however, there were no new songs). It ran at the SIGNATURE THEATRE, 11/3/97–12/7/97. Previews from 10/28/97), and was much-acclaimed. A New York run was speculated upon, but never happened.

NORTH SHORE CENTER FOR THE PERFORMING ARTS, Skokie, Ill. Not a stage production, but a radio performance, recorded by Theatres on the Air for a 10/4/98 broadcast on WFMT Chicago. DIRECTOR: Cecilie D. Keenan. Tyne Daly and Charles Durning were to star, but Miss Daly canceled at the last minute, and Felicia Fields stepped in.

LONG WHARF THEATRE, New Haven, 3/5/99–4/4/99. The new 1997 version, but further updated. It was now 90 minutes long, with no intermission, and it had two new songs—"I'm Just Movin'" (by Stephen Schwartz) and "Traffic Jam" (by James Taylor). "If I Could've Been," which originally closed Act I, was now the fourth song. DIRECTOR: Christopher Ashley (replacing David Petrarca, who quit before the show opened). It was going to open on 11/13/98, but the date got put back. *Cast*: Alix Korey, John Herrera, Ken Prymus, Rex Robbins, Emily Skinner.

The 1999 update was PRESENTED BY the American Theatre Company, 11/20/00. Previews from 11/14. DIRECTOR: Brian Russell; MUSICAL DIRECTOR: Marc Eliot. Closing date was extended from 12/16/00 to 1/14/01. The same company presented it again, at the METROPOLIS PERFORMING ARTS CENTER, Arlington Heights, Ill., 2/22/01–3/18/01.

761. *A Year with Frog and Toad*

A children's musical about a pair of amphibian friends. This show was significant in that it brought professional children's theatre to Broadway, awakening interest among the 3-10 year olds.

Before Broadway. Robert Sella was in one of several readings that led up to this show's premiere at the CHILDREN'S THEATRE COMPANY, Minneapolis, in 8/02. Then it had a sell-out run at the NEW VICTORY THEATRE, New York, 11/17/02–12/1/02. Previews from 11/15/02. DIRECTOR: David Petrarca; SETS: Adrianne Lobel (she was the daughter of the author of the Frog and Toad books, Arnold Lobel). *Cast*: Mark Linn-Baker, Jay Goede, Danielle Ferland, Kate Reinders (Jennifer Gambatese took her role for Broadway), Frank Vlastnik. Plans for Broadway for the summer of 2002 were put off until 4/03. Broadway rehearsals began on 3/17/03, at the New 42nd Street Studios.

The Broadway Run. CORT THEATRE, 4/13/03–6/15/03. 15 previews from 4/2/03. 73 PERFORMANCES. The Children's Theatre Company production, PRESENTED BY Bob Boyett, Adrianne Lobel, Michael Gardner, Lawrence Horowitz, and Roy Furman; MUSIC: Robert Reale; LYRICS/BOOK: Willie Reale; Based on the *Frog and Toad* books by Arnold Lobel; DIRECTOR: David Petrarca; CHOREOGRAPHER: Daniel Pelzig; SETS: Adrianne Lobel; COSTUMES: Martin Pakledinaz; LIGHTING: James F. Ingalls; SOUND: Rob Milburn & Michael Bodeen; MUSICAL DIRECTOR: Linda Twine; ORCHESTRATIONS: Irwin Fisch; CAST RECORDING on a private label by the producers; PRESS: Barlow — Hartman Public Relations; CASTING: Cindy Tolan; GENERAL MANAGERS: 101 Productions; COMPANY MANAGERS: David Auster & Heidi Neven; PRODUCTION STAGE MANAGER: Michael J. Passaro; STAGE MANAGER: Michelle Bosch; ASSISTANT STAGE MANAGER: Jason Brouillard. *Cast*: BIRDS: Danielle Ferland, Jennifer Gambatese, Frank Vlastnik.

FROG: Jay Goede (2) ☆, *Jonathan Rayson* (from 5/14/03 while Mr. Goede was out with appendicitis), *Jay Goede* (from 5/30/03); TOAD: Mark Linn-Baker (1) ☆; SNAIL: Frank Vlastnik; TURTLE: Danielle Ferland; MOUSE: Jennifer Gambatese; LIZARD: Frank Vlastnik; SQUIRRELS: Danielle Ferland & Jennifer Gambatese; YOUNG FROG: Jennifer Gambatese; FATHER FROG: Frank Vlastnik; MOTHER FROG: Danielle Ferland; MOLES: Danielle Ferland, Jennifer Gambatese, Frank Vlastnik. *Understudies*: Mole/Mother Frog/Mouse/Squirrel: Kate Manning; Turtle/Young Frog/Bird: Kate Manning; Bird/FatherFrog/Frog/Lizard/Mole/

Snail/Toad: Jonathan Rayson. *Orchestra*: PIANO: Linda Twine; BASS/TUBA: Linc Milliman; DRUMS/PERCUSSION: James Saporito; GUITAR/BANJO: Brian Koonin; WOODWINDS: Eddie Salkin & Dan Block; TRUMPET: Brian Pareschi; TROMBONE: Art Baron. *Act I*: "A Year with Frog and Toad" (Birds, Frog, Toad), "It's Spring" (Frog, Toad, Birds), "Seeds" (Toad)," "The Letter" (Snail), "Getta Loada Toad" (Toad, Frog, Turtle, Mouse, Lizard), Underwater Ballet (Orchestra), "Alone" (Frog), "The Letter" (reprise) (Snail), "Cookies" (Frog, Toad, Birds). *Act II*: Entr'acte (Orchestra); "The Kite" (Birds, Frog, Toad), "A Year with Frog and Toad" (reprise) (Birds), "He'll Never Know" (Toad & Frog), "Shivers" (Young Frog, Father Frog, Mother Frog, Toad, Frog), "Snow Ballet" (Orchestra), "The Letter" (reprise) (Snail), "Down the Hill" (Frog, Toad, Moles), "I'm Coming Out of My Shell" (Snail), "Toad to the Rescue" (Toad & Moles), "Merry Almost Christmas" (Toad, Frog, Moles), Finale (Birds, Frog, Toad).

Reviews were kind. It didn't do well at the box-office. Closing was announced on 6/3/03. It received Tony Nominations for musical, score, and book.

After Broadway. There were plans for a tour in the 2004–2005 season.

762. *The Yearling*

Jody is a twelve year old boy in Northern Florida just after the Civil War, who comes of age through his experiences with a pet fawn, which is shot at the end.

Before Broadway. A year before the show opened Barbra Streisand recorded "I'm All Smiles" on her "People" album. The numbers "Boy Thoughts," "Growing Up is Learning to Say Goodbye" and "Spring is a New Beginning" were not used. The show opened for tryouts at the Shubert Theatre, Philadelphia, 11/9/65–11/27/65. Herbert Ross replaced Lloyd Richards as director, but is not credited. Likewise Vernon Lusby replaced Ralph Beaumont as choreographer, and Larry Wilcox replaced Hershy Kay as orchestrator. Joe E. Marks was in the show during tryouts but didn't come with it to Broadway, whereas Carmen Alvarez was introduced after the Boston tryout opening night. "My Pa (My Love)" was cut before Broadway. The Broadway opening date was moved back from 12/27/65 to 1/3/66, then on 12/6/65 the official Broadway opening night was brought forward to 12/10/65 because there was no more money for tryouts.

The Broadway Run. ALVIN THEATRE, 12/10/65–12/11/65. 11 previews from 12/1/65. 3 PERFORMANCES. PRESENTED BY Lore Noto; MUSIC: Michael Leonard; LYRICS: Herbert Martin; BOOK: Herbert Martin & Lore Noto; BASED ON the 1938 Pulitzer Prize–winning novel of the same name by Marjorie Kinnan Rawlings, which had been filmed in 1946, straight (i.e. not as a musical), with Gregory Peck, Jane Wyman, Claude Jarman Jr., and Forrest Tucker; DIRECTOR: Lloyd Richards; CHOREOGRAPHER: Ralph Beaumont; SETS/COSTUMES: Ed Wittstein; LIGHTING: Jules Fisher; MUSICAL DIRECTOR/VOCAL ARRANGEMENTS: Julian Stein; ORCHESTRATIONS: Larry Wilcox; DANCE MUSIC ARRANGEMENTS: David Baker; CAST RECORDING on Mercury; PRESS: Harvey B. Sabinson, Lee Solters, David Powers; GENERAL MANAGER: Norman Maibaum; COMPANY MANAGER: Morton Zolotow; PRODUCTION STAGE MANAGER: Mortimer Halpern; STAGE MANAGER: Edward Julien; ASSISTANT STAGE MANAGER: Frank Bouley. *Cast:* JODY BAXTER: Steve Sanders (5); EZRA "PENNY" BAXTER, JODY'S FATHER: David Wayne (1) ☆; ORA BAXTER, JODY'S MOTHER: Dolores Wilson (2) ☆; FODDER-WING: Peter Falzone (6); MA FORRESTER: Fay Sappington; BUCK FORRESTER: Allan Louw (8); ARCH FORRESTER: Rodd Barry; PACK FORRESTER: Roy Barry; GABBY FORRESTER: Bob La Crosse; MILLWHEEL FORRESTER: Tom Fleetwood; LEM FORRESTER: Robert Goss (7); MRS. HUTTO: Carmen Mathews (3) ☆; OLIVER HUTTO: David Hartman (9); EULALIE: Janet Campano; TWINK: Carmen Alvarez (4) ☆; DOC WILSON: Gordon B. Clarke (10); PREACHER: Frank Bouley; CAPTAIN: David Sabin; TOWNSPEOPLE: Loyce Baker, Lynette Bennett, Vito Durante, Anthony Endon, Harrison Fisher, Lois Grandi, Scott Hunter, Bobbi Lange, Ruth Lawrence, Barbara Miller, Martin Ross, Herbert Sanders, Bella Shalom, Ted Sprague, Myrna Strom, Mimi Wallace, Trudy Wallace. *Standbys:* Jody/Fodder-Wing: Bryant

Fraser; Ora: Lizabeth Pritchett. **Understudies:** Twink: Mimi Wallace; Buck/Millwheel/Lem/Oliver/Doc: David Sabin; Eulalie: Lois Grandi; Arch/Pack/Gabby: Vito Durante & David Sabin; Ma: Barbara Miller. **Act I: Scene 1** The Baxter clearing: "Let Him Kick up His Heels" (Penny & Ora); **Scene 2** The Forrester clearing: "Boy Talk" (Jody & Fodder-Wing), "Bear Hunt" (Penny, Jody, The Forresters), "Some Day I'm Gonna Fly" (Jody, Fodder-Wing, The Forresters); **Scene 3** The woods: "Lonely Clearing" (Penny); **Scene 4** The Hutto house: "Everything in the World I Love" (Jody & Mrs. Hutto); **Scene 5** The town of Volusia: "I'm All Smiles" (Twink), "I'm All Smiles" (reprise) (Oliver); **Scene 6** The glen; **Scene 7** The woods; **Scene 8** The Forrester clearing; **Scene 9** The Baxter cabin: "The Kind of Man a Woman Needs" (Ora), "What a Happy Day" (Ora, Jody, Doc, Buck, Millwheel), "What a Happy Day" (reprise) (Jody, Doc, Buck, Millwheel). **Act II: Scene 1** The Baxter cabin; the week before Christmas: "Ain't He a Joy?" (Penny & Jody), "Why Did I Choose You?" (Penny & Ora), "One Promise (Come True)" (Ora); **Scene 2** Volusia: "One Promise (Come True)" (reprise) (Ora & Townspeople), "Bear Hunt" (reprise) (Entire Company); **Scene 3** Wharf: "Everything in the World I Love" (reprise) (Penny, Jody, Mrs. Hutto, Oliver, Twink, Townspeople); **Scene 4** The Baxter cabin: "What a Happy Day" (reprise) (Jody); **Scene 5** The Baxter cabin: "Nothing More" (Penny & Jody); **Scene 6** The runaway; **Scene 7** The Baxter clearing: "Everything Beautiful" (Ora).

Being from the man (Lore Noto) who brought us *The Fantasticks*, it was highly anticipated on Broadway, but reviews were terrible. It lost $375,000. Mercury Records, who were going to record the cast album (but never did) invested (and lost) $100,000.

After Broadway. ATLANTA THEATRE OF THE STARS, 1985. This has been the only revival of note. NEW BOOK: Herbert Martin; DIRECTOR: Lucia Victor. **Cast:** John Cullum, D'Jamin Bartlett.

763. *Your Arms Too Short to Box with God*

A soaring celebration in song and dance, a black gospel musical without intermission.

Before Broadway. Originally developed by Vinnette Carroll's Urban Arts Corps (Anita MacShane, production director), for presentation at the SPOLETO FESTIVAL OF TWO WORLDS, Italy, in 1975. That year it had its U.S. premiere at FORD'S THEATRE, Washington, DC, 11/4/75. 168 PERFORMANCES. It had the same crew as for the later Broadway run, except ORCHESTRATIONS: Billy Wilson. **Cast:** Lamar Alford, Salome Bey, Alex Bradford, Sharron Brooks, Maryce Carter, Billy Dorsey, Thomas Jefferson Fouse Jr., Cardell Hall, Delores Hall, William Hardy Jr., Jan Hazell, Aisha Khabeera, Michelle Murray, Stanley Perryman, Zola Shaw, Alwin Taylor. **Act I:** "(There's a) Stranger in Town," "Do You Know Jesus?"/"He's a Wonder," "Just a Little Bit of Jesus Goes a Long Way," "Hail the Savior, Prince of Peace," "Alone," "There Are Days I'd Like to Be," "Be Careful Whom You Kiss," "Your Arms Too Short to Box with God," "Give Us Barabbas," "Why Did I Do It?," "See How They Done My Lord," "Somebody Here Don't Believe in Jesus," "What Have I Done to Thee?," "The Hour of Darkness," "Were You There?," "Can't No Grave Hold My Body Down." **Act II:** "Didn't I Tell You," "When the Power Comes," "Following Jesus," "I Love You So Much," "On That Day," "How Can I Make It?," "Everybody Has His Own Way," "I Know He'll Look Out for Me," "The Band."

The Broadway Run. LYCEUM THEATRE, 12/22/76–11/13/77; EUGENE O'NEILL THEATRE, 11/16/77–1/1/78. 5 previews from 12/20/76. Total of 429 PERFORMANCES. The Ford's Theatre production, PRESENTED BY Frankie Hewitt & The Shubert Organization, in association with Theatre Now; MUSIC/LYRICS: Alex Bradford; ADDITIONAL MUSIC & LYRICS: Micki Grant; CONCEIVED BY: Vinnette Carroll, from the *Book of Matthew*; DIRECTOR: Vinnette Carroll; CHOREOGRAPHER: Talley Beatty; SETS/COSTUMES: William Schroder; SET SUPERVISOR: Michael J. Hotopp; LIGHTING: Gilbert V. Hemsley Jr.; CONDUCTOR: Eddie Brown; ORCHESTRATIONS/DANCE MUSIC: H.B. Barnum; CHORAL DIRECTOR/CHORAL ARRANGEMENTS: Chapman Roberts; PRESS: Henry Luhrman Associates; GENERAL MANAGEMENT: Theatre Now; PRODUCTION STAGE MANAGER: Haig Shepherd; STAGE MANAGER: Robert

Charles. **Cast:** Salome Bey, Clinton Derricks-Carroll, David St. Charles (*Derek Williams*), Sheila Ellis, Delores Hall, William Hardy Jr., Hector Jaime Mercado, Mabel Robinson, William Thomas Jr., Deborah Lynn Bridges, Sharron Brooks, Thomas Jefferson Fouse Jr., Michael Gray, Cardell Hall, Bobby Hill, Lidell Jackson (*Adrian Bailey*), Edna M. Krider, Leon Washington, Marilynn Winbush. **Swing Dancers:** Thelma Drayton & Ralph Farrington. **Musicians:** KEYBOARDS: Denzil A. Miller Jr.; DRUMS: Howard L. Grate; PERCUSSION: Howard Hirsch; HORNS: Bob Fortunato; GUITAR: Van J. Gibbs; REEDS: Pat Perrone; BASS: Thomas Michael Stevens. "Beatitudes" (composed by Micki Grant) (Company), "We're Gonna Have a Good Time" (composed by Micki Grant) (Mr. Derricks-Carroll & Company), "(There's a) Stranger in Town" (Mr. Derricks-Carroll, Mr. Hill, Company) [later Mr. Hardy & Company], "Do You Know Jesus?"/"He's a Wonder" (Mr. Fouse & Company), "Just a Little Bit of Jesus Goes a Long Way" (Delores Hall & Company) [later Miss Ellis & Company], "We Are the Priests and Elders" (composed by Micki Grant) (Messrs Hardy, Derricks-Carroll, Hill, Gray), "Something is Wrong in Jerusalem" (composed by Micki Grant) (Miss Bey, Miss Robinson, Company), "It Was Alone" (Mr. Thomas & Mr. St. Charles) [later Mr. Williams, Mr. Fouse, Company], "I Ain't Had My Fill" (Mr. Derricks-Carroll & Mr. St. Charles), "Be Careful Whom You Kiss" (Miss Bey & Company), "I Know I Have to Leave Here" (Mr. Hardy & Company) [later Mr. Williams, Mr. Fouse, Company, and the number was tagged on to the earlier "It Was Alone"], "Trial" (composed by Micki Grant) (Company) [this number was added during the run], "It's Too Late" (composed by Micki Grant) (Company), Judas Dance (composed by H.B. Barnum) (Mr. Mercado), "Your Arms Too Short to Box with God" (Delores Hall & Company) [later Delores Hall, Cardell Hall, Company], "Give Us Barabbas" (Company), "See How They Done My Lord" (Miss Bey & Company), "Come on Down" (Miss Ellis, Mr. Derricks-Carroll, Mr. Gray), "That's What the Bible Say" (Mr. Gray & Company) [this number was dropped during the run], "Were You There When They Crucified My Lord?" (Miss Bey) [this number was dropped during the run], "Can't No Grave Hold My Body Down" (Mr. Hill & Company) [later Mr. Derricks-Carroll, Mr. Williams, Company], "Beatitudes" (reprise) (Mr. Hill & Company), "Didn't I Tell You" (Mr. Hardy & Company), "When the Power Comes" (Mr. Hardy & Company), "As Long as I Live" (Miss Bey) [this number was dropped during the run], "Everybody Has His Own Way" (Messrs Derricks-Carroll, Gray, Fouse), "I Love You So Much, Jesus" (Delores Hall), "I Left My Sins Behind Me" (Delores Hall & Company) [this number was dropped during the run], "On That Day" (Mr. Derricks-Carroll, Mr. Fouse, Mr. Hill, Mr. Gray) [this number was dropped during the run], "The Band" (Mr. Hardy & Company) [later Mr. Hardy, Delores Hall, Miss Ellis, Company].

Reviews were divided, but generally good. Delores Hall won a Tony, and the show was also nominated for book, direction of a musical, and choreography.

764. *Your Arms Too Short to Box with God (1980 Broadway revival)*

This time it had an intermission.

Before Broadway. This Broadway run was part of tour that opened on 1/19/79, in Hartford, Conn., and closed in 3/80, in Los Angeles (it closed in order to prepare for Broadway). Grenoldo Frazier was musical director on this tour.

The Broadway Run. AMBASSADOR THEATRE, 6/2/80–9/14/80; BELASCO THEATRE, 9/16/80–10/12/80. 4 previews. Total of 149 PERFORMANCES. PRESENTED BY Tom Mallow, in association with James Janek; MUSIC/LYRICS: Alex Bradford; ADDITIONAL MUSIC & LYRICS: Micki Grant; CONCEIVED BY: Vinnette Carroll, from the *Book of Matthew*; DIRECTOR: Vinnette Carroll; CHOREOGRAPHER: Talley Beatty; SETS/COSTUMES: William Schroder; LIGHTING: Richard Winkler; SOUND: Abe Jacob; MUSICAL DIRECTOR: Michael Powell; ORCHESTRATIONS/DANCE MUSIC: H.B. Barnum; PRESS: Max Eisen, Irene Gandy, Barbara Glenn, Francine L. Trevens; GENERAL MANAGER: James Janek; COMPANY MANAGER: Sheila R. Phillips; PRODUCTION STAGE MANAGER: Robert Borod; STAGE MANAGER: Robert Charles; ASSISTANT STAGE MANAGER:

Ralph Farrington. **Cast:** Adrian Bailey, Julius Richard Brown, Cleavant Derricks, Sheila Ellis, Ralph Farrington, Jamil K. Garland, Elijah Gill, William-Keebler Hardy Jr., Jennifer-Yvette Holliday, Linda James, Garry Q. Lewis, Linda Morton, Jai Oscar St. John, Kiki Shepard, Leslie Hardesty Sisson, Ray Stephens, Quincella Swyningan, Faruma S. Williams, Marilynn Winbush, Linda E. Young. **Swing Dancers**: Adrian Bailey & Linda James. **Company Musicians**: PIANO: Michael Powell; DRUMS: Howard Grate; ORGAN/ORGAN SYNTHESIZER: Robert E. Wootten Jr.; PERCUSSION: Juan J. Gutierrez; GUITAR/GUITAR SYNTHESIZER: Henry Grate; BASS: Jerry Beckles; TRUMPET/FLUGELHORN: David Schneck & Jimmy Owens; SAX/FLUTE: Pat Perrone. **Act I**: "Beatitudes" (composed by Micki Grant) (Company), "We're Gonna Have a Good Time" (Mr. Brown, Mr. Derricks, Company), "(There's a) Stranger in Town" (Miss Ellis & Company), "Do You Know Jesus?"/"He's a Wonder" (Mr. Garland & Company), "Just a Little Bit of Jesus Goes a Long Way" (Miss Holliday), "We Are the Priests and Elders" (composed by Micki Grant) (Messrs Brown, Derricks, Hardy, St. John), "Something is Wrong in Jerusalem" (composed by Micki Grant) (Miss Ellis & Miss Swyningan), "It Was Alone"/"I Know I Have to Leave Here" (Miss Holliday & Company), "Be Careful Whom You Kiss" (Miss Ellis & Miss Swyningan), "Trial" (composed by Micki Grant) (Company), "It's Too Late" (composed by Micki Grant) (Company), "Judas Dance" (composed by H.B. Barnum) (Mr. Farrington), "Your Arms Too Short to Box with God" (Miss Holliday & Company), "Give Us Barabbas" (Company), "See How They Done My Lord" (Miss Ellis & Company), "Come on Down" (Miss Young, Mr. Garland, Mr. St. John), "Can't No Grave Hold My Body Down" (Mr. Stephens & Company), "Beatitudes" (reprise) (Mr. Derricks & Company). **Act II**: "Didn't I Tell You" (Mr. Brown, Mr. Derricks, Company), "When the Power Comes" (Company), "Everybody Has His Own Way" (Messrs Brown, Derricks, Stephens), "Down by the Riverside" (traditional) (Mr. Derricks & Company), "I Love You So Much, Jesus" (Miss Holliday), "The Band" (Company).

Note: all songs composed by Alex Bradford, unless otherwise stated.

Note: the roles performed by Mr. Derricks & Mr. Brown in "We're Gonna Have a Good Time," "Didn't I Tell You" and "Everybody Has His Own Way" are alternated.

Reviews were good, but the show was generally reckoned to be a little smooth by now.

765. *Your Arms Too Short to Box with God (1982 Broadway revival)*

The Broadway Run. ALVIN THEATRE, 9/9/82–11/7/82. 11 previews. 69 PERFORMANCES. PRESENTED BY Barry & Fran Weissler, in association with Anita MacShane & the Urban Arts Theatre; MUSIC/LYRICS: Alex Bradford; ADDITIONAL MUSIC & LYRICS: Micki Grant; CONCEIVED BY: Vinnette Carroll, from the Book of Matthew; DIRECTION & CHOREOGRAPHY RE-STAGED BY: Ralf Paul Haze; SETS/COSTUMES: William Schroder; LIGHTING: Richard Winkler; SOUND: Rod Shepard & Jim Esher; MUSICAL DIRECTOR/ARRANGEMENTS: Michael Powell; ORCHESTRATIONS/DANCE MUSIC: H.B. Barnum; PRESS: Burnham — Callaghan Associates; GENERAL MANAGERS: Alecia A. Parker & Patricia M. Morinelli; COMPANY MANAGER: Stephanie S. Hughley; PRODUCTION STAGE MANAGER: Robert Borod; STAGE MANAGER: Jonathan Weiss; ASSISTANT STAGE MANAGER: Leslie Hardesty Sisson. **Cast:** Patti LaBelle, Al Green, Julius Richard Brown, Nora Cole, Jamil K. Garland, Elijah Gill, L. Michael Gray, Ralf Paul Haze, Cynthia Henry, Bobby Hill, Rufus E. Jackson, Elmore James, Linda James, Tommi Johnson, Janice Nunn Nelson, Dwayne Phelps, Quincella Swyningan, Kiki Shepard, Leslie Hardesty Sisson, Marilynn Winbush. **Act I**: "Beatitudes" (Company), "We're Gonna Have a Good Time" (Miss LaBelle & Company), "Me and Jesus" (Mr. Green & Company), "(There's a) Stranger in Town" (Mr. Green), "Running for Jesus" (Miss Nelson & Company), "We Are the Priests and Elders" (Messrs Brown, Hill, Gray, James), "Something is Wrong in Jerusalem" (Miss Cole & Quincella), "It Was Alone"/"I Know I Have to Leave Here" (Mr. Gill & Mr. Johnson), "Be Careful Whom You Kiss" (Mr. Gill, Mr. Haze, Miss Cole, Quincella), "Trial" (Company), "It's Too Late" (Company), "Judas Dance" (Mr. Haze), "Your Arms Too Short to Box with God" (Miss LaBelle & Company), "Give Us Barabbas" (Company), "See How They Done My Lord" (Miss Cole & Company), "Come on Down" (Messrs Gray, Garland, James), "Veil of the Temple" (Miss LaBelle & Company), "Can't No Grave Hold My Body Down" (Mr. Gray, Quincella, Mr. Gill, Company), "Beatitudes" (reprise) (Miss LaBelle, Mr. Green, Company). **Act II**: "Didn't I Tell You" (Mr. Green & Company), "Couldn't Keep it to Myself" (Mr. Green & Company), "When the Power Comes" (Mr. Green & Company), "Everybody Has His Own Way" (Messrs Green, Brown, Hill, Johnson), "Down by the Riverside" (Mr. Gray, Mr. Green, Company), "I Love You So Much, Jesus" (Miss LaBelle), "As Long as I Live" (Mr. Johnson), "On That Day" (Mr. Hill & Company), "The Band" (Company).

Reviews were generally good. Al Green was nominated for a Tony.

After Broadway. OFF BROADWAY REVIVAL. BEACON THEATRE, 6/18/96–6/30/96. 1 preview. 15 PERFORMANCES. PRESENTED BY Sal Michaels, Arthur Katz, and Anita MacShane; ADDITIONAL MUSIC/CHORAL DIRECTOR: Rev. Melvin C. Dawson; CHOREOGRAPHER: Phaze Farrington; SETS/COSTUMES: William Schroder. **Cast:** Raquelle Chavis, Aubrey Lynch, Stephanie Mills, Derrick Minter, Teddy Pendergrass, BeBe Winans. Prologue, "Truly Blessed," "Beatitudes," "We're Gonna Have a Good Time," "(There's a) Stranger in Town," "Miracle Dance," "We Are the Priests and Elders," "Something is Wrong in Jerusalem," "It Was Alone"/"I Know I Have to Leave Here," "Be Careful Whom You Kiss," "What Have You Done?," "Trial," "It's Too Late," "Judas Dance," "You Better Stop," "Your Arms Too Short to Box with God," "Give Us Barabbas," "Were You There?," "See How They Done My Lord," "Come on Down," "Veil of the Temple," "Funeral Oration," "Can't No Grave Hold My Body Down," "Beatitudes" (reprise), "When I Think of the Goodness of Jesus," "Because He Lives."

766. *You're a Good Man, Charlie Brown*

"A day made up of little moments picked from all the days of Charlie Brown, from Valentine's Day to the baseball season, from wild optimism to utter despair, all mixed with the lives of his friends (human and non-human) and strung together on the string of a single day, from bright uncertain morning to hopeful starlit evening." None of the human characters is older than 6 (although the actors were). Lucy is a crabby and authoritarian little girl; Schroeder is an infant musical prodigy; Patty is sweet and innocent; Linus, Lucy's little brother, hugs a blanket; Charlie is perplexed, uncertain, and always put-upon. Charlie's highly imaginative pet beagle is Snoopy who pretends he is a World War I air ace in search of the Red Baron.

Before Broadway. Charles Schulz began drawing his first cartoon strip, "Li'l Folks," in 1947, for a St. Paul, Minn. newspaper. In 1950 United Features Syndicate contracted with him for the rights, and changed the name of the strip to "Peanuts." It debuted on 10/2/50 and was syndicated in seven daily newspapers. Charlie Brown, Patty and Shermy were the first characters. Snoopy was added later in 1950. Schroeder arrived in 1951, Lucy and Linus in 1952, and Linus's security blanket in 1954. In 1965 an animated special for TV won an Emmy, and in 1966 came the TV special *The Great Pumpkin, Charlie Brown*. Clark Gesner had written several songs based on Schulz's characters, and MGM had produced a children's record album of them. On the basis of the success of this album, Arthur Whitelaw persuaded MGM to co-finance the Off Broadway stage musical.

The Off Broadway hit (with no comma in the title, but with one in the title song) had four very successful years at THEATRE 80 ST. MARKS, 3/7/67–2/14/71. 1,597 PERFORMANCES. It was one of Off Broadway's longest-running musicals. They made up the show as they went along. It had the same crew as for the subsequent Broadway run, except CHOREOGRAPHER: Marc Breaux; PRESS: Max Eisen, Carl Samrock, Jeanne Merrick; COMPANY MANAGER: Larry Goossen; STAGE MANAGERS: Ed Royce & Chuck Brummit. **Cast:** LINUS: Bob Balaban, *Albert Sanders,*

Gene Kidwell, George Ryland; CHARLIE: Gary Burghoff, *Sean Simpson, Bob Lydiard, Alfred Mazza*; PATTY: Karen Johnson, *Vicki Lewis, Karen Johnson, Lorna Luft, Merry Flershem*; SCHROEDER: Skip Hinnant, *Jimmy Dodge, Carter Cole*; SNOOPY: Bill Hinnant, *Don Potter*; LUCY: Reva Rose, *Boni Enten, Kay Cole, Ann Gibbs, Corie Simms*.

TOUR. Opened on 6/1/67, at the Little Fox Theatre, San Francisco. **Cast**: CHARLIE: Wendell Burton.

TOUR. Opened on 10/18/67, at the Playhouse, Toronto. **Cast**: CHARLIE: Alan Lofft & David Rhys Anderson.

TOUR. Opened on 12/18/67, in Boston. **Cast**: CHARLIE: Jim Ricketts.

LONDON. Opened on 2/1/68. **Cast**: CHARLIE: David Rhys Anderson; LUCY: Boni Enten; SNOOPY: Don Potter.

TOUR. Opened on 3/12/68, at the Ivar Theatre, Los Angeles. **Cast**: CHARLIE: Gary Burghoff; LUCY: Judy Kaye; PATTY: Nicole Jaffe; ALSO WITH: Russ Caldwell, Hal James Pederson, Robert Towers.

TOUR. Opened on 12/23/68, at the Coconut Grove Playhouse, Miami. **Cast**: CHARLIE: Ken Kube, *Bob Lydiard, Richard Whelan*.

TOUR. Opened on 9/17/69, at the American Theatre, St. Louis, and closed on 4/15/70, at the Vest Pocket Theatre, Detroit. In 1971 this tour went to Broadway (the subject of this article). **Cast**: CHARLIE: Alan Lofft.

TOUR. Opened on 9/17/70, and closed on 12/13/70, at the Mendelssohn Auditorium, Ann Arbor. **Cast**: CHARLIE: Richard Whelan.

TOUR. Opened on 9/24/71, and closed on 12/11/71.

The Broadway Run. JOHN GOLDEN THEATRE, 6/1/71–6/26/71. 15 previews from 5/21/71. 31 PERFORMANCES. PRESENTED BY Arthur Whitelaw & Gene Persson; MUSIC/LYRICS: Clark Gesner; BOOK: John Gordon (this was really Clark Gesner and the original Off Broadway cast); BASED ON Charles M. Schulz's comic strip *Peanuts*; DIRECTOR: Joseph Hardy; ASSISTANT DIRECTOR/CHOREOGRAPHER: Patricia Birch; SETS/COSTUMES: Alan Kimmel; LIGHTING: Jules Fisher; MUSICAL SUPERVISOR/ARRANGEMENTS/ADDITIONAL MUSICAL MATERIAL: Joseph Raposo; MUSICAL DIRECTOR: Jack Holmes; PIANO: Ronald Clairmont; PERCUSSION: Lou Nazzaro; ORIGINAL OFF BROADWAY CAST RECORDING on MGM; PRESS: Max Eisen, Warren Pincus, Milly Schoenbaum; GENERAL MANAGER: Marvin A. Krauss; COMPANY MANAGER: John Corkill; STAGE MANAGERS: Barbara Tuttle & Jason Holt. **Cast:** LINUS: Stephen Fenning; CHARLIE BROWN: Dean Stolber; PEPPERMINT PATTY: Lee Wilson; SCHROEDER: Carter Cole; SNOOPY: Grant Cowan; LUCY VAN PELT: Liz O'Neal. **Standbys**: Male Roles: Jason Holt; Female Roles: Merry Flershem. **Act I**: "You're a Good Man, Charlie Brown" (Entire Company), "Schroeder" ("Moonlight Sonata") (Lucy & Schroeder), "Snoopy" (Snoopy, Charlie, Lucy), "My Blanket and Me" (Linus), "The Kite" (Charlie), "Dr. Lucy" ("The Doctor is In") (Lucy & Charlie), "Book Report" (Charlie, Lucy, Linus, Schroeder). **Act II**: "The Red Baron" (Snoopy), "T-E-A-M" ("The Baseball Game") (Entire Company), "Glee Club Rehearsal" (Entire Company) [not on the original cast album, but replaced for Broadway with a bit of Act I underscored dialog between Lucy & Linus called "Queen Lucy"], "Little Known Facts" (Lucy, Linus, Charlie), "Suppertime" (Snoopy & Charlie), "Happiness" (Entire Company).

Broadway reviews were very good.

After Broadway. NBC TV. 2/9/73. NBC. **Cast**: CHARLIE: Wendell Burton; SNOOPY: Bill Hinnant; SCHROEDER: Mark Montgomery; LINUS: Barry Livingston; PATTY: Noelle Matlovsky; LUCY: Ruby Persson.

Snoopy! A sequel (but not a direct one), *Snoopy!*, about Snoopy and his bird friend Woodstock, was first produced as a tour, opening on 12/9/75, at the Little Fox Theatre, San Francisco, and closing on 7/5/76, in Marin County, Calif. PRESENTED BY Arthur Whitelaw, Michael L. Grace, and Susan Bloom; MUSIC: Larry Grossman; LYRICS: Hal Hackady; BOOK: Warren Lockhart, Arthur Whitelaw, Michael L. Grace; BASED ON Charles M. Schulz's cartoon character; MUSICAL DIRECTORS: John Olson & Gus Gustavson, *Lawrence Blank*. **Cast**: CHARLIE BROWN: James Gleason; PEPPERMINT PATTY: Pamela Myers; SALLY: Randy Kallan; SNOOPY: Don Potter; WOODSTOCK: Cathy Cahn; LINUS: Jimmy Dodge; LUCY: Janelle Pulis. **Standbys**: Rhoda Butler Blank, John Forman. The musical numbers sometimes changed order according to the production, or some might be cut. **Act I**: Overture (Orchestra), "The World According to Snoopy" (Ensemble), "Sit Up! Lie Down! Roll Over! Play Dead!" ("Snoopy's Song") (Snoopy & Ensemble), "Woodstock's Theme" (Orchestra), "Edgar Allan Poe" (Patty, Lucy, Sally, Linus, Charlie), "Mother's Day" (Snoopy), "I Know Now" (Lucy, Sally, Patty), "Vigil" (Linus), "Clouds" (Ensemble), "Where Did That Little Dog Go?" (Charlie), "Dime a Dozen" (Lucy, Patty, Sally, Snoopy), "Daisy Hill" (Snoopy), Entr'acte (Orchestra). **Act II**: "Bunnies" (Snoopy), "The Great Writer" (Snoopy), "Poor Sweet Baby" (Patty), "Don't Be Anything Less (Than Everything You Can Be)" (Charlie, Linus, Sally, Patty), "The Big Bow-Wow!" (Snoopy), "Just One Person" (Ensemble), "Bows" (Ensemble). Other numbers used during certain productions: "Friend," "It Was a Dark and Stormy Night," "Wishy-Washy," "When Do the Good Things Start?."

Snoopy! ran Off Broadway, at LAMB'S THEATRE, 12/20/82–5/1/83. 4 previews. 152 PERFORMANCES. PRESENTED BY Gene Persson, in association with Paul D. Hughes, Martin Markinson, Donald Tick, and United Media Productions; DIRECTOR: Arthur Whitelaw; CHOREOGRAPHER: Marc Breaux; SETS/COSTUMES: David Graden; LIGHTING: Ken Billington; MUSICAL DIRECTOR/ADDITIONAL ORCHESTRATIONS: Ronald Melrose. **Cast**: PATTY: Vicki Lewis, *Lorna Luft* (from 2/21/83; a new number "Hurry Up, Face" was added for her); CHARLIE: Terry Kirwin; LUCY: Kay Cole; LINUS: Stephen Fenning; SALLY: Deborah Graham; WOODSTOCK: Cathy Cahn; SNOOPY: David Garrison, *Jason Graae* (from 2/21/83). **Standbys**: Nina Hennessey & Jason Graae.

Snoopy! first ran in London, at the DUCHESS THEATRE, 9/20/83–11/11/83. MUSICAL DIRECTOR: Stuart Pedlar. **Cast:** Nicki Croyden, Teddy Kempner, Susie Blake, Robert Locke, Anthony Best, Zoe Bright, Mark Hadfield.

767. *You're a Good Man, Charlie Brown (Broadway revival)*

An average day in the life of Charlie Brown. Patty was cut, and replaced by Sally, Charlie's little sister (a new character created by Mike Mayer). 17 of the original 42 vignettes were cut, and 23 new vignettes were written by Charles Schultz & adapted by Mike Mayer. It was updated, with Mike Mayer and Clark Gesner removing obviously outdated material.

Before Broadway. On 7/16/98 it was announced that there would be a Broadway revival in 3/99, preceded by a national tour opening in Skokie, Ill., on 11/18/98 (previews from 11/3/98), with Aldo Scrofani to produce with Fox Theatricals (Mr. Scrofani did not make it to Broadway). On 8/18/98 it was being rumored that Anthony Rapp was going to play Charlie (which he did), and by 9/21/98 that Roger Bart was going to be Snoopy (which he was). Rehearsals began in Chicago, on 10/12/98. By 10/29/98 the Broadway opening had been announced for the middle of 2/99, after a three-month pre–Broadway tour. There was an open press rehearsal on 10/30/98. It got good reviews in the Chicago papers. The production then tried out in Detroit in 12/98. The production cost $3 million; it lost its major backer, Columbia Artists Management, in mid–December, 1998, leaving the show $1.5 million short. It canceled its out of town tryout in Boston and moved the Broadway opening date up to 2/4/99 (from 2/11/99). It was going to open at the Longacre, but with the closing of *Bring in da Noise, Bring in da Funk* at the Ambassador, it was announced in 11/98 that *Charlie Brown* would open there instead.

The Broadway Run. AMBASSADOR THEATRE, 2/4/99–6/13/99. 13 previews from 1/23/99. 150 PERFORMANCES. PRESENTED BY Michael Leavitt, Fox Theatricals, Jerry Frankel, and Arthur Whitelaw & Gene Persson, in association with Larry Payton, and by arrangement with the Tams-Witmark Music Library; MUSIC/LYRICS/BOOK: Clark Gesner; ADDITIONAL MATERIAL/MUSICAL SUPERVISOR/ARRANGEMENTS: Andrew Lippa; BASED ON Charles M. Schulz's comic strip *Peanuts*; DIRECTOR: Michael Mayer; CHOREOGRAPHER: Jerry Mitchell; SETS: David Gallo; COSTUMES: Michael Krass; LIGHTING: Kenneth Posner; SOUND: Brian Ronan; MUSICAL DIRECTOR/CONDUCTOR: Kimberly Grigsby; NEW ORCHESTRATIONS: Michael Gibson; CAST RECORDING on RCA, made on

1/20/99, and released on 3/9/99; PRESS: Richard Kornberg & Associates; CASTING: Binder Casting; GENERAL MANAGEMENT: Nina Lannan & Associates; COMPANY MANAGER: Amy Beth Jacobs; PRODUCTION STAGE MANAGER: James Harker; STAGE MANAGER: Allison Sommers; ASSISTANT STAGE MANAGER: Doan Mackenzie. *Cast:* SALLY: Kristin Chenoweth; SCHROEDER: Stanley Wayne Mathis; LINUS: B.D. Wong; SNOOPY: Roger Bart; LUCY VAN PELT: Ilana Levine; CHARLIE BROWN: Anthony Rapp. *Standbys*: Charlie/Schroeder: Doan Mackenzie & Mark Price; Linus: Doan Mackenzie; Snoopy: Mark Price; Lucy/Sally: Kirsten Wyatt. *The Band*: PIANO/KEYBOARD: Kimberly Grigsby; VIOLIN/VIOLA: Jill Jaffe; BASS: Maryann McSweeney; PERCUSSION: Joseph Mowatt; REEDS: Christine MacDonnell. *Act I*: "You're a Good Man, Charlie Brown" (Company) (add material by Andrew Lippa), "Schroeder" (Lucy & Schroeder), "Snoopy" (Snoopy), "My Blanket and Me" (Linus), "The Kite" (Charlie), "The Doctor is In" (Lucy & Charlie), "Beethoven Day" (new song by Andrew Lippa) (Schroeder), "Rabbit Chasing" (this pantomime had a new score) (Sally & Snoopy), "Book Report" (Charlie, Lucy, Linus, Schroeder). *Act II*: "The Red Baron" (this melodrama had same dialogue, but new musical underscoring) (Snoopy), "My New Philosophy" (new song by Mr. Lippa) (Sally & Schroeder), "T.E.A.M. (The Baseball Game" (Charlie & Company), "Glee Club Rehearsal" (Company), "Little Known Facts" (Lucy, Linus, Charlie), "Suppertime" (Snoopy), "Happiness" (Company).

Note: there was some new music ("half a number," they said), composed by Mr. Lippa, which preceded the opening number.

Broadway reviews were very good. The show won Tonys for Roger Bart and Kristin Chenoweth, and was nominated for revival of a musical and direction of a musical. On 5/12/99 it was announced that it would tour, but it never happened. Charles Schulz died on 2/12/99.

After Broadway. *Snoopy! The Musical* was revived in London, at the 70-seat JERMYN STREET THEATRE, 2/19/03–3/1/03. Previews from 2/17/03. DIRECTORS/CHOREOGRAPHERS: Joseph Pitcher & Claire Winsper. *Cast:* SNOOPY: Stephen Carlisle.

Snoopy! had a benefit concert for the Pied Piper's Children's Theatre of New York City, 4/12/04, at PETER NORTON SYMPHONY SPACE. PRESENTED BY Sutton Foster, Jamie McGonnigal, Linda Gabler, Jonathan Ross, and Matthew Stocke; DIRECTOR: Ben Rimalower; MUSICAL DIRECTOR: Seth Rudetsky. *Cast*: HOST: John Tartaglia; SNOOPY: Christian Borle; PATTY: Sutton Foster; LINUS: Hunter Foster; SALLY: Jennifer Cody; LUCY: Ann Harada; CHARLIE BROWN: Deven May; WOODSTOCK: McKinney Danger-James.

There was a 21st anniversary production of *Snoopy!*, at the NEW PLAYERS THEATRE, London, 7/21/04. PRESENTED BY Morning Vicar Productions. *Cast:* SNOOPY: Robin Armstrong; ALSO WITH: Sarah Lark, Stuart Piper, Alex Woodhall, Clare Louise Connelly, Steven Kynman, Kellie Ryan.

768. *Yours Is My Heart*

An operetta set in 1900. A Chinese prince is in love with a Parisian opera singer. He then moves back to China, where he tries to marry the singer and defy Chinese tradition.

Before Broadway. Franz Lehar's *Das Land des Lachelns* (*Land of Smiles*), with a German libretto by Ludwig Herzer & Fritz Loehner, and adapted from *Die gelhe Jacke,* by Victor Leon, opened at THEATER AN DER WIEN, Vienna, 2/9/23. Its London opening was on 5/8/31, at the THEATRE ROYAL, DRURY LANE, with Richard Tauber. In the USA it was tried twice by the Shuberts, first as *Prince Chu Chan*, and later as *Land of Smiles*. Both productions closed on the road. The story didn't make Broadway until 1946, where it was designed to showcase songs by Franz Lehar, notably "Yours is My Heart, Alone," which the show revolved around.

The Broadway Run. SHUBERT THEATRE, 9/5/46–10/5/46. 36 PERFORMANCES. PRESENTED BY Arthur Spitz, in association with Continental Music Publishing Company, Inc.; MUSIC: Franz Lehar; LYRICS/BOOK: Ira Cobb & Karl Farkas; BASED ON *Land of Smiles*, by Harry Graham, Ira Cobb, Karl Farkas; DIRECTOR: Theodore Bache; DIALOGUE DIRECTOR: Monroe Manning; CHOREOGRAPHER: Henry Shwarze; SETS: H.A.

(Heinz) Condell; LIGHTING: Milton Lowe; MUSICAL DIRECTOR: George Schick; ARRANGEMENTS/ADAPTED BY: Felix Guenther; PRESS: Karl Bernstein & Martha Dreiblatt; GENERAL MANAGER: Jacob L. Steisel; COMPANY MANAGER: Charles Stewart; STAGE MANAGER: Monroe Manning; ASSISTANT STAGE MANAGER: Edward Groag. *Cast:* GUY: Monroe Manning; LUCILLE: Helene Whitney; LOU: Jane Mackle; PIERRE: Harold Lazaron; FERNAND D'ORVILLE: Alexander d'Arcy (3); YVONNE: Natalye Greene; FIFI: Dorothy Karrol; MARIE: Jean Heisey; ARCHIBALD MASCOTTE, IMPRESARIO: Sammy White (4); CLAUDETTE VERNAY, PRIMA DONNA: Stella Andreva (2); BUTLER: Harvey Kier; PRINCE SOU CHONG: Richard Tauber (1) ☆, *John Hendrick*; HUANG WEI, CHINESE AMBASSADOR: Edward Groag; PRINCE TSCHANG, SOU CHONG'S UNCLE: Arnold Spector; HSI FUENG, MINISTER OF FINANCE: Fred Keating (6); PRINCESS MI, SOU CHONG'S SISTER: Lillian Held (5); MASTER OF CEREMONIES: Albert Shoengold; HIGH PRIEST: Fred Briess; LI TSI, CHINESE BRIDE: Beatrice Eden; SOLO DANCERS: Trudy Groth, Henry Shwarze, Haydee Morini, Wayne Lamb, Alberto Feliciano; SINGING ENSEMBLE: Fred Briess, Edwin Budana, Natalye Greene, Jean Heisey, Julie Jefferson, Dorothy Karrol, Harvey Kier, Harold Lazaron, Phyllis Lockard, Jane Mackle, Scotty Miller, Albert Shoengold, Helene Whitney, Isabella Wilson; DANCE ENSEMBLE: Elfi Duka, Helen Farrell, Eleanore Gregory, Mary Kane, Athena Kellar, Sonia Levanskaya, Sondra Lipton, Margaret McCallion, Carol Percy, Gloria Stevens, Estelle Tamus, Edythe A. Uden, Joanna Vischer, Geraldine Wyss. *Act I*: Drawing-room of Claudette Vernay's Paris apartment: Music Box and Waltz (dance) (Ensemble), "Goodbye, Paree" (Fernand & Ensemble), "Free as the Air" (Claudette & Ensemble), "Chinese Melody" (Claudette), "Patiently Smiling" (Sou Chong), "A Cup of China Tea" (Claudette & Sou Chong), "Upon a Moonlight Night in May" (Sou Chong & Ensemble), Finale (Claudette & Sou Chong). *Act II*: Hall in Sou Chong's palace in Peiping; six weeks later: Chinese Ceremony (dance) (Entire Ensemble): a/ Master of Ceremonies (Henry Shwarze); b/ Sword Dance (Wayne Lamb & Alberto Feliciano); c/ Dance of the Girls (Dance Ensemble); d/ Chinese Puppet Dance (Trudy Groth & Dance Ensemble) [end of Chinese Ceremony dance sequence]; "Love, What Has Given You This Magic Power?" (Claudette & Sou Chong), "Men of China" (Mi & Dance Ensemble), "Chingo-Pingo" (Mi, Fernand, Dance Ensemble), "Yours is My Heart, Alone" (l: Harry B. Smith) (Sou Chong), Wedding Ceremony (dance) (Entire Ensemble), Finale (Claudette & Sou Chong). *Act III*: Room in Sou Chong's palace; the following day: "Upon a Moonlight Night in May" (reprise) (Claudette, Trudy Groth, Ensemble), "Paris Sings Again" (by French composer Paul Durant) (Claudette), Opium Ballet (Henry Schwarze, Mascotte, Fernand, Dance Ensemble) [cut during run], "Ma Petite Cherie" (Mi & Fernand), "Chingo-Pingo" (reprise) (Mi) [added during run], Finale (Claudette, Mi, Sou Chong, Archibald, Fernand).

Richard Tauber, whose singing was the main attraction, got good reviews, but he was the only part of the show that did. He developed throat problems just after the show started, and on 9/19/46 came down with laryngitis. John Hendrick went on for him, and continued to play the role with the exception of only three more Tauber performances. However, the show without Mr. Tauber was not the show that was promised, and it closed when he couldn't continue.

769. *Ziegfeld Follies of 1943*

This was the 25th (and longest-running) in the series of revues that began in 1907 as *Follies of*... [and then the year], and which from 1911 was called *Ziegfeld Follies of*... [and then the year]. Produced by Florenz Ziegfeld, the series was famous for its opulent sets, showgirls, farces, and songs. The last four—1934, 1936, 1943 and 1957—were produced after Flo Ziegfeld's death. This was comedian Milton Berle's first show with his name above the title. It opened with an elaborate chorus line of dancing boys in tuxedos; one of them fell out of step and flat on his face. This was Milty, who then chased the dancers off stage and went into his monologue: "See what happens when the Shuberts try to put on a Follies? This never would have happened if Ziggy were around today. How do you like the costumes? They're left over from *Blossom Time* and *The Student Prince*." This joke referred to the Shuberts' reputation for cutting production costs.

The Broadway Run. WINTER GARDEN THEATRE, 4/1/43–1/25/44; IMPERIAL THEATRE, 1/25/44–7/22/44. Total of 553 PERFORMANCES. The Messrs Shubert (Lee & J.J. Shubert), in association with Alfred Bloomingdale & Lou Walters, by arrangement with Billie Burke Ziegfeld, PRESENT a National Institution Glorifying the American Girl; MUSIC: Ray Henderson; ADDITIONAL MUSIC: Dan White & Baldwin "Beau" Bergersen; LYRICS: Jack Yellen; ADDITIONAL LYRICS: Buddy Burston; SKETCHES BY: various writers; DEVISED BY: John Murray Anderson; ENTIRE PRODUCTION STAGED BY: John Murray Anderson; ASSISTANT TO JOHN MURRAY ANDERSON: Saint Subber; DIALOGUE DIRECTORS: Arthur Pierson & Fred de Cordova; CHOREOGRAPHER: Robert Alton; ADDITIONAL CHOREOGRAPHY: Jack Cole; SETS: Watson Barratt; COSTUMES: Miles White; MUSICAL DIRECTOR: John McManus; ORCHESTRATIONS: Don Walker; PRESS: C.P. Greneker; COMPANY MANAGER: Phil Adler; STAGE MANAGERS: Fred de Cordova & Danny Brennan. *Cast:* Milton Berle (1), Ilona Massey (2) (*Sara Ann McCabe* from 5/31/43), Arthur Treacher (3), Jack Cole (4), Sue Ryan (comedienne-singer) (5), Nadine Gae (dancer) (6), Tommy Wonder (dancer) (7), Dean Murphy (8), Christine Ayres (9), The Rhythmaires (singing quartet: Robert Bay, Don Weissmuller, Robert Shaw, Victor Griffin)) (10), Jack McCauley (11), Imogene Carpenter (singer-pianist) (12), Jaye Martin (13), Katherine Meskill (14), Bil & Cora Baird (15), Arthur Maxwell (16), Charles Senna (17), The Jansleys (18) [led by Jerry Jansley], Ben Yost's Vi-Kings (19) (male sextet: Edmund Lyndeck, Feodore Tedick, Manfred Hecht, Howard Jackson, Edward Hayes, Robert Rippy), Ray Long (20), Mary Ganley (21), Patricia Hall (22), Penny Edwards (23), Dixie Roberts (24), Rebecca Lee, Virginia Miller, Ruth Rowan; THE ZIEGFELD FOLLIES SHOW GIRLS: Bea Bailey, Doris Brent, Veronica Byrnes, Josine Cagle, Betty Douglas, Eleanor Hall, Yvonne Kummer, Renee Riley, Betty Stuart, Rose Teed); THE ZIEGFELD FOLLIES DANCING GIRLS: Carolyn Ayres, Mary Alice Bingham, Virginia Cheneval, Skippy Cekan, Grace de Witt, Gretchen Houser, Marilyn Hightower, Jerry Koban, Kay Lewis, Mary McDonnell, Bubbles Mandel, Janie New, Marianne O'Brien, Rosaleen Simpson, Mimi Walthers, Ila Marie Wilson, Doris York; THE ZIEGFELD FOLLIES MESSIEURS: Jim Barron, Bob Copsey, Ray Cook, David Gray, Arthur Grahl, Bruce Davison, Howard Ludwig, Michael Pober, Tom Smith. *Act I: Scene 1* Prologue (by Jerry Seelen & Lester Lee). With NADINE GAE, TOMMY WONDER, IMOGENE CARPENTER, JAYE MARTIN: (a) Vignette (after Cole Porter). CHRISTINE AYRES, Mary Ganley, Dixie Roberts, Michael Pober, Penny Edwards, Jim Barron, Howard Ludwig, Ben Yost's Vi-Kings; (b) Vignette (after Ernest Hemingway): THE HERO: Jack McCauley; THE BELLRINGER: Jerry Jansley; (c) Vignette (after William Saroyan): A CHARACTER: Manfred Hecht; ANOTHER CHARACTER: Charles Senna; STILL ANOTHER CHARACTER: Bil Baird; (d) Vignette (after Irving Berlin): Ziegfeld Follies Showgirls, Ziegfeld Follies Dancing Girls, Ziegfeld Follies Dancing Boys; *Scene 2* Something for the Berles (Milton Berle); *Scene 3* "Thirty-Five Summers Ago" (sung by ILONA MASSEY). Jaye Martin, The Ziegfeld Follies Show Girl (without Doris Brent), BEN YOST'S VI-KINGS; *Scene 4* Good God Godfrey (by Bud Pearson & Les White) [this sketch was dropped during the run]: MR. TAPPAN: Jack McCauley; MRS. TAPPAN: Katherine Meskill; GODFREY: Arthur Treacher; *Scene 5* "This is It." Sung by ARTHUR MAXWELL & IMOGENE CARPENTER. Danced by NADINE GAE, Penny Edwards, Patricia Hall, Dixie Roberts, Mary Ganley, The Ziegfeld Follies Dancing Girls & Boys, THE RHYTHMAIRES, TOMMY WONDER; *Scene 6* Counter Attack (by Charles Sherman & Harry Young): CECIL: MILTON BERLE; MR. ANDREWS: Jack McCauley; MRS. ANDREWS: Sue Ryan; *Scene 7* "The Wedding of a Solid Sender" (dance). Choreographed by Jack Cole. Composed & arranged by Baldwin Bergersen. THE GROOM: JACK COLE; THE BRIDE: Rebecca Lee; BRIDESMAIDS: Virginia Miller & Ruth Rowan; CONGREGATION: Carolyn Ayres, Mary McDonnell, Mimi Walthers, Marilyn Hightower; *Scene 8* The Merchant of Venison (rich butcher J. PIERSWIFT ARMOUR — played by MILTON BERLE, who, during food rationing, deposits a porterhouse steak into a safe surrounded by guards with tommy guns): "Meat for Sale" (Milton Berle); *Scene 9* "Love Songs

Are Made in the Night" (sung by ILONA MASSEY & Jaye Martin): (a) Romantic Ballet (NADINE GAE & THE RHYTHMAIRES); (b) Rhythmic Ballet (CHRISTINE AYRES, Ray Long, Ensemble); *Scene 10* SUE RYAN (m: Dan White; l: Buddy Burston); *Scene 11* BEN YOST'S VI-KINGS. ????? [sic]; *Scene 12* "Come up and Have a Cup of Coffee" (sung by ARTHUR MAXWELL, IMOGENE CARPENTER, Ben Yost's Vi-Kings, The Ziegfeld Follies Show Girls). Danced by Dixie Roberts, Mary Ganley, Patricia Hall, Penny Edwards, The Rhythmaires, The Ziegfeld Follies Dancers, NADINE GAE, TOMMY WONDER; *Scene 13* Love's a-Poppin' (by Ray Golden & Sid Kuller). Introduction by Katherine Meskill. Spoof of *Private Lives* & Olsen & Johnson's show *Hellzapoppin'*. GERTRUDE OLSEN: ILONA MASSEY; PERRY JOHNSON: MILTON BERLE; CRUMPET: ARTHUR TREACHER; *Scene 14* Carmen in Zoot. Prologue, with Jaye Martin & Imogene Carpenter. "The Saga of Carmen" (m: Dan White; l: Buddy Burston) (jive version of *Carmen*). Sung by SUE RYAN). A FORTUNE TELLER: Christine Ayres; A SMUGGLER: Ray Long; THE BULL: Nadine Gae; A TOREADOR: Tommy Wonder; MICHALA: ILONA MASSEY; DON JOSE: ARTHUR TREACHER; MATADORS: The Rhythmaires; CARMEN: SUE RYAN; PICADORS: Ben Yost's Vi-Kings; ESCAMILLO: MILTON BERLE and ENTIRE COMPANY. *Act II: Scene 1* "Swing Your Lady, Mr. Hemingway." Sung & danced by SUE RYAN & Ray Long, The Rhythmaires, Christine Ayres, Doris Brent, Jack McCauley, Marilyn Hightower, Nadine Gae, Tommy Wonder, Ensemble; *Scene 2* THE JANSLEYS (acrobats); *Scene 3* Once a Butler (by Lester Lawrence) [sketch dropped during the run]: HIMSELF: ARTHUR TREACHER; HIS WIFE: Katherine Meskill; MR. SMITH: Jack McCauley; *Scene 4* DEAN MURPHY (impressionist, he did the Roosevelts — FDR & Eleanor — and Wendell Willkie); *Scene 5* "Back to the Farm" (m: Dan White; l: Buddy Burston). Sung by SUE RYAN, with Christine Ayres & the Ziegfeld Follies Show Girls; *Scene 6* Mr. Grant Goes to Washington (by Joseph Erens): CHARLIE GRANT: MILTON BERLE; MARY GRANT: Katherine Meskill; BELL BOY: Charles Senna; HOTEL MANAGER: Jack McCauley; *Scene 7* "Hindu Serenade" (dance). Based on the style of an Oriental dancer named Shankar. Sung by ILONA MASSEY & Jaye Martin. Danced by JACK COLE & Rebecca Lee, Virginia Miller, Ruth Rowan; *Scene 8* BIL & CORA BAIRD (puppeteers); *Scene 9* Sutton Interlude (by William Wells): AIR RAID WARDEN: ARTHUR TREACHER; STROLLER: KATHERINE MESKILL; HUSBAND: JACK McCAULEY; 2ND STROLLER: Doris Brent; *Scene 10* "Hep Hot and Solid Sweet" (song & dance). Sung by the RHYTHMAIRES. Danced by NADINE GAE, TOMMY WONDER, Ziegfeld Follies Dancing Girls; *Scene 11* "The Micromaniac" (by Harold J. Rome). Sung by MILTON BERLE; *Scene 12* "Hold that Smile" (sung by NADINE GAE, TOMMY WONDER, JAYE MARTIN, IMOGENE CARPENTER. Danced by Mary Ganley, MILTON BERLE, ILONA MASSEY, ARTHUR TREACHER, and the Entire Company).

Reviews were divided, but mostly bad. The show won a Donaldson Award for sets.

After Broadway. Between 1943 and the next real Ziegfeld Follies there was a gap of 13 years. In 1955 Jack Entratter, operator of the Sands Hotel, Las Vegas, put on a few editions of the Ziegfeld Follies there.

There was also a movie — *Ziegfeld Follies*, 1945. DIRECTOR: Vincente Minnelli. *Cast:* FLO ZIEGFELD: William Powell; ALSO WITH: Fred Astaire, Judy Garland, Lucille Ball, Cyd Charisse, Gene Kelly, Esther Williams, Fannie Brice, Virginia O'Brien, Marion Bell, Lena Horne.

770. *Ziegfeld Follies of 1957*

Before Broadway. *Ziegfeld Follies of 1956*, the 26th revue in the series, opened for tryouts on 4/16/56, at the Shubert Theatre, in Boston, and closed on 5/12/56, at the Shubert Theatre, Philadelphia, never making its Winter Garden engagement on Broadway, because it was so bad. Tallulah Bankhead lampooned an airline stewardess in "High and Flighty" (Miss Lillie took the role in the 1957 edition). Tallulah Bankhead also read Dorothy Parker, lampooned *Damn Yankees* baseball language, and reprised her TV skit "The Subway." "Large Talk" was another sketch used later in the 1957 edition. PRESENTED by Richard Kollmar & James W. Gardiner; MUSIC/LYRICS/SKETCHES: Arnold Horwitt, Albert Hague, Ronny Graham, Richard Lewine, Alton Rinker, Floyd Huddleston, Jerry

Bock, Larry Holofcener, Irving Berlin; SKIT DIRECTOR: Christopher Hewett; CHOREOGRAPHER: Jack Cole; SETS/COSTUMES: Raoul Pene du Bois; LIGHTING: Peggy Clark; MUSICAL DIRECTOR: Anton Coppola. **Cast**: Tallulah Bankhead, Carol Haney, Joan Diener, Mae Barnes, Elliott Reid, David Burns, Matt Mattox, Beryl Towbin, Don Crichton, Tim Kirby, Beatrice Arthur, Julie Newmar, Lee Becker, Larry Kert, Jay Harnick, Svetlana McLee, Preshy Marker, Mort Marshall, Stuart Hodes. The show lost $400,000. The sets and costumes were magnificent, however, so they were used in a revamped 1957 edition, called the Golden Jubilee Edition, which wasn't quite as bad as the 1956 edition, but it was still bad (and it did make Broadway). Certain numbers were cut on 2/18/57, during the Washington, DC tryout: "Don't Tell a Soul" (by Romoff & Rogers), "Follies Nocturne" (by Bernie Wayne), "Golden Anniversary" (by Myers & Lawrence), "Hazards of the Profession" (by Fuller & Barer), and "Producer's Office" (by Myers & Lawrence). "Stay on the Subject" (by Fuller & Barer), "Time Magazine" (by Grant, Jeffries, Wilson), and the sketches "Bea and Sympathy" (by Charles Scheuer) and "Supermarket" (by David Rogers) were cut later, but before Broadway.

The Broadway Run. WINTER GARDEN THEATRE, 3/1/57–6/15/57. 123 PERFORMANCES. PRESENTED BY Mark Kroll & Charles Conaway; MUSIC/LYRICS/SKETCHES: various writers; SKETCH EDITOR: Arnold Auerbach; DIRECTOR: John Kennedy; CHOREOGRAPHER: Frank Wagner; SETS/COSTUMES: Raoul Pene du Bois; LIGHTING: Paul Morrison; MUSICAL DIRECTOR: Max Meth; ORCHESTRATIONS: Russell Bennett, Bill Stegmeyer, Joe Glover, Bob Noelneter; DANCE MUSIC COMPOSER: Rene Wiegert; VOCAL ARRANGEMENTS: Earl Rogers; PRESS: Karl Bernstein, Anne Sloper, Bob Feinberg; COMPANY MANAGER: Morry Efron; PRODUCTION STAGE MANAGER: Milton Stern; STAGE MANAGER: Bruce Laffey; ASSISTANT STAGE MANAGER: William Hellinger. **Act I: Scene 1** "Bring on the Girls" (m: Richard Myers; l: Jack Lawrence) (Ziegfeldians & Ensemble); **Scene 2** Double Indemnity (by Alan Jeffreys & Maxwell Grant): SECRETARY: Charlotte Foley; MR. WEDGECLIFFE: Billy De Wolfe (2); LOLA LA MOUNDSVILLE: Jane Morgan (4); **Scene 3** "If You Got Music" (m: Colin Romoff; l: David Rogers) [danced & sung by Harold Lang (3), Helen Wood, Ensemble]; **Scene 4** Milady Dines Alone (by Beatrice Lillie): THE LADY: Beatrice Lillie (1) ☆; WAITER: Bruce Laffey; **Scene 5** "(You Bring Out) The Lover in Me" (m: Philip Springer; l: Carolyn Leigh) [sung by Micki Marlo (*Paula Wayne*)]. Note: this song was replaced during the run by "Mangoes" (m/l: Dee Libby & Sid Wayne) (sung by Micki Marlo, assisted by Ron Cecill, Allan Craine, Mel Davidson, Tommy Franko, Chuck Green, Hugh Lambert, Jack Leigh, Ed Powell, James Stevenson, Gene Varrone; **Scene 6** High and Flighty (by Arnie Rosen & Coleman Jacoby): HOSTESS: Beatrice Lillie (1) ☆; PASSENGERS: John Philip, Bob & Larry Leslie, Bette Graham, Robert Feyti; BETTY: Mary Jane Doerr; **Scene 7** "I Don't Wanna Rock" (m: Colin Romoff; l: David Rogers) [a take-off on the Elvis phenomenon]: JUVENILE DELINQUENT: Billy De Wolfe (2); TENTH STREET SHEIKS: Vicki Barrett, James Brooks, Wisa D'Orso, Chuck Green, Nancy Hachenberg, Hugh Lambert, Julie Marlowe, Ed Powell, Lou Richards, James Stevenson, Rod Strong, Gene Varrone; **Scene 8** Jay Marshall (comedy, prestidigitation, ventriloquism) [act dropped during run]; **Scene 9** "Music for Madame" (m: Richard Myers; l: Jack Lawrence): THE BOY: Harold Lang (3); THE GIRL: Helen Wood; MAITRE D': John Philip; Ziegfeldians & Dancers; **Scene 10** "Intoxication" (m: Dean Fuller; l: Marshall Barer) [sung by Beatrice Lillie (1) ☆]: ESCORT: Allen Conroy; **Scene 11** Dramatically Speaking [monologue performed by Billy De Wolfe (2)]; **Scene 12** "Song of India:" THE RAJAH: John Philip; HIS FAVORITE: Beatrice Lillie (1) ☆; ASSISTED BY: Dancers & The Ziegfeldians. **Act II: Scene 1** "Two a Day on the Milky Way" (m: Dean Fuller; l: Marshall Barer) [sung & danced by Harold Lang (3) & Ensemble]: AGENT: Bob Leslie; **Scene 2** Large Talk (by David Rogers): 1ST GIRL: Charlotte Foley; 2ND GIRL: Susan Shaute; LUCILLE: Beatrice Lillie (1) ☆; HARRIET: Billy De Wolfe (2); **Scene 3** "Salesmanship" (m: Philip Springer; l: Carolyn Leigh) [sung by Jane Morgan (4), Micki Marlo (*Paula Wayne*), Carol Lawrence (5), with the Ziegfeld Girls]; **Scene 4** Kabuki Lil (by Beatrice Lillie): KABUKI LIL: Beatrice Lillie (1) ☆; **Scene 5** "Honorable Mambo" (m: Dean Fuller; l: Marshall Barer) [sung & danced by Carol Lawrence (5) & Ensemble]; **Scene 6** "Miss Follies" (m: Colin Romoff; l: David Rogers) [sung by Billy De Wolfe (2), Chuck Green, Ed Pow-

ell, James Stevenson, Gene Varrone, The Ziegfeld Girls]; **Scene 7** "Make Me" (by Tony Velone, Larry Spier, Ulpio Minucci) [sung by Jane Morgan (4) & The Ziegfeldians) [cut soon after opening]; **Scene 8** "Miss (All You Don't Catch) Follies of 192-" (m/l: Herman Hupfeld) [sung by Beatrice Lillie (1) ☆]: PAGE GIRL: Nancy Hachenberg; **Scene 9** Jay Marshall [dropped during the run]; **Scene 10** Song: "An Element of Doubt" (m: Sammy Fain; l: Howard Dietz) [sung by Harold Lang (3) & Micki Marlo (*Paula Wayne*) [cut soon after the opening]; **Scene 11** Sketch & Song: "My Late, Late Lady" (m: Dean Fuller; l: Marshall Barer) [a take-off of *My Fair Lady*, whose composers Lerner & Loewe were not amused]: ANNOUNCER: Ed Powell; THE ORIGINAL CAST: Beatrice Lillie (1) ☆, Billy De Wolfe (2), John Philip; **Scene 12** Finale (m: Richard Myers; l: Jack Lawrence) (Entire Company).

ZIEGFELDIANS: Billie Bensing, Robert Feyti, Tony Franco, Bette Graham, Chuck Green, Faith Hilton, Frances Koll, Ed Powell, Susan Shaute, James Stevenson, Gene Varrone, Paula Wayne; DANCERS: Vicki Barrett, Bob Bernard, James Brooks, Ron Cecill, Ruth Chamberlain, Allen Conroy, Allan Craine, Dorothy D'Honau, Mary Jane Doerr, Wisa D'Orso, Nancy Hachenberg, Marcia Hewitt, Hugh Lambert, Jack Leigh, Julie Marlowe, Ted Monson, Lou Richards, Sylvia Shay, Rod Strong, Merritt Thompson, Gini Turner, Shirley Vincent, *Mel Davidson*; ZIEGFELD GIRLS: Roberta Brown, Denise Colette, Ann Drake, Charlotte Foley, Pat Gaston, Nancy Westbrook, Barbara Hall, Gloria Kristy. **Understudies**: For Mr. De Wolfe: Gene Wesson; For Miss Morgan: Frances Koll; For Miss Marlo: Paula Wayne; For Mr. Lang: Ron Cecill; For Miss Wood: Mary Jane Doerr; For Miss Lawrence: Vicki Barrett; For Mr. Philip: Gene Varrone; For Mr. Powell/Mr. Feyti: Bruce Laffey; For Miss Foley: Susan Shaute; For Miss Shaute: Nancy Hachenberg.

It got terrible Broadway reviews, but still lasted three months. It was the last in the *Ziegfeld Follies* series. During the run Pat Gaston married asbestos millionaire Tommy Manville. Also during the run Micki Marlo went out to a party, got a black eye, and was replaced for a while by Paula Wayne. Bea Lillie was nominated for a Tony.

After Broadway. TOUR. The 1957 Broadway production was revised, and parts of the 1956 edition were added to it, and it opened for a tour on 9/12/57, at the Royal Alexandra Theatre, Toronto. It was planning to return to Broadway after the tour, as *Ziegfeld Follies of 1958*, but the tour closed on 10/12/57, at the Shubert Theatre, Cincinnati, and ideas of Broadway were a thing of the past for the *Ziegfeld Follies*. OTHER CONTRIBUTORS TO THE SCORE: David Rogers, Colin Romoff, Herbert Hartig; SKITS BY: David Rogers, Ira Wallach, Eddie Davis, Loney Lewis; DIRECTOR: Mervyn Nelson; CHOREOGRAPHER: Bob Copsey; SETS: Raoul Pene du Bois; MUSICAL DIRECTOR: Ray O'Brien. **Cast**: Kaye Ballard, Paul Gilbert, Micki Marlo, Paul Copsey & JoBee Ayers, Patrice Helene & Jan Howard, Ketty Lester, Lord Buckley, Loney Lewis, Jimmy Roma, Sara Aman, Lew Herbert, Richard Curry. MUSICAL NUMBERS were (alphabetically): "Be Bop Lullaby" (m: Ralph Strain; l: Marshall Barer), "Go Bravely On," "The Happiest Millionaire" (m: Paul Klein; l: Fred Ebb), "Honorable Mambo" (from 1957 edition), "It's Silk, Feel It" (m: Dean Fuller; l: Marshall Barer), "The Kiss that Rocked the World" (by Joe & Noel Sherman), "Lonesome is as Lonesome Does," "The Parade is Passing Me By," "Mangoes" (from 1957 edition), "Miss Follies (from the 1957 edition), "One More Samba" (m: Gerald Alters), "Play, Mr. Bailey" (by Biff Jones & Chuck Meyer), "A Pretty Girl is Like a Melody" (by Irving Berlin), "Somebody's Keeping Score" (m: Sammy Fain; l: Jack Barnett), "When Papa Would Waltz" (m: Jerry Bock; l: Larry Holofcener) [from the 1956 edition], "A Ziegfeld Show" (m: Otis Clements).

NEW EDITION. In 1960 Mrs. Florenz Ziegfeld Jr. and The Shuberts produced a new edition, in the round, at St. John Terrell's summer stock musical tent, LAMBERTVILLE, NJ. DIRECTOR: Max Meth; Hank Ladd directed the sketches, under the personal direction of Bobby Clark; CHOREOGRAPHERS: Jim Russell & Gordon Micunis; COSTUMES: Bernie Joy. It flopped. **Cast**: Bert Wheeler, Hank Ladd, Connie Sawyer, India Adams, Helen Wood, Bob Brooks, Lee Davis, Jim Russell, Tom Dillon, Kiko de Brazil.

NEW EDITION. In 1960 Tibor Rudas devised a new edition, and presented an Australian tour. Billie Burke (Flo Ziegfeld's widow) appeared at the premiere in Sydney. DIRECTOR: Clyde Collins; CHOREOGRAPHERS: Anna & Tibor Rudas; SETS: Angus Winneke. **Cast**: Barney

Grant, Lee Davis, Edith Dahl, The Coquettes, Evelyn Rose, Rita Moreno & Ann, The Dandinis, Ulk & Maor, The Taboris, The Diors, Peter Crago, Rosemary Butler, Marie-Claire, Patricia Smith, Eileen O'Connor, James Vaughn.

771. *Zorba*

Set in a bouzouki circle at the present time; in Piraeus; and in Crete in 1924. About Zorba, a life-loving Greek peasant in Crete, and his relationship with a studious young man, Nikos, who has inherited an abandoned mine in Crete. A youth kills himself in a terminal fit of unrequited love for a young widow, whereupon the widow is stoned to death by the vengeful family. Hortense is the coquettish French woman of dubious livelihood who is in love with Zorba. The mine proves to be inoperable. Zorba teaches Nikos how to live in the moment, the joy of life.

Before Broadway. There were no stage productions of the Zorba story before this, only the straight 1964 Michael Cacoyannis movie with Anthony Quinn and Lila Kedrova (who would both star in the 1983 Broadway revival — see below; Alan Bates played Basil and Irene Pappas played the Widow). Herschel Bernardi came up with idea to make a musical out of the story. He and Joseph Stein secured Hal Prince as producer/director, and then Kander & Ebb came in for the score. It tried out for three weeks at the Shubert Theatre, New Haven, from 10/7/68, and got good reviews. Boston followed.

The Broadway Run. IMPERIAL THEATRE, 11/17/68–8/9/69. 12 previews. 305 PERFORMANCES. PRESENTED BY Harold Prince, in association with Ruth Mitchell; MUSIC: John Kander; LYRICS: Fred Ebb; BOOK: Joseph Stein; BASED ON the 1946 novel *Zorba the Greek*, by Nikos Kazantzakis; DIRECTOR: Harold Prince; CHOREOGRAPHER: Ronald Field; SETS: Boris Aronson; COSTUMES: Patricia Zipprodt; LIGHTING: Richard Pilbrow; MUSICAL DIRECTOR: Harold Hastings; ORCHESTRATIONS: Don Walker; DANCE MUSIC ARRANGEMENTS: Dorothea Freitag; CHURCH BELLS RECORDED IN Irapetra, Crete; CAST RECORDING on Capitol; PRESS: Mary Bryant, David Rothenberg, Ellen Levene; CASTING: Shirley Rich; PRODUCTION CONSULTANT: Vassili Lambrinos; GENERAL MANAGER: Carl Fisher; COMPANY MANAGER: Warren O'Hara; PRODUCTION STAGE MANAGER: Ruth Mitchell; STAGE MANAGER: James Bronson; ASSISTANT STAGE MANAGER: Bob Burland. **Cast:** CONSTABLE: David Wilder; NIKOS: John Cunningham (3); ALEXIS: Alex Petrides (10); HORTENSE: Maria Karnilova (2) ☆; MANOLAKO: James Luisi (6); PANAYOTIS: Nat Horne; THE WIDOW: Carmen Alvarez (4); MIMIKO: Al DeSio (8); KONSTANDI: Joseph Alfasa (12); SOFIA: Marsha Tamaroff; KYRIAKOS: Jerry Sappir; THE LEADER: Lorraine Serabian (5); KANAKIS: Ali Hafid; KOSTANTINOS: Angelo Saridis; MARINA: Alicia Helen Markarian; FIVOS: Gerrit de Beer; EFTERPI: Lee Hooper; ZORBA: Herschel Barnardi (1) ☆; LOUKAS: Loukas Skipitaris (9); MEROPI: Juliette Durand; ARISTOS: Charles Kalan; GEORGI: Johnny La Motta; ANTONIS: Anthony Marciona; TASSO: Susan Marciona; THANOS: Lewis Gundunas (11); PAVLI: Richard Dmitri; FATHER ZACHARIA: Gerard Russak; ALIKI: Miriam Welch; MAVRODANI: Paul Michael (7); CHYRISTO: Louis Garcia; ZACHARIAS: Edward Nolfi; BELLY DANCER: Jemela Omar (13); OLD MAN: Robert Bernard; KATAPOLIS: Richard Nieves; DESPO: Nina Dova; IRINI: Connie Burnett; ATHENA: Peggy Cooper; GRIGORIS: Wayne Boyd; VASSILIS: Martin Meyers; INSTRUMENTAL INTERLUDE SOLOISTS: Jerry Sappir, Ali Hafid, Angelo Saridis. **Understudies:** Zorba: James Luisi; Hortense: Nina Dova; Nikos: Loukas Skipitaris; Widow: Lee Hooper; Leader: Peggy Cooper; Manalako: Johnny La Motta; Mavrodani: David Wilder; Mimiko: Louis Garcia; Loukas/Alexis: Richard Nieves; Konstandi: Martin Meyers; FEMALE DANCERS: Anna Maria Fanizzi; MALE DANCERS: Terry Violino. *Act I*: *Scene 1* A bouzouki circle: "Life Is (What You Do While You're Waiting to Die)" (Leader & Company); *Scene 2* A waterfront cafe in Piraeus: "The First Time" (Zorba); *Scene 3* The exterior of a village cafe, adjacent shops, and village church in Crete: "The Top of the Hill" (Leader & Chorus); *Scene 4* The garden of Hortense's inn: "No Boom Boom" (Hortense, Zorba, Nikos, Admirals), "Vive la Difference" (Admirals & Dancers); *Scene 5* Hortense's bedroom; *Scene 6* The entrance to the mine: "The Butterfly" (Nikos, Leader, Widow, Chorus);

Scene 7 Exterior of Hortense's inn; the next morning: "Goodbye, Canavaro" (Hortense & Zorba); *Scene 8* Interior of a cafe in Khania: "Belly Dance" (Jemela), "Grandpapa (Zorba's Dance)" (Zorba, Leader, Chorus), "Only Love" (Hortense), "The Bend of the Road" (Leader & Chorus), "Only Love" (reprise) (Leader); *Scene 9* Interior and exterior of the Widow's home; dusk of the next day. *Act II*: *Scene 1* The village square: "Bells" (Dancers); *Scene 2* Exterior of the cottage in Hortense's garden: "Y'assou" (Nikos, Zorba, Hortense, Leader, Chorus); *Scene 3* A road: "Why Can't I Speak?" (Widow & Girl); *Scene 4* The village square; *Scene 5* The entrance to the mine: "Mine Celebration" (Zorba & Company); *Scene 6* Hortense's bedroom: "The Crow" (Leader & Women), "Happy Birthday (to Me)" (Hortense); *Scene 7* The road leading out of the village: "I Am Free" (Zorba); *Scene 8* A bouzouki circle: "Life Is" (reprise) (Leader & Company).

The show was capitalized at $500,000, and it had a $2 million advance at the Broadway box-office. It was the first Broadway show to charge $15 for Saturday night orchestra seats. Reviews were divided, but mostly very good. The two stars began fighting, missed performances through sickness and other reasons, and business dropped off. Rather than fire them, Hal Prince closed the show. It won a Tony for sets, and was also nominated for musical, direction of a musical, choreography, costumes, and for Lorraine Serabian, Maria Karnilova, and Herschel Bernardi.

After Broadway. TOUR. Opened on 12/26/69, in Philadelphia. **Cast:** ZORBA: John Raitt; HORTENSE: Barbara Baxley; LEADER: Chita Rivera; NIKOS: Gary Krawford; WIDOW: Marsha Tamaroff. "Bells" was dropped, "Y'assou" was replaced with "Bouboulina" (Zorba, Hortense, Leader, Chorus), and "Why Can't I Speak?" was replaced with "That's a Beginning" (Widow, Nikos, Leader).

TOUR. Opened on 9/11/70, at the Bushnell Theatre, Hartford, Conn., and closed on 5/18/71, at the Memorial Auditorium, Worcester, Mass., after 217 performances in 118 cities. PRESENTED BY Tom Mallow; DIRECTOR: Ruth Mitchell; CHOREOGRAPHER: George Martin; MUSICAL DIRECTOR: Albert L. Fiorillo. **Cast:** ZORBA: Michael Kermoyan; NIKOS: Thom Koutsoukos; HORTENSE: Vivian Blaine; FATHER ZACHARAIA: Christopher Cable.

772. *Zorba (Broadway revival)*

Before Broadway. This revival tried out as tour, opening on 1/25/83, at the Forrest Theatre, Philadelphia. It had the same basic crew as for the Broadway run which followed the tour. It had the same cast too, except SOPHIA/CROW: Theresa Rakov (she also understudied The Woman). Tori Brenno (and not Danielle R. Striker) was a swing.

The Broadway Run. BROADWAY THEATRE, 10/16/83–9/1/84. 14 previews. 354 PERFORMANCES. PRESENTED BY Barry & Fran Weissler, Kenneth — John Productions; MUSIC: John Kander; LYRICS: Fred Ebb; BOOK: Joseph Stein; BASED ON the novel *Zorba the Greek*, by Nikos Kazantzakis; DIRECTOR: Michael Cacoyannis; CHOREOGRAPHER: Graciela Daniele; SETS: David Chapman; COSTUMES: Hal George; LIGHTING: Marc B. Weiss; SOUND: T. Richard Fitzgerald; MUSICAL SUPERVISOR: Paul Gemignani; MUSICAL DIRECTOR: Randolph Mauldin; ORCHESTRATIONS: Don Walker; DANCE MUSIC ARRANGEMENTS: Thomas Fay; CAST RECORDING on RCA; PRESS: Fred Nathan & Associates; CASTING: Howard Feuer & Jeremy Ritzer; GENERAL MANAGEMENT: National Artists Management; COMPANY MANAGER: Robert H. Wallner; PRODUCTION STAGE MANAGER: Peter Lawrence; STAGE MANAGER: Jim Woolley; ASSISTANT STAGE MANAGER: James Lockhart. **Cast:** THE WOMAN: Debbie Shapiro (5) ☆, *Angelina Fiordellisi* (during Miss Shapiro's illness); KONSTANDI/TURKISH DANCER/RUSSIAN ADMIRAL: Frank De Sal; THANASSAI/FRENCH ADMIRAL: John Mineo; ITALIAN ADMIRAL/YORGO: Richard Warren Pugh; ENGLISH ADMIRAL/PRIEST: Paul Straney; CONSTABLE: Raphael LaManna; ATHENA: Suzanne Costallos; NIKO: Robert Westenberg (3) ☆, *Jeff McCarthy*; ZORBA: Anthony Quinn (1) ☆; DESPO: Panchali Null; MARIKA: Angelina Fiordellisi; KATINA: Susan Terry; VASSILAKAS: Chip Cornelius; MARINAKOS: Peter Marinos; MIMIKO: Aurelio Padron (7) ☆; KATAPOLIS: Peter Kevoian; SOPHIA: Pamela Trevisani; MAVRODANI: Charles Karel (6) ☆; PAVLI: Thomas

David Scalise; MANOLAKAS: Michael Dantuono (8) ☆; THE WIDOW: Taro Meyer (4) ☆; MADAME HORTENSE: Lila Kedrova (2) ☆, *Vivian Blaine* (1/10/84–1/30/84), *Lila Kedrova* (from 1/31/84); MARSALIAS: Rob Marshall; ANAGNOSTI: Tim Flavin (9) ☆, *Jim Litten*; MARIA/CAFE WHORE: Karen Giombetti; MONKS: Rob Marshall, John Mineo, Peter Marinos, Peter Kevoian; CROWS: Suzanne Costallos, Panchali Null, Angelina Fiordellisi, Pamela Trevisani. *Standbys*: Zorba: Charles Karel & James Lockhart; Hortense: Suzanne Costallos; The Woman: Angelina Fiordellisi; Niko: Michael Dantuono; The Widow: Susan Terry; Mavrodani: James Lockhart; Mimiko: John Mineo; Manolakas: Chip Cornelius. *Swings*: Jim Litten & Danielle R. Striker. *Musicians:* KEYBOARDS: Antony Geralis; ON-STAGE BOUZOUKI: Foto Gonis; DUMBEG: Eddie Kochak; BOUZOUKI: Angelo Saridis; ACCORDION: Charles Sauss; PERCUSSION: David Tancredi. *Act I: Scene 1* A market place, Piraeus: "Life Is" (The Woman & Company); *Scene 2* A cafe, Piraeus: "The First Time" (Zorba); *Scene 3* A Crete village: "The Top of the Hill" (The Woman & Company); *Scene 4* Hortense's garden: "No Boom Boom" (Hortense, Admirals, Zorba, Niko); *Scene 5* Interior of Hortense's inn: "Vive la Difference" (Admirals), *Scene 6* The mine site: "Mine Song" (Company); *Scene 7* A village street: "The Butterfly" (Widow, Niko, The Woman), "Goodbye, Canavaro" (Hortense, Zorba, Niko); *Scene 8* A bar in Piraeus: "Grandpapa" (additional choreography: Theodore Pappas) (Zorba, The Woman, Company); *Scene 9* A village street: "Only Love" (Hortense), "The Bend of the Road" (The Woman), "Only Love" (reprise) (The Woman). *Act II: Scene 1* Hortense's garden: "Y'assou" (Company), "Woman" (Zorba); *Scene 2* The widow's house: "Why Can't I Speak"/"That's a Beginning" (Widow, Niko, The Woman); *Scene 3* The church square: Easter Dance (Company); *Scene 4* Entrance to the mine: Miners' Dance (Men); *Scene 5* Hortense's bedroom: "The Crow" (The Woman, Crows, Monks), "Happy Birthday" (Hortense); *Scene 6* The port, Piraeus: "I Am Free" (Zorba).

The show got generally great reviews, and Anthony Quinn got raves. Lila Kedrova won a Tony Award.

After Broadway. Tour. Opened on 9/5/84, at the Kennedy Center, Washington, DC (where it ran until 10/14/84), and closed on 8/3/86, at the Westbury Music Fair, NY. It had the same basic crew as for Broadway, except MUSICAL DIRECTOR: Al Cavaliere; PRODUCTION SUPERVISOR: Joel Grey. As for the cast Messrs Quinn, Karel, Pugh, Padron, De Sal, LaManna and Straney all reprised, as did Misses Kedrova and Null. Angelina Fiordellisi now played the Widow, Donna Theodore played the Woman, and Robert Westenberg played Niko. Leila Martin played Sister/Crow and understudied Hortense.

After Broadway. NORTH SHORE MUSIC THEATRE, Beverly, Mass., 10/4/01–10/21/01. Previews from 10/2/01. DIRECTOR: Richard Sabellico; CHOREOGRAPHER: Danny Buraczeski; MUSICAL DIRECTOR: Darren R. Cohen. Olympia Dukakis & Louis Zorich were announced for the leads, but pulled out. *Cast*: ZORBA: Ron Holgate; HORTENSE: Anita Gillette; WIDOW: Glory Crampton; NIKOS: Franc D'Ambrosio.

A planned 40-week national tour, to open in fall 2003, produced by Alan Lichtenstein, and directed by Sammy Dallas Bayes, and starring Topol, did not happen, even though 22 weeks worth of tour had been set. There wasn't enough demand.

Appendix:
Other Musicals

This appendix includes the great majority of shows from 1943 through 2004 that did not run on Broadway or otherwise did not meet the criteria laid out in the preface of this book for inclusion as a Broadway musical.

Shows listed here that played in a Broadway theatre were not musicals or musical revues, as such. They might be plays with music, or some form of special presentation. In any case, the reason for consignment to this appendix is explained in each instance.

Some shows were just too early or too late chronologically to be included in the main text of this book (which runs between March 31, 1943, and December 31, 2004). However, those that were still running when *Oklahoma!* opened in 1943 are included in this appendix, as are some 2005 Broadway musicals and some of the more important non–Broadway ones that opened that year.

In addition, most of the pre–*Oklahoma!* shows that later had non-Broadway revivals are also listed in this appendix. If the revivals played Broadway, then the original runs are, of course, always discussed in the main part of this book.

As for shows that did not play in a Broadway theatre, we are looking primarily at Off Broadway and Off Off Broadway shows, both of which I have almost always abbreviated to OB in this appendix, deliberately avoiding distinguishing between OB and OOB, partly because non–Broadway shows are not the thrust of this book, and partly because, for the few times this abbreviation is used, the game of distinction is not worth the candle.

Also in this appendix are shows that were destined for Broadway but closed during out-of-town tryouts (or, as they say, "closed on the road") or, as a few shows have done, closed during previews in the actual Broadway theatre scheduled for the official run, which is as close as you come without actually opening on Broadway.

Some other regional shows are listed, especially famous ones that the reader might think had a Broadway run (but didn't).

A good number of British shows are listed, most of which played in London, either in a West End theatre or in a fringe theatre. Many British shows did go to Broadway, of course, in which case they are in the main part of this book. But most did not (or may have played Off Broadway), and the majority of these are listed in this appendix.

If you are looking for a show and cannot find it either in the main part of the book or in the appendix, then try the index. There may well be some extraneous reference to it under the heading of another show.

I want to stress that this appendix is not exhaustive, nor are the contents within each appendix entry meant to be — and not simply because of space. The space factor alone would make it impossible to discuss these musicals in the same depth as the Broadway shows. But also, there are simply too many non–Broadway shows. The list is in fact endless, and growing more endless every day.

Entries are organized as follows: ***Title*** (and within some shows there will be *alternative titles* for that show); a brief indicator of what type of production it was (play with music; revue; etc.) unless it was a regular musical, in which case there is no such indicator; a brief synopsis of the show; theatre or other venue (this will be a New York theatre unless otherwise specified); dates it ran and number of previews (prev) and performances (perf), and usually when previews began; and different theatres where it was staged during its run (if there was more than one theatre involved). Sometimes there is only the opening date, with the word "opened" omitted as being understood. Credits follow, in roughly this order: producer (p); composer (m); lyricist (l); librettist (b for book); idea; conceived by (concept); director (d); choreographer (ch); set/scenic designer (set); costume designer (cos); lighting designer (light); sound designer (sound); musical supervisor (ms); musical director (md); orchestrator (orch); arranger (arr); and a few management credits.

Most often, there is some sort of cast list, usually not complete; the "musical numbers"; other notes perhaps; revivals and tours information; award information; and review information.

A La Carte see # 534

773. *A La Carte*. Revue. Savoy, London, 6/17/48. m: Charles Zwar; l/b: Alan Melville; d: Henderson Storie; md: Peter Yorke. Cast: Hermione Baddeley, Dickie Henderson, Jean Telfer

774. *A ... My Name Is Alice*. Mildly feministic topical musical revue about women. Material by: Marta Kauffman & David Crane, Doug Katsaros & David Zippel, Carol Hall, Amanda McBroom, Susan Birkenhead, Anne Meara, Glen Roven & June Siegel, Cassandra Medley (the "Ms. Mae" sketch), etc.; conceived by: Joan Micklin Silver & Julianne Boyd. There were 2 readings at American Place Theatre, 11/2/83 (12 perf) and 2/24/84–3/11/84 (12 perf). d: Joan Micklin Silver & Julianne Boyd; ch: Yvonne Adrian; set: Adrianne Lobel; md: Jan Rosenberg. Cast: Lynnie Godfrey, Randy Graff, Polly Pen, Alaina Reed, Grace Roberts. Then it was revised, and had its first real run, at Village Gate Upstairs, 4/8/84– 2/17/85 (prev from 3/30/84). p: Anne Wilder, Douglas F. Goodman, Rosita Sarnoff, by special arrangement with The Women's Project; d: Joan Micklin Silver & Julianne Boyd; ch: Edward Love; set: Adrianne Lobel; md: Michael Skloff. Cast: Roo Brown, Randy Graff, Mary Gordon Murray, Alaina Reed, Charlaine Woodard. It won an Obie Award. There was a sequel, *A...My Name Is Still Alice*, with material by Craig Carnelia, Douglas Bernstein, Alaina Reed Hall, Doug Katsaros, Michael John La Chiusa, Amanda McBroom, Stephen Schwartz, June Siegel, Mary Bracken Phillips, etc. It opened at the Old Globe Theatre, San Diego, 5/14/92. d: Joan Micklin Silver & Julianne Boyd; ch: Liza Gennaro; md: Henry Aronson. Cast: Roo Brown, Randy Graff, Alaina Reed Hall, Mary Gordon Murray, Nancy Ticotin. The sequel ran again at Second Stage, 10/13/92–1/3/93. 84 perf. d: Joan Micklin Silver; ch: Hope Clarke; md: Ian Herman. Cast: Roo Brown, Laura Dean, Cleo King, KT Sullivan, Nancy Ticotin. It then toured. These 2 *Alice* shows amalgamated to form *A...My Name Will Always Be Alice*, which had a run at the Barrington Stage Company, Massachusetts. This new show was re-named *Alice Revisited*, and opened at American Stage Festival, Milford, NH, on 8/17/95. d: Julianne Boyd; ch: Hope Clarke; set: Jim Noone; md: Joel Framm. Cast: Barbara Walsh, Heather MacRae, Cheryl Howard, Gwen Stewart, Marguerite MacIntyre

775. *Abby's Song*. Set in Whispering Pines, Montana. About young daughter of Montana shepherd. City Center, 11/14/99– 11/28/99. 19 perf. m: Elliot Wilensky; l/b: Mary Pat Kelly; d/ch: Randy Skinner; set: Bill Clarke; cos: David C. Woolard; sound: Scott Lehrer; md: Stephen Bates; orch: Michael Gibson. Cast: Jackie Angelescu, Paul Sorvino. "An Ordinary Town," "Woman's Work," "Fly a Rainbow," "More than Ever," "Wolf Song," "I Am Home," "Another Girl Who's Just Like Me," "There's a Price," "You Just Gotta Be You," "She Left without a Word," "A Little Girl in the Night," "Beyond," "I Did It," "An Angel Has a Message," "A Mother's Heart," "Pass the Wine," "The Revelation," "How Do You Follow a Star?," "Who is This Child?," "Abby's Song," "One Small Voice."

776. *Abi Gezunt*. Yiddish. Set in a Catskills hotel. Also called *As Long as You're Healthy*. Second Avenue, 10/8/49. p/d: Jacob Kalich; m: Joseph Rumshinsky; l: Molly Picon; b: Jacob Kalich & Sholom Perlmutter; ch: Lillian Shapero. Cast: Molly Picon, Julius Adler, Irving Jacobson, Henrietta Jacobson. "Mama Loshen," "Tzimmers Polka"

777. *Abie's Irish Rose*. Set on 2 fictitious islands, Tornados and Manhattan. Jewish Rep, 4/29/00–5/21/00. 9 prev. 15 perf. m/d/orch: Doug Katsaros; l: Richard Engquist & Frank Evans; b: Ron Sproat; set: Jim Morgan; light: Mary Jo Dondlinger. Cast: Keith Lee Grant, Carla Woods, Heather MacRae, Steven Rose. "Two Islands," "Omens," "That Was Him," "Rainbow," "A Bit of a Surprise," "That Girl," "Something Else," "What's Going On?," "Crazy Mixed Up Me," "Somewhere in the World," "Liberal," "All for Her," "Welcome to Manhattan," "Nice While it Lasted," "The Way it's S'posed to Be," "Late Night TV," "He Used to Whistle," "Wasted on the Young"

778. *About Face*. Army. Traveled around camps. 1944. Frank Loesser wrote most of m/l. Cast: Jules Munshin. "Dogface," "Gee, But it's Great to Be in the Army," "PX Parade," "When He Comes Home," "First Class Private Mary Brown," "One Little WAC," "Why Do they Call a Private a Private?"

779. *Abracadabra*. Lyric, Hammersmith, London, 12/18/83–1/21/84. m/l: Wood/Black; based on Abba's songs. Cast: Elaine Paige

780. *Absolutely Freeee*. Frank Zappa musical revue. Garrick, 5/24/67. p: Herb Cohen. Cast: Frank Zappa & Mothers of Invention

781. *Absolutely Rude*. Comedy Cellar, 10/17/91–12/1/91. m/l: Rick Crom; d: John McMahon. Cast: Rick Crom, Virginia McMath. "Tacky Opening Number," "Party Line," "Guardian Angels," "If I Only Were the Pope," "Urge Dirge," "First Ladies First," "You Don't Need Me Any More," "Cole Porter's Star Trek," "Close That Show!," "One Last Prince," "Sondheim's Oklahoma," "Tacky Closing Number"

782. *Abyssinia*. CSC Rep, 4/3/87– 4/18/87. 14 perf. m/l/b: Ted Kociolek & James Racheff; from novel *Marked by Fire*, by Joyce Carol Thomas; d: Tazewell Thompson; ch consultant: Julie Arenal. Cast: Jennifer Leigh Warren (as Abyssinia Jackson), Tina Fabrique, Cheryl Freeman, Zelda Pulliam. "Rise and Fly," "Abyssinia," "Lift up Your Voice!," "There Has to Be a Reason," "I Have Seen the Wind," "Cry," "Pickin' up the Pieces," "Honey and Lemon." Goodspeed, 6/8/88. Cast: Tina Fabrique, Cheryl Freeman, Noreen Crayton (as Abyssinia), Vanessa Williams

783. *Ace of Clubs*. Sailor falls for nightclub singer at *Ace of Clubs* nightclub in gangster-ridden Soho. Palace, Manchester, England, 5/16/50 (3 weeks); toured; the Cambridge, London, 7/7/50–1/6/51 (211 perf). p: Tom Arnold; w/d: Noel Coward; ch: Freddie Carpenter; md: Mantovani. Cast: Patricia Kirkwood, Graham Payn, Jean Carson, Raymond Young, Myles Eason, June Whitfield, Vivien Merchant, Elwyn Brook-Jones, Jack Lambert. "Top of the Morning," "My Kind of Man," "This Could Be True," "Nothing Can Last Forever," "Something About a Sailor," "I'd Never, Never Know," "Three Juvenile Delinquents," "Sail Away," "Josephine," "Would You Like to Stick a Pin in My Balloon?," "In a Boat on a Lake with My Darling," "I Like America," "Why Does Love Get in the Way?," "Evening in Summer," "Time for Baby's Bottle," "Chase Me, Charlie"

784. *Adam*. Harry DeJur, 1/23/83– 2/6/83. 12 perf. p: New Federal Theatre; m/l: Richard Ahlert; b: June Tansey; d: Don Evans. "Walk Just a Few Feet," "Give Me the Power," "When I'm Your Woman," "He Should Have Been Mine," "Mr. Harlem," "We Got Grounds," "Good Ole Boys," "I Never Thought I'd See the Day," "Let's Do it for Adam," "We Kept the Faith," "Look Who's Coming to Harlem"

785. *The Adventures of Mr. Toad*. Haymarket, Basingstoke, England, 12/84; Theatre Royal, Winchester, 1/85; Bloomsbury, London, 12/86–1/87. w: Piers Chater-Robinson; from Kenneth Grahame's book *The Wind in the Willows*. "Hang Spring Cleaning," "Messing About," "Introducing Mr. Toad," "Let's Jump Aboard," "Weasels Reign," "Mr. Toad," "Breakfast," "A Duty to Perform," "Ducks Ditty," "Goodbye Toad," "Toad Hall," "Off a-Bashing," "Toad Has Gone to Prison"

786. *Aesop's Fables*. Rock musical. Previously ran in Chicago. Mercer-Brecht, 8/17/72– 9/19/72. 59 perf. p/m: William Russo; text: Jon Swan; based on Aesop's Fables. Cast: Performing Ensemble of the Chicago Free Theatre

787. *After the Ball*. An operette (musical play). Royal Court, Liverpool, England, 3/1/54; toured; Globe, London, 6/10/54– 11/20/54 (188 perf). m/l/b: Noel Coward; from Oscar Wilde's *Lady Windermere's Fan*; d: Robert Helpmann & Noel Coward; ch: Robert Helpmann; set/cos: Doris Zinkeisen; cast recording on Philips. Cast: Graham Payn, Vanessa Lee, Irene Browne, Mary Ellis, Peter Graves, Marion Grimaldi, Lois Green, Andrew Sachs. "Oh, What a Century it's Been," "I Knew That You Would Be My Love," "Mr. Hopper's Chanty," "Sweet Day," "Stay on the Side of the Angels," "Creme de la Creme," "Light Is the Heart," "May I Have the Pleasure?," "I Offer You My Heart," "Why Is it the Woman Who Pays?," "Aria," "Go, I Beg You," "London at Night," "Clear, Bright Morning," "All My Life Ago," "Oh, What a Season This Has Been," "Farewell Song," "Something on a Tray," "Faraway Land." Lambertville, NJ, 8/2/55. p: John Terell's Music Circus. Good Shepherd Faith Church, NYC, 6/7/93 (1 concert perf). d: Sheila Smith. Cast: Tammy Grimes, Paula Laurence, Patrick Quinn, SuEllen Estey. Irish Rep, NYC, 12/16/04. Prev from 12/7/04. add material: Barry Day; d/set: Tony Walton; ch: Lisa Shriver; light: Brian Nason; md: Mark Hartman. Cast: Kristin Huxhold, Mary Illes, Paul Carlin, David Staller, Kathleen Widdoes, Drew Eshelman, Elizabeth Inghram

788. *After the Fair*. Set in Melchester & London, 1897. York Theatre Co., 7/15/99– 8/8/99. 18 prev from 6/30/99. 30 perf. m: Matthew Ward; l/b: Stephen Cole; from story by Thomas Hardy; d: Travis L. Stockley; set: James Morgan; cos: Michael Bottari & Ronald Case; md/add orch: Georgia Stitt; orch: David Siegel; cast recording on Varese Sarabande. Cast: James Ludwig, Michele Pawk, David Staller, Jennifer Piech. "World at My Window," "After the Fair," "Just in Case," "Charles' Letter," "And Then," "Beloved," "Summer Fancy," "Another Letter Montage," "Idiots! Lunatics!," "This is Not the End," "Nothing Will Ever Be the Same," "A Spot of Tea," "Between the Lines," "There's a Woman"/"What is Real," "Men and Wives," "Your Words Were Music." King's Head, London, 2000

789. *After the Show*. Late night revue. St. Martin's, London, 4/30/51. 24 perf. p: John Regan; m: Norman Dannatt & John Pritchett; w: Peter Myers & Alec Grahame. Cast: Beryl Reid, Robert Dorning, Suzanne Wilde

790. *Ah, Men*. An entertainment of the male experience. South Street, 5/11/81–5/24/81. 14 prev. 14 perf. p: Jay Garon; w/d: Paul Shyre; set/cos: Eldon Elder. Cast: Jane White, Jack Betts, Curt Dawson, Stephen Lang. "Ah, Men," "Man is for the Woman Made," "When After You Pass My Door," "My First," "Last Minute Waltz," "Truck Stop," "Illusions," "Daddy Blues"

791. *Airs on a Shoestring*. Intimate revue, successor to *Penny Plain*. Royal Court, London (the show re-opened this theatre), 4/22/53. 777 perf. p/dev: Laurier Lister; m: Richard Addinsell, John Pritchett, Madeleine Dring, Arthur Benjamin; l: Michael Flanders & Donald Swann (i.e. Flanders & Swann), Charlotte Mitchell, Madeleine Dring, Jerry Mann; ch: Alfred Rodrigues; md: John Pritchett. Cast: Moyra Fraser, Max Adrian, Sally Rogers, Betty Marsden, Denis Quilley. "Airs on a Shoestring," "The Model Models," "Taken as Red," "Sing High, Sing Low," "Jamaican Rumba," "Mediterranean," "Fly Customers"

792. *The Al Chemist Show*. Los Angeles Actors Theatre, 1980. m/l: Steve Allen. Cast: Georgia Brown, James Booth. "I Depend on Me"

793. *Aladdin*. Pantomime version of American TV musical. Coliseum, London, 12/17/59. 145 perf. m/l: Cole Porter; d/ch: Robert Helpmann; set/cos: Loudon Sainthill. Cast: Bob Monkhouse, Doretta Morrow, Ronald Shiner, Ian Wallace, Alan Wheatley, Milton Reid. "I Am Loved." There have been many productions of several different versions of *Aladdin*, most of them pantomimes

794. *Aladdin*. Lyric, Hammersmith, London, 12/21/79. m/l: Sandy Wilson; cast recording on President. Cast: Elisabeth Welch, Aubrey Woods, Joe Melia, Michael Sadler, Belinda Long, Christine McKenna, Cass Allen, Ernest Clark. "The Spell," "Aladdin," "The Proclamation," "It is Written in the Sands," "There and Then," "Love's a Luxury," "Dream About Me," "Chopsticks," "All I Did," "Wicked," "Life in the Laundry," "Give Him the Old Kung Fu"

795. *Aldersgate '88: A Musical Celebration*. Inspirational musical revue, preceded by one-act concert Earl Wrightson in *Songs of the Spirit*. Avery Fisher Hall, 2/21/88. 1 perf. p: NY Conference of the United Methodist Church & Dr. Warren L. Danskin; m/l: Paul Trueblood; d: Jack Eddleman; md: Eric Stern. Cast: June Angela, Earl Grandison, Walter Willison. "I Want to Make a Diff'rence," "The Aldersgate Connection," "Let the Ladies Do It," "Quintessential Methodist," "Don't Be a Stranger," "There Is One"

796. *Alec Wilder: Clues to a Life*. Vineyard, 2/3/82–2/21/82. 20 perf. conceived by: Barbara Zinn & Elliot Weiss; d: Norman Rene; ch: Louise Quick. Cast: Christine Andreas, D'Jamin Bartlett, Keith David, Craig Lucas. "A Child is Born," "The Echoes of Mind," "That's My Girl," "Unbelievable," "Give Me Time," "Where Is the One?," "Moon and Sand," "I'd Do It All Again," "Lovers and Losers," "I'll Be Around," "While We're Young," "The Wrong Blues," "I've Been There," "Rain, Rain," "Blackberry Winter," "Trouble Is a Man," "It's So Peaceful in the Country," "I See It Now"

797. *Alias Jimmy Valentine*. Set in Bowery, NY, and in Willow Run, Idaho, in 1912. Musical Theatre Works, 2/25/88– 3/13/88. 8 prev. 8 perf. m/l: Bob Haber & Hal Hackady; b: Jack Wrangler; from O. Henry short story *A Retrieved Reformation*; d: Charles Repole; ch: Sam Viverito; md: Arnold Gross. Cast: Kurt Peterson, Katharine Buffaloe, Lillian Graff, Dick Decareau, Denise Lor, Thomas Ruisinger, Faith Prince. "Winner Take All," "Jimmy's Comin' Back," "What's Your Hurry?," "I'm Free," "Flim-Flam," "You're So Good, John," "Miss Invisible," "She'll Get You Yet," "That Girl," "Dink's Lament," "Leave It to Me," "Today Is on Me," "Love Is a Four-Letter Word," "Small Town," "I'm Gettin' Off Here," "I Love You, Jimmy Valentine"

Alice in Concert see # 2805, this appendix

798. *Alice in Wonderland*. Play with mus. Virginia Theatre, Broadway, 12/23/82– 1/9/83. 18 prev. 21 perf. p: Sabra Jones, Anthony D. Marshall, WNET/Thirteen; m: Richard Addinsell; adapted m/ms: Jonathan Tunick; from Lewis Carroll's stories; adapted for the stage by: Eva Le Gallienne & Florida Friebus; conceived by: Eva Le Gallienne; d: Eva Le Gallienne & John Strasberg; movement: Bambi Linn; set: John Lee Beatty; cos: Patricia Zipprodt (nominated for Tony); light: Jennifer Tipton; sound: Jack Mann; puppets: The Puppet People; conductor: Les Scott; m: Steven Suskin. Cast: Marti Morris, Kate Burton (Alice), Mary Stuart Masterson (Small White Rabbit/4 of Hearts/Alice understudy), John Miglietta, Nicholas Martin, James Valentine, Rebecca Armen, Curt Dawson, John Heffernan, Geddeth Smith, Claude-Albert Saucier, Edward Zang, Richard Sterne, Josh Clark, MacIntyre Dixon, Nicholas Martin, Geoff Garland, Robert Ott Boyle, Steve Massa, Skip Harris, Cliff Rakerd, Marti Morris, John Seidman, Brian Reddy, Richard Woods, Edward Hibbert, Mary Louise Wilson, Eva Le Gallienne (White Queen: Joan White on Tues

evenings & Weds matinees). 1st ran as *Alice in Wonderland and Through the Looking Glass*, at the Civic Repertory Theatre, 12/12/32, then moved to the New Amsterdam, 1/30/33–5/6/33. 127 perf. Cast: Alice: Josephine Hutchinson

799. *Alice in Wonderland*. Adult version of the Lewis Carroll novel. Has full nudity. Kirk, 1/29/04. Prev from 1/12/04. m/l: Taywah; William Osco adapted it as a stage musical from his movie, and also dir; ch: Tania L. Pearson; set: Josh Iacovelli; cos: Laura Frecon; light: Chris Hudacs

800. *Alice Through the Looking Glass*. Stratford Festival, England, 1994. m: Keith Thomas. Cast: Barbara Byrne, Sarah Polley. "Into the Looking Glass," "Tweedle Dum and Tweedle Dee," "Walrus and the Carpenter," "The Wood of Namelessness," "Lion and Unicorn," "Drummers!," "Humpty Dumpty's Song," "All the King's Men," "Jabberwocky," "A-Sittin' on a Gate," "Alice Crowned Queen," "Looking Glass Song," "Oyster Riddle Song," "Mad Dinner Party," "Alice Returns," "Farewell Song"

801. *Alison*. Rock musical. Closed before Broadway, 1968. m/l: Larry Norman, Herb Hendler, Ken Mansfield. "Curious," "I Want to Run Out from Under My Skin," "Love on Haight Street," "Mary Jane," "We All," "Wake Up to Me Gently"

802. *Alive, Alive Oh*. Theatre Four, 10/28/94–12/18/94. 4 prev. 35 perf. Irish songs, poetry, vaudeville, drama, pantomime. p: Irish Rep; conceived by/w/starred: Milo O'Shea & Kitty Sullivan

803. *All Cloned Up*. Dangers of human cloning. King's Head, London, 2001. p/w: Mike Bennett; d: Alkis Kritikos. Cast: Gemma Bassett, Andy Cresswell, Mary Savva, Tom Leick, Ben Graves. 1st ran at Wimbledon Studio Theatre; then 5 weeks at the Grace, Battersea

804. *All in Love*. Martinique Theatre, 11/10/61–3/11/62. 141 perf. m: Jacques Urbont; l/b: Bruce Geller; from Sheridan's *The Rivals*; d: Tom Brennan; light: Jules Fisher; orch: Jonathan Tunick; cast recording on Mercury. Cast: David Atkinson, Gaylea Byrne, Lee Cass, Christina Gillespie, Mimi Randolph, Charles Kimbrough, Dom De Luise. "To Bath Derry O," "Poor," "What Can It Be?," "Odds," "I Love a Fool," "A More Than Ordinary Glorious Vocabulary," "Women Simple," "The Lady Was Made to Be Loved," "The Good Old Ways," "Honour," "I Found Him," "Daydreams," "Don't Ask Me," "Why Wives," "Quickly," "All in Love." Mayfair, London, 3/64. 22 perf. Cast: Annie Ross, Peter Pratt, Peter Gilmore, Ronnie Barker, James Fox, Mary Millar

805. *All Kinds of Giants*. Cricket, 12/18/61– 12/31/61. 16 perf. m/l: Sam Pottle & Tom Whedon; d: Peter Conlow; md: Milton Setzer. Cast: Bill Hinnant, Richard Morse, Claiborne Cary, Ralph Purdum. "State of the Kingdom," "My Prince," "Paint Me a Rainbow," "Logic!," "If I Were Only Someone," "To Be a King," "Suddenly Stop and Think," "My Star," "All Kinds of Giants," "Friends," "Here We Are," "Be Yourself"

806. *The All Night Strut!* Musical entertainment, using 22 old songs. Theatre Four, 10/4/79–10/7/79. 7 prev. 6 perf. conceived by/d/ch: Fran Charnas. Cast: Andrea Danford, Jess Richards, Tony Rich, Jana Robbins. Previously ran in Cleveland & Boston

807. *All of the Above*. Musical entertainment. Perry Street, 7/14/82–7/18/82. 7 perf. w: Michael Eisenberg; d: Tony Berk; light: Victor En Yu Tan; md: Ed Ellner. Cast: Ann Morrison, Linda Gelman, Ed Ellner. "A Cry from the Coast," "Be My Bland Romantic Lead," "Born Again," "California Love," "Dancin' Shoes," "For Alice," "It Just Ain't a Party Without You," "Memories of Kong," "My Heart's Intact," "New Year's Eve at the Computer Center," "School on Saturday Night," "Talk to My Machine," "The Dictator Who Ran Away," "Willy's Prize," "Your Show"

808. *All Shook Up*. About a magical jukebox and a leather-jacketed stranger in a small town. Set in 1955. Commissioned by Elvis Presley's estate, and, although Elvis is not a character in the show, there are about 20 Elvis songs in it. Goodspeed. 5/13/04– 6/6/04. Developmental run. b: Joe DiPietro. Cast: Manley Pope, Jennifer Gambatese, Jonathan Hadary, Leah Hocking, Nikki M. James, Ashton Holmes, John Jellison, Alix Korey, Katy Grenfell. World premiere at Cadillac Palace, Chicago, 1/13/05–1/23/05. Prev from 12/19/04. p: Jonathan Pollard, Bernie Kukoff, Clear Channel Entertainment, Harbor Entertainment, Stanley Buchthal, Miramax Films, in assoc with Eric Falkenstein, Nina Essman/Nancy Nagel Gibbs, Karen Jason, Barney Rosenzweig; d: Christopher Ashley; ch: Ken Roberson (replacing Jodi Moccia); Sergio Trujillo (helped with ch); set: David Rockwell; cos: David C. Woolard; light: Donald Holder. Cast: Cheyenne Jackson (Jarrod Emick was going to play this role, but understudy Mr. Jackson was announced on 10/29/04), Jennifer Gambatese, Jonathan Hadary, Leah Hocking, Nikki M. James, John Jellison, Alix Korey, Mark Price, Sharon Wilkins, Paul Castree, Curtis Holbrook, Michelle Kittrell, Anika Larsen, John Eric Parker, Jenny-Lynn Suckling. Palace, Broadway, 3/24/05. Prev from 2/20/05

809. *All That Glitters*. Neil, a songwriter, has to choose between marrying rich woman & poor girl he really loves. Williams College, 3/49. 3 perf. m/l: Stephen Sondheim (his 2nd show at the college); based on play *Beggar on Horseback*, by George S. Kaufman & Marc Connelly. Cast: Ronald Moir, Betty Dissell. "When I See You," "I Must Be Dreaming," "I Love You, etc.," "I Need Love," "Let's Not Fall in Love"

810. *All You Need Is Love*. Revue of Beatles songs. Queen's, London, 5/29/01– 9/1/01. Prev from 5/21/01. m/l: Lennon & McCartney; dev/d: Jon Miller & Pete Brooks; ch: Nigel Charnock & Kate Prince; set/cos: Laura Hopkins; light: Chris Ellis; sound: Rick Clarke

811. *All's Fair*. Closed before Broadway, 1968. m/l: Dick Stern & Lou Carter. "All's Fair," "America, America, America," "Berger, Boozer and Digby," "A Brand New World," "He's My Son," "I Think I'm Going to Faint," "My American," "What's Happened to Love," "You Can't Take a Man Out of Romance"

812. *Almos' a Man*. Musical drama. Set in Arkansas in 1933. Soho Rep, NYC, 4/12/85– 5/5/85. 20 perf. w: Paris Barclay; from short story by Richard Wright; d: Tazewell Thompson; md: Dianne Adams. Cast: La Donna Mabry, Todd A. Rolle, Todd Oleson

813. *Almost Like Being in Love: The Lerner and Loewe Songbook*. Tour. Opened in Englewood, NJ, 11/5/98. Cast: Diahann Carroll, David Bedella, Jonathan Dokuchitz, Jordan Leeds, David White

814. *Almost Like Being in Love: The Lost Songs of Alan Jay Lerner*. Intimate late-night one-hour cabaret revue. Terrace Cafe, Royal National, London, 5/25/01–6/16/01. dev/d: Hugh Wooldridge; md: Stuart Barr. Cast: Sian Phillips, Anita Dobson, Clive Carter, Matt Rawle, John Standing, Anna Francolini

815. *Altar Boyz*. About a Christian pop group. Dodger Stages Stage IV, 3/1/05. Prev from 2/15/05. p: Ken Davenport & Robyn Goodman. m/l: Gary Adler & Michael Patrick Walker; b: Kevin del Aguila; conceived by Michael Kessler & Ken Davenport; d: Stafford Arima; ch: Christopher Gattelli; set: Anna Louizos; cos: Gail Brassard; light: Natasha Katz; md/orch: Lynne Shankel & Doug Katsaros. Cast: Ryan Duncan, David Josefsberg, Andy Karl, Tyler Maynard. A developmental run in 2004 had same cast except Scott Porter, who joined for the 2005 OB run

816. *Always*. The ultimate love story. About Edward VIII & Mrs. Simpson. Victoria Palace, London, 6/10/97–7/26/97. Prev from 5/20/97. m/l/b: William May & Jason Sprague; add b material: Frank Hauser; d: Frank Hauser & Thommie Walsh; cast recording on Warners. Cast: Clive Carter, Jan Hartley, Shani Wallis, Sheila Ferguson, David McAlister. "Long May You Reign," "Someone Special," "I Stand Before My Destiny," "Why?," "Love's Carousel," "If Always Were a Place," "This Time Around," "It's the Party of the Year," "Hearts Have Their Reasons," "Reason for Life is to Love," "The Montage," "The Invitation Is for Two," "Always." Began as workshop in Victorian Arts Centre, Australia

817. *Always … Patsy Cline*. Musical bio. Variety Arts, 6/24/97–12/7/97. 16 prev from 6/9/97. 192 perf. w/d: Ted Swindley; add material: Ellis Nassour; sound: Peter J. Fitzgerald; md: Vicki Masters; cast recording on MCA. Cast: Tori Lynn Palazola, Margo Martindale. "Honky Tonk Merry-Go-Round," "Back in Baby's Arms," "Anytime," "Walkin' After Midnight," "I Fall to Pieces," "It Wasn't God Who Made Honky Tonk Angels," "Come on In," "Your Cheatin' Heart," "She's Got You," "San Antonio Rose," "Lovesick Blues," "Sweet Dreams," "Three Cigarettes in an Ashtray," "Crazy," "Seven Lonely Days," "If I Could See the World," "Just a Closer Walk with Thee," "Blue Moon of Kentucky," "Gotta a Lot of Rhythm in My Soul," "Faded Love," "True Love"

818. *Am I Asking Too Much?* Fashion Institute Auditorium, 4/3/79–4/14/79. 11 perf. w/d: Ken Rubenstein. Cast: Judith Jamison, Fae Rubenstein, Charles "Cookie" Cook (also ch tap dancing)

819. *Amahl and the Night Visitors*. Crippled boy journeys with Wise Men to Bethlehem on orig Christmas Day. City Center, 2/21/52 (2 months after TV debut. It was originally written for TV. p: NYC Opera; m/l/d: Gian-Carlo Menotti; md: Thomas Schippers. Cast: Chet Allen, Rosemary Kuhlmann. Theatre of the Riverside Church, 11/30/79. d: David K. Manion. Kennedy Center, 12/12/89–12/17/89. d: Gian-Carlo Menotti

820. *The Amazing Adele*. Dealt with clairvoyance. Set during a summer in Atlantic City in 1930s. Pre-Broadway tryouts from 12/26/55, Shubert, Philadelphia. Closed 1/21/56, Shubert, Boston. Never made Broadway. p: Albert Selden & Morton Gottlieb; m/l: Albert Selden; b: Anita Loos; from French play by Pierre Barrillet & Jean-Pierre Gredy; d/ch: Herbert Ross; book d: Jack Landau; set: Oliver Smith; cos: Thomas Becher; asst cos: Patricia Zipprodt; light: Peggy Clark; mus continuity: Donald Pippin. Cast: Tammy Grimes, Johnny Desmond, Jeri Archer, Babe Hines, Peggy Cass, Cris Alexander, Dagmar, Don De Leo, Joey Faye, Enid Markey, Grover Dale, Alvin Beam. "Atlantic City Welcomes You," "What Kind of Grandma Are You?," "My Luck Has Changed," "Saturday Night," "Now Is the Time," "The Amazing Adele," "Treat 'em Rough," "You Belong," "Go and Get Yourself a Yo-Yo," "Yo-Yo Dance," "Under the Boardwalk Ballet," "Count on Me," "I Wonder," "Go Away Devil," "Never Again," "Who Needs It"

821. *The Amazing Adventures of Tense Guy*. Comedy with mus. Set in NYC & Planet America Corporation. Paradise, 6/8/94–7/1/94. 3 prev. 12 perf. m/l/b: Alan Ball; d: Matthew Lenz. Cast: Kyle Shannon

822. *The Amazons*. Nottingham Playhouse, England, 4/7/71–5/8/71. 21 perf. m: John Addison; l: David Heneker; b: Michael Stewart; from play by Arthur Pinero; d: Philip Wiseman; ch: Irving Davies; md: Denys Rawson. Cast: Fiona Mathieson. "There's Nothing Wrong with England," "My Boys," "West End Is the Worst End," "On Parade" (replaced with "Knees Up, My Boys"), "Whatever Can Have Happened," "Let's Stick Together," "We Shall See What We Shall See," "I'm Only Following My Instructions" (cut, and replaced with "On Parade"), "A Nice Young Fellow," "Don't Follow the Music," "She Hates Me," "Afternoon Tea," "I Thought as Much," "The Coast Is Clear," "Eurhythmics," "Gymnastics" (same melody as "Eurythmics"), "We're Models at Madame Tussauds" (cut, and replaced with "A Stag Party"), "Three Pretty Daughters." Two numbers were cut during tryouts: "Tweenwayes' Proposal Song" and "De Grival's Proposal Song"

823. *America*. Radio City Music Hall, 3/13/81–9/7/81. 11 prev from 3/6/81. 264 perf. p/conceived by/d: Robert F. Jani; orig m/l: Tom Bahler & Mark Vieha; special material & dial: Harvey Jacobs; principals staged by Frank Wagner; ch by Violet Holmes (dir of the Rockettes), Linda Lemac, Frank Wagner; set: Robert Guerra; cos: Michael Casey; light: Ken Billington; md: Tom Bahler; organists: Robert Maidhof & George Wesner. Cast: Jeff Johnson, Iris Revson, Mark Morales, Reed Jones, Wendy Edmead, The Rockettes. "Fifty Great Places All in One Place," "The Spirit of America"

824. *America Dreaming.* Music theatre piece. Vineyard, 12/8/94–1/8/95. 12 prev. 20 perf. m: Tan Dun; w: Chiori Miyagawa; d: Michael Mayer; ch: Doug Varone. Cast: Billy Crudup, Liana Pai, Ann Harada, Virginia Wing, Beth Dixon

825. *America Kicks Up Its Heels.* Playwrights Horizons Mainstage, 2/9/83– 3/27/83. 28 perf. m/l: William Finn; b: Charles Rubin; d: Mary Kyte & Ben Levit; ch: Mary Kyte; set/cos: Santo Loquasto; light: Frances Aronson; md: Michael Starobin. Cast: Patti LuPone, Dick Latessa, Lenora Nemetz, Alexandra Korey, Robin Boudreau, Robert Dorfman, Peggy Hewett. "All of Us Are Niggers," "Put It Together," "A Better World," "America, Kick Up Your Heels," "Push and Pull," "All Fall Down," "The Happiest Moment of My Life," "Sex Stories in Hard Times," "Nobody's Ever Gonna Step on Me," "Why," "It Was Fun," "My Day Has Come," "Papa Says"

826. *American Ballroom Theatre.* Joyce, 4/9/91–4/21/91. 16 perf. d: Richard Corley; ch: Patricia Birch, John Roudis, Peter Di Falco, Graciela Daniele, Gary Pierce

827. *The American Dance Machine.* Dance revue. Century Theatre/Alpha Company, 6/14/78–12/3/78. 198 perf. p: Lee Theodore, Louis K. Sher, Gloria Sher; d: Lee Theodore; md: David Baker & David Krane. Dancers: American Dance Machine (Steven Gelfer, Don Johanson, Patti Mariano, Joseph Pugliese, Liza Gennaro, Helena Andreyko, Louise Hickey, Derek Wolshonak, Janet Eilber, Zan Charisse), who danced selections from 15 Broadway musicals: Excerpt from *Gentlemen Prefer Blondes,* "Terrific Rainbow" (from *Pal Joey*), "Popularity" (from *George M*), "June is Bustin' Out All Over" (from *Carousel*), "Whip Dance" (from *Destry Rides Again*), "All Aboard for Broadway" (from *George M*), "Charleston" (from *The Boy Friend*), excerpts from *Shenandoah* & *Cabaret,* "Rich Kid's Rag" (from *Little Me*), "If the Rain's Gotta Fall" (from *Half a Sixpence*), "Satin Doll" (from TV), "Monte Carlo Crossover" & "Up Where the People Are" (from *The Unsinkable Molly Brown*), "Come to Me, Bend to Me" & "Funeral Dance" (from *Brigadoon*), "Quadrille" (from *Can-Can*), "You Can Dance with Any Girl at All" (from *No, No, Nanette*), "Clog Dance" (from *Walking Happy*). Then it toured all over USA. City Center, 2/4/86–2/16/86. 16 perf. md/orch: James Raitt. Cast: Dick Cavett (special guest host), Aja Major, Tinka Gutrick, Harold Cromer, Kelby Kirk. Several changes in the musical numbers

828. *American Enterprise.* Musical bio of robber-baron George Pullman. St. Clements, 4/13/94–4/23/94. 1 prev on 4/12. 15 perf. m/l/b: Jeffrey Sweet; d: Patricia Birch; md: Betsy Riley. Cast: John Romeo, Betsy Riley. "Shall We Plant a Tree?," "Porters on a Pullman Train," "Leave a Light," "It's a Trust," "The Columbian Exposition," "Maggie Murphy," "Step by Step," "The Pullman Strike"

829. *An American Family.* Play with mus. Set in Lower East Side, NYC, from about 1900 to the Great Depression. Theatre Four, 11/12/00–1/21/01. 7 prev. 64 perf. p: Folksbiene Yiddish Theatre; w: Miriam Kressyn; d: Eleanor Reissa; set: Vicki Davis; md: Zalmen Mlotek. Cast: Mina Bern

American Hamburger League see # 486.

830. *American Passion.* Joyce, 7/10/83. 42 prev. 1 perf. p: Stuart Ostrow; m/l: Willie Fong Young & Fred Burch; b: Fred Burch; d/ch: Patricia Birch; cos: William Ivey Long; sound: Otts Munderloh; md/orch: Timothy Graphenreed. Cast: Laura Dean, Don Kehr, Todd Graff, Taryn Grimes. "American Passion," "Romance is the Way," "There Ain't No Virgins in Queens," "Gospel According to Rock," "Limo to the Plaza," "Trashin' & Tourin'," "Loud Enough," "Concert Tonight," "Balcony of the Faithful," "Shirts," "In the Hallway," "We'll Sleep with the Radio On," "Hi," "I Light a Light"

831. *American Princess.* INTAR, 9/23/82–10/10/82. 15 perf. m/l: Jed Feuer & Leonard Orr; d: Jed Feuer; ch: Daniel Joseph Giagni; sound: T. Richard Fitzgerald. Cast: Merilee Magnuson, Mary Testa. "Hail Professor," "With That Hand," "Yes, I'm Here," "The Perfect Man," "Back to Me," "Wake Up Late," "Family Man," "You've Gone Too Far," "That Hand is Still," "Gotta Stop Her," "I Think"

832. *American Rhapsody: A New Musical Revue.* Triad, 11/10/00–5/27/01. Prev from 10/25/00. 231 perf. songs: George & Ira Gershwin; text/starred: KT Sullivan & Mark Nadler; d: Ruth Leon; ch: Donald Saddler

833. *Americana.* Revue highlighting 100 years of American mus. Theatre East, 9/18/96–1/26/97. 9 prev. 69 perf. w/arr: John A. Mezzano Jr; d: Sharon Hillegas

834. *America's Sweetheart.* Set in Hollywood. Broadhurst, Broadway, 2/10/31– 6/6/31. 135 perf. m: Richard Rodgers; l: Lorenz Hart; b: Herbert Fields; book d: Monty Woolley; set: Donald Oenslager; md: Alfred Goodman; orch: Russell Bennett. Cast: Jack Whiting, Gus Shy, Harriette Lake (i.e. Ann Sothern). "Mr. Dolan Is Passing Through," "In Californ-i-a," "My Sweet," "I've Got Five Dollars," "Sweet Geraldine," "There's So Much More," "We'll Be the Same," "How About It," "Innocent Chorus Girls of Yesterday," "A Lady Must Live," "You Ain't Got No Savoir Faire," "Two Unfortunate Orphans," "I Want a Man," "Tennessee Dan." Theatre Off Park. 12/10/95–12/11/95. 2 perf. 2nd in series of concert revivals of Rodgers & Hart musicals (*I Married an Angel* was 1st — see this appendix). Series ended with death of dir Albert Harris. mus restoration: James Stenborg. Cast: Ed Dixon, Jarrod Emick, Alison Fraser, Liz Larsen

835. *America's Sweetheart.* Set in the Al Capone days in Chicago. Hartford, Conn., 1985. p: Hartford Stage; m: Robert Waldman; l: Alfred Uhry; b: John Weidman & Alfred Uhry; based on John Kobler's bio *Capone*; d: Gerald Freedman; ch: Graciela Daniele; md: Liza Redfield. Cast: Stephen Vinovich, KT Sullivan, Nicholas Gunn, Tom Robbins, Donna English, K.K. Preece

836. *The Amorous Flea.* Musical version of Moliere's *School for Wives.* East 78th Street Playhouse, 2/27/64; The York, 3/20/64–5/10/64. Total of 93 perf. m/l: Bruce Montgomery; b: Jerry Devine; d: Jack Sydow; cos: Donald Brooks; orch: Lou Busch. Cast: Lew Parker, Imelda De Martin. "All About Me," "Learning Love," "There Goes a Mad Old Man," "Dialogue on Dalliance," "March of the Vigilant Vassals," "Lessons on Life," "Man Is a Man's Best Friend," "The Other Side of the Wall," "Closeness Begets Closeness," "It's a Stretchy Day," "When Time Takes Your Hand," "The Amorous Flea"

837. *Anansi and the Strawberry Queen.* Folk rock fairy tale musical about adventures of black & white allegorical characters. London, 1974. 19 perf. m/l: Ilona Sekacz & Manley Young. Cast: Eddie Grant, Paul Carter, Grace Hutchinson, Janet Wilson

The Anastasia Affair; The Anastasia Game see # 27.

838. *Anchorman.* Blues operetta. Theatre Four, 2/11/88–2/28/88. 20 perf. m: Julius Hemphill; w/d: Paul Carter Harrison. Cast: Giancarlo Esposito, Peter De Maio, Al Freeman Jr, Micki Grant

839. *And Another Thing.* Revue. Fortune, London, 10/6/60. 229 perf. p: Anna Deere Wiman & Charles Ross; m: Charles Zwar; l: Alan Melville; sk: Ted Dicks & Myles Rudge; add items: Lionel Bart, Barry Cryer, Robert Tanitch, Christopher Dandy; dev/d: Charles Ross; ch: Lionel Blair & Bob Stevenson. Cast: Bernard Cribbins, Anna Quayle, Lionel Blair, Donald Hewlett, Anton Rodgers, Joyce Blair. "Grouse re Strauss"

840. *And God Created Great Whales.* Musical theatre piece. Bessie Schonberg, 6/1/00–6/25/00. 9 prev. 13 perf; 45 Bleecker, 8/30/00–10/1/00. 30 perf. p: Foundry Theatre; m/w: Rinde Eckert; d: David Schweizer. Cast: Rinde Eckert, Nora Cole

841. *... And in This Corner.* Musical revue. Downstairs at the Upstairs, 2/12/64– 9/19/64. 410 perf. p/conceived by: Michael McWhinney & Rod Warren; d: Jonathan Lucas. Cast: Bill Brown, Marian Mercer, Virgil Curry, Carol Morley

842. *And So to Bed.* Comedy with mus. Royal Court, Liverpool, England, 8/20/51; toured; New Theatre, London, 10/17/51; Strand, 12/10/51–7/26/52. Total of 323 perf. p: Jack De Leon; m/l: Vivian Ellis; from 1926 comedy by J.B. Fagan (in which Yvonne Arnaud played Mrs. Pepys); d/ch: Wendy Toye; set: Stanley Moore; md: Mantovani. Cast: Samuel Pepys: Leslie Henson; King Charles II: Keith Michell; Also with: Betty Paul, Eileen Way, Denis Quilley, Jessie Royce Landis, Gwen Nelson, Dilys Lay (later Dilys Laye). "Ayre and Fa-La," "A Chine of Beef," "Beauty Retire," "Rigaudon," "Gaze Not on Swans," "Love Me Little, Love Me Long," "Amo, Amas," "Sarabande," "And So to Bed," "Moppety Mo," "Catch," "Bartholomew Fair." The straight play had run on Broadway in 1927, and was not revived in NY until 1975, at Stage 73

And the World Goes 'Round see # 2810, this appendix.

843. *Androcles and the Lion.* Greek tailor

befriends lion. York Theatre Co., 4/12/02–1/14/02. Part of *Musicals in Mufti* series. m/l: Richard Rodgers; b: Peter Stone; from Shaw's play

844. *Andy Capp*. Royal Exchange, Manchester, England, 6/29/82–8/21/82; Aldwych, London, 9/28/82–1/22/83. 3 prev. 99 perf. m: Alan Price; l: Alan Price & Trevor Peacock; b: Trevor Peacock; based on Reg Smythe's *Daily Mirror* cartoon strip; d: Braham Murray; ch: Sue Lefton; md: Michael Dixon. Cast: Tom Courtenay, Alan Price, Val McLane, John Bardon, Stanley Fleet, Vivienne Ross, Eve Matheson (*Fiona Mathieson*). "On My Street," "We're Waiting," "Good Evening," "I Ought to Be Ashamed of Myself," "Good Old Legs," "I Have a Dream," "Oh, Gawd, Men…Beasts," "Points of View," "Spend! Spend! Spend!," "Don't Tell Me That Again," "Frozen Moments," "I Could Not Have Dreamed Him," "Goin' to Barcelona," "Hermione," "When You've Lived in Love with Someone," "Mr. Scrimmett," "The Trouble with People," "It's Better to Be in Simple Harmony," "The Wedding"

845. *Angel Levine*. Jewish Rep, 5/6/95–5/28/95. 24 perf. m/l/b: Phyllis K. Robinson; from Bernard Malamud's story; d: Peter Bennett; ch: Hope Clarke; light: Spencer Mosse. Cast: Michael Ingram, Jordan Leeds, Marilyn Sokol, Andre De Shields, Tina Fabrique, Reggie Phoenix. "The Name Is Levine," "Come Spring," "Black Is the Color of Night," "It's a Gift," "Only Believe," "Can It Happen," "Nobody Believes in Me," "You Can't Sing the Blues When You Tango," "Something to Live For," "I'm Only Human," "Hand Song," "Come to the Wild Side," "God Made the Grass Be Green," "Making a Living"

846. *Angelina's Pizzeria*. Theatre for the New City, 5/14/92–5/31/92. 12 perf. w: Eddie Di Donna, Crystal Field, T. Scott Lilly, Mark Marcante, Michael Vazquez; d: Mark Marcante. Cast: the writers (but not Mr. Di Donna)

847. *Angry Housewives*. Discontented wives conspire to form rock band. Minetta Lane, 9/7/86–1/3/87. 15 prev. 137 perf. p: M Square Entertainment, Mitchell Maxwell, Alan J. Schuster, Marvin R. Meit, Alice Field; m/l: Chad Henry; b: A.M. Collins; d: Mitchell Maxwell; ch: Wayne Cilento; set: David Jenkins; sound: Otts Munderloh; md: Jonny Bowden; add arr: Mark Hummel. Cast: Vicki Lewis, Michael Manasseri, Carolyn Casanave, Camille Saviola, Nicholas Wyman, Lee Wilkof, Mary Munger, Lorna Patterson, Michael Lembeck. "Think Positive," "It's Gonna Be Fun," "Generic Woman," "Not at Home," "First Kid on the Block." Previously ran at Pioneer Square, Seattle, and Organic Theatre, Chicago

848. *Animal Farm*. England, 1984. w: Richard Peaslee & Adrian Mitchell; adapted by/d: Peter Hall; from George Orwell's novel. Revised in 2000. Ran in USA in 2002. Cast: Melota Marshall, Aaron Hendry

849. *Ann Reinking…Music Moves Me*. Musical revue. Joyce, 12/23/84–1/6/85. 3 prev. 17 perf. p: Lee Gross Assocs; orig material/ms: Larry Grossman; d/ch: Alan Johnson; light: Ken Billington; md: Ronald Melrose; orch: Joseph Gianono, Michael Gibson, Harold Wheeler. Cast: Ann Reinking, Gary Chryst, Reed Jones, Michael Kubala, Sara Miles, Christina Saffran, Rob Marshall. "Another Mr. Right," "Anything Goes," "Ballin' the Jack," "Higher and Higher," "Hit Me with a Hot Note," "I Can't Turn You Loose," "If Love Were All," "Isn't It Romantic," "Just Once," "Moonlight Sonata," "Music Moves Me," "Nowhere to Run," "Oh, Baby, Won't You Please Come Home," "Rescue Me," "Satin Doll," "Sing, Sing, Sing," "Stompin' at the Savoy," "Tea for Two," "Unchained Melody," "Why Not?," "Wild Women," "You and Me"

850. *Ann Veronica*. Belgrade Theatre, Coventry, England, 2/6/69–3/1/69; toured; the Cambridge, London, 4/17/69–5/24/69. 44 perf. m: Cyril Ornadel; l/d: David Croft; b: Frank Wells & Ronald Gow; from H.G. Wells's novel about suffragettes; ch: Alfred Rodrigues; set/cos: Peter Rice; md: Grant Hossack; cast recording on CBS. Cast: Dorothy Tutin (title role-replaced before London by *Mary Millar*), Peter Reeves, Hy Hazell, Mary Millar (*Janet Mahoney*), Charles West, Arthur Lowe, Jacquie Toye, Joan Cooper, Ian Lavender, John Inman (as a waiter). "A Whole Person," "I Don't See What Else I Could Have Said," "Maternity," "Opportunity," "Sweep Me Off My Feet," "Ann Veronica," "One Man's Love," "Chemical Attraction," "I Couldn't Do a Thing Like That," "Why Can't I Go to Him?," "They Can't Keep Us Down," "Stand in Line," "Home Sweet Home," "Glad to Have You Back," "If I Should Lose You," "You're a Good Man," "Too Much Meat"

851. *Anne of Green Gables*. Orphan girl grows up in tiny village of Avonlea, PEI, at turn of 20th century. City Center, 12/21/71–1/2/72. 16 perf. m: Norman Campbell; l: Donald Harron & Norman Campbell; add l: Mavor Moore & Elaine Campbell; adapted by Donald Harron from L.M. Montgomery's novel; d/ch: Alan Lund; md/orch: John Fenwick. Cast: Gracie Finley, Kathryn Watt, Lloyd Malenfant, Jack Northmore, Bill Hosie, George Merner, Elizabeth Mawson, Peter Mews, Roma Hearn, Glenda Landry, Sharlene McLean, Barbara Barsky, Patti Toms, Lynn Marsh, Deborah Miller, Jeff Hyslop, George Juriga, Dan Costain, Andre Denis, John Powell, Calvin McRea. "Great Workers for the Cause," "Where Is Matthew Going?," "Gee, I'm Glad I'm No One Else (but Me)," "We Clearly Requested," "The Facts," "Where'd Marilla Come From?," "Humble Pie," "Oh, Mrs. Lynde!," "Back to School Ballet," "Avonlea We Love Thee," "Wondrin'," "Did You Hear?," "Ice Cream," "The Picnic," "Where Did the Summer Go To?," "Kindred Spirits," "Open the Window!," "The Words," "Nature Hunt Ballet," "I'll Show Him," "General Store," "Pageant Song," "If It Hadn't Been for Me," "Anne of Green Gables." Originally produced by Canadian National Musical Theatre, at Charlottetown, PEI, 7/65. A hit in Canada & London (where it opened at New Theatre, 4/16/69, and starred Hiram Sherman & Polly James)

852. *Annie*. Unrelated to *Little Orphan Annie* or the Broadway musical. Westminster Theatre, London, 7/27/67–12/9/67. 156 perf; re-ran there 2/1/68–8/31/68. 242 perf. m: William L. Reed; l/b: Alan Thornhill; d: Henry Cass; ch: Denny Bettis. Cast: Annie: Margaret Burton; Also with: Denny Bettis, Angela Richards, Gerard Hely, Bill Kenwright. "Our Town," "Annie," "Right for You," "Remember, Bill," "Ribbons and Such," "Walking Out," "My Cousin in London," "I Don't Like Your Hat," "It Fair Takes Your Breath Away," "Knock, Knock, Knock," "Good Morning," "I Keeps Myself to Myself," "A Cup of You and Me," "Who's the Dictator, Jim Parks?," "We're Going to Shake the Country," "Betwixt and Between," "Open Your Heart," "Sheep! Sheep!—Come the Day," "The Appeasement Parade," "Mending Things," "A Basinful of Revolution"

853. *Anonymous*. Set in Rome & NY. AMAS, 10/25/84–11/18/84. 16 perf. w/d: Vincenzo Stornaiuolo; add English l/md: Jack Everly; ch: Gui Andrisano. Cast: Dirk Lumbard, Tug Wilson. "Anonymous"

854. *Another Evening with Harry Stoones*. A Jeff Harris revue. Gramercy Arts Theatre, 10/21/61. 1 perf. md: Abba Bogin. Cast: Diana Sands, Dom De Luise, Barbra Streisand (her NY debut)

855. *ANTA Album*. Series of benefits mounted by the American National Theatre and Academy (ANTA). Began in 1947. Ended in the mid 50s. There was a master (or mistress) of ceremonies, and sketches & songs, all relevant in some way to the past Broadway season

856. *Antiques*. Variations on theme of the generation gap. Mercer O'Casey, 6/19/73–6/24/73. 8 perf. m/l: Alan Greene & Laura Manning; special material: Dore Schary; d: Mario Martone; ch: Jeffrey K. Neill. Cast: Charles Hudson, Laura Manning, Richard Marr, Betty Oakes, Molly Stark, Eugene Smith, Ward Smith. "Antiques," "The Pill," "They Don't Write Songs Like That Any More," "Rent-a-Grandma," "To Love Again," "Papa Bird," "Don't Grow Old Gracefully," "Bridges," "Grandma's Diary," "The Hey Ma, You Were Right Cantata," "The Red Kimono," "Oh, What a Time We Had," "We Got Married," "Look Underneath," "Love Is Everything," "Conversations," "Victims of the Past," "Solutions." Previously produced on cable TV

857. *Any Minute Now*. About nuclear arms proliferation. Scotland, 1982. m/l: David MacLennan & David Anderson. Theatre Royal, Stratford East, London, 1/26/83–2/12/84. p: Wildcat Stage Prods

858. *Anything Cole*. Musical revue of Cole Porter songs. Harold Clurman, 2/17/93–3/7/93. 20 perf. d: Tom Klebba; ch: Lynnette Barkley; md: Robert A. Berman. Cast: Elizabeth Green, David Lowenstein, Wendy Oliver, Jane Wasser

859. *Ape Over Broadway*. A new gorilla musical, set in NYC & in Deepest, Darkest Africa. Bert Wheeler, 3/12/75–3/23/75. 11 perf. m/l: Stephen Ross & Bill Vitale; b: Mary McCartney & Bart Andrews; from orig idea & story by Andrew Herz; d/ch: Jeffrey K. Neill. Cast: Norb Joerder, Jim Cyrus, Barbara Coggin, Curt Ralston, Robert Lydiard, Freyda-Ann Thomas, Jacqueline Reilly, Robert Calvert,

Phyllis Ward. "Nude-Lewd," "The Star Number," "Broadway," "I've Had Everything But a Man," "The Man-Eating Ape Waltz," "Saga of Men and Marriage," "An Ape Can Save the World," "Mixed-Up Media," "I'm in Like with You," "Flamingo Fuss," "Triangle Song," "Just Whistle," "My Friend," "Ape Over Broadway"

860. *Apple Pie.* Woman hounded out of Nazi Germany only to be degraded by American anti-feminist attitudes & actions. Anspacher, 1/27/76–3/21/76. 72 perf. p: NY Shakespeare Festival; m/l: Nicholas Myers; b: Myrna Lamb; d: Joseph Papp; movement: Lynne Weber; set: David Mitchell; light: Pat Collins; md: Liza Redfield. Cast: Stephanie Cotsirilos, Lucille Patton, Spain Logue, Robert Guillaume (*Alan Weeks*), Joseph Neal, Lee Allen, Robert Polenz. "Yesterday is Over," "I'm Lise," "Waltz of Lise's Childhood," "Father's Waltz," "Men Come with Guns," "Hundsvieh," "Mother's March," "The Trial," "Marshall's Blues," "The Counterman," "America—We're in New York," "The Victim Dream," "The Stockboy Blues," "The Too Much Motet," "The Mating Dance," "Love Scene," "The Doctor," "Lise Dear," "The Wedding," "Gun Scene," "Harry's Rag," "Freedom Anthem," "Reified Expression," "Yesterday Is Over" (reprise), "Break-up Rag," "Marshall's Reply," "Survival Song," "Final Judgment"

861. *Applemando's Dreams.* One-act family opera set in middle of nowhere. Little boy uses dreams to create colorful images to brighten his world. Vineyard, 12/26/94–12/31/94. 12 afternoon perf. m: James Kurtz; b: Barbara Zinn Krieger; from book by Patricia Polacco; d/ch: Lisa Brailoff; cos: David Brooks. Cast: Joey Hannon, Jackie Angelescu. Tribeca Performing Arts Center (who produced, with the Vineyard Theatre), 3/18/00–4/2/00. 2 prev from 3/11/01. 6 perf. d/ch: John Ruocco. Cast: Reed Van Dyk, J.T. Cromwell

862. *April Song.* Stock tryouts. 1980. m/l: Mitch Leigh; d: Albert Marre. Cast: Glynis Johns

863. *Arabian Nights.* Jones Beach, 1954 (2 seasons). m/l: Carmen Lombardo & John Jacob Loeb; ch: Rod Alexander. Cast: Lauritz Melchior, William Chapman, Helena Scott. "What a Party," "It's Great to Be Alive," "A Thousand and One Nights," "The Hero of All My Dreams," "A Whale of a Story," "Marry the One You Love," "How Long Has It Been?," "Teeny Weeny Genie." Same venue, 7/2/67–9/3/67. 63 perf. p: Guy Lombardo; ch: Yurek Lazowski. Cast: Lee Cass, Judy Knaiz, Linda Bennett, Robert LuPone

864. *Arc de Triomphe.* Play with mus. 20 years in life of French opera singer. Phoenix, London, 11/9/43–5/20/44. 222 perf. p: Tom Arnold & Ivor Novello; m/b: Ivor Novello; l: Christopher Hassall & Ivor Novello; d: Leontine Sagan; ch: Keith Lester; set: Joseph Carl; cos: Cecil Beaton, etc; md: Harry Acres. Cast: Mary Ellis, Raymond Lovell, Peter Graves, Elisabeth Welch, Harcourt Williams, Gwen Floyd, Netta Westcott. "Shepherd Song," "Man of My Heart," "Easy to Live With," "I Wonder Why," "Apache Ballet," "Josephine," "Waking or Sleeping," "Royal France," "Paris Re-

minds Me of You," "Dark Music," "The Phantom Court," "Vision Duet," "Jeanne d'Arc" (opera sequence incorporating "France Will Rise Again")

865. *archy and friends.* Set in newspaper office. Asolo State Theatre, Fla., 8/6/78. 15 perf. m/l: John Franceschina; conceived by/d/ch: Jim Hoskins; set: Jeff Dean. Cast: Evan S. Perry (Don Marquis), Don Fahrer (archy), Janet Nawrocki (mehitabel), James St. Clair (bill, the rogue tomcat), Jeff King (hoarse, the theatre cat)

archy and mehitabel see # 627.

866. *archy & mehitabel.* Town Hall, 3/11/96. 1 perf. d: Kirsten Sanderson; ch: Michael Lichtefeld; md: Albin Konopka & James Stenborg. Cast: archy: Lee Wilkof; mehitabel: Taylor Dayne; big bill: Timothy Warmen; tyrone: Bill Buell. "What Do We Care?," "Toujours Gai," "Queer Little Insect," "Bragging Flea," "Trio," "My Real Romance," "Lightning Bug Song," "Flotsam and Jetsam," "Come to Me-Ow," "Suicide Song," "Actor Cat," "Romeo and Juliet," "A Woman Wouldn't Be a Woman," "Lullaby," "The Rescue," "Pretty Kitty," "The Way She Used to Be," "Roun' in a Circle," "Ladybug Song," "Song of the Moth"

867. *Are You Lonesome Tonight?* Tribute to Elvis. Phoenix, London, 7/13/85. m/l: various authors; b: Alan Bleasdale. Cast: Martin Shaw, Simon Bowman, Stacey Zuckerman

868. *Area 51.* Sci-fi musical, set in secret lab beneath Nevada desert. Sanford Meisner, 3/2/00–3/25/00. 16 perf. m/l: Noel Katz; d/ch: Gary Slavin; md: Jono Mainelli

869. *Around the World in 80 Days.* Summer musical spectacle, not related to Broadway show of same name. Jones Beach, 6/22/63. p: Guy Lombardo; m: Sammy Fain; l: Harold Adamson; b: Sig Herzig; from Jules Verne novel; d/ch: June Taylor. Cast: Fogg: Fritz Weaver; Fix: Dom De Luise; Passepartout: Robert Clary; Dancing Ensemble included: Kathryn Doby. "March of the Grenadiers," "Long Live the English Scene," "Have You Heard About Phileas Fogg?," "Hide Your Sister," "I'm a Sleuth," "Sidewalks of Paris," "I Hate to Travel," "Sky Symphony," "Fiesta in Spain," "Are We Talking About the Same Thing," "Lloyds of London," "His Little World," "One-Woman Man," "Once I Wondered," "Dance of Sacrifice," "Around the World," "Hong Kong," "Barbary Coast," "Carry On," "Way Out West," "Indian Raid," "I Love to Travel," "Burning of the *Henrietta*." Same venue, 6/27/64– 9/6/64. 70 perf. Cast: David Atkinson, Dom De Luise, Robert Clary, Mercedes Ellington, Bob Bernard, Fernando Grahal

870. *The Art of Living.* Anglo-American intimate revue. Criterion, London, 8/18/60. 197 perf. p: Oscar Lewenstein & Wolf Mankowitz; m: Monty Norman & David Heneker; l/sk: Monty Norman, David Heneker, Julian More; add sk: Johnny Speight; from writings of Art Buchwald; dev/d: Laurier Lister; ch: George Baron. Cast: Hiram Sherman, Carole Shelley, Graham Stark, Edward Woodward, Judy Bruce. "Neapolitan Nostalgia"

871. *Arthur: The Musical.* Musical of the Dudley Moore film (screenplay by Steve Gordon). Goodspeed, 1992. m: Michael Skloff; l/b: David Krane & Marta Kauffman; d: Joseph Billone; ch: Tony Stevens; md: Tim Stella. Cast: Greg Edelman, Michael Allison, Carolee Carmello, David Cryer, Jane Kean, Leslie Feagan. "A Child Is Born," "Hold That Thought," "We'll Get Through This," "Love in Bergdorf Goodman," "Really Great Mood," "Carried Away," "Coney Island," "Memory of Tonight," "I Love a Romance," "You Can't Have Everything," "Magical Night," "What I Never Knew," "Champagne," "Can I Live Without the Man," "A Job I Highly Recommend," "What Am I Doing Here?," "One More Day," "Try to Remember It All"

872. *Asinumali!* South African play (not a musical). 5 men thrown into Leeuwkop Prison, outside Johannesburg, during 1983 rent strike. Jack Lawrence, Broadway, 4/23/87–5/17/87. 9 prev. 29 perf. w/d: Mbongeni Ngema (nominated for a Tony for direction of a play). Involved in its NY presentation were Paul Simon, Miriam Makeba, Harry Belafonte, Hamilton Fish III. The title is Zulu for "We have no money." Cast: Solomzi Bhisholo, Thami Cele, Bongani Hlophe, Bheki Mqadi, Bhoyi Ngema. Produced previously, at the Mitzi Newhouse, 9/10/86–9/14/86. 9 perf

873. *At the Drop of a Hat.* Intimate 2-character revue ("an after-dinner farrago"). New Lindsey Theatre, Notting Hill, London, 12/31/56. 26 perf. A hit. Fortune, London, 1/24/57. 733 perf. Cast: Michael Flanders & Donald Swann (who also wrote most of m/l). "Song of Reproduction," "The Hog Beneath the Skin" (The Warthog), "A Transport of Delight," "Youth of the Heart" (l: Sydney Carter), "Greensleeves," "The Wompom," "Sea Fever," "A Gnu" (The Gnu Song), "Judgment of Paris," "A Song of the Weather," "The Reluctant Cannibal," "In the Bath," "Design for Living," "Tried by the Centre Court," "Misalliance," "Kokoraki" (A Greek Song), "Madeira, M'Dear?," "The Hippopotamus" (The Hippopotamus Song, or "Mud, Mud, Glorious Mud"). John Golden, Broadway, 10/8/59–5/14/60. 216 perf. p: Alexander H. Cohen & Joseph I. Levine. Generally great reviews. Tour opened 10/26/60, at the Playhouse, Wilmington, Del. Closed 3/11/61, at the O'Keefe, Toronto. A sequel, *At the Drop of Another Hat*, ran at the Booth, Broadway, 12/27/66–4/9/67. 1 prev on 12/26/66. 104 perf. Flanders & Swann again. "The Gas Man Cometh," "From Our Bestiary," "Bilbo's Song," "Slow Train," "Thermodynamic Duo," "Sloth," "More Songs for Our Time," "In the Desert," "Los Olvidados," "Motor Perpetuo," "A Song of Patriotic Prejudice," "All Gall," "Horoscope," "Armadillo Idyll," "Twenty Tons of TNT," "Ill Wind," "Food for Thought," "Prehistoric Complaint," "Twice Shy"

At the Grand see # 264.

874. *At the Lyric.* Lyric, Hammersmith, London, 12/23/53. m: Kenneth Leslie-Smith, Charles Zwar, Donald Swann; l: Alan Melville & Paul Dehn; d/cos: William Chappell. Cast: Hermione Baddeley, Dora Bryan, Eric Berry,

Ian Carmichael, Rachel Roberts, Myles Eason, Shirley Eaton, Vivienne Martin

875. *At Wit's End*. Irreverent one-man musical evening based on the 3 autobiographies of Oscar Levant (*A Smattering of Ignorance*, *The Unimportance of Being Oscar*, and *Memoirs of an Amnesiac*). Michael's Pub, 10/8/91–11/2/91. 1 prev. 27 perf. p: Lawrence Kasha, Ronald A. Lachman, Warner/Chappell Music Group, in co-operation with June Levant; w: Joel Kimmel; d: Barbara Karp. Cast: Oscar: Stan Freeman. Previously presented in extensive tour

876. *At Wit's End*. Set in 1929. About the wits of the Algonquin Round Table & the founding of the *New Yorker* magazine. Dorothy Parker, Tallulah Bankhead, George S. Kaufman & Edna Ferber perform a play in the Algonquin Hotel's lobby to commemorate 10th anniversary of their 1st luncheon there. Florida Stage, 2001. m: Michael Duff; l/b: Cheri Coons. Northlight, Skokie, Ill., 5/21/03–6/22/03. Prev from 5/14/03. d: Joe Leonardo; ch: Marla Lampert. Cast: Dorothy: Sara Davis; Harold Ross: Sean Fortunato; Alexander Woollcott: Blake Hammond; Robert Benchley: George Keating; Edna Ferber: Iris Lieberman; Jane Grant: Susie McGonagle; Tallulah: Carrie McNulty; Helen Hanes: Marci Medwed; George: Jason Sperling; Marc Connelly: Stephen Wallem

877. *The Athenian Touch*. Courtesan in love with Socrates in Athens. Jan Hus, 1/14/64. 1 perf. m/l: Willard Straight & David Eddy; b: Arthur Goodman; d/ch: Alex Palermo. Cast: Butterfly McQueen, Marion Marlowe, Will Richter. "There Goes Time," "The Singer and the Song," "What is a Woman?," "Look Away," "All We Need to Know"

878. *Atomic Opera*. Music theatre piece tracing evolution of Atomic Age. Ohio Theatre, 10/25/91–11/3/91. 10 perf. created by: Kevin Malony, Michele Elliman, John O'Malley; d: Kevin Malony (d). Cast: Michele Elliman, John O'Malley

879. *Autumn's Here*. Set in Sleepy Hollow, NY, in 1819. Schoolmaster Ichabod Crane, his rivalry with Brom Bones for the hand of Katrina Van Tassel, and his disappearance after his encounter with the legendary, fearful Headless Horseman. Bert Wheeler, 10/25/66–12/31/66. 80 perf. p: Bob Hadley; m/l/b: Norman Dean; from *The Legend of Sleepy Hollow*, by Washington Irving; d/ch: Hal Le Roy. Cast: Bob Riehl, Fred Gockel, Karin Wolfe, John Johann. "Sleepy Hollow," "Boy, Do I Hate Horse Races," "Me and My Horse," "Autumn's Here," "Song of the Thirteen Colonies," "Patience," "For the Harvest Safely Gathered," "Who Walks Like a Scarecrow," "This Is the Girl for Me," "Do You Think I'm Pretty?," "Fine Words and Fancy Phrases," "Private Hunting Ground," "It's a Long Road Home," "Brom and Katrina," "Dark New England Night," "Dutch Country Table," "You Never Miss the Water," "Any Day Now," "You May Be the Someone," "Beware as You Ride Through the Hollow," "The Chase"

880. *Avenue X*. An a cappella musical. Set in Brooklyn in 1963. The Studio, 6/3/93–6/13/93. 14 perf. m/l: Ray Leslee; d: Mark Brokaw; set: Loy Arcenas; md: Chapman Roberts. Cast: Ellis E. Williams. "Where is Love?," "A Thousand Summer Nights," "Serves You Right," "Woman of the World," "She's Fifteen," "Stay with Me, Baby," "Where Are You Tonight?," "Why," "Follow Me," "Moonlight in Old Sicily," "Till the End of Time." Playwrights Horizons, 1/28/94– 4/3/94. 77 perf. Cast: Chuck Cooper, Alvaleta Guess, Roger Mazzeo

881. *Awf'lly Nice*. Musical revue. Broadway tryouts at Shubert, New Haven, 9/7/64–9/12/64. Never made Broadway. m/l: Frank Stuart & Tom McKee; sk: Frank Orefice. Cast: Marie Wilson, Julie Gibson, Joan Dexter, Bhaskar

882. *Babalooney*. Musical revue. Visiting troupe from Evanston, Ill. presented comic & musical numbers. Provincetown Playhouse, 2/15/84–3/4/84. 24 perf. p: Practical Theatre Co.; orig m: Larry Schanker & Practical Theatre Co.; d: Brad Hall

883. *Babes in Arms*. Shubert Theatre, Broadway, 4/14/27–10/23/37. Majestic Theatre, Broadway, 10/25/37–12/18/37. Total of 289 perf. m: Richard Rodgers; l: Lorenz Hart; b: Rodgers & Hart; d: Robert Sinclair; ch: George Balanchine. Cast: Mitzi Green, Alfred Drake (in his Broadway debut, playing Marshall Blackstone), the Nicholas Brothers (i.e. Fayard & Harold Nicholas), Wynn Murray. Chorus: Dan Dailey (Broadway debut), Robert Rounseville. "Where or When," "Babes in Arms" (sung by Alfred Drake), "I Wish I Were in Love Again," "All Dark People," "Way Out West," "My Funny Valentine," "Johnny One Note," "Imagine," "All at Once," "The Lady is a Tramp," "You Are So Fair." Filmed in 1939, with Judy Garland & Mickey Rooney. NY revival, OB, 1950–51. From the late 1950s a new libretto by George Oppenheimer became standard stock prod version, sanitized, cutting racial & other controversial issues. In 1985 this version aimed at (but failed to get to) Broadway. Tried out at Music Hall, Tarrytown, NY, 6/26/85–8/9/85. d: Ginger Rogers; ch: Randall Skinner; md/orch: Bruce Pomahac. "Manhattan" & "Mountain Greenery" were added. Cast: Randy Skinner, Karen Ziemba, James Brennan, Michele Franks, Donna Theodore, Joy Hodges, Kim Morgan. Revived in 1989 in concert at Lincoln Center/Avery Fisher Hall to benefit Starlight Foundation. p/conductor: Evans Haile; b: George Oppenheimer; adapted: Tommy Krasker; d: Sarah Louise Lazarus; ch: Charles Repole. Cast: Judy Blazer, Gregg Edelman, Jason Graae, Donna Kane, Judy Kaye, Anita Morris, Philip Bosco. Repeated 2/17/90, at State Theatre, New Brunswick, NJ, with Jim Walton replacing Mr. Edelman & Olympia Dukakis as host replacing Anita Morris & Phil Bosco. The new prod ran in 1993 at St. Peters Theatre. d: Christopher Catt; ch: Jeff Peters. Cast: Mark Modano, Melissa Broder, Lizzie Yawitz. John Guare did concert adaptation for *Encores!* series at City Center, 2/11/99–2/14/99. 5 perf. d/ch: Kathleen Marshall; set: John Lee Beatty; cos: Toni-Leslie James; light: Peter Kaczorowski; md: Rob Fisher; cast recording on DRG. Cast: Priscilla Lopez, Thommie Walsh, Perry Laylon Ojeda, Donna McKechnie, Don Correia, Erin Dilly, Jessica Stone, Kevin Cahoon, Matt McGrath, Michael McCormick. Goodspeed did revised version, 8/2/02–10/5/02. Prev from 7/12/02. It had a new (tougher) book by Joe DiPietro. d: Greg Ganakas; ch: Randy Skinner. Cast: Leslie Kritzer, Kenneth Kantor, Rena Strober, Bradford Anderson, Marie Lillo (playing a new character, Mabel Lancaster). "Blue Moon" (not written for any particular musical show) was interpolated. In 11/02 Randy Skinner was to have directed John Guare's version at Kennedy Center, but it was called off. Freud Playhouse, UCLA, Calif. 9/10/03–9/21/03. Prev from 9/9/03. Part of *Reprise!* series. d: Glenn Casale; ch: Dan Mojica; md: Gerald Sternbach. Cast: Joey McIntyre & Jodi Benson (Neil Patrick Harris & Rachel York were going to star)

884. *Babes in the Wood*. Orpheum, 12/28/64–2/7/65. 45 perf. w/d: Rick Besoyan; based on *A Midsummer Night's Dream;* ch: Ralph Beaumont; set/light: Paul Morrison. Cast: Ruth Buzzi, Danny Carroll, Carol Glade, Elmarie Wendel, Kenneth McMillan. "This State of Affairs," "A Lover Waits," "I'm Not for You," "Old Fashioned Girl," "Love Is Lovely," "Babes in the Wood," "Anyone Can Make a Mistake," "There's a Girl," "Little Tear," "Helena," "Midsummer Night," "Moon Madness," "The Alphabet Song"

885. *Babes in the Wood*. Pantomime. Palladium, London, 12/21/65. m/l: The Shadows; b: David Croft; cast recording on Columbia. Cast: Mike Sammes Singers, Frank Ifield, Angie Millar, Eddie Lester. "The King's Theme," "Robbers' Song," "I Only Want to Be with You," "Down with Tyranny," "We Hate School," "My Love," "Marion's Song to the Babes," "Don't Be Afraid," "Nottingham Fair," "There'll Be Another Spring," "We're Gonna Find 'Em," "Lincoln Green," "Then Came She," "The Tick Tock Song"

886. *Babes in Toyland*. Majestic, Broadway, 10/13/1903. 192 perf. m: Victor Herbert; l/b: Glen MacDonough. Jolson's 59th Street Theatre, 12/23/29–1/11/30. 32 perf. d: Milton Aborn; md: Louis Kroll. Cast: Barry Lupino. Imperial, 12/20/30–1/10/31. 33 perf. d: Milton Aborn. Cast: Ruth Gillette. "It's Fun to Feel We're Young," "It's Toyland," "Slumber Song," "Toyland, Toyland," "Toymaker's Song," "Your Heart is Where You Are," "Zim-Zam-Zumble," "March of the Toys." An entirely new version was written by William Mount-Burke of the Light Opera of Manhattan, with Alice Hammerstein Mathias. 11/29/78–1/21/79. p: LOOM; d/md: William Mount-Burke; set: Jerry Gotham; light: Peggy Clark. Cast: Jeanne Beauvais, Julio Rosario, Georgia McEver. Another new adaptation was written by Ellis Weiner, based on an orig idea by Barry Weissler, and called *The Babes in Toyland* (i.e. with a definite article). Felt Forum, 12/21/79–1/1/80. 16 perf. p: Barry & Fran Weissler; new m & l: Shelly Markham & Annette Leisten; d: Munson Hicks; ch: Tony Stevens; set/cos: Michael J. Hotopp & Paul de Pass; puppets: Sid & Marty Krofft; orchestral arr: Kirk Nurock. Cast: Mark Holleran, Roger Lawson,

Michael Calkins, Debbie McLeod, Edward T. Jacobs. "Big Baby," "It's a Sweet Life," "Something Must Be Done," "Don't Cry, Bo Peep," "Bare Facts," "Step Out in Front," "Dream Toyland," "The Two of Us," "The March of the Wooden Soldiers"

887. *Back Country*. Set in 1894 in rustic tavern near Hays, Kansas. Closed on the Road. Cohoes Music Hall, Cohoes, NY, 8/15/78; Wilbur, Boston, 9/8/78–9/24/78; never made Broadway. p: Eugene V. Wolsk & Harvey Granat; m: Stanley Walden; l/b: Jacques Levy; based on 1907 play *Playboy of the Western World*, by J.M. Synge; d: Jacques Levy; ch: Margo Sappington; set: Peter Larkin; light: Neil Peter Jampolis; md: Susan Romann. Cast: Ken Marshall, Suzanne Lederer, Harry Groener, Stuart Germain, Barbara Andres, Rex Everhart, Terri Treas, Pamela Pilkenton. "Mother of Spring," "Little Girl Again," "Child of the Devil," "Mr. Moon and Lady Fire," "Heaven on My Mind," "Hay Pitchin'," "The Western Slope," "All the Men in My Life," "Diamond Jim Brady," "The Fiddler's Tune," "As a Boy," "Too Much Pain," "As a Girl," "Old Man," "Through the Shadows"

888. *Back in My Life*. Revue of songs of Nancy Ford & Gretchen Cryer. Stage Left, 4/10/89–4/22/89. 13 perf. Cast: Gretchen & Robin Cryer

889. *Back on the Boulevard*. Musical revue. Kaufman, 9/6/96–9/29/96. 6 prev. 19 perf. p: Lucille Lortel; set: Michael Anania; light: F. Mitchell Dana; md: Dick Gallagher. Cast: Liliane Montevecchi

890. *Back to Bacharach and David*. Musical revue showcasing hits of Burt Bacharach & Hal David. Club 53, 3/25/93–5/25/93. Prev from 3/11/93. 69 perf. d: Kathy Najimy. Cast: Melinda Gilb, Steve Gunderson (also conceived/arr), Sue Mosher, Lillias White. "A House is Not a Home," "Alfie," "Always Something There to Remind Me," "Anyone Who Had a Heart," "Close to You," "Do You Know the Way to San Jose," "I'll Never Fall in Love Again," "Just Don't Know What to Do with Myself," "Message to Michael," "Promises Promises," "This Guy's in Love with You," "Trains and Boats and Planes," "24 Hours from Tulsa," "Walk on By," "What the World Needs Now"

891. *A Backers' Audition*. Set in living room of wealthy Park Avenue angel who is producing her 1st Broadway show. Manhattan Theatre Club Upstage, 12/13/83–1/29/84. 48 perf. w: Douglas Bernstein & Denis Markell; idea/d: Martin Charnin; ch: Janie Sell. Cast: Barbara Barrie, Douglas Bernstein, Mary D'Arcy, Scott Robertson. Manhattan Theatre Club, 3/26/85–3/31/85. 8 perf. d: Daniel Gerroll. Cast: Mary Ann Dorward, Nathan Lane, Beau Gravitte, John Horton, Phyllis Newman, Scott Robertson, William Roy (also md), Claudette Sutherland. American Jewish Theatre, 11/21/92–12/20/92. 31 perf. d: Leonard Foglia. Cast: Sheila Smith, Tom Ligon, Gretchen Kingsley

892. *Bagels and Yox*. American-Yiddish revue. Bagels were given to the audience in intermission. Holiday Theatre, 9/12/51–

2/12/52. 204 perf. p: Al Beckman, John Pransky, Brandt Theatres; m/l: Sholom Secunda & Hy Jacobson; add l: Millie Alpert; light: Bruno Maine; md: Irv Carroll; mus arr: Jerome Goldstein; piano: Curt Bell. Cast: Larry Alpert, Lou Saxon, the Barton Brothers, Marty Drake, Rickie Layne & Velvel, Mary Forrest, Patrice Helene, Jan Howard (*Kurt Jons*). "Bagels and Yox," "Such a Good-Looking Boy," "Chi-ri-bim, Chi-ri-bom," "Sholem Aleichem," "Inimitably Yours," "Let's Dance a Frailichs"

893. *Bags*. Three Muses, 4/6/82–4/25/82. 18 perf. m/md: Robert Mitchell; l/b: Elizabeth Perry; d/ch: Wally Strauss; set: John Falabella. Cast: Peggy Atkinson, Maggy Gorrill, Susan Kaslow, Tiger Haynes, Audre Johnston, Michael Zaslow. "It's Mine," "I Was Beautiful," "Lady Wake Up," "This is Where We Met," "So Much for Marriage," "Honky Jewish Boy," "Out on the Streets," "Lucky Me," "Schwesters," "Freedom Song"

894. *Baker's Dozen*. A Julius Monk revue. Plaza 9, 1/9/64–10/6/64. 469 perf. w several songs: William Roy; d/ch: Frank Wagner. Cast: Ruth Buzzi, Jamie Ross, Barbara Cason, Gerry Matthews. "Baker's Dozen"

895. *The Baker's Wife*. A baker's young wife runs off with another man, but returns to the baker. Based on the French play & film *La Femme du Boulanger*, by Marcel Pagnol & Jean Giono. In 1952 Cy Feuer & Ernest H. Martin were ready to make this as a musical, with Frank Loesser writing m/l, Abe Burrows book, and Bert Lahr starring, but it fell through. Over the years Zero Mostel was talked about as lead, but nothing happened until David Merrick took it on as a big musical, with m/l by Stephen Schwartz and book by Joseph Stein, which toured the country starring Topol, en route to Broadway. The tour opened on 5/11/76, at Dorothy Chandler Pavilion, L.A. d: John Berry; ch: Dan Siretta, *Robert Tucker*; set: Jo Mielziner (his last; he died as this show took to the road); cos: Theoni V. Aldredge; light: Jennifer Tipton; md: Robert Billig; orch: Don Walker; dance mus: Daniel Troob. Cast: Carole Demas (*Loni Ackerman, Patti LuPone*), Topol (*Paul Sorvino*), Portia Nelson, Bill Mullikin, Teri Ralston, Keene Curtis, Charles Rule (who replaced Benjamin Rayson before the tour began), Pierre Epstein, Timothy Jerome, Gordon Connell, Kurt Peterson. "Chanson," "Merci, Madame," "Gifts of Love," "The Baking," "Bread," "Not in the Market," "Serenade," "Meadowlark," "Perfect Every Time," "Any Day Now," "Endless Delights," "The Luckiest Man in the World," "What's a Man to Do?," "If I Have to Live Alone," "Where is the Warmth?." Other musical numbers used at various times: "Welcome to Concorde," "A Little Taste of Heaven," "Proud Lady," "Something's Got to Be Done," "Romance." Herschel Bernardi was almost brought in to replace Topol in California. Topol wasn't working out, and finally quit in Washington, to be replaced 2 weeks before the show's demise by Paul Sorvino. Closed at Kennedy Center, 11/13/76, canceling its scheduled 11/21/76 Broadway opening at the Mar-

tin Beck. The songs were so good that theatre companies produced it all over the country. Stephen Schwartz and Joseph Stein made constant improvements, and the show was finally produced in NY (but OB), but it failed. 3/24/85–4/14/85. Prev from 3/20/85. 20 perf. p: York Theatre Co.; d: Stephen Schwartz; ch: Lynne Taylor-Corbett; set: James Morgan; light: Mary Jo Dondlinger. Cast: Jack Weston, Gabriel Barre, Gail Pennington, Kevin Gray. Trevor Nunn produced an "improved" version in London, 10/27/89, but it too failed. Stephen Schwartz, Joseph Stein, and Gordon Greenberg revised it, as an amalgamation of the best parts of the 1976 orig and the 1989 London prod. The Goodspeed Opera House, Conn. 11/7/02–12/1/02. d: Gordon Greenberg; ch: Warren Carlyle; md: Georgia Stitt. Cast: Lenny Wolpe (as Aimable, the baker), Christiane Noll (as Genevieve, his wife), Michael Medeiros (as Barnaby), Laurent Giroux. Paper Mill Playhouse, NJ, 4/13/05–5/15/05 (limited run). d: Gordon Greenberg; ch: Christopher Gattelli. Cast: Lenny Wolpe, Alice Ripley, Max von Essen. This version slightly revised by Mr. Schwartz & Mr. Stein.

896. *Balancing Act*. Actor finds happiness in well-balanced life. Westside, 6/15/92–8/2/92. 16 prev from 6/2/92. 56 perf; Douglas Fairbanks (Sun nights only from 8/9; Dan Goggin's *Nunsense* was playing there rest of the time). m/l/b: Dan Goggin; d: Tony Parise & Dan Goggin; md: Michael Rice. Cast: Craig Wells (*Robert Stella*), Nancy E. Carroll, Diane Fratantoni (*Cindy Benson*), Christine Toy, J.B. Adams, Suzanne Hevner. "Life is a Balancing Act," "Next Stop: New York City," "Home Sweet Home," "Play Away the Blues," "My Bio is a Blank," "A Tough Town," "I Left You There," "A Twist of Fate," "A Casting Call," "The Fifth from the Right," "You Heard it Here First," "A Long, Long War," "The Woman of the Century," "Welcome, Bienvenue," "Where is the Rainbow?," "I Am Yours," "That Kid's Gonna Make It," "Chew Chewy Chow," "Hollywood 'n' Vinyl," "California Suite," "I Knew the Music." Previously ran at Seven Angels Theatre, Waterbury, Conn.

897. *The Ball*. Set in Paradise Ballroom. Duo, 9/16/93. Re-ran 5/5/94–6/26/94. 32 perf. m: Bronwen Jones; l/b/d: Michael Alasa

898. *Ballad for Bimshire*. Black musical. Love between NY playboy & native girl. Set in Barbados. Mayfair, 10/15/63–12/15/63. 74 perf. p: Ossie Davis; m/l: Irving Burgie; b: Irving Burgie & Loften Mitchell; d: Ed Cambridge; ch: Talley Beatty. Cast: Christine Spencer, Ossie Davis, Frederick O'Neal, Miriam Burton, Bobby Dean Hooks. "Ballad for Bimshire," "Street Cries," "'Fore Day Noon in the Mornin'," "Lately I've Been Feeling So Strange," "Deep in My Heart," "Have You Got Charm?," "Hail Britannia," "Welcome Song," "Belle Plain," "I'm a Dandy," "Silver Earring," "My Love Will Come By," "Chicken's a Popular Bird," "Vendor's Song," "Pardon Me, Sir," "Yesterday Was Such a Lovely Day," "The Master Plan," "Chant," "We Gon' Jump Up"

899. *The Ballad of Baby Doe*. Big hit,

about silver mining. NYC Opera, 1958. m/l: Douglas Moore & John Latouche. Cast: Beverly Sills, Walter Cassel. "Augusta's Aria," "Farewell Song," "Letter Song," "Silver Song," "Warm as the Autumn Light," "Willow Song"

900. *The Ballad of Irving the Frog ... and Other Stories.* 10 orig stories, each with puppets, solicited from schoolteachers across the USA. Vital Children's Theatre Co., 10/11/03–11/23/03. p: Striking Viking Story Pirates; m: Eli Bolin; l: Eli Bolin, Lee Overtree, Drew Callander; d: Lee Overtree. Cast: Drew Callander, Liz Bangs, Dan Mahoney, Megan O'Meara, Laura Hernandez, Jacob Rossmer, Peter Russo, Kristen Schaal, Dylan Ris, Sam Reiff-Pasarew

901. *The Ballad of Johnny Pot.* Hippy Johnny Appleseed plants marijuana all over the place. Theatre Four, 4/26/71–5/9/71. 16 perf. m/l: Clinton Ballard & Carolyn Richter; d: Joshua Shelley; ch: Jay Norman; set/light: Lloyd Burlingame; cos: Alvin Colt; md: Harrison Fisher. Music performed by Bandana. Cast: Sara: Betty Buckley; Johnny Pot: John Bennett Perry (David Carradine played him in previews); Also with: Robert Berdeen. "The Ballad of Johnny Pot," "A Carol," "Head Down the Road," "How Wonderful it Is," "Little Sparrows," "Find My Way Alone"

902. *Ballet Ballads.* 3 one-act dance & song plays. Maxine Elliott's, 5/9/48. 6 perf. Presented by ANTA; producer: Nat Karson (for the Experimental Theatre); m: Jerome Moross; l/b: John Latouche; d: Mary Hunter. 1. *Susanna and the Elders.* Set during a revival meeting. The Parson takes the sermon from the story of Susanna and the Elders as found in the *Apocrypha.* ch: Katherine Litz. Cast: Susanna the Dancer: Katherine Litz; Susanna the Singer: Sheila Vogelle; The Elders: Moe: Frank Seabolt; Joe: Robert Trout; The Parson: Richard Harvey. 2. *Willie the Weeper.* Set in Willy's untidy mind. ch: Paul Godkin. Cast: Singing Willie: Robert Lenn; Dancing Willie: Paul Godkin; Cocaine Lil: Sono Osato, *Olga Lunick.* 3. *The Eccentricities of Davy Crockett.* Davy told his tall tales, and various people remembered him and his exploits. ch: Hanya Holm. Cast: Davy: Ted Lawrie; Sally Ann: Barbara Ashley; Also with: Arlouine Goodjohn, Olga Lunick. "I've Got Me," "My Yellow Flower," "Ridin' on the Breeze." Music Box Theatre, Broadway, 5/18/48–7/10/48. 62 perf. p: T. Edward Hambleton. It got generally great reviews. East 74th Street Theatre, 1/3/61–2/5/61. 40 perf. p: Ethel Watt. Cast: Carmen de Lavallade, Ellen Graff

903. *Ballet Russes.* Love affair between Vaslav Nijinsky & Serge Diaghilev, 1909–1923. American Theatre of Actors, 1/6/94–1/15/94. 6 perf. m/l: David Reiser; b: Bernard Myers; d: Karen Berman; ch: Oleg Briansky. Cast: Petter Jacobsson, Carmen De Michael. "Le Dieu Bleu," "Golden Slave," "Something Wonderful," "When You're Intimate with the Czar," "When You're in Love," "Les Sylphides," "Afternoon of a Faun," "I'm Through with You," "We Need Money," "Petrouchka," "Le Spectre de la Rose," "He's So Near," "Rite of Spring," "Les Sirenes"

904. *Bamboche!* Moroccan-style dance revue. 54th Street Theatre, Broadway, 10/22/62–10/28/62. 8 perf. p: Stephen Papich, Dorothy Gray, Ludwig Gerber; creator/d: Katherine Dunham; set/cos: John Pratt; md: Leslie Harnley. Cast: Katherine Dunham, Bessie Griffin, Katherine Dunham Dancers, Royal Troupe of Morocco. Robert Guillaume was one of the singers. "Yanvalou," "Bamboche!" "The Diamond Thief." The name Bamboche is Haitian Creole for "get together and have a good time"

905. *Band in Berlin.* Play with mus. The Comedian Harmonists were a sextet of Jews & non-Jews (Ari Leshnikoff, Erich Collin, Harry Frommermann, Roman Cycowski, Robert Biberti, Erwin Bootz) in Germany, 1927–35, forced to disband by Nazis. Helen Hayes, Broadway, 3/7/99–3/21/99. 19 prev from 2/19/99. 17 perf. p: Robert V. Straus, Jeffrey Ash, Randall L. Wreghitt, Gayle Francis, Marcia Roberts, DLT Entertainment/ZDF Enterprises, by special arr with Arts at St. Ann's & American Music Festival; w: Susan Feldman; conceived by Susan Feldman, Patricia Birch, Wilbur Pauley; d/ch: Patricia Birch; set: Douglas W. Schmidt; cos: Jonathan Bixby & Gregory Gale; light: Kirk Bookman; puppets: Stephen Kaplin. Cast: Herbert Rubens, The Hudson Shad (Mark Bleeke, Timothy Leigh Evans, Hugo Munday, Peter Becker, Wilbur Pauley, Robert Wolfinsky). "Good Night, Sweetheart," "A New Spring Will Come to the Homeland," "Dearest Isabella from Castille," "My Little Green Cactus," "Stormy Weather," "Happy Days Are Here Again," "The Spring is Here," "Village Music," "Tea for Two," "What's Happening in Lisbon?," "It Don't Mean a Thing if it Ain't Got That Swing," "Creole Love Call," "*Barber of Seville* Overture," "Night and Day," "A Little Spring Melody," "Uncle Bumba from Columba Dances the Rhumba," "Whistle While You Work," "Love Comes, Love Goes," "Baby," "The Old Cowboy," "The Last Roundup," "Auf Wiederseh'n, My Dear." See also *Harmony* (in this appendix)

906. *The Banker's Daughter.* Set in elegant NY, 1837–57. Jan Hus, 1/22/62–3/18/62. 68 perf. m/l: Sol Kaplan & Edward Eliscu; based on Dion Boucicault's *Streets of New York;* d: David Brooks; set: Kim Swados; light: Jules Fisher. Cast: David Daniels, Helena Scott, Lloyd Gough, Phil Leeds. "One More Day," "Gentlemen's Understanding," "Such a Beautiful World," "Genteel," "In a Brownstone Mansion," "Both Ends Against the Middle," "The Sun Rises," "Father's Daughter," "Say No More," "More than One More Day," "Nero, Caesar, Napoleon," "Sleep, O Sleep," "Unexpectedly," "In Time," "Head in the Stars," "It's So Heart-warming"

907. *Bar Mitzvah Boy.* Eliot runs away from his very expensive bar mitzvah. Palace, Manchester, England, 9/25/78; Her Majesty's, London, 10/31/78–1/6/79. Prev from 10/20/79. 77 perf. m: Jule Styne; l: Don Black; b: Jack Rosenthal; based on TV play by Jack Rosenthal; d: Martin Charnin; ch: Peter Gennaro; md: Alexander Faris. Cast: Joyce Blair, Vivi-

enne Martin, Ray C. Davis, Benny Lee, Barry Martin, Harry Towb, Barbara Rosenblat, Erica Yorke. "Why?," "If Only a Little Bit Sticks," "The Bar Mitzvah of Eliot Green," "This Time Tomorrow," "Thou Shalt Not," "The Harolds of This World," "We've Done Alright," "You Wouldn't Be You," "Where is the Music Coming From?," "The Sun Shines Out of Your Eyes," "I've Just Begun"

908. *The Bar That Never Closes.* Astor Place, 12/3/72–12/31/72. 33 perf. m: Tom Mandel; l: Louisa Rose, John Braswell, Tom Mandel; sk: Marco Vassi; b: Louisa Rose; conceived by: John Braswell & Louisa Rose; d: John Braswell; md: Cathy MacDonald & Tom Mandel. Cast: Sara Parker, Jennie Mortimer, Lane Binkley. "Walking with You, Two by Two," "Do It," "Recipe for Love," "Kaleidoscope," "I Don't Think I'll Ever Love You," "Dear Dear," "Tears of Ice," "Circus of Jade," "Precious Little Darkness"

909. *Das Barbecu.* Set in Texas. Minetta Lane, 11/10/94–12/4/94. 18 prev from 10/25. 30 perf. p: Thomas Viertel, Steven Baruch, Richard Frankel, Jack Viertel, Dasha Epstein, Margery Klain, Leavitt/Fox/Mages, Daryl Roth; m: Scott Warrender; l/b: Jim Luigs; inspired by Wagner's *Ring* cycle; d: Christopher Ashley; ch: Stephen Terrell; set/cos: Eduardo Sicangco; light: Frances Aronson; sound: T. Richard Fitzgerald; ms: Michael Kosarin; md: Jeff Halpern; orch: Bruce Coughlin; cast recording on Varese Sarabande. Cast: Carolee Carmello, Julie Johnson. "A Ring of Gold in Texas," "What I Had in Mind," "Hog-Tie Your Man," "Makin' Guacamole," "Rodeo Romeo," "County Fair," "Public Enemy Number One," "A Little House for Me," "River of Fire," "If Not fer You," "Slide a Little Closer," "Barbecue for Two," "After the Gold is Gone," "Wanderin' Man," "Turn the Tide"

910. *Bare: The Musical.* High schoolers growing up at a Catholic boarding school. American Theatre of Actors (Chernuchin Theatre), 4/19/04–5/27/04. Prev from 3/25/04. m: Damon Intrabartolo; l: Jon Hartmere Jr.; b: Jon Hartmere Jr. & Damon Intrabartolo; d: Kristin Hanggi; set: David Gallo; cos: David C. Woolard

911. *Barnardo.* Dr. Barnardo & his children's homes. Royalty, London, 5/21/80–6/29/80. 43 perf. w/d: Ernest Maxin; d: Barry Westcott. Cast: Dr. Thomas Barnardo: James Smillie; Also with: Fiona Fullerton, John Arnatt. "Cor," "My Son," "Lovely Hot Pies," "London's East End," "Snuggle Up," "Girls Are Luverly." *Panned by the critics.* 1980 studio recording, but not by cast. A musical about Barnardo, to star Tommy Steele, was rumored in 1967, but never happened

912. *El Barrio '92.* Also called *El Barrio USA.* Musical comedy revue on life in NY through Hispanic eyes. Village Gate, 7/8/92. b: Angel Salazar & Andrew Smith. Cast: Angel Salazar (also d), Daphne Rubin-Vega, J.J. Ramirez, Kenya Bennett

913. *Baseball, Sex and Other Facts of Life.* Musical revue. Kraine, 5/6/98–5/17/98. 12 perf. m: Paul V. Patanella; l/b/d: Gayden Wren; md: Stephen O'Leary

914. *Bashville.* Open Air Theatre, Regent's Park, London, 8/2/83–8/24/83. p: New Shakespeare Co.; m: Denis King; l: Benny Green; adapted by David William & Benny Green from George Bernard Shaw's play *The Admirable Bashville;* d: David William; ch: Gillian Gregory; md: Anthony Bowles; cast recording on TER. Cast: Douglas Hodge, James Cairncross, Peter Woodward, Christina Collier, Joan Davies. "Fancy Free," "8-9-10," "Lydia," "One Pair of Hands," "A Gentleman's True to His Code," "Because I Love Her," "Take the Road to the Ring," "Hymn to Law and Order," "Black Man's Burden," "He is My Son," "Bashville's Boats Are Burned." Same venue, same crew, 7/31/84. Cast: Richard Rees, Felicity Jane Goodson, Peter Woodward, James Cairncross, Noreen Berry, Natasha Richardson. Odyssey Theatre Ensemble, California, 3/30/85. Revised. d: John Allison. Cast: James Reeder, Lauri Landry

915. *Basin Street.* Set in 1917, in Storyville, New Orleans. New Federal Theatre, 9/8/83–9/25/83. 15 perf. m/l: Turk Murphy & Michael Hulett; cos: Judy Dearing; ms: Danny Holgate; orch: Turk Murphy & Danny Holgate. Cast: Sandra Reaves-Phillips, Alexana Ryer. "Call the Children Home," "All that it Takes," "Sporting House Professor Blues," "Blue Book," "Song of My Fathers," "Lady Gets Me There," "Miss Lulu White," "Chicago Drag," "The Ham Kick," "Don't Much Matter Any More," "Naked Dance"

916. *Bat Boy: The Musical.* Darkly comic musical about half boy, half bat. Union Square, 3/21/01–12/2/01 (closed early, after 257 perf, a victim of 9/11). 21 prev from 3/3/01. m/l: Laurence O'Keefe; b/story: Keythe Farley & Brian Flemming; based on cartoon in the *Weekly World News;* d: Scott Schwartz; ch: Christopher Gattelli; set: Richard Hoover & Bryan Johnson; cos: Fabio Toblini; light: Howell Binkley; md: Alex Lacamoire; orch: Laurence O'Keefe & Alex Lacamoire. Cast: Bat Boy: Deven May; Also with: Kaitlin Hopkins, Sean McCourt, Kerry Butler, Kathy Brier. "Hold Me, Bat Boy," "Christian Charity," "Ugly Boy," "Whatcha Wanna Do?," "A Home for You," "Another Dead Cow," "Dance with Me, Darling," "Ruthie's Lullaby," "Show You a Thing or Two," "Comfort and Joy," "A Joyful Noise," "Let Me Walk Among You," "Three Bedroom House," "Children, Children," "More Blood," "Inside Your Heart," "Apology to a Cow," "Revelations," "I Imagine You're Upset." Before NY it had an L.A. prod & many workshops & readings, and was revised. Later got several regional prods. Shaftesbury, London, 9/18/04–1/15/05. Prev from 8/18/04. d: Mark Wing-Davey; md: Ian Vince-Gatt. Cast: Deven May, Emma Williams, Maurey Richards, Rebecca Vere. "Ugly Boy" was replaced with "Hey, Freak!" and "Inside Your Heart" by "Mine, All Mine." There was another new song, "What You Wanna Do." There was a new UK cast recording. Filmed in 2005. d: John Landis

917. *Bats.* Dark comedy with mus. Nat Horne, 9/9/93–9/26/93. 12 perf. m: James Merrillat; l: John B. Kenrick & James Merrillat; w: Fred Gormley; d: David Ness

918. *Bayou Legend.* Set in 1800s. Church of St. Paul & St. Andrew, 1/10/75–1/26/75. 12 perf. m/l: Jack Landron; b: Owen Dodson; d: Shauneille Perry; ch: Deborah Allen; set: C. Richard Mills; md: Neal Tate. Cast: Yvette Johnson, Clinton Turner Davis, Jack Landron, Edward Love

919. *Be Kind to People Week.* A smiling musical. Set in NYC. Belmont, 3/23/75–6/29/75. 100 perf. The Quinton Raines prod, presented by. J. Arthur Elliot; w: Jack Bussins & Ellsworth Olin; d: Quinton Raines; ch: Bobby Lee; md: Jeremy Stone. Cast: Alan Kass, Bobby Lee, Naura Hayden, Kenneth Cory, Alan Kass, Nell N. Carter, Grenoldo Frazier, Maureen Moore. "Whatever Happened to the Good Old Days?," "I Will Give Him Love," "Mad About You, Manhattan," "All I Got is You," "I Need You," "To Love is to Live," "Black is Beautiful," "A Smile is Up," "You're Divine," "Be Kind to People Week"

920. *Beach Blanket Babylon.* A campy show. Longest running US musical revue. San Francisco, 6/7/74. w: Steve Silver

921. *Beatlemania.* Concert-style revue, a "rockumentary." Winter Garden, Broadway, 5/31/77–1979. Prev from 5/26/77 after out-of-town tryout; Lunt-Fontanne, Broadway, 3/1/79–10/17/79. Total of 920 perf were recorded through 9/1/79; additional perfs took place on irregular & unrecorded schedule during final weeks of run, for a total of 1,006 perf. It never scheduled a formal opening night (*New York Times* reviewed it 6/17/77; reviews were generally good). By agreement with League of New York Theatres and Producers, opening date has been set (for the record) at 5/31/77. p: David Krebs & Steven Leber; m/l: Beatles; conceived by: Steven Leber, David Krebs, Jules Fisher; editorial content: Robert Rabinowitz, Bob Gill, Lynda Obst; set: Robert D. Mitchell; sound: Abe Jacob; prod super/light: Jules Fisher (Tony nomination for lighting); ms: Sandy Yaguda; special consultant: Murray the K. Cast: Joe Pecorino (rhythm guitar), Mitch Weissman (bass guitar), Leslie Fradkin (lead guitar), Justin McNeill (drums). 4 Beatles impersonators sing & play Beatles hits. At same time 2,000 slide projections of figures of the day–Marilyn Monroe, Martin Luther King, Doris Day, JFK, etc., were flashed between & during songs onto backdrop screen, and a tickertape neon sign showed headlines from Beatle era. Effect was a documentary of the period & traced the lads from Liverpool roots to international sages & gurus. A staff of 36 writers, photographers, researchers, graphic designers & film editors was hired to assemble imagery. 4 successful touring companies were launched. Filmed in 1981

922. *The Beautiful and the Damned.* Shaftesbury, London, 5/10/04. Prev from 4/28/04. w: Les Reed, Roger Cook, Kit Hesketh Harvey; d/ch: Craig Revel Horwood; set/cos: Christopher Woods; md: John Owen Edwards; orch: Larry Blank. Cast: Michael Praed, Helen Anker. About F. Scott Fitzgerald and his wife Zelda

923. *Beautiful Dreamer.* Madison Avenue Playhouse, 12/27/60–1/18/61. 24 perf. m:

Stephen Foster; w: William Engvick. Cast: Foster: James Morris; Also with: Carolyn Maye, Don Liberto, Jeanne Schlegel

924. *The Beautiful Game.* Set in Belfast in the 1960s. Cambridge Theatre, London, 9/26/00–9/1/01. m: Andrew Lloyd Webber; l/b: Ben Elton; cast recording on Telstar. Cast: Michael Shaeffer, Josie Walker, Ben Goddard, Frank Grimes, Diane Pilkington, Hannah Waddingham, Dale Meeks, Oliver Segal, David Shannon, Alex Sharp. "The Beautiful Game," "Clean the Kit," "Don't Like You," "God's Own Country," "Let Us Love in Peace," "The Final," "Off to the Party," "Our Kind of Love," "Happiest Day," "To Have and to Hold," "First Time," "I'd Rather Die on My Feet than Live on My Knees," "The Selection," "Dead Zonc," "If This is What We're Fighting For," "All the Love I Have"

925. *Becoming.* Variety. Circle in the Square Downtown, 6/15/76–6/16/76. 6 prev. 2 perf. w: Gail Edwards & Sam Harris; d/ch: John Mineo. Cast: Norman Meister, Ann Sward, Gail Edwards. "It Feels So Good to Be Alive Today," "Believe in You," "It's Not Easy to Change Your Life," "Goin' Back to That Feelin'," "Mama," "Valentine Song," "Lonely Times," "Lordy," "Choices," "Birthday Song," "From Now On," "Let it Be Today," "Love Me Lightly," "Freer Love," "Look Inside," "Let's Get Started." Developed at Univ of Miami, Fla

926. *Bed and Sofa.* Set in Moscow, 1926. Vineyard, 1/16/95–3/10/95. 16 prev. 40 perf. m: Polly Pen; b: Laurence Klavan; based on 1926 film by Abram Room; d: Andre Ernotte; ch: Loni Ackerman; set/cos: G.W. Mercier; md: Alan Johnson; orch: John McKinney; cast recording on Varese Sarabande. Cast: Terri Klausner, Michael X. Martin, Jason Workman, Martin Moran, Polly Pen

927. *Beehive.* Musical revue. 1960s women singers with beehive hairstyles. Village Gate Upstairs, 3/30/86–8/23/87. Prev from 3/11/86. 600 perf. conceived by/d: Larry Gallagher; ch: Leslie Dockery; md: Skip Brevis. Cast: Pattie Darcy (*Julee Cruse*), Alison Fraser (*B.J. Jefferson*), Jasmine Guy (*Debbie Lyons*), Adriane Lenox (*Carol Lynn Maillard, Adriane Lenox*), Gina Taylor (*Cookie Watkins*), Laura Theodore (*Jessie Richards*). "Name Game," "My Boyfriend's Back," "Sweet Talkin' Guy," "One Fine Day," "Will You Still Love Me Tomorrow," "Remember Walking in the Sand," "I Hear a Symphony," "It's My Party," "You Don't Own Me," "Judy's Turn to Cry," "Where the Boys Are," "Beehive Dance," "Beat Goes On," "Downtown," "To Sir with Love," "Wishin' and Hopin'," "Don't Sleep in the Subway," "You Don't Have to Say You Love Me," "Beehive Boogie," "River Deep, Mountain High," "Proud Mary," "Respect," "A Natural Woman," "Me and Bobby McGee." Previously ran OOB at Sweetwaters. There was an 8/2/04 workshop of a musical called *Beehive on Broadway*, about the 1987 show. p: Jeffrey Richards & Michael Rothfeld; b: Jim Geoghan; d/ch: Debbie Allen

928. *The Beggar's Opera.* Written as a satirical ballad opera (see also *The Beggar's Holiday* and, more importantly, *The Threepenny Opera* both in the main part of this book) by John

Gay, in England, in 1728. Dr. John Christopher Pepusch arr the tunes. 1st prod in NY in 1750, and many times since. Frederic Austin re-set the airs (the musical is composed of a series of airs) and also composed add mus. His version 1st appeared OB, at the Greenwich Village Theatre, 12/29/20. 37 perf. This adaptation ran at 48th Street Theatre, Broadway, 3/28/28–4/28/28. 36 perf. Cast: Macheath: George Baker. City Center, 3/13/57–3/24/57. 15 perf. Adapted/d: Richard Baldridge; set: Watson Barratt; light: Jean Rosenthal; prod super: Burt Shevelove. Cast: Beggar Poet: Peter Turgeon; Filch: Charles Bolender; Macheath: Jack Cassidy; Matt of the Mint: Robert Burr; Jemmy the Twitcher: Hal England; Crooked Finger Jack: Maurice Edwards; Wat Dreary: Francis Barnard (this character became Walt Dreary in *The Threepenny Opera*); Nimming Ned: J.C. McCord; Slippery Sam: Jack de Lon; Bob Booty: David Nillo; Tom Tizzle: William Inglis; Polly Peachum: Shirley Jones; Mr. Peachum: George S. Irving; Mrs. Peachum: Zamah Cunningham; Mr. Lockit: George Gaynes; Lucy Lockit: Jeanne Beauvais; Mrs. Coaxer: Paula Laurence; Jenny Diver: Constance Brigham; Dolly Trull: Maria Karnilova; Mrs. Vixen: Anita Cooper; Mrs. Slammekin: Adnia Rice; Suky Tawdry: Shirley Chester; Molly Brazen: Charlotte Ray. "Let Us Take the Road," "My Heart Was So Free," "Where I Laid on Greenland Coast," "Virgins Are Like the Fair Flower," "Our Polly is a Sad Slut," "The Turtle Thus with Plaintive Crying," "'tis Woman that Seduces All Mankind," "Through All the Employments of Life," "Hanging is My Only Sport," "O, What a Pain it is to Part," "No Power on Earth Can E'er Divide," "Man May Escape from Rope and Gun," "Why, How Now, Madam Flirt?," "Is Then His Fate Decreed, Sir?," "Fill Every Glass," "The Ways of the World," "If the Heart of a Man," "Youth's a Season Made for Joys," "When Young at the Bar," "In the Days of My Youth," "At the Tree I Shall Suffer with Pleasure," "I'm Like a Skiff on the Ocean Toss'd," "Come, Sweet Lass," "The Charge Was Prepar'd," "Would I Might Be Hanged," "Since Laws Were Made for Every Degree," "See the Conquering Hero." Chelsea Theatre Center of Brooklyn, 3/21/72–4/16/72. 29 perf; McAlpin Roof Theatre, 5/30/72–12/10/72. 224 perf. new m/l: Ryan Edwards; d: Gene Lesser; set: Robert U. Taylor; cos: Carrie F. Robbins; md: Richard Parrinello. Cast: Macheath: Stephen D. Newman, *Timothy Jerome* (from 5/30/72), *Peter Lombard* (from 9/72); Polly: Kathleen Widdoes, *Leila Martin* (from 7/5/72); Mr. Peachum: Gordon Connell, *Rex Robbins* (from 10/72), *Jerrold Ziman, Tom Batten*; Mrs. Peachum: Jeanne Arnold, *Mary Louise Wilson* (from 7/5/72), *Charlotte Jones* (from 10/17/72); Dolly: Joan Nelson, *Jill Eikenberry*; Lockit: Reid Shelton, *Ralston Hill* (from 5/30/72); Lucy: Marilyn Sokol, *June Gable, June Helmers* (from 9/19/72), *June Gable* (from 10/24/72); Suki: Irene Frances Kling; Jenny: Tanny McDonald. Billy Rose Theatre, 12/22/73–12/31/73. 6 perf in rep. p: City Center Acting Co.; d: Gene Lesser; set: Robert Yodice; cos:

Carrie F. Robbins; light: Martin Aronstein; md: Roland Gagnon. Cast: Filch: Norman Snow; Peachum: David Ogden Stiers; Mrs. Peachum/Betty Coaxer: Mary Lou Rosato; Polly: Cynthia Herman; Macheath: Kevin Kline; Jemmy Twitcher: Peter Dvorsky; Harry Paddington: Joel Colodner; Walt: David Schramm; Jenny Diver: Mary-Joan Negro; Lockit: Sam Tsoutsouvas; Lucy Lockit: Patti LuPone. Ohio Theatre, NY, 10/22/93–11/14/93. 21 perf. New m/l. p: Tony Geballe. Cast: Macheath: Kenneth Talberth. There was a 1975 sequel, *Polly* (qv this section)

929. *The Believers (The Black Experience in Song)*. Set in "The Gone Years" & "The Then and Now Years." Garrick, 5/9/68–2/2/69. 310 perf. d: Barbara Ann Teer. Cast: Josephine Jackson (also w) & Joseph A. Walker (also w). "African Sequence," "Believers' Chants," "This Old Ship," "Where Shall I Go?," "What Shall I Believe in Now?," "I Just Got in the City," "City Blues," "You Never Really Know," "Early One Morning Blues," "Daily Buzz," "Children's Games," "School Don't Mean a Damn Thing," "I'm Gonna Do My Things," "Where Do I Go from Here?," "Burn This Town," "Learn to Love"

930. *Belinda Fair*. 19th-century girl joins Army disguised as her cousin & falls in love with colonel. Saville, London, 3/25/49; Strand, 6/10/49–7/16/49. Total of 131 perf. m: Jack Strachey; l/b: Eric Maschwitz & Gilbert Lennox; d: Charles Goodner; ch: Pauline Grant; md: Walter Stiasny. Cast: Adele Dixon, Geoffrey Hibbert, John Battles, Daphne Anderson, Stella Moray, David Croft, Ferdy Mayne

931. *Bella*. Satire on whodunits, set in 1930s. Gramercy Arts, 11/16/61–11/19/61. 6 perf. m/l: Jane Douglas & Tom O'Malley; d: Richard C. Schank. Cast: Dodo Denney, Will B. Able, Gloria LeRoy, Ruth Jaroslow. "On the Seashore By the Sea," "It isn't the Same," "All About Evelyn," "Could Be," "Time," "The Seven Seas," "Hand in Hand," "Love Doesn't Grow on Trees," "I'm Happy," "My Card," "Kiss Me," "Madame from Paree," "Big, Big," "Take a Chance," "Way Down in Li'l Old Texas," "For Love or Money"

932. *Belle*. Music-hall musical, also called *The Ballad of Dr. Crippen*. About Dr. Crippen, the murderer. King's Theatre, Southsea, England, 4/10/61; Brighton; Strand, London, 5/4/61–6/10/61. 44 perf. p: Wolf Mankowitz, Bob Swash, Kenneth Wagg; m/l/md: Monty Norman; b: Wolf Mankowitz; from play by Beverley Cross; d: Val May; ch: Michael Charnley; set: Loudon Sainthill; cast recording on TER. Cast: Patricia Burke (*Rose Hill*), Nicolette Roeg, George Benson, Jerry Desmonde, Davy Kaye, Virginia Vernon, Bill Owen, Jenny Till. "Ballad of Dr. Crippen," "Fifty Years Ago," "Bird of Paradise," "Meet Me at the Strand," "You Are Mine," "Devil's Bandsman," "Ain't it a Shame," "Song of the Future," "Belle," "Lovely London," "Bravest of Men," "A Pint of Wallop," "Fairy Godmother," "Walking with You," "I Can't Stop Singing," "Don't Ever Leave Me," "Minstrel Show," "You Can't Beat a British Crime"

933. *La Belle*. Set in 1860s, at Theatre des Varietes, Paris. Show within a show, in which some of the actors stage updated musical version of Helen of Troy saga. Shubert, Philadelphia, 8/13/62–8/25/62. 16 perf. Did not make intended Broadway run. p: Gerard Oestreicher; m: William Roy (based on themes by Offenbach); l: Marshall Barer; b: Brendan Gill (based on libretto by Bill Hoffman); d: Albert Marre; ch: Todd Bolender; set/light: Ed Wittstein; cos: Robert Fletcher; md: Pembroke Davenport; dance mus: Genevieve Pitot; orch: Philip J. Lang. Cast: Paris: George Segal; Calchas: Howard Da Silva; Menelaus: Menasha Skulnik; Helen: Joan Diener; Agamemnon: Thayer David; Graphis: Mimi Turque; Diana: Marilyn D'Honau; Chorus: Mickey Gunnersen, Carmen Morales, Louis Polacek. "It isn't the Way You Play the Game," "How Will I Know?," "I'm Called the King," "There is No Such Thing as Love," "Play Nice," "Golden Crowns of Greece," "Vengeance" (ballet), "Go to the Mountains," "This is the Night," "Transformation," "Oh! What a Ball!," "The Canard," "Night Music," "No One is Perfect," "I Give Up," "I'll Fall in Love Again," "No Sad Songs for Me," Finale

934. *Belle Epoque*. Story of Toulouse-Lautrec. Mitzi Newhouse, 11/21/04. m/l/b: Martha Clarke & Charles L. Mee; translated by: Michael Feingold; d: Martha Clarke; ch: Rebecca Wender; set: Robert Israel; cos: Jane Greenwood; light: Christopher Akerlind; sound: Scott Stauffer; md/orch: Jill Jaffe. Cast: Mark Povinelli, Nina Goldman, Rebecca Wender, Robert Wersinger, Michael Stuhlbarg, Joyce Chittick

935. *Belle Starr*. Also known as *The Piecefull Palace*. American musical. Palace, London, 1969. 16 perf. Part of UK tour. m/l: Steve Allen. Cast: Betty Grable, Ray Chiarella. "Belle," "Gee, You're Pretty"

936. *Bells of St. Martin's*. Revue. St. Martin's, London, 8/29/52. 107 perf. w/d: W. Lyon-Shaw; ch: Peter Glover. Cast: Hattie Jacques, Douglas Byng, Roma Milne, Pamela Hill, Richard Waring

937. *Le Bellybutton*. Porno-musical. Diplomat Cabaret, 4/2/76–4/25/76. 28 perf. m/l/b/d: Scott Mansfield; ch: Katherine Hull & Louise Quick; set: David Chapman; md: Ken Werner. Cast: Marilyn Chambers, Alan Scott, Jim Sbano, Thommie Bush, Jessie Hill, Adrienne Frimet, Larry Kingery, Debbie Kinney, Alan Lee Kootsher, Billy Padgett, Paulette Sanders, Suzanne Walker. "Jenny," "Marilyn's Theme"

938. *Below the Belt*. A Rod Warren cabaret revue. Upstairs at the Downstairs, 6/21/67–10/8/67. d: Sandra Devlin. Cast: Richard Blair, Genna Carter, Madeline Kahn, Robert Rovin, Lily Tomlin. "And in this Corner...," "The Game is Up," "Just for Openers." All musical numbers collected & updated from previous Warren revues

939. *Ben Bagley's Shoestring Revues*. Equity Library, 10/15/70–11/1/70. 22 perf. Based on revues by Mr. Bagley; d/ch: Miriam Fond; special dance ch: Bick Goss; md: Bob Waxman. Cast: Jay Bonnell. "Man's Inhumanity to Man," "Queen of Spain," "Garbage,"

"Good Little Girls," "Lest We Forget," "Medea in Disneyland," "On a Shoestring," "Auf Wiedersehen," "Rochelle Hudson Tango," "Time to Say Goodnight"

940. *Berlin.* About the Berlin Airlift. Theatre 315 (OB's new venue), 9/10/03–9/27/03. p: O Prods; m/l/b: Erik Orton; d: Jamibeth Margolis; ch: Jody Ripplinger; set: Doug Ellis; cos: Brenda Phelps; light: Edward Pierce; sound: Tony Angelini; md: Rick Bertone. Cast: Tregoney Shepherd, Nicole Riding, Edward Prostak, Joe Konicki, Jeff Austin, Richard Todd Adams

941. *Berlin to Broadway with Kurt Weill.* Musical revue. Theatre de Lys (where Mr. Weill's *The Threepenny Opera* ran for so long in the 1950s), 10/1/72–2/11/73. 152 perf. d: Donald Saddler; set: Herbert Senn & Helen Pond; light: Thomas Skelton. Cast: Ken Kercheval (the Guide on this musical voyage), Jerry Lanning, Judy Lander, Margery Cohen, Hal Watters. Excerpts from *The Threepenny Opera, The Rise and Fall of the City of Mahagonny, Marie Galante, Happy End, Johnny Johnson, Knickerbocker Holiday, Lady in the Dark, One Touch of Venus, Love Life, Street Scene, Lost in the Stars.* Triad, 8/19/00–12/2/00. 10 prev from 8/11/00. 121 perf. d/ch: Hal Simons; cos: Suzy Benzinger; md/arr: Eric Stern. Cast: Michael Winther

942. *Bernadette.* Dominion, London, 6/21/90. w: Gwyn & Maureen Hughes. Cast: Ruthie Henshall, Nick Curtis, Lottie Mayor. "Watch Me Begin," "Show Me the Way," "Only Fools," "Ignore a Child," "Who Are You?," "Like a Child," "Bernadette's a Liar," "Idle Minds," "Don't Turn Away," "Have Another," "Girl Like Me," "It Was an Illusion," "Love Goes On," "Bernadette"

943. *Bessie Speaks.* Bessie Smith songs. Henry Street Settlement, 10/27/94–11/20/94. 16 perf. p: New Federal Theatre; w: China Clark; d: Dwight R.B. Cook; ch: Louis Johnson; md: Grenoldo Frazier; cos: Judy Dearing. Cast: Debbi Blackwell Cook

944. *Best Foot Forward.* Set in small Pennsylvania univ town in spring 1940. College boy invites movie star to be date at prom, and, for publicity purposes, she accepts. Ethel Barrymore, Broadway, 10/1/41–7/4/42. 326 perf. p/d: George Abbott; Richard Rodgers (also p-uncredited); m/l: Hugh Martin & Ralph Blane; b: John Cecil Holm; ch: Gene Kelly; set: Jo Mielziner; cos: Miles White; md: Archie Bleyer; orch: Donald Walker & Hans Spialek. Cast: Rosemary Lane, Nancy Walker (Broadway debut), June Allyson, Danny Daniels, Lou Wills Jr., Stanley Donen. "Don't Sell the Night Short," "Three Men on a Date," "That's How I Love the Blues," "The Three Bs," "Every Time," "The Guy Who Brought Me," "I Know You By Heart," "Shady Lady-Bird," "Buckle Down, Winsocki," "My First Promise," "What Do You Think I Am," "Just a Little Joint with a Juke Box," "Where Do You Travel?," "I'd Gladly Trade." Filmed in 1943, with Lucille Ball, Nancy Walker, June Allyson, Eileen Barton. Stage 73, 4/2/63–10/13/63. 224 perf. p: Arthur Whitelaw, Buster Davis, Joan D'Incecco, Lawrence Baker Jr.; d/ch: Danny Daniels;

set/cos: Jack Fletcher; light: Jules Fisher; md: Buster Davis; dance mus arr: William Goldenberg. Cast: Liza Minnelli (stage debut, as Ethel Hofflinger), Ronald Walken (became Christopher Walken), Kay Cole, Glenn Walken, Paula Wayne. Partially new score: "Wish I May" [from the movie version of *Best Foot Forward*], "Three Men on a Date," "That's How I Love the Blues," "Three Bs," "Every Time," "Alive and Kicking" [from movie], "The Guy Who Brought Me," "Shady Lady-Bird," "Buckle Down, Winsocki," "You're Lucky" [from movie], "What Do You Think I Am?," "Raving Beauty" [from stage musical *Meet Me in St. Louis*], "Just a Little Joint with a Juke Box," "You are for Loving" [from *Meet Me in St. Louis*]. Theatre at St. Peter's, 3/19/04–3/21/04. Part of *Musicals in Mufti* series. p: York Theatre Co.; adapted by: David Ives; d: Jay Binder; ch: Kelli Barclay; cos: Carrie Robbins; md: Michael Dansicker. Cast: Leah Hocking, Jim Stanek, Jim Bohon, Jen Cody. 89-year-old original composer Hugh Martin wrote a new song for this prod, "Up to My Eyebrows"

945. *Best of Times: The Showtunes of Jerry Herman.* Vaudeville Theatre, London, 11/17/98–12/19/98. Prev from 11/13/98. conceived by: Paul Gilger; d/ch: Bill Starr. Cast: Kathryn Evans, Lindsay Hamilton, Sarah Payne, Garth Bardsley, Jamie Golding, James Followell. It developed into *Showtune: the Jerry Herman Songbook*

946. *Bet Your Life.* Psychic jockey marries American heiress. New Theatre, Oxford, England, 12/4/51 (2 weeks); Manchester from 12/18/51 (8 weeks); Hippodrome, London, 2/18/52–10/25/52. 362 perf. m: Kenneth Leslie-Smith & Charles Zwar; l/b: Alan Melville; d: Richard Bird; ch: George Carden; md: Bretton Byrd; cast recording on Blue Pear. Cast: Arthur Askey, Julie Wilson (*Noele Gordon*), Sally Ann Howes, Brian Reece. "I Want a Great Big Hunk of Male," "Now is the Moment," "What Care I?," "I Love Being in Love," "Ta Ever So," "Eat, Drink and Be Merry," "I Love Him as He Is," "All on Account of a Guy," "Don't Look Now"

947. *Betjemania.* Musical entertainment based on works of affable poet laureate John Betjeman. Orange Tree, Richmond, Surrey, England, 1976. m: John Gould; l: John Betjeman; b/dev: David Benedictus & John Gould. Cast: Gay Soper, Barry Stokes. 55 min long; expanded to 2 hours; the Key, Peterborough; the Shaw, London, 12/8/76. Cast recording on TER. Cast: Gay Soper, Barry Stokes, John Gould, Rowland Davies. "Cornish Cliffs," "Our Padre," "Christmas," "Dorset," "Slough," "In Westminster Abbey," "In a Bath Tea Shop," "Cat Hill," "Eunice," "Sun and Fun." 1977 tour. Revived, 1980, for City of London Festival

948. *Betting on Bertie.* Like the Broadway musical *By Jeeves* (but in no other way connected) this musical was taken from P.G. Wodehouse's stories. In 1968 Frank Loesser got together with P.G. Wodehouse & Guy Bolton to talk about a Jeeves musical. Mr. Loesser persuaded Wodehouse & Bolton to hire Robert

Wright & George "Chet" Forrest to do the mus, while Mr. Wodehouse wrote lyr (his last). Bolton & Wodehouse wrote libretto. Mr. Loesser died, and Wright & Forrest put the show on hold. Eventually revived by Walter Willison, with a view to Broadway in fall 1997. A fall 96 workshop at the Hasty Pudding, Cambridge, Mass., was canceled when actor Keene Curtis fell ill. However, on 10/15/96 (P.G. Wodehouse's birthday) there was a staged reading. Emily Loesser (Frank's daughter) was going to be in it, but she went to *By Jeeves* instead. Cast: Jeeves: Keene Curtis; Bertie: Douglas Holmes; Also with: Judy Kaye, Diane J. Findlay, Jack Eddleman, Emily Skinner, Sam Reni. Another reading took place 4/14/97, at the Promenade (OB). p: Michael Frazier; md: Jack Lee. Cast: Jeeves: Simon Jones; Bertie: Douglas Holmes; Also with: Sally Mayes, Timothy Jerome, Diane J. Findlay, Anne Van Cleave, Ben George, Steve Asciolla, Sam Reni. The show did not progress from there

949. *Betty Blokk-Buster Follies.* Revue. Bijou, Balmain, Sydney, 1975. Cast recording on Festival. Cast: Reg Livermore. "Family of Man," "Money Money," "Captain Jack," "Matrimony," "Long Tall Glasses," "Walk on the Wild Side," "Is That All There Is?," "Ticking," "Celluloid Heroes," "The Show Must Go On," "Train"

950. *BETTY RULES.* Book musical/performance piece, self-styled an "alterna-musical." Chronicles real-life ups & downs of band BETTY, formed in 1985, and fronted by Amy Ziff, Elizabeth Ziff & Alyson Palmer. Magic Theatre, San Francisco, 2001. The trio w/performed. NY debut at the Zipper, 10/15/02–3/30/03. Prev from 9/21/02. d: Michael Greif; set/light: Kevin Adams; sound: David Arnold. Cast recording

951. *Beyond the Fringe.* Satirical revue with mus, orig conceived & prod by Jonathan Bassett for the Edinburgh Festival. Fortune Theatre, London, 5/10/61. 1,189 perf. d: Eleanor Fazan. Writers/Cast: Dudley Moore, Peter Cook, Jonathan Miller, Alan Bennett. John Golden Theatre, Broadway, 10/27/62–5/30/64. 4 prev from 10/22/62. 667 perf. The Nine O'clock Theatre production, presented by Alex Cohen, William Donaldson, Donald Albery; d: Alex Cohen; set: John Wyckham; light: Ralph Alswang. Cast: Dudley Moore, Peter Cooke, Jonathan Miller (*Paxton Whitehead* from 1/8/64), Alan Bennett. Understudies: Hugh Alexander & Brendan Burke. "Man Bites God," "Deutscher Chansons," "And the Same to You" (Dud's piano solo), "Little Miss Britten," "Weill Song" (added in 1964). Milton Smith (stage tech) was nominated for a Tony. On 1/8/64 the name of the show on Broadway changed to *Beyond the Fringe 1964*, and was billed as a new edition. The U.S. tour opened at the Huntington Hartford Theatre, Hollywood, 8/5/63. Cast: Patrick Horgan, Paxton Whitehead (*Patrick Hamilton* from 1/8/64), Patrick Carter, William Christopher. The tour closed on 3/14/64, at the O'Keefe, Toronto, and resumed there on 5/11/64. *Beyond the Fringe '65.* Ethel Barrymore Theatre, 12/15/64–1/9/65. 30 perf. Cast: James Valentine, Joel

Fabiani, Robert Cessna, Donald Cullen. Years later Pete and Dud wrote a two-man musical revue, *Behind the Fringe*, which ran in London. p: Bernard Delfont. It also ran on Broadway, at the Plymouth, 11/14/73–11/30/74 (438 perf), as *Good Evening*. p: Alex Cohen & Bernard Delfont; d: Jerry Adler; set/cos/light: Robert Randolph. "Madrigal," "Die Flabbergast," "One Leg Too Few," "Chanson," "The Kwai Sonata," "Tea for Two." "Resting" was added during the run. Pete & Dud won a Special Tony. It toured

952. Beyond the Rainbow. Italian musical. Set in Italian mountain village of San Crispino. Rome, Italy, 1974. Ran 3½ years (as *Aggiungi un posto a tavola*). m: Armando Trovajoli; l: Iaia Fastri; adapted by Pietro Garinei & Sandro Giovannini from British novel *After the Deluge*, by David Forrest. Cast: Father Silvestro: Johnny Dorelli. Adelphi, London, 11/9/78 (6 months). English l: Leslie Bricusse. Cast: Johnny Dorelli, Roy Kinnear. "Come Join Us at the Table," "Pity," "Ding Dong Song," "Throw it Away," "A Time for Love," "Consolation," "Love According to Me," "A Tiny Art," "San Crispino," "Clementina," "I Want You," "Beyond the Rainbow"

953. Big as Life. Univ of Wisconsin, 1948. m/l: Jerrold Bock (Jerry Bock's 1st effort) & Jack Royce. "Everybody Loses," "Great Wisconsin," "Stairway Lullaby," "Why Sing a Love Song?"

954. Big Bad Burlesque. Burlesque revue. Orpheum, 8/14/79–11/18/79. 16 prev. 112 perf. d: Celeste Hall; ch/conceived mus numbers: Don Brockett; md: Jim Walton. Cast: Tamara Brandy, Nina David, Danny Herman, Eva Parmelee, Jim Walton. "Big Bad Burlesque," "Glamour Girls," "School Days," "Flora and Fauna," "Wonderful Burlesque Days"

955. The Big Bang. 2 producers of new musical at backers' audition. Douglas Fairbanks, 3/1/00–4/16/00. 17 prev from 2/15/00. 55 perf. m: Jed Feuer; l/b/d: Boyd Graham; set: Edward T. Gianfrancesco; md: Albert Ahronheim. Cast: Jed Feuer & Boyd Graham. "Big Bang," "Free Food and Frontal Nudity," "Pyramid," "Viva la Diva," "Wake Up, Caesar," "Hell of a Job," "Coliseum," "Emperor Man," "Number One," "Cantata," "A New World," "Cooking for Henry," "True Tale of Pocahontas," "Today's Just Yesterday's Tomorrow," "Freedom," "Potato," "Two Asian Ladies," "We're Gonna Fly," "Loving Him," "The Twentieth Century"

956. Big Ben. Light opera. Opera House, Manchester, England, 4/19/46 (2 weeks); tour; Adelphi, London, 7/17/46–12/14/46. 172 perf. p: C.B. Cochran; m: Vivian Ellis; l/b: A.P. Herbert; d/ch: Wendy Toye; set: Rolf Gerard & Doris Zinkeisen; md: Charles Prentice. Cast: Gabrielle Brune (*Noele Gordon*), Lizbeth Webb, David Davies, Joy Adams, Natasha Wills

957. Big Boy. Theatre Royal, Newcastle, England, 6/19/45; tour; Saville, London, 9/12/45–2/16/46. 174 perf. m: Carroll Gibbons; l: Douglas Furber; add l: Fred Emney; b: Douglas Furber, Fred Emney, Max Kester; d: Frank Adey; ch: Freddie Carpenter; md:

Harold Collins. Cast: Richard Hearne, Fred Emney, Carol Raye, Pamela Harrington

958. Big City Rhythms. Musical revue. Triad, 1/29/96–2/26/96. 5 perf. m/l: Barry Kleinbort. Cast: Marcia Lewis, Melanie Vaughan, Lewis Cleale, Eric Michael Gillett

959. Big Noise of '92: Diversions from the New Depression. Musical revue. Cherry Lane, 12/16/91. 9 prev from 12/4. 1 perf. Cast: Neilan Tyree (also p)

960. Big Sin City. Ashcroft, Croydon, England, 2/13/78; tour; Roundhouse, London, 5/30/78–6/3/78. Prev from 5/23. 6 perf. p: Bill Kenwright; w: the Heather Brothers (Neil, Lea & John); d: Bill Kenwright & Brian Peck; md: John Heather. Cast: Myra Sands, Ian Bartholomew, Deena Payne, Jack Wild, Nicholas Chagrin, Lea Heather. "Big Sin City," "They're Sending Us Down," "It Must Be Love," "Twenty-Four Hours," "The Pleasure Pit," "Hots for Louie," "K.I.D.S.," "Without You Here by My Side," "Everything Money Can Buy," "It'll Be Me," "Revenge," "The Knife Fight"

961. The Big Winner. In Yiddish, with narration in English. Set in 1910 in Jewish town in Russia. Eden, 10/20/74–2/2/75. 119 perf. m/l: Sol Kaplan & Wolf Younin; w: Sholem Aleichem; adapted/d: David Opatoshu; ch: Sophie Maslow; set/cos: Jeffrey B. Moss; md: Jack Easton. Cast: Bruce Adler, David Opatoshu, Cheryl Hartley. "How Can I Tell Him She Loves Me?," "We're the People," "Lottery Celebration," "Money, Wealth, Gold," "It's Delicious," "I Am the Tailor's Daughter," "The Tango," "In-Laws," "Love Song," "Winners, Losers," "Wedding Dance." Re-done as a comedy with mus, at Folksbiene, 10/22/88–3/12/89. 48 perf. new adaptation: I.D. Berkowitz; new m/l: Haim Elisha & Miriam Kressyn; d: Rinn Elisha. Cast: Mina Bern. Simcha Kruger (English narration)

962. Billy. Palace, Manchester, England, 3/22/74–4/13/74; Theatre Royal, Drury Lane, London, 5/1/74. Prev from 4/25. 904 perf. m: John Barry; l: Don Black; b: Dick Clement & Ian La Frenais; from novel *Billy Liar*, by Keith Waterhouse & Willis Hall; d: Patrick Garland; ch: Onna White. Cast: Michael Crawford (*Roy Castle*), Elaine Paige (*Marianne Price*), Gay Soper, Billy Boyle, Bryan Pringle (*George Sewell*). "Ambrosia," "And," "Some of Us Belong to the Stars," "Happy to Be Themselves," "The Witch," "Lies," "It Were All," "Green Hills," "Aren't You Billy Fisher?," "Is This Where I Wake Up?," "Billy," "Remembering," "Any Minute Now," "Lady from L.A.," "I Missed the Last Rainbow"

963. Billy Bishop Goes to War. Canadian play with music, based on the life of Canadian World War I air ace Billy Bishop. Vancouver East Cultural Centre, 11/78. m/w/d: John Gray & Eric Peterson. "(We're) Off to Fight the Hun," "Canada at War," "The Good Ship *Caledonia*," "Buried Alive in the Mind," "December Nights," "The RE-7," "Nobody Shoots No-One in Canada," "Lady St. Helier," "My First Solo Flight," "In the Sky," "As Calm as the Ocean," "Friends Ain't S'posed to Die," "General Sir Hugh M. Trenchard," "The

Empire Soiree." Kreeger Theatre, Washington, DC. p: Arena Stage Theatre. Morosco Theatre, Broadway, 5/29/80–6/7/80. 7 prev. 12 perf. p: Mike Nichols & Lewis Allen; set: David Gropman; light: Jennifer Tipton. Cast: Eric Peterson & John Gray. Theatre de Lys, 6/17/80–8/24/80. 78 perf. Cast: Eric Peterson (*Cedric Smith* from 8/12/80 — he had been playing the role at matinees), John Gray (*Ross Douglas* from 8/12/80 — he had been playing the role at matinees). Comedy Theatre, London, 6/3/81–7/13/81

964. Billy Elliot — The Musical. Highly-anticipated musical version of the 2000 movie, created by Lee Hall, and dir by Stephen Daldry, set in North East of England during miners' strike of 1980s. Billy, son of macho single father, discovers ballet. It was Elton John's idea to do a musical of it. Jamie Bell, star of the movie, expressed no interest in reprising. It was due to try out at the Tyne Theatre, Newcastle, England, from 11/29/04, then to go on to the West End, to open at the Victoria Palace on 3/11/05 (prev from 2/05). However, the Newcastle Opera House (as the venue was more popularly called) closed in 6/04, thus changing the schedule. Opened for prev at Victoria Palace, 3/31/05. m: Elton John; l/b: Lee Hall; d: Stephen Daldry; ch: Peter Darling; set: Ian MacNeil; cos: Sue Blane; ms: Martin Koch. Cast: Liam Mower, James Lomas, George McGuire (all as Billy), Hayden Gwynne (Julie Walters had been approached to reprise her screen role), Ann Emery (who replaced Anne Rogers just before the show opened in the West End), Joe Caffrey, Trevor Fox, Steve Elias. "Electricity," "Express Yourself," "Grandma's Song," "When We Were Kings"

965. Billy Noname. Set in Bay Alley, USA, 1937–1970. Fatherless black child grows up & out of American city slum. Truck & Warehouse Theatre, 3/2/70–4/12/70. 48 perf. m/l: Johnny Brandon; d: Lucia Victor; ch: Talley Beatty; cast recording on Roulette. Cast: Donnie Burks, Roger Lawson, Hattie Winston, Alan Weeks, Eugene Edwards, Glory Van Scott, Urylee Leonardos, Andy Torres. "King Joe," "Billy Noname," "A Different Drummer," "Hello World," "At the End of the Day," "I Want to Live," "Color Me White," "Mother Earth," "The Dream," "Black Boy," "Burn, Baby, Burn," "Get Your Slice of Cake"

966. The Biograph Girl. Gardner Centre, Brighton, England, 10/21/80–11/1/80; Phoenix, London, 11/19/80–1/10/81. 57 perf. m/l: David Heneker & Warner Brown; b: Warner Brown; d: Victor Spinetti; ch: Irving Davies; md: Michael Reed; cast recording on TER. Cast: Mary Pickford: Sheila White; D.W. Griffith: Bruce Barry; Lillian Gish: Kate Revill; Dorothy Gish: Sally Brelsford; Mack Sennett: Guy Siner: Also with: Jane Hardy. "Moving Picture Show," "Working in Flickers," "That's What I Get All Day," "Moment I Close My Eyes," "Diggin' Gold Dust," "Every Lady Needs a Master," "I Just Wanted to Make Him Laugh," "I Like to Be the Way I Am in My Own Front Parlour," "Beyond Babel," "A David Griffith Show," "More than a Man," "The Industry," "Gentle Fade," "Nineteen Twenty Five," "Biograph Girl," "One of the Pioneers," "Put it on the Tissue Paper"

967. *Birds of Paradise*. Set on fictional Harbor Island. Theatre professional joins forces with amateur group for prod of Chekhov's *The Seagull*. Promenade, 10/26/87–11/15/87. 29 prev from 10/2/87. 24 perf. m: David Evans; l: Winnie Holzman; b: David Evans & Winnie Holzman; d: Arthur Laurents; ch: Linda Haberman; light: Jules Fisher; md: Frederick Weldy; orch: Michael Starobin. Cast: Barbara Walsh, Mary Beth Piel, Andrew Hill Newman, J.K. Simmons, Donna Murphy, Todd Graff, John Cunningham, Crista Moore. "So Many Nights," "Diva," "Every Day is Night," "Somebody," "Coming True," "It's Only a Play," "She's Out There," "Birds of Paradise," "Imagining You," "Penguins Must Sing," "You're Mine," "Things I Can't Forget," "After Opening Night," "Chekhov," "Something New." Previously produced in NY Univ's theatre program

968. *A Bistro Car on the CNR*. Set in a Bistro car (a converted baggage car) on the *Rapido* on its final trip from Toronto to Montreal. Playhouse, 3/23/78–5/14/78. 21 prev. 61 perf. p: Jeff Britton & Bob Bisaccia; m/l: Patrick Rose, Merv Campone, Richard Ouzounian; dial: D.R. Andersen; d: Richard Ouzounian; ch: Lynne Gannaway; set/cos: John Falabella; md: John Clifton. Cast: Tom Wopat, Marcia McClain, Patrick Rose, Henrietta Valor. "C.N.R.," "25 Miles," "Guitarist," "Passing By," "Madame la Chanson," "Oh, God! I'm 30," "Ready or Not," "Sudden Death Overtime," "Bring Back Swing," "Yesterday's Lover," "Four Part Invention," "Nocturne," "La Belle Province," "Dewey and Sal," "Here I Am Again," "Street Music," "Other People's Houses," "Genuine Grade A Canadian Superstar," "I Don't Live Anywhere Anymore," "Somebody Write Me a Love Song." Previously ran in Canada

969. *The Bitch*. Little Theatre, London, 8/16/76–9/4/76. w: Hereward Brown & Ian Senior; from story by Roald Dahl; d: Roy Russell-Pattison; md: Martin Jacklin. Cast: June Shand, Kevin Whately, Leon Head, Jeremy Arnold

970. *Bits and Pieces XIV*. A Julius Monk cabaret revue. Plaza 9, 10/9/64–6/5/65. 426 perf. p: Thomas Hammond; ch: Frank Wagner. Cast: Gerry Matthews, Jamie Ross, Barbara Cason. "Feathered Friends" (m: Marvin Hamlisch; l: Howard Liebling), "Alexander's Discount Rag" (m: Stan Lebowsky; l: Fred Tobias), "Peanut Butter Affair" (m/l: Clark Gesner), "Ballad for a Park" (l: Clark Gesner), "The Game is Over!" (m: Stan Lebowsky; l: Fred Tobias). Many other numbers by William F. Brown & Michael Brown. Dick Dana wrote sketch "Conference Call"

971. *Bittersuite*. Songs of experience. Quaigh, 1/20/84–2/18/84. 24 perf. m: Elliot Weiss; l: Mike Champagne; d: Bert Michaels. Cast: Claudia Casson, Del Green, Anthony Mucci, Theresa Rakov, Richard Roemer. "The Bittersuite," "Life that Jack Built," "You're Not Getting Older," "John's Song," "Win and Lose," "Fathers and Sons," "Mama Don't Cry,"

"Snap Back," "The Apology," "Dungcons and Dragons," "Twentieth Reunion," "I'll Be There," "How Little We've Learned," "World without End," "Flight of the Phoenix." Duplex, 4/5/87. d: Mike Champagne; cos: Judy Dearing; md: Elliot Weiss. Cast: Claudia Casson-Jellison, Joy Franz, John Jellison, Joseph Neal. Palsson's Supper Club, 10/5/87–5/2/88. 211 perf. d: Mike Champagne; md: Elliot Weiss. Cast: Suzanne Blakeslee, David Edwards, Barbara Marineau, Byron Nease. Alix Korey & Stephen Berger (alternates). A new edition, *Bittersuite — One More Time*, ran at Palsson's, 5/16/88–6/12/88. 18 perf. Cast: David Edwards, SuEllen Estey, Roger Neil, Barbara Scanlon. m/l were revised, some new songs, some old ones were cut

972. *Black Broadway*. A Newport Jazz Festival mus entertainment. Featured musical numbers (from period 1899–1946) introduced by black performers. Town Hall, 5/4/80–5/24/80. 3 prev. 24 perf. p: George Wein, Honi Coles, Robert Kimball, Bobby Short; md: Frank Owens; orch: Dick Hyman. Cast: Gregory Hines, John W. Bubbles, Nell Carter, Carla Earle, Honi Coles, Adelaide Hall, Terri Griffen, Bobby Short, Edith Wilson, Elisabeth Welch, Mercedes Ellington, Charles "Cookie" Cook, Leslie "Bubba" Gaines, Wyetta Turner. 1st prod for 1 concert perf by the Newport Jazz Festival at Avery Fisher Hall, 1/24/79

973. *Black Nativity*. 41st Street Theatre, 12/11/61; the York 1/9/62–1/28/62. Total of 59 perf. w: Langston Hughes; d: Vinnette Carroll; ch: Louis Johnson; light: Martin Aronstein. Cast: Alex Bradford, Madeline Bell, Howard Sanders. Tour opened 10/14/63, Shubert, Boston. Closed 1/12/64, Chicago. Cast: Hope Clarke, Matt Cameron, Ed Hall, Alex Bradford Singers. Criterion, London, 8/14/62; Phoenix, 9/10/62; Piccadilly, 2/26/63. d: Vinnette Carroll; ch: Cristyne Lawson & Ronald Frazier; cos: Bill Hargate. Rest of cast: Vinnette Carroll, Cristyne Lawson, Ronald Frazier, Alex Bradford, Madeline Bell. Kennedy Center, 12/20/94–1/1/95

974. *Blackberries*. Minstrel-vaudeville spectacular celebrating enormous contributions made to American musical comedy. AMAS, 1984. conceived by/b: Joseph George Caruso; sk: Billy K. Wells; add material/dial/d: Andre De Shields; ch: Andre De Shields & Gui Andrisano; cos: Mardi Philips; ms: Joel Silberman. Cast: Clent Bowers, Christina Britton, Ellia English, Mardi Philips

975. *Blackamoor*. Set in Madrid in mid–17th century. AMAS, 10/13/88–11/6/88. 17 perf. m: Ulpio Minucci; l: Helen Kromer; from novel *I, Juan de Pareca*, by Elizabeth Borton de Trevino; d: Kent Paul; ch: Barry McNabb. Cast: Christopher Innvar, David Jackson, Keelee Seetoo, Ruthanna Graves. "Spanish Serenade," "In Madrid," "We Do Absolutely Nothing," "I Like to Paint By Early Light," "Home with the King," "We Can't Turn Back," "It's All Over for Us," "Will I Be Caught?," "You're Wearing the Autumn So Well," "Had We Been Free," "Black Is," "Remembrance," "Free"

976. *Blackbirds of Broadway: A Harlem*

Rhapsody. Downtown Cabaret, Bridgeport, Conn. p: Richard & Susan Hallinan; m/l: various artists; conceived by: David Coffman & Marion J. Caffey; based on the Blackbird revues of the 20s & 30s, produced by Lew Leslie (a white man); d/ch: Marion J. Caffey. "Memories of You," "Doin' the New Low Down," "Let the Good Times Roll," "Papa de Da Da," "Your Mother's Son-in-Law," "He May Be Your Man," "Dinah," "Porgy," "Exactly Like You," "Some of These Days," "I Can't Give You Anything But Love," "On the Sunny Side of the Street," "St. James Infirmary," "St. Louis Blues," "Original Black Bottom Dance," "Shim Sham Shimmy Dance," "Minnie the Moocher," "Man from Harlem," "Darktown Strutters' Ball," "I Got it Bad and That Ain't Good," "Woman," "My Handy Man," "Elijah Rock," "Stormy Weather," "Lenox Ave Tap," "Until the Real Thing Comes Along," "Bye Bye Blackbird." The musical & dance numbers are interspersed with several jazz poems written by Langston Hughes. It has played regionally

977. *The Blacksmith's Folly*. Set in Russian village at turn of 20th century. Folksbiene, 11/1/97–1/18/98. 47 perf. m: Zalmen Mlotek; l/b: Michael Greenstein; from play by David Pinski; translated by: Pearl Krupit; d: Daniel Banks; cos: Gail Cooper-Hecht. Cast: Kelli Kolodny, Ibi Kaufman, Mina Bern, Felix Fibich

978. *Blackstone*. Magnificent musical magic show, performed by Harry Blackstone, son of the noted magician Blackstone. Majestic, Broadway, 5/19/80–8/17/80. 104 perf. d/ch: Kevin Carlisle; set: Peter Wolf; cos: Winn Morton; light: Martin Aronstein; ms: Milton Setzer; orch: Richard Bellis; magic d: Charles Reynolds

979. *Blame It On The Movies*. Musical revue of numbers from 40 years of movies. Criterion Center Stage Left, 5/16/89–5/17/89. 3 perf. p: Roger Berlind, Franklin R. Levy, Gregory Harrison; orig m/l: Billy Barnes; conceived by/compiled by/d: Ron Abel, Billy Barnes, David Galligan; ch: Larry Hyman; md: Ron Abel. Cast: Sandy Edgerton, Christine Kellogg, Bill Hutton, Barbara Sharma

980. *Blast!* Musical spectacle. Featured 60-member drum & bugle corps & presented its own rendition of military marches. Brainchild of Indiana bandleader James Mason. Began in London, opened as tour in Boston on 8/22/00, then to Broadway Theatre, Broadway, 4/17/01–9/23/01. 13 prev from 4/5/01. 173 perf. Composers & lyricists featured include Maurice Ravel, Leonard Bernstein, Samuel Barber, Aaron Copeland, Stephen Sondheim, James Mason, John Vanderkloff, Chuck Mangione. Featured the Star of Indiana Drum Corps. d: James Mason; ch: Jim Moore, George Pinney, John Vanderkloff; set/cos: Mark Thompson; light: Hugh Vanstone; md/orch: James Prime. Divided reviews. Won 1st ever Special Tony for Special Theatrical Event. Also nominated for ch. Spawned sequel, *Blast II: Shockwave*, which played 1st at Disneyworld's Epcot Theatre, Fla., until 8/24/02, then it went on tour

981. *Bless the Bride*. Lucy Veracity Willow, apparently doomed to marry noble numbskull

Thomas Trout, finds true love with dashing French actor Pierre Fontaine. Adelphi, London, 4/26/47–6/11/49. 886 perf. p: C.B. Cochran; m: Vivian Ellis; l/b: A.P. Herbert; d/ch: Wendy Toye; set/cos: Tanya Moiseiwitsch; md: Michael Collins; cast recording on AEI. Cast: Georges Guetary, Lizbeth Webb, Betty Paul, Pamela Carroll, Brian Reece, Peter Lupino, Babatunde Macaulay, Anona Winn, Natasha Wills, John Turner. "Too Good to Be True," "Any Man But Thomas T," "Oh, What Will Mother Say?," "I Was Never Kissed Before," "God Bless the Family," "Ma Belle Marguerite," "The Silent Heart," "Bless the Bride," "Ducky," "Table for Two," "This is My Lovely Day," "Bless the Sea," "Bobbing-Bobbing," "Come Dance, My Dear," "Croquet, Croquet," "En Angleterre," "Les Demoiselles," "The Englishman," "A Fable for Two," "The Fish," "Here's a Kiss for One and Twenty," "Mon Pauvre Petit Pierre," "My Big Moment," "Summer," "This Man Could Never Be a Spy," "To France," "Twenty-One Candles," "A Consomme," "Where is *The Times?*" Stoll, London, 7/10/51–7/18/51. 23 perf. d: Maxwell Wray; ch: Izna Roselli; md: Tom Lewis. Cast: Valerie Lawson, Terry O'Donovan, Peter Croft, Gavin Gordon, Babatunde MacCaulay. In 1967 an album was cut (but a show was not produced) on Music For Pleasure, with studio cast including Peggy Mount, Leslie Fyson, Charles Young, Mary Millar

982. *Blitz!* Lionel Bart's follow up to *Oliver*. Set in London during the blitz. About the Blitzstein family. Regal Cinema, Edmonton, London, 4/13/62; Adelphi, London, 5/8/62–9/14/63. 568 perf. p: Donald Albery, by arr with Jack Hylton; m/l/d: Lionel Bart; b: Lionel Bart & Joan Maitland; ch: Peter Wright; set: Sean Kenny; md: Marcus Dods; orch: Bob Sharples; cast recording on EMI. Cast: Grazina Frame (*Toni Eden*), Bob Grant, Toni Palmer, Amelia Bayntun, Graham James, Anna Tzelniker (Vera Lynn sang this role on the recording), Tom Kempinski (*Jonathan Burn*), Edward Caddick, Bernard Stone. "Our Hotel," "Tell Him — Tell Her," "I Want to Whisper Something," "The Day After Tomorrow," "We're Going to the Country," "Another Morning," "Who's this Geezer Hitler?," "Be What You Wanna Be," "Opposites," "Far Away," "Petticoat Lane," "Down the Lane," "So Tell Me," "Mums and Dads," "Who Wants to Settle Down," "Is This Gonna Be a Wedding?," "Duty Calls," "Bake a Cake," "Leave it to the Ladies," "As Long as This is England." In NY it played OB the same year

983. *Blitzstein!* Program of songs. Provincetown Playhouse, 11/30/66–12/4/66. 5 prev. 7 perf. p: Herbert Dorfman, Stage Assocs, C.K. Wilson; m/l: Marc Blitzstein; d: Ellen Pahl. Singers: Mira Gilbert, Norman Friesen. Piano: Peter Basquin

984. *Blockheads.* 1984 Mermaid, London, 10/17/84–11/3/84. m/l: Kay Cole, Whitelaw, Peskanov, et al; ch: Kay Cole; based on Laurel & Hardy

985. *Blondel.* Set in the 1180s; about Richard the Lion Heart & his minstrel Blondel. Theatre Royal, Bath, England, 9/8/83; then Manchester; Old Vic, London, 11/9/83–1/14/84. Prev from 10/31/83. 87 perf; Aldwych, 1/20/84–9/2/84. 278 perf. p: Cameron Mackintosh; m: Stephen Oliver; l/b: Tim Rice; d: Peter James; ch: Anthony Van Laast; md: Martin Koch; cast recording on MCA. Cast: Paul Nicholas, Stephen Tate, David Burt, Kevin Williams, David Alder, Tracy Booth, Maria Friedman. "Blondel and Fiona," "Least of My Troubles," "Lionheart," "No Rhyme or Richard," "Assassin's Song," "Running Back for More," "Blondel in Europe," "Saladin Days," "I Can't Wait to Be King," "Blondel's Search," "The Cell," "Westminster Abbey," "I'm a Monarchist"

986. *Blood.* Returning Vietnam War vet. Martinson, 3/7/71–3/21/71. 14 perf. p: NY Shakespeare Festival; m/l: Doug Dyer, etc; conceived by/d: Doug Dyer; loosely based on the *Oresteia*; clothes: Theoni V. Aldredge; ms: John Morris; md: Patrick Fox. Cast: Mary Boylan, Christopher Cox, Doug Dyer, Patrick Fox. "High Lonesome," "Hear the Guns," "Gas Can," "I Dreamt About My Home," "Don't Call Us," "Monkey in a Tree," "Minute by Minute," "Hail to the Blood"

987. *Blood Red Roses.* Anti-war play with songs. Set during Crimean War, 1854–55, in England & the Crimean Peninsula. John Golden, Broadway, 3/22/70. 9 prev. 1 perf. p: Seymour Vall & Louis S. Goldman, in assoc with Rick Mandell & Bjorn I. Swanstrom; m: Michael Valenti; l/b: John Lewin; d: Alan Schneider; ch: Larry Fuller; set: Ed Wittstein; cos: Deidre Cartier; light: Tharon Musser; asst light: Ken Billington; md: Milton Setzer; orch: Julian Stein & Abba Bogin. Cast: Jeannie Carson, Philip Bruns, Jess Richards, Sydney Walker, Ronald Drake, Lowell Harris, Jay Gregory, Charles Abbott, William Tost, Bill Gibbens. Standby: Frances Sternhagen (for Miss Carson). "The Cream of English Youth," "A Garden in the Sun," "In the Country Where I Come From," "Song of How Mucked up Things Are," "Song of Greater Britain," "Black Dog Rum," "The English Rose," "O Rock Eternal," "Soldiers Anthem" (also seen as "Soldier's Prayer"), "Blood Red Roses," "The Fourth Light Dragoons," "Song of the Fair Dissenter Lass"

988. *Blue.* Play with jazz-flavored tunes. Woman follows career of jazz singer Blue Williams. Gramercy, 6/28/01–9/16/01. 98 perf. m: Nona Hendryx; l: Nona Hendryx & Charles Randolph-Wright; b: Charles Randolph-Wright; d: Sheldon Epps; set: James Leonard Joy. Cast: Phylicia Rashad, Michael McElroy, Messeret Stroman, Kevyn Morrow. Paper Mill Playhouse, NJ, 1/8/03–2/9/03. Cast: Leslie Uggams, Michael McElroy

989. *Blue for a Boy: What Shall We Do with the Body?* Musical romp. Theatre Royal, Birmingham, England, 8/14/50 (2 weeks); tour; His Majesty's, London, 11/30/50–6/28/52. 664 perf. p: Emile Littler; m: Harry Parr Davies; l: Harold Purcell; adapted/d: Austin Melford; revival of 1930 musical *It's a Boy*, based on play *Hurrah, eine Junge!*, by Franz Arnold & Ernest Bach; ch: Joan Davis; set: Edward Delaney. Cast: Fred Emney, Richard Hearne, Jessie Hitter (*Bertha Belmore, Benita Lydal*), Austin Melford

990. *Blue Plate Special.* Manhattan Theatre Club Upstage, 10/18/83–11/27/83. 47 perf. m/l: Harris Wheeler & Mary L. Fisher; b: Tom Edwards; d: Art Wolff; ch: Douglas Norwick; set: David Jenkins. Cast: Gretchen Cryer, Ron Holgate, Tina Johnson, Mary Gordon Murray. "Morning Glory Mountain," "At the Bottom Lookin' Up," "Never Say Never," "Halfway to Heaven," "Satisfaction Guaranteed," "Blue Plate Special," "Twice as Nice," "All-American Male," "Honky Tonk Queens," "I Ain't Lookin' Back," "I'm Gonna Miss Those Tennessee Nights"

991. *Blues in Rags.* Musical theatre piece utilizing pantomime, skits & song. Henry Street Settlement, 4/4/91–4/21/91. 4 prev. 11 perf. m: Nick Kosco; w/d: Marketa Kimbrell. Cast: Ariel Joseph, Marcia Donalds, Jennifer Johnson

992. *Bob's Your Uncle.* Musical farce. Liverpool, England, 5/15/48; toured; Saville, London, 5/5/48–3/19/49. 363 perf. m: Noel Gay; l: Frank Eyton; b: Austin Melford; d: Leslie Henson & Austin Melford; ch: Beatrice Appleyard; md: Mantovani. Cast: Leslie Henson, Austin Melford, Lionel Blair (as a waiter). "He Loves Me," "Like Me a Little Bit More," "We'll Start as We Mean to Go On," "With a Girl Like You," "Call it Love"

993. *Boccaccio.* Set in a villa outside Florence, 1348. Plague refugees flee city & pass time in country, telling stories, usually of ribald nature. Edison, Middle Broadway, 11/24/75–11/30/75. 48 prev. 7 perf. p: Rita Fredricks, Theatre Now, Norman Kean; m: Richard Peaslee; dramatized/l: Kenneth Cavander; based on stories from *The Decameron*, by Giovanni Boccaccio; d: Warren Enters; ch: Julie Arenal; set: Robert U. Taylor; cos: Linda Fisher; light: Patrika Brown; md: Ken Bichel; orch: Walt Levinsky & Richard Peaslee. Cast: Michael Zaslow, Virginia Vestoff, Armand Assante, Caroline McWilliams, D'Jamin Bartlett, Jill Choder, Munson Hicks, Richard Bauer. Standbys: Sheilah Rae & Michael Forella. "Masetto's Song," "Nuns Song," "God is Good," "Now My Season's Here," "Only in My Song," "Egano D'Galluzzi," "The Men Who Have Loved Me," "In the Garden," "Lucky Anichino," "Pretend You're Living," "Devil in Hell," "The She Doctor," "Lover Like a Blind Man," "If You Had Seen," "Love Was Just a Game," "Madonna Isabella," "My Holy Prayer," "Hold Me Gently." Previously ran at Arena Stage, Washington, DC

994. *The Body in the Seine.* Closed before Broadway, 1954. Cast: Alice Pearce, Barbara Ashley. m/l: David Lippincott. "But Wonderful," "Chacun a Son Gout," "Where Do I Go From Here?," "Why Can't You Be You?." Cast recording made (unreleased) on the Alden Shaw label

995. *Body Shop.* Set in small-town strip club. Westbeth, 11/19/94–12/17/94. 15 perf. m/l/b: Walter Marks; d: Sue Lawless; ch: Tony Stevens; cos: Franne Lee. Cast: Donna Drake, Beth Glover. "Desire," "Maybe it's Not Too Late," "You're a Natural," "Suffer," "Esmeralda," "My Turn," "Class Act," "A Matter of Time," "Mr. Maybe," "The Woman in Me," "Find a Way," "Virtual Sexuality." Same venue, 1/18/95–3/26/95. 9 prev. 41 perf. Few cast changes; "Esmeralda" was replaced with "Angelina"

996. *Body Work*. Christ's Hospital, Edinburgh, 3/18/87. w: Richard Stilgoe. Cast: Maria Friedman, Lonnie Donegan, Isla St. Clair, Jake Thackray, Chichester Cathedral Choir, Chas & Dave. "How Are You Today?," "Bodywork," "Take Two of These," "This May Be Too Early," "Don't Go," "They Never Ask Us," "Life Passes Me By," "I Am Tomorrow," "Kiss of Life," "Everybody"

997. *Bon Voyage*. Black comedy musical farce. Set in 18th century. Ocean liner cruise goes wrong. Tabernacle, Notting Hill, London, 12/13/00–12/17/00. w: Alexander & Nat Waugh (sons of Auberon Waugh & grandsons of Evelyn Waugh). 1st ran in London in 1998

998. *Bonanza Bound*. Set in Cruickshank Town, during 1898 Alaska goldrush. Shubert, Philadelphia, 12/26/47–1/3/48. Aimed for Broadway, but failed. p: Herman Levin, Paul Feigay, Oliver Smith; m: Saul Chaplin; l: Betty Comden & Adolph Green; d: Charles Friedman; ch: Jack Cole; set: Oliver Smith; cos: Irene Sharaff; light: Peggy Clark; md: Lehman Engel; orch: Philip Lang; cast recording on Columbia (unreleased). Cast: Allyn Ann McLerie, George Coulouris, Adolph Green, Jack Cole, Carol Raye, Gwen Verdon (as the Gambling Dancer, performing "Gambling Dance"), Ted Thurston, Hal Hackett, Johnny Silver. "Little Fish," "Vein of Gold," "No Mind of Your Own," "Tell Me Why," "Fill 'er Up," "The Versatile Da Vincis," "Misunderstood," "Up in Smoke," "Bonanza," "Cruickshank March," "Somewhere in the Snow," "(I Know It's) True," "Spring," "This Was Meant to Be," "Inspiration"

999. *The Bone Room*. Man glues bones in Museum of Natural History, and has nervous breakdown as result of male menopause. Experimental musical in limited run as OB workshop prod, 1975. m: Harvey Schmidt; l: Tom Jones. Cast: Ray Stewart, Susan Watson. "Postcards," "A Wonderful Way to Die," "Will We Ever Know Each Other?," "Wishes Don't Wash Dishes"

1000. *Boobs! The Musical: The World According to Ruth Wallis*. Musical revue of the post—WWII risque songs of the songwriter/comedienne. Triad, 5/19/03–11/30/03. Prev from 5/8/03. p: Michael Whaley & Lawrence Leritz; b: Steve Mackes; d: Donna Drake; ch: Lawrence Leritz; cast recording on MOL. "Pizza," "The Dinghy Song," "All the Clowns." Dillon's, 12/19/03. Had a modified set design by Eric Harriz. There were some new cast members, including Gennifer Flowers (1/21/04–1/31/04; *Leslie Ann Hendricks*)

1001. *Boots with Strawberry Jam*. Musical bio. Nottingham Playhouse, England, 2/28/68. Did not go to London. m/l/b: Johnny Dankworth & Benny Green; d: Wendy Toye; md: Iwan Williams. Cast: Ellen Terry/Mrs. Patrick Campbell: Cleo Laine; George Bernard Shaw: John Neville; Also with: Rosemary Martin

1002. *Bordello*. Queen's, London, 4/18/74–5/24/74. 41 perf. m: Al Frisch; l: Julian More & Bernard Spiro; b: Julian More; d: John Cox. Cast: Stella Moray, Paddy Glynn, Jacquie Toye, Judy Cannon, Angela Easterling, Lynda Bellingham, Brenda Kempner, Angela Ryder. "A Place Like This," "Bordello," "Yourself," "A Country Bride," "Simple Pleasures," "Can-Can," "Family Life," "If You Should Leave Me," "All the Time in the World," "I Love Me," "Girl in Cabin 54," "The Way I See It," "What Does it Take?"

1003. *Born to Rumba*. Duo, 5/8/91–5/25/91. 12 perf. m/l: Michelangelo Alasa, David Welch; d: Michelangelo Alasa. "Roses," "No You Can't," "Santiago," "Dark Perfect Stranger," "Loving for Sale," "Gonna Catch Me a Dream," "Rumba," "Off to Hollywood," "Strange Times," "Havana," "Dreamers." Sequel, *Beyond Born to Rumba!*, opened at the Duo, 11/15/96. m/l/b/d: Michelangelo Alasa

1004. *Born to Sing!* Union Square, 8/8/96–12/1/96. 8 prev from 7/31/96. 133 perf. Sequel to *Mama, I Want to Sing* (see this appendix). m/ms: W. Naylor; l/b: Vy Higgensen & Ken Wydro; d: Ken Wydro. Cast: Lisa Fischer. "Lead Us On," "Sweeping Through the City," "Is My Living in Vain," "Give the Child a Break," "And the Winner Is," "Your Time Will Come," "Born to Sing," "Harmony," "Who Needs Who?," "Take a Stand," "Sky's the Limit," "Who You Gonna Blame?," "Attention Must Be Paid," "Face to Face," "Take the High Way"

1005. *Borscht Capades*. English-Yiddish musical revue. Royale, Broadway, 9/17/51–12/2/51. 90 perf. p: Hal Zeiger; d: Mickey Katz; ch: Ted Adair & Belle Didjah; set/light: Charles Elson; md: Max Pollack; special mus for dances: Joseph Rumshinsky. Cast: Mickey Katz, Phil Foster, Joel Kaye, Dave Barry, The Barry Sisters, Patsy Abbott, Jack Hilliard. "Yiddish Mule Train," "Lighting of the Sabbath Candles," "Geshray of de vilde Katchke"

1006. *Bounce*. About real-life eccentric, roguish & flamboyant brothers Addison & Wilson Mizner (Addison was gay), con men, adventurers, entrepreneurs, real estate speculators, who helped develop Boca Raton, Fla. Called "a vaudeville" because the lifespan of the Mizners was same as that of American vaudeville–1860s to 1920s. In 1953 the book *The Legendary Mizners*, by Alvah Johnston, came out. Steve Sondheim talked with Oscar Hammerstein II about doing a musical based on the book. It was a definite project until 1956, when David Merrick sent Sondheim a script written by Sam Behrman, of Irving Berlin's unproduced musical *Sentimental Guy*, based on same book (other tentative titles for Berlin show were *The Mizner Story* & *Wise Guy*). All that Sondheim's project had was the number "Afternoon in Benicia," depicting Mrs. Mizner's genteel afternoon tea, and other bits of script, so he let the project die. 3 songs from Berlin's *Sentimental Guy* were later recorded on Varese Sarabande's CD "*Unsung Irving Berlin*," viz. "You're a Sucker for a Dance," "You're a Sentimental Guy," and "Love Leads to Marriage." "Go Home and Tell it to Your Wife" was a 4th song

intended for the Berlin show. When *Passion* was in previews, in 1994, Sondheim asked John Weidman to read Johnston's book. They began working on the musical, which they called *Wise Guys*. Commissioned by Kennedy Center in 1995 to open there in fall 1996, as their 1st prod of 96–97. That didn't happen. Re-scheduled for Kennedy Center, 6/30/97. However, the Kennedy Center gig was postponed until mid 1997–98. A reading was planned for 2/97, to be followed by workshop prod in late spring, and full prod in fall 1997. On 3/27/97, at Raw Space rehearsal studios, 890 Broadway, a private showcase presentation reading of full script & 2 songs was held for audience of major Broadway producers. Sondheim & Weidman were there, as were producers Scott Rudin & Roger Berlind. p: Ira Weitzman; d: Lori Steinberg. Cast: Wilson: Victor Garber; Addison: Patrick Quinn; Their Mother: Cass Morgan; Paris Singer: Howard McGillin; Also with: Bob Ari, Candy Buckley, Nick Cokas, Randy Graff, Dee Hoty, Tom Ikeda, Greg Jbara, Norm Lewis, Michael McGrath, Robert Westenberg. On 9/23/97 newspaper rumors began that Sam Mendes would dir Kennedy Center run in spring 1998, followed by Broadway run in fall. Sondheim denied these rumors. He said a reading—not a workshop–might happen in 10/97, but only of Act I. On 11/8/97 another reading did take place, with most of Act I, including songs written so far:— the opening number, which was actually 4 songs (one of them being "Wise Guys"), followed by "Benicia," "Gold," "Next to You," "Addison's Trip Around the World," "Dowagers," "The Good Life" & "The Game." p: Ira Weitzman; d: Lori Steinberg; md: Paul Gemignani; accompanist: David Evans. Cast: Wilson: Victor Garber; Addison: Nathan Lane; Mama Mizner: Debra Monk; Also with: Ray Wills, Gregory Jbara, William Parry, Randy Graff. Another workshop planned for 5/98, and Washington premiere in 2/99. On 1/4/99 it was announced that Sam Mendes would dir Broadway prod, possibly in fall 1999, starring Garber & Lane. New workshop planned for spring 1999, with Rudin & Berlind to prod, with Dodger Theatricals & Kennedy Center. On 4/30/99 there was secret reading of script & score, and on 5/7/99 it was announced there would be fall 1999 workshop. On 9/13/99 Broadway opening date of 4/27/00 was announced, but with no theatre specified. Garber & Lane to star. On 9/24/99 it was announced Christopher Wilson had joined cast, in multiple roles, and on 9/27/00 Candy Buckley & Lauren Ward were announced. On 10/19/99 entire cast was confirmed. A month-long fall workshop did take place, at New York Theatre Workshop, 10/29/99–11/20/99. At some perfs only Act I was shown, and at others only parts of Act II. Scott Rudin was backer. d: Sam Mendes. Cast: Wilson: Victor Garber; Addison: Nathan Lane; Mama Mizner: Candy Buckley (Debra Monk was originally going to play this role); Paris Singer: Michael Hall; Also with: Lauren Ward, Christopher Wilson, Kevin Chamberlin, Nancy Opel, Brooks Ashmanskas, Jessica Boevers, Jessica Molaskey, William Parry, Clarke Thorell, Ray Wills. It was expected to go to Broadway, but workshop failed. There were several problems; Sondheim said it was a waste of time. On 10/29/99 it was announced that the producers had canceled Broadway plans. The project languished, Sam Mendes dropped out, then it got going again. On 3/12/00 Hal Prince was announced as new dir, and the title was changed to *Gold*. The Goodman Theatre, Chicago, was then planned as 1st venue for full prod. At that point Scott Rudin, who had lost money at the workshop & who was now out of the picture as far as the prod was concerned, threatened to sue, claiming he owned the rights. Hal Prince backed out. On 11/20/01 Sondheim & Weidman filed $5 million countersuit against Rudin for malicious interference. The very next day Rudin filed $8 million counter-countersuit, claiming breach of contract & fraud. This high-profile battle settled out of court. Rudin was to get $160,000 if the show was ever produced. This would cover his expenses at 1999 workshop. By 9/02 the show was 95 per cent finished, according to Hal Prince, who was now back in. He called the script "robust," and said that the creators were polishing it. On 10/31/02 Richard Kind & Howard McGillin were offered the leads at the Goodman, and on 11/1/02 Faith Prince (no relation to Hal) was announced. In early 2003 the name was changed again, to *Bounce*. Long-awaited song list announced on 6/24/03. Goodman, Chicago, 6/30/03–8/3/03 (closing date put back from 7/19/03, then from 7/26/03). Prev from 6/20/03 (date put back from 6/13/03). m/l: Stephen Sondheim; b: John Weidman; d: Harold Prince; ch: Michael Arnold; set: Eugene Lee; cos: Miguel Huidor; light: Howell Binkley; sound: Duncan Edwards; md: David Caddick; dance mus arr: Robert Nassif. Cast: Addison: Richard Kind; Wilson: Howard McGillin; Nellie, the gold rush dance hall girl: Michele Pawk (Faith Prince had originally been scheduled); Mama: Jane Powell; Lansing "Papa" Mizner: Herndon Lackey; Hollis Bessemer: Gavin Creel; Also with: Sean Blake, Marilyn Bogetich, Tom Daugherty, Jeff Dumas, Deanne Dunagan, Nicole Grothues, Rick Hilsabeck, Jeff Parker, Harriet Nzinga Plump, Jenny Powers, Craig Ramsay, Jacquelyn Ritz, Fred Zimmerman. Act I: "Bounce" (Wilson & Addison), "Opportunity" (Papa, Addison, Wilson, Mama), "Gold!" (Prospector, Wilson, Mama, Addison, Alaskans), "Gold!" (reprise) (Poker Players), "What's Your Rush?" (Nellie), "Next to You" (Addison, Wilson, Mama), "Addison's Trip Around the World" (Addison, Salesmen, Guatemalans, Servants), "What's Your Rush?" (reprise) (Wilson & Mrs. Yerkes), "Alaska" (Mrs. Yerkes & Wilson), "New York Sequence" (Wilson, Nellie, Reporters, Photographer, Ketchel, Armstrong, Jockey, Gamblers, Policemen, Wilson's Women), "(You Are) The Best Thing that Ever Has Happened to Me" (Wilson & Nellie) [moved here from Act II during tryouts], "Isn't He Something?" (Mama), "Bounce" (reprise) (Addison). Act II: "The Game" (Addison, Nellie, Wilson, Promoter), "Talent" (Hollis), "You" (Addison, Hollis, Aristocrats), "Addison's City" (Hollis, Wilson,

Addison, Nellie), "Boca Raton" (Boca Girl, Sportsmen, Fashion Models, Yachtsmen, Caruso, Salvador Dali, Wilson, Addison, Nellie, Hollis, Prospector, Varmints, Bobby Jones, Mae West, Princess Ghika, Chorus), "Last Flight" (Addison & Wilson), "Bounce" (reprise) (Wilson & Addison). Mixed reviews. Kennedy Center, Washington, DC, 10/21/03–11/16/03. Rehearsals began 9/03, in NYC. Prev from 10/6/03. "Alaska" was cut between Chicago & Washington runs. Act I was now 15 mins shorter. Same basic cast as in Chicago. Disastrous reviews, nixing Broadway plans. Cast recording made by Nonesuch in Washington, DC, 11/10/03–11/11/03, & released 5/4/04 (date put back from 4/27/04). On 5/9/04 there was to be a one-night only benefit concert in NYC for the Actors' Fund, with orig cast, but it was canceled

1007. *Box Office of the Damned*. Set in & around a theatre box office. CSC Theatre, 6/3/94. m/l/b/md: Michael James Ogborn; d/ch: Barry McNabb; Cast: Kristin Chenoweth, Mark Agnes. "A Season You'll Never Forget," "Please Hold," "Festival Fever," "Just Say No," "Viva la Matinee," "I'm in the Show," "We See it All," "Our Exchange Policy," "Remember Me," "One Ticket," "Stranger," "Daddy Long Legs," "Curtain Speech," "Late," "Clerk 2 Clerk"

1008. *Boy Meets Boy*. Set in London & Paris, Dec. 1936. American correspondent & English nobleman find each other. Actors Playhouse, 9/17/75–11/14/76. 463 perf. m/l: Billy Solly; b: Billy Solly & Donald Ward; d: Ron Troutman; ch: Robin Reesen; md: David Friedman. Cast: Joe Barrett, David Gallegly, Bobby Bowen, Mary-Ellen Hanlon, Kathy Willinger. "Boy Meets Boy," "Giving it up for Love," "Me," "The English Rose," "Marry an American," "It's a Boy's Life," "Does Anybody Love You?," "You're Beautiful," "Just My Luck," "It's a Dolly," "What Do I Care," "Clarence's Turn"

1009. *Boy on the Straight-Back Chair*. Drama with mus. St. Clement's Church, 2/14/69–3/22/69. 43 perf. m: Orville Stoeber; w: Ronald Tavel; d: Lee von Rhau. Cast: Kevin O'Connor, Gloria LeRoy

1010. *Boyband*. The story of a band. Gielgud, London, 6/8/99–8/14/99. p/m/l/b: Steve Levine, Aron Friedman, Nicky Graham; d: Peter Roew; ch: Emma Victoria. Cast: Bryan Murray, Kevin Andrew, Tom Ashton, Daniel Crossley, Damian Flood, Stepps

1011. *Brainchild*. A "musical in the mind." Forrest, Philadelphia, 3/25/74–4/6/74. Aimed at Broadway, it never made it. p: Adela Holzer; m: Michel Legrand; l: Hal David; b/d: Maxine Klein; set: Kert Lundell; cos: Joseph G. Aulisi; light: Thomas Skelton; md: Thomas Pierson. Cast: Tovah Feldshuh, Nancy Ann Denning, Dorian Harewood, Louise Hoven, Gene Lindsey, Signa Joy, Barbara Niles, Mark Siegel, Ben Harney, Marilyn Pasekoff. "I'm Tired of Me," "No Faceless People," "First Time I Heard a Bluebird," "I Know You Are There," "Don't Talk, Don't Think," "Low Bottom Woman," "I've Been Starting Tomorrow," "Let Me Think for You," "I Never Met a Rus-

sian I Didn't Like," "Sally Ensalada," "Let Me Be Your Mirror," "Just a Little Space Can Be a Growing Place," "What is It?," "Don't Pull up the Flowers," "Everything that Happens to You"

1012. *El Bravo!* Set in El Barrio, somewhere in NYC, about a modern day Robin Hood called Pepe de Marco (El Bravo). Entermedia, 6/16/81–7/26/81. 48 perf. p: Kenneth Waissman, Edward Mezvinsky, Sidney Shlenker; m/l: John Clifton; b: Jose Fernandez & Tom Schiera; based on story by Jose Fernandez & Kenneth Waissman; d/ch: Patricia Birch; set: Tom Lynch; cos: Carrie F. Robbins; light: Neil Peter Jampolis; sound: Tom Morse; ms: Louis St. Louis; md: Herbert Kaplan; orch: Michael Gibson & Gary Anderson. Cast: Aurelio Padron, Dennis Daniels, Michael Jeter, Vanessa Bell, Frank Kopyc, Yamil Borges, Olga Merediz, Duane Bodin, Jesse Corti, Alaina Warren Zachary, Jenifer Lewis, Quitman Fludd III, Ray Stephens, Chamaco Garcia, Charlie Serrano, Ray DeMattis, Keith Jochim, Starr Danias, Lenka Peterson, S.J. Davis, Julia Lema, Stephen Jay, Leilani Jones, Greg Rosatti. "El Bravo," "Cuchifrito Restaurant," "Que Pasa, My Love?," "Honest John's Game," "Chiquita Bonita," "Shoes," "Hey Chico," "Criminal," "He Says," "Talent Contest," "Gotta Get Out," "Adios Barrio," "Fairy Tales," "Torture," "That Latin Lure," "Congratulations!," "Bailar!," "And Furthermore"

1013. *Breakfast at Tiffany's*. Same story as successful 1961 movie; writer fascinated by eccentric neighbor, Holly Golightly. The most anticipated Broadway show of 1966–67, but it never opened. m/l: Bob Merrill; based on Truman Capote's novella; ch: Michael Kidd; set: Oliver Smith; cos: Freddy Wittop; light: Tharon Musser; md: Stanley Lebowsky. Forrest, Philadelphia, 10/15/66. 2 acts; 25 scenes. Then entitled *Holly Golightly*. "I've Got a Penny," "Holly Golightly," "So Here We Are Again," "Traveling," "Freddy Chant," "Holly Golucci," "Scum-Dee-Dum," "Lament for Ten Men," "My Nice Ways," "Home for Wayward Girls," "You've Never Kissed Her," "Bessie's Blues," "Who Needs Her," "Nothing is New in New York," "The Bachelor," "The Rose," "Breakfast at Tiffany's." Note: "Moon River" was never in this show, at any stage. Boston (1 month). Still called *Holly Golightly*. After Truman Capote refused to do a libretto, Nunnally Johnson wrote one, but that was rejected (Bob Merrill's score was mostly to Nunnally Johnson's book). Abe Burrows then came aboard, as librettist/dir (Josh Logan had rejected the idea), but it was still obvious the show was in trouble. Edward Albee was called in to re-write book & said some unkind things about Abe Burrows, who left. Joe Anthony then took over as dir. Larry Kert & others joined & others were dropped. Diahann Carroll was orig choice for Holly, but Mary Tyler Moore was thought to be big draw. But she didn't work out, and it was rumored that Tammy Grimes was waiting to take over. However, Mary Tyler Moore did go to Broadway. Majestic, Broadway, 12/12/66, 2 acts; 15 scenes. Now called *Breakfast at Tiffany's*. On 12/14/66, after 4 prev, producer

David Merrick announced its closure in most dramatic terms, thus canceling scheduled 12/26/66 official Broadway opening. Several actors made transition from Philly to NY, others didn't (in which case the Broadway previews actor is in italics, while several characters were cut entirely. Cast: Jeff Claypool: Richard Chamberlain; Holly: Mary Tyler Moore; Mr. Buckley: James Olson (new role for NY); Mr. Moss: William Stanton; Voice: John Anania; O.J. Berman: Martin Wolfson; O.J.'s Assistant: Richard Terry; Guests: John Anania, Justin McDonough, Henry LeClair, John Aman, Scott Schultz, Feodore Tedick, Robert Donahue; Rusty Trawler: Brooks Morton, *Thayer David*; Mag Wildwood: Sally Kellerman; The Cat: Louis; Doc Golightly: Art Lund; Joe Bell: Charles Welch (in NY this character became Joe Howard); Messenger: John Sharpe; Bar Patrons: William Stanton, John Sharpe, Mitchell Thomas; Jose Ybarra: Mitchell Gregg (in NY this character became Carlos, as played by *Larry Kert*); Patrick O'Connor: Robert Donahue (new role for NY); Sheila Fezzonetti: Paula Bauersmith (new role for NY); Announcer: Justin McDonough; Hospital Attendant: Paul Solen; Giovanni's Girls: Sally Hart, Maryann Kerrick, Marybeth Lair (new characters for NY); Giovanni: Paul Michael (new character for NY); Prison Guard/Detective: Robert Donahue (roles cut for NY); Singers: Sally Hart, Lee Hooper, Maryann Kerrick, Marybeth Lair, John Anania, Henry LeClair, Robert Donahue, Bob Gorman, Justin McDonough, Richard Terry, *John Aman, Scott Schultz, Feodore Tedick*; Dancers: Barbara Beck, Trudy Carson, Judith Dunford, Carolyn Kirsch, Priscilla Lopez, Debe Macomber, Pat Trott, *Bud Fleming, Teak Lewis, Dom Salinaro, John Sharpe, Paul Solen, William Stanton, Kent Thomas, Mitchell Thomas*. Understudies: Holly: Sally Kellerman; Jeff: Justin McDonough; Doc: Robert Donahue; Mag: Maryann Kerrick. "Holly Golightly," "Breakfast at Tiffany's," "When Daddy Comes Home," "Freddy Chant," "Lament for Ten Men," "Home for Wayward Girls," "Who Needs Her?," "You've Never Kissed Her," "Lulamae," "Stay with Me," "I'm Not the Girl," "Grade 'A' Treatment," "Ciao, Cumpare," "Better Together," "Same Mistakes"

Brief Encounter see # 1979, this appendix

1014. *A Brief History of White Music.* Soulful look (by black performers) at white pop music. Village Gate, 11/19/96–9/7/97. Prev from 10/17/96. p: Gene Wolsk, Rad Prods, Art D'Lugoff; conceived by: DeeDee Thomas & David Tweedy; d/ch: Ken Roberson. Cast: Wendy Edmead, James Alexander, Deborah Keeling. "Who Put the Bomp," "Bei Mir Bist du Schoen," "I Got a Gal in Kalamazoo," "That'll Be the Day," "Teenager in Love," "Where the Boys Are," "Leader of the Pack," "Walk Like a Man," "Love Potion No. 9," "Blue Suede Shoes," "Love Me Tender" (medley), "Jailhouse Rock," "California Dreamin'," "Monday Monday," "Surfin' USA," "I Got You Babe," "Itsy Bitsy Teeny Weenie Yellow Polka Dot Bikini," "These Boots Are Made for Walkin'," "Do Wah Diddy Diddy," "Son of a

Preacher Man," "To Sir with Love," "Downtown," "She Loves You," "I Wanna Hold Your Hand," "With a Little Help from My Friends," "Sgt Pepper's Lonely Hearts Club Band," "Imagine," "We Can Work it Out"

1015. *Bright Lights, Big City.* Frustrated writer-husband tries to find himself in NYC night spots. New York Theatre Workshop, 2/24/99–3/21/99. 27 prev from 1/31/99. 31 perf. m/l/b: Paul Scott Goodman; based on novel by Jay McInerney; d/ch: Michael Greif; set: Paul Clay; cos: Angela Wendt; light: Blake Burba; sound: Jon Weston; md/orch: Richard Barone. Cast: Paul Scott Goodman, Patrick Wilson, Carla Bianco, Natascia Diaz, Jerry Dixon, Kerry O'Malley. "Bright Lights, Big City," "I Love Drugs," "1984"/"Heartbreak," "Missing," "Beautiful Sunday," "Coma Baby"/ "Gotham Magazine," "Can I Come Over, Please," "Fact and Fiction," "You Don't Show Me Your Stories Anymore," "I Hate the French," "Brother," "Monstrous Events," "Odeon"/"Club Crawl," "I Wanna Have Sex Tonight," "Forest Hills, 9 a.m.," "Happy Birthday, Darling," "New Literature," "Walk," "To Model," "So Many Little Things," "It's Great to Be Back in the City," "Thinkers and Drinkers"/"Kindness," "Perfect Feeling," "Tonight I Am Happy," "You Couldn't Handle It, Jamie," "Come On," "Wednesday," "Heart and Soul," "The Letter," "Bad Blow," "Camera Wall," "How About Dinner at My Place?," "My Son," "Mummies at the Met," "Are You Still Holding My Hand?," "Stay in My Life," "Wordfall." Peter Lewis Auditorium, Guggenheim, NY, 9/14/03–9/15/03. Concert. Part of *Works and Process* series. Cast: Maya Days, Norm Lewis, Gavin Creel, Liz Larsen, Eden Espinosa, Sarah Litzsinger, AnnMarie Milazzo

1016. *Brighton Rock.* About a 17-year-old gangster. Almeida, Islington, London (their 1st musical), 10/5/04–11/13/04. Prev from 9/20/04. m: John Barry; l: Don Black (Grahame Greene wrote the orig lyrics, but they were not used); b: Giles Havergal; from an idea by John Barry; based on Grahame Greene's novel; d: Michael Attenborough (Richard's son. Richard played Pinkie in the 1947 movie); ch: Karen Bruce; set: Lez Brotherston; Steven Edis (md/arr). Cast: Pinkie: Michael Jibson; Also with: Sophia Ragavelas, Nick Lumley, Harriet Thorpe

1017. *Bring in the Morning.* Set in the ghetto of Cougar's mind. Variety Arts, 4/23/94–6/5/94. 36 prev. 16 perf. p: Jeff Britton & Edgar M. Bronfman; m: Gary William Friedman; l/adapted: Herb Schapiro; based on writings of young people in Poets in Public Service program; d: Bertin Rowser & Michele Assaf; ch: Michele Assaf (ch); md: Louis St. Louis; orch: Dianne Adams McDowell & Michael Gibson; set: Ken Foy; cos: Robert Mackintosh; light: Ken Billington. Cast: Cougar: Sean Grant; Also with: Yassmin Alers, Imelda de los Reyes. "Come into My Jungle," "Bring in the Morning," "Let it Rain," "You (Tu)," "Not Your Cup of Tea," "Ghetto of My Mind," "Funky Eyes," "Another Cry," "I'm on My Way," "Never Stop Believing," "Something is Wrong with Everyone Today," "Missing Per-

son," "Light of Your Love (La Luz de tu Amor)," "Hector's Dream," "Trip," "Glory of Each Morning," "Deliver My Soul," "I Want to Walk in a Garden"

1018. *Broadway Babylon: The Musical That Never Was!* Songs from other Broadway musicals. Paper Moon Cabaret, 5/18/84–6/9/84. 2 prev. 20 perf. p/conceived & created by: Chris Adams & David Agress; d/ch: Susan Stroman. Cast: Josie de Guzman, Scott Bakula, Melinda Gilb

1019. *Broadway Dandies.* Musical romp through NY. International Cabaret, 12/17/74–12/22/74. 8 perf. p/d: Robert Johnnene; ch: Henry Le Tang; md: Don Whisted. Cast: Robert Fitch, Janet Saunders, Suzi Swanson, Hal James Pederson. "On Broadway," "Lullaby of Broadway," "Give Our Regards to Broadway," "Wilkommen," "Cabaret," "Carousel," "Standing on the Corner," "Big Spender," "Ten Cents a Dance," "I'm All Smiles," "Let's Dance," "Ain't Misbehavin'," "Honeysuckle Rose," "Adelaide's Lament," "Summertime," "I Never Has Seen Snow," "Night and Day," "Too Darn Hot," "Sisters," "Aquarius," "Send in the Clowns," "That's Entertainment," "Another Opening"

1020. *Broadway for Peace.* Concert in the interests of peace. Philharmonic Hall, NY, 1/21/68. m/l: Leonard Bernstein, Betty Comden & Adolph Green. Cast: Barbra Streisand, Leonard Bernstein. "So Pretty"

1021. *Broadway Opry '79.* Series of country music concerts. St. James, Broadway, 7/27/79–8/2/79. 6 perf. creative d: Jonas McCord; set/light: Michael J. Hotopp & Paul de Pass. Cast: Tanya Tucker, Floyd Cramer, Don Gibson, Mickey Newbury, Waylon Jennings, The Crickets, The Waylors

1022. *Broadway Scandals of 1928.* Upstairs at O'Neals, 7/7/82–8/15/82. 3 prev. 39 perf. p: Jefrey Silverman & Walter Willison; m/md: Jefrey Silverman; l/scenario/conceived by/d: Walter Willison; ch: Jo Anna Lehmann & Gwen Hillier Lowe. Cast: Texas Guinan: Jessica James, *Diane J. Findlay*; Also with: Jefrey Silverman, Walter Willison, Jo Anna Lehmann, Rose Scudder, Gwen Hillier Lowe (*Eva Grant*), Kenny D'Aquila, Bill Johnson. "Scandals," "Let's Go Boating," "Picture Me with You," "Nobody Needs a Man as Bad as That!," "Charleston Under the Moon," "When You Come to the End of Your Rainbow," "Happy Jest Bein' with Me," "Blowing Bubbles in the Bathtub," "I Gotta Hear a Song," "A Good Ol' Mammy Song," "Things Have Never Been Better," "That Man at the Piano," "Sodomangamor," "I Couldn't Say," "Tango," "Give a Girl a Break!," "Broadway Wedding," "Better Bein' Loved," "Maizie," "Scandals Finale." See also *Options* in this appendix

1023. *Broadway Sings the Old Potato.* Children's musical. Set during Hannukah. Peter Norton Symphony Space, 11/24/03–11/30/03. p: 6–10 Prods; m: Gail C. Bluestone; l/b: Eileen Bluestone Sherman (based on her 1984 picture book of same name); d/ch: Randy Skinner (Ben Vereen had been scheduled). Cast: Matt Jacoby, B.J. Crosby, Debbie Gravitte, Frank Gorshin, Charlotte Rae, Sky Jarrett, Molly Ephraim. It had been a TV special in 1990

1024. *Broadway '68*. Musical revue. Songs from Broadway musicals that opened in 67–68 season. La Mama, 2/12/98–3/7/98. 12 perf. conceived by/d: Scott Wittman; ch: Joey Pizzi & Adam Shankman; ms: Dick Gallagher. Cast: Annie Golden, Laura Kenyon, Maggie Moore, Paul Dobie, Ned Hannah, Beau & Debbie Gravitte

1025. *Broken Toys!* Set in bedroom & attic of suburban house. Young girl falls in love with toy soldier who comes to life, man-sized. Orpheum, 4/15/82–5/1/82. 9 perf. m/l/b: Keith Berger; d: Carl Haber. Cast: Elizabeth Wren Arthur (*Debra Greenfield*), Keith Berger, Oona Lind, Johnny Zeitz. Actors Playhouse, 7/19/82–8/15/82. 19 prev. 29 perf. "This Life's the Right One for Me," "We're on a Shelf in Your Attic," "Play with Me," "Broken and Bent," "Let's Play, Let's Say," "I Don't Play with Humans," "Prayer Song," "Johnny Space," "Choo Choo Rap," "Lady, Ride with Me," "Not of Her World," "Kangaroo Court," "I Don't Think I Like This Game," "Temperance Song," "So, You Wanna Be a Toy," "I Got That Other-Lady's-with-My-Baby Feeling," "Ain't Worth a Dime," "Rag Doll Rag," "Funny Wind-Up Toy," "Left Alone to Be," "Weird Fun," "Wind-Up in New York City"

1026. *Brooklyn Bridge*. The building of Brooklyn Bridge. Presented on the 100th anniversary. Quaigh, 8/17/83–9/11/83. 4 prev. 28 perf. p: Dorothy Chansky, with Bridge Theatre Prod Co.; m: Scott MacLarty; l/b: Dorothy Chansky; d: Marjorie Melnick; ch: Missy Whitchurch; md: Harrison Fisher. "Brooklyn," "Love Means," "Can I Do It All?," "Bridge to the Future," "Cash Politics," "The Roebling Plan," "When You're the Only One," "Ain't No Women There," "Every Day for Four Years," "Man in the Window," "All that I Know"

1027. *Brownstone*. Set in & around NYC brownstone apartment building during course of one year, from autumn to autumn. Hudson Guild, 5/23/84–6/24/84. 35 perf. m/l: Peter Larson & Josh Rubins; d: Andrew Cadiff; ch: Cheryl Carty; md: Yolanda Segovia; orch: Harold Wheeler. Cast: Maureen McGovern, Loni Ackerman, Lenny Wolpe, Ralph Bruneau, Kimberly Farr. "Someone's Moving In," "Fiction Writer," "I Just Want to Know," "There She Goes," "We Should Talk," "Camouflage," "Thanks a Lot," "Neighbors Above, Neighbors Below," "I Wasn't Home for Christmas," "What Do People Do?," "Not Today," "The Water Through the Trees," "You Still Don't Know," "Babies on the Brain," "Almost There," "Don't Tell Me Everything," "One of Them," "Spring Cleaning," "Fiction Writer Duet," "He Didn't Leave It Here," "It isn't the End of the World," "See That Lady There," "Since You Stayed Here," "We Came Along Too Late," "Hi There, Joan," "It's a Funny Thing," "Nevertheless," "Someone's Moving Out." Presented again, 10/18/86–12/6/86. 69 perf, by Roundabout. d: Andrew Cadiff (d); set: Loren Sherman; md: Don Jones; sound: Peter Fitzgerald. Cast: Liz Callaway, Rex Smith, Ben Harney, Ernestine

Jackson, Kimberly Farr. Cast recording finally released in 6/03

1028. *The Bubbly Black Girl Sheds Her Chameleon Skin*. A black Broadway dancer from childhood to adulthood. Playwrights Horizons, 6/20/00–7/16/00. 29 prev from 5/26. 32 perf. m/l/b: Kirsten Childs; d: Wilfredo Medina; ch: A.C. Ciulla; set: David Gallo; cos: David C. Woolard; sound: Jon Weston; md: Fred Carl. Cast: La Chanze, Natalie Venetia Belcon, Cheryl Alexander, Darius de Haas, Duane Boutte, Jerry Dixon, Jonathan Dokuchitz, Felicia Finley. "Welcome to My L.A.," "Sweet Chitty Chatty," "Smile, Smile," "I Am in a Dance Class," "The Skate," "Sticks and Stones," "Walk on the Water," "Pass the Flame," "War is Not Good," "Brave New World," "Give it Up," "Belle of the Ball," "Beautiful Bright Blue Sky," "Legacy," "The Argument," "Wonderland," "Who's That Bubbly Black Girl?," "Secretarial Pool," "Pretty," "Three Dance Classes," "Director Bob," "Come with Me," "Granny's Advice," "Listen!," "There Was a Girl." Partially developed during 1998 National Music Theatre Conference at Eugene O'Neill Theatre Center, Waterford, Conn.

1029. *The Buccaneer*. Old-fashioned boys' magazine threatened by American comics. New Watergate, London, 9/8/53. w: Sandy Wilson; d: Lloyd Lamble; ch: John Heawood. Cast: Rachel Roberts, Bill Nagy. "Good Clean Fun," "Captain Fairbrother," "It's Commercial," "Unromantic Us," "Facts of Life," "You'll Find Out," "Something's Missing," "For Adults Only," "Oh, What a Beautiful Brain," "Read All About It," "Just Another Man," "Just Another Girl," "In the Good Old USA," "Learn to Do One Thing Well," "Why Did it Have to be Spring?," "Behind the Times," "Just Pals." Theatre Royal, Brighton, 8/22/55; Southsea, Hampshire; Lyric, Hammersmith, 9/8/55–2/4/56. 170 perf; then a few other London theatres; Apollo, London, 2/22/56–3/17/56. 29 perf. d: William Chappell; ch: William Chappell & Honor Blair; set: Peter Snow; md: Charles Zwar; cast recording on HMV. Cast: Kenneth Williams, Ronald Radd, Billie Love

1030. *The Buck Stops Here*. Set 1894–1953. AMAS, 10/27/83–11/20/83. 16 perf. m/l/conceived by: Richard A. Lippman; add l/b: Norman J. Fedder; d: Reggie Life; ch: Tim Millett; add m/md: Lea Richardson. Cast: Harry Truman: Harris Shore; Bess: Alexana Ryer. "The 33rd President," "If You Try," "My Best Friend," "That Boy's Not Good Enough for You," "Haberdashery Blues," "When Will You Learn," "I Believe in the Man," "The Buck Stops Here," "My One Day," "Dear Dad," "Simple, But Not an Ordinary Man," "Never Look Back," "This Time We're Clapping for You"

1031. *Budgie*. Cambridge Theatre, London, 10/18/88 (3 months). m: Mort Shuman; l: Don Black; b: Keith Waterhouse & Willis Hall; based on TV series of early 1970s (which starred Adam Faith as loser Ronald "Budgie" Bird & Iain Cuthbertson as sleazy Soho night club owner, Charlie Endell); cast recording on

MCA. Cast: Adam Faith, Anita Dobson, Caroline O'Connor, John Turner, Philip Cox, Richard Calkin, Julian Littman. "They're Naked and They Move," "Thank You, Mr. Endell," "There is Love and There is Love," "If You Want to See Palermo Again," "In One of My Weaker Moments," "Mary, Doris and Jane," "Why Not Me?," "If it Wasn't for the Side Effects," "Old Compton Street," "If That Baby Could Talk," "Winners and Losers," "I Like That in a Man," "Budgie"

1032. *Bugles at Dawn*. Set in the Civil War. Chernuchin, 10/10/82–10/24/82. 12 perf. m/l: Mark Barkan & David Vando; suggested by Stephen Crane's *The Red Badge of Courage*; d: Robert Pesola. Cast: Joseph Breen, Jay Devlin, Nancy Ringham, Peggy Atkinson, Mimi Bessette. "Marching to Victory," "Blow, Bugles, Blow," "More is Less," "Covered in the Rear," "Run," "Give Me Love," "Picture Perfect," "Annie's Song," "Dream," "Life's Odyssey," "Flag of Death"

1033. *Bugsy Malone*. Set in NY in 1929. Her Majesty's, London, 5/26/83–2/11/84. 300 perf. m/l: Paul Williams; b: Mickey Dolenz; based on movie by Alan Parker. "Bugsy Malone," "Tomorrow," "I'm Feeling Fine," "My Name is Tallulah," "Ordinary Fool," "Fat Sam's Grand Slam," "You Give a Little Love"

1034. *A Bundle of Nerves*. Satire on major neuroses of our time. Musical revue. Top of the Gate, 3/13/83–4/10/83. 33 perf. m: Brian Lasser; l: Geoff Leon & Edward Dunn; d/ch: Arthur Faria; cos: David Toser; md: Clay Fullum; orch: Steven Margoshes. Cast: Gary Beach, Vicki Lewis. "A Bundle of Nerves," "The News," "She Smiled at Me," "Boogey Man," "Flying," "Old Enough to Know Better," "Studs," "That's What'll Happen to Me," "I Don't Know How to Have Sex," "Fatality Hop," "Waiting," "After Dinner Drinks," "Slice of Life," "What Do You Do," "Connie," "I'm Afraid," "That Sound"

1035. *Burlesque on Parade*. Revue. Village Theatre, 12/10/63–12/29/63. 33 perf. m/md: David Fleischmann; l: Eric Blau; ch: Elna Laun. Cast: Blaze Starr, Dick Dana, Ken Martin, June Knight, Paul Brown, Charlie Robinson (also d), Jean Carroll, Thelma Pelish, Pam Burrell, Judy Cassmore, Altovise Gore, Robert St. Clair

1036. *The Burning Boat*. Unsuccessful love affair in English seaside town during music festival. Royal Court, London, 3/10/55–3/19/55. 12 perf. p: Laurier Lister; w: Nicholas Phipps & Geoffrey Wright; d: Murray MacDonald; md: Leonard Hancock. Cast: Bruce Trent, Marion Grimaldi, Marie Ney, Michael Gough, John Abineri, John Bennett, Anthea Askey

1037. *Busker Alley*. Set in London's West End theatre district just before WWII. Opened at the Macauley, Louisville, 4/7/95. Closed in Tampa 10/8/95, after star Tommy Tune broke left foot, thus canceling its scheduled 11/16/95 Broadway opening. However, it had been beset by problems from its very beginning. p: Barry & Fran Weissler, Jujamcyn Theatres/TV ASAHI, PACE Theatrical Group; m/l: Richard M. Sherman & Robert B. Sherman); b: A.J. Carothers; based on 1938 British film *St. Mar-*

tin's Lane, written by Clemence Dane; d/ch: Jeff Calhoun; set: Tony Walton; cos: Willa Kim; light: Richard Pilbrow; sound: Brian Ronan; md: John McDaniel; orch: William David Brohn. Cast: Tommy Tune, Brent Barrett, Darcie Roberts, Marcia Lewis, Robert Nichols, Laurie Gamache, Brad Aspel, Michael Berresse, Paige Price, Mark Santoro. Previously performed as *Stage Door Charley*, and *Buskers*

1038. *Buskers*. Stage Arts Theatre, 4/27/86. w/d: Howard Goldberg; ch: Lillo Way. Cast: Tony Azito, Sasha Charnin, Kimberly Hall, JoAnn M. Hunter, Phil La Duca, Anthony Marciona, Kelly Woodruff. "Power in the Air," "I Walk Alone," "All of My Love," "Pain in My Heart," "Born to Love," "Love at First Sight," "Alien Love," "Soap is Good for You," "I Know What Love Can Bring," "Maybe I'm Lonely"

1039. *Buy Bonds, Buster!* About troop entertaining & the drives for war-bonds in early 1940s. Theatre de Lys, 6/4/72. 1 perf. m/b: Jack Holmes; l/conceived by: Bill Conklin & Bob Miller; d: John Bishop; ch: Bick Goss; set: William Pitkin; md: Shelly Markham. Cast: SuEllen Estey, Winston DeWitt Hemsley, Virginia Martin, Rick Podell, Pamela Hunt, Jane Robertson. "Pearl," "So Long for Now," "The Freedom Choo-Choo," "Dreamboat from Dreamland," "These Are Worth Fighting For," "The Woogie Boogie," "Canteen Serenade," "Donuts for Defense," "Now and Then," "Master Race Polka," "Us Two," "When the Bluebirds Fly All Over the World," "Buy Bonds, Buster," "My G.I. Joey," "O Say Can You See." Previously ran in Atlanta

1040. *Buzzsaw Berkeley*. Set in Grave Hollow, USA, in 1939. WPA, 8/1/89–8/27/89. 19 prev. 8 perf. A WPA Silly Series presentation. m/l: Michael John La Chiusa; d: Christopher Ashley. Cast: Ethyl Eichelberger, Becky Gelke, Vicki Lewis, Keith Reddin, Peter Bartlett, John Hickok, Shauna Hicks

1041. *By Bernstein*. Musical cabaret tribute to Leonard Bernstein. Westside. 11/23/75–12/7/75. 40 prev. 17 perf. conceived by: Betty Comden & Adolph Green; d: Michael Bawtree; light: Marc B. Weiss; md: Clay Fullum; orch: Thomas Pierson. Cast: Jack Bittner, Janie Sell, Kurt Peterson, Ed Dixon, Patricia Elliott, Jim Corti, Margery Cohen. Songs written by Leonard Bernstein for various shows but which were dropped in production. "Welcome," "Gabey's Comin'," "Lonely Me," "Say When," "Like Everybody Else," "I'm Afraid it's Love," "Another Love," "I Know a Fellow," "It's Gotta Be Bad to Be Good," "Dream with Me," "Another Love" (reprise), "Ringaroundarosy," "Captain Hook's Soliloquy," "The Riobamba," "The Intermission's Great," "The Story of My Life," "Ain't Got No Tears Left," "The Collie's Dilemma," "In There," "Spring Will Come Again," "Here Comes the Sun"

1042. *By Hex*. About the Amish in Lancaster County, Pa. Tempo Playhouse, 6/18/56. 40 perf. p: Julie Bovasso; m/l: Howard Blankman; d: Bill Penn; ch: Ed Balin. Cast: Ken Cantril, Wynne Miller, Tom Mixon. "Market Day," "Shunned," "Ferhuddled and Ferhexed," "Wonderful Good," "Wonderful Bad," "Antiques," "What is Love?," "I Can Learn," "Only a

Man," "An Amishman," "I Have Lived," "I Know My Love," "The Trouble with Me," "Something New," "It Takes Time." Revived in summer theatre, 1967. Cast: Marianne Weicksel, Fred Vanderpoel

1043. *By Jupiter*. Set in Ancient Greece. Shubert, Broadway, 6/3/42–6/12/43. 427 perf. p: Dwight Deere Wiman, Richard Rodgers, Richard Kollmar; m/l/b: Richard Rodgers & Lorenz Hart; based on Julian F. Thompson's *The Warrior's Husband*; d: Josh Logan; ch: Robert Alton; set/light: Jo Mielziner; cos: Irene Sharaff; md: Johnny Green; orch: Don Walker; voc arr: Johnny Green & Buck (Clay) Warnick. Cast: Ray Bolger, Constance Moore (*Nanette Fabray* from 2/43), Benay Venuta, Vera-Ellen, Mark Dawson, Robert Hightower, Jayne Manners, Rose Inghram, Bertha Belmore, Babs Heath. "For Jupiter and Greece," "Jupiter Forbid," "Life with Father," "Nobody's Heart (Belongs to Me)," "The Gateway of the Temple of Minerva," "Here's a Hand," "No, Mother, No," "The Boy I Left Behind Me," "Ev'rything I've Got," "Bottoms Up," "Careless Rhapsody," "Wait 'til You See Her" (dropped a month after Broadway opening), "Now that I've Got My Strength." The last original show written by Rodgers & Hart together. Folded when Ray Bolger quit to entertain troops in Far East. Theater Four, 1/19/67–4/30/67. 118 perf. add material: Fred Ebb; d: Christopher Hewett; ch: Ellen Ray; set: Herbert Senn & Ellen Pond; md: Milton Setzer; orch: Abba Bogin; cast recording on RCA. Cast: Bob Dishy, Sheila Sullivan, Emory Bass, Debra Lyman. 4/5/02–4/7/02, part of the York Theatre Co.'s *Musicals in Mufti* series. d: Ted Sod. Cast: Kevin Cahoon, Klea Blackhurst, Burke Moses, Merwin Goldsmith

1044. *By Strouse*. Musical revue. Ballroom, 2/1/78–4/30/78. 156 perf. p: Norman Kean; m/d: Charles Strouse; l: Lee Adams & Martin Charnin; ch: Mary Kyte. Cast: Gary Beach, Donna Marshall, Maureen Moore, Gail Nelson. Collection of Strouse songs from various shows, including *Bye Bye Birdie*, *All American*, *Golden Boy*, *It's a Bird, It's a Plane, It's Superman*, *Applause*, *Annie*, *Charlie and Algernon*, and the unproduced shows *Hunky Dory*, *Palm Beach*, *The Borrowers*, *Marjorie Morningstar*, and other works. "Stick Around," "A Lot of Living to Do," "Immigration and Naturalization Rag," "This is the Life," "Colorful," "What a Country," "N.Y.C.," "Don't Forget 127th Street," "I'm Not in Philadelphia," "Half of Life," "One Boy," "One Last Kiss," "We Love You, Conrad," "Born Too Late," "Bye Bye Birdie," "How Lovely to Be a Woman," "Livin' Alone," "Some Bright Morning," "Marjorie Morningstar," "Welcome to the Theatre," "But Alive," "In a Silly Mood," "One of a Kind," "Good Friends," "Everything's Great," "Hunky Dory," "You're Never Fully Dressed without a Smile," "Put on a Happy Face," "Tomorrow," "Once Upon a Time," "Lorna's Here," "Night Song," "Those Were the Days," "Applause," "A Broadway Musical"

1045. *Cabalgata*. Spanish musical cavalcade. Interpretation of Iberian folklore in song, dance & spoken word. Broadway Theatre,

Broadway, 7/7/49–9/10/49. 76 perf. p: Sol Hurok; d/ch/cos: Daniel Cordoba; set: Luis Marquez; md/orch/arr: Ramon Bastida. Cast: Carmen Vazquez, Pepita Marco, Floriana Alba, Pilar Calvo, Aurea Reyes, Jose Toledano, Paco Fernandez, Manuel Medina, Paco Millet, Violeta Carrillo, Maria Castan, Pepita Durango. Organized by Daniel Cordoba in Madrid in 1942. Came to NY after 7 years in Spain, Latin America & West of USA

1046. *Le Cabaret Risque*. Set in Paris nightclub in 1930s. Time Cafe, 10/1/92–10/15/92. 3 perf. p: Le Cirque Gregoire; w: Robin Noble; songs: Timothy J. Anderson & Debra Kaye; guest ch: Peter Di Falco; md: Debra Kaye. Cast: Robert Cardazone, Debra Kaye, Suzanne Gregoire, Ian Betts, J.S. Anderson. "Le Cabaret Risque," "Room of Madagascar," "Je ne t'aime pas," "Taunting Song," "Lolaboa's Boa," "Wonderful Nightmare"

1047. *Cabin in the Sky*. The struggle between the Lord & the Devil's henchmen for the soul of Little Joe Jackson. Martin Beck, Broadway, 10/25/40–3/8/41. 156 perf. p: Albert Lewis & Vinton Freedley; m: Vernon Duke; l: John Latouche & Ted Fetter; b: Lynn Root; based on Lynn Root's story "Little Joe;" d/ch: George Balanchine; dial d: Albert Lewis; set/cos: Boris Aronson; md: Max Meth; voc arr: Hugh Martin. Cast: Ethel Waters, Todd Duncan, Dooley Wilson, Katherine Dunham, Rex Ingram, Archie Savage, Roger Ohardieno, Lawaune Kennard (she became Lawaune Ingram), Talley Beatty, Lavinia Williams, Candido Vicenty. The first major musical to play the Martin Beck, and Ethel Waters' only book musical. "The General's Song," "Pay Heed," "Taking a Chance on Love" [the big hit], "Cabin in the Sky," "Holy Unto the Lord," "Dem Bones," "Do What You Wanna Do," "My Old Virginia Home (on the Nile)," "Love Me Tomorrow," "Love Turned the Light Out," "Honey in the Honeycomb," "Savannah." Filmed, with Ethel Waters, in 1943. Unsuccessful revised OB revival, at Greenwich Mews, 1/21/64–3/1/64. 47 perf. d: Brian Shaw; ch: Pepe DeChazza. Cast: Rosetta Le Noire, Ketty Lester, Joseph Attles, Albert Popwell. "Wade in the Water," "We'll Live All Over Again" [written for 1940 prod but never used], "The Man Upstairs" [new to this show], "Taking a Chance on Love," "Cabin in the Sky," "Great Day" [written for this prod], "Do What You Wanna Do," "Not a Care in the World" [originally written by Duke & Latouche for the show *Banjo Eyes*], "Not So Bad to Be Good" [new to this show], "Love Me Tomorrow," "Love Turned the Light Out," "Livin' it Up" [written for this prod], "Honey in the Honeycomb," "Savannah." Note: "My Old Virginia Home," from the 1940 prod, was cut from this prod. Sol Goldman 14th Street YMHA, 10/21/03–11/9/03. Part of the *Musicals Tonight!* series. Cast: Leslee Warren, Tyrone Grant, Glenne Townsend, Joe Wilson, Thursday Farrar

1048. *Cafe a Go Go*. Set in 1960s London. 31 rock songs. Premiered at Kings Head, London, 1990, as *A Slice of Saturday Night*, and moved to the Strand. Americanized as *Fab!*, and ran at Alcazar, San Francisco. Re-named again, as *Cafe a Go Go*. Cafe a Go Go (in the Edison Hotel), 7/13/03. Prev from 6/7/03. p: Joe & Daniel Corcoran; m/l: The Heather Brothers; d: John Hadden; ch: Susan Dibble

1049. *Cafe Puttanesca*. About prostitutes saying goodbye to one of their own in an Amsterdam bar in 1946. m/l: Michael Ogborn; b: Michael Ogborn & Terence J. Nolen. It began with a Philadelphia workshop, produced by the Arden Theatre, 11/11/02–11/22/02. d: Terence J. Nolen; md: Bryan Loudermilk. Cast: Jeffrey Coon, Kate Shindle, Anne Robinson, Mary Martello, Rebecca Robbins. "My Mother's Frying Pan," "Artists and Models," "Au Revoir l'Amour," "Oh, How I Miss the Kaiser," "Rasputin and the Russian Nun," "Ou Apres la Guerre." It was a cabaret-style show back then, and was revised and expanded into a book musical. World premiere at the Arden, Philadelphia, 9/16/03–11/2/03. Prev from 9/11/03. d: Michael Ogborn & Terence J. Nolen; set: Bob Phillips; cos: Karen Gilmer; light: James Leitner; sound: Nick Rye. Cast: Tracie Higgins, Mary Martello, Jilline Ringle, Tony Braithwaite, Elisa Matthews, Vince Di Mura (md/at piano). After Philly it was re-vamped, two songs–"The Company You Keep" and "The Gypsy in My Purse"—were added and one was taken out. A second cast, also rehearsed in Philadelphia (by Mr. Nolen), opened at the City Theatre, Pittsburgh, 11/20/03–12/28/03. ch: Deidre Finnegan; sound: Nick Rye & Elizabeth Atkinson. Cast: Lenora Nemetz, Jilline Ringle, Daniel Krell, Megan Hilty, Stephanie Riso, Thomas Wesley Douglas (played piano on stage)

1050. *Cage Me a Peacock*. Strand, London, 6/18/48–12/6/48; the Cambridge, London, 12/6/48–4/9/49. Total of 337 perf. p: Linnit & Dunfee; m: Eve Lynd; l/b: Noel Langley; add l: Adam Leslie; d: Charles Hickman; ch: David Paltenghi; set/cos: Berkeley Sutcliffe; md: Philip Martell. Cast: Yolande Donlan, Linda Gray (*Eve Lynd*), Ballard Berkeley, David Paltenghi, Valerie Lawson

1051. *Calamity Jane*. Short run stage version of 1953 Doris Day movie. Jane saves her local theatre, the Golden Garter. London, 1962. m: Sammy Fain; l: Paul Francis Webster. "Deadwood Stage," "Black Hills of Dakota," "Windy City," "Secret Love," "Higher than a Hawk." A UK tour of same musical opened in Northampton, 9/9/02. adapted by Charles K. Freeman from James O'Hanlon's screenplay; d: Ed Curtis; ch: Craig Revel Horwood; md: Adam Goodman. Cast: Toyah Wilcox, Alasdair Harvey, Kellie Ryan, Ian Gareth Jones. After 9 months on the road it ran at the Shaftesbury, London, 6/26/03 (prev from 6/19/03). Randy Skinner revised the book of this last production, and there were plans for a 2005 prod, d/ch by Mr. Skinner

1052. *Call It Love?* Revue. Wyndham's, London, 6/22/60. 5 perf. p: Donald Albery; m/l: Sandy Wilson; w: Robert Tanitch; d: Toby Robertson; set/cos: Felix Harbord; orch: Arthur Birkby; cast recording on TER. Cast: Derek Waring, Richard Owens, Suzanne Neve, Norman Warwick, Lally Bowers. "Love Play," "Love

Song in Rag," "I Know, Know, Know," "Hate Each Other Cha-Cha," "Call it Love?"

1053. *Call Me Ethel!* One-woman musical evening. Susan Bloch. 6/8/89–10/8/89. 67 perf. w: Christopher Powich & Rita McKenzie; d: Christopher Powich; md: Peter Blue. Cast: Rita McKenzie as Ethel Merman

1054. *Cam Jansen*. 10-year-old girl uses photographic memory to solve crimes. Lamb's, 11/12/04–11/28/04. Prev from 11/6/04. p: TheatreWorks/USA; m: Laurence O'Keefe; l/b: Nell Benjamin; based on series of popular children's books by David A. Adler; d: Gordon Greenberg; ch: Jody Ripplinger; md: Vadim Feichtner. Cast: Kate Weatherhead, Jill Abramovitz, Miguel Cervantes

1055. *Cambodia Agonistes*. Music-theatre epic. St. Clements, 10/28/92–11/29/92. 29 perf. p; Pan Asian Rep; m/l: Louis Stewart & Ernest Abuba; d: Tisa Chang. Cast: June Angela, John Baray, Ron Nakahara, Richard Ebihara

1056. *Cambridge Circus*. Comedy revue. New Arts Theatre Club, London, 7/10/63. p: Michael White; w: Hugh McDonald & Bill Oddie; add material: Terry Jones & Chris Stuart-Clarke, etc; d: Humphrey Barclay; cast recording on Parlophone. Similar to *Beyond the Fringe* in that it was devised from a Cambridge University revue (this one was called *A Clump of Plinths*), by ex-grads John Cleese, Bill Oddie, Tim Brooke-Taylor, Graham Chapman, David Hatch, Jo Kendall, Jonathan Lynn, all of whom were in the cast. Bring Out the Beast, Cloak and Dagger, "London Bus," Stage Coach, Final Episode, "Traffic Island," "Patients, For the Use of," "Scatty," How Black Was My Valley, "Boring Straight Song," "BBCBC," "Sing Sing," Humor without Tears, "I Wanna Hold Your Handel," Prophet, "West End Saga," "Music-Hall 1600," "Those Were the Days," "Pride and Joy," To Bury Caesar, "On Her Majesty's Service," Banana, "Bigger than Both of Us," "Judge Not," Foot Note. Plymouth Theatre, Broadway, 10/6/64–10/24/64. 2 prev from 10/3/64. 23 perf. p: Sol Hurok, David Black, Jay Julien, Andre Goulston; d: Humphrey Barclay. Same cast as London. Mostly great reviews. This prod transferred OB, to Square East, 10/28/64–1/13/65. 90 perf. A new edition, *New Cambridge Circus*, ran at Square East, 1/14/65–3/21/65. 78 perf. Same cast

1057. *Camille Claudel*. About the French sculptress and her mentor/lover Rodin. Goodspeed, 8/14/03–9/7/03. Developmental run, closed to critics, but open to paying public. Sold out. On opening night at Goodspeed power went out over the Northeast, but by Act II it was back on. b: Frank Wildhorn; d: Gabriel Barre; ch: Mark Dendy; set: Walt Spangler; cos: Constance Hoffman; light: Howell Binkley; sound: Mark Menard; md: Jeremy Roberts; orch: Jonathan Tunick. Cast: Camille Claudel: Linda Eder [Mrs. Frank Wildhorn in real life]; Rodin: Michael Nouri; Paul, Camille's brother: Matt Bogart; Mme Claudel: Rita Gardner (Joan Copeland was going to play role); M. Claudel: Milo O'Shea; Also with: John Paul Almon, Timothy W. Bish, Nick Cavarra, Margaret Ann Gates, Natalie

Hill, Mayumi Miguel, Tracy Miller, Tricia Paoluccio, Darren Ritchie, Shonn Wiley. There had been a 1988 French film of same name, starring Isabelle Adjani. The plan was to get the stage musical to Broadway in 2002–03 season, but that didn't happen. By 4/03 it was being planned for Broadway in spring 2004, to be presented by Clear Channel Entertainment. Polly Bergen, Matt Bogart, Milo O'Shea & Michael Nouri were all in negotiations for roles. Lori McKelvey also wrote m/l/b of an unrelated musical about the heroine, called *M. Claudel*, which had 2 industry readings at the Theatre at St. Clement's on 3/22/04. p: Kevin Duda; d: Henry Fonte; ch: Todd Underwood; md: Gillian Berkowitz. Cast: Janine LaManna, Eartha Kitt, Michael Berry, Anne Kanengeiser, Joe Vincent

1058. *Canciones de Mi Padre: A Romantic Evening in Old Mexico*. Mexican musical revue. City Center, 2/88. p: James M. Nederlander & Jerome Minskoff; d/ch: Michael Smuin; set: Tony Walton; light: Jules Fisher; asst light: Peggy Eisenhauer. Cast: Linda Ronstadt, Danny Valdez. Minskoff, Broadway, 7/12/88–7/30/88. 18 perf

1059. *Candles, Snow and Mistletoe*. Musical celebration of Christmas & Chanukah for whole family. When Santa loses his ho-ho-ho, Sharon, Lois, Bram & Elephant, embark on musical adventure to North Pole to take him true spirit of holiday season. Palace, Broadway, 12/27/93–12/30/93. 3 prev from 12/26/93. 7 perf. p: James L. & James M. Nederlander, Stewart F. Lane, Nickelodeon; w: Mark Saltzman; mus arr: Glen Roven; md: Rick Fox. Cast: Sharon Hampson, Lois Lilienstein, Bram Morrison, Line Roberge. "We Need a Little Christmas" (by Jerry Herman), "Silver Bells" (by Ray Evans & Jay Livingstone), "Ring Them Bells" (by John Kander & Fred Ebb), "With Bells On" (by Dolly Parton), "Have Yourself a Merry Little Christmas" (by Hugh Martin & Ralph Blane), "Rudolph the Red Nosed Reindeer" (by Johnny Marks)

1060. *Cannibal! The Musical*. Kraine, 3/3/01–8/4/01. p: Saturday Players; w: Trey Parker; d: Joan Eileen Murray; adapted by Lisa Gardner from the 1996 movie

1061. *Capitol Cakewalk*. Story of Warren Harding as told by a Harlem theatre. Dimson, 2/21/90–3/18/90. 16 perf. m: Terry Waldo; l: Lou Carter; b: Elmer Kline & Perry Arthur Kroeger; d: Tom O'Horgan; ch: Wesley Fata. Cast: Adrian Bailey, Minnette Coleman. "The Only Crime," "My Ohio," "Harry and Jesse Soft Shoe," "Nomination," "Normalcy," "Warren Harding March," "Shack Stomp," "A Louse in the White House," "Too Late to Love," "Summer of '23," "Hoi-Ya," "You're the Prez"

1062. *Capitol Steps*. Musical political satire. John Houseman, 2/13/97–6/29/97. Prev from 2/5/97. p: Eric Krebs & Anne Strickland Squadron; w/conceived by/d/starred: Bill Strauss & Elaina Newport. A sequel, *Capitol Steps: When Bush Comes to Shove*, ran 5/16/02–8/31/02, at the John Houseman. p: Eric Krebs

1063. *Caprice*. Alhambra, Glasgow, Scotland, 10/24/50 (2 weeks); toured. Did not make West End. p: Jack Waller; m: Geoffrey

Wright; l: Sandy Wilson; add numbers: Joseph Tunbridge & Jack Waller; add l: Sonny Miller; b: Michael Pertwee; from *French for Love*, by Marguerite Steen & Derek Patmore. Cast: Sally Ann Howes, Guido Lorraine

1064. *The Captain's Boy*. Pirate musical. Wings, 3/2/96–5/4/96. 3 prev. 26 perf. m: Christopher Jackson; l/b: Clint Jefferies; suggested by book *Sodomey and the Pirate Tradition*; d: Jeffrey Corrick

1065. *Captains Courageous*. Set in 1928 in various spots on North Atlantic & in Gloucester, Mass. Ford's, Washington, DC, 9/21/92. m: Frederick Freyer; l/b: Patrick Cook; based on 1937 movie, starring Spencer Tracy, which in turn was based on book by Rudyard Kipling; d/ch: Graciela Daniele; set: Christopher Barreca; cos: Ann Hould-Ward; light: Jules Fisher & Peggy Eisenhauer; sound: Peter Fitzgerald; md: James Kowal. Cast: John Dossett, Don Chastain, Frank Di Pasquale, George Kmeck, Joseph Kolinski, Michael Mandell, John Mineo, Ric Ryder. Manhattan Theatre Club Stage 1, 2/16/99–4/4/99. 40 prev from 1/12/99. 56 perf. d: Lynne Meadow; ch: Jerry Mitchell; set: Derek McLane; cos: Catherine Zuber; sound: Otts Munderloh; md: Robert Gustafson; orch: Jonathan Tunick. Cast: Treat Williams (*Rich Hebert*), Michael Mulheren, George Kmeck, Pete Herber, Dick Decareau, Michael DeVries, Michael X. Martin, Norm Lewis, Brandon Espinoza, Jason Opsahl. "I'm Harvey Ellesworth Cheyne," "Out on the Sea," "Little Fish," "Not So Bad," "I Married a Woman," "I Make up This Song," "A Hundred Years Ago," "Goodnight, Sweet Molly," "She Waits for Me," "That's Where I'm Bound," "Jonah," "You Never Saw," "Song of the Sea," "Grand Banks Sequence"/"Not This Year," "Regular Fellas," "I'm Home"

1066. *Captive*. Gothic musical based on true story of woman abducted by Seneca Indians, in Rochester area of NY, in 1759. Mint Space, 4/18/97–5/4/97. 12 perf. m/md: Robert Collister; l/b: Leslie Collins; d: Mark-Leonard Simmons. Cast: Christina Seymour, Joseph Melendez, Adam Matalon

1067. *A Captured Claus*. Christmas musical. St. Peter's. 11/24/95–12/31/95. 7 prev. 39 perf. m: Joe Raposo; l/b: Nick Raposo; based on L. Frank Baum short story; d: Michael John Murnin; ch: Jennifer Roth; md: Steve Steiner. Cast: Steve Steiner, Susan Stringer

1068. *The Card*. Go-getter becomes mayor in the Potteries of 1900. Theatre Royal, Bristol, England, 6/7/73–6/30/73; Queen's, London, 7/24/73–11/3/73. Prev from 7/12/73. 130 perf. p: Cameron Mackintosh; m/l: Tony Hatch & Jackie Trent; b: Willis Hall & Keith Waterhouse; from Arnold Bennett's novel; d: Val May; ch: Gillian Lynne; md: Ray Holder. Cast: Marti Webb, Millicent Martin, Jim Dale, Michael Malnick, John Savident, Eleanor Bron (*Dinah Sheridan*), Joan Hickson. "Hallelujah," "Nine Till Five," "Lead Me," "Universal White Kid Gloves," "Nobody Thought of It," "Moving On," "That Once a Year Feeling," "Come Along and Join Us," "That's the Way the Money Grows," "I Could Be the One," "The Card," "Opposite Your Smile," "Nothing Suc-

ceeds Like Success," "The Right Man," "You'll Do," "Rents," "Time to Spend," "Is It Just Me?," "If Only." The show, with new lyr by Anthony Drewe, did revival tour in 1994, with Hayley Mills, Jessica Martin, Peter Duncan, Cameron Blakely, Jane Lowe

1069. *The Carefree Heart*. Set in the France of Louis XIV. Tour only. Opened 9/30/57, Cass, Detroit. Closed 10/26/57, Hanna, Cleveland. p: Lynn Loesser & Shamus Locke; m/l/b: Robert Wright & George Forrest; d: H.C. Potter; ch: Dania Krupska; set: Oliver Smith; cos: Miles White; light: Peggy Clark; md: Samuel Krachmalnick; orch: Don Walker. Cast: Melville Cooper, Susan Johnson, Jack Carter, Allen Case, Rosemary O'Reilly, Michael Kermoyan, Jack Bittner, Jacquelyn McKeever, Virginia Martin. "She's Appealing, She's Alluring," "I Would Love You Still," "Bane of My Life," "To Cook My Gander's Goose," "I Am Your Man," "Bleed and Purge," "Rich Man, Poor Man," "Formula, Formulae, Formulorum," "To the Clinic," "The Carefree Heart," "Aristotle," "At the Bottom of It–Love," "Would I Were," "Anatomy." Ran as *The Love Doctor* (with new lyr by Douglas Byng) at the Piccadilly, London, 10/12/59. 16 perf. d: Albert Marre; ch: Todd Bolender; md: Alexander Faris; light: John Wyckham. Cast: Ian Carmichael, Joan Heal, Douglas Byng, Felix Felton, Eleanor Drew, Peter Gilmore, Richard Wordsworth, Philip Locke, Michael Darbyshire, Patricia Routledge, Anna Sharkey

A Caribbean Rhapsody see # 44, Main Book

1070. *Carissima*. Set in Venice & NY. Palace, London, 3/10/48–4/23/49. 488 perf. m: Hans May; l/b: Eric Maschwitz; from story by Armin Robinson; d: Reginald Tate; ch: Alan Carter & Joan Davis; cos: Norman Hartnell, etc; md: Walter Stiasny. Cast: Guido Lorraine, Frederick Schiller, Lester Ferguson (*Bruce Trent, Robert Shackleton*), Hugh Dempster (*Peter Haddon*), Shirl Conway, Maxine Audley (*Rosemary Morgan*), Sonya Hana. Made for BBC-TV & shown 11/25/50, with Edmund Purdom, Dino Galvani, Barbara Kelly, Rosemary Morgan, David Davies; and again 5/18/59, with Ginger Rogers, Warren Mitchell, Lizbeth Webb

1071. *Carmen's Place (A Fantasy)*. Set in NY, using excerpts from Bizet's opera *Carmen*. Castillo, 3/27/98–5/10/98. 34 perf. m: Fred Newman & Annie Roboff; l: Fred Newman; d: Gabriele Kurlander

1072. *Carricknabauna*. Irish folk revue. Adaptation of Padraic Colum's poetry & ballads in form of folk play with mus. Greenwich Mews, 3/30/67–4/16/67. 3 prev. 21 perf. d: Larry Arrick. Cast: Martyn Green, Anne Draper, Tanny McDonald, Rosemary McNamara. "When You Were a Lad," "Carricknabauna," "Tonight You See My Face," "No Bird that Sits," "Sean O'Dwyer," "Cheap Jack," "One Came Before Her," "Toymaker," "The Terrible Robber Men," "Birds that Left the Cage," "Over the Hills and Far Away." Previously produced, in part, in Dublin, as *The Road Round Ireland*

1073. *Carry On London*. Revue of sketches,

based on film series. Birmingham Hippodrome, 1973; Victoria Palace, London, 10/4/73–3/75. Huge success. m: Richard Holmes; w: Talbot Rothwell, Dave Freeman, Eric Merriman; add material: Ian Grant; d: Alan West; comedy d: Bill Robertson; ch: Tommy Shaw. Cast: Sid James, Barbara Windsor, Kenneth Connor, Bernard Bresslaw, Jack Douglas, Peter Butterworth. "Round About Victoria!!," "What a Carry On!," "Carry On, Girls," "Emergency Ward 99 and a Bit," "Deauville 1900," "Elizabethan Madrigals," "London Night Out," "Curtain Time at the Royal Standard Music Hall," "Carry On London," "Hello Dollies," "Be Prepared," "Cleopatra's Palace on the Nile," "Cleopatra's Boudoir," "Smile"

1074. *Cartoons for a Lunch Hour*. Perry Street, 11/28/78–12/3/78. 12 perf. m/add l: Rudy Stevenson; l/b: Loften Mitchell; d: Akin Babatunde; ch: Frank Hatchett. Cast: Clinton Derricks-Carroll, Charlene Harris, Brenda Mitchell, Rick Odums, Arlena Rolant, Christopher Wynkoop. "Come on in This House," "This Angel's Arrivin'," "Wanna Go to Heaven," "Ain't You Ashamed?," "Heaven Come and Help Us Out," "I Am the President," "Stay Ahead of the People," "I'm Here," "Heaven in Your Eyes," "Just a Little Italian Girl," "There's a New Place," "A Party at Peter's Place"

1075. *Casino Paradise*. Cabaret opera. Ballroom, 6/7/92–6/23/92. 18 perf. m/l: William Bolcom & Arnold Weinstein; md: Roger Trefousse. Cast: Joan Morris, Andre De Shields, Steven Goldstein

1076. *Casper*. About Casper the friendly ghost. Shaftesbury, London, 12/13/99–2/26/00. Prev from 12/4/99. m: Henry Marsh & Phil Pickett; l/b/d: David H. Bell. Cast: Siobhan Moore. "Rattle Me Bones," "Guys in Orange," "Twelve Hours Till Tomorrow," "Act Strong," "Up to No Good," "Casper," "Bad Relations," "Friendship," "Have a Night Out," "More," "I Could Love a Man Named Stinkie," "Livin' in Harmony," "The Battle"

1077. *The Cast Aways*. Theatre troupe captured by Barbary pirates in 1819 Mediterranean. Marymount Manhattan College, 9/19/75–9/28/75. 12 perf. m: Don Pippin; l: Steve Brown; b/d: Anthony J. Stimac; from play *She Would Be a Soldier*, by Mordecai Noah; ch: Gene Kelton. Cast: Reid Shelton, Marie Santell, Peter Boyden, Patti Perkins. "All the World's a Hold," "I Won't Love a Soldier Boy," "The Chase," "Let's Mop up These Yankees and Go Back Home," "Bring Out Old Glory," "My Love," "She Would Be a Soldier," "Whipperwill," "Call Back the Times," "If I Had Wings," "Isn't She," "This Dawn." Re-ran as *Castaways*, at the Promenade, 2/7/77. 13 prev. 1 perf. Modified score; book changed by Anthony J. Stimac, Dennis Andersen & Ron Whyte. p: Jeff Britton; d: Tony Tanner. Cast: Joel Kramer, Maureen Maloney, Kathleen Widdoes, June Squibb, Stephen James, Gibby Brand, Wayne Sherwood

1078. *Caste*. On 10/10/55 two musicals, both named *Caste*, opened in different parts of England. The Worthing prod (at the Connaught), Allon Bacon's musicalization of Tom

Robertson's play *Caste*, ran a week. d: Reginald Long; ch: Tommy McLennan. Cast: Cherry Lind, Peter Byrne, Mercy Haystead. It went on to the West End as *She Smiled at Me* (qv). The other, by Ronald Hill & Bill Owen, ran 2 weeks at the Theatre Royal, Windsor. d: John Counsell; ch: Bill Owen. Cast: Leslie Henson, Sara Gregory, Betty Paul, Bill Shine, Bill Owen. Did not make London

Cat and Mouse *see* # 187, Main Book

1079. *The Cat and the Fiddle*. Musical romance. Set in Brussels. Globe, Broadway, 10/15/1931; George M. Cohan, 5/24/32–9/24/32. Total of 395 perf. p: Max Gordon; m: Jerome Kern; l/b: Otto Harbach; d: Jose Ruben; ch: Albertina Rasch; md: Victor Baravalle; orch: Jerome Kern & Robert Russell Bennett. Cast: George Metaxa, Bettina Hall, Odette Myrtil, Eddie Foy Jr., Jose Ruben, Lawrence Grossmith. "The Night Was Made for Love," "The Breeze Kissed Your Hair," "Love Parade," "Try to Forget," "Poor Pierrot," "Passionate Pilgrim," "She Didn't Say Yes," "A New Love is Old," "One Moment Alone," "Oh! Cha Cha." Filmed in 1934. Cast: Jeanette MacDonald, Ramon Novarro. Carnegie/Weill Hall, 1990. Concert. Cast: Olga Talyn, Jason Graae, Judy Kaye, Cris Groenendaal, Davis Gaines, Paige O'Hara

1080. *Catch Me If I Fall*. A sculptor & his problems. Promenade, 11/12/90–11/18/90. Prev from 10/24/90. 8 perf. m/l/b: Barbara Schottenfeld; d: Susan Einhorn; add staging: Stuart Ross; set/cos: G.W. Mercier; light: Richard Nelson; md: Joseph Church; orch: Joe Gianono. Cast: James Judy, David Burdick, Sal Viviano. "Catch Me if I Fall," "Business is an Art," "Love that Came Before," "Sometimes at Night," "I Want You to Be…," "Home Never Leaves You," "When You Live in New York," "Isn't it Strange," "Never or Now"

1081. *Catch My Soul*. Musical of *Othello*. Ahmanson, L.A., 1967. m: Ray Pohlman & Emil Dean Zoghby; l/b: Jack Good; ch: Andre Tayir. Cast: William Marshall, Jerry Lee Lewis, Julienne Marie, Gerrianne Raphael, William Jordan. "Goats and Monkeys," "Wedding Chant," "Ballad of Catch My Soul," "Drunk," "If Wives Do Fall," "Cannikins," "Put Out the Light," "You Told a Lie," "Very Well — Go To," "Willow," "Seven Days and Nights," "Why," "Black on White," "Death Chant," "Othello," "Working on a Building," "Wash Us Clean," "Eat the Bread, Drink the Wine," "Book of Prophecy," "That's What God Said," "Chug a Lug," "I Found Jesus," "Looking Back," "Open Our Eyes," "Lust of the Blood," "Tickle His Fancy," "Run Shaker Life." Roundhouse, London, 3/5/68. Cast recording on Polydor (1970). Cast: P.P. Arnold, Lance LeGault, Dorothy Vernon, Jeffrey Wickham, Jack Good, Sharon Gurney, P.J. Proby, Emil Dean Zoghby. Filmed in 1974, with Richie Havens, Lance LeGault, Season Hubley, Susan Tyrrell

1082. *Catchpenny Twist*. Play with songs. Soho Rep, NYC, 1/27/84–2/19/84. 20 perf. m/l: Shaun Davey & Stewart Parker; w: Stewart Parker; d: Marlene Swartz; md: Michael John La Chiusa. Cast: Gerald Finnegan, Steven Culp, Deborah Walsh, Katherine Leask

1083. *The Cats' Pajamas*. Revue. Sheridan Square Playhouse, 5/31/62–7/1/62. 34 perf. d: Herb Sufrin; md: Arthur Siegel & Monte Aubrey. Cast: The Stewed Prunes (Richard Libertini, MacIntyre Dixon, Sylvia Lord). See also (in this appendix) *Stewed Prunes*

1084. *Catskills on Broadway*. Humorous borscht-belt revue. Lunt-Fontanne, Broadway, 12/5/91–1/3/93. 23 prev. 452 perf. w: Mal Z. Lawrence, Dick Capri, Marilyn Michaels; d: Barry Levitt. Cast: Freddie Roman (also conceived), Marilyn Michaels (*Louise DuArt*), Mal Z. Lawrence, Dick Capri. During illnesses guest performers included Julie Budd, Henny Youngman, Nipsey Russell

1085. *The Caucasian Chalk Circle*. Vineyard/Dimson, 8/8/95–8/26/95. 20 perf. m: Fabian Obispo; w: Bertolt Brecht; d: Chito Jao Garces. Cast: Rona Figueroa, Virginia Wing. "Down to the Abyss," "I Shall Be Waiting," "To the War My Weary Way I'm Wending," "I Shall Have to Take You," "Song of the Rotten Bridge," "Stay in the Middle of the War," "Song of Injustice," "Every Pleasure Costs Full Measure," "If He Walked in Golden Shoes"

1086. *La Cava: The Musical*. Set in 8th-century Morocco. Prostitute ("cava") sets out to destroy king. Victoria Palace, London, 6/8/00–7/22/00. Prev from 5/22/00; Piccadilly, 8/21/00–2/3/01. m: Laurence O'Keefe; add m: Stephen Keeling; l: John Claflin & Laurence O'Keefe; add l: Shaun McKenna; b: Dana Broccoli; d: Steven Dexter. Cast: Oliver Tobias, Julie-Alanah Brighten, Paul Keating

1087. *Celebration*. A theatre festival celebrating the black experience, a musical journey from beginning of African-American tradition to the present, with songs, poems, excerpts & stories by various authors. No connection to Broadway musical. American Place, 1/1/86–2/23/86. 31 perf. conceived by/d: Shauneille Perry. Cast: Carolyn Byrd, Fran Salisbury, Clebert Ford, Andre Robinson Jr.

1088. *Celebrity Sondheim*. Henry Miller's Theatre, 12/2/02–1/6/03. 10 special concert perfs. m/l: Stephen Sondheim; md/pianist: Paul Ford; light: Eric Cornwell; sound: Otts Munderloh. Cast: Mandy Patinkin

1089. *Censored*. Dance theatre piece. Set in world of film noir mystery. Ohio Theatre, NY, 4/3/97–4/21/97. 4 prev. 13 perf. Last perf was at Lincoln Center's Alice Tully Hall. w/conceived by/d: Brian Jucha; ch: the Company; sound: Darron L. West. Cast: Sheryl Dold, Will Keenan, Kristen Lee Kelly, Cheryl Lewis, Jennifer Pace, Allan Tibbetts

1090. *Censored Scenes from King Kong*. Comic extravaganza with mus. Edinburgh Festival, Scotland, 1977. Open Space Theatre, 10/21/77–12/10/77. m/md: Andy Roberts; l/b: Howard Schuman; d: Colin Bucksey; ch: David Toguri; set: Mike Porter. Cast: Little Nell. "Ha-Cha," "Banana Oil," "He Ain't Scared of Nothin'," "Number One," "Soft Shoe Freak," "Other Side of the Wall." Princess (OB), 3/6/78–3/9/78. 11 prev. 5 perf. p: Michael White & Eddie Kulukundis; same basic crew as for British prods, except cos: Jennifer von Mayrhauser. Cast: Stephen Collins,

Peter Riegert, Alma Cuervo, Chris Sarandon, Edward Love, Carrie Fisher

1091. *The Challenge*. Shaw, London, 7/19/92. m/l: various authors; b: Stephen Clarke; cast recording on TER. Cast: Nicolas Colicos, Clive Rowe, Caroline O'Connor, Audrey Halliday. "Mediterranean Sea," "From Nothing to Something," "Aphrodite Hears," "Love Must Change," "Bull Inside My China Shop," "Love Has Got a Sting in Its Tail," "Bull by the Horns," "Every Year," "If I Ever See That Face Again," "The Moment is Here," "Revenge," "Closer and Closer," "I've Had Enough," "Four Sicilian Princesses," "Positive Thought," "If I Tell You"

1092. *Champeen!* Harry DeJur, 3/18/83–4/17/83. 24 perf. p: New Federal Theatre; m/l/b/d: Melvin Van Peebles; ch: Louis Johnson. Cast: Ruth Brown, Sandra Reaves-Phillips, Ted Ross, Manette La Chance, Melvin Van Peebles. "You Had Me Anyhow," "Like a Dream," "Come to Mama," "Opportunity Knockout," "World's a Stage," "Gimme a Pigfoot," "Home," "Tain't Nobody's Bizness if I Do," "Knockout"

1093. *A Change in the Heir*. Set in a castle, once upon a time. Rival factions vying for the crown bring up their children disguised as members of the opposite sex. Edison, Middle Broadway, 4/29/90–5/13/90. 23 prev. 17 perf. p: Stewart F. Lane; m: Dan Sticco; l: George H. Gorham; b: Dan Sticco & George H. Gorham; d/ch: David H. Bell; set: Michael Anania & Ron Kadri; cos: David Murin; md: Rob Bowman; orch: Robby Merkin. Cast: Brooks Almy, Brian Sutherland, J.K. Simmons, David Gunderman, Connie Day, Mary Stout, Judy Blazer, Jeffrey Herbst, Jan Neuberger, Jennifer Smith. "Here I Am," "The Weekend," "Exactly the Same as it Was," "Look at Me," "Take a Look at That," "I Tried and I Tried and I Tried," "Can't I?," "When," "A Fairy Tale," "An Ordinary Family," "Happily Ever After, After All," "Shut up and Dance," "Duet," "Hold That Crown," "By Myself." Previously produced at New Tuners, Chicago

1094. *Changes*. DC Black Rep, Washington, 12/6/73. 47 perf. m/l/md: Valerian E. Smith; b/d: Motojicho; ch: Louis Johnson & Mike Malone. Cast: Clyde-Jacques-Barrett, Kiki Shepard. "Can't Be Nobody Else," "Amy's Song," "Mississippi Mud," "Intangible Things," "She Noticed Me," "Change Your Name," "Yoyo," "Understand Me," "My Mother's Face"

1095. *Changes*. 2 couples & the changes in their relationships. No dialogue. Theatre de Lys, 2/19/80–2/24/80. 7 perf. m: Addy Fieger; l: Danny Apolinar; conceived by/d: Dorothy Love; ch: Ronn Forella; cos: Miles White; sound: Bill Merrill; md: Richard Nelson. Cast: Kelly Bishop, Irving Allen Lee, Larry Kert, Trina Parks. "Changes," "Have I Got a Girl for You," "Have I Got a Guy for You," "Happy New Year," "Isn't This Fun," "Is This the Way," "Keep Love Away," "All of a Sudden it's Spring," "Man About Town," "Running Out of Time," "Ideal Deal," "Merry Christmas to Me"

1096. *Chantecler*. Set in barnyard & surrounding forest in Gascony. 47th Street Theatre, 11/18/81–11/29/81. 12 perf. m: Michael R. Colichio; l/b: Anthony A. Piano; based on Edmond Rostand's play; d: Edward Berkeley; ch: Nora Peterson; md: Robert Goldstone. Cast: Gary Barker, Ralph Bruneau, Kate Dezina, D. Michael Heath

1097. *Chapeau.* Closed before Broadway, 1977. m/l: Robert Waldman & Alfred Uhry. Cast: Brooks Baldwin & Daniel Corcoran. "Surprises"

1098. *Chaplin.* Music Center Pavilion, L.A. Opened 8/12/83 for 8-week limited run; closed 9/24/83, canceling scheduled 11/10/83 Broadway opening at Mark Hellinger. p: Raymond Katz, Sandy Gallin, James M. Nederlander, Arthur Rubin, David Susskind; m/l/b: Anthony Newley & Stanley Ralph Ross; d: Michael Smuin; ch: Michael Smuin & Claudia Asbury; set: Douglas W. Schmidt; cos: Willa Kim; light: Ken Billington. Cast: Charlie Chaplin: Anthony Newley; Oona/Lita/Paulette Goddard: Andrea Marcovicci; Also with: Kathy Andrini, Marsha Bagwell, Mary Leigh Stahl, Thom Sesma. "A Little Bit of Power and Powder and Paint," "Me and You," "Joyeux Noel," "Love," "Sydney's Hymn," "Heel and Toe and Away We Go," "Funny Man," "American Dream," "Madame Butterfingers," "Doing the Charlie Chaplin," "If Only You Were Here," "Bonne Nuit, Papa," "My Private Life," "Thanks for Nothing," "Dinner with W.R.," "One Man Band," "Remember Me." Houston's Theatre Under the Stars, summer 1985. p/d: Anthony Newley. It failed again

1099. *Charley's Tale.* Musical Theatre Works, 3/26/86–4/12/86. 2 prev. 12 perf. m: Donald Johnston; l/b: Tricia Tunstall; ch: Marcia Milgrom Dodge; light: Victor En Yu Tan. Cast: Tim Ewing, Rex D. Hays, Suzanne Lukather, Sal Mistretta, William Nabel, Marianne Tatum. "Better off Alone," "Ain't Got Time," "Close Your Eyes," "Mushrooms and Mozart," "If I Weren't a Beast," "We Can Do Better," "Greenwich Village Girls," "Look at Me," "Charley"

1100. *Charlie Girl.* Golders Green Hippodrome, London, 11/25/65–12/4/65; Adelphi, London, 12/15/65–3/27/71. 2,202 perf. m/l: David Heneker & John Taylor; b: Hugh Williams, Margaret Williams, Ray Cooney; d: Wallace Douglas; ch: Alfred Rodrigues; md: Donald Elliott. Cast: Anna Neagle (*Evelyn Laye*), Joe Brown (*Gerry Marsden*), Derek Nimmo, Hy Hazell (*Patricia Burke*), Stuart Damon, Christine Holmes (*Stephanie Voss*). "Most Ancestral Home of All," "Bells Will Ring," "Charlie Girl," "I Love Him, I Love Him," "What Would I Get From Being Married," "Let's Do a Deal," "My Favorite Occupation," "What's the Magic," "When I Hear Music, I Dance," "I 'ates Money," "The Part of a Lifetime," "Like Love," "That's It," "Washington," "Fish 'n Chips," "Society Twist," "You Never Know What You Can Do," "I Was Young," "Liverpool." Victoria Palace, London, 1986 (6 months). Cast: Cyd Charisse, Paul Nicholas, Dora Bryan, Mark Wynter, Nicholas Parsons

1101. *Charlotte Sweet.* Set in Victorian music hall days. Chernuchin, 4/13/82–5/1/82.

16 perf. m: Gerald Jay Markoe; b: Michael Colby; d: Edward Stone; ch: Dennis Dennehy; md: Polly Pen. Cast: Mara Beckerman, Timothy Landfield, Michael McCormick, Michael Dantuono, Alan Brasington, Sandra Wheeler, Christopher Seppe, Virginia Seidel, Polly Pen. "At the Music Hall," "Charlotte Sweet," "A Daughter for Valentine's Day," "Forever," "Liverpool Sunset," "Layers of Underwear," "Quartet Agonistes," "Circus of Voices," "Keep it Low," "Bubbles in Me Bonnet," "Vegetable Reggie," "My Baby and Me," "A-Weaving," "Your High Note!," "Katinka," "The Darkness," "On it Goes," "You See in Me a Bobby," "A Christmas Buche," "The Letter" (Me Charlotte Dear), "Dover," "Good Things Come," "It Could Only Happen in the Theatre," "Lonely Canary," "Queenly Comments," "Surprise! Surprise!," "The Reckoning," "Farewell to Auld Lang Syne." Westside Arts Center/ Cheryl Crawford Theatre, 8/12/82–11/7/82. 8 prev. 102 perf. md: Jan Rosenberg. Cast: Mara Beckerman, Nicholas Wyman (*Timothy Landfield*) Michael McCormick, Alan Brasington (*Jeff Keller*), Merle Louise, Sandra Wheeler (*Lynn Eldredge*), Christopher Seppe, Virginia Seidel, Polly Pen. Standby: Michael Dantuono.

1102. *Chase a Rainbow.* Writer tries to make up his mind between vocation & money. Theatre Four, 6/12/80–6/15/80. 8 prev. 6 perf. m/l/b: Harry Stone; d: Sue Lawless; ch: Bick Goss; light: Patrika Brown; md: John Franceschina. Cast: Ted Pugh, Suzanne Dawson, Virginia Sandifur. "Let's Hear it for Me," "The People You Know," "You've Gotta Have a Passion," "Everything Happens for the Best," "Out of Love," "Big City," "The Happiest People," "Have a Good Day," "Listen, Little Boy," "I'm in Showbiz," "Life on the Rocks," "To Be or Not to Be," "I've Been Around the Horn," "My Meadow," "All the Years," "Listen World"

1103. *Cherry.* OB, 1969. Never opened. m/l: Tom Baird & Ron Miller; based on *Bus Stop*, by William Inge. "Something to Believe In." It did finally make it to production, at NY Public Library, 5/8/72–5/10/72

1104. *Chez Garbo.* Set in Greta Garbo's East Side living room. Duo, 5/26/95–6/18/95. m: Michelangelo Alasa & David Welch; l/b/d: Michelangelo Alasa. Cast: Garbo: Lynne Charnay; Young Garbo: Michelle Powers. "Never," "I See Myself," "I Have Always Collected," "Just Let Me Love You," "Where Does One Turn To?," "An Artist Till the End," "As I Do," "Roses," "In a Perfect World," "How You've Changed," "Dreamers," "It's Not Like We Have Forever"

1105. *Chic.* Revue. About being chic. Orpheum, 5/19/59–5/23/59. 6 perf. m/l: Lester Judson, Raymond Taylor, Frank Slay, Bob Crewe, Fred Piscariello, Julian Stein, Murray Grand; d: Richard Altman; ch: Jim Russell; cos: Theoni Vachlioti Aldredge; md: Dorothea Freitag. Cast: Beatrice Arthur, Emory Bass, Bob Dishy, Eileen Rodgers, Virginia de Luce. "Chic," "Julie is Mine," "Tallahassee Lassie"

1106. *Children of Adam.* Musical revue. Chelsea Westside Cabaret, 8/17/77–10/9/77. 9 prev. 62 perf. m/l: Stan Satlin; conceived by/d: John Driver; ch: Ruella Frank; md: Jimmy

Wisner. Cast: Carole Schweid, Elizabeth Lathram, Robert Polenz, Karen Philipp, Gene Bua, Roger Rathburn. "Dreams," "Mr. & Mrs. Myth," "What's Your Name?," "Move Along," "Sex is Animal," "It's Really You," "Walkin'," "You've Got to Die to Be Born Again," "Rise in Love," "The Wedding," "Flowers and the Rainbow," "Life," "It Ain't Easy/Equilib," "Sleep, My Child," "I Must Go Now," "Like a Park on Sunday," "Part of the Plan," "I Can Feel," "Sleepin' Around," "Wooden People," "Cacophony," "Maybe You Can See Yourself," "Just a Feeling (My Spirit Awakening)," "No More Games," "I Can Make It/Song Song," "Sweetest Songs Remain to Be Sung," "Children of Adam"

1107. *Children of Eden.* Biblical story. Prince Edward, London, 1/8/91. 103 perf. m/l: Stephen Schwartz; b: John Caird; cast recording on London. Cast: Ken Page, Martin Smith, Ruthie Henshall, Shezwae Powell, Kevin Colson, Frances Ruffelle. "Let There Be," "Spark of Creation," "A World without You," "Lost in the Wilderness," "Close to Home," "Children of Eden," "Civilized Society," "Return of the Animals," "In Whatever Time We Have," "Hardest Part of Love," "Ain't it Good," "In the Beginning," "Tree of Knowledge," "Perfect," "A Ring of Stones," "Death of Abel," "Mark of Cain," "Gathering Storm," "Precious Children." Very expensive failure. US premiere at Paper Mill Playhouse, NJ. 1998. d: Robert Johanson; ch: Dawn Di Pasquale; set: Michael Anania; md: Danny Kosarin. Cast: Hunter Foster, Darius de Haas, Stephanie Mills, Adrian Zmed, Kelli Rabke

1108. *Children's Letters to God.* Quotes letters from real kids. Lamb's, 6/30/04. Prev from 6/19/04. p: Carolyn Rossi Copeland, in assoc with Lamb's Theatre Co.; m: David Evans; l: Douglas Cohen; based on best-selling book of same name by Stuart Hample; d: Stafford Arima; ch: Patti Wilcox; set: Anna Louizos, cos: Gail Brassard; light: Kirk Bookman; sound: Peter Hylenski

1109. *Chippy.* Set in West Texas, 1930s–1960s. John Jay, 7/27/94–7/30/94. 4 perf. m/l: Jo Harvey Allen, Terry Allen, Butch Hancock, Joe Ely, Wayne Hancock, Jo Carol Pierce; d: Evan Yionoulis; set: Terry Allen & Donald Eastman; sound: Darron L. West. Cast: Jo Harvey Allen, Terry Allen, Joe Ely, Butch & Wayne Hancock, Jo Carol Pierce

1110. *Chitty Chitty Bang Bang.* London Palladium, 4/16/02. Prev from 3/17/02. Richard & Robert Sherman (score of orig movie, plus new songs by them); originally adapted for screen by Roald Dahl, for 1968 movie dir by Ken Hughes, and starring Dick Van Dyke & Sally Ann Howes; adapted for stage by: Jeremy Sams; from Ian Fleming's children's book; d: Adrian Noble; ch: Gillian Lynne; set/cos: Anthony Ward; Cast: Caractacus Potts: Michael Ball, *Gary Wilmot* (from 3/16/04); Also with: Nichola McAuliffe, Anton Rodgers, Richard O'Brien (*Paul O'Grady, Peter Polycarpou, Derek Griffiths, Wayne Sleep*), Brian Blessed (*Victor Spinetti*), Emma Williams. London's most expensive show ever (over 5 million pounds). On 4/17/02 the computer which enabled the car to fly broke down & the perf was canceled. Moved to the Dominion. New cast as of 3/16/04: Potts: Gary Wilmot; Grandpa: Tony Adams; Truly Scrumptious: Scarlett Strallen; Baron Bomburst: Christopher Biggins; Baroness: Louise Gold; Child Catcher: Lionel Blair. UK tour opened at Liverpool Philharmonic Hall, 10/27/03. Cast: Michael Ball. Plans for the Hilton Theatre (formerly the Ford Center for the Performing Arts), Broadway, 4/28/05. Prev from 3/27/05. p: Barbara Broccoli, Eon Prods, Frederick M. Zollo, Nicolas Paleologos; d: Adrian Noble; ch: Gillian Lynne; set/cos: Anthony Ward; light: Mark Henderson; sound: Andrew Bruce; md: Robert Scott. orch: Chris Walker; gm: Alan Wasser & Assocs. Cast: Potts: Raul Esparza; Grandpa Potts; Philip Bosco; Bomburst: Marc Kudisch; Truly Scrumptious: Erin Dilly; Baroness Bomburst: Jan Maxwell; Child Catcher: Kevin Cahoon (Meat Loaf had been scheduled); Goran: Chip Zien; Boris: Robert Sella; Also with: Dirk Lumbard, Ken Kantor, J.B. Adams, Kurt von Schmittou, Robert Creighton, Rick Faugno. "You Two," "Them Three," "Toot Sweets," "Think Vulgar," "Hushabye Mountain," "Come to the Funfair," "Me Ol' Bamboo," "Posh," "Hushabye Mountain" (reprise), "Chitty Chitty Bang Bang," "Truly Scrumptious," "Chitty Chitty Bang Bang" (reprise), Entr'acte, "Vulgarian National Anthem," The Roses of Success," "Kiddy-Widdy-Winkies," "Team work," "Chu-Chi Face," "The Bombie Samba," "Doll on a Music Box," "Truly Scrumptious" (reprise)

1111. *Choices*. Young man journeys to mythical land of Edentine. One Dream, 11/12/92–11/15/92. 5 perf. m/l: Michael Filak & Howard Danzinger; d: Andrew Barrett; md: Neil Ginsberg. Cast: Andrea Bianchi, Anthony Inneo, Alisa Reyes

1112. *The Chosen*. Set in 1940s, in Williamsburg, Brooklyn. Jewish teenagers grow up as friends, despite their parents' differing views on faith & doctrine. Second Avenue, 1/6/88–1/10/88. 52 prev from 11/15/87. 6 perf. co-p/d: Mitchell Maxwell; m: Philip Springer; l: Mitchell Bernard; b: Chaim Potok (based on his novel); ch: Richard Levi; set: Ben Edwards; cos: Ruth Morley; light: Thomas R. Skelton; md: Eric Stern; orch: Samuel Matlovsky. Cast: George Hearn, Gerald Hiken, Daniel Marcus, Lynnette Perry, Patricia Ben Peterson, Tia Riebling, Joey Rigol, Mimi Turque, Anny De Gange, Jeff Gardner, Tracy Katz, Kevin Ligon, Paul Haber, Patricia Wilcox. "Play to Win," "Words," "Holy Little World," "Ladder to the Lord," "The Prince and Me," "A Woman of Valor," "Wake Us with Your Song," "Our New Jerusalem," "The Chosen," "Tune in My Heart," "Tear Down the Wall," "Silence"

1113. *Christina Alberta's Father*. Vineyard, 4/21/94–5/29/94. 40 perf. m/l/b: Polly Pen; based on novel by H.G. Wells; d: Andre Ernotte; ch: Lynne Taylor-Corbett; md: Paulette Haupt; orch: Lawrence Yurman. Cast: Marla Schaffel, Alma Cuervo, Tina Johnson, Don Mayo, Andy Taylor. "Sleep Little Red Object," "Court of Conscience," "Alone in the World," "A Rock and a Body," "Waiting,"

"Early Amphibians," "I Am Reeling," "My World," "Running About," "Where is the Lost and Found of London?," "Uneasy Armchairs," "Later Amphibians," "Christina Albert and I," "Tra-La-Lee," "Daybreak," "Here is Love," "First Night of Summer"

1114. *The Christmas Bride*. Musical romance. William Redfield, 12/8/88–12/18/88. 12 perf. m/l: Noel Katz; b: Margit Ahlin; based on *The Battle of Life*, by Charles Dickens; d: Al D'Andrea. Cast: Lee Winston

1115. *A Christmas Carol*. Holiday benefit for Actors Fund of America. Hudson, Broadway, 12/10/90. 1 perf. 1st theatrical perf at the Hudson since 1965. Charles Dickens's play — i.e. not a musical. p/d: Zoe Caldwell; mus by & performed by David Amram. Cast: Narrators: Zoe Caldwell & Christopher Plummer; Scrooge: Jason Robards Jr.; Also with: David Rasche, Eli Wallach, Hume Cronyn, Richard Kiley, E.G. Marshall, Anne Jackson, Julie Harris, Maureen Stapleton, Lindsay Crouse

1116. *A Christmas Carol*. New musical version of Dickens story. Westbeth, 12/4/92–12/20/92. 14 perf. m/l: Douglas Yetter & Michael Hulett; d: Margaret Mancinelli-Cahill. Cast: Pamela Brown, Nick Plakias. "Spirit of Christmas," "Ours for the Keeping," "Link by Link," "Christmas at Home," "Hand in Hand and Arm in Arm," "Take My Heart," "Nightmare," "Touch My Robe," "Anything at All," "Family Christmas Recipe," "Yes or No," "It All Goes Around"

1117. *A Christmas Carol*. Tour. Opened 12/10/93, Clowes, Indianapolis. Closed 12/29/93, Fort Wayne. m: Michel Legrand; l/b: Sheldon Harnick; from Dickens' story. Cast: Scrooge: Douglas E. Holmes. "Spirit of Christmas," "Icy Ebenezer," "Bah! Humbug!," "Thank Heaven for Christmas," "Bells of Christmas Day," "Christmas Eve," "Partners," "Penny by Penny," "My Two Feet Polka," "Close Were We," "Yes and No," "One Family," "Balancing the Books," "Let There Be Time," "One More Chance"

1118. *A Christmas Carol*. The famous NY presentation of Charles Dickens' story, running every year, 1994–2003. p: Nickelodeon Family Classics & Madison Square Garden; m: Alan Menken; l: Lynn Ahrens; b: Mike Ockrent & Lynn Ahrens; d: Mike Ockrent (*Susan Stroman* in 2002); ch: Susan Stroman; set: Tony Walton; cos: William Ivey Long; light: Jules Fisher & Peggy Eisenhauer; sound: Tony Meola; md: Paul Gemignani; orch: Michael Starobin; dance mus arr: Glen Kelly; cast recording on Columbia. "The Years Are Passing By," "Jolly, Rich and Fat" ("A Jolly Good Time"), "Nothing to Do with Me," "Street Song," "Link by Link," "Lights of Long Ago," "God Bless Us Everyone," "A Place Called Home," "Mr. Fezziwig's Annual Christmas Ball," "Abundance and Charity," "Christmas Together," "Dancing on Your Grave," "Yesterday, Tomorrow and Today." Paramount, Madison Square Garden (the 5,100-seat theatre), 12/1/94–1/1/95. 14 prev from 11/23. 71 perf; 11/30/95–12/31/95. 88 perf; 11/22/96–1/5/97. 90 perf; 11/18/97–1/4/98. 96 perf; 11/27/98–12/27/98. 69 perf; 11/26/99–12/30/99. 64 perf;

11/24/00–12/31/00. 63 perf; 11/23/01–12/29/01; 11/29/02–12/29/02; 11/28/03–12/27/03. Actors who played Scrooge: Walter Charles (94), Terrence Mann (95), Tony Randall (96), Hal Linden & Roddy McDowall (alternating in 97), Roger Daltrey (98), Tony Roberts (99), Frank Langella (00), Tim Curry (01), F. Murray Abraham (02), Jim Dale (03). From the 1995 production onwards the numbers were slightly different (and this new line-up would become standard): "The Years Are Passing By" was cut; there was a new song, "You Mean More to Me," immediately before "Street Song;" and another new song (replacing a reprise of "The Years Are Passing By"), before the Final Medley–"London Town Carol"

1119. *Christy*. Bert Wheeler, 10/14/75–11/16/75. 40 perf. p: Joseph Lillis & Joan Spiro; m: Lawrence J. Blank; l/b: Bernie Spiro; based on *The Playboy of the Western World*, by J.M. Synge; d/set: Peter David Heth; ch: Jack Estes; md: Robert Billig. Cast: John Canary, Betty Forsyth, Alexander Sokoloff. "Christy," "To Please the Woman in Me," "Until the Likes of You," "Picture Me," "Morning After" (m: Robert Billig), "One Fell Swoop," "All's Fair," "The Heart's a Wonder," "Down the Hatch," "Gallant Little Swearers"

1120. *Chrysanthemum*. Melodrama in ragtime. Chrysanthemum Brown becomes white slave in London in 1913. New Lindsey, London, 3/14/56–4/30/56. 40 perf. m: Robb Stewart; l/b: Neville Phillips & Robin Chancellor; d: John Regan. Cast: Colin Croft. "Alexander," "Watch Your Step," "Sorry You've Been Troubled," "How Can I Find My Love?," "Saturday Night," "No More Love Songs," "Shanghai Lil," "Mary Ann," "Thanks to the Weather," "Is This Love?," "I Love a Game," "Fire Brigade." Opera House, Manchester, 9/8/58; toured; Apollo, London, 11/13/58–2/18/59. Total of 148 perf. d: Eleanor Fazan; ch: Alfred Rodrigues; set/light: Disley Jones; md: Roy Lowe. Cast: Pat Kirkwood, Hubert Gregg (Pat Kirkwood's husband in real life), Vivien Grant, Josephine Blake, Greta Hanby, Judy Carne. Royal Poinciana Playhouse, Palm Beach, 1/22/62. d: Jack Sydow; ch: Ellen Ray. Cast: Sherry Lambert, Ginger Prince, Patrice Munsel

1121. *The Cincinnati Saint*. Playhouse 91, 10/23/93–11/14/93. 23 perf. p: Jewish Rep; m/md/orch: Raphael Crystal; l: Richard Engquist; b: Norman Lessing; based on play *36*; d: Ran Avni; ch: Helen Butleroff; cos: Gail Cooper-Hecht. Cast: Robert Ari, Ellen Foley, Jonathan Hadley, Steve Sterner

1122. *Cinderella*. This Rodgers & Hammerstein musical started out on CBS-TV in the USA on 3/31/57. d: Ralph Nelson. Cast: Julie Andrews, Jon Cypher, Howard Lindsay, Ilka Chase, Kaye Ballard, Alice Ghostley, Dorothy Stickney, Edith Adams (this prod was shown again on 12/5/04). Then it played on the stage. Coliseum, London, 12/18/58–4/11/59. 160 perf. 1st pantomime at the Coliseum since 1944. Book much altered from US TV version, and character of Buttons was added (Tommy Steele's West End debut). p: Harold Fielding; b: Joseph Schrank; d: Freddie Carpenter; ch: Tommy Linden; set/cos: Loudon Sainthill; light: Michael Northen; md: Bobby Howell; orch: Robert Russell Bennett & Ronnie Hanmer. Cast: Yana, Tommy Steele, Bruce Trent, Jimmy Edwards, Enid Lowe, Betty Marsden, Kenneth Williams. "In My Own Little Corner," "Your Majesties," "Boys and Girls Like You and Me," "Impossible," "Ten Minutes Ago," "Stepsisters' Lament," "Do I Love You Because You're Beautiful?," "When You're Driving Through the Moonlight," "A Lovely Night." Adelphi, London, 12/22/60. 101 perf. p: Harold Fielding, by arrangement with Jack Hylton; d: Freddie Carpenter; ch: Sidonie Darrell; set/cos: Loudon Sainthill. Cast: Joan Heal, Jimmy Edwards, Ted Rogers, Gillian Lynne. In USA, CBS re-made it for TV, 2/22/65, with Lesley Anne Warren, Stuart Damon, Walter Pidgeon, Celeste Holm. New York State Theatre, 11/9/93–11/21/93. 14 perf; 11/9/95–11/19/95 (return engagement). 12 perf. p: NYC Opera; adapted b: Steve Allen; adapted for stage/d: Robert Johanson; ch: Robert Johanson & Sharon Halley; set: Henry Bardon; cos: Gregg Barnes; light: Jeff Davis; sound: Abe Jacob; conductor: Eric Stern, *Rob Fisher* (for return engagement); orch: Robert Russell Bennett. Cast: Fairy Godmother: Sally Ann Howes; Stepmother: Nancy Marchand, *Jean Stapleton* (for return engagement); Joy, Cinderella's Stepsister: Alix Korey; Portia, Cinderella's other Stepsister: Jeanette Palmer; Cinderella: Crista Moore, *Rebecca Baxter* (for return engagement); Queen: Maria Karnilova, *Jane Powell* (for return engagement); King: George S. Irving; Prince: George Dvorsky. Overture, "The Prince Is Giving a Ball," "In My Own Little Corner," "Your Majesties," "The Loneliness of Evening" (orig cut from *South Pacific*), "My Best Love" (orig cut from *Flower Drum Song*), "Impossible!," "It's Possible," "The Gavotte," "Ten Minutes Ago," "Stepsisters' Lament," "Waltz for a Ball," "If I Weren't King" (cut from 1957 TV version), "Do I Love You Because You're Beautiful?," "When You're Driving Through the Moonlight," "A Lovely Night," "Royal Wedding." Madison Square Garden, 5/1/01–5/13/01. 13 perf. This revised version was adapted by Tom Briggs from teleplay by Robert L. Freedman, which was broadcast on 11/2/98. Presented by Radio City Entertainment; p: NETworks; d: Gabriel Barre; ch: Ken Roberson; set: James Youmans; cos: Pamela Scofield; light: Tim Hunter; sound: Duncan Edwards; ms/arr: Andrew Lippa; md: John Mezzio; orig orch: Robert Russell Bennett; new orch: David Siegel. Cast: Fairy Godmother: Eartha Kitt; Cinderella: Jamie-Lynn Sigler; Prince Christopher: Paolo Montalban; Stepmother: Everett Quinton; Lionel: Victor Trent Cook; King Maximilian: Ken Prymus; Chorus: Jason Ma, Karine Plantadit-Bageot, Christeena Michelle Riggs, Ron J. Todorowski. "The Sweetest Sounds" (from *No Strings*), "The Prince is Giving a Ball," "In My Own Little Corner," "Fol-de-Rol," "Impossible," "The Transformation," "It's Possible," "The Gavotte," "The Cinderella Waltz," "Ten Minutes Ago," "Stepsisters' Lament," "Do I Love You Because You're Beau-

tiful?," "When You're Driving Through the Moonlight," "A Lovely Night," "The Search," "There's Music in You" (from the movie *Main Street to Broadway*). There have been other shows called *Cinderella*

1123. *Cindy*. Kitchen girl makes it to the Plaza, in re-working of Cinderella story. Gate, 3/19/64–6/21/64. 110 perf. m/l: Johnny Brandon; d/ch: Marvin Gordon. Cast: Cindy Kreller: Jacqueline Mayro; Also with: Johnny Harmon (*Tommy Karaty*), Thelma Oliver, Dena Dietrich. Orpheum, 9/24/64–12/13/64. 94 perf. Cast: Cindy: Kelly Wood. Cricket, 1/19/65–5/2/65. 114 perf. d: Ruth Nastasi; musical numbers re-staged by: Tommy Karaty. Cast: Cindy: Isabelle Farrell. "Once Upon a Time," "Let's Pretend," "Is There Something to What He Said?," "Papa, Let's Do It Again," A Genuine Feminine Girl," "Cindy," "Think Mink," "Tonight's the Night," "If You've Got It, You've Got It," "The Life that I Planned for Him," "If it's Love," "Got the World in the Palm of My Hands," "Call Me Lucky," "Laugh It Up." London, 1968

1124. *Cindy-Ella: I Gotta Shoe*. For children. Fairy godmother helps girl get into movies. Garrick, London, 12/17/62 (matinees only). p: Michael Codron; m: Peter Knight & Ron Grainer; l: Caryl Brahms & Ned Sherrin; b: Johnny Clarke; d: Colin Graham; set: Tony Walton; cast recording on DRG. All-black cast: Cleo Laine, Elisabeth Welch, Cy Grant, George Browne. "I Gotta Shoe," "Troubles of the World," "Motherless Child," "Shine Shine Shoe," "Nobody Knows the Trouble I've Seen," "You're Worried Now," "You Gotta Look Disdainful," "Git Along Home, Cindy Cindy," "High Summer Day," "Look on Me with a Loving Eye," "Raise a Ruckus," "Plenty Good Room," "Cindy-Ella," "Swing Low Sweet Chariot," "Nobody's Business," "De Midnight Special," "Hush-a-Bye." Tried for Broadway, opening at Central Library Theatre, Toronto, 12/10/64, but closed on the road. London, 1974. 27 perf. Cast: June Page, Harry Meacher, Sam Dale

1125. *Cinema Toast*. Salute to great movie songs. Duplex, 8/04. md: Michael Holland. Cast: Scott Coulter

1126. *City Canyons*. Set in Oklahoma & NY's East Village, 1960–78. Gene Frankel, 4/30/00–4/21/00. 13 perf. m: Steve McConnaughey; l: Steve McConnaughey & Tribor Lloyd; b: Tribor Lloyd; add m/l: Michael Quenneville; d/ch: Rajendra Ramoon Maharaj; md: William Foster McDaniel. Cast: Steve Asciolla, Samara Dunn, Richard V. Licata, Marshall Pailet. "Life Slowly Circles," "Bright Lights Fever," "The Gospel," "A Feeling I Know," "Walking Down St. Mark's Place," "The Lost Child," "Troubled Waters," "Rough Justice," "Let it Burn," "Moonthreads," "Losing Proposition," "Black Butterfly," "Violent Boogie," "I'll Do Anything," "Treasures of the Snow," "Barbeque," "Seen into His Dreams," "Body Wants Body," "Into the Night," "Virgil's Lullaby"

1127. *City of Dreams*. Prince in 1889 Vienna has affair with 16-year-old girl which threatens to tear down Empire. Lambs, 3/10/03. 2 concert

perf. m: Joseph Zellnick; l/b: David Zellnick; d: Chris Smith. Cast: Raul Esparza, Alison Fraser, Nancy Anderson, Adam Heller, Danielle Ferland, Tom Zemon. Previously ran in Cardiff, Wales

1128. *Clams on the Half Shell*. Bette Midler showcase revue. Also known as *Bette Midler's Clams on the Half Shell*. Minskoff, Broadway, 4/14/75–6/21/75. 13 prev. 67 perf. d/ch: Joe Layton; assoc ch: Andre De Shields; set/cos: Tony Walton; light: Beverly Emmons; md: Don York. Cast: Bette Midler, Lionel Hampton, Michael Powell Ensemble, The Hartlettes

1129. *The Class*. Ballet musical. Songs were fantasies of the players. Downstairs at City Center, 4/28/78–4/30/78. 4 perf. orig m: Andrew Asch; conceived by/d/ch: Jack Johnson. Cast: Rico Costa, Gisele Ferrari, Debra Lynn Jones, Donna McEntee, Robert Raimondo, Charles C. Sheek, Gloria Szymkowicz, Whitney Wiemer

1130. *Cliff: The Musical*. Musical bio of Cliff Richard. Cliff was not in it. Prince of Wales, London, 3/14/03–5/10/03. Prev from 3/12/03. m/l/b: Mike Read, Trevor Payne, Colin Rozee; d: Trevor Payne. Preceded by a one month UK tour

1131. *Climb High*. Young man aspires to become Broadway actor. m/l/b: Stephen Sondheim (while student at Williams College)

1132. *Close Enough for Jazz*. Musical comedy revue. Wonderhorse, 6/18/81–6/28/81. 12 perf. p/d: David J. Rothkop; m: Scott Steidl; l/b: Joseph Keenan; creators: Joseph Keenan & David J. Rothkopf; ch: Mary Duncan; md: Douglas Bernstein. Cast: Susan J. Baum, Stephen Berenson, Mary Duncan, Debra Jacobs, Nina Hennessey, Dietrich Snelling, Joe Joyce

1133. *Closer Than Ever*. Musical revue. Cherry Lane, 11/6/89–7/1/90. 24 prev from 10/17/89. 288 perf. m: David Shire; l: Richard Maltby Jr.; b: Steven Scott Smith; d: Steven Scott Smith & Richard Maltby Jr.; ch: Marcia Milgrom Dodge; light: Natasha Katz. Cast: Brent Barrett (*Jim Walton* from 5/90), Sally Mayes, Richard Muenz (*Craig Wells* from 5/90), Lynne Wintersteller, Patrick Scott Brady (also md). "Doors," "She Loves Me Not," "You Wanna Be My Friend?," "What Am I Doin'?," "The Bear, the Tiger, the Hamster and the Mole," "Like a Baby," "Miss Byrd," "The Sound of Muzak," "One of the Good Guys," "There's Nothing Like It," "Life Story," "Next Time," "I Wouldn't Go Back," "Three Friends," "Fandango," "There," "Patterns," "Another Wedding Song," "If I Sing," "Back on Base," "March of Time," "Fathers of Fathers," "It's Never That Easy/I've Been Here Before," "Closer than Ever." Previously ran at Williamstown, Mass.

1134. *Closer to Heaven*. Arts Theatre, London, 5/31/01–10/13/01. Prev from 5/15/01. m/l: Neil Tennant & Chris Lowe (The Pet Shop Boys, Britain's most successful musical duo ever); b: Jonathan Harvey; d: Gemma Bodinetz; ch: Peter Darling; md: Chris Nightingale. "My Night," "Something Special," "Closer to Heaven," "In Denial," "Call Me Old-Fashioned," "Nine Out of Ten," "It's Just

My Little Tribute to Caligula, Darling!," "Hedonism," "Friendly Fire," "Shameless," "Vampires," "Out of My System," "K-Hole," "For All of Us," "Positive Role Model"

1135. *Clownaround*. Also called *Gene Kelly's Clownaround*. Combination circus/musical touring arena show starring Ruth Buzzi & cast of 70 (Troy Garza made his professional debut). Opened 4/27/72, Oakland Coliseum. Closed 5/6/72, Cow Palace, San Francisco. m/l: Moose Charlap & Alvin Cooperman; d: Gene Kelly. Complex set by Irish designer Sean Kenny

1136. *The Club*. Musical spoof of attitudes & personalities in 1905 London men's clubs. 4 elegant gentlemen (played by women) & the club's employees sing condescending songs about women & joke about women. Songs from 1894–1905. Satire on sexism. Westbeth, 1976. w: Eve Merriam; d: Tommy Tune (his debut); md: Alexandra Ivanoff. Then workshopped & revised at Lenox Arts Center, Mass. Circle in the Square Downtown 10/14/76. 674 perf. Actresses were billed using not first names but initials (real identities are in parentheses): J.J. Hafner (Julie J.), G. Hodes (Gloria), C. Monferdini (Carole), J. Beretta (Joanne), M. Dell (Marlene). "A Woman is Only a Woman, But a Good Cigar is a Smoke"

1137. *Club XII*. Musical adaptation of *Twelfth Night*, set in hot dance club. Westbeth, 12/8/90–12/15/90. 10 perf. p: Edgar Lansbury, John Wulp, Shubert Organization; m/l: Ron Hanning, Randy Weiner, Sasha Lewis; d/ch: Patricia Birch; set: Douglas Schmidt; light: Jules Fisher; cos: Willa Kim

1138. *Clue: The Musical*. Featured a murder, 6 suspects & a hard-nosed female detective (played by Denny Dillon) set at Boddy Manor. Players, 12/3/97–12/28/97. 17 prev. 29 perf from 11/18/97. m: Galen Blum, Wayne Barker, Vinnie Martucci; l: Tom Chiodo; b/d/ch: Peter De Pietro; based on the Parker Brothers' board game "Clue;" orch: Wayne Barker. Cast: Robert Bartley, Wysandria Woolsey, Ian Knauer. "The Game," "Life is a Bowl of Pits," "Everyday Devices," "Once a Widow," "Corridors and Halls," "The Murder," "She Hasn't Got a Clue," "Seduction Deduction," "Foul Weather Friend," "Don't Blame Me," "Final Clue"

1139. *The Cockeyed Tiger*. Set in Club Kishka, at Broome & Houston Streets, NYC. The Last, Final, Farewell Performance Tour of a nightclub performer worried about tigers as an endangered species. Astor Place, 1/13/77–1/16/77. 5 perf. p: James J. Wisner; m/l: Bert Kalmar & Harry Ruby; new songs: Nicholas Meyers & Eric Blau; w/d: Eric Blau; ch: Gemze de Lappe & Buzz Miller. Cast: Janet McCall, Joseph Neal, Elly Stone, Jack Scalici. "Littleflea Hop," "God is Good to Me," "Tyger, Tyger," "Whoopie," "Hold Me Thusly," "My Dream of the South of France," "It's a Long, Long March to Kansas City," "We're Together at Kishka," "Good Times," "You've Got to Be a Tiger, Tiger," "We're Four of the Three Musketeers," "Tulip Told Tale," "Show Me a Rose," "America I Like You," "Daddy Oh!," "You Were a Hell of a Crowd Tonight"

1140. *Cockles and Champagne*. Revue. Saville, London, 5/29/54. 126 perf. m/l: David Heneker & Sam Coslow, etc; w: Maureen Stevens; dev/d: Cecil Landeau; asst d: Christopher Hewett; ch: Paddy Stone, etc. Almost totally female cast: Patricia Burke, Renee Houston, Phyllis Neilson-Terry, Fenella Fielding (this was the show that launched her), Miriam Karlin, Elizabeth Seal, Frances King. "Darling, They're Playing Our Song"

1141. *The Cocoanuts*. A show within a show. Lyric Theatre, Broadway, 12/8/25–8/7/26. 276 perf. p: Sam H. Harris; m/l: Irving Berlin; b: George S. Kaufman; book d: Oscar Eagle; ch: Sammy Lee. Cast: Marx Brothers, Margaret Dumont. "The Guests," "The Bellhops," "Family Reputation" (replaced during the run with "Why Do You Want to Know Why?"), "Lucky Boy," "Why Am I a Hit with the Ladies?" (replaced during the run with "Gentlemen Prefer Blondes"), "A Little Bungalow" (replaced during the run with "Ting-a-Ling"), "Florida by the Sea," "Monkey Doodle Doo," "Five O'clock Tea," "They're Blaming the Charleston," "We Should Care," "Minstrel Days," "Tango Melody," "The Tale of a Shirt." Century Theatre, Broadway, 5/16/27–5/28/27. 16 perf. Mostly same cast & crew. "A Little Bungalow" & "Everyone in the World is Doing the Charleston" were restored. "Gentlemen Prefer Blondes" & "Ting-a-Ling" were dropped. "We Should Care" was dropped in favor of a reprise of "Why Do You Want to Know Why?." American Jewish Theatre, 5/12/96–6/23/96. 17 prev from 4/27/96. 49 perf; American Place Theatre, 8/15/96–1/5/97. 22 prev from 7/27/96. 165 perf. adapted by/d/ch: Richard Sabellico. Cast: Laurie Gamache, Celia Tackaberry, Michael McGrath, Michael Berresse, Peter Slutsker (later known as Peter Marx). "Florida by the Sea," "The Bellhops," "Pack up Your Sins and Go to the Devil" (not in the orig), "A Little Bungalow," "With a Family Reputation," "Lucky Boy," "We Should Care," "Always" (cut from the orig), "Five O'clock Tea," "Tango Melody," "We Work While You Sleep" (not in the orig), "When My Dreams Come True" (from the 1929 film), "Shaking the Blues Away" (not in the orig), "Tale of a Shirt"

1142. *Cole*. Tribute to Cole Porter. Mermaid, London, 7/2/74. m/l: Cole Porter; b: Benny Green & Alan Strachan; cast recording on RCA. Cast: Angela Richards, Peter Gale, Julia McKenzie, Kenneth Nelson, Rod McLennan, Lucy Fenwick, Una Stubbs, Bill Kerr, Ray Cornell, Elizabeth Power. Rochester, Mich., 4/20/78. 37 perf. d/ch: John Sharpe

1143. *Colette*. Play with mus about the French author. Set between 1873 & 1954. Ellen Stewart Theatre, 5/6/70–8/2/70. 14 prev. 101 perf. p: Cheryl Crawford; 3 songs & incidental m: Harvey Schmidt & Tom Jones; w: Elinor Jones (Tom Jones's wife); d: Gerald Freedman; cos: Theoni V. Aldredge. Cast: Colette: Zoe Caldwell; Also with: Mildred Dunnock (*Ruth Nelson* from 6/30/70), Keene Curtis (*Tom Aldredge*), Barry Bostwick. Same venue, 10/14/70–10/18/70. 9 prev. 7 perf. Cast: Fenella Fielding, Ruth Nelson, Erik Rhodes. The play with music idea was then scrubbed, and Har-

vey Schmidt & Tom Jones spent the next 5 years writing (among other things) a real musical covering 64 years (1890–1954) in the life of Colette. "There's Another World," "Come to Life," "Do Not Hold On," "Semiramis," "Do it for Willy," "Claudine Sequence," "Why Can't I Walk Through That Door?," "Music Hall," "Dream of Egypt," "I Miss You," "La Vagabonde," "Music Hall Scandal," "Curiosity," "Riviera Nights," "Oo-La-La," "Something for the Summer," "Something for the Winter," "Madame Colette," "Be My Lady," "The Room is Filled with You," "Victory," "Growing Older," "Joy." In 1980 Harry Rigby started to prod the Jones/Schmidt musical for Broadway, and announced Debbie Reynolds for the role. Nothing happened, though, until 1981, when Mr. Rigby hired Diana Rigg for pre-Broadway tour, which opened 2/9/82, at Fifth Avenue Theatre, Seattle. d: Dennis Rosa; ch: Carl Jablonski; set: John Conklin; cos: Raoul Pene du Bois; light: Gilbert V. Hemsley Jr.; md: Larry Blank; orch: Larry Wilcox; dance mus arr: David Krane. Cast: Colette: Diana Rigg; Also with: Robert Helpmann, Marta Eggerth, John Reardon, Martin Vidnovic, Marti Stevens. Then the tour went to Auditorium, Denver, where it closed 3/20/82, losing $1.5 million & failing to make NY. *Colette* was revised into a smaller version, *Colette Collage: Two Musicals About Colette*. 1st half was *Willy*, about Colette's marriage to Henri Gauthier-Villars. "Joy," "Come to Life," "A Simple Country Wedding," "Do it for Willy," "Willy Will Grow Cold," "The Claudines," "Why Can't I Walk Through the Door?," "Music Hall," "Dream of Egypt," "I Miss You," "La Vagabonde," "Love is Not a Sentiment Worthy of Respect," "Now I Must Walk Through That Door." 2nd half was *Maurice*, about Colette's marriage to Maurice Goudeket. "Autumn Afternoon," "Riviera Nights," "Ooo-La-La," "Something for the Summer," "Madame Colette," "You Could Hurt Me," "Be My Lady," "The Room is Filled with You," "Growing Older." York Theatre Company, 3/31/83–4/17/83. 20 perf. d: Fran Soeder; ch: Janet Watson; set: James Morgan; cos: Sigrid Insull; light: Mary Jo Dondlinger; md: Eric Stern. Cast: Jana Robbins, Timothy Jerome. St. Peter's Church, NY, 5/3/91–5/19/91. 28 perf. p: Musical Theatre Works; d: Tom Jones & Harvey Schmidt; ch: Janet Watson & Scott Harris; set/cos: Ed Wittstein; light: Mary Jo Dondlinger; md: Norman Weiss. Cast: Betsy Joslyn, Kenneth Kantor, Ralston Hill, James J. Mellon, Mary Setrakian

1144. *Colette*. Stables Theatre, Wavendon, England, 11/13/79–11/17/79. 2 prev. 3 perf. It was called *Cleo Colette* then. After title change it opened at the Alexandra, Birmingham, England, 9/2/80 (2 weeks); Comedy, London, 9/24/80–11/8/80. 47 perf. w: Johnny Dankworth; d: Wendy Toye. Cast: Cleo Laine, Kenneth Nelson, John Moffatt (Narrator-role played initially by Johnny Dankworth). "You Can Be Sure of Spring," "He's a Captain," "I'm Special," "Ambitious," "Paree!," "Our Relationship," "Alone with Myself," "Attention Will Wander," "You've Got to Do What You've Got to Do," "We'll Stick Together," "I Never Make the Same Mistake," "Little Girl," "Nothing Special," "A Little Touch of Powder," "Love with Someone Younger," "Will He Ever Be Back?," "Little Red Room"

1145. *The Collected Works of Billy the Kid.* Homespun Billy the Kid story with background of folk music, orig written as poem & subsequently adapted by its author into a play. Lepercq Space, Brooklyn Academy of Music, 10/13/75–10/19/75. 10 perf. m: Alan Laing; l/w: Michael Ondaatje; d: John Wood. Cast: Neil Munro, Patricia Collins. Previously prod by Neptune Theatre Co. of Nova Scotia

1146. *The Color Purple.* Girl struggles to find herself. Alliance, Atlanta, 9/17/04–10/17/04. Prev from 9/9/04. World premiere. p: The Alliance Theatre, by special arr with Creative Battery & Scott Sanders Prods; m: Brenda Russell, Allee Willis, Stephen Bray; b: Marsha Norman; based on Pulitzer Prize-winning novel by Alice Walker, and on the 1985 Steven Spielberg movie that starred Oprah Winfrey, Whoopi Goldberg, and Danny Glover; d: Gary Griffin; ch: Donald Byrd (replaced Ken Roberson); set: John Lee Beatty; cos: Paul Tazewell; light: Brian MacDevitt; sound: Jon Weston. Cast: Felicia P. Fields, La Chanze, Saycon Sengbloh, Adriane Lenox, Kingsley Leggs. Plans for Broadway in fall 2005 were postponed to spring 2006

1147. *Come Spy with Me.* New Theatre, Oxford, England, 4/28/66 (2 weeks); Brighton; Golders Green; the Whitehall, London, 5/31/66–7/22/67. 468 perf. w: Bryan Blackburn; d: Ned Sherrin; ch: Irving Davies; set: Disley Jones; cast recording on Decca. Cast: Danny La Rue, Barbara Windsor, Jenny Logan, Riggs O'Hara, Janet Mahoney, Valerie Walsh, Rose Hill, Richard Wattis. "File on Dr. Fink," "Come Spy with Me," "Ups and Downs," "Look at Me Now," "A Far Better Thing," "Welfare State," "Don't Say a Word," "Fancy Free," "The Whole Truth," "Assassinating Rhythm," "Female and Feminine," "What's His Name?," "You're the Greatest"

Come What May see # 573, Main Book

1148. *Comedy.* Musical commedia. Colonial, Boston, 11/6/72–11/18/72. Canceled scheduled 11/28 Broadway opening at the Martin Beck. p: Edgar Lansbury, Stuart Duncan, Joseph Beruh; m/l: Hugo (Peretti) & Luigi (Creatore) & George David Weiss; b/d: Lawrence Carra; based on 1622 commedia dell'arte sketch *The Great Magician*, by Basilio Locatelli, set on island of Arcadia, where inept ruler tries to turn place into tourist attraction; ch: Stephen Reinhardt; set/cos: William Pitkin; light: Roger Morgan; md: Joseph Stecko; arr: Mel Marvin. Cast: George Lee Andrews, Joseph Bova, SuEllen Estey, Merwin Goldsmith, George S. Irving, Marc Jordan, Bill McCutcheon, Marty Morris, Joseph R. Sicari, John Witham, Diane Findlay, Marilyn Saunders, Lana Shaw, Bobby Lee. "Comedy," "Open Your Heart," "Gotta Hang My Wash Out to Dry," "A Friend is a Friend," "Where is My Love?," "Sacrifice," "God Bless the Fig Tree," "Smile, Smile, Smile," "Magnetic," "Love is Such a Fragile Thing," "Breakin' the Spell,"

"Whirlwind Circle." Revised as *Smile, Smile, Smile,* and toured summer circuit. Eastside Playhouse, 4/4/73–4/8/73. 7 perf. d: Robert Simpson. Cast: Rudy Tronto, Chip Zien, Diane Findlay, Marilyn Saunders, Bobby Lee, Joseph Neal, SuEllen Estey, Gary Beach, Virginia Pulos, Donna Liggitt Forbes

1149. *Comedy of Errors.* Comic operetta, adapted from Shakespeare. Arts Theatre, London, 3/28/56–5/12/56. 36 perf. m: Julian Slade; w: Lionel Harris & Robert McNabb; d: Lionel Harris; set/cos: Hutchinson Scott; md: Myer Fredman. Cast: Frederick Jaeger, David Peel, Bernard Cribbins, Patricia Routledge, Jane Wenham, David Bird, Lally Bowers, David Dodimead. 1st shown on BBC, 5/16/54 & 5/20/54. d: Lionel Harris; set: James Bould; md: Eric Robinson. Cast: Richard Vernon, James Cairncross, David Peel, Joan Plowright, Jane Wenham, David Bird, Lally Bowers, Patricia Routledge, Patrick Horgan. ITV showed 1956 musical on 5/21/56. Same cast & crew except md: Dennis Ringrove

1150. *Comedy Tonight.* Revue. Lunt-Fontanne, Broadway, 12/18/94–12/25/94. 6 prev from 12/14. 8 perf. p: Alexander Cohen & Max Cooper; Dorothy Loudon's special material written by: Bruce Vilanch; d: Alex Cohen; ch: Albert Stephenson; cos: Alvin Colt; light: Richard Nelson; md: Peter Howard. Cast: Dorothy Loudon, Joy Behar, Mort Sahl, Michael Davis. "Fifty Percent." Pre-Broadway tryout featured new song, "Three," by John Kander & Fred Ebb. Reviews were not good. Previously ran at Rich Forum, Stamford, Conn.

1151. *The Committee.* Revue with some music. Mostly skits about follies of present-day living. Material changed nightly. Grew out of improvs by the performers. Henry Miller's, Broadway, 9/16/64–11/7/64. 5 prev from 9/12/64. 61 perf. p: Arthur Cantor; d: Alan Myerson; set/light: Ralph Alswang; incidental m: Ellsworth Milburn. Cast: Hamilton Camp, Scott Beach, Garry Goodrow, Larry Hankin, Ellsworth Milburn, Dick Stahl, Irene Riordan, Kathryn Ish

1152. *A Connecticut Yankee...* 1950s doo-wop singer transported back to Camelot. An Equity-approved showcase. Unrelated to Broadway prods except for Mark Twain source. Judith Anderson, 11/19/98–11/29/98. m/md: W. Scott Warfel; l/b/d: Craig L. Davis; ch: Kristin Brigitte Hughes

1153. *Conrack.* Set on island of Yamacraw & in Beaufort, SC, 1969. AMAS, 10/15/87–11/8/87. 16 perf. m: Lee Pockriss; l: Anne Croswell; b: Granville Burgess; based on novel *The Water is Wide,* by Pat Conroy; d: Stuart Ross; ch: Sheila D. Barker. Cast: Peggy Alston, Lisa Boggs, Herb Lovelle, Tarik Winston. "Find Me a Body," "Bye Bye Conrack," "The Water is Wide," "Hey, I'm Talkin' to You, Beethoven!," "Southern Charm," "Tune in Tomorrow," "One Night to Howl," "A Regular Family," "Hopes an' Dreams," "City Lights." Arena Stage, Washington, DC, 2/29/92. d: Lonny Price; ch: Gregg Burge; md: Tim Weil. Cast: Patrick Cassidy, Tina Fabrique, Pamela Isaacs, Larry Marshall, Baakari Wilder

1154. *The Contrast.* Eastside Playhouse,

11/27/72–12/17/72. 24 perf. p: Peter Cookson; m: Don Pippin; l: Steve Brown; based on 1787 comedy by American Indian author Royall Tyler; adapted by/d: Anthony Stimac; ch: Bill Guske; set: David Chapman; light: C. Murawski; md: Dorothea Freitag. Cast: Connie Danese, Elaine Kerr, Gene Kelton, Patti Perkins, Pamela Adams, Ty McConnell. "A Woman Rarely Ever," "A House Full of People," "Keep Your Little Eye Upon the Main Chance, Mary," "So, They Call it New York," "Dear Lord Chesterfield," "A Sort of Courting Song," "So Far," "She Can't Really Be," "That Little Monosyllable," "It's Too Much," "Wouldn't I," "A Hundred Thousand Ways," "I Was in the Closet"

1155. *Conundrum.* Christian musical. Set on Shadow Planet. Historical Glad Tidings Tabernacle, 11/4/99–12/4/99. 18 perf. w: Dr. Stace Gaddy; d/set: Mark Todd Bruner; ch: Michael Leonard James; conductor: Mark Adamy. Cast: Michael Leonard James, Stace Gaddy, Ana Mercedes Torres. "Number Five," "What's it Like?," "Crayons and Make Believe," "Slam," "Party," "Peek-a-Boo," "A Time of Peace," "Maybe it's Love," "Will You Be Mine?," "Tell Me Why," "Look into Your Soul," "Stand Up," "Mama," "Suddenly," "With You," "Life Has Begun"

1156. *Cookin' at the Cookery: The Music and Times of Alberta Hunter.* Play with mus. Melting Pot, 1/22/03. Prev from 1/14/03. w/d: Marion J. Caffey. Cast: Ann Duquesnay, Debra Walton. Alberta Hunter, famous jazz singer, quit music business aged 61, after her mother died, and went into nursing. Ran regionally before coming to NYC. San Jose Rep, 7/2/03–8/03/03. set: Dale F. Jordan; cos: Marilyn A. Wall; ms/arr: Danny Holgate; md: George Caldwell. Cast: Ann Duquesnay, Janice Lorraine

1157. *Cool Off.* Bored young housewife sells soul to Devil for night on town. Pre-Broadway tryouts at the Forrest, Philadelphia, 3/31/64–4/4/64. 7 perf. Never made Broadway. p: Barbara Griner; m/l: Howard Blankman; b: Jerome Weidman; d: Herbert Machiz; ch: Bob Herget; set: Stewart Chaney; md: John Lesko; dance mus: Genevieve Pitot. Cast: Stanley Holloway, Hermione Baddeley, Stuart Damon, Sheila Sullivan, Jane Connell (understudy for Miss Baddeley). "Cuckoo," "Suburbia," "Can This Be Why We Came Here?," "Cool Off," "A Matter of Pride," "Take Care," "Warm Up," "At My Age," "Ballad of the Dauntless Courier," "Only Wonderful," "Where Do We Go From Here?," "For the Life of Me," "Bessie's Bossa Nova," "Witch Hazel," "Plenty of Zip," "A Dream Ago"

1158. *The Coolest Cat in Town.* Senior Dance Night & following day at Midville High School gym. Elvis-type rock star returns to old haunts 20 years later. City Center Downstairs, 6/22/78–7/9/78. 8 perf. 21 perf. m/l: Diane Leslie & William Gleason; d: Frank Carucci; ch: Mary Lou Crivello; md: Bob Goldstone. Cast: Joey Faye, Michael Hayward-Jones, Christopher Callan, Lennie Del Duca Jr., William Parry, Maura Silverman, Bill Britten, Pamela Ann Wilson, Mary Lou Crivello, Danny

Rounds. "Disco Rag," "Born to Rock and Roll," "Superstar," "One Kiss," "Suspended Animation," "Lost My Cool," "Rock Back the Clock," "The Bob Will Never Die," "Let's Live it Over Again," "You're My Last Chance," "Hula Hoop," "Coolest Cat in Town," "Mr. Know it All," "So What?." Previously produced in a Brooklyn high school

1159. *Copacabana.* Set in nightclub in 1940. Palace, Manchester, England, 5/5/94; Prince of Wales, London, 6/23/94. m/l/b: Barry Manilow, Bruce Sussman, Jack Feldman. Cast: Jenny Logan, Nicola Dawn, Richard Lyndon, Duncan Smith, Gary Wilmot. "Copacabana," "Dancin' Fool," "Night on the Town," "Lola," "Ay Caramba!," "Sweet Heaven," "This Can't Be Real," "Welcome to Havana," "El Bravo!," "Call Me Mr. Lucky," "Big City Blues." A tour of *Barry Manilow's Copacabana* opened in Pittsburgh, 6/17/00, with Franc D'Ambrosio, Darcie Roberts, Philip Hernandez, Gavin MacLeod (*Dale Radunz* from 11/00), Beth McVey

1160. *Copacabana Revue.* Series of revues–1942, 1944, 1945, 1946, 1947, 1950, 1952, 1953, 1955. Joe E. Lewis was staple in early ones. Sophie Tucker was in 44. Georgia Gibbs starred in 53. Scores by authors such as Eddie DeLange, Irving Actman, Charles Tobias, Nat Simon, Carl Sigman, Bob Hilliard, Dave Mann, Lyn Duddy

1161. *Corkscrews!* Slightly twisted revue. Tomi/Terrace Theatre, 10/6/82–10/24/82. 15 perf. m: Arthur Siegel; l/sk: Tony Lang; d/ch: Miriam Fond. Cast: Tony Aylward. "I'm into Music," "The Daily Grind," "Let it All Hang Out," "You Have a Friend," "Make it Another," "Family that Plays Together," "People," "Greetings," "Psychotic Overtures," "Not Getting Murdered Today," "Up the Hill There," "I'm Not Queer," "I Like Me," "What I Need the Most," "Golden Age," "Last Minority," "Free Advice," "Looking for Love"

1162. *Corn.* Chelsea Playhouse, 4/2/97–5/24/97. 8 prev. 40 perf. m/l: Virgil Young; add m & l: Lance Cruce & Mary Rodriguez; b: Charles Ludlam; d: Everett Quinton; md: Lance Cruce. Cast: Everett Quinton

1163. *Costa Packet.* A candy-floss entertainment. Skit on travel-agent racket. Theatre Royal, Stratford East, London, 10/5/72–12/9/72. 65 perf. p: Theatre Workshop; m/l: Lionel Bart; b: Frank Norman & Alan Klein; d: Joan Littlewood; ch: Judith Paris; md: David Gold. Cast: Avis Bunnage, Gaye Brown, Larry Dann, Ken Hill, Judith Paris, Maxwell Shaw, Valerie Walsh

1164. *Cotton Club.* Series of revues. Started 1931 at the famous Harlem nightclub. Only ones to fall within post–1943 era are 1956 & 1958 editions. The last starred Cab Calloway & the Four Step Brothers. Mr. Calloway had starred in most editions going back to the very beginning. Benny Davis had written or co-written scores for several editions, and did so in 1958

1165. *Cotton Patch Gospel.* Lambs, 10/21/81–4/11/82. 193 perf. m/l: Harry Chapin; b: Tom Key & Russell Treyz; based on book *The Cotton Patch Version of Matthew and John*, by Clarence Jordan; d: Russell Treyz; set/cos: John Falabella; light: Roger Morgan; md: Tom Chapin. Cast: Tom Key, The Cotton Patch String Band. "Somethin's Brewin' in Gainesville," "I Did It," "Mama is Here," "It isn't Easy," "Sho' Nuff," "Turn it Around," "When I Look Up," "Are We Ready?," "We Got to Get Organized," "We're Gonna Love It," "Jubilation," "I Wonder." Riverside Church, 11/12/97–12/7/97. 2 prev. 26 perf. p: Melting Pot Theatre Co.; d: Danny Peak; md: Steve Steiner. Cast: John C. Havens, Mimi Bessette, Kevin Fox

1166. *The Count of Monte Cristo.* London, 1974. 28 perf. m: Ian Armit (based on contemporary French songs); w: Ken Hill; from Alexandre Dumas novel. Cast: Toni Palmer, Bill Zappa

1167. *Cowardy Custard.* Noel Coward revue. Mermaid, London, 7/10/72. 344 perf. dev/d: Gerald Frow, Alan Strachan, Wendy Toye; md: John Burrows; cast recording on RCA. Cast: Patricia Routledge (*Julia McKenzie*), Maggie Grant (*Una Stubbs*), Jonathan Cecil (*Hugh Walters*), Peter Gale, Anna Sharkey, Laurel Ford, John Moffatt, Geoffrey Burridge, Tudor Davies, Elaine Delmar, Derek Waring. "If Love Were All," "I'll See You Again," "Has Anybody Seen Our Ship?," "Kiss Me," "Go Slow, Johnny," "Tokay," "Dearest Love," "Could You Please Oblige Us with a Bren Gun?," "Come the Wild, Wild Weather," "Any Little Fish," "A Room with a View," "Beatnik Love Affair," "Poor Little Rich Girl," "Louisa," "Mad About the Boy," "The Stately Homes of England," "Twentieth Century Blues," "I Went to a Marvellous Party," "Mrs. Worthington," "Why Must the Show Go On?," "London is a Little Bit of Alright," "What Ho, Mrs. Brisket!," "Saturday Night at the Rose & Crown," "London at Night," "Alice is at it Again," "The Passenger's Always Right," "Useful Phrases," "Why Do the Wrong People Travel?," "Mad Dogs and Englishmen," "Nina," "I Like America," "Bronxville Darby and Joan," "Darjeeling," "Let's Do It," "Nothing Can Last Forever," "Would You Like to Stick a Pin in My Balloon?," "Dance, Little Lady," "Forbidden Fruit," "Sigh No More." Theatre 1010, 5/10/91–6/10/91. 14 perf. d: David Dunn Bauer; ch: Hal Simons

1168. *Cowboy.* StageArts, 4/29/87–5/24/87. 20 perf. m/l: Richard Riddle; from idea by Ronnie Claire Edwards; d: Robert Bridges; ch: Robert Bridges & Dennis Dennehy; md: Wendell Kindberg. Cast: George Ball, Ilene Kristen, Carolyn DeLany, Dennis Edenfield, Richard Browne, Joyce Fleming, Audrey Lavine, Ken Lundie, Michael Mann. "Hunker Down Cowboy," "It Seems to Me," "I'll Dream Your Dream," "Oh, Oh, Cowboy," "Light Doesn't Last That Long," "Singin' to 'em," "Goin' East," "She's a Shame"

1169. *Cowboys!* Set on the Straight Arrow Ranch. Wings, 9/21/00–10/21/00. 5 prev. 20 perf. m: Paul L. Johnson; l/b: Clint Jefferies; d: Jeffery Corrick; ch: Kate Swan. "Where Men are Men," "One Thing I Can Do Good," "War Dance," "I Fall to Faded Pieces After Midnight," "When Your Sweet Dreams Drive Me Crazy," "Nothin' at All," "Lonesome Cowpoke," "Everything's Bigger in Texas," "Gringo's Lament," "Girl from Texarkana," "Ain't Never Had a Kiss Like His," "Make the Switch," "I Ain't No Good for You," "Apache Dance," "Cloggin' onto Broadway', "Always Get My Man"

1170. *Cowgirls.* Set in Hiram Hall, a country/western music hall in Rexford, Kansas. Minetta Lane, 4/1/96–1/5/97. 16 prev from 3/19/96. 321 perf. p: Denise Cooper, Susan Gallin, Rodger Hess, Suki Sandler; m/l/conceived by: Mary Murfitt; b: Betsy Howie; d/ch: Eleanor Reissa; set: James Noone; cos: Catherine Zuber; md: Pam Drews Phillips. Cast: Rhonda Coullet, Mary Murfitt, Betsy Howie. "Three Little Maids," "Jesse's Lullaby," "Ode to Connie Carlson," "Sigma Alpha Iota," "Ode to Jo," "From Chopin to Country," "Kingdom of Country," "Songs My Mama Sang," "Heads or Tails," "Love's Sorrow," "Looking for a Miracle," "Don't Call Me Trailer Trash," "Honky Tonk Girl," "Every Saturday Night," "Don't Look Down," "They're All Cowgirls To Me," "Saddle Tramp Blues," "It's Time to Come Home," "We're a Travelin' Trio," "Sunflower," "Concert Medley," "House Rules," "Cowgirls." Previously produced by Caldwell Theatre Co., Boca Raton; Berkshire Theatre Festival; and Old Globe, San Diego

1171. *Cradle Song.* Musical Theatre Works, 3/8/89–4/2/89. 8 prev. 21 perf. m/l: Jan Mullaney & Mary Bracken Phillips; d: Anthony J. Stimac; set: Richard Ellis. Cast: Mary Bracken Phillips, Paul Ukena Jr., Carole Schweid, Keith Charles. "Father's Day," "Choices," "Beautiful Baby," "Hickory Dickory Dock," "He Was Just Here," "Kick the Machine," "Is It Anybody's Business But My Own," "Nobody's Perfect," "I Wouldn't Trade a Minute"

1172. *Cranford.* Theatre Royal, Stratford East, London, 11/11/75–12/6/75. Prev from 11/5/75. 26 perf. p: Theatre Workshop; m: Carl Davis; l/b: Joan Littlewood & John Wells; from novel by Mrs. Gaskell; d: Joan Kemp-Welch; set: Dee Greenwood; md: Trevor T. Smith. Cast: Penelope Lee, Richard Tonge, Bill Shine, Ed Devereaux, Stephanie Voss, Pamela Charles, Tony Bateman. Thames TV showed a prod on 12/28/76. d: Pamela Lonsdale. Cast: Judy Cornwell, Ann Beach, Pamela Charles, Aubrey Woods

1173. *Crazy Now.* Musical revue. Eden, 9/10/72. 1 perf. m: Norman Sachs; l/b: Richard Smithies & Maura Cavanagh; d/ch: Voight Kempson. Cast: Carla Benjamin, William Buell, John Scoullar, Rosalie, Glenn Mure. "Crazy Now," "Marginal People," "Tears," "Algae," "Beautiful," "Hard Times," "Get Naked," "Dirty Mind," "Regulation Purple," "Something to Do with My Hands"

1174. *The Crooked Mile.* 2 rival gangs in Soho. Opera House, Manchester, England, 8/11/59 (2 weeks); Liverpool; the Cambridge, London, 9/10/59–1/30/60. 164 perf. m: Peter Greenwell; l/b: Peter Wildeblood (from his book *West End People*); d: Jean Meyer; ch: John Heawood; set/cos: Reginald Woolley; md: Kenneth Alwyn; orch: Gordon Langford; cast recording on HMV. Cast: Jack MacGowran,

Elisabeth Welsh, Millicent Martin, Elwyn Brook-Jones, Anton Rodgers, Norman Warwick, Alan Thomas, John Larsen, Jacqueline Murray, Edgar K. Bruce, Lita Tovey, John Heawood. "Requiem for Joe," "Someone Else's Baby," "Lolly-By," "Going Up," "If I Ever Fall in Love Again," "Buy a Ticket," "This is War," "Horticulture," "The Crooked Mile," "Cousin Country," "Meet the Family," "Spare a Penny," "The War on Saturday Night," "I'll Wait," "Other People's Sins," "Free," "Down to Earth"

1175. *Crossroads Cafe*. 18th Street Playhouse, 11/3/83–11/20/83. 12 perf. d: Carole Start. Cast: Tommy Re, Lynne McCall, John C. Introcaso (also m/l). "Ain't Doin' Nothin' Wrong," "Searching for That Sunset," "Rainy Day Blues," "Lovely Ladies," "Fool Inside of Me," "Give Before You Die," "Three O'clock in the Mornin'," "You Wanna Go to Broadway," "Woman's Work Ain't Never Done," "When I Dream," "Good Mornin', Mr. Sunshine," "Crossroads Cafe"

1176. *Crowns*. Second Stage, 2002. Based on volume of photos of African-American women in their Sunday hats, by photographer Michael Cunningham & journalist Craig Marberry. Played with gospel music. w/d: Regina Taylor; ch: Ronald K. Brown; md: Daryl Waters. Cast: Lillias White, Lawrence Clayton

Cry the Beloved Country see # 409, Main Book

1177. *The Crystal Heart*. American musical fantasy. Set in mid 19th century. London, 1957. Cast: Gladys Cooper. East 74th Street, 2/15/60–2/21/60. 8 perf. m/l: Baldwin Bergersen & William Archibald; d/ch: William Archibald; md: Baldwin Bergersen. Cast: Mildred Dunnock, John Stewart, Virginia Vestoff. "A Year is a Day," "A Monkey When He Loves," "Handsome Husbands," "Yes, Aunt," "A Girl with a Ribbon," "I Must Paint," "I Wanted to See the World," "Fireflies," "How Strange the Silence," "When I Drink with My Love," "Desperate," "Lovely Island," "Bluebird," "Agnes and Me," "Madam, I Beg You!," "My Heart Won't Learn," "Tea Party," "Lovely Bridesmaids," "It Took Them," "D-o-g"

1178. *Cummings and Goings*. Special musical event, celebrating poetry of e.e. cummings. Top of the Village Gate, 2/26/84–3/11/84. 5 perf. m: Ada Janik; d/ch: Nina Janik; orch: Steve Margoshes. Cast: Nina Hennessey, Bruce Hubbard, Elisa Fiorillo, Sharon Brown, Raymond Patterson

1179. *Cupid and Psyche*. John Houseman, 9/24/03–10/26/03. Prev from 9/17/03. m: Jihwan Kim; l/b: Sean Hartley; d: Timothy Childs; ch: Dev Janki; set: David Swayze. Cast: Barret Foa, Deborah Lew, Logan Lipton (Deven May was going to play this role), Laura Marie Duncan. Before this run it had been developed at BMI Lehman Engel Musical Theatre Workshop, and had played at various venues throughout the USA. There were OB plans for a bigger venue in 2004

1180. *Curley McDimple*. Big-hit spoof of Shirley Temple movies, about child star in movies in 1934. Bert Wheeler, 11/22/67–1/25/70. 931 perf. m/l/d: Robert Dahdah; b: Mary Boylan & Robert Dahdah. Cast: Curley: Bayn Johnson (alternated with Sunny Leigh); Alice: Bernadette Peters, *Joyce Nolen*; Butterfly McQueen (joined cast 5/9/68, in role written for her; when she left, in 68–69, role was cut); Also with: Helon Blount. "A Cup of Coffee," "I Try," "Curley McDimple," "Love is the Loveliest Love Song," "Are There Any More Rosie O'Gradys?," "Dancing in the Rain," "Be Grateful for What You've Got," "At the Playland Jamboree," "I've Got a Little Secret," "You Like Monkey, You," "Stars and Lovers," "The Meanest Man in Town," "Something Nice is Going to Happen," "Swing-a-Ling," "Hi de hi de hi, Hi de hi de ho." Plaza 9 Music Hall, 6/26/72–8/20/72. 96 perf. d: Robert Dahdah; md: Horace Diaz. Cast: Robbi Morgan, Mary Boylan, Lynn Brossman, Don Emmons, George Hillman, Jane Stuart, Richard Durham

1181. *Curtain Going Up*. Musical revue. Closed out of Town, 1952. p/d: Mervyn Nelson; m/l: Michael Brown; sk: Wax Wilk & George Axelrod, Mel Brooks, etc; set/light: Peggy Clark; md: Milton Rosenstock; orch: Don Walker. Cast: Marilyn Cantor (Eddie Cantor's daughter), Larry Storch (debut), Barbara Ashley, Patricia Hammerlee, Phil Leeds, Skeet Guenther. "I Love You, I Love You, I Love You," "Lizzie Borden," "Swamp Boy (Swamp Girl)"

1182. *Custody*. Set in early 1950s, in a Connecticut boarding school for girls. Westbeth, 4/19/91–4/28/91. 12 perf. m/l: Marsha Singer & Sandra Hochman; based on portion of novel *Walking Papers*, by Sandra Hochman; d: Mina Yakim. "Dance of Custody," "Throwaway Kid," "We Have to Love Each Other," "Cherry Lawn," "Watercolor Girl," "Doin' It," "It Hurts Like a Razor Strap," "Missing You," "Stargazers," "Friendship is the Most Important Thing," "There Was Something Wrong with Your Head," "Sum of My Dreams"

1183. *Cut the Ribbons*. Mother-daughter musical. Westside Theatre Downstairs, 9/20/92–10/11/92. Prev from 9/8/92. 40 perf. p: George & Phase Three Prods; m: Cheryl Hardwick & Mildred Kayden; add m: Nancy Ford; l: Mae Richard; d: Sue Lawless; ch: Sam Viverito; md: Sande Campbell; set/light: Michael Hotopp. Cast: Georgia Engel, Barbara Feldon, Donna McKechnie. "She Loves You," "Kick Me Again," "Mommy Number Four," "Let Her Go," "Door is Closed," "A Period Piece," "Lookin' Good," "It's a Party," "Because of Her," "Try Not to Need Her," "Balancing," "Mom Will Be There," "Am I Ready for This?," "Instinct," "T'ai Chi," "Bed," "Isabel," "That Woman in the Mirror," "Where's My Picture," "I Dare You Not to Dance," "Her Career," "I Just Can't Move in Her Shadow," "Cut the Ribbons"

1184. *Cybele: A Love Story*. Set in Ville d'Avray, a small suburb of Paris, in 1956. Judith Anderson, 11/7/96–11/17/96. 1 prev. 11 perf. m/l/adapted by: Paul Dick; from book by Bernard Eschasseriaux; d: Lisa Brailoff; set: Donald L. Brooks. Cast: Allison Baker, Jack Fletcher, Monika Kendall, Tony Meindl. "Stones from a Star," "Another Night, Another Moon, Another Shore," "I Had a Future," "We Touch a Lot," "No Greater Joy," "Lonely Chil-

dren," "Ring That Bell," "Be a Daffodil," "And Now it's My Turn," "I Knew He Wouldn't Be Coming Back to Begin With," "A Kiss on My Brow," "Each Sunday," "Knife into You," "I'll Tell You My Name," "Eighteen/Thirty Four," "Meant to Be Married," "Come to the Fair," "Pierre, My Love," "Sensitive, So Sensitive," "How Could You," "My Best Christmas," "Follow Forever," "A Real Man," "Happier with Her," "Memory of a Dark Mind," "Town Talk," "Cybele"

Daarlin' Juno see # 367, Main Book

1185. *Daddy Goodness*. Set in Louisiana during Sweet Summer. London, 1972. 24 perf. m: David Lindup & Jeff Martins; l: Joan Maitland & Mark Heath; based on 1968 Negro Ensemble Company OB prod of same name by Richard Wright & Louis Sapin, which had opened 6/4/68 (64 perf). Cast: Willie Payne, Mark Heath, Faye Chance, Monica Hall. Orig play was used again as basis for another musical of same name which opened 8/16/79, Forrest, Philadelphia. Closed 10/7/79, National, Washington, DC, without making intended Broadway. p: Ashton Springer & Motown; new m/l: Ken Hirsch & Ron Miller; new b: Ron Miller & Shauneille Perry; d: Israel Hicks, *Phil Oesterman*; ch: Louis Johnson, *Mike Malone*; set: Santo Loquasto; light: Jennifer Tipton; ms: Danny Holgate; md: Lea Richardson; orch: Robert M. Freedman. Cast: Clifton Davis, Freda Payne, Ted Ross, Rod Perry, Mabel Robinson, Dan Strayhorn, Sandra Reaves-Phillips, Raymond Bazemore. "Goodness Don't Come Easy When You're Bad," "I Got Religion," "Hungry," "Spread Joy," "Lottie's Purification," "We'll Let the People Decide," "One More Step," "People Make Me Cry," "I Don't Want to Do it Alone No More," "Daddy's Decision," "Don't Touch That Dial," "You're Home." See also *Louisiana Summer* (this appendix)

1186. *Dad's Army*. Nostalgic music & laughter show of Britain's finest hour. Shaftesbury, London, 10/1/75. m/l: Jimmy Perry & David Croft; based on British TV series; cast recording on Warners. Cast: Arthur Lowe, Ian Lavender, Clive Dunn, John Le Mesurier, Bill Pertwee, Arnold Ridley, Pamela Cundell, John Bardon, Joan Cooper. "Put That Light Out," "Carry on on the Home Front," "Command Post," "When Can I Have a Banana Again?," "The King is Still in London," "Lords of the Air," "Siegfried Line," "We'll Meet Again," "A Nightingale Sang in Berkeley Square," "Radio Personalities of 1940," "Home Town," "The Beach"

1187. *Dames at Sea*. One-act spoof revue of Dick Powell — Ruby Keeler type musicals. Cafe Cino, 1966. p: Jordan Hott; m: Jim Wise; l/b: George Haimsohn & Robin Miller; d: Robert Dahdah. It was re-written & expanded, and re-opened 12/20/68 at the Bouwerie Lane; moved to Theatre de Lys, where it closed 5/10/70. Total of 575 perf. d/ch: Neal Kenyon; cast recording on Columbia. Cast: Bernadette Peters (*Pia Zadora* from 6/17/69, *Bonnie Franklin* from 7/69, *Barbara Sharma* from 12/5/69, *Loni Zoe Ackerman* from 2/24/70), Steve Elmore. Other actors in the show at some stage include: Janie Sell, Carol Morley, David Christmas (the original Dick), Tamara Long. "Wall Street," "It's You," "Broadway Baby," "That Mister Man of Mine," "Choo-Choo Honeymoon," "Sailor of My Dreams," "Singapore Sue," "Good Times Are Here to Stay," "Dames at Sea," "The Beguine," "Raining in My Heart," "There's Something About You," "Echo Waltz," "Star Tar," "Let's Have a Simple Wedding." Mirroring the musical, Bernadette Peters (playing a Ruby Keeler clone called Ruby from Centerville, Utah who lands a chorus job in a Broadway-bound musical called *Dames at Sea*) became a star after this. In the story they lose their theatre & the show proceeds on deck of battleship. Plaza 9 Music Hall, 9/23/70–1/31/71. 170 perf. Cast: Dick: Kurt Peterson; Ruby: Leland Palmer; Janie Sell & Carol Morley reprised, Raymond Thorne. Tour opened 6/25/69, San Francisco. Cast: Ruby: Marti Rolph. Duchess, London, 8/27/69. Cast: Ruby: Sheila White; Mona: Joyce Blair. Tour opened 3/10/70, Hollywood. Cast: Ruby: Barbara Sharma; Dick: Ron Husmann. Televised in 1972. Cast: Ann-Margret, Anne Meara, Ann Miller. Paper Mill Playhouse, NJ, 1973. Cast: Bernadette Peters. Asolo, Sarasota. Successful run. Lambs, 6/12/85–2/9/86. 9 prev. 278 perf. d/ch: Neal Kenyon; set/cos: Peter Harvey; light: Roger Morgan; md: Janet Aycock. Cast: Donna Kane, Richard Sabellico (*Robert Fitch* from 1/21/85), Dorothy Stanley, George Dvorsky, Dirk Lumbard. Harold Clurman, 12/2/94–12/11/94. 13 perf. d: Bob Bogdanoff; ch: Mark Santoro. Cast: Mona: Sally Ann Swarm; Ruby: Kristin Chenoweth

1188. *Dance on a Country Grave*. Hudson Guild, 4/21/77. w: Kelly Hamilton; based on Thomas Hardy's *Return of the Native;* d: Robert Brewer. Cast: Sam Freed, Donna Theodore, Mike Dantuono, Fiddle Viracola, Gail Kellstrom, Kevin Kline

1189. *Dance wi' Me: The Fatal Twitch*. NY Shakespeare Festival one-act comedy with mus. Freewheeling fantasies of young & engaging urban loser. Set in 1950s. Anspacher, 6/10/71–7/18/71. 53 perf. Cast: Greg Antonacci (also w/m), Johnny Bottoms, Judy Allen, Joel Zwick (also d). Mayfair (OB), as *Dance With Me*, 1/23/75–1/4/76. 396 perf. Cast: Greg Antonacci (*Peter Riegert* from 7/10/75), Johnny Bottoms (nominated for a Tony), Joel Zwick (also d/ch — Tony nomination for ch), Annie Abbott, Patricia Gaul. Previously produced by La Mama

1190. *The Dancing Heiress*. American musical. Opera House, London, 3/15/60. 15 perf. p: Robert Lavin & Yvette Schumer; m/l: Murray Grand; b: Jack Fletcher & Murray Grand; d: John Heawood. Cast: Millicent Martin, Jill Ireland, Norman Bowler, Judy Collins, Lally Bowers, Peter Bayliss

1191. *Dancing in the Streets*. About housing situation in Washington. Boston, 1943 (2 weeks). m/l: Vernon Duke & Howard Dietz. Mary Martin turned down *Oklahoma!* to do this. Also in cast: Ernest Cossart. "Dancing in the Streets," "Got a Bran' New Daddy," "Indefinable Charm," "Irresistible You"

1192. *The Dancing Years*. Revival of Ivor Novello's old musical. London, 1968. Cast: June Bronhill

1193. *Danny and Sylvia: A Musical Love Story*. Musical love story about Danny Kaye & his wife Sylvia Fine. After a 3/01 workshop, it opened 10/01 and played 66 perf in venues in the Washington, DC area. p: The American Century Theatre (TACT), of Virginia; m: Bob Bain; l/b: Bob McElwaine; d: Jack Marshall. Mr. McElwaine was Danny Kaye's publicist for a long time. Cast: Danny: Brian Childers. Used classic Kaye numbers like "Minnie the Moocher," "Anatol of Paris" & "Tchaikovsky," as well as two dozen new songs. TACT produced its NY debut, at the Chashama, 9/5/02–9/22/02. 13 perf. p: TACT; d/ch: Thommie Walsh. Cast: Danny: Brian Childers; Sylvia: Perry Payne

1194. *Dark Horses*. Musical revue. Upstairs at the Downstairs, 12/30/67. p/d: Rod Warren; m/l: David Finkle & Bill Weeden, Gene Bissell, Drey Shepperd, Ed Kresley, etc; sk: Kenny Solms & Gail Parent, Bob Lerner, Rod Warren, Drey Shepperd, Sidney Davis; ch: Ed Kresley; md: Edward Morris. Cast: Carol Richards, Richard Blair, Janie Sell

1195. *Dark of the Moon*. Legend with mus. John, a witch-boy (his mother was a witch & his father a buzzard) lives high up in the Smokey Mountains & consorts with witch girls. When he spies Barbara Allen in the valley he makes pact with Conjur Woman to make him human so he can marry Barbara. If she should prove untrue within a year, then he will become a witch again. They marry & produce a witch child which is burned by the midwives. At a religious festival Barbara is induced by her Christian kin to surrender herself to Marvin Hudgens in order to break the spell. Barbara dies & John goes back to the witches. 46th Street Theatre, Broadway, 3/14/45–12/15/45. 318 perf. p: Messrs Shubert; m: Walter Hendl; written by 2 very young novice playwrights Howard Richardson & William Berney; based on old English folk song "Barbara Allen;" d: Robert E. Perry; ch: Esther Junger; set/light: George Jenkins. Cast: Carol Stone, Richard Hart, Georgia Simmons, John Gifford, Gar Moore, James Lanphier, Conrad Janis, Marjorie Belle (i.e. Marge Champion). Carnegie Hall Playhouse, 2/26/58–5/10/58. d: Norman Roland; ch: Barton Mumaw. Cast: John Brachitta, Ann Hillary, Norman Roland, Conrad Bain. Mercer — Shaw Arena, 4/3/70–6/14/70. 86 perf. d/set: Kent Broadhurst. Cast: Chandler Hill, Margaret Howell (*Claudia Jennings* from 5/19/70), Rue McLanahan (*Shirley Bodtke*). Pearl, 6/7/90–6/16/90. 12 perf. d: Jay Michaels. Cast: Mark Edward Lang, Claudia Lane

1196. *Darwin's Theories*. Madison Avenue Playhouse, 10/19/60–10/20/60. 2 perf. m/l: Darwin Venneri; sk: Alan Alda; ch: Louis Johnson. Cast: Alan Alda, James Coco, Patricia Fay, Austin Colyer, Darwin Venneri

1197. *A Dash of Rosemary!* 3-actor conceptual revue of life of singer Rosemary Clooney (George Clooney's aunt). 2 actresses play Rosie, one older, one younger, and one actor plays all male roles. Equity Library, 3/5/03–3/16/03. w: Douglas Kempsen & Kathy Weese; d: Douglas Kempsen; ch: Kathy Weese; md: Jeffrey Buchsbaum. In 3/02 Jill Roberts & Nicole Fenstad played Rosie

1198. *Davy Jones' Locker*. Marionette musical. Set on deserted Bahamas island, aboard Capt. Fletcher Scorn's ship & in Davy Jones' Locker. Bil Baird, 12/24/72–3/11/73. 79 perf. m/l: Mary Rodgers; b: Arthur Birnkrant & Waldo Salt; d: Lee Theodore; md: Alvy West. Same venue, 10/15/76–1/16/77. 97 perf. d: Bill Dreyer. Done regularly since, including at Orpheum, 12/20/87–1/3/88. 28 perf

1199. *Day Dreams: The Music and Magic of Doris Day*. Musical bio. INTAR, 7/92–8/2/92. 28 perf. p: Gerald A. Goehring & Daniel E. Heffernan; orig m & l: David Levy & Darren Cohen; b: Jim Murphy; d/ch: Helen Butleroff; md/orch: Darren Cohen. Cast: Patty Carver, Christopher Scott, Michelle Opperman, Marijane Sullivan, Jeannine Moore, Danny Rutigliano, Steve Fickinger. "You've Got Something," "Girl Back Home," "In My Hands," "Girl You Always Wanted to Be," plus some Doris Day standards

1200. *A Day in the Life of Just About Everyone*. Examination of one man's life in the present era. Bijou, 3/9/71–3/14/71. 8 perf. m/l: Earl Wilson Jr.; d: Tom Panko; cos: Miles White; orch: Don Pippin. Cast: Earl Wilson Jr., June Gable, DeMarest Grey. "If I Could Live My Life Again," "View from My Window," "Fare Thee Well," "Safe," "When I Was a Child," "Goin' Home," "Out of Town," "Everybody Loves a Single Girl," "What Do I Do Now?," "Faces without Names," "Paper Tiger," "The People in the Street," "The Man I Could Have Been." Stuart Oesterman presented successful regional prod

1201. *Days of Hope*. Hampstead Theatre, London, 4/12/91. m/l: Howard Goodall; b: Renata Allen; cast recording on TER. Cast: Darryl Knock, Una Stubbs, John Turner, Nicholas Caunter. "Days of Hope," "Harvest," "Market Day," "Democracy," "Long Live Death," "Scarborough Fair," "Say, Gypsy, Say," "Song of the English Volunteer," "If Not Today," "Lorca," "Antonio," "Song of the Brigades," "In Old Madrid"

1202. *Dazy*. AMAS, 2/12/87–3/8/87. 16 perf. m: Lowell E. Mark; l/conceived by: Norman Simon; b: Allan Knee; d: Philip Rose; ch: Clarence Teeters; set: Clarke Dunham; cos: Gail Cooper-Hecht; light: Ken Billington; md: Jeffrey Roy. Cast: Leah Hocking, Peter Gunther, Peter Lind Harris. "Streets," "You Can Own the Whole World," "It Takes Time," "Better Get a Grip," "Where Did the World Go?," "In the Rainbow of My Mind," "Love Got in the Way," "Who Am I?," "Layin' in the Sand," "Some of it's Good," "Other Side of Time," "A Mother's Love Song"

1203. *Dean*. Casino, London, 8/30/77–10/1/77. 35 perf. p: Steven Bentinck; m: Robert Campbell; l/b: John Howlett; d: Robert H. Livingston; ch: Noel Tovey; md: Clive Chaplin. Cast: James Dean: Glenn Conway; Elia Kazan, etc: Murray Kash; Pier Angeli/Natalie Wood/Elizabeth Taylor: Anna Nicholas; Hedda Hopper, etc: Betty Benfield; Also with: Kenneth Caswell

1204. *Dear Anyone.* Birmingham Rep, England, 9/9/83–10/8/83; the Cambridge, London, 11/8/83–1/14/84. Prev from 10/28/83. 65 perf. m: Geoff Stephens; l: Don Black; b: Jack Rosenthal; d: David Taylor; ch: Tudor Davies; set: Ralph Koltai & Nadine Baylis; md: Chris Walker. Cast: Jane Lapotaire, Stubby Kaye, Stephanie Voss, Myra Sands. "I Don't Know the Answer," "I'll Put You Together Again," "You'd Be Amazed," "Sleeping Like a Baby Now," "Shortcomings," "What About Us?," "One-Sided Love," "Dear Anyone," "All Rocked Out," "Don't Stop Him if You've Heard It," "Why the Panic?," "Have You Heard About Pandora?," "Orange County," "My Turn"

1205. *Dear Miss Phoebe.* Set during Napoleonic Wars. Theatre Royal, Birmingham, England, 7/31/50; toured; Phoenix, London, 10/13/50–6/16/51. 283 perf. p: Emile Littler; m: Harry Parr Davies; l/b: Christopher Hassall; from J.M. Barrie's *Quality Street;* d: Charles Hickman; ch: Freddie Carpenter; set: Doris Zinkeisen; md: Philip Martell. Cast: Carol Raye, Gretchen Franklin, Peter Graves, Olga Lindo, Jean Telfer, Noel Dyson. "Whisper While You Waltz," "(I Leave My Heart in an) English Garden," "Living a Dream," "Spring Will Sing a Song for You," "All's Well Tonight," "Livvy's 'ad One of her Turns," "After the Ball," "Marry and Carry Me Home"

1206. *Dear Oscar.* Play with mus (although billed as a musical). Set in London, 1883 & 1894. Playhouse, Broadway, 11/16/72–11/19/72. 14 prev from 11/3/72. 5 perf. p: Mary W. John; m: Addy O. Fieger; l/b: Caryl Gabrielle Young; set: William Pitkin; cos: Mary McKinley; light: David F. Segal; ms: Hal Hastings; md: Arnold Gross. Cast: Oscar Wilde: Richard Kneeland; Lord Alfred: Russ Thacker; Also with: Jane Hoffman, Nancy Cushman, Jack Bittner, Gary Krawford, Tommy Breslin, Len Gochman, Garnett Smith, Edward Penn. "We Like Things the Way They Are," "Tite Street," "Oscar Wilde Has Said It," "Wot's 'is Name," "Poor Bosie," "Perfect Understanding," "Swan and Edgar's," "If I Could," "If I 'ad 'alf," "We Dare You," "We'll Have a Party," "We're Only Lovers," "For Woman," "When Did You Leave Me?," "Good, Good Times," "There, Where the Young Men Go"

1207. *Dear Piaf.* Musical revue of Edith Piaf songs, in English. Mama Gail's, 12/19/75–2/14/76. 74 perf. p: Ira Rubin; adapted m: Ken Guilmartin; translated/adapted l: Lucia Victor; d: Dorothy Chernuck. Cast: Irene Datcher, Linda Fields, Michael Calkins, Lou Rodgers, Michael Tartel, Norman Carey (pianist)

1208. *Dearest Enemy.* Set in NYC, 1776. Knickerbocker, Broadway, 9/18/25–5/22/26. 286 perf. m: Richard Rodgers; l: Lorenz Hart; b: Herbert Fields; d: John Murray Anderson. Cast: Charles Purcell, Detmar Poppen, Helen Ford. "Heigh-Ho Lackaday," "War is War," "I Beg Your Pardon," "Cheerio," "Full Blown Roses," "The Hermits," "Here in My Arms," "Gavotte," "I'd Like to Hide It," "Where the Hudson River Flows," "Bye and Bye," "(You Must Be) Old Enough to Love," "Sweet Peter,"

"Here's a Kiss." Mainstage. 9/7/99–9/18/99. 16 perf. Part of *Musicals Tonight!* series. p: Mel Miller; d: Thomas Mills; md: Mark W. Hartman. Cast: Stephen Carter-Hicks, Joe Cassidy, Rita Harvey, Nanne Puritz, Celia Tackaberry, Daniel Bogart, Leslie Kritzer

1209. *The Death of Von Richthofen as Witnessed from Earth.* Play with songs. Set in 1918, during WWI. Estelle R. Newman, 7/29/82–9/5/82. 9 prev. 45 perf. p: Joseph Papp & NY Shakespeare Festival; m/l/b/d: Des McAnuff; ch: Jennifer Muller; set: Douglas W. Schmidt; cos: Patricia McGourty; light: Richard Nelson; sound: Bill Dreisbach; md: Michael S. Roth; orch: Michael Starobin. Cast: John Vickery, Bob Gunton, Peggy Harmon, Brent Barrett, Robert Westenberg, Mark Linn-Baker, Davis Gaines, Tad Ingram. "All I Wanted was a Cup of Tea," "Our Red Knight," "Good Luck," "Speed," "Sweet Eternity', "Take What You Can," "If I Have the Will," "I've Got a Girl," "England — the U.K.," "Save the Last Dance," "Here We Are," "Congratulations," "Stand up for the Fatherland," "Sitting in the Garden," "It's All Right, God," "Four White Horses," "1918," "Dear Icarus," "Sarah," "I Don't Ask About Tomorrow," "April Twenty-One," "The Skies Have Gone Dry"

1210. *Debbie Does Dallas.* Off-color satirical play with mus. Small-town girl wants to be Dallas Cowboys cheerleader. Jane Street, 10/29/02–2/15/03. 22 prev from 10/8/02. 126 perf. songs: Erica Schmidt, Andrew Sherman, Tom Kitt, Jonathan Callicut; conceived by: Susan L. Schwartz; adapted/d: Erica Schmidt; ch: Jennifer Cody; based on infamous adult movie of same name; ms: Tom Kitt; cast recording on Sh-K-Boom (released 11/02). Cast: Sherie Rene Scott, Caitlin Miller, Mary Catherine Garrison, Tricia Paoluccio, Jama Williamson, Del Pentecost, Paul Fitzgerald, Jon Patrick Walker. Began as part of 2001 NY International Fringe Festival

1211. *The Decameron.* East 74th Street Theatre, 4/12/61–5/14/61. 39 perf. m/l: Edward Earle & Yvonne Tarr; from Boccaccio's stories. Cast: Jan Miner, Bob Roman. "Deceive Me," "I Know, I Know," "Come Sweet Love." A 1973 musical, *Decameron '73* (no connection), ran in England. m/l: Joe Griffiths; created by: Peter Coe

1212. *The Decline and Fall of the Entire World as Seen Through the Eyes of Cole Porter Revisited.* Revue of Cole Porter songs from 1929 to 1945. Generally known as *Cole Porter Revisited.* Square East, 3/30/65–11/25/65. 273 perf. p: Ben Bagley; light: Jules Fisher. Cast: Carmen Alvarez, Harold Lang, Kaye Ballard, Bill Hickey, Elmarie Wendel. London, 1966. A 2nd edition, *New Cole Porter Revue,* ran at Square East, 12/22/65–2/27/66. 76 perf. ch: Buddy Schwab. Cast: Dody Goodman, Bobby Short, Danny Meehan, Carol Arthur, Jane Manning, Virginia Vestoff

1213. *The Decline of the (Middle) West.* Set around Crystal Palace Nightclub, St. Louis, in 1950s & early 1960s. The Supper Club, 5/3/95–5/13/95. 12 perf. p: Jujamcyn Theatres; l: Fran Landesman; b: Arnold Weinstein; d: Susan H. Schulman; md: Michael Rafter. Cast:

Robert Michael Baker, Anita Gillette, Paul Harman, Betsy Joslyn, Michele Pawk

Delilah see # 729, Main Book

1214. *Delphi or Bust.* Musical spoof of Greek mythology. Theatre Row, 12/3/98–12/20/98. 16 perf. p: AMAS; m: Gerald Jay Markoe; l/b: Michael Colby; d/ch: Christopher Scott; md: Steven Silverstein. Cast: Colleen Hawks, Ken Prymus, Tia Riebling, Jill Geddes. "We Greeks Have a Myth for it All," "Oracle at Delphi," "To Help You Through the Night," "Believe Her," "Give Me a Chance," "This Has Got to Stop," "Fate Can Be Funny"

1215. *Dementos.* Theatre Guinevere, 10/13/83–11/12/83. 42 perf. p: The Production Company; d: Theodore Pappas. Cast: Joanne Beretta, Pi Douglass, Jane Galloway, Annie Golden, Patrick Jude, Jimmy Justice, Roger Lawson, Charlaine Woodard. "Crazy Crazy," "Hotel del Rio," "I Saw God," "Hustlers, Hookers, Whores," "It's a Job," "Lowlife," "Dreams," "I'd Like to Spray the World," "High Class Bums," "Just Like You," "Never Had a Home," "Let Me Out," "New York is a Party," "God Save the City"

1216. *Demi-Dozen.* Nightclub revue, 1958. p: Julius Monk; m/l: Cy Coleman, Carolyn Leigh, Portia Nelson. Cast: Jane Connell, Gordon Connell. "Sunday in New York," "You Fascinate Me So"

1217. *The Demon Barber.* Musical version of Sweeney Todd story. Lyric, Hammersmith, London, 12/10/59–1/9/60. 39 perf. p: J. Baxter Somerville, John Roberts, Bernard Delfont; m: Brian Burke; l/b: Donald Cotton; d: Colin Graham; set: Disley Jones; md: Anthony Bowles. Cast: Todd: Roy Godfrey; Mrs. Lovett: Barbara Howett; Ragg: Leighton Camden; Johanna Oakley: Maureen Hartley; Fogg: Barry Humphries; Also with: Ian Paterson, Trevor Griffiths, James Maxwell, Richard Curnock, Joan Kennedy

1218. *Desire Under the Elms.* American folk opera. City Center, 1/11/89–1/15/89. 3 perf. p: NY Opera Repertory Theatre; m: Edward Thomas; libretto: Joe Masteroff; based on Eugene O'Neill's play; d: David Gately; set: Michael Anania; conductor: Leigh Gibbs Gore. Cast: Nicholas Solomon, Judy Kaye, James Schwisow

1219. *Dessa Rose.* Set in the south in 19th century. About a runaway slave and the woman who helps her escape. Mitzi E. Newhouse, 3/21/05. Prev from 2/17/05. m: Stephen Flaherty; l: Lynn Ahrens; based on novel *Dessa Rose;* d/ch: Graciela Daniele; set: Loy Arcenas; light: Jules Fisher & Peggy Eisenhauer; md: David Holcenberg; orch: Bill Brohn & Christopher Jahnke. Cast: La Chanze, Michael Hayden, Rachel York, Rebecca Eichenberger, Tina Fabrique, Kecia Lewis, Norm Lewis, James Stovall, William Parry, Eric Jordan Young, David Hess. Originally had a reading in 6/02 with La Chanze and Donna Murphy; a workshop at Lincoln Center Theatre, summer 2003

1220. *The Devil's Music: The Life and Blues of Bessie Smith.* Play with mus. Theatre 3, 1/26/01–3/3/01. 6 prev. 28 perf. p: Melting Pot Theatre Co.; w: Angelo Parra; d: Joe Brancato. Cast: Miche Braden

1221. *Diamond Lil*. American Conservatory Theatre, San Francisco, 1/27/88. w: Mae West; adapted: Paul Blake & Dennis Powers; d: Paul Blake; set: Douglas W. Schmidt; md: Harper McKay. Cast: Gretchen Wyler, Peter Donat, Gina Ferrall, Harper McKay, Drew Eshelman

1222. *Diamond Studs: The Life of Jesse James*. Saloon musical based on career of Jesse James & other Western characters. Westside, 1/14/75–8/3/75. 232 perf. p: Chelsea Theatre Center of Brooklyn; orig m/l: Bland Simpson & Jim Wann; b: Jim Wann; d: John L. Haber; ch: Patricia Birch; design adviser: Larry King; mus consultant: Mel Marvin. Cast: Jim Wann, Bland Simpson, John Foley, Joyce Cohen, Mike Sheehan, Frances Tamburro, Bill Hicks, Scott Bradley, Tommy Thompson, Jim Watson, Jan Davidson, Mike Craver, Rick Simpson, Madelyn Smoak. "Jesse James Robbed This Train," "These Southern States that I Love," "The Year of Jubilo," "Unreconstructed Rebel," "Mama Fantastic," "Saloon Piano," "I Don't Need a Man to Know I'm Good," "Northfield, Minnesota," "King Cole," "New Prisoner's Song," "K.C. Line," "Cakewalk into Kansas City," "When I Was a Cowboy," "Pancho Villa," "Put it Where the Moon Don't Shine," "Sleepy Time Down South," "Bright Morning Star," "When I Get the Call"

1223. *Diamonds*. Musical revue. Celebration of baseball. From works of more than 40 authors & songwriters. Circle in the Square Downtown, 12/16/84–3/31/85. Prev from 11/23/84. 122 perf. b: John Weidman, Budd Abbott & Lou Costello, Sean Kelly, Arthur Masella, John Lahr, etc; d: Harold Prince; ch: Theodore Pappas; set: Tony Straiges; cos: Judith Dolan; light: Ken Billington; sound: Tom Morse; md: Paul Gemignani. Cast: Loni Ackerman, Susan Bigelow, Jackee Harry, Scott Holmes, Dick Latessa, Chip Zien. Understudy: Zelda Pulliam. "Winter in New York" (m: John Kander; l: Fred Ebb), "In the Cards," "Favorite Sons," "Song for a Pinch Hitter," "Vendors" (m: Cy Coleman; l: Betty Comden & Adolph Green), "What You'd Call a Dream," "He Threw Out the Ball," "Hundreds of Hats" (m: Jonathan Sheffer; l: Howard Ashman), "1919" (by Jim Wann), "Let's Play Ball" (by Gerard Alessandrini), "The Boys of Summer," "Song for a Hunter College Graduate" (m: Jonathan Sheffer; l: Howard Ashman), "Stay in Your Own Back Yard," "Diamonds Are Forever" (m: John Kander; l: Fred Ebb)

1224. *Dick Deterred*. A Watergate musical parody of Richard III. Bush, London, 2/25/74. Prev from 2/12/74; ICA Terrace Theatre, 3/4/74–4/27/74. Did not go to West End. m/md: Graham Field; l/b: David Edgar; d: Michael Wearing; ch: Sue Lefton. Cast: Gregory Floy, Deborah Grant. In NY it ran at West Bank Cafe, 9/24/83–11/5/83. 8 prev. 19 perf. p: Lily Turner; d: George Wolf Reily; md: William Schimmel. Cast: Steve Pudenz. "Welcome Washington," "Gonna Win," "Don't Let Them Take Checkers Away," "You Are Bugging Me," "Expletive Deleted," "It's the End"

1225. *The Difficult Woman*. Set in Buenos Aires at turn of 19th century. Barbizon-Plaza, 4/25/62–4/27/62. 3 perf. m/l: Richard Freitas,

Morty Neff, George Mysels; from play by Conrado Nale Roxlo. Cast: Joyce Orlando. "Siesta," "The Hangman's Plea," "Milonga," "Dream Ballet," "I Won't Take No for an Answer," "Throw the House Out the Window"

1226. *Digging for Apples*. Musical revue. Washington Square, 9/27/62. 28 perf. w/d: James E. Butler & Robert Bowers. Cast: Bob Cotton & Gretchen Vanaken (both also ch)

1227. *Dime a Dozen*. Musical revue. Plaza 9, 10/18/62–12/21/63. 728 perf. p/conceived by: Julius Monk; musical numbers by: William Roy, Tom Whedon, Bruce Williamson, Bud McCreery, Bart Howard, Sam Pottle, Jay Foote, Allison Roulston, William F. Brown, etc; d/ch: Frank Wagner; cos: Donald Brooks. Cast: Ceil Cabot, Gerry Matthews, Jack Fletcher, Mary Louise Wilson, Rex Robbins, Susan Browning. "Dime a Dozen," "Someone Like You," "Battle Hymn of the Rialto," "Slow Down Moses," "Johnny Come Lately," "Thor," "Le Spot Hot"

1228. *Dinah! Queen of the Blues*. Set in famous jazz club Birdland, 1963. Westside Arts Center/Cheryl Crawford Theatre, 12/27/83–1/15/84. 24 perf. co-p/d: Woodie King Jr.; w: Sasha Dalton & Ernest McCarthy; cos: Judy Dearing. Cast: Sasha Dalton. "I Wanna Be Loved," "Dinah Washington," "Blow Soft Winds," "Dream," "Lover Come Back to Me," "Salty Papa Blues," "Evil Gal Blues," "I Don't Hurt Anymore," "The Blues Ain't Nothin'," "This Can't Be Love," "Blow Top Blues # 1," "Mixed Emotions," "I Could Write a Book," "Teach Me Tonight," "This Bitter Earth," "Love for Sale," "Am I Asking Too Much," "Make Someone Happy," "What a Diff'rence a Day Makes," "Unforgettable"

1229. *Dinah Was*. Bio of blues singer Dinah Washington. WPA, 3/12/98–5/3/98. 12 prev. 42 perf. w: Oliver Goldstick; d: David Petrarca; ch: George Faison; cos: Paul Tazewell; ms/orch: Jason Robert Browne. Cast: Dinah: Yvette Freeman; Also with: Adriane Lenox. "Bad Luck," "Showtime," "Baby, You Got What it Takes," "Slick Chick on the Mellow Side," "What a Diff'rence a Day Makes," "I Wanna Be Loved," "Long John Blues," "I Won't Cry Anymore," "Come Rain or Come Shine," "This Bitter Earth," "Sometimes I'm Happy," "A Rockin' Good Way," "I Don't Hurt Anymore." Gramercy, 5/28/98–1/3/99. 242 perf. Lillias White replaced Yvette Freeman

1230. *Dirty Rotten Scoundrels*. 2 con men on the Riviera. Old Globe, San Diego, 9/22/04–11/7/04. Prev from 9/15/04; Imperial, Broadway, 3/3/05. Prev from 1/31/05. p: West Egg Entertainment, Producers 4, David Brown, Roy Furman, Amanda Lipitz, Jay Harris, Chase Mishkin, Ruth Hendel, Dede Harris/Sharon Karmazin, Scott Prisand, Debra Black, Clear Channel Entertainment, Harvey Weinstein, by arr with MGM ON Stage; m/l: David Yazbek; b: Jeffrey Lane; based on the novel *King of the Mountain*, and upon the 1964 Marlon Brando-David Niven movie *Bedtime Story*, and, most specifically and recently, upon the 1988 movie re-make, *Dirty Rotten Scoundrels*, with Michael Caine and Steve Martin; d: Jack O'Brien; ch: Jerry Mitchell; set: David Rockwell; cos: Gregg Barnes; light: Kenneth Posner; sound: Acme

Sound Partners; md: Ted Sperling; orch: Harold Wheeler; dance mus arr: Zane Mark. Cast: John Lithgow, Norbert Leo Butz, Joanna Gleason, Gregory Jbara, Sara Gettelfinger, Sheri Rene Scott, Timothy J. Alex, Andrew Asnes, Roxane Barlow, Joe Cassidy, Julie Connors, Rachel de Benedet, Laura Marie Duncan, Sally Mae Dunn, Rick Faugno, Tom Galantich, Jason Gillman, Greg Graham, Amy Heggins, Grason Kingsberry, Rachelle Rak, Tony Yazbeck. "Overture, "Give Them What They Want," "What Was a Woman to Do?," "Great Big Stuff," "Chimp in a Suit," "Oklahoma?," "All About Ruprecht," "What Was a Woman to Do?" (reprise), "Here I Am," "Nothing is Too Wonderful to Be True," "The Miracle," "Entr'acte," "Ruffhousin' mit Shuffhausen," "Like Zis/Like Zat," "The More We Dance," "Love is My Legs, and You Are My Love, So You Are My Legs, My Love," "Love Sneaks In," "Like Zis/Like Zat" (reprise), "Above the Waist," "The Soap," "Dirty, Rotten," "Give Them What They Want" (reprise)

1231. *Disappearing Act*. Gay musical revue. 47th Street Theatre, 9/4/96–10/6/96. 10 prev. 39 perf. m/l: Mike Oster; d/ch: Mark Frawley; cos: Gregg Barnes; sound: Jim Van Bergen; md: Ron Roy. Cast: Michael McElroy, Jamie MacKenzie, Branch Woodman. "Fear and Self-Loathing," "They Say Men Who Like Their Men," "Gentrification," "Just Go Shopping," "I Had to Laugh," "A Secret," "Children Are a Blessing," "Friendly Vacation," "Let Me In," "Something's Wrong with This Picture," "Rants and Raves," "I Slept with a Zombie," "The Ride Home," "Looks Like it Might Rain," "Dance Floor," "All Tied Up on the Line," "In Here," "Dear Diary," "What Do Ya Know," "Fruits of Domestic Bliss," "Old Flame," "In Our Community," "Someone I Missed," "Ounce of Prevention," "Ordinary Day," "Trio for Three Buddies," "Faded Levi Jacket," "Disappearing Act"

1232. *Dispatches*. Rock-war musical. Cabaret Theatre, 4/19/79–6/10/79. 77 perf. p: Joseph Papp; adapted/composed/d: Elizabeth Swados; based on book by Michael Herr; light: Jennifer Tipton. Cast: Penelope Bodry, Joan Macintosh, William Parry, David Schechter, Gedde Watanabe (Timm Fujii standby). "Crazy," "Thou Shalt Not Be Afraid," "Breathing In," "There Were the Faces," "The Ground Was Always in Play," "Helicopter, Helicopter," "Stoned in Saigon," "Beautiful for Once," "Tiger Lady," "Prayers in the Delta," "Quakin' and Shakin'," "Six Fucking Shades of Green," "I See a Road," "Take the Glamor Out of War," "This War Gets Old," "Back in the World Now," "Freezing and Burning"

1233. *Diss Diss and Diss Dat*. Rap musical. Based on real life group Funke Natives. New Federal, 10/29/03–11/30/03. d: Rajendra Ramoon Maharaj; conceived by Woodie King Jr. Cast: McKenzie Frye, Jonathan "Jas" Anderson, Du Kelly, Amber Efe, Rodney Gilbert, Bryan Taronn-Jones. "Small Talk on 125th Street," "Da Boom and da Bipp," "Urban Contemporary Jeep Music," "Warning," "Praise the Songs," "Riding the Wave"

1234. *Diversions*. Revue. Downtown Theatre, 11/7/58–1/18/59. 85 perf. p: New Princess Co.; w/d: Steven Vinaver; md: Carl Davis. Cast: Aline Brown, Thom Molinaro, Nancy Dussault, Cy Young, Peter Feldman, Gubi Mann. There were some cast changes: Peg Murray, Jack Eddleman, Bill Howe, Cynthia Price, Barbara Gilbert

Divorce Me, Darling! see # 75, Main Book

1235. *The Dixie Dewdrop*. Country musical. INTAR Stage 2, 8/15/86–9/14/86. 28 perf. p/d: Thomas J. Carroll; w: R. Santinelli & Patrick Sky. Cast: Ralph P. Martin (as Uncle Dave Macon), Gilles Malkine

1236. *Do It Again!* A "Gershwin musicade;" cabaret-style collection of songs with mus by George & lyr by Ira. Promenade, 2/18/71–2/28/71. 14 perf. conceived by/d: Bert Convy. Cast: Margaret Whiting, Clifton Davis, Robin Benson, Susan Long, Marion Ramsey

1237. *Do Somethin', Addy Man: The Black Alcestis*. London-Caribbean musical. Theatre Royal, Straford East, London, 9/13/62–10/6/62. 25 perf. m/d: George Browne; l/b: Jack Russell; dev/d/set: Herbert Marshall; ch: Harold Holness. Cast: The Ira Aldridge Players (including Alaba Peters & Harold Holness)

1238. *Do You Know the Milky Way?* Play with mus. Billy Rose, Broadway, 10/16/61–10/28/61. 16 perf. p: Ninon Tallon, Paul Feigay, Dick Button, Vancouver International Festival; m/l: Alex Fry & Lyon Phelps; b: Karl Wittlinger; set: Colin Low; cos: Norman Bel Geddes & Edith Lutyens; light: Lee Watson. Cast: Hal Holbrook, George Voskovec. Revived, but without the mus, at Gramercy Arts Theatre, 3/14/63–6/2/63. 94 perf

1239. *Doctor Doctor*. Musical comedy revue. Players, 3/26/97–4/20/97. 9 prev from 3/18/97. 31 perf. p: Barter Theatre; m/l: Peter Ekstrom; add l & material: David de Boy; d: Richard Rose; md: Albert Ahronheim. Cast: James Weatherstone, Buddy Crutchfield, Jill Geddes, Nancy Johnston, Albert Ahronheim. "The Human Body," "Oh Boy, How I Love My Cigarettes," "The Consummate Picture," "I'm a Well-Known Respected Practitioner," "Tomorrow," "World of My Own," "And Yet I Lived On," "Willie," "Right Hand Song," "Please, Dr. Fletcher," "Take it off Tammy," "It's My Fat," "Nine Long Months Ago," "Hymn," "Medicine Man Blues," "Private Practice," "Nurse's Care," "I'm Sure of It," "I Loved My Father," "Jesus is My Doctor," "Bing Bang Boom!," "Eighty Thousand Orgasms," "Good Ole Days of Sex," "Do I Still Have You?," "I Hope I Never Get"

1240. *Doctor Dolittle*. Huge, lavish, complex prod. London Apollo, Hammersmith, 7/14/98–6/5/99. Prev from 6/29/98. p/d: Steven Pimlott; m/l/b: Leslie Bricusse (Lerner & Lowe originally meant to have written It); based on Hugh Lofting's stories & on Leslie Bricusse's 1967 film with Rex Harrison; ch: Aletta Collins; set/cos: Mark Thompson; light: Hugh Vanstone; characters created by Jim Henson Workshop. Cast: Dolittle: Phillip Schofield; Polynesia the Parrot, voice only: Julie Andrews; Also with: Sarah Jane Hassell, Bryan Smith. "My Friend the Doctor," "The Vegetarian," "Talk to the Animals," "Doctor Dolittle," "You're Impossible," "I've Never Seen Anything Like It," "Beautiful Thing," "When I Look into Your Eyes," "Like Animals," "After Today," "Fabulous Places," "Where Are the Words?," "I Think I Like You," "Save the Animals," "Something in Your Smile," "Voice of Protest." It then toured the UK. US tour, summer 2005. p: Pittsburgh CLO. This prod was different to the London one

1241. *Dr. Jekyll and Mr. Hyde*. Paper Mill Playhouse, NJ, 11/4/98. m: Phil Hall; l/b: David Levy & Leslie Eberhard; based on Robert Louis Stevenson's novella; d/ch: Philip Wm McKinley; set: Michael Anania; light: Kirk Bookman; md: Jim Coleman; orch: Michael Gibson. Cast: Richard White (Jekyll), Marc Kudisch (Hyde), Christopher Eid, Peter Cormican, Glory Crampton, Regina O'Malley, Bill Kocis, William Ryall, Judy McLane, Gwendolyn Jones. "Two Sides of London," "Under the Skin," "Rest Now, My Friend," "In Your Eyes," "Pushing Back the Sky," "Hot House Rose," "Stranger," "Speak My Heart," "Another Man," "Life at the Bottom of the Glass," "I Am the Night," "Love Treats Us All the Same," "Jekyll's Discovery," "Waltz Montage," "Once More," "Take What You Can Get," "A Father's Song," "Tell Me it's Not True," "Jekyll's Soliloquy," "Voices Rushing Through My Head," "Lily's Ditty"

1242. *Dr. Selavy's Magic Theatre*. About mental illness & therapy. Mercer-O'Casey, 11/23/72–3/25/73. 144 perf. The Lenox Arts Center production (in Mass., where it 1st ran that summer). p: Lyn Austin & Oliver Smith; m/l: Stanley Silverman & Tom Hendry; conceived by/d/set: Richard Foreman. Cast: Ron Faber (*Barry Primus*), Denise Delapenha, Jessica Harper. "I Live By My Wits," "Bankrupt Blues," "Future for Sale," "Life on the Inside," "The More You Get," "Money in the Bank," "Doesn't it Bug You?," "Dusky Shadows," "Poor Boy," "Dearest Man," "Where You Been Hiding Till Now," "What Are You Proposing?," "Party's Gonna End," "Let's Hear it for Daddy Moola." St. Clement's Theatre, 1/27/84–2/18/84. 3 prev. 20 perf. p: Music Theatre Group. Cast: David Patrick Kelly, Annie Golden, Jessica Harper, Kathi Moss, Dara Norman, Roy Brocksmith

1243. *Dogs*. One of 9 dogs escaped from NYC pound adopted by the Mayor. Perry Street, 8/10/83–8/14/83. 7 prev from 8/4. 9 perf. p: Provincetown Theatre Ensemble in Exile; m/l: James Stewart Bennett; d: Charles G. Horne. "Tricks," "Jail Song," "Somehow I Must Find a Way," "I Hate Dogs," "I'm the Master of the City," "Dance at the Ritz," "I Got a Plan," "Don't Take Away All My Friends"

1244. *The $ Value of Man*. Leperq Space, 5/9/75–5/18/75. 8 perf. The Byrd Hoffman Foundation production. p: Brooklyn Academy of Music; m: Michael Galasso; w/d: Christopher Knowles & Robert Wilson; ch: Andrew De Groat. Cast of 60

1245. *The Don Juan and the Non Don Juan*. Vineyard–26th Street, 12/5/91–12/29/91. m/l: Neil Radisch, James Milton, David Goldstein; based on writings by Marvin Cohen; d: Evan Yionoulis; md: Dale Rieling. Cast: Karen Mason, Polly Pen, Vicki Lewis, Joseph Adams, Monica Carr. "Intangible Tom," "Obituary," "I'll Be Gone," "Married," "You're Fired," "Love is the Way that We Live"

1246. *The Donkey Show*. A Midsummer night's disco. Shakespeare in a 1970s disco setting. El Flamingo. Opened 8/18/99 (prev from 8/10/99) for 6-week run, but kept going. p: Jordan Roth; created/d: Diane Paulus & Randy Weiner; set: Scott Pask; cos: David C. Woolard. "A Fifth of Beethoven," "Also Sprach Zarathustra," "Car Wash," "Dance with Me," "Disco Circus," "Don't Leave Me This Way," "I Love the Night Life," "Never Knew Love Like This Before," "I'm Your Boogie Man," "Knock on Wood," "Ring My Bell," "Salsation," "That's the Way of the World," "You Sexy Thing," "We Are Family"

1247. *Don't Bother Me, I Can't Cope*. A musical entertainment. Black revue about the black in white man's world. Songs & dances with some musical themes borrowed from ballads, calypso, gospel music, etc. Playhouse, Middle Broadway, 4/19/72–6/11/72. 63 perf; Edison, 6/13/72–10/26/74. 1,002 perf. An Urban Arts Corps production. p: Edward Padula, Arch Lustberg, Ford's Theatre Society, Washington, DC; m/l: Micki Grant (nominated for Tony for score); b: Micki Grant & Vinnette Carroll (nominated for Tony); conceived by/d: Vinnette Carroll [if you count the Edison as a Broadway theatre, some sources say Miss Carroll was 1st black woman to direct a Broadway musical (although, Katherine Dunham did, 30 years earlier, with *A Tropical Revue*), and she was nominated for a Tony]; ch: George Faison; set: Richard A. Miller; set super: Neil Peter Jampolis; cos: Edna Watson; cos super: Sara Brook; light: B.J. Sammler; light super: Ken Billington; md/arr: Danny Holgate. Cast: Alex Bradford, Hope Clarke, Micki Grant, Bobby Hill, Arnold Wilkerson. Singers: Alberta Bradford, Charles Campbell, Marie Thomas. Dancers: Thommie Bush, Gerald G. Francis, Ben Harney, Leona Johnson. Musicians: Drums: Danny Holgate & Herb Lovelle; Bass: John Lucien; Guitar/Flute: Rudy Stevenson. Nominated for Tony for best musical. 1st produced in workshop form OOB at Vinnette Carroll's Urban Arts Corps Theatre. Then to Washington, DC, Philadelphia & Detroit, before opening at the Playhouse. Musical numbers (including those added during the run — and the order of the songs did change throughout the course of the run): "I Gotta Keep Movin'," "Harlem Intro," "Lock up the Dog," "Harlem Street," "Lookin' Over From Your Side," "Don't Bother Me, I Can't Cope," "When I Feel Like Movin'," "Help," "Love Power," "Children's Rhymes," "Ghetto Life," "So Long, Sammy," "You Think I Got Rhythm?," "Time Brings About a Change," "So Little Time," "Thank Heaven for You," "Show Me That Special Gene," "My Love's So Good," "Men's Dance," "They Keep Coming," "My Name is Man," "All I Need," "Questions," "Love Mississippi," "It Takes a Whole Lot of Human Feeling," "Good Vibrations," "Storefront Church," "Prayer," "Sermon," "Fighting for Pharaoh," "We've Gotta Keep Movin'." Won Grammy for orig cast recording. Several tours, 3 in 1976. Tour actors included: Nell Carter, Charlaine Woodard, Leslie Dockery, Billy Dorsey, Clinton Derricks. "The Billie Holiday Song," and "Universe in Mourning" were new songs for the tours

1248. *Don't Step on My Olive Branch.* Israeli musical revue in English. Playhouse, Broadway, 11/1/76–11/14/76. 16 prev. 16 perf. p: Yael Company & Norman Kean; m/l: Ron Eliran; b: Harvey Jacobs; d/ch: Jonathan Karmon; md: David Krivoshei. Cast: Rivka Raz, Ron Eliran, Gail Benedict, Karen Di Bianco, Carla Farnsworth, David Kottke. "Moonlight," "World's Greatest Magical Act," "I Believe," "Only Love," "My Land," "We Love a Conference," "Come with Me," "Tired Heroes," "Have a Little Fun," "I Hear a Song," "I Live My Life in Color," "Young Days," "Somebody's Stepping on My Olive Branch," "It Was Worth It," "Jerusalem"

1249. *Don't Walk on the Clouds.* St. Clements Church, 11/18/71–12/11/71. 7 prev. 21 perf. m/l: John Aman; b: Marvin Gordon & Terry Miller; conceived by/d: Marvin Gordon. Cast: John Aman. "Processional," "Love it or Leave It," "Swinger Boogie," "Love and the World Will Be Yours," "Dante and Da Vinci Rag," "Make Music and Love," "What Am I Bid?," "Be My Brother," "Who Am I Now?," "Ultimate Trip," "Blood Bath," "Summer of Love," "Let's Get Our Heads Together," "Don't Walk on the Clouds"

1250. *Dorian.* Musical adaptation of Oscar Wilde's *The Picture of Dorian Gray*. Set in London, 1882–1900. Saval, 3/10/90. m/l: Michael Rubell & Nan Barcan; d: Robert Petito; ch: Irene Rubell; set: Joseph A. Varga. Cast: William Broderick, Elaine Terriss, Lorraine Serabian. "Art is Forever," "Creation," "Temptation," "Men on My Mind," "American Girls," "You Are the Magic," "I Love Him," "You Must Remember," "Night at the Theatre," "My Perfection," "Lady Can't Act," "Till I Met You," "A Perfect Tragedy," "Picture of Dorian Gray," "Dissipation," "Marriage," "For Old Time's Sake," "Jim's Song," "Prince Charming," "We Knew How to Live," "Chatter," "Confession"

1251. *Dorian.* Musical adaptation of Oscar Wilde's *The Picture of Dorian Gray*. Goodspeed, 4/11/00–6/4/00. m/l: Richard Gleaves; d: Gabriel Barre; set: James M. Youmans; cos: Pamela Scofield; md: Stephen Oremus. Cast: Sutton Foster, Tom Stuart, Nancy Anderson

1252. *Dorian Gray.* Judith Anderson, 9/17/96–10/6/96. 1 prev. 16 perf. m: Gary David Levinson; l/b: Allan Rieser; based on Oscar Wilde's novella *The Picture of Dorian Gray*; d: Don Price. Cast: Brian Duguay, Tom Rocco, Gerrianne Raphael, Mary Setrakian. "Beauty Past All Dreaming," "Discover the Man You Are," "I Would Give My Soul for That," "Counterfeit Love," "Marriage," "Love that Lives Forever," "Don't Throw Your Love Away," "What Will Happen to Me Now?," "Dorian Gray," "Take Care of Your Heart," "What Dark November Thoughts"/"Let Me Believe in You," "The Prayer," "Blue Gate Fields Hotel," "As Long as There Are Men,"

"Stay," "We Are But Patters of Paint," "I'll Call My Soul My Own"

1253. *Double Dublin.* Irish revue. Little Theatre, Broadway, 12/26/63–12/28/63. Prev from 12/24/63. 4 perf. p: Josephine Forrestal Prods; material by cast; song editor: David Nillo; set/light: Helen Pond & Herbert Senn; md: Baldwin Bergersen; prod super: Gus Schirmer Jr. Cast: Noel Sheridan, John Molloy, Deirdre O'Callaghan, Patricia Brogan. Numbers sung by Deirdre O'Callaghan: "Gaelic Air," "The Green Bushes," "Dublin Saunter" (written by Leo Maguire), "I Was Strolling"

1254. *Double Entry.* 2 one-act musicals by Jay Thompson. Martinique Theatre, 2/20/61–4/9/61. 56 perf. d: Bill Penn; Brooks Morton & Rita Segree at pianos. *The Bible Salesman* starred Rosetta Le Noire, Garrett Morris, Ted Lambrinos; set in Texas. "Same Old Summer," "Miss Lucy Long," "The Question Is," "Sure Gets Lonesome," "I Wish You Could." *The Oldest Trick in the World* starred Rosetta Le Noire, Jane Connell, Doreese DuQuan; set on 8th Avenue, NYC. "Sweep," "Kinda Sorta Doin' Nothing," "The Oldest Trick in the World," "White Slavery Fandango," "All the Young Men"

1255. *Double Feature.* Romantic problems of 2 couples. Set in NYC. Long Wharf, New Haven, 1979. w: Jeffrey Moss; d: Mike Nichols; ch: Tommy Tune; cos: Michel Stuart. Theatre at St. Peter's Church 10/8/81–10/13/81. 7 perf. d: Sheldon Larry; ch: Adam Grammis; cos: Patrizia von Brandenstein; light: Marilyn Rennagel; md: Michael Lee Stockler; orch: Michael Starobin. Cast: Pamela Blair, Carole Shelley, Stephen Vinovich, Don Scardino, Michael Kubala, Tina Paul. "Just as It Should Be," "Double Feature," "When I Met Her," "What if I Asked You for a Dance?," "How's it Gonna End?," "Just One Step at a Time" [this dance number featured the feet of Niki Harris & Albert Stephenson (see *A Day in Hollywood/A Night in the Ukraine*—in main part of this book)], "Our Last Dance Together," "A Little Bit of This"

1256. *Double Identity.* Set in Russia, in 1913. Folksbiene, 10/28/95–1/14/96. m: Ben Schaechter; l/b: Miriam Hoffman; based on Sholem Aleichem's *Hard to Be a Jew* (see this appendix); d: Bryna Wasserman. Cast: Steve Sterner

1257. *Double Trouble.* Yiddish. About twin sisters, one a prostitute ex-con. Clinton, 1949. m: S. Solomon; l/b: H. Hoffenberg; add m/l: Lou Weissman. Cast: Paul Burstein, Lillian Lux

1258. *Down! Down! Down! 30 Seconds to Hell.* Comedy with mus based on 1970s disaster films. Grove Street Playhouse, 11/3/99–11/21/99. 3 prev. 12 perf. m/set: Clark Gesner; w: Garet Scott; d/sound: Kevin Thomsen; ch: Kevin Pettito

1259. *Down in the Valley.* Folk opera. Univ. of Indiana, 1948. m/l: Kurt Weill & Arnold Sundgaard. Cast: Marion Bell, James Welch. "The Lonesome Dove"

1260. *Downriver.* Musical Theatre Works, 1/9/85–1/27/85. 2 prev. 12 perf. p/d: Michael

Maurer; m/l: John Braden; b: Jeff Tambornino; based on *The Adventures of Huckleberry Finn*, by Mark Twain; ch: Mary Jane Houdina; set: Karl Eigsti; light: Neil Peter Jampolis. Cast: Huck: John Scherer; Tom: Todd Heughens; Also with: Ted Forlow, Helon Blount. "Bound Away," "'til Our Good Luck Comes Along," "It's a Hard Life," "You've Brightened up My Day," "River Rats," "Just Like Love," "Downriver," "Every Other Saturday Night," "Shine Down, Lord"

1261. *Dracula.* Theatre Royal, Stratford East, London, 11/26/74–2/1/75. 77 perf. m: Ian Armit; l/b/d: Ken Hill. Cast: Sylveste McCoy, Valerie Walsh, Geoffrey Freshwater, Marianne Price, Melody Kaye, Larry Dann

1262. *Dragons.* Fractured fairy tale with a wicked contemporary spin, a musical parable about democracy. Luna Stage, Montclair, NJ, 11/15/03–12/21/03. Prev from 11/13/03. m/l/b: Sheldon Harnick; d: James Glossman; ch: Susan Ancheta; set: Fred Kinney; cos: Bettina Bierly; light: Richard Currie; md: Stephen Randoy. Cast: Susan Ancheta, Anita Rundles, Paul Murphy, Garth Kravits, Jake Speck, Catherine Rogers, Seleena Harkness, Kirk Mouser, Kenneth Boys, Michael Aquino, Nellie Beavers, Cecily Ellis, Paul Whelihan. This was its professional Equity premiere, although it had been playing at university settings since the late 1980s (beginning with Northwestern), and a revised version had played at the Univ of Michigan

1263. *Drake's Dream.* Funtastic musical adventure for all the family. Connaught, Worthing, England, 10/26/77–11/10/77. Shaftesbury, London, 12/7/77. m/l: Lynne & Richard Riley; b: Simon Brett; d: Nicholas Young; md: Peter Martin. Cast: Paul Jones (Sir Francis Drake), David Burt, Nicholas Denney. "At the Court of Queen Elizabeth," "I've Always Had a Dream," "Let's Get Going," "Take a Little Time," "When the Winds Command Us Away," "She Plays a Dangerous Game," "Between Today and Tomorrow," "Waiting isn't Easy," "Gold," "Nova Albion," "God of the Craters," "Spice of Life," "Sailing Around." Moved to the Westminster, London, in revised version by Ken Hill (also d), 2/1/78–3/4/78. Total West End run of 82 perf

1264. *Drat!* Set in Plasterville, Iowa & in NYC. McAlpin Rooftop, 10/18/72. 8 prev. 1 perf. m/md: Steven Metcalf; l/b/conceived by/d: Fred Bluth; mus arr: Donald Pippin. Cast: Bonnie Franklin, Jane Connell, Gary Gage, Walter Bobbie, Carol Swarbrick. "Little Fairies," "Early Bird Eddy," "Walkin' in the Rain," "Friday, Friday," "My Geranium," "Kick it Around," "You and I," "Where is the Man for Me?," "Frightened of the Dark," "Desperation Quintet," "Drat!," "Has Anyone Here Seen My Daddy?," "Lean on Me," "Sally," "Bye and Bye," "The Chase"

1265. *Dream a Little Dream.* Story of the Mamas and the Papas. Village Theatre (formerly the Village Gate), 4/23/03–8/31/03. 21 prev from 4/2/03. 147 perf. Called *Dream a Little Dream*, then *California Dreamin'*, then back to orig title. p: Eric Nederlander; w: Denny "Papa" Doherty & Paul Ledoux; d:

Randal Myler; set: Walt Spangler; cos: David C. Woolard; light: Peter Kaczorowski. Originally ran in Toronto in 6/01

1266. *Dream True: My Life with Vernon Dexter*. Set in Wyoming over 4 decades beginning in 1945. Vineyard, 3/24/98–5/8/98. 25 prev. 22 perf. m: Ricky Ian Gordon; l/b/d: Tina Landau; orch: Jonathan Tunick. Cast: Jeff McCarthy, Judy Kuhn, Alex Bowen, Jessica Molaskey, Steven Skybell, Daniel Jenkins. "Wyoming Intro," "Kingdom of Addo," "Finding Home," "We Will Always Walk Together," "The Way West," "Best Years of Our Lives," "Ka Da Bing," "God is There," "Space," "Peter's Dream," "Dream True," "Have a Nice Day," "The Best for You," "Crick Crack," "Pride," "This is How it Goes," "Wyoming," "Hold On"

1267. *Dreamstuff*. Musical update of Aladdin tale, set in NYC. Samuel Beckett, 1/22/97–3/9/97. 28 prev. 22 perf. m/l: Sal Lombarde; b/d: John Pantozzi; ch: Pamela Sousa; md/orch: Barry Levitt. Cast: Joshua Tucker (*Evan Ferrante*), Carol Woods, Aileen Quinn (*Kathleen Riley*). "Cityscape," "It's Magic if You Believe," "I Have a Boy/I Need a Boy," "Can't You Just See Me?," "It Was Only Yesterday," "All My Life," "Mom, I'm Sorry," "Lights and Music," "I Am Killam," "Three Unique Things," "Guilt and Pain," "My Master," "Get By," "Flying," "A Job and a Drink," "Time." 1st performed in 2 acts, the prod was altered during the run to be performed without intermission

1268. *A Drifter, the Grifter & Heather McBride*. Ad agency dropout, ne'er-do-well & Hoosier maid in romantic triangle in folksy setting. 47th Street, 6/20/82–6/27/82. 11 prev. 9 perf. p: Popcorn Prods; m: Bruce Petsche; l/b: John Gallagher; d: Dick Sasso; ch: George Bunt; md: Jeremy Harris. Cast: Ronald Young, Elizabeth Austin, Diane Findlay. "Getaway," "Remember the Dream," "Fat Luigi," "Holding the Bag," "Just Our Way of Doing Business," "Find a Way," "Tippity Top," "Tiny International Empire," "Honesty," "I Dream," "Fly with Me," "Little Little," "Hair-Pulling Ballet," "Hey, Kiddo, You're Through," "Again"

1269. *The Drunkard: The Fallen Saved*. 13th Street Theatre, 4/13/70–5/24/70. 48 perf. p/adapted by/d: Bro Herrod; orig mus numbers/md: Barry Manilow; based on W.H.S. Smith's (straight, i.e. non-musical) melodrama (1st produced by P.T. Barnum in 1843); ch: Carveth Wells. Cast: Marie Santell, Christopher Cable, Joy Garrett, Donna Sanders, Lou Vitacco. "Something Good Will Happen Soon," "Whispering Hope," "Don't Swat Your Mother, Boys," "Good is Good," "Have Another Drink," "Curse of an Aching Heart," "Garbage Can Blues," "Julia's Song," "Do You Wanna Be Saved?." Revived (straight) on Broadway, 3/10/34. 277 perf. And again (straight) in 1937–38 in L.A., for very long run. Cherry Lane, 8/6/86–8/24/86. 21 perf. p: Light Opera of Manhattan; d: Raymond Allen; cos: Jerry Gotham; md: Todd Ellison. This time only standard (non-Barry Manilow) numbers were used

1270. *Du Barry Was a Lady*. Washroom attendant dreams he's Louis XV wooing Madame Dubarry. 46th Street Theatre, Broadway, 12/6/39–12/12/40. 408 perf. p: Buddy De Sylva; m/l: Cole Porter; b: Herbert Fields & Buddy De Sylva; d: Edgar MacGregor; ch: Robert Alton; set/cos: Raoul Pene du Bois; md: Gene Salzer; orchestral arr: Hans Spialek; add arr: Russell Bennett & Ted Royal; choral arr: Hugh Martin. Cast: Bert Lahr, Ethel Merman, Betty Grable, Benny Baker. "Where's Louie?," "Ev'ry Day a Holiday," "It Ain't Etiquette," "When Love Beckoned (in Fifty-Second Street)," "Come on In," "Dream Song," "Mesdames et Messieurs," "Gavotte," "But in the Morning, No!," "Do I Love You?," Danse Victoire, "Danse Erotique," "Du Barry Was a Lady," Danse Tzigane, "Give Him the Oo-La-La," "Well, Did You Evah?," "It Was Written in the Stars," "L'Apres Midi d'un Boeuf," "Katie Went to Haiti," "Friendship." "What Have I?" & "In the Big Money" were cut. 5th-longest running Broadway musical of 1930s. Filmed in 1943. Cast: Lucille Ball, Gene Kelly, Red Skelton. Equity Library Theatre, 5/4/72–5/21/72. 22 perf. d: Marvin Gordon. Cast: Danny De Vito, Diane Findlay. City Center, 2/15/96–2/17/96. 4 concert perf. Part of *Encores!* series. adapted by: David Ives & Walter Bobbie; d: Charles Repole; ch: Kathleen Marshall; set: John Lee Beatty; md: Rob Fisher. Cast: Faith Prince, Robert Morse, Bruce Adler, Liz Larsen, Ruth Williamson, Scott Waara, Eugene Fleming, Burke Moses, Michael McGrath, Dick Latessa, Donald Trump (as IRS agent), Danny Burstein, Ken McMullen, Beth McVey, Karen Murphy, Elizabeth Walsh, Mamie Duncan-Gibbs, Sean Grant, Colton Green, Troy Myers, Aimee Turner, Susan Pfau, Clif Thorn, Joseph Webster, Elizabeth Mills

1271. *The Duenna*. Comic operetta. Bristol Old Vic, England, 1954. m/l: Julian Slade & Dorothy Reynolds; adapted/d: Lionel Harris; from operetta by Richard Brinsley Sheridan. The Westminster, London, 7/28/54. 124 perf. set/cos: Tom Lingwood. Cast: Joyce Carey, Joan Plowright, Patricia Routledge, Elizabeth West, Gerald Cross, Victor Maddern, Jane Wenham. Brought Mr. Slade to notice of London public

1272. *Dumas and Son*. Dorothy Chandler Pavilion, L.A., 1967. m/l: Robert Wright & George Forrest (adapted from music of Camille Saint-Saens); b: Jerome Chodorov; d: Joseph Anthony. Cast: Inia Te Wiata (as the novelist), Constance Towers, Frank Porretta, Edward Everett Horton, Hermione Gingold, Gregory Morton

1273. *Durante*. Tour. Opened at Blum Appel, St. Lawrence Centre, Toronto, 8/12/89. Closed 11/26/89, Shubert, L.A. Its San Francisco run was interrupted & canceled by earthquake. Did not make Broadway. m/l: various writers; b: Frank Peppiatt & John Aylesworth; add dial: Caroline Peppiatt; based on life & times of comedian Jimmy Durante; d: Ernest O. Flatt; ch: Toni Kaye; md: Grant Sturiale; dance & vocal arr: David Krane & Grant Sturiale; special consultant: Mrs. Maggie Durante. Cast: Jimmy: Lonny Price; Also with: Evan Pappas, Ralph Small, B. Alan Geddes, Joel Blum, Jane Johanson, David Gibb, Ira Denmark, Bob Riddell, Michel La Fleche, Melodee Finlay, Brian Hill, Terri Turai, Risa Waldman. "Grandpa's Spells," "People Would Laugh," "Who Will Be with You When I'm Far Away," "What a Day!," "Put Your Arms Around Me, Honey," "I'll Do the Strutaway," "Courtship Ballet," "Hello, Hello, Hello," "Jimmy, the Well-Dressed Man," "Whispering," "Challenge," "I Know Darn Well I Can Do without Broadway," "Llamas in the Bahamas," "Don't Lose Your Sense of Humor," "You Gotta Start off Each Day with a Song," "I Love Ya, Love Ya, Love Ya," "Bill Bailey," "Goodnight, Goodnight," "Toot Toot Tootsie," "Did You Ever Get the Feeling?," "What Do I Have to Say?," "One Room Home," "Partners," "Inka Dinka Doo," "We're the Men," "A Razz a Ma Tazz," "September Song"

1274. *Dynamite Tonight*. Comic opera. Group of people caught in bunker during a war. York Theatre, NY, 3/15/64. 1 perf. p: Actors Studio; m: William Bolcom; b: Arnold Weinstein; d: Paul Sills & Arnold Weinstein; art curtain design: Andy Warhol, etc. Cast: Gene Wilder, George Gaynes, Lou Gilbert, Barbara Harris. The Martinique, 3/15/67–3/26/67. 15 perf. p: Paul Libin; light: F. Mitchell Dana. Cast: George Gaynes, Lou Gilbert, Allyn Ann McLerie, Gene Troobnick, Alvin Epstein

1275. *Earnestly Yours*. Rainbow, Reading, England, 11/30/60. w: Michael Wild. Cast: Jean Logue, Ken Paul. "Fancy Meeting You," "Going to Tea with Algy," "Earnestly Yours," "A Handbag," "Cousin Earnest," "Fairer than a Rose," "One Name," "Such Friends," "When Love Has Gone," "Let's Kiss and Make Up," "Where's That Baby?"

1276. *Earthlight*. Play with mus. Garrick, 1/17/71–3/21/71. 56 perf. mus w/performed by Pure Love & Pleasure (this group was replaced by Shaker); created by: Allan Mann & The Earthlight Ensemble; d: Allan Mann

1277. *Eastward Ho!* Mermaid, London, 10/17/62. 55 perf. m/l: George Chapman & John Marton; based on Ben Jonson's play. Revised & revived, 7/7/81–8/15/81. 45 perf. at the Mermaid. adapted by: Robert Chetwyn, Howard Schuman, Nick Bicat; new m: Nick Bicat; new l: Howard Schuman (new l); d: Robert Chetwyn; ch: Charles Augins; md: Tony Britten. Cast: Richard O'Brien

1278. *Eating Raoul*. Sex, murder & cannibalism satirized. Union Square, 5/13/92–5/24/92. 24 prev from 4/21/92. 14 perf. p: Max Weitzenhoffer, Stewart F. Lane, Joan Cullman, Richard Norton; m: Jed Feuer; l: Boyd Graham; b: Paul Bartel (based on his screenplay with Richard Blackburn); d: Toni Kotite; ch: Lynn Taylor-Corbett; set: Loren Sherman; cos: Franne Lee; light: Peggy Eisenhauer; sound: Peter Fitzgerald; md: Albert Ahronheim; orch: Joseph Gianono. Cast: Raoul: Adrian Zmed; Also with: Courtenay Collins, Eddie Korbich, Cindy Benson, Susan Wood, Lovette George, David Masenheimer. "Meet the Blands," "A Small Restaurant," "La La Land," "Swing, Swing, Swing," "Happy Birthday, Harry," "You

Gotta Take Pains," "The Thought Occurs," "Sexperts," "Empty Bed," "Basketball," "Tool for You," "Think About Tomorrow," "Hot Monkey Love," "Momma Said," "Lovers in Love," "Mary," "Eating Raoul," "Mucho Macho Trio," "One Last Bop"

1279. *Ed Linderman's Broadway Jukebox.* Musical revue of great songs that were commercial failures. John Houseman, 7/19/90–9/2/90. 15 prev from 7/6/90. 53 perf. p: Eric Krebs; conceived by/super: Ed Linderman; d/ch: Bill Guske; set: James Morgan. Cast: Robert Michael Baker, Beth Leavel, Susan Flynn, Gerry McIntyre, Amelia Prentice, Sal Viviano

1280. *Eleanor & Hick.* Set in Albany, Hyde Park & Washington, 1932–62. John Houseman, 6/26/97–6/29/97. 4 perf. p: David Kersten, Eric Krebs, Aboveground Theatre; m/l/b/md: Tom Wilson Weinberg; d: Deborah Block. Cast: Eleanor & Franklin Roosevelt: Todd Waddington; Also with: Elena Bennett, John Boone. "Brace up the Nation," "One of the Boys/Interview," "A Tent to Sleep In," "Lovely Little File," "New National Anthem," "My Way with Women," "I'd Rather Be with You," "Love Sub Rosa," "Secret World," "Sunrise at Hyde Park," "Only Four to Go"

1281. *Elegies—A Song Cycle.* Revue of William Finn's songs. Formerly called *Looking* Up. Mitzi E. Newhouse, 3/24/03–3/30/03. Prev from 3/2/03. 9 perf (Sun & Mon only; limited run). d: Graciela Daniele; md: Vadim Feichtner; cast recording on Fynsworth Alley. Cast: Christian Borle, Betty Buckley, Carolee Carmello, Michael Rupert, Keith Byron Kirk (Norm Lewis had been rumored for role). "Looking Up Quintet," "Mister Choi & Madame G," "Mark's All-Male Thanksgiving," "Only One," "Joe Papp," "Peggy Hewitt & Mysty Del Giorno," "Passover," "Infinite Joy," "Ballad of Jack Eric Williams (and Other 3-Named Composers)," "My Dogs," "14 Dwight Ave., Natick, Massachusetts," "Then the Earth Stopped Turning," "Goodbye," "Boom Boom," "Looking Up." A hit. Same venue, 4/14/03–4/19/03. 7 perf. Arts Theatre, London, 11/7/04 & 11/14/04 (2 concert perfs). UK premiere. d: Jamie Lloyd. Cast: Deven May, John Barrowman

1282. *The Elephant Piece.* Play Ground, 2/7/91–2/24/91. 12 perf. m/l/b: Darryl Curry; d: Al D'Andrea. Cast: Margit Ahlin, Angela Bullock, Lee Winston. "Akatu Akate," "You'll See," "Baby," "Gimme," "I'm Smellin' Just Like a Rose," "Whaddya Want?"

1283. *Eli's Comin'.* Vineyard, 4/11/01–7/14/01. 26 prev. 70 perf. m/l: Laura Nyro; created by Bruce Buschel & Diane Paulus; d: Diane Paulus; set: G.W. Mercier; cos: Linda Cho; md: Joe Rubenstein. Cast: Judy Kuhn, Mandy Gonzalez, Anika Noni Rose, Wilson Jermaine Heredia, Ronnell Bey. "Stoned Soul Picnic," "New York Tendaberry," "Captain Saint Lucifer," "Luckie," "Buy and Sell," "Money," "Eli's Comin'," "The Wind," "Blowin' Away," "Sweet Blindness," "The Confession," "Captain for Dark Mornings," "I Am the Blues," "Poverty Train," "Been on a Train," "Stoney End," "Emmie," "Mother's Spiritual," "Brown Earth," "And When I Die"

1284. *Elizabeth and Essex.* South Street, 1/31/80–3/9/80. 24 perf. p: Encompass Theatre; m: Doug Katsaros; l: Richard Engquist; b: Michael Stewart & Mark Bramble; based on Maxwell Anderson's play *Elizabeth the Queen;* d: Nancy Rhodes; ch: Sharon Halley. Cast: Estelle Parsons, Richard White, Florence Lacey. "Fa La," "As You Are," "Cheers," "I'll Be Different," "Gloriana," "Gossip," "First to Know," "Ireland," "Love Knots," "Not Now," "She's a Woman," "The Lady Lies," "All I Remember is You." Chancel of Heavenly Rest, 5/23/84–6/2/84. 16 perf. p: York Theatre Co.; d: Sondra Lee; ch: Onna White; set: James Morgan; cos: Willa Kim; light: Mary Jo Dondlinger; md: Doug Katsaros. Cast: Evelyn Lear, Dennis Parlato, George Dvorsky, Willy Falk, Jan Pessano, Lisa Vroman.

1285. *Elvis.* Astoria, London, 12/5/77. m/l: various writers; b: Jack Good & Ray Cooney. Cast: Timothy Whitnall, James Proby (i.e. P.J. Proby), Shakin' Stevens. "Tupelo Mississippi Flash," "Yesterday," "World without Love," "Tiger Man," "I Wanna Hold Your Hand," "All Around the World," "Six-Five Special," and several Elvis songs

1286. *Elvis: A Rockin' Remembrance.* Musical bio. Beacon, 6/6/89–6/30/89. 31 perf. w: Robert Rabinowitz; d/ch: Patricia Birch; set: Douglas W. Schmidt; cos: Jeanne Button; light: Jules Fisher & Peggy Eisenhauer; sound: Otts Munderloh. Cast: Terry Mike Jeffrey (also md), Johnny Seaton, Julian Whitaker, Helena Andreyko, Carol Denise Smith

1287. *Elvis: The Legend Lives!* Musical review [sic] of life & mus of Elvis Presley. Palace, Broadway, 1/31/78–4/30/78. 101 perf. title m: Doc Pomus & Bruce Foster; d: Jim Sotos & Harry Scarpelli; light: Barry Arnold; md: Peter Dino. Cast: Elvis: Rick Saucedo; Ed Sullivan: Will Jordan; The Jordanaires (Elvis's old backing group), D.J. Fontana (Elvis's old drummer)

1288. *The Emperor of My Baby's Heart.* Set in 1941. Theatre of the Riverside Church, 6/7/84–6/24/84. 12 perf. m/l: Mark Barkan & Lawrence Du Kor; d: David Gold. Cast: Robert Grossman, Adam Heller, Lauree Taradash. "Your Time is My Time," "Time is Money," "Sweet Nightingale," "Star that Never Got to Shine," "Humanity," "No Yesterdays," "In the Beginning," "Boogie Woogie Boy from Brooklyn," "You Could Be the One," "I'm Not the Man I Used to Be," "Emperor of My Baby's Heart"

1289. *Enchanting Melody.* Yiddish folk musical. Folksbiene, 11/24/64–3/14/65 (weekend perfs only). m: Henoch Kon; b: Itzik Manger; d: David Licht

1290. *Encore: 50 Golden Years of Showstoppers.* Radio City Music Hall, 3/26/82–9/6/82. 288 perf. p: Robert F. Jani, for Radio City Music Hall Prods for its Golden Jubilee Spectacular; d: Robert Jani; ch: Adam Grammis, Shozo Nakano, Geoffrey Holder, Linda Lemac, Frank Wagner, Violet Holmes; set: Charles Lisanby; light: Ken Billington; md: Tom Bahler. Cast: Wendy Edmead, Tom Garrett, Michael Kubala, Kuniko Narai, Deborah Phelan, Justin Ross, Luis Villanueva, Karen Ziemba, the Rockettes. "Encore" (m: Stan Lebowsky; l: Fred Tobias), "Ohka-No-Zu (Cherry Blossom)," "Rhapsody in Blue" (m: George Gershwin), "Showstoppers" (m: John Kander; l: Fred Ebb), "Bolero" (m: Maurice Ravel), "There Are No Girls Like Show Girls" (m: Don Pippin; l: Sammy Cahn), "That's Entertainment" (m: Arthur Schwartz; l: Howard Dietz), "You're at the Music Hall" (m: Don Pippin; l: Sammy Cahn)

1291. *Endangered Species.* Music theatre piece. Majestic, 10/2/90–10/14/90. 14 perf. p: Brooklyn Academy of Music, Music Theatre Group, Circus Flora; conceived by/d: Martha Clarke; text was Walt Whitman's *Leaves of Grass;* adapted by: Robert Coe; light: Paul Gallo. Cast: Flora Baldini, Paul Guilfoyle, Eileen Henry, Judy Kuhn

1292. *Enter the Guardsman.* Set in & around a theatre. Donmar Warehouse, London, 9/17/97–10/18/97. Prev from 9/11/97. p: in assoc with The Really Useful Co.; m/orch: Craig Bohmler; l: Marion Adler; b: Scott Wentworth; based on Ferenc Molnar's play; d: Jeremy Sams. Cast: Janie Dee, Nicky Henson, Angela Richards. "Tonight Was Like the First Night," "Chopin," "My One Great Love," "Language of Flowers," "Drama," "The Actor's Fantasy," "You Have the Ring," "Enter the Guardsman," "True to Me," "She's a Little Off," "I Can't Go On," "Waiting in the Wings," "They Die," "The Long Run," "Art Imitating Life." Vineyard/Dimson (OB), 5/9/00–6/4/00. 12 prev. 15 perf. d: Scott Wentworth; md: Nicholas Archer. Cast: Robert Cuccioli, Marla Schaffel, Mark Jacoby, Derin Altay, Kate Dawson, Rusty Ferracane, Buddy Crutchfield

1293. *'Erb.* Manchester University, England, 12/22/69–1/24/70. p: 69 Theatre Company; m/l/b: Trevor Peacock; from W. Pett Ridge's book. Strand, London, 4/7/70–5/9/70. 38 perf. p: Richard Pilbrow; d: Braham Murray; ch: Deborah Grant, Nicklas Grace, Braham Murray; md: Gordon Mackie. Cast: Trevor Peacock (as 'Erb), Nicklas Grace, Deborah Grant

1294. *Erik and the Snow Maidens.* Musical fantasy. Eighty-Eight's, 1/6/97–3/97. w/d: John Richard Thompson. Cast: Erik: Elena Bennett

1295. *Ernest.* Set in England in 1895. Jose Quintero, 6/30/00–7/9/00. 7 perf. m: Vance Lehmkuhl; l/b/d: Gayden Wren; based on *The Importance of Being Ernest*, by Oscar Wilde; md: Stephen O'Leary

1296. *Ernest in Love.* Gramercy Arts, 5/4/60 (2 months). Good reviews. p: Noel Behn & Robert Kamlot; m: Lee Pockriss; l/b: Anne Croswell; based on Oscar Wilde's *The Importance of Being Ernest;* d: Harold Stone; ch: Frank Derbas. Cast: Leila Martin, John Irving, Gerrianne Raphael. "Come, Raise Your Cup," "How Do You Find the Words?," "The Hat," "Mr. Bunbury," "Perfection," "A Handbag is Not a Proper Mother," "A Wicked Man," "Metaphorically Speaking," "You Can't Make Love," "Lost," "My First Impression," "Muffin Song," "My Eternal Devotion," "Ernest in Love." Theatre Off Park, 5/14/80. d: Jay

Stephens. All Souls Church, 1/27/94–2/6/94. 10 perf. p: All Souls Players; d: Jeffrey K. Neill; md: Joyce Hitchcock. Gerrianne Raphael, who had played Cicely in 1960, now played Lady Bracknell

1297. *Etiquette.* Musical revue with manners. s.n.a.f.u., 12/5/82–12/26/82. 8 perf. m: John Braden; l: John Braden & William H. Hoffman; add l: Emily Post; d: John Vaccaro. Cast: Billy Barnes, Cindy Benson, Jerry Cunliffe, Marcia McClain

1298. *Eubie Blake: A Century of Music.* All-star tribute to the jazz pianist; benefit for Eubie Blake Cultural Center, Baltimore. Unrelated to Broadway show *Eubie!* Kennedy Center, 1/20/83

1299. *Evangeline.* Play with mus. Blackpool, England, 2/18/46; then Glasgow & Edinburgh; the Cambridge, London, 3/14/46–3/30/46. 32 perf. m: George Posford & Harry Jacobson; l: Eric Maschwitz; b: Romney Brent; from *Nymph Errant,* by James Laver; d: Val Guest & Frances Day; ch: William Chappell & Therese Langfield; set: Joseph Carl; md: Philip Martell. Cast: Jon Pertwee, Guy Rolfe, Frances Day, Jo Keene, Gwen Bateman, Sebastian Cabot, Sonya Hana, The Modernaires. See also *Nymph Errant,* in this appendix

1300. *The Evangelist.* Set in St. Joseph, Mo., Omaha, and Des Moines, summer 1924. Wonderhorse, 3/31/82–4/18/82. 16 perf. p: Marvin Kahan; w: Al Carmines; d: William Hopkins; ch: Ellen Krueger; set: Peter Harrison; md: Ernest Lehrer. Cast: Paul Farin, Keith Baker, Kate Ingram, Judith Moore, Donna Bullock. "Hymns from the Darkness," "Everything God Does is Perfect," "Holy Ghost Ride," "I Was a Black Sheep," "Remember Joplin," "Omaha, I'm Here," "Cardboard Madonna," "Blame it on the Moon," "The Brother Blues," "Buds of May," "Men are Men," "We're Going to Des Moines," "I Am an Evangelist," "Navajo Woman," "Raven the Magnet," "Home"

1301. *An Evening with Joan Crawford.* Orpheum, 1/28/81–2/8/81. Prev from 1/20/81. 15 perf. m: Joseph Church & Nick Branch; conceived by/d: Julian Neil; ch: Sydney Smith; md: Joseph Church. Cast: Joan: Lee Sparks; Also with: Joyce Fullerton. "Blame it All on Me," "The Devil's Song," "Hollywood Lullaby," "Give 'em Hell," "Too Much Money Blues," "Except, of Course, Men," "You're One of a Kind," "Ain't No Place Like Home," "Take a Vacation," "What's it Like to Be a Legend." Previously produced at the New York Theatre Ensemble

1302. *Every Beat Face Ain't Beautiful.* Chelsea Playhouse, 12/1/96–12/21/96. 1 prev. 20 perf. Written & performed by homeless & formerly homeless people with AIDS. "Hustlin'," "Husband Material," "Duelin' Divas," "The Walk," "Love Me in the Daylight," "One Night in Manhattan." See also *I Make Me a Promise,* in this appendix

1303. *Every Good Boy Deserves Favor.* Play with mus. Set in asylum in Russia in 1970s. m: Andre Previn; w: Tom Stoppard. In 1974 Mr. Previn asked Mr. Stoppard if he would write a work that included an orchestra on stage. In

1976 Mr. Stoppard met Victor Fainberg & based it on him. It was prod in 1977. Re-done at Kimmel Center for the Performing Arts, Philadelphia, 11/20/02–11/26/02. d: Jiri Zizka. Cast: Richard Easton

1304. *Everybody's Gettin' into the Act.* Vaudeville revue. Vignettes of contemporary life & love. Actors Playhouse, 9/27/81–10/25/81. 33 perf. w: Bob Ost; d/ch: Darwin Knight. Cast: Ann Hodapp, Bill McCauley (also md), Ross Petty. "Everybody's Gettin' into the Act," "That First Hello," "Perfection," "Too Good," "So Close," "Steppin' Back," "I'm Available," "Love Me Just a Little Bit," "Looks Like Love," "You Never Take Me Anywhere," "It Always Seems to Rain," "Never, Never," "Keepin' it Together," "Alive and … Well," "Don't I Know You?." First produced OOB

Exactly Like You see # 735, Main Book

1306. *Exchange.* Topical cabaret-style musical entertainment with dissent motif. Mercer-O'Casey, 2/8/70. 1 perf. m/l: Mike Brandt, Michael Knight, Robert J. Lowery; d: Sondra Lee; set: Peter Harvey; cos: Stanley Simmons. Cast: Mike Brandt, Igors Gavon, Darwin Knight, Megan Kay, Pamela Talus, Penelope Bodry. "All Over My Mind," "Why Don't You Believe Me?," "Flower Song," "Santa Barbara," "Puddles," "Pied Piper," "I Can Make It"

1307. *Exiles.* Mixed-media musical. INTAR Stage Two, 12/9/82–1/2/83. 16 perf. p: INTAR Hispanic American Theatre; m/l: Elliot Sokolov, Louis Milgrom, Ana Maria Simo; d: Maria Irene Fornes. Cast: Anita Keal, Karen Ludwig, Jose Antonio Maldonado, Rebecca Schull, Nicole Baptiste, Jose Febus, Maria Garcia. "Hurricane of Revolution," "Did I See You?," "Do You See This Card?," "Got Your Letter," "Memory is an Art," "Icebergs Collide," "A Sleeping Black Panther"

1308. *Exit Music.* Village Theatre, 7/8/93–7/26/93; 17 perf. m: James Merrillat; l: Dick Paqual; based on story *Me and the Girls,* by Noel Coward; d: Brian Meister; ch: Karin Baker; md: Mark Wagner. "Perfect Mate for Me," "Easy Target for Love," "The Grandest View," "Me and the Girls," "Don't Write Any More Songs," "Secrets," "Never Lonely," "Dancing on Air," "I'll Show You How," "The Rest of My Life," "I'm in Demand," "Time to Celebrate," "I Meant to Be Beautiful," "Where Do We Play?," "You'll Get a Boot Out of Italy," "To Say Goodbye"

1309. *Expresso Bongo.* The 1st rock 'n roll musical. "Bongo" Herbert Rudge (bongo player) is discovered in London coffee bar in 1956 & becomes star. Loosely based on rise of rock 'n roll star Tommy Steele. Theatre Royal, Nottingham, England. 3/24/58; toured; Saville, London, 4/23/58–1/24/59. 316 perf. p: Oscar Lewenstein & Neil Crawford; m: David Heneker & Monty Norman; l: Julian More, Monty Norman, David Heneker; b: Wolf Mankowitz & Julian More; based on Wolf Mankowitz's story; d/ch: William Chappell; set: Loudon Sainthill; cos: Jocelyn Rickards; md: Burt Rhodes. Cast: Paul Scofield (his 1st musical), Millicent Martin, Hy Hazell, James Kenney (as Bongo), Meier Tzelniker, Elizabeth Ashley, Victor Spinetti, Aubrey Morris, Barry

Cryer, Charles Gray, Hilda Fenemore, Rosaline Haddon, Susan Hampshire, Anna Sharkey, Jill Gascoigne. "Time," "Don't You Sell Me Down the River," "Shrine on the Second Floor," "Spoil the Child," "Seriously," "I Am," "I Never Had it So Good," "Gravy Train," "Nausea," "I've Bought It," "He's Got Something for the Public," "Nothing is for Nothing," "There's Nothing Wrong with British Youth Today." Filmed in 1959. w: Wolf Mankowitz; d: Val Guest. Cast: Cliff Richard (as Bongo), Laurence Harvey, Yolande Donlan, Hermione Baddeley, Sylvia Syms, Meier Tzelniker, Wolf Mankowitz (as Sandwich Man)

1310. *F. Jasmine Addams.* Sister of 12-year-old Southern girl in 1945 is getting married. Circle in the Square, 10/27/71–10/31/71. 6 perf. m/l: G. Wood; b: Carson McCullers, G. Wood, Theodore Mann; based on Miss McCullers' 1950 play *The Member of the Wedding;* d: Theodore Mann; ch: Patricia Birch; cos: Joseph G. Aulisi; md: Liza Redfield; arr: Luther Henderson. Cast: Theresa Merritt, Neva Small, Johnny Doran, Northern J. Calloway, William Le Massena. "How About You and Me?," "If I Had a …," "Miss Pinhead," "Baby, That's Love," "Did I Make a Good Impression?," "Good as Anybody," "The We of Me," "Travelin' On," "Sunshine Tomorrow," "F. Jasmine Addams," "How Sweet is Peach Ice Cream," "Do Me a Favor," "Another Day," "Quite Suddenly"

1311. *Fables in Slang: A Ragtime Revue.* Musical revue, featuring songs of Ragtime era. Theatre 3, 4/21/99–5/29/99. 6 prev. 36 perf. p: Melting Pot Theatre; w: Gene Jones; based on writing of George Ade; d: Nick Corley; ch: Jennifer Paulson Lee; md: Peter Muir. Cast: Nancy Anderson, Gene Jones

1312. *The Fabulous La Fontaine.* Set in France in 17th century. Riverwest, 2/2/90–2/24/90. 21 perf. l/b/conceived by: Owen S. Rackleff; mus adapted from *The Carnival of the Animals,* by Camille Saint-Saens; d: Dennis Deal. Cast: Patti Perkins. "King of Beasts," "Elephant Duo," "There Was a Bird," "Funny Moment," "Paths of Glory," "Fable of the Fossil," "The Frog and the Rat," "I'm a Pisces," "Wife and Mistress," "Age Has its Hour," "Lion in Love"

1313. *The Faggot.* Vignettes of homosexual lives & attitudes in songs & sketches. Judson Poets' Theatre, 4/13/73. 21 perf. Cast: Al Carmines (also m/l/d), Ira Siff, Essie Borden, Lou Bullock, Bill Reynolds, David Pursley, Julie Kurnitz, Philip Owens, David Summers, Peggy Atkinson, Marilyn Child, Tony Clark (*Reathel Bean*), Frank Coppola, Lee Guilliatt, Bruce Hopkins. Truck & Warehouse Theatre, 6/18/73–11/25/73. 182 perf. p: Bruce Mailman & Richard Lipton. "Women with Women—Men with Men," "The Hustler: A Five-Minute Opera," "I'll Take My Fantasy," "Hari Krishna," "Desperation," "A Gay Bar Cantata," "Nookie Time," "Your Way of Loving," "Ordinary Things," "Art Song," "What is a Queen?"

1314. *Fairy Tales.* Musical revue. WPA, 5/20/97–6/21/97. 14 prev. 20 perf. m/l: Eric Lane Barnes. "Flying Dreams," "Gay Guys," "You're the Bottom," "God Hates Fags,"

"Grace," "Heaven to Me," "When You Meet an Angel," "Anniversary Five," "American Beauty," "A Hummingbird," "Keepers of the Light." London, 1997. Earlier version ran at Duplex Cabaret, NY earlier in 96–97

1315. *Faith Journey*. Musical look at Civil Rights Movement, based on life of Martin Luther King, using traditional & contemporary songs. Lamb's, 7/21/94–1/5/95. 193 perf. m/md: George Broderick; l: George Broderick & Clarence Cuthbertson; b: Clarence Cuthbertson; d: Chuck Patterson; ch: Barry Carrington. Cast: Craig Anthony Grant. "Somebody's Knocking," "I Made a Vow," "Over My Head," "Best of Both Worlds," "Should I Wait?," "Decide," "Don't Take Your Love," "One Day," "We Got a Movement," "By Any Means Necessary," "To Be Loved for Who I Am," "Help Me Find a Way," "I Wanna Be Ready," "Ain't Gonna Let Nobody Turn Me 'round," "Woke up This Morning," "There's a War in Mississippi," "We Shall Overcome," "My Country 'tis of Thee," "Freedom," "Walk Together," "I Find a Friend in You," "I Miss You." Ran previously at Circle Rep, from 1/28/93. d/ch: Bernard Marsh; md: Ladd Johnson. Cast: Mark Hall

1316. *Fallen Angel*. Rock musical. La Mama, 3/27/92–4/12/92. 11 perf. m/l/b: William L. Boesky; d: Rob Greenberg. Cast: Jonathan Goldstein, Michael McCoy, Amy Correia. "Coming and Going," "More than You Know," "Falling in Line," "Till I'm Gone," "Southbound Train," "Hey Lady," "Silo," "Fallen Angel," "Unveil My Eyes," "All Right." Circle in the Square Downtown, 4/14/94–5/11/94. 16 prev from 4/1/94. 32 perf. p: Peter Holmes a Court, Rodger Hess, Back Row Prods; d: Rob Greenberg. Cast: Jonathan Goldstein, Corey Glover, Shannon Conley, Susan Gibney, George Coe

1317. *Fallout*. Revue. Renata, 5/20/59. m/l: Martin Charnin, Robert Kessler, Paul Nassau; sk: Martin Charnin, etc; d: Harvey Stuart; ch: Buddy Schwab; set/cos/light: Fred Voelpel. Cast: Grover Dale (*Kip Carlisle*), Paul Dooley (*Tom O'Horgan*), Charles Nelson Reilly, Virginia Vestoff

Falsettoland see # 200, Main Book

1318. *Fame: The Musical*. Set in NY's legendary High School of the Performing Arts. Hopes & dreams of aspiring stars. Cambridge Theatre, London, 6/27/95–9/28/96. m: Steven Margoshes; l: Jacques Levy; Dean Pitchford & Michael Gore wrote the title song "Fame," which was in the movie; b: Jose Fernandez; conceived & developed by/d: David da Silva; inspired by hit film & subsequent TV series. Victoria Palace, 11/11/97–1/17/98; Prince of Wales, 10/15/98–1/16/99; Victoria Palace, 10/3/00–9/8/01; the Cambridge, 9/20/01–8/02; Aldwych, 9/4/02–1/31/04. Ran at the Little Shubert (OB), 11/11/03–6/27/04, as *Fame on 42nd Street*. 40 prev from 10/7/03; 264 perf. p: Richard Martini, Allen Spivak, Dodger Stage Holding, in assoc with Father Fame Foundation; d: Drew Scott Harris; ch: Lars Bethke; set: Norbert Kolb; cos: Paul Tazewell; light: Ken Billington; sound: Christopher "Kit" Bond; cast recording on Q Records. Cast:

Jenna Coker, Nancy Hess, Emily Corney, Peter Reardon, Cheryl Freeman, Christopher J. Hanke, Michael Kary, Nicole Leach, Gannon McHale, Dennis Moench, Q Smith, Shakiem Evans, Jose Restrepo, Sara Schmidt, *Marque Lynch*. "Hard Work," "I Want to Make Magic," "Can't Keep it Down," "Dance Class," "Tyrone's Rap," "There She Goes," "Fame," "Let's Play a Love Scene," "Bring on Tomorrow," "The Teacher's Argument," "Pray I Make P.A.," "The Junior Festival," "Think of Meryl Streep," "Mabel's Prayer," "Dancin' on the Sidewalk," "These Are My Children," "Reconnecting with Iris," "In L.A."

1319. *Fancy Free*. Prince of Wales, London, 5/15/51. 369 perf. m/l: Norman Newell & Coates; b: Barbara Gordon & Basil Thomas; d: Charles Henry; ch: Joan Davis. Cast: Pat Kirkwood, Tommy Trinder, Alan and Blanche Lund, Jennifer Jayne, Jean Bayless, Jack Parnell & His Music Makers, The George Mitchell Quintette. Unrelated to the Leonard Bernstein ballet that led to *On the Town*, or with the later British musical of the same name (with score by Elizabeth Quinn & book by Sam Cree, that ran in Belfast from 3/26/63)

1320. *The Fantasticks*. An OB prod, it ran 42 years, the longest-running American musical of all time. A couple of fathers pretend to quarrel so their children will get together. When this doesn't work they arrange with outlaw El Gallo to stage the mock rape of The Girl, so The Boy can prove his valor. Sullivan Street Playhouse, 5/3/60–1/13/02. 17,162 perf. m: Harvey Schmidt; l/b: Tom Jones; based on Edmond Rostand's 1894 play Les Romanesques; d: Word Baker; set: Ed Wittstein; md: Julian Stein, *Dorothy Martin*; cast recording on MGM. Cast (replacement dates are those the actor took over): Narrator (character later re-named El Gallo): Jerry Orbach, Gene Rupert, Bert Convy, John Cunningham, Don Stewart 1/63, David Cryer, Keith Charles 10/63, John Boni 1/13/65, Jack Mette 9/14/65, George Ogee, Keith Charles, Tom Urich 8/30/66, John Boni 10/5/66, Jack Crowder 6/13/67, Nils Hedrick 9/19/67, Keith Charles 10/9/67, Robert Goss 11/7/67, Joe Bellomo 3/11/68, Michael Tartel 7/8/69, Donald Billett 6/70, Joe Bellomo 2/15/72, David Rexroad 6/73, David Snell 12/73, Hal Robinson 4/2/74, Chapman Roberts 7/30/74, David Brummel 2/18/75, David Rexroad 8/31/75, Roger Brown 9/30/75, David Rexroad 9/1/76, Joseph Galiano 10/14/76, Keith Charles 3/22/77, Joseph Galiano 4/5/77, Douglas Clark 5/2/78, Joseph Galiano 5/23/78, Richard Muenz 10/78, Joseph Galiano 2/20/79, George Lee Andrews 11/27/79, Sal Provenza 5/13/80, Lance Brodie 9/8/81, Roger Neil 5/17/83, Sal Provenza 8/9/83, Hal Robinson, David Brummel 1/29/85, Dennis Parlato 5/7/85, Michael Licata 6/87, George Lee Andrews 6/87, Robert Vincent Smith 8/18/87, David Brummel 12/25/90, Michael Licata 1/8/91, Kenneth Kantor 2/12/91, Scott Willis 3/26/91, Michael Scott, Michael X. Martin, Kim Moore 3/17/92, Christopher Innvar 92–93, Paul Blankenship 92–93, Robert Vincent Smith by 93–94, John Savarese by 94–95, Christopher Coucill by 96–97, John Savarese

10/7/97, Paul Blankenship from 2/99); The Girl (character later re-named Luisa): Rita Gardner, Carla Huston, Liza Stuart 12/61, Eileen Fulton, Alice Cannon 9/62, Royce Lenelle, B.J. Ward 12/1/64, Leta Anderson 7/13/65, Carole Demas 11/22/66, Anne Kaye 5/28/68, Carolyn Mignini 7/29/69, Virginia Gregory 7/27/70, Leta Anderson, Marti Morris 3/7/72, Sharon Werner 8/1/72, Sarah Rice 6/24/74, Cheryl Horne 7/1/75, Sarah Rice 7/29/75, Betsy Joslyn 3/23/76, Kathy Vestuto 7/18/78, Betsy Joslyn 8/8/78, Kathryn Morath 11/28/78, Debbie McLeod 4/17/79, Joan Wiest 10/9/79, Marti Morris 11/6/79, Carole-Ann Scott 5/20/80, Beverly Lambert 9/2/80, Judith Blazer 12/1/80, Elizabeth Bruzzese 8/15/81, Virginia Gregory 12/7/82, Karen Culliver 12/4/84, Virginia Gregory 11/12/85, Jennifer Lee 12/2/85, Lorrie Harrison 11/4/86, Glory Crampton 11/10/87, Kate Suber 11/15/88, Sharen Camille 11/7/89, Marilyn Whitehead 1/23/90, Debbie Pavelka by 93–94, Natasha Harper by 94–95, Lisa Mayer 94–95, Kristin Chenoweth 94–95, Jennifer Westfeldt by 95–96, Christine Long 95–96, Sara Schmidt by 96–97, Gina Schuh-Turner 10/7/97, Natasha Harper 1/25/00), Elizabeth Cherry; The Boy (character later re-named Matt): Kenneth Nelson, Gino Conforti, Jack Blackton 10/63, Paul Giovanni, Ty McConnell, Richard Rothbard, Gary Krawford, Bob Spencer 9/5/64, Erik Howell 6/28/66, Gary Krawford 12/12/67, Steve Skiles 2/6/68, Craig Carnelia 1/69, Erik Howell 7/18/69, Samuel D. Ratcliffe 8/5/69, Michael Glenn-Smith 5/26/70, Jimmy Dodge 9/20/70, Geoffrey Taylor 8/31/71, Erik Howell 3/14/72, Michael Glenn-Smith 6/13/72, Phil Killian 7/4/72, Richard Lincoln 9/72, Bruce Cryer 7/24/73, Phil Killian 9/11/73, Michael Glenn-Smith 6/17/74, Ralph Bruneau 10/29/74, Bruce Cryer 9/30/75, Jeff Knight 7/19/77, Michael Glenn-Smith 1/9/79, Christopher Seppe 3/6/79, Howard Lawrence 12/29/81, Bill Perlach 2/5/85, Paul Blankenship 12/22/87, Neil Nash 3/15/88, Matthew Eaton Bennett 5/30/89, Neil Nash 1/23/90, Rex Nockengust 7/31/90, Kevin R. Wright 11/6/90, Christopher Scott, Rex Nockengust 5/7/91, Christopher Scott 92–93, Richard Roland by 93–94, Josh Miller by 94–95, Darren Romeo by 95–96, Eric Meyersfield 95–96, Charles Hagerty 11/99); The Boy's Father (character later re-named Hucklebee): William Larsen, Lore Noto himself played this role 1971–1986; The Girl's Father (character later re-named Bellomy): Hugh Thomas; The Mute (character later re-named Prentice): Richard Stauffer; The Old Actor (character later re-named Henry Albertson): Thomas Bruce (i.e. Tom Jones), F. Murray Abraham began a short stint playing the Old Actor in 6/67; The Man Who Dies (character later re-named Mortimer): George Curley; The Handyman: Jay Hampton. Understudy for the Girl from the beginning to 5/31/69: Sybil Lamb. "Try to Remember" [the big hit], "Much More," "Metaphor," "Never Say No," "It Depends on What You Pay," "Soon it's Going to Rain," "Rape Ballet," "Happy Ending," "This Plum is Too Ripe," "I Can See It," "Plant a Radish," "Round and

Round," "They Were You." Originally titled *Joy Comes to Dead Horse*, the name was changed, and it 1st ran at Barnard College's Minor Latham Theatre (Susan Watson was The Girl), and picked up by producer Lore Noto. Then it began its phenomenal OB run. On 11/5/66 it played its 2,718th performance, passing *My Fair Lady* as the longest-running-ever NY musical. Special Tony award in 1992. Present at the last night were Lore Noto, Tom Jones, Harvey Schmidt, Rita Gardner, F. Murray Abraham, Ed Wittstein, and George Curley. The 1st of many tours opened 4/4/61, at Del Prado, Chicago. md: Michael Cohen. Cast: Narrator: John McLeod; Girl: Mimi Turque; Boy: Tom Ayre. Apollo Theatre, London, 9/7/61. 44 perf. Cast: El Gallo: Terence Cooper; Matt: Peter Gilmore; Luisa: Stephanie Voss; Bellomy: Timothy Bateson; Hucklebee: Michael Barrington; Prentice: Melvyn Hayes; Mortimer: John Cater; Henry: John Wood. It has played all over the world, in various languages, for example: *Los fantastickos*, the Spanish premiere. San Pol Theatre, Madrid, 10/23/97. Translator: Ana Maria Bordeguer; d: James Cook; md: Juan Jimenez

1321. *Fashion.* Royal Playhouse, 1/20/59–3/3/59. 50 perf. w: Anna Cora Mowatt. Cast: Enid Markey, Will Geer. "Come, Birdie, Come," "Take Back the Heart," "Not for Joe"

1322. *Fashion.* Comedy within musical, set on Long Island. Greenwich Mews, 1973; McAlpin Rooftop, 2/17/73–4/13/73. 62 perf; Little Hippodrome, 4/17/73–5/12/73. 32 perf. p: R. Scott Lucas; m: Don Pippin; l: Steve Brown; based on play by Anna Cora Mowatt; adapted by/d: Anthony Stimac; set: Robert U. Taylor; md: Susan Romann. Cast: Mary Jo Catlett, Ty McConnell, Sandra Thornton, Susan Romann, Henrietta Valor, Jan Buttram, Rhoda Butler (understudy *Patti Perkins* from 3/5/74). "You See Before You What Fashion Can Do," "It Was for Fashion's Sake," "Good Old American Way," "What Kind of Man is He?," "My Daughter the Countess," "Take Me," "Why Should They Know About Paris?," "Meet Me Tonight," "A Life without Her"

1323. *Father's Inheritance.* Folksbiene, 10/11/90–1/13/91. 39 perf. Based on Jacob Gordin's *The Charlatan*; d: Yevgeny Lanskoye; ch: Felix Fibich; set: Brian P. Kelly. Cast: Zypora Spaisman, Emile Groovets (also m/l/adapted), Julie Alexander. "We Are 76 Years Old Today," "Laugh Brother, Laugh Sister," "Goodbye Odessa," "I'll Sing a Little Song," "Wheel of Fortune Turns," "Love is a Heavenly Song," "Money is Only Paper," "I Can Swear by Heaven," "There Are Such Daughters," "In a Lucky Hour"

1324. *Feast Here Tonight.* Bluegrass musical. Vineyard, 6/14/89–6/30/89. 12 perf. Returned 11/22/89–12/17/89. 30 perf. d: Gloria Muzio. Cast: Daniel Jenkins (also m/l), Susan Glaze, Cass Morgan, Patrick Tovatt. "My Soul Was Born to This Land," "Where You Been," "This World," "December Light," "Back Way Home," "David," "Pumpkin Pie," "Hound Dog," "Little Rabbit," "Home on the Hill," "If You Knew Eula Well," "Mason Boys," "Breath of an Angel"

1325. *Feathertop.* Set in Massachusetts in mid–1700s. WPA, 10/17/84–11/18/84. 38 perf. m/l: Skip Kennon; b: Bruce Peyton; from short story by Nathaniel Hawthorne; d: Susan H. Schulman; ch: Michael Lichtefeld; md: Sand Lawn. Cast: Alexandra Korey, Stephen Bogardus, David Barron, Laura Dean, Jason Graae, Charles Bari. "The New World," "Here I Am," "They Had to Change," "Spring Day," "Home," "One Two Three," "Better," "Happily the Days Are Running By," "Marvelous, Curious and Strange," "Something Different," "It's Only the Best Yet"

1326. *Feeling No Pain.* Closed before Broadway, 1973. m/l: Leslie Bricusse. Cast: Steve Lawrence. "Hello, Los Angeles"

1327. *Femme Fatale.* Psychological mystery musical with all-female cast. American Ballet Theatre, 2/23/00–3/4/00. 10 perf. m: Keith Herrmann; l/b: Barry Harman; based on novel *The Haunted Hotel,* by Wilkie Collins; d: Barry Harman; ch: D.J. Salisbury. Cast: Priscilla Lopez, Christiane Noll, Natalie Toro, Darcy Pulliam, Mindy Cooper, Teri Gibson, Cindy Marchionda

1328. *Fermat's Last Tango.* Theatre at St. Peter's, NY, 11/21/00–12/31/00. 18 prev. 30 perf. p: York Theatre Co.; m/orch: Joshua Rosenbloom; l: Joanne Sydney Lessner & Joshua Rosenbloom; b: Joanne Sydney Lessner; inspired by work of Princeton math professor Andrew Wiles and French mathematician Pierre de Fermat; d: Mel Marvin; ch: Janet Watson; set: James Morgan; md: Milton Granger; cast recording on Original Cast Records. Cast: Jonathan Rabb, Gilles Chiasson, Christianne Tisdale, Chris Thompson, Edwardyne Cowan, Mitchell Kantor, Carrie Wilshusen. "Press Conference I," "You're a Hero Now," "Beauty of Numbers," "Tell Me Your Secret," "Sing We to Symmetry," "Welcome to the AfterMath," "Your Proof Contains a Hole," "I Dreamed," "Press Conference II," "My Name," "All I Want for My Birthday," "Game Show," "Math Widow," "I'll Always Be There (Fermat's Last Tango)," "Relay Race," "I'm Stumbling," "Oh, It's You," "Press Conference III." European premiere of *O ultimo tango de Fermat* (translated by Cesar Viana), at Teatro de Trinidade, Lisbon, 1/8/04 (after a brief tour of Portuguese university towns beginning 11/13/03 in Porto)

1329. *The Fickle Finger of Lady Death.* Musical fable. Parks Tour/Puerto Rican Traveling Theatre, 7/28/94–8/28/94. 29 perf. w: Eduardo Rodriguez-Solis; translator: Carlos Morton; d: Jorge Huerta. Cast: Tony Chiroldes

1330. *The Fields of Ambrosia.* Set in Deep South of USA, 1918. George Street Playhouse, New Brunswick, NJ, 3/6/93. m: Martin Silvestri; l/b: Joel Higgins; based on screenplay *The Traveling Executioner,* by Garrie Bateson; d: Gregory S. Hurst; ch: Lynne Taylor-Corbett; set: Deborah Jasien; cos: Hilary Rosenfeld; md: Sariva Goetz; orch: Harold Wheeler. Cast: Joel Higgins, Eddie Korbich, Robert Ousley, Christine Andreas, Peter Samuel. "Ball and Chain," "The Fields of Ambrosia," "How Could This Happen?," "Who Are You?," "Step Right Up," "Too Bad," "That Rat is Dead,"

"Alone," "Card Game," "The Gallows," "Do it for Me," "All in This Together," "The Gateway," "The Breakout." Aldwych, London, 1/15/96. 23 perf. md: Mark Warman. Cast: Joel Higgins, Christine Andreas, Marc Joseph, Michael Fenton Stevens, Mark Heenehan, Roger Leach, Cliff Brayshaw, Peter Gallagher, Henry Webster, Morgan Deare, Kevin Rooney

1331. *Fiesta in Madrid.* Set in Madrid in 19th cent. Wealthy apothecary infatuated with 2 beautiful girls. In Spanish. City Center, 5/28/69–6/15/69. 23 perf. Adapted by Tito Capobianco from the zarzuela *La Verbena de la Paloma,* by Tomas Breton; conceived by/d: Tito Capobianco; ch: Teresa. Cast: Teresa, Kay Creed, Franco Iglesias, Muriel Greenspon, Henrietta Valor. "Fiesta in Madrid," "The Tarantula," "Flamenco Song," "Streets of Madrid," "Best Woman in the World," "You Are the Only One for Me"

1332. *The Fifth Season.* Set in a 7th Avenue showroom. NY garment district. Eden, 10/12/75–1/25/76. m/l: Dick Manning; adapted in Yiddish & English by: Luba Kadison; from play of same name by Sylvia Regan; d: Joseph Buloff; set/cos: Jeffrey B. Moss; md: Renee Solomon. Cast: Joseph Buloff, David Carey, Evelyn Kingsley, Stan Porter, Miriam Kressyn. "Believe in Yourself," "My Son, the Doctor," "Goodbye," "The Fifth Season," "Friday Night" (l: Luba Kadison), "Mom! You Don't Understand," "How Did This Happen to Me?," "From Seventh Avenue to Seventh Heaven"

1333. *Fifty Million Frenchmen.* Lyric, Broadway, 11/27/29–7/5/30. 254 perf. m/l: Cole Porter; b: Herbert Fields; d: Ray Goetz; book d: Monty Woolley. Cast: William Gaxton, Genevieve Tobin, Helen Broderick, Thurston Hall, Lester Crawford. "A Toast to Volstead," "You Do Something to Me," "The American Express," "You've Got That Thing," "Find Me a Primitive Man," "Where Would You Get Your Coat?," "Do You Want to See Paris?," "At Longchamps Today," "The Happy Heaven of Harlem," "Why Shouldn't I Have You?," "It isn't Done," "I'm in Love," "The Tale of an Oyster," "Paree, What Did You Do to Me?," "You Don't Know Paree," "I'm Unlucky at Gambling." Filmed (not a musical) in 1931. Cast: Helen Broderick, William Gaxton. Florence Gould Hall, 1991. Concert. p: Alliance Francaise; d: Larry Carpenter. Cast: Jean LeClerc, Peggy Cass, Karen Ziemba, Scott Waara, Jason Graae, Susan Powell, Howard McGillin, Kay McClelland, Kim Criswell. See also *Paris '31*

1334. *Final Solutions.* Musical drama. The plight of Jews in the Soviet Russia of the day. Felt Forum, 3/11/68. 1 perf. p: American League for Russian Jews; orig m: Jacques Belasco; w: Jan Hartman; d: Gene Lasko; ch: Valerie Bettis. Cast: Marian Seldes, Leonardo Cimino, John Heffernan, Tony Lo Bianco

1335. *Fings Ain't Wot They Used T'Be.* Set among Soho low-lifes. Theatre Royal Stratford East, London, 2/17/59–4/18/59. 63 perf. p: Theatre Workshop; m/l: Lionel Bart; b: Frank Norman; d: Joan Littlewood; ch: Jean Newlove; set: John Bury; cos: Margaret Bury. Cast:

Richard Harris, Ann Beach, James Booth, Howard Goorney, Glynn Edwards, Yootha Joyce, Edward Caddick, Dudley Sutton, Shelagh Delaney, Clive Barker. Revised version, same venue, 12/22/59; Garrick, London, 2/11/60–2/22/62. 897 perf. Same basic crew except p: Theatre Workshop & Donald Albery; md: Ronnie Franklin, *Kenneth Moule*. Certain actors reprised: Glynn Edwards (*Bryan Pringle*), Yootha Joyce, James Booth (*Maurice Kaufmann*), Edward Caddick. New members of the cast: Miriam Karlin, Barbara Windsor, George Sewell, Wallas Eaton, Toni Palmer, Paddy Joyce, Tom Chatto. "G'night Dearie," "Fings Ain't Wot They Used t'Be," "Laying Abaht," "Where it's Hot," "The Ceilin's Comin' Dahn," "Contempery," "Polka Dots," "Meatface," "Where Do Little Birds Go?," "Big Time," "Carve Up!," "Cop a Bit of Pride," "The Student Ponce"

1336. *Finkel's Follies*. Musical revue. John Houseman, 12/15/91–1/1/92. Prev from 8/29/91. 19 perf; Westside Theatre Downstairs, 1/30/92–3/8/92. 46 perf. p: Eric Krebs; m/l: Elliot Finkel & Philip Namanworth; conceived by: Fyvush Finkel; adapted by/d: Robert H. Livingston; orch: Ian Finkel. Cast: Fy Finkel, Mary Ellen Ashley. "You Were Meant for Me," "Not on the Top," "That Something Special," "The Fiddle"

1337. *Fire Angel*. Wimbledon Theatre, London, 2/25/77–3/12/77; Her Majesty's, 3/24/77–5/7/77. Prev from 3/17/77. 42 perf. p: Ray Cooney; m: Roger Haines; l/b: Paul Bentley; from Shylock story; d: Braham Murray; ch: Arlene Phillips; md: Anthony Bowles. Cast: Gaye Brown, Colm Wilkinson (*Paul Bentley*)

Fire of Flowers see # 2511, this appendix

1338. *The Fishkin Touch*. Set in NYC in 1910. Playhouse 91, 6/6/98–6/29/98. 7 prev. 16 perf. p: Jewish Rep; m: Greg Armbruster; l: Lenore Skenazy; b: David Javerbaum; d: Alan Fox; cos: Gail Cooper-Hecht; md: Christopher McGovern. Cast: Mike Burstyn, Joan Copeland, Carolann Page, Jordan Leeds, Beth Thompson. "Poor Old Oedipus," "Mama," "Idol of the Yiddish Matinee," "Families Are," "The Usual," "Adam, Adam, Adam," "Levin," "Glass Slipper," "The Scarlet Aleph," "Finkelberg's," "Oh, Juliet," "Who Would Want to Be an Actress," "Down," "Emerald Eyes," "Mrs. Rosenbloom," "All We Want is for You," "Outlaw Mama," "Boy Meets Girl," "A Yiddish Kiss," "Reflected in My Heart," "Koogelplatz"

1339. *5-6-7-8 ... Dance!* Musical revue. Radio City Music Hall, 6/15/83–9/5/83. 149 perf. m/l: Wally Harper & David Zippel; b: Bruce Vilanch; d/ch: Ron Field; set: Tom H. John; cos: Lindsay W. Davis; ms: Wally Harper; md: Thomas Helm; orch: Bill Byers. Cast: Sandy Duncan, Don Correia, Bill Irwin, Armelia McQueen, Ken Sacha, Marge Champion, The Rockettes (dir by Violet Holmes). Dancers included: Eydie Fleming, Ciscoe Bruton II. "Life is a Dance," "5-6-7-8 ... Dance!," "It's Better with a Band," "You Mustn't Kick It Around," "It Only Happens When I Dance with You," "Bad Habits," "It's Not What You Weigh," "Sing, Sing, Sing," "Make Way for Tomorrow," "I'm Flying," "She Just Loves Las Vegas!," "Dance with Me," "Neverland," "Tea for Two," "I Love to Dance," "Tres Moutarde," "La Cumparcita," "The Continental," "Our Love is Here to Stay," "Broadway Rhythm," "Body Language"

1340. *The Fix*. One man's meteoric rise and fall. Donmar Warehouse, London, 5/12/97–6/14/97. Prev from 4/25/97. Donmar's 1st world premiere of an American musical. p: Donmar Warehouse & Cameron Mackintosh; m: Dana P. Rowe; l/b: John Dempsey; d: Sam Mendes. Cast: John Barrowman, Krysten Cummings, Philip Quast, Kathryn Evans, David Firth. "One Two Three," "Embrace Tomorrow," "Control," "America's Son," "I See the Future," "Lonely is a Two-Way Street," "Simple Word," "Alleluia," "Dangerous Games," "Two Guys at Harvard," "First Came Mercy," "Bend the Spoon," "Cleaning House," "Upper Hand," "Spin," "The Ballad of Bobby 'Cracker' Barrel," "Child's Play," "Mistress of Deception"

1341. *Flamenco Puro*. Flamenco singers, dancers & guitarists. Mark Hellinger, Broadway, 10/19/86–11/30/86. 13 prev. 40 perf. p: Mel Howard & Donald K. Donald; conceived by/d/set: Claudio Segovia & Hector Orezzoli; sound: T. Richard Fitzgerald. Previously ran in Seville, 1980; Paris, 1984; Gusman Center, Miami. After Broadway it went on national tour

1342. *Fledermaus*. City Center, 5/19/54–6/6/54. 15 perf. p: NY City Center Light Opera Co.; m: Johann Strauss; b: Carl Haffner & Richard Genee; l/English b: Ruth & Thomas Martin; d: Glenn Jordan; ch: Robert Pagent; cos: John Boyt; light: Jean Rosenthal; md: Thomas Martin. Cast: Rosalinda: Gloria Lind & Guen Omeron; Alfredo: Thomas Leech & Harold R. Brown; Also with: Adelaide Bishop, Jack Russell, Carl Nicholas, John Tyers, Stanley Carlson, Lidija Franklin, Donald Gramm, Thomas R. Powell, Bob Pagent, Coley Worth, Stanley Bakis, Hill Eller, Alan James, Don Ratka, James Spicer, George Tucker, Marilyn Bladd, Rina Falcone, Barbara Ford, Ellen Gleason, Sheila Mathews, Dorothy Mirr, Gloria Sacks, Greta Thormsen, Rose Virga, Benjamin Bajorek, Dawin Emanuel, Russell Goodwin, Charles Kuestner, James Martindale, Roland Miles, Benjamin Plotkin, William W. Reynolds, Joseph Tanner. "Darling Rosalinda," "We Are Going to a Party," "When These Lawyers Don't Deliver," "Come Along to the Ball," "Oh Dear, It Breaks My Heart," "What a Joy to Be Here," "Chacun a son Gout," "My Friends, Your Kind Attention," "Laughing Song," "How Engaging, How Exciting," "Emperor Waltz," "Voice of My Homeland," "Sing to Love," "Ah, Happy Day," "Ever Since I Was a Baby," "Vengeance is Mine." 1st ran in NY in 1879, and in English in 1885. See also *Rosalinda* (in this appendix). This 1954 version was one of many over the years, but it is probably still the best remembered by people today

1343. *Florodora*. AMDA Studio I, 2/20/81–3/15/81. 20 perf. p: Jerry Bell; m/l: Leslie Stuart, Paul Rubens, Ernest Boyd-Jones; b: Owen Hall; book adaptation/d: Lester Malizia; ch: Denny Shearer. Cast: Mary D'Arcy, Theresa Rakov, Ian Michael Towers, Byron Conner

Flowers for Algernon see # 130, Main Book

1344. *Floyd Collins*. Floyd is trapped in Kentucky cave (in Barren County) for 2 weeks, from 1/30/25. Skeets Miller is the reporter who interviews him while he's stuck there (Floyd died). Philadelphia, 4/13/94. Prev from 4/9/94. Commissioned by American Musical Theatre Festival in Philadelphia. m/l: Adam Guettel (son of Mary Rodgers & grandson of Richard Rodgers); b/add l/d: Tina Landau; ch: John De Luca; md: Ted Sperling. Cast: Floyd: Jim Morlino; Skeets: Martin Moran; Also with: Mary Beth Peil, Jason Danieley, Stephen Lee Anderson, Theresa McCarthy, Nick Plakias. Redeveloped & ran OB, 3/3/96–3/24/96. 28 prev from 2/9/96. 25 perf. p: Playwrights Horizons; d: Tina Landau; md: Ted Sperling; orch: Bruce Coughlin; cast recording on Nonesuch. Cast: Floyd: Christopher Innvar; Skeets: Martin Moran; Also with: Stephen Lee Anderson, Don Chastain, Cass Morgan, Jason Danieley, Michael Mulheren, Brian d'Arcy James, Jesse Lenat, Theresa McCarthy. "The Call," "'tween a Rock an' a Hard Place," "Lucky," "Daybreak," "I Landed on It," "Blue Eyes," "Heart an' Hand," "Riddle Song," "Is That Remarkable?," "The Carnival," "Through the Mountain," "Git Comfortable," "Family Hymn," "The Dream," "How Glory Goes," "Ballad of Floyd Collins." A concert reunion was produced, 1/23/03–1/26/03, by Playwrights Horizons. West Coast Ensemble Theatre, L.A., 2/11/05–4/3/05. Prev from 2/8/05. d: Richard Israel; ch: Cate Caplin; set: Evan Bartoletti; md: Johanna Kent

1345. *Fly Blackbird*. Conflict between those blacks who want immediate equality & those who want to wait. Mayfair, 2/5/62–5/27/62. 127 perf. m/l: C. Jackson & James Hatch; ch: Talley Beatty; light: Jules Fisher; md: Gershon Kingsley. Racially mixed cast: Micki Grant, Robert Guillaume, Avon Long, Michael Kermoyan, Helon Blount, William Sugihara. "Ev'rything Comes to Those Who Wait," "Now," "Big Betty's Song," "I'm Sick of the Whole Damn Problem," "Who's the Fool?," "The Right Way," "Couldn't We?," "The Housing Cha-Cha," "Natchitoches, Louisiana," "Fly Blackbird," "The Gong Song," "Rivers to the South," "Lilac Tree," "Twilight Zone," "Love Elixir," "Mister Boy," "Old White Tom," "Wake Up"

1346. *Flypaper*. Set in a Greenwich Village tavern. 224 Waverly Place, 11/8/90–11/25/90. 18 perf. m/l/b: Cheryl Paley & Larry Pellegrini. Cast: Cheryl Paley, James Loren

1347. *The Fol-De-Rols*. Variety show. St. Martin's, London, 1/1/51. 117 perf. m: Wolseley Charles, Harry Tait, Ross Parker; l/sk: Greatrex Newman; add l: Philip Whitley. Cast: June Powell, David Nixon (compere), Cyril Wells, Kathleen West, Charles Stewart. 26 items on the bill. "The Dresden Music Box"

1348. *Follies Burlesque '67*. Musical in burlesque style. Group of women visit Paris. Players, 5/3/67–5/14/67. 4 prev; 16 perf. m/l: Sol Richman; b: Stanley Richman; d: Dick Richards; ch: Paul Morokoff. Cast: Mickey Hargitay, Claude Mathis. "Oooh Lah Lah," "Scratch My Back," "Rabbit Habit," "The More I Hold You," "Tell Me"

1349. *The Follies of 1910.* Revue. Carnegie Hall Playhouse, 1/12/60–1/24/60. 14 perf. w/conceived by: Albert Moritz; d: Saul Swimmer. Cast: Albert Moritz, Susan Watson, Rhoda Levine, Michael Fesco, June L. Walker

1350. *Follow That Girl.* Began as *Christmas in King Street* at Theatre Royal, Bristol, 12/24/52–1/31/53. p: Bristol Old Vic Co.; d: Denis Carey; ch: Elizabeth West; set/cos: Hutchinson Scott; at pianos: Julian Slade & Harold Britton. Cast: James Cairncross, Dorothy Reynolds, John Neville, Kenneth Cope, Elizabeth West, Pat Heywood, Norman Rossington. Revived, same Bristol venue, 12/24/58–2/21/59. Same producer & dir; set/cos: Peter Rice; at pianos: Julian Slade & Margaret Tudor-Evans. Cast: James Cairncross, Patricia Routledge, Emrys James, John Woodvine, Donald Pickering, Philip Bond, John Rolfe. In 1960 it was adapted from the orig by Bernard Grun, and changed name to *Follow That Girl.* Vaudeville Theatre, London, 3/17/60–9/17/60. 211 perf. p: Linnit & Dunfee; m/md: Julian Slade; l: Dorothy Reynolds & James Cairncross; b: Julian Slade & Dorothy Reynolds; d: Denis Carey; ch: Basil Pattison; set/cos: Hutchinson Scott; cast recording on HMV. Cast: Peter Gilmore, Susan Hampshire, James Cairncross, John Davidson, Patricia Routledge, Grazina Frame, John Baddeley, Philip Guard, Newton Blick, Marion Grimaldi, Bridget Armstrong. "Tra La La," "Where Shall I Find My Love?," "I'm Away," "Follow That Girl," "Solitary Stranger," "Life Must Go On," "Three Victorian Mermaids," "Doh, Ray, Me," "Song and Dance," "Taken for a Ride," "Shopping in Kensington," "Waiting for Our Daughter," "Lovely Meeting You at Last," "Victoria! Victoria!," "One, Two, Three, One," "Evening in London." *Christmas Back in King Street* was produced at Theatre Royal, Bristol, 12/24/72–2/10/73. p: Bristol Old Vic Co.; d: David Phethean; ch: Lynn Brit. Cast: James Cossins, June Barrie. *Follow That Girl* was revived at Theatre Museum, Covent Garden, 4/16/00 & 4/18/00. d/ch: Stewart Nichols; md: Rowland Lee. Cast: Leigh Jones, Rosie Jenkins, Marion Grimaldi

1351. *Follow the Star.* Nativity musical. Chichester Festival Theatre, England, 12/24/74–1/11/75. m: Jim Parker; l/b: Wally K. Daly. Westminster Theatre, London, 12/2/75–2/8/76. 88 perf. d/ch: Wendy Toye; md: Bryan Bennett; cast recording on Philips. Cast: Robert Dorning, Lewis Fiander. "Clap Your Hands," "I've Always Wanted a Baby," "I'm Going to Be a Star," "Follow the Star," "Home," "We Won't Let the Baby Die," "Let Him Come In," "A Baby's Been Born," "We'll Always Love Him," "Clap Your Hands, Be Cheery." Westminster Theatre, 12/2/76–1/29/77. d: Max Howard; ch: Sheila Holt; md: Alan Gout. Cast: Aubrey Morris, Robert Dorning. 1979 TV version. p/d: Wendy Toye. Cast: Robert Dorning & Lewis Fiander

1352. *For Love or Money.* Musical entertainment. Circle Rep, 3/29/77–4/10/77. 9 perf. m/l: Jason McAuliffe & Jay Jeffries; d: Susan Lehman; md: Daniel Glosser. Cast: Kate Kelly, Jason McAuliffe, Kenneth Kimmins, Sharon Madden. "Other Alternatives," "Geography," "That Happy Melody," "Brief Encounter," "Confessional," "Where Have I Been All My Life?," "Snap Decision," "Taboo or Not Taboo," "Counterpoint," "Mama's Cooking," "Living Love"

1353. *Forbidden Broadway.* Comedy musical satire of the current Broadway season. Palsson's Supper Club, 1/15/82–8/30/1987. 2,332 perf. l/conceived by/d: Gerard Alessandrini. Cast: Gerard Alessandrini, Nora Mae Lyng, Bill Carmichael, Fred Barton, Chloe Webb, Jason Alexander, Doug Voet, Patrick Quinn, Davis Gaines, Herndon Lackey, Roxie Lucas, Susan Terry. It started as a 15-minute club spot (classified as Off Off Broadway), but soon grew into a full review with four singers and a pianist. On 5/4/82 it was re-classified as Off Broadway. It became a big deal for performers to see themselves spoofed. The show would revise itself from time to time: 10/27/83 ("1984 version"), 1/29/85 ("1985 version"), 6/11/86 ("1986 version"), 6/26/87 ("1987 version"). The tour opened at the Comedy Store, Los Angeles, on 4/26/83. p: Playkill Productions (Peter Brash & Melissa Burdick). Cast: Gerard Alessandrini, Fred Barton, Bill Carmichael, Dee Hoty, Chloe Webb. The "Second Edition," or *Forbidden Broadway 1988* (on 5/31/89 its name changed to *Forbidden Broadway 1989*) ran at Theatre East, 9/15/88–12/24/89. 534 perf. p: Jonathan Scharer; d: Gerard Alessandrini; ch: Roxie Lucas. Cast: Roxie Lucas, Michael McGrath, David B. McDonald, Toni DiBuono, Philip Fortenberry. There was a Summer Shock Edition in 6/89. London's Fortune Theatre ran *Forbidden Broadway,* 3/2/89–5/20/89. The 3rd NY edition, called *Forbidden Broadway 1990* (and later *Forbidden Broadway 1991*), was a continuation of the previous run at Theatre East, 1/23/90–6/9/91 (prev from 1/16/90; 576 perf). Cast: Suzanne Blakeslee, Jeff Lyons, Marilyn Pasekoff, Bob Rogerson, Philip Fortenberry (these last two replaced by Herndon Lackey & Brad Ellis). This edition targeted the *Miss Saigon* controversy, Mandy Patinkin, *Aspects of Love,* and Topol, among other subjects. *Forbidden Broadway 1991* became *Forbidden Broadway 1991½* and ran at Theatre East, 6/20/91–1/12/92. 237 perf. Cast: Mary Denise Bentley, Suzanne Blakeslee, Brad Ellis, Herndon Lackey, Jeff Lyons. For 56 perf (11/19/91–1/5/92) it was known as *Forbidden Christmas.* Cast: Suzanne Blakeslee, Brad Ellis, Leah Hocking, Herndon Lackey, Michael McGrath. A 10th-anniversary edition, *Forbidden Broadway 1992,* opened 4/6/92, and featured excerpts from previous shows. Cast: Brad Ellis, Leah Hocking, Alix Korey, Michael McGrath, Patrick Quinn. From 12/1/92–12/27/92 it was technically called *Forbidden Broadway Featuring Forbidden Christmas,* and then became *Forbidden Broadway 1993.* 1/12/93–9/19/93. Prev from 1/7/93. Cast: Suzanne Blakeslee, Brad Ellis, Dorothy Kiara, Craig Wells. *Forbidden Broadway 1994* ran at Theatre East, 11/11/93–1/2/94. d: Suzanne Blakeslee. Cast: Suzanne Blakeslee, Brad Ellis, Christine Pedi, Craig Wells. *Forbidden Hollywood* was a musical spoof of Hollywood performers and films, and ran at the Triad Theatre, 3/10/96–9/1/96. 28 prev from 2/16/96. 201 perf. w/created by: Gerard Alessandrini; d/ch: Gerard Alessandrini & Phillip George; cos: Alvin Colt; md: Fred Barton. Cast: Fred Barton, Toni DiBuono, Michael McGrath, Christine Pedi, Lance Roberts. *Forbidden Broadway Strikes Back* ran at the Triad, from 10/16/96. Prev from 9/5/96. Then it ran at the Stardust, 6/26/97–9/20/98. Total of 850 perf. w/ created/d: Gerard Alessandrini; ch: Phillip George; set: Bradley Kaye; cos: Alvin Colt; md: Matthew Ward. Cast: Bryan Batt, David Hibbard, Donna English (*Lori Hammel*), Christine Pedi. *Forbidden Broadway Cleans Up Its Act!* ran at the Stardust, 11/17/98–8/30/00. 754 perf. d: Gerard Alessandrini & Phillip George; ch: Phillip George; cos: Alvin Colt; Cast recording on DRG (who do all the series' recordings). Cast: Bryan Batt, Lori Hammel, Edward Staudenmayer, Kristine Zbornik. *Forbidden Broadway Cleans Up Its Act!* ran at the Jermyn Theatre, London (extended run), then moved to the West End's Albery Theatre, 8/3/99–9/5/99. Prev from 7/29/99. Cast: Christine Pedi. *Forbidden Broadway 2001: A Spoof Odyssey* ran at the Stardust, from 11/18/00 (prev from 10/30/00), then at the Douglas Fairbanks from 5/10/01 (prev from 5/8/01) (no break in the performance schedule). d: Phillip George & Gerard Alessandrini; ch: Phillip George; cos: Alvin Colt; md: Brad Ellis. Cast: Felicia Finley, Danny Gurwin, Tony Nation, Christine Pedi, *Carter Calvert, Robert Gallagher, Joel Carlton.* *Forbidden Broadway Summer Shock!* Douglas Fairbanks, 7/5/04–9/15/04. Parodies of *Wicked, Assassins, Thoroughly Modern Millie, Lion King, Avenue Q,* and *Hairspray.* d: Gerard Alessandrini. Cast: Jennifer Simard, David Benoit, Valerie Fagan, Michael West. *Forbidden Broadway SVU: Special Victims Unit.* Douglas Fairbanks. 12/16/04. Prev from 10/16/04. Spoof of such musicals as *Wicked, Assassins, Avenue Q, Movin' Out, Boy from Oz, Dracula, Bombay Dreams.* *Forbidden Vegas.* Westin Causarina Hotel & Spa, Las Vegas, 1/18/05. Prev from 11/19/04. w/d: Gerard Alessandrini; ch: Gerry McIntyre; cos: Alvin Colt; md: Kim Douglas Steiner. Cast: Michael West, Eric Lee Johnson, Valerie Fagan, Carter Calvert

1354. *Forever Plaid.* Very successful OB revue. The Plaids are a (mythical) group (like the real-life Four Freshmen), who are killed in 1964 in a collision with a busload of convent girls who are on their way to see the Beatles on the *Ed Sullivan Show.* A benevolent god allows them one night on earth to perform the show they were headed to almost 30 years earlier. Steve McGraw's, 5/20/90–6/12/94. Prev from 5/4/90. 1,811 perf. p: Gene Wolsk & Steven Suskin; m/l: various songwriters (several hit songs from several decades); conceived by/d/ch: Stuart Ross; set: Neil Peter Jampolis; md: James Raitt; cast recording on RCA. Cast: Stan Chandler (*Paul Binotto, Ryan Perry*), David Engel (*Gregory Jbara, John Ganun, Tom Cianfichi*), Jason Graae (*Larry Raben, Dale Sandish, Michael Winther, David Benoit, Daniel Eli Friedman*), Guy Stroman (*Drew Geraci, Neil

Nash, Robert Lambert). "Three Coins in the Fountain," "Moments to Remember," "Catch a Falling Star," "Cry," "Love is a Many-Splendored Thing," "Undecided," "Heart and Soul." Gene Wolsk caught it at McGraw's and poured in money to extend the run. George Bush invited the quartet to the White House. 1st tour opened 3/12/91, Washington, DC. p: Gene Wolsk, Laura Stein, Steven Suskin; md: Seth Rudetsky. Cast: Paul Binotto, Gregory Jbara, Michael Winther, Neil Nash. 2nd tour opened 5/12/91, St. Louis. Cast: Dan Brunson, Tom Cianfichi, Buck Dietz, Alan Souza. 3rd tour opened 10/9/91, Boston Park Plaza Hotel. md: Ron Roy. Cast: Dale Sandish (*Robert Lambert*), David Benoit (*Bruce Moore*), Leo Daignault (*Roy Chicas*), Jeff Bannon (*Jeffrey Korn*). Another tour ran during 1992–93 season. md: Steven Freeman. Cast: Stan Chandler, David Engel, Larry Raben, Guy Stroman. A special holiday edition opened at Pasadena Playhouse, 11/10/01. d: Stuart Ross. Cast: Leo Daignault, John-Michael Flate, Steve Gunderson, Michael Winther

1355. *Forever Young: The Music of Bob Dylan.* Bob Dylan songs. American Conservatory Theatre, San Francisco. created/d: Craig Slaight; mus arr: Naomi Sanchez. Part of the Young Conservatory program. Royal National, London, 7/16/03–7/22/03. d: Craig Slaight; md: Krista Wigle

1356. *Fortuna.* Life in a Naples tenement. Maidman, 1/3/62–1/7/62. 5 perf. m/l: Francis Thorne & Arnold Weinstein; based on play *Fortuna con 'F' maiuscula,* by Eduardo De Filippo & Armando Curcio; d: Arnold Weinstein; gm: Ben Bagley. Cast: Gabriel Dell, Jane Connell, Patricia Birch. "Angelica," "Life is a Long Winter's Day," "Million Goes to Million," "Speak in Silence," "Speech"

1357. *The Forty-Nine Years.* Drama with mus. Set in a Victorian house in Arlington, Vermont. Raw Space, 6/19/97–7/13/97. 23 perf. w/composed: Elizabeth Swados; d: Estelle Parsons. Cast: Kathryn Grody, Estelle Parsons

1358. *Found in a Handbag.* Musical of *The Importance of Being Earnest.* Theatre Royal, Margate, England, 11/18/57. Did not go to London. m/l: Allon Bacon. The Paris, Brighton, 1958. Theatre South East, Eastbourne, 2/1/68

1359. *Four Baboons Adoring the Sun.* Play with mus. Set in Sicily. Vivian Beaumont, Broadway, 3/18/92–4/19/92. 26 prev from 2/22/92. 38 perf. p: Lincoln Center; m: Stephen Edwards; w: John Guare; d: Peter Hall; set: Tony Walton; cos: Willa Kim; md: Michael Barrett. Cast: Stockard Channing, James Naughton, Eugene Perry

1360. *4 Guys Named Jose ... and Una Mujer Named Maria!* Musical revue. Anthology of popular Latin songs. 4 Latino men put on a show in midwinter Omaha, to counteract Latino stereotypes. Blue Angel, 9/18/00–3/4/01. Prev from 8/25/00. 191 perf. p: Enrique Iglesias & Dasha Epstein; m/l/conceived by: David Coffman & Dolores Prida; b: Dolores Prida; d: Susana Tubert; ch: Maria Torres; sound: T. Richard Fitzgerald; ms/arr: Oscar Hernandez; Cast recording on DRG. Cast:

Philip Anthony, Lissette Gonzalez, Henry Gainza, Allen Hidalgo, Ricardo Puente

1361. *The Four Musketeers.* Theatre Royal, Drury Lane, London, 12/5/67–1/18/69. 462 perf. p: Bernard Delfont; m: Laurie Johnson; l: Herbert Kretzmer; b: Michael Pertwee; d: Peter Coe; ch: Donald McKayle; set: Sean Kenny; cos: Loudon Sainthill; md: Derek New; cast recording on Philips. Cast: Harry Secombe, Kenneth Connor, Jeremy Lloyd, Elizabeth Larner, Stephanie Voss, John Junkin, Glyn Owen, Aubrey Woods. "A Little Bit of Glory," "Think Big," "What Love Can Do," "There's a New Face in the Old Town," "Got a Lot of Love to Give," "If You Are Looking for a Man," "Masquerade," "Give Me a Man's Life," "Baden-Baden," "Strike While the Iron is Hot," "I Was Only Doing it for You," "Cherchez la Femme," "Nobody's Changing Places with Me," "If You Are Looking for a Girl," "There Comes a Time"

1362. *4 Steps to Heaven.* Musical celebration of 4 great rock stars. Their songs (title inspired by Eddie Cochran's "Three Steps to Heaven"). Piccadilly, London, 8/2/99–9/25/99. Prev from 7/27/99. Cast: Reuben Gershon (Buddy Holly), Peter Howarth (Roy Orbison), Rebel Dean (Elvis), Kloud White (Eddie Cochran)

1363. *Four Thousand Brass Halfpennies.* Mermaid, London, 7/8/65. Prev from 7/5/65. In rep. m: Kenny Graham; l: Gerald Frow; b: Bernard Miles; from John Dryden's *Amphitryon*; d: Denys Palmer; md: Denny Wright. Cast: Denise Coffey, James Bolam, Freddie Jones, Rosamund Burne, Jennifer Clulow, Timothy Bateman, Sally Miles

1364. *Four to the Bar.* After-dinner entertainment. Arts Theatre Club, London, 12/14/61; Criterion, London, 2/24/62. Total of 144 perf. p: Charles Ross & Rick Rydon; m/l: various; b: Alan Bleasdale; d: Charles Ross; cast recording on Philips. Cast: Ian Wallace, Rose Hill, Peter Reeves, Bryan Blackburn. "Uproarious Devon," "Strike," "Li-chee Fair"

1365. *1491.* A "romantic speculation" about Christopher Columbus. Also called *Meredith Willson's 1491.* Opened 9/2/69, Dorothy Chandler Pavilion, L.A. Closed 12/13/69, Curran, San Francisco. p: Edwin Lester (for Civic Light Opera); based on idea by Ed Ainsworth; m/l: Meredith Willson; b: Meredith Willson & Richard Morris; d: Richard Morris; ch: Danny Daniels. Cast: John Cullum, Jean Fenn, Chita Rivera, Gino Conforti, Bruce Gordon, Joseph Mell, Kathryn Hays, Steve Arlen. "Why Not?"

1366. *Fourth Avenue North.* Revue. Madison Avenue Playhouse, 9/27/61–9/28/61. 2 perf. m/l: Bart Howard & Murray Grand, etc; d: Michael Batterberry. Cast: Linda Lavin, Alice Nunn, Gerrianne Raphael, Clint Anderson. "So Long as He Loves You"

1367. *Fourtune.* About a young singing group. Actors Playhouse, 4/27/80–11/23/80. 241 perf. m: Ronald Melrose; l/b: Bill Russell; d: Ron Troutman; ch: Troy Garza; asst ch: Cynthia Onrubia; set: Harry Silverglat; md: Janet Hood. Cast: Ken Arthur, Gail Hebert, Barbara Richardson, Justin Ross. "Rich and Famous," "Women in Love," "Fantasy"/"Funky

Love," "No One Ever Told Me Love Would Be So Hard," "I'd Rather Be a Fairy than a Troll," "Complications," "On the Road," "What Do I Do Now?," "Making It," "I'll Try it Your Way," "Fortune"

1368. *Foxy.* Palace, Watford, England, 4/28/77–5/21/77. Unrelated to Broadway show. m/l: Tony Sharpe & Jill Racy; b: Roger Deeley. Cast: Foxy: Christian Roberts

1369. *Francis.* In 12th-century Umbria St. Francis of Assisi, on his deathbed, looks back on his life. St. Peter's Church, 12/22/81–1/24/82. 30 perf. m: Steve Jankowski; l: Kenny Morris; b: Joseph Leonardo; d: Frank Martin; set: Neil Bierbower; md: Larry Esposito; cm: George Elmer. Cast: John Dossett, KC Wilson, Lloyd Battista, Tanny McDonald, Donna Murphy, Kenny Morris, Cris Groenendaal, Tom Rolfing. "Miracle Town," "Legend of Old Rufino," "Legend of King Arthur," "I'm Ready Now!," "The Fire in My Heart," "Ballet San Damiano," "For the Good of Brotherhood," "New Madness," "Bidding the World Farewell," "Oh, Brother," "All the Time in the World," "Walking All the Way to Rome," "Two Keys," "Road to Paradise," "Francis," "Praises to the Sun" (Canticle of Our Brother Son)

1370. *Frank Gagliano's City Scene.* Play with mus. Fortune, 3/10/69–3/23/69. 16 perf. m: Mildred Kayden; l/w: Frank Gagliano; d: Neil Israel. 2 one-act plays strung together: *City Scene I: Paradise Gardens East* was set in an apartment on NY's Upper East Side. "Harmony," "Beat of the City," "I'll Bet You're a Cat Girl," "Gussy and the Beautiful People," "Look at My Sister," "Black and Blue Plumps," "That's Right, Mr. Syph," "The Incinerator Hour." *City Scene II: Conerico Was Here to Stay* was straight play previously produced 3/3/65, at the Cherry Lane. Set on NYC subway platform. Cast for both: Terry Kiser, Raul Julia, Lenny Baker, Dominic Chianese, Lynn Milgrim, Fran Stevens, M.K. Douglas

1371. *Frankie.* Set now, in NYC & the Catskills. York Theatre Co., 10/6/89–10/29/89. 24 perf. m/l: Joseph Turrin & Gloria Nissenson; b: George Abbott; based on Mary Shelley's *Frankenstein*; d: George Abbott & Donald Saddler; set: James Morgan; cos: Beba Shamash; md: Arthur M. Greene. Cast: Gil Rogers, Ellia English, Casper Roos, Colleen Fitzpatrick, Mark Zimmerman, Kim Moore, Richard White, Elizabeth Walsh, Howard Pinhasik, Ron Wisniski

1372. *Free as Air.* Set on tiny & unknown Channel Island of Terhou. Grand, Leeds, England, 4/8/57; toured; Savoy, London, 6/6/57–6/7/58. 417 perf. p: Linnit & Dunfee; m: Julian Slade; l/b: Julian Slade & Dorothy Reynolds; d: Denis Carey; ch: Mark Stuart; set: Patrick Robertson; md: Philip Martell; cast recording on Oriole. Cast: Gillian Lewis, John Trevor, Dorothy Reynolds, Michael Aldridge, Patricia Bredin (*Bunty Turner*), Joyce Carpenter (*Anna Dawson*), Vincent Charles, Josephine Tewson, Gerald Harper, Howard Goorney, Len Rossiter. "Many Ways to Skin a Cat," "I'm up Early," "Let the Grass Grow," "Rollin' in Gold," "Money isn't Everything," "Nothing But Sea and Sky," "The Boat's In," "Larceny and Love,"

"Ebenezer McAfee III," "A Man from the Mainland," "Talk to Me, Baby," "Free as Air," "This is My Night to Howl," "Her Mummy Doesn't Like Me Anymore," "Bon Vivant," "Girl from London," "I'd Like to Be Like You," "It's Easy When You Know How," "Testudo," "Run, Run, Run, Cinderella," "I've Got My Feet on the Ground," "I'm Way Ahead of the Game," "A Case of Rape," "Holiday Island," "In Loving Memory," "Geraldine," "We're Holding Hands," "Terhou"

1373. *Free to Be You and Me.* OB musical revue. 6/13/02–6/30/02. Based on cult album of same name, with songs by Marlo Thomas, Peter Stone, Herb Gardner, Carl Reiner, Carol Hall, Sheldon Harnick, Shel Silverstein; d: Douglas Carter Beane; md: Sam Davis. Cast: Robert Ari, Debbie Gravitte, Daphne Rubin-Vega, Keith Nobbs

1374. *Freefall.* A Rod Warren revue. Upstairs at the Downstairs, 3/20/69. d: Ronny Graham; ch: Bruce Becker; md: Jerry Goldberg. Cast: Bud Cort (*James Catusi*), Warren Burton, Patti Deutsch, Judy Engles, Brandon Maggart

1375. *French Without Tears.* London, 1960. m/l: Robert Stolz & Paul Dehn; based on Terence Rattigan's play. Cast: Donald Sinden (his only book musical)

1376. *Frere Jacques.* Young man returns to Brooklyn relatives after being raised by Tibetan monks. Theatre 802, 6/6/68–6/16/68. 13 perf. w: Gerard Singer; d: Richard Balin; md: Harry Goodman. Cast: David Tabor, Nina Dova, Pamela Hall, Carolyn Dahl. "I Remember," "A Kiss is a Poem," "Keep the Cool," "Smile and Be Gracious," "Frere Jacques Rock," "You Can't Judge the World," "Love of a Woman," "Julie," "Heffley & Browne Secretarial School"

1377. *Frimbo.* Revue of railroad lore staged in train platform area of Grand Central Station. Grand Central Terminal Tracks 39–42, 11/9/80. 23 prev. 1 perf. p/conceived/adapted/d: John L. Haber; m/md: Howard Harris; l: Jim Wann; based on book *All Aboard with E.M. Frimbo*, by Rogers E.M. Whitaker & Anthony Hiss; set: Karl Eigsti & Fred Buchholz; cos: Patricia McGourty. Cast: Richard B. Shull, Deborah May, Larry Riley, Pattie Darcy, Cass Morgan, Pauletta Pearson. "The Frimbo Special," "Ballad of Frimbo," "The Train," "Going Home," "Lady by Choice," "I Hate Trains," "Gone Everywhere but Home," "Siberia," "Home to Steam," "Names of the Trains"

1378. *From Brooks with Love.* Harold Clurman, 3/30/83–4/2/83. 4 perf. m: George Koch & Russ Taylor; l/b: Wayne Sheridan; d: William Michael Maher. Cast: Richard Sabellico. "The Main Floor," "Shopping," "Love is a Feeling," "Customer's Nightmare," "Showbiz," "Eggs," "It's Nice," "A New Kind of Husband," "Let's Go," "Will They Remember," "Move Over, You Guys"

1379. *From Israel with Love.* Hebrew musical revue. Palace, Broadway, 10/2/72–10/8/72. 2 prev. 8 perf. d: Avi David. "Israel, Israel," "From the South Good Will Come," "Call for Freedom," "Three Legs," "We Take Whatever Comes," "Jerusalem of Gold," "Natasha," "A Beach Song," "The Parachutist,"

"My Dear Son," "Havanagila," "I Am Dying," "A Song of Peace." Previously produced in Israel

1380. *From My Hometown.* 3 strangers arrive in NYC from Detroit, Memphis & Philadelphia, with one goal in mind — to sing at famous Apollo Theatre. Milwaukee Rep, 1998. Over 30 R & B classics, plus 6 orig songs by Lee Summers, Ty Stephens, Will Barow; b: Lee Summers, Ty Stephens, Herbert Rawlings Jr.; conceived by: Lee Summers. Kirk (OB), 6/19/03–7/12/03. Prev from 6/10/03. p: AMAS; d: Kevin Ramsey; ch: Kevin Ramsey & Leslie Dockery; set: Matthew Myhrums; cos: Deborah A. Cheretun; md/voc arr: Jo Lynn Burks. Cast: Kevin R. Free, Andre Garner, Rodney Hicks. Gramercy, 7/22/04–8/21/04. 12 prev from 7/12/04. 36 perf. p: Lee Summers, in assoc with Leonard Soloway & Steven M. Levy; Same cast & crew

1381. *From the Hip: Siamese Twin Variations.* Inspired by story of Hilton Sisters. HERE, 10/16/97–11/15/97. 3 prev. 11 perf. p: Burning Boy Theatre Co. & Independent Art HERE; m/l: Maggie Moore; b/d: Blair Fell. Cast: Maggie Moore: Sissy Sheraton; Amy Ziff: Sassy Sheraton. Opened same day *Side Show* opened on Broadway

1382. *From the Second City.* Revue with mus. 1st of several Second City prods OB (they were normally out of Chicago, and improvised, whereas this one was fully scripted). Royale, Broadway, 9/26/61–12/9/61. 1 prev on 9/25/61. 87 perf. p: Max Liebman, Paul Sills, Bernard Sahlins, Howard Alk; m: William Mathieu; d: Paul Sills; set/light: Frederick Fox. Cast: Alan Arkin, Barbara Harris (nominated for a Tony), Howard Alk, Severn Darden (nominated for a Tony), Paul Sand, Mina Kolb, Gene Troobnick, Andrew Duncan. "Second City Symphony," "Tempo," "I Got Blues," "Minstrel Show." Eastside Playhouse, 10/14/69–11/9/69. 31 perf. p: Bernard Sahlins; m/md: Fred Kaz; lyr for "Flower Song:" Sandy Holt; d: David Lynn. Cast: J.J. Barry, Pamela Hoffman, Ira Miller

1383. *From This Day Forward.* Plot-driven revue using over 60 Stephen Schwartz songs. Don't Tell Mama, 3/02; ran again in 7/02 (10 weeks total). Created by Robert Jay Cronin, with the permission & supervision of Stephen Schwartz. p: Ergo Theatre Co. Expanded & ran again, 9/20/02–10/13/02. md: Mark Hartman

1384. *Fun City.* Musical revue. Program built around Lynne Carter's female impersonations. Jan Hus, 3/6/68–3/31/68. 31 perf. p: Jack Irving; w/d: David Rogers. Cast: Joan Porter (*Cari Stevens*), Mel Edwards, Dee Robinson, Ted Tingling. "Fun City"

1385. *Funny Face.* Alvin, Broadway, 11/22/27–6/23/28. 250 perf. p: Alex A. Aarons & Vinton Freedley; m: George Gershwin; l: Ira Gershwin; b: Fred Thompson & Paul Gerard Smith; d: Edgar MacGregor; md: Alfred Newman. Cast: Adele Astaire, Fred Astaire, William Kent, Victor Moore. "Birthday Party," "Once," "Funny Face," "High Hat," "s'Wonderful," "Let's Kiss and Make Up," "In the Swim," "She Loves and He Loves," "Tell the

Doc," "What Am I Gonna Do?," "The Babbit and the Bromide." Ford's, Washington, DC, 1/2/74. 23 perf. Revised version. adapted/d: Neal Du Brock; set/light: David F. Segal. Cast: Susan Watson, Tony Tanner, Ronald Young, Pat Lysinger

1386. *Funny Feet.* Revue. Spoof of pro dancing. Lamb's, 4/21/87–7/19/87. 12 prev from 4/11/87. 103 perf. set/cos: Lindsay W. Davis. Cast: Bob Bowyer (also conceived/d/ch), Irene Cho, Sandra Chinn. "Baby Bobby's Backyard," "Les Jazz Chics" "Molotov Brothers," "The Buttercups," "Smile," "Big Ballet in the Sky"

1387. *Funzapoppin'.* Olsen & Johnson vaudeville revue, similar to *Laffin' Room Only*, *Sons O' Fun*, and *Hellzapoppin'.* Madison Square Garden, 6/30/49–7/31/49. 37 perf. p: Arthur M. Wirtz; m/l: Olsen & Johnson, Chuck Gould, Perry Martin; conceived by: Olsen & Johnson, Arthur M. Wirtz; d: Olsen & Johnson; ch: Catherine & Carl Littlefield; md: Jack Pfeiffer; mus arr: Paul Van Loan. Cast: Ole Olsen & Chic Johnson, Marty May, Nirska, Gloria Gilbert, Bill Hayes, the Berry Brothers, June Johnson (Chic's daughter), J.C. Olsen (Chic's son). "Oh, What a Night for a Party," "Jungle Rhythm," "I'd Like to Be a Baby Sitter for a Baby Like You," "It's a Great Wide Wonderful World," "Swing on the Corner," "Six-Gun Joe from Cicero," "How Down," "Funzapoppin'"

1388. *The Gambler.* Comedy Theatre, London, 7/3/86. Cast: Peter Brewis, Bob Goody, Mel Smith (all also m/l/b), Paul Brown, Philip Davis. "Get Your Life," "Ten Thousand Quid," "I've Sailed Through Hell," "Shaking in the Shadows"

1389. *The Game Is Up.* Cabaret revue. Upstairs at the Downstairs, 9/29/64–3/6/65. 260 perf. p/conceived by: Rod Warren; m/l/sk mostly by Rod Warren; d: Jonathan Lucas. Cast: Richard Blair, R.G. Brown, Virgil Curry, Judy Knaiz, Marian Mercer, Carol Morley. "The Game is Up," "Sunday Television," "Freedom," "Beth," "What's in a Name?," "76 Foolish Things," "Tinsel," "Discotheque," "Hip Hooray," "Tokyo, Mon Amour," "Forgotten Words," "Loves Labours Lost," "I'm the Girl," "The Doll Song," "Adam Clayton Powell." Replaced by new edition, 3/11/65. 132 perf. And by 3rd edition, 6/15/65–10/16/65. New musical numbers for 3rd edition included: "Camp," "Counterpoint," "I Like the Job," "Lady Bird." New cast members were Ruth Buzzi & Linda Lavin

1390. *The Gates of Paradise.* Musical play. Set in Paradise Automat. Neill Gallery, 11/25/77–12/18/77. 12 perf. p: Fantasy Factory; m/l/d: Bill Vitale; b: Ed Kuczewski; ch: Jay Fox. Cast: Lorraine Davidson, Ed Kuczewski. "Falling Star," "Dying Is," "Bad Trip," "Seamy Side of Heaven," "Passing Through Exotic Places"

1391. *Gavin and the Monster.* Westminster Theatre, London, 11/17/81–1/23/82. 78 perf. m: Kathleen Johnson; l/b: Hugh Steadman Williams; d: Denise Coffey; ch: Pauline Grant; md: Paul Abrahams. Cast: Matthew Ryan, Thick Wilson, Joan Heal, Elaine White, Ann-Marie Gwatkin, Frances Ruffelle

1392. *Gay Company*. A Try-Sexual Musical revue. Little Hippodrome, 10/29/74–2/23/75. m/l: Fred Silver; d: Sue Lawless. Cast: Candice Earley, Rick Gardner, Robert Tananis, Cola Pinto, Gordon Ramsey. "Beginners' Guide to Cruising," "Handsome Stranger," "True Confession," "I Met My Love," "Phantom of the Opera," "Two Strangers," "Freddy Liked to Fugue." Re-ran as *In Gay Company*, at Upstairs at Jimmy's, 4/4/75–4/13/75. Prev from 3/28/75. 8 perf. Partially new score & some old cast (Robert Tananis, Rick Gardner, Gordon Ramsey) and some new: Ann Hodapp, Bob Gorman.

1393. *Gay Divorce*. Mimi goes to England to arrange plot to begin divorce from boring husband. Ethel Barrymore, Broadway (1st musical to play this theatre). Opened 11/29/32. Moved to the Shubert, 1/16/33, and closed there 7/1/33. Total of 248 perf. m/l: Cole Porter; b: Dwight Taylor; based on the unproduced play *The Adorable Adventure*, by J. Hartley Manners; d: Howard Lindsay; set: Jo Mielziner; md: Gene Salzer; orch: Hans Spialek & Russell Bennett. Cast: Fred Astaire (the only stage prod Fred performed in without sister Adele, and his last time on Broadway), Claire Luce, Luella Geer, Erik Rhodes, Eric Blore. "After You, Who?," "Why Marry Them?," "Salt Air," "I Still Love the Red, White and Blue," "Night and Day," "How's Your Romance?," "What Will Become of Our England?," "I've Got You on My Mind," "Mister and Missus Fitch," "You're in Love." Filmed in 1934, as *The Gay Divorcee*, with Fred Astaire & Ginger Rogers. Cherry Lane, 4/3/60–4/24/60. 25 perf. p: Noel Behn & New Princess Co.; conceived by/d: Gus Schirmer Jr.; ch: Joan Mann; set: Helen Pond & Herbert Senn. Cast: Bea Arthur, Sigyn, Mary Jane Doerr, Arny Freeman, Frank Aletter, Emory Bass. Equity Library, 3/9/78–3/26/78. 20 perf. d: Robert Brink; ch: Helen Butleroff. Cast: Mike Brennan, Jeri Kansas, Richard Sabellico, Bob Ari, Sonja Stuart. Kaufman, 2/24/87–3/29/87. 39 perf. adapted: Robert Brittan; d: Robert Brink; ch: Helen Butleroff; set: James Morgan; md: David Schaefer. Cast: Ray DeMattis, Debra Dickinson, Richard Lupino, Joaquin Romaguera, Karen Ziemba. Carnegie Hall, 6/9/93–6/16/93. 6 perf in concert. d: John McGlinn. Cast: Rebecca Luker, John Driver, Robert Westenberg, Maureen Brennan, Judy Kaye, Paige Price. Several songs were also used in *The New Yorkers* (see this appendix)

1394. *Gay's the Word*. Series of set pieces with dialogue & sub-plot. Ivor Novello's last musical (he died while performing in his own *King's Rhapsody*, 3/5/51). Palace, Manchester, England, 10/17/50 (3 weeks); toured; Saville, London, 2/16/51–5/3/52. 504 perf. p: Tom Arnold; m/b: Ivor Novello; l: Alan Melville; conceived by/d: Jack Hulbert; ch: Irving Davies & Eunice Crowther; set: Edward Delaney; cos: Berkeley Sutcliffe; md: Robert Probst. Cast: Cicely Courtneidge (this musical was written for her by Mr. Novello; she played an old actress who opens a theatre school by the seaside; she was replaced by *Doris Hare*), Lizbeth Webb, Thorley Walters (*Brian Reece*), Carl

Jaffe, June Laverick, Elizabeth Seal. "Ruritania," "Guards of the Parade," "Bees are Buzzin'," "An Englishman in Love," "Everything Reminds Me of You," "Father Thames," "Finder, Please Return," "Gaiety Glad," "If Only He'd Looked My Way," "It's Bound to Be Right on the Night," "Matter of Minutes," "On Such a Night as This," "Vitality," "Sweet Thames"

1395. *Genesis: Music and Miracles for a New Age*. Based on medieval mystery plays. LuEsther Hall, 1/17/89–1/22/89. 50 prev from 11/29/88. 8 perf. m/md: Michael Ward; l/b: A.J. Antoon & Robert Montgomery; d: A.J. Antoon; ch: Lynne Taylor-Corbett; set/cos: John Conklin. Cast: Stephen Bogardus, Mindy Cooper, Braden Danner, Mary Munger, Tina Paul, Russ Thacker, Christine Toy

1396. *Gentlemen, Be Seated!* A musical entertainment Re-telling of events that led up to Civil War, in the form of minstrel show. City Center, 10/10/63–11/10/63. 3 perf in rep. p: NYC Opera; m: Jerome Moross; l: Edward Eager; b: Jerome Moross & Edward Eager; d: Robert Turoff; ch: Paul Draper; set: William Pitkin; light: Jules Fisher. Cast: Dick Shawn, Alice Ghostley, Avon Long, Charles Atkins, Carol Brice, Richard Krause, Paul Draper. "Grand March," "In the Sunny Old South," "Freedom Train," "Waltzing in the Shadow," "Fare You Well," "Why Ain't We Got a Dome?," "Tap Dance Drill," "O, The Picnic in Manassas," "Mocking Bird," "Shiloh," "The Ballad of Belle Boyd," "I Spy," "It's the Witching Hour By the Old Water Tower," "I'm a Pinkerton Man," "Belle Boyd, Where Have You Been?," "'mancipation," "Pardon, Ma'am," "Look Who I Am, Surprise, Surprise!," "This isn't a Gentleman's War Anymore," "The Contraband Ball," "Gentlemen, Be Seated," "It's Quiet on the Potomac Tonight," "The Ballad of Stonewall Jackson," "I'm Matthew P. Brady, the Cameraman," "Miss Dorothea Dix," "I Can't Remember," "From Atlanta to the Sea," "What Has Become of Beauty?," "Have You Seen Him, Did He Pass This Way?," "This Was the War, What Did it Do for Me and You?"

1397. *Gentlemen Prefer Anything*. Theatre Royal, Stratford East, London, 1/20/74–3/2/74. 34 perf. p: Theatre Workshop; m/md: Ian Armit; songs: Tony Macaulay; b/d: Ken Hill. Cast: James Booth, Jenny Logan, Roy Starr, Myvanwy Jenn, Diane Langton

1398. *George Gershwin Alone*. One-man play with mus. Helen Hayes, Broadway, 4/30/01–7/24/01. 16 prev from 4/17/01. 96 perf. m: George Gershwin; l: Ira Gershwin; w/ starred: Hershey Felder; d: Joel Zwick; set: Yael Pardess. Mostly negative reviews. Developed at Tiffany Theatre, L.A.

1399. *Gertrude Stein's First Reader*. Revue. 4 performers playing children are led in games, recitations & songs by a pianist (Ann Sternberg). Astor Place, 12/15/69–1/18/70. 40 perf. m: Ann Sternberg; l: Gertrude Stein; conceived by/d: Herbert Machiz; based on Miss Stein's writings. Cast: Joy Garrett, Sandra Thornton, Frank Giordano, Michael Anthony. "Sunshine," "Wild Flowers," "A Dog," "Writing Lesson," "Johnny and Jimmy," "Blackberry

Vine," "Big Bird," "Three Sisters Who Are Not Sisters," "Be Very Careful," "New World," "Jenny," "How They Do Do," "Soldier," "Baby Benjamin," "In a Garden"

1400. *Get on Board — The Jazz Train*. Revue. Opened for pre–Broadway tryouts 9/10/62, Her Majesty's, Montreal. Closed 9/22/62, Royal Alexandra, Toronto. Never made Broadway. p: Manning Gurian; orig m: J.C. Johnson; d: Mervyn Nelson; ch: Herbert Harper. Cast: Gilbert Adkins, Rosalie Maxwell, Danny Barker, Thelma Oliver, Rawn Spearman, Albert Popwell, Rosalind Cash, Barbara Teer

1401. *Get Thee to Canterbury*. A musical "medieval happenynge." Sheridan Square Playhouse, 1/25/69–2/9/69. 20 perf. m/l: Paul Hoffert & David Secter; freely adapted by Jan Steen & David Secter from Chaucer's *Canterbury Tales*; d: Jan Steen. Cast: Travis Hudson, Will B. Able, Shev Rodgers, Marc Jordan. "Get Thee to Canterbury," "The Journey," "Take a Pick," "Death Beware," "Buy My Pardons," "Canter Banter," "Ballad of Sir Topaz," "A Simple Wife," "Shadows," "Where Are the Blossoms?," "Everybody Gets it in the End." Previously produced, in part, as a straight play, in Canada

1402. *Get Used to It*. Musical revue on gay life. Courtyard Playhouse, 3/4/92–5/31/92. 78 perf. w/d: Tom Wilson Weinberg; ch: Jack Matter. Cast: Sebastian Herald, John O'Brien, Todd Whitley, Wayne Barker (piano)

1403. *Ghosts: Live from Galilee*. Opera about the Scottsboro Boys trail in Georgia in 1930s. La Mama, 2/11/93–2/28/93. 16 perf. m: Genji Ito; libretto: Edgar Nkosi White; d: George Ferencz. Cast: Jonathan Goldstein, Lynnard Edwin Williams, Phyllis Nannyoung

1404. *Gift of the Magi*. Set in Greenwich Village in December 1906. Stony broke husband & wife sacrifice most cherished possessions to give each other Christmas present. Players, 12/1/75–1/4/76. 16 prev. 48 perf. m/l/b: Ronnie Britton; based on O. Henry's short story; d: M.T. Knoblauh. Cast: Mary Saunders, William Brockmeier, Paige O'Hara, Bill March. "Magi Waltz," "There You Go Again," "The Gift," "Della's Desire," "Mr. James Dillingham Young," "Day After Day," "Kids Are Out," "Sullivan Street Flat," "Beautiful Children," "You'd Better Tell Her!," "Washington Square," "Till Tomorrow," "Quiet Morning," "Brave You," "A Penny Saved," "I've Got Something Better," "Pretty Lady," "He Did It, She Did It," "Make Him Think I'm Still Pretty"

1405. *The Gift of Winter*. Offers comic explanation of the history of snow. TADA, 12/14/90–12/31/90. 4 prev. 30 perf. m/l: David Evans & Faye Greenberg; b: Michael Slade; based on book by John Leach & Jean Rankin; d: James Learned. Cast: Colin Fisher, Sean Nelson, and 22 other performers aged 8–16

1406. *Gifts of the Magi*. Set in NYC, 12/23/1905–12/25/1905. Lamb's Club Little Theatre, 1984 (from then on every Christmas it has been a musical holiday tradition at Lamb's). m/l: Randy Courts & Mark St. Germain; based on O. Henry stories. "Star of the

Night," "Gifts of the Magi," "Jim and Della," "Christmas to Blame," "How Much to Buy My Dream?," "The Restaurant," "Once More," "Bum Luck," "Greed," "Pockets," "Same Girl," "Gift of Christmas." Directors have included: Carolyn Rossi Copeland, Stephen A. Zorthian, Sonya Baehr, Scott Harris, Christopher Catt; ch have included: Piper Pickrell, Ricarda O'Conner, Janet Watson, Terpsie Toon; musical directors have included: Steven M. Alper, Randy Courts, Lynn Crigler. Players have included: Cissy Rebich, Rebecca Renfroe, Scott Waara, Gabriel Barre, Michael Calkins, Paul Jackel, Gordon Stanley, Lou Williford, Eddie Korbich

1407. The Gilded Cage. The Production Company, 1/9/83–1/30/83. 19 perf. conceived/d: James Milton; ch: Marcia Milgrom Dodge; md: Polly Pen. Cast: Marianne Tatum, Tom McKinney, Robert Stillman, Polly Pen. "There's a Broken Heart for Every Light on Broadway," "Always Do as People Say You Should," "You Naughty Man," "Little Birdies Learning How to Fly," "Put on Your Tatta, Little Girlie," "Bird in a Gilded Cage," "Take Back Your Gold," "A Good Cigar is a Smoke," "Nobody," "She Was One of the Early Birds," "Je Ne Sais Pa Pa," "She is More to Be Pitied than Censured," "Sawing a Woman in Half," "In the Baggage Car Ahead," "Waitin' for the Evenin' Mail," "Kiss a Lonely Wife," "Absinthe Frappe." See also *Ragtime*, in the main part of this book

1408. The Gingerbread Man. Towngate Theatre, Basildon, England, 12/13/76–1/8/77. w: David Wood; d: Jonathan Lynn; ch: Ronnie Stevens; md: Peter Pontzen. Cast: Herr von Cuckoo: Ronnie Stevens; Salt: Tim Barker; Pepper: Pearly Gates; Gingerbread Man: Jack Chissick; Old Bag: Veronica Clifford; Sleek, the mouse: Keith Varnier. Old Vic, London, 12/13/77–1/7/78. Cameron Mackintosh & David Wood prod this & all subsequent prods. Same basic crew as for 1976 prod. Cast: Ronnie Stevens, Tim Barker, Cheryl Branker, Andrew Secombe, Vivienne Martin, Keith Varnier. Old Vic, from 12/17/78. Same basic crew again, except ch: Neil Fitzwilliam. Cast: Larry Dann, Tim Barker, Cheryl Branker, Neil Fitzwilliam, Judith Bruce, Keith Varnier. Royalty, London, 12/18/79–1/12/80. 38 matinees. ch: Geoffrey Ferris. Cast: Bernard Cribbins, Tim Barker, Pepsi Maycock, Tony Jackson, Jacqueline Clark, Keith Varnier. The Westminster, London, 11/18/80. d: Paddy McIntyre; md: Peter Pontzen. Cast: Ronnie Stevens, Larry Dann, Pepsi Maycock, Tony Jackson, Vivienne Martin, Keith Varnier. The Westminster, 11/22/82–1/15/83. 64 matinees. d: David Wood; ch: Paddy McIntyre. Cast: Clive Dunn, Larry Dann, Joan-Ann Maynard, Tony Jackson, Stephanie Voss, Keith Varnier. The Bloomsbury, London, 12/6/84. d: David Wood; ch: Geoffrey Ferris; md: Lesley Hayes. Cast: Ronnie Stevens, Tim Barker, Joan-Ann Maynard, Peter Duncan, Jacqueline Clark, Keith Varnier

1409. A Girl Called Jo. Opera House, Manchester, England, 11/22/55 (2 weeks); Piccadilly, London, 12/15/55–4/14/56. 141 perf. p:

Linnit & Dunfee; m: John Pritchett & Stanley Meyers; l/b: Peter Myers, Alec Grahame, David Climie; based on Louisa May Alcott's *Little Women;* d: Denis Carey; ch: Michael Charnley; set/cos: Hutchinson Scott; md: Mark Lubbock. Cast: John Brooke: Edward Woodward; Also with: Joan Heal, Marion Grimaldi, Denis Quilley, Noel Dyson, Gwen Nelson, Bessie Love, Peter Dyneley

1410. Girl Crazy. Alvin, Broadway, 10/14/30–6/6/31. 272 perf. p: Alex A. Aarons & Vinton Freedley; m: George Gershwin; l: Ira Gershwin; b: Guy Bolton & Jack McGowan; d: Alexander Leftwich; ch: George Hale; set: Donald Oenslager; md: Earl Busby; orch: Russell Bennett. Cast: Ginger Rogers, Ethel Merman (debut), Willie Howard, Lew Parker. "Bidin' My Time," "The Lonesome Cowboy Won't Be Lonesome Now," "Could You Use Me?," "Bronco Busters," "Barbary Coast," "Embraceable You," "Sam and Delilah," "I Got Rhythm," "Land of the Gay Caballero," "But Not for Me," "Treat Me Rough," "Boy, What Love Has Done to Me," "(When it's) Cactus Time in Arizona." Led to *Crazy for You* (see main part of this book). Equity Library, 3/13/86–4/6/86. 32 perf. d: Stephen Bonnell

1411. Girls, Girls, Girls. Public, 9/9/80–10/4/80. 30 perf. A NY Shakespeare Festival prod. p: Joseph Papp; m/md: Cheryl Hardwick; l/b: Marilyn Suzanne Miller; d: Bob Balaban; ch: Graciela Daniele. Cast: Valri Bromfield, Frances Conroy, Anne De Salvo, Judith Ivey. "The Betty Song," "High School," "Punk," "Lovers," "Credit Card," "Divorce," "Planet of No Thigh Bulge," "Street Lady," "Man/Woman"

Give My Regards to Broadway see # 398, Main Book

1412. Glad to See You. About USO troop entertainment overseas. Opened 11/13/44, Shubert, Philadelphia, for Broadway tryouts, and got bad reviews. Folded 1/6/45, Opera House, Boston. p: David Wolper; m/l: Jule Styne & Sammy Cahn; b: Eddie Davis & Fred Thompson; d: Busby Berkeley; ch: Valerie Bettis; set: Howard Bay. Cast: Jane Withers, Eddie Davis, Gene Barry, Joseph Macaulay, Jayne Manners, June Knight, Sammy White, Olga Lunick. "B, Apostrophe K, Apostrophe Lyn," "I'm Laying Away a Buck," "I Murdered Them in Chicago," "I'll Hate Myself in the Morning," "I Lost My Beat," "Grown-Ups are the Stupidest People," "Ladies Don't Have Fun," "Guess I'll Hang My Tears Out to Dry"

1413. The Globe Revue. Revue. Successor to *The Lyric Revue.* Globe, London, 7/10/52. 234 perf. m/l: Noel Coward, Donald Swann, Paul Dehn, Arthur Macrae, Charles Zwar, Richard Addinsell; d/ch/cos: William Chappell; set: Loudon Sainthill; md: Norman Hackforth. Cast: Graham Payn, Dora Bryan, Joan Heal, Ian Carmichael, Jeremy Hawk, Diana Decker, Myles Eason, Irlin Hall, George Benson. "Give Me the Kingston By-Pass," "(There Are) Bad Times Just Around the Corner"

1414. The Glorious Age. Light look at the Dark Ages. Theatre Four, 5/11/75–5/18/75. 14 perf. m/l: Cy Young; b: Cy Young & Mark

Gordon; d: John-Michael Tebelak; cos: Jennifer von Mayrhauser. Cast: Laurie Faso, Don Scardino, Carol Swarbrick, D'Jamin Bartlett, Susan Willis, Clyde Laurents, Stuart Pankin. "Glorious Age," "The Turn My Life is Taking," "Must Be a Witch in Town," "Future Looks Promising," "Maybe There's a Place," "La La La," "Child of the Shade"

1415. The Glorious Days. Built around flashbacks in the mind of wartime ambulance driver after being stunned by blast in air raid. She was Nell Gwynn, Queen Victoria, and her own mother, Lillian Grey, musical comedy star. Palace, London, 2/28/53. 357 perf. m: Harry Parr Davies; l: Harold Purcell; b: Robert Nesbitt. Cast: Anna Neagle, Peter Graves, Olaf Olsen, James Carney, Patrick Holt, Albert Chevalier, Beryl Marsden, John Williamson

1416. Go Fight City Hall. Yiddish-American. Set 1948–1961 in Brooklyn. Mayfair, 11/2/61–1/14/62. 77 perf. p: Irving Jacobson & Julius Adler; m/l: Murray Rumshinsky & Bella Mysell. Cast: Irving Jacobson, Henrietta Jacobson, Bruce Adler, Fyvush Finkel

1417. Goblin Market. Vineyard, 10/17/85–12/22/85. 58 perf; Circle in the Square Downtown, 4/13/86–6/29/86. Prev from 4/9/86. 95 perf. m: Polly Pen; adapted by: Peggy Harmon & Polly Pen; from Christina Rossetti's poem; d: Andre Ernotte; set: William Barclay. Cast: Terri Klausner (*Sharon Scruggs*), Ann Morrison. "Come Buy, Come Boy," "We Must Not Look," "Mouth So Charmful," "Do You Not Remember Jeanie?," "Sleep, Laura, Sleep," "The Sisters," "Some There Are Who Never Venture," "Mirage," "Passing Away," "Here They Come," "Like a Lilly," "Lizzie, Lizzie, Have You Tasted?," "Two Doves"

1418. God Bless Coney. Set on 7/14/64, on beach at Coney Island. Orpheum, 5/3/72–5/5/72. 13 prev. 3 perf. p: Paul B. Reynolds; w: John Glines; d: Bob Schwartz; md: Robert Rogers. Cast: Bill Hinnant, Ann Hodapp, Marcia Lewis, Liz Sheridan, Johnny La Motta, William Francis. "Subway to Coney," "Seagulls," "Throw Out the Lifeline," "Love Life," "Eight-Horse Parlay," "Man and Wife," "Goodbye Hives," "He Looked at Me," "The Coney Island," "Intermission Rag," "Here We Are," "God Bless All the Misfits," "Music Hall Medley," "Here Comes the Rabbi," "God Bless Coney"

1419. God Bless You, Mr. Rosewater. Foundation president doles out millions in unusual way. Entermedia, 10/14/79–11/25/79. 49 perf. p: Edith Vonnegut; m: Alan Menken; l/b/d: Howard Ashman; add l: Dennis Green; w: Kurt Vonnegut; ch: Mary Kyte; md: David Friedman; cm: Steven Suskin. Cast: Frederick Coffin, Janie Sell, Jonathan Hadary, Anne De Salvo. "The Rosewater Foundation," "Look Who's Here," "Since You Came to This Town," "A Poem by William Blake," "I, Eliot Rosewater." Previously produced at WPA. Concert reading in NY, 3/7/03. Cast: Carolee Carmello, Jim Walton, David Pittu, Robin Skye. York Theatre Co., NY, 4/1/05–4/3/05

1420. God Is a (Guess What?). Morality play with mus. Mark's Playhouse, 12/17/68–1/12/69. 32 perf. p: Negro Ensemble Co.; m:

Coleridge-Taylor Perkinson; w: Ray McIver; d: Michael A. Schultz. Cast: Julius W. Harris, Clarice Taylor, Hattie Winston, Rosalind Cash, Esther Rolle. "God Will Take Care," "Sit Down Song"

God's Trombones *see* # 2659, this appendix
Godsong *see* # 2659, this appendix

1421. Gogo Loves You. The training of a cocotte. Theatre De Lys, 10/9/64–10/10/64. 2 perf. m/l: Claude Leveillee & Gladys Shelley; b: Anita Loos; based on French comedy *L'ecole des cocottes*; d: Fred Weintraub; light: Jules Fisher. Cast: Judy Henske, Arnold Soboloff, Dorothy Greener. "Parnasse," "Prima Donna," "Bazoom," "He Can, I Can," "Go-Go," "There is No Difference," "Keep in Touch," "My Uncle's Mistress," "Happy Love Affair," "Tell Me the Story of Your Life," "Woman Makes the Man," "Life is Lovely," "College of L'Amour," "Savoir Faire," "Quelle Heure est-il?"

1422. The Golden Age. An entertainment in words & music of the Elizabethan Age, showing what life was like then. Lyceum, Broadway, 11/18/63–11/23/63. 7 perf. dev: Richard Johnson; d: Douglas Campbell. Cast: Douglas Campbell, Nancy Wickwire, Betty Wilson, Douglas Rain, Lester Rawlins, James Stover, Gordon Myers

1423. Golden Bat. Japanese rock celebration. Sheridan Square Playhouse, 7/21/70–11/29/70. 152 perf. p: Kermit Bloomgarden & Arthur Cantor; m/md: Itsuro Shimoda; l/d: Yutaka Higashi. The Tokyo Kid Brothers & all-Japanese cast & crew. "America, America," "Home," "I Like Girls," "Western Movies," "North-Northwest," "American Rock," "Rock, Crane's Town," "I Like," "Love, Love, Love." Came from Tokyo; in USA first played at Cafe La Mama

1424. Golden City. Set in South African goldrush of 1880s. Adelphi, London, 6/15/50–10/14/50. 140 perf. p: Stephen Mitchell; w: John Tore; d: Michael Benthall; ch: Robert Helpmann; set: Audrey Cruddas; md: Philip Green. Cast: Edmund Purdom, Eleanor Summerfield, Norman Lawrence, Muriel Brunskill, Leila Roth, Moyra Fraser, Anne Rogers. "Golden City"

1425. The Golden Land. Yiddish. Jewish immigrant songwriter arrives in 1908 & makes good (somewhat based on Irving Berlin). Second Avenue, 10/17/43. p: Judah Bleich; m: Al Olshanetsky; l: Jacob Jacobs; b: Julie Berns. Cast: Leo Fuchs, Dinah Halpern, Wolf Barzell

1426. The Golden Land. English-Yiddish. Norman Thomas, 10/27/84–3/31/85. 70 perf. p: Art D'Lugoff & Moishe Rosenfeld; created by: Zalmen Mlotek & Moishe Rosenfeld; d: Howard Rossen; light: Victor En Yu Tan; md: Zalmen Mlotek. Cast: Bruce Adler (*Bernardo Hiller*), Betty Silberman, Joanne Borts, Phyllis Berk, Avi Hoffman. "Ellis Island," "Give Me Your Tired, Your Poor," "Fifty Fifty," "Wheels Turn Quickly," "Working Women," "Rebel Girl," "Ballad of the Triangle Fire," "Elegy on the Triangle Fire Victims," "Bread and Roses," "Long Live Columbus," "Three Cheers for Yankee Doodle," "Yankee Doodle Rides Uptown," "Flag of Freedom," "She'll Be Coming

from the Mountains," "Fun Downtown-Uptown," "I Am a Boarder at My Wife's House," "When Rosie Lived on Essex Street," "God and His Judgment Are Right," "Where Shall We Find the Witnesses?," "The Wedding," "I Bring You Greetings from the Trenches," "Steam," "Joe and Paul's," "Levine and His Flying Machine," "How Do I Make a Living?," "Brother Can You Spare a Dime?," "As Long as You Are Healthy," "Everything is Spoiled," "Buy Cigarettes," "Rumania," "Yiddle with His Fiddle," "Dear Brothers Help," "The Jewish People Live." Second Avenue, 11/11/85–7/13/86. 18 prev. 277 perf. p: Sherwin M. Goldman, Moishe Rosenfeld, Westport Prods; d: Jacques Levy; ch: Donald Saddler. Cast: Bruce Adler, Joanne Borts, Phyllis Berk, Avi Hoffman, Neva Small, Marc Krause

1427. The Golden Screw. Folk rock musical. Folk music in 1st half & hard rock in 2nd. Rock 'n roll singer rises to top. Provincetown Playhouse, 1/30/67–3/5/67. 40 perf. m/l/b: Tom Sankey; d: James Grove; cast recording on Atlantic. Cast: Janet Day, Murray Paskin, Patrick Sullivan, Jack Hopper. "2,000 Miles," "Beautiful People," "Trip Tack Talking Blues," "Can I Touch You?," "That's Your Thing, Baby" "I Can't Remember"

1428. The Golden Touch. Royal Lyceum, Edinburgh, Scotland, 4/5/60; Glasgow; Piccadilly, London, 5/5/60–5/14/60. 12 perf. p: Michael Codron & Neil Crawford; m: James Gilbert; l/b: Julian More; d/ch: Paddy Stone; set: Hugh Casson. Cast: Sergio Franchi, Gary Cockrell, Stella Claire, Ian Kaye, Nita Howard, Cec Linder, Patricia Laffan, Michael Coles, Frank Thornton

1429. Golf: The Musical. Musical revue. John Houseman, 11/19/03. p: Eric Krebs; m/l: Michael Roberts; d/ch: Christopher Scott; set: James Joughin; cos: Bernard Grenier; light: Aaron Spivey; md: Ken Lundie. Cast: Joel Blum, Trisha Rapier, Christopher Sutton, Sal Viviano. "A Show About Golf," "The History of Golf," "Who Plays Celebrity Golf?," "Scratch Golfer," "Plaid," "The Golfer's Psalm," "Tiger Woods," "A Great Lady Golfer," "Let's Bring Golf to the Gulf," "My Husband's Playing Around," "The Golfing Museum," "The Road to Heaven," "No Blacks, No Chicks, No Jews," "The Ballad of Casey Martin," "Pro Shop Polyphony," "Golf's Such a Naughty Game," "Presidents and Golf," "The Beautiful Time," "I'm Going Golfing Tomorrow." Cast recording released 4/1/04

1430. Gone with the Wind. 2-part, 9-hour stage extravaganza. Also called *Margaret Mitchell's Gone with the Wind*. Imperial, Tokyo, 1966. This show inaugurated the theatre. p: Kazuo Kikuta & Toho Company (they owned theatrical rights to the novel). They then commissioned Joe Layton to d/ch, with Harold Rome to do m/l (book was done by Kikuta, in Japanese). It was then called *Scarlett*, and opened 1/2/70, in Tokyo. Harold Fielding put it on—in English—as *Gone with the Wind*, at Drury Lane Theatre, London, with new book by Horton Foote, 5/3/72. 397 perf. Cast: Harve Presnell, June Ritchie. Panned by NY critics who came to see it. Then to USA, and

opened 8/28/73, Dorothy Chandler Pavilion, L.A., and not in the more appropriate Atlanta, as had been planned. Closed 11/24/73, Curran, San Francisco. d: Joe Layton; set: David Hays; cos: Patton Campbell; light: H.R. Poindexter; md: Jay Blackton; dance & choral arr: Trude Rittman; orch: Keith Amos. Cast: Rhett: Pernell Roberts; Scarlett: Lesley Ann Warren; Ashley: Terence Monk; Melanie: Udana Power; Belle: Ann Hodges; Mammy: Theresa Merritt; Prissy: Cheryl Robinson. Then toured USA, but folded after 3 months of bad business, canceling scheduled Broadway opening of 4/1/74. "Today's the Day," "Cakewalk," "We Belong to You," "Scarlett," "Bonnie Blue Flag," "Bizarre Hymn," "Virginia Reel," "Quadrille," "Two of a Kind," "Blissful Christmas," "My Soldier," "Tomorrow is Another Day," "Ashley Departure," "Where is My Soldier Boy?," "Why Did They Die?," "Johnny is My Darling," "Lonely Stranger," "Atlanta Burning," "If Only," "How Often (How Often)," "Gone with the Wind," "How Lucky," "A Southern Lady," "Marrying for Fun," "Brand New Friends," "Miss Fiddle-Dee-Dee," "Blueberry Eyes," "Bonnie Gone," "It Doesn't Matter Now." In 1976 Lucia Victor directed a production in Dallas, followed by 3 other cities, but it folded. David Selznick had toyed with idea of a musical of the film back in 1959, but nothing came of it

1431. Good. Play with mus. Professor becomes Nazi in pre-War Germany. Booth, Broadway, 10/13/82–1/30/83. 125 perf. p: Royal Shakespeare Co.; w: C.P. Taylor; d: Howard Davies; light: Beverly Emmons; md: Michael Dansicker. Cast: Alan Howard, Felicity Dean. Previously produced in London

1432. The Good Companions. Diverse group of strangers meet on road during Great Depression in England & form concert party. The 1957 film, dir by J. Lee Thompson, starred Eric Portman & Celia Johnson. Palace, Manchester, England, 6/7/74–6/22/74; Her Majesty's, London, 7/11/74–2/15/75. Prev from 7/3/74. 252 perf. m: Andre Previn; l: Johnny Mercer; b: Ronald Harwood; from J.B. Priestley's novel; d: Braham Murray; ch: Jonathan Taylor; md: Marcus Dods; cast recording on DRG. Cast: John Mills, Judi Dench, Celia Bannerman (*Marti Webb*), Hope Jackman, Ray C. Davis, Christopher Gable, Malcolm Rennie. "Camaraderie," "The Pools," "Footloose," "Pleasure of Your Company," "Stage Struck," "Slippin' Around the Corner," "Good Companions," "A Little Travelling Music," "And Point Beyond," "Darkest Before the Dawn," "Susie for Everybody," "Ta, Luv," "I'll Tell the World," "Stage Door John," "Dance of Life," "All Mucked Up," "Goodbye Dicky Doos," "Great North Road," "On My Way." York Theatre Co., 10/5/01–10/7/01. Part of *Musicals in Mufti* series. d: Susan H. Schulman. Cast: Brian Murray, Mary Stout, Michael McGrath. There were plans to take it further, into a genuine OB prod

1433. Good Luck. 2 love matches in Miami. Anderson Yiddish Theatre, 10/17/64–1/3/65. 117 perf. m/l: Sholom Secunda & Jacob Jacobs; d: Max Perlman. Cast: Jacob Jacobs, Max Perlman, Bruce Adler, Fyvush Finkel, Miriam

Kressyn, Susan Walters, Gita Galina, Thelma Mintz, Rose Greenfield, Seymour Rechtzeit

1434. *Good News.* Yiddish. Naval officer loses memory, and 2 girls contend for him. Unrelated to Broadway musical. Second Avenue Theatre, 9/27/44. 200 perf. p/d: Menasha Skulnik; m: Joseph Rumshinsky; l/b: Isidor Lillian; ch: Valentina Belova. Cast: Menasha Skulnik, Miriam Kressyn, Willie Secunda

1435. *The Good Old Bad Old Days.* Musical satire on contemporary scene. Prince of Wales, London, 12/20/72–9/15/73. Prev from 12/13/72. 309 perf. p: Bernard Delfont; m/l/b: Leslie Bricusse & Anthony Newley; d: Anthony Newley; ch: Paddy Stone; set: Disley Jones; md: Robert Mandell; cast recording on EMI. Cast: Anthony Newley, Caroline Villiers, Paul Bacon, Julia Sutton, Fred Evans, Terry Mitchell, Bill Kerr, Keith Chegwin, Wendy Barry. "The Good Old Bad Old Days," "Fool Who Dared to Dream," "Wisdom of the World," "Thanksgiving Day," "Today," "Tomorrow," "Yesterday," "It's a Musical World," "I Do Not Love You," "A Cotton Pickin' Moon," "Good Things in Life," "The People Tree," "We've Got a Cure for Everything on Broadway"

1436. *A Good Swift Kick.* Musical revue, with satirical songs. Variety Arts Theatre, 7/29/99–8/8/99. 19 prev from 7/13/99. 13 perf. p: Sandy Faison, Chase Mishkin, Steven M. Levy, Leonard Soloway; m/l: John Forster; d: Paul Kreppel; ch: Murphy Cross; set: Kenneth Foy; light: Jason Kantrowitz; sound: Peter Fitzgerald; md: John DiPinto. Cast: D'Monroe, David Naughton, Wanda Houston, Jim Newman, Elisa Surmont. "In the Closet," "Tone Deaf," "The PAC Man," "Helium," "Legacy," "One Billion Little Emperors," "Whole," "Ballad of Robert Moses," "Fusion," "Way Down Deep," "A Mismatch Made in Hell," "Spores," "Bye Bye Future," "The Big Mac Tree," "Tragique Kingdom," "Entering Marion," "Nothing Ventured, Nothing Lost," "Virtual Vivian," "Co dependent with You," "Passing." Previously produced at Goodspeed

1437. *Good Time Johnny.* Birmingham Rep, England, 12/16/71. m: James Gilbert; l: Julian More & James Gilbert; b: Julian More; d/ch: Alan Lund; md: Red Reid. Cast: Eric Flynn, Joan Sims, Ronnie Barker (*John Baddeley*)

1438. *The Good Times Are Killing Me.* Play with mus. Set in mid–1960s, in working-class neighborhood. Second Stage, 3/26/91–6/23/91. 106 perf. w: Lynda Barry; d: Mark Brokaw; md: Steve Sandberg. Cast: Lauren Gaffney, Ruth Williamson, Kathleen Dennehy, Ray DeMattis, Peter Appel

1439. *Good Vibrations.* Beach Boys musical (but not a biography), using more than 30 songs by Brian Wilson and the Beach Boys. Eugene O'Neill, Broadway, 2/2/05 (date put back from 1/13/05 and 1/27/05). Prev from 12/20/04 (date put back from 12/4/04). Presented by Dodger Theatricals; b: Richard Dresser; d/ch: John Carrafa (his first Broadway job handling both chores. On 1/6/05 David Warren was brought in to help with direction).

It began in 11/03, and at that stage Don Scardino was going to be the director, but he dropped out. 1st presented as a workshop at New York Stage & Film on the Campus, at Vassar College, 7/29/04–8/1/04. p: NJC Prods, Michael Watt, Dodger Stage Holding; d/ch: John Carrafa. Cast: David Larsen, Justin Guarini (out of the show as of 11/10/04), Tituss Burgess, Heath Calvert, Tom Deckman, Elizabeth Fye, Geoffrey Hemingway, Julie Martell, Tyler Maynard, Megan McGinnis, Nina Negri, Julie Reiber, Jose Restrepo, Jonathan Richard Sandler, Krysta Rodriguez, Allison Spratt, Emily Toress, Haneefah Wood. Broadway cast: Eddie: Tituss Burgess; Bobby: David Larsen; Caroline: Kate Reinders; Dave: Brandon Wardell; Marcella: Jessica-Snow Wilson; Also with: Tracee Beazer, Milena Govich, Chad Kimball, John Jeffrey Martin. "Fun Fun Fun" (opening number)

1440. *The Good Woman of Setzuan.* Pulse Ensemble, 3/13/98–4/5/98. 3 prev. 15 perf. m: Michael Rice; l: Michael Rice & Eric Bentley; b: Eric Bentley; from the Brecht play; d: Alexa Kelly; ch: Barry McNabb. Cast: Angelina Fiordellisi

1441. *Goodbye Mr. Chips.* Chichester Festival Theatre, England, 8/11/82–10/2/82. 38 perf in rep. m/l: Leslie Bricusse; b: Roland Starke; from James Hilton's novel but more specifically from movie musical made from it in 1969, starring Pet Clarke & Peter O'Toole; d: Patrick Garland & Christopher Selbie; ch: Lindsay Dolan; md: John Owen Edwards; cast recording on TER. Cast: John Mills, Colette Gleason, Nigel Stock, Paul Hardwick. "Roll Call," "Fill the World with Love," "Would I Had Lived My Life Then," "Schooldays," "That's a Boy," "Where Did My Childhood Go?," "Boring," "Take a Chance," "Walk Through the World," "When I Am Older," "The Miracle," "A Day Has a Hundred Pockets," "You and I," "What a Lot of Flowers," "When I Was Younger," "Goodbye Mr. Chips," "London is London," "And the Sky Smiled"

1442. *The Gorey Details.* A musicale. Sketches with songs inspired by Edward Gorey's macabre work. Century Center for the Performing Arts, 10/16/00–12/10/00. 16 prev from 10/3/00. 65 perf. p: Ken Hoyt & Kevin McDermott, in assoc with Brent Peek; m/orch: Peter Matz; l/b: Edward Gorey; d/ch: Daniel Levans; set: Jesse Poleschuck; cos: Martha Bromelmeier; md: Bruce W. Coyle. Cast: Alison Crowley, Daniel C. Levine, Christopher Youngsman, Kevin McDermott

1443. *The Gospel According to Al.* Celebration of Al Carmines' 20 years in theatre. Wonderhorse, 10/14/82–10/24/82. 12 perf. Theatre songs by Al; d: William Hopkins; set: Peter Harrison. Cast: Georgia Creighton, Kate Ingram, Tad Ingram, Cathleen Axelrod, Paul Farin. "Sometimes the Sky is Blue," "Good Old Days," "It's a Man's World," "My Old Man," "A Woman Needs Approval Now and Then," "It's Nice to Cuddle in a Threesome," "New Boy in Town," "Ordinary Thing," "Disposable Woman," "Montgomery Moon," "Dummy Juggler," "I'm Peculiar That Way," "I Am My Beloved," "I Forget and I Remember," "Nos-

talgia," "Fifty Years of Making People Laugh," "Forgiveness," "I'm Innocence," "World is Yours," "God Bless Us All"

1444. *Gotta Getaway!* Radio City Music Hall, 6/16/84–9/3/84. 2 prev from 6/8/84. 149 perf. p/artistic d: Patricia Morinelli; orig m: Marc Eliot, Chip Orton, Gene Palumbo, Marc Shaiman, Eric Watson; conceived & created by: Stephen Nisbet & James Lecesne; w: James Lecesne; d: Larry Fuller; ch: Larry Fuller & Marianne Selbert; set: Eduardo Sicangco; cos: Michael Casey; md: Gene Palumbo; orch: Michael Gibson & Bill Brohn; conductor: Robert Billig. Cast: Liliane Montevecchi, Tony Azito, Loretta Devine, Alyson Reed, Ron & Joy Holiday, The Rockettes, Arminae Azarian, Ellia English, Connie Kunkle, Jacqueline Reilly, Bonnie Schon, Freida Williams, Ciscoe Bruton, John Clonts, Joe DeGunther, Brian Feehan, Darrell Greene, Marc Hunter, David-Michael Johnson, Robert Kellett, Lacy Darryl Phillips, Jeff Shade, Paul Solen, Alan Stuart, John M. Wiltberger. "Gotta Getaway" (by Glen Roven), "I'm Throwing a Ball Tonight," "Use Your Imagination," "Too Marvelous for Words," "This Heart of Mine," "Bubble Bubble," "La Cumparsita," "Here in Minipoora," "Hot VooDoo," "Hello Beautiful," "Le Dernier Pierrot," "Folies Bergere," "Stairway to Paradise," "Higher and Higher," "Come to the Super Market in Old Peking," "Peking Ballet," "Once You've Seen a Rainbow," "Manhattan," "Take Good Care of That Lady"

1445. *Grab Me a Gondola.* Aspiring Hollywood actress & young reporter during film festival. Theatre Royal, Windsor, England, 10/30/56. p: John Counsell; m: James Gilbert; l: Julian More & James Gilbert; b: Julian More. Lyric, Hammersmith, London, 11/27/56–12/26/56. 22 perf. p: Donald Albery & Neil Crawford; d: John Counsell & Eleanor Fazan; ch: Eleanor Fazan; set: Hal Henshaw & Stanley Moore; md: Stanley Myers, *Alan Abbott*. Lyric, London, 12/26/56–7/12/58. 673 perf. Cast recording on HMV. Cast: Joan Heal, Denis Quilley, Joyce Blair (*Mary Preston*), Una Stubbs, Jay Denyer, Ina de la Haye (*Hope Jackman*), Donald Hewlett, Peter Brett, Jane Wenham, Guido Lorraine, Peter Gilmore. "Grab Me a Gondola," "That's My Biography," "Plain in Love," "Motor Car is Treacherous," "Cravin' for the Avon," "Bid Him a Fond Goodbye," "Star Quality," "A Man, not a Mouse," "Lonely in a Crowd," "Jimmy's Bar," "Chianti," "What Are the Facts?," "Rig o' the Day," "When I Find That Girl," "Rockin' at the Cannonball." The hit of the London year. 1st produced by Windsor Rep

1446. *Graham Crackers.* Small revue. Upstairs at the Downstairs, 1/23/63–7/16/63. 286 perf. m/l mostly by David Shire & Richard Maltby Jr.; conceived by/d: Ronny Graham; ch: Lee Becker. Cast: Bob Kaliban, Bill McCutcheon, McLean Stevenson, Pat Stanley (*Ann Fraser*). "Crossword Puzzle," "The Sound of Muzak," "Lovely Light," "A Doodlin' Song" (m: Cy Coleman; l: Carolyn Leigh). The sketch "Psychological Warfare" was written by Woody Allen

1447. *The Grand Music Hall of Israel.* Jewish revue. Palace, Broadway, 2/6/68–3/31/68. 64 perf. p: Lee Guber & Shelly Gross; d/ch: Jonathan Karmon; light: Jules Fisher; md: Itzchak Graziani. Cast: Helena Hendel, Ilan & Ilanit, The Carmelim, Geula Gill & The High Willows (Miss Gill nominated for Tony as featured actress), Nishri, Boaz & Nechemia, Alice & Hannan, The Karmon Histadruth Ballet. "Israeli Rhapsody," "Dance of the Fisherman," "Hassidic," "Sabre Dance," "The Feats of the Kibbutz." Then it toured. A new edition, *The New Music Hall of Israel*, ran in 1969 (see this appendix). The orig re-ran at Felt Forum, 1/4/73–1/14/73. 15 perf. d/ch: Jonathan Karmon; md: Rafi Paz. Cast: Myron Cohen

1448. *A Grand Night for Singing: The Rodgers & Hammerstein Revue.* Musical revue in 2 acts. Rainbow & Stars, 3/2/93–4/10/93. 60 perf. p: Gregory Dawson & Steve Paul; m: Richard Rodgers; l: Oscar Hammerstein II; conceived by/d: Walter Bobbie; add staging: Pamela Sousa; set: Tony Walton; cos: Martin Pakledinaz; light: Natasha Katz; md/arr: Fred Wells; orch: Michael Gibson & Jonathan Tunick. Cast: Martin Vidnovic, Jason Graae, Victoria Clark, Karen Ziemba, Lynne Wintersteller. Standbys: Rebecca Eichenberger & James Hindman. Expanded & ran at Criterion Center Stage Right, 11/17/93–1/1/94. 41 prev from 10/13/93. 52 perf. p: Roundabout Theatre Co., by special arr with Gregory Dawson & Steve Paul; cast recording on Varese Sarabande. Alyson Reed took over from Karen Ziemba, but otherwise cast (and crew) remained the same. Suzzanne Douglas replaced Miss Reed on 12/14/93. "Carousel Waltz"/"So Far"/"(It's a) Grand Night for Singing," "Surrey with the Fringe on Top," "Stepsister's Lament," "We Kiss in a Shadow," "Hello, Young Lovers," "A Wonderful Guy," "I Cain't Say No," "Maria," "Do I Love You Because You're Beautiful?," "Honey Bun," "Gentleman is a Dope," "Don't Marry Me," "I'm Gonna Wash That Man Right Out of My Hair," "If I Love You," "Shall We Dance?," "That's the Way it Happens," "All at Once You Love Her," "Some Enchanted Evening," "Oh, What a Beautiful Mornin'," "Wish Them Well," "The Man I Used to Be," "It Might as Well Be Spring," "Kansas City," "When the Children Are Asleep"/"I Know it Can Happen Again"/"My Little Girl," "It's Me," "Love Look Away," "When You're Driving Through the Moonlight"/"A Lovely Night," "Something Wonderful," "This Nearly Was Mine," "Impossible"/"I Have Dreamed." It got good reviews. Tony nominations for musical & book

1449. *El Grande de Coca-Cola.* Cabaret-style revue with running time of 1 hour. Purposefully bad entertainment performed in gibberish versions of Spanish, French & German. Don Pepe Hernandez is small-time impresario in town of Trujillo, Honduras. He has promised a parade of international stars, but none have showed up. Borrowing money from his uncle, the manager of local Coca-Cola bottling plant, he rents flea-bitten nightclub & hires relatives to play the missing talent. It all goes wrong, of course. Mercer Arts Center/ Oscar Wilde Room, 2/13/73; Plaza 9, 8/10/73–

4/13/75. Total of 1,114 perf. Developed by British comedy troupe Low Moan Spectacular (i.e. the cast of this show) as they toured Europe. It actually opened as *El Coca-Cola Grande*, but name changed 2/21/73. set: Mischa Petrow. Cast: Alan Shearman, Sally Willis, Ron House, Diz White, John Neville-Andrews. Revised & revived at Village Gate Downstairs, 1/22/86–4/6/86. Prev from 1/10/86. 86 perf. d: Ron House, Diz White, Alan Shearman; ch: Anne Gunderson. Cast: Diz White, Rodger Bumpass, Alan Shearman, Ron House, Olga Merediz

1450. *Grandpa.* Revue about growing older. 92nd Street YM-YWHA/Kaufman Auditorium, 1/23/77–3/27/77. 20 perf. p/w/set: Judith Martin; m: Donald Ashwander. Cast: Donald Ashwander, Irving Burton, Jeanne Michels, Judith Martin, Virgil Roberson. "Getting Older," "Stolen Sneakers," "It's Just Not Fair," "Bubble Gum," "A Great Big Kiss," "When You're Older," "Growing Up," "Changing"

1451. *The Great American Backstage Musical.* Set in NY, London, and on the battlefields of Europe, 1939–45. Matrix, L.A., 12/2/76. m/l: Bill Solly. "I Got the What?," "Crumbs in My Bed," "Cheerio!," "You Should Be Being Made Love To," "Star of the Show," "When the Money Comes In," "News of You," "I Could Fall in Love," "Ba-Boom!," "I'll Wait for Joe." Regent, London, 8/8/78. Silver Lining (OB), 9/15/83–10/1/83. 5 prev. 18 perf. Cast: Mark Fotopoulos, Paige O'Hara, Bob Amaral

1452. *Great Balls of Fire: The Jerry Lee Lewis Story.* Cambridge Theatre, London, 10/6/99–12/18/99. Prev from 10/1/99. w: Todd Wm. Ristau & Richard Cameron; d: Simon Usher. Cast: Billy Geraghty

1453. *The Great Debate.* Musical revue on question of creation vs evolution. Lambs, 7/22/99–8/15/99. 2 prev 14 perf. m/l/b: Mona Johnian; d: Patty Freeman; ch: Jamie Collins; md: Paul Johnian. Cast: Jamie Collins, Tom Schmidt, Elizabeth Chiang. "Creation," "Reach Out to God," "Rebel Heart," "Time Will Tell the Story," "Big Apple," "Evolution/Revolution," "Signature of God," "Mr. Einstein," "The Question," "Song of the Agnotheist," "Reason Logic," "God of Second Chance," "On Wings of Love," "Lion's Song," "This is the Land," "O Ethiopian," "Don't Let the Vision Fade"

1454. *Great Expectations.* Yvonne Arnaud, Guildford, England, 12/24/75–1/31/76; toured in England, and (from 4/6/76) in Canada. m: Cyril Ornadel; l: Hal Shaper; b: Hal Shaper & Trevor Preston; from Charles Dickens' novel; d: Alan Lund; ch: Bob Stevenson; md: John Burrows. Cast: Leonard Whiting, Colin Douglas, George A. Cooper, Joy Nichols, Janet Mahoney, Lesley-Anne Down, Moira Lister, Ronald Radd

1455. *The Great Gilly Hopkins.* New Victory, 4/15/98–4/26/98. m/l/b: David Paterson & Steve Liebman; based on book by Katherine Paterson; d: J. Daniel Herring

1456. *The Great Hall.* Set on Ellis Island, 1921. Sanford Meisner, 6/6/97–6/28/97. 21

perf. m/l: David W. Radulich; b: Thomas J. O'Shaughnessy; d/ch: Cynthia M. Mazzant. Cast: Rick Alessa, Nicole Scrofani

1457. *The Great Macdaddy.* Odyssey with mus. St. Mark's Playhouse, 2/12/74–4/17/74. 72 perf. p: Negro Ensemble Co.; m: Coleridge-Taylor Perkinson; w: Paul Carter Harrison; d: Douglas Turner Ward; ch: Dianne McIntyre; light: Ken Billington. Cast: Phylicia Ayers-Allen, Marjorie Barnes, Adolph Caesar, David Downing (*Cleavon Little*), Al Freeman Jr. (*Robert Hooks* from 3/4/74), Alton Lathrop, Hattie Winston. Revived in St. Croix & St. Thomas, Virgin Islands, a prod that went to Theatre de Lys (OB), 4/5/76–5/22/76 (press date 4/13/76). Same d/ch; light: Sandra L. Ross. Cast: Charles Brown, Bill Mackey, Barbara Montgomery, Charles Weldon, Lynn Whitfield, Reyno, Graham Brown, Frankie R. Faison

1458. *The Great Ostrovsky.* About David Ostrovsky, a larger than life figure from the Yiddish theatre of the 1920s. Prince Music Theatre, Philadelphia, 3/13/04–4/4/04. Prev from 3/6/04. m/l: Cy Coleman; b: Avery Corman. Cast: Bob Gunton, Louise Pitre. There had been a private reading at the same venue, 12/15/03. d: Douglas C. Wager; ch: Patricia Birch. Alan King was at one time going to star. Earlier known as *Ostrovsky* and *It's Good to Be Alive*

1459. *Great Scot.* About Scottish poet Robert Burns. Theatre Four, 11/10/65–12/12/65. 38 perf. m/l: Don McAfee & Nancy Leeds; d: Charles Tate; set/cos: Herbert Senn & Helen Pond; md: Joe Raposo. Cast: Allan Bruce, Charlotte Jones, Joleen Fodor, Jack Eddleman, Mary Jo Gillis. "You're the Only One," "Great Scot," "I'll Find a Dream Somewhere," "He's Not for Me," "That Special Day," "Original Sin," "I'll Still Love Jean," "Where is That Rainbow?," "Princes Street," "Happy New Year," "That Big-Bellied Bottle," "He Knows Where to Find Me," "I Left a Dream Somewhere," "We're Gonna Have a Wedding"

1460. *The Great Waltz.* Dealt with rivalry of the 2 Strausses. Huge show; cost $246,000. Center Theatre, Broadway, 9/22/34–6/8/35. 298 perf. p: Max Gordon; m: Johann Strauss Sr. & Johann Strauss Jr.; l: Desmond Carter; b: Moss Hart; based on an English version of the Viennese musical *Waltzes from Vienna*; d: Hassard Short; ch: Albertina Rasch; mus arr: Erich Wolfgang Korngold. Cast: Marion Claire, Marie Burke, Alexandra Danilova. Ensemble included: Meg Mundy, May Muth. "You Are My Song," "Love Will Find You," "Like a Star in the Sky," "With All My Heart," "While You Love Me," "Danube So Blue." Re-ran 8/5/35–9/16/35. 49 perf. Music Center, L.A., 7/27/65. new b: Jerome Chodorov; add mus adaptation & l: Robert Wright, George Forrest, Forman Brown. Never made it to NY, although it did have a 605-perf run in London from 1970. "Blue Danube," "Two by Two," "Where Would I Be?," "A Waltz with Wings," "Teeter-Totter Me," "Radetzky March," "Love and Gingerbread," "An Artist's Life," "Enchanted Wood," "The Gypsy Told Me," "Philosophy of Life"

1461. *The Green Bird*. Philosophical comedy with mus. Set in city of Monterotondo, Serpentina's garden, the Ogre's mountain lair, and other fabulous places. Yale Rep, 12/2/93. w: Carlo Gozzi; Albert Bermel & Ted Emery translated from Carlo Gozzi's *L'augellino belverde*; d: Vincent Gracieux; md: Eric Jensen. Cast: Felicity Jones (also cos), Angela Lewis, Vincent Gracieux, Dominique Serrand, Eric Jensen. New Victory, NYC, 3/7/96–3/24/96. 15 perf. p: Theatre for a New Audience; orig m/orch: Elliot Goldenthal; d: Julie Taymor; set: Christine Jones & Julie Taymor; cos: Constance Hoffman; light: Donald Holder; sound: Bob Belecki. Cast: Didi Conn, Myriam Cyr, Ken Barnett, Ned Eisenberg, Lee Lewis, Kristine Nielsen, Sebastian Roche, Sophia Salguero, Priscilla Shanks, Derek Smith, Bruce Turk, Trellis Stepter, Erico Villanueva, Andrew Weems. La Jolla Playhouse, Calif., 1996. Cort, Broadway, 4/18/00–6/4/00. 16 prev from 4/1/00. 56 perf. p: Theatre For a New Audience, Nina Lannan, OSTAR Enterprises; lyr to "Oh Foolish Heart:" David Suehsdorf; add text: Eric Overmyer; d/mask & puppet design: Julie Taymor; ch: Daniel Ezralow; set: Christine Jones; cos: Constance Hoffman; light: Donald Holder; sound: Jon Weston; md: Rick Martinez; vocal d: Joseph Church. Cast: Didi Conn, Ken Barnett, Ramon Flowers, Sarah Jane Nelson, Meredith Patterson, Sophia Salguero, Erico Villanueva, Reg E. Cathey, Ned Eisenberg, Edward Hibbert, Lee Lewis, Katie MacNichol, Kristine Nielsen, Sebastian Roche, Derek Smith, Bruce Turk, Andrew Weems. Understudy: Jan Leslie Harding. Tony nominations for cos & Derek Smith

1462. *The Green Heart*. Variety Arts, 4/10/97–5/4/97. 40 prev from 2/25/97. 40 perf. m/l: Rusty Magee; b: Charles Busch; based on story by Jack Ritchie; d: Kenneth Elliott; ch: Joey McKneely; set: James Noone; cos: Robert Mackintosh; md: Joe Baker. Cast: John Ellison Conlee, Alison Fraser, Don Goodspeed, Julie J. Hafner, Karyn Quackenbush, Ruth Williamson, David Andrew Macdonald, Karen Trott, Lovette George. "Our Finest Customer," "I'm Poor," "Picture Me," "I Can't Recall," "Till Death Do They Part," "Tropical Island Breezes," "Easy Life," "Get Used to It," "Why Can't We Turn Back the Clock?," "Horns of an Immoral Dilemma," "I'm the Victim Here," "The Green Heart," "What's it Gonna Take (to Make it Clear Across the Lake)?"

1463. *Green Pond*. 2 couples vacationing on South Carolina coast, summer 1976. Chelsea Theatre Center/Brooklyn Academy of Music, 11/22/77–12/18/77. 32 perf. press date 11/30/77. m/orch: Mel Marvin; l/b: Robert Montgomery; d: David Chambers; set/cos: Marjorie Kellogg. Cast: Christine Ebersole, Stephen James, Stephanie Cotsirilos, Richard Ryder. "Green Pond," "Pleasant Company," "Daughter," "I Live Alone," "Eyes of Egypt," "How We Get Down," "Alligator Meat," "Priceless Relics," "Woman to Woman," "Brother to Brother," "Hurricane," "Hard to Love," "On the Ground at Last." Westside Theatre, Manhattan, 12/7/77–12/18/77. Previously ran at Stage South, SC

1464. *Greenwich Village Follies*. Revue. New Follies, 6/10/76; The Gate, 9/8/76; Cricket, 11/17/76. m/l/vignettes/conceived by/d: Ronnie Britton. Cast: Linda David, Gregory Cook, Jacqueline Carol, Marisa Lyon, Danny Freedman

1465. *Greenwich Village, USA*. Revue. One Sheridan Square, 9/28/60–12/11/60. 87 perf. Cast: Pat Finley, Ken Urmston, James Pompeii

1466. *Ground People*. Drama with mus. Set in Mississippi Delta in 1920. American Place, 4/21/90–5/20/90. 20 prev. 19 perf. w: Leslie Lee; d: Walter Dallas. Cast: Ron Richardson, Frances Foster

1467. *Groundhog*. Mentally disturbed homeless man versus the system. Manhattan Theatre Club, 4/14/92–5/17/92. 40 perf. m/w/d: Elizabeth Swados; light: Natasha Katz. Cast: Stephen Lee Anderson, Anne Bobby, Bill Buell, Gilles Chiasson. "Weather Report # 1," "Cooper Square," "Project Heal," "One More Day," "Willard Scott," "Abduction," "Weather Report # 2," "Street People," "Groundhog is Going to Trial," "My Movie of the Week," "Who Will it Be?," "Flight to Health," "Bellevue and the Judge," "Testimony," "Experts," "This isn't How I Imagined a Trial to Be," "Just Trust Me," "Yes/No," "Doctor's Canon," "Bill and Willa," "Danilo's Rap," "Sweet Bitter Candy," "Hey Groundhog," "Why Did I Forget," "Ten Year Blues," "Harmonica Man," "Weather Report # 3," "If I Am Released," "Closing Arguments," "The Judge's Decision," "Battle Hymn of Groundhog," "Groundhog Has Won," "Lawyer's Lament," "Open the Door," "Groundhog is Becoming Important," "Hearing Voices," "Pay Phone," "ACLU," "Rewrite Your Own Story," "Hymn to Spring," "Weather Report # 4," "What Could I Have Done?," "Someone is Discovering Something"

1468. *Grover's Corners*. Tour. World premiere 7/22/87, Marriott's Lincolnshire Theatre. Closed 11/11/87. m: Harvey Schmidt; l/b: Tom Jones; based on Thornton Wilder's play *Our Town;* d: Dominic Missimi; set/light: John & Diane Williams; cos: Nancy Missimi; md: Kevin Stites; orch: David Siegel. Cast: Tom Jones, Harvey Schmidt, Deanna Wells. "Our Town," "A Hearty Breakfast," "Someplace," "Maybe," "Evening," "Day After Day," "It isn't Hard to Get Married," "I Noticed You," "I Only Want Somebody to Love Me," "Snapshots/Photographs," "Time Goes By," "Do Not Hold On," "Birthday Girl," "A Star is Mighty Good Company," "Goodbye World," "Conclusion"

1469. *The Grub Street Opera*. Set in Wales in 1731. Greenwich House, NYC, 5/30/86–6/22/86. 16 perf. w: Henry Fielding; world premiere of a new score by Anthony Bowles; d: Anthony Bowles; set: Alison Ford; md: Robert Grusecki. Cast: Richard T. Alpers, Colleen Fitzpatrick, Avril Gentles, Nita Novy, Steve Sterner, Lee Winston

1470. *Guilt Without Sex*. Musical expose. Theatre Arielle, 1991. p: Eric Krebs; based on book by Marilyn Sokol & Ken Friedman; d: Bob Goldstone; consultant: Sue Lawless. Cast: Marilyn Sokol

1471. *Gulliver's Travels*. Mermaid, London, 12/15/75–1/17/76. m/l: Mike D'Abo; b: William Rushton; based on book by Jonathan Swift; d: David Toguri & William Rushton; set: Sean Kenny; cos: Ruth Maskell; md: Roy Civil. Cast: Mike D'Abo, William Rushton, Larry Dann

1472. *Gunmetal Blues*. Theatre Off Park, 3/27/92–5/10/92. 46 perf. m/l: Craig Bohmler & Marion Adler; b: Scott Wentworth; d: Davis Hall. Cast: Daniel Marcus, Michael Knowles, Marion Adler, Scott Wentworth. "Welcome to This," "Don't Know What I Expected," "Facts," "Well-to-Do Waltz," "Spare Some Change," "Mansion Hill," "Shadowplay," "Skeletons," "Blonde Song," "Childhood Days," "Take a Break," "Not Available in Stores!" "Gunmetal Blues," "I'm the One that Got Away," "Jenny," "Put it on My Tab," "The Virtuoso"

1473. *Gunslinger*. Phoenix, Leicester, England, 6/10/76–7/3/76. songs: Joss Buckley; b: Richard Crane; d: Peter Moss; md: Ian Smith. Cast: Joss Buckley. Theatre Royal, Stratford East, London, 3/9/77. 34 perf;, and again, 4/5/77–4/30/77. 25 perf. p: Theatre Workshop; d: Rhys McConnochie; ch: Geoffrey Saunders; md: Martin Duncan. New cast

1474. *The Gypsy Baron*. Comic opera. City Center, 11/14/44–12/10/44. 20 perf in rep. p: NYC Opera; m: Johann Strauss; George Mead revised & adapted into English Ignaz Schnitzer's original Viennese libretto to *Der Zigeunerbaron*, which had been based on the story *Saffi*, by Mor Jokai; d: William Wymetal; dial d: Jessie Royce Landis; ballet ch: Helen Playova; set: Heinz A. Condell; conductor: Laszlo Halasz. Cast: Polyna Stoska, William Horne, Marguerite Piazza. City Center, 4/15/45–4/28/45. 4 perf in rep. City Center, 10/6/45–11/10/45. 4 perf in rep. p: NYC Opera; d: Leopold Sachse; ch: Carl Randall; md: Julius Rudel; conductor: Laszlo Halasz. Cast: Gordon Dilworth, Brenda Lewis. 1st NY run was at the Casino, 2/15/1886. 86 perf

1475. *Gypsy Pasion*. [note spelling]. Story of the gypsies of Andalucia & their inspiration–flamenco. Town Hall, 4/22/92–5/3/92. 15 perf. p: Andalucia Prods & Roy A. Somlyo; traditional m/l; b/d: Tomas Rodriguez-Pantoja; ch: Gitanos de Jerez; set: David Sumner; cos: Mercedes Muniz; light: Tom Sturge; sound: Otts Munderloh. Cast: Manuel Morao, Lorenzo Galvez, Manuel Moneo, Sara Baras, Carmen de la Jeroma, Pepe de la Joaquina, Luis Moneo, Antonio Moreno, Juan Antonio Ogalla, Concha Vargas, Estefania Aranda, Manuela Nunez, Mercedes Ruiz, Patricia Valdes. Plymouth, Broadway, 11/17/92–1/2/93. 55 perf. Good reviews

1476. *Haarlem Nocturne*. Cabaret revue. Latin Quarter, 11/18/84–12/30/84. 15 prev. 49 perf. p: Barry & Fran Weissler; conceived by: Andre De Shields; w/d: Andre De Shields & Murray Horwitz; set: David Chapman; cos: Jean-Claude Robin; light: Marc B. Weiss; sound: Bill Dreisbach; md/orch: Marc Shaiman. Cast: Andre De Shields, Debra Byrd, Ellia English, Marc Shaiman, Freida Williams. "Love in the Morning," "Wishful Thinking,"

"New York is a Party," "Jungle Hip Hop," "Sweet Dreams Are Made of This," "What Becomes of the Broken-Hearted," "Love's Sad Glance," "Secret Love," "Say it Again," "Heads or Tails," "Hit the Road, Jack," "Waterfaucet Blues," "Streetcorner Symphony," "Bad Boy," "Mary Mack," "Pastiche," "Harlem Nocturne" [sic], "Louie," "B.Y.O.B.," "Now is the Time." Cabaret Downstairs at La Mama, 1/19/84. Originally ran at B.Y.O.B.

1477. Halala! Zulu musical in English. Name means "Congratulations." Douglas Fairbanks, 2/12/86–3/9/86. The Izulu Dance Theatre production, in its world premiere. p: Eric Krebs; w/d: Welcome Msomi; ch: Thuli Dumakude. Cast: Thuli Dumakude, Lorraine Mahlangu, Mandla Msomi, Seth Sibanda, Linda Tshabalala, Michael Xulu. "Koze Kubenini," "Sonqoba," "Bayakhala," "The Halala Song"

1478. Half in Earnest. Adaptation of Oscar Wilde's *The Importance of Being Earnest*. Belgrade Theatre (a brand new theatre then), Coventry, England, 3/27/58–4/12/58. Did not go to London, but toured instead. m/l/b: Vivian Ellis; d: Bryan Bailey; md: William Blezard. Cast: Marie Lohr, Bryan Johnson, Brian Reece, Stephanie Voss, Phyllida Sewell, Patrick O'Connell. "Tea Time," "So Romantic," "Cloakroom at Victoria," "Foolish Love," "German Lesson," "How Do You Propose to Propose?," "There's No Friend Like a New Friend." Bucks County Playhouse, Pa., 6/17/57–6/29/57. d: Ezra Stone; md: George Bauer. Cast: Jack Cassidy, Emory Bass, Anna Russell, Mimi Strongin. Wrexham, England, 9/28/64. p: Welsh Theatre Co.; then toured. d: Warren Jenkins; md: Michael Tubbs. Cast: Elaine Taylor

1479. Half-Past Wednesday. Orpheum, 4/6/62–4/7/62. 2 perf. Ran again, 4/28/62–4/29/62. 4 perf. p/d: Hal Raywin; m/l: Nita Jonas & Robert Colby; b: Anna Marie Barlow; based on *Rumpelstiltskin;* ch: Gene Bayliss; light: Jules Fisher; md: Julian Stein. Cast: Dom De Luise, Sean Garrison. "What's the Fun of Being King?," "You're the Sweet Beginning," "Who? Where? What?," "Spinning Song," "Jumping Jehosephat," "If You Did It Once," "How Lovely, How Lovely," "Grandfathers," "To Whit — To Woo," "Companionship," "We Know a Secret"

1480. Halloween. Set in an asylum. Pre-Broadway tryouts at Bucks County Playhouse, New Hope, Pa., 9/20/72–10/1/72. Canceled scheduled 10/30/72 Broadway opening at Martin Beck. p: Albert W. Selden & Jerome Minskoff; m/l: Mitch Leigh, Joe Darion, Sidney Michaels; based on Sidney Michaels' unproduced play *Saltpeter in the Rhubarb*; d: Albert Marre; ch: Bert Michaels; set/light: Howard Bay; md: John Lesko. Cast: David Wayne, Dick Shawn, Margot Moser, Felix Silla. Introducing Billy Barty. "Bazoom," "A Strange Variation of Love," "In the Autumn of the Night," "Love in a Barbershop"

1481. Hamelin: A Musical Tale from Rats to Riches. The Pied Piper tale as a rock musical. Set in Hamelin on 6/26/1284. Circle in the Square Downtown, 10/31/85–11/24/85. 46 perf. m/l: Richard Jarboe & Harvey Shield; b:

Richard Jarboe, Harvey Shield, Matthew Wells; d: Ron Nash; ch: Jerry Yoder; ms: Ronald Melrose. Cast: Patrick Hamilton. "We're Rats," "The Mayor Doesn't Care," "Doing My Job," "Rat Trap," "Easy for Me," "What a Day," "Paradise," "Charismatic," "Better Keep Your Promise," "Follow the Music Man," "Feel the Beat," "Serving the People," "Mother," "Gold," "I'll Remember," "You've Outstayed Your Welcome." Previously ran OOB at Musical Theatre Works

1482. A Hand Is on the Gate. Evening of black poetry & folk songs. Delacorte, 8/15/66. 1 perf. p: NY Shakespeare Festival; m/l: William Lee & Stuart Scharf; light: Jules Fisher. Longacre, Broadway, 9/21/66–10/8/66. 2 prev. 21 perf. light: Jules Fisher; cast recording on Verve/Folkways. Cast: James Earl Jones, Moses Gunn, Cicely Tyson, Josephine Premice (nominated for a Tony), Leon Bibb (nominated for a Tony), Roscoe Lee Browne (also d), Gloria Foster. "'buked and Scorned," "Jane Jane," "All Hid," "Careless Love," "Dink's Song," "The Ballad of Rudolph Reed," "Harlem Sweeties," "Glory Glory," "Rocks and Gravel." New version, by Roscoe Lee Browne, *A Hand is On the Gate '76*, ran at Afro-American Studio, from 3/5/76. d: Ernie McClintock

1483. Hang Down Your Head and Die. Revue by David Wright. The evils of capital punishment. Mayfair, 10/18/64. 1 perf. d/ch: Braham Murray; set: Fred Voelpel. Cast: Michael Berkson, David Garfield, Jordan Charney, Gerome Ragni, Remak Ramsay, Nancy Tribush, Jill O'Hara, Charles Gray, James Rado, George Marcy. Previously ran in Oxford & London, England

1484. Hang On to the Good Times. Musical revue. Collection of songs from Nancy Ford-Gretchen Cryer concerts, records & musicals (*Shelter* and *I'm Getting My Act Together and Taking it on the Road*), 1967–1980. The Space at City Center, 1/22/85–2/24/85. 39 perf. p: Manhattan Theatre Club; m/l: Nancy Ford & Gretchen Cryer; conceived by: Richard Maltby Jr., Gretchen Cryer, Nancy Ford; d: Richard Maltby Jr.; ch: Kay Cole; set: James Morgan; light: Mary Jo Dondlinger; md: Cheryl Hardwick; orch: Cheryl Hardwick & Steven Margoshes. Cast: Terri Klausner, Don Scardino, Charlaine Woodard, Cass Morgan. "Big Bill Murphy," "In a Simple Way I Love You," "Strong Woman Number," "You Can Never Know My Mind," "Do Whatcha Gotta Do," "Too Many Women in My Life," "You Can Kill Love," "She's My Girl," "Dear Tom," "Happy Birthday," "Goin' Home with My Children," "Mary Margaret's House in the Country," "White Trash Motel," "Last Day at the Job," "The News," "Rock Singer," "Put in a Package and Sold," "Lonely Lady," "Blackberry Wine," "Old Friend" "Hang on to the Good Times"

1485. Hannah … 1939. Set in dress factory in Nazi-occupied Prague in 1939. Vineyard, 5/17/90–6/17/90. 39 perf. m/l/b: Bob Merrill; d: Douglas Aibel; ch: Tina Paul; set: G.W. Mercier; md: Stephen Milbank. Cast: Julie Wilson, Tony Carlin, Richard Thomsen, Patti Perkins, Lori Wilner, Mary Setrakian, Neva

Small, Leigh Beery. "Ah! Our Germans," "The Pearl We Called Prague," "Martina," "Wear a Little Grin," "Kissed on the Eyes," "Things Will Be Different," "We Dance," "Hannah Will Take Care of You," "Learn About Life," "Someday," "Gentle Afternoon," "So Good to See You," "Who is Hannah?"

1486. Hannah Senesh. Play with mus. Cherry Lane, 1985. m: Steven Lutvak; add m: Elizabeth Swados & David Schechter; w/d: David Schechter; developed in collaboration with Lori Wilner; from diaries of Hannah Senesh (or Senesz), Hungarian Jewish freedom fighter parachuted into Hungary in 1944, caught by Hungarian police, tortured, and executed without talking; cos: David Woolard; light: Vivien Leone. Cast: Lori Wilner, David Schechter, John Fistos. Susan Gabriel (understudy). "Rainbow Song," "Eli, Eli," "Blessed is the Match," "Soon," "Shtil di Nacht," "Zog Nit Keyn Mol," "One, Two, Three"

1487. Hans Andersen. Set in 1830s Denmark. London Palladium, 12/19/74. p: Harold Fielding & Louis Benjamin; m/l: Frank Loesser & Marvin Laird; b: Beverley Cross; based on 1952 movie *Hans Christian Andersen*, starring Danny Kaye; d: Freddie Carpenter; ch: Gillian Lynne; set: Tim Goodchild. Cast: Tommy Steele, Milo O'Shea, Bob Todd, Lila Kaye, Willoughby Goddard, Geoffrey Toone, Colette Gleason, Sarah Bennett. "Ecclesiasticus," "Don't Talk to Me About Those Happy Days," "I'm Hans Christian Andersen," "For Hans Tonight," "Thumbelina," "Inchworm," "Anywhere I Wander," "This Town," "Wonderful Copenhagen," "The Ugly Duckling," "No Two People," "The King's New Clothes." Ran at the Palladium every year, the last being 12/17/77. Cast: Tommy Steele, Sally Ann Howes, Anthony Valentine, Lila Kaye

1488. Hans Christian Andersen. American Conservatory Theatre, San Francisco, 8/31/00–9/7/00. World premiere. m/l: Frank Loesser; b: Sebastian Barry; based on film; d/ch: Martha Clarke; cos: Jane Greenwood; light: Paul Gallo; md: Constantine Kitsopoulos. Cast: John Glover, Karen Trott, Dashiell Eaves, Galina Alexandrova, Teri Hansen

1489. Hans Christian Andersen. Stage version of 1952 movie; no new music. Maine State Music Theatre, Brunswick, Me, 6/4/03–6/21/03. m/l: Frank Loesser; b/mus arr: Maury Yeston; d: Charles Abbott. Cast: Ken Barnett, Amy Bodnar, Linda Romoff, David Hibbard. By 2/04 it was aiming for London's West End

1490. Happy as a King. Musical frolic. Grand, Blackpool, England, 4/6/53; toured; Princes, London, 5/23/53–6/13/53. 26 perf. p: Jack Hylton; m/l: Ross Parker; b: Austin Melford & Fred Emney; d: Richard Bird; ch: Joan Davis; set: George Ramon; md: Eric Rogers. Cast: Fred Emney, Shani Wallis, Dickie Henderson, Lloyd Pearson (*Austin Melford*), Warren Mitchell, Greta Unger

1491. Happy as a Sandbag: All the Fun of the 1940s. Compilation musical revue of war-years songs. Ambassadors, London, 1975

1492. Happy Holiday. Christmas show of fun, mystery & song. New Theatre, Oxford, England, 11/2/54; toured; Palace, London, 12/22/54–1/15/55. 31 perf. p: Emile Littler; m: George Posford; l/b: Eric Maschwitz; based on *The Ghost Train*, by Arnold Ridley; d: Peter Cotes; ch: Felicity Gray; set/cos: Berkeley Sutcliffe; md: Philip Martell. Cast: Marie Burke, Reg Dixon, Austin Melford, Janet Brown, Erica Yorke, Sheila Bernette, Betty McDowell, Faye Weldon

1493. The Happy Hypocrite. Set in Regency England. Bouwerie Lane, 9/5/68–9/19/68. 17 perf. m/l: James Bredt & Edward Eager; d/add material: Tony Tanner; light: Jules Fisher. Cast: Rosemarie Heyer, Howard Girven, John Aman. "Street Song," "Deep in Me," "Amorous Arrow," "Echo Song," "Miss Mere," "Mornings at Seven," "Song of the Mask," "(It's) Almost Too Good to Be True," "Wedding Pantomime," "Don't Take Sides," "Hell Hath No Fury," "I Must Smile," "Once, Only Once," "Face of Love"

1494. Hard Job Being God. Rock musical based on *Genesis* & other Old Testament books. Edison, Middle Broadway, 5/15/72–5/20/72. 7 prev from 5/10/72. 7 perf. p: Bob Yde & Andy Wiswell; m/l: Tom Martel; d: Bob Yde; ch: Lee Theodore; set/sm: Ray Wilke; cos: Mary Whitehead; light: Patrika Brown; sound: Bill Sandreuter; md: Roy Bittan. Cast: Gini Eastwood, Stu Freeman, Tom Martel, Anne Sarofeen, John Twomey. The Band: Keyboard: Roy Bittan; Bass: Pete Gries; Drums: Steve Merola; Guitar: Harry Rumpf. "Hard Job Being God," "Wherever You Go," "Famine," "Buy a Slave," "Prayer," "Moses's Song," "The Ten Plagues," "Passover," "The Eleven Commandments," "Tribes," "Ruth," "Festival," "Hail, David," "A Very Lonely King," "You're on Your Own," "A Psalm of Peace," "I'm Countin' on You," "Shalom L'Chaim!," "Amos Gonna Give You Hell," "What Do I Have to Do?"

1495. Hard Times. Circus musical. Belgrade Theatre, Coventry, England, 11/6/73–11/17/73. m/l: Christopher Tookey [film critic for the *Daily Mail*] & Hugh Thomas; b: Charles Sturridge & Hugh Thomas; based on Charles Dickens' novel; d: Charles Sturridge; ch: John Broome; md: John Royston Mitchell. Cast: Victor Spinetti, Deborah Grant, Paul Humpoletz, Linal Haft. Theatre Royal, Haymarket, London, 6/6/00–8/26/00. Prev from 5/19/00. d: Christopher Tookey. Cast: Brian Blessed, Roy Hudd

1496. Hard to Be a Jew. Set in big city in Czarist Russia, 1913–14. Eden, 10/28/73–2/10/74. 129 perf; re-ran 4/13/74–5/5/74. 32 perf. m: Sholom Secunda; l: Yitzchok Perlov; w: Sholem Aleichem; adapted: Joseph Buloff & David Licht; d: David Licht; ch: Pearl Lang; set/cos: Jeffrey B. Moss; md: Renee Solomon. Cast: Joseph Buloff, David Carey, Zvee Scooler, Bruce Adler, Miriam Kressyn. "Romance," "Russian Waltz," "Candle Blessing." See also *Double Identity* (in this appendix)

1497. Hark! Musical revue. Series of songs about youth, love & more specific phenomena of present day. Mercer O'Casey, 5/22/72–10/1/72. 152 perf. m/l: Dan Goggin, Marvin Solley, Robert Lorick; d: Darwin Knight. Cast: Jack Blackton, Dan Goggin, Danny Guerrero,

Sharron Miller, Elaine Petricoff, Marvin Solley. "Hark!," "Take a Look," "George," "Smart People," "Six Little Kids," "Sun Down," "The Outstanding Member," "How Am I Doin', Dad?," "All Good Things," "Molly," "I See the People," "Pretty Jack," "What's Your Sun Sign, Mr. Simpson?," "A Dying Business," "Waltz with Me, Lady"

1498. Harlem Song. Song & dance evening. History of Harlem music, from Jazz Age to modern day. Used photos & projections. Apollo, 8/4/02–12/29/02. 146 perf. Prev from 7/8/02. p: George C. Wolfe, Frank Wildhorn, John Schreiber Group, David Goodman, Margo Lion, Daryl Roth, Herb Alpert, Whoopi Goldberg; m/l/md: Daryl Waters & Zane Mark; d: George C. Wolfe; ch: Ken Roberson; set: Riccardo Hernandez; cos: Paul Tazewell; light: Jules Fisher & Peggy Eisenhauer; cast recording released 11/26/02 on Columbia/Legacy. Cast: B.J. Crosby, Queen Esther, Rosa Arredona, Rosa Curry, Gabriel Croom, Randy Andre Davis, Zoie Morris, David St. Louis, Keith Lamelle Thomas, Charles E. Wallace. "Well, Alright Then," "Drop Me off in Harlem," "Donnies Inn Kids," "Tarzan of Harlem," "Shakin' the African," "For Sale," "A Train," "Doin' the Niggerati Rag," "Hungry Blues," "Miss Linda Brown," "Here You Come with Love," "Time is Winding Up," "King Joe," "Joe the Bomber," "Fable of Rage in the Key of Jive," "Apple Honey," "Dream Deferred," "Shake," "Tree of Life." Toward end of 2002 there was great effort made to save the show. There were plans to bring it back every year

1499. Harmony. The story (based on fact) of the Comedian Harmonists, 6 young men in 1920s Germany who rose from unemployed street musicians to world-famous entertainers who made a dozen movies & sold millions of records, but because they were mixture of Jews & gentiles ran afoul of Nazis. La Jolla Playhouse, Calif., 1997. m: Barry Manilow; l/b: Bruce Sussman; d: David Warren. Cast: Rebecca Luker, Danny Burstein. Broadway plans for spring 1999 and then fall 1999 never materialized because they couldn't find suitable theatre. Backers' audition in 12/99. d: David Warren (assisted by Des McAnuff). Cast: Christiane Noll. In 2001 Barry Manilow tried to persuade the Goodman, in Chicago, to take it, but it didn't happen. With renewed plans for Broadway by winter 2004, it planned to open at the Forrest, Philadelphia, on 12/17/03, a week later than the expected 12/10/03, after prevs that were meant to have begun 12/2/03 (a week later than the expected 11/25/03), and it was due to close 1/3/04. This Philly run was to have replaced the previously scheduled run at Parker Playhouse, Fort Lauderdale, 10/21/03–1/4/04 (rehearsals from 9/1/03). p: Mark Schwartz, in assoc with Garry C. Kief, Brent Peck, Richard Jay-Alexander; d: David Warren; ch: Peter Pucci; md: David Chase. Cast: Brian D'Arcy James, Stephen Buntrock, Bradley Dean, Aaron Lazar, David Turner, Thom Christopher Warren. Also with: Kate Baldwin, Janine LaManna, Heather Ayers, Joe Dellger, Ian Knauer, Elizabeth Loyacano, April

Nixon, Josh Rhodes, Alex Sanchez, Jennifer Zimmerman. Broadway plans were now for winter 2004. However, the Philly run was canceled, due to lack of money. So, it was shelved, but not for long. It got new producers (Coats Guiles, Daniel Karslake, Beth Smith, Tara Schoen Fishman), a fresh look, its script was re-done. On 8/9/04 rehearsals for a 4-week workshop began, and full rehearsals began 8/16/04. md: David Chase. The same six stars as before, except that David Ayers replaced Stephen Buntrock. Basically the same supporting cast. Private industry presentations 9/9/04–9/10/04. This time it was aiming for a spring 2005 Broadway opening. See also *Band in Berlin* (this appendix)

1500. Harmony Close. King's, Glasgow, Scotland, 9/11/56 (2 weeks), then toured. p: Stephen Mitchell; m/l: Ronald Cass & Charles Ross; d: John Fernald; ch: Hazel Gee. Cast: Dennis Lotis, Derek Tansley, Carol Raye, Harry Landis, David Lander, Peter Gilmore. Theatre Royal, Brighton, 3/19/57 (2 weeks); Bournemouth; Lyric, Hammersmith, London, 4/17/57–6/8/57. 62 perf. d: Charles Ross; ch: Ross Taylor; set: Neil Hobson; cos: Michael Whittaker; md: Leonard Morris. Cast: Barbara Ferris, Bernard Cribbins, Zack Matalon, Colin Croft, Betty Huntley Wright, Rose Hill

1501. Harvest Time. New Lindsey, London, 2/21/57. m/d: Jack Sherman; l: Geoffrey Venis; ch: Norman Simpson. Cast: Norman Simpson, David Kernan, Diane Todd

1502. Hats Off to Ice. Icetravaganza. Center Theatre, 6/22/44–4/27/46. 889 perf. p: Sonart Prods (Sonja Henie & Arthur M. Wirtz); m/l: James Littlefield & John Fortis; d: William H. Burke & Catherine Littlefield; skating d: May Judels; ch: Catherine & Dorothie Littlefield; set: Bruno Maine; cos: Grace Houston. Principal Skaters: Freddie Trenkler, Carol Lynne, The Brandt Sisters, Lucille Page, Rudy Richards, Claire Wilkins, Bob Ballard, Peggy Wright, Paul Castle, Jean Sturgeon. "Hats off to Ice," "Love Will Always Be the Same," "You've Got What it Takes," "Isle of the Midnight Rainbow," "With Every Star," "Headin' West," "Here's Luck"

1503. Havana Under the Sea. Ghost of aristocratic lady condemned to wander for eternity among sunken ruins of Havana. INTAR, 3/11/03. Prev from 2/28/03. Classic Cuban songs, with English libretto. w: Abilio Estevez; translated/adapted into English: Caridad Svich; d: Max Ferra; cos: Willa Kim; md: Meme Solis. Cast: Doreen Montalvo, Meme Solis

1504. Have a Nice Day! Musical spoof of Nixon-era youth traveling shows. Theatre East, 4/18/96–5/26/96. 5 prev. 31 perf. conceived by/w/arr: Rick Lewis; d: Frank H. Latson; ch: Susan Streater

1505. Have I Got a Girl for You! The Frankenstein Musical. Send-up of movie *The Bride of Frankenstein* & others in genre. Set a long time ago, in a Bavarian forest just east of Hollywood. Inroads, 2/10/85–3/3/85. 16 perf. m/l/md: Dick Gallagher; b: Joel Greenhouse & Penny Rockwell; d: Bruce Hopkins; ch: Felton Smith; set: Herman C. Arnhold; cos: Kenneth M. Yount. Cast: Rick Stanley, Chris Tanner,

Semina De Laurentis, Susan Borneman. "Peasants Song," "Don't Open the Door," "Always for Science," "Hollywood," "Last Lullaby," "The Way I Look at You," "I Love Me," "Have I Got a Girl for You!," "If This is How it Ends," "The Opera," "I'll Take it From Here." Revised & revived at Second Avenue Theatre, 10/29/86–1/4/87. 8 prev; 78 perf. Main crew as before, except set: Harry Darrow; md: Michael Rice. Cast: Gregory Jbara, Walter Hudson, Angelina Fiordellisi, Semina De Laurentis, Dennis Parlato. Some numbers were deleted, others added: "Girlfriends for Life," "The Monster's Song," "Mary's Lament," "Something"

1506. *Have I Got One for You*. Musical fairy tale of romance among toads, moles, princes & princesses. Theatre Four, 1/7/68. 1 perf. m/l: Jerry Blatt & Lonnie Burstein; d: Roberta Sklat; light: Peter Hunt; cast recording on ABC-Paramount. Cast: Gloria De Haven, Dick O'Neill, John Michael King. "The Toad's Lament," "Fly Away," "Have I Got a Girl for You," "Imagine Me," "The Chicken Song," "I Should Stay," "My Dream is Through," "A Nice Girl Like You," "So It Goes"

1507. *Head Over Heels*. Harold Clurman, 12/15/81–1/3/82. 22 perf. m: Albert T. Viola; l: William S. Kilborne Jr.; b: William S. Kilborne Jr. & Albert T. Viola; based on play *The Wonder Hat*, by Kenneth Sawyer Goodman & Ben Hecht; d: Jay Binder; ch: Terry Rieser; set/cos: John Falabella; ms/orch: John Clifton; md: Herbert Kaplan; assoc p: Joseph M. Sutherin. Cast: John Cunningham, Elizabeth Austin, Gwyda DonHowe. "New Loves for Old," "Perfection," "I'm in Love," "Aqua Vitae," "Nowhere," "Castles in the Sand," "As If," "Couldn't He Be You?," "Lullaby to Myself"

1508. *The Heart's a Wonder*. Westminster Theatre, London, 9/18/58. 44 perf. w: Nuala & Mairin O'Farrell; based on *The Playboy of the Western World*, by J.M. Synge; d: Denis Carey; ch: Josie MacAvin & Patricia Ryan; set/cos: Micheal MacLiammoir. Cast: Una Collins, Milo O'Shea, Dermot Kelly, Joe Lynch, Ann O'Dwyer

1509. *Hearts Are Trumps*. Theatre Royal, Birmingham, England, 10/19/43 (2 weeks); Manchester, 11/13/43 (2 weeks). Did not make London. m: Leon Carroll, Jack Waller, Joseph Tunbridge; l: Ian Grant & Robert Fyle; b: Robert Fyle; based on *The Best People*, by Avery Hopgood & David Grey. Cast: Hermione Baddeley, Wylie Watson

1510. *Hearts Delight Follies '69*. Closed before Broadway, 1969. m/l: Bob Crewe. Cast: Bobby Dimple, Darvana Payne. "American Moon"

1511. *Heat Lightning*. About an Elvis-obsessed wannabe rock star. Kirk, 3/5/03–4/20/03. Prev from 2/25/03. p: Steve Griggs; m/l: George Griggs; b: Steve Griggs & Paul Andrew Perez; inspired by myth of Cephalus & Procris, from Ovid's *Metamorphoses*; d: Paul Andrew Perez; ch: Jennifer Dell; set: Leo T. Van Allen. Cast: Colleen Sexton, Laura Marie Duncan

1512. *Heathcliff*. Began as concept album,

1995, recorded by Cliff Richard, Olivia Newton-John & Kristina Nichols. Academy, Birmingham, England, 10/16/96. m: John Farrar; l: Tim Rice; b: Frank Dunlop. Cast: Cliff Richard, Helen Hobson, Darryl Knock, Jimmy Johnston. "A Misunderstood Man," "Sleep of the Good," "Each to His Own," "Had to Be," "When You Thought of Me," "Dream Tomorrow," "Choosing When it's Too Late," "Be with Me Always," "Nightmare." In 1997 the show moved to London

Heaven on Earth see # 502, Main Book
Heaven Sent see # 524, Main Book

1513. *Hedwig and the Angry Inch*. Rock 'n roll glam-punk drag musical bio. The action spans Berlin, a Kansas trailer park & Madison Square Garden TGIF restaurant. The angry inch is the 1 inch left of Hedwig's penis after botched sex-change operation from man to woman. Westbeth, 2/27/97–3/31/97. 10 prev. 17 perf. m/l: Stephen Trask; b: John Cameron Mitchell; d: Peter Askin; ch: Jerry Mitchell; set: James Youmans. Cast: Hedwig Schmidt/ Tommy Gnosis: Jerry Mitchell; Yitzak: Miriam Shor. The band Cheater (Stephen Trask — the leader — Scott Bilbrey, David McKinley & Chris Wielding) played the Angry Inch. "Tear Me Down," "Origin of Love," "Sugar Daddy," "Angry Inch," "Wig in a Box," "Wicked Little Town," "The Long Gift," "Hedwig's Lament," "Exquisite Corpse," "Midnight Radio." Public; Fez; Squeezebox; 1907 Hotel Riverview (at that point re-named the Jane Street Theatre), 2/14/98–4/9/00. 12 prev from 2/1/98. 857 perf. Jerry Mitchell & Stephen Trask were on stage for full 90 mins, Mr. Mitchell as star & Mr. Trask as keyboardist. Mr. Mitchell was replaced by Michael Cerveris, then by Ally Sheedy, Matt McGrath, Kevin Cahoon, and Asa Somers (Donovan Leitch alternate). Jeremy Chatzky replaced Scott Bilbrey in band. A movie was made. Playhouse, London, 9/19/00–11/4/00. Prev from 9/8/00. Cast: Michael Cerveris (Nathan Taylor on Mon evenings). Victoria, San Francisco, 11/22/02. d: Jason Eagan. Cast: Kevin Cahoon (*Asa Somers* 3/12/03–3/23/03). City Theatre, Pittsburgh, 5/1/03–6/27/03. Huge success. d: Brad Rouse. Cast: Anthony Rapp, Sarah Siplak. Moved to Hartford Stage, Conn., 8/2/03–8/17/03

1514. *The Heebie Jeebies*. Musical tribute to Vet, Connee & Martha Boswell (the Boswell Sisters), reprising their many hits. Westside Arts Theatre Downstairs, 6/18/81–7/19/81. 37 perf. p: Spencer Tandy, Joseph Butt, Peter Alsop; w: Mark Hampton & Stuart Ross; from orig idea by Mark Hampton; script & prod adviser: Vet Boswell; d/ch: Stuart Ross; set: Michael Sharp; cm: George Elmer. Cast: Memrie Innerarity, Audrey Lavine, Nancy McCall. "The Heebie Jeebies," "Spend an Evening in Caroline," "Sentimental Gentleman from Georgia," "Nights When I Am Lonely," "St. Louis Blues," "I'm Gonna Cry," "Dinah," "That's How Rhythm Was Born," "We're on the Highway to Heaven," "We Gotta Put the Sun Back in the Sky," "Life is Just a Bowl of Cherries," "Sing a Little Jingle," "Crazy People," "Nothing is Sweeter than You," "When I Take My Sugar to Tea," "The Music Goes Round

and Round," "Let Yourself Go," "You Oughta Be in Pictures," "Rock n' Roll," "These Foolish Things," "Until the Real Thing Comes Along," "Darktown Strutters Ball," "Minnie the Moocher's Wedding Day," "Goin' Home," "Shout, Sister, Shout," "The Object of My Affection," "Everybody Loves My Baby." Previously ran at Berkshire Theatre Festival

1515. *Helen*. AMAS, 11/30/78. 12 perf. m/l: Johnny Brandon; b/d: Lucia Victor; based on Helen of Troy; ch/cos: Bernard Johnson; md: Danny Holgate. Cast: Jean Du Shon, Fran Salisbury, Pauletta Pearson, Paul Binotto. "Nothing Ever Happens in Greece," "Come on and Dance," "Somethin' Doin'," "Bring it on Home," "Bite Your Tongue," "There Are Ways of Gettin' Things Done," "Diplomacy," "You've Got It," "Do Us a Favor," "Dance of the Golden Apple," "Helen," "Hold on Tight," "Do What You Must," "Somebody Touched Me," "You Never Know the Mind of a Woman," "Good or Bad"

1516. *Hello Again*. Mitzi Newhouse, 1/30/94–3/27/94. 45 prev from 12/30/93. 65 perf. m/l/b: Michael John La Chiusa; suggested by *La Ronde*, by Arthur Schnitzler; d/ch: Graciela Daniele; set: Derek McLane; cos: Toni-Leslie James; light: Jules Fisher & Peggy Eisenhauer; md: David Evans; orch: Michael Starobin. Cast: Judy Blazer, Donna Murphy (*Saundra Santiago*), Carolee Carmello, Malcolm Gets, Michele Pawk, John Cameron Mitchell, Michael Park, Dennis Parlato, John Dossett (*Bob Stillman* during illness), David A. White. "Hello Again," "Zei Gezent," "I Gotta Little Time," "We Kiss," "In Some Other Life," "Story of My Life," "At the Prom," "Ah Meinen Zeit," "Tom," "Listen to the Music," "Montage," "Safe," "The One I Love," "Silent Movie," "Rock with Rock," "Angel of Mercy," "Mistress of the Senator," "The Bed Was Not My Own." 1st workshopped 8/27/93–8/29/93. Cast: Tom Hulce, Robert Duncan McNeill, Barbara Walsh, Harold Perrineau Jr., Juliet Lambert, Peter Friedman. Revived in London, 2001

1517. *Hello Charlie*. Anderson Yiddish Theatre, 10/23/65–1/6/66. 129 perf. m/l: Maurice Rayuch & Jacob Jacobs. Cast: Susan Walters, Gita Galina, Jacob Jacobs (also p), Max Perlman (also d)

1518. *Hello Muddah, Hello Fadduh*. Musical revue. Life in Florida retirement community frames songs written by Allan Sherman (who died in 1973). Circle in the Square Downtown, 12/5/92–6/27/93. 235 perf. m/l: Allan Sherman; w/conceived by: Douglas Bernstein & Rob Krausz; d/ch: Michael Leeds; md: David Evans; sound: Tom Morse. Cast: Stephen Berger, Tovah Feldshuh, Jason Graae, Paul Kreppel (*Scott Robertson* from 12/92), Mary Testa (*Leslie Klein* from 12/92). "Hello Muddah, Hello Fadduh," "One Hippopotami," "Jump Down, Spin Around," "Down the Drain" (m: Albert Hague). Triad, 8/2/01–11/18/01. 124 perf. d: Rob Krausz

1519. *Hello, Solly!* Yiddish musical revue. Carnegie Hall, 9/10/66–9/11/66. 3 perf. p: Hal Zeiger; md: Al Hausman. Cast: Mickey Katz, Larry Best. Henry Miller, Broadway. 4/4/67–5/28/67. 68 perf

1520. *Hellzapoppin.* Olsen & Johnson vaudeville "scream-lined revue." 46th Street Theatre, Broadway, 9/22/38. m: mostly by Sammy Fain; l: mostly by Charles Tobias; d: Edward Duryea Dowling. "Hellz-a-poppin'," "Fuddle Dee Duddle" (Funny Little Tune), "A Bedtime Story," "Strollin' Through the Park," "Abe Lincoln," "Shaganola," "It's Time to Say Aloha," "Harem on the Loose," "Ole Man Mose," "When You Look in Your Looking Glass." Despite being roasted by critics (except Walter Winchell), the show was smash hit. Moved (due to boost in press from Winchell) to Winter Garden, 11/28/38. On 12/11/39 it became known as *The New Hellzapoppin'* (although the show did not take a break at this point). New numbers: "I Tank I Go Home," "Mosquito," "Up High," "We Won't Let it Happen Here," "Balloon," "Boomps-a-Daisy," "When McGregor Sings Off Key," "Scarem Harem," "Now You See it — Now You Don't," "Over the Rainbow," "Havana for a Night," "Surprise Party," "Now Comes the Time." Added during run: "Any Bonds for Sale?." On 11/25/41 it moved again, to the Majestic, and closed there 12/17/41, Total of 1,404 perf (longest-running Broadway musical up to then). Toured with Jackie Gleason & Lew Parker. Filmed in 1941, with Olsen & Johnson, and Martha Raye. The show led to a sort of sequel, *Sons o' Fun* (1941-q.v.). *Hellzapoppin* was revived as *Hellzapoppin '67*, at Garden of Stars, Expo '67, Montreal, 7/1/67–9/16/67. p: Alex Cohen; m/l: Marian Grudeff & Raymond Jessel; d: Jerry Adler. Cast: Soupy Sales, Johnny Melfi, Luba Lisa, Claiborne Cary, Betty Madigan (who replaced Gretta Thyssen), Jackie Alloway, Brandon Maggart, Jack Fletcher, Ted Thurston, Susanna Clemm, Will B. Able, Graziella. *Hellzapoppin* (without the '67 tag after it), billed as "a musical circus," opened 11/22/76, Mechanic, Baltimore. Then on to the National, Washington, DC, but closed in Boston 1/22/77, never reaching intended Broadway. p: Alex Cohen; m: Jule Styne & Hank Beebe; l: Carolyn Leigh & Bill Heyer; one additional song ("Bouncing Back for More," cut from *Wildcat*) by Cy Coleman & Carolyn Leigh; d: Abe Burrows, *Jerry Adler*; ch: Donald Saddler (Tommy Tune also had a hand); set: Robert Randolph; cos: Alvin Colt; sound: Jack Shearing; ms: Elliot Lawrence; orch: Ralph Burns; dance mus: Gordon Lowry Harrell. Cast: Jerry Lewis, Lynn Redgrave, Herb Edelman, Joey Faye, Brandon Maggart, Jill Choder, Robert Fitch, Tom Batten, Mace Barrett, Justine Johnston, Bob Harvey, The Volantes, Bob Williams, Mercedes Ellington, Marie Berry, Susan Danielle, Gwen Hillier, P.J. Mann, Tudi Roach, Fred Siretta, Lisa Guignard. "Hellzapoppin," "A Husband, a Lover, a Wife," Eighth Avenue," "Once I've Got My Cane," "Hello, Mom," "Back to Him," "A Hymn to Her," "A Miracle Happened," "One to a Customer." There were legal problems between the producer & Jerry Lewis (it was claimed Jerry didn't rehearse properly)

1521. *Help!! Desk.* About the corporate computer revolution. Producers Club II, 11/18/97–12/6/97. 4 prev. 11 perf. m/l: Keith Edwards & Elizabeth Edwards. Cast: Chev Rodgers. "Help Desk Rhapsody," "Never Tell 'em Your Name," "Beeps in the Night," "Darwin Jive," "Changes," "Never Admit that You're Wrong," "Old Guy's Song," "Slash and Burn," "The Questionnaire," "Choices," "Half Man, Half Machine," "My Old Friend Mac," "Rainbow Comes After the Storm," "It Ain't Got No Soul," "Secrets," "Miranda"

1522. *Help, Help, the Globolinks!* 70-minute one-act opera for children. Globolinks are green aliens who invade earth. The only way to chase one away is to play music. Hamburg, Germany, 12/21/68. Commissioned by Hamburg Opera. w/d: Gian-Carlo Menotti. City Center, NYC, 1969. Cast: Judith Blegen, Richard Best

1523. *Henry the 8th at the Grand Ole Opry.* Musical comedy revue. Chronicled the life of the king through country music. Palsson's, 9/15/87–11/15/87. 46 perf. w/d: Alan Bailey. Cast: William Mesnick, Jennifer Smith, Linda Miles, Linda Kerns (*Deborah Unger*)

1524. *Her Excellency.* Alhambra, Glasgow, Scotland, 4/19/49 (2 weeks); toured; London Hippodrome, 6/22/49; Saville, 9/21/49–1/29/50. 252 perf total. m: Manning Sherwin & Harry Parr Davies; l: Harold Purcell; b: Archie Menzies & Harold Purcell (b); add dial: Max Kester; d: Jack Hulbert; ch: Bert Stimmel & Jack Hulbert; cos: Berkeley Sutcliffe; md: Robert Probst. Cast: Cicely Courtneidge, Thorley Walters, Eleanor Summerfield, Patrick Barr, Austin Trevor, Billy Dainty, Eleanor Fazan, Tucker McGuire

1525. *Here Lies Jenny.* Musical revue about a saloon singer. Zipper, 5/27/04–10/3/04. Prev from 5/7/04. 92 perf. m: Kurt Weill; l: various authors; conceived by/d: Roger Rees; ch: Ann Reinking; set: Neil Patel; light: Frances Aronson; sound: Tony Meola. Cast: Bebe Neuwirth, Ed Dixon

1526. *Herringbone.* Play with songs. Southern-born youth driven by evil spirit to career as performer. Previously produced at the St. Nicholas Theatre, Chicago. Playwrights Horizons, 6/30/82–8/27/82. m: Skip Kennon; l: Ellen Fitzhugh; b: Tom Cone (based on his play); d: Ben Levit; ch: Theodore Pappas; light: Frances Aronson. Cast: David Rounds (all 10 roles, male & female), Skip Kennon (at the piano). "Herringbone," "Uncle Billy," "God Said," "Little Mister Tippy Toes," "George," "The Cheap Exit," "What's a Body to Do?," "The Chicken and the Frog," "Ten Years"

1527. *Herschel and the Jester.* True story of jester in Ukraine. Yiddish Art Theatre, 12/12/48. m: Joseph Rumshinsky; based on Moshe Livshitz's story of the same name; d: Maurice Schwartz; ch: Selma Schneider. Cast: Maurice Schwartz, Boris Auerbach, Sara Gingold

1528. *Hexen.* Chamber musical. 2 witches live out the 8th of their 9 lives. Tribeca Lab, 2/4/93–2/27/93. 12 perf. w/adapted/d: Danny Ashkenasi; orig German script: Peter Lund. Cast: Kimberly Gambino, Priscilla Quinby

1529. *Hey, Love.* Cabaret revue on songs of Mary Rodgers. Eighty-Eights, 3/24/93–6/23/93. p: Music Theatre Group; conceived by/d: Richard Maltby Jr.; md: Patrick S. Brady; cast recording on Varese Sarabande. Cast: Karen Mason, Marcus Lovett, Mark Waldrop. Brought back by the Musical Theatre Group, to the Rainbow & Stars, as *3 of Hearts*, 9/3/96–9/28/96. 40 perf. d: Mark Waldrop. Cast: Faith Prince, Mark Waldrop, Jason Workman. Used the song "Who Knows" (m: Mary Rodgers & Steve Sondheim; l: Mr. Sondheim & Martin Charnin), which had been cut from *Hot Spot*, but with new lyrics by Mark Waldrop. It also used "Don't Laugh," the big song from *Hot Spot* (same writers), but it was now called "I Know" (add lyr by Mr. Maltby)

1530. *Hey, Ma … Kaye Ballard.* Promenade, 2/27/84–4/22/84. 16 prev. 62 perf. p: Karl Allison & Brian Bantry; conceived by/orig m & l: David Levy & Leslie Ebenhard; w: Kaye Ballard; d: Susan H. Schulman; cos: William Ivey Long; md: Robert Billig; special mus arr: Arthur Siegel. Cast: Kaye as herself, telling life story & singing songs. "Up There," "Someone Special," "Nana," "You Made Me Love You," "Thinking of You," "Supper Club," "Without a Song," "Nobody but You," "Teeny Tiny," "Hey, Ma," "Lazy Afternoon," "Always You," "You Don't Need It," "Down in the Depths," "Cookin' Breakfast," "Old Tunes," "All the Magic Ladies"

1531. *Hi, Paisano!* Set in NYC. York Playhouse, 9/30/61–10/1/61. 3 perf. m/l: Robert Holton & June Carroll; b: Ernest Chambers; conceived by/d: Vassili Lambrinos; md: Joseph Stecko. Cast: David Canary, Marie Santell, Paula Wayne

1532. *Hi, Yank!* Army Show, 1944. m/l: Frank Loesser, Hy Zaret, Jack Hill. Cast: David Brooks, Joshua Shelley. "Classification Blues," "Little Red Rooftops," "The Most Important Job," "Yank, Yank, Yank," "My Gal and I," "Saga of a Sad Sack." Toured camps

1533. *High Diplomacy.* Westminster Theatre, London, 6/5/69–11/1/69. 172 perf. m: William L. Reed & George Fraser; l/b: Alan Thornhill & Hugh Steadman Williams; d: Henry Cass; ch: Virginia Mason; md: John W. Daley. Cast: Patricia Bredin, Muriel Smith

The High Life see # 242, Main Book

1534. *High Society.* Victoria Palace, London, 1/25/87–1/16/88. Not connected to the Broadway musical, except both came from the 1956 movie. The Vereinigten Buehnen Wien bought the rights & put it on in Vienna, 6/3/98–8/1/98. Another unconnected prod toured UK, 1996, with Natasha Richardson

1535. *High Spirits.* Intimate musical revue (no connection to the Noel Coward play). Hippodrome, London, 5/23/53. 125 perf. m: John Pritchett & Ronald Cass; d: William Chappell; md: Van Phillips. Cast: Cyril Ritchard, Diana Churchill, Ian Carmichael, Dilys Lay (later Laye), Leslie Crowther, Patrick Cargill, Joan Sims, Ronnie Stevens. "Honky-Tonk Blues"

1536. *The Highest Yellow.* About Van Gogh's psychiatrist, Dr. Felix Rey. Signature Theatre, Arlington, Va., 10/26/04–12/12/04. m/l: Michael John La Chiusa; d: Eric Schaeffer. Cast: Jason Danieley, Judy Kuhn

1537. *Hijinks!* Opera singer's arrival & adventures in USA. Cheryl Crawford, 12/17/80–

1/18/81. 7 prev. 37 perf. p: Chelsea Theatre Center; m/l: Robert Kalfin, Steve Brown, John McKinney; based on idea by William Bolcom, David Brooks, Robert Kalfin, Arnold Weinstein & on Clyde Fitch's 1901 play *Captain Jinks of the Horse Marines;* d: Robert Kalfin; ch: Larry Hayden; md: Michael O'Flaherty. Cast: Joseph Kolinski, Evalyn Baron, Michael Connolly, Randall Easterbrook, Scott Ellis, Elaine Petricoff, Michael O'Flaherty. "Love's Old Sweet Song," "Star Spangled Banner," "Capt. Jinks of the Horse Marines," "Will You Love Me in December as You Do in May?," "Beautiful Dreamer," "Silver Threads Among the Gold," "Whispering Hope," "Auld Lang Syne," "Wait Till the Sun Shines, Nellie"

1538. *The Hired Man.* Set in Cumberland in 1896 & 1914. Farmhand tries to become miner in order to support family. Nuffield, Southampton, England, 2/2/84–2/25/84. m: Howard Goodall; l/b: Melvyn Bragg (based on his novel); d: David Gilmore; set: Roger Glossop. Cast: Phyllis Logan. Revised & ran at Haymarket, Leicester, 7/19/84; Astoria, London, 10/31/84–3/23/85. 164 perf. p: Andrew Lloyd Webber (*Melvyn Bragg* & *Laurie Marsh*); d: David Gilmore; ch: Anthony Van Laast; set: Martin Johns; cast recording on Polydor. Cast: Julia Hills. "Song of the Hired Man," "Fill it to the Top," "Now for the First Time," "Who Will You Marry, Then?," "Time Passing," "I Wouldn't Be the First," "Fade Away," "What a Fool I've Been," "If I Could," "Men of Stone," "You Never See the Sun," "Gathering of Soldiers," "So, Tell Your Children," "No Choir of Angels." In the USA it ran at INTAR, 11/3/88–11/13/88; 47th Street Theatre, 11/17/88–12/18/88. 33 perf. Presented by the Heritage Players; p/d: Brian Aschinger; ch: Rodney Griffin; md: Ann Crawford. Cast: Paul Avedisian, Ray Collins, Nick Corley, Richard Lupino, Carolyn Popp. A concert was done in London in 1992, with several members of the orig cast

1539. *Hiroshima.* Play with mus. Theatre for the New City, 10/2/97–11/2/97. 4 prev. 16 perf. m: Yoko Ono; w/d: Ron Destro

1540. *His Master's Voice.* Half Moon, London, 10/13/77–11/19/77. w/md: David Anderson; d: Stuart Mungall. Cast: Michelle Collins, Gary Sheil

1541. *His Monkey Wife.* Hampstead Theatre Club, London, 12/20/71–1/15/72. Prev from 12/13/71. 28 perf. w: Sandy Wilson; from novel by John Collier; d: Basil Coleman; ch: David Drew; md: Richard Holmes; cast recording on President. Cast: Bridget Armstrong, Roland Curran, Myvanwy Jenn, June Ritchie, Sally Mates, Robert Swann, Jeffrey Wickham, Jonathan Elsom. "Home and Beauty and You," "In Boboma Tonight," "Don't Rush Me," "Who is She?," "Dear Human Race," "Leave it All to Smithers," "Mad About Your Mind," "His Monkey Wife," "A Girl Like You," "Doing the Chimpanzee," "Live Like the Blessed Angels"

1542. *A History of the American Film.* Play with mus. Eugene O'Neill Memorial Theatre Center, Waterford, Conn., 8/12/76. 2 perf. m: John J. Gaughan Jr.; l/b: Christopher Durang

(Tony nomination for book); d: Peter Mark Schifter. Cast: Cynthia Herman, Jerry Zaks, Gale Garnett, Gary Bayer, Dianne Wiest. Official world premiere at Hartford Stage Co., Conn., 3/11/77. 44 perf. d: Paul Weidner; set: Hugh Landwehr; cos: Claire Ferraris; light: John McLain; md/accompanist: Richard De-Rosa. Cast: Jerry Zaks, Alice White, Cynthia Herman. Then it was a Center Theatre Group prod at Mark Taper Forum, L.A. 38 perf in rep with Sam Shepard's *Angel City*. d: Peter Mark Schifter; set: John Conklin; cos: Joe I. Tompkins; light: F. Mitchell Dana. Cast: Udana Power, Robert Walden, June Gable, Alice Playten, Richard Lenz, Jane Connell, Teri Ralston, Roger Robinson, Barry Dennen, Frank O'Brien, Lu Leonard, Gordon Connell. Arena Stage, Washington, D.C., 5/13/77. 46 perf. d/ch: David Chambers; set: Tony Straiges; light: William Mintzer. Cast: April Shawhan, Gary Bayer, Swoosie Kurtz, Joan Pape. Ran on Broadway, at ANTA, 3/30/78–4/16/78. 19 prev. 21 perf. p: Judith Gordon, Richard S. Bright, Marc Howard, Sheila-Barbara-Dinah Prods; m: Mel Marvin; d: David Chambers; ch: Graciela Daniele; set: Tony Straiges; cos: Marjorie Slaiman; light: William Mintzer; sound: Lou Shapiro; md: Clay Fullum; orch: Robert M. Freedman. Cast: Maureen Anderman, Gary Bayer, Walter Bobbie, Jeff Brooks, Bryan Clark, David Cromwell, David Garrison, Ben Halley Jr., Swoosie Kurtz, Kate McGregor-Stewart, Joan Pape, April Shawhan, Brent Spiner, Eric Weitz, Mary Catherine Wright, Robert Fisher (onstage pianist). "The Silent Years," "Minstrel Song," "Shanty Town Romance," "They Can't Prohibit Love," "We're in a Salad," "Euphemism," "Ostende Nobis Tosca," "The Red, the White and the Blue," "Pretty Pin-Up," "Apple Blossom Victory," "Isn't it Fun to Be in the Movies," "Search for Wisdom"

1543. *Hit Me with a Hot Note!— The Duke Ellington Songbook.* Tour opened Englewood, NJ, 2/6/99. Cast: Marilyn McCoo, Billy Davis Jr., Stacie Precia (*Angela Robinson* from 3/25/99), Cindy Marchionda (*Kyla Grogan* from 3/25/99), Abe Clark, Chad Borden

1544. *Hit the Lights!* Pop/rap musical fantasy. Vineyard, 12/21/93–1/9/94. 20 perf. m: Jon Giluntin; l/b: Michele Lowe; add m: Chris Hajian; d: Lisa Peterson; ch: Lynne Taylor-Corbett; light: Peter Kaczorowski. Cast: Annie Golden, John Sloman, Andrea Frierson, Ann Harada, Michael Mandell, Jason Danieley, Michael O'Gorman

1545. *Hobo.* Set in NY. Gate, 4/10/61–5/7/61. 32 perf. w: John Dooley. Cast: Ronald Holgate, Elmarie Wendel, Ned Wertimer, Rita Howell. "Nuthin' for Nuthin'," "Cindy," "Julie," "Bleecker Street," "On the Day When the World Goes Boom," "Good for Nothing," "Little Birds," "Who Put Out the Light that Lit the Candle that Started the Fire that Started the Flame Deep Down in My Heart"

1546. *Holiday on Broadway.* Variety revue. Mansfield, Broadway. 4/27/48–5/1/48. 6 perf. p: Al Wilde. Cast: Billie Holiday, Slam Stewart Trio, Cozy Cole

1547. *The Hollow Crown.* An entertain-

ment by & about the kings & queens of England–music, poetry, speeches, letters & other writings from the chronicles, from plays, and in the monarchs' own words; also mus concerning them and by them. Henry Miller's, Broadway, 1/29/63–3/9/63. 46 perf. p: Bonard Prods, by arr with Royal Shakespeare Theatre; dev/d: John W. Barton; md: Brian Priestman. Cast: John W. Barton, Max Adrian, Paul Hardwick, Dorothy Tutin. "Agincourt Song," "The King's Hunt," "Here's a Health Unto His Majesty," "The Vicar of Bray," "Ballad to an Absent Friend." On 12/30/63 a tour opened at the McCarter, Princeton, NJ, and closed at the University of Maryland College Park, 4/25/64. Cast: John Nettleton, John Werner, Michael Gough, Ann Firbank. Brooklyn Academy of Music, 4/21/74–4/28/74. Prev from 4/18/74. 7 perf in rep. p: Royal Shakespeare Theatre. Cast: Michael Redgrave, Paul Hardwick, Sara Kestelman; same venue, same producers, 5/1/76. 2 perf. Cast: Brenda Bruce, Jeffrey Dench. Princess of Wales, Toronto, 1/27/04–2/29/04. p: Ed & David Mirvish. Cast: Vanessa Redgrave, Ian Richardson, Donald Sinden, Alan Howard

1548. *Hollywood Opera.* The Ballroom, 3/13/85–5/18/85. 4 prev. 40 perf. m/l/conceived by/d: Barry Keating; add l: David Schechter; ch: Stuart Ross. Cast: Camille Saviola (*Lynn Eldredge*), Perry Arthur (also puppets), Mary-Cleere Haran. "Hollywood Opera," "D'Oyly Carte Blanche," "Citizen Kong," "Three Phases of Eve," "Opera in 3-D," "Delle Rose's Turn," "Das Exorcist," "How Now Voyager," "Tippy's Immolation"

1549. *Home Again, Home Again.* Set between 1925 & the present. Opened for Broadway tryouts 3/12/79, American Shakespeare Theatre, Stratford, Conn. Closed 4/14/79, Royal Alexandra, Toronto, canceling scheduled 4/26/79 Broadway opening at the Mark Hellinger (it was due to replace *Sarava*, which moved to the Broadway). Previously titled *Home Again*. m/l: Cy Coleman & Barbara Fried; b: Russell Baker; d: Gene Saks; ch: Onna White; set: Peter Larkin; cos: Jane Greenwood; light: Neil Peter Jampolis; md: Stanley Lebowsky; orch: Jim Tyler; dance mus arr: Cy Coleman. Cast: Dick Shawn, Ronny Cox, Lisa Kirk (her part was written out), Mike Kellin, Teri Ralston, Anita Morris, Rex Everhart, Jeannine Taylor, Robert Polenz, Mordecai Lawner, Tim Waldrip, William Morrison, Bob Freschi, Susan Cella, Lisa Guignard, Dirk Lumbard, Bill Nabel, Karen Tamburelli, Maggy Gorrill, Ron Schwinn. "America is Bathed in Sunlight," "When the Going Gets Tough," "I'm Your Guy," "All for Love," "When it Comes to Loving," "Home Again," "What'll It Take?," "Big People," "Traveling Together," "Winter Rain," "The Way I See It"

1550. *Home Fires.* Set during WWII; used period songs. Playhouse 91, 12/9/92–1/3/93. 28 perf. p: Light Opera of Manhattan; w: Linda Thorsen Bond & William Repicci; d: Robert Stewart; md: Jeffrey Buchsbaum

1551. *Honk!* Watermill, Newbury, England, 1997. m: George Stiles; l/b: Anthony Drewe; from *The Ugly Duckling*, by Hans Christian

Andersen. "A Poultry Tale (of Folk Down on the Farm)," "Joy of Motherhood," "Different," "Hold Your Head up High," "Look at Him," "Play with Your Food," "Every Tear a Mother Cries," "Wild Goose Chase," "It Takes All Sorts," "Together," "Now I've Seen It All," "Warts and All," "The Blizzard," "Transformation." Scarborough, Yorks, 1997, for Christmas season. d: Julia McKenzie. Olivier, London, 12/16/99–3/25/00. Prev from 12/11/99. d: Julia McKenzie. Helen Hayes, Nyack, NJ, 2/12/00 (US premiere). d: Gordon Greenberg; ch: Scott Wise & John MacInnis; sound: Peter Fitzgerald; md: Kimberly Grigsby. Cast: Alison Fraser, Gavin Creel, Nancy Anderson, Evalyn Baron

1552. *Hoofers.* Wooden O, 1/20/82–2/20/82. 12 perf. w: Clif Dowell & Eduardo Angulo; d: Clif Dowell; ch: Tod Miller & Germaine Salsberg; md: Fraser Hardin. Cast: Richard Atkins, Tod Miller, Virginia Seidel. "Wedding Cake," "Watch After Jill," "When Love Looks into Your Heart," "Hoofers," "Mailman's Valentine," "Jack of All Trades," "Have We Gotta Show," "I Gotta Tango to Do," "Yankee Come Home," "At the Savoy Grill," "Why Should a Guy Cry," "Syncopated Lady," "Women," "One Jack"

1553. *The Hoofers.* Musical entertainment with tap & rhythm dancers, singing, comedy & mime. Mercury, 7/29/69–10/12/69. 88 perf. m: Tiny Grimes Band; conceived by/co-ord: Leticia Jay; d: Derby Wilson; md: Tiny Grimes. Cast: Sandman Sims, Derby Wilson, Lon Chaney, Leticia Jay, Tiny Grimes. "You Gotta Go Tap Dancing Tonight"

1554. *Hooray for Daisy.* Daisy was a cow. Theatre Royal, Bristol, England, 12/23/59–2/20/60. p: Bristol Old Vic; m: Julian Slade; l/b: Julian Slade & Dorothy Reynolds; d: Denis Carey; ch: Basil Pattison; set/cos: Jane Graham; at pianos: Julian Slade & Martin Goldstein. Cast: James Cairncross, Leonard Rossiter, Annette Crosbie, Dorothy Reynolds, Angus Mackay, Peter Gilmore, Susan Engel, John Davidson, Peter Bowles. Lyric Opera House, Hammersmith, 12/20/60–1/28/61. 51 perf. Same crew, except p: Linnit & Dunfee. Cast: Dorothy Reynolds, Eleanor Drew, Edward Hardwick, Robin Hunter, Angus Mackay, Paddy Frost, John Davidson, Anna Dawson. "Wine is a Thing," "She's Coming on the 4.48," "I Feel as if I'd Never Been Away," "Nice Day," "No Lullaby," "Soft Hoof Shuffle," "If Only You Needed Me," "How, When and Where," "See You on the Moon," "Going Up," "He's Got Absolutely Nothing," "Tring-a-Ling," "It Won't Be the Same," "Madam, Will You Dine?," "I'm Sorry," "Let's Do a Duet," "Personally"

1555. *Hooray! It's a Glorious Day ... and All That.* Set in NYC. Theatre Four, 3/9/66–3/20/66. 15 perf. m: Arthur Gordon; l: Ethel Bieber, Maurice Teitelbaum, Charles Grodin; b: Maurice Teitelbaum & Charles Grodin; d: Charles Grodin; ch: Sandra Devlin; set/cos: Peter Harvey; light: Jules Fisher; md: Peter Fuchs; orch: Gershon Kingsley. Cast: Ron Holgate, Mina Kolb, Joan Eastman, Lou Criscuolo, Joy Franz, Jaclynn Villamil. "He's a-

Comin'," "I Hope He's Not Ashamed of Me," "Happy," "What's a Gang without a Guy Named Muggsy?," "I Wish I Knew," "Love Was a Stranger to Me," "Tap Dance," "Nasality," "The Wonderland of Love," "Dear Diary," "For Example," "It's a Glorious Day," "Panic Ballet," "Inspirational Song," "You're Gorgeous, You're Fantastic," "Everything Happens for the Best"

1556. *Horizons.* Musical drama. Horizons is a lodging house for teenagers. Riverwest, 12/10/84–12/30/84. 21 perf. m/l: Carlos Davidson & Kathleen True; b: Jack Adolfi; d: Paul Eisenman; ch: Ron Bohmer; md: J.T. Thomas. Cast: Deborah Smith, Clayton Prince, Ron Bohmer. "I See the Light," "I See the Streetlights," "Your Time Has Come," "Turned off to Turning On," "Ladies of the Night," "Why Can't it Be?," "Listen to the Children," "Grow Up, Little Girl," "Don't Live in Yesterday"

1557. *Horseman, Pass By.* A musical celebration. Fortune, 1/15/69–2/16/69. 37 perf. m: John Duffy; l/b: Rocco Bufano & John Duffy; from the writings & spirit of W.B. Yeats; d: Rocco Bufano; ch: Rhoda Levine. Cast: Barbara Barrie, Will Geer, Clifton Davis, George Hearn, Terry Kiser, Laurence Luckinbill (*Ken Kercheval*), Novella Nelson, Maria Tucci. "What Then? (Dead Man's Tango)," "This Great Purple Butterfly," "Brown Penny," "Girl's Song," "A Soldier Takes Pride in Saluting His Captain," "Before the World Was Made," "Last Confession," "Mad as the Mist and Snow," "Crazy Jane on the Day of Judgment," "Her Anxiety," "Salley Gardens," "Soulless a Faery Dies," "A Drunken Man's Praise of Sobriety," "To an Isle in the Water," "Consolation," "For Anne Gregory," "Three Songs to the One Burden" ("Henry Middleton"), "Final Choral Blessing"

1558. *Hot Grog.* Blackbeard story set in 1718 in coastal Carolina. Musical Theatre Lab, Kennedy Center, 3/15/77. 12 perf. m/l: Bland Simpson & Jim Wann; b: Jim Wann; d: Edward Berkeley; ch: Patricia Birch; cos: Hilary Rosenfeld; light: Joan Arhelger; md: Jeff Waxman. Cast: Edward Teach, alias Blackbeard: Frederick Coffin; Anne Bonney, the girl pirate: Cassandra Morgan; Also with: Kathi Moss, Mimi Wallace. Phoenix, NYC, 10/6/77–10/23/77. 28 perf. Same basic crew as before except set/light: James Tilton. Cast: Anne: Mimi Kennedy; Blackbeard: Louis Zorich; Also with: Patrick Hines, Kathi Moss, Mary Bracken Phillips. "Seizure to Roam," "Got a Notion," "Come on Down to the Sea," "Hot Grog," "The Pirate's Life," "The Difference is Me," "Change in Direction," "Heaven Must Have Been Smiling," "Hack 'em," "Treasure to Bury/One of Us," "Sea Breeze," "Skye Boat Song," "Marooned," "The Head Song," "Drinking Fool," "Bound Away"

1559. *Hot Klezmer.* Musical revue. American Jewish Theatre, 3/31/98–4/5/98. 24 prev from 3/7/98. 8 perf. compositions: Harold Seletsky & Mary Feinsinger; d: Michael Leeds; ch: Arte Phillips. Cast: Harold Seletsky, Mary Feinsinger, Ellis Berger

1560. *A Hot Minute.* Background singers dream of their "hot minute" in the spotlight. Bottom Line, 7/6/89–8/31/89. 28 perf.

conceived by/w: Melanie Mintz; d: Wayne Cilento. Cast: Vivian Cherry, Pattie Darcy, Annie Golden, John Martin Green, Jon Fiore

1561. *Hot Sake ... with a Pinch of Salt.* Set in Brooklyn & in Japan, in 1959. AMAS, 10/23/86–11/16/86. 16 perf. m: Jerome I. Goldstein; l/b: Carol Baker & Lana Stein; based on *A Majority of One*, by Leonard Spigelgass; d: William Martin; ch: Audrey Tischler; md: Neal Tate. Cast: Alvin K.U. Lum, Laurie Katzmann. "Fridays," "Pictures of You," "Here We Go Again," "How Do You Do," "Another Martini," "Trust No One," "How Was Your Day?," "I Found a Friend," "Moon Watching," "Let the Flowers Find Me," "All or Nothing Woman," "Sake," "What Good Does Loneliness Do?," "You Who Have Taught Me to Love," "A Nice Man Like That"

1562. *Hot September.* Shubert, Boston. Tryouts 9/14/65–10/9/65. Canceled scheduled 10/20/65 Broadway opening at the Alvin. p: Leland Hayward & David Merrick; m/l: Kenny Jacobson & Rhoda Roberts; b: Paul Osborn & Josh Logan; from William Inge's play *Picnic;* d: Josh Logan; ch: Danny Daniels; set: Oliver Smith; cos: Theoni V. Aldredge; md: Milton Rosenstock; orch: Philip J. Lang. Cast: Sean Garrison, Sheila Sullivan (who replaced Kathryn Hays), Betty Lester (who replaced Patricia Roe), Lovelady Powell, Eddie Bracken, Lee Lawson, John Stewart, Paula Trueman, Gene Castle, Kay Cole, Ronn Forella. "Another Crummy Day," "Hey, Delilah," "Whistle of a Train," "Golden Moment," "Come on Strong," "Somethin' More," "Live," "What Do You Do?," "Tell Me the Truth," "Show Me Where the Good Times Are," "Frug," "This Town," "A Guy Like Me," "Who Needs It?," "Hot September Dance," "Rosemary's Soliloquy," "Tell Me the Truth" (reprise), "You," "I Got it Made," "Somethin' More" (reprise), "Goodbye Girls," "I Blew It," "Golden Moment" (reprise). See also in this appendix *Show Me Where the Good Times Are*

1563. *Hot Voodoo Massage.* Troupe Theatre/Fantasy Factory, 12/22/78–1/7/79. 12 perf. m/l/d/ch: Bill Vitale; b: Ed Kuczewski

1564. *Hotel for Criminals.* Exchange, 12/30/74–1/12/75. 16 perf. w/d: Richard Foreman; m: Stanley Silverman; md: Roland Gagnon. Cast: Ken Bell, Paul Ukena, Lisa Kirchner, Paul Ukena Jr.

1565. *Hotel Passionato.* Set in Paris in 1912. Attempted adultery in hotel, complicated by appearance of various interested parties. East 74th Street Theatre, 10/22/65–10/31/65. 11 perf. p: Slade Brown; m/l: Philip Springer & Joan Javits; b: Jerome J. Schwartz; d: Michael Ross. Cast: Lee Cass, Roger Hamilton, The Kane Triplets, Linda Lavin, Phil Leeds, Marian Mercer, Robert Rovin, Paul Sand, Ned Wertimer, Jo Anne Worley. "Not Getting Any Younger," "What a Curious Girl," "Hotel Passionato," "Don't," "What a Night!"

1566. *Houdini: La Magia del Amor.* Through-sung musical. Teatro Benito Juarez, Mexico City, 11/5/97 (world premiere). p: Antonio Calvo & OCESA; m: Antonio Calvo; l: Patricia Perrin; b: Rafael Perrin, Patricia Perrin, Antonio Calvo; d: Rafael Perrin; ch:

Guillermo Telez; set: Monica Raya; cos: Oriet Fernandez. Cast: Enrique Chi, Lorena de la Garza. "Bola de cristal," "El rey de la magia," "Siempre te amare," "Fe," "Bienvenidos a Coney Island," "La confesion," "Que injusticia," "Por ti mi vida doy," "Las tres bodas," "El farmaceutico," "Te de tila," "Metamorfosis," "Letras y palabras," "La explicacion," "La audicion," "En el hospital," "Mi decision," La magia del amor," "Scotland Yard," "Levitacion," "Cruzando dimensiones," "El telegrama/ La muerte de Cecilia," "El mensaje oculto," "Las mediums," "La camara china de tortura," "La muerte de Houdini," "Hagase tu voluntad." Cast recording. Broadway aspirations

1567. ***House of Cards***. Players, London, 1/26/63. m/b: Peter Greenwell; l: Peter Wildeblood; based on David Margashack's translation of Ostrovsky's *Even a Wise Man Stumbles*; d: Vida Hope; set: Reginald Woolley. Cast: Patrick Mower, Geoffrey Hibbert, Francis Egerton, Stella Moray. Revised by Peter Greenwell & Peter Wildeblood, and with add dial by Guy Morgan, and ran at Wimbledon Theatre, 9/17/63; then Golders Green; Phoenix, London, 10/3/63–10/26/63. 27 perf. d: Vida Hope; ch: Terry Gilbert; set: Reginald Woolley; md: Michael Moores. Cast: Patrick Mower, Geoffrey Hibbert, Philip Hinton, Stella Moray, Douglas Byng, Terry Gilbert

1568. ***The House of Leather***. Ante-bellum rock musical. Set in New Orleans whorehouse, and at Donny Brook's Farm, outside the city, during and after Civil War. Ellen Stewart, 3/18/70. 1 perf. m/l: Dale F. Menten & Frederick Gaines; b: Frederick Gaines; md: Dale F. Menten; cast recording on Capitol. Cast: Barry Bostwick, Peter De Anda, Jonelle Allen. "House of Leather Theme," "Do You Recall the House of Leather?," "Armies of the Right," "God is Black," "Sherman's March to the Sea"

1569. ***The House of Martin Guerre***. Goodman, Chicago, 6/21/96. m/l: Leslie Arden; b: Leslie Arden & Anna Theresa Cascio; d: David Petrarca; ch: David Marques; md: Jeffrey Klitz. Cast: Guy Adkins, Hollis Resnik, Kevin Gudahl, Anthony Crivello, Kingsley Leggs. "The House of the Guerres," "The Wedding Night," "Eight Years," "Lullaby," "Seasons Pass," "It isn't That Easy for Me," "Martin's Home," "Devils and Doubts," "The World is Changing," "Something isn't Right," "Martin Couldn't Be Happier/Nothing Can Prepare You," "I've Had Enough," "Nothing to Do but Wait," "Why Are You Still Crossing Me?," "The Way of the World," "No Life at All," "Everything is True," "The Night I Won't Forget," "Monsieur Coras," "A Shred of Doubt," "Beautiful Day for a Hanging," "Arnaud's Apology"

1570. ***The Housewives' Cantata***. 3 sisters & the men in their lives. Part I set in 1962; Part II in 1972. Theatre Four, 2/17/80–3/9/80. 24 perf. p: Cheryl Crawford & Eryk Spektor; m: Mira J. Spektor; l: June Siegel; b: Willy Holtzman; d/ch: Rina Elisha; cos: Judy Dearing. Cast: Patti Karr, Foresby Russell, Sharon Talbot, William Perley. "Dirty Dish Rag," "Sex," "Song of the Bourgeois Beatnik," "Early Morn-

ing Rain" (l: Charline Spektor), "Little Women," "Adultery Waltz," "Divorce Lament," "Suburban Rose," "Song of the Open Road," "Legs," "M.C.P.," "Daughter's Lullaby," "Guinevere Among the Grapefruit Peels," "Apartment Lament," "Middle Aged," "Mr. Fixer," "White House Resident," "A New Song"

1571. ***How Do You Do, I Love You***. Closed before Broadway, 1967. m/l: David Shire & Richard Maltby Jr. Cast: Phyllis Newman, Barbara Cook. "One Step." Came from summer circuit

1572. ***How I Survived High School***. Jan Hus, 6/9/86–6/23/86. 12 perf. p: Robert Nicholas; m: Glenn Slater; d/co-w: Michael Taubenslag; ch: Tammy Thomas. Cast: Scott Fried, Nancy Pothier, Joe Buffington, Orlando Powers. "High School," "Shy Couple," "Wondering," "By Myself," "V.D.," "Lonely," "Please Don't Tell My Father," "Where," "Child Abuse," "Hi, Grandma," "Living a Dream," "Friendship," "Virgin," "View from the Hill," "Life"

1573. ***How to Be a Jewish Mother***. Jewish mother & her relationship with various people (all played by Godfrey Cambridge). Comedy with mus. Morris A. Mechanic Theatre, Baltimore, 12/11/67 (1 week). p: Jon-Lee & Seymour Vall; m: Michael Leonard; l: Herbert Martin; conceived by/sk: Seymour Vall; based on 1965 book by Dan Greenburg; d: Frederick Rolf, *Avery Schreiber*; ch: Doug Rogers; set: Robert Randolph; cos: Michael Travis; light: John J. Moore; md: Julian Stein. Cast: Molly Picon, Godfrey Cambridge. Standbys: Naomi Riseman & Tiger Haynes. "Once the Man You Laughed At," "Laugh a Little," "Since The Time We Met," "The Wedding Song," "Child You Are (Man You'll Be)." Hudson, Broadway, 12/28/67–1/13/68. 12 prev from 12/8/67. 21 perf. Renee Taylor & Joseph Bologna replaced Seymour Vall on sketches but were uncredited. d: Avery Schreiber. Broadway reviews were very bad

1574. ***How to Get Rid of It***. Set in NY. An ever-growing corpse represents a dying marriage. Astor Place, 11/17/74–11/24/74. 9 perf. m: Mort Shuman; l/b/d: Eric Blau; based on Eugene Ionesco's *Amedee*; light: Ian Calderon; psm: G. Allison Elmer [i.e. George Elmer]. Cast: Matt Conley, James Doerr, Joe Masiell, Carol L. Hendrick, Lorrie Davis, Joseph Neal, Janet McCall, Vilma Vaccaro, Muriel Costa-Greenspon. "Mind Your Business," "I Am a Vietnam Veteran," "What an Evening," "Amedee, Amedee, It isn't Too Late," "The Late, Late Show"

1575. ***How to Steal an Election***. Satire of American political chicanery from George Washington's administration to the present. Pocket, 10/13/68–12/22/68. 89 perf. m/l: Oscar Brand. Cast: Bill McCutcheon, Clifton Davis, Ed Crowley, Del Hinkley, Carole Demas, Thom Koutsoukos. "The Plumed Knight," "Clay and Frelinghuysen," "Get on the Raft with Taft," "Silent Cal," "Nobody's Listening," "(Comes) the Right Man," "How to Steal an Election," "Van Buren," "Tippecanoe and Tyler Too," "Charisma," "Lincoln and Soda," "Lincoln and Liberty," "Grant," "Law and Order,"

"Lucky Lindy," "Down Among the Grass Roots," "Get Out the Vote," "Mr. Might've Been," "We're Gonna Win," "More of the Same"

1576. ***Howard Crabtree's When Pigs Fly***. Gay musical revue. Douglas Fairbanks, 8/14/96–8/15/98. 15 prev from 8/1/96. 840 perf. m: Dick Gallagher; l/sk/d: Mark Waldrop; conceived by Howard Crabtree & Mark Waldrop; cos: Howard Crabtree; md: Philip Fortenberry; cast recording on RCA. Cast: David Pevsner, John Treacy Egan, Stanley Bojarski, Jay Rogers, Michael West. "When Pigs Fly," "You've Got to Stay in the Game," "Torch," "Light in the Loafers," "Coming Attractions with Carol Ann," "Not All Man," "Patriotic Finale," "Wear Your Vanity with Pride," "Hawaiian Wedding Day," "Shaft of Love," "Sam and Me," "Bigger is Better," "Laughing Matters," "Over the Top." Mr. Crabtree died 6/28/96, 5 days after finishing work on this prod

1577. ***Huckleberry Finn***. Unfinished Kurt Weill & Maxwell Anderson musical (Mr. Weill died). 1950. "Apple Jack," "The Catfish Song," "Come In, Mornin'," "River Chanty," "This Time Next Year"

1578. ***The Hunchback of Notre Dame***. Quasimusical. Charles Ludlam, 4/24/91–6/23/91. 54 perf. m/l/cos: Mark Bennett & Everett Quinton; freely adapted from Victor Hugo's novel. Cast: Hapi Phace, Bobby Reed, Mark Bennett, Everett Quinton

1579. ***The Hunchback of Notre Dame***. Westbeth, 4/22/93–5/15/93. 19 perf. m/l: Byron Janis & Hal Hackady; b: Anthony Scully; d: Brian Murray; ch: Karen Azenberg; md: Tom Fay; set: Bob Phillips; cos: Franne Lee; light: Nancy Collings; sound: Peter Fitzgerald. Cast: Steve Barton, Leslie Castay, Ed Dixon, Laura Kenyon, Brian Sutherland, Nick Wyman, Tony Capone, Anne Rickenbacher, Joyce Chittick. "Notre-Dame Prelude," "Welcome to Paris," "A Little Love," "Because of Me," "A Kiss Like That," "Auction," "Let Me Make Love to You," "Like Any Man," "I'll Die Happy," "Keep an Eye on Me," "You Are More," "I Can't Lose You," "Steal Another Day," "Sanctuary," "Look at Me," "It's Better with a Man," "Madonna Mia," "Esmeralda," "On to Notre Dame," "All That's Left of Love"

1580. ***Hundreds of Hats***. Musical revue focusing on lyr of Howard Ashman, including many songs cut from plays & films. WPA, 5/25/95–7/2/95. 19 prev. 21 perf. m: Alan Menken, Jonathan Sheffer, Marvin Hamlisch; l: Howard Ashman; conceived by/d: Michael Mayer. Cast: John Ellison Conlee, Nancy Opel. "Hero," "In Our Hands," "Thirty Miles from the Banks of the Ohio," "Firestorm Consuming Indianapolis," "Rhode Island Tango," "Belle," "Skid Row," "Song for a Hunter College Graduate," "Thank God for the Volunteer Fire Brigade," "Cheese Nips," "A Little Dental Music," "Aria for a Cow," "Hundreds of Hats," "Growing Boy," "Les Poissons," "Maria's Song," "Suddenly Seymour," "Since You Came to This Town," "A Day in the Life of a Fat Kid in Philly," "Part of Your World," "Somewhere that's Green," "Disneyland," "Your Day Begins

Tonight," "A Magician's Work," "Babkak Omar Aladdin Kassim," "Daughter of Prospero," "Kiss the Girl," "How Quick They Forget," "Poor Unfortunate Souls," "We'll Have Tomorrow," "Proud of Your Boy," "High Adventure," "Sheridan Square," "Daughter of God"

1581. *The Hunting of the Snark*. Prince Edward, London, 10/24/91. Cast: Cliff Richard, Roger Daltrey, Julian Lennon, Deniece Williams, Mike Batt (also w), Art Garfunkel. "Children of the Sky," "The Escapade," "Midnight Smoke," "The Pig Must Die," A Delicate Combination," "As Long as the Moon Can Shine," "The Vanishing"

1582. *Hysterical Blindness: And Other Southern Tragedies That Have Plagued My Life So Far*. Trials of a Tennessee Baptist coping with mother's psychosomatic illness & trying to break into showbiz at same time. Playhouse on Vandam, 5/19/94. Prev from 4/20/94. m/l/md: Joe Patrick Ward; w: Leslie Jordan; developed/d: Carolyne Barry; ch: Mark Knowles. Cast: Storyteller: Leslie Jordan, *Mark Baker*; Also with: Mary Bond Davis. "Keep Smilin' Through," "Pessimistic Voices," "The Trashy Effeminate Hoodlum," "Just the Way We're Bred"

I, Anastasia see # 27, Main Book

1583. *I and Albert*. The life of Queen Victoria. Piccadilly, London, 11/6/72. 120 perf. m/l: Charles Strouse & Lee Adams; b: Jay Allen. Cast: Polly James, Lewis Fiander, Sven-Bertil Taube, Aubrey Woods. "Vivat! Vivat Regina!," "It Has All Begun," "Leave it Alone," "This Gentle Land," "This Noble Land," "I and Albert," "Enough," "All Glass," "Genius of Man," "His Royal Highness," "Just You and Me," "Widow at Windsor," "No One to Call Me Victoria," "When You Speak with a Lady," "Go it, Old Girl." Originally called *H.R.H.*, it had been optioned as such by David Merrick, and Julie Andrews had turned it down

1584. *I Can't Keep Running in Place*. 6 women in sessions with their psychiatrist. La Mama, 2/21/80. m/l/b: Barbara Schottenfeld; d: Susan Einhorn; ch: Dennis Dennehy; light: Victor En Yu Tan. Cast: SuEllen Estey, Bev Larson, Melinda Tanner, Catherine Wolfe, Eva Charney, Anna Korzen, Maggie Anderson. "I'm Glad I'm Here," "Don't Say Yes if You Want to Say No," "I Can't Keep Running in Place," "I'm on My Own," "More of Me to Love," "I Live Alone," "I Can Count on You," "Penis Envy," "Get the Answer Now," "What if We…," "Almost Maybes and Perhapses," "Where Will I Be Next Wednesday Night?." Westside Arts Theatre, 5/14/81–10/25/81. 208 perf. Same crew as above, except ch: Baayork Lee. Cast: Evalyn Baron, Helen Gallagher, Bev Larson, Jennie Ventriss, Marcia Rodd, Joy Franz, Mary Donnet

1585. *I Dreamt I Dwelt in Bloomingdale's*. Absurd rock fable. Girl imagines living in Bloomingdale's Department Store. Provincetown Playhouse, 2/12/70–2/15/70. 14 prev. 6 perf. m/l: Ernest McCarty & Jack Ramer; d: David Dunham; set: Ed Wittstein; clothes by Bloomingdale's. Performed by The Wet Clam. Cast: Lucy Saroyan, Linda Rae Hager, Michael

Del Medico, Liz Otto, Richard Darrow. "Ballad of Dry Dock Country," "Who Will I Be?," "I Dreamt I Dwelt in Bloomingdale's," "Any Spare Change?," "Brown Paper Bag," "Naomi," "Smart"

1586. *I Feel Wonderful*. Musical revue. 21-year-old Jerry Herman's 1st show. It interrupted the run of *Threepenny Opera* at Theatre De Lys, 10/18/54–11/28/54. 48 perf. p: Sidney S. Oshrin; m/l/d: Jerry Herman; sk: Barry Alan Grael; ch: Frank Wagner; set/cos: Romain Johnston; md: Wally Levine; gm: Harry Herman. Cast: Phyllis Newman, Janie Janvier, Rita Tanno, Tom Mixon, Bob Miller, Rebecca Barksdale, John Bartis, Joan Coburn, Nina Dova, Albie Gaye, Barry Alan Grael, Ed Holleman, Sherry McCutcheon, Richard Tone

1587. *I Got a Song*. View of life & times through lyr of E.Y. Harburg. Pre-Broadway tryouts at Studio Arena, Buffalo, 9/26/74–10/20/74. 34 perf. Did not make Broadway. m: Harold Arlen, Vernon Duke, Sammy Fain, Burton Lane, Jay Gorney, Earl Robinson; b: E.Y. Harburg & Fred Saidy; d: Harold Stone; ch: Geoffrey Holder; set: R.J. Graziano; cos: Theoni V. Aldredge; light: Thomas Skelton; md: Marty Henne. Cast: D'Jamin Bartlett, Alan Brasington, Norma Donaldson, Bonnie Franklin, Miguel Godreau, Gilbert Price

1588. *I Have a Dream*. Play with mus. Included several hymns. Set 1955–1968. Ambassador, Broadway, 9/20/76–12/5/76. 80 perf. adapted: Josh Greenfield; based on words of Dr. Martin Luther King Jr.; conceived by/d: Robert Greenwald; light: Martin Aronstein; md: Fred Gripper. Cast: Billy Dee Williams (*Moses Gunn* from 11/30/76), Leata Galloway, Clinton Derricks-Carroll, Sheila Ellis, Judyann Elder, Ramona Brooks, Millie Foster. 1st produced at Ford's Theatre, Washington, DC, 4/5/76. New Federal Theatre, 12/22/85–1/12/86. 24 perf. d: Woodie King Jr.; cos: Judy Dearing. Cast: Bruce Strickland (as Martin)

1589. *I Hear Music … of Frank Loesser and Friends*. Jo Sullivan recaps songs of her career written by her late husband, Frank Loesser, and others (George Gershwin, Richard Rodgers, Kurt Weill, Stephen Sondheim, Giacomo Puccini, Jule Styne, etc). Ballroom Theatre, 10/29/84–12/2/84. 10 prev. 32 perf. p: Henry Luhrman; d: Donald Saddler; gowns: Robert Mackintosh; md: Colin Romoff. Cast: Jo Sullivan, Colin Romoff, Greg Utzig, Brian Slawson, Douglas Romoff, Ed Joffe

1590. *I Knock at the Door*. Billy Munk, 4/12/76–4/14/76. 4 perf. m/l: Paul Dick; w: Sean O'Casey; adapted: Paul Shyre; d: Ron Nash; md: Sal Sicari. Cast: Margo Lacey, Richard Ianni, Kevin Hunter, Lisa Hall, Norman Weiler, William Fredericks, Jonathan Howard Jones, Susan J. Baum. "Last Shake o' the Bag," "Ounce of Cavendish Cut Plug," "My Love Goes Down," "Little Boy Blue," "Cock Robin," "There Was a Funny Man," "White Bum," "An Irish Ireland," "The Brook"

1591. *I Love a Piano*. Musical revue of 64 Irving Berlin songs. The story follows a piano through the 20th-century, as it is bought, sold, abandoned, then found again. conceived by/w: Ray Roderick & Michael Berkeley; d/ch: Ray

Roderick; mus arr: Michael Berkeley. 1st played in summer stock in upstate NY, in early 1990s. Producer Kevin McCollum invited Ray Roderick to stage it in 1996, at the Ordway Center, St. Paul, Minn, where it ran 12 weeks. Rewritten & ran again at Auditorium, Denver, from 8/13/02. p: Denver Center Attractions; set: Larry Gruber; md: John Glaudini. Cast: Jeffry Denman

1592. *I Love You, You're Perfect, Now Change*. Comic musical revue for hopeful heterosexuals. Covers spectrum of male-female relationships in 1990s. Westside Theatre Upstairs, 8/1/96. Prev from 7/15/96. p: James Hammerstein, Bernie Kukoff, Jonathan Pollard; l/b: Joe DiPietro; d: Joel Bishoff; set: Neil Peter Jampolis; md: Tom Fay; cast recording on Sarabande. Cast: Jordan Leeds (*Danny Burstein, Adam Grupper, Gary Imhoff, Adam Grupper; Jordan Leeds, Bob Walton, Jordan Leeds, Darrin Baker, Danny Burstein, Jordan Leeds*), Robert Roznowski (*Kevin Pariseau, Adam Hunter, Sean Arbuckle, Frank Baiocchi, Colin Stokes*), Melissa Weil (*Cheryl Stern, Mylinda Hull, Melissa Weil, Evy O'Rourke, Marylee Graffeo, Cheryl Stern, Marylee Graffeo, Janet Metz, Anne Bobby, Janet Metz*), Jennifer Simard (*Erin Leigh Peck, Kelly Anne Clark, Andrea Chamberlain, Lori Hammel, Andrea Chamberlain, Amanda Watkins, Karyn Quackenbush, Marissa Burgoyne, Andrea Chamberlain, Karyn Quackenbush, Sandy Rustin*). Began as hourlong straight revue of sketches called *Love Lemmings*, which eventually played at Village Gate. Producer Ted Rawlings got Joe DiPietro to make it into musical. Still without music it opened at American Stage Co., Teaneck, NJ, changed its name, then got composer, Jimmy Roberts. Long Wharf, New Haven, 1995–96. Then to Westside, where it became longest-running musical revue in NY history (in 2001 it beat *Smokey Joe's Cafe*), and 3rd-longest-running OB musical of all time (behind *The Fantasticks* & *Nunsense*). On 10/21/03 it celebrated its 3,000th perf, and was still running at the end of 2004. "Cantata for a First Date," "A Stud and a Babe," "Single Man Drought," "Why? 'cause I'm a Guy!," "Tear Jerk," "I Will Be Loved Tonight," "Hey There, Single Guy/Gal," "He Called Me," "Wedding Vows," "Always a Bridesmaid," "Baby Song," "Marriage Tango," "On the Highway of Love," "Waiting Trio," "Shouldn't I Be Less in Love with You," "I Can Live with That," "I Love You, You're Perfect, Now Change." Played over 150 cities throughout the world, including the Comedy Theatre, London, 7/28/99–9/25/99. Prev from 7/22/99. d: Joel Bishoff. Cast: Clive Carter, Shona Lindsay, Gillian Kirkpatrick, Russell Wilcox. Marines Memorial Theatre, San Francisco, 2004. d: Jeff Bishoff. Cast: Jennifer Simard, Darrin Baker, Anne Bobby, Daniel Tatar. Jermyn Street, London, 3/3/05–3/26/05 (limited run; prev from 3/1/05). d: Phil Willmott; mdL Anthony England. Cast: Lucy Hunter-James, John Payton, Mark Hilton, Jo Cook

1593. *I Make Me a Promise*. Written & performed by kids of formerly homeless people living with AIDS. Selected songs from earlier musical *Blocks*, by Jonathan Larson & Hal Hackady. McGinn/Cazale, 9/10/97–9/27/97. 16 perf. p: Theatre Project at Housing Works & Broadway Arts/Theatre for Young Audiences; m: Christine Talbott & Jonathan Larson; l: Marisa Peluso & Hal Hackady; d: Victoria McElwaine; md: Christine Talbott. "Make Your Own Music," "Nobody's Home," "Parents for Sale," "Go Home, Little Girl," "I Live in a Castle," "Reasons to Fail," "I'm Alright," "Castle of a Better Reality." See also *Every Beat Face Ain't Beautiful*, in this appendix

1594. *I Married an Angel*. Set in Budapest, 1938. Shubert, Broadway, 5/11/38–2/25/39. 338 perf. m: Richard Rodgers; l: Lorenz Hart; b: Rodgers & Hart; from Hungarian play by John Vaszary; d: Josh Logan (Broadway debut as dir); ch: George Balanchine; set: Jo Mielziner. Cast: Dennis King, Vera Zorina, Vivienne Segal, Walter Slezak, Audrey Christie. "Did You Ever Get Stung?," "I Married an Angel," "I'll Tell the Man in the Street," "How to Win Friends and Influence People," "Spring is Here," "Angel without Wings," "A Twinkle in Your Eye," "At the Roxy Music Hall." Filmed in 1942, with Nelson Eddy & Jeanette MacDonald. Town Hall, 5/17/86–5/19/86. 3 perf in concert. p: New Amsterdam Theatre Co.; d: Rick Lombardo; md: Gregory J. Dlugos. Cast: Kurt Peterson, Virginia Seidel, Phyllis Newman, Karen Ziemba, Maggie Task, Lee Lobenhofer, Ralph Farnworth. It was planned to present a series of Rodgers & Hart revivals at Theatre Off Park , in staged concert version. The first was *I Married an Angel*, 10/29/95–10/30/95. 2 perf. d: Albert Harris; ch: Joey McKneely; md: James Stenborg. Cast: Brent Barrett, Victoria Clark, Robert Creighton, Kim Criswell, Jason Graae, Edmund Lyndeck, Marin Mazzie. Next in series was *America's Sweetheart* (see this appendix). 14th Street Y, 9/12/00–9/24/00. 16 perf. Part of the *Musicals Tonight!* series. p: Mel Miller; d/ch: Thomas Mills; md: Mark Hartman. Cast: Kathy Fitzgerald, Nanne Puritz

1595. *I Paid My Dues*. Musical celebration of labor. Used many standard songs. Astor Place, 4/20/76–5/23/76. 20 perf. l/b: Eric Blau; md: David Frank; d: George Allison Elmer. Cast: Joe Morton, Christopher Cable, Linda Rios. Went to Queens, NY; then to Ford's Theatre, Washington, DC (which began 20-city tour)

1596. *I Sent a Letter to My Love*. Set in 1954, in small Ohio town. Brother & sister inadvertently send love letters to each other. Primary Stage, 1/18/95–2/19/95. 21 prev. 13 perf. m: Melissa Manchester; l: Jeffrey Sweet & Melissa Manchester; b: Jeffrey Sweet; from novel by Bernice Rubens; d: Patricia Birch; set: James Noone; sound: Jim Van Bergen; orch: Doug Besterman. Cast: Lynne Wintersteller, Robert Westenberg, John Hickok. "Across the Lake," "God Never Closes a Door," "What I Am," "Lady Seeks Gentleman," "Grass Between My Toes," "Your Prince," "Very Truly Yours," "Rosy Red," "Perfect Timing," "I Never Knew," "Someone in a Chair," "The Day I Meet My Friend," "Last Night," "Change in

the Air." North Shore Musical Theatre, Mass., 9/3/02–9/22/02. d: Patricia Birch; set: Jim Morgan; cos: Susan E. Picinich; light: Kirk Bookman; md: Phil Reno. Cast: Cass Morgan, Diana Canova, Kevin Earley, Bethe B. Austin, David Garrison (Stephen Bogardus had been scheduled but went into Broadway revival of *Man of La Mancha*)

1597. *I Want You*. Maidman, 9/14/61–9/16/61. 3 perf. m/l: Joe Crayham, Stefan Kanfer, Jess J. Korman; d: Theodore J. Flicker; ch: Rhoda Levine. Cast: Al Mancini, Joshua Shelley. "Ain't it Funny," "I Want You," "Loyal American," "A Perfect Man," "Remarkable," "The Street"

1598. *I Will Come Back*. Players. 2/10/98–5/3/98. new songs: Hugh Martin & Timothy Gray; w/d: Timothy Gray. Cast: Judy Garland: Tommy Femia; Also with: Kristine Zbornik. "I Will Come Back," "Come on In," "They Don't Write 'em Like That Anymore," "Smile," "La Cucaracha," "Zing Went the Strings of My Heart," "After You've Gone," "Two is Company," "Optimism," "Somewhere Out There," "Meet Me in St. Louis," "Boy Next Door," "Trolley Song," "Rock-a-Bye Your Baby with a Dixie Melody," "Just in Time," "Happy Days Are Here Again," "Get Happy," "Over the Rainbow"

1599. *Identical Twins from Baltimore*. Playhouse 91, 6/14/95–7/9/95. 9 prev. 16 perf. m/l: Dan Alvy; b: Marc Mantell; d/ch: Bill Castellino; set: Michael Bottari & Ronald Case. Cast: Rose McGuire, Adriane Lenox, Mary Stout. "Take the Picture," "New York, Get Ready for Us," "Famous for Fifteen Minutes," "This Night," "One-Sided Love," "I'm on Your Side," "Movie Moguls," "Love Gets in the Way," "Everyone's Here," "Interrogation," "Another Chance," "The Girls Are Back," "I Made it to the Top"

1600. *If You Please*. Revue. Pre-Broadway tryouts at the Curran, San Francisco, 11/28/50–12/2/50. 6 perf. Did not make Broadway. Cast: Frank Fay (also p/m/l/w/d), Maurice Kelly. "Don't Look Now," "Kiss Hello and Not Goodbye," "Ta-Hy-Ta-Ho-Tahiti," "What's a Girl to Do," "Wrapped in Arms"

1601. *I'll Die If I Can't Live Forever*. A stage-struck revue. The Improvisation, 10/31/74–2/2/75. 81 perf. m/l/ch: Joyce Stoner. Cast: Maureen Maloney, Gail Johnston, Don Bradford. "The Improvisation," "Joys of Manhattan Life," "Where Would We Be without Perverts?," "My Life's a Musical Comedy," "We're Strangers Who Sleep Side by Side," "The Roommate Beguine," "A is For," "Take Me!," "Ode to Electricity," "There's Always Someone Who'll Tell You 'No'," "Twenty-Four Hours from This Moment," "I'm in Love," "I'm So Bored," "My Place or Yours?," "Who Do We Thank!," "Let's Have a Rodgers and Hammerstein Affair," "Less is More and More," "I Hate Football," "They Left Me," "It's Great to Be Gay," "I'll Die if I Can't Live Forever," "The Great White Way"

1602. *I'm Getting My Act Together and Taking It on the Road*. Big hit about women's lib. 39-year old pop singer auditions for comeback in front of her dubious manager. Public,

6/14/78. Prev from 5/16/78. 226 perf; Circle in the Square Downtown, 12/16/78–3/15/81. 939 perf. p: Joseph Papp at the NY Shakespeare Festival; m: Nancy Ford; l/b: Gretchen Cryer; d: Word Baker. Cast: Heather: Gretchen Cryer, *Virginia Vestoff* (from 5/29/79), *Betty Aberlin* (from 11/30/79), *Gretchen Cryer* (from 1/18/80), *Carol Hall* (from 2/19/80), *Betty Buckley* (from 4/1/80), *Carol Hall* (from 6/10/80), *Anne Kaye* (from 10/14/80), *Nancy Ford* (from 10/21/80), *Phyllis Newman* (from 1/20/81), *Gretchen Cryer* (from 3/10/81); Joe: Joel Fabiani, *Steven Keats* (from 5/29/79), *George Hosmer* (from 9/25/79), *Orson Bean* (from 3/3/81); Also with: Margot Rose (*Jackee Harry*), Betty Aberlin (*Anne Kaye, Betty Aberlin*), Don Scardino (*Michael Ayr, Jake Turner, James Mellon, Mark Buchan*), Scott Berry, Bob George, Dean Swenson, Lee Grayson. "Natural High," "Smile," "In a Simple Way I Love You," "Miss America," "Strong Woman Number," "Dear Tom," "Old Friend," "Put in a Package and Sold," "Feel the Love," "Lonely Lady," "Happy Birthday." A tour began 3/12/80. Cast: Gretchen Cryer (*Phyllis Newman, Betty Aberlin, Donna McKechnie* from 10/21/80, *Nancy Linari* from 1/27/81, *Gretchen Cryer*), Mark Hutter (*Howard Platt, Peder Melhuse, Orson Bean* from 2/8/81). Apollo, London, 3/31/81. Cast: Diane Langton, Ben Cross

1603. *Imaginary Friends*. Play with mus. The feud between the two writers. Globe, San Diego, 9/21/02–11/3/02. m: Marvin Hamlisch; l: Craig Carnelia; w: Nora Ephron; d: Jack O'Brien; ch: Jerry Mitchell; set: Michael Lavine; cos: Robert Morgan; light: Kenneth Posner; sound: Jon Weston; md: Ron Melrose. Cast: Mary McCarthy: Cherry Jones; Lillian Hellman: Swoosie Kurtz. Ethel Barrymore, Broadway, 12/12/02–2/16/03. 20 prev from 11/25/02. 76 perf

1604. *The Immigrant*. A young Jew comes through Galveston instead of Ellis Island, and struggles to become part of 1909 Texas rural life. Set in Hamilton, Texas, 1909–1942. CAP21, 9/13/00–10/8/00. 6 prev. 21 perf. p: Collaborative Arts Project 21; m/orch: Steven M. Alper; l: Sarah Knapp; b: Mark Harelik; based on the 1985 smash hit regional play of the same name, written by Mark Harelik & Randal Myler; d: Randal Myler. Cast: Evan Pappas, Cass Morgan, Walter Charles, Jacqueline Antaramian. "The Stars." "A Stranger Here," "Simply Free," "Changes," "Travel Light," "Through His Eyes," "People Change Hard," "I Don't Want It," "Take the Comforting Hand of Jesus," "Padadooly," "The Sun Comes Up," "Candlesticks," "Safe and Sound," "Where Would You Be?," "No Place to Go," "The Comforting Hand." It played in Denver & Coconut Grove in 2002. Dodger Stages Stage IV, 11/4/04–11/28/04. 19 prev from 10/19/04. 29 perf. p: HELLO Entertainment. Same crew as for 2000. Cast: Adam Heller, Jacqueline Antaramian, Walter Charles, Cass Morgan

1605. *Imperfect Chemistry*. Musical comedy about baldness. Minetta Lane, 8/15/00–10/1/00. 10 prev. 46 perf. m/story: Albert Tapper; l/b: James Racheff; d/ch: John Ruocco. Cast: John Jellison, Brooks Ashmanskas, Ken

Barnett, Amanda Watkins, Sara Schmidt. "Avalon," "Dream Come True," "Serious Business," "I Love Problems," "It's All Written in Your Genes," "Ahhhh," "St. Andrews," "Leave Your Fate to Fate," "Hell to Pay," "Loxagane," "Big Hair," "E-Mail Love Notes," "Bub's Song," "Chaos Ballet"

1606. *The Importance.* Ambassadors, London, 5/31/84–6/23/84. 8 prev. 29 perf. w: John Hugh Dean (i.e. Sean O'Mahoney); based on Oscar Wilde's *The Importance of Being Earnest*; d: Tony Craven; ch: Sheila O'Neill; md: Bryan Bennett. Cast: David Firth, Sheila Bernette

1607. *In a Pig's Valise.* Set in & around the Heartbreak Hotel at the corner of Neon and Lonely. Center Stage, Baltimore, 6/3/86. m/l: August Darnell & Eric Overmyer; d: Mark Harrison; ch: Marcia Milgrom Dodge; set: Hugh Landwehr; cos: Jess Goldstein; light: Pat Collins; sound: Janet Kalas; md: Mike Huffman. Cast: Yamil Borges, Michael McCormick, Steve Pudenz, Sheila Pearce, Alan Brasington. "Neon Heart," "Kiss Me Deadly," "The Skulk," "Three-Fingered Glove," "Balkan Boogie," "Mango Culo," "Talent Scout," "Nuevo Nuevo," "Shrimp Louie," "Put Your Legs on My Shoulders," "Never Judge a Thriller," "Prisoner of Genre," "If I was a Fool to Dream," "No More Magic Kingdoms," "Doin' the Denouement." Second Stage, 1/11/89–3/5/89. 57 perf. d/ch: Graciela Daniele; set: Bob Shaw; light: Peggy Eisenhauer; md: Peter Schott. Cast: Nathan Lane, Thom Sesma, Michael McCormick

1608. *In Circles.* Free-form one-act play with mus. Cherry Lane, 11/5/67–5/12/68. 222 perf. Presented by Franklin DeBoer; p: Judson Poets Theatre; m: Al Carmines; w: Gertrude Stein; d: Lawrence Kornfeld. Cast: Arlene Rothlein, Al Carmines (*David Tice*), Elaine Summers (*Lee Guilliatt*). Gramercy Arts Theatre, 6/25/68–8/11/68. 4 prev. 56 perf. Basically same cast. Ran in tandem with another, one-man program, *Songs by Carmines* (i.e. Al Carmines)

1609. *In Dahomey.* Revised version of 1903 musical (1st full-length Broadway musical written & performed by black artists). Set in Gatorville, Florida, and Dahomey, West Africa. Harry DeJur, 6/23/99–7/25/99. 5 prev. 25 perf. m: Will Marion Cook; l: Paul Laurence Dunbar, James Weldon Johnson, Alex Rogers; new b/d: Shauneille Perry; inspired by characters of Jesse A. Shipp; ch: Chiquita Ross Glover; set: Robert Joel Schwartz; md: Julius P. Williams. Cast: Trini Parks, Keith Lee Grant, Charles Reese, Jim Jacobson, LaTrice Verrett, Tonya Alexander, Cedric D. Cannon, Kim Sullivan, Shirley Verrett, Brian Chandler, Lucio Fernandez. "Swing Along," "I Want to Be an Actor Lady," "Cecelia's Lament," "Molly Green," "Bon-Bon Buddy," "Brown Skin Baby of Mine," "I'm a Jonah Man," "Colored Aristocracy," "Emancipation Day," "Morning Dawn," "I'd Rather Be," "Cake Walk," "The Czar," "My Dahomian Queen," "African Aristocracy," "I May Be Crazy But I Ain't No Fool," "Caboccers," "Same Old Sigh," "Dahomian Bye and Bye"

1610. *The In-Gathering.* Set in the Caroli-

nas, Louisiana, Mississippi, 1862–1865. The Duke Theatre, 9/19/00–10/1/00. 2 prev. 10 perf. p: New Professional Theatre; m: Daryl Waters; l: Daryl Waters & John Henry Redwood; b: John Henry Redwood; d/ch: Hope Clarke. Cast: Ann Duquesnay, Rosena M. Hill, Kimberly JaJuan, Nancy Ringham. "Dawn," "Don't Answer Me," "Do You Remember?," "Heaven Right Here on Earth," "Lead Me," "Movin'," "A Boy," "Gather Together," "Dance of Congo Square," "There's a Chill in the Air, January," "Life is a Party," "I Knew a Girl," "What's Wrong with You?," "I'm My Own Woman"

1611. *In Gay New Orleans.* Set in New Orleans, 1829–1835. Pre-Broadway tryouts at the Colonial, Boston. 12/25/46–1/31/47. Did not make Broadway. p/l/b: Forbes Randolph; m: Carl Fredrickson; ch: Felicia Sorel; set: Watson Barratt; orch: Robert Russell Bennett; md: Ray Kavanaugh. Cast: Janie Janvier, Catherine Ayers, Jeanne Grant, Maria Gambarelli. "New Orleans Saga," "Don't Pull the Wool Over My Eyes," "Just to Say that I Love You," "What Would You Do?," "Now and Forever More," "House on a Cloud," "Wind from the Bayou," "Forever Spring," "Love Came By," "What Kind of Noise Annoys an Oyster?," "Don't Break the Spell." It seemed a shame to waste the sets, so they were used again, for the Broadway prod of *Louisiana Lady*

In Someone Else's Sandals see # 334, Main Book

1612. *In the Nick of Time.* Topical revue of song & skits. Stage 73, 6/1/67–6/18/67. 22 perf. d: Earl Durtham. Cast: Ted Pugh, Sue Lawless

In the Pocket see # 1783, this appendix

In Trousers see # 200, Main Book

1613. *Inappropriate.* A life experience musical. Fool's Company, 3/21/96–3/24/96. 6 perf. m/l: Ben Baze, Shelton Becton, Debra Byrd, Seth Jaslow, Lonnie McNeil; conceived by: A. Michael De Sisto & Lonnie McNeil; adapted by Lonnie McNeil from creative memoirs of De Sisto School alumni, of Stockbridge, Mass.; d/ch: Lonnie McNeil. Theatre Row, 12/1/99–2/27/00. 9 prev from 11/23/99. 103 perf. new m & l: Michael Sottile; d: Ray Leeper & Michael Sottile; ch: Ray Leeper. "Our World Within," "Let Me Be the One," "Dear Dad," "Feels Good," "Real," "A Good Boy," "I Wonder," "The Dream," "Mexico," "Kaleidoscope," "Lost," "Found — the Discovery," "Everything that You Are." Soon after opening Lonnie McNeill died of AIDS

1614. *Les Incroyables.* French musical revue featuring Les Incroyables (female impersonators). Kaptain Banana, 6/1/93. d: Jean-Marie Riviere. Cast: Daniel Rohou, Gilles Jean, Michel Prosper. On 9/27/94 a new edition opened at the Blue Angel

1615. *Infertility.* In cabaret form. Don't Tell Mama, 2/16/03–2/19/03. m/l: Chris Neuner (based on his experiences); d: Dan Foster; md: Steven Ray Watkins. Cast: Rich Affannato, Jenni Frost, Larry Picard, Stacey Plaskett, Sharon Wheatley. "You've Got Parts," "I've Got Sperm in My Pocket and I'm Talking to Eileen," "Finding a Father," "Birth Control

Trilogy," "Il Mio Sperma Funziona nell'Abbondanza"

1616. *Innocent as Hell.* American musical. Lyric, Hammersmith, London, 6/29/60. 13 perf. p: Thane Parker; w: Andrew Rosenthal; d: Vida Hope; md: Gordon Franks. Cast: Anne Francine, Hy Hazell, Patricia Laffan, Totti Truman Taylor

1617. *Instant Marriage.* Piccadilly, London, 8/1/64–6/19/65. 366 perf. p: Donald Albery & Brian Rix; m: Laurie Holloway; l/b: Bob Grant; d: Eleanor Fazan, *Bob Grant*; ch: Rae Landor; set: Disley Jones; cos: M. Berman, Ltd. Cast: Joan Sims (*Patsy Rowlands*), Stephanie Voss, Carmel Cryan, Harold Goodwin, Richard Wordsworth (*Rex Garner*), Derek Tansley, Paul Whitsun-Jones, Alan Rothwell, Wallas Eaton. Had its origins earlier in 1964, at the Gaumont State, Kilburn, where it had played as *Don't Ask Me — Ask Dad*

1618. *Instant Replay.* A Rod Warren musical revue. Upstairs at the Downstairs, 8/6/68. Cast: Warren Burton, Larry Moss, George Poulos, Jeanette Landis, Lily Tomlin

1619. *Ionescopade.* Vaudeville musical taken from the works of Eugene Ionesco. Theatre Four, 4/25/74–5/5/74. 14 perf. p: Kermit Bloomgarden & Roger Ailes; m/l: Mildred Kayden; conceived by/d: Robert Allan Ackerman. Cast: Joseph Abaldo, Gary Beach, Connie Danese, Bob Morrisey. "Salutations," "The Two Robertas," "Surprising People," "Maid to Marry," "Fire," "Madeleine," "Cooking Lesson," "Mother Peep," "The Leader," "Cirque-o-Pade," "The Auto Salon," "Josette," "Bobby Watson and Family," "The Peace Conference," "Knocks," "Flying," "Wipe Out Games" Previously produced by New Repertory Co.

1620. *Iphigenia.* Rock musical. Public, 12/16/71–4/16/72. 139 perf. p: NY Shakespeare Festival; m: Goatleg; freely based on Euripides' story; adapted by: Doug Dyer, Peter Link, Gretchen Cryer; d: Gerald Freedman; cos: Theoni V. Aldredge. Cast: Agamemnon: Manu Tupou; Clytemnestra: Madge Sinclair; as Iphigenia there were various actresses: Nell Carter, Leata Galloway, Margaret Dorn, Bonny Guidry, Marta Heflin, Patricia Hawkins, Andrea Marcovicci, Marion Ramsey, Sharon Redd, Pamela Pentony, Lynda Lee Lawley, Julienne Marshall. "What Has Your Tongue to Tell?," "On a Ship with Fifty Oars," "This New Land," "Lead Me On," "And Now," "Only Stone," "I Wonder," "Crown Us with the Truth." It had 2 parts, *The Wedding of Iphigenia* (dealing with the sacrifice of Iphigenia by Agamemnon in Aulis), and *Iphigenia in Concert* (in which her character is fragmented & performed by a rock chorus of 12 women, and deals with the rituals of her life in Tauris before her escape)

1621. *Ipi-Tombi.* South African folk dances, songs & rituals, mostly of village life. Harkness, Middle Broadway, 1/12/77–2/13/77. 17 prev. 39 perf. The Bertha Egnos prod, presented by A. Deshe (Pashanel) & Topol, by arr with Ray Cooney Prods, and Academy Theatre & Brooke Theatre, Johannesburg; orig m/conceived by/dev: Bertha Egnos; l: Gail Lakier; ch: Sheila Wartski; add ch: Neil McKay & members of the cast; set: Elizabeth MacLeish;

American set super: Robert Mitchell; cos super: Susan Wain; American cos super: David Toser; light: Timothy Heale & John Wain; American light super: Jeremy Johnson; sound: Sander Hacker; cast recording on Ashtree/Audio Fidelity; press: Max Eisen & Barbara Glenn; gm: Ralph Roseman; psm: Patrick Horrigan; sm: Barbara Dilker; asm: Andre Love. Cast: Count Wellington Judge, Daniel Pule, Jabu Mbalo, Matthew Bodibe, Gideon Bendile, Elliot Ngubane, Andrew Kau, Sam Hlatshwayo, Philip Gama, David Mthethwa, Shadrack Moyo, Junior Tshabalala, Simon Nkosi, Ali Lerefolo, Martha Molefe, Dorcas Faku, Lydia Monamodi, Busi Dlamini, Zelda Funani, Thembi Mtshali, Linda Tshabalala, Betty-Boo Hlela, Dudu Nzimande, Coreen Pike, Nellie Khumalo. Chief Drummer: Junior Tshabalala; Drummers: Ali Lerefolo & Simon Nkosi. The Program: Act I: Overture: "Ipi-Tombi" (Where Are the Girls). Scene 1: Village of Tsomo: "Sesiyahamba" (We Are Going About Our Labors), "Hamba Bhekile" (Let the Drinks Be Served), "Uthando Luphelile" (Love is Lost, Love is Gone), "Madiwa-Madiwa" (Calling for Rain), "Qhobosha" (The Unfaithful One Will Die), Mokhibo (The Sotho Girls Dance), "Ntaba Zenkuya" (The Mountains Are High), "Orgy, the Temptress," "Moriva," "Shamanile," Shangaan (A Dance of Happiness). Scene 2: The Baptism (conflict between villagers & witch doctor). Scene 3: "Nadia" (Song of Hope). Scene 4: E'Goli (The City of Gold): "Emdudeni" (Street Sweepers), "Oo-Le-Le," A Xhosa Proposition (a Xhosa girl converses with a man in the 'click' language of the Xhosa tongue), The Refuse Collectors (Johannesburg workers doing their job at the double), "Arieni" (Let's Dance), Gum Boot Dance, "Ipi-Tombi." Act II: Scene 1: Sunday on the Mines: "Bayakhala" (The Child, Zulu). Scene 2: The Township Wedding: "Mama Tembu's Wedding," "Baby Baby," "Phata Phata" (Touch Touch), "Wishing," "Zimbaba," "Baby Baby" (reprise). Scene 3: Workday on the Mine: "Shosholoza" (A Work Song), "Going Home." Scene 4: The Warriors (fierce dance in prelude to battle). First produced 3/74, at the Brooke, Johannesburg, and then in London. Revived at Cambridge Theatre, London, 5/12/81–6/13/81

1622. *Irrationals.* About bright, troubled high-school students. American Theatre of Actors, 11/10/04. Prev from 11/6/04. m: Edward Thomas; l/b: Jon Marans; d: Martin Platt; ch: Cjay Hardy-Philip; set: Bill Clarke. Cast: Rodney Hicks, Jim Walton

1623. *Irving Berlin Ragtime Revue.* Musical revue. Mint Theatre Co., 7/21/94–7/31/94. 8 perf. d: Robert Dahdah; ch: Craig Meade; set/light: Donald L. Brooks. Cast: Matthew Bigtree, Carla Hall

1624. *Is Paris Flaming?* French musical revue, originally called *Paris en folie.* Riverwest, 1983. w: Alain Marcel; translator: Mort Shuman; d/ch: Fred Weiss. Cast: David L. Carson, Larry Goodsight, Steven Joseph

1625. *Is Your Doctor Really Necessary?* Theatre Royal, Stratford East, London, 2/14/73–4/21/73. 68 perf. p: Theatre Workshop; m/l: Tony Macaulay; b/d: Ken Hill; ch:

Judith Paris; md: Ian Armit. Cast: Maxwell Shaw, Diane Langton, Brian Murphy, Avis Bunnage, Larry Dann, Toni Palmer, Valerie Walsh

1626. *Isabel's a Jezebel.* Duchess, London, 12/15/70. 61 perf. m: Galt MacDermot; l/b: William Dumaresq; cast recording on United artists. Cast: Sharon Campbell, Frank Aiello. "More than Earth, More than Air," "Down by the Ocean," "Oh, Fish in the Sea," "Isabel's a Jezebel," "In Another Life," "Nothing," "Sand," "Oh, Mummy's Darling," "God, It Matters Now," "The Saddest Moon," "Mama Don't Want No Baby," "These Are the Things," "Use My Name," "The Moon Should Be Rising Soon," "Weeds in the Wind," "My God, When I Think," "Hah," "Love Knows No Season," "So Ends Our Night"

1627. *It Ain't Over 'Til the Fat Lady Sings.* The musical comedy troupe Capitol Steps in a musical revue. Douglas Fairbanks, 6/6/00–9/2/00. 12 prev. 92 perf. p: Eric Krebs; conceived by/w/d: Bill Strauss & Elaina Newport; md: Howard Breitbart. Cast: Elaina Newport, Linda Rose Payne (also cos), Bill Strauss

1628. *The IT Girl.* Jazz Age Cinderella musical, set in and around 1927, in the era of Clara Bow. Jonathan Waltham, dashing owner of department store, tries to discover perfect girl with special "something," in advertising campaign. He finds Betty Lou Spence, a poor shopgirl, who falls for him. BroadHollow, Long Island, 9/12/98–10/4/98. p: York Theatre Co.; m: Paul McKibbin; l: B.T. McNicholl; b: B.T. McNicholl & Michael Small; based on *It,* the 1927 movie that made a star of Clara Bow; d: Trent Jones; md: Jeff Marder. Cast: Maureen O'Leary, Adrian Bewley. "Black and White World," "Why Not?," "Stand Straight and Tall," "It," "Mama's Arms," "What to Wear," "A Perfect Plan," "Coney Island," "Woman and Waif," "Stay with Me"/"Left-Hand Arrangement," "Step into Their Shoes," "Out at Sea," "How Do You Say?," "You're the Best Thing that Ever Happened to Me." Theatre at St. Peter's, 5/3/01–5/27/01. 19 prev from 4/17/01. 29 perf. p: York Theatre Co.; d: B.T. McNicholl; prod consultant: Jerry Zaks; set: Mark Hayden; md: Albin Konopka; cast recording made on Jay 5/21/01 (not released until 10/1/02). Cast: Betty Lou: Jean Louisa Kelly; Waltham: Jonathan Dokuchitz; Also with: Jessica Boevers, Stephen DeRosa, Susan M. Haefner, Danette Holden. Good reviews. 11/04. Prev from 9/04. p: Jonathan C. Herzog & James Simon; ch: Robert Bianca; d: B.T. McNicholl; prod super: Jerry Zaks

1629. *It's a Wonderful Life! The Musical.* Beef and Boards Dinner Theatre, Indianapolis, 1990. m: John Kroner; l: Walter Willison; b: Doug Holmes; based on movie; d: Douglas E. Stark. Cast: George: Lee Chew; Clarence: Doug Holmes. Another, unrelated musical, *It's a Wonderful Life,* but based on same film, opened 12/15/91 at Toby's Dinner Theatre, Columbia, Md. m/l: David Nehls; b: Michael Tilford; d: Toby Orenstein. Cast: George: Stephen Schmidt. See also *A Wonderful Life* (this appendix). Not to be confused with a new version, written by Steve Brown & Matthew

Francis, which had a semi-staged reading at the Riverside Studios, Hammmersmith, London, 2/17/05, which was aiming at the West End

1630. *It's Better with a Band.* Topical revue of songs with lyrics by David Zippel. Don't Tell Mama, 2/2/83–2/26/83. 16 perf. m: various writers, including Wally Harper & Doug Katsaros; d: Joseph Leonardo. Cast: Patrick Quinn, Catherine Cox, Jenifer Lewis, Nancy LaMott, Alyson Reed (standby). "It's Better with a Band," "Camel Song," "You'll Never See Me Run," "Loud is Good," "The Ingenue," "What I Like is You," "God's Gift to Women," "Why Don't We Run Away," "Until Tomorrow," "I Can't Remember Living without Loving You," "Horsin' Around," "Forget It," "I Reach for a Star," "Time on Our Side," "I Was Born to Be a Slide Trombone," "Another Mr. Right," "I'm Singin' a Song for Myself." Sardi's Club Room, 3/29/83–4/30/83. 47 perf. Scott Bakula replaced Patrick Quinn. Donna Murphy replaced Alyson Reed as standby. Expanded & 70 percent revised, and ran at Prince Music Theatre, Philadelphia, 9/21/02–10/6/02. Prev from 9/18/02. d: Joe Leonardo; md: Christopher Marlowe. Cast: John Barrowman, Sally Mayes, Marva Hicks, Judy Blazer. "You Can Always Count on Me," "Another Mr. Right," "It Started with a Dream," "Go the Distance," "Reflections," "It's Better with a Band"

1631. *It's Karate, Kid!* Spoof of the *Karate Kid* movies. Teatro La Tea, 12/2/04–12/18/04. m/l/b: Travis Kramer; add lyr: Tom Oster; d: Jake Hirzel; ch: Jennifer L. Mudge. Cast: Matthew Simpkins, Sarah Hubbard, Jennifer Byrne, Charles Duff, Kevin Kirkwood, Andrew Rannells, Thomas Lash. "Wax On! Wax Off!," "A ... My Name is Ali," "We Are the Bitchkicks"

1632. *It's Not Where You Start...* Musical tribute to Dorothy Fields. 41 songs written by the late lyricist/librettist. All Souls Unitarian Church, 1/20/75–1/23/75. 3 perf. conceived by/d: Tran William Rhodes; ch: Don Madison. Cast: Barbara Coggin, Don Madison, Tran William Rhodes, Norb Joerder, Paul Merrill

1633. *It's Spring.* An entertainment. Radio City Music Hall, 3/14/80–4/13/80. 56 perf. p/conceived by: Robert F. Jani; orig m: Sammy Cahn & Don Pippin; d/ch: Dru Davis & Howard Parker; Rockettes ch: Violet Holmes; set: John William Keck; light: Ken Billington; exec md: Don Pippin; orch: Philip J. Lang. Cast: Rockettes, Vienna Boys Choir, The New Yorkers, Famous People Players

1634. *It's Toast.* NYC Parks, 8/3/96–9/15/96. 13 perf. p: Theatre for the New City (this marked their 25th anniversary of street prods in NYC); m: Christopher Cherney; l/d: Crystal Field. Cast: Crystal Field

1635. *It's Up in the Air.* Spoof of the inflight experience. Vital Theatre Co., 9/12/99–9/26/99. 3 perf. w/d: Michael Schloegl

1636. *It's Wilde!* Theatre East, 5/21/80–5/25/80. 7 perf. m/orch: Randy Klein; l/b/d: Burton Wolfe; ch: Buck Heller; set: John Falabella. Cast: Oscar Wilde: Ross Petty; Also with: Betty Jamison. "Times Divine," "I Need One Man," "Masses of Masses," "Exquisite Passions," "Jailhouse Blues," "It's Wilde!," "Our Special Love," "Poor Teddy Bear," "Reach for the Sky," "Get Thee to Bed," "Rape Me," "Love Please Stay," "You Are My Gold"

1637. Jack. Tokyo, 1982. Based on life of choreographer Jack Cole. p: American Dance Machine; ch: Ed Kresley. Cast: Wayne Cilento

1638. Jack and Jill. Jazz musical. Riverwest, 3/25/85–4/14/85. 20 perf. m/l: Hal Schaefer & Bob Larimer; d: Miriam Fond. Cast: Lara Teeter, Raymond Thorne, Sheila Smith, Ernestine Jackson, Edye Byrde. "J-a-z-z," "The First Time I Heard Ella," "Black and White People," "The First Time I Heard Ellington," "After All," "In Between Gigs." Theatre Arielle, 4/27/93–4/30/93. 4 perf. d: Miriam Fond. Cast: Michael Scott, Julia Lema, Raymond Thorne, Sheila Smith

1639. Jack the Ripper. Set on the corner of Flower & Dean Street, Whitechapel. Players, London, 6/25/74; Ambassadors, 9/17/74. Prev from 9/6/74; the Cambridge, 2/17/75–4/12/75. Total of 228 perf. m: Ron Pember; l/b: Ron Pember & Denis de Marne; d/set/cos: Reginald Woolley; md: Tim Higgs. "Saturday Night," "Ordinary Girl," "God Bless Us," "Street Song," "Sing Sing," "Jack the Lad," "Goodbye Day," "The Ripper's Gonna Get Yer," "There's a Boat Coming In," "Sir Charles Warren and Queen Victoria," "The Grass on the Other Side," "Suspects," "There Ain't Any Work Today," "Look at Them," "What Will This Mean to Me?," "Step Across the River," "The Chase," "Oh, Goodnight." U.S. premiere at Lederer Theatre Downstairs, 3/13/79. 43 perf. d/ch: Ron Pember. Cast: Neva Small

1640. Jackie Mason: Laughing Room Only. Comedy with mus. Also known as *Laughing Room Only*. Mr. Mason plays himself trying to put on a $10 million Broadway musical for $19.99. Brooks Atkinson, Broadway, 11/19/03–11/30/03. 31 prev from 10/23/03. 14 perf. p: Jill Rosenfeld, Jon Stoll, James Scibelli, in assoc with Sidney Kimmell & John Morgan; m: Doug Katsaros; w: Dennis Blair; conceived by: Digby Wolfe; d: Robert Johanson; ch: Michael Lichtefeld; set: Michael Anania; cos: Thom Heyer; light: Paul D. Miller; md: Joseph Baker. Cast: Jackie Mason, Darrin Baker, Robert Creighton, Barry Finkel, Ruth Gottschall, Cheryl Stern. "Million Dollar Musical," "French Chanteuse," "This Jew Can Sing," "Frieda from Fresno," "Only in Manhattan," "Starbucks," "Comedy Ambulance," "Jackie's Signature Song," "I Need a Man," "Perfect," "Jew Gentile Tap Off," "Tea Time," "Musical Chairs." The show was panned

1641. The Jackie Wilson Story. 25 songs of the era, including Mr. Wilson's big ones—"Lonely Teardrops," "Doggin' Around," "Higher and Higher." Black Ensemble Theatre, Chicago, 2000 (ran over 2 years, to packed houses). Cast: Jackie: Chester Gregory II. 8-city national tour. Apollo, Harlem, 4/6/03–4/27/03. Prev from 4/3/03. 19 perf. d: Jackie Taylor. Cast: Jackie: Chester Gregory II; Jackie's Mother: Melba Moore; Also with: Eva D, Tony Duwon, Rueben D. Echoles

1642. Jack's Holiday. Jack the Ripper visits NYC in 1891 as member of acting company.

Playwrights Horizons, 3/5/95–3/26/95. 28 prev from 2/10/95. 25 perf. m: Randy Courts; l: Mark St. Germain & Randy Courts; b: Mark St. Germain; d: Susan H. Schulman; ch: Michael Lichtefeld; cos: Catherine Zuber; orch: Douglas Besterman. Cast: Allen Fitzpatrick, Judy Blazer, Herb Foster, Alix Korey, Mark Lotito, Michael X. Martin, Michael Mulheren, Dennis Parlato, Anne Runolfsson. "Changing Faces," "City of Dreams," "Tricks of the Trade," "Never Time to Dance," "The Line," "What I Almost Said," "The Hands of God," "You Never Know Who's Behind You," "What Land is This?," "Stage Blood," "If You Will Dream of Me," "Don't Think About It," "All You Want is Always"

1643. Jacob's Journey. Albery, London, 1973. Ran as a forepiece to *Joseph and the Amazing Technicolor Dreamcoat*. p: Robert Stigwood; m: Andrew Lloyd Webber; l: Tim Rice; dial: Ray Galton & Alan Simpson. Cast: Jacob: Kevin Williams; Leah: Joan Heal; Rachel: Joanna Wake; God: Paul Brooke; Laban: Ian Trigger; Isaac: Alex McEvoy; Esau: Peter Blake; Rebecca: Alison Groves; Also with: Sam Cox, Roy North, Frank Vincent, Maynard Williams

1644. Jailhouse Rock. About jailbird Vince Everett who becomes a rocker. Piccadilly, London, 4/19/04–4/23/05. Prev from 3/26/04. Adapted for stage by Alan Janes; based on 1957 Elvis movie; d: Rob Bettinson; ch: Drew Anthony; set: Adrian Rees; ms: David Mackay. Cast: Vince: Mario Kombou; Also with: Lisa Pearce, Roger Alborough, Gilz Terera. Before going to London, it tried out in Plymouth and Manchester. The song "Jailhouse Rock" not in it — the producers couldn't get the rights

1645. Jam on the Groove. A hip-hop musical. Minetta Lane, 11/16/95–2/11/96. 10 prev from 11/7/95. 90 perf. conceived by/created/w/composed/ch: GhettOriginal Prods; light: Peter Kaczorowski. Cast: Peter "Bam Bam" Arizmendi, Leon "Mr. Twister" Chesney, Steve "Mr. Wiggles" Clemente, "Crazy Legs," Gabriel "Kwikstep" Dionisio, Kenny "Ken Swift" Gabbert, Tamara Gaspard, Antoine "Doc" Jenkins, Risa Kobatake, Adesola "D'Incredible" Osakalumi, Jorge "Fabel" Pabon, Jerry "Flow Master" Randolph, Roger "Orko" Romero, Ereine "Honet Roc Well" Valencia

1646. The James Joyce Memorial Liquid Theatre. Audience-participation revue. Began with concerts & games, then the audience passed, eyes closed, through a maze while being offered demonstrations of affection & other physical sensations. The last part is dancing. Solomon R. Guggenheim Museum, 10/11/71–3/15/72. 189 perf. m: Jack Rowe, Robert Walter, Lance Larsen; conceived by/d: Steven Kent; md: Jack Rowe. Cast: Steven Kent, Jack Rowe, Lance Larsen, Robert Walter, and many others. Previously produced by Company Theatre of L.A.

1647. Jane Eyre. Unrelated to Broadway show, except that it was based on the Bronte novel. Theatre Royal, Windsor, England, 6/13/61 (3 weeks). Did not go to London. m: Monty Stevens; l: Hal Shaper; b: Roy Harley

Lewis & Hal Shaper; d: John Counsell; ch: Margaret Maxwell; md: Anthony Bowles. Cast: Jane: Diane Todd; Mrs. Fairfax: Jean Anderson; Gregory: Michael Bates; Rochester: Terence Cooper; Leah: Vivienne Martin. Same venue, 7/10/73–8/18/73. d: Joan Riley; ch: Hazel Gee; md: John Pritchett. Diane Todd & Jean Anderson reprised. Rochester: Gordon Clyde

1648. Jane Eyre. Not related to Broadway show. Studio Arena, Buffalo, and GeVa, Rochester, NY (from 9/4/90). m: David Clark; l/b/d: Ted Davis; ch: Jim Hoskins; light: F. Mitchell Dana; md: Corinne Aquilina. Cast: Charlotte/Jane: Maryann Plunkett; Rochester: Charles Pistone; Mrs. Ingram/Miss Scatcherd: Maureen Sadusk; Also with: Peter Samuel

1649. Jayson. Set in a cartoon world remarkably similar to our own. 45th Street Theatre, 7/10/98–8/16/98. 12 prev from 6/26/98. 33 perf. m/l: Ron Romanovsky & Paul Phillips; b: Jeff Krell (based on his comic); d: Jay Michaels; ch: Kyle Craig; md/orch: Simon Deacon. Cast: Brian Cooper. "I May Not Be Much," "A Friend Like Me," "I'm Here," "Video Boys," "My Mother's Clothes," "Always a Friend (Never a Lover)," "Baby, Take Advantage of Me," "All We Have to Do," "Promise of Love," "Authentic," "All You Had to Do," "Dr. Love," "He Wasn't Talking to Me," "Let's Do Lunch," "Follow Your Heart," "Success"

1650. The Jazz Singer. Musical about Al Jolson. p: Hy Juter & Marvin A. Krauss. m/l: Will Holt; b: Sherman Yellen. Cast: Sam Harris. By 9/98 the producers had raised enough money to bring it OB, and it was scheduled to open on Broadway 1/7/99 (prev from 12/17/98). Tommy Tune was being talked of as dir. Then it lost its big investor, and the show was shelved. On 8/13/04 it re-surfaced as *Broadway Man*, for a one-day stay at the Theatre Building, Chicago, as part of Stages 2004: a Festival of New Musicals

1651. The Jazz Singer. Jewish Rep, 10/23/99–11/21/99. 8 prev 22 perf. Standard songs from the period were used; b/d: Richard Sabellico; based on 1925 play by Samson Raphaelson (it had later been filmed with Neil Diamond & Laurence Olivier); ch: Kirby Ward; md/orch: Christopher McGovern. Cast: Evalyn Baron, Beth Leavel, James Murtaugh, Ric Ryder, Raymond Thorne, Reuben Schafer

1652. Jazzbo Brown. Set in Harlem in 1924. City Lights, 6/24/80–8/24/80. 44 perf. m/l/b: Stephen H. Lemberg; d/ch: Louis Johnson; asst ch: Mercedes Ellington; ms/orch: Luther Henderson. Cast: Andre De Shields, Chris Galloway, Jerry Jarrett, Zulema, Ned Wright, Rodney Green. "Jazzbo Brown," "Broadway," "I'm Bettin' on You," "Million Songs," "Born to Sing," "He Had the Callin'," "Bump Bump Bump," "The Same Old Tune," "When You've Loved Your Man," "The Best Man," "Give Me More," "When I Die," "Dancin' Shoes," "Precious Patterns," "Funky Bessie," "Harlem Follies," "First Time I Saw You," "Pride and Freedom," "Take a Bow"

1653. Jean Seberg. Olivier, London, 12/1/83–4/3/84. p: National Theatre; m: Marvin Hamlisch; l: Christopher Adler. A flop

1654. *Jekyll and Hyde*. Unrelated to Broadway musical. George Street Playhouse, NJ, 3/14/90. m: Norman Sachs; l: Mel Mandel; b: Leonora Thuna; d: Gregory S. Hurst; ch: Lynne Taylor-Corbett; set: Deborah Jasien; md: Joel Silberman; orch: Larry Hochman. Cast: John Cullum, Cady Huffman, Rebecca Baxter, Celia Tackaberry, Jon Vandertholen, David Sabin, Jamie Ross, James Judy, Terrence Currier

1655. *Jekyll and Hyde*. Modern-day nerd takes substance in order to become cool cat. Unrelated to Broadway musical. Promenade, 6/25/90–7/22/90. 45 perf, plus 6 special perf: 10/27/90–10/28/90 & 11/3/90–11/4/90). p: Theaterworks USA; m: Michael Skloff; l/b: David Crane & Marta Kauffman; d: Jay Harnick; ch: Helen Butleroff; md: Wayne Abravanel. Cast: Christopher Scott. "A Better Man," "The Experiment," "Home Away from Home," "I Bought a Bicycle," "I'll Never Be a Lady," "In a Far-Off Corner of My Mind," "Know What I Mean?," "The Life I Wanted," "My World," "No Ordinary Day," "Nothing Like a Spot of Tea," "Our Time Together," "Quite Like Him," "Something Very Very Good," "What's the Matter with Me?," "You're Not Alone," "What If…," "New Kid"

1656. *Jekyll in Chamber*. Music-theatre piece. Mazur, 3/7/91–3/23/91. 1 prev. 14 perf. p: Playwrights' Preview Prods; m/md: Brad Ellis; b/d: Joann Green. Cast: Frank Licato. "Hospital Board," "It's Over Now," "Letting Go," "Love Has Come of Age," "A New Life," "No One Knows Who I Am," "No One Must Ever Know," "Once Upon a Dream-Boy," "Once Upon a Dream-Girl," "Possessed," "Retribution," "Seduction," "Someone Like You," "This is the Moment," "Till You Came into My Life," "Transformation," "We Still Have Time"

1657. *The Jello Is Always Red*. Musical revue. York Theatre Co., 6/11/98–6/28/98. 11 prev from 6/3/98. 21 perf. m/l: Clark Gesner; d: James Morgan; md: Winston Clark; cast recording on Harbinger. Cast: Clark Gesner, Neal Young, Celia Gentry. "The Jello is Always Red," "Hey There, Let's All Have a Little Fun," "There is Always Some More Toothpaste in the Tube," "It's Very Warm in Here," "Humpty Doo," "Peanut Butter Affair," "Roses," "Where Do All the Chickens Come From?," "I Love a Lad," "Bird in a Cage"

1658. *Jelly Roll! The Music and the Man*. 47th Street Theatre, 8/10/94–3/30/95; Kaufman, 4/1/95–7/3/95. Total of 294 perf. m/l: Jelly Roll Morton; b: Vernel Bagneris; ch: Pepsi Bethel. Cast: Jelly (solo perf): Vernel Bagneris, *Marion J. Caffey* (during vacation). A previous version ran at Michael's Pub for nearly a year

1659. *Jenny Jones*. Brighton Hippodrome, England, 9/12/44; London Hippodrome, 10/2/44–12/44. 153 perf. m: Harry Parr Davies; l: Harold Purcell; b: Ronald Gow; from stories of Rhys Davies; add dial: "John Jowett" (i.e. Ronald Millar); d: Hugh Miller; ch: Wendy Toye; cos: Norman Hartnell, etc; md: Bobby Howell. Cast: Nona Wynne

1660. *Jericho…* Musical legend. 18th Street Playhouse, 11/11/84–11/28/84. 12 perf. p:

Greensboro Civil Rights Fund; m: Buck Brown; l/b: Judy Brussell; d: Jerry Campbell. Cast: Buck Brown, Eugene Kay, Mark Cohen, Mimi Wyche. "Spinning Song," "But I Hear," "A Decent Job," "In Good Old Colony Times," "Jericho Cotton Mill Blues," "Devoted to the Cause," "One Step at a Time," "My Son," "If It All Were True," "A Kind of Power," "Come Back to Brooklyn," "Gentle People," "We Have to Lead the Fight," "Nothing Left But the Rope," "Our Kids," "The Union is Behind Us," "Jericho Massacre," "Nothing Else to Do," "We Are No Longer Strangers," "Beware the Thunder and the Light"

1661. *Jerico-Jim Crow*. Musical play. The story of black America done through traditional songs & dramatic readings. The Sanctuary, 1/12/64–4/26/64. 32 perf. p: Greenwich Players, CORE, NAACP, SNCC; w: Langston Hughes (he also wrote 2 of the songs: "Such a Little King" & "Freedom Land"); d: Alvin Ailey & William Hairston. Cast: Joseph Attles, Rosalie King, William Cain, Lamont Washington, Micki Grant. Greenwich Mews, 3/9/68–5/5/68. 5 perf (weekends only). p: Stella Holt; d: Alvin Ailey & William Hairston; Cast: Joseph Attles, Rosalie King

1662. *Jerry Springer — The Opera*. Comedy musical. About the American TV talk show host. National, London, 4/29/03–9/30/03. Prev from 4/9/03; it was a huge hit, and moved to the West End, to the Cambridge, London. Prev from 10/14/03. Closed 2/19/05. 609 perf. 398,000 people saw it at the Cambridge. p: Allan McKeown & Avalon U.K. Prods; m: Richard Thomas; l/b: Richard Thomas & Stewart Lee. Cast: Jerry: Michael Brandon (until 7/10/04. *David Soul* from 7/22/04); Satan: David Bedella; God: Benjamin Lake; Also with: Alison Jiear, Valda Aviks. "Overly-Tune," "Audience Very Plainsong," "Ladies and Gentlemen," "Have Yourselves a Good Time," "Bigger than Oprah Winfrey," "Foursome Guest," "I Been Seein' Someone Else," "Chick with a Dick," "Talk to the Hand," "Adverts 1," "Intro to a Diaper Man," "Diaper Man," "Montel Comes Dirty," "This is My Jerry Springer Moment," "Mama, Gimme Smack in the Asshole," "I Wanna Sing Something Beautiful," "Adverts 2," "The First Time I Saw Jerry," "Backstage Scene," "Poledancer," "I Just Wanna Dance," "It Has No Name," "Some Are Descended from Angels," "Jerrycam," "Clan Entrance — End of Act I," "Gloomy Nurses," "Purgatory Dawning," "Eat Excrete," "The Haunting," "Him am the Devil," "Every Last Mother Fucker Must Go Down," "Grilled and Roasted," "Transition Music," "Once in Happy Realms of Lights," "Fuck You Talk," "Satan Spate," "Adam and Eve and Mary," "Where Were You?," "Behold God," "It Ain't Easy Being Me Parts 1 & 2," "Marriage of Heaven and Hell," "The Big Cheesy Jerry Springer Moment," "Jerry, It is Finished," "Jerry Eleison," "Please Don't Die," "Take Care," "Finale de Grand Fromage," "Playout." After workshops in USA, it first came to big notice at the Edinburgh Fringe Festival, Scotland, in concert form, in summer 2002. In U.S. it was going to try out at the Orpheum, San Francisco, from

2/28/05, then on to Broadway, 10/20/05, d: Stewart Lee. However, on 8/11/04 it was announced that producer Allan McKeown had dropped out, saying it was too expensive (he was going to fund more than half of the $11-13 million cost). It now aimed for a spring 2006 Broadway opening. The London run was bedeviled by a March 2004 *Daily Mail* article erroneously stating that the show was in trouble and was going to close. The production sued the paper, but lost audiences. In 11/04 Richard Dreyfuss was approached to replace David Soul in London. On 1/8/05 the BBC aired it on TV, 2.4 million people saw it, and a record 45,000 complaints were received, as well as threats of lawsuits, and actual death threats to BBC executives. Tour began in Manchester in 10/05

Jerry's Boys see # 356, Main Book

1663. *The Jewish Gypsy*. Set in Czarist Russia. Town Hall, 10/9/83–12/26/83. 5 prev. 65 perf. p: Shalom Yiddish Musical Comedy Theatre; m/l: Martin Moskowitz & Moshe Sachar; d: Michael Greenstein; ch: Derek Wolshonak; md: Renee Solomon. Cast: Yankele Alperin, Reizl Bozyk, Bill Badolato. "Play Gypsy," "My Yiddish Gypsy," "A Good Week," "I Don't Agree," "What a Pair," "Yearning," "To Your Health," "Let There Be Peace," "When Love Calls," "Life is So Beautiful," "The Dream," "No! No! No!," "Wish Me Luck," "Together," "I Want to Be a Jewish Girl"

1664. *Jimmy & Billy*. Satire on Jimmy Carter & his brother. Westside Theatre Upstairs, 12/10/78. 1 perf. p/l/b: David I. Levine; m: David I. Levine & Pat Curtis; d/ch: Robert Pagent; md: John Lesko. Cast: Joan Dunham, Laurie Franks, Gary Holcombe. Previously ran in Norfolk, Va.

1665. *Jingle Jangle*. Shaw, London, 11/22/82–11/27/82. m: Geoff Morrow; l: Hal Shaper; b: Hal Shaper & Geoff Morrow. Cast: Norman Wisdom. "The Biggest Star," "Anyone but Gerald," "I Lied," "The Three of Us," "Me, Myself and I," "Jingle Jangle," "You've Come to the Right Place," "I Might Have Been with Him," "Good Time," "Being Number One," "Maybe Sham," "The Missing Years," "I'm Wilde, You're Crazy"

1666. *Jo*. *Little Women* set to music. Orpheum, 2/12/64–4/5/64. 63 perf. m/l: William Dyer & Don Parks; d: John Bishop; ch: Chele Abel & Gerald Teijelo. Cast: Susan Browning, Joy Hodges, April Shawhan, Karin Wolfe (Jo), Mimi Randolph. "Harmony, Mass.," "Deep in the Bosom of the Family," "Hurry Home," "Let's Be Elegant or Die!," "Castles in the Air," "Friendly Polka," "Time Will Be," "What a Long, Cold Winter!," "Moods," "Afraid to Fall in Love," "A Wedding! A Wedding!," "I Like," "Genius Burns," "If You Find a True Love," "Nice as Any Man Can Be," "More than Friends," "Taking the Cure"

1667. *Joan*. Musical interpretation of Joan of Arc, as told in contemporary terms. Circle in the Square, 6/19/72–8/14/72. 64 perf. m/l/b/d: Al Carmines; ch: Gus Solomons Jr. Cast: Lee Guilliatt (Joan), Essie Borden, David Vaughan, Julie Kurnitz, Tracy Moore, Al Carmines (pianist). "Praise the Lord," "Come on, Joan," "It's So Nice," "Go Back" (ch by Phyllis MacBryde), "They Call Me the Virgin Mary," "Salve Madonna," "The Woman I Love," "Ira, My Dope Fiend," "A Country of the Mind," "I Live a Little," "What, I Wonder," "The Religious Establishment" (ch by David Vaughan), "In My Silent Universe," "Take Courage, Daughter," "Rivers of Roses," "I'm Madame Margaret the Therapist" (ch by David Vaughan), "Look at Me, Joan," "Despair," "Faith is Such a Simple Thing"

1668. *Job: A Circus.* Musical resetting of biblical Job story under the big top. Under One Roof Theatre, 1/9/92–2/2/92. 19 perf. m/conceived by/d: Elizabeth Swados. Cast: Mary Dino, Michael Gunst, Jeff Hess, Alan Mintz, Stephen Ringold (they all did clown routines, along with Gabriel Barre)

1669. *Jockies.* Play with mus. Set in NYC. Promenade, 4/11/77–4/17/77. 8 perf. p: Jule Styne & Joseph Kipness; m: Bernardo Segall; w: Frank Spiering & Milton Katselas; d: Milton Katselas; ch: Gerald Arpino. Cast: Chick Vennera, Al Mancini, Thaao Penghlis

1670. *Joey.* Theatre Royal, Bristol, England, 12/26/62–2/1/63. p: Old Vic Theatre Co.; w: Ron Moody; d: Tony Robertson; ch: Peter Darrell; md: Ray Holder. Cast: Ron Moody (Joey the Clown, i.e. Joey Grimaldi, famous clown), Jimmy Handley, Rod McLennan, Aleta Morrison, Nicholas Smith. Revised & re-staged in London in 1966 as *The Great Grimaldi*, then as *Joey, Joey*. Cast: Ron Moody, Vivienne Martin

1671. *john & jen.* Lives of a brother & sister. Set in the USA & Canada, 1952–72. Lamb's Little Theatre, 6/1/95–10/1/95. Prev from 5/16/95. m: Andrew Lippa; l: Tom Greenwald; b: Tom Greenwald & Andrew Lippa; d: Gabriel Barre; orch: Jason Robert Brown. Cast: James Ludwig, Carolee Carmello (*Michele Pawk*). "Welcome to the World," "Christmas," "Think Big," "Dear God," "Hold Down the Fort," "Timeline," "Out of My Sight," "Run and Hide," "Old Clothes," "Little League," "Just Like You," "Bye Room," "What Can I Do?," "Smile of Your Dreams," "Graduation," "The Road Ends Here," "That Was My Way," "Every Goodbye is Hello." Previously ran at Goodspeed

1672. *John, Paul, George, Ringo … and Bert.* Musical documentary about the Beatles. Everyman, Liverpool, England, 5/15/74. w: Willy Russell. Cast: George Costigan (Bert), Bernard Hill (John), Trevor Eve (Paul), Phillip Joseph (George), Anthony Sher (Ringo), Robin Hooper (Brian Epstein), Barbara Dickson (singer/pianist). Won several awards. Lyric, London, 8/15/74. p: Robert Stigwood & Michael Codron; d: Alan Dossor

1673. *Johnny Guitar: The Lounge Western.* Century Center for the Performing Arts, 3/23/04–5/16/04. Prev from 3/9/04 (the scheduled first prev of 3/4/04 was canceled). 79 perf. m: Joel Higgins & Martin Silvestri; l: Joel Higgins; b: Nicholas Van Hoogstraten; based on 1954 Nicholas Ray movie western, with Joan Crawford, Mercedes McCambridge, Sterling Hayden; cast recording done on 5/17/04. Cast: Steve Blanchard, Judy McLane, Ann Crumb, Robert Evan. "Branded a Tramp," "Tell Me a Lie," "Johnny Guitar." It had had a 11/02 reading with Steve Blanchard, Michele Pawk, Joanna Glushak

1674. *Johnny Johnson.* Comedy legend with music. Set in 1917, and some years later, in America & France. 44th Street Theatre, Broadway, 11/19/36–1/16/37. 68 perf. p: Group Theatre; m/orch: Kurt Weill; l/b: Paul Green; d: Lee Strasberg; set: Donald Oenslager; md: Lehman Engel. Cast: Lee Strasberg, Lee J. Cobb, Jules Garfield (i.e. John Garfield), Eliza Kazan, Sanford Meisner, Luther Adler, Morris Carnovsky, Roman Bohnen, Bob Lewis, Russell Collins, Albert Dekker, Joseph Pevney. Revived 5/2/41 & again 10/21/56. Edison, Middle Broadway, 4/11/71. 10 prev from 4/1/71. 1 perf. p: Timothy Gray, Robert Fletcher, Midge La Guardia; d: Jose Quintero; ch: Bertram Ross; set: Peter Harvey; cos: Robert Fletcher; light: Roger Morgan; md: Joseph Klein. Cast: Ralph Williams (as Johnny), Alice Cannon, Paul Michael, June Helmers, Bob Lydiard, Christopher Klein, James Billings, Gordon Minard, Charlotte Jones, Norman Chase, Wayne Sherwood, Clay Johns, Alexander Orfaly, Nadine Lewis, Norman Riggins. "Over in Europe," "Democracy's Call," "Up Chickamauga Hill," "Johnny's Melody," "Aggie's Song," "Oh Heart of Love," "Farewell, Goodbye," "The Sergeant's Chant" (new to this prod), "Valentine's Tango," "You're in the Army Now," "Johnny's Oath," "Song of the Goddess," "Song of the Wounded Frenchmen," "Tea Song," "Cowboy Song," "Johnny's Dream," "Song of the Guns," "Music of the Stricken Redeemer," "Army Song," "Mon Ami, My Friend," "Allied High Command," "Laughing Generals," "The Battle," "Prayer: In Times of War and Tumults," "No Man's Land," "The Psychiatry Song," "Hymn to Peace," "Johnny Johnson's Song," "How Sweetly Friendship Binds" (cut from this prod), "Oh Heart of Love" (reprise). York Theatre Co., 10/20/00–10/22/00. Part of *Musicals in Mufti* series. d: Michael Montel; md: Jeffrey Smith. Cast: Perry Laylon Ojeda, Sherry Boone, Mark Aldrich

1675. *Johnny Pye and the Foolkiller.* Set in Martinsville, USA, and other places, 1928–1955. Orphan grows up trying to solve riddle. Lambs Little Theatre, 3/22/88–4/2/88. 14 perf. m: Randy Courts; l: Mark St. Germain & Randy Courts; b: Mark St. Germain; from short story by Stephen Vincent Benet; d: Paul Lazarus; ch: Patrice Soriero; set: William Barclay; md: Steven M. Alper. Cast: Ed Dixon, Scott Waara. "The Fool," "Shower of Sparks," "I Can See Him," "Goodbye Johnny," "Opportunity Knocks," "The Weasel," "I Can See Him" (reprise), "Challenge to Love," "One Good Reason," "Married with Children," "Land Where There is No Death," "Time Passes," "Never Felt Better in My Life." Revised, and ran again, same theatre, 10/31/93–12/12/93. Prev from 10/21/93. 54 perf. d: Scott Harris; ch: Janet Watson; set: Peter Harrison; md: Steven M. Alper; orch: Douglas Besterman. Cast: Daniel Jenkins, Spiro Malas, Kaitlin Hopkins, Tanny McDonald, Ralston Hill, Mark Lotito, Michael Ingram. "Another Day," "Goodbye Johnny," "Shower of Sparks," "Occupations," "Handle with Care," "The End of the Road," "Challenge to Love," "The Barbershop," "Married with Children," "The Land Where There is No Death," "Time Passes," "Never Felt Better in My Life," "Epilogue (The Answer)"

1676. *Johnny the Priest.* London priest's relationship with delinquent who he gets into the Navy & who then steals a telescope. Wimbledon Theatre, London, 3/25/60; Princes, London, 4/19/60–4/30/60. 14 perf. Players' Ventures (Don Gemmell & Reginald Woolley) presented the Players Theatre prod, by arr with Jack Hylton; m: Antony Hopkins; l/b: Peter Powell; from play *The Telescope*, by R.C. Sherriff; d: Norman Marshall; sct: Reginald Woolley; md: Alan Harris; cast recording on Decca (not released until 1983). Cast: Rev. Richard Highfield: Jeremy Brett; Johnny: Bunny May; Also with: Stephanie Voss, Jenny Wren, Hope Jackman, Norman Warwick, Phyllida Sewell. "The Maybury Story," "Hellfire," "Johnny the Priest," "Bound Over," "Vicarage Tea," "Be Not Afraid," "I'm Your Girl," "Rooftops," "Johnny Earn Peanuts," "A Boy Called Johnny," "Stormy Evening," "A Tanner's Worth of Tune"

1677. *Joie de Vivre.* New Theatre, Oxford, England, 5/3/60 (2 weeks); toured; Queen's, London, 7/14/60–7/16/60. 4 perf. m: Robert Stolz; l: Paul Dehn; b: Terence Rattigan (from his play *French Without Tears*); d: William Chappell; ch: Ross Taylor; set: Peter Rice; cos: M. Berman, Ltd; md: Michael Steyn. Cast: Barrie Ingham, Jill Martin, Anna Sharkey, Joan Heal, John Moore, Harold Kasket, Donald Sinden, Terence Alexander

1678. *Joley.* Pre-Broadway tryouts at Northstage Theatre, Glen Cove, Long Island, 3/2/79–4/22/79. Did not make Broadway. m/l: Milton Delugg & Herbert Hartig; d: Jay Harnick; ch: George Bunt; set: David Chapman; light: Marc B. Weiss; md: Liza Redfield. Cast: Al Jolson: Larry Kert; Georgie Jessel: Gibby Brand; Louella Parsons: Dorothy Stanley; Also with: Merwin Goldsmith, Jerry Jarrett, Joleen Fodor, Eileen Casey, Dana Moore, Diana Broderick, Gloria Hodes. "I'm Just Wild About Harry," "You Ain't Seen Nuthin' Yet," "Darktown Strutters Ball," "Rock-a-bye Your Baby," "Toot-Toot Tootsie," "Alabamy Bound," "Mammy," "Sonny Boy," "Ruby," "Oh! You Beautiful Doll"

Jollyanna see # 217, Main Book

1679. *Jolson & Company.* Musical bio of Al Jolson. The story revolves around 1949 interview Jolson gave to Barry Gray at Winter Garden. The singer's life in flashbacks. Standard Jolson songs. York Theatre Co., 12/9/99–1/2/00. 19 prev from 11/23/99. 29 perf. p: Ric Wanetik; dev: Stephen Mo Hanan & Jay Berkow; d/ch: Jay Berkow; set: James Morgan; cos: Gail Baldoni; light: Ann Marie Duggan; md: Peter Larson. Jolson: Stephen Mo Hanan; Also with: Nancy Anderson, Robert Ari. Century Center for the Performing Arts, 9/29/02–12/22/02. 19 prev from 9/12/02. 97 perf. Same basic cast & crew. Set box-office record for advance sales at that theatre. Coconut Grove Playhouse, Miami, 2/17/04–3/7/04. Same basic cast and crew

1680. *Jolson: The Musical.* Life of Al Jolson. Victoria Palace, London, 1996 (2 years). Won an Olivier. m/l: various authors; b: Francis Essex & Rob Bettinson. Cast: Brian Conley, Brian Greene, John Bennett, Sally Ann Triplett. "Mammy," "Swanee," "Rockabye Your Baby," and all the famous Jolson songs. In 1998 it came to the USA, for tour. Opened 10/6/98, Cleveland. Cast: Mike Burstyn. Her Majesty's, Sydney, 2/10/00. Cast: Rob Guest, Leonie Page

1681. *Jonah.* Play with mus. American Place, 2/15/66–3/6/66. 24 perf. w: Paul Goodman. Cast: Earle Hyman, Ruth Jaroslow, Sorrell Booke, Richard Frisch. Not related to comedy of same name by T.J. Spencer, which ran at Stage 73 in 1967, or another, later musical (see below)

1682. *Jonah.* Martinson Hall, 3/20/90–3/25/90. 40 prev from 2/13/90. 8 perf. Based on Robert Nathan's novel; adapted by/composed by/d: Elizabeth Swados (this was her 5th biblical cantata); ch: Bill Castellino; cos: Judy Dearing; whale design: Tobi Kahn; light: Beverly Emmons. Cast: Jake Ehrenreich

1683. *Jorrocks: The Happiest Man Alive.* Wimbledon Theatre, London, 8/13/66; New Theatre, London, 9/22/66–2/25/67. 181 perf. p: Donald Albery; m/l: David Heneker; b: Beverley Cross; from novels by R.S. Surtees; d: Val May; ch: Irving Davies; md: Kenneth Alwyn; cast recording on EMI. Cast: Joss Ackland (as John Jorrocks), Thelma Ruby, Paul Eddington, Cheryl Kennedy, Michael Malnick, Bernard Lloyd, Willoughby Goddard, Richard Stilgoe (as Benjamin), Gay Soper, Heather Chasen, Olivia Breeze

1684. *Joy.* An Oscar Brown Jr. Brazilian-music come-together. Several Oscar Brown songs. New Theatre, 1/27/70–7/26/70. 208 perf. light: F. Mitchell Dana. Cast: Oscar Brown Jr., Jean Pace, Sivuca

1685. *A Joyful Noise.* Play with mus. Humorous look at 1st perf of Handel's "Messiah." Unrelated to Broadway show. Lamb's, 2/17/00–3/25/00. 7 prev from 2/11/00. 44 perf. w: Tim Slover; d: Robert Smyth. Cast: Handel: Tom Stephenson. First ran in San Diego

1686. *The Joys of Sex: A Naughty New Musical.* 4 characters sing about sex. Variety Arts, 5/12/04–6/13/04. Prev from 4/9/04. p: Ben Sprecher & William P. Miller; m: David Weinstein; l: Melissa Lewis; b: Melissa Lewis & David Weinstein; d: Jeremy Dobrish; ch: Lisa Shriver; set: Neil Patel; cos: David C. Woolard; light: Donald Holder; sound: T. Richard Fitzgerald. Cast: Ron Bohmer, Jenelle Lynn Randall, David Josefsberg, Stephanie Kurtzuba

1687. *J.P. Morgan Saves the Nation.* Site-specific musical tracing Morgan's life, performed in front of Federal Hall, J.P. Morgan Bank Building, and NY Stock Exchange. Wall & Broad Streets, 6/6/95–7/16/95. m: Jonathan Larson; l/b: Jeffrey M. Jones. Cast: James Judy

1688. *Juba.* Based on life of street dancer William Henry Lane. Dimson, 2/7/91–3/10/91. 31 perf, preceded by 6 special workshop pre-

views at the Samuel Beckett, 9/19/90–9/23/90). p: AMAS Musical Theatre; m: Russell Walden; l/b: Wendy Lamb; d: Sheldon Epps; ch: Mercedes Ellington; set: James Leonard Joy; md: Ted Kociolek. Cast: James Brennan, Katherine Buffaloe, Ken Prymus, Terri White, Kevin Ramsey, Steve Boles, Mark Dovey. The workshop had: Lawrence Clayton, Evan Matthews, Jane Bodle, Michael McCormick, Ken Prymus, Brenda Pressley, Paul Kassel, Edwin Louis Battle. "Juba," "Every Step You Take," "The Gift," "No Irish Need Apply," "Today is the Day," "Kick up Your Heels," "It Wouldn't Be Fair," "A Long Way," "Here and Now," "Next Time We Meet," "Listen to Me," "The Eighth Wonder," "My Blue-Eyed Gal," "Heartless," "This isn't What I Expected," "Take Heart," "He's Our Man," "Rivals"

1689. *Jubilee.* Set in a country threatened with insurrection in 1935. Imperial, Broadway, 10/12/35–3/7/36. 169 perf. p: Sam H. Harris & Max Gordon; m/l: Cole Porter; b: Moss Hart; d: Hassard Short & Monty Woolley; ch: Albertina Rasch; set: Jo Mielziner; cos: Irene Sharaff & Connie DePinna; md: Frank Tours; orch: Russell Bennett. Cast: Mary Boland (*Laura Hope Crews*), June Knight, Melville Cooper, Montgomery Clift. "Our Crown (National Anthem)," "(We're off to) Feathermore," "Why Shouldn't I?," "The Kling-Kling Bird on the Divi-Divi Tree," "When Love Comes Your Way," "What a Nice Municipal Park," "Begin the Beguine," "My Most Intimate Friend," "A Picture of Me without You," "Ev'rybod-ee Who's Anybod-ee," "Judgment of Paris," "Swing That Swing," "Sunday Morning, Breakfast Time," "Mr. and Mrs. Smith," "Gay Little Wives," "Me and Marie," "Just One of Those Things," Jubilee Presentation. Town Hall, 3/2/86–3/3/86. 2 concert perf. d/ch: James Brennan; md: Gregory J. Dlugos. Cast: Alyson Reed, Rebecca Luker, Davis Gaines, Patrick Quinn, Roderick Cook, John Remme, Reed Jones, Paula Laurence, Carole Shelley. Revived in NY, as part of the *Musicals Tonight!* series, 10/6/04–10/17/04. Cast: Patti Perkins, Ed Schiff, Sebastian La Cause, Melissa Lone

1690. *Jubilee Girl.* Bristol Hippodrome, England, 3/5/56; toured; Victoria Palace, London, 6/14/56–7/14/56. 53 perf. m: Alexander Kevin (i.e. A.K. Kaplan); l/b: Robin Fordyce & David Rogers; d: Bert Stimmel, *Leslie Bricusse* & *Frederick Raphael, George Hall* & *Caspar Wrede*; ch: Bert Stimmel, *Alfred Rodrigues, Peter Darrell*; set/cos: Loudon Sainthill. Cast: Fenella Fielding, George Benson, Marie Lohr (*Joyce Barbour*), Lizbeth Webb (*Maureen Quinney*), Irene Handl

1691. *Judy: A Garland of Songs.* Musical celebration of Judy Garland & her career. Upstairs at Channel VII, 5/9/74. Conceived by/d: Jeffrey K. Neill; md/mus adaptations: Wendell Kindberg. Cast: Barbara Coggin, Peter Marinos, Patricia Moline, Tim Sheahan, Norb Joerder (narrator). All Souls Fellowship Hall, 2/24/84–3/10/84. 8 perf. Cast: Diana Daniel, Edwin Decker, Helen Eckard, Steven Fickinger, Debra Kelman, Richard K. Smith

1692. *Junebug Graduates Tonight.* Jazz

allegory. Chelsea Theatre Center, 2/26/67–3/3/67. 5 prev. 5 perf. w: Archie Shepp; d: Robert Kalfin. "Dispensable," "Juney Graduates Tonight," "Hollow Days, Mellow Days," "They 4-F'd My Billy," "You Could've Been a Big-Time Pimp," "I'm a Virgin," "Let Freedom Ring," "I Dig Action," "Poor Foolish Frightened Boy," "Allah," "Hey Now," "Scorin' Makes a Girl Seem Old," "Blame the Reds," "My Man Don't Love Me"

1693. *Junie B. Jones.* First grader writes everything down in her "top-secret personal beeswax" diary. 1 hour long. Lucille Lortel, 7/14/04–8/20/04. The Free Summer Theatre production, presented by Theatreworks/USA; m: Zina Goldrich; l/b: Marcy Heisler; based on popular series of books by Barbara Park; d: Peter Flynn; ch: Dev Janki; md: Kimberly Grigsby. Cast: Jill Abramovitz

1694. *Just a Night Out! A Musical Love Story.* Leader of small jazz singing group has romances with his backup singers. Top of the Village Gate, 2/16/92–4/12/92. Prev from 1/23/92. 65 perf. p: Negro Ensemble Co.; b: Richard & Susan Turner; score included numbers by Cole Porter, and Betty Comden & Adolph Green; d/ch: Leslie Dockery; set: Lisa Watson. Cast: Diane Weaver, Rufus James, Tonya Alexander, Zenzele Scott, Charlene Fitzpatrick, Bruce Butler, Juju Harty. "Just a Night Out!," "Everything Costs Money in New York," "Here We Go Again," "Don't Go to Strangers," "What is She Doing Here," "Let's Get One Thing Straight," "Showtime is Mine," "That Woman is Me," "Lovely Ladies"

1695. *Just for Love.* A musical presentation, an anthology of love. Provincetown Playhouse, 10/17/68–10/20/68. 6 perf. p: Seymour Vall; orig m & l: Michael Valenti; dev: Jill Showell & Henry Comor; d: Henry Comor; md: George Taros. Cast: Henry Comor, Jacqueline Mayro, Jill Showell, Steve Perry. "Just for Love," "Come Live with Me," "Two Strings to a Bow," "What is Love?," "Jenny Kissed Me"

1696. *Just for Openers.* Cabaret revue. Upstairs at the Downstairs, 11/3/65. Conceived by: Rod Warren (also most of the score); d: Sandra Devlin. Cast: Betty Aberlin, Richard Blair, Fannie Flagg, Madeline Kahn. "Just for Openers," "The Dolly Sisters," "Where Did We Go Wrong?," "America the Beautiful," "You're a Big Boy Now," "Mr. Know-it-All" (m: William Goldenberg; l: Larry Alexander)

1697. *Just So.* Set on the world's 1st day. Pennsylvania Stage Co., Allentown, 9/19/84. m/orch: Doug Katsaros; l: David Zippel; b: Mark St. Germain; based on *Just So* stories, by Rudyard Kipling; conceived by/d: Julianne Boyd; set: Atkin Pace; cos: Ann Hould-Ward; light: Craig Miller; md: Paul Sullivan. Cast: Larry Marshall, Bebe Neuwirth, Clent Bowers, Tina Johnson. "Just So," "The Whole World Revolves Around You," "Arm in Arm in Harmony," "Chill Out!," "Camel's Blues," "Eat, Eat, Eat," "Desert Dessert," "Itch, Itch, Itch," "Everything Under the Sun," "Gospel According to the Leopard," "My First Mistake," "The Answer Song," "I've Got to Know," "I Have Changed." Jack Lawrence, 12/3/85–12/8/85. 30 prev from 11/7/85. 6 perf. d: Julianne Boyd;

ch: David Storey; cos: Ann Hould-Ward; md: David Friedman. Cast: Andre De Shields, Keith Curran, Teresa Burrell, Tom Robbins, Tina Johnson, Tico Wells, Jason Graae

1698. *Just So.* Goodspeed, 11/5/98. American premiere. p: Goodspeed, in assoc with Cameron Mackintosh; m: George Stiles; l/b: Anthony Drewe; story: Anthony Drewe & George Stiles; adapted from *Just So* stories by Rudyard Kipling; d: Lou Jacob; ch: Jennifer Paulson Lee; set: David Gallo; sound: Tony Meola; md: Michael O'Flaherty. Cast: Gabriel Barre, Amy Bodnar, Katy Grenfell. "A World of Possibilities," "Just So," "Another Tempest," "There's No Harm in Asking," "The Limpopo River," "Living on This Island," "Thick Skin," "Parsee Cake Walk," "The Crime," "Pick up Your Hooves and Trot," "We Want to Take the Ladies Out," "Jungle Light," "Putting on Appearances," "The Argument," "Roll Up, Roll Up," "Leaps and Bounds," "Wait a Bit," "Take Your Time," "Please Don't Touch My Stove," "Little One, Come Hither," "Does the Moment Ever Come?," "If the Crab." Previously ran in UK

1699. *Kaboom.* Lampoon of American institutions. Bottom Line, 5/1/74. 1 perf. m: Doris Schwerin; l/b: Ira Wallach; d/ch: Don Price; set: Peter Harvey; md: Arnold Gross; orch: Eddie Sauter. Cast: James Donahue, Marjorie Barnes, Bernice Massi, Jack Blackton, Matthew Tobin. "Supermarket," "Buying and Selling," "High School Diplomas," "Busy Lady," "Ritual," "Ave Nelson," "Velvet Vest," "Existential," "Time Was," "Mother Darling," "I'm Gonna Make It," "While They Were Sleeping," "Sex, Sex, Sex," "Is it Too Late?," "On Her Own," "God is Smiling on You"

1700. *Ka-Boom!* After a nuclear explosion the survivors put on a show called *Creation, Part II.* Carter, 11/20/80–1/19/81. 16 prev. 71 perf. m: Joe Ercole; l/b: Bruce Kluger; d: John-Michael Tebelak; ch: Lynne Gannaway; md: John Lehman. Cast: Ken Ward, Fannie Whitehead, Andrea Wright, John Hall, Terry Barnes, Judith Bro. "Now We Pray," "Maybe for Instance," "Smile," "Let Me Believe in Me," "Ballad of Adam and Eve," "The Soft Spot," "The Light Around the Corner," "Let the Show Go On!"

1701. *The Kafka Project.* Musical theatre work based on 6 stories, diaries & letters of Franz Kafka. Ohio Theatre, NY, 1/7/98–1/10/98. 5 perf. m/l: Christopher Drobny; conceived by/d: Devon Allen

1702. *Kaleidoscope.* Musical revue. Provincetown Playhouse, 6/13/57. m/l: Martin Charnin, Murray Grand, Sheldon Harnick, Tom Jones, David Rogers, etc; sk: Lee Adams, Louis Botto, Mickey Deems, Tom Jones, Mike Stewart, etc; ch: Ed Balin; asst ch: Joe Layton; d of sk & blackouts: Paul Mazursky. Cast: Mickey Deems, Wisa D'Orso, Maria Karnilova, Erin Martin, Tom Mixon, Kenneth Nelson, John Smolko

Katherine Dunham and Her Company see # 44, Main Book

1703. *Keep Your Hair On.* Apollo, London, 2/13/58–3/1/58. 20 perf. p: A.K. Kaplan; m: John Addison; dev/l/d: John Cranko; set/cos: Tony Armstrong Jones & Desmond Heeley; md: Anthony Bowles. Cast: John Turner, Betty Marsden, Rachel Roberts, Barbara Windsor, Steve Arlen, Adrienne Marsh, Eric Thompson

1704. *Ken Murray's Hollywood.* Program of commentary & home movies of the stars. John Golden, Broadway, 5/10/65–5/22/65. 16 perf. A Nine O'clock Theatre prod, presented by Alex Cohen & Arthur Whitelaw; conceived by/narrator: Ken Murray; set/light: Ralph Alswang; mus arr/played piano: Armin Hoffman

Kern Goes to Hollywood see # 354, Main Book

1705. *Kerouac.* Musical bio of writer Jack Kerouac. Theatre East, 4/10/97. m: Shelley Gartner; l: Benita Green & Reena Heenan; b: Reena Heenan; d: James B. Nicola. Cast: Robert Maier

1706. *Kes — The Musical.* Set in northern industrial town. A boy, Billy Casper, learns something of life from fate of pet bird. Octagon, Bolton, England, 9/14/95 (ran the season). m/l: Terry Davies; add l/b: Lawrence Till; from Barry Hines's novel *A Kestrel for a Knave.* Cast: Darren Southworth. "Always Fleeing," "You and Me," "A Lifetime of Saturday Nights," "Kes"

1707. *Kicks & Co.* Sex & racial problems on campus of black Freedman University, Chicago, caused by the Devil (Mr. Kicks). Pre-Broadway tryouts at Arie Crown Theatre, Chicago, 10/11/61–10/14/61. 4 perf. Did not make Broadway. w: Oscar Brown Jr.; d: Lorraine Hansberry; ch: Donald McKayle. Cast: Mr. Kicks: Burgess Meredith; Hazel Sharpe: Nichelle Nichols; Also with: Al Freeman Jr., Miriam Burton, Lonnie Sattin, Jan Goldin, Gino Conforti, Mercedes Ellington, Jack Eddleman, Carmen Morales, Thelma Oliver. "Mr. Kicks," "What's in it for Me?," "Lucky Guy," "Hooray for Friday," "While I Am Still Young," "Opportunity, Please Knock," "Turn the Other Cheek," "Hazel's Hips," "I'll Get You Killed," "The Comb is Hot," "Beautiful Girl," "Love is Like a Newborn Child," "Virtue is its Own Reward," "Most Folks are Dopes," "Call of the City," "World Full of Gray"

1708. *The Kid from Stratford.* Palace, Manchester, England, 8/10/48 (3 weeks); toured; Princes', London, 9/30/48; Winter Garden, London, 12/13/48–4/23/49. Total of 235 perf. m: Manning Sherwin; add m: Joseph Tunbridge; l/b: Barbara Gordon & Basil Thomas; d: William Mollison; ch: Pauline Grant; md: Louis Voss. Cast: Arthur Askey, Eunice Gayson, Alfred Marks, Peter Glaze

1709. *King David.* New Amsterdam, Broadway (the prod re-opened this old, 1903, and now fully-restored, theatre. Its last prod had been in 1937; between then & 1982 it had been a movie theatre before closing down), 5/18/97–5/23/97. 3 prev from 5/15/97. 6 perf. Disney concert musical, a biblical oratorio. m: Alan Menken; l/b: Tim Rice; d: Mike Ockrent; set: Tony Walton; cos: William Ivey Long; light: David Agress; sound: Jonathan Deans; md: Michael Kosarin; orch: Doug Besterman. Cast: David: Marcus Lovett; Bathsheba: Alice Ripley; Joab: Stephen Bogardus; Saul: Martin Vidnovic; Goliath: Bill Nolte; Michal: Judy Kuhn; Jonathan: Roger Bart; Also with: Timothy Shew, Anthony Galde, Timothy Robert Blevins, Michael Goz, Kristen Behrendt, Michael DeVries, Michael X. Martin, Karen Murphy, Joan Barber. "Israel and Saul," "Samuel Confronts Saul," "Samuel Anoints David," "The Enemy Within," "There is a View," "Psalm 8," "Genius from Bethlehem," "Valley of Elah," "Goliath of Gath," "Sheer Perfection," "Saul Has Slain His Thousands," "You Have it All," "Psalm 23," "Hunted Partridge on the Hill," "Death of Saul," "How Are the Mighty Fallen," "This New Jerusalem," "David and Michal," "The Ark Brought to Jerusalem," "Never Again," "How Wonderful the Peace," "Off Limits," "Warm Spring Night," "When in Love," "Uriah's Fate Sealed," "Atonement," "The Caravan Moves On," "Death of Absalom," "Absalom, My Absalom," "Solomon," "David's Final Hours," "The Long, Long Day." Reviews were not good. Dallas, Texas, 12/15/04–12/17/04 and Irving, Texas, 12/18/04–12/19/04. d: Cheryl Denson

1710. *King Kong.* African jazz musical. Princes, London, 2/23/61. 201 perf. p: Jack Hylton; m: Todd Matshikiza; l: Pat Williams; b: Harry Bloom; d: Leon Gluckman; ch: Arnold Dover; cast recording on Decca. Cast: Nathan Mdledle, Sophie Mqcina, Stephen Moloi. "Sad Times — Bad Times," "King Kong," "Back of the Moon," "The Earth Turns Over," "Damn Him!," "Be Smart, Be Wise," "Crazy Kid," "Quickly in Love," "Death Song"

1711. *King Mackerel & The Blues Are Running.* Songs & stories of the Carolina coast. West Bank Downstairs, 2/9/95–3/19/95. 30 perf. w: Bland Simpson & Jim Wann; add material: Jerry Leath Mills, Cass Morgan, John Dos Passos; d: John L. Haber. Cast: The Coastal Cohorts (Don Dixon, Bland Simpson, Jim Wann). "King Mackerel & The Blues Are Running," "Timeless," "Ain't That Something?," "Rushing the Season," "Down by the Edge of the Sea," "Georgia Rose," "Sand Mountain Song," "Shag Baby," "Maco Light," "To Catch a King," "Home on the River," "A Mighty Storm," "I'm the Breeze," "Beautiful Day"

1712. *King of Schnorrers.* Yiddish. Set in 1791, in the East End of London. The arrogant king of Sephardic beggars, his pretty daughter, and the lowly but resourceful young artisan who is in love with her. Harold Clurman, 10/9/79–11/3/79. 30 perf; Playhouse, Broadway, 11/28/79–1/13/80. Prev from 11/21/79. 63 perf. m/l/b: Judd Woldin; freely based on Israel Zangwill's novella; d/ch: Grover Dale; set: Adrianne Lobel; md: Hank Ross (*Robert Billig* on Broadway). Cast: Sophie Schwab, Lloyd Battista, Paul Binotto, Ralph Bruneau, Philip Casnoff, Ed Dixon. "Hail to the King," "Chutzpah," "I'm Only a Woman," "Just for Me," "I Have Not Lived in Vain," "The Fine Art of Schnorring," "Tell Me," "What Do You Do?," "Sephardic Lullaby," "Each of Us." 1st ran at George Street Playhouse, Brunswick, NJ, as *Petticoat Lane.* Re-done as *Tatterdemalion* (see this appendix)

1713. *King of the Whole Damn World!* Set

in Greenwich Village in 1940. Jan Hus, 4/12/62–5/20/62. 43 perf. m/l: Robert Larimer; b: George Panetta (from his 1958 OB play *Comic Strip*); d: Jack Ragotzy. Cast: Alan Howard, Tom Pedi, Joseph Macaulay, Kenneth McMillan. "What to Do?," "Poor Little Boy," "King of the World," "Who's Perfect?," "Far Rockaway"

King Solomon and the Cobbler *see* # 334, Main Book

1714. *Kingdom Coming*. Roundhouse, London, 5/21/73–6/2/73. Prev from 5/10/73. 14 perf. m: Bill Snyder; l: Stanley Baum; b/add l: David Climie & Ronnie Cass; d: John Acevski; ch: Joanne Steuer; md: Ed Coleman. Cast: John Bluthal, Antonia Ellis, Aubrey Morris, John Bay

1715. *Kings*. An evening of dance & drama. Alvin, Broadway, 9/27/76–10/18/76. 4 consecutive Mon evenings only. p: Dancehouse, Inc. & Philip Rose; ch: Lynne Taylor; set: John Falabella; cos: Ben Benson; light: Thomas Skelton. Part I: *Oedipus.* w: Sophocles; adapted by: John Cullum. Cast: Oedipus: John Cullum; Also with: Casper Roos, Paul Myrvold, Graham Brown, E. Allan Stevens, Carol Mayo Jenkins, William Duell, Ed Preble, Lisa Casko, Samantha Gold. Part II: *Medea.* m: Alban Berg; ch: Norman Walker. Cast: Medea: Emily Frankel; Also with: David Anderson, John Cullum, Stephen Casko. Part III: *Theseus & Hippolyta.* Adapted from Mary Renault's novel *Bull from the Sea.* m: Miloslav Kabelac & Arvo Part; d/ch: Emily Frankel. Cast: John Cullum, Emily Frankel

1716. *Kings and Clowns*. Birmingham Rep, England, 1/19/78–2/11/78; Phoenix, London, 3/1/78–4/1/78. Prev from 2/17/78. 34 perf. p: Triumph Prods (Duncan C. Weldon & Louis I. Michaels), Hillard Elkins, S. Spencer Davies; m/l/b: Leslie Bricusse; d: Mel Shapiro; ch: Gillian Gregory; set: John Napier; cos: John Napier & Ann Curtis; md: Ed Coleman. Cast: Frank Finlay, Dilys Watling, Anna Quayle, Maureen Scott, Ray C. Davis, June Shand

1717. *King's Rhapsody*. Set in the royal court of Murania, to which Nikki is the dissolute heir. The big hit of the London stage in 1949. Palace, London, 9/15/49–10/6/51. 881 perf. p: Tom Arnold; m/l/b: Ivor Novello; d: Murray MacDonald; ch: Pauline Grant; set: Edward Delaney; cos: Frederick Dawson; md: Harry Acres. Cast: Nikki: Ivor Novello (his last starring role—he died 3/5/51, after a perf), *Barry Sinclair, Jack Buchanan*; Also with: Vanessa Lee (this made her a star), Zena Dare, Phyllis Dare, Olive Gilbert, Robert Andrews, Denis Martin, Netta Westcott, Pamela Harrington, John Young (*Gawn Grainger*). "The Dancing Lesson," "Birthday Greetings," "Some Day My Heart Will Awake," "National Anthem," "Fly Home Little Heart," "Mountain Dove," "If This Were Love," "The Mayor of Perpignan," "The Gates of Paradise," "Take Your Girl," "The Violin Began to Play," "Muranian Rhapsody," "Coronation Hymn," "The Years Together." Filmed in 1953. p/d: Herbert Wilcox; w: Pamela Bower & Christopher Hassall. Cast: Errol Flynn, Anna Neagle, Patrice Wymore. On 7/17/57 the BBC showed

a version, adapted & dir by Douglas Moodie. Cast: Nikki: Griffith Jones; Also with: Vanessa Lee, Denis Jones, David Hemmings

1718. *Kiss Me Quick Before the Lava Reaches the Village*. Set in Greenwich Village & Hollywood. Musical Theatre Works, 10/26/88–11/13/88. 8 prev. 21 perf. m/l: Peter Ekstrom; d: Anthony J. Stimac; ch: Frank Ventura; set: James Noone; md: Albert Ahronheim. Cast: Donna English, Ray Wills, Bill Buell. "Lava Line," "Look at Me!," "Not Yet," "Bring Me a Man," "Will She Still Love Me Now?," "Roll Me Over," "Boom Boom Boom," "Tell Me Moon," "God Bless a Boy that I Love"

1719. *Kiss Now*. Episodic variations on the word "kiss." Martinique Theatre, 4/20/71–4/23/71. 4 perf. m/l: William S. Fischer & Maxine Klein; conceived by/d: Maxine Klein; ch: Sandra Caprin; orch: Bill Brohn. Cast: Sandra Caprin, Louise Hoven. "This City is a Kisser," "Travelin' Man," "The June Taylor," "Too Tired to Love," "Try the Sky," "Death Dance," "No Touch Mine," "Strawberry Day," "Touch Kiss," "Rodeo," "French Thing Tango," "Kabuki Rock," "Kiss Now"

1720. *Kittiwake Island*. Life on a small island. Martinique Theatre, 10/12/60–10/16/60. 7 perf. p: Joseph Beruh & Lawrence Carra; m: Alec Wilder; l/b: Arnold Sundgaard; d: Lawrence Carra. Cast: Kathleen Murray, Lainie Kazan, Joe Lautner, David Canary. "Were This to Prove a Feather in My Hat," "I'd Gladly Walk to Alaska," "The Smew Song," "Never Try Too Hard," "Robinson Crusoe," "If Love's Like a Lark," "When a Robin Leaves Chicago," "It's So Easy to Say," "Kittiwake Island"

1721. *Klenosky Against the Slings and Arrows of Outrageous Fortune*. Theatre East, 9/12/67–9/24/67. 12 perf. Score by the sole actor William J. Klenosky

1722. *Knickerbocker Holiday*. Set in Washington Irving's study in 1809, and at the Battery in 1647. Ethel Barrymore, Broadway, 10/19/38; 46th Street Theatre, 2/13/39–3/11/39. Total of 168 perf. p: The Playwrights' Co.; m/orch: Kurt Weill; l/b: Maxwell Anderson; inspired by Washington Irving's *Knickerbocker History of New York*; d: Josh Logan; set: Jo Mielziner. Cast: Walter Huston, Ray Middleton, Robert Rounseville, Clarence Nordstrom, Richard Kollmar, Dow Fonda. "Introduction & Washington Irving Song," "Clickety-Clack," "It's a Law" (replaced during run by "Hush-Hush"), "There's Nowhere to Go but Up," "It Never Was You," "How Can You Tell an American?," "Will You Remember Me?," "One Touch of Alchemy," "The One Indispensable Man," "Young People Think About Love," "September Song" [the big hit], "Ballad of the Robbers," "We Are Cut in Twain," "To War!," "Our Ancient Liberties," "Romance and Musketeer," "The Scars," Dance of the Algonquins, "Dirge for a Soldier," "No, Ve Vouldn't Gonto Do It." Filmed in 1944 with Nelson Eddy & Charles Coburn. Town Hall, 4/19/77–4/30/77. 16 perf. Part of *Broadway in Concert* series. p: Richard Grayson, John Bowab, Joseph Harris; d: John Bowab; light: Ken Billington; md: Bill Brohn.

Cast: Pieter Stuyvesant: Richard Kiley; Irving: Kurt Peterson; Also with: John Dorrin, Gene Varrone, Elliott Savage, Eric Brotherson, Walter Charles, Ed Evanko, Alyson Bristol, Maureen Brennan, John Leslie Wolfe, Gerard Russak, Genette Lane, Maida Meyers, Susan Rush, Clay Causey, Ed Dixon, Orrin Reiley

1723. *The Knife*. All-singing British musical, set in Winchester. Newman (part of the Public Theatre, NYC), 2/12/87–4/5/87. 60 perf. World premiere. m: Nick Bicat; b/d: David Hare; l: Tim Rose Price; ch: Graciela Daniele; set: Hayden Griffin; cos: Jane Greenwood; light: Tharon Musser; sound: Otts Munderloh; md: Michael Starobin; orch: Chris Walker. Cast: Mandy Patinkin, Cass Morgan, William Parry, Tim Shew, Mary Elizabeth Mastrantonio, Mary Gordon Murray, Mary Testa, Lisa Vroman, Louisa Flaningam, Ronn Carroll, Kevin Gray, Mary Gutzi, Dennis Parlato. "To Be at Sea," "Hello Jeremy," "Agnus Dei," "Miserere," "Between the Sheets," "Blow Slow Kisses," "The Gay Rap," "Men's Eyes," "The Shape I'm In," "You're Not Unique," "Macumba," "Someone Who Touches Me," "Africa," "Shadows Dance Behind You," "The Knife," "Hello Peter, We're Going Out," "What Would You Do in My Place?," "When I Was a Man," "At Least There Are Parties," "The Open Sea," "Ache in Acorn," "What You Mean to Me"

1724. *Kookaburra*. "An Australian musical"—actually a play with mus. Pavilion, Bournemouth, England, 10/19/59; toured; Prince's, London, 11/26/59–1/9/60. 42 perf. p: John Forbes-Sempill Prods, by arr with Jack Hylton; m/l: Eric Spear; w: Charles Macarthur Hardy; from book & orig play by Joyce Dennys; d: John Forbes-Sempill. Cast: Maggie Fitzgibbon, Gordon Boyd, Julia Shelley, Harry H. Corbett

1725. *The Kosher Widow*. Anderson, 10/31/59–1/10/60. 87 perf. m/l: Sholom Secunda & Molly Picon. Cast: Molly Picon, Irving Jacobson, Henrietta Jacobson (also ch/set). "All I Want, Baby, Is You," "Am Yisroel Chai!," "The Hutska," "No Greater Love"

1726. *Kumquats*. The world's first erotic puppet revue. Village Gate, 11/15/71–1/2/72. 53 perf. p: Cosmo Richard Falcon & Wayland Flowers; m: Gustavo Motta; l/b: Cosmo Richard Falcon; creator/set: Wayland Flowers; d: Nicholas Coppola; md: Michael Leonard. "In the Name of Love," "Kumquats," "At the Library," "American Dream Girl," "Irma's Candy Heaven," "The Sensuous Woman," "The Story of Oooh!." It had sketches with titles such as: "Legs!," "The Evil Fairy and the Hippie," "The Wee Scotsman," "Madame Meets a Midget"

1727. *Kuni-Leml: Or the Mismatch*. Set in Odessa, Ukraine, before & during holiday of Purim, in 1880. Jewish Rep, 6/9/84–7/29/84. 30 perf. m/orch: Raphael Crystal; l: Richard Engquist; b: Nahma Sandrow; based on *The Fanatic: or The Two Kuni-Lemls*, a farce by Avrom Goldfadn; d: Ran Avni; ch: Haila Strauss; set: Joel Fontaine; cos: Karen Hummel. Cast: Daniel Marcus, Jack Savage, Mark Zeller, Barbara McCulloh, Gene Varrone, Scott

Wentworth, Susan Victor, Stuart Zagnit. "Celebrate!," "The Boy is Perfect," "Carolina's Lament," "The World is Getting Better," "Cuckoo," "The Matchmaker's Daughter," "A Meeting of the Minds," "A Little Learning," "Nothing Counts But Love," "What's My Name?," "Purim Song," "Do Horses Talk to Horses?" "Lovesongs and Lullabies," "Be Fruitful and Multiply." Moved to the Audrey Wood, 10/9/84–4/21/85. 5 prev. 298 perf. gm: Dorothy Olim & George Elmer. Cast: Steve Sterner, Adam Heller (*Jack Savage*), Barbara McCulloh (*Patricia Ben Peterson*), Gene Varrone, Scott Wentworth (*Adam Heller*), Susan Friedman (*Liz Larsen*), Stuart Zagnit, Mark Zeller. Theatre 91, 10/24/98–11/22/98. 8 prev. 22 perf. p: Jewish Rep; d: Ran Avni; ch: Haila Strauss; md: David Wolfson. Cast: Jay Brian Winnick, Joel Newsome, David Brummel, Paul Harman, Jodie Langel, Danny Gurwin

1728. *A Kurt Weill Cabaret.* Musical cabaret. Used several Weill songs. Edison, Middle Broadway, 5/4/76–5/25/76. 3 perf. p: Norman Kean; conceived by/d: Will Holt; md: William Cox. Cast: Will Holt, Dolly Jonah. Bijou, 11/5/79–11/15/79 (alternated with *Mummenschanz* during this 1st run), and again 12/26/79–12/31/79; 1/4/80–3/8/80; 5/6/80–6/1/80. Total of 72 perf. Cast: Martha Schlamme, Alvin Epstein (*Leonard Frey* 2/11/80–3/8/80), Steven Blier (at piano). Roundabout Stage One, 12/15/81–12/27/81. 16 perf. Cast: Martha Schlamme, Alvin Epstein. Harold Clurman, 12/20/84–4/21/85. Prev from 12/17/84. 130 perf. Cast: Martha Schlamme, Alvin Epstein. Steven Blier on piano (*Harry Huff* from 1/1/85)

1729. *The L.A. Scene.* Duo, 2/15/90–3/17/90. 15 perf. m/l: Jorge Mirkin, Bronwen Jones, Elias Miguel Munoz; d: Mary Lisa Kinney. "Once Upon a Time in the City of Angels," "Song for Little Sister," "Sugar Cane Drinks," "Returning," "Always See the Light," "L.A. Boulevard"

1730. *La-Di-Da-Di-Da.* Farcical musical. Opera House, Blackpool, England, 3/15/43 (2 weeks); Victoria Palace, London, 3/30/43–10/16/43. 318 perf. m: Noel Gay; add dial: Barry Lupino & Arty Ash; based partly on *That's a Pretty Thing*, by Stanley Lupino; d: Lupino Lane; ch: Buddy Bradley, John Regan, Fred A. Leslie; md: Mantovani. Cast: Lupino Lane, Wallace Lupino, Greta Fayne

1731. *Ladies and Gentlemen, Jerome Kern.* An evening of Kern songs. Harold Clurman, 6/9/85–6/30/85. 6 prev. 22 perf. conceived by/d: William E. Hunt; ch: Valarie Pettiford; md: Hank Levy. Cast: Delores Hall, Louise Edeiken (*Audrey Lavine*), Michele Pigliavento, John Scherer (*Edward Prostak*)

1732. *Lady at the Wheel.* Arts Theatre, Cambridge, England, 11/9/53. p: Cambridge University Musical Comedy Club; m/l: Leslie Bricusse & Robin Beaumont; b: Frederick Raphael & Lucienne Hill. Lyric Hammersmith, London, 1/23/58–2/15/58. 28 perf. d: Wendy Toye; ch: Wendy Toye & Tommy Linden; cos: Motley. Cast: Maggie Fitzgibbon, Peter Gilmore, Bernard Cribbins, Malcolm McDonald. The Westminster, London, 2/19/58–3/22/58. 37 perf

1733. *Lady Audley's Secret.* Eastside Playhouse, 10/3/72–10/8/72. 8 perf. p: Haila Stoddard & Arnold H. Levy; m: George Goehring; l: John Kuntz; adapted by Douglas Seale from novel by Mary Elizabeth Braddon; d: Douglas Seale; ch: George Bunt; light: Lawrence Metzler; md: John Cina. Cast: Donna Curtis, Russell Nype, Danny Sewell, Douglas Seale, June Gable, Richard Curnock, Rick Atwell, Michael Serrecchia, Virginia Pulos. "English Country Life," "A Mother's Wish is a Daughter's Duty," "Winter Rose," "Comes a Time," "That Lady in Eng-a-land," "Civilized," "Dead Men Tell No Tales," "Pas de Deux," "An Old Maid," "Repose," "Audley Family Honor," "La-de-da-da," "I Knows What I Knows," "How? What? Why?," "Firemen's Quartet," "Forgive Her, Forgive Her." This prod had begun at the Goodman, Chicago, 5/24/71. 34 perf

1734. *Lady, Be Good!* Liberty, Broadway, 12/1/24–9/12/25. 330 perf. p: Alex A. Aarons & Vinton Freedley; m: George Gershwin; l: Ira Gershwin; b: Guy Bolton & Fred Thompson; book d: Felix Edwardes; ch: Sammy Lee; set: Norman Bel Geddes; orch: Robert Russell Bennett, Charles N. Grant, Paul Lannin, Stephen Jones, Max Steiner, William Daly. Cast: Fred & Adele Astaire. "Hang on to Me," "Fascinating Rhythm," "So Am I," "Oh, Lady Be Good!," "The Half-of-it-Dearie Blues," "Little Jazz Bird," "Swiss Miss" (l: Ira Gershwin & Arthur Jackson). "The Man I Love" was dropped before Broadway. The 1st teaming of the Gershwin brothers, and the show that made a star of Fred Astaire. First called *Black-Eyed Susan*. Revived in London, 1968. Cast: Aimi Macdonald, Lionel Blair

1735. *Lady Day: A Musical Tragedy.* Set in the eye of the Black Nation, and concerning Billie Holiday. Chelsea Theatre Center of Brooklyn, 10/25/72–11/5/72. 8 prev from 10/17/72. 24 perf. m/l: Archie Shepp, Stanley Cowell, Cal Massey, Aishah Rahman; d: Paul Carter Harrison; set: Robert U. Taylor; cos: Randy Barcelo; md: Stanley Cowell. Cast: Cecelia Norfleet, Rosetta Le Noire, Roger Robinson, Signa Joy, Madge Sinclair. Dee Dee Bridgewater (understudy). "Tears of This Fool," "Looking for Someone to Love," "Billie's Blues," "Strange Fruit," "Blues for the Lady," "God Bless the Child," "Lover Man," "Big Daddy"

The Lady from Paris see # 463, Main Book

1736. *Lady in the Dark.* *Allure* magazine editor Liza can't decide whether to marry publisher, and comes to realize the man who can cure her neuroses is cynical ad manager because he is only one who can complete the song "My Ship," which Liza had learned as a child but is now unable to finish. Alvin, Broadway, 1/23/41–6/15/41. 162 perf; took hiatus until 9/2/41, so star Gertrude Lawrence might rest; re-opened 9/2/41, again at the Alvin, and finally closed 5/30/42 (after add 305 perf). p: Sam H. Harris; m/orch/arr: Kurt Weill; l: Ira Gershwin; b: Moss Hart (he originally conceived it as straight play for Katharine Cornell); d: Hassard Short & Moss Hart; ch: Albertina Rasch; set: Harry Horner; cos: Irene Sharaff; md: Maurice Abravanel. Cast: Gertrude Lawr-ence, Victor Mature (*Willard Parker*), Danny Kaye (*Eric Brotherson*), Macdonald Carey (*Walter Coy, Hugh Marlowe*), Ron Field (Broadway debut in chorus), Scott Merrill (one of the replacement Albertina Rasch Dancers). "Oh, Fabulous One in Your Ivory Tower," "The World's Innamorata," "One Life to Live," "Girl of the Moment," "It Looks Like Liza," "Mapleton High Chorale," "This is New," "The Princess of Pure Delight," "The Woman at the Altar," "Greatest Show on Earth," "The Dance of the Tumblers," "The Best Years of His Life," "Tschaikowsky," "The Saga of Jenny," "My Ship." Originally called *I Am Listening*. Following a tour, the show returned to Broadway (the Broadway Theatre) 2/27/43–5/15/43. 83 perf. Filmed in 1944, with Ray Milland & Ginger Rogers. Playhouse, Nottingham, England, 12/9/81. Cast: Celeste Holm, Kenneth Nelson, Don Fellows, Jeremy Hawk. City Center, 5/4/94–5/7/97. 4 concert perfs. Part of *Encores!* series. adapted by/d: Larry Carpenter; ch: Daniel Pelzig; set: John Lee Beatty; md: Rob Fisher. Cast: Christine Ebersole, Joe Morton, Betsy Joslyn, Carole Shelley, Frank Converse, Susan Cella. London, 1997

1737. *Lady of Mexico.* Operetta. Set in Mexico in 1531. Blackfriars', 10/16/62–12/9/62. 56 perf. m/l: Rev. Joseph Roff & Sister Mary Francis; d: Walter Cool. Cast: Mary O'Malley, Jorge Rios

1738. *The Lady or the Tiger.* Orange Tree, Richmond, London, 8/5/75–8/24/75. m/l/b: Jeremy Paul & Michael Richmond; d: Michael Richmond. Revised and re-ran at same theatre, 12/20/75–12/28/75; Fortune, London, 2/3/76–3/20/76. Prev from 1/30/76. 52 perf. p: John Gale & David Conville. Cast: Kate Crutchley, Vernon Joyner, Gordon Reid, John Morton

1739. *Lady Windermere's Fan.* London, 1954. adapted by Noel Coward from Oscar Wilde's play. Cast: Vanessa Lee, Mary Ellis

1740. *The Land of Dreams.* Play with mus. Folksbiene, 11/11/89–3/18/90. 45 perf. m/l: Raphael Crystal & Miriam Kressyn; w: Nahum Stutchkoff; adapted by: Miriam Kressyn; translator: Simcha Kruger; d: Bryna Wortman; set: Brian P. Kelly

1741. *The Land of the Christmas Stocking.* Play with mus. Duke of York's, London, 12/19/46–1/19/47. m: Mabel Buchanan; w: Henry D.G. Foord & Mabel Buchanan; d: Patrick Ide. Cast: Wee Willie Winkie: June Nield. Same venue, 12/18/47–1/18/48. d: Maxwell Wray. Cast: Wee Willie Winkie: Jimmy Crabbe; Contrary Mary (a new character): Jean Marsh. Same venue, 12/27/48–1/22/49. Cast: Wee Willie Winkie: Robin Netscher. Certain characters were played by the same actors in all 3 prods: Tilly: Patsy Ann Hedges; Angelina: Jean Brown; Simpcy: Sydney Bromley; Dandy Diddle: Greta Unger; Dame Foot: Eleanor Hallam

1742. *The Land of the Dinosaurs.* Theatre Royal, Stratford East, London, 10/3/74–11/16/74. Subsequently performed at matinees until 1/4/75. m: Ian Armit; l/b/d: Ken Hill. Cast: Larry Dann, Marianne Price, Melody Kaye

1743. *Larry the Lamb in Toytown.* Started

as *Toyland*, at the Swan, Worcester, 12/26/69–1/17/70. w: David Wood & Sheila Ruskin; from books of S.G. Hulme Beaman; d: John Hole; ch: Sonia Davis. Larry: Marcia King. After name change played at the Shaw, London, 12/12/73. d: David Wood; ch: Maurice Lane; md: Peter Pontzen. Cast: Larry: Melody Kaye; Dennis the Dachshund: Paul Henley; Mayor of Toytown: Geoffrey Lumsden; Ernest the Policeman: Norman Warwick

1744. *The Last Empress*. Korean musical. New York State Theatre, 8/15/97–8/24/97. Limited run of 12 perf. m: Hee Gab Kim; l: InJa Yang; b: Mun Yol Yi; adapted by: Kwang Lim Lim; d: Ho Jin Yun; add m/orch: Peter Casey. Cast of over 80, including Taewon Yi Kim (as Queen Min, who was assassinated in 1895). Returned 8/4/98–8/23/98. 24 perf

1745. *The Last Five Years*. Artistic couple meet, fall in love, and separate. Minetta Lane, 3/3/02–5/5/02. 73 perf. m/l/: Jason Robert Brown; d: Daisy Prince; md: Thomas Murray. Cast: Sherie Rene Scott, Norbert Leo Butz, Nicole Van Giesen, D.B. Bonds. "Still Hurting," "Jamie's Song," "See, I'm Smiling," "Moving Too Fast," "A Part of That," "The Schmuel Song," "A Summer in Ohio," "The Next Ten Minutes," "A Miracle Would Happen"/"When You Come Home to Me," "Climbing Uphill," "If I Didn't Believe in You," "I Can Do Better than That," "Nobody Needs to Know," "Goodbye Until Tomorrow"/"I Could Never Rescue You." First prod at Northlight Theatre Co., Skokie, Ill., 5/23/01

1746. *The Last Minstrel Show*. Set in the Variety Theatre, Cincinnati, on the night of 3/15/26, when blacks picketed the theatre when the last minstrel show played there. Several songs from 1920s. Pre-Broadway tryouts. Opened 3/20/78, Wilbur, Boston; on to the Playhouse, Wilmington, Del., 3/30/78; closed 4/30/78, New Locust, Philadelphia. Never made Broadway. w: John Taylor Ford; d: Donald McKayle; set: Edward Burbridge; light: Ian Calderon; md/orch: Howard Roberts. Cast: Gregory Hines, Tucker Smallwood, Clebert Ford, Ralston Hill, Roger Alan Brown, Della Reese

1747. *The Last Musical Comedy*. Riverwest, 2/12/88–3/5/88. 2 perf. m/l: Arthur Siegel & Tony Lang; d/ch: Pamela Hunt. Cast: Donna English, Eddie Korbich, Mark Esposito, Michael DeVries. "Last Overture," "Last Opening," "Last Hometown Song," "Last Soubrette Song," "Last Love Duet," "Last Hate Song," "Last Soft Shoe," "Last Production Number," "Last Waltz," "Last Dream Ballet," "Last Jazz Specialty," "Last Torch Song," "Last Tap Dance," "Last Seduction Song," "Last Soliloquy," "Last Eleven O'clock Number," "Last Finale"

1748. *The Last Savage*. Opera. The Met, 1964. Lasted only a few perfs. m/l: Gian-Carlo Menotti. Cast: Nicolai Gedda, Teresa Stratas. "How Can My Lips Deny It?"

1749. *The Last Session*. Former rock star is forced to defend his past and confront his future. Currican, 5/8/97–8/31/97. 111 perf; 47th Street Theatre, 10/17/97–3/1/98. 17 prev from 10/3/97. 154 perf. m/l: Steve Schalchlin;

b: Jim Brochu; d: Mike Wills. "Save Me a Seat," "Preacher and the Nurse," "Somebody's Friend," "The Group," "Going it Alone," "At Least I Know What's Killing Me," "Friendly Fire," "Connected," "When You Care"

1750. *The Last Starfighter*. Sci-fi musical. A teenage video-game player saves the universe. Storm, 10/15/04–10/30/04. World premiere. m/l: Skip Kennon; b: Fred Landau; inspired by 1984 movie of same name, written by Jonathan Betuel; d: Peter Dobbins; ch: Jennifer Paulson Lee; set: Todd Ivins. Cast: Joseph Kolinski, William Parry, Paul Jackel

1751. *The Last Supper*. St. Luke's, 3/22/00–4/21/00. 8 perf. m/orch: Gary William Friedman; l/b: Thomas Mitz; conceived by: Andrew Krey; d: Nancy Rhodes; md: Glenn Gordon. Cast: David Sitler (as Leonardo Da Vinci, upon whose painting this was based). "Visions," "Stand Like a Rock," "God Has a Plan for Me," "How Deep is Your Gaze?," "All I Can Do is Love You," "How Beautiful Upon the Mountain," "You Are the Light," "If It Was Easy," "Didn't You Know?"

Last Sweet Days (of Isaac) see # 623, Main Book

1752. *The Late Great Ladies of Blues and Jazz*. John Houseman, 6/16/87–7/17/87. 2 prev. 23 perf. Cast: Sandra Reaves-Phillips (also concept/w)

1753. *Laugh a Lifetime*. Satirical musical revue. Norman Thomas, 10/22/78–12/3/78. 20 perf. p: Lively and Yiddish Co. Cast: Shimon Dzigan (also d), Ben Bonus, Mina Bern

1754. *Laughs and Other Events*. Revue. Ethel Barrymore, Broadway, 10/10/60–10/15/60. 8 perf. p: Martin Tahse; from book by Stanley Holloway; d: Tony Charmoli; set/light: John Robert Lloyd. Cast: Stanley Holloway, Baliol Holloway

1755. *The Laundry Hour*. Cabaret-style musical revue. Spiritual adventure from the fervent 1960s to today's loss of the liberal leading edge. Public, 8/4/81–8/9/81. 8 perf. p: NY Shakespeare Festival; m/md: Paul Schierhorn; l/sk: Mark Linn-Baker & Lewis Black; d: William Peters; ch: Rick Elice. Cast: Mark Linn-Baker, Lewis Black, Paul Schierhorn

1756. *Lautrec*. Bio of the painter. Shaftesbury, London, 4/6/00–6/17/00. Prev from 3/27/00. m/l: Charles Aznavour; English l: Dee Shipman; b: Shaun McKenna; d: Rob Bettinson. Cast: Sevan Stephan, Hannah Waddingham

Lawyers, Lovers and Lunatics see # 735, Main Book

1757. *L'Chaim to Life*. Yiddish musical revue. Town Hall, 11/5/86–12/21/86. Prev from 10/29/86. 48 perf. By Sholom Secunda, Max Perlman, Jacob Jacobs, Joseph Rumshinsky, Ben Bonus, Paul Anka, Edith Piaf, etc; d/light: Neil Steinberg; ch/cos: Eber Lobato; md: Renee Solomon. Cast: Mina Bern, Jackie Jacob. "Shalom Aleichem," "Roumania, Roumania," "La Vie en Rose," "C'est Si Bon," "Valentine," "Bei Mir Bist du Shayn," "Chiribin," "My Way"

1758. *Leave It to Beaver Is Dead*. Public Theatre's Other Stage, 3/29/79–4/7/79. 15 perf. p: Joseph Papp; m: Larry David & Des

McAnuff; w/d: Des McAnuff; set: Jennifer von Mayrhauser; cos: Heidi Landesman; light: Victor En Yu Tan; md: Larry David. Cast: Mandy Patinkin, Brent Spiner, Maury Chaykin, Saul Rubinek, Dianne Wiest

1759. *Leave It to Charley*. Yiddish. Misadventures of milkman Charley Cucumber. Second Avenue, 2/13/49. p: Menasha Skulnik; m: Abe Ellstein; l: Isidor Lillian & Jacob Jacobs; b: Louis Freiman & Isidor Friedman; d: Menasha Skulnik & Isador Goldstein; ch: Lillian Shapero. Cast: Menasha Skulnik, Leon Liebgold, Lilly Lilliana, Anna Teitelbaum, Yetta Zwerling. "I Can't Describe it (But I Know What I Want)," "Charley Knows His History," "I'm Not in a Hurry (I Got Plenty of Time)"

1760. *Leave It to Jane*. Set in Atwater College. Longacre, Broadway, 8/28/17. 167 perf. m: Jerome Kern; l/b: Guy Bolton & P.G. Wodehouse; based on play *The College Widow*, by George Ade. "Good Old Atwater," "Great Big Land," "Wait Till Tomorrow," "Just You Watch My Step," "Leave it to Jane," "Siren's Song," "Medley of College Songs," "There is it Again," "Cleopatterer," "Crickets Are Calling," "What I'm Longing to Say," "Sir Galahad," "Sun Shines Brighter. Sheridan Square Playhouse, 5/25/59. 928 perf. d: Lawrence Carra; ch: Mary Jane Doerr; set: Lloyd Burlingame; md: Joseph Stecko. Cast: Ollie Mitchell; George Segal, *Austin O'Toole*; Sally: Lee Thornberry, *Lainie Kazan, Jean Hilzinger*; Also with: Kathleen Murray (*Laurie Franks*, 59–60, while Miss Murray was on leave), Art Matthews (*John Stratton*), Angelo Mango (*Chuck Floyd*), Dorothy Stinnette (*Joy Claussen, Jeanne Allen*), Dorothy Greener, Al Checco (*Bert Pollock*), A Goodspeed production aimed at (but not getting to) Broadway, opened at Goodspeed 10/2/85, and closed at Royal Poinciana Playhouse, Palm Beach, Fla., 1/18/86. d: Thomas Gruenewald; ch: Walter Painter; set: James Leonard Joy; md: Lynn Crigler. Cast: Rebecca Luker, Faith Prince, Michael Waldron, Gary Gage, Nick Corley, Iris Revson, Jack Doyle. Equity Library, 3/9/89–4/2/89. 32 perf. d: Lynnette Barkley; ch: Niki Harris; md: Ethyl Will. Cast: Wendy Oliver

1761. *Leave It to Me!* Set in Paris & Russia. Imperial, Broadway, 11/9/38–7/15/39. 291 perf. p: Vinton Freedley; m/l: Cole Porter; b: Bella & Samuel Spewack (based on their play *Clear All Wires*); d: Sam Spewack; ch: Robert Alton; set: Albert Johnson; cos: Raoul Pene du Bois; md: Robert Emmett Dolan; orch: Donald J. Walker. Cast: Sophie Tucker, William Gaxton, Victor Moore, Mary Martin (Broadway debut as Dolly Winslow, singing "My Heart Belongs to Daddy"), George Tobias, Gene Kelly (as one of the secretaries to Mr. Goodhue). "How Do You Spell Ambassador?," "We Drink to You, J.H. Brody," "Vite, Vite, Vite," "(I'm) Taking the Steppes to Russia" (Gene Kelly was in this), "Get Out of Town," "When it's All Said and Done," "Most Gentlemen Don't Like Love" (Gene Kelly was in this), "I Want to Go Home," "Comrade Alonzo," "From Now On," "My Heart Belongs to Daddy," "Tomorrow," "Far Away," "From the USA to the USSR." Again at the Imperial, 9/4/39–9/16/39. 16 perf.

A few notable cast replacements: Mary Martin was replaced by *Mildred Fenton*; Gene Kelly by *Joel Friend*; George Tobias by *Eugene Sigaloff*. Equity Library, 3/10/88–4/3/88. 32 perf. d: Howard Rossen; ch: David Storey. Cast: Mary Ellen Ashley, Mary Brienza, Gerry Burkhardt, Mary-Kathleen Gordon, Caitlin Larsen. 14th Street Y, 3/20/01–4/1/01. 16 perf. Part of the *Musicals Tonight!* series. p: Mel Miller; d/ch: Thomas Mills; md/voc arr: Mark Hartman. Cast: Gordon Connell, Barbara McCulloh, Kenny Morris, John Wasiniak, J. Michael McCormack, Robin Baxter

1762. Leaves of Grass. Anthology of Walt Whitman's works arranged as lyr & set to music. Theatre Four, 9/12/71–10/24/71. 49 perf. m/adapted: Stan Harte Jr.; d: Stan Harte Jr. & Bert Michaels; ch: Bert Michaels; set: David Chapman; md: Karen Gustafson; arr: Bill Brohn. Cast: Yolande Bavan, Lynn Gerb, Scott Jarvis, Joe Masiell. "Come Said My Soul," "There is That in Me," "Song of the Open Road," "Give Me," "Who Makes Much of a Miracle?," "Tears," "Twenty-Eight Men," "A Woman Waits for Me," "As Adam," "Do You Suppose," "Enough," "Dirge for Two Veterans," "How Solemn," "Oh Captain! My Captain!," "Pioneers," "Song of Myself," "Excelsior," "In the Prison," "Twenty Years," "Unseen Buds," "Goodbye, My Fancy," "Thanks," "I Hear America Singing"

1763. Legacy. Harold Clurman, 6/10/94–6/19/94. 10 perf. p: AMAS; m/l: Holly B. Francis & Arden Altino; developed by AMAS/Eubie Blake Youth Theatre; d: James L. Moody; ch: Felicia Kennerly; set/cos: the Company; md: Holly B. Francis. "Conditions of the World," "Star-Spangled Banner," "Once Upon a Time," "Paycheck Away from the Streets," "We've Got Something Goin' On," "Good Morning Heart Ache," "Isn't That the Way," "Running," "Let's Learn to Be Friends," "If We're Supposed to Be in Love," "Never E-Nuff Time," "But This Is"

1764. Legends in Concert. Musical concert-style revue. 9 show-biz legends impersonated. Academy Theatre, 5/10/89–5/28/89. Prev from 5/4/89. 22 perf. p/created/d: John Stuart; ch: Inez Mourning; md: Kerry McCoy. Cast: Jack Benny: Eddie Carroll; Buddy Holly: George Trullinger; Liberace: Daryl Wagner; Jolson: Clive Baldwin; Marilyn Monroe: Katie LaBourdette; John Lennon: Randy Clark; Judy Garland: Julie Sheppard; Nat "King" Cole: Donny Ray Evins; Elvis: Tony Roi

1765. Lennon. Musical bio. Entermedia, 10/5/82–10/26/82. 25 perf. The Liverpool Everyman Theatre production. w/d: Rob Eaton; sound: Tom Morse. Cast: Robert LuPone, Gusti Bogok, John Jellison, David Patrick Kelly. Previously ran in Liverpool & Sheffield, England. There was another, unrelated, musical bio of John Lennon, with same title, that ran at the Astoria, London, from 11/2/85

1766. Lennon. Formerly called *The Lennon Project*. 10 actors play John at different times of his life. 30 Lennon songs. World premiere at the Orpheum, San Francisco, 4/12/05–5/14/05; Colonial, Boston, 5/31/05–6/25/05; Broadhurst, Broadway, 7/21/05 (prev from 7/7/05).

p: Allan McKeown, Edgar Lansbury, Don Scardino, in assoc with Clear Channel Entertainment, by arrangement with Yoko Ono; m/l: John Lennon; conceived by/b/d: Don Scardino; ch: Joe Malone; set: John Arnone; cos: Jane Greenwood; light: Natasha Katz. Cast: Terrence Mann, Will Chase, Chuck Cooper, Julie Danao, Mandy Gonzalez, Marcy Harriell, Michael Potts, Julia Murney, Chad Kimball. "India, India," "I Don't Want to Lose You," "Cookin' in the Kitchen of Love"

1767. Lenny and the Heartbreakers: A New American Opera. Newman, 12/22/83–1/8/84. 14 prev from 12/7/83. 20 perf. m/l: Scott Killian, Kim D. Sherman, Kenneth Robins; d/ch: Murray Louis & Alwin Nikolais. Cast: Nancy Ringham, Joanna Glushak. "The First Last Supper," "Study of the Human Figure," "A Light Thing," "I'm a Rocket Tonight," "Interesting Use of Space," "There's Art in My Revenge," "Lonely in Space," "Lenny and the Heartbreakers"

1768. Leonard Bernstein's Theatre Songs. Program of songs with mus by Mr. Bernstein, from *On the Town, Trouble in Tahiti, Wonderful Town, Candide, West Side Story.* Theatre de Lys, 6/28/65 –9/12/65. 88 perf. conceived by/d: Will Holt; light: Jules Fisher. Cast: Trude Adams (*Lee Beery* from 8/17/65), Don Francks (*Will Holt* from 8/17/65), Micki Grant

Let 'Em Eat Cake see # 497, Main Book
Let 'Em Rot see # 735, Main Book

1769. Let Me Hear the Melody. Philadelphia, 1951. m/l: George Gershwin. Cast: Melvyn Douglas, Anthony Quinn. "Hi-Ho" (the 1st publication of this song, previously cut from *Shall We Dance*)

1770. Let's Do It! Festival Theatre, Chichester, England, 1994. m/l: Noel Coward & Cole Porter; b: Robin Ray & Dick Vosburgh. Cast: David Kernan, Liz Robertson, Louise Gold, Pat Kirkwood, Peter Greenwell, Robin Ray. "My Heart Belongs to Daddy," "Matelot," "Blow Gabriel Blow," "Mrs. Worthington," "The Physician," "It's De-Lovely," "Chase Me Charlie," "You Don't Know Paree," "London Bride," "I Happen to Like New York," "I'm Throwing a Ball Tonight," "I've Been to a Marvelous Party," "Useless Useful Phrases," "Nina," "You're the Top," "I Wonder What Happened to Him," "Mad Dogs and Englishmen," "20th-Century Blues"

1771. Let's Face It! Set in 1941, on Decoration Day weekend. Imperial, Broadway, 10/29/41–3/20/43. Vacationed 7/18/42–8/17/42. 547 perf. p: Vinton Freedley; m/l: Cole Porter; add l: Sylvia Fine & Max Liebman; b: Herbert & Dorothy Fields; from 1925 play *The Cradle Snatchers*, by Russell Medcraft & Norma Mitchell (a play that featured Humphrey Bogart); d: Edgar MacGregor; ch: Charles Walters; set: Harry Horner; md: Max Meth; orchestral arr: Hans Spialek, Donald J. Walker, Ted Royal. Cast: Danny Kaye (his 1st starring role; *Jose Ferrer* from 2/43), Benny Baker, Eve Arden (her understudy was Carol Channing, who went on only once; *Carol Goodner* from 7/42), Vivian Vance, Nanette Fabray, Joseph Macaulay, Garry Davis. "Milk, Milk, Milk," "A Lady Needs a Rest," "Jerry, My Soldier Boy," "Let's

Face It!," "Farming," "Ev'rything I Love," "Ace in the Hole," "You Irritate Me So," "Baby Games," "A Fairy Tale" [dropped when Mr. Kaye left], "Rub Your Lamp," "Cuttin' a (Persian) Rug," "I've Got Some Unfinished Business with You," "Let's Not Talk About Love," "A Little Rumba Numba," "I Hate You, Darling," "Melody in Four F" [when Mr. Kaye left this was replaced with "It Ain't Etiquette"]. Filmed in 1943, with Bob Hope & Betty Hutton. Jule Styne & Sammy Cahn wrote 4 new songs for the film. AMDA (OB), 4/18/77–5/1/77. 12 perf. adapted/d/ch: Jeffrey K. Neill; light: Peggy Moran; md: Wendell Kindberg. Cast: Martha Daly, Geraldine Hanning, Renee Orin, Norman Beim

1772. Let's Sing Yiddish. Set in a European shtetl between the World Wars. Brooks Atkinson, Broadway, 11/9/66–1/29/67. 1 prev on 11/8/66. 107 perf. p: Ben Bonus; based on humor & Yiddish folklore of Itzik Manger, featuring art songs by Mr. Manger; d: Mina Bern; md: Renee Solomon. Cast: Mina Bern, Ben Bonus, Susan Walters, Max Bozyk, Rose Bozyk. "Once Upon a Shtetl," "Castle Garden," "Life in the Shop," "On the Subway," "Encounter in the Park," "Wishful Thinking," "American in Israel," "Let's Sing Yiddish"

1773. A Letter for Queen Victoria. Opera. ANTA, Broadway, 3/22/75–4/6/75. 3 prev. 18 perf. p: Byrd Hoffman Foundation; m: Alan Lloyd & Michael Galasso; add text: Christopher Knowles, Cynthia Lubar, Stefan Brecht, James Neu; b/d: Robert Wilson; ch: Andrew de Groat; set/cos: Peter Harvey; light: Beverly Emmons & Carol Mullins; sound: R.O. Willis; md: Michael Galasso; cm: C. Edwin Knill. Entr'actes by Robert Wilson & Christopher Knowles. Singers: Sheryl Sutton, Cynthia Lubar, George Ashley, Stefan Brecht, Kathryn Cation, Alma Hamilton, Christopher Knowles, James Neu, Robert Wilson. Dancers: Andrew de Groat & Julia Busto. Musicians: Michael Galasso, Susan Korngold, Kevin Byrnes, Laura Epstein, Kathryn Cation. Also with the Byrd Hoffman School of Byrds. Tony nomination for score

1774. Liberty Ranch! Long after Goldsmith & slightly to the West. Greenwich Theatre, London, 7/18/72–8/12/72. 26 perf. p: Robert Stigwood; m: John Cameron; l/conceived by: Caryl Brahms & Ned Sherrin; b: Dick Vosburgh; from Oliver Goldsmith's play *She Stoops to Conquer;* d/ch: Gillian Lynne; cos: Berkeley Sutcliffe; md: Barry Booth. Cast: Elizabeth Seal, David Kernan, Bill Kerr, Derek Griffiths

1775. Lie Down, I Think I Love You. Strand, London, 10/14/70–10/24/70. 13 perf. p: Daniel Rees; m/l: Ceredig Davies; b/d: John Gorrie; ch: Geoffrey Cauley; set/cos: Hutchinson Scott; md: David Cullen. Cast: Ray Brooks, Vanessa Miles, Tim Curry, Lynn Dalby, Ray Davis, Antonia Ellis

1776. Lies and Legends: The Musical Stories of Harry Chapin. Musical revue. "Story songs" by the late Harry Chapin. Village Gate, 4/24/85–6/30/85. 14 prev. 79 perf. conceived by: Joseph Stern; d: Sam Weisman; ch: Tracy Friedman; md: Stephen Chapin & Tom Chapin. Cast: John Herrera (*Mark Fotopoulos*), Joanna

Glushak, Martin Vidnovic, Ron Orbach, Terri Klausner. "Salt and Pepper," "Mr. Tanner," "The Rock," "Taxi," "Get on with It," "Bananas," "Shooting Star," "Sniper," "Dance Band on the Titanic," "Mail Order Annie," "Odd Job Man," "Dreams Go By," "Tangled-Up Puppet," "Cat's in the Cradle," "Halfway to Heaven," "Better Place to Be." Previously ran in Chicago

1777. *The Life and Adventures of Nicholas Nickleby.* Aldwych, London, 6/5/80. m/l: Stephen Oliver. Cast: Rose Hill, Lila Kaye, Sharon Bower, Andrew Hawkins, John Woodvine. "London," "Home in Devonshire," "Dotheboys Hall," "Journey to Portsmouth," "Sir Mulberry Hawk," "At the Opera," "Christmas Carol." Done on TV in 1982; same cast

1778. *Life Is Not a Doris Day Movie.* Musical revue. Set at a bus stop at the tip of Manhattan. Showbiz aspirants wish someone would give them a chance. In Act II they show what they can do if someone did. Top of the Gate, 6/25/82–7/25/82. 17 prev from 6/10/82. 37 perf. m: Stephen Graziano; l/b: Boyd Graham; d: Norman Rene; ch: Marcia Milgrom Dodge; md: Jim Cantin. Cast: Boyd Graham, Mary Testa, Neva Small, Olga Merediz (understudy). "Waiting for the Bus of Life," "Don't Cry for Me," "Oh, William Morris," "The Last Thing that I Want to Do is Fall in Love," "You'll Be Sorry," "Little Girl — Big Voice," "I'm So Fat," "It's a Doris Day Morning," "Singer Who Moves Well," "Not Mr. Right," "Think of Me"

1779. *Life with the Lyons.* Musical comedy adaptation of the radio program. Hippodrome, Blackpool, England, 6/28/52. Never made the West End. d: Jack Hulbert; ch: Jack Hulbert & Archie Savage; md: Robert Probst. Cast: Bebe Daniels, Ben Lyon, Barbara Lyon, Richard Lyon, Mollie Weir, Diana Dors (as Peaches La Rue)

1780. *Light in the Piazza.* Set in Florence & Rome, in 1953. Young Italian man & young American girl have romance, but girl's mother is opposed for unknown reasons. Intiman, Seattle, 6/14/03–7/19/03. Prev from 5/31/03. m/l: Adam Guettel; b: Craig Lucas; from 1960 novel by Elizabeth Spencer; d: Craig Lucas; ch: Pat Graney; set: Loy Arcenas; cos: Catherine Zuber; light: Christopher Akerlind; sound: Acme Sound Partners; md: Ted Sperling; orch: Ted Sperling & Adam Guettel. Cast: Victoria Clark, Celia Keenan-Bolger, Patti Cohenour, Kelli O'Hara, Mark Harelik, Glenn Seven Allen. Goodman, Chicago, 1/20/04–2/22/04 (closing date extended from 2/15/04). Prev from 1/10/04. d: Bartlett Sher; ch: Marcela Lorca; set: Michael Yeargan; cos: Catherine Zuber; light: Christopher Akerlind; md: Ted Sperling. Same basic cast. Vivian Beaumont, Broadway, 4/18/05. Prev from 3/17/05 (date brought forward by a day). Cast: Victoria Clark (reprising her role as the mother), Kelli O'Hara (this time as Clara; in Chicago she had played Franca); Franca: Sarah Uriarte Berry; Also with: Michael Berresse, Beau Gravitte, Matthew Morrison. "Aiutami," "The Beauty Is," "The Joy You Feel," "Love to Me"

1781. *Light, Lively and Yiddish.* Set in the shtetl, NYC, and Israel. Belasco, Broadway,

10/27/70–1/10/71. 8 prev from 10/20/70. 87 perf. p: Sol Dickstein; m: Eli Rubinstein; l/text: Abram Shulman, Wolf Younin, Sylvia Younin; adapted into musical: Ben Bonus; d: Mina Bern; ch: Felix Fibich; md: Renee Solomon. Cast: Ben Bonus, Mina Bern, Miriam Kressyn, Reizl Bozyk, Harry Endicott. "It's Hard to Be a Jewish Woman," "Nobody Told Me This," "Where is Justice?," "A Joyful Song," "Light, Lively and Yiddish," "The Song of My Generation," "Israel," "Shoe Shine Boy," "A Letter," "The Day Will Come"

1782. *Lightin' Out.* About Mark Twain & his characters. Judith Anderson, 11/20/92–12/20/92. 13 prev. 18 perf. m/l: Walt Stepp & John Tucker; d: Kevin Cochran. Cast: Gordon Stanley, Robert Tate, Tony Fair, Karen Looze. "Nothin' Left but You," "Mother, I Am Not a Christian," "So Says I," "Ain't No Trouble," "Blue Jeans and Misery," "Don't Take off Your Mask in Bricksville," "I'll Be Gone to Freedom," "Home is a State of Mind," "Belle of New York," "Rip Around," "It Was Kinda Lazy and Jolly," "Murderer's Home," "Satan's Song"

1783. *Like Jazz: A New Kind of Musical.* Celebration of jazz and its artists, it featured 16 orig songs. Mark Taper Forum, L.A., 12/4/03–1/25/04. Prev from 11/21/03. m: Cy Coleman; l: Alan & Marilyn Bergman and Larry Gelbart; d: Gordon Davidson; ch: Patricia Birch; set/light: D. Martyn Bookwalter; cos: Judith Dolan; sound: Jon Gottlieb & Phillip G. Allen; md: Tom Kubis. Cast: Patti Austin (*Jennifer Holliday* for 5 perf, 12/28/03–12/31/03), Lillias White, Harry Groener. It evolved from a "Portraits in Jazz" concert at the Kennedy Center. After L.A. it was revised, and by 2/05 was re-named *In The Pocket*, and headed for Broadway, hopefully by spring 2006. p: Transamerica; d: Dirk Decloedt (debut); ch: Maurice Hines

1784. *The Likes of Us.* Based on life of Dr. Barnardo, Victorian founder of children's charity homes. London. 1st effort by Andrew Lloyd Webber & Tim Rice. Ran way out of the West End & failed

1785. *The Lily White Boys.* Gang members rise in society (except one — played by Philip Locke). Theatre Royal, Birmingham, England, 1/18/60; Royal Court, London, 1/27/60–3/5/60. 46 perf. p: The English Stage Co., Oscar Lewenstein, Wolf Mankowitz; m: Tony Kinsey & Bill Le Sage; songs: Christopher Logue; w: Harry Cookson; d: Lindsay Anderson; ch: Eleanor Fazan; set: Sean Kenny; md: Anthony Bowles. Cast: Albert Finney, Monty Landis, Georgia Brown, Shirley Ann Field, Ann Lynn, Willoughby Goddard, Ronnie Stevens

1786. *Linda.* Country musical. Set in Dead Man's Gulch, Colorado. Charles Ludlam, 4/14/93–5/30/93. 42 perf. p: Ridiculous Theatrical Co.; m/l: Mark Bennett & Everett Quinton; d: David Ganon. Cast: Chris Tanner, Grant Neale, Lisa Herbold, Everett Quinton. "Lizzie the Lezzie," "A Whole Lotta Them," "I'm Gonna Cry, Cry, Cry," "No Flies on You," "There's Gotta Be a Place," "Heatin' up This Hell-Hole Tonight," "End of the Line, Lady," "Ain't No Sin," "The Girl I Love," "Peace of Mind"

1787. *Lisbon Story.* Play with mus. WWII spy story. Imperial, Brighton, England, 5/31/43 (2 weeks); London Hippodrome, 6/17/43–7/8/44. 492 perf; Stoll, London, 10/17/44–12/2/44. 44 perf. m: Harry Parr Davies; l: Harold Purcell. Cast: Patricia Burke, Noele Gordon, Jack Livesey, Albert Lieven, John Turner. "Someday We Shall Meet Again," "Pedro the Fisherman," "Song of the Sunrise," "Madame Louisa," "Never Say Goodbye," "Music at Midnight," "Serenade for Sale," "Carnival Song." Filmed in 1946. d: Paul Stein. Cast: David Farrar, Patricia Burke, Richard Tauber, Harry Welchman, Noele Gordon, Stephane Grappelli

1788. *Listen to My Heart: The Songs of David Friedman.* Upstairs at Studio 54, 10/23/03–12/7/03. 16 prev from 10/9/03. 52 perf. d: Mark Waldrop; set: Michael Anania; cos: Markas Henry; light/sound: Matt Berman. Cast: Alix Korey, Anne Runolfsson, Joe Cassidy, Allison Briner, Michael Hunsaker, David Friedman (at piano). Cast album recorded live. "Trust the Wind," "You're Already There," "What I Was Dreaming Of," "My White Knight," "He Comes Home Tired," "If You Love Me, Please Don't Feed Me," "I'm Not My Mother," "You'll Always Be My Baby," "Two Different Worlds," "Open Your Eyes to Love," "Live it Up," "Trick of Fate," "Listen to My Heart," "The Gift of Trouble," "Catch Me," "I Can Hold You," "My Simple Christmas Wish," "We Can Be Kind," "Only My Pillow Knows," "Nothing in Common," "What I'd Had in Mind," "If I Were Pretty," "We Live on Borrowed Time," "You're There," "As Long as I Can Sing," "Help is on the Way"

1789. *Listen to the Wind.* Musical for children. Oxford Playhouse, England, 12/15/54. m/l: Vivian Ellis; b: Angela Ainley Jeans; d: Peter Hall; ch: Michael Holmes; set/cos: Disley Jones. Cast: Vivienne Martin, Derek Francis. "When I Grow Up," "Timothy's Under the Table," "Listen to the Wind," "I'm a Naughty Gale Bird," "Palace of the Wind," "Whistle Down the Chimney," "It's Nice to Be Home Again," "I Used to Rock," "Twinkle, Twinkle, Little Star," "When They Grow Up." Arts Theatre, London, 12/16/55–1/21/56. 48 perf. Same basic crew. Cast: Ronald Barker, Edward Atienza, Roderick Cook, Anne Lascelles, Miriam Karlin, Peter Jeffrey, Clive Revill. King's Head, London, 1997. Cast: Paula Wilcox. Cast recording on Jay

1790. *Little by Little.* The lives and loves of 3 friends from childhood. Eighty-Eight's, 3/20/95–5/1/95. 7 Monday perfs. m: Brad Ross; l: Ellen Greenfield & Hal Hackady; b: Ellen Greenfield & Annette Jolles; d: Annette Jolles. Cast: Michael Gruber, Tia Speros, Sarah Uriarte. "Little By Little," "Friendship and Love," "Homework," "Tag," "Life and All That," "Starlight," "Popcorn," "Just Between Us," "I'm Not," "A Little Hustle," "Rainbows," "Nocturne," "Yes," "The Schmooze," "Take the World Away," "Okay," "If You Only Knew," "If You Loved Me," "Tell Me," "I Ought to Cry," "So it Goes," "I'm a Rotten Person," "Journey that Never Ends." York Theatre Co., 1/21/99–2/28/99. 9 prev from 1/13/99. 45 perf. d:

Annette Jolles; set: James Morgan; light: Mary Jo Dondlinger; md: Vincent Trovato; cast recording on Varese Sarabande. Cast: Liz Larsen, Christiane Noll, Darrin Baker. John Houseman Studio II Theatre, 5/8/03–5/19/03. d: Jess McLeod; md: Brian Cimmet. Cast: David Niles, Erin Leigh Peck, Lauren Rubin

A Little Doll Laughed see # 217, Main Book

1791. *Little Fish*. Neurotic New Yorker (played by Jennifer Laura Thompson) reflects on life, tries to quit smoking and exercise regularly & tries to find man of her dreams in big city. Second Stage, 2/13/03–3/9/03. Prev from 1/22/03. 29 perf. m/l/b: Michael John LaChiusa; d/ch: Graciela Daniele; set: Riccardo Hernandez; cos: Toni-Leslie James; light: Peggy Eisenhauer; sound: Scott Lehrer; md: Dan Lipton; orch: Bruce Coughlin. Cast: Jennifer Laura Thompson, Lea De Laria, Marcy Harriell (La Chanze had played this role in the workshop), Jesse Tyler Ferguson, Hugh Panaro, Celia Keenan-Bolger, Eric Jordan Young, Ken Marks. "Days," "Robert," "It's a Sign," "The Pool," "Winter is Here," "Short Story," "Perfect," "John Paul," "He," "Cigarette Dream," "Flotsam," "I Ran," "By the Way," "Remember Me," "It Feels Good," "Little Fish," "Poor Charlotte," "Simple Creature," "In Twos and Threes"

1792. *Little Ham*. A Harlem jazzical. Full title is *Langston Hughes' Little Ham*. Set in 1936 in Harlem. Little Ham (Hamlet Hitchcock Jones) is small-time mobster. George Street Playhouse, NJ, 1987. Producer Eric Krebs began the project in 1985. After George Street it was revised through several drafts, then presented again, by arr with AMAS Musical Theatre, as test run, at 99-seat Hudson Guild Theatre (OOB), 11/14/01–1/6/02. Cast: Andre Garner (title role), D'Ambrose Boyd, Venida Evans, Jerry Gallagher, Julia Lema, Joy Styles, Leigh Summers, Richard Vida, Joe Wilson Jr. (all of whom would reprise in later, 2002, OB prod). Good reviews. John Houseman, 9/26/02–12/1/02. 17 prev from 9/12/02. 76 perf. m: Judd Woldin; l: Judd Woldin & Richard Engquist; b: Dan Owens; based on play of same name by Langston Hughes; d: Eric Riley; ch: Leslie Dockery; set: Edward T. Gianfrancesco; cos: Bernard Grenier; light: Richard Latta; md: David Alan Bunn; orch: Luther Henderson. New cast members: Brenda Braxton, Adrian Bailey, Cheryl Alexander, Monica Patton. "I'm Gonna Hit Today," "It's All in the Point of View," "Stick with Me, Kid," "No," "Get Yourself Some Lovin'," "That Ain't Right," "Cuttin' Out," "Room for Improvement," "Get Back," "Harlem, You're My Girl," "Angels," "Big Ideas," "It's a Hulluva Big Job," "Wastin' Time," "Say Hello to Your Feet"

1793. *Little Kit*. Family opera. Set in London in mid–19th century. Vineyard/26th Street, 12/17/97–12/23/97. 14 perf. m: Charles Greenberg; libretto: Barbara Zinn Krieger; from novel *Little Kit, or the Industrious Flea Circus Girl*, by Emily Arnold McCully; d: Lisa Brailoff. Cast: Jackie Angelescu, William Ryall, Kirk McDonald, Erin Dilly, Tina Johnson, Steven Ted Beckler. Tribeca Performing Arts Center, 3/10/99–3/28/99. 3 prev. 7 perf. p:

Vineyard Theatre; d/ch: John Ruocco. Cast: Abigail Hardin, Don Mayo, Laurie Gamache

1794. *A Little Like Magic*. Canadian puppet show with black light effects (i.e. performers invisible in black costumes), which played Broadway as part of world tour. Lyceum, 10/26/86–12/7/86. 49 perf. p: Famous People Players; conceived by/d: Diana Lynn Dupuy; light: Ken Billington. "A Little Like Magic," "Aruba Liberace," "Aquarium," "Sorcerer's Apprentice," "Bear and Bee," "Concertino for Carignan," "Viva Las Vegas," "The Gambler," "Theme from *Superman*," "Music of 007," "Battle Hymn of the Republic," "Divertissement," "Night on Bald Mountain," "Fossils," "The Swan," "Billie Jean," "Part-Time Lover," "That's Entertainment," "New York, New York," "42nd Street," "Ease on Down the Road," "Don't Rain on My Parade," "Send in the Clowns," "Night They Invented Champagne," "Get Me to the Church on Time," "Oklahoma!," "Can-Can," "Lullaby of Broadway," "Give My Regards to Broadway"

1795. *Little Mary Sunshine*. Big Jim Warrington of the Forest Rangers rescues his girl Mary Potts, owner of the Colorado Inn, from the clutches of lecherous Indian Yellow Feather. Orpheum, 11/18/59; Cherry Lane, 3/30/59–9/2/62. Total of 1,143 perf. p: Howard Barker, Cynthia Baer, Robert Chambers; m/l/b: Rick Besoyan; d: Ray Harrison & Rick Besoyan; ch: Ray Harrison; based largely on 1924 operetta *Rose Marie*, and set in Colorado Rockies early in 20th century. Capt. Cast: Jim: William Graham, *Dick Hoh*; Mary: Eileen Brennan, *Marian Mercer, Margaret Hall, Joleen Fodor*; Yellow Feather: Ray James, *Anthony Falco, Marc Destin*; Cpl Billy Jester, a Forest Ranger: John McMartin, *Dom De Luise, Edward Miller*; Nancy Twinkle, Little Mary's maid: Elmarie Wendel, *Sonja Savig, Kathy Lake*. "The Forest Rangers," "Little Mary Sunshine," "Look for a Sky of Blue," "You're the Fairest Flower," "In Izzenschnooken on the Lovely Essenzook Zee," "Playing Croquet," "How Do You Do?," "Tell a Handsome Stranger," "Once in a Blue Moon," "Colorado Love Call," "Every Little Nothing," "What Has Happened," "Such a Merry Party," "Say, Uncle!," "Me, a Big Heap Indian," "Naughty, Naughty Nancy," "Mata Hari," "Do You Ever Dream of Vienna?," "A Shell Game," "Coo Coo." 1st OB show to have full cast recording. Comedy Theatre, London, 5/17/62. 42 perf. d/ch: Paddy Stone. Cast: Patricia Routledge, Joyce Blair, Bernard Cribbins, Terence Cooper, John Harvey, Erik Chitty, Edward Bishop. Equity Library, 2/12/70–3/1/70. 22 perf. d: Larry Whiteley. Cast: Eleanor Rogers, Jon Peck, Fran Brill. In 2002 a prod began that was destined for Broadway in 2003–04. Actress Sarah Rice & husband John Hiller had acquired Broadway rights and (as MadjaLook Prods) produced readings 7/18/02 & 7/19/02, and 8/20/02 & 8/22/02, at Chelsea Studios, Manhattan. d: Jamie Rocco; ch: Sharon Halley; set: Howard Baker; cos: Gregg Barnes; md: Jonathan Tunick; orch: Arnold Goland. Cast: Jim: Chuck Wagner; Mary: Sarah Rice; Chief Brown Bear of the Kadota Indians: Chapman Roberts; Billy:

Mike Daisey; Mme Ernestine von Liebedich, an opera singer: Marni Nixon; Nancy: Tari Kelly; Gen. Uncle Oscar Fairfax, Ret., a Washington diplomat: Hal Robinson; Yellow Feather, Chief Brown Bear's son: Doug Wynn; Fleet Foot, an Indian guide: Edmund Fitzpatrick. Capitalized at $10 million. However, this project fell through, and the rights changed hands. There was a private reading on 7/11/03. Cast: Mary: Kristin Chenoweth; Jim: Craig Bierko; Ernestine: Christine Ebersole; Brown Bear: George Merritt; Billy: Chris Fitzgerald; Fleet Foot: Kim Chan; Yellow Feather: Sterling Brown; Oscar: Edward Hibbert; Nancy: Erin Dilly

1796. *The Little Prince*. Harold Clurman, 12/28/82–1/2/83. 3 prev. 5 perf. p: Joseph Tandet; adapted by: Ada Janik; from book *Le Petit Prince*, by Antoine de Saint-Exupery; d: Maggie L. Harrer. Cast: Charles Coleman, Andre De Shields, William Parry

1797. *The Little Prince*. 28th Street Theatre, 10/6/93–10/24/93. 5 prev. 11 perf; John Houseman, 10/28/93–1/2/94. 68 perf. m: Rick Cummins; l/b: John Scoullar; from Saint-Exupery's book; d: William Martin; light: Beverly Emmons. Cast: Prince: Daisy Eagan, *Ramzi Khalaf*; Aviator: Howard Kaye, *Joseph Mahowald*; Also with: Merwin Goldsmith (*Mike Champagne*), Natascia Diaz. "I Fly," "44 Sunsets," "Enough," "Such a Lot to Do," "What a Beautiful," "I Love You, Goodbye," "Fly Away," "Admire Me," "Days Go So Quickly," "The Snake," "Some Otherwhere," "Sunset Stories," "Day After Day," "This Lovely Song," "All the Stars Will Laugh"

1798. *The Little Prince and the Aviator*. French aviator meets alien in Sahara. Set in the Sahara, in Paris, and on Asteroid B6-12, during 1911–1928. Closed during Broadway previews at the Alvin (1/1/82–1/17/82), canceling its 1/20/82 Broadway opening. The courts said the theatre owners (the Nederlanders) forced the closure, and the producer, A. Joseph Tandet, was awarded $1,000,000. m: John Barry; l: Don Black; b: Hugh Wheeler; from Antoine de Saint-Exupery's 1943 book *Le Petit Prince* (*The Little Prince*); d: Jerry Adler; ch: Billy Wilson; flying: Foy; set: Eugene Lee; light: Roger Morgan; md: David Friedman; orch: Don Walker. Cast: Aviator: Michael York; Prince: Anthony Rapp; Also with: Ellen Greene, Janet Eilber, Mark Dovey, Robert Hoshour, Brooks Almy, Chip Garnett, Alan Gilbert. "Par Avion," "Power Comes, Power Goes," "I Pity the Poor Parisiennes," "Making Every Minute Count," "Made for Each Other," "Wind, Sand and Stars," "First Impressions," "A Day Will Never Be the Same," "I've Got You to Thank for All This," "I Don't Regret a Thing," "We Couldn't, We Mustn't, We Won't," "Watch Out for the Baobabs," "I Like My Misfortunes to Be Taken Seriously," "The Volcano Song," "More than Just a Pretty Flower," "Playground of the Planets," "It Was You," "Grain of Sand," "Sunset Song," "Little Prince," "Stars Will Be Laughing"

1799. *The Little Rascals*. Goodspeed, 1987. m/l: Joe Raposo. Cast: Ronn Carroll, Betsy Joslyn. "Not Much of a Dog"

1800. *The Little Show and Friends*. The intimate revues of Howard Dietz & Arthur Schwartz. All Souls Church, 4/24/87–5/10/87. 15 perf. p/conceived by: Tran William Rhodes; d: David McNitt; ch: Linda Panzer; md: Joyce Hitchcock & David Lahn. Cast: Jim Bumgardner, Siobhan Fallon, Marion Markham

1801. *Little White Lies*. The Walter Donaldson songbook. Eighty Eight's, 8/7/94–9/25/94. 7 perf. d/arr: David Berk; md: Dick Gallagher. Cast: Harvey Evans, Rosemary McNamara, Sam Stoneburner, Margaret Wright

1802. *Little Women*. Small musical. Virginia Theatre, Broadway, 1/23/05 (re-scheduled from 1/20/05 because of Presidential inauguration). Prev from 12/7/04 (date put back from 12/2/04). p: Randall L. Wreghitt, Dani Davis, Ken Gentry, Chase Mishkin, Ruben Brache, in assoc with Theatre Previews at Duke & Lisa Vioni; m: Jason Howland; l: Mindi Dickstein; b: Allan Knee; based on Louisa May Alcott's 1868 classic Civil War-era novel of the same name set in New England; d: Susan H. Schulman; ch: Michael Lichtefeld; set: Derek McLane; cos: Catherine Zuber; light: Kenneth Posner (replacing David Lander); sound: Peter Hylenski (replacing Tony Meola); md: Andrew Wilder; orch: Kim Scharnberg; cast recording on Ghostlight, made on 2/28/05, and released early 4/05. Cast: Marmee: Maureen McGovern; Jo March: Sutton Foster; Aunt March: Janet Carroll; Prof. Baker: John Hickok; Laurie: Danny Gurwin; John Brooke: Jim Weitzer; Mr. Laurence: Robert Stattel; Meg: Jenny Powers (replaced Amy Rutberg); Beth: Megan McGinnis; Amy: Amy McAlexander; Also with: Christopher Gunn, Larisa Shukiss, Julie Foldesi, Andrew Varela, Anne Kanengeiser. "An Operatic Tragedy," "Better," "Our First Dreams," "Here Alone," "Could You," "I'd Be Delighted," "Take a Chance on Me," "Better" (reprise), "Off to Massachusetts," "Five Forever," "More Than I Am," "Take a Chance on Me" (reprise), "Astonishing," "The Weekly Volcano Press," "Off to Massachusetts (reprise), "How I Am," "Some Things Are Meant to Be," "The Most Amazing Thing," "Days of Plenty', "The Fire Within Me," "Small Umbrella in the Rain," "Sometimes When You Dream." It had started in 1998. The songwriters then were Kim Oler & Allison Hubbard, and their work was seen in at least one public reading in NYC. By 2/01 Jason Howland & Mindi Dickstein were in, and the show had a sold-out workshop as part of the *Theatre Previews* series at Duke Univ., Durham, NC. Cast: Jo: Kerry O'Malley; John Brooke: Robert Bartley; Beth: Megan McGinnis; Laurie: Joe Machota; Mr. Laurence: Robert Stattel. All these actors went on to do further readings on 4/6/01–4/8/01. By mid–2001 Susan H. Schulman had come aboard as dir. The Broadway date had originally been planned for 4/04, after Theatre Previews at Duke, NC, 1/03–2/04, and then New Haven for 3/04, but Sutton Foster was not available until 9/04, and the producers wanted her for Jo. So none of those gigs happened. After industry presentations in spring 2004, rehearsals began 9/7/04, and it finally tried out

at the Reynolds Theatre, at Duke, 10/13/04–10/31/04. Prev from 10/7/04, and at New Haven, 11/11/04–11/21/04. Then on to Broadway. Capitalized at $5.6 million

1803. *The Littlest Revue*. A Ben Bagley intimate musical revue. Phoenix, 5/22/56–6/17/56. 32 perf. m/l: Vernon Duke, Ogden Nash, Sol Berkowitz, Sheldon Harnick, John Latouche, Charles Strouse, Lee Adams, Kenward Elmslie, John Strauss, Sydney Shaw, Sammy Cahn; sk: Nat Hiken, Billy Friedberg, Eudora Welty ("Bye-Bye Brevoort"), Mike Stewart ("Give My Regards to Mott St." & "Two Cents Worth of Plain"), George Baxt, Bud McCreery, Allan Manings, Bob Van Scoyk; d: Paul Lammers; ch: Charles Weidman (with Danny Daniels); cos: Alvin Colt; md: Will Irwin; orch: John Strauss. Cast: Charlotte Rae, Tammy Grimes, Joel Grey, Larry Storch, George Marcy, Beverlee Bozeman, Dorothy Jarnac. "Born Too Late," "Good Little Girls," "Madly in Love," "You're Far from Wonderful," "Game of Dance," "The Shape of Things" (by Harnick), "Summer is a-Comin' In," "I Lost the Rhythm" (by Strouse), "Spring Doth Let Her Colors Fly" (by Strouse & Adams)

1804. *Live from New York*. One-woman show starring Gilda Radner as her *Saturday Night Live* characters. Winter Garden, Broadway, 8/2/79–9/22/79. 52 perf. p/d: Lorne Michaels; ch: Patricia Birch; md: Howard Shore. Cast also featured Don Novello (as father Guido Sarducci). "Let's Talk Dirty to the Animals," "Goodbye Saccharine," "If You Look Close"/"Gimme Mick," "The Way We Were," "Honey"

1805. *Livin' the Life*. Set in Hannibal, Missouri, around 1850. Phoenix, 4/27/57–5/19/57. 25 perf. m/l: Jack Urbont & Bruce Geller; b: Dale Wasserman & Bruce Geller; based on Mark Twain stories; d: David Alexander; ch: John Butler; set: William & Jean Eckart; cos: Alvin Colt; light: Klaus Holm; md: Anton Coppola; orch: Hershy Kay & Joe Glover; add mus arr: Ralph Burns, Jack Easton, James Mundy, Sy Oliver; dance mus: Genevieve Pitot; choral arr: Jacques Urbont. Cast: Muff Potter: Stephen Elliott; Aunt Polly: Alice Ghostley; Injun Joe: James Mitchell; Bill Anders: Edward Villella; Ben Rogers: Kevin Carlisle; Tom Sawyer: Timmy Everett; Alfred Noble: Loren Hightower; Amy Lawrence: Lee Becker; Judge Thatcher: Jack De Lon; Emmy Harper: Marijane Maricle; Huckleberry Finn: Richard Ide. "Someone," "Whiskey Bug," "Livin' the Life," "Steamboat," "Take Kids," "Probably in Love," "Don't Tell Me," "All of 'em Say," "Late Love," "Ain't It a Shame," "Supersational Day," "Nightmare Ballet," "MacDougal's Cave"

1806. *Living for Pleasure*. Garrick, London, 7/10/58. 379 perf. m: Richard Addinsell; l/sk: Arthur Macrae; d: William Chappell; set/cos: Peter Rice; cast recording on HMV. Cast: George Rose, Daniel Massey, Janie Marden, Dora Bryan, Susan Beaumont, Patience Collier, Lynda Baron, Clemence Bettany, Dany Clare. "Living for Pleasure," "Alone with a Love Song," "The Lady," "Mr. Wrong," "No

Ball," "Dustbin Follies," "Sloane Street Ladies," "The Pretty Miss Brown," "Friends," "No Better than I Should Be"

1807. *Liza of Lambeth*. Shaftesbury, London, 6/8/76–9/11/76. Prev from 6/4/76. 110 perf. m: Cliff Adams; l/b: William Rushton & Berny Stringle; d: Berny Stringle; ch: Michele Hardy; set: Christopher Morley; md: John Burrows. Cast: Angela Richards, Stella Tanner, Paddy Glynn, Pamela Cundell, Kenneth Caswell, Ron Pember, Patricia Hayes, Bryan Marshall, Michael Robbins. "Husbands," "Liza," "I've Got a Talent," "Liza of Lambeth's Mum," "Prince of Wales," "Is This All?," "Good Bad Time," "Who in His Right Mind," "Tricky Finish," "Whatever Happens to a Man," "Beautiful Colours," "Why Can't We Choose," "I Know I Shouldn't Like It," "Between Ourselves," "A Little Bit on the Side"

1808. *A Load of Old Sequins*. Donmar Warehouse, London, 6/17/87. w: Dillie Keane, Adele Anderson, Marilyn Cutts. Cast: Dillie Keane, Adele Anderson, Fascinating Aida, Denise Wharmby. "Boring," "Yuppies," "Shattered Illusions," "Song of the Homesick Traveller," "Another Man," "My Dream Man," "Jealousy," "Sew on a Sequin," "Taboo"

1809. *Lock Up Your Daughters*. Set in the village of London, 1735. Mermaid, London, 5/28/59–12/5/59. 330 perf. p/b: Bernard Miles; m: Laurie Johnson; l: Lionel Bart; bawdy adaptation of Henry Fielding's *Rape Upon Rape;* d: Peter Coe; ch: Gilbert Vernon; set: Sean Kenny; md: Colin Beaton. Cast: Hilaret: Stephanie Voss; Ramble: Frederick Jaeger; Justice Squeezum: Richard Wordsworth; Mrs. Squeezum: Hy Hazell; Also with: Brendan Barry, Terence Cooper, Robin Wentworth, John Sharp, Barry Jackson. "All's Well," "A Proper Man," "It Must Be True," "Red Wine and a Wench," "'tis Plain to See," "On the Side," "When Does the Ravishing Begin?," "Lovely Lover," "Lock up Your Daughters," "There's a Plot Afoot," "Mister Jones," "(On a) Sunny Sunday Morning," "If I'd Known You," "Is This the Happy Ending?," "I'll Be There." It was such a success that the run was considerably extended. Shubert, New Haven, 4/27/60. d: Alfred Drake; ch: Rhoda Levine; set: Sean Kenny; cos: Fred Voelpel; md: Max Goberman. Shubert, Boston, 5/7/60. Closed there before hoped for Broadway gig. Cast: Hilaret: Nancy Dussault; Ramble: Frederick Jaeger; Sotmore: George S. Irving; Constant: John Michael King; Mrs. Squeezum: Hy Hazell; Watchmen: Alfred Toigo & Jamie Ross; Also with: Robin Wentworth. Mermaid, London, 5/17/62. 111 perf. d: Richard Wordsworth; ch: Denys Palmer; md: Derek New. Cast: Squeezum: Bernard Miles; Ramble: Peter Gilmore; Hilaret: Sally Smith; Mrs. Squeezum: Hy Hazell; Sotmore: Joss Ackland. Her Majesty's, 8/16/62–11/30/63. 553 perf. Some cast changes: *Richard Wordsworth* replaced Bernard Miles; *David Lloyd Meredith* replaced Joss Ackland; *Stephanie Voss* replaced Sally Smith. The Varsity (OB), 8/14/68–9/7/68. d: Carl Ritchie; ch: Shirlee Dodge; md: W. Bernard Windt. Cast: Amanda McBroom, Danny Davis. Mermaid, London, 3/31/69–

6/14/69. 69 perf. p/d: Bernard Miles; set: Sean Kenny; md: Derek New. Cast: Squeezum: Russell Hunter; Hilaret: Anna Dawson. Goodspeed, 3/30/82–6/12/82. d: Bill Gile; ch: George Bunt; set: Vittorio Cappece; md: John Miner. Cast: Squeezum: Carleton Carpenter; Dora: Kaye Walbye; Hilaret: Dena Olstad

1810. *Lolita, My Love.* Pre-Broadway tryouts at the Shubert, Philadelphia, 2/16/71–2/27/71. 1 prev on 2/15/71. Terrible reviews. Closed for revisions & re-ran at the Shubert, Boston, 3/23/71–3/27/71. Prev from 3/18/71. Canceled scheduled 3/30/71 Broadway opening at the Mark Hellinger. p: Norman Twain; m: John Barry; l/b: Alan Jay Lerner; from novel & movie *Lolita*, written by Vladimir Nabokov; *Noel Willman* replaced Tito Capobianco as dir; ch: Dan Siretta (taking over from Danny Daniels, who took over from Jack Cole); set: Ming Cho Lee; light: Jules Fisher; dance mus arr: John Morris. Cast: Lolita: Denise Nickerson (replacing Annette Ferra); Also with: Dorothy Loudon, John Neville (Richard Burton had rejected the role), Leonard Frey. "Lolita," "Going, Going, Gone," "In the Broken Promise Land of Fifteen," "The Same Old Song," "Mother Needs a Boyfriend," "Dante, Petrarch and Poe," "Sur les Quais," "Charlotte's Letter," "Farewell, Little Dream," "Have You Got What You Came With?," "At the Bed-D-By Motel," "Tell Me, Tell Me," "Buckin' for Beardsley," "Beardsley School for Girls," "It's a Bad, Bad World," "How Far Is It to the Next Town?"

1811. *London Days & New York Nights.* Jason's Park Royal Theatre, 10/27/83–11/20/83. 20 perf. m: Jason McAuliffe; l: Fran Landesman, etc; d: Jeff Golding; ch: Marcia Milgrom Dodge; md: Rick Lewis. Cast: Nancy Johnston, Joseph Kolinski, Scott Robertson. "London Days & New York Nights," "Yankee Doodle Londoner," "Jaywalkin'," "A Song Whose Time Has Come," "Against the Time," "I'll Sing a Different Song Tomorrow," "May the Force Be with You," "I Will Never Be the Same," "Best Way to Have the Blues," "One Night Stand," "Code of the West," "I Live in a Dive," "Half-Remembered Melody," "When Did the End Begin?," "Who's New?," "A Permanent Romance," "Brief Encounter," "There's Something Worse than Living Alone," "Ending up Alone," "Dying a Little a Lot Alone," "Big Dreams," "Where Have I Been All My Life?," "Crystal Palaces," "Best of Friends"

1812. *The London Music Hall.* Musical revue. Opened in Halifax, Nova Scotia on pre–Broadway tour, but closed 5/28/77, Boston. p: David Stones; dev/d: John Gratton; ch: Irving Davies. Cast: Jimmy Edwards, The New Faces, Tessie O'Shea

1813. *The Londoners.* Theatre Royal, Stratford East, London, 3/27/72–5/20/72. 63 perf. p: Theatre Workshop; m/l: Lionel Bart; b: Stephen Lewis; from novel *Sparrers Can't Sing*, by Stephen Lewis; d: Joan Littlewood. Cast: Yootha Joyce, Brian Murphy, Walter Plinge (i.e. Lionel Bart as Charlie), Stephen Lewis, Bob Grant, Rita Webb

1814. *Lone Star Love, or the Merry Wives of Windsor, Texas.* Musical comedy. Re-set-

ting of Shakespeare's into a post–Civil War Texas setting. Alley, Houston, 1988. m/l: Jack Herrick; conceived by/adapted: John L. Haber. Aimed for Broadway, but never got there. Repertory Theatre of St. Louis, 1989; Playhouse in the Park, Cincinnati, 1994; two developmental workshops in NYC, backed by Dodger Theatricals and the Kennedy Center; Great Lakes Theatre Festival, Cleveland, 10/18/01–11/4/01; John Houseman, NYC, 12/8/04–2/6/05. Prev from 11/23/04. p: AMAS Musical Theatre; d: Michael Bogdanov; ch: Randy Skinner; cast recording on PS Classics, made on 3/2/05. Cast: Gary Sandy (*Joseph Mahowald* from 1/21/05), Tracee Beazer, Clarke Thorell, Beth Leavel, Jay O. Sanders, Dan Sharkey, Kevin Bernard, Stacia Fernandez, Shane Braddock, Drew McVety, Stacey Harris, Harriett Foy

1815. *Long Road Home.* Set in a small church south of Memphis. Hudson Guild, 11/16/00–12/17/00. 5 prev. 28 perf. p: Overture Theatre Co.; m/arr: Kathy Sommer; l/b/d: Barry Harman; ch: D.J. Salisbury; cos: Toni-Leslie James; md: Wendy Bobbitt-Cavett. Cast: Brenda Braxton, Charles Gray, Jamie Danielle Jackson, Joseph Siravo, Saundra McClain. "Take a Look at My Heart," "Ask Him," "Virgil and Me," "Come-Back-to-Bed-Babe Eyes," "A Bottle to Remind Me," "I Want This Tomorrow," "Twelve Steppin' Out," "Call Patty," "So I Think I Might Have Lied," "Sure as Christmas," "Dump Another Load on Me," "Walk in My Shoes," "I Know Myself Better," "Life Slipping Away," "Long Road Home"

1816. *Look Me Up.* Cabaret musical revue of nostalgia. Collection of song & dance numbers with mus written during & near the 1920s. Plaza 9 Music Hall, 10/7/71–5/21/72. 12 prev. 394 perf. p/d: Costas Omero; b/conceived by: Laurence Taylor; ch: Bob Tucker; md: Horace Diaz. Cast: Ted Agress, Zan Charisse, Kevin Christopher, Connie Day (*Marilyn Cooper*), Mary Lynn Kolas, Linda Kurtz, Don Liberto, Jeff Richards, Virginia Seidel. "Running Wild," "Hallelujah," "Get Happy," "Happy Feet," "Someone to Watch Over Me," "Making Whoopee," "Button up Your Overcoat," "You Made Me Love You," "Bidin' My Time," "Can't Help Lovin' That Man," "Strike up the Band," "Drums in My Heart," "It Had to Be You," "If You Knew Susie," "Thinking of You," "The Best Things in Life Are Free," "Glad Rag Doll," "Yes Sir, That's My Baby," "Baby Face," "Aba Daba Honeymoon," "Manhattan," "How Long Has This Been Going On?," "Great Day"

1817. *Look Out, It's Sir.* Theatre Royal, Stratford East, London, 7/17/75. p: Theatre Workshop; songs: Alan Klein; b: Stephen Lewis; d: Victor Spinetti; md: Ian Armit. Cast: Barry Martin, Thick Wilson, Dennis Egan, Steve Lowe, Valerie Walsh, Jenny Logan, Myvanwy Jenn

1818. *Look Where I'm At!* Man in the middle is equally disenchanted with hippies & hard-hats. Theatre Four, 3/5/71–3/7/71. 5 perf. m/l: Jordan Ramin, Frank H. Stanton, Murray Semos; adapted by: James Leasor from Thorne Smith's novel *Rain in the Doorway;* d/ch: Wakefield Poole; orch: Wally Harper; arr: Sid

Ramin; md: Jack Lee. Cast: Ron Husmann, Martin Ross, Mary Bracken Phillips. "Change of Scene," "What a Day for a Wonderful Day," "Partners," "Who Does She Think She Is?," "Look Where I'm At!," "Never, Never Leave Me," "Money isn't Everything, But," "The Me I Want to Be," "Little Sparrow"

1819. *Look Who's Here!* Revue. Fortune, London, 1/21/60. 148 perf. p: Anna Deere Wiman & Charles Ross; w: Ted Dicks, David Edwards, Richard Waring, Julian Slade, John O'Hare, Charlotte Mitchell, Neville McGrah, Dick Vosburgh, Tony Tanner, Charles Ross, Adrian Slade, Robin Miller; dev/d: Charles Ross; ch: Bob Stevenson; set: Michael Young. Cast: Anna Quayle, Donald Hewlett, Nyree Dawn Porter, Tony Tanner, Dennis Wood, Sonia Graham, Barbara Young. Not the 1916 show of the same name, but it is the show that was first presented at Leatherhead Rep in 1959, as *Let's Go Mad*

1820. *Lord of the Dance.* Dance musical. An Irish prod. Conflict between good & evil. Radio City Music Hall, 3/4/97–3/17/97. p/created/ch: Michael Flatley; d: Arlene Phillips. Cast: Michael Flatley, Bernadette Flynn

1821. *The Lord of the Rings.* Princess of Wales, Toronto, 3/23/06 (prev from 2/2/06). p: Kevin Wallace & Saul Zaentz; m: A.R. Rahman & Varttina; b: Shaun McKenna; based on JRR Tolkien's trilogy of the same name; d: Matthew Warchus; set/cos: Rob Howell; ms: Christopher Nightingale. It was originally goign to open in London in 10/05, capitalized at 8 million pounds, but never did

1822. *Lost.* Spooky operatic musical. A modern Hansel & Gretel tale, set in the Great Smokey Mountains. Connelly, 9/4/03–9/14/03. p: Inverse Theatre Co.; m: Jessica Grace Wing; l/b: Kirk Wood Bromley; d: Rob Urbinati. 1st ran at International Fringe Festival. Jessica Grace Wing died 7/19/03, aged 31. of colon cancer, and never heard it performed all the way through

1823. *Lost Highway: The Music and Legend of Hank Williams.* Used 25 songs by the country music legend who died 1/1/53, age 29. Old Globe, San Diego, 8/28/92. m: Mark Harelik & Dan Wheetman; l/b: Randal Myler & Mark Harelik; d: Randal Myler. Cast: Mark Harelik, Michael Bryan French, Dan Wheetman. Ran, in slightly differing versions, with slightly differing titles, in different parts of the country, such as Ryman Auditorium, Nashville & Mark Taper Forum, L.A. Alabama Shakespeare Festival, 8/13/99–9/19/99. Prev from 8/10/99. d: Kent Gash. Cast: Jason Petty & Alex Kilgore (alternated). Cleveland Playhouse produced it at the Bolton, 9/24/02–10/20/02, still with Jason Petty as Hank. Manhattan Ensemble Theatre, 1/19/03–2/23/03. Prev from 12/9/02. There were no perfs 2/2/03–2/10/03. d: Randal Myler. Cast: Jason Petty. Little Shubert, 3/26/03–7/20/03. Cast recording made on Fynsworth alley, 6/16/03 & released 8/5/03

1824. *Lotta: The Best Thing Evolution's Ever Come Up With.* Play with mus. About a magically gifted woman. Public, 10/18/73–12/2/73. 54 perf. p: NY Shakespeare Festival; w/songs: Robert Montgomery; d: David Chambers; ch: Dennis Nahat; set: Tom H. John. Cast: Dale Soules, Irene Cara, MacIntyre Dixon, Bette Henritze, Jill Eikenberry, Clay Fullum (on piano)

1825. *Louisiana Purchase.* Imperial, Broadway, 5/28/40–6/14/41. 444 perf. p: Buddy De Sylva (Irving Berlin also p, but was uncredited); m/l: Irving Berlin; b: Morrie Ryskind; from story by Buddy De Sylva; d: Edgar MacGregor; ch: George Balanchine; orch: Russell Bennett. Cast: William Gaxton, Victor Moore, Vera Zorina, Irene Bordoni, Carol Bruce, Hugh Martin, Ralph Blane. "Apologia," "Sex Marches On," "Louisiana Purchase," "Tomorrow is a Lovely Day," "Outside of That, I Love You," "You're Lonely and I'm Lonely," "Dance with Me (Tonight at the Mardi Gras)," "Latins Know How," "What Chance Have I (with Love)?," "The Lord Done Fixed up My Soul," "Fools Fall in Love," "You Can't Brush Me Off." Mr. Berlin's return to Broadway after 7 years. Filmed in 1941, with Bob Hope, Vera Zorina, Irene Bordoni, Victor Moore. Carnegie Hall, 6/19/96–6/23/96. 6 perf. d: Scott Baron; md: Rob Fisher; cast recording on DRG. Cast: Taina Elg, George S. Irving, Judy Blazer, Merwin Goldsmith, Michael McGrath, Debbie Gravitte

1826. *Louisiana Summer.* AMAS, 10/28/82–11/21/82. 16 perf. m: Rocky Stone; l: Robert Wexler; b: Robert & Bradley Wexler; d: Robert Stark; ch: Keith Rozie; set: Tom Barnes; md: Lea Richardson. "Cutting in the Cane," "Silent Summer Nights," "Pictures in the Sky," "Busy Days," "Country Harmony," "Train Song," "Voodoo Dance," "Alligator Romp," "Louisiana Summer," "Louisiana Cajun Man," "Black Annie," "My Friend." See also *Daddy Goodness* (this appendix)

1827. *Loungeville, Volume 1 ... Music to Watch Girls By.* Musical revue. Rainbow & Stars, 11/18/97–12/6/97. 30 perf. d: Ted Pappas; md: Joe McGinty. Cast: Ellen Foley, Linda Hart, Jessica Molaskey, Richard Muenz

1828. *Love.* Musical version of *Luv,* Murray Schisgal's 1964 Broadway hit. Aubrey Wood, 4/15/84–4/29/84. 17 prev. 27 perf. p: Haila Stoddard, Joy Klein, Maggie Minskoff; m: Howard Marren; l: Susan Birkenhead; b: Jeffrey Sweet; d: Walton Jones; ch: Ed Nolfi; light: Ruth Roberts; md: Uel Wade. Cast: Nathan Lane, Stephen Vinovich, Judy Kaye. "Polyarts U," "Paradise," "Carnival Ride," "The Chart," "Ellen's Lament," "Somebody," "Yes, Yes, I Love You," "Love," "What a Life!," "Lady," "If Harry Weren't Here," "Do I Love Him?," "Harry's Resolution." Revised as *What About Luv?,* and ran at the Lyric, Hammersmith, London, 4/8/87–5/2/87. "Harry's Letter," "Why Bother?," "Paradise," "My Brown Paper Hat," "Do I Love Him?" The revised version was revived (as *What About Love?*) by York Theatre Co., 12/22/91–1/19/92. Prev from 12/6/91. d: Patricia Birch; md: Tom Helm. Cast: Austin Pendleton, Judy Kaye, David Green

1829. *Love and Let Love.* Set in Illyria. Sheridan Square Playhouse, 1/3/68–1/14/68. 14 perf. m/l: Stanley Jay Gelber, John Lollos, Don Christopher; based on *Twelfth Night;* adapted by/d: John Lollos; ch: Rhoda Levine; ms/orch: Arthur Rubinstein. Cast: Marcia Rodd, Virginia Vestoff, John Cunningham. "I've Got a Pain," "If She Could Only Feel the Same," "Dancing Rogue," "Will He Ever Know?," "I Like It," "Man is Made for Woman," "Epistle of Love," "Love Lesson," "I'll Smile," "I Will Have Him," "Write Him a Challenge," "She Called Me Fellow," "They'll Say I've Been Dreaming," "How Do I Know You're Not Mad, Sir?," "I Found My Twin," "Some Are Born Great"

1830. *Love and Maple Syrup.* Canadian revue in French & English. Compiled from Canadian writers & composers. Orig French title: *L'Amour et Sucre d'Erable.* Mercer-Hansberry, 1/7/70–1/18/70. 15 perf. w: Louis Negin. Cast: Louis Negin, Bill Schustik, Sandra Caron. "Love and Maple Syrup" (by Gordon Lightfoot). Previously ran in Washington, DC

1831. *Love and Shrimp.* About 3 women. Ballroom, 11/4/92–11/15/92. 15 perf. p/d: Marilyn Shapiro; m/l: Shelly Markham & Judith Viorst; md: Shelley Markham (md). Cast: Eileen Barnett, Bonnie Franklin, Mariette Hartley

1832. *Love from Judy.* About an orphan & her secret benefactor. Hippodrome, Coventry, England, 8/26/51; toured; Saville, London, 9/25/52–1/23/54. 594 perf. p: Emile Littler; m: Hugh Martin; l: Hugh Martin & Timothy Gray; b: Eric Maschwitz; from Jean Webster's play *Daddy Long Legs;* d: Charles Hickman; ch: Pauline Grant; set: Berkeley Sutcliffe; md: Philip Martell. Cast: Jean Carson (*June Whitfield*), Adelaide Hall, Johnny Brandon, Bill O'Conner, June Whitfield (*Myra de Groot*), Barbara Deeks (*Barbara Windsor*), Heather Lee. "Daddy Long Legs," "Go and Get Your Old Banjo," "Love from Judy," "My True Love," "I Ain't Going to Marry," "Dum Dum Dum," "Goin' Back to School," "Here We Are," "I Never Dream When I Sleep," "It's Better Rich," "It's Great to Be an Orphan," "Mardi Gras," "A Touch of Voodoo," "What Do I See in You?," "Kind to Animals." This was the show that made Jean Carson a star. North American premiere as part of the *Musicals Tonight!* series, 11/11/03–11/23/03. d: Thomas Mills; md: James Stenborg. Cast: Vanessa Lemonides, Julian Reboledo

1833. *Love in the Snow.* Musical romance. Set in mythical Scandinavian country of Olafland in 1872. Pre-Broadway tryouts opened at the Bushnell, Hartford, Conn., 3/15/46, and closed at the Forrest, Philadelphia, 4/6/46. p: Messrs Shubert; m: Ralph Benatzky; l/b: Rowland Leigh. Cast: Robert Pitkin, Robert Douglas, Raymond Bailey, Le Roi Operti, Allegra Varron. Allyn & Anthony, the dancers, joined the show after the opening, and were given 2 dance specialties. "Love in the Snow"

1834. *Love in Two Countries.* Two one-act musicals: *That Pig of a Molette,* and *A Question of Faith.* Theatre at St. Peter's, 3/20/91–4/13/91. 26 perf. p: Musical Theatre Works; m: Thomas Z. Shepard; l: Sheldon Harnick; d: Michael Montel; ch: Karen Azenberg; md: Albert Ahronheim. Cast: Scott Robertson, Elizabeth Walsh, SuEllen Estey, Bill Carmichael

1835. *Love Is a Ball.* Revue. Opened for pre-Broadway tryouts, 9/27/65, Civic Auditorium, San Jose. Closed 10/25/65, Civic Auditorium, Fort Worth. p: Robert T. Gaus & San Francisco Contemporary Dancers Foundation; m: Henry Mancini, Stan Kenton, Dave Brubeck, John Lewis, Franz Waxman; conceived by/d/ch: J. Marks; special material/new l: James Thurber, Jules Feiffer, J. Marks. Cast: Alice Ghostley, J. Marks

1836. *Love, Janis: The Songs, the Soul of Janis Joplin.* Bay Street Theatre, Sag Harbor, Long Island, 7/19/00–8/6/00. conceived & adapted by/d: Randal Myler; md: Sam Andrew (he had been one of Janis's band). Cast: Catherine Curtin, Cathy Richardson, Andra Mitrovich. There were two Janises, one singing & one talking (i.e. the private Janis, narrating the life). Janis's sister, Laura Joplin, happened to catch a perf of Randal Myler's show *Lost Highway* (about Hank Williams — see this appendix) and asked him to write similar show about Janis. She had Janis's correspondence from 1967–70 period & Mr. Myler used this as basis of his musical. Village Theatre, 4/22/01–1/5/03. 13 prev from 4/10/01. 713 perf. sound: Tony Meola. Among the actresses who played Janis were: Amelia Campbell, Cathy Richardson, Andra Mitrovich, Kristen Lee Kelly, Orfeh, Laura Brannigan, Amy Jo Johnson, Sass Jordan, Katrina Chester, Dana Fuchs, Kate Forbes, Wendy Hoopes. Charged the highest ticket prices for an OB show. Hurt by 9/11/01 attack on NYC, it was going to close in 10/01, but Eric Nederlander, owner of Village Theatre, gave the show a break on the rent, thus enabling it to continue. Before Sag Harbor the show had played at Denver Center Theatre Company, and at the Royal George, Chicago

1837. *Love Lemmings: A Comic Leap into the Dating Abyss.* Revue. Village Gate/Top of the Gate, 4/3/91–8/4/91. 13 prev. 101 perf. m/l: Eric Thoroman & Joe DiPietro; d: Melia Bensussen. Cast: John Daggett, Steve Ahern, Helen Greenberg, Becky Borczon (*Kathryn Rosseter*)

1838. *Love! Love! Love!* All-American musical 'bout love & other things. Astor Place, 6/15/77–7/3/77. 25 perf. w/composed: Jimmy Brandon; d/ch: Buck Heller; md: Clark McClellan. Cast: Michael Calkins, Pat Lundy, Glory Van Scott, Neva Rae Powers, Mel Johnson Jr. "Great-All-American Power-Driven-Engine," "Searching for Love," "Battle of Chicago," "Where Did the Dream Go," "I Am You," "Consenting Adults," "Come on In," "Preacher Man," "Age is a State of Mind," "Searching for Yesterdays," "Somewhere Along the Road," "Reach Out," "Love! Love! Love!," "Empty Spaces," "Look All Around You," "Find Someone to Love," "Streets of Bed-Stuy," "What is There to Say?," "Mothers Day," "Lovin'," "What Did We Do Wrong?," "Law and Order," "Middle-Class-Liberal-Blues"

1839. *Love Makes Things Happen.* Compilation of the hits of Kenneth "Babyface" Edmonds, with the setting an office romance. Tour, 2002. w: David E. Tabert & Babyface; d: David E. Tabert. Cast: Dawn Robinson,

Kevon Edmonds (Babyface's brother). "It Hurts Like Hell," "Superwoman," "End of the Road," "Ready or Not," "Soon as I Get Home," "Love Makes Things Happen," "I Just Met Heaven"

1840. Love Match. Previously called *The Loving Couple*. Opened for pre–Broadway try-outs, 11/3/68, Palace West, Phoenix, Ariz. Closed 1/4/69, Ahmanson, L.A., canceling scheduled 2/69 Broadway opening. m/l: David Shire & Richard Maltby Jr.; b: Christian Hamilton; d/ch: Danny Daniels. Cast: Teenage Queen Victoria: Patricia Routledge; Prince Albert: Laurence Guittard (replaced Max von Sydow); Also with: Michael Allinson, Hal Linden, Patricia Ripley, Bill Hinnant, Rex Robbins, Ronald Drake, Marilyn D'Honau. "These Two Hands," "Coronation Parade," "Play It Again," "Packing Song," "As Plain as Daylight," "I Hear Bells," "I (Think) I May Want to Remember Today," "A Meaningful Life," "The Grand Diversion," "I Won't Sleep a Wink Tonight," "Waiting for Morning Alone," "Beautiful," "I Don't Believe It," "A Word of Love," "Mine," "A Woman Looking for Love," "The Little Part of Me That's Mine," "Never Again," "The World and You"

1841. Love Me, Love My Children. Rock musical. Runaway girl joins youth culture in big city & is disillusioned by it. Mercer-O'Casey, 11/3/71–4/23/72. 187 perf. w: Robert Swerdlow; d: Paul Aaron; ch: Elizabeth Swerdlow; set: Jo Mielziner; cos: Patricia Quinn Stuart; voc arr: Robert de Cormier. Cast: Don Atkinson, Salome Bey, Jacqueline Britt, Ed Evanko (*Mike Perrier*), Michon Peacock, Patsy Rahn (*Margaret Castleman*). "Don't Twist My Mind," "Reflections," "Fat City," "Leave the World Behind," "Face to Face," "Let Me Down," "Walking in the World," "Gingerbread Girl," "You're Dreaming," "Running Down the Sun." Originally a Canadian play

1842. Love on the Dole. Musical play. Nottingham Playhouse, England, 7/21/70. m: Alan Fluck; l: Robert A. Gray; b: Terry Hughes; from play by Ronald Gow & Walter Greenwood, which had been adapted from novel of same name by Walter Greenwood; d/ch: Gillian Lynne; set: Patrick Robertson; md: Barry Booth. Cast: Angela Richards, Eric Flynn, Glyn Houston, Lila Kaye, Ivan Beavis. "Hanky Park," "Is it Always to Be Tomorrow?," "My Favorite Music," "Long Trousers," "Move Yourself, Horse," "Pawnshop Door," "If You Can't Trust Your Bookie," "You'll Never Get Out without Me," "The Spirits," "That Clock," "I'm on Your Side," "I Don't Give up Easily," "There May Never Be a Next Time," "Little Piece of Paper," "Beyond the Hill," "Tiger By the Tail," "Was She Once Young?." Not recorded. Rhoda McGraw, Woking, England, 1995. p: Stewart Nicholls. Some new material & an amateur (but brilliant) cast including Lori Tingay (Sally, the heroine) & Jill Payne

1843. The Love Racket. Opera House, Manchester, 9/43; toured; Victoria Palace, London, 10/21/43–4/1/44; Prince's, London, 4/8/44–7/8/44. Total of 324 perf; toured; Adelphi, London, 12/23/44–1/45. 36 perf. m: Noel Gay; l: Frank Eyton, Barbara Gordon,

Basil Thomas, Leslie Gibbs; b: Stanley Lupino; add dial: Arty Ash; add numbers: Hubert Gregg & Freddie Bretherton; d: William Mollison; ch: Freddie Carpenter; md: Freddie Bretherton. Cast: Arthur Askey, Finlay Currie, Hugh Morton, Greta Unger, Sylvia Peters, Alison Fearnley

1844. Lovers. Really gay musical revue. Players, 1/27/75–5/11/75. 118 perf. m: Steve Sterner; l/b/d: Peter del Valle. Cast: Martin Rivera, Michael Cascone, John Ingle, Richard Ryder (*Robert Sevra*), Reathel Bean, Gary Sneed. "Lovers," "Look at Him," "Make It," "I Don't Want to Watch TV"/"Twenty Years," "Somebody, Somebody Hold Me," "Belt and Leather," "There is Always You," "Hymn," "Somehow I'm Taller," "Role-Playing," "Argument," "Where Do I Go From Here?," "The Trucks," "Don't Betray His Love," "You Came to Me as a Young Man." Originally produced OB by Tosos

1845. Lovers & Keepers. Set in Florida, 1939–1962 INTAR, 4/4/86–5/4/86. 33 perf. m: various composers; l/b/d: Maria Irene Fornes. Cast: Jesse Corti, Josie de Guzman, Tomas Milian. "My House," "Farewell," "Now He's Looking," "You Ruined It," "When You Walk in the Shadows," "I Think of You," "Yes, We Can"

1846. A Lover's Rhapsody. Highlights from the 1935–51 musicals of Ivor Novello. Kraine, 3/4/94–3/20/94. 15 perf. d: Jerry Bell. Cast: Michael Dantuono. "Glamorous Night," "Music in May," "Gates of Paradise," "A Matter of Minutes," "Waking or Sleeping," "Man of My Heart," "Easy to Live With," "Love is My Reason," "Manchuko," "Fly Home, Little Heart," "Love Made the Song," "What Do You Mean?," "Night May Have its Sadness," "When I Curtsied to the King," "Dark Music," "Mountain Dove"/"If This Were Love," "Shine Through My Dreams," "When it's Spring in Vienna," "Singing Waltz," "Paris Reminds Me of You," "Fold Your Wings," "*Dancing Years* Highlights," "Wait for Me," "Why is There Ever Goodbye?," "Someday My Heart Will Awake," "Take Your Girl," "We'll Gather Lilacs," "Keep the Home Fires Burning"

1847. Lovesong. Revue. Top of the Village Gate, 10/5/76–10/24/76. 24 perf. m: Michael Valenti; w/orch: Michael Valenti; based on words in love themes by James Agee, Lord Byron, A.E. Houseman, John Lewin, Dorothy Parker, Sir Walter Raleigh, Christina Rossetti, Richard Brinsley Sheridan; conceived by: Henry Comor; md: John Montgomery; md: David Krane; cm: Mark Bramble. Cast: Jess Richards, Melanie Chartoff, Sigrid Heath, Ty McConnell. "What is Love?," "Did Not," "When I Was One and Twenty," "Bid Me Love," "A Birthday," "Sophia," "Many a Fairer Face," "Maryann," "When We're Married," "To My Dear and Loving Husband," "I Remember," "April Child," "Song," "What is a Woman Like?," "Let the Toast Pass," "Echo," "Open All Night," "A Rondelay," "Just Suppose," "Young I Was," "Jenny Kiss'd Me," "Indian Summer," "The Fair Dissenter Lass," "Blood Red Roses," "So, We'll Go No More a-Roving," "An Epitaph"

1848. Lucky Boy. Play with mus. Wimbledon Theatre, London, 8/31/53; Winter Garden, London, 9/22/53–9/24/53. 3 perf. m: George Melachrino; w/set: Ian Douglas; d: Lloyd Lamble. Cast: Doris Hare, Harry Welchman

1849. Lucky Stiff. Playwrights Horizons, 4/25/88–5/8/88. 27 prev from 4/1/88. 15 perf. m: Stephen Flaherty; l/b: Lynn Ahrens; from novel *The Man Who Broke the Bank at Monte Carlo*, by Michael Butterworth; d: Thommie Walsh; set: Bob Shaw; light: Beverly Emmons; md: Jeffrey Saver. Cast: Ron Faber, Paul Kandel, Barbara Rosenblat, Michael McCarty (*Erick Devine*), Mary Testa, Stuart Zagnit, Patty Holley, Stephen Stout, Julie White, Frank Zagottis. "Something Funny's Going On," "Good to Be Alive," "Lucky," "Monte Carlo!," "Times Like This," "Fancy Meeting You Here." Revived in London in 1997. Theatre at St. Peter's, NYC, 10/24/03–10/26/03. 5 perf. Concert version, part of the *Musicals in Mufti* series. p: York Theatre Co.; d: Graciela Daniele; md: David Loud. Cast: Mary Testa, Paul Kandel, Malcolm Gets, Janet Metz, Erick Devine, Stuart Zagnit, Emily Skinner

1850. Lullabye and Goodnight. Musical romance about prostitutes. Newman, 2/9/82–3/7/82. 30 perf. w/d: Elizabeth Swados; ch: Ara Fitzgerald; set: David Jenkins; cos: Hilary Rosenfeld; light: Marcia Madeira. Cast: Gail Boggs, Josie de Guzman, Jesse Corti, Olga M. Merediz, Bruce Hubbard, Cliff Lipson (understudy). "Gentlemen of Leisure," "I Am Sick of Love," "When a Pimp Meets a Whore," "The Moth and the Flame," "Why We Do It," "Wife Beating Song," "You're My Favorite Lullabye," "Turn Her Out," "You Gave Me Love," "Let the Day Perish When I Was Born," "Lies Lies Lies," "Sub-Babylon," Sweet Words," "The Nightmare Was Me"

1851. The Lullaby of Broadway: Or Harry Who? Musical tribute to Harry Warren. Boltax, 11/20/79–12/16/79. 36 perf. d: Judith Haskell; md: Jeremy Harris; ch: Eleanore Treiber. Cast: SuEllen Estey, Josie O'Donnell, Jess Richards, Scott Robertson

1852. Lust. Set in London in 1661. Theatre Royal, Haymarket, London, 7/19/93. m/l/b: The Heather Brothers (Neil, Lea, John, Charles); freely adapted from William Wycherley's *The Country Wife*. Cast: Mark White, Christina Bolton. "Lust," "Art of Deceiving," "Serve the Dog Right," "I Live for Love," "A Pox on Love and Wenching," "Somewhere Out There," "Ladies of Quality," "Husbands Beware," "Why Did You Have to Come into My Life?," "What a Handsome Little Fellow," "Captain's Jig," "Wait and See," "Dear Sir," "Ode to the One I Love," "China," "Come Tomorrow," "A Little Time in the Country," "The Master Class," "One of You," "Vengeance," "We Thank You." Walnut Street Theatre, Philadelphia, from 5/3/95, and then (with same cast & crew) OB, at the John Houseman, 6/23/95–8/5/95. 32 prev. 27 perf. d: Bob Carlton; ch: Barry Finkel; light: F. Mitchell Dana. Cast: Jennifer Lee Andrews, Judith Moore, Barry Finkel. "A Little Time in the Country" was cut

1853. *Lyle*. Musical fable about a crocodile. McAlpin Rooftop, 3/20/70–3/22/70. 4 perf. m/l: Janet Gari & Toby Garson; from *The House on East 88th* Street & other books by Bernard Waber; d: Marvin Gordon; cos: Winn Morton. Carleton Carpenter was Lyle in previews, but during actual run the role was played by Steve Harmon. Rest of cast: Joey Faye, Jack Fletcher, Stanley Grover. "Always Leave 'em Wanting More," "I Can't Believe it's Real," "Generation Gap," "I Belong," "Me, Me, Me," "Alternate Parking," "Try to Make the Best of It," "Loretta," "Look at Me," "Crocodiles Cry," "On the Road," "Lyle's Turn," "Suddenly You're a Stranger," "Everybody Wants to Be Remembered," "Lyle," "Things Were Much Better in the Past," "We Belong." New version, *Lyle the Crocodile*, ran in Albany, NY, in 1987. m/l/b: Charles Strouse; d/ch: Barbara Siman; md: Louis St. Louis. Cast: John Thomas Maguire III. It went on to the Lyric, Hammersmith, London, 12/3/87–1/9/88

1854. *Lypsinka Is Harriet Craig!* Semi-musical adaptation by "S.P. Ellbound" of 1950 Joan Crawford movie. Mother, 8/20/97–9/28/97. 15 perf. Re-ran 1/29/98–3/8/98. 17 perf. d: Kevin Malony. Cast: Harriet Craig: John "Lypsinka" Epperson

1855. *The Lyric Revue*. Intimate revue. Lyric, Hammersmith, London, 5/24/51. Big hit. Globe, London, 9/26/51. 314 perf. p: Company of Four; m/l: Arthur Macrae, Charles Zwar, Donald Swann, Richard Addinsell, Gerard Bryant, Cole Lesley, Graham Payn; d/ch: William Chappell; set/cos: Loudon Sainthill. Cast: Graham Payn, Dora Bryan, Joan Heal, Roberta Huby, Ian Carmichael, Jeremy Hawk, George Benson, Irlin Hall, Myles Eason. Noel Coward contributed one quartet: "Don't Make Fun of the Fair." Other numbers: "Let's Ignore It," "This Seems to Be the Moment," "Portrait of a Lady," "Ornamental Orientals," "Modern Trends," "Something for the Kiddies," "Revival"

1856. *Lysistrata*. Play with mus. Semi-musical version of Aristophanes' comedy of Athenian women withholding sex from husbands until they agree to stop waging war. Brooks Atkinson, Broadway, 11/13/72–11/18/72. 35 prev. 8 perf. p: David Black & David Seltzer; m: Peter Link; adapted/d: Michael Cacoyannis; set: Robin Wagner; cos: Willa Kim; light: Jules Fisher; sound: Abe Jacob; md: Henry "Bootsie" Normand; psm: Mortimer Halpern. Cast: Melina Mercouri, Evelyn Russell, Priscilla Lopez, Madeleine Le Roux, Nai Bonet, Marylou Sirinek, Emory Bass, Jane Connell, Gordon Connell, Mary Jo Catlett, Jack Fletcher, Joseph Palmieri, Philip Bruns, Joy Franz, Stephen Macht, Patti Karr, John Bentley. "A Woman's Hands," "On, On, On," "Oh, What a Siege That Was," "As I Choose," "Many the Beasts," "Are We Strong?," "A Cavalry Captain," "Lysistrata," "To Touch the Sky," "Eels Are a Girl's Best Friend," "Let Me Tell You a Litle Story," "You Out There," "Kalimera"

1857. *Lyz!* Set in NYC. Samuel Beckett, 1/7/99–1/31/99. 3 prev. 13 perf. m: Jim Cowdery; l/b: Joe Lauinger; from *Lysistrata*, by Aristophanes; d: John Rue. Cast: Jill Paxton. "The Gods," "The Answer is No," "Fire in the Belly," "Song of Peace," "Fanged Tango," "Women's Chants," "Battle of the Choruses," "We Can't Finish," "I'll Do Anything," "Bug Song," "Reconciliation," "We All Gotta Stand," "Kindness and Love"

1858. *Ma Rainey's Black Bottom*. Not a musical, but often, erroneously, listed as such. OB, 1984. Cast: Aleta Mitchell, Charles S. Dutton, Theresa Merritt, Scott Davenport-Richards, Robert Judd, Joe Seneca, Leonard Jackson

1859. *Mack the Knife … The Life and Music of Bobby Darin*. Theatre at St. Peter's, 6/22/03–8/10/03. 13 prev from 6/11/03. 56 perf. created by: Chaz Esposito & James Haddon; d/starred: Chaz Esposito; md: James Haddon

1860. *Mackey of Appalachia*. Set in Slatey Fork, WV, in Oct. 1900. Blackfriars, 10/6/65–11/23/65. 48 perf. w/d: Walter Cool. Cast: James Bormann. "Mackey of Appalachia," "I Wonder Why," "Love Me Too," "You're Too Smart," "Love Will Come Your Way," "It's Sad to Be Lonesome," "How We Would Like Our Man," "Lonely Voice," "My Love, My Love," "Blue and Troubled," "My Little Girl," "Go up to the Mountain," "There's Got To Be Love," "We Got Troubles," "Gotta Pay," "Only a Day Dream," "Things Ain't as Nice," "We Are Friends"

1861. *The Mad Show*. Musical revue based on *Mad* magazine. New Theatre, 1/9/66–9/10/67. 871 perf. p: Ivor David Balding (for the Establishment Theatre Co.); m: Mary Rodgers; l: Marshall Barer, Larry Siegel, Steven Vinaver, Norm Deploom (i.e. Stephen Sondheim), etc; b: Larry Siegel & Stan Hart; dev/d: Steven Vinaver; set/cos: Peter Harvey; md: Joe Raposo. Cast: Linda Lavin, MacIntyre Dixon, Dick Libertini, Paul Sand, Jo Anne Worley. Others during the run: Marcia Rodd, Carol Morley, Mitzi McCall, Reni Santoni, David Steinberg, Charlie Brill, Marilyn Cooper, Fiddle Viracola. "You Never Can Tell," "Eccch!," "The Real Thing," "Misery Is," "Hey, Sweet Momma," "Well, It Ain't," "Hate Song," "Looking for Someone," "The Gift of Maggie," "The Boy from…" (l: Norm Deploom). Sketches: Academy Awards, Saboteurs, Babysitter, Handle with Care, Primers, Football in Depth, Kiddie TV, Snappy Answers, Getting to Know You, The Irving Irving Story. Several different touring companies

1862. *Madame Aphrodite*. About a rooming house on Euclid Avenue. Orpheum, 12/29/61–1/7/62. 13 perf. m/l: Jerry Herman (his 2nd OB musical); b: Tad Mosel; d: Robert Turoff; set: David Ballou; cos: Patricia Zipprodt; light: Lee Watson; md: Peg Foster. Cast: Nancy Andrews, Jack Drummond, Mona Paulee, Cherry Davis. "I Don't Mind," "Sales Reproach," "Beat the World," "Miss Euclid Avenue," "Beautiful" (later re-worked as "A Little More Mascara" for *La Cage aux Folles*), "You I Like," "And a Drop of Lavender Oil," "The Girls Who Sit and Wait," "Afferdytie," "There Comes a Time," "Only Love," "Take a Good Look Around," "Where Do I Go from Here?"

1863. *Maddie*. Young San Francisco wife in 1981 possessed by spirit of madcap showgirl killed in 1920s before she could fulfill dream of stardom. Salisbury Playhouse, England, 9/96. m: Stephen Keeling; l: Shaun McKenna; b: Shaun McKenna & Steven Dexter; based on Jack Finney's novel *Marion's Wall*; d: Martin Connor. Cast: Summer Rognlie, Graham Bickley, Kevin Colson, Lynda Baron, Louise Davidson, Paddy Glynn. "Don't Look Back," "Knick Knacks," "Ghost," "I'll Find Time for You," "Easy," "The Time of My Life," "Star," "One More Day," "I've Always Known," "From Now On," "Afraid," "At the Gates," "If Not for Me." It was roundly panned. There was a 7-month delay getting to the West End because one of the major backers pulled out. Over 100 *Daily Telegraph* readers came in as sponsors. Lyric, London. 9/29/97–11/8/97. Prev from 9/22/97. cast recording on Dress Circle. The story was also basis for Glenn Close film *Maxie*

1864. *Mademoiselle Colombe*. Theatre Off Park, 12/9/87–1/17/88. 12 prev. 28 perf. m/l: Michael Valenti & Edward Dulchin; from Louis J. Kronenberger's English-language adaptation of Jean Anouilh's play; d: Albert Harris; cos: Lindsay W. Davis; md: Rod Derefinko. Cast: Tammy Grimes, Joaquin Romaguera, David Cryer, Dick Decareau, Georgia Creighton, Lisa Vroman, Elizabeth Walsh, Keith Buterbaugh, Tom Galantich. "Goddess of Love," "Two Against the World," "Only So Much I Can Give," "This Bright Morning," "More than One Man in Her Life," "And if I Tell You that I Want You," "She's an Actress," "The Color Red," "Why Did it Have to Be You?," "Years from Now," "From This Day"

1865. *Madison Avenue: The Subliminal Musical*. Lone Star. Opened 10/31/92, as dinner theatre; on 12/29/92 changed status to OB cabaret; closed 2/7/93. 48 perf as cabaret. p: Paul Streitz; m: Gary Cherpakov & Robert Moehl; l: Paul Streitz & Gary Cherpakov; d/ch: David C. Wright. Cast: Randi Cooper, Sarah Laine Terrell. "Women on the Move," "A Woman at Home," "Something for Me," "All a Matter of Strategy," "Thirty Seconds," "Client Service," "L.A. Freeway," "Office Romance," "Typical American Consumer," "Residuals," "Leonardo's Lemonade," "Lennie's Lemonade," "Leonard's Lemonade," "It's Not a Commercial, It's Art," "Squeeze, Squeeze, Squeeze," "The Look," "Upper East Side Blues," "Madison Avenue"

1866. *The Madwoman of Central Park West*. One-woman show with Phyllis Newman. Studio Arena, Buffalo, 4/6/79. 34 perf. World premiere. m/l: Peter Allen, Leonard Bernstein, Jerry Bock & Sheldon Harnick, Martin Charnin, John Clifton, Betty Comden & Adolph Green, John Kander & Fred Ebb, Ed Kleban, Jack Feldman, Jule Styne, Bruce Sussman, Stephen Sondheim, Carole Bayer Sager, Joe Raposo, Phyllis Newman, Mary Rodgers, Barry Manilow; b: Phyllis Newman & Arthur Laurents; d: Arthur Laurents; cos: Florence Klotz; light: Ken Billington; md: Herbert Kaplan. "Up, Up, Up," "My Mother Was a Fortune Teller," "Cheerleader," "What Makes

Me Love Him?," "Don't Laugh," "No One's Toy," "Some People," "Better," "Don't Wish," "Copacabana," "My New Friends," "List Song." 22 Steps, 6/13/79–8/25/79. 86 perf. cos: Theoni V. Aldredge. "Some People" was dropped

1867. *Maggie.* Shaftesbury Theatre, London, 10/12/77–11/19/77. Prev from 10/7/77. 42 perf. m/l/b: Michael Wild; from J.M. Barrie's *What Every Woman Knows*; d: Tom Hawkes; ch: Sally Gilpin; md: John White. Cast: Anna Neagle, Peter Gale, Anna Sharkey, Clifton Todd, Leonard Fenton, Barrie Sinclair (*Charles Stapley*). "Maggie," "I Can See the Stars," "I Never Laughed in My Life," "London Waltz," "If I Ever Really Love," "Do You Remember?," "Till the End of Time," "Just an Idea," "I Just Took a Look at Me"

1868. *Maggie May.* About a Liverpool prostitute. Opera House, Manchester, England, 8/19/64 (4 weeks); Adelphi, London, 9/22/64–12/4/65. 501 perf. m/l: Lionel Bart; b: Alun Owen; d: Ted Kotcheff; ch: Paddy Stone; set: Sean Kenny; md: Marcus Dods; cast recording on Decca. Cast: Rachel Roberts (*Georgia Brown, Judith Bruce*), Kenneth Haigh, Andrew Keir, Barry Humphries, Billy Boyle, Fred Evans, John Junkin, Julia McKenzie (in chorus & understudied the lead). "Ballad of the Liver Bird," "Lullaby," "I Love a Man," "Casey," "Shine You Swine," "Dey Don't Do Dat t'Day," "I Told You So," "Right of Way," "Stroll On," "Away from Home," "Maggie, Maggie May," "Leave Her, Johnny, Leave Her," "Land of Promises," "Carryin' On," "There's Only One Union," "It's Yourself," "The World's a Lovely Place," "I'm Me," "We Don't All Wear d'Same Size Boots." In 1964 Judy Garland recorded album *Maggie May* on Capitol, with some of the songs from the show

1869. *The Magic of Frederick Loewe.* Musical revue. Wings, 10/9/03–10/19/03. 12 perf. p: Bandwagon; d: Jerry Bell; ch: Heather Rosario & Jerry Bell; md: Eddie Guttman. "A Waltz was Born in Vienna," "May I Suggest Romance," "Why Can't This Night Last Forever?," "To Whom it May Concern," "Night Can Be Blind," "There Had to Be the Waltz," "Here We Go Again," "Life of the Party." An earlier version, *The Lost Music of Frederick Loewe*, was produced by Bandwagon in 5/02

1870. *The Magic of Jolson!* Musical tribute to Al Jolson, including an impersonation of him in some of his famous numbers. Provincetown Playhouse, 4/9/75–4/13/75. 5 perf. p/b/add l: Pearl Sieben; add m: Richard DeMone; conceived by/d: Isaac Dostis. Cast: Norman Brooks, Linda Gerard, John Medici

Magic to Do see # 418, Main Book

1871. *The Magnificent Christmas Spectacular.* Christmas program. Radio City Music Hall, 11/25/79–1/6/80. Prev from 11/14/79. 93 perf. p/conceived by: Robert F. Jani; exec md: Donald Pippin; d/ch: Dru Davis & Howard Parker; Rockettes ch: Violet Holmes; light: Ken Billington. Huge cast which included: Jane Krakowski, Dee Dee Knapp, Kay Walbye, Marie Santell, Nina Hennessey, Dale Kristien. Repeated over the years

1872. *Mahagonny.* About imaginary American city founded by criminals. Anderson, 4/28/70–5/3/70. 69 prev. 8 perf. m/l: Kurt Weill & Bertolt Brecht; based on 1930 opera *The Rise and Fall of the City of Mahagonny*, by Weill & Brecht; adapted into English by: Arnold Weinstein; d: Carmen Capalbo; set: Robin Wagner; cos: Ruth Morley; light: Thomas Skelton; md: Samuel Matlovsky; cast recording on Atlantic. Cast: Barbara Harris, Estelle Parsons, Frank Porretta (who replaced Mort Shuman), Louis St. Louis, Jack De Lon, Keith Kaldenberg, Alexander Orfaly. The American premiere of Weill & Brecht's *The Little Mahagonny*, translated by Michael Feingold, was on 5/13/70, at Yale Rep. 22 perf. d: Michael Posnick; set/cos: Santo Loquasto. Cast: Stephanie Cotsirilos, Jack Litten, Henry Winkler

1873. *Mahalia.* Henry Street Playhouse, 5/31/78–6/11/78. 14 perf. orig m: John Lewis; l/b: Don Evans; based on *Just Mahalia Baby*, the life of gospel singer Mahalia Jackson, written by Laurraine Goreau; d: Oz Scott; md: Luther Henderson. Cast: Esther Marrow, Nat Adderley, Loretta Devine, Otis Sallid, Chuck Patterson, Al Perryman. Hartman, Stamford, Conn., 4/1/82. d: Gerald Freedman; ch: Talley Beatty; ms: Joyce Brown. Cast: Esther Marrow. Unrelated to Broadway show *Truly Blessed*, and to *Sing, Mahalia, Sing* (see this appendix)

1874. *Maid of the Mountains.* Revival of 1916 show, revised by Harry Parr Davies. Palace, London, 1972. orig m: H. Fraser-Simpson; orig l: Harry Graham; orig b: Frederick Lonsdale. "Friends Have to Part," "My Life is Love," "Love Will Find a Way," "Over There and Over Here"

1875. *Maid to Measure.* Revue. London, 1948. m/l: Hugh Wade & Leigh Stafford. Cast: Jessie Matthews, Tommy Fields. "Time May Change"

1876. *The Maiden of Ludmir.* Yiddish musical. True story, set in Ukraine in 19th century. Folksbiene, 10/19/96 1/27/97. 57 perf. m/l: John Clifton & Miriam Hoffman; d: Robert Kalfin; cos: Gail Cooper-Hecht; md: Herbert Kaplan. Cast: Mina Bern

1877. *Make Me an Offer.* Set in world of antique dealers in Portobello Road. Theatre Royal, Stratford East, London, 10/17/59–11/21/59. 36 perf. p: Theatre Workshop; m/l: David Heneker & Monty Norman; b: Wolf Mankowitz (from his novel of same name); d: Joan Littlewood; set: Voytek; cos: Susan Yelland; md: Gareth Davies. Cast: Daniel Massey, Victor Spinetti, Sheila Hancock, Milton Sills, Martin Lawrence, Dilys Laye, Meier Tzelniker, Diana Coupland, Roy Kinnear, Wally Patch. New Theatre, London, 12/16/59–6/18/60. 267 perf. p: Oscar Lewenstein & Donald Albery; otherwise same crew & cast (Martin Miller replaced Meier Tzelniker during an absence). Cast recording on AEI. "The Pram Song," "Portobello Road," "Dog Eat Dog," "I Want a Lock-Up," "If I Was a Man," "Business is Business," "Americans' Entrance," "Concerning Fleas," "All Big Fleas," "Fanfare for Fleas," "You Gotta Have Capital," "Love Him," "Make Me an Offer," "Whatever You Believe," "It's Sort of Romantic," "Knock-Out"

1878. *The Make Over.* Comedy with mus. Harold Clurman, 9/10/93–10/3/93. 16 perf. p: Riverside Theatre Workshop; m: Steven Silverstein & Hershel Dwellingham; l: Bianca Miller & Luigia M. Miller; w: Luigia M. Miller; d/ch: Alberto Guzman; md: Michael Lavine. "Miracles of Change," "What Fools These Mortals Be," "Phantom of Avenue D," "My Jolly Jelly Roll," "Electrocution Rock," "Let Me Sing," "When You Can't See Clearly," "Gotta Get Back Home," "Center of the World," "Brand Old Me," "Silence Finds"

1879. *Make Someone Happy: The Jule Styne Revue.* Rainbow & Stars, 1993. p: Steve Paul & Greg Dawson; d: Fred Greene; cos: Gail Cooper-Hecht. Cast: Gregg Edelman, Ann Hampton Callaway, David Garrison, Jay Leonhart, Kay McClelland, William Roy (also md)

1880. *Making Tracks.* Set 1865–1999, in Japan & various parts of USA. Taipei Theatre, 1/30/99–2/20/99. 5 prev. 17 perf. m: Woody Pak; l: C. Matthew Eddy & Brian Yorkey; b: Matthew Eddy, Brian Yorkey, Welly Yang; conceived by: Welly Yang; d: Lenny Leibowitz. Cast: Aiko Nakasone, Welly Yang, Mimosa. "One More Mile," "Making Tracks," "Pearl River," "Picture Perfect," "So Now I See You," "Voices of Angels," "Dance the World Away," "Earth, Sand, Wind, Sky," "Fly Away," "Open Spaces," "The Lucky One," "Wings Like a Dove," "The New Frontier"

Mama see # 331, Main Book

1881. *Mama, I Want to Sing.* AMAS, 12/3/80. 13 perf. m: Richard Tee; l: Vy Higgensen & Ken Wydro; b: Vy Higgensen; d: Duane L. Jones. Cast: Steve Bland, Ursuline Kairson, Andrew Frierson, Ann Duquesnay, Crystal Johnson. Heckscher Theatre, 3/25/90. It was still playing in rep into 1990s, with *Mama, I Want to Sing—Part II*, which opened 2/2/90. m/l: Wesley Naylor, Vy Higgensen, Ken Wydro; d: Ken Wydro. Cast: Doris Troy. "The Spirit of Your Father," "The Lord is Blessing Me," "Faith," "Sermon," "Because He Lives," "Something Pretty," "Finding a Man Ain't Easy," "We Belong Together," "Bless You, My Children," "Stay Close to the Music," "Long Distance Love," "New Life on the Planet," "Mt. Calvary Baptism Day," "Sister Carrie's Song," "The Promise of the Future," "To Love is to Serve," "Please Understand," "Something to Remember Me By," "Where is My Mommy, Please," "Alone on the Road," "Going Home." The sequel was *Born to Sing* (see this appendix)

1882. *The Mambo Kings.* 2 Cuban brothers in NY in 1949 trying to become recording stars. Pre-Broadway tryout at Golden Gate, San Francisco, 5/24/05–6/19/05 (the month-long tryout at the Oriental, Chicago, from 2/7/05 was canceled). p: Daryl Roth & Jordan Roth; m: Carlos Franzetti; l/d: Arne Glimcher; b: Arne Glimcher & Oscar Hijuelos; based on Pulitzer Prize-wining novel *The Mambo Kings Play Songs of Love*, by Oscar Hijuelos, and on the 1992 movie (*The Mambo Kings*) made from it by Arne Glimcher, and starring Armand Assante & Antonio Banderas; ch: Sergio Trujillo; cos: Ann Roth; light: Jules Fisher & Peggy

Eisenhauer. Broadway Theatre, Broadway, 8/18/05 (prev from 7/18/05) (opening date put back from 3/29/05). Cast: Billy Dee Williams, Esai Morales, Albita, Justina Machado. A 2004 NY workshop featured Anthony Crivello, Ivan Fernandez, Leah Hocking, Natascia Diaz, Priscilla Lopez, Alton White

1883. *Man Better Man*. A foreign play, set in Trinidad, at turn of 20th century. Village boy tries to become champ at game of sticks to impress girl he loves. St. Mark's Playhouse, 7/2/69–7/20/69. 23 perf. p: Negro Ensemble; m: Coleridge-Taylor Perkinson; w: Errol Hill; d: Douglas Turner Ward. Cast: David Downing, Rosalind Cash, Hattie Winston, Julius W. Harris, Esther Rolle, Richard Roundtree (in chorus). "Tiny, the Champion," "I Love Petite Belle," "One, Two, Three," "Man Better Man," "Me Alone," "Girl in the Coffee," "Briscoe, the Hero" (a reprise of "Tiny, the Champion")

1884. *The Man from the East*. Franco-Japanese rock operetta. Roundhouse, London, 1973. m/l/d: Stomu Yamashita. Brooklyn Academy of Music, 10/23/73–10/28/73. 8 perf

1885. *Man in the Moon*. A Bil & Cora Baird puppet show. Biltmore, Broadway, 4/11/63–4/21/63. 7 perf. p: Arthur Cantor & Joseph P. Harris; m/l: Jerry Bock & Sheldon Harnick; b: Arthur Burns; d: Gerald Freedman. "Look Where I Am," "Itch to Be Rich," "Worlds Apart," "Ain't You Never Been Afraid?," "Oh, Treacherous Men"

1886. *Man of Magic*. About Houdini. Opera House, Manchester, England, 10/22/66–11/5/66; Piccadilly, London, 11/16/66–3/11/67. 135 perf. p: Harold Fielding; m: Wilfred Wylam (i.e. Wilfred Josephs); l/b: John Morley & Aubrey Cash; d: Peter Ebert; ch: Norman Maen; cos: Loudon Sainthill; md: Jan Cervenka; cast recording on CBS. Cast: Stuart Damon, Judith Bruce, Stubby Kaye, Joan Miller (*Doris Hare*), Gaye Brown, Colin Welland. "Man of Magic," "Man in the Crowd," "Fantabulous," "Man that Captured My Heart," "Suddenly," "Sling the Gin," "Conquer the World," "Take Your Medicine," "Like No Other Man," "The Earth is the Lord's," "You Can't Keep a Good Man Down," "This He Knows," "Say Your Name"

1887. *A Man of No Importance*. Set in Dublin in 1963. Mitzi E. Newhouse, 10/10/02–12/29/02. Prev from 9/12/02. 93 perf. m/voc arr: Stephen Flaherty; l: Lynn Ahrens; b: Terrence McNally; based on 1994 film with Albert Finney as closet homosexual with passion for Oscar Wilde (the musical's title is a play on Wilde's *A Woman of No Importance*); d: Joe Mantello; ch: Jonathan Butterell; set: Loy Arcenas; cos: Jane Greenwood; light: Donald Holder; sound: Scott Lehrer; md: Ted Sperling; orch: William David Brohn & Christopher Jahnke; cast recording on Jay (recorded 12/16/02; released 4/8/03). Cast: Roger Rees, Faith Prince, Ronn Carroll, Luther Creek, Michael McCormick, Jessica Molaskey, Martin Moran, Sally Murphy, Charles Keating, Barbara Marineau, Patti Perkins. "A Man of No Importance," "Burden of Life," "Going Up," "Princess," "First Rehearsal," "Streets of Dublin," "Books," "Man in the Mirror," "Love

Who You Love," "Our Father," "Confession," "The Cuddles Mary Gave," "Art," "Confusing Times," "Tell Me Why," "Welcome to the World." Joe Mantello had directed a reading at Lincoln Center Theatre in 3/01. Later played in London

1888. *Man on the Moon*. Little Theatre, 1/29/75–2/1/75. 21 prev. 5 perf. p: Andy Warhol & Richard Turley; m/l/b: John Phillips; d: Paul Morrissey; ch unbilled; set: John J. Moore; cos: Marsia Trinder; light: Jules Fisher; sound: Gary Harris; md: Karen Gustafson; arr: Michael Gibson & Jim Tyler. Cast: Genevieve Waite, Monique Van Vooren, Dennis Doherty, Harlan S. Foss, Eric Lang, Mark Lawhead, E. Lynn Nickerson. "Boys from the South," "Midnight Deadline Blastoff," "Mission Control," "Speed of Light," "Though I'm a Little Angel," "Girls," "Canis Minor Bolero Waltz," "Starbust," "Penthouse of Your Mind," "Champagne and Kisses," "Star Stepping Stranger/Convent," "My Name is Can," "American Man on the Moon," "Welcome to the Moon," "Sunny, Sunny Moon," "Love is Coming Back," "Truth Cannot Be Treason," "Place in Space," "Family of Man," "Yesterday I Left the Earth," "Stepping to the Stars." Its orig title, when it was being developed by the then producer Michael Butler & the then dir Michael Bennett, was *Space*. Dennis Doherty replaced top-billed John Phillips (Genevieve Waite's husband), and this left Mr. Doherty's role open, which then went to Harlan Foss. It was roundly panned

1889. *Man with a Load of Mischief*. Set at a wayside inn in early 19th-century England. Prince's mistress has romantic rendezvous with nobleman, but instead falls in love with his valet. Jan Hus, 11/6/66–6/4/67; Provincetown Playhouse, from 5/17/67. Total of 241 perf. p: Donald H. Goldman; m: John Clifton; l: John Clifton & Ben Tarver; b: Ben Tarver; adapted from play by Ashley Dukes (produced on Broadway in 1925 for 16 perf); d: Tom Gruenewald; ch: Noel Schwartz; set/light: Joan Larkey; md: Sande Campbell. Cast: Reid Shelton, Raymond Thorne, Virginia Vestoff, Alice Cannon. "Wayside Inn," "The Rescue," "Goodbye, My Sweet," "Romance," "Lover Lost," "Once You've Had a Little Taste," "Hulla-Baloo-Balay," "You'd Be Amazed," "A Friend Like You," "(Come to the) Masquerade," "Man with a Load of Mischief," "What Style!," "A Wonder," "Make Way for My Lady!," "Forget," "Any Other Way," "Little Rag Doll." Ran in London, 1968, starring Julia McKenzie. Equity Library, 5/9/74–5/26/74. 19 perf. d: Joseph F. Leonardo. Cast: Avril Gentles, Edward Penn, Gloria Zaglool. Theatre at St. Peter's, 10/31/03–11/2/03. 5 perf. Part of the *Musicals in Mufti* series. p: York Theatre Co.; d: Michael Montel. Cast: Stephen Bogardus, Lenny Wolpe, Holly Holcomb, Frank Vlastnik, Diane Sutherland, Laura Kenyon

1890. *Mandrake*. Set in Florence during early 16th century. Theatre Royal, Bristol, England, 5/28/69–6/21/69. p: Bristol Old Vic Co.; m: Anthony Bowles; l/b: Michael Alfreds; based on *Mandragola*, by Machiavelli; d: Val May; ch: Geraldine Stephenson; set: Karen

Mills; cos: Charles Alty; md: Brian Gascoigne. Cast: Jonathan Lynn, Roger Davenport, Sandra Michaels, Paul Shelley, Sarah Atkinson, Margaret Burton, Cindy Wells, Ian Paterson, Julia McCarthy, Edward Caddick, Tom Marshall, Irene Hamilton. Criterion, London, 4/16/70–4/25/70. 12 perf. p: Donald Albery; d: Edward Caddick; md: David Cullen. Rest of crew basically same. Same cast except that Irene Hamilton's role was cut, and a few new ones added. Soho Rep (NYC), 4/13/84–5/6/84. 20 perf. d: Anthony Bowles; set: Joseph A. Varga; md: Michael Rafter. Cast: Steve Sterner, Mary Testa

1891. *Manhattan Moves*. All-dancing theatrical entertainment, with recorded score. American Place, 12/17/92–1/24/93. 45 perf. d/ch: Michael Kessler. Cast: Michael Kessler, Melinda Jackson, Adrienne Armstrong

1892. *Manhattan Rhythm*. Savoy, 7/21/82–8/14/82. 27 perf. conceived by/d/ch: Jon Devlin. Cast: Jon Devlin & his Company. "Love for Sale," "Manhattan Rhythm Blues," "Take Five," "One O'clock Jump," "In the Mood," "Star Trek Medley," "Spanish Cape," "Hey Good Lookin'," "9 to 5," "Physical," "Fame," "Celebration"

1893. *Manhattan Serenade*. Revue based on mus of Louis Alter. AMAS, 4/18/85–5/12/85. 16 perf. l: Frank Loesser, Stanley Adams & others; new l: Stanley Adams & Karen Cottrell; compiler/arr/md: Alfred Heller; w: Karen Cottrell & Alfred Heller; d/ch: Bob Rizzo. Cast: Sally Ann Swarm, Michele Pigliavento. "Manhattan Serenade," "Melody from the Sky," "Blue Shadows," "New Love for Old Love," "My Kinda Love," "That Tired Feeling," "Throw it Out the Window," "Blow Hot, Blow Cold," "You Turned the Tables on Me," "The Rain Falls on Everybody," "Wonderworld," "Autumn Night," "Something's Come Over Me," "Love Me as I Am," "The Blues Are Brewin'," "Hello Manhattan!," "Star Crazy," "We Worked the Whole Thing Out," "Seeing Things"

1894. *Manhattan Showboat*. Radio City Music Hall, 6/30/80–10/15/80. 191 perf. p/conceived by: Robert F. Jani; orig m/l: Donald Pippin, Sammy Cahn, Nan Mason; dial: Stan Hart; special material: Nan Mason; principals staged by: Frank Wagner; ch: Linda Lemac, Howard Parker, Debra Pigliavento, Frank Wagner; Rockettes' ch: Violet Holmes; set: Robert Guerra; cos: Frank Spencer & Michael Casey; light: David F. Segal; exec md: Don Pippin; mus routining: Stan Lebowsky; orch: Elman Anderson, Michael Gibson, Arthur Harris, Philip J. Lang. Cast: Karen Anders, Louis Carry, Thomas Ruisinger, Steven Williford, Tony Moore, Buddy Crutchfield, Lou Ann Csaszar, Laurie Stephenson. "Love is a Simple Thing" and "He Takes Me off His Income Tax" (both from *New Faces of 1952*), "Manhattan Showboat" and "There Are No Girls Quite Like Show Girls" (both with music by Don Pippin and lyrics by Sammy Cahn), "Right Here," (m: Don Pippin; l: Nan Mason)

1895. *Marathon '33*. Comedy with mus. ANTA, 12/22/63–2/1/64. 48 perf. p: Actors Studio; m: Conrad Janis & His Tailgate 5; w:

June Havoc; set: Peter Larkin; light: Tharon Musser; prod super: Lee Strasberg. Cast: Julie Harris, Lee Allen, Gabriel Dell, Conrad Janis, Peter Masterson, Olive Deering, Brooks Morton, Logan Ramsey, Don Fellows, Pat Randall, Iggie Wolfington, Ralph Waite, Richard Bradford, Lonny Chapman, John Strasberg, Joe Don Baker

March of the Falsettos see # 200, Main Book

1896. *Marching with Johnny*. Emphasized Labor's contribution to the War. Touring musical headed for Broadway, but closed in Philadelphia, 1943. m/l: Jay Gorney, Henry Meyers, Edward Eliscu. Cast: Beatrice Kay, David Brooks. "Let's End the Beguine." Most of the material for this show came from two 1941 failures — *They Can't Get You Down* & *The New Meet the People 1941*

1897. *Mardi Gras*. New Orleans lawyer's society girlfriend doesn't want to marry him because he is not as romantic as his ancestors Jean Lafitte the pirate & Lucky Lafitty the gambler. Jones Beach, 6/26/65–9/5/65. 68 perf. p: Guy Lombardo; m/l: John Jacob Loeb & Carmen Lombardo; b: Sig Herzig; d/ch: June Taylor; set/light: George Jenkins; orch: Philip J. Lang. Cast: David Atkinson, Karen Shepard, Juanita Hall, Ralph Purdum, Ruth Kobart, Phil Leeds, Gail Johnston, Mercedes Ellington, Steven Boockvor. "Mardi Gras Waltz," "I'd Know that Smile," "Mumbo Jumbo," "We're Wanted," "When I Take My Lady," "When My Man Sails Home," "Someone I Could Love," "Come Along Down," "The Kind of a Girl (for Me)," "We're Gonna See the Voodoo Queen." Same venue, 7/8/66–9/4/66. 54 perf. light: Peggy Clark. In the cast David Atkinson, Karen Shepard, Ralph Purdum & Gail Johnston all reprised. Louis Armstrong & Guy Lombardo both appeared. Lynne Broadbent was in the chorus

1898. *Mardi Gras*. Prince of Wales, London, 3/18/76–9/18/76. Prev from 3/10/76. 212 perf. p: Bernard Delfont & Richard M. Mills; m/l: Ken Howard & Alan Blaikley; b: Melvyn Bragg; d: Clifford Williams; ch: Paddy Stone; md: Ray Cook; cast recording on EMI. Cast: Aubrey Woods, Nicky Henson, Lon Sattin, Miquel Brown, Gaye Brown, Dana Gillespie, Marsha Hunt. "Mardi Gras," "Everything About You," "From Now On," "Isn't it a Nice Sensation," "I Call the Tune," "That's That," "The Second Line," "Love Keeps No Season," "New Orleans," "Everybody's Moving," "I Can See it All," "Make Jazz," "Celandine's Blues," "When I Feel the Spirit Move Me," "The Calinda," "Love's Fool"

1899. *Marigold*. Her Majesty's, Aberdeen, Scotland, 5/4/59; toured; Savoy, London, 5/27/59; Saville, London, 7/13/59–8/1/59. Total of 77 perf. m: Charles Zwar; l/b: Alan Melville; based on romantic play by F.R. Pryor & L. Allen Harker; d: Murray MacDonald; ch: Malcolm Goddard; set: Hutchinson Scott; md: Robert Probst; cast recording on HMV. Cast: Jeremy Brett, Sally Smith, Sophie Stewart, Jean Kent, William Dickie, Aubrey Morris, Anna Dawson. "Romance at the Manse," "Love Can't Be Learned," "New Bohemian Polka," "Accord-

ing to Mr. Payton," "Always Ask Your Heart," "Princes Street," "Her Majesty's Health," "Wonderful View," "Reel," "Present Day Youth," "Fashionable Pair." This promising musical died when it had to move to the Saville

1900. *Marilyn*. Pop opera, closely modeled on *Evita*. Marilyn Monroe's life told through "Camera," her one true lover. This is not *Marilyn: An American Fable*, the Broadway musical. Adelphi, London, 3/17/83–7/30/83. Produced by Americans in London, and written by Eddie Garson. It had an interesting score, a very good first act, and a great perf by leading lady Stephanie Lawrence

1901. *The Marital Bliss of Francis & Maxine*. Dance theatre, set in NY in the Roaring 20s. Ohio Theatre, NY, 9/4/97–9/14/97. 11 perf. p: Fay Simpson Dance Theatre; m: Earl Wentz; conceived by/ch/starred: Bill Torres & Fay Simpson; d: Deborah Kampmeier

1902. *Marlene*. Revue-type play with mus, about Marlene Dietrich's 1969 farewell tour in Paris; set in her dressing room. Coliseum, Oldham, England, 10/3/96. w: Pam Gems; b: Alois Haider; conceived by: Martin Flossman. Cast: Sian Phillips, Mary Diveny, Margaret Whitton. Score included big Dietrich hits, e.g. "See What the Boys in the Back Room Will Have," "Falling in Love Again," "Lili Marlene." Moved to London, 1997, Cort, Broadway, 4/11/99–5/2/99. 15 prev from 3/30/99. 25 perf. p: Ric Wanetik & Frederick B. Vogel; d: Sean Mathias; set: John Arnone; cos: David C. Woolard; light: Mark Jonathan; sound: Peter J. Fitzgerald; md: Kevin Amos. Same cast. Tony nominations for book & Sian Phillips

1903. *The Marriage Contract*. Yiddish comedy with mus. Set in Tel-Aviv, in early 1950s. Folksbiene, 10/19/91–1/12/92. 39 perf. w: Ephraim Kishon; d: Howard Rossen

1904. *Marry Me a Little*. One-act all-sung revue with NY theme, using relatively unknown Stephen Sondheim songs written between 1954 & 1973 for Broadway but never used there. Set in Brooklyn apartment house on a Saturday night. 2 young people dream alone & finally meet. Production Company, 10/29/80 (3 months). d: Norman Rene; ch: Don Johanson. It has a cast recording. Cast: Suzanne Henry, Craig Lucas (also conceived/developed with Norman Rene). "Two Fairy Tales," "Saturday Night," "What More Do I Need?," "The Girls of Summer," "Silly People," "Uptown/Downtown," "Can That Boy Fox Trot," "All Things Bright and Beautiful," "Bang!," "Who Could Be Blue"/"Little White House," "Your Eyes Are Blue," "So Many People," "A Moment with You," "Marry Me a Little," "Pour le Sport," "It Wasn't Meant to Happen," "Happily Ever After," "There Won't Be Trumpets." Same cast played at Actors Playhouse, NY, 3/12/81–5/31/81. 96 perf. King's Head, London, 6/12/82–7/24/82. Cast: Martin Connor, Mandy Moore. York Theatre Co., 1/16/87–2/7/87. 20 perf. d: Stephen Lloyd Helper; ch: Liza Gennaro-Evans; md: Sand Lawn. Cast: Liz Callaway, John Jellison. Holy Trinity, 11/19/92–12/13/92. 19 perf. p: Triangle Theatre Co.; d: Alex Dmitriev. Revived in London, 1996. Popular in regional theatre in USA

1905. *The Marry Month of May*. One-act musical. West Bank, 4/26/88–4/30/88. 4 perf. m/l: Peter Ekstrom; b: Katharine Houghton; d: Charlotte Moore. Cast: Jerome Dempsey

1906. *Martin Guerre*. Hartford Stage Co, Conn., 1992. Pre-dates famous (non-Broadway) French prod. The 2 are unrelated. m: Roger Ames; l/b: Laura Harrington; d: Mark Lamos; ch: Liza Gennaro; light: Jennifer Tipton; md: Sue Anderson. Cast: Patrick Cassidy, Malcolm Gets, Walter Charles, Peter Samuel, Beth Fowler, Judy Kuhn, Cris Groenendaal, John Aller, Bill Badolato, Joan Susswein Barber, Kyle Craig, Peter Reardon. See also *The House of Martin Guerre* (in this appendix)

1907. *Martin Guerre*. Musical love story. Set in French village of Artigat, in 1560; Bertrande de Rols, young wife of Martin Guerre, believes him to have been killed during troubles sweeping France as rise of Protestantism challenges established Catholic religion. Having Protestant sympathies, Bertrande persuades Arnaud du Thil to take her husband's name to prevent her being married off to Catholic suitor who she despises. Prince Edward, London, 7/10/96. p: Cameron Mackintosh; m: Claude-Michel Schoenberg; l: Edward Hardy & Stephen Clarke; add l: Herbert Kretzmer & Alain Boublil; b: Alain Boublil & Claude-Michel Schoenberg; d: Declan Donnellan; set: Nick Ormerod. Cast: Julia Sutton, Jerome Pradon, Susan Jane Tanner, Martin Turner. "Working on the Land," "Where's the Child?," "Martin Guerre," "Here Comes the Morning," "Sleeping on Our Own," "When Will Someone Hear?," "Louison," "Welcome Home," "Tell Me to Go," "Bethlehem," "All I Know," "The Courtroom," "Me," "Someone," "The Impostors," "The Last Witness," "I Will Make You Proud," "The Madness," "The Reckoning," "Land of the Fathers," "Live with Somebody You Love," "Your Wedding Day," "The Deluge," "I'm Martin Guerre," "Without You as a Friend," "Death Scene," "God's Anger," "How Many Tears," "Welcome to the Land," "Don't," "The Holy Fight," "The Revelation," "The Day Has Come," "Who?," "All that I Love," "The Impostor's Here," "The Verdict," "Justice Will Be Done," "Why?," "The Killing," Kennedy Center, 12/23/99–1/16/00. See also *The House of Martin Guerre* (in this appendix)

1908. *Marty*. Huntington Theatre Co., Boston. 10/18/02–11/24/02. p: Jim Weissenbach & Waxman Williams Entertainment; m: Charles Strouse; l: Lee Adams; b: Rupert Holmes; based on 1955 film, written by Paddy Chayefsky, and starring Ernie Borgnine as homely, unassuming Bronx butcher who wins new lease of life through unexpected romance; d: Mark Brokaw; ch: Rob Ashford; set: Robert Jones; cos: Jess Goldstein; light: Mark McCullough. Cast: Marty: John C. Reilly; Also with: Barbara Andres, Jennifer Frankel, Cheryl McMahon, Anne Torsiglieri, Jim Bracchitta, Shannon Hammons, Evan Pappas, Matt Ramsey, Marilyn Pasekoff. The musical had been in development for years, Mark Brokaw directing previous readings. Jim Weissenbach acquired rights from Chayefsky estate on strength of

Jason Alexander, who was going to star (he didn't, as it turned out). For a while Robert Longbottom was going to be dir. In 2000 Rupert Holmes replaced Aaron Sorkin as librettist, and wrote entirely new book from scratch without having read Mr. Sorkin's. John C. Reilly took singing lessons for the role. Broke box-office records at the Huntington; hoped for Broadway in fall 2003 (but didn't make it). By 8/04, after a successful workshop that month, it was back on track for 2005 (the producers turned down an offer of the Barrymore, wanting a bigger Broadway theatre)

1909. *Mary Poppins.* Rehearsals began 7/19/04. Tried out at Bristol Hippodrome, England, 9/18/04–11/6/04. Prev from 9/15/04; Prince Edward, London, 12/15/04. Prev from 12/6/04. p: Cameron Mackintosh & Disney Theatricals; m/l: Robert & Richard Sherman (the songs were from the movie, but reworked); add m/l: George Stiles & Anthony Drewe; b: Julian Fellowes; d: Sir Richard Eyre; ch: Matthew Bourne; set/cos: Bob Crowley; cast album released 4/4/05, on First Night. Cast: Mary: Laura Michelle Kelly (Joanna Riding was long tipped for title role, as were Miss Kelly & Ruthie Henshall); Bert: Gavin Lee; Mr. Banks: Alex Jennings; Mrs. Banks: Janie Dee; Also with: David Haig, Linzi Hateley, Rosemary Ashe, Jenny Galloway, Julia Sutton. New songs: "Practically Perfect," "Anything Can Happen (If You Let It)." In London persons under age 3 were banned (it was too scary). It opened in London to mostly raves and to an advance ticket sale of $20 million

1910. *Masada.* A love story, set in Warsaw during WWII, when a group of actors recreated the Masada story. Los Angeles, 1998. Charity benefit concert. p: Shuki Levy, Anita Mann, Barry Brown; m: Shuki Levy; l: David Goldsmith; b: Glenn Berenbeim. Cast: Jon Voight, Rita Moreno, Davis Gaines. Tried out at the Ford Center for the Performing Arts, Chicago, for 5 weeks from 9/19/04. d: Timothy Sheader; ch: David Parsons; set: David Mitchell; cos: Ann Hould-Ward; light: Ken Billington; sound: Peter Fitzgerald; md: Edward G. Robinson; gm: Alan Wasser Assocs. Broadway ambitions for 12/04 were not realized

1911. *Masquerade.* London, 1948. m/l: George Posford & Eric Maschwitz; based on biographical play *David Garrick*, by Tom Robertson

1912. *Masquerade.* Stage/West, West Springfield, Mass., 12/7/74. 27 perf. World premiere. m/l/md: Thomas Babbitt; b/d: John Ulmer; based on Carlo Goldoni's *The Servant of Two Masters*; ch: Judith Haskell

1913. *Masquerade.* Young Vic, London, 3/5/82. 31 perf. m/l: Rod Argent; d: Frank Dunlop; adapted from story by Kit Williams

1914. *Mass.* Also known as *Leonard Bernstein's Mass.* Theatre piece for singers, players & dancers. Kennedy Center, 9/8/71 (the show was created for the opening of this theatre). m: Leonard Bernstein; texts from the liturgy of the Roman Catholic mass; English texts: Stephen Schwartz & Leonard Bernstein. Kennedy Center, 6/5/72–6/17/72. 2 prev. p: John F. Kennedy Center for the Performing Arts & Sol

Hurok; d: Gordon Davidson; ch: Alvin Ailey; set: Oliver Smith; cos: Frank Thompson; light: Gilbert V. Hemsley Jr.; sound: Richard Guy; md: Maurice Peress; cast recording on Columbia. Cast: Alan Titus & David Cryer alternated, Cheryl Barnes, Jacqueline Britt, Jane Coleman, Margaret Cowie, Ed Dixon, Lowell Harris, Lee Hooper, Larry Marshall, John Bennett Perry, Mary Bracken Phillips, Neva Small, the Alvin Ailey Dance Theatre (including Judith Jamison, Hector Mercado, Leland Schwantes), Norman Scribner Choir, Berkshire Boys' Choir. "A Simple Song," "I Don't Know," "Easy," "Gloria Tibi," "Thank You," "The Word of the Lord," "God Said," "Non Credo," "Hurry," "World without End," "I Believe in God," "Our Father," "I Go On," "Things Get Broken," "Secret Songs." Philadelphia Academy of Music, 6/19/72–6/24/72; Metropolitan Opera House, NYC, 6/28/72–7/22/72. 2 prev. 22 perf. NY reviews were not that good. For the 10th anniversary of the opening of the Kennedy Center it ran there again, 9/10/81–9/27/81

1915. *A Mass Murder in the Balcony of the Old Ritz-Rialto.* Elysian Playhouse, 11/14/75–12/21/75. 20 perf. m/l/d: Bill Vitale. Cast: Ed Kuczewski (also b), Prima Stephen, Martin Rivera (also ch), Claudia Tompkins. "Shadow Song," "Slumming," "42nd Street," "Popcorn and Piss," "Dope," "Dope Rag," "Musical Chairs," "The Old Days," "Sung-Fu," "Time to Go Home, Vernon," "Pink Lady," "The Comic," "When You're Shot in the Movies"

1916. *Mata Hari.* Very costly David Merrick anti-war failure about famous spy & French intelligence officer who hunted her down. Previously titled *Facade.* Pre-Broadway tryouts opened chaotically on 11/18/67, at the National, Washington, DC, and closed there 12/9/67, canceling its scheduled, next, Philadelphia opening, and its 1/13/68 Broadway opening at the Alvin. m/l: Edward Thomas & Martin Charnin; b: Jerome Coopersmith; d: Vincente Minnelli; ch: Jack Cole; set/light: Jo Mielziner; cos: Irene Sharaff; md: Colin Romoff; orch: Robert Russell Bennett. Cast: Marisa Mell, Pernell Roberts, Jack Holmes, Martha Schlamme, W.B. Brydon, Mark Dempsey, George Marcy, Nadine Lewis, Blythe Danner, Dominic Chianese, Reiko Sato, Paul Glaser, Altovise Gore. "Is this Fact?," "Everyone Has Something to Hide," "How Young You Were Tonight," "I'm Saving Myself for a Soldier," "Maman," "The Choice is Yours," "Sextet," "Not Now, Not Here," "Hello, Yank!," "In Madrid," "I Don't See Him Very Much Any More," "You Have No Idea," "The Arrest," "Interrogation and Ballet," "There Is No You," "There Will Be Love Again." Theatre de Lys, 12/11/68–12/15/68. 7 perf. Now known as *Ballad for a Firing Squad.* p: Edward Thomas; d: Martin Charnin; cos: Theoni V. Aldredge. Several of the same songs. Cast: Renata Vaselle, James Hurst, Liz Sheridan, Dominic Chianese, George Marcy, Neva Small. A revised version of *Mata Hari* was prod by the York Theatre Co., at St. Peter's, 1/25/96–2/4/96. 13 prev from 1/12. 12 perf. Part of *Musicals in Mufti* series. d: Martin Charnin; ch:

Michele Assaf; set: James Morgan; light: Mary Jo Dondlinger. Cast: Jack Fletcher, Marguerite MacIntyre, Robin Skye, Judith Thiergaard, Julia K. Murney

1917. *Matador.* Queen's, London, 4/16/91. m/l: Mike Leander & Edward Seago; b: Peter Lukes; cast recording on Epic. Cast: Tom Jones, Robert Powell, John Barr. "There's No Way Out of Here," "To Be a Matador," "I Was Born to Be Me," "Only Other People," "Manolete! Belmonte! Joselito!," "A Boy from Nowhere," "Wake Up, Madrid," "I'll Take You Out to Dinner," "This Incredible Journey," "Don't Be Deceived," "I'll Dress You in Mourning," "Dance with Death," "A Panama Hat"

1918. *The Match Girls.* Factory workers strike at Bryant & May match company. Leatherhead Theatre Club, England, 11/23/65 (2 weeks). m: Tony Russell; l/b: Bill Owen; d/ch: Gillian Lynne; md: Ian MacPherson. Cast: Vivienne Martin, Julia Sutton, Sonia Fox, Cheryl Kennedy, Olivia Breeze, Eric Flynn, David Henderson-Tait, Ray Davis. Globe, London, 3/1/65–6/11/65. 119 perf. p: Geoffrey Russell & Bernard Delfont; cast recording on AEI. Same basic crew. Same cast except that Prunella Ransome took over from Sonia Fox, Marion Grimaldi from Anna Barry, Gerard Hely from Eric Flynn, Kim Grant from David Henderson-Tait. "Phosphorous," "Look at That Hat," "Look Around Me," "Men," "Something About You," "My Dear Lady," "We're Gonna Show 'em," "Cockney Sparrers," "Life of Mine," "I Long to See the Day," "Comes a Time," "Waiting"

1919. *A Match Made in Heaven.* Set in miller's yard in 1910. Town Hall, 10/30/85–12/29/85. 6 prev. 54 perf. p: Yiddish Musical Theatre of New York; orig m/b: Jack Rechtzeit; new l: I. Alper; English translation: David Ellin; mus arr: Alexander Lustig; d: Yankele Alperin; ch: Derek Wolshonak. Cast: Monica Tesler, Eleanor Reissa, Yankele Alperin, Reizl Bozyk, David Ellin, Dean Badolato

1920. *The Matinee Kids.* BTA, 3/10/81–3/20/81. 9 prev. 15 perf. m: Brian Lasser; l: Garry Bormet, Gary Gardner, Brian Lasser; b: Garry Bormet & Gary Gardner; conceived by/d: Garry Bormet & Brian Lasser; ch: Carol Marik; set: Nancy Winters. Cast: Karen Mason, Liz Callaway. "Lucky Love," "Just to Look at Him," "A Couple of Years from Now," "Footprints," "Hi!," "Lucky Baby," "Hold Me," "First to Walk Away"

1921. *A Matter of Opinion.* Trial of realists vs fantasists, with rhymed dialogue. Players, 9/30/80–10/5/80. 2 prev. 8 perf. m: Harold Danko & John Jacobson; l/b: Mary Elizabeth Hauer; d/ch: Shari Upbin; ms: Harold Danko; md: John Jacobson. Cast: Andy Bey, Suzanne Smart, Janet Bliss. "Not Every Day Can Be a Day of Shine," "No Thank You from a Mocking Sun," "The Average Man," "Free Time," "Hobo's Song," "Gotta Pretend," "The Sandman," "Just the Facts," "I Am Here," "Matter of Opinion," "Hooray for the Judge"

1922. *A Matter of Time.* The New Year refuses to come in one year. Set on 12/31/75. Playhouse, 4/27/75. 1 perf. m/l: Philip F. Margo; d/ch: Tod Jackson; light: Martin Aronstein; sound: Jack Shearing; md: Arnold Gross. Cast: David-James Carroll, Glory Van Scott, Joe Masiell, Carol Estey, Joyce Nolen, Leland Schwantes, Ronnie De Marco, Elliot Lawrence, Miriam Welch, Jane Robertson. "Me God, Please God," "It's Not Easy Being Next," "Snake," "If This Were My World," "A Matter of Time," "This Moment," "Don't Let Me Bother You," "Sex is a Spectator Sport," "I Can Give You Music," "This is Your Year 1976," "The Devil in Your Eyes," "I Am the Next"

1923. *Maybe I'm Doing It Wrong*. Also called *Randy Newman's Maybe I'm Doing it Wrong*. Production Company, 3/22/81–4/13/81. 3 prev. 17 perf. m/l: Randy Newman; conceived by/d: Joan Micklin Silver. Cast: Deborah Rush, Mark Linn-Baker, Patti Perkins, Treat Williams. "My Old Kentucky Home," "Birmingham," "Political Science," "Jolly Coppers on Parade," "Caroline," "Maybe I'm Doing it Wrong," "Simon Smith and the Amazing Dancing Bear," "Debutante's Ball," "Love Story," "Tickle Me," "It's Money that I Love," "God's Song (That's Why I Love Mankind)," "Sail Away," "Yellow Man," "Rider in the Rain," "Rollin'," "You Can leave Your Hat On," "Old Man," "Davy the Fat Boy," "Marie," "Short People," "I'll Be Home." See *The Middle Of Nowhere*, in this appendix

1924. *Maybe That's Your Problem*. Roundhouse, London, 6/16/71–7/3/71. 18 perf. m: Walter Scharf; l: Don Black; b: Lionel Chetwynd; d: Ted Miller; ch: Virginia Mason; md: Gordon Rose. Cast: Elaine Paige, Harold Kasket, Al Mancini

1925. *Mayor*. Musical revue. Top of the Gate, 5/13/85–10/21/85. 15 prev. 183 perf. p: Martin Richards, Jerry Kravat, Mary Lea Johnson with the New York Music Company/Sid Bernstein; m/l: Charles Strouse; b: Warren Leight; based on book *Mayor*, by Edward I. Koch, former Mayor of NYC; d: Jeffrey B. Moss; ch: Barbara Siman; set/cos: Randy Barcelo; md: Michael Kosarin; orch: Christopher Bankey; cast recording by New York Music Co. Cast: The Mayor: Lenny Wolpe; Also with: Douglas Bernstein, Marion J. Caffey, Nancy Giles, Ken Jennings, Ilene Kristen, Kathryn McAteer, Keith Curran. Susan Cella (understudy). "Mayor," "You Can Be a New Yorker Too!," "You're Not the Mayor," "March of the Yuppies," "Hootspa," "Isn't it Time for the People," "What You See is What You Get," "I Want To Be the Mayor," "The Last 'I Love New York' Song," "Good Times," "We Are One," "How'm I Doin'?," "My City." Latin Quarter, 10/23/85–1/5/86. 70 perf. Various musical numbers & sketches were added: "Critics," "Alternate Side," "Coalition," "Testimonial Dinner." "Ballad" was originally between "In the Park" & "On the Telephone." Keith Curran was replaced by *John Sloman* for this run. During run Lenny Wolpe was replaced by *Scott Robertson*, and *John Sloman* stood in for Ken Jennings during illness

1926. *Me, Myself and I*. Orange Tree, Richmond, Surrey, England, 12/10/82–12/18/82; and 12/29/82–1/29/83. m: Paul Todd; l/b: Alan Ayckbourn; d: Kim Grant; md: Chris Tingley.

Cast: Rosemary Williams, Jill Martin. Originally produced as 3 one-act pieces in 1981

1927. *The Medium & the Telephone*. Gian-Carlo Menotti was commissioned by Columbia University to write one-act chamber work *The Medium*. Madame Flora (known as Baba), lives with teenage daughter Monica and mute assistant, Toby. The trio con mourning parents into believing Flora can contact dead children. At one séance, in her parlor, Flora feels a hand on her throat and thinks it's Toby. She fires him, and when he returns she thinks he is a ghost & shoots him. Premiered 5/8/46 at Columbia's Brander Matthews Theatre. d: Gian-Carlo Menotti; set: Oliver Smith. Cast: Flora: Claramae Turner; Monica: Evelyn Keller; Toby: Leo Coleman. Producers Efrem Zimbalist Jr. & Chandler Cowles wanted to get it onto Broadway, as part of the Ballet Society's one-act opera season, but in order to do this Gian-Carlo Menotti had to write a curtain raiser, which he did, calling it *The Telephone* (subtitled *L'amour a trois*), a 22-minute comic opera telling the story of Lucy (played by Marilyn Cotlow), who is so obsessed by the phone that Ben, her suitor (played by Frank Rogier) is forced to call her on his rival, the telephone, to propose. The double bill opened OB at the Hecksher on 2/18/47, with orig cast of *The Medium* intact, except that Marie Powers (alternating with Mary Davenport) was now Flora. The double bill moved to Broadway's Ethel Barrymore, 5/1/47–11/1/47. 211 perf. p: Chandler Cowles & Efrem Zimbalist Jr. and Edith Lutyens; d: Gian-Carlo Menotti; light: Jean Rosenthal; md: Emanuel Balaban. Musical number (in *The Medium*): "The Black Swan." Horace Armistead won a Tony for sets. Aldwych, London, 4/29/48–5/22/48. 26 perf. With Broadway cast. City Center, 12/7/48–1/1/49. 40 perf. d: Gian-Carlo Menotti; set/cos: Horace Armistead; light: Jean Rosenthal; md: Emanuel Balaban. Cast of *The Telephone*: Maria D'Attili & Paul King. Cast of *The Medium*: Flora: Marie Powers & Margery Mayer; Monica: Evelyn Keller & Derna de Lys; Toby: Leo Coleman; Mr. Gobineau: Paul King; Mrs. Nolan: Virginia Beeler; Mrs. Gobineau: Derna de Lys & Maria D'Attili. Arena Theatre, in the Edison Hotel, 7/19/50–10/14/50. 102 perf. 3rd in series of 4 revivals (also including *The Show-Off*, *Julius Caesar* and *Arms and the Man*). Broadway's 1st experience with theatre-in-the-round or arena theatre. d: Gian-Carlo Menotti. Cast of *The Medium*: Toby: Leo Coleman; Flora: Zelma George; Monica: Evelyn Keller (Derna de Lys in matinees). Edith Gordon & Paul King starred in *The Telephone*. *The Medium* was filmed in 1951, with Marie Powers, Leo Coleman, Anna Maria Alberghetti. *The Telephone* ran at Sadlers Wells, in London, in 1959. Cast: Frederick Sharp, June Bronhill

1928. *Medium Rare*. Big hit revue. Happy Medium, Chicago, 6/29/60–6/9/62. 1,210 perf. Score: Cy Coleman & Carolyn Leigh, Jerry Bock & Sheldon Harnick, Charles Strouse & Lee Adams; d: Bill Penn. Cast: Jerry Stiller (*Bob Dishy, Marc London*), Jean Arnold (*Ann Mitchell*), Anne Meara (*Diane Ladd, Cindy Whitsell*). "The Tempo of the Times" (by Coleman & Leigh)

1929. *Meeow!!* A mad musical meringue. Cabaret Theatre, 3/2/71–4/2/71. 48 perf. Adapted by A. Devon; from Lewis Carroll's stories. Cast: MacIntyre Dixon (also d), Jay Bonnell, Howard Girven

1930. *Meet Me in Victoria*. Opera House, Blackpool, England, 3/6/44; toured; Victoria Palace, London, 4/8/44–7/8/44 (117 perf); re-ran there 10/14/44–1/27/45 (134 perf). m: Noel Gay; l: Frank Eyton; b: Lupino Lane & Lauri Wylie; from story by H.F. Maltby; add dial: Ted Kavanagh; d: Lupino Lane; ch: Max Rivers; md: Mantovani. Cast: Lupino Lane, Wallace Lupino, Lauri Lupino Lane

1931. *Meet the People*. Small edition of fast-moving tropical revue of same name that ran on Broadway in 1940 (starring Nanette Fabray & Peggy Ryan). Café Theatre of the Hotel Paramount, 1955. m/l: Jay Gorney, Henry Meyers, Edward Eliscu. Cast: Mickey Calin, Janet Gaylord. "You and Your Broken Heart!"

1932. *Meg and Mog Show*. Arts Theatre, London, 12/10/81. m/l/b: David Wood; based on books by Helen Nicoll & Jan Pienkowski; d: Tony Wreddon & David Wood; ch: Pamela Power; set/cos: Jan Pienkowski & Vikie Le Sache; md: Peter Pontzen. Cast: Meg: Maureen Lipman; Mog: Vincent Osborne; Also with: Pamela Power, Tim Bannerman. Same venue, from 4/83. d: David Wood; ch: Sue Weston; md: Peter Pontzen. Same basic cast, except Meg: Amanda Barrie

1933. *The Megilla of Itzik Manger*. Set in present, in small town in Eastern Europe; adaptation of Book of Esther. Partly in Yiddish. John Golden, Broadway, 10/9/68–12/15/68. 2 prev. 78 perf. p: Zvi Kolitz, Solomon Sagall, Alice Peerce; m: Dov Seltzer; l/b: Shmuel Bunim, Hayim Hefer, Itzik Manger, Dov Seltzer; English commentaries: Joe Darion; d: Shmuel Bunim; light: Eldon Elder; md: Max Meth. Cast: Mike Burstein, Pesach Burstein, Lillian Lux, Susan Walters (*Evelyn Kingsley* for the re-opening), Zisha Gold, Ariel Furman. "The Tailor's Megilla," "Song of the Walnut Tree," "Fly Little Bird," "A Mother's Tears," "Lechaim." Previously ran in Jaffa & Tel-Aviv. Longacre, 4/19/69–4/26/69. 12 perf. *Evelyn Kingsley* replaced Susan Walters; *Abba Bogin* replaced Max Meth as md

1934. *Memphis Store-Bought Teeth*. Traveler returns home & helps re-enact amorous incident that took place 15 years earlier. Orpheum, 12/29/71. 1 perf. p/l/b: D. Brian Wallach; m: E. Don Alldredge; d: Marvin Gordon; md: Rene Wiegert. Cast: Jerry Lanning, J.J. Jepson, Alice Cannon, Travis Hudson. "Quiet Place," "It's Been a Hard Life," "Where Have I Been?," "The Lord Bless and Keep You," "Fanny Dear," "My Final Fling," "When I Leave," "That's What a Friend is For," "Nothing Seems the Same," "Something You Really Want," "Nicest Part of Me," "Something to Hold on To"

1935. *Men Women and Why It Won't Work*. Set in city & suburbs. Mama Gail's, 10/22/75–11/8/75. 12 perf. m/l: David Warrack & June Siegel; b: June Siegel & Miriam Fond; d/ch: Miriam Fond; md: John R. Williams; cos: Danny Morgan. Cast: Ann Hodapp, Gail

Oscar, Garrett M. Brown, Leila Holliday, Arne Gundersen, Charles Maggiore, Barbara Lea. "What Do We Do?," "Temporary Woman Blues," "Let's Spend an Hour," "It's Great to Be Single Again," "Morris," "Lonely Woman," "It's Love! So What?," "Best of Both Possible Worlds," "Take Me—Find Me"

1936. *Menopause, the Musical*. Hot-flashy musical. Group of women in Bloomingdales talk about ups & downs of middle age. 28 revised tunes from 1960s & 70s. Orlando, Fla., 3/28/01. p: Mark Schwartz & Jeanie Linders; b: Jeanie Linders; d: Kathleen Lindsay. A hit. Moved to West Palm Beach, then to NY, first to Theatre Four, 4/4/02–9/22/02. Prev from 3/5/02. Then to Playhouse 91, from 9/27/02. d: Kathleen Lindsay; ch: Patty Bender; set: Jesse Poleschuck; cos: Martha Bromelmeier; light: Michael Gilliam; sound: Johanna Doty; md: Corinne Aquilina. Cast: Lynn Eldredge, Joy Lynn Matthews, Carolann Page, Sally Ann Swarm. On 8/3/04 it played its 1,000th perf. Coronet, West Hollywood, Calif. 10/30/03. p: TOC Prods & Entertainment Events; d/ch: Patty Bender; mus & voc arr: C.T. Hollis. Cast: Michele Mais, Myra McWethy, Rende Rae Norman, Lisa Robinson

1937. *The Mermaid Wakes*. Set in the Caribbean. Triplex, 2/9/91–3/3/91. 3 prev. 14 perf. mus by: the performers: Judy Bennett, Barington Antonio Burke-Green (also co-ch), Natalie Carter, Percy Pitzu, Silindile Sokutu (also co-ch); m/d: Elizabeth Swados; based on book by Lora Berg

1938. *Mermaids*. Hartley House, 4/2/88–5/8/88. 20 perf. p: On Stage Prods; m/l: Robert J. Gardner & Terry Bovin; b: Robert J. Gardner & Monica Hayes; d: Monica Hayes; based on Hans Christian Andersen's *The Little Mermaid*; ch: Rhonda Hayes; cos/puppets: Robert J. Gardner; md: Terry Bovin. Cast: Kimberly Campbell, Catherine Dyer, Kathleen R. Delaney, Dennis Figueroa, Carol Cornicelli. "Mermaid Jubilee," "Someday," "Prince's Jubilee," "Sailor Boy," "So Unaware," "Seahorse Song," "Briny Bubbles," "Dark and Briny Ocean," "Are You Willing?," "Mysterious Maiden," "Diddle Dee"

1939. *The Merry Gentleman*. Christmas entertainment. Tale of an Edwardian Christmas. Theatre Royal, Bristol, England, 12/24/53. p: Bristol Old Vic Co.; m/md: Julian Slade; l/b: Dorothy Reynolds & Julian Slade; d: Lionel Harris; ch: Elizabeth West. Cast: Dorothy Reynolds, Pat Heywood, Bob Harris, Alan Dobie, Barbara Leigh Hunt, Gillian Lewis, Patricia Routledge, Patrick Horgan, Joan Plowright, Donald Harron, Jane Wenham, James Cairncross, Norman Rossington. Revised & ran at Little Theatre, Bristol, 12/23/70 (8 weeks). Everyman, Cheltenham, 12/15/79–1/12/80. d: John David. Cast: Jeremy Irons, Sally Adcock. Theatre Royal, Bristol, 12/23/83–2/4/84. d: John David. Cast: June Barrie

1940. *Meshuggah-Nuns!* One of the many sequels to *Nunsense*. 4 of the Little Sisters of Hoboken from the orig—Sisters Mary Hubert, Robert Anne, Mary Amnesia, and Mother Superior, are on board S.S. *Delicious*, the "apple

of the Eden line." When the troupe playing *Fiddler on the Roof* falls sick, the nuns do a revue. Chanhassen Dinner Theatre's Fireside Theatre, Minneapolis, 9/19/02. Prev from 9/6/02. m/l/b/d: Dan Goggin. "Say it in Yiddish," "My Fat is My Fortune," "If I Were Catholic." Helen Hayes Theatre, Nyack, NY, 1/31/04–2/15/04. Cast: Rachel Cohen, Carolyn Droscoski, Bonnie Lee, Jeanne Tinker, Michael J. Farina.

1941. *Metropolis*. Piccadilly, London, 3/8/89–9/2/89. m: Joseph Brooks; l/b: Dusty Hughes & Joseph Brooks; add material: David Firman. Cast: Judy Kuhn, Graham Bickley, Megan Kelly, Jonathan Adams, Brian Blessed, Lucy Dixon. "Hold Back the Night," "The Machines Are Beautiful," "Children of Metropolis," "One More Morning," "It's Only Love," "Bring on the Night," "You Are the Light," "The Sun," "There's a Girl Down Below," "This is Life," "Listen to Me," "Haven't You Finished with Me?," "Let's Watch the World Go to the Devil," "Metropolis"

1942. *Miami*. Musical in progress. Set in Miami in 1950s. Playwrights Horizons, 1/1/86–2/2/86. 39 workshop perf. m/l: Jack Feldman & Bruce Sussman; b: Wendy Wasserstein; d: Gerald Gutierrez; ch: Larry Hyman; set: Heidi Landesman; cos: Ann Hould-Ward; light: Richard Nelson; md: David Bishop. Cast: Royana Black, Phyllis Newman, Stephen Pearlman, Marcia Lewis, Chevi Colton, Bill Badolato, John Cunningham, Jane Krakowski, Joanna Glushak

1943. *Miami Beach Monsters*. Set in Florida & Hollywood. Triad, 10/23/99–2/12/00. Involved in the creation were: Helen Butleroff, Georgia Bogardus Holof, Robert Leahy, George Robert Minkoff, Ellen M. Schwartz, Carol Spero, Dan Berkowitz, Michael Brown, Dick Gallagher, David Mettee, Steven Silverstein, David Strickland. d/ch: Helen Butleroff; md: David Strickland. Cast: Steve Elmore, Diane J. Findlay, Laurie Gamache, Craig Mason, Richard Rowan, Jimmy Spadola

1944. *The Middle of Nowhere*. Set in bus depot in Louisiana in 1969. Stranded travelers fantasize musical revue with Randy Newman songs. Astor Place, 11/20/88–12/11/88. Prev from 11/17/88. 24 perf. w/conceived by/d/ch: Tracy Friedman; set: Loren Sherman; md: Jonny Bowden. Cast: Roger Robinson, Vondie Curtis-Hall, Michael Arkin, Diana Castle, Tony Hoylen. "I Think it's Going to Rain Today," "Simon Smith," "Yellow Man," "Davy the Fat Boy," "Lonely at the Top," "Lovers Prayer," "Old Kentucky Home," "Tickle Me," "Maybe I'm Doing it Wrong," "They Just Got Married," "Short People," "Song for the Dead," "Baltimore," "I'm Different," "It's Money that I Love," "Sigmund Freud's Impersonation," "You Can Leave Your Hat On," "Old Man," "Sail Away," "Marie," "Rednecks," "Mr. President," "Louisiana 1927." See *Maybe I'm Doing It Wrong*, in this appendix

1945. *Mighty Fine Music*. Revue of songs of Burton Lane. T.O.M.I., 1983. w/d: Brent Wagner. Cast: Burton Lane, David Lowenstein, Lisa Merrill McCord, Douglas Tompos

1946. *Mike*. Story of Mike Todd. Walnut Street, Philadelphia, 3/26/88. m: Mitch Leigh; l: Lee Adams; b: Thomas Meehan; d: Sue Lawless; ch: Tony Stevens; set: Kenneth Foy; cos: Waldo Angelo; light: Ken Billington. Cast: Mike: Michael Lembeck; Also with: Robert Morse, Loni Ackerman, Bob Amaral, Colleen Dunn, Leslie Easterbrook, Robert Fitch, Patrick Hamilton, K. Craig Innes, Eddie Korbich, Alex Kramarevsky, Sal Mistretta, K.K. Preece, Mimi Quillin

1947. *A Millionaire in Trouble*. Yiddish. Town Hall, 1/16/80–3/2/80. 55 perf. m/l: Alexander Lustig & Yankele Alperin; d: Yankele Alperin; ch: Felix Fibich; md: Renee Solomon. Cast: Chaim Levin, Diane Cypkin, Raquel Yossifon, Solo Moise. "Promises and Love," "How Do You Do," "A Happy Life," "Many Trades," "Mazel Tov," "Hard to Be a Pauper"

1948. *Ministry of Progress*. An ordinary man does an extraordinary thing. Play with mus. Jane Street, 3/4/04–3/28/04. Prev from 2/17/04. p: Terry Schnuck; 7 different composers did orig score; d: Kim Hughes. Cast: Jason Scott Campbell, Jennifer McCabe. In 1991 Kim Hughes was handed a 15-page one-act play by Wm. Charlie Morrow, that had been on radio on Thanksgiving Day, 1987, on WBAI out of NYC, and she developed it from that. A 40-min version was successfully produced

1949. *Mirette*. Little girl in Paris in 1890s helps mother run boarding house for actors, and inspired by the Great Bellini, she dreams of being tight-rope walker. She also helps him overcome fear that drove him from the high wire. Goodspeed, 8/1/96. m: Harvey Schmidt; l: Tom Jones; b: Elizabeth Diggs; based on children's book *Mirette on the High Wire*, by Emily Arnold McCully; d: Drew Scott Harris; ch: Janet Watson; set: James Morgan; cos: Suzy Benzinger; md/voc arr: Gary Adler. Cast: Kelly Mady, Marsha Bagwell, Kelley Swaim, Steve Barton, Gerry Vichi. "Madame Gateau's Colorful Hotel," "I Like it Here," "Someone in the Mirror," "Irkutsk," "Practicing," "Learning Who You Are," "Keep Your Feet Upon the Ground," "If You Choose to Walk Upon the Wire," "The Great Bellini," "Sometimes You Just Need Someone," "Madame Gateau's Desolate Hotel." Same venue, 7/1/98–9/18/98. d: Andre Ernotte; ch: Janet Watson; set: Neil Patel; cos: Suzy Benzinger; md: Michael O'Flaherty; voc arr: Gary Adler. Cast: Cassandra Kubinski, Marsha Bagwell, Steve Pudenz, Michael Hayward-Jones, Bob Freschi. "Sitting on the Edge," "Madame Gateau's Colorful Hotel," "Maybe," "Someone in the Mirror," "Irkutsk," "Practicing," "Learning Who You Are," "Juggling," "The Show Goes On," "Feet Upon the Ground," "Clouk & Claire," "If You Choose to Walk Upon the Wire," "She isn't You," "The Great God Pan," "The Great Bellini," "Sometimes You Just Need Someone," "Madame Gateau's Desolate Hotel," "All of a Sudden." See also *The Show Goes On* (in this appendix)

1950. *The Misanthrope*. Comedy with mus. Anspacher, 10/4/77–11/27/77. 62 perf. m/l: Jobriath Boone, Margaret Pine, Arthur Bienstock; based on Moliere's play, as translated by Richard Wilbur; d: Bill Gile; cos: Carrie F. Robbins; md: Allen Shawn; orch: Robert Rodgers & Bill Brohn. Cast: Seth Allen, John Bottoms, Helen Gallagher, John McMartin, Josh Mostel, William Parry, Virginia Vestoff. "Symphonie," "Be Witness to My Madness," "Paris," "Double," "He Loves to Make a Fuss," "Madam," "The Other Day I Went to an Affair," "Second Best," "I Love You More," "Altogether Too Outrageous," "How Dare You?" "I Confess"

1951. *Mis-Guided Tour*. Revue. Downtown Theatre, 10/12/59–11/28/59. 56 perf. p/w/d: James Allen Reid; md: Margaret Foster. Cast: Leo Bloom, Michael Fesco, Ruth Buzzi, Maureen McNalley, Jean Sincere

1952. *Miss Emily Adam*. Theatre Marquee, 3/29/60–4/16/60. 21 perf. m/l: Sol Berkowitz & James Lipton; based on orig story *Rosemary and the Planet*, by Winthrop Palmer. Cast: Cherry Davis, Bob Fitch. "Home," "Storm Ballet," "All Aboard," "It's Positively You," "Once Upon a Time," "Talk to Me," "Love Is," "Fun," "Dear Old Friend," "I, Your Valentine," "At the Ball"

1953. *Miss Moffat*. Unsuccessful Broadway tryout at the Shubert, Philadelphia, 10/7/74–10/17/74. p: Eugene V. Wolsk, Joshua Logan, Slade Brown; m/l: Albert Hague & Emlyn Williams; b: Josh Logan & Emlyn Williams; based on *The Corn is Green*, by Emlyn Williams but relocated from Wales to American South of early 20th century (this play was done straight in 1940, and filmed in 1946, with Bette Davis); d: Josh Logan; ch: Donald Saddler; set/light: Jo Mielziner; cos: Robert Mackintosh; md: Jay Blackton. The lead role was turned down by Mary Martin & Katharine Hepburn before Miss Davis took it (her only book musical). Others in cast: Dody Goodman, David Sabin, Marion Ramsey, Avon Long, Lee Goodman, Anne Francine, Gil Robbins, Dorian Harewood, Giancarlo Esposito. "A Wonderful Game," "Pray for the Snow," "Here in the South," "Tomorrow," "There's More to a Man than His Head," "Time's a-Flyin'," "You Don't Need a Nail File in a Cornfield," "The Words Unspoken," "Peekaboo, Jehovah," "Go, Go, Morgan," "I Can Talk Now," "If I Weren't Me," "What Could Be Fairer than That?," "The Debt I Owe," "I Shall Experience it Again." Scheduled for 44-week cross-country tour to end on Broadway in fall 1975. The Baltimore premiere (it was due to run there 9/9/74–9/21/74) was canceled because Miss Davis was limping around in pain during rehearsals, and was hospitalized in late 8/74. It finally opened in Philly, but Miss Davis couldn't continue after 15 perf. The show cost half a million, but the producers had insured against Miss Davis doing something like this. Indianapolis Civic Theatre, 1/83 (2 weeks). p: Josh Logan. Starred Ginger Rogers with mostly non-Equity cast

1954. *Miss Truth*. Apollo, 6/5/79–6/17/79. 16 perf. d/ch: Louis Johnson. Cast: Glory Van Scott (also w), Loretta Abbott, Loretta Devine. "Disco," "Miss Truth," "Children Are for Loving," "I Sing the Rainbow," "Self-Made Woman," "My Religion," "Do Your Thing,"

Miss Truth," "Shame," "This is a Very Special Day," "Freedom Diet," "Lift Every Voice and Sing"

1955. *Miss Waters to You*. Life & travels of Ethel Waters from 1917 to 1960. AMAS, 2/24/82–3/20/82. 17 perf. mus from Miss Waters' repertoire; b: Loften Mitchell; based on concept by Rosetta Le Noire; d: Billie Allen; ch: Keith Rozie; set: Tom Barnes; light: Gregg Marriner; md/arr/special material: Luther Henderson. Cast: Mary Louise, Luther Henderson, Jeff Bates, Yolanda Graves, Lee Winston, Leon Summers Jr., Melodee Savage, Denise Morgan, Ronald Mann

1956. *Missionaries*. Sung-through musical (i.e. no spoken libretto). About nuns murdered in El Salvador in 1980. Brooklyn Academy of Music/Majestic, 11/4/97–11/8/97. 5 perf. p: BAM/NY Stage & Film Company, Ron Kastner; m/conceived by/d: Elizabeth Swados; ch: Kay Voyce; light: Beverly Emmons. Cast: Josie de Guzman

1957. *Mister Venus*. Opera House, Manchester, England, 9/29/58; then Liverpool; Prince of Wales, London, 10/23/58–11/8/58. 16 perf. m: Trevor H. Stanford & Norman Newell; l: Norman Newell; b: Ray Galton & Johnny Speight; d: Charles Reading; ch: Paddy Stone & Irving Davies; md: Bob Lowe. Cast: Frankie Howerd, Anton Diffring, Judy Bruce, Amelia Bayntun (*Myra de Groot*), June Grant, Alexander Dore, C. Denier Warren, Gavin Gordon, Vincent Charles, Aidan Turner, Bill Owen

1958. *The Mitford Girls*. Globe, London, 10/8/81–1/9/82. m: Peter Greenwell; l: various authors; b: Caryl Brahms & Ned Sherrin; cast recording on Philips. Cast: Gay Soper, Julia Sutton, Patricia Michael, Lucy Fenwick, Patricia Hodge, Colette Gleason, Oz Clarke. "Thanks for the Memory," "Ukulele Lady," "Imagination," "Other People's Babies," "Let's Do It," "Why Do People Fall in Love?," "Why Fall for Love?," "The Controversial," "I'll Fall in Love," "Think of Being Rich," "Find Your Partner and Dance," "Children of the Ritz," "Why Love?," "Strange Forces," "I Danced with a Man," "Travelling Light," "Gangway," "September Song"

1959. *Mixed Doubles*. A Rod Warren cabaret revue. Upstairs at the Downstairs, 10/19/66–7/1/67. 428 perf. m/l: Rod Warren, etc; d/ch: Robert Audy. Cast: Madeline Kahn, Robert Rovin, Janie Sell. "Mixed Doubles," "Walter Kerr," "Sartor Sartoris," "Bon Voyeur," "Ronald Reagan," "Physical Fitness," "In Old Chicago," "Bobby the K," "Best Wishes"

1960. *Moby Dick*. Paul Mazur, 2/12/86–3/1/86. 16 perf. p: York Theatre Co.; m/md: Doug Katsaros; b: Mark St. Germain; based on Herman Melville's novel; d: Thomas Gardner; light: Mary Jo Dondlinger. Cast: Ed Dixon, Dennis Parlato, Steven Blanchard. "The Sea," "The Sermon," "What Makes Ye Go a-Whaling?," "Morning to Ye," "Ahab," "After Ye/Setting Sail," "The Doubloon," "Eight Bells," "Stand by Me," "The Whiteness," "Every Morning," "The Will," "First Hunt," "White Whale," "Ahab and the Carpenter," "My Boy," "I Will Stay with You," "Mild Day," "Final Chase"

1961. *Moby Dick*. Piccadilly, London, 3/17/92. m: Hereward Kaye & Robert Longden; l/b: Robert Longden; add l: Hereward Kaye; based on Herman Melville's novel. Cast: Leigh McDonald, Dawn Spence, Mark White, Jackie Crawford. "Parents Day," "In Old Nantucket," "Ahab's Curse," "Love Will Always," "Punish Us," "People Build Walls," "Pequod," "At Sea One Day," "Building America," "Living Shadows," "Mr. Starbuck," "Heave Away," "Can't Keep Out the Night," "A Whale of a Tale," "Daily Massacre," "Ship Ahoy!," "Shadows of the Deep," "Storm," "The Whale's Revenge," "Save the Whale"

1962. *Mod Donna*. Space age musical soap. Bored married couple's sexual adventures with another couple. Public, 4/24/70–6/7/70. 56 perf. Part of the NY Shakespeare Festival's indoor schedule of 3 programs (others: *Stomp & Sambo*). m/l: Susan Hulsman Bingham & Myrna Lamb; d: Joseph Papp; light: Martin Aronstein; md: Dorothea Freitag. Cast: April Shawhan, June Gable, Liz Gorrill. "Trapped," "Earthworms," "All the Way Down," "Liberia," "The Morning After," "Food is Love," "Earth Dance," "Take a Knife," "Now!," "We Are the Whores"

1963. *Moll Flanders*. Lyric, Hammersmith, London, 4/23/93. m/l: George Stiles & Paul Leigh; b: Claire Luckham; cast recording on First Night. Cast: Clare Burt, Angela Richards, Issy Van Randwyck, Darryl Knock, Peter Woodward. "Let Us Tell a Tale," "Moll's Prayer," "The Seduction," "Her Love Made Her Rich," "Life of a Sailor," "Lapdogs," "Sailing to Virginia," "Never Look Back," "Mr. Honest," "Fits and Starts," "The Hour is Late," "Damn, Damn, Damn!," "I Shall Work Alone," "Hang, Hang, Hang!," "Child of Newgate," "The Love Birds Fly." Not to be confused with a musical of the same name, that did not play in London, with m/l by Iwan Williams, and with book by Michael Rudman, that ran at Nottingham Playhouse for a season from 6/22/66. Maggie Jordan played Moll in that one, and Donald Sumpter played a Fop. Ronald Magill & John Neville dir

1964. *The Molly Maguires*. Community of Irish coalminers in Pennsylvania in 1877 is infiltrated by Pinkerton man. BMI Lehman Engel Musical Theatre Workshop, 1990. m/l: Sid Cherry; b: William Strzempek. Many subsequent readings & workshops. In 10/92 a full-length version was presented in series of staged readings for 2 weeks at Playwrights Horizons, culminating in 4 public perfs. World premiere at Media Theatre for the Performing Arts, Media, Pa., 9/8/96–10/6/96. Workshop, 5/3/99–6/10/99. p: Bill Haber & Kathleen Raitt; d: Dan Foster; ch: Joey McKneely. Cast: Ciaran Sheehan, Jane Bodle, John Jellison, Robert Du Sold, Rich Hebert, Karen Murphy, Ken Jennings, Martin Moran, Christopher Innvar. "The Molly Maguires," "This One Chance," "Passin' Through," "Down, Down," "Whose Turn Now?"/"Wedding Dance," "Take Another Look," "Father, Tell Me," "Thankin' Franklin Gowen," "Do You Trust Him?," "Brothers," "One More Ton," "Watching and Waiting," "An Eye for an Eye," "There's a Wind

Comin' In," "Hey, McKenna," "The Man I Know," "If That's the Way They Want It," "Love Will." Plans for Broadway on 3/17/00, with Eugene Lee (set) & Santo Loquasto (cos), but it did not proceed

1965. Moms. Musical play. Based on life of comedienne Jackie "Moms" Mabley (1894–1975). Astor Place, 8/4/87–12/13/87. 152 perf. m/l/ms: Grenoldo Frazier; w: Ben Caldwell; based on concept by Clarice Taylor; d: Walter Dallas. There had been an earlier version of *Moms* at the Hudson Guild in 1986, featuring Clarice Taylor

1966. Money. Musical play for cabaret. Upstairs at the Downstairs, 7/9/63. 214 perf. m: Sam Pottle; l/b: David Axelrod & Tom Whedon; d: Ronny Graham. Cast: David Rounds, Barbara Quaney, Jon Stone, George Coe. "She Just Walked In," "A Man with a Problem," "Beautiful Day," "Commitment," "How Can I Tell?," "San Fernando," "Give a Cheer," "The Philanthropist's Progress," "Who Wants to Work?"

1967. A Month of Sundays. About an excursion boat & its passengers. Pre-Broadway tryouts opened 12/25/51, Shubert, Boston. Closed 1/26/52, Forrest, Philadelphia. p: Carly Wharton; m: Albert Selden; l/b/d: B.G. (Burt) Shevelove; based on play *Excursion*, by Victor Wolfson; ch: Anna Sokolow; set/light: Jo Mielziner; md: Lehman Engel; orch: Ted Royal; dance mus arr: David Baker. Cast: Nancy Walker, Richard Kiley, Gene Lockhart, Buddy Schwab, Michael Dominico, Richard France, Virginia Bosler, Elizabeth Logue, Urylee Leonardos, Eddie Phillips, Richard Loo, Henry Beckman, Robert St. Clair, Bob Kennedy, Estelle Loring. "Looking for a Bluebird," "Semi Tropical Island," "So Right," "You Have to Have Love"

1968. Month of Sundays. Survivors of a Flood-to-be are towed to Paradise by a whale, on the rather remarkable house of Carrousel Jones (played by Gil Robbins). Theatre de Lys, 9/16/68–9/22/68. 8 perf. m/l: Maury Laws & Jules Bass; b: Romeo Muller (based on his play *The Great Git-Away);* d: Stone Widney. Cast: Pamela Hall, Martha Schlamme, Dan Resin, Patti Karr, Joe Morton, John Bennett Perry. "How Far Can You Follow?," "I Won't Worry," "Communicate," "Part of the Crowd," "We Know Where We've Been," "Summer Love," "Who Knows Better than I?," "Words Will Pay My Way," "Elbow Room," "My First Girl," "Flower, I Don't Need You Any More," "It's Out of My Hands," "The Wedding." Previously produced by the Tyrone Guthrie Theatre, Minneapolis

1969. Monty Python's Spamalot. Also called *Spamalot.* Stage musical re-working of the film *Monty Python and the Holy Grail.* Shubert, Chicago, 12/21/04–1/23/05 (closing date extended from 1/16/05); Shubert, Broadway, 3/17/05 (date put back from 3/10/05). Prev from 2/14/05 (date put back from 2/7/05). p: Ostar Boyett Productions; m: John DuPrez; l: Eric Idle; d: Mike Nichols; ch: Casey Nicholaw; set/cos: Tom Hatley; light: Hugh Vanstone; sound: Acme Sound Partners; md: Todd Ellison; orch: Larry Hochman; mus arr: Glen

Kelly; cast recording on Decca Broadway, made on 2/7/05, and released in spring 2005. *Cast:* Sir Lancelot: Hank Azaria; King Arthur; Tim Curry; Sir Robin: David Hyde Pierce; Patsy, et al: Michael McGrath; Lady of the Lake: Sara Ramirez; Sir Bedevere: Steve Rosen; Sir Galahad: Douglas Sills (bowed out on 11/18/04, and replaced within 2 days by Christopher Sieber); Ensemble: Jesse Tyler Ferguson (dropped before Broadway), John Bolton, Jennifer Frankel, Lisa Gajda, Thomas Cannizzaro, Brad Bradley, Emily Hsu, Jenny Hill, James Ludwig, Rick Spaans. "Fish Schlapping Song," "King Arthur's Song," "I Am Not Dead Yet," "Come with Me," "The Song that Goes Like This," "Burn Her," "All for One," "Knights of the Round Table" (from the movie), "The Song that Goes Like This" (reprise), "Find Your Grail," "The Cow Song" ("Fetchez la Vache"), "Run Away," "Always Look on the Bright Side of Life," "Brave Sir Robin" (from the movie), "You Won't Succeed on Broadway," "The Diva's Lament," "Where Are You?," "Here Are You," "His Name is Lancelot," "I'm All Alone," "The Song that Goes Like This" (reprise), "The Holy Grail," "Find Your Grail Finale–Medley." Another song from the movie, "He's Going to Tell," was dropped in Chicago

1970. Moonwalk. City Center, 11/28/70–12/6/70. 8 perf. m/l/performed: The Open Window. Cast: Annie Abbott, Tommy Breslin. "Ready to Go," "Moonwalk," "Grand Tour of the Planets," "Moonrock Candy Freak-Out," "Earth Fall"

More Canterbury Tales see # 113, Main Book

1971. More Than You Deserve. Musical comment on Vietnam War. Public, 11/21/73–1/13/74. 63 perf. p: NY Shakespeare Festival; m/l: Jim Steinman & Michael Weller; d: Kim Friedman; ch: Scott Salmon; light: Martin Aronstein; sound: Abe Jacob; md: Steve Margoshes. Cast: Leata Galloway, Marybeth Hurt, Larry Marshall, Meat Loaf, Kim Milford, Terry Kiser, Fred Gwynne, Dale Soules, Kimberly Farr. "Give Me the Simple Life," "Could She Be the One?," "Where Did it Go?," "Mama, You Better Watch Out for Your Daughter," "O, What a War," "More than You Deserve," "Song of the City of Hope," "To Feel So Needed," "Go, Go, Go Guerrillas," "What Became of the People We Were?," "If Only," "Midnight Lullaby," "Song of the Golden Egg"

1972. Morning Sun. Play with mus. Set in the Southwest in 1870. Phoenix, 10/6/63–10/13/63. 9 perf. m: Paul Klein; l/b: Fred Ebb; based on story by Mary Deasy; d: Daniel Petrie; ch: Donald Saddler; set: Eldon Elder; cos: Patricia Zipprodt; light: Eldon Elder & Martin Aronstein; md: John Strauss. Cast: Bert Convy, Patricia Neway, Jan Tanzy, Ave Maria Megna, Joan August, Stuart Hodes, Carole Demas, Sammy Bayes. "Morning Sun," "This Heat!," "Tell Me Goodbye," "New Boy in Town," "Good as Anybody," "Mr. Chigger," "Pebble Waltz," "Follow Him," "Missouri Mule," "Square Dance," "Seventeen Summers," "It's a Lie," "My Sister-in-Law," "Why?," "That's Right!," "For Once in My Life," "Thad's Journey," "All the Pretty Little Horses," "I Seen it with My Very Own Eyes"

1973. Moses, My Love. Judith Anderson, 10/30/98–11/15/98. 16 perf. m/l: Paul Dick; based on the Five Books of Moses; d: Marc Geller. Cast: Walter Willison. "In the Reeds of the River," "To Build Tomorrow," "Welcome, Warm Welcome," "Out of the Wilderness," "The Time Has Come," "Green Gardens," "So Can We," "Let My People Go," "Believe in Miracles," "Song By the Sea," "On Wings of Eagles," "The Ten Commandments," "Little Giant"

1974. Most Men Are. Theatre Off Park, 2/3/95–2/11/95. 3 prev. 6 perf. m/l/b/md: Stephen Dolginoff; d: Daniel Simmons. "You Won't Die Alone," "What If," "Something Bound to Begin," "The Perfect Place on Christopher Street," "I Couldn't Care Less," "Away," "When I Come Home at Night," "Gotta Get Outta Here," "Most Men Are," "Better Not to Know," "Maybe Some Weekend"

1975. The Mother of Us All. Musical story of Susan B. Anthony. Guggenheim Museum, 1972. A Lenox Arts Center prod. p: Lyn Austin, Orin Lehman, Hale Matthews, Oliver Smith; m: Virgil Thomson; text: Gertrude Stein; d: Elizabeth Keen & Roland Gagnon; set: Oliver Smith; cos: Patricia Zipprodt; md: Roland Gagnon. Cast: Judith Erickson & Phyllis Worthington (alternated), Lynne Wickenden, Olivia Buckley, Wayne Turnage, Gene West

1976. A Mother's Kisses. Satire on momism. Pre-Broadway tryout opened 9/23/68, Shubert, New Haven. Closed 10/19/68, Mechanic, Baltimore, canceling scheduled 10/29/68 Broadway opening at 46th Street Theatre. m/l: Richard Adler (he replaced Bob Merrill on lyr); adapted by: Bruce Jay Friedman (from his own novel); d: Gene Saks; ch: Onna White; set: William & Jean Eckart; cos: Alvin Colt; light: Tharon Musser. Cast: Bea Arthur, Bill Callaway, Bernadette Peters (left during rehearsals), Carl Ballantine, Rudy Bond, Alan North, Ned Wertimer, Renee Roy, Kate Wilkinson, Ruth Jaroslow, Daniel Goldman, Arthur Anderson, Martin Wolfson (left during rehearsals), Maggie Worth, Maggie Task, Del Horstmann, Taylor Reed, John Johann. "There Goes My Life," "Look at Those Faces," "With a Little Help from Your Mother," "Left by the Wayside," "When You Gonna Learn?," "We've Got Meg," "Where Did the Summer Go?," "People of Passionate Nature," "They Won't Regret It," "I Told Them We Were Lovers," "I Have a Terrible Secret," "A Course in Your Mother"

1977. Movie Buff. Fantasy of nostalgia for 1930s movies. Actors Playhouse, 3/14/77–4/3/77. 3 prev. 21 perf. m: John Raniello; l: John Raniello & Hiram Taylor; b: Hiram Taylor; d: Jim Payne; ch: Jack Dyville; md: Donald G. Jones. Cast: Jim Richards, Mark Waldrop, Mary Travizo, Deborah Carlson, Nancy Rich, Keith Curran, Charlie Scatamacchia, Nora Cole. "Silver Screen," "Something to Believe In," "Movietown USA," "Movie Stars," "May I Dance with You?," "Song of Yesterday," "The Movie Cowboy," "All-Talking, All-Singing, All-Dancing," "Coming Attractions," "Tomorrow"

1978. Moving On. 70th birthday celebration for Stephen Sondheim, using his m/l. Bridewell, London, 7/00. Cast: Angela Richards, Robert Meadmore, Linzi Hateley, Geoffrey Abbott, Belinda Long. "Our Time," "Opening Doors," "Move On," "I Know Things Now," "Everybody Says Don't," "Take Me to the World," "Who Wants to Live in New York," "What More Do I Need?," "Me and My Town," "Another Hundred People," "Broadway Baby," "Someone is Waiting," "Multitudes of Amys," "No, Mary Ann," "Johanna," "I Do Like You," "Old Friends," "Side by Side," "Loving You," "Not a Day Goes By," "So Many People," "The Miller's Son," "Goodbye for Now," "I Wish I Could Forget You," "Pretty Women," "Ah, But Underneath," "In Buddy's Eyes," "Water Under the Bridge," "There Won't Be Trumpets," "With So Little to Be Sure Of." The show was re-titled *Opening Doors,* and as such ran at Zankel Hall, NY, 10/5/04–10/9/04. Prev from 9/30/04. d: David Kernan; ch: James Scott Wise; set: Walt Spangler; cos consultant: Jane Greenwood; sound: Peter Hylenski; md/piano: Rob Berman; mus arr: Jason Carr. Cast: Gregg Edelman, Victoria Clark, Jan Maxwell (Carolee Carmello was meant to have played the role, but she went into *Mamma Mia* on Broadway), Kate Baldwin, Eric Jordan Young

1979. *Mr. and Mrs.* Alias *Brief Encounter.* Palace, Manchester, England, 11/14/68 (3 weeks); Palace, London, 12/11/68–1/18/69. 44 perf. p: George W. George & Frank Granat; m/l/b: John Taylor; based on Noel Coward's plays *Fumed Oak* and *Still Life;* d: Ross Taylor; ch: Norman Maen & Ross Taylor; md: Derek New. Cast: John Neville, Honor Blackman, Hylda Baker

1980. *Mr. Burke, M.P.* A chimp goes into politics. Mermaid, London, 10/6/60–12/10/60. 114 perf. m/l/b: Gerald Frow; d: Sally Miles; ch: Denys Palmer; set: Michael Richardson; cast recording on DRG. Cast: Mr. Burke: Peter Clegg; Also with: Ron Pember, Brian Rawlinson, John Turner, Raf de la Torre, Sally Miles, Timothy West, The Vipers (played the mus; Wally Whyton, a member of this group, played the Commentator, and also arr the mus). "It's a Rat Race," "Marriage of Convenience," "Ninety Five Percent of Me Loves You," "You're Going to Be Caught"

Mr. Pickwick see # 545, Main Book

1981. *Mr. Shakespeare and Mr. Porter.* Absurdist musical comedy incorporating Cole Porter songs from *Macbeth, King Lear, As You Like It, Measure for Measure, Hamlet,* and *Midsummer Night's Dream.* Medicine Show, 1992. b/conceived by: Barbara Vann & James Barbosa; d: Barbara Vann, Deloss Brown, Harvey Cort; md: Randy Redd. Cast: Lisa Haim, James Barbosa, Barbara Vann, Mark J. Dempsey, Morton Banks

1982. *Mrs. Patterson.* Play with mus. Set in 1920, in Kentucky. National, Broadway, 12/1/54–2/26/55. 102 perf. p: Leonard Sillman; incidental m: James Shelton; l/w: Charles Sebree & Greer Johnson; d: Guthrie McClintick; set/cos: Raoul Pene du Bois; md: Abba Bogin; orch: George Siravo. Cast: Enid Markey (*Estelle Winwood*), Avon Long, Terry Carter. Most of

the numbers were sung by Eartha Kitt (playing Teddy Hicks): "Mrs. Patterson," "Tea in Chicago," "If I Was a Boy," "My Daddy is a Dandy," "Be Good, Be Good, Be Good" (The Devil Song). "I Wish I Was a Bumble Bee" was sung by Helen Dowdy (playing Bessie Bolt)

1983. *Mrs. Tucker's Pageant.* Theatre Royal, Stratford East, London, 9/21/81–10/31/81. 49 perf. m: Alan Klein; l/b/d: Ken Hill. Cast: Judith Bruce, Peggy Mount, Larry Dann

1984. *Mrs. Wilson's Diary.* Affectionate lampoon of PM Harold Wilson, as imagined through diary of his wife, Mary. Criterion, London, 1967. m: Jeremy Taylor; l: John Wells; b: Richard Ingrams & John Wells; d: Joan Littlewood; md: Arthur Greenslade. Cast: Bill Walls, Myvanwy Jenn, Stephen Lewis, Peter Reeves, Bob Grant, Sandra Caron, Howard Goorney. "Here I Kneel," "Who Are the Bastards Now?," "The Terrible Mr. Brown," "Why Should I Worry?," "What Would They Say?," "Harold and Me," "One Man Band," "Cocoa Time"

1985. *Murderous Instincts.* Murder mystery among the rich in Puerto Rico. Salsa musical. Savoy, London, 10/7/04–1/29/05. Prev from 9/10/04. m: Alberto Carrion; l/b: Cinda Fox; d: Bob Carlton; ch: Jhesus Aponte (the famous Salsa dancer); set/cos: Dinah England. Cast: Nichola McAuliffe, Kevin Colson

1986. *Music at Midnight.* His Majesty's, London, 11/10/50–11/18/50. 11 perf. m: Jacques Offenbach; l: Harold Purcell; b: Guy Bolton; d: Wallace Douglas; md: Ludo Philipp. Cast: Joan Heal, Austin Trevor, Genevieve Guitry, George Benson, Ballard Berkeley, Moyra Fraser

1987. *Music-Hall Sidelights.* Theatrical scrapbook drawn from Colette's *L'envers du music-hall.* Lion, 10/26/78–11/12/78. 19 perf. w: Jack Heifner; d: Garland Wright; light: Frances Aronson. Cast: Cathy Bates, Jane Galloway, James McLure, Gene Nye

1988. *Music! Music!* Cavalcade of American Music [1895 to present] with Footnotes by Alan Jay Lerner. City Center, 4/11/74–5/12/74. 4 prev. 37 perf. d: Martin Charnin; ch: Tony Stevens; set: David Chapman; cos: Theoni V. Aldredge; light: Martin Aronstein; md/voc arr: John Lesko; orch: Elliot Lawrence, with Al Cohn & William Elton; dance mus arr: Wally Harper. Cast: Gene Nelson (replaced Dan Dailey), Larry Kert, Karen Morrow, Donna McKechnie, Robert Guillaume, Will MacKenzie, Gail Nelson (who replaced 6th-billed star Jonelle Allen), Ted Pritchard, Arnold Soboloff, Russ Thacker, Renee Baughman, Michon Peacock, Tom Offt. Reviews were very divided

1989. *Musical Chairs.* About "model Jewish ghetto" of Theresienstadt, in Czechoslovakia, during WWII, which Nazis populated with artists, musicians, actors & professors, to show the world how well they were treating the Jews. Unrelated to 1980 Broadway musical. El Portal Center for the Performing Arts, North Hollywood, 8/24/01. Prev from 8/16/01. d: Jules Aaron; ch: Kay Cole. Cast: Joel Hirschhorn, Jennifer Carter

1990. *A Musical: Madame Bovary.* Judith Anderson, 11/16/95–11/26/95. 1 prev. 10 perf.

m/l/adapted by: Paul Dick; from novel by Gustave Flaubert; d: Ed Setrakian; ch: Artemis Preeshl. Cast: Jennifer Little

1991. *The Musical of Musicals — A Musical.* 5 musicals in one. June can't pay her rent to evil landlord. Will handsome hero come to her aid? Tells the same story but in varying styles of different musical theatre songwriters-Rodgers & Hammerstein, Steve Sondheim, Jerry Herman, Andrew Lloyd Webber, and Kander & Ebb. Theatre at St. Peter's, 12/16/03–1/18/04. Prev from 12/2/03. p: York Theatre Co. m: Eric Rockwell; l: Joanne Bogart; b: Eric Rockwell & Joanne Bogart; d: Pamela Hunt; set: James Morgan; light: Mary Jo Dondlinger; cast recording on Jay Records. Cast: Craig Fols, Lovette George, Eric Rockwell, Joanne Bogart. It was a hit, but had to vacate the theatre. Theatre at St. Peter's, 6/10/04–10/2/04. 14 prev from 5/24/04. 194 perf (longest run of any show prod by York Theatre Co.). Same basic cast & crew. Dodger Stages, 2/10/05 (prev from 2/2/05)

1992. *A Musical Timepiece.* All-music musical. 4 people search, find, touch, trust, love, enjoy — then lose each other. Equity Library, 10/19/70–10/21/70. 3 perf. w: Alan Foster Friedman; d: Allen R. Belknap. Cast: Jeanne Allen, George Lee Andrews, Thomas Inghram, Ellen Wells

1993. *Mutiny!* The *Bounty* story. Piccadilly, London, 7/18/85. m/l: David Essex & Richard Crane; cast recording on Telstar. Cast: David Essex, Frank Finlay, Patrick Clancy, Nicola Blackman, Neville Jason, David Oakley. "New World," "Friends," "The Storm," "Failed Cape Horn," "Saucy Sal," "The Lash," "Welcome," "Tahiti," "Bread Fruit," "Will You Come Back?," "Hell," "Freedom," "Falling Angels Riding," "I'll Go No More a-Roving"

1994. *My Friend Yossel.* Yiddish. Restaurant owner frames man & almost ruins his life. Second Avenue, 3/3/44. p: Menasha Skulnik; m: Sholom Secunda; l: Isidor Lillian; b: Isidor Friedman & William Siegel; d: Mike Wilensky; ch: Valentina Belova. Cast: Menasha Skulnik, Yetta Zwerling, Miriam Kressyn, Jacob Zanger, Michal Michalesko

1995. *My Gentleman Pip.* Opera House, Harrogate, England, 1968. Did not go to London. w: Jack Sherman & Geoffrey Venis; from Charles Dickens' *Great Expectations;* d: Brian Howard. Cast: Jess Conrad, John Shorter, Jill Howard, Jan Wilson, Paul Greenwood, Simon Cuff. Theatre Royal, Northampton, 12/26/69 (4 weeks). d: Willard Stoker. Cast: Jess Conrad, Ivan Stafford, Maria Aitken

1996. *My Heart Is in the East.* Jewish Rep, 5/28/83–6/26/83. 23 perf. m/l: Raphael Crystal & Richard Engquist; b: Linda Kline; inspired by life & times of 12th-century Spanish poet Judah Halevy; d: Ran Avni

1997. *My L.A.* Limited run revue that never made it to Broadway. Los Angeles, 1951. m/l: Sammy Fain, Paul F. Webster, Bob Hilliard. "Heaven Help Us," "On the Seventh Day He Rested," "Our Little Gray Home in the Red," "Something for the Books," "That's My L.A.," "Twist My Arm," "A Thousand Burning Bridges"

1998. *My Life with Albertine*. Playwrights Horizons, 3/13/03–3/30/03. Prev from 2/18/03. 22 perf. m: Ricky Ian Gordon; l: Richard Nelson & Ricky Ian Gordon; b/d: Richard Nelson; based on section of *Remembrance of Things Past*, by Marcel Proust; set: Thomas Lynch; md: Charles Prince; cast recording released on PS Classics, 10/7/03. Cast: Kelli O'Hara, Brent Carver, Emily Skinner, Chad Kimball, Donna Lynne Champlin, Brooke Sunny Moriber, Ken Barnett, Jim Poulos. Amy Spanger dropped out before the opening

1999. *My Lucky Day*. Yiddish. Second Avenue, 1952. m/l: Joseph Rumshinksy. Cast: Edmund Zayenda, Selma Kaye. "My Lucky Day." Not to be confused with 1951 British musical of same name by John Dellacey, which didn't make the West End (this was a revised version of *Under the Lilacs*, and Stephanie Voss was in it*)

2000. *My Mama the General*. Set on Suez Canal during Six-Day War. Burstein, 1973. m/l: Nurit Hirsch & Lillian Lux; b: Eli Shagi; d: Israel Valin; ch: Baruch Blum; md: Elliot Finkel. Cast: Lillian Lux, Pesach Burstein, Natalie Rogers, Baruch Blum. "Galiciano Caballero," "Shalom Suez," "My Son," "Look at Mama, the General!," "How Did I Get into This?," "Peace Will Come"

2001. *My Old Friends*. Set in the Golden Days Retirement Home. La Mama, 11/23/79. m/l/b: Mel Mandel & Norman Sachs; d: Philip Rose; ch: Bob Tucker; ms: Norman Sachs. Cast: Allen Swift, Leslie Barrett, Grace Carney, Maxine Sullivan (nominated for a Tony). "(Thank God) I'm Not Old," "My Old Friends," "For Two Minutes," "What We Need Around Here," "Oh, My Rose," "I Bought a Bicycle," "Battle at Eagle Rock," "Dear Jane," "Only Place for Me," "I Work with Wood," "Mambo '52," "A Little Starch Left," "Our Time Together," "You've Got to Keep Building." Orpheum, 1/12/79–4/8/79. 100 perf. 22 Steps, 4/12/79–5/27/79. 54 perf

2002. *My Wife and I*. Set before TV, in 1939. Boy runs away from home, but returns safely. Theatre Four, 10/10/66–10/22/66. 6 prev. 8 perf. m/l/b: Bill Mahoney; d: Tom Ross Prather; ch: Darwin Knight; md/arr: James Reed Lawlor. Cast: Helon Blount, Carol-Leigh Jensen. "Confusion," "Busy, Busy Day," "They've Got to Complain," "My Wife and I," "Pay, Pay, Pay," "I've Got a Problem," "It's Pouring," "I'll Come By," "Dad Got Girls," "Baltimore," "The Principle of the Thing," "Please, God," "I Really Love You," "I'll Try to Smile," "Family Tree," "Why Grow Old"

2003. *The Mysteries*. South African prod of Bible stories based on the Miracle Plays. Wilton's Music Hall, London, 6/01. Sold out. Queen's, London, 2/26/02–5/18/02. Prev from 2/22/02; Peacock Theatre, London, 3/3/03–3/8/03

2004. *Naked Boys Singing*. Musical revue. Musical spectacle of male nudity. Actors' Playhouse, 7/22/99–3/7/04. Prev from 7/2/99; Theatre 4, 3/10/04–9/5/04; John Houseman, 9/17/04. Score: various authors; Conceived by/d: Robert Schrock; ch: Jeffry Denman; md:

Stephen Bates. "Gratuitous Nudity," "Naked Maid," "Bliss," "Window to Window," "Fight the Urge," "Robert Mitchum," "Jack's Song," "Members Only," "Perky Little Porn Star," "Kris, Look What You've Missed," "Muscle Addiction," "Nothin' But the Radio On," "The Entertainer," "Window to the Soul," "Naked Boys Singing." Originally presented by Celebration Theatre, L.A.

2005. *Naked Revolution*. Four-act opera imagining Lenin & George Washington. The Kitchen, 10/4/97–10/18/97. 1 prev. 9 perf. m: Dave Soldier; l/b: Maita Di Niscemi; d: David Herskovits; cos: Kay Voyce. Cast: Tony Boutte, Dina Emerson, Jimmy Justice, Robert Osborne, Oleg Riabets

2006. *Napoleon*. Shaftesbury, London, 10/17/00–2/3/01. Prev from 9/30/01. m/l/b: Timothy Williams & Andrew Sabiston; d: Francesca Zambello; ch: Denni Sayers; set: Michael Yeargen; cos: Marie-Jeanne Lecca; light: Rick Fisher; sound: Martin Levan; ms: Seann Alderking; md: David Charles Abell; orch: Jonathan Tunick. Cast: Paul Baker, Anastasia Barzee, Nigel Richards, David Burt, Teddy Kempner

2007. *Narnia*. Haft, 1/7/91–1/20/91. 1 prev. 14 perf. p: New York State Theatre Institute; m/l: Thomas Tierney & Ted Drachman; based on book *The Lion, the Witch and the Wardrobe*, by C.S. Lewis; d: Shela Xoregos. Cast: Marlene Goudreau. "Doors and Windows," "Turkish Delight," "Narnia," "All of These," "Hot and Bothered," "At Last it's Christmas," "Murder Today," "From the Inside Out," "Deep Magic," "A Field of Flowers," "Catch Me if You Can," "To Make the World Right Again," "The Days Danced By"

2008. *Nash at Nine*. A "wordsical" without intermission. Helen Hayes, Broadway, 5/17/73–6/2/73. 5 prev from 5/1/73. 21 perf. p: Les Schecter, Barbara Schwei, SRO Enterprises, Arnold Levy; m: Milton Rosenstock; l/verses: Ogden Nash; conceived by/d: Martin Charnin; set: David Chapman; cos: Theoni V. Aldredge; light: Martin Aronstein; md: Karen Gustafson; ms/orch: John Morris; press: Frank Goodman, Arlene Wolf, Susan L. Schulman; gm: Sherman Gross; psm: Janet Beroza; sm: Mary Porter Hall. Cast: E.G. Marshall, Bill Gerber, Richie Schechtman, Virginia Vestoff, Steve Elmore. Standbys: For Mr. Marshall/Mr. Elmore: John Stratton; For Miss Vestoff: June Gable; For Mr. Gerber/Mr. Schechtman: Jess Richards. Tour opened 1/28/75, Ford's Theatre, Washington, DC., 1/28/75, and closed 3/16/75, Mechanic, Baltimore. Cast: Craig Stevens, Harvey Evans, Jane Summerhays, John Stratton

2009. *Nashville New York*. Revue. King's Head, London, 11/12/79. m: Vernon Duke & Kurt Weill; l: Ogden Nash; b/d: Robert Cushman; cast recording on TER. Cast: Leueen Willoughby, Christopher Benjamin, Robert Cushman, Bryan Murray. "The Theatre is a Lady," "Turn Me Loose on Broadway," "The Trouble with Women," "Just Like a Man," "What is Bibbidi-Bobbidi-Boo in Sanskrit?," "I'm Glad I'm Not a Man," "Four Prominent So-and-Sos," "Decline and Fall of a Roman

Umpire," "Musical Zoo," "A Drink with Something in It," "Madly in Love," "Columbus," "Fly Now and Pay Later," "You're Far from Wonderful," "Love is Still in Town," "My Daddy," "Sweet Bye and Bye," "Born Too Late," "That's Him," "Suppose I Darken Your Door," "Round About"

2010. *The National Lampoon Show*. Satirical revue. New Palladium, 3/2/75–7/6/75. 180 perf. Music composed & performed by Paul Jacobs; words & music by the cast (overlooked by Sean Kelly); d: Martin Charnin; light: Lowell Sherman; sound: Abe Jacob. Cast: John Belushi, Bill Murray, Gilda Radner, Harold Ramis, Brian Doyle-Murray

2011. *National Lampoon's Class of '86*. Musical revue. Village Gate Downstairs, 5/22/86–7/6/86. 6 prev from 5/16/86. 53 perf. head w: Andy Simmons; d: Jerry Adler; ch: Nora Brennan. Cast: Rodger Bumpass, Annie Golden. "Cocaine," "Yuppie Love," "They Lost the Revolution," "My Bod is for God," "I Got It," "The President's Dream," "Don't Drop the Bomb," "Apartheid Lover," "The Ticker"

2012. *National Lampoon's Lemmings*. Musical revue/satire. Village Gate, 2/5/73–11/25/73. Prev from 1/25/73. 350 perf. p/d: Tony Hendra; m: Paul Jacobs & Christopher Guest; words/l: various authors; light: Beverly Emmons; sound: Abe Jacob; md: Paul Jacobs. Cast: John Belushi, Chevy Chase, Garry Goodrow, Christopher Guest, Paul Jacobs, Alice Playten, Mary-Jennifer Mitchell

2013. *Naughty Girl*. Musical screwball comedy. Studio 1, 4/23/98–4/26/98. 5 perf. m: Christopher Seppe & Jeffrey Lodin; l: Christopher Seppe & Scott Hayes; b: Scott Hayes; ch: Nancy Lemenager. Cast: Michelle Du Pre, Amy Frankel, Brandon Savage

2014. *A Naughty Knight*. The Duke Theatre, 5/20/01–6/17/01. 16 prev. 17 perf. p: Jewish Rep; m/l: Chuck Strand; b/d: William Martin; based on Mark Twain's *A Medieval Romance*; ch: Dennis Dennehy; md: Steven Silverstein

2015. *Naughty Marietta*. Set in New Orleans in 1780. New York Theatre, Broadway, 11/7/1910. 136 perf. p: Oscar Hammerstein; m: Victor Herbert; l/b: Rida Johnson Young. Jolson's 59th Street Theatre, 10/21/29–11/2/29. 16 perf. d: Milton Aborn; md: Louis Kroll. Cast: Roy Cropper, Ilse Marvenga; Erlanger, 11/16/31–11/28/31. 16 perf—it returned 12/7/31–12/12/31, for a further 8 perf. Cast: Roy Cropper, Detmar Poppen, Ilse Marvenga. Filmed in 1935, with Nelson Eddy & Jeanette MacDonald. Light Opera of Manhattan, 11/12/75. 12 perf. Cast: Georgia McEver, Jeanne Beauvais, Joanne Jamieson. Same show, same crew, same cast, opened again, 12/29/76. New York State Theatre, 8/31/78–9/10/78. 14 perf. new l/b based on the orig: Frederick S. Roffman; d: Gerald Freedman; ch: Graciela Daniele; set: Oliver Smith; cos: Patricia Zipprodt; light: Ken Billington; md: John Mauceri. Cast: Gianna Rolandi, Alan Titus, James Billings, Russ Thacker, Brooks Morton, Don Yule, Harlan Foss, Rita Metzger, Robert Brubaker. "It Never, Never Can Be Love," "This Brave New Land," "Tramp, Tramp,

Tramp," "Taisez-Vous," "All I Crave is More of Life," "Italian Street Song," "Naughty Marietta," "If I Were Anyone Else But Me," "New Orleans Jeunesse Doree," "You Marry a Marionette," "'neath the Southern Moon," "Loves of New Orleans," "It's Pretty Soft for Silas," "Live for Today," "The Sweet By and By," "I'm Falling in Love with Someone," "Ah, Sweet Mystery of Life." This prod returned to the same venue, 8/30/79–9/2/79. 6 perf. This time it was adapted & dir by Jack Eddleman. Rest of crew basically the same. Cast: Elizabeth Hynes, Howard Hensel, Alan Titus, Susanne Marsee, Lara Teeter, James Billings, Don Yule, Harlan Foss, Bob Brubaker, Candace Itow. A new adaptation by Theodore Pappas (also d/ch) ran at New York State Theatre, 8/30/88–9/11/88. 14 perf. p: NYC Opera; set: Oliver Smith; conductor: Scott Bergeson. Cast: Richard White, Susanne Marsee, William Ledbetter, Don Yule, John Lankston, James Billings

2016. *Naughty Naught '00*. Musical satire. American Music Hall, 1/23/37–5/30/37. 128 perf; same venue, 1/24/39. 42 perf. p: John & Jerrold Krimsky; m: Richard Lewine; l: Ted Fetter; b: John Van Antwerp (i.e. John & Jerrold Krimsky); d: Morgan Lewis. "Goodbye Girls, Hello Yale," "Naughty-Naught," "Love Makes the World Go Round," "Zim-Zam-Zee," "Pull the Boat for Eli," "Coney-by-the-Sea," "Mother isn't Getting Any Younger," "When We're in Love," "What's Good About Good Morning?," "Just Like a Woman." Revived in cabaret style at the Old Knickerbocker Music Hall, 10/19/46–11/2/46. 21 perf. p: Paul Killiam & Oliver Rea; d: Ted Fetter; md: Richard Lewine. Cast: John Cromwell, Teddy Hart, Ottilie Kruger

2017. *Nefertiti*. About the Egyptian queen. Pre-Broadway tryouts 9/20/77–10/22/77, Blackstone, Chicago. Canceled scheduled 11/10/77 Broadway opening at the Minskoff. p: Sherwin M. Goldman; m: David Spangler; l/b: Christopher Gore; add b material: Joe Masteroff; d: Jack O'Brien; ch: Daniel Lewis; light: Gilbert V. Hemsley Jr.; md: John De Main; dance mus arr: Wally Harper. Cast: Andrea Marcovicci, Robert LuPone, Michael Nouri, Marilyn Cooper, Benjamin Rayson, Michael V. Smartt, Jane White, Patrick Kinser-Lau, Jane White, G. Eugene Moose, Ann Crumb. "Diary of a Dying Princess," "Lama Su Apapi," "Penmut's Apology," "Everything is Possible," "Breakfast at Thebes," "Father," "Pardon Me a Minute," "Beautiful Has Come," "Whatever Happened to Me?," "It Happens Very Softly," "Legions of the Night," "Light Will Shine," "Under the Sun," "The New World," "A Free Translation," "Someone Was Here," "Another Free Translation," "Dinner at Thebes," "Take off the Sandal." First produced in 1976 at La Mama, as *Brothers*

2018. *Nell!* Richmond Theatre, England, 4/8/70–4/25/70; toured until 5/23/70. Never went to London. p: Frederic Piffard & Tony Hatch; m/l: John Worth; b: John Worth & Philip Mackie; d: Mark Kingston; ch: Tom Merrifield & Peter Walker; md: Tony Hatch. Cast: Nell Gwynne: Jackie Trent; Mrs. Gwynne:

Hermione Baddeley; Charles II: Stuart Damon; Also with: Jean Challis, Michael Elwick

2019. *Nellie*. Musical bio of Nellie Bly. Set in NYC & Pittsburgh in the 1890s. Greenwich Street, 5/22/97–6/1/97. 10 perf. m: Jaz Dorsey; l: Jaz Dorsey & Bernice Lee; b: Bernice Lee; d: Scott Pegg; md: James Mironchik. Cast: Jeanine Serralles. "Nellie Don't Go," "Been There, Done That," "Alone," "What Choices Are Left for Me?," "Why Did Ya Go?," "Come Luv," "Papa's Song," "Always Remember," "Mexico," "Check it Out," "Gettin' Ready for Love," "Happy Am I," "We Don't Waste Food," "You Are There," "Easy Breeze," "Woman Who Acts Like a Man," "Mother of the Bride," "Away with Age," "Could I?," "Nellie Paves the Way," "Still Be Me?," "International Reporters Song," "Look at Me!," "And I Know." Lambs, 6/3/99–6/13/99. 3 prev. 9 perf. d: Patricia Heuermann; ch: Andrea Andresakis; set/light: Nadine Charlsen; md: Kenneth Faulkner-Alexander. Cast: Becky Lillie. See also *Nellie Bly*, in the main part of this book

2020. *Neverland*. Musical Theatre Lab, Kennedy Center, 4/26/77. 8 perf. w: Jim Steinman; based on Peter Pan story, by J.M. Barrie (but not in any other way connected to any of the Broadway musicals); d: Barry Keating; ch: Ed Kresley; md: Paul Jacobs. Cast: Barry Keating, Richard Dunne, Larry Dilg, Baxter Harris, Johanna Albrecht, Ellen Foley, Mark Kapitan, Tim Millett, Toby Parker, Rodney Reiner, Robert Rhys, Brian Destazio, Don Swanson. "The Formation of the Pack," "City Night," "Midnight Serenade," "Bat Out of Hell," "Heaven Can Wait," "The Hunt," "The Assassins' Song," "Gids," "Dance in My Pants," "The Malediction," "Kingdom Come," "The Annihilation"

2021. *Nevertheless They Laugh*. Set in circus in Europe at the turn of 20th century. Lambs Club, 3/24/71–3/28/71. 5 perf. m/orch: Richard Lecsak; l/b: LaRue Watts; based on *He Who Gets Slapped*, by Leonid Andreyev; d/ch: Tod Jackson. Cast: David Holliday, Bernadette Peters, Marilyn Child, Bill Starr, Lu Leonard, Dick Korthaze. "You Must Forget," "No One Will Know," "Can You Love?," "Believe," "Nevertheless They Laugh," "One Simple Song," "I Don't Understand It," "More than You," "Once and for All," "More than Me," "I Charmed the Wine"

2022. *New American Musical Writers Festival*. Sheridan Square Playhouse, 7/18/92–7/27/92. 8 perf. 3 musicals: *Some Summer Night*: m/l: Joel Adlen & Steve Josephson; d: Joe Miloscia; md: Maria Delgado. Cast: Lora Jeanne Martens, Daniel Ely, Joseph Ricci. *Jungle Queen Debutante*: m/l: Thomas Tierney; d: Gene Foote; md: Wendy Bobbitt. Cast: Nora Brennan, Linda Gabler, Peter Kapetan, Nancy Leach, B.K. Kennelly, Tom Souhrada, Andy Taylor. *Finale!*: m/l/d: Robert Ost; md: C. Colby Sachs. Cast: Edwin Bordo, Jo Ann Cunningham, Helen Hanft

2023. *A New Brain*. Mitzi E. Newhouse, 6/18/98–8/23/98. 40 prev from 5/14/98. 78 perf. m/l: William Finn; b: William Finn & James Lapine; d/ch: Graciela Daniele; set: David Gallo; cos: Toni-Leslie James; light:

Peggy Eisenhauer; sound: Tony Meola; md: Ted Sperling; orch: Michael Starobin; cast recording on RCA. Cast: Christopher Innvar (*Norm Lewis*), Malcolm Gets (*Lewis Cleale*), Mary Testa, Liz Larsen, Kristin Chenoweth, Chip Zien, John Jellison, Penny Fuller. "The Specials Today," "911 Emergency," "I Have So Many Songs," "Heart and Music," "There's Trouble in His Brain," "Mother's Gonna Make Things Fine," "Be Polite to Everybody," "I'd Rather Be Sailing," "Family History," "Gordo's Law of Genetics," "And They're Off," "Roger Arrives," "Just Go," "Operation Tomorrow," "Poor, Unsuccessful and Fat," "Sitting Becalmed in the Lee of Cutty Hunk," "Craniotomy," "An Invitation to Sleep in My Arms," "Change," "Yes," "In the Middle of the Room," "I Am the Nice Nurse," "Throw it Out," "Really Lousy Day in the Universe," "Brain Dead," "Whenever I Dream," "Eating Myself up Alive," "The Music Still Plays On," "Don't Give In," "You Boys Are Gonna Get Me in Such Trouble," "The Homeless Lady's Revenge," "Time," "Time and Music," "I Feel So Much Spring"

2024. *New Jersey Trapezoid*. Love in the age of corporate scandal. Set in Aug. 2004 in NJ. It is an allusion to the Bermuda Triangle, which, with pirates, figues in the story. Theater Three, 10/30/04–11/14/04. Prev from 10/28/04. m/l/b: Tom Kleh; d: Jeff Edgerton; md: Linda Dowdell

2025. *The New Meet the People of 1944*. Closed before Broadway, 1944. Revised edition of the revue *The New Meet the People* (1941), which did make Broadway. m/l: Jay Gorney, Edward Eliscu, Henry Myers. "Four Rivers," "Damn the Torpedoes"

2026. *The New Moon*. Operetta. Set in New Orleans in 1788. Young man on run from French authorities. *The New Moon* is a boat. Imperial, Broadway, 9/19/28; Casino, 11/18/29–12/14/29. Total of 509 perf. p: Laurence Schwab & Frank Mandel; m: Sigmund Romberg; l: Oscar Hammerstein II; b/d: Oscar Hammerstein II, Frank Mandel, Lawrence Schwab; based on the life of Robert Misson, a French aristocrat; set: Donald Oenslager. Cast: Evelyn Herbert, Robert Halliday. "Marianne," "The Girl on the Prow," "Gorgeous Alexander," "An Interrupted Love Song," "Tavern Song" (Red Wine), "Softly, as in a Morning Sunrise," "Stouthearted Men" (Liberty Song), "One Kiss," "Ladies of the Jury," "Wanting You," "Funny Little Sailor Man," "Lover, Come Back to Me," "Love is Quite a Simple Thing," "Try Her Out at Dancing," "Never (for You)." Filmed in 1930, with Lawrence Tibbett & Grace Moore, and again in 1940, with Jeanette MacDonald & Nelson Eddy. Carnegie Hall, 8/18/42–9/6/42. 24 perf. p/md: Joseph S. Tushinsky; d/ch: John Pierce. Cast: Ruby Mercer, Wilbur Evans, Hope Emerson, Gene Barry, Teddy Hart, Doris Patston, Viola Essen, Peter Birch. City Center, 5/17/44–6/24/44. 44 perf. p: Perry Frank for Belmont Operetta Company; d: Jose Ruben; ch: Charles Weidman; set: Oliver Smith; md: Charles Blackman. Cast: Dorothy Kirsten, John Hamill, Laurence Hayes, Earl Wrightson, Zoya Leporsky, Ralph

Sassano, Elizabeth Houston, Ann Jackson, Betty Leighton, Jeanne Beauvais. Town Hall, 11/23/81. 1 benefit perf as *The New Moon in Concert*. Cast: Estelle Parsons, Debbie Shapiro, Allan Jones, John Reardon, Russ Thacker, Meg Bussert. Done many times before & since. Robert Johanson adapted l/b, and this new prod ran at New York State Theatre, 8/26/86–9/7/86. 16 perf, with a few numbers omitted. d/ch: Robert Johanson; set: Michael Anania. Cast: David Rae Smith, Davis Gaines, Leigh Munro, Muriel Costa-Greenspon, John Lankston, Jack Harrold. This new prod re-ran at the same venue, 7/19/88–7/24/88. 7 perf, without Davis Gaines

2027. *The New Music Hall of Israel*. New edition of vaudeville revue *The Grand Musical Hall of Israel* (see this appendix). In Hebrew, Yiddish & English. Lunt-Fontanne, Broadway, 10/2/69–11/29/69. 9 prev. 68 perf. p: Leon H. Gildin; d/ch: Jonathan Karmon; md: Rafi Paz. Cast: Germaine Onikowski, The Karmon Dancers, Geula Gill

A New Tomorrow see # 2301, this appendix
New York City Street Show *see* # 2511, this appendix

2028. *New York Rock*. Set in NYC. WPA Theatre, 3/3/94–4/17/94. 42 perf. m/l/b: Yoko Ono; d: Philip Oesterman; ch: Kenneth Tosti; md/orch: Jason Robert Brown. Cast: Jan Horvath, Lynnette Perry, Walter O'Neil, Evan Ferrante

2029. *A New York Romance*. One-woman musical, set in NYC. Altered Stages, 5/31/94–6/5/94. 7 perf. conceived by/w/arr: Mary Setrakian; d: Drew Scott Harris. Cast: Maddy Madison: Mary Setrakian

2030. *A New York Summer*. Musical celebration of NYC & the Music Hall. Radio City Music Hall, 5/31/79–9/26/79. 203 perf. p/d: Robert F. Jani; creative d: Tom Bahler; special cos for the Rockettes: Bob Mackie; exec md: Donald Pippin; ch: Dru Davis, Violet Holmes, Louis Johnson, Linda Lemac, Howard Parker. Cast: Karen Anders, Tim Cassidy, Anthony Falco, John Hallow, John J. Martin, Christina Saffran, the Rockettes

2031. *The New Yorkers*. Linhart, 11/13/94–11/27/94. 10 perf. p: Musical Theatre Works; m/l: Cole Porter; b: Herbert Fields; based on story by Peter Arno & E. Ray Goetz; d: Anthony J. Stimac; ch: Lois Englund; md: Milton Granger; arr: Milton Granger & Louis St. Louis. Cast: Sean McDermott, Wynn Harmon, Jeanne Jones, Patti Perkins, Jack Savage, Raymond Thorne, Emily Hsu. "Just One of Those Things," "Go into Your Dance," "Where Have You Been?," "Say it with Gin," "I Happen to Like New York," "I'm Getting Myself Ready for You," "Love for Sale," "Most Gentlemen Don't Like Love," "Rap-a-Tap on Wood," "Ev'rybodee Who's Anybodee," "But He Never Said He Loved Me," "You're Too Far Away," "Sing Sing for Sing Sing," "The Extra Gal," "When Love Comes Your Way," "Let's Fly Away," "Take Me Back to Manhattan," "It Only Happens in Dreams"

2032. *Newsical: All the News That's Fit to Spoof*. Satire, "the ever-changing new topical musical comedy." Updated songs & material every week. Upstairs at Studio 54, 10/7/04. Prev from 9/10/04. p: Fred M. Caruso; creator: Rick Crom; d/ch: Donna Drake; sets: Peter P. Allburn; cos: David Kaley; light/sound: Michael Flink; md: Ed Goldscheider. Cast: Kim Cea, Jeff Skowron, Stephanie Kurtzuba, Todd Alan Johnson

2033. *The Next President*. "A musical salmagundi." Bijou, Broadway, 4/9/58–4/19/58. 13 perf. p/d: Frank B. Nichols; set: Lee Watson. Cast: Mort Sahl, The Jimmy Giuffre Three (Mr. Giuffre, Bob Brookmeyer, Jim Hall), Anneliese Widman, The Folk Singers: David Allen, Erik Darling, Robin Howard, Dylan Todd, Mary Allin Travers, Donald Vogel, Stan Watt, Caroly Wilcox. Program: The Status Quo, The Chorus of Collective Conscience (Folk Singers), "Cry Holy" (Folk Singers), "A Night-to-Night Report of the News, with Complete Flexibility as to Foreign Policy" (Mort Sahl), The Jimmy Giuffre Three, "Gotta Dance" (by Anneliese Widman), "Deep Blue Sea" (Folk Singers), Mort Sahl, A Brand New Attitude with the Same Old Prejudices, "He's Gone Away" (Folk Singers), "The Green Country" (Jimmy Giuffre Three), "Cloudy Morning" (David Allen), Animation (by Anneliese Widman), Mort Sahl, Press Conference (by Mort Sahl & Folk Singers)

2034. *The Next-to-the-Last Revue*. Musical revue. Sam's Dream Street Cabaret, 10/6/04–10/23/04. Prev from 9/30/04. p: Jim Kierstead; conceived by/d: Martin Charnin; md: Brandon Sturiale. Cast: Melanie Adelman, Michael Diliberto, Elizabeth Inghram, Jenny Neale, Christopher Totten

2035. *Nickleby and Me*. Theatre Royal, Stratford East, London, 12/16/75–1/24/76. Prev from 12/8/75. 44 perf. m: Ron Grainer; l/b: Caryl Brahms & Ned Sherrin; d: Ned Sherrin; ch: Bon Howe; md: Michael Reeves. Cast: Peter Bayliss, Ann Beach, David Firth, Ed Devereaux, Rosemary Williams. Chichester Festival Theatre, 12/15/81–1/9/82. Revised version. add l: Herbert Chappell; d: Ned Sherrin; ch: Lindsay Dolan; md: Chris Walker. Cast: Alfred Marks, David Firth, Aubrey Woods, Alexandra Bastedo

2036. *A Night in Venice*. Strauss operetta. Senator's daughter infatuated with street singer in Venice in 1750. Eastside Playhouse, 5/5/82–5/30/82. 28 perf. p: Light Opera of Manhattan; m: Johann Strauss; l: Alice Hammerstein Mathias; b: William Mount-Burke & Alice Hammerstein Mathias; based freely on idea by Zell & Richard Genee; d/md: William Mount-Burke; ch: Jerry Gotham. Cast: Sylvia Lanka. First produced in Berlin in 1883

2037. *Night of the Hunter*. Ex-con Harry Powell, with "Love" tattooed on one hand and "Hate" on the other, pretending to be a preacher, terrorizes his late partner's West Virginia family in order to find missing loot. Began as a 1998 concept album on Fynsworth Alley label. Stephen Cole won a 2000 Kleban Award, and after workshops at Vineyard Theatre (d: Lonny Price) and Goodman Theatre, (d: Robert Falls), and an April 2003 workshop starring Ron Raines, it had its world premiere at Willows Theatre Co., Concord, Calif. (this theatre was Broadway-size), 9/24/04–10/24/04. Prev from 9/20/04. m: Claibe Richardson (died of cancer in 2003); l/b: Stephen Cole; based on 1953 novel of same name by Davis Grubb, and on 1955 movie, dir by Charles Laughton, and starring Robert Mitchum & Shelley Winters; d: John Bowab; ch: Diana Baffa-Brill; set: Ray Klausen; cos: Loran Watkins; md: Daniel Freyer. Cast: Brian Noonan, Lynne Wintersteller. Aiming for Broadway in 2005 or 2006

2038. *The Night They Invented Champagne: The Lerner & Loewe Revue*. Rainbow & Stars, 7/6/93–8/28/93. 80 perf. p: Steve Paul & Gregory Dawson; d: Deborah R. Lapidus. Cast: Maureen Brennan, Eddie Korbich, Juliet Lambert, Martin Vidnovic

2039. *Nightclub Cantata*. Revue. Top of the Gate, 1/9/77–5/15/77. 145 perf. The Music-Theatre Performing Group/Lenox Arts Center production (previously prod at Westbeth & at Lenox Arts Center, Stockbridge, Mass.); m/conceived by/d: Elizabeth Swados; l: various writers; set: Patricia Woodbridge; light: Cheryl Thacker. Cast: Karen Evans, Paul Kandel, Shelley Plimpton, Elizabeth Swados, David Schechter. "Things I Didn't Know I Loved," "To the Harbormaster," "Adolescents," "Decisions," "In Dreams Begin Responsibilities," "Are You with Me?," "Waking This Morning," "The Ballad of the Sad Cafe," "Isabella," "Waiting," "On Living"

2040. *The Nightingale*. Prince's, London, 7/15/47–8/30/47. 55 perf. m/md: Kennedy Russell; l/b: Michael Martin-Harvey & Sax Rohmer; add l: Max Kester; d: Jack Hulbert; ch: Anthony Burke; set/cos: Berkeley Sutcliffe. Cast: Pearl o' the Moon: Mimi Benzell; Also with: Gavin Gordon, Rosaline Haddon, Fabia Drake, Kenneth Kove, Sonya Hana

2041. *Nightingale*. Opera based on Hans Christian Andersen's fairy tale. Lyric, Hammersmith, London, 12/22/82–1/29/83. Prev from 12/18/82. m/l: Charles Strouse; cast recording on Jay. Cast: Sarah Brightman, Susannah Fellows, Jill Pert, Grant Smith, Michael Heath. "Perfect Harmony," "Why Am I So Happy?," "Take Us to the Forest," "Who Are These People?," "Never Speak Directly to an Emperor," "Nightingale," "The Emperor is a Man," "I Was Lost," "Charming," "A Singer Must Be Free," "Mechanical Bird," "Please Don't Make Me Hear That Song Again," "Rivers Cannot Flow Upwards," "We Are China," "Death Duet," "Nobody Ever Sang for Me"

2042. *Nightmare Alley*. Rise & fall of con artist in 1930s. Primary Stages Theatre 3, 11/16/96–12/1/96. 1 prev. 15 perf. Co-prod with the Directors' Co. m/l/b/orch: Jonathan Brielle; based on novel by William Lindsay Gresham; d/ch: Danny Herman; set: Michael Hotopp; cos: Catherine Zuber; md: Phil Reno. Cast: Willy Falk, Vicki Frederick, Sarah E. Litzsinger, Nick Jolley, Ken Prymus, Nancy Lemenager. "Ten in One," "Someday, Sometime," "Tough Cookies," "Questions," "Kid," "Shuffle the Cards," "Whatever it Takes," "Lucky Heart," "Human Nature," "This is Not What I Had Planned," "Science," "Indecent Exposure," "All Will Come to You," "Cross

That River," "Hit 'em Where it Hurts," "Nobody Home," "I Still Hear it All," "Don't You Love to Watch What People Do," "Unpredictable You," "Get Her to Do It," "Nightmare Alley," "Song of the Road"

2043. *Nightsong.* A musical mosaic, program of songs. Village Gate Downstairs, 11/17/77–12/4/77. 35 perf. d: Dan Early; set: Harry Silverglat. Cast: Ron Eliran (also m/l); Holly T. Lipton, Dian Sorel, Joy Kohner. "Looking at Us," "My Land," "Dusty Roads," "Butterfly Child," "I Hear a Song," "Come with Me," "Who Am I?," "Nightsong," "Lady Vagabond," "Music in the City," "Come, Elijah, Come," "Grain of Sand," "All in the Name of Love," "Sweet Fantasy," "Have a Little Fun," "Moments by the Sea," "Young Days," "It Was Worth It," "I Believe"

2044. *Nite Club Confidential.* Set during Eisenhower era. Ballroom, 5/10/84–9/23/84. 156 perf. p: CHS Prods, Greentrack Entertainment, Sidney L. Shlenker, Joseph Stein Jr., Barbara M. Friedman; w/new songs/d/ch: Dennis Deal; standard songs by Johnny Mercer, Sammy Fain, Arthur Schwartz, Frank Loesser, Murray Grand, Jimmy Van Heusen, Beau Bergersen, Harold Rome, Harold Arlen, June Carroll & Arthur Siegel, etc; conceived by: Dennis Deal, with Albert Evans & Jamie Rocco; ms: Albert Evans; gm: Dorothy Olim & George Elmer. Cast: Fay De Witt (*Eileen Fulton* from 8/30/84 after Miss De Witt broke her leg), Stephen Berger. "Nite Club," "Something's Gotta Give," "Goody Goody," "Nothing Can Replace a Man," "I Thought About You," "French with Tears," "That Old Black Magic," "The Long Goodbye," "Ev'rybody's Boppin'," "The Other One," "Dressed to Kill," "Dead End Street." Previously produced OOB at Riverwest

2045. *No Bed for Bacon.* Theatre Royal, Bristol, England, 6/9/59 (3 weeks). p: Old Vic Theatre Trust; m: Malcolm Williamson; l/b: Ned Sherrin & Caryl Brahms; from novel by Caryl Brahms & S.J. Simon; d: Frank Dunlop; set/cos: Carl Toms; md: Gareth Davies. Cast: Michael Bates, Lally Bowers, Marion Grimaldi, Robert Lang, John Woodvine, John Rolfe, Derek Godfrey, Peter Jeffrey, Donald Pickering. Revised, with new mus by Tom Gregory & John Scott, at the Ashcroft, Croydon, 9/14/63 (2 weeks); Golders Green, London, 9/28/63. d: Michael Ashton; ch: Geraldine Stephenson; md: Ian MacPherson. Cast: Angela Baddeley, Tony Bateman, Vivienne Martin, William Rushton, Richard Wordsworth

No Bed of Roses see # 328, Main Book

2046. *The No-Frills Revue.* Comedy treatment of the theatre & other subjects. Musical Theatre Works, 10/8/87–10/25/87. 16 perf; Cherry Lane, 11/25/87–5/22/88. 207 perf. m/l: Marshall Brickman, Martin Charnin, Ronny Graham, Marvin Hamlisch, Ron Melrose, Kirk Nurock, Harold Arlen, etc; conceived by/d: Martin Charnin; sk: Thomas Meehan, etc. Cast: Sasha Charnin, Bob Stillman. The Martin Charnin songs were: "The No-Frills Revue," "Stools," "Someone's Got to Do It," "I Know Where the Bodies Are Buried," "The

Nine Supreme Chords," "Tippy Tappy" (m: Mr. Hamlisch; l: Mr. Charnin), "Come on Midnight" (m: Mr. Arlen; l: Mr. Charnin), "Yes! We Have the Manuscripts"

2047. *No In Between.* A musical mindscape. Don't Tell Mama, 8/26/96–9/5/96. 7 perf. orig songs: Elliot Weiss & Mike Champagne; b: Mike Champagne; d: Dan Held. Cast: Marc Eliot, Robin Gray, Brooke Marie Procida. "No In Between," "Alan's Song," "Haven't We Met," "I Don't Remember Christmas," "You Can Always Count on Me," "Side by Side by Side," "I'm Gonna Live Forever," "You Are There," "Not a Day Goes By"

2048. *No Shoestrings.* Musical revue. Upstairs at the Downstairs, 10/11/62. 66 perf. Musical numbers by Ronald Cass, Arthur Siegel, Richard Addinsell, Tchaikovsky, Lawrence Grossman, Peter Myers, Bud McCreery, Michael McWhinney, etc; conceived by/d: Ben Bagley; d/ch: Robert Haddad; md/arr: Dorothea Freitag. Cast: Danny Carroll, Jane Connell, Larry Holofcener, Bill McCutcheon, Patti Regan, June Squibb. "It's a Great Little World," "Hoffa Love is Better than None," "A Pawn for Wernher von Braun"

2049. *No Trams to Lime Street.* Richmond Theatre, England, 9/8/70–9/26/70; then toured. Never made the West End. p: Bill Kenwright & David Gordon; m/l: Marty Wilde & Ronnie Scott; add material: Leo Aylen; based on TV play by Alun Owen; d: Maurice Stewart; ch: Roy Pannell; md: Del Newman. Cast: Bill Kenwright, Frazer Hines, Edward Evans, Virginia Stride

2050. *No Way to Treat a Lady.* Hudson Guild, 5/27/87–7/5/87. 14 prev. 27 perf. m/l/b: Douglas J. Cohen; based on William Goldman's novel, which was turned into a movie with Rod Steiger & Lee Remick; d: Jack Hofsis; ch: Christopher Chadman; set: David Jenkins; light: Beverly Emmons; md: Uel Wade; orch: Danny Troob. Cast: Stephen Bogardus, Peter Slutsker, June Gable, Liz Callaway. "Five More Minutes," "A Very Funny Thing," "So Far So Good," "Safer in My Arms," "I've Been a Bad Boy," "The First Move," "I Hear Humming," "Killer on the Line," "The Next Move," "Whose Hands," "You're Getting Warmer," "Front Page News," "Female Encounters," "Once More from the Top," "One of the Beautiful People," "Still," "Sarah's Touch," "I've Noticed a Change," "A Close Call." St. Peter's Church, 12/11/96–2/2/77. 14 prev. 44 perf. Somewhat revised score. p: York Theatre Co.; d: Scott Schwartz; ch: Daniel Stewart; set: James Morgan; cos: Yvonne De Moravia; light: Mary Jo Dondlinger; md: Wendy Bobbitt; orch: David Siegel; cast recording on Varese Sarabande. Cast: Adam Grupper, Alix Korey, Paul Schoeffler, Marguerite MacIntyre

2051. *Noddy in Toyland.* Children's play with mus. Stoll, London, 12/23/54–1/22/55. m: Philip Green; add songs: R.C. Noel-Johnson; based on characters created by Enid Blyton; d: Andre Van Gyseghem. Cast: Noddy: Bunny May; Big Ears: David Keir; Mr. Plod: Peter Elliott; Mr. Tubby Bear: Terry Johnson; Mrs. Tubby Bear: Sylvia Ellis; Also with: Oscar Quitak, Bruno Barnabe, Timothy Grey,

Michael Maguire. Prince's, 12/22/55; Stoll, 12/22/56; Prince's, 12/23/57; Victoria Palace, 12/23/58; Prince's, 12/23/59; Scala, 12/21/62

2052. *Noel and Gertie.* About Noel Coward & Gertrude Lawrence. King's Head, London, 5/9/83–6/4/83. m/l: Noel Coward; dev: Sheridan Morley. Cast: Patricia Hodge, Simon Cadell. "Someday I'll Find You," "Mrs. Worthington," "Dance Little Lady," "We Were Dancing," "You Were There," "Has Anybody Seen Our Ship?," "Men About Town," "I Travel Alone," "Sail Away," "I'll See You Again." 1st produced at Hong Kong Festival, 1982. Donmar Warehouse, London, 8/26/86. Cast: Lewis Fiander, Patricia Hodge. Cast recording on Jay. York Theatre Co. (OB), 1993. Re-vamped & re-titled *If Love Were All.* Bay Street Theatre, Sag Harbor, Long Island; Lucille Lortel Theatre (OB), 6/10/99–9/5/99. 27 prev from 5/18/99. 101 perf. adapted/d: Leigh Lawson; ch: Niki Harris; set/cos: Tony Walton; md/orch: Tom Fay. Cast: Harry Groener, Twiggy. In 2002 Sheridan Morley dir his own revival at the Jermyn Street, London, 8/19/02–9/7/02. ch: Irving Davies; md: Stuart Pedlar. Cast: Annabel Leventon, John Watts

2053. *Noel Coward's Sweet Potato.* Revue. Ethel Barrymore, Broadway, 9/29/68–10/12/68. 20 prev. 17 perf; Booth, 11/1/68–11/23/68. 27 perf. p: Robert L. Steele; m/l: Noel Coward. From a conception by Roderick Cook; d: Lee Theodore; ch: Lee Theodore & Robert Tucker; set: Helen Pond & Herbert Senn; cos: David Toser; light: Peter Hunt; ms/arr: Fred Werner; md/voc arr: Charles Schneider. Cast: George Grizzard, Dorothy Loudon (*Mary Louise Wilson* from 11/1/68), Carole Shelley, Arthur Mitchell, Robert LuPone, Ian Tucker, Bonnie Schon, Tom Kneebone, Stephen Reinhardt. "Useful Phrases," "Mad Dogs and Englishmen," "A Bar on the Piccola Marina," "Mad About the Boy," "A Room with a View," "Don't Put Your Daughter on the Stage, Mrs. Worthington," "Sweet Potato" (dance)

2054. *Northern Boulevard.* Set on Northern Boulevard, Jackson Heights, Queens, NY, Oct. 1941–Oct. 1981. AMAS, 2/14/85–3/10/85. 16 perf. m/l: Carleton Carpenter; d: William Martin; ch: Dennis Dennehy; cos: Judy Dearing. Cast: Alice Cannon, Rosetta Le Noire. "Get up and Dance," "He Loves Her," "Half a World Away," "Plus One," "Growing," "Northern Boulevard," "Living in Luxury," "Master," "Priorities," "A Silver Song," "Fathers and Sons," "Let's Not Miss the Boat," "Whoa, Baby!"

2055. *Nostalgia Tropical.* Afro-Cuban musical revue. Playhouse 91, 2/10/93–3/28/93. 49 perf. conceived by/d: Max Ferra; cos: Randy Barcelo; light: Jennifer Tipton. Cast: Meme Solis (also md), Victor Sterling. Re-opened at the Blue Angel, 6/9/93

Not So New Faces of '82 and '84 see # 486, Main Book

2056. *Not Tonight, Benvenuto!* About Cellini. Carter, 6/5/79. 35 prev. 1 perf. co-p/d: Jim Payne; m/l/b: Virgil Engeran; ch: Robin Reseen; set: James Morgan; ms: Larry Hochman. Cast: Ron Wyche, Marion Markham. "How Do You Do," "Can't Make Love without You,"

"Who Can Control the Human Heart?," "Poppin'," "This is Our World," "Gonna Get Right Some Day," "Wedding Ball"

2057. ***Not While I'm Eating.*** Musical revue. Madison Avenue Playhouse, 12/19/61–12/20/61. 2 perf. m: Arthur Siegel; l/sk: Arthur Sherman (l/sk); d: Warren Enters; ch: Tom Panko; cos: Stanley Simmons; md: Milton Greene. Cast: Wisa D'Orso, Buzz Halliday

2058. ***Notre Dame de Paris.*** French-Canadian musical that took the French-speaking world by storm. This is the French title for Victor Hugo's book which in English is called *The Hunchback of Notre Dame*. Palais des Congres, Paris, 9/18/98. m: Richard Cocciante; l: Luc Plamondon; d: Gilles Maheu; ch: Martino Muller; cast recording on Pomme Music. Cast: Quasimodo: Garou; Esmeralda: Noa; Also with: Daniel Lavoie, Bruno Pelletier, Patrick Fiori, Julie Zenatti. 1st presented as CD in 11/97, then in 1/98 as concept album. After Paris it toured France, Belgium, Switzerland & French Canada, then Toronto. On 1/21/00 it had U.S. debut, at Paris Hotel, Las Vegas (English l: Will Jennings). Cast: Douglas Storm, Francis Ruivivar, Jessica Grove. Dominion, London, 5/23/00–10/6/01. Prev from 5/15/00. Cast: Quasimodo: Garou; Esmeralda: Tina Arena

2059. ***Now.*** Topical musical revue. Cherry Lane, 6/5/68–6/23/68. 22 perf. m: John Aman; l/sk: George Haimsohn; conceived by/d: Marvin Gordon; md: Barry Manilow. Cast: John Aman, Frank Andre (*Richard Granat*), Sue Lawless, Ted Pugh, Lauree Berger, Rosalind Harris. Opened after shooting & before death of Bobby Kennedy, and "Bobby Baby" was cut. A skit satirizing Andy Warhol, who had recently been injured in assassination attempt, was not cut. "Come Along with Us," "Space Idiocy," "Save a Sinner Tonight," "Acre of Grass," "Sidney," "Peonies," "Flower Children," "The Third Lady," "Leather Love," "Minimal," "Climb up Here with Daddy on the Boom Boom," "Beautiful People," "California Style," "Now"

2060. ***Now Is the Time for All Good Men.*** Set in Bloomdale, Indiana (population 973). Theatre de Lys, 9/26/67–12/31/67. 22 prev. 112 perf. p: David Cryer & Albert Poland; m: Nancy Ford; l/b: Gretchen Cryer; d: Word Baker; md: Stephen Lawrence; cast recording on Columbia. Cast: Sally Niven (who was really Gretchen Cryer), David Cryer (*John Bennett Perry*), Art Wallace (*Murray Olson*), Murray Olson (*John Long*), Anne Kaye (*Judy Allen*), Regina Lynn, Judy Frank, Donna Curtis, David Sabin, Margot Hanson, John Bennett Perry, Steve Skiles. "We Shall Meet in the Great Hereafter," "Keep 'em Busy, Keep 'em Quiet," "What's in the Air?," "Tea in the Rain," "What's a Guy Like You Doin' in a Place Like This?," "Halloween Hayride," "Campfire Songs," "See Everything New," "All Alone," "He Could Show Me," "Washed Away," "Stuck-Up," "My Holiday," "On My Own," "It Was Good Enough for Grandpa," "A Simple Life," "A Star on the Monument," "Rain Your Love on Me." Equity Library, 4/29/71–5/16/71. 2 prev. 14 perf. d: Ronald Roston; md:

John R. Williams. Cast: Judy Knaiz, Marcia O'Brien. The score was a little different

2061. ***The Nuclear Family.*** All improvised, no score on paper. Created in 2001 at the World Domination TheatreSports Tournament in Atlanta. Then to NY, at 45 Bleecker Street, then to HERE (4 months), then to the Zipper, 9/10/03. Prev from 8/29/03. md: Matt Cohen. Cast: Jimmy Bennett, John Gregorio, Stephen Guarino

2062. ***Nunsense.*** Phenomenally successful comedy hit. 5 nuns are only survivors of tragedy at convent Little Sisters of Hoboken, N.J. ("Little Hobos"); all other sisters had died of food poisoning when Sister Julia "Child of God" cooked up some bad vichyssoise. The 5 sisters were out playing bingo & are now staging benefit to raise money to bury the others. Cherry Lane, 12/12/85–2/23/86. Prev from 12/3/85; Sheridan Square Playhouse/Circle Rep, from 2/27/86; Douglas Fairbanks, 9/8/86–10/16/94. Total of 3,672 perf. w/d: Dan Goggin; ch: Felton Smith; set: Barry Axtell; light: Susan A. White; md: Michael Rice. In 1981, as a joke from a Dominican brother friend of his, Dan Goggin received a mannequin dressed as Dominican nun, and he began designing a line of humorous greeting cards with photos of a friend, dental assistant Marilyn Farina, in nun's clothing. She would appear in this habit at stores to promote the product, and Goggin would write material for her. They sold 200,000 cards by end of year. In 1983 this developed into 15-minute cabaret act *The Nunsense Story*, with contributions from Steven Hays. Included monks & nuns, and ran 38 weeks in basement of the Duplex, a cabaret in Greenwich Village, starring Marilyn Farina. As the nuns were the ones getting the laughs, Goggin decided to re-write & expand it as full-length musical, and developed it at workshop in Baldwin School in 1985. Opened at the Cherry Lane, but reviews were not great. However, audiences loved it. Cast: Christine Anderson (*Helen Baldassare*), Marilyn Farina (*Travis Hudson, Mary-Pat Green, Julie J. Hafner*), Vicki Belmonte (*Edwina Lewis, Nancy Johnston*), Semina De Laurentis (*Nancy Johnston, Susan Gordon-Clark, Nancy Hillner*), Suzi Winson. Standby: Karen Ziemba. Understudy: Susan Gordon-Clark. "Nunsense is Habit-Forming," "A Difficult Transition," "Benedicte," "The Biggest Ain't the Best," "Playing Second Fiddle," "So You Want to Be a Nun," "Turn up the Spotlight," "Lilacs Bring Back Memories," "Tackle That Temptation with a Time Step," "Growing up Catholic," "We've Got to Clean Out the Freezer," "Just a Coupl'a Sisters," "Soup's On (The Dying Nun Ballet)," "I Just Want to Be a Star," "The Drive-In," "I Could've Gone to Nashville," "Gloria in Excelsis Deo," "Holier than Thou." Fortune, London, 3/23/87–1/16/88. Cast: Honor Blackman. Triad, 11/17/95–12/31/95. 55 perf. Cast: Nancy E. Carroll, Jennifer Perry, Lin Tucci, Robin Taylor, Kim Galbraith. 20th-anniversary tour in fall 2003. p: Scott M. Robbins; d: Dan Goggin; ch: Felton Smith. Cast: Kaye Ballard, Georgia Engel, Mimi Hines, Darlene Love, Lee Meriwether. Several sequels (see below)

2063. ***Nunsense II: The Second Coming.*** Sequel to *Nunsense*, set 6 weeks after events of 1985 orig. Hamilton Pavilion, Seven Angels, Waterbury, Conn., 11/20/92. d: Dan Goggin; ch: Felton Smith. Cast: Christine Anderson, Semina De Laurentiis, Mary Gillis, Kathy Robinson, Lyn Vaux. Ran in some regional theatres from 1992 on. Ran OB, as *Nunsense 2: The Sequel*, at the Douglas Fairbanks, 10/31/94–2/26/95. Prev from 10/21/94. d: Dan Goggin; ch: Felton Smith; md: Michael Rice. Cast: Nancy E. Carroll, Semina De Laurentis (*Amanda Buterbaugh*), Carolyn Droscoski, Susan Emerson (*Elizabeth Dargan Doyle*), Terri White. "Jubilate Deo," "Nunsense, the Magic Word," "Winning is Just the Beginning," "Prima Ballerina," "The Biggest Still Ain't the Best," "I've Got Pizazz," "The Country Nun," "Look Ma, I Made It," "The Padre Polka," "The Classic Queens," "A Hat and Cane Song," "Angeline," "We're the Nuns to Come To," "What Would Elvis Do?," "Yes, We Can," "I Am Here to Stay," "Oh Dear, What a Catastrophe," "No One Ever Cared The Way You Do," "Gloria in Excelsis Deo," "There's Only One Way to End Your Prayers." Both this show, and *Nunsense*, have played all over the world, especially reproductions of the orig. Another sequel, *Sister Amnesia's Country Western Jamboree* (also known as *Sister Amnesia's Nunsense Jamboree*); then another, *Nutcrackers* (a Christmas show); then came *Nunsense A-Men!*

2064. ***Nunsense A-Men!*** Brazil, 1995. Another sequel, of sorts, to *Nunsense* & *Nunsense II* (see above). This, all-male version (male actors dressed as nuns) debuted in Brazil & ran there for years. 47th Street Theatre (OB), 6/23/98–1/3/99. 12 prev from 6/13/98. 225 perf. d: Dan Goggin; ch: Felton Smith; md: Leo P. Carusone. Cast: David Titus, Greg White, Lothair Eaton, Doan Mackenzie, Danny Vaccaro, Tom Dwyer. Same score as orig. A later sequel was *Meshuggah-Nuns* (see above)

2065. ***Nymph Errant.*** Equity Library, 3/11/82–4/4/82. 32 perf. m/l: Cole Porter; b: Romney Brent; from novel by James Laver; d: Clinton J. Atkinson; ch: Dennis Dennehy; md: Donald Sosin. Cast: Kathleen Mahony-Bennett, Lynne Charnay, Avril Gentles, Boncellia Lewis, Lil Arbogast. See also *Evangeline*, in this appendix

2066. ***O Marry Me!*** Set in England in 1806. Gate, 10/27/61–11/12/61 (21 perf). From Oliver Goldsmith's *She Stoops to Conquer*; d: Michael Howard; set/light: Herbert Senn & Helen Pond. Cast: Elly Stone, Chevi Colton. "I Love Everything That's Old," "Time and Tide," "The Kind of Man," "Ale House Song," "Proper Due," "Be a Lover," "Perish the Baubles," "The Meeting," "Fashions," "Say Yes, Look No," "Let's All Be Exactly and Precisely What We Are," "Braggart Song," "O Marry Me!," "Betrayed," "Motherly Love," "Morality"

2067. ***O, Oysters!!!*** An Eric Blau cabaret revue. Village Gate, 1/26/61–4/16/61. 104 perf. Jacques Brel wrote some of the music. Cast: Elly Stone, Jon Voight, Louise Troy, Danny Meehan

2068. *O Pioneers!* Play with mus. Set on the plains of Nebraska in the 1890s. Women's Project, 5/2/01–5/13/01. 1 prev. 12 perf. m/orch: Kim D. Sherman; l/adapted by: Darrah Cloud; from 1913 novel by Willa Cather; d: Richard Corley; set: Loy Arcenas; light: Dennis Parichy; md: Kimberly Grigsby. Cast: Todd Cerveris

2069. *O Sappho, O Wilde!* Comedy revue with mus. Duplex, 8/1/90–8/15/90. 3 perf. d: Bill Cosgriff. Cast: Lisa Goodman, Jo Anna Rush

2070. *O Say Can You See!* Spoof of Hollywood's old patriotic musicals. Provincetown Playhouse, 10/8/62–11/4/62. 24 perf. p: Greenville Co.; m: Jack Holmes; l/b: Bill Conklin & Bob Miller; d/ch: Ray Harrison; book d: Cynthia Baer; light: Jules Fisher. Cast: Jan Chaney, Sally Ackerman, Mike Douglas, Marcia Rodd, Elmarie Wendel. "The Freedom Choo-Choo is Leaving Today," "Dreamboat from Dreamland," "The Dogface Jive," "Us Two," "Take Me Back to Texas," "Doughnuts for Defense," "Canteen Serenade," "These Are Worth Fighting For," "Someone a Lot Like You," "Veronica Takes Over," "Buy Bonds, Buster, Buy Bonds," "Chico-Chico Chico-Layo Tico-Tico Pay-Pa-Payo Buena Vista de Banana by the Sea," "Flim Flam Flooey," "When the Bluebirds Fly All Over the World," "Just the Way You Are," "My G.I. Joey," "O Say Can You See!"

2071. *Oba Oba.* Brazilian extravaganza. Named for a famous showcase in Rio de Janeiro. Ambassador, Broadway, 3/29/88–5/8/88. 11 prev. 53 perf. p/conceived by: Franco Fontana; ch: Roberto Abrahao; sound: Peter Fitzgerald; md: Wilson Mauro. Cast: Nilze Carvalho, Eliana Estevao, Toco Preto, Jaime Santos. *Oba Oba '90,* ran at Marquis, Broadway 3/15/90–4/22/90. 11 prev. 45 perf, then resumed tour. *Oba Oba '93,* ran at Marquis, 10/1/92–11/11/92. 24 prev. 45 perf. Mostly favorable reviews

2072. *O'Casey's Knock.* Set in 19th-century Dublin. Judith Anderson, 11/6/97–11/16/97. 5 prev. 7 perf. m/l/b: Paul Dick; from novel *Knock at the Door,* by Sean O'Casey; d: Ron Nash. Cast: Stephen Lloyd Webber

2073. *Occasional Grace.* Play with mus. St. Peter's/Universalist Church, 2/27/91–3/16/91. 3 prev. 9 perf. p: Anne Hamburger; w: Michael Ahn, Neena Beber, Magdalia Cruz, Talvin Wilks; d: Bill Rauch; light: Brian Aldous. "Angels," "Safe," "Sinner," "It Don't Mean Nothing," "Jesus Was a Working Man," "Being Alive," "I'm in Love with an Angel," "Nothing but the Grace," "Get Right Church"

2074. *The Odd Potato.* One-act children's musical. Concert version. Set during Hannukah. Peter Norton Symphony Space, 11/24/03–11/30/03. p: 6-10 Prods; m: Gail C. Bluestone; l/b: Eileen Bluestone Sherman; d: Ben Vereen. Cast: Mark Jacobs, Melba Moore, Charlotte Rae, Molly Ephraim

Odyssey see # 318, Main Book

2075. *Oedipus — Private Eye.* Ancient Greek myth re-set in 1940s. Musical Theatre Works, 2/3/95–2/12/95. 10 perf. m: Matthew Sklar; l/b/d: Chad Beguelin; ch: Patricia

Wilcox. Cast: George Merrick, Andrew Driscoll, Lynnette Perry, Gwen Stewart

2076. *Of Mice and Men.* Musical drama based on John Steinbeck's play. Provincetown Playhouse, 12/4/58–1/8/59. 37 perf. m: Alfred Brooks; l: Ira J. Bilowit; adapted by: Ira J. Bilowit & Wilson Lair; d: Jerome Eskow; incidental dance movement: Zoya Leporska. Cast: George: Leo Penn; Lennie: Art Lund; Curly's Wife: Jo Sullivan; Candy: John F. Hamilton. "Nice House We Got Here," "No Ketchup," "We Got a Future," "Buckin' Barley," "Curly's Wife," "Wanta, Hope to Feel at Home," "Lemme Tell Ya," "Just Someone to Talk To," "Dudin' Up," "Nice Fella," "Why Try Hard to Be Good?," "Never Do a Bad Thing," "We Got a Future" (reprise), "Is There Some Place for Me?," "A Guy, a Guy, a Guy," "Strangeley," "Candy's Lament"

2077. *Oh, Boy!* Princess, Broadway, 2/20/17; Casino, 11/19/17–3/30/18. Total of 463 perf. m: Jerome Kern; l/b: Guy Bolton & P.G. Wodehouse; d: Edward Royce. Cast: Marion Davies, Tom Powers, Edna May Oliver. "Let's Make a Night of It," "You Never Knew About Me," "A Package of Seeds," "An Old-Fashioned Wife," "A Pal Like You," "Till the Clouds Roll By," "A Little Bit of Ribbon," "The First Day of May," "Koo-La-Loo," "Rolled into One," "Oh, Daddy, Please," "Nesting Time in Flatbush," "Words are Not Needed (Every Day)," "Flubby Dub, the Cave Man." Park Royal, 11/29/79–12/22/79. 20 perf. d: Donnis Honeycutt; ch: Daniel Levans; md: David Krane. Cast: Julie Wilder, Greg Minahan, Lauren Goler, Elaine Swann, Gene Paul Rickard. York Theatre Company prod it as the 40th in its *Musicals in Mufti* series, 10/17/03–10/19/03. d: Simon Jones. Cast: Hunter Bell, Viola Harris, Randy Redd, Jim Stanek

2078. *Oh, Johnny.* WWII pilot recruited for secret mission behind lines in China. Players, 1/10/82. 13 prev. 1 perf. m/l: Gary Cherpakov & Paul Streitz; d/ch: Alan Weeks; md: Robert Marks. Cast: Michael Crouch. Previously ran OOB at Off Center Theatre

2079. *Oh Me, Oh My, Oh Youmans.* Tribute to Vincent Youmans. Wonderhorse, 1/14/81–1/31/81. 20 perf. conceived by/d: Darwin Knight; md: Sand Lawn. Cast: Jo Ann Cunningham, Todd Taylor, Sally Woodson, Ronald Young

2080. *Oh! My Papa!* Garrick, London, 7/16/57. 45 perf. m: Paul Burkhard; w: Juerg Amstein & Erik Charell; English adaptation: Elizabeth Montagu; d: Warren Jenkins; set: Patrick Robertson; cos: Rosemary Vercoe. Cast: Peter O'Toole, Robert Lang, Sonia Rees, Phyllida Sewell, Phyllida Law, Gwen Nelson, Paul Curran, Angela Sturdee

2081. *Oh! Oh! Obesity!* New Federal Theatre, 6/7/84–6/24/84. 15 perf. m/l/story: Gerald W. Deas; d: Bette Howard. Cast: Sandra Reaves-Phillips, Reginald VelJohnson. "Oh! Oh! Obesity," "I Don't Eat a Thing," "You've Got to Stay Real Cool," "Han-Some," "You're Gonna Need Somebody," "If de Boot Don't Fit You Can't Wear It," "Jellybread Falls on Jellyside Down," "I'm Fat," "Everybody Wants to Be a Star," "Gym Jam Boogie," "I Fried All Night Long"

2082. *Oh, What a Night.* Featured 1970s songs. Manchester, England. Sold out. London Apollo, Hammersmith, 8/5/99–10/16/99. Prev from 7/27/99. d/ch: Kim Gavin. Cast: Kid Creole, Will Mellor, John Altman, Michael Howe, Michelle McSween

2083. *Oil City Symphony.* Musical revue. Graduates have reunion in honor of favorite teacher. Circle in the Square Downtown, 11/5/87–5/7/89. 11 prev. 626 perf. The Oil City Symphony in recital, with refreshments afterwards. By & with Mike Craver, Debra Monk (*Michelle Horman*), Mark Hardwick, Mary Murfitt (*Kathy Beaver*). d: Larry Forde; light: Natasha Katz; sound: Otts Munderloh. "Count Your Blessings," "Musical Moments," "Baby, It's Cold Outside," "The End of the World," "In the Sweet By and By," "My Old Kentucky Rock and Roll Home." Previously ran in Dallas & Baltimore. A "replugged" version ran at Danny's Skylight Cabaret, 10/19/00–12/31/00. p: George Gordon; d: Mary Murfitt. Cast: Mike Craver, John DePinto, Mary Ehlinger, Mary Murfitt

2084. *Okay U.S.A.* Army Show, 1944. From the Special Services Division in military establishments. m/l: Frank Loesser. "I Was Down Texas Way," "My Chicago," "The Tall Pines," "Tonight in San Francisco," "A Trip Round the USA," "You're OK, USA!," "When He Comes Home"

2085. *Old Bucks and New Wings.* Mayfair, 11/5/62–11/11/62. 8 perf. m/l/d: Harvey Lasker. Cast: Harland Dixon, Kathryn Doby, Beverly Ann Paulsen, Rex Weber, Charlie Dale, Joe Smith, Ted Lambrinos, Flip Wilson, Mary Mon Toy. "Our Business is News," "So, So Sophie," "That Was Your Life," "That Day Will Come," "Sweet Memories," "You Made It Possible, Dear," "Stand up and Cheer," "Let's Bring Back Showbusiness"

2086. *Ole!* Greenwich Mews, 3/18/59–4/18/59. 35 perf. p: Village Presbyterian Church & Brotherhood Synagogue; based on the zarzuela *La Chulapona;* from English adaptation by Tracy Samuels & Max Leavitt; d: Max Leavitt; ch: Ruthanna Boris. Cast: Ruth Kobart, Gino Conforti. "Isabel," "Girls of Madrid," "La Chulapona," "El Pelele," "In the Hills of Andalusia," "Free for All," "Love is a Game," "Ole!"

2087. *Olympus on My Mind.* Set in ancient Thebes (Greece) during the course of a 41-hour day. Actors Outlet, 5/2/86; Lambs, 7/15/86–1/10/87. 207 perf. m: Grant Sturiale; l/b/d: Barry Harman; suggested by *Amphitryon,* by Heinrich von Kleist (1807); ch: Pamela Sousa. Cast: Peter Kapetan, Andy Spangler (*Danny Weathers*), Keith Bennett (*David Andrew White*), Elizabeth Austin (*Rusty Riegelman*), Martin Vidnovic (*Tom Wopat*), Jason Graae (*John Scherer*), Peggy Hewett (*Naz Edwards*), Emily Zacharias (*Susan Powell*), Lewis J. Stadlen (*Charles Repole*). "Welcome to Greece," "Heaven on Earth," "The Gods on Tap," "Surprise!," "Wait 'til it Dawns," "I Know My Wife," "It Was Me," "Back So Soon?," "Wonderful," "At Liberty in Thebes," "Jupiter Slept Here," "Back to the Play," "Don't Bring Her Flowers," "General's Pandemonium," "Olympus is a Lonely Town," "A Star is Born," "Final Sequence"

2088. *On Second Avenue.* Yiddish-English musical revue. Norman Thomas, 10/25/87–1/10/88. 54 perf. created by: Zalmen Mlotek & Moishe Rosenfeld; songs: Moishe Rosenfeld, Zalmen Mlotek, Sholem Aleichem, Joseph Rumshinsky, Sholom Secunda, Molly Picon, Itzik Manger, etc; d: Isaiah Sheffer; light: Victor En Yu Tan. Cast: Bruce Adler, Joanne Borts. Went on to national tour

2089. *On the Level.* Royal Court, Liverpool, England, 2/25/66–3/12/66; Saville, London, 4/19/66–7/30/66. 118 perf. p: Martin Landau; m: Ron Grainer; l/b: Ronald Millar; d: Wendy Toye; ch: Wendy Toye & Malcolm Clare; md: Ed Coleman. Cast: Angela Richards, Rod McLennan, Leslie Phillips (*Barrie Ingham*), Sheila White, Gary Bond, Irlin Hall, Bernard Sharpe, John Horsley, Robert Cawdron, Phyllida Law. "Three Crazy Letters," "Strangely Attractive," "Bleep Bleep," "Thermodynamically Yours," "Very Good Friend," "My Girl at the Dance," "Let's Make the Most of Now," "Where the Action Is," "Nostalgia," "Love Gets Younger Every Year," "Peaceful," "On the Level," "And Then I'll Go," "Chorale"

2090. *On the Lock-In.* Episodes of prison life in musical form. NY Shakespeare Festival, 4/14/77–6/5/77. 62 perf-press date 4/27/77. w: David Langston Smyrl; conceived by/d: Robert Macbeth; set: Karl Eigsti; md: George Stubbs. Cast: David Langston Smyrl, Billy Barnes, Alan Weeks, Don Jay. "Whatever it Happens to Be," "Dry Mouth with No Water," "Born to Lose," "Sister Paradise," "Peace Will Come," "Circumstances," "42nd Street Blues," "Talkin' Blues," "Marlene," "Alone"

2091. *On the Prowl.* Actors Outlet, 11/9/88–12/3/88. 5 prev. 11 perf. m/l/b: John Chibbaro & Claudia-Jo Allmand; ch: Marvin Gordon. Cast: Claudia-Jo Allmand, Tony Di Benedetto (also d). "Crazy," "On the Prowl," "If I Say Yes," "Closer to Me," "We're Just Like Children," "I Cry Tears," "I Forget About Romance," "Tailpipe," "Once There Was Love in Me," "Dancing Alone," "Tell Me," "Please Let Me Prove," "This is What I'll Do"

2092. *On the Record.* Three people's lives are changed. More than 50 Disney songs. Tour only, opened 11/19/04–11/21/04, Palace, Cleveland. Prev from 11/9/04. Then on with tour. Closed 7/31/05, Buell, Denver. d/ch: Robert Longbottom; set: Robert Brill; cos: Gregg Barnes; light: Natasha Katz; ms/arr: David Chase. Cast: Emily Skinner (*Kaitlin Hopkins*), Brian Sutherland

2093. *On the Road to Victory.* Boogie-woogie musical revue. All Souls Church, 2/27/97–3/16/97. 6 prev. 9 perf. add m/l/adapted by/d: Michael Tester; ms/orch: Steve Steiner; md: Christine Talbott

2094. *Once Around the City.* Good-hearted heiress cheated out of home where she shelters homeless men. 7/10/01–7/22/01. 16 perf. m: Robert Reale; l/b: Willie Reale; d: Mark Linn-Baker; ch: Jennifer Muller; set: Adrianne Lobel; cos: Paul Tazewell; light: Donald Holder; sound: Jon Weston; md/orch: Rick Fox. Cast: William Parry, Anna Stone,

Patrick Garner, Joe Grifasi, Geoffrey Nauffts, Anne Torsiglieri, Jane Bodle

2095. *Once on a Summer's Day.* Relationship between Lewis Carroll & Alice. Ensemble Studio, 12/7/84–12/23/84. 26 perf. Same venue, 1/10/85–2/11/85. 28 perf. m: Jeffrey Lunden; l/b: Arthur Perlman; d: John Henry Davis; ch: Elizabeth Keen; md: Ronald Clay Fullum. Cast: Kim Morris, Carolyn Mignini, Martin Moran, Nicholas Wyman, David Purdham, Mimi Wyche, Polly Pen, David Green, Kay Walbye (understudy). "Once on a Summer's Day," "Don't Depend on Watches," "The Angles of Geometry," "Wonderland," "Fairy Child," "No," "The Music Box," "See What Mr. Dodgson Gave Me," "The Tea Party," "Jabberwocky," "The Equation Cannot Be Solved," "The Trial," "Rules Shall Not Be Broken"

2096. *Once Upon a Song.* Coconut Grove Playhouse, Miami, 1990. World premiere of new piece using old & new Anthony Newley material. m/l: Anthony Newley; b: Leslie Bricusse, Herbert Kretzmer, Ian Fraser, Stanley Ralph Ross; conceived by: Anthony Newley & Arnold Mittelman; d: Arnold Mittelman; ch: Tony Stevens; md: Louis St. Louis; orch: Michael Gibson. Cast: Anthony Newley, Bertilla Baker, Tracy Venner, Sean Dooley

2097. *Once Upon a Time...* Pantomime/nursery rhyme show, journey into magic world of make-believe. Duke of York's, London, 12/21/72–1/20/73. 26 matinees. p: David Frost; m: Roger Webb; l/b: Norman Newell; d/ch: Gillian Lynne; set/cos: Tony Walton; md: Martin Goldstein. Cast: Tim Curry, Tony Robinson, Kerry Gardner, Roger Webb, Joyce Grant, Patsy Rowlands. "Ding, Dong, Bell," "Three Bears," "Three Famous Pussy Cats," "Owl and the Pussy Cat," "Wicked," "Little Red Riding-hood," "Queen of Hearts," "Pat-a-Cake," "Make Your Own Rainbow," "Scarecrow Song," "Here We Go Round the Mulberry Bush," "Silver Sleigh," "All the Fun of the Fair"

2098. *Once Upon a Time in New Jersey.* Set in 1950s Hoboken. Vinnie, a deli worker longs for co-worker who is in love with Vinnie's no-good brother Rocco. Rocco finds himself target of hit man & changes places with Vinnie. Director's Co., 6/25/03–6/30/03. m: Stephen Weiner; l/b: Susan DiLallo; d/ch: Patricia Birch. Cast: Nick Cavarra, Orfeh, Melanie Vaughan

2099. *One Foot Out the Door.* 3 people meet in group therapy. Trocadero Cabaret & Don't Tell Mama, 3/5/93–10/3/93. 41 perf. m/l/b/md: Stephen Dolginoff; d: Cheryl Katz. Cast: Laurie Alyssa Myers, Kyle Dadd, Garth Kravits, Elizabeth Richmond. "Therapy," "Here I Am," "Barbie and Ken," "One Foot Out the Door," "Not Anymore," "Like the Skyline," "My Deepest Thoughts"

2100. *One for My Baby: Johnny Mercer.* 90-song salute to Johnny Mercer. All Souls Unitarian Church, 10/20/78–11/30/78. 10 perf. narrator/d/voc orch: Tran William Rhodes; ch: Randy Fields; md: Joyce Hitchcock

2101. *One for the Money, Etc.* Revival of selected excerpted highlights from Nancy Hamilton (sk) & Morgan Lewis (m) revues of

1939, 1940 & 1946. Eastside Playhouse, 5/24/72–6/11/72. 23 perf. d/ch: Tom Panko; set/cos: Fred Voelpel; light: Judy Rasmuson; md: Peter Howard. Cast: Pamela Adams, Georgia Engel, Joy Garrett, Pat Lysinger, Liz Otto. See # 697, Main Book

2102. *125th Street.* Set during one of the "Amateur Nights" at Apollo Theatre, Harlem in 1969. Shaftesbury, London, 9/17/02–1/11/03. Prev from 8/30/02. w: Alan Jones; d: Rob Bettinson

2103. *One Man Band.* South Street, 6/12/85–7/28/85. 8 prev. 38 perf. m/l: Marc Eliot & Larry Hochman; b: James Lecesne; d: Jack Hofsis; set: Lawrence Miller; cos: William Ivey Long; light: Natasha Katz; sound: Tony Meola. Cast: James Lecesne, Kay Cole, Judy Gibson, Vanessa Williams. "Hey, Lady," "Somewhere Out There," "Moonlight," "One Silk Shirt," "Atlantic City," "Singin' a Song," "Female Animal," "The Perfect Life," "One Man Band"

2104. *One Mo' Time.* An evening of 1920s black vaudeville. About the difficulties faced by blacks in showbiz, in particular those of the real-life Bertha Williams, who was in New Orleans in 1926, at the Lyric Theatre, to perform "One Mo' Time." Village Gate Downstairs, 10/22/79–2/6/83. 1,372 perf. m/l: Vernel Bagneris, etc; conceived by/d: Vernel Bagneris; cast recording on Warners. Cast: Sylvia "Kuumba" Williams (*Carol Woods* from 7/81), Vernel Bagneris (*Bruce Strickland* from 7/80), Topsy Chapman (*Peggy Alston* from 7/81), John Stell (*James "Red" Wilcher* from 7/81), Thais Clark (*Frozine Jo Thomas* from 7/81). "He's Funny That Way," "Everybody Loves My Baby," "Kitchen Man," "I've Got What It Takes." Originally performed in New Orleans by the New Experience Players. Tour opened 7/2/80, Philadelphia. Cast: Sandra Reaves-Phillips, Jackee Harry, Deborah Burrell, Vernel Bagneris, Red Wilcher. Cambridge Theatre, London, 7/14/81. Orig NY cast; moved to the Phoenix. A sequel, *And Further Mo'*, set a year later, opened at the Crossroads, New Brunswick, NJ, as part of 89–90 season. d: Vernel Bagneris. Cast: Sandra Reaves-Phillips. "Beautiful Doll," "Messing Around," "What's Your Price?," "Salty Dog," "One Hour Mama," "Wild Women," "Positively No," "Shake it and Break It," "Had to Give up Gym," "Here Comes the Hot Tamale Man," "Pretty Doll," "Come on In," "My Man," "Revival Day," "Baby, Won't You Please Come Home," "Funny Feather," "West Indies Blues," "Boot it Boy," "Alabamy Bound," "Home Sweet Home," "(A) Hot Time in the Old Town (Tonight)." As *Further Mo'* it moved to OB's Village Gate 5/17/90–10/14/90. 174 perf. sound: Peter Fitzgerald. Revived, 3/6/02–3/24/02, at Longacre, Broadway. ch: Eddie D. Robinson; set: Campbell Baird; light: John McKernon; cos: Toni-Leslie James; sound: Kurt Kellenberger; md: Orange Kellin. Cast: Vernel Bagneris, Rosalind Brown, B.J. Crosby, Wally Dunn, Roz Ryan, Carol Woods

2105. *One More Song/One More Dance.* Modern ballet revue, with songs. Joyce, 12/21/83–12/31/83. 14 perf. p: Lee Gross Assocs;

created/d: Grover Dale; set: Lawrence Miller; cos: Albert Wolsky; light: Richard Nelson; md/new dance mus/voc arr: Joel Silberman; dance mus/voc arr: Mark Hummel. Cast: Ann Reinking, Gary Chryst, Jeff Calhoun, Stephen Jay

2106. *One Night Stand.* Successful stage & movie composer is going to commit suicide at 10 o'clock that night, and invites an audience to see song & dance show which will explain why. Closed after 8 Broadway previews at the Nederlander, 10/20/80–10/25/80). p: Joseph Kipness, Lester Osterman, Joan Cullman, James M. Nederlander, Alfred Taubman; m: Jule Styne; l/b: Herb Gardner; d: John Dexter; ch: Peter Gennaro; set: Robin Wagner; cos: Patricia Zipprodt; sound: Otts Munderloh; md: Eric Stern; orch: Philip J. Lang; dance mus arr: Marvin Laird. Cast: Jack Weston, Charles Kimbrough, Catherine Cox, Brandon Maggart, Kate Mostel, Charles Levin, William Morrison, Christopher Balcom, Terri Treas, Paul Binotto, Steven Boockvor, Kerry Casserly, Cheryl Clark, Ida Gilliams, John Mineo, Sonja Stuart, Kathrynann Wright. "Everybody Loves Me," "There Was a Time (Part I)," "A Little Traveling Music, Please," "Go Out Big," "Some Day Soon," "For You," "I Am Writing a Love Song," "Gettin' Some," "Somebody Stole My Kazoo," "We Used to Talk Once," "The 'Now' Dance," "Long Way from Home," "Too Old to Be So Young," "There Was a Time (Part II)," "Here Comes Never"

2107. *One Night Stand.* Coliseum, Oldham, England, 5/16/81–6/13/81; Apollo, London, 7/21/81–8/29/81. 47 perf. m/l/b: Mike Harding; d: Kenneth Alan Taylor; ch: Sheila Carter; md: Chris Monks. Cast: Patricia Winslow, Candice Hartley

2108. *One of a Kind.* Yiddish. Norman Thomas, 10/12/80–12/28/80. 33 perf. p: Ben Bonus; m/l/d: Leo Fuchs; w: Al Springer; based on play by Louis Freiman & William Gunther. Cast: Leo Fuchs, Mina Bern, Sylvia Feder, Evelyn Kingsley

2109. *One Shining Moment.* Closed in Chicago, 1983. m/l: Leslie Bricusse & Allan Jay Friedman. Cast: Kevin Anderson. "Imitate the Sun"

2110. *Only a Kingdom.* About King Edward VIII's marriage to Mrs. Simpson. Pasadena Playhouse, Calif., 11/6/98–12/20/98. m/l: Judith Shobow Steir; d: Scott Schwartz

2111. *Only Fools Are Sad.* Yiddish. Edison, Middle Broadway, 11/22/71–3/26/72. 8 prev from 11/13/71. 144 perf. p: Yaacov Agmon; b: Dan Almagor; based on old Hassidic songs & parables; d: Yossi Yzraely; cos: Herbert Senn & Helen Pond. Cast: Danny Litanny, Galia Ishay, Don Maseng, Shlomo Nitzan, Michal Noy, Aviva Schwarz. "Once There Was a Melody," "Tell Me What the Rain is Saying" (dropped during run), "Forest, Forest" (dropped during run), "Bim-Bam-Bom," "Angel, Angel...," "Only Fools Are Sad," "And God Said Unto Jacob." Previously ran in Tel-Aviv as *Ish Hassid Haya* (*Once There Was a Hassid*)

2112. *Only the Lonely.* Roy Orbison story. Playhouse, Liverpool, 7/26/93. p: Bill Kenwright; m/l: various writers. Cast: Larry Branson, Christina Fry

2113. *Opal.* Set in lumber camp in Oregon, 1904. Lambs, 3/12/92–5/3/92. Prev from 3/4/92. 63 perf. m/l/b: Robert Nassif Lindsey; d: Scott Harris; set: Peter Harrison; cos: Michael Bottari; md: Joshua Rosenblum. Cast: Reed Armstrong, Mimi Bessette, Louisa Flaningam, Regina O'Malley, Marni Nixon, Pippa Winslow. George Street Playhouse, NJ, 2/18/95. d/ch: Lynn Taylor-Corbett. Cast: Opal: Jackie Angelescu

2114. *An Open Heart.* Comic look at life through the eyes of a man during a one-minute life-changing trauma. Cherry Lane, 3/17/04–4/25/04. Prev from 3/4/04. w: Robby Benson. Cast: Robby Benson, Karla De Vito (his wife in real life), Stan Brown

Opening Doors see # 1978, this appendix

2115. *Opening Night.* AMAS, 4/21/83–5/15/83. 15 perf. w: Corliss Taylor-Dunn & Sandra Reaves-Phillips; d: William Michael Maher; ch: Mabel Robinson; set: Larry Fulton; cos: Judy Dearing; md: Grenoldo Frazier. Cast: Avery Sommers, Dan Strayhorn. "Mr. Playwright," "I Don't Have a Name," "Mommy Says," "You're My Friend," "New Beginnings," "New York City Cockroach Blues," "We're Almost There," "How Many Rainbows," "The Man I Want to Be," "Take a Chance," "Cause a Sensation," "Nobody's Blues," "Keep Holding On," "I Love the Dance," "Opening Night," "Let Me Show You a New Way to Love"

2116. *Operation Sidewinder.* Play with songs. Vivian Beaumont, 3/12/70–4/25/70. 52 perf. p: Repertory Theater of Lincoln Center; w: Sam Shepard; mus composed & performed by the Holy Modal Rounders; d: Michael A. Schultz; set: Douglas W. Schmidt; cos: Willa Kim; light: John Gleason. Cast: Andy Robinson, Garrett Morris, Philip Bosco. "Do it Girl," "Float Me Down Your Pipeline," "Generalonely," "Catch Me," "Euphoria," "Synergy," "Don't Leave Me Dangling in the Dust," "Alien Song," "Bad Karma," "I Disremember Quite Well," "C.I.A. Men"

2117. *Options.* An evening of song. Songwriting team creates musical. Circle Rep, 7/11/85–7/12/85. 17 prev from 6/13/85. 2 perf. m: Jefrey Silverman; l/b: Walter Willison; d/ch: Michael Shawn; tap ch: Brenda Buffalino. Cast: Julie Budd, Jefrey Silverman, Walter Willison, Jo Anna Rush. "Give a Girl a Break!," "Life Don't Always Work Out," "He's an Acrobat," "Bareback Rider," "Bubbles in the Bathtub," "Perfect Strangers," "Options," "The Kinda Girl I Am," "The Front Page," "The Man at the Piano," "I Leave You with a Little Song." See also *Broadway Scandals of 1928* in this appendix

2118. *Oranges and Lemons.* Revue. London, 1948. m/l: Flanders & Swann/Sandy Wilson; w: Laurier Lister. Cast: Max Adrian, Elisabeth Welch, Diana Churchill

Orfeo see # 169, Main Book

2119. *Orwell That Ends Well.* Musical revue & social satire in skits & songs. Village Gate Downstairs, 3/4/84–6/3/84. 10 prev from 3/1/84. 110 perf. p: Bernard Sahlins & Art D'Lugoff; m: Fred Kaz; d: Bernard Sahlins. Cast: Original Chicago Second City Co. "Cul-

ture Quiz," "Pirates," "Margaret Thatcher," "Who Gives a Damn"

2120. *Oscar of the Waldorf.* Musical suite in 3 parts. Waldorf Astoria, 1/14/98. 1 perf. p: The Waldorf Astoria & Sage Hill; m/b: Rob La Rocco; l: Sam Austin; d: Patrick Trettenero. Cast: Walter Willison, Diane Findlay, Willy Falk, Rob Sutton, Sean Lough

2121. *Our Day Out.* Underprivileged kids on a day out. Young Vic, London, 8/30/83–9/30/83. m/l: Willy Russell, Bob Eaton, Chris Mellor; b: Willy Russell. First seen on BBC-2 in 1977

2122. *Our House.* Love story, based on music of 1980s rock group Madness. Cambridge Theatre, London, 10/28/02–8/16/03. w: Tim Firth; d: Matthew Warchus; ch: Peter Darling. Cast: Ian Reddington (*Suggs* until 6/14/03), Michael Jibson. "It Must Be Love," "Our House." In addition, 2 songs were written specially for this show. Toured in 2004

2123. *Our Lady of the Harbor Bar & Grill.* Performance piece. Don't Tell Mama, 5/6/88–6/30/88. 16 perf. w: Bruce Hopkins; songs by several well-known writers; md: Paul Greenwood. Cast: Bruce Hopkins. "The Universe Song," "And I Am Telling You," "Lilacs," "My Buddy," "The Way I See It"

2124. *Our Lan'.* Folk-drama with mus. Recently freed slaves try to establish community on land in Georgia granted them by General Sherman during Civil War, only to find land reverting to orig owners after war. Royale, Broadway, 9/27/47–11/1/47. 47 perf. p: Eddie Dowling & Louis J. Singer; m/l partly by Theodore Ward & Joshua Lee; d: Eddie Dowling. Cast: Muriel Smith, William Veasey, William Marshall, Mary Lewis, Urylee Leonardos. "Hoe, Boy, Hoe," "Cotton Song"

2125. *Our Man Crichton.* A butler takes command on desert island. Palace, Manchester, England, 11/23/64–12/12/64; Shaftesbury, London, 12/21/64–6/26/65. 208 perf. p: Bernard Delfont; m: David Lee; l/b: Herbert Kretzmer; based on J.M. Barrie's play *The Admirable Crichton;* d: Clifford Williams; ch: Denys Palmer; md: Burt Rhodes; cast recording on Parlophone. Cast: Kenneth More, Millicent Martin, David Kernan, Patricia Lambert, George Benson, Anna Barry, Dilys Watling, Glyn Worsnip. "Tweeny!," "Yes, Mr. Crichton," "Our Kind of People," "Down with the Barriers," "Were I as Good," "London, London–My Home Town," "Let's Find an Island," "Doesn't Travel Broaden the Mind," "I Tries," "Yesterday's World," "Little Darlin'," "I Never Looked for You," "Oh! For a Husband; Oh! For a Man," "Nobody Showed Me How," "My Time Will Come"

2126. *Our Sinatra.* Full-length celebration revue of Frank's music. Oak Room, Algonquin Hotel, 1999. Officially opened at Blue Angel, 12/19/99. Prev from 12/8/99. Moved to Reprise Room, at Dillon's, 8/13/00–7/28/02. Total of 1,096 perf. p: Jack Lewin; m/l: various writers; conceived by cast members Eric Comstock, Christopher Gines (Billy Stritch during Mr. Gines' vacation), Hilary Kole; d: Kurt Stamm; light: Jeff Nellis; prod super: Richard Maltby Jr. Birdland, 11/20/03–3/14/04. Prev from

11/12/03. 142 perf. p: Jack Lewin; d: Kurt Stamm. Cast: Hilary Kole, Tony DeSare, Adam James

2127. *Out of Bounds*. Theatre Royal, Bristol, England, 12/26/73–2/16/74. p: Bristol Old Vic Co.; w: Julian Slade; based on *The Schoolmistress*, by Arthur Pinero; d: Val May; ch: Bob Stevenson; md: Neil Rhoden. Cast: Anna Quayle, David Ryall (*Nigel Stock*), June Barrie

2128. *Out of the Blue*. Shaftesbury, London, 11/4/94. m: Shun-Ichi Tokura; l/b: Paul Sand. Cast: David Burt, Greg Ellis, Meredith Braun. "Let Me Go," "Is This a Test?," "You Are All I See," "Only Believe," "Years Pass," "Something to See Me Through," "On Your Side," "Last Time We Met," "The Magic Spell," "Message from a Dark Day," "What Can I Hope For?," "Tell Him," "What is That?," "At Sunrise," "Let us Be Perfectly Clear," "Hot Summer's Day," "Into the Light," "The Enemy Machine"

2129. *Out of the Blue*. The Icarus legend set in nudist colony. 30th Street Theatre, 1999. m/l/b: William Benton; d/ch: David Swan; md: Darren R. Cohen. "It's up to Us," "Here Come the Tourists," "An 'I Love You' Song," "It's the Clothes that Make the Man," "That's What You Bid," "The Story," "A Formal Affair," "Summer Song—Someone Fell," "I Just Can't Wait," "I've Got a Case on You', "You Are an Ass," "Conversation," "Real Life Musical Comedy," "Piney Spine," "Vicinity of Love," "What Am I Gonna Do?," "Could That Be Right?," "It's up to You"

2130. *Out of This World*. Unrelated to Cole Porter musical which opened on Broadway within a week of this revue closing in London. London Palladium, 10/18/50–12/16/50. 112 perf, twice-nightly. Cast: Frankie Howerd, Nat Jackley, the Tiller Girls

2131. *Over Forty*. Billie Holiday, 2/17/89. p: Marjorie Moon. Cast: Janyse M. Singleton. "Over Forty," "When We Were Young," "Why Did We Part?," "Ignite My Love," "Another Life to Come," "We Need Our Men," "Someone to Say I Love You," "Beat the Clock," "A Litle Age Sits Well," "In My Life"

2132. *Over the Moon*. Revue. London, 1953. m/l: Vivian Ellis; Harold Rome (a song of his was used). Cast: Cicely Courtneidge

2133. *The Overtons*. A Vincent Lawrence comedy with 1 song. Problems caused to a marriage by another woman. Booth, Broadway, 2/6/45–7/7/45. 174 perf. p: Paul Czinner; m/l: Jerome & Archie Gottler; d: Elisabeth Bergner; cos: Hattie Carnegie. Cast: Arlene Francis, Glenda Farrell, Jack Whiting. "Two Hearts in Danger"

2134. *Oy Mama! Am I in Love!* Set in Poland in 1905, and in NYC in 1923. Town Hall, 11/28/84–12/30/84. 5 prev. 55 perf. p: Shalom Yiddish Musical Comedy Theatre; m/l: Ed Linderman & Yakov Alper; d: Michael Greenstein; ch: Derek Wolshonak; md: Barry Levitt. Cast: Mary Soreanu, Max Perlman, Yankele Alperin, Reizl Bozyk, Shifra Lerer, Sandy Levitt, Eleanor Reissa, Alec Timmerman

2135. *Oz: A Twisted Musical*. New take on *The Wizard of* Oz. Paper Mill Playhouse, NJ,

2002. m/l: Bill Francoeur; b: Tim Kelly. Created by drama department of High Tech High School, Bergen, NJ. Originally done as a showcase at Playhouse 91. Producers Club II, Manhattan, 7/16/03–8/9/03. d: Alex Perez; sound/md: Rod Shepard. Same cast as at HTHS

2136. *Pacific 1860*. Noel Coward South Pacific romance operetta. Set in Samolo. Visiting diva has romance with planter's son. Theatre Royal, Drury Lane, London, 12/19/46–4/12/47. 129 perf. w/d: Noel Coward; set/cos: Gladys E. Calthrop; md: Mantovani. Cast: Mary Martin, Graham Payn, Sylvia Cecil, Irlin Hall, Daphne Anderson, Gwen Bateman, Carl Jaffe. "His Excellency Regrets," "If I Were a Man," "Uncle Harry," "Dear Madam," "Salvador," "My Horse Has Cast a Shoe," "Bright Was the Day," "One, Two, Three," "I Never Knew," "I Saw No Shadow," "Invitation to the Waltz," "I Wish I Wasn't Such a Big Girl," "Pretty Little Bridesmaid," "Mother's Lament," "This is a Changing World," "Fumfumbolo," "This is a Night for Lovers," "The Toast Music." Re-done 1/31–2/2/03, by York Theatre Co. (in NYC) as part of the *Musicals in Mufti* series

2137. *Pacific Paradise*. Maori-language musical revue. Palace, Broadway, 10/16/72–10/21/72. 2 prev. 5 perf. p: Irving Sudrow; d: Jack Regas. "Karanga Tia," "Ti Tiro Mai," "Taku Patu," "Karu," "Koroki," "Pa Aki Kini," "E Pare Ra." Previously ran in NZ

2138. *Pageant*. Musical comedy beauty pageant, with the contestants played by male actors, with audience picking "Miss Glamouresse 1991" each night. Riverwest, 11/1/86–12/21/86. 3 prev. 45 perf. m: Albert Evans; l/b: Bill Russell & Frank Kelly; conceived by/d/ch: Robert Longbottom; co-ch: Tony Parise; md: Glen Kelly. Cast: Rex Carlton, Bill Fabris, Russell Giesenschlag, Edward Marona, John Salvatore, Dick Scanlan, Lawrence Raiken. "Natural Born Females," "Something Extra," "One Smile at a Time," "Don't Be Afraid," "More than a Woman," "Pageant Days," "Nighty Night," "We're on Our Way," "It's Gotta Be Venus," "Beauty Work," "Goodbye," "A Pretty Life," "Girl Power." Blue Angel, 5/2/91–6/27/92. 10 prev from 4/23/91. 462 perf. md/orch: James Raitt. Cast: Randl Ask, David Drake, Russell Garrett, Jo Joyce, John Salvatore, Dick Scanlan, J.T. Cromwell. King's Head, London; Vaudeville, London, 8/1/00–9/30/00. Prev from 7/26/00. d: Bill Russell; ch: Warren Carlyle; set: Nigel Hook; cos: Gregg Barnes; md: Elliot Davis. Cast: Lionel Blair

2139. *Painting It Red*. Trials & travails of modern relationships. Holy Trinity, 10/7/93–10/31/93. 20 perf. m: Gary Rue; l: Leslie Ball; d: Michael Ramach. Cast: Andy Taylor

2140. *Panama Hattie*. Set in Panama City. 46th Street Theatre, Broadway, 10/30/40–1/3/42. 501 perf. p: Buddy De Sylva; m/l: Cole Porter; b: Herbert Fields & Buddy De Sylva; d: Edgar MacGregor; ch: Robert Alton; set/cos: Raoul Pene du Bois; md: Gene Salzer; orchestral arr: Russell Bennett, Hans Spialek, Don Walker; voc arr: Lynn Murray. Cast: Ethel Merman (1st time her name alone had been

above title), Arthur Treacher, Betty Hutton, June Allyson, Vera Ellen, Pat Harrington, Joan Carroll, Betsy Blair. "Join it Right Away," "Visit Panama," "American Family," "My Mother Would Love You," "I've Still Got My Health," "Fresh as a Daisy," "Welcome to Jerry," "Let's Be Buddies," "I'm Throwing a Ball Tonight," "I Detest a Fiesta," "Who Would Have Dreamed," "Make it Another Old-Fashioned, Please," "All I've Got to Get Now is My Man," "You Said It," "God Bless the Women." Not long after the opening Miss Merman began short-lived marriage to Bill Smith. When Betty Hutton got measles on 5/19/41, her understudy, June Allyson, went on for her for 4 days, and was "discovered." Filmed in 1942, with Ann Sothern, Red Skelton & Lena Horne. Adelphi, London, 1/25/45–4/21/45. 100 perf. d: Teddy Beaumont; ch: Wendy Toye; cos: Norman Hartnell; md: Harold Collins. Cast: Bebe Daniels, Max Wall. Condensed TV prod, 1954. Cast: Ethel Merman, Art Carney. Equity Library, 1/15/76–2/1/76. 22 perf. adapted by: Charles Abbott & Fredric Dehn; d: Charles Abbott; ch: Roger Braun; md: Eileen La Grange. Cast: Mary Ellen Ashley, Christopher Wynkoop, May Keller, Lynn Martin. In 1976 Ann Miller starred on tour

2141. *Paper Moon*. Paper Mill Playhouse, NJ, 9/8/93. m: Larry Grossman; l: Ellen Fitzhugh & Carol Hall; b: Martin Casella; based on novel *Addie* Pray, by Joe David Brown, and also on movie *Paper Moon*; d: Matt Casella; ch: Alan Johnson; set: Michael Anania; md: Steve Marzullo. Cast: Christine Ebersole, Gregory Harrison, Roxie Lucas, Mary Stout, Kathryn Kendall, Ruth Gottschall, Joe Locarro, John Dossett. Goodspeed, 6/26/96. d: Martin Casella; ch: John Carrafa; md: Michael O'Flaherty. Cast: Lindsay Cummings, Joanna Pacitti, Mark Zimmerman. "Another Little Child," "I Recollect Him," "The Wida' Waltz," "Pretty Like Your Mam," "Goin' Along," "I Do What I Can (With What I Got)," "Boy-Oh-Boy," "How Many Times?," "Doin' Business," "Someday, Baby," "Rabbity Stew," "Who Belongs to Us?," "You with Me?," "Girls Like Us"

2142. *Parade*. Revue. Players, 1/12/60–4/10/60. 95 perf. m/l/d/at piano: Jerry Herman; ch: Richard Tone; cast recording on Kapp. Cast: Dody Goodman, Charles Nelson Reilly, Richard Tone, Fia Karin, Lester James. "Overture" (Orchestra), "(There's No Tune Like a) Show Tune," "Save the Village" (Miss Goodman), "Your Hand in Mine" (Mr. James & Miss Karin), "Confession to a Park Avenue Mother" (Mr. Reilly), "(Wonderful World of the) Two-a-Day" (Mr. Tone), "Just Plain Folks" (Miss Goodman & Mr. Reilly), "The Antique Man" (Mr. James), "The Next Time I Love" (Miss Karin), "Your Good Morning" (Mr. James & Miss Karin), "Maria in Spats" (Miss Goodman playing Maria Callas begging for a booking at the Palace now that she's been banished from so many opera houses), "Another Candle" (Miss Karin), "Jolly Theatrical Season" (tongue-in-cheek look by Miss Goodman & Mr. Reilly at Broadway shows such as *J.B.*, *Juno*, and *The World of Suzie Wong*), Finale: "Parade" (Company). Started life as *Nightcap*, which Mr. Herman put on at the Showplace, where he was working as pianist. Lawrence Kasha asked him to expand it & it became *Parade*. *Nightcap* also had "Bosom Buddies" & "Gooch's Song"

2143. *Paradise!* Atlanta family finds itself stranded on an island paradise in the ocean, this weekend. Playwrights Horizons, 9/28/85–10/6/85. 21 prev from 9/4/85. 14 perf. m: Robert Forrest; l/b: George C. Wolfe; d/ch: Theodore Pappas; set: James Noone; cos: David C. Woolard; light: Frances Aronson; md: David Loud. Cast: Jerry Lanning (*Steven Vinovich*), Danielle Ferland, Ben Wright, Charlaine Woodard, Tommy Hollis, Janice Lynde. "This Could Be the End," "We're Needed Here," "Take Me Away," "Something's Gonna Happen Really Strange Tonight," "On Mahaneyheya," "Doom is Due at Dawn," "Mama Will Be Waiting with the Dawn," "Welcome to Paradise," "Who is This Woman," "Secrets Men Should Know," "The Last Paradise," "You've Got to Let Go," "This is Not the End." Previously ran in Cincinnati

2144. *Paradise Island*. Hawaiian summer musical fantasy. Jones Beach, 1961. 75 perf. p: Guy Lombardo; m/l/b: Guy Lombardo & John Jacob Loeb. Cast: William Gaxton, Arthur Treacher. "Beyond the Clouds," "The Coconut Wireless," "It's a Great Day for Hawaii," "Never Any Time to Play," "Paradise Island"

2145. *Pardon My French*. Revue. Prince of Wales, London, 9/23/53. 758 perf. d: Dick Hurran; ch: Hazel Gee. Cast: Frankie Howerd, Winifred Atwell

2146. *Paris Lights: The All-Star Literary Genius Expatriate Revue*. Musical celebration in their own words, i.e. by those in Paris in the 1920s. American Place, 1/11/80–2/3/80. 24 perf–press date 1/24/80. m/idea/orch: William Russo; b: Michael Zettler & George Ferencz; d: George Ferencz; ch: Jane Summerhays; set: Bill Stabile; md: Michael Ward. Cast: Alice B. Toklas/Edna St. Vincent Millay: Margery Cohen; Josephine Baker: Rhetta Hughes; Gertrude Stein: Trisha Long; Charles Lindbergh: Christopher Murray; Zelda Fitzgerald: Jane Summerhays; James Joyce/Scott Fitzgerald: Nicholas Wyman; Hemingway: James York. "Haschich Fudge," "First Fig," "Mariposa," "Let Her Be," "If I Could Tell You"

2147. *Paris '90*. One-woman show. Booth, Broadway, 3/4/52; John Golden, 4/21/52–5/17/52. Total of 87 perf. p/d: Alden S. Blodget; m/l: Kay Swift; sk: Cornelia Otis Skinner; set: Donald Oenslager; md: Nathaniel Shilkret; orch: Robert Russell Bennett. Cast: Cornelia Otis Skinner. "Moonlight on Notre Dame," "From a Window on the Seine," "Saint Lazare," "Madame Arthur." Tour opened 9/20/52, Erie Theatre, Schenectady, NY. Closed 4/11/53, Shubert, Washington, DC

2148. *Paris '31*. AMAS Musical Theatre, 11/2/89–11/26/89. 22 perf. m/l: Cole Porter; b/d: John Fearnley; ch: Robert Longbottom. Cast: Thelma Carpenter. "Dizzy Baby," "Bad Girl in Paree," "Quelque Chose," "Find Me a Primitive Man," "You Don't Know Paree,"

"Paree," "What Did You Do to Me?," "I'm in Love," "Let's Do It," "You Do Something to Me," "Bull Dog," "Why Shouldn't I Have You?," "Queen of Terre Haute," "After You," "Let's Fly Away," "The Heaven Hop," "Don't Look at Me That Way," "They All Fall in Love," "I Worship You," "You Can Do No Wrong," "I'm Unlucky at Gambling," "Vivienne," "Why Don't We Try Staying at Home," "Let's Step Out." See also *Fifty Million Frenchmen* in this appendix

2149. *Paris to Piccadilly*. Revue. Prince of Wales, London, 4/12/52. 846 perf. p: Bernard Delfont & Dick Hurran. Cast: Norman Wisdom

2150. *A Party with Comden and Green*. Intimate revue of Comden & Green songs, starring the famous song-writing (not married to each other) couple. Cherry Lane, 11/10/58 (Mon nights only); John Golden, Broadway, 12/23/58–1/24/59. 38 perf; John Golden again, 4/16/59–5/23/59. 44 perf. Morosco, Broadway, as *A Party with Betty Comden and Adolph Green*, 2/10/77–4/30/77. 92 perf

2151. *The Passing Show*. Musical revue. 16th edition of *The Passing Show* since the 1st in 1912. Opened 11/9/45, Bushnell, Hartford, Conn. Closed 2/17/46, Erlanger, Chicago. Failed to make Broadway. p: Messrs Shubert; m/l: Irving Actman, etc; d: Russell Mack; set: Watson Barratt. Cast: Willie Howard, Sue Ryan, Bobby Morris, Richard Buckley. During the run Myrtill & Pacaud joined the cast with the number "Rhapsody in Diamonds"

2152. *Passion Flower Hotel*. Palace, Manchester, England, 7/30/65; Prince of Wales, London, 8/24/65–1/1/66. 148 perf. m: John Barry; l: Trevor Peacock; b: Wolf Mankowitz; based on novel by "Rosalind Erskine;" d/cos: William Chappell; ch: Peter Gordeno; md: Richard Holmes. Cast: Francesca Annis, Nicky Henson, Pauline Collins, Joan Ryan, Sylvia Tysick, Jane Birkin, Hilary Dwyer, Bill Kenwright, Bunny May, Jonathan Burn (*Julian Holloway*), Jenny Till. "School Song," "A Little Hammer," "What a Question," "What Does This Country Need Today?," "The Syndicate," "Naughty, Naughty," "How Much of the Dream Comes True?," "Tick Which Applies," "Passion Flower Hotel," "A Great Big Nothing," "I Love My Love," "Beastly, Beastly," "Something Different," "Don't Stop the Show"

2153. *Passionate Extremes*. Musical Theatre Works, 9/28/88–10/16/88. 8 prev. 13 perf. m: George Cochran Quincy; b: Thayer Q. Burch; d: Mark S. Herko; set: James Noone; md: Eric Barnes. Cast: Panchali Null, James Hindman, Marianne Tatum, SuEllen Estey. "Ocean Liner Aria," "Kiss," "New York State of Devotion," "Maternal Memories," "My Innocent Boy," "I Can See the Light," "I'll Make Her Happy," "When You Find a Love"

2154. *Peace*. Minstrel musical set in Heaven & on Earth. Astor Place, 1/27/69–7/13/69. 109 perf. m/l: Al Carmines, Katherine Lee Bates, Tim Reynolds; based on play by Aristophanes; d: Lawrence Kornfeld; ch: Arlene Rothlein. Cast: Essie Borden, Julie Kurnitz (*Carol Fox* from 5/6/69), Reathel Bean, Arlene Rothlein, Lee Crespi (*Violet Santangelo* from 5/20/69).

"America the Beautiful," "Just Sit Around," "Peace Anthem," "Summer's Nice," "Things Starting to Grow Again," "Up in Heaven"

2155. *The Pearl Necklace*. Jewish State Theatre of Bucharest's production of Jewish folk songs, which played in rep with the straight play *The Dybbuk*. Brooklyn Academy of Music, 9/21/72–10/1/72. 14 perf. w: Israel Berkovici

2156. *Pearls*. Musical adaptation of Jacob Gordin's play *Mirele Efros*. Jewish Rep, 6/29/85–8/1/85. 30 perf. w: Nathan Gross; d: Ran Avni; ch: Haila Strauss. Cast: Gloria Hodes, Richard Frisch, Rosalind Elias, Judy Kuhn (*Susan Friedman*). "Mud," "A Promise is a Promise," "I Don't Like the Match," "A Simple Child," "Wedding in the Rain," "My Sabbath Bride," "Live and Let Live," "Save Me," "What's the Difference?," "Ask for a Star," "Look in the Mirror," "Her Little Boy," "Pearls," "A Mother's Love"

2157. *The Peep Show*. Musical show. Palladium, London, 10/30/51. 48 perf. d: Charles Henry; ch: Joe Latona, Anne Negus, Barbara Aitken; set: Charles Reading. Cast: Vera Lynn, Edmundo Ros & his Rumba Band, The George Mitchell Choir, Gillian Lynne

2158. *Peg*. Also called *Peg o' My Heart*. Set in Sussex in 1913. Yvonne Arnaud, Guildford, England, 3/8/84–3/31/84; Phoenix, London, 4/12/84–8/11/84. 6 prev. 146 perf. Panned by the critics. p: Louis Busch Hager; m/l: David Heneker; b: Robin Miller & Ronald Millar; from 1912 play *Peg o' My Heart*, by J. Hartley Manners; d: Ian Judge; ch: Sheila Falconer; md: Kevin Amos. Cast: Sian Phillips, Julia Sutton, Patricia Michael, Ann Morrison, Martin Smith, Liza Sadovy, John Hewer, David McAlister, Kim Smith, Edward Duke. "A Matter of Minutes," "Pretty Dresses," "Peg and Jerry," "The Steamers Go By," "Peg o' My Heart," "There's a Devil in Me," "Fishing Fleet," "How Would You Like Me?," "I Want to Dance," "Little Brick," "Three of a Kind," "Manhattan Hometown," "When a Woman Has to Choose," "Who Needs 'em." Came to USA later in 1984, but closed in NH after limited run. Cast: Ann Morrison, George Ede. Not to be confused *Peg*, Peggy Lee's one-woman show of 1983

2159. *Peg o' My Heart*. Pretty Irish colleen leaves NY for English stately home. Irish Rep, 5/22/03–7/6/03. Prev from 5/13/03. based on J. Hartley Manners' 1912 play; d: Charlotte Moore; set: James Morgan; cos: David Toser; light: Mary Jo Dondlinger; md/arr: Eddie Guttman. Cast: Kathleen Early, Jonathan Hadley (*Chris Orbach* from 7/1/03)

2160. *Peggy Sue Got Married*. Shaftesbury, London, 8/20/01–10/13/01. Prev from 8/4/01. m: Bob Gaudio; l: Jerry Leichtling; b: Arlene Sarner & Jerry Leichtling; based on film of the same name, written by Jerry Leichtling & Arlene Sarner; d: Kelly Robinson; ch: Sergio Trujillo; set: Ruari Murchison. Cast: Ruthie Henshall, Andrew Kennedy, Gavin Lee

2161. *Pendragon*. Set in Britain in the Dark Ages. City Center, 10/25/95–10/28/95. 3 perf. p: Sir Andrew Lloyd Webber & National Youth Music Theatre; m/l/b/d: Peter Allwood, Joanna

Horton, Jeremy James Taylor, Frank Whateley; md: Peter Allwood. Cast: Nick Saich

2162. ***The Penny Friend***. Cockney shopgirl imagines she is modern Cinderella. Stage 73, 12/26/66–1/22/67. 32 perf. p: Thomas Hammond; m/l/b: William Roy; based on play *A Kiss for Cinderella*, by J.M. Barrie; d: Benno D. Frank. Cast: Cinderella: Bernadette Peters; Also with: Charlotte Fairchild, Jamie Ross, Michael Wager, Georgia Creighton. "The Penny Friend," "She Makes You Think of Home," "Who Am I, Who Are You," "Feet," "I Am Going to Dance," "How Doth the Apple Butterfly," "The Diagnostician," "The Great Unknown," "Won't You Come to the Party?," "Adios," "Time We Were Dancing," "Utterly Delicious," "Full and Productive Day," "The World Today"

2163. ***Penny Plain***. Intimate revue. St. Martin's, London, 6/28/51 (ran over a year). m/l: Hugh Martin, Richard Addinsell, Flanders & Swann, Joyce Grenfell, Paul Dehn, Nicholas Phipps; dev/d/set: Laurier Lister; ch: Bert Stimmel; md: John Pritchett. Cast: Joyce Grenfell, Elisabeth Welch, Max Adrian, Desmond Walter-Ellis, Rose Hill, Moyra Fraser, June Whitfield, Julian Orchard. "Janette," "Joyful Noise," "Surley Girls," "A Moment with Tennyson"

2164. ***People Are Wrong!*** Young NY couple move to the country. Vineyard, 11/4/04–12/11/04 (prev from 10/27/04) (closing date extended from 11/27/04). p: Vineyard Theatre & Target Margin Theater; The music, by Julia Greenberg & Stephen Trask, was orig written for the NY Theatre workshop staging of Kate Moira Ryan's *Cavedweller*. l: Julia Greenberg & Robin Goldwasser; d: David Herskovits; ch: Jody Ripplinger; set: G.W. Mercier; md: Jeremy Chatzky & Joe McGinty. Cast: John Flansburgh. Developed in concert versions at Joe's Pub and P.S. 122

2165. ***People Be Heard***. Play with mus written by Quincy Long, about a school board controversy about evolution in a small town. Playwrights Horizons, 9/23/04–10/10/04. Prev from 8/31/04. m: Michael Roth; d: Erica Schmidt; ch: Peter Pucci; set: Christine Jones; cos: Michelle Phillips; md: Michael Roth & Steve Tarshis. Cast: Annie Golden, John Schuck, Dashiell Eaves

2166. ***Perchance to Dream***. A family over several generations, starting from Regency times. London Hippodrome, 4/21/45–10/11/48. 1,022 perf. p: Tom Arnold; m/l/b: Ivor Novello; d: Jack Minster; ch: Keith Lester & Frank Staff; set: Joseph Carl; md: Harry Acres. Cast: Ivor Novello, Margaret Rutherford, Roma Beaumont, Muriel Barron, Robert Andrews, Olive Gilbert. "When the Gentlemen Get Together," "Love is My Reason for Living," "The Meeting," "The Path My Lady Walks," "A Lady Went to Market Fair," "When I Curtsied to the King," "Highwayman Love," "The Triumph of Spring" (ballet), "Autumn Lullaby," "A Woman's Heart," "We'll Gather Lilacs," "The Victorian Wedding," "The Glo-Glo," "The Elopement," "Ghost Finale"

2167. ***Pere Goriot***. Set in Paris in 1820. Theatre of the Riverside Church, 2/15/85–3/3/85. 12 perf. m: Gary Levinson; b/d: Alan Mokler;

based on novel by Balzac. Cast: Richard Frisch. "Today's the Day," "So Nice," "The Love Letter," "The New World," "My Own Way of Loving," "Don't Come Back," "How Can We Know?," "Joy," "What Are Fathers For?," "I Dreamed"

2168. ***The Perils of Scobie Prilt***. New Theatre, Oxford, England, 1963. p: Donald Albery; w: Julian More & Monty Norman; incidental m: William Russo; d: Peter Brook; ch: Lee Becker; set: Rolf Gerard; md: Burt Rhodes. Cast: Mike Sarne, Nyree Dawn Porter, Nigel Davenport, Arthur Mullard, Roddy Maude Roxby. Did not make the West End

2169. ***Personals***. Musical revue. About classified lonelyhearts ads in NY. Minetta Lane, 11/24/85–7/13/86. 19 prev from 11/8/85. 265 perf. m: William Dreskin, Seth Friedman, Alan Menken, Stephen Schwartz, Joel Phillip Friedman, Michael Skloff; l/b: David Krane, Marta Kauffman, Seth Friedman; d: Paul Lazarus; ch: D.J. Giagni; set: Loren Sherman; cos: Ann Hould-Ward; light: Richard Nelson; sound: Otts Munderloh; md: Michael Skloff. Cast: Nancy Opel, Jeff Keller, Laura Dean (*Liz Larsen*), Jason Alexander (*Marcus Olson*), Trey Wilson (*Hal Robinson*), Dee Hoty. "Nothing to Do with Love," "After School Special," "Mama's Boys," "A Night Alone," "I Think You Should Know," "Second Grade," "Imagine My Surprise," "I'd Rather Dance Alone," "Moving in with Linda," "A Little Happiness," "I Could Always Go to You," "The Guy I Love," "Michael," "Picking up the Pieces," "Some Things Don't End." Apollo, London, 6/15/00–7/29/00. Prev from 6/13/00. d: Dion McHugh. Cast: Cameron Blakely, Marcus Allen Cooper, Carmen Cusack, Christina Fry, Martin Callaghan, Vicki Simon. Altered Stages, 4/20/01–5/6/01. 14 perf. p: Ergo Theatre Co.; d/ch: Robert Jay Cronin; md/arr: Charles Alterman. Cast: Jedediah Cohen, Anika Larsen, Hazel Anne Raymundo, Todd Alan Crain, Johanna Pinzler, Joe Farrell. Not the musical cabaret show of the same name that ran at American Place, 5/8/80. 12 perf. p: The Women's Project; m/l: Michael Ward & Rose Leiman Goldemberg. Cast: Julianne Boyd

2170. ***Pete 'n' Keely***. Comic musical. About a divorced couple of singing sweethearts (based on Steve Lawrence & Eydie Gorme) who haven't spoken since their divorce 5 years ago, and are now brought back together for a TV special. Set in 1968. John Houseman, 12/14/00–3/11/01. 13 prev from 12/2/00. 96 perf. m/l: Mark Waldrop & Patrick Brady; b: James Hindman; conceived by James Hindman, Mark Waldrop, Patrick Brady; d: Mark Waldrop; ch: Keith Cromwell; set: Ray Klausen; cos: Bob Mackie; light: F. Mitchell Dana; sound: Jon Weston; md/arr: Patrick S. Brady. Cast: Sally Mayes, George Dvorsky. Guest stars: Jo Anne Worley, Phyllis Diller, Charo, Cousin Brucie. Songs of the 50s & 60s, and new ones by Mark Waldrop & Patrick Brady: "Kid Stuff," "Tony and Cleo," "Too Fat to Fit," "Wasn't it Fine," "Have You Got a Lot to Learn," "Hello, Egypt!." It started with a workshop at CAP21, in NYC, in 2/00, dir by Mark Waldrop, then had a 1st staging at Springfield,

Mass, 4/25/00–5/4/00. d: Mark Waldrop. Cast: Sally Mayes, George Dvorsky

2171. ***The Petrified Prince***. Set in Slavonia in 1807. Martinson, 12/18/94–1/15/95. 16 prev from 12/6/94. 32 perf. m/l: Michael John La Chiusa; b: Edward Gallardo; based on screenplay by Ingmar Bergman; d: Harold Prince; ch: Rob Marshall; set: James Youmans; cos: Judith Dolan; light: Howell Binkley; md: Jason Robert Browne; orch: Jonathan Tunick. Cast: Loni Ackerman, Gabriel Barre, Geoffrey Blaisdell, Marilyn Cooper, Timothy Jerome, George Merritt, Mindy Cooper, Wendy Edmead, Amy N. Heggins, Darren Lee, David Masenheimer, Dana Moore, Troy Myers, Casey Nicholaw, Daisy Prince, Candy Buckley, Cynthia Sophiea. "Move," "There Are Happy Endings," "His Family Tree," "The Easy Life," "Abbe's Appearance," "Samson's Thoughts," "Pointy's Lament," "A Woman in Search of Happiness," "Napoleon's Nightmare," "Dormez-Vous," "One Little Taste," "Never Can Tell," "Look Closer, Love," "Stay," "Without Me," "The Animal Song," "Samson's Epiphany," "Fernando's Suicide," "Addio, Bambino," "What the Prince is Saying," "I Would Like to Say"

2172. ***Pets***. Musical revue. Judith Anderson, 3/18/93–4/4/93. 16 perf. conceived by/d/ch: Helen Butleroff; md/orch: Albert Ahronheim. Cast: Tim Connell, Cheryl Stern. "Pets," "Take Me Home with You," "Don't Worry 'bout Me," "I Walk ze Dogs," "Just Do it without Me," "Cat in the Box," "There's a Bagel on the Piano," "Perpetual Care," "Cool Cats," "Dear Max," "First Cat," "What About Us?," "Peculiar," "Franklin," "Mice of Means," "Night of the Iguana," "If You Can Stay," "All in a Day's Work." Theatre East, 7/27/95–9/24/95. 11 prev from 7/19/95. 68 perf. New cast

2173. ***PFC Mary Brown***. Army show, 1944. Toured camps during WWII. m/l: Frank Loesser. "First Class Private Mary Brown," "The WAC Hymn"

2174. ***The Phantom Tollbooth***. Boy drives his toy car through toy tollbooth into fantasy world called The Land of Wisdom, accompanied by his dog Tock and a humbug. They try to save the Princesses Rhyme & Reason. Harwich Junior Theatre, Cape Cod, Mass., 8/6/02–8/23/02. m: Arnold Black; l: Sheldon Harnick; adapted by Norton Juster's from his children's book; d: James P. Byrne; md: Robert Wilder. 1st conceived as an opera. Mr. Black died in 2001, so Mr. Harnick found himself doing mus as well

2175. ***Phil the Fluter***. Palace, London, 11/15/69–2/28/70. 123 perf. p: Harold Fielding; m/l: David Heneker & Percy French; d: Wallace Douglas; ch: Gillian Lynne; md: Ray Cook. Cast: Phil McHugh: Stanley Baxter; Also with: Mark Wynter, Sarah Atkinson, Evelyn Laye, Billie Love. "They Don't Make Them Like That Anymore," "You Like It," "If I Had a Chance," "Mama," "A Favour for a Friend," "Good Morning," "How Would You Like Me," "Abdoul Abulbul Ameer," "I Shouldn't Have to Be the One to Tell You," "Follow Me," "Are You Right There, Michael?," "That's Why the Poor Man's Dead," "Wonderful Woman." Started at the Gaiety, Dublin, as *The Golden*

Years, adapted by Donal Giltinan & Beverley Cross from Mr. Giltinan's radio play. Changed name on move to London

2176. *Philemon*. Clown masquerades as Christian zealot, and is martyred. Based on true event in Antioch in 287 AD. Portfolio Studio, 1/3/75–1/26/75. 12 perf. m: Harvey Schmidt; l/b: Tom Jones; d: Lester Collins (i.e. Harvey Schmidt); md: Ken Collins (i.e. Tom Jones). Cast: Dick Latessa, Leila Martin, Michael Glenn-Smith, Drew Katzman, Virginia Gregory, Howard Ross, Kathrin King Segal. "Within This Empty Space," "The Streets of Antioch Stink," "Gimme a Good Digestion," "Don't Kiki Me," "I'd Do Most Anything to Get Out of Here and Go Home," "He's Coming/Antioch Prison," "Name: Cockian," "I Love Order," "My Secret Dream," "I Love His Face," "Sometimes/The Protest," "The Nightmare," "The Greatest of These," "The Confrontation," "How Free I Feel," "How Easy to Be Scornful," "Come with Me," "The Vision: I See a Light." Re-ran 4/8/75–5/18/75. 48 perf. The York Theatre Co. produced it 1/11/91–2/3/91. 23 perf. d: Fran Soeder; md: Norman Weis; set: James Leonard Joy; cos: Mariann Verheyen; light: Natasha Katz. Cast: Michael Tucci, Kenneth Kantor, Kim Crosby, Kathryn McAteer, Jean Tafler, Joel Malina

2177. *Phinney's Rainbow*. College, 1948. m/l: Stephen Sondheim. "How Do I Know?," "Phinney's Rainbow," "Still Got My Heart"

2178. *Phoenix '55*. Small musical revue. Phoenix, 4/23/55–7/17/55. 97 perf. m/l: David Baker & David Craig; sk: Ira Wallach; from idea by Nicholas Benton & Stark Hesseltine; d: Marc Daniels; ch: Boris Runanin (nominated for Tony); cos: Alvin Colt (nominated for Tony); md: Buster Davis. Cast: Nancy Walker (nominated for Tony), Harvey Lembeck, Gemze de Lappe, Kenneth Harvey, Joshua Shelley, Marge Redmond, Dick Korthaze, Louise Hoff, Rain Winslow, Bob Bakanic, Shellie Farrell, Elton Warren, Jay Harnick. Remembered chiefly for satirical sketch on Ed Murrow called "Upper Birth." "It Says Here," "Tomorrow is Here," "All Around the World," "Never Wait for Love," "Down to the Sea," "This Tuxedo is Mine," "Just Him," "The Charade of the Marionettes," "A Funny Heart," "Suburban Retreat." Reviews were very good

2179. *Piaf ... A Remembrance*. Play with mus. About Edith Piaf, the French singer. Playhouse, Broadway, 2/14/77–3/6/77. 16 prev. 24 perf. w: David Cohen; conceived by: Millie Janz; d: Lee Rachman; set/light: Ralph Alswang; md: John Marino. Cast: Piaf: Juliette Koka; Marcel Cerdan, her boxer boyfriend: Lou Bedford; Also with: Edmund Lyndeck. "Padam," "L'accordeoniste," "Milord," "La vie en rose," "Les trois cloches," "Hymne a l'amour," "Non, Je ne regrette rien," and other Piaf numbers. Another straight play, called *Piaf*, played in London in 1980, and on Broadway, at the Plymouth, 2/5/81–6/28/81. 165 perf. Both prods starred Jane Lapotaire (this show achieved a certain notoriety when the character "peed" on stage). Elaine Paige starred in London revival

at the Piccadilly (opened 12/13/93). This show is unrelated to Juliette Koka's one-woman show *Piaf ... Remembered* (1993)

2180. *Piano Bar*. Set at Sweet Sue's, a pub near Grand Central Station. Very little dialogue, but much singing. Westside, 6/8/78–9/24/78. 8 prev. 133 perf. m/l: Rob Fremont & Doris Wilens; d: Albert Takazauckas; ch: Nora Peterson; md: Joel Silberman; arr: Philip J. Lang. Cast: Kelly Bishop, Joel Silberman, Richard Ryder, Steve Elmore, Karen De Vito, Jim McMahon. "Sweet Sue's," "Today," "Pigeon-Hole Time," "Congratulations," "Believe Me," "Everywhere I Go," "Nobody's Perfect," "One, Two, Three," "Moms and Dads," "Meanwhile, Back in Yonkers," "It's Coming Back to Me," "Tomorrow Night"

2181. *Pick a Number XV*. Julius Monk revue. Plaza 9 Room, Hotel Plaza, 10/14/65. m/l: William F. Brown, Stan Lebowsky, Claibe Richardson, Fred Tobias, Walter Marks, etc; ch: Frank Wagner. Cast: Lee Beery, Rex Robbins, Bill Hinnant, Liz Sheridan, John Keatts, Elizabeth Wilson, John Svar, Nancy Parell. "Happiness is a Bird," "New York is a Summer Festival" (m: Harvey Schmidt; l: Tom Jones), "Almost a Love Song" (by Clark Gesner), "Societus Magnificat: An Oratorio" (by Clark Gesner)

2182. *Picking Up the Pieces*. Eighty Eights, 6/92–7/26/92. m/l: Skip Kennon, Richard Engquist, Ellen Fitzhugh, Terrence McNally, David Spencer; d: Sarah Louise Lazarus. Cast: Joseph Kolinski, Maureen Silliman, Jane Smulyan, Skip Kennon. 4 mini-musicals. Their musical numbers were: *Plaisir d'Amour*: "Love at First Sight," "Vows/The First Year," "Loads of Time," "It was Like Fire." *Did You Ever Have One of Those Years?*: "Did You Ever Have One of Those Years?," "That's the Good News," "What's a Body," "Picking up the Pieces," "We'll Do it Again." *Fairy Tales and Legends*: "Small Words," "Spring Day," "As I'd Like to Be," "I Had to Come from Somewhere." *The Music of Love*: "The Music of Love," "Time and Time Again," "I Almost Cry," "A Mother (Louise)," "It's All Too Beautiful," "It's Only the Best Yet," "So, When the Time Comes"

2183. *Pieces of Eight*. Apollo, London, 9/23/59. p: Michael Codron & Neil Crawford; m: Laurie Johnson, Edward Scott, Lance Mulcahy; l: Lenny Adelson & John Law; sk: Peter Cook, Sandy Wilson, Lance Mulcahy, Harold Pinter (including "The Last to Go"), John Law; dev: Michael Codron & Paddy Stone; d: Paddy Stone; set: Tony Walton; light: Richard Pilbrow. Cast: Kenneth Williams, Fenella Fielding, Valerie Walsh, Josephine Blake, Myra de Groot, Peter Reeves. "The Power of Love," "High Society" (dance numbers)

2184. *Pieces of Eight*. Downstairs at the Upstairs, 1960. m/l: Robert Kessler & Martin Charnin. "Clandestine," "Orientale"

2185. *The Pied Piper*. Theatre Royal, Stratford East, London, 12/19/62–1/12/63. 42 perf. p: Duncan Stanley & Gordon Vivian; m/md: James Stevens; l: Gordon Vivian & James Stevens; b: Gordon Vivian; d: Robert Atkins; ch: Lennie Mayne; set: David Marshall. Cast: Gilbert Wynne, Howard Marion Crawford,

Anna Sharkey, John Bay, Victor Winding. Not the same as earlier British musical with same name, by David Croft & Cyril Ornadel, which ran in Worthing, from 12/24/58, for 4 weeks. Gerald Flood was in that one. There was another British musical *The Piper of Hamelin*, by Geoff White & Chris Ball, which ran at Liverpool Playhouse, 7/6/84–7/27/84

2186. *Pigjazz, II*. Satirical musical revue based on the lives & experiences of the cast. Actors Playhouse, 11/16/81–12/20/81. 30 perf. p/d: Michael Nee; md: Paul Sklar; written by the cast: Gretchen Alan Aurthur, Glenn Kramer, Michael Nee, Stephen Pell. "When You're Not the Same" "I Have No Name," "Miya Sama Dinah Shore," "Did You Notice?," "Phantom Affair," "Love is a Crazy Thing," "Yes, Yes, Yes," "Bad Bar Bebop," "Job Hunting in Sodom," "It's the Loneliness, I Think," "East Indian Love Call," "Too Hot to Handel," "The Movie Guide to Love," "Cheatin'," "I Only Want the Best," "Thank God"

2187. *Pilgrim's Progress*. Gate, 3/20/62–3/25/62. 8 perf. w: Edwin Greenberg; d: Ted Vermont. Cast: Don Gunderson. "Ballad of Bedford Gaol," "Take My Hand in Friendship," "Girls Who Sell Orangeade," "Sing Out in the Streets." Revised by Jane McCulloch, as *Pilgrim*, at Birmingham Rep, from 7/14/75, then toured; Edinburgh Festival, 8/25/75 (3 weeks); then toured; Roundhouse, London, 10/15/75–11/8/75. d: Toby Robertson; ch: Robert North; md: Neil Rhoden. Cast: Christian: Paul Jones; Faithful: Ben Cross. *Pilgrim's Progress*, a different British musical of the same name, ran at the Yvonne Arnaud, Guildford, 3/26/74–4/6/74 (it did not go to London). m: Carl Davis; l/b: Jan McCulloch; again, based on John Bunyan's book. Faithful: Ben Cross

2188. *Pimpernel*. Unrelated to the later Broadway prod, *The Scarlet Pimpernel*, except that it, too, was based on Baroness Orczy's novel. Gramercy Arts, 1/6/64–1/8/64. 3 perf. p: Gerald Krone & Dorothy Olim; m: Mimi Stone; l/b: William Kaye; d: Malcolm Black; ch: Sandra Devlin; set/light: Lloyd Burlingame; cos: Sonia Lowenstein; md: Robert Rogers; arr: Julian Stein. Cast: Percy: David Daniels; Marguerite: Leila Martin; Armand: John Canemaker; Chauvelin: William Larsen; Also with: Jane Lillig, Stephen Pearlman, Dick Latessa, Buff Shurr, John Cunningham. "This is England," "Dangerous Game," "A la Pimpernel," "Le Croissant," "Touch of Paris," "Everything's Just Divine," "A Woman," "Le Bon Mot," "As if I Weren't There," "Liberty, Equality, Fraternity," "Love of Long Ago," "What a Day for Me," "I'm Seeing Things," "Sing, Jacques, Sing," "Nose Ahead"

2189. *The Pink Jungle*. Satire of beauty industry. Alcazar, San Francisco, 10/14/59. 3 weeks; Detroit; Shubert, Boston, 12/2/59–12/12/59. p: Paul Gregory; written by Leslie Stevens as (straight) comedy, with 4 incidental songs by Vernon Duke, but it mutated into large-scale musical on the road; based on *Carousel*; d: Joe Anthony, Leslie Stevens; ch: Matt Mattox. Cast: Ginger Rogers, Agnes Moorehead, Matt Mattox, Leif Erickson, Ray Hamilton, Maggie Hayes, Bruce Peter Yarnell.

"Nobody but Tess," "A Hundred Women in One," "There Was I," "Chic Talk," "Persian Room-Ba," "Free as the Air," "Just Like Children," "It's Tough to Be a Girl," "It's Tough to Be a Man," "Brian," "Paris in New York," "Where Do You Go When You Arrive?." Folded after star Ginger Rogers had given her notice to quit because she wasn't being paid. Canceled its 1/14/60 Broadway opening date at the 54th Street Theatre

2190. *Pinocchio.* Puppet musical. Bil Baird, 12/15/73–4/21/74. 134 perf. p: Bil Baird; m: Mary Rodgers; l: Sheldon Harnick; b: Jerome Coopersmith; based on book by C. Collodi; d: Lee Theodore; light: Peggy Clark. Cast: Olga Felgemacher, Bob Gorman, Marcia Rodd. It then toured through 5/26/74

2191. *Pins and Needles.* Musical revue. Labor Stage, 11/27/37. 1,108 perf. p: International Ladies Garment Workers Union; m/l: Harold Rome; sk: Marc Blitzstein, etc; d: Charles Friedman. Cast: ILGWU members (the ILGWU had bought the Princess Theatre and renamed it). "Why Sing of Skies Above?" (Sing Me a Song of Social Significance), "Four Little Angels of Peace," "Chain Store Daisy," "Not Cricket to Picket," "I've Got the Nerve to Be in Love," "One Big Union for Two," "Bertha the Sewing Machine Girl," "What Good is Love?," "Back to Work," "Sunday in the Park," "G-Man," "Status Quo," "Cream of Mush," "Nobody Makes a Pass at Me," "Doing the Revolutionary," "Mene Mene Tekel." On 4/20/39 it was re-titled *Pins and Needles 1939,* and brought in several new sketches & actors to keep it up to date; then on 6/26/39 it moved to the Windsor, with another name change— *New Pins and Needles* on 11/25/39. Closed 6/22/40. Longest-running Broadway musical up to that time. Under the orig title, it was revived by Roundabout Theatre, 5/19/67– 3/24/68. 214 perf. d: Gene Feist; ch: Larry Life; md: Mary Chaffee. Cast: Zaida Coles, Loretta Long, Ellen March, Susan Stevens, Roger Lawson, Elaine Tishler, Joe Abramski, Richard Allan, David Baker, John Byrd, Larry Life. Stage One, 5/30/78–12/17/78. 226 perf. press date 7/6/78. p: Roundabout; d: Milton Lyon; ch: Haila Strauss. Cast: Trudy Bayne, David Berman, Randy Graff, Tom Offt, Elaine Petricoff, Phyllis Bash. The Jewish Rep revived it in concert form (with some material never before heard), 3/27/03, 3/30/03, 3/31/03. d: Gary John La Rosa. Cast: Karen Mason, Jim Walton

The Piper of Hamelin see # 2185, this appendix

2192. *Piper's Song.* A promising young man's world falls apart, only to be put back together by a lunatic crew of street people. Gene Frankel, 8/4/03–8/25/03. Prev from 8/2/03. p: Rockhill Prods; m/l/b: John Ryerson; d: Susan Streater

2193. *The Pirate.* Set in Town Square of village of Calvados; in Panama City; in Manuela's sitting room. Neighborhood House, 11/15/74–11/23/74. 5 perf. m/l: Cole Porter; b: Lawrence Kasha & Hayden Griffin; based on 1942 comedy by S.N. Behrman & on 1948 musicalized movie made from it by Albert

Hackett & Frances Goodrich; d/ch: Jeffrey K. Neill. Cast: Norb Joerder, Cynthia Meryl, Jeffrey Wallach, Patricia Brooks

2194. *Pleasures and Palaces.* About Catherine the Great & Potemkin (who fails to take power in Russia, flees to the USA, and takes the name Benedict Arnold), and John Paul Jones hired to fight the Turks in 1787. Previously called *Ex-Lover.* Opened 3/11/65, Fisher, Detroit. Closed 4/10/65, canceling scheduled 5/10/65 Broadway opening at the Lunt-Fontanne. Lost $450,000. p: Frank Loesser & Allen B. Whitehead; m/l: Frank Loesser (his last musical); b: Frank Loesser & Sam Spewack; based on Sam Spewack's *Once There Was a Russian,* a 1961 failed comedy (1 perf, 2/18/61, at the Music Box, starring Francoise Rosay, Albert Salmi, Julie Newmar, Walter Matthau); d/ch: Bob Fosse. Cast: Potemkin: Jack Cassidy (replaced Alfred Marks); Countess Sura: Phyllis Newman; Catherine: Hy Hazell; Also with: John McMartin, Leon Janney, Mort Marshall, Eric Brotherson, Sammy Smith, Woody Romoff, John Anania, Kathryn Doby, Gene Gavin, Leland Palmer, Barbara Sharma, Michael Quinn. "Salute," "I Hear Bells," "My Lover is a Scoundrel," "To Marry," "Hail Majesty," "Thunder and Lightning," "To Your Health," "Turkish Delight," "What is Life?," "Neither the Time Nor the Place," "In Your Eyes," "Truly Loved" which was later used in London stage prod of *Hans Christian Andersen*), "The Sins of Sura," "Hoorah for Jones," "Propaganda," "Barabanchik," "Ah, To Be Home Again," "Pleasures and Palaces," "Tears of Joy," "Far, Far, Far Away"

2195. *The Plot Against the Chase Manhattan Bank.* Revue. Theatre East, 11/26/63– 12/8/63. 15 perf. m/l: Richard R. Wolf & Frank Spiering Jr.; sk: Carl Larsen; d: Tom Gruenewald. Cast: Renee Gorsey

2196. *The Plotters of Cabbage Patch Corner.* Swan, Worcester, England, 12/26/70. w: David Wood; d: Mick Hughes; ch: Wendy Nightingale; md: Phil Wilby. Cast: Marcia King, Richard Carrington. Shaw, London, 12/15/71. p: Eddie Kulukundis; d: Jonathan Lynn; md: Peter Pontzen. Cast: Julia McKenzie, Ben Aris

2197. *Pocahontas.* American musical. About the American Indian princess Lyric, Hammersmith, London, 11/63 (1 week). w: Kermit Goell. Cast: Anita Gillette, Isabelle Lucas

2198. *The Point!* Mermaid, London, 12/16/76. Harry Nilsson (w/starred/sang his songs)

2199. *A Political Party.* Revue. 41st Street Theatre, 9/26/63–10/13/63. 14 perf. Cast: Jean Anne (also co-w/cos), Arch Lustberg (also d), Daniel Ruslander (also md), Bill Holter

2200. *Polly.* John Gay's 1729 sequel to *The Beggar's Opera.* Macheath is saved from hanging & transported to West Indies, followed by Polly; he becomes pirate; she becomes a whore. Brooklyn Academy of Music, 5/8/75– 5/25/75. 32 perf. newly realized m: Mel Marvin; adapted by/d: Robert Kalfin; cos: Carrie F. Robbins; md: Clay Fullum. Cast: Macheath: Stephen D. Newman; Polly Peachum: Betsy Beard; Jenny: Patricia Elliott; Also with: Alex Orfaly, Fran Stevens, William J. Coppola, Richard Ryder, Igors Gavon, Lucille Patton

2201. *Poor Little Lambs.* Set in Yale. Theatre at St. Peter's Church, 3/14/82–3/16/82. 73 perf. p: Richmond Crinkley; w: Paul Rudnick; d: Jack Hofsis; ch: Peter Anastos; set: David Jenkins; cos: William Ivey Long; light: Beverly Emmons; sound: T. Richard Fitzgerald. Cast: Bronson Pinchot, Albert Macklin, David Naughton, Kevin Bacon, Miles Chapin, William Thomas Jr., Gedde Watanabe. "Mother of Men," "When My Sugar Walks Down the Street," "I Married an Angel," "Love for Sale," "Good Night, Poor Harvard," "We're Saving Ourselves for Yale," "You'll Have to Put a Nightie on Aphrodite," "The Whiffenpoof Song"

2202. *Pop.* Free musical adaptation of *King Lear.* Players, 4/3/74. 9 prev. 1 perf. m/md: Donna Cribari; l/b: Larry Schiff & Chuck Knull; d: Allen R. Belknap; add l/ch: Ron Spencer. Cast: Frank W. Kopyc, Karen Magid. "Hail Hio," "Guess What from Guess Who," "Here I Go Bananas!," "Love is…," "Friends," "Locker of Love," "Cindelia," "Heroes," "No One Listens," "Her Song," "Hollow Faces," "See the Light," "Dad," "Revolution Now," "We Shall Release You," "Wedding Song"

2203. *Popkiss.* Arts Theatre, Cambridge, England, 5/16/72; toured; Globe, London, 8/22/72–10/14/72. Prev from 8/10. 60 perf. p: Donald Albery & Ina Hunter; m/l: John Addison & David Heneker; b: Michael Ashton; based on farce *Rookery Nook,* by Ben Travers; d: Richard Cottrell. Cast: Daniel Massey, Patricia Hodge, Joan Sanderson, John Standing, Isla Blair, Bernard Horsfall, Mary Millar

2204. *Poppy.* Pantomime parody. About the Opium Wars. Unrelated to the 1923 W.C. Fields musical. Barbican, London, 9/25/82 (opened in rep). p: Royal Shakespeare Co.; m: Monty Norman; l/b: Peter Nichols; d: Terry Hands; ch: David Toguri; md: David Caddick. Cast: Roger Allam, Julia Hills, Geoffrey Hutchings, Bernard Lloyd, Seeta Indrani. Adelphi, 11/14/83. 97 perf. "The Emperor's Greeting," "The Good Old Days," "Why Must I?," "If You Want to Make a Killing," "John Companee," "Poppy," "The China Clipper," "The Bounty of the Earth," "They All Look the Same to Us," "Rock-a-Bye Randy," "Rat-Tat-Tat-Tat," "The Blessed Trinity." Revised, and revived at the Adelphi, London, 11/14/83– 2/18/84. Prev from 11/9/83. 97 perf. d: Terry Hands; ch: Onna White; md: Ian MacPherson. Cast: Nichola McAuliffe, David Firth, Geoffrey Hutchins, Antonia Ellis, Alfred Marks. The revised version ran again, at Half Moon, London, 1988

2205. *The Portable Pioneer and Prairie Show.* Set in Minnesota in late 1800s. Ford's Theatre, Washington, DC, 2/11/75. 40 perf. m/md: Mel Marvin; l: David Chambers & Mel Marvin; b/d: David Chambers; ch: Dennis Nahat; light: Spencer Mosse. Cast: Lyle Swedeen. Theatre of Riverside Church, 2/5/97– 3/2/97. 2 prev. 23 perf. p: Melting Pot Theatre Co.; d: Lori Steinberg. Cast: Sean McCourt

2206. *Porterphiles.* Revue of lesser-known Cole Porter songs. York Theatre Co., 12/19/02– 1/12/03. Prev from 12/3/02. dev/md: Judy Brown; d/set: James Morgan; ch: Barry McNabb; light: Mary Jo Dondlinger. Cast: Lynne Halliday, Ricky Russell, Stephen Zinnato

2207. *Portrait of Jenny*. Harry DeJur, 11/26/82–12/19/82. 7 prev. 7 perf. p: New Federal Theatre; m/l: Howard Marren & Enid Futterman; adapted by: Enid Futterman & Dennis Rosa; from novel by Robert Nathan; d/ch: Dennis Rosa; orch: William D. Brohn. Cast: Brent Barrett, Donna Bullock, Bob Freschi. "Winter of the Mind," "Where I Come From," "Hammerstein's Music Hall," "My City," "Wish," "Alhambra Nights," "Secrets," "Portrait of Jenny," "A Green Place," "Remember Today," "Paris," "Time Stands Still in Truro," "I Love You"

2208. *Postcards on Parade*. About a postcard collector. York Theatre Co., 4/14/00–4/19/00. 6 prev. no perfs. m: Steven Taylor; l/b: Kenward Elmslie; d: Clayton Phillips; ch: Andy Blankenbuehler; set: James Morgan; light: Mary Jo Dondlinger. Cast: Jennifer Allen, John Hillner, Mark Lotito, Randy Redd

2209. *Potholes*. Musical revue. Cherry Lane, 10/9/79–10/21/79. 15 perf. m: Ted Simons; l/b: Elinor Guggenheimer; d: Sue Lawless; ch: Wayne Cilento; set: Kenneth Foy. Cast: Jill Cook, Brandon Maggart, Carol Morley, Lee Roy Reams, Samuel E. Wright. "Lost New York," "Can You Type?," "Madison Avenue," "Giant," "Yoga and Yogurt," "Network," "Looking for Someone," "Typical New Yorkers"

Poverty Is No Crime see # 2514, this appendix

2210. *Preppies*. Farcical machinations over an inheritance, in so-called 'preppy' culture. Promenade, 8/18/83–10/2/83. 9 prev. 52 perf. m/l: Gary Portnoy & Judy Hart Angelo; b: David Taylor & Carlos Davis; d/ch: Tony Tanner; set: David Jenkins; cos: Patricia McGourty; cm: George Elmer. Cast: Kathleen Rowe McAllen, Bob Walton, Beth Fowler, John Scherer, Tia Riebling, Karyn Quackenbush. "People Like Us," "Chance of a Lifetime," "One Step Away," "Summertime," "Fairy Tales," "Bells," "Moving On," "Our Night," "We've Got Each Other," "Gonna Run," "No Big Deal," "Worlds Apart," "Bring on the Loot." Originally produced by Goodspeed

2211. *A Present from the Corporation*. Opened 5/67 as *And Was Jerusalem*, at the Oxford University Experimental Theatre Club, England. Revised & re-named, and ran at the Swan, Worcester, 11/14/67 (2 weeks). p: Worcester Rep. Fortune, London, 11/30/67–12/2/67. 3 perf. m/md: John Gould; l/d: David Wood; b: Michael Sadler; set/cos: Patricia Thomas. Cast: Maggie Slater: Julia McKenzie; Also with: Gay Soper

2212. *The Present Tense*. Topical satirical revue. Park Royal Cabaret Theatre, 10/4/77–10/23/77. 24 perf. p: The Comedy Club; m/l: several writers, inc. Lee S. Wilkoff; head w: Jeff Sweet; d: Stephen Rosenfeld; set/cos: Paul de Pass. Cast: Lee S. Wilkoff, Barbara Brummel, Chris Carroll, Jim Cyrus, Lianne Kressin, Michael Nobel. "Cautiously Optimistic," "Yankee Man," "Margaret," "Come to Cuba," "Song for a Crowded Cabaret," "Love Me or Leave Me," "Man on a Subway," "Possum Pie," "Sklip, Dat, Doobee"

2213. *The President's Daughter*. Yiddish-American musical comedy. Set in Flatbush, NY. Billy Rose, Broadway, 11/3/70–1/3/71. 4 prev from 10/27/70. 72 perf. p/l/d: Jacob Jacobs; m/md: Murray Rumshinsky; b: H. Kalmanov; ch: Henrietta Jacobson; set: Barry Arnold. Cast: Jacob Jacobs, Michele Burke. "Women's Liberation," "The President's Daughter," "I Have What You Want," "A Lesson in Yiddish," "Everything is Possible in Life," "Welcome, Mr. Golden!," "Stiochket," "Without a Mother," "Love at Golden Years," "If Only I Could Be a Kid Again," "An Old Man Shouldn't Be Born," "We Two," "What More Do I Need?," "What Would You Do?"

2214. *Pretty Faces: The Large and Lovely Musical*. Set in beauty pageant to elect "Miss Global Glamour Girl." Actors Outlet, 10/21/90–12/2/90. Prev from 10/19/90. 49 perf. p: Tommy De Maio; m/l/b: Robert W. Cabell; d/ch: Gene Foote. Cast: Lynn Halverson, Michael Winther, Charles Mandracchia. "Taking Chances," "42-32-42," "How Do You Like Your Men?," "Furs, Fortune, Fame, Glamour," "Too Plump for Prom Night," "Heartbreaker," "What's Missing in My Life?," "Pretty Faces," "Daddy Doesn't Care," "Solo for the Telephone," "Global Glamour Girls," "Woman that I Am," "Purple Hearted Soldiers," "Song for Jesus," "Are You the One?," "On with the Show," "Tears and Tears Ago," "This Moment is Mine"

2215. *Prettybelle*. Southern widow, on finding that husband was a bigot, sets out to right wrongs done to her community. Opened 2/1/71, Shubert, Boston. Closed 3/6/71, canceling scheduled 3/15/71 Broadway opening at the Majestic. p: Alex Cohen; m/l: Jule Styne & Bob Merrill; b: Bob Merrill; based on 1970 novel *Prettybelle, a Lively Tale of Rape and Resurrection*, by Jean Arnold; d/ch: Gower Champion; set: Oliver Smith; md: Peter Howard. Cast: Angela Lansbury, Jon Cypher, Mark Dawson, Charlotte Rae, Peter Lombard, William Larsen, Bert Michaels, Michael Jason, Joe Morton, Igors Gavon, Maggie Task. "Manic Depressives," "Policeman's Hymn," "Prettybelle," "To a Small Degree," "You Ain't Hurtin' Your Ole Lady None," "How Could I Know (What Was Going On)?," "I Never Did Imagine," "New Orleans Poon," "In the Japanese Gardens," "An Individual Thing," "I Met a Man," "The No-Tell Motel," "I'm in a Tree," "When I'm Drunk I'm Beautiful"

2216. *Pretzels*. Revue. Theatre Four, 12/16/74–3/30/75. 120 perf. The Phoenix Theatre production, presented by Burry Fredrik & Walter Boxer; m/l: John Forster; w: Jane Curtin, Fred Grandy, Judy Kahan; d: Patricia Carmichael; light: Ken Billington. Cast: Jane Curtin (*Jane Ranallo* from 3/18/75), John Forster, Judy Kahan (*Sandy Faison* from 3/18/75), Timothy Jerome. Tour opened 5/5/75, Detroit, with Jane Curtin, Timothy Jerome, Christopher Bankey, Sandy Faison. "Pretzels," "Take Me Back," "Sing and Dance," "The Cockroach Song," "Classical Music," "The Reunion"

2217. *Prime Time*. AMAS, 4/9/87–5/3/87. 16 perf. m/l: Johnny Brandon; d/ch: Marvin

Gordon; md: Joyce Brown. Cast: Eddie Simon, Elly Barbour. "The Six O'clock News," "A Blonde in Bed," "Make Way for One More Dream," "It's a Jungle Out There," "A Very Good Night," "Get off My Back," "A Reason for Living," "Nobody Ever Hears What I've Got to Say," "You Blow Hot and Cold," "Leading My Own Parade"

2218. *Prime Time Prophet*. Musical satire of televangelism. Players, 6/10/93–7/25/93. 8 prev from 6/1/93. 54 perf. m/l/b: Kevin Connors; b: Randy Buck; md: David Wolfson. Cast: Beth Glover, Marcus Maurice, David Brand, Jonathan Hadley, Janet Aldrich. "The Devil to Pay," "Hot Shot," "The Award," "Saved!," "Heavenly Party," "Expect a Miracle," "So Help Me God," "Homesick for Hell," "Leap of Faith," "Step into the Light," "Diva Supreme," "Tina Seeks Solace," "Tips from Tina," "Necessarily Evil," "How Does She Do It?," "Tina's Finest Hour," "Armageddon"

2219. *Primrose*. London, 1924. 225 perf. m: George Gershwin; l: Ira Gershwin & Desmond Carter; b: George Grossmith & Guy Bolton. "Naughty Baby," "Boy Wanted." It never played Broadway. 1st ever North American run was in concert, as part of *Musicals Tonight!* series, 12/2/03–12/21/03. d: Thomas Mills; md: Barbara Anselmi

2220. *The Prince and the Pauper*. Judson Hall, 10/12/63. 158 perf. p: Joseph Beinhorn; m: George Fischoff; l/b: Verna Tomasson; d: David Shanstrom; ch: Bick Goss. Cast: John Davidson, Carol Blodgett, Joan Shepard, Robert McHaffey. "Garbage Court Round," "In a Storybook," "I've Been a-Begging," "Why Don't We Switch?," "Do This, Do That," "The Prince is Mad," "Oh, Pity the Man," "With a Sword in My Buckle," "Ev'rybody Needs Somebody to Love," "The Tree and the Sun," "King Foo-Foo the First," "Coronation Song"

2221. *The Prince and the Pauper*. Fifth Avenue, Seattle, 2001. m/l: Marc Eliot & Judd Woldin; b: Ivan Menchell. Cast: Marc Kudisch

2222. *The Prince and the Pauper*. Lambs, 6/16/02. Prev from 6/7/02. On hiatus from 10/21/02. Resumed 11/27/02, with some cast changes. After a limited run it closed 1/5/03. p: Carolyn Rossi Copeland, Marian Lerman Jacobs, Leftfield Prods; m/l: Neil Berg; add l: Bernie Garzia; b: Bernie Garzia & Ray Roderick; based on Mark Twain's novel; Ray Roderick; cast recording on Jay (released 11/29/02). Cast: Dennis Michael Hall, Gerard Canonico (*Jimmy Dieffenbach*). Lambs, 6/4/03–8/31/03. 102 perf. Cast: Rob Evan, Dennis Michael Hall, Jimmy Dieffenbach, Alison Fischer, Leslie Castay. 1st ran in Westchester, NY., 1996, after which Bernie Garzia was brought in, then it played in Queens

2223. *The Prince of Grand Street*. Set in & around Lower East Side of Manhattan, 1908. Opened 3/8/78, Forrest, Philadelphia. Closed 4/15/78, Shubert, Boston, canceling scheduled 5/11/78 Broadway opening at the Palace. p: Robert Whitehead, Roger L. Stevens, Shubert Organization; m/l/b: Bob Merrill (his last musical); d: Gene Saks; ch: Lee Theodore; set: David Mitchell; light: Thomas Skelton; cos: Jane Greenwood; md: Colin Romoff. Based on life of actor Boris Thomashevsky (re-named Nathan Rashumsky in the musical). Cast: Robert Preston (his last musical), Sam Levene, Neva Small, Werner Klemperer, David Margulies, Bernice Massi, Sammy Smith, Alan Manson, Addison Powell, Alexander Orfaly, Richard Muenz, Walter Charles, Darlene Anders, Steven Gelfer, Susan Edwards. "A Grand Street Tivoli Presentation," "Fifty Cents," "I Know What it is to Be Alone," "I'm a Star," "Do I Make You Happy," "Stay with Me," "Sew a Button," "The Prince of Grand Street," "A Place in the World," "The Youngest Person I Know," "What Do I Do Now?." "Where Does Love Go?" was added late in Boston run. It did not have its 1st NY showing until it was revived, in concert, by Jewish Rep, 5/29/03–6/2/03. This prod had newly found & re-constructed scenes. adapted by: Walter Willison; d: Barry Kleinbort; md: Christopher Denny. Cast: Nathan: Mike Burstyn; Leah: Brooke Sunny Moriber; Also with: Kenneth Kantor, David Brummel

2224. *Privates on Parade*. Play with mus. Set in Singapore & Malaya in 1948. Female impersonator is part of British secret service regiment on entertainment duty. Aldwych, London, 2/17/77. 208 perf. m: Denis King; l: Peter Nichols; based on comedy by Peter Nichols. Cast: Denis Quilley, Joe Melia, Neil McCaul, Ben Cross, Simon Jones, David Daker, Nigel Hawthorne. "S.A.D.U.S.E.A.," "Les Girls," "Danke Schon," "Western Approaches Ballet," "The Little Things We Used to Do," "Black Velvet," "Better Far than Sitting This Life Out," "The Price of Peace," "Could You Please Inform Us," "Privates on Parade," "The Latin American Way," "Sunnyside Lane." American premiere at Long Wharf Theatre, New Haven, 5/24/79. 37 perf. d: Arvin Brown; ch: Malcolm Goddard; set: David Jenkins; md: Thomas Fay. Cast: Jim Dale, Gavin Reed, Joe Grifasi, Alvin K.U. Lum. Christian C. Yegen Theatre, NYC, 8/22/89–10/15/89. 30 prev from 7/26/89. 64 perf. p: Roundabout Theatre; d: Larry Carpenter; ch: Daniel Pelzig; set: Loren Sherman; cos: Lindsay W. Davis; light: Marcia Madeira; md: Philip Campanella. Cast: Jim Dale, Simon Jones, Donald Burton, John Curry, Gregory Jbara, Donna Murphy, Tom Matsusaka, Edward Hibbert, Jim Fyfe, Ross Bickell, Stephen Lee

2225. *Prizes*. AMAS, 4/26/89–5/21/89. 20 perf. m/l: Charles DeForest; d: Lee Minskoff; ch: Margo Sappington. Cast: Luther Fontaine, Doug Okerson, Mary Stout, Darcy Thompson, Karen Ziemba. "Awards," "Thank You Very Much," "It Always Worked," "I'm Not Ready for You," "Run a Little Faster," "Is There Any Other Way to Live?," "All the Rest is Bullshit," "I Am the One," "I Don't Need Anybody," "Prizes"

2226. *Prodigal*. Young Australian can't resist temptations of big city. Theatre at St. Peter's, 3/12/02–3/31/02. 24 perf. p: York Theatre Co.; m: Mathew Frank; l/b: Dean Bryant; d/set: James Morgan. Cast: Christian Borle, Kerry Butler, Alison Fraser, David Hess, Joshua Park, Mathew Frank. "Picture Postcard Place," "Happy Families," "Run with the Tide," "Brand

New Eyes," "When I Was a Kid," "My Boy," "Out of Myself," "Set Me Free," "Epiphany," "Love Them and Leave Them Alone," "Where Does it Get You," "Maddy's Piece," "Lullaby." Originally prod in Australia

2227. *The Prodigal Sister*. Theatre de Lys, 11/25/74–12/29/74. 8 prev. 42 perf. p: Woodie King Jr.; m: Micki Grant; l: J.E. Franklin & Micki Grant; b: J.E. Franklin; d: Shauneille Perry; ch: Rod Rogers; set: C. Richard Mills; cos: Judy Dearing; md: Neal Tate. Cast: Frances Salisbury, Paula Desmond, Esther Brown, Frank Carey, Ethel Beatty, Leonard Jackson, Louise Stubbs, Yolande Graves. "Slip Away," "Talk, Talk, Talk," "Ain't Marryin' Nobody," "If You Know What's Good for You," "First Born," "Woman Child," "Big City Dance," "Sister Love," "Hot Pants Dance," "Remember Caesar," "Superwoman," "Flirtation Dance," "Look at Me," "I Been up in Hell," "Thank You, Lord," "Remember," "Celebration," "The Prodigal Has Returned." Originally presented at New Federal Theatre, 7/11/74

2228. *Professionally Speaking*. Musical revue. St. Peter's Church, 5/22/86–6/15/86. 7 prev. 37 perf. p: Frederic Block, Irving Welzer, Kate Harper; m/l: Peter Winkler, Ernst Muller, Frederic Block; d: Tony Tanner; md: Bruce W. Coyle. Cast: Marilyn Pasekoff, Meg Bussert, David Ardao, Jilana Devine, Dennis Bailey, Hal Davis, Kathy Morath. Understudies: Joan Jaffe & Sel Vitella. "The Doctor's Out Today," "Malpractice," "Three Doctors' Wives," "A Doctor's Prayer," "Guadalajara," "The Lawyer's Out Today," "Malpractice II," "Equitable Distribution Waltz," "Lawyerman," "What Price Have I Paid?," "First Let's Kill All the Lawyers," "The Teacher's Out Today," "The Best Part-Time Job in Town," "Emmylou Lafayette and the Football Team," "Tamara Queen of the Nile," "Stupidly in Love," "I Hate It," "Remember There Was Me," "Who the Hell Do These Wise Guys Think They Are?," "Over the Hill"

2229. *Prom Queens Unchained*. Contest for queen of 1950s high school prom. Village Gate, 6/30/91–8/18/91. 57 perf. m: Keith Herrmann; l: Larry Goodsight; b: Stephen Witkin; d/ch: Karen Azenberg; md: Stuart Malina. Cast: Ron Kurowski, Sandra Purpuro, David Brummel, Susan Levine. "Down the Hall," "That Special Night," "Dustbane: the Ballad of Minka," "Eat the Lunch," "Most Likely," "The Venulia"/"Seeing Red," "The Perfect Family," "Corsage," "Squeeze Me in the Rain," "Going All the Way," "Sherry's Theme," "Give Your Love"

2230. *Promenade*. Satire on the world seen through the eyes & values of a pair of convicts. Promenade, 6/4/69–1/18/70. 259 perf. This show opened the Promenade Theatre. p: Edgar Lansbury & Joseph Beruh; m/md: Al Carmines; l/b: Maria Irene Fornes; d: Lawrence Kornfeld; set: Rouben Ter-Arutunian; cos: Willa Kim; light: Jules Fisher; orch: Eddie Sauter. Cast: Alice Playten, Madeline Kahn, Shannon Bolin (*Mary Jo Catlett* from 9/23/69), Ty McConnell (*Kenneth Carr* from 9/15/69), Gilbert Price, George S. Irving, Glenn Kezer.

"Promenade Theme," "Dig, Dig, Dig," "Unrequited Love," "Isn't That Clear?," "Don't Eat It," "Four," "Chicken is He," "A Flower," "Apres Vous," "Bliss," "The Moment Has Passed," "Thank You," "Clothes Make the Man," "Cigarette Song," "Two Little Angels," "Passing of Time," "Capricious and Fickle," "Crown Me," "Mr. Phelps," "Madeline," "Spring Beauties," "A Poor Man," "Why Not," "Finger Song," "Little Fool," "Czardas," "Laughing Song," "A Mother's Love," "Listen, I Feel," "I Saw a Man," "All is Well in the City." Theatre Off Park, 10/11/83–10/29/83. 16 perf. d: Albert Harris; set: Leo B. Meyer; cos: Tony Chase; light: Martin Friedman; md: John R. Williams. Cast: Bill Buell, Georgia Creighton, Tim Ewing, Susan Feldon, Jason Graae, Jim Hindman, Regina O'Malley

2231. *Promised Land*. Lamb's Little Theatre, 10/10/91. w: George Fischoff; based on Moses & the Exodus; d: Peter Bennett; ch: Mercedes Ellington; set: Peter Harrison. Cast: Dana Cote, Michael Oberlander, Wendy Oliver, Francis Ruivivar, Jahneen

2232. *The Proposition*. Satirical musical revue. Bitter End, 4/19/68–4/20/68. 2 perf. d/w: Jeremy Leven. Cast: Fred Grandy, Paul Jones

2233. *The Proposition*. Revue. Improvised entirely from suggestions supplied by audience at each perf, tending to be topical & comic. Gramercy Arts, 3/24/71; Mercer-Shaw Arena, from 4/28/71. Previously produced in Cambridge, Mass., 1968. Somewhat re-structured for a new edition beginning 9/16/71, and again for later edition beginning 9/13/72. conceived by: Allan Albert. Cast: Josh Mostel (*Sam Jory*), Karen Welles, Jane Curtin. Finally closed 4/14/74, after 1,109 perf. Actors Playhouse, 5/3/78–5/21/78. 24 perf. Cast: Raymond Baker, Timothy Hall, Anne Cohen, Deborah Reagan

2234. *Pull Both Ends*. A vehicle for the TV dance group The Young Generation. Set in Christmas cracker factory threatened with takeover. Manchester, England, 6/14/72; Piccadilly, London, 7/18/72–8/19/72. 36 perf. m/l: John Schroeder & Anthony King; b: Brian Comport; d: Leslie Lawton; ch: Nigel Lythgoe; md: Alyn Ainsworth. Cast: Gerry Marsden, Christine Holmes, Keith Smith, Judy Bowen, Miles Greenwood, Liz Robertson, The Young Generation. "Every Morning," "What About People?," "After All (We're Women)," "A Tiny Touch," "Particular Woman," "Some Kind of Love," "Decisions," "Put a Little Smile," "Wallflowers," "If You Knew the Way I Feel," "Get the World to Dance," "Here I Am," "Strike," "Little Leather Book," "There's Something About Her," "Oh, Joe," "Can This Be Love"?," "We're Ready," "Pullin' Together"

2235. *The Pursuit of Love*. Theatre Royal, Bristol, England, 5/24/67–6/20/67. Did not go to London. p: Bristol Old Vic Co.; m/l/b: Julian Slade; based on Nancy Mitford's novel; d: Val May; ch: Denys Palmer; md: Grant Hossack. Cast: Aubrey Woods, Lewis Fiander, Edward de Souza, Norman Comer, Stella Moray

2236. *Put It in Writing*. Small revue. Theatre de Lys, 5/13/63–6/2/63. 24 perf. p: Lucille Lortel; material: Fred Ebb, Martin Charnin, etc. d: Bill Penn; ch: Joyce Trisler; cos: Audre; ms: Gershon Kingsley; md: Gordon Connell. Cast: Jane Connell, Buzz Halliday, Brandon Maggart, Jack Blackton, Bill Hinnant. "Walking Down the Road." Tour began 6/28/62, Happy Medium, Chicago. md: Harry Fuchs. Cast: Jeanne Arnold, Jack Blackton, Bob Dishy

2237. ***A Quarter for the Ladies Room***. A musical eyeview. Ladies in powder room sing of men in their lives. Village Gate, 11/12/72. 7 prev. 1 perf. m: John Clifton & Arthur Siegel; l: Ruth Batchelor; d: Darwin Knight; cos: Miles White; md: Karen Gustafson; arr: Bill Brohn. Cast: Helon Blount, Benay Venuta, Norma Donaldson. "First Quarter," "Turn Around," "Married Man," "Gemini," "Feel at Home," "My Lover and His Wife," "Baby Dolls," "The Princess," "Nice Ladies," "Woman Power," "When Will the Music Be Gone?," "When the Time Comes," "Why Don't I Leave Him?," "Talk to Me," "Last Quarter"

2238. ***Queen of Hearts***. Based on life of Princess Diana. Grove Street, 10/7/98–11/1/98. 20 perf. m/l: Claudia Perry; b: Stephen Stahl; d: Christopher Casoria; ch: Marian Akana; md: Charles Eversole. Cast: Diana: Kendra Munger; Charles: James A. Walsh; Dodi: Tony Sicuso; Raine/Camilla: Debbie Clydesdale. "Way of the World," "Who You Are," "Backbone of Steel," "Nothing Ever Happens to Me," "A Fairy Tale Come True," "Her Royal Highness," "Future King of England," "Moment to Moment," "The Walls Are Closing In," "Time to Let Go," "The New Me," "Queen of Hearts," "You're My World," "Its My Time." Harold Clurman, 3/26/99–4/11/99. 3 prev. 13 perf. The score was slightly rearranged, and some numbers cut & others added. d: Stephen Stahl; ch: Phil La Duca; md: Allan Kashkin. Cast: Diana: Paula Leggett Chase; Charles: James A. Walsh; Dodi: Tom Schmid; Camilla: Annie Edgerton; Also with: Derin Altay, Bill Quinlan

2239. ***Queenie***. Comedy Theatre, London, 6/22/67–7/8/67. 20 perf. p: Bernard Delfont & Arthur Lewis; m: Ted Manning & Marvin Laird; l/b: Ted Willis (wrote book in rhyming couplets); d: Arthur Lewis; ch: Leo Kharibian; set/cos: Hutchinson Scott; md: Leo Mole. Cast: Vivienne Martin, Bill Owen, Cheryl Kennedy, Paul Eddington, Simon Oates, Julia McKenzie (in chorus). It was panned. It had started at the Yvonne Arnaud, Guildford, as *The Ballad of Queenie Swann* (opened 5/30/67)

2240. ***Quick, Quick, Slow***. Birmingham Rep, England, 8/20/69–9/27/69 (in rep). m: Monty Norman; l: Julian More; b: David Turner; from the TV play *Way Off Beat*, by David Turner; d: Peter Dews; ch: Virginia Mason; md: Grant Hossack. Cast: John Baddeley, Stella Moray

2241. ***A Quiet Place***. 3-act opera. 1984. m/l: Leonard Bernstein & Stephen Wadsworth. Cast: Robert Galbraith, Beverly Morgan. Incorporated the short opera *Trouble in Tahiti*

2242. ***Quilt: A Musical Celebration***. Theatre at St. Peter's, 6/6/94–6/13/94. 2 perf.

m/md: Michael Stockler; add m: Robert Lindner; l: Jim Morgan; based on stories that inspired panels of the NAMES Project AIDS Quilt; d: John Margulis. Cast: Angela Bullock, Sara Krieger, Nancy Ringham, Ty Taylor, Russ Thacker, Lillias White, Matt Zarley. "Something Beautiful," "At a Distance," "Hot Sex," "Living with the Little Things," "In the Absence of Angels," "Could You Do Me a Favor," "I Believe in You," "Victims of AIDS," "One Voice"

2243. ***Quilters***. Story of American pioneer women as suggested by patterns in their quilts. Jack Lawrence, 9/25/84–10/14/84. 5 prev. 24 perf. m/l/d: Barbara Damashek; based on book *The Quilters: Women and Domestic Art*, by Patricia Cooper & Norman Bradley Allen. Cast: Lenka Peterson, Evalyn Baron, Alma Cuervo, Rosemary McNamara. "Pieces of Lives," "Rocky Road," "Little Babes that Sleep All Night," "Thread the Needle," "Cornelia," "The Windmill Song," "Are You Washed in the Blood of the Lamb?," "The Butterfly," "Gren," "Hoedown," "Quiltin' and Dreamin'," "Every Log in My House," "Land Where We'll Never Grow Old," "Who Will Count the Stitches?," "The Lord Don't Rain Down Manna," "Dandelion," "Everything Has a Time," "Hands Around." Tony nominations: musical, score, book, dir of a musical, Lenka Peterson, Evalyn Baron. Previously ran at Denver Theatre Center, and in Washington, DC, and L.A.

2244. ***The Quiz Kid***. Royal Court, Liverpool, 7/27/59; toured; Lyric, Hammersmith, London, 9/8/59–10/3/59. 31 perf. m/l/b: Jimmy & Nina Thompson; add m/md: John Pritchett; d/ch: Alfred Rodrigues. Cast: Jimmy Thompson, Barry Cryer, Patricia Lancaster, Roderick Cook, Murray Kash, Diana Decker, Doris Hare, Sally Williams, Ben Aris, Tristram Jellinek, Julia Sutton, Kim Grant

2245. ***R Loves J***. Chichester Festival, England, 7/11/73 (in rep). It did not make the West End. m: Alexander Faris; l: Julian More; b: Peter Ustinov; d/ch: Wendy Toye; md: Peter L. Collins. Cast: Topol, Rosemary Williams, David Watson, Anna Dawson, Gemma Craven

2246. ***Rabbit Sense***. Musical adaptation of *Uncle Remus* tales. Tada, 7/19/91–8/12/91. 35 perf. m/l: John Kroner & Gary Gardner; b: Davidson Lloyd; d: James Learned; md: Wendell Smith. "Grab Some Magic," "What's a Kid to Do?," "Ballad of Brer Rabbit," "Boss Bear," "Skedaddle," "Brer Fox Trot," "The Magic's in You" (by Joel Gelpe)

2247. ***Rabboni***. The life of Yeshua (Jesus). Perry Street, 6/13/85–8/25/85. 88 perf. w: Jeremiah Ginsberg; d/ch: Alan Weeks; set: Nancy Winters; md: Neal Tate. Cast: Paul Clark, Scott Elliott, Roumel Reaux (*Steve Cupo*). "The Shepherd of Old," "If I Have No Love," "I Am the Way, the Truth and the Light," "O Jerusalem Jerusalem," "Last Days of Rome," "My God, My God," "Rabboni"

2248. ***Rachael Lily Rosenbloom — And Don't You Ever Forget It!*** Would-be star from Fulton Fish Market in Manhattan winds up as gossip columnist. She spells her name "Rachael" to compensate for lost "a" in Barbra Streisand. Broadhurst, Broadway, 11/26/73–

12/1/73 (closed after 8 prev, and did not officially open). p: Robert Stigwood & Ahmet Ertegun; m/l: Paul Jabara; b: Paul Jabara & Tom Eyen; d: Tom Eyen; ch: Tony Stevens (but was replaced by Grover Dale, despite official billing); set: Robin Wagner; cos: Joseph G. Aulisi; light: Jules Fisher; sound: Abe Jacob; ms: Gordon Lowry Harrell. Bette Midler turned it down. Cast: Ellen Greene, Anita Morris, Carole Bishop, Jozella Reed, Thomas Walsh, Michon Peacock, Jane Robertson, Judy Gibson, Andre De Shields, Richard Cooper Bayne, Kenneth Carr, Anthony White, Wayne Cilento, Rhoda Farber, Marion Ramsey, Paul Jabara. "Dear Miss Streisand," "Me and My Perch," "Gorgeous Lily," "Get Your Show Rolling," "Hollywood! Hollywood!," "East Brooklyn Blues," "Broadway Rhythm," "Hollywood is Dying," "Broadway I Love You," "Silver Diamond Rhinestone Glasses," "Party Sickness," "Take Me Savage," "Change in Raquel," "Ocho Rios," "Cobra Woman," "Things," "One Man," "We'll Be There"

2249. ***Radiant Baby***. Newman, 3/2/03–3/23/03. Prev from 2/1/03. 25 perf. m: Debra Barsha; l: Ira Gasman, Debra Barsha, Stuart Ross; b: Stuart Ross; based on John Gruen's 1993 bio of artist Keith Haring, who died from AIDS in 1990, aged 31; d: George C. Wolfe; ch: Fatima Robinson. Cast: Daniel Reichard, Kate Jennings Grant, Billy Porter. One of Mr. Haring's paintings was of a shining, crawling baby

2250. ***Radio City Music Hall Christmas Spectacular***. Annual holiday revue. Radio City Music Hall, 1987. m/l: Billy Butt. Cast: The Rockettes. "It's Christmas in New York." Another prod ran 11/7/96–1/5/97. d/ch: Robert Longbottom

2251. ***Radio Gals***. Set in Cedar Ridge, Ark., in late 1920s. John Houseman, 10/1/96–11/3/96. 17 prev from 9/17/96. 39 perf. m/l/b: Mike Craver & Mark Hardwick; d/ch: Marcia Milgrom Dodge; sound: Tom Morse. Cast: Carole Cook, Klea Blackhurst, Rosemary Loar. "Wedding of the Flowers," "Sunrise Melody," "Aviatrix Love Song," "Horehound Compound," "If Stars Could Talk," "When it's Sweetpea Time in Georgia," "Dear Mr. Gershwin," "Tranquil Boxwood," "Faeries in My Mother's Flower Garden," "A Fireside, a Pipe, a Pet," "Edna Jones the Elephant Girl," "Paging the Ether," "Royal Radio," "Weather Song," "Buster, He's a Hot Dog Now," "Why Did You Make Me Love You?," "Kittens in the Snow," "Old Gals," "A Gal's Got to Do What a Gal's Got to Do," "NBC Broadcast." Previously prod by Arkansas Rep

2252. ***Radio Times***. Queen's, London, 1992. m: Noel Gay; l: various authors; b: Abi Grant; cast recording on Polydor. Cast: Kathryn Evans, Jeff Shankley, Tony Slattery, Ian Bartholomew, James Bullen. "Turn on the Music," "Laughing at the Rain," "Just One More," "Hello to the Sun," "Let the People Sing," "Someone Else," "There's Something About a Soldier," "Ali Baba's Camel," "Run, Rabbit, Run," "All for the Love of a Lady," "My Thanks to You," "Song of Tomorrow"

Rag Dolly see # 567, Main Book

2253. ***A Rag on a Stick and a Star***. About

Theodore Herzl, Israel's founder. Theatre Row, 9/10/92. m/l: Elliot Weiss & Eric Blau; d: Richard Ziman. Cast: Daniel Neiden, William Youmans, David Pevsner, Jeff Gardner. "Oh, Lead Us Now," "Wishing for a Victory," "Farewell Soft Life," "A Rag on a Stick and a Star," "On the Way Home to the Old Land," "Abdullah," "In the Wildest Dream," "We Have Come So Far," "Let Them Bleed," "This is My Promise," "We Are Dancing in the Temple"

2254. ***The Ragged Child***. Set in London in 1850–51. Sadlers Wells, London, 1/20/88. m: David Nield; l/b: Jeremy James Taylor & Frank Whateley. Triplex (OB), 4/15/93–4/17/93. 5 perf. ch: Wendy Cook. Cast: Greg Morton, Laurence Taylor, Timothy Goodwin, Tom Hollis, Michael Dovey. Slightly revised m/l: "Opening Sentence," "Botany Bay," "Ballad of Joe Cooper," "Now, Ain't That a Bloomin' Shame," "There'll Come a Day," "Sores of London," "Deep Below the City Streets," "Let Them Starve," "Work, Boys, Work," "London Town," "There's a Friend for Little Children," "Here's to the Bootblacks," "Home Sweet Home," "Come Sway," "Closing Sentence"

2255. ***Rainbow***. Man killed in Vietnam, and his search for his place in the Universe, as seen through pastiche of rock songs. Orpheum, 12/18/72–1/28/73. 48 perf. p/b: James & Ted Rado; m/l: James Rado; d: Joe Donovan; set/light: James Tilton; cos: Nancy Potts; sound: Abe Jacob; md: Steven Margoshes. Cast: Gregory V. Karliss, Meat Loaf, Marie Santell, Marcia McClain, Kay Cole, Janet Powell. "Who Are We?," "Questions, Questions," "Song to Sing," "What Can I Do for You?," "People Stink," "Give Your Heart to Jesus," "Joke a Cola," "Mama Loves You," "I Want to Make You Cry," "I Am a Cloud," "A Garden for Two," "Starry Cold Night," "O.K., Goodbye," "Deep in the Dark," "You Live in Flowers," "I Don't Hope for Great Things," "Globligated," "Be Not Afraid," "Ten Days Ago," "Oh, Oh, Oh," "Moosh, Moosh," "The Man," "The World is Round," "Stars and Bars," "I Am Not Free," "We Are the Clouds," "How Dreamlike," "Somewhere Under the Rainbow," "Star Song"

2256. ***Rainbow***. Romantic musical adventure, set in & around Fort Independence, Mo.; and during the Gold Rush, in & around a small mining town in California, in the days of '49. Gallo, Broadway, 11/21/28–12/15/28. 29 perf. p: Philip Goodman; m: Vincent Youmans; l/d: Oscar Hammerstein II; b: Laurence Stallings & Oscar Hammerstein II; ch: Busby Berkeley; md: Max Steiner. Cast: Libby Holman, Harland Dixon, Charles Ruggles, Brian Donlevy. "On the Golden Trail," "My Mother Told Me Not to Trust a Soldier," "Virginia," "I Want a Man," "Soliloquy," "I Like You as You Are," "The One Girl," "Let Me Give All My Love to Thee," "Diamond in the Rough," "Who Wants to Love Spanish Ladies," "Hay! Straw!," "The Bride Was Dressed in White." Off Center, 4/23/86–5/5/86. 12 perf. Revised version. add l: Harold Adamson, Buddy De Sylva, Edward Heyman, Bud McCreery, J. Russell Robbison; new b: Conn Fleming; d: Robert Brewer; ch:

David Storey. Cast: Lee Lobenhofer, Teri Bibb, Debbie Shapiro. "On the Golden Trail," "I Want a Man," "West Wind," "I Like You as You Are," "Rise 'n Shine," The Primping Dance, "Time on My Hands," "Virginia," "Let Me Give All My Love to Thee," "The One Girl," "He Came Along," "Diamond in the Rough," "Mean Man," "You're Everywhere," "Drums in My Heart"

2257. ***The Rainbow Rape Trick***. Bert Wheeler, 4/13/75–4/15/75. 4 perf. m: Ann K. Lipson; l: Ann K. Lipson & Greg Reardon; b: Greg Reardon; d: Robert Davison; ch: Robin Raseen. Cast: Bob Bosco, Deidre Lynn, Jerry Rodgers, Jeremy Stockwell, John Blanda, Jean Greer, Lois Hathaway, Vincent Millard, Patrick O'Sullivan, Anthony Dileva, Joseph Tripolino. "Zip Community," "Free," "Itch to Be a Witch," "Stay with Me," "Little Blue Star," "Three Fierce Men," "Act Like a Villager," "Empty World of Power"

2258. ***Rainbow Square***. Set in post-war occupied Vienna. Stoll, London, 9/21/51–1/26/52. 146 perf. m: Robert Stolz; l/b: Guy Bolton & Harold Purcell; d: Robert Nesbitt; ch: Hazel Gee; cos: Hardy Amies, etc. Cast: Bill Travers, Martha King, Gloria Lane, Alfred Marks, Vera Pearce, Bruce Trent, Martin Benson, Andrea Malandrinos, Sonnie Hale, Arnold Diamond, George Margo. "Rainbow Square," "What a Day," "Who Knows," "You're So Easy to Know," "You'll Still Belong to Me," "Fabulous," "My Sunday Girl," "The Show Must Go On," "Bells of St. Veronica"

2259. ***Ram in the Thicket***. Musical vignettes based on Bible stories, juxtaposed with modern issues such as AIDS & abortion. Judith Anderson, 8/31/94–9/18/94. 24 perf. m/md: Steve Rue; l: Steve Rue & Michael Criss; b: Bill Johnson & Michael Criss; d: L. Keith White; ch: Jamie Waggoner. "Blood Religion," "The Shadrach and Meshach Show," "The Jonah Cliche," "Let's Do the Confessional," "Trying to Get Back on My Feet Again," "Smelly Demon Swine," "A Mother with Sons," "Together So Long," "Out on My Own," "King David"

2260. ***Rap Master Ronnie***. A partisan revue. Top of the Gate, 10/3/84–11/10/84. 49 perf. p: Rosita Sarnoff; m/add l: Elizabeth Swados; l: Garry Trudeau; d: Caymichael Patten; ch: Ronni Stewart; set: Neil Peter Jampolis; cos: David Woolard. Cast: Ronald Reagan: Reathel Bean; Also with: Ernestine Jackson, Mel Johnson Jr., Catherine Cox, Richard Ryder. "Rap Master Ronnie," "Take That Smile off Your Face," "The Class of 1984," "You're Not Ready," "The Majority," "Self-Made Man," "O Grenada," "Nine to Twelve," "Thinking the Unthinkable," "Cheese," "Facts," "The Empire Strikes First," "New Year's in Beirut, 1983," "The Roundup," "Something for Nothing"

2261. ***The Rat Pack***. A hit musical entertainment. About Frank Sinatra, Dean Martin & Sammy Davis Jr., and hangers-on. Set over the course of an evening at the Sands night club in Vegas during the time the boys were filming *Oceans Eleven*. Theatre Royal, Haymarket, London, 3/18/03. Cast: Frank: Stephen Triffitt;

Sammy: George Long; Dean: Mark Adams. "New York, New York," "That's Amore," "Fly Me to the Moon," "That Old Black Magic," "Memories Are Made of This," "My Way." Strand, 7/1/03. Prev from 6/26/03. Previously had successful UK tour & runs at the Peacock & Palladium. Canadian tour opened in Canada 9/03, as *Direct from Vegas—The Rat Pack*. North American premiere in Toronto, 9/04. d/ch: Mitch Sebastian; md: Barry Robinson

2262. ***Rats***. Musical revue. Van Buren, 10/18/82–11/6/82. 6 prev. 12 perf. p: Tom O'Shea; m/md: Vivian Krasner; l/b: Roy Doliner; d/ch: Don Swanson. It claimed NOT to be based on a book by T.S. Eliot. Cast: Roy Doliner, George Merritt, Yvette Freeman, Gerry Martin, Ken Ward. "Does Broadway Need Some More Rats?," "Acting and Hustling," "Rodents," "The Night I Bit John Simon," "Mr. Sondheim," "Never Have a Book," "Never Left Home," "We Ate the Money," "Under the Spotlight," "Test Tube Baby," "Write About Me," "Crastine," "The Rat-a-Tat Tap," "Like Liza Does," "I'd Know How to Be Big," "Cheese Medley"

2263. ***Raze the Roof***. Musical revue. Opened 9/17/48, Curran, San Francisco. Closed 3/12/49, American Theatre, St. Louis. Did not make Broadway. p: Maurice Duke; special songs & material: Snag Werris; d: Jerry Lester & Maurice Duke; ch: Ray Malone. Cast: Jerry Lester, Wiere Brothers, Bobb Sherwood & His Orchestra. "California Medley," "An Odd Moment," "Hey Look, I'm Dancin'," "Spots Before Your Eyes," "Continental Pandemonium," "Call for Herbert Tillson," "Royal Garden Blues," "Pardon Me, Pretty Baby," "Rhythmic Charm," "Poono in Persia," "Dancing Feet," "Rum-Rum-Rumba Fantasy," "The House of Sherwood"

2264. ***Ready or Not***. INTAR, 4/23/87–5/17/87. 16 perf. p: City Troupe; m/l/b: Michael Smit; d: Tim Vode. Cast: Michael DeVries, Mark Roland, Pamela McLernon, Colleen Fitzpatrick, Melinda Tanner. "Watery Blue," "They're Going Sailing," "A Way of Showing I Love You," "Does He Think of Her?," "Daddy," "From Here to Here," "Villains of History," "Grandfather Clock in the Hall," "It Didn't Used to Be This Way," "Am I Nuts," "State Fair," "Ready or Not," "I Have to Tell You," "Take the Boat," "I Knew I Could Fly," "The Fog," "Jenny"

2265. ***The Real Ambassadors***. Musical play. Monterey Jazz Festival, 1962. Cast: Louis Armstrong & Carmen McRae doing Dave Brubeck numbers

2266. ***Real Life Funnies***. Manhattan Theatre Club Upstage, 2/11/81–3/1/81. songs: Alan Menken; based on idea by Lawrence Kraman; from Stan Mack's comic strip; adapted by/d: Howard Ashman; ch: Douglas Norwick; md: Larry Hochman; light: Frances Aronson. Cast: Pamela Blair, Gibby Brand, Merwin Goldsmith, Janie Sell, Dale Soules, Chip Zien

2267. ***The Real McCoy***. About the Hatfield-McCoy feud. Cap21 Studio 1, 4/28/99–5/1/99. 5 perf. m/l: David Loud; b: Gene P. Bissell & Joan Ross Sorkin; d: Michael Unger; ch: Tony Parise; md: David Holcenberg

2282 *Appendix* (Reuben)

2268. *Really Rosie*. Children's musical based on the cartoon character. Musical Theatre Lab, Kennedy Center, 10/17/78. 12 perf. m: Carole King; l/b: Maurice Sendak; d/ch: Patricia Birch; md: Glen Roven. Cast: Tisha Campbell, Mary K. Lombardi, Christine Langner. "Really Rosie," "(My) Simple Humble Neighborhood," "Alligators All Around," "One Was Johnny," "Pierre," "Screaming and Yelling," "The Awful Truth," "Very Far Away," "Avenue P," "Chicken Soup with Rice." Chelsea Theatre Center Upstairs, NY, 9/30/80–11/23/80; American Place, 11/26/80–6/13/81. Total of 274 perf. set: Douglas W. Schmidt; cos: Carrie F. Robbins; light: John Gleason; md: Joel Silberman. Cast: Tisha Campbell, Bibi Humes, Lara Berk

2269. *The Rebbitzen from Israel*. Yiddish. Mayfair, 1972. m/l: Lili Amber; based on play by L. Freiman (i.e. Louis Freiman); ch: Yona Aloni; md: Elliot Finkel. Cast: Pesach Burstein (also adapted/d/ch), Lillian Lux, Rina Ellis. "Where Were You," "I'm in Love," "I Should Live So," "Love is International," "Ladies Should Be Beautiful," "I Wish it Was Over," "Tel-Aviv"

2270. *Rebecca, the Rabbi's Daughter*. Yiddish. Town Hall, 11/4/79–1/6/80. 84 perf. orig m & l: Abraham Ellstein; b: William Siegel; d: Michael Greenstein; md: Renee Solomon; ch: Felix Fibich. Cast: David Ellin, David Carey (also co-p), Shifra Lerer, Yankele Alperin. "My Dreams," "Everyone Has a Right to Love," "Forget Me Not," "When a Jew Sings," "How Good it Is," "I Want to Be a Bride"

2271. *The Red Blue-Grass Western Flyer Show*. A Grand Ole Opry musical play. St. Clement's Church, 5/2/75–5/11/75. 12 perf. m: Clint Ballard Jr.; l/b: Conn Fleming; d: Robert Brewer; ch: Dennis Grimaldi; asst ch: Baayork Lee; set: John Falabella. Cast: Kate Wilkinson, Maurice Copeland, Barbara Coggin

2272. *Red, Hot and Blue!* Alvin, Broadway, 10/29/36–4/10/37. 183 perf. p: Vinton Freedley; m/l: Cole Porter; b: Howard Lindsay & Russel Crouse; d: Howard Lindsay; ch: George Hale; set: Donald Oenslager; md: Frank Tours; orchestral arr: Russell Bennett. Cast: Jimmy Durante, Ethel Merman, Bob Hope, Paul & Grace Hartman, Lew Parker. "At Ye Olde Coffee Shoppe in Cheyenne," "It's a Great Life," "Perennial Debutantes," "Ours," "Down in the Depths on the 90th Floor," "Carry On," "You've Got Something," "It's De-Lovely," "A Little Skipper from Heaven Above," "Five Hundred Million," "Ridin' High," "We're About to Start Big Rehearsin'," "Hymn to Hymen," "What a Great Pair We'll Be," "You're a Bad Influence on Me" (replaced during run by "The Ozarks are Calling Me Home"), "Red, Hot and Blue." Equity Library, 1/5/84–1/29/84. 24 perf. adapted by: Gerry Matthews; d: Christopher Catt; ch: Patti D'Beck & Jerry Yoder; light: Natasha Katz; dance mus arr: Stephen Flaherty. Cast: Christine Anderson, Susan Cella. "I'm Throwing a Ball Tonight," "Down in the Depths on the 90th Floor," "Red, Hot and Blue," "A Little Skipper from Heaven Above," "You're a Bad Influence on Me," "How'm I Ridin'?," "You've

Got Something," "It's De-Lovely," "Goodbye, Little Dream, Goodbye," "Let's Do It," "When All's Said and Done," "Dizzy Baby." Goodspeed, 10/13/00–12/31/00. Revised by/d: Michael Leeds; ch: Andy Blankenbuehler; set: Kenneth Foy; orch: Dan DeLange; cos: Ann Hould-Ward; light: Ken Billington; dance mus arr/add voc arr: David Loud. Cast: Debbie Gravitte, Peter Reardon, Stephanie Kurtzuba, Beth Glover

2273. *The Red Shoes*. Unrelated to 1993 Broadway prod, except that it was also based on the Hans Christian Andersen fairy tale. Yale Rep's Children's Theatre, 4/19/70. 2 perf. m: Bruce Trinkley; l/b: Michael Feingold; d/starred: Carmen de Lavallade

2274. *The Red White and Black*. A left-of-center "musical roll call" (political satire). Players, 3/30/71. 1 perf. m/md: Brad Burg; l/b/d: Eric Bentley; conceived by: John Dillon. Cast: Rob Farkas, Marilyn Sokol, The History of Russia (rock group). Previously ran at Cafe La Mama

2275. *Red, White and Blue*. An American Legion revue. Opened 10/7/50, Paramount, L.A. Closed 1/20/51, Opera House, Chicago, without making Broadway. m/l: Robert Wright & George Forrest, David Rose (also md), Sammy Cahn, Al Rinker, Leo Robin, Victor Young, Bob Hilliard, Hal Borne, etc. d: LeRoy Prinz & Owen Crump. Cast: Larry Storch, Gale Sherwood, Bob Carroll, Paul Haakon (also ch), Bobby Van, Virginia Lee. Guest star for opening week in L.A.: George Jessel

2276. *Reefer Madness*. Parody of 1936 anti-drug film. Variety Arts, 10/7/01–10/28/01. 25 perf. p: James L. Nederlander, Verna Harrah, Nathaniel Kramer, Terry Allen Kramer, Dead Old Man Productions; m: Dan Studney; l: Kevin Murphy; b: Kevin Murphy & Dan Studney; d: Andy Fickman; ch: Paula Abdul; set: Walt Spangler; md: David Manning. Cast: Gregg Edelman, Roxane Barlow, Kristen Bell, Michele Pawk, Robert Torti, Jennifer Gambatese, Michael Seelbach. "Reefer Madness!," "Romeo and Juliet," "The Stuff," "Down at the Ol' Five-and-Dime," "Jimmy Takes a Hit," "The Orgy," "Lonely Pew," "Listen to Jesus, Jimmy," "Lullaby," "Dead Old Man," "Jimmy on the Lam," "The Brownie Song," "Little Mary Sunshine," "Murder," "Tell 'em the Truth"

2277. *A Reel American Hero*. About the influence of 1930s & 40s music on the America of today. New Rialto, Broadway. Opened 3/25/81. Closed there 3/29/81 (after 5 prev, no actual perfs). p: Gerald Paul Hillman; m: Gordon Kent & Stephanie Peters; l: Gerald Paul Hillman & Stephanie Peters; b: Judy GeBauer & Burt Vinocur; d: Nancy Tribush Hillman; ch: George Bunt; set/light: Harry Silverglat Darrow; orch: Gordon Kent; md: Roger Neil. Cast: Vidya Kaur, Peter Newman, Roxanna White, Jess Richards, Hillary Bailey. "I Want to Be Somebody," "What's Gone Wrong," "Garter Song," "Lili is a Lady with a Suitcase up Her Sleeve," "Ratta Tat Tat," "Sugar Daddy Blues," "Dance with Me," "You Mustn't Eat People," "Monster Medley," "The Movie Game of Make Believe," "The Gunfighter," "Fly,

Eagle, Fly," "I'll Be Waitin'," "Here's a Love Song," "Hero Time." Previously produced OOB by Chareeva

2278. *Rendezvous*. Comedy Theatre, London, 5/1/52. 28 perf. m: Jack Lemkow; adapted/add m/l: Michael Trefford; based on Finn Boe's Norwegian revue with a plot; d: Tor Lemkow. Cast: Diana Dors, Chili Bouchier, Tutte Lemkow, Jacqueline Giovanni, Robert Dorning

2279. *Requiem*. Religious musical. Concert version. St. Thomas's Episcopal Church, Manhattan, 2/24/85. m/l: Andrew Lloyd Webber. Cast: Sarah Brightman, Placido Domingo, Paul Miles-Kingston. "Pie Jesu." Televised 4/5/85

2280. *Restoration*. Royal Court, London, 7/21/81–9/5/81. 62 perf. m: Edward Bond & Nick Bicat; l/b/d: Edward Bond; md: Terry Davies. Cast: Simon Callow, Nicholas Ball, Irene Handl

2281. *Return to the Forbidden Planet: Shakespeare's Forgotten Rock 'n Roll Masterpiece*. Life on space ship & on forbidden planet of D'Illyria, in 2024. Bubble Touring Theatre, London, 1983. b/d: Bob Carlton; based loosely on 1950s film *The Forbidden Planet*, itself based loosely on Shakespeare's *The Tempest*. 20 rock songs from the '60s, by various composers, including: "Born to Be Wild," "Don't Let Me Be Misunderstood," "Gloria," "Go Now," "Good Golly Miss Molly," "Good Vibrations," "Great Balls of Fire," "I Can't Turn You Loose," "I Heard it Through the Grapevine," "I'm Gonna Change the World," "It's a Man's World," "Mr. Spaceman," "Monster Mash," "Oh, Pretty Woman," "Only the Lonely," "Robot Man," "Shake Rattle and Roll," "Shakin' All Over," "She's Not There," "Tell Her," "Telstar," "Who's Sorry Now?," "Teenager in Love," "Wipeout," "Young Girl," "The Young Ones." Tricycle, London, 12/21/84–2/2/85; toured thereafter; Cambridge Theatre, London, 9/18/89. 1,516 perf. Won an Olivier for Best Musical (beating *Miss Saigon*). Cast recording on Virgin. Cast: Christian Roberts, Tim Barron, Nicky Furre, Kate Edgar, John Ashby, Ben Fox, Patrick Moore. Theatre Royal, Sydney, 1991. Variety Arts (NY), 10/23/91–4/26/92. Prev from 9/27/91. 245 perf. d: Bob Carlton; md: Kate Edgar. Cast: Robert McCormick, Steve Steiner, Gabriel Barre, Allison Briner, Louis Tucci, Erin Hill, David La Duca, James Doohan

2282. *Reuben, Reuben*. An almost totally sung opera. Reuben, the hero, son of a circus performer known as The Human Dart (who, as the show opens, has just jumped to his death because of world tension), is suffering from aphonia, i.e. he can't speak unless approached with love. Reuben is encouraged to jump to his death too, by a shady barkeeper who has taken an insurance policy out on his life. Reuben learns to communicate with the aid of a girl. Shubert, Boston. Opened 10/10/55. Closed there 10/22/55, canceling scheduled 11/8/55 NYC opening at ANTA. p: Cheryl Crawford; m/l/orch: Marc Blitzstein; d: Robert Lewis; ch: Hanya Holm; set/cos: William & Jean Eckart; asst set: Patricia Zipprodt & Pat Campbell; md: Samuel Krachmalnick; orch assts: Hershy Kay & Bill Stegmeyer; choral d: Abba Bogin. Cast: Reuben: Eddie Albert; Countess: Kaye Ballard; Also with: Evelyn Lear, Josephine Lang, George Gaynes, Timmy Everett, Anita Darian, Karen Anders, Al Checco, Tony Gardell, Edmund Gaynes, Enzo Stuarti, Nina Varela, Sondra Lee, Crandall Diehl, Sara Dillon, Billie Allen, Skeet Guenther, Evelyn Page, Allen Case. "Thank You," "Never Get Lost," "Tell it to Bart," "It's in the Cards," "Shave and a Haircut," "Song of the Arrow," "Cop's Lament," "Such a Little While," "Have Yourself a Night," "San Gennaro," "With a Woman to Be," "The Hills of Amalfi," "Rose Song," "Miracle Song," "Sleep," "Love at the First Word," "The Spot," "Mystery of the Flesh," "Yeth, Yeth," "Moment of Love," "Ballet," "There Goes My Love," "Be with Me," "Mother of the Bridegroom," "Upstairsy," "Musky and Whiskey," "Reuben Talks," "We Got a Pact," "Monday Morning Blues." Over 300 of the audience left at end of Act I during opening night

2283. Reunion. Play with mus. Set in spring 1978, in Student/Faculty lounge off main hallway to auditorium on 3rd day of rehearsal for reunion show. Cubiculo, 5/12/78–5/28/78. 12 perf. m/l: Ron Roullier, Melvin H. Fredman, Robert Kornfeld; d/ch: Jeffrey K. Neill. Cast: Wendell Kindberg, Lou Corato, Geraldine Hanning, Brian Watson, Peter Rivera, Beverly Wideman, Eleanor Reissa. "Today," "Young Dreams," "Childhood," "Golden Days," "Reunion," "I'm Gonna Make It," "That Moment is Now," "Give Me Love," "The Great Wind"

2284. Reunion. Musical epic in miniature set in a theatre on 4/14/1890; featured songs of the period. Theatre Row, 3/26/99–5/16/99. 10 prev. 41 perf. p: AMAS; b: Jack Kyrieleison; story: Jack Kyrieleison & Ron Holgate; d: Ron Holgate; trad mus arr: Michael O'Flaherty. Cast: Donna Lynne Champlin

2285. Rhinestone. Richard Allen Center, 11/16/82–12/5/82. 6 prev. 20 perf. m/l: Sam Waymon & Bill Gunn; d: Bill Gunn; ch: George Faison; set: Peter Harvey; md: Sam Waymon. Cast: Pauletta Pearson, Joe Morton. "Black Narcissus," "Money Was Made to Spend," "I'll See You in Jail, Old Pal," "Miss Grab-it-All," "Blue Skies," "Our Brazilian Friends," "Rhinestone," "They'll Never Know You," "Palm Gardens," "Freedom is My Name," "Doin' the Low Low Down," "Give Us Men," "This Love," "We Both Agree"

2286. Richard Rodgers' Broadway. New revue for families & children. Company of Equity performers sang Rodgers songs. 50-minutes long. Lucille Lortel, 11/30/02–12/15/02 (weekends only). p: Inside Broadway; d/ch: Marlo Hunter; mus arr: Daniel Harris. Cast: Dean Nigro, Christopher Sloan, Joy Suprano, Suzannah Taylor

2287. Ride! Ride! Theatre Royal, Nottingham, 3/2/76; toured; Westminster Theatre, London, 5/20/76–7/24/76. 76 perf. m: Penelope Thwaites; l/b: Alan Thornhill; d: Peter Coe; ch: Larry Oaks; set: Cameron Johnson; md: Raymond Bishop; cast recording on Grapevine. Cast: Richard Owens, Brendan Barry, Caroline Villiers, Jane Martin, Gordon

Gostelow. "The Whole Wide World," "It's Exciting to Be Alive," "Which is Which?," "Strange City," "The Garden of England," "Why Me?," "He Knows My Name," "A Nice Little Change of Air," "One by One," "Everyone is Needed"

2288. Ride the Winds. Play with mus (even though it was listed as a musical). Set in old Japan. Bijou, 5/16/74–5/18/74. 3 perf. m/l/b: John Driver; d: Lee D. Sankowich; ch: Jay Norman. Cast: Chip Zien, Irving Lee, Sab Shimono, Nate Barnett, Tom Matsusaka, Elaine Petricoff, Alex Orfaly. "Run, Musashi, Run," "The Emperor Me," "The Gentle Buffoon," "Those Who Speak," "Flower Song," "You're Loving Me," "Breathing the Air," "Remember That Day," "Tengu," "Ride the Winds," "Are You a Man?," "Every Days," "Loving You," "Pleasures," "Some Day I'll Walk," "That Touch"

2289. Ring-A-Levio. Studio Arena, Buffalo, 1/4/73 (world premiere). 30 perf. m: Lance Mulcahy; l: Jason Darrow; b: Donald Ross; d: Paul Aaron; ch: Tony Stevens; set/cos: David F. Segal; md: Rod Derefinko; orch: Arthur B. Rubinstein. Cast: Camila Ashland, Alan Brasington, Mary Jane Houdina

2290. Rip Van Winkle. Closed before Broadway, 1953. m/l: Edwin McArthur & Morton Da Costa. "Now He's Gone," "Stolen Moments"

2291. The Rise of David Levinsky. Set at turn of 20th century, the loss of belief in the American Dream. American Jewish Theatre, 3/12/83–4/24/83. p: Eric Krebs; m: Bobby Paul; l/b: Isaiah Sheffer; based on novel by Abraham Cahan; d: Sue Lawless; ch: Bick Goss; set: Kenneth Foy; md: John Franceschina. Cast: Lawrence Asher, Robert Ott Boyle, Norman Golden, Mickey Hartnett, Eva Charney, Clarke Evans. "Who is This Man?," "500 Pages," "Grand Street," "In America," "The Boarder," "The Transformation," "Sharp," "Two of a Kind," "Little Did I Know," "Hard Times," "Credit Face," "500 Garments," "The Garment Trade," "Some Incredible Guy," "Just ... Like ... Me," "Be Flexible," "A Married Man," "Little Did We Know," "Bittersweet," "Survival of the Fittest," "A View from the Top." John Houseman, 1/12/87–2/8/87. 16 prev from 12/25/86. 31 perf. Basically same crew, except md: Lanny Myers. Cast: Larry Kert, Avi Hoffman, Bruce Adler, Judith Cohen, Larry Raiken, Eleanor Reissa, David Vosburgh, Lynne Wintersteller

2292. The River. OB, 1977. Never produced. m/l: David Shire & Richard Maltby Jr. "It's Never That Easy," "Song of Me," "Travel"

2293. The River. A musical revelation. Water celebrated in its various forms. Promenade, 1/13/88–1/31/88. 22 prev. 22 perf. m/l: Peter Link; d/ch: Michael Shawn. Cast: Jerry Dixon, Lawrence Hamilton. "Genesis," "Didn't it Rain," "One Drop Alone," "Put the Fire Out," "A Still Small Voice," "The Stream," "Lead Me to the Water," "The River's in Me," "The River," "The Waterfall," "Run, River, Run," "This is All I Ask," "Love Runs Deeper than Pride." The show then had 6 interludes, with various musical numbers in each inter-

lude. Previously prod by The Triplex, Manhattan Community College/CUNY

2294. Riverdance. Irish dance, music, and song show, with over 100 performers. Radio City Music Hall, 3/13/96–3/17/96. 8 perf. Returned 10/2/96–10/20/96. 21 perf. m: Bill Whelan; d: John McColgan; set: Robert Ballagh; cos: Jen Kelly; md: David Hayes. Returned 9/25/97–10/12/1997, and again 9/24/98–10/11/98. 23 perf. As *Riverdance — On Broadway* it ran at the Gershwin, Broadway, 3/16/00–8/26/01. 13 prev from 3/3/01. 605 perf. p: Moya Doherty; d: John McColgan; ch: Mavis Ascott, Jean Butler, Colin Dunne, Michael Flatley, Maria Pages, Moscow Folk Ballet Co., Tarik Winston; set: Robert Ballagh; cos: Joan Bergin. Principal dancers: Pat Roddy & Eileen Martin. Maria Pages performed flamenco firedance/Andalucia; other featured performers were Tsidii LeLoka (*Michel Bell* from 12/10/00) & Brian Kennedy (*Michael Londra* from 12/5/00). Also featured were The Irish Dance Troupe; The Riverdance Band, Singers, Tappers & Drummers; Moscow Folk Ballet; Amanzi (from Southern Africa). Sara Clancy (*Kira Deegan* from 5/23/01) was female soloist; Liam Neeson's voice was heard

2295. Riverwind. About a "tourist rest" called Riverwind, on the banks of the Wabash, in Indiana. Middle-aged woman tries to recapture spirit of romance by returning with husband to place they spent their honeymoon. Actors Playhouse, 12/12/62–1/5/64. 443 perf. m/l: John Jennings; d: Adrian Hall; light: Jules Fisher; md: Joseph Stecko; arr: Abba Bogin. Cast: Helon Blount, Lawrence Brooks, Elizabeth Parrish, Dawn Nickerson, Brooks Morton, Lovelady Powell (*Millie Slavin*). "Riverwind," "Wishing Song," "American Family Plan," "Sew the Buttons On," "Almost, But Not Quite," "Laughing Face." Equity Library, 5/3/73–5/20/73. 19 perf. d: Jeff Hamlin; add ch: Lynne Gannaway; md: Danny Troob. Cast: Helon Blount, Marty Morris, Lynn Grossman

2296. The Road to Hollywood. A Bob Hope/Bing Crosby/Dorothy Lamour-type musical. Theatre Guinevere, 3/13/84–4/21/84. 42 perf. p: The Production Co., by special arr with Norman Twain; m/l: Rob Preston & Michael Pace; b: Walter Bobbie & Michael Pace; d: Word Baker; ch: Lynnette Barkley; md: Rob Preston; orch: Dan DeLange. Cast: Michael Pace, Kay Cole, Scott Fless, Camille Saviola (*Nora Mae Lyng*), Bebe Neuwirth, Maggie Task. "I Can't Sit Still," "Schleppin'," "Hey Kid," "The Beast in Me," "Hot Ice," "Don't Spill the Beans," "I've Got My Eye on You," "When the Right One Comes Along," "Opening Night," "I Don't Care," "She's a Star." Goodspeed, 8/8/02–9/8/02. d: Lawrence Yurman; ch: Casey Nicholaw; set: John Lee Beatty; cos: David C. Woolard; light: Ken Billington; sound: Tony Meola. Cast: Jeff Edgerton, Tom Plotkin, Laura Griffith, Kena Tangi Dorsey, Leah Hocking, Jamie Day, Christopher Innvar, Cynthia Darlow, Peter Van Wagner, Phillip Huber

2297. Robert and Elizabeth. Grand, Leeds, England, 9/9/64 (2 weeks) as *The Barretts and Mr. Browning*; Manchester (3 weeks); Lyric,

London (by which time its name had changed), 10/20/64–2/4/67. 948 perf. p: Martin Landau; m: Ron Grainer; l/b: Ronald Millar; based on *The Barretts of Wimpole Street*, by Rudolph Besier; d/ch: Wendy Toye. Cast: Robert: Keith Michell, *Kevin Colson*; Elizabeth: June Bronhill, *Jane Fyffe*; Edmund Moulton-Barrett: John Clements, *Donald Wolfit*; Also with: Angela Richards, Stella Moray, Sarah Badel, Rod McLennan, Jeremy Lloyd. "Here on the Corner of Wimpole Street," "The World Outside," "The Moon in My Pocket," "I Said Love," "The Real Thing," "In a Simple Way," "I Know Now," "Escape Me Never," "Pass the Eau-de-Cologne," "I'm the Master Here," "Hate Me, Please," "The Girls that Boys Dream About," "Long Ago I Loved You," "What the World Calls Love," "Woman and Man," "Frustration." No Broadway offers. First ran in USA in 1974, at the Forum, Chicago. Brunswick Music Theatre, Maine, 8/21/78–9/2/78. d: Charles Abbott; ch: Dennis Grimaldi. Cast: Mark Jacoby, Carol Wilcox, Herndon Lackey. Paper Mill Playhouse, NJ, 10/30/82–12/19/82. d: Robert Johanson; md: Jim Coleman. Cast: Mark Jacoby, Leigh Beery, Ron Randell, Eleanor Glockner. Chichester Festival, England, 1987. Cast: Mark Wynter, Gaynor Miles, John Savident

2298. Roberta. All-American fullback inherits modiste's shop & finds girl (really a princess). New Amsterdam, Broadway, 11/18/33–7/21/34. 295 perf. p: Max Gordon; m: Jerome Kern; l/b: Otto Harbach; add l: Dorothy Fields; based on novel "Gowns by Roberta," by Alice Duer Miller; d: Hassard Short (he replaced Jerome Kern, and refused credit); ch: Jose Limon (John Lonergan was uncredited); set: Clark Robinson; md: Victor Baravalle; orch: Robert Russell Bennett. Cast: Lyda Roberti, Bob Hope, Fay Templeton, Tamara, George Murphy, Sydney Greenstreet, Ray Middleton, Fred MacMurray. "Let's Begin," "Alpha Beta Pi," "You're Devastating," "Yesterdays," "Something's Got to Happen," "The Touch of Your Hand," "I'll Be Hard to Handle," "Hot Spot," "Smoke Gets in Your Eyes," "Don't Ask Me Not to Sing." Filmed in 1935. Cast: Fred Astaire, Ginger Rogers, Irene Dunne. Studio Arena, Buffalo, 10/12/72. 30 perf. d: William Gile; ch: Bick Goss. Cast: Lilia Skala, Bonnie Franklin, Tricia O'Neil, Lee Roy Reams. All Soul's Church, 4/19/85–5/5/85. 16 perf. d: Jeffrey K. Neill; md: Wendell Kindberg. Cast: Norb Joerder (also set)

2299. Robin Hood. Romantic comic opera. Chicago, 1890. p: The Bostonians; w: Reginald de Koven & Harry B. Smith; b: Harry B. Smith. It flopped. During the subsequent tour it arrived in Detroit, where public reception was so favorable it suddenly became a hit. Standard Theatre, NY, 9/28/1891. 2 engagements of 35 & 42 perf. Revived in 1900 & 1902 & many times since then, becoming immensely popular all over the country. Adelphi, Broadway, 11/7/44–11/18/44. 15 perf. p: R.H. Burnside & The Shuberts; d: R.H. Burnside; set: United Studios; cos: Veronica. Cast: Robin Hood: Robert Field; Also with: George Lipton, Frank Farrell, Harold Patrick, Wilfred Glenn, Jerry

Robinson, Edith Herlick, Barbara Scully, Zamah Cunningham, Margaret Spencer. "The Milkmaid's Song," "Come the Bowmen in Lincoln Green," "My Dream Has Come True," "I Am the Sheriff of Nottingham," "Churning," "It Takes Nine Tailors to Make a Man," "Brown October Ale," "O, Promise Me," "The Tinker Song," "See the Little Lambkins Play," "The Forest Song," "The Serenade," "Revenge is Mine," "The Armorer's Song," "When a Maiden Weds," "The Legend of the Chimes"

2300. Robin's Band. AMAS, 4/14/88–5/8/88. 16 perf. m/l: Maija Kupris. Cast: Kecia Lewis-Evans, Herb Lovelle, Kelly Hinman. "There's Got to Be a Place," "Shuffle Boogie," "I Don't Have a Clue," "You've Got to Pay the Price," "Robin's Song," "Get it Before it Comes Out," "Something New," "Give it to Me Now," "In Sherwood," "Little Boy Blue," "Don't it Feel Right," "Where We Want to Be"

2301. Rock Nativity. Newcastle University Theatre, England, 12/18/74–1/25/75. p: Cameron Mackintosh & Veronica Flint-Shipman; m/l: Tony Hatch & Jackie Trent; b: David Wood; d: Gareth Morgan; ch: Teddy Green; md: Iwan Williams. Cast: Teddy Green, Chris Hallam, George Irving. Revised & re-produced, same theatre, same producers, same dir, but with different cast, 10/29/75 (2 weeks), then toured (by the end of the tour it was known as *A New Tomorrow*). ch: Arlene Phillips; md: Tim Higgs

2302. Rockbound. Sci-fi musical. South Street, 10/29/85–11/16/85. 16 perf. m/l: Roberta Baum & C.J. Critt; d: Dennis Deal; md: Jonny Bowden. "Rockabound Rap," "Here in My Hands," "After the Sadness," "Hugs and Kisses," "What Does One Life Mean?," "Basic Love," "Chain of Lies," "Return to the Light," "I Don't Want to Be in Love," "Life Times," "It Doesn't Stop Here"

2303. Rodgers and Hart: A Celebration. Program of 98 songs (in part or in toto) by Richard Rodgers & Lorenz Hart. Helen Hayes, Broadway, 5/13/75–8/16/75. 22 prev. 108 perf. p: Lester Osterman, Richard Horner, World-Vision Enterprises; conceived by: Richard Lewine & John Fearnley; d: Burt Shevelove; ch: Donald Saddler; asst ch: Arthur Faria; set: David Jenkins; cos: Stanley Simmons; light: Ken Billington; md/voc arr: Buster Davis; principal orch & dance mus arr: Luther Henderson; add orch: Jim Tyler, Bill Brohn, Robert Russell Bennett. Cast: Barbara Andres, Mary Sue Finnerty, Jimmy Brennan, Laurence Guittard, Wayne Bryan, Stephen Lehew, David-James Carroll, Jim Litten, Jamie Donnelly, Virginia Sandifur, Tovah Feldshuh, Rebecca York. Standbys: Kevin Daly, Pamela Peadon, David Thome, Judi Rolin. Triangle, 10/3/91–10/27/91. 20 perf. d: Michael Ramach; md: Stuart Rosenthal. Different cast

2304. The Rodgers and Hart Revue. A musical songbook. Rainbow & Stars, 10/29/91–11/23/91. 40 perf. p/conceived by: Steve Paul & Greg Dawson. Cast: Elaine Stritch, Margaret Whiting, Judy Kuhn, Jason Graae, Fred Wells (also md)

2305. Roleplay. Village Theatre Company, 1992. m/l: Adryan Russ & Doug Haverty;

d/set: Henry Fonte; ch: Karen Luschar; md: Mark York. Cast: Alyson Reim, Kimberly Schultheiss. Originally ran at the Group Repertory Theatre. After the Village Theatre it ran at Florida Studio Theatre. Revised, as *Inside Out*, and ran at Cherry Lane, 11/7/94–1/1/95. Prev from 10/28/94. 74 perf. m: Adryan Russ; l: Adryan Russ & Doug Haverty; b: Doug Haverty; d: Henry Fonte; cos: Gary Slavin; md: Suzan Ott. Cast: Ann Crumb, Cass Morgan, Julie Prosser, Kathleen Mahony-Bennett. "Inside Out," "Thin," "Let it Go," "I Can See You Here," "If You Really Loved Me," "Yo, Chlo," "Behind Dena's Back," "No One Inside," "Grace's Nightmare," "All I Do is Sing," "Never Enough," "I Don't Say Anything," "The Passing of a Friend," "Things Look Different," "Do it at Home," "Reaching Up"

2306. Romance. Leeds Playhouse, England, 7/28/71–8/14/71; toured; Duke of York's, London, 9/28/71–10/2/71. Prev from 9/23/71. 6 perf. p/m/l/d: Charles Ross; b: John Spurling; ch: Sally Gilpin; md: Alan Leigh. Cast: Bill Simpson, Joyce Blair, Lynn Dalby, Jess Conrad

2307. Romance in Candlelight. Theatre Royal, Brighton, England, 8/8/55; toured; Piccadilly, London, 9/15/55–11/12/55. 53 perf. m/l: Sam Coslow; b: Eric Maschwitz; from play *By Candlelight (Bei Kerzenlicht)*, by Siegfried Geyer & Karl Farkas; d: Richard Bird; ch: Phyllis Blakston; set/cos: Doris Zinkeisen; md: Alexander Faris. Cast: Sally Ann Howes, Roger Dann, Patricia Burke

2308. Romance in Hard Times. Set in NY soup kitchen during Great Depression. Anspacher Theatre (NY Shakespeare Festival), 5/31/89–6/18/89. 19 perf. m/l/b: William Finn; d: David Warren; ch: Marcia Milgram Dodge. Cast: Rufus Bonds Jr., Vondie Curtis-Hall, Andi Henig, Peggy Hewett, Timothy Jerome, Alix Korey, James Stovall, Lillias White. "Harvey," "Standing in Line," "Out of Here," "Harvey Promised to Change the World," "The Supreme Court Saved from Fire," "Goodbye," "Charity Quartet," "Love Song," "Eleanor Roosevelt: A Discussion of Soup," "I Never Said I Didn't Love You," "You Got Me Grinding My Teeth," "That's Enough for Me," "Places I Fainted from Hunger/Time Passes," "All Fall Down," "The Good Times Are Here," "Feeling Rich," "Hold My Baby Back," "Hennie Soup," "I Don't Want to Feel What I Feel," "The Prosperity Song," "A Gaggle of Celebrities," "I'll Get You Out of My Life," "How Could You Do This to Someone Who Robbed for You," "Blame it on These Times," "You Can't Let Romance Die." Newman, 12/28/89–12/31/89. 46 prev from 11/14/89. 6 perf. Cast: Rufus Bonds Jr., Stacey Lynn Brass, Lawrence Clayton, Victor Trent Cook, Cleavant Derricks, J.P. Dougherty, Ray Gill, Peggy Hewett, Alix Korey, Michael Mandell, Amanda Naughton, Melodee Savage, John Sloman, James Stovall, Lillias White

Romany Love see # 281, Main Book

2309. Romeo and Juliet: The Musical. Paris, 1/01. m/l: Gerard Presgurvic; based on Shakespeare's play. Cast recording sold over 6 million copies. English-language version had same mus, but lyr by Don Black, and book by Don Black & David Freeman. Piccadilly, London, 11/4/02–2/8/03. Prev from 10/12/02. d: Andrew Freeman; ch: Redha; set/cos: David Roger; mus arr: John Cameron. Cast: Romeo: Andrew Bevis; Juliet: Lorna Want; Also with: Louise Davidson, Jane McDonald, Tim Walton

2310. Rondelay. Set in Vienna in 1905 & 1906. Hudson West, 11/5/69–11/14/69. 11 perf. m/l: Hal Jordan & Jerry Douglas; based on *La Ronde*, (*Der Reige*) by Arthur Schnitzler; d: William Francisco; ch: Jacques D'Amboise; set/cos: Raoul Pene du Bois; light: Neil Peter Jampolis; md: Karen Gustafson; orch: Philip J. Lang; prod co-ord: F. Mitchell Dana. Cast: Barbara Lang, Carole Demas, Louise Clay, Paxton Whitehead, Shawn Elliott, Gwyda DonHowe. "Rondelay," "Lovers of the Lamplight," "One Hundred Virgins," "Angel Face," "Tonight You Dance with Me," "Easy," "The First Kiss," "Afterward," "She Deserves Me," "Closer," "Honor," "The Answer," "Failure," "Success," "The Days of My Youth," "I've Got a Surprise for You," "Reidhof's," "Champagne," "Dessert," "Masquerade," "When Lovers Fall in Love," "What You Are," "A Castle in India," "Back to Nature," "Saint Genesius," "Opera Star," "Not So Young Love," "Auf Wiedersehen," "Gusto," "Happy Ending," "I'll Show You the World Tonight," "Reflections," "Before Breakfast," "Give and Take"

2311. Rosa. St. Clement's, 5/10/78–5/12/78. 12 perf. m: Baldwin Bergersen; l/b: William Archibald; from play by Brenda Forbes; d: Patricia Carmichael; ch: Roger Preston-Smith; cos: Danny Morgan; md: Robert Colston. Cast: John Deyle, Jill Harwood, Everett McGill, Kathleen Swan, Steve Vinovich. "Rosa," "I Am Royal," "Fame," "Let Us Charm Each Other," "From the Bottom of the Sea," "Dear Friend," "Before it's Too Late"

2312. Rosalinda. 44th Street Theatre, Broadway, 10/28/42; Imperial, Broadway, 5/24/43; 44th Street Theatre, 10/4/43; 46th Street Theatre, 10/15/43–1/22/44. Total of 521 perf. p: Lodewick Vroom for the New Opera Co., under supervision of Max Reinhardt; new l: Paul Kerby; adapted by Gottfried Reinhardt & John Meehan Jr., from the Max Reinhardt hit version of Johann Strauss Jr.'s 1874 operetta *Die Fledermaus*; d: Gottfried Reinhardt (although Felix Brentano was credited); ch: George Balanchine; set: Oliver Smith; light: Jean Rosenthal; md: Erich Wolfgang Korngold. Cast: Dorothy Sarnoff, Oscar Karlweis, Gene Barry, Ernest McChesney, Virginia MacWatters, Shelly Winter (as Fifi–Miss Winter later became Shelley Winters), Jose Limon. Chorus: Jeanne Beauvais, Diana Corday

2313. The Rose and the Ring. Musical adaptation of famous fireside pantomime by William Makepeace Thackeray. Theatre Royal, Stratford East, London, 12/21/64–1/30/65. m/l/b/md: John Dalby; d: Adrian Rendle & David Thompson; ch: Geraldine Stephenson. Cast: Thelma Ruby, Julian Somers, Nicholas Smith, Gerald Campion

2314. Rose Marie. Imperial, Broadway, 9/2/24–1/16/26. 557 perf. The 4th-longest running musical of the 1920s. p: Arthur Hammerstein; m: Rudolf Friml & Herbert Stothart; l/b: Otto Harbach & Oscar Hammerstein II; book d: Paul Dickey; orch: Robert Russell Bennett. Cast: Mary Ellis, Dennis King. "Vive la Canadienne," "Hard-Boiled Herman," "Rose Marie," "The Mounties Song," "Lak Jeem," "Indian Love Call," "Pretty Things," "Why Shouldn't We?," "Totem Tom-Tom," "Only a Kiss," "One Man Woman," "The Door of Her Dreams." Theatre Royal, Drury Lane, London, 1925. 581 perf. Century Theatre, Broadway, 1/24/27–3/5/27. 48 perf. p: Arthur Hammerstein; d: Paul Dickey & Arthur Hammerstein. Cast: Ethel Louise Wright, Paul Donah. Filmed in 1928 (a silent film, it had no songs of course, but it did star Joan Crawford); again in 1936, with Jeanette MacDonald & Nelson Eddy, but was very different to the stage prod. Stoll, London, 1942. Paper Mill Playhouse, NJ, 1943. Cast: Rosemarie Brancato, Donald Gage. Los Angeles Civic Light Opera, 1950. Cast: Patrice Munsel, Wally Cassell. London, 1951 (on ice). d: Gerald Palmer; ch: Beatrice Livesey. Filmed again in 1954, with Howard Keel & Ann Blyth. Victoria Palace, London, 8/22/60. 135 perf. p: Tom Arnold & Leslie A. Macdonnell; d: Freddie Carpenter; ch: Ross Taylor. Cast: Stephanie Voss, David Whitfield, Gillian Lynne, Ronnie Stevens, Maggie Fitzgibbon, Andy Cole

2315. Roundabout. Saville, London, 8/4/49–8/27/49. 27 perf. m: Edward Horan; l: Frank Eyton & Ken Attiwill; b: Austin Melford & Ken Attiwill; d: Dick Hurran; ch: Beatrice Appleyard; set/cos: Berkeley Sutcliffe; md: Robert Busby. Cast: Bobby Howes, Pat Kirkwood, Marilyn Hightower, Jerry Desmonde. Started life at Theatre Royal, Birmingham, 6/6/49, as *Hat in the Air*, then toured; then changed name for London debut

2316. Roundheads and Peakheads. Play with mus. Classic, 5/23/84–6/10/84. 16 perf. orig m/md: Charles Robbins Mills; l/w: Bertolt Brecht; d: Jerry Roth. Cast: Livia Ann (also ch), Elizabeth Bove, Kristin Reeves. Ran again, as *Roundheads and the Pointheads*, at the Cubiculo, 3/26/85–4/14/85. 21 perf. new orig m/l: Hanns Eisler; md: Erich K. Rausch. Cast: Bill Maloney, Amy Brentano, Laura Tewksbury. "Change the World," "Urging of the Flesh," "Poverty, Chastity, Obedience"

2317. Royal Flush. Wicked dowager queen & her sorcery. Opened for pre–Broadway tryouts 12/30/64, Shubert, New Haven; then 1/5/65, Royal Alexandra, Toronto; then 1/20/65–1/23/65, Shubert, Philadelphia. p: L. Slade Brown; b: Jay Thompson & Robert Schlitt; from Nina Savo's novel *The Green Bird*. Jack Cole started as d/ch, but was replaced in both capacities by Martyn Green, who was then replaced by June Havoc (d) and Ralph Beaumont (ch). set/cos: Raoul Pene du Bois; light: Jules Fisher; md: Skip Redwine. Cast: Mickey Deems (who had replaced Eddie Foy prior to New Haven), Kaye Ballard, Jodi Williams, Louis Edmonds, Allen Knowles, Al DeSio, Fred Kimbrough, Jane Connell, Donna Baccala, John Aristedes, Altovise Gore, Kenneth Nelson, Dick O'Neill, Luigi Gasparinetti.

"Right, Right, Right," "The Edge of the World," "She's Sweet," "Bye Bye," "The Road to Hell," "Lotus Blossom," "You'll Be Something," "Just Reach Out and Touch Me," "Magic Time," "Try a Little," "No Happy Ending"

2318. R.S.V.P. Topical revue. The problems of living in NYC. Theatre East, 8/24/82–12/26/82. 127 perf. m/l/sk: Rick Crom; d: Word Baker & Rod Rogers; md: Glen Kelly. Cast: Christopher Durham (*Christopher Tracy* from 9/29/82), John Fucillo, Lianne Johnson, Julie Sheppard (*Jeri Winbarg* from 9/21/82), John Wyatt

2319. Rumpelstiltskin. Town Hall, 5/23/73–5/24/73. 4 perf. Ran in rep with *Treasure Island* (see this appendix). m: Philip Fleischman & Joan Shepherd; l/d: Evan Thompson; b: Joan Shepherd. Cast: David Burrow, Nancy Temple, Bill Steele, Evan Thompson, Chester Thornhill, Joan Shepherd (Rumpelstiltskin). "Traveling Troubadour," "Killer-Diller Miller," "Never," "Down by the Mill," "A Woman in the Palace," "Straw into Gold," "What Will You Give Me?," "A Love Match," "Guess My Name"

2320. Russell Patterson's Sketchbook. Revue. Maidman, 2/6/60–2/7/60. 3 perf. m/md: Ruth Cleary Patterson; d: Hudson Fausett; ch: Nelle Fisher. Cast: Anita Gillette, Margaret Gathright, Jan Leighton, Jen Nelson, Gaby Monet, Ralph Lowe, Jerry Bergen, Marlene Manners, Michael Dominico

2321. Ruthless! Set in Small Town, USA, and in NYC. The would-be child star as monster. Musical Theatre Works, 10/16/91–11/2/91. 12 perf (as a one-act); Players, 5/6/92–1/24/93. 40 prev from 3/13/92. 302 perf (as a 2-act). m: Marvin Laird; l/b/d: Joel Paley; md: Marvin Laird & Dennis Buck; set: Jeffrey Rathaus & James Noone; cos: Gail Cooper-Hecht & Jeffrey Rathaus. Cast: Joel Vig (*Sylvia Miles*), Susan Mansur (*Adinah Alexander*). "Born to Entertain," "Pippi Song," "Kisses and Hugs," "I Hate Musicals," "A Penthouse Apartment," "It Will Never Be That Way Again," "Ruthless." 3 numbers were cut when it moved to the Players: "Tap Shoes," "My Poodle Puddles" & "Sleep Now My Child"

2322. Sadie Is a Lady. Yiddish. Woman claims reward for foundling. Second Avenue, 1/29/50. p: Irving Jacobson; m: Joseph Rumshinsky; l: Molly Picon; b: Louis Freiman; d: Jacob Kalich; ch: Lillian Shapero. Cast: Molly Picon, Julius Adler, Henrietta Jacobson, Irving Jacobson. "My Street," "Monkey Business," "Sadie is a Lady"

2323. Safari 300. Revue of black musical history, from African chants to rock 'n roll. Mayfair, 7/12/72–8/1/72. 29 perf. p: Richie Havens; w: Tad Truesdale; d: Hugh Gittens; ch: Lari Becham; md: Scat Wilson. Cast: Tad Truesdale, Lari Becham. "Dombaye," "Little Black Baby," "Johnny Too Bad," "Voodoo," "Baron Samedi," "This Little Light," "Cakewalk," "Song of Sorrow," "Goin' to Chicago," "Cotton Club Revue," "Younger Men Grow Older," "My Children Searching," "Doin' it By the Book," "Get it Together," "The Man and the Message," "What Have We Done?," "It's Rainin'," "Rock 1975," "Return to Africa"

2324. *A Saint She Ain't*. Each character based on Hollywood legend. King's Head, London, 4/21/99; Apollo, London, 9/22/99–1/15/00. Prev from 9/16/99. m: Denis King; l/b: Dick Vosburgh; loosely based on Moliere's *Le Cocu Imaginaire*. Cast: Brian Greene, Gavin Lee, Jessica Martin, Barry Cryer, Pauline Daniels. "Mr. Moliere," "The Navy's in Town," "My All-American Gal," "A Saint She Ain't," "I Love to Hold Rose with the Rolled Hose and the Shing-Shing-Shingled Hair," "I Only Dig That Jive," "You're the Only Star in My Heaven," "Manitowoc," "There Oughta Be a Way," "The Joke's on Me," "Can't Help Dancing," "The Banana for My Pie." US debut at Berkshire Theatre Festival, 7/31/02–8/10/02. 1 prev 7/30/02. Moved to Westport Country Playhouse, 8/30/02–9/14/02. Prev from 8/28/02. d: Eric Hill. Cast: Christina Marie Norrup (who replaced Kate Levering before show started there), P.J. Benjamin, Allison Briner, Lovette George, Joel Blum

2325. *Saint Tous*. Music theatre piece based on life of Haiti's revolutionary hero, Toussaint L'Ouverture. La Mama, 1991. m: Andre De Shields & Thaddeus Pinkston; l/b/conceived by/d: Andre De Shields; ch: Fletcher L. Nickerson; md: Thaddeus Pinkston. Cast: Andre De Shields, Cheryl Alexander, Regge Bruce Ashanti. "The Trouble in Saint Domingue," "Challenge of a Dream," "Voodoo Babble," "Shine On," "Tragic Mulatto," "Cum Sancto Spiritu," "Alleluia Deo Gratis," "Gloria," "Emperor's Anthem," "B-U-Wit-Me?," "Measure of Life," "Mercy Saint Tous"

2326. *Saints*. Good Shepherd-Faith Church, 6/30/76–7/11/76. 10 perf. m: William Penn; b/l: Merle Kessler; d: Edward Berkeley; ch: Nora Peterson; md: Bob Goldstone. Cast: Jane Altman, Jill Eikenberry, Dean Pitchford, Terry Quinn, Tom Tofel, Marti Rolph. "I Am the Sign," "In the Sweet By and By," "The Old Rabbit Hole," "Stand By Me," "O My Soul," "Bastard for the Lord," "The Ladies Come from Baltimore," "See the River Flow," "Sweet Jesus, Blessed Savior"

2327. *Salad Days*. 2 ex-university students, about to be married, hire Victorian piano on wheels belonging to a bum, only to find piano has power to make people dance. Theatre Royal, Bristol, England, 6/1/54. 46 perf. p: Bristol Old Vic Co.; m: Julian Slade; l/b: Julian Slade & Dorothy Reynolds; d: Denis Carey; ch: Elizabeth West; set: Patrick Robertson; at pianos: Julian Slade & Harold Britton. Cast: Alan Dobie, Eleanor Drew, Basil Henson, Dorothy Reynolds, Pat Heywood, Norman Rossington, Bob Harris, Eric Porter, Christine Finn. It had been slated to fill 3-week gap in that theatre's schedule. Theatre Royal, Brighton, 7/26/54. p: Linnit & Dunfee, who then took it to Vaudeville Theatre, London, 8/5/54–2/27/60. 2,283 perf. Became London's longest ever running musical up to that time. Same basic crew, with addition of cos: Alvary Williams. Cast: Eleanor Drew, Dorothy Reynolds, James Cairncross (replaced Eric Porter), Newton Blick (replaced Alan Dobie), Michael Aldridge (replaced Basil Henson), Pat Heywood, Christine Finn, Joe Greig (replaced Norm Rossington). "Hush-Hush," "Out of Breath," "Sand in My Eyes," "I Sit in the Sun," "It's Easy to Sing," "Oh! Look at Me," "The Time of My Life," "We Said We Wouldn't Look Back." Theatre du Rond, Paris, 1957. French adaptation by: Christian Duvaleix & Marianne Fournier. The English version tried out in NY, OB, at the Barbizon-Plaza, 11/10/58–1/18/59. d: Barry Morse. Cast: Barbara Franklin, Richard Easton, Eric Christmas. It had new musical number, "Let's Take a Stroll Through London," but it didn't have what American audiences wanted. Princes, London, 12/26/61–1/27/62. 46 perf. p: Linnit & Dunfee and Jack Hylton; d: Julian Slade; ch: Diana Murdoch. Cast: Alan Hockey, Sheila Chester, Derek Holmes, Pat Michael, Richard Fraser, Roddy Maude Roxby, Bob Harris. Lyric, Hammersmith, London, 8/18/64–9/19/64. 39 perf. d: Jasmine Dee. Cast: Belinda Carroll, Olivia Breeze, John Inman, Lynn Dalby. Theatre Royal, Windsor, 3/23/76; Duke of York's, London, 4/14/76–8/7/76. d: David Conville; ch: Wayne Sleep. Cast: Bill Kerr, Sheila Steafel, Elizabeth Seal. Yorkshire TV aired a prod on 1/2/83, with screenplay by Julian Slade. Cast: Ian Richardson, Ann Beach

2328. *The Salad of the Mad Cafe*. Satirical revue with mus. Masque, 3/31/64–4/12/64. 16 perf. Cast: Danny Logan (also d/w), Marguerite Davis, Susan Murphy

2329. *Salon*. Duo, 4/3/87–4/26/87. 12 perf. m/l: David Welch & Michael Alasa; d: Michael Alasa & Christopher Markle. Cast: Lynne Charnay, Juliette Koka, Mark Lotito, Jody Walker-Lichtig. "Paris," "An Adventure," "What Remains," "Seek and Ye Shall Find," "Images," "Don't Let Go of His Arm," "Paris is About to Fall," "Joie de Vivre," "Come the Revolution," "Salon," "Bibi Paco," "Always," "New York is About to Fall," "Where Do We Go From Here?," "In Between the Lines," "Something to Remember You By"

2330. *Salvation*. Enacted rock concert without intermission. Village Gate, 3/11/69 (6 months). m/l: Peter Link & C.C. Courtney; d: Peter Link. Cast: C.C. Courtney, Joe Morton, Marta Heflin, Edloe, Annie Rachel, Chapman Roberts. "Salvation," "In Between," "Let the Moment (Slip By)," "Gina," "If You Let Me Make Love to You (Then Why Can't I Touch You?)," "There Ain't No Flies on Jesus," "Daedalus," "Forever," "Let's Get Lost in Now," "Tomorrow is the First Day of the Rest of My Life." Jan Hus, 9/24/69–4/19/70. 239 perf. d: Paul Aaron. Cast: C.C. Courtney (*Barry Bostwick, Jim Hall*), Yolande Bavan, Peter Link (*Clifford Lipson*), Joe Morton (*Northern J. Calloway, George Turner*), Boni Enten, Annie Rachel, Marta Heflin (*Bette Midler*), Chapman Roberts (*Northern J. Calloway*)

2331. *Sambo*. Black opera with white spots. Public, 12/12/69–1/11/70. 37 perf. p: NY Shakespeare Festival; part of Festival's indoor schedule of 3 programs (others: *Stomp & Mod Donna*). m/l: Ron Steward & Neal Tate; d: Gerald Freedman; set: Ming Cho Lee; light: Martin Aronstein; ms: John Morris. Cast: Hattie Winston, Jenny O'Hara, Ron Steward, Camille Yarbrough, Gerri Dean. "Sing a Song of Sambo," "Hey Boy," "I Am Child," "Baddest Mammy-Jammy," "Sambo Was a Bad Boy," "Be Black," "Let's Go Down," "The Eternal Virgin," "Boy Blue," "Black Man," "Son of Africa." Mobile Theatre, 7/14/70–8/8/70, after playing parks & playgrounds of the 5 NY boroughs. Ron Steward was only one of orig cast left. d: Michael Shchuktz; light: Lawrence Metzler; ch: Tommy Jonsen; set: Ming Cho Lee

2332. *Sancocho*. About Puerto Ricans in NY. LuEsther Hall, 3/28/79–4/1/79. 31 prev. 7 perf. p: Joseph Papp; m/l: Jimmy Justice & Ramiro (Ray) Ramirez; d/ch: Miguel Godreau; md: Jimmy Justice. Cast: Terri Lombardozzi, Hector Jaime Mercado, Ray Ramirez, Beth Shorter, Dan Strayhorn, Pamela Pilkenton, Avery Sommers

2333. *Sandhog*. A ballad in 3 acts & 16 scenes. About NY tunnel-builders in the 1880s. Phoenix, 11/29/54–1/2/55. 48 perf. m/l: Earl Robinson & Waldo Salt; based on short story *St. Columba and the River*, by Theodore Dreiser; d: Howard Da Silva; ch: Sophie Maslow; set/light: Howard Bay; orch: Hershy Kay; psm: Bernard Gersten; cm: Carl Fisher. Cast: Jack Cassidy, Alice Ghostley, Yuriko, John Carter, David Hooks, Leon Bibb, Paul Ukena, Michael Kermoyan, David Brooks, Gordon Dilworth, Betty Oakes, David Winters. "Come Down," "Some Said They Were Crazy," "Stand Back," "Hey Joe," "Johnny's Cursing Song," "Come and Be Married," "Johnny-O," "Good Old Days," "Song of the Bends," "By the Glenside," "High Air," "Work Song," "28 Men," "Sandhog Song," "Sweat Song," "Fugue on a Hot Afternoon in a Small Flat," "T-w-i-n-s," "Katie O'Sullivan," "Sing Sorrow," "You Want to Mourn," "Ma, Ma, Where's My Dad?," "Greathead Shield," "Waiting for the Men," "Ring Iron," "Oh, Oh, Oh, O'Sullivan"

2334. *Sands of the Negev*. Yiddish. President, Broadway, 10/19/54–12/12/54. 64 perf. b: Yigal Mossensohn; adapted by: Shimon Wincelberg; d: Boris Tumarin; ch: Ora Braunstein. Cast: Gregory Morton, Si Oakland, Sylvia Davis

2335. *The Sap of Life*. One Sheridan Square, 10/2/61–11/12/61. 49 perf. m/l: David Shire & Richard Maltby Jr.; md: Julian Stein. Cast: Kenneth Nelson, Jerry Dodge. "Saturday Morning," "Charmed Life," "Fill up Your Life with Sunshine," "Watching the Big Parade Go By," "The Love of Your Life," "A Hero's Love," "She Loves Me Not," "Time and Time Again"

2336. *Sarah, Plain and Tall*. Young woman leaves home for American prairie of late 1800s. Lucille Lortel, 7/17/02–8/14/02. Prev from 7/11/02. Free-tickets. p: Theatreworks/USA; m: Laurence O'Keefe; l: Nell Benjamin; based on children's novel by Patricia McLachlan; adapted by Julia Jordan; d: Joe Calarco; set: Michael Fagin. Cast: Sarah: Becca Ayers; Also with: Trisha Jeffrey, John Lloyd Young, Debra Wiseman, Herndon Lackey. There had been a TV version, starring Glenn Close

2337. *Sarita*. Set in South Bronx, 1939–49. INTAR (International Arts Relations), 1/18/84–

2/19/84. 35 perf. m/md: Leon Odenz; l/b/d: Maria Irene Fornes. Cast: Rodolfo Diaz. "He Was Thinking of You," "I'm Lonely," "A Woman Like You," "You Are Tahiti," "His Wonderful Eye," "Here Comes the Night," "The Letter"

2338. *Satchmo: America's Musical Legend.* The national tour opened 7/14/87, at the Theatre of the Performing Arts, New Orleans, and closed on 10/4/87, at the Colonial, Boston. Failed to make Broadway. p: Kenneth Feld; m/l/b/d: Jerry Bilik; ch: Maurice Hines; light: Thomas R. Skelton. Cast: Louis Armstrong: Byron Stripling; Also with: James Rowan, Matilda A. Haywood, Ebony Jo-Ann, Julio Monge, Quincella, Allyson Tucker

2339. *Saturday Night.* Brooklyn youth dreams of fame & fortune across the river, but finds happiness at home. Set in pre-Depression 1929. Stephen Sondheim's 1st full score written for a Broadway show. Written in 1954, it came to a grinding halt in 1955 when producer Lemuel Ayers died. Revivified, but put aside when Mr. Sondheim began work on *West Side Story*, then on *Gypsy*, and Jule Styne was set to produce it for a 12/59 opening at the 46th Street Theatre, with Bob Fosse as dir. During auditions Mr. Sondheim withdrew it. b: Julius J. Epstein; based on play *Front Porch in Flatbush*, by Julius J. Epstein & Philip G. Epstein. "Saturday Night," "Class," "Delighted, I'm Sure," "Love's a Bond," "Isn't It?," "In the Movies," "Exhibit A," "A Moment with You," "Montana Chem," "So Many People," "One Wonderful Day," "I Remember That," "Love's-a-Bond Blues," "All for You," "(It's) That Kind of Neighborhood," "What More Do I Need?." Bridewell, London, 12/11/97. Cast: Gavin Lee, Ashleigh Sendin, Anna Franciolini. Second Stage (NYC), 2/17/00–3/26/00. 31 prev from 1/21/00. 45 perf. d/ch: Kathleen Marshall; set: Derek McLane; cos: Catherine Zuber; light: Donald Holder; sound: Scott Lehrer; md: Rob Fisher; orch: Jonathan Tunick. Cast: Christopher Fitzgerald, David Campbell, Kirk McDonald, Rachel Ulanet, Lauren Ward, David White, Clarke Thorell, Frank Vlastnik, Natascia A. Diaz, Andrea Burns

2340. *Saturn Returns; A Concert.* A staged song cycle. LuEsther Hall, 3/31/98–4/12/98. 18 prev. 16 perf. m/l: Adam Guettel; d: Tina Landau; light: Blake Burba; md: Ted Sperling; orch: Don Sebesky & Jamie Lawrence. Cast: Annie Golden, Jose Llana. "Saturn Returns: The Flight," "Icarus," "Migratory IV," "Pegasus," "Jesus, the Mighty Conqueror," "Children of the Heavenly King," "At the Sounding," "Build a Bridge," "Sisyphus," "Life is but a Dream," "Every Poodle," "Hero and Leander," "Come to Jesus," "How Can I Lose You," "Great Highway," "There's a Land," "Awaiting You," "The Return"

2341. *Saturnalia.* Belgrade Theatre, Coventry, England, 8/4/71. p: Charles Ross; w/d: Ron Moody; ch: Sheila O'Neil; md: Anthony Bowles. Cast: Ron Moody, Gemma Craven, Vivienne Martin, Weston Gavin

2342. *Sauce Tartare.* London, 1949. 443 perf. m/l: Fase & Parsons; b: Cecil Landreau. Cast: Ronald Frankau, Renee Houston, Claude Hulbert. Led to sequel, *Sauce Piquante*, in 1950. 67 perf. Cast: Moira Lister, Douglas Byng (also w), Norman Wisdom, Audrey Hepburn, Bob Monkhouse, Muriel Smith, Adele Leigh, Jean Bayless

2343. *Saucy Jack and the Space Vixens.* Intergalactic musical. Queen's, London, 3/23/98–6/6/98. Prev from 3/18/98. m: Robin Forrest & Jonathan Croose; b: Charlotte Mann; add m: Adam Meggido; add l: Michael Fidler. Cast: Catherine Porter, David Ashley. Preceded by UK tour

2344. *The Savage Routine of Living.* Set in San Francisco coffee house, 1960. One Dream Theatre, 10/7/93–10/31/93. 16 perf. p/w/d: Jim Farmer. Cast: Jim Farmer, Jane Grenier

2345. *Savings.* Set in the lobby of the Neighborhood Savings Bank. INTAR Stage 2, 5/18/85–6/9/85. Prev from 5/15/85. 24 perf. m/md: Leon Odenz; l/b: Dolores Prida; d: Max Ferra. "There Goes the Neighborhood," "Savings," "Iron Pumping," "Woman," "Good Afternoon," "Aerobics," "Make Me Believe," "One Last Song," "We Won't Be Moved." First, it had a staged reading, 10/7/84

2346. *Say Hello to Harvey.* Toronto, 9/14/81–10/14/81. Canceled scheduled Washington & then Broadway openings. m/l/b: Leslie Bricusse; based on Mary Chase's 1945 comedy *Harvey*, about the giant rabbit; d: Mel Shapiro; ch: Donald Saddler; set/light: Neil Peter Jampolis; cos: Olga Dimitroff; ms: Ian Fraser; md: Milton Rosenstock; orch: Billy Byers. Cast: Donald O'Connor, Patricia Routledge, Judy Sabo, Patricia Arnell, Mary Leigh Stahl, Janet McCall, Jack Davidson, Jim Betts, Mark Esposito, Karen Giombetti, Sherry Lambert, Claudia Shell. "Smalltown, USA," "The Wednesday Forum," "We Like the Very Same Things," "That Brother of Mine," "Dr. Chumley," "I'd Rather Look at You," "Do Your Own Thing," "Sue," "Bring it to the Bar," "Elwood P. Dowd," "Say Hello to Harvey," "A Lousy Life," "Be Glad," "The Perfect Person," "One Last Fling," "Human Beings"

2347. *Say It with Music.* Salute to Irving Berlin & his music. Lincoln Center Library Theatre, 12/26/79–12/28/79. 4 perf. created by/d: Jeffrey K. Neill; md: Wendell Kindberg. Cast: Richard P. Bennett, Sean McNickle, Mimi Moyer, Ken Seiter, Rima Starr, Karen Stefko. Rainbow & Stars, 7/7/92–9/26/92. 120 perf. p: Steve Paul & Greg Dawson; d: Neal Kenyon; md: Fred Wells; gm: George Elmer. Cast: Kaye Ballard, Liz Callaway, Jason Graae, Jay Leonhart, Fred Wells, Ron Raines, Joe Cocuzzo

2348. *Say When.* Reminiscences of 1920s from point of view of 1970s. Plaza 9, 12/4/72–12/9/72. 7 perf. m/l: Arnold Goland & Keith Winter; d/ch: Zoya Leporska. Cast: Bill Berrian, Andrea Duda, Gerrianne Raphael, Anita Darian, Sharron Miller, Michael Misita

2349. *Sayonara.* Paper Mill Playhouse, NJ, 9/16/87. m: George Fischoff; l: Hy Gilbert; b: William Luce; adapted from novel by James Michener; d: Robert Johanson; ch: Susan Stroman; set: Michael Anania. Cast: Colleen Fitzpatrick, Christopher Wynkoop, June Angela, Lyd-Lyd Gaston, Robert Hoshour, Valerie Lau-Kee, Christine Toy, Kevin B. Weldon

2350. *Scandals.* Workshop, 1983. Michael Bennett's last orig project, but he canceled it after several developmental workshops. He died 4 years later. Choreographer Jerry Mitchell worked on it with him

2351. *Scapa.* All-male musical. Adelphi, London, 3/8/62–4/14/62. 44 perf. p; S.A. Gorlinsky; adapted by Hugh Hastings from his play *Seagulls Over Sorrento*; d/ch: George Carden; md: Derek New. Cast: Haggis: Edward Woodward; Also with: Pete Murray, Timothy Grey

2352. *Scapin.* Musical version of Moliere's 1671 French comedy about a quick-witted scoundrel. Classic Stage Co., 1/12/93–3/7/93. 9 prev. 48 perf. m/l: Rusty Magee; b: Shelly Berc & Andrei Belgrader; d: Andrei Belgrader; set: Anita Stewart. Cast: Stanley Tucci, Michael McCormick, Mary Testa. "Scapin," "Another Girl," "Heir to My Fortune," "The Way I Got," "Vile Thing," "Gypsy Song," "Money and Family." Seattle, 9/18/02–10/12/02. d: Christopher Bayes. Cast: David V. Scully

2353. *School.* Birmingham Rep, England, 11/19/57. p: Sir Barry Jackson; m: Christopher Whelen; l/b: Redmond Phillips; from play by Tom Robertson; d: Douglas Seale; ch: Margaret Maxwell; md: Doris Watkins. Cast: Pamela Beesley (*Jane Wenham*), Eleanor Drew, Diana Barrington, Sonia Fraser, Arthur Pentelow, Michael Blakemore. Prince's, London, 3/4/58–3/15/58. 22 perf. Same crew, except md: Robert Probst. Several cast members reprised. New members: Jean Bayless, Bunty Turner

2354. *The School of Jolly Dogs.* New revue of classic songs from English music hall, 1856–1908. Home for Contemporary Theatre and Art, 12/2/87–12/19/87. 2 prev. 12 perf. Cast: Becky Borczon, Randy Rollison (also d), Kenneth Tosti (also ch)

2355. *Scrambled Feet.* Musical revue satirizing Broadway season. Village Gate Upstairs, 6/11/79–6/7/81. 831 perf. w: John Driver & Jeffrey Haddow; d: John Driver. Cast: Roger Neil, Jeffrey Haddow, John Driver, Evalyn Baron, Hermione the Duck. Ran originally as showcase at the Shirtsleeves, NY, then at the St. Nicholas, Chicago. Filmed for TV in 1984 with 3 of the orig cast (Messrs Driver, Haddow, and Neil), and with Madeline Kahn in women's roles

2356. *Scrooge: The Holiday Musical.* Alexandra Theatre, Birmingham, England, 11/9/92. 99 perf. Leslie Bricusse (m/l/b); based on Charles Dickens's *A Christmas Carol*. "The Beautiful Day," "A Better Life," "A Christmas Carol," "Christmas Children," "Christmas Joys," "December the 25th," "Father Christmas," "Good Times," "Happiness," "I Hate Christmas," "I Like Life," "I'll Begin Again," "It's Not My Fault," "Make the Most of This World," "Thank You Very Much." Finally went to London in 1996. set: Paul Farnsworth. Starbright, Las Vegas (Vegas's first Equity theatre, and this was the show that opened it), 12/9/03–12/24/03. Cast: Davis Gaines (Scrooge). Oriental Theatre, Chicago, 10/26/04–11/7/04, then toured. p: Bill Kenwright; d: Bob

Tomson; ch: Lisa Kent; set: Paul Farnsworth; Cast: Richard Chamberlain

2357. *The Secret Annex*. An Anne Frank musical. Playhouse 91, 9/8/95–9/24/95. 4 prev. 16 perf. m: William Charles Baton; l/b: Robert K. Carr; d: Dom Ruggiero. Cast: Lydia Gladstone. "We Are God's Forgotten People," "Forever Friends," "Day and Night," "The Final Hour," "Pieces of My Life," "Anne's Song," "World Beyond the Pane," "Mother's Love," "These Four Walls," "On My Side," "My Darling, Close Your Eyes," "Summer Afternoons," "Living in New York," "The Man I've Become," "The Power of Dreams"

2358. *The Secret Diary of Adrian Mole*. Phoenix Arts Centre, Leicester, England, 9/6/84; Wyndham's, London, 12/12/84. songs: Ken Howard & Alan Blaikley; b: Sue Townsend; d: Graham Watkins; md: Mark Warman. Cast: Sheila Steafel

2359. *The Secret Garden*. Palace, Watford, England, 3/13/82. p: Theatre in Education Group; m: Sharon Burgett; l: Diana Matterson & Sue Beckwith-Smith; b: Alfred Shaughnessy; based on Frances Hodgson Burnett's novel. Salisbury Playhouse, 4/28/83–5/21/83. d: David Horlock; ch: Angela Hardcastle; set: Richard Marks; cos: Barbara Wilson; md: Rob Mitchell. Cast: Mary: Sara Markland; Archie: Richard Bartlett; Colin: Richard Charles; Mrs. Medlock: Mary Griffiths. It was the recording of this prod that inspired Heidi Landesman to write her own version of *The Secret Garden* for Broadway in 1991

2360. *The Secret Garden*. Not connected to the 1982 Watford prod or the 1991 Broadway prod. King's Head, London, 1/16/87–5/30/87. m: Stephen Markwick; l/b: Diana Morgan; based on novel by Frances Hodgson Burnett. Cast: Peter Gale, Toby Morton, Angela Rook, Tony Watkins. "Get Up, Miss Mary," "Other Little Girls," "Misselthwaite Hall," "The Secret Garden," "Give it a Try," "Lillian," "Nightfolk," "The Little Rajah," "Roses," "Dai and I," "That's Spring," "The Finale," "Playout," "It's Over for Good," "Give Her a Chance"

2361. *The Secret Life of Walter Mitty*. Players, 10/26/64–1/3/65. 96 perf. m/l: Leon Carr & Earl Shuman; b: Joe Manchester; based on James Thurber's story about middle-aged daydreamer who imagines himself in various heroic roles; d: Mervyn Nelson; ch: Bob Arlen; set/light: Lloyd Burlingame. Cast: Mitty: Marc London; Peninnah: Christopher Norris; Also with: Cathryn Damon, Rudy Tronto, Rue McClanahan. "The Secret Life," "The Walter Mitty March," "By the Time I'm Forty," "Walking with Peninnah," "Aggie," "Drip, Drop, Tapoketa," "Don't Forget," "Marriage is for Old Folks," "Hello, I Love You, Goodbye," "Willa," "Confidence," "Two Little Pussycats," "Fan the Flame," "She's Talking Out Her Problems," "You're Not," "Lonely Ones." Equity Library, 1/11/73–1/28/73. 19 perf. d: Jerry Grant; md: John R. Williams. Cast: Matthew Tobin, Laura Dean, Nancy Trumbo, Don Croll, Glen McClaskey

2362. *Secrets Every Smart Traveler Should Know*. Musical revue. Triad, 10/30/97; Ibis, 11/14/98–2/21/00. Total of 953 perf. songs/sk: Murray Grand, etc; d: Patrick Quinn; cast recording on RCA. Cast: Michael McGrath, Liz McConahay, Kathy Fitzgerald, James Darrah, John Sloman, Jay Leonhart, Charles Alterman. "Secrets Every Smart Traveler Should Know," "Naked in Pittsburgh," "Star Search," "This is Your Captain Speaking," "Private Wives," "Seeing America First," "What Did I Forget?," "See it Now," "Red Hot Lava," "Paradise Found," "Border Guard," "Traveling Light"

2363. *Secrets of the Lava Lamp*. An entertainment. Manhattan Theatre Club Upstage, 4/24/85–5/11/85. 18 perf. w: Adriana Trigiani; adapted from characters & stories created by Camille Saviola; d/ch: Stuart Ross; md: Joel Silberman. Cast: Camille Saviola, Scott Robertson. "There's No Business Like Show Business," "Three Coins in the Fountain," "River Deep Mountain High," "Moments to Remember," "Catch a Falling Star," "Papa Loves Mambo"

2364. *Selma*. Louis Abron Arts for Living Center, 2/16/84–3/4/84. 15 perf. m/l/b: Thomas Isaiah Butler; d: Cliff Roquemore; ch: Charles Lavont Williams; cos: Judy Dearing; md: Neal Tate. Cast: Ernie Banks, Ronald Wyche. "Nature's Child," "Working in the Name of King," "Martin, Martin," "Niggerwoman," "The Time is Now," "Pull Together," "You're My Love," "Isn't it Wonderful," "Tell Us, Martin," "Do You Lie?," "Pick up Your Weapon," "Boycott Trial Song," "I Can Feel Him," "When Will It End?," "Higher," "I Hate Colored People," "Children of Love," "Selma," "Selma March," "We Shall Overcome"

2365. *Senator Joe*. Rock opera. Set in, about & around the minds of Wisconsin Communist-hunter Joe McCarthy and those involved with him in the early 1950s. Closed 1/7/89 after 3 Broadway previews (beginning 1/3/89), at the Neil Simon. p: Adela Holzer & Chester Fox; m/d: Tom O'Horgan; b: Perry Arthur Kroeger; ch: Wesley Fata; set: Bill Stabile; cos: Randy Barcelo; md: Gordon Lowry Harrell; orch: Jimmy Vivino. Cast: J.P. Dougherty, Ric Ryder. "The 50s," "Cold War," "Hysteria," "Microfilm," "Black and Blue," "Where the War Left Us," "Dirt Between My Fingers," "Three First Ladies," "Communism," "Almighty American," "Dealing in Wheeling," "Charisma," "Rape of Liberty," "The Weakest Point," "The Briefcase," "What He Needs I Got," "Ism # 1," "Take a Professor," "Ism # 2," "Jeannie," "Was There Love," "Joe's Liver," "Cocktail Party," "Jungle of Lies," "Personal President," "What's My Lie," "The Wedding," "Slow as the Moon," "What's up for You," "Book Burning," "Mamie and Bess Bicker," "I Knew a Man," "Twenty Years of Treason," "Have You No Shame," "Time Heals All Wounds," "See it Now," "Pussyfootin'," "Haunted Television," "Boozin' and Barfin'," "The Telephone," "The Army," "Make Up," "Ron and Bobby," "The Hearings," "Flashback," "Aftermath," "America." Mrs. Holzer went to jail for her questionable methods in raising money for the show

2366. *Senor Discretion Himself*. Fichlander Main Stage, Arena Stage, Washington, DC, 4/15/04–5/23/04. Prev from 4/9/04. Frank Loesser spent 2 years working on it, and by 1968 had come up with an unfinished book about a small-town, middle-aged Mexican baker (it had caused him problems) and 17 musical numbers. He died in 1969. Workshopped in 1985 but nothing came of it. Mr. Loesser's widow, Jo Sullivan, was so pleased with the Arena's staging of *Guys and Dolls* that she gave permission to produce this musical. Enhanced by Culture Clash, a trio of Chicano artists (Richard Montoya, Ric Salinas, Herbert Siguenza). Based on a story by Budd Schulberg; d: Charles Randolph-Wright; ch: Dorianna Sanchez; orch: Larry Hochman; md: Brian Cimmet. Cast: Shawn Elliott. "I Cannot Let You Go," "You Don't Understand Me"

2367. *Sensations*. Update of *Romeo and Juliet*, with drugs & violence. Theatre Four, 10/25/70–11/8/70. 16 perf. m/l: Wally Harper & Paul Zakrzewski; d: Jerry Dodge; set: William & Jean Eckart; md: Jack Lee. Cast: John Savage, Judy Gibson, Marie Santell, Joe Masiell. "Lonely Children," "Sensations," "Good Little Boys," "Power," "Up and Down," "Oh, My Age," "War is Good Business," "The Kill," "Lying Here," "I Cannot Wait," "Sounds," "Morning Sun," "In Nomine Dei"

2368. *Serenade the World: The Music and Words of Oscar Brown Jr.* Musical revue of the music of the R & B legend. John Houseman, 7/29/03–9/27/03. p/conceived by: Eric Krebs; d: Stephen Henderson. Cast: Genovis Albright. "Signifying Monkey," "But I Was Cool," "Forty Acres and a Mule," "Joy," "Column of Birds"

2369. *Sex Tips for Modern Girls*. Musical revue about the woman's point of view. Susan Bloch, 10/5/86–11/9/86. 41 perf. Collectively created by Edward Astley, Susan Astley, Kim Seary, John Sereda, Hilary Strang, Christine Willes, Peter Eliot Weiss. d: Susan Astley; md: John Sereda. Cast: Kim Seary, Christine Willes, Hilary Strang, Edward Astley. All songs by John Sereda, unless noted: "Ordinary Women," "Motherload," "Go for It," "Who Will Be There," "Easy for Them to Say," "Baby Baby," "Penis Envoy" (add l: Gary Fisher), "Up to My Tits in Water" (by Kim Seary & Adrian Smith), "Victim of Normality," "Oh! K-Y Chorale (or, Beyond the Labia Majora)," "More and More." Originally prod by Touchstone Theatre, Vancouver. 41 perf. After the NY prod it was re-cast, and re-ran at Actors' Playhouse, 12/19/86–5/3/87. 157 perf. Same basic crew, except md: Kevin Wallace. Cast: Julie Ridge, Laura Turnbull, Briana Burke, Alan Harrison

2370. *Sextet*. Play with mus. About hetero & homosexual relationships among 6 people in a NYC apartment. Bijou, 3/3/74–3/10/74. 14 prev from 2/20. 9 perf. p: Balemar Prods & Lawrence E. Sokol; m: Lawrence Hurwitt; l: Lee Goldsmith; b: Harvey Perr & Lee Goldsmith; d/ch: Jered Barclay; asst ch: Mary Jane Houdina; set: Peter Harvey; cos: Zoe Brown; light: Marc B. Weiss; sound: Gary Harris; md/orch: David Frank. Cast: Dixie Carter, Harvey Evans, Jerry Lanning, Robert Spencer, Mary Small, John Newton. "Nervous," "What the Hell Am I Doing Here?," "Keep on Dancing," "Spunk," "Visiting Rights," "Going-Staying," "I Wonder," "Women and Men," "I Love You All the Time," "Hi," "It'd Be Nice," "Roseland," "How Does it Start?," "Someone to Love"

2371. Sgt. Pepper's Lonely Hearts Club Band on the Road. Rock spectacle, based on the Beatles film. Beacon, 11/17/74–1/5/75. 66 perf. p: Robert Stigwood & Brian Avnet; m/l: Lennon & McCartney (the show used Beatles songs); conceived & adapted by: Robin Wagner & Tom O'Horgan; d: Tom O'Horgan; set: Robin Wagner; cos: Randy Barcelo; light: Jules Fisher; sound: Abe Jacob; md: Gordon Lowry Harrell. Cast: Ted Neeley, Alaina Reed, Kay Cole, Edward Q. Barton, William Parry, Allan Nicholls, B.G. Gibson

2372. Shabbatai. Set in Ottoman Empire, 1639–76. American Jewish Theatre, 4/22/95–5/28/95. 41 perf. m/l/b: Michael Shubert & Michael Edwin; ch: Joe Locarro. Cast: Rex Hays, Romain Fruge, Ken Jennings. "Tikkun," "Bad Boy," "A Good Man," "Messiah?," "Not Another False Messiah," "Why Shabbatai," "Life Sucks When You're Jewish," "People Would Rather Listen to Lies," "Redemption Through Sin," "Bad Love," "Let's Talk Turkey," "The Place No One Ever Goes," "Good Old Ways," "Confession," "It's All How You Look at Things," "The Apostasy"

2373. Shades of Harlem. Cabaret re-creation of an evening at the Cotton Club in 1920s, with period music augmented by new numbers. Village Gate Downstairs, 8/21/84–4/6/85. 3 prev. 258 perf. p: Tony Conforti, Jerry Saperstein, Brian Winthrop; created by: Jeree Palmer; d: Mical Whitaker; ch: Ty Stephens. Cast: Branice McKenzie, Ty Stephens, Jeree Palmer. "Shades of Harlem," "Take the 'A' Train," "I Love Harlem," "Sweet Georgia Brown," "Satin Doll," "I Got it Bad and That Ain't Good," "Black Coffee," "The Jitterbug," "Harlem Hop," "At a Georgia Camp Meetin'," "If You Wanna Keep Your Man," "Diga Diga Doo," "Stowaway," "I'm Just Simply Full of Jazz," "My Man," "On the Sunny Side of the Street," "Body and Soul," "I Got Rhythm," "Perdido," "It Don't Meana Thing," "God Bless the Child"

2374. Shanghai Lil's. Set in San Francisco's Chinatown during WWII. St. Clement's, 4/22/97–5/10/97. 5 prev. 22 perf. p: Pan Asian Rep; m: Louis Stewart; l/b: Lilah Kan; d/ch: Tisa Chang; md: Eric K. Johnston. Cast: Jeanne Sakata, Steven Eng. "Dream Time Hour," "Uncertain Times," "Growing Up is So Exciting," "It's Really a Home," "Is it Really Possible?," "At Shanghai Lil's," "It's Time to Dance," "I'm Confused By My Feelings for Him," "Tai Chi Ballet," "Moon Song." Returned 10/15/97–11/8/97. 3 prev. 25 perf. Cast: Blossom Lam, Michael Mann

2375. Share My Lettuce. Diversion with mus. Each actor wore a different color. Lyric, Hammersmith, London, 8/21/57. 285 perf; the Comedy, London, 9/25/57; Garrick, London, 1/27/58. p: Michael Codron; m: Keith Statham & Patrick Gowers; l/b: Bamber Gascoigne; d: Eleanor Fazan; set: Disley Jones; md: Anthony Bowles; cast recording on AEI. Cast: Maggie Smith (orange), Kenneth Williams (lettuce

green), Roderick Cook (grey), Philip Gilbert (blue), Johnny Greenland (maroon), Heather Linson (violet), Barbara Evans (pink), Kenneth Mason (brown). "Colours," "Sez We," "Lute Song," "Voices of Evening," "Accelerando," "Trapped," "Love's Cocktail," "Wallflower Waltz," "Behind Bars," "Bubble Man," "Menu," "Dancing Partners," "Party Games," "Colour Calls"

2376. Sharon. Playhouse 91, 5/8/93–5/30/93. 9 prev. 15 perf. m: Franklin Micare; l/b/d: Geraldine Fitzgerald; based on *Sharon's Grave,* by John B. Keane; ch: Pamela Sousa. Cast: Kurt T. Johns, David K. Thome. "For the Money," "Song of Sharon," "It's a Sin," "Rim of a Rainbow," "Hear the Birds," "I'm Blest," "Two Eyes," "God Bless Everyone," "Grand Man," "That's How it Goes," "Dreaming," "Let's Pretend," "Boots on the Floor," "The Man Below," "Sharon's Waltz"

2377. She Shall Have Music. Musical version of *The Country Wife.* Theatre Marquee, 1/22/59; 41st Street Theatre, 2/17/59–3/15/59 (54 perf). m/l: Dede Meyer; d: Louis MacMillan; ch: Tao Strong; md: Julian Stein. Cast: Cherry Davis, Betty Oakes (*Marie Haines*), Lawrence Weber (*Pat Tolson*), Rudy Tronto. "No True Love," "Someday, Maybe," "Moi," "Wonder Where My Heart Is," "Who Are You?," "Basic," "Maud, the Bawd," "She Shall Have Music," "One Sweet Moment," "Who Needs It?," "If I Am to Marry You"

2378. She Smiled at Me. Connaught, Worthing, 1/16/56 (1 week); St. Martin's, London, 2/2/56–2/4/56. 4 perf. Began in Worthing as *Caste* (see this appendix). d: Jack Williams; ch: Thurza Rogers; md: Harry Tait. Cast: Jean Kent (took over the Cherry Lind role), Peter Byrne & Mercy Haystead (reprised), William Peacock (*Robin Bailey*), Hugh Paddick. "A Military Man," "Wouldn't It Be Fun?," "Marry for Love," "Shall We Fall in Love?," "She Smiled at Me," "Life is an Empty Thing," "Music Hall"

2379. Sheba. Set in Jerusalem, 960 B.C. Jewish Rep, 1/11/96–3/24/96. 9 prev. 63 perf. m: Gary William Friedman; l/b: Sharleen Cooper Cohen; d/ch: Tony Stevens. Cast: Ernestine Jackson, Natasha Rennalls, Tamara Tunie, Joseph Sinaro. "Begging the Question," "Song of Solomon," "I Question You," "How Does a King Decide," "You'll Be King," "Water Wears the Stone," "The Names," "Give and Take," "You Are the One," "Night of Love," "Moment in the Sun," "God of Our Fathers," "Mysteries," "Child of Mine," "Come with Me," "Solomon Decide," "You Fill My Arms." Not to be confused with a later musical with the same name, based on *Come Back, Little Sheba,* which had m/l by Lee Goldsmith and book by Cliff Ballard Jr. That one ran at White Barn, Westport, Conn., 8/31/01. d: Leslie B. Cutler; ch: Donald Saddler; md: Glen Clugston; orch: Ralph Burns. Cast: Donna McKechnie

2380. The Sheik of Avenue B. Ragtime & jazz era musical comedy revue with songs of the period. Set during the fall of 1932. Town Hall, 11/22/92–12/27/92. Prev from 10/28/92. 54 perf. w/conceived by: Isaiah Sheffer; d/ch:

Dan Siretta; md: Lanny Meyers. Cast: Paul Harman, Michele Ragusa, Virginia Sandifur, Larry Raiken

2381. Sheila's Day. Drama with mus. Set in South Africa & America, 1965–1972. Brooklyn Academy of Music/Carey Playhouse, 6/2/93–6/6/93. 7 perf. w: Duma Ndlovu; d: Mbongeni Ngema; ch: Thuli Dumakude; light: Victor En Yu Tan. Cast: Gina Breedlove, Thuli Dumakude, Ebony Jo-Ann. New Victory, 1/5/96–1/21/96. 4 prev. 17 perf. re-staged by: Kenneth Johnson. Cast: Gina Breedlove, Thuli Dumakude, Ebony Jo-Ann, Fuschia Walker, Irene Datcher (also md)

2382. Sheridan Square. Cabaret-style play with mus. Duplex, 6/5/99–7/31/99. 17 perf. p: Langston County Players; w/conceived by: Phil Geoffrey Bond; add material: Tim Cahill; d: Joseph Verlezza; md: Brett Kristofferson. Cast: Phil Geoffrey Bond, Al Centauri, Tim Cahill. "Sheridan Square," "The Miller's Son," "Shitty People," "Let Me Sing," "Before the Parade Passes By," "How Lucky Can You Get," "You're Mine," "Making Love Alone," "I Don't Remember Christmas," "The Portrait"

2383. Sherlock Holmes — The Musical. The Cambridge, London, 4/24/89–7/8/89. m/l: Leslie Bricusse; cast recording on BMG. Cast: Liz Robertson, Julia Sutton, Ron Moody, Derek Waring, Colin Bennett. "Anything You Want to Know," "The Best of You, The Best of Me," "Down the Apples 'n Pears," "Halcyon Days," "Her Face," "I Shall Find Her," "London is London," "Look Around You," "The Lord Abides in London," "A Lousy Life," "A Million Years Ago, or Was it Yesterday?," "Men Like You," "No Reason," "Sherlock Holmes," "Vendetta," "Without Him There Can Be No Me." Bristol Old Vic, 3/16/93. Cast: David Oakley, Marilyn Cutts, Robert Powell, James Head, Roy Barraclough

2384. Shindig. City Center Downstairs, 4/12/79–4/15/79. 6 perf. Title song: Louis St. Louis; conceived by/d: Anthony J. Ingrassia; ms: Martin Silvestri; md: Jimmy & Tommy Wynbrandt. Cast: Paul Binotto, Jimmy & Tommy Wynbrandt

2385. Shlemiel the First. Yiddish. Set in village of Chelm. First done at Yale Rep, 4/12/74, with Kurt Kasznar. John Jay, 7/7/94–7/9/94. 4 perf. Part of Lincoln Center's Serious Fun Festival. m/orch: Hankus Netsky; l: Arnold Weinstein; based on play by Isaac Bashevis Singer; conceived by/adapted: Robert Brustein; d/ch: David Gordon; cos: Catherine Zuber; md: Zalmen Mlotek. Cast: Larry Block, Charles Levin, Marilyn Sokol

2386. Shockheaded Peter: A Junk Opera. Slovenelt Peter is very bad boy who comes to sticky end. Portrayed by actors & puppets. New Victory, 10/14/99–10/31/99. 15 perf. m: The Tiger Lilies (a London trio); Martyn Jacques adapted lyr from Heinrich Hoffmann's 1844 unpleasant poems *Struwwelpeter;* d: Phelim McDermott & Julian Crouch; md: Martyn Jacques. Piccadilly, London, 2/19/01–4/28/01. Prev from 2/14/01; Albery, London, 4/11/02–6/15/02. Prev from 4/4/02. Olivier Award for Best Entertainment. 37 Arts Theatre, NY, 1/14/05. Phelim McDermott & Julian Crouch (d). Orig OB cast. This latter prod opened OB at the Little Shubert, 2/22/05 (prev from 2/11/05)

2387. *The Shoemaker and the Peddler.* East 74th Street Theatre, 10/14/60–11/13/60. 43 perf. m/l: Frank Fields & Armand Aulicino; based on Sacco & Vanzetti story; d: Lee Nemetz. Cast: James Bosotina, Jose Duval, Anita Darian. "Headlines," "Is This the Way?," "Sometimes I Wonder," "Remember, Remember," "Guilty!"

2388. *Shoemaker's Holiday.* Set in 16th-century London. Orpheum, 3/2/67–3/5/67. 2 prev. 6 perf. p/d: Ken Costigan; m: Mel Marvin; l/b: Ted Berger; based on Elizabethan comedy by Thomas Dekker; ch: Myrna Galle; md: Elman Anderson. Cast: Jerry Dodge, Gail Johnston, Judy Knaiz, Tom Urich, Sue Lawless, Penny Gaston. "Cold's the Wind," "What Do We Care if it Rains," "A Poor Man at Parting," "Who Gives a Hey," "Where is the Knight for Me," "When a Maid Wears Purple Stockings," "Down a Down Down Derry," "Gather Ye Rosebuds," "Ribbons I Will Give Thee," "My Lovely Lad," "Trowl the Bowl," "The Wonder of the Kingdom," "The Recipe for Husbandry," "The Shaking of the Sheets," "Would that I," "Everythin' is Tinglin'," "What a Life"

2389. *Shoestring '57.* Nightclub revue. Barbizon Plaza, 11/5/56–2/17/57. 119 perf. p: Ben Bagley; m/l: Philip Springer, Carolyn Leigh, Moose Charlap, Norman Gimbel, Harvey Schmidt, Mike Stewart, Charles Strouse, etc; sk: Tom Jones & Lee Adams, etc; d: Paul Lammers, ch: Danny Daniels; md/pianist: Dorothea Freitag. Cast: Dody Goodman, George Marcy, Fay De Witt, Dorothy Greener, Patricia Hammerlee, Diki Lerner, Paul Mazursky. "Love is a Feeling," "There's Always One Day More"

2390. *Shoestring Revue.* A Ben Bagley revue. President, 2/28/55–5/22/55. 100 perf. m/l: David Baker & Sheldon Harnick, etc; sk: mostly by Mike Stewart; d: Christopher Hewett; md: Charles Strouse. Cast: Dody Goodman, Dorothy Greener, Peter Conlow, Mel Larned, Chita Rivera, Bea Arthur, Rhoda Kerns, Arte Johnson, Sheldon Harnick, Charles Strouse. "Someone's Been Sending Me Flowers"

2391. *Shoop Shoop Shoop Shoop.* Doo-wop musical. Producers Club, 6/30/99–8/28/99. w/d: Gil Rambach; md: Jess Jurkovic

2392. *Shoot Up at Elbow Creek.* Orange Tree, Richmond, England, 8/13/76–9/12/76. w: Keith Strachan, Roy Truman, Leslie Stewart; d: Michael Richmond; ch: Scott Martyn & Tanith Banbury. Cast: Tanith Banbury, Scott Martyn. Greenwich Theatre, London, 8/16/77–9/17/77. 28 perf. d/ch: Christie Dickason; md: Keith Strachan. Cast: Thick Wilson

2393. *Shootin' Star.* Musical story of Billy the Kid, in 2 acts & 7 scenes. Set in Lincoln County, NM, ca. 1880. Opened 4/4/46, Shubert, New Haven. Closed 4/27/46, Shubert, Boston, without making Broadway. p: Max Liebman & Joseph Kipness; m/l: Bob Russell & Sol Kaplan; b: Walter Hart, Louis Jacobs, Halsted Welles; d: Halsted Welles; md: Pembroke Davenport; orch: Hershy Kay. Cast:

Billy: David Brooks; Amy: Doretta Morrow; Also with: Howard Da Silva, Bernice Parks, Elline Walther, Nelle Fisher. "Saga of Billy the Kid," "Footloose," "Kid Stuff," "Friendly Country," "What Do I Have to Do?," "Mighty Big Dream," "Sometime Tomorrow," "It's a Cold, Cruel World," "Free," "Nothin'," "I'm Paying You"

2394. *The Shop on Main Street.* Set in town of Sabinov, Eastern Czechoslovakia, in mid-June, 1942. Jewish Rep, 12/14/85–1/12/86. 27 perf. m/l: Saul Honigman & Bernard Spiro; based on novel by Ladislav Grosman; d: Fran Soeder; ch: Janet Watson; set: James Leonard Joy; cos: Mardi Philips. Cast: Gregg Edelman, Olga Talyn, Kenneth Kantor, Lilia Skala. "The Shop on Main Street," "Mark Me Tomorrow," "Someone to Do For," "I Feel Like a Woman," "Better Days"

2395. *Shotgun Wedding.* Closed before Broadway. 1950. m/l: Glenn Hughes & Nicholas Russo. Cast: Christie Nicholas. "Houseboat on the Mississippi," "In Love at Last," "There's a Ring Around the Moon"

2396. *The Show Goes On.* "A portfolio of theatre songs by the authors of *The Fantasticks* and other shows" [i.e. Harvey Schmidt & Tom Jones]. Theatre at St. Peter's Church, 12/17/97–3/1/98. Prev from 12/10/97. 88 perf. p: York Theatre Co.; d: Drew Scott Harris; ch: Janet Watson; set: James Morgan; cos: Suzy Benzinger; light: Mary Jo Dondlinger. Cast: Harvey Schmidt, Tom Jones, Jo Ann Cunningham, Emma Lampert, J. Mark McVey. "Come on Along," "Try to Remember," "Mr. Off-Broadway," "Everyone Looks Lonely," "I Know Loneliness Quite Well," "Story of My Life," "The Holy Man and the New Yorker," "It's Gonna Be Another Hot Day," "I Can Dance," "Desseau Dance Hall," "Flibberty-Gibbet," "Melisande," "Simple Little Things," "I Do! I Do!," "The Honeymoon is Over," "My Cup Runneth Over," "Celebration," "Orphan in the Storm," "Survive," "Under the Tree," "Fifty Million Years Ago," "Decorate the Human Face," "Where Did it Go?," "Wonderful Way to Die," "The Room is Filled with You," "Time Goes By," "Goodbye World," "The Show Goes On" (title song from *Mirette*— for which see this appendix)

2397. *Show Me Where the Good Times Are.* Set in 1913 in NYC's Lower East Side. Edison, Middle Broadway, 3/5/70. p: Lorin E. Price & Barbara Lee Horn; m/l: Kenneth Jacobson & Rhoda Roberts. They took the title & title song from a previous flop, *Hot September* (see this appendix). b: Leonora Thuna; suggested by Moliere's *Le Malade Imaginaire;* d: Morton Da Costa; ch: Bob Herget; set: Tom John; light: Neil Peter Jampolis; md: Karen Gustafson; orch: Philip J. Lang; cast recording on RCA Victor. Cast: Cathryn Damon, Neva Small, Arnold Soboloff, John Bennett Perry, Mitchell Jason, Christopher Hewett, Edward Earle, Austin Colyer, Denny Martin Flinn. "How Do I Feel?," "He's Wonderful," "Look Up," "Show Me Where the Good Times Are," "You're My Happiness," "Cafe Royale Rag," "Staying Alive," "One Big Happy Family," "Follow Your Heart," "Look Who's Throwing

a Party," "When Tomorrow Comes," "The Test," "I'm Not Getting Any Younger," "Who'd Believe?." Playhouse 91, 6/5/93–6/27/93. 9 prev. 15 perf. p: Jewish Rep; d: Warren Enters; ch: Dennis Grimaldi. Cast: Robert Ari, Lauren Mitchell, Gabriel Barre

2398. *Show Time.* Vaudeville show. Broadhurst, Broadway, 9/16/42–4/3/43. 342 perf (every night, plus 5 matinees weekly). p/conceived by: Fred F. Finklehoffe Jr. Cast: George Jessel, Jack Haley, Ella Logan, Con Colleano, The De Marcos (Tony & Renee), The Berry Brothers, Bob Williams & his dog act. Organized on the Pacific Coast, where it ran 5 months in L.A. & San Francisco. Miss Logan's numbers included: "Strip Polka," "Something I Dreamed Last Night," "Tipperary," "You Take the High Note and I'll Take the Low Note" (with Mr. Haley)

2399. *The Showgirl.* Set in Brooklyn & Paris in 1945, 1925 and 1934. Town Hall, 10/24/82–1/2/83. 60 perf. p: Raymond Ariel & David Carey; m/l: Nellie Casman & Yankele Alperin; b: Samuel Steinberg; add m: Alexander Lustig; new mus numbers: Yankele Alperin; English narration: Roz Regalson; d: Michael Greenstein; ch: Yankele Kaluski; set: Lydia Pincus-Gani; md: Renee Solomon. Cast: Mary Soreanu, Karol Feldman, Lydia Saxton, Shifra Lerer, Yankele Alperin, Adrian Mandel, Reizl Bozyk, Michael Michalovic, David Carey, David Ellin, Karol Latowicz, Hallie Lightdale, Orly Jaffe. "Excuse Me, Sir," "Childishness," "A Jewish Song," "Today Is a Holiday," "Purim," "I'll Always Remember You," "Shteytl," "I Love the Theatre," "French Medley," "I Will Wait for You," "Just a Little Bit of Health," "Five Cents." It closed to go on tour

2400. *Showing Off.* Musical revue. Steve McGraw's (formerly Palsson's), 5/18/89–10/15/89. 3 prev from 5/15. 17 perf. w: Douglas Bernstein & Denis Markell; d/ch: Michael Leeds; md: Stephen Flaherty. Cast: Douglas Bernstein, Donna Murphy (*Bebe Neuwirth*), Veanne Cox, Mark Sawyer. "Showing Off," "72nd Street," "I Don't Get It," "They're Yours," "Michele," "Rental Cruelty," "How Things Change," "Take de Picture," "Old Fashioned Song"

2401. *The Showman.* Theatre Royal, Stratford East, London, 10/6/76–11/20/76. 47 perf. p: Theatre Workshop; m: Roland Hase; l/b: Herbert Shield; from *The Bells*, by Leopold Lewis; d/ch: Tommy Shaw; md: Terry White. Cast: Ron Moody, June Shand, Judith Bruce

2402. *Showtune: The Jerry Herman Songbook.* Musical revue. Also known as *Jerry Herman's Showtune.* Helen Hayes, Nyack, NY, 10/12/02–10/27/02. p: Jenny Sanchez; conceived by: Paul Gilger; d/ch: Joey McKneely; md: James Followell; pianist: Bobby Peaco. Cast: Donna McKechnie, Martin Vidnovic, Paul Harman, Tom Korbee, Russell Arden Koplin, Sandy Binion. Excerpts from the shows: *Milk and Honey*–"Shalom;" *Hello, Dolly!*–"Before the Parade Passes By," "Hello, Dolly!," "It Only Takes a Moment," "It Takes a Woman," "Put on Your Sunday Clothes;" *Mame*–"Bosom Buddies," "If He Walked into My Life," "It's Today," "Mame," "The Man in the Moon," "My Best Girl," "Open a New Window," "That's How Young I Feel," "We Need a Little Christmas," "What Do I Do Now?;" *Dear World*– "And I Was Beautiful," "Kiss Her Now," "I Don't Want to Know," "One Person;" *Mack and Mabel*– "Big Time," "Hundreds of Girls," "I Promise You a Happy Ending," "I Won't Send Roses," "Look What Happened to Mabel," "Movies Were Movies," "Tap Your Troubles Away," "Time Heals Everything," "Wherever He Ain't;" *The Grand Tour*– "I'll Be Here Tomorrow;" *A Day in Hollywood/A Night in the Ukraine*– "Just Go to the Movies," "Nelson;" *La Cage aux Folles*– "A Little More Mascara," "The Best of Times," "I Am What I Am," "Song of the Sand," "With You on My Arm." By 10/02 Jerry Herman was looking at the Helen Hayes on Broadway, or OB, at the Harold Clurman. Instead, it played the Theatre at St. Peter's (OB), 2/27/03–4/13/03. 11 prev from 2/18. 53 perf. Same crew & cast, except Karen Murphy replaced Donna McKechnie

2403. Siamsa. Traditional Celtic rituals, dancing & folk music presented in context of an Irish village festival. Palace, Broadway, 9/27/76–10/2/76. 8 perf. dev/d: Pat Ahern; ch: Patricia Hanafin. Cast: National Folk Theatre of Ireland

2404. Sid Caesar and Company: Does Anyone Know What I'm Talking About? Musical special. Originally presented by Art D'Lugoff at the Village Gate, 6/22/89. 72 perf. John Golden, Broadway, 11/1/89–11/5/89. 6 prev. 5 perf. p: Ivan Bloch, Harold Thau, Larry Spellman; orig songs/d: Martin Charnin; set/light: Neil Peter Jampolis; md: Elliot Pinkel. Cast: Sid Caesar, Lee Delano, Linda Hart, Lubitza Gregus, Peter Shawn, Laura Turnbull, Erick Devine, Carolyn Michel

2405. Side by Side by Seymour Glick. Musical comedy revue. West End Theatre, NY, 5/15/98–6/8/98. 16 perf. m/l/b: Steve Allen; d: Robert Armin; md: Steve Liebman. Cast: Robert Armin, Steve Liebman

2406. Sigh No More. Piccadilly, London, 1945. 212 perf. m/l/d: Noel Coward; ch: George Garden, Sheila Nicholson, Wendy Toye; set: G.E. Calthrop. Cast: Joyce Grenfell, Cyril Ritchard, Madge Elliott, Graham Payn, Gail Kendall, Mantovani & his Orchestra. "I Wonder What Happened to Him," "Indian Army Officer," "Matelot," "Music Hath Charms," "Never Again," "Nina," "Parting of the Ways," "Sigh No More," "That is the End of the News," "Wait a Bit, Joe," "Oh, Mr. Du Maurier" (by Richard Addinsell & Miss Grenfell)

2407. The Sign in Sidney Brustein's Window. Pressures on idealistic young Greenwich Village newspaper publisher. Longacre, Broadway, 10/15/64–1/10/65. 101 perf. w: Lorraine Hansberry. Cast: Sidney: Gabriel Dell; Iris: Rita Moreno; Max: Dolph Sweet; Mavis: Alice Ghostley (Tony award). At this stage it was a straight play. It did not have a musical score, except that "The Wally O'Hara Campaign Song," written by Ernie Sheldon, was recorded by the Moonshiners, and the voice of Joan Baez came courtesy of Vanguard Records. But that was it, musically speaking. The play was re-

vived, again at the Longacre, 1/26/72–1/29/72. 9 prev. 5 perf. This time it was a play with mus, having been adapted by Robert Nemiroff & Charlotte Zaltzberg to include songs presented as a comment on the action by the chorus. m/orch: Gary William Friedman; l: Ray Errol Fox; d: Alan Schneider; ch: Rhoda Levine; cos: Theoni V. Aldredge. Cast: Sidney: Hal Linden; Iris: Zohra Lampert; Max: Dolph Sweet; Mavis: Frances Sternhagen; David: William Atherton; Gloria: Kelly Wood; Also with: Richard Cox, Arnetia Walker, Pendleton Brown, John Danelle, Mason Adams. "Can a Flower Think?," "In Another Life," "Mountain Girl," "To the People," "While There's Still Time," "Things as They Are," "Sweet Evenin'." Richard Allen Center, NY, 1/24/80–2/10/80. Cast: Victor Arnold

2408. Signs Along the Cynic Route. Revue. Actors' Playhouse, 12/14/61–3/4/62. 93 perf. m/l: Will Holt; sk: Will Holt & Dolly Jonah. Cast: Will Holt, Dolly Jonah, Robert Barend

2409. Simply Cole Porter. Musical revue. Perry Street, 6/4/94–6/26/94. 4 prev. 20 perf. Conceived & performed by Deborah Ausemus & J. Kent Barnhart; d: Francis J. Cullinan

2410. Sing a Rude Song. Greenwich Theatre, London, 2/18/70; Garrick, London, 5/26/70. 71 perf. m/arr: Ron Grainer; l/b: Caryl Brahms & Ned Sherrin; add material: Alan Bennett; d: Ned Sherrin; ch: Virginia Mason; md: Alfred Ralston. Cast: Marie Lloyd: Barbara Windsor; Also with: Denis Quilley (*Ian Paterson*), Maurice Gibb, Harry Towb, Irlin Hall, Jacquie Toye, Derek Griffiths

2411. Sing Hallelujah! Musical gospel revue without dialogue. Playhouse in the Park, Cincinnati, 7/21/87. conceived by: Worth Gardner & Donald Lawrence; d: Worth Gardner; light: Kirk Bookman; sound: Otts Munderloh; md: Donald Lawrence. Cast: Curtis Blake, Carrie Scott, Clarence Snow, Patricia Ann Everson, Ann Nesby. "Sing Hallelujah!," "Everybody Ought to Know," "We Can't Go on This Way," "Right Now," "New World," "I'm Just Holdin' On," "Oh Happy Day," "The Question Is." Village Gate Downstairs (NYC), 11/3/87–1/3/88. 72 perf. Rose Clyburn took over from Carrie Scott

2412. Sing Happy! Showcase of work of John Kander & Fred Ebb. Special single benefit perf for American Musical and Dramatic Academy and the George Junior Republic. Avery Fisher Hall, 1978. d/ch: Tony Stevens; md: Paul Gemignani; sound: T. Richard Fitzgerald. Cast: Cy Coleman, Anita Gillette, Joel Grey, Jerry Herman, Larry Kert, Charles Strouse, Chita Rivera, Jack Gilford, John Raitt, Lotte Lenya, Liza Minnelli, Gwen Verdon (assisted by Obba Babatunde), Henrietta Jacobson, Susan Danielle, Angelique Ilo, Frank Mastrocola, Roger Minami, Gena Ramsel, Michael Serrecchia

2413. Sing, Israel, Sing. A mixture of Yiddish & Israeli folklore, humor & art songs tied together as events taking place in a kibbutz in Israel; in Yiddish. Brooks Atkinson, Broadway, 5/11/67–5/21/67. 14 perf— actually perfs were suspended in order to translate the book into English and add material). p: Ben Bonus; b:

Wolf Younin; d: Mina Bern. Cast: Mina Bern, Ben Bonus, Susan Walters, Rose Bozyk, Max Bozyk. Re-ran 6/7/67–6/11/67. 8 perf, in English. "The Dream," "Only I and You," "Song of the Rain," "Sing, Israel, Sing," "The Bride Sings," "Guard of Israel"

2414. Sing, Mahalia, Sing. About Mahalia Jackson, the gospel singer. Opened as national tour, 3/26/85, Warner Theatre, Washington, DC. Closed 9/1/85, Paramount, Oakland, Calif., without making intended Broadway opening. orig m & l: Richard Smallwood, George Faison, Wayne Davis; b/d/ch: George Faison; cos: Nancy Potts; light: Thomas Skelton; ms: Timothy Graphenreed. Cast: Jennifer Holliday (Esther Marrow alternated twice weekly)

2415. Sing Me Sunshine! Set in 1934, in England. AMAS, 2/9/84–3/4/84. 16 perf. m/l: Johnny Brandon; b: Robert E. Richardson & Johnny Brandon; based on *Peg 'o My Heart*, by J. Hartley Manners; d: Jack Timmers; ch: Henry Le Tang; cos: Gail Cooper-Hecht; dance mus arr: Timothy Graphenreed. Cast: Jan Horvath. "The H'Elegant Homes of H'England," "Ruined," "A Long, Long Time," "When a Gentleman's Well-Dressed," "Nothing Like a Friend," "All Alone," "The Education of Peg," "That's What Living's All About," "Where is Away?," "You Can Do It," "Changes," "Down My Street," "That is What I Give You," "Peg," "Sing Me Sunshine," "Where Do I Stand?"

2416. Sing Muse! About Helen of Troy. Van Dam, 12/6/61–1/7/62. 39 perf. m/l: Joe Raposo & Erich Segal; d: Bill Penn; md: Jerry Goldberg. Cast: Karen Morrow, Brandon Maggart. "Helen, Quit Your Yellin'," "I Am a Traveling Poet," "O Pallas Athene," "Your Name May Be Paris," "Sing Muse!," "You're in Love," "The Wrath of Achilles," "No Champagne," "Business is Bad," "In Our Little Salon for Two," "Fame!," "We'll Find a Way," "Tonight's the Fight," "I'm to Blame"

2417. Sisterella. Black American Cinderella story. Musical Theatre Works, 11/8/95–11/19/95. 13 perf. p: Michael Jackson; m/l/b: Larry Hart; d: David Simmons; md: Matthew Sklar. Cast: Rain Pryor. Pasadena Playhouse, 1996. Regent, Melbourne, Australia, from 3/7/98, at a cost of $A6.5 million, backed by Michael Jackson & Kevin Jacobsen. Cast recording financed by Michael Jackson

2418. Sisters of Mercy. Musical journey into the words of Leonard Cohen. Theatre de Lys, 9/25/73–10/7/73. 15 perf. conceived by/d: Gene Lesser; add m/md: Zizi Mueller; set: Robert U. Taylor; cos: Carrie F. Robbins. Cast: Gale Garnett, Emily Bindiger, Michael Calkins, Nicholas Surovy, Pamela Paluzzi, Rosemary Radcliffe. "Winter Lady," "War Song," "Bird on a Wire," "Tonight Will Be Fine," "Hey, That's No Way to Say Goodbye," "One of Us Cannot Be Wrong," "Famous Blue Raincoat," "The Singer Must Die," "Nancy," "Diamonds in the Mine," "You Know Who I Am," "Chelsea Song," "Suzanne," "Works of Charity," "Love Calls You By Your Name," "Priests," "Dress Rehearsal Rag," "Sisters of Mercy," "So Long, Marianne"

2419. Sit Down and Eat Before Our Love

Gets Cold. West Side Y Arts Center, 5/3/85–5/17/85. 9 prev. 11 perf. d: Anthony McKay; ch: David Storey; md: David Loud. Cast: Bev Larson, Barbara Schottenfeld (also w), John Wesley Shipp. "First Child by 33," "Boy to Love," "I Don't Want Any More Good Friends," "Legalese," "How Did I Come Across?," "Losing Touch," "Simple Things," "I Don't Want to Hold Back," "Sit Down and Eat Before Our Love Gets Cold," "I'm So Happy for Her," "I Want You to Be," "Why Should We Talk," "Why Do I Only," "Revisions," "When You Find Somebody"

2420. *Six*. Charles Strouse's musical topical revue without intermission. Cricket, 4/12/71–4/18/71. 8 perf. p: Slade Brown; d: Peter Coe; md: Wally Harper. Cast: Lee Beery, Gail Nelson, Gilbert Price, Hal Watters, Johanna Albrecht, Alvin Ing. "What is There to Sing About?," "The Garden," "Love Song," "Six," "Coming Attractions," "The Invisible Man," "The Critic," "Trip," "The Beginning," "The Dream"

2421. *The Six Million Dollar Musical*. Set in the 1970s. Producers Club, 10/12/00–10/21/00. 6 perf. Cast: John Cecil (also w), John Carlton, Doreen Barnard, John Wake, Denise Clark, Jeromy Barber, Jamie Smith

2422. *Six Pairs of Shoes*. Cabaret story with mus. Playhouse, London, 4/10/44–4/29/44. 23 perf. m: Mark Lubbock, Eric Spear, Billy Mayerl, Z. Karazinski, Harry Roy; l: Paddy Browne, Max Kester, Frank Eyton, Diana Morgan; b: Monica Disney Ullman; d: Leontine Sagan; md: Harry Roy. Cast: Monica Disney Ullman, Paddy Browne, Moira Lister

2423. *Skirts!* US Army Air Force revue. The Cambridge, London, 1944. m/l: Frank Loesser & Harold Rome. "Jumping to the Juke Box," "The Little Brown Suit my Uncle Bought Me," "My Pin-Up Girl" (all those by Mr. Rome), "Skirts!" (by Mr. Loesser)

2424. *Skits-Oh-Frantics!* Revue of songs, dances, stand-up monologues, and burlesque routines. Bert Wheeler, 4/2/67–4/16/67. 17 perf. p: Bob Hadley; m/l/md: Bernie Wayne. Cast: Hank Ladd (also d), Bobbi Baird, Patti Karr

2425. *Sky High*. Musical extravaganza sending up various musical entertainment forms. Players Theatre, 6/28/79–7/29/79. 27 prev. 38 perf. p: E. David Rosen; m/l: Ann Harris; w/d: Brian O'Hara; ch: The Harris Sisters; set/cos: Angel Jack; add m & arr: Frederic Harris. Cast: Richard Di Pasquale, Ann Harris, Eloise Harris, Jayne Anne Harris, Lulu Belle Harris, Angel Jack, Brian O'Hara. "Rainbow," "Behold the Coming of the Sun," "I'm Betting on You," "Singing Mermaids," "South American Way," "Queen Cobra," "Let's Go to the Dogs," "Toast of the Town," "Opium Song," "I'm Lazy," "Miss America," "Hot as Hades," "Champagne Song"

2426. *Skye*. Musical fairy tale. Equity Library, 2/1/71–2/3/71. 3 perf. m/l: Ben Finn, Avery Corman, Dan Rustin; d: James Curtan; md: Wendell Kindberg. Cast: Jay Kirsch. "The Isle of Skye," "Ring, Ring the Bell," "The Fairie Piper," "Underneath a Dragon Moon," "Only One Shadow"

2427. *Skyline*. Set in the Skyline Cafe, on Columbus Avenue, NYC. American Theatre of Actors, 1/6/83–1/29/83. 19 perf. m/b: Sonny Casella; d: Dennis Dennehy & Sonny Casella; ch: Dennis Dennehy. Cast: Lawrence Clayton, Carole-Ann Scott, Pi Douglass, Wendy Laws, Michael Piatkowski, Donna M. Pompei

2428. *Slay It with Music*. Musical chiller. Set in Hollywood in 1968. Actors Outlet, 10/13/89–11/1/89. 4 prev. 12 perf. m/l: Paul Katz & Michael Colby; d: Charles Repole; ch: Dennis Dennehy; md: Phil Reno. Cast: Janet Metz, Susan Bernstein, Virginia Sandifur, Louisa Flaningam. "Whatever Happened to…?," "Second Chance/Slasher Movie," "I Gotta Get Her Back," "Sisters," "Anything," "In Love," "You're There When I Need You," "Got it All," "Two Actresses Practicing Their Art," "I Know a Secret," "Slay it with Music," "Trapped," "More than Just a Movie Fan," "That's a Wrap/Second Chance," "Now We Can't Miss"

2429. *Sleak*. Deams Street, Manchester, England, 1977; Ernie's, Mathew Street, Liverpool, 7/12/77–7/15/77; Royal Court, London, 7/20/77. 4 perf; Royal Court, 9/12/77 (3 weeks); Roundhouse, London, 10/4/77–10/29/77. 23 perfs. m/l/b: C.P. Lee; d: Charlie Hanson. Cast: Norman Sleak: Jimmy Hibbert; Also with: C.P. Lee, Gordon Kaye. In the USA it was prod OB, at Privates

2430. *A Slice of Saturday Night*. King's Head, London, 8/1/89–8/26/89; Arts Theatre, 9/27/89; Strand, London, 9/6/93. m/l: The Heather Brothers. Cast: David Easter, Sarah Jane Hassell, James Powell, Charlotte Edwards. "A Slice of Saturday Night," "Seventeen," "Don't Touch Me," "Twiggy," "Cliff," "Love on Our Side," "What Do I Do Now?," "What Do You Do?," "If You Wanna Have Fun," "The Long Walk Back," "Wham Bam," "The Boy of My Dreams," "It Wouldn't Be Saturday Night without a Fight," "I Fancy You," "Sentimental Eyes," "Heartbreaker," "Oh, So Bad," "Please Don't Tell Me," "Lies," "Baby, I Love You," "Last Saturday Night"

2431. *Smile*. Musical revue. Unrelated to the 1986 Broadway show, this was about Charlie Chaplin (the title came from the famous song from his 1952 movie *Limelight*). Amsterdam, Netherlands, 1/21/98. p: Eugene Chaplin (Charlie's son); conceived by: Koos Mark; dance sequences created by: Caroline O'Connor & Mark Adams

2432. *Smilin' Through*. Musical version of the stage & film hit. Yvonne Arnaud, Guildford, England, 3/29/72–4/22/72; toured; Prince of Wales, London, 7/5/72–7/29/72. 28 perf. m/l: John Hanson; b: John Hanson & Constance Cox; d/ch: David Gardiner; md: Derek Taverner; cast recording on Philips. Cast: John Hanson, Lauverne Gray, Diana Jane Argyle, Carol Doree, Glyn Worsnip. "When You're Young," "Smilin' Through," "Why Did I Leave Ireland," "If You Really Loved Me," "You, Who Have Never Known Love," "Who Wants to Be Free," "We're Not Going Home Tonight!," "There's Nothing Like a Wedding," "The Best Man," "The Luckiest Girl in the World', "A Quiet Girl," "Will You Love, Hon-

our and Obey?," "The Time Will Come," "Why Must I Leave You?," "Give Me Your Hand"

2433. *Smiling the Boy Fell Dead*. Cherry Lane, 4/19/61–5/7/61. 22 perf. m: David Baker; l: Sheldon Harnick; b: Ira Wallach; set: Herbert Senn & Helen Pond; cos: Theoni V. Aldredge; light: David Hays; md: Julian Stein. Cast: Danny Meehan, Warren Wade, Joseph Macaulay, Louise Larrabee, Justine Johnston, Phil Leeds, Claiborne Cary, Gino Conforti, Ted Beniades. "Sons of Greentree," "Let's Evolve," "The ABCs of Success," "If I Felt Any Younger (Today)," "More than Ever Now," "I've Got a Wonderful Future," "Small Town," "Heredity-Environment," "The Gatsby Bridge March," "A World to Win," "The Wonderful Machine," "Temperance Polka," "Day Dreams," "Dear Old Dad," "Me and Dorothea," "Two by Two"

2434. *Smiling Through*. About a music hall singer during the War. Set in London, 1940–44. Theatre Four, 2/2/93–2/6/93. 15 prev from 1/21/93. 6 perf. p: Lois Teich; songs: various writers; b: Ivan Menchell; d/ch: Patricia Birch; set: James Morgan; sound: Otts Munderloh. Cast: Vicki Stuart, Jeff Woodman. "Don't Dilly Dally on the Way," "Nobody Loves a Fairy," "Underneath the Arches," "All Our Tomorrows," "Wish Me Luck," "No One Believes…," "The Deepest Shelter in Town," "Dancing with My Shadow," "I'm Gonna Get Lit Up," "We'll Meet Again," "The White Cliffs of Dover," "A Nightingale Sang in Berkeley Square." Previously prod by Pennsylvania Stage Company & Emelin Theatre in Mamaroneck, NY

2435. *Smith*. Set at Baggett Nitrates, Tenafly, NJ. Hard-working botanist finds himself projected into new identity as hero of musical comedy, from which he cannot escape. Eden, 5/19/73–6/2/73. Prev from 4/30/73. 18 perf. p: Jordan Hott; m/l: Matt Dubey & Dean Fuller; d: Neal Kenyon; ch: Michael Shawn; set: Fred Voelpel; cos: Winn Morton; light: Martin Aronstein; sound: Peter J. Fitzgerald; md: Richard Parrinello; orch: Jonathan Tunick; dance mus arr: John Berkman; choral arr: Dean Fuller. Cast: Don Murray, Virginia Sandifur, Mort Marshall, Carol Morley, David Horwitz, Lou Criscuolo, Michael Tartel, David Vosburgh, Bonnie Walker, Ted Thurston, Patricia Garland, Renee Baughman, Nicholas Dante, Bonnie Hinson, Guy Spaull. "Boy Meets Girl," "There's a Big Job Waiting for You," "To the Ends of the Earth," "Balinasia," "Onh-Honh-Honh!," "Police Song," "You Need a Song," "How Beautiful it Was," "Island Ritual," "People Don't Do That," "You're in New York Now," "It Must Be Love," "Song of the Frog," "G'bye," "Melody"

2436. *Smoke on the Mountain*. Gospel musical comedy. Set on a Saturday night in June 1938 in Mount Pleasant Baptist Church, Mount Pleasant, NC. Lambs, 5/10/90–6/30/91. 11 prev. 452 perf. Note: it was raised from OOB to OB status on 8/14/90, after 120 perf. w: Connie Ray; conceived by/d: Alan Bailey; set: Peter Harrison; md: John Foley & Mike Craver. Cast: Reathel Bean, Linda Kerns (*Susan Mansur*), Connie Ray, Kevin Chamberlin, Dan Manning, Jane Potter, Robert Olsen. "The Church in the Wildwood," "A Wonderful Time up There," "Meet Mother in the Skies," "No Tears in Heaven," "Christian Cowboy," "Jesus is Mine," "I'll Live a Million Years," "Everyone Home but Me," "Bringing in the Sheaves," "Whispering Hope," "Smoke on the Mountain," "I'll Fly Away," "When the Roll is Called up Yonder." Lamb's, 6/18/98–9/12/98. Prev from 6/6/98. 79 perf. d: Alan Bailey; set: Peter Harrison; light: Mary Jo Dondlinger; md: John Foley; arr: Mike Craver & Mark Hardwick. Cast: Constance Barron, Sean Dooley

2437. *Smoke Rings*. Musical revue. Harold Clurman, 11/4/92–11/8/92. 5 perf. w: Blanche Blakeny, Drew Pacholyk, William Perry Morgan. Cast: Jane Brockman, Candy Joseph, Ray Luetters, Dewey Moss

2438. *Snapshot*. Hudson Guild, 1/9/80–2/10/80. 30 perf. m: Herbert Kaplan; l: Mitchell Bernard; d: Thomas Gruenewald; md: Bruce Coyle. Cast: John Cunningham, Patti Karr, Helon Blount. "Snapshot," "Someday," "Watching the News," "Ballad of Sheldon Roth," "Point of View," "Queen of Hollywood," "Tell Me I'm Good," "Little Girl," "What Marriage Is," "Snapshot II"

2439. *The Snicker Factor*. Political satire. American Place, 2/9/87–2/20/87. 7 perf. m/md: Adrienne Torf; conceived by/d: Suzanne Bennett & Liz Diamond. Cast: Alma Cuervo, Edward Baran, Nancy Giles

2440. *Snow White and the Seven Dwarfs*. Radio City Music Hall, 10/18/79–11/18/79. 38 perf; brief tour; re-ran (slightly modified), same theatre, 1/11/80–3/9/80. 68 perf. movie mus: Frank Churchill; stage mus: Jay Blackton; l: Larry Morey & Joe Cook; based on Disney movie; adapted for stage by Joe Cook; d/ch: Frank Wagner; light: Ken Billington; exec md: Donald Pippin; orch: Philip J. Lang. Cast: Mary Jo Salerno, Richard Bowne, Anne Francine, Yolande Bavan, Lauren Lipson, Don Potter, Clifford Fearl, Norb Joerder, Kenneth Kantor, Caryl Tenney. "Welcome to the Kingdom," "I'm Wishing," "One Song," "With a Smile and a Song," "Whistle While You Work," "Heigh-Ho," "Bluddle-Iddle-Um-Dum" (The Washing Song), "Will I Ever See Her Again?," "The Dwarf's Yodel Song" (The Silly Song), "Some Day My Prince Will Come"

2441. *So Long, 174th Street*. David, a Bronx high school boy, works as druggist's assistant while taking 1st steps toward being actor. The musical numbers are reserved for David's fantasies. Wanda is his girlfriend. Set in NYC at the present time (i.e. 1976) and in late 1930s. Harkness, Middle Broadway, 4/27/76–5/9/76. 6 prev. 16 perf. p: Frederick Brisson, Harkness Organization & Wyatt Dickerson; m/l: Stan Daniels; b: Joseph Stein (based on his 1963 comedy *Enter Laughing*, from Carl Reiner's 1958 autobiographical novel); d: Burt Shevelove; ch: Alan Johnson; asst ch: Graciela Daniele; set: James Riley; cos: Stanley Simmons; light: Richard Nelson; md: John Lesko; orch: Luther Henderson; dance mus arr: Wally Harper; press: Solters & Roskin; prod super: Stone Widney; gm: Ralph Roseman; cm: John

A. Caruso; psm: Mortimer Halpern; sm: Bryan Young; asm: Jack Magradey. Cast: Robert Morse, Gene Varrone, Joe Howard, Freda Soiffer, Robert Barry, Richard Marr, David Berk, Nancy Killmer, Mitchell Jason, Loni Ackerman, Lawrence John Moss, Sydney Blake, Chuck Beard, Michael Blue Aiken, Barbara Lang (replaced Marian Winters during tryouts), George S. Irving, Lee Goodman, James Brennan, Jill Cook, Meribeth Kisner, Denise Mauthe, Rita Rudner, William Swiggard, Claudia Asbury, Jack Magradey. "David Kolowitz, the Actor," "It's Like," "(I'm) Undressing Girls with My Eyes," "Bolero on Rye," "Whoever You Are," "Say the Words," "You," "My Son the Druggist," "You Touched Her," "Men," "Boy Oh Boy," "The Butler's Song," "Being with You," "If You Want to Break My Father's Heart," "So Long 174th Street." Got 5 pans & a rave. Revised version by Mel Miller ran OB, at American Place, 3/7/99–3/23/99. 4 prev. 11 perf. Part of *Musicals Tonight!* series. In 2 acts, featuring 3 songs not heard in the 1976 prod–"The Man I Can Love," "Hot Cha Cha," "Ladies' Hats." d: Thomas Mills; md: Mark W. Hartman. Cast: George S. Irving, Kenny Raskin, Rachel Lynn Ricca, Jana Robbins, KT Sullivan, Sally Wilfert

2442. *So, Who Needs Marriage?* Gardner Centre, Brighton, England, 5/8/75–5/24/75. 17 perf. p: Brighton Festival; w: Monty Norman; d: Roger Redfarn; ch: Irving Davies; md: Bryan Bennett. Cast: Eric Flynn, Diana Coupland, June Ritchie, Jon Pertwee. It then toured; did not go to the West End

2443. *Soap*. Lion, 9/11/82–9/26/82. 16 perf. m/l: Aaron Egigian & David Man. Cast: Cindy Benson. "Martha by the Pyramids," "Born Blonde," "Share," "I'm the Only One That's Home," "Grovel," "Red Rover," "At the Singles Bar," "Early Efforts," "The Girl Who Has Everything," "The Days of My Lives," "The Good Stuff," "Weren't We Together," "Four Sides of the Coin"

2444. *Softly*. 1965. Never Produced. m/l: Harold Arlen & Martin Charnin; b: Hugh Wheeler. "That's a Fine Kind o' Freedom"

Solomon/Solomon see # 334, Main Book
Some Like It Hot see # 668, Main Book

2445. *Some Other Time*. 2 one-act musicals shown together. Library & Museum of Performing Arts, 5/4/70–5/5/70. 2 perf. p: Equity Library; d: Richard Mogavero. Cast: Hal Watters, Jessica Hull, Suellen Esty, Joan Maniscalco, Penny White, Christopher Barrett. The 1st play was *Les Jardins Publiques*, set in a park in provincial France in 1900. m/l: Mark Lamos & Philip Killian. "Les Jardins Publiques," "Sunday Morning," "Listen to the Band," "So Happy," "How Funny and Old," "You, My Dear," "Strange Frightening Feeling." The 2nd was *And I Bet You Wish You Was Me Now*, set in a small Mississippi town. m/l: Jane Staab & Philip Killian. "Lovely Music," "Ellisville," "Xylophone Man," "Lily," "Hope Chest," "And I Bet You Wish You Was Me Now"

Someone in April see # 118, Main Book

2446. *Someone Sort of Grandish*. Musical tribute to E.Y. "Yip" Harburg (featured 59 of

his songs). All Souls Unitarian Church, 1/22/76–1/26/76. 6 perf. Cast: Tran William Rhodes (also conceived/d), Kirby Lewellen (also ch), Hester Lewellen, Dana Coen, Linda Lipson

2447. *Something for the Boys*. Diverse heirs inherit ranch in Texas, but Army is maneuvering next door. Alvin, Broadway, 1/7/43–1/8/44. 422 perf. Rave reviews. p: Mike Todd; m/l: Cole Porter; b: Herbert & Dorothy Fields; d: Hassard Short; book d: Herbert Fields; ch: Jack Cole; set: Howard Bay; md/choral arr: William Parson; orch: Hans Spialek, Don Walker, Russell Bennett, Ted Royal. Cast: Ethel Merman, Paula Lawrence, Bill Johnson, Betty Garrett, Jed Prouty, Anita Alvarez, Betty Bruce, Bill Callahan, Allen Jenkins, Jack Cassidy & Dody Goodman (in chorus). "Announcement of Inheritance," "See that You're Born in Texas," "When My Baby Goes to Town," "Something for the Boys," "When We're Home on the Range," "Could it Be You?," "Hey, Good Lookin'," "He's a Right Guy," "The Leader of a Big Time Band," "I'm in Love with a Soldier Boy," "There's a Happy Land in the Sky," "By the Mississinewah." Betty Garrett played the lead for a week when Ethel Merman was sick. Glasgow, Scotland, Christmas 1943; London, 3/44. ADMA' Studio One, NYC, 11/27/81–12/20/81. 20 perf. p: Jerry Bell; d/ch: Tod Jackson; md: Bruce Kirle. Cast: Austin Adams, Karen Babcock, Carleton Carpenter, Patti Karr, Frank Kosik, Wade Laboissonniere, Rosemary Loar, Virginia Martin, Scott Willis

2448. *Something in the Air*. Theatre Royal, Birmingham, England, 8/24/43 (3 weeks); Palace, London, 9/23/43–7/8/44. 336 perf; toured; Palace, 10/5/44–2/24/45. 163 perf. m: Manning Sherwin; l: Max Kester & Harold Purcell; b: Arthur Macrae, Archie Menzies, Jack Hulbert; d: Jack Hulbert; ch: Buddy Bradley & Jack Hulbert; cos: Norman Hartnell, etc; md: Robert Probst. Cast: Jack Hulbert, Cicely Courtneidge, Ronald Shiner

2449. *Something Nasty in the Woodshed*. Theatre Royal, Stratford East, London, 10/18/65–11/6/65. 20 perf. m: Nick Transem; l: Irving Manley; b/d: Adrian Rendle; based on novel *Cold Comfort Farm*, by Stella Gibbons; ch: Denys Palmer; set/cos: Disley Jones; md: Anthony Bowles. Cast: Jennifer Jayne, Peter Brookes, Rosemary Nichols

2450. *Something Wonderful*. Celebration of lyricist Oscar Hammerstein II (1895–1960), on what would have been his 100th birthday. Gershwin, Broadway, 7/12/95. 1 perf. p: Rodgers & Hammerstein Organization/Livent (U.S.)/Bert Fink; md: Eric Stern & Catherine Matejka. Cast: Theodore S. Chapin (host), Maureen McGovern, Liz Callaway, Joel Blum, Garth Drabinsky, William Hammerstein, Audra McDonald, Doug LaBrecque, Rebecca Luker, Michel Bell, Dorothy Stanley, Jonathan Dokuchitz, Schuyler G. Chapin. "A Cockeyed Optimist," "Oh, What a Beautiful Mornin'," "Can I Forget You?," "A Wonderful Guy," "Stan' up and Fight," "All er Nothin'," "All the Things You Are," "Something Wonderful," "Suddenly Lovely"

2451. *Something Wonderful: A Richard Rodgers Celebration in Song*. Town Hall,

6//3/05 (one night only concert). Cast: Heather MacRae, KT Sullivan, Craig Rubano, Mark Nadler

2452. *Sondheim: A Celebration at Carnegie Hall*. Gala benefit. Carnegie Hall, 6/10/92. 1 perf. w: David Thompson; d: Scott Ellis; ch: Susan Stroman; md: Paul Gemignani; cast recording on RCA. Cast: Bill Irwin, Madeline Kahn, Patti LuPone, Dorothy Loudon, Betty Buckley, Liza Minnelli, Karen Ziemba, Victor Garber, Daisy Eagan, Richard Muenz, James Naughton, Robert La Fosse, George Lee Andrews, Bernadette Peters, Stephen Sondheim, Maureen Moore

2453. *Sondheim Tonight*. Barbican, London, 5/17/98. m/l: Stephen Sondheim; b: Hugh Wooldridge. Cast: David Kernan, Elaine Stritch, Maria Friedman, Millicent Martin, Clive Rowe, Len Cariou, Michael Ball, Cleo Laine, Julia McKenzie, Steve Sondheim, Dame Edna Everage, Ned Sherrin. "Overture for Stephen Sondheim," "Comedy Tonight," "March to the Treaty House," "Next," "The Ballad of Sweeney Todd," "Night Waltz," "Losing My Mind," "Not While I'm Around," "Send in the Clowns," "Stavisky Suite," "A Very Short Violin Sonata," "The Ladies Who Lunch," "More," "A Salute to Stephen Sondheim," "Company," "Barcelona," "Good Thing Going," "Not a Day Goes By," "Never Do Anything Twice," "Variations on a Theme (Katie Malone)," "Beautiful Girls," "Loving You," "Broadway Baby," "Being Alive," "Another Hundred People," "Sunday in the Park with George"

2454. *Song for a Saturday*. Play with mus. Set in 1946. American Jewish Theatre, 5/9/87–6/28/87. 28 prev. 17 perf. m/l: Jule Styne & Don Black; b: Jack Rosenthal; d: Robert Kalfin; ch: Larry Hayden; cos: Gail Cooper-Hecht; md: Buster Davis. Cast: Mary Gutzi, Michael Callan, Mary Stout, Michael Cone, Eleanor Reissa. "Always Me," "The Cohens Are Coming," "Why," "If Only a Little Bit Sticks," "I'm Grown Up," "This Time Tomorrow," "The Howards of the World," "We've Done Alright," "Simcha," "You Wouldn't Be You," "Kill Me," "Why Did I Do It?," "Only Myself to Blame," "That's Grown Up," "Hamakom," "I've Just Begun"

2455. *A Song for Cyrano*. Opened 6/18/73, Westport Country Playhouse, Conn. Closed 9/16/73, Pocono Playhouse, Mountainhome, Pa., without making Broadway. p/d: Jose Ferrer; m/l: Robert Wright & George Forrest; h: Jose Ferrer (he used the name "J. Vincent Smith"). Cast: Jose Ferrer, Willi Burke, Don McKay, Edmund Lyndeck, Keith Kaldenberg, Marshall Borden, Helon Blount, Adam Petroski

2456. *Song Night in the City*. Musical revue, with songs & dances on theme of romance. Orpheum, 1980. p/md: Karen Manno; conceived/d: John Braswell; add arr: The Song Night Band

2457. *The Song of Jacob Zulu*. Drama with mus. Set in South Africa in the 1980s. Plymouth, Broadway, 3/24/93–5/9/93. 11 prev from 3/17/93. 53 perf. p: Steppenwolf Theatre Co.; m: Ladysmith Black Mambazo; l/w: Tug

Yourgrau; d: Eric Simonson. Cast: Garry Becker, K. Todd Freeman, Danny Johnson, Erika L. Heard, Gary DeWitt Marshall, Tania Richard, Zakes Mokae

2458. *Song of Singapore*. Zany melodrama set on Singapore waterfront in 1941. 17 Irving Place, 5/23/91–6/30/92. 18 prev from 5/7/91. 459 perf. p: Steven Baruch, Richard Frankel, Thomas Viertel, Allen Spivak, Larry Magid; m/l: Eric Frandsen, Robert Hipkens, Michael Garin, Paula Lockheart; d: A.J. Antoon; set: John Lee Beatty; light: Peter Kaczorowski; cast recording on DRG. Cast: Donna Murphy (*Jaquey Maltby, Andrea Green*), Cathy Foy, Eric Frandsen, Michael Garin, Robert Hipkens. "Song of Singapore," "Inexpensive Tango," "I Miss My Home in Haarlem," "You Gotta Do What You Gotta Do," "The Rose of Rangoon," "Necrology," "Sunrise," "Never Pay Musicians What They're Worth," "Harbor of Love," "I Can't Remember," "I Want to Get Offa This Island," "Foolish Geese," "Serve it Up," "Fly Away Rose," "I Remember," "Shake, Shake, Shake," "We're Rich." Chichester, England (ran there twice); Mayfair, London, 7/2/01–9/9/01. Prev from 6/28/01. d: Roger Redfarn. Cast: Issy Van Randwyck

Songbook see # 457, Main Book

2459. *Songs for a New World*. Musical revue, or song-cycle. Series of tunes loosely focused on change, newness & discovery. WPA, 10/11/95–11/5/95. 15 prev. 12 perf. m/l: Jason Robert Browne; d: Daisy Prince; ch: Michael Arnold; orch: Brian Besterman & Jason Robert Browne. Cast: Brooks Ashmanskas, Andrea Burns, Jessica Molaskey, Billy Porter. "The New World," "On the Deck of a Spanish Sailing Ship, 1492," "Just One Step," "I'm Not Afraid of Anything," "The River Won't Flow," "The Stars and the Moon" [the hit], "She Cries," "The Steam Train," "The World Was Dancing," "Surabaya-Santa," "Christmas Lullaby," "King of the World," "I'd Give it All for You," "Flagmaker, 1775," "Flying Home," "Hear My Song." Crepe de Paris Dinner Cabaret, Seattle, 9/5/02–10/12/02. d: Bill Berry; md: R.J. Tancioco. Cast: Louis Hobson, Ann Evans, Anna Lauris, Ty Willis

2460. *Songs of Addiction*. Evening of poetry, music & humor. Broome Street, 5/8/91–5/26/91. 2 prev. 21 perf. m/l: Dave Hall & Robert Douglas Walters; d: Cheryl Katz. Cast: Lisa Lyons, Marcia Mintz, Cathy Diane Tomlin

2461. *Songs of Paradise*. Susan Stein Shiva Theatre (NY Shakespeare Festival & Joseph Papp Yiddish Theatre), 1/23/89–5/21/89. 8 prev from 1/17/89. 134 perf. m: Rosalie Gerut; b: Miriam Hoffman & Rena Berkowicz Borow; based on biblical poetry of Itzik Manger; d: Avi Hoffman; ch: Eleanor Reissa. Cast: Adrienne Cooper, Rosalie Gerut, Avi Hoffman, David Kener, Eleanor Reissa. "The Twilight," "Khave and the Apple Tree," "Odem and Khave Duet," "Song of Blessings," "The Farewell Song." Astor Place, 11/13/89–12/10/89. Prev from 11/3/89. 32 perf. Harry Peerce replaced David Kener during this run

2462. *Songs on a Shipwrecked Sofa*. Vineyard, 5/21/87–6/21/87. 30 perf. m/l/b: Polly

Pen & James Milton; based on poems by Mervyn Peake; d: Andre Ernotte. Cast: Alma Cuervo. "O'er Seas that Have No Beaches," "Pygmies, Palms and Pirates," "The Sunlight," "Dear Children," "It is Most Best," "Lean Sideways on the Wind," "The Men in Bowler Hats," "I Cannot Give the Reasons," "All Flowers that Die," "I Have My Price," "Leave the Stronger and the Lesser Things to Me," "The Threads Remain"

2463. *Songs You Might Have Missed*. Featuring songs cut from shows, songs from unproduced shows, or songs that were just overlooked. Steve McGraw's, 10/5/90–10/26/90. 4 perf; 3/11/91–4/1/91. 4 perf. Cast: Alix Korey

2464. *Sons o' Fun*. Olsen & Johnson Vaudeville revue. Winter Garden, Broadway, 12/1/41; 46th Street Theatre, 3/29/43–8/9/43. Total of 742 perf. p: Messrs Shubert; m/l: Jack Yellen & Sammy Fain; add m & l: Jay Livingston & Ray Evans; sk: Ole Olsen & Chic Johnson; d/light: Edward Duryea Dowling; ch: Robert Alton; set: Raoul Pene du Bois; prod super: Harry Kaufman; md: John McManus; voc arr: Pembroke Davenport. Cast: Ole Olsen & Chic Johnson, Carmen Miranda, Ella Logan, Frank Libuse, Joe Besser. "The Joke's on Us," "It's a New Kind of Thing," "Happy in Love," "Thank You, South America," "Thank You, North America," "It's a Mighty Fine Country We Have Here," "Hi-Ho, the Hoe-Down Way," "Manuelo," "Tete a Tete," "Let's Say Goodnight with a Dance"

2465. *Soon*. Rock opera. Group of young musicians come to NY & achieve popular success, but suffer from it. Ritz, Middle Broadway, 1/12/71–1/13/71. 21 prev, 3 perf. p: Bruce W. Stark & Sagittarius Prods (Edgar M. Bronfman & Henry S. White); m/l: Joseph Martinez Kookoolis & Scott Fagan; b: Robert Greenwald, Joseph Martinez Kookoolis, Scott Fagan (all uncredited); based on orig story by Joseph Martinez Kookoolis & Scott Fagan; adapted by: Martin Duberman; d: Robert Greenwald (uncredited); add staging: Gerald Freedman; ch: Fred Benjamin; set: Kert Lundell; cos: David Chapman; light: Jules Fisher; audio design: Jack Shearing; md: Louis St. Louis; voc arr: Louis St. Louis & Jacqueline Penn; orch: Howard Wyeth & Jon Huston. Cast: Barry Bostwick, Marta Heflin, Dennis Belline, Richard Gere (6th billed, as Michael), Joseph Campbell Butler, Peter Allen, Marion Ramsey, Leata Galloway, Vicki Sue Robinson, Rita Pamela Pentony, Nell Carter, Del Hinkley, Singer Williams, Michael Jason, John C. Nelson, Angus Cairns, Larry Spinelli, Paul Eichel, Tony Middleton, Pendleton Brown. Pitshit: Richard Apuzzo, Tim Case, Sonny Coppola, Adam Ippolito, Louis St. Louis. "Let the World Begin Again," "In Your Hands," "I See the Light"/"Gentle Sighs," "Roll Out the Morning," "Everybody's Running," "Henry is Where it's At," "Music, Music," "Glad to Know Ya," "Rita Cheeta," "Henry's Dream Theme," "To Touch the Sky," The Chase: "Everybody's Running" (reprise), "Marketing, Marketing," "Sweet Henry Loves You," "One More Time," "Straight," "Wait," "Faces, Names, Places," "Annie's Thing," "Doing the High," "Soon,"

"Country Store Living," "What's Gonna Happen to Me?," "On the Charts," "Molecules," "So Much that I Know," "Child of Sympathy," "Frustration," "It Won't Be Long." Peter Allen replaced Scott Fagan in the lead during previews. Divided reviews, mostly bad. This was the prod that re-established the Ritz as a legit (limited) Broadway theatre (it had been a radio & TV studio since 1939, and in 1990 would become the Walter Kerr Theatre)

2466. *Sophie.* Jewish Rep, 10/17/87–11/22/87. 20 perf. m: Debra Barsha; l/b: Rose Leiman Goldemberg; based on life of Sophie Tucker, but not in any other way connected to 1963 Broadway show of same name; d: Louis O. Erdmann; ch: Eugenia V. Erdmann. Cast: Sophie: Judith Cohen; Anna: Lorraine Goodman; Papa/Ziegfeld: Adam Heller; Mollie: Ernestine Jackson. "Soup," "Nice Girls Don't Do That," "Gonna Be Somebody," "Keep Movin'," "De Bluebells," "My Man," "Don't Forget Your Mama," "Pushcart Sellers," "Black Up," "My Terms," "We Still Love Her," "She'll Thank Me," "Playing the Part of the Maid," "Sophie's Love Song," "You Think it's Easy to Love Her," "She's Comin' to Town," "How Many?," "The Looka Song," "Sophie's Waltz," "What Do Women Want?," "Baby Pictures," "One Night Stands," "Mollie's Song"

2467. *Soul Train.* Classic soul hits. Victoria Palace, London, 6/22/99–9/4/99. Prev from 6/16/99. dev: Mark Clements & Michael Vivian. Cast: Sheila Ferguson, Sharon Benson, Danny John-Jules

2468. *Space Is So Startling.* Westminster Theatre, London, 12/19/62. 51 perf. m: Herbert Allen, Richard Hadden, Cecil Broadhurst; l/b: Peter & Anthony Howard; d: Martin Flutsch; cast recording on Philips. Cast: Herbert Allen, Cecil Broadhurst, Ilene Godfrey, John Sayre, Tom Kennedy. "Sleep On!," "Millions of Years Ago," "Why Worry?," "It Would Help a Lot to Squat," "Any Moment Now," "We've Got to Be First," "What do the Eyes of the Millions Seek?," "Have You a Place for Me up There?," "If Only," "Sportsmen of the World," "Space is So Startling," "Where's That Basket?," "Do You See What I See?," "Peace Be Upon You," "It Works!," "The World Can Be One Family"

2469. *Space Trek, a Musical Parody.* Set aboard the Spaceship *Merchandise.* Chelsea Playhouse, 2/16/97–3/9/97. 5 prev from 2/13/97. 29 perf. p: Joyce M. Sarner; m/l: Rick Crom; b: Marc Lipitz; d: Vincent Sassone; ch: Karen Molnar; md: John Bowen. Cast: Capt. Slim Quirk: Jason Hayes; Capt. Christian Spike: Hank Jacobs; Mr. Schlock: Shawn Sears; Lt Yomama: Michelle Merring; Dr. Moans: Randy Lake; Chief Engineer Sloshy: Billy Sharpe; Ensign Chicks-Love: Adam Wald; Ensign Bambi: Stephanie Jean. "Captain of the Ship," "Shoulda Been, Coulda Been Mine," "The Ballad of Happy Planet," "Hello Boys," "The Problem with Us," "Ensign's Lament," "Picnic on a Planet," "Amour Time," "To Be a Captain," "Brain Drain," "Spike's Turn," "Got to Get a Life"

Spamalot see Monty Python's Spamalot

2470. *Sparrow in Flight.* Based on life of Ethel Waters. AMAS, 11/2/78–11/19/78. 12 perf.

conceived by Rosetta Le Noire; d: Dean Irby; ch/cos: Bernard Johnson. Cast: Ethel Ayler, Charles Brown, Don Paul, Pauletta Pearson, Fran Salisbury, Sandra Phillips, William "Gregg" Hunter, Mary Louise

2471. *The Special.* Set in Montreal in 1980. Jewish Rep, 10/19/85–11/17/85. 27 perf. m/md: Galt MacDermot; l/b: Mike Gutwillig; d: Ran Avni; ch: Haila Strauss. Cast: Paul Ukena, Sam Stoneburner, Adam Heller, Patricia Ben Peterson, Olga Merediz, Mina Bern, Steve Sterner. "What's So Special About a Special?," "The Situation in Quebec," "There is an Old Tradition," "Quebec, Oui!," "Non, Merci!," "Longue Vie a la Famille!," "Cote-St.-Jacques," "Will You Be My Yvette?," "Married Yet," "We Say Oui!," "J'pas Capable!," "A Ruling is a Ruling," "It isn't Easy to Be a Jew," "Alleluia, Alleluia," "On My Heart," "A Special!," "What Will People Think?," "I Don't Want that You Don't Want," "Notre Pere," "Shema," "God's Favorite Choice," "Raise a Glass to Love," "Ess ees mein Kind," "Swing Your Heart out le Bon Dieu"

2472. *Speed Gets the Poppys.* Stylized musical melodrama with strong anti-drug message. Set on the Poppys' farm. Mercer-Brecht, 7/25/72–7/30/72. 7 perf. m/l: Lorenzo Fuller & Lila Levant; d/ch: Charles Abbott. Cast: Edward Penn, Robin Field, Anita Keal. "What is a Melodrama?," "Living Next Door to the Sun," "Instant Magic," "Caught," "Whatever Happened to Tomorrow?," "Take it from a Pal," "I'll Bring the Roses," "Speed Won't Get Me," "What Real True Friends Are For," "Try, Try Again," "My Moustache is Twitchin'," "An Old-Fashioned Chase," "Good Triumphs Over Evil"

2473. *Spend Spend Spend.* Rags to riches story. West Yorkshire Playhouse, England; Piccadilly, London, 10/12/99–8/5/00. Prev from 10/5/99. Cast: Barbara Dickson (*Diane Langton* from 7/24/00), Steve Houghton, Rachel Leskovac, Mary Stockley

2474. *A Spinning Tale.* Fantasy loosely based on Rumpelstiltskin story. Playhouse 91, 2/20/90–5/11/90. 92 perf. p/set: Mariner James Pezza; m/orch: C.E. Kemeny; l/b: C.E. Kemeny & A. Kemeny; d: Jack Ross & C.E. Kemeny. Cast: Sally O'Shea (also ch). "A Spinning Tale," "Fall Under the Spell," "The Last Elf Aria," "Another Life," "Remember the Time," "Hello, Stranger!," "Straw into Gold," "Locked and Secluded," "Spin! Spin! Spin!," "Gold! Gold!"/"I Have a Little Secret," "Together as One," "The Shadow," "What's in a Name," "Precious to Me," "Never Met a Man I Didn't Like," "Ah, Sweet Youth!," "Trust Me Tango," "You Get What You Give." Previously produced on a tour of Connecticut theatres

2475. *The Spitfire Grill.* Percy, a female ex-con, goes to Gilead, a small Wisconsin town, to try to start anew. She works at the *Spitfire Grill,* a restaurant run by Hannah. It is basically the story of their relationship. George Street Playhouse, NJ, 11/29/00–12/23/00. Prev from 11/25/00. m/orch: Jacques Valcq; l: Fred Alley; b: Jacques Valcq & Fred Alley; based on 1996 film of same name written by David Lee Zlotoff; d: David Saint; ch: Luis Perez; set: Michael Anania; cos: Theoni V. Aldredge;

light: Howell Binkley. Cast: Beth Fowler, Garrett Long, Janet Metz, Susan Mansur, Armand Schultz. "Ring Around the Moon," "Something's Cooking at the Spitfire Grill," "Out of the Frying Pan," "When Hope Goes," "Ice and Snow," "The Colors of Paradise," "Digging Stone," "This Wide Woods," "Forgotten Lullaby," "Shoot the Moon," "Come Alive Again," "Wild Bird," "Shine," "Way Back Home." Had hopes for Broadway run. Fred Alley died 5/1/01, aged 38. Duke on 42nd Street, 10/2/01–10/14/01. 15 perf. Prev from 9/7/01. p: Playwrights Horizons. Same basic crew except sound: Scott Stauffer; md: Andrew Wilder. Cast: Liz Callaway, Mary Gordon Murray, Phyllis Somerville, Garrett Long, Steven Pasquale, Armand Schultz, Stephen Sinclair. Cast recording made 12/17/01 & released 4/22/02, on Triangle Road. Florida Stage, Manalapan, 6/28/02–9/1/02. Prev from 6/25/02. d: Bill Castellino; set: Michael Anania; light: Jim Fulton; md: Christopher McGovern. Cast: Kathryn Blake, Heather Ayers, Melinda Tanner. Milwaukee (home town of the authors), fall 2002. Cast: Garrett Long, Phyllis Somerville, Kate Weatherhead, Elizabeth Moliter, Robert Boles. Southern California Theatre, 10/29/02–12/1/02. On 11/21/02 Kathryn Blake stepped in for a sick Misty Cotton on 24 hours notice

2476. *Splendora.* Young man returns (in guise of a woman) to East Texas town of Splendora to face his past after 15-year absence. American Place, 11/9/95–11/19/95. 9 prev from 11/1/95. 14 perf. m: Stephen Hoffman; l: Mark Campbell; b: Peter Webb; based on novel by Edward Swift; d: Jack Hofsis; ch: Robert La Fosse; set: Eduardo Sicangco; cos: William Ivey Long; light: Richard Nelson; md: Sariva Goetz; orch: Michael Gibson. Cast: Evalyn Baron, KT Sullivan, Laura Kenyon, Nancy Johnston, Michael Moore. "In Our Hearts," "How Like Heaven," "Don't Get Me Started," "Pretty Boy," "Poor Sad Thing," "A Hymn to Her," "Up at Dawn," "In Small and Simple Ways," "Warms My Soul," "Dear Heart," "How Little I Know," "Good Hearts Rejoice," "Promise Me One Thing," "I Got Faith in You," "All the Time in the World," "A Man Named Dewey," "Grateful." Previously produced, in this prod, by the Bay Street Theatre, Sag Harbor, Long Island. Revised & revived at Chelsea Playhouse, 2/8/00–3/26/00. 9 prev. 33 perf. d/ch: Donna Drake; md: Jeffrey Biering. Cast: Kristine Zbornik

2477. *Spook Scandals.* President, Broadway, 12/8/44–12/9/44. 2 perf. p: The Michael Todd Midnight Players, members of the casts of the recent prods *Catherine Was Great, Mexican Hayride* and *Pick-up Girl* (only *Mexican Hayride* being a musical); conceived by/d: Jerry Sylvon. Basically it comprised 3 one-act plays: *The Gobi Curse,* by Arthur Gondra; *The Coffin Room,* by Al Henderson; and *The Blind Monster,* by Jerry Sylvon. Songs & comic acts were added to the program between these plays. orig m: Sergio DeKarlo; ch: Paul Haakon, Marta Nita, Paul Reyes; light: Sammy Lambert. Cast: Don De Leo, Gedda Petry, Al Henderson, Dean Myles, Mila Niemi, Eva Reyes, Kendal Bryson

2478. *Spoon River Anthology*. Dramatic reading of the verse of Edgar Lee Masters. Set in Spoon River, Ill., at turn of 20th century. Booth, Broadway, 9/29/63–11/16/63; Belasco, 11/18/63–1/4/64. Total of 111 perf. p: Joseph Cates; m: Naomi Caryl Hirshhorn; l/conceived by/d: Charles Aidman; light: Jules Fisher. Cast: Charles Aidman, Robert Elston, Betty Garrett, Joyce Van Patten. "He's Gone Away," "Illinois," "Soldier, Oh Soldier," "Times Are Getting Hard, Boys," "The Water is Wide," "Paper of Pins," "Freedom," "Three Nights Drunk," "Far Away from Home," "In the Night," "Mornin's Come," "God Bless the Moon," "Sow Took the Measles," "Who Knows Where I'm Goin'," "My Rooster," "I Am, I Am," "A Horse Named Bill," "Spoon River." Orig prod by Theatre Group, University extension, UCLA. Prod many times since around the world, one of the latest being the 2002 prod at Theatre West, L.A. d: Betty Garrett & Joyce Van Patten (mostly Miss Van Patten). Cast: Lee Meriwether, Bridget Hanley, Drew Katzman

2479. *Spotlight*. Set between 1955 and the present. National, Washington, DC, 1/11/78–1/14/78. Canceled Broadway opening at the Palace. p: Sheldon R. Lubliner & David Black; m: Jerry Bresler; l: Lyn Duddy; b: Richard Seff (he replaced Leonard Starr, upon whose story the libretto was based); d: David Black; ch: Tony Stevens; set: Robert Randolph; cos: Robert Mackintosh; md: Jack Lee; dance mus arr: Wally Harper; cm: Steven Suskin. Cast: Gene Barry, Lenora Nemetz, D'Jamin Bartlett, Polly Rowles, Marc Jordan, David-James Carroll, James Braet, Michon Peacock. Carleton Carpenter (standby for Gene Barry). "No Regrets," "What Am I Bid?," "Spotlight," "You Need Someone," "Round and Round," "Tricks of the Trade," "Notice Me," "Everything," "Didn't You Used to Be Him?," "Such a Business," "The Stranger in the Glass," "You Are You," "Where is Everybody?." This is the one where a reviewer said "Gene Barry dances like an arthritic pugilist"

2480. *Spring in Brazil*. Opened 10/1/45, Shubert, Boston. Closed 1/12/46, Great Northern, Chicago, failing to make Broadway. p: Monte Proser & the Shuberts; m/l: Robert Wright & George Forrest; b: Philip Rapp; d: John Murray Anderson; ch: Marjery Fielding; set: Howard Bay. Cast: Milton Berle, Christine Ayres (*Dorothy De Winter*), Rose Marie (*Mary Healy*), John Cherry (*Harry Sothern*), Bernice Parks (*Marion Colby*), Gene Blakeley (*Jack Collins*), Don Arres (*Dean Campbell*), Randolph Symonette (*Howard Hoffman*), Roger Ohardieno, Joseph Macaulay, Jack McCauley, Morton J. Stevens, Talley Beatty, LaVerne French, Jack Cassidy. "Fernando," "Our Day," "Little Ol' Boy," "Chi-ni-gui-chi," "Riot in Rio," "Spring in Brazil," "Frenetica," "Samba at Daybreak," "The Bean of the Coffee Tree," "New Worlds," "Rough, Rugged and Robust," "Arupan Ballet," "Carnival in Rio"

2481. *Squonk*. An entertainment. P.S. 122, 6/11/99–8/28/99. 60 perf. p: William Repicci & Michael Minichiello; m: Jackie Dempsey with Squonk; l: Jana Losey with Jackie Dempsey; Steve O'Hearn & Jackie Dempsey created,

in collaboration with orig NY Squonk Ensemble (Casi Pacilio, Kevin Kornicki, Jana Losey, T. Weldon Anderson); d: Tom Diamond; ch: Jana Losey; set/puppets/cos: Steve O'Hearn; md: Jackie Dempsey. The cast (Miss Dempsey, Mr. O'Hearn, Mr. Anderson, Mr. Kornicki) all played instruments on stage. Jana Losey was vocalist. It picked up additional producers & moved to Broadway's Helen Hayes, 2/29/00–3/26/00. 24 prev from 2/8/00. 32 perf. But it was too small a prod for Broadway

2482. *Stag Movie*. Blue movie is filmed in motel room near Kennedy Airport. Gate, 1/3/71–3/21/71. 89 perf. p: Robert L. Steele; m/md: Jacques Urbont; l/b: David Newburge; d: Bernard Barrow; ch: Doug Rogers. Cast: Hy Anzell, Brad Sullivan (*Gene GeBauer* from 3/2/71), Adrienne Barbeau, Josip Elic. "Stag Movie," "Looking at the Sun," "I Want More Out of Life than This," "Grocery Boy," "Splendor in the Grass," "It's So Good," "Get in Line," "Try a Trio," "Get Your Rocks off Rock," "We Came Together"

2483. *Stages*. New cabaret musical. Panache Encore, 4/13/88–5/25/88. 1 prev. 12 perf. m/conceived by: Elaine Chelton; add m: Leslie Harnley; l: Elaine Chelton & Tony Michael Pann; d/ch/set: Jim Coleman. Cast: Tony Michael Pann, Ann Brown, Barry Burns, Brooks Almy, Elly Barbour. "Showtime Tonight," "What Could Go Wrong," "Queen of the Bus and Trucks," "Tonight I Get That Chance Again," "My Magnificent Career," "My Nerves Are Shot to Hell," "In the Footlights," "The Trouble with Men," "Blue Violets," "My Old Friend," "I'm Coming Back Again," "One More Beat of the Drum," "Where Did the Magic Go?"

2484. *Staggerlee*. R & B musical. Set at local corner bar, in Deep South, in late 1950s. Second Avenue, 3/18/87–6/28/87. 32 prev from 2/27/87. 86 perf. m/l: Allen Toussaint; b/d/add l: Vernel Bagneris; based on New Orleans folk tale about bold young man's romance with young girl against wishes of her scheming mother; ch: Pepsi Bethel. Cast: Adam Wade, Juanita Brooks, Ruth Brown, Marva Hicks, Reginald Veljohnson, Carol Sutton. "Iko Iko," "Night People," "Staggerlee," "Discontented Blues," "With You in Mind," "Big Chief," "Mardi Gras Time," "A Pimp Like That," "You Knew I Was No Good," "Lover of Love," "Saved by Grace," "Happy Time," "Victims of the Darkness," "Devil's Disguise," "Our Monkey Don't Stop No Show," "Ruler of My Heart," "Going Down Slowly," "Lighting a Candle," "Knocking Myself Out," "We're Gonna Do It Good," "Let's Live it Up"

2485. *Stand and Deliver*. A bawdy ballad. Royal Lyceum, Edinburgh, Scotland, 9/20/72; Roundabout, London, 10/24/72–11/5/72. Prev from 10/21. 14 perf. m/l/story: Monty Norman; b: Wolf Mankowitz; d/ch: Wendy Toye; md: Robert Stewart. Cast: Nicky Henson, Derek Godfrey, Anna Dawson, Paul Hardwick, James Cairncross

2486. *Standup Shakespeare*. Musical revue. Shakespearian dialogue & lyr applied to jazzy love songs & other modern subjects. Theatre 890, 4/4/87–4/5/87. 2 perf. p: Shubert Organization; m: Ray Leslee; conceived by/md: Ray

Leslee & Kenneth Welsh; words: William Shakespeare; d: Mike Nichols; set: John Arnone. Cast: Kenneth Welsh, Taborah Johnson, Thomas Young

2487. *Star and Garter*. Burlesque revue. Music Box, Broadway, 6/24/42–12/4/43. 1 prev. 609 perf. p: Mike Todd; m/l: Irving Berlin, Al Dubin, Harold Rome, Harold Arlen, Johnny Mercer, etc; d: Hassard Short; ch: Al White Jr.; set: Harry Horner; cos: Irene Sharaff; md: Raymond Sinatra. Cast: Bobby Clark, Gypsy Rose Lee (a big investor), Pat Harrington, Richard Rober, Joe Lyons. "Star and Garter Girls," "Clap Your Hands," "Les Sylphides avec la Bumpe," "In the Malamute Saloon," "The Girl on the Police Gazette," "Bunny" (replaced during run by "Money"), "For a Quarter," "Don't Take on More than You Can Do," "I Can't Strip to Brahms," "Blues in the Night," "Robert the Roue," "I Don't Get It," "Brazilian Nuts"

2488. *Star Maker*. King's, Glasgow, Scotland, 2/13/56 (2 weeks); toured. Never made the West End. p: Bernard Delfont; m: Cyril Ornadel; l: David Croft; b: Ian Stuart Black; add songs: Harold Purcell & John Aldis, and Knight & Friedman; d: Jack Hulbert; ch: Mark Stuart; cos: Berkeley Sutcliffe; md: Harold Collins. Cast: Jerry Wayne, Jack Hulbert, June Laverick, Cicely Courtneidge, Peter Gilmore, Gladys Henson, Una Stubbs

2489. *Starboard Home*. Set aboard ship in English Channel & North Atlantic, New Year's Eve, 1899. Sardi's, 9/12/99; Triad, 11/7/99–12/19/99 (Sun nights only). m/md: Chuck Muckle; l/b: David Eisner; d: Charles Michel; ch: Patrick Loy. Cast: Jill Geddes (*Kathy Brier*), Seth Teter, Matt Walton, Kelly King. "At Sea," "Wake up and Love," "Lie, Lie, Lie," "Decisions, Decisions," "Looking for the Joy," "Take Care," "Fit for the Fight," "Piccadilly Posh," "Singularly Unprepared," "No More," "Never Mind," "The Time and Place," "Lexi's Lament," "Little One," "Take the Turn"

2490. *Starlight Roof*. Revue. Hippodrome, London, 1947 (18 months). m: George Melachrino; l: Eric Maschwitz & Matt Brooks. Cast: Barbara Perry, Fred Emney, Vic Oliver, Julie Andrews (London debut). "South America, Take it Away" (Harold Rome's song from *Call Me Mister*)

2491. *Starmania*. Rock opera, France's biggest musical theatre hit. 1st released as concept album in 1978. Palais des Congres, Paris, 4/10/79. m: Michel Shepherd; l: Luc Plamondon; d: Tom O'Horgan. Cast: France Gall, Daniel Balavoine, Diane Dufresne, Nanette Workman. New, reduced, version opened in Paris, 9/15/88. In 1992 Tim Rice wrote English lyr for studio recording led by Cyndi Lauper, Tom Jones, and Celine Dion. It was called "Tycoon." A new prod opened at the Mogador, Paris, 9/28/93. d: Lewis Furey. It has been prod in several countries, notably Canada

2492. *Stars in Your Eyes*. Set in Milford & Bloomfield, 2 small American towns, in 1862. The Man in the Moon plays Cupid. Not connected to the 1939 musical comedy by Arthur Schwartz & Dorothy Fields. Cherry Lane, 10/24/99–11/28/99. 27 prev from 10/1/99. 39

perf. m/l/b: Chip Meyrelles; d: Gabriel Barre; ch: Jennifer Paulson Lee; set: James Youmans; sound: Brian Ronan; md: Georgia Stitt. Cast: James Stovall, Heather MacRae, Crista Moore, David M. Lutken, Barbara Walsh, John Braden, Christy Carlson Romano. "Endless Possibilities," "Somebody (More or Less) Like Me," "Can't Say for Sure," "That's What They Said," "I'm Leigh Hunt-Smith," "Another Day," "Dance by Numbers," "Must Be Something," "Saturn Rising," "Stars in Your Eyes," "I've Got a Light on You," "Men!," "Thinking the Impossible," "Ordinary Jo," "The Best of Everything," "Why Do We Dance?," "Conventional Wisdom," "Take Me to Heart"

2493. Startime. Revue. Unrelated to 1944 Broadway show. London Palladium, 3/30/59. 48 perf. dev/d: Robert Nesbitt. Cast: Frankie Vaughan, Roy Castle, The Kaye Sisters

2494. *Starting Here, Starting Now*. Musical revue. Barbarann Theatre Restaurant, 3/7/77–6/19/77. 120 perf. m: David Shire; l/d: Richard Maltby Jr.; ch: Ethel Martin; cos: Stanley Simmons; md: Robert W. Preston. Cast: Loni Ackerman, George Lee Andrews, Margery Cohen. "The Word is Love," "Starting Here, Starting Now," "A Little Bit Off," "I Think I May Want to Remember Today," "Beautiful," "We Can Talk to Each Other," "Across the River," "Crossword Puzzle," "Autumn," "I Don't Remember Christmas," "I Don't Believe It," "I Hear Bells," "I'm Going to Make You Beautiful," "Pleased with Myself," "Hey There Fans," "Girl of the Minute," "(I'm a) Girl You Should Know," "Travel," "Watching the Parade Go By," "Flair," "What About Today?" (l: David Shire), "One Step," "Song of Me," "Today is the First Day of the Rest of My Life," "A New Life Coming." This was a new edition of an eclectic revue previously produced as *Theatre Songs by Maltby & Shire*, at the Manhattan Theatre Club. Orange Tree, Richmond, Surrey, England, 8/17/84–9/15/84

2495. Stempenyu. Musical drama. Central Synagogue, 11/14/73–3/17/74. 66 perf. p: Folksbiene Ensemble; m: Dov Seltzer; based on Sholem Aleichem's writings; d: Shmuel Bunim. Folksbiene, 10/23/93–1/17/94. new adaptation: Dora Wasserman; m: Eli Rubinstein; d: Bryna Turetsky; ch: Felix Fibush. Cast: Mina Bern, Julie Alexander

2496. Step into My World. AMAS, 2/16/89–3/19/89. 24 perf. m/l: Micki Grant; conceived by/developed/d: Ronald G. Russo. Cast: Jeffrey Dobbs (also ch), Deborah Woodson, Jennifer Bell. "Step into My World," "This Time," "How to Say Goodbye," "Togetherness," "It's Lonely," "The Women," "Like a Lady," "They Keep Coming," "We're Gonna Have a Good Time," "Back Home," "Mysteries and Miracles," "Fighting for the Pharaoh," "The World Keeps Going Round," "American Dream," "Bright Lights," "Who's Gonna Teach the Children," "First Born," "Workin' for the Man," "Look at That Sky," "Keep Steppin'"

2497. *Stepping Out*. Play with mus. Set in the hall of a North London church. John Golden, Broadway, 1/11/87–3/15/87. 29 prev. 72 perf. p: James M. Nederlander, Shubert Organization, Jerome Minskoff, Elizabeth I.

McCann, Bill Kenwright; w: Richard Harris; d/ch: Tommy Tune; ch assoc: Marge Champion; set: David Jenkins; cos: Neil Spisak; light: Beverly Emmons; sound: Otts Munderloh; ms/arr: Peter Howard. Cast: Pamela Sousa, Victoria Boothby, Cherry Jones, Marcell Rosenblatt, Carole Shelley, Janet Eilber, Don Amendolia, Meagen Fay, Sheryl Sciro, Carol Woods. Standbys: Candace Tovar, Roo Brown, Nancy Callman, Susanna Frazer, Gwen Shepherd, David Doty. Re-done, more as a musical. UK tour; then the Albery, London, 10/28/97–2/28/98. Prev from 10/8/97. m: Denis King; l: Mary Stewart-David; b: Richard Harris; d: Julia McKenzie; ch: Tudor Davies. Cast: Liz Robertson, Sharon D. Clarke

2498. Sterling Silver. Cabaret revue of humorous songs. Village Gate, 3/7/79–3/11/79. 1 prev. 6 perf. p: David Silberg; m/l: Frederick Silver; d: Sue Lawless; ch: Bick Goss; set: Kenneth Foy; light: Michael J. Hotopp. Cast: Lee Roy Reams, Karen Jablons, Roger Berdahl, Alan Brasington, Cynthia Meryl. "The Age of Elegance," "Rainbow, Rainbow," "Twelve Days After Christmas," "Visiting Hours," "Wooing in the Woods," "A Simple Song," "Waiting in the Wings," "Very New York," "I Do Like London," "When You Are on the Coast," "A Matter of Position," "Someone in My Life," "Closing Time," "Days of the Dancing"

2499. Stewed Prunes. Intimate revue. Circle in the Square, 12/5/60; Showplace, 12/14/60. p: Jim Paul Eilers. By & starring MacIntyre Dixon, Linda Segal, Richard Libertini. See also (in this appendix) *The Cats' Pajamas*

2500. *The Stiffkey Scandals of 1932*. Revised version of *A Life in Bedrooms*. Queen's, London, 6/12/69–6/21/69. 12 perf. m/l: David Wood; b: David Wright; d: Patrick Garland; ch: Jo Cook; set: Patrick Robertson; md: Carl Davis. Cast: Annie Ross, Sheila Ruskin, Peter Bowles, Jerome Willis

2501. Stomp. Multimedia protest rock musical environment entertainment. Series of song numbers, skits, movies & other happenings blended into a topical satire. Public, 11/16/69; recessed 2/1/70; re-opened 2/17/70; finally closed 4/19/70. 161 perf. Part of the NY Shakespeare Festival's indoor schedule of 3 programs (others: *Sambo* & *Mod Donna*). Conceived & performed by the 23 members of The Combine (group of former University of Texas students led by Doug Dyer)

2502. Stomp. An evening that featured spirited dancing to the percussive sounds of non-traditional, everyday objects used as instruments. Unique combination of percussion, movement, and visual comedy. Brighton, England, 1991. created by/d: Luke Cresswell & Steve McNicholas. Cast: Luke Cresswell, Nick Dwyer. Toured 39 countries (10 million people saw it), including a very long stint at the OB theatre, the Orpheum, from 2/27/94. Prev from 2/18/94. It celebrated its 10th year in 2004. Opened for 1st time in London's West End, at the Vaudeville, 9/24/02, and broke all box-office records for that theatre

2503. A Stoop on Orchard Street. Set around 1910, in NYC's Lower East Side. Immigrant life through Ellis Island. Mazer, 8/7/03.

Prev from 7/8/03. p/m/l/b: Jay Kholos; d: Lon Gary; ch: Jason Summer & Tom Berger; set/cos: Jason Lee Courson; md: Tom Berger. Cast: Lon Gary. A non-Equity prod, it had an advance sale of $350,000. Began with workshop in Nashville in fall 2002

2504. Stop in the Name of Love. 1960s songs. Piccadilly, London, 8/15/88. Cast: The Singlettes

2505. Story Theater. Play with mus. Also called *Paul Sills' Story Theater*. Originally presented at the Mark Taper Forum, L.A., and elsewhere. Ambassador, Broadway, 10/26/70–7/3/71. 14 prev from 10/19/70. 243 perf. p: Zev Bufman, City Center of Music & Drama, Shubert Organization, Theatre Development Fund; add m & l: Hamid Hamilton Camp; from fairy tales of Paul Sills & from those of the Brothers Grimm; d: Paul Sills; set: Michael Devine; cos: Stephanie Kline; light: H.R. Poindexter; cast recording on Columbia. Cast: Peter Bonerz (*Peter Boyle* from 12/70, *MacIntyre Dixon* from 2/71), Hamilton Camp, Melinda Dillon, Mary Frann, Valerie Harper (*Linda Lavin* from 12/70, *Valerie Harper*), Richard Libertini, Paul Sand (won a Tony), Richard Schaal (*Charles Bartlett* from 12/70), Lewis Arquette (alternate). *Paula Kelly* & *Avery Schreiber* were two of the replacements in 4/71. "A Lot Can Happen in a Day," "I'll Be Your Baby Tonight" (m/l: Bob Dylan), "Fixin' to Die Rag" (m/l: Joe McDonald), "About Time," "Dear Landlord" (m/l: Bob Dylan), "Here Comes the Sun" (m/l: George Harrison). From 4/22/71 it alternated with another Paul Sills show — Ovid's *Metamorphoses,* which was love stories & mythical romances from the works of Ovid, presented in story, mime, dance & song. Same cast as for *Story Theatre.* 35 perf. mus composed & performed by The True Brethren; l/translated/adapted: Arnold Weinstein). Toured 53 cities, 12/25/72–1/27/73

2506. Stovepipe Hat. About Abe Lincoln. Closed in Boston after 10 days total pre–Broadway tryouts in New Haven & Boston, 1944. m/l: Harold Spina & Edward Heyman. Cast: Bob Kennedy, Ann Warren. "The Great Man Says," "Lady Lovely," "Softly My Heart is Singing"

2507. Strange Feet. A site-specific play with mus. Dinosaurs give primordial perspective on mysteries of the planet. U.S. Customs House, 3/16/93–4/11/93. 24 perf. w: Mac Wellman; m: David Van Tieghem; d: Jim Simpson. Cast: Jan Leslie Harding, Steve Mellor

2508. Straws in the Wind. A theatrical look-ahead. American Place, 2/21/75–3/22/75. 33 perf. m/l: Cy Coleman, Betty Comden, Adolph Green, Galt MacDermot, Stephen Schwartz, Peter Stone, etc; d: Phyllis Newman; asst ch: Otis A. Sallid; set: Peter Harvey; cos: Ruth Morley. Cast: Tovah Feldshuh, Carol Jean Lewis, Brandon Maggart, Josh Mostel, George Pentecost

2509. Streakin'. Revue. "A fun-filled musical flashback to the outrageous 70s." 40 hit songs from the period, and a real-life streaker on stage. Wichita, Kansas, 2001 (5 months). w: Jamie Rocco & Albert Evans; d/ch: Jamie Rocco. It was begun in 1995. El Flamingo, NY,

4/02. Successful run. Babalu Restaurant & Cabaret, NY, 5/2/03. Prev from 4/17/03; originally only for 8 weeks, but had 2 extensions. md: John DiPinto; d/ch: Jamie Rocco. Cast: Tari Kelly. Closed for hiatus 6/28/03; resumed in fall 2003

2510. *Street Dreams.* St. Clement's, 5/15/84–6/2/84. 21 perf. The Lenox Arts Center production; m: William Eaton; w: Mitchell Ivers; d/ch: Peter Gennaro; light: Marilyn Rennagel; md: Nick Diminno & Grant Sturiale. Cast: Ray Contreras

2511. *Street Jesus.* American street musical. Provincetown Playhouse, 11/16/74–1/4/75. 52 perf. m: Chris Staudt & Peter Copani; l/b/conceived by/d: Peter Copani; md: Ed Vogel. Cast: Angela Martin, Michael D. Knowles, Vernon Spencer, Aixa Clemente, Robin Cantor, Larry Campbell, Regina Cashone, Joe Garrambone, Anita Tomaino, Mari Weiner. "Bad but Good," "The Good News," "Manufacture and Sell," "Today Will Be," "Strawberries, Pickles and Ice Cream," "Hail, Hail," "If Jesus Walked the Earth Today," "Who Can Say," "Down on Me," "Wait and See," "God's in the People," "Street Jesus," "Flame of Life," "Corruption," "For the Good Times," "Special Man," "A Better Day," "Friends," "In the Name of Love," "Make Them Hate," "Riot," One of Us," "Love is Beautiful." Re-vamped as *Fire of Flowers,* and ran at the Provincetown Playhouse, 1/29/76–2/29/76. 17 prev. 38 perf. Cast: Larry Campbell, Sylvia Miranda, Val Reiter, Gwen Sumter. Re-vamped again, as *New York City Street Show,* at Actors Playhouse, 4/28/77–5/15/77. 21 perf. It had a new cast & modified score

2512. *Streetheat.* Cabaret revue. Studio 54, 1/27/85–2/24/85. Based on orig concept by Michele Assaf & Rick Atwell; d/ch: Rick Atwell; set/cos: Franne Lee. Cast: Vicki Lewis, Tico Wells. "We Paint Life," "Uptown Dreamer's Express," "Hold On," "To Dance is to Fly," "Power," "I'm a Wow," "Lucky Louie," "Full Circle," "Streetheat," "I Want a Real Man," "The King Becomes a Clown," "Nirvana," "Danger, Men Working," "Today I Found Me," "The Power Lies Within"

2513. *The Streets of Gold.* Set on NYC's Lower East Side, in 1911. Manhattan Center Ballroom, 11/25/77–12/11/77. 12 perf. m: Ted Simons; l/b: Marvin Gordon; d: Scott Redman; ch: Tony Masullo; md: Harrison Fisher. Cast: Nancy Diaz, Stuart Silver. "Streets of Gold," "Greenhorn," "Tammany," "The Old Ways," "Pogrom Ballet," "Coney Island," "This Time"

2514. *The Streets of London.* An old Dion Boucicault melodrama. Also known as *Poverty is No Crime.* Theatre Royal, Stratford East, London, 3/18/80–4/12/80. m/songs: Gary Carpenter & Ian Barnett. d: Diane Cilento; md: Ian Barnett. Cast: William Squire, Nicholas Smith, David Mallinson, Elspet Gray, Patsy Byrne. Her Majesty's, London, 10/21/80–1/31/81. 122 perf. d: Diane Cilento; ch: Noel Tovey; md: Roger Moffatt. Cast: William Squire, Royce Mills, David Mallinson, Helen Cherry, Patsy Byrne

2515. *The Streets of New York.* Maidman, 10/29/63–8/2/64. 318 perf. p: Gene Dingenary

& Jane Gilliland; m: Richard B. Chodosh; l/b: Barry Alan Grael; based on play by Dion Boucicault. Cast: David Cryer, Gail Johnston. "If I May," "Arms for the Love of Me," "Love Wins Again"

2516. *Strider: The Story of a Horse.* Play with mus. Chelsea Theatre Center, 5/31/79–11/11/79. 189 perf. adapted by Mark Razovsky from Leo Tolstoy's story *Kholstomer: The Story of a Horse*; m: Mark Rozovsky & S. Vetkin; orig Russian l: Uri Riashentsev; English-language prod based on translation by Tamara Bering Sunguroff; adapted with add mus by Normal L. Berman; new English l: Steve Brown; d: Robert Kalfin & Lynne Gannaway; md: Normal L. Berman. Cast: Gerald Hiken, John Brownlee, Skip Lawing, Igors Gavon, Gordon Gould, Katherine Mary Brown, Roger De Koven, Pamela Burrell (nominated for a Tony), Nina Dova. "Darling's Romance," "Live Long Enough" (added during Broadway run), "Oh, Mortal," "Serpuhovsky's Romance," "Serpuhovsky's Song," "Song of the Herd," "Troika" (dropped during Broadway run), "Warm and Tender." Ran as *Strider* at Broadway's Helen Hayes Theatre, 11/14/79–5/18/80. 214 perf. Taina Elg replaced Pamela Burrell on 2/5/80. Revived OB in 1993. ch: Michele Assaf

2517. *Strike a Light!* Leeds Arts Centre, England, 1961. m: Gordon Caleb; l/b: Joyce Adcock. Revived, with additional songs by John Taylor & add dial by Frank Lawton, at the Alhambra, Glasgow, 4/7/66–4/16/66; toured; Piccadilly, London, 7/5/66–7/30/66. 30 perf. d/ch: Ross Taylor; set: Disley Jones; md: George Michie. Cast: Jeannie Carson, Evelyn Laye, John Fraser, Josephine Blake, Ben Aris

2518. *Striking 12.* Folk-rock musical. A "rewired" version of *The Little Match Girl,* by Hans Christian Andersen. Christmas scrooge-type reformed by blonde selling light bulbs. Prince Music Theatre, Philadelphia, 11/20/02–12/31/02. w: Brendan Milburn, Rachael Sheinkin, Brenda Vigoda; performed by GrooveLily (Brenda Vigoda — vocals & electric violin; Gene Lewin — vocals & drums; Brendan Milburn — vocals & keyboards). Old Globe, San Diego, 12/10/03–12/31/03. Prev from 12/6/03. d: Ted Sperling. Leonard Nimoy Thalia Theatre at the Peter Norton Symphony Space, NYC, 9/11/04–9/12/04. 3 perf. p: Melting Pot Theatre Co. One of their "Preludes: New Musicals in Concert" series. TheatreWorks, Palo Alto, 12/04–1/8/05. Album on PS Classics

2519. *Strip!* Burlesque revue. Explored the stripper behind the strip. Village Gate. 6/30/87–7/5/87. 8 perf. p/d: Phil Oesterman

2520. *Strip for Action.* A burlesque show entertains at the Brooklyn Navy Yard. Opened 3/17/56, Shubert, New Haven. Closed 4/14/56, Nixon, Pittsburgh, without making Broadway. m/l: Jimmy McHugh & Harold Adamson; based on play by Howard Lindsay & Russel Crouse; d: Don Hershey; cos: Miles White; md: Buster Davis. Cast: Yvonne Adair, Jerome Courtland, Joey Faye, Danny Dayton, Hal Linden, Dana Elcar, Jack Whiting, Sue Ann Langdon. "Chaps from Annapolis," "Strip for Action," "Dame Crazy," "Too Young to Go Steady," "Kicking up a Storm," "I Just Found

Out About Love," "Rock and Roll Bump," "Love Me as Though There Was No Tomorrow," "(I Just Wanna Be a) Song and Dance Man," "(My) Papa from Panama," "Good Old Days of Burlesque"

2521. *Struttin'.* AMAS, 2/11/88–3/6/88. 16 perf. m/l/b/d: Lee Chamberlin; md: Neal Tate. Cast: Roumel Reaux, David Lowenstein, Valerie Macklin

2522. *Studio.* Musical based on life of Serge Diaghilev. Duo, 4/14/88–5/7/88. 12 perf. m/md: David Welch; l/b/d/set: Michael Alasa. Cast: Jody Walker-Lichtig, Mark Lotito, Tony Loudon, Jon Spano

2523. *Suburb.* City-dwellers consider move to the 'burbs. Theatre at St. Peter's, 3/1/01–3/25/01. 19 prev from 2/13/01. 29 perf. This prod following readings at the York Theatre Co., in 5/00 & 6/00. p: York Theatre Co.; m: Robert S. Cohen; l: David Javerbaum; b: David Javerbaum & Robert S. Cohen; d: Jennifer Uphoff Gray; ch: John Carrafa; md: Jeffrey R. Smith; orch: Larry Hochman. Cast: Jacquelyn Piro, James Ludwig, Dennis Kelly, Alix Korey, Adinah Alexander. "Directions," "Mow," "Do it Yourself," "Suburb," "Not Me," "Barbecue," "The Girl Next Door," "Ready or Not," "Commute," "Mall," "Duet," "Handy," "Walkin' to School," "Bagel Shop Quartet," "Trio for Four," "Everything Must Go," "Someday." Developed by Musical Theatre Works. West Coast premiere at Long Beach Playhouse, Calif., 10/11/02–11/23/02. d: Martin Lang. Cast: Alix Korey, Nancy Anderson, Sandy Binion

2524. *Suburban Strains.* Stephen Joseph Theatre-in-the-Round, Scarborough, England, 1/18/80–2/9/80; same venue, 2/2/81–3/14/81. 31 perf, with somewhat different cast. m/md: Paul Todd; l/b/d: Alan Ayckbourn. Roundabout, London, 1981

2525. *Suddenly the Music Starts.* Revue. AMAS, 5/3/79–5/20/79. 12 perf. w: Johnny Brandon; d: Sam Gonzales; ch: Henry Le Tang & Lucia Victor; assoc ch: Eleanor Le Tang; md: Neal Tate; dance mus arr: Danny Holgate. Cast: William "Gregg" Hunter, Mary Louise, Andy Torres. "Suddenly the Music Starts," "My Home Town," "Faces in a Crowd," "Funky People," "Super Bad," "I'll Scratch Your Back," "Goodnight," "Boogie Woogie Ball," "Talk Your Feelings," "Your Love is My Love," "Dancing Dan," "Dance! Dance! Dance!," "Whole Lotta Real Good Feeling," "Remember Someone," "Everybody's Doing the Disco," "Guides," "Stuff," "Syncopatin'," "Kansas City Blues," "Manhattan Lullaby," "One Day at a Time," "You," "It's My Turn Now," "Strolling Down Broadway"

2526. *Suds.* The Rocking '60s musical soap opera. Set in 1960s laundromat. 51 songs from the period. Criterion Center Stage Left, 9/25/88–12/4/88. 23 prev 81 perf. co-p/d: Will Roberson; created by/w: Melinda Gilb, Steve Gunderson, Bryan Scott; ch: Javier Belasco; md: William Doyle. Cast: Melinda Gilb, Steve Gunderson, Christine Sevec, Susan Mosher. Previously produced at the Old Globe, San Diego

2527. *Suffragette!* Trinity Theatre, 5/13/82–

5/29/82. 12 perf. m/l: Josh Rubins; md: Mary L. Rodgers; ch: Lisa Brailoff. Cast: Alice Cannon, Kimberly Farr, Jane Milne

2528. *Sullivan and Gilbert*. Comedy with mus. Set in 1890, mostly at London's Savoy Theatre. Actors Outlet, 12/6/84–12/16/84. 15 perf. w: Kenneth Ludwig; using m/l of Sir Arthur Sullivan & W.S. Gilbert; d: Larry Carpenter; set: John Falabella. Cast: Gilbert: George Ede; Sullivan: Jonathan Moore; Also with: Gary Krawford. Kennedy Center, 9/7/88–10/9/88. Cast: Fritz Weaver, Noel Harrison

2529. *Summer of '42*. A boy's passage into adulthood. Set on an island off the coast of New England, in summer 1942. Mountain View Center for the Arts, 6/23/01; Variety Arts, 12/18/01–1/27/02. 47 perf. Quite a different score from the Mountain View Center prod. m/l: David Kirshenbaum; b: Hunter Foster; based on movie of same name, written by Herman Raucher, and in turn based on his novel; d/ch: Gabriel Barre; assoc ch: Jennifer Cody; set: James Youmans; md: Lynne Shankel. Cast: Kate Jennings Grant, Ryan Driscoll, Greg Stone, Celia Keenan-Bolger, Megan Valerie Walker, Brett Tabisel, Jason Marcus, Bill Kux, Erin Webley. "Here and Now," "Will That Ever Happen to Me?," "You're Gonna Miss Me," "Little Did I Dream," "The Walk," "Like They Used To," "I Think I Like Her," "The Heat," "The Movies," "Man Around the House," "Someone to Dance with Me," "Unfinished Business," "Make You Mine," "The Drugstore," "The Campfire," "Promise of the Morning," "Oh Gee, I Love My G.I.," "The Dance." Originally prod at Goodspeed, 8/10/00

2530. *Summer 69*. Music of 1969 by various writers. Theatre 80, 6/24/99–8/8/99; Douglas Fairbanks, 8/16/99–10/10/99. Total of 110 perf. b: Bill Van Horn, Leer Paul Leary, Ellen Michelmore; d: Bruce Lumpkin

2531. *Summer Song*. Life of Anton Dvorak (whose music was used). Princes, London, 2/16/56. l: Eric Maschwitz; b: Eric Maschwitz & Hy Kraft; cast recording on Philips. Cast: Sally Ann Howes, Laurence Naismith, Edric Connor. "I Loved My Love," "Just Around the Corner," "Once a Year is Not Enough," "Be She Dark, Be She Fair," "Cotton Tail," "No One Told Me," "Sing Me a Song," "Saturday Girl," "One Boy Sends You a Rose," "Dvorak's Letter Home," "Deep Blue Evening," "Summer Song," "Small Town Sweetheart," "New York '93," "I'll Be Remembering." The show failed

2532. *Sung and Unsung Sondheim*. Tribute to Stephen Sondheim. The Space at City Center, 1/28/85. 1 perf. p: Manhattan Theatre Club. Cast: Patricia Elliott, John McMartin

Sunset see # 550, Main Book

2533. *The Sunset Gang*. Set in Florida retirement home. Jewish Rep, 4/25/92–5/24/92. m/l: L. Russell Brown & Warren Adler; d: Edward M. Cohen; ch: Ricarda O'Conner. Cast: Irving Burton, Shifra Lerer, Alfred Toigo, Chevi Colton, Sheila Smith, Gene Varrone. "What's Wrong, Bill?," "Maybe it's Me," "I Miss My Mama," "It's Too Late for Love," "Don't Tell Me This isn't Love," "Red

Eye Express," "I Wish I Could Explain," "From September to December"

2534. *Sunset Salome*. Musicalization of *Salome* as re-written by Norma Desmond (the character from *Sunset Boulevard*). Set in Whispering Sands Hospital for the Criminally Insane, in Palm Springs. HERE, 4/5/96–4/28/96. 2 prev. 10 perf. m: Max Kinberg; b: Peter Wing Healey; d: Laurence J. Geddes; cos: Willa Kim. Cast: Michael McQuary, Peter Wing Healey

2535. *The Sunshine Train*. Gospel musical. Abbey, 6/15/72–12/17/72. 224 perf. conceived by/d: William E. Hunt. Cast: The Gospel Starlets, The Carl Murray Singers. "The Sunshine Train," "Near the Cross," "On My Knees Praying," "Thank You, Lord," "Just Look Where I Come From," "His Eye is on the Sparrow," "Troubled Waters," "Swing Low," "Beams of Heaven," "We Need More Love," "Jesus Loves Me," "All the World to Me," "Judgment Day," "Higher," "Come by Here," "Peace," "Stand up for Jesus," "God Be with You"

2536. *The Survival of St. Joan*. Medieval rock opera, in which none of the characters sing. What would have happened if Joan of Arc had been set free. Phyllis Anderson, 2/28/71–3/14/71. 17 perf. m: Hank & Gary Ruffin; l/b: James Lineberger; conceived by/d: Chuck Gnys; set/cos: Peter Harvey; light: Thomas Skelton; ms: Stephen Schwartz. Cast: F. Murray Abraham, Lenny Baker, Gretchen Corbett. Music performed by Smoke Rise

2537. *Susan B!* Martin, 11/24/81–11/29/81. 8 perf. m: Thomas Tierney; l: Ted Drachman; b: Jules Tasca; d: John Henry Davis; ch: Haila Strauss; set: Jack Stewart; md: Harrison Fisher. Cast: Lillian Byrd, Frank Groseclose

2538. *The Swan Down Gloves*. A Shakespearian gallimaufry, or pantomime. About Sir Walter Raleigh. Royal Shakespeare Theatre, Stratford-on-Avon, England, 1/12/81. 3 perf. p: Royal Shakespeare Co.; m/md: Nigel Hess; l: Bille Brown & Nigel Hess; b: Bille Brown; d: Ian Judge; ch: David Toguri. Cast: Joe Melia, Bille Brown, Sinead Cusack, Derek Godfrey, Barbara Leigh Hunt, Julia Tobin, Brenda Bruce. "With the Sun Arise," "Everything's Going to Be Fine," "Catastrophe," "Let's Be Friends," "Make Your Own World," "How's the Way?," "Going into Town," "Stuck in a Muddle," "Best Foot Forward," "Muck," "Any Old Rose," "Fire Down." Aldwych, London, 12/22/81. 22 perf. Mostly same cast, but not Brenda Bruce

2539. *Swan Esther*. Young Vic, London, 12/17/83–1/7/84. 26 perf. p: Robert Stigwood & David Land; m: Nick Munns; l/b: J. Edward Oliver; d: Frank Dunlop; ch: Jeff Thacker; md: Gareth Valentine. Cast: Amanda Redman, Stephen Lewis. Revised & ran at the Theatre Royal, Windsor, from 4/30/85; then toured. p: Bill Kenwright

2540. *Swan Song*. Mystery with mus. Set on stage of Cambridge Arts Theatre, London. Masur, 10/31/86–11/22/86. 16 perf. p: York Theatre Co.; m: Gioacchino Rossini; w: John Greenwood & Jonathan Levi; based on Edmund Crispin's novel. Cast: Brent Barrett,

Ron Randell, Tony Tanner (also d), Richard Lupino, Jack Eddleman

2541. *Sweeney Todd*. Unrelated to famous Broadway show. Royal Ballet Co., London, 1959. m: Malcolm Arnold; ch: John Cranko

2542. *Sweeney Todd*. Unrelated to Broadway show. Croydon, England, 6/25/68. p: Terence Fitzgerald & Henry McCarthy; m: John Britten; l: David Cumming; b/d: Ben Hawthorne. Cast: Todd: Michael Wisher; Mistress Lovett: Miranda Marshall

2543. *Sweet Adeline*. Addie Schmidt is the daughter of a Hoboken beergarden owner in 1898. This is the story of her 3 loves. After Tom Martin goes away to fight in the Spanish American war, Addie Belmont (as she is now known) becomes a Broadway star and falls for wealthy socialite James Day. But his family disapproves and she winds up happily with composer Sid Barnett. Hammerstein's, Broadway, 9/3/29–3/22/30. 234 perf. p: Arthur Hammerstein (Oscar's uncle); m: Jerome Kern; l/b: Oscar Hammerstein II; d: Reginald Hammerstein (Oscar's brother); ch: Danny Dare. Cast: Helen Morgan, Robert Chisholm. "'twas Not So Long Ago," "Here Am I," "Spring is Here," "Out of the Blue," "Naughty Boy," "Oriental Moon," "Mollie O'Donahue," "Why Was I Born?," "The Sun About to Rise," "Some Girl is on Your Mind," "Don't Ever Leave Me," "Indestructible Kate." Filmed in 1935, with Irene Dunne. Revived in concert at Town Hall, 5/20/85, and again, in concert at City Center, 2/13/97–2/16/97. 5 perfs. adapted by: Norman Allen; d: Eric D. Schaeffer; ch: John De Luca; orch: Robert Russell Bennett. Cast: Patti Cohenour, Tony Randall, MacIntyre Dixon, Dorothy Loudon, Stephen Bogardus, Kristi Lynes, Gary Beach, Hugh Panaro, Jacquelyn Piro, Timothy Robert Blevins

2544. *Sweet and Low*. Revue. Ambassadors, London, 6/10/43. m/l: Charles Zwar, Geoffrey Wright, Alan Melville. Cast: Hermione Gingold. Led to 2 sequels, at the same theatre, and with the same star—*Sweeter and Lower* (2/27/44–2 years) & *Sweetest and Lowest* (5/9/46)

2545. *Sweet Bye and Bye*. Set on 7/4/2076, in NY. Opened 10/10/46, Shubert, New Haven. Closed 11/5/46, Erlanger, Philadelphia. Did not get to Broadway. In 2 acts & 13 scenes. p: Nat Karson; m/l: Vernon Duke & Ogden Nash; b: S.J. Perelman & Al Hirschfeld; d: Curt Conway; ch: Fred Kelly; set: Boris Aronson; md: Charles Blackman. Cast: Dolores Gray (replaced Pat Kirkwood during rehearsals), Walter O'Keefe, Robert Strauss, Fred Hearn, Gene Sheldon (*Erik Rhodes*), Percy Helton, Le Roi Operti. "Sweet Bye and Bye," "An Old Fashioned Tune," "Yes, Yes," "Diana," "Good Deed for Today," "Factory Ballet," "Low and Lazy," "Breakfast in Bed," "Crisp and Crunchy," "Let's Be Young," "Roundabout" Hymn," "My Broker Told Me So," "Just Like a Man," "It's Good," "Where is Bundy?," "We Love Us," "Eskimo Bacchante"

2546. *Sweet Feet*. Musical satire on 1940s Hollywood. New Theatre, 5/25/72–5/28/72. 6 perf. m/l/d: Don Brockett; b: Dan Graham. Cast: Dan Graham, Marty Goetz, Lenora

Nemetz, Scott Burns, Florence Lacey. "Sweet Feet," "Your Eyes Danced," "Is This Love?," "Making a Star," "The Show Must Go On," "The Kind of a Woman," "Boompies"

2547. *Sweet Miani.* Lampoon of Hollywood's old South Sea musicals. Players, 9/25/62–10/13/62. 22 perf. p: Edmund Brophy & Donald Currie; m/l: Ed Tyler; b: Stuart Bishop; d: Louis MacMillan. Cast: Sheila Smith, Virgil Curry, Isabelle Farrell. "Middle of the Sea," "Legend of the Islands," "Black Pearls," "Going Native," "A Honey to Love," "Sailing," "Not Tabu," "Maluan Moon," "Canticle to the Wind," "Homesick in Our Hearts," "Just Sit Back and Relax," "Forever and Always," "Turoola," "Miani," "Ritual of Ruku," "Silvery Days," "Code of the Licensed Pilot," "Warm Breezes at Twilight," "Far Away Island"

2548. *Sweet Song.* A theatricalized song cycle. Perry Street, 8/8/90–8/12/90. 5 perf. m: Ricky Ian Gordon; l: from the poetry of various famous poets; d: Fabrizio Melano. Cast: Angelina Reaux

Sweet Will see # 619, Main Book

2549. *Sweet Yesterday.* Empire, Edinburgh, Scotland, 3/26/45; toured; Adelphi, London, 6/21/45–12/8/45. 196 perf. m: Kenneth Leslie-Smith; l: Philip Leaver, James Dyrenforth, Max Kester; b: Philip Leaver; d: Esme Church; md: Herbert Lodge. Cast: Hugh Morton, Webster Booth, Doris Hare, Gwen Lewis

2550. *Sweetheart Mine.* King's, Southsea, England, 7/1/46; toured; Victoria Palace, London, 8/1/46–4/12/47. 323 perf. m: Noel Gay; l: Frank Eyton; b: Lauri Wylie & Lupino Lane; based on play *My Old Dutch*, by Albert Chevalier & Arthur Shirley; d: Lupino Lane; ch: Dorothy MacAusland; md: Marcel Gardner. Cast: Lupino Lane, Lauri Lupino Lane, Barry Lupino, Wallace Lupino, Vernon Kelso, Billy Russell

2551. *Sweethearts: Nostalgic Musical Memories of Jeanette MacDonald & Nelson Eddy.* Actors Playhouse, 12/7/88–1/22/89. 54 perf. Cast: Antoinette Mille, Walter Adkins. Previously presented at Pantages Center, Tacoma, Wash.

2552. *A Swell Party — The Cole Porter Songbook.* Musical revue. Sylvia and Danny Kaye Playhouse, 10/9/97–10/12/97. 4 perf. p: Jeffrey Finn Prods; d/ch: Patricia Wilcox; md: Fred Wells; light: T. Richard Fitzgerald. Cast: Melba Moore, Jerry Christakos, Jennifer Lee Andrews, Denise Nolin, Abe Sylvia

2553. *Swing.* Set between a college prom in 1937 & a Broadway hotel on VJ Night, 1945. Playhouse, Wilmington, Del., 2/25/80; Kennedy Center, 3/5/80–3/29/80. 34 perf. Failed to make Broadway. p: Stuart Ostrow & Edgar M. Bronfman; m: Robert Waldman; l: Alfred Uhry; b: Conn Fleming; d: Stuart Ostrow; ch: Kenneth Rinker; set: Robin Wagner; cos: Patricia Zipprodt; light: Richard Pilbrow; md: Peter Howard; orch: Eddie Sauter. Cast: Paul Binotto, Paul Bogaev, Jerry Colker, Janet Eilber, Robert LuPone, Pat Lysinger, Adam Redfield, Debbie Shapiro, Mary Catherine Wright, John Hammil, Tim Flavin. "Swing," "Good from Any Angle," "Michigan Bound," "The Real Thing," "Marilyn," "A Piece of Cake," "Home," "Miliaria Rubra," "One Hundred Percent Cockeyed," "All Clear," "A Girl Can Go Wacky," "The Doowah Diddy Blues," "If You Can't Trot Don't Get Hot," "Dream Time"

2554. *Swing.* Carey Playhouse, 10/20/87–11/1/87. 15 perf. p: Brooklyn Academy of Music; conceived by/d: Elizabeth Swados. Cast: Connie Alexander

2555. *Swing: The Big Band Musical.* Bigband revue. North Carolina School of the Arts, 1993–94 season. p: Ron Kumin (who organized pre–Broadway tryouts in Winston-Salem); conceived by/d/ch: Randy Skinner; md/orch: Scot Wooley; set: Bill Clarke; cos: Michael Bottari & Ronald Case; light: Jeremy Kumin. Cast: Margaret Whiting, Debra Ann Draper, Wendy Edmead, Robert H. Fowler, Susan M. Haefner, Frantz G. Hall, Cheryl Howard, Tina Johnson, Marcus Neville, Randy Skinner, Tom Stuart, Sean Frank Sullivan, Elizabeth Ward

2556. *Swingtime Canteen.* Set in 1944, onstage at concert for 8th Air Force in London. Used 1940s standards. Blue Angel, 3/14/95–11/26/95. Prev from 2/24/95. b: Linda Thorsen Bond, William Repicci, Charles Busch; special material: Dick Gallagher; d: Kenneth Elliott; ch: Barry McNabb; cos: Robert Mackintosh; md: Lawrence Yurman. Cast: Alison Fraser, Emily Loesser, Maxene Andrews (i.e. one of the Andrews Sisters — from 9/95). Previously produced at Bay Street Theatre, Sag Harbor, NY

2557. *The Taffetas.* Musical journey through the Fabulous 1950s. Westbeth, 8/5/88; Cherry Lane, 10/12/88–1/1/89. 5 prev. 90 perf. p: Arthur Whitelaw, James Shellenberger, Select Entertainment. Top of the Gate, 2/1/89–4/9/89. 3 prev. 67 perf. Add p: Harold D. Cohen; conceived by/md: Rick Lewis; d: Steven Harris; ch: Tina Paul; light: Ken Billington. Cast: Jody Abrahams, Karen Curlee, Tia Speros, Melanie Mitchell

2558. *Take It Easy.* Set on a college campus in 1944. Judith Anderson, 3/21/96–6/30/96. 13 prev from 3/8/96. 104 perf. m/l/b: Raymond Fox; d: Collette Black. Cast: Kristin Hughes, Christian Anderson, Stephanie Kurtzuba. "We're in the Army," "Who Cares," "Take it Easy," "An Old Time Girl," "Just One More Time," "It's All Right," "I Think I'm Falling for You," "I'll Remember Spring," "Funny," "The Night When We Were Young," "Say Farewell," "Worry About the Blues Tomorrow," "Home Front Farm Brigade," "Home for Christmas," "Our Yesterday," "Looking for the Sunshine"

2559. *Take It from Us.* Variety revue. Adelphi, London, 10/30/50. 580 perf. orig m: Freddie Bretherton; sk: Frank Muir & Denis Norden; ch: Bert Stimmel. Cast: Jimmy Edwards, Joy Nichols, Dick Bentley, Wallas Eaton. "Out of a Dream," "What a Sphinx"

2560. *Taking a Chance on Love: The Lyrics and Life of John Latouche.* Musical revue. York Theatre Co., 3/2/2000–3/26/00. 17 prev from 2/17/00. 29 perf. m/l: various writers; dev: Erick Haagensen; d/set: James Morgan; cos: Suzy Benzinger; md: Jeffrey R. Smith. Cast: Terry Burrell, Jerry Dixon, Donna English, Eddie Korbich

2561. *Taking My Turn.* About old people. Entermedia, 6/9/83–1/8/84. 10 prev. 245 perf. m: Gary William Friedman; l: Will Holt; conceived by/d: Robert H. Livingston; set: Clarke Dunham; cos: Judith Dolan; md: Barry Levitt; orch: Gary William Friedman. Cast: Margaret Whiting, Tiger Haynes, Mace Barrett, Marni Nixon, Cissy Houston, Ted Thurston, Sheila Smith, Victor Griffin. "This is My Song," "Somebody Else," "Fine for the Shape I'm In," "Two of Me," "I Like It," "I Never Made Money from Music," "Vivaldi," "Do You Remember?," "In April," "Pick More Daisies," "Taking Our Turn," "Sweet Longings," "I Am Not Old," "Good Luck to You," "It Still isn't Over"

2562. *The Tale of Madame Zora.* Dramatization with mus of life of Zora Neale Hurston, black novelist & folklorist. Set in Hurstonville, Florida, in the 1960s. Ensemble Studio, 2/18/86–3/1/86. 14 perf. m/l: Olu Dara & Aishah Rahman; d: Glenda Dickerson; ch: Dianne McIntyre. Cast: Stephanie Berry, Keith David

2563. *Tales of Tinseltown.* Set in Hollywood in 1932–36. Musical Theatre Works, 8/8/85–8/31/85. 19 perf. m: Paul Katz; l/b: Michael Colby; d: Rick Lombardo; ch: Dennis Dennehy; md: James Stenborg. Cast: Elizabeth Austin, Olga Talyn, Jason Graae, Nora Mae Lyng. "Tinseltown Tattletale," "I Belong to Hollywood," "Let's Go," "I Can Sing," "All Over the Place," "Hollywood Sign," "In Broken-Promise Land," "I Knew It," "Jungle Fever," "So This is the Movies," "Alphabet Soup," "At Sea," "Just Laugh it Away," "It's Mine," "Oh, the Scandal!," "Dream of Hollywood," "I'll Stand By You," "I'm Beautiful," "Take Two," "Ruin Them," "Stars in My Eyes," "Expose." George Street Playhouse, NJ, 1/6/89. d: Larry Carpenter; ch: Baayork Lee; md: Steve Alper. Cast: Laura Kenyon, Patricia Ben Peterson, Evan Pappas, Robert Dorfman, Janice Lynde, Nat Chandler, Kathryn Kendall, Mark Bove

2564. *Tallulah.* Musical based on life of actress Tallulah Bankhead. Tomi Terrace, 6/13/83–6/25/83. 4 prev. 12 perf. m: Arthur Siegel; l: Mae Richard; b: Tony Lang; d/ch: David Holdgrive. Cast: Helen Gallagher, Joel Craig. "Darling," "Tallulah," "When I Do a Tap Dance for You," "I've Got to Try Everything Once," "You're You," "I Can See Him Clearly," "Tallulahbaloo," "The Party is Where I Am," "Stay Awhile," "It's a Hit," "If Only He Were a Woman," "Love is on Its Knees," "Don't Ever Book a Trip on the IRT," "You Need a Lift!." Westside Arts Center/Cheryl Crawford Theatre, 10/30/83–12/6/83. 19 prev. 42 perf. A few changes to crew & cast: set/cos: John Falabella; light: Ken Billington; Russell Nype was now in the cast. Revised as *Tallulah's Party*, and opened OB at the Kaufman, 3/10/98. d: Latifah Taormina; ch: Jerome Vivona; md: Jeffrey Buchsbaum; arr: Doug Katsaros. Cast: Tovah Feldshuh, Alan Gilbert, Bobby Clark, Robert Cary

2565. *Tallulah Hallelujah!* An imagination of the life of actress Tallulah Bankhead. Set during a USO show in 1956. Douglas Fairbanks, 9/19/00–12/31/00. 23 prev. 97 perf. p:

Eric Krebs & Chase Mishkin; m/l: several writers; w: Tovah Feldshuh (with Larry Amoros & Linda Selman); d: William Wesbrooks; cos: Carrie Robbins; md/arr: Bob Goldstone. Cast: Tallulah: Tovah Feldshuh; Meredith Willson: Bob Goldstone; Corp. Chapman: Mark Deklin

2566. *Tallulah Tonight!* Solo performance by Helen Gallagher, without intermission. American Place, 3/16/88–4/3/88. 22 perf. orig m/l: Bruce W. Coyle & Tony Lang; w: Tony Lang; d: Wynn Handman

2567. *Tambourines to Glory.* A gospel-singing play with mus. About a gospel church in Harlem. Little Theatre, Broadway, 11/2/63–11/23/63. 24 perf. m: Jobe Huntley; l: Langston Hughes (he also adapted from his novel); d: Nikos Psacharopoulos. Cast: Louis Gossett, Hilda Simms, Robert Guillaume, Rosetta Le Noire, Clara Ward, Micki Grant, Joseph Attles, Rosalie King, Theresa Merritt, Alma Hubbard. "Nobody Knows the Trouble I've Seen," "O, What Blessings to Receive," "Traveling Show," "The New York Blues," "Moon Outside My Window," "Scat with Me," "As I Go," "Just to Be a Flower in the Garden of the Lord," "I've Come Back to the Fold," "I'm Goin' to Testify," "Away from Temptation," "Devil, Devil, Take Yourself Away," "Yes, Ma'am," "Fix Me," "Just Trust in Him," "God's Got a Way," "Let the Church Say Amen," "God's Love Can Save," "If You've Got a Tambourine, Shake it for the Glory of God" (Tambourines to Glory)

Tango Apasionado see # 169, Main Book
2568. *Tania.* New York Theatre Ensemble, 11/5/75–12/14/75. 30 perf. m/l: Paul Dick; b: Mario Fratti; d: Ron Nash. Cast: Norah Foster, Cynthia Haynes, Marsha Bonine, Jane Kerns, Norman Lewis, Denis Jones, Marcy Olive, Walter George Alton, Lee Torchia, Akki Onyango. "To Start a Revolution," "There'll Come a Day," "Fire and Joy," "The American Dream," "I Sing Woman," "Man in a Cage," "Hail Alma Mater," "The Wall," "The Shoot Out"

2569. *Tap Dogs.* Dance theatre piece. Variations on art of tap-dancing by 9-member Australian cast. Previously produced in Sydney, and on tour in North America. Union Square, 3/16/97–8/24/97. 14 prev from 3/5/97. 184 perf. p: Back Row Prods, Peter Holmes a Court, Columbia Artists Management, Richard Frankel, Marc Routh, by arrangement with Dein Perry & Nigel Triffitt; m: Andrew Wilkie; created/ch: Dein Perry; d/set: Nigel Triffitt. Cast: Dein Perry, Darren Disney, Billy Burke

2570. *Tapestry: The Music of Carole King.* Musical revue. Union Square, 1/26/93–3/7/93. 23 prev. 19 perf. d: Jeffrey Martin; ch: Ron NaVarre; set: David Jenkins; md: Kathy Sommer. Cast: Mary Gutzi, Frank Mastrone. "Up on the Roof," "Will You Love Me Tomorrow?," "Tapestry," "Natural Woman"

2571. *Tarot.* Symbolic adventures of a Fool (played by Joe McCord) among characters representing various cards in Tarot deck, in form of rock-mime musical (no singing or talking). Brooklyn Academy of Music. 12/11/71–12/20/71. 13 perf; Circle in the Square, 3/4/72–4/4/72 (38 perf). m/l: Tom Constanten &

Touchstone; conceived by The Rubber Duck (i.e. Joe McCord, who also dir with Robert Kalfin). Cast: Yolande Bavan, Rubber Duck

2572. *Tars and Spars.* Army Revue. Toured country during WWII to recruit people for Coast Guard. 1944. m/l: Vernon Duke & Howard Dietz. Cast: Victor Mature, Sid Caesar, Gower Champion. "Apprentice Seaman," "Arm in Arm," "Civilian," "Farewell for a While," "Palm Beach," "Silver Shield"

2573. *Tatterdemalion.* Re-vamping of *King of the Schnorrers* (see this appendix). Douglas Fairbanks, 10/27/85–11/17/85. 19 prev from 10/10. 25 perf. p/d: Eric Krebs; m/l/b: Judd Woldin; add l: Susan Birkenhead; based on Israel Zangwill's novella *The King of the Schnorrers*; ch: Mary Jane Houdina; set: Ed Wittstein; ms: Peter Howard; md: Edward G. Robinson; orch: Robert M. Freedman & Judd Woldin. Cast: Annie McGreevey, Ron Wisniski, Stuart Zagnit, KC Wilson. "Petticoat Lane," "Ours," "Chutzpah," "Tell Me," "Born to Schnorr," "I Have Not Lived in Vain," "A Man is Meant to Reason," "Blood Lines," "Leave the Thinking to Men," "It's Over," "Murder," "Dead," "I'm Only a Woman," "An Ordinary Man," "Well Done, Da Costa," "Each of Us"

2574. *The Tattooed Countess.* Set in Maple Valley, Iowa, in the summer of 1897. Barbizon-Plaza, 4/3/61–4/6/61. 4 perf. w: Countess Dowell; based on novel by Carl Van Vechten. Cast: Irene Manning, Travis Hudson, John Stewart. "Home Town Girl," "You Take Paris," "How She Glows," "Rolling Stone," "Tattooed Woman," "Too Old for Love," "Autumn," "Got to Find My Way"

2575. *Telecast.* St. Bart's Playhouse, 2/8/79–3/3/79. 28 perf—no formal opening took place, yet perfs prior to 2/15/79 were termed previews. p: Harve Bronstein; m/l: Martin Silvestri & Barry Harman; d: Barry Harman & Wayne Cilento; ch: Wayne Cilento; light: Jane Reisman & Neil Peter Jampolis. Cast: Matt Landers, Carolyn Kirsch, Jana Schneider. "The Whole World Will Be Watching," "Don't Ask!," "Ordinary Guy," "Every Thursday Night," "Izzie's Story," "Sure of His Love," "The Silent Spot," "I've Arrived," "A Lot of Heart," "Host of Hosts," "Something Else," "Don't Wait Up," "The Finale," "I Caught a Glimpse of a Man," "In One," "I'm Nothing without You"

Tell Me on a Sunday see # 648, Main Book
2576. *The Temporary Mrs. Smith.* A fading Hollywood star has financial problems. Wilmington, Del., 1946. m/l: Arthur Siegel & Jeff Bailey. Cast: Luba Malina, Howard St. John. "Lovely Me"

2577. *The Ten Commandments: The Spectacle Musical.* The biblical story. Palais des Sports, Paris, 2000. Then known as Les dix commandements. m: Pascal Obispo; d: Eli Chouraqui. Kodak, Hollywood, 9/27/04. Prev from 9/18/04. new m: Patrick Leonard; New l: Maribeth Derry; d: Robert Iscove; set: Giantito Burchiellaro; cos: Azria. Cast: Moses: Val Kilmer; Ramses: Kevin Earley; Nefertari: Lauren Kennedy; Joshua: Adam Lambert; Bithia: Luba Mason. 50 dancers & singers. Reviews were luke-warm, and the show did not

catch on in USA. National tour due to begin at Radio City Music Hall, NYC, 1/18/05 (38 perf), costing $10–15 million, was canceled

2578. *Ten Nights in a Barroom.* Musical melodrama. Set in New England, about 1850. Greenwich Mews, 10/1/62–10/28/62. 32 perf. m/l: Stanley Silverman & Martin Sherman; from play by W.W. Pratt; d: Robert Alvin. Cast: Martha Velez, Ronald Stuart

2579. *Ten Percent Revue.* Gay musical revue. Susan Bloch. 4/13/88–6/5/88. 78 perf. p: Laura Green; m/l: Tom Wilson Weinberg; d: Scott Green. Cast: Lisa Bernstein, Trish Kane (*Rainie Cole*), Timothy Williams (*James Humphrey*), Valerie Hill (*Helena Snow*), Robert Tate, Cathleen Riddley. "Flaunting It," "Best Years of My Life," "Wedding Song," "Home," "Not Allowed," "Safe Sex Slut," "Homo Haven Fighting Song," "Obituary," "And the Supremes," "Before Stonewall," "We're Everywhere." Actors Playhouse, 6/7/88–11/6/88. 16 prev. 176 perf

2580. *Terra Incognita.* Opera for the theatre. Set in Spanish town where Columbus first set sail for New World. INTAR, 3/19/97–4/13/97. 6 prev. 15 perf. m: Roberto Sierra; libretto/d: Maria Irene Fornes; cos: Willa Kim; md: Stephen Gosling

2581. *Tess's Last Night.* Mazer, 1/16/03–2/9/03. m/l: Joel Weiss; b/d: David L. Williams; based on Thomas Hardy's novel *Tess of the D'Urbevilles* (setting updated to a children's theatre in New York). Cast: Carrie Libling

2582. *Tess of the D'Urbervilles.* Savoy, London, 11/10/99–1/8/00. Prev from 10/30/99. m: Stephen Edwards; l: Justin Fleming; adapted/d: Karen Louise Hebden; from Thomas Hardy's novel. Cast: Alasdair Harvey, Jonathan Monks, Philippa Healey & Poppy Tiernay (alternated as Tess), Diane Pilkington. Preceded by short regional tour

2583. *Thank God! The Beat Goes On.* Gospel musical. Beacon, 10/14/97–10/26/97. 1 prev. 13 perf. p/story/conceived by: Barry Singer; orig m/b/d: Loren Dean Harper; set/light: Ron Nash. Cast: Alyson Williams, The Whispers

2584. *That 5 a.m Jazz.* Play with mus. Astor Place, 10/19/64–1/10/65. 94 perf. m/l: Will Holt; d: Michael Kahn; ch: Sandra Devlin; set: Lloyd Burlingame. Part I: modern day Adam & Eve. Part II: western hero meets former girlfriend. Cast: James Coco, Ruth Jaroslow, Jerry Jarrett, Dolly Jonah, Lester James. "Some Sunday," "Gonna Get a Woman," "Sweet Time," "Nuevo Laredo," "Those Were the Days"

2585. *That Hat!* Theater Four, 9/23/64. 1 perf. w: Cy Young; based on French farce *Le chapeau de paille d'Italie*; d/ch: Dania Krupska; md: Gerald Alters. Cast: Pierre Olaf, Carmen Alvarez, Elmarie Wendel, Merle Louise, Barbara Sharma. "Italian Straw Hat," "It's All Off," "Sound of the Night," "I Love a Man," "My, It's Been Grand," "The Mad Ballet"

2586. *That Thing at the Cherry Lane.* Revue. Cherry Lane, 5/18/65–5/22/65. 6 perf. w: Jeff Steve Harris; d: Bill Penn; set/cos/light: Fred Voelpel; ms: Abba Bogin; md: Natalie

Charlson. Cast: John C. Becher, Hugh Hurd, Gloria Bleezarde, Jo Anne Worley, Evelyn Russell, Conrad Fowkes, Jayme Mylroie (understudy). "The Long Song," "Beat This!," "Lady Bird," "Ragtime," "Tears," "Olympics," "Scotch on the Rocks," "You Won't Believe Me," "Minnesota," "Blues," "Safety in Numbers," "Communication," "To Belong," "Jersey," "The New York Coloring Book"

2587. *That's Entertainment.* Although the characters have names, it is a bookless, revue-type anthology of Dietz-Schwartz songs from past shows. Edison, Middle Broadway, 4/14/72–4/16/72. 5 prev from 4/8/72; 4 perf. p: Gordon Crowe & J. Robert Breton; m: Arthur Schwartz; l: Howard Dietz; d: Paul Aaron; ch: Larry Fuller; set/light: David F. Segal; cos: Jane Greenwood; md/orch/arr: Luther Henderson; psm: May Muth; sm: Herman Magidson. Cast: David Chaney, Jered Holmes, Judith Knaiz, Michon Peacock, Vivian Reed, Scotty Salmon, Bonnie Schon, Michael Vita, Alan Weeks. "We Won't Take It Back," "Hammacher Schlemmer, I Love You," "Come, Oh, Come," "I'm Glad I'm Single," "You're Not the Type," "Miserable with You," "Something to Remember You By," "Hottentot Potentate," "Day After Day," "Fly By Night," "Everything," "Blue Grass," "Fatal Fascination," "White Heat," "Right at the Start of It," "Confession," "Smoking Reefers," "How High Can a Little Bird Fly?," "Keep off the Grass," "I See Your Face Before Me," "Experience," "Two-Faced Woman," "Foolish Face," "Be Myself," "That's Entertainment," "You and the Night and the Music," "Louisiana Hayride," "Dancing in the Dark," "Triplets," "High and Low," "How Low Can a Little Worm Go?," "Absent-Minded," "High is Better than Low," "If There is Someone Lovelier than You," "I've Made a Habit of You," "I Guess I'll Have to Change My Plan," "New Sun in the Sky," "Farewell My Lovely," "Alone Together," "Shine on Your Shoes"

2588. *That's Life.* Musical revue celebrating Jewish life. Playhouse 91, 8/1/94–4/30/95. 292 perf. p: Jewish Rep; m/l: Dick Gallagher, Ben Schaechter, June Siegel, etc; conceived by/d/ch: Helen Butleroff; cos: Gail Cooper-Hecht. Cast: Steve Sterner. "Endangered Species," "It's Beyond Me," "My Calling," "A Share of Paradise," "Mama, I Wanna Sit Downstairs," "We Could All Be Jewish if We Tried a Little Harder," "I Can Pass," "Bei Mir Bist du Rap," "Fathers and Sons." 1st produced by Jewish Rep, OOB, 6/4/94. Re-ran at Theatre East, 7/26/97–5/17/88. 144 perf. New cast

2589. *That's the Ticket.* About politics. Opened for pre–Broadway previews, 9/24/48, Shubert, Philadelphia. Closed there 10/2/48, without making Broadway. p: Joseph Kipness, John Pransky & Al Beckman; m/l: Harold Rome; b: Julius J. & Philip G. Epstein; d: Jerome Robbins; ch: Paul Godkin; md: Lehman Engel; set: Oliver Smith; cos: Miles White; light: Peggy Clark; orch: Don Walker & Robert Russell Bennett. Cast: Leif Erickson, Loring Smith, Kaye Ballard, Edna Skinner, Rod Alexander, Marc Breaux, Jack C. Carter, George S. Irving, Gisella Svetlik, Royal Dano, Kaz Kokic, Herbert Ross, Gay Laurence, Shel-

lie Farrell, Marijane Maricle, Eleanor Boleyn. "I Shouldn't Love You," "The Money Song," "Take off the Coat," "You Never Know What Hit You (When it's Love)"

2590. *That's What You Said.* Improvisational musical revue. Chicago City Limits, 7/20/95–6/22/96. 293 perf. d: Paul Zuckerman; md: Gary Adler. Cast: Gary Adler, John Cameron Telfer

2591. *Theda Bara and the Frontier Rabbi.* Set in Hollywood in 1917. Jewish Rep, 1/9/93–1/31/93. 9 prev. 15 perf. m/l: Bob Johnston & Jeff Hochhauser; d/ch: Lynne Taylor-Corbett; md: Michael Rafter; orch: Steve Margoshes. Cast: Jonathan Brody, Frank Di Pasquale. "Father, I Have Sinned," "There Are So Many Things that a Vampire Can't Do," "Frontier Rabbi," "It's Like a Movie," "Velcome to Shul," "Bolt of Love," "If She Comes Back Again," "Waiting for the Kiss to Come," "Oh, Succubus"

They All Laughed see # 502, Main Book

2592. *They Don't Make 'Em Like That Anymore.* Cabaret revue designed for impressionist Arthur Blake doing various Hollywood stars. Plaza 9 Music Hall, 6/6/72–6/25/72. 8 prev. 24 perf. m/l/sk: Hugh Martin & Timothy Gray; d: Timothy Gray; light: Beverly Emmons. Rest of cast: Clay Johns, Luba Lisa

2593. *They Wrote That?* The songs of Barry Mann & Cynthia Weil. McGinn-Cazale, 2/5/04–3/14/04. d: Richard Maltby Jr.; md: Fed Mollin. Cast: Mann & Weil, Moeisha McGill, Jenelle Lynn Randall, Deb Lyons, Daria Hardeman (understudy)

2594. *The Thing About Men.* Man finds that his wife is cheating on him, moves out to live with his friend, who just happens to be the other man. Promenade, 8/27/03–2/15/04. Prev from 8/6/03. p: Jonathan Pollard, Bernie Kukoff, Tony Converse; m: Jimmy Roberts; l/b: Joe DiPietro; based on 1985 German movie *Maenner* (*Men*) by Doris Doerrie; d: Mark Clements; ch: Rob Ashford; cast recording made 2/23/04 on DRG, and released 4/6/04. Cast: Marc Kudisch (until 2/8/04; *Graham Rowat*), Ron Bohmer, Leah Hocking, Daniel Reichard (*Danny Gurwin* stood in 10/03–12/03), Jennifer Simard. Originally called *Men*, there was a 12/02 reading, with Marc Kudisch, Christopher Sieber, Michele Pawk, Jennifer Simard, Daniel Reichard

2595. *13 Days to Broadway.* Announced for Broadway, 1983; never produced. m/l: Cy Coleman & Barbara Fried. "You There in the Back Row"

2596. *This Is the Army.* Army Emergency Relief Fund all-soldier musical revue. Broadway Theatre, Broadway, 7/4/42–9/26/42. 113 perf. p: Uncle Sam; m/l: Irving Berlin; dial: James MacColl; d: Staff Sgt Ezra Stone & Josh Logan. Cast: Pvt Burl Ives, Pvt Gary Merrill, Pvt Julie Oshins, Sgt Irving Berlin, Pvt Hayden Rorke. 300 soldiers took part. "Military Minstrel Show," "This is the Army, Mr. Jones," "The Army's Made a Man Out of Me," "I Left My Heart at the Stage Door Canteen," "Mandy," "I'm Getting Tired So I Can Sleep," "Oh, How I Hate to Get up in the Morning," "American Eagles," "This Time." Filmed in

1943, with Ronald Reagan in the cast, then toured overseas until 10/22/45. Earned $9,561,501, including film & music sales. On Broadway opening night Kate Smith paid $10,000 for two seats

2597. *This Love.* Musical revue. Duplex. 11/4/99–12/16/99. 9 perf. m/l: Brett Kristofferson; conceived by/d: Dawn M.J. Bates. Cast: Jesse Tyler Ferguson, Rebecca Burton. "This Love," "Every Day," "Get Me Where I Wanna Go," "Crazy Life of Me," "I Know You', "Something in the Way," "Happy Birthday to Me," "All the Time," "Done with Playing the Fool," "What I Do for My Man," "I Remember Moons," "Being Me," "Nothing More to Say', "City of Men," "Every Day with You," "Miki Go," "Faint and Familiar Song"

2598. *This Was Burlesque.* Musical satire in 2 acts with small score (by Sonny Lester & Bill Grundy), based on stripper Ann Corio's recollections of her famous 1930s show *This is Burlesque*, as told by her to Joe DiMona, and suggested by Eddie Jaffe. Casino East, 3/6/62. Presented by Miss Corio's husband, ex-Pittsburgh Steeler Michael Iannucci. b/d: Ann Corio; ch: Paul Brandeaux. An all-new version ran there 12/4/63–3/7/65. 1509 perf for both versions combined. Hudson Theatre, Broadway, 3/16/65–6/6/65. 124 perf. ch: Paul Morokoff (1st season), *Paul Brandeaux*. Cast: Ann Corio, Steve Mills, Harry Conley, Dick Bernie, the Burley Cuties (including Nicole Jaffe, Barbara Rhoades, Rita O'Connor). "Hello Everybody," "Bill Bailey," "St. James Infirmary," "Les Poules," "Powder My Back," "Evolution of Dance." Hudson West, 2/11/70–5/3/70. 106 perf. d/ch: Richard Barstow. Cast: Ann Corio, Steve Mills. Susan Stewart was one of the Burley Cuties. Several theatres throughout country; revived at the Princess, Broadway, 6/23/81–7/17/81. 8 prev. 28 perf. p: MPI Prods & Jeff Satkin; d: Ann Corio; ch: Fred Albee. Ann Corio led the cast. The show continues to play throughout country, its last perf being in St. Petersburg, Fla., in 1991. Banned in Chicago, Boston & Hoboken. HBO filmed it during long run at Playhouse, Paramus, N.J. Ann Corio died in 1999

2599. *This Week in the Suburbs.* Inner Circle, 6/5/83–6/26/83. 6 perf. m/l: Douglas Cohen & Susan DiLallo. Cast: Ron Orbach. "Welcome to the Neighborhood," "Suburban Calendar," "Car Pool Mother of the Year," "Tennis," "Chalktalk," "I'm the Best Volunteer," "Newspaper Boy," "I Met Him at the Mall," "Used," "Waiting for the 5.03," "Jogging," "Community Theatre," "For the Children," "Real Estate," "It's Better in the Burbs"

2600. *Thomas and the King.* Henry II's relationship with Archbishop Thomas Becket. Her Majesty's, London, 10/16/75. m: John Williams; l: James Harbert; b: Edward Anhalt; cast recording on TER. Cast: Caroline Villiers, Lewis Fiander, Tom Saffery, Richard Day-Lewis, Michael Sammes, James Smilie. "Look Around You," "Am I Beautiful?," "Man of Love," "The Question," "What Choice Have I?," "We Shall Do It," "Improbable as Spring," "Power," "'tis Love," "Sincerity," "The Test," "Replay the Game," "A New Way to Turn,"

"Will No One Rid Me?," "So Many Other Worlds"

2601. *Those Were the Days*. Musical revue in Yiddish & English. Edison, Middle Broadway, 11/7/90–2/24/91. 18 prev from 10/23/90. 126 perf. p: Moe Septee, Emanuel Azenberg, Victor H. Potamkin, Zalmen Mlotek, Moishe Rosenfeld; m/l: Ben Bonus, Sammy Cahn, Jacob Jacobs, Itzik Manger, Gioacchino Rossini, Joseph Rumshinsky, Sholom Secunda, etc; scenes: Sholem Aleichem & I.L. Peretz; conceived by: Zalmen Mlotek & Moishe Rosenfeld; d/ch: Eleanor Reissa (Tony nomination for director of a musical); cos: Gail Cooper-Hecht; md: Zalmen Mlotek; gm: Leonard Soloway. Cast: Bruce Adler (Tony nomination), Mina Bern, Eleanor Reissa, Robert Abelson, Lori Wilner, The Golden Land Klezmer Orchestra. Understudies & Standbys: For Mr. Adler: Stuart Zagnit; For Mr. Abelson: Norman Atkins; For Miss Bern: Shifra Lerer; For Miss Reissa/Miss Wilner: Sandra Ben Dor. "The Wedding," "Those Were the Days," "The Palace of the Czar," "Yiddish International Radio Hour," "Figaro's Aria" (from *The Barber of Seville*), "My Yiddishe Mame," "Bei Mir Bist du Schoen," "Rumania, Rumania"

2602. *Thoughts*. Musical celebration of memories of growing up in the South as the son of a black preacher. Theatre de Lys, 3/19/73–4/8/73. 24 perf. p: Arthur Whitelaw, Seth Harrison, Dallas Alinder, Peter Kean; w: Lamar Alford; add l: Megan Terry & Jose Tapla; d: Michael Schultz; cos: Stanley Simmons; light: Ken Billington; mus arr: David Horowitz. Cast: Barbara Montgomery, Howard Porter, Robin Lamont. "Blues Was a Pastime," "At the Bottom of Your Heart," "Ain't That Something," "Trying Hard," "Separate but Equal," "Gone," "Bad Whitey," "Thoughts," "Strange Fruit," "I Can Do it Myself," "Walking in Strange and New Places," "Music in the Air," "Sunshine," "Many Men Like You," "Roofs"

2603. *3 from Brooklyn*. Special revue. Set on a Brooklyn street, in present. Homage to Brooklyn as seen through eyes of cab driver. Helen Hayes, Broadway, 11/19/92–12/27/92. 8 prev from 11/12/92. 45 perf. p: Michael Frazier, Larry Spellman, Don Ravella; orig m/l: Sandi Merle & Steve Michaels; conceived by/d: Sal Richards; set: Charles E. McCarry; light: Phil Monat; sound: Raymond D. Schilke; md: Steve Michaels; press: Judy Jacksina; gm: Michael Frazier Prods; cm: Peter Bogyo; psm: Laura Kravets; sm: Bern Gautier. Cast: The BQE Dancers (Guy Richards, John Michaels, Damon Rusignola), Raymond Serra (as "Cosmo the Cabbie"), Adrianne Tolsch, Roslyn Kind, Bobby Alto & Buddy Mantia, Sal Richards. Broadway reviews were not good

2604. *Three Guys Naked from the Waist Down*. A trio of stand-up comics (for which "naked from the waist down" is showbiz slang) tries to make it big time. Minetta Lane, 2/5/85–6/30/85. 20 prev 160 perf. p: James B. Freydberg, Stephen Wells, Max Weitzenhoffer, Richard Maltby Jr.; m: Michael Rupert; l/b: Jerry Colker; d: Andrew Cadiff; ch: Don Bondi; set: Clarke Dunham; cos: Tom McKinley; light: Ken Billington; sound: Tony Meola; md: Henry Aronson; orch: Michael Starobin; cast recording on Polydor. Cast: John Kassir, Jerry Colker, Scott Bakula. Peter Samuel (general understudy). "Promise of Greatness," "Angry Guy/Lovely Day," "Don't Wanna Be No Superstar," "Operator," "Screaming Clocks," "The History of Stand-Up Comedy," "Dreams of Heaven," "Kamikaze Kabaret," "The American Dream," "What a Ride," "Hello Fellas," "A Father Now," "Three Guys Naked from the Waist Down Theme," "I Don't Believe in Heroes Anymore." Previously produced at PlayMakers Rep, Chapel Hill, NC. Ran at Donmar Warehouse, London, 1/13/89–2/26/89

2605. *3 Musketeers?* Theatre Royal, Margate, England, 5/31/62. m: Kenny Graham; l/b: Gerald Frow; based loosely on book by Dumas (but unrelated to Broadway musical). Cast: Athos: Powell Jones; D'Artagnan: Patrick Crean; Aramis: Christopher Tranchell; Mme Bonacieux: Zoe Randall; Also with: Emma Young, Louanne Harvey, Rosemary Croft, Tony Beckley. Lyric, Hammersmith, London, 1/30/63–3/2/63. 11 perf. d: Sally Miles; set: Tony Carruthers; light: Mick Hughes. Cast: Athos: Jack Tweddle; Porthos: Anthony Paul; Aramis: Christopher Owen; D'Artagnan: Christopher Tranchell; Cardinal/Prime Minister: Brian Hewlett; De Rochefort: Patrick Crean; Milady: Sasha Waddell; Mme Bonacieux: Zoe Randall; Also with: Powell Jones, Emma Young, Louanne Harvey, Rosemary Croft

2606. *The Three Musketeers*. Unrelated to Broadway musical. Newcastle Playhouse, England, 12/20/78–1/20/79. p: Tynewear Theatre Co.; m/l: Ian Armit & Roger Haines; b: Ken Hill; d: John Blackmore; ch: Sheila Falconer; md: Mike Stanley

2607. *The Three Musketeers*. Royal Exchange, Manchester, England, 6/25/79–7/21/79. m/l: Derek Griffiths; b: Braham Murray & Derek Griffiths; based on Dumas novel, but otherwise unrelated to Broadway musical; d: Braham Murray; ch: Michele Hardy; md: Nigel Hess. Cast: Athos: Derek Griffiths; Aramis: Trevor Peacock; Also with: Barry Martin, Keith Varnier, Nigel Hess

2608. *The 3hree Musketeers*. San Jose, Calif., 3/9/01–3/25/01. m: George Stiles; l: Paul Leigh (after Anthony Drewe had refused the job in the early 1990s); b: Peter Raby; based on Dumas novel, but otherwise unrelated to Broadway musical; d: Dianna Shuster; ch: Dottie Lester-White; set: J.B. Wilson; orch: William David Brohn. Cast: D'Artagnan: Jim Stanek; Athos: Alton Fitzgerald White; Constance: Sutton Foster; Milady de Winter: Rachel de Benedet; Bonacieux: Gerald Hiken; Porthos: Fred Inkley; Aramis: Robert Mamanna; Richelieu: James Carpenter. The musical numbers (interspersed with "Expositions") included: "Riding to Paris," "For a While," "The Challenges," "Any Day," "It's a Funny Thing Being a Hero," "Count Me In," "Paris By Night," "Shadows," "Doing Very Well without You," "Gentlemen," "The Life of a Musketeer," "Ride On!," "Ghosts," "Time," "No Gentleman," "Who Could Have Dreamed of You?," "A Good Old-Fashioned War," "Take a Little Wine," "The Inspector," "Beyond the Walls." It had been in the works since 1989 (its name was changed from *The Three Musketeers* in 8/00). After workshops in London in 1994 & 1995, and failed attempt to get to the West End, it toured Denmark in concert version in 6/97, with British cast; Florida workshop, 6/99. d: Francis Matthews. There were more readings in America, then it opened (in German), in rep, in Switzerland, on 2/26/00

2609. *The 3p Off Opera*. Musical parody of *The Threepenny Opera*. Half Moon Theatre, London, 7/12/74. m/l: Murray Head; b: Billy Colvill; add material: Tim Rice & Johnny Clarke; d: Guy Sprung. Cast: Macheath: Will Knightley; Also with: Jeff Chiswick, Pamela Moisewitsch

2610. *3 Postcards*. Set in a NY restaurant. Circle Rep. 11/16/94–12/11/94. 16 prev from 11/2/94. 31 perf. New revision of a 1987 musical (produced by Playwrights Horizons, 5/14/87; 22 perf). m/l: Craig Carnelia; b: Craig Lucas; d/ch: Tee Scatuorchio; cos: Toni-Leslie James. Cast: Steve Freeman (also md), David Pittu, Amanda Naughton. "She Was K.C.," "What the Song Should Say," "See How the Sun Shines," "I've Been Watching for You," "3 Postcards," "The Picture in the Hall," "A Minute," "I'm Standing in This Room"

2611. *Three Star Gypsy*. Announced for Broadway, 1992, but closed before NY. m/l: Leslie Bricusse. "The Eleven O'clock Song," "Love Letter to Broadway"

2612. *Three Waltzes*. 3 separate acts, set in 1867, 1900, 1937, with mus by (resp): Johann Strauss Sr., Johann Strauss Jr., and Oscar Strauss. Based on opera *Drei Walzer*, by Paul Knepler & Armin Robinson. Originally prod as *Les Trois Valses*, for Paris Expo of 1937. Majestic, Broadway, 12/25/37–4/9/38. 122 perf. Princes, London, 1945. 189 perf. "Springtime is in the Air," "My Heart Controls My Head," "Vienna Gossip," "Do You Recall?," "To Live is to Love," "The Only One," "Paree," "Can-Can," "Scandal," "Our Last Waltz Together," "The Three Waltzes"

2613. *A Thrill a Moment*. Set at Mickey's Place (bar & restaurant). Louis Abrons Arts for Living Center, 4/19/89–5/28/89. 30 perf. p: New Federal Theatre; song book: William "Mickey" Stevenson; d/ch: Edward Love; md: Grenoldo Frazier. Cast: Adrian Bailey, Kiki Shepard, Allison Williams. "Nothing's Too Good for My Baby," "He Was Really Saying Something," "Needle in a Haystack," "Playboy," "Devil with the Blue Dress," "Pride and Joy," "One of These Days," "Love Me All the Way," "Got to Be a Miracle," "Dancing in the Street," "Wild One," "My Baby Loves Me," "Truly Yours," "A Thrill a Moment," "It Takes Two"

2614. *Thrill Me: The Leopold and Loeb Story*. Nathan Leopold & Richard Loeb were the famous thrill killers who shocked Chicago in the 1920s (the Leopold & Loeb murders). Midtown International Theatre Festival, 7/16/03–8/3/03. World premiere. p: Jim Kirkstead; m/l/b: Stephen Dolginoff; d: Martin Charnin. Cast: Nathan: Christopher Totten;

Richard: Matthew Morris. York Theatre Co., 5/16/05–6/26/05 (limited run). d: Sheryl Keller

2615. *Thunder Knocking on the Door.* Blues fable. Set in 1966 rural Alabama. Alabama Shakespeare Festival, 10/1/96. p: Mitchell Maxwell & Ted Tulchin; m: Keb' Mo' & Anderson Edwards; l/b/add m: Keith Glover; d: Marion McClinton; ch: Ken Roberson; md: Olu Dara. Cast: Harriett D. Foy, Charles Weldon, Shawana Kemp, Victor Mack, Lester Purry. "All Around the World," "Good, Good Lovin'," "Evil (is Going On)," "I Just Wanna Make Love to You," "The Sky is Crying," "Tell Me," "Three O'clock Blues," "Suffering with the Blues," "Someday After a While," "I Need Your Love So Bad." Arena Stage, Washington, DC. Cincinnati Playhouse. Trinity Rep, Providence, RI, 2/15/02–3/24/02. d: Marion McClinton. Cast: Leslie Uggams, Chuck Cooper. Minetta Lane (OB), 6/20/02–7/28/02. 18 prev from 6/4. 44 perf. p: Ted Tulchin & Benjamin Mordecai; d: Oskar Eustis; set: Eugene Lee; cos: Toni-Leslie James; light: Natasha Katz; cast recording on DLP (recorded 7/7/02–7/8/02). Cast: Leslie Uggams, Chuck Cooper, Peter J. Fernandez, Marva Hicks, Michael McElroy

2616. *Thundercats Live!* Cartoon superstars come to life. Madison Square Garden, 10/2/87–10/4/87. 6 perfs. w/d/ch: Nancy Gregory. Cast: Greg Carrillo, Evel, Billy Richardson

2617. *A Thurber Carnival.* Play with mus. ANTA, 2/26/60–6/25/60. 127 perf; 9/5/60–11/26/60. 96 perf. p: Michael Davis, Helen Bonfils, Haila Stoddard; m: Don Elliott; based on writings of James Thurber; conceived by/d: Burgess Meredith; assoc d: James Starbuck; set: Marvin Reiss; light: Paul Morrison. Cast: Peggy Cass, Tom Ewell, Alice Ghostley, John McGiver, Peter Turgeon, Paul Ford, Wynne Miller, Charles Braswell, Margo Lungreen, Don Elliott Quartet. "Word Dance," "Gentleman Shoppers." Tour began 9/22/61, Center, Norfolk, Va.; closed 4/28/62, Music Hall, Kansas City. d: James Starbuck. Cast: Imogene Coca, King Donovan, Elaine Swann, Arthur Treacher. Savoy, London, 4/11/62. 27 perf. d: Willard Stoker; mus p: Johnny Dankworth. Cast: Tom Ewell, Betty Marsden, David Bauer. Equity Library, NYC, 2/9/84–2/26/84. 22 perf

2618. *tick, tick ... BOOM!* Jane Street, 6/13/01–1/6/02. 24 prev from 5/23/01. 215 perf. m/l/b: Jonathan Larson; book adapted by David Auburn; based on the life of Mr. Larson, the creator of *Rent*; d: Scott Schwartz; ch: Christopher Gattelli; md: Stephen Oremus. Cast: Raul Esparza (*Joey McIntyre*), Amy Spanger (*Molly Ringwald, Natascia Diaz* from 10/30/01), Jerry Dixon. "30/90," "Green Green Dress," "Johnny Can't Decide," "Sunday," "No More," "Therapy," "Play Game," "Real Life," "Sugar," "See Here Smile," "Come to Your Senses," "Why," "Louder than Words." Cut from the show was "Theatre is Dead." Began as solo presentations in 1990, dir by David Saint, and starring Jonathan Larson, and was then called variously *30/90* (i.e. turning 30 in 1990) and *Boho Days*, then developed into a musical revue. National tour opened 1/7/03,

Majestic, Dallas. Closed 6/8/03, Wilbur, Boston. d: Scott Schwartz; ch: Christopher Gattelli (ch); md: Randy Cohen. Cast: Wilson Cruz, Christian Campbell (*Joey McIntyre* 5/27/03–6/8/03), Nicole Ruth Snelson. George Street Theatre, NJ. 3/16/04–4/18/04 (closing extended from 4/11/04). d: David Saint; ch: Christopher Gattelli (ch); Anna Louizos (set); md: Randy Cohen. Cast: Sarah Litzsinger, Colin Hanlon, Stephen Bienskie

2619. *Tickles by Tucholsky.* Original songs & sketches written by Kurt Tucholsky for Berlin cabaret in the 1920s & 30s. Theatre Four, 4/26/76–5/9/76. 24 prev. 16 perf. translated/adapted: Louis Golden & Harold Poor; conceived by/d: Moni Yakim. Cast: Helen Gallagher, Joe Masiell, Jana Robbins, Joseph Neal, Jerry Jarrett. "The Song of Indifference," "Rising Expectations," "Tickles," "Christmas Shopping," "Brown-Shirted Cowboy," "German Evening," "Lovers," "Waldemar," "How to Get Rich," "Lullaby," "Waiting," "Follow Schmidt," "Lamplighters," "Heartbeat," "It's Your Turn," "I'm Out," "Over the Trenches"

2620. *The Tiger Rag.* Musical chronicle. Cherry Lane, 2/16/61–2/26/61. 14 perf. m: Kenneth Gaburo; l/b: Seyril Schochem; ch: Peter Conlow; light: Jules Fisher. Cast: Nancy Andrews, Patricia Roe, Logan Ramsey. "Honeysuckle Vine," "Traveling Song," "Tiger Rag Blues," "Apache," "Slewfoot Shuffle," "My Father was a Peculiar Man"

2621. *Ti-Jean and His Brothers.* Morality fable with mus. Set in West Indies. NY Shakespeare Festival outdoor program, 8/9/72–9/27/72. 2 prev. 15 perf. m/l: Andre Tanker & Derek Walcott; b/d: Derek Walcott; ch: George Faison; md: Patti Brown. Cast: Dennis Hines, Deborah Allen, Madge Sinclair, Gail Boggs

2622. *Time and Again.* Artist goes back in time to seek his muse. Set in NY in the 1880s & the present. City Center Stage II, 1/30/01–2/18/01. Prev from 1/9/01. 24 perf. The Manhattan Theatre Club production; m/l: Walter Edgar Kennon; b: Jack Viertel; based on 1970 novel by Jack Finney; add story material: James Hart; d: Susan H. Schulman; ch: Rob Ashford; set: Derek McLane; cos: Catherine Zuber; light: Ken Billington; sound: Brian Ronan; md: Kevin Stites. Cast: Laura Benanti (*Betsi Morrison* during Miss Benanti's illness), Lewis Cleale, Christopher Innvar, Joseph Kolinski, David McCallum, Julia Murney, Lauren Ward, Melissa Rain Anderson, Eric Michael Gillett, Ann Arvia, Patricia Kilgarriff, Amy Walsh. "Standing in the Middle of the Road," "At the Theatre," "Who Would Have Thought It," "She Dies," "The Lady in the Harbor," "Carrara Marble," "The Music of Love," "Who Are You, Anyway?," "What of Love?," "For Those You Love," "The Marrying Kind," "The Fire," "Time and Time Again," "The Right Look," "I Know This House." Developed in readings at 1993 National Theatre Conference, at Eugene O'Neill Theatre Center. World premiere at Old Globe, San Diego, 1995

2623. *Time and the Wind.* John Houseman, 7/27/95–9/2/95. 12 prev. 27 perf. p: Eric

Krebs, John Houseman Theatre Center, AMAS; m/md: Galt MacDermot; l: Norman Matlock; d/ch: Louis Johnson. Cast: Carl Hall. "Time and the Wind," "I Came to Town," "Gentle Rain," "By the Time I Forget Her," "My Key Don't Fit the Lock," "I Am Not Gone," "There Are Times," "They Didn't Ask," "When You Love Really," "Tell Her You Care," "When I Was a Child," "I Was Taught to Love," "Flowers for Her Hair," "I Love You," "True Love's Hand," "Goodbye," "According to Plan"

2624. *Time, Gentlemen, Please.* British musical revue. Strollers Theatre-Club, 11/4/61. p: John Krimsky & The Players Theatre of London; d: Don Gammell (London), Fred Stone (NY); ch: Tony Bateman. On 1/16/62 a new program of songs was introduced. Cast: Fred Stone, Joan Sterndale Bennett, Tony Bateman

2625. *Times and Appetites of Toulouse-Lautrec.* Set 11/24/1864–9/9/1901, in Paris. American Place, 12/5/85–12/15/85. 18 perf. l: Michael Feingold (based on French originals); b: Jeff Wanshel; d: John Ferraro; ch: Priscilla Lopez; md: Russell Walden. Cast: Lonny Price, MacIntyre Dixon, Ron Faber, June Gable, Priscilla Lopez. "Freckled Fanny," "Can-Can," "Under a Bridge at Night," "Mademoiselle de Paris," "It's Not as Good as Love," "Along the Seine"

2626. *Tip-Toes.* Liberty, Broadway, 12/28/25–6/12/26. 194 perf. p: Alex A. Aarons & Vinton Freedley (they gave their names to the Alvin Theatre); m: George Gershwin; l: Ira Gershwin; b: Guy Bolton & Fred Thompson; ch: Sammy Lee. Cast: Jeanette MacDonald, Robert Halliday. "Waiting for the Train," "Nice Baby," "Looking for a Boy," "Lady Luck," "When Do We Dance?," "These Charming People," "That Certain Feeling," "Sweet and Low-Down," "Our Little Captain," "It's a Great Little World," "Nightie-Night," "Tip-Toes." The Goodspeed production, presented by Brooklyn Academy of Music at the Helen Carey Playhouse, 3/24/79–4/8/79. 5 prev from 3/21/79. 19 perf. p: Warren Pincus; d: Sue Lawless; ch: Dan Siretta; md: William Cox. Cast: Russ Thacker, Georgia Engel, Bob Gunton, Jana Robbins, Nicole Barth, Jon Engstrom, Susan Danielle

2627. *T.N.T.* Musical send-up of California cults (Tricephalous Neurosyllogistic Training). Players, 4/22/82–4/25/82. 7 prev. 6 perf. w: Richard Morrock; d: Frank Carucci; ch: Mary Lou Crivello. Cast: Steven F. Hall, Mary Ann Dorward, Regis Bowman, Gabriel Barre, Mary Garripoli. "Why?," "Tricephalous You," "Life is a Four-Letter Word," "A Casual Kind of Thing," "Previous Lives," "Where Have I Been," "Mantra," "Id Superego," "Longing for Someone," "I'm OK, You're OK," "Meat Market," "The Secret of Life"

2628. *To Be or Not to Be ... What Kind of a Question Is That?* American-Israeli topical musical revue. Barbizon Plaza, 10/19/70–11/15/70. 32 perf. d/ch: Marvin Gordon; md: Eli Rubinstein. Cast: Denise Lor, Evelyn Kingsley, Mark Stuart. "The Wolf and the Lamb," "I'm in Love with a Flyer," "Tilibim,"

"Tel-Aviv I Love You," "Chiribim," "Haifa Melody," "The Eighth Day"

2629. *To Broadway with Love.* Musical extravaganza. Ran twice a day and had a completely different cast each perf. Texas Pavilion's Music Hall, NY World's Fair, 4/21/64. p: George Schaefer, Angus G. Wynne Jr., Compass Fair, Inc.; title theme/orig m: Jerry Bock & Sheldon Harnick; conceived by/d: Morton Da Costa; ch: Donald Saddler; md: Franz Allers; adapted by/mus arr: Philip J. Lang. Cast: Carmen Alvarez, Kelly Brown, Millie Slavin. "To Broadway with Love," "Old Folks at Home," "Dixie," "Till the Clouds Roll By," "Over There," "Lullaby of Broadway," "There's No Business Like Show Business," "Hey, Look Me Over"

2630. *To Live Another Summer, to Pass Another Winter.* Israeli musical revue, about Israel's emergence as a nation. Helen Hayes, Broadway, 10/21/71–1/8/72; Lunt-Fontanne, 1/10/72–3/19/72. 14 prev. Total of 173 perf. p: Leonard Soloway; m: Dov Seltzer & David Krivoshei; l: Hayim Hefer; d/ch: Jonathan Karmon; set: Neil Peter Jampolis. Cast: Rivka Raz, Hanan Goldblatt, David Devon. "Son of Man" (translated by David Axelrod), "The Sacrifice," "What Are the Basic Things?" (translated by Lillian Burstein), "The Grove of Eucalyptus" (m/l: Naomi Shemer; translated by George Sherman), "Mediterranee," "When My Man Returns" (m: George Moustaki), "Better Days," "To Live Another Summer, To Pass Another Winter," "Noah's Ark" (replaced midway through run with "I Never Wanted to Be a Hero"), "Give Me a Star" (m: David Krivoshei). Tour opened 4/4/72, Boston, and closed 4/30, Forrest, Philadelphia

2631. *To Whom It May Concern.* Musical celebration. Churchgoers sing their thoughts during a service. St. Stephen's Church, 12/16/85–3/23/86. 19 prev from 11/19/85. 106 perf. w: Carol Hall; d: Geraldine Fitzgerald; ch/md: Michael O'Flaherty. Cast: Michael O'Flaherty, Gretchen Cryer, Carol Hall, Louise Edeiken, Becky Gelke, Guy Stroman, Kecia Lewis-Evans, George Gerdes, Al DeCristo. "When I Consider the Heavens," "Truly My Soul," "Blessed Be God," "Holy God," "Miracles," "We Were Friends," "Sandy," "Make a Joyful Noise," "Ain't Nobody Got a Bed of Roses," "We Believe," "I Only Miss the Feeling," "My Sort of Ex Boyfriend," "Jenny Rebecca," "Skateboard Acrobats," "In the Mirror's Reflection," "Ain't Love Easy," "Walk in Love," "Who Will Dance with the Blind Dancing Bear," "To Whom it May Concern." Previously presented at the summer festival at Williamstown, Mass.

2632. *Together Again for the First Time.* Jo Sullivan & Emily Loesser (her stage debut) in celebration of Broadway musicals. Kaufman, 2/27/89–3/26/89. 13 prev from 2/17/89. 30 perf. p: Martin R. Kaufman; conceived by: Barry Kleinbort & Colin Romoff; d: Barry Kleinbort; md: Colin Romoff; cos: William Ivey Long

2633. *'Toinette.* Set in Paris in 1961. Marquee, 11/20/61–12/16/61. 31 perf. m/l: Dede Meyer; based on Moliere's *Le Malade Imagi-*

naire; d: Curt Conway; ch: Harry Woolever; md: David Shire. Cast: Logan Ramsey, Ellie Wood, Paul Dooley. "Rags," "Bonjour," "Come on Outside and Get Some Air," "Why Shouldn't I?," "A Father Speaks," "A Lullaby," "Honest Honore," "Someone to Count On," "Fly Away," "'Toinette," "Madly in Love with You Am I," "Beat, Little Pulse," "Even a Doctor Can Make a Mistake," "Small Apartment," "You're the Most Impossible Person"

2634. *Tokyo Can Can.* Set in Tokyo, after WWII. St. Clement's, 6/4/96–6/22/96. 8 prev. 12 perf. m: Saburo Iwakawa; l/b/d: Yutaka Okada; ch: Lois Englund; md: Kuni Mikami. Cast: Bruce Alan Johnson, Melanie May Po, Reggie Lee, Christine Toy

2635. *Tom Brown's Schooldays.* Ashcroft Theatre, Croydon, England, 11/6/71. At that stage called *Young Tom*, an amateur prod. p: Joe Vegoda; m: Chris Andrews; l/b: Jack & Joan Maitland; based on 1857 novel by Thomas Hughes. Changed name; Cambridge Theatre, London, 5/9/72–7/15/72. 76 perf. Very bad reviews. p: Richard M. Mills & Harold Davidson; d: Peter Coe; ch: Leo Kharibian; md: Alan Braden; cast recording on Decca. Cast: Tom: Adam Walton; Dr. Arnold: Roy Dotrice; Also with: Leon Greene, Jill Martin, Ray Davis, Judith Bruce, Michael Darbyshire, Keith Chegwin. "Petticoat Government," "I Like My Children Around," "Head Up," "In the Swim," "My Way," "Three Acres and a Cow," "Where is He?," "What is a Man?," "Young Tom," "Have a Try," "Six of the Best," "If I Had a Son," "A Boy's Point of View," "Vision of Youth," "Warwickshire Home," "One for Your Nose," "Hold Me," "The Ballad of the Great White Horse"

2636. *Tomfoolery.* Criterion, London, 6/5/80. m/l: Tom Lehrer. Cast: Jonathan Adams, Martin Connor, Tricia George, Robin Ray. "Be Prepared," "Poisoning Pigeons," "I Wanna Go Back to Dixie," "My Home Town," "Pollution," "Bright College Days," "Fight Fiercely Harvard," "The Elements," "Folk Song Army," "In Old Mexico," "She's My Girl," "When You Are Old and Grey," "Wernher von Braun," "Who's Next," "I Got it From Agnes," "National Brotherhood Week," "So Long Mom," "Send the Marines," "Hunting Song," "Irish Ballad," "New Math," "Silent E," "Oedipus Rex," "I Hold Your Hand in Mine," "Masochism Tango," "Old Dope Peddler," "The Vatican Rag," "We Will All Go Together When We Go." Village Gate Upstairs, NYC, 12/14/81–3/28/82. 27 prev. 120 perf. p: Cameron Mackintosh & Hinks Shimberg, in spite of Art D'Lugoff; adapted by: Cameron Mackintosh & Robin Ray; d: Gary Pearle & Mary Kyte; set: Tom Lynch; md: Eric Stern. Cast: Donald Corren, Jonathan Hadary, Joy Franz, MacIntyre Dixon. Equity Library, 1/5/89–1/29/89. 24 perf. d/ch: Pamela Hunt. Cast: Don Bradford, Jack Doyle, Patricia Masters, John Remme, Bob McDowell (piano/md)

2637. *Tomorrow's Broadway: A Look Back.* Musical revue. Set at the future 1999 Tony Awards show, and is a retrospective view of the last 10 years of Broadway (i.e. 1989–1999). Baldwin, 2/17/88–2/28/88. 10 perf. m/l:

Tony Tanner, David Bruen, Vince Morton; conceived by: Leslie Welles & Robert Carson; d: David Bruen; md: Vince Morton. Cast: Leslie Welles, Robert Carson

2638. *Tonight at 8:30.* Nine one-act plays with mus (performed in 3 separate programs). National, Broadway, 11/24/36–3/9/37. 118 perf. p: John C. Wilson; plays/m/l/d: Noel Coward. Cast: Gertrude Lawrence, Graham Payn. National, Broadway, 2/20/48–3/14/48. 26 perf. This time only 6 plays (in 2 programs). p: Homer Curran, Russell Lewis, Howard Young; d: Noel Coward; ch: Richard Barstow; md: Frank Tours. Cast: Gertrude Lawrence, Graham Payn, Booth Colman

2639. *Tonight's the Night.* The "Rod Stewart musical." A mechanic sells his soul to be as cool as Rod. Based on Mr. Stewart's hits. Victoria Palace, London, 11/03–10/9/04 (it closed early). w/d: Ben Elton. Cast: Tim Hower. Despite bad reviews, it was popular. There was a UK tour in 2005

2640. *Too Jewish.* Rock musical comedy revue. Westside Theatre Downstairs, 9/7/95–2/18/96. 189 perf. w/conceived by: Avi Hoffman; md: Ben Schaechter. Cast: Avi Hoffman. 1st prod OOB, 1/15/95. After Westside it ran 6 months in Florida, then did national tour. PBS TV showed it, 12/3/02 & 12/8/02. There was a sequel, *Too Jewish Two*, 4/28/98–5/17/98. Prev from 4/18/98. p: Jewish Rep; d: Avi Hoffman

2641. *Too Many Girls.* Set in 1939 in New England, and at Pottawatomie College, NM. Imperial, Broadway, 10/18/39; Broadway Theatre, 4/22/40–5/18/40. Total of 249 perf. p/d: George Abbott; m: Richard Rodgers; l: Lorenz Hart; b: George Marion Jr.; ch: Robert Alton; cos: Raoul Pene du Bois; md: Harry Levant; orch: Hans Spialek; voc arr: Hugh Martin. Cast: Desi Arnaz, Eddie Bracken, Van Johnson, Richard Kollmar, Mary Jane Walsh, Leila Ernst, Mildred Law, Diosa Costello. "Heroes in the Fall," "Tempt Me Not," "My Prince," "Pottawatomie," "'cause We Got Cake," "Love Never Went to College," "Spic and Spanish," "I Like to Recognize the Tune," "Look Out," "Sweethearts of the Team," "She Could Shake the Maracas," "I Didn't Know What Time It was," "Too Many Girls," "Give it Back to the Indians." Filmed 1940, with Lucille Ball & Ann Miller. Equity Library, 3/12/87–4/5/87. 2 prev. 30 perf. d: Stephen G. Hults; ch: Larry Hayden; md: Jay Dias. Cast: Bryan Batt

2642. *Touch.* Episodes of life among companionship-seeking youth in modern communes. Village Arena, 11/8/70; the Martinique, 6/1/71. m/l: Kenn Long & Jim Crozier; b: Amy Saltz & Kenn Long; d: Amy Saltz; cast recording on AMPEX. Cast: Kenn Long. "Declaration," "Windchild," "City Song," "Sitting in the Park," "I Don't Care," "Goodbyes," "Come to the Road," "Reaching, Touching," "Quiet Country," "Susan's Song," "Tripping," "Alphagenesis"

2643. *Tough at the Top.* Adelphi, London, 7/1/49–11/26/49. 154 perf. p: C.B. Cochran & Anthony Vivian; m: Vivian Ellis; l/b: A.P. Herbert; d/ch: Wendy Toye; set/cos: Oliver Messel; md: Michael Collins. Cast: Carol Raye,

Gwen Nelson, George Tozzi, Eddie Byrne, Peter Lupino, Geoffrey Bayldon, Anita Bolster

2644. *Toulouse*. Set in Paris in 1891. Ukrainian Hall, 9/14/81–9/27/81. 12 perf. p: Ronnie Britton & Robert Speller; w/d: Ronnie Britton; ch: Robert Speller; md: Keith Ripka. Cast: Toulouse-Lautrec: Richard Rescingno; Also with: Beverly Gold, Molly Stark, Charlotte d'Amboise

2645. *Tour de Four*. Musical revue. Writers' Stage, 6/18/63–6/30/63. 16 perf. m/l/sk: June Carroll & Arthur Siegel, etc; conceived by/d: Tom Eyen; md: Natalie Charlson. Cast: Lyle O'Hara, Paul Blake, Carol Fox, Carl Crow. "Tour de Four"

2646. *Township Fever*. Set in South Africa, 1987. Majestic, 12/19/90–1/20/91. 30 prev from 11/23/90. 39 perf. The Committed Artists production, presented in assoc with Brooklyn Academy of Music; m/l/b/conceived by/d/ch/orch: Mbongeni Ngema. Cast: Sindiswa Dlathu, Bhoyi Ngema, Mabonga Khumalo, John Lata, Sbusiso Ngema, Mamthandi Zulu, Themba Mbonani, Clara Reyes. "One Blood," "Township Fever," "Blazing Like Fire," "Beautiful Little Mama," "Times of War," "Corruption," "South Africa," "Mandela," "Freedom Charter"

2647. *The Traveling Music Show*. Her Majesty's, London, 3/28/78. m/l: Leslie Bricusse & Anthony Newley; cast recording on CBS. Cast: Bruce Forsyth, Derek Griffiths, Valerie Welsh, Katie Budd. "On a Wonderful Day Like Today," "Nothing Can Stop me Now," "The Candy Man," "Feeling Good," "My Way," "The Ladies Love Me," "London is London," "Talk Your Way Out of It," "King of the Castle," "I Wanna Be Rich," "Gonna Build a Mountain," "Typically English," "The Joker," "The Good Old Bad Old Days," "Someone Nice Like You," "Who Can I Turn To?," "If I Ruled the World," "On the Boards," "When You Gotta Go"

2648. *Treasure Island*. Town Hall, 5/21/73–5/23/73. 4 perf. Ran in rep with *Rumpelstiltskin*. m/l/md: John Clifton; b: Tom Tippett; from Robert Louis Stevenson's novel; d: Evan Thompson. Cast: Jim: Joan Shepherd; Silver: Chester Thornhill. "Treasure Island," "I'll Buy Me a Ship," "Gold," "That's What I Would Do," "Honest Sailors," "Yo-Ho," "Let's Be Friends." Tour opened 1/20/75, DuPont Playhouse, Wilmington, Del., and closed 3/8/75, Shubert, New Haven. Same crew; same cast, except Silver: Christopher Cable

2649. *Treasure Island*. Musical adventure. Mermaid, London, 12/17/73–2/2/74. m: Cyril Ornadel; l: Hal Shaper; b: Bernard Miles & Josephine Wilson; from Robert Louis Stevenson's novel; d: Josephine Wilson; ch: Terry Gilbert & Denys Palmer; md: John Burrows; cast recording on Prestige. Cast: Jim: Roger Eden; Silver: Bernard Miles; Also with: Nicholas Smith, Gary Raymond, Spike Milligan. "Treasure Island," "The Admiral Benbow Inn," "Fifteen Men on a Dead Man's Chest," "Find That Boy," "Shipmates, Partn'rs and Pals," "Land Ho," "Deepwater Sailors," "Cheese," "Cap'n Silver," "Far Away from England," "Never Get Caught." Mermaid, 12/16/74; New London Theatre, 12/18/75

2650. *Treasure Island*. Birmingham Rep, England, 12/21/84–2/9/85. m: Denis King; l/b: Willis Hall; from Robert Louis Stevenson's novel; d: Clive Perry; ch: Kenn Oldfield; md: Ed Coleman. Cast: John Barr, Eileen Gourlay, Bob Grant, Jack Douglas

2651. *Trelawny*. Theatre Royal, Bristol, England. 1/12/72–2/26/72. p: Bristol Old Vic Co.; m/l: Julian Slade; b: Aubrey Woods, George Powell, Julian Slade; from Arthur Wing Pinero's play *Trelawny of the Wells*. Sadler's Wells, London, 6/27/72. Prev from 6/21/72. p: Cameron Mackintosh. Prince of Wales, London, 8/3/72–12/2/72. 177 perf. d: Val May; ch: Bob Stevenson; md: Neil Rhoden; cast recording on TER. Cast: Hayley Mills (*Gemma Craven*), Ian Richardson, Timothy West (*Max Adrian, Roland Culver*), Rosamund Greenwood (*Joyce Carey*), John Parker (*Teddy Green*), Philip Hinton. "Pull Yourself Together," "Walking On," "Ever of Thee," "Trelawny of the Wells," "On Approval," "Rules," "Back to the Wells," "Old Friends," "The One Who isn't There," "We Can't Keep 'em Waiting," "Two Fools," "Life." Bristol Old Vic, 1972. 171 perf. Same basic cast

2652. *Trevallion*. Comic opera. Palace, London, 3/21/56–3/24/56. 4 perf. m: Roy Phillips; l: Philip Phillips; b: Philip Phillips & Malcolm Morley; d: Malcolm Morley; md: Charles Brill. Cast: Anne Lascelles

2653. *The Trials of Oz*. Play with mus. Anderson, 12/19/72–12/31/72. 15 perf. songs: John Lennon, Yoko Ono, Mick Jagger, etc; w: Geoff Robertson; based on 1971 Old Bailey trial of controversial publication *Oz*; d: Jim Sharman; cos: Joseph G. Aulisi; light: Jules Fisher. Cast: Cliff DeYoung, Greg Antonacci, Harry Gold, Leata Galloway (understudy). "Oranges and Lemons," "Rupert Bear Song," "If You Can't Join 'em, Beat 'em," "Dirty is the Funniest Thing I Know," "Masquerade Ball," "The Love's Still Growing," "Give Me Excess of It," "Schoolboy Blues," "The Justice Game," "God Save Us"

2654. *Trixie True, Teen Detective*. Set in mid–1940s; teenaged pulp fiction detective heroine of Cherry Hill, NJ. Theatre de Lys, 12/7/80–2/15/81. 6 prev from 12/4/80. 86 perf. w: Kelly Hamilton; d: Bill Gile; ch: Arthur Faria; set: Michael J. Hotopp & Paul de Pass; cos: David Toser; light: Craig Miller; md: Robert Fisher; orch: Eddie Sauter. Cast: Kathy Andrini, Marilyn Sokol, Gene Lindsey. "Trixie's on the Case!," "This is Indeed My Lucky Day," "Most Popular and Most Likely to Succeed," "Mr. and Mrs. Dick Dickerson," "Juvenile Fiction," "A Katzenjammer Kind of Song," "You Haven't Got Time for Love," "In Cahoots," "The Mystery of the Moon," "The Secret of the Tapping Shoes," "Rita from Argentina," "Trixie True Teen Detective!"

2655. *Troubadour*. Cambridge Theatre, London, 12/19/78–2/24/79. 76 perf. p/l/b: Michael Lombardi; m: Ray Holder; d: James Fortune; ch: David Drew; md: Denys Rawson. Cast: Andrew C. Wadsworth, Kim Braden. "The Wife-Beating Song," "Troubadour," "Panic in the Palace," "Melancholy Lover," "Onward to Jerusalem," "We Must

Have Jerusalem," "Mary's Child," "Woman, Whoever You Are"

2656. *Troubadour*. Life of Francis of Assisi, set 1205–1225. Riverwest, 1990. m/l/b: Bert Draesel & John Martin; d: John Margulis; ch: Paul Nunes; md: Howard Kilik. Cast: Christopher Mellon. "The Troubadour," "Who Can Benefit You Most?," "There Must Be Something More," "You Can't Have Me," "The Rule/Called to the Simple Life," "Listen to the Voice," "An Unusual Normal," "There is a Mystery," "There is a Time," "This is the Man," "Every Day," "Soon," "And We Were One," "It Was Magnificent," "Let There Be Books," "Praised Be My Lord." Revised & re-presented by the Ubu Repertory, 5/25–8/3/91. d/md: D.J. Maloney

2657. *Trouble in Tahiti*. One-act, 7-scene opera. Brandeis University, Waltham, Mass, 6/12/52. m/l: Leonard Bernstein. Playhouse, Broadway, 4/19/55–5/28/55. 49 perf as the 1st segment of the 3-part production *All in One*. p: Charles Bowden & Richard Barr; set/light: Eldon Elder; cos: Pat Campbell. The other 2 parts were Paul Draper doing his one-man dance program, and a one-act play by Tennessee Williams, *27 Wagons Full of Cotton* (dir by Vincent J. Donehue, and starring Maureen Stapleton, Myron McCormick, Felice Orlandi). As for Bernstein's opera, the cast included: Dinah: Alice Ghostley; Sam: John Tyers; Also with: Constance Brigham, John Taliaferro, James Tushar. d: David Brooks. See also *A Quiet Place*. *Trouble in Tahiti* was revived at City Center, running 4/6/58–4/18/58. 3 perf in rep with opera *Tale for a Deaf Ear*, by Mark Bucci. d: Michael Pollock; set: Andreas Nomikos. Cast: Beverly Wolff, David Atkinson, Naomi Collier, William Metcalf, Stanley Kolk

2658. *Truckload*. Lyceum, Broadway, 9/6/75–9/11/75 (prevs only). Closed during previews, canceling scheduled opening night of 9/23/75. p: Adela Holzer, Shubert Organization, Dick Clark; m/l: Louis St. Louis & Wes Harris; b: Hugh Wheeler; conceived by: Patricia Birch & Louis St. Louis; d/ch: Patricia Birch; set: Douglas W. Schmidt; cos: Carrie F. Robbins; light: John Gleason. Cast: Debbie Allen, Cheryl Barnes, Donnie Burks, Jose Fernandez, Ilene Graff, Sherry Mathis, Kelly Ward, Laurie Prange, Doug McKeown, Kenneth S. Eiland, Ralph Strait, Rene Enriquez, Louis St. Louis & the All Night Drivers, Chris Callan (standby). "Truckload," "Find My Way Home," "Cumbia/Wedding Party," "Step-Mama," "Look at Us," "Standing in This Phone Booth," "Amelia's Theme," "I Guess Everything Will Turn Out All Right," "Rest Stop," "Boogie Woogie Man," "Ricardo's Lament," "Hash House Habit," "Dragon Strikes Back," "Bonnie's Song," "Pour Out Your Soul," "Jesus is My Main Man," "There's Nothing Like Music," "Hello Sunshine"

2659. *Trumpets of the Lord*. Musical adaptation by Vinnette Carroll of James Weldon Johnson's *God's Trombones*, presented as revival meeting, built around sermons by Mr. Johnson which tell story of Biblical characters, with help of gospel music. Astor Place, 12/21/63; One Sheridan Square, 1/22/64–5/17/64. Total of 160 perf. p: Theodore Mann & Will B. Sandler; d: Donald McKayle; set: Ed Wittstein. Cast: Al Freeman Jr. (*Ed Hall*), Cicely Tyson. "So Glad I'm Here," "Call to Prayer," "Listen Lord — a Prayer," "Amen Response," "In His Care," "The Creation," "God Lead Us Along," "Noah Built the Ark," "Run Sinner Run," "Didn't It Rain," "The Judgment Day," "In That Great Gettin'-up Mornin'," "Soon One Morning," "There's a Man," "Go Down Death," "He'll Understand," "Were You There?," "Calvary," "Crucifixion," "Reap What You Sow," "I Shall Not Be Moved," "We Are Soldiers," "Woke up This Morning," "Let My people Go," "We Shall Overcome," "Jacob's Ladder," "God Be with You." Brooks Atkinson, Broadway, 4/29/69–5/3/69. 7 perf. p: Circle in the Square; d: Theodore Mann; set: Marsha Eck; light: Jules Fisher; md: Howard Roberts. Cast: Cicely Tyson, Bernard Ward, Theresa Merritt, Lex Monson. The musical *God's Trombones* ran at the Church of St. Paul & St. Andrew, 4/11/75–4/27/75. 12 perfs. Cast: John Barracuda (also d), Dee Dee Levant, Fran Salisbury, Juliet Seignious (also ch). Revived as *Godsong*, at AMAS, from 3/4/76. adapted by/d: Tad Truesdale. Cast: Ernie Adano, Ruth Brisbane. *God's Trombones* was re-done at Town Hall, 4/16/82 –4/18/82. 3 perf. d: James Petis. Cast: Maxwell Glanville (as the pastor). And again, at New Federal Theatre, from 10/4/89. 45 perf. Cast: Rhetta Hughes, Lex Monson, Theresa Merritt. Tribeca Performing Arts Center, 2/5/97–2/9/97. 5 perf. d: Woodie King Jr. Cast: Trazana Beverly, Todd Davis, Theresa Merritt

2660. *The Truth About Ruth: The Musical Memoirs of a Bearded Lady*. Actors Playhouse, 6/28/94–7/94. m: Brad Ellis; l/b: Peter Morris; d/ch: Phillip George; md: Pete Blue. Cast: Ruth: Peter Morris (*Tom DiBuono*); The Men in Her Life: David Lowenstein. "The Truth About Ruth," "Hit That High Note," "Home, Sweet Home," "Hello, Hello," "Love Nest," "You're Unique," "Bang," "Dear Ruth"/"Ruth's Hit Parade," "This is the Place to Be," "Face the Fact," "Let Me Possess You," "Low," "If I Were Beautiful." Previously a one-act cabaret show at the Duplex, under the title *The Remarkable Ruth Fields*

2661. *Try It, You'll Like It*. Yiddish. Mayfair, 3/14/73–5/27/73. 87 perf. m/l: Alexander Olshenetsky & Jacob Jacobs. Cast: Jacob Jacobs (also d). "Try it, You'll Like It"

Tsk, Tsk, Tsk see # 534, Main Book

2662. *Tune the Grand Up!* Bruno Walter Auditorium, 12/18/78–12/20/78. 3 perf. p: Stage Directors & Choreographers Workshop Foundation/Sally E. Parry & Peter M. Paulino; m/l: Jerry Herman; add dial: Mary McCartney; d/ch: Jeffrey K. Neill; md/adapted/at piano: Wendell Kindberg. Cast: Barbara Coggin, Norb Joerder, Edna Manilow, Ed Penn, Maitland Peters, Lisa M. Steinman, John Vought, Ruth E. Kramer, Lou Corato, Jim Jeffrey, Joan Kobin, Joan Susswein

2663. *Tuscaloosas's Calling Me … But I'm Not Going!* Musical revue. The case for living in NYC, in songs and sketches. Top of the Gate, 12/1/75; Westside Theatre, 12/26/75–

12/12/76. Total of 429 perf. The Quintal production; m: Hank Beebe; l: Bill Heyer; d: James Hammerstein & Gui Andrisano; md: Jeremy Harris. Cast: Patti Perkins, Renny Temple (*Chip Zien*), Len Gochman (*Ted Pritchard, Paul Kreppel*). "Only Right Here in New York City," "I Dig Myself," "Cold Cash," "Things Were Out," "Central Park on a Sunday Afternoon," "New York from the Air," "Backwards', "Delicatessen," "Everything You Hate is Right Here," "Fugue for a Menage a Trois," "Poor," "Graffiti," "Singles Bar," "Astrology" "New York 69," "Tuscaloosa's Calling Me, But I'm Not Going"

2664. *Twang!!* About Robin Hood. Palace, Manchester, England, 11/3/65; Shaftesbury, London, 12/20/65–1/29/66. 43 perf. p: Bernard Delfont; m/l: Lionel Bart; b: Lionel Bart & Harvey Orkin; d: Joan Littlewood, *Burt Shevelove*; ch: Paddy Stone; set/cos: Oliver Messel; md: Kenneth Moule, *Gareth Davies*; cast recording on TER. Cast: Barbara Windsor, Toni Eden, Bob Grant, James Booth, Ronnie Corbett, Long John Baldry, Bernard Bresslaw, Maxwell Shaw, Howard Goorney, Ben Aris, Clive Barker, Terry Williams. "Welcome to Sherwood," "What Makes a Star," "Make an Honest Woman of Me," "To the Woods," "Roger the Ugly," "Dreamchild," "With Bells On," "Twang!!," "Unseen Hands," "Sighs," "You Can't Catch Me," "Follow Your Leader," "Wander," "Whose Little Girl Are You?," "I'll Be Hanged"

2665. *Twanger*. Vandam, 11/15/72–12/10/72. 2 prev. 24 perf. m/l/b/ch: Ronnie Britton; d: Walter Ash; mus arr: Gordon Harrell. Cast: Becky Thatcher McSpadden. "Wanna Get Married," "Five Minutes Ago," "Have You Seen the Princess?," "Impossibility," "A Sister and a Brother," "To Win a Prince," "Twanger!," "Normal, Normal, Normal," "Tiny Light," "Forest of Silver," "But I Love You"

2666. *The 25th Annual Putnam County Spelling Bee*. 6 young people on the point of puberty trying to become adults. Workshop prod by Barrington Stage Co., Mass, who also prod the world premiere, at Sheffield, Mass, in 7/04. Second Stage, 2/7/05–3/20/05. Prev from 1/11/05. m/l: William Finn; conceived by: Rebecca Feldman; b: Rachael Sheinkin. Cast: Jesse Tyler Ferguson, Celia Keenan-Bolger, Jose Llana. By 2/05 it was aiming for Broadway

2667. *Twenty Fingers, Twenty Toes*. Musical bio of the the Siamese twins, the Hilton Sisters. Set 1925–1929 in carnivals & vaudeville houses across USA. WPA, 12/19/89–1/21/90. 35 perf. m/l: Michael Dansicker; b: Michael Dansicker & Bob Nigro; d: Bob Nigro; ch: Ken Prescott; md: Dick Gallagher. Cast: Daisy: Ann Brown; Violet: Maura Hanlon; Also with: Roxie Lucas, Paul Kandel, Ken Prymus. "We Don't Have a Mother," "Bluebirds," "Sign on the Dotted Line," "Feet," "Doubletalk," "Twenty Fingers, Twenty Toes," "Natural Harmony," "We'll Always Be Together," "Nothin's Gonna Stay the Same Forever," "Abracadabra," "Cooperation," "Two Different People," "Bad," "The Clock is Ticking." Theatre at St. Peter's, NYC, 10/15/04–

10/17/04. Part of *Musicals in Mufti* series. p: York Theatre Co.; d: Jay Binder; md: Lawrence Yurman. Cast: Jenna Coker, Alicia Sable, Beth McVey, Paul Kandel, James Stovall, Mark Price. See also *Side Show*, in the main part of this book

2668. *Twenty Minutes South*. Players Theatre, England, 5/10/55. Re-staged at Theatre Royal, Birmingham, 6/27/55; Nottingham, from 7/4/55; St. Martin's, London, 7/13/55–10/8/55. 101 perf. m/md: Peter Greenwell; l/b: Maurice Browning; d: Hattie Jacques; set/cos: Reginald Woolley. Cast: Totti Truman Taylor, George Woodbridge, Margaret Burton (*Daphne Anderson*), John Le Mesurier, Brian Blades

2669. *22 Years*. A Jeff Britton/Manhattan Theatre Club rockumentary. Notorious mass-murderer Charles Manson (played by Frank Girardeau) and his family shown as innocent victims. Stage 73, 12/9/71–1/29/72. 40 perf. d/w: Robert Sickinger. Several songs, including 2 written by Manson himself. Cast: King Morton, Joan Grove

2670. *Two*. Set in small Illinois towns of Dwight and Beardstown. Vandam, 4/15/82–4/25/82. 12 perf. m/l: Misha Segal & Fredricka Weber; b: Fredricka Weber; d: Raymond Homer; orch: Doug Katsaros. Cast: Evelyn Page, Joe Godfrey, Charles C. Welch, Fredricka Weber. "Illinois," "It Might Fall Off," "I've Got a Secret," "I'll Be a Hairstylist to the Movie Stars," "Ain't She Sweet," "Do the Opposite," "One Door Opens," "Don't Lose That Spark"

2671. *2 by 5*. Retrospective musical cabaret revue of works of John Kander & Fred Ebb. Village Gate Downstairs, 10/19/76–12/5/76. 57 perf. m/l: Kander & Ebb; conceived by/d: Seth Glassman. Cast: D'jamin Bartlett, Kay Cummings, Danny Fortus, Shirley Lemmon, Scott Stevensen. "Cabaret," "Wilkommen," "Yes," "Sing Happy," "Mein Herr," "Seeing Things," "The World Goes Round," "Love Song," "The Money Song," "Sign Here," "My Own Best Friend," "Losers," "Military Man," "Only Love," "Why Can't I Speak," "Me and My Baby," "Isn't This Better?," "Home," "Maybe This Time," "Ring Them Bells," "Mr. Cellophane," "(Walking) Among My Yesterdays," "I Don't Remember You," "Class," "Broadway, My Street," "New York, New York," "On Stage," "Ten Percent," "Razzle Dazzle," "A Quiet Thing," "Cabaret" (reprise)

2672. *Two Cities*. Palace, London, 2/27/69–4/5/69. 44 perf. p/l: Jeff Wayne; m: Jeff Wayne; b: Constance Cox; based on *A Tale of Two Cities*, by Charles Dickens; d: Vivian Matalon; ch: Jaime Rogers; md: Ian MacPherson; cast recording on Columbia. Cast: Carton: Edward Woodward (Keith Michell had once been touted for the role); Mme Defarge: Nicolette Roeg; Also with: Kevin Colson, Leon Greene, Elizabeth Power. "The Best of Times," "Tender Love and Patience," "Independent Man, What Would You Do?," "Look Alike," "And Lucy is Her Name," "Golden-Haired Doll," "Suddenly," "The Time is Now," "The Machine of Dr. Guillotine," "Two Different People," "Only a Fool," "Will We Ever Meet Again?," "Knitting Song," "Long Ago," "It's a Far, Far Better Thing"

2673. *Two for Fun*. Revue. Madison Avenue Playhouse. 2/13/61–3/19/61. 35 perf. Conceived, staged by, and starring Mata & Hari

Two for the Money see # 697, Main Book

2674. *Two Hearts Over Easy*. Love & fantasies of gay man & divorced woman who meet every Sunday for brunch. 1994 Actors Playhouse, 8/24/94–9/25/94. 39 perf. w/d: Robert W. Cabell; md: Seth Osburn. Cast: Maggie Wirth, Melanie Dimitri, Bill Ebbesmeyer, Randy Weiss

2675. *Two If by Sea*. Parallels between contemporary youth rebellion & the American Revolution. Circle in the Square, 2/6/72. 1 perf. m/l: Tony Hutchins & Priscilla B. Dewey; d: Charles Werner Moore. Cast: Kay Cole, Judy Gibson, John Stratton. "The American Revolution," "Paul Revere," "Wouldn't It Be Fine?," "Daddy's Footsteps," "There'll Be a Tomorrow," "Stamp Out the Tea Tax," "Melt it Down," "Tea Dance," "We're a Young Country," "Law Breakers," "You Can't Turn off the Stars," "Be More Aggressive," "Throw the Egg," "People Who Live on Islands," "Two if By Sea, I Think," "Lanterns"

2676. *Two Pianos Four Hands*. Play with music. Used classical pieces. Promenade, 10/30/97–5/10/98. 231 perf. creators/performers: Ted Dykstra & Richard Greenblatt; d: Gloria Muzio; light: Tharon Musser. Originally prod at Tarragon Theatre, Toronto

2677. *2008½: A Spaced Oddity*. Truck & Warehouse, 1/19/74–3/2/74. 21 perf. m: Gary William Friedman; l/b/d: Tom Eyen; ch: Julie Arenal. Cast: Theatre of the Eye Repertory Company (including Andre De Shields)

2678. *Tyger*. Celebration of William Blake. New Theatre, London, 7/20/71. m: Mike Westbrook; l/b: Adrian Mitchell; cast recording on RCA. Cast: Denis Quilley, John Moffatt, Jane Wenham, Sarah Atkinson, Maureen Lipman. "London Song," "Three Bloody Cheers," "A Man Must Be Happy," "Box 505," "The Children of Blake," "A Poison Tree," "The Destroyers of Jerusalem," "Happy Birthday, William Blake," "If You Can," "Poetry," "Joy," "I See Thy Form"

2679. *T. Zee*. Royal Court, London, 8/10/76–9/11/76. Prev from 8/6/76. 38 perf. p: Michael White; m/l/b: Richard O'Brien & Richard Hartley; d: Nicholas Wright; md: Richard Hartley. Cast: Warren Clarke, Richard O'Brien, Diane Langton, Arthur Dignam

2680. *Uhuruh*. Topical musical cabaret revue. City Center Downstairs, 3/20/72–3/25/72. 8 perf. Cast: Danny Duncan (also w/d/ch), Blondell Breed, Alice Alexander. Originally produced in San Francisco

2681. *Umbatha: The Zulu Macbeth*. New York State Theatre, 7/21/97–7/27/97. 6 perf. The Johannesburg Civic Theatre prod. w/d: Welcome Msomi; based on William Shakespeare's play; ch: Thuli Dumakude, Mdudzi Zwane, Mafika Mgwazi. Cast: Thabani Patrick Tshanini, Dieketseng Mnisi

2682. *The Umbrellas of Cherbourg*. Sung-through show, with few actual songs. Set 1957–1963. Cabaret Theatre, 2/1/79–3/4/79. 36 perf. p: Joseph Papp; m/orch: Michel Legrand; English translation: Sheldon Harnick

& Charles Burr; b: Jacques Demy; based on 1964 French movie *Les Parapluies de Cherbourg*; d: Andrei Serban; cos: Jane Greenwood; sound: Otts Munderloh; md: Steven Margoshes. Cast: Stefanianne Christopherson, Dean Pitchford, Stephen Bogardus, Laurence Guittard, Michael Pearlman, Joe Palmieri, Marc Jordan, Lizabeth Pritchett, Maureen Silliman. London, 1980. 3 prev. 9 perf

2683. *Umoja*. South African dance show. 2002 Shaftesbury, London, 11/15/01–2/6/02. Prev from 11/12/01. Because of complaints from residents about noise of drums, the show had to close. Queen's, 6/18/02–8/31/02. Prev from 6/5/02; New London Theatre, 9/6/02–2/8/03 (the producers had stated that the show would run as long as *Cats*), replaced with revival of *Joseph and the Amazing Technicolor Dreamcoat*

2684. *Under the Bridge*. Hobo becomes caretaker to homeless children in 1953 Paris. Zipper, 1/6/05–2/20/05. Prev from 12/1/04. m: David Pomeranz; l/b: Kathie Lee Gifford; based on 1950s book by Natalie Savage Carlson; d: Eric Schaeffer; set: Jim Kronzer; cos: Anne Kennedy; light: Chris Lee; sound: Kai Harada; md: Paul Raiman; orch: Brian Besterman. Cast: Ed Dixon, Florence Lacey, Jacquelyn Piro, Tamra Hayden

2685. *Under the Counter*. Comedy with mus. About a retired actress in London. Leeds, England, 9/11/45; toured; Phoenix, London, 11/22/45–7/5/47. 665 perf. m: Manning Sherwin; l: Harold Purcell; w: Arthur Macrae; d: Jack Hulbert; ch: Jack Hulbert & John Gregory; cos: Norman Hartnell, etc; md: Robert Probst. Cast: Cicely Courtneidge (*Florence Desmond*), Thorley Walters, Irene Handl, Francis Roberts. "Everywhere," "No-one's Tried to Kiss Me," "Let's Get Back to Glamour," "Ai Yi Yi." Shubert, Broadway, 10/3/47–10/25/47. 27 perf. Cast: Cicely Courtneidge, Wilfred Hyde-White, Thorley Walters, Ballard Berkeley, Francis Roberts. After Broadway, Miss Courtneidge & Mr. Walters took the show to the Royal, Sydney, from 1/3/48. It then went on to NZ & South Africa

2686. *Underneath the Arches*. A musical celebration of old British vaudevillians the Crazy Gang (Bud Flanagan, Chesney Allen, Nervo & Knox, Monsewer Eddie Grey). Prince of Wales, London, 3/4/81–5/20/81. A Chichester Festival Theatre prod. m/l: various authors; b: Patrick Garland, Brian Glanville, Roy Hudd; cast recording on TER. Cast: Julia Sutton, Billy Gray, Roy Hudd, Chris Melville, Christopher Timothy, Chesney Allen, Peter Glaze. "Just for Laughs," "The Boers Have Got My Daddy," "Umbrella Man," "Mr. Right," "Flanagan," "The Old Bull and Bush," "Underneath the Arches," "Five Little Broken Blossoms," "Siegfried Line," "Run, Rabbit, Run," "Maybe it's Because I'm a Londoner," "Music, Maestro, Please," "Strolling"

2687. *Underworld*. Scheduled for Broadway, 1962, but never produced. m/l: Jerome Moross, Lester Judson, John Hollander. "Love Me"

2688. *Unfair to Goliath*. Satirical revue on Israeli themes. Cherry Lane, 1/25/70–3/29/70. 75 perf. m/l: Menachem Zur & Herbert Apple-

man; w: Ephraim Kishon; based on writings of Ephraim Kishon, newspaper columnist on a Tel Aviv daily paper; d: Ephraim Kishon & Herbert Appleman. Cast: Jay Devlin, Hugh Alexander, Corinne Kason. "The Danger of Peace is Over," "In the Reign of Chaim," "What Kind of Baby?," "A Parking Meter Like Me," "The Sabra," "The Famous Rabbi," "When Moses Spake to Goldstein," "The Rooster and the Hen," "What Abraham Lincoln Once Said," "The Song of Sallah Shabeti"

2689. *An Unfinished Song*. Complexities of falling in love. Provincetown Playhouse, 2/10/91–3/3/91. 12 prev from 2/1/91. 24 perf. m/l/b: James J. Mellon; d: Simon Levy. Cast: Joanna Glushak, Robert Lambert, Beth Leavel, Aloysius Gigl, Ken Land. "Things We've Collected," "Balance the Plate," "Crossing Boundaries," "The Frying Pan," "Being Left Out," "As I Say Goodbye," "Hobby Horses"/"How Could I Let You Leave Me," "New Hampshire Nights," "Blonde Haired Babies," "Is That Love," "An Unfinished Song," "We Were Here"

2690. *The Unicorn*. Madrigal fable for chorus & dancers. NYC Ballet, 1957. Limited run. Score: Gian-Carlo Menotti

2691. *Unsung Cole*. 32 obscure songs of Cole Porter. Circle Rep, 6/23/77–9/4/77. 3 prev. 75 perf. conceived by/d/voc arr: Norman L. Berman; ch: Dennis Grimaldi; set: Peter Harvey; md: Leon Odenz. Cast: Anita Morris (*Margery Cohen* from 7/3/77), Mary Louise, John Sloman, Maureen Moore, Gene Lindsey. "Pick Me up and Lay Me Down," "Farming," "Thank You So Much, Mrs. Lowsborough — Goodbye," "The Great Indoors," "The Tale of an Oyster," "Poor Young Millionaire," "A Lady Needs a Rest," "Ours," "Lost Liberty Blues," "Olga," "The Queen of Terre Haute," "Almiro" (orig l: Rene Pujil; adapted by Brian Ross), "Dancin' to a Jungle Drum," "Take Me Back to Manhattan"/"I Happen to Like New York," "Why Don't We Try Staying Home?," "Give Me the Land," "Abracadabra," "When the Hen Stops Laying," "That's Why I Love You," "Nobody's Chasing Me," "I'm Getting Myself Ready for You," "Just Another Page in Your Diary," "Goodbye, Little Dream, Goodbye," "After You, Who?," "Down in the Depths," "Love for Sale," "I've Got Some Unfinished Business with You," "Kate the Great," "If Ever Married I'm," "Red Hot and Blue," "Swingin' the Jinx Away," "Friendship." The idea of using these Porter songs came to a more concrete fruition with the Broadway musical *Happy New Year*

2692. *Unsung Musicals*. A celebration of unrecorded Broadway musicals, including: *Drat! The Cat!*, *The First*, *La Strada*, *Sherry!*, *The Vamp*, *Foxy*, and *A Broadway Musical*. Sylvia & Danny Kaye Playhouse, 11/13/94. 1 perf. p: Jeffrey Finn Prods & Varese Sarabande Theatricals; d/ch: Niki Harris; md: Tom Fay. Cast: Christine Baranski, Laurie Beechman, Liz Callaway, Jason Graae, Timothy Jerome, Liz Larsen, Mary McCatty, Harry Groener, Crista Moore, Lynnette Perry, Sal Viviano, Lee Wilkof, Lynne Wintersteller, Michelle Nicastro

2693. *Unzippin' My Doo Dah (and Other

National Priorities). Musical comedy revue. Irreverent look at national & international politics. John Houseman, 7/15/98–9/5/98. 5 prev from 7/9. 63 perf. p: Eric Krebs; w/conceived by/d: Bill Strauss & Elaina Newport; NY staging by: Mark Waldrop. Cast: Capitol Steps musical comedy troupe

2694. *Up Against It*. Set in 1960s, in mythical place not unlike England. Male friends, victimized by women, plot to assassinate female prime minister. LuEsther Hall, 12/4/89–12/17/89. 41 prev from 11/14/89. 16 perf. m/l: Todd Rundgren; from unproduced 1967 Joe Orton screenplay for the Beatles, which was rejected, re-written, but ultimately unproduced; adapted by: Tom Ross; d: Kenneth Elliott; ch: Jennifer Muller; md: Tom Fay; orch: Doug Katsaros. Cast: Philip Casnoff, Alison Fraser, Roger Bart, Mindy Cooper, Toni DiBuono, Scott Carollo. "When Worlds Collide," "Parallel Lines," "Free," "Male and Twenty-One," "The Smell of Money," "If I Have to Be Alone," "Up Against It," "Life is a Drag," "Lilly's Address," "Love in Disguise," "You'll Thank Me in the End," "Maybe I'm Better Off," "From Hunger," "Entropy"

2695. *Up Eden*. Free adaptation of Mozart's *Cosi fan tutte*. Set in mythical Utopian community of Beam, in the USA. Jan Hus, 11/27/68–12/1/68. 7 perf. m/l: Robert Rosenblum & Howard Schuman; d: John Bishop; ch: Patricia Birch; md: Jack Lee; dance mus/orch: Wally Harper. Cast: Blythe Danner, Robert Balaban. "Remember Me Smiling," "A Playboy's Work Is Never Done," "No More Edens"

2696. *Up from Paradise*. Jewish Rep, 10/25/83–11/6/83. 12 prev. 12 perf. m: Stanley Silverman; l/b: Arthur Miller; d: Ran Avni. Cast: Len Cariou, Austin Pendleton, Alice Playten, Walter Bobbie, Paul Ukena Jr., Lonny Price. "The Lord is a Hammer of Light," "How Fine it Is," "When Night Starts to Fall," "Bone of Thy Bones," "Hallelujah," "The Center of Your Mind," "It's Just Like I Was You," "Recitative," "But if Something Leads to Good," "I'm Me, We're Us," "Curses," "Lonely Quartet," "How Lovely is Eve," "I Am the River and Waltz," "All of That Made for Me," "As Good as Paradise," "It Was So Peaceful Before There Was Man," "It Comes to Me," "I Don't Know What is Happening to Me," "Why Can't I See God?," "All Love," "Passion," "Nothing's Left of God," "Never See the Garden Again"

2697. *Upstairs at O'Neal's*. Satirical revue. O'Neal's, 43rd Street, 10/28/82–7/2/83. 14 prev. 308 perf. p: Martin Charnin, Michael O'Neal, Patrick O'Neal, Ture Tufvesson; conceived by/d: Martin Charnin; ch: Ed Love; md: David Krane. Cast: Richard Ryder, Bebe Neuwirth, Douglas Bernstein, Michon Peacock (*Carole Schweid* from 12/27/82). "Upstairs at O'Neal's" (by Mr. Charnin), "Stools" (by Mr. Charnin), "Cancun," "Something," "I Furnished My One-Room Apartment," "Little H and Little G," "The Ballad of Cy and Beatrice," "Signed, Peeled, Delivered," "The Feet," "The Soldier and the Washerworker," "Soap Operetta," "Talkin' Morosco Blues" (l: Murray Horwitz; guitar

accompaniment: Willie Nininger), "All I Can Do is Cry," "Cover Girls," "Boy, Do We Need it Now" (by Charles Strouse)

2698. *Urban Blight*. Revue of life in NY. OB, 1978. m: David Shire; l: Richard Maltby Jr.; based on idea by John Tillinger. Cast: Faith Prince, Rex Robbins. "Don't Fall for the Lights," "Life Story," "Miss Byrd," "Aerobicantata," "One of the Good Guys," "There's Nothing Like It," "Three Friends," "You Wanna Be My Friend," "Three Friends Chaser." City Center Stage 1, 6/19/88–7/1/88. 12 perf. p: Manhattan Theatre Club; Ed Kleban wrote an additional song, "Self Portrait"; d: John Tillinger & Richard Maltby Jr.; ch: Charles Randolph-Wright; set: Heidi Landesman; light: Natasha Katz; ms: Joel Silberman; conductor: Michael Skloff. Cast: Larry Fishburne, Nancy Giles, Oliver Platt, Faith Prince, Rex Robbins, John Rubinstein, E. Katherine Kerr. Later revamped as *Closer Than Ever* (qv)

Use Your Imagination see # 524, Main Book

Used Faces of 2004 see # 486, Main Book

2699. *Utamaro*. Japan's first full-scale, orig, Broadway-type musical. Picaresque tale about the colorful 19th-century artist. Kennedy Center, 2/17/88–2/18/88

2700. *Utopia!* Set in April & October, 1962. Folksbiene, 5/6/63–5/12/63. 11 perf. w: William Klenosky; d: Cecil Reddick. "The Ballad of Utopia," "You've Got the Devil in Your Eyes," "I Work for Pravda," "The Masses Are Asses," "All You Need is a Little Love"

2701. *Utterly Wilde!!!* Musical bio of Oscar Wilde. Set at Hotel d'Alsace, Paris, 1899. Next Stage Co., 3/22/95–3/26/95. 5 perf. m/l: John Franceschina; created/starred: Marc H. Glick. "Deja Vu," "Two Loves," "I Want to Make Magic," "Wasted Days," "Dearest of All Boys," "Romantic Experience," "Joshua," "To My Wife," "I'll Never Give up on Bosie," "The Ballad of Reading Gaol"

2702. *Vagabond Stars*. Songs & routines of the Yiddish theatre. First musical presented by the Jewish Rep. 1980. m: Raphael Crystal; l: Alan Poul; b: Nahma Sandrow. Revived at Queens Theatre in the Park, 4/24/92–5/24/92. 15 perf. d: Christopher Catt; ch: Tom Polum. Cast: Fred Goldberg, Guylaine Laperriere, Eugene Flam. Revived in concert form by the Jewish Rep, 5/29/02–6/2/02, in Manhattan. d: Ran Avni. Cast: Stuart Zagnit

2703. *Valmouth*. New Shakespeare Theatre, Liverpool, England, 9/16/58; Lyric, Hammersmith, London, 10/2/58–12/13/58 (84 perf.). p: Michael Codron; m/l/b: Sandy Wilson; based on Ronald Firbank's novel; d: Vida Hope; ch: Harry Naughton; set/cos: Tony Walton; light: John Wyckham; md: Neville Meale; orch: Arthur Birkby. Cast: Bertice Reading, Aubrey Woods, Peter Gilmore, Fenella Fielding, Doris Hare, Patsy Rowlands, Roderick Jones, Marcia Ashton. "Valmouth," "Magic Fingers," "Mustapha," "I Loved a Man," "All the Girls Were Pretty," "What Do I Want with Love?," "Just Once More," "Lady of the Manor," "Big Best Shoes," "Niri-Esther," "Cry of the Peacock," "Little Girl Baby," "Cathedral of Clemenza," "Only a Passing Phase," "Where

the Trees Are Green with Parrots," "My Talking Day," "I Will Miss You," "Pimpipi's Song of Love," "What Then Can Make Him Come So Slow." Saville, London, 1/27/59–4/25/59. 102 perf. Cleo Laine took over role of Mrs. Yajnavalkya from Bertice Reading. Rest of crew & cast basically same. York Playhouse (OB), 10/6/60–10/16/60. 14 perf. p: Gene Andrewski, Barbara Griner, Morton Segal; d: Vida Hope; ch: Harry Naughton; set/cos: Tony Walton; md/orch: Julian Stein. Cast: Anne Francine, Elly Stone, Constance Carpenter, Rhoda Levine, Philippa Bevans, Femi Taylor, Alfred Toigo, Bertice Reading, Ralston Hill. Chichester Festival, England, 1982 (in rep). d: John Dexter; ch: Lindsay Dolan; md: John Owen Edwards. Cast: Bertice Reading, Fenella Fielding, Doris Hare, Robert Helpmann, Cheryl Kennedy (*Sue Withers*), Robert Meadmore, Mark Wynter, Jane Wenham, Marcia Ashton, Femi Taylor

2704. *Vamps and Rideouts*. Hudson Guild, 2/4/82–2/13/82. 12 perf. m: Jule Styne; material adapted by: Phyllis Newman & James Pentecost; conceived by: Phyllis Newman; d: James Pentecost; ch: Dennis Dennehy; md: Eric Stern. Cast: Phyllis Newman, George Lee Andrews, Pauletta Pearson. "It's a Perfect Relationship," "I Met a Girl," "People," "Long Before I Knew You," "The Party's Over," "Let's See What Happens," "I'm the Greatest Star," "Never Never Land," "Just in Time," "Little Rock," "My Fortune is in My Face," "Some People," "Let Me Entertain You," "Together"

2705. *Vanessa*. Pulitzer Prize-winning opera. The Met. Performed on limited basis from 1/15/58. m/l: Samuel Barber; b/d: Gian-Carlo Menotti; set: Cecil Beaton. Cast: Eleanor Steber, Rosalind Elias, Nicolai Gedda, Regina Resnik, Giorgio Tozzi, George Cehanovsky. "Do Not Utter a Word," "Must the Winter Come So Soon," "Under the Willow Tree," "To Leave, To Break"

2706. *Vanity Fair*. Bristol Hippodrome, England, 10/16/62; toured; Queen's, London, 11/27/62–1/26/63 (70 perf.). p: Linnit & Dunfee; m: Julian Slade; l: Robin Miller; b: Robin Miller & Alan Pryce-Jones; based on novel of same name by William M. Thackeray; d: Lionel Harris; ch: Norman Maen; cos: Motley; md: Michael Moores. Cast: Sybil Thorndike (in her 1st musical, at age 80), Frances Cuka, George Baker, Naunton Wayne, John Stratton, Joyce Carey, Michael Aldridge, Annette Andre. "Vanity Fair," "I'm No Angel," "There He Is," "Alone the Orphan," "Dear Miss Crawley," "The Wickedest Man in the World," "Mama," "The Chatham Farewell," "Advice to Women," "Billy Boy Comes Marching Home Again," "How to Live Well on Nothing a Year," "Someone to Believe In," "Rebecca," "Forgive Me," "La Vie Boheme." Its book was revised by Constance Cox, and the show was re-presented at Cheltenham's Everyman Theatre, in 1967, with Vivienne Martin. It played Liverpool in 1968, Perth in 1969, Guildford in 1971 (with June Ritchie, Patricia Michael, Christopher Biggins, Joan Heal), and Worthing in 1974. Not to be confused with an earlier musical of the same name, written by Kenneth Rose, and produced at the Kidderminster Playhouse, in England, on 4/25/60

2707. *The Ventriloquist*. Quaigh, 4/19/83–5/8/83. 18 perf. m/l: Eddie Garson; b: Steven Otfinoski; d: Will Lieberson. Cast: Eddie Garson. "The Ventriloquist," "Hello World," "How Far Will You Go?," "Thirty Days," "Just Because He's Made of Wood," "I'm the Ventriloquist, He's the Dummy"

2708. *Very Warm for May*. Alvin, Broadway, 11/17/39–1/6/40. 59 perf. p: Max Gordon; m: Jerome Kern; l/b: Oscar Hammerstein II; d: Oscar Hammerstein II & Vincente Minnelli; ch: Albertina Rasch; set/cos: Vincente Minnelli; md: Robert Emmett Dolan; orch: Russell Bennett. Cast: Grace McDonald, Donald Brian, Jack Whiting, Eve Arden, Avon Long, Jack Whiting, Richard Quine, Max Showalter, Hiram Sherman, Vera Ellen, Webb Tilton, June Allyson, Billie Worth. "In Other Words Seventeen," "Me and the Roll and You," "All the Things You Are," "May Tells All," "Heaven in My Arms," "That Lucky Fellow," "L'Histoire de Madame de la Tour," "That Lucky Lady," "The Strange Case of Adam Standish" (ballet), "In the Heart of the Dark," "All in Fun," "High up in Harlem." Equity Library Theatre, 3/7/85–3/31/85. 30 perf. d: Worth Howe; md: Lawrence W. Hill. Cast: Doug Tompos. Ran in concert at Carnegie Hall, 10/19/94–10/23/94. 6 perf. d/conductor: John McGlinn. Cast: Edward Albert, Gregory Jbara, Brent Barrett, Donna Lynne Champlin, Marguerite Shanon, Karl duHoffmann, James Ludwig, Jeanne Lehman

2709. *La Vie Parisienne*. Set in Paris in 1866. 44th Street Theatre, 11/5/41–11/11/41. 7 perf in rep. New English version of Jacques Offenbach's operetta (1st heard in Paris, 1866, and on Broadway, at the Bijou, 3/18/1884) by Felix Brentano & Louis Verneuil, after French original by Henri Meilhac & Ludovic Halevy; new l: Marion Farquhar; d: Felix Brentano; ch: Igor Schwezoff; conductor: Antal Dorati; chorus master: Herbert Winkler. Cast: John Tyers, Gemze de Lappe. Broadway Theatre, Broadway, 11/10/42–12/7/42. 17 perf in rep. add dial: Frank Torloff & Leo Riskin; md: Paul Breisach. Cast: Wilbur Evans, Patricia Neway, Margit De Kova. City Center, 1/12/45–2/10/45. 37 perf. p: Yolanda Mero-Irion for the New Opera Co.; d: Ralph Herbert; ch: Leonide Massine; conductor: Antal Dorati. Cast: Lillian Andersen, Edward Roecker. London, 1961. City Center, 3/10/64–3/15/64. 8 perf. p: Sol Hurok; d: Jean-Louis Barrault. Cast: The Theatre Francais (Jean-Louis Barrault, Jean Paredes, Suzy Delair, Jean Desailly, Pierre Bertin, etc)

2710. *Viet Rock*. Series of vignettes in protest against Vietnam War. Yale Drama School, 10/11/66; the Martinique, 11/10/66–12/31/66. 62 perf. p: Jordan Charney; w/d: Megan Terry. Cast: Gerome Ragni (*Stephen Pearlman*), Jordan Charney, Seth Allen

2711. *A View from Under the Bridge*. Revue. Second City at Square East. 8/5/64–10/25/64. 94 perf. p: Alan Arkin, David Arkin, Paul Sills, David Shepard, etc; d: Sheldon Patinkin; set: Ralph Alswang. Cast: Alan Arkin, Severn Darden, Barbara Dana

2712. *Vintage '60*. Satirical revue with very little music. Brooks Atkinson, Broadway, 9/12/60–9/17/60. 8 perf. p: David Merrick, Zev Bufman, George Skaff, Max Perkins; m/l: various writers; d: Michael Ross; ch: Jonathan Lucas; set/cos: Fred Voelpel; md: Gershon Kingsley. Cast: Barbara Heller, Fay De Witt, Dick Patterson, Mickey Deems, Bert Convy, Bonnie Scott, Michele Lee, Emmaline Henry, Larry Billman. "The Time is Now," "More," "All American," "Isms" (l: Sheldon Harnick), "Five Piece Band," "Down in the Streets," "Convention," "Do it in Two," "Dublin Town" (l: Fred Ebb & Lee Goldsmith), "Forget Me" (l: Sheldon Harnick), "Tranquilizers," "Afraid of Love." There was a fuss when Vice-President Richard Nixon and his wife Pat were lampooned, and no corresponding Democrat was

2713. *Violet*. Playwrights Horizons. Musical drama. 3/11/97–4/6/97. 29 prev from 2/14. 32 perf. m: Jeanine Tesori; l/b: Brian Crawley; based on Doris Betts' short story *The Ugliest Pilgrim;* d: Susan H. Schulman; ch: Kathleen Marshall; set: Derek McLane; cos: Catherine Zuber; light: Peter Kaczorowski; sound: Tony Meola; md: Michael Rafter; cast recording on Resmirandaj. Lauren Ward starred as the badly disfigured young Southerner hoping for a miraculous cure in 1964. Rest of cast: Michael McElroy, Michael Medeiros, Cass Morgan, Paula Newsome, Stephen Lee Anderson, Michael Park, Amanda Posner, Kirk McDonald, Roz Ryan, Robert Westenberg. "On My Way," "Luck of the Draw," "Question and Answer," "All to Pieces," "Let it Sing," "Who'll Be the One (If Not Me)?," "Lonely Stranger," "Anyone Would Do," "Lay Down Your Head," "Hard to Say Goodbye," "Promise Me, Violet," "Raise Me Up," "Down the Mountain," "Look at Me," "That's What I Could Do." The papers gave it very good reviews, except *New York Times*, which killed its chances for Broadway transfer. In 11/98 it began national tour in Seattle, where it was well-received

2714. *Virtue in Danger*. Restoration romp. New Theatre, Oxford, England, 4/2/63; Mermaid, London, 4/10/63; Strand, London, 6/3/63–6/29/63. Total of 121 perf. m: James Bernard; l/b: Paul Dehn; d/ch: Wendy Toye; md: Michael Moores. Cast: Patricia Routledge, Lewis Fiander, Jane Wenham, Barrie Ingham, Richard Wordsworth, Patsy Byrne, John Moffatt, Alan Dudley, Basil Hoskins, Harold Innocent, Gwen Nelson, Kim Grant. "Don't Call Me Sir," "Fortune, Thou Art a Bitch," "I'm in Love with My Husband," "Hurry Surgeon!," "Conscience, Thou Art a Bore," "Let's Fall Together," "Nurse, Nurse, Nurse!," "Say the Word," "Fire a Salute," "Put Him in the Dog House," "The Hoyden Hath Charms," "Wait a Little Longer, Lover," "Why Do I Feel What I Feel?," "Stand Back, Old Sodom!," "O, Take This Ancient Mansion"

2715. *The Visit*. Dark comedy of revenge. Claire Zachanassian, former prostitute, and now, after 7 marriages the richest woman in the world, pays visit to her impoverished home town, from which she was driven out in disgrace by the villagers when she was 17. With promise of financing village, she tempts village

to kill Anton Schill, the man who ruined her when she was a girl. Goodman, Chicago, 10/1/01–11/3/01. Prev from 9/21/01). p: Harry Brown, Elizabeth Williams, Anita Waxman, Kevin McCollum; m: John Kander; l: Fred Ebb; b: Terrence McNally; based on 1956 play of same name, by Swiss playwright Friedrich Duerenmatt, and on 1963 film with Ingrid Bergman & Anthony Quinn; d: Frank Galati; ch: Ann Reinking; set: Derek McLane; cos: Susan Hilferty; light: Brian MacDevitt; sound: Rob Milburn & Michael Bodeen; md: David Loud. Cast: Chita Rivera, Guy Adkins (John McMartin had been 1st choice), McKinley Carter, Cristen Paige, Mark Jacoby, Steven Sutcliffe, Ami Silvestri, Jim Corti, Scott Calcagno, Adam Pelty, Bernie Yvon. In this prod Claire had a wooden leg, so it's not a dancing part. Well-received in Chicago. A planned Broadway prod for 2000 failed to happen after Angela Lansbury backed out, and it was booked for the Public's Newman Theatre, Feb.–March 2004, with a new, revised book by Mr. McNally, and some new songs. Cast: Chita Rivera, Frank Langella (again, Mr. McMartin was 1st choice). However, in 8/03 major investors Jeffrey Seller & Kevin McCollum backed out, and it was canceled

2716. *The Vocal Lords*. Play with doo-wop mus. St. in Brooklyn & Manhattan, between late 1950s and late 1990s. St. Clement's, 5/9/01–6/2/01. 27 perf. p: The Checkhov Theater Ensemble; w: Eric Winick; d: Floyd Rumohr; md: Kelly Ellenwood

2717. *Volpone*. Mark Taper Forum, L.A., 3/9/72. 54 perf. m/l: Jack Rowe, Timothy & Holly Near, Cordes Langley; from Ben Jonson's play, re-set in San Francisco, in 1872; d: Edward Parone; set: Ming Cho Lee; light: Martin Aronstein. Cast: Avery Schreiber, Sam Waterston, Jack Rowe, Herb Edelman, John Schuck, William Schallert, Joyce Van Patten, Marian Mercer, Adam West, Ezra Stone

2718. *Voyeurz*. Whitehall, London, 7/22/96. w: Michael Lewis & Peter Rafelson. Cast: Krysten Cummmings. "Insatiable," "Sin," "Sex on a Train," "The Hole," "So Confused," "Swing," "Where Did Love Go?," "Are You Insane?," "Go for the Kill," "Cruel and Unusual," "I'd Die for You," "Stand Back," "Evil," "Can't Talk Now," "Dreamtime"

2719. *Waiting in the Wings*. Play about aging, with mus. London, 1960. Ran 9 months & toured. Cast: Sybil Thorndike, Graham Payn. m/l: Noel Coward. "Come the Wild, Wild Weather," "Oh, Mister Kaiser"

2720. *Waking Up to Beautiful Things*. St. Clement's Church. 4/23/75–4/27/75. 10 perf. m/l: Jeffrey Roy; d: Jeffrey Wachtel; light: Gary Porto. Cast: Deborah Magid, Joanne Young, Norman Begin, Richard Eber, Marcia Savella. "I Know a Song," "The Good Thing," "Getting There," "Natural Kind of Love," "Let the Bad Times Stumble," "Time in the Snow," "Love Day," "Open All Night," "Don't Play with Fire," "We'll Build a Castle," "Waking up to Beautiful Things"

2721. *Walk Down Mah Street!* Topical musical revue on racial subjects. Players, 6/12/68–10/6/68. 135 perf. m/l: Norman Curtis & Patricia Taylor Curtis; special material: James Taylor, etc; d/ch: Patricia Taylor Curtis. Cast: Denise Delapenha. "We're Today," "Walk Down Mah Street," "If You Wanna Get Ahead," "Just One More Time," "I'm Just a Statistic," "Someday, If We Grow Up," "Basic Black," "What Shadows We Are," "Want to Get Retarded?," "Teeny Bopper," "Flower Child," "For Four Hundred Years," "Don't Have to Take it Any More," "Lonely Girl," "Clean up Your Own Back Yard," "Walk, Lordy, Walk"

2722. *A Walk on the Wild Side.* Set in 1931 in East Texas & in New Orleans. Musical Theatre Works, 1/14/88–1/31/88. 20 perf. w: Will Holt; from Nelson Algren's novel of same name; d/ch: Pat Birch; ms: Louis St. Louis. Cast: Rhonda Coullet, John Mineo, Kathi Moss, KC Wilson. "Stay Way from Waycross," "Shut Out the Night," "That Old Piano Roll," "Don't Put Me Down for the Common Kind," "The Life We Lead," "The Rex Cafe," "Ingenuity," "When It Gets Right Down to Evening," "Cawfee Man," "Turtle Song," "A Walk on the Wild Side," "Loew's State and Orpheum," "Little Darling," "Night Time Women," "Strongman's Song," "Since the Night I Stood in the Dancehall Door," "The Way Home," "That Boy Can Read," "Heaviest Fight in New Orleans," "We Been in Love," "So Long"

2723. *Wally Pone.* Unity, London, 7/18/58. m/l/b: Lionel Bart; based on *Volpone,* by Ben Jonson; d/set/cos: Bernard Sarron. Cast: Bernard Goldman, Morris Perry

2724. *Wandering Stars.* Yiddish. Town Hall, 10/22/96–10/27/96. 7 perf. p: Jewish Theatre of Warsaw; w: Sholem Aleichem; adapted/d: Szymon Szurmiej

2725. *Wanted.* Comic reversal of attitude toward supposed good guys & bad guys, in episodes from history of American outlawry. Cherry Lane, 1/19/72–3/26/72. 79 perf. m/l: Al Carmines & David Epstein; b: David Epstein; d: Lawrence Kornfeld. Cast: Reathel Bean (Billy the Kid), Cecelia Cooper, Frank Coppola (John Dillinger), June Gable, Merwin Goldsmith, Lee Guilliatt (Ma Barker), Peter Lombard (Jesse James). "I Am the Man," "Outlaw Man," "Jailhouse Blues," "Guns Are Fun," "Wahoo!," "I Want to Blow up the World," "As I'm Growing Older"

2726. *Watch Out, Angel!* Closed before Broadway. 1945. m/l: Josef Myrow, Eddie DeLange, Jerry Seelen. Cast: Carol Haney, Lester Allen. "It's a Great Life if You Weaken," "Watch Out, Angel!"

2727. *The Water Babies.* Royalty, London, 7/25/73–9/73. 62 perf. p: Tom Arnold; m/l/b: John Taylor; from Charles Kingsley's book; d/ch: Ross Taylor; md: Phil Phillips. Cast: Hope Jackman, Jessie Matthews

2728. *Water Coolers.* Musical revue set in corporate office environment. Dillons, 10/14/02–12/22/02. Prev from 9/27/02. 80 perf. w: Thomas Mitchell Allen, Joe Allen, Marya Grandy, E. Andrew Sensenig; d: William Westbrook; ch: Timothy Albrecht; md: Michael Lavine. Cast: Peter Brown, Marya Grandy, Adam Mastrelli, Kurt Robbins, Elena

Shaddow. "Gather 'round," "Panic Monday," "In My Cube," "The Paranoia Circus," "P.C.," "The Great Pretender," "A Song of Acceptance," "And Hold Please," "The IT Cowboy," "In Windows 2525," "Who Will Buy," "One Rung Higher," "Chat Room," "A Love Song," "What You Want," "Just Another Friday," "Many Paths." "I Bought a Palm" was cut during prev. A fall 2003 tour was expected. Miracle Theatre, Coral Gables, Fla., 7/7/04–9/5/04. d: David Arisco

2729. *The Water Gipsies.* Play with mus. About canal folk. Theatre Royal, Nottingham, England, 8/2/54; toured; Winter Garden, London, 8/31/55–3/24/56. 239 perf. p: Peter Saunders; m: Vivian Ellis; l/b: A.P. Herbert; d: Charles Hickman; ch: Narice Allen; set: Berkeley Sutcliffe; md: Jack Coles; cast recording on HMV. Cast: Dora Bryan, Doris Hare, Pamela Charles, Peter Graves, Vivienne Martin, Wallas Eaton. "It Would Cramp My Style," "When I'm Washing Up," "I Should Worry," "This is Our Secret," "Castles and Hearts and Roses," "He Doesn't Care," "You Never Know with Men," "Peace and Quiet," "Little Boat," "Why Should Spring Have All the Flowers?"

2730. *The Waves.* New York Theatre Workshop, 4/27/90–6/2/90. 37 perf. m/l: David Bucknam; w: David Bucknam & Lisa Peterson; from Virginia Woolf's novel; d: Lisa Peterson. Cast: Catherine Cox, Diane Fratantoni, Aloysius Gigl, John Jellison, Sarah Rice, John Sloman

2731. *The Way It Is!!!* Adult musical. New Lincoln Theatre, 12/2/69–1/20/70. 60 prev only. m/l: Buddy Bregman, Michael Greer, Kelly Montgomery; b/conceived by: Jerry Clark; d: Buddy Bregman; ch: Eddie Gasper; md: Jack Lee; orch: Wally Harper. Cast: Gene Foote, Deborah Bush, Jacqueline Britt, Milton Earl Forrest. "Adam and Eve," "Superman," "Pornography," "Tune of the Hickory Stick," "The Vice-President and the Call Girl," "The Way It Is"

2732. *W.C.* About W.C. Fields. Opened 6/15/71, Painters Mill Music Fair, Owing Mills, Md. Closed 7/25/71, Westbury Music Fair, NY. Did not make intended Broadway. p: David Black, with Lee Guber & Shelly Gross; m/l: Al Carmines; b: Milton Sperling & Sam Locke; d: Richard Altman; ch: Bob Herget. Cast: Mickey Rooney, Bernadette Peters, Virginia Martin, Gary Oakes, Rudy Tronto, Jack Bittner, David Vaughan, Sam Stoneburner, Martin J. Cassidy

2733. *We Shall.* Play with mus. Theatre Guinevere, 1/22/87–2/8/87. 15 perf. p/w: Karmyn Lott; d: Anderson Johnson. Cast: Jeffrey Harmon, PaSean Wilson. "Let the Church Say Amen," "Woke up This Morning," "These Blessings," "I'm on My Way," "Whose Side Are You On?," "Ain't Gonna Let Nobody," "Why the King of Love is Dead," "Never Turn Back," "We Shall"

2734. *We Take the Town.* Opened 2/19/62, Shubert, New Haven. Closed 3/17/62, Shubert, Philadelphia (30 perfs). It was scheduled to open on Broadway at the Broadway Theatre on 4/5/62, but canceled. p: Stuart Ostrow (his debut); m/l: Harold Karr & Matt Dubey; b: Felice Bauer & Matt Dubey; based on 1934

movie *Viva Villa!,* written by Ben Hecht & starring Wally Beery; d: Alex Segal; ch: Donald Saddler; set: Peter Larkin; cos: Motley; light: Tharon Musser; orch: Robert Russell Bennett & Hershy Kay. Cast: Pancho Villa: Robert Preston; Also with: Carmen Alvarez, Pia Zadora (one of the children), John Cullum, Mark Lenard, Romney Brent, Gerald Teijelo, Ken Urmston, Mike Kellin, Kathleen Widdoes. Art Lund (understudy for Villa). Jerome Robbins thought of replacing dir Segal but decided against it. "Viva Villa!," "Silverware," "I Marry You," "I Don't Know How to Talk to a Lady," "How Does the Wine Taste?" (which Barbra Streisand was to record on Columbia), "Good Old Porfirio Diaz," "I've Got a Girl," "The Only Girl," "A Wedded Man," "When?"

2735. *We Will Rock You.* Showcase of Queen's 25 greatest hits (i.e. no new music). Set in future where musical instruments are banned. Some youngsters rebel. Dominion, London, 5/14/02–1/3/03. p: Queen, Robert de Niro, Phil McIntyre; w: Ben Elton; d: Christopher Renshaw; ch: Arlene Phillips; cast recording made 5/03. Cast: Nigel Planer. Took 6 years to bring to the stage; cost 7.5 million pounds. US debut (open-ended run) at Paris Theatre des Arts, Las Vegas, 9/8/04. Prev from 8/16/04. p: Jane Rosenthal; d: Ben Elton; set/cos: Mark Fisher. Cast: Rich Hebert, Douglas Crawford, Jason Wooten. 10 shows a week here (instead of the 8 specified by a legit theatre). In fall 2004 opened in Sydney, Moscow and Cologne. Canadian premiere in Toronto, 5/05. p: Ed & David Mirvish; d: Christopher Renshaw

2736. *We'd Rather Switch.* Revue. Mermaid, London, 5/2/69. m/l: Larry Crane; adapted sk: Walter M. Berger; from idea by Mario Manzini; md: Lorenzo Fuller. Cast: Ron Collins, Patricia Sandberg, Martha Wilcox. "We'd Rather Switch," "Villains Aren't Bad Anymore," "The Strangest Show on Earth," "Mod Man of Manhattan," "A Man is Good for Something After All," "Make Me Over," "Let's Do It All Over Again," "Let's All Sing," "I'm Going Down the River and Have Myself a Damn Good Cry," "Greatest Show on Earth," "The Golden Fang." Ran OB, 1969. Cast: Maureen Sadusk, Karen Lynn, Diana Goble

2737. *Wedding in Paris.* Romantic musical play. Grand, Blackpool, England, 3/9/54; Bradford; Hippodrome, London, 4/3/54–4/2/55. 411 perf. p: George & Alfred Black; m: Hans May; l: Sonny Miller; b: Vera Caspary; d: Charles Hickman; ch: Walter Gore; cos: Motley; md: Alexander Faris. Cast: Anton Walbrook (*Francis Lederer*), Evelyn Laye, Jeff Warren. "A Wedding in Paris," "It's News," "The French Lesson," "The Young in Heart," "The Simple Things of Life," "It Only Took a Moment," "I Have Nothing to Declare but Love," "The Streets of Gay Paree," "A Man is a Man is a Man," "How Do I Know it's Love?," "I Must Have Been Crazy," "Strike Another Match," "In the Pink"

2738. *A Wedding in Shtetel.* Set in village of Brinitze, Russia, before WWI, and in Kretshma, in the town of Zhmerkinka. Eden, 2/9/75–3/2/75. 12 perf. m: H. Wohl; b: William Siegel; adapted by: Lillian Lux; d: Pesach Burstein; md: Renee Solomon. Cast: David Carey, Pesach Burstein, Mike Burstein, Lillian Lux. "An Actor's Life," "Without Him," "Sing a Happy Song"

2739. Weekend. Boy and girl in facing Manhattan apartments meet and fall in love. Theatre at St. Peter's Church, 10/24/83–10/31/83. 8 prev. 8 perf. p: Donald Rubin; w: Roger Lax; d/ch: David H. Bell. Cast: Gregg Edelman, Justin Ross, Carole-Ann Scott, Louise Edeiken. "Thank God it's Friday," "Lip Service," "This Song's for You," "Big Date Tonight," "Lover Sweet Lover," "The Man Next Door," "What's On?," "Let's Have Dinner and Dance," "Hangin' Out the Window," "Saturday is Just Another Day," "Lucky Woman," "It's Sad to Say," "Once You Take the Feeling Out," "See What Happens," "Where is She Now?," "Cuddle In," "Baby It Must Be Love," "Wake-Up Call," "A Man Wakes Up," "Seven Years Later," "I Have Me," "I'll Never Want You Again," "Word Gets Around," "Dragon Lady," "What Time is It?," "Sunday Makes a Difference"

2740. Welcome Back to Salamanca. INTAR, 6/8/88–7/10/88. m/l: Fernando Rivas & Magdalia Cruz; d: George Ferencz; light: Beverly Emmons. Cast: Sheila Dabney, Willie C. Barnes. "Blood," "Secret Jungle," "Give Us the Story," "Making it Happen," "I'm the Meat Man," "The Food Chain," "1999," "Cuchi," "Magic," "Sweet China Eyes," "Island," "Maria's Lament," "The Pot"

2741. We'll Meet Again. Musical journey through England during WWII. American & British period songs. 45th Street Theatre, 7/27/95–10/1/95. 6 prev from 7/22. 77 perf. conceived by/d: Johnny King; w: Vicki Stuart; set: James Morgan; cos: Oleg Cassini; md: Paul Katz. Cast: Vicki Stuart, Paul Katz. Theatre at St. Peter's, 5/23/96–6/30/96. 40 perf. p: York Theatre Co.

2742. We're Civilized? Jan Hus, 11/8/62–11/24/62. 22 perf. m/l: Ray Haney & Alfred Aiken; d: Martin B. Cohen; ch: Bhaskar. Cast: Roy Bhaskar, Marty Ross, Karen Black, Diane Findlay, Robert E. Fitch. "Brewing the Love Potion," "Too Old," "J.B. Pictures, Inc.," "Me Atahualpa," "No Place to Go," "I Like," "You Can Hang Your Hat Here," "Witch Song," "Mother Nature," "Bad if He Does, Worse if He Don't," "Yankee Stay," "We're Civilized"

2743. We're Home. Set in small city park on an evening this spring. Vineyard, 10/19/84–11/11/84. 24 perf. m/l: Bob Merrill; adapted by: Douglas Aibel & Stephen Milbank; conceived by/d: Douglas Aibel; ch: Pamela Sousa; md: Stephen Milbank. Cast: Peter Frechette, Rita Gardner, Larry Keith, Ann Talman. "I'm in a Tree," "Nine O'clock," "Here I Am," "Make Yourself Comfortable," "Traveling," "You Are a Woman," "I'm Naive," "My Place," "My Red Riding Hood," "Mira," "The Girl with Too Much Heart," "A Woman in Love," "Stay with Me," "People Watchers," "Nothing is New in New York," "The Rich," "Party People," "I've Got a Penny," "To a Small Degree," "How Could I Know?," "Knights on White Horses," "Breakfast at Tiffany's," "Home for Wayward

Girls," "Company of Men," "She Wears Red Feathers," "There's a Pawnshop on the Corner in Pittsburgh, Pennsylvania," "Sunshine Girls," "Flings," "Grade 'A' Treatment," "Staying Young," "We're Home," "Better Together," "But Yours," "Waltz," "When Daddy Comes Home," "Do You Ever Go to Boston?," "Alone in the World," "People"

2744. We're Just Not Practical. Theatre Royal, Stratford East, London, 1/23/61–2/11/61. 21 perf. p: Theatre Workshop; m: Ronnie Franklin; l: Ronnie Franklin & John Junkin; b: Marvin Kane; d: Joan Littlewood; ch: Jean Newlove; set: John Bury; cos: David Walker. Cast: Brian Murphy, Barbara Ferris, John Junkin, Roy Kinnear, Sean Lynch, Amelia Bayntun, Glynn Edwards. Did not go to West End

2745. Wet Paint. Musical revue. Renata, 4/12/65–4/24/65. 16 perf. Material by Sheldon Harnick, Anne Croswell, Martin Charnin, Paul Sand, Ronny Graham, Dolly Jonah, Bob Hilliard, Paul Lynde, etc; d: Michael Ross; ch: Rudy Tronto; md: Gerald Alters. Cast: Paul Sand, Bill McCutcheon, Gene Allen, Linda Lavin, Hank Garrett, Isobel Robbins

2746. What a Crazy World. Pop musical. Theatre Royal, Stratford East, London, 10/30/62–12/15/62. 48 perf. p: Theatre Workshop; m/l/b: Alan Klein; d: Gerry Raffles; set: John Bury; md: Malcolm Sircom. Cast: Barry Bethell, Cheryl Kennedy, Brian Murphy, Avis Bunnage, Larry Dann, Glynn Edwards. Ran again, for a season, at the same theatre, from 5/28/75. d: Larry Dann; md: Ian Armit. Cast: Melody Kaye, Tony Scannell, Kim Smith, Jenny Logan. Filmed in 1963. p/d: Michael Carreras. Cast: Susan Maugham, Joe Brown and the Bruvvers, Harry H. Corbett, Avis Bunnage, Grazina Frame, Marty Wilde, Alan Klein, Freddy and the Dreamers

2747. What a Killing. Folksbiene, 3/27/61. 1 perf. b: Fred Hebert; based on story by Jack Waldron; ch: Bob Hamilton. Cast: Paul Hartman, Al Mancini, Lou Wills Jr., John Anania, Judy Lynn, John Carter, Chanin Hale. "The Chicago that I Know," "I'm a Positive Guy," "Out of Luck with Luck," "Here I Come," "Nobody Cheats Big Mike," "A Rag, a Bone, and a Hank of Hair," "Face the Facts," "Pride in My Work," "What a Killing"

2748. What a Swell Party! The Cole Porter Revue. Rainbow & Stars, 7/23/91–8/31/91. 60 perf. p/conceived by: Greg Dawson & Steve Paul; d: Fred Greene. Cast: Terri Klausner, Bruce Coyle (also md)

2749. What Goes Up …! Theatre Royal, Stratford East, London, 9/17/63–10/26/63. 42 perf. m: Murray Graham; l: Frank Benoit; b: Brian O'Connor; d: Peter Cotes; ch: Bob Stevenson; set: John Bury; cos: Una Collins; md: Thomas Erskine. Cast: Anna Sharkey, David Watson

2750. What This Country Needs. About computers & their errors. Music Box, Hollywood, Calif., 7/28/65. m/l: Ray Golden; b: Ray Golden & Jack Marlowe

2751. What Would Esther Williams Do in a Situation Like This? About a Staten Island family. Village Theatre, 2/6/91–3/3/91. 17 perf. m/l: Jimmy Flynn; d: Steven Yuhasz

2752. What You Will. Set at the Club Illyria during WWII. Connelly, 3/29/01–4/21/01. 7 prev. 17 perf. p: Moonwalk Theatre Co.; m: Andrew Sherman & Rusty Magee; w: William Shakespeare; d: Gregory Wolfe; ch: Lars Rosager; md: Rusty Magee; light: David Sherman. Cast: Rusty Magee

2753. Whatever Happened to Baby Jane? Musical thriller. Two aging showbiz sisters. Blanche has mysterious accident, and is crippled. Jane, former child-star from vaudeville days, and now an alcoholic, always dreaming of Las Vegas comeback, becomes her caretaker, and tortures & torments her sister, while Blanche, now confined to wheelchair, tries to escape. Blanche is now a former star of MGM musicals (in book & film she was a former dramatic actress). Hobby Center, Houston, 10/9/02–10/27/02. p: Theatre Under the Stars/Michael Rose; m: Lee Pockriss; l: Hal Hackady; b: Henry Farrell; inspired by 1960 novel & 1962 film (with Bette Davis & Joan Crawford); d: David Taylor; ch: Dan Siretta; set: Jerome Sirlin; cos: Eduardo Sicangco; light: Richard Winkler; sound: Beth Berkley; md: Michael Biagi; orch: Chris Walker. Cast: Jane: Millicent Martin; Blanche: Leslie Denniston. "What Would I Do without You?," "Four Walls," "Cos You're There, Blanche!," "Talent," "Two Who Move as One," "Sisters," "I Still Have Tomorrow," "He's Here," "When Am I Gonna Be Me?," "If This House Could Talk," "Do I Care," "Let's Have a Party," "Her." The show, in development since 1994, had a London workshop and a full concert reading at Brighton, England

2754. Whatnot. Musical vaudeville. Set in mythical town of Whatnot Springs, USA, curio capital of the world. Theatre at St. Peter's, 9/5/90–10/6/90. 34 perf. p: Musical Theatre Works; m/l/md/orch: Dick Gallagher; w/conceived by: Mark Waldrop & Howard Crabtree; d/ch: Mark Waldrop; set: James Noone; cos: Howard Crabtree. Cast: Howard Crabtree, Jennifer Smith, Mark Lazore. "Shine," "Put it on a Whatnot Shelf," "Bugs," "Blue Flame," "Hat and Cane," "When I Stop the Show," "Just Desserts," "Teach it How to Dance," "Gamblin' Heart"

2755. What's a Nice Country Like You Doing in a State Like This? A red, white & blue revue, a political musical satire. St. Peter's Gate, 1973. Transferred to American Place Theatre's cabaret stage, before finding the nightclub Upstairs at Jimmy's, where it opened 4/19/73. Prev from 4/2/73. A new edition immediately succeeded the old one without a break, on 3/25/74. The whole show (both editions combined) ran a total of 543 perf, closing 5/12/74. m: Cary Hoffman; l/b: Ira Gasman; d/ch: Miriam Fond. Cast: Betty Lynn Buckley, Sam Freed, Priscilla Lopez, Barry Michlin, Bill LaVallee. "Liberal's Lament," "I'm in Love with…," "Massage a Trois," "Changing Partners," "Crime in the Streets," "Street People," "It's Getting Better," "I Like Me," "Male Chauvinist," "Johannesburg," "But I Love New York," "Why Do I Keep Going to the Theatre?," "A Mugger's Work is Never Done," "Farewell First Amendment," "Why

Johnny?," "The Right Place at the Right Time," "Love Story," "I'm Not Myself Anymore," "People Are Like Porcupines," "On a Scale of One to Ten," "Threesome," "Come On, Daisy," "Whatever Happened to the Communist Menace?." Tour opened at the Happy Medium, Chicago, 2/28/74, and closed there 4/21/74. Cast: Gary Beach, Alan Brasington, Wendie Cohen, Bill LaVallee, Carla Oleck. Another tour opened at Theatre in the Dell, Toronto, 6/10/74, and moved 3/17/75, to the Firehall Restaurant. Cast: Trudy Desmond, Claude Tessier, Martin Short. Another tour opened at the Meeting House Cabaret, L.A., 10/30/74, with Suzanne Astor, Trudy Desmond, Michael Scott, Bill LaVallee, Lorry Goldman. A sequel, *What's a Nice Country Like You Still Doing in a State Like This?* ran OOB at American Place Theatre, 10/21/84–11/11/84. 10 prev. 21 perf. Same basic crew. Cast: Brent Barrett, Krista Neumann. Several of the same musical numbers. Actors Playhouse, 7/31/85–2/9/86. 252 perf. d/ch: Suzanne Astor Hoffman; md/add arr: Dean Johnson. Cast: Missy Baldino, Jane Brucker (*Patty Granau* from 9/3/85), Steve Mulch, Hugh Panaro, Rob Resnick. A revised version of the orig ran at the Theatre Row, NY, 11/23/96–1/5/97. 45 perf. p: Anne Strickland Squadron & Eric Krebs. Cast: Janine LaManna, David Edwards, Sean McCourt, Vontress Mitchell, Karyn Quackenbush. "Liberal's Lament," "Church & State," "One Night Stand," "Be Frank," "Farewell First Amendment," "Button A," "Militia Song," "I'm in Love," "M.C.P.," "Last One of the Boys," "Coffee Bar Suite," "Honky," "Coalition," "Farrakhan," "Fill 'er Up," "Reality Check," "Pee Wee," "I'm Not Myself (Anymore)," "Watch Your Language," "Homeless Suite," "Rights of Bill," "How Do I Say I Love You?," "New York Suite," "(Come On) Daisy"

2756. ***When in Rome.*** Set in Rome. Andy & Nicky are young married couple. Nicky writes risque best-selling novel, *Rock-a-Bye Baby*, and Andy cannot believe she made it all up. Adelphi, London, 12/26/59. p: Jack Hylton; m: Kramer; l/b: Pietro Garinei & Sandro Giovannini; English l: Eric Shaw; English b: Ted Willis & Ken Ferrey; d: Harold French. Cast: Dickie Henderson, June Laverick, Eleanor Summerfield, John Hewer, Teddy Green, Leo Britt. "Call it Primavera," "Stop" (dance number), "Ballarello"

2757. ***Where or When...*** Musical revue. Theatre Row, 12/8/94–12/18/94. m: Richard Rodgers; l: Lorenz Hart; conceived by/d: Stephen Pickover; ch: Robin Reseen; md/arr: Nathan Matthews. Cast: Sonja Stuart, Jay Poindexter

2758. ***Whispers on the Wind.*** Young middle-westerner succeeds in rock business in NY. Theatre de Lys, 6/3/70–6/10/70. 13 prev. 9 perf. m/l: Lor Crane & John B. Kuntz; d: Burt Brincker-hoff; ms/orch: Arthur Rubinstein; mus consultant: Wally Harper. Cast: David Cryer, Nancy Dussault, Mary Louise Wilson, Patrick Fox. "Whispers on the Wind," "Midwestern Summer," "Why and Because," "Is There a City?," "Neighbors," "Things Are Going Nicely," "It Won't Be Long," "Prove I'm Really Here"

2759. ***Whistle Down the Wind.*** The Barn, Beauchamp House, Gloucestershire, England, 1992. m/b: Andrew Lloyd Webber; l: Jim Steinman; based on 1961 British film of same name, which had been based on novel by Mary Hayley Bell. The 1st workshop of this musical opened in 4/92/92, performed by the Beauchamp Music Group. Also that month it was performed at the First UK Festival of Musicals, at Buxton. New Olympus Theatre, Gloucester, 10/92; Adam Smith Theatre, Kirk-caldy, Scotland, 8/93, and also at the George Square Theatre, Edinburgh, as part of the Edinburgh Fringe Festival; Sadlers Wells, London, 12/93; West Yorkshire Playhouse, Leeds, 7/94; Riverside Theatre, London, 12/94. The first draft (with new book by Patricia Knop, and now set in Louisiana) premiered at the National, Washington, DC, 12/12/96, closing at Kennedy Center, 2/9/97. d: Harold Prince; ch: Joey McKneely; set: Andrew Jackness; cos: Florence Klotz; light: Howard Binkley; sound: Martin Levan; ms: Michael Reed; md: Patrick Vaccariello; orch: David Cullen & Andrew Lloyd Webber. Cast: Timothy Nolen, Timothy Shew, Lacey Hornkohl, Davis Gaines, David Lloyd Watson. The intended Broadway opening of 6/15/97, which had been postponed, was now canceled. Aldwych, London, 7/1/98–1/6/01. Prev from 6/22/98. d: Gale Edwards; set/cos: Peter J. Davison. Cast: Lottie Mayor, Marcus Lovett, Nicolas Colicos, Patricia Knop, Gale Edwards, Laurel Ford, Christopher Howard, John Turner, James Graeme. "Vaults of Heaven," "Whistle Down the Wind," "No Matter What," "If Only," "When Children Rule the World," "Cold," "A Kiss is a Terrible Thing to Waste," "Try Not to Be Afraid," "Wrestle with the Devil," "Tire Tracks and Broken Hearts," "Unsettled Scores," "I Never Get What I Pray For," "Home By Now," "It Just Doesn't Get Any Better than This," "The Vow," "Safe Haven," "Long Overdue for a Miracle," "Annie Christmas," "Charlie Christmas," "The Hunt," "Nature of the Beast"

2760. ***White Christmas.*** Savoy, London. Due to open 10/8/01 (prev from 9/24/01), but it was canceled. p: John Gore; m/l: Irving Berlin; based on film

2761. ***White Christmas.*** Ex-veteran entertainment duo teams with girl duo at Vermont lodge owned by the boys' former general. Curran, San Francisco, 11/9/04–1/1/05 (closing extended from 12/26/04). Prev from 11/3/04. m/l: Irving Berlin; b: David Ives; adapted by Paul Blake from the 1954 movie starring Bing Crosby, Danny Kaye, Rosemary Clooney, and Vera-Ellen, and with a screenplay by Norman Krasna, Norman Panama and Melvin Frank; d: Walter Bobbie; ch: Randy Skinner; set: Anna Louizos; cos: Carrie Robbins; light: Ken Billington; sound: Acme Sound Partners; md: Rob Berman; orch: Larry Blank; dance mus & voc arr: Bruce Pomahac. Cast: Brian d'Arcy James, Anastasia Barzee, Jeffry Denman, Meredith Patterson, Susan Mansur. Orig ran at Muny, St. Louis, with Karen Mason & Lee Roy Reams

2762. ***White Cotton Sheets.*** Set in Southern hotel on hot August night in 1931. One Dream

Theatre, 1993. d: Michael Sexton. Cast: Tom Judson (also m/l/b), Bobby Reed, Dori Kiplock

2763. ***The White House.*** Play with mus. About the presidents. Henry Miller's, 5/19/64–6/6/64. 1 prev on 5/18/64. 23 perf. p: Fryer, carr & Harris (i.e. Robert Fryer, Lawrence Carr & Joseph Harris), Gilbert Miller, Helen Bonfils, & Morty Gottlieb; m: Lee Hoiby; l/b: A.E. Hotchner; d: Henry Kaplan; set/cos: Ed Wittstein; light: Jules Fisher. Cast: Eric Berry, James Daly, Nancy Franklin, Helen Hayes, Bette Henritze, Fritz Weaver, Sorrell Booke, Gene Wilder

2764. ***White Lies.*** Musical comedy revue inspired by weekly tabloid headlines. Steve McGraw's, 5/29/92 (off-hour schedule). p: Michael Gill; songs: Keith Thompson & Douglas Carter Beane; sk: Douglas Carter Beane; d/ch: Greg Ganakas. Cast: Nancy Johnston, Jennifer Smith

2765. ***White Widow.*** Set in Sicily. INTAR, 12/4/93–12/19/93. 13 perf. m/l/b: Paul Dick; based on play *Mafia*, by Mario Fratti; d: John Margulis. Cast: William Broderick, Diana Di Marzio. "The Stoning," "Fish Lemon Chickens," "Bel Paese," "The Game," "The Letter," "Law, Order, Justice," "Two Young People in Love," "Basic Sicilian," "Music for a Murder," "We Mourn," "Donna Cinzia's Love," "Four Proverbs," "So Little Time," "Don't You Understand?," "Not I," "To Build Tomorrow," "Time to Prepare for Donna Cinzia," "Only Yesterday," "All for You"

2766. ***Who Plays Wins.*** Vaudeville, London, 9/26/85. w/starred: Peter Skellern & Richard Stilgoe. "Two Pals in Harmony," "Love is the Sweetest Thing," "The Curate and the Priest," "SAS," "Mr. James," "Laugh at the Lover," "You're a Lady"

2767. ***Whoop-Dee-Doo.*** Gay musical revue satirizing the *Follies*. Also known as *Howard Crabtree's Whoop-Dee-Doo*. Actors Playhouse, 6/29/93–2/20/94. 258 perf. conceived by/created by/developed by: Charles Catanese, Howard Crabtree, Dick Gallagher, Phillip George, Peter Morris, Mark Waldrop; d: Phillip George. Cast: Howard Crabtree, David Lowenstein, Peter Morris. "Whoop-Dee-Doo," "Stuck on You," "Teach it How to Dance," "Elizabeth," "Nancy: the Unauthorized Musical," "Tough to Be a Fairy," "Blue Flame," "A Soldier's Musical," "It's a Perfect Day," "Last One Picked," "As Plain as the Nose on My Face," "I Was Born This Way," "You Are My Idol," "The Magic of Me," "My Turn to Shine," "Less is More"

2768. ***Whores, Wars & Tin Pan Alley.*** Evening of songs by Kurt Weill. Bitter End, 6/16/69–8/17/69. 72 perf. p: Allen Swift. Cast: Martha Schlamme, Alvin Epstein. Included songs from *Johnny Johnson*, *The Happy End*, *The Threepenny Opera*, etc

2769. ***Who's Pinkus? Where's Chelm?*** Jeannetta Cochran Theatre, England, 1/3/67–1/11/67. 10 perf. p: London Traverse Theatre Co.; m: Monty Norman; l: Cecil P. Taylor & Monty Norman; b: Cecil P. Taylor; add material/d: Charles Marowitz; ch: Tutte Lemkow. Cast: Bernard Bresslaw, David Lander, Nancy Nevinson

2770. *Who's Who, Baby?* Set on the island of Manuella. Players, 1/29/68–2/11/68. 16 perf. m/l: Johnny Brandon; b: Gerald Frank; d/ch: Marvin Gordon. Cast: Jacqueline Mayro, Gloria Kaye, Glory Van Scott, Erik Howell, Frank Andre, Tommy Breslin. "Island of Happiness," "That'll Be the Day," "Come-Along-a-Me, Babe," "Nothin's Gonna Change," "There Aren't Many Ladies in the Mile End Road," "Syncopatin'," "Voodoo," "How Do You Stop Loving Someone?," "Drums," "Feminine-inity," "That's What's Happening, Baby," "Me," "Nobody to Cry To"

2771. *Why Do Fools Fall in Love?* Three women claim to be the widow of 50s rock star Frankie Lymon (who died of a heroine overdose in 1968). m/l: Tina Andrews & Stanley Bennett Clay; b: Tina Andrews (based on the movie written by her. The movie starred Halle Berry); d/ch: Wayne Cilento. A 2003 workshop starred Darius de Haas as Lymon. A Pasadena Playhouse, Calif., prod, 10/8/04–11/14/04, was canceled

2772. *Why Do I Deserve This?* Musical revue in German (also called *Womit haben wir das verdient?*). Previously produced in Dusseldorf. Barbizon-Plaza, 1/18/66–1/29/66. 12 perf. Cast: Lore Lorentz, Kay Lorentz (also d)

2773. *The Wicked World of Bel Ami*. Set in late 19th-century Paris. Theatre Royal, Stratford East, London, 4/13/89–5/13/89. m: Jacques Offenbach; l/b: Ken Hill; from Guy de Maupassant's novel

2774. *Wild Grows the Heather*. Palace, Manchester, England, 3/13/56 (3 weeks); then Edinburgh; London Hippodrome, 5/3/56–5/26/56. 28 perf. p: Jack Waller; m: Robert Lindon (i.e. Jack Waller & Joseph Tunbridge); l: William Henry (i.e. Ralph Reader); b: Hugh Ross Williamson; from J.M. Barrie's play *The Little Minister*; d: Ralph Reader; ch: Gilbert Vernon; m: Lew Stone, *Michael Collins*. Cast: David Keir, Patrick Newell

2775. *Wild Men!* A musical ... sort of. Westside Theatre Downstairs, 5/6/93–6/27/93. 15 prev from 4/23. 59 perf. m/l: Mark Nutter; d: Rob Riley; ch: Jim Corti; md: Lisa Yeargan. Cast: George Wendt, Rob Riley. "Come Away," "What Stuart Has Planned," "True Value," "Oooh, That's Hot," "We're Wild Men," "Lookit Those Stars," "It's You," "My Friend, My Father," "Get Pissed," "Now I Am a Man"

2776. *Wild Thyme*. Prima donna falls in love with railway porter. Theatre Royal, Bath, England. 5/23/55; toured; Duke of York's, London, 7/14/55–8/27/55. 52 perf. p: Laurier Lister; m/md: Donald Swann; b: Philip Guard; d/ch: Wendy Toye; set: Ronald Searle. Cast: Gwen Nelson, Jane Wenham, Denis Quilley, Betty Paul, Ronald Ward (*Colin Gordon*), Julian Orchard

2777. *Wild, Wild Women*. A western musical, set in Aggroville, about the Earps & the Clantons. Mountview Theatre School, England, 7/17/81; Orange Tree, Richmond, 12/11/81–12/19/81, then again 12/30/81–1/23/82. m/md: Nola York; l/b/d: Michael Richmond; ch: Marcia King. Cast: Gaye Brown, Marcia King. "Peaceable Haven," "Aggroville," "Wild, Wild Women," "Ooh La La," "The Stars Already Know." Theatre Royal, Windsor, 5/11/82–5/29/82; Astoria, London, 6/15/82. 29 perf. md: Stuart Pedlar. Cast: Susannah Fellows, Marcia King

2778. *Wilder*. Erotic chamber musical, set in a Depression-era brothel. Wilder, an old man, looks back on his life. Peter J. Sharp, 10/26/03–11/14/03. Prev from 10/14/03. World premiere. p: Playwrights Horizons; m/l: Jack Herrick & Mike Craver; b: Erin Cressida Wilson (based on her play *Cross-Dressing in the Depression*); d: Lisa Portes; ch: Jane Comfort; set/cos: G.W. Mercier; light: Jane Cox; sound: Tom Morse. Cast: John Cullum, Jack Herrick, Mike Craver, Lacey Kohl, Jeremiah Miller. Mr. Herrick & Mr. Craver were members of the Red Clay Ramblers. Unanimously bad reviews

2779. *Wildest Dreams*. A musical entertainment. Everyman Theatre, Cheltenham, England, 9/20/60–10/1/60. m: Julian Slade; l/b: Julian Slade & Dorothy Reynolds; d: Nicholas Garland; ch: Basil Pattison; at pianos: Julian Slade & Courtenay Kenny. Cast: Denis Quilley, Anna Dawson, Edward Hardwicke, Dorothy Reynolds, Angus Mackay, John Davidson. Tour. Revised. Vaudeville, London, 8/3/61–10/7/61. 76 perf. p: David Hall; d: Nicholas Garland; ch: Basil Pattison; cast recording on HMV. Same basic cast, except Denis Quilley was replaced by *John Baddeley*, Dorothy Reynolds by *Rosamund Burne*. There were other cast changes, and some characters were deleted & others added. "Nelderham," "Mrs. Birdview's Minuet," "Please, Aunt Harriet," "Till Now," "Girl on the Hill," "Zoom, Zoom, Zoom," "Here Am I," "Wildest Dreams," "Red or White," "You Can't Take Any Luggage with You," "A Man's Room," "I'm Holding My Breath," "Quite Something," "Green/Oxblood Hill," "There's a Place We Know," "The Days Go By," "When You're Not There," "This Man Loves You." Tour. Cast: Tony Adams, Ben Aris, Gillian Royale, Roberta Huby. Everyman, 1970. Cast: Sarah Atkinson, Janet Hargreaves, Marc Urquhart, Brian Gilman

2780. *Will the Mail Train Run Tonight?* Musical parody of the old-fashioned melodrama, set in New York State in the 1890s. New Bowery, 1/9/64–1/17/64. 8 perf. p/d: Jon Baisch; m: Alyn Heim; l/b: Malcolm L. LaPrade; based on play by Hugh Nevill; ch: Lynne Fippinger. Cast: Fred Jackson, Naomi Riseman, Barbara Cole. "So Much to Be Thankful For," "Dearer to Me," "Nature's Serenade," "Honeymoon Choo-Choo," "Hickory Dickory," "Comes the Dawn," "Paper Matches," "To Dream or Not to Dream," "Prudence Have Faith," "Villainy," "Three Cowards Craven," "Vengeance," "This Decadent Age," "Heroism," "A Slip of a Girl," "Remember Him," "I'll Walk Alone," "The Fall of Valor," "Age of Miracles," "Bitter Tears: No Sacrifice"

2781. *Williams and Walker*. Set in 1910, backstage at Majestic Theatre, NYC, in dressing-room of Bert Williams. American Place, 2/27/86–6/1/86. 87 perf. p: American Place Theatre & Henry Street Settlement's New Federal Theatre; w: Vincent D. Smith; d: Shauneille Perry; cos: Judy Dearing. Cast: Bert Williams: Ben Harney; George Walker: Vondi Curtis-Hall; Pianist/Musical Director: Neal Tate. "Magnetic Rag," "Constantly," "Bon Bon Buddy," "Somebody Stole My Gal," "Let it Alone," "Everybody Wants to See the Baby," "Save Your Money, John," "Nobody," "I'd Rather Have Nothin' All of the Time," "I May Be Crazy but I Ain't No Fool," "I'm a Jonah Man," "Original Rag," "Chocolate Drop"

2782. *Willie Stark*. Kennedy Center, 5/9/81–5/29/81. 24 perf. Commissioned by Kennedy Center, and produced jointly by them and the Houston Grand Opera; w: Carlisle Floyd; based on *All the King's Men*, by Robert Penn Warren; d: Harold Prince; ch: Frances Patrelle; set: Eugene Lee; cos: Judith Dolan; light: Ken Billington; md: John De Main & Hal France. Cast: Timothy Nolen, David Vosburgh

2783. *The Wind Blows Free*. Closed before Brodway 1959, after trying out on the summer circuit. m/l: Alec Wilder & Arnold Sundgaard. "Douglas Mountain," "Where Do You Go?"

2784. *The Wind in the Willows*. Alhambra, Bradford, England, 9/26/83. m/md: Derek Taverner; l/b: Carol Crowther; based on Kenneth Grahame's characters; d: Graham Ashe; ch: Kim Joyce. Cast: Mole: Kim Joyce; Toad: David Bluestone, *Kim Joyce*. Then toured UK

2785. *The Wind in the Willows*. Theatre Royal, Plymouth, England, 11/22/84. m: Denis King; l/b: Willis Hall; based on Kenneth Grahame's characters. It then ran at Bath & Guildford; Sadler's Wells, London, 1/15/85–2/10/85. d: Roger Redfarn; ch: Michele Hardy; md: Barry Westcott. Cast: Rat: Patrick Cargill; Mole: Melvin Hayes; Badger: Donald Hewlett; Toad: Terry Scott

2786. *The Wind in the Willows*. New 42nd Street Inc., 5/29/98–6/14/98. 18 perf. The Syracuse stage prod, in assoc with Syracuse University. m/l/add text/md/voc arr/orch: Dianne Adams & James McDowell; add l: Geraldine Clark & Katharine Clark; adapted by Geraldine Clark from Kenneth Grahame's book; d: Geraldine Clark & Anthony Salatino. Cast: Eric Collins, Timothy A. Fitz-Gerald, Michael Poignand, Lee Zarrett. "Wind in the Willows," "Song of the River," "Things with Wheels," "Song of the Wild Wood," "It's Time to Take Toad in Hand," "Dulce Domum," "I, Glorious Toad," "Mercy-Justice," "The End of Toad," "Joy Shall Be Yours in the Morning," "Missing Him," "The Triumph of Toad," "Weapons Underscore," "Stoats Forever," "Battle Song"

2787. *The Window Man*. One Dream Theatre, 4/28/94. m: Bruce Barthol & Greg Pliska; l/text/set: Matthew Maguire; based on 1982 murder of Asian-American youth by unemployed Detroit auto worker; md: Genji Ito. Cast: Angela Bullock, Frank Deal

2788. *Windy City*. Play with mus about a gambler and his problems in Chicago. Opened 4/18/46, Shubert, New Haven. Closed 6/6/46, Great Northern, Chicago. Did not make intended Broadway. p: Richard Kollmar; m/l: Walter Jurman & Paul Francis Webster; b: Philip Yordan; d: Edward Reveaux; ch: Katherine Dunham; set/light: Jo Mielziner; md: Charles Sanford; orch: Don Walker; voc arr: Clay Warnick; ballet mus: Dorothea Freitag. Cast: Al Shean, Frances Williams, John Conte, Joey Faye, Loring Smith, Susan Miller, Tom Pedi, Betty Jane Smith, Florence Lessing, Lili St. Cyr, Jerry Ross. "State Street," "Don't Ever Run Away from Love," "Gambler's Lullaby," "As the Wind Bloweth," "It's the Better Me," "Out on a Limb," "Nightfall on State Street," "It's Time I Had a Break," "Mrs. O'Leary's Cow," "Where Do We Go from Here?." The book was completely re-written after the New Haven opening, and Kay Stewart & Grover Burgess joined the cast. Also during re-staging various dance numbers were cut–"Lady of the Evening," "The Beggar," "Frankie's Wife." "The Little Girl" was substituted

2789. Windy City. Set in Chicago in 1929. Bristol Hippodrome, England, 6/15/82; Victoria Palace, London, 7/20/82–2/26/83. 12 prev. 250 perf. m: Tony Macaulay; l/b: Dick Vosburgh; from play *The Front Page*, by Ben Hecht & Charles MacArthur; d: Peter Wood; md: Anthony Bowles; cast recording on Angel. Cast: Diane Langton, Victor Spinetti, Dennis Waterman, Anton Rodgers, Tracy Booth, Amanda Redman, Bob Sessions. "Hey, Hallelujah," "Wait Till I Get You on Your Own," "Saturday," "No One Walks Out on Me," "Windy City," "Round in Circles," "(I Can) Just Imagine It," "I Can Talk to You," "Perfect Casting," "Water Under the Bridge," "Born Reporter," "The Day I Quit this Rag," "Long Night Again Tonight," "Stamp! Stamp! Stamp!," "Ten Years From Now," "The Times We Had." In USA it ran at Marriot's Lincolnshire Theatre, 2/2/84–4/22/84. d/ch: David H. Bell; md: Kevin Stites. Cast: Paula Scrofano

2790. Winged Victory. Drama with mus. 44th Street Theatre, Broadway, 11/20/43–5/20/44. 212 perf. Part of cross-country tour, presented by US Army Air Forces for benefit of Army Emergency Relief. incidental mus/arr: Sgt David Rose; conceived/w/d: Moss Hart; set: Sgt Harry Horner; cos: Sgt Howard Shoup; light: Sgt Abe Feder; cast recording on Decca. The show followed 3 "ordinary men"–played by Pvt Don Taylor, Pfc Edmond O'Brien, and Cpl Marc Daniels–through training & into combat. Rest of the 350-member cast included: Pvt Barry Nelson, Pvt Lee J. Cobb, Pvt Philip Bourneuf, Sgt George Reeves, Phyllis Avery, Elisabeth Fraser, Olive Deering, Pvt Red Buttons, Sgt Kevin McCarthy, Pvt Alan Baxter, Pvt Whitner Bissell, Pvt Hayes Gordon, Cpl Gary Merrill, Pfc Edward McMahon, Cpl Jerry Hilliard Adler, Sgt Victor Young, Sgt Ray Middleton, Pvt William Marshall, Pvt Alfred Ryder, Pvt Karl Malden, S/Sgt Peter Lind Hayes, Pfc Martin Ritt, Pvt Henry Slate, 2nd Lt Donald Beddoe, Pvt John Tyers. "My Dream Book of Memories," "Winged Victory." 5 big revolving stages. A bad show that got a great reception. James M. Nederlander was on the prod staff. Filmed in 1944

2791. Wings. Set on a mountain top. Eastside Playhouse, 3/16/75–3/23/75. 9 perf. w: Robert McLaughlin & Peter Ryan; based on

Aristophanes' *The Birds;* d: Robert McLaughlin; ch: Nora Christiansen; set: Karl Eigsti; md: Larry Hochman; orch: Bill Brohn. Cast: Mary Sue Finnerty, David Kolatch, David Pursley, Maureen Sadusk, Barbara Rubenstein. "Call of the Birds," "The Human Species," "Time to Find Something to Do," "You'll Regret It!," "The Wall Song," "Take to the Air," "The Great Immortals," "Wings," "We're Gonna Make It"

2792. Wings. Musical drama. Newman, 2/23/93–4/18/93. 16 prev. 47 perf. m/l: Jeffrey Lunden & Arthur Perlman; based on play by Arthur Kopit; d: Michael Maggio. Cast: Rita Gardner, Hollis Resnik, William Brown. "Catastrophe," "Globbidge," "Wait-Stop-Hold-Cut," "My Name Then," "All in All," "Make Your Naming Powers," "I'll Come Back to That," "Yum Yummy Yum," "Tither," "I Don't Trust Him," "Malacats," "Needle," "Out on the Wing," "I Wonder What's Inside," "Let Me Call You Sweetheart," "A Recipe for Cheesecake," "Like the Clouds," "Preparing for Flight," "Snow," "Wings"

Winner Take All *see* # 523, Main Book

2793. Winnie the Pooh. Puppets. Set in & around the 100-Acre Wood. Bil Baird Puppet Theatre, 11/23/67–5/19/68. 185 perf. m: Jack Brooks; adapted by A.J. Russell from A.A. Milne's stories; d: Fania Sullivan; md: Alvy West. 3/7/69–4/27/69. 58 perf; 3/28/70–5/16/70. 48 perf. From then on it was part of the repertoire, performed practically every year. Lee Theodore dir in 1972. There was also a Christmas musical based on the stories, which ran at the Phoenix, London, 12/17/70–1/16/71, adapted by & with add mus by Julian Slade. d: Malcolm Farquhar. Cast: Pooh: Jimmy Thompson; Christopher Robin: Jasper Jacob; Also with: Julian Orchard, Zulema Dene. Same venue, from 12/16/71; from 12/18/72. 52 perf. Cast: Ronald Radd, Frank Thornton, Maria Charles, John O'Farrell; from 12/14/74; from 12/16/75

2794. Wish Me Mazel-Tov. Town Hall, 10/19/80–1/11/81. 84 perf. m: D. Blitenthal & Alexander Lustig; l: Yankele Alperin; b: Moshe Tamir; d: Michael Greenstein; ch: Yankele Kaluski; set/cos: Adina Reich; md: Renee Solomon; arr: Horia Alexander & Alexander Lustig. Cast: Mary Soreanu, Reizl Bozyk, Raquel Yossifon, David Carey, Shelly Pappas, Mark Rubin. "Yafo Ballet," "Honesty's the Hard Way," "Daliah," "A Yiddish Yingele," "Ver S'iz Avek," "Soldier's Dance," "Whatever You Want," "We Went Forth," "My Dearest," "God Will Provide," "Peace," "I Need a Husband," "Mazel-Tov"

2795. The Witches of Eastwick. Theatre Royal, Drury Lane, London, 7/18/00–2/24/01. Prev from 6/24/00. p: Cameron Mackintosh; m: Dana P. Rowe; l/b: John Dempsey; from novel by John Updike; d: Eric Schaeffer; ch: Bob Avian. Cast: Maria Friedman, Rosemary Ashe, Peter Jobach, Caroline Sheen, Rebecca Thornhill, Stephen Tate, Clarke Peters, Lucie Arnaz, Joanna Riding, Ian MacShane (Michael Crawford had been scheduled for this role). "Eastwick Knows," "Make Him Mine," "I Love a Little Town," "Eye of the Beholder," "Wait-

ing for the Music to Begin," "Words, Words, Words," "Dirty Laundry," "I Wish I May," "Another Night at Darryl's," "Something," "Dance with the Devil," "Evil," "Loose Ends," "Who's the Man," "The Wedding," "Look at Me." Opened to much fanfare, as the new mega-musical, but got divided reviews & failed. Re-vamped, and with cast changes, and for a more intimate feel, moved to the Prince of Wales, 3/23/01–10/27/01. Total of 504 perf. New cast: Clarke Peters, Josefina Gabrielle, Rebecca Thornhill, Joanna Riding. In 2002 it ran 3 months in Australia, at the Princess, Melbourne. On 3/13/03 there was a private industry reading in Manhattan. d: Gabriel Barre. Cast: Alix Korey, Emily Skinner

2796. With a Little Help from My Friends. Beatles compilation. Duke of York's, London, 7/31/81–8/8/81

2797. Without Rhyme or Reason. Closed before Broadway, 1948. m/l: John Alton & Fred Hillebrand. "I Worry About You"

2798. The Wizard of Oz. Majestic, 1/20/1903. 293 perf. The earliest Broadway musical prod of Frank Baum's story; starred Montgomery & Stone (i.e. Dave Montgomery & Fred Stone) in their theatrical debut. Bil Baird's Puppet Theatre, 11/27/68–3/2/69. 114 perf; 4/7/69–4/8/69. 4 perf. d: Bil Baird & Arthur Cantor; md: Alvy West. This show became part of the marionettes' repertoire, and was prod by them again in 1971, for 65 perf. 1975 came *The Wiz* (see the main part of this book). A new musical, *The Wizard of Oz*, based on the 1939 movie with Judy Garland, opened at Paper Mill Playhouse, NJ, 1992. m: Harold Arlen; l: E.Y. Harburg; b: John Kane; adapted by: Robert Johanson; d/ch: Robert Johanson & James Rocco; set: Michael Anania; cos: Gregg Barnes; light: Tim Hunter; md: Jeff Rizzo. Cast: Kelli Rabke, Evan Bell, Eddie Bracken, Mark Chmiel, Elizabeth Franz, Michael Hayward-Jones, Judith McCauley, Michael O'Gorman. This prod finally made it to NY, to the Theatre at Madison Square Garden, 5/15/97–6/8/97. 15 prev from 5/7/97. 45 perf. p: Tim Hawkins; d: Robert Johanson; ch: Jamie Rocco; set: Michael Anania; cos: Gregg Barnes; light: Tim Hunter; md: Jeff Rizzo; orch: Larry Wilcox. Cast: Dorothy: Jessica Grove; Toto: Plenty; Aunt Em/Glinda: Judith McCauley; Uncle Henry: Roger Preston Smith; Scarecrow/Hunk: Lara Teeter; Tinman/Hickory: Michael Gruber; Lion/Zeke: Ken Page; Witch/Almira Gulch: Roseanne [i.e. Roseanne Barr]; Prof. Marvel/Wizard: Gerry Vichi. Ensemble: Maggie Keenan-Bolger, Patrick Boyd, Christine De Vito, Danielle Lee Greaves, M. Kathryn Quinlan, D.J. Salisbury, Dana Scarborough. "Over the Rainbow," "Cyclone," "Come Out, Come Out," "Ding Dong, the Witch is Dead," "Follow the Yellow Brick Road," "If I Only Had a Brain"/"Heart"/"The Nerve," "We're off to See the Wizard," "Lions, Tigers and Bears," "Poppies"/"Optimistic Voices," "Merry Old Land of Oz," "King of the Forest," "March of the Winkies." Broadway reviews were not good. Same venue, 5/1/98–5/31/98. 38 perf. Same crew; same cast except Henry: Bob Dorian; Tinman: Dirk Lumbard;

Witch: Eartha Kitt; Wizard: Mickey Rooney. Same venue, 5/6/99–5/16/99. 22 perf. Same basic crew. Cast: Dorothy: Jessica Grove; Toto: Plenty; Em: Judith McCauley; Henry: Tom Urich; Scarecrow: Casey Colgan; Tinman: Dirk Lumbard; Lion: Francis Ruivivar; Witch: Jo Anne Worley; Wizard: Mickey Rooney

2799. *A Woman Called Truth*. Play with musical score of American slave songs. Open Eye, 1/19/91–2/17/91. 10 perf. w: Sandra Fenichel Asher. Cast: Patricia R. Floyd (as Sojourner Truth), Kim Bey

2800. *The Woman in White*. Workshop of Act I, plus a couple of songs from Act II was performed at Andrew Lloyd Webber's Sydmonton Festival, 7/11/03–7/13/03. d: Trevor Nunn; Simon Lee conducted a a 6-piece orchestra. Cast: Anne Hathaway, Laura Michelle Kelly, Kevin McKidd, Roger Allam, Kevin Colson. Palace, London, 9/15/04. Prev from 8/28/04. m: Andrew Lloyd Webber; l/b: l: David Zippel; b: Charlotte Jones; freely based on novel by Wilkie Collins; d: Trevor Nunn; md: Simon Lee. Cast: Count Fosco: Michael Crawford (*Michael Ball* from 2/22/05, replacing Mr. Crawford, who had flu; *Michael Crawford* 4/31/05–5/28/05); Marian Halcombe: Maria Friedman; The Woman in White: Angela Christian; Walter Hartright: Martin Crewes; Laura Fairlie: Jill Paice; Sir Percival Glyde: Oliver Darley; Also with: Anne Hathaway. Prologue, "I Hope You Like it Here," "Perspective," "Trying Not to Notice," "I Believe My Heart," "Lammastide," "You See I Am No Ghost," "A Gift for Living Well," "The Holly and the Ivy," "All for Laura," "The Document," "Act One Finale," "If I Could Only Dream This World Away," "The Nightmare," "Fosco Tells of Laura's Death/The Funeral/ London," "Evermore without You," "Lost Souls," "If Not for Me for Her," "You Can Get Away with Anything," "The Seduction," "The Asylum," "Back to Limeridge," Finale. Reviews were divided, but the show did very well. The single "I Believe My Heart" went to top of UK charts. It was scheduled to open at the Minskoff, on Broadway, 11/10/05, at a cost of $10–12 million. Same crew as in London. Cast: Maria Friedman. However, it was put back to spring 2006, with a pre–Broadway run at the LaSalle Bank Theatre (formerly the Shubert), Chicago, 11/15/05–1/8/06

2801. *The Wonder Years*. Musical revue. Lives of a half dozen baby boomers from birth to year 2019, the 50th anniversary of the Woodstock rock concert. Top of the Gate, 5/25/88–6/12/88. 17 prev. 23 perf. p: Russ Thacker & Dwight Frye; m/l: David Levy; based on idea by Leslie Eberhard; d/ch: David Holdgrive; cos: Kenneth M. Yount; light: Ken Billington. Cast: Alan Osburn, Louisa Flaningam, Adam Bryant, Meghan Duffy, Lenny Wolpe, Kathy Morath. "Baby Boom Babies," "Thru You," "Another Elementary School," "First Love," "Teach Me How to Fast Dance," "The Wonder Years," "Flowers from the Sixties," "Pushing Thirty," "The Girl Most Likely"

2802. *A Wonderful Life*. Arena Stage, Washington, 11/21/91. m: Joe Raposo; l/b: Sheldon Harnick; based on 1946 movie *It's a Won-*

derful Life; d: Douglas C. Wager; ch: Joey McKneely; set: Thomas Lynch; md: Jeffrey Saver. Cast: Casey Biggs, Scott Wise, Richard Bauer, James Hindman, Jeffrey V. Thompson. "Christmas Gifts." Broadway plans never materialized, except as a benefit for the Actors Fund of America, at the New Amsterdam, 12/13/04

2803. *The Wonderful World of Burlesque*. Musical creation of the best in burlesque, past & present. Mayfair, 4/28/65. p/d: LeRoy C. Griffith; ch: Guy Martin. Cast: Yolanda Moreno, Barbara Curtis

2804. *Wonderland*. King's Head, Islington, London, 6/25/81–8/1/81. 35 perf. p: Dan Crawford; m/md: Dave Brown; l/b: William Fairchild; d: Lou Stein; ch: Tudor Davies. Cast: David Firth, Don Fellows, Oliver Pierre, Sandra Dickinson, Christina Matthews

2805. *Wonderland in Concert*. Newman, 12/27/79–12/29/79. 3 perf. p: NY Shakespeare Festival; from Lewis Carroll's books *Alice in Wonderland* & *Through the Looking Glass*; m/add l/d: Elizabeth Swados; light: Jennifer Tipton; sound: Bill Dreisbach. Cast: Alice: Meryl Streep; Also with: Gloria Hodes, William Parry, Karen Evans, Rodney Hudson, Joanna Peled, Paul Kreppel, Joan Macintosh, Jim McConaughty. Re-done as *Alice in Concert*, again with Meryl Streep, at the Anspacher, 12/29/80–1/25/81. 32 perf. p/d: Joseph Papp; m/l/md: Elizabeth Swados; ch: Graciela Daniele; cos: Theoni V. Aldredge. Rest of cast: Betty Aberlin, Richard Cox, Rodney Hudson, Amanda Plummer, Mark Linn-Baker. "What There Is," "The Rabbit's Excuse," "Down Down Down," "Drink Me," "Goodby Feet," "The Rabbit's House," "Bill's Lament," "Caterpillar's Advice," "Beautiful Soup," "Wow Wow Wow," "Pretty Piggy," "Cheshire Puss," "If You Knew Time," "No Room, No Room," "Starting Out Again," "White Roses Red," "Alphabet," "Red Queen," "Never Play Croquet," "Mock Turtle Lament," "Lobster Quadrille," "Eating Mushrooms," "Child of Pure Unclouded Brow," "Jabberwocky," "Bird Song," "Humpty Dumpty," "Tweedledum and Tweedledee," "The Walrus and the Carpenter," "The White Queen," "The White Knight," "An Aged, Aged Man," "The Examination," "The Lion and the Unicorn," "Queen Alice," "What is a Letter?"

2806. *Wonderworld*. Musical spectacle put on 4 times a day at 1964 World's Fair. m/l: Jule Styne & Stanley Styne; ch: Michael Kidd (assisted by Tony Mordente). Cast: Chita Rivera, Gretchen Wyler

2807. *Woody Guthrie's American Song*. Musical revue. Theatre 3, 12/2/98–1/9/99. 6 prev. 36 perf. songs/writings: Woody Guthrie; conceived & adapted by/d: Peter Glazer; md/orch: Jeff Waxman. Cast: Ernestine Jackson, David M. Lutken. "Hard Travelin'," "Oklahoma Hills," "Dust Storm Disaster," "I Ain't Got No Home," "Bound for Glory," "Dust Bowl Refugee," "Do-Re-Mi," "Worried Man," "Ain't Gonna Be Treated That Way," "End of My Line," "Grand Course Dam," "Pastures of Plenty," "New York Town," "Hard, Ain't it Hard," "I Don't Feel at Home on the Bowery No More," "Talkin' Subway," "Union Maid," "Sinking of the Reuben James," "Nine

Hundred Miles," "Deportee," "Better Work"/ "Lonesome Valley," "Another Man Done Gone," "This Land is Your Land"

2808. *Words and Music*. Sammy Cahn (1915–1993) sings his own songs & discusses his career in embellished one-man show. John Golden, Broadway, 4/16/74–8/3/74. 11 prev from 4/12/74. 127 perf. p: Alexander H. Cohen & Harvey Granat; d: Jerry Adler; set/cos: Robert Randolph; light: Marc B. Weiss; md: Sammy Cahn & Richard Leonard. Rest of cast: Kelly Garrett (*Kay Cole*), Jon Peck, Shirley Lemmon, Richard Leonard. Standbys: Christine Andreas & William James. Rave reviews. Kelley Garrett was poached from the show by Gower Champion for *Mack and Mabel*. Tour opened 9/26/75, Ann Arbor. Closed 1/11/76, L.A. Cast: Sammy Cahn, Martha Danielle, Sydnee Devitt, Paul Eichel. William James (standby). Originally prod for 2 perfs at 92nd Street "Y"

2809. *Working Out with Leona*. Musical comedy lampoon featuring many cast members who were HIV positive. Sanford Meisner, 8/31/93–10/3/93 (40 perf). Jewel Box, 11/10/93. p: HIV Ensemble; m: Paul Radelat & Michael Capece; l/d/ch: Nelson Jewell; b: Nelson Jewell & Mary Lee Miller; md: Michael Capece. "Sell Sell Sell," "Doing it Every Day," "Secretary Spread," "Wish I Were a Beauty," "Pump That Iron," "Leona's Nightmare," "When Will They Find Out?," "Yesterday, Today and Tomorrow," "It'll All Work Out," "Yoga Song," "Touch of Love"

2810. *The World Goes 'Round ... with Kander and Ebb*. Successful revue featuring songs of John Kander & Fred Ebb. Whole Theatre, Montclair, NJ, 6/6/89. conceived by: Susan Stroman, Scott Ellis, David Thompson; d: Scott Ellis; ch: Susan Stroman (her 1st major ch job); orch: David Krane. Cast: Brent Barrett, Karen Mason, Paige O'Hara, Jim Walton, Karen Ziemba. Re-titled *And the World Goes 'round: The Songs of Kander and Ebb*, and ran at Westside Theatre, 3/18/91–3/8/92. Prev from 3/5/91. 408 perf. Cast: Bob Cuccioli, Karen Mason, Karen Ziemba, Brenda Pressley (*Terry Burrell*), Jim Walton (*Joel Blum*). Re-titled again, as *The World Goes 'round*, and went on tour starting 9/27/92, Cincinnati, and including stint at Kennedy Center (6/1/93–6/27/93). New cast: Joel Blum, Shelley Dickinson, Marin Mazzie, John Ruess, Karen Ziemba

2811. *World of Illusion*. A mime's view of Man's world, in fables, with mus & narration. Actors Playhouse, 6/24/64–8/23/64. p: Jay Stanwyck. Cast: Lionel Shepard (also d/w), Lily Tomlin

2812. *The World of Kurt Weill*. Musical tribute to the composer. Theatre Arielle, 7/7/92–8/1/92. 28 perf. conceived by/performed by: Juliette Koka

2813. *The World of Paul Slickey*. Musical comedy of manners. Jack Oakham, alias Paul Slickey, is a despicable gossip columnist on the *Daily Rocket*. Pavilion, Bournemouth, England, 4/14/59; toured; Palace, London, 5/5/59–6/13/59. 47 perf. p: David Pelham; m: Christopher Whelen; l/b/d: John Osborne; ch: Kenneth Macmillan; md: Anthony Bowles. Cast: Paul Slickey: Dennis Lotis; Also with: Marie Lohr, Philip Locke, Harry Welchman, Adrienne Corri, Maureen Quinney, Jack Watling, Geoffrey Webb, Ben Aris, Anna Sharkey, Aidan Turner. It was panned

2814. *The World of Wallowitch*. Musical revue. Skylight Lounge/Hamburger Harry's, 7/8/87. m/l: John Wallowitch; d: Charles Maryan; md: Ken Lundie. Cast: Ken Lundie (*John Wallowitch*), Melissa Eddy, Betsy Ann Leadbetter

2815. *The World's My Oyster*. Actors Playhouse, 7/31/56–9/2/56. m/l: Carley Mills & Lorenzo Fuller; d: Jed Duane; md: Lorenzo Fuller. Cast: Lorenzo Fuller, Ned Wright, Butterfly McQueen, Moses LaMarr. "Shoeshine," "Rich Enough to Be Rude," "Footprints in the Sand," "Moola Makes the Hula Feel Much Cooler," "A Thing Like This," "The World in a Jug," "The Finer Things of Life," "I Set My Heart on One Love," "Just Before I Go to Sleep," "This is the Life for Me," "It's the Human Thing to Do," "The Devil is a Man You Know"

2816. *Worzel Gummidge*. Birmingham Rep, England, 12/12/80–2/21/81. m: Denis King; l/b: Keith Waterhouse & Willis Hall; based on characters created by Barbara Euphan Todd, and on TV series made from them, about a scarecrow; d: Clive Perry; ch: Geraldine Stephenson; md: Ray Bishop. Cast: Jon Pertwee, Geoffrey Bayldon, Michael Ripper, Una Stubbs, Denis Holmes. Cambridge, London, 12/18/81–2/27/82. 79 perf. Cast: Jon Pertwee, Geoffrey Bayldon, Norman Mitchell, Una Stubbs, Bill Pertwee

2817. *The Would-Be Gentleman*. Comedy with music. Booth, Broadway, 1/9/46–3/16/46. 77 perf. p: Michael Todd; m: Jean-Baptiste Lully (adapted by Jerome Moross); adapted by Bobby Clark from comedy *Le Bourgeois Gentilhomme*, by Moliere (not credited) [not a faithful musical reproduction of Moliere's play by any means. Extracts from other Moliere plays were included]; d: John Kennedy; set: Howard Bay; cos: Irene Sharaff. Cast: Donald Burr, Alex Fisher, Fred Werner, Ann Thomas, Rand Elliot, Albert Henderson, Bobby Clark, Ruth Harrison, Constance Brigham, Mary Godwin, Lewis Pierce, Edith N. King, Earle MacVeigh, Frederic Persson, Gene Barry, Eleanore Whitney, Leonard Elliott, John Heath, LeRoi Operti (*Jerome Collamore*), Lester Towne, June Knight, Gregory Bemko, David Gindin, James Nassy, Eric Silberstein, Max Tartasky

2818. *Wren*. Musical celebration of 17th century. Mayfair, London, 6/25/78. 34 perf. m: David Adams & Chuck Mallett; l/b: David Adams; add material/d: Ken Hill. Cast: Christopher Wren: Steve Grives. Also prod at the Park Lane Hotel, as *Wren, Pepys & Charlie Too*. d: David Adams; ch: Gillian Gregory; set: Derek Cousins; md: David Green. Cast: Wren: Brian Ralph; Nell: Carol Cleveland

2819. *Wrong Way Up*. Rock musical. History of a rebel from teenage to adulthood. Belt, 10/20/04–12/15/04 (Weds only). p: The Zipper & Joshua P. Weiss; w/starred: Robert Whaley

& Tony Grimaldi; d: Andrew Grosso; md: Frank Spitznagel; ch: Thomas Mills. Previously seen at the NY Performance Works Theatre, since when it was revised

2820. *Wuthering Heights*. McGinn/Cazale. 9/13/92–9/27/92. 16 perf. m/l/b: Paul Dick; from Emily Bronte's novel; d: Jack Horner; ch: Jean Shepard; md: Christopher McGovern. Cast: John La Londe, Beth Thompson, Steve Gray. "Hymn to the House," "Dance on the Moor," "Heathcliff's Love," "From Now On," "More Like a Lady," "Never Seen Anything Like it Before," "I Can Hardly Belive it's You," "If I Were Edgar," "Dusting Now?," "Go if You Want," "Caught," "Hymn to Her," "Choose Love," "I Love Him," "Will I Wake Tomorrow?," "I Thought Only of You," "From the Very First Day," "Come with Me," "A Life without Love," "Twenty Years from Now," "Never to Go," "Be There," "Wuthering Heights." Min, 10/22/99–11/7/99. 16 perf. d/ch: David Leidholdt; md: Peter C. Mills. Cast: William Thomas Evans, Jennifer Featherston. Another, unrelated musical of same story, ran at Paper Mill Playhouse, NJ, during 1998–99 season. w/d: Robert Johanson; set: Michael Anania; cos: Gregg Barnes. Cast: David Ledingham, Libby Christopherson

2821. *Yakety Yak*. Half Moon, London. 11/15/82–12/18/82. m/l: Jerry Leiber & Mike Stoller. Astoria, London, 1/18/83

Yellow Drum see # 266, Main Book

2822. *Yes, God Is Real*. Set in Casino City, in 1985. Apollo, 3/5/88–5/26/88. 20 perf. w: James M. Brown; d: Al (Suavae) Mitchell; md: Thomas Jennings. Cast: Betty Graves Scott, Rev. Charles Lyles, Wendy Mason, Bill Greene. "Come to the Casino," "Yes, God is Real"

2823. *Yiddle with a Fiddle*. Yiddish musical in English. Set in Poland in 1936. Adventures of father and daughter (disguised as boy). Town Hall, 10/28/90–12/30/90. Prev from 10/24/90. 62 perf. m: Abraham Ellstein; l/b: Isaiah Sheffer; based on 1936 movie *Yitl midn Fidl*, by Joseph Green; d: Ran Avni; ch: Helen Butleroff; md: Lanny Meyers. Cast: Yiddle: Emily Loesser; Also with: Robert Michael Baker, Susan Flynn, Mitchell Greenberg, Michael Ingram, Patricia Ben Peterson, Danny Rutigliano, Steve Sterner, Andrea Green, Steve Fickinger, Rachel Black. "Come Gather 'round," "If You Wanna Dance," "Music, It's a Necessity," "Yiddle with a Fiddle," "New Rhythm," "Help is on the Way!," "I'll Sing," "Hard as a Nail," "Man to Man," "Oh Mama, Am I in Love," "Traveling First Class Style," "Badchen's Verses," "Only for a Moment," Wedding Bulgar (dance), "Warsaw!," "How Can the Cat Cross the Water?," "Stay Home Here with Me," "Take it from the Top," "To Tell the Truth," "We'll Sing." Previously prod in West Orange, NJ. American Jewish Theatre, 4/19/97–5/25/97. d: Lori Steinberg; ch: Naomi Goldberg; md: Lanny Meyers. Cast: Aileen Quinn, Sean McCourt, Mark Lotito, Philip Hoffman, Regina O'Malley

2824. *Yoshe Kalb*. Yiddish musical drama. Eden, 10/22/72–1/7/73. 95 perf. m/l: Maurice Rauch & Isaac Dogim; w: I.J. Singer; adapted by/d: David Licht; md: Renee Solomon. Cast:

Warren Pincus, Isaac Dogim, Miriam Kressyn, David Opatoshu, Reizl Bozyk, Shifra Lerer, Jacob Ben-Ami. "Song of Joy," "The Three Good Deeds"

2825. *You Don't Miss the Water*. Music-theatre work. Vineyard/26th Street, 6/6/97–6/29/97. 12 prev. 13 perf. m: Deidre L. Murray; l: Cornelius Eady; conceived by/d: Evan Yionoulis; set/cos: G.W. Mercier. Cast: Andrea Frierson Toney, Brenda Pressley

2826. *You Never Know*. Set in 1938 in Baron Romer's drawing-room. Winter Garden, Broadway, 9/21/38–11/26/38. 78 perf. p: Messrs Shubert; m/l: Cole Porter; b/add l/book d: Rowland Leigh; based on play *By Candlelight*, by Siegfried Geyer; ch: Robert Alton; md: John McManus; orch: Hans Spialek; add orch: Claude Austin, Maurice DePackh, Menotti Salta, Don Walker. Cast: Clifton Webb, Rex O'Malley, Toby Wing, Lupe Velez, Libby Holman, Grace & Paul Hartman, Gus Schirmer Jr. "I Am Gaston," "Au Revoir, Cher Baron," "By Candlelight," "Maria," "You Never Know," "Ladies' Room," "What is That Tune," "For No Rhyme or Reason," "Alpha to Omega," "Don't Let it Get You Down," "What Shall I Do?," "Let's Put it to Music," "At Long Last Love," "Take Yourself a Trip," "Yes, Yes, Yes," "Gendarme," "No (You Can't Have My Heart)," "Good Evening, Princess." 1st NY revival in 1969, at Stage Directors and Choreographers Workshop; adapted by: Rowland Leigh. Eastside Playhouse, 3/12/73–3/18/73. 8 perf. d/ch: Robert Troie. Cast: Baron Romer: Dan Held; Also with: Lynn Fitzpatrick, Rod Loomis. "By Candlelight," "Maria," "I'm Going in for Love," "I'm Back in Circulation," "From Alpha to Omega," "You've Got That Thing," "What Shall I Do?," "For No Rhyme or Reason," "At Long Last Love," "Greek to You," "You Never Know," "Ridin' High," "They All Fall in Love"

2827. *You Say What I Mean But What You Mean Is Not What I Said*. An a cappella musical. CSC, 1/15/97–2/9/97. 6 prev. 22 perf. m/conceived by: Grisha Coleman; add m/arr: Jonathan Stone; d: Talvin Wilks. Cast: Grisha Coleman. "Tell it Like it Is," "The Moment that I Saw It," "Afrokode," "Ain't Got a Gal," "Nobody Knows…," "Country Lament," "Madame X," "Title Song," "O Little Child," "One Born, One Gone"

2828. *Young Abe Lincoln*. York Theatre, 4/3/61–4/8/61. 18 perf, including 3 matinees daily; Eugene O'Neill, Broadway, 4/25/61–5/6/61. 27 perf, including 12 matinees weekly; York Theatre, 5/10/61–6/24/61. 48 perfs, which did not include 34 perf touring in NYC schools. p: Arthur Shimkin, for the Little Golden Theatre; m/md: Victor Ziskin; l: Arnold Sundgaard; b: Richard N. Bernstein & John Allen; d: Jay Harnick; ch: Rhoda Levine; set/cos/light: Fred Voelpel. Cast: Abe: Darrell Sandeen; Also with: Jack Kauflin (*Ken Kercheval*), Travis Hudson (*Joan Kibrig*). "The Same Old Me," "Cheer Up!," "You Can Dance," "Someone You Know," "(I Wanna Be) A Little Frog in a Little Pond," "Clarey Grove (Song)," "Don't P-P-Point Them Guns (at Me)," "The Captain Lincoln March" (The

Drill Song), "Run, Indian, Run" (Run Injuns), "Welcome Home March," "Vote for Lincoln," "Frontier Politics." Town Hall, 2/13/71. 1 perf. d: Jay Harnick; set: Fred Voelpel

2829. *Young Rube*. Musical Theatre Works, 4/12/89–4/30/89. 8 prev. 21 perf. m/l: Matty Selman; d: Mark Herko; ch: Margie Castleman. Cast: Joan Jaffe, Robert Polenz, Keith Savage. "Boob McNutt," "Funny," "Everybody's Here Tonight," "My Crazy Right Hand," "A Real Torch Song," "We're Counting on You," "Big Parade," "Candy Kid," "Lowell High," "Mixing Metaphors," "Your Crazies," "Do it the Hard Way"

2830. *The Young Visitors*. Hippodrome, Bristol, England, 11/27/68; Piccadilly, London, 12/23/68–2/15/69. 63 perf. p/d: Martin Landau; m: Ian Kellam; l/b: Michael Ashton; add songs: Richard Kerr & Joan Maitland; based on Daisy Ashford's novella for children; ch: Malcolm Clare; md: Alexander Faris. Cast: Alfred Marks, Jan Waters, Anna Sharkey, Frank Thornton, Barry Justice, Clive Morton

2831. *Your Own Thing*. The now-generation rock musical suggested by *Twelfth Night*. Twin brother & sister shipwrecked on Manhattan Island, and because they are dressed alike create confusion. Slide images were presented. Orpheum, 1/13/68–4/5/70. 933 perf. p: Zev Bufman & Dorothy Love; m/l: Hal Hester & Danny Apolinar; b/d: Donald Driver. Cast: Viola: Leland Palmer, *Sandy Duncan*; Also with: Rusty Thacker (*Raul Julia*), Marian Mercer (*Marcia Rodd* shortly after opening), Danny Apolinar, Igors Gavon, Tom Ligon, Ed Lauter (John Wayne's voice). "The Flowers," "I'm Me," "Come Away, Death," "I'm on My Way to the Top," "The Now Generation," "The Middle Years," "Don't Leave Me," "I'm Not Afraid," "She Never Told Her Love," "What Do I Know?," "(When You're) Young and in Love," "Your Own Thing," "Be Gentle." First OB play to win NY Drama Critics Circle award. Great reviews, and sold to Hollywood, but they never filmed it. Several tours 1968–1971. Cast on these tours included: Sheree North, Gretchen Wyler, Leland Palmer, Renata Vaselle, Marcia Rodd, Paula Kelly, Russ Thacker, Priscilla Lopez, Sandy Duncan. Comedy, London, 2/6/69 (6 weeks). Cast: Jill Choder, Carleton Carpenter, June Compton

2832. *You're Gonna Love Tomorrow*. One-act revue. Greenwich Playhouse, London, 2000. m/l: Stephen Sondheim. Cast: George Hearn, Judy Kaye, Angela Lansbury, Stephen Sondheim. "Isn't It:." Originally ran 3/13/83, as *A Stephen Sondheim Evening*, at Sotheby Parke Bernet, NY, as part of the Whitney Museum of American Art Composers' Showcase

2833. *Yours, Anne*. Set in Amsterdam, June 12, 1942–Aug. 4, 1944. Playhouse 91, 10/13/85–12/1/85. Prev from 9/21/85. p: John Flaxman; m: Michael Cohen; b: Enid Futterman; from book *Anne Frank: The Diary of a Young Girl*, and play by Frances Goodrich & Albert Hackett; d: Arthur Masella; ch: Helena Andreyko; set: Franco Colavecchia; cos: Judith Dolan; light: Beverly Emmons; sound: Jack Mann; md: Dan Strickland; orch: James Stenborg.

Cast: Trini Alvarado, Merwin Goldsmith, Betty Aberlin, George Guidall. "Dear Kitty: I Am Thirteen Years Old," "Dear Kitty: It's a Dangerous Adventure," "An Ordinary Day," "Schlaf," "She Doesn't Understand Me," "Dear Kitty: In the Night," "They Don't Have To," "Hollywood," "Dear Kitty: I Have a Nicer Side," "We Live with Fear," "A Writer," "I'm Not a Jew," "The First Chanukah Night," "Dear Kitty: It's a New Year/We're Here," "Dear Kitty: My Sweet Secret," "My Wife," "Dear Kitty: I Am Longing," "I Remember," "I Think Myself Out," "Nightmare," "For the Children," "Something to Get up For," "Dear Kitty: I Am a Woman," "When We Are Free," "Dear Kitty: I Still Believe"

2834. *Zanna, Don't!* A pop musical fairy tale. Set in magical high school where universe is homosexual instead of straight. Zanna is fashionably hip androgynous teenager with super powers. Rodney Kirk, 10/17/02–11/3/02. Prev from 10/8/02. p: AMAS Musical Theatre, Jack M. Dalgleish, Stephanie Joel; m/l: Tim Acito; add l/b: Alexander Dinelaris; d/ch: Devanand Janki; md/orch: Edward G. Robinson. Before this it had public readings in Manhattan in 2/00 & 6/00, and one at Yale Cabaret Theatre. Re-ran at the John Houseman, 3/20/03–6/29/03. 17 prev from 3/5/03. 119 perf. Cast: Jai Rodriguez. "Who's Got Extra Love?," "I Think We Got Love," "I Ain't Got Time," "Ride 'em," "Zanna's Song," "Be a Man," "Don't Ask, Don't Tell," "Fast," "I Could Write Books," "Don't You Wish We Could be in Love," "Whatcha Got?," "Do You Know What it's Like," "'tis a Far, Far Better Thing I Do"/"Blow Winds," "Straight to Heaven," "Someday You Might Love Me." Cast recording made 6/9/03 on PS Classics & released 10/7/03. Despite being a hit, it cost $750,000, and couldn't sustain itself financially, and had to close, thus pointing up a major weakness in theatre. The name changed to *Zanna!*, and a Broadway prod was talked about for early 2005. p: Jack M. Dalgleish; d: Eric Schaeffer; md: Edward G. Robinson

2835. *Zenda*. Update of Anthony Hope's novel *The Prisoner of Zenda*. Richard Rassendyl is British song-and-dance man with troupe playing in Zenda, who impersonates lookalike King Rudolph and falls for King's fiancee, Flavia, which pleases the King's mistress, Athena (new role written for this musical). King & Athena disappear & Richard continues to play King & new husband. Curran, San Francisco, 8/5/63; L.A.; closed 11/16/63, at the Civic Auditorium, Pasadena, canceling scheduled 11/26/63 Broadway opening at Mark Hellinger. p: Edwin Lester & his San Francisco Civic Light Opera Company; m/l: Vernon Duke (his last score) & Martin Charnin, etc; b: Everett Freeman; d: George Schaefer; ch: Jack Cole; set: Harry Horner; cos: Miles White; md: Pembroke Davenport. Cast: Richard/King: Alfred Drake; Falavia: Anne Rogers; Athena: Chita Rivera; Also with: Susan Luckey, Carmen Mathews, Bob Avian (chorus). Lawrence Brooks (Alfred Drake's understudy). "My Royal Majesty," "The Night is Filled with Wonderful Sounds," "Alone at

Night," "Now the World Begins Again," "Zenda," "A Whole Lot of Happy," "Here and There," "I Wonder What He Meant By That," "When Athena Dances," "Yesterday's Forgotten," "Let Her Not Be Beautiful," "Artists," "Born at Last," "No Ifs! No Ands! No Buts!," "Why Not?," "Enchanting Girls," "Words, Words, Words!"

2836. *Ziegfeld*. London Palladium, 4/26/88. m/l: various authors; b: Ned Sherrin & Alistair Beaton. Cast: Len Cariou, Louise Gold, Fabienne Guyon, Geoffrey Hutchings. "A Pretty Girl is Like a Melody," "Who," "It Had to Be You," "Nobody," "Shine on, Harvest Moon," "My Man," "Mister Gallagher and Mr. Shean," "More than You Know," "Hot and Bothered," "I'm Always Chasing Rainbows," "Make Believe," "Stairway to Paradise"

Ziegfeld Follies of 1956 see # 770, Main Book

Ziegfeld Follies of 1958 see # 770, Main Book

2837. *Zip Goes a Million*. Musical extravaganza. Window cleaner (the locale was changed to Lancashire for the benefit of British audiences) goes to USA and has to spend million in order to inherit 8 million. 1951 Hippodrome, Coventry, England. 9/4/53. 2 weeks; Palace, Manchester, 9/17/53. 4 weeks. The first half was broadcast on BBC Radio; Palace, London, 10/20/51–2/7/53. 544 perf. p: Emile Littler; m: George Posford; l/b: Eric Maschwitz; from book *Brewster's Millions*, by B.G. McCutcheon, and 1907 play by Winchell Smith & Byron Ongley; d: Charles Hickman; ch: Pauline Grant. Cast: George Formby (it was written for him; this was his West End musical comedy debut), Sara Gregory, Wallas Eaton, Warde Donovan, Barbara Perry, Ian Stuart. "Ordinary People," "I Owe You," "Saving up for Sally," "The Thing About You," "Thou Art for Me," "It Takes Me Time to Fall in Love," "Running Away to Land," "Trouble with My Heart," "The Story of Chiquita." After 8 months George Formby had a heart attack & was replaced by *Reg Dixon* on 4/28/52. After London the show toured for 2 years with Mr. Dixon (replaced by *Charlie Chester*). Theatre Museum, 2001. Cast: Gavin Lee, Zoe Curlett, Louise Davidson, Alison Carter, Richard Owens, Andrew Halliday, Brian Greene, Richard Colton. Unrelated to the 1919 Jerome Kern musical of same name, which closed out of town

2838. *Zipp!* Covers 100 musicals in 90 mins. Duchess, London, 2/4/03–4/5/03. Prev from 1/23/03. dev: Steven Dexter & Gyles Brandreth; d/ch: Carole Todd. Cast: Gyles Brandreth. Rave reviews. Previously ran in Edinburgh

2839. *Zombie Prom*. Set during the nuclear 1950s. Variety Arts, 4/9/96–4/19/96. 17 prev from 3/22. 11 perf. m: Dana P. Rowe; l/b: John Dempsey; based on story by John Dempsey & Hugh M. Murphy; d: Philip Wm McKinley; ch: Tony Stevens; light: Richard Nelson; sound: Abe Jacob; orch: Michael Gibson. Cast: Karen Murphy, Jessica-Snow Wilson, Natalie Toro, Richard Muenz, Jeff Skowron. "Enrico Fermi High," "Ain't No Goin' Back," "Jonny

Don't Go," "Good as it Gets," "The C Word," "Rules, Regulations and Respect," "Blast from the Past," "That's the Beat for Me," "Voice in the Ocean," "It's Alive," "Where Do We Go from Here," "Trio (Case Closed)," "Then Came Jonny," "Come Join Us," "How Can I Say Goodbye," "Easy to Say," "Expose," "Isn't It?," "Forbidden Love," "The Lid's Been Blown," "Zombie Prom"

2840. *Zombies from the Beyond*. Musical spoof, set in & around Milwaukee Space Center, in 1955. Players, 10/23/95–12/24/95. Prev from 10/11. p: Colin Cabot; m/l/b: James Valcq; d/ch: Pam Kriger; light: Ken Billington; md: Andrew Wilder. Cast: Matt McClanahan, Susan Gottschalk. "The Sky's the Limit," "The Rocket-Roll," "Second Planet on the Right," "Blast off Baby," "Atomic Feet," "Big Wig," "In the Stars," "Secret Weapon," "Zombies from the Beyond," "Dateline: Milwaukee," "The American Way," "I Am a Zombie," "The Last Man on Earth," "Breaking the Sound Barrier," "Keep Watching the Skies"

2841. *Zona, the Ghost of Greenbrier*. Courtroom drama with songs. Based on actual events. Set in & around Lewisburg, W. Va., in 1897. Hudson Guild. 3/10/00–4/16/00. 9 prev. 27 perf. p: Abingdon Theatre Co.; w: Jan Buttram; d: James F. Wolk; ch: Deborah Roshe; cos: Pamela Scofield; md: Philip Cunningham. Cast: Elizabeth Dean. "Silver Dagger," "Shady Grove"

2842. *Zoot Suit*. Drama with mus. Set 1942–1944 in barrios of L.A., San Quentin prison, and in the mind of Henry Reyna. Loosely based on actual anti-Chicano events revolving around the Sleepy Lagoon Murder Case of 1942 and the Zoot Suit Riots of 1943. Winter Garden, Broadway. 3/25/79–4/29/79. 17 prev. 41 perf. m/l: Lalo Guerrere & Daniel Valdez; w/d: Luis Valdez; ch: Patricia Birch; sound: Abe Jacob. Cast: Edward James Olmos (nominated for a Tony), Daniel Valdez, Charles Aidman, Richard Jay-Alexander, Helena Andreyko. "Zoot Suit," "Los Chucos Suaves," "Vamos a Bailar," "Chicas Patas Boogie." Produced first, successfully, at Mark Taper Forum, L.A.

2843. *Zuleika*. Arts Theatre, Cambridge, England, 10/25/54. p: Cambridge University Musical Comedy Club; m: Peter Tranchell; l/b: James Ferman; suggested by Max Beerbohm's novella *Zuleika Dobson*. Next ran at Opera House, Manchester, 3/5/57; toured; Saville, London, 4/11/57–7/27/57. 124 perf. p: Donald Albery; d: Alfred Rodrigues, *Peter Powell* & *Eleanor Fazan*; set/cos: Osbert Lancaster; md: Ron Grainer, *Charles Mackerras*. Cast: Diane Cilento (*Mildred Mayne*), Patricia Routledge, Roderick Cook, Philip Bond, Peter Murray, Patricia (later Patsy) Rowlands

2844. *The Zulu and the Zayda*. Comedy with mus. About prejudice in South Africa. Cort, Broadway, 11/10/65–4/16/66. 24 prev from 10/18/65. 179 perf. p: Dore Schary & Theodore Mann; w: Howard Da Silva & Felix Leon; m/l: Harold Rome (his last Broadway show); based on 1959 short story *The Zulu and the Zeide*, by Dan Jacobson; d: Dore Schary; set: William & Jean Eckart. Cast: Menasha Skulnik, Ossie Davis, Lou Gossett, Joe Silver, John Pleshette, Yaphet Kotto. "Tkambuza," "Crocodile Wife," "It's Good to Be Alive," "The Water Wears Down the Stone," "Rivers of Tears," "Like the Breeze Blows," "Out of This World," "Some Things," "Zulu Love Song," "L'Chayim" ("May Your Heart Stay Young"), "How Cold, Cold an Empty Room." Divided reviews. Paper Mill Playhouse, NJ, 1966. d/star: Menasha Skulnik

Bibliography

Three separate sources were vital to this book. All differed from one another in many respects, and each offered masses of information not found in the others. These sources were *Theatre World*, *Best Plays* (also known, at least in the early days, as Burns Mantle) and *Playbill*. You cannot do a book like this unless you ransack these sources.

Theatre World began in the mid–1940s, and got better and better as a production, the way annuals do; then in the late 1990s, it began to deteriorate. Although still an annual, and still following the mandate of covering that year's plays, its publication dates have become erratic. By the time an edition would hit the streets, some years had gone by, and it had lost its immediacy, if not its relevance. To make matters worse, *Theatre World* is no longer as accurate or as carefully prepared as it has been in the past.

Best Plays began long before the mid–1940s, and also got better and better. *Playbill* has been going an awfully long time. With the first two of these publications it meant consulting every edition from 1943 (actually before that) to the present, and that meant first finding them, which was not always easy. *Theatre World* especially, although easily available from libraries or through inter-library loan, has almost invariably had its *Oh, Calcutta!* photos ripped out by some desperate young pornographer, leaving gaps throughout the volume, including some musicals. One has to overcome this. *Playbill* is a much more complicated story. There is a *Playbill* issued each week during the run of a show (cast changes during the week are indicated by a slip inserted into the program), and the program is the only sure way of keeping up with cast changes during a show. However it is impossible to consult every *Playbill* for every musical ever produced on Broadway. The best you can hope for reasonably is one or two per show. The earlier *Playbills*, especially, are simply not generally available, except in the Lincoln Center Library, and even then not all. I did the best I could.

A word of warning: all three of these publications have to get their information from somewhere, usually from the production itself–or rather from a production's spokesperson. Usually it is correct, but not always. Things happen during previews, sometimes quite drastic changes, and those previews may be where the periodical gets its information. Sometimes *Best Plays'* Broadway opening night looks quite different from *Theatre World's*, which in turn may only vaguely resemble *Playbill's*. One must be alert.

The other print sources I consulted most often are listed in this bibliography. I also consulted countless oral sources — actors, crew members, and miscellaneous persons.

Abbott, George. *Mister Abbott.* New York: Random House, 1963.

Bailey, Pearl. *Talking to Myself.* New York: Harcourt Brace Jovanovich, 1971.

Baral, Robert. *Revue: A Nostalgic Reprise of the Great Broadway Period.* New York: Fleet Publishing Corp., 1962.

Billman, Larry. *Film Choreographers and Dance Directors.* Jefferson, N.C.: McFarland, 1987.

Blum, Daniel. *A Pictorial History of the American Theatre, 1860–1985.* Updated by John Willis. New York: Crown, 1986.

Bordman, Gerald. *American Musical Comedy.* New York: Oxford University Press, 1982.

_____. *American Musical Revue.* New York: Oxford University Press, 1985.

_____. *American Musical Theatre—A Chronicle.* New York: Oxford University Press, 1978.

_____. *The Oxford Companion to American Theatre.* New York: Oxford University Press, 1984.

Brown, Gene. *Show Time: A Chronology of Broadway and the Theatre from its Beginnings to the Present.* New York: Macmillan, 1997.

Chapman, John (ed). *Theatre '53.* New York: Random House, 1953.

Ganzl, Kurt. *The British Musical Theatre*, vol. ii (1915–1984). New York: Oxford University Press, 1986.

Green, Stanley. *Broadway Musicals Show by Show.* 5th edition. Milwaukee: Hal Leonard, 1996.

Grubb, Kevin Boyd. *Razzle Dazzle: The Life and Work of Bob Fosse.* New York: St. Martin's Press, 1989.

Hay, Peter. *Broadway Anecdotes.* New York: Oxford University Press, 1989.

Hirschhorn, Clive. *The Hollywood Musical.* New York: Portland House/Redd International, 1991.

Ilson, Carol. *Harold Prince.* Ann Arbor, Mich.: UMI Research Press, 1989.

Kazan, Elia. *A Life.* New York: Knopf, 1988.

Kimball, Robert (ed). *Cole.* New York: Holt, Rinehart, Winston, 1971.

Laufe, Abe. *Broadway's Greatest Musicals.* New York: Funk & Wagnalls, 1969.

Leiter, Samuel L. *The Encyclopedia of the New York Stage, 1940–50.* Westport, Conn.: Greenwood Press, 1992.

Lewine, Richard, and Alfred Simon. *Songs of the Theater: A Definitive Index to the Songs of the Musical Stage.* New York: H.W. Wilson, 1984.

Logan, Joshua. *Josh.* New York: Delacorte Press, 1976.

Mandelbaum, Ken. *Not Since Carrie: 40 Years of Musical Flops.* New York: St. Martin's Press, 1991.

Mordden, Ethan. *Beautiful Mornin': The Broadway Musical in the 1940s.* New York: Oxford University Press, 1999.

_____. *Comin' Up Roses: The Broadway Musical in the 1950s.* New York: Oxford University Press, 1998.

Nathan, George Jean. *The Theatre Book of the Year.* 1942–51. New York: Alfred A. Knopf.

The New York Times Directory of the Theatre. New York: Arno, 1971.

Norton, Richard C. *A Chronology of American Musical Theatre.* New York: Oxford University Press, 2002. 3 vols.

Players' Guide. New York: Paul L. Ross, 1964.

Rodgers & Hammerstein: The Illustrated Songbook. New York: Universe/Hal Leonard, 1998.

Sheward, David. *It's a Hit: The Back Stage Book of Longest Running Broadway Shows, 1884 to the Present.* New York: Back Stage Books, 1994.

Stubblebine, Donald J. *Broadway Sheet Music: A Comprehensive Listing 1918–1993.* Jefferson, N.C.: McFarland, 1996.

Suskin, Steven. *Berlin, Kern, Rodgers, Hart, and Hammerstein: A Complete Song Catalogue.* Jefferson, N.C.: McFarland, 1990.

_____. *More Opening Nights on Broadway: A Critical Quotebook of the Musical Theatre, 1965–1981.* New York: Schirmer, 1997.

_____. *Opening Night on Broadway.* New York: Schirmer, 1990.

Sutherland, Susan. *Teach Yourself About Musicals.* London: Hodder & Stoughton (Teach Yourself Books), 1998.

Taymor, Julie, with Alexis Greene. *The Lion King: Pride Rock on Broadway.* New York: Disney Editions, 1997.

Wearing, J.P. *The London Stage, 1940–1949.* Metuchen, N.J.: Scarecrow Press, 1991.

_____. *The London Stage, 1950–1959.* Metuchen, N.J.: Scarecrow Press, 1993.

Wlaschin, Ken. *Gian-Carlo Menotti on Screen.* Jefferson, N.C.: McFarland, 1999.

Best Plays
Internet Broadway Theatre Database
Internet Theatre Database
The New York Times
Phantom on Broadway Internet database
Playbill
Playbill on the Internet
Theatre World
Theatre World Annual, 1950–64

Song Index

References are to entry numbers

Personnel Index

References are to entry numbers

893

Alk, Howard 1382
All, Harriet 255
Allagree, Andrew 462
Allam, Roger 140, 450, 2204, 2800
Allan, Gene 63
Allan, Jed 9, 508
Allan, Lewis 71, 343
Allan, Richard 2191
Allan, Ted 139, 503
Allard, Martine 687
Allburn, Peter P. 2032
Alldredge, E. Don 1934
Alleman, Beverly 372
Allen, April 217
Allen, B.J. 442
Allen, Barbara 108
Allen, Beau 57
Allen, Betty 189, 629, 712
Allen, Betty Lou 231
Allen, Billie 117, 231, 470, 1955, 2282
Allen, Bob 744
Allen, Bobby 598
Allen, Carolyn 362
Allen, Cass 794
Allen, Chesney 2686
Allen, Chet 819
Allen, Christopher 357
Allen, Clifford 287, 302, 334
Allen, Clint 60
Allen, Crystal 552
Allen, David 364, 2033
Allen, Deborah (Debbie) 5, 92, 119, 126, 271, 569, 571, 675, 738, 918, 927, 2621, 2658
Allen, Devon 1701
Allen, Domenick 68
Allen, Douglas 494, 624
Allen, Elizabeth 178, 228, 242, 389, 626
Allen, Evans 491
Allen, Fred 690
Allen, G. Brandon 216
Allen, Gene 2745
Allen, Georgia 576
Allen, Glenn Seven 1780
Allen, Guy 302, 303
Allen, Harry 289
Allen, Herbert 2468
Allen, Ivan 251
Allen, Jack 383, 509
Allen, Jay Presson (Jay Allen) 97, 101, 568, 1583
Allen, Jeanne 1760, 1992
Allen, Jeffrey 276, 466
Allen, Jennifer 128, 275, 401, 404, 2208
Allen, Jimmy 32
Allen, Jo Harvey 1109
Allen, Joe 2728
Allen, John (librettist) 2828
Allen, John (psm) 27, 199, 218, 329, 519, 689
Allen, John (singer) 720, 741
Allen, Jonelle 209, 245, 282, 419, 700, 719, 1568, 1988
Allen, Judy 1189, 2060
Allen, June 447
Allen, Keith 101, 657
Allen, Lee 119, 237, 860, 1895
Allen, Leigh 269, 654, 698
Allen, Lester 2726
Allen, Lewis 12, 92, 286, 477, 963
Allen, Malcolm 15, 439, 456, 468, 473
Allen, Mana 644
Allen, Marc III 406
Allen, Marianna 443
Allen, Mark 20, 73
Allen, Martin (Marty) 320, 329, 333, 390, 496, 636
Allen, Matt 507
Allen, Mel 164
Allen, Michael K. 372, 486
Allen, Narice 2729
Allen, Nina 582
Allen, Norman 286, 2543

Allen, Norman Bradley 2243
Allen, Patricia 504
Allen, Penny 508
Allen, Peter 59, 77, 388, 1866, 2465
Allen, Phillip G. (Phil) 359, 1783
Allen, Rae 110, 163, 193, 204, 508, 511, 529
Allen, Ralph G. 319, 669
Allen, Raymond (Ray) 174, 398, 479, 639, 677, 728, 752, 1269
Allen, Renata 1201
Allen, Richard 569
Allen, Rita 266
Allen, Robert 629
Allen, Ross 47, 128, 567
Allen, Roy 408
Allen, Sandra 220, 671
Allen, Sanford 38, 132, 363, 671
Allen, Scott 136, 376
Allen, Sean 199, 286, 422
Allen, Seth 357, 1950, 2710
Allen, Steve 650, 792, 935, 1122, 2405
Allen, Stuart 512, 582
Allen, Sylvia 649
Allen, Terry 1109
Allen, Theodore 599
Allen, Thomas Mitchell 2728
Allen, Timothy 557
Allen, Tyrees 3
Allen, Valerie 53
Allen, Vicki 144
Allen, Virginia 81, 105, 199
Allen, Vivienne 504, 531
Allen, Whitney 236, 351
Allen, William 351
Allen, Woody 235, 1446
Allen, Zelda 249
Allende, Fernando 422
Allentuck, Max 49, 63, 242, 245, 309, 333, 412, 458, 466, 496, 570, 609
Aller, John 128, 132, 381, 460, 526, 568, 673, 1906
Allerick, Stephen 397
Allers, Franz 25, 80, 105, 106, 124, 289, 372, 377, 444, 470, 472, 474, 528, 549, 629, 2629
Allers, Roger 397
Alley, Fred 2475
Alleyn, Barbara 503
Allgood, Anne 350, 460, 532, 598, 653
Allingham, William 349
Allinson, Judi 105
Allinson, Michael 98, 144, 472, 474, 510, 1840
Allison, Bernie 596
Allison, Fred 490
Allison, Jerry 91
Allison, Jimmy 212, 433, 597
Allison, John 914
Allison, Karl 1530
Allison, Mary Ellen 658
Allison, Michael 871
Allison, Patti 18, 77, 544
Allison, Ruth 677
Allison, Steve 104
Allison, Ted 14
Allison, Thom 375, 580
Allison, Wana 273, 289, 316, 411, 444, 579, 606, 723
Allman, Janet 661
Allman, Jennifer 661
Allmand, Claudia-Jo 2091
Allmon, Clint 57
Allocca, Christine 452
Allott, Nicholas 507
Alloway, Jacqueline (Jackie) 199, 245, 1520
Alloy, Albert (Al) 83, 179, 378, 471, 682, 740
Alloy, Tony 340
Allred, John 694
Allsbrook, Bill 30, 97
Allsopp, Clarence 72
Allwood, Peter 2161

Allwyn, Marilyn 179, 210
Ally, Victoria 466
Allyn & Anthony 1833
Allyn, Reed 378, 531
Allyson, June 259, 494, 944, 2140, 2708
Almack, Richard 282
Almagor, Dan 334, 2111
Almass, Tim 522
Almberg, John 414, 609, 615
Almedilla, Joan 359, 450, 452
Almon, John Paul 112, 635, 1057
Almquist, Leasen Beth 26
Almy, Brooks 22, 264, 466, 467, 530, 551, 672, 1093, 1798, 2483
Alon, Meir 334
Aloni, Yona 2269
Alonso, Maria Conchita 381
Aloysius, Paul 657
Alper, I. 1919
Alper, Steven M. (Steve) 22, 253, 1406, 1604, 1675, 2563
Alper, Yakov 2134
Alperin, Yankele 1663, 1919, 1947, 2134, 2270, 2399, 2794
Alpers, Richard T. 1469
Alpert, Anita 42
Alpert, Chris 283
Alpert, Herb 352, 1498
Alpert, Larry 390, 892
Alpert, Michael 184, 193, 502, 557, 570, 588, 712, 724
Alpert, Millie 892
Alsop, Lamar 298
Alsop, Peter 1514
Alston, Barbara 7, 97, 562
Alston, Peggy 1153, 2104
Alstrom, Ed 387
Alswang, Ralph 127, 156, 245, 252, 392, 539, 594, 643, 701, 721, 951, 1151, 1704, 2179, 2711
Altay, Derin 198, 631, 1292, 2238
Alter, Louis 538, 1893
Alter, Rosalie 411
Alterman, Charles 2169, 2362
Alterman, Michael 547
Alters, Gerald 84, 201, 288, 361, 770, 2585, 2745
Altino, Arden 1763
Altman, Caroline 524
Altman, Jane 696, 2326
Altman, John 2082
Altman, Richard 559, 1105, 2732
Altman, Robert 66, 532
Altman, Ruth 75
Altmark, Lois 446
Altner, Harry 71
Alto, Bobby 2603
Alton, John 2797
Alton, Robb 198
Alton, Robert 29, 195, 297, 384, 437, 531, 729, 769, 1043, 1270, 1761, 2140, 2464, 2641, 2826
Alton, Walter George 2568
Altschuler, A. Robert 267, 538
Altshul, Sara 456
Alty, Charles 1890
Alvarado, Rachel 514
Alvarado, Trini 253, 596, 644, 2833
Alvarez, Anita 11, 62, 209, 210, 243, 522, 2447
Alvarez, Carmen 31, 96, 340, 396, 406, 529, 736, 762, 771, 1212, 2585, 2629, 2734
Alvarez, Isay 452
Alvarez, Pilar 686
Alvarez, Sandy 397
Alvarez, Tomas 444
Alvarez, Tony 198
Alvers, Zinaida 131
Alvies, Betty Jo 257
Alvin, Farah 268, 405, 492, 605
Alvin, Robert 2578
Alvy, Dan 1599

Alwine, Bon 91
Alwyn, Celine 74
Alwyn, Kenneth 286, 1174, 1683
Alyson, Eydie 205, 403, 450
Alzado, Peter 45
Amado, Jorge 604
Aman, John 81, 170, 282, 453, 497, 654, 1013, 1249, 1493, 2059
Aman, Sara 217, 372, 549, 770
Amant, Saint 549
Amanzi 2294
Amaral, Bob 240, 275, 397, 561, 1451, 1946
Amarino, Michael 588
Amaro, Richard 169, 355, 429
Amato, Anthony 597
Amato, Evelyn 128
Amber, Iris 36
Amber, Lili 2269
Amber, Michael 545
Ambler, Jim 225, 605
Ambler, William 505, 690
Ambrose, Martin 43, 322, 353, 365, 369
Ambrose, Stuart 735
Ambroziak, Monika 445
Ambudkar, Utkarsh 439
Ameche, Don 212, 258, 306, 310, 494, 636, 692
Amendolia, Don 477, 535, 758, 2497
Amendum, Dominick 510
Amerson, Tammy 198
Ames, Ed 120, 624
Ames, Florenz 34, 497, 504
Ames, Jerry 32
Ames, Joyce 302
Ames, Kenneth 551
Ames, Kenston 295, 753
Ames, Lionel 93
Ames, Nancy 379
Ames, Paul V. 25, 29, 370
Ames, Roger 1906
Ames, Suzanne 243
Amick, Alan 373
Amidon, Charise 369
Amies, Hardy 2258
Amigo, Norma 224
Amirante, Robert (Bob) 128, 136
Ammon, Richard 304, 473, 474
Ammons, Albert 149, 715
Ammons, Rosalind 286
Amobi, Johnny 363
Amodeo, Paul 606
Amore, Bob 128
Amoros, Larry 2567
Amoroso, Jack 413
Amos, Keith 16, 439, 619, 1430
Amos, Kevin 522, 1902, 2158
Amos, Ruth 711
Amphlett, Carole 657
Amphlett, Chrissie 77
Ampill, Joanna 359, 450, 452
Amram, David 1115
Amsden, Jeffrey 268
Amstein, Juerg 2080
Amsterdam, Morey 71, 314, 601
Amundsen, Monte 100, 367
Amy Beth 450
Amyot, Shaun 26, 569, 611
Anagnostou, Arthur 106, 474
Anania, John 30, 100, 137, 257, 304, 399, 641, 677, 1013, 2194, 2747
Anania, Michael 30, 107, 114, 125, 132, 136, 163, 174, 202, 222, 237, 248, 274, 279, 387, 402, 423, 438, 444, 459, 491, 493, 510, 521, 530, 544, 547, 584, 622, 624, 630, 639, 654, 666, 758, 889, 1093, 1107, 1218, 1241, 1640, 1788, 2026, 2141, 2349, 2475, 2798, 2820
Anastos, Peter 132, 173, 237, 2201
Anbri, Christiana 22, 23, 450, 653
Ancheta, Susan 220, 452, 1262
Andahazy, Lorand 124
Andahazy, Shirley 124

Dacre, Harry 638, 705
Dadd, Kyle 2099
Daenen, John 30
Dafgek, Nancy 136, 299, 414
Dagarvarian, Michele 596
Daggett, John 1837
Daggett, Larry 569
Daggett, Tommy 644
Dagmar 396, 820
Dagny, Robert 528
Dahdah, Robert 1180, 1187, 1623
Dahl, Arlene 30, 55, 454
Dahl, Carolyn 1376
Dahl, Edith 770
Dahl, James 495
Dahl, Joyce 302
Dahl, Roald 969, 1110
Dahlem, Stephen (Steve) 128, 746
Dahms, Gail 669
Daigle, Kenneth M. 206
Daignault, Leo 236, 1354
Dailey, Dan 104, 327, 883, 1988
Dailey, Peter F. 444
Daily, Jerry 249
Daily, Willis 556
Dainton, Scott 128
Dainty, Billy 1524
Dais, Michael 676
Daisey, Mike 1795
Daisy 106
Daker, David 2224
Dakin, Linnea 248, 659
Dakin, Phil 10
Dalby, John 2313
Dalby, Lynn 1775, 2306, 2327
Dalco, Matthew 507
Daldry, Stephen 964
Dale, Charles (Charlie) 83, 471, 2085
Dale, Clamma 557
Dale, Grover 63, 223, 270, 286, 355, 396, 418, 419, 456, 505, 592, 598, 609, 644, 722, 736, 820, 1317, 1712, 2105, 2248
Dale, Jim 47, 112, 438, 510, 1068, 1118, 2224
Dale, Lenn 411
Dale, Mary 165
Dale, Nancy 466
Dale, Neil 657
Dale, Patricia 377
Dale, Sam 1124
Daleo, Mona 33, 246
Daley, Bob *see* Daley, Robert
Daley, George 456
Daley, Jack 629
Daley, John W. 1533
Daley, Joseph 586
Daley, R.F. 38, 128, 132, 140, 275, 607, 673
Daley, Robert (Bob) 73, 256, 294, 407, 458, 722, 729, 749
Dalgleish, Jack M. 2834
Dali, Farid 357
Dalian, Kent 283
Dalio, Marc G. 50
Dall, Evelyn 224
Dallas, Dorothy 652
Dallas, Lorna 629, 652
Dallas, Robert 758
Dallas, Walter 1466, 1965
Dalle, Peter 424
Dallessio, Rich 375
Dallimore, Chloe 134, 561
Dally, Francoise 553
Dalmatoff, Michael 131
Dalmes, Mony 722
D'Aloia, Chuck 593
Dalrymple, Jean 108, 119, 195, 273, 463, 522, 555, 597
Dalsey, Christine 237
Dalsey, Pat 237
Dalton, Buddy 172
Dalton, Devin 544
Dalton, Doris 614, 682
Dalton, Gerry 237

Dalton, Kathie 45, 97, 105, 144, 222
Dalton, Nancy 360, 513, 737
Dalton, Peter 503
Dalton, Sasha 1228
Dalton, Stanley 755
Dalton, T. Michael 128, 651
Dalton, Timothy 240
Daltrey, David 362
Daltrey, Roger 475, 746, 1118, 1581
Daltry, Faith 549
Daly, Caroline 22
Daly, Christine M. 40
Daly, Erin 22
Daly, James 2763
Daly, Kevin 494, 2303
Daly, Martha 1771
Daly, Patricia 248
Daly, Tyne 96, 103, 278, 279, 758, 760
Daly, Wally K. 1351
Daly, William 497, 1734
Dalziel, Raymond 736
Damaino, Tami Tappan *see* Tappan, Tami
Daman, John 688
Damane, David Aron (David Damane) 61, 395, 719
Damashek, Barbara 2243
D'Amato, Anthony 267
D'Amato, Ernie 384
d'Amboise, Charlotte 109, 126, 128, 134, 148, 153, 164, 355, 513, 540, 675, 2644
d'Amboise, Christopher 312, 514, 648
D'Amboise, Jacques 539, 627, 2310
D'Ambrosio, Franc 544, 673, 772, 1159
Damian, Michael 363
D'Amico, Dennis 337
D'Amico, Marcus 424, 509
Damien, Alexandra 97
Damkoehler, William 719
Damon, Cathryn 78, 95, 145, 201, 218, 232, 422, 627, 729, 2361, 2397
Damon, Lisa 584, 654
Damon, Mark 206
Damon, Stuart 78, 105, 178, 214, 235, 341, 416, 1100, 1122, 1157, 1886, 2018
Damrongsri, Mark 374
Damsel, Charles 415
Dana, Barbara 2711
Dana, Dick *see* Dana, Richard
Dana, F. Mitchell (Mitch) 29, 125, 275, 362, 423, 501, 510, 544, 592, 622, 654, 749, 889, 1274, 1542, 1648, 1684, 1852, 2170, 2310
Dana, Leora 293
Dana, Nick 13, 310, 505
Dana, Paige 128
Dana, Richard (Dick) "Gabby" 37, 224, 447, 707, 970, 1035
Danao, Julie P. Relova (Julie Danao) 3, 580, 605, 1766
Dance, Bill 160
Danckaert, Jan 450
D'Ancona, Miranda 15
Dandinis, The 770
Dando, Catherine 412
D'Andrea, Al 1114, 1282
D'Andrea, Carole 736, 737
Dandridge, Dorothy 119, 556
Dandridge, Merle 3, 359, 580
Dandy, Christopher 839
Dane, Clemence 1037
Dane, Eddie 444
Dane, Faith 276, 480, 597
Danek, Michael 136, 155
Danelle, Joe 2407
Daneman, Paul 105
Danese, Connie 22, 494, 1154, 1619
Danford, Andrea 806
Danforth, William 70
Dangcil, Linda 136, 539
D'Angeles, Evan 527, 580
D'Angelo, Beverly 283, 587

Danger-James, McKinney 767
D'Angerio, Joseph 118
Dangler, Anita 161
Danias, Starr 517, 1012
Daniecki, John 579
Daniel, Billie 231
Daniel, Billy Lynn 556
Daniel, Davide 728
Daniel, Diana 1691
Daniel, Gary 540
Daniel, Lenny 128, 351
Daniel, Leslie 144, 521
Daniel, Ven 605
Daniele, Graciela 26, 133, 138, 144, 153, 169, 222, 260, 309, 331, 362, 431, 459, 479, 505, 518, 548, 562, 569, 583, 644, 739, 760, 772, 826, 835, 1065, 1219, 1281, 1411, 1516, 1542, 1607, 1723, 1791, 1849, 2015, 2023, 2441, 2805
Danieley, Jason 82, 112, 125, 236, 237, 521, 654, 711, 1344, 1536, 1544
Danielian, Barry 229, 462
Danielian, Leon 649
Danielle, Marlene 128, 403, 434, 604, 738
Danielle, Martha 196, 513, 581, 654, 2808
Danielle, Susan 136, 1520, 2412, 2626
Danielli, Fred 104, 741
Daniels, Annabel 657
Daniels, Bebe 228, 1779, 2140
Daniels, Billy 89, 256, 303, 441
Daniels, Charlie 141, 725
Daniels, Cicily 122, 580
Daniels, Danny 9, 22, 25, 43, 62, 313, 331, 378, 421, 664, 687, 734, 944, 1365, 1562, 1803, 1810, 1840, 2389
Daniels, David 103, 120, 502, 549, 654, 906, 2188
Daniels, Dennis 136, 260, 465, 581, 631, 661, 1012
Daniels, Edgar 210, 487
Daniels, Edward 439
Daniels, Gregory 29
Daniels, Jacqueline 504
Daniels, Jeffrey (Jeff) 260, 657
Daniels, Kaipo 373, 374
Daniels, Leon 93
Daniels, Marc 154, 2178, 2790
Daniels, Moe 397, 403
Daniels, Monique 580
Daniels, Nikki Renee 3, 405, 492
Daniels, Pauline 2324
Daniels, Salie 368
Daniels, Sharon 459
Daniels, Stan 265, 2441
Daniels, Tracy 544
Daniels, Veronique 580
Daniels, Walker 282
Daniels, William 402, 511, 615
Danielson, Nick 207
Danilova, Alexandra 500, 649, 1460
Danis, Amy 82, 403
Danko, Harold 1921
Dankworth, Jacqueline 443
Dankworth, Johnny 1001, 1144, 2617
Dann, Larry 503, 1163, 1261, 1408, 1471, 1625, 1742, 1983, 2746
Dann, Roger 503, 2307
Dannatt, Norman 789
Dannehl, David 198, 533, 631
Danner, Blythe 125, 223, 1916, 2695
Danner, Braden 450, 510, 657, 1395
Danner, Dorothy 45, 630
Danner, Harry 42, 579, 666, 666
Dannheiser, Adam 153
Danns, David 126
Dano, Lazar 372
Dano, Paul Franklin 569
Dano, Royal 209, 698, 2589
Danot, Eric 362
Danova, Cesare 264
Dansby, William 672

Dansicker, Michael 4, 167, 944, 1431, 2667
Danskin, Warren L. 795
Dante, Dino 505
Dante, Nikolas (Nicholas) 15, 30, 136, 334, 2435
Dante, Ron 5, 63, 400
Dantine, Helmut 103, 463
Danton, Ray 521
D'Antonakis, Fleury 178, 333, 347
Dantuono, Michael (Mike) 109, 228, 229, 239, 696, 772, 1101, 1188, 1846
Danvers, Lindsey 128
Danvers, Marie (Marie-Laurence Danvers) 544
Danyl, Gloria 447, 720
Danzig, Evelyn 695
Danzinger, Howard 1111
D'Aquila, Kenny 1022
Dara, Olu 2562, 2615
Darby, Joan 549
Darby, Kenn 671
Darby, Prudence 87, 146, 263, 274, 414, 587
Darby, Ra Joe 565
Darbyshire, Michael 545, 1069, 2635
D'Arc, Victor 587
Darcel, Denise 222, 500, 534
d'Arcy, Alexander 768
Darcy, Don 555
D'Arcy, Eamon 605
Darcy, Georgine 243, 497
D'Arcy, Jean 249
Darcy, John 597
D'Arcy, Mary 172, 466, 544, 639, 670, 891, 1343
Darcy, Pattie (later Pattie Darcy Jones) 387, 645, 927, 1377, 1560
D'Arcy, Richard 10, 67, 69, 80, 300, 332, 404, 512, 632
d'Arcy James, Brian *see* James, Brian d'Arcy
Darden, Michael 210, 682
Darden, Severn 1382, 2711
Dare, Coy 451
Dare, Danny 2543
Dare, Phyllis 1717
Dare, Robert G. 618
Dare, Thelma 20, 377, 458
Dare, Zena 472, 1717
Dare Thomas, Barbara *see* Thomas, Barbara Dare
Darewski, Herman 503
Dargan Doyle, Elizabeth *see* Doyle, Elizabeth Dargan
Darian, Anita 372, 600, 629, 2282, 2348, 2387
Darin, Bobby 689, 699
Darion, Joe 333, 425, 426, 427, 428, 429, 627, 1480, 1933
Darken, Nanci 470
Darley, Oliver 2800
Darling, Candy 190, 730, 744
Darling, Denver 215
Darling, Erik 2033
Darling, Jane 648
Darling, Jean 123
Darling, Jennifer 322, 417, 503
Darling, Peter 112, 443, 964, 1134, 2122
Darlow, Cynthia 267, 2296
Darnay, Toni 456, 466, 597
Darnell, August 1607
Darnell, Catrin 128
Darnell, Deede 449
Darnell, Rick 343
Darnell, Robert 326, 610
Darnutzer, Don 343
Darr, Deborah (formerly Deborah St. Darr) 111, 185, 610, 654
Darrah, James 62, 305, 2362
Darrell, Peter 1670, 1690
Darrell, Sidonie 1122
Darrenkamp, John 152
Darrieux, Danielle 15, 55, 144

Ferrone, Dan 652
Ferrugiari, Glenn 136
Ferry, John 654
Ferry, Robert 427
Ferry, Stephen 377
Ferry Williams, Diane *see* Williams, Diane Ferry
Fesco, Michael 235, 258, 341, 485, 1349, 1951
Festa, John Joseph 128
Fetcher, Tom 44
Fetter, Danny 397
Fetter, Ted 72, 421, 1047, 2016
Feuer, Cy 1, 25, 75, 108, 136, 137, 273, 323, 331, 399, 466, 511, 515, 546, 636, 641, 734, 741, 745, 895
Feuer, Howard 47, 59, 259, 414, 438, 675, 772
Feuer, Jed 831, 955, 1278
Feyder, Jacques 121
Feyhe, B. 678
Feyti, Robert 677, 770
ffolkes, David 14, 80, 217, 614, 642, 741, 742
Fialkov, Max 650
Fian, Robbee 719
Fiander, Lewis 615, 1351, 1583, 2052, 2235, 2600, 2714
Fibich, Felix 977, 1323, 1781, 1947, 2270, 2495
Fichman, Joel S. 89
Fickinger, Steven (Steve) 515, 1199, 1691, 2823
Fickman, Andy 2276
Fiddlin' Irving 296
Fidler, Michael 2343
Fiedler, John 464
Fieger, Addy O. 1095, 1206
Field, Alice 847
Field, Amy 657
Field, Carol 127
Field, Crystal 846, 1634
Field, Graham 1224
Field, Katie 193
Field, Leonard 556
Field, Morey 613
Field, Robert 153, 171, 444, 723, 2299
Field, Robin 2472
Field, Ron (Ron; Ronnie) 29, 30, 75, 97, 98, 100, 121, 228, 243, 257, 376, 377, 379, 414, 442, 443, 496, 513, 538, 540, 568, 618, 626, 629, 654, 771, 1339, 1736
Field, Shirley Ann 1785
Fielder, Sean C. 85
Fielder, Thom 548
Fielding, Anne 367, 519
Fielding, Fenella 1140, 1143, 1690, 2183, 2703
Fielding, Harold 65, 286, 466, 598, 1122, 1430, 1469, 1487, 1886, 2175
Fielding, Henry 1469, 1809
Fielding, Marjery 681, 2480
Fields, Benny 655
Fields, Bradley Steven *see* Steven-Fields, Bradley
Fields, Chip 183, 303
Fields, Clare 57
Fields, Dorothy 5, 24, 25, 26, 34, 59, 66, 83, 95, 121, 230, 354, 435, 446, 482, 577, 609, 669, 674, 675, 678, 711, 723, 724, 725, 758, 1632, 1771, 2298, 2447, 2492
Fields, Felicia P. 760, 1146
Fields, Frank 2387
Fields, Heather 142
Fields, Herbert (Herb) (actor) 20, 232, 329, 360, 378, 455, 487, 626, 629, 707
Fields, Herbert (librettist) 24, 25, 26, 34, 95, 121, 150, 446, 577, 722, 758, 834, 1208, 1270, 1333, 1771, 2031, 2140, 2447
Fields, Hilary 136
Fields, Howie 490

Fields, J. Michael 341
Fields, Joan 707
Fields, Joe (actor) 7
Fields, John 425
Fields, Joseph A. (Joe) (librettist) 219, 220, 243, 244, 250, 407, 758, 759
Fields, Julius C. 210, 302, 372, 377, 382, 603, 629, 736
Fields, Linda 1207
Fields, Lynn 286, 370
Fields, Nilyne 518
Fields, Peter 415
Fields, Randy 2100
Fields, Richard 623
Fields, Sandie 417
Fields, Thor 106, 373
Fields, Tommy 1875
Fields, W.C. 2204, 2732
Fields, William 367, 408, 451, 664
Fierstein, Harvey 101, 102, 207, 283, 285, 388
Fife, Ashlee 668
Figg, David M. 621
Fighera, Frank 675
Figman, Max 728
Figne, S. 688
Figueroa, Dennis 1938
Figueroa, Rona 450, 452, 492, 1085
Filak, Michael 1111
Filali, Marianne 138
Filderman, Alan 311, 431, 518
Filiato, Phillip 15
Filiberto, J. de Dios *see* de Dios Filiberto, J.
Filipov, Alexander 517
Filkins, Shellie 104
Fillhart, Tammie 293
Finch, David 99
Finch, Patricia (Pat) 24, 202, 505, 654, 722
Finch, Peter 620
Finch, Richard 605
Finck, Arthur 503
Finck, David 400, 675, 735
Finck, Herman 469
Finclair, Barry 4
Finders, Matt 608
Findlay, Diane J. (Diane Findlay) 147, 173, 302, 369, 423, 449, 948, 1022, 1148, 1268, 1270, 1943, 2120, 2742
Findley, Danielle 22
Fine, C. Robert 270
Fine, Michelle 39
Fine, Sidney 466, 467
Fine, Sylvia 1193, 1771
Finegan, Bill 493
Fineman, Carol R. 85, 514
Fineman, Karen 140, 450, 562
Finger, Leonard 502, 591
Fink, Bert 510, 2450
Fink, Dann 450
Fink, Dave 140
Fink, John 615
Fink, Katherine 575
Finkel, Barry 312, 385, 635, 1640, 1852
Finkel, Elliot 1336, 2000, 2269
Finkel, Fyvush (Fy) 204, 205, 403, 1336, 1416, 1433
Finkel, Ian 4, 164, 305, 381, 1336
Finkel, Joshua 381, 450
Finkelstein, Joan 568
Finkle, David 326, 334, 1194
Finklehoffe, Fred F. (Jr.) 20, 386, 2398
Finkler, Marion 567
Finlay, Frank 1716, 1993
Finlay, Melodee 1273
Finlayson, Robert 544
Finley, Felicia 3, 198, 395, 645, 750, 1028, 1353
Finley, Gracie 851
Finley, Patte (formerly Pat Finley) 302, 1465
Finn, Ben 2426

Finn, Christine 2327
Finn, Frank 444, 454
Finn, George 654
Finn, Jeffrey 148, 2552, 2692
Finn, Kenneth (Ken) 112, 467
Finn, Kevin 363
Finn, Robyn 22
Finn, Terry 443
Finn, William 169, 200, 825, 1281, 2023, 2308, 2666
Finnegan, Deidre 1049
Finnegan, Gerald 1082
Finneran, Katie 99, 396, 476
Finnerty, Mary Sue 292, 2303, 2791
Finney, Albert 22, 1785, 1887
Finney, Jack 1863, 2622
Finney, Mary 214, 243, 291, 420
Finnie, Ross 128
Fiordallisi, Mary Anne 669, 772, 1440, 1505
Fiore, Dominic 651
Fiore, James (Jim) 436, 499
Fiore, Jon 1560
Fiore, Roland 478
Fiorella, Al 252
Fiorentino, Imero 490
Fiori, Patrick 2058
Fiorillo, Albert L. (Jr.) 472, 473, 691, 718, 771
Fiorillo, Elisa 696, 1178
Fiorito, John 459
Fiorito, Ted 59
Fippinger, Lynn 2780
Firbank, Ann 1547
Firbank, Ronald 2703
Firman, David 128, 1941
Firth, David 39, 544, 634, 1340, 1606, 2035, 2204, 2804
Firth, Tazeena 181, 198
Firth, Tim 2122
Fisch, Irwin 761
Fischelli, Camille 582
Fischer, Alfred 748
Fischer, Alison 2222
Fischer, Bobby 132
Fischer, Howard 654, 751
Fischer, Jane 217, 291, 504
Fischer, Juliet 514
Fischer, Kurt 580
Fischer, Lisa 1004
Fischer, Loretta 681
Fischer, Lori 395
Fischer, Martin 164
Fischer, Mary 262
Fischer, William S. 1719
Fischoff, George 246, 2220, 2231, 2349
Fiser, Don 454
Fish, Hamilton III 872
Fishburne, Larry 2698
Fisher, Alex 2817
Fisher, Anne 150
Fisher, Bruce 586
Fisher, Carl 27, 97, 103, 147, 163, 204, 211, 218, 222, 238, 344, 487, 519, 529, 621, 689, 736, 754, 771, 2333
Fisher, Carrie 340, 1090
Fisher, Chester 539
Fisher, David "Dudu" 450
Fisher, Eddie 754
Fisher, Fred 5, 59, 340, 638
Fisher, Gary 2369
Fisher, George 470, 633
Fisher, Harrison 762, 901, 1026, 2513, 2537
Fisher, Irving 103, 601
Fisher, J.W. 118
Fisher, Jacqueline 336, 654
Fisher, Jerry 486
Fisher, Joely 99, 268
Fisher, Jules 17, 28, 39, 56, 59, 85, 101, 113, 122, 133, 134, 138, 168, 169, 178, 241, 255, 264, 280, 282, 283, 286, 309, 313, 329, 350, 352, 357, 362, 388, 431, 444, 449, 456, 476, 489,

494, 545, 547, 568, 569, 583, 586, 587, 599, 609, 648, 654, 663, 699, 732, 750, 752, 762, 766, 804, 906, 921, 944, 967, 1058, 1065, 1118, 1137, 1212, 1219, 1286, 1345, 1396, 1421, 1447, 1479, 1482, 1493, 1498, 1516, 1555, 1768, 1810, 1856, 1882, 1888, 2070, 2230, 2248, 2295, 2317, 2371, 2465, 2478, 2620, 2653, 2659, 2763
Fisher, Kate 351, 450
Fisher, Linda 654, 993
Fisher, Lola 95, 211, 470, 472, 503, 540
Fisher, M. Anthony 60, 338
Fisher, Mark 2735
Fisher, Mary Helen 460
Fisher, Mary L. 990
Fisher, Michael James 106
Fisher, Nelle 255, 421, 512, 522, 573, 723, 2320, 2393
Fisher, Paula Heil 164
Fisher, Rick 2006
Fisher, Robert (librettist) 449
Fisher, Robert (Rob) (musical director) 12, 96, 103, 120, 134, 211, 256, 396, 398, 438, 495, 522, 524, 532, 562, 599, 705, 759, 883, 1122, 1270, 1542, 1736, 1825, 2339, 2654
Fisher, William 33
Fishko, Robert S. 157, 499, 551
Fishman, Al 547
Fishman, Lisa 705
Fishman, Tara (Tara Schoen Fishman) 439, 1499
Fisk, Kimberly 324
Fiske, Louise 471
Fiss, Thomas Michael 236
Fistos, John 1486
Fitch, Bob *see* Fitch, Robert
Fitch, Clyde 1537
Fitch, Edith 124
Fitch, Elaine 284
Fitch, Robert E. (Bob) 22, 29, 144, 177, 218, 240, 251, 306, 389, 407, 414, 422, 472, 562, 618, 626, 689, 752, 1019, 1187, 1520, 1946, 1952, 2742
Fitch, Thelma 284
Fite, Beverly 46
Fite, David E. 143
Fite, Mark 143
Fitts, Debbie 755
Fitts, Dudley 262
Fitz, Richard 631
Fitzgerald, Allen 671
Fitzgerald, Ara 1850
Fitzgerald, Barry 182, 209
Fitzgerald, Christopher (Chris) 17, 747, 1795, 2339
Fitzgerald, Ed 126, 687
Fitzgerald, Ella 724
Fitzgerald, F. Scott 922
Fitzgerald, Fern 133, 136
Fitzgerald, Geraldine 367, 424, 682, 2376, 2631
Fitzgerald, Kate 68
Fitzgerald, Kathy 561, 679, 1594, 2362
Fitzgerald, Lillian 71
Fitzgerald, Paul 282, 489, 1210
Fitzgerald, Peter J. 6, 16, 58, 61, 96, 101, 102, 115, 140, 188, 191, 200, 206, 229, 278, 305, 311, 330, 356, 388, 395, 423, 434, 462, 475, 541, 568, 591, 678, 688, 700, 717, 725, 732, 752, 817, 1027, 1065, 1278, 1436, 1551, 1579, 1902, 1910, 2071, 2104, 2435
Fitzgerald, Richard *see* Fitzgerald, T. Richard
Fitzgerald, Robert 262
Fitzgerald, Scott *see* Fitzgerald, F. Scott
Fitzgerald, T. Richard (Richard Fitzgerald) 23, 50, 82, 92, 177, 216, 228,

Mahoney, Will 209
Mahony, Sean 568
Mahony-Bennett, Kathleen (Kathy) 29, 498, 2065, 2305
Mahowald, Joseph 82, 351, 444, 450, 450, 1797, 1814
Maibaum, Norman 15, 154, 196, 762
Maidhof, Robert 823
Maidy, Kelly 746
Maier, Barbara 664
Maier, Marcia 46, 273, 332, 384, 601, 741
Maier, Robert 1705
Maier, Tommy 690
Maika, Michele 450
Mai-Lan 137
Mailer, Norman 569
Maillard, Carol Lynn 146, 183, 197, 345, 927
Mailman, Bruce 1313
Maiman, Henry 349
Main, Laurie 214
Main, Marjorie 440, 464
Main, Norman 18
Mainbocher 103, 522, 536, 652, 758
Maine, Bruno 892, 1502
Mainelli, Jono 868
Maio, Frank J. 106, 440, 452
Mais, Michele 593, 1936
Maison, Gil 314
Maitland, Jack 2635
Maitland, Joan 982, 1185, 2635, 2830
Maitland, Michael 422, 592
Maitland, Richard (Dick) 396, 609
Maitland, Ruth 494
Maitner, Rob 726
Majer, Joseph 728
Major, Aja 128, 385, 827
Major, William 323
Makarova, Natalia 517
Makeba, Miriam 602, 872
Maker, Gregory (Greg) 197, 319, 656
Makkonen, Kip 311
Mako 526
Mal 268
Malakhow, Justin A. 88
Malambos, Los 86
Malamud, Bernard 31, 845
Malandrinos, Andrea 2258
Malas, Spiro 444, 448, 460, 505, 1675
Malbin, Elaine 120, 377, 470
Malcolm, Christopher 588, 589
Malcolm, Graeme 3, 375
Malcolm, John 704
Malcolm-Smith, George 32
Malden, Karl 276, 471, 2790
Maldonado, J. 134
Maldonado, Jose Antonio 1307
Maleitzke, Peter 700
Malek, David 128
Malekos, Nick 133, 417, 674
Malenfant, Lloyd 851
Malenke, Jennifer 339
Maleson, Leon 401, 659
Malfitano, Catherine 600, 664
Malfitano, Elena 82
Malfitano, Jan 506
Malidon, Lisette 236
Malina, Joel 592, 2176
Malina, Luba 425, 433, 446, 2576
Malina, Robert 7
Malina, Stuart 462, 2229
Malinou, Selma 9
Malizia, Lester 1343
Malki, Mourad 357
Malkin, Seth 112
Malkine, Gilles 1235
Mall, Benjamin 122
Mallard, David E. 673
Mallardi, Michelle 351
Mallardy, Claire 379
Mallen, Dave 504
Malleson, Miles 105
Mallet, David 363
Mallett, Chuck 2818

Mallin, Vera 316
Mallinson, David 2514
Mallory, Henry 721
Mallory, Lisa Ann 724
Mallory, Victoria 120, 222, 402, 737
Mallory, William 506
Mallow, Tom 25, 47, 91, 132, 168, 197, 245, 275, 338, 547, 648, 672, 691, 718, 755, 756, 764, 771
Malloy, Judy 635
Malm, Mia 228, 584, 644
Malmuth, Ravah 406
Malneck, Matt (Matty) 188, 538, 656
Malnick, Michael 243, 1068, 1683
Malo, Gina 516
Malone, Bettye 469, 576
Malone, Dale 273, 508, 509, 710, 722
Malone, Deborah 755
Malone, Elizabeth 24
Malone, Howard 14, 104
Malone, Joe 1766
Malone, Kay 127
Malone, Ken 175, 179
Malone, Michael (early 70s actor) 439
Malone, Michael (late 90s actor) 229, 693
Malone, Mike 578, 682, 1094, 1185
Malone, Ray 95, 2263
Malone, Richard 135
Maloney, Bill 2316
Maloney, D.J. 2656
Maloney, Kristin 322
Maloney, Maureen 261, 1077, 1601
Maloney, Peter 125
Maloney, Russell 642
Malony, Kevin 878, 1854
Maloof, Donald 105
Malory, Thomas 105
Malosh, Timothy 452
Maltby, H.F. 1930
Maltby, Jacquey 109, 140, 356, 624, 631, 654, 2458
Maltby, Richard Jr. 5, 6, 41, 58, 161, 230, 367, 452, 486, 489, 648, 1133, 1446, 1484, 1529, 1571, 1840, 2126, 2292, 2335, 2494, 2593, 2604, 2698
Maltz, Maxwell *see* Ashley, Clayton
Malvin, Arthur 669
Mamanna, Robert D. 450, 2608
Mamas and the Papas, The 1265
Mambazo, Ladysmith Black *see* Ladysmith Black Mambazo
Mamoulian, Rouben 34, 123, 408, 504, 555, 556, 597, 599, 636
Man, Christopher (Chris) 646
Man, David 2443
Manabat, Jake 580
Manahan, George 673
Manasse, Jon 38, 375
Manasseri, Mark 510
Manasseri, Michael 510, 847
Manche, Daniel 492
Manchester, Joe 2361
Manchester, Mary 629
Manchester, Melissa 168, 648, 673, 1596
Mancina, Mark 397
Mancinelli-Cahill, Margaret 1116
Mancini, Al 654, 1597, 1669, 1924, 2747
Mancini, Henry 188, 732, 1835
Mancuso, Sam 625
Mandagaran, Oscar 226
Mandan, Robert 30, 324, 417, 419
Mandel, Adrian 2399
Mandel, Bubbles 769
Mandel, Frank 174, 259, 494, 2026
Mandel, Lisa 671
Mandel, Mel 1654, 2001
Mandel, S.R. 597
Mandel, Tom 908
Mandela, Nelson 602
Mandelbaum, Ken 271, 354, 438, 501
Mandelker, Philip 147, 246

Mandell, Michael 343, 1065, 1544, 2308
Mandell, Rick 986, 987
Mandell, Robert 1435
Mandell, Steve 585
Mander, Peter 742
Mandia, John 448
Mandra, Barbara 228, 669
Mandracchia, Charles 264, 754, 2214
Mandrella, Anne 134
Mandvi, Aasif 507
Manera, Richard 526
Manes, Steve 418
Maney, Richard 14, 25, 46, 67, 105, 157, 158, 243, 251, 404, 413, 453, 463, 472, 614, 632, 655, 710, 711
Manfredi, Nino 594
Manfredini, Harry 551
Mangano, Nick 499
Manger, Itzik 1289, 1772, 1933, 2088, 2461, 2601
Mangione, Chuck 980
Mango, Angelo 78, 341, 1760
Manhart, Grant 191
Manhattan Rhythm Kings, The 626
Manheim, Ralph 699
Manilow, Barry 1159, 1269, 1499, 1866, 2059
Manilow, Edna 2662
Manim, Mannie 602
Manings, Allan 484, 1803
Manion, David K. 819
Maniscalco, Joan 2445
Mankes, Karen 586
Mankiewicz, Joseph 30
Mankiewicz, Tom 246
Manko, Dorothy 614
Mankoff, Allan 481
Mankowitz, Wolf 545, 592, 699, 870, 932, 1309, 1785, 1877, 2152, 2485
Manley, Iris 629
Manley, Irving 2449
Manley, Mark 56, 77, 205, 263
Manley, Sandra (Sandy) 160, 615, 668, 755
Mann, Alan 292
Mann, Alison 295, 639
Mann, Allan 1276
Mann, Andrea 446, 601
Mann, Anita 1910
Mann, Barry 168, 645, 2593
Mann, Buddy 255
Mann, Cecile 62, 582
Mann, Charlotte 2343
Mann, Daniel 217, 528
Mann, David (Dave) 19, 1160
Mann, Delbert 710
Mann, Edward 16
Mann, Elizabeth 700
Mann, Ethel 638
Mann, Fred C. III 168, 442, 675
Mann, Friederike 748
Mann, Gubi 1234
Mann, Heinrich 559
Mann, Howard 257
Mann, Jack "Peanuts" 447, 522
Mann, Jack 41, 147, 181, 222, 261, 265, 277, 307, 319, 337, 344, 402, 443, 448, 491, 510, 515, 526, 610, 634, 672, 687, 705, 738, 753, 760, 798, 2833
Mann, Jerry 504, 505, 791
Mann, Joan 62, 69, 336, 497, 536, 643, 701, 1393
Mann, June 224
Mann, Karen 673
Mann, Michael 47, 135, 237, 276, 301, 318, 664, 721, 1168, 2374
Mann, Miriam 509
Mann, Nancy 237, 301
Mann, P.J. 136, 318, 1520
Mann, Patrick 345
Mann, Peggy 613
Mann, Ronald 1955
Mann, Shirley Jean 466

Mann, Stuart 273, 365, 372
Mann, Sylvia 204
Mann, Terrence V. 39, 47, 50, 128, 355, 450, 547, 562, 568, 589, 607, 1118, 1766
Mann, Theodore 21, 532, 743, 1310, 2659, 2844
Mann, Tommy 508
Manners, Bernard 66, 197, 477
Manners, J. Hartley 1393, 2158, 2159, 2415
Manners, Jayne 11, 83, 1043, 1412
Manners, Loraine 70
Manners, Marlene 2320
Mannes, Marya 166
Manning, Carla 719
Manning, Carol 334
Manning, Dan 12, 2436
Manning, David 25, 422, 2276
Manning, Dick 1332
Manning, Doncharles 604
Manning, Frankie 66
Manning, Irene 171, 174, 2574
Manning, Jack 140, 178, 606
Manning, Jane 1212
Manning, Joanne 153, 234, 732
Manning, Kate 761
Manning, Laura 856
Manning, Linda 22
Manning, Monroe 768
Manning, Phyllis 224, 666
Manning, Richard 664
Manning, Rick 260, 381, 388, 428
Manning, Robin 688
Manning, Ruth 456
Manning, Samuel L. (Sam) 117
Manning, Ted 2239
Manning, Tony 736
Mannion, Elizabeth 664
Mannis, Sandra 174
Manno, Dana 197
Manno, Karen 2456
Manocherian, Jennifer 122, 350
Manoff, Dinah 387
Manon, Sylvia 420
Manos, Chris 533
Manos, Dean 672
Manos, Judy 672
Manou, Diana 128
Manough, Anthony 359, 397
Mansfield, Bowling H. 629
Mansfield, Irving 654
Mansfield, Karl 186
Mansfield, Ken 801
Mansfield, Laurie 91
Mansfield, Richard 666
Mansfield, Scott 937
Mansfield, Vicki (formerly Victoria) 621, 667
Mansfield, Wendy 136, 719
Manship, George 413
Manson, Alan 104, 237, 2223
Manson, Allison Renee (Allison R. Manson) 146, 345, 675
Manson, Charles 2669
Manson, Eddy 702
Mansour, George 357
Mansur, Susan 57, 164, 735, 2321, 2436, 2475, 2761
Mantegna, Joe 253, 282, 760
Mantell, Joe 93
Mantell, Marc 1599
Mantello, Joe 39, 747, 1887
Mantelman, Roy 446
Mantia, Buddy 2603
Mantinan, Alejandra 686
Mantovani 783, 842, 992, 1730, 1930, 2136, 2406
Mantz, Delphine T. 724
Manuel, Caren Lyn 88, 450, 580
Manuel, Paul 450, 738
Manulis, Martin 192
Manus, Robin 669
Manville Dresselhuys, Lorraine *see* Dresselhuys, Lorraine Manville

Mastrogiorgio, Danny 153
Mastrone, Frank 58, 128, 198, 256, 351, 450, 544, 605, 2570
Masullo, Tony 2513
Masuzzo, Dennis 111, 548
Mata & Hari 384, 2673
Matalon, Adam 128, 1066
Matalon, Vivian 82, 687, 2672
Matalon, Zack 341, 1500
Matassa, Cosmo 311
Mate, James 317, 446
Matejka, Catherine 2450
Matera, Pat 196, 204, 737
Mates, Sally 1541
Mather, Ted 657
Mathers, Jack 692
Mathes, Martha 108, 214, 243, 458, 528
Matheson, Douglas 512
Matheson, Eve 844
Matheson, Murray 502
Mathews, Carmen 15, 110, 155, 156, 173, 334, 670, 762, 2835
Mathews, George 179, 365, 704
Mathews, Jimmy 669
Mathews, John 317, 613
Mathews, Joyce 14
Mathews, Kevin 451
Mathews, Norman 129
Mathews, Sheila 81, 175, 464, 500, 629, 1342
Mathews, Tony 343
Mathias, Alice Hammerstein 444, 886, 2036
Mathias, Philip 273, 654
Mathias, Sean 1902
Mathibe, Eddie 602
Mathibe, Master Amos 602
Mathieson, Fiona 822, 844
Mathieu, William 1382
Mathis, Bonnie 302
Mathis, Brian 611
Mathis, Claude 1348
Mathis, Lee 547
Mathis, Sherry 402, 465, 2658
Mathis, Stanley Wayne (Stanley W. Mathis) 352, 380, 395, 397, 502, 599, 759, 767
Mathison, Cameron 547
Mathon, A. 684, 685
Matias, Fiely 22
Matkin, Terry 362
Matlock, Harry 723
Matlock, Norman 532, 571, 719, 2623
Matlock, Victoria 236, 351
Matlovsky, Navarre 47, 376
Matlovsky, Noelle 766
Matlovsky, Samuel 53, 273, 370, 1112, 1872
Matlovsky, Stanley 699
Matos Rodriguez, G.H. 226, 684, 685, 686
Matosich, Frank Jr. 622
Matoto, Cristina 375
Matray, Ernst 534
Matray, Maria 534
Matricardi, Lisa 607, 759
Matsey, Jeff 666
Matshikiza, Todd 1710
Matsios, Christine 273, 378, 415
Matson, David 425
Matson, Jill 58, 159, 562
Matson, Ruthena 71
Matson, Vera 586
Matsui, Blythe 220
Matsui, Rumi 527
Matsumoto, Paul 452
Matsuoka, V.V. 373
Matsusaka, Tom 422, 526, 2224, 2288
Mattaliano, Al 136
Matter, Jack 1402
Matterson, Diana 2359
Mattes, Jay 381
Matteson, Pamela 22
Matteson, Ruth 444, 454, 536

Matthaei, Konrad 245, 692
Matthau, Celia Celnik 691
Matthau, Walter 273, 302, 393, 2194
Matthew, Ed 533
Matthew, Jack 110, 211, 372, 396, 529, 603
Matthews, Anderson 585
Matthews, Art 33, 55, 251, 422, 511, 1760
Matthews, Artie 705
Matthews, Bert 528
Matthews, Billy 51, 53, 108, 245, 273, 379, 692
Matthews, Brian 155
Matthews, Christine 137, 372, 737, 2804
Matthews, Debra 118
Matthews, Denese 91
Matthews, Dorothy 192, 346
Matthews, Edward 231, 555
Matthews, Elisa 1049
Matthews, Ellen 202, 250, 620
Matthews, Evan 1688
Matthews, Francis 2608
Matthews, Gerald 649
Matthews, Gerry (actor) 511, 894, 970, 1227
Matthews, Gerry (writer) 2272
Matthews, Hale 292, 1975
Matthews, Inez 119, 231, 408, 556
Matthews, Jessie 1875, 2727
Matthews, Jon 596
Matthews, Joy Lynn 431, 467, 1936
Matthews, Lester 174
Matthews, Melle 654
Matthews, Nathan 2757
Matthews, Scott 604
Matthews, Tommy 80, 171
Matthews, Tony 123, 410
Matthews, Y. Yvonne 557
Matthews, Yvette 136
Matthias, Martin 657
Mattingly, Hedley 509
Mattioli, Louis 283, 659
Mattis, Dorothy Jeanne 214
Mattis, Jack 300
Mattise, Rudy 93
Mattox, Harold 536
Mattox, Jean 606
Mattox, Matt 32, 81, 121, 232, 353, 415, 519, 606, 612, 698, 729, 739, 770, 2189
Mattson, Eric 123, 124
Mattson, Wayne 407, 465, 691
Mature, Victor 1736, 2572
Matwiow, Paul 72
Matz, Jerry 206, 593
Matz, Peter 21, 51, 56, 78, 264, 287, 321, 348, 414, 495, 598, 745, 758, 1442
Mau, Lester J.N. 526
Mauceri, John 111, 112, 467, 475, 517, 648, 664, 2015
Maude Roxby, Roddy 2168, 2327
Maude, Margery 472
Maudslay, Susan 494
Mauer, Gary 450, 544
Maugham, Dora 284
Maugham, Somerset 597
Maugham, Susan 2746
Mauldin, Anna 582
Mauldin, Bill 697
Mauldin, Joe B. 91
Mauldin, Mildred Ann 574, 698
Mauldin, Randolph 772
Maule, Michael 24, 411, 444, 505
Maulsby, Viki 613
Maultsby, Carl 311, 345, 381
Maung, Kavin 526
Maung, Khin-Kyaw 526
Maupassant, Guy de 31, 2773
Mauree, Leta 554
Maurel, Michael 120
Maurer, Michael 193, 282, 337, 495, 496, 692, 727, 1260

Maurette, Marcelle 27
Mauri, Joe 396
Maurice, Marcus 2218
Maurice, Michael A. 696
Mauriello, Julianna Rose 280, 507
Mauro, Bellavia 726
Mauro, Buzz 39
Mauro, Dana Lynn 58, 148, 660
Mauro, Ernest (Ernie) 495, 553
Mauro, Wilson 2071
Maurstad, Toralv 649
Maury, Richard F. 484, 485, 643
Mauthe, Denise 2441
Mauzey, Alli 285
Mavimbela, Thandani 602
Mawson, Elizabeth 851
Max, Harry 342
Max, Jacqueline 666
Maxie 199
Maxim, John 272
Maxin, Ernest 911
Maxine, Irene 12
Maxmen, Mimi 147
Maxon, Normand 217
Maxon, Richard 33, 106, 303, 304, 331, 414, 472, 473, 668
Maxtone-Graham, John 81
Maxwell, Arthur 8, 383, 389, 437, 769
Maxwell, Bob 739
Maxwell, Frank 416, 654
Maxwell, James 1217
Maxwell, Jan 140, 308, 653, 653, 1110, 1978
Maxwell, Kelley 248
Maxwell, Margaret 1647, 2353
Maxwell, Marilyn 480
Maxwell, Marshall 396
Maxwell, Mitchell 54, 72, 88, 164, 552, 847, 1112, 2615
Maxwell, Robert E. Jr. (Bob) 187, 739
Maxwell, Roberta 649
Maxwell, Rosalie 382, 633, 1400
Maxwell, Victoria 54, 72, 88, 164, 552, 657
Maxwells, The 447
May, Aeva 128
May, Billy 689
May, Bunny 1676, 2051, 2152
May, Charles 294
May, Daniel 220
May, Deborah 1377
May, Deven 711, 767, 916, 1179, 1281
May, Earl 59
May, Elaine 621, 674
May, Hans 1070, 2737
May, James (Jim) 101, 119, 170, 450, 671
May, Joe 464
May, Linda 128
May, Marty 24, 36, 163, 211, 534, 1387
May, Mitchell 194, 558
May, Susan 288, 448, 722
May, Val 211, 932, 1068, 1683, 1890, 2127, 2235, 2651
May, William 432, 816
Mayall, Rik 359
Mayans, Nancy 366, 493
Maybaum, Robert 111, 302, 584
Mayberry, Arthur 383, 582
Mayberry, Dave 362
Maycock, Pepsi 1408
Maye, Anita 55
Maye, Carolyn 202, 372, 411, 425, 458, 923
Maye, Charlotte 195
Mayehoff, Eddie 149, 195, 582
Mayer, Charles 205
Mayer, Clementine 748
Mayer, Edwin Justus 212
Mayer, Ella 317, 582, 677
Mayer, Lee 224
Mayer, Lisa A. 50, 78, 125, 128, 380, 759, 1320
Mayer, Margery 1927
Mayer, Michael 511, 693, 714, 767, 824, 1580

Mayer, Neal 450
Mayer, Timothy S. 477
Mayer, Val 205
Mayerl, Billy 2422
Mayers, Lloyd 651
Mayerson, Frederic H. 285, 338, 403, 608, 645
Mayerson, Rhoda 403
Mayes, Doris 231
Mayes, Sally 96, 622, 725, 735, 948, 1133, 1630, 2170
Mayfield, Julian 408
Mayforth, Leland 105, 620
Mayhew, Billy 5
Mayla 36
Maynard, Gaylord 86
Maynard, Joan-Anne 1408
Maynard, Ruth 508
Maynard, Tyler 424, 815, 1439
Mayne, Ferdy 495, 930
Mayne, Lennie 2185
Mayne, Mildred 2843
Mayo Jenkins, Carol see Jenkins, Carol Mayo
Mayo, Don 171, 332, 378, 428, 429, 514, 607, 1113, 1793
Mayo, John 524
Mayo, Larry 224
Mayo, Phyllis 421
Mayo, Robert 638
Mayo, Virginia 222, 259, 494
Mayo, Win 458, 636
Mayor, Lottie 543, 743, 942, 2759
Mayorals, The (Hector & Elsa Maria) 684, 685
Mayro, Jacqueline 33, 55, 96, 276, 1123, 1695, 2770
Mays, Willie 71
Mazard, Salome 159
Mazey, Duane F. 391
Mazin, Stan 42, 313
Mazur, Kenneth 263
Mazurki, Mike 273, 502
Mazursky, Paul 1702, 2389
Mazza, Alfred 766
Mazzant, Cynthia M. 1456
Mazzello, Joe 306
Mazzello, Mary 652
Mazzeo, Roger 115, 880
Mazzie, Marin 60, 82, 185, 338, 380, 429, 443, 521, 524, 537, 569, 743, 750, 752, 1594, 2810
Mazzini, Herb 55
Mazzocchetti, Germano 341
Mazzolini, Joe 415
Mazzone and the Abbott Dancers 314
Mbalo, Jabu 1621
Mbambo, Nonhlanhla 602
Mdledle, Nathan 1710
Meacher, Harry 1124
Meachum, Roy 22
Mead, George 1474
Mead, Lewis (Lew) 2, 375, 523, 726, 759
Mead, Shepherd 323, 324
Mead, William (Will) 136, 738
Meade, Bettye 371
Meade, Bill see Meade, William
Meade, Claire 740
Meade, Craig 1623
Meade, Gardiner 529
Meade, Marie Louise 346
Meade, Norman 586
Meade, William (Bill Meade) 4, 139, 164, 305, 385, 428, 605, 656
Meader, George 574
Meadmore, Robert 82, 106, 414, 1978, 2703
Meadow, Lynne 1065
Meadows, Arlene 347
Meadows, Audrey 310, 707
Meadows, Carol Lee 78, 179, 240, 380, 440, 562
Meadows, Christine 111
Meadows, Kristen 203